New Internati

DISCIPLE'S STUDY BIBLE

PRESENTED TO

BY ______

ON ______

CERTIFICATE
OF
MARRIAGE

THIS CERTIFIES THAT

AND

WERE UNITED IN

HOLY MATRIMONY

ON

AT

OFFICIANT

WITNESS

WITNESS

BIRTHS

BORN ON

AT

BORN ON

AT

BORN ON

AT

BORN ON

AT

BORN ON

AT

BORN ON

AT

BAPTISMS

BAPTIZED ON

AT *BY*

BAPTIZED ON

AT *BY*

BAPTIZED ON

AT *BY*

BAPTIZED ON

AT *BY*

BAPTIZED ON

AT *BY*

BAPTIZED ON

AT *BY*

MARRIAGES

TO

ON *AT*

TO

ON *AT*

TO

ON *AT*

TO

ON *AT*

TO

ON *AT*

TO

ON *AT*

DEATHS

ON

ON

ON

ON

ON

ON

OCCASIONS TO REMEMBER

New International Version

DISCIPLE'S STUDY BIBLE

New International Version

DISCIPLE'S STUDY BIBLE

STUDY FEATURES:

27 Major Bible Doctrines
Annotated from Genesis to Revelation
Summarized, Indexed, and Traced in Church History

24 Pages of Full-Color Illustrations on Doctrine and Chronology

Theological Introductions to Each Book of the Bible

Glossary of Theological Terms

Concordance

Life Helps

8 Pages of Full-Color Maps with Map Index

BROADMAN & HOLMAN PUBLISHERS
Nashville, Tennessee

Disciple's Study Bible

Color	*Binding*	*ISBN*	*Holman Code*
Black	Genuine	1-55819-023-6	4670-33
Black	Genuine Indexed	1-55819-024-4	4670-34
Burgundy	Genuine	1-55819-025-2	4670-35
Burgundy	Genuine Indexed	1-55819-026-0	4670-36
Black	Bonded	1-55819-015-5	4670-25
Black	Bonded Indexed	1-55819-016-3	4670-26
Burgundy	Bonded	1-55819-021-X	4670-31
Burgundy	Bonded Indexed	1-55819-022-8	4670-32
Galilean Blue	Bonded	1-55819-366-9	4671-12
Galilean Blue	Bonded Indexed	1-55819-367-7	4671-13
Dusty Rose	Bonded	1-55819-162-3	4670-38
Dusty Rose	Bonded Indexed	1-55819-163-1	4670-39
Blue	Hardcover	1-55819-014-7	4670-24
Blue	Hardcover Indexed	1-55819-161-5	4670-37
Slate	Bonded	1-55819-368-5	4671-14
Slate	Bonded Indexed	1-55819-369-3	4671-15

Printed in the United States of America
6 7 8 9 97 96 95 94

You will be pleased to know that a portion of the purchase price of your new NIV Bible has been provided to the International Bible Society to help spread the gospel of Jesus Christ around the world!

DISCIPLE'S STUDY BIBLE

Table of Contents

How to Use Your Disciple's Study Bible

"If you hold to my teachings, you are really my disciples" (Jn 8:31).

Disciples of Jesus Christ continue to learn of Him and hold to His teachings. The *Disciple's Study Bible* is designed to invite readers to become disciples of Jesus Christ and to help disciples enter a new stage of learning from and commitment to Christ's teachings. To help you organize and understand the teachings of the Bible, these teachings are presented under twenty-seven major headings. Each of these headings represents one major biblical theme or doctrine.

The *Disciple's Study Bible* presents a challenging opportunity for you to study God's Word and decide through the leadership of the Holy Spirit what the Bible teaches about each doctrine and how you can apply the doctrinal teachings to your life. To help you get started in your study of the great Bible doctrines, the following paragraphs will provide an overview of the *Disciple's Study Bible,* suggest ways to study a Bible doctrine, and encourage you to begin a life-long learning activity to become a better disciple of Jesus Christ.

OVERVIEW OF THE *DISCIPLE'S STUDY BIBLE*

Fourteen helpful features are available to you in your study Bible. Each gives you needed information as you study the Bible in depth to determine its teachings.

1. New International Version Bible Text

The Bible text is the basic part of the *Disciple's Study Bible.* The New International Version (NIV) is an accurate, beautiful, and easy-to-read translation of God's inspired Word. As you read it, ask the Holy Spirit to help you understand and apply the teaching of the Word to your life. The Bible text is God's Word. All other parts of the *Disciple's Study Bible* are human-produced helps, seeking to guide you in learning and applying God's Word.

2. Theological Introductions to Bible Books

At the beginning of each book of the Bible you find an introduction to that book. Each introduction has four sections: Theological Setting; Theological Outline, Theological Conclusions, and Contemporary Teaching. The Theological Setting will help you understand the circumstances of the original readers of the book and the questions God's chosen writer attempted to answer while writing the inspired text. The outline is designed to help you follow the sequence of thought within the book and see the basic teachings of the book. Theological conclusions summarize briefly the major issues raised and taught by the inspired writer, while the contemporary teaching section gives you suggestions for applying the book to your daily life.

3. Doctrinal Notes

Doctrinal notes appear below the Bible text, center column references, and NIV text notes. These represent the best thinking of contemporary students of God's Word seeking to explain the teaching of the Bible passage. Each of the doctrinal notes has four parts:

A. **Bold face** numbers indicate the passage being discussed in the note that follows.

B. **WORDS** in bold face capital letters indicate one of the twenty-seven major doctrines studied in the *Disciple's Study Bible.*

C. **Words** in bold face capital and lower case letters indicate a sub-topic under the major doctrine. These represent an outline of the major doctrine. The outline listing sub-topics can be found in the Doctrinal Reference Index, where italic type is used for words appearing in the doc*trinal note headings.*

D. Words following the bold face dash (**—**) provide a Doctrinal Note written by a contemporary evangelical scholar seeking to show what the passage contributes to the understanding of the sub-topic of the major doctrine. The Doctrinal Notes often have "See Note on (Bible reference)." This directs you to other passages of Scripture and Doctrinal Notes, where you can find related information on the major doctrine. These help you find immediate help in developing a more comprehensive understanding of the Bible's teaching on an eternal truth or principle. A more complete listing of related references appears in the Doctrinal Reference Index.

4. NIV Text Notes

Raised bold face letters in the Bible text direct you to the bottom of the right hand column for an NIV Text Note. These notes indicate alternative ways of translating the original Hebrew, Aramaic, or Greek text; more literal translations of the original text; or readings of ancient manuscripts that differ from the manuscript used for the NIV translation of the verse. In the New Testament, Text Notes also indicate the Old Testament source of quotations cited by New Testament writers.

5. NIV Center Column References

The NIV Center Column References give you the needed information to explore concepts and specific words in other parts of the Bible. These references are located in the center column between the columns of Bible text. When more space is required, the references are continued at the bottom of the right hand column of the Bible text just above the NIV Text Notes. The illustration shows how the system can be used in studying Genesis 11:27—12:1.

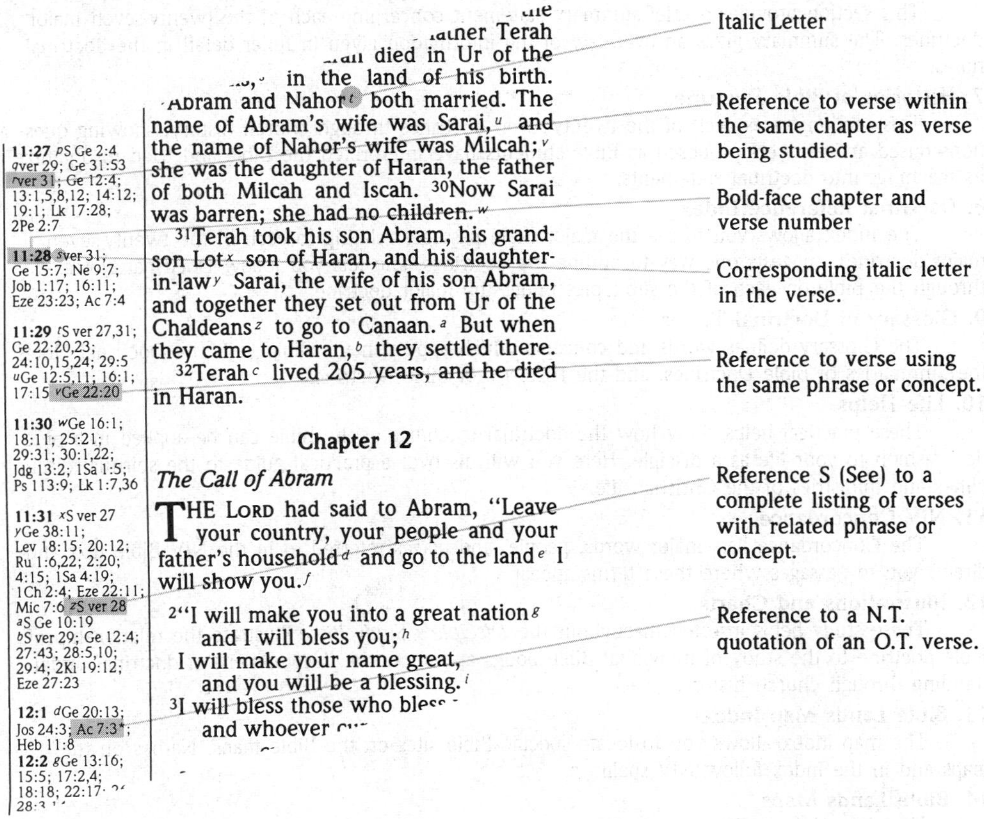

11:27 [p]S Ge 2:4 [q]ver 29; Ge 31:53 [r]ver 31; Ge 12:4; 13:1,5,8,12; 14:12; 19:1; Lk 17:28; 2Pe 2:7
11:28 [s]ver 31; Ge 15:7; Ne 9:7; Job 1:17; 16:11; Eze 23:23; Ac 7:4
11:29 [t]S ver 27,31; Ge 22:20,23; 24:10,15,24; 29:5 [u]Ge 12:5,11; 16:1; 17:15 [v]Ge 22:20
11:30 [w]Ge 16:1; 18:11; 25:21; 29:31; 30:1,22; Jdg 13:2; 1Sa 1:5; Ps 113:9; Lk 1:7,36
11:31 [x]S ver 27 [y]Ge 38:11; Lev 18:15; 20:12; Ru 1:6,22; 2:20; 4:15; 1Sa 4:19; 1Ch 2:4; Eze 22:11; Mic 7:6 [z]S ver 28 [a]S Ge 10:19 [b]S ver 29; Ge 12:4; 27:43; 28:5,10; 29:4; 2Ki 19:12; Eze 27:23
12:1 [d]Ge 20:13; Jos 24:3; Ac 7:3* Heb 11:8
12:2 [g]Ge 13:16; 15:5; 17:2,4; 18:18; 22:17 ...
28:3 ...

... the
... father Terah
... died in Ur of the
... in the land of his birth.
Abram and Nahor[t] both married. The
name of Abram's wife was Sarai,[u] and
the name of Nahor's wife was Milcah;[v]
she was the daughter of Haran, the father
of both Milcah and Iscah. 30Now Sarai
was barren; she had no children.[w]
31Terah took his son Abram, his grandson Lot[x] son of Haran, and his daughter-in-law[y] Sarai, the wife of his son Abram,
and together they set out from Ur of the
Chaldeans[z] to go to Canaan.[a] But when
they came to Haran,[b] they settled there.
32Terah[c] lived 205 years, and he died
in Haran.

Chapter 12

The Call of Abram

THE LORD had said to Abram, "Leave your country, your people and your father's household[d] and go to the land[e] I will show you.[f]

2"I will make you into a great nation[g]
and I will bless you;[h]
I will make your name great,
and you will be a blessing.[i]
3I will bless those who bless ...
and whoever ...

Italic Letter

Reference to verse within the same chapter as verse being studied.

Bold-face chapter and verse number

Corresponding italic letter in the verse.

Reference to verse using the same phrase or concept.

Reference S (See) to a complete listing of verses with related phrase or concept.

Reference to a N.T. quotation of an O.T. verse.

A. In verse 28 a raised italic letter *s* appears beside "Chaldeans."

B. In the center column the bold face number **11:28** appears, followed by the corresponding raised italic letter *s*, followed by "ver 31" and six other references.

C. In verse 31 Chaldeans appears in the text as in verse 28, again followed by a raised italic letter *Z*.

D. In the center column the bold face number **11:31** appears, again followed by the corresponding raised italic letter. There you then read "S ver 28." The "S" stands for "See" and directs you to the place (ver 28) where a larger number of references related to the key word or phrase (in this case "Chaldeans") occurs. The "S" in the center column reference system always directs you to another place in the system where the main or "head entry" for the word or phrase can be found. In this case, Genesis 11:28 represents the "head entry."

E. Starting from the "head entry," follow the chain of references through the Bible to study the word or phrase in more detail. In this instance you will want to read Genesis 11:28,31; 15:7; Nehemiah 9:7; Job 1:17; 16:11; Ezekiel 23:23; Ac 7:4.

F. In Genesis 12:1 a raised italic *f* appears after "I will show you." In the center column, you will discover a series of references including "Ac 7:3*". The asterisk (*) indicates the Old Testament verse (Ge 12:1) is quoted in the New Testament verse (Ac 7:3).

6. Summaries of Bible Doctrines

This section provides a brief summary statement concerning each of the twenty-seven major doctrines. The summary gives an overview of the information given in fuller detail in the doctrinal notes.

7. Histories of Bible Doctrines

This section traces each of the twenty-seven doctrines through church history, showing questions raised and answers proposed as Bible students have interpreted the Bible and tried to organize its teachings into doctrinal statements.

8. Doctrinal Reference Index

The Index allows you to see the major Bible passages relating to each of the twenty-seven major doctrines, suggests one way to outline the doctrines, and lets you follow Doctrinal Notes through the Bible on each of the sub-topics under the major doctrine.

9. Glossary of Doctrinal Terms

The Glossary defines words and concepts which appear in the Bible text, the Doctrinal Notes, the Summaries of Bible Doctrines, and the Histories of Bible Doctrines.

10. Life Helps

These practical helps show how the doctrinal teachings of the Bible can be applied in a practical fashion to your life as a disciple. Here you will discover a practical guide to the spiritual disciplines and ministries of the Christian life.

11. NIV Concordance

The Concordance lists major words, people, and places referred to in the NIV Bible text and directs you to passages where these terms appear.

12. Illustrations and Charts

These study helps inserted throughout the *Disciple's Study Bible* illustrate the relationship of Bible doctrine to the study of individual Bible books and show the development of doctrinal understanding through church history.

13. Bible Lands Map Index

The map index allows you to locate specific Bible sites on the Bible maps. Names on the maps and in the index follow NIV spellings.

14. Bible Lands Maps

The eight Holman Bible Lands Maps provide a handy reference to locate Bible events and to understand the nature of the land in which God's great historical acts occurred.

STUDYING A BIBLE DOCTRINE

By studying Bible doctrines, you can follow Christ's command, enrich your spiritual life, and build a spiritual and doctrinal basis for making daily decisions. With the *Disciple's Study Bible* you can approach the study of Bible doctrine in a variety of ways. "Guide to Studying a Bible Theme or Doctrine" (Life Helps, p. 1772) is an excellent starting point. As you begin your study, you will want to have a notebook in which you can record the results of your study and preserve your notes for later reference.

1. Studying a Bible Book

Doctrinal study may begin with the study of one Bible book. This method involves the following steps:

A. Read the theological introduction to the book. List in your notebook the major doctrines you can expect to find in the book. Choose one doctrine for thorough study.

B. Read the Bible book through from chapter one onwards. As you finish the chapter, read the Doctrinal Notes, if any, on the doctrine you have chosen to study.

C. Note the major sub-topics of the doctrine noted in the Doctrinal Notes. Use the sub-topics to develop your own outline of the doctrine. Does your reading of the Bible text suggest other sub-topics which should be included in the outline? When you have developed your outline, you will want to compare it with that listed in the Doctrinal Reference Index.

D. Use your outline to write your own summary of the book's teaching on the doctrine. Use the Doctrinal Notes as guidelines, but base your conclusions on the Bible text.

E. Write a personal commitment to action based on the doctrine. Refer to the Life Helps for assistance and ideas.

2. Doctrine Study Based on Life Needs

Events in daily life often raise questions about God, the world, the church, discipleship, evil and suffering, evangelism, or other areas of Christian belief. Your own intellectual, emotional, and spiritual experiences may raise an interest in a particular doctrine. In this case you can take the following steps:

A. Find the doctrine in the Doctrinal Reference Index.

B. Scan the outline of the doctrine to see which sub-topics are most important in meeting your present need.

C. Use the Index to find Bible passages which relate to the sub-topic(s) in which you are interested.

D. Read each Bible passage. Write in your notebook your understanding of the teaching of the passage in relationship to the topic you are studying.

E. Read the Doctrinal Notes on your topic. Do they help you add to or change your original understanding of the passage. Note this in your notebook.

F. When you have read all the Bible texts listed in the Index on a sub-topic, summarize in your notebook what you think the Bible teaches on the topic.

G. Read the Summary of the Bible Doctrine in the front of your *Disciple's Study Bible.* Alter your summary in light of what you have read.

H. Look at the History of the Doctrine in the back of your *Disciple's Study Bible.* Does this answer some of your questions and help you complete your summary of the doctrine?

I. Make a final rewrite of your summary. Then apply your understanding of the doctrine to the life need which originally led you to study the doctrine. Write in your notebook a prayer to God expressing gratitude for teaching you what you have learned and committing yourself to an action which you think is the biblical response to your situation.

3. Practical Concerns

You may start doctrinal study from practical questions such as How do I study a Bible book? How do I know God's will? How can I give my personal testimony? What is my part in my church's ministry? You will want to turn immediately to the Life Helps section for help in answering such questions. The Life Helps will lead you to doctrinal topics you will need to explore. Follow the steps listed under Doctrine Study Based on Life Needs.

Wherever you start your study, you will want to pay most attention to the Bible text. Write your own summary based on the Bible text. Then use Doctrinal Notes, Summaries, and Histories in the *Disciple's Study Bible* to refine your own summary. A term you do not understand may be in the Glossary of Doctrinal Terms. If not, you will need to look in a Bible dictionary. If you want to trace a particular biblical word or phrase, you can use the concordance and Center Column Reference system to follow the term through the Bible. To make a complete study, you will need an exhaustive or complete concordance.

Whichever way you find best in your study of Bible doctrine, you will want to learn the meaning of the doctrine and then hold fast to that doctrine by expressing it in your daily life. As life presents new decisions and questions, you will want to review the doctrine to deepen your understanding and to guide your decision-making. This underlines the importance of writing your conclusions in a notebook you can keep and refer back to.

LIFE-LONG DOCTRINAL LEARNING

The *Disciple's Study Bible* can serve you the rest of your life. Chart out a plan now to study each of the twenty-seven major doctrines within the next year, five years, or even ten years. Read through the Table of Contents to see the helps available to you as you study. As questions and personal needs arise, review these helps. Determine where you are in the stages of growth as a Christian disciple and monitor your growth in discipleship. Write in your notebook a specific goal in doctrinal study for each month of the year. Set up one day each month to check on your progress toward accomplishing your goals. When your life situation leads you to alter your plan so you can study a doctrine of more immediate interest, revise your plan of study to allow for this. Whatever alterations you make, hold fast to daily study of God's Word so you can keep your commitment to hold fast to Christ's teaching and so you can continue to mature as Christ's disciple.

The editorial staff of Holman Bible Publishers sends the *Disciple's Study Bible* to you with the prayer that God will use it to strengthen Christ's disciples and churches and will help you find His will and His place of service for you in His ministry. We encourage your questions concerning this study Bible and would like to hear ways you and your church use the Bible to disciple God's people.

The twenty-seven doctrines that are the focus of the Disciple's Study Bible are grouped under six major categories. The annotations at the bottom of the Bible text pages, the Outlines of the Doctrines, the Summaries of the Doctrines, the Histories of the Doctrines, selected charts, and the Doctrinal Reference Index all follow the sequence shown below. The sequence shows the six major categories, the order of the doctrines within the six categories, and identifies the page number on which you may find each doctrine in the Outlines, Summaries, Histories, and Doctrinal Reference Index.

Alphabetical Listing
of Doctrines

Doctrine	Category
Christian Ethics	God's Saving Purpose
Church, The	God's People
Church Leaders	God's People
Creation	The World
Discipleship	God's Saving Purpose
Education	God's People
Election	God's Saving Purpose
Evangelism	The Church and the World
Evil and Suffering	The World
Family	God's People
God	The Trinitarian God
History	Knowledge of God
Holy Scripture	Knowledge of God
Holy Spirit	The Trinitarian God
Humanity	The World
Jesus Christ	The Trinitarian God
Last Things	God's Saving Purpose
Miracle	The World
Missions	The Church and the World
Ordinances	God's People
Prayer	God's People
Proclamation	God's People
Revelation	Knowledge of God
Salvation	God's Saving Purpose
Sin	The World
Stewardship	God's Saving Purpose
Worship	God's People

Outlines of the Doctrines

These outlines of each of the 27 doctrines show the points about the doctrine that are annotated in the Bible text. The outlines are the basis for the Summaries of the Doctrines (pp. 1663–1702) and are expanded with Scripture references to substantiate each point in the Doctrinal Reference Index.

THE TRINITARIAN GOD

GOD

I. GOD IS UNIQUE IN NATURE
- A. He is Constant in *Nature*
- B. He is the *One* true *God*
- C. He is *Holy*
- D. He is *Transcendent*
- E. He is *Immanent*
- F. He is *Eternal*
- G. He is *Spirit*
- H. He is One in three, *Trinity*
- I. He reveals Himself in *Glory*

II. GOD IS INTIMATE
- A. He is *Living*
- B. He is *Personal*
- C. He is *Jealous*

III. GOD RELATES TO US AND TO HIS WORLD
- A. He is *Creator*
- B. He is *Judge*
- C. He is *Father*

IV. GOD HAS DISTINCTIVE QUALITIES
- A. He is *Love*
- B. He relates in *Mercy*
- C. He saves in *Grace*
- D. He is *Righteous*
- E. His *Goodness* is unequalled
- F. His *Faithfulness* can be trusted
- G. His *Justice* is impartial and fair
- H. He reacts to sin in *Wrath*
- I. He has perfect *Wisdom*
- J. He has all *Power*
- K. His *Presence* is always, everywhere available

V. GOD WORKS IN HIS WORLD
- A. He redeems as *Savior*
- B. He fulfills His purposes in *Sovereignty*

JESUS CHRIST

I. JESUS IS THE MESSIAH OF ISRAEL
- A. Scripture *Foretold* His coming
- B. *John* the Baptist prepared the way
- C. He *Fulfilled* Old Testament teachings and hopes
- D. He was the expected Messiah, the *Christ*
- E. He was the expected *Prophet* like Moses

II. JESUS WAS GOD IN HUMAN FLESH
- A. His *Virgin Birth* was through the Spirit
- B. He was holy and thus *Sinless*
- C. He performed God's *Miracles*
- D. He displayed divine *Authority*
- E. He is the *Son of God*
- F. He is the *Son of Man*
- G. He is the *Wisdom of God*
- H. He is the eternal *Word of God*
- I. He is *Lord*
- J. The *Resurrection* showed His divine nature
- K. He endured physical and emotional *Suffering*
- L. He is the Old Testament *I Am*
- M. He is *God*

III. JESUS WAS A HUMAN BEING LED BY GOD'S SPIRIT
- A. He experienced human *Birth*
- B. He endured *Temptation* as all humans do
- C. He experienced *Death* as humans do.

IV. JESUS FULFILLED GOD'S PURPOSES
- A. In His *Teaching*
- B. As God's *Servant*
- C. As God's *Shepherd*
- D. In His *Glory*

E. As the *Truth* of God
F. As the *Light* to God
G. By completing His *Mission*
H. As the *Bread of Life*
I. In His *Love*
J. As the *Cornerstone*

V. JESUS PROVIDES SALVATION
A. As *Redeemer*
B. As *Savior*
C. As *Lamb of God*
D. As the *Life*
E. As our *Priest*
F. In His *Atonement* for us
G. As our *Hope*

VI. JESUS CONTINUES TO MINISTER FOR US
A. In heaven after His *Ascension*
B. Through *Intercession* for us

VII. JESUS IS THE ETERNAL KING
A. He was *Preexistent*
B. He is the *Son of David*
C. He introduced the *Kingdom of God*
D. We await His *Final Coming*
E. He is the Judge in final *Judgment*
F. Misunderstanding made the messianic *Secret* necessary
G. He is the expected *King*

HOLY SPIRIT

I. THE HOLY SPIRIT IS REVEALED
A. *Promised* by God
B. Revealed at *Pentecost*
C. Described by specific *Vocabulary*

II. THE HOLY SPIRIT WORKS FOR GOD'S PURPOSES
A. In *Creation*
B. In *Redemption*
C. In Messianic *Hope*
D. In *Jesus*
E. In *The Twelve*
F. In *Revelation*

III. THE HOLY SPIRIT EMPOWERS GOD'S PEOPLE
A. Undergirds the *Church*
B. Unites a *Fellowship*
C. *Energizes* for mission
D. Guides in *Mission*
E. Calls and equips *Leaders*
F. *Teaches* His people

IV. THE HOLY SPIRIT LEADS INDIVIDUALS
A. *Fills* Christians
B. *Convicts* sinners
C. *Regenerates* believers
D. Permanently *Indwells* the saved
E. *Protects* the endangered
F. Gives *Security*
G. Gives *Gifts* to every believer
H. *Transforms* the faithful
I. May be *Resisted*
J. *Guides* the believer
K. Must be *Obeyed*
L. *Intercedes* in prayer for the believer

V. THE SPIRIT IS GOD
A. *Presence of God*
B. *Personal*
C. Acts in divine *Freedom*
D. Third of the *Trinity*

THE WORLD

CREATION

I. THE DIVINE AGENT OF CREATION
A. *Personal Creator*
B. *Jesus Christ*
C. *The Trinity*

II. WHY GOD CREATES
A. For *Praise*
B. For *Covenant* Relationship
C. For *Redemption*

III. HOW GOD CREATES
A. In *Sovereignty* as Lord
B. In *Freedom*
C. In *Love*
D. With *Purposeful* intent
E. With *Power*
F. For *Order*
G. In *Progressive* manner
H. In *Continuous* work

IV. WHAT GOD CREATES
A. *Earth*
B. *Persons*
C. *Nature*
D. *Miracles*
E. Moral Limitations leading to *Judgment*
F. *Justice* Through Freedom
G. *New Creation*

V. OUTCOMES OF GOD'S CREATION
A. It is *Good*
B. Freedom allows *Sin*
C. *Evil* exists
D. *Confidence* in humans
E. *Hope*

MIRACLE

I. DEFINITION OF MIRACLE
A. *God's Working*
B. *Exception* to ordinary experience
C. Biblical *Vocabulary* of Miracles
D. Worked through various *Methods*

II. PURPOSE OF MIRACLES
A. God's work of *Continual Creation*
B. *Redemption* of God's People
C. *Revelation* of God
D. Elicit *Praise*
E. Execute God's *Judgment*
F. Show God's *Power*

III. CONTEXT OF MIRACLES
A. World of *Nature*
B. Response of *Faith*

IV. AGENTS OF MIRACLES
- A. Humans as *Instruments*
- B. Jesus *Christ*
- C. The *Evil* One

EVIL AND SUFFERING

I. THE ORIGIN OF EVIL AND SUFFERING
- A. The *Divine Origin*
- B. *Satan* as originator
- C. *Human Origin*
- D. *Natural Origin*

II. TYPES OF EVIL AND SUFFERING
- A. *Deserved*
- B. *Testing*
- C. *Redemptive*

III. GOD'S RELATION TO EVIL AND SUFFERING
- A. *Punishment*
- B. *Providence*
- C. *God's Compassion*
- D. *God's Present Help*
- E. *God's Future Help*

IV. CHRISTIAN RESPONSE TO EVIL AND SUFFERING
- A. *Repentance*
- B. *Rejoicing*
- C. *Endurance*
- D. *Compassion*
- E. *Humility*
- F. *Comfort*
- G. *Worship*
- H. *Prayer*
- I. *Vindication*

HUMANITY

I. GOD'S CREATION OF HUMANITY
- A. The *Image of God*
- B. For *Responsibility*
- C. With *Moral Consciousness*
- D. With *Potentiality*
- E. With *Worth*

II. NATURE OF GOD'S HUMAN CREATION
- A. *Human Nature*
- B. *Physical Nature*
- C. *Spiritual Nature*
- D. *Intellectual Nature*
- E. *Psychological Nature*

III. EXPERIENCES OF HUMAN LIFE
- A. *Life*
- B. *Birth*
- C. *Childhood and Youth*
- D. *Marriage*
- E. *Celibacy*
- F. *Parenthood*
- G. *Work*
- H. *Age*

IV. TERMINATION OF HUMAN LIFE
- A. *Death*
- B. *Nature of Death*
- C. *Death and Sin*
- D. *Attitudes to Death*
- E. *Burial*

V. INTERACTIONS OF HUMAN LIFE
- A. *Relationships*
- B. *Relationship to God*
- C. *Community Relationships*
- D. *Family Relationships*
- E. *Relationship to Nature*
- F. *Commitment* in Relationships

SIN

I. DEFINITION OF SIN
- A. *Transgression* of Law
- B. *Covenant Breach*
- C. *Violation* of God's Character
- D. *Unbelief*
- E. *Missing the Mark*
- F. *Against God*
- G. *Self-centeredness*
- H. *Unfaithfulness*

II. ORIGIN OF SIN
- A. *Universal Nature*
- B. Result of *Individual Choice*
- C. *Satan*

III. CHARACTERISTICS OF SIN
- A. *Disobeying* God
- B. *Lawlessness*
- C. *Unrighteousness*
- D. *Lack of Faith*
- E. *Evil Desire*
- F. *Rebellion*
- G. *Hypocrisy*
- H. *Violence*
- I. *Pride*
- J. *Responsibility*
- K. *Serious* in Nature
- L. *Tempting*

IV. CONSEQUENCES OF SIN
- A. *Slavery* to Sin
- B. Personal *Depravity*
- C. Spiritual *Blindness*
- D. *Moral Insensitivity*
- E. *Guilt*
- F. *Death*
- G. *Alienation* from God
- H. *Estrangement* from Others
- I. *Shame*

V. GOD'S INTERVENTION
- A. *Judgment*
- B. *Punishment*
- C. *Discipline*
- D. *Forgiveness*

KNOWLEDGE OF GOD

HOLY SCRIPTURE

I. WHAT SCRIPTURE IS
- A. God's *Word*
- B. *God's Initiative*

C. *Inspired* by God
D. Communicates God's *Purpose*

II. HOW GOD COMMUNICATES HIS MESSAGE
A. *Visions*
B. *Oracle*
C. *Gospel*
D. Through the *Spirit*
E. Through *Eyewitnesses*

III. HOW SCRIPTURE CAME TO US
A. *Writing*
B. *Collection*
C. *Canonization*

IV. SCRIPTURE IS *AUTHORITATIVE*

V. WHY WE HAVE SCRIPTURE
A. *Redemption*
B. *Hope*
C. *Commitment*
D. *Inspiration*
E. *Obedience*
F. Right *Relationship* with God and others
G. *Unity*
H. *Powerful*

REVELATION

I. GOD TAKES THE INITIATIVE
A. In Specific *Events*
B. Through *Divine Presence*
C. In *Jesus Christ*
D. By the Holy *Spirit*
E. Through His *Word*
F. Through *Persons*
G. Through His *Messengers*
H. Through His *Angels*
I. Through *Dreams*
J. Through *Inspiration*
K. Through *Visions*
L. Through *Oracles*
M. Through *Signs*
N. Through *History*
O. In *Worship*
P. *In Nature*

II. GOD TELLS US WHO HE IS
A. As *Author of Creation*
B. As *Author of Life*
C. As *Author of Hope*
D. As *Author of Grace*
E. As *Author of Love*
F. In the essence of *God's Nature*
G. In His *Actions*

III. GOD REVEALS HIS INTENTIONS AND PURPOSES
A. *Fellowship* with His people
B. *Faithfulness* among His people
C. *Commitment* from His people

HISTORY

I. TIME AND ETERNITY
A. God acts in human *Time*
B. Time is *Linear*, not cyclical
C. God knows and directs the *Future*
D. History's time is not *Eternal*

II. GOD AND POLITICAL HISTORY
A. *God's People* stand in history's center
B. God concentrated on *National* history
C. God is active in international *Politics*
D. God's *Deliverance* is part of history
E. God's *Kingdom* is first revealed in history
F. God's concern is *Universal* history

III. HISTORY AND MEANING
A. *Faith* gains understanding of meaning
B. God's *Promise* gives history meaning
C. History's *Moral* foundation gives meaning
D. History involves divine *Judgment*
E. History points to *Hope*
F. *Geography* does not limit God

IV. HISTORY AND HUMANITY
A. God works in *Individual* history
B. God gives and limits *Freedom*
C. God works through *God's Leaders*

V. HISTORY AND WORSHIP
A. History leads to *Praise*
B. *Worship* celebrates God's acts in history
C. *Confession* of belief recites history
D. *Narrative* teaches history

VI. HISTORY AND GOD
A. *God* is active in history
B. *God's Will* is revealed in history
C. God's *Intentions*, not human ones, guide history
D. God's *Presence* is known in history
E. God controls the history of *Nature*
F. God's *Salvation* occurs in history
G. *Knowledge* of God comes through history

GOD'S SAVING PURPOSE

ELECTION

I. DEFINITION
A. Based on *God's Initiative*
B. Based on *God's Purpose*
C. Based on *God's Promise*
D. Done *In Christ*

II. ELECTION AND GOD
A. *Providence*
B. *Presence*
C. *Sovereignty*
D. *Freedom*
E. *Love*
F. *Faithfulness*
G. *Foreknowledge*
H. *Mercy*

III. ELECTED COMMUNITIES
A. *Israel*
B. *Other Nations*
C. *The Church*
D. *God's Servants*
E. *Remnant*

IV. ELECTION EXPRESSED IN COMMUNITIES
A. As *Blessing*
B. In *Worship*
C. In *Leadership*
D. As *Responsibility*
E. In *Mission*
F. In *Testing*
G. As *Protection*

V. ELECTION AND INDIVIDUALS
A. *Predestination*
B. *Free Will*
C. *Righteousness*
D. *Faith*
E. *Prayer*
F. *Perseverance*
G. *Personal*

VI. ELECTION AND JUDGMENT
A. *Eternal Security*
B. *Condemnation*
C. *Divine Justice*
D. *Forgiveness*

SALVATION

I. *DEFINITION* OF SALVATION

II. DIVINE PROVISION OF SALVATION
A. The Divine *Preparation*
B. The Divine *Initiative*
C. The Divine *Grace* behind Salvation

III. THE WORK OF CHRIST IN SALVATION
A. *Atonement*
B. *Redemption*
C. *Justification*
D. *Vindication*
E. *Sanctification*
F. *Reconciliation*
G. *Glorification*

IV. BIBLICAL IMAGES OF SALVATION
A. *As Adoption*
B. *As Being in Christ*
C. *As Cleansing*
D. *As Deliverance*
E. *As New Birth*
F. *As Refuge*
G. *As Rest*

V. HUMAN RESPONSE TO SALVATION
A. *Human Freedom*
B. *Acceptance*
C. *Belief*
D. *Confession*
E. *Fear of God*
F. *Knowledge of God*
G. *Love of God*
H. *Obedience*
I. *Repentance*
J. *Remembrance*

VI. BENEFITS OF SALVATION
A. *Blessing*
B. *Eternal Life*
C. *Forgiveness*
D. *Healing*
E. *Joy*
F. *Renewal*

DISCIPLESHIP

I. *NATURE* OF DISCIPLESHIP

II. PREPARATION FOR DISCIPLESHIP
A. Christian *Conversion*
B. *Enabling power*
C. *Training*
D. *Priesthood* of believers
E. Ministry of the *Laity*
F. *Women* in ministry

III. GUIDELINES FOR DISCIPLESHIP
A. *God's leadership*
B. *Covenant* agreement
C. *Kingdom of God*
D. *Lordship of Christ*
E. Guidance of the *Holy Spirit*
F. Assisted by *Spiritual Leaders*

IV. PURPOSE FOR DISCIPLESHIP
A. *God's Purposes*
B. *Neighbor Love*
C. *Influence*
D. Active *Involvement*
E. Service *Rewarded*

V. FOCUS OF DISCIPLESHIP
A. Needs of *Persons*
B. The *Poor*
C. The *Hungry*
D. The *Homeless*
E. The *Oppressed*
F. The *Sick*
G. The *Handicapped*
H. *The Fallen*

CHRISTIAN ETHICS

I. PERSONAL CHARACTER IN SOCIETY
A. Integrity of *Character* through relationship with God
B. *Covetousness* lies at the heart of idolatry
C. Truth and trustworthiness yields *Honesty*
D. *Language* reflects character
E. God requires *Obedience*
F. *Righteousness* involves right relationship with God
G. *Prayer* shapes character

II. SOCIAL VALUES
A. Christians have a *Covenant* with God
B. God's *Justice* involves personal and social accountability
C. God expresses His will through *Moral Imperatives*
D. God expresses His will through *Moral Limits*
E. God expects stewardship of *Property Rights*
F. Chaos exists without *Social Order*

G. Love of Neighbor should dictate *Social Relationships*
H. Corporate *Worship* yields positive social values

III. SOCIAL PROBLEMS
A. *Murder* denies sacredness of human life
B. *Theft* contradicts right to property
C. *Alcohol* abuse affects character and relationships

IV. AREAS OF APPLICATION
A. Christians have *Citizenship* in the world
B. Both *Church and State* have claims on Christians
C. *Ecology* issues concern Christians
D. Christians care about the people's *Health*
E. Prejudice in *Race Relations* challenges the church
F. God created *The State*
G. *War* calls for the application of *Peace*

STEWARDSHIP

I. GOD'S PLAN OF STEWARDSHIP
A. *Management* assigned to humans
B. Recognition of *God's Ownership*
C. Christian Values of Stewardship
1. *Life-style*
2. *Work*
3. *Attitudes*
4. *Purpose of Possessions*
5. *Sacrificial Giving*
D. Christian use of possessions
1. *Care of Family*
2. *Care of Needy*
3. *Service to God*
4. *Support* of the *Ministry*
5. Payment of *Taxes*

II. A GIVING GOD EXPECTS A GIVING PEOPLE
A. Biblical practices of giving
1. *Tithe*
2. *Sacrifice Giving*
3. *Vows*
4. Giving for the *House of God*
5. *Storehouse* giving
6. *Giving in Worship*
B. *Rewards* for faithful stewardship

LAST THINGS

I. THE SHAPE OF THE FUTURE
A. The *Day of the Lord*
B. The *Coming Kingdom*
C. The *Last Days*
D. The *Age to Come*
E. *Church Age*

II. DEATH AND RESURRECTION
A. *Believers' Death*
B. *Unbelievers' Death*
C. *Intermediate State*
D. *Believers' Resurrection*
E. *Unbelievers' Resurrection*
F. The *Resurrection Body*

III. THE RETURN OF CHRIST
A. *Return Promises*
B. *Return Signs*
C. *Return Attitudes*
D. *Return Purposes*
E. Events surrounding
1. *Rapture* of Church
2. *Great Tribulation*
3. *Millennium*

IV. THE ETERNAL STATE
A. *Judgment*
B. *Heaven*
C. *Hell*

V. THE SIGNIFICANCE
A. *History's Goal*
B. *Creation's Redemption*
C. *Salvation's Completion*
D. *Church's Consummation*
E. *Evil's End*
F. *Humanity Restored*
G. *Satan's Defeat*
H. God's *Kingdom Established*

VI. IMPLICATIONS FOR TODAY'S LIVING
A. *Inspires Hope*
B. *Purity*
C. *Encourages Faithfulness*
D. *Demands Preparedness*

GOD'S PEOPLE

THE CHURCH

I. OLD TESTAMENT CONCEPTS
A. *Covenant People*
B. *Remnant*
C. *God's Community*

II. NEW TESTAMENT CONCEPTS
A. *Body of Christ*
B. Images
1. The *Bride* of Christ
2. The *True Israel*

III. PURPOSE OF THE CHURCH
A. Bring about *God's Kingdom*
B. *Intention of Christ*

IV. FUNCTIONING OF THE CHURCH
A. *Discipline*
B. *Fellowship*
C. *Practice*
D. *Covenant* keeping
E. *Servant*hood
F. *Saints*

V. FORM OF THE CHURCH
A. *Redeemed of All Ages*
B. *People of God*
C. *Local Body*

ORDINANCES

I. BAPTISM
A. *Background of Baptism*
B. Meaning
1. *Baptism as Cleansing*

2. *Baptism as Unity*
3. *Baptism as Death*
4. *Baptism as New Life*

C. *Form of Baptism*
D. *Baptismal Candidate*
E. Administrator
1. *Baptism by John*
2. *Baptism by Jesus*
3. *Baptism by Holy Spirit*

F. Authority for Baptism
1. *Baptism Commanded*
2. *Baptism in Jesus' Name*
3. *Baptism as Confession*

II. LORD'S SUPPER

A. *Background of Lord's Supper*
B. *Institution of Lord's Supper*
C. Meaning
1. *Lord's Supper as New Covenant*
2. *Lord's Supper as Humility*
3. *Lord's Supper as Death and Resurrection*
4. *Presence in the Lord's Supper*

D. *Observance of Lord's Supper*

WORSHIP

I. THE ESSENCE OF WORSHIP

A. *Praise*
B. *Service*

II. THE *IMPORTANCE* OF WORSHIP

III. WARNINGS ABOUT *FALSE* WORSHIP

IV. THE COMPONENTS OF WORSHIP

A. Attitudes
1. *Reverence*, awe, and adoration
2. *Humility*, weeping, and fasting
3. Faith, submission, and *Obedience*
4. *Thanksgiving*
5. *Rejoicing*

B. Practice
1. *Sacrifice*
2. Sacred *Buildings*
3. *Priesthood*
4. *Calendar*
5. *Prayer*
6. *Proclamation* of God's Word
7. *Music*
8. Sense of *Community*

C. Participation
1. *Corporate*
2. *Individual*

PROCLAMATION

I. CONTENT OF PROCLAMATION

A. Definition of *Gospel*
B. Simplicity and *Clarity* of the Gospel
C. *Central Theme* of the Gospel
D. *Divine Source* of the Gospel

II. NATURE OF PROCLAMATION

A. *Authoritative* declaration
B. Declared by God's Chosen *Proclaimer*
C. Qualities of the Proclaimer
1. *Called* by God
2. *Compulsion*
3. *Anointing*
4. *Fearless*

III. RESULTS OF PROCLAMATION

A. Brings *Unbelievers* to God
B. Leads to *Faith*
C. *Rejection* is possible
D. Benefits Believers
1. *Instruction*
2. *Reproof*
3. *Exhortation* and encouragement
4. *Growth* and perseverance

PRAYER

I. THE FOUNDATION OF PRAYER

A. *Universality of* Prayer
B. Prayer and the nature of God
1. *Holiness of God*
2. *Mercy of God*
3. *Love of God*
4. *Sovereignty of God*
5. *Faithfulness of God*
6. *Honor of God*
7. *Righteousness of God*

C. Importance of prayer
1. *Command of God*
2. *Biblical Characters*
3. *Jesus' Example*

II. PURPOSE OF PRAYER

A. *Fellowship with God*
B. Ascertain and do *Will of God*
C. Experience *God's Presence*
D. Spiritual *Growth*
E. To receive God's *Answer*
F. To receive *Instruction*
G. To receive *Salvation*
H. To advance God's *Kingdom Growth*
I. To *Inquire* of God
J. To Intercede in *Politics*

III. HELPS IN PRAYER

A. *Holy Spirit Helps* in prayer
B. *Holy Spirit Guides* in Prayer
C. Prayer *In Christ* our Advocate

IV. TYPES OF PRAYER

A. *Confession*
B. *Praise*
C. *Thanksgiving*
D. *Petition*
E. *Intercession*
F. *Commitment*
G. For *Forgiveness*
H. *Confidence*

V. MODES OF PRAYING

A. *Worship*
B. *Blessing*
C. *Curse*
D. *Oath*
E. *Vow*

F. *Lament*
G. *Music*

VI. BIBLICAL PRINCIPLES IN PRAYING
A. *Hindrances* in praying
B. Praying *In Jesus' Name*
C. Proper Attitudes in Praying
1. *Faith*
2. *Humility*
3. *Sincerity* and Earnestness
4. *Repentance*
5. *Responsiveness*
D. Procedures in Praying
1. Regular and continuous *Persistence*
2. *Ordered* prayer

VII. PERSONAL AND COMMUNITY PRAYER
A. *Personal* prayer
B. *Family* prayer
C. *Corporate* prayer
D. *Church* prayers

CHURCH LEADERS

I. AUTHORITY OF CHURCH LEADERS

II. ORDINATION

III. EARLIEST LEADERS
A. *The Twelve*
B. *Apostle* as Eye Witness
C. *Disciple*
D. *Prophet*

IV. CHURCH OFFICERS
A. *Pastor and Overseer*
B. *Elder*
C. *Deacon*
D. *Teacher*
E. *Evangelist*
F. *Widow*
G. *Minister*
H. *Priest*

V. LEADERS OF OPPOSITION
A. *False Apostle*
B. *False Prophet*

EDUCATION

I. WHY EDUCATION?
A. *Commanded*
B. *Essential* to wholeness
C. *Qualified Teachers*

II. TEACHERS IN THE BIBLE
A. *God* as teacher
B. *Moses* as teacher
C. *Law* as teacher
D. *Priests* as teachers
E. *Prophets* as teachers
F. *Parents* as teachers
G. *Jesus* as teacher
H. *Disciples* as teachers
I. *Evangelists* as teachers
J. *Missionaries* as teachers
K. The *Spirit* as teacher
L. *Scribes and Pharisees* as teachers
M. *Pastors* as teachers
N. *Christians* as teachers
O. *False Teachers* as teachers

III. AIMS OF EDUCATION
A. *Wisdom*
B. *Guidance* for living
C. *Happiness*
D. *Correction*
E. *Social Order*
F. *Spiritual Renewal*
G. *Moral Purity*
H. To communicate *Tradition*
I. *Effective Witnessing*
J. *Self-preservation*

IV. EDUCATIONAL METHODS
A. *Discipline*
B. *Example*
C. *Instruction*
D. *Object Lessons*
E. *Parables*
F. *Questions*
G. *Scripture Study*
H. *Symbolism*
I. *Repetition*
J. *Participation*
K. *Obedience*

FAMILY

I. GOD'S PREPARATION FOR FAMILY
A. Creation of *Personhood*
B. Creation of *Sexual Nature*
C. Creation of *Social Persons*
D. Creation of *Environment* for living
E. Goodness of *Creation*

II. GOD'S PURPOSES FOR MARRIAGE AND FAMILY
A. *Companionship*: mutual submission
B. Sexual fulfillment: *One Flesh*
C. *Childbearing*
D. *Education* and discipline
E. *Economic Support*
F. *Symbolic Nature* for faith
G. *Temporal* not eternal
H. *Single*

III. HUMAN FAILURE TO FULFILL GOD'S PLAN
A. *Disobedience* to God
B. *Female Subordination*
C. *Intermarriage*
D. *Parental Failure*
E. Family favoritism, deceit, *Conflict*
F. *Rejecting Parents*
G. Destructive *Sexual Sin*
H. *Violence* in family relationships
I. Polygamy and concubines: *Multiple Wives*
J. *Divorce*
K. *God's Judgment* on families for sin

IV. HUMAN FULFILLMENT OF GOD'S PLAN
A. *Accepting Covenant* relationship
B. *Covenant Marriage*

C. *New Selfhood* in Christ
D. Healthy *Sexual Fulfillment*
E. Fulfilling family *Role Relationships*
F. *Social Concern* for others
G. *Mutual Respect*
H. *Continuing Growth*

V. QUALITIES OF MATURITY
A. Perspective on *Priorities*
B. Mutual *Need Fulfillment*
C. *Accepted Grace*

VI. ESSENTIAL FACTORS IN STRONG FAMILIES
A. *Bible Study*
B. Family *Worship*
C. Commitment to effective *Communication*
D. Practicing principles of *Conflict Resolution*
E. Developing *Friendships*
F. *Authentic Love*
G. *Forgiveness*
H. *Shared Joy*

THE CHURCH AND THE WORLD

EVANGELISM

I. THE MEANING OF EVANGELISM
A. As seen in the *Gospel*
B. *God's Provision* of Salvation
C. *Universality* For all People

II. THE MOTIVES OF EVANGELISM
A. God's *Call to Evangelize*
B. Give *Glory to God*
C. *Love* for People
D. *Obedience* to Christ
E. Eternal *Rewards* Promised

III. THE REASONS FOR EVANGELISM
A. *Lostness* of Humanity
B. *Christ*, Humanity's Only *Hope*
C. God's *Salvation* of People
D. God *Involves* His People

IV. THE THEOLOGY OF EVANGELISM
A. Based in the *Work of Christ*
B. God's *Judgment* on Sin
C. The *Call to Salvation* through Repentance and Faith
D. *Results* of Salvation
E. Includes *Follow-up*

V. EXAMPLES OF EVANGELISM
A. *Mass* Evangelism
B. *Personal* Evangelism
C. *Social Action* in Evangelism
D. *Teaching* Evangelism

VI. HOW EVANGELISM IS PRACTICED
A. *In the Church*
B. Through *Worship* experiences
C. *In the Marketplace*
D. *In the Home*
E. Through *Confrontation*
F. Through Personal *Testimony*
G. Through *Persecution*

VII. SUPPORT FOR EVANGELISM
A. *Power* of God
B. Power of the *Holy Spirit*
C. Power of *Holy Life*
D. Power of *Prayer*

MISSIONS

I. GOD IS THE *SOURCE* OF MISSIONS

II. HUMANITY IS THE *SCOPE* OF MISSIONS

III. REDEMPTION IS THE PURPOSE OF MISSIONS
A. A biblical *Command*
B. Consistent with God's *Call*
C. On the risen Lord's *Authority*
D. Based on the gospel *Message*
E. Given *Power* by the Holy Spirit
F. *Nature* found in reconciliation, ministry, fellowship

IV. MESSENGERS ARE THE INSTRUMENTS OF MISSIONS
A. *Sending* Messengers is God's Work
B. Early missionaries and churches are *Examples*
C. Human *Means* are needed in missions

V. MISSIONS YIELD HISTORICAL AND ETERNAL *RESULTS*

DISCIPLE'S STUDY BIBLE

Editors-in-Chief	*Johnnie Godwin, Roy Edgemon*
General Editor	*Trent C. Butler*
Associate Editors	*William Stephens, Avery Willis*
Editorial Staff	*Claude King, Candace Morris*
Design Artist	*Jody Waldrup*

CONTRIBUTORS

Bible Book Introductions

Genesis	*Dan G. Kent*
Exodus	*William B. Tolar*
Leviticus	*D. Waylon Bailey*
Numbers	*Gleason L. Archer*
Deuteronomy	*R. Dennis Cole*
Joshua	*Marten H. Woudstra*
Judges	*Bobby D. Box*
Ruth	*Gerald L. Keown*
1 & 2 Samuel	*Joe O. Lewis*
1 & 2 Kings	*John H. Traylor, Jr.*
1 & 2 Chronicles	*Hayes P. Wicker, Jr.*
Ezra, Nehemiah	*D. C. Martin*
Esther	*Trent C. Butler*
Job	*Ralph L. Smith*
Psalms	*Alton H. McEachern*
Proverbs	*Harry B. Hunt, Jr.*
Ecclesiastes	*Bill G. Bruster*
Song of Songs, Isaiah	*Russell Lester*
Jeremiah	*Joseph Edward Coleson*
Lamentations	*Joel F. Drinkard, Jr.*
Ezekiel	*J. W. Lee*
Daniel	*J. J. Owens*
Hosea	*Billy K. Smith*
Joel	*J. Kenneth Eakins*
Amos	*Robert L. Cate*
Obadiah	*W. H. Bellinger, Jr.*
Jonah	*Fred M. Wood*
Micah	*R. K. Harrison*
Nahum	*W. H. Bellinger, Jr.*
Habakkuk	*Samuel Y. C. Tang*
Zephaniah	*F. B. Huey, Jr.*
Haggai	*Gary V. Smith*
Zechariah	*Paul L. Redditt*
Malachi	*Gary V. Smith*
Matthew	*Clair M. Crissey*
Mark	*William L. Lane*
Luke	*Virtus E. Gideon*
John	*R. Alan Culpepper*
Acts	*Brian L. Harbour*
Romans	*Harold S. Songer*
1 Corinthians	*James T. Draper, Jr.*
2 Corinthians	*R. E. Glaze, Jr.*
Galatians	*William H. Vermillion*
Ephesians	*Charles D. Page*
Philippians	*Daniel Vestal*
Colossians	*David W. Perkins*
1 Thessalonians	*Herschel H. Hobbs*
2 Thessalonians	*Leon Morris*
1 Timothy	*D. L. Lowrie*
2 Timothy	*James H. Semple*
Titus	*Ted Sisk*
Philemon	*Thomas Dale Lea*
Hebrews	*Robert J. Dean*
James	*William M. Pinson, Jr.*
1 & 2 Peter	*Clayton K. Harrop*
1, 2, & 3 John	*Billy E. Simmons*
Jude	*William L. Blevins*
Revelation	*William Stephens*

Theological Annotations and Summaries of Doctrines

The Trinitarian God

God	*J. Terry Young*
Jesus Christ	*William L. Hendricks*
Holy Spirit	*Fisher Humphreys*

The World

Creation	*Fred M. Wood*
Miracle	*J. Estill Jones*
Evil and Suffering	*Warren McWilliams*
Humanity	*Robert L. Cate*
Sin	*Billy E. Simmons*

God's People

The Church	*D. Waylon Bailey*
Ordinances	*Wayne Ward*
Worship	*James T. Draper, Jr.*
Proclamation	*James T. Draper, Jr.*
Prayer	*T. W. Hunt*
Church Leaders	*David E. Garland*

Knowledge of God

Holy Scripture	*Daniel G. Bagby*
Revelation	*Daniel G. Bagby*
History	*Trent C. Butler*

God's Saving Purpose

Election	*J. Alfred Smith*
Salvation	*Delos Miles*
Discipleship	*C. W. Scudder*
Christian Ethics	*William M. Tillman, Jr.*
Stewardship	*Cecil A. Ray*
Last Things	*Jerry W. Batson*
Education	*Lucien E. Coleman, Jr.*
Family	*John C. Howell*

The Church and the World

Evangelism	*Lewis A. Drummond*
Missions	*A. Clark Scanlon*

Histories of Bible Doctrines

God, Holy Spirit, Miracle, Evil and Suffering, Church Leaders	*Reggie McNeal*
Jesus Christ, Ordinances	*Hugh Wamble*
Creation, Sin	*Walter O. Draughoh, III*
Humanity	*Mark DeVine*
Holy Scripture, Revelation, Salvation, Last Things, Worship, Proclamation	*Timothy George*
History	*Mark Fountain*
Election	*Paul A. Basden*
Discipleship	*Donald L. Morcom*
Christian Ethics	*Joon-Sik Park*
The Church, Evangelism	*Mark E. Dever*
Prayer	*James Leo Garrett, Jr.*
Education	*Jack D. Terry, Jr.*
Family	*Diana S. Richmond Garland*
Missions	*Barbara J. Bruce*
Stewardship	*Candace Morris*

Editorial Consultants

Michael Allen
Wayne Allen
Tal D. Bonham
L. Russ Bush, III
Robert O. Byrd
Michael Fink
Jack Graham
Brian Harbour
James E. Harvey
Lawson Hatfield
Kenneth Hemphill
John Hewett
Leonard H. Hill
Herschel H. Hobbs
David L. Jester
Milford Misener
Don Moore
Winfred Moore
Bob Norman
David Perkins
James L. Pleitz
James Semple
Robert B.Sloan
Ralph L. Smith
Ralph M. Smith
James Taulman
Ronald Tonks
J. H. Traylor, Jr.
Daniel G. Vestal
Perry F. Webb, Jr.
Bill Weber
Fred H. Wolfe

PREFACE

THE NEW INTERNATIONAL VERSION is a completely new translation of the Holy Bible made by over a hundred scholars working directly from the best available Hebrew, Aramaic and Greek texts. It had its beginning in 1965 when, after several years of exploratory study by committees from the Christian Reformed Church and the National Association of Evangelicals, a group of scholars met at Palos Heights, Illinois, and concurred in the need for a new translation of the Bible in contemporary English. This group, though not made up of official church representatives, was transdenominational. Its conclusion was endorsed by a large number of leaders from many denominations who met in Chicago in 1966.

Responsibility for the new version was delegated by the Palos Heights group to a self-governing body of fifteen, the Committee on Bible Translation, composed for the most part of biblical scholars from colleges, universities and seminaries. In 1967 the New York Bible Society (now the International Bible Society) generously undertook the financial sponsorship of the project—a sponsorship that made it possible to enlist the help of many distinguished scholars. The fact that participants from the United States, Great Britain, Canada, Australia and New Zealand worked together gave the project its international scope. That they were from many denominations—including Anglican, Assemblies of God, Baptist, Brethren, Christian Reformed, Church of Christ, Evangelical Free, Lutheran, Mennonite, Methodist, Nazarene, Presbyterian, Wesleyan and other churches—helped to safeguard the translation from sectarian bias.

How it was made helps to give the New International Version its distinctiveness. The translation of each book was assigned to a team of scholars. Next, one of the Intermediate Editorial Committees revised the initial translation, with constant reference to the Hebrew, Aramaic or Greek. Their work then went to one of the General Editorial Committees, which checked it in detail and made another thorough revision. This revision in turn was carefully reviewed by the Committee on Bible Translation, which made further changes and then released the final version for publication. In this way the entire Bible underwent three revisions, during each of which the translation was examined for its faithfulness to the original languages and for its English style.

All this involved many thousands of hours of research and discussion regarding the meaning of the texts and the precise way of putting them into English. It may well be that no other translation has been made by a more thorough process of review and revision from committee to committee than this one.

From the beginning of the project, the Committee on Bible Translation held to certain goals for the New International Version: that it would be an accurate translation and one that would have clarity and literary quality and so prove suitable for public and private reading, teaching, preaching, memorizing and liturgical use. The Committee also sought to preserve some measure of continuity with the long tradition of translating the Scriptures into English.

In working toward these goals, the translators were united in their commitment to the authority and infallibility of the Bible as God's Word in written form. They believe that it contains the divine answer to the deepest needs of humanity, that it sheds unique light on our path in a dark world, and that it sets forth the way to our eternal well-being.

The first concern of the translators has been the accuracy of the translation and its fidelity to the thought of the biblical writers. They have weighed the significance of the lexical and grammatical details of the Hebrew, Aramaic and Greek texts. At the same time, they have striven for more than a word-for-word translation. Because thought patterns and syntax differ from language to language, faithful communication of the meaning of the writers of the Bible demands frequent modifications in sentence structure and constant regard for the contextual meanings of words.

A sensitive feeling for style does not always accompany scholarship. Accordingly the Committee on Bible Translation submitted the developing version to a number of stylistic consultants. Two of them read every book of both Old and New Testaments twice—once before and once after the last major revision—and made invaluable suggestions. Samples of the translation were tested for clarity and ease of reading by various kinds of people—young and old, highly educated and less well educated, ministers and laymen.

Concern for clear and natural English—that the New International Version should be idiomatic but not idiosyncratic, contemporary but not dated—motivated the translators and consultants. At the same time, they tried to reflect the differing styles of the biblical writers. In view of the international use of English, the translators sought to avoid obvious Americanisms on the one hand and obvious Anglicisms on the other. A British edition reflects the comparatively few differences of significant idiom and of spelling.

As for the traditional pronouns "thou," "thee" and "thine" in reference to the Deity, the translators judged that to use these archaisms (along with the old verb forms such as "doest," "wouldest" and "hadst") would violate accuracy in translation. Neither Hebrew, Aramaic nor Greek uses special pronouns for the persons of the Godhead. A present-day translation is not enhanced by forms that in the time of the King James Version were used in everyday speech, whether referring to God or man.

For the Old Testament the standard Hebrew text, the Masoretic Text as published in the latest editions of *Biblia Hebraica,* was used throughout. The Dead Sea Scrolls contain material bearing on an earlier stage of the Hebrew text. They were consulted, as were the Samaritan Pentateuch and the ancient scribal traditions relating to textual changes. Sometimes a variant Hebrew reading in the margin of the Masoretic Text was followed instead of the text itself. Such instances, being variants within the Masoretic tradition, are not specified by footnotes. In rare cases, words in the consonantal text were divided differently from the way they appear in the Masoretic Text. Footnotes indicate this. The translators also consulted the more important early versions—the Septuagint; Aquila, Symmachus and Theodotion; the Vulgate; the Syriac Peshitta; the Targums; and for the Psalms the *Juxta Hebraica* of Jerome. Readings from these versions were occasionally followed where the Masoretic Text seemed doubtful and where accepted principles of textual criticism showed that one or more of these textual witnesses appeared to provide the correct reading. Such instances are footnoted. Sometimes vowel letters and vowel signs did not, in the judgment of the translators, represent the correct vowels for the original consonantal text. Accordingly some words were read with a different set of vowels. These instances are usually not indicated by footnotes.

The Greek text used in translating the New Testament was an eclectic one. No other piece of ancient literature has such an abundance of manuscript witnesses as does the New Testament. Where existing manuscripts differ, the translators made their choice of readings according to accepted principles of New Testament textual criticism. Footnotes call attention to places where there was uncertainty about what the original text was. The best current printed texts of the Greek New Testament were used.

There is a sense in which the work of translation is never wholly finished. This applies to all great literature and uniquely so to the Bible. In 1973 the New Testament in the New International Version was published. Since then, suggestions for corrections and revisions have been received from various sources. The Committee on Bible Translation carefully considered the suggestions and adopted a number of them. These were incorporated in the first printing of the entire Bible in 1978. Additional revisions were made by the Committee on Bible Translation in 1983 and appear in printings after that date.

As in other ancient documents, the precise meaning of the biblical texts is sometimes uncertain. This is more often the case with the Hebrew and Aramaic texts than with the Greek text. Although archaeological and linguistic discoveries in this century aid in understanding difficult passages, some uncertainties remain. The more significant of these have been called to the reader's attention in the footnotes.

In regard to the divine name *YHWH,* commonly referred to as the *Tetragrammaton,* the translators adopted the device used in most English versions of rendering that name as "LORD" in capital letters to distinguish it from *Adonai,* another Hebrew word rendered "Lord," for which small letters are used. Wherever the two names stand together in the Old Testament as a compound name of God, they are rendered "Sovereign LORD."

Because for most readers today the phrases "the LORD of hosts" and "God of hosts" have little meaning, this version renders them "the LORD Almighty" and "God Almighty." These renderings convey the sense of the Hebrew, namely, "he who is sovereign over all the 'hosts' (powers) in heaven and on earth, especially over the 'hosts' (armies) of Israel." For readers unacquainted with Hebrew this does not make clear the distinction between *Sabaoth* ("hosts" or "Almighty") and *Shaddai* (which can also be translated "Almighty"), but the latter occurs infrequently and is always footnoted. When *Adonai* and *YHWH Sabaoth* occur together, they are rendered "the Lord, the LORD Almighty."

As for other proper nouns, the familiar spellings of the King James Version are generally retained. Names traditionally spelled with "ch," except where it is final, are usually spelled in this translation with "k" or "c," since the biblical languages do not have the sound that "ch" frequently indicates in English—for example, in *chant.* For well-known names such as Zechariah, however, the traditional spelling has been retained. Variation in the spelling of names in the original languages has usually not been indicated. Where a person or place has two or more different names in the Hebrew, Aramaic or Greek texts, the more familiar one has generally been used, with footnotes where needed.

To achieve clarity the translators sometimes supplied words not in the original texts but required by the context. If there was uncertainty about such material, it is enclosed in brackets. Also for the sake of clarity or style, nouns, including some proper nouns, are sometimes substituted for pronouns, and vice versa. And though the Hebrew writers often shifted back and forth between first, second and third personal pronouns without change of antecedent, this translation often makes them uniform, in accordance with English style and without the use of footnotes.

Poetical passages are printed as poetry, that is, with indentation of lines and with separate stanzas. These are generally designed to reflect the structure of Hebrew poetry. This poetry is normally characterized by parallelism in balanced lines. Most of the poetry in the Bible is in the Old Testament, and scholars differ regarding the scansion of Hebrew lines. The translators determined the stanza divisions for the most part by analysis of the subject matter. The stanzas therefore serve as poetic paragraphs.

As an aid to the reader, italicized sectional headings are inserted in most of the books. They are not to be regarded as part of the NIV text, are not for oral reading, and are not intended to dictate the interpretation of the sections they head.

The footnotes in this version are of several kinds, most of which need no explanation. Those giving alternative translations begin with "Or" and generally introduce the alternative with the last word preceding it in the text, except when it is a single-word alternative; in poetry quoted in a footnote a slant mark indicates a line division. Footnotes introduced by "Or" do not have uniform significance. In some cases two possible translations were considered to have about equal validity. In other cases, though the translators were convinced that the translation in the text was correct, they judged that another interpretation was possible and of sufficient importance to be represented in a footnote.

In the New Testament, footnotes that refer to uncertainty regarding the original text are introduced by "Some manuscripts" or similar expressions. In the Old Testament, evidence for the reading chosen is given first and evidence for the alternative is added after a semicolon (for example: Septuagint; Hebrew *father*). In such notes the term "Hebrew" refers to the Masoretic Text.

It should be noted that minerals, flora and fauna, architectural details, articles of clothing and jewelry, musical instruments and other articles cannot always be identified with precision. Also measures of capacity in the biblical period are particularly uncertain (see the table of weights and measures following the text).

Like all translations of the Bible, made as they are by imperfect man, this one undoubtedly falls short of its goals. Yet we are grateful to God for the extent to which he has enabled us to realize these goals and for the strength he has given us and our colleagues to complete our task. We offer this version of the Bible to him in whose name and for whose glory it has been made. We pray that it will lead many into a better understanding of the Holy Scriptures and a fuller knowledge of Jesus Christ the incarnate Word, of whom the Scriptures so faithfully testify.

The Committee on Bible Translation

June 1978
(Revised August 1983)

Names of the translators and editors may be secured
from the International Bible Society,
translation sponsors of the New International Version.
P.O. Box 62970, Colorado Springs, Colorado, 80962-2970

BOOKS OF THE BIBLE
in Alphabetical Order

The books in the New Testament are indicated by *italics.*

Books of the Bible

Old Testament

New Testament

5. God brings reconciliation through trial, confession, acceptance of responsibility, and forgiveness. (41:53—45:28)
6. God leads and rules even in a foreign kingdom. (46:1—47:31)
7. The patriarchal blessings belong to the tribes of Israel. (48:1—49:33)
8. Israel must responsibly fulfill the charges of the patriarchs. (50:1-14)
9. God renews His promises to a forgiving, faithful people. (50:15-26)

Theological Conclusions

The book of Genesis expresses how God's people received their identity. It shows God's people that:

1. Our God and only our God is Creator. Others may make the claim, but only Yahweh, God of Israel, has maintained His care for the entire world to prove He is its Creator and Sustainer.

2. Our trouble results from human rebellion—sin—not from God's imperfection, immorality, or lack of concern. God created us and His world "very good." Sin is immoral and person-centered.

3. Our potential is great, for we are formed in God's image and given responsibility to care for God's universe.

4. Our sin faces God's punishment. He neither ignores those He created nor tolerates their sin. Our sin hurts us, other people, and our relationship with God. He seeks constantly to restore relationships with us, but cares enough for us to teach us the danger of sin by punishing us for our sin.

5. Our hope lies in God's redemption. The Lord started in the very beginning to work to redeem us from sin. He began to deal with those who would respond to Him and eventually selected one person and his family to be His channels of redemption to all people. Carefully, patiently, He worked with Abraham, his family, and eventually his many descendants to make the blessings of redemption possible to all (12:2-3). Such redemption rests on God's grace and love, not on human efforts or rights.

6. Our identity centers in missions. From the beginning God has worked to bless all peoples. God's people are blessed so they can be a blessing to all nations. God chose or elected His people to achieve His missionary purpose.

7. Our God remains in control of the world. The power struggles among nations may make it appear other gods have control, but the long run of history will show only God makes and fulfills promises for His people. He acts according to His own moral nature. He is not arbitrary or capricious, malicious or cruel, impotent or uncaring. He works redemptively in our history to restore sinful, needy people to Himself.

8. Our identity centers in the extended family. God works out His promises and purposes despite our family quarrels.

9. The Creator God reveals Himself through gracious acts, through repeated and consistent mercies, and through utmost faithfulness to His promises and purposes. He not only rewards those who respond to Him; He blesses far in excess of what we deserve. In the Old Testament, too, the story of the Lord's dealing with us is a story of grace.

Contemporary Teaching

Genesis calls God's people today to understand our identity anew. We are creatures of the one Creator God. As such, we need to accept responsibility to care for the world God created for us, to join in God's missionary purpose of blessing all nations, and to live as faithful family members of God's people. We should recognize our sin as rebellion against the good Creator God. We should look to Him for grace and redemption. We should let Him lead us to abandon the ways of hatred and jealousy for His way of love. In faith, we should follow the examples of Abraham, Jacob, and Joseph. We should let the sovereign God rule our own history while we serve Him and His people.

We should place our complete trust in this sovereign God, instead of in some other supposed resource such as our own abilities, intelligence, or material goods. The Lord is not limited by any rival, weakness, or circumstance.

Knowing Him will make us different from those around us who do not know Him. It will make a difference in the way we relate to others. They are His people, too—at least potentially so. They are also created in His image. We should do nothing that damages them or hinders their relationship with Him. We should be especially considerate of the disadvantaged, the oppressed, and the less fortunate.

God is a God who comes to us. He reaches out to us, even in this world of today. He speaks to us. He is still looking for modern Noahs, Abrahams, Josephs, and yes, even Jacobs, who will respond to what He wants to do through them.

Chapter 1

The Beginning

IN the beginning[a] God created[b]
the heavens[c] and the earth.[d]
2Now the earth was[a] formless[e]
and empty,[f] darkness was over the
surface of the deep,[g] and the Spirit
of God[h] was hovering[i] over the
waters.

3And God said,[j] "Let there be light,"
and there was light.[k] 4God saw that
the light was good,[l] and he separated the light from the darkness.[m]
5God called[n] the light "day," and
the darkness he called "night."[o]
And there was evening, and there
was morning[p]—the first day.
6And God said,[q] "Let there be an expanse[r] between the waters[s] to
separate water from water." 7So
God made the expanse and separated the water under the expanse
from the water above it.[t] And it
was so.[u] 8God called[v] the expanse
"sky."[w] And there was evening,
and there was morning[x]—the second day.
9And God said, "Let the water under the
sky be gathered to one place,[y] and
let dry ground[z] appear." And it
was so.[a] 10God called[b] the dry
ground "land," and the gathered

1:1 [a]Ps 102:25; Pr 8:23; Isa 40:21; 41:4,26; Jn 1:1-2 [b]ver 21,27; Ge 2:3 [c]ver 6; Ne 9:6; Job 9:8; 37:18; Ps 96:5; 104:2; 115:15; 121:2; 136:5; Isa 40:22; 42:5; 51:13; Jer 10:12; 51:15 [d]Ge 14:19; 2Ki 19:15; Ne 9:6; Job 38:4; Ps 90:2; 136:6; 146:6; Isa 37:16; 40:28; 42:5; 44:24; 45:12, 18; Jer 27:5; 32:17; Ac 14:15; 17:24; Eph 3:9; Col 1:16; Heb 3:4; 11:3; Rev 4:11; 10:6
1:2 [e]Isa 23:1; 24:10; 27:10; 32:14; 34:11 [f]Isa 45:18; Jer 4:23 [g]Ge 8:2; Job 7:12; 26:8; 38:9; Ps 36:6; 42:7; 104:6; 107:24; Pr 30:4 [h]Ge 2:7; Job 33:4; Ps 104:30; Isa 32:15 [i]Dt 32:11; Isa 31:5 **1:3** [j]ver 6; Ps 33:6,9; 148:5; Heb 11:3 [k]2Co 4:6*; 1Jn 1:5-7 **1:4** [l]ver 10,12,18,21,25,31; Ps 104:31; 119:68; Jer 31:35 [m]ver 14; Ex 10:21-23; Job 26:10; 38:19; Ps 18:28; 104:20; 105:28; Isa 42:16; 45:7
1:5 [n]ver 8,10; Ge 2:19,23 [o]Ps 74:16 [p]ver 8,13,19,23,31
1:6 [q]S ver 3 [r]S ver 1; Isa 44:24; 2Pe 3:5 [s]ver 9; Ps 24:2; 136:6
1:7 [t]Ge 7:11; Job 26:10; 38:8-11,16; Ps 68:33; 148:4; Pr 8:28 [u]ver 9,11,15,24 **1:8** [v]S ver 5 [w]Job 9:8; 37:18; Ps 19:1; 104:2; Isa 40:22; 44:24; 45:12; Jer 10:12; Zec 12:1 [x]S ver 5
1:9 [y]Job 38:8-11; Ps 33:7; 104:6-9; Pr 8:29; Jer 5:22; 2Pe 3:5 [z]Ps 95:5; Jnh 1:9; Hag 2:6 [a]S ver 7 **1:10** [b]S ver 5

[a]2 Or possibly *became*

1:1 GOD, Eternal—The first verse of the Bible simply presents us with God. The rest of the Bible is an expansion on the theme of who God is, what He is like, and what He is doing. God has no beginning—He is eternal; He is without beginning and without ending. He brings about the beginning of all else through His power as Creator. The eternity of God is difficult for the human mind to understand since we are so rooted in time and are accustomed to measuring life by the passage of time. Eternity is not simply unlimited time, forever extending backwards and forwards. Eternity is another dimension of existence and belongs solely to God. Time itself is a creation of God. Time is the experience of a succession of events and experiences for a created being. God existed in the dimension of eternity when He had not created time. As eternal, God stands above time just as He stands above matter and persons whom He also has created. But He may also choose to interact with persons or things within time. In this passage, we see the beginning of all things, but not the beginning of God, for He was already living when time came into being. If God had a beginning, He too would be a creature, and we would want to worship the one who brought Him into existence. We human creatures cannot explain the existence of God. His existence will always be a mystery to the human mind.

1:1–2 HOLY SPIRIT, Creation—The Spirit of God participated in the creation of the world. The Hebrew word *ruach* may refer to God's Spirit, the spirit of a person, breath, or wind. Scholars are divided about whether the reference here is to the Spirit of God creating or to God's breath blowing across the waters. The eternal Spirit of God was certainly present at the creation. The Spirit is everywhere associated with power and life, both of which are important in creation. This reference to the Spirit should not conceal the metaphor used here. God's breath-like Spirit moved or hovered over the waters which covered the earth. God's Spirit thus kept the chaotic forces in check. Only a few verses associate the Spirit with creation. He is more often associated with individual persons. Other references to the Spirit creating include Job 33:4; 34:14–15; Ps 33:6; 104:30.

1:1 CREATION, Personal Creator—The world came into being through the perfect will of a free, personal, self-existing Spirit (Jn 4:24). Creation included the entire material world we experience—the earth on which we live and all the space of the heavens with the heavenly bodies. God's creative acts are introduced by a special verb (Hebrew *bara'*) of which God is always the subject. The verb separates God's way of creating from all human experiences and comparisons. Creation is a uniquely divine act which humans cannot perfectly imitate. The verb never has an object naming material out of which God creates. He creates from nothing. Other verbs are used to describe God's shaping preexistent materials into new forms. Creation is God's sovereign act motivated only by His will and done without hindrance from any other power or being. See note on Dt 32:6.

1:1–3 EVIL AND SUFFERING, Divine Origin—God created a good world. God did not create any part of the world to be intrinsically evil but left evil as a possibility, since He wanted humans to be free to love and serve Him. Such freedom required the possibility of sin and its evil consequences. As Creator, God is responsible for the world in which evil occurs. He allows evil; but being good, He does not act in an evil way. Evil is whatever or whoever disrupts the goodness of God's world. The direct cause of evil and suffering may be human beings, or Satan, or demons. These are all created beings who can cause evil and suffering. Evil and suffering were not part of the original creation but are a perversion of that created order. Evil is not an eternal power or person equal to God.

1:2 CREATION, Earth—The world was at first formless and empty. The deep (Hebrew *tehom*), the frightening chaotic waters covered in darkness, posed no threat to God as chaotic elements did to the creator gods in the myths of Israel's neighbors. His Spirit hovered over them in complete control. The Hebrew text involves a wordplay. Spirit (Hebrew *ruach*) also means breath and wind. God's Spirit is pictured as God blowing the wind over the troubled waters. The deep, dark elements of life which humans fear have been under God's control since creation began.

1:2 REVELATION, Author of Creation—The Maker of life disclosed in the acts of creation His very nature. He is a God of order and purpose who moves in all the created order to direct what He makes. As Author of all that is made, He is like an inventor hovering over His creation, shaping it to conform to His designs. The beauty, order, and majesty of the created world show God is a God of order, power, and design.

1:3—2:25 GOD, Creator—This extended passage is the Bible's primary account of God's work as Creator of the universe. God has both the sovereign power and the purposive intelligence to bring forth creation in an orderly, designed fashion, so that it is pleasing to Him. When God created, He got what He wanted. Nothing is said in this passage about how God created the world and all of its creatures. Genesis only says that God spoke and it happened. The word of God was the effective tool or instrument of God for creating, blessing, or chastising. This passage gives us a religious truth, that God created through His word. In creating, God brought things into existence out of nothingness. He did not take previously existing matter and transform it into new kinds of material objects. He began with nothing and ended with the whole of existence

waters[c] he called "seas."[d] And
God saw that it was good.[e]
11 Then God said, "Let the land
produce vegetation:[f] seed-bearing
plants and trees on the land that
bear fruit with seed in it, according
to their various kinds.[g]" And it
was so.[h] 12 The land produced vegetation: plants bearing seed according to their kinds[i] and trees bearing fruit with seed in it according to
their kinds. And God saw that it
was good.[j] 13 And there was evening, and there was morning[k] —
the third day.

14 And God said, "Let there be lights[l] in
the expanse of the sky to separate
the day from the night,[m] and let
them serve as signs[n] to mark seasons[o] and days and years,[p] 15 and
let them be lights in the expanse of
the sky to give light on the earth."
And it was so.[q] 16 God made two
great lights—the greater light[r] to
govern[s] the day and the lesser light
to govern[t] the night.[u] He also
made the stars.[v] 17 God set them in
the expanse of the sky to give light
on the earth, 18 to govern the day
and the night,[w] and to separate
light from darkness. And God saw
that it was good.[x] 19 And there was
evening, and there was morning[y]
—the fourth day.

1:10 [c]Ps 33:7 [d]Job 38:8; Ps 90:2; 95:5 [e]S ver 4 **1:11** [f]Ps 65:9-13; 104:14 [g]ver 12,21, 24,25; Ge 2:5; 6:20; 7:14; Lev 11:14,19,22; Dt 14:13,18; 1Co 15:38 [h]S ver 7 **1:12** [i]S ver 11 [j]S ver 4 **1:13** [k]S ver 5 **1:14** [l]Ps 74:16; 136:7 [m]S ver 4 [n]Jer 10:2 [o]Ps 104:19 [p]Ge 8:22; Jer 31:35-36; 33:20, 25 **1:15** [q]S ver 7 **1:16** [r]Dt 17:3; Job 31:26; Jer 43:13; Eze 8:16 [s]Ps 136:8 [t]Ps 136:9 [u]Job 38:33; Ps 74:16; 104:19; Jer 31:35; Jas 1:17 [v]Dt 4:19; Job 9:9; 38:7,31-32; Ps 8:3; 33:6; Ecc 12:2; Isa 40:26; Jer 8:2; Am 5:8 **1:18** [w]Jer 33:20,25 [x]S ver 4 **1:19** [y]S ver 5 **1:20** [z]Ps 146:6 [a]Ge 2:19 **1:21** [b]S ver 1 [c]Job 3:8; 7:12; Ps 74:13; 148:7; Isa 27:1; Eze 32:2 [d]Ps 104:25-26 [e]S ver 11 [f]S ver 4 **1:22** [g]ver 28; Ge 8:17; 9:1,7,19; 47:27; Lev 26:9; Eze 36:11 **1:23** [h]S ver 5 **1:24** [i]Ge 2:19 [j]S ver 11 [k]S ver 7 **1:25** [l]Ge 7:21-22;

20 And God said, "Let the water teem
with living creatures,[z] and let birds
fly above the earth across the expanse of the sky."[a] 21 So God created[b] the great creatures of the sea[c]
and every living and moving thing
with which the water teems,[d] according to their kinds, and every
winged bird according to its kind.[e]
And God saw that it was good.[f]
22 God blessed them and said, "Be
fruitful and increase in number and
fill the water in the seas, and let the
birds increase on the earth."[g]
23 And there was evening, and there
was morning[h]—the fifth day.

24 And God said, "Let the land produce
living creatures[i] according to their
kinds:[j] livestock, creatures that
move along the ground, and wild
animals, each according to its
kind." And it was so.[k] 25 God made
the wild animals[l] according to
their kinds, the livestock according
to their kinds, and all the creatures
that move along the ground according to their kinds.[m] And God saw
that it was good.[n]
26 Then God said, "Let us[o] make
man[p] in our image,[q] in our likeness,[r] and let them rule[s] over the

Jer 27:5 [m]S ver 11 [n]S ver 4 **1:26** [o]Ge 3:5,22; 11:7; Ps 100:3; Isa 6:8 [p]Isa 45:18 [q]ver 27; Ge 5:3; 9:6; Ps 8:5; 82:6; 89:6; 1Co 11:7; 2Co 4:4; Col 1:15; 3:10; Jas 3:9 [r]Ac 17:28-29 [s]Ge 9:2; Ps 8:6-8

---

brought into being out of His powerful word.

1:3—2:1 CREATION, Progressive—God moved from the general to the specific and from the lower to the higher in His creative process. He was active for six days and rested on the seventh. Many contend the "day" (Hebrew *yom*) should be understood as meaning an unspecified period of time rather than a twenty-four hour period. The sun and the moon, which mark the change from evening to morning, were not created until the fourth day. Day means hours of light contrasted to night's hours of darkness (1:5). In the Hebrew Bible, day (*yom*) refers to a longer, unspecified period (2:4; 35:3; Lev 14:57; 2 Sa 22:1; Ps 137:7; Jer 18:17; Hos 10:14; Na 3:17). Differences of opinion here often turn on the reference to "evening and morning" as well as on *yom*. Taking these words figuratively, the account can more easily be harmonized with theories of a vast age for the earth and a gradual development of life. Taken literally, the account would point to a much younger universe and a more rapid origin of life. In either view the creation of the universe and of life is a miraculous act of love by the sovereign God. God as an orderly, purposeful Creator is the central emphasis.

1:12,18,21,25,31 CREATION, Good—The recurring phrase "it was good" stands in contrast with accounts of creation from pagan cultures that picture the world as a dangerous place to be escaped. The biblical record portrays a world that can be enjoyed because of the many wonderful things God has provided for His creatures. Anything which might threaten humans stands directly under God's control (vv 2,21). God did not create an evil world. Human rebellion led to the introduction of hardship and pain.

1:22,28 SALVATION, Blessing—God's salvation is His blessing. God blessed the creatures of the sea, the birds of the air, and the man and woman whom He had created. He told them to be fruitful and multiply. An added blessing to the man and woman was to fill the earth and subdue it. They were given stewardship over the rest of God's creation. Compare 5:2. Saved persons are stewards of God's blessings.

1:26–29 HUMANITY, Image of God—Human beings are created to be like God. Some degree of physical likeness is implied by the use of identical terms to describe likeness between Adam and his son Seth. See 5:3. The divine image is of far more significance than this, however. It clearly includes authority and responsibility insofar as the natural world is concerned. The image of God may also be revealed in the male-female relationship of love and commitment. God is revealed through the loving commitment of one human being for another.

1:26–28 REVELATION, Author of Life—The creation of human beings was God's crowning work. He bestowed upon them the unique characteristics of God, by making them "in His own *tselem*" (likeness, image of same). Thus man and woman reflect and reveal the Creator's characteristics. God took control of creation (from void to order and form, v 2). Likewise He created humans to take an unfinished and untamed creation and direct and subdue it as God would.

1:26–31 STEWARDSHIP, Management—All of creation is God's work and reflects His character. Therefore, it is good. All people are special, for He made us in His image to represent Him in the world. As humans, we hold a special place of importance and service in God's perfect plan. God placed humans in charge of His material world to manage and care for it. Under God's authority we must fulfill His purpose in our lives. Being a manager for God is the foundation of stewardship. See note on 39:2–6. Sin, however, corrupts God's perfect order. It distorts our likeness to God. It causes us to try to take over God's primary ownership and authority. See note on Ps 24:1. Material possessions are neither good nor bad in themselves. Selfish misuse of possessions is sinful (Mt 25:4).

fish of the sea and the birds of the
air,[t] over the livestock, over all the
earth,[b] and over all the creatures
that move along the ground."

27So God created[u] man[v] in his own
image,[w]
in the image of God[x] he created
him;
male and female[y] he created
them.[z]

28God blessed them and said to
them,[a] "Be fruitful and increase in
number;[b] fill the earth[c] and subdue it. Rule over[d] the fish of the
sea and the birds of the air and over
every living creature that moves on
the ground.[e]"
29Then God said, "I give you every seed-bearing plant on the face
of the whole earth and every tree
that has fruit with seed in it. They
will be yours for food.[f] 30And to all
the beasts of the earth and all the
birds of the air and all the creatures
that move on the ground—everything that has the breath of life[g] in
it—I give every green plant for
food.[h]" And it was so.
31God saw all that he had made,[i]
and it was very good.[j] And there
was evening, and there was morning[k]—the sixth day.

Chapter 2

THUS the heavens and the earth
were completed in all their vast
array.[l]
2By the seventh day[m] God had finished
the work he had been doing; so on
the seventh day he rested[c] from all
his work.[n] 3And God blessed the
seventh day and made it holy,[o] because on it he rested[p] from all the
work of creating[q] that he had done.

Adam and Eve

4This is the account[r] of the heavens
and the earth when they were created.[s]

When the LORD God made the earth
and the heavens— 5and no shrub of the
field had yet appeared on the earth[d] and
no plant of the field had yet sprung up,[t]
for the LORD God had not sent rain on the
earth[d][u] and there was no man to work
the ground, 6but streams[e] came up from
the earth and watered the whole surface
of the ground— 7the LORD God formed[v]
the man[f][w] from the dust[x] of the
ground[y] and breathed into his nostrils
the breath[z] of life,[a] and the man became
a living being.[b]
8Now the LORD God had planted a garden in the east, in Eden;[c] and there he
put the man he had formed. 9And the
LORD God made all kinds of trees grow
out of the ground—trees[d] that were

1:26 [t]Ps 8:8 **1:27** [u]S ver 1 [v]Ge 2:7; Ps 103:14; 119:73 [w]S ver 26 [x]Ge 5:1 [y]Ge 5:2; Mt 19:4*; Mk 10:6*; Gal 3:28 [z]Dt 4:32 **1:28** [a]Ge 33:5; Jos 24:3; Ps 113:9; 127:3,5 [b]S Ge 17:6 [c]S ver 22; Ge 6:1; Ac 17:26 [d]ver 26; Ps 115:16 [e]Ps 8:6-8 **1:29** [f]Ge 9:3; Dt 12:15; Ps 104:14; 1Ti 4:3 **1:30** [g]Ge 2:7; 7:22 [h]Job 38:41; Ps 78:25; 104:14, 27; 111:5; 136:25; 145:15; 147:9 **1:31** [i]Ps 104:24; 136:5; Pr 3:19; Jer 10:12 [j]S ver 4; 1Ti 4:4 [k]S ver 5 **2:1** [l]Dt 4:19; 17:3; 2Ki 17:16; 21:3; Ps 104:2; Isa 44:24; 45:12; 48:13; 51:13 **2:2** [m]Dt 5:14 [n]ver 2-3; Ex 20:11; 31:17; 34:21; Jn 5:17; Heb 4:4* **2:3** [o]Ex 16:23; 20:10; 23:12; 31:15; 35:2; Lev 23:3; Ne 9:14; Isa 58:13; Jer 17:22 [p]Ps 95:11; Heb 4:1-11 [q]S Ge 1:1 **2:4** [r]Ge 5:1; 6:9; 10:1; 11:10,27; 25:12,19; 36:1,9; 37:2 [s]Ge 1:1; Job 38:8-11 **2:5** [t]Ge 1:11 [u]Job 38:28; Ps 65:9-10; Jer 10:13 **2:7** [v]Isa 29:16; 43:1,21; 44:2 [w]S Ge 1:27 [x]Ge 3:19; 18:27; Job 4:19; 10:9; 17:16; 34:15; Ps 90:3; Ecc 3:20; 12:7 [y]Ge 3:23; 4:2; Ps 103:14; Jer 18:6; 1Co 15:47 [z]S Ge 1:2; Job 27:3; Isa 2:22 [a]S Ge 1:30; Isa 42:5; Ac 17:25 [b]Job 12:10; 32:8; 33:4; 34:14; Ps 104:29; Isa 57:16; Eze 37:5; 1Co 15:45* **2:8** [c]ver 10,15; Ge 3:23,24; 4:16; 13:10; Isa 51:3; Eze 28:13; 31:9,16; 36:35; Joel 2:3 **2:9** [d]Eze 31:8

[b]*26* Hebrew; Syriac *all the wild animals* [c]*2* Or *ceased*; also in verse 3 [d]*5* Or *land*; also in verse 6 [e]*6* Or *mist* [f]*7* The Hebrew for *man (adam)* sounds like and may be related to the Hebrew for *ground (adamah)*; it is also the name *Adam* (see Gen. 2:20).

1:27 FAMILY, Personhood—The image of God is the basis for defining human personhood. We are created with the capacity for relationship with God as Creator and with each other as fellow humans. This makes family life possible. The divine image makes human beings different from all God's other earthly creations.

1:27–28 FAMILY, Sexual Nature—In God's creative purpose, human life is inherently sexual since maleness and femaleness define the physical nature of humans. Human sexuality describes all feelings about being a man or a woman that develop from infancy on through adult years. These feelings contribute to our understanding of masculine and feminine roles in marriage and family as well as in all of society. Sexuality also refers to the various ways in which sexual desires are accepted and expressed in human relationships. Numerous Bible passages celebrate the gift of sexuality as a blessing to human life. Other passages illustrate how one's sexual nature can be expressed in exploitive and sinful ways. Doctrinally, sex ought not to be considered to be evil because of God's judgment on the wrong uses of it. Human sexual nature is God's idea and is to be used in accordance with His purposes for it.

2:4 HISTORY, Linear—Biblical history is an account of the created world and its generations. "Account" (Hebrew *toledoth*) gives the literary and theological pattern to Genesis (5:1; 6:9; 10:1; 11:10,27; 25:12,19; 36:1,9; 37:2). *Toledoth* means both an account of a people's history and the generations of people who participate in the history. The Bible focuses upon earthly activities rather than heavenly ones as did many of Israel's neighbors. The Bible points to God's new acts to relate to new generations of people, whereas other religions focused on repeated acts in the divine world which determined the fate of the human world. Thus creation is not a mythical fight among the gods but an earthly action by the one God to prepare a place for the human creatures with whom He wished to relate in freedom and love.

2:4–17 FAMILY, Environment—The first chapters of Genesis introduce the theme of appreciation for the physical environment. Contrary to later philosophies which taught that matter was evil, the Bible positively identifies God as the Creator of the earth and all that is within it. Human life has been given an environment conducive to growth and entrusted with responsibility for using it well. This stewardship of the land and its resources is even more essential today for families to be able to survive materially and economically. See 1:28–31.

2:7 HUMANITY, Physical Nature—People are distinguished from the rest of God's animal kingdom in that they are in His image. See note on 1:26–29. The terms used here to describe humanity, however, are the same words used in 1:20,24 to describe other forms of animal life. Furthermore, since God formed His people from dust, any basis for human pride in creation is eliminated. What makes human dust live is God's breath. Life comes as His gift and not as our right.

2:8–24 GOD, Grace—God placed the newly created man in a garden especially created and designed as a comfortable home for him. God created woman to be his companion, to share life with him in a complementary, mutually-fulfilling relationship. The grace of God and the righteousness of God

pleasing to the eye and good for food. In
the middle of the garden were the tree of
life[e] and the tree of the knowledge of
good and evil.[f]
10 A river[g] watering the garden flowed
from Eden;[h] from there it was separated
into four headwaters. 11 The name of the
first is the Pishon; it winds through the
entire land of Havilah,[i] where there is
gold. 12 (The gold of that land is good; aro-
matic resin[g][j] and onyx are also there.)
13 The name of the second river is the Gihon; it winds through the entire land of
Cush.[h] 14 The name of the third river is
the Tigris;[k] it runs along the east side of
Asshur. And the fourth river is the
Euphrates.[l]
15 The LORD God took the man and put
him in the Garden of Eden[m] to work it
and take care of it. 16 And the LORD God
commanded the man, "You are free to eat
from any tree in the garden;[n] 17 but
you must not eat from the tree of the
knowledge of good and evil,[o] for when
you eat of it you will surely die."[p]
18 The LORD God said, "It is not good
for the man to be alone. I will make a
helper suitable for him."[q]
19 Now the LORD God had formed out of
the ground all the beasts of the field[r] and
all the birds of the air.[s] He brought them
to the man to see what he would name
them; and whatever the man called[t]
each living creature,[u] that was its name.
20 So the man gave names to all the livestock, the birds of the air and all the
beasts of the field.
But for Adam[i] no suitable helper[v] was
found. 21 So the LORD God caused the man
to fall into a deep sleep;[w] and while he

2:9 [e]Ge 3:22,24; Pr 3:18; 11:30; S Rev 2:7 [f]Eze 47:12
2:10 [g]Nu 24:6; Ps 46:4; Eze 47:5 [h]S ver 8
2:11 [i]Ge 10:7; 25:18
2:12 [j]Nu 11:7
2:14 [k]Ge 41:1; Da 10:4 [l]Ge 15:18; 31:21; Ex 23:31; Nu 22:5; Dt 1:7; 11:24; Jos 1:4; 2Sa 8:3; 1Ki 4:21; 2Ki 23:29; 24:7; 1Ch 5:9; 18:3; 2Ch 35:20; Jer 13:4; 46:2; 51:63; S Rev 9:14
2:15 [m]S ver 8
2:16 [n]Ge 3:1-2
2:17 [o]Ge 3:11,17 [p]Ge 3:1,3; 5:5; 9:29; Dt 30:15,19; Jer 42:16; Eze 3:18; S Ro 5:12; S 6:23
2:18 [q]Pr 31:11; 1Co 11:9; 1Ti 2:13
2:19 [r]Ps 8:7 [s]S Ge 1:20 [t]S Ge 1:5 [u]Ge 1:24
2:20 [v]Ge 3:20; 4:1 **2:21** [w]Ge 15:12; 1Sa 26:12; Job 33:15

[g]*12* Or *good; pearls* [h]*13* Possibly southeast Mesopotamia [i]*20* Or *the man*

are both seen in 2:16–17 where God instructed Adam and Eve concerning what was considered right and wrong. On the one hand, God desired for them a rich and full life. On the other hand, God expected them to live in the ways of righteousness that He set forth. God's requirements for people are more than arbitrary rules by which we must live. God's requirements are designed to bring the greatest good to us. Doing what is declared right by God is always in our own best interest. That is God's gracious intent.

2:9 LAST THINGS, Believers' Resurrection—The tree of life apparently represents the availability of eternal life for the couple in the garden. From the beginning God's purpose for humans was life not death. He created humans with the freedom to sin and choose death.

2:10–14 HISTORY, Linear—The Bible locates all God's actions in time and space. Human history is the arena of divine action even with the first people. The first couple did not lose a place in heaven and have to settle for earth. They were made from and belonged to earth. They lost intimacy with God and cooperation with one another and the environment, but God's intention was always an earthly history with His creatures.

2:15 HUMANITY, Work—Human work was a part of God's original intent for His people. It is a divine gift and is not to be viewed as a punishment. In human work God was sharing a part of His responsibility to care for the world He created. Labor is a normal part of the responsibility of God's people.

2:16–17 EVIL AND SUFFERING, Human Origin—As a creation of God, human beings are free but have limits. Eating from the tree of the knowledge of good and evil was prohibited. Evil entered human history when human beings refused to obey. The misuse of human freedom is frequently the direct cause of human suffering. Suffering may sometimes be a divine punishment for sin. See note on 3:14–24.

2:16–17 HUMANITY, Moral Consciousness—Divine commandments and the gift of freedom to choose whether or not to obey established the basis for the moral consciousness. Commands without the freedom to choose turn people into automatons. Freedom without divine guidance provides the basis for an utterly unstable life and society.

2:16–17 SALVATION, Human Freedom—Adam's freedom and God's sovereignty exist side by side in the doctrine of salvation. God the Creator tells us what is best for us, but we are free to accept or rebel against His direction. Our freedom makes salvation necessary. His sovereignty makes salvation possible.

2:16–17 CHRISTIAN ETHICS, Moral Limits—Our ethical freedom carries responsibility. We must consider limitations God sets on us so we will not infringe upon the freedom of other people or take God's rights to ourselves.

2:17 HUMANITY, Death—From the beginning death has been understood as the consequence of disobedience to God. Only later was it clearly revealed that the ultimate form of death is spiritual death, the separation from God. See Ro 8:1–13.

2:18 EVIL AND SUFFERING, Divine Origin—The whole created world was good. See note on 1:1–3. Creation of woman reinforces the overall goodness of creation. It was not good for man to be alone. Man was not evil, but he was incomplete and needed "a helper suitable" for him. The good God provided for the man's need.

2:18 HUMANITY, Marriage—God intended marriage to meet the basic human need of love and companionship. The expression describing this companion literally means "a helper corresponding to him" or "a helper alongside of him," a beautiful description of the relationship which God intends between husband and wife.

2:18–24 FAMILY, Companionship—One of God's basic purposes for marriage is companionship. Companions help one another, are suitable or compatible for one another, and are able to stand alongside and share their personal lives. The unique quality of this companion was demonstrated when Adam could not find a creature corresponding to himself among the animals he was commissioned to name. Built from a portion of man's side, the suitable companion shares the same physical nature. The basic implication of the text focuses on the similarity of man and woman and on their mutual need for each other. Because of their similarity, the man and woman can marry and establish a one-flesh union that takes priority over all other family relationships.

2:18 FAMILY, Social Persons—Human life is inherently social and needs human relationships for satisfactory development. Marriage is the fundamental response to this need, but more generally human beings need interaction with other people to become whole persons. The larger family context of parents, brothers and sisters, spouse, children, and in-laws is the basic social unit within which personality development takes place. The Bible, therefore, contains many positive and negative examples of family life to instruct God's people concerning social life in families.

2:21–25 HUMANITY, Marriage—The first song in the Bible was sung by the man in joyous celebration of God's gift of a wife to him. Ideal marriage still produces this kind of rejoicing. From the very act of creation, unity within the marriage relationship is set forth in terms of oneness. The absence of shame in this relationship points to the goodness of this whole relationship, including the gift of sex. Although the first couple had no parents, the intention that marriage should take

was sleeping, he took one of the man's
ribs[j] and closed up the place with flesh.
22 Then the LORD God made a woman
from the rib[k][x] he had taken out of the
man, and he brought her to the man.
23 The man said,

"This is now bone of my bones
and flesh of my flesh;[y]
she shall be called[z] 'woman,[l] '
for she was taken out of man.[a] "

24 For this reason a man will leave his father and mother and be united[b] to his wife, and they will become one flesh.[c]
25 The man and his wife were both naked,[d] and they felt no shame.

Chapter 3

The Fall of Man

NOW the serpent[e] was more crafty than any of the wild animals the LORD God had made. He said to the woman, "Did God really say, 'You must not eat from any tree in the garden'?[f] "
2 The woman said to the serpent, "We
may eat fruit from the trees in the garden,[g] 3 but God did say, 'You must not eat
fruit from the tree that is in the middle of
the garden, and you must not touch it, or
you will die.' "[h]
4 "You will not surely die," the serpent
said to the woman.[i] 5 "For God knows
that when you eat of it your eyes will be
opened, and you will be like God,[j]
knowing good and evil."
6 When the woman saw that the fruit of
the tree was good for food and pleasing to
the eye, and also desirable[k] for gaining
wisdom, she took some and ate it. She
also gave some to her husband,[l] who
was with her, and he ate it.[m] 7 Then the
eyes of both of them were opened, and
they realized they were naked;[n] so they
sewed fig leaves together and made coverings for themselves.[o]
8 Then the man and his wife heard the

2:22 [x]1Co 11:8,9, 12; 1Ti 2:13
2:23 [y]Ge 29:14; Eph 5:28-30 [z]S Ge 1:5 [a]1Co 11:8
2:24 [b]Mal 2:15 [c]Mt 19:5*; Mk 10:7-8*; 1Co 6:16*; Eph 5:31*
2:25 [d]Ge 3:7, 10-11; Isa 47:3; La 1:8
3:1 [e]Job 1:7; 2:2; 2Co 11:3; Rev 12:9; 20:2 [f]S Ge 2:17
3:2 [g]Ge 2:16
3:3 [h]S Ge 2:17
3:4 [i]S Jn 8:44; 2Co 11:3
3:5 [j]S Ge 1:26; 14:18,19; Ps 7:8; Isa 14:14; Eze 28:2
3:6 [k]Jas 1:14-15; 1Jn 2:16 [l]Nu 30:7-8; Jer 44:15,19,24 [m]2Co 11:3; 1Ti 2:14
3:7 [n]Ge 2:25 [o]ver 21

[j]21 Or *took part of the man's side* [k]22 Or *part* [l]23 The Hebrew for *woman* sounds like the Hebrew for *man.*

precedence over child-parent ties is clearly stated. The new relationship of marriage becomes the primary one.

2:24 FAMILY, One Flesh—The Hebrew and Greek terms usually translated "flesh" refer to the whole human being rather than merely to the sensual or physical aspect of human nature. Becoming one flesh is established through sexual union, but the implications of the term are more than sexual. Sexual union creates a spiritual and psychological interrelationship in which the participants establish a bond that is more than physical. The one-flesh union, therefore, establishes a bonding of personhood which is fundamental to marriage permanence. The one-flesh union does not destroy the personhood of either partner but celebrates the unity of their self-giving to each other in love. This concept has a mystical quality, but it symbolizes the depth of the marriage relationship. See Mt 19:6; Mk 10:6–9; Eph 5:28–31.

3:1–13 EVIL AND SUFFERING, Human Origin—The entrance of evil and suffering into human history was due to the sin of the man and woman. The serpent provided the temptation for sin, but the origin of the serpent's wickedness is not specifically explained here. The serpent questioned the relationship between sin and death (3:4). Knowing good and evil (3:4,22) is not merely an awareness of the difference between right and wrong. Adam and Eve already had an awareness of right and wrong, since they knew of God's command not to eat from the tree of the knowledge of good and evil. Knowing good and evil suggests having the prerogative or power to determine what is right or wrong behavior. By eating of the tree's fruit in direct disobedience, the man and the woman usurped God's right to determine what is good and evil. Only God has the right to define good and evil.

3:4–24 SIN, Death—Here sin was introduced into human history. For the first time Adam and Eve were confronted with options and the consequences relating to sin. The serpent offered the woman the choice of disobeying God's direct command. He clouded the issue by distorting the consequences associated with this act of disobedience. "You will not surely die" (v 4) must be interpreted as, at best, a half truth. Certainly physical death was not an immediate consequence of this action, but this act of disobedience surely introduced the potential for death into the history of the human race. Spiritual death or separation from God did enter human history. Compare 2:17. The account makes no hint that God was in any way responsible for sin's introduction into the world. Satan is the one who introduced sin when he beguiled Eve, but the Bible does not teach that human sin had its origin with him either. Sin's origin is to be found in the rebellious actions of Adam and Eve. Since that fateful action sin has infected humanity like a terrible disease. Because of their actions, Adam and Eve were driven from the presence of God. Sin not only infected them, but it also affected their environment. "Cursed is the ground because of you; through painful toil you will eat of it all the days of your life" (v 17). From the blessings of Paradise to the reality of earning their bread by the sweat of their brow was their sentence for sin. Beyond their environment, their disobedience had also affected their longevity. Though there is no explicit statement relative to life expectancy prior to their sin, afterwards God explicitly told them that because of their sin they would die. Thus, because of sin, human history has been inflicted with sorrow, suffering, and ultimately death. Sin originated with one act of disobedience in Eden, but its consequences have been pervasive in all aspects of life throughout history.

3:6 SIN, Individual Choice—Sin's long, melancholy reign over humankind began with the very first humans. The Bible offers no philosophical explanation for the origin of sin. Instead, the Bible narrates the sin of earth's first inhabitants. It assumes a world in which sin is possible and temptation is present. The fateful choice of the woman combined with her husband's willingness to share in her choice is as close as it comes to explaining the origin of sin. This account shows sin to be individual in nature. Each individual must bear responsibility for choosing to sin. See note on Ro 5:12–21.

3:8–24 GOD, Judge—The judgment of God comes certainly, if not swiftly, when we disobey God. Sometimes God moves swiftly in bringing judgment; sometimes He moves slowly; but He always moves to judge sin. God prefers that His judgment be positive and redemptive rather than negative and vindictive. Even in judgment God is loving rather than vengeful. God tempered His judgment of Adam and Eve by providing more adequate clothing for them than they could provide for themselves. Though He drove them out of their sheltered place in the Garden, they were not driven beyond the reach of His loving concern for their well-being. Their work now became difficult toil, and life was to be punctuated by suffering. Life was still possible in God's world. God would still give them a harvest for their labor. The whole story of redemption that emerges as the Bible progresses is proof of God's continuing interest in people despite their sin. God's judgment should be understood in the light of His grace. If His judgment were not

sound of the LORD God as he was walking[p] in the garden in the cool of the day,
and they hid[q] from the LORD God among
the trees of the garden. 9But the LORD
God called to the man, "Where are
you?"[r]

10He answered, "I heard you in the
garden, and I was afraid[s] because I was
naked;[t] so I hid."

11And he said, "Who told you that you
were naked?[u] Have you eaten from the
tree that I commanded you not to eat
from?[v]"

12The man said, "The woman you put
here with me[w]—she gave me some fruit
from the tree, and I ate it."

13Then the LORD God said to the woman, "What is this you have done?"

The woman said, "The serpent deceived me,[x] and I ate."

14So the LORD God said to the serpent,
"Because you have done this,

"Cursed[y] are you above all the
livestock
and all the wild animals!
You will crawl on your belly
and you will eat dust[z]
all the days of your life.
15And I will put enmity
between you and the woman,
and between your offspring[m][a] and
hers;[b]
he will crush[n] your head,[c]
and you will strike his heel."

16To the woman he said,

"I will greatly increase your pains in
childbearing;
with pain you will give birth to
children.[d]
Your desire will be for your husband,

3:8 [p]Lev 26:12; Dt 23:14 [q]Job 13:16; 23:7; 31:33; 34:22,23; Ps 5:5; 139:7-12; Isa 29:15; Jer 16:17; 23:24; 49:10; Rev 6:15-16 **3:9** [r]Ge 4:9; 16:8; 18:9; 1Ki 19:9,13 **3:10** [s]Ex 19:16; 20:18; Dt 5:5; 1Sa 12:18 [t]Ge 2:25 **3:11** [u]Ge 2:25 [v]S Ge 2:17 **3:12** [w]Ge 2:22 **3:13** [x]Ro 7:11; 2Co 11:3; 1Ti 2:14 **3:14** [y]Dt 28:15-20 [z]Ps 72:9; Isa 49:23; 65:25; Mic 7:17 **3:15** [a]Jn 8:44; Ac 13:10; 1Jn 3:8 [b]Ge 16:11; Jdg 13:5; Isa 7:14; 8:3; 9:6; Mt 1:23; Lk 1:31; Gal 4:4; Rev 12:17 [c]Ro 16:20; Heb 2:14 **3:16** [d]Ps 48:5-6; Isa 13:8; 21:3; 26:17; Jer 4:31; 6:24; Mic 4:9; 1Ti 2:15

[m]*15* Or *seed* [n]*15* Or *strike*

tempered by His grace, there would be no salvation for any of us.

3:8–13 REVELATION, Divine Presence—To communicate God's presence, the Bible often speaks of God as if He has a human form. Here God was present in the garden He made, seeking His creatures, who had chosen to disobey His rules for living. The God who reveals Himself is also the Creator who seeks His creatures and their welfare. Having trusted them with all He made, He is still available to save whatever we destroy: trust, creation, His hopes and plans.

3:9–20 EVANGELISM, Call to Salvation—Immediately after the sin and fall of our first parents, God sought them out and called them to salvation. He expressed His divine judgment against sin, invited them to confess their rebellion, and then "covered" them. The call to salvation always starts with God's initiative. He calls *all* sinners to Himself. We can rely upon God to call people as we witness to them concerning His salvation.

3:12–13 HUMANITY, Relationship to God—Although clearly subservient to God in the relationship of creature-Creator, human beings are also free to make their own choices. This, too, is God's gift. Further, even though we regularly seek to escape the blame and guilt of our own acts, we have the inner awareness that the choice to rebel was ultimately our own.

3:14–19 CREATION, Judgment—Moral law operates in God's creation. Rebellion against God brings punishment and ultimate death. Human dominion over creation is not absolute. God set limits which humans must obey or suffer the consequences. Creation is God's gift and retains an element of God's mystery which humans can never know. The doctrine of creation presents a call to humans to trust God and not seek absolute freedom. Human pain, broken relationships, a nonproductive environment, occupational toil are all related to human rebellion and not to God's original intention for human life. They represent God's gracious alternative to the expected sentence of immediate death. The Creator set up a moral world in which wrongdoing ultimately receives its proper recompense. He also reacted and reacts to wrongdoing in grace, providing hope even in light of human sin.

3:14–24 EVIL AND SUFFERING, Punishment—God had warned the man that sin would lead to death (2:17). The serpent had questioned God's warning. See note on 3:1–13. As illustrated here, some human suffering is deserved as the consequence of human sin. A moral, just God punishes sin and rewards obedience. Physical pain (3:16–17) and physical death (3:19,22) are examples of deserved suffering for the man and the woman. Human work and sex are not evil. They were part of life in God's good creation, but they became associated with pain through God's punishment of human sin.

3:15 JESUS CHRIST, Foretold—Christians read the Old Testament in light of the full revelation in Jesus, the Messiah. He gives deeper meaning and new light to the Old Testament intention. The doctrine of Jesus Christ finds its roots in these deeper meanings seen in light of Christ's ministry. This is the first foregleam of the gospel. The seed or offspring of the woman is Jesus (Gal 4:4). The bruising of His heel is the crucifixion. The crushing of the serpent is the provisional overcoming of the evil one by the cross (Heb 2:14) and the ultimate overcoming at the final appearing of Christ (Rev 20:10). Christians are encouraged by the victory of Christ, from the first to the last of our Bible (Ro 16:20).

3:15 SALVATION, Preparation—This has been called the first gospel. Its good news is that the seed of the woman will crush the head of the serpent-tempter. The verse is messianic in principle, presenting a picture of the conflict which climaxed on the cross.

3:15 LAST THINGS, Satan's Defeat—The connection of serpent imagery with Satan is clearly established in Rev 12:9. The infliction of a fatal wound to the head points to the victory of Christ at the cross (Jn 12:31; Heb 2:14). Satan's final defeat is revealed in Rev 20:7–10.

3:16 FAMILY, Female Subordination—In this passage female subordination is introduced into the one-flesh relationship that previously (Ge 1—2) had been one of shared authority over the physical world. The judgment on Eve included increased pain in childbearing and subordination to the husband for whom she had desire that leads to childbearing. Since Eve had not yet given birth, this judgment explained the pain associated with the joy of becoming a mother. The condition that her sexual desire be for her husband alone influenced some interpreters to propose that sexuality was in some way involved in the "fall." This idea is not based upon the biblical text. It is more probable that this condition is related to the previous one on childbearing. Even though childbirth is associated with pain and pregnancy as the result of sexual union, the wife is to continue to desire sexual relations with her husband. See 1 Co 7:3–5. Since Eve had refused to obey God's instructions given through Adam, he was to rule over her. Such subordination was not in the original purpose of God for marriage but is a consequence of Eve's failure to obey God. The three conditions here are not specifically discussed in the remainder of the Old Testament. The New Testament makes one specific reference only to the last condition (1 Ti 2:13–14). However, the relationship of the gospel to the "fall," to submission, and to marriage is basic to an understanding of the husband-wife relationship as taught in the New Testament. See note on Eph 5:21.

and he will rule over you.[e]”

17 To Adam he said, “Because you listened to your wife and ate from the tree
about which I commanded you, ‘You
must not eat of it,’[f]

“Cursed[g] is the ground[h] because of
you;
through painful toil[i] you will eat of
it
all the days of your life.[j]
18 It will produce thorns and thistles[k] for
you,
and you will eat the plants of the
field.[l]
19 By the sweat of your brow[m]
you will eat your food[n]
until you return to the ground,
since from it you were taken;
for dust you are
and to dust you will return.”[o]

20 Adam[o] named his wife Eve,[p][p] because she would become the mother of
all the living.
21 The LORD God made garments of skin
for Adam and his wife and clothed
them.[q] 22 And the LORD God said, “The
man has now become like one of us,[r]
knowing good and evil. He must not be
allowed to reach out his hand and take
also from the tree of life[s] and eat, and
live forever.” 23 So the LORD God banished him from the Garden of Eden[t] to
work the ground[u] from which he had
been taken. 24 After he drove the man out,
he placed on the east side[q] of the Garden
of Eden[v] cherubim[w] and a flaming
sword[x] flashing back and forth to guard
the way to the tree of life.[y]

Chapter 4

Cain and Abel

ADAM[o] lay with his wife[z] Eve,[a] and
she became pregnant and gave birth
to Cain.[r][b] She said, “With the help of
the LORD I have brought forth[s] a man.”
2 Later she gave birth to his brother
Abel.[c]

Now Abel kept flocks, and Cain
worked the soil.[d] 3 In the course of time
Cain brought some of the fruits of the soil
as an offering[e] to the LORD.[f] 4 But Abel
brought fat portions[g] from some of the
firstborn of his flock.[h] The LORD looked
with favor on Abel and his offering,[i] 5 but
on Cain and his offering he did not look
with favor. So Cain was very angry, and
his face was downcast.
6 Then the LORD said to Cain, “Why are

3:16 [e]1Co 11:3; Eph 5:22 **3:17** [f]S Ge 2:17 [g]Ge 5:29; Nu 35:33; Ps 106:39; Isa 24:5; Jer 3:1; Ro 8:20-22 [h]Ge 6:13; 8:21; Isa 54:9 [i]Ge 29:32; 31:42; Ex 3:7; Ps 66:11; 127:2; Ecc 1:13 [j]Ge 47:9; Job 5:7; 7:1; 14:1; Ecc 2:23; Jer 20:18 **3:18** [k]Job 31:40; Isa 5:6; Heb 6:8 [l]Ps 104:14 **3:19** [m]Ps 104:23 [n]Ge 14:18; Dt 8:3, 9; 23:4; Ru 1:6; 2:14; 2Th 3:10 [o]S Ge 2:7; S Job 7:21; S Ps 146:4; 1Co 15:47; Heb 9:27 **3:20** [p]S Ge 2:20; 2Co 11:3; 1Ti 2:13 **3:21** [q]S ver 7 **3:22** [r]S Ge 1:26 [s]S Ge 2:9; S Rev 2:7 **3:23** [t]S Ge 2:8 [u]S Ge 2:7 **3:24** [v]S Ge 2:8 [w]Ex 25:18-22; 1Sa 4:4; 2Sa 6:2; 22:11; 1Ki 6:27; 8:6; 2Ki 19:15; 2Ch 5:8; Ps 18:10; 80:1; 99:1; Isa 37:16; Eze 10:1; 28:16 [x]Job 40:19; Ps 104:4; Isa 27:1 [y]S Ge 2:9 **4:1** [z]ver 17,25 [a]S Ge 2:20 [b]Heb 11:4; 1Jn 3:12; Jude 1:11 **4:2** [c]Mt 23:35; Lk 11:51; Heb 11:4; 12:24 [d]S Ge 2:7 **4:3** [e]Lev 2:1-2; Isa 43:23; Jer 41:5 [f]Nu 18:12 **4:4** [g]Lev 3:16; 2Ch 29:35 [h]Ex 13:2,12; Dt 15:19 [i]Heb 11:4

[o]*20,1* Or *The man* [p]*20 Eve* probably means *living.* [q]*24* Or *placed in front* [r]*1 Cain* sounds like the Hebrew for *brought forth* or *acquired.* [s]*1* Or *have acquired*

3:17–19 HUMANITY, Work—Work itself was not the punishment for sin. Rather, the difficult, frustrating, and unremitting toil which comes from dealing with an unresponsive environment became the lot of humanity. The unrelieved nature of this kind of labor led ultimately to the grave, re-emphasizing human mortality.

3:20–24 HUMANITY, Human Nature—The very names of our primeval ancestors indicate their human nature. Adam literally means “man” or “mankind,” and Eve means “life.” Adam’s name distinguished him from the animals, reflecting his nature as belonging to a separate category. Originally created in God’s image, people have marred the image of God through their sin. But the human nature has remained. We are people, living people. Though we may act both demonic and beastly, we are still human. That makes us different from either animals or demons.

3:20 HISTORY, Linear—History finds unity in one God relating to one family of people. History has meaning because its subjects share common traits and a common heritage.

4:1–2 HUMANITY, Birth—The birth of children is the natural and expected outcome of human marriage. Each person born develops individual characteristics and personalities, not being merely a copy of either parent or of other family members.

4:1–2 FAMILY, Childbearing—Bearing and nurturing children is one of the biblical purposes for marriage and sexuality. Sexual intercourse makes conception possible, but ultimately conception and birth depend on “the help of the Lord.” See Pr 5:15–19; 1 Co 7:3–5. Having a large family was important to the Hebrew people for a number of reasons. Farming and herding required the help of sons, and having sons gained a father respect from his neighbors. Both men and women valued children as God’s blessing to their marriage. See notes on Ps 127:3–5; 128:3–6. Compare 1 Sa 1:18–20. Women interpreted barrenness as a curse or failure (Ge 30:1–2) since nothing was known about the possible sterility of the male as well as the female. Sterility of one or both marriage partners affects many marriages. Rather than being God’s judgment, human health factors are usually involved. Seeking corrective medical treatment is legitimate, but accepting an uncorrectable situation in grace is also an appropriate Christian response to such a situation. Childbearing is still a fundamental purpose for marriage, but planning the time and number of children is consistent with responsible Christian parenthood. Controlling conception is not discussed in the Bible. Being fruitful (1:28) does not demand unlimited reproduction. In the Western world, but increasingly all over the world, Christian couples are making informed decisions about family planning based upon their Christian faith.

4:2–11 STEWARDSHIP, Giving in Worship—Not all gifts are equally pleasing to God. What we give and how we give it—our attitude and purpose—are both important. By saying, “If you do what is right . . .”, God indicated to Cain what he needed to do to make his gift acceptable. Giving is vital in each person’s relationship to God. See note on Mt 5:23–24.

4:3–7 WORSHIP, Individual—See note on Ex 33:9–11. When people worship, they naturally bring an offering from the produce of their labor. God does not accept all worship acts. The Bible does not say why Cain’s worship was unacceptable. If we fail to please God with our worship, we have His promise that we will be accepted if we do what is right. The Christian knows Christ gave Himself once for all as a sacrifice for us. Through Christ and only through Him our worship will always be accepted.

4:6–12 SIN, Individual Choice—Cain’s jealousy and anger determined his decision to kill his brother. These sinful emotions erupted when God accepted Abel’s sacrifice but did not look with favor upon Cain’s. Nothing in the passage would lead one to assume that Cain was in any way coerced into killing his brother. He had to bear responsibility for his sinful

you angry?[j] Why is your face downcast?
7If you do what is right, will you not be
accepted? But if you do not do what is
right, sin is crouching at your door;[k] it
desires to have you, but you must master
it.[l]"

8Now Cain said to his brother Abel,
"Let's go out to the field."[t] And while
they were in the field, Cain attacked his
brother Abel and killed him.[m]

9Then the LORD said to Cain, "Where
is your brother Abel?"[n]

"I don't know,[o]" he replied. "Am I
my brother's keeper?"

10The LORD said, "What have you
done? Listen! Your brother's blood cries
out to me from the ground.[p] 11Now you
are under a curse[q] and driven from the
ground, which opened its mouth to receive your brother's blood from your
hand. 12When you work the ground, it
will no longer yield its crops for you.[r]
You will be a restless wanderer[s] on the
earth.[t]"

13Cain said to the LORD, "My punishment is more than I can bear. 14Today
you are driving me from the land, and I
will be hidden from your presence;[u] I
will be a restless wanderer on the earth,[v]
and whoever finds me will kill me."[w]

15But the LORD said to him, "Not so[u];
if anyone kills Cain[x], he will suffer vengeance[y] seven times over.[z]" Then the
LORD put a mark on Cain so that no one
who found him would kill him. 16So Cain
went out from the LORD's presence[a] and
lived in the land of Nod,[v] east of Eden.[b]

17Cain lay with his wife,[c] and she became pregnant and gave birth to Enoch.
Cain was then building a city,[d] and he
named it after his son[e] Enoch. 18To
Enoch was born Irad, and Irad was the
father of Mehujael, and Mehujael was the
father of Methushael, and Methushael
was the father of Lamech.

19Lamech married[f] two women,[g] one
named Adah and the other Zillah. 20Adah
gave birth to Jabal; he was the father of
those who live in tents and raise livestock. 21His brother's name was Jubal; he
was the father of all who play the harp[h]
and flute.[i] 22Zillah also had a son, Tubal-Cain, who forged[j] all kinds of tools
out of[w] bronze and iron. Tubal-Cain's sister was Naamah.

23Lamech said to his wives,

"Adah and Zillah, listen to me;
wives of Lamech, hear my words.
I have killed[x][k] a man for wounding
me,
a young man for injuring me.
24If Cain is avenged[l] seven times,[m]
then Lamech seventy-seven
times.[n]"

25Adam lay with his wife[o] again, and
she gave birth to a son and named him
Seth,[y][p] saying, "God has granted me another child in place of Abel, since Cain
killed him."[q] 26Seth also had a son, and
he named him Enosh.[r]

At that time men began to call on[z] the
name of the LORD.[s]

4:6 [j]Jnh 4:4 **4:7** [k]Ge 44:16; Nu 32:23; Isa 59:12 [l]Job 11:15; 22:27; Ps 27:3; 46:2; S Ro 6:16 **4:8** [m]Mt 23:35; Lk 11:51; 1Jn 3:12; Jude 1:11 **4:9** [n]S Ge 3:9 [o]S Jn 8:44 **4:10** [p]Ge 9:5; 37:20,26; Ex 21:12; Nu 35:33; Dt 21:7, 9; 2Sa 4:11; Job 16:18; 24:2; 31:38; Ps 9:12; 106:38; Heb 12:24; Rev 6:9-10 **4:11** [q]Dt 11:28; 2Ki 2:24 **4:12** [r]Dt 28:15-24 [s]Ps 37:25; 59:15; 109:10 [t]ver 14 **4:14** [u]2Ki 17:18; Ps 51:11; 139:7-12; Jer 7:15; 52:3 [v]ver 12; Dt 28:64-67 [w]Ge 9:6; Ex 21:12, 14; Lev 24:17; Nu 35:19,21,27,33; 1Ki 2:32; 2Ki 11:16 **4:15** [x]Eze 9:4,6 [y]Ex 21:20 [z]ver 24; Lev 26:21; Ps 79:12 **4:16** [a]Jude 1:11 [b]S Ge 2:8 **4:17** [c]S ver 1 [d]Ps 55:9 [e]Ps 49:11 **4:19** [f]Ge 6:2 [g]Ge 29:28; Dt 21:15; Ru 4:11; 1Sa 1:2 **4:21** [h]Ge 31:27; Ex 15:20; 1Sa 16:16; 1Ch 25:3; Ps 33:2; 43:4; Isa 16:11; Da 3:5 [i]Job 21:12; 30:31; Ps 150:4 **4:22** [j]Ex 35:35; 1Sa 13:19; 2Ki 24:14 **4:23** [k]Ge 9:5-6; Ex 20:13; 21:12; 23:7; Lev 19:18; 24:17; Dt 27:24; 32:35 **4:24** [l]Dt 32:35; 2Ki 9:7; Ps 18:47; 94:1; Isa 35:4; Jer 51:56; Na 1:2 [m]S ver 15 [n]Mt 18:22 **4:25** [o]ver 1 [p]Ge 5:3; 1Ch 1:1 [q]ver 8 **4:26** [r]Ge 5:6; 1Ch 1:1; Lk 3:38 [s]Ge 12:8; 13:4; 21:33; 22:9; 26:25; 33:20; 35:1; Ex 17:15; 1Ki 18:24; Ps 116:17; Joel 2:32; Zep 3:9; S Ac 2:21

[t]*8* Samaritan Pentateuch, Septuagint, Vulgate and Syriac; Masoretic Text does not have *"Let's go out to the field."* [u]*15* Septuagint, Vulgate and Syriac; Hebrew *Very well* [v]*16* *Nod* means *wandering* (see verses 12 and 14). [w]*22* Or *who instructed all who work in* [x]*23* Or *I will kill* [y]*25* *Seth* probably means *granted.* [z]*26* Or *to proclaim*

jealousy and anger and for the resulting sinful act. He could not blame his parents. No matter how unjust life appears to be or how badly our ancestors handled life, we cannot lay our sin on someone else's shoulders. Each of us must bear responsibility for our own personal sinful actions.

4:10–12 EVIL AND SUFFERING, Punishment—Cain suffered less than he deserved for his murder of Abel. God had warned Cain earlier about his attitude (4:6–7). No human witnessed and punished Cain's crime. God noted it as He does all crime. Eventually all criminals must face God's judgment no matter how well they escape human punishment.

4:14–15,25 SALVATION, Grace—The mark on Cain was an indication of God's grace and protection. Seth was given by God as a replacement for Abel. Divine grace is behind, before, beneath, and operating in salvation.

4:15–26 HISTORY, Promise—History according to secular definitions is limited to description of human activities and interpretation of human causes and motivations. Biblical history centers on divine motivation by focusing on promises God gives people and fulfills for them. The promise to Cain led to geographic and cultural expansion of the human race. It also led to history carried out without concern for God's presence. History thus has two types of subjects—those who move away from God and those who call on God. The interaction of the two form the basis for divine deliverance of His people.

4:17–22 HUMANITY, Potentiality—The rebellious line of Cain is portrayed as making great advances in various areas of civilization. Rather than being an indication of the evil nature of civilization, testimony is made of the great potential of all humans. Human accomplishment is not necessarily to be measured by the spirituality of a person. On the other hand, many great accomplishments are prostituted by those who lack the spiritual character to use them properly and who turn them to evil purposes.

4:23–24 SIN, Depravity—Sin grew rapidly in the human race. Lamech killed a young man who had simply injured him. The poetic form of the text indicated the depravity of Lamech's character as he bragged about his sinful act. Similarly, we are often tempted to demand more justice than we are due. Both divine and civil law attempt to restrain our sinful impulses and dispense a balanced judgment. Sin is never a cause for bragging. It causes only God's wrath and judgment.

4:26 PRAYER, Petition—The word "Enosh," like the word "Adam," (2:7) means "man," but implies weakness and dependency. This recognition of need in the naming of Enosh opens the history of prayer in the Bible. Later, Abram (12:8; 13:4) and Elijah (1 Ki 18:24) would call on the name of the Lord. The Lord promises to be near to all who call on Him (Ps 145:18).

Chapter 5

From Adam to Noah

THIS is the written account[t] of Adam's
line.[u]
When God created man, he made him
in the likeness of God.[v] 2 He created
them[w] male and female[x] and blessed
them. And when they were created, he
called them "man.[a] "
3 When Adam had lived 130 years, he
had a son in his own likeness, in his own
image;[y] and he named him Seth.[z] 4 After
Seth was born, Adam lived 800 years and
had other sons and daughters. 5 Altogether, Adam lived 930 years, and then he
died.[a]
6 When Seth had lived 105 years, he
became the father[b] of Enosh.[b] 7 And after he became the father of Enosh, Seth
lived 807 years and had other sons and
daughters. 8 Altogether, Seth lived 912
years, and then he died.
9 When Enosh had lived 90 years, he
became the father of Kenan.[c] 10 And after
he became the father of Kenan, Enosh
lived 815 years and had other sons and
daughters. 11 Altogether, Enosh lived 905
years, and then he died.
12 When Kenan had lived 70 years, he
became the father of Mahalalel.[d] 13 And
after he became the father of Mahalalel,
Kenan lived 840 years and had other sons
and daughters. 14 Altogether, Kenan lived
910 years, and then he died.
15 When Mahalalel had lived 65 years,
he became the father of Jared.[e] 16 And after he became the father of Jared, Mahalalel lived 830 years and had other sons
and daughters. 17 Altogether, Mahalalel
lived 895 years, and then he died.
18 When Jared had lived 162 years, he
became the father of Enoch.[f] 19 And after
he became the father of Enoch, Jared
lived 800 years and had other sons and
daughters. 20 Altogether, Jared lived 962
years, and then he died.

5:1 [t]S Ge 2:4 [u]1Ch 1:1 [v]S Ge 1:27; Col 3:10
5:2 [w]Ge 1:28 [x]S Ge 1:27; Mt 19:4; Mk 10:6; Gal 3:28
5:3 [y]S Ge 1:26; 1Co 15:49 [z]S Ge 4:25; Lk 3:38
5:5 [a]S Ge 2:17; Heb 9:27
5:6 [b]S Ge 4:26; Lk 3:38
5:9 [c]1Ch 1:2; Lk 3:37
5:12 [d]1Ch 1:2; Lk 3:37
5:15 [e]1Ch 1:2; Lk 3:37
5:18 [f]1Ch 1:3; Lk 3:37; Jude 1:14
5:21 [g]1Ch 1:3; Lk 3:37
5:22 [h]ver 24; Ge 6:9; 17:1; 24:40; 48:15; 2Ki 20:3; Ps 116:9; Mic 6:8; Mal 2:6
5:24 [i]S ver 22 [j]2Ki 2:1,11; Ps 49:15; 73:24; 89:48; Heb 11:5
5:25 [k]1Ch 1:3; Lk 3:36
5:29 [l]1Ch 1:3; Lk 3:36 [m]S Ge 3:17; Ro 8:20
5:32 [n]Ge 7:6,11; 8:13 [o]Lk 3:36 [p]Ge 6:10; 9:18; 10:1; 1Ch 1:4; Isa 65:20
6:1 [q]S Ge 1:28
6:2 [r]Job 1:6 *fn*; 2:1 *fn* [s]ver 4 [t]Dt 21:11 [u]S Ge 4:19
6:3 [v]Job 34:14; Gal 5:16-17 [w]Isa 57:16; 1Pe 3:20 [x]Job 10:9; Ps 78:39; 103:14; Isa 40:6
6:4 [y]Nu 13:33 [z]ver 2

21 When Enoch had lived 65 years, he
became the father of Methuselah.[g] 22 And
after he became the father of Methuselah,
Enoch walked with God[h] 300 years and
had other sons and daughters. 23 Altogether, Enoch lived 365 years. 24 Enoch
walked with God;[i] then he was no more,
because God took him away.[j]
25 When Methuselah had lived 187
years, he became the father of Lamech.[k]
26 And after he became the father of Lamech, Methuselah lived 782 years and
had other sons and daughters. 27 Altogether, Methuselah lived 969 years, and then
he died.
28 When Lamech had lived 182 years,
he had a son. 29 He named him Noah[c] [l]
and said, "He will comfort us in the labor
and painful toil of our hands caused by
the ground the LORD has cursed.[m]" 30 After Noah was born, Lamech lived 595
years and had other sons and daughters.
31 Altogether, Lamech lived 777 years,
and then he died.
32 After Noah was 500 years old,[n] he
became the father of Shem,[o] Ham and
Japheth.[p]

Chapter 6

The Flood

WHEN men began to increase in number on the earth[q] and daughters
were born to them, 2 the sons of God[r]
saw that the daughters of men[s] were
beautiful,[t] and they married[u] any of
them they chose. 3 Then the LORD said,
"My Spirit[v] will not contend with[d] man
forever,[w] for he is mortal[e];[x] his days
will be a hundred and twenty years."
4 The Nephilim[y] were on the earth in
those days—and also afterward—when
the sons of God went to the daughters of
men[z] and had children by them. They

[a] 2 Hebrew *adam* [b] 6 *Father* may mean *ancestor*; also in verses 7-26. [c] 29 *Noah* sounds like the Hebrew for *comfort*. [d] 3 Or *My spirit will not remain in* [e] 3 Or *corrupt*

5:1–3 HUMANITY, Image of God—The same terms are used to describe people being in God's image as are used to describe Seth being in Adam's image. See note on 1:26–29. The Bible emphasizes that people are the creatures of God the Creator. At the same time, life is passed on from parent to child in the normal life processes of conception and birth.

5:1–32 HISTORY, Linear—See notes on 2:4; 4:15–26. Genealogy is a basic form of biblical history telling. Genealogy shows how one generation expands its influence and abilities or how history continues through the centuries from one generation to another. All human events and generations are not the subject of biblical history. The Bible centers on events in which God gave identity to His people and worked out His purposes with them. Human hope of escape from the problems of history does not constitute history's theme (v 29). God's acts to deliver His faithful people gain the center of attention.

5:24 SALVATION, Grace—Enoch did not have to die because God took him (Heb 11:5). Although we must die, God's grace permits us to enjoy sweet fellowship with Him here and hereafter.

5:24 LAST THINGS, Believers' Death—Death as the outcome of life is stated eight times in this chapter of Genesis. This verse, however, breaks the pattern. Personal existence after physical death was not clearly taught in the early biblical literature. This verse indicates a basis for that belief even in these early genealogies. In this and other ways God revealed that our life extends beyond this world.

5:24 PRAYER, Fellowship with God—Practically every activity of the time required walking, and the term came to refer to the entire course of life itself. Enoch's life was spent in the company of God. See note on 1 Jn 1:3.

5:29 SIN, Estrangement—As a sign of their painful separation from God, humans continually seek comfort from other human sources. Future generations may offer new hope to the world. They cannot solve our sin problem. Bringing children into the world does not relieve sin's curse and make life easier.

were the heroes of old, men of renown.[a]
5 The LORD saw how great man's wickedness on the earth had become,[b] and
that every inclination of the thoughts of
his heart was only evil all the time.[c] 6 The
LORD was grieved[d] that he had made
man on the earth, and his heart was filled
with pain. 7 So the LORD said, "I will wipe
mankind, whom I have created, from the
face of the earth[e]—men and animals,
and creatures that move along the
ground, and birds of the air—for I am
grieved that I have made them.[f]" 8 But
Noah[g] found favor in the eyes of the
LORD.[h]

9 This is the account[i] of Noah.

Noah was a righteous man, blameless[j]
among the people of his time,[k] and he
walked with God.[l] 10 Noah had three
sons: Shem,[m] Ham and Japheth.[n]
11 Now the earth was corrupt[o] in God's
sight and was full of violence.[p] 12 God
saw how corrupt[q] the earth had become,
for all the people on earth had corrupted
their ways.[r] 13 So God said to Noah, "I
am going to put an end to all people, for
the earth is filled with violence because
of them. I am surely going to destroy[s]
both them and the earth.[t] 14 So make
yourself an ark of cypress[f] wood;[u] make
rooms in it and coat it with pitch[v] inside
and out. 15 This is how you are to build it:
The ark is to be 450 feet long, 75 feet
wide and 45 feet high.[g] 16 Make a roof for
it and finish[h] the ark to within 18
inches[i] of the top. Put a door in the side
of the ark and make lower, middle and
upper decks. 17 I am going to bring floodwaters[w] on the earth to destroy all life
under the heavens, every creature that
has the breath of life in it. Everything on
earth will perish.[x] 18 But I will establish
my covenant with you,[y] and you will enter the ark[z]—you and your sons and
your wife and your sons' wives with you.
19 You are to bring into the ark two of all
living creatures, male and female, to keep
them alive with you.[a] 20 Two[b] of every
kind of bird, of every kind of animal and
of every kind[c] of creature that moves
along the ground will come to you to be
kept alive.[d] 21 You are to take every kind
of food that is to be eaten and store it
away as food for you and for them."

6:4 [a]Ge 11:4 **6:5** [b]Ge 38:7; Job 34:26; Jer 1:16; 44:5; Eze 3:19 [c]Ge 8:21; Ps 14:1-3 **6:6** [d]Ex 32:14; 1Sa 15:11,35; 2Sa 24:16; 1Ch 21:15; Isa 63:10; Jer 18:7-10; Eph 4:30 **6:7** [e]Eze 33:28; Zep 1:2,18 [f]ver 17; Ge 7:4,21; Dt 28:63; 29:20 **6:8** [g]Eze 14:14 [h]Ge 19:19; 39:4; Ex 33:12,13,17; 34:9; Nu 11:15; Ru 2:2; Lk 1:30; Ac 7:46 **6:9** [i]S Ge 2:4 [j]Ge 17:1; Dt 18:13; 2Sa 22:24; Job 1:1; 4:6; 9:21; 12:4; 31:6; Ps 15:2; 18:23; 19:13; 37:37; Pr 2:7 [k]Ge 7:1; Ps 37:39; Jer 15:1; Eze 14:14, 20; Da 10:11; S Lk 1:6; Heb 11:7; 2Pe 2:5 [l]S Ge 5:22 **6:10** [m]Lk 3:36 [n]S Ge 5:32 **6:11** [o]Dt 31:29; Jdg 2:19 [p]Ps 7:9; 73:6; Eze 7:23; 8:17; 28:16; Mal 2:16 **6:12** [q]Ex 32:7; Dt 4:16; 9:12,24 [r]Ps 14:1-3 **6:13** [s]Dt 28:63; 2Ki 8:19; Ezr 9:14; Jer 44:11 [t]ver 17; Ge 7:4,21-23; Job 34:15; Isa 5:6; 24:1-3; Jer 44:27; Eze 7:2-3 **6:14** [u]Heb 11:7; 1Pe 3:20 [v]Ex 2:3 **6:17** [w]Ps 29:10 [x]S ver 7,S 13; 2Pe 2:5 **6:18** [y]Ge 9:9-16; 17:7; 19:12; Ex 6:4; 34:10,27; Dt 29:13,14-15; Ps 25:10; 74:20; 106:45; Isa 55:3; Jer 32:40; Eze 16:60; Hag 2:5; 1Pe 3:20 [z]Ge 7:1,7,13 **6:19** [a]Ge 7:15 **6:20** [b]Ge 7:15 [c]S Ge 1:11 [d]Ge 7:3

[f] *14* The meaning of the Hebrew for this word is uncertain. [g] *15* Hebrew *300 cubits long, 50 cubits wide and 30 cubits high* (about 140 meters long, 23 meters wide and 13.5 meters high) [h] *16* Or *Make an opening for light by finishing* [i] *16* Hebrew *a cubit* (about 0.5 meter)

6:5–8 GOD, Wrath—In the days of Noah, God's sternest measures were required if He was to show His true nature in redemptive love that brings forth righteousness. The wrath of God is not a release of pent-up emotion, such as we might experience as humans. The wrath of God is God's firm commitment to accomplish His righteous purposes. While He is patient and long-suffering in dealing with us as sinners, He will respond in sterner ways of judgment and retribution when necessary. When people do not properly respond to God's loving and gracious ways of dealing with them, the hand of God that blesses becomes the hand that chastises, or destroys if necessary. God does not ride a roller coaster of emotional changes so that He is loving one moment and wrathful at another. God is constant, patient and loving, but also faithful and just. He does what is necessary to accomplish His purpose. See Jas 1:17.

6:5 EVIL AND SUFFERING, Human Origin—Evil is frequently due to the human heart. Evil includes not only external public actions that oppose the will of God but also internal secret intentions. The human moral will did not and does not improve with passing generations. Humans do not naturally choose to do good. We are more inclined to do evil. See note on 8:21–22.

6:5 SIN, Depravity—As God viewed the progression toward evil within humanity, He was grieved that He had even created them. This text indicates that humanity's natural bent is toward evil. In theology this is referred to as depravity. Depravity can be defined as moral crookedness or perversion. Whether or not depravity is the cause of sin or sin the cause of depravity is not discussed here. What is plain, however, is that when humanity is left to its own inclinations, the result is sin. The cause of depravity is not discussed at length in the Bible. There are passages that can be interpreted to mean that humanity's depravity is inherited. See notes on Ps 51:5; Eph 2:1–3. Other texts seem to affirm that depravity is due to human choice. See notes on Eze 18:1–32; Ro 1:18–25. Whatever one's conclusion, the Bible teaches conclusively that humanity's depraved condition results in universal sin.

6:6–13 EVIL AND SUFFERING, Punishment—God's response to human evil can be radical punishment. God chose to destroy the created order dominated by human sin. God experiences grief, sorrow, and disappointment over our failure to do His will, but this does not turn Him from punishing sinners. Even in punishment His grace leads to reward for faithful obedience and a new start. See note on Ex 22:22–27.

6:8 SALVATION, Grace—God's grace is His undeserved favor. He favors those who like Noah are upright in character and conduct and can be used in His purposes. Compare 5:24.

6:9 HISTORY, Linear—See note on 2:4. History gains meaning from God's actions to overcome what grieves Him by creating new life opportunities for those who please Him. History thus is an ongoing account of judgment and deliverance as God seeks to establish His purposes on earth.

6:9,22 CHRISTIAN ETHICS, Moral Imperatives—The key to the description of Noah is that he obligated himself to the commands of God. As God's creatures, we live under heavenly expectations of conduct. God places imperatives upon us which it is our duty to perform. As Christians, we will walk through life with God. We also walk with other people, taking society's expectations into account. We must be righteous, living so that the consequences of our actions bear just results for other people both in the short-term and over the long haul of life. Our ethical decisions thus include theological, societal, relational, and consequential aspects. A one-sided basis for ethics is not sufficient to meet biblical standards.

6:9 PRAYER, Fellowship with God—See note on 5:24.

6:18 THE CHURCH, Covenant People—God's covenant promise first came as God announced devastating judgment. As God's covenant people, we owe our existence to God's mercy. In His mercy He seeks to purify and redeem us. See note on 9:8–17.

22 Noah did everything just as God commanded him.[e]

Chapter 7

THE LORD then said to Noah, "Go into
the ark, you and your whole family,[f]
because I have found you righteous[g] in
this generation. 2 Take with you seven[j] of
every kind of clean[h] animal, a male and
its mate, and two of every kind of unclean
animal, a male and its mate, 3 and also
seven of every kind of bird, male and female, to keep their various kinds alive[i]
throughout the earth. 4 Seven days from
now I will send rain[j] on the earth[k] for
forty days[l] and forty nights,[m] and I will
wipe from the face of the earth every living creature I have made.[n]"
5 And Noah did all that the LORD commanded him.[o]
6 Noah was six hundred years old[p]
when the floodwaters came on the earth.
7 And Noah and his sons and his wife and
his sons' wives entered the ark[q] to escape the waters of the flood. 8 Pairs of
clean and unclean[r] animals, of birds and
of all creatures that move along the
ground, 9 male and female, came to Noah
and entered the ark, as God had commanded Noah.[s] 10 And after the seven
days[t] the floodwaters came on the earth.
11 In the six hundredth year of Noah's
life,[u] on the seventeenth day of the second month[v]—on that day all the springs
of the great deep[w] burst forth, and the
floodgates of the heavens[x] were opened.
12 And rain fell on the earth forty days and
forty nights.[y]
13 On that very day Noah and his sons,[z]
Shem, Ham and Japheth, together with
his wife and the wives of his three sons,
entered the ark.[a] 14 They had with them
every wild animal according to its kind,
all livestock according to their kinds, every creature that moves along the ground
according to its kind and every bird according to its kind,[b] everything with
wings. 15 Pairs of all creatures that have
the breath of life in them came to Noah
and entered the ark.[c] 16 The animals going in were male and female of every living thing, as God had commanded
Noah.[d] Then the LORD shut him in.
17 For forty days[e] the flood kept coming
on the earth, and as the waters increased
they lifted the ark high above the earth.
18 The waters rose and increased greatly
on the earth, and the ark floated on the
surface of the water. 19 They rose greatly
on the earth, and all the high mountains
under the entire heavens were covered.[f]
20 The waters rose and covered the mountains to a depth of more than twenty feet.[k,l] [g] 21 Every living thing that
moved on the earth perished—birds,
livestock, wild animals, all the creatures
that swarm over the earth, and all mankind.[h] 22 Everything on dry land that had
the breath of life[i] in its nostrils died.
23 Every living thing on the face of the
earth was wiped out; men and animals
and the creatures that move along the
ground and the birds of the air were
wiped from the earth.[j] Only Noah was
left, and those with him in the ark.[k]
24 The waters flooded the earth for a
hundred and fifty days.[l]

Chapter 8

BUT God remembered[m] Noah and all
the wild animals and the livestock

6:22 [e]Ge 7:5,9,16; Ex 7:6; 39:43; 40:16,19,21,23,25, 27,29,32 **7:1** [f]S Ge 6:18; Mt 24:38; Lk 17:26-27; Heb 11:7; 1Pe 3:20; 2Pe 2:5 [g]Ge 6:9; Eze 14:14 **7:2** [h]ver 8; Ge 8:20; Lev 10:10; 11:1-47; Dt 14:3-20; Eze 44:23; Hag 2:12; Ac 10:14-15 **7:3** [i]Ge 6:20 **7:4** [j]Ge 8:2 [k]1Ki 13:34; Jer 28:16 [l]Nu 13:25; Dt 9:9; 1Sa 17:16; 1Ki 19:8 [m]ver 12,17; Ex 24:18; 32:1; 34:28; Dt 9:9,11, 18,25; 10:10; Job 37:6,13; Mt 4:2 [n]S Ge 6:7,13 **7:5** [o]S Ge 6:22 **7:6** [p]S Ge 5:32 **7:7** [q]S Ge 6:18 **7:8** [r]S ver 2 **7:9** [s]S Ge 6:22 **7:10** [t]S ver 4 **7:11** [u]S Ge 5:32 [v]Ge 8:4,14 [w]S Ge 1:7; Job 28:11; Ps 36:6; 42:7; Pr 8:24; Isa 51:10; Eze 26:19 [x]Ge 8:2; 2Ki 7:2; Ps 78:23; Isa 24:18; Mal 3:10 **7:12** [y]S ver 4; S 1Sa 12:17; S Job 28:26 **7:13** [z]Ge 8:16; 1Pe 3:20; 2Pe 2:5 [a]S Ge 6:18 **7:14** [b]S Ge 1:11 **7:15** [c]ver 8-9; Ge 6:19 **7:16** [d]S Ge 6:22 **7:17** [e]S ver 4 **7:19** [f]Ps 104:6 **7:20** [g]Ge 8:4-5; 2Pe 3:6 **7:21** [h]S Ge 6:7,13; 2Pe 3:6 **7:22** [i]S Ge 1:30 **7:23** [j]Job 14:19; 21:18; 22:11,16; Ps 90:5; Isa 28:2; Mt 24:39; Lk 17:27; 1Pe 3:20; 2Pe 2:5 [k]Heb 11:7 **7:24** [l]Ge 8:3; Job 12:15 **8:1** [m]Ge 9:15; 19:29; 21:1; 30:22; Ex 2:24; Nu 10:9; Ru 4:13; 1Sa 1:11,19; 2Ki 20:3; 1Ch 16:15; Ne 1:8; 5:19; 13:14,22,31; Job 14:13; Ps 105:42; 106:4; Lk 1:54,72

[j]2 Or *seven pairs*; also in verse 3 [k]20 Hebrew *fifteen cubits* (about 6.9 meters) [l]20 Or *rose more than twenty feet, and the mountains were covered*

7:1—9:17 MIRACLE, Redemption—These miracles should generate in us the same wonder and amazement that they generated in the first witnesses. Miracles have redemptive purpose. They display God's power and purpose to save and judge. Disappointed with human sin, God brought a unique flood to destroy the sinners, but He also miraculously rescued one family and representative animals to start over again. The emphasis is on God's saving mercy even as He remains sovereign Lord of creation. To perform His miracles, God used the natural order—rain and rainbow, animals. He used the persons He wished to save to announce, to cooperate in, and to interpret the miracle. He caused all to happen according to His timing for His purposes. A wonderful part of this miracle is God's solemn promise never to repeat it.

7:1,5 CHRISTIAN ETHICS, Moral Imperatives—See note on 6:9,22.

7:1,7; 9:1–2 FAMILY, Accepting Covenant—In the midst of a generation corrupting God's world, Noah and his family were found faithful enough to be spared the judgment of destruction by flood. After the waters receded, God established His covenant with Noah and his family. This covenant reaffirmed the creative intent of God for humans and included a new and powerful declaration of the value of life created in the image of God. Accepting covenant relationships with God by families is central to God's requirements throughout the Old Testament. It finds its ultimate fulfillment in the acceptance of the covenant of grace in Jesus Christ. See note on Eph 5:21.

7:15,22 CREATION, Judgment—God loved His creation; but when it defied His moral standards, He knew He must vindicate His holiness by sending punishment. Because creation was good, however, He wished to preserve it. He established propagation as His method of perpetuating His creation. Even as He punished sinners, He made provision for propagation of the species to continue. We can be certain God's world will go on today until He wills to consummate history with Christ's return. The world is so constituted that it adjusts to any shock or tragedy. God controls creation's destiny.

8:1 GOD, Faithfulness—God faithfully kept His promise to Noah that he and his family would be saved during the flood that destroyed all the rest of mankind. God always remembers His promises and is faithful to His people. His faithfulness is the outgrowth of two of the basic attributes of God: love and righteousness.

that were with him in the ark, and he
sent a wind over the earth,[n] and the waters receded. 2Now the springs of the
deep and the floodgates of the heavens[o]
had been closed, and the rain[p] had
stopped falling from the sky. 3The water
receded steadily from the earth. At the
end of the hundred and fifty days[q] the
water had gone down, 4and on the seventeenth day of the seventh month[r] the ark
came to rest on the mountains[s] of Ararat.[t] 5The waters continued to recede
until the tenth month, and on the first
day of the tenth month the tops of the
mountains became visible.

6After forty days[u] Noah opened the
window he had made in the ark 7and sent
out a raven,[v] and it kept flying back and
forth until the water had dried up from
the earth.[w] 8Then he sent out a dove[x] to
see if the water had receded from the surface of the ground. 9But the dove could
find no place to set its feet because there
was water over all the surface of the
earth; so it returned to Noah in the ark.
He reached out his hand and took the
dove and brought it back to himself in the
ark. 10He waited seven more days and
again sent out the dove from the ark.
11When the dove returned to him in the
evening, there in its beak was a freshly
plucked olive leaf! Then Noah knew that
the water had receded from the earth.[y]
12He waited seven more days and sent
the dove out again, but this time it did
not return to him.

13By the first day of the first month of
Noah's six hundred and first year,[z] the
water had dried up from the earth. Noah
then removed the covering from the ark
and saw that the surface of the ground
was dry. 14By the twenty-seventh day of
the second month[a] the earth was completely dry.

15Then God said to Noah, 16"Come out
of the ark, you and your wife and your
sons and their wives.[b] 17Bring out every
kind of living creature that is with you—
the birds, the animals, and all the creatures that move along the ground—so
they can multiply on the earth and be
fruitful and increase in number upon
it."[c]

18So Noah came out, together with his
sons and his wife and his sons' wives.[d]
19All the animals and all the creatures
that move along the ground and all the
birds—everything that moves on the
earth—came out of the ark, one kind after another.

20Then Noah built an altar to the
LORD[e] and, taking some of all the clean
animals and clean[f] birds, he sacrificed
burnt offerings[g] on it. 21The LORD
smelled the pleasing aroma[h] and said in
his heart: "Never again will I curse the
ground[i] because of man, even though[m]
every inclination of his heart is evil from
childhood.[j] And never again will I destroy[k] all living creatures,[l] as I have
done.

22"As long as the earth endures,
seedtime and harvest,[m]
cold and heat,
summer and winter,[n]
day and night
will never cease."[o]

Chapter 9

God's Covenant With Noah

THEN God blessed Noah and his sons,
saying to them, "Be fruitful and increase in number and fill the earth.[p]
2The fear and dread of you will fall upon
all the beasts of the earth and all the birds
of the air, upon every creature that moves
along the ground, and upon all the fish of

[m]21 Or *man, for*

8:1 [n]Ex 14:21; Jos 2:10; 3:16; Job 12:15; Ps 66:6; Isa 11:15; 44:27; Na 1:4
8:2 [o]S Ge 7:11 [p]S Ge 7:4
8:3 [q]S Ge 7:24
8:4 [r]S Ge 7:11 [s]Ge 7:20 [t]2Ki 19:37; Jer 51:27
8:6 [u]Ge 7:12
8:7 [v]Lev 11:15; Dt 14:14; 1Ki 17:4, 6; Job 38:41; Ps 147:9; Pr 30:17; Isa 34:11; Lk 12:24 [w]ver 11
8:8 [x]Job 30:31; Ps 55:6; 74:19; SS 2:12,14; Isa 38:14; 59:11; 60:8; Jer 48:28; Eze 7:16; Hos 7:11; 11:11; Na 2:7; Mt 3:16; 10:16; Jn 1:32
8:11 [y]ver 7
8:13 [z]S Ge 5:32
8:14 [a]S Ge 7:11
8:16 [b]S Ge 7:13
8:17 [c]S Ge 1:22
8:18 [d]1Pe 3:20; 2Pe 2:5
8:20 [e]Ge 12:7-8; 13:18; 22:9; 26:25; 33:20; 35:7; Ex 17:15; 24:4 [f]S Ge 7:8 [g]Ge 22:2, 13; Ex 10:25; 20:24; 40:29; Lev 1:3; 4:29; 6:8-13; Nu 6:11; Jdg 6:26; 11:31; 1Sa 20:29; Job 1:5; 42:8
8:21 [h]Ex 29:18,25; Lev 1:9,13; 2:9; 4:31; Nu 15:3,7; 2Co 2:15 [i]S Ge 3:17 [j]Ge 6:5; Ps 51:5; Jer 17:9; Mt 15:19; Ro 1:21 [k]Jer 44:11 [l]Ge 9:11,15; Isa 54:9
8:22 [m]Jos 3:15; Ps 67:6; Jer 5:24 [n]Ps 74:17; Zec 14:8 [o]S Ge 1:14
9:1 [p]S Ge 1:22

8:20 PRAYER, Thanksgiving—In view of the destruction of animal life in the flood, this sacrifice was very precious. Noah's gratitude was expressed by offering something very valuable to him. Noah, Abraham, Isaac, and Jacob built altars (12:8; 26:25; 35:7) in gratitude. See notes on 12:7–8; Lev 1:9.

8:21–22 EVIL AND SUFFERING, Natural Origin—The evil of human hearts (6:5) continued after the flood. In His grace God decided to bear with human evil rather than destroy all life. Human evil is thus an ongoing part of life in God's creation until Christ comes again. Such evil does not threaten the natural order. God maintains control of His creation and promises the regular coming and going of the seasons of the year. God did not promise we would never have natural disasters. He did assert His control of nature.

8:21 SIN, Depravity—Though the Bible presents no philosophical or systematic arguments concerning humanity's depravity or the cause of it, the fact of the universality of sin is everywhere affirmed in the Bible. Through Adam's sin, sin and death entered the world, bringing condemnation to all humans. See note on 6:5; Ro 5:12–21.

8:21 SALVATION, Grace—All persons since Noah have been blessed because of God's covenant with Noah. See note on Heb 11:7.

8:22 CREATION, Hope—God promised those who survived the flood that the forces of nature would act with predictable harmony. People would, therefore, be able to plan for the future with assurance that sowing and reaping would still be a reality. The constant factors of creation remain in God's hand as a way of offering hope to His people.

8:22 HISTORY, Promise—History gains stability and continuity through God's promises not through human accomplishments.

9:1–6 HUMANITY, Responsibility—A part of being in God's image is responsibility. See note on 1:26–29. That responsibility focuses upon the fact that only God can give life. It also involves humanity's responsible use of procreating powers. Beyond this, human responsibility includes the proper exercise of control over all the rest of the world and its creatures. For a treatment of the relationship between life and blood, see note on Lev 17:11.

the sea; they are given into your hands.[q]
3Everything that lives and moves will be
food for you.[r] Just as I gave you the green
plants, I now give you everything.[s]
4"But you must not eat meat that has
its lifeblood still in it.[t] 5And for your lifeblood I will surely demand an accounting.[u] I will demand an accounting from
every animal.[v] And from each man, too, I
will demand an accounting for the life of
his fellow man.[w]

6"Whoever sheds the blood of man,
by man shall his blood be shed;[x]
for in the image of God[y]
has God made man.

7As for you, be fruitful and increase in
number; multiply on the earth and increase upon it."[z]
8Then God said to Noah and to his sons
with him: 9"I now establish my covenant
with you[a] and with your descendants after you 10and with every living creature
that was with you—the birds, the livestock and all the wild animals, all those
that came out of the ark with you—every
living creature on earth. 11I establish my
covenant[b] with you:[c] Never again will
all life be cut off by the waters of a flood;
never again will there be a flood to destroy the earth.[d]"
12And God said, "This is the sign of the
covenant[e] I am making between me and
you and every living creature with you, a
covenant for all generations to come:[f] 13I
have set my rainbow[g] in the clouds, and
it will be the sign of the covenant between me and the earth. 14Whenever I
bring clouds over the earth and the rainbow[h] appears in the clouds, 15I will remember my covenant[i] between me and
you and all living creatures of every kind.
Never again will the waters become a
flood to destroy all life.[j] 16Whenever the
rainbow[k] appears in the clouds, I will see
it and remember the everlasting covenant[l] between God and all living creatures of every kind on the earth."
17So God said to Noah, "This is the
sign of the covenant[m] I have established
between me and all life on the earth."

The Sons of Noah

18The sons of Noah who came out of
the ark were Shem, Ham and Japheth.[n]
(Ham was the father of Canaan.)[o]
19These were the three sons of Noah,[p]
and from them came the people who
were scattered over the earth.[q]
20Noah, a man of the soil, proceeded[n]
to plant a vineyard. 21When he drank

9:2 [q]S Ge 1:26 **9:3** [r]S Ge 1:29 [s]S Ac 10:15; Col 2:16 **9:4** [t]Lev 3:17; 7:26; 17:10-14; 19:26; Dt 12:16, 23-25; 15:23; 1Sa 14:33; Eze 33:25; Ac 15:20,29 **9:5** [u]Ge 42:22; 50:15; 1Ki 2:32; 2Ch 24:22; Ps 9:12 [v]Ex 21:28-32 [w]Ge 4:10 **9:6** [x]S Ge 4:14; S Jdg 9:24; S Mt 26:52 [y]S Ge 1:26 **9:7** [z]S Ge 1:22 **9:9** [a]ver 11; S Ge 6:18 **9:11** [b]ver 16; Isa 24:5; 33:8; Hos 6:7 [c]S ver 9 [d]S Ge 8:21 **9:12** [e]ver 17; Ge 17:11 [f]Ge 17:12; Ex 12:14; Lev 3:17; 6:18; 17:7; Nu 10:8 **9:13** [g]ver 14; Eze 1:28; Rev 4:3; 10:1 **9:14** [h]S ver 13 **9:15** [i]S Ge 8:1; Ex 2:24; 6:5; 34:10; Lev 26:42, 45; Dt 7:9; Ps 89:34; 103:18; 105:8; 106:45; Eze 16:60 [j]S Ge 8:21 **9:16** [k]ver 13 [l]S ver 11; Ge 17:7, 13,19; 2Sa 7:13; 23:5; Ps 105:9-10; Isa 9:7; 54:10; 55:3; 59:21; 61:8; Jer 31:31-34; 32:40; 33:21; Eze 16:60; 37:26; S Heb 13:20 **9:17** [m]S ver 12 **9:18** [n]S Ge 5:32; Lk 3:36 [o]ver 25-27; Ge 10:6,15 **9:19** [p]Ge 5:32 [q]S Ge 1:22; 10:32; 11:4,8,9

[n]*20* Or *soil, was the first*

9:4–11 CHRISTIAN ETHICS, Moral Limits—Ethical limits can be defined through contracts. God made covenants or contracts with His people outlining the limits of life acceptable to God. Because God is good, we know the limits He establishes are good for us. We must honor life in all His creatures. See note on Dt 12:23–25.

9:7 HISTORY, Linear—Human procreation and family life cause history to continue. This basic human reality is based on God's creative act and blessing. Israel's neighbors celebrated divine procreation populating the heavenly world and establishing the natural elements. Israel's God celebrated human procreation fulfilling His purposes.

9:8–17 GOD, Personal—God expresses His relationship to people in terms of the covenant, a solemn personal promise or agreement. God initiates the covenant and chooses to be gracious to His chosen ones. The covenant is the outward expression of the inward disposition of the heart of God. Through the covenant announced here, God showed that He is personally interested in all mankind to come and that He has a benevolent disposition towards all.

9:8–17 CREATION, Hope—This divine promise or covenant guarantees the continuity of human life and of creation. God has committed Himself to a stable world in which He is working to establish His kingdom. Humans can plan for the future, assured life will continue on earth until Christ comes.

9:8–17 THE CHURCH, Covenant People—God fulfills His promises. See note on 6:18. What God promised to do for Noah, He did. God bases His work with His people on His own grace, not on any goodness which the people might possess or perform. A covenant establishes a relationship. In ancient times covenants were prevalent among many peoples. A covenant could be established among equal partners or, more often, between superior and inferior parties. Victorious kings established covenants with defeated kings. The covenants between such parties defined the relationship to be maintained and the requirements to be placed on each party. Remarkably God's covenant with Noah required no stipulations. God freely enters into relationship with His people. He wishes to know His own and to be known by them. This first explicit biblical covenant revealed God to be a covenant-making God seeking to bless all people. Thus it prepared the way for all other covenants. The Lord is involved intimately with the whole earth. He created the world, sent the waters of the flood, and made a covenant with the earth and all its inhabitants. God blesses His people with promises which are sure and unwavering. The people were afraid of every rain cloud, but the Lord gave a sign of His constant care and vigilance. This everlasting covenant remains in effect. God continues to guard His creation. The rainbow is a sign of God's unfailing care. The promise does not prohibit God from finally judging His universe. See note on Ex 19:4–8.

9:12–16 REVELATION, Author of Grace—The covenant of grace reveals God as the Author of creation and hope. He made a commitment to redeem creation and offered a sign for all to see. Human beings are thus reminded daily of the covenant God makes and which we forget. God offered here another window through which we may gaze at His heart: He does not wish to destroy what He has made. He wishes to redeem, save, and sustain all that He makes. The ancients looked upon many of nature's signs as revelation of God's work. The Bible sees the rainbow as a symbol of hope and forgiveness. God is ever present to keep on bringing back to life His dream and plan for human beings. Each day and night are clear reminders of His power and His caring presence in the universe: without the presence of good as God's constant revealed intention in the world, people would despair. The earliest revelation of the Divine is also immediately associated with His commitment. He is a God who keeps His promises, even if people do not.

9:18–19 HISTORY, Linear—See notes on 5:1–32; 10:1–32.

9:20–27 HISTORY, Moral—History rests on a moral foundation. Ham's immodest treatment of his father brought

some of its wine,[r] he became drunk and
lay uncovered inside his tent. 22 Ham, the
father of Canaan, saw his father's nakedness[s] and told his two brothers outside.
23 But Shem and Japheth took a garment
and laid it across their shoulders; then
they walked in backward and covered
their father's nakedness. Their faces were
turned the other way so that they would
not see their father's nakedness.
24 When Noah awoke from his wine
and found out what his youngest son had
done to him, 25 he said,

"Cursed[t] be Canaan![u]
The lowest of slaves
will he be to his brothers.[v]"

26 He also said,

"Blessed be the LORD, the God of
Shem![w]
May Canaan be the slave[x] of
Shem.[o]
27 May God extend the territory of
Japheth[p];[y]
may Japheth live in the tents of
Shem,[z]
and may Canaan be his[q] slave."

28 After the flood Noah lived 350 years.
29 Altogether, Noah lived 950 years, and
then he died.[a]

Chapter 10

The Table of Nations

THIS is the account[b] of Shem, Ham
and Japheth,[c] Noah's sons,[d] who
themselves had sons after the flood.

The Japhethites

10:2–5pp — 1Ch 1:5–7

2 The sons[r] of Japheth:
Gomer,[e] Magog,[f] Madai, Javan,[g] Tubal,[h] Meshech[i] and
Tiras.
3 The sons of Gomer:
Ashkenaz,[j] Riphath and Togarmah.[k]
4 The sons of Javan:
Elishah,[l] Tarshish,[m] the Kittim[n]
and the Rodanim.[s] 5 (From these
the maritime peoples spread out
into their territories by their clans
within their nations, each with its
own language.)[o]

The Hamites

10:6–20pp — 1Ch 1:8–16

6 The sons of Ham:
Cush,[p] Mizraim,[t] Put[q] and
Canaan.[r]
7 The sons of Cush:
Seba,[s] Havilah,[t] Sabtah, Raa-
mah[u] and Sabteca.
The sons of Raamah:
Sheba[v] and Dedan.[w]

8 Cush was the father[u] of Nimrod,[x]
who grew to be a mighty warrior on the
earth. 9 He was a mighty[y] hunter[z] before
the LORD; that is why it is said, "Like
Nimrod, a mighty hunter before the
LORD." 10 The first centers of his kingdom
were Babylon,[a] Erech,[b] Akkad and Calneh,[c] in[v] Shinar.[w][d] 11 From that land he
went to Assyria,[e] where he built Nineveh,[f] Rehoboth Ir,[x] Calah 12 and Resen,
which is between Nineveh and Calah;
that is the great city.

13 Mizraim was the father of
the Ludites, Anamites, Lehabites,
Naphtuhites, 14 Pathrusites, Casluhites (from whom the Philistines[g]
came) and Caphtorites.[h]
15 Canaan[i] was the father of
Sidon[j] his firstborn,[y][k] and of
the Hittites,[l] 16 Jebusites,[m] Amorites,[n] Girgashites,[o] 17 Hivites,[p]

9:21 [r]Ge 19:35 **9:22** [s]Hab 2:15 **9:25** [t]Ge 27:12 [u]ver 18; Ex 20:5; Ps 79:8; Isa 14:21; Jer 31:29; 32:18 [v]Ge 25:23; 27:29, 37,40; 37:10; 49:8; Nu 24:18; Jos 9:23 **9:26** [w]Ge 14:20; Ex 18:10; Ps 7:17 [x]1Ki 9:21 **9:27** [y]Ge 10:2-5 [z]Eph 2:13-14; 3:6 **9:29** [a]S Ge 2:17 **10:1** [b]Ge 2:4 [c]S Ge 5:32 [d]ver 32; 1Ch 1:4 **10:2** [e]Eze 38:6 [f]Eze 38:2; 39:6; Rev 20:8 [g]Eze 27:19 [h]Isa 66:19; Eze 27:13; 32:26 [i]Eze 39:1 **10:3** [j]Jer 51:27 [k]Eze 27:14; 38:6 **10:4** [l]Eze 27:7 [m]Ps 48:7; 72:10; Isa 2:16; 23:1,6,10, 14; 60:9; 66:19; Jer 10:9; Eze 27:12, 25; 38:13; Jnh 1:3 [n]Nu 24:24; Isa 23:12; Jer 2:10; Eze 27:6; Da 11:30 **10:5** [o]Ge 9:27 **10:6** [p]2Ki 19:9; 2Ch 12:3; 16:8; Isa 11:11; 18:1; 20:3; 43:3; Jer 46:9; Eze 30:4, 9; 38:5; Na 3:9; Zep 2:12; 3:10 [q]Eze 27:10; 38:5 [r]S Ge 9:18 **10:7** [s]Isa 43:3 [t]S Ge 2:11 [u]Eze 27:22 [v]Ge 25:3; 1Ki 10:1; 2Ch 9:1; Job 1:15; 6:19; 16:11; Ps 72:10,15; Isa 60:6; Jer 6:20; Eze 27:22; 38:13; Joel 3:8 [w]1Ch 1:32; Isa 21:13; Jer 25:23-24; 49:8; Eze 27:15,20; 38:13 **10:8** [x]Mic 5:6 **10:9** [y]2Ch 14:9; 16:8; Isa 18:2 [z]Ge 25:27; 27:3 **10:10** [a]Ge 11:9; 2Ch 36:17; Isa 13:1; 47:1; Jer 21:2; 25:12; 50:1 [b]Ezr 4:9 [c]Isa 10:9; Am 6:2 [d]Ge 11:2; 14:1; Zec 5:11 **10:11** [e]Ps 83:8; Mic 5:6 [f]2Ki 19:36; Isa 37:37; Jnh 1:2; 3:2,3; 4:11; Na 1:1; Zep 2:13 **10:14** [g]Ge 21:32, 34; 26:1,8; Jos 13:2; Jdg 3:3; Isa 14:31; Jer 47:1,4; Am 9:7 [h]Dt 2:23; 1Ch 1:12 **10:15** [i]S Ge 9:18 [j]ver 19; Jos 11:8; Jdg 10:6; Isa 23:2,4; Jer 25:22; 27:3; 47:4; Eze 28:21; 32:30; Joel 3:4; Zec 9:2 [k]Ex 4:22; Nu 1:20; 3:2; 18:15; 26:5; 33:4 [l]Ge 15:20; 23:3,20; 25:10; 26:34; 27:46; 49:32; Nu 13:29; Jos 1:4; 1Sa 26:6; Eze 16:3 **10:16** [m]Jdg 19:10; 1Ch 11:4; Ezr 9:1 [n]Ex 3:8; Nu 13:29; 21:13; 32:39; Dt 1:4; Jos 2:10; 2Ch 8:7 [o]Ge 15:18-21; Dt 7:1 **10:17** [p]Ge 34:2; 36:2; Ex 3:8; Dt 7:1; Jdg 3:3

[o]*26* Or *be his slave* [p]*27 Japheth* sounds like the Hebrew for *extend.* [q]*27* Or *their* [r]*2 Sons* may mean *descendants* or *successors* or *nations*; also in verses 3, 4, 6, 7, 20-23, 29 and 31. [s]*4* Some manuscripts of the Masoretic Text and Samaritan Pentateuch (see also Septuagint and 1 Chron. 1:7); most manuscripts of the Masoretic Text *Dodanim* [t]*6* That is, Egypt; also in verse 13 [u]*8 Father* may mean *ancestor* or *predecessor* or *founder*; also in verses 13, 15, 24 and 26. [v]*10* Or *Erech and Akkad—all of them in* [w]*10* That is, Babylonia [x]*11* Or *Nineveh with its city squares* [y]*15* Or *of the Sidonians, the foremost*

disgrace and servitude to his family. The moral basis of history derives from the moral nature and purposes of God, who directs history.

9:21 CHRISTIAN ETHICS, Alcohol—The ugly side of the use of alcohol became apparent early in human existence. Drunkenness is wrong not only for what it does to the individual but also because of its effects on family relationships.

9:24–27 PRAYER, Petition—What seems to be a strange prayer was a recognition before God of the character of these sons. The closely knit family structure of patriarchal days rendered it likely that godliness would be propagated (18:19; Ps 103:17), as well as ungodliness (Ex 20:5). Future generations are responsible for their own sin. Of all Ham's sons, it was the Canaanites whose Baal worship would plague future Israel.

10:1–32 HISTORY, Universal—History involves nations not just individuals. The table of nations uses genealogical forms to describe the rise of international powers and rivals. Nations are not eternal realities but historical developments rising out of God's call to individuals to be fruitful. The table of nations witnesses to God's universal interest. No matter how narrow the biblical story may appear as it focuses on the one family of Abraham, its universal context provides theological interpretation for the narrow focus. See notes on 5:1–32; 9:7.

Arkites, Sinites, 18Arvadites,[q]
Zemarites and Hamathites.[r]

Later the Canaanite[s] clans scattered
19and the borders of Canaan[t] reached
from Sidon[u] toward Gerar[v] as far as
Gaza,[w] and then toward Sodom, Gomorrah, Admah and Zeboiim,[x] as far as La-
sha.

20These are the sons of Ham by their
clans and languages, in their territories
and nations.

The Semites

10:21–31pp — Ge 11:10–27; 1Ch 1:17–27

21Sons were also born to Shem, whose
older brother was[z] Japheth; Shem was
the ancestor of all the sons of Eber.[y]

22The sons of Shem:
Elam,[z] Asshur,[a] Arphaxad,[b] Lud
and Aram.[c]
23The sons of Aram:
Uz,[d] Hul, Gether and Meshech.[a]
24Arphaxad was the father of[b] Shelah,
and Shelah the father of Eber.[e]
25Two sons were born to Eber:
One was named Peleg,[c] because
in his time the earth was divided;
his brother was named Joktan.
26Joktan was the father of
Almodad, Sheleph, Hazarmaveth,
Jerah, 27Hadoram, Uzal,[f] Diklah,
28Obal, Abimael, Sheba,[g]
29Ophir,[h] Havilah and Jobab. All
these were sons of Joktan.

30The region where they lived stretched
from Mesha toward Sephar, in the eastern hill country.

31These are the sons of Shem by their
clans and languages, in their territories
and nations.

32These are the clans of Noah's sons,[i]
according to their lines of descent, within
their nations. From these the nations
spread out over the earth[j] after the
flood.

Chapter 11

The Tower of Babel

NOW the whole world had one language[k] and a common speech. 2As
men moved eastward,[d] they found a
plain in Shinar[e][l] and settled there.
3They said to each other, "Come, let's
make bricks[m] and bake them thoroughly." They used brick instead of stone,[n]
and tar[o] for mortar. 4Then they said,
"Come, let us build ourselves a city, with
a tower that reaches to the heavens,[p] so
that we may make a name[q] for ourselves
and not be scattered[r] over the face of the
whole earth."[s]

5But the LORD came down[t] to see the
city and the tower that the men were
building. 6The LORD said, "If as one people speaking the same language[u] they
have begun to do this, then nothing they
plan to do will be impossible for them.
7Come, let us[v] go down[w] and confuse
their language so they will not understand each other."[x]

8So the LORD scattered them from
there over all the earth,[y] and they
stopped building the city. 9That is why it
was called Babel[f][z]—because there the
LORD confused the language[a] of the
whole world.[b] From there the LORD scattered[c] them over the face of the whole
earth.

10:18 [q]Eze 27:8 [r]1Ch 18:3 [s]Ge 12:6; 13:7; 50:11; Ex 13:11; Nu 13:29; 14:25; 21:3; 33:40; Dt 1:7; Jdg 1:1 **10:19** [t]Ge 11:31; 12:1; 13:12; 17:8; 24:3; 26:34; 27:46; 28:1,6,8; 31:18; 35:6; 37:1; Lev 25:38 [u]S ver 15; Ge 49:13; Jos 19:28; Jdg 1:31; 18:28; 2Sa 24:6 [v]2Ch 14:13 [w]Dt 2:23; Jos 10:41; 11:22; 15:47; Jdg 1:18; 6:4; 16:1,21; 1Sa 6:17; Jer 25:20; 47:1; Am 1:6; Zep 2:4 [x]Ge 14:2; Dt 29:23 **10:21** [y]ver 24; Nu 24:24 **10:22** [z]Ge 14:1; Isa 11:11; 21:2; Jer 25:25; 49:34; Eze 32:24; Da 8:2 [a]Nu 24:22,24; Eze 27:23 [b]Lk 3:36 [c]Jdg 3:10; 1Ki 11:25; 19:15; 20:34; 22:31; 2Ki 5:1; 8:7 **10:23** [d]Ge 22:21; Job 1:1; Jer 25:20; La 4:21 **10:24** [e]S ver 21; Lk 3:35 **10:27** [f]Eze 27:19 **10:28** [g]1Ki 10:1; Job 6:19; Ps 72:10, 15; Isa 60:6; Eze 27:22 **10:29** [h]1Ki 9:28; 10:11; 1Ch 29:4; Job 22:24; 28:16; Ps 45:9; Isa 13:12 **10:32** [i]S ver 1 [j]S Ge 9:19 **11:1** [k]ver 6 **11:2** [l]S Ge 10:10 **11:3** [m]Ex 1:14; 5:7; Jer 43:9 [n]Isa 9:10; Am 5:11 [o]Ge 14:10 **11:4** [p]Dt 1:28; 6:10; 9:1; Job 20:6; Jer 51:53 [q]Ge 6:4 [r]Dt 30:3; 1Ki 22:17; Est 3:8; Ps 44:11; Jer 31:10; 40:15; Eze 6:8; Joel 3:2 [s]S Ge 9:19; Dt 4:27

11:5 [t]ver 7; Ge 18:21; Ex 3:8; 19:11,18,20; Ps 18:9; 144:5 **11:6** [u]S ver 1 **11:7** [v]S Ge 1:26 [w]S ver 5 [x]Ge 42:23; Dt 28:49; Isa 28:11; 33:19; Jer 5:15; 1Co 14:2,11 **11:8** [y]S Ge 9:19; Dt 32:8; S Lk 1:51 **11:9** [z]S Ge 10:10 [a]Ps 55:9 [b]Ac 2:5-11 [c]Isa 2:10,21; 13:14; 24:1

[z]*21* Or *Shem, the older brother of* [a]*23* See Septuagint and 1 Chron. 1:17; Hebrew *Mash* [b]*24* Hebrew; Septuagint *father of Cainan, and Cainan was the father of* [c]*25 Peleg* means *division.* [d]*2* Or *from the east*; or *in the east* [e]*2* That is, Babylonia [f]*9* That is, Babylon; *Babel* sounds like the Hebrew for *confused.*

11:1–9 MIRACLE, Continual Creation—God's creative powers were not put in retirement after the first seven days of world history. He continued to use His powers even in responding to human sin to accomplish His ultimate creative purposes. He did not intend for a major part of the world to remain uninhabited. Human pride and arrogance produced the Tower of Babel. God responded in limited judgment. He scattered the human population throughout the earth and brought about the diversity of human languages. This miraculous judgment created a new human situation demanding a new stage in God's missionary work to redeem all people.

11:1–9 HUMANITY, Potentiality—God's own estimate of human potentiality is one of the highest compliments paid to humankind anywhere in the Bible (v 6). Cooperative efforts which are unified and unrestricted can have almost unlimited results. The attainments of the age of Babel bear testimony of a highly advanced technology. Such attainments in contemporary times can just as certainly be used in an attempt to thwart God's purposes for His human creatures. The common linguistic heritage of humanity serves as an additional evidence for the interrelatedness of all people. See 3:20.

11:4 SIN, Rebellion—God created humans to have fellowship with Him and enjoy the privileges of serving their Creator. Instead people chose to serve their own pride and egotism. Rather than trusting God to protect them and preserve their community, they took matters in their own hands. Rebellion against God on the individual or community level is sin. We are called to trust the Creator, not to usurp His place.

11:9 HISTORY, God—Biblical history is the narrative of God's acts. The secular historian would describe political events, personalities, and strategies to explain international communication problems and power blocks. The Bible sees God's purposes and actions behind all major epochs of history. This God-centered interpretation comes from personal spiritual experience and faith. Such an interpretation does not meet the secular historian's criteria of concrete, empirical evidence. It does provide an inspired view of history with continuity and unity based on a grand view of divine sovereignty and human freedom. Behind human, empirical historical causes stands the divine Causer. Compare 9:19; 10:32.

From Shem to Abram

11:10–27pp — Ge 10:21–31; 1Ch 1:17–27

10This is the account[d] of Shem.

Two years after the flood, when Shem
was 100 years old, he became the father[g]
of Arphaxad.[e] 11And after he became the
father of Arphaxad, Shem lived 500 years
and had other sons and daughters.
12When Arphaxad had lived 35 years,
he became the father of Shelah.[f] 13And
after he became the father of Shelah, Arphaxad lived 403 years and had other
sons and daughters.[h]
14When Shelah had lived 30 years, he
became the father of Eber.[g] 15And after
he became the father of Eber, Shelah
lived 403 years and had other sons and
daughters.
16When Eber had lived 34 years, he became the father of Peleg.[h] 17And after he
became the father of Peleg, Eber lived
430 years and had other sons and daughters.
18When Peleg had lived 30 years, he
became the father of Reu.[i] 19And after
he became the father of Reu, Peleg lived
209 years and had other sons and daughters.
20When Reu had lived 32 years, he became the father of Serug.[j] 21And after he
became the father of Serug, Reu lived 207
years and had other sons and daughters.
22When Serug had lived 30 years, he
became the father of Nahor.[k] 23And after
he became the father of Nahor, Serug
lived 200 years and had other sons and
daughters.
24When Nahor had lived 29 years, he
became the father of Terah.[l] 25And after
he became the father of Terah, Nahor
lived 119 years and had other sons and
daughters.
26After Terah had lived 70 years, he
became the father of Abram,[m] Nahor[n]
and Haran.[o]

27This is the account[p] of Terah.

Terah became the father of Abram, Nahor[q] and Haran. And Haran became the
father of Lot.[r] 28While his father Terah
was still alive, Haran died in Ur of the
Chaldeans,[s] in the land of his birth.
29Abram and Nahor[t] both married. The
name of Abram's wife was Sarai,[u] and
the name of Nahor's wife was Milcah;[v]
she was the daughter of Haran, the father
of both Milcah and Iscah. 30Now Sarai
was barren; she had no children.[w]
31Terah took his son Abram, his grandson Lot[x] son of Haran, and his daughter-
in-law[y] Sarai, the wife of his son Abram,
and together they set out from Ur of the
Chaldeans[z] to go to Canaan.[a] But when
they came to Haran,[b] they settled there.
32Terah[c] lived 205 years, and he died
in Haran.

Chapter 12

The Call of Abram

THE LORD had said to Abram, "Leave
your country, your people and your

11:10 [d]S Ge 2:4 [e]Lk 3:36
11:12 [f]Lk 3:35
11:14 [g]Lk 3:35
11:16 [h]Lk 3:35
11:18 [i]Lk 3:35
11:20 [j]Lk 3:35
11:22 [k]Lk 3:34
11:24 [l]Lk 3:34
11:26 [m]Lk 3:34 [n]Jos 24:2 [o]2Ki 19:12; Isa 37:12; Eze 27:23
11:27 [p]S Ge 2:4 [q]ver 29; Ge 31:53 [r]ver 31; Ge 12:4; 13:1,5,8,12; 14:12; 19:1; Lk 17:28; 2Pe 2:7
11:28 [s]ver 31; Ge 15:7; Ne 9:7; Job 1:17; 16:11; Eze 23:23; Ac 7:4
11:29 [t]S ver 27,31; Ge 22:20,23; 24:10,15,24; 29:5 [u]Ge 12:5,11; 16:1; 17:15 [v]Ge 22:20
11:30 [w]Ge 16:1; 18:11; 25:21; 29:31; 30:1,22; Jdg 13:2; 1Sa 1:5; Ps 113:9; Lk 1:7,36
11:31 [x]S ver 27 [y]Ge 38:11; Lev 18:15; 20:12; Ru 1:6,22; 2:20; 4:15; 1Sa 4:19; 1Ch 2:4; Eze 22:11; Mic 7:6 [z]S ver 28 [a]S Ge 10:19 [b]S ver 29; Ge 12:4; 27:43; 28:5,10; 29:4; 2Ki 19:12; Eze 27:23
11:32 [c]Jos 24:2

[g] *10 Father* may mean *ancestor*; also in verses 11-25.
[h] *12,13* Hebrew; Septuagint (see also Luke 3:35, 36 and note at Gen. 10:24) *35 years, he became the father of Cainan. 13And after he became the father of Cainan, Arphaxad lived 430 years and had other sons and daughters, and then he died. When Cainan had lived 130 years, he became the father of Shelah. And after he became the father of Shelah, Cainan lived 330 years and had other sons and daughters*

11:10–26 HUMANITY, Life—The genealogies of the Bible affirm that the process of life is both ongoing and natural. Generation follows generation. God planned it that way and used the process to produce Abram, whom God would use to fulfill His saving purposes.

11:10,27 HISTORY, Linear—See note on 2:4. The genealogies of Shem and Terah link the history of God's chosen people to universal history. By nature people of God have no claim to superiority over other people. God's sovereign choice led to biblical history focusing on one people. Uniquely, Israel's history does not center on an eternal people in a land given from creation centering on a temple built at the beginning of time. God began His special history of election and salvation with a shepherd family on the move rather than with a kingly or priestly family settled in an institution.

12:1–3 GOD, Savior—By calling Abram to a mission of blessing, God revealed His intent to be the gracious Savior. The gracious redemptive purpose of God begins to emerge with this passage. In His grace, He chooses to save His sinful creatures. The climax of the redemptive purpose of God came in all that God did through the life of Jesus Christ, His own Son.

12:1–2 REVELATION, Commitment—God revealed to Abram plans for humans and for God for the immediate present and the far future. Human beings are regularly invited to participate in God's great plans. The first step of faith brings us to discover our own promised land. The God who reveals is always beckoning His people into the next great horizon of His purposes (13:1,14–15).

12:1–7 ELECTION, God's Initiative—Abram did not choose God. God chose Abram to fulfill His purposes. Abram responded with obedience to the invitation of God to become the father of a people whom God would use to bless all the people of the earth.

12:1–3 SALVATION, Blessing—God promised to bless Abraham by making him a great nation and by blessing all peoples of the earth through him. Compare 14:19–20; 17:16–20; 18:18; 22:17–18; 24:1,31,35,60. Believers are beneficiaries of this promised blessing. See note on 1:22,28.

12:1–5 DISCIPLESHIP, God's Leadership—Abraham is a classic example of one who trusted God's leadership and served obediently according to God's commands. In a real sense he was the first disciple, the father of Israel, and the example of faith. God promised to give Abraham a place of honor and to make him a channel of blessing for all the people on earth. Discipleship is a call to follow God and bless others.

12:1–3 THE CHURCH, Covenant People—God's people began as homeless wanderers depending in faith on God's promises. The establishment of Israel's monarchy brought a great nation, blessing, an opportunity to bless the nations. It did not fulfill God's purpose. Only Jesus Christ, His church, and final judgment can do that.

12:1–7 EVANGELISM, God's Provision—The grand design of salvation began in God's gracious provision. The Lord God made a covenant with Abraham, thus creating the

father's household[d] and go to the land[e] I
will show you.[f]

2“I will make you into a great
nation[g]
and I will bless you;[h]
I will make your name great,
and you will be a blessing.[i]
3I will bless those who bless you,
and whoever curses you I will
curse;[j]
and all peoples on earth
will be blessed through you.[k]”

4So Abram left, as the LORD had told
him; and Lot[l] went with him. Abram
was seventy-five years old[m] when he set
out from Haran.[n] 5He took his wife Sarai,[o] his nephew Lot, all the possessions
they had accumulated[p] and the people[q]
they had acquired in Haran, and they set
out for the land of Canaan,[r] and they arrived there.
6Abram traveled through the land[s] as
far as the site of the great tree of Moreh[t]
at Shechem.[u] At that time the Canaanites[v] were in the land. 7The LORD appeared to Abram[w] and said, “To your offspring[i] I will give this land.[x]”[y] So he
built an altar there to the LORD,[z] who
had appeared to him.

8From there he went on toward the
hills east of Bethel[a] and pitched his
tent,[b] with Bethel on the west and Ai[c]
on the east. There he built an altar to the
LORD and called on the name of the
LORD.[d] 9Then Abram set out and continued toward the Negev.[e]

12:1 [d]Ge 20:13; 24:4,27,40 [e]S Ge 10:19 [f]Ge 15:7; 26:2; Jos 24:3; Ac 7:3*; Heb 11:8 **12:2** [g]Ge 13:16; 15:5; 17:2,4; 18:18; 22:17; 26:4; 28:3,14; 32:12; 35:11; 41:49; 46:3; 47:27; 48:4,16,19; Ex 1:7; 5:5; 32:13; Dt 1:10; 10:22; 13:17; 26:5; Jos 11:4; 24:3; 2Sa 17:11; 1Ki 3:8; 4:20; 1Ch 27:23; 2Ch 1:9; Ne 9:23; Ps 107:38; Isa 6:13; 10:22; 48:19; 51:2; 54:3; 60:22; Jer 33:22; Mic 4:7 [h]Ge 24:1,35; 25:11; 26:3; 28:4; Ex 20:24; Nu 22:12; 23:8,20; 24:9; Ps 67:6; 115:12; Isa 44:3; 61:9; 65:23; Mal 3:12 [i]Ge 22:18; Isa 19:24; Jer 4:2; Hag 2:19; Zec 8:13 **12:3** [j]Ge 27:29; Ex 23:22; Nu 24:9; Dt 30:7 [k]Ge 15:5; 18:18; 22:18; 26:4; 28:4,14; Dt 9:5; Ps 72:17; Isa 19:25; Ac 3:25; Gal 3:8* **12:4** [l]S Ge 11:27 [m]Ge 16:3,16; 17:1,17,24; 21:5 [n]S Ge 11:31 **12:5** [o]S Ge 11:29 [p]ver 16; Ge 13:2,6; 31:18; 46:6 [q]Ge 14:14; 15:3; 17:23; Ecc 2:7 [r]Ge 11:31; 16:3; Heb 11:8 **12:6** [s]Heb 11:9 [t]Ge 35:4; Dt 11:30; Jos 24:26; Jdg 7:1; 9:6 [u]Ge 33:18; 37:12; Jos 17:7; 20:7; 24:1; Jdg 8:31; 21:19; 1Ki 12:1; Ps 60:6; 108:7 [v]S Ge 10:18 **12:7** [w]Ge 17:1; 18:1; 26:2; 35:1; Ex 6:3; Ac 7:2 [x]Ex 3:8; Nu 10:29; Dt 30:5; Heb 11:8 [y]Ge 13:15,17; 15:18; 17:8; 23:18; 24:7; 26:3-4; 28:13; 35:12; 48:4; 50:24; Ex 6:4,8; 13:5,11; 32:13; 33:1; Nu 11:12; Dt 1:8; 2:31; 9:5; 11:9; 34:4; 2Ki 25:21; 1Ch 16:16; 2Ch 20:7; Ps 105:9-11; Jer 25:5; Eze 47:14; Ac 7:5; Ro 4:13; Gal 3:16* [z]S Ge 8:20; 13:4 **12:8** [a]Ge 13:3; 28:11,19; 35:1,8,15; Jos 7:2; 8:9; 1Sa 7:16; 1Ki 12:29; Hos 12:4; Am 3:14; 4:4 [b]Ge 26:25; 33:19; Heb 11:9 [c]Jos 7:2; 12:9; Ezr 2:28; Ne 7:32; Jer 49:3 [d]S Ge 4:26; S 8:20 **12:9** [e]Ge 13:1,3; 20:1; 24:62; Nu 13:17; 33:40; Dt 34:3; Jos 10:40 **12:10** [f]Ge 41:27,57; 42:5; 43:1; 47:4,13; Ru 1:1; 2Sa 21:1; 2Ki 8:1; Ps 105:19 [g]Ge 41:30,54, 56; 47:20; Ps 105:16 **12:11** [h]S Ge 11:29 [i]ver 14; Ge 24:16; 26:7; 29:17; 39:6 **12:13** [j]Ge 20:2; 26:7 **12:14** [k]S ver 11 **12:16** [l]S ver 5; Ge 24:35; 26:14; 30:43; 32:5; 34:23; 47:17; Job 1:3; 31:25

Abram in Egypt

12:10–20Ref— Ge 20:1–18; 26:1–11

10Now there was a famine in the
land,[f] and Abram went down to Egypt to
live there for a while because the famine
was severe.[g] 11As he was about to enter
Egypt, he said to his wife Sarai,[h] “I know
what a beautiful woman[i] you are.
12When the Egyptians see you, they will
say, ‘This is his wife.’ Then they will kill
me but will let you live. 13Say you are my
sister,[j] so that I will be treated well for
your sake and my life will be spared because of you.”
14When Abram came to Egypt, the
Egyptians saw that she was a very beautiful woman.[k] 15And when Pharaoh's officials saw her, they praised her to Pharaoh, and she was taken into his palace.
16He treated Abram well for her sake, and
Abram acquired sheep and cattle, male
and female donkeys, menservants and
maidservants, and camels.[l]

[i]7 Or *seed*

---

particular race (the Jews) through whom Jesus Christ, the Savior, would come. Salvation always emerges out of the wisdom, power, action, and grace of a loving God. He alone is the provider of redemption.

12:1–3 MISSIONS, Source—God's purpose and actions provide the ultimate source for our missionary teaching and actions. With this chapter, Genesis moves beyond the universal primeval history of God's dealing with all humankind to election of an individual person and nation. Through personal contact, judgment, and the flood, God had sought to bring humanity into willing, loving relation with their Maker. People continued to rebel, however. Finally God took a new direction. With Abraham, God began to carry out His purpose through one man, his family, and his descendants. While He worked through one family, God made His universal purpose clear. He wanted to bless the whole human race. In faith Abraham accepted God's challenging call and proved a blessing to other nations. As God had promised, Abraham's descendants became the great nation Israel. Israel often forgot their blessings were for the purpose of blessing others. They fell into sin and followed false gods (Isa 1:2–20). Finally, God accomplished His missionary purpose through Christ. All believers in Him become sons of Abraham and children of the Heavenly Father. See Gal 3:7–9. As believers we can follow Abraham's faithful example or easily forget we have been blessed to bless others. In Lk 24:44–49, Christ showed His disciples how the Law of Moses, the Prophets, and the Psalms all referred to Him. He then related that fulfillment to a missionary challenge in Lk 24:47–49. The seed thought of missions is here. All nations are to be blessed in Christ Jesus—the God-Man, Son of Abraham and Son of David as well as Son of God. From the beginning, God loved the whole world. See Jn 3:16–18.

12:2–3 JESUS CHRIST, Foretold—Abraham was blessed of God. In turn his descendants bless the earth. The primary descendant (seed) of Abraham is Jesus (Gal 3:16). The promise of God to Abraham comes also to those who have faith in Jesus. God's blessings stretch beyond the faithful to others. Compare Ge 17:19; 18:18; 22:18; 26:4; 28:14.

12:6–8 WORSHIP, Prayer—The building of an altar refers to worship. Prayer is part of that worship. We may not hear God speak audibly to us today, but He does speak to us in the experience of worship through His Spirit and His Word. See notes on PRAYER, Worship.

12:7–8 PRAYER, Thanksgiving—Abram built these altars in gratitude for God's promise that the land would be given to his descendants. It symbolized his recognition of God. Compare 13:3–4,18. An altar was often a gesture of recognition or gratitude (26:25). Later leaders also built altars to the Lord. See note on Jos 8:30–31.

12:10–20 SIN, Punishment—Abram feared the Egyptians would kill him, so he lied concerning his relationship with his wife Sarai. Because of his lie, the Pharaoh took Sarai into his palace and gave special favors to Abram. To protect Sarai, whom He had chosen for a special role, God intervened and inflicted serious diseases on the household of Pharaoh. Through this experience, Abram and Sarai learned the seriousness of deception and the power of God to intervene to insure His purposes are realized. Deception is a sin that endangers the well-being of the deceived and deceiver.

17But the LORD inflicted[m] serious diseases on Pharaoh and his household[n] because of Abram's wife Sarai. 18So Pharaoh summoned Abram. "What have you done to me?"[o] he said. "Why didn't you tell me she was your wife?[p] 19Why did you say, 'She is my sister,'[q] so that I took her to be my wife? Now then, here is your wife. Take her and go!" 20Then Pharaoh gave orders about Abram to his men, and they sent him on his way, with his wife and everything he had.

Chapter 13

Abram and Lot Separate

SO Abram went up from Egypt[r] to the Negev,[s] with his wife and everything he had, and Lot[t] went with him. 2Abram had become very wealthy[u] in livestock[v] and in silver and gold.

3From the Negev[w] he went from place to place until he came to Bethel,[x] to the place between Bethel and Ai[y] where his tent had been earlier 4and where he had first built an altar.[z] There Abram called on the name of the LORD.[a]

5Now Lot,[b] who was moving about with Abram, also had flocks and herds and tents. 6But the land could not support them while they stayed together, for their possessions were so great that they were not able to stay together.[c] 7And quarreling[d] arose between Abram's herdsmen and the herdsmen of Lot. The Canaanites[e] and Perizzites[f] were also living in the land[g] at that time.

8So Abram said to Lot,[h] "Let's not have any quarreling between you and me,[i] or between your herdsmen and mine, for we are brothers.[j] 9Is not the whole land before you? Let's part company. If you go to the left, I'll go to the right; if you go to the right, I'll go to the left."[k]

10Lot looked up and saw that the whole plain[l] of the Jordan[m] was well watered, like the garden of the LORD,[n] like the land of Egypt,[o] toward Zoar.[p] (This was before the LORD destroyed Sodom[q] and Gomorrah.)[r] 11So Lot chose for himself the whole plain of the Jordan and set out toward the east. The two men parted company: 12Abram lived in the land of Canaan,[s] while Lot[t] lived among the cities of the plain[u] and pitched his tents near Sodom.[v] 13Now the men of Sodom[w] were wicked and were sinning greatly against the LORD.[x]

14The LORD said to Abram after Lot had parted from him, "Lift up your eyes from where you are and look north and south, east and west.[y] 15All the land that you see I will give to you and your offspring[j] forever.[z] 16I will make your offspring like the dust of the earth, so that if anyone could count the dust, then your offspring could be counted.[a] 17Go, walk through the length and breadth of the land,[b] for I am giving it to you."[c]

18So Abram moved his tents and went to live near the great trees of Mamre[d] at Hebron,[e] where he built an altar to the LORD.[f]

Chapter 14

Abram Rescues Lot

AT this time Amraphel king of Shinar,[k][g] Arioch king of Ellasar, Kedor-

12:17 [m]2Ki 15:5; Job 30:11; Isa 53:4, 10 [n]1Ch 16:21; Ps 105:14 **12:18** [o]Ge 20:9; 26:10; 29:25; 31:26; 44:15 [p]Isa 43:27; 51:2; Eze 16:3 **12:19** [q]Ge 20:5; 26:9 **13:1** [r]Ge 45:25 [s]S Ge 12:9 [t]S Ge 11:27 **13:2** [u]S Ge 12:5; 26:13; Pr 10:22 [v]Ge 32:15; Job 1:3; 42:12 **13:3** [w]S Ge 12:9 [x]S Ge 12:8 [y]Jos 7:2 **13:4** [z]S Ge 12:7 [a]S Ge 4:26 **13:5** [b]S Ge 11:27 **13:6** [c]S Ge 12:5; 33:9; 36:7 **13:7** [d]Ge 26:20,21; Nu 20:3 [e]S Ge 10:18 [f]Ge 15:20; 34:30; Ex 3:8; Jdg 1:4 [g]Ge 12:6; 34:30 **13:8** [h]S Ge 11:27 [i]Pr 15:18; 20:3 [j]Ge 19:9; Ex 2:14; Nu 16:13; Ps 133:1 **13:9** [k]Ge 20:15; 34:10; 47:6; Jer 40:4 **13:10** [l]1Ki 7:46; 2Ch 4:17 [m]Nu 13:29; 33:48 [n]Ge 2:8-10; Isa 51:3; Eze 31:8-9 [o]Ge 46:7 [p]Ge 14:2; 19:22,30; Dt 34:3; Isa 15:5; Jer 48:34 [q]Dt 29:23; Job 39:6; Ps 107:34; Jer 4:26 [r]Ge 14:8; 19:17-29 **13:12** [s]S Ge 10:19 [t]S Ge 11:27 [u]S ver 10; Ge 19:17,25,29 [v]Ge 14:12 **13:13** [w]Ge 19:4; Isa 1:10; 3:9 [x]Ge 18:20; 19:5; 20:6; 39:9; Nu 32:23; 1Sa 12:23; 2Sa 12:13; Ps 51:4; Eze 16:49-50; 2Pe 2:8 **13:14** [y]Ge 28:14; 32:12; 48:16; Dt 3:27; 13:17; Isa 54:3 **13:15** [z]S Ge 12:7; Gal 3:16* **13:16** [a]S Ge 12:2; 16:10; 17:20; 21:13,18; 25:16; Nu 23:10 **13:17** [b]ver 15; Nu 13:17-25 [c]S Ge 12:7; 15:7 **13:18** [d]Ge 14:13,24; 18:1; 23:17,19; 25:9; 49:30; 50:13 [e]Ge 23:2; 35:27; 37:14; Nu 13:22; Jos 10:3,36; Jdg 1:10; 1Sa 30:31; 2Sa 2:1,3,11; 1Ch 11:1 [f]S Ge 8:20 **14:1** [g]S Ge 10:10

[j]*15* Or *seed*; also in verse 16 [k]*1* That is, Babylonia; also in verse 9

13:1–13 HISTORY, Narrative—Israel's authoritative Scripture is historical narrative in form rather than theological discussion of doctrine or catechetical list of teaching. The narrative centers on persons of minor or no significance for secular historians of the biblical period. Biblical history is concerned with the spiritual experiences of chosen people with God rather than with the political history of powerful nations. Only as international politics intersects with the working out of God's purposes do international institutions and personalities receive notice in biblical history. Abram moved from Mesopotamia through Canaan to Egypt, but no kings, pharaohs, or international events were named. Rather Abram's ability to bring blessing or cursing on nations and individuals is the focus. History is the story of God's blessing (12:2–3) and promise (13:14–17).

13:4 WORSHIP, Prayer—See note on 12:6–8.

13:7–12 CHRISTIAN ETHICS, War and Peace—War and conflict are as ancient as humanity. For ages, people have acted upon the conciliatory impulses of God to seek peace. The distribution of goods and wealth is a major area of dispute leading to conflict. The willingness to compromise even to the extent of giving up economic advantages often leads to peace.

13:13 SIN, Moral Insensitivity—The sin of the men of Sodom is not elaborated here. Homosexuality was one aspect of their sin (19:4–5), but more was involved. Sin had produced a moral insensitivity on their part. The emphasis here is on the blatant character of their sin. God's people should neither profit (14:21–24) nor live with (19:1–29) such people, for moral insensitivity is contagious (19:26,30–38).

13:14–17 ELECTION, God's Promise—God's election of Abram had a purpose. Through Abram's seed all nations would be blessed (12:1–3). God's election also brought Abram the promise of land acquisition so the elect nation would have a homeland. Election of Israel thus rested on God's initiative and promise, not on human action or merit.

14:1–24 HISTORY, Deliverance—A major international war apparently occupied center stage for biblical history here, but international consequences were not drawn. The narrative focused on God's deliverance of His chosen people and Abram's faithfulness to his oath under God.

14:1–16 CHRISTIAN ETHICS, War and Peace—Political domination often leads to dissatisfaction and rebellion. The Bible often describes rebellion and war as facts of human life without making a moral judgment concerning their justification or their evil character. Robbery and looting often associated with warfare cannot be justified. See note on 13:7–12.

laomer[h] king of Elam[i] and Tidal king of
Goiim 2 went to war against Bera king of
Sodom, Birsha king of Gomorrah, Shinab
king of Admah, Shemeber king of Zeboiim,[j] and the king of Bela (that is, Zoar).[k]
3 All these latter kings joined forces in the
Valley of Siddim[l] (the Salt Sea[l][m]). 4 For
twelve years they had been subject to
Kedorlaomer,[n] but in the thirteenth year
they rebelled.

5 In the fourteenth year, Kedorlaomer[o]
and the kings allied with him went out
and defeated the Rephaites[p] in Ashteroth
Karnaim, the Zuzites in Ham, the
Emites[q] in Shaveh Kiriathaim 6 and the
Horites[r] in the hill country of Seir,[s] as
far as El Paran[t] near the desert. 7 Then
they turned back and went to En Mishpat
(that is, Kadesh),[u] and they conquered
the whole territory of the Amalekites,[v] as
well as the Amorites[w] who were living in
Hazazon Tamar.[x]

8 Then the king of Sodom, the king of
Gomorrah,[y] the king of Admah, the king
of Zeboiim[z] and the king of Bela (that is,
Zoar)[a] marched out and drew up their
battle lines in the Valley of Siddim[b]
9 against Kedorlaomer[c] king of Elam,[d] Tidal king of Goiim, Amraphel king of Shinar and Arioch king of Ellasar—four
kings against five. 10 Now the Valley of
Siddim[e] was full of tar[f] pits, and when
the kings of Sodom and Gomorrah[g] fled,
some of the men fell into them and the
rest fled to the hills.[h] 11 The four kings
seized all the goods[i] of Sodom and
Gomorrah and all their food; then they
went away. 12 They also carried off
Abram's nephew Lot[j] and his possessions,
since he was living in Sodom.

13 One who had escaped came and reported this to Abram the Hebrew.[k] Now
Abram was living near the great trees of
Mamre[l] the Amorite, a brother[m] of Eshcol[m] and Aner, all of whom were allied
with Abram. 14 When Abram heard that
his relative[n] had been taken captive, he
called out the 318 trained[o] men born in
his household[p] and went in pursuit as far
as Dan.[q] 15 During the night Abram divided his men[r] to attack them and he routed them, pursuing them as far as Hobah,
north of Damascus.[s] 16 He recovered[t] all
the goods[u] and brought back his relative
Lot and his possessions, together with the
women and the other people.

17 After Abram returned from defeating
Kedorlaomer[v] and the kings allied with
him, the king of Sodom[w] came out to
meet him in the Valley of Shaveh (that is,
the King's Valley).[x]

18 Then Melchizedek[y] king of Salem[n][z]
brought out bread[a] and wine.[b] He was
priest of God Most High,[c] 19 and he
blessed Abram,[d] saying,

"Blessed be Abram by God Most
High,[e]
Creator[o] of heaven and earth.[f]
20 And blessed be[p] God Most High,[g]
who delivered your enemies into
your hand."

Then Abram gave him a tenth of everything.[h]

21 The king of Sodom[i] said to Abram,
"Give me the people and keep the
goods[j] for yourself."

22 But Abram said to the king of
Sodom,[k] "I have raised my hand[l] to the
LORD, God Most High,[m] Creator of heav-
en and earth,[n] and have taken an oath
23 that I will accept nothing belonging to
you,[o] not even a thread or the thong of a
sandal, so that you will never be able to
say, 'I made Abram rich.' 24 I will accept
nothing but what my men have eaten and
the share that belongs to the men who

14:1 [h]ver 4,9,17 [i]S Ge 10:22 **14:2** [j]S Ge 10:19 [k]S Ge 13:10 **14:3** [l]ver 8,10 [m]Nu 34:3,12; Dt 3:17; Jos 3:16; 12:3; 15:2,5; 18:19 **14:4** [n]S ver 1 **14:5** [o]S ver 1 [p]Ge 15:20; Dt 2:11,20; 3:11, 13; Jos 12:4; 13:12; 17:15; 1Ch 20:4 [q]Dt 2:10 **14:6** [r]Ge 36:20; Dt 2:12,22 [s]Ge 32:3; 33:14, 16; 36:8; Dt 1:2; 2:1,5,22; Jos 11:17; 24:4; 1Ch 4:42; Isa 34:5; Eze 25:8; 35:2; Am 1:6 [t]Ge 21:21; Nu 10:12; 12:16; 13:3,26; Hab 3:3 **14:7** [u]Ge 16:14; 20:1; Nu 13:26; 20:1; 32:8; Dt 1:2; Jos 10:41; Jdg 11:16; Ps 29:8 [v]Ex 17:8; Nu 13:29; 14:25; 24:20; Dt 25:17; Jdg 3:13; 6:3; 10:12; 12:15; 1Sa 14:48; 15:2; 28:18; 2Sa 1:1; 1Ch 4:43; Ps 83:7 [w]Nu 13:29; Dt 1:4; Jos 2:10; 13:4 [x]2Ch 20:2; Eze 48:28 **14:8** [y]S Ge 13:10 [z]Dt 29:23; Hos 11:8 [a]S Ge 13:10 [b]S ver 3 **14:9** [c]S ver 1 [d]S Ge 10:22 **14:10** [e]S ver 3 [f]Ge 11:3 [g]ver 17,21 [h]Ge 19:17,30; Jos 2:16; Ps 11:1 **14:11** [i]ver 16,21 **14:12** [j]S Ge 11:27 **14:13** [k]Ge 37:28; 39:14,17; 40:15; 41:12; 43:32; Ex 3:18; 1Sa 4:6; 14:11 [l]ver 24; S Ge 13:18 [m]Nu 13:23; 32:9; Dt 1:24 **14:14** [n]ver 12 [o]Dt 4:9; Pr 22:6 [p]S Ge 12:5 [q]Dt 34:1; Jdg 18:29; 1Ki 15:20 **14:15** [r]Jdg 7:16 [s]Ge 15:2; 2Sa 8:5; 1Ki 20:34; 2Ki 16:9; Isa 7:8; 8:4; 10:9; 17:1; Jer 49:23,27; Eze 27:18; Am 1:3-5 **14:16** [t]1Sa 30:8,18 [u]S ver 11 **14:17** [v]S ver 1 [w]S ver 10 [x]2Sa 18:18 **14:18** [y]Ps 110:4; Heb 5:6; 7:17,21 [z]Ps 76:2; Heb 7:2 [a]S Ge 3:19 [b]Jdg 9:13; 19:19; Est 1:10; Ps 104:15; Pr 31:6; Ecc 10:19; SS 1:2 [c]ver 22; Ps 7:8,17; Da 7:27 **14:19** [d]Heb 7:6 [e]ver 18 [f]ver 22; S Ge 1:1; 24:3; Jos 2:11; Ps 148:5; Mt 11:25 **14:20** [g]S Ge 9:26; S 24:27 [h]Ge 28:22; Dt 14:22; 26:12; Lk 18:12; Heb 7:4 **14:21** [i]S ver 10 [j]S ver 11 **14:22** [k]S ver 10 [l]Ex 6:8; Nu 14:30; Dt 32:40; Ne 9:15; Eze 20:5; Da 12:7; Rev 10:5-6 [m]S ver 18 [n]S ver 19 **14:23** [o]1Sa 15:3, 19; 2Ki 5:16; Est 8:11; 9:10,15

[l] *3* That is, the Dead Sea [m] *13* Or *a relative*; or *an ally* [n] *18* That is, Jerusalem [o] *19* Or *Possessor*; also in verse 22 [p] *20* Or *And praise be to*

14:13 THE CHURCH, Covenant People—A covenant establishes a relationship between individuals or between groups of people. "Allied with Abram" can be literally translated "they were lords of the covenant of Abram." Here we see the basic meaning of covenant as establishing a relationship treaty or agreement. Abram aided his allies according to the covenant stipulations. They came to him because they expected him to fulfill his covenant obligations. See note on 9:8–17.

14:14 FAMILY, Education—The household in biblical times included the primary family, servants, other family members, and persons entrusted with various responsibilities for maintaining the household. Thus, in the household of Abram children of servants were educated as soldiers from their youth. Education is a basic task of the household. The Wisdom Literature of the Old Testament is particularly focused on the nurture and education of children in the household. See Pr 4:1–7; 22:6; 29:15,17. In the New Testament, Paul encouraged fathers in the task of education (Eph 6:4).

14:17–24 JESUS CHRIST, Priest—See note on Heb 7:25.

14:18–20 PRAYER, Blessing—Blessing is God's constant provision of daily needs through His invisible presence in our lives. Prayer for blessing is a recognition of God as the provider of food, health, work, and all other available resources. Worship involves asking God for blessing, acknowledging His blessing, and blessing Him or praising Him for being the Source of blessing.

14:20–24 STEWARDSHIP, Tithe—Tithing began before the Old Testament tithe law was established. It was common among many religions. Abraham gave the first tithe recorded in Scripture as a worshipful act of gratitude to God for help in battle. See note on Nu 18:21–32.

went with me—to Aner, Eshcol and
Mamre.[p] Let them have their share."

Chapter 15

God's Covenant With Abram

AFTER this, the word of the LORD came
to Abram[q] in a vision:[r]

"Do not be afraid,[s] Abram.
I am your shield,[q] [t]
your very great reward.[r] [u]"

2But Abram said, "O Sovereign LORD,[v]
what can you give me since I remain
childless[w] and the one who will inherit[s]
my estate is Eliezer of Damascus?[x]"
3And Abram said, "You have given me no
children; so a servant[y] in my household[z] will be my heir."
4Then the word of the LORD came to
him: "This man will not be your heir, but
a son coming from your own body will be
your heir.[a]" 5He took him outside and
said, "Look up at the heavens and count
the stars[b]—if indeed you can count
them." Then he said to him, "So shall
your offspring be."[c]
6Abram believed the LORD, and he
credited it to him as righteousness.[d]
7He also said to him, "I am the LORD,
who brought you out[e] of Ur of the Chaldeans[f] to give you this land to take possession of it."[g]
8But Abram said, "O Sovereign LORD,[h]
how can I know[i] that I will gain possession of it?"[j]
9So the LORD said to him, "Bring me a
heifer,[k] a goat and a ram, each three
years old,[l] along with a dove and a young
pigeon.[m]"
10Abram brought all these to him, cut
them in two and arranged the halves opposite each other;[n] the birds, however,
he did not cut in half.[o] 11Then birds of
prey came down on the carcasses,[p] but
Abram drove them away.
12As the sun was setting, Abram fell
into a deep sleep,[q] and a thick and dreadful darkness came over him. 13Then the
LORD said to him, "Know for certain that
your descendants will be strangers in a
country not their own, and they will be
enslaved[r] and mistreated four hundred
years.[s] 14But I will punish the nation
they serve as slaves, and afterward they
will come out[t] with great possessions.[u]
15You, however, will go to your fathers[v]
in peace and be buried at a good old

14:24 [p]S Ge 13:18 **15:1** [q]1Sa 15:10; 2Sa 7:4; 1Ki 6:11; 12:22; Jer 1:13; Eze 3:16; Da 10:1 [r]Ge 46:2; Nu 12:6; 24:4; Ru 1:20; Job 33:15 [s]Ge 21:17; 26:24; 46:3; Ex 14:13; 20:20; 2Ki 6:16; 2Ch 20:15,17; Ps 27:1; Isa 7:4; 41:10,13-14; 43:1, 5; Jer 1:8; Hag 2:5 [t]Dt 33:29; 2Sa 22:3,31; Ps 3:3; 5:12; 18:2; 28:7; 33:20; 84:11; 119:114; 144:2; Pr 2:7; 30:5 [u]Ps 18:20; 37:25; 58:11; Isa 3:10 **15:2** [v]ver 8; Isa 49:22; Jer 44:26; Eze 5:11; 16:48 [w]Ac 7:5 [x]S Ge 14:15 **15:3** [y]Ge 24:2,34 [z]S Ge 12:5 **15:4** [a]Gal 4:28 **15:5** [b]Job 11:8; 35:5; Ps 8:3; 147:4; Jer 33:22 [c]S Ge 12:2; S Jer 30:19; Ro 4:18*; Heb 11:12 **15:6** [d]Ps 106:31; Ro 4:3*,20-24*; Gal 3:6*; Jas 2:23* **15:7** [e]Ge 12:1; Ex 20:2; Ac 7:3; Heb 11:8 [f]S Ge 11:28; Ac 7:4 [g]S Ge 13:17; 17:8; 28:4; 35:12; 48:4; Ex 6:8; Dt 9:5 **15:8** [h]S ver 2 [i]Lk 1:18 [j]Dt 12:20; 19:8 **15:9** [k]Nu 19:2; Dt 21:3; Hos 4:16; Am 4:1 [l]1Sa 1:24 [m]Lev 1:14; 5:7,11; 12:8 **15:10** [n]ver 17; Jer 34:18 [o]Lev 1:17; 5:8 **15:11** [p]Dt 28:26; Jer 7:33 **15:12** [q]S Ge 2:21 **15:13** [r]Ex 1:11; 3:7; 5:6,10-14, 18; 6:5; Dt 5:15; Job 3:18 [s]ver 16; Ex 12:40; Nu 20:15; Ac 7:6,17; Gal 3:17 **15:14** [t]Ge 50:24; Ex 3:8; 6:6-8; 12:25; Nu 10:29; Jos 1:2; Ac 7:7* [u]Ex 12:32-38 **15:15** [v]Ge 47:30; 49:29; Dt 31:16; 2Sa 7:12; 1Ki 1:21; Ps 49:19

[q] *1* Or *sovereign* [r] *1* Or *shield; / your reward will be very great* [s] *2* The meaning of the Hebrew for this phrase is uncertain.

15:1–21 HISTORY, Promise—Promise for the future rather than accomplishment in the present is the emphasis of biblical history. God's promises give His people visions and goals on which to center life. Promises concern the basic life needs—family, the future, land, economic security, peace, death. Promise-centered theology is the foundation for faith-based relationship with God. Biblical history narrates God's faithfulness and human faith. Compare 12:1–3,7; 13:14–17; 17:1–27; 18:10,18; 22:15–18; 24:7; 26:3–6,24; 28:4, 13–15; 35:11–13; 46:3–4; 48:3–4; 50:24.

15:1–21 ELECTION, Righteousness—The God who elects is also the God who rewards the elected for responsible commitment. The reward to Abram was more than the prosperity of owning large amounts of land. Because Abram trusted God, God rewarded him with the status and standing of the righteous man. Election of the individual is thus closely tied to faith and righteousness as the expected life-style of the elect.

15:2–3 PRAYER, Faith—Abram expressed his deepest concerns to God, resulting in a relationship of faith (v 6). Prayer is genuine dialogue concerning life's biggest problems.

15:6 SALVATION, Justification—With just five Hebrew words this verse summarizes the Old Testament understanding of the salvation relationship. Humans hear God's promise and believe (Hebrew *he'emin*), that is lean on God or trust His word. *God credits faith as righteousness*, just as a priest judged a sacrifice acceptable (Lev 7:18; 17:4; Nu 18:27). That means obedient trust in God—not a gift, offering, or good work—is the only requirement for a person to be given a saving relationship with God. See notes on Hab 2:4; Ro 1:16–17; 3:21–31; 4:1–25.

15:7–16 REVELATION, Faithfulness—Abram, as any new follower, began to wonder about God's promises and to seek concrete evidence that God was at work in his life. He, like us, asked for a sign or tangible proof that God was present in his future. The journey of faith involves both the excitement of trying new plans and the fear that we are not in control of our destiny. Faith is learned by trying to be faithful to the revelation God gives us. God addressed the man of faith and fear in a dream and made known His purposes. Dreaming was an active experience of contact with God throughout the patriarchs' lives.

15:13–16 GOD, Sovereignty—God's sovereignty includes His ability to accomplish His purposes across hundreds of years of history yet to come. God renewed and further defined His covenant with Abraham, promising Abraham that even though suffering and adverse circumstances would prevail for a time, nevertheless God would achieve His goals. As God exercises His sovereignty in history, He does not simply manipulate the peoples of the earth as pawns on a chessboard. He works in a way that takes into account the freedom of will that He has granted to all people. The sovereignty of God is always directed by His own will and His own purposes. God is doing something in history, not simply responding to what humans do. As the One who alone has the power to create, God has the right and the power to work in and through the various peoples of the earth to accomplish His will. We may not always understand what God is doing, but we can know that God is in control of His world and will finally accomplish His own righteous, redemptive purposes. See note on Ro 8:28. Life for us has meaning and purpose because our lives are linked to His.

15:15 HUMANITY, Death—Death is the natural conclusion of life and is to be faced as a normal experience. Under normal conditions, death is expected to come at the end of a long life. Long life and peaceful death marked the life blessed by God. Then the person was ready to rest with those who went before and let a new generation enjoy the blessings of life. See notes on Lev 10:1–2; Jos 23:14.

age.[w] 16In the fourth generation[x] your
descendants will come back here,[y] for
the sin of the Amorites[z] has not yet
reached its full measure."
17When the sun had set and darkness
had fallen, a smoking firepot with a blazing torch[a] appeared and passed between
the pieces.[b] 18On that day the LORD
made a covenant with Abram[c] and said,
"To your descendants I give this land,[d]
from the river[t] of Egypt[e] to the great
river, the Euphrates[f]— 19the land of
the Kenites,[g] Kenizzites, Kadmonites,
20Hittites,[h] Perizzites,[i] Rephaites,[j]
21Amorites, Canaanites, Girgashites and
Jebusites."[k]

Chapter 16

Hagar and Ishmael

NOW Sarai,[l] Abram's wife, had borne
him no children.[m] But she had an
Egyptian maidservant[n] named Hagar;[o]
2so she said to Abram, "The LORD has
kept me from having children.[p] Go, sleep
with my maidservant; perhaps I can build
a family through her."[q]
Abram agreed to what Sarai said. 3So
after Abram had been living in Canaan[r]
ten years,[s] Sarai his wife took her Egyptian maidservant Hagar and gave her to
her husband to be his wife. 4He slept
with Hagar,[t] and she conceived.
When she knew she was pregnant, she
began to despise her mistress.[u] 5Then Sarai said to Abram, "You are responsible
for the wrong I am suffering. I put my
servant in your arms, and now that she
knows she is pregnant, she despises me.
May the LORD judge between you and
me."[v]
6"Your servant is in your hands,[w]"
Abram said. "Do with her whatever
you think best." Then Sarai mistreated[x]
Hagar; so she fled from her.
7The angel of the LORD[y] found Hagar
near a spring[z] in the desert; it was the
spring that is beside the road to Shur.[a]
8And he said, "Hagar,[b] servant of Sarai,
where have you come from, and where
are you going?"[c]
"I'm running away from my mistress
Sarai," she answered.
9Then the angel of the LORD told her,
"Go back to your mistress and submit to
her." 10The angel added, "I will so increase your descendants that they will be
too numerous to count."[d]
11The angel of the LORD[e] also said to
her:

"You are now with child
  and you will have a son.[f]
You shall name him[g] Ishmael,[u] [h]

15:15 [w]Ge 25:8; 35:29; Ex 23:26; Dt 34:7; Jos 14:11; Jdg 8:32; 1Ch 29:28; Job 5:26; 21:23; 42:17; Ps 91:16; Pr 3:16; 9:11; Isa 65:20 **15:16** [x]S ver 13; Ex 12:40 [y]Ge 28:15; 46:4; 48:21; 50:24; Ex 3:8,17 [z]Lev 18:28; Jos 13:4; Jdg 10:11; 1Ki 21:26; 2Ki 16:3; 21:11; Eze 16:3 **15:17** [a]Jdg 7:16, 20; 15:4,5 [b]S ver 10 **15:18** [c]Ge 17:2,4, 7; Ex 6:4; 34:10, 27; 1Ch 16:16; Ps 105:9 [d]S Ge 12:7 [e]Nu 34:5; Jos 15:4, 47; 1Ki 8:65; 2Ki 24:7; 2Ch 7:8; Isa 27:12; Jer 37:5; 46:2; La 4:17; Eze 30:22; 47:19 [f]S Ge 2:14 **15:19** [g]Nu 24:21; Jdg 1:16; 4:11,17; 5:24; 1Sa 15:6; 27:10; 30:29; 1Ch 2:55 **15:20** [h]S Ge 10:15; S Dt 7:1 [i]S Ge 13:7 [j]S Ge 14:5 **15:21** [k]S Ge 10:16; Jos 3:10; 24:11; Ne 9:8 **16:1** [l]S Ge 11:29 [m]S Ge 11:30; Lk 1:7,36; Gal 4:24-25 [n]Ge 21:9; 24:61; 29:24,29; 31:33; 46:18 [o]ver 3-4,8, 15; Ge 21:14; 25:12 **16:2** [p]Ge 29:31; 30:2 [q]Ge 19:32; 30:3-4,9-10 **16:3** [r]S Ge 12:5 [s]S Ge 12:4 **16:4** [t]S ver 1 [u]Ge 30:1; 1Sa 1:6 **16:5** [v]Ge 31:53; Ex 5:21; Jdg 11:27; 1Sa 24:12,15; 26:10,23; Ps 50:6; 75:7 **16:6** [w]Jos 9:25 [x]Ge 31:50 **16:7** [y]ver 11; Ge 21:17; 22:11,15; 24:7,40; 31:11; 48:16; Ex 3:2; 14:19; 23:20,23; 32:34; 33:2; Nu 22:22; Jdg 2:1; 6:11; 13:3; 2Sa 24:16; 1Ki 19:5; 2Ki 1:3; 19:35; Ps 34:7; Zec 1:11; S Ac 5:19 [z]ver 14; Ge 21:19 [a]Ge 20:1; 25:18; Ex 15:22; 1Sa 15:7; 27:8 **16:8** [b]S ver 1 [c]S Ge 3:9 **16:10** [d]S Ge 13:16 **16:11** [e]S ver 7; S Ac 5:19 [f]S Ge 3:15 [g]Ge 12:2-3; 18:19; Ne 9:7; Isa 44:1; Am 3:2; Mt 1:21; Lk 1:13,31 [h]Ge 17:19; 21:3; 37:25,28; 39:1; Jdg 8:24

[t] *18* Or *Wadi* [u] *11* *Ishmael* means *God hears.*

15:18 THE CHURCH, Covenant People—God's promises remain secure through trials and throughout time. The Lord reaffirmed His relationship with Abraham by promising an heir. The Old Testament often refers to making a covenant as "cutting" a covenant. The terminology probably goes back to events such as recorded in Ge 15 and Jer 34. God reaffirms individuals with sagging hopes and unfulfilled dreams. When life seems unbearable and God's promises appear remote, the Lord encourages His people. Before giving an heir, God promised Abraham would be the father of a great multitude of people who would inhabit the land for years to come. When possibilities seem most remote, God often gives the greatest gifts to His people. God's covenants grow out of His love for His creation and His determination to create a people who will respond freely in love and faithfulness. In making covenants God makes basic promises to His people, establishing Himself as the God of promise. Through history He continues to make promises. Many are not directly tied to the covenants He makes, but all grow out of His covenant commitment to His people.

16:1–2 REVELATION, Faithfulness—Humans too often forget God's revelation or lose faith in it. The promise that Abram would have children was suspected by husband and wife, who began to make their own plans in order to produce offspring. Both Abram and Sarai chose to have a stepchild. The ensuing story of Ishmael and the grief his birth caused is a constant reminder that plans outside of God's intention cause people harm. God's people must trust the revelation God gives and wait for Him to lead into the future. He is faithful, but we must be patient. God makes His will known according to His timing as He knows we need it.

16:1–16 FAMILY, Multiple Wives—Abram's taking of Hagar as a concubine upon Sarai's instructions resulted in hostility between Sarai and Hagar. Sarai acted upon her disbelief in God's promise of a son and gave her handmaiden to Abram so that she might bear a child in Sarai's stead. Using a servant girl as a concubine was common among the patriarchs of Israel. She remained a slave, but any children born from her union with her master had the same status as a child born to the legitimate wife. The clearest illustration is in the family of Jacob (Ge 29:31—30:24). It was not uncommon for a man who had no heirs to have children by a concubine in order to keep his family name alive. Even though having multiple wives was not based upon any specific word of God, such polygamy was practiced by the leaders and kings of Israel and Judah with Solomon having the largest number of wives and concubines. In his situation the intermarriages were often for political advantage and ultimately contributed to his spiritual separation from God. See note on 1 Ki 11:1–9. The historical examples are never set up as authoritative instructions for God's people in all generations to follow. One spouse for a lifetime is the biblical teaching.

16:10 ELECTION, Providence—God preserved Hagar and her son by His providence and promised descendants too numerous to count. See note on 17:1–27.

16:11 EVIL AND SUFFERING, God's Compassion—Suffering is emotional as well as physical. Disturbed human relationships cause suffering. God's angel told the desperate Hagar that she would name her son "Ishmael," meaning "God hears." God is aware of our suffering and identifies compassionately with our anguish. See note on 21:8–20.

for the LORD has heard of your
misery.[i]
12He will be a wild donkey[j] of a man;
his hand will be against everyone
and everyone's hand against him,
and he will live in hostility
toward[v] all his brothers.[k]"

13She gave this name to the LORD who
spoke to her: "You are the God who sees
me,[l]" for she said, "I have now seen[w]
the One who sees me."[m] 14That is why
the well[n] was called Beer Lahai Roi[x];[o] it
is still there, between Kadesh[p] and Bered.
15So Hagar[q] bore Abram a son,[r] and
Abram gave the name Ishmael[s] to the
son she had borne. 16Abram was eighty-
six years old[t] when Hagar bore him Ishmael.

Chapter 17

The Covenant of Circumcision

WHEN Abram was ninety-nine years
old,[u] the LORD appeared to him[v]
and said, "I am God Almighty[y];[w] walk
before me and be blameless.[x] 2I will confirm my covenant between me and you[y]
and will greatly increase your numbers."[z]
3Abram fell facedown,[a] and God said
to him, 4"As for me, this is my covenant
with you:[b] You will be the father of many
nations.[c] 5No longer will you be called
Abram[z]; your name will be Abraham,[a][d]
for I have made you a father of many nations.[e] 6I will make you very fruitful;[f] I
will make nations of you, and kings will
come from you.[g] 7I will establish my covenant[h][i] as an everlasting covenant[j][k]
between me and you and your descendants after you for the generations to
come, to be your God[l] and the God of
your descendants after you.[m] 8The whole
land of Canaan,[n] where you are now an
alien,[o] I will give as an everlasting possession to you and your descendants after
you;[p] and I will be their God.[q]"
9Then God said to Abraham, "As for
you, you must keep my covenant,[r] you
and your descendants after you for the
generations to come.[s] 10This is my covenant with you and your descendants after you, the covenant you are to keep:
Every male among you shall be circum-

16:11 [i]Ge 29:32; 31:42; Ex 2:24; 3:7,9; 4:31; Nu 20:16; Dt 26:7; 1Sa 9:16 **16:12** [j]Job 6:5; 11:12; 24:5; 39:5; Ps 104:11; Jer 2:24; Hos 8:9 [k]Ge 25:18 **16:13** [l]Ps 139:1-12 [m]Ge 32:30; 33:10; Ex 24:10; 33:20, 23; Nu 12:8; Jdg 6:22; 13:22; Isa 6:5 **16:14** [n]S ver 7 [o]Ge 24:62; 25:11 [p]S Ge 14:7 **16:15** [q]S ver 1 [r]Ge 21:9; Gal 4:22 [s]Ge 17:18; 25:12; 28:9 **16:16** [t]S Ge 12:4 **17:1** [u]S Ge 12:4 [v]S Ge 12:7 [w]Ge 28:3; 35:11; 43:14; 48:3; 49:25; Ex 6:3; Ru 1:20; Job 5:17; 6:4,14; 22:21; 33:19; 36:16; Isa 13:6; Joel 1:15; Mic 6:9 [x]S Ge 5:22; 20:5; Dt 18:13; 1Ki 3:6; 9:4; Job 1:1; Ps 15:2; 18:23; 78:72; 101:2 **17:2** [y]S Ge 15:18; S 22:16-18 [z]S Ge 12:2 **17:3** [a]ver 17; Ge 18:2; 19:1; 33:3; Ex 18:7; Nu 14:5; Jos 5:14; 7:6; Jdg 13:20; Eze 1:28; 3:23 **17:4** [b]S Ge 15:18 [c]ver 16; S Ge 12:2; 25:23 **17:5** [d]ver 15; Ge 32:28; 35:10; 37:3,13; 43:6; 46:2; 1Ki 18:31; 2Ki 17:34; 1Ch 1:34; Ne 9:7; Isa 48:1; S Jn 1:42 [e]Ro 4:17* **17:6** [f]Ge 1:28; 22:17; 26:22; 28:3; 35:11; 41:52; 47:27; 48:4; 49:22; Lev 26:9; Dt 7:13 [g]ver 16, 19; Ge 18:10; 21:1; 36:31; Isa 51:2; Mt 1:6 **17:7** [h]S Ge 15:18; Lev 26:9,15 [i]S Ge 6:18 [j]S Heb 13:20 [k]S Ge 9:16 [l]Ex 6:7; 20:2; 29:45,46; Lev 11:44-45; 18:2; 22:33; 25:38; 26:12,45; Nu 15:41; Dt 4:20; 7:6,21; 29:13; 2Sa 7:24; Jer 14:9; Rev 21:7 [m]Ro 9:8; Gal 3:16 **17:8** [n]S Ge 10:19 [o]Ge 23:4; 28:4; 35:27; 37:1; Ex 6:4; 1Ch 29:15 [p]S Ge 12:7; S 15:7 [q]S ver 7; Jer 31:1 **17:9** [r]Ge 22:18; Ex 19:5; Dt 5:2 [s]Ge 18:19

[v]12 Or *live to the east / of* [w]13 Or *seen the back of* [x]14 *Beer Lahai Roi* means *well of the Living One who sees me.* [y]1 Hebrew *El-Shaddai* [z]5 *Abram* means *exalted father.* [a]5 *Abraham* means *father of many.*

16:13 GOD, Presence—The name for God that Hagar used in this passage literally means the God who sees. Hagar was in a moment of severe personal crisis. As the angel of the Lord confronted her, she realized that she was not alone, that God saw her in her time of distress. This awareness of God's presence is not neutral or indifferent, but is positive and gracious. Not only was God with Hagar, but He also provided support and the promise of blessing.

16:13 PRAYER, Thanksgiving—Hagar's gratitude gave God another name. In the dialogue of prayer we recognize that God is aware of us as individuals.

17:1–8 REVELATION, Word—God was seen by Abram, who immediately fell down in reverence. Abram's experience is not described further. A vision experience at a place of worship or a dream may be meant. The Bible's interest is in the fact that God speaks to His people and reveals His will. The how of the revelation is often ignored. The revelation showed that God is the faithful God of covenant. It declared God's purpose for years to come. The Lord unveiled at this moment an entire geographical and spiritual plan for the ages. At the same time, God revealed that it is His nature to take unknown people and places and to transform them into creative participants of His will.

17:1–27 ELECTION, Predestination—The electing God changed Abram's name to Abraham and presented him with an everlasting covenant. He promised Sarah would give birth to a son named Isaac. He called the elect people to obedience in bearing the covenant sign. The young son, Isaac, had been predestined prior to his birth to fulfill God's will as the family of promise. God did not ignore or condemn Ishmael. Instead, He promised to bless him. He elected Isaac as the one through whom He would fulfill His promises. Election involves God's sovereign, free choice of people to use for His purposes, not exclusion from His mercy, care, and salvation.

17:1,10 CHRISTIAN ETHICS, Obedience—Two general ethical expectations (v 1) on Abraham provided a basis for the specific expectation (v 10). The pattern is the same for contemporary people of God. General principles for ethical decision making built on a covenant relationship give direction for specific circumstances. See note on 6:9,22.

17:1–21 THE CHURCH, Covenant People—God is able to establish relationships and carry out His promises. God's promises are everlasting. His promises are not bound by limitations common to human beings. These verses contain the ideal of the covenant relationship in any age. God desires to be our God. He wants us to be His people. All people may know God because of His grace. We may be the covenant people of God because God freely bestows His grace. God wants His people to respond to His grace with obedience. As the Lord called Abraham to keep the covenant, He calls us to obey the divine will. When obedience is commanded, the Lord takes the responsibility for maintaining the relationship. God initiates the covenant and keeps it. God blesses and cares for all people. God blessed both Isaac and Ishmael. However, God established His everlasting covenant with Isaac.

17:3,17 PRAYER, Humility—The position a person takes before God reflects the person's attitude. Abram fell facedown in humble dependence. He was not only a man of faith (15:6); he was humble. Biblical giants often fall prostrate in prayer (Mk 14:35; Rev 4:10; 5:8).

17:6 HISTORY, Politics—God's history with a chosen family had larger purposes in view. Political history grew out of the history of God's promises to a family. A theology of history must always keep in view God's focus on the individual and on the larger structures of society. See note on 15:1–21.

17:6,16 CHRISTIAN ETHICS, The State—See note on Ro 13:1–7.

cised.[t] 11You are to undergo circumcision,[u] and it will be the sign of the covenant[v] between me and you. 12For the
generations to come[w] every male among
you who is eight days old must be circumcised,[x] including those born in your
household or bought with money from a
foreigner—those who are not your offspring. 13Whether born in your household or bought with your money, they
must be circumcised.[y] My covenant in
your flesh is to be an everlasting covenant.[z] 14Any uncircumcised male, who
has not been circumcised[a] in the flesh,
will be cut off from his people;[b] he has
broken my covenant.[c]"

15God also said to Abraham, "As for Sarai[d] your wife, you are no longer to call
her Sarai; her name will be Sarah.[e] 16I
will bless her and will surely give you a
son by her.[f] I will bless her so that she
will be the mother of nations;[g] kings of
peoples will come from her."

17Abraham fell facedown;[h] he
laughed[i] and said to himself, "Will a son
be born to a man a hundred years old?[j]
Will Sarah bear a child at the age of ninety?"[k] 18And Abraham said to God, "If
only Ishmael[l] might live under your
blessing!"[m]

19Then God said, "Yes, but your wife
Sarah will bear you a son,[n] and you will
call him Isaac.[b][o] I will establish my covenant with him[p] as an everlasting covenant[q] for his descendants after him.
20And as for Ishmael, I have heard you: I
will surely bless him; I will make him
fruitful and will greatly increase his numbers.[r] He will be the father of twelve rulers,[s] and I will make him into a great
nation.[t] 21But my covenant[u] I will establish with Isaac, whom Sarah will bear to
you[v] by this time next year."[w] 22When
he had finished speaking with Abraham,
God went up from him.[x]

23On that very day Abraham took his
son Ishmael and all those born in his
household[y] or bought with his money,
every male in his household, and circumcised them, as God told him.[z] 24Abraham
was ninety-nine years old[a] when he was
circumcised,[b] 25and his son Ishmael[c]
was thirteen; 26Abraham and his son Ishmael were both circumcised on that same
day. 27And every male in Abraham's
household[d], including those born in his
household or bought from a foreigner,
was circumcised with him.

Chapter 18

The Three Visitors

THE LORD appeared to Abraham[e] near
the great trees of Mamre[f] while he
was sitting at the entrance to his tent[g] in
the heat of the day. 2Abraham looked up[h]
and saw three men[i] standing nearby.
When he saw them, he hurried from the
entrance of his tent to meet them and
bowed low to the ground.[j]

3He said, "If I have found favor in your
eyes,[k] my lord,[c] do not pass your servant[l] by. 4Let a little water be brought,
and then you may all wash your feet[m] and
rest under this tree. 5Let me get you
something to eat,[n] so you can be refreshed and then go on your way—now
that you have come to your servant."

17:10 [t]ver 23; Ge 21:4; Lev 12:3; Jos 5:2,5,7; Jn 7:22; Ac 7:8; Ro 4:11 **17:11** [u]Ex 12:48; Dt 10:16 [v]S Ge 9:12; Ro 4:11 **17:12** [w]S Ge 9:12 [x]Ge 21:4; Lev 12:3; Jos 5:2; S Lk 1:59 **17:13** [y]Ex 12:44,48 [z]S Ge 9:16 **17:14** [a]ver 23 [b]Ex 4:24-26; 12:15, 19; 30:33; Lev 7:20,25; 17:4; 18:29; 19:8; 20:17; Nu 9:13; 15:30; 19:13; Dt 17:12; Jos 5:2-8; Job 38:15; Ps 37:28 [c]Eze 44:7 **17:15** [d]S Ge 11:29 [e]S ver 5 **17:16** [f]S ver 6; S Isa 29:22 [g]S ver 4; Ge 24:60; Gal 4:31 **17:17** [h]S ver 3 [i]Ge 18:12; 21:6 [j]S Ge 12:4 [k]Ge 18:11,13; 21:7; 24:1,36; Jer 20:15; Lk 1:18; Ro 4:19; Gal 4:23; Heb 11:11 **17:18** [l]S Ge 16:15 [m]Ge 21:11 **17:19** [n]S ver 6,21; Ge 18:14; 21:2; 1Sa 1:20 [o]S Ge 16:11; Mt 1:21; Lk 1:13,31 [p]Ge 26:3; 50:24; Ex 13:11; Dt 1:8 [q]S Ge 9:16; S Gal 3:16 **17:20** [r]S Ge 13:16 [s]Ge 25:12-16 [t]Ge 25:18; 48:19 **17:21** [u]Ex 34:10 [v]S ver 19 [w]Ge 18:10,14 **17:22** [x]Ge 18:33; 35:13; Nu 12:9 **17:23** [y]S Ge 12:5 [z]S ver 10,S 14 **17:24** [a]S Ge 12:4 [b]Ro 4:11 **17:25** [c]Ge 16:16 **17:27** [d]Ge 14:14 **18:1** [e]S Ge 12:7; Ac 7:2 [f]S Ge 13:18 [g]Ge 19:1; 23:10, 18; 34:20,24; Ru 4:1; Ps 69:12; Heb 11:9 **18:2** [h]Ge 24:63 [i]ver 16,22; Ge 19:1,10; 32:24; Jos 5:13; Jdg 13:6-11; Hos 12:3-4; Heb 13:2 [j]S Ge 17:3; S 43:28 **18:3** [k]Ge 19:19; 39:4; Ru 2:2, 10,13; 1Sa 1:18; Est 2:15 [l]Ge 32:4,18,20; 33:5 **18:4** [m]Ge 19:2; 24:32; 43:24; Jdg 19:21; 2Sa 11:8; S Lk 7:44 **18:5** [n]Jdg 13:15; 19:5

[b]19 *Isaac* means *he laughs.* [c]3 Or *O Lord*

17:14 GOD, Wrath—This was a warning that whoever did not follow the commandment of God concerning circumcision would be subject to the wrath of God. God views His will for His people quite seriously. Those who want the blessings of God must fulfill the expectations of God. This is not simply an arbitrary or a vindictive stance on God's part. It is a recognition of the serious nature of the covenant relationship of God with His people. They must be His people truly responding to Him in faithful obedience. To fail God in basic requirements is to put oneself in jeopardy. God desires to bless us, but on His own terms, and in the context of His own purposes. God does not belong to us—we belong to Him. We exist for His benefit, not the other way around.

17:16,21 EVANGELISM, God's Provision—The covenant promise of God to Abraham began to be fulfilled miraculously in the promised birth of Isaac. Through Isaac, and later Jacob and his twelve sons, the Jewish nation was born through whom came the Messiah, Jesus Christ, who brought redemption to all. The history of God's actions is a *salvation* history.

17:17–18 PRAYER, Faith—Abraham's embarrassed laughter did not originate from unbelief; his attitude was the same as in v 3. The prayer that Ishmael might live indicated Abraham's concern for his son and his submission to God's will. Faith means being ready to do things God's way.

17:20 HISTORY, Universal—The one God works through all history not just a small segment of it. While electing Abraham's family and then Isaac as His covenant messengers through whom He would work out His purposes, God continued to guide destinies of other peoples such as Ishmael, whose descendants have been prominent in Near Eastern history to this day (25:12–18). Only as Abraham influenced other nations positively could the original calling and blessing be fulfilled (12:1–3).

18:1—19:29 REVELATION, Messengers—God surprised even Abraham, communicating through messengers (human beings who deliver God's message) who arrived unexpectedly. The ancient near eastern custom of hospitality is clear here, for it was an offense not to offer food and shelter to the stranger at the door. The Hebrew text provokes mystery by alternating singular and plural references to the guests after introducing the section with God's appearance in the same language of 17:1. The messengers were men who could leave, Abraham then being alone with God (v 22). The messengers could eat and have their feet washed. Messenger and angel is the same word in the Hebrew (*mal'ak*). The disbelief of both future parents underscores God's ability to carry out His revealed plans even with limited faith.

"Very well," they answered, "do as
you say."

6So Abraham hurried into the tent to
Sarah. "Quick," he said, "get three
seahs[d] of fine flour and knead it and bake
some bread."[o]

7Then he ran to the herd and selected a
choice, tender calf[p] and gave it to a servant, who hurried to prepare it. 8He then
brought some curds[q] and milk[r] and the
calf that had been prepared, and set these
before them.[s] While they ate, he stood
near them under a tree.

9"Where is your wife Sarah?"[t] they
asked him.

"There, in the tent,[u]" he said.

10Then the LORD[e] said, "I will surely
return to you about this time next year,[v]
and Sarah your wife will have a son."[w]

Now Sarah was listening at the entrance to the tent, which was behind
him. 11Abraham and Sarah were already
old and well advanced in years,[x] and Sarah was past the age of childbearing.[y] 12So
Sarah laughed[z] to herself as she thought,
"After I am worn out and my master[f][a] is
old, will I now have this pleasure?"

13Then the LORD said to Abraham,
"Why did Sarah laugh and say, 'Will I
really have a child, now that I am old?'[b]
14Is anything too hard for the LORD?[c] I
will return to you at the appointed time
next year[d] and Sarah will have a son."[e]

15Sarah was afraid, so she lied and said,
"I did not laugh."

But he said, "Yes, you did laugh."

Abraham Pleads for Sodom

16When the men[f] got up to leave, they
looked down toward Sodom, and Abraham walked along with them to see them
on their way. 17Then the LORD said,
"Shall I hide from Abraham[g] what I am
about to do?[h] 18Abraham will surely become a great and powerful nation,[i] and
all nations on earth will be blessed
through him. 19For I have chosen him[j],
so that he will direct his children[k] and
his household after him to keep the way
of the LORD[l] by doing what is right and
just,[m] so that the LORD will bring about
for Abraham what he has promised
him."[n]

20Then the LORD said, "The outcry
against Sodom[o] and Gomorrah is so

18:6 [o]Ge 19:3; 2Sa 13:8 **18:7** [p]1Sa 28:24; Lk 15:23 **18:8** [q]Isa 7:15,22 [r]Jdg 4:19; 5:25 [s]Jdg 6:19 **18:9** [t]S Ge 3:9 [u]Ge 24:67; Heb 11:9 **18:10** [v]S Ge 17:21; 21:2; 2Ki 4:16 [w]S Ge 17:6; Ro 9:9* **18:11** [x]S Ge 17:17; Lk 1:18 [y]S Ge 11:30; Ro 4:19; Heb 11:11-12 **18:12** [z]S Ge 17:17 [a]1Pe 3:6 **18:13** [b]S Ge 17:17 **18:14** [c]Job 42:2; Isa 40:29; 50:2; 51:9; Jer 32:17,27; S Mt 19:26; Ro 4:21 [d]S ver 10 [e]S Ge 17:19; Ro 9:9*; Gal 4:23 **18:16** [f]S ver 2 **18:17** [g]Am 3:7 [h]Ge 19:24; Job 1:16; Ps 107:34 **18:18** [i]S Ge 12:2; Gal 3:8* **18:19** [j]Ge 17:9 [k]Dt 4:9-10; 6:7 [l]Jos 24:15; Eph 6:4 [m]Ge 22:12,18; 26:5; 2Sa 8:15; Ps 17:2; 99:4; Jer 23:5 [n]S Ge 16:11; S Isa 14:1 **18:20** [o]Isa 1:10; Jer 23:14; Eze 16:46

[d]*6* That is, probably about 20 quarts (about 22 liters)
[e]*10* Hebrew *Then he* [f]*12* Or *husband*

18:10–14 HUMANITY, Birth—While producing offspring is the normal experience of marriage and love, it is also to be understood as the gift of God. See 17:15–16.

18:10,18 ELECTION, Righteousness—Covenant-making between God and Abraham was based on the genuine trust Abraham placed in God's promises and the compassion God had for His people. God expected the elect people to live in justice and rightousness. This was directly opposite of the world's way as seen in Sodom and Gomorrah. God's righteous way includes intercession for the immoral world, thus blessing the nations. Election and mission are theological partners.

18:14 GOD, Sovereignty—God has the capability of doing what He wills, even though what He wills surpasses the limits of normal human expectations. God's sovereignty means He had the authority and the power to give Sarah a son even though she was past ninety years of age. He who made the normal functions can also alter them when necessary for His own purposes. Miraculous intervention usually is for the purpose of revelation. It is God's way of showing He is doing something important. Otherwise, the very precise and orderly way the laws of nature work is also an expression of the sovereign will of God. As sovereign God, He has chosen for all aspects of life in His universe to operate in a well defined, ordered, and regular way. The alternative would be a world of chaos and uncertainty.

18:14 PRAYER, Sovereignty of God—God is omnipotent. The limitations of prayer are not caused by any lack of power on God's part. He answers prayer in ways that best conform to His perfect will.

18:16—19:29 EVIL AND SUFFERING, Punishment—What humans call evil may be God's action in punishing and disciplining sinners. Sodom and Gomorrah clearly deserved God's punishment. In grace, He agreed to spare the city for ten righteous persons, but ten could not be found. In love for Abraham, God spared Lot's family. They soon showed they had adopted the sinful habits of their environment. God's discipline is controlled by grace even as it brings deserved suffering.

18:16–33 MISSIONS, Scope—Since Abraham was to be a channel of God's blessing to all peoples, God brought Abraham into His confidence concerning His coming judgment and destruction of Sodom and Gomorrah. In interceding for the cities, Abraham carried out his call to bring blessing to the nations. In sharing His intentions and purposes with Abraham, God began His missionary work of using humans to teach and practice missions. Even in wrath and judgment God was seeking to carry out His announced intention of blessing all peoples. God's scope of activity may seem to be, but never is, limited at any one moment. God had elected Abraham. That election meant blessing. The purpose of being blessed is to bless others. A cardinal truth appears repeatedly in the Bible. We are blessed to bless; we are saved to serve. Note the missionary and redemptive element here. From the first book of the Bible, God included all peoples in His promise (12:1; Gal 3:8).

18:18–19 EVANGELISM, Results—God created His people to be a blessing for others. The evangelistic call has always been central to the identity of God's people. Through Abraham's seed came the promised Savior, Jesus Christ. He lived out Israel's calling. In Him all the nations shall be blessed. Blessing is a result of salvation.

18:19 HISTORY, Moral—History is communication between God and His chosen people to ensure proper moral behavior by the people and fulfillment of the promises by God. Biblical history ties promise and obedience together tightly.

18:19 CHRISTIAN ETHICS, Moral Imperatives—Following God's moral expectations always carries the responsibilities of conveying those expectations to one's family. Our moral development begins through family habits and expectations long before we can learn God's expectations through reading His Word. His expectations are not unreasonable demands of a tyrant. They are the perfect guidelines of the heavenly Father leading to righteousness and justice.

18:19 EDUCATION, Parents—Parents are responsible for providing religious and moral instruction for their sons and daughters. This God-given responsibility is to be taken as seriously as the obligation to provide food, clothing, and shelter. When parents neglect this teaching task, God is forgotten, values become corrupt, and society as a whole suffers decline. See note on Dt 6:1–10.

18:20–33 GOD, Justice—The grace and justice of God may appear to be contradictory traits to the human mind. The

great[p] and their sin so grievous[q] 21that I
will go down[r] and see if what they have
done is as bad as the outcry that has
reached me. If not, I will know."

22The men[s] turned away and went toward Sodom,[t] but Abraham remained
standing before the LORD.[g][u] 23Then
Abraham approached him and said: "Will
you sweep away the righteous with the
wicked?[v] 24What if there are fifty righteous people in the city? Will you really
sweep it away and not spare[h] the place
for the sake of the fifty righteous people
in it?[w] 25Far be it from you to do such a
thing[x]—to kill the righteous with the
wicked, treating the righteous[y] and the
wicked alike.[z] Far be it from you! Will
not the Judge[i][a] of all the earth do
right?"[b]

26The LORD said, "If I find fifty righteous people in the city of Sodom, I will
spare the whole place for their sake.[c]"

27Then Abraham spoke up again:
"Now that I have been so bold as to speak
to the Lord, though I am nothing but dust
and ashes,[d] 28what if the number of the
righteous is five less than fifty? Will you
destroy the whole city because of five
people?"

"If I find forty-five there," he said, "I
will not destroy it."

29Once again he spoke to him, "What
if only forty are found there?"

He said, "For the sake of forty, I will
not do it."

30Then he said, "May the Lord not be
angry,[e] but let me speak. What if only
thirty can be found there?"

He answered, "I will not do it if I find
thirty there."

31Abraham said, "Now that I have
been so bold as to speak to the Lord, what
if only twenty can be found there?"

18:20 [p]Ge 19:13
[q]S Ge 13:13
18:21 [r]S Ge 11:5
18:22 [s]S ver 2
[t]Ge 19:1 [u]ver 1;
Ge 19:27
18:23 [v]Ex 23:7;
Lev 4:3,22,27;
Nu 16:22;
Dt 27:25;
2Sa 24:17;
Ps 11:4-7; 94:21;
Eze 18:4; 2Pe 2:9
18:24 [w]ver 26;
Jer 5:1
18:25 [x]Ge 44:7,17;
Dt 32:4; Job 8:3-7;
34:10 [y]Isa 5:20;
Am 5:15; Mal 2:17;
3:18 [z]Dt 1:16-17
[a]Jdg 11:27;
Job 9:15; Ps 7:11;
94:2; Heb 12:23
[b]Ge 20:4; Dt 32:4;
2Ch 19:7; Ezr 9:15;
Ne 9:33; Job 8:3,
20; 34:10; 36:23;
Ps 58:11; 75:7;
94:2; 119:137;
Isa 3:10-11;
Eze 18:25; Da 4:37;
9:14; Mal 2:17;
Ro 3:6
18:26 [c]S ver 24
18:27 [d]S Ge 2:7;
S Job 2:8
18:30 [e]ver 32;
Ge 44:18; Ex 32:22
18:32 [f]S ver 30;
Jdg 6:39 [g]Jer 5:1
18:33 [h]Ex 31:18
[i]S Ge 17:22
[j]Ge 31:55
19:1 [k]S Ge 18:2;
Heb 13:2 [l]Ge 18:22
[m]S Ge 11:27
[n]S Ge 18:1
[o]S Ge 17:3; 48:12;
Ru 2:10; 1Sa 25:23;
2Sa 14:33; 2Ki 2:15
19:2 [p]S Ge 18:4;
Lk 7:44 [q]Jdg 19:15,
20
19:3 [r]Ge 33:11
[s]Job 31:32
[t]Ex 12:39
[u]S Ge 18:6
19:4 [v]S Ge 13:13
19:5 [w]S Ge 13:13;
Lev 18:22;
Dt 23:18;
Jdg 19:22;
Ro 1:24-27
19:6 [x]Jdg 19:23

He said, "For the sake of twenty, I will
not destroy it."

32Then he said, "May the Lord not be
angry, but let me speak just once more.[f]
What if only ten can be found there?"

He answered, "For the sake of ten,[g] I
will not destroy it."

33When the LORD had finished speaking[h] with Abraham, he left,[i] and Abraham returned home.[j]

Chapter 19

Sodom and Gomorrah Destroyed

THE two angels[k] arrived at Sodom[l] in
the evening, and Lot[m] was sitting in
the gateway of the city.[n] When he saw
them, he got up to meet them and bowed
down with his face to the ground.[o] 2"My
lords," he said, "please turn aside to your
servant's house. You can wash your feet[p]
and spend the night and then go on your
way early in the morning."

"No," they answered, "we will spend
the night in the square."[q]

3But he insisted[r] so strongly that they
did go with him and entered his house.[s]
He prepared a meal for them, baking
bread without yeast,[t] and they ate.[u] 4Be-
fore they had gone to bed, all the men
from every part of the city of Sodom[v]—
both young and old—surrounded the
house. 5They called to Lot, "Where are
the men who came to you tonight? Bring
them out to us so that we can have sex
with them."[w]

6Lot went outside to meet them[x] and
shut the door behind him 7and said, "No,
my friends. Don't do this wicked thing.
8Look, I have two daughters who have

[g]22 Masoretic Text; an ancient Hebrew scribal tradition *but the LORD remained standing before Abraham* [h]24 Or *forgive*; also in verse 26
[i]25 Or *Ruler*

Bible shows us they are never contradictory. They are complementary; each completes the other. The righteousness of God prompted Him to consider bringing judgment upon the extreme wickedness of Sodom and Gomorrah. On the other hand, Abraham's plea for righteous people who might live in the city evoked the promise of God that if just ten righteous people were found there God would spare the cities. This does not mean that the wicked would go unpunished. It does mean that God would not destroy the righteous in a destruction meant as judgment for the wicked. Sparing ten righteous persons had a greater value in God's eyes than destroying all of the wicked of the two cities. Judgment is held in reserve until people reject grace and redemption. A righteous God must act justly. God Himself is the standard of justice. It is the very nature of God to do what is right in all circumstances. God will not do what is wrong, for that would contradict His own nature and will. We cannot always easily determine what is right and what is wrong in any given set of circumstances. We can rest assured that God, in His infinite wisdom, will always do what is right.

18:23–32 PRAYER, Persistence—Importunity, or persistence, may not result in the request being granted but in a deeper learning about God. God knew at the beginning of Abraham's prayer that He could not spare Sodom. The Lord's patience with Abraham's persistence demonstrated that it is all right to ask for something outside God's immediate will if the request is within the character of God. Sparing Sodom would have been within the character of God if there had been any possibility of reform. That possibility had been exhausted; Sodom had passed a point of no return. Continued toleration could not have brought repentance, even if there had been a significant number of witnesses to God's righteousness. Abraham asked in ignorance; he did not possess God's knowledge that there were not even ten righteous in Sodom. He began with a dwarfed conception of God but ended with a magnificent conception of God.

19:1–29 HISTORY, Judgment—Judgment is part of God's history, for humans do not consistently cooperate to achieve God's purposes. God works in history to eliminate that which ignores His moral will (13:13). Judgment occurs in communication with God's faithful people (18:16–33) and in mercy (19:16). In historical judgment, God's people see the holy, righteous, and just side of God's character.

never slept with a man. Let me bring
them out to you, and you can do what you
like with them. But don't do anything to
these men, for they have come under the
protection of my roof."[y]
9"Get out of our way," they replied.
And they said, "This fellow came here as
an alien,[z] and now he wants to play the
judge![a] We'll treat you worse than
them." They kept bringing pressure on
Lot and moved forward to break down
the door.
10But the men[b] inside reached out and
pulled Lot back into the house and shut
the door. 11Then they struck the men
who were at the door of the house, young
and old, with blindness[c] so that they
could not find the door.
12The two men said to Lot, "Do you
have anyone else here—sons-in-law, sons
or daughters, or anyone else in the city
who belongs to you?[d] Get them out of
here, 13because we[e] are going to destroy
this place. The outcry to the LORD against
its people is so great[f] that he has sent us
to destroy it."[g]
14So Lot went out and spoke to his
sons-in-law, who were pledged to marry[j]
his daughters. He said, "Hurry and get
out of this place, because the LORD is
about to destroy the city![h]" But his
sons-in-law thought he was joking.[i]
15With the coming of dawn, the angels
urged Lot, saying, "Hurry! Take your wife
and your two daughters who are here, or
you will be swept away[j] when the city is
punished.[k]"
16When he hesitated, the men grasped
his hand and the hands of his wife and of
his two daughters[l] and led them safely
out of the city, for the LORD was merciful
to them.[m] 17As soon as they had brought
them out, one of them said, "Flee for
your lives![n] Don't look back,[o] and don't
stop anywhere in the plain![p] Flee to the
mountains[q] or you will be swept away!"
18But Lot said to them, "No, my
lords,[k] please! 19Your[l] servant has found
favor in your[l] eyes,[r] and you[l] have
shown great kindness[s] to me in sparing
my life. But I can't flee to the mountains;[t] this disaster will overtake me,
and I'll die. 20Look, here is a town near
enough to run to, and it is small. Let me
flee to it—it is very small, isn't it? Then
my life will be spared."
21He said to him, "Very well, I will
grant this request[u] too; I will not overthrow the town you speak of. 22But flee
there quickly, because I cannot do anything until you reach it." (That is why the
town was called Zoar.[m][v])
23By the time Lot reached Zoar,[w] the
sun had risen over the land. 24Then the
LORD rained down burning sulfur[x] on
Sodom and Gomorrah[y]—from the LORD
out of the heavens.[z] 25Thus he overthrew those cities[a] and the entire
plain,[b] including all those living in the
cities—and also the vegetation in the
land.[c] 26But Lot's wife looked back,[d] and
she became a pillar of salt.[e]
27Early the next morning Abraham got
up and returned to the place where he
had stood before the LORD.[f] 28He looked
down toward Sodom and Gomorrah, toward all the land of the plain, and he saw
dense smoke rising from the land, like
smoke from a furnace.[g]
29So when God destroyed the cities of
the plain,[h] he remembered[i] Abraham,
and he brought Lot out of the catastrophe[j] that overthrew the cities where Lot
had lived.[k]

19:8 [y]Jdg 19:24; 2Pe 2:7-8 **19:9** [z]Ge 23:4 [a]S Ge 13:8; Ac 7:27 **19:10** [b]S Ge 18:2 **19:11** [c]Dt 28:28-29; 2Ki 6:18; Ac 13:11 **19:12** [d]S Ge 6:18 **19:13** [e]Ex 12:29; 2Sa 24:16; 2Ki 19:35; 1Ch 21:12; 2Ch 32:21 [f]Ge 18:20 [g]1Ch 21:15; Ps 78:49; Jer 21:12; 25:18; 44:22; 51:45 **19:14** [h]Nu 16:21; Rev 18:4 [i]Ex 9:21; 1Ki 13:18; Jer 5:12; 43:2; Lk 17:28 **19:15** [j]Nu 16:26; Job 21:18; Ps 58:9; 73:19; 90:5 [k]Rev 18:4 **19:16** [l]2Pe 2:7 [m]Ex 34:6; Ps 33:18-19 **19:17** [n]1Ki 19:3; Jer 48:6 [o]ver 26 [p]S Ge 13:12 [q]S ver 19; S Ge 14:10; Mt 24:16 **19:19** [r]S Ge 6:8; S 18:3 [s]Ge 24:12; 39:21; 40:14; 47:29; Ru 1:8; 2:20; 3:10 [t]S ver 17,30 **19:21** [u]1Sa 25:35; 2Sa 14:8; Job 42:9 **19:22** [v]S Ge 13:10 **19:23** [w]S Ge 13:10 **19:24** [x]Job 18:15; Ps 11:6; Isa 30:33; 34:9; Eze 38:22 [y]Dt 29:23; Isa 1:9; 13:19; Jer 49:18; 50:40; Am 4:11 [z]S Ge 18:17; S Lev 10:2; S Mt 10:15; Lk 17:29 **19:25** [a]S ver 24; Eze 26:16; Zep 3:8; Hag 2:22 [b]S Ge 13:12 [c]Ps 107:34; Isa 1:10; Jer 20:16; 23:14; La 4:6; Eze 16:48 **19:26** [d]S ver 17 [e]Lk 17:32 **19:27** [f]Ge 18:22 **19:28** [g]Ge 15:17; Ex 19:18; Rev 9:2; 18:9 **19:29** [h]S Ge 13:12 [i]S Ge 8:1 [j]2Pe 2:7 [k]Ge 14:12; Eze 14:16

[j]14 Or *were married to* [k]18 Or *No, Lord;* or *No, my lord* [l]19 The Hebrew is singular. [m]22 *Zoar* means *small.*

19:12–19,29 GOD, Grace—The grace of God sometimes works in our lives in ways that we do not understand at the time. That is because God sees and knows things that we are not aware of. Surely Lot did not see the destruction of his hometown as an act of grace. Only looking back at the event could it be so understood. God seeks what is best for us as a loving heavenly Father, the picture of God that is developed so powerfully in the teaching of Jesus. In justice He destroyed the wicked cities to protect His chosen ones. Thus He showed His grace and mercy to them. The kindness and love of God always go beyond what we truly deserve from Him.

19:13,24–26 GOD, Wrath—God's wrath comes in judgment upon those who do not repent of their sins and turn to Him. How soon that judgment comes and how that wrath is expressed is not for us to determine. God's judgment came dramatically and decisively on Sodom and Gomorrah. The fact that God has not dealt just as openly and dramatically with other persons or cities does not mean that God will not act in judgment on them. In His grace God often delays the exercise of His wrath to let His grace achieve positive results. God attempts through His grace and His wrath to bring people to repentance, faith, and responsible action. Wrath is God's last resort. It is neither right nor loving for God simply to let sin go unpunished in the lives of those who will not respond to Him in faith. It is not right because God does not contradict His own basic character by continuing to overlook sin. It is not loving because God will not let people have reason to believe sin is not serious. God's actions lead us to take Him seriously when He demands our repentance and right living.

19:23–29 MIRACLE, Redemption—Miraculous judgment works toward redemption of God's people. Sin had engulfed Sodom and Gomorrah. God responded in miraculous judgment. Only Lot and his two daughters escaped the destruction of the two cities. As limited as redemption appears in the story, there is evidence of God's mercy. Lot's greedy choice threatened the future of his whole people. In allowing him to escape, God preserved an entire nation.

19:27 PRAYER, God's Presence—Abraham was conscious that God knew all his actions. This phrase, "before the LORD" is frequently used of persons acting in the consciousness of God's presence in their lives (1 Sa 15:33; 23:18).

Lot and His Daughters

30Lot and his two daughters left Zoar[l]
and settled in the mountains,[m] for he was
afraid to stay in Zoar. He and his two
daughters lived in a cave. 31One day the
older daughter said to the younger, "Our
father is old, and there is no man around
here to lie with us, as is the custom all
over the earth. 32Let's get our father to
drink wine and then lie with him and
preserve our family line[n] through our father."[o]

33That night they got their father to
drink wine, and the older daughter went
in and lay with him. He was not aware of
it when she lay down or when she got
up.[p]

34The next day the older daughter said
to the younger, "Last night I lay with my
father. Let's get him to drink wine again
tonight, and you go in and lie with him so
we can preserve our family line through
our father."[q] 35So they got their father to
drink wine[r] that night also, and the
younger daughter went and lay with him.
Again he was not aware of it when she
lay down or when she got up.[s]

36So both of Lot's daughters became
pregnant by their father.[t] 37The older
daughter had a son, and she named him
Moab[n];[u] he is the father of the Moabites[v] of today. 38The younger daughter
also had a son, and she named him Ben-
Ammi[o]; he is the father of the Ammonites[w] of today.

Chapter 20

Abraham and Abimelech

20:1–18Ref — Ge 12:10–20; 26:1–11

NOW Abraham moved on from there[x]
into the region of the Negev[y] and
lived between Kadesh[z] and Shur.[a] For a
while[b] he stayed in Gerar,[c] 2and there
Abraham said of his wife Sarah, "She is
my sister.[d]" Then Abimelech[e] king of
Gerar sent for Sarah and took her.[f]

3But God came to Abimelech[g] in a
dream[h] one night and said to him, "You
are as good as dead[i] because of the woman you have taken; she is a married
woman."[j]

4Now Abimelech had not gone near
her, so he said, "Lord, will you destroy an
innocent nation?[k] 5Did he not say to me,
'She is my sister,[l]' and didn't she also
say, 'He is my brother'? I have done this
with a clear conscience[m] and clean
hands.[n]"

6Then God said to him in the dream,
"Yes, I know you did this with a clear
conscience, and so I have kept[o] you from
sinning against me.[p] That is why I did
not let you touch her. 7Now return the
man's wife, for he is a prophet,[q] and he
will pray for you[r] and you will live. But if
you do not return her, you may be sure
that you and all yours will die."[s]

8Early the next morning Abimelech
summoned all his officials, and when he
told them all that had happened, they
were very much afraid. 9Then Abimelech
called Abraham in and said, "What have
you done to us? How have I wronged you
that you have brought such great guilt
upon me and my kingdom? You have
done things to me that should not be
done.[t]" 10And Abimelech asked Abraham, "What was your reason for doing
this?"

11Abraham replied, "I said to myself,
'There is surely no fear of God[u] in this
place, and they will kill me because of my
wife.'[v] 12Besides, she really is my sister,[w] the daughter of my father though
not of my mother; and she became my
wife. 13And when God had me wander[x]
from my father's household,[y] I said to
her, 'This is how you can show your love
to me: Everywhere we go, say of me, "He
is my brother." ' "

14Then Abimelech[z] brought sheep and
cattle and male and female slaves and
gave them to Abraham,[a] and he returned
Sarah his wife to him. 15And Abimelech
said, "My land is before you; live wherever you like."[b]

16To Sarah he said, "I am giving your
brother a thousand shekels[p] of silver.

19:30 [l]ver 22; S Ge 13:10 [m]S ver 19; S Ge 14:10 **19:32** [n]S Ge 16:2 [o]ver 34,36; Ge 38:18 **19:33** [p]ver 35 **19:34** [q]S ver 32 **19:35** [r]Ge 9:21 [s]ver 33 **19:36** [t]S ver 32 **19:37** [u]Ge 36:35; Ex 15:15; Nu 25:1; Isa 15:1; 25:10; Jer 25:21; 48:1; Eze 25:8; Zep 2:9 [v]Nu 22:4; 24:17; Dt 2:9; Jdg 3:28; Ru 1:4,22; 1Sa 14:47; 22:3-4; 2Sa 8:2; 2Ki 1:1; 3:4; Ezr 9:1; Ps 108:9; Jer 48:1 **19:38** [w]Nu 21:24; Dt 2:19; 23:3; Jos 12:2; Jdg 3:13; 10:6,7; 1Sa 11:1-11; 14:47; 1Ch 19:1; 2Ch 20:23; 26:8; 27:5; Ne 2:19; 4:3; Jer 25:21; 40:14; 49:1; Eze 21:28; 25:2; Am 1:13 **20:1** [x]Ge 18:1 [y]S Ge 12:9 [z]S Ge 14:7 [a]S Ge 16:7 [b]Ge 26:3 [c]Ge 26:1, 6,17 **20:2** [d]ver 12; S Ge 12:13 [e]ver 14; Ge 21:22; 26:1 [f]S Ge 12:15 **20:3** [g]Nu 22:9,20 [h]Ge 28:12; 31:10, 24; 37:5,9; 40:5; 41:1; Nu 12:6; Dt 13:1; Job 33:15; Da 2:1; 4:5 [i]Ex 10:7; 12:33; Ps 105:38 [j]ver 7; Ge 26:11; 1Ch 16:21; Ps 105:14 **20:4** [k]S Ge 18:25 **20:5** [l]S Ge 12:19 [m]S Ge 17:1 [n]Ps 7:8; 25:21; 26:6; 41:12 **20:6** [o]1Sa 25:26,34 [p]S Ge 13:13; Ps 41:4; 51:4 **20:7** [q]Dt 18:18; 34:10; 2Ki 3:11; 5:3; 1Ch 16:22; Ps 105:15 [r]ver 17; Ex 8:8; Nu 11:2; 12:13; 1Sa 7:5; 1Ki 13:6; Job 42:8; Jer 18:20; 37:3; 42:2 [s]S ver 3; S Ps 9:5 **20:9** [t]S Ge 12:18; 34:7 **20:11** [u]Ge 42:18; Ne 5:15; Job 31:23; Ps 36:1; Pr 16:6 **20:12** [v]S Ge 12:12; 31:31 [w]S Ge 12:13 **20:13** [x]Dt 26:5; 1Ch 16:20; Isa 30:28; 63:17 [y]S Ge 12:1 **20:14** [z]S ver 2 [a]Ge 12:16 **20:15** [b]Ge 13:9; S 45:18

[n]*37 Moab* sounds like the Hebrew for *from father.*
[o]*38 Ben-Ammi* means *son of my people.*
[p]*16* That is, about 25 pounds (about 11.5 kilograms)

19:32–35 CHRISTIAN ETHICS, Alcohol—Drunkenness allows a person to be manipulated by other persons for their selfish interests. No purpose justifies intoxicating and manipulating another person. See notes on 9:21; Ps 104:14–15.

20:1–9 SIN, Judgment—God's intervention can prevent sin against His people even though they deceive and are guilty. Living in a sinful environment does not justify deception. Nor does it justify expecting God to save us from the consequences of our sin. God may act to achieve His purposes, but He is not bound to act just because we claim to be His people. See note on 12:10–20.

20:4–6 GOD, Justice—God's justice is not a blind, arbitrary, mechanical reaction to evil or the appearance of evil. God's justice takes into account the circumstances involved in each individual situation. Instead of pouring harsh judgment upon Abimelech for unwittingly taking Abraham's wife, God tempered His judgment with understanding and mercy. We can always count on God to understand our circumstances at any given time. He is a loving heavenly Father, just as Jesus taught. This does not mean, however, that we can manipulate God or make flimsy excuses for our disobedience. God's justice is informed by His perfect knowledge of us. We cannot deceive God, but we can depend upon Him to deal with us justly.

This is to cover the offense against you before all who are with you; you are completely vindicated."

17 Then Abraham prayed to God,[c] and God healed Abimelech, his wife and his slave girls so they could have children again, 18 for the LORD had closed up every womb in Abimelech's household because of Abraham's wife Sarah.[d]

Chapter 21

The Birth of Isaac

NOW the LORD was gracious to Sarah[e] as he had said, and the LORD did for Sarah what he had promised.[f] 2 Sarah became pregnant and bore a son[g] to Abraham in his old age,[h] at the very time God had promised him.[i] 3 Abraham gave the name Isaac[q][j] to the son Sarah bore him. 4 When his son Isaac was eight days old, Abraham circumcised him,[k] as God commanded him. 5 Abraham was a hundred years old[l] when his son Isaac was born to him.

6 Sarah said, "God has brought me laughter,[m] and everyone who hears about this will laugh with me." 7 And she added, "Who would have said to Abraham that Sarah would nurse children? Yet I have borne him a son in his old age."[n]

Hagar and Ishmael Sent Away

8 The child grew and was weaned,[o] and on the day Isaac was weaned Abraham held a great feast. 9 But Sarah saw that the son whom Hagar the Egyptian had borne to Abraham[p] was mocking,[q] 10 and she said to Abraham, "Get rid of that slave woman[r] and her son, for that slave woman's son will never share in the inheritance with my son Isaac."[s]

11 The matter distressed Abraham greatly because it concerned his son.[t] 12 But God said to him, "Do not be so distressed about the boy and your maidservant. Listen to whatever Sarah tells you, because it is through Isaac that your offspring[r] will be reckoned.[u] 13 I will make the son of the maidservant into a nation[v] also, because he is your offspring."

14 Early the next morning Abraham took some food and a skin of water and gave them to Hagar.[w] He set them on her shoulders and then sent her off with the boy. She went on her way and wandered in the desert of Beersheba.[x]

15 When the water in the skin was gone, she put the boy under one of the bushes. 16 Then she went off and sat down nearby, about a bowshot away, for she thought, "I cannot watch the boy die." And as she sat there nearby, she[s] began to sob.[y]

17 God heard the boy crying,[z] and the angel of God[a] called to Hagar from heaven[b] and said to her, "What is the matter, Hagar? Do not be afraid;[c] God has heard the boy crying as he lies there. 18 Lift the boy up and take him by the hand, for I will make him into a great nation.[d]"

19 Then God opened her eyes[e] and she saw a well of water.[f] So she went and filled the skin with water and gave the boy a drink.

20 God was with the boy[g] as he grew up. He lived in the desert and became an archer. 21 While he was living in the Desert of Paran,[h] his mother got a wife for him[i] from Egypt.

The Treaty at Beersheba

22 At that time Abimelech[j] and Phicol the commander of his forces[k] said to Abraham, "God is with you in everything you do.[l] 23 Now swear[m] to me here before God that you will not deal falsely with me or my children or my descendants.[n] Show to me and the country where you are living as an alien the same kindness I have shown to you."[o]

24 Abraham said, "I swear it."

25 Then Abraham complained to Abimelech about a well of water that Abimelech's servants had seized.[p] 26 But Abimelech said, "I don't know who has

[q]3 *Isaac* means *he laughs.* [r]12 Or *seed* [s]16 Hebrew; Septuagint *the child*

20:17 [c]S ver 7; Job 42:9 **20:18** [d]Ge 12:17 **21:1** [e]1Sa 2:21 [f]S Ge 8:1; S 17:16, 21; 18:14; Gal 4:23; Heb 11:11 **21:2** [g]S Ge 17:19; S 30:6 [h]Gal 4:22; Heb 11:11 [i]S Ge 18:10 **21:3** [j]S Ge 16:11; S 17:19; Jos 24:3 **21:4** [k]Ge 17:10, 12; Ac 7:8 **21:5** [l]S Ge 12:4; Heb 6:15 **21:6** [m]Ge 17:17; Job 8:21; Ps 126:2; Isa 12:6; 35:2; 44:23; 52:9; 54:1 **21:7** [n]S Ge 17:17 **21:8** [o]1Sa 1:23 **21:9** [p]S Ge 16:15 [q]Ge 39:14; Gal 4:29 **21:10** [r]Ge 39:17 [s]Ge 25:6; Gal 4:30* **21:11** [t]Ge 17:18 **21:12** [u]Mt 1:2; Ro 9:7*; Heb 11:18* **21:13** [v]ver 18; S Ge 13:16 **21:14** [w]S Ge 16:1 [x]ver 31,32; Ge 22:19; 26:33; 28:10; 46:1,5; Jos 15:28; 19:2; Jdg 20:1; 1Sa 3:20; 1Ch 4:28; Ne 11:27 **21:16** [y]Jer 6:26; Am 8:10; Zec 12:10 **21:17** [z]Ex 3:7; Nu 20:16; Dt 26:7; Ps 6:8 [a]S Ge 16:7 [b]Ge 22:11,15 [c]S Ge 15:1 **21:18** [d]ver 13; S Ge 17:20 **21:19** [e]Nu 22:31 [f]S Ge 16:7 **21:20** [g]Ge 26:3,24; 28:15; 39:2,21,23; Lk 1:66 **21:21** [h]S Ge 14:6 [i]Ge 24:4,38; 28:2; 34:4,8; Jdg 14:2 **21:22** [j]S Ge 20:2 [k]ver 32; Ge 26:26 [l]ver 23; Ge 26:28; 28:15; 31:3,5,42; 39:2,3; 1Sa 3:19; 16:18; 2Ch 1:1; Ps 46:7; Isa 7:14; 8:8,10; 41:10; 43:5 **21:23** [m]ver 31; Ge 25:33; 26:31; 31:53; Jos 2:12; 1Ki 2:8 [n]1Sa 24:21 [o]S ver 22; Jos 2:12 **21:25** [p]Ge 26:15, 18,20-22

20:17–18 HISTORY, Universal—See note on 17:20. The moral foundation of history is not limited to God's people. God works out His universal purposes on a moral foundation, also. He honors the moral integrity of unbelieving rulers while at the same time protecting His own people and using them to bless others.

20:17 PRAYER, Intercession—Abimelech's healing depended on the prayer of the one offended, however unconscious the offense. See note on Nu 12:10–14.

21:1,12–13 ELECTION, God's Purpose—God had a purpose for the birth of Isaac and Ishmael. Each one had a separate and distinct purpose. Each one had to learn dependence upon God to reach God's purpose for his life. In electing a people to bear covenant promise, God did not ignore all others. See note on 17:1–27.

21:8–20 EVIL AND SUFFERING, God's Compassion—God acts in love even with people outside His elect. God's response to Ishmael's suffering reflects the meaning of Ishmael's name—God hears. See note on 16:11.

21:13 HISTORY, Universal—See note on 17:20.

21:22–34 HISTORY, Worship—Biblical history described potential international incidents to teach about God rather than to provide detailed accounts of political history. The confrontation of Abraham and Abimelech showed how God blessed international relations through Abraham (12:3) and introduced the history of a sacred worship place. Worship and the place of worship were of more concern to biblical history than were a political treaty. Compare 46:1; 1 Sa 8:2; 2 Ki 23:8; Am 5:5; 8:14.

done this. You did not tell me, and I heard about it only today."

27 So Abraham brought sheep and cattle and gave them to Abimelech, and the two men made a treaty.[q] 28 Abraham set apart seven ewe lambs from the flock, 29 and Abimelech asked Abraham, "What is the meaning of these seven ewe lambs you have set apart by themselves?"

30 He replied, "Accept these seven lambs from my hand as a witness[r] that I dug this well.[s]"

31 So that place was called Beersheba,[t][t] because the two men swore an oath[u] there.

32 After the treaty[v] had been made at Beersheba,[w] Abimelech and Phicol the commander of his forces[x] returned to the land of the Philistines.[y] 33 Abraham planted a tamarisk tree[z] in Beersheba, and there he called upon the name of the LORD,[a] the Eternal God.[b] 34 And Abraham stayed in the land of the Philistines[c] for a long time.

Chapter 22

Abraham Tested

SOME time later God tested[d] Abraham. He said to him, "Abraham!"

"Here I am,"[e] he replied.

2 Then God said, "Take your son,[f] your only son, Isaac, whom you love, and go to the region of Moriah.[g] Sacrifice him there as a burnt offering[h] on one of the mountains I will tell you about.[i]"

3 Early the next morning[j] Abraham got up and saddled his donkey. He took with him two of his servants and his son Isaac. When he had cut enough wood for the burnt offering, he set out for the place God had told him about. 4 On the third day Abraham looked up and saw the place in the distance. 5 He said to his servants, "Stay here with the donkey while I and the boy go over there. We will worship and then we will come back to you.[k]"

6 Abraham took the wood for the burnt offering and placed it on his son Isaac,[l] and he himself carried the fire and the knife.[m] As the two of them went on together, 7 Isaac spoke up and said to his father Abraham, "Father?"

"Yes, my son?" Abraham replied.

"The fire and wood are here," Isaac said, "but where is the lamb[n] for the burnt offering?"

8 Abraham answered, "God himself will provide[o] the lamb[p] for the burnt offering, my son." And the two of them went on together.

9 When they reached the place God had told him about,[q] Abraham built an altar[r] there and arranged the wood[s] on it. He bound his son Isaac and laid him on the altar,[t] on top of the wood. 10 Then he reached out his hand and took the knife[u] to slay his son.[v] 11 But the angel of the LORD[w] called out to him from heaven,[x] "Abraham! Abraham!"[y]

"Here I am,"[z] he replied.

12 "Do not lay a hand on the boy," he said. "Do not do anything to him. Now I know that you fear God,[a] because you have not withheld from me your son, your only son.[b]"

21:27 [q]ver 31,32; Ge 26:28,31; 31:44,53 **21:30** [r]Ge 31:44, 47,48,50,52; Jos 22:27,28,34; 24:27; Isa 19:20; Mal 2:14 [s]ver 25; Ge 26:25,32 **21:31** [t]S ver 14 [u]S ver 23,S 27 **21:32** [v]S ver 27 [w]S ver 14 [x]S ver 22 [y]S Ge 10:14 **21:33** [z]1Sa 22:6; 31:13 [a]S Ge 4:26 [b]Ex 15:18; Dt 32:40; 33:27; Job 36:26; Ps 10:16; 45:6; 90:2; 93:2; 102:24; 103:19; 146:10; Isa 40:28; Jer 10:10; Hab 1:12; 3:6; Heb 13:8 **21:34** [c]S Ge 10:14 **22:1** [d]Ex 15:25; 16:4; 20:20; Dt 8:2,16; 13:3; Jdg 2:22; 3:1; 2Ch 32:31; Ps 66:10; Heb 11:17; Jas 1:12-13 [e]ver 11; Ge 31:11; 46:2; 1Sa 3:4,6,8; Isa 6:8 **22:2** [f]ver 12,16; Jn 3:16; Heb 11:17; 1Jn 4:9 [g]2Ch 3:1 [h]S Ge 8:20 [i]ver 9 **22:3** [j]Jos 8:10 **22:5** [k]Ex 24:14 **22:6** [l]Jn 19:17 [m]ver 10; Jdg 19:29 **22:7** [n]Ex 29:38-42; Lev 1:10; Rev 13:8 **22:8** [o]ver 14 [p]ver 13; S Jn 1:29 **22:9** [q]ver 2 [r]S Ge 4:26; S 8:20 [s]Lev 1:7; 1Ki 18:33 [t]Heb 11:17-19; Jas 2:21 **22:10** [u]S ver 6 [v]ver 3; S Ge 18:19 **22:11** [w]S Ge 16:7 [x]S Ge 21:17 [y]Ge 46:2 [z]S ver 1 **22:12** [a]S Ge 18:19; 42:18; Ex 18:21; 1Sa 15:22; Job 1:1; 37:24; Pr 8:13; Jas 2:21-22 [b]S ver 2; Jn 3:16; 1Jn 4:9

[t]31 *Beersheba* can mean *well of seven* or *well of the oath.*

21:33 GOD, Eternal—From Ge 1:1 we infer the eternity of God. Here is the Bible's first direct statement of His eternity. The idea of God as eternal suggests He is supreme, uncaused. See notes on 1:1; Ex 20:1–7. We need not seek for any greater being. None exists.

22:1–18 EVIL AND SUFFERING, Testing—God tested Abraham's faith by commanding him to offer Isaac as a sacrifice. God did not seek to make Abraham sin. He presented Abraham an opportunity to clarify his loyalty to God. Did Abraham love Isaac more than God? Sometimes our suffering is not due to God punishing us but to God placing us in a situation where our faith is challenged and can grow.

22:1–18 REVELATION, Author of Hope—The test of Abraham revealed the kind of God who called Abraham to follow. He is not a God who wants wasteful human sacrifice although other gods in the area were known for requiring it. He is a giver of life and purpose, not one who authors destruction and death. God wants good, is good, and gives life, rather than takes it. The test was revealed through direct conversation between God and Abraham. As usual in the Bible, the how of the conversation is not described. V 3 may point back to a night vision. A messenger (Hebrew *mal'ak*) delivered God's message in the center of the action (vv 11,15). The messenger was from heaven and thus an angel. See note on 18:1—19:29. Angels normally appeared in the middle of events rather than at the beginning in biblical narrative.

22:1–19 CHRISTIAN ETHICS, Moral Imperatives—Total allegiance to and trust in God is the foundation for the Bible's ethical teachings. Because we know God is good, we do not ask questions here about the morality of God in asking Abraham to sacrifice his only son, the son of promise. Rather, we ask if we are trusting enough to obey our good God's most radical demands on us. Ultimately, God alone required the sacrifice of an only Son of Himself.

22:8 SALVATION, Justification—Abraham's faith manifested itself in obedience, illustrated by his offering his son Isaac as a burnt offering in accordance with God's command. Even so, his answer to Isaac was that God would provide the lamb for the sacrifice. See note on Jn 1:29.

22:9–14 MIRACLE, Faith—All of Isaac's life is a miracle. Born to aging parents (18:11) after God's promise, he miraculously escaped being slaughtered by his own father. The provision of the substitute ram may have appeared as a mere circumstance to another with less faith than Abraham. But the great man of faith saw God's provision and named that place "The Lord Will Provide." We may not understand how and why God acts sometimes, but we can count on Him to provide for us if we faithfully obey Him. Such obedience may let us recognize God's miracle.

22:12 SALVATION, Fear of God—Reverential fear or awe is a proper human response to God's salvation. God knew that Abraham feared Him when he showed his willingness to offer Isaac.

13Abraham looked up and there in a
thicket he saw a ram[u] caught by its
horns.[c] He went over and took the ram
and sacrificed it as a burnt offering instead of his son.[d] 14So Abraham called[e]
that place The LORD[f] Will Provide. And
to this day it is said, "On the mountain of
the LORD it will be provided.[g]"
15The angel of the LORD[h] called to
Abraham from heaven[i] a second time
16and said, "I swear by myself,[j] declares
the LORD, that because you have done
this and have not withheld your son, your
only son,[k] 17I will surely bless you[l] and
make your descendants[m] as numerous as
the stars in the sky[n] and as the sand on
the seashore.[o] Your descendants will
take possession of the cities of their enemies,[p] 18and through your offspring[v] all
nations on earth will be blessed,[q] because you have obeyed me."[r]
19Then Abraham returned to his servants, and they set off together for Beersheba.[s] And Abraham stayed in Beersheba.

Nahor's Sons

20Some time later Abraham was told,
"Milcah is also a mother; she has borne
sons to your brother Nahor:[t] 21Uz[u] the
firstborn, Buz[v] his brother, Kemuel (the
father of Aram), 22Kesed, Hazo, Pildash,
Jidlaph and Bethuel.[w]" 23Bethuel became
the father of Rebekah.[x] Milcah bore
these eight sons to Abraham's brother
Nahor.[y] 24His concubine,[z] whose name
was Reumah, also had sons: Tebah, Ga-
ham, Tahash and Maacah.

Chapter 23

The Death of Sarah

SARAH lived to be a hundred and
twenty-seven years old. 2She died at
Kiriath Arba[a] (that is, Hebron)[b] in the land
of Canaan, and Abraham went to mourn
for Sarah and to weep over her.[c]
3Then Abraham rose from beside his
dead wife and spoke to the Hittites.[w][d]
He said, 4"I am an alien and a stranger[e]
among you. Sell me some property for a
burial site here so I can bury my dead.[f]"
5The Hittites replied to Abraham,
6"Sir, listen to us. You are a mighty
prince[g] among us. Bury your dead in the
choicest of our tombs. None of us will
refuse you his tomb for burying your
dead."
7Then Abraham rose and bowed down
before the people of the land, the Hittites.
8He said to them, "If you are willing to let
me bury my dead, then listen to me and
intercede with Ephron son of Zohar[h] on
my behalf 9so he will sell me the cave of
Machpelah,[i] which belongs to him and
is at the end of his field. Ask him to sell it
to me for the full price as a burial site
among you."
10Ephron the Hittite was sitting among
his people and he replied to Abraham in
the hearing of all the Hittites[j] who had
come to the gate[k] of his city. 11"No, my
lord," he said. "Listen to me; I give[x][l]
you the field, and I give[x] you the cave
that is in it. I give[x] it to you in the presence of my people. Bury your dead."
12Again Abraham bowed down before
the people of the land 13and he said to
Ephron in their hearing, "Listen to me, if
you will. I will pay the price of the field.
Accept it from me so I can bury my dead
there."
14Ephron answered Abraham, 15"Listen to me, my lord; the land is worth four
hundred shekels[y] of silver,[m] but what is

22:13 [c]S ver 8 [d]S Ge 8:20; Ro 8:32 **22:14** [e]Ex 17:15; Jdg 6:24 [f]Isa 30:29 [g]ver 8 **22:15** [h]S Ge 16:7 [i]S Ge 21:17 **22:16** [j]Ex 13:11; 32:13; 33:1; Isa 45:23; 62:8; Jer 22:5; 44:26; 49:13; 51:14; Am 6:8; Lk 1:73; Heb 6:13 [k]S ver 2 **22:17** [l]S Ge 12:2 [m]Heb 6:14* [n]S Ge 15:5; Ex 32:13; Dt 7:7; 28:62 [o]S Ge 12:2; S 26:24; Hos 1:10; Ro 9:27; Heb 11:12 [p]Ge 24:60; Est 9:2 **22:18** [q]S Ge 12:2, 3; Ac 3:25*; Gal 3:8* [r]S ver 10; Ge 17:2,9; Ps 105:9 **22:19** [s]Ge 21:14; 26:23; 28:10 **22:20** [t]S Ge 11:29 **22:21** [u]S Ge 10:23 [v]Job 32:2; Jer 25:23 **22:22** [w]Ge 24:15, 47; 25:20 **22:23** [x]Ge 24:15 [y]S Ge 11:29 **22:24** [z]Ge 25:6; 35:22; 36:12; Jdg 8:31; 2Sa 3:7; 1Ki 2:22; 11:3; 1Ch 1:32; SS 6:8 **23:2** [a]Jos 14:15; 15:13; 20:7; 21:11 [b]ver 19; S Ge 13:18 [c]Ge 24:67 **23:3** [d]S Ge 10:15 **23:4** [e]S Ge 17:8; 19:9; Ex 2:22; Lev 25:23; Ps 39:12; 105:12; 119:19; Heb 11:9, 13 [f]Ge 49:30; Ac 7:16 **23:6** [g]Ge 14:14-16; 24:35 **23:8** [h]Ge 25:9 **23:9** [i]ver 17,19; Ge 25:9; 47:30; 49:30; 50:13 **23:10** [j]ver 18 [k]S Ge 18:1; Dt 22:15; 25:7; Jos 20:4; Ru 4:11; 2Sa 15:2; 2Ki 15:35; Ps 127:5; Pr 31:23; Jer 26:10; 36:10 **23:11** [l]2Sa 24:23 **23:15** [m]Eze 45:12

[u]*13* Many manuscripts of the Masoretic Text, Samaritan Pentateuch, Septuagint and Syriac; most manuscripts of the Masoretic Text *a ram behind* ⌞*him*⌟ [v]*18* Or *seed* [w]*3* Or *the sons of Heth*; also in verses 5, 7, 10, 16, 18 and 20 [x]*11* Or *sell* [y]*15* That is, about 10 pounds (about 4.5 kilograms)

22:14 GOD, Grace—Preparing to offer Isaac as a sacrifice, Abraham learned that God is a gracious God, who will provide for us what He expects from us. We are not relieved of our responsibility. Indeed, we are required to act in faith, as Abraham did. When we commit ourselves to doing what God asks of us, God will work within us and around us so that we can carry out His will for us. He does not make impossible, unreasonable demands of us.

22:15–18 HISTORY, Promise—See note on 15:1–21.

22:15–18 ELECTION, Faith—The story of Abraham's willingness to sacrifice his only son illustrates his complete trust in God and thus also the true meaning of being a member of God's elect. This story reminds Christians of Jesus Christ, the obedient and sacrifical Lamb who made the supreme sacrifice for the salvation of the world. God elects people of faith.

22:16–18 MISSIONS, Nature—No more moving account exists in the Bible than this account of Abraham's willingness to sacrifice his own son—his only son—and God's providing a substitute. Two lessons shine clearly in the chapter: God does not require human sacrifice, and He does demand absolute obedience (22:11–12). Missionary work is by nature obedience to God. Abraham was willing to sacrifice his own son, the agent through whom God promised to work out His missionary purpose of blessing for the nations. God commanded and accepted Abraham's substitutionary sacrifice of a ram for his son. In his obedience, Abraham proved equal to the missionary task set before him. He obeyed God rather than men. Abraham's obedience allowed God to bless him and use his descendants to bless all of the nations or peoples of the earth. The biblical principle is that being blessed, we are to bless in return. Knowing the Savior, we are to share Him. God's purpose in the world is a redemptive and missionary purpose.

22:18 EVANGELISM, Results—See note on 18:18–19.

22:20–24 HISTORY, Universal—See note on 11:10,27.

23:1–2 HUMANITY, Attitudes to Death—Although death is the natural outcome of life, it is also natural to grieve over the loss of a beloved companion.

23:3–20 HUMANITY, Burial—The proper burial of the dead is important. It demonstrates the unity and ongoing nature of the family, providing a place for succeeding generations to return and remember their roots.

that between me and you? Bury your
dead."
16Abraham agreed to Ephron's terms
and weighed out for him the price he had
named in the hearing of the Hittites: four
hundred shekels of silver,[n] according to
the weight current among the merchants.[o]
17So Ephron's field in Machpelah[p]
near Mamre[q]—both the field and the
cave in it, and all the trees within the
borders of the field—was deeded 18to
Abraham as his property[r] in the presence
of all the Hittites[s] who had come to
the gate[t] of the city. 19Afterward Abraham
buried his wife Sarah in the cave in
the field of Machpelah[u] near Mamre
(which is at Hebron[v]) in the land of Canaan.[w]
20So the field and the cave in it
were deeded[x] to Abraham by the Hittites
as a burial site.[y]

Chapter 24

Isaac and Rebekah

ABRAHAM was now old and well advanced
in years,[z] and the LORD had
blessed[a] him in every way.[b] 2He said to
the chief[z] servant[c] in his household, the
one in charge of all that he had,[d] "Put
your hand under my thigh.[e] 3I want you
to swear[f] by the LORD, the God of heaven[g]
and the God of earth,[h] that you will
not get a wife for my son[i] from the
daughters of the Canaanites,[j] among
whom I am living,[k] 4but will go to my
country and my own relatives[l] and get a
wife for my son Isaac.[m]"
5The servant asked him, "What if the
woman is unwilling to come back with
me to this land?[n] Shall I then take your
son back to the country you came
from?[o]"
6"Make sure that you do not take my
son back there,"[p] Abraham said. 7"The
LORD, the God of heaven,[q] who brought
me out of my father's household and my
native land[r] and who spoke to me and
promised me on oath, saying, 'To your
offspring[a][s] I will give this land'[t]—he
will send his angel before you[u] so that
you can get a wife for my son from there.
8If the woman is unwilling to come back
with you, then you will be released from
this oath[v] of mine. Only do not take my
son back there."[w] 9So the servant put his
hand under the thigh[x] of his master[y]
Abraham and swore an oath to him concerning
this matter.
10Then the servant took ten of his master's
camels[z] and left, taking with him all
kinds of good things[a] from his master.
He set out for Aram Naharaim[b][b] and
made his way to the town of Nahor.[c]
11He had the camels kneel down near the
well[d] outside the town; it was toward
evening, the time the women go out to
draw water.[e]
12Then he prayed, "O LORD, God of my
master Abraham,[f] give me success[g] today,
and show kindness[h] to my master
Abraham. 13See, I am standing beside this
spring, and the daughters of the towns-

23:16 [n]2Sa 24:24; Jer 32:9; Zec 11:12 [o]2Sa 14:26
23:17 [p]S ver 9 [q]S Ge 13:18
23:18 [r]S Ge 12:7 [s]ver 10 [t]S Ge 18:1
23:19 [u]S ver 9 [v]S Ge 13:18; Jos 14:13; 1Ch 29:27 [w]Ge 49:31
23:20 [x]Jer 32:10 [y]S Ge 10:15; 35:29; 47:30; 49:30; 50:5, 13
24:1 [z]S Ge 17:17; Jos 23:1 [a]Ge 12:2; Gal 3:9 [b]ver 35
24:2 [c]S Ge 15:3 [d]Ge 39:4-6 [e]ver 9; Ge 47:29
24:3 [f]Ge 47:31; 50:25 [g]ver 7 [h]S Ge 14:19; S Nu 20:14 [i]Dt 7:3; 2Co 6:14-17 [j]S Ge 10:15-19 [k]ver 37
24:4 [l]S Ge 12:1; Jdg 14:3 [m]S ver 29; S Ge 21:21
24:5 [n]ver 39 [o]Heb 11:15
24:6 [p]ver 8
24:7 [q]ver 3 [r]Ge 12:1 [s]Ro 4:13; Gal 3:16* [t]S Ge 12:7 [u]S Ge 16:7
24:8 [v]ver 41; Jos 2:12,17,20; 9:20 [w]S ver 6
24:9 [x]S ver 2 [y]Ge 32:4; 33:8
24:10 [z]ver 19; 1Ki 10:2; 1Ch 12:40; Isa 30:6 [a]ver 22,30,47,53; Ge 43:11; 45:23 [b]Nu 23:7; Dt 23:4; Jdg 3:8 [c]S Ge 11:29
24:11 [d]Ex 2:15 [e]ver 13; Ge 29:2, 9-10; Ex 2:16; 1Sa 9:11; Jn 4:7
24:12 [f]ver 27,42, 48; Ge 26:24; 28:13; 31:42,53; 32:9; 43:23; 46:3; Ex 3:6,15,16; 4:5; 1Ki 18:36; Ps 75:9; 94:7 [g]ver 21,40,51,56; Ge 27:20; Ne 1:11 [h]S Ge 19:19; Jos 2:12; Job 10:12

[z]2 Or *oldest* [a]7 Or *seed* [b]10 That is, Northwest Mesopotamia

23:17–20 HISTORY, God's People—Biblical history centers on significant moments for God's people rather than for international relationships. Sarah's death gave opportunity for Abraham to gain legal deed to a piece of land in the Promised Land. Thus God's promise of land (12:7) began to be fulfilled.

24:1–67 ELECTION, Providence—God works out His elected will in the routines of human life. The human relationships and actions involved in securing a wife for the son of promise worked successfully because God blessed them to work out His purpose in electing Abraham and Isaac. God's providential guiding and human plans and actions work together in a way beyond human understanding to accomplish God's election.

24:1–67 DISCIPLESHIP, God's Leadership—The choice of a wife for Isaac is a beautiful picture of God's leadership and the obedient following of His servant, Abraham. Following the death of Sarah, Abraham still had to arrange for the marriage of Isaac, the heir of God's promise. Abraham instructed his oldest and most trusted servant how to seek a wife for Isaac. The servant took an oath to follow Abraham's instructions and prayed that God would give him success in his mission. His prayer was answered. Following both human and divine leadership is a part of discipleship. God also led Isaac (v 63). Divine leadership is essential for any disciple contemplating marriage.

24:1–67 FAMILY, Covenant Marriage—The marriage of Isaac and Rebekah is a classic example of covenant marriage. Abraham, Isaac's father, wanted his son to marry a woman within the covenant community of Israel and dispatched his trusted servant to go back to the town of Nahor to find such a wife. The covenant concept of marriage is not discussed at length in the Bible, but it is basic to an understanding of the meaning of marriage among the people of God. To covenant together as fellow believers in Christ is one of the grounds for stability in marriage. See notes on Mal 2:13–16; 2 Co 6:14–18.

24:3,7,50 GOD, Sovereignty—God's sovereignty is more than sheer power or absolute authority. It is His capability of achieving His purposes in ways that do not violate the very conditions of life that He has created. God has given to each person the right of self-determination, or free will, which God does not violate. God did not force Rebekah or Rebekah's family into accepting Abraham's proposal that Rebekah become the wife of Isaac. God's sovereignty worked in gentle, persuasive ways to win a positive response based on faith and personal acceptance, a free choice on the part of Rebekah and her family, but a response that leaves us in awe at the power of the sovereign grace of God.

24:7 HISTORY, Promise—See note on 15:1–21.

24:12–27 PRAYER, Petition—Prayer can include specific requests, particularly when the request involves the participation of other people in the fulfillment of God's purposes. Praise and worship are the proper responses when God fulfills our requests. Through prayer we become aware of God's initiative in working in our lives.

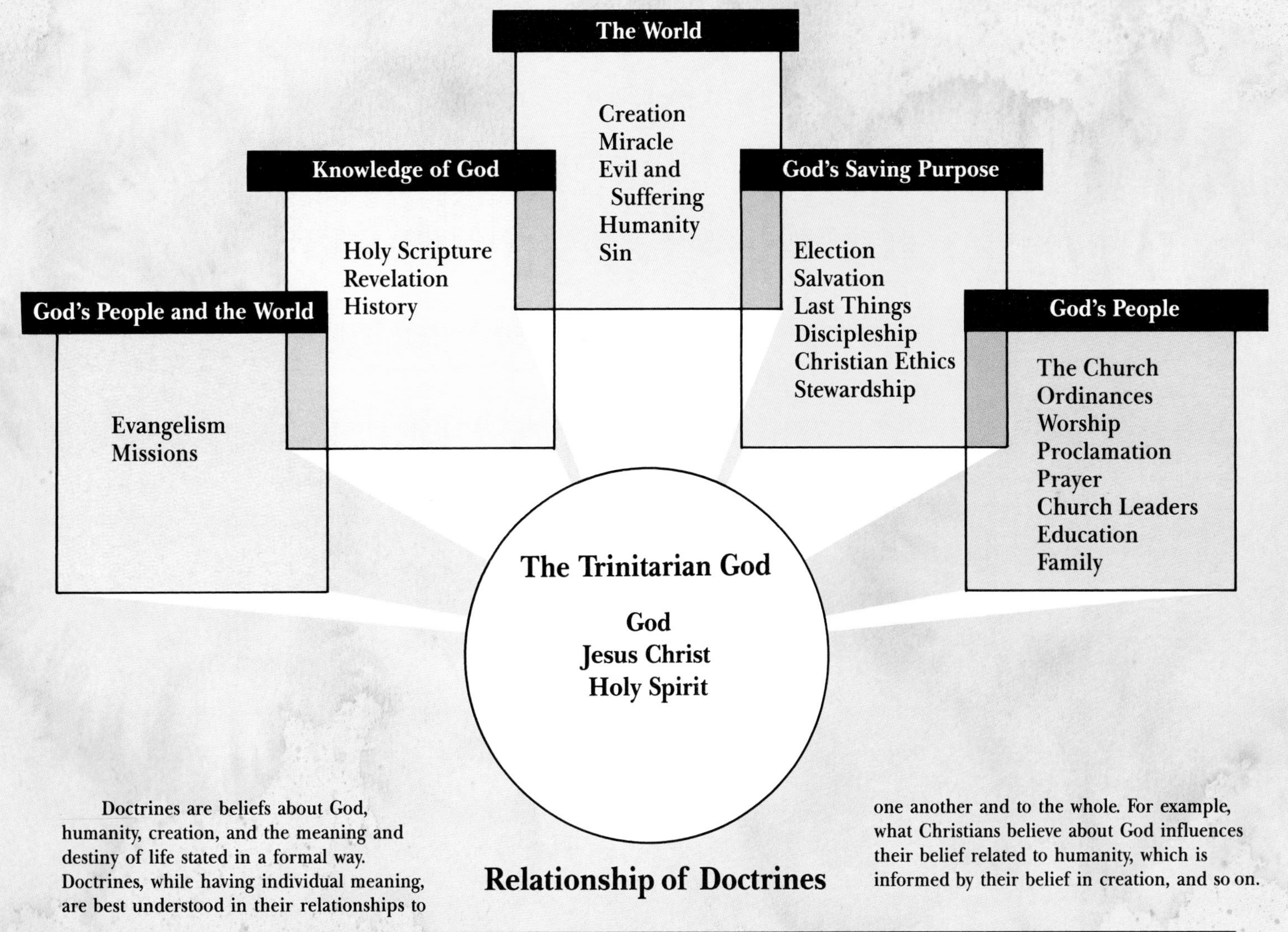

Relationship of Doctrines

Doctrines are beliefs about God, humanity, creation, and the meaning and destiny of life stated in a formal way. Doctrines, while having individual meaning, are best understood in their relationships to one another and to the whole. For example, what Christians believe about God influences their belief related to humanity, which is informed by their belief in creation, and so on.

Pentateuch

BIBLICAL HISTORY

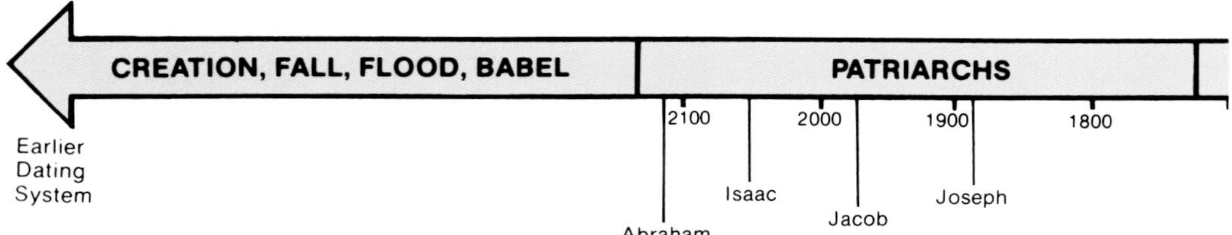

ANCIENT HISTORY

WORLD HISTORY

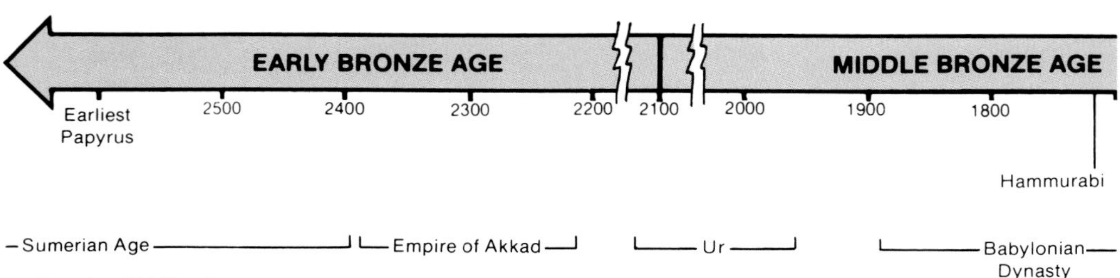

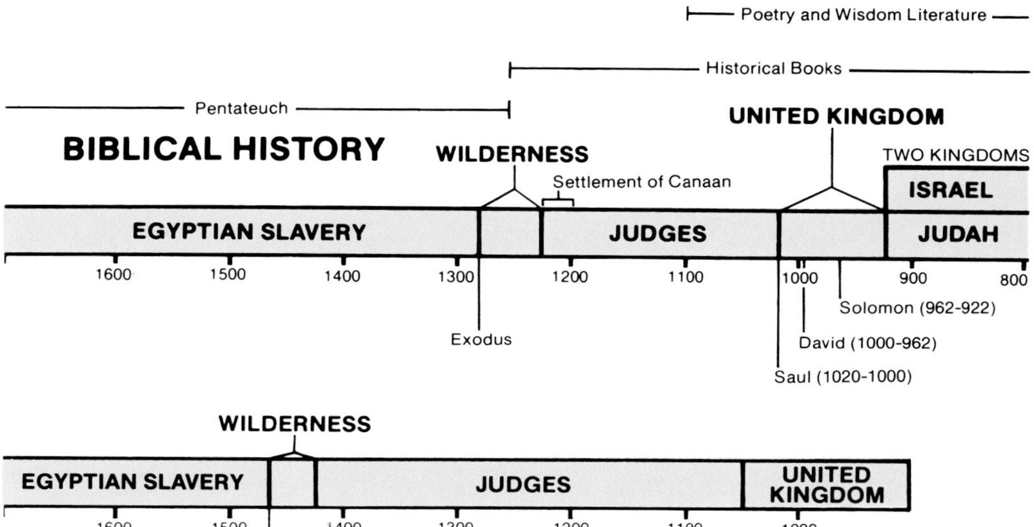
Poetry and Wisdom Literature
Historical Books
Pentateuch
BIBLICAL HISTORY
UNITED KINGDOM
WILDERNESS
TWO KINGDOMS
Settlement of Canaan
ISRAEL
EGYPTIAN SLAVERY
JUDGES
JUDAH
1600
1500
1400
1300
1200
1100
1000
900
800
Solomon (962-922)
Exodus
David (1000-962)
Saul (1020-1000)
WILDERNESS
EGYPTIAN SLAVERY
JUDGES
UNITED KINGDOM
1600
1500
1400
1300
1200
1100
1000
Exodus

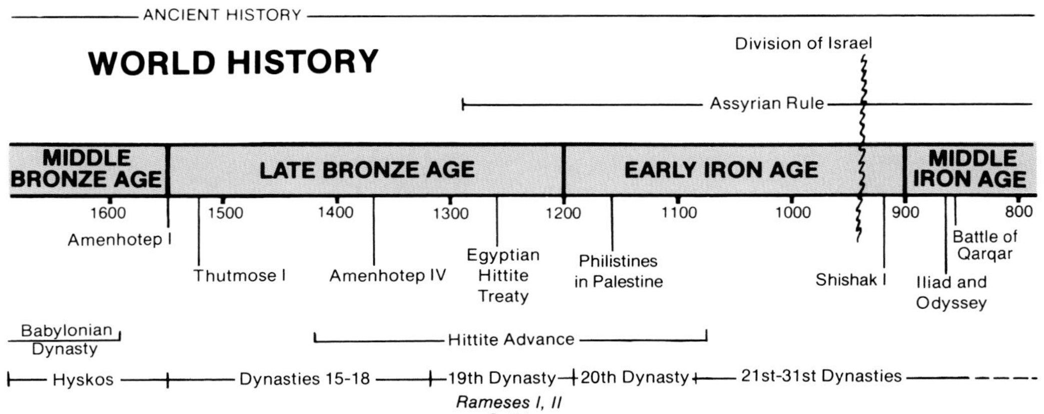
ANCIENT HISTORY
WORLD HISTORY
Division of Israel
Assyrian Rule
MIDDLE BRONZE AGE
LATE BRONZE AGE
EARLY IRON AGE
MIDDLE IRON AGE
1600
1500
1400
1300
1200
1100
1000
900
800
Amenhotep I
Thutmose I
Amenhotep IV
Egyptian Hittite Treaty
Philistines in Palestine
Shishak I
Battle of Qarqar
Iliad and Odyssey
Babylonian Dynasty
Hittite Advance
Hyskos
Dynasties 15-18
19th Dynasty
20th Dynasty
21st-31st Dynasties
Rameses I, II
Seti I
Merneptah

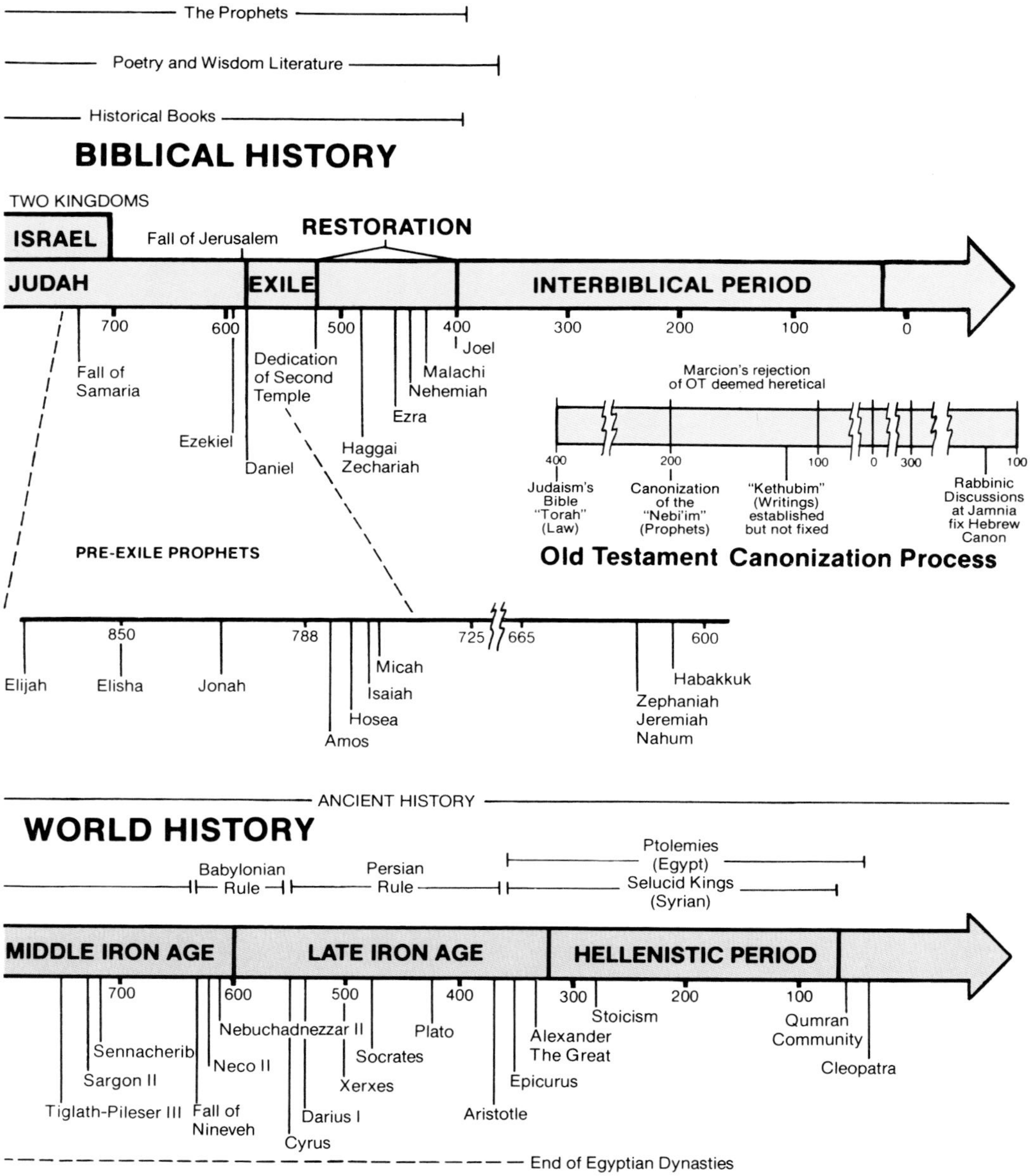

The Prophets

Poetry and Wisdom Literature

Historical Books

BIBLICAL HISTORY

TWO KINGDOMS

ISRAEL

Fall of Jerusalem

RESTORATION

JUDAH | **EXILE** | **INTERBIBLICAL PERIOD**

700 600 500 400 300 200 100 0

Fall of Samaria

Ezekiel

Daniel

Dedication of Second Temple

Haggai Zechariah

Ezra

Nehemiah

Malachi

Joel

Marcion's rejection of OT deemed heretical

400 200 100 0 300 100

Judaism's Bible "Torah" (Law)

Canonization of the "Nebi'im" (Prophets)

"Kethubim" (Writings) established but not fixed

Rabbinic Discussions at Jamnia fix Hebrew Canon

Old Testament Canonization Process

PRE-EXILE PROPHETS

850 788 725 665 600

Elijah

Elisha

Jonah

Amos

Hosea

Isaiah

Micah

Zephaniah Jeremiah Nahum

Habakkuk

ANCIENT HISTORY

WORLD HISTORY

Babylonian Rule

Persian Rule

Ptolemies (Egypt)

Selucid Kings (Syrian)

MIDDLE IRON AGE | **LATE IRON AGE** | **HELLENISTIC PERIOD**

700 600 500 400 300 200 100

Tiglath-Pileser III

Sargon II

Sennacherib

Fall of Nineveh

Neco II

Nebuchadnezzar II

Cyrus

Darius I

Xerxes

Socrates

Plato

Aristotle

Epicurus

Alexander The Great

Stoicism

Qumran Community

Cleopatra

End of Egyptian Dynasties

people are coming out to draw water.[i]
14May it be that when I say to a girl,
'Please let down your jar that I may have
a drink,' and she says, 'Drink,[j] and I'll
water your camels too'[k]—let her be the
one you have chosen for your servant
Isaac.[l] By this I will know[m] that you
have shown kindness to my master."

15Before he had finished praying,[n] Rebekah[o] came out with her jar on her
shoulder. She was the daughter of Bethuel[p] son of Milcah,[q] who was the wife of
Abraham's brother Nahor.[r] 16The girl
was very beautiful,[s] a virgin;[t] no man
had ever lain with her. She went down to
the spring, filled her jar and came up
again.

17The servant hurried to meet her and
said, "Please give me a little water from
your jar."[u]

18"Drink,[v] my lord," she said, and
quickly lowered the jar to her hands and
gave him a drink.

19After she had given him a drink, she
said, "I'll draw water for your camels[w]
too,[x] until they have finished drinking."
20So she quickly emptied her jar into the
trough, ran back to the well to draw more
water, and drew enough for all his camels.[y] 21Without saying a word, the man
watched her closely to learn whether or
not the LORD had made his journey successful.[z]

22When the camels had finished drinking, the man took out a gold nose ring[a]
weighing a beka[c] and two gold bracelets[b] weighing ten shekels.[d] 23Then he
asked, "Whose daughter are you?[c]
Please tell me, is there room in your father's house for us to spend the night?[d]"

24She answered him, "I am the daughter of Bethuel, the son that Milcah bore to
Nahor.[e]" 25And she added, "We have
plenty of straw and fodder,[f] as well as
room for you to spend the night."

26Then the man bowed down and worshiped the LORD,[g] 27saying, "Praise be to
the LORD,[h] the God of my master Abraham,[i] who has not abandoned his kindness and faithfulness[j] to my master. As
for me, the LORD has led me on the journey[k] to the house of my master's relatives."[l]

28The girl ran and told her mother's
household about these things.[m] 29Now
Rebekah had a brother named Laban,[n]
and he hurried out to the man at the
spring. 30As soon as he had seen the nose
ring, and the bracelets on his sister's
arms,[o] and had heard Rebekah tell what
the man said to her, he went out to the
man and found him standing by the camels near the spring. 31"Come, you who
are blessed by the LORD,"[p] he said.
"Why are you standing out here? I have
prepared the house and a place for the
camels."

32So the man went to the house, and
the camels were unloaded. Straw and fodder[q] were brought for the camels, and
water for him and his men to wash their
feet.[r] 33Then food was set before him,
but he said, "I will not eat until I have
told you what I have to say."

"Then tell us," ⌊Laban⌋ said.

34So he said, "I am Abraham's servant.[s] 35The LORD has blessed[t] my master abundantly,[u] and he has become
wealthy.[v] He has given him sheep and
cattle, silver and gold, menservants and
maidservants, and camels and donkeys.[w]
36My master's wife Sarah has borne him a
son in her[e] old age,[x] and he has given
him everything he owns.[y] 37And my
master made me swear an oath,[z] and
said, 'You must not get a wife for my son
from the daughters of the Canaanites, in
whose land I live,[a] 38but go to my father's family and to my own clan, and get
a wife for my son.'[b]

39"Then I asked my master, 'What if
the woman will not come back with
me?'[c]

40"He replied, 'The LORD, before
whom I have walked,[d] will send his angel with you[e] and make your journey a
success,[f] so that you can get a wife for
my son from my own clan and from my
father's family.[g] 41Then, when you go to
my clan, you will be released from my
oath even if they refuse to give her to
you—you will be released from my
oath.'[h]

42"When I came to the spring today, I
said, 'O LORD, God of my master Abraham, if you will, please grant success[i] to
the journey on which I have come. 43See,
I am standing beside this spring;[j] if a
maiden[k] comes out to draw water and I
say to her, "Please let me drink a little
water from your jar,"[l] 44and if she says
to me, "Drink, and I'll draw water for
your camels too," let her be the one the
LORD has chosen for my master's son.'[m]
45"Before I finished praying in my

c22 That is, about 1/5 ounce (about 5.5 grams)
d22 That is, about 4 ounces (about 110 grams)
e36 Or *his*

24:13 iS ver 11,43; Ge 29:8
24:14 jver 18,46 kver 19 lver 44 mJos 2:12; Jdg 6:17, 37; 1Sa 14:10; 1Ki 13:3; Ps 86:17; Isa 38:7; Jer 44:29
24:15 nver 45 oS Ge 22:23 pS Ge 22:22 qS Ge 11:29 rS Ge 11:29
24:16 sS Ge 12:11 tDt 22:15-21
24:17 uver 45; 1Ki 17:10; Jn 4:7
24:18 vS ver 14
24:19 wS ver 10 xver 14
24:20 yver 46
24:21 zS ver 12
24:22 aver 47; Ge 41:42; Isa 3:21; Eze 16:11-12 bS ver 10
24:23 cver 47 dJdg 19:15; 20:4
24:24 ever 29,47; S Ge 11:29
24:25 fver 32; Jdg 19:19
24:26 gver 48,52; Ex 4:31; 12:27; 1Ch 29:20; 2Ch 20:18
24:27 hGe 14:20; Ex 18:10; Ru 4:14; 1Sa 25:32; 2Sa 18:28; 1Ki 1:48; 8:56; Ps 28:6; 41:13; 68:19; 106:48; Lk 1:68 iS ver 12 jver 49; Ge 32:10; 47:29; Jos 2:14; Ps 98:3 kver 21 lS ver 12,48; S Ge 12:1
24:28 mGe 29:12
24:29 nver 4; Ge 25:20; 27:43; 28:2,5; 29:5,12,13
24:30 oS ver 10; Eze 23:42
24:31 pGe 26:29; Ps 115:15
24:32 qS ver 25 rS Ge 18:4
24:34 sS Ge 15:3
24:35 tS Ge 12:2 uver 1 vS Ge 23:6 wS Ge 12:16
24:36 xS Ge 17:17 yGe 25:5; 26:14
24:37 zGe 50:5,25 aver 3
24:38 bS Ge 21:21
24:39 cS ver 5
24:40 dS Ge 5:22 eS Ge 16:7 fS ver 12 gS Ge 12:1
24:41 hS ver 8
24:42 iS ver 12
24:43 jS ver 13 kPr 30:19; Isa 7:14 lS ver 14
24:44 mver 14

24:26 WORSHIP, Individual—Individual worship may occur as a spontaneous response to God's presence in daily activities. See note on Ex 33:9–11.

24:40–42 HUMANITY, Relationship to God—All life is lived under the guidance of God. The people of God expect God's concern with and direction over the issues of life. See note on 24:62–67 for an understanding of marriage.

heart,[n] Rebekah came out, with her jar
on her shoulder.[o] She went down to the
spring and drew water, and I said to her,
'Please give me a drink.'[p]
46"She quickly lowered her jar from
her shoulder and said, 'Drink, and I'll water your camels too.'[q] So I drank, and she
watered the camels also.[r]
47"I asked her, 'Whose daughter are
you?'[s]
"She said, 'The daughter of Bethuel[t]
son of Nahor, whom Milcah bore to
him.'[u]
"Then I put the ring in her nose[v] and
the bracelets on her arms,[w] 48and I
bowed down and worshiped the LORD.[x] I
praised the LORD, the God of my master
Abraham,[y] who had led me on the right
road to get the granddaughter of my master's brother for his son.[z] 49Now if you
will show kindness and faithfulness[a] to
my master, tell me; and if not, tell me, so
I may know which way to turn."
50Laban and Bethuel[b] answered, "This
is from the LORD;[c] we can say nothing to
you one way or the other.[d] 51Here is Rebekah; take her and go, and let her become the wife of your master's son, as
the LORD has directed.[e]"
52When Abraham's servant heard what
they said, he bowed down to the ground
before the LORD.[f] 53Then the servant
brought out gold and silver jewelry and
articles of clothing[g] and gave them to Rebekah; he also gave costly gifts[h] to her
brother and to her mother. 54Then he and
the men who were with him ate and
drank and spent the night there.
When they got up the next morning,
he said, "Send me on my way[i] to my
master."
55But her brother and her mother replied, "Let the girl remain with us ten
days or so;[j] then you[f] may go."
56But he said to them, "Do not detain
me, now that the LORD has granted success[k] to my journey. Send me on my
way[l] so I may go to my master."
57Then they said, "Let's call the girl
and ask her about it."[m] 58So they called
Rebekah and asked her, "Will you go
with this man?"
"I will go,"[n] she said.
59So they sent their sister Rebekah on
her way,[o] along with her nurse[p] and
Abraham's servant and his men. 60And
they blessed[q] Rebekah and said to her,

24:45 [n]1Sa 1:13 [o]ver 15 [p]S ver 17; Jn 4:7
24:46 [q]ver 18-19 [r]ver 20
24:47 [s]ver 23 [t]S Ge 22:22 [u]S ver 24 [v]S ver 22 [w]S ver 10; Isa 3:19; Eze 16:11-12
24:48 [x]S ver 26 [y]S ver 12 [z]S ver 27
24:49 [a]S ver 27
24:50 [b]Ge 22:22 [c]Ps 118:23 [d]Ge 31:7,24,29,42; 48:16
24:51 [e]S ver 12
24:52 [f]S ver 26
24:53 [g]Ge 45:22; Ex 3:22; 12:35; 2Ki 5:5 [h]S ver 10, 22
24:54 [i]ver 56,59; Ge 30:25
24:55 [j]Jdg 19:4
24:56 [k]S ver 12 [l]S ver 54
24:57 [m]Jdg 19:3
24:58 [n]Ru 1:16
24:59 [o]S ver 54 [p]Ge 35:8
24:60 [q]Ge 27:4,19; 28:1; 31:55; 48:9, 15,20; Jos 22:6 [r]S Ge 17:16 [s]Ge 22:17; Ps 127:5; Pr 27:11
24:61 [t]S Ge 16:1; 30:3; 46:25
24:62 [u]S Ge 16:14 [v]S Ge 12:9
24:63 [w]Jos 1:8; Ps 1:2; 77:12; 119:15,27,48,97, 148; 143:5; 145:5 [x]Ge 18:2
24:64 [y]Ge 31:17, 34; 1Sa 30:17
24:65 [z]Ge 38:14; SS 1:7; 4:1,3; 6:7; Isa 47:2
24:67 [a]Ge 31:33 [b]S Ge 18:9 [c]Ge 25:20; 49:31 [d]Ge 29:18,20; 34:3; Jdg 16:4 [e]Ge 23:1-2
25:2 [f]Jer 25:25 [g]Ge 36:35; 37:28, 36; Ex 2:15; Nu 22:4; 25:6,18; 31:2; Jos 13:21; Jdg 6:1,3; 7:1; 8:1, 22,24; 9:17; 1Ki 11:18; Ps 83:9; Isa 9:4; 10:26; 60:6; Hab 3:7 [h]Job 2:11; 8:1
25:3 [i]S Ge 10:7 [j]S Ge 10:7
25:4 [k]Isa 60:6
25:5 [l]S Ge 24:36
25:6 [m]S Ge 22:24 [n]S Ge 21:10,14 [o]Ge 29:1; Jdg 6:3, 33; 1Ki 4:30; Job 1:3; Eze 25:4
25:7 [p]ver 26; Ge 12:4; 35:28; 47:9,28; 50:22,26; Job 42:16
25:8 [q]S Ge 15:15 [r]ver 17; Ge 35:29; 49:29,33; Nu 20:24; 31:2; Dt 31:14; 32:50; 34:5
25:9 [s]Ge 35:29; 47:30; 49:31

"Our sister, may you increase
to thousands upon thousands;[r]
may your offspring possess
the gates of their enemies."[s]

61Then Rebekah and her maids[t] got
ready and mounted their camels and
went back with the man. So the servant
took Rebekah and left.
62Now Isaac had come from Beer Lahai
Roi,[u] for he was living in the Negev.[v]
63He went out to the field one evening to
meditate,[g][w] and as he looked up,[x] he
saw camels approaching. 64Rebekah also
looked up and saw Isaac. She got down
from her camel[y] 65and asked the servant,
"Who is that man in the field coming to
meet us?"
"He is my master," the servant answered. So she took her veil[z] and covered herself.
66Then the servant told Isaac all he had
done. 67Isaac brought her into the tent[a]
of his mother Sarah,[b] and he married Rebekah.[c] So she became his wife, and he
loved her;[d] and Isaac was comforted after his mother's death.[e]

Chapter 25

The Death of Abraham

25:1–4pp — 1Ch 1:32–33

ABRAHAM took[h] another wife, whose
name was Keturah. 2She bore him
Zimran,[f] Jokshan, Medan, Midian,[g] Ishbak and Shuah.[h] 3Jokshan was the father
of Sheba[i] and Dedan;[j] the descendants
of Dedan were the Asshurites, the
Letushites and the Leummites. 4The sons
of Midian were Ephah,[k] Epher, Hanoch,
Abida and Eldaah. All these were descendants of Keturah.
5Abraham left everything he owned to
Isaac.[l] 6But while he was still living, he
gave gifts to the sons of his concubines[m]
and sent them away from his son Isaac[n]
to the land of the east.[o]
7Altogether, Abraham lived a hundred
and seventy-five years.[p] 8Then Abraham
breathed his last and died at a good old
age,[q] an old man and full of years; and he
was gathered to his people.[r] 9His sons
Isaac and Ishmael buried him[s] in the

[f]55 Or *she* [g]63 The meaning of the Hebrew for this word is uncertain. [h]1 Or *had taken*

24:62–67 HUMANITY, Marriage—Ancient marriages were usually arranged by the parents. Such marriages stressed the initial commitment of each partner to marriage even without knowing the partner. The love which follows upon this kind of commitment is an enduring love, not to be confused with contemporary images of romantic love.

25:1–18 HISTORY, Universal—See notes on 2:4; 10:1–32; 17:20.

25:7–11 HUMANITY, Burial—The proper burial of a loved one in the family burial plot was a fitting end of a long, full life. It was the responsibility of those who survived to fulfill this obligation. Yet even when death comes, life for the survivors goes on under the guidance of God. See note on 23:3–20.

cave of Machpelah[t] near Mamre,[u] in the
field of Ephron[v] son of Zohar the Hittite,[w] 10the field Abraham had bought
from the Hittites.[i][x] There Abraham was
buried with his wife Sarah. 11After Abraham's death, God blessed his son Isaac,[y]
who then lived near Beer Lahai Roi.[z]

Ishmael's Sons

25:12–16pp — 1Ch 1:29–31

12This is the account[a] of Abraham's
son Ishmael, whom Sarah's maidservant,
Hagar[b] the Egyptian, bore to Abraham.[c]

13These are the names of the sons of
Ishmael, listed in the order of their birth:
Nebaioth[d] the firstborn of Ishmael, Kedar,[e] Adbeel, Mibsam, 14Mishma, Dumah,[f] Massa, 15Hadad, Tema,[g] Jetur,[h]
Naphish and Kedemah. 16These were the
sons of Ishmael, and these are the names
of the twelve tribal rulers[i] according to
their settlements and camps.[j] 17Alto-
gether, Ishmael lived a hundred and thirty-seven years. He breathed his last and
died, and he was gathered to his people.[k]
18His descendants[l] settled in the area
from Havilah to Shur,[m] near the border of
Egypt, as you go toward Asshur. And they
lived in hostility toward[j] all their brothers.[n]

Jacob and Esau

19This is the account[o] of Abraham's
son Isaac.

Abraham became the father of Isaac,
20and Isaac was forty years old[p] when he
married Rebekah[q] daughter of Bethuel[r]
the Aramean from Paddan Aram[k][s] and
sister of Laban[t] the Aramean.[u]

21Isaac prayed to the LORD on behalf of
his wife, because she was barren.[v] The
LORD answered his prayer,[w] and his wife
Rebekah became pregnant. 22The babies
jostled each other within her, and she
said, "Why is this happening to me?" So
she went to inquire of the LORD.[x]

23The LORD said to her,

"Two nations[y] are in your womb,
 and two peoples from within you
 will be separated;
one people will be stronger than the
 other,
 and the older will serve the
 younger.[z]"

24When the time came for her to give
birth,[a] there were twin boys in her
womb.[b] 25The first to come out was
red,[c] and his whole body was like a hairy
garment;[d] so they named him Esau.[l][e]
26After this, his brother came out,[f] with
his hand grasping Esau's heel;[g] so he
was named Jacob.[m][h] Isaac was sixty
years old[i] when Rebekah gave birth to
them.

27The boys grew up, and Esau became
a skillful hunter,[j] a man of the open
country,[k] while Jacob was a quiet man,

25:9 [t]S Ge 23:9 [u]S Ge 13:18 [v]Ge 23:8 [w]Ge 49:29; 50:13 **25:10** [x]S Ge 10:15 **25:11** [y]S Ge 12:2 [z]S Ge 16:14 **25:12** [a]S Ge 2:4 [b]S Ge 16:1 [c]S Ge 17:20; 21:18 **25:13** [d]Ge 28:9; 36:3 [e]Ps 120:5; SS 1:5; Isa 21:16; 42:11; 60:7; Jer 2:10; 49:28; Eze 27:21 **25:14** [f]Jos 15:52; Isa 21:11; Ob 1:1 **25:15** [g]Job 6:19; Isa 21:14; Jer 25:23 [h]1Ch 5:19 **25:16** [i]Ge 17:20 [j]S Ge 13:16; Ps 83:6 **25:17** [k]S ver 8 **25:18** [l]S Ge 17:20; 21:18 [m]S Ge 16:7 [n]Ge 16:12 **25:19** [o]S Ge 2:4 **25:20** [p]ver 26; Ge 26:34; 35:28 [q]S Ge 24:67 [r]S Ge 22:22 [s]Ge 28:2,5,6; 30:20; 31:18; 33:18; 35:9,26; 46:15; 48:7 [t]S Ge 24:29 [u]Ge 31:20,24; Dt 26:5 **25:21** [v]S Ge 11:30 [w]Ge 30:17,22; 1Sa 1:17,23; 1Ch 5:20; 2Ch 33:13; Ezr 8:23; Ps 127:3 **25:22** [x]Ex 18:15; 28:30; 33:7; Lev 24:12; Nu 9:6-8; 27:5,21; Dt 17:9; Jdg 18:5; 1Sa 9:9; 10:22; 14:36; 22:10; 1Ki 22:8; 2Ki 3:11; 22:13; Isa 30:2; Jer 21:2; 37:7,17; Eze 14:7; 20:1,3 **25:23** [y]S Ge 17:4 [z]S Ge 9:25; 48:14, 19; Ro 9:11-12* **25:24** [a]Lk 1:57; 2:6 [b]Ge 38:27 **25:25** [c]1Sa 16:12 [d]Ge 27:11 [e]Ge 27:1,15 **25:26** [f]Ge 38:29 [g]Hos 12:3 [h]Ge 27:36; 32:27; Dt 23:7; Jos 24:4; Ob 1:10,12 [i]S ver 7,S 20 **25:27** [j]S Ge 10:9 [k]ver 29; Ge 27:3,5

[i]*10* Or *the sons of Heth* [j]*18* Or *lived to the east of* [k]*20* That is, Northwest Mesopotamia [l]*25* *Esau* may mean *hairy*; he was also called Edom, which means *red.* [m]*26* *Jacob* means *he grasps the heel* (figuratively, *he deceives*).

25:19 HISTORY, Linear—See note on 2:4.
25:19–34 FAMILY, Conflict—The family of Isaac and Rebekah demonstrates sibling rivalry and parental favoritism as illustrations of family conflict. Jacob shrewdly conned his impetuous twin brother Esau into selling the birthright which was legitimately Esau's because he was born first. Later, Rebekah contrived with Jacob to deceive Isaac, who favored Esau (ch 27). This event represents many other biblical narratives of family discord and conflict. See 29:15–30; 30:1–34; 37:2–30; 2 Sa 15:1—19:8. Even among God's chosen ones, conflict can develop in family relationships. Such experiences can make Christians more dependent on the loving grace of God for forgiveness and strength in seeking to bring harmony and reconciliation to family life. Christians also have family problems; it is wrong to allow them to go on without letting the teachings of God's Word help bring about resolution of conflict.
25:21 HUMANITY, Birth—See note on 18:10–14.
25:21 PRAYER, Intercession—Intercession is prayer to God on behalf of another person. God responds to faithful intercession.
25:22–23 REVELATION, Word—Rebekah sought God's explanation, probably at first unaware of twins in her womb, yet facing apparent childbirth pains that seemed to threaten her life. She went to find God's answer to her question. Apparently she went to a place of worship seeking an answer. God provides ways for people to determine His will. Prayer is the direct access to God seeking His direction. God answers prayer and thus reveals Himself.
25:22–23 PRAYER, Petition—Petition may ask for understanding of life's perplexing situations and problems. Rebekah gained perspective on the future history of her family through prayer.
25:23 HISTORY, Universal—Birth stories rather than battle announcements are featured in early biblical history because it centers on God's chosen family rather than the secular historian's chosen power struggles. All history writing is interpretation of a small portion of historical events. The choice of events depends on the element of history emphasized. The Bible's inspired narrative focuses on God's use of a family to work out His blessings for the nations (12:1–3). As such, the Bible often points to reversals of normal human expectations such as the importance of the younger son rather than the older.
25:23 ELECTION, Other Nations—Edom became Israel's despised enemy (Ps 137:7). Their existence was still part of God's elective plan. Custom placed the older son in family leadership even when the brothers were twins. God's election chose the younger son to carry out His covenant purposes, while not ignoring the older. The election conflict with custom introduced a life of conflict for Jacob. Election does not protect the elect from life's problems.
25:27–28 HUMANITY, Parenthood—The partiality of parents toward one child or another establishes the basis for future conflict and difficulties.

staying among the tents. 28Isaac, who had a taste for wild game,[l] loved Esau, but Rebekah loved Jacob.[m]

29Once when Jacob was cooking some stew,[n] Esau came in from the open country,[o] famished. 30He said to Jacob, "Quick, let me have some of that red stew![p] I'm famished!" (That is why he was also called Edom.[n])[q]

31Jacob replied, "First sell me your birthright.[r]"

32"Look, I am about to die," Esau said. "What good is the birthright to me?"

33But Jacob said, "Swear[s] to me first." So he swore an oath to him, selling his birthright[t] to Jacob.

34Then Jacob gave Esau some bread and some lentil stew.[u] He ate and drank, and then got up and left.

So Esau despised his birthright.

Chapter 26

Isaac and Abimelech

26:1-11Ref— Ge 12:10-20; 20:1-18

NOW there was a famine in the land[v]—besides the earlier famine of Abraham's time—and Isaac went to Abimelech king of the Philistines[w] in Gerar.[x] 2The LORD appeared[y] to Isaac and said, "Do not go down to Egypt;[z] live in the land where I tell you to live.[a] 3Stay in this land for a while,[b] and I will be with you[c] and will bless you.[d] For to you and your descendants I will give all these lands[e] and will confirm the oath I swore to your father Abraham.[f] 4I will make your descendants[g] as numerous as the stars in the sky[h] and will give them all these lands,[i] and through your offspring[o] all nations on earth will be blessed,[j] 5because Abraham obeyed me[k] and kept my requirements, my commands, my decrees[l] and my laws.[m]" 6So Isaac stayed in Gerar.[n]

7When the men of that place asked him about his wife, he said, "She is my sister,[o]" because he was afraid to say, "She is my wife." He thought, "The men of this place might kill me on account of Rebekah, because she is beautiful."

8When Isaac had been there a long time, Abimelech king of the Philistines[p] looked down from a window and saw Isaac caressing his wife Rebekah. 9So Abimelech summoned Isaac and said, "She is really your wife! Why did you say, 'She is my sister'?[q]"

Isaac answered him, "Because I thought I might lose my life on account of her."

10Then Abimelech said, "What is this you have done to us?[r] One of the men might well have slept with your wife, and you would have brought guilt upon us."

11So Abimelech gave orders to all the people: "Anyone who molests[s] this man or his wife shall surely be put to death."[t]

12Isaac planted crops in that land and the same year reaped a hundredfold,[u] because the LORD blessed him.[v] 13The man became rich, and his wealth continued to grow until he became very wealthy.[w] 14He had so many flocks and herds and servants[x] that the Philistines envied him.[y] 15So all the wells[z] that his father's servants had dug in the time of his father Abraham, the Philistines stopped up,[a] filling them with earth.

16Then Abimelech said to Isaac, "Move away from us;[b] you have become too powerful for us.[c]"

17So Isaac moved away from there and encamped in the Valley of Gerar[d] and settled there. 18Isaac reopened the wells[e] that had been dug in the time of his father Abraham, which the Philistines had stopped up after Abraham died, and he gave them the same names his father had given them.

19Isaac's servants dug in the valley and discovered a well of fresh water there. 20But the herdsmen of Gerar quarreled[f] with Isaac's herdsmen and said, "The water is ours!"[g] So he named the well Esek,[p] because they disputed with him.

25:28 [l]Ge 27:3,4, 9,14,19 [m]Ge 27:6; 37:3
25:29 [n]2Ki 4:38-40 [o]S ver 27
25:30 [p]ver 34 [q]Ge 32:3; 36:1,8, 8-9,19; Nu 20:14; Dt 23:7; Ps 137:7; Jer 25:21; 40:11; 49:7
25:31 [r]Dt 21:16-17; 1Ch 5:1-2
25:33 [s]S Ge 21:23; S 47:31 [t]Ge 27:36; Heb 12:16
25:34 [u]ver 30
26:1 [v]S Ge 12:10; S Dt 32:24 [w]S Ge 10:14; Jdg 10:6 [x]S Ge 20:1
26:2 [y]S Ge 12:7 [z]Ge 46:3 [a]S Ge 12:1
26:3 [b]Ge 20:1 [c]S Ge 21:20; 27:45; 31:3,5; 32:9; 35:3; 48:21; Ex 3:12; 33:14-16; Nu 23:21; Dt 31:23; Jos 1:5; Isa 43:2; Jer 1:8,19; Hag 1:13 [d]ver 12; S Ge 12:2 [e]S Ge 12:7; Ac 7:5 [f]S Ge 17:19
26:4 [g]ver 24; Ge 48:4 [h]S Ge 12:2; S Nu 10:36 [i]S Ge 12:7 [j]S Ge 12:3; Ac 3:25*; Gal 3:8
26:5 [k]S Ge 18:19 [l]Ps 119:80,112; Eze 18:21 [m]Lev 18:4,5,26; 19:19,37; 20:8,22; 25:18; 26:3; Nu 15:40; Dt 4:40; 6:2; 11:1; 1Ki 2:3
26:6 [n]S Ge 20:1
26:7 [o]S Ge 12:13
26:8 [p]S Ge 10:14
26:9 [q]S Ge 12:19
26:10 [r]S Ge 12:18
26:11 [s]1Sa 24:6; 26:9; Ps 105:15 [t]S Ge 20:3
26:12 [u]Mt 13:8 [v]S ver 3
26:13 [w]S Ge 13:2; S Dt 8:18
26:14 [x]S Ge 12:16; S 24:36; 32:23 [y]Ge 37:11
26:15 [z]S Ge 21:30 [a]S Ge 21:25
26:16 [b]ver 27; Jdg 11:7 [c]Ex 1:9; Ps 105:24-25
26:17 [d]S Ge 20:1
26:18 [e]S Ge 21:30 **26:20** [f]S Ge 13:7 [g]Ge 21:25

[n]*30 Edom* means *red.* [o]*4* Or *seed* [p]*20 Esek* means *dispute.*

26:1–33 HISTORY, Worship—See notes on 20:17–18; 21:22–34.

26:2,24 HISTORY, Promise—See note on 15:1–21.

26:2–33 ELECTION, Righteousness—Because of Abraham's faithful obedience to God, He renewed His covenant with Isaac. The covenant assured Isaac God would be with him, his descendants would be as numerous as the stars, possess much land, and be the source of blessings for all nations. For Isaac, blessing was clearly evident (v 13). Election may lead to worldly possessions but does not necessarily do so. The necessary result of election is God's presence.

26:4 EVANGELISM, Results—See note on 18:18–19.

26:5 CHRISTIAN ETHICS, Obedience—Biblical ethics is founded in a covenant relationship God initiated with His people. He promises salvation and expects obedience. The faithfulness of one generation leads to the renewal of the covenant with the next. See note on 17:1,10.

26:12–16 STEWARDSHIP, Rewards—In the Old Testament period, people often identified faithfulness to God and personal prosperity. Wealth was considered a reward for faithfulness. Job discovered the deeper truth that we cannot judge a person's religion by a bank account. God does bless His faithful people, but His blessings are not always in material form. Isaac's prosperity provoked anger and envy from those living around him, as is often the case today. See note on Lk 6:38.

26:18–23 CHRISTIAN ETHICS, War and Peace—The human struggle over limited natural resources leads to conflict and, at times, to war. Compromise and refusal to demand one's rights can lead to peace. See note on 13:7–12.

21Then they dug another well, but they
quarreled[h] over that one also; so he
named it Sitnah.[q] 22He moved on from
there and dug another well, and no one
quarreled over it. He named it Rehoboth,[r][i] saying, "Now the LORD has giv-
en us room[j] and we will flourish[k] in the
land."

23From there he went up to Beersheba.[l] 24That night the LORD appeared to
him and said, "I am the God of your father Abraham.[m] Do not be afraid,[n] for I
am with you;[o] I will bless you and will
increase the number of your descendants[p] for the sake of my servant Abraham."[q]

25Isaac built an altar[r] there and called
on the name of the LORD.[s] There he
pitched his tent, and there his servants
dug a well.[t]

26Meanwhile, Abimelech had come to
him from Gerar, with Ahuzzath his personal adviser and Phicol the commander
of his forces.[u] 27Isaac asked them, "Why
have you come to me, since you were
hostile to me and sent me away?[v]"

28They answered, "We saw clearly that
the LORD was with you;[w] so we said,
'There ought to be a sworn agreement
between us'—between us and you. Let
us make a treaty[x] with you 29that you
will do us no harm,[y] just as we did not
molest you but always treated you well
and sent you away in peace. And now you
are blessed by the LORD."[z]

30Isaac then made a feast[a] for them,
and they ate and drank. 31Early the next
morning the men swore an oath[b] to each
other. Then Isaac sent them on their way,
and they left him in peace.

32That day Isaac's servants came and
told him about the well[c] they had dug.
They said, "We've found water!" 33He
called it Shibah,[s] and to this day the
name of the town has been Beersheba.[t] [d]

34When Esau was forty years old,[e] he
married Judith daughter of Beeri the Hittite, and also Basemath daughter of Elon
the Hittite.[f] 35They were a source of
grief to Isaac and Rebekah.[g]

Chapter 27

Jacob Gets Isaac's Blessing

WHEN Isaac was old and his eyes
were so weak that he could no longer see,[h] he called for Esau his older
son[i] and said to him, "My son."

"Here I am," he answered.

2Isaac said, "I am now an old man and
don't know the day of my death.[j] 3Now
then, get your weapons—your quiver and
bow—and go out to the open country[k] to
hunt some wild game for me. 4Prepare
me the kind of tasty food I like[l] and
bring it to me to eat, so that I may give
you my blessing[m] before I die."[n]

5Now Rebekah was listening as Isaac
spoke to his son Esau. When Esau left for
the open country[o] to hunt game and
bring it back, 6Rebekah said to her son
Jacob,[p] "Look, I overheard your father
say to your brother Esau, 7'Bring me
some game and prepare me some tasty
food to eat, so that I may give you my
blessing in the presence of the LORD before I die.'[q] 8Now, my son, listen carefully and do what I tell you:[r] 9Go out to the
flock and bring me two choice young
goats,[s] so I can prepare some tasty food
for your father, just the way he likes it.[t]
10Then take it to your father to eat, so
that he may give you his blessing[u] before
he dies."

11Jacob said to Rebekah his mother,
"But my brother Esau is a hairy man,[v]
and I'm a man with smooth skin. 12What
if my father touches me?[w] I would appear
to be tricking him and would bring down
a curse[x] on myself rather than a blessing."

13His mother said to him, "My son, let
the curse fall on me.[y] Just do what I
say;[z] go and get them for me."

14So he went and got them and brought
them to his mother, and she prepared
some tasty food, just the way his father

[q]21 *Sitnah* means *opposition.* [r]22 *Rehoboth* means *room.* [s]33 *Shibah* can mean *oath* or *seven.* [t]33 *Beersheba* can mean *well of the oath* or *well of seven.*

26:21 [h]S Ge 13:7
26:22 [i]Ge 36:37 [j]Ps 18:19; Isa 33:20; 54:2; Am 9:11 [k]S Ge 17:6
26:23 [l]S Ge 22:19
26:24 [m]S Ge 24:12 [n]S Ge 15:1; S Jos 8:1 [o]S Ge 21:20 [p]S ver 4 [q]ver 4; Ge 17:7; S 22:17; 28:14; 30:27; 39:5; Dt 13:17
26:25 [r]S Ge 8:20 [s]S Ge 4:26; S Ac 2:21 [t]S Ge 21:30
26:26 [u]S Ge 21:22
26:27 [v]S ver 16
26:28 [w]S Ge 21:22 [x]S Ge 21:27; Jos 9:6
26:29 [y]Ge 31:29, 52 [z]S Ge 24:31
26:30 [a]Ge 31:54; Ex 18:12; 24:11; 1Sa 20:27
26:31 [b]S Ge 21:23, 27
26:32 [c]S Ge 21:30
26:33 [d]S Ge 21:14
26:34 [e]S Ge 25:20 [f]S Ge 10:15; 28:9; 36:2; Jos 3:10; 1Sa 26:6; 1Ki 10:29
26:35 [g]Ge 27:46; 28:8; Job 7:16
27:1 [h]Ge 48:10; Dt 34:7; 1Sa 3:2 [i]S Ge 25:25
27:2 [j]Ge 47:29; 1Ki 2:1
27:3 [k]S Ge 25:27
27:4 [l]S Ge 25:28 [m]ver 10,25,31; S Ge 24:60; 49:28; Dt 33:1; Heb 11:20 [n]ver 7
27:5 [o]S Ge 25:27
27:6 [p]S Ge 25:28
27:7 [q]ver 4
27:8 [r]ver 13,43
27:9 [s]1Sa 16:20 [t]S Ge 25:28
27:10 [u]S ver 4
27:11 [v]Ge 25:25
27:12 [w]ver 22 [x]S Ge 9:25
27:13 [y]Mt 27:25 [z]S ver 8

26:25 PRAYER, Thanksgiving—See note on 12:7–8.

27:1–40 HUMANITY, Family Relationships—Jealousy between children, plus parental partiality, breeds dishonesty and deception. The consequences are a divided family, frequently producing hatred, lack of trust, and dissolution of the family itself. See note on 25:27–28.

27:1–40 HISTORY, Promise—God worked in history in many ways to accomplish His purposes, miracles being one of His ways. The passing of the promise to the younger son Jacob occurred through the deceptive practices of family members. God did not cause the deception but worked out His purposes in it. In the midst of life's moral and physical complexities God mysteriously works out His historical purposes. Faith testifies to God's working through human freedom but does not claim to know how God works.

27:1—28:9 CHRISTIAN ETHICS, Character—God works His redemptive plan with humans who do not always obey Him. Rebekah and Jacob did not depend on God to provide the promised blessing (25:23). They deceived Esau and his blind father Isaac. Following cultural patterns, the patriarch's words of blessing became family law. Jacob obtained the desired blessing through unethical means. He also gained his brother's death-threatening anger, a violently-upset father, and separation from his mother and home. The Bible realistically describes the results of unethical choices and lets the reader decide, in this instance, if the gains were worth the loss. Persons of true character do not have to bear the name deceiver (27:36; NIV footnote). They please God with their lives and trust Him to provide His promised blessings.

liked it.[a] 15Then Rebekah took the best
clothes[b] of Esau her older son,[c] which
she had in the house, and put them on
her younger son Jacob. 16She also covered
his hands and the smooth part of his neck
with the goatskins.[d] 17Then she handed
to her son Jacob the tasty food and the
bread she had made.

18He went to his father and said, "My
father."

"Yes, my son," he answered. "Who is
it?"[e]

19Jacob said to his father, "I am Esau
your firstborn.[f] I have done as you told
me. Please sit up and eat some of my
game[g] so that you may give me your
blessing."[h]

20Isaac asked his son, "How did you
find it so quickly, my son?"

"The LORD your God gave me success,[i]" he replied.

21Then Isaac said to Jacob, "Come near
so I can touch you,[j] my son, to know
whether you really are my son Esau or
not."

22Jacob went close to his father Isaac,[k]
who touched[l] him and said, "The voice
is the voice of Jacob, but the hands are
the hands of Esau." 23He did not recognize him, for his hands were hairy like
those of his brother Esau;[m] so he blessed
him. 24"Are you really my son Esau?" he
asked.

"I am," he replied.

25Then he said, "My son, bring me
some of your game to eat, so that I may
give you my blessing."[n]

Jacob brought it to him and he ate; and
he brought some wine and he drank.
26Then his father Isaac said to him,
"Come here, my son, and kiss me."

27So he went to him and kissed[o]
him[p]. When Isaac caught the smell of his
clothes,[q] he blessed him and said,

"Ah, the smell of my son
 is like the smell of a field
 that the LORD has blessed.[r]
28May God give you of heaven's dew[s]
 and of earth's richness[t] —
 an abundance of grain[u] and new
 wine.[v]
29May nations serve you
 and peoples bow down to you.[w]
Be lord over your brothers,
 and may the sons of your mother
 bow down to you.[x]
May those who curse you be cursed
 and those who bless you be
 blessed.[y]"

30After Isaac finished blessing him and
Jacob had scarcely left his father's presence, his brother Esau came in from
hunting. 31He too prepared some tasty
food and brought it to his father. Then he
said to him, "My father, sit up and eat
some of my game, so that you may give
me your blessing."[z]

32His father Isaac asked him, "Who are
you?"[a]

"I am your son," he answered, "your
firstborn, Esau.[b]"

33Isaac trembled violently and said,
"Who was it, then, that hunted game and
brought it to me?[c] I ate it just before you
came and I blessed him—and indeed he
will be blessed![d]"

34When Esau heard his father's words,
he burst out with a loud and bitter cry[e]
and said to his father, "Bless[f] me—me
too, my father!"

35But he said, "Your brother came deceitfully[g] and took your blessing."[h]

36Esau said, "Isn't he rightly named Jacob[u]?[i] He has deceived[j] me these two
times: He took my birthright,[k] and now
he's taken my blessing!"[l] Then he
asked, "Haven't you reserved any blessing for me?"

37Isaac answered Esau, "I have made
him lord over you and have made all his
relatives his servants, and I have sustained him with grain and new wine.[m] So
what can I possibly do for you, my son?"

38Esau said to his father, "Do you have
only one blessing, my father? Bless me
too, my father!" Then Esau wept aloud.[n]

39His father Isaac answered him,[o]

"Your dwelling will be
 away from the earth's richness,
 away from the dew[p] of heaven
 above.[q]
40You will live by the sword
 and you will serve[r] your brother.[s]
But when you grow restless,
 you will throw his yoke
 from off your neck.[t]"

Jacob Flees to Laban

41Esau held a grudge[u] against Jacob[v]
because of the blessing his father had

27:14 [a]S Ge 25:28
27:15 [b]ver 27; SS 4:11 [c]S Ge 25:25
27:16 [d]ver 22-23
27:18 [e]ver 32
27:19 [f]ver 32 [g]S Ge 25:28 [h]S ver 4
27:20 [i]S Ge 24:12
27:21 [j]ver 12
27:22 [k]Ge 45:4 [l]ver 12
27:23 [m]ver 16
27:25 [n]S ver 4
27:27 [o]Ge 31:28, 55; 33:4; 48:10; Ex 4:27; 18:7; Ru 1:9; 1Sa 20:41; 2Sa 14:33; 19:39 [p]Heb 11:20 [q]S ver 15 [r]Ps 65:9-13
27:28 [s]Dt 33:13; 2Sa 1:21; Job 18:16; 29:19; Pr 3:20; Isa 26:19; Hos 14:5; Hag 1:10; Zec 8:12 [t]ver 39; Ge 49:25; Lev 26:20; Dt 33:13 [u]Ps 65:9; 72:16 [v]ver 37; Nu 18:12; Dt 7:13; 33:28; 2Ki 18:32; Ps 4:7; Isa 36:17; Jer 31:12; 40:10
27:29 [w]2Sa 8:14; Ps 68:31; 72:11; Isa 19:21,23; 27:13; 45:14,23; 49:7,23; 60:12,14; 66:23; Jer 12:17; Da 2:44; Zec 14:17-18 [x]S Ge 9:25; S 25:23; S 37:7 [y]ver 33; Ge 12:3
27:31 [z]S ver 4
27:32 [a]ver 18 [b]ver 19
27:33 [c]ver 35 [d]S ver 29
27:34 [e]Heb 12:17 [f]Ex 12:32
27:35 [g]Jer 9:4; 12:6 [h]ver 19,45
27:36 [i]S Ge 25:26 [j]Ge 29:25; 31:20, 26; 34:13; 1Sa 28:12 [k]S Ge 25:33 [l]Heb 12:16-17
27:37 [m]S ver 28; Dt 16:13; Ezr 6:9; Isa 16:10; Jer 40:12
27:38 [n]Ge 29:11; Nu 14:1; Jdg 2:4; 21:2; Ru 1:9; 1Sa 11:4; 30:4; Heb 12:17
27:39 [o]Heb 11:20 [p]ver 28 [q]Ge 36:6
27:40 [r]2Sa 8:14 [s]S Ge 9:25 [t]2Ki 8:20-22
27:41 [u]Ge 37:4; 49:23; 50:15; 1Sa 17:28 [v]Ge 31:17; 32:11; Hos 10:14

[u]*36 Jacob* means *he grasps the heel* (figuratively, *he deceives*).

27:27–29 PRAYER, Will of God—Isaac's prayer was answered according to God's intention not according to Isaac's full understanding. Blessing is the key type of prayer in the stories of Israel's ancestors. Blessing here refers to agricultural fertility and national power. See note on 14:18–20. Compare 12:1–3.

27:29 ELECTION, Providence—Isaac was deceived into blessing Jacob against his intention. His actions still fulfilled God's elective purposes. Election works out in the mysterious providence of God rather than through human planning and strategy. See note on 24:1–67.

27:41 HUMANITY, Family Relationships—The Hebrew word for Esau's attitude has a fundamental concept of rejection. Deep and divisive problems within a family lead members

given him. He said to himself, "The days
of mourning[w] for my father are near; then
I will kill[x] my brother Jacob."[y]
42When Rebekah was told what her
older son Esau[z] had said, she sent for her
younger son Jacob and said to him, "Your
brother Esau is consoling himself with
the thought of killing you.[a] 43Now then,
my son, do what I say:[b] Flee at once to
my brother Laban[c] in Haran.[d] 44Stay
with him for a while[e] until your brother's fury subsides. 45When your brother is
no longer angry with you and forgets
what you did to him,[f] I'll send word for
you to come back from there.[g] Why
should I lose both of you in one day?"
46Then Rebekah said to Isaac, "I'm disgusted with living because of these Hittite[h] women. If Jacob takes a wife from
among the women of this land,[i] from
Hittite women like these, my life will not
be worth living."[j]

Chapter 28

SO Isaac called for Jacob and blessed[v] [k]
him and commanded him: "Do not
marry a Canaanite woman.[l] 2Go at once
to Paddan Aram,[w] [m] to the house of your
mother's father Bethuel.[n] Take a wife for
yourself there, from among the daughters
of Laban, your mother's brother.[o] 3May
God Almighty[x] [p] bless[q] you and make
you fruitful[r] and increase your numbers[s] until you become a community of
peoples. 4May he give you and your descendants the blessing given to Abraham,[t] so that you may take possession of
the land[u] where you now live as an
alien,[v] the land God gave to Abraham."
5Then Isaac sent Jacob on his way,[w] and
he went to Paddan Aram,[x] to Laban son
of Bethuel the Aramean,[y] the brother of
Rebekah,[z] who was the mother of Jacob
and Esau.
6Now Esau learned that Isaac had
blessed Jacob and had sent him to Paddan
Aram to take a wife from there, and that
when he blessed him he commanded
him, "Do not marry a Canaanite woman,"[a] 7and that Jacob had obeyed his father and mother and had gone to Paddan
Aram. 8Esau then realized how displeasing the Canaanite women[b] were to his
father Isaac;[c] 9so he went to Ishmael[d]
and married Mahalath, the sister of Nebaioth[e] and daughter of Ishmael son of
Abraham, in addition to the wives he already had.[f]

Jacob's Dream at Bethel

10Jacob left Beersheba[g] and set out for
Haran.[h] 11When he reached a certain
place,[i] he stopped for the night because
the sun had set. Taking one of the stones
there, he put it under his head[j] and lay

[v] *1* Or *greeted* [w] *2* That is, Northwest Mesopotamia; also in verses 5, 6 and 7 [x] *3* Hebrew *El-Shaddai*

27:41 [w]Ge 50:4, 10; Nu 20:29 [x]ver 42 [y]Ob 1:10
27:42 [z]Ge 32:3,11; 33:4 [a]ver 41
27:43 [b]S ver 8 [c]S Ge 24:29 [d]S Ge 11:31
27:44 [e]Ge 31:38, 41
27:45 [f]S ver 35 [g]S Ge 26:3
27:46 [h]S Ge 10:15 [i]S Ge 10:15-19 [j]S Ge 26:35; S Job 7:7
28:1 [k]S Ge 24:60 [l]Ge 24:3
28:2 [m]S Ge 25:20 [n]S Ge 25:20 [o]S Ge 21:21; S 24:29
28:3 [p]S Ge 17:1 [q]Ge 48:16; Nu 6:24; Ru 2:4; Ps 129:8; 134:3; Jer 31:23 [r]S Ge 17:6 [s]S Ge 12:2
28:4 [t]S Ge 12:2,3 [u]S Ge 15:7 [v]S Ge 17:8
28:5 [w]S Ge 11:31 [x]Hos 12:12 [y]S Ge 25:20 [z]S Ge 24:29
28:6 [a]S ver 1
28:8 [b]S Ge 10:15-19 [c]S Ge 26:35
28:9 [d]S Ge 16:15 [e]S Ge 25:13 [f]S Ge 26:34
28:10 [g]S Ge 21:14 [h]S Ge 11:31
28:11 [i]S Ge 12:8 [j]ver 18

to substitute rejection for acceptance. Acceptance is the only basis for family life. Rejection frequently simmers below the surface until grief or loss brings it to the light. Respect and love for parents often keeps the lid on such rejection until the parent's death. Rejection and hatred of others establishes the foundation for the possibility of more violent acts. See Mt 5:21–24.

27:41–45 SIN, Estrangement—Jacob and his mother deceived Esau and Isaac to steal the birthright of inheritance (25:31–34) and final legal blessing (27:1–36). This action, of course, caused a serious rift between them. Jacob had to leave home to keep Esau from killing him. Relationships cannot be built on greed, self-interest, partiality, and deception. Such sinful attitudes, motives, and actions bring estrangement and separation to people who should enjoy the support and love God intended His people to give one another.

28:1–4 ELECTION, Free Will—Isaac had unintentionally blessed Jacob (27:27–29). When Jacob was forced to flee from Esau's wrath, Isaac gave Jacob an intentional blessing. The blessing promised Jacob fruitful and numerous descendants who would possess the land in which they now lived as aliens. The free act of Isaac reinforced God's elective purposes. God uses free human decisions to fulfill His intentions.

28:3 GOD, Sovereignty—Isaac's prayerful blessing of Jacob is a beautiful expression of faith in the benevolent sovereignty of God. Isaac recognized that God could bring good things to pass in the life of his son through whom the covenant people of God would grow. Isaac frankly recognized that without the blessing of God, the future is left to chance and subject to hostile forces and human failure.

28:3–4 PRAYER, Will of God—Isaac prayed for the preservation of the covenant made with Abraham (12:1–3). Part of prayer is to ask that the known will of God be done in our personal and community actions and relationships.

28:4 HISTORY, Promise—See note on 15:1–21.

28:10–22 MIRACLE, Revelation—Jacob's dream proved to be a confirmation of God's presence and purpose. The Old Testament treats dreams as instruments of revelation. In Jacob's confusion and fear and guilt he needed a fresh revelation of God's will. God spoke through the instrument of the dream.

28:10–22 HUMANITY, Spiritual Nature—Physical and emotional stress frequently lead a person to seek God. The spiritual nature of the most disobedient of people may be awakened in such a confrontation. Awareness of God's presence changes our lives, bringing new devotion and stewardship of life to God.

28:11–13 REVELATION, Dreams—Jacob arrived at a holy sanctuary where Abraham had originally set up an altar (12:8). At such places of worship, gods were supposed to protect those present, and divine revelations were received. Apparently Jacob did not recognize this as an ancient sanctuary. He saw it as the only available place to sleep. His experience proved it was a house of God (Hebrew *Beth'el*). The dream which followed was stunning to Jacob. He was addressed by the God of his father Isaac. In those ancient days gods were thought to have control only over specific territories. Once a pilgrim crossed a boundary, another god's authority supposedly took over. God here revealed that He has no boundaries. He could follow Jacob even into hiding, and He would make a covenant with him despite his treachery. God surprised him by being more powerful and more available than he expected. The dream was a picture without words showing access to God was available in that holy place. The angelic messengers reenforced the idea that God wanted to communicate with Jacob. God's speech did not interpret the dream. It reaffirmed Jacob as recipient of the promises to Abraham and Isaac.

down to sleep. 12He had a dream[k] in
which he saw a stairway[y] resting on the
earth, with its top reaching to heaven,
and the angels of God were ascending
and descending on it.[l] 13There above it[z]
stood the LORD,[m] and he said: "I am the
LORD, the God of your father Abraham
and the God of Isaac.[n] I will give you and
your descendants the land[o] on which
you are lying.[p] 14Your descendants will
be like the dust of the earth, and you[q]
will spread out to the west and to the
east, to the north and to the south.[r] All
peoples on earth will be blessed through
you and your offspring.[s] 15I am with
you[t] and will watch over you[uv] wherever you go,[w] and I will bring you back to
this land.[x] I will not leave you[y] until I
have done what I have promised
you.[z]"[a]

16When Jacob awoke from his sleep,[b]
he thought, "Surely the LORD is in this
place, and I was not aware of it." 17He
was afraid and said, "How awesome is
this place![c] This is none other than the
house of God;[d] this is the gate of heav-
en."

18Early the next morning Jacob took
the stone he had placed under his head[e]
and set it up as a pillar[f] and poured oil
on top of it.[g] 19He called that place Bethel,[a][h] though the city used to be called
Luz.[i]

20Then Jacob made a vow,[j] saying, "If
God will be with me and will watch over
me[k] on this journey I am taking and will
give me food to eat and clothes to wear[l]
21so that I return safely[m] to my father's
house,[n] then the LORD[b] will be my
God[o] 22and[c] this stone that I have set up
as a pillar[p] will be God's house,[q] and of
all that you give me I will give you a
tenth.[r]"

Chapter 29

Jacob Arrives in Paddan Aram

THEN Jacob continued on his journey
and came to the land of the eastern
peoples.[s] 2There he saw a well in the
field, with three flocks of sheep lying near
it because the flocks were watered from
that well.[t] The stone[u] over the mouth of
the well was large. 3When all the flocks
were gathered there, the shepherds
would roll the stone[v] away from the
well's mouth and water the sheep.[w]
Then they would return the stone to its
place over the mouth of the well.

4Jacob asked the shepherds, "My
brothers, where are you from?"[x]

"We're from Haran,[y]" they replied.

5He said to them, "Do you know Laban, Nahor's grandson?"[z]

"Yes, we know him," they answered.

6Then Jacob asked them, "Is he well?"

"Yes, he is," they said, "and here
comes his daughter Rachel[a] with the
sheep.[b]"

7"Look," he said, "the sun is still high;
it is not time for the flocks to be gathered.
Water the sheep and take them back to
pasture."

8"We can't," they replied, "until all
the flocks are gathered and the stone[c]
has been rolled away from the mouth of

28:12 [k]S Ge 20:3; 37:19 [l]Jn 1:51 **28:13** [m]S Ge 12:7; 35:7,9; 48:3 [n]S Ge 24:12; 48:16; 49:25; 50:17 [o]S Ge 12:7 [p]Ge 46:4; 48:21 **28:14** [q]Ge 26:4 [r]S Ge 12:2; S 13:14; S 26:24 [s]S Ge 12:3; Ac 3:25; Gal 3:8 **28:15** [t]S Ge 21:20 [u]Ps 121:5,7-8 [v]ver 20 [w]ver 22; Ge 35:3 [x]ver 21; S Ge 15:16; 30:25; 31:30 [y]Dt 31:6,8; Jos 1:5; Ne 4:14; Ps 9:10 [z]Lev 26:42 [a]Ps 105:10 **28:16** [b]1Ki 3:15; Jer 31:26 **28:17** [c]Ex 3:5; 19:21; Jos 5:15; Ps 68:24,35 [d]ver 22; Ge 32:2; 1Ch 22:1; 2Ch 3:1 **28:18** [e]ver 11 [f]ver 22; Ge 31:13, 45,51; 35:14; Ex 24:4; Jos 24:26, 27; Isa 19:19 [g]Lev 8:11; Jos 4:9 **28:19** [h]S Ge 12:8 [i]Ge 35:6; 48:3; Jos 16:2; 18:13; Jdg 1:23,26 **28:20** [j]Ge 31:13; Lev 7:16; 22:18; 23:38; 27:2,9; Nu 6:2; 15:3; Dt 12:6; Jdg 11:30; 1Sa 1:21; 2Sa 15:8 [k]S ver 15 [l]1Ti 6:8 **28:21** [m]Jdg 11:31 [n]S ver 15 [o]Ex 15:2; Dt 26:17; Jos 24:18; Ps 48:14; 118:28 **28:22** [p]S ver 18; 1Sa 7:12 [q]S ver 17 [r]S Ge 14:20; S Nu 18:21; Lk 18:12 **29:1** [s]S Ge 25:6 **29:2** [t]S Ge 24:11 [u]ver 3,8,10 **29:3** [v]S ver 2 [w]ver 8 **29:4** [x]Ge 42:7; Jdg 19:17 [y]S Ge 11:31 **29:5** [z]S Ge 11:29 **29:6** [a]Ge 30:22-24; 35:16; 46:19,22 [b]Ex 2:16 **29:8** [c]S ver 2

[y]*12* Or *ladder* [z]*13* Or *There beside him*
[a]*19 Bethel* means *house of God.* [b]*20,21* Or *Since God . . . father's house, the LORD* [c]*21,22* Or *house, and the LORD will be my God, 22then*

28:13–15 HISTORY, Promise—See note on 15:1–21.
28:14 JESUS CHRIST, Foretold—The blessing promised to Abraham was carried on through Isaac (17:19; 18:18–19; 21:12). From Isaac the promise of God's blessing was extended through Jacob (28:14) and fulfilled through Jesus (Gal 3:16; Heb 6:14). The descendants of God through Jesus are still blessed of God (Ge 12:2–3; Jn 17:20–26).
28:16–22 WORSHIP, Buildings—Originally God was to be worshiped wherever He was known to appear (Ge 12:7). In the wilderness God led Israel to construct a tabernacle as the central worship place (Ex 25:8). In the Promised Land the people worshiped at a multiplicity of local sanctuaries (1 Sa 7:15–17; 9:12; 10:3,5,8,17). God eventually chose Jerusalem (Dt 12:5) as the proper place for worship and sacrifice (1 Ki 8). There David brought the ark (2 Sa 6:12), and Solomon built the Temple (1 Ki 5:3–5; 6:38). Synagogue worship gradually developed during the Exile or later from the people's desire to worship even though the destruction of the Temple and/or geographical isolation from Jerusalem made traditional Temple worship impossible. Compare Ps 137; Eze 8:1. In the synagogues prayers were offered as a substitute for sacrifice. However, the synagogue was primarily a place of instruction, rather than worship. The Jews had a passionate belief that the *Temple in Jerusalem was God's* only earthly habitation. This kept the synagogue in a subordinate position as long as the Temple stood. In the New Testament it was not considered important where the Christians worshiped. They knew that the Lord Jesus was with them always and everywhere. Buildings are not inherently sacred or secular. All structures and places belong equally to God. Corporate worship was shared in homes, in the open country, wherever Christians met. The expectation of the Lord's return discouraged the building of special places of worship. Compare Ex 3:12,18; Dt 12:4–14; 1 Ki 8:62–66; 1 Ch 22:1–19; Ps 26:8; 134:1–3; Ecc 5:1–7; Lk 24:52–53; Jn 4:19–24; Ac 2:41–47; 3:8; 16:13; 17:2, 17,22; 18:1–8.
28:20–21 PRAYER, Vow—A vow or an oath is a pledge of faithfulness expressed in specific ways. A covenant originates in God; a vow is a human response of faithfulness to God's faithfulness. Later, the Law made the taking of a vow entirely voluntary, but if a vow was made, it was binding (Dt 23:21–23). Regulations for vows are spelled out in Nu 30.
28:22 STEWARDSHIP, Tithe—Jacob made a vow to tithe. A vow is a solemn, holy promise that is binding. This is the second biblical reference to the tithe, occurring before the commandment to tithe. See notes on 14:20–24; Lev 27:30–33; Nu 18:21–32; Dt 12:6–18; 14:22–29; 26:1–15.
29:1–30 HISTORY, God's People—Biblical history changes its geographical focus to follow God's people, who form the center of interest for biblical history. See notes on 27:1–40; 1 Ch 29:29–30.

the well. Then we will water[d] the
sheep."
9While he was still talking with them,
Rachel came with her father's sheep,[e] for
she was a shepherdess. 10When Jacob
saw Rachel[f] daughter of Laban, his
mother's brother, and Laban's sheep, he
went over and rolled the stone[g] away
from the mouth of the well and watered[h]
his uncle's sheep.[i] 11Then Jacob kissed[j]
Rachel and began to weep aloud.[k] 12He
had told Rachel that he was a relative[l] of
her father and a son of Rebekah.[m] So she
ran and told her father.[n]
13As soon as Laban[o] heard the news
about Jacob, his sister's son, he hurried to
meet him. He embraced him[p] and kissed
him and brought him to his home, and
there Jacob told him all these things.
14Then Laban said to him, "You are my
own flesh and blood."[q]

Jacob Marries Leah and Rachel

After Jacob had stayed with him for a
whole month, 15Laban said to him, "Just
because you are a relative[r] of mine,
should you work for me for nothing? Tell
me what your wages[s] should be."
16Now Laban had two daughters; the
name of the older was Leah,[t] and the
name of the younger was Rachel.[u] 17Leah
had weak[d] eyes, but Rachel[v] was lovely
in form, and beautiful.[w] 18Jacob was in
love with Rachel[x] and said, "I'll work for
you seven years in return for your younger daughter Rachel."[y]
19Laban said, "It's better that I give her
to you than to some other man. Stay here
with me." 20So Jacob served seven years
to get Rachel,[z] but they seemed like only
a few days to him because of his love for
her.[a]
21Then Jacob said to Laban, "Give me
my wife. My time is completed, and I
want to lie with her.[b]"
22So Laban brought together all the
people of the place and gave a feast.[c]
23But when evening came, he took his
daughter Leah[d] and gave her to Jacob,
and Jacob lay with her. 24And Laban gave
his servant girl Zilpah[e] to his daughter as
her maidservant.[f]
25When morning came, there was
Leah! So Jacob said to Laban, "What is
this you have done to me?[g] I served you
for Rachel, didn't I? Why have you deceived me?[h]"
26Laban replied, "It is not our custom
here to give the younger daughter in marriage before the older one.[i] 27Finish this
daughter's bridal week;[j] then we will
give you the younger one also, in return
for another seven years of work.[k]"
28And Jacob did so. He finished the
week with Leah, and then Laban gave
him his daughter Rachel to be his wife.[l]
29Laban gave his servant girl Bilhah[m] to
his daughter Rachel as her maidservant.[n]
30Jacob lay with Rachel also, and he loved
Rachel more than Leah.[o] And he worked
for Laban another seven years.[p]

Jacob's Children

31When the LORD saw that Leah was
not loved,[q] he opened her womb,[r] but
Rachel was barren. 32Leah became pregnant and gave birth to a son.[s] She named
him Reuben,[e][t] for she said, "It is because the LORD has seen my misery.[u]
Surely my husband will love me now."
33She conceived again, and when she
gave birth to a son she said, "Because the
LORD heard that I am not loved,[v] he gave
me this one too." So she named him Simeon.[f][w]
34Again she conceived, and when she
gave birth to a son she said, "Now at last
my husband will become attached to
me,[x] because I have borne him three
sons." So he was named Levi.[g][y]
35She conceived again, and when she
gave birth to a son she said, "This time I
will praise the LORD." So she named him
Judah.[h][z] Then she stopped having children.[a]

Chapter 30

WHEN Rachel saw that she was not
bearing Jacob any children,[b] she
became jealous of her sister.[c] So she said

29:8 [d]S Ge 24:13 29:9 [e]Ex 2:16 29:10 [f]ver 16 [g]S ver 2 [h]S Ge 24:11 [i]ver 3; Ex 2:17 29:11 [j]ver 13 [k]Ge 33:4; 42:24; 43:30; 45:2,14-15; 46:29; 50:1,17; Ru 1:9 29:12 [l]ver 15 [m]S Ge 24:29 [n]Ge 24:28 29:13 [o]S Ge 24:29 [p]Ge 33:4; 45:14-15,14; 48:10; Ex 4:27; 18:7; Lk 15:20 29:14 [q]Ge 2:23; 37:27; Jdg 9:2; 2Sa 5:1; 19:12-13; 20:1; Ne 5:5; Isa 58:7 29:15 [r]ver 12 [s]Ge 30:28,32; 31:7,41 29:16 [t]ver 17,23, 28,30; Ge 30:9; 35:23; 47:30; 49:31; Ru 4:11 [u]ver 9-10 29:17 [v]S ver 16 [w]S Ge 12:11 29:18 [x]S Ge 24:67 [y]ver 20,27,30; Ge 30:26; Hos 12:12 29:20 [z]S ver 18; Ge 31:15 [a]SS 8:7; Hos 12:12 29:21 [b]Jdg 15:1 29:22 [c]Jdg 14:10; Isa 25:6; Jn 2:1-2 29:23 [d]S ver 16 29:24 [e]Ge 30:9 [f]S Ge 16:1 29:25 [g]S Ge 12:18 [h]S Ge 27:36 29:26 [i]Jdg 15:2; 1Sa 14:49; 18:17, 20; 2Sa 6:23 29:27 [j]Jdg 14:12 [k]S ver 18; Ge 31:41 29:28 [l]S ver 16; S Ge 4:19 29:29 [m]Ge 30:3; 35:22; 49:4; Dt 22:30; 1Ch 5:1 [n]S Ge 16:1 29:30 [o]S ver 16 [p]S ver 20 29:31 [q]ver 33; Dt 21:15-17 [r]S Ge 11:30; S 16:2; Ru 4:13; 1Sa 1:19; Ps 127:3 29:32 [s]Ge 30:23; Ru 4:13; 1Sa 1:20 [t]Ge 37:21; 46:8; 48:5,14; 49:3; Ex 6:14; Nu 1:5,20; 26:5; Dt 33:6; Jos 4:12; 1Ch 5:1,3 [u]S Ge 16:11 29:33 [v]S ver 31 [w]Ge 34:25; 46:10; 48:5; 49:5; Ex 6:15; Nu 1:6,22; 34:20; 1Ch 4:24; Eze 48:24 29:34 [x]Ge 30:20; 1Sa 1:2-4 [y]Ge 34:25; 46:11; 49:5-7; Ex 2:1; 6:16,19; Nu 1:47; 3:17-20; 26:57; Dt 33:8; 1Ch 6:1,16; 23:6-24,13-14 **29:35** [z]Ge 35:23; 37:26; 38:1; 43:8; 44:14,18; 46:12; 49:8; 1Ch 2:3; 4:1; Isa 48:1; Mt 1:2-3 [a]Ge 30:9 **30:1** [b]S Ge 11:30; Isa 49:21; 54:1 [c]S Ge 16:4; Lev 18:18

[d]17 Or *delicate* [e]32 *Reuben* sounds like the Hebrew for *he has seen my misery*; the name means *see, a son.* [f]33 *Simeon* probably means *one who hears.* [g]34 *Levi* sounds like and may be derived from the Hebrew for *attached.* [h]35 *Judah* sounds like and may be derived from the Hebrew for *praise.*

29:18–21 HUMANITY, Marriage—True human love involves and is based upon life commitment. It can also lead people to work long and hard to establish a lifelong relationship. Love leads to self-sacrifice.

29:31 HUMANITY, Birth—The birth of children is a gift of life from God. See note on 18:10–14.

29:31—30:24 HISTORY, Promise—The promise of a large family began to be realized. Human intrigue, physical barrenness, and family relationship problems appear to be the immediate factors involved. The Bible's inspired narrative points to God's work as the guiding factor. In so doing the Bible does not hold the actions up as a moral example but shows how God can accomplish His purposes despite the weaknesses of His people. See notes on 25:23; 27:1–40.

29:35 PRAYER, Personal—The name "Judah" (Hebrew *yehudah*) was intended to suggest the Hebrew word for "praise" (*yehodeh*). His very naming was a prayer of gratitude.

to Jacob, "Give me children, or I'll die!"
2 Jacob became angry with her and said,
"Am I in the place of God,[d] who has kept
you from having children?"[e]
3 Then she said, "Here is Bilhah,[f] my
maidservant.[g] Sleep with her so that she
can bear children for me and that through
her I too can build a family."[h]
4 So she gave him her servant Bilhah as
a wife.[i] Jacob slept with her,[j] 5 and she
became pregnant and bore him a son.
6 Then Rachel said, "God has vindicated
me;[k] he has listened to my plea and giv-
en me a son."[l] Because of this she
named him Dan.[i] [m]
7 Rachel's servant Bilhah[n] conceived
again and bore Jacob a second son. 8 Then
Rachel said, "I have had a great struggle
with my sister, and I have won."[o] So she
named him Naphtali.[j] [p]
9 When Leah[q] saw that she had
stopped having children,[r] she took her
maidservant Zilpah[s] and gave her to Jacob as a wife.[t] 10 Leah's servant Zilpah[u]
bore Jacob a son. 11 Then Leah said,
"What good fortune!"[k] So she named
him Gad.[l] [v]
12 Leah's servant Zilpah bore Jacob a
second son. 13 Then Leah said, "How happy I am! The women will call me[w] happy."[x] So she named him Asher.[m] [y]
14 During wheat harvest,[z] Reuben
went out into the fields and found some
mandrake plants,[a] which he brought to
his mother Leah. Rachel said to Leah,
"Please give me some of your son's mandrakes."
15 But she said to her, "Wasn't it
enough[b] that you took away my husband? Will you take my son's mandrakes
too?"
"Very well," Rachel said, "he can
sleep with you tonight in return for your
son's mandrakes."[c]
16 So when Jacob came in from the
fields that evening, Leah went out to
meet him. "You must sleep with me,"
she said. "I have hired you with my son's
mandrakes."[d] So he slept with her that
night.
17 God listened to Leah,[e] and she became pregnant and bore Jacob a fifth son.
18 Then Leah said, "God has rewarded me
for giving my maidservant to my husband."[f] So she named him Issachar.[n] [g]
19 Leah conceived again and bore Jacob
a sixth son. 20 Then Leah said, "God has
presented me with a precious gift. This
time my husband will treat me with hon-
or,[h] because I have borne him six sons."
So she named him Zebulun.[o] [i]
21 Some time later she gave birth to a
daughter and named her Dinah.[j]
22 Then God remembered Rachel;[k] he
listened to her[l] and opened her womb.[m]
23 She became pregnant and gave birth to
a son[n] and said, "God has taken away my
disgrace."[o] 24 She named him Joseph,[p] [p]
and said, "May the LORD add to me another son."[q]

Jacob's Flocks Increase

25 After Rachel gave birth to Joseph, Jacob said to Laban, "Send me on my way[r]
so I can go back to my own homeland.[s]
26 Give me my wives and children, for
whom I have served you,[t] and I will be
on my way. You know how much work
I've done for you."
27 But Laban said to him, "If I have
found favor in your eyes,[u] please stay. I
have learned by divination[v] that[q] the
LORD has blessed me because of you."[w]
28 He added, "Name your wages,[x] and I
will pay them."
29 Jacob said to him, "You know how I
have worked for you[y] and how your livestock has fared under my care.[z] 30 The
little you had before I came has increased
greatly, and the LORD has blessed you
wherever I have been.[a] But now, when
may I do something for my own household?[b]"
31 "What shall I give you?" he asked.
"Don't give me anything," Jacob replied. "But if you will do this one thing
for me, I will go on tending your flocks
and watching over them: 32 Let me go
through all your flocks today and remove
from them every speckled or spotted
sheep, every dark-colored lamb and every
spotted or speckled goat.[c] They will be
my wages.[d] 33 And my honesty will testify
for me in the future, whenever you check
on the wages you have paid me. Any goat
in my possession that is not speckled or

30:2 [d]Ge 50:19; Dt 32:35; 2Ki 5:7 [e]S Ge 16:2 **30:3** [f]ver 7; S Ge 29:29 [g]S Ge 24:61 [h]Ge 16:2 **30:4** [i]ver 9,18 [j]Ge 16:3-4 **30:6** [k]Ps 35:24; 43:1 [l]ver 23; Ge 21:2; Ru 4:13; 1Sa 1:20 [m]Ge 46:23; 49:16-17; Nu 26:42-43; Jos 19:40-48; Jdg 1:34; 13:2; 18:2; Jer 4:15; 8:16; Eze 48:1 **30:7** [n]S ver 3 **30:8** [o]Ge 32:28; Hos 12:3-4 [p]Ge 35:25; 46:24; 49:21; Nu 1:42; 26:48; Dt 33:23; Jdg 4:6; 5:18; 1Ch 7:13 **30:9** [q]S Ge 29:16 [r]Ge 29:35 [s]Ge 29:24 [t]S ver 4 **30:10** [u]Ge 46:18 **30:11** [v]Ge 35:26; 46:16; 49:19; Ex 1:4; Nu 1:24; 26:18; Jos 4:12; 1Ch 5:11; 12:8; Jer 49:1 **30:13** [w]Ps 127:3 [x]Ru 4:14; Ps 127:4-5; Lk 1:48 [y]Ge 35:26; 46:17; 49:20; Nu 1:40; 26:47; Dt 33:24; Jos 19:24-31; 1Ch 7:30-31 **30:14** [z]Ex 34:22; Jdg 15:1; Ru 2:23; 1Sa 6:13; 12:17 [a]ver 15,16; SS 7:13 **30:15** [b]Nu 16:9, 13; Isa 7:13; Eze 34:18 [c]Ge 38:16; Eze 16:33; Hos 9:1 **30:16** [d]S ver 14 **30:17** [e]S Ge 25:21 **30:18** [f]S ver 4 [g]Ge 46:13; 49:14; Nu 1:8,28,29; 26:25; Dt 27:12; 33:18; Jos 17:10; 19:17; 21:6,28; Jdg 5:15; 10:1; 1Ch 7:1 **30:20** [h]S Ge 29:34; 1Pe 3:7 [i]Ge 35:23; 46:14; 49:13; Nu 1:30; 26:27; 34:25; Dt 33:18; Jdg 5:18 **30:21** [j]Ge 34:1; 46:15 **30:22** [k]S Ge 8:1 [l]S Ge 25:21 [m]S Ge 11:30 **30:23** [n]S ver 6; S Ge 29:32 [o]Isa 4:1; 25:8; 45:17; 54:4; Lk 1:25 **30:24** [p]S Ge 29:6; 32:22; 33:2,7; 35:24; 37:2; 39:1; 49:22-26; Dt 33:13 [q]Ge 35:17; 1Sa 4:20 **30:25** [r]S Ge 24:54 [s]S Ge 28:15

30:26 [t]S Ge 29:18 **30:27** [u]Ge 33:10; 50:4; Est 2:15 [v]Ge 44:5,15; Lev 19:26; Nu 22:7; 23:23; 24:1; Jos 13:22; 2Ki 17:17; Jer 27:9 [w]ver 30; S Ge 26:24; 31:38; Dt 28:11; 2Sa 6:11 **30:28** [x]S Ge 29:15 **30:29** [y]Ge 31:6 [z]Ge 31:38-40 **30:30** [a]S ver 27 [b]1Ti 5:8 **30:32** [c]ver 33,35,39,40; Ge 31:8, 12 [d]S Ge 29:15

[i]6 *Dan* here means *he has vindicated.* [j]8 *Naphtali* means *my struggle.* [k]11 Or *"A troop is coming!"* [l]11 *Gad* can mean *good fortune* or *a troop.* [m]13 *Asher* means *happy.* [n]18 *Issachar* sounds like the Hebrew for *reward.* [o]20 *Zebulun* probably means *honor.* [p]24 *Joseph* means *may he add.* [q]27 Or possibly *have become rich and*

30:27–30 ELECTION, Other Nations—Laban learned through actions forbidden to Israel (Lev 19:26; Dt 18:10,14) that his rich blessings from God came through his association with Jacob. Covenant and election brought blessings to all associated with Jacob (27:29). Other nations were not the elect through whom God chose to work. God was concerned for them and was seeking to bless them.

spotted, or any lamb that is not dark-colored,[e] will be considered stolen.[f]”
34“Agreed,” said Laban. “Let it be as
you have said.” 35That same day he removed all the male goats that were
streaked or spotted, and all the speckled
or spotted female goats (all that had white
on them) and all the dark-colored
lambs,[g] and he placed them in the care
of his sons.[h] 36Then he put a three-day
journey[i] between himself and Jacob,
while Jacob continued to tend the rest of
Laban's flocks.

37Jacob, however, took fresh-cut
branches from poplar, almond[j] and
plane trees[k] and made white stripes on
them by peeling the bark and exposing
the white inner wood of the branches.[l]
38Then he placed the peeled branches[m]
in all the watering troughs,[n] so that they
would be directly in front of the flocks
when they came to drink. When the
flocks were in heat[o] and came to drink,
39they mated in front of the branches.[p]
And they bore young that were streaked
or speckled or spotted.[q] 40Jacob set apart
the young of the flock by themselves, but
made the rest face the streaked and
dark-colored animals[r] that belonged to
Laban. Thus he made separate flocks for
himself and did not put them with Laban's animals. 41Whenever the stronger
females were in heat,[s] Jacob would place
the branches in the troughs in front of the
animals so they would mate near the
branches,[t] 42but if the animals were
weak, he would not place them there. So
the weak animals went to Laban and the
strong ones to Jacob.[u] 43In this way the
man grew exceedingly prosperous and
came to own large flocks, and maidservants and menservants, and camels and
donkeys.[v]

Chapter 31

Jacob Flees From Laban

JACOB heard that Laban's sons[w] were
saying, “Jacob has taken everything
our father owned and has gained all this
wealth from what belonged to our father.”[x] 2And Jacob noticed that Laban's
attitude toward him was not what it had
been.[y]

3Then the LORD said to Jacob, “Go
back[z] to the land of your fathers and to
your relatives, and I will be with you.”[a]

4So Jacob sent word to Rachel and Leah
to come out to the fields where his flocks
were. 5He said to them, “I see that your
father[b]'s attitude toward me is not what
it was before,[c] but the God of my father
has been with me.[d] 6You know that I've
worked for your father with all my
strength,[e] 7yet your father has cheated[f]
me by changing my wages[g] ten times.[h]
However, God has not allowed him to
harm me.[i] 8If he said, ‘The speckled
ones will be your wages,’ then all the
flocks gave birth to speckled young; and if
he said, ‘The streaked ones will be your
wages,’[j] then all the flocks bore streaked
young. 9So God has taken away your father's livestock[k] and has given them to
me.[l]

10“In breeding season I once had a
dream[m] in which I looked up and saw
that the male goats mating with the flock
were streaked, speckled or spotted. 11The
angel of God[n] said to me in the dream,[o]
‘Jacob.’ I answered, ‘Here I am.’[p] 12And
he said, ‘Look up and see that all the male
goats mating with the flock are streaked,
speckled or spotted,[q] for I have seen all
that Laban has been doing to you.[r] 13I
am the God of Bethel,[s] where you
anointed a pillar[t] and where you made a
vow[u] to me. Now leave this land at once
and go back to your native land.[v]’ ”

14Then Rachel and Leah replied, “Do
we still have any share[w] in the inheritance of our father's estate? 15Does he not
regard us as foreigners?[x] Not only has he
sold us, but he has used up what was paid
for us.[y] 16Surely all the wealth that God
took away from our father belongs to us
and our children.[z] So do whatever God
has told you.”

17Then Jacob put his children and his
wives[a] on camels,[b] 18and he drove all
his livestock ahead of him, along with all
the goods he had accumulated[c] in Paddan Aram,[r][d] to go to his father Isaac[e] in
the land of Canaan.[f]

19When Laban had gone to shear his
sheep,[g] Rachel stole her father's household gods.[h] 20Moreover, Jacob deceived[i]
Laban the Aramean[j] by not telling him
he was running away.[k] 21So he fled[l]
with all he had, and crossing the

30:33 [e]S ver 32 [f]Ge 31:39
30:35 [g]S ver 32 [h]Ge 31:1
30:36 [i]Ge 31:22; Ex 3:18; 5:3; 8:27
30:37 [j]Jer 1:11 [k]Eze 31:8 [l]ver 38, 41
30:38 [m]S ver 37 [n]Ex 2:16 [o]ver 41; Jer 2:24
30:39 [p]ver 41 [q]S ver 32
30:40 [r]S ver 32
30:41 [s]S ver 38 [t]S ver 37
30:42 [u]Ge 31:1,9, 16,43
30:43 [v]S Ge 12:16
31:1 [w]Ge 30:35 [x]S Ge 30:42
31:2 [y]ver 5
31:3 [z]ver 13; Ge 32:9; Dt 30:3; Isa 10:21; 35:10; Jer 30:3; 42:12 [a]S Ge 21:22; S 26:3
31:5 [b]ver 29,42,53; Ge 43:23; Da 2:23 [c]ver 2 [d]S Ge 21:22; S 26:3
31:6 [e]Ge 30:29
31:7 [f]Lev 6:2; Am 8:5 [g]S Ge 29:15 [h]ver 41; Nu 14:22; Job 19:3 [i]ver 52; S Ge 24:50
31:8 [j]S Ge 30:32
31:9 [k]Job 39:2; Eze 31:6 [l]S Ge 30:42
31:10 [m]S Ge 20:3
31:11 [n]S Ge 16:7 [o]S Ge 20:3 [p]S Ge 22:1; S Ex 3:4
31:12 [q]S Ge 30:32 [r]Ex 3:7
31:13 [s]Ge 28:10-22 [t]S Ge 28:18 [u]S Ge 28:20 [v]S ver 3
31:14 [w]2Sa 20:1; 1Ki 12:16
31:15 [x]Dt 15:3; 23:20; Ru 2:10; 2Sa 15:19; 1Ki 8:41; Ob 1:11 [y]S Ge 29:20
31:16 [z]S Ge 30:42
31:17 [a]S Ge 27:41 [b]S Ge 24:63-64
31:18 [c]S Ge 12:5 [d]S Ge 25:20 [e]Ge 35:27 [f]S Ge 10:19
31:19 [g]Ge 38:12, 13; 1Sa 25:2,4,7; 2Sa 13:23 [h]ver 30, 32,34-35; Ge 35:2; Jos 24:14; Jdg 17:5; 18:14,17,24,30; 1Sa 7:3; 19:13; 2Ki 23:24; Hos 3:4
31:20 [i]S Ge 27:36 [j]S Ge 25:20 [k]ver 27
31:21 [l]ver 22; Ex 2:15; 14:5; 1Ki 18:46; 19:3; Jer 26:21

[r]*18* That is, Northwest Mesopotamia

31:1–55 CHRISTIAN ETHICS, Moral Limits—Those sensitive to the ordinary events of life can recognize when injustice occurs. Refusal to abide by wage agreements is outside acceptable moral limits in all societies. Theft and deception are wrong in themselves and thus are not proper responses to unethical behavior. Agreements are the proper basis for relationships, particularly when the parties represent different cultures. This account relates that Jacob had been sensitive and was becoming more sensitive to the leadership of God. Many of his rough edges were being worn off through his encounters with Laban. Such is the work of God in our lives as others become in God's hands formative instruments for shaping our character. Even these who work for our God need His disciplining hand as they may try to press too far in imposing moral limits upon us.

River,[s] [m] he headed for the hill country of
Gilead.[n]

Laban Pursues Jacob

22On the third day[o] Laban was told
that Jacob had fled.[p] 23Taking his relatives[q] with him[r], he pursued Jacob for
seven days and caught up with him in the
hill country of Gilead.[s] 24Then God came
to Laban the Aramean[t] in a dream at
night and said to him,[u] "Be careful not to
say anything to Jacob, either good or
bad."[v]
25Jacob had pitched his tent in the hill
country of Gilead[w] when Laban overtook
him, and Laban and his relatives camped
there too. 26Then Laban said to Jacob,
"What have you done?[x] You've deceived
me,[y] and you've carried off my daughters
like captives in war.[z] 27Why did you run
off secretly and deceive me? Why didn't
you tell me,[a] so I could send you away
with joy and singing to the music of tambourines[b] and harps?[c] 28You didn't even
let me kiss my grandchildren and my
daughters good-by.[d] You have done a
foolish thing. 29I have the power to harm
you;[e] but last night the God of your father[f] said to me, 'Be careful not to say
anything to Jacob, either good or bad.'[g]
30Now you have gone off because you
longed to return to your father's house.[h]
But why did you steal[i] my gods?[j]"
31Jacob answered Laban, "I was afraid,
because I thought you would take your
daughters away from me by force.[k] 32But
if you find anyone who has your gods, he
shall not live.[l] In the presence of our
relatives, see for yourself whether there
is anything of yours here with me; and if
so, take it." Now Jacob did not know that
Rachel had stolen the gods.[m]
33So Laban went into Jacob's tent and
into Leah's tent[n] and into the tent of the
two maidservants,[o] but he found nothing.[p] After he came out of Leah's tent, he
entered Rachel's tent. 34Now Rachel had
taken the household gods[q] and put them
inside her camel's saddle[r] and was sitting on them. Laban searched[s] through
everything in the tent but found nothing.
35Rachel said to her father, "Don't be
angry, my lord, that I cannot stand up
in your presence;[t] I'm having my
period.[u]" So he searched but could not
find the household gods.[v]
36Jacob was angry and took Laban to
task. "What is my crime?" he asked Laban. "What sin have I committed[w] that
you hunt me down?[x] 37Now that you
have searched through all my goods,
what have you found that belongs to your
household?[y] Put it here in front of your
relatives[z] and mine, and let them judge
between the two of us.[a]
38"I have been with you for twenty
years now.[b] Your sheep and goats have
not miscarried,[c] nor have I eaten rams
from your flocks. 39I did not bring you
animals torn by wild beasts; I bore the
loss myself. And you demanded payment
from me for whatever was stolen[d] by day
or night.[e] 40This was my situation: The
heat consumed me in the daytime and
the cold at night, and sleep fled from my
eyes.[f] 41It was like this for the twenty
years[g] I was in your household. I worked
for you fourteen years for your two
daughters[h] and six years for your
flocks,[i] and you changed my wages[j] ten
times.[k] 42If the God of my father,[l] the
God of Abraham[m] and the Fear of Isaac,[n]
had not been with me,[o] you would surely
have sent me away empty-handed. But
God has seen my hardship and the toil of
my hands,[p] and last night he rebuked
you.[q]"
43Laban answered Jacob, "The women
are my daughters, the children are my
children, and the flocks are my flocks.[r]
All you see is mine. Yet what can I do
today about these daughters of mine, or
about the children they have borne?
44Come now, let's make a covenant,[s]
you and I, and let it serve as a witness
between us."[t]
45So Jacob took a stone and set it up as
a pillar.[u] 46He said to his relatives,
"Gather some stones." So they took
stones and piled them in a heap,[v] and
they ate there by the heap. 47Laban called
it Jegar Sahadutha,[t] and Jacob called it
Galeed.[u] [w]
48Laban said, "This heap[x] is a witness

31:21 [m]S Ge 2:14 [n]ver 23,25; Ge 37:25; Nu 26:30; 32:1; Dt 3:10; Jos 12:2; Jer 22:6
31:22 [o]S Ge 30:36 [p]S ver 21
31:23 [q]ver 37 [r]Ex 14:9 [s]S ver 21
31:24 [t]S Ge 25:20 [u]S Ge 20:3 [v]S Ge 24:50
31:25 [w]S ver 21
31:26 [x]S Ge 12:18 [y]S Ge 27:36 [z]Ge 34:29; 1Sa 30:2-3
31:27 [a]ver 20 [b]Ex 15:20; Jdg 11:34; 1Sa 10:5; 2Sa 6:5; Ps 68:25; Isa 24:8; Jer 31:4 [c]S Ge 4:21
31:28 [d]ver 55; S Ge 27:27; Ru 1:14; Ac 20:37
31:29 [e]S ver 7; S Ge 26:29 [f]S ver 5 [g]S Ge 24:50
31:30 [h]S Ge 28:15; Job 29:2 [i]Ge 44:8 [j]S ver 19
31:31 [k]S Ge 20:11
31:32 [l]Ge 44:9 [m]S ver 19
31:33 [n]Ge 24:67 [o]S Ge 16:1 [p]ver 37
31:34 [q]S ver 19 [r]S Ge 24:63-64 [s]ver 37; Ge 44:12
31:35 [t]Ex 20:12; Lev 19:3,32; Dt 21:18; 27:16; Jer 35:18 [u]Lev 15:19-23 [v]ver 19
31:36 [w]1Sa 19:5; 20:32 [x]1Sa 23:23; 24:11
31:37 [y]ver 33 [z]ver 23 [a]Dt 1:16; 16:18
31:38 [b]S Ge 27:44 [c]S Ge 30:27
31:39 [d]Ge 30:33 [e]Ex 22:13
31:40 [f]Ps 132:4; 2Co 11:27
31:41 [g]S Ge 27:44 [h]Ge 29:30 [i]S Ge 30:32 [j]S Ge 29:15 [k]S ver 7
31:42 [l]S ver 5; S Ex 3:15 [m]S Ge 24:12 [n]ver 53; Ge 46:1 [o]S Ge 21:22; Ps 124:1-2 [p]S Ge 3:17 [q]S Ge 24:50
31:43 [r]Ge 30:32,42
31:44 [s]S Ge 21:27 [t]S Ge 21:30
31:45 [u]S Ge 28:18
31:46 [v]ver 48,51, 52
31:47 [w]S Ge 21:30
31:48 [x]S ver 46

[s] *21* That is, the Euphrates [t] *47* The Aramaic *Jegar Sahadutha* means *witness heap.* [u] *47* The Hebrew *Galeed* means *witness heap.*

31:30–35 GOD, One God—Old Testament people lived among people who worshiped many gods. For hundreds of years God struggled with the Israelites, trying to help them see that the gods of the nations were no more than figments of the imagination or fetishes carved out of wood and stone. See notes on Ex 20:1–7; Dt 6:4–9. The Bible laughs at such "gods" who can be stolen and carried around. People continue to devote their entire energy and attach *supreme value to things they can steal and carry* around.

31:36 SIN, Estrangement—Jacob met a master deceiver in his father-in-law Laban (29:13–25) and continued on the path of deception (30:25–43) he had first practiced with Esau. See note on 27:41–45. The result was flight (31:1–35) and anger (v 36). Finally, reason and family loyalty prevailed, producing a treaty or covenant (v 44). Still, complete separation was the final result of such selfish deception. Sin never improves relationships with other people.

31:42 ELECTION, Providence—Laban intended to unjustly rob and exploit Jacob, sending him away empty-handed. God's providence in election protected Jacob, turning evil human intention into blessing. God's purposes in election will ultimately prevail over human plans. See note on 25:23.

between you and me today."[y] That is
why it was called Galeed. 49It was also
called Mizpah,[v][z] because he said, "May
the LORD keep watch between you and
me when we are away from each other.
50If you mistreat[a] my daughters or if you
take any wives besides my daughters,
even though no one is with us, remember
that God is a witness[b] between you and
me."[c]

51Laban also said to Jacob, "Here is this
heap,[d] and here is this pillar[e] I have set
up between you and me. 52This heap is a
witness, and this pillar is a witness,[f] that
I will not go past this heap to your side to
harm you and that you will not go past
this heap[g] and pillar to my side to harm
me.[h] 53May the God of Abraham[i] and
the God of Nahor,[j] the God of their father, judge between us."[k]

So Jacob took an oath[l] in the name of
the Fear of his father Isaac.[m] 54He offered
a sacrifice[n] there in the hill country and
invited his relatives to a meal.[o] After
they had eaten, they spent the night
there.

55Early the next morning Laban kissed
his grandchildren and his daughters[p] and
blessed[q] them. Then he left and returned
home.[r]

Chapter 32

Jacob Prepares to Meet Esau

JACOB also went on his way, and the
angels of God[s] met him. 2When Jacob
saw them, he said, "This is the camp of
God!"[t] So he named that place Mahanaim.[w][u]

3Jacob sent messengers[v] ahead of him
to his brother Esau[w] in the land of Seir,[x]
the country of Edom.[y] 4He instructed
them: "This is what you are to say to my
master[z] Esau: 'Your servant[a] Jacob says,
I have been staying with Laban[b] and
have remained there till now. 5I have cattle and donkeys, sheep and goats, menservants and maidservants.[c] Now I am
sending this message to my lord,[d] that I
may find favor in your eyes.[e]' "

6When the messengers returned to Jacob, they said, "We went to your brother
Esau, and now he is coming to meet you,
and four hundred men are with him."[f]

7In great fear[g] and distress[h] Jacob divided the people who were with him into
two groups,[x][i] and the flocks and herds
and camels as well. 8He thought, "If Esau
comes and attacks one group,[y] the
group[y] that is left may escape."

9Then Jacob prayed, "O God of my father Abraham,[j] God of my father Isaac,[k]
O LORD, who said to me, 'Go back to your
country and your relatives, and I will
make you prosper,'[l] 10I am unworthy of
all the kindness and faithfulness[m] you
have shown your servant. I had only my
staff[n] when I crossed this Jordan, but
now I have become two groups.[o] 11Save
me, I pray, from the hand of my brother
Esau, for I am afraid[p] he will come and
attack me,[q] and also the mothers with
their children.[r] 12But you have said, 'I
will surely make you prosper and will
make your descendants like the sand[s] of
the sea, which cannot be counted.[t]' "

13He spent the night there, and from
what he had with him he selected a gift[u]
for his brother Esau: 14two hundred female goats and twenty male goats, two
hundred ewes and twenty rams,[v] 15thirty
female camels with their young, forty
cows and ten bulls, and twenty female

31:48 [y]S Ge 21:30; Jer 29:23; 42:5 **31:49** [z]Jos 11:3; Jdg 10:17; 11:29 **31:50** [a]Ge 16:6 [b]Dt 31:19; Jos 24:27; Jdg 11:10; 1Sa 12:5; 20:14,23, 42; Job 16:19; Jer 29:23; 42:5; Mic 1:2 [c]S Ge 21:30; S Dt 4:26; S Jer 7:11 **31:51** [d]S ver 46 [e]S Ge 28:18 **31:52** [f]S Ge 21:30 [g]S ver 46 [h]S ver 7; S Ge 26:29 **31:53** [i]S Ge 24:12 [j]S Ge 11:27 [k]S Ge 16:5 [l]S Ge 21:23,27 [m]S ver 42 **31:54** [n]Ge 46:1; Ex 24:5; Lev 3:1 [o]S Ge 26:30 **31:55** [p]S ver 28; Ru 1:9 [q]S Ge 24:60; S Ex 39:43 [r]Ge 18:33 **32:1** [s]S Ge 16:11; 2Ki 6:16-17; 1Ch 21:15; Ps 34:7; 35:5; 91:11; Da 6:22 **32:2** [t]S Ge 28:17 [u]Jos 13:26,30; 21:38; 2Sa 2:8,29; 17:24; 19:32; 1Ki 2:8; 4:14; 1Ch 6:80 **32:3** [v]Nu 21:21; Jdg 11:17 [w]S Ge 27:41-42 [x]S Ge 14:6; S Nu 24:18 [y]S Ge 25:30; S 36:16 **32:4** [z]S Ge 24:9 [a]S Ge 18:3 [b]Ge 31:41 **32:5** [c]S Ge 12:16 [d]S Ge 24:9 [e]Ge 33:8,10,15; 34:11; 47:25,29; 50:4; Ru 2:13 **32:6** [f]Ge 33:1 **32:7** [g]ver 11 [h]Ge 35:3; Ps 4:1; 77:2; 107:6 [i]ver 10; Ge 33:1 **32:9** [j]S Ge 24:12 [k]S Ge 28:13 [l]S Ge 26:3; 31:13 **32:10** [m]S Ge 24:27 [n]Ge 38:18; 47:31; Nu 17:2 [o]S ver 7 **32:11** [p]S ver 7 [q]Ge 43:18; Ps 59:2 [r]S Ge 27:41 **32:12** [s]S Ge 22:17; 1Ki 4:20,29 [t]S Ge 12:2; S 13:14; Hos 1:10; Ro 9:27 **32:13** [u]ver 13-15,18,20,21; Ge 33:10; 43:11,15,25,26; 1Sa 16:20; Pr 18:16; 21:14 **32:14** [v]Nu 7:88

[v]49 *Mizpah* means *watchtower.* [w]2 *Mahanaim* means *two camps.* [x]7 Or *camps*; also in verse 10 [y]8 Or *camp*

32:1–30 HUMANITY, Spiritual Nature—Fear may open a person's spiritual nature to God and create a desire to be blessed. In the Old Testament a changed name indicates a changed nature. The transformed nature gives a new spiritual basis for facing future anxieties and fears. Having seen God face to face does not necessarily change the future, but it does change the nature of the one who faces the future.

32:1–2 REVELATION, Angels—Revelation helps God's people prepare for life's dark, struggling moments. God sent two messengers to reassure Jacob. Their appearance is not described. How Jacob recognized them we do not know. They encouraged him, letting him know God was with him. The presence of angels represented God's presence with His people.

32:3—33:17 FAMILY, Conflict Resolution—The experience of Jacob and Esau provides an illustration of bitter conflict between brothers resolved in later years by the desire of both brothers to overcome the hostility. Family treachery can be overcome when the victim takes the initiative in offering forgiveness. See 45:1–15; Mt 5:23–24. Contemporary families may not use the same methods Jacob and Esau used to resolve conflicts. We can and must demonstrate the same willingness to overcome family hostilities through forgiveness and reconciliation.

32:9–12 PRAYER, Faithfulness of God—Jacob based his prayer on God's faithfulness to His past actions and to His word.

32:10 GOD, Grace—Jacob had worked long and hard for what he had, but he recognized the very ability to work was itself a gift from God's grace. Jacob confessed he had nothing he could call his own. Everything he had in life was a precious gift from God. Rather than brag about personal accomplishments, faithful Christians seek to praise and thank God for His abounding grace in giving us all we have.

32:12,28 ELECTION, Prayer—As Jacob prepared to leave Laban and return home, fears overpowered him. He feared confronting his brother, Esau. In anguish and distress he prayed to the God of Abraham and Isaac for protection from the retributive hand of Esau. In this prayer Jacob appealed to the election promises that God had made to his fathers. In wrestling with God, Jacob gained assurance of victory. Election leads the elect to struggle with God in prayer.

donkeys and ten male donkeys.[w] 16He
put them in the care of his servants, each
herd by itself, and said to his servants,
"Go ahead of me, and keep some space
between the herds."[x]
17He instructed the one in the lead:
"When my brother Esau meets you and
asks, 'To whom do you belong, and
where are you going, and who owns all
these animals in front of you?' 18then you
are to say, 'They belong to your servant[y]
Jacob. They are a gift[z] sent to my lord
Esau, and he is coming behind us.' "
19He also instructed the second, the
third and all the others who followed the
herds: "You are to say the same thing to
Esau when you meet him. 20And be sure
to say, 'Your servant[a] Jacob is coming behind us.' " For he thought, "I will pacify
him with these gifts[b] I am sending on
ahead;[c] later, when I see him, perhaps
he will receive me."[d] 21So Jacob's gifts[e]
went on ahead of him, but he himself
spent the night in the camp.

Jacob Wrestles With God

22That night Jacob got up and took his
two wives, his two maidservants and his
eleven sons[f] and crossed the ford of the
Jabbok.[g] 23After he had sent them across
the stream, he sent over all his possessions.[h] 24So Jacob was left alone,[i] and a
man[j] wrestled with him till daybreak.
25When the man saw that he could not
overpower him, he touched the socket of
Jacob's hip[k] so that his hip was
wrenched as he wrestled with the man.
26Then the man said, "Let me go, for it is
daybreak."
But Jacob replied, "I will not let you go
unless you bless me."[l]
27The man asked him, "What is your
name?"
"Jacob,"[m] he answered.

32:15 [w]S Ge 13:2; 42:26; 45:23
32:16 [x]Ge 33:8
32:18 [y]S Ge 18:3 [z]S ver 13
32:20 [a]S Ge 18:3 [b]S ver 13; 1Sa 9:7; 2Ki 8:8; Jer 40:5 [c]1Sa 25:19 [d]Ge 33:10; Ex 28:38; Lev 1:4; Mal 1:8
32:21 [e]S ver 13
32:22 [f]S Ge 30:24 [g]Nu 21:24; Dt 2:37; 3:16; Jos 12:2
32:23 [h]S Ge 26:14
32:24 [i]Da 10:8 [j]S Ge 18:2
32:25 [k]ver 32
32:26 [l]Hos 12:4
32:27 [m]S Ge 25:26
32:28 [n]Isa 1:26; 56:5; 60:14; 62:2, 4,12; 65:15 [o]S Ge 17:5 [p]S Ge 30:8
32:29 [q]Ex 3:13; 6:3; Jdg 13:17 [r]Jdg 13:18 [s]Ge 25:11; 35:9; 48:3
32:30 [t]S Ge 16:13; 1Co 13:12
32:31 [u]Jdg 8:9
32:32 [v]ver 25
33:1 [w]S Ge 32:6 [x]S Ge 32:7
33:2 [y]ver 6 [z]S Ge 30:24
33:3 [a]ver 6,7; S Ge 17:3; 37:7-10; 42:6; 43:26; 44:14; 48:12; 1Sa 20:41 [b]2Ki 5:10,14
33:4 [c]S Ge 27:41-42 [d]S Ge 29:11; Lk 15:20 [e]S Ge 27:27
33:5 [f]S Ge 18:3; Ge 48:9; Ps 127:3; Isa 8:18

28Then the man said, "Your name[n]
will no longer be Jacob, but Israel,[z][o] because you have struggled with God and
with men and have overcome."[p]
29Jacob said, "Please tell me your
name."[q]
But he replied, "Why do you ask my
name?"[r] Then he blessed[s] him there.
30So Jacob called the place Peniel,[a]
saying, "It is because I saw God face to
face,[t] and yet my life was spared."
31The sun rose above him as he passed
Peniel,[b][u] and he was limping because of
his hip. 32Therefore to this day the Israelites do not eat the tendon attached to the
socket of the hip,[v] because the socket of
Jacob's hip was touched near the tendon.

Chapter 33

Jacob Meets Esau

JACOB looked up and there was Esau,
coming with his four hundred men;[w]
so he divided the children among Leah,
Rachel and the two maidservants.[x] 2He
put the maidservants and their children[y]
in front, Leah and her children next, and
Rachel and Joseph[z] in the rear. 3He himself went on ahead and bowed down to
the ground[a] seven times[b] as he approached his brother.
4But Esau[c] ran to meet Jacob and embraced him; he threw his arms around
his neck and kissed him.[d] And they
wept.[e] 5Then Esau looked up and saw
the women and children. "Who are these
with you?" he asked.
Jacob answered, "They are the children God has graciously given your servant.[f] "
6Then the maidservants and their chil-

[z]28 *Israel* means *he struggles with God.*
[a]30 *Peniel* means *face of God.* [b]31 Hebrew *Penuel,* a variant of *Peniel*

32:22–32 MIRACLE, God's Working—This manifestation of God's working made a lasting impression on Jacob. Again he was confused, afraid, and filled with guilt. He needed fresh assurance of God's presence. The story represents an intense spiritual struggle. Like the earlier dream (28:10–22) the event occurred during the night hours. Jacob recognized it as a revelation of God.

32:24–30 REVELATION, Messengers—Jacob, struggling with his life and purposes, waited alone at the border of his old home. Suddenly he was confronted with a messenger with whom he struggled for hours. Only later did He realize the messenger was more than another man. He was God. The Hebrew prepares for this surprise by using "man" only once (v 24), and there the word may mean "someone." Jacob left town as an arrogant, insensitive young man. He returned to Israel a limping leader who had come face to face with his Maker and had become a man with purpose. He would become a nation. Here we see God's ability to use a messenger to interact with and convey the divine message to His chosen servant. For the recipient, revelation was unexpected and difficult, resulting in physical injury as well as spiritual growth. To struggle with God's messenger was to struggle and see the God of the messenger. Compare 16:7–13; 18:1—19:29; 32:1–2.

32:24 PRAYER, Sincerity—Both the earnestness and the contentiousness (Hos 12:3) of Jacob's nature are seen in his struggle with the angel. God's patience is seen in that He allowed the struggle to continue. Prayer is an earnest struggle with God. Prayer is not a fight against God. It is a dialogue in which we are determined to know God's direction for life.

32:30 GOD, Holy—After Jacob wrestled with a strange man, he understood he was in the presence of God. He marvelled that he had seen the face of God and yet had lived. This was Jacob's understanding of the holiness of God. Holiness is that awesome boundary between what is human and what is divine. God, and only God, is holy. The basic meaning of the word holy was "separate." To call God holy is to say that God is separate from all else. Jacob was saying that it was a sheer miracle for a sinful man to look upon the holy God and live. See notes on Ex 3:5–6; 19:10–24; Lev 11:44–45.

33:1–10 HUMANITY, Image of God—The forgiveness and acceptance which people see in another's face may remind them of God. Forgiveness is not a natural human trait but one which is more Godlike than human. The best way to reflect God to others is to forgive them freely, expecting nothing in return.

dren[g] approached and bowed down.[h]
7Next, Leah and her children[i] came and
bowed down.[j] Last of all came Joseph
and Rachel,[k] and they too bowed down.
8Esau asked, "What do you mean by all
these droves I met?"[l]
"To find favor in your eyes, my lord,"[m]
he said.
9But Esau said, "I already have plenty,[n] my brother. Keep what you have for
yourself."
10"No, please!" said Jacob. "If I have
found favor in your eyes,[o] accept this
gift[p] from me. For to see your face is like
seeing the face of God,[q] now that you
have received me favorably.[r] 11Please accept the present[s] that was brought to
you, for God has been gracious to me[t]
and I have all I need."[u] And because Jacob insisted,[v] Esau accepted it.
12Then Esau said, "Let us be on our
way; I'll accompany you."
13But Jacob said to him, "My lord[w]
knows that the children are tender and
that I must care for the ewes and cows
that are nursing their young.[x] If they are
driven hard just one day, all the animals
will die. 14So let my lord go on ahead of
his servant, while I move along slowly at
the pace of the droves[y] before me and
that of the children, until I come to my
lord in Seir.[z]"
15Esau said, "Then let me leave some
of my men with you."
"But why do that?" Jacob asked. "Just
let me find favor in the eyes of my
lord."[a]
16So that day Esau started on his way
back to Seir.[b] 17Jacob, however, went to
Succoth,[c] where he built a place for himself and made shelters for his livestock.
That is why the place is called Succoth.[c]
18After Jacob came from Paddan
Aram,[d][d] he arrived safely at the[e] city of
Shechem[e] in Canaan and camped within
sight of the city. 19For a hundred pieces of
silver,[f] he bought from the sons of Hamor,[f] the father of Shechem,[g] the plot
of ground[h] where he pitched his tent.[i]
20There he set up an altar[j] and called it
El Elohe Israel.[g]

Chapter 34

Dinah and the Shechemites

NOW Dinah,[k] the daughter Leah had
borne to Jacob, went out to visit the
women of the land. 2When Shechem[l]
son of Hamor[m] the Hivite,[n] the ruler of
that area, saw her, he took her and violated her.[o] 3His heart was drawn to Dinah[p]
daughter of Jacob,[q] and he loved[r] the
girl and spoke tenderly[s] to her. 4And
Shechem said to his father Hamor, "Get
me this girl as my wife."[t]
5When Jacob heard that his daughter
Dinah had been defiled,[u] his sons were
in the fields with his livestock; so he kept
quiet about it until they came home.
6Then Shechem's father Hamor went
out to talk with Jacob.[v] 7Now Jacob's
sons had come in from the fields as soon
as they heard what had happened. They
were filled with grief[w] and fury,[x] because Shechem had done a disgraceful
thing in[h] Israel[y] by lying with Jacob's
daughter—a thing that should not be
done.[z]
8But Hamor said to them, "My son Shechem has his heart set on your daughter.
Please give her to him as his wife.[a] 9In-
termarry with us; give us your daughters
and take our daughters for yourselves.[b]
10You can settle among us;[c] the land is
open to you.[d] Live in it, trade[i] in it,[e]
and acquire property in it.[f]"
11Then Shechem said to Dinah's father
and brothers, "Let me find favor in your
eyes,[g] and I will give you whatever you
ask. 12Make the price for the bride[h] and
the gift I am to bring as great as you like,

33:6 [g]ver 2 [h]S ver 3
33:7 [i]ver 2 [j]S ver 3 [k]S Ge 30:24
33:8 [l]Ge 32:14-16 [m]S Ge 24:9; S 32:5
33:9 [n]ver 11; S Ge 13:6
33:10 [o]S Ge 30:27; S 32:5 [p]S Ge 32:13 [q]S Ge 16:13 [r]S Ge 32:20
33:11 [s]1Sa 25:27; 30:26 [t]Ge 30:43 [u]S ver 9 [v]Ge 19:3
33:13 [w]ver 8 [x]Isa 40:11; Jer 31:8
33:14 [y]Ex 12:38 [z]S Ge 14:6
33:15 [a]S Ge 32:5
33:16 [b]S Ge 14:6
33:17 [c]Jos 13:27; Jdg 8:5,6,8,14, 14-16,15,16; 1Ki 7:46; 2Ch 4:17; Ps 60:6; 108:7
33:18 [d]S Ge 25:20 [e]S Ge 12:6
33:19 [f]Ge 34:2; Jdg 9:28; Ac 7:16 [g]Ge 34:2; Jos 24:32 [h]Ge 34:10,16,21; 47:27; Jn 4:5 [i]S Ge 12:8
33:20 [j]S Ge 4:26; S 8:20
34:1 [k]S Ge 30:21
34:2 [l]S Ge 33:19 [m]S Ge 33:19 [n]S Ge 10:17 [o]Dt 21:14; 2Sa 13:14
34:3 [p]ver 26 [q]ver 19 [r]S Ge 24:67 [s]Ge 50:21; Isa 14:1; 40:2
34:4 [t]S Ge 21:21
34:5 [u]ver 2,13,27; Ge 35:22; 49:4; Dt 27:20; 33:6; 1Ch 5:1
34:6 [v]Jdg 14:2-5
34:7 [w]1Co 5:2 [x]Ge 39:19; 49:6-7; 2Sa 12:5; 13:21; Est 7:7; Pr 6:34 [y]Dt 22:21; Jdg 19:23; 20:6; 2Sa 13:12; Jer 29:23 [z]S Ge 20:9
34:8 [a]S Ge 21:21; Dt 21:11
34:9 [b]ver 16,21; Dt 7:3; Jos 23:12
34:10 [c]ver 23; Ge 46:34; 47:6,27 [d]S Ge 13:9 [e]Ge 42:34 [f]S Ge 33:19
34:11 [g]S Ge 32:5
34:12 [h]Ex 22:16; Dt 22:29; 1Sa 18:25

[c]*17 Succoth* means *shelters.* [d]*18* That is, Northwest Mesopotamia [e]*18* Or *arrived at Shalem, a*
[f]*19* Hebrew *hundred kesitahs*; a kesitah was a unit of money of unknown weight and value.
[g]*20 El Elohe Israel* can mean *God, the God of Israel* or *mighty is the God of Israel.* [h]*7* Or *against*
[i]*10* Or *move about freely*; also in verse 21

33:18—34:31 HISTORY, Narrative—History can be written with little direct reference to God. It can describe human emotions—love, jealousy, revenge, grief, anger—roused by emotion-loaded words: defile (Hebrew *timme'*), 34:5,13,27; Lev 5:3; 11:24—12:5; 15:4-32; Nu 19:7-22; disgraceful (Hebrew *nebalah*), Ge 34:7; Dt 22:21; Jos 7:15; Jdg 19:23-24; 20:6,10; disgrace (Hebrew *cherpah*), Ge 34:14; 1 Sa 11:2. Biblical history is concerned with the reputation and feelings of God's people and readily shows the scheming, pragmatic side of life. With this people God works in history to secure important worship places like Shechem (Jdg 9; Jos 20:7; 24:1-32; Ps 60:6; Hos 6:9). See notes on Ge 13:1-13; 29:31—30:24.

33:20 PRAYER, Worship—The altar's name proclaims God as the God of Israel. Compare 32:28. See note on 12:7-8.

34:1-31 CHRISTIAN ETHICS, War and Peace—Marriage and sexual relationships may lead to conflicts which erupt into war. Individual agreements should lead to peace, but human greed and vengeance lead to violation of agreements and war. Our goals should not be to satisfy our greed or to gain absolute justice for ourselves. Our goal should be to reach satisfactory agreements of peace and to abide by them. See note on 13:7-12.

34:1-31 FAMILY, Sexual Sin—Rape, the forced, sexual violation of a woman, is one of the most graphic examples of the misuse of God's gift of sexuality. The consequences of Shechem's violation of Dinah brought death and destruction on the men of the city even though Shechem wanted to marry Dinah after his sexual experience with her. Dinah's brothers justified deceit, plundering, and murder because of what had happened to her. The sexual sin created destructive effects for many people unrelated to the actual sexual crime. See 2 Sa 13:1-21. In all ages rape is "a thing that should not be done."

and I'll pay whatever you ask me. Only
give me the girl as my wife."
13Because their sister Dinah had been
defiled,[i] Jacob's sons replied deceitfully[j]
as they spoke to Shechem and his father
Hamor. 14They said to them, "We can't
do such a thing; we can't give our sister
to a man who is not circumcised.[k] That
would be a disgrace to us. 15We will give
our consent to you on one condition[l]
only: that you become like us by circum-
cising all your males.[m] 16Then we will
give you our daughters and take your
daughters for ourselves.[n] We'll settle
among you and become one people with
you.[o] 17But if you will not agree to be
circumcised, we'll take our sister[j] and
go."
18Their proposal seemed good to Hamor and his son Shechem. 19The young
man, who was the most honored[p] of all
his father's household, lost no time in doing what they said, because he was delighted with Jacob's daughter.[q] 20So Hamor and his son Shechem went to the
gate of their city[r] to speak to their fellow
townsmen. 21"These men are friendly toward us," they said. "Let them live in our
land and trade in it;[s] the land has plenty
of room for them. We can marry their
daughters and they can marry ours.[t]
22But the men will consent to live with us
as one people only on the condition that
our males be circumcised,[u] as they themselves are. 23Won't their livestock, their
property and all their other animals become ours?[v] So let us give our consent to
them, and they will settle among us.[w]"
24All the men who went out of the city
gate[x] agreed with Hamor and his son
Shechem, and every male in the city was
circumcised.
25Three days later, while all of them
were still in pain,[y] two of Jacob's sons,
Simeon[z] and Levi,[a] Dinah's brothers,
took their swords[b] and attacked the unsuspecting city,[c] killing every male.[d]
26They put Hamor and his son Shechem
to the sword[e] and took Dinah[f] from Shechem's house and left. 27The sons of Jacob came upon the dead bodies and looted the city[g] where[k] their sister had been
defiled.[h] 28They seized their flocks and
herds and donkeys[i] and everything else
of theirs in the city and out in the fields.[j]
29They carried off all their wealth and all
their women and children,[k] taking as
plunder[l] everything in the houses.[m]
30Then Jacob said to Simeon and Levi,
"You have brought trouble[n] on me by
making me a stench[o] to the Canaanites
and Perizzites, the people living in this
land.[p] We are few in number,[q] and if
they join forces against me and attack me,
I and my household will be destroyed."
31But they replied, "Should he have
treated our sister like a prostitute?[r]"

Chapter 35

Jacob Returns to Bethel

THEN God said to Jacob, "Go up to
Bethel[s] and settle there, and build
an altar[t] there to God,[u] who appeared to
you[v] when you were fleeing from your
brother Esau."[w]
2So Jacob said to his household[x] and to
all who were with him, "Get rid of the
foreign gods[y] you have with you, and purify yourselves and change your clothes.[z]
3Then come, let us go up to Bethel,
where I will build an altar to God,[a] who
answered me in the day of my distress[b]
and who has been with me wherever I
have gone.[c]" 4So they gave Jacob all the
foreign gods they had and the rings in
their ears,[d] and Jacob buried them under
the oak[e] at Shechem.[f] 5Then they set
out, and the terror of God[g] fell upon the
towns all around them so that no one pursued them.[h]
6Jacob and all the people with him
came to Luz[i] (that is, Bethel) in the land
of Canaan.[j] 7There he built an altar,[k]
and he called the place El Bethel,[l] because it was there that God revealed

34:13 [i]S ver 5 [j]S Ge 27:36 **34:14** [k]Ge 17:14; Jdg 14:3; 1Sa 31:4; Isa 52:1 **34:15** [l]1Sa 11:2 [m]ver 22; Ex 12:48 **34:16** [n]S ver 9 [o]S Ge 33:19 **34:19** [p]Ge 49:3; 1Ch 11:21 [q]ver 3 **34:20** [r]S Ge 18:1 **34:21** [s]S Ge 33:19 [t]S ver 9 **34:22** [u]S ver 15 **34:23** [v]ver 28; S Ge 12:16 [w]S ver 10 **34:24** [x]S Ge 18:1 **34:25** [y]Jos 5:8 [z]S Ge 29:33 [a]S Ge 29:34 [b]Ge 49:5; Mal 2:16 [c]Jdg 18:7,10,27; Eze 38:11 [d]Ge 49:7 **34:26** [e]S ver 7; Ge 48:22 [f]ver 3 **34:27** [g]2Ki 21:14 [h]S ver 5 **34:28** [i]Ge 43:18 [j]S ver 23 **34:29** [k]S Ge 31:26 [l]Nu 14:3; 31:9,53; Dt 2:35; Jos 7:21 [m]2Ki 8:12; Isa 13:16; La 5:11; Am 1:13; Zec 14:2 **34:30** [n]Ge 43:6; Ex 5:23; Nu 11:11 [o]Ex 5:21; 6:9; 1Sa 13:4; 27:12; 2Sa 10:6; 1Ch 19:6 [p]S Ge 13:7 [q]Ge 35:26; 46:27; Ex 1:5; Dt 10:22; 26:5; 1Ch 16:19; Ps 105:12 **34:31** [r]ver 2 **35:1** [s]S Ge 12:8 [t]S Ge 4:26; 8:20 [u]ver 3 [v]S Ge 12:7 [w]ver 7; Ge 27:43 **35:2** [x]Ge 18:19; Jos 24:15 [y]S Ge 31:19; S Jos 24:14 [z]Ex 19:10,14; Nu 8:7,21; 19:19 **35:3** [a]ver 1 [b]S Ge 32:7; S Jdg 2:15 [c]S Ge 26:3 **35:4** [d]S Ge 24:22; Ex 32:3; 35:22; Jdg 8:24; Pr 25:12 [e]ver 8 [f]S Ge 12:6 **35:5** [g]Ex 15:16; 23:27; Dt 2:25; Jos 2:9; 1Sa 7:10; 13:7; 14:15; 2Ch 14:14; 17:10; 20:29; Ps 9:20; Isa 19:17; Zec 14:13 [h]Ps 105:14

35:6 [i]S Ge 28:19 [j]S Ge 10:19 **35:7** [k]S Ge 8:20 [l]Ge 28:19

[j]17 Hebrew *daughter* [k]27 Or *because* [l]7 *El Bethel* means *God of Bethel.*

35:1 HUMANITY, Spiritual Nature—Developing our spiritual nature requires worship and obedience.

35:2 GOD, One God—Jacob commanded his household to get rid of their foreign gods—their false gods. He recognized that all other gods are crude human attempts to counterfeit the one, true God. Humans have fashioned many symbols for God and have developed many different ideas about gods. God is known only where He makes Himself known. Jacob was trying to purify the religious practices of his household by putting away all other ideas and images of God. Getting them out of the house was one thing. Getting them out of the minds and hearts of the Israelites was quite another! Modern gods may be more subtle, but they are *just as tempting—and just as false*: *sensualism, money, pleasure, drugs, sports,* etc. Many of us serve them wholeheartedly and end up just as empty as those who worshiped a block of stone or wood. There is only one God. He has no competitors, not even of lesser rank.

35:3 GOD, Faithfulness—Jacob called his family to join him in worship of the one true God at Bethel, where Jacob had encountered God before. God had been faithful to Jacob wherever he had gone. God heard and blessed him everywhere he went. Later Israelites came to think of God as localized in the tabernacle or in the Temple. When they were carried into captivity, they felt that they were alone, away from God, and could not worship Him. See Ps 137:1–4. This was still a problem in the day of Jesus. See Jn 4:19–24.

35:7 PRAYER, Thanksgiving—See note on 12:7–8. Prayer and symbolism are parts of worship expressing gratitude for past history with God.

himself to him[m] when he was fleeing from
his brother.[n]
8Now Deborah, Rebekah's nurse,[o]
died and was buried under the oak[p] below Bethel.[q] So it was named Allon
Bacuth.[m]
9After Jacob returned from Paddan
Aram,[n] [r] God appeared to him again and
blessed him.[s] 10God said to him, "Your
name is Jacob,[o] but you will no longer be
called Jacob; your name will be Israel.[p]"[t] So he named him Israel.
11And God said to him, "I am God Almighty[q]; [u] be fruitful and increase in
number.[v] A nation[w] and a community of
nations will come from you, and kings
will come from your body.[x] 12The land I
gave to Abraham and Isaac I also give to
you, and I will give this land to your descendants after you.[y]"[z] 13Then God
went up from him[a] at the place where he
had talked with him.
14Jacob set up a stone pillar[b] at the
place where God had talked with him,
and he poured out a drink offering[c] on it;
he also poured oil on it.[d] 15Jacob called
the place where God had talked with him
Bethel.[r] [e]

The Deaths of Rachel and Isaac

35:23–26pp — 1Ch 2:1–2

16Then they moved on from Bethel.
While they were still some distance from
Ephrath,[f] Rachel[g] began to give birth
and had great difficulty. 17And as she was
having great difficulty in childbirth, the
midwife[h] said to her, "Don't be afraid,
for you have another son."[i] 18As she
breathed her last—for she was dying—
she named her son Ben-Oni.[s] [j] But his
father named him Benjamin.[t] [k]
19So Rachel died and was buried on the
way to Ephrath[l] (that is, Bethlehem[m]).
20Over her tomb Jacob set up a pillar, and
to this day[n] that pillar marks Rachel's
tomb.[o]
21Israel moved on again and pitched his
tent beyond Migdal Eder.[p] 22While Israel
was living in that region, Reuben went in
and slept with his father's concubine[q]
Bilhah,[r] and Israel heard of it.

Jacob had twelve sons:
23The sons of Leah:[s]
Reuben the firstborn[t] of Jacob,
Simeon, Levi, Judah,[u] Issachar
and Zebulun.[v]
24The sons of Rachel:
Joseph[w] and Benjamin.[x]
25The sons of Rachel's maidservant Bilhah:[y]
Dan and Naphtali.[z]
26The sons of Leah's maidservant Zilpah:[a]
Gad[b] and Asher.[c]
These were the sons of Jacob,[d] who
were born to him in Paddan Aram.[e]

27Jacob came home to his father Isaac[f]
in Mamre,[g] near Kiriath Arba[h] (that is,
Hebron),[i] where Abraham and Isaac had
stayed.[j] 28Isaac lived a hundred and
eighty years.[k] 29Then he breathed his
last and died and was gathered to his people,[l] old and full of years.[m] And his sons
Esau and Jacob buried him.[n]

Chapter 36

Esau's Descendants

36:10–14pp — 1Ch 1:35–37
36:20–28pp — 1Ch 1:38–42

THIS is the account[o] of Esau (that is,
Edom).[p]
2Esau took his wives from the
women of Canaan:[q] Adah daughter
of Elon the Hittite,[r] and Oholibamah[s] daughter of Anah[t] and granddaughter of Zibeon the Hivite[u]—
3also Basemath[v] daughter of Ishmael
and sister of Nebaioth.[w]
4Adah bore Eliphaz to Esau, Basemath bore Reuel,[x] 5and Oholibamah
bore Jeush, Jalam and Korah.[y] These
were the sons of Esau, who were
born to him in Canaan.
6Esau took his wives and sons and
daughters and all the members of his
household, as well as his livestock
and all his other animals and all the
goods he had acquired in Canaan,[z]
and moved to a land some distance

35:7 [m]S Ge 28:13 [n]S ver 1 **35:8** [o]Ge 24:59 [p]ver 4 [q]S Ge 12:8; 1Sa 10:3 **35:9** [r]S Ge 25:20 [s]S Ge 28:13; S 32:29 **35:10** [t]S Ge 17:5 **35:11** [u]S Ge 17:1 [v]S Ge 12:2 [w]S Ge 12:2 [x]S Ge 17:6 **35:12** [y]S Ge 28:13 [z]S Ge 12:7; S 15:7 **35:13** [a]S Ge 17:22 **35:14** [b]S Ge 28:22 [c]Ex 29:40; Lev 23:13; Nu 6:15, 17; 15:5; 28:7,14; 2Sa 23:16; 2Ch 29:35 [d]S Ge 28:18 **35:15** [e]S Ge 12:8 **35:16** [f]ver 19; Ge 48:7; Ru 1:2; 4:11; 1Sa 17:12; Mic 5:2 [g]S Ge 29:6 **35:17** [h]Ge 38:28; Ex 1:15 [i]S Ge 30:24 **35:18** [j]1Sa 4:21; 14:3 [k]ver 24; Ge 42:4; 43:16,29; 45:12,14; 49:27; Nu 1:36; Dt 33:12 **35:19** [l]S ver 16 [m]Ge 48:7; Jos 19:15; Jdg 12:8; 17:7; 19:1,18; Ru 1:1,19; 1Sa 17:12; Mic 5:2 **35:20** [n]Jos 4:9; 7:26; 8:28; 10:27; 1Sa 6:18 [o]1Sa 10:2 **35:21** [p]Jos 15:21 **35:22** [q]S Ge 22:24 [r]S Ge 29:29; S 34:5; S Lev 18:8 **35:23** [s]S Ge 29:16 [t]Ge 43:33; 46:8 [u]S Ge 29:35 [v]S Ge 30:20 **35:24** [w]S Ge 30:24 [x]S ver 18 **35:25** [y]Ge 37:2 [z]S Ge 30:8 **35:26** [a]Ge 37:2 [b]S Ge 30:11 [c]S Ge 30:13 [d]S Ge 34:30; 46:8; Ex 1:1-4 [e]S Ge 25:20 **35:27** [f]Ge 31:18 [g]S Ge 13:18 [h]Ge 23:2; Jos 15:54; Jdg 1:10; Ne 11:25 [i]S Ge 13:18 [j]S Ge 17:8 **35:28** [k]S Ge 25:7, 20 **35:29** [l]S Ge 25:8 [m]S Ge 15:15 [n]S Ge 23:20; S 25:9 **36:1** [o]S Ge 2:4 [p]S Ge 25:30 **36:2** [q]Ge 28:8-9 [r]Ge 26:34 [s]ver 14, 18 [t]ver 25; 1Ch 1:40 [u]ver 24; S Ge 10:17; 1Ch 1:40 **36:3** [v]ver 4,10,13, 17 [w]S Ge 25:13 **36:4** [x]S ver 3; 1Ch 1:35 **36:5** [y]ver 14,18; 1Ch 1:35 **36:6** [z]Ge 12:5

[m]*8 Allon Bacuth* means *oak of weeping.* [n]*9* That is, Northwest Mesopotamia; also in verse 26
[o]*10 Jacob* means *he grasps the heel* (figuratively, *he deceives*). [p]*10 Israel* means *he struggles with God.*
[q]*11* Hebrew *El-Shaddai* [r]*15 Bethel* means *house of God.* [s]*18 Ben-Oni* means *son of my trouble.*
[t]*18 Benjamin* means *son of my right hand.*

35:9–12 ELECTION, God's Promise—When Jacob obeyed God and returned to Bethel, God renewed His election promise, assuring Jacob that He would grant him the land, protection, and prosperity that had been promised to his fathers. Blessing in election included a "community of nations."
35:29 HUMANITY, Burial—A normal part of family responsibilities at the time of the death of a loved one is providing the proper burial. This final service is not only an obligation but also an aid to the grief process.

36:1,9 HISTORY, Universal—See note on 2:4. The structure of Genesis according to "accounts" or generations begins with heaven and earth (2:4), includes the patriarchs (11:27; 25:19; 37:2), and extends to the related peoples of Ishmael (25:12) and Esau. For later Israel the inclusion of Esau was an important lesson, for his descendants the Edomites became Israel's hated enemies (Ps 137:7). Biblical history concentrates on the chosen people but always with a universal perspective.

from his brother Jacob.[a] 7Their possessions were too great for them to
remain together; the land where they
were staying could not support them
both because of their livestock.[b] 8So
Esau[c] (that is, Edom)[d] settled in the
hill country of Seir.[e]

9This is the account[f] of Esau the father
of the Edomites[g] in the hill country of
Seir.

10These are the names of Esau's sons:
Eliphaz, the son of Esau's wife
Adah, and Reuel, the son of Esau's
wife Basemath.[h]
11The sons of Eliphaz:[i]
Teman,[j] Omar, Zepho, Gatam
and Kenaz.[k]
12Esau's son Eliphaz also had a concubine[l] named Timna, who bore
him Amalek.[m] These were grandsons of Esau's wife Adah.[n]
13The sons of Reuel:
Nahath, Zerah, Shammah and
Mizzah. These were grandsons of
Esau's wife Basemath.[o]
14The sons of Esau's wife Oholibamah[p] daughter of Anah and granddaughter of Zibeon, whom she bore
to Esau:
Jeush, Jalam and Korah.[q]
15These were the chiefs[r] among Esau's
descendants:
The sons of Eliphaz the firstborn of
Esau:
Chiefs Teman,[s] Omar, Zepho,
Kenaz,[t] 16Korah,[u] Gatam and
Amalek. These were the chiefs
descended from Eliphaz[u] in
Edom;[v] they were grandsons of
Adah.[w]
17The sons of Esau's son Reuel:[x]
Chiefs Nahath, Zerah, Shammah
and Mizzah. These were the
chiefs descended from Reuel in
Edom; they were grandsons of
Esau's wife Basemath.[y]
18The sons of Esau's wife Oholiba-
mah:[z]
Chiefs Jeush, Jalam and Korah.[a]
These were the chiefs descended
from Esau's wife Oholibamah
daughter of Anah.
19These were the sons of Esau[b] (that
is, Edom),[c] and these were their chiefs.[d]

20These were the sons of Seir the Horite,[e] who were living in the region:
Lotan, Shobal, Zibeon, Anah,[f]
21Dishon, Ezer and Dishan. These
sons of Seir in Edom were Horite
chiefs.[g]
22The sons of Lotan:

36:6 [a]Ge 27:39
36:7 [b]S Ge 13:6
36:8 [c]Dt 2:4 [d]S Ge 25:30 [e]S Ge 14:6
36:9 [f]S Ge 2:4 [g]ver 1,43
36:10 [h]S ver 3
36:11 [i]ver 15-16; 1Ch 1:45; Job 2:11; 4:1 [j]Jer 49:7,20; Eze 25:13; Am 1:12; Ob 1:9; Hab 3:3 [k]ver 15
36:12 [l]S Ge 22:24 [m]Ex 17:8,16; Nu 24:20; Dt 25:17,19; 1Sa 15:2; 27:8 [n]ver 16
36:13 [o]S ver 3
36:14 [p]S ver 2 [q]S ver 5
36:15 [r]ver 19,40; Ex 15:15 [s]Job 2:11; Jer 49:7; Eze 25:13; Am 1:12; Hab 3:3 [t]S ver 11
36:16 [u]S ver 11 [v]Ge 32:3; Ex 15:15; Nu 20:14; 33:37 [w]ver 12
36:17 [x]1Ch 1:37 [y]S ver 3
36:18 [z]S ver 2 [a]S ver 5
36:19 [b]1Ch 1:35 [c]S Ge 25:30 [d]S ver 15
36:20 [e]S Ge 14:6 [f]ver 29
36:21 [g]ver 30
36:24 [h]S ver 2 [i]Jos 15:19 [j]Job 1:14
36:25 [k]S ver 2 [l]S ver 2
36:29 [m]ver 20
36:30 [n]ver 21
36:31 [o]S Ge 17:6
36:33 [p]Isa 34:6; 63:1; Jer 49:13,22
36:34 [q]Jer 49:7; Eze 25:13; Ob 1:9
36:35 [r]S Ge 25:2 [s]S Ge 19:37; Nu 21:11; 22:1; Dt 1:5; Jdg 3:30; Ru 1:1,6
36:37 [t]Ge 26:22

Hori and Homam.[v] Timna was
Lotan's sister.
23The sons of Shobal:
Alvan, Manahath, Ebal, Shepho
and Onam.
24The sons of Zibeon:[h]
Aiah and Anah. This is the Anah
who discovered the hot
springs[w][i] in the desert while he
was grazing the donkeys[j] of his
father Zibeon.
25The children of Anah:[k]
Dishon and Oholibamah[l] daughter of Anah.
26The sons of Dishon[x]:
Hemdan, Eshban, Ithran and Keran.
27The sons of Ezer:
Bilhan, Zaavan and Akan.
28The sons of Dishan:
Uz and Aran.
29These were the Horite chiefs:
Lotan, Shobal, Zibeon, Anah,[m]
30Dishon, Ezer and Dishan. These
were the Horite chiefs,[n] according to their divisions, in the land
of Seir.

The Rulers of Edom

36:31–43pp — 1Ch 1:43–54

31These were the kings who reigned in
Edom before any Israelite king[o]
reigned[y]:
32Bela son of Beor became king of
Edom. His city was named Dinhabah.
33When Bela died, Jobab son of Zerah
from Bozrah[p] succeeded him as
king.
34When Jobab died, Husham from the
land of the Temanites[q] succeeded
him as king.
35When Husham died, Hadad son of
Bedad, who defeated Midian[r] in
the country of Moab,[s] succeeded
him as king. His city was named
Avith.
36When Hadad died, Samlah from
Masrekah succeeded him as king.
37When Samlah died, Shaul from Rehoboth[t] on the river[z] succeeded
him as king.
38When Shaul died, Baal-Hanan son of
Acbor succeeded him as king.
39When Baal-Hanan son of Acbor died,

[u] *16* Masoretic Text; Samaritan Pentateuch (see also Gen. 36:11 and 1 Chron. 1:36) does not have *Korah.*
[v] *22* Hebrew *Hemam,* a variant of *Homam* (see 1 Chron. 1:39) [w] *24* Vulgate; Syriac *discovered water;* the meaning of the Hebrew for this word is uncertain. [x] *26* Hebrew *Dishan,* a variant of *Dishon*
[y] *31* Or *before an Israelite king reigned over them*
[z] *37* Possibly the Euphrates

Hadad[a] succeeded him as king.
His city was named Pau, and his
wife's name was Mehetabel
daughter of Matred, the daughter
of Me-Zahab.

40These were the chiefs[u] descended
from Esau, by name, according to their
clans and regions:

Timna, Alvah, Jetheth, 41Oholiba-
mah, Elah, Pinon, 42Kenaz, Teman, Mibzar, 43Magdiel and Iram.
These were the chiefs of Edom,
according to their settlements in
the land they occupied.

This was Esau the father of the
Edomites.[v]

Chapter 37

Joseph's Dreams

JACOB lived in the land where his father
had stayed,[w] the land of Canaan.[x]

2This is the account[y] of Jacob.

Joseph,[z] a young man of seventeen,[a]
was tending the flocks[b] with his brothers, the sons of Bilhah[c] and the sons of
Zilpah,[d] his father's wives, and he
brought their father a bad report[e] about
them.

3Now Israel[f] loved Joseph more than
any of his other sons,[g] because he had
been born to him in his old age;[h] and he
made a richly ornamented[b] robe[i] for
him.[j] 4When his brothers saw that their
father loved him more than any of them,
they hated him[k] and could not speak a
kind word to him.

5Joseph had a dream,[l] and when he
told it to his brothers,[m] they hated him all
the more.[n] 6He said to them, "Listen to
this dream I had: 7We were binding
sheaves[o] of grain out in the field when
suddenly my sheaf rose and stood upright, while your sheaves gathered
around mine and bowed down to it."[p]

8His brothers said to him, "Do you intend to reign over us? Will you actually
rule us?"[q] And they hated him all the
more[r] because of his dream and what he
had said.

9Then he had another dream,[s] and he
told it to his brothers. "Listen," he said,
"I had another dream, and this time the
sun and moon and eleven stars[t] were
bowing down to me."[u]

10When he told his father as well as his
brothers,[v] his father rebuked[w] him and
said, "What is this dream you had? Will
your mother and I and your brothers actually come and bow down to the ground
before you?"[x] 11His brothers were jealous of him,[y] but his father kept the matter in mind.[z]

Joseph Sold by His Brothers

12Now his brothers had gone to graze
their father's flocks near Shechem,[a]
13and Israel[b] said to Joseph, "As you
know, your brothers are grazing the
flocks near Shechem.[c] Come, I am going
to send you to them."

"Very well," he replied.

14So he said to him, "Go and see if all
is well with your brothers[d] and with the
flocks, and bring word back to me." Then
he sent him off from the Valley of Hebron.[e]

When Joseph arrived at Shechem, 15a
man found him wandering around in the
fields and asked him, "What are you looking for?"

16He replied, "I'm looking for my
brothers. Can you tell me where they are
grazing their flocks?"

17"They have moved on from here,"
the man answered. "I heard them say,
'Let's go to Dothan.[f]'"

So Joseph went after his brothers and
found them near Dothan. 18But they saw
him in the distance, and before he
reached them, they plotted to kill him.[g]

19"Here comes that dreamer!"[h] they
said to each other. 20"Come now, let's
kill him and throw him into one of these
cisterns[i] and say that a ferocious animal[j] devoured him.[k] Then we'll see
what comes of his dreams."[l]

21When Reuben[m] heard this, he tried
to rescue him from their hands. "Let's

36:40 [u]S ver 15
36:43 [v]S ver 9
37:1 [w]S Ge 17:8 [x]S Ge 10:19
37:2 [y]S Ge 2:4 [z]S Ge 30:24 [a]Ge 41:46; 2Sa 5:4 [b]Ge 46:32; 1Sa 16:11; 17:15; Ps 78:71; Am 7:15 [c]Ge 35:25 [d]Ge 35:26 [e]1Sa 2:24
37:3 [f]S Ge 17:5 [g]S Ge 25:28 [h]Ge 43:27; 44:20 [i]ver 23,31,32; 2Sa 13:18-19 [j]Ge 43:34; 45:22; 1Sa 1:4-5; Est 2:9
37:4 [k]S ver 24; S Ge 27:41; Ac 7:9
37:5 [l]S Ge 20:3; S 28:12 [m]ver 10 [n]ver 8
37:7 [o]Ru 2:7,15 [p]ver 9,10; Ge 27:29; 42:6,9; 43:26,28; 44:14; 50:18; 2Sa 1:2; 9:6
37:8 [q]Ge 41:44; 42:10; 44:16,18; 48:22; 49:26; Dt 33:16 [r]ver 5
37:9 [s]S ver 7; Ge 28:12 [t]Rev 12:1 [u]Dt 4:19; 17:3
37:10 [v]ver 5 [w]Ru 2:16; Ps 9:5; 68:30; 106:9; 119:21; Isa 17:13; 54:9; Zec 3:2 [x]S ver 7; S Ge 9:25; S 33:3
37:11 [y]Ge 26:14; Ac 7:9 [z]Lk 2:19,51
37:12 [a]S Ge 12:6
37:13 [b]S Ge 17:5 [c]Ge 33:19
37:14 [d]1Sa 17:18 [e]S Ge 13:18
37:17 [f]2Ki 6:13
37:18 [g]1Sa 19:1; 2Ch 24:21; Ps 31:13,20; 37:12, 32; S Mt 12:14; Mk 14:1; Ac 23:12
37:19 [h]S Ge 28:12
37:20 [i]ver 22; Jer 38:6,9 [j]ver 33; Lev 26:6,22; Dt 32:24; 2Ki 17:25; Eze 34:25 [k]ver 31-33; S Ge 4:10 [l]Ge 50:20
37:21 [m]S Ge 29:32

[a]39 Many manuscripts of the Masoretic Text, Samaritan Pentateuch and Syriac (see also 1 Chron. 1:50); most manuscripts of the Masoretic Text *Hadar*
[b]3 The meaning of the Hebrew for *richly ornamented* is uncertain; also in verses 23 and 32.

37:1–17 ELECTION, God's Promise—Joseph incurred the wrath of his brothers when he shared his dreams of his leadership above them. The dreams revealed God's election of Joseph to save his family and famine-stricken nations from extinction. God reveals His election promise and purposes to His elect people in different ways.

37:2–11 HUMANITY, Childhood and Youth—Youthful dreams are a normal part of the process of growing up. Some dreams (like those of Joseph) may be revelatory. Unfortunately, in Joseph's case, the recounting of his dreams flamed the resentment already present due to parental partiality. Only the passage of time can determine the true nature of adolescent dreams.

37:2 HISTORY, Linear—See note on 2:4. Jacob is the climactic figure in patriarchal history, for he gave his name Israel to the nation. His "account" deals with his sons much more than with Jacob, showing the family-centered content of Israel's early history.

37:5–11 MIRACLE, Nature—Joseph's entire life bears witness to God's providential care. His marvelous dreams and his ability to interpret dreams (41:1–36) mark him as God's revealer. Yet few of his wise actions move beyond the realm of nature. God used him to accomplish His purpose.

not take his life," he said.[n] 22"Don't
shed any blood. Throw him into this cistern[o] here in the desert, but don't lay a
hand on him." Reuben said this to rescue
him from them and take him back to his
father.[p]
23So when Joseph came to his brothers,
they stripped him of his robe—the richly
ornamented robe[q] he was wearing—
24and they took him and threw him into
the cistern.[r] Now the cistern was empty;
there was no water in it.
25As they sat down to eat their meal,
they looked up and saw a caravan of Ishmaelites[s] coming from Gilead.[t] Their
camels were loaded with spices, balm[u]
and myrrh,[v] and they were on their way
to take them down to Egypt.[w]
26Judah[x] said to his brothers, "What
will we gain if we kill our brother and
cover up his blood?[y] 27Come, let's sell
him to the Ishmaelites and not lay our
hands on him; after all, he is our brother,[z] our own flesh and blood.[a]" His
brothers agreed.
28So when the Midianite[b] merchants
came by, his brothers pulled Joseph up
out of the cistern[c] and sold[d] him for
twenty shekels[c] of silver[e] to the Ishmaelites,[f] who took him to Egypt.[g]
29When Reuben returned to the cistern
and saw that Joseph was not there, he
tore his clothes.[h] 30He went back to his
brothers and said, "The boy isn't there!
Where can I turn now?"[i]
31Then they got Joseph's robe,[j] slaughtered a goat and dipped the robe in the
blood.[k] 32They took the ornamented
robe[l] back to their father and said, "We
found this. Examine it to see whether it is
your son's robe."
33He recognized it and said, "It is my
son's robe! Some ferocious animal[m] has
devoured him. Joseph has surely been
torn to pieces."[n]
34Then Jacob tore his clothes,[o] put on
sackcloth[p] and mourned for his son
many days.[q] 35All his sons and daughters
came to comfort him,[r] but he refused to
be comforted.[s] "No," he said, "in
mourning will I go down to the grave[d] [t]
to my son.[u]" So his father wept for him.
36Meanwhile, the Midianites[e] [v] sold
Joseph[w] in Egypt to Potiphar, one of Pharaoh's officials, the captain of the guard.[x]

Chapter 38

Judah and Tamar

At that time, Judah[y] left his brothers
and went down to stay with a man of
Adullam[z] named Hirah.[a] 2There Judah
met the daughter of a Canaanite man
named Shua.[b] He married her and lay
with her; 3she became pregnant and gave
birth to a son, who was named Er.[c] 4She
conceived again and gave birth to a son
and named him Onan.[d] 5She gave birth
to still another son and named him Shelah.[e] It was at Kezib that she gave birth
to him.
6Judah got a wife for Er, his firstborn,
and her name was Tamar.[f] 7But Er, Judah's firstborn, was wicked in the LORD's
sight;[g] so the LORD put him to death.[h]
8Then Judah said to Onan, "Lie with
your brother's wife and fulfill your duty to
her as a brother-in-law to produce offspring for your brother."[i] 9But Onan
knew that the offspring would not be his;
so whenever he lay with his brother's
wife, he spilled his semen on the ground
to keep from producing offspring for his
brother. 10What he did was wicked in the
LORD's sight; so he put him to death
also.[j]
11Judah then said to his daughter-in-

37:21 [n]Ge 42:22 **37:22** [o]S ver 20 [p]ver 29-30 **37:23** [q]ver 3 **37:24** [r]S ver 4; Ge 49:23; Jer 38:6; 41:7; Eze 22:27 **37:25** [s]S Ge 16:11 [t]S Ge 31:21; S SS 4:1 [u]Jer 8:22; 22:6; 46:11 [v]Ge 43:11; Ex 30:23; Ps 45:8; Pr 7:17; SS 1:13; Mt 2:11 [w]ver 28; Ge 39:1; Ps 105:17 **37:26** [x]S Ge 29:35 [y]S Ge 4:10 **37:27** [z]Ge 42:21 [a]S Ge 29:14 **37:28** [b]S Ge 25:2 [c]Jer 38:13 [d]Ex 21:16 [e]Lev 27:5; Mt 26:15 [f]S Ge 16:11 [g]ver 36; Ge 39:1; 45:4-5; Ps 105:17; Jer 12:6; Ac 7:9 **37:29** [h]ver 34; Ge 44:13; Nu 14:6; Jos 7:6; 2Sa 1:11; 2Ki 2:12; 5:7; 11:14; 22:11; Job 1:20; 2:12; Isa 36:22; 37:1; Jer 36:24; 41:5; Joel 2:13 **37:30** [i]ver 22 **37:31** [j]S ver 3 [k]Rev 19:13 **37:32** [l]S ver 3 **37:33** [m]S ver 20 [n]Ge 42:13,38; 44:20,28 **37:34** [o]S ver 29 [p]2Sa 3:31; 1Ki 20:31; 21:27; 2Ki 6:30; 19:1,2; Job 16:15; Ps 69:11; Isa 3:24; 15:3; 22:12; 32:11; 37:1; Jer 48:37; 49:3; Joel 1:13 [q]Ge 50:3,10,11; Nu 20:29; Dt 34:8 **37:35** [r]Job 2:11; 15:11; 16:5; 42:11 [s]2Sa 12:17; Ps 77:2; Jer 31:15 [t]Ge 42:38; 44:22, 29,31 [u]2Sa 12:23 **37:36** [v]S Ge 25:2 [w]S ver 28 [x]Ge 39:1; 40:3; 41:10,12; 1Sa 22:14 **38:1** [y]S Ge 29:35 [z]Jos 12:15; 15:35; 1Sa 22:1; 2Sa 23:13; 2Ch 11:7 [a]ver 12, 20

38:2 [b]ver 12; 1Ch 2:3 **38:3** [c]ver 6; Ge 46:12; Nu 26:19 **38:4** [d]ver 8,9; Ge 46:12; Nu 26:19 **38:5** [e]Nu 26:20 **38:6** [f]ver 11,13 **38:7** [g]S Ge 6:5 [h]ver 10; Ge 46:12; Lev 10:1-2; 1Ch 2:3 **38:8** [i]Dt 25:5-6; Ru 4:5; Mt 22:24-28 **38:10** [j]S ver 7; Dt 25:7-10

[c]*28* That is, about 8 ounces (about 0.2 kilogram)
[d]*35* Hebrew *Sheol* [e]*36* Samaritan Pentateuch, Septuagint, Vulgate and Syriac (see also verse 28); Masoretic Text *Medanites*

37:34–35 HUMANITY, Attitudes to Death—The deep inner grief of a person may be shown outwardly. The torn garment and the wearing of sackcloth were common signs of grief in Old Testament times. Grief may be so intense as almost to bring death itself to the mourner. Further, death will eventually unite loved ones in the common experience of the grave. The New Testament offers genuine hope to those grieving. See 1 Co 15:54–57.

37:35 LAST THINGS, Intermediate State—See note on Isa 14:9.

38:1–10 FAMILY, Disobedience—By Hebrew law, if a man died and left no children, his brother was required to marry the widow and father children who would bear the name of the deceased brother (Dt 25:5–6). Under the patriarchal family structure of that time, *neither the widow nor the brother could refuse the demand* of the head of the family to fulfill this obligation. So Onan took Tamar as a second wife and had intercourse with her but withdrew before ejaculation in order that she not become pregnant. He did not want to father a child that would not bear his own name. This disobedience resulted in his death. Compare Dt 25:7–10; Ru 4:1–12. Unfortunately, the experience of Onan has been identified with masturbation. (Masturbation in the past was called Onanism.) The punishment on him has been interpreted to show God's displeasure with self-stimulation. This interpretation misrepresents the passage under consideration. The Bible does not speak specifically about the issue of masturbation in this passage or in any other. Attitudes toward masturbation must be informed by general principles of biblical teachings about sexuality rather than from the experience of Onan.

38:6–10 EVIL AND SUFFERING, Punishment—Human suffering may be directly related to human sin. Sin brings death (2:17). At times death may be delayed; other times death comes quickly. God punishes sin. Onan sinned by refusing to fulfill his duties to his brother's wife according to the tradition of his people and later biblical law (Dt 25:5–10).

law[k] Tamar,[l] "Live as a widow in your
father's house[m] until my son Shelah[n]
grows up."[o] For he thought, "He may
die too, just like his brothers." So Tamar
went to live in her father's house.
12 After a long time Judah's wife, the
daughter of Shua,[p] died. When Judah had
recovered from his grief, he went up to
Timnah,[q] to the men who were shearing
his sheep,[r] and his friend Hirah the
Adullamite[s] went with him.
13 When Tamar[t] was told, "Your father-in-law is on his way to Timnah to
shear his sheep,"[u] 14 she took off her widow's clothes,[v] covered herself with a
veil[w] to disguise herself, and then sat
down[x] at the entrance to Enaim, which
is on the road to Timnah.[y] For she saw
that, though Shelah[z] had now grown up,
she had not been given to him as his
wife.
15 When Judah saw her, he thought she
was a prostitute,[a] for she had covered
her face. 16 Not realizing[b] that she was
his daughter-in-law,[c] he went over to her
by the roadside and said, "Come now, let
me sleep with you."[d]
"And what will you give me to sleep
with you?"[e] she asked.
17 "I'll send you a young goat[f] from my
flock," he said.
"Will you give me something as a
pledge[g] until you send it?" she asked.
18 He said, "What pledge should I give
you?"
"Your seal[h] and its cord, and the staff[i]
in your hand," she answered. So he gave
them to her and slept with her, and she
became pregnant by him.[j] 19 After she
left, she took off her veil and put on her
widow's clothes[k] again.
20 Meanwhile Judah sent the young goat
by his friend the Adullamite[l] in order to
get his pledge[m] back from the woman,
but he did not find her. 21 He asked the
men who lived there, "Where is the
shrine prostitute[n] who was beside the
road at Enaim?"
"There hasn't been any shrine prostitute here," they said.
22 So he went back to Judah and said, "I
didn't find her. Besides, the men who
lived there said, 'There hasn't been any
shrine prostitute here.' "
23 Then Judah said, "Let her keep what
she has,[o] or we will become a laughingstock.[p] After all, I did send her this
young goat, but you didn't find her."
24 About three months later Judah was
told, "Your daughter-in-law Tamar is
guilty of prostitution, and as a result she
is now pregnant."
Judah said, "Bring her out and have
her burned to death!"[q]
25 As she was being brought out, she
sent a message to her father-in-law. "I am
pregnant by the man who owns these,"
she said. And she added, "See if you recognize whose seal and cord and staff
these are."[r]
26 Judah recognized them and said,
"She is more righteous than I,[s] since I
wouldn't give her to my son Shelah.[t]"
And he did not sleep with her again.
27 When the time came for her to give
birth, there were twin boys in her
womb.[u] 28 As she was giving birth, one of
them put out his hand; so the midwife[v]
took a scarlet thread and tied it on his
wrist[w] and said, "This one came out
first." 29 But when he drew back his hand,
his brother came out,[x] and she said, "So
this is how you have broken out!" And he
was named Perez.[f][y] 30 Then his brother,
who had the scarlet thread on his wrist,[z]
came out and he was given the name
Zerah.[g][a]

Chapter 39

Joseph and Potiphar's Wife

NOW Joseph[b] had been taken down to
Egypt. Potiphar, an Egyptian who
was one of Pharaoh's officials, the captain
of the guard,[c] bought him from the Ishmaelites who had taken him there.[d]
2 The LORD was with Joseph[e] and he
prospered, and he lived in the house of
his Egyptian master. 3 When his master
saw that the LORD was with him[f] and
that the LORD gave him success in everything he did,[g] 4 Joseph found favor in his
eyes[h] and became his attendant. Potiphar put him in charge of his household,[i] and he entrusted to his care everything he owned.[j] 5 From the time he put
him in charge of his household and of all
that he owned, the LORD blessed the
household[k] of the Egyptian because of

38:11 [k]S Ge 11:31 [l]S ver 6 [m]Ru 1:8 [n]ver 14,26 [o]Ru 1:13 **38:12** [p]S ver 2 [q]ver 14; Jos 15:10, 57; 19:43; Jdg 14:1, 2; 2Ch 28:18 [r]S Ge 31:19 [s]S ver 1 **38:13** [t]S ver 6 [u]S Ge 31:19 **38:14** [v]ver 19 [w]S Ge 24:65 [x]Jer 3:2 [y]S ver 12 [z]S ver 11 **38:15** [a]Jdg 11:1; 16:1 **38:16** [b]Ge 42:23 [c]Lev 18:15; 20:12; Ru 1:6 [d]Ge 39:7, 12; 2Sa 13:11 [e]S Ge 30:15 **38:17** [f]Jdg 15:1 [g]ver 20 **38:18** [h]ver 25; 1Ki 21:8; Est 3:12; 8:8; SS 8:6; Isa 49:16; Jer 22:24; Hag 2:23; 2Co 1:22; Eph 1:13 [i]S Ge 32:10; S Ex 4:2 [j]S Ge 19:32 **38:19** [k]ver 14 **38:20** [l]S ver 1 [m]ver 17 **38:21** [n]S Ge 19:5; Lev 19:29; Dt 22:21; 23:17; 2Ki 23:7; Hos 4:14 **38:23** [o]ver 18 [p]Ex 32:25; Job 12:4; Jer 20:7; La 3:14 **38:24** [q]Lev 20:10, 14; 21:9; Dt 22:21, 22; Jos 7:25; Jdg 15:6; 1Sa 31:12; Job 31:11,28; Eze 16:38 **38:25** [r]S ver 18 **38:26** [s]1Sa 24:17 [t]S ver 11 **38:27** [u]Ge 25:24 **38:28** [v]S Ge 35:17 [w]ver 30 **38:29** [x]Ge 25:26 [y]Ge 46:12; Nu 26:20,21; Ru 4:12,18; 2Sa 5:20; 6:8; 1Ch 2:4; 9:4; Isa 28:21; Mt 1:3 **38:30** [z]ver 28 [a]Ge 46:12; 1Ch 2:4; Ne 11:24 **39:1** [b]S Ge 30:24 [c]S Ge 37:36 [d]S Ge 37:25 **39:2** [e]S Ge 21:20, 22; Jos 1:5; 6:27; Jdg 1:19; 1Sa 18:14; Ac 7:9 **39:3** [f]S Ge 21:22 [g]ver 23; 1Sa 18:14; 2Ki 18:7; 2Ch 20:20; Ps 1:3; 128:2; Isa 33:6 **39:4** [h]S Ge 6:8; S 18:3 [i]Ge 47:6; 1Ki 11:28; Pr 22:29 [j]ver 8,22; Ge 40:4; 42:37 **39:5** [k]2Sa 6:11

[f]29 *Perez* means *breaking out.* [g]30 *Zerah* can mean *scarlet* or *brightness.*

39:2–6 HISTORY, God—God's acts in history were not confined to military or political acts. Economic success resulted from divine action in the life of His faithful servant. Such actions carried out the call to bless the nations (12:1–3). Again this shows that biblical history writing was faith interpretation of events, at times ignoring the human factors involved to concentrate on God's acts and purposes.

39:2–6 STEWARDSHIP, Management—Joseph's role as manager-steward for Potiphar illustrates the biblical concept of stewardship. The master/owner entrusted the steward to manage the household. In the Old and New Testaments, steward denotes the management role God has assigned us. As trustees for God, we act in responsible freedom—free to make decisions, yet accountable for those decisions. We respond to God either in rejection or in love, but we are always accountable for how we respond. Every steward is to be faithful in all matters.

Joseph.[l] The blessing of the LORD was
on everything Potiphar had, both in the
house and in the field.[m] 6So he left in
Joseph's care everything he had;[n] with
Joseph in charge, he did not concern himself with anything except the food he ate.
Now Joseph was well-built and handsome,[o] 7and after a while his master's
wife took notice of Joseph and said,
"Come to bed with me!"[p]
8But he refused.[q] "With me in
charge," he told her, "my master does
not concern himself with anything in the
house; everything he owns he has entrusted to my care.[r] 9No one is greater in
this house than I am.[s] My master has
withheld nothing from me except you,
because you are his wife. How then could
I do such a wicked thing and sin against
God?"[t] 10And though she spoke to Joseph day after day, he refused[u] to go to
bed with her or even be with her.
11One day he went into the house to
attend to his duties,[v] and none of the
household servants[w] was inside. 12She
caught him by his cloak[x] and said,
"Come to bed with me!"[y] But he left his
cloak in her hand and ran out of the
house.[z]
13When she saw that he had left his
cloak in her hand and had run out of the
house, 14she called her household servants.[a] "Look," she said to them, "this
Hebrew[b] has been brought to us to make
sport of us![c] He came in here to sleep
with me, but I screamed.[d] 15When he
heard me scream for help, he left his
cloak beside me and ran out of the
house."[e]
16She kept his cloak beside her until
his master came home. 17Then she told
him this story:[f] "That Hebrew[g] slave[h]
you brought us came to me to make sport
of me. 18But as soon as I screamed for
help, he left his cloak beside me and ran
out of the house."
19When his master heard the story his
wife told him, saying, "This is how your
slave treated me," he burned with anger.[i] 20Joseph's master took him and put
him in prison,[j] the place where the
king's prisoners were confined.
But while Joseph was there in the prison, 21the LORD was with him;[k] he
showed him kindness[l] and granted him
favor in the eyes of the prison warden.[m]
22So the warden put Joseph in charge of
all those held in the prison, and he was
made responsible for all that was done
there.[n] 23The warden paid no attention
to anything under Joseph's[o] care, because the LORD was with Joseph and gave
him success in whatever he did.[p]

Chapter 40

The Cupbearer and the Baker

SOME time later, the cupbearer[q] and
the baker[r] of the king of Egypt offended their master, the king of Egypt.
2Pharaoh was angry[s] with his two officials,[t] the chief cupbearer and the chief
baker, 3and put them in custody in the
house of the captain of the guard,[u] in the
same prison where Joseph was confined.
4The captain of the guard[v] assigned them
to Joseph,[w] and he attended them.
After they had been in custody[x] for
some time, 5each of the two men—the
cupbearer and the baker of the king of
Egypt, who were being held in prison—
had a dream[y] the same night, and each
dream had a meaning of its own.[z]
6When Joseph came to them the next
morning, he saw that they were dejected.
7So he asked Pharaoh's officials who were
in custody[a] with him in his master's
house, "Why are your faces so sad today?"[b]
8"We both had dreams," they answered, "but there is no one to interpret
them."[c]
Then Joseph said to them, "Do not interpretations belong to God?[d] Tell me
your dreams."
9So the chief cupbearer[e] told Joseph
his dream. He said to him, "In my dream
I saw a vine in front of me, 10and on the
vine were three branches. As soon as it
budded, it blossomed,[f] and its clusters
ripened into grapes. 11Pharaoh's cup was
in my hand, and I took the grapes,
squeezed them into Pharaoh's cup and
put the cup in his hand."
12"This is what it means,[g]" Joseph
said to him. "The three branches are
three days.[h] 13Within three days[i] Pharaoh will lift up your head[j] and restore
you to your position, and you will put
Pharaoh's cup in his hand, just as you

39:5 [l]S Ge 26:24 [m]Dt 28:3; Ps 128:4
39:6 [n]Ge 24:2 [o]S Ge 12:11; Ex 2:2; 1Sa 9:2; 16:12; 17:42; Est 2:7; Da 1:4
39:7 [p]S Ge 38:16; Pr 7:15-18
39:8 [q]Pr 6:23-24 [r]S ver 4
39:9 [s]Ge 41:33,40 [t]S Ge 13:13; S Nu 22:34
39:10 [u]Est 3:4
39:11 [v]Ex 18:20; Dt 1:18 [w]ver 14
39:12 [x]2Sa 13:11; Pr 7:13 [y]S Ge 38:16 [z]ver 15; Pr 5:8; 2Ti 2:22
39:14 [a]ver 11 [b]S Ge 14:13 [c]S Ge 21:9 [d]Dt 22:24,27
39:15 [e]S ver 12
39:17 [f]Ex 20:16; 23:1,7; Dt 5:20; Ps 101:5 [g]S Ge 14:13 [h]Ge 21:10
39:19 [i]S Ge 34:7; S Est 1:12
39:20 [j]Ge 40:3; 41:10; Ps 105:18
39:21 [k]S Ge 21:20 [l]S Ge 19:19 [m]Ex 3:21; 11:3; 12:36; Est 2:9; Ps 106:46; Pr 16:7; Da 1:9
39:22 [n]S ver 4
39:23 [o]S Ge 21:20; S Nu 14:43 [p]S ver 3
40:1 [q]ver 9,13,21; Ne 1:11 [r]ver 16,20
40:2 [s]Pr 16:14,15; 19:12 [t]Ge 41:10; Est 2:21
40:3 [u]S Ge 37:36; S 39:20
40:4 [v]S Ge 37:36 [w]S Ge 39:4 [x]ver 7; Ge 42:17
40:5 [y]S Ge 20:3 [z]Ge 41:11
40:7 [a]S ver 4 [b]Ne 2:2
40:8 [c]Ge 41:8,15 [d]Ge 41:16,25,28, 32; Dt 29:29; Da 2:22,28,47
40:9 [e]S ver 1
40:10 [f]Isa 27:6; 35:1-2; Hos 14:7
40:12 [g]ver 16; Ge 41:12,15,25; Da 2:36; 4:19 [h]ver 18
40:13 [i]ver 19,20; Jos 1:11; 3:2; Ezr 8:32; Ne 2:11 [j]ver 19

39:9 SIN, Responsibility—Joseph recognized his responsibility to refuse the advances of Potiphar's wife. Political or business expediency never justifies sinful action. Individuals are responsible for their own acts of sin and must accept the responsibility ro refrain from sin. To refrain from sin does not guarantee immediate success in earthly ventures. It *may lead to* greater hardship, *as in Joseph's case.*

***39:21–23* GOD, Grace**—God's grace was with Joseph in the disaster of his being sold into slavery and his imprisonment on false charges. In this instance God changed disastrous circumstances into a blessing for Joseph. In the following chapters Joseph rose to a place of prominence, second only to Pharaoh in all of Egypt. A gracious and sovereign God can use any or all circumstances to further His cause or bless His people. See note *on Ro 8:28.* God does not cause all things that happen. In His grace God can use calamities to work out blessing and victory. God uses what we view as evil to work out His purpose in the lives of His people.

used to do when you were his cupbearer.[k] 14But when all goes well with you,
remember me[l] and show me kindness;[m]
mention me to Pharaoh[n] and get me out
of this prison. 15For I was forcibly carried
off from the land of the Hebrews,[o] and
even here I have done nothing to deserve
being put in a dungeon."[p]

16When the chief baker[q] saw that Joseph had given a favorable interpretation,[r] he said to Joseph, "I too had a
dream: On my head were three baskets[s]
of bread.[h] 17In the top basket were all
kinds of baked goods for Pharaoh, but the
birds were eating them out of the basket
on my head."

18"This is what it means," Joseph said.
"The three baskets are three days.[t]
19Within three days[u] Pharaoh will lift off
your head[v] and hang you on a tree.[i][w]
And the birds will eat away your flesh."[x]

20Now the third day[y] was Pharaoh's
birthday,[z] and he gave a feast for all his
officials.[a] He lifted up the heads of the
chief cupbearer and the chief baker[b] in
the presence of his officials: 21He restored the chief cupbearer[c] to his position,[d] so that he once again put the cup
into Pharaoh's hand,[e] 22but he hanged[j]
the chief baker,[f] just as Joseph had said
to them in his interpretation.[g]

23The chief cupbearer, however, did
not remember Joseph; he forgot him.[h]

Chapter 41

Pharaoh's Dreams

WHEN two full years had passed,
Pharaoh had a dream:[i] He was
standing by the Nile,[j] 2when out of the
river there came up seven cows, sleek
and fat,[k] and they grazed among the
reeds.[l] 3After them, seven other cows,
ugly and gaunt, came up out of the Nile
and stood beside those on the riverbank.
4And the cows that were ugly and gaunt
ate up the seven sleek, fat cows. Then
Pharaoh woke up.[m]

5He fell asleep again and had a second
dream: Seven heads of grain,[n] healthy
and good, were growing on a single stalk.
6After them, seven other heads of grain
sprouted—thin and scorched by the east
wind.[o] 7The thin heads of grain swallowed up the seven healthy, full heads.
Then Pharaoh woke up;[p] it had been a
dream.

8In the morning his mind was troubled,[q] so he sent for all the magicians[r]
and wise men of Egypt. Pharaoh told
them his dreams, but no one could interpret them for him.[s]

9Then the chief cupbearer said to Pharaoh, "Today I am reminded of my shortcomings.[t] 10Pharaoh was once angry
with his servants,[u] and he imprisoned
me and the chief baker in the house of
the captain of the guard.[v] 11Each of us
had a dream the same night, and each
dream had a meaning of its own.[w] 12Now
a young Hebrew[x] was there with us, a
servant of the captain of the guard.[y] We
told him our dreams, and he interpreted
them for us, giving each man the interpretation of his dream.[z] 13And things
turned out exactly as he interpreted them
to us: I was restored to my position, and
the other man was hanged.[j][a]"

14So Pharaoh sent for Joseph, and he
was quickly brought from the dungeon.[b]
When he had shaved[c] and changed his
clothes,[d] he came before Pharaoh.

15Pharaoh said to Joseph, "I had a
dream, and no one can interpret it.[e] But
I have heard it said of you that when you
hear a dream you can interpret it."[f]

16"I cannot do it," Joseph replied to
Pharaoh, "but God will give Pharaoh the
answer he desires."[g]

17Then Pharaoh said to Joseph, "In my
dream I was standing on the bank of the
Nile,[h] 18when out of the river there came
up seven cows, fat and sleek, and they
grazed among the reeds.[i] 19After them,
seven other cows came up—scrawny and
very ugly and lean. I had never seen such
ugly cows in all the land of Egypt. 20The
lean, ugly cows ate up the seven fat cows
that came up first. 21But even after they
ate them, no one could tell that they had
done so; they looked just as ugly as before. Then I woke up.

22"In my dreams I also saw seven
heads of grain, full and good, growing on
a single stalk. 23After them, seven other
heads sprouted—withered and thin and
scorched by the east wind. 24The thin
heads of grain swallowed up the seven

[h] *16* Or *three wicker baskets* [i] *19* Or *and impale you on a pole* [j] *22,13* Or *impaled*

40:13 [k]S ver 1 **40:14** [l]1Sa 25:31; Lk 23:42 [m]S Ge 19:19; 1Sa 20:14,42; 2Sa 9:1; 1Ki 2:7 [n]ver 23; Ge 41:9; Ecc 9:15 **40:15** [o]S Ge 14:13 [p]Ge 39:20; Job 13:27 **40:16** [q]S ver 1 [r]S ver 12 [s]Am 8:1-2 **40:18** [t]ver 12 **40:19** [u]ver 13 [v]S ver 13 [w]ver 22; Dt 21:22-23; Est 2:23; 7:10 [x]Dt 28:26; 1Sa 17:44; 2Sa 21:10; 1Ki 14:11; 16:4; 21:24; Eze 39:4 **40:20** [y]S ver 13 [z]Mt 14:6-10 [a]Est 2:18; Mk 6:21 [b]S ver 1 **40:21** [c]S ver 1 [d]2Ki 25:27; Jer 52:31 [e]ver 13 **40:22** [f]S ver 19 [g]Ge 41:13; Ps 105:19 **40:23** [h]S ver 14; S Ecc 1:11 **41:1** [i]S Ge 20:3 [j]ver 17; S Ge 2:14; Ex 1:22; 2:5; 7:15 **41:2** [k]ver 26; Jer 5:28 [l]ver 18; Ex 2:3; Job 40:21; Isa 19:6 **41:4** [m]ver 7 **41:5** [n]Jos 13:3; 2Ki 4:42; 1Ch 13:5; Isa 23:3; Jer 2:18 **41:6** [o]Ex 10:13; 14:21; Job 6:26; 11:2; 15:2; Ps 11:6; 48:7; Isa 11:15; 27:8; Jer 4:11; 18:17; Eze 19:12; 27:26; Hos 12:1; 13:15; Jnh 4:8 **41:7** [p]ver 4 **41:8** [q]Job 7:14; Da 2:1,3; 4:5,19 [r]Ex 7:11,22; Da 1:20; 2:2,27; 4:7; 5:7 [s]ver 24; S Ge 40:8; Da 4:18 **41:9** [t]S Ge 40:14 **41:10** [u]S Ge 40:2 [v]S Ge 37:36; S 39:20 **41:11** [w]Ge 40:5 **41:12** [x]S Ge 14:13; 39:17 [y]S Ge 37:36; 40:4 [z]S Ge 40:12 **41:13** [a]S Ge 40:22 **41:14** [b]Ps 105:20 [c]Isa 18:2,7 [d]S Ge 35:2; 45:22; Ru 3:3; 2Sa 12:20 **41:15** [e]S Ge 40:8 [f]S Ge 40:12; Da 4:18; 5:16 **41:16** [g]S Ge 40:8 **41:17** [h]S ver 1 **41:18** [i]S ver 2

41:1–32 EVIL AND SUFFERING, Providence—God may use what humans see as disaster to accomplish His purposes. People suffered famine, but God provided a way to survive famine while using the situation to gain the position He wanted Joseph to have. What appears to be evil in the short-term may prove to be God's leadership for good in the long run. See notes on 45:4–11; 50:20.

41:16,25,28,32 GOD, Sovereignty—God has many ways of making Himself known to people. In this case God, in His sovereignty over all of life, spoke to Pharaoh through his dream as interpreted by Joseph. God sometimes speaks through the strong feelings of the heart, the words spoken by a faithful prophet or preacher, the reading of a written message (Scripture or otherwise), or through dreams. Just as not all spoken or written words are a message from God, not all dreams are a word from God.

good heads. I told this to the magicians,
but none could explain it to me.[j]"
25Then Joseph said to Pharaoh, "The
dreams of Pharaoh are one and the
same.[k] God has revealed to Pharaoh
what he is about to do.[l] 26The seven
good cows[m] are seven years, and the sev-
en good heads of grain are seven years; it
is one and the same dream. 27The seven
lean, ugly cows that came up afterward
are seven years, and so are the seven
worthless heads of grain scorched by the
east wind: They are seven years of
famine.[n]
28"It is just as I said to Pharaoh: God
has shown Pharaoh what he is about to
do.[o] 29Seven years of great abundance[p]
are coming throughout the land of Egypt,
30but seven years of famine[q] will follow
them. Then all the abundance in Egypt
will be forgotten, and the famine will ravage the land.[r] 31The abundance in the
land will not be remembered, because
the famine that follows it will be so severe. 32The reason the dream was given
to Pharaoh in two forms is that the matter
has been firmly decided[s] by God, and
God will do it soon.[t]
33"And now let Pharaoh look for a discerning and wise man[u] and put him in
charge of the land of Egypt.[v] 34Let Pharaoh appoint commissioners[w] over the
land to take a fifth[x] of the harvest of
Egypt during the seven years of abundance.[y] 35They should collect all the food
of these good years that are coming and
store up the grain under the authority of
Pharaoh, to be kept in the cities for
food.[z] 36This food should be held in reserve for the country, to be used during
the seven years of famine that will come
upon Egypt,[a] so that the country may not
be ruined by the famine."
37The plan seemed good to Pharaoh
and to all his officials.[b] 38So Pharaoh
asked them, "Can we find anyone like
this man, one in whom is the spirit of
God[k]?"[c]
39Then Pharaoh said to Joseph, "Since
God has made all this known to you,[d]
there is no one so discerning and wise as
you.[e] 40You shall be in charge of my palace,[f] and all my people are to submit to
your orders.[g] Only with respect to the
throne will I be greater than you.[h]"

Joseph in Charge of Egypt

41So Pharaoh said to Joseph, "I hereby
put you in charge of the whole land of
Egypt."[i] 42Then Pharaoh took his signet
ring[j] from his finger and put it on Joseph's finger. He dressed him in robes[k]
of fine linen[l] and put a gold chain
around his neck.[m] 43He had him ride in a
chariot[n] as his second-in-command,[l][o]
and men shouted before him, "Make
way[m]!"[p] Thus he put him in charge of
the whole land of Egypt.[q]
44Then Pharaoh said to Joseph, "I am
Pharaoh, but without your word no one
will lift hand or foot in all Egypt."[r]
45Pharaoh gave Joseph[s] the name Zaphe-
nath-Paneah and gave him Asenath
daughter of Potiphera, priest[t] of On,[n][u]
to be his wife.[v] And Joseph went
throughout the land of Egypt.
46Joseph was thirty years old[w] when he
entered the service[x] of Pharaoh king of
Egypt. And Joseph went out from Pharaoh's presence and traveled throughout
Egypt. 47During the seven years of abundance[y] the land produced plentifully.
48Joseph collected all the food produced
in those seven years of abundance in
Egypt and stored it in the cities.[z] In each
city he put the food grown in the fields
surrounding it. 49Joseph stored up huge
quantities of grain, like the sand of the
sea;[a] it was so much that he stopped
keeping records because it was beyond
measure.
50Before the years of famine came, two
sons were born to Joseph by Asenath
daughter of Potiphera, priest of On.[b]
51Joseph named his firstborn[c] Manasseh[o][d] and said, "It is because God has
made me forget all my trouble and all my
father's household." 52The second son he
named Ephraim[p][e] and said, "It is because God has made me fruitful[f] in the
land of my suffering."
53The seven years of abundance in
Egypt came to an end, 54and the seven
years of famine[g] began,[h] just as Joseph
had said. There was famine in all the other lands, but in the whole land of Egypt
there was food. 55When all Egypt began
to feel the famine,[i] the people cried to
Pharaoh for food. Then Pharaoh told all
the Egyptians, "Go to Joseph and do what
he tells you."[j]
56When the famine had spread over the

k *38* Or *of the gods* l *43* Or *in the chariot of his second-in-command*; or *in his second chariot* m *43* Or *Bow down* n *45* That is, Heliopolis; also in verse 50 o *51 Manasseh* sounds like and may be derived from the Hebrew for *forget.* p *52 Ephraim* sounds like the Hebrew for *twice fruitful.*

41:24 *j*S ver 8 **41:25** *k*S Ge 40:12 *l*S Ge 40:8; Isa 46:11; Da 2:45 **41:26** *m*S ver 2 **41:27** *n*S Ge 12:10 **41:28** *o*S Ge 40:8 **41:29** *p*ver 47 **41:30** *q*ver 54; Ge 45:6,11; 47:13; Ps 105:16 *r*ver 56; S Ge 12:10 **41:32** *s*Da 2:5 *t*S Ge 40:8 **41:33** *u*ver 39 *v*S Ge 39:9 **41:34** *w*Est 2:3 *x*Ge 47:24,26; 1Sa 8:15 *y*ver 48; Ge 47:14 **41:35** *z*ver 48 **41:36** *a*ver 56; Ge 42:6; 47:14 **41:37** *b*Ge 45:16; Est 2:4; Isa 19:11 **41:38** *c*Nu 27:18; Dt 34:9; Da 2:11; 4:8,8-9,18; 5:11,14 **41:39** *d*Da 2:11; 5:11 *e*ver 33 **41:40** *f*1Ki 4:6; 2Ki 15:5; Isa 22:15; 36:3 *g*S Ge 39:9; Ps 105:21-22; Ac 7:10 *h*Est 10:3 **41:41** *i*ver 43,55; Ge 42:6; 45:8,13, 26; Est 8:2; Jer 40:7; Da 6:3 **41:42** *j*S Ge 24:22; Est 3:10; 8:2,8 *k*1Sa 17:38; 18:4; 1Ki 19:19; Est 6:8, 11; Da 5:29; Zec 3:4 *l*Ex 25:4; Est 8:15; Da 5:29 *m*Ps 73:6; SS 4:9; Isa 3:18; Eze 16:11; Da 5:7,16,29 **41:43** *n*Ge 46:29; 50:9; Isa 2:7; 22:18 *o*Est 10:3 *p*Est 6:9 *q*S ver 41 **41:44** *r*S Ge 37:8; Est 10:2; Ps 105:22 **41:45** *s*Est 2:7 *t*Ex 2:16 *u*Eze 30:17 *v*ver 50; Ge 46:20,27 **41:46** *w*S Ge 37:2 *x*1Sa 8:11; 16:21; Pr 22:29; Da 1:19 **41:47** *y*ver 29 **41:48** *z*S ver 34 **41:49** *a*S Ge 12:2 **41:50** *b*S ver 45 **41:51** *c*Ge 48:14, 18,20; 49:3 *d*Ge 46:20; 48:1; 50:23; Nu 1:34; Dt 33:17; Jos 4:12; 17:1; 1Ch 7:14 **41:52** *e*Ge 46:20; 48:1,5; 50:23; Nu 1:32; 26:28; Dt 33:17; Jos 14:4; Jdg 5:14; 1Ch 7:20; 2Ch 30:1; Ps 60:7; Jer 7:15; Ob 1:19 *f*S Ge 17:6 **41:54** *g*S Ge 12:10 *h*Ac 7:11 **41:55** *i*Dt 32:24; 2Ch 20:9; Isa 51:19; Jer 5:12; 27:8; 42:16; 44:27 *j*S ver 41; Jn 2:5

41:38–39 HOLY SPIRIT, Leaders—The Spirit helps God's people plan to avoid crisis. God not only empowered Joseph to interpret Pharaoh's dreams, but also He gave Joseph a long-range plan to prevent disaster. Even the foreign ruler recognized Joseph's plan as divinely inspired. The divine Spirit was "in" Joseph. Just as human breath (Hebrew *ruach*) is in a person forming an essential part of the person, so God's Spirit (*ruach*) formed an essential part of Joseph. God gives His people Spirit-inspired leaders to lead them through crises.

whole country, Joseph opened the storehouses and sold grain to the Egyptians,[k]
for the famine[l] was severe throughout
Egypt.[m] 57And all the countries came to
Egypt to buy grain from Joseph,[n] because
the famine was severe in all the world.[o]

Chapter 42

Joseph's Brothers Go to Egypt

WHEN Jacob learned that there was
grain in Egypt,[p] he said to his
sons, "Why do you just keep looking at
each other?" 2He continued, "I have
heard that there is grain in Egypt. Go
down there and buy some for us,[q] so that
we may live and not die."[r]

3Then ten of Joseph's brothers went
down to buy grain[s] from Egypt. 4But Jacob did not send Benjamin,[t] Joseph's
brother, with the others, because he was
afraid that harm might come to him.[u] 5So
Israel's sons were among those who went
to buy grain,[v] for the famine was in the
land of Canaan[w] also.[x]

6Now Joseph was the governor of the
land,[y] the one who sold grain to all its
people.[z] So when Joseph's brothers arrived, they bowed down to him with
their faces to the ground.[a] 7As soon as
Joseph saw his brothers, he recognized
them, but he pretended to be a stranger
and spoke harshly to them.[b] "Where do
you come from?"[c] he asked.

"From the land of Canaan," they replied, "to buy food."

8Although Joseph recognized his brothers, they did not recognize him.[d] 9Then
he remembered his dreams[e] about them
and said to them, "You are spies![f] You
have come to see where our land is unprotected."[g]

10"No, my lord,[h]" they answered.
"Your servants have come to buy food.[i]
11We are all the sons of one man. Your
servants[j] are honest men,[k] not spies.[l]"

12"No!" he said to them. "You have
come to see where our land is unprotected."[m]

13But they replied, "Your servants[n]
were twelve brothers, the sons of one
man, who lives in the land of Canaan.[o]
The youngest is now with our father, and
one is no more."[p]

14Joseph said to them, "It is just as I
told you: You are spies![q] 15And this is
how you will be tested: As surely as Pharaoh lives,[r] you will not leave this place
unless your youngest brother comes
here.[s] 16Send one of your number to get
your brother;[t] the rest of you will be
kept in prison,[u] so that your words may
be tested to see if you are telling the
truth.[v] If you are not, then as surely as
Pharaoh lives, you are spies![w]" 17And he
put them all in custody[x] for three days.

18On the third day, Joseph said to
them, "Do this and you will live, for I fear
God:[y] 19If you are honest men,[z] let one
of your brothers stay here in prison,[a]
while the rest of you go and take grain
back for your starving households.[b] 20But
you must bring your youngest brother to
me,[c] so that your words may be verified
and that you may not die." This they proceeded to do.

21They said to one another, "Surely we
are being punished because of our brother.[d] We saw how distressed he was
when he pleaded with us for his life, but
we would not listen; that's why this distress[e] has come upon us."

22Reuben replied, "Didn't I tell you not
to sin against the boy?[f] But you wouldn't
listen! Now we must give an accounting[g]
for his blood."[h] 23They did not realize[i]
that Joseph could understand them,[j]
since he was using an interpreter.

24He turned away from them and began to weep,[k] but then turned back and
spoke to them again. He had Simeon tak-
en from them and bound before their
eyes.[l]

25Joseph gave orders to fill their bags
with grain,[m] to put each man's silver
back in his sack,[n] and to give them provisions[o] for their journey.[p] After this was
done for them, 26they loaded their grain
on their donkeys[q] and left.

27At the place where they stopped for
the night one of them opened his sack to
get feed for his donkey,[r] and he saw his
silver in the mouth of his sack.[s] 28"My
silver has been returned," he said to his
brothers. "Here it is in my sack."

Their hearts sank[t] and they turned to
each other trembling[u] and said, "What is
this that God has done to us?"[v]

29When they came to their father Jacob
in the land of Canaan,[w] they told him all
that had happened to them.[x] They said,
30"The man who is lord over the land
spoke harshly to us[y] and treated us as
though we were spying on the land.[z]
31But we said to him, 'We are honest
men; we are not spies.[a] 32We were
twelve brothers, sons of one father. One
is no more, and the youngest is now with
our father in Canaan.'[b]

33"Then the man who is lord over the
land said to us, 'This is how I will know
whether you are honest men: Leave one
of your brothers here with me, and take
food for your starving households and
go.[c] 34But bring your youngest brother to
me so I will know that you are not spies
but honest men.[d] Then I will give your

41:56 [k]S ver 36 [l]S Ge 12:10 [m]S ver 30
41:57 [n]Ge 42:5; 47:15 [o]S Ge 12:10
42:1 [p]Ac 7:12
42:2 [q]Ge 43:2,4; 44:25 [r]ver 19,33; Ge 43:8; 47:19; Ps 33:18-19
42:3 [s]ver 10; Ge 43:20
42:4 [t]S Ge 35:18 [u]ver 38
42:5 [v]S Ge 41:57 [w]ver 13,29; Ge 31:18; 45:17 [x]S Ge 12:10; S Dt 32:24; Ac 7:11
42:6 [y]S Ge 41:41; S Ne 5:14 [z]S Ge 41:36 [a]S Ge 33:3
42:7 [b]ver 30 [c]S Ge 29:4
42:8 [d]Ge 37:2
42:9 [e]S Ge 37:7 [f]ver 14,16,30; Dt 1:22; Jos 2:1; 6:22 [g]ver 12
42:10 [h]S Ge 37:8 [i]S ver 3
42:11 [j]ver 13; Ge 44:7,9,16,19,21, 31; 46:34; 47:3 [k]ver 15,16,19,20,34 [l]ver 31
42:12 [m]ver 9
42:13 [n]S ver 11 [o]S ver 5; Ge 46:31; 47:1 [p]ver 24,32,36; S Ge 37:30,33; 43:7,29,33; 44:8; Jer 31:15
42:14 [q]S ver 9
42:15 [r]1Sa 17:55 [s]S ver 11; Ge 43:3, 5,7; 44:21,23
42:16 [t]ver 15 [u]ver 19 [v]S ver 11 [w]S ver 9
42:17 [x]S Ge 40:4
42:18 [y]S Ge 20:11; S 22:12; Lev 19:14; 25:43; 2Sa 23:3
42:19 [z]S ver 11 [a]ver 16 [b]S ver 2
42:20 [c]S ver 15
42:21 [d]Ge 37:26-28 [e]Ge 45:5
42:22 [f]Ge 37:21-22 [g]S Ge 9:5 [h]Ge 45:24
42:23 [i]Ge 38:16 [j]S Ge 11:7
42:24 [k]S Ge 29:11 [l]S ver 13; Ge 43:14, 23
42:25 [m]Ge 43:2 [n]ver 27,35; Ge 43:12,18,21; 44:1,8 [o]Jer 40:5 [p]Ge 45:21,23
42:26 [q]S Ge 32:15; 44:13; 45:17; 1Sa 25:18; Isa 30:6
42:27 [r]Jdg 19:19; Job 39:9; Isa 1:3 [s]S ver 25
42:28 [t]Jos 2:11; 5:1; 7:5 [u]Mk 5:33 [v]Ge 43:23
42:29 [w]S ver 5 [x]Ge 44:24
42:30 [y]ver 7 [z]S ver 9
42:31 [a]ver 11
42:32 [b]S ver 13
42:33 [c]S ver 2
42:34 [d]S ver 11

brother back to you,[e] and you can trade[q]
in the land.[f]' "
35As they were emptying their sacks,
there in each man's sack was his pouch of
silver![g] When they and their father saw
the money pouches, they were frightened.[h] 36Their father Jacob said to them,
"You have deprived me of my children.
Joseph is no more and Simeon is no
more,[i] and now you want to take Benjamin.[j] Everything is against me![k]"
37Then Reuben said to his father, "You
may put both of my sons to death if I do
not bring him back to you. Entrust him to
my care,[l] and I will bring him back."[m]
38But Jacob said, "My son will not go
down there with you; his brother is
dead[n] and he is the only one left. If harm
comes to him[o] on the journey you are
taking, you will bring my gray head down
to the grave[r][p] in sorrow.[q]"

Chapter 43

The Second Journey to Egypt

NOW the famine was still severe in the
land.[r] 2So when they had eaten all
the grain they had brought from Egypt,[s]
their father said to them, "Go back and
buy us a little more food."[t]
3But Judah[u] said to him, "The man
warned us solemnly, 'You will not see my
face again unless your brother is with
you.'[v] 4If you will send our brother along
with us, we will go down and buy food
for you.[w] 5But if you will not send him,
we will not go down, because the man
said to us, 'You will not see my face again
unless your brother is with you.[x]' "
6Israel[y] asked, "Why did you bring
this trouble[z] on me by telling the man
you had another brother?"
7They replied, "The man questioned us
closely about ourselves and our family. 'Is
your father still living?'[a] he asked us. 'Do
you have another brother?'[b] We simply
answered his questions. How were we to
know he would say, 'Bring your brother
down here'?"[c]
8Then Judah[d] said to Israel[e] his father,
"Send the boy along with me and we will
go at once, so that we and you and our
children may live and not die.[f] 9I myself
will guarantee his safety; you can hold me
personally responsible for him.[g] If I do
not bring him back to you and set him
here before you, I will bear the blame[h]
before you all my life.[i] 10As it is, if we
had not delayed,[j] we could have gone
and returned twice."
11Then their father Israel[k] said to
them, "If it must be, then do this: Put
some of the best products[l] of the land in
your bags and take them down to the
man as a gift[m]—a little balm[n] and a little
honey, some spices[o] and myrrh,[p] some
pistachio nuts and almonds. 12Take double the amount[q] of silver with you, for
you must return the silver that was put
back into the mouths of your sacks.[r] Perhaps it was a mistake. 13Take your brother also and go back to the man at once.[s]
14And may God Almighty[s][t] grant you
mercy[u] before the man so that he will let
your other brother and Benjamin come
back with you.[v] As for me, if I am bereaved, I am bereaved."[w]
15So the men took the gifts and double
the amount of silver,[x] and Benjamin also.
They hurried[y] down to Egypt and presented themselves[z] to Joseph. 16When
Joseph saw Benjamin[a] with them, he
said to the steward of his house,[b] "Take
these men to my house, slaughter an animal and prepare dinner;[c] they are to eat
with me at noon."
17The man did as Joseph told him and
took the men to Joseph's house.[d] 18Now
the men were frightened[e] when they
were taken to his house.[f] They thought,
"We were brought here because of the
silver that was put back into our sacks[g]
the first time. He wants to attack us[h] and
overpower us and seize us as slaves[i] and
take our donkeys.[j]"
19So they went up to Joseph's steward[k]
and spoke to him at the entrance to the
house. 20"Please, sir," they said, "we
came down here the first time to buy
food.[l] 21But at the place where we
stopped for the night we opened our
sacks and each of us found his silver—the
exact weight—in the mouth of his sack.
So we have brought it back with us.[m]
22We have also brought additional silver
with us to buy food. We don't know who
put our silver in our sacks."
23"It's all right," he said. "Don't be
afraid. Your God, the God of your father,[n] has given you treasure in your
sacks;[o] I received your silver." Then he
brought Simeon out to them.[p]
24The steward took the men into Joseph's house,[q] gave them water to wash

42:34 [e]S ver 24 [f]Ge 34:10
42:35 [g]S ver 25 [h]Ge 43:18
42:36 [i]S ver 13 [j]S ver 24 [k]Job 3:25; Pr 10:24; Ro 8:31
42:37 [l]S Ge 39:4 [m]Ge 43:9; 44:32
42:38 [n]Ge 37:33 [o]ver 4 [p]S Ge 37:35 [q]Ge 44:29,34; 48:7
43:1 [r]S Ge 12:10
43:2 [s]Ge 42:25 [t]S Ge 42:2
43:3 [u]ver 8; Ge 44:14,18; 46:28 [v]S Ge 42:15
43:4 [w]S Ge 42:2
43:5 [x]S Ge 42:15; 44:26; 2Sa 3:13
43:6 [y]ver 8,11; S Ge 17:5 [z]S Ge 34:30
43:7 [a]ver 27; Ge 45:3 [b]S Ge 42:13; 44:19 [c]S Ge 42:15
43:8 [d]S ver 3; S Ge 29:35 [e]S ver 6 [f]S Ge 42:2; Ps 33:18-19
43:9 [g]1Sa 23:20 [h]Ge 44:10,17 [i]S Ge 42:37; Phm 1:18-19
43:10 [j]Ge 45:9
43:11 [k]S ver 6 [l]S Ge 24:10 [m]S Ge 32:13 [n]S Ge 37:25; Eze 27:17 [o]Ex 30:23; 1Ki 10:2; Eze 27:22 [p]S Ge 37:25
43:12 [q]ver 15; Ex 22:4,7; Pr 6:31 [r]S Ge 42:25
43:13 [s]ver 3
43:14 [t]S Ge 17:1 [u]Dt 13:17; Ps 25:6 [v]S Ge 42:24 [w]2Sa 18:33; Est 4:16
43:15 [x]ver 12 [y]Ge 45:9,13 [z]Ge 47:2,7; Mt 2:11
43:16 [a]S Ge 35:18 [b]ver 17,24,26; Ge 44:1,4,12; 2Sa 19:17; Isa 22:15 [c]ver 31; Lk 15:23
43:17 [d]S ver 16
43:18 [e]Ge 42:35 [f]Ge 44:14 [g]S Ge 42:25 [h]S Ge 32:11 [i]Ge 44:9,16,33; 50:18 [j]Ge 34:28
43:19 [k]ver 16
43:20 [l]S Ge 42:3
43:21 [m]S ver 15; S Ge 42:25
43:23 [n]S Ge 24:12; S 31:5; Ex 3:6 [o]Ge 42:28 [p]S Ge 42:24
43:24 [q]S ver 16

[q]34 Or *move about freely* [r]38 Hebrew *Sheol*
[s]14 Hebrew *El-Shaddai*

42:38 HUMANITY, Attitudes to Death—See note on 37:34–35.

43:23 GOD, Sovereignty—Joseph attributed his own act of loving-kindness to God Himself. See 42:25. Many times God performs His own acts of grace through human instrumentality. That does not reduce the human element of love and generosity, for the human element is very real. It does emphasize the leadership of God as He exercises His sovereignty in human affairs to achieve His own purposes and bless His people.

their feet[r] and provided fodder for their
donkeys. 25They prepared their gifts[s] for
Joseph's arrival at noon,[t] because they
had heard that they were to eat there.
26When Joseph came home,[u] they presented to him the gifts[v] they had brought
into the house, and they bowed down before him to the ground.[w] 27He asked
them how they were, and then he said,
"How is your aged father[x] you told me
about? Is he still living?"[y]
28They replied, "Your servant our father[z] is still alive and well." And they
bowed low[a] to pay him honor.[b]
29As he looked about and saw his
brother Benjamin, his own mother's
son,[c] he asked, "Is this your youngest
brother, the one you told me about?"[d]
And he said, "God be gracious to you,[e]
my son." 30Deeply moved[f] at the sight of
his brother, Joseph hurried out and
looked for a place to weep. He went into
his private room and wept[g] there.
31After he had washed his face, he
came out and, controlling himself,[h] said,
"Serve the food."[i]
32They served him by himself, the
brothers by themselves, and the Egyptians who ate with him by themselves,
because Egyptians could not eat with Hebrews,[j] for that is detestable to Egyptians.[k] 33The men had been seated before him in the order of their ages, from
the firstborn[l] to the youngest;[m] and they
looked at each other in astonishment.
34When portions were served to them
from Joseph's table, Benjamin's portion
was five times as much as anyone else's.[n]
So they feasted[o] and drank freely with
him.

Chapter 44

A Silver Cup in a Sack

NOW Joseph gave these instructions to
the steward of his house:[p] "Fill the
men's sacks with as much food as they
can carry, and put each man's silver in
the mouth of his sack.[q] 2Then put my
cup,[r] the silver one,[s] in the mouth of
the youngest one's sack, along with the
silver for his grain." And he did as Joseph
said.
3As morning dawned, the men were
sent on their way with their donkeys.[t]
4They had not gone far from the city
when Joseph said to his steward,[u] "Go
after those men at once, and when you
catch up with them, say to them, 'Why
have you repaid good with evil?[v] 5Isn't
this the cup[w] my master drinks from and
also uses for divination?[x] This is a wicked thing you have done.' "
6When he caught up with them, he repeated these words to them. 7But they
said to him, "Why does my lord say such
things? Far be it from your servants[y] to
do anything like that![z] 8We even brought
back to you from the land of Canaan[a] the
silver[b] we found inside the mouths of
our sacks.[c] So why would we steal[d] silver or gold from your master's house? 9If
any of your servants[e] is found to have it,
he will die;[f] and the rest of us will become my lord's slaves.[g]"
10"Very well, then," he said, "let it be
as you say. Whoever is found to have it[h]
will become my slave;[i] the rest of you
will be free from blame."[j]
11Each of them quickly lowered his
sack to the ground and opened it. 12Then
the steward[k] proceeded to search,[l] beginning with the oldest and ending with
the youngest.[m] And the cup was found in
Benjamin's sack.[n] 13At this, they tore
their clothes.[o] Then they all loaded their
donkeys[p] and returned to the city.
14Joseph was still in the house[q] when
Judah[r] and his brothers came in, and
they threw themselves to the ground before him.[s] 15Joseph said to them, "What
is this you have done?[t] Don't you know
that a man like me can find things out by
divination?[u]"
16"What can we say to my lord?[v]" Judah[w] replied. "What can we say? How
can we prove our innocence?[x] God has
uncovered your servants'[y] guilt. We are
now my lord's slaves[z]—we ourselves
and the one who was found to have the
cup.[a]"
17But Joseph said, "Far be it from me to
do such a thing![b] Only the man who was
found to have the cup will become my
slave.[c] The rest of you, go back to your
father in peace."[d]
18Then Judah[e] went up to him and
said: "Please, my lord,[f] let your servant
speak a word to my lord. Do not be angry[g] with your servant, though you are
equal to Pharaoh himself. 19My lord asked
his servants,[h] 'Do you have a father or a
brother?'[i] 20And we answered, 'We have
an aged father, and there is a young son
born to him in his old age.[j] His brother
is dead,[k] and he is the only one of his
mother's sons left, and his father loves
him.'[l]
21"Then you said to your servants,[m]
'Bring him down to me so I can see him
for myself.'[n] 22And we said to my lord,[o]
'The boy cannot leave his father; if he

43:24 [r]S Ge 18:4
43:25 [s]S Ge 32:13 [t]ver 16
43:26 [u]S ver 16 [v]S Ge 32:13; Mt 2:11 [w]S Ge 33:3
43:27 [x]S Ge 37:3 [y]S ver 7
43:28 [z]Ge 44:24, 27,30 [a]Ge 18:2; Ex 18:7 [b]S Ge 37:7
43:29 [c]S Ge 35:18 [d]S Ge 42:13 [e]Nu 6:25; Ps 67:1; 119:58; Isa 30:18-19; 33:2
43:30 [f]Jn 11:33,38 [g]S Ge 29:11
43:31 [h]Ge 45:1; Isa 30:18; 42:14; 63:15; 64:12 [i]S ver 16
43:32 [j]S Ge 14:13; Gal 2:12 [k]Ge 46:34; Ex 8:26
43:33 [l]S Ge 35:23 [m]S Ge 42:13; 44:12
43:34 [n]S Ge 37:3; S 2Ki 25:30 [o]Lk 15:23
44:1 [p]S Ge 43:16 [q]S Ge 42:25
44:2 [r]ver 5,10,12, 16 [s]ver 8
44:3 [t]Jdg 19:9
44:4 [u]S Ge 43:16 [v]Ps 35:12; 38:20; 109:5; Pr 17:13; Jer 18:20
44:5 [w]S ver 2 [x]S Ge 30:27; Dt 18:10-14
44:7 [y]S Ge 42:11 [z]S Ge 18:25
44:8 [a]S Ge 42:13 [b]ver 2 [c]S Ge 42:25; S 43:15 [d]Ge 31:30
44:9 [e]S Ge 42:11 [f]Ge 31:32 [g]S ver 10; S Ge 43:18
44:10 [h]S ver 2 [i]ver 9,17,33 [j]S Ge 43:9
44:12 [k]S Ge 43:16 [l]S Ge 31:34 [m]S Ge 43:33 [n]ver 2
44:13 [o]S Ge 37:29 [p]S Ge 42:26
44:14 [q]Ge 43:18 [r]ver 16; S Ge 29:35; S 43:3 [s]S Ge 33:3
44:15 [t]S Ge 12:18 [u]S Ge 30:27
44:16 [v]ver 22,24; S Ge 37:8 [w]S ver 14 [x]Ps 26:6; 73:13 [y]S Ge 42:11 [z]S Ge 43:18 [a]S ver 2
44:17 [b]S Ge 18:25 [c]S ver 10 [d]S Ge 43:9
44:18 [e]S Ge 29:35 [f]S ver 16 [g]S Ge 18:30
44:19 [h]S Ge 42:11 [i]S Ge 43:7
44:20 [j]S Ge 37:3 [k]S Ge 37:33 [l]S Ge 42:13
44:21 [m]S Ge 42:11 [n]S Ge 42:15
44:22 [o]S ver 16

44:18–33 HUMANITY, Family Relationships—The ultimate in loving commitment is realized when one person offers to bear the punishment of another. Compare Judah's actions in 37:26–27.

leaves him, his father will die.'[p] 23But
you told your servants, 'Unless your youngest brother comes down with you, you
will not see my face again.'[q] 24When we
went back to your servant my father,[r] we
told him what my lord[s] had said.[t]
25"Then our father said, 'Go back and
buy a little more food.'[u] 26But we said,
'We cannot go down. Only if our youngest brother is with us will we go. We
cannot see the man's face unless our
youngest brother is with us.'[v]
27"Your servant my father[w] said to us,
'You know that my wife bore me two
sons.[x] 28One of them went away from
me, and I said, "He has surely been torn
to pieces."[y] And I have not seen him
since.[z] 29If you take this one from me too
and harm comes to him, you will bring
my gray head down to the grave[t][a] in
misery.'[b]
30"So now, if the boy is not with us
when I go back to your servant my father[c] and if my father, whose life is
closely bound up with the boy's life,[d]
31sees that the boy isn't there, he will
die.[e] Your servants[f] will bring the gray
head of our father down to the grave[g] in
sorrow. 32Your servant guaranteed the
boy's safety to my father. I said, 'If I do
not bring him back to you, I will bear the
blame before you, my father, all my
life!'[h]
33"Now then, please let your servant
remain here as my lord's slave[i] in place
of the boy,[j] and let the boy return with
his brothers. 34How can I go back to my
father if the boy is not with me? No! Do
not let me see the misery[k] that would
come upon my father."[l]

Chapter 45

Joseph Makes Himself Known

THEN Joseph could no longer control
himself[m] before all his attendants,
and he cried out, "Have everyone leave
my presence!"[n] So there was no one
with Joseph when he made himself
known to his brothers. 2And he wept[o] so
loudly that the Egyptians heard him, and
Pharaoh's household heard about it.[p]
3Joseph said to his brothers, "I am Joseph! Is my father still living?"[q] But his
brothers were not able to answer him,[r]
because they were terrified at his presence.[s]
4Then Joseph said to his brothers,
"Come close to me."[t] When they had
done so, he said, "I am your brother Joseph, the one you sold into Egypt![u] 5And
now, do not be distressed[v] and do not be
angry with yourselves for selling me
here,[w] because it was to save lives that
God sent me ahead of you.[x] 6For two
years now there has been famine[y] in the
land, and for the next five years there will
not be plowing and reaping. 7But God
sent me ahead of you to preserve for you
a remnant[z] on earth and to save your
lives by a great deliverance.[u][a]
8"So then, it was not you who sent me
here, but God.[b] He made me father[c] to
Pharaoh, lord of his entire household and

44:22 [p]S Ge 37:35
44:23 [q]S Ge 42:15; S 43:5
44:24 [r]S Ge 43:28 [s]S ver 16 [t]Ge 42:29
44:25 [u]S Ge 42:2
44:26 [v]S Ge 43:5
44:27 [w]S Ge 43:28 [x]Ge 46:19
44:28 [y]S Ge 37:33 [z]Ge 45:26,28; 46:30; 48:11
44:29 [a]S Ge 37:35 [b]S Ge 42:38
44:30 [c]S Ge 43:28 [d]1Sa 18:1; 2Sa 1:26
44:31 [e]S ver 22 [f]S Ge 42:11 [g]S Ge 37:35
44:32 [h]S Ge 42:37
44:33 [i]S ver 10; S Ge 43:18 [j]Jn 15:13
44:34 [k]S Ge 42:38 [l]Est 8:6
45:1 [m]S Ge 43:31 [n]2Sa 13:9
45:2 [o]S Ge 29:11 [p]ver 16; Ac 7:13
45:3 [q]S Ge 43:7 [r]ver 15 [s]Ge 44:20; Job 21:6; 23:15; Mt 17:6; Mk 6:49-50
45:4 [t]Ge 27:21-22 [u]Ge 37:28
45:5 [v]Ge 42:21 [w]Ge 42:22 [x]ver 7-8; Ge 50:20; Job 10:12; Ps 105:17
45:6 [y]S Ge 41:30
45:7 [z]2Ki 19:4,30, 31; Ezr 9:8,13; Isa 1:9; 10:20,21; 11:11,16; 46:3; Jer 6:9; 42:2; 50:20; Mic 4:7; 5:7; Zep 2:7 [a]S ver 5; Ge 49:18; Ex 15:2; 1Sa 14:45; 2Ki 13:5; Est 4:14; Isa 25:9; Mic 7:7
45:8 [b]ver 5 [c]Jdg 17:10; 2Ki 6:21; 13:14

[t]*29* Hebrew *Sheol*; also in verse 31 [u]*7* Or *save you as a great band of survivors*

45:4–11 EVIL AND SUFFERING, Providence—God can use adversity to accomplish His long-term goals for His people. Joseph recognized that God had guided him to Egypt as a slave so he could save many lives. Joseph's temporary suffering (37:12–28; 39:1–20; 40:23) was part of God's larger providential plan for the Hebrews. We can complain about suffering or seek ways to serve God through suffering.

45:5–9 GOD, Grace—God knew ahead of time about the coming famine and in His grace took steps to provide for the needs of His people. God's overflowing grace and amazing sovereign power are both seen in this passage in a dramatic way. The absence of bitterness in Joseph's heart was itself a work of God's grace. See 49:22–25. A boy sold into Egyptian slavery who rose to the number two political position in Egypt was a testimony to God's sovereign power. God's rescue of a people who might have otherwise starved to death is a tribute to His long-term wisdom as well as His mighty power to deliver His people.

45:5 REVELATION, Events—The brothers interfered with God's plan for Israel and his children, but even their destructive work could not ruin God's redemptive plans. Looking back, Joseph understood that God transformed brotherly rivalry into redemptive work for an entire population. God works in specific events to redeem whatever human beings try to destroy. His involvement may be hard to see in the event itself. Later reflection lets us see the event as revelation. The Bible does not recount all events of Israel's history but only those which God led them *to see as His specific revelation.* God *led in* the specific events, in the interpretation of the events, and in the memory of and recording of the events. This led to the production of an inspired Bible text as permanent revelation.

45:5–7 HISTORY, Intentions—See note on 39:2–6. God can use bad human intentions to accomplish His will. His purposes can be accomplished despite human sin. Joseph's brothers jealously sought to punish him. God used their actions to prepare Joseph for deliverance of his people in famine.

45:5 DISCIPLESHIP, God's Leadership—God's leadership may perplex us. He led Joseph via a slaves' prison. The prison setting made it possible for Joseph to come to Pharaoh's attention. He recognized that God had been guiding his life to bless many people through him, including the brothers who had sold him into slavery. See 37:1—45:28. The account is punctuated with references to God's blessing and leadership in his life. See 39:2–4,20–23; 41:15–16,25,28,32,39–40. God's people should expect God to be at work in our lives. We should recognize and acknowledge His leadership. See note on 48:15–16,21.

45:7–8 ELECTION, God's Purpose—His brothers, by their evil deed, meant to harm Joseph; but Joseph wanted them to know that God had elected him for slavery and suffering so that the children of Israel would be saved and delivered as a remnant unto God. Election seeks a faithful remnant to realize God's purposes. Those purposes and their earthly realization are not always visible even to the eyes of faith.

45:7–8 SALVATION, Preparation—What happened to Joseph in Egypt saved his father and brothers from destruction, along with their families and flocks. It set the stage for the Exodus from Egypt. Salvation history was in the making.

ruler of all Egypt.[d] 9Now hurry[e] back to
my father and say to him, 'This is what
your son Joseph says: God has made me
lord of all Egypt. Come down to me; don't
delay.[f] 10You shall live in the region of
Goshen[g] and be near me—you, your
children and grandchildren, your flocks
and herds, and all you have.[h] 11I will provide for you there,[i] because five years of
famine[j] are still to come. Otherwise you
and your household and all who belong to
you will become destitute.'[k]

12"You can see for yourselves, and so
can my brother Benjamin,[l] that it is
really I who am speaking to you.[m] 13Tell
my father about all the honor accorded
me in Egypt[n] and about everything you
have seen. And bring my father down
here quickly.[o]"

14Then he threw his arms around his
brother Benjamin and wept, and Benjamin[p] embraced him,[q] weeping. 15And
he kissed[r] all his brothers and wept over
them.[s] Afterward his brothers talked
with him.[t]

16When the news reached Pharaoh's
palace that Joseph's brothers had come,[u]
Pharaoh and all his officials[v] were
pleased.[w] 17Pharaoh said to Joseph, "Tell
your brothers, 'Do this: Load your animals[x] and return to the land of Canaan,[y]
18and bring your father and your families
back to me. I will give you the best of the
land of Egypt[z] and you can enjoy the fat
of the land.'[a]

19"You are also directed to tell them,
'Do this: Take some carts[b] from Egypt for
your children and your wives, and get
your father and come. 20Never mind
about your belongings,[c] because the best
of all Egypt[d] will be yours.' "

21So the sons of Israel did this. Joseph
gave them carts,[e] as Pharaoh had commanded, and he also gave them provisions for their journey.[f] 22To each of
them he gave new clothing,[g] but to Benjamin he gave three hundred shekels[v] of
silver and five sets of clothes.[h] 23And this
is what he sent to his father: ten donkeys[i] loaded with the best things[j] of
Egypt, and ten female donkeys loaded
with grain and bread and other provisions
for his journey.[k] 24Then he sent his
brothers away, and as they were leaving
he said to them, "Don't quarrel on the
way!"[l]

45:8 [d]S Ge 41:41 **45:9** [e]S Ge 43:15 [f]Ge 43:10; Ac 7:14 **45:10** [g]Ge 46:28, 34; 47:1,11,27; 50:8; Ex 8:22; 9:26; 10:24; 47:1 [h]Ge 46:6-7 **45:11** [i]Ge 47:12; 50:21 [j]S Ge 41:30 [k]Ps 102:17 **45:12** [l]S Ge 35:18 [m]Mk 6:50 **45:13** [n]S Ge 41:41 [o]S Ge 43:15; Ac 7:14 **45:14** [p]S Ge 35:18 [q]S Ge 29:13 **45:15** [r]S Ge 29:11; Lk 15:20 [s]S Ge 29:11,13; S 46:4 [t]ver 3 **45:16** [u]S ver 2; Ac 7:13 [v]Ge 50:7 [w]S Ge 41:37 **45:17** [x]S Ge 42:26 [y]S Ge 42:5 **45:18** [z]ver 20; Ge 20:15; 46:34; 47:6,11,27; Jer 40:4 [a]Ezr 9:12; Ps 37:19; Isa 1:19 **45:19** [b]ver 21,27; Ge 46:5; Nu 7:3-8 **45:20** [c]Ge 46:6,32 [d]S ver 18 **45:21** [e]S ver 19 [f]S Ge 42:25 **45:22** [g]S Ge 24:53 [h]S Ge 37:3; S 41:14; Jdg 14:12, 13; 2Ki 5:22 **45:23** [i]S Ge 42:26 [j]S Ge 24:10 [k]S Ge 42:25 **45:24** [l]Ge 42:21-22 **45:25** [m]Ge 13:1 [n]Ge 42:29 **45:26** [o]S Ge 41:41 [p]S Ge 44:28; 1Ki 10:7 **45:27** [q]S ver 19 **45:28** [r]Lk 16:31 [s]S Ge 44:28 **46:1** [t]ver 5 [u]S Ge 21:14 [v]S Ge 31:54 [w]S Ge 31:42 **46:2** [x]S Ge 17:5 [y]S Ge 15:1 [z]S Ge 22:1 **46:3** [a]S Ge 28:13 [b]S Ge 15:1 [c]Ge 26:2 [d]S Ge 12:2 [e]Ex 1:7 **46:4** [f]S Ge 15:16; S 28:13 [g]ver 29; Ge 45:14-15; 50:1 **46:5** [h]S Ge 21:14 [i]ver 1 [j]S Ge 45:19 **46:6** [k]S Ge 45:20 [l]S Ge 12:5 [m]Nu 20:15; Dt 26:5; Jos 24:4; Ps 105:23; Isa 52:4; Ac 7:15 **46:7** [n]Ge 13:10 [o]ver 6; Ge 45:10 **46:8** [p]S Ge 35:26; Ex 1:1; Nu 26:4 [q]S Ge 29:32 **46:9** [r]Ex 6:14; Nu 1:20; 26:7; 1Ch 5:3 [s]Nu 26:5;

25So they went up out of Egypt[m] and
came to their father Jacob in the land of
Canaan.[n] 26They told him, "Joseph is still
alive! In fact, he is ruler of all Egypt."[o]
Jacob was stunned; he did not believe
them.[p] 27But when they told him everything Joseph had said to them, and when
he saw the carts[q] Joseph had sent to carry him back, the spirit of their father Jacob revived. 28And Israel said, "I'm convinced![r] My son Joseph is still alive. I
will go and see him before I die."[s]

Chapter 46

Jacob Goes to Egypt

So Israel[t] set out with all that was his,
and when he reached Beersheba,[u] he
offered sacrifices[v] to the God of his father Isaac.[w]

2And God spoke to Israel[x] in a vision
at night[y] and said, "Jacob! Jacob!"

"Here I am,"[z] he replied.

3"I am God, the God of your father,"[a]
he said. "Do not be afraid[b] to go down to
Egypt,[c] for I will make you into a great
nation[d] there.[e] 4I will go down to Egypt
with you, and I will surely bring you back
again.[f] And Joseph's own hand will close
your eyes.[g]"

5Then Jacob left Beersheba,[h] and Israel's[i] sons took their father Jacob and
their children and their wives in the
carts[j] that Pharaoh had sent to transport
him. 6They also took with them their livestock and the possessions[k] they had acquired[l] in Canaan, and Jacob and all his
offspring went to Egypt.[m] 7He took with
him to Egypt[n] his sons and grandsons
and his daughters and granddaughters—
all his offspring.[o]

8These are the names of the sons of
Israel[p] (Jacob and his descendants) who
went to Egypt:

Reuben the firstborn[q] of Jacob.

9The sons of Reuben:[r]
Hanoch, Pallu,[s] Hezron and Carmi.

10The sons of Simeon:[u]
Jemuel,[v] Jamin, Ohad, Jakin, Zohar[w] and Shaul the son of a Canaanite woman.

1Ch 5:3 [t]Nu 26:6 **46:10** [u]S Ge 29:33; Nu 26:14 [v]Ex 6:15; Nu 26:12 [w]Nu 26:13

[v]*22* That is, about 7 1/2 pounds (about 3.5 kilograms)

46:3–4 HISTORY, Promise—God's promises may relate to the Promised Land, but He acted to fulfill the promises outside the land. Geography does not limit His control of history.

46:3–4 ELECTION, Other Nations—Election does not have geographical limits. Jacob could leave the Promised Land under the electing God's guidance, another indication of the worldwide scope of God's election purposes.

46:8–27 HISTORY, Linear—See note on 5:1–32. Biblical history is more than a history of heroes. Genealogical lists consistently show the scope of people of God continuing from one generation to the next. The Bible shows how God formed a people for Himself in the midst of normal human circumstances including famine, migration, and the passing of generations.

11The sons of Levi:[x]
Gershon,[y] Kohath[z] and Merari.[a]
12The sons of Judah:[b]
Er,[c] Onan,[d] Shelah, Perez[e] and
Zerah[f] (but Er and Onan had
died in the land of Canaan).[g]
The sons of Perez:[h]
Hezron and Hamul.[i]
13The sons of Issachar:[j]
Tola, Puah,[w][k] Jashub[x][l] and
Shimron.
14The sons of Zebulun:[m]
Sered, Elon and Jahleel.
15These were the sons Leah bore to Jacob in Paddan Aram,[y][n] besides his
daughter Dinah.[o] These sons and daughters of his were thirty-three in all.

16The sons of Gad:[p]
Zephon,[z][q] Haggi, Shuni, Ezbon,
Eri, Arodi and Areli.
17The sons of Asher:[r]
Imnah, Ishvah, Ishvi and Beriah.
Their sister was Serah.
The sons of Beriah:
Heber and Malkiel.
18These were the children born to Ja-
cob by Zilpah,[s] whom Laban had given
to his daughter Leah[t]—sixteen in all.

19The sons of Jacob's wife Rachel:[u]
Joseph and Benjamin.[v] 20In
Egypt, Manasseh[w] and Ephraim[x]
were born to Joseph[y] by Asenath
daughter of Potiphera, priest of
On.[a][z]
21The sons of Benjamin:[a]
Bela, Beker, Ashbel, Gera, Naaman, Ehi, Rosh, Muppim, Huppim
and Ard.[b]
22These were the sons of Rachel[c] who
were born to Jacob—fourteen in all.

23The son of Dan:[d]
Hushim.[e]
24The sons of Naphtali:[f]
Jahziel, Guni, Jezer and Shillem.
25These were the sons born to Jacob by
Bilhah,[g] whom Laban had given to his
daughter Rachel[h]—seven in all.

26All those who went to Egypt with Jacob—those who were his direct descendants, not counting his sons' wives—numbered sixty-six persons.[i] 27With the two
sons[b] who had been born to Joseph in
Egypt,[j] the members of Jacob's family,
which went to Egypt, were seventy[c] in
all.[k]

28Now Jacob sent Judah[l] ahead of him
to Joseph to get directions to Goshen.[m]
When they arrived in the region of
Goshen, 29Joseph had his chariot[n] made
ready and went to Goshen to meet his
father Israel.[o] As soon as Joseph appeared before him, he threw his arms
around his father[d] and wept[p] for a long
time.[q]
30Israel[r] said to Joseph, "Now I am
ready to die, since I have seen for myself
that you are still alive."[s]
31Then Joseph said to his brothers and
to his father's household, "I will go up
and speak to Pharaoh and will say to him,
'My brothers and my father's household,
who were living in the land of Canaan,[t]
have come to me.[u] 32The men are shepherds;[v] they tend livestock,[w] and they
have brought along their flocks and herds
and everything they own.'[x] 33When
Pharaoh calls you in and asks, 'What is
your occupation?'[y] 34you should answer,
'Your servants[z] have tended livestock
from our boyhood on, just as our fathers
did.'[a] Then you will be allowed to settle[b] in the region of Goshen,[c] for all
shepherds are detestable to the Egyptians.[d]"

Chapter 47

JOSEPH went and told Pharaoh, "My father and brothers, with their flocks
and herds and everything they own, have
come from the land of Canaan[e] and are
now in Goshen."[f] 2He chose five of his
brothers and presented them[g] before
Pharaoh.
3Pharaoh asked the brothers, "What is
your occupation?"[h]
"Your servants[i] are shepherds,[j]"
they replied to Pharaoh, "just as our fathers were." 4They also said to him, "We
have come to live here awhile,[k] because
the famine is severe in Canaan[l] and your
servants' flocks have no pasture.[m] So
now, please let your servants settle in Goshen."[n]
5Pharaoh said to Joseph, "Your father
and your brothers have come to you, 6and
the land of Egypt is before you; settle[o]
your father and your brothers in the best

46:11 [x]S Ge 29:34; S Nu 3:17 [y]Ex 6:16; Nu 3:21; 4:38 [z]Ex 6:16; Nu 3:27; 1Ch 23:12 [a]Ex 6:19; Nu 3:20, 33; 4:29; 26:57; 1Ch 6:19
46:12 [b]S Ge 29:35 [c]S Ge 38:3 [d]S Ge 38:4 [e]S Ge 38:29 [f]S Ge 38:30 [g]S Ge 38:7; Nu 26:19 [h]1Ch 2:5; Mt 1:3 [i]Nu 26:21
46:13 [j]S Ge 30:18 [k]Nu 26:23; Jdg 10:1; 1Ch 7:1 [l]Nu 26:24
46:14 [m]S Ge 30:20
46:15 [n]S Ge 25:20; 29:31-35 [o]S Ge 30:21
46:16 [p]S Ge 30:11; S Nu 1:25 [q]Nu 26:15
46:17 [r]S Ge 30:13
46:18 [s]Ge 30:10 [t]S Ge 16:1
46:19 [u]S Ge 29:6 [v]Ge 44:27
46:20 [w]S Ge 41:51 [x]S Ge 41:52 [y]Nu 26:28-37 [z]S Ge 41:45
46:21 [a]Nu 26:38-41; 1Ch 7:6-12; 8:1 [b]Nu 26:40; 1Ch 8:3
46:22 [c]S Ge 29:6
46:23 [d]S Ge 30:6 [e]Nu 26:42
46:24 [f]S Ge 30:8
46:25 [g]Ge 30:8 [h]S Ge 24:61
46:26 [i]ver 5-7; Ex 1:5; Dt 10:22
46:27 [j]S Ge 41:45 [k]S Ge 34:30; Ac 7:14
46:28 [l]S Ge 43:3 [m]S Ge 45:10
46:29 [n]S Ge 41:43 [o]ver 1,30; S Ge 32:28; 47:29, 31 [p]S Ge 29:11 [q]S ver 4; Lk 15:20
46:30 [r]S ver 29 [s]S Ge 44:28
46:31 [t]S Ge 42:13 [u]S Ge 45:10
46:32 [v]Ge 47:3 [w]S Ge 37:2 [x]S Ge 45:20
46:33 [y]Ge 47:3
46:34 [z]S Ge 42:11 [a]Ge 47:3 [b]S Ge 34:10 [c]S Ge 45:10 [d]S Ge 43:32
47:1 [e]S Ge 42:13 [f]S Ge 46:31
47:2 [g]S Ge 43:15
47:3 [h]Ge 46:33 [i]S Ge 42:11 [j]Ge 46:32
47:4 [k]Ru 1:1 [l]S Ge 12:10 [m]1Ki 18:5; Jer 14:5-6; Joel 1:18 [n]Ge 46:34
47:6 [o]S Ge 34:10

[w]*13* Samaritan Pentateuch and Syriac (see also 1 Chron. 7:1); Masoretic Text *Puvah* [x]*13* Samaritan Pentateuch and some Septuagint manuscripts (see also Num. 26:24 and 1 Chron. 7:1); Masoretic Text *Iob* [y]*15* That is, Northwest Mesopotamia [z]*16* Samaritan Pentateuch and Septuagint (see also Num. 26:15); Masoretic Text *Ziphion* [a]*20* That is, Heliopolis [b]*27* Hebrew; Septuagint *the nine children* [c]*27* Hebrew (see also Exodus 1:5 and footnote); Septuagint (see also Acts 7:14) *seventy-five* [d]*29* Hebrew *around him*

47:5–6 HISTORY, Universal—God's direction of history overrode normal tabus and prejudices to accomplish His will. Egyptians hated shepherds, but God's chosen shepherds gained special privilege from Egypt's all-powerful ruler.

part of the land.[p] Let them live in Goshen. And if you know of any among them with special ability,[q] put them in charge of my own livestock.[r] "

7Then Joseph brought his father Jacob in and presented him[s] before Pharaoh. After Jacob blessed[e] Pharaoh,[t] 8Pharaoh asked him, "How old are you?"

9And Jacob said to Pharaoh, "The years of my pilgrimage are a hundred and thirty.[u] My years have been few and difficult,[v] and they do not equal the years of the pilgrimage of my fathers.[w]" 10Then Jacob blessed[f] Pharaoh[x] and went out from his presence.

11So Joseph settled his father and his brothers in Egypt and gave them property in the best part of the land,[y] the district of Rameses,[z] as Pharaoh directed. 12Joseph also provided his father and his brothers and all his father's household with food, according to the number of their children.[a]

Joseph and the Famine

13There was no food, however, in the whole region because the famine was severe; both Egypt and Canaan wasted away because of the famine.[b] 14Joseph collected all the money that was to be found in Egypt and Canaan in payment for the grain they were buying,[c] and he brought it to Pharaoh's palace.[d] 15When the money of the people of Egypt and Canaan was gone,[e] all Egypt came to Joseph[f] and said, "Give us food. Why should we die before your eyes?[g] Our money is used up."

16"Then bring your livestock,[h]" said Joseph. "I will sell you food in exchange for your livestock, since your money is gone.[i]" 17So they brought their livestock to Joseph, and he gave them food in exchange for their horses,[j] their sheep and goats, their cattle and donkeys.[k] And he brought them through that year with food in exchange for all their livestock.

18When that year was over, they came to him the following year and said, "We cannot hide from our lord the fact that since our money is gone[l] and our livestock belongs to you,[m] there is nothing left for our lord except our bodies and our land. 19Why should we perish before your eyes[n]—we and our land as well? Buy us and our land in exchange for food,[o] and we with our land will be in bondage to Pharaoh.[p] Give us seed so that we may live and not die,[q] and that the land may not become desolate."

20So Joseph bought all the land in Egypt for Pharaoh. The Egyptians, one and all, sold their fields, because the famine was too severe[r] for them. The land became Pharaoh's, 21and Joseph reduced the people to servitude,[g][s] from one end of Egypt to the other. 22However, he did not buy the land of the priests,[t] because they received a regular allotment from Pharaoh and had food enough from the allotment[u] Pharaoh gave them. That is why they did not sell their land.

23Joseph said to the people, "Now that I have bought you and your land today for Pharaoh, here is seed[v] for you so you can plant the ground.[w] 24But when the crop comes in, give a fifth[x] of it to Pharaoh. The other four-fifths you may keep as seed for the fields and as food for yourselves and your households and your children."

25"You have saved our lives," they said. "May we find favor in the eyes of our lord;[y] we will be in bondage to Pharaoh."[z]

26So Joseph established it as a law concerning land in Egypt—still in force today—that a fifth[a] of the produce belongs to Pharaoh. It was only the land of the priests that did not become Pharaoh's.[b]

27Now the Israelites settled in Egypt in the region of Goshen.[c] They acquired property there[d] and were fruitful and increased greatly in number.[e]

28Jacob lived in Egypt[f] seventeen years, and the years of his life were a hundred and forty-seven.[g] 29When the time drew near for Israel[h] to die,[i] he called for his son Joseph and said to him, "If I have found favor in your eyes,[j] put your hand under my thigh[k] and promise that you will show me kindness[l] and faithfulness.[m] Do not bury me in Egypt, 30but when I rest with my fathers,[n] carry me out of Egypt and bury me where they are buried."[o]

"I will do as you say," he said.

31"Swear to me,"[p] he said. Then Joseph swore to him,[q] and Israel[r] worshiped as he leaned on the top of his staff.[h][s]

47:6 pS Ge 13:9; S 45:18 qEx 18:21, 25; Dt 1:13,15; 2Ch 19:5; Ps 15:2 rS Ge 39:4
47:7 sS Ge 43:15 tver 10; 2Sa 14:22; 19:39; 1Ki 8:66
47:9 uS Ge 25:7 vS Ge 3:17; Ps 39:4; 89:47 wJob 8:9; Ps 39:12
47:10 xS ver 7
47:11 yS Ge 45:10, 18 zEx 1:11; 12:37; Nu 33:3,5
47:12 aS Ge 45:11
47:13 bS Ge 12:10; S 41:30
47:14 cS Ge 41:36 dS Ge 41:34; Ex 7:23; 8:24; Jer 43:9
47:15 ever 16,18 fS Ge 41:57 gver 19; Ex 16:3
47:16 hver 18,19 iver 15
47:17 jEx 14:9 kS Ge 12:16
47:18 lS ver 15 mS ver 16
47:19 nS ver 15 oS ver 16 pver 21, 25 qS Ge 42:2
47:20 rS Ge 12:10
47:21 sS ver 19
47:22 tver 26 uDt 14:28-29
47:23 vIsa 55:10; 61:11 wNe 5:3
47:24 xS Ge 41:34
47:25 yS Ge 32:5 zS ver 19
47:26 aS Ge 41:34 bver 22
47:27 cS Ge 45:10, 18 dS Ge 33:19 eS Ge 1:22; S 12:2; S 17:6
47:28 fPs 105:23 gS Ge 25:7
47:29 hS Ge 46:29 iS Ge 27:2 jS Ge 32:5 kS Ge 24:2 lS Ge 19:19 mS Ge 24:27; Jdg 1:24; 2Sa 2:6
47:30 nS Ge 15:15 oS Ge 23:20; S 25:9; S 29:16; 50:25; Ex 13:19; Jos 24:32; Ac 7:15-16
47:31 pGe 21:23; Jos 2:20; Jdg 15:12; 1Sa 24:21; 30:15 qS Ge 24:3 rS Ge 46:29 sS Ge 32:10; Heb 11:21 fn 1Ki 1:47

e7 Or *greeted* **f**10 Or *said farewell to* **g**21 Samaritan Pentateuch and Septuagint (see also Vulgate); Masoretic Text *and he moved the people into the cities* **h**31 Or *Israel bowed down at the head of his bed*

47:26–27 HISTORY, Promise—See note on Ex 1:1–7.
47:29–30 HUMANITY, Burial—Many images are used to describe the experience of death. The ultimate desire of those about to die was to be buried in the family burial ground, so that the family might be reunited in death. It remained for the New Testament to point out the ultimate nature of reunion in death. See 1 Co 15:54–57.

Chapter 48

Manasseh and Ephraim

SOME time later Joseph was told, "Your father is ill." So he took his two sons Manasseh and Ephraim[t] along with him. 2When Jacob was told, "Your son Joseph has come to you," Israel[u] rallied his strength and sat up on the bed.

3Jacob said to Joseph, "God Almighty[1][v] appeared to me at Luz[w] in the land of Canaan, and there he blessed me[x] 4and said to me, 'I am going to make you fruitful and will increase your numbers.[y] I will make you a community of peoples, and I will give this land[z] as an everlasting possession to your descendants after you.'[a]

5"Now then, your two sons born to you in Egypt[b] before I came to you here will be reckoned as mine; Ephraim and Manasseh will be mine,[c] just as Reuben[d] and Simeon[e] are mine. 6Any children born to you after them will be yours; in the territory they inherit they will be reckoned under the names of their brothers. 7As I was returning from Paddan,[1][f] to my sorrow[g] Rachel died in the land of Canaan while we were still on the way, a little distance from Ephrath. So I buried her there beside the road to Ephrath" (that is, Bethlehem).[h]

8When Israel[i] saw the sons of Joseph,[j] he asked, "Who are these?"

9"They are the sons God has given me here,"[k] Joseph said to his father.

Then Israel said, "Bring them to me so I may bless[l] them."

10Now Israel's eyes were failing because of old age, and he could hardly see.[m] So Joseph brought his sons close to him, and his father kissed them[n] and embraced them.[o]

11Israel[p] said to Joseph, "I never expected to see your face again,[q] and now God has allowed me to see your children too."[r]

12Then Joseph removed them from Israel's knees[s] and bowed down with his face to the ground.[t] 13And Joseph took both of them, Ephraim on his right toward Israel's left hand and Manasseh on his left toward Israel's right hand,[u] and brought them close to him. 14But Israel[v] reached out his right hand and put it on Ephraim's head,[w] though he was the younger,[x] and crossing his arms, he put his left hand on Manasseh's head, even though Manasseh was the firstborn.[y]

15Then he blessed[z] Joseph and said,

"May the God before whom my fathers
Abraham and Isaac walked,[a]
the God who has been my shepherd[b]
all my life to this day,
16the Angel[c] who has delivered me from all harm[d]
—may he bless[e] these boys.[f]
May they be called by my name
and the names of my fathers
Abraham and Isaac,[g]
and may they increase greatly
upon the earth."[h]

17When Joseph saw his father placing his right hand[i] on Ephraim's head[j] he was displeased; so he took hold of his father's hand to move it from Ephraim's head to Manasseh's head. 18Joseph said to him, "No, my father, this one is the firstborn; put your right hand on his head."[k]

19But his father refused and said, "I know, my son, I know. He too will become a people, and he too will become great.[l] Nevertheless, his younger brother will be greater than he,[m] and his descendants will become a group of nations.[n]" 20He blessed[o] them that day[p] and said,

"In your[k] name will Israel[q]
pronounce this blessing:[r]
'May God make you like Ephraim[s]
and Manasseh.[t]' "

So he put Ephraim ahead of Manasseh.

21Then Israel said to Joseph, "I am about to die, but God will be with you[1][u] and take you[1] back to the land of your[1] fathers.[v] 22And to you, as one who is

48:1 [t]S Ge 41:52; Heb 11:21
48:2 [u]ver 8,9,11, 14,20
48:3 [v]S Ge 17:1 [w]S Ge 28:19 [x]S Ge 28:13; S 32:29
48:4 [y]S Ge 12:2; S 17:6 [z]S Ge 12:7; S 28:13 [a]S Ge 15:7
48:5 [b]S Ge 41:50-52 [c]1Ch 5:1 [d]S Ge 29:32 [e]S Ge 29:33
48:7 [f]S Ge 25:20 [g]S Ge 42:38 [h]Ge 35:19; Ru 1:2; 1Sa 16:4
48:8 [i]S ver 2 [j]ver 10
48:9 [k]S Ge 33:5 [l]S Ge 24:60
48:10 [m]S Ge 27:1 [n]S Ge 27:27 [o]S Ge 29:13
48:11 [p]S ver 2 [q]S Ge 44:28 [r]Ge 50:23; Job 42:16; Ps 103:17; 128:6
48:12 [s]Ge 50:23; Job 3:12 [t]S Ge 19:1; S 33:3; 37:10
48:13 [u]Ps 16:8; 73:23; 110:1; Mt 25:33
48:14 [v]S ver 2 [w]ver 17,18 [x]S Ge 25:23 [y]S Ge 29:32; S 41:51
48:15 [z]S Ge 24:60 [a]S Ge 5:22 [b]Ge 49:24; 2Sa 5:2; Ps 23:1; 80:1; Isa 40:11; Jer 23:4
48:16 [c]S Ge 16:7 [d]S Ge 24:50; 2Sa 4:9; Ps 71:4; Jer 15:21; Da 3:17 [e]S Ge 28:3 [f]1Ch 5:1; Eze 47:13; Heb 11:21 [g]S Ge 28:13 [h]S Ge 12:2; S 13:14
48:17 [i]ver 13 [j]S ver 14
48:18 [k]S ver 14
48:19 [l]Ge 17:20 [m]S Ge 25:23 [n]S Ge 12:2
48:20 [o]S Ge 24:60 [p]Heb 11:21 [q]S ver 2 [r]Lev 9:22; Nu 6:23; Dt 10:8; 21:5 [s]Nu 2:18; Jer 31:9 [t]S Ge 41:51; Nu 2:20; 10:23; Ru 4:11
48:21 [u]S Ge 26:3 [v]S Ge 15:16; S 28:13; Dt 30:3; Ps 126:1; Jer 29:14; Eze 34:13

[1]3 Hebrew *El-Shaddai* [1]7 That is, Northwest Mesopotamia [k]20 The Hebrew is singular. [1]21 The Hebrew is plural.

48:3–20 ELECTION, Providence—See note on 31:42. The blind Jacob worked out God's election intention despite Joseph's protests.

48:4 HISTORY, Promise—See note on 15:1–21.

48:15–16,21 DISCIPLESHIP, God's Leadership—God continues to lead His people from generation to generation. Speaking as the bearer of God's grace and promise, Jacob, aged and about to die, blessed Joseph and promised the continued blessing of God. God's aging leaders should be consciously active in passing the mantle of leadership from one generation to the next. See note on 45:5.

***48:15–20 PRAYER, Blessing**—The patriarchal blessing was the family's way of transmitting religious tradition to a new* generation (vv 3–4). Foreign birth did not rob Joseph's sons of family blessings. They, too, could become heirs of God's original blessing to Abraham (12:1–7). Control of the blessing did not rest with Joseph or Jacob. Mysteriously, God led to the proper blessing for each son. The blessing tied the new generation to the Promised Land, not to Egypt; and to Yahweh, God of Israel, for fertility, not to Baal. It promised deliverance in the future parallel to deliverance received by Jacob. The prayer of blessing was thus instruction, commitment, confession of faith, *and petition. See* note on 14:18–20. Compare 49:1–27; Dt *33:1–29;* Mt 19:13; Mk 10:16; Lk 24:50.

48:17–20 HISTORY, Universal—See note on 25:23.

over your brothers,[w] I give the ridge of land[m][x] I took from the Amorites with my sword[y] and my bow."

Chapter 49

Jacob Blesses His Sons

49:1–28Ref — Dt 33:1–29

THEN Jacob called for his sons and said: "Gather around so I can tell you what will happen to you in days to come.[z]

2"Assemble[a] and listen, sons of Jacob;
listen to your father Israel.[b]

3"Reuben, you are my firstborn,[c]
my might, the first sign of my strength,[d]
excelling in honor,[e] excelling in power.
4Turbulent as the waters,[f] you will no longer excel,
for you went up onto your father's bed,
onto my couch and defiled it.[g]

5"Simeon[h] and Levi[i] are brothers—
their swords[n] are weapons of violence.[j]
6Let me not enter their council,
let me not join their assembly,[k]
for they have killed men in their anger[l]
and hamstrung[m] oxen as they pleased.
7Cursed be their anger, so fierce,
and their fury,[n] so cruel![o]
I will scatter them in Jacob
and disperse them in Israel.[p]

8"Judah,[o][q] your brothers will praise you;
your hand will be on the neck[r] of your enemies;
your father's sons will bow down to you.[s]
9You are a lion's[t] cub,[u] O Judah;[v]
you return from the prey,[w] my son.
Like a lion he crouches and lies down,
like a lioness—who dares to rouse him?
10The scepter will not depart from Judah,[x]
nor the ruler's staff from between his feet,
until he comes to whom it belongs[p][y]
and the obedience of the nations is his.[z]
11He will tether his donkey[a] to a vine,
his colt to the choicest branch;[b]
he will wash his garments in wine,
his robes in the blood of grapes.[c]
12His eyes will be darker than wine,
his teeth whiter than milk.[q][d]

13"Zebulun[e] will live by the seashore
and become a haven for ships;
his border will extend toward Sidon.[f]

14"Issachar[g] is a rawboned[r] donkey
lying down between two saddlebags.[s][h]
15When he sees how good is his resting place
and how pleasant is his land,[i]
he will bend his shoulder to the burden[j]
and submit to forced labor.[k]

16"Dan[t][l] will provide justice for his people
as one of the tribes of Israel.[m]
17Dan[n] will be a serpent by the roadside,
a viper along the path,[o]
that bites the horse's heels[p]
so that its rider tumbles backward.

18"I look for your deliverance,[q]
O LORD.[r]

19"Gad[u][s] will be attacked by a band of raiders,

48:22 [w]Ge 37:8 [x]Jos 24:32; Jn 4:5 [y]S Ge 34:26 **49:1** [z]Nu 24:14; Dt 31:29; Jer 23:20; Da 2:28,45 **49:2** [a]Jos 24:1 [b]ver 16,28; Ps 34:11 **49:3** [c]S Ge 29:32; S 41:51 [d]Dt 21:17; Ps 78:51; 105:36 [e]S Ge 34:19 **49:4** [f]Isa 57:20; Jer 49:23 [g]S Ge 29:29; S 34:5 **49:5** [h]S Ge 29:33 [i]Ge 29:34 [j]S Ge 34:25; S Pr 4:17 **49:6** [k]Ps 1:1; Pr 1:15; Eph 5:11 [l]S Ge 34:26 [m]Jos 11:6,9; 2Sa 8:4; 1Ch 18:4 **49:7** [n]Ge 34:7 [o]Ge 34:25 [p]Jos 19:1,9; 21:1-42 **49:8** [q]S Ge 29:35 [r]Dt 28:48 [s]S Ge 9:25; 1Ch 5:2 **49:9** [t]Nu 24:9; Ps 7:2; 10:9; Eze 19:5; Mic 5:8 [u]Eze 19:2 [v]Rev 5:5 [w]ver 27; Nu 23:24; Job 38:39; Ps 17:12; 22:13; 104:21 **49:10** [x]Nu 24:17,19; Jdg 1:1-2; 20:18; 1Ch 5:2; 28:4; Ps 60:7; 108:8 [y]Eze 21:27 [z]Ps 2:9; 72:8-11; 98:3; 110:2; Isa 2:4; 26:18; 42:1,4; 45:22; 48:20; 49:6; 51:5 **49:11** [a]Jdg 5:10; 10:4; Zec 9:9 [b]Dt 8:8; 2Ki 18:32 [c]Dt 32:14; Isa 63:2 **49:12** [d]SS 5:12 **49:13** [e]S Ge 30:20 [f]S Ge 10:19 **49:14** [g]S Ge 30:18 [h]Jdg 5:16; Ps 68:13 **49:15** [i]Jos 19:17-23 [j]Eze 29:18 [k]1Ki 4:6; 5:13; 9:21; Isa 14:2; 31:8 **49:16** [l]Ge 30:6 [m]S ver 2 **49:17** [n]Jdg 18:27 [o]Jer 8:17; Am 9:3 [p]ver 19 **49:18** [q]S Ge 45:7; Ps 40:1-3 [r]Ps 119:166,174 **49:19** [s]S Ge 30:11

[m]22 Or *And to you I give one portion more than to your brothers—the portion* [n]5 The meaning of the Hebrew for this word is uncertain. [o]8 *Judah* sounds like and may be derived from the Hebrew for *praise.* [p]10 Or *until Shiloh comes;* or *until he comes to whom tribute belongs* [q]12 Or *will be dull from wine, / his teeth white from milk* [r]14 Or *strong* [s]14 Or *campfires* [t]16 *Dan* here means *he provides justice.* [u]19 *Gad* can mean *attack* and *band of raiders.*

49:1–28 HISTORY, God's People—History is not an unchanging way for all God's people. Various parts of God's people have various gifts, opportunities, and challenges. The different prospects for the tribes of Israel mirror the different histories of God's people through the ages. See note on 25:23.

49:1–28 *ELECTION,* Predestination—The patriarch under divine guidance pronounced the tribal fortunes before tribes were formed or the nation settled in the land. God knows the future, but His knowledge is not a causative factor which prohibits the exercise of human freedom. Election involves the mystery of God's foreknowledge and God's decision to respond in free relationship to free humans He created.

49:1–28 PRAYER, Blessing—See note on 48:15–20. Prayer reaches into the future as well as seeking help for the present. Jacob's blessing gave national identity to his future descendants as they formed the nation Israel. Differing characteristics and locations did not separate the tribes, for the blessing of Abraham tied them to a joint mission under the one God. Each had a role to play. Reading Jacob's blessing on them would call each new generation to fulfill that role under the Creator of nature and of the nation.

49:5–7 CHRISTIAN ETHICS, War and Peace—Persons dedicated to anger, war, and violence do not receive blessings. Improper human attitudes are the basic cause of war. See note on 13:7–12.

49:10 JESUS CHRIST, Foretold—Jesus was a descendant of Judah (Lk 3:33). The triumphant Christ is called "the Lion of the tribe of Judah" (Rev 5:5). Shiloh (NIV footnote) remains a common name used among Christians to remind us of His promised first coming and final coming.

but he will attack them at their
heels.[t]

20"Asher's[u] food will be rich;[v]
he will provide delicacies fit for a
king.[w]

21"Naphtali[x] is a doe set free
that bears beautiful fawns.[v] [y]

22"Joseph[z] is a fruitful vine,[a]
a fruitful vine near a spring,
whose branches[b] climb over a
wall.[w]

23With bitterness archers attacked him;[c]
they shot at him with hostility.[d]
24But his bow remained steady,[e]
his strong arms[f] stayed[x] limber,
because of the hand of the Mighty One
of Jacob,[g]
because of the Shepherd,[h] the Rock
of Israel,[i]
25because of your father's God,[j] who
helps[k] you,
because of the Almighty,[y] [l] who
blesses you
with blessings of the heavens above,
blessings of the deep that lies
below,[m]
blessings of the breast[n] and
womb.[o]
26Your father's blessings are greater
than the blessings of the ancient
mountains,
than[z] the bounty of the age-old
hills.[p]
Let all these rest on the head of
Joseph,[q]
on the brow of the prince among[a]
his brothers.[r]

27"Benjamin[s] is a ravenous wolf;[t]
in the morning he devours the
prey,[u]
in the evening he divides the
plunder."[v]

28All these are the twelve tribes of Israel,[w] and this is what their father said to
them when he blessed them, giving each
the blessing[x] appropriate to him.

The Death of Jacob

29Then he gave them these instructions:[y] "I am about to be gathered to my
people.[z] Bury me with my fathers[a] in
the cave in the field of Ephron the Hittite,[b] 30the cave in the field of Machpelah,[c] near Mamre[d] in Canaan, which
Abraham bought as a burial place[e] from
Ephron the Hittite, along with the field.[f]
31There Abraham[g] and his wife Sarah[h]
were buried, there Isaac and his wife Rebekah[i] were buried, and there I buried
Leah.[j] 32The field and the cave in it were
bought from the Hittites.[b] [k]"

33When Jacob had finished giving instructions to his sons, he drew his feet up
into the bed, breathed his last and was
gathered to his people.[l]

Chapter 50

JOSEPH threw himself upon his father
and wept over him and kissed him.[m]
2Then Joseph directed the physicians in
his service to embalm his father Israel. So
the physicians embalmed him,[n] 3taking a
full forty days, for that was the time required for embalming. And the Egyptians
mourned for him seventy days.[o]

4When the days of mourning[p] had
passed, Joseph said to Pharaoh's court,[q]
"If I have found favor in your eyes,[r]
speak to Pharaoh for me. Tell him, 5'My
father made me swear an oath[s] and said,
"I am about to die;[t] bury me in the tomb
I dug for myself[u] in the land of Canaan."[v] Now let me go up and bury my
father;[w] then I will return.'"

6Pharaoh said, "Go up and bury your
father, as he made you swear to do."

7So Joseph went up to bury his father.
All Pharaoh's officials[x] accompanied him
—the dignitaries of his court[y] and all the
dignitaries of Egypt— 8besides all the
members of Joseph's household and his
brothers and those belonging to his father's household.[z] Only their children
and their flocks and herds were left in
Goshen.[a] 9Chariots[b] and horsemen[c]
also went up with him. It was a very large
company.

10When they reached the threshing
floor[c] of Atad, near the Jordan, they lamented loudly and bitterly;[d] and there
Joseph observed a seven-day period[e] of
mourning[f] for his father.[g] 11When the
Canaanites[h] who lived there saw the
mourning at the threshing floor of Atad,
they said, "The Egyptians are holding a
solemn ceremony of mourning."[i] That is

49:19 [t]ver 17
49:20 [u]S Ge 30:13 [v]Isa 25:6 [w]Job 29:6
49:21 [x]S Ge 30:8 [y]Job 39:1
49:22 [z]Ge 30:24 [a]S Ge 17:6; Ps 128:3; Eze 19:10 [b]Ps 80:10
49:23 [c]1Ch 10:3 [d]S Ge 27:41; S 37:24
49:24 [e]Job 29:20 [f]Ps 18:34; Isa 63:12 [g]Ps 132:2,5; Isa 1:24; 10:34; 49:26; 60:16 [h]S Ge 48:15 [i]Dt 32:4,15,18,31; 1Sa 2:2; 2Sa 22:32; Ps 18:2,31; 19:14; 78:35; 89:26; 144:1; Isa 17:10; 26:4; 30:29; 44:8; Hab 1:12
49:25 [j]S Ge 28:13 [k]Ex 18:4; Ps 27:9 [l]S Ge 17:1 [m]S Ge 27:28 [n]Isa 66:11 [o]Dt 7:13; 28:4; Ps 107:38; Pr 10:22
49:26 [p]Hab 3:6 [q]1Ch 5:1; Eze 47:13 [r]S Ge 37:8
49:27 [s]Ge 35:18; Jdg 20:12-13 [t]Hab 1:8; Zep 3:3 [u]S ver 9 [v]Nu 31:11; Dt 2:35; Jos 7:21; 8:2; 22:8; Jdg 8:24
49:28 [w]S ver 2 [x]S Ge 27:4
49:29 [y]Ge 50:16 [z]S Ge 25:8 [a]S Ge 15:15; 50:25; 2Sa 2:32; 19:37 [b]S Ge 25:9
49:30 [c]S Ge 23:9 [d]S Ge 13:18 [e]S Ge 23:4 [f]S Ge 23:20
49:31 [g]Ge 25:9 [h]Ge 23:19 [i]S Ge 24:67 [j]S Ge 23:20; S 29:16
49:32 [k]S Ge 10:15
49:33 [l]S Ge 25:8; Ac 7:15
50:1 [m]S Ge 29:11; S 46:4
50:2 [n]ver 26; 2Ch 16:14; Mt 26:12; Mk 16:1; Jn 19:39-40
50:3 [o]S Ge 37:34; S Dt 1:3
50:4 [p]S Ge 27:41 [q]ver 7 [r]S Ge 30:27; S 32:5
50:5 [s]S Ge 24:37 [t]ver 24 [u]2Sa 18:18; 2Ch 16:14; Isa 22:16; Mt 27:60 [v]Ge 47:31 [w]Mt 8:21
50:7 [x]Ge 45:16 [y]ver 4
50:8 [z]ver 14 [a]S Ge 45:10
50:9 [b]S Ge 41:43
50:10 [c]Nu 15:20; Ru 3:2; 2Sa 24:18; 1Ki 22:10 [d]2Sa 1:17; 3:33; 2Ch 35:25; Eze 32:16; Ac 8:2 [e]1Sa 31:13; Job 2:13; Eze 3:15 [f]S Ge 27:41; S Lev 10:6 [g]S Ge 37:34
50:11 [h]S Ge 10:18 [i]S Ge 37:34

[v]21 Or *free; / he utters beautiful words* [w]22 Or *Joseph is a wild colt, / a wild colt near a spring, / a wild donkey on a terraced hill* [x]23,24 Or *archers will attack . . . will shoot . . . will remain . . . will stay* [y]25 Hebrew *Shaddai* [z]26 Or *of my progenitors, / as great as* [a]26 Or *the one separated from* [b]32 Or *the sons of Heth* [c]9 Or *charioteers*

49:26–27 HISTORY, Promise—God began *fulfilling His promises in a foreign land. Israel gained possessions,* grew in *number, and blessed the nations.* Compare 12:1–3.
49:29–33 HUMANITY, Burial—See note on 47:29–30.

50:1–3 **HUMANITY, Attitudes to Death**—Embalming of the dead was a practice of Egypt. Grief over death did not prevent the reverent care for the body of the loved one.

why that place near the Jordan is called
Abel Mizraim.[d]
12So Jacob's sons did as he had commanded them:[j] 13They carried him to
the land of Canaan and buried him in the
cave in the field of Machpelah,[k] near
Mamre,[l] which Abraham had bought as
a burial place from Ephron the Hittite,[m]
along with the field.[n] 14After burying his
father, Joseph returned to Egypt, together
with his brothers and all the others who
had gone with him to bury his father.[o]

Joseph Reassures His Brothers

15When Joseph's brothers saw that
their father was dead, they said, "What if
Joseph holds a grudge[p] against us and
pays us back for all the wrongs we did to
him?"[q] 16So they sent word to Joseph,
saying, "Your father left these instructions[r] before he died: 17'This is what you
are to say to Joseph: I ask you to forgive
your brothers the sins[s] and the wrongs
they committed in treating you so badly.'[t] Now please forgive the sins of the
servants of the God of your father.[u]"
When their message came to him, Joseph
wept.[v]
18His brothers then came and threw
themselves down before him.[w] "We are
your slaves,"[x] they said.
19But Joseph said to them, "Don't be
afraid. Am I in the place of God?[y] 20You
intended to harm me,[z] but God intended[a] it for good[b] to accomplish what is
now being done, the saving of many
lives.[c] 21So then, don't be afraid. I will
provide for you and your children.[d]" And
he reassured them and spoke kindly[e] to
them.

The Death of Joseph

22Joseph stayed in Egypt, along with all
his father's family. He lived a hundred
and ten years[f] 23and saw the third generation[g] of Ephraim's[h] children.[i] Also the
children of Makir[j] son of Manasseh[k]
were placed at birth on Joseph's
knees.[e] [l]
24Then Joseph said to his brothers, "I
am about to die.[m] But God will surely
come to your aid[n] and take you up out of
this land to the land[o] he promised on
oath to Abraham,[p] Isaac[q] and Jacob."[r]
25And Joseph made the sons of Israel
swear an oath[s] and said, "God will surely come to your aid, and then you must
carry my bones[t] up from this place."[u]
26So Joseph died[v] at the age of a hundred and ten.[w] And after they embalmed
him,[x] he was placed in a coffin in Egypt.

50:12 [j]Ge 49:29 **50:13** [k]S Ge 23:9 [l]S Ge 13:18 [m]S Ge 25:9 [n]S Ge 23:20 **50:14** [o]ver 8 **50:15** [p]S Ge 27:41 [q]ver 17; S Ge 9:5; 37:28; Zep 3:11; 1Pe 3:9 **50:16** [r]Ge 49:29 **50:17** [s]S Mt 6:14 [t]S ver 15 [u]S Ge 28:13 [v]S Ge 29:11 **50:18** [w]S Ge 37:7 [x]S Ge 43:18 **50:19** [y]S Ge 30:2; S Ex 32:34; Ro 12:19; Heb 10:30 **50:20** [z]Ge 37:20 [a]Isa 10:7; Mic 4:11-12 [b]Ro 8:28 [c]S Ge 45:5; Est 4:14 **50:21** [d]S Ge 45:11 [e]S Ge 34:3; Eph 4:32 **50:22** [f]S Ge 25:7; Jos 24:29 **50:23** [g]Job 42:16 [h]S Ge 41:52 [i]S Ge 48:11 [j]Nu 26:29; 27:1; 32:39,40; 36:1; Dt 3:15; Jos 13:31; 17:1; Jdg 5:14 [k]S Ge 41:51 [l]S Ge 48:12 **50:24** [m]ver 5 [n]Ru 1:6; Ps 35:2; 106:4; Isa 38:14 [o]S Ge 15:14 [p]S Ge 13:17 [q]S Ge 17:19 [r]S Ge 12:7; S 15:16 **50:25** [s]S Ge 24:37 [t]S Ge 49:29 [u]S Ge 47:29-30; Heb 11:22 **50:26** [v]Ex 1:6 [w]S Ge 25:7 [x]S ver 2

[d]*11 Abel Mizraim* means *mourning of the Egyptians.*
[e]*23* That is, were counted as his

50:12–14 HUMANITY, Burial—See note on 47:29–30.
50:15–19 EVIL AND SUFFERING, Endurance—Other people may cause us to suffer even when we do not deserve such treatment. Injustice by others does not give us the right to retaliate. Joseph refused to play God and seek revenge on his brothers. God is the One who punishes. He can work through human injustice to bring blessing to us and to fulfill His purposes. See notes on Mt 5:38–48; Ro 12:14–21.
50:17–21 SALVATION, Forgiveness—God's salvation is His forgiveness. The way Joseph forgave his brothers is comparable to the way God forgives us.
50:19–21 HISTORY, Intentions—See note on 45:5–7.
50:20 EVIL AND SUFFERING, Providence—Joseph recognized that God's providential plan for his life included the brothers' intentions and his own temporary suffering. The theme of divine providence permeates the entire story of Joseph (chs 37—50) and illustrates God's ability to guide the course of history. Our sufferings often have a purpose within God's providence. See notes on 41:1–32; 45:4–11.
50:20 ELECTION, Providence—See note on 31:42. In 45:7–8 Joseph showed he had no malice against his brothers for selling him into slavery. The brothers had not understood or believed Joseph. When their father died, they expected Joseph to seek revenge. He reminded them that God used the actions intended for harm to fulfill His election plan for the saving of many lives. God's purposes are always good.
50:24–25 HISTORY, Promise—God's promises are sure, so God's people can set goals and make commitments in light of divine promises.
50:25 REVELATION, Divine Presence—Divine revelation can be expected in future events. Joseph knew that the God who had constantly redeemed his life would also be present for the next generation. God's visitation would provide instruction and guidance of His unfinished purposes for Joseph's descendants. Our past experience of God gives us confidence He will be present in the future.
50:26 HUMANITY, Attitudes to Death—See note on 50:1–3.

Exodus

Theological Setting

The Hebrew people lived in Egypt for about four hundred years (12:40; Ge 15:13). From the status of honored and welcomed guests (Ge 45:17-20) when they first came to Egypt about the eighteenth century BC, they had been demoted to the level of a feared foreign element. From a Pharaoh who elevated Joseph to second in command, the Egyptians had come to have a king who "did not know Joseph" (Ex 1:8). Living in the northeast part of the country in the Nile delta called "Goshen," the Israelites were at the doorway where foreign armies would enter to conquer, pillage, rape, and kill. Nationalistic rulers saw these non-Egyptians as a possible threat to their national security. Thus, the Egyptians felt a need to change the Hebrews' status and to stop their population growth. Discrimination and oppression came upon the Hebrews in Egypt.

How do people keep their identity intact, their religion vital, and their heritage precious in an alien country and culture? Israel, with its shepherding heritage and simple faith in the God of Abraham, Isaac, and Jacob, faced sophisticated culture and an enticing religious system in Egypt. Deities abounded. Religious pluralism flourished. Polytheism was broad-minded and inclusive. New gods and religions could be accommodated (and absorbed) alongside the old ones. Polytheistic thinking expressed itself in a variety of ways—from the sacred Nile to the sun deity, from sacred monkeys and baboons to the deified Pharaoh, from sacred beetles to sacred bulls. All forms of life took on mystical and magical meaning. Music and ceremony were beautiful and attractive. Temples were well furnished and attended by numerous priests and priestesses administering magnificent rituals polished by centuries of aesthetic refinement. All of life was saturated and regulated by religion. The Pharaoh himself was regarded as a god. Everyone in the land had to give obeisance to him. Not to do so was not only sacrilege, it was treason!

How do a simple people maintain their own simple faith in an unseen, invisible God, with no pompous ceremony nor system of priests, in a situation like Egypt? When that faith teaches "covenant" and "promise," how long can people believe it when they become subjugated by others? How do enslaved people keep on believing in their God when they are not the victors?

The Israelites had several options in Egypt. 1. Through the centuries they could have given up their uniqueness and their faith in the God of Abraham, Isaac, and Jacob to become polytheists like the Egyptians. Without question, some must have done that! (3:13). It would seem logical to them to convert to the victorious gods of their adopted land. 2. Another option was to hold to henotheism letting the God of their fathers be only one of many gods. They could believe in and worship Him but not deny the existence of other gods. 3. Yet another option for the Israelites was that of monotheism. By living apart from the main culture of Egypt in their own enclaves, they could keep traditions and customs unique. Very likely there were Israelites in all three categories when Moses came on the scene.

In such a religious situation God called Moses to serve. It is difficult to know his precise dates, but surely it was no earlier than 1450 B.C. and no later than 1250 B.C.. Egypt was at a zenith in military power and political glory. The pyramids were over a thousand years old. Engineering, architecture, and medicine were all extremely well advanced. Two powerful Pharaohs ruled during that era, and both have been suggested as the "Pharaoh of the Exodus": Thutmosis III (1490-1435 B.C.) and Ramses II (1290-1224 B.C.). With great God-given natural gifts, a brilliant mind and a courageous spirit, a rich heritage and a life-transforming experience at the burning bush, Moses sought to bring a renewed concept of the covenant-making, covenant-keeping God of their fathers to an oppressed people. Some of them must have wondered if He really existed at all, if He would not or could not help them! Did He care for His people? Was their heritage of the Abrahamic covenant only an ancient tradition or a vital reality?

Moses faced incredible problems convincing his own people, to say nothing of the Pharaoh, that they should leave Egypt. He overcame opposition, resentment, misunderstanding, and all the problems associated with leading a slave people. He led them through some of the most desolate country on the earth. He faced rebellion and apostasy by his fellow Israelites. He received the most famous and far-reaching code of laws the world has ever known. He would become for the Hebrew people the most influential person of the entire Old Testament.

The Book of Exodus would remind the Hebrew people as they entered and settled in Canaan, and also in later years, how the God of their fathers had delivered them from bondage when they were an oppressed people, how He kept His promise to Abraham, how He covenanted with them at Sinai, and how He tabernacled in their midst. It would remind them that He was a holy God who demanded first place in their lives with no images or idols. It would remind them of His might and power to cause plagues, divide the sea, bring water from a rock, and shake a mountain with His awesome presence. Because He acted in such mighty deliverance, He had the right to demand their utmost loyalty and obedience.

Theological Outline

Exodus: God Mightily Delivers His People

- I. God Saves His People. (1:1—4:17)
  - A. God's people face oppression in fear. (1:1-22)
  - B. God raises up a deliverer for His oppressed people. (2:1—4:17)
    - 1. God's future leader is born and providentially cared for. (2:1-10)
    - 2. Self-styled justice does not protect God's chosen leader. (2:11-22)
    - 3. God hears the groaning of His people and remembers His covenant. (2:23-25)
    - 4. God calls His leader to a difficult task. (3:1—3:10)
    - 5. The chosen leader offers excuses to avoid God's assignment. (3:11—4:12)
    - 6. In anger, the Lord appoints a helper for His leader. (4:13-17)
- II. God Sends His Leader on a Difficult Mission. (4:18—7:2)
  - A. God uses all means to accomplish His will against an ungodly ruler. (4:18-26)
  - B. God fulfills His angry promise to provide a helper for His leader. (4:27-31)
  - C. God's leader delivers God's message to pagan leaders. (5:1-23)
  - D. God promises deliverance to a deaf people. (6:1-9)
  - E. God reaffirms His insecure leaders. (6:10—7:2)
- III. God Reveals Himself in Punishing His Enemy. (7:3—12:30)
  - A. God is sovereign over enemy powers. (7:3-13)
  - B. Miracles do not bring belief. (7:14-25)
  - C. Enemy powers seek compromise not conversion. (8:1-15)
  - D. God's power convinces enemy religious leaders. (8:16-19)
  - E. Political deceit cannot defeat God's purposes. (8:20-32)
  - F. God's power is superior to Egyptian religious symbols. (9:1-7)
  - G. God's power affects people as well as animals. (9:8-12)
  - H. Terror and admission of sin are not adequate responses to the actions of the only God. (9:13-35)
  - I. God's saving acts are to be taught to coming generations. (10:1-20)
  - J. God's will must be followed completely. (10:21-29)
  - K. God distinguishes between His people and His enemies when He punishes. (11:1-10)
  - L. God judges other gods but preserves an obedient people. (12:1-13)
  - M. God's people are to remember and celebrate His deliverance. (12:14-28)
  - N. God punishes His proud, stubborn enemies. (12:29-30)
- IV. God Reveals Himself by Delivering His People from Bondage. (12:31—15:21)
  - A. God delivers and blesses His people and those who join them. (12:31-51)
  - B. God instructs His people to remember, celebrate, and teach His mighty salvation. (13:1-16)
  - C. God leads and protects His obedient people. (13:17-22)
  - D. God gains glory and evokes faith by saving His troubled people. (14:1-31)
  - E. God's people praise Him for their deliverance. (15:1-21)
- V. God Provides for His Doubting, Complaining People. (15:22—18:27)
  - A. God promises healing to an obedient people. (15:22-27)
  - B. God reveals His glory and tests His people's faith while meeting their needs. (16:1-36)
  - C. Doubting people test God's presence. (17:1-7)
  - D. God delivers His people and permanently curses their enemy. (17:8-16)
  - E. Foreign relatives testify to God's superiority over all gods. (18:1-12)
  - F. God's people must have effective teaching and administrative leadership. (18:13-27)
- VI. God Covenants with His People. (19:1—20:21)
  - A. God's covenant is based upon His act of deliverance and upon the people's obedience as a kingdom of priests. (19:1-8)

B. God prepares His people for His coming down to make a covenant. (19:9-15)
C. God's awesome presence confirms His covenant. (19:16-25)
D. The Ten Commandments are God's covenant ground rules for life with Him. (20:1-17)
E. Awestruck people need a human mediator with the holy God. (20:18-21)

VII. God Gives Civil, Ceremonial, and Criminal Laws to Help His People. (20:22—23:33)
A. Instructions for acceptable worship (20:22-26)
B. How Hebrew slaves are to be treated (21:1-11)
C. What is to be done with a person who injures or kills another person (21:12-32)
D. Justice for damage done to another's property (21:33—22:15)
E. Justice when a virgin is seduced (22:16-17)
F. Punishment for sorcery, bestiality, and idolatry (22:18-20)
G. Care for the stranger, widow, orphan, and poor (22:21-27)
H. Respect for God and human rulers, dedication of children, and being holy (22:28-31)
I. Practice honesty; do not hurt the righteous or innocent. (23:1-9)
J. Keep the sabbatic year, the sabbath day, and sacred occasions. (23:10-19)
K. God will provide spiritual guidance. (23:20-33)

VIII. God and His People Must Ratify the Covenant. (24:1-18)
A. The people commit themselves to do God's will. (24:1-11)
B. God ratifies the covenant with His holy presence. (24:12-18)

IX. God Plans to be Present with His People. (25:1—31:17)
A. As their hearts move them, people are to give for God's worship place. (25:1-7)
B. God will dwell among His people in His place of holy worship. (25:8—27:21)
C. God's minister mediates His holy presence for a holy people. (28:1—29:37)
D. People respond to the holy presence with sacrificial giving. (29:38—30:38)
E. Craftsmen respond to the holy presence by dedicating God-given skills. (31:1-11)
F. People respond to the holy presence by sabbath worship. (31:12-17)

X. God Restores a Sinful People. (31:18—34:35)
A. God provides guidelines for life in His presence. (31:18)
B. An impatient people break the covenant by making and worshiping other gods. (32:1-6)
C. God reacts against a disobedient people in wrath. (32:7-10)
D. Intercessory prayer brings divine repentance. (32:11-14)
E. Judgment comes to a disobedient people through God's chosen leaders. (32:15-29)
F. A mediator's majestic intercession is not sufficient. (32:30-35)
G. God withdraws His immediate presence from a sinful people. (33:1-4)
H. Mourning and repentance even by a disobedient people catch God's attention. (33:5-6)
I. Worship at God's chosen place is an essential element in restoring the covenant. (33:7-11)
J. The unseeable presence of God reaffirms the covenant relationship. (33:12-23)
K. God renews His covenant with His people. (34:1-35)
   1. God reveals His forgiving nature. (34:1-7)
   2. The mediator asks God for His presence, forgiveness, and renewal. (34:8-9)
   3. God renews His covenant with its demand for worship of Him alone. (34:10-28)
   4. The covenant mediator reflects the presence of God with His people. (34:29-35)

XI. God Honors the Obedience of His People with His Holy Presence. (35:1—40:38)
A. God gives His people specific requirements. (35:1-19)
B. Obedient people provide resources and skills needed for God's work. (35:20—36:7)
C. Obedient people use their resources to build God's dwelling place. (36:8—39:43)
D. The leader of God's people prepares for worship. (40:1-33)
E. God's presence fills the worship place continually for His obedient people. (40:34-38)

Theological Conclusions

The Book of Exodus brings a new awareness to God's people of His redemptive power and His rightful claim upon their lives by emphasizing these teachings:

1. God is Covenant-maker and Covenant-keeper.
2. God is Lord of history.
3. God is the compassionate Deliverer of the oppressed.
4. God calls and uses committed leaders.
5. God is holy and demands righteous living.
6. God cares about worship and dwells among His obedient people.

Exodus depicts God as a covenant-making God who keeps His covenant. He is the God of Abraham, Isaac, and Jacob who made a covenant with them and with their descendants. He kept His part of the covenant. He is a covenant-renewing God. When people sin and fail to keep their part of the covenant, He will forgive and renew if they repent and are willing to renew it.

The book also depicts God as the living God who is Lord or Master of history. He is not only God of personal meditation and individual belief but also the One who introduced Himself by the personal name Yahweh to Moses. He is Lord over nations and nature, over land and sea. He introduced Himself to the Egyptians with the plagues and the victory at the sea. He revealed Himself and worked in history to carry out His purposes. The book expressed the desire for God's people to know and do that purpose, that will, that mission in history. God wanted His people to become a kingdom of priests revealing His greatness to all other nations and handing down the witness to His saving deeds to all generations.

The book also depicts God as loving, gracious, and compassionate. Not only was He God Almighty (El Shaddai) with awesome power. He heard His people when they groaned and cried in Egypt. He cared that they suffered. He responded to their prayers. He moved to deliver them. He is a redeeming God. Adherence to the Passover rituals as recorded in Exodus would serve as an annual reminder that their God was mighty to deliver them. They would have their theology shaped by the facts of history and not by idle human speculations.

The Book of Exodus teaches that God calls and uses committed leaders. Not only do Moses and Aaron make their contributions, but so does Jethro (or Reuel), the father-in-law of Moses. To lead a group of former slaves through desert areas and to help them develop into a nation of people with identity and purpose is one of history's greatest success stories in leadership. It shows what God can do through dedicated, faithful leaders who refuse to give up when difficulties arise.

The book depicts God as holy. As such, He demands that His people be holy also. The Ten Commandments brilliantly show what a relationship to God and to others should be (20:1-17). True religion must include both. God is a jealous God who will allow no other gods or idols. Ethical and moral living are the results of our relationship to God.

Exodus also teaches that God cares about His worship. He gave directions on the designing and building of the tabernacle. The tabernacle was located in the center of the camp to symbolize His centrality in their lives, but it was *His presence* that made the real difference. The great God chose to tabernacle *with* His people. He was no distant god, far removed from human existence. He was in their midst.

Contemporary Teaching

The Book of Exodus centers our attention on an act of deliverance by Yahweh, the only living God who is Ruler over nations and individuals, kings and slaves, people and things, land and sea, history and nature. It shows what He can do through and with the life of just one person.

He is the God who acts in history to reveal Himself and to redeem His people. He is not a myth of pagan superstition nor a fictitious figment of idle Oriental speculation. He is Lord of history and has a purpose for people. This realization shaped ancient Israel's theology and influences ours today.

The God who acted in history to deliver Israel from Egypt is the same God who acted in history during the Roman Empire in the Person of Jesus Christ to redeem us today! We are slaves to sin, and He sets us free by his grace and power. It was no accident that Jesus chose to use two elements of the Passover meal to institute the Lord's Supper. Both observances symbolize death and deliverance. Both reflect mankind's plight and God's mighty deed of grace and love in redemption.

Exodus leads us: (1) to recognize that people are oppressed today; (2) to realize that God cares and is working to redeem them; (3) to be open to hear His call and to be willing to obey Him whenever and wherever He wants us to serve; (4) to understand that He is still a covenant-making and a covenant-keeping God; (5) to accept the fact that our part of the covenant means obedience to Him; (6) to trust God to lead, to guide, and to provide for us as we follow Him day by day; (7) to know that a Holy God calls for a holy people; (8) to thank God for revealing His commandments and inspiring His word to be put into written form; (9) to see that God demands ethical conduct and compassionate treatment for the dispossessed, the helpless, and the needy; (10) to know that He is a just God who still punishes sin; (11) to commit ourselves to lives of intercessory prayer for sinful people; (12) to realize that God was, and still is, a compassionate, gracious, forgiving Lord; (13) to know that God will meet with His people when they gather to worship if they will meet His requirements; (14) to understand that only when He is present is there true worship; (15) to put God at the center of our lives; and (16) to live with deep gratitude and in genuine humility because of His deliverance from our bondage of sin.

Chapter 1

The Israelites Oppressed

THESE are the names of the sons of Israel[a] who went to Egypt with Jacob,
each with his family: 2Reuben, Simeon,
Levi and Judah; 3Issachar, Zebulun and
Benjamin; 4Dan and Naphtali; Gad and
Asher.[b] 5The descendants of Jacob numbered seventy[a] in all;[c] Joseph was already in Egypt.

6Now Joseph and all his brothers and
all that generation died,[d] 7but the Israelites were fruitful and multiplied greatly
and became exceedingly numerous,[e] so
that the land was filled with them.

8Then a new king, who did not know
about Joseph, came to power in Egypt.[f]
9"Look," he said to his people, "the Israelites have become much too numerous[g]
for us.[h] 10Come, we must deal shrewdly[i] with them or they will become even
more numerous and, if war breaks out,
will join our enemies, fight against us and
leave the country."[j]

11So they put slave masters[k] over them
to oppress them with forced labor,[l] and
they built Pithom and Rameses[m] as store
cities[n] for Pharaoh. 12But the more they
were oppressed, the more they multiplied
and spread; so the Egyptians came to
dread the Israelites 13and worked them
ruthlessly.[o] 14They made their lives bitter with hard labor[p] in brick[q] and mortar and with all kinds of work in the
fields; in all their hard labor the Egyptians
used them ruthlessly.[r]

15The king of Egypt said to the Hebrew
midwives,[s] whose names were Shiphrah
and Puah, 16"When you help the Hebrew
women in childbirth and observe them
on the delivery stool, if it is a boy, kill
him; but if it is a girl, let her live."[t]
17The midwives, however, feared[u] God
and did not do what the king of Egypt had
told them to do;[v] they let the boys live.
18Then the king of Egypt summoned the
midwives and asked them, "Why have
you done this? Why have you let the boys
live?"

19The midwives answered Pharaoh,
"Hebrew women are not like Egyptian
women; they are vigorous and give birth
before the midwives arrive."[w]

20So God was kind to the midwives[x]
and the people increased and became
even more numerous. 21And because the
midwives feared[y] God, he gave them
families[z] of their own.

22Then Pharaoh gave this order to all
his people: "Every boy that is born[b] you
must throw into the Nile,[a] but let every
girl live."[b]

Chapter 2

The Birth of Moses

NOW a man of the house of Levi[c] married a Levite woman,[d] 2and she became pregnant and gave birth to a son.
When she saw that he was a fine[e] child,
she hid him for three months.[f] 3But
when she could hide him no longer, she
got a papyrus[g] basket for him and coated
it with tar and pitch.[h] Then she placed
the child in it and put it among the
reeds[i] along the bank of the Nile. 4His
sister[j] stood at a distance to see what
would happen to him.

5Then Pharaoh's daughter went down
to the Nile to bathe, and her attendants
were walking along the river bank.[k] She
saw the basket among the reeds and sent
her slave girl to get it. 6She opened it and
saw the baby. He was crying, and she felt
sorry for him. "This is one of the Hebrew
babies," she said.

7Then his sister asked Pharaoh's
daughter, "Shall I go and get one of the
Hebrew women to nurse the baby for
you?"

8"Yes, go," she answered. And the
girl went and got the baby's mother.

1:1 [a]S Ge 46:8
1:4 [b]Ge 35:22-26; Nu 1:20-43
1:5 [c]S Ge 46:26
1:6 [d]Ge 50:26; Ac 7:15
1:7 [e]ver 9; S Ge 12:2; Dt 7:13; Eze 16:7
1:8 [f]Jer 43:11; 46:2
1:9 [g]S ver 7 [h]S Ge 26:16
1:10 [i]Ge 15:13; Ex 3:7; 18:11; Ps 64:2; 71:10; 83:3; Isa 53:3 [j]Ps 105:24-25; Ac 7:17-19
1:11 [k]Ex 3:7; 5:10, 13,14 [l]S Ge 15:13; Ex 2:11; 5:4; 6:6-7; Jos 9:27; 1Ki 9:21; 1Ch 22:2; Isa 60:10 [m]S Ge 47:11 [n]1Ki 9:19; 2Ch 8:4
1:13 [o]ver 14; Ge 15:13-14; Ex 5:21; 16:3; Lev 25:43,46,53; Dt 4:20; 26:6; 1Ki 8:51; Ps 129:1; Isa 30:6; 48:10; Jer 11:4
1:14 [p]Dt 26:6; Ezr 9:9; Isa 14:3 [q]S Ge 11:3 [r]Ex 2:23; 3:9; Nu 20:15; 1Sa 10:18; 2Ki 13:4; Ps 66:11; 81:6; Ac 7:19
1:15 [s]S Ge 35:17
1:16 [t]ver 22
1:17 [u]ver 21; Pr 16:6 [v]1Sa 22:17; Da 3:16-18; Ac 4:18-20; 5:29
1:19 [w]Lev 19:11; Jos 2:4-6; 1Sa 19:14; 2Sa 17:20
1:20 [x]Pr 11:18; 22:8; Ecc 8:12; Isa 3:10; Heb 6:10
1:21 [y]S ver 17 [z]1Sa 2:35; 2Sa 7:11,27-29; 1Ki 11:38; 14:10
1:22 [a]S Ge 41:1 [b]ver 16; Ac 7:19
2:1 [c]S Ge 29:34 [d]ver 2; Ex 6:20; Nu 26:59
2:2 [e]S Ge 39:6 [f]Heb 11:23
2:3 [g]Isa 18:2 [h]Ge 6:14 [i]S Ge 41:2; S Job 8:11; Ac 7:21
2:4 [j]Ex 15:20
2:5 [k]Ex 7:15; 8:20

[a]*5* Masoretic Text (see also Gen. 46:27); Dead Sea Scrolls and Septuagint (see also Acts 7:14 and note at Gen. 46:27) *seventy-five* [b]*22* Masoretic Text; Samaritan Pentateuch, Septuagint and Targums *born to the Hebrews*

1:1–7 HISTORY, Promise—See note on Ge 46:8–27.
1:7–21 ELECTION, God's Promise—God had promised Abraham, Isaac, Jacob, and Joseph that their offspring would be fruitful and multiply. Even under the most oppressive living conditions in Egypt as slaves, this promise was kept. Not even the evil, powerful, genocidal hand of Pharaoh could prevent the population increase of the Israelites.
1:8–14 EVIL AND SUFFERING, Human Origin—Political greed, injustice, and oppression cause much human suffering. God controls the direction of history. He does not interfere in every national incident to prevent tyrants from gaining control. Rather He respects human freedom. Mistreatment by other humans and human institutions causes much of our suffering. God works to liberate the oppressed and create a people of His own. See note on 2:23–25.
1:8—2:10 HISTORY, Intentions—Human rulers, no matter how powerful, cannot fulfill their intentions in opposition to God's purposes. The new Egyptian ruler sought to limit Israel's power and privileges. He ended up preparing the way for educating God's chosen deliverer.
1:20–21 GOD, Grace—God blesses those who are responsive to Him and do His will. Because the midwives followed the inner promptings of God to spare the Hebrew male babies, God blessed them with families of their own. God's grace always reaches out to bless, in some way, those who are obedient and faithful to God. God is not an automatic blessing-dispensing machine who can be manipulated for our own purposes. Nor should we think that our good works buy God's favor. God does bless those who respond favorably to Him.
2:1–10 HUMANITY, Family Relationships—The normal loving relationships within a family can be used by God even when the people involved are unaware of it.

9Pharaoh's daughter said to her, "Take
this baby and nurse him for me, and I
will pay you." So the woman took the baby
and nursed him. 10When the child grew
older, she took him to Pharaoh's daughter
and he became her son. She named[l] him
Moses,[c] saying, "I drew[m] him out of the
water."

Moses Flees to Midian

11One day, after Moses had grown up,
he went out to where his own people[n]
were and watched them at their hard labor.[o] He saw an Egyptian beating a Hebrew, one of his own people. 12Glancing
this way and that and seeing no one, he
killed the Egyptian and hid him in the
sand. 13The next day he went out and
saw two Hebrews fighting. He asked the
one in the wrong, "Why are you hitting
your fellow Hebrew?"[p]
14The man said, "Who made you ruler
and judge over us?[q] Are you thinking of
killing me as you killed the Egyptian?"
Then Moses was afraid and thought,
"What I did must have become known."
15When Pharaoh heard of this, he tried
to kill[r] Moses, but Moses fled[s] from
Pharaoh and went to live in Midian,[t]
where he sat down by a well. 16Now a
priest of Midian[u] had seven daughters,
and they came to draw water[v] and fill the
troughs[w] to water their father's flock.
17Some shepherds came along and drove
them away, but Moses got up and came
to their rescue[x] and watered their
flock.[y]

2:10 [l]1Sa 1:20 [m]2Sa 22:17
2:11 [n]Ac 7:23; Heb 11:24-26 [o]S Ex 1:11
2:13 [p]Ac 7:26
2:14 [q]S Ge 13:8; Ac 7:27*
2:15 [r]Ex 4:19 [s]S Ge 31:21 [t]Heb 11:27
2:16 [u]Ex 3:1; 18:1 [v]S Ge 24:11 [w]S Ge 30:38
2:17 [x]1Sa 30:8; Ps 31:2 [y]S Ge 29:10
2:18 [z]Ex 3:1; 4:18; 18:1,5,12; Nu 10:29
2:20 [a]Ge 18:2-5
2:21 [b]Ex 4:25; 18:2; Nu 12:1
2:22 [c]Jdg 18:30 [d]S Ge 23:4; Heb 11:13
2:23 [e]Ac 7:30 [f]Ex 4:19 [g]S Ex 1:14 [h]ver 24; Ex 3:7,9; 6:5; Nu 20:15-16; Dt 26:7; Jdg 2:18; 1Sa 12:8; Ps 5:2; 18:6; 39:12; 81:7; 102:1; Jas 5:4
2:24 [i]S Ge 8:1 [j]S Ge 9:15; 15:15; 17:4; 22:16-18; 26:3; 28:13-15; Ex 32:13; 2Ki 13:23; Ps 105:10,42; Jer 14:21
2:25 [k]Ex 3:7; 4:31; Lk 1:25
3:1 [l]S Ex 2:18; Jdg 1:16 [m]S Ex 2:16 [n]ver 12; Ex 17:6; 19:1-11,5; 33:6; Dt 1:2,6; 4:10; 5:2; 29:1; 1Ki 19:8; Mal 4:4 [o]Ex 4:27; 18:5; 24:13; Dt 4:11,15
3:2 [p]S Ge 16:7; S Ex 12:23; S Ac 5:19

18When the girls returned to Reuel[z]
their father, he asked them, "Why have
you returned so early today?"
19They answered, "An Egyptian rescued us from the shepherds. He even
drew water for us and watered the flock."
20"And where is he?" he asked his
daughters. "Why did you leave him? Invite him to have something to eat."[a]
21Moses agreed to stay with the man,
who gave his daughter Zipporah[b] to Moses in marriage. 22Zipporah gave birth to
a son, and Moses named him Gershom,[d][c] saying, "I have become an
alien[d] in a foreign land."
23During that long period,[e] the king of
Egypt died.[f] The Israelites groaned in
their slavery[g] and cried out, and their
cry[h] for help because of their slavery
went up to God. 24God heard their groaning and he remembered[i] his covenant[j]
with Abraham, with Isaac and with Jacob.
25So God looked on the Israelites and was
concerned[k] about them.

Chapter 3

Moses and the Burning Bush

NOW Moses was tending the flock of
Jethro[l] his father-in-law, the priest
of Midian,[m] and he led the flock to the far
side of the desert and came to Horeb,[n]
the mountain[o] of God. 2There the angel
of the LORD[p] appeared to him in flames

[c]10 *Moses* sounds like the Hebrew for *draw out.*
[d]22 *Gershom* sounds like the Hebrew for *an alien there.*

2:11–15 CHRISTIAN ETHICS, Justice—Injustice surrounds us daily. We must seek God's path toward justice. We only compound the injustice when we attempt to take matters into our own hands. Murder is not the proper way to deal with injustice.

2:23–25 GOD, Righteous—Because He is righteous, God comes to the aid of the victims of suffering and injustice. The righteous and faithful God remembered His covenant with Abraham and his descendants. He had been slow to intervene in their period of slavery in Egypt because the nation was growing rapidly and in the crucible of hardship was developing the hardness that would be necessary when God would bring them into the Promised Land. God's "concern" for the Israelites was not a mere passing observation. It was expressed concretely as God initiated their deliverance from Egyptian captivity.

2:23–25 EVIL AND SUFFERING, God's Compassion—We do not suffer alone. God is aware of all we suffer. God identified with the Hebrews' slavery and suffering. His empathy with our situation leads to His direct involvement with us and our eventual liberation, though liberation may come only in the resurrection. See note on 3:7–10.

2:23–24 PRAYER, Mercy of God—The Bible repeatedly emphasizes that God hears the cry or groaning of the oppressed (3:7,9; 22:22–23; Ro 8:23; Jas 5:4).

2:24 THE CHURCH, Covenant People—God's covenant promises transcend geographical boundaries and human limitations. God's people are never alone and never forgotten. In His own time and His own way, the Lord remembers His people. Years may pass, and circumstances may change; but God's steadfast love endures forever.

3:1—4:31 EVANGELISM, Involves—When God is about to redeem people, He first calls someone to declare His word. God called Moses to speak this word to Pharaoh. After the burning bush experience, Moses completely involved himself in declaring God's word that Israel might be redeemed from their Egyptian bondage. God uses people who are willing to be involved in the needs of others. Involved people are His plan in evangelism.

3:2 MIRACLE, Nature—The Creator continues to control His created world. He can use any part of the natural order to reveal His presence. Some Bible students have attempted to analyze how God performed this miracle. They have identified the bush as one having scarlet berries or bright red leaves which caught and reflected the sun's rays. If God worked this way, the miracle would be in His timing and in inspiring Moses to recognize His presence. The sovereign God of creation is able to act in and use His creation as He chooses. He may well have chosen to set the bush on fire without burning up the bush. The fire would communicate to Moses the holiness and purity of God. However God chose to act in this case, He accomplished His purpose of gaining Moses' attention to call him to lead His people out of slavery. The miracle at the bush began the miracle of the Exodus. See note on Jdg 6:17.

3:2–6 REVELATION, Events—The messenger from God appeared in a flame. The messenger and God Himself could not be distinguished. See note on Ge 32:24–30. The messenger appeared, but God spoke. See note on Ge 18:1—19:29. Moses was afraid to look at God. Compare Ge 32:30. Burning bushes in the hot desert were not unusual events. The unusual for this bush was that it was not burned up. Moses found himself in the presence of the living God, who spoke to him,

of fire[q] from within a bush.[r] Moses saw
that though the bush was on fire it did
not burn up. 3So Moses thought, "I will
go over and see this strange sight—why
the bush does not burn up."
4When the LORD saw that he had gone
over to look, God called[s] to him from
within the bush,[t] "Moses! Moses!"
And Moses said, "Here I am."[u]
5"Do not come any closer,"[v] God said.
"Take off your sandals, for the place
where you are standing is holy ground."[w]
6Then he said, "I am the God of your
father, the God of Abraham, the God of
Isaac and the God of Jacob."[x] At this,
Moses hid[y] his face, because he was
afraid to look at God.[z]
7The LORD said, "I have indeed seen[a]
the misery[b] of my people in Egypt. I have
heard them crying out because of their
slave drivers, and I am concerned[c] about
their suffering.[d] 8So I have come down[e]
to rescue them from the hand of the
Egyptians and to bring them up out of
that land into a good and spacious land,[f]
a land flowing with milk and honey[g]—
the home of the Canaanites, Hittites,

3:2 [q]Ex 19:18; 1Ki 19:12 [r]ver 4; Ex 2:2-6; Dt 33:16; Mk 12:26; Lk 20:37; Ac 7:30 **3:4** [s]Ex 19:3; Lev 1:1 [t]Ex 4:5 [u]Ge 31:11; 1Sa 3:4; Isa 6:8 **3:5** [v]Jer 30:21 [w]S Ge 28:17; Ac 7:33* **3:6** [x]S Ge 24:12; S Ex 4:5; Mt 22:32*; Mk 12:26*; Lk 20:37*; Ac 3:13; 7:32* [y]1Ki 19:13 [z]Ex 24:11; 33:20; Jdg 13:22; Job 13:11; 23:16; 30:15; Isa 6:5 **3:7** [a]1Sa 9:16 [b]ver 16; S Ge 16:11; 1Sa 1:11; Ne 9:9; Ps 106:44 [c]S Ex 2:25; Ac 7:34* [d]S Ex 1:10 **3:8** [e]S Ge 11:5; Ac 7:34* [f]S Ge 12:7; S 15:14 [g]ver 17; Ex 13:5; 33:3; Lev 20:24; Nu 13:27; Dt 1:25; 6:3; 8:7-9; 11:9; 26:9; 27:3; Jos 5:6; Jer 11:5; 32:22; Eze 20:6

Amorites, Perizzites, Hivites[h] and Jebusites.[i] 9And now the cry of the Israelites
has reached me, and I have seen the way
the Egyptians are oppressing[j] them. 10So
now, go. I am sending[k] you to Pharaoh to
bring my people the Israelites out of
Egypt."[l]
11But Moses said to God, "Who am I,[m]
that I should go to Pharaoh and bring the
Israelites out of Egypt?"
12And God said, "I will be with you.[n]
And this will be the sign[o] to you that it is
I who have sent you: When you have
brought the people out of Egypt, you[e]
will worship God on this mountain.[p]"
13Moses said to God, "Suppose I go to
the Israelites and say to them, 'The God
of your fathers has sent me to you,' and

[h]Jos 11:3; Jdg 3:3; 2Sa 24:7 [i]S Ge 15:18-21; Ezr 9:1 **3:9** [j]S Ex 1:14; S Nu 10:9 **3:10** [k]Ex 4:12; Jos 24:5; 1Sa 12:8; Ps 105:26; Ac 7:34* [l]Ex 6:13,26; 12:41,51; 20:2; Dt 4:20; 1Sa 12:6; 1Ki 8:16; Mic 6:4 **3:11** [m]Ex 4:10; 6:12,30; Jdg 6:15; 1Sa 9:21; 15:17; 18:18; 2Sa 7:18; 2Ch 2:6; Isa 6:5; Jer 1:6 **3:12** [n]S Ge 26:3; S Ex 14:22; Ro 8:31 [o]Nu 26:10; Jos 2:12; Jdg 6:17; Ps 86:17; Isa 7:14; 8:18; 20:3; Jer 44:29 [p]S ver 1; Ac 7:7

[e] *12* The Hebrew is plural.

revealing both the nature of God and His purpose for Moses and the nation. Unless Moses had been alert to a slightly different occurrence in his daily routine, he could have missed the revelation. His willingness to explore a specific event led him into a divine-human encounter which changed his plans for life. God reveals Himself to those who are alert in the routine of their day, who in the ordinary tending of their schedule suddenly discover the Presence. God turns the ordinary into the miraculous to reveal Himself and His will. Lives are redirected by the One who prepares us (even in the wilderness) to use our gifts in His will.

3:4 PRAYER, Responsiveness—Prayer is a response to God's call. Moses placed himself at God's disposal, as did Samuel (1 Sa 3:4,10), Isaiah (Isa 6:8), Ananias (Ac 9:10), and Paul (Ac 26:19).

3:5–6 GOD, Holy—The holiness of God is the absolute difference between God and man. Holiness belongs to God alone. Anything else called holy is so because of its association with God. The ground on which Moses stood was called holy because God was present and speaking to Moses through the burning bush. Moses exhibited fear at the presence of God. Holiness makes us mindful of our lowly status as a creature compared to the Almighty One, who created us and holds our life in His hands.

3:6 LAST THINGS, Believers' Resurrection—The hope of individual life after death is not clearly described in the Old Testament for the most part. The basis of such hope, however, is found in a person's relation to God. Jesus used this statement to teach belief in resurrection to Sadducees and scribes who accepted only the authority of the five books of Moses (Lk 20:37–38). The living God was and is still called the God of Abraham, Isaac, and Jacob centuries after their physical death, but God is the God of the living, not the dead. Those who die in faith, therefore, continue a relationship with God that reaches past the grave. The hope of individual existence beyond death is the basis for a belief in the resurrection of the dead. This belief became clearer to the people of God as His revelation of truth progressed.

3:7 GOD, Love—God is not distant, blind, or indifferent to the needs of His people. He is a God of compassion and love. While the love of God is a major New Testament theme, it is also a significant idea in the Old Testament. The whole story of redemption from Egyptian slavery, sojourn to the Promised Land, and subsequent development into a nation is a testimony of God's never-ending love for His people.

3:7–10 EVIL AND SUFFERING, God's Present Help—God's concern for the Hebrews' suffering led to His choice of Moses to help liberate them. God often uses human beings to bring about His desired results. The story of the Exodus from Egypt illustrates God's willingness to work in and through human beings to alleviate unjust suffering.

3:9 PRAYER, Mercy of God—See note on 2:23–24.

3:12–16 GOD, Personal—The name of God is a single Hebrew word from the verb "to be" which is translated as "I AM WHO I AM" or "I WILL BE WHAT I WILL BE." In Hebrew the name is composed of only four consonants, YHWH, because ancient Hebrew script did not contain vowels. Today no one is certain how the name was pronounced. The Hebrews so reverenced the name of God they never pronounced it for fear of mispronouncing it. In their great reverence for the name of God, they substituted another word (Hebrew *'adonai*), translated Lord, for this personal, covenant name for God. Today, scholars think that the name was pronounced Yahweh. Many translations of the Bible translate the name in all capital letters as LORD. Two important ideas grow out of the disclosure of God's personal name in this passage. For one, God is declared to be a personal God. He is not an impersonal force, like gravity. In biblical times, the disclosure of one's name was a very personal act, that disclosed one's very nature. God here shows His love for the Hebrew people by initiating a personal, intimate relationship in the disclosure of His name to them. The Almighty Sovereign Creator has stooped to reveal His intimate, personal name to people whom He has chosen to be His people. In the second place, the personal name of God suggests that He is a living God, not a dead object or abstract idea. There is a certain mystery to "I AM WHO I AM." This name suggests that He is eternal, without beginning and without ending. God made it clear that He was the same God who had been with the Hebrew people from their beginning, from the call of Abraham.

3:12–18 WORSHIP, Buildings—See note on Ge 28:16–22.

3:13–14 PRAYER, Petition—Some petition is inquiry. Moses' inquiry led to the revelation of God's self-identity in His self-existence.

they ask me, 'What is his name?'[q] Then
what shall I tell them?"
14God said to Moses, "I AM WHO I AM.[f]
This is what you are to say to the Israelites: 'I AM[r] has sent me to you.'"
15God also said to Moses, "Say to the
Israelites, 'The LORD,[g] the God of your
fathers[s]—the God of Abraham, the God
of Isaac and the God of Jacob[t]—has sent
me to you.' This is my name[u] forever,
the name by which I am to be remembered from generation to generation.[v]
16"Go, assemble the elders[w] of Israel
and say to them, 'The LORD, the God of
your fathers—the God of Abraham, Isaac
and Jacob[x]— appeared to me and said: I
have watched over you and have seen[y]
what has been done to you in Egypt.
17And I have promised to bring you up
out of your misery in Egypt[z] into the land
of the Canaanites, Hittites, Amorites, Perizzites, Hivites and Jebusites—a land
flowing with milk and honey.'[a]
18"The elders of Israel will listen[b] to
you. Then you and the elders are to go to
the king of Egypt and say to him, 'The
LORD, the God of the Hebrews,[c] has
met[d] with us. Let us take a three-day
journey[e] into the desert to offer sacrifices[f] to the LORD our God.' 19But I know
that the king of Egypt will not let you go
unless a mighty hand[g] compels him. 20So
I will stretch out my hand[h] and strike the
Egyptians with all the wonders[i] that I
will perform among them. After that, he
will let you go.[j]
21"And I will make the Egyptians favorably disposed[k] toward this people, so
that when you leave you will not go empty-handed.[l] 22Every woman is to ask her
neighbor and any woman living in her
house for articles of silver[m] and gold[n]
and for clothing, which you will put on
your sons and daughters. And so you will
plunder[o] the Egyptians."[p]

Chapter 4

Signs for Moses

MOSES answered, "What if they do
not believe me or listen[q] to me
and say, 'The LORD did not appear to
you'?"
2Then the LORD said to him, "What is
that in your hand?"
"A staff,"[r] he replied.
3The LORD said, "Throw it on the
ground."
Moses threw it on the ground and it
became a snake,[s] and he ran from it.
4Then the LORD said to him, "Reach out
your hand and take it by the tail." So Moses reached out and took hold of the
snake and it turned back into a staff in his
hand. 5"This," said the LORD, "is so that
they may believe[t] that the LORD, the God
of their fathers—the God of Abraham,
the God of Isaac and the God of Jacob—
has appeared to you."
6Then the LORD said, "Put your hand
inside your cloak." So Moses put his hand
into his cloak, and when he took it out, it
was leprous,[h] like snow.[u]
7"Now put it back into your cloak," he
said. So Moses put his hand back into his
cloak, and when he took it out, it was
restored,[v] like the rest of his flesh.
8Then the LORD said, "If they do not
believe[w] you or pay attention to the first
miraculous sign,[x] they may believe the
second. 9But if they do not believe these
two signs or listen to you, take some water from the Nile and pour it on the dry
ground. The water you take from the river will become blood[y] on the ground."
10Moses said to the LORD, "O Lord, I
have never been eloquent, neither in the
past nor since you have spoken to your
servant. I am slow of speech and
tongue."[z]
11The LORD said to him, "Who gave
man his mouth? Who makes him deaf or

3:13 qS Ge 32:29 **3:14** rEx 6:2-3; Jn 8:58; Heb 13:8; Rev 1:8; 4:8 **3:15** sGe 31:42; Da 2:23 tS Ge 24:12 uEx 6:3,7; 15:3; 23:21; 34:5-7; Lev 24:11; Dt 28:58; Ps 30:4; 83:18; 96:2; 97:12; 135:13; 145:21; Isa 42:8; Jer 16:21; 33:2; Hos 12:5 vPs 45:17; 72:17; 102:12 **3:16** wEx 4:29; 17:5; Lev 4:15; Nu 11:16; 16:25; Dt 5:23; 19:12; Jdg 8:14; Ru 4:2; Pr 31:23; Eze 8:11 xS Ge 24:12 yEx 4:31; 2Ki 19:16; 2Ch 6:20; Ps 33:18; 66:7 **3:17** zS Ge 15:16; 46:4; Ex 6:6 aS ver 8 **3:18** bEx 4:1,8,31; 6:12,30 cS Ge 14:13 dNu 23:4,16 eS Ge 30:36 fEx 4:23; 5:1,3; 6:11; 7:16; 8:20, 27; 9:13; 10:9,26 **3:19** gEx 4:21; 6:6; 7:3; 10:1; 11:9; Dt 4:34; 2Ch 6:32 **3:20** hEx 6:1,6; 7:4-5; 9:15; 13:3,9, 14,16; 15:6,12; Dt 4:34,37; 5:15; 7:8; 26:8; 2Ki 17:36; 2Ch 6:32; Ps 118:15-16; 136:12; Isa 41:10; 63:12; Jer 21:5; 51:25; Da 9:15 iEx 4:21; 7:3; 11:9, 10; 15:11; 34:10; Nu 14:11; Dt 3:24; 4:34; 6:22; Ne 9:10; Ps 71:19; 72:18; 77:14; 78:43; 86:10; 105:27; 106:22; 135:9; 136:4; Jer 32:20; Mic 7:15; Ac 7:36 jEx 11:1; 12:31-33 **3:21** kS Ge 39:21 lEx 11:2; 2Ch 30:9; Ne 1:11; Ps 105:37; 106:46; Jer 42:12 **3:22** mJob 27:16-17 nEx 11:2; 12:35; Ezr 1:4,6; 7:16; Ps 105:37 oS Ge 15:14; Eze 39:10 pEze 29:10 **4:1** qS Ex 3:18

4:2 rver 17,20; Ge 38:18; Ex 7:19; 8:5,16; 14:16,21; 17:5-6, 9; Nu 17:2; 20:8; Jos 8:18; Jdg 6:21; 1Sa 14:27; 2Ki 4:29 **4:3** sEx 7:8-12,15 **4:5** tver 31; S Ex 3:6; 14:31; 19:9 **4:6** uLev 13:2,11; Nu 12:10; Dt 24:9; 2Ki 5:1,27; 2Ch 26:21 **4:7** v2Ki 5:14; Mt 8:3; Lk 17:12-14 **4:8** wS Ex 3:18 xver 30; Jdg 6:17; 1Ki 13:3; Isa 7:14; Jer 44:29 **4:9** yEx 7:17-21 **4:10** zS Ex 3:11

f *14* Or *I WILL BE WHAT I WILL BE* g *15* The Hebrew for *LORD* sounds like and may be derived from the Hebrew for *I AM* in verse 14. h *6* The Hebrew word was used for various diseases affecting the skin—not necessarily leprosy.

3:14–17 SALVATION, Initiative—God takes the initiative in salvation. He gave His divine name to Moses at Sinai, along with His plan for deliverance.

3:16–22 HISTORY, Promise—History can be deceiving. Present conditions may hide God's promises. God is faithful to His promises and at the proper time encourages His people with new promises. No matter how we suffer in the present, we can trust God's promises to deliver and save His people at the right time.

4:10–12 HUMANITY, Potentiality—The potential of individuals is generally far greater than most are willing to acknowledge. Human potential is a gift of God and can be realized by His power.

4:10–12 REVELATION, Divine Presence—Revelation does not force human agreement and commitment. Compare Ge 32:22–32. Moses had already questioned God as to His identity and power (3:13; 4:1). Here he excused himself as unfit for the call. God revealed Himself as patient, yet caringly angry that Moses used every excuse not to serve. Patiently God reminded the sheepherder that the Creator has formed all human gifts and can release them for His purposes. Even more encouraging, God revealed He would continue to reveal His presence as Moses fulfilled his mission.

4:10–13 PRAYER, Sovereignty of God—Moses had a tendency to argue with God. What God has made, God can direct. Refusal to follow God's answer to prayer may bring God's anger.

mute?[a] Who gives him sight or makes
him blind?[b] Is it not I, the LORD? 12Now
go;[c] I will help you speak and will teach
you what to say."[d]
13But Moses said, "O Lord, please send
someone else to do it."[e]
14Then the LORD's anger burned[f]
against Moses and he said, "What about
your brother, Aaron the Levite? I know
he can speak well. He is already on his
way to meet[g] you, and his heart will be
glad when he sees you. 15You shall speak
to him and put words in his mouth;[h] I
will help both of you speak and will teach
you what to do. 16He will speak to the
people for you, and it will be as if he were
your mouth[i] and as if you were God to
him.[j] 17But take this staff[k] in your
hand[l] so you can perform miraculous
signs[m] with it."

Moses Returns to Egypt

18Then Moses went back to Jethro his
father-in-law and said to him, "Let me go
back to my own people in Egypt to see if
any of them are still alive."
Jethro said, "Go, and I wish you well."
19Now the LORD had said to Moses in
Midian, "Go back to Egypt, for all the
men who wanted to kill[n] you are
dead.[o]" 20So Moses took his wife and
sons,[p] put them on a donkey and started
back to Egypt. And he took the staff[q] of
God in his hand.
21The LORD said to Moses, "When you
return to Egypt, see that you perform before Pharaoh all the wonders[r] I have giv-
en you the power to do. But I will harden
his heart[s] so that he will not let the people go.[t] 22Then say to Pharaoh, 'This is
what the LORD says: Israel is my firstborn
son,[u] 23and I told you, "Let my son go,[v]
so he may worship[w] me." But you refused to let him go; so I will kill your
firstborn son.' "[x]
24At a lodging place on the way, the
LORD met ⌊Moses⌋[i] and was about to kill[y]
him. 25But Zipporah[z] took a flint knife,
cut off her son's foreskin[a] and touched
⌊Moses'⌋ feet with it.[j] "Surely you are a
bridegroom of blood to me," she said.
26So the LORD let him alone. (At that time
she said "bridegroom of blood," referring
to circumcision.)
27The LORD said to Aaron, "Go into the
desert to meet Moses." So he met Moses
at the mountain[b] of God and kissed[c]
him. 28Then Moses told Aaron everything
the LORD had sent him to say, and also
about all the miraculous signs he had
commanded him to perform.
29Moses and Aaron brought together all
the elders[d] of the Israelites, 30and Aaron
told them everything the LORD had said to
Moses. He also performed the signs[e] before the people, 31and they believed.[f]
And when they heard that the LORD was
concerned[g] about them and had seen
their misery,[h] they bowed down and
worshiped.[i]

Chapter 5

Bricks Without Straw

AFTERWARD Moses and Aaron went to
Pharaoh and said, "This is what the
LORD, the God of Israel, says: 'Let my
people go,[j] so that they may hold a festival[k] to me in the desert.' "
2Pharaoh said, "Who is the LORD,[l]

4:11 [a]Lk 1:20,64 [b]Ps 94:9; 146:8; Mt 11:5; Jn 10:21 4:12 [c]S Ex 3:10 [d]ver 15-16; Nu 23:5; Dt 18:15, 18; Isa 50:4; 51:16; Jer 1:9; Mt 10:19-20; Mk 13:11; S Lk 12:12 4:13 [e]Jnh 1:1-3 4:14 [f]Nu 11:1,10, 33; 12:9; 16:15; 22:22; 24:10; 32:13; Dt 7:25; Jos 7:1; Job 17:8 [g]ver 27; 1Sa 10:2-5 4:15 [h]ver 30; Nu 23:5,12,16; Dt 18:18; Jos 1:8; Isa 51:16; 59:21; Jer 1:9; 31:33 4:16 [i]Ex 7:1-2; Jer 15:19; 36:6 [j]Nu 33:1; Ps 77:20; 105:26; Mic 6:4 4:17 [k]S ver 2 [l]ver 20; Ex 17:9 [m]Ex 7:9-21; 8:5,16; 9:22; 10:12-15, 21-23; 14:15-18,26; Nu 14:11; Dt 4:34; Ps 74:9; 78:43; 105:27 4:19 [n]Ex 2:15 [o]Ex 2:23; Mt 2:20 4:20 [p]Ex 2:22; 18:3; Ac 7:29 [q]S ver 2 4:21 [r]S Ex 3:19,20 [s]Ex 7:3,13; 8:15; 9:12,35; 10:1,20, 27; 11:10; 14:4,8; Dt 2:30; Jos 11:20; 1Sa 6:6; Ps 105:25; Isa 6:10; 63:17; Jn 12:40; Ro 9:18 [t]Ex 8:32; 9:17 4:22 [u]S Ge 10:15; Dt 32:6; Isa 9:6; 63:16; 64:8; Jer 3:19; 31:9; Hos 11:1; Mal 2:10; Ro 9:4; 2Co 6:18 4:23 [v]Ex 5:1; 7:16 [w]S Ex 3:18 [x]Ge 49:3; Ex 11:5; 12:12,29; Nu 8:17; 33:4; Ps 78:51; 105:36; 135:8; 136:10 4:24 [y]Nu 22:22 4:25 [z]S Ex 2:21

[a]Ge 17:14; Jos 5:2,3 4:27 [b]S Ex 3:1 [c]S Ge 27:27; S 29:13 4:29 [d]S Ex 3:16 4:30 [e]S ver 8 4:31 [f]S Ex 3:18 [g]S Ex 2:25 [h]S Ge 16:11 [i]S Ge 24:26 5:1 [j]S Ex 4:23 [k]S Ex 3:18 5:2 [l]Jdg 2:10; Job 21:15; Mal 3:14

[i]24 Or *Moses' son*; Hebrew *him* [j]25 Or *and drew near ⌊Moses'⌋ feet*

4:14,24 GOD, Wrath—The biblical writers did not hesitate to ascribe to God very human emotions, such as anger. This is an expression suggesting God's firmness and the seriousness with which He views His will. Moses' continued excuse-making was unreasonable resistance to the will of God, and God became quite firm in His dealing with Moses. We ought not interpret this as God having lost control of Himself. This simply expressed the intensity of God's will in this situation.

4:14–15 HUMANITY, Family Relationships—Family relationships can be used to aid family members in serving God.

4:21 GOD, Sovereignty—God has revealed His sovereign power in human history. He has shown that He has earthly rulers like Pharaoh in His power. Moses needed this assurance as he prepared to meet Pharaoh. God gave the assurance in two ways: (1) He would perform miracles to help Moses; (2) He would harden Pharaoh's heart so that Pharaoh could experience all God's power so the Egyptians might know He was the sovereign God, ruling all countries and all history (7:3–5). Through five plagues Pharaoh hardened his own heart (7:13, 14,22; 8:15,19,32; 9:7). Compare 9:34,35; 13:15. Then God became the subject, hardening Pharaoh's heart (9:12; 10:1, 20,27; 11:10; 14:4,8,17). Here we see the dynamic interplay between human freewill and divine sovereignty. Pharaoh retained the freedom to harden his heart, refusing to do what God commanded. Behind it all, God showed His control over all participants of human history by using Pharaoh to accomplish His purpose and to reveal Himself fully to His people and to the Egyptians. In all this, the just and righteous God did not do evil or injustice. Pharaoh remained responsible for his refusal to cooperate in achieving God's purposes. God's people gained assurance that God can accomplish His purposes anywhere and any way He chooses. He is the ultimate cause of all that occurs because He is the only Sovereign God. See note on Jdg 9:23–24,56–57.

4:22 ELECTION, Love—When Pharaoh refused to liberate Israel, God's firstborn son, God's judgment destroyed Pharaoh's firstborn son. God is a God of grace and judgment. He offers grace to His chosen and judgment to those who reject Him. Election is based on God's parental love.

4:31 PRAYER, Corporate—See note on 2:23–24. Prayer belongs to community worship as much as individual piety. Prayer and humble worship are proper responses to God's merciful actions.

5:1–23 EVIL AND SUFFERING, Divine Origin—We humans are quick to blame God for our troubles. God does permit wicked, godless people like Pharaoh to bring suffering and injustice on other people. God's people need faith and patience to wait for God's liberating actions. See note on 3:7–10.

that I should obey him and let Israel go? I
do not know the LORD and I will not let
Israel go."[m]

3Then they said, "The God of the Hebrews has met with us. Now let us take a
three-day journey[n] into the desert to offer sacrifices to the LORD our God, or he
may strike us with plagues[o] or with the
sword."

4But the king of Egypt said, "Moses
and Aaron, why are you taking the people
away from their labor?[p] Get back to your
work!" 5Then Pharaoh said, "Look, the
people of the land are now numerous,[q]
and you are stopping them from
working."

6That same day Pharaoh gave this order
to the slave drivers[r] and foremen in
charge of the people: 7"You are no longer
to supply the people with straw for making bricks;[s] let them go and gather their
own straw. 8But require them to make
the same number of bricks as before;
don't reduce the quota.[t] They are lazy;[u]
that is why they are crying out, 'Let us go
and sacrifice to our God.'[v] 9Make the
work harder for the men so that they
keep working and pay no attention to
lies."

10Then the slave drivers[w] and the foremen went out and said to the people,
"This is what Pharaoh says: 'I will not
give you any more straw. 11Go and get
your own straw wherever you can find it,
but your work will not be reduced[x] at
all.'" 12So the people scattered all over
Egypt to gather stubble to use for straw.
13The slave drivers kept pressing them,
saying, "Complete the work required of
you for each day, just as when you had
straw." 14The Israelite foremen appointed by Pharaoh's slave drivers were beat-
en[y] and were asked, "Why didn't you
meet your quota of bricks yesterday or
today, as before?"

15Then the Israelite foremen went and
appealed to Pharaoh: "Why have you
treated your servants this way? 16Your
servants are given no straw, yet we are
told, 'Make bricks!' Your servants are being beaten, but the fault is with your own
people."

17Pharaoh said, "Lazy, that's what you
are—lazy![z] That is why you keep saying,
'Let us go and sacrifice to the LORD.'
18Now get to work.[a] You will not be giv-
en any straw, yet you must produce your
full quota of bricks."

19The Israelite foremen realized they
were in trouble when they were told,
"You are not to reduce the number of
bricks required of you for each day."
20When they left Pharaoh, they found
Moses and Aaron waiting to meet them,
21and they said, "May the LORD look
upon you and judge[b] you! You have made
us a stench[c] to Pharaoh and his officials
and have put a sword[d] in their hand to
kill us."[e]

God Promises Deliverance

22Moses returned to the LORD and said,
"O Lord, why have you brought trouble
upon this people?[f] Is this why you sent
me? 23Ever since I went to Pharaoh to
speak in your name, he has brought trouble upon this people, and you have not
rescued[g] your people at all."

Chapter 6

THEN the LORD said to Moses, "Now
you will see what I will do to Pharaoh: Because of my mighty hand[h] he will
let them go;[i] because of my mighty hand
he will drive them out of his country."[j]
2God also said to Moses, "I am the

5:2 [m]Ex 3:19
5:3 [n]S Ge 30:36 [o]Lev 26:25; Nu 14:12; Dt 28:21; 2Sa 24:13
5:4 [p]S Ex 1:11; 6:6-7
5:5 [q]S Ge 12:2
5:6 [r]S Ge 15:13
5:7 [s]S Ge 11:3
5:8 [t]ver 14,18 [u]ver 17 [v]Ex 10:11
5:10 [w]ver 13; Ex 1:11
5:11 [x]ver 19
5:14 [y]ver 16; Isa 10:24
5:17 [z]ver 8
5:18 [a]S Ge 15:13
5:21 [b]S Ge 16:5 [c]S Ge 34:30 [d]Ex 16:3; Nu 14:3; 20:3 [e]S Ex 1:13; S 14:11
5:22 [f]Nu 11:11; Dt 1:12; Jos 7:7
5:23 [g]Jer 4:10; 20:7; Eze 14:9
6:1 [h]S Ex 3:20; S Dt 5:15 [i]S Ex 3:20 [j]Ex 11:1; 12:31,33, 39

5:19—6:12 HISTORY, Promise—See note on 3:16–22.
5:22–23 PRAYER, Intercession—Various emotions and motives may lead us to pray. Moses was frustrated with the people and impatient for God to act. He pleaded with God to act for His people. God responded with a renewed call to service and a promise to act.
6:1–8 GOD, Justice—An already bad situation was turning worse for the Hebrews. God reassured Moses that He was in control and justice would certainly be done soon. God's covenant promises had not been forgotten. The previously hardened heart of Pharaoh would be changed. Justice may not always come as soon as we think it should, but we can be sure that it will come. God will always complete His promises and vindicate His people.
6:1–8 EVIL AND SUFFERING, God's Present Help—See note on 3:7–10.
6:1–5 REVELATION, Commitment—God invited Moses to observe history in the making as He disclosed His plans and actions. Moses not only received the revelation from God but was prepared to recognize God's power in events about to occur. God rehearsed with Moses a history of His revelation to the forefathers, reminding Moses that He was the same God whose plans had been developing for generations. He was known historically by different names, but He remained the same Divine Presence who gave purpose to earlier Israelite leaders. The name of a person represents the nature and character in the Bible. To explain and give one's name was to reveal the central aspect of one's personality and nature. God was still committed to His covenant with Abraham. God's revelation builds off past revelations, prepares His chosen leader to interpret present actions, and builds a path to future revelations. God reveals Himself when His people need Him.
6:2–3 GOD, One God—The Lord revealed to Moses that the God named YHWH in 3:14 is the same God who called Abraham, Isaac, and Jacob. God revealed Himself gradually as He dealt with His people. Moses had a dimension of what he knew about God that Abraham did not have. The people of Jesus' day would have a dimension of knowledge about God that Moses did not have. That is not to say that earlier information was wrong. It is only saying that earlier information was not as complete as later information. This does not imply that each generation knows more about God. Some generations refuse to learn about God at all. Others have to learn the basic truths all over again. God did not choose to reveal everything about Himself at once.
6:2–8 ELECTION, Sovereignty—Moses was told to

LORD.[k] 3I appeared to Abraham, to Isaac
and to Jacob as God Almighty,[k l] but by
my name[m] the LORD[l n] I did not make
myself known to them.[m] 4I also established my covenant[o] with them to give
them the land[p] of Canaan, where they
lived as aliens.[q] 5Moreover, I have heard
the groaning[r] of the Israelites, whom the
Egyptians are enslaving, and I have remembered my covenant.[s]
6"Therefore, say to the Israelites: 'I am
the LORD, and I will bring you out from
under the yoke of the Egyptians.[t] I will
free you from being slaves to them, and I
will redeem[u] you with an outstretched
arm[v] and with mighty acts of judgment.[w]
7I will take you as my own people, and I
will be your God.[x] Then you will know[y]
that I am the LORD your God, who
brought you out from under the yoke of
the Egyptians. 8And I will bring you to
the land[z] I swore[a] with uplifted hand[b]
to give to Abraham, to Isaac and to Jacob.[c] I will give it to you as a possession.
I am the LORD.' "[d]
9Moses reported this to the Israelites,
but they did not listen to him because of
their discouragement and cruel bondage.[e]
10Then the LORD said to Moses, 11"Go,
tell[f] Pharaoh king of Egypt to let the Israelites go out of his country."[g]
12But Moses said to the LORD, "If the
Israelites will not listen[h] to me, why
would Pharaoh listen to me, since I speak
with faltering lips[n]?"[i]

Family Record of Moses and Aaron

13Now the LORD spoke to Moses and
Aaron about the Israelites and Pharaoh
king of Egypt, and he commanded them
to bring the Israelites out of Egypt.[j]
14These were the heads of their families[o]:[k]

The sons of Reuben[l] the firstborn
son of Israel were Hanoch and Pallu,
Hezron and Carmi. These were the
clans of Reuben.

15The sons of Simeon[m] were Jemuel, Jamin, Ohad, Jakin, Zohar and
Shaul the son of a Canaanite woman.
These were the clans of Simeon.
16These were the names of the
sons of Levi[n] according to their
records: Gershon,[o] Kohath and Merari.[p] Levi lived 137 years.
17The sons of Gershon, by clans,
were Libni and Shimei.[q]
18The sons of Kohath[r] were Amram, Izhar, Hebron and Uzziel.[s] Kohath lived 133 years.
19The sons of Merari were Mahli
and Mushi.[t]

These were the clans of Levi according to their records.
20Amram[u] married his father's sister Jochebed, who bore him Aaron
and Moses.[v] Amram lived 137 years.
21The sons of Izhar[w] were Korah,
Nepheg and Zicri.
22The sons of Uzziel were Mishael,
Elzaphan[x] and Sithri.
23Aaron married Elisheba, daughter of Amminadab[y] and sister of
Nahshon,[z] and she bore him Nadab
and Abihu,[a] Eleazar[b] and Ithamar.[c]
24The sons of Korah[d] were Assir,
Elkanah and Abiasaph. These were
the Korahite clans.
25Eleazar son of Aaron married one
of the daughters of Putiel, and she
bore him Phinehas.[e]

6:2 *k*ver 6,7,8,29; Ex 3:14,15; 7:5,17; 8:22; 10:2; 12:12; 14:4,18; 16:12; Lev 11:44; 18:21; 20:7; Isa 25:3; 41:20; 43:11; 49:23; 60:16; Eze 13:9; 25:17; 36:38; 37:6,13; Joel 2:27 **6:3** *l*S Ge 17:1 *m*S Ex 3:15; 2Sa 7:26; Ps 48:10; 61:5; 68:4; 83:18; 99:3; Isa 52:6 *n*Ex 3:14; Jn 8:58 **6:4** *o*S Ge 6:18; S 15:18 *p*S Ge 12:7; Ac 7:5; Ro 4:13; Gal 3:16; Heb 11:8-10 *q*S Ge 17:8 **6:5** *r*S Ex 2:23; Ac 7:34 *s*S Ge 9:15 **6:6** *t*ver 7; Ex 3:8; 12:17,51; 16:1,6; 18:1; 19:1; 20:2; 29:46; Lev 22:33; 26:13; Dt 6:12; Ps 81:10; 136:11; Jer 2:6; Hos 13:4; Am 2:10; Mic 6:4 *u*Ex 15:13; Dt 7:8; 9:26; 1Ch 17:21; Job 19:25; Ps 19:14; 34:22; 74:2; 77:15; 107:2; Isa 29:22; 35:9; 43:1; 44:23; 48:20; Jer 15:21; 31:11; 50:34 *v*S Ex 3:19, 20; S Jer 32:21; Ac 13:17 *w*Ex 3:20; Ps 9:16; 105:27 **6:7** *x*S Ge 17:7; S Ex 34:9; Eze 11:19-20; Ro 9:4 *y*S ver 2; 1Ki 20:13,28; Isa 43:10; 48:7; Eze 39:6; Joel 3:17 **6:8** *z*S Ge 12:7; Ex 3:8 *a*Jer 11:5; Eze 20:6 *b*S Ge 14:22; Rev 10:5-6 *c*Ps 136:21-22 *d*Lev 18:21 **6:9** *e*S Ge 34:30; Ex 2:23 **6:11** *f*ver 29 *g*S Ex 3:18 **6:12** *h*S Ex 3:18 *i*Ex 4:10 **6:13** *j*S Ex 3:10 **6:14** *k*Ex 13:3; Nu 1:1; 26:4 *l*S Ge 29:32 **6:15** *m*S Ge 29:33 **6:16** *n*S Ge 29:34 *o*S Ge 46:11 *p*Nu 3:17; Jos 21:7; 1Ch 6:1,16 **6:17** *q*Nu 3:18; 1Ch 6:17 **6:18** *r*Nu 3:27; 1Ch 23:12 *s*Nu 3:19; 1Ch 6:2,18 **6:19** *t*Nu 3:20,33; 1Ch 6:19; 23:21 **6:20** *u*1Ch 23:13 *v*Ex 2:1-2; Nu 26:59 **6:21** *w*1Ch 6:38 **6:22** *x*Lev 10:4; Nu 3:30; 1Ch 15:8; 2Ch 29:13 **6:23** *y*Ru 4:19,20; 1Ch 2:10 *z*Nu 1:7; 2:3; Mt 1:4 *a*Ex 24:1; 28:1; Lev 10:1 *b*Lev 10:6; Nu 3:2,32; 16:37, 39; Dt 10:6; Jos 14:1 *c*Ex 28:1; Lev 10:12,16; Nu 3:2; 4:28; 26:60; 1Ch 6:3; 24:1 **6:24** *d*ver 21; Nu 16:1; 1Ch 6:22,37 **6:25** *e*Nu 25:7,11; 31:6; Jos 24:33; Ps 106:30

k3 Hebrew *El-Shaddai* **l**3 See note at Exodus 3:15. **m**3 Or *Almighty, and by my name the LORD did I not let myself be known to them?* **n**12 Hebrew *I am uncircumcised of lips*; also in verse 30 **o**14 The Hebrew for *families* here and in verse 25 refers to units larger than clans.

inform Pharaoh that only God is sovereign Lord. Human rulers are subservient to God. Only God is all-powerful. He has determined to, can, and will fulfill His purposes in election. His basic purpose is to let all people know Him as God.

6:2–8 SALVATION, As Deliverance—See note on 3:14–17. God's salvation is deliverance. He frees us from every bondage. His deliverance arises out of His covenant relationship with His people. Compare 13:14.

6:4–5 THE CHURCH, Covenant People—Because of His covenant relationship with His people, the Lord remained faithful to His promises and His people. See note on Ge 17:1–21. Moses needed to be reminded of God's work with the covenant community. God does not need to be reminded that He is God and we are His people. He always remembers us. See note on 2:24.

6:5 GOD, Love—God heard and remembered. His hearing and remembering are not distant, disinterested functions. Rather, they are personal experiences that call forth remedial action and are expressions of His abiding love. Having remembered His covenant promises to His people, He was moving to keep that covenant alive and fresh. God's love does not ebb and flow; it is constant and continuing. We may sometimes pass through dark and trying times, but that does not mean that God has forgotten us, or that He no longer loves us. We can rest assured God has a reason why He has not yet acted in our behalf. His love will reach out to us according to His knowledge of what is best.

6:6 SALVATION, Redemption—God's salvation is His redemption of His people. "Redeem" (Hebrew *ga'al*) means to deliver or set free by paying a price. The Exodus from Egypt is God's greatest act of redemption in the Old Testament. He redeemed a slave people and set them free. See note on Heb 9:12,15.

6:14–25 HUMANITY, Life—See note on Ge 11:10–26.

These were the heads of the Levite families, clan by clan.

26It was this same Aaron and Moses to whom the LORD said, "Bring the Israelites out of Egypt[f] by their divisions."[g] 27They were the ones who spoke to Pharaoh[h] king of Egypt about bringing the Israelites out of Egypt. It was the same Moses and Aaron.[i]

Aaron to Speak for Moses

28Now when the LORD spoke to Moses in Egypt, 29he said to him, "I am the LORD.[j] Tell Pharaoh king of Egypt everything I tell you."

30But Moses said to the LORD, "Since I speak with faltering lips,[k] why would Pharaoh listen to me?"

Chapter 7

THEN the LORD said to Moses, "See, I have made you like God[l] to Pharaoh, and your brother Aaron will be your prophet.[m] 2You are to say everything I command you, and your brother Aaron is to tell Pharaoh to let the Israelites go out of his country. 3But I will harden Pharaoh's heart,[n] and though I multiply my miraculous signs and wonders[o] in Egypt, 4he will not listen[p] to you. Then I will lay my hand on Egypt and with mighty acts of judgment[q] I will bring out my divisions,[r] my people the Israelites. 5And the Egyptians will know that I am the LORD[s] when I stretch out my hand[t] against Egypt and bring the Israelites out of it."

6Moses and Aaron did just as the LORD commanded[u] them. 7Moses was eighty years old[v] and Aaron eighty-three when they spoke to Pharaoh.

Aaron's Staff Becomes a Snake

8The LORD said to Moses and Aaron, 9"When Pharaoh says to you, 'Perform a miracle,[w] then say to Aaron, 'Take your staff and throw it down before Pharaoh,' and it will become a snake."[x]

10So Moses and Aaron went to Pharaoh and did just as the LORD commanded. Aaron threw his staff down in front of Pharaoh and his officials, and it became a snake. 11Pharaoh then summoned wise men and sorcerers,[y] and the Egyptian magicians[z] also did the same things by their secret arts:[a] 12Each one threw down his staff and it became a snake. But Aaron's staff swallowed up their staffs. 13Yet Pharaoh's heart[b] became hard and he would not listen[c] to them, just as the LORD had said.

The Plague of Blood

14Then the LORD said to Moses, "Pharaoh's heart is unyielding;[d] he refuses to let the people go. 15Go to Pharaoh in the morning as he goes out to the water.[e] Wait on the bank of the Nile[f] to meet him, and take in your hand the staff that was changed into a snake. 16Then say to him, 'The LORD, the God of the Hebrews, has sent me to say to you: Let my people go, so that they may worship[g] me in the desert. But until now you have not listened.[h] 17This is what the LORD says: By this you will know that I am the LORD:[i] With the staff that is in my hand I will strike the water of the Nile, and it will be changed into blood.[j] 18The fish in the Nile will die, and the river will stink;[k] the Egyptians will not be able to drink its water.'"[l]

19The LORD said to Moses, "Tell Aaron, 'Take your staff[m] and stretch out your hand[n] over the waters of Egypt—over the streams and canals, over the ponds and all the reservoirs'—and they will turn to blood. Blood will be everywhere in Egypt, even in the wooden buckets and stone jars."

20Moses and Aaron did just as the LORD had commanded.[o] He raised his staff in the presence of Pharaoh and his officials and struck the water of the Nile,[p] and all the water was changed into blood.[q] 21The fish in the Nile died, and the river smelled so bad that the Egyptians could not drink its water. Blood was everywhere in Egypt.

22But the Egyptian magicians[r] did the same things by their secret arts,[s] and

6:26 [f]S Ex 3:10 [g]Ex 7:4; 12:17,41, 51
6:27 [h]Ex 5:1 [i]Nu 3:1; Ps 77:20
6:29 [j]S ver 2
6:30 [k]S Ex 3:11
7:1 [l]S Ex 4:16 [m]Ex 4:15; Ac 14:12
7:3 [n]S Ex 4:21; Ro 9:18 [o]S Ex 3:20; S 10:1; Ac 7:36
7:4 [p]ver 13,16,22; Ex 8:15,19; 9:12; 11:9 [q]S Ex 3:20; Ac 7:36 [r]S Ex 6:26
7:5 [s]S Ex 6:2 [t]Ex 3:20; Ps 138:7; Eze 6:14; 25:13
7:6 [u]ver 2,10,20; Ge 6:22
7:7 [v]Dt 31:2; 34:7; Ac 7:23,30
7:9 [w]Dt 6:22; 2Ki 19:29; Ps 78:43; 86:17; 105:27; 135:9; Isa 7:11; 37:30; 38:7-8; 55:13; S Jn 2:11 [x]Ex 4:2-5
7:11 [y]Ex 22:18; Dt 18:10; 1Sa 6:2; 2Ki 21:6; Isa 2:6; 47:12; Jer 27:9; Mal 3:5 [z]S Ge 41:8; 2Ti 3:8 [a]ver 22; Ex 8:7,18; S Mt 24:24
7:13 [b]S Ex 4:21 [c]S ver 4
7:14 [d]ver 22; Ex 8:15,32; 9:7; 10:1,20,27
7:15 [e]Ex 8:20 [f]S Ge 41:1
7:16 [g]S Ex 3:18 [h]S ver 4
7:17 [i]S Ex 6:2; 14:25 [j]ver 19-21; Ex 4:9; Rev 11:6; 16:4
7:18 [k]Isa 19:6 [l]ver 21,24; Ps 78:44
7:19 [m]S Ex 4:2 [n]Ex 14:21; 2Ki 5:11
7:20 [o]S ver 6 [p]Ex 17:5 [q]Ps 78:44; 105:29; 114:3; Hab 3:8
7:22 [r]S Ge 41:8 [s]S ver 11; S Mt 24:24

7:3–5,13,22 GOD, Sovereignty—See note on 4:21. As God began to move against Pharaoh, Pharaoh's heart was hardened, just as God had predicted. The approach of God to Pharaoh had the opposite effect, at first, from what God ultimately wanted. He wanted the Egyptians to recognize His sovereign power (v 5). How often has God's approach to a lost sinner only seemed to make him more determined in his opposition to God. We may not understand, but God knows what He is doing.

7:5 HISTORY, Universal—God seeks to introduce Himself and His power to all people, not just to a chosen few.

7:5 EVANGELISM, Glory to God—The redemption of people always brings glory to God and makes others aware of His greatness and grace. God's people should engage in witnessing, leading others to Jesus Christ, that God may be glorified. This is the supreme motive to evangelize and share Christ.

7:8–13 MIRACLE, Revelation—Moses grew to manhood in the court of Pharaoh. He certainly would have learned of the magicians in Egypt. The Bible admits that God's enemies have powers to perform extraordinary feats. It does not say whether the Egyptian magicians used sleight of hand or possessed demonic powers. At the outset of the struggle between Moses and Pharaoh the magicians apparently duplicated the feats of Moses and Aaron. In each instance, however, the sign Moses and/or Aaron performed proved superior to that of the magicians. Miracles are properly understood as signs of God's sovereignty. The miracles do not have to be overwhelmingly convincing to all people. Pharaoh refused to respond to the miracles. Eyes of faith see God revealing His power and sovereignty.

Pharaoh's heart[t] became hard; he would
not listen to Moses and Aaron, just as the
LORD had said. 23Instead, he turned and
went into his palace, and did not take
even this to heart. 24And all the Egyptians
dug along the Nile to get drinking water[u], because they could not drink the
water of the river.

Chapter 8

The Plague of Frogs

25SEVEN days passed after the LORD
struck the Nile. 1Then the LORD said
to Moses, "Go to Pharaoh and say to him,
'This is what the LORD says: Let my people
go, so that they may worship[v] me. 2If you
refuse to let them go, I will plague your
whole country with frogs.[w] 3The Nile will
teem with frogs. They will come up into
your palace and your bedroom and onto
your bed, into the houses of your officials
and on your people,[x] and into your ovens
and kneading troughs.[y] 4The frogs will go
up on you and your people and all your
officials.' "

5Then the LORD said to Moses, "Tell
Aaron, 'Stretch out your hand with your
staff[z] over the streams and canals and
ponds, and make frogs[a] come up on the
land of Egypt.' "

6So Aaron stretched out his hand over
the waters of Egypt, and the frogs[b] came
up and covered the land. 7But the magicians did the same things by their secret
arts;[c] they also made frogs come up on
the land of Egypt.

8Pharaoh summoned Moses and Aaron
and said, "Pray[d] to the LORD to take the
frogs away from me and my people, and I
will let your people go to offer sacrifices[e]
to the LORD."

9Moses said to Pharaoh, "I leave to you
the honor of setting the time[f] for me to
pray for you and your officials and your
people that you and your houses may be
rid of the frogs, except for those that remain in the Nile."

10"Tomorrow," Pharaoh said.

Moses replied, "It will be as you say, so
that you may know there is no one like
the LORD our God.[g] 11The frogs will leave
you and your houses, your officials and
your people; they will remain only in the
Nile."

12After Moses and Aaron left Pharaoh,
Moses cried out to the LORD about the
frogs he had brought on Pharaoh. 13And
the LORD did what Moses asked.[h] The
frogs died in the houses, in the courtyards
and in the fields. 14They were piled into
heaps, and the land reeked of them. 15But
when Pharaoh saw that there was relief,[i]
he hardened his heart[j] and would not
listen to Moses and Aaron, just as the
LORD had said.

The Plague of Gnats

16Then the LORD said to Moses, "Tell
Aaron, 'Stretch out your staff[k] and strike
the dust of the ground,' and throughout
the land of Egypt the dust will become
gnats." 17They did this, and when Aaron
stretched out his hand with the staff and
struck the dust of the ground, gnats[l]
came upon men and animals. All the dust
throughout the land of Egypt became
gnats. 18But when the magicians[m] tried to
produce gnats by their secret arts,[n] they
could not. And the gnats were on men
and animals.

19The magicians said to Pharaoh, "This
is the finger[o] of God." But Pharaoh's
heart[p] was hard and he would not listen,[q] just as the LORD had said.

The Plague of Flies

20Then the LORD said to Moses, "Get
up early in the morning[r] and confront
Pharaoh as he goes to the water and say
to him, 'This is what the LORD says: Let
my people go, so that they may worship[s]
me. 21If you do not let my people go, I
will send swarms of flies on you and your

7:22 [t]ver 13,S 14; Ex 8:19; Ps 105:28
7:24 [u]S ver 18
8:1 [v]Ex 3:12,18; 4:23; 5:1; 9:1
8:2 [w]Ps 78:45; 105:30; Rev 16:13
8:3 [x]Ex 10:6 [y]Ex 12:34
8:5 [z]S Ex 4:2; 7:9-20; 9:23; 10:13,21-22; 14:27 [a]S Ex 4:17
8:6 [b]Ps 78:45; 105:30
8:7 [c]S Ex 7:11; S Mt 24:24
8:8 [d]ver 28; Ex 9:28; 10:17; Nu 21:7; 1Sa 12:19; 1Ki 13:6; Jer 42:2; Ac 8:24 [e]ver 25; Ex 10:8,24; 12:31
8:9 [f]Ex 9:5
8:10 [g]Ex 9:14; 15:11; Dt 3:24; 4:35; 33:26; 2Sa 7:22; 1Ki 8:23; 1Ch 17:20; 2Ch 6:14; Ps 71:19; 86:8; 89:6; 113:5; Isa 40:18; 42:8; 46:9; Jer 10:6; 49:19; Mic 7:18
8:13 [h]Jas 5:16-18
8:15 [i]Ecc 8:11 [j]S Ex 7:14
8:16 [k]S Ex 4:2
8:17 [l]Ps 105:31
8:18 [m]Ex 9:11; Da 5:8 [n]S Ex 7:11
8:19 [o]Ex 7:5; 10:7; 12:33; 31:18; 1Sa 6:9; Ne 9:6; Ps 8:3; 33:6; Lk 11:20 [p]S Ex 7:22 [q]S Ex 7:4
8:20 [r]Ex 7:15; 9:13 [s]S Ex 3:18

8:1–2 REVELATION, Events—The God of Abraham took initiative to release His people by sending His messenger Moses to Pharaoh. God knew the king's cold heart (7:14) and was prepared to use many forces in His creation to pressure the unbelieving Pharaoh to let Israel go. This is the beginning of the series of plagues which occurred in Egypt and is one of the strongest pictures of God's revelation of His concern and commitment to Israel and to His plans for His children. The plagues show revelation may occur through any part of God's created order and that destructive events may bring revelation. Moses acted throughout the section as the spokesman for the Almighty God, the One whose name and nature had just been revealed to Moses near the mountain. Events need to be interpreted by God's chosen representative before other people understand them as revelation.

8:10 GOD, One God—*To the Egyptians* (and probably *many of the Israelites,* too) Yahweh was just one more among the many gods. Moses used this incident as an opportunity to disclose that the God of the Israelites was unique. As Moses accurately predicted, God was shown to surpass the gods whom the Egyptians claimed to be in competition with Yahweh. The other "gods" were shown to be empty, useless ideas that have no reality. God is one of a kind; there is none other like Him. See 12:12; note on Ge 35:2.

8:19 MIRACLE, Revelation—At this point the magicians admitted defeat. They were unable to duplicate the feat and sensed God's power at work. Even they recognized the powerful presence of God. Yet Pharaoh refused to bow to God's power. Each of the succeeding plagues, flies (8:24), illness and death of cattle (9:6), boils (9:10), hail (9:23), locusts (10:13), darkness (10:22), and death of the firstborn (12:29) pointed to God's power over creation. Moses, man of faith, sought to provoke Pharaoh's obedience to God. Each time Pharaoh "hardened his heart." Miracles are agents of revelation only to those who believe.

officials, on your people and into your
houses. The houses of the Egyptians will
be full of flies, and even the ground
where they are.
22“ ‘But on that day I will deal differently with the land of Goshen,[t] where
my people live;[u] no swarms of flies will
be there, so that you will know[v] that I,
the LORD, am in this land. 23I will make a
distinction[p] between my people and your
people.[w] This miraculous sign will occur
tomorrow.’ ”
24And the LORD did this. Dense swarms
of flies poured into Pharaoh’s palace and
into the houses of his officials, and
throughout Egypt the land was ruined by
the flies.[x]
25Then Pharaoh summoned[y] Moses
and Aaron and said, “Go, sacrifice to your
God here in the land.”
26But Moses said, “That would not be
right. The sacrifices we offer the LORD
our God would be detestable to the Egyptians.[z] And if we offer sacrifices that are
detestable in their eyes, will they not
stone us? 27We must take a three-day
journey[a] into the desert to offer sacrifices[b] to the LORD our God, as he commands us.”
28Pharaoh said, “I will let you go to offer sacrifices to the LORD your God in the
desert, but you must not go very far. Now
pray[c] for me.”
29Moses answered, “As soon as I leave
you, I will pray to the LORD, and tomorrow the flies will leave Pharaoh and his
officials and his people. Only be sure that
Pharaoh does not act deceitfully[d] again
by not letting the people go to offer sacrifices to the LORD.”
30Then Moses left Pharaoh and prayed
to the LORD,[e] 31and the LORD did what
Moses asked: The flies left Pharaoh and
his officials and his people; not a fly remained. 32But this time also Pharaoh
hardened his heart[f] and would not let
the people go.

Chapter 9

The Plague on Livestock

THEN the LORD said to Moses, “Go to
Pharaoh and say to him, ‘This is what
the LORD, the God of the Hebrews, says:
“Let my people go, so that they may worship[g] me.” 2If you refuse to let them go
and continue to hold them back, 3the
hand[h] of the LORD will bring a terrible
plague[i] on your livestock in the field—
on your horses and donkeys and camels
and on your cattle and sheep and goats.
4But the LORD will make a distinction between the livestock of Israel and that of
Egypt,[j] so that no animal belonging to
the Israelites will die.’ ”
5The LORD set a time and said, “Tomorrow the LORD will do this in the land.”
6And the next day the LORD did it: All the
livestock[k] of the Egyptians died,[l] but
not one animal belonging to the Israelites
died. 7Pharaoh sent men to investigate
and found that not even one of the animals of the Israelites had died. Yet his
heart[m] was unyielding and he would not
let the people go.[n]

The Plague of Boils

8Then the LORD said to Moses and Aaron, “Take handfuls of soot from a furnace
and have Moses toss it into the air in the
presence of Pharaoh. 9It will become fine
dust over the whole land of Egypt, and
festering boils[o] will break out on men
and animals throughout the land.”
10So they took soot from a furnace and
stood before Pharaoh. Moses tossed it
into the air, and festering boils broke out
on men and animals. 11The magicians[p]
could not stand before Moses because of
the boils that were on them and on all the
Egyptians. 12But the LORD hardened Pharaoh’s heart[q] and he would not listen[r] to
Moses and Aaron, just as the LORD had
said to Moses.

The Plague of Hail

13Then the LORD said to Moses, “Get
up early in the morning, confront Pharaoh and say to him, ‘This is what the
LORD, the God of the Hebrews, says: Let
my people go, so that they may worship[s]
me, 14or this time I will send the full
force of my plagues against you and
against your officials and your people, so
you may know[t] that there is no one
like[u] me in all the earth. 15For by now I
could have stretched out my hand and
struck you and your people[v] with a

8:22 [t]S Ge 45:10 [u]Ex 9:4,6,26; 10:23; 11:7; 12:13; 19:5; Dt 4:20; 7:6; 14:2; 26:18; 1Ki 8:36; Job 36:11; Ps 33:12; 135:4; Mal 3:17 [v]Ex 7:5; 9:29
8:23 [w]Ex 9:4,6; 10:23; 11:7; 12:13, 23,27
8:24 [x]Ps 78:45; 105:31
8:25 [y]ver 8; Ex 9:27; 10:16; 12:31
8:26 [z]S Ge 43:32
8:27 [a]S Ge 30:36 [b]S Ex 3:18
8:28 [c]S ver 8; S Jer 37:3; Ac 8:24
8:29 [d]ver 15; Ex 9:30; 10:11; Isa 26:10
8:30 [e]ver 12; Ex 9:33; 10:18
8:32 [f]S Ex 7:14
9:1 [g]S Ex 8:1
9:3 [h]Ex 7:4; 1Sa 5:6; Job 13:21; Ps 32:4; 39:10; Ac 13:11 [i]Lev 26:25; Ps 78:50; Am 4:10
9:4 [j]ver 26; S Ex 8:23
9:6 [k]ver 19-21; Ex 11:5; 12:29 [l]Ps 78:48-50
9:7 [m]S Ex 7:22 [n]Ex 7:14; 8:32
9:9 [o]Lev 13:18,19; Dt 28:27,35; 2Ki 20:7; Job 2:7; Isa 38:21; Rev 16:2
9:11 [p]S Ex 8:18
9:12 [q]S Ex 4:21 [r]S Ex 7:4
9:13 [s]S Ex 3:18
9:14 [t]S Ex 8:10 [u]Ex 15:11; 1Sa 2:2; 2Sa 7:22; 1Ki 8:23; 1Ch 17:20; Ps 35:10; 71:19; 86:8; 89:6; Isa 46:9; Jer 10:6; Mic 7:18
9:15 [v]Ex 3:20

[p]23 Septuagint and Vulgate; Hebrew *will put a deliverance*

8:22–23 ELECTION, *Other Nations*—Even the elements of nature moved to bring judgment and punishment upon Pharaoh and those who disobeyed God, so He could reveal His election power and purpose to foreign people in a foreign land. The heart of election is the distinction between God’s people and other people. Sin and unbelief lead to the doctrine of election, wherein God selects, delivers, and trains a people to be His own in the midst of an unbelieving world. See Ro 9:17.

8:30–31 PRAYER, Will of God—Prayer is God’s means of executing His will on the earth. The plagues occurred at the initiative of God; the cessation of the plagues came in answer to prayer.

9:4–7,26 ELECTION, Mercy—In Goshen, where the chosen of God lived, God mercifully preserved the elect from the destructive hail, which punished unbelieving Pharaoh and his people. The doctrine of election is built on God’s merciful desire to save people from the death all deserve.

plague that would have wiped you off the
earth. 16 But I have raised you up[q] for this
very purpose,[w] that I might show you my
power[x] and that my name might be proclaimed in all the earth. 17 You still set
yourself against my people and will not
let them go. 18 Therefore, at this time tomorrow I will send the worst hailstorm[y]
that has ever fallen on Egypt, from the
day it was founded till now.[z] 19 Give an
order now to bring your livestock and everything you have in the field to a place of
shelter, because the hail will fall on every
man and animal that has not been
brought in and is still out in the field, and
they will die.' "

20 Those officials of Pharaoh who
feared[a] the word of the LORD hurried to
bring their slaves and their livestock inside. 21 But those who ignored[b] the word
of the LORD left their slaves and livestock
in the field.

22 Then the LORD said to Moses,
"Stretch out your hand toward the sky so
that hail will fall all over Egypt—on men
and animals and on everything growing
in the fields of Egypt." 23 When Moses
stretched out his staff toward the sky, the
LORD sent thunder[c] and hail,[d] and lightning flashed down to the ground. So the
LORD rained hail on the land of Egypt;
24 hail fell and lightning flashed back and
forth. It was the worst storm in all the
land of Egypt since it had become a nation.[e] 25 Throughout Egypt hail struck everything in the fields—both men and animals; it beat down everything growing in
the fields and stripped every tree.[f] 26 The
only place it did not hail was the land of
Goshen,[g] where the Israelites were.[h]

27 Then Pharaoh summoned Moses and
Aaron. "This time I have sinned,"[i] he
said to them. "The LORD is in the right,[j]
and I and my people are in the wrong.
28 Pray[k] to the LORD, for we have had
enough thunder and hail. I will let you
go;[l] you don't have to stay any longer."

29 Moses replied, "When I have gone
out of the city, I will spread out my
hands[m] in prayer to the LORD. The thunder will stop and there will be no more
hail, so you may know that the earth[n] is
the LORD's. 30 But I know that you and
your officials still do not fear[o] the LORD
God."

31 (The flax and barley[p] were destroyed, since the barley had headed and
the flax was in bloom. 32 The wheat and
spelt,[q] however, were not destroyed, because they ripen later.)

33 Then Moses left Pharaoh and went
out of the city. He spread out his hands
toward the LORD; the thunder and hail
stopped, and the rain no longer poured
down on the land. 34 When Pharaoh saw
that the rain and hail and thunder had
stopped, he sinned again: He and his officials hardened their hearts. 35 So Pharaoh's heart[r] was hard and he would not
let the Israelites go, just as the LORD had
said through Moses.

Chapter 10

The Plague of Locusts

THEN the LORD said to Moses, "Go to
Pharaoh, for I have hardened his
heart[s] and the hearts of his officials so

[q] *16 Or have spared you*

9:16 [w]Pr 16:4 [x]Ex 14:4,17,31; Ps 20:6; 25:11; 68:28; 71:18; 106:8; 109:21; Ro 9:17*
9:18 [y]ver 23; Jos 10:11; Ps 78:47-48; 105:32; 148:8; Isa 30:30; Eze 38:22; Hag 2:17 [z]ver 24; Ex 10:6
9:20 [a]Pr 13:13
9:21 [b]S Ge 19:14; Eze 33:4-5
9:23 [c]Ex 20:18; 1Sa 7:10; 12:17; Ps 18:13; 29:3; 68:33; 77:17; 104:7 [d]S ver 18; Rev 8:7; 16:21
9:24 [e]S ver 18
9:25 [f]Ps 105:32-33; Eze 13:13
9:26 [g]S ver 4; Isa 32:18-20 [h]Ex 10:23; 11:7; 12:13; Am 4:7
9:27 [i]ver 34; Ex 10:16; Nu 14:40; Dt 1:41; Jos 7:11; Jdg 10:10; 1Sa 15:24; 24:17; 26:21 [j]Ps 11:7; 116:5; 119:137; 129:4; 145:17; Jer 12:1; La 1:18
9:28 [k]Ex 8:8; Ac 8:24 [l]S Ex 8:8
9:29 [m]ver 33; 1Ki 8:22,38; Job 11:13; Ps 77:2; 88:9; 143:6; Isa 1:15 [n]Ex 19:5; Job 41:11; Ps 24:1; 50:12; 1Co 10:26
9:30 [o]S Ex 8:29
9:31 [p]Dt 8:8; Ru 1:22; 2:23; 2Sa 14:30; 17:28; Isa 28:25; Eze 4:9; Joel 1:11
9:32 [q]Isa 28:25
9:35 [r]S Ex 4:21
10:1 [s]S Ex 4:21

9:16 HISTORY, Universal—See note on 7:5.

9:16 MISSIONS, Authority—God raised up Pharaoh to demonstrate His power. Egyptian religion considered Pharaoh a god. The Exodus proved only the true God of Israel possessed divine power. God's deeper purpose in the Exodus was that His name might be declared in all the earth. Knowing that God wants His name known in all the earth provides authority for missions as Christians declare His name, love, and power. From the very beginning of the Bible, God is never presented as a tribal god or one who is confined to certain geographic territory. He is the God of all the earth, who acts so all peoples of the earth may know Him.

9:20 HISTORY, Universal—See note on 7:5. God honored the trusting actions of Egyptians as well as Israelites.

9:20–21,25,30 EVANGELISM, Lostness—Those who do not have faith or who ignore God's Word lose everything. They are lost to the good things of life, to joy and happiness, and to God Himself. Lostness is the greatest of human tragedies. God's people should be burdened and dedicated to share with others the danger in ignoring the Word of God and refusing to have Jesus Christ in their lives.

9:27 GOD, Righteous—Pharaoh finally began to see that the God of Moses and the Hebrew people was right—righteous—and that Pharaoh and the Egyptians were sinners in the wrong. Pharaoh evidently interpreted the plagues that had come on them as the judgment of God. Pharaoh was now ready, but only temporarily, to yield to Moses and his God. That God is in the right and thus righteous becomes evident even to His enemies.

9:33 PRAYER, Will of God—See note on 8:30–31.

9:34 SIN, Rebellion—Pharaoh's sin was that of rebellion against the directive of God as delivered through Moses. When the thunder, rain, and hail stopped, he changed his mind and rebelled once more. Rebellion against God's holy will is always sin in every generation. See note on Ge 11:4. The Bible says Pharaoh hardened his heart. In other words he deliberately set himself against the purposes of God. After each plague, Pharaoh seemed to bend somewhat toward God's purposes, but in the end he stiffened his will to go against God. When people harden their hearts against the purposes of God, no power on earth can alter their mindset. God in His sovereignty has given each person the right to rebel against His will. In Pharaoh's case God gave him repeated opportunities to repent of his wickedness. In fact each plague represented an opportunity for Pharaoh to soften his heart toward God. However, each time he refused. People can ignore the pleadings of God's Spirit until their hearts become hardened against the will of God to the extent that it may appear God has stopped pleading with them. In reality, the problem rests with the person. See note on Ro 1:26–32.

10:1–2 HISTORY, Confession—God's mighty historical acts of salvation are not performed in every generation. Each generation has the responsibility to share historical memories with the next. Such confession keeps the power of God's acts

that I may perform these miraculous
signs[t] of mine among them 2that you
may tell your children[u] and grandchildren how I dealt harshly[v] with the Egyptians and how I performed my signs
among them, and that you may know that
I am the LORD."[w]
3So Moses and Aaron went to Pharaoh
and said to him, "This is what the LORD,
the God of the Hebrews, says: 'How long
will you refuse to humble[x] yourself before me? Let my people go, so that they
may worship me. 4If you refuse[y] to let
them go, I will bring locusts[z] into your
country tomorrow. 5They will cover the
face of the ground so that it cannot be
seen. They will devour what little you
have left[a] after the hail, including every
tree that is growing in your fields.[b] 6They
will fill your houses[c] and those of all your
officials and all the Egyptians—something neither your fathers nor your forefathers have ever seen from the day they
settled in this land till now.' "[d] Then
Moses turned and left Pharaoh.
7Pharaoh's officials said to him, "How
long will this man be a snare[e] to us? Let
the people go, so that they may worship
the LORD their God. Do you not yet realize that Egypt is ruined?"[f]
8Then Moses and Aaron were brought
back to Pharaoh. "Go, worship[g] the
LORD your God," he said. "But just who
will be going?"
9Moses answered, "We will go with
our young and old, with our sons and
daughters, and with our flocks and herds,
because we are to celebrate a festival[h] to
the LORD."
10Pharaoh said, "The LORD be with
you—if I let you go, along with your
women and children! Clearly you are
bent on evil.[r] 11No! Have only the men
go; and worship the LORD, since that's
what you have been asking for." Then
Moses and Aaron were driven out of
Pharaoh's presence.
12And the LORD said to Moses, "Stretch
out your hand[i] over Egypt so that locusts
will swarm over the land and devour

10:1 [t]S Ex 3:19; S 7:3; Jos 24:17; Ne 9:10; Ps 74:9; 105:26-36
10:2 [u]Ex 12:26-27; 13:8,14; Dt 4:9; 6:20; 32:7; Jos 4:6; Ps 44:1; 71:18; 78:4,5; Joel 1:3 [v]1Sa 6:6 [w]S Ex 6:2
10:3 [x]1Ki 21:29; 2Ki 22:19; 2Ch 7:14; 12:7; 33:23; 34:27; Job 42:6; Isa 58:3; Da 5:22; Jas 4:10; 1Pe 5:6
10:4 [y]Ex 8:2; 9:2 [z]Dt 28:38; Ps 105:34; Pr 30:27; Joel 1:4; Rev 9:3
10:5 [a]Ex 9:32; Joel 1:4 [b]ver 15
10:6 [c]Joel 2:9 [d]S Ex 9:18
10:7 [e]Ex 23:33; 34:12; Dt 7:16; 12:30; 20:18; Jos 23:7-13; Jdg 2:3; 8:27; 16:5; 1Sa 18:21; Ps 106:36; Ecc 7:26 [f]S Ge 20:3; S Ex 8:19
10:8 [g]S Ex 8:8
10:9 [h]S Ex 3:18
10:12 [i]Ex 7:19
10:13 [j]ver 21-22; Ex 4:17; 8:5,17; 9:23; 14:15-16, 26-27; 17:5; Nu 20:8 [k]ver 4; 1Ki 8:37; Ps 78:46; 105:34; Am 4:9; Na 3:16
10:14 [l]Dt 28:38; Ps 78:46; Isa 33:4; Joel 1:4; 2:1-11,25; Am 4:9
10:15 [m]Dt 28:38; Ps 105:34-35; Joel 1:4; Am 7:2; Mal 3:11
10:16 [n]S Ex 8:25 [o]S Ex 9:27
10:17 [p]1Sa 15:25 [q]S Ex 8:8
10:18 [r]S Ex 8:30
10:20 [s]S Ex 4:21
10:21 [t]Dt 28:29
10:22 [u]Ps 105:28; Isa 13:10; 45:7; 50:3; Rev 16:10
10:23 [v]S Ex 8:22; Am 4:7
10:24 [w]S Ex 8:8 [x]ver 8-10 [y]S Ge 45:10

everything growing in the fields, everything left by the hail."
13So Moses stretched out his staff[j]
over Egypt, and the LORD made an east
wind blow across the land all that day and
all that night. By morning the wind had
brought the locusts;[k] 14they invaded all
Egypt and settled down in every area of
the country in great numbers. Never before had there been such a plague of locusts,[l] nor will there ever be again.
15They covered all the ground until it was
black. They devoured[m] all that was left
after the hail—everything growing in the
fields and the fruit on the trees. Nothing
green remained on tree or plant in all the
land of Egypt.
16Pharaoh quickly summoned[n] Moses
and Aaron and said, "I have sinned[o]
against the LORD your God and against
you. 17Now forgive[p] my sin once more
and pray[q] to the LORD your God to take
this deadly plague away from me."
18Moses then left Pharaoh and prayed
to the LORD.[r] 19And the LORD changed
the wind to a very strong west wind,
which caught up the locusts and carried
them into the Red Sea.[s] Not a locust was
left anywhere in Egypt. 20But the LORD
hardened Pharaoh's heart,[s] and he
would not let the Israelites go.

The Plague of Darkness

21Then the LORD said to Moses,
"Stretch out your hand toward the sky so
that darkness[t] will spread over Egypt—
darkness that can be felt." 22So Moses
stretched out his hand toward the sky,
and total darkness[u] covered all Egypt for
three days. 23No one could see anyone
else or leave his place for three days. Yet
all the Israelites had light in the places
where they lived.[v]
24Then Pharaoh summoned Moses and
said, "Go,[w] worship the LORD. Even your
women and children[x] may go with you;
only leave your flocks and herds behind."[y]

[r] *10* Or *Be careful, trouble is in store for you!*
[s] *19* Hebrew *Yam Suph*; that is, Sea of Reeds

---

alive among the people and helps each generation know God.

10:2 EDUCATION, Moses—Israel's strong educational tradition is woven like a golden thread through the pages of the Old Testament. Even before the Exodus, Moses was reminded of the importance of telling future generations the story of God's mighty acts. *In every generation*, what God does in the lives of His people should become a part of the spiritual heritage passed on to children and grandchildren.

10:3–7 EVANGELISM, Judgment—Although God is gracious, loving, and patient, He also judges rebellious, sinful people. The Scriptures make this clear countless times. Those who refuse His salvation and stubbornly reject His will inevitably experience God's judgment. Their lives result in ruin.

10:16–17 SALVATION, Human Freedom—Pharaoh was free at any time to let Israel go. He was no robot in the hands of God. Yet God was determined to deliver His people. Compare 13:15. Here and elsewhere the freedom of the ruler of Egypt and the sovereignty of God were joined together in a great collision (4:21; 5:2; 7:14; 8:15,19,32; 9:7,16–17,34; 11:9–10; 14:17; Ro 9:17–18). When we misuse or abuse our freedom, like this Pharaoh misused and abused his freedom, we collide with God's power. If we harden our hearts as did the Pharaoh, God may choose to further harden our hearts (Ex 10:20). We should remember that God is the Potter, and we are the clay (Ro 9:19–29).

10:17–18 SALVATION, Forgiveness—God forgave Pharaoh's sin in answer to the prayer of Moses. He will forgive us our sins if we ask Him. See note on Ge 50:17–21.

10:23 ELECTION, Mercy—See note on 9:4–7,26.

25But Moses said, "You must allow us
to have sacrifices and burnt offerings[z] to
present to the LORD our God. 26Our livestock too must go with us; not a hoof is to
be left behind. We have to use some of
them in worshiping the LORD our God,
and until we get there we will not know
what we are to use to worship the
LORD."
27But the LORD hardened Pharaoh's
heart,[a] and he was not willing to let
them go. 28Pharaoh said to Moses, "Get
out of my sight! Make sure you do not
appear before me again! The day you see
my face you will die."
29"Just as you say," Moses replied, "I
will never appear[b] before you again."

Chapter 11

The Plague on the Firstborn

NOW the LORD had said to Moses, "I
will bring one more plague on Pharaoh and on Egypt. After that, he will let
you go[c] from here, and when he does, he
will drive you out completely.[d] 2Tell the
people that men and women alike are to
ask their neighbors for articles of silver
and gold."[e] 3(The LORD made the Egyptians favorably disposed[f] toward the people, and Moses himself was highly regarded[g] in Egypt by Pharaoh's officials and by
the people.)
4So Moses said, "This is what the LORD
says: 'About midnight[h] I will go throughout Egypt.[i] 5Every firstborn[j] son in
Egypt will die, from the firstborn son of
Pharaoh, who sits on the throne, to the
firstborn son of the slave girl, who is at
her hand mill,[k] and all the firstborn of
the cattle as well. 6There will be loud
wailing[l] throughout Egypt—worse than
there has ever been or ever will be again.
7But among the Israelites not a dog will
bark at any man or animal.' Then you will
know that the LORD makes a distinction[m]
between Egypt and Israel. 8All these officials of yours will come to me, bowing
down before me and saying, 'Go,[n] you
and all the people who follow you!' After
that I will leave."[o] Then Moses, hot with
anger, left Pharaoh.
9The LORD had said to Moses, "Pharaoh will refuse to listen[p] to you—so that
my wonders[q] may be multiplied in
Egypt." 10Moses and Aaron performed all
these wonders before Pharaoh, but the
LORD hardened Pharaoh's heart,[r] and he
would not let the Israelites go out of his
country.

Chapter 12

The Passover

12:14–20pp — Lev 23:4–8; Nu 28:16–25; Dt 16:1–8

THE LORD said to Moses and Aaron in
Egypt, 2"This month is to be for you
the first month,[s] the first month of your
year. 3Tell the whole community of Israel
that on the tenth day of this month each
man is to take a lamb[t][t] for his family,
one for each household.[u] 4If any household is too small for a whole lamb, they
must share one with their nearest neighbor, having taken into account the number of people there are. You are to determine the amount of lamb needed in accordance with what each person will eat.
5The animals you choose must be year-old
males without defect,[v] and you may take
them from the sheep or the goats. 6Take
care of them until the fourteenth day of
the month,[w] when all the people of the
community of Israel must slaughter them
at twilight.[x] 7Then they are to take some
of the blood[y] and put it on the sides and

[t]3 The Hebrew word can mean *lamb* or *kid*; also in verse 4.

10:25 [z]S Ge 8:20; S Ex 18:12
10:27 [a]S Ex 4:21
10:29 [b]Ex 11:8; Heb 11:27
11:1 [c]S Ex 3:20 [d]S Ex 6:1
11:2 [e]S Ex 3:21,22
11:3 [f]S Ge 39:21 [g]Dt 34:11; 2Sa 7:9; 8:13; 22:44; 23:1; Est 9:4; Ps 89:27
11:4 [h]Ex 12:29; Job 34:20 [i]Ex 12:23; Ps 81:5
11:5 [j]S Ex 4:23 [k]Isa 47:2
11:6 [l]Ex 12:30; Pr 21:13; Am 5:17
11:7 [m]S Ex 8:22
11:8 [n]Ex 12:31-33 [o]Heb 11:27
11:9 [p]S Ex 7:4 [q]S Ex 3:20
11:10 [r]S Ex 4:21; Ro 2:5
12:2 [s]ver 18; Ex 13:4; 23:15; 34:18; 40:2; Dt 16:1
12:3 [t]Mk 14:12; 1Co 5:7 [u]ver 21
12:5 [v]Ex 29:1; Lev 1:3; 3:1; 4:3; 22:18-21; 23:12; Nu 6:14; 15:8; 28:3; Dt 15:21; 17:1; Heb 9:14; 1Pe 1:19
12:6 [w]ver 19; Lev 23:5; Nu 9:1-3, 5,11; Jos 5:10; 2Ch 30:2 [x]Ex 16:12; Dt 16:4, 6
12:7 [y]ver 13,23; Eze 9:6

11:3 HISTORY, Promise—See note on 3:16–22. God works in history to gain the recognition and resources His people need to accomplish His purposes and fulfill His promises.

11:7 ELECTION, Israel—The loud wailing throughout Egypt over the death of Egypt's firstborn sons contrasted with the silence and peace of both persons and animals, even dogs, in Israel. This indicated that God is a God of distinction and choice. His people are the chosen or elected ones free from the wrath experienced by those who saw Pharaoh as lord. Even Pharaoh was helpless in saving his firstborn son, the heir apparent to Pharaoh's throne of power. Election is a doctrine seeking to formulate for human understanding the historical experience that God distinguishes one people from another.

12:1–28 HISTORY, Time—Israel apparently emphasized the content of time rather than its simple duration. Special meaning was attached to worship festivals celebrating both agricultural achievements and memories of God's historical acts. Such acts gave rise to the order of the calendar. Time was determined and ordered according to God's acts and human worship in response to those acts. Israel is apparently the first people to use a seven-day worship week lasting from sabbath to sabbath. Israel depended on God's actions (Ge 1:1—2:4) to set time sequences.

12:1—13:16 CHRISTIAN ETHICS, Moral Imperatives—Obeying God solidifies each individual's resolve in being a covenant person. Obedience to God also communicates to future generations by action and word-of-mouth that obedience is the best way to live life. Obedience and celebration are two complementary sides of life in covenant with God.

12:1—13:16 WORSHIP, Calendar—See note on 16:23–30.

12:3–4 FAMILY, Worship—In preparation for hastily leaving Egyptian captivity, families were commanded to prepare a Passover meal which would give sustenance for the journey and also be an occasion of worshiping God through the blood sacrifice of the lamb. The Passover was established as a family worship ritual celebrated in the home reminding the Jewish people of their deliverance by God from bondage (12:43–49). Family worship should be the unifying center of the family. *Christians no longer* celebrate the Passover ritual, but we must find ways to teach children our basic beliefs in the family setting.

tops of the doorframes of the houses
where they eat the lambs. 8That same
night[z] they are to eat the meat roasted[a]
over the fire, along with bitter herbs,[b]
and bread made without yeast.[c] 9Do not
eat the meat raw or cooked in water, but
roast it over the fire—head, legs and inner parts.[d] 10Do not leave any of it till
morning;[e] if some is left till morning,
you must burn it. 11This is how you are to
eat it: with your cloak tucked into your
belt, your sandals on your feet and your
staff in your hand. Eat it in haste;[f] it is
the LORD's Passover.[g]

12"On that same night I will pass
through[h] Egypt and strike down[i] every
firstborn[j]—both men and animals—and
I will bring judgment on all the gods[k] of
Egypt. I am the LORD.[l] 13The blood will
be a sign for you on the houses where
you are; and when I see the blood, I will
pass over[m] you. No destructive plague
will touch you when I strike Egypt.[n]

14"This is a day you are to commemorate;[o] for the generations to come you
shall celebrate it as a festival to the LORD
—a lasting ordinance.[p] 15For seven days
you are to eat bread made without
yeast.[q] On the first day remove the yeast
from your houses, for whoever eats anything with yeast in it from the first day
through the seventh must be cut off[r]
from Israel. 16On the first day hold a sacred assembly, and another one on the
seventh day. Do no work[s] at all on these
days, except to prepare food for everyone
to eat—that is all you may do.

17"Celebrate the Feast of Unleavened
Bread,[t] because it was on this very day
that I brought your divisions out of
Egypt.[u] Celebrate this day as a lasting ordinance for the generations to come.[v]
18In the first month[w] you are to eat bread
made without yeast, from the evening of
the fourteenth day until the evening of
the twenty-first day. 19For seven days no
yeast is to be found in your houses. And
whoever eats anything with yeast in it
must be cut off[x] from the community of
Israel, whether he is an alien[y] or native-
born. 20Eat nothing made with yeast.
Wherever you live,[z] you must eat unleavened bread."[a]

21Then Moses summoned all the elders
of Israel and said to them, "Go at once
and select the animals for your families
and slaughter the Passover[b] lamb. 22Take
a bunch of hyssop,[c] dip it into the blood
in the basin and put some of the blood[d]
on the top and on both sides of the doorframe. Not one of you shall go out the
door of his house until morning. 23When
the LORD goes through the land to strike[e]
down the Egyptians, he will see the
blood[f] on the top and sides of the doorframe and will pass over[g] that doorway,
and he will not permit the destroyer[h] to
enter your houses and strike you down.

24"Obey these instructions as a lasting
ordinance[i] for you and your descendants. 25When you enter the land[j] that
the LORD will give you as he promised,
observe this ceremony. 26And when your
children[k] ask you, 'What does this ceremony mean to you?' 27then tell them, 'It
is the Passover[l] sacrifice to the LORD,
who passed over the houses of the Israelites in Egypt and spared our homes when
he struck down the Egyptians.' "[m] Then
the people bowed down and worshiped.[n]
28The Israelites did just what the LORD
commanded[o] Moses and Aaron.

29At midnight[p] the LORD[q] struck
down all the firstborn[r] in Egypt, from the
firstborn of Pharaoh, who sat on the
throne, to the firstborn of the prisoner,
who was in the dungeon, and the firstborn of all the livestock[s] as well. 30Phar-
aoh and all his officials and all the Egyptians got up during the night, and there
was loud wailing[t] in Egypt, for there was
not a house without someone dead.

The Exodus

31During the night Pharaoh summoned
Moses and Aaron and said, "Up! Leave
my people, you and the Israelites! Go,
worship[u] the LORD as you have request-

12:8 [z]ver 10; Ex 16:19; 23:18; 34:25; Lev 7:15; Nu 9:12 [a]Dt 16:7; 2Ch 35:13 [b]Nu 9:11 [c]ver 19-20; Ex 13:3; Dt 16:3-4; 1Co 5:8 **12:9** [d]Ex 29:13,17,22; Lev 3:3 **12:10** [e]S ver 8; Ex 13:7; 29:34; Lev 22:30; Dt 16:4 **12:11** [f]ver 33; Dt 16:3; Isa 48:20; 52:12 [g]ver 13,21,27,43; Lev 23:5; Nu 9:2,4; 28:16; Dt 16:1; Jos 5:10; 2Ki 23:21,23; 2Ch 30:1; Ezr 6:19; Isa 31:5; Eze 45:21 **12:12** [h]Am 5:17 [i]Isa 10:33; 31:8; 37:36 [j]ver 29; S Ex 4:23; 13:15 [k]Ex 15:11; 18:11; Nu 33:4; 2Ch 2:5; Ps 95:3; 97:9; 135:5; Isa 19:1; Jer 43:12; 44:8 [l]S Ex 6:2 **12:13** [m]S ver 11, 23; Heb 11:28 [n]S Ex 8:23 **12:14** [o]Ex 13:9; 23:14; 32:5 [p]ver 17,24; Ex 13:5,10; 27:21; Lev 3:17; 10:9; 16:29; 17:7; 23:14; 24:3; Nu 18:23 **12:15** [q]Ex 13:6-7; 23:15; 34:18; Lev 23:6; Nu 28:17; Dt 16:3; 1Co 5:7 [r]S Ge 17:14 **12:16** [s]Nu 29:35 **12:17** [t]Ex 23:15; 34:18; Dt 16:16; 2Ch 8:13; 30:21; Ezr 6:22; Mt 26:17; Lk 22:1; Ac 12:3 [u]ver 41; S Ex 6:6, 26; 13:3; Lev 19:36 [v]Lev 3:17 **12:18** [w]S ver 2 **12:19** [x]S Ge 17:14 [y]Nu 9:14; 15:14; 35:15; Dt 1:16; Jos 8:33 **12:20** [z]Lev 3:17; Nu 35:29; Eze 6:6 [a]Ex 13:6 **12:21** [b]S ver 11; Mk 14:12-16 **12:22** [c]Lev 14:4,6; Nu 19:18; Ps 51:7 [d]Heb 11:28 **12:23** [e]Isa 19:22 [f]S ver 7; Rev 7:3 [g]S ver 13 [h]S Ge 16:7; Isa 37:36; Jer 6:26; 48:8; 1Co 10:10; Heb 11:28 **12:24** [i]S ver 14 **12:25** [j]S Ge 15:14; Ex 3:17 **12:26** [k]Ex 10:2 **12:27** [l]S ver 11 [m]S Ex 8:23 [n]S Ge 24:26 **12:28** [o]ver 50 **12:29** [p]S Ex 11:4 [q]S Ge 19:13 [r]S Ex 4:23 [s]S Ex 9:6 **12:30** [t]S Ex 11:6 **12:31** [u]S Ex 8:8

12:12 GOD, One God—See note on 8:10. As God finally broke Pharaoh's resistance, He also brought judgment upon the gods of the Egyptians, showing them to be worthless. In so doing He revealed His own unique position as the sovereign Lord of the world.

12:24–27 EDUCATION, Symbolism—Whenever the Passover meal has been observed in Jewish homes down through the centuries, its symbolism has been used to retell the story of the Exodus from Egypt. See 13:8,14. The combination of sensory experiences—taste, touch, sight, sound, and smell—contribute to a vivid and memorable learning experience, enabling small children to grasp significant truths in concrete form long before they are able to understand abstract ideas. Christians have a similar teaching opportunity each time they break bread and pass the cup in observance of the Lord's Supper.

12:27 ELECTION, Worship—Election leads the elect to worship. The Passover feast was to be observed as a historical reminder of God's electing action, destroying those who rejected Him in Egypt and saving Israel. Worship looks to God's mercy in election and deliverance and not to human pride.

12:29–42 HISTORY, Deliverance—See notes on 11:3; Ge 15:1–21. The Exodus event delivered Israel from slavery and created a nation. The event became for Israel the primary evidence of God's ability and will to intervene in history. The Exodus was not limited to Israelites. Others went up with them, showing again God's universal interest and purpose.

ed. 32Take your flocks and herds,[v] as you have said, and go. And also bless[w] me."

33The Egyptians urged the people to hurry[x] and leave[y] the country. "For otherwise," they said, "we will all die!"[z] 34So the people took their dough before the yeast was added, and carried it on their shoulders in kneading troughs[a] wrapped in clothing. 35The Israelites did as Moses instructed and asked the Egyptians for articles of silver and gold[b] and for clothing.[c] 36The LORD had made the Egyptians favorably disposed[d] toward the people, and they gave them what they asked for; so they plundered[e] the Egyptians.

37The Israelites journeyed from Rameses[f] to Succoth.[g] There were about six hundred thousand men[h] on foot, besides women and children. 38Many other people[i] went up with them, as well as large droves of livestock, both flocks and herds. 39With the dough they had brought from Egypt, they baked cakes of unleavened bread. The dough was without yeast because they had been driven out[j] of Egypt and did not have time to prepare food for themselves.

40Now the length of time the Israelite people lived in Egypt[u] was 430 years.[k] 41At the end of the 430 years, to the very day, all the LORD's divisions[l] left Egypt.[m] 42Because the LORD kept vigil that night to bring them out of Egypt, on this night all the Israelites are to keep vigil to honor the LORD for the generations to come.[n]

Passover Restrictions

43The LORD said to Moses and Aaron, "These are the regulations for the Passover:[o]

"No foreigner[p] is to eat of it. 44Any slave you have bought may eat of it after you have circumcised[q] him, 45but a temporary resident and a hired worker[r] may not eat of it.

46"It must be eaten inside one house; take none of the meat outside the house. Do not break any of the bones.[s] 47The whole community of Israel must celebrate it.

48"An alien living among you who wants to celebrate the LORD's Passover must have all the males in his household circumcised; then he may take part like one born in the land.[t] No uncircumcised[u] male may eat of it. 49The same law applies to the native-born and to the alien[v] living among you."

50All the Israelites did just what the LORD had commanded[w] Moses and Aaron. 51And on that very day the LORD brought the Israelites out of Egypt[x] by their divisions.[y]

Chapter 13

Consecration of the Firstborn

THE LORD said to Moses, 2"Consecrate to me every firstborn male.[z] The first offspring of every womb among the Israelites belongs to me, whether man or animal."

3Then Moses said to the people, "Commemorate this day, the day you came out of Egypt,[a] out of the land of slavery, because the LORD brought you out of it with a mighty hand.[b] Eat nothing containing yeast.[c] 4Today, in the month of Abib,[d] you are leaving. 5When the LORD brings you into the land of the Canaanites,[e] Hittites, Amorites, Hivites and Jebusites[f]—the land he swore to your forefathers to give you, a land flowing with milk and honey[g]—you are to observe this ceremony[h] in this month: 6For seven days eat bread made without yeast and on the seventh day hold a festival[i] to the LORD. 7Eat unleavened bread during those seven days; nothing with yeast in it is to be seen among you, nor shall any yeast be seen anywhere within your borders. 8On that day tell your son,[j] 'I do this because

[u]40 Masoretic Text; Samaritan Pentateuch and Septuagint *Egypt and Canaan*

12:32 [v]Ex 10:9,26 [w]Ge 27:34
12:33 [x]S ver 11 [y]S Ex 6:1; 1Sa 6:6 [z]S Ge 20:3; S Ex 8:19
12:34 [a]Ex 8:3
12:35 [b]S Ex 3:22 [c]S Ge 24:53
12:36 [d]S Ge 39:21 [e]S Ex 3:22
12:37 [f]S Ge 47:11 [g]Ex 13:20; Nu 33:3-5 [h]Ge 12:2; Ex 38:26; Nu 1:46; 2:32; 11:13,21; 26:51
12:38 [i]Nu 11:4; Jos 8:35
12:39 [j]Ex 3:20; 11:1
12:40 [k]Ge 15:13; Ac 7:6; Gal 3:17
12:41 [l]S Ex 6:26 [m]S Ex 3:10
12:42 [n]Ex 13:10; Lev 3:17; Nu 9:3; Dt 16:1,6
12:43 [o]S ver 11 [p]ver 48; Nu 9:14; 15:14; 2Ch 6:32-33; Isa 14:1; 56:3,6; 60:10
12:44 [q]S Ge 17:12-13
12:45 [r]Lev 22:10
12:46 [s]Nu 9:12; Ps 22:14; 34:20; 51:8; Pr 17:22; Jn 19:36*
12:48 [t]ver 49; Lev 19:18,34; 24:22; Nu 9:14; 10:32 [u]Eze 44:7
12:49 [v]Lev 24:22; Nu 15:15-16,29; Dt 1:16
12:50 [w]ver 28
12:51 [x]S Ex 3:10; S 6:6 [y]S Ex 6:26
13:2 [z]ver 12,13,15; Ex 22:29; 34:20; Lev 27:26; Nu 3:13; 8:17; 18:15; Dt 15:19; Ne 10:36; Lk 2:23*
13:3 [a]ver 14; Ex 7:4; Lev 26:13; Nu 1:1; 9:1; 22:5; 26:4; Dt 4:45; 5:6; Ps 81:10; 114:1 [b]S Ex 3:20 [c]S Ex 12:8
13:4 [d]S Ex 12:2
13:5 [e]ver 11 [f]S Ex 3:8 [g]S Ex 3:8 [h]Ex 12:25-26
13:6 [i]S Ex 12:15-20
13:8 [j]S Ex 10:2; Ps 78:5-6

12:38,48 EVANGELISM, Mass—When many people are redeemed, as were the Israelites out of Egypt, masses will often be inspired and follow. This is the power of mass evangelism. See Guide to Mass Evangelism, pp. 1835–1837.

12:46 JESUS CHRIST, Foretold—The Passover lamb was to be perfect, having no broken bones (Nu 9:12). Jn 19:36 connects Jesus to the Passover and to the title Lamb of God (Jn 1:36). The New Testament reads the Old Testament through the eyes of faith. Christians reading the Bible both forwards and backwards, historically and theologically, see the powerful purpose of God tied together in these biblical figures.

13:1 REVELATION, Actions—The setting aside of the firstborn in Egypt was to be a constant reminder to the children of God that God is the Giver of life and the Redeemer who saved them from slavery. All around Israel's camps were the cries of Egyptians who had just lost their beloved firstborn. Yet the Israelites retained their own first child, as a gift never to be taken lightly. This child, by God's direct revelation, was to be set aside as a special gift of grace from God and for God. This resulted in every firstborn son becoming an agent of God's revelation reminding each new parent of God's saving actions. God later offered this sacrifice Himself as Christ was given to redeem His people.

13:1–16 HISTORY, Worship—The Exodus event became the central feature of Israel's worship. Thus Israel became the first people known to center worship on historical memory rather than agricultural need or mythical reenactment. Worship included memory, education, and moral commitment.

13:5,11 GOD, Faithfulness—God fulfilled His promises. He finally delivered the children of Israel out of captivity. Once into the Promised Land of Canaan, the people were to preserve the memory that God was faithful to His promises. Time and distance do not dim God's memory or diminish His promises. Each new generation needs to hear their parents' testimony to this.

of what the LORD did for me when I came out of Egypt.' 9This observance will be for you like a sign on your hand[k] and a reminder on your forehead[l] that the law of the LORD is to be on your lips. For the LORD brought you out of Egypt with his mighty hand.[m] 10You must keep this ordinance[n] at the appointed time[o] year after year.

11"After the LORD brings you into the land of the Canaanites[p] and gives it to you, as he promised on oath[q] to you and your forefathers,[r] 12you are to give over to the LORD the first offspring of every womb. All the firstborn males of your livestock belong to the LORD.[s] 13Redeem with a lamb every firstborn donkey,[t] but if you do not redeem it, break its neck.[u] Redeem[v] every firstborn among your sons.[w]

14"In days to come, when your son[x] asks you, 'What does this mean?' say to him, 'With a mighty hand the LORD brought us out of Egypt, out of the land of slavery.[y] 15When Pharaoh stubbornly refused to let us go, the LORD killed every firstborn in Egypt, both man and animal. This is why I sacrifice to the LORD the first male offspring of every womb and redeem each of my firstborn sons.'[z] 16And it will be like a sign on your hand and a symbol on your forehead[a] that the LORD brought us out of Egypt with his mighty hand."

Crossing the Sea

17When Pharaoh let the people go, God did not lead them on the road through the Philistine country, though that was shorter. For God said, "If they face war, they might change their minds and return to Egypt."[b] 18So God led[c] the people around by the desert road toward the Red Sea.[v] The Israelites went up out of Egypt armed for battle.[d]

19Moses took the bones of Joseph[e] with him because Joseph had made the sons of Israel swear an oath. He had said, "God will surely come to your aid, and then you must carry my bones up with you from this place."[w][f]

20After leaving Succoth[g] they camped at Etham on the edge of the desert.[h] 21By day the LORD went ahead[i] of them in a pillar of cloud[j] to guide them on their way and by night in a pillar of fire to give them light, so that they could travel by day or night. 22Neither the pillar of cloud by day nor the pillar of fire by night left[k] its place in front of the people.

Chapter 14

THEN the LORD said to Moses, 2"Tell the Israelites to turn back and encamp near Pi Hahiroth, between Migdol[l] and the sea. They are to encamp by the sea, directly opposite Baal Zephon.[m] 3Pharaoh will think, 'The Israelites are wandering around the land in confusion, hemmed in by the desert.' 4And I will harden Pharaoh's heart,[n] and he will pursue them.[o] But I will gain glory[p] for myself through Pharaoh and all his army, and the Egyptians will know that I am the LORD."[q] So the Israelites did this.

5When the king of Egypt was told that the people had fled,[r] Pharaoh and his officials changed their minds[s] about them and said, "What have we done? We have let the Israelites go and have lost their services!" 6So he had his chariot made ready and took his army with him. 7He

13:9 [k]Isa 44:5 [l]ver 16; Dt 6:8; 11:18; Pr 3:3; Mt 23:5 [m]S Ex 3:20
13:10 [n]S Ex 12:14 [o]Ps 75:2; 102:13
13:11 [p]S ver 5 [q]S Ge 22:16; Dt 1:8 [r]S Ge 12:7; S 17:19; Ps 105:42-45
13:12 [s]S Ge 4:4; Lev 27:26; Nu 3:13; 18:15,17; Lk 2:23*
13:13 [t]ver 15; Lev 27:11 [u]Ex 34:20; Isa 66:3 [v]Nu 3:46-47 [w]Nu 18:15
13:14 [x]S Ex 10:2 [y]Ex 20:2; Dt 7:8; 28:68
13:15 [z]S ver 2
13:16 [a]S ver 9
13:17 [b]Ex 14:11; Nu 14:1-4; Dt 17:16; Hos 11:5
13:18 [c]Ex 15:22; Ps 136:16; Eze 20:10 [d]Jos 1:14; 4:13
13:19 [e]Jos 24:32; Ac 7:16; Heb 11:22 [f]S Ge 47:29-30
13:20 [g]S Ex 12:37 [h]Nu 33:6
13:21 [i]Ex 32:1; 33:14; Dt 2:7; 31:8; Jdg 4:14; 5:4; Ps 68:7; 77:20; Jer 2:2; Hab 3:13 [j]Ex 14:19,24; 24:16; 33:9-10; 34:5; 40:38; Nu 9:16; 12:5; 14:14; Dt 1:33; Ne 9:12,19; Ps 78:14; 99:7; 105:39; Isa 4:5; 1Co 10:1
13:22 [k]Ne 9:19
14:2 [l]Nu 33:7; Jer 44:1; Eze 29:10 [m]ver 9
14:4 [n]S Ex 4:21 [o]ver 8,17,23; Ps 71:11 [p]S Ex 9:16; Ro 9:17,22-23 [q]S Ex 6:2; Eze 32:15
14:5 [r]S Ge 31:21 [s]Ps 105:25

[v] *18* Hebrew *Yam Suph*; that is, Sea of Reeds
[w] *19* See Gen. 50:25.

13:13–15 SALVATION, Redemption—Israel's redemption was founded on the death of the firstborn in Egypt (11:1—12:30). The offering of a lamb foreshadowed the offering of the Son of God on the cross for our redemption (Jn 1:29). Compare Ex 34:20. See note on 6:6.

13:21–22 REVELATION, Divine Presence—The childlike people who left Egypt needed a visible evidence that God was present in their journey. To guide and reassure them, God provided a sign before them day and night: cloud and pillar of fire. Thus God showed Himself constantly to His children, revealing at the same time His compassion for their anxiety on this journey and His understanding of the limitations of their faith. Newborn followers today usually require a concrete sign of God's presence or activity in their lives. Similarly Moses apparently needed several reassuring miracles before he would follow. See note on 4:10–12. Sadly, the concrete signs of God's revealing presence did not keep Israel in the wilderness from complaining.

13:21 DISCIPLESHIP, God's Leadership—God chooses the way in which He will lead those who serve Him. He always will choose appropriate leadership in ways His servants will be able to follow. He may use clearly visible signs, or He may use only the small voice that speaks to our hearts.

14:1—15:18 REVELATION, History—Historical actions datable on the calendar and locatable on the map are the central points of God's revelation. The Exodus event is the Old Testament's closest parallel to the divine revelation on the Roman cross and in the empty tomb. In unique historical acts God showed He was more than a philosophical idea. He had personal power to deliver and save His people in the crises of life. In historical actions for which He had prepared chosen interpreters God introduced to Egypt and to Israel His power, sovereignty, and commitment to His people. Egypt refused to acknowledge Him as God and died. Israel responded to revelation in faith and praise and gained freedom and new identity. Crossing the sea showed God has power over history, over human armies, and over nature.

14:1—15:18 CHRISTIAN ETHICS, War and Peace—God's might enters into the conflict of this world on the side of right and justice.

14:4,18 HISTORY, Universal—See note on 7:5. God revealed His universal power and introduced Himself to the Egyptians through the Exodus. God works in history to let people know who He is and to call them to be His people.

14:4,18,25 EVANGELISM, Glory to God—Even as God judges a people who reject His gracious salvation, He brings glory to Himself. See note on 7:5.

took six hundred of the best chariots,[t]
along with all the other chariots of Egypt,
with officers over all of them. 8The LORD
hardened the heart[u] of Pharaoh king of
Egypt, so that he pursued the Israelites,
who were marching out boldly.[v] 9The
Egyptians—all Pharaoh's horses[w] and
chariots, horsemen[x] and troops[x]—pursued the Israelites and overtook[y] them as
they camped by the sea near Pi Hahiroth,
opposite Baal Zephon.[z]

10As Pharaoh approached, the Israelites
looked up, and there were the Egyptians,
marching after them. They were terrified
and cried[a] out to the LORD. 11They said
to Moses, "Was it because there were no
graves in Egypt that you brought us to the
desert to die?[b] What have you done to us
by bringing us out of Egypt? 12Didn't we
say to you in Egypt, 'Leave us alone; let
us serve the Egyptians'? It would have
been better for us to serve the Egyptians
than to die in the desert!"[c]

13Moses answered the people, "Do not
be afraid.[d] Stand firm and you will see[e]
the deliverance the LORD will bring you
today. The Egyptians you see today you
will never see[f] again. 14The LORD will
fight[g] for you; you need only to be
still."[h]

15Then the LORD said to Moses, "Why
are you crying out to me?[i] Tell the Israelites to move on. 16Raise your staff[j] and
stretch out your hand over the sea to divide the water[k] so that the Israelites can
go through the sea on dry ground. 17I will
harden the hearts[l] of the Egyptians so
that they will go in after them.[m] And I
will gain glory through Pharaoh and all
his army, through his chariots and his
horsemen. 18The Egyptians will know
that I am the LORD[n] when I gain glory
through Pharaoh, his chariots and his
horsemen."

19Then the angel of God,[o] who had
been traveling in front of Israel's army,
withdrew and went behind them. The
pillar of cloud[p] also moved from in front
and stood behind[q] them, 20coming between the armies of Egypt and Israel.
Throughout the night the cloud brought
darkness[r] to the one side and light to the
other side; so neither went near the other all night long.

21Then Moses stretched out his hand[s]
over the sea,[t] and all that night the LORD
drove the sea back with a strong east
wind[u] and turned it into dry land.[v] The
waters were divided,[w] 22and the Israelites went through the sea[x] on dry
ground,[y] with a wall[z] of water on their
right and on their left.

23The Egyptians pursued them, and all
Pharaoh's horses and chariots and horsemen[a] followed them into the sea. 24Dur-
ing the last watch of the night the LORD
looked down from the pillar of fire and
cloud[b] at the Egyptian army and threw it
into confusion.[c] 25He made the wheels of

14:7 [t]Ex 15:4 **14:8** [u]S Ex 11:10 [v]Nu 33:3; Ac 13:17 **14:9** [w]Ge 47:17 [x]ver 6-7,25; Jos 24:6; Isa 43:17 [y]Ex 15:9 [z]ver 2 **14:10** [a]Ex 15:25; Jos 24:7; Ne 9:9; Ps 5:2; 34:17; 50:15; 107:6,28 **14:11** [b]S Ex 5:21; 16:3; 17:3; Nu 11:1; 14:22; 20:4; 21:5; Dt 9:7 **14:12** [c]S Ex 5:21; 15:24; 17:2; Ps 106:7-8 **14:13** [d]S Ge 15:1 [e]1Sa 12:16; 2Ch 20:17 [f]ver 30 **14:14** [g]ver 25; Ex 15:3; Dt 1:30; 3:22; 20:4; Jos 10:14; 23:3,10; 2Sa 5:24; 2Ch 20:29; Ne 4:20; Ps 24:8; 35:1; Isa 42:13; Jer 41:12 [h]1Sa 12:16; Ps 37:7; 46:10; 116:7; Isa 28:12; 30:15; Zec 2:13 **14:15** [i]Jos 7:10 **14:16** [j]S Ex 4:2 [k]ver 27; Isa 10:26 **14:17** [l]Ex 4:21 [m]S ver 4 **14:18** [n]S Ex 6:2; Eze 32:15 **14:19** [o]S Ge 16:7; Isa 63:9 [p]S Ex 13:21; 1Co 10:1 [q]Isa 26:7; 42:16; 49:10; 52:12; 58:8 **14:20** [r]Jos 24:7 **14:21** [s]S Ex 7:19 [t]S Ex 4:2; Job 26:12; Isa 14:27; 23:11; 51:15; Jer 31:35; Ac 7:36 [u]S Ge 41:6; Ex 15:8; 2Sa 22:16; 1Ki 19:11; Job 38:1; 40:6; Jer 23:19; Na 1:3 [v]S ver 22; S Ge 8:1 [w]2Ki 2:8; Ps 74:13; 78:13; 114:5; 136:13; Isa 63:12 **14:22** [x]ver 16; Nu 33:8; Jos 24:6; Isa 43:16; 63:11; 1Co 10:1 [y]ver 21,29; S Ex 3:12; 15:19; Dt 31:6-8; Jos 3:16,17; 4:22; Ne 9:11; Ps 66:6; 77:19; 106:9; Isa 11:15; 41:10; 43:5; 44:27; 50:2; 51:10; 63:13; Jer 46:28; Na 1:4; Heb 11:29 [z]Ex 15:8; Jos 3:13; Ps 78:13 **14:23** [a]ver 7 **14:24** [b]S Ex 13:21; 1Co 10:1 [c]Ex 23:27; Jos 10:10; 1Sa 5:9; 7:10; 14:15; 2Sa 5:24; 2Ki 7:6; 19:7

x9 Or *charioteers*; also in verses 17, 18, 23, 26 and 28

14:10 PRAYER, Mercy of God—Prayer is appropriate in every situation and mood of life. Israel cried in terror to God. He heard the cry of the oppressed. See note on 2:23–24.

14:11–12 SIN, Lack of Faith—The Hebrews exhibited a lack of faith in God as they cringed in fear before Pharaoh and his army. Though God had led them up to this point, in the moment of crisis their faith waivered. They feared God had forsaken them. Failure to trust God is the root of all sin.

14:13 HISTORY, God—God can and does work in history despite the fear and unbelief of His people. He acts to accomplish His will and to elicit faith from His people. The historical initiative remains with God.

14:13,30 SALVATION, Initiative—The Exodus of Israel from slavery in Egypt was the great Old Testament example of God's saving action in history. "Saved" (Hebrew *hoshia'*), also the root for "deliverance," means "to be wide and spacious" or "to develop without hindrance." It thus signified freedom or victory. Here it referred to God's victory over the Pharaoh and the freedom Israel gained through her deliverance from Egypt. The important point here is the victory of God, not the drowning of the Egyptians. This historic victory of God established His Lordship beyond dispute. Salvation is the work of God. Besides Him, there is no Savior (Isa 43:11; Jer 14:8; Hos 13:4). The Exodus points beyond itself to the continuation of God's saving action in history. It became the basis for the hope that God would one day complete what He had begun. That day came when Jesus, the One greater than Moses, led the new Exodus, delivering us from our bondage to sin (Heb 3:3).

14:15–16 DISCIPLESHIP, God's Leadership—God's will is not always what His people anticipate or desire. God did not simply fight the Egyptians and give their land and power to Israel. Instead, He provided an escape for His people which led through the wilderness. God provides a way for His disciples to do His will when they are obedient. It has been said that when God closes a door He will open a window. In this case He opened a way through the sea on dry ground.

14:21 HOLY SPIRIT, Vocabulary—The Holy Spirit is not mentioned in Israel's greatest experience of deliverance—the Exodus victory over Egypt. God did use the east wind, wind being the same Hebrew word (*ruach*) as spirit.

14:21 MIRACLE, Redemption—God's redemption from Egyptian bondage was the central miracle for Israel. The crossing of the sea created identity and faith for God's people. Frightened rebels (14:10–12) came to believe in God's redemptive purpose (v 31). How? The Scripture clearly attests God's miraculous use of His created nature. The wind blew back and dried up the waters. The event came at God's time through the obedience of God's prophet. Moses stretched out his hand, and God brought the strong east wind. Israel crossed, and Moses stretched out his hand bidding the waters to return. The Egyptians were drowned. Israel was redeemed. The important event is God's victory. That day the Lord saved Israel (v 30). God had introduced Himself on the international scene and to His chosen people through the miraculous action in history.

their chariots come off[y] so that they had
difficulty driving. And the Egyptians said,
"Let's get away from the Israelites! The
LORD is fighting[d] for them against
Egypt."[e]
26Then the LORD said to Moses,
"Stretch out your hand over the sea so
that the waters may flow back over the
Egyptians and their chariots and horsemen." 27Moses stretched out his hand
over the sea, and at daybreak the sea
went back to its place.[f] The Egyptians
were fleeing toward[z] it, and the LORD
swept them into the sea.[g] 28The water
flowed back and covered the chariots and
horsemen—the entire army of Pharaoh
that had followed the Israelites into the
sea.[h] Not one of them survived.[i]
29But the Israelites went through the
sea on dry ground,[j] with a wall[k] of water on their right and on their left. 30That
day the LORD saved[l] Israel from the
hands of the Egyptians, and Israel saw the
Egyptians lying dead on the shore. 31And
when the Israelites saw the great power[m]
the LORD displayed against the Egyptians,
the people feared[n] the LORD and put
their trust[o] in him and in Moses his
servant.

Chapter 15

The Song of Moses and Miriam

THEN Moses and the Israelites sang
this song[p] to the LORD:

"I will sing[q] to the LORD,
for he is highly exalted.
The horse and its rider[r]
he has hurled into the sea.[s]
2The LORD is my strength[t] and my
song;
he has become my salvation.[u]
He is my God,[v] and I will praise him,
my father's God, and I will exalt[w]
him.
3The LORD is a warrior;[x]
the LORD is his name.[y]
4Pharaoh's chariots and his army[z]
he has hurled into the sea.
The best of Pharaoh's officers
are drowned in the Red Sea.[a]
5The deep waters[a] have covered them;
they sank to the depths like a
stone.[b]

6"Your right hand,[c] O LORD,
was majestic in power.
Your right hand,[d] O LORD,
shattered[e] the enemy.
7In the greatness of your majesty[f]
you threw down those who opposed
you.
You unleashed your burning anger;[g]
it consumed[h] them like stubble.
8By the blast of your nostrils[i]
the waters piled up.[j]
The surging waters stood firm like a
wall;[k]
the deep waters congealed in the
heart of the sea.[l]

9"The enemy boasted,

14:25 [d]S ver 14 [e]S ver 9; Dt 32:31; 1Sa 2:2; 4:8 **14:27** [f]Jos 4:18 [g]ver 28; Ex 15:1, 21; Dt 1:40; 2:1; 11:4; Ps 78:53; 106:11; 136:15; Heb 11:29 **14:28** [h]ver 23; Ex 15:19; Jos 24:7 [i]S ver 27; Ex 15:5; Jdg 4:16; Ne 9:11 **14:29** [j]ver 21,S 22; Jos 24:11; 2Ki 2:8; Ps 74:15 [k]Ps 78:13 **14:30** [l]ver 29; 1Sa 14:23; 1Ch 11:14; Ps 44:7; 106:8,10,21; Isa 43:3; 50:2; 51:9-10; 60:16; 63:8,11 **14:31** [m]S Ex 9:16; Ps 147:5 [n]Ex 20:18; Dt 31:13; Jos 4:24; 1Sa 12:18; Ps 76:7; 112:1 [o]S Ex 4:5; Ps 22:4; 40:3; 106:12; Jn 2:11; 11:45 **15:1** [p]Nu 21:17; Jdg 5:1; 2Sa 22:1; 1Ch 16:9; Job 36:24; Ps 59:16; 105:2; Rev 15:3 [q]Jdg 5:3; Ps 13:6; 21:13; 27:6; 61:8; 104:33; 106:12; Isa 12:5,6; 42:10-11,10; 44:23 [r]Dt 11:4; Ps 76:6; Jer 51:21 [s]S Ex 14:27 **15:2** [t]Ps 18:1; 59:17 [u]S Ge 45:7; Ex 14:13; Ps 18:2, 46; 25:5; 27:1; 62:2; 118:14; Isa 12:2; 33:2; Jnh 2:9; Hab 3:18 [v]S Ge 28:21 [w]Dt 10:21; 2Sa 22:47; Ps 22:3; 30:1; 34:3; 35:27; 99:5; 103:19; 107:32; 108:5; 109:1; 118:28; 145:11; 148:14; Isa 24:15; 25:1; Jer 17:14; Da 4:37

15:3 [x]S Ex 14:14; Rev 19:11 [y]S Ex 3:15 **15:4** [z]Ex 14:6-7; Jer 51:21 **15:5** [a]S Ex 14:28 [b]ver 10; Ne 9:11 **15:6** [c]Ps 16:11; 17:7; 21:8; 63:8; 74:11; 77:10; 89:13; 98:1; 118:15; 138:7 [d]S Ex 3:20; S Job 40:14 [e]Nu 24:8; 1Sa 2:10; Ps 2:9 **15:7** [f]Dt 33:26; Ps 150:2 [g]Ps 2:5; 78:49-50; Jer 12:13; 25:38 [h]Ex 24:17; Dt 4:24; 9:3; Ps 18:8; 59:13; Heb 12:29 **15:8** [i]S Ex 14:21; Ps 18:15 [j]Jos 3:13; Ps 78:13; Isa 43:16 [k]S Ex 14:22 [l]Ps 46:2

[y]25 Or *He jammed the wheels of their chariots* (see Samaritan Pentateuch, Septuagint and Syriac)
[z]27 Or *from* [a]4 Hebrew *Yam Suph*; that is, Sea of Reeds; also in verse 22

14:29–31 HISTORY, Faith—God's participation in history is not immediately recognized by all people. God uses an interpreter like Moses to announce His historical intentions and explain His acts as divine direction of history. Only by faith do people accept an event in history as God's act. Without faith they search for strictly natural causes. Biblical writers looked beyond the natural cause to the ultimate Cause. Human eyes see military victory. Faith sees divine salvation.

15:1–18 GOD, One God—Both the sovereignty and the wrath of God are extolled in the Song of Moses and the Israelites. They confessed their deliverance as a mighty and gracious act of the sovereign God, Yahweh. His reign was permanently established (v 18); His wrath had slain those who opposed Him (v 7); His power and uniqueness were clearly seen (v 11). Who could duplicate such a miraculous deliverance? No other "god" could compare. He is the one and only true God. See note on 12:12.

15:1–21 EVIL AND SUFFERING, God's Present Help—God helped the Hebrews escape suffering in Egypt by miraculously opening a path through the sea (14:21–22). Like Moses and Miriam, we can praise God for His help in alleviating suffering. Like the Hebrews, we can trust God as our Liberator and Companion.

15:1–21 HISTORY, Worship—Historical deliverance leads people to praise the Deliverer. Such praise appropriates the historical act as important for the individual life, as revealing of God's nature, as evidence of God's uniqueness, and as basis for hope in future divine acts.

15:1–21 WORSHIP, Praise—See note on 1 Ch 6:31–32. One of the earliest evidences of music in worship is found in these verses. Compare Ge 4:21. This is a song of praise and thanksgiving to God. From the beginning this has been a significant part of worship. Worship is not a casual matter of observing like a spectator. It involves the personal activity of the worshiper. Praise is a positive, specific act of gratitude, in which the worshiper reaches out to God. We can define worship as pure adoration in which the redeemed person meditates upon the perfection and provision of God and praises Him. This is the natural response of believing individuals to God's revelation of Himself. Compare 2 Sa 22; 1 Ch 29:10–20; Ps 9:1–20; 29:1–2; 34:1–3; 150; Isa 12:1–6; 44:23; Eze 3:12; Eph 5:19; Col 3:16.

15:1–18 PRAYER, Praise—Corporate praise is the appropriate response of God's people to His saving actions. Praise extols God's character and His works. It looks to past, present, and future. Such prayers may come to be written down and preserved as means of teaching God's people. Prayer points ultimately to participation in God's kingdom.

15:2 SALVATION, Initiative—See note on 14:13,30.

'I will pursue,[m] I will overtake
them.
I will divide the spoils;[n]
I will gorge myself on them.
I will draw my sword
and my hand will destroy them.'
10But you blew with your breath,[o]
and the sea covered them.
They sank like lead
in the mighty waters.[p]

11"Who among the gods is like you,[q]
O LORD?
Who is like you—
majestic in holiness,[r]
awesome in glory,[s]
working wonders?[t]
12You stretched out[u] your right hand
and the earth swallowed them.[v]

13"In your unfailing love you will lead[w]
the people you have redeemed.[x]
In your strength you will guide them
to your holy dwelling.[y]
14The nations will hear and tremble;[z]
anguish[a] will grip the people of
Philistia.[b]
15The chiefs[c] of Edom[d] will be terrified,
the leaders of Moab will be seized
with trembling,[e]
the people[b] of Canaan will melt[f]
away;
16 terror[g] and dread will fall upon
them.
By the power of your arm
they will be as still as a stone[h]—
until your people pass by, O LORD,
until the people you bought[c][i]
pass by.[j]
17You will bring[k] them in and plant[l]
them
on the mountain[m] of your
inheritance—
the place, O LORD, you made for your
dwelling,[n]
the sanctuary,[o] O Lord, your hands
established.

18The LORD will reign
for ever and ever."[p]

19When Pharaoh's horses, chariots and
horsemen[d] went into the sea,[q] the LORD
brought the waters of the sea back over
them, but the Israelites walked through
the sea on dry ground.[r] 20Then Miriam[s]
the prophetess,[t] Aaron's sister, took a
tambourine in her hand, and all the women
followed her, with tambourines[u] and
dancing.[v] 21Miriam sang[w] to them:

"Sing to the LORD,
for he is highly exalted.
The horse and its rider[x]
he has hurled into the sea."[y]

The Waters of Marah and Elim

22Then Moses led Israel from the Red
Sea and they went into the Desert[z] of
Shur.[a] For three days they traveled in the
desert without finding water.[b] 23When
they came to Marah, they could not drink
its water because it was bitter. (That is
why the place is called Marah.[e][c]) 24So
the people grumbled[d] against Moses, saying,
"What are we to drink?"[e]
25Then Moses cried out[f] to the LORD,
and the LORD showed him a piece of
wood. He threw[g] it into the water, and
the water became sweet.

There the LORD made a decree and a
law for them, and there he tested[h] them.
26He said, "If you listen carefully to the
voice of the LORD your God and do what
is right in his eyes, if you pay attention

15:9 [m]Ex 14:5-9; Dt 28:45; Ps 7:5; La 1:3 [n]Jdg 5:30; Isa 9:3; 53:12; Lk 11:22 **15:10** [o]Job 4:9; 15:30; Isa 11:4; 30:33; 40:7 [p]ver 5; Ne 9:11; Ps 29:3; 32:6; 77:19 **15:11** [q]S Ex 8:10; Ps 77:13; S Isa 46:5 [r]Lev 19:2; 1Sa 2:2; 1Ch 16:29; Ps 99:3; 110:3; Isa 6:3; Rev 4:8 [s]S Ex 14:4; Ps 4:2; 8:1; 26:8; Isa 35:2; 40:5 [t]S Ex 3:20 **15:12** [u]S Ex 7:5 [v]Nu 16:32; 26:10; Dt 11:6; Ps 106:17 **15:13** [w]Ne 9:12; Ps 77:20 [x]S Ex 6:6; Job 33:28; Ps 71:23; 106:10; Isa 1:27; 41:14; 43:14; 44:22-24; 51:10; 63:9; Tit 2:14 [y]ver 17; Ps 68:16; 76:2; 78:54 **15:14** [z]ver 16; Ex 23:27; Dt 2:25; Jos 2:9; 5:1; 9:24; 1Sa 4:7; Est 8:17; Ps 48:6; 96:9; 99:1; 114:7; Eze 38:20 [a]Isa 13:8 [b]Ps 83:7 **15:15** [c]S Ge 36:15 [d]Dt 2:4 [e]Nu 22:3; Ps 114:7 [f]Jos 2:9,24 **15:16** [g]S ver 14; S Ge 35:5 [h]1Sa 25:37 [i]Ps 74:2; 2Pe 2:1 [j]Dt 2:4 **15:17** [k]Ex 23:20; 32:34; 33:12 [l]2Sa 7:10; Ps 44:2; 80:8,15; Isa 5:2; 60:21; Jer 2:21; 11:17; 24:6; Am 9:15 [m]Dt 33:19; Ps 2:6; 3:4; 15:1; 78:54, 68; 133:3; Da 9:16; Joel 2:1; Ob 1:16; Zep 3:11 [n]S ver 13; Ps 132:13-14 [o]Ps 78:69; 114:2 **15:18** [p]S Ge 21:33; Ps 9:7; 29:10; 55:19; 66:7; 80:1; 102:12; 145:13; La 5:19 **15:19** [q]S Ex 14:28 [r]S Ex 14:22 **15:20** [s]ver 21; Ex 2:4; Nu 12:1; 20:1; 26:59; 1Ch 4:17; 6:3 [t]Jdg 4:4; 2Ki 22:14; 2Ch 34:22; Ne 6:14; Isa 8:3; Eze 13:17 [u]S Ge 31:27; 1Sa 18:6; Ps 81:2; Isa 30:32 [v]S Ge 4:21; Jdg 11:34; 21:21; 1Sa 18:6; 2Sa 6:5,14,16; Ps 30:11; 149:3; 150:4; SS 6:13; Jer 31:4,13 **15:21** [w]1Sa 18:7 [x]Am 2:15; Hag 2:22 [y]S Ex 14:27 **15:22** [z]Ps 78:52 [a]S Ge 16:7 [b]Ex 17:1, 3; Nu 20:2,5; 33:14; Ps 107:5 **15:23** [c]Nu 33:8; Ru 1:20 **15:24** [d]S Ex 14:12; 16:2; 7:3; Nu 14:2; Jos 9:18; Ps 78:18,42; 106:13,25; Eze 16:43 [e]Mt 6:31 **15:25** [f]S Ex 14:10 [g]2Ki 2:21; 4:41; 6:6 [h]S Ge 22:1; Jdg 3:4; Job 23:10; Ps 81:7; Isa 48:10 **15:26** [i]Ex 23:22; Dt 11:13; 15:5; 28:1; Jer 11:6

[b] *15* Or *rulers* [c] *16* Or *created* [d] *19* Or *charioteers* [e] *23* *Marah* means *bitter.*

15:13,18 DISCIPLESHIP, God's Leadership—Confidence, expectation, and faith in God's leadership are essential in the victorious living and service of God's people. We can be faithful disciples even though the dry wilderness stretches before us because we have confidence in God's eternal kingdom.

15:21 PRAYER, Praise—All God's people, men and women, individually and as a community, can praise God.

15:24 SIN, Disobeying—Even though God had given them victory over the Egyptians, the people of Israel rebelled against Moses' leadership. They grumbled because they had no fresh water to drink. How easy it is for God's people to be rebellious in little things even after a great victory. Trust in God is a continuous attitude of life, not a luxury reserved for good times.

15:25 PRAYER, Petition—See note on 5:22–23. God may answer prayer by calling on us *to act.*

15:26 GOD, Love—God promised a special blessing to His people if they would be faithful and obedient to Him. God promised His people that He would not bring upon them the diseases or plagues that the Egyptians had suffered. The stern display of mighty force upon the Egyptians must have made a deep impression on the Israelites. God wanted them to remember that the powerful, sovereign God of the Exodus is also the God of tender, loving care. God prefers to be known as the God of love. That love is more clearly understood against the background of what God is like when His love is thwarted.

15:26 EVIL AND SUFFERING, Deserved—God can bring disease on people to punish them for disobedience. God's basic work, however, is healing His people. This does not mean all disease results from God's punishment of individual sin. It does not mean God heals every disease of His people. It does mean God's basic nature is love and His eternal occupation is healing His people. He wants us to trust and obey Him in a world plagued by suffering.

15:26 CHRISTIAN ETHICS, Moral Imperatives—God's imperatives are set out to help us, not to rob us of life's joys.

to his commands and keep[i] all his
decrees,[j] I will not bring on you any of the
diseases[k] I brought on the Egyptians, for I
am the LORD, who heals[l] you."
27 Then they came to Elim, where there
were twelve springs and seventy palm
trees, and they camped[m] there near the
water.

Chapter 16

Manna and Quail

THE whole Israelite community set out
from Elim and came to the Desert of
Sin,[n] which is between Elim and Sinai,
on the fifteenth day of the second month
after they had come out of Egypt.[o] 2 In
the desert the whole community grumbled[p] against Moses and Aaron. 3 The Israelites said to them, "If only we had died
by the LORD's hand in Egypt![q] There we
sat around pots of meat and ate all the
food[r] we wanted, but you have brought
us out into this desert to starve this entire
assembly to death."[s]
4 Then the LORD said to Moses, "I will
rain down bread from heaven[t] for you.
The people are to go out each day and
gather enough for that day. In this way I
will test[u] them and see whether they will
follow my instructions. 5 On the sixth day
they are to prepare what they bring in,
and that is to be twice[v] as much as they
gather on the other days."
6 So Moses and Aaron said to all the Israelites, "In the evening you will know
that it was the LORD who brought you out
of Egypt,[w] 7 and in the morning you will
see the glory[x] of the LORD, because he
has heard your grumbling[y] against him.
Who are we, that you should grumble
against us?"[z] 8 Moses also said, "You will
know that it was the LORD when he gives
you meat to eat in the evening and all the
bread you want in the morning, because
he has heard your grumbling[a] against
him. Who are we? You are not grumbling
against us, but against the LORD."[b]
9 Then Moses told Aaron, "Say to the
entire Israelite community, 'Come before
the LORD, for he has heard your grumbling.'"
10 While Aaron was speaking to the
whole Israelite community, they looked
toward the desert, and there was the glory[c] of the LORD appearing in the cloud.[d]
11 The LORD said to Moses, 12 "I have
heard the grumbling[e] of the Israelites.
Tell them, 'At twilight you will eat meat,
and in the morning you will be filled with
bread. Then you will know that I am the
LORD your God.'"[f]
13 That evening quail[g] came and covered the camp, and in the morning there
was a layer of dew[h] around the camp.
14 When the dew was gone, thin flakes
like frost[i] on the ground appeared on the
desert floor. 15 When the Israelites saw it,
they said to each other, "What is it?" For
they did not know[j] what it was.
Moses said to them, "It is the bread[k]
the LORD has given you to eat. 16 This is
what the LORD has commanded: 'Each
one is to gather as much as he needs.
Take an omer[f][l] for each person you
have in your tent.'"
17 The Israelites did as they were told;
some gathered much, some little. 18 And

15:26 [j]Ex 19:5-6; 20:2-17; Dt 7:12 [k]Dt 7:15; 28:27, 58-60; 32:39; 1Sa 5:6; Ps 30:2; 41:3-4; 103:3 [l]Ex 23:25-26; 2Ki 20:5; Ps 25:11; 103:3; 107:20; Jer 30:17; Hos 11:3 **15:27** [m]Nu 33:9 **16:1** [n]Ex 17:1; Nu 33:11,12 [o]S Ex 6:6; 12:1-2 **16:2** [p]S Ex 15:24; 1Co 10:10 **16:3** [q]Ex 17:3; Nu 14:2; 20:3 [r]Nu 11:4,34; Dt 12:20; Ps 78:18; 106:14; Jer 44:17 [s]S Ge 47:15; Dt 8:3 **16:4** [t]ver 14-15; Dt 8:3; Ne 9:15; Ps 78:24; 105:40; S Jn 6:31* [u]S Ge 22:1 **16:5** [v]ver 22; Lev 25:21 **16:6** [w]S Ex 6:6 **16:7** [x]ver 10; Ex 24:16; 29:43; 33:18,22; 40:34; Lev 9:6; Nu 16:19, 42; Dt 5:24; 1Ki 8:11; Ps 63:2; Isa 6:3; 35:2; 40:5; 44:23; 60:1; 66:18; Eze 1:28; 10:4; 43:5; Hab 2:14; Hag 2:7; Jn 11:40 [y]ver 12; Nu 11:1, 18; 14:2,27,28; 17:5 [z]Nu 16:11 **16:8** [a]ver 7 [b]Nu 23:21; Dt 33:5; Jdg 8:23; 1Sa 8:7; 12:12; S Mt 10:40; Ro 13:2; 1Th 4:8 **16:10** [c]S ver 7; Jn 11:4 [d]Ex 13:21; 40:34-35; 1Ki 8:10; 2Ch 7:1; Eze 10:4 **16:12** [e]S ver 7 [f]S Ex 6:2; S 20:2 **16:13** [g]Nu 11:31; Ps 78:27-28; 105:40; 106:15 [h]Nu 11:9 **16:14** [i]ver 31; Nu 11:7-9; Dt 8:3, 16; Ps 105:40 **16:15** [j]Dt 8:16 [k]S ver 4; Ne 9:20; S Jn 6:31 **16:16** [l]ver 32,36

[f]*16* That is, probably about 2 quarts (about 2 liters); also in verses 18, 32, 33 and 36

16:1–36 EVIL AND SUFFERING, Testing—As God's people we do not always have everything we want. We can trust God to supply needs, not desires. Times of want test us to see if faith or complaint is the dominant mood of life.

16:3–8 REVELATION, Events—God revealed Himself in miracles in response to human complaint. The people's weak faith showed itself as food and water ran scarce. Moses faced a rebelling group of freed slaves. God provided for their needs with miraculous use of all creation's elements available to Him. The revelation in miracle became at the same time a test of faith. The people had to work to gather the daily food and had to obey instructions to have sabbath food. Thus God revealed His faithfulness to His covenant and His care for Israel. In Israel's wilderness classroom revelation occurred every day. Still they complained. Daily revelation does not guarantee faith.

16:4 CHRISTIAN ETHICS, Moral Imperatives—The twists and turns of life ought not be perceived by the Christian as the acts of a capricious God. Rather, they are challenges to our attention skills, testing if we are seeking the will of God. Following God's commands develops our character. Mourning and lamenting are proper ways to seek God's will in times of danger and/or loss. See notes on PRAYER, Petition, Lament

16:6 SALVATION, Initiative—See note on 14:13,30. Hardship sometimes causes persons who have been saved to doubt. God often takes the initiative to remove that doubt and display anew His saving power.

16:7,10 GOD, Glory—The glory of God is the manifestation of His presence and of His unique nature. At times this glory was manifested physically as in the cloud in the desert. This manifestation of the glory of God could inspire loving awe on the part of the faithful people of God, and it could inspire fear on the part of the enemies of Israel.

16:13 MIRACLE, Nature—God's provision for feeding Israel in the wilderness is described as His control of natural events. The manna followed the dew. The quails were blown in by the wind (Nu 11:31). Attempts have been made to identify the manna with a sweet juice coming from the tamarisk tree which forms small round grains. Verse 31 offers a comparison with coriander seed. If this explanation is correct, the miracle appears to be in the amount, the regularity, and the necessity of Israel's obedience in collecting measured amounts. Miracle does not have to transcend the laws of nature. It may be God using natural occurrences in a specific setting to meet His people's needs and reveal His purposes. Another possibility is that God creatively intervened in His created order to provide special food for His people in a special historical crisis. The miracle is God's provision for His people. The how is God's free choice of the way He wants to operate in His creation. The importance for us is to recognize God's grace and mercy in saving His people. See note on Jdg 6:17.

when they measured it by the omer, he
who gathered much did not have too
much, and he who gathered little did not
have too little.[m] Each one gathered as
much as he needed.
19Then Moses said to them, "No one is
to keep any of it until morning."[n]
20However, some of them paid no attention to Moses; they kept part of it until
morning, but it was full of maggots and
began to smell.[o] So Moses was angry[p]
with them.
21Each morning everyone gathered as
much as he needed, and when the sun
grew hot, it melted away. 22On the sixth
day, they gathered twice[q] as much—two
omers[g] for each person—and the leaders
of the community[r] came and reported
this to Moses. 23He said to them, "This is
what the LORD commanded: 'Tomorrow
is to be a day of rest, a holy Sabbath[s] to
the LORD. So bake what you want to bake
and boil what you want to boil. Save
whatever is left and keep it until
morning.' "
24So they saved it until morning, as
Moses commanded, and it did not stink
or get maggots in it. 25"Eat it today," Moses said, "because today is a Sabbath to
the LORD. You will not find any of it on
the ground today. 26Six days you are to
gather it, but on the seventh day, the Sabbath,[t] there will not be any."
27Nevertheless, some of the people
went out on the seventh day to gather it,
but they found none. 28Then the LORD
said to Moses, "How long will you[h] refuse to keep my commands[u] and my instructions? 29Bear in mind that the LORD
has given you the Sabbath; that is why on
the sixth day he gives you bread for two
days. Everyone is to stay where he is on
the seventh day; no one is to go out."
30So the people rested on the seventh
day.
31The people of Israel called the bread
manna.[i v] It was white like coriander
seed and tasted like wafers made with
honey. 32Moses said, "This is what the
LORD has commanded: 'Take an omer of
manna and keep it for the generations to
come, so they can see the bread I gave
you to eat in the desert when I brought
you out of Egypt.' "
33So Moses said to Aaron, "Take a jar
and put an omer of manna[w] in it. Then
place it before the LORD to be kept for the
generations to come."
34As the LORD commanded Moses, Aaron put the manna in front of the Testimony,[x] that it might be kept. 35The Israelites ate manna[y] forty years,[z] until they
came to a land that was settled; they ate
manna until they reached the border of
Canaan.[a]
36(An omer[b] is one tenth of an
ephah.)[c]

Chapter 17

Water From the Rock

THE whole Israelite community set out
from the Desert of Sin,[d] traveling
from place to place as the LORD commanded. They camped at Rephidim,[e] but
there was no water[f] for the people to
drink. 2So they quarreled with Moses and
said, "Give us water[g] to drink."[h]
Moses replied, "Why do you quarrel
with me? Why do you put the LORD to the
test?"[i]
3But the people were thirsty[j] for
water there, and they grumbled[k] against

16:18 [m]2Co 8:15* **16:19** [n]ver 23; Ex 12:10 **16:20** [o]ver 24 [p]Ex 32:19 **16:22** [q]S ver 5 [r]Ex 34:31 **16:23** [s]S Ge 2:3; S Ex 20:8; Dt 5:13-14 **16:26** [t]ver 23 **16:28** [u]Jos 9:14; Ps 78:10; 106:13; 107:11; 119:1; Jer 32:23 **16:31** [v]S ver 14 **16:33** [w]Heb 9:4; Rev 2:17 **16:34** [x]Ex 25:16, 21,22; 27:21; 31:18; 40:20; Lev 16:13; Nu 1:50; 7:89; 10:11; 17:4,10; Dt 10:2; 1Ki 8:9; 2Ch 5:10 **16:35** [y]Jn 6:31,49 [z]Nu 14:33; 33:38; Dt 1:3; 2:7; 8:2-4; Jos 5:6; Jdg 3:11; Ne 9:21; Ps 95:10; Am 5:25 [a]Jos 5:12 **16:36** [b]S ver 16 [c]Lev 5:11; 6:20; Nu 5:15; 15:4; 28:5 **17:1** [d]S Ex 16:1 [e]ver 8; Ex 19:2; Nu 33:15 [f]Nu 20:5; 21:5; 33:14 **17:2** [g]Nu 20:2; 33:14; Ps 107:5 [h]S Ex 14:12 [i]Dt 6:16; Ps 78:18, 41; 106:14; Mt 4:7; 1Co 10:9 **17:3** [j]S Ex 15:22 [k]S Ex 15:24

[g]*22* That is, probably about 4 quarts (about 4.5 liters)
[h]*28* The Hebrew is plural.
[i]*31* *Manna* means *What is it?* (see verse 15).

16:20 SIN, Transgression—Though the people had been told not to keep manna overnight, some of them paid no attention to the command. Because they transgressed the command of God, Moses was angry with them. Consciously disobeying God's command for your life or the life of the community of faith is sin. We cannot expect Him to provide for us when we refuse to follow Him.

16:23–30 WORSHIP, Calendar—God told Israel to set apart the sabbath as a special time of rest. God had set the example for such a special time during the days of creation (Ge 2:2–3). Subsequent to this passage the Ten Commandments stipulated the setting apart of a special day to worship (Ex 20:8–11). The sabbath was the most sacred day of the week for the Jew. It was cherished and hallowed by the worship of the Lord (Lev 23:3; Dt 5:12–15). The national worship of Israel culminated in the annual Festival of Passover, Festival of Unleavened Bread, and Festival of Weeks (Ex 12:1—13:16; 23:14–17; 34:18–26; Lev 23:4–38; Nu 28:16—29:39; Dt 16:1–17). The Day of Atonement (Ex 30:10; Lev 16; 23:26–32; 25:9; Nu 29:7–11) rose to special prominence as a time of special repentance and confessional worship. Later, worship was offered daily in the Temple. In the New Testament the early church continued to hold a special day of worship. Shortly after the ascension of the Lord Jesus, the early church began to worship on the first day (the Lord's Day) instead of the seventh (the sabbath). The reason for this was both practical and theological. The early Christians continued to worship at the Temple or in the synagogue on the sabbath until persecution drove them away. It seems logical that they would move their special day to the day on which they celebrated their Lord's resurrection, the first day (Ac 20:7). This pattern was well-established within a few years (1 Co 16:2; Rev 1:10). Of course, they continued to worship the Lord daily (Ac 2:46–47). Diverse attitudes about holy days remained (Ro 14:5–6), but Paul clearly forbid Christians to judge one another on the basis of the day or manner of their worship (Col 2:16–17) as long as Christ was truly worshiped. The important thing is that they lived "to the Lord" every day (Ro 14:7–8).

17:1–7 DISCIPLESHIP, God's Leadership—The whole Israelite community was united in obedience to God's command. When they found no water to drink on the way God had commanded, they began to quarrel with their leader, Moses, and to demand water to drink. They began to question God's leadership and to threaten Moses. Moses continued to obey God, and God affirmed him as leader with the miracle of the rock at Horeb. God assists and affirms His leaders when they are obedient in following His leadership.

17:2–3 SIN, Rebellion—See note on 15:24.

Moses. They said, "Why did you bring us
up out of Egypt to make us and our children and livestock die[l] of thirst?"
4Then Moses cried out to the LORD,
"What am I to do with these people?
They are almost ready to stone[m] me."
5The LORD answered Moses, "Walk on
ahead of the people. Take with you some
of the elders of Israel and take in your
hand the staff[n] with which you struck
the Nile,[o] and go. 6I will stand there before you by the rock at Horeb.[p] Strike[q]
the rock, and water[r] will come out of it
for the people to drink." So Moses did
this in the sight of the elders of Israel.
7And he called the place Massah[j][s] and
Meribah[k][t] because the Israelites quarreled and because they tested the LORD
saying, "Is the LORD among us or not?"

The Amalekites Defeated

8The Amalekites[u] came and attacked
the Israelites at Rephidim.[v] 9Moses said
to Joshua,[w] "Choose some of our men
and go out to fight the Amalekites. Tomorrow I will stand on top of the hill
with the staff[x] of God in my hands."
10So Joshua fought the Amalekites as
Moses had ordered, and Moses, Aaron
and Hur[y] went to the top of the hill. 11As
long as Moses held up his hands, the Israelites were winning,[z] but whenever he
lowered his hands, the Amalekites were
winning. 12When Moses' hands grew
tired, they took a stone and put it under
him and he sat on it. Aaron and Hur held
his hands up—one on one side, one on
the other—so that his hands remained
steady till sunset.[a] 13So Joshua overcame
the Amalekite[b] army with the sword.
14Then the LORD said to Moses,
"Write[c] this on a scroll as something to
be remembered and make sure that Joshua hears it, because I will completely blot
out[d] the memory of Amalek[e] from under
heaven."
15Moses built an altar[f] and called[g] it
The LORD is my Banner. 16He said, "For
hands were lifted up to the throne of the
LORD. The[l] LORD will be at war against
the Amalekites[h] from generation to generation."[i]

Chapter 18

Jethro Visits Moses

NOW Jethro,[j] the priest of Midian[k]
and father-in-law of Moses, heard of
everything God had done for Moses and
for his people Israel, and how the LORD
had brought Israel out of Egypt.[l]
2After Moses had sent away his wife
Zipporah,[m] his father-in-law Jethro received her 3and her two sons.[n] One son
was named Gershom,[m] for Moses said, "I
have become an alien in a foreign
land";[o] 4and the other was named Eliezer,[n][p] for he said, "My father's God was
my helper;[q] he saved me from the sword
of Pharaoh."
5Jethro, Moses' father-in-law, together
with Moses' sons and wife, came to him
in the desert, where he was camped near
the mountain[r] of God. 6Jethro had sent
word to him, "I, your father-in-law Jethro, am coming to you with your wife and
her two sons."
7So Moses went out to meet his father-in-law and bowed down[s] and
kissed[t] him. They greeted each other
and then went into the tent. 8Moses told
his father-in-law about everything the
LORD had done to Pharaoh and the

[j]7 *Massah* means *testing.* [k]7 *Meribah* means *quarreling.* [l]16 Or *"Because a hand was against the throne of the LORD, the* [m]3 *Gershom* sounds like the Hebrew for *an alien there.* [n]4 *Eliezer* means *my God is helper.*

17:3 [l]S Ex 14:11 **17:4** [m]Nu 14:10; 1Sa 30:6; S Jn 8:59 **17:5** [n]S Ex 4:2; S 10:12-13 [o]Ex 7:20 **17:6** [p]S Ex 3:1 [q]Nu 20:8 [r]Nu 20:11; Dt 8:15; Jdg 15:19; 2Ki 3:20; Ne 9:15; Ps 74:15; 78:15-16; 105:41; 107:35; 114:8; Isa 30:25; 35:6; 43:19; 48:21; 1Co 10:4 **17:7** [s]Dt 6:16; 9:22; 33:8; Ps 95:8 [t]Nu 20:13,24; 27:14; Ps 81:7; 106:32 **17:8** [u]S Ge 36:12 [v]S ver 1 **17:9** [w]Ex 24:13; 32:17; 33:11; Nu 11:28; 27:22; Dt 1:38; Jos 1:1; Ac 7:45 [x]S Ex 4:17 **17:10** [y]ver 10-12; Ex 24:14; 31:2 **17:11** [z]Jas 5:16 **17:12** [a]Jos 8:26 **17:13** [b]ver 8 **17:14** [c]Ex 24:4; 34:27; Nu 33:2; Dt 31:9; Job 19:23; Isa 30:8; Jer 36:2; 45:1; 51:60 [d]Ex 32:33; Dt 29:20; Job 18:17; Ps 9:5; 34:16; 109:15; Eze 18:4 [e]ver 13; S Ge 36:12; Nu 24:7; Jdg 3:13; 1Sa 30:17-18; Ps 83:7 **17:15** [f]S Ge 8:20 [g]S Ge 22:14 **17:16** [h]Nu 24:7; 1Sa 15:8,32; 1Ch 4:43; Est 3:1; 8:3; 9:24 [i]Est 9:5 **18:1** [j]S Ex 2:18 [k]S Ex 2:16 [l]S Ex 6:6 **18:2** [m]S Ex 2:21 **18:3** [n]S Ex 4:20; Ac 7:29 [o]Ex 2:22 **18:4** [p]1Ch 23:15 [q]S Ge 49:25; S Dt 33:29 **18:5** [r]S Ex 3:1 **18:7** [s]S Ge 17:3; S 43:28 [t]S Ge 29:13

17:4–6 PRAYER, Petition—See note on 15:25. God shows His faithfulness even to a disobedient, grumbling people.

17:6–7 MIRACLE, Nature—God may work miracles for rebellious people (vv 2–3). Just as the people needed food (see note on 16:13) in the wilderness, they also needed water. Water was there. God used Moses to show the water to them. Rebels cannot expect God to answer their demands with a miracle. We can marvel at God's grace when He chooses to supply our needs miraculously despite our rebellious attitudes. God works miracles in His way, in His timetable, for whom He chooses. He may work through the processes and laws of His created world, or He may choose to work uniquely outside the normal patterns of nature. Both ways of working are miraculous because God is at work to reveal Himself and His purposes. The center of miracle is that human beings in faith are made aware of God at work in His world.

17:8–16 CHRISTIAN ETHICS, War and Peace—What justifies retaliation? To what extent is the child of God allowed self defense? This passage shows one instance where God approved retaliation. Passages such as this must be brought into tension with those of the New Testament speaking of peace. See notes on Jos 6:1–27; Jdg 1:1–36. To get a clearer perspective for interpretation and application of this passage, we need to have a sense of the total biblical description of the nature and person of God. He is a God who demands justice from His enemies and from His chosen people as they revert to paganism. He is also a God whose ultimate goal is *shalom* or peace. The history of redemption running through the Bible underscores this idea. Thus, even in the battles and the wars God makes a covenant aimed at making peace. His people, at their best, will be seeking to make this peace happen, too.

18:1–12 ELECTION, Other Nations—See note on 8:22–23. Moses gave his two sons names to indicate the electing action of God in choosing Israel even when they were aliens in a foreign land. Jethro, the Midianite priest, could worship along with the elect Israel because he confessed faith in God. Election is not an exclusive doctrine seeking to prohibit people from worship. It is a confessing doctrine pointing to God's initiative in bringing people to worship Him.

18:8–10 SALVATION, As Deliverance—God's deliverance is His rescue—His salvation. Like Jethro, we should all praise (literally, "bless") God for His deliverance. God's salvation is something to shout and sing about. These verses repeat the same verb (Hebrew *hitstsil*) four times. It means "to snatch away, rescue, deliver." Salvation is God's good action in

Egyptians for Israel's sake and about all
the hardships[u] they had met along the
way and how the LORD had saved[v] them.
9 Jethro was delighted to hear about all
the good things[w] the LORD had done for
Israel in rescuing them from the hand of
the Egyptians. 10 He said, "Praise be to
the LORD,[x] who rescued you from the
hand of the Egyptians and of Pharaoh,
and who rescued the people from the
hand of the Egyptians. 11 Now I know that
the LORD is greater than all other gods,[y]
for he did this to those who had treated
Israel arrogantly."[z] 12 Then Jethro, Moses' father-in-law,[a] brought a burnt offering[b] and other sacrifices[c] to God, and
Aaron came with all the elders of Israel to
eat bread[d] with Moses' father-in-law in
the presence[e] of God.
13 The next day Moses took his seat to
serve as judge for the people, and they
stood around him from morning till evening. 14 When his father-in-law saw all
that Moses was doing for the people, he
said, "What is this you are doing for the
people? Why do you alone sit as judge,
while all these people stand around you
from morning till evening?"
15 Moses answered him, "Because the
people come to me to seek God's will.[f]
16 Whenever they have a dispute,[g] it is
brought to me, and I decide between the
parties and inform them of God's decrees
and laws."[h]
17 Moses' father-in-law replied, "What
you are doing is not good. 18 You and
these people who come to you will only
wear yourselves out. The work is too
heavy for you; you cannot handle it
alone.[i] 19 Listen now to me and I will
give you some advice, and may God be
with you.[j] You must be the people's representative before God and bring their
disputes[k] to him. 20 Teach them the decrees and laws,[l] and show them the way
to live[m] and the duties they are to perform.[n] 21 But select capable men[o] from
all the people—men who fear[p] God,
trustworthy men who hate dishonest
gain[q]—and appoint them as officials[r]
over thousands, hundreds, fifties and
tens. 22 Have them serve as judges for the
people at all times, but have them bring
every difficult case[s] to you; the simple
cases they can decide themselves. That
will make your load lighter, because they
will share[t] it with you. 23 If you do this
and God so commands, you will be able
to stand the strain, and all these people
will go home satisfied."
24 Moses listened to his father-in-law
and did everything he said. 25 He chose
capable men from all Israel and made
them leaders[u] of the people, officials
over thousands, hundreds, fifties and
tens.[v] 26 They served as judges[w] for the
people at all times. The difficult cases[x]
they brought to Moses, but the simple
ones they decided themselves.[y]
27 Then Moses sent his father-in-law on
his way, and Jethro returned to his own
country.[z]

Chapter 19

At Mount Sinai

IN the third month after the Israelites
left Egypt[a]—on the very day—they
came to the Desert of Sinai.[b] 2 After they
set out from Rephidim,[c] they entered the

18:8 [u]Nu 20:14; Ne 9:32 [v]Ex 15:6, 16; Ps 81:7
18:9 [w]Jos 21:45; 1Ki 8:66; Ne 9:25; Ps 145:7; Isa 63:7
18:10 [x]S Ge 9:26; S 24:27
18:11 [y]S Ex 12:12; S 1Ch 16:25 [z]S Ex 1:10; S Lk 1:51
18:12 [a]S Ex 3:1 [b]Ex 10:25; 20:24; Lev 1:2-9 [c]Ge 31:54; Ex 24:5 [d]S Ge 26:30 [e]Dt 12:7
18:15 [f]S ver 19; S Ge 25:22
18:16 [g]Ex 24:14 [h]ver 15; Lev 24:12; Nu 15:34; Dt 1:17; 2Ch 19:7; Pr 24:23; Mal 2:9
18:18 [i]Nu 11:11, 14,17; Dt 1:9,12
18:19 [j]Ex 3:12 [k]ver 15; Nu 27:5
18:20 [l]Dt 4:1,5; 5:1; Ps 119:12,26, 68 [m]Ps 143:8 [n]S Ge 39:11
18:21 [o]S Ge 47:6; Ac 6:3 [p]S Ge 22:12 [q]Ex 23:8; Dt 16:19; 1Sa 12:3; Ps 15:5; Pr 17:23; 28:8; Ecc 7:7; Eze 18:8; 22:12 [r]Nu 1:16; 7:2; 10:4; Dt 16:18; Ezr 7:25
18:22 [s]Lev 24:11; Dt 1:17-18 [t]Nu 11:17; Dt 1:9
18:25 [u]Nu 1:16; 7:2; 11:16; Dt 16:18 [v]Dt 1:13-15
18:26 [w]Dt 16:18; 2Ch 19:5; Ezr 7:25 [x]Dt 1:17 [y]ver 22
18:27 [z]Nu 10:29-30
19:1 [a]S Ex 6:6 [b]Nu 1:1; 3:14; 33:15
19:2 [c]S Ex 17:1

---

snatching us away from dangers that threaten us.

18:10–11 PRAYER, Praise—People do not have to be direct recipients of God's actions to praise Him. Hearing of what God has done for loved ones and friends leads us to praise.

18:13–24 DISCIPLESHIP, Laity—Moses received good advice from his father-in-law Jethro, the priest of Midian. Moses was trying to do too much for the people and did not allow them to do enough for themselves. Jethro advised him to choose capable and trustworthy men to share the judging responsibility. This change would remove the strain from Moses' life and also please the people. The more difficult decisions would still be brought to Moses for his wise judgment. Ministers today would do well to heed Jethro's advice as Moses did. He decided to share his ministry with others. God later told Moses that Israel was to be a kingdom of priests (Ex 19:6). Likewise, Christians are called "to be a holy priesthood." See note on 1 Pe 2:5,9–10.

18:16 CHRISTIAN ETHICS, Moral Limits—God's commands form the basis for settling human disputes. Every society must have a just system for settling disputes, or everyone will feel free to ignore moral limits placed on us by the rights of others. See notes on Dt 4:1–8; 17:8–13.

18:17–26 EVIL AND SUFFERING, Comfort—Emotional and physical fatigue are kinds of suffering we may endure unconsciously. Jethro helped relieve Moses' fatigue by recommending he appoint judges to relieve his work load. The simple delegation of authority and division of labor helped Moses and the Hebrews. As Christians, we can often alleviate suffering by giving helpful advice and sharing responsibilities.

18:20 CHRISTIAN ETHICS, Moral Imperatives—Teaching and demonstration are part of God's mechanism to have character expectations placed before us. We are obligated to learn God's moral expectations and obey them.

19:1–6 GOD, Sovereignty—From His position as the sovereign Lord who had delivered them out of Egypt, God told the Israelites that He would once again reaffirm the covenant first made with Abraham. He promised that if Israel would be faithful and obedient, He would bless and use them as a kingdom of priests to the world. Because God initiated the call of Abraham and executed the deliverance of Israel from captivity, He had a perfect right as sovereign Lord to place demands upon Israel in return for their continued favor from God. His commands outlined the boundaries of the covenant relationship. They thus pointed to God's grace in letting His people know the way of life in relationship with Him.

19:2–3 REVELATION, Commitment—God invited Moses to come up the mountain, symbolically closer to the heavens and to God. The revealing Lord chose Moses for this special revelation, for he had been from the beginning of the Exodus the one through whom God disclosed His plans. God chose the place where He first revealed Himself to Moses (3:12). Sacred places often become locations of revelation, though revelation is never limited to one place.

Desert of Sinai, and Israel camped there
in the desert in front of the mountain.[d]
3Then Moses went up to God,[e] and
the LORD called[f] to him from the mountain and said, "This is what you are to say
to the house of Jacob and what you are to
tell the people of Israel: 4'You yourselves
have seen what I did to Egypt,[g] and how
I carried you on eagles' wings[h] and
brought you to myself.[i] 5Now if you obey
me fully[j] and keep my covenant,[k] then
out of all nations you will be my treasured
possession.[l] Although the whole earth[m]
is mine, 6you[o] will be for me a kingdom
of priests[n] and a holy nation.'[o] These are
the words you are to speak to the Israelites."
7So Moses went back and summoned
the elders[p] of the people and set before
them all the words the LORD had commanded him to speak.[q] 8The people all
responded together, "We will do everything the LORD has said."[r] So Moses
brought their answer back to the LORD.
9The LORD said to Moses, "I am going
to come to you in a dense cloud,[s] so that
the people will hear me speaking[t] with
you and will always put their trust[u] in
you." Then Moses told the LORD what the
people had said.
10And the LORD said to Moses, "Go to
the people and consecrate[v] them today
and tomorrow. Have them wash their
clothes[w] 11and be ready by the third
day,[x] because on that day the LORD will
come down[y] on Mount Sinai[z] in the

19:2 [d]S ver 17; S Ex 3:1; Dt 5:2-4 **19:3** [e]Ex 20:21 [f]S Ex 3:4; S 25:22; Ac 7:38 **19:4** [g]Dt 29:2; Jos 24:7 [h]Dt 32:11; Ps 103:5; Isa 40:31; Jer 4:13; 48:40; Rev 12:14 [i]Dt 33:12; Isa 31:5; Eze 16:6 **19:5** [j]Ex 15:26; Dt 6:3; Ps 78:10; Jer 7:23 [k]S Ge 17:9; S Ex 3:1 [l]S Ex 8:22; S 34:9; S Dt 8:1; S Tit 2:14 [m]S Ex 9:29; 1Co 10:26 **19:6** [n]Isa 61:6; 66:21; S 1Pe 2:5 [o]Ge 18:19; Lev 11:44-45; Dt 4:37; 7:6; 26:19; 28:9; 29:13; 33:3; Isa 4:3; 62:12; Jer 2:3; Am 3:2 **19:7** [p]Ex 18:12; Lev 4:15; 9:1; Nu 16:25 [q]Ex 4:30; 1Sa 8:10

19:8 [r]Ex 24:3,7; Dt 5:27; 26:17 **19:9** [s]ver 16; Ex 20:21; 24:15-16; 33:9; 34:5; Dt 4:11; 2Sa 22:10,12; 2Ch 6:1; Ps 18:11; 97:2; 99:7; Mt 17:5 [t]Dt 4:12,36; Jn 12:29-30 [u]S Ex 4:5 **19:10** [v]ver 14,22; Lev 11:44; Nu 11:18; 1Sa 16:5; Joel 2:16; Heb 10:22 [w]S Ge 35:2; Rev 22:14 **19:11** [x]ver 16 [y]S Ge 11:5 [z]ver 3,20; S Ex 3:1; 24:16; 31:18; 34:2,4,29,32; Lev 7:38; 26:46; 27:34; Nu 3:1; Dt 10:5; Ne 9:13; Gal 4:24-25

[o]5,6 Or *possession, for the whole earth is mine.* [6]*You*

19:3–8 CHRISTIAN ETHICS, Moral Imperatives—God's saving actions show His nature and establish His right to set up moral demands on His people. His demands lead His people to be holy, an example of morality before all other people. As such, they can be priests, mediating God's will and way to all other peoples. His demands are not unreasonable. His people readily accept them.

19:3–6 MISSIONS, Means—Eagles often push young eaglets out of the nest to teach them to fly. On the first attempts, the mother eagle swoops underneath, gathers them to safety and carries them on her strong wings. God did the same in rescuing Israel from Egypt. Having known the nature, the care, and the love of God, Israel was to be a missionary nation to others. God carefully spelled out His missionary strategy here. As Creator, He is the universal God to whom all nations belong. He could use His power to force all nations to be His. Instead, He chose to use personal missionary means. He called Israel to be a special people, a holy, priestly nation. They were to mediate between God and all other nations, seeking to bring all people to obey God, keep His covenant, and be His people. Today, as God's people we face the same mandate to be His missionary means. As God's chosen, redeemed, priestly nation (1 Pe 2:9), will we share His message with the peoples of the world? 2 Ki 7:9 and Eze 33:6 warn us of the spiritual danger of having a message of good news and a warning of danger, but not sharing it.

19:4 HISTORY, God's People—God's historical acts had a goal—the creation of His covenant people. God's call for obedience rested on His saving acts.

19:4–8 THE CHURCH, Covenant People—God continues to make for Himself a people even through difficult circumstances and throughout long periods of time. After the sojourn in Egypt, the contest with the Pharaoh, and the Exodus, the Lord brought the people of Israel out of Egypt. The promises which He made to Abraham, Isaac, and Jacob were relevant for the people of a later day. God had made a covenant with the created order (Ge 9:8–17) and with the patriarchs (Ge 17:1–21). At Sinai, He extended the covenant to the people whom He delivered from bondage in Egypt. God desires to make *all people His people.* All the earth belongs to God (Ex 19:5). Instead of excluding, God includes. Israel's history became one of self-exclusion: the Northern Kingdom, then Judah, until only a remnant remained. Ultimately Jesus established the church as His holy remnant. He includes all people in His plans to redeem and to save. The Lord intended to make a treasured possession of the people with whom He entered into covenant. Israel would become the special people of God, people through whom God could work His great work of salvation. Covenant people are people of responsibility. In the Old Testament, the emphasis in the concepts of covenant and election falls on responsibility and service rather than on privilege and power. God promised to make His people His own particular treasure, a kingdom of priests, and a holy nation. Each promise implies its own responsibility toward God. God desires that His covenant people in every age bring other people to know Him. The term "holy" describes that which is set apart for service. The concept of holiness implies both negative and positive ideas. Those who are devoted to God must allow God to remove us from the destructive power of sin. The major emphasis, however, is positive. God desires His covenant people to set themselves apart for His service. Every covenant must be sealed by commitment. Only dedicated people will serve God. God does not force people into His covenant. He allows them to choose to be His people.

19:5–8 DISCIPLESHIP, Priesthood—All God's people share a common vocation. We are priests, dedicated to revealing the holy God to all the world. As priests we must accept witnessing, teaching, worshiping, and interceding responsibilities for the nations. Priests should not be self-centered. We are to be God-centered and people-centered. Our task is to witness and pray until all people know and serve God. Holy living is an important part of that witness. Israel promised to accept the identity as holy priests, but they did not act on their promise. To be part of God's kingdom we must function as His priests.

19:5 DISCIPLESHIP, Covenant—God's people live in covenant relationship with Him. They serve God under the conditions of the covenant. Christian disciples still find moral and spiritual guidance from the basic moral law of Ex 20:1–17 as we serve God's purposes.

19:10–24 GOD, Holy—God wanted the people to learn at the outset the vast qualitative difference between God and humans. God is holy, and we are not. People must humble themselves and purify themselves in the presence of a holy God. Human sin is the opposite of divine holiness. Sinfulness prevents us from looking upon the holiness of God, lest the intensity of God's holiness destroy the sinner. An analogy would be one's trying to look on the sun with the naked eye—you would quickly be blinded. We can approach God only on God's terms. We must show respect for God and must come in the manner He prescribes. The privilege of approaching God is itself a gift of God's grace and must not be taken lightly. The thunder and lightning, the thick cloud, the loud trumpet, and the earthquake that shook the mountain (vv 16–19) gave dramatic reinforcement to the awesomeness and mystery of the otherness of the holiness of God.

19:10–11 PRAYER, Holiness of God—Those who appear in the presence of the Lord should show their respect in outward appearance as well as inward attitude.

sight of all the people. 12Put limits[a] for
the people around the mountain and tell
them, 'Be careful that you do not go up
the mountain or touch the foot of it. Whoever touches the mountain shall surely be
put to death. 13He shall surely be stoned[b]
or shot with arrows; not a hand is to be
laid on him. Whether man or animal, he
shall not be permitted to live.' Only when
the ram's horn[c] sounds a long blast may
they go up to the mountain."[d]

14After Moses had gone down the
mountain to the people, he consecrated
them, and they washed their clothes.[e]
15Then he said to the people, "Prepare
yourselves for the third day. Abstain[f]
from sexual relations."

16On the morning of the third day
there was thunder[g] and lightning, with a
thick cloud[h] over the mountain, and a
very loud trumpet blast.[i] Everyone in
the camp trembled.[j] 17Then Moses led
the people out of the camp to meet with
God, and they stood at the foot of the
mountain.[k] 18Mount Sinai was covered
with smoke,[l] because the LORD descended on it in fire.[m] The smoke billowed up
from it like smoke from a furnace,[n] the
whole mountain[p] trembled[o] violently,
19and the sound of the trumpet grew
louder and louder. Then Moses spoke and
the voice[p] of God answered[q] him.[q]

20The LORD descended to the top of
Mount Sinai[r] and called Moses to the top
of the mountain. So Moses went up 21and
the LORD said to him, "Go down and
warn the people so they do not force their
way through to see[s] the LORD and many
of them perish.[t] 22Even the priests, who
approach[u] the LORD, must consecrate[v]
themselves, or the LORD will break out
against them."[w]

23Moses said to the LORD, "The people
cannot come up Mount Sinai,[x] because
you yourself warned us, 'Put limits[y]
around the mountain and set it apart as
holy.' "

24The LORD replied, "Go down and
bring Aaron[z] up with you. But the priests
and the people must not force their way
through to come up to the LORD, or he
will break out against them."[a]

25So Moses went down to the people
and told them.

Chapter 20

The Ten Commandments

20:1-17pp — Dt 5:6-21

AND God spoke[b] all these words:[c]

2"I am the LORD your God,[d]
who brought you out[e] of
Egypt,[f] out of the land of slavery.[g]

19:12 [a]ver 23 **19:13** [b]Heb 12:20* [c]Jos 6:4; 1Ch 15:28; Ps 81:3; 98:6 [d]ver 21; Ex 34:3 **19:14** [e]S Ge 35:2 **19:15** [f]1Sa 21:4; 1Co 7:5 **19:16** [g]1Sa 2:10; Isa 29:6 [h]S ver 9 [i]Heb 12:18-19; Rev 4:1 [j]S Ge 3:10; 1Sa 13:7; 14:15; 28:5; Ps 99:1; Heb 12:21 **19:17** [k]S ver 2; Dt 4:11 **19:18** [l]Ex 20:18; Ps 104:32; Isa 6:4; Rev 15:8 [m]S Ex 3:2; 24:17; Lev 9:24; Dt 4:11, 24,33,36; 5:4; 9:3; 1Ki 18:24,38; 1Ch 21:26; 2Ch 7:1; Ps 18:8; Heb 12:18 [n]S Ge 19:28; Rev 9:2 [o]Jdg 5:5; 2Sa 22:8; Ps 18:7; 68:8; Isa 2:19; 5:25; 41:15; 64:1; Jer 4:24; 10:10; Mic 1:4; Na 1:5; Hab 3:6,10; Hag 2:6 **19:19** [p]S ver 9; Dt 4:33; Ne 9:13 [q]Ps 81:7 **19:20** [r]S ver 11 **19:21** [s]Ex 24:10-11; Nu 4:20; 1Sa 6:19 [t]S ver 13 **19:22** [u]Lev 10:3 [v]1Sa 16:5; 2Ch 29:5; Joel 2:16 [w]ver 24; 2Sa 6:7 **19:23** [x]ver 11 [y]ver 12 **19:24** [z]Ex 24:1,9 [a]ver 22 **20:1** [b]Dt 10:4 [c]Ne 9:13; Ps 119:9; 147:19; Mal 4:4 **20:2** [d]S Ge 17:7; Ex 16:12; Lev 19:2; 20:7; Isa 43:3; Eze 20:19 [e]S Ge 15:7 [f]S Ex 6:6 [g]Ex 13:3; Eze 20:6

[p]*18* Most Hebrew manuscripts; a few Hebrew manuscripts and Septuagint *all the people* [q]*19* Or *and God answered him with thunder*

19:17–25 REVELATION, Messengers—Revelation comes in unexpected ways. Moses, the great servant of God, had just learned God's organizational plan for Israel from a Midianite priest. Then God instructed Moses to go and get Aaron that he might also see the greatness of the God of Israel.

20:1–7 GOD, One God—The first four of the Ten Commandments deal with the nature of God. In the first commandment, Israel was to recognize no other God (v 3). Yahweh alone is God. The God who brought Israel out of captivity will not tolerate the worship of any other deity. The second commandment (vv 4–6) forbids making any kind of idol that would become an object of worship, or reverence. Only God is to receive our worship, adoration, and trust. This commandment is reinforced with the declaration that God is a jealous God; that is, He takes Himself seriously and will not tolerate any divided allegiance. God's demand for total allegiance to Himself was also reinforced by the warning that He punishes even the fourth generation for the sin of the fathers. See note on Eze 18:25–32. God impressed upon the people the seriousness of His righteousness that would not tolerate any compromise. Even as God warned Israel concerning the wrath of His righteous nature, He stressed that the dominant feature of His nature is His love. He will express His love to a thousand generations of those who honor Him, not just four generations as in the case of His wrath. The third commandment (v 7) forbids the misuse of God's name. God does not take Himself lightly or casually, and neither must those who want His favor. See note on 15:1–18. The fourth commandment demands that the Sabbath day be regarded as holy because of its association with the holy God.

20:1–17 SIN, Transgression—The Old Testament teaches that transgression of the law is sin. The question of the Old Testament law as relevant for New Testament Christians is sometimes raised. Which, if any, of the Old Testament laws is the Christian who is "under grace" to keep? The person who would discount God's revelation in the Old Testament may be attempting to avoid some reality of life. Jesus affirmed that He did not come to destroy the law but to fulfill it (Mt 5:17). That is to say He came to give the Old Testament its true meaning. He did not mean ceremonial and sacrificial laws were valid for the church. Christ's sacrificial death ended the validity of the sacrificial system. Therefore, the entire Bible must be understood and interpreted in the light of the revelation in Christ. When this is done and the person approaches the law in the spirit of Christ, there will be no problem concerning how much of the Old Testament revelation pertains to the Christian.

20:1–17 REVELATION, Commitment—Revelation brings more than an awesome sense of divine presence. It may bring renewed assurance of God's commitment and call for human obedience. At Sinai, God revealed who He is and what He wants His people to be. The value of these words is that they reveal not only the identifying characteristics of God's people but also the very heart of the Maker of all life, His intentions for human existence, and His hopes for the quality of life He wished to share.

20:2–11 HUMANITY, Relationship to God—People are expected to be rightly related to God. This relationship is based upon obedience to God's commands.

20:2 SALVATION, As Deliverance—God's name should be associated with His great acts of deliverance. He is the God who saves us by His mighty deeds. He introduced Himself in the Ten Commandments as the Deliverer from Egypt. See note on 14:13,30. God's deliverence precedes His demands.

The Ten Commandments and Related Doctrines

Commandment	Passage	Related Old Testament Passages	Related New Testament Passages	Jesus' Teachings	Related Doctrines
You shall have no other Gods before me	Ex 20:3; Dt 5:7	Ex 20:23, 34:14; Dt 6:4, 13-14; 2 Ki 17:35; Ps 81:9; Je 25:6, 35:15	Ac 5:29	Mt 4:10, 6:33, 22:37-40	CREATION, Sovereignty; ELECTION, Sovereignty; GOD, One God; REVELATION, God's Nature; WORSHIP, Praise
You shall not make for yourself an idol	Ex 20:4-6; Dt 5:8-10	Ex 32:8, 34:17; Lev 19:4, 26:1; Dt 4:15-20, 7:25, 32:21; Ps 115:4-7; Isa 44:12-20	Ac 17:29-31; 1 Co 8:4-6, 10:14; Col 3:5; 1 Jn 5:21	Mt 6:24; Lk 16:13	GOD, Jealous; WORSHIP, False
You shall not misuse the name of the Lord	Ex 20:7; Dt 5:11	Ex 22:28; Lev 18:21, 19:12, 22:2, 24:16; Eze 39:7	Ja 5:12	Mt 5:33-37, 6:9, 23:16-22	GOD, Holy; HUMANITY, Relationship to God; WORSHIP, Reverence
Remember the Sabbath day by keeping it holy	Ex 20:8-11; Dt 5:12-15	Ge 2:3; Ex 16:23-30, 31:13-16, 35:2-3; Lev. 19:30; Isa 56:2; Jer 17:21-27	Heb 10:25	Mt 12:1-13; Mk 2:23-27, 3:1-6; Lk 6:1-11	ELECTION, Worship; CHRISTIAN ETHICS, Worship
Honor your father and your mother	Ex 20:12; Dt 5:16	Ex 21:17; Lev 19:3; Dt 21:18-21, 27:16; Pr 6:20	Eph 6:1-3; Col 3:20	Mt 15:4-6, 19:19; Mk 7:9-13; Lk 18:20	CHRISTIAN ETHICS, Character; FAMILY, Role Relationships; STEWARDSHIP, Care of Family
You shall not murder	Ex 20:13; Dt 5:17	Ge 9:6; Lev 24:17; Nu 35:33; Ec 3:3	Ro 13:9-10; Ja 2:11	Mt 5:21-24, 19:18, 26:52; Mk 10:19; Lk 18:20	CHRISTIAN ETHICS, Murder; CREATION, Persons; HUMANITY, Worth, Moral Consciousness, Relationships; SIN, Violence
You shall not commit adultery	Ex 20:14; Dt 5:18	Lev 18:20, 20:10; Dt 22:22; Nu 5:12-31; Pr 6:29, 32	Ro 13:9-10; 1 Co 6:9; Heb 13:4; Ja 2:11	Mt 5:27-30, 19:18; Mk 10:19; Lk 18:20	FAMILY, Sexual Sin; HUMANITY, Moral Consciousness Marriage, Relationships; SIN, Evil Desire; CHRISTIAN ETHICS, Character
You shall not steal	Ex 20:15; Dt 5:19	Lev 19:11, 13; Eze 18:7	Ro 13:9-10; Eph 4:28	Mt 19:18; Mk 10:19; Lk 18:20	CHRISTIAN ETHICS, Honesty, Theft; HUMANITY, Moral Consciousness, Relationships; SIN, Selfishness
You shall not give false testimony	Ex 20:16; Dt 5:20	Ex 23:1, 7; Lev 19:11; Ps 15:2, 101:5; Pr 10:18; Jer 9:3-5; Zec 8:16	Eph 4:25, 31; Col 3:9; Tit 3:2	Mt 5:37, 19:18; Mk 10:19; Lk 18:20	CHRISTIAN ETHICS, Honesty; HUMANITY, Moral Consciousness, Relationships; SIN, Unrighteousness
You shall not covet	Ex 20:17; Dt 5:21	Dt 7:25; Job 31:24-28; Ps 62:10	Ro 7:7, 13:9; Eph 5:3-5; Heb 13:5; Ja 4:1-2	Lk 12:15-34	CHRISTIAN ETHICS, Covetousness; HUMANITY, Moral Consciousness, Relationships; SIN, Evil Desire

Denominational Perspectives on Major Doctrines

	Baptist	Catholic	Churches of Christ	Episcopal	Lutheran	Methodist	Pentecostal	Presbyterian
GOD	There is one and only one living and true God who reveals Himself to us as Father, Son, and Holy Spirit, with distinct personal attributes, but without division of nature, essence, or being.	The one God is three by reason of three inner personal principles, Father, Son (Word), and Holy Spirit. One God beyond time and space is perfect and changeless. God created freely from love.	Speaking where the Bible speaks and remaining silent where the Bible is silent, Churches of Christ prefer not to use the word "Trinity." While believing in Father, Son, and Holy Spirit, stress is on the Son, Jesus Christ.	"In unity of this Godhead there be three persons, of one substance, power, and eternity, the Father, the Son, and the Holy Ghost."	There is one Divine Essence, God; and yet there are three Persons of the same essence and power, co-eternal—Father, Son, Holy Ghost.	The three persons of the Godhead are "one in substance, power and eternity." God is infinite in power, wisdom, and goodness." He is spirit and personal, creator and sustainer, and has revealed Himself as Father, Son, and Spirit.	God is ultimate authority. The one true God has revealed himself in three personalities: Father, Son, and Holy Spirit. All three are essential in revealing the one, inseparable God.	God made Himself known to us in three Persons: Father, Son, and Holy Spirit. The three persons are one true, eternal God, the same in substance, equal in power and glory, though distinguished by personal properties.
HOLY SCRIPTURE	The Holy Bible was written by men divinely inspired and is the record of God's self-revelation to humanity. It has God for its author, salvation for its end, and truth without any mixture of error for its matter.	The Bible teaches without error those truths which God wishes to reveal to all people for their eternal salvation. The church in her creeds summarizes basic doctrines of the Bible. Both Old and New Testaments and Apocrypha are believed divinely inspired.	Scripture is true, inspired, and completely sufficient for doctrine. Both Old and New Testaments are canonical, but the New Testament is primary as it reveals Christ.	The Word of God is the written record of God's self-revelation and of God's acts in history. Must be seen in the context of reason and tradition. Includes Old and New Testaments and Apocrypha.	The Scriptures are the Word of God, reliable, trustworthy, and understood through the Holy Spirit. Several confessional statements interpreting Scripture "participate in the normative authority of Scripture."	The sixty-six books of the Bible contain all things necessary to salvation. The Bible is the primary source and guideline for doctrine. Tradition, experience, and reason interact with Scripture in understanding God's Word.	The Bible as the written revelation of God in Christ is inspired by the Holy Spirit and is authoritative.	The sixty-six books of the Bible are the primary source of knowledge about God and His intentions for persons. As the inspired record of God's revelation, Scriptures contain instruction to salvation.
SALVATION	Salvation involves redemption of sinners who accept Jesus Christ as Lord and Savior. In its broadest sense, salvation includes regeneration, sanctification, and glorification.	Original sin interfered with God's plan for humanity. God sent His Son to save humanity from original sin and sins committed. Jesus saved humanity by His life and death and by rising from the dead and ascending into heaven. All who believe Jesus and are sorry for sins are saved.	All persons are sinful and need salvation but do not merit it. God offers salvation and persons may decide to accept or reject it. Salvation comes through faith in Bible teachings and Jesus, repentance, and baptism. Apostasy is an option.	Redemption was wrought and wholeness of life is seen in the life, death, resurrection of Jesus Christ. Individuals respond to God's salvation through baptism and spend a lifetime appropriating God's grace.	Salvation is God's gift offered to all people by the Holy Spirit through the preaching of God's Word.	Salvation comes by the grace of God upon a person's decision to say yes to God's gracious offer of salvation. Good works are a sign of salvation. Christians may renounce salvation (commit apostasy) or achieve a temporary state of holy perfection.	All persons need salvation to restore relationship with God because of sin. Salvation involves three stages including repentance and salvation, sanctification, and baptism of the Holy Spirit evidenced by speaking in tongues.	All persons are sinful and need salvation. We do not earn salvation; rather God elects some persons to salvation. These cannot refuse His offer (irresistible grace). God saves those who by faith repent and put their trust in Christ.

Denominational Perspectives on Major Doctrines

	Baptist	Catholic	Churches of Christ	Episcopal	Lutheran	Methodist	Pentecostal	Presbyterian
BAPTISM	Christian baptism is the immersion of a believer in water in the name of the Father, Son, and Holy Spirit symbolizing the believer's death to sin, burial of old life, and resurrection to new life in Christ.	Baptism is the sacrament of spiritual regeneration by which a person is incorporated into life with Christ and His church, given grace and cleansed from original and personal sin. It is administered by pouring water over the person, or the person is immersed in water.	Baptism is necessary for the remission of sins, to place one in Christ, and to place one in the church. The mode is immersion for believers only.	Baptism is the sacrament in which we say yes to God's prior act of grace toward us in Jesus Christ. Baptism is the preferred form, though pouring is often used. Both adults and infants are baptized.	Baptism plants the seed of salvation and may be administered by sprinkling. Other means of baptism using water and the Word of God are also accepted.	Baptism is a sacrament, a sign of God's grace by which He works within us to strengthen and confirm our faith. Infants are baptized as an initiation into Christian community by sprinkling, pouring or immersion.	Baptism is a sacred ordinance to be obeyed but it does not save. Believers are baptized by immersion.	A visible sign of God's word portraying Christ's redemption, baptism is administered by sprinkling or pouring water on adults. Baptism is the sign and seal of our ingrafting into Christ.
LORD'S SUPPER	The Lord's Supper is a symbolic act of obedience whereby members of the church, through partaking of the bread and fruit of the vine, memorialize the death of Christ and anticipate His second coming.	The Eucharist or mass is the central act of worship. The sacrament reenacts Christ's death and resurrection in ritual form. The actual body and blood of Christ are believed to be present in the elements (transubstantiation). Celebrated daily.	The Lord's Supper is an ordinance with a threefold meaning including: memorial meal commanded by Christ, proclamation of Christ's death for sins, and a time for examination of commitment to Christ. Observed only on Sunday at the church, each week.	The Holy Eucharist is the sacrament commanded by Christ for the continual remembrance of His life, death, and resurrection until His coming again. The elements of bread and wine are received by those claiming Christ as Savior.	Holy Eucharist is one of three sacraments including baptism and absolution. Celebrated corporately, Eucharist is the Real Presence of the body and blood of Christ through sacramental union. When received in faith, grace through the Eucharist works forgiveness of sin, life, and salvation.	The Lord's Supper is a sign of love that Christians should share and a sacrament of our redemption by Christ's death. As a symbol, represents Christ's work of atonement. As a sacrament, the Spirit of God works through the bread and grape juice to call to mind Christ's death. Open to all Christians.	The Lord's Supper is a command of Christ to be obeyed in remembrance of Christ's death and sacrifice on the cross. The elements are symbolic of the spilled blood and broken body. The supper is a time for individual examination and may be accompanied by foot washing.	The Lord's Supper is a sacrament in that the Spirit of God works in the believer who recalls Christ's work of redemption, reflects on his or her commitment to Christ, and participates in the priesthood of believers by passing the bread and cup. The Lord is the host of the supper and all who trust Him may partake.

Old Testament Doctrines

	Doctrines	Genesis	Exodus	Leviticus	Numbers	Deuteronomy	Joshua	Judges	Ruth	1 Samuel	2 Samuel	1 Kings	2 Kings	1 Chronicles	2 Chronicles	Ezra	Nehemiah	Esther	Job	Psalms	Proverbs	Ecclesiastes	Song of Songs	Isaiah	Jeremiah	Lamentations	Ezekiel	Daniel	Hosea	Joel	Amos	Obadiah	Jonah	Micah	Nahum	Habakkuk	Zephaniah	Haggai	Zechariah	Malachi
	God	●	●	●	●	●	●	●	●	●	●	●	●	●	●	●	●	●	●	●	●	●		●	●	●	●	●	●	●	●	●	●	●	●	●	●	●	●	●
The Trinitarian God	Jesus	●	●		●	●								●					●	●	●			●	●		●	●	●				●	●					●	●
	Holy Spirit	●	●		●	●		●		●	●	●	●	●	●		●		●	●				●			●	●		●				●				●	●	
	Creation	●		●		●								●			●		●	●	●	●		●	●		●		●		●		●							●
	Miracle	●	●				●	●		●		●	●				●		●	●				●	●			●		●			●	●						
The World	Evil and Suffering	●	●	●		●	●	●	●	●	●	●	●	●	●	●	●	●	●	●	●	●		●	●	●	●	●	●	●	●		●	●		●		●	●	●
	Humanity	●	●	●	●	●	●	●	●	●	●	●	●	●	●	●	●		●	●	●	●	●	●	●	●	●	●	●	●	●	●	●	●	●	●			●	●
	Sin	●	●	●	●	●	●	●		●	●	●	●	●	●	●	●		●	●	●	●		●	●	●	●	●	●		●		●	●	●	●	●	●	●	●
	Holy Scripture		●	●		●	●				●	●	●	●	●	●	●			●	●	●		●	●	●	●	●	●					●	●	●	●		●	●
Knowledge of God	Revelation	●	●	●	●	●	●	●	●	●	●	●	●	●	●	●	●	●	●	●	●	●		●	●	●	●	●	●	●	●	●	●	●	●	●	●	●	●	●
	History	●	●	●	●	●	●	●	●	●	●	●	●	●	●	●	●	●		●	●	●		●	●		●	●	●	●	●		●	●	●	●	●	●	●	
	Election	●	●	●	●	●	●	●		●	●	●	●	●	●	●	●			●				●	●	●	●	●	●	●	●		●	●			●	●	●	●
	Salvation	●	●	●	●	●	●	●	●	●	●	●		●	●	●	●		●	●	●	●		●	●	●	●	●	●	●	●		●	●	●	●	●	●	●	●
God's Saving Purpose	Discipleship	●	●	●	●	●		●		●	●		●	●							●			●	●					●	●			●				●		
	Christian Ethics	●	●	●	●	●	●	●		●	●	●	●	●	●	●	●		●	●	●	●		●	●	●	●	●	●		●	●		●	●	●	●	●	●	●
	Stewardship	●	●	●	●	●					●		●	●	●	●	●			●	●	●					●				●			●						●
	Last Things	●	●							●	●	●		●	●				●	●	●	●		●			●	●	●	●	●		●				●			●
	The Church	●	●	●	●	●	●	●			●	●	●	●	●	●	●		●	●				●	●	●	●	●	●	●	●			●			●	●	●	●
	Ordinances			●									●																											
	Worship	●	●	●	●	●		●		●	●	●	●	●	●	●	●			●		●		●	●		●		●	●	●			●			●	●	●	●
God's People	Proclamation					●																		●	●				●	●	●		●	●	●	●			●	
	Prayer	●	●	●	●	●	●	●	●	●	●	●	●	●	●	●	●	●	●	●	●	●		●	●	●	●	●	●	●	●		●	●		●			●	●
	Church Leaders				●																																			
	Education	●	●	●		●	●						●		●		●		●	●	●			●	●		●		●					●				●		●
	Family	●	●	●	●	●	●	●	●	●	●	●		●	●	●	●	●	●	●	●		●	●	●		●		●					●						●
God's People and the World	Evangelism	●	●					●	●	●		●	●		●					●				●	●		●	●			●		●	●		●	●		●	●
	Missions	●	●												●					●				●									●							

3"You shall have no other gods before[r] me.[h]
4"You shall not make for yourself an
idol[i] in the form of anything in
heaven above or on the earth
beneath or in the waters below.
5You shall not bow down to
them or worship[j] them; for I,
the LORD your God, am a jealous God,[k] punishing the children for the sin of the fathers[l]
to the third and fourth generation[m] of those who hate me,
6but showing love to a thousand[n] ⌞generations⌟ of those
who love me and keep my commandments.
7"You shall not misuse the name of
the LORD your God, for the
LORD will not hold anyone guiltless who misuses his name.[o]
8"Remember the Sabbath[p] day by
keeping it holy. 9Six days you
shall labor and do all your
work,[q] 10but the seventh day is
a Sabbath[r] to the LORD your
God. On it you shall not do any
work, neither you, nor your son
or daughter, nor your manservant or maidservant, nor your
animals, nor the alien within
your gates. 11For in six days the
LORD made the heavens and the
earth,[s] the sea, and all that is
in them, but he rested[t] on the
seventh day.[u] Therefore the
LORD blessed the Sabbath day
and made it holy.
12"Honor your father and your mother,[v] so that you may live long[w]
in the land[x] the LORD your God
is giving you.
13"You shall not murder.[y]
14"You shall not commit adultery.[z]
15"You shall not steal.[a]
16"You shall not give false testimony[b]
against your neighbor.[c]

20:3 [h]ver 23; Ex 34:14; Dt 6:14; 13:10; 2Ki 17:35; Ps 44:20; 81:9; Jer 1:16; 7:6,9; 11:13; 19:4; 25:6; 35:15 **20:4** [i]ver 5,23; Ex 32:8; 34:17; Lev 19:4; 26:1; Dt 4:15-19,23; 27:15; 2Sa 7:22; 1Ki 14:9; 2Ki 17:12; Isa 40:19; 42:8; 44:9 **20:5** [j]Ex 23:13,24; Jos 23:7; Jdg 6:10; 2Ki 17:35; Isa 44:15,17,19; 46:6 [k]Ex 34:14; Dt 4:24; Jos 24:19; Na 1:2 [l]S Ge 9:25; S Lev 26:39 [m]Ex 34:7; Nu 14:18; Jer 32:18 **20:6** [n]Ex 34:7; Nu 14:18; Dt 7:9; Jer 32:18; Lk 1:50; Ro 11:28 **20:7** [o]Ex 22:28; Lev 18:21; 19:12; 22:2; 24:11,16; Dt 6:13; 10:20; Job 2:5,9; Ps 63:11; Isa 8:21; Eze 20:39; 39:7; S Mt 5:33 **20:8** [p]S Ex 16:23; 31:13-16; 35:3; Lev 19:3,30; 26:2; Isa 56:2; Jer 17:21-27; Eze 22:8 **20:9** [q]Ex 23:12; 31:13-17; 34:21; 35:2-3; Lev 23:3; Lk 13:14 **20:10** [r]S Ge 2:3; Ex 31:14; Lev 23:38; Nu 28:9; Isa 56:2; Eze 20:12, 20 **20:11** [s]Ge 1:3-2:1 [t]S Ge 2:2 [u]Ex 31:17; Heb 4:4 **20:12** [v]S Ge 31:35; S Dt 5:16; Mt 15:4*; 19:19*; Mk 7:10*; 10:19*; Lk 18:20*; Eph 6:2 [w]Dt 6:2; Eph 6:3 [x]Dt 11:9; 25:15; Jer 35:7 **20:13** [y]S Ge 4:23; Mt 5:21*; 19:18*; Mk 10:19*; Lk 18:20*; Ro 13:9*; Jas 2:11* **20:14** [z]Lev 18:20; 20:10; Nu 5:12,13,29; Pr 6:29,32; Mt 5:27*; 19:18*; Mk 10:19*; Lk 18:20*; Ro 13:9*; Jas 2:11* **20:15** [a]Lev 19:11,13; Eze 18:7; Mt 19:18*; Mk 10:19*; Lk 18:20*; Ro 13:9* **20:16** [b]Lev 19:11; Jer 9:3,5 [c]Ex 23:1,7; Lev 19:18; Ps 50:20; 101:5; 119:29; Mt 19:18*; Mk 10:19; Lk 3:14*; 18:20*

[r]3 Or *besides*

20:5–6 EVIL AND SUFFERING, Deserved—Sin brings consequences to the sinner and to many other people. This was especially true in a time when several generations lived in the same house. Such consequences are seen theologically as God's punishment on sin. The major biblical emphasis lies on individual responsibility and punishment (Eze 18:1–32), but the further consequences cannot be ignored. The sinner brings deserved consequences on loved ones. This should be a sufficient warning against sin.

20:6 CHRISTIAN ETHICS, Moral Limits—God's ethical ideals have no limits in time and scope of application. God's love for His people is the reason He sets out moral limits for us.

20:7 CHRISTIAN ETHICS, Language—Misuse of God's name is more than profanity. Misuse includes the profane life-style of a child of God. We who bear God's name must not give other people reason to lose respect for His name.

20:8–12 CHRISTIAN ETHICS, Moral Imperatives—Worship is integral to a balanced perspective on life. Honor and respect for parents are appropriate behavior by children, no matter their ages. Worship and parental respect add moral strength to individuals and society at large.

20:12–17 GOD, Sovereignty—God wants His lordship in the lives of His people to carry over into their daily relationships. The last six commandments deal with human relationships just as the first four deal with one's relationship to God. As sovereign Lord, God can make whatever demands He pleases. As a righteous God, He must demand of us that we conform to His standards of right and wrong. As a loving God, He has shaped these six commandments to work for our own best interests in life. These commandments are not just arbitrary rules imposed by a demanding God; they are wise admonitions from one who loves us and wants the best for us. God would be less than loving if He did not give to us these basic steps to order our human relationships.

20:12 HUMANITY, Family Relationships—The basis for a stable society is a stable family. As originally given to the adult men of Israel, this command demanded a special respect for the old people of the community.

20:12 FAMILY, Role Relationships—The word translated "honor" suggests the idea of taking parents seriously, giving them importance in one's life, and paying attention to their place in our lives. The commandment to honor father and mother is based upon the covenant relationship between God and His people (20:1–2) and has a direct application to the covenant community of faith. Its original setting refers mainly to adults and aging parents. As a principle for effective living in the family, it has a universal quality that strengthens family relationships even among people who do not know the Lord. For believers, it is a direct word from God to which we must respond and for which we are accountable. See Eph 6:1–3. This commandment gives high regard to the mother. She is placed in a position equal to the father in receiving honor from her children (Lev 19:3; Dt 5:16).

20:13–17 HUMANITY, Community Relationships—A stable society must be built upon respect for life, property, sexual commitments, and trustworthiness. Personal contentment furnishes the basis for this kind of stability.

20:13–17 DISCIPLESHIP, Neighbor Love—The second table of the Ten Commandments sets a high standard for serving the best interests and well-being of a neighbor. God's people are to respect and protect their neighbor's life, marriage or home, property, and good name. We are not even to desire anything that belongs to a neighbor. See notes on Lev 19:1–2,9–19; Mt 22:37–40.

20:13 CHRISTIAN ETHICS, Murder—This verse forms the central reference point regarding the sacredness of life in the Old Testament. The major emphasis of the commandment is that life is a gift from God and its stewardship is to be guarded carefully. Though generally the application is that there should be no vengeful killing (e.g. murder), the statement still puts the burden of proof upon anyone who takes another's life in whatever circumstances. To take life away from another lightly was perceived as an attempt at taking the place of God as Controller of life.

20:15 CHRISTIAN ETHICS, Theft—Persons in most societies can own their own property. We must understand that God, however, is the ultimate Owner. To take property from someone is a violation of their personhood.

20:16 CHRISTIAN ETHICS, Language—A word spoken cannot be called back, whether a word of truth or falsehood.

17“You shall not covet[d] your neighbor’s house. You shall not covet
your neighbor’s wife, or his
manservant or maidservant, his
ox or donkey, or anything that
belongs to your neighbor.”

18When the people saw the thunder
and lightning and heard the trumpet[e]
and saw the mountain in smoke,[f] they
trembled with fear.[g] They stayed at a distance 19and said to Moses, “Speak to us
yourself and we will listen. But do not
have God speak[h] to us or we will die.”[i]
20Moses said to the people, “Do not be
afraid.[j] God has come to test[k] you, so
that the fear[l] of God will be with you to
keep you from sinning.”[m]
21The people remained at a distance,
while Moses approached the thick darkness[n] where God was.

Idols and Altars

22Then the LORD said to Moses, “Tell
the Israelites this: ‘You have seen for
yourselves that I have spoken to you from
heaven:[o] 23Do not make any gods to be
alongside me;[p] do not make for yourselves gods of silver or gods of gold.[q]
24“ ‘Make an altar[r] of earth for me and
sacrifice on it your burnt offerings[s] and
fellowship offerings,[s] your sheep and
goats and your cattle. Wherever I cause
my name[t] to be honored, I will come to
you and bless[u] you. 25If you make an altar
of stones for me, do not build it with
dressed stones, for you will defile it if you
use a tool[v] on it. 26And do not go up to
my altar on steps, lest your nakedness[w]
be exposed on it.’

Chapter 21

“THESE are the laws[x] you are to set
before them:

20:17 [d]Lk 12:15; Ro 7:7*; 13:9*; Eph 5:3; Heb 13:5 **20:18** [e]Ex 19:16-19; Dt 4:36; Isa 58:1; Jer 6:17; Eze 33:3; Heb 12:18-19; Rev 1:10 [f]S Ex 19:18 [g]S Ge 3:10; S Ex 14:31; S 19:16 **20:19** [h]Job 37:4,5; 40:9; Ps 29:3-4 [i]Dt 5:5,23-27; 18:16; Gal 3:19 **20:20** [j]S Ge 15:1 [k]S Ge 22:1 [l]Dt 4:10; 6:2,24; 10:12; Ps 111:10; 128:1; Pr 1:7; Ecc 12:13; Isa 8:13 [m]Job 1:8; 2:3; 28:28; Pr 3:7; 8:13; 14:16; 16:6 **20:21** [n]S Ex 19:9; Dt 5:22; Ps 18:9; 68:4; 97:2; Isa 19:1 **20:22** [o]Dt 5:24,26; Ne 9:13 **20:23** [p]S ver 3 [q]Ex 22:20; 32:4,8, 31; 34:17; Dt 29:17-18; Ne 9:18 **20:24** [r]Ex 27:1; 40:29; Nu 16:38; Dt 27:5; Jos 8:30; 2Ki 16:14; 2Ch 4:1; Ezr 3:2; Eze 43:13 [s]S Ge 8:20; S Ex 18:12 [t]Dt 12:5; 16:6,11; 26:2; 1Ki 9:3; 2Ki 21:4,7; 2Ch 6:6; 12:13; Ezr 6:12 [u]S Ge 12:2; 22:17 **20:25** [v]Jos 8:31; 1Ki 6:7 **20:26** [w]Eze 43:17 **21:1** [x]Ex 24:3; 34:32; Dt 4:14; 6:1 **21:2** [y]Ex 22:3 [z]ver 7; Jer 34:8,14 **21:5** [a]Dt 15:16 **21:6** [b]Ex 22:8-9; Dt 17:9; 19:17; 25:1 [c]Ps 40:6 [d]Job 39:9; 41:4 **21:10** [e]1Co 7:3-5 **21:12** [f]ver 15,17; S Ge 4:14,23; Ex 31:15; Lev 20:9, 10; 24:16; 27:29; Nu 1:51; 35:16, 30-31; Dt 13:5; 19:11; 22:22; 27:16; Job 31:11;

Hebrew Servants

21:2–6pp — Dt 15:12–18
21:2–11Ref — Lev 25:39–55

2“If you buy a Hebrew servant,[y] he is
to serve you for six years. But in the seventh year, he shall go free,[z] without paying anything. 3If he comes alone, he is to
go free alone; but if he has a wife when
he comes, she is to go with him. 4If his
master gives him a wife and she bears
him sons or daughters, the woman and
her children shall belong to her master,
and only the man shall go free.
5“But if the servant declares, ‘I love my
master and my wife and children and do
not want to go free,’[a] 6then his master
must take him before the judges.[t][b] He
shall take him to the door or the doorpost
and pierce[c] his ear with an awl. Then he
will be his servant for life.[d]
7“If a man sells his daughter as a servant, she is not to go free as menservants
do. 8If she does not please the master
who has selected her for himself,[u] he
must let her be redeemed. He has no
right to sell her to foreigners, because he
has broken faith with her. 9If he selects
her for his son, he must grant her the
rights of a daughter. 10If he marries another woman, he must not deprive the
first one of her food, clothing and marital
rights.[e] 11If he does not provide her with
these three things, she is to go free, without any payment of money.

Personal Injuries

12“Anyone who strikes a man and kills
him shall surely be put to death.[f] 13How-
ever, if he does not do it intentionally,
but God lets it happen, he is to flee to a
place[g] I will designate. 14But if a man
schemes and kills another man deliber-

Pr 20:20; S Mt 26:52 **21:13** [g]Nu 35:10-34; Dt 4:42; 19:2-13; Jos 20:9

[s]24 Traditionally *peace offerings* [t]6 Or *before God*
[u]8 Or *master so that he does not choose her*

Dishonest reports, slander, exaggerating the truth—all distort the character of the teller and the one reported upon. To establish justice, society must be able to believe the words of its members.

20:17 CHRISTIAN ETHICS, Covetousness—The core attitude for stealing is coveting. The inner character damage done by coveting is severe. The society God intends for His people is based on love for neighbors, not envy. See notes on Dt 22:1–4; 27:17.

20:20 SALVATION, Fear of God—Salvation is the fear of God, with fear meaning reverential respect and awe for God. God wants to help us with our struggle against sin (Heb 12:3–4), not to frighten us or fill us with terror and anxiety. See note on Ps 85:9. Saved persons have a sense of reverence for God and His power.

20:22—23:19 CHRISTIAN ETHICS, Moral Limits—The covenant code provides timeless guidelines for societal relationships. Particular *emphasis is on the vertical* (God to *person) and horizontal* (person to person) relationships. See notes on Ge 6:9,22; 17:1,10; Lev 19:1–18.

20:24–26 WORSHIP, Sacrifice—The mechanics of worship occupy an important place in biblical revelation. The sacrifices to the Lord, the place of such sacrifice, the priests who administer the sacrifices, the times and seasons stipulated, as well as the ingredients of the ritual of worship began to unfold here. The important thing is to realize that some form, some ritual or regulation, generally accompanies worship. A ritual for worship must be planned and designed. Worship may be individual (Ge 24:26–27) or corporate (1 Ch 29:20). In either case it is never consistently haphazard or casual. Definite patterns of worship are seen in Scripture. Such worship is directed to the one true God. God does not tolerate practices which people might confuse with worship practices of other gods or life-styles opposed to the holy God.

21:12–14 CHRISTIAN ETHICS, Murder—Accidental killing differs from murder and must be dealt with through different processes of the legal system. Murder is so serious a crime the Bible sets up the death penalty as the proper legal response. See notes on Lev 24:17–22; Nu 35:6–34; Dt 25:1–3.

ately,[h] take him away from my altar and put him to death.[i]

15"Anyone who attacks[v] his father or his mother must be put to death.

16"Anyone who kidnaps another and either sells[j] him or still has him when he is caught must be put to death.[k]

17"Anyone who curses his father or mother must be put to death.[l]

18"If men quarrel and one hits the other with a stone or with his fist[w] and he does not die but is confined to bed, 19the one who struck the blow will not be held responsible if the other gets up and walks around outside with his staff; however, he must pay the injured man for the loss of his time and see that he is completely healed.

20"If a man beats his male or female slave with a rod and the slave dies as a direct result, he must be punished, 21but he is not to be punished if the slave gets up after a day or two, since the slave is his property.[m]

22"If men who are fighting hit a pregnant woman and she gives birth prematurely[x] but there is no serious injury, the offender must be fined whatever the woman's husband demands[n] and the court allows. 23But if there is serious injury, you are to take life for life,[o] 24eye for eye, tooth for tooth,[p] hand for hand, foot for foot, 25burn for burn, wound for wound, bruise for bruise.

26"If a man hits a manservant or maidservant in the eye and destroys it, he must let the servant go free to compensate for the eye. 27And if he knocks out the tooth of a manservant or maidservant, he must let the servant go free to compensate for the tooth.

28"If a bull gores a man or a woman to death, the bull must be stoned to death,[q] and its meat must not be eaten. But the owner of the bull will not be held responsible. 29If, however, the bull has had the habit of goring and the owner has been warned but has not kept it penned up[r] and it kills a man or woman, the bull must be stoned and the owner also must be put to death. 30However, if payment is demanded of him, he may redeem his life by paying whatever is demanded.[s] 31This law also applies if the bull gores a son or daughter. 32If the bull gores a male or female slave, the owner must pay thirty shekels[y] [t] of silver to the master of the slave, and the bull must be stoned.

33"If a man uncovers a pit[u] or digs one and fails to cover it and an ox or a donkey falls into it, 34the owner of the pit must pay for the loss; he must pay its owner, and the dead animal will be his.

35"If a man's bull injures the bull of another and it dies, they are to sell the live one and divide both the money and the dead animal equally. 36However, if it was known that the bull had the habit of goring, yet the owner did not keep it penned up,[v] the owner must pay, animal for animal, and the dead animal will be his.

Chapter 22

Protection of Property

"If a man steals an ox or a sheep and slaughters it or sells it, he must pay back[w] five head of cattle for the ox and four sheep for the sheep.

2"If a thief is caught breaking in[x] and is struck so that he dies, the defender is not guilty of bloodshed;[y] 3but if it happens[z] after sunrise, he is guilty of bloodshed.

"A thief must certainly make restitution,[z] but if he has nothing, he must be sold[a] to pay for his theft.

4"If the stolen animal is found alive in his possession[b]—whether ox or donkey or sheep—he must pay back double.[c]

5"If a man grazes his livestock in a field or vineyard and lets them stray and they graze in another man's field, he must make restitution[d] from the best of his own field or vineyard.

6"If a fire breaks out and spreads into thornbushes so that it burns shocks[e] of grain or standing grain or the whole field, the one who started the fire must make restitution.[f]

7"If a man gives his neighbor silver or goods for safekeeping[g] and they are stolen from the neighbor's house, the thief, if he is caught, must pay back double.[h] 8But if the thief is not found, the owner of the house must appear before the judges[a] [i] to determine whether he has laid his hands on the other man's property. 9In all cases of illegal possession of an ox, a donkey, a sheep, a garment, or any other lost property about which somebody says, 'This is mine,' both parties are to bring their cases before the judges.[j]

21:14 [h]Ge 4:8; Nu 35:20; 2Sa 3:27; 20:10; Heb 10:26 [i]Dt 19:11-12; 1Ki 2:28-34
21:16 [j]Ge 37:28 [k]Ex 22:4; Dt 24:7
21:17 [l]S ver 12; S Dt 5:16; Mt 15:4*; Mk 7:10*
21:21 [m]Lev 25:44-46
21:22 [n]ver 30
21:23 [o]Lev 24:19; Dt 19:21
21:24 [p]S ver 23; Mt 5:38*
21:28 [q]ver 32; Ge 9:5
21:29 [r]ver 36
21:30 [s]ver 22
21:32 [t]Ge 37:28; Zec 11:12-13; Mt 26:15; 27:3,9
21:33 [u]Lk 14:5
21:36 [v]ver 29
22:1 [w]Lev 6:1-7; 2Sa 12:6; Pr 6:31; S Lk 19:8
22:2 [x]Job 24:16; Jer 2:34; Hos 7:1; Mt 6:19-20; 24:43 [y]Nu 35:27
22:3 [z]ver 1 [a]S Ex 21:2; S Mt 18:25
22:4 [b]1Sa 12:5 [c]S Ge 43:12
22:5 [d]ver 1
22:6 [e]Jdg 15:5 [f]ver 1
22:7 [g]ver 10; Lev 6:2 [h]S Ge 43:12
22:8 [i]S Ex 21:6
22:9 [j]ver 8; Dt 25:1

[v]*15* Or *kills* [w]*18* Or *with a tool* [x]*22* Or *she has a miscarriage* [y]*32* That is, about 12 ounces (about 0.3 kilogram) [z]*3* Or *if he strikes him* [a]*8* Or *before God*; also in verse 9

21:23–25 EVIL AND SUFFERING, Endurance—Violent revenge is not the answer to evil and suffering. God limited retaliation or revenge in proportion to the injury. Traditionally known as *lex talionis* (Latin for law of retaliation), the "eye for eye" principle kept Hebrews from seeking extreme forms of revenge. Jesus later criticized the desire for revenge. See note on Mt 5:38–48.

The one whom the judges declare[b] guilty
must pay back double to his neighbor.
10"If a man gives a donkey, an ox, a
sheep or any other animal to his neighbor
for safekeeping[k] and it dies or is injured
or is taken away while no one is looking,
11the issue between them will be settled
by the taking of an oath[l] before the LORD
that the neighbor did not lay hands on
the other person's property. The owner is
to accept this, and no restitution is required. 12But if the animal was stolen
from the neighbor, he must make restitution[m] to the owner. 13If it was torn to
pieces by a wild animal, he shall bring in
the remains as evidence and he will not
be required to pay for the torn animal.[n]
14"If a man borrows an animal from his
neighbor and it is injured or dies while
the owner is not present, he must make
restitution.[o] 15But if the owner is with
the animal, the borrower will not have to
pay. If the animal was hired, the money
paid for the hire covers the loss.[p]

Social Responsibility

16"If a man seduces a virgin[q] who is
not pledged to be married and sleeps with
her, he must pay the bride-price,[r] and
she shall be his wife. 17If her father absolutely refuses to give her to him, he must
still pay the bride-price for virgins.
18"Do not allow a sorceress[s] to live.
19"Anyone who has sexual relations
with an animal[t] must be put to death.
20"Whoever sacrifices to any god[u] other than the LORD must be destroyed.[c][v]
21"Do not mistreat an alien[w] or oppress him, for you were aliens[x] in Egypt.
22"Do not take advantage of a widow
or an orphan.[y] 23If you do and they cry
out[z] to me, I will certainly hear their
cry.[a] 24My anger will be aroused, and I
will kill you with the sword; your wives
will become widows and your children
fatherless.[b]
25"If you lend money to one of my people among you who is needy, do not be
like a moneylender; charge him no interest.[d][c] 26If you take your neighbor's cloak
as a pledge,[d] return it to him by sunset,
27because his cloak is the only covering
he has for his body. What else will he
sleep in?[e] When he cries out to me, I will
hear, for I am compassionate.[f]
28"Do not blaspheme God[e][g] or
curse[h] the ruler of your people.[i]
29"Do not hold back offerings[j] from
your granaries or your vats.[f]
"You must give me the firstborn of
your sons.[k] 30Do the same with your cattle and your sheep.[l] Let them stay with
their mothers for seven days, but give
them to me on the eighth day.[m]
31"You are to be my holy people.[n] So
do not eat the meat of an animal torn by
wild beasts;[o] throw it to the dogs.

22:10 [k]S ver 7 **22:11** [l]Lev 6:3; 1Ki 8:31; 2Ch 6:22; Heb 6:16 **22:12** [m]ver 1 **22:13** [n]Ge 31:39 **22:14** [o]ver 1 **22:15** [p]Lev 19:13; Job 17:5 **22:16** [q]Dt 22:28 [r]S Ge 34:12 **22:18** [s]S Ex 7:11; Lev 19:26,31; 20:27; Dt 18:11; 1Sa 28:3; 2Ch 33:6; Isa 57:3 **22:19** [t]Lev 18:23; 20:15; Dt 27:21 **22:20** [u]S Ex 20:23; 34:15; Lev 17:7; Nu 25:2; Dt 32:17; Ps 106:37 [v]Lev 27:29; Dt 13:5; 17:2-5; 18:20; 1Ki 18:40; 19:1; 2Ki 10:25; 23:20; 2Ch 15:13 **22:21** [w]Ex 23:9; Lev 19:33; 24:22; Nu 15:14; Dt 1:16; 24:17; Eze 22:29 [x]Dt 10:19; 27:19; Zec 7:10; Mal 3:5 **22:22** [y]ver 26; Dt 10:18; 24:6,10, 12,17; Job 22:6,9; 24:3,21; Ps 68:5; 146:9; Pr 23:10; Isa 1:17; Jer 7:5,6; 21:12; 22:3; Eze 18:5-9,12; Zec 7:9-10; Mal 3:5; Jas 1:27 **22:23** [z]Lk 18:7 [a]Dt 10:18; 15:9; 24:15; Job 34:28; 35:9; Ps 10:14,17; 12:5; 18:6; 34:15; Jas 5:4 **22:24** [b]Ps 69:24; 109:9; La 5:3 **22:25** [c]Lev 25:35-37; Dt 15:7-11; 23:20; Ne 5:7,10; Ps 15:5; Eze 18:8 **22:26** [d]S ver 22; Pr 20:16; Eze 33:15; Am 2:8 **22:27** [e]Dt 24:13, 17; Job 22:6; 24:7; 29:11; 31:19-20; Eze 18:12,16 [f]Ex 34:6; Dt 4:31; 2Ch 30:9; Ne 9:17; Ps 99:8; 103:8; 116:5; 145:8; Joel 2:13; Jnh 4:2 **22:28** [g]S Ex 20:7 [h]2Sa 16:5,9; 19:21; 1Ki 21:10; 2Ki 2:23; Ps 102:8 [i]Ecc 10:20; Ac 23:5* **22:29** [j]Ex 23:15,16,19; 34:20,26; Lev 19:24; 23:10; Nu 18:13; 28:26; Dt 18:4; 26:2,10; 1Sa 6:3; Ne 10:35; Pr 3:9; Mal 3:10 [k]S Ex 13:2; Nu 8:16-17; Lk 2:23 **22:30** [l]Ex 34:19; Dt 15:19 [m]Ge 17:12; Lev 12:3; 22:27 **22:31** [n]Ex 19:6; Lev 19:2; 22:31; Ezr 9:2 [o]Lev 7:24; 17:15; 22:8; Dt 14:21; Eze 4:14; 44:31

[b]*9* Or *whom God declares* [c]*20* The Hebrew term refers to the irrevocable giving over of things or persons to the LORD, often by totally destroying them.
[d]*25* Or *excessive interest* [e]*28* Or *Do not revile the judges* [f]*29* The meaning of the Hebrew for this phrase is uncertain.

22:20 WORSHIP, False—In its essence sin perverts good things. Real and genuine worship can be perverted into false worship. We are always in danger of placing some person or object in the place of supreme worship that belongs only to God. That is precisely why God told Abraham to sacrifice Isaac. Abraham's obedient response showed that God was more important to him than even his only son Isaac (Ge 22:12). In Scripture, worship always has God as the object. The manner and attitude of worship is to be reverential. False worship is worship done in an improper way, with an improper attitude, or to an improper object. Compare Dt 29:18; 1 Sa 13:9–13; 2 Ki 17:25–41; Isa 1:10–17; Am 5:21–27; Mal 1:6–14; Col 2:20–23; Jude 11–13; Rev 13:4–15.

22:21 DISCIPLESHIP, Homeless—God's people are to protect foreigners in our midst without property and to treat them properly. Human rights are to be a concern for those who serve the purposes of God. See note on 23:9.

22:22–24 GOD, Wrath—A loving God made provision for the protection of the vulnerable, widows, and orphans. These were pitiably helpless in ancient times and to some degree still are. As an expression of the righteousness of His nature, God warns against committing evil acts in taking advantage of the helpless. While the term *anger* is used forcefully here, it has a positive as well as negative connotation. God is not only opposing what is wrong, but He is also vigorously *upholding what is* right, the gracious *protection of those who* cannot protect *themselves.*

22:22–27 EVIL AND SUFFERING, Comfort—God insisted that the Hebrews be concerned about groups such as widows, orphans, and the poor. These might suffer because of neglect or oppression by the rich and powerful. God is compassionate and identifies with these oppressed groups just as He identified with the suffering Hebrews in Egypt. See note on 2:23–25.

22:22–23 PRAYER, Mercy of God—See note on 2:23–24.

22:25–27 DISCIPLESHIP, Poor—The people of God are to show compassion toward those who find it necessary to borrow money. Nothing is to be taken and kept as collateral that the person needs for his or her well-being. God is compassionate and hears the cries of the needy. He expects us to be just as compassionate. We should alleviate poverty, not cause it. See 23:6,10.

22:28 CHRISTIAN ETHICS, Language—Anger must be expressed in appropriate ways. Misusing God's name or asking for God's curse on a political leader are not appropriate expressions. To curse a ruler is to ask God to destroy a system He established to provide justice. Only God has the right to decide who deserves His curse of destruction. See notes on 20:7, 16.

22:31 CHRISTIAN ETHICS, Health—Many and varied are the characteristics of God's holy people. One is obedience. God protected His people from food which might be contaminated.

Chapter 23

Laws of Justice and Mercy

"DO not spread false reports.[p] Do
not help a wicked man by being a
malicious witness.[q]
2"Do not follow the crowd in doing
wrong. When you give testimony in a
lawsuit, do not pervert justice[r] by siding
with the crowd,[s] 3and do not show favoritism[t] to a poor man in his lawsuit.
4"If you come across your enemy's[u] ox
or donkey wandering off, be sure to take
it back to him.[v] 5If you see the donkey[w]
of someone who hates you fallen down
under its load, do not leave it there; be
sure you help him with it.
6"Do not deny justice[x] to your poor
people in their lawsuits. 7Have nothing to
do with a false charge[y] and do not put an
innocent[z] or honest person to death,[a]
for I will not acquit the guilty.[b]
8"Do not accept a bribe,[c] for a bribe
blinds those who see and twists the
words of the righteous.
9"Do not oppress an alien;[d] you yourselves know how it feels to be aliens, because you were aliens in Egypt.

Sabbath Laws

10"For six years you are to sow your
fields and harvest the crops, 11but during
the seventh year let the land lie unplowed and unused.[e] Then the poor
among your people may get food from it,
and the wild animals may eat what they
leave. Do the same with your vineyard
and your olive grove.
12"Six days do your work,[f] but on the
seventh day do not work, so that your ox
and your donkey may rest and the slave
born in your household, and the alien as
well, may be refreshed.[g]
13"Be careful[h] to do everything I have
said to you. Do not invoke the names of
other gods;[i] do not let them be heard on
your lips.[j]

The Three Annual Festivals

14"Three times[k] a year you are to celebrate a festival to me.
15"Celebrate the Feast of Unleavened
Bread;[l] for seven days eat bread made
without yeast, as I commanded you. Do
this at the appointed time in the month of
Abib,[m] for in that month you came out of
Egypt.
"No one is to appear before me
empty-handed.[n]
16"Celebrate the Feast of Harvest[o]
with the firstfruits[p] of the crops you sow
in your field.
"Celebrate the Feast of Ingathering[q] at
the end of the year, when you gather in
your crops from the field.[r]
17"Three times[s] a year all the men are
to appear before the Sovereign LORD.
18"Do not offer the blood of a sacrifice
to me along with anything containing
yeast.[t]
"The fat of my festival offerings must
not be kept until morning.[u]
19"Bring the best of the firstfruits[v] of
your soil to the house of the LORD your
God.
"Do not cook a young goat in its
mother's milk.[w]

God's Angel to Prepare the Way

20"See, I am sending an angel[x] ahead
of you to guard you along the way and to
bring you to the place I have prepared.[y]
21Pay attention to him and listen[z] to
what he says. Do not rebel against him;

23:1 [p]S Ge 39:17; Mt 19:18; Lk 3:14 [q]S Ex 20:16; Dt 5:20; 19:16-21; Ps 27:12; 35:11; Pr 19:5; Ac 6:11 **23:2** [r]ver 3,6,9; Lev 19:15,33; Dt 1:17; 16:19; 24:17; 27:19; 1Sa 8:3 [s]Job 31:34 **23:3** [t]Dt 1:17 **23:4** [u]Ro 12:20 [v]Lev 6:3; 19:11; Dt 22:1-3 **23:5** [w]Dt 22:4 **23:6** [x]S ver 2; Dt 23:16; Pr 22:22 **23:7** [y]S Ex 20:16; S Eph 4:25 [z]Mt 27:4 [a]S Ge 18:23 [b]Ex 34:7; Dt 19:18; 25:1 **23:8** [c]S Ex 18:21; Lev 19:15; Dt 10:17; 27:25; Job 15:34; 36:18; Ps 26:10; Pr 6:35; 15:27; 17:8; Isa 1:23; 5:23; Mic 3:11; 7:3 **23:9** [d]S ver 2; S Ex 22:21; Lev 19:33-34; Eze 22:7 **23:11** [e]Lev 25:1-7; Ne 10:31 **23:12** [f]S Ex 20:9; Lk 13:14 [g]Ge 2:2-3 **23:13** [h]Dt 4:9,23; 1Ti 4:16 [i]ver 32; Dt 12:3; Jos 23:7; Ps 16:4; Zec 13:2 [j]Dt 18:20; Jos 23:7; Ps 16:4; Hos 2:17 **23:14** [k]ver 17; S Ex 12:14; 34:23, 24; Dt 16:16; 1Ki 9:25; 2Ch 8:13; Eze 46:9 **23:15** [l]S Ex 12:17; Mt 26:17; Lk 22:1; Ac 12:3 [m]S Ex 12:2 [n]S Ex 22:29 **23:16** [o]Lev 23:15-21; Nu 28:26; Dt 16:9; 2Ch 8:13 [p]S Ex 22:29; S 34:22 [q]Ex 34:22; Lev 23:34,42; Dt 16:16; 31:10; Ezr 3:4; Ne 8:14; Zec 14:16 [r]Lev 23:39; Dt 16:13; Jer 40:10 **23:17** [s]S ver 14 **23:18** [t]Ex 34:25; Lev 2:11 [u]S Ex 12:8 **23:19** [v]S Ex 22:29; S 34:22; S Nu 18:12 [w]Ex 34:26; Dt 14:21 **23:20** [x]S Ge 16:7 [y]Ex 15:17 **23:21** [z]Dt 18:19; Jer 13:15

23:1–2 CHRISTIAN ETHICS, Language—Language properly used is related to justice. God's people must value justice over personal fame and popularity. We must be willing to help unpopular causes if they are just. See note on 20:7.
23:6 DISCIPLESHIP, Poor—Injustice against anyone is wrong, but the Bible has a special word concerning the poor because poor people have difficulty securing justice in the courts. God warns His people not to pervert justice, especially in regard to the poor. Court systems with all their expense and red tape must always be accessible to the poor and must protect the rights of the poor. Court systems must not protect only the rich and educated who know how to work the system.
23:9 DISCIPLESHIP, Homeless—This warning is against *mistreating* foreigners by taking legal advantage of them through both harsh and unjust treatment in the courts. Such persons are a special kind of homeless and require a special kind of protection. God's people concern themselves with the rights of homeless foreigners as well as all other human rights. See note on 22:21.
23:14–32 WORSHIP, Calendar—See note on 16:23–30.
23:19 PRAYER, Worship—God is worthy of the best and the first of all we produce (Dt 18:4). The Feast of Firstfruits was instituted (Lev 23:9–14) specifically for harvest time to let God's people express gratitude.
23:20–33 HISTORY, Promise—God's promises prepared His people to recognize His acts in history. This promise was connected with moral and spiritual expectations. His historical promises were related to the needs and potential of His people; thus He looked to a period of years before the land would be completely conquered.
23:20–31 REVELATION, Angels—The faithful God revealed again that He intended to be a constant presence to Israel and to guard His children and guide them into His plans. The angel of God in the early Scriptures usually symbolizes God's concrete presence in an event. Angels often took a recognizable human form which interpreted the unseeable God. See note on Ge 18:1—19:29. Here the angel is identified with God Himself, whose name (nature and identity) was in the messenger. The angelic messenger had God's power to forgive. God used concrete ways to show His people He would neither forsake nor abandon them. He also indicated His specific plans for a nation with certain borders to be established. Thus God did not limit revelation to teachings or commandments. Revelation dealt with concrete historical needs and plans of His people.

he will not forgive[a] your rebellion,[b]
since my Name[c] is in him. 22If you listen
carefully to what he says and do[d] all that
I say, I will be an enemy[e] to your enemies and will oppose those who oppose
you. 23My angel will go ahead of you and
bring you into the land of the Amorites,
Hittites, Perizzites, Canaanites, Hivites
and Jebusites,[f] and I will wipe them out.
24Do not bow down before their gods or
worship[g] them or follow their practices.[h] You must demolish[i] them and
break their sacred stones[j] to pieces.
25Worship the LORD your God,[k] and his
blessing[l] will be on your food and water.
I will take away sickness[m] from among
you, 26and none will miscarry or be barren[n] in your land. I will give you a full
life span.[o]

27"I will send my terror[p] ahead of you
and throw into confusion[q] every nation
you encounter. I will make all your enemies turn their backs and run.[r] 28I will
send the hornet[s] ahead of you to drive
the Hivites, Canaanites and Hittites[t] out
of your way. 29But I will not drive them
out in a single year, because the land
would become desolate and the wild animals[u] too numerous for you. 30Little by
little I will drive them out before you,
until you have increased enough to take
possession[v] of the land.

31"I will establish your borders from
the Red Sea[g] to the Sea of the Philistines,[h] and from the desert to the River.[i][w] I will hand over to you the people
who live in the land and you will drive
them out[x] before you. 32Do not make a
covenant[y] with them or with their gods.
33Do not let them live in your land, or
they will cause you to sin against me, because the worship of their gods will certainly be a snare[z] to you."

Chapter 24

The Covenant Confirmed

THEN he said to Moses, "Come up to
the LORD, you and Aaron,[a] Nadab
and Abihu,[b] and seventy of the elders[c]
of Israel. You are to worship at a distance,
2but Moses alone is to approach[d] the
LORD; the others must not come near.
And the people may not come up with
him."

3When Moses went and told the people
all the LORD's words and laws,[e] they responded with one voice, "Everything the
LORD has said we will do."[f] 4Moses then
wrote[g] down everything the LORD had
said.

He got up early the next morning and
built an altar[h] at the foot of the mountain
and set up twelve stone pillars[i] representing the twelve tribes of Israel. 5Then
he sent young Israelite men, and they offered burnt offerings[j] and sacrificed
young bulls as fellowship offerings[j][k] to
the LORD. 6Moses[l] took half of the

23:21 [a]Dt 29:20; 2Ki 24:4; La 1:17 [b]Nu 17:10; Dt 9:7; 31:27; Jos 24:19; Ps 25:7; 78:8,40, 56; 106:33; 107:11; 1Jn 5:16 [c]S Ex 3:15 **23:22** [d]S Ex 15:26 [e]S Ge 12:3; Isa 41:11; Jer 30:20 **23:23** [f]Nu 13:29; 21:21; Jos 3:10; 24:8,11; Ezr 9:1; Ps 135:11 **23:24** [g]S Ex 20:5 [h]Lev 18:3; 20:23; Dt 9:4; 12:30-31; Jer 10:2 [i]Ex 34:13; Nu 33:52; Dt 7:5; 12:3; Jdg 2:2; 2Ki 18:4; 23:14 [j]Lev 26:1; Dt 16:22; 1Ki 14:23; 2Ki 3:2; 10:26; 17:10; 2Ch 14:3; Isa 27:9 **23:25** [k]Mt 4:10 [l]Lev 26:3-13; Dt 7:12-15; 28:1-14 [m]S Ex 15:26 **23:26** [n]Lev 26:3-4; Dt 7:14; 28:4; Mal 3:11 [o]S Ge 15:15; Dt 4:1,40; 32:47; Ps 90:10 **23:27** [p]S Ge 35:5; S Ex 15:14 [q]S Ex 14:24; Dt 7:23 [r]2Sa 22:41; Ps 18:40; 21:12 **23:28** [s]Dt 7:20; Jos 24:12 [t]Ex 33:2; 34:11,24; Nu 13:29; Dt 4:38; 11:23; 18:12; Jos 3:10; 24:11; Ps 78:55 **23:29** [u]Dt 7:22 **23:30** [v]Jos 23:5 **23:31** [w]S Ge 2:14; Dt 34:2; Ezr 4:20 [x]Dt 7:24; 9:3; Jos 21:44; 24:12, 18; Ps 80:8 **23:32** [y]S Ge 26:28; Ex 34:12; Dt 7:2; Jos 9:7; Jdg 2:2; 1Sa 11:1; 1Ki 15:19; 20:34; Eze 17:13 **23:33** [z]S Ex 10:7 **24:1** [a]S Ex 19:24 [b]S Ex 6:23 [c]ver 9; Nu 11:16 **24:2** [d]Nu 12:6-8 **24:3** [e]S Ex 21:1; Gal 3:19 [f]S Ex 19:8; Jos 24:24 **24:4** [g]S Ex 17:14 [h]S Ge 8:20 [i]S Ge 28:18; S Dt 27:2 **24:5** [j]Lev 1:3 [k]S Ge 31:54 **24:6** [l]Ex 14:15; 32:31; Ps 99:6

[g]31 Hebrew *Yam Suph*; that is, Sea of Reeds
[h]31 That is, the Mediterranean [i]31 That is, the Euphrates [j]5 Traditionally *peace offerings*

23:22–33 CHRISTIAN ETHICS, War and Peace—Only an obedient people can expect God's protection from enemies. The Bible speaks of God using human warfare to establish His purposes for His people. It does not thereby justify any people who call themselves God's people entering into war and demanding or expecting God to fight for them. The Bible speaks of God's initiative, not human initiative. See note on 14:1—15:18.

23:24 SIN, Against God—Moses admonished the people to avoid idolatry by demolishing the heathen altars of the people with whom they came in contact. Idolatry is a sin against the true God because it replaces God with an inferior material or being from His creation. Other gods can be destroyed and certainly do not deserve our honor, worship, or service. Not to destroy false gods is sin.

23:33 SIN, Against God—Close fellowship with sinful people leads us to follow their practices, replacing the true God with an inadequate substitute. Avoiding wrong associations prevents the sin of worshiping other gods. See note on 23:24.

24:1–11 REVELATION, Word—Many phases of revelation appear here. Revelation occurred in the context of worship with an altar symbolizing God's presence. Direct revelation was limited to Moses alone. No one else could approach the holy God. Thus revelation for the people came through God's chosen mediator. The people recognized the oral laws Moses reported to them as God's revealed will. They accepted the written Book of the Covenant as *God's authoritative revelation. They agreed revelation placed a demand* on their lives. A *covenant ceremony* of commitment symbolized the recognition of and commitment to revelation. Committed people were allowed to see God, though precisely what they saw is not indicated. The path to God, not God Himself, is described. Revelation thus brings worship, fellowship, and commitment. To be of lasting significance revelation took written form.

24:1–11 THE CHURCH, Covenant People—The Lord's words must be heard and obeyed. At Sinai, the people of Israel heard the commands of the Lord and agreed to keep the covenant. A ceremony sealed the people's commitment to God. In times of worship, people make important commitments which continue through life. By offering sacrifices and by sprinkling blood on the altar, they showed a serious dedication of themselves to the Lord. "The Book of the Covenant" contained the commands and stipulations of the Lord to be followed by the people of the covenant.

24:3,7 CHRISTIAN ETHICS, Worship—Affirming obedience to God's ethical requirements in a corporate context reinforces our resolve to carry out that ethical obedience. Worship should not only place demands on us but also provide us opportunity to respond to God's demands.

24:4 HOLY SCRIPTURE, Inspired—God is the Author of Holy Scripture. At points Scripture says God wrote (31:18; 32:16; 34:28; Dt 4:13; 9:10). Most often humans wrote under God's leadership. Their personalities and distinctive literary styles show up. This enhances the richness of the text and *reveals God's character* as One who reveals Himself through human messengers. The end result is the preservation of God's Word for future generations to study, learn, and obey.

blood[m] and put it in bowls, and the other
half he sprinkled[n] on the altar. 7Then he
took the Book of the Covenant[o] and read
it to the people. They responded, "We
will do everything the LORD has said; we
will obey."[p]
8Moses then took the blood, sprinkled
it on the people[q] and said, "This is the
blood of the covenant[r] that the LORD has
made with you in accordance with all
these words."
9Moses and Aaron, Nadab and Abihu,
and the seventy elders[s] of Israel went
up 10and saw[t] the God of Israel.
Under his feet was something like a pavement made of sapphire,[k][u] clear as the
sky[v] itself. 11But God did not raise his
hand against these leaders of the Israelites; they saw[w] God, and they ate and
drank.[x]
12The LORD said to Moses, "Come up
to me on the mountain and stay here, and I will give you the tablets of stone,[y] with the law and commands I have written for their instruction."
13Then Moses set out with Joshua[z] his
aide, and Moses went up on the mountain[a] of God. 14He said to the elders,
"Wait here for us until we come back to you. Aaron and Hur[b] are with you, and anyone involved in a dispute[c] can go to them."
15When Moses went up on the mountain, the cloud[d] covered it, 16and the glory[e] of the LORD settled on Mount Sinai.[f]
For six days the cloud covered the mountain, and on the seventh day the LORD called to Moses from within the cloud.[g]
17To the Israelites the glory of the LORD
looked like a consuming fire[h] on top of the mountain. 18Then Moses entered the
cloud as he went on up the mountain. And he stayed on the mountain forty[i] days and forty nights.[j]

24:6 [m]Heb 9:18 [n]Lev 1:11; 3:2,8, 13; 5:9; Mt 26:28 **24:7** [o]2Ki 23:2,21; Heb 9:19 [p]Ex 19:8; Jer 40:3; 42:6,21; 43:2 **24:8** [q]Heb 9:19; 1Pe 1:2 [r]Lev 26:3; Dt 5:2-3; Jos 24:25; 2Ki 11:17; Jer 11:4, 8; 31:32; 34:13; Zec 9:11; S Mt 26:28; S Lk 22:20; Heb 9:20* **24:9** [s]S ver 1 **24:10** [t]S Ge 16:13; Nu 12:6; Isa 6:1; Eze 1:1; 8:3; 40:2; S Jn 1:18 [u]Job 28:16; Isa 54:11; Eze 1:26; 10:1 [v]Rev 4:3 **24:11** [w]S ver 10; S Ex 3:6; S 19:21 [x]Eze 44:3; Mt 26:29 **24:12** [y]Ex 31:18; 32:15-16; 34:1,28, 29; Dt 4:13; 5:22; 8:3; 9:9,10,11; 10:4; 2Co 3:3 **24:13** [z]S Ex 17:9 [a]S Ex 3:1 **24:14** [b]S Ex 17:10 [c]Ex 18:16 **24:15** [d]S Ex 19:9; Mt 17:5 **24:16** [e]S Ex 16:7; Lev 9:23; Nu 14:10; 1Sa 4:21, 22; Eze 8:4; 11:22 [f]S Ex 19:11 [g]Ps 99:7 **24:17** [h]S Ex 15:7; S 19:18; Heb 12:18, 29 **24:18** [i]1Ki 19:8 [j]S Ge 7:4; Mt 4:2 **25:2** [k]Ex 35:21,22, 26,27,29; 36:2; 2Ki 12:4; 1Ch 29:5, 7,9; 2Ch 24:10; 29:31; Ezr 2:68; Ne 7:70-72; 2Co 8:11-12; 9:7 **25:4** [l]Ex 28:4-8 **25:5** [m]Nu 4:6,10 [n]Dt 10:3 **25:6** [o]Ex 27:20; 30:22-32; 35:28; 39:37; Nu 4:16 [p]Ex 30:1,7,35; 31:11; 35:28; Lev 16:12; Nu 4:16; 7:14;

Chapter 25

Offerings for the Tabernacle

25:1–7pp — Ex 35:4–9

THE LORD said to Moses, 2"Tell the Israelites to bring me an offering. You
are to receive the offering for me from
each man whose heart prompts[k] him to
give. 3These are the offerings you are to
receive from them: gold, silver and
bronze; 4blue, purple and scarlet yarn[l]
and fine linen; goat hair; 5ram skins dyed
red and hides of sea cows[l];[m] acacia
wood;[n] 6olive oil[o] for the light; spices
for the anointing oil and for the fragrant
incense;[p] 7and onyx stones and other
gems to be mounted on the ephod[q] and
breastpiece.[r]
8"Then have them make a sanctuary[s]
for me, and I will dwell[t] among them.
9Make this tabernacle and all its furnishings exactly like the pattern[u] I will show
you.

The Ark

25:10–20pp — Ex 37:1–9

10"Have them make a chest[v] of acacia
wood—two and a half cubits long, a cubit
and a half wide, and a cubit and a half
high.[m] 11Overlay[w] it with pure gold, both
inside and out, and make a gold molding
around it. 12Cast four gold rings for it and
fasten them to its four feet, with two
rings[x] on one side and two rings on the
other. 13Then make poles of acacia wood

2Ch 13:11 **25:7** [q]Ex 28:4,6-14; 29:5; Jdg 8:27; Hos 3:4 [r]Lev 8:8 **25:8** [s]Ex 36:1-5; Lev 4:6; 10:4,7; 21:12,23; Nu 3:28; Heb 9:1-2 [t]Ex 29:45; Lev 26:11-12; Nu 5:3; Dt 12:11; 1Ki 6:13; Zec 2:10; 2Co 6:16 **25:9** [u]ver 40; Ex 26:30; 27:8; 31:11; 39:32,42,43; Nu 8:4; 1Ch 28:11,19; Ac 7:44; Heb 8:5 **25:10** [v]Dt 10:1-5; 1Ki 6:19; Heb 9:4 **25:11** [w]ver 24; Ex 30:3 **25:12** [x]ver 26; Ex 30:4

[k]*10* Or *lapis lazuli* [l]*5* That is, dugongs
[m]*10* That is, about 3 3/4 feet (about 1.1 meters) long and 2 1/4 feet (about 0.7 meter) wide and high

24:12 EDUCATION, Law—"Law" and "instruction" grew out of the same root Hebrew word. See note on Pr 13:14. The Law given to Moses is not merely the subject matter of his teaching, but is a direct expression of the mind of God, the Law (*Torah*) itself being regarded as a teacher. In a similar sense, the Bible serves as teacher for the people of God today. See note on Ps 19:7–11.

25:1—31:18 GOD, Holy—God gave instructions to Moses concerning the way in which Israel was to worship Him through sacrifices, offerings, and ceremonies. The people must understand that they do not approach God on their own terms, but are to approach Him obediently in the way prescribed by God Himself. Priests were to be consecrated and ordained. Various implements for worship were to be ceremonially cleansed and declared holy since they were to be used in worshiping the holy God. These items do not become holy in and of themselves. Through the prescribed ceremonies, God imparted His own holiness to them since they were dedicated to Him through the purification ritual He had prescribed. Even Aaron and his sons, as priests, ceremonially cleansed themselves before approaching the altar of God to minister. God's people must not take His sovereign holiness lightly.

25:1—30:38 REVELATION, Divine Presence—God revealed Himself in special ways to Moses (20:19–21; 24:2; 33:7–23). He also provided the people a holy place which symbolized His continual presence with them (25:8; 29:44–46). Only the priests worshiped in the tent in ways and times God specified. They represented Israel's grateful response to God's presence and performed rites leading to Israel's atonement. This passage indicates that approaching God's presence is not a common or ordinary experience. God prescribes the way in which people may approach Him. Jesus provided eternal redemption on the cross doing away with the priestly manner of atonement. Thus Jesus is the revelation of and means to God's saving presence today.

25:1–8 STEWARDSHIP, House of God—Building and maintaining the "house of God" is an important part of biblical faith. The house of God symbolizes God's presence among His people. It is a place of prayer and public worship to God. God calls us to have willing hearts, so we will make freewill offerings to contribute to the construction of a worship building. The New Testament reflects little attention to building since the early churches usually met in homes or available public places.

and overlay them with gold.[y] 14 Insert the poles[z] into the rings on the sides of the chest to carry it. 15 The poles are to remain in the rings of this ark; they are not to be removed.[a] 16 Then put in the ark the Testimony,[b] which I will give you.

17 "Make an atonement cover[n][c] of pure gold—two and a half cubits long and a cubit and a half wide.[o] 18 And make two cherubim[d] out of hammered gold at the ends of the cover. 19 Make one cherub on one end and the second cherub on the other; make the cherubim of one piece with the cover, at the two ends. 20 The cherubim[e] are to have their wings spread upward, overshadowing[f] the cover with them. The cherubim are to face each other, looking toward the cover. 21 Place the cover on top of the ark[g] and put in the ark the Testimony,[h] which I will give you. 22 There, above the cover between the two cherubim[i] that are over the ark of the Testimony, I will meet[j] with you and give you all my commands for the Israelites.[k]

The Table

25:23–29pp — Ex 37:10–16

23 "Make a table[l] of acacia wood—two cubits long, a cubit wide and a cubit and a half high.[p] 24 Overlay it with pure gold and make a gold molding around it. 25 Also make around it a rim a handbreadth[q] wide and put a gold molding on the rim. 26 Make four gold rings for the table and fasten them to the four corners, where the four legs are. 27 The rings are to be close to the rim to hold the poles used in carrying the table. 28 Make the poles of acacia wood, overlay them with gold[m] and carry the table with them. 29 And make its plates and dishes of pure gold, as well as its pitchers and bowls for the pouring out of offerings.[n] 30 Put the bread of the Presence[o] on this table to be before me at all times.

The Lampstand

25:31–39pp — Ex 37:17–24

31 "Make a lampstand[p] of pure gold and hammer it out, base and shaft; its flowerlike cups, buds and blossoms shall be of one piece with it. 32 Six branches are to extend from the sides of the lampstand—three on one side and three on the other. 33 Three cups shaped like almond flowers with buds and blossoms are to be on one branch, three on the next branch, and the same for all six branches extending from the lampstand. 34 And on the lampstand there are to be four cups shaped like almond flowers with buds and blossoms. 35 One bud shall be under the first pair of branches extending from the lampstand, a second bud under the second pair, and a third bud under the third pair—six branches in all. 36 The buds and branches shall all be of one piece with the lampstand, hammered out of pure gold.[q]

37 "Then make its seven lamps[r] and set them up on it so that they light the space in front of it. 38 Its wick trimmers and trays[s] are to be of pure gold. 39 A talent[r] of pure gold is to be used for the lampstand and all these accessories. 40 See that you make them according to the pattern[t] shown you on the mountain.

Chapter 26

The Tabernacle

26:1–37pp — Ex 36:8–38

"MAKE the tabernacle[u] with ten curtains of finely twisted linen and blue, purple and scarlet yarn, with cherubim[v] worked into them by a skilled craftsman. 2 All the curtains are to be the same size[w]—twenty-eight cubits long and four cubits wide.[s] 3 Join five of the curtains together, and do the same with the other five. 4 Make loops of blue material along the edge of the end curtain in one set, and do the same with the end curtain in the other set. 5 Make fifty loops on one curtain and fifty loops on the end curtain of the other set, with the loops opposite each other. 6 Then make fifty gold clasps and use them to fasten the curtains together so that the tabernacle is a unit.[x]

7 "Make curtains of goat hair for the tent over the tabernacle—eleven altogether. 8 All eleven curtains are to be the same size[y]—thirty cubits long and four cubits wide.[t] 9 Join five of the curtains together into one set and the other six into another set. Fold the sixth curtain double at the front of the tent. 10 Make fifty loops along the edge of the end curtain in one set and also along the edge of

25:13 [y]ver 28; Ex 27:6; 30:5; 37:28
25:14 [z]Ex 27:7; 40:20; 1Ch 15:15
25:15 [a]1Ki 8:8
25:16 [b]S Ex 16:34; Heb 9:4
25:17 [c]ver 21; Lev 16:13; Ro 3:25
25:18 [d]Ex 26:1,31; 36:35; 1Ki 6:23,27; 8:6; 2Ch 3:10-13; Heb 9:5
25:20 [e]S Ge 3:24 [f]Ex 37:9; 1Ki 8:7; 1Ch 28:18; Heb 9:5
25:21 [g]ver 10-15; Ex 26:34; 40:20; Dt 10:5 [h]S Ex 16:34; Heb 9:4
25:22 [i]Nu 7:89; 1Sa 4:4; 2Sa 6:2; 22:11; 2Ki 19:15; 1Ch 13:6; 28:18; Ps 18:10; 80:1; 99:1; Isa 37:16 [j]S Ex 19:3; 29:42; 30:6,36; Lev 1:1; 16:2; Nu 17:4 [k]Jer 3:16
25:23 [l]ver 30; Ex 26:35; 40:4,22; Lev 24:6; Nu 3:31; 1Ki 7:48; 1Ch 28:16; 2Ch 4:8,19; Eze 41:22; 44:16; Heb 9:2
25:28 [m]S ver 13
25:29 [n]Nu 4:7
25:30 [o]Ex 35:13; 39:36; 40:4,23; Lev 24:5-9; Nu 4:7; 1Sa 21:4-6; 1Ki 7:48; 1Ch 23:29
25:31 [p]Ex 26:35; 31:8; 35:14; 39:37; 40:4,24; Lev 24:4; Nu 3:31; 1Ki 7:49; 2Ch 4:7; Zec 4:2; Heb 9:2; Rev 1:12
25:36 [q]ver 18; Nu 8:4
25:37 [r]Ex 27:21; 30:8; Lev 24:3-4; Nu 8:2; 1Sa 3:3; 2Ch 13:11
25:38 [s]S ver 37; Nu 4:9
25:40 [t]S ver 9; Ac 7:44; Heb 8:5*
26:1 [u]Ex 29:42; 40:2; Lev 8:10; Nu 1:50; Jos 22:19, 29; 2Sa 7:2; 1Ki 1:39; Ac 7:44; Heb 8:2,5; 13:10; S Rev 21:3 [v]S Ex 25:18
26:2 [w]ver 8
26:6 [x]ver 11
26:8 [y]ver 2

[n]17 Traditionally *a mercy seat* [o]17 That is, about 3 3/4 feet (about 1.1 meters) long and 2 1/4 feet (about 0.7 meter) wide [p]23 That is, about 3 feet (about 0.9 meter) long and 1 1/2 feet (about 0.5 meter) wide and 2 1/4 feet (about 0.7 meter) high [q]25 That is, about 3 inches (about 8 centimeters) [r]39 That is, about 75 pounds (about 34 kilograms) [s]2 That is, about 42 feet (about 12.5 meters) long and 6 feet (about 1.8 meters) wide [t]8 That is, about 45 feet (about 13.5 meters) long and 6 feet (about 1.8 meters) wide

25:17–22 PRAYER, Mercy of God—*The ongoing prayer relationship is based on God's atonement of His people showing His mercy to them.* Only an atoned people are ready to live in God's holy presence. Without atonement a person needs to pray in repentance for forgiveness. Compare Heb 9:13–14; 1 Jn 4:10.

the end curtain in the other set. 11Then make fifty bronze clasps and put them in the loops to fasten the tent together as a unit.[z] 12As for the additional length of the tent curtains, the half curtain that is left over is to hang down at the rear of the tabernacle. 13The tent curtains will be a cubit[u] longer on both sides; what is left will hang over the sides of the tabernacle so as to cover it. 14Make for the tent a covering[a] of ram skins dyed red, and over that a covering of hides of sea cows.[v] [b]

15"Make upright frames of acacia wood for the tabernacle. 16Each frame is to be ten cubits long and a cubit and a half wide,[w] 17with two projections set parallel to each other. Make all the frames of the tabernacle in this way. 18Make twenty frames for the south side of the tabernacle 19and make forty silver bases[c] to go under them—two bases for each frame, one under each projection. 20For the other side, the north side of the tabernacle, make twenty frames 21and forty silver bases[d]—two under each frame. 22Make six frames for the far end, that is, the west end of the tabernacle, 23and make two frames for the corners at the far end. 24At these two corners they must be double from the bottom all the way to the top, and fitted into a single ring; both shall be like that. 25So there will be eight frames and sixteen silver bases—two under each frame.

26"Also make crossbars of acacia wood: five for the frames on one side of the tabernacle, 27five for those on the other side, and five for the frames on the west, at the far end of the tabernacle. 28The center crossbar is to extend from end to end at the middle of the frames. 29Overlay the frames with gold and make gold rings to hold the crossbars. Also overlay the crossbars with gold.

30"Set up the tabernacle[e] according to the plan[f] shown you on the mountain.

31"Make a curtain[g] of blue, purple and scarlet yarn and finely twisted linen, with cherubim[h] worked into it by a skilled craftsman. 32Hang it with gold hooks on four posts of acacia wood overlaid with gold and standing on four silver bases.[i] 33Hang the curtain from the clasps and place the ark of the Testimony behind the curtain.[j] The curtain will separate the Holy Place from the Most Holy Place.[k] 34Put the atonement cover[l] on the ark of the Testimony in the Most Holy Place. 35Place the table[m] outside the curtain on the north side of the tabernacle and put the lampstand[n] opposite it on the south side.

36"For the entrance to the tent make a curtain[o] of blue, purple and scarlet yarn and finely twisted linen—the work of an embroiderer.[p] 37Make gold hooks for this curtain and five posts of acacia wood overlaid with gold. And cast five bronze bases for them.

Chapter 27

The Altar of Burnt Offering

27:1–8pp — Ex 38:1–7

"BUILD an altar[q] of acacia wood, three cubits[x] high; it is to be square, five cubits long and five cubits wide.[y] 2Make a horn[r] at each of the four corners, so that the horns and the altar are of one piece, and overlay the altar with bronze. 3Make all its utensils of bronze—its pots to remove the ashes, and its shovels, sprinkling bowls,[s] meat forks and firepans.[t] 4Make a grating for it, a bronze network, and make a bronze ring at each of the four corners of the network. 5Put it under the ledge of the altar so that it is halfway up the altar. 6Make poles of acacia wood for the altar and overlay them with bronze.[u] 7The poles are to be inserted into the rings so they will be on two sides of the altar when it is carried.[v] 8Make the altar hollow, out of boards. It is to be made just as you were shown[w] on the mountain.

The Courtyard

27:9–19pp — Ex 38:9–20

9"Make a courtyard[x] for the tabernacle. The south side shall be a hundred cubits[z] long and is to have curtains of finely twisted linen, 10with twenty posts and twenty bronze bases and with silver hooks and bands on the posts. 11The north side shall also be a hundred cubits long and is to have curtains, with twenty posts and twenty bronze bases and with silver hooks and bands on the posts.

12"The west end of the courtyard shall be fifty cubits[a] wide and have curtains, with ten posts and ten bases. 13On the east end, toward the sunrise, the courtyard shall also be fifty cubits wide. 14Curtains fifteen cubits[b] long are to be on one side of the entrance, with three posts and three bases, 15and curtains fifteen cubits long are to be on the other side, with three posts and three bases.

26:11 [z]ver 6
26:14 [a]Nu 3:25 [b]Nu 4:25
26:19 [c]ver 21,25, 32; Ex 38:27
26:21 [d]S ver 19
26:30 [e]Ex 40:2; Nu 9:15 [f]S Ex 25:9
26:31 [g]Nu 4:5; 2Ch 3:14; Mt 27:51; Lk 23:45; Heb 9:3 [h]S Ex 25:18
26:32 [i]S ver 19
26:33 [j]Ex 27:21; 35:12; 40:3,21; Lev 16:2; Nu 3:31; 4:5; 2Ch 3:14 [k]Lev 16:2,16; 1Ki 6:16; 7:50; 8:6; 2Ch 3:8; 5:7; Eze 41:4; Heb 9:2-3
26:34 [l]Ex 25:21; 30:6; 37:6; Lev 16:2; Heb 9:5
26:35 [m]S Ex 25:23; Heb 9:2 [n]S Ex 25:31
26:36 [o]Ex 35:15; 40:5,28 [p]Ps 45:14; Eze 16:10; 26:16; 27:7
27:1 [q]S Ex 20:24; S 40:6; S 1Ki 8:64
27:2 [r]Ex 29:12; 30:2; 37:25; Lev 4:7; 1Ki 1:50; 2:28; Ps 118:27; Jer 17:1; Eze 43:15; Am 3:14; Zec 9:15
27:3 [s]Nu 7:13; 1Ki 7:40,45; 2Ki 12:13 [t]Nu 4:14; 1Ch 28:17; Jer 52:18
27:6 [u]S Ex 25:13
27:7 [v]Ex 25:14,28
27:8 [w]S Ex 25:9
27:9 [x]Ex 35:17; 40:8,33; Lev 6:16, 26; Eze 40:14; 42:1

[u]*13* That is, about 1 1/2 feet (about 0.5 meter) [v]*14* That is, dugongs [w]*16* That is, about 15 feet (about 4.5 meters) long and 2 1/4 feet (about 0.7 meter) wide [x]*1* That is, about 4 1/2 feet (about 1.3 meters) [y]*1* That is, about 7 1/2 feet (about 2.3 meters) long and wide [z]*9* That is, about 150 feet (about 46 meters); also in verse 11 [a]*12* That is, about 75 feet (about 23 meters); also in verse 13 [b]*14* That is, about 22 1/2 feet (about 6.9 meters); also in verse 15

16"For the entrance to the courtyard, provide a curtain[y] twenty cubits[c] long, of blue, purple and scarlet yarn and finely twisted linen—the work of an embroiderer[z]—with four posts and four bases. 17All the posts around the courtyard are to have silver bands and hooks, and bronze bases. 18The courtyard shall be a hundred cubits long and fifty cubits wide,[d] with curtains of finely twisted linen five cubits[e] high, and with bronze bases. 19All the other articles used in the service of the tabernacle, whatever their function, including all the tent pegs for it and those for the courtyard, are to be of bronze.

Oil for the Lampstand

27:20–21pp — Lev 24:1–3

20"Command the Israelites to bring you clear oil[a] of pressed olives for the light so that the lamps may be kept burning. 21In the Tent of Meeting,[b] outside the curtain that is in front of the Testimony,[c] Aaron and his sons are to keep the lamps[d] burning before the LORD from evening till morning. This is to be a lasting ordinance[e] among the Israelites for the generations to come.

Chapter 28

The Priestly Garments

"HAVE Aaron[f] your brother brought to you from among the Israelites, along with his sons Nadab and Abihu,[g] Eleazar and Ithamar,[h] so they may serve me as priests.[i] 2Make sacred garments[j] for your brother Aaron, to give him dignity and honor.[k] 3Tell all the skilled men[l] to whom I have given wisdom[m] in such matters that they are to make garments for Aaron, for his consecration, so he may serve me as priest. 4These are the garments they are to make: a breastpiece,[n] an ephod,[o] a robe,[p] a woven tunic,[q] a turban[r] and a sash. They are to make these sacred garments for your brother Aaron and his sons, so they may serve me as priests. 5Have them use gold, and blue, purple and scarlet yarn, and fine linen.[s]

The Ephod

28:6–14pp — Ex 39:2–7

6"Make the ephod[t] of gold, and of blue, purple and scarlet yarn, and of finely twisted linen—the work of a skilled craftsman. 7It is to have two shoulder pieces attached to two of its corners, so it can be fastened. 8Its skillfully woven waistband[u] is to be like it—of one piece with the ephod and *made with gold, and with blue, purple and* scarlet yarn, and with finely twisted linen.

27:16 [y]Ex 40:33 [z]Ex 36:37
27:20 [a]S Ex 25:6
27:21 [b]Ex 28:43; 29:42; 30:36; 33:7; Lev 1:1; 6:26; 8:3, 31; Nu 1:1; 31:54; Jos 18:1; 1Ki 1:39 [c]S Ex 16:34 [d]S Ex 25:37 [e]Ex 29:9; 30:21; Lev 3:17; 16:34; 17:7; Nu 18:23; 19:21; 1Sa 30:25
28:1 [f]Lev 8:30; Ps 99:6; Heb 5:4 [g]S Ex 6:23; 24:9 [h]S Ex 6:23 [i]Lev 8:2; 21:1; Nu 18:1-7; Dt 18:5; 1Sa 2:28; Heb 5:1
28:2 [j]Ex 29:5,29; 31:10; 35:19; 39:1; Lev 8:7-9,30; 16:32; Nu 20:26-28 [k]ver 40
28:3 [l]Ex 31:6; 35:10,25,35; 36:1 [m]Ex 31:3; Dt 34:9; Isa 11:2; 1Co 12:8; S Eph 1:17
28:4 [n]ver 15-30 [o]S Ex 25:7 [p]ver 31-35 [q]ver 39; Lev 10:5 [r]ver 37
28:5 [s]Ex 25:4
28:6 [t]S Ex 25:7
28:8 [u]Ex 29:5
28:9 [v]SS 8:6; Isa 49:16; Hag 2:23
28:12 [w]Dt 33:12; Job 31:36 [x]ver 29; Ex 30:16; Nu 10:10; 31:54; Jos 4:7; Zec 6:14
28:15 [y]S Ex 25:7
28:17 [z]Eze 28:13; Rev 21:19-20
28:20 [a]Eze 1:16; 10:9; Da 10:6
28:21 [b]Jos 4:8 [c]Rev 21:12

9"Take two onyx stones and engrave[v] on them the names of the sons of Israel 10in the order of their birth—six names on one stone and the remaining six on the other. 11Engrave the names of the sons of Israel on the two stones the way a gem cutter engraves a seal. Then mount the stones in gold filigree settings 12and fasten them on the shoulder pieces of the ephod as memorial stones for the sons of Israel. Aaron is to bear the names on his shoulders[w] as a memorial[x] before the LORD. 13Make gold filigree settings 14and two braided chains of pure gold, like a rope, and attach the chains to the settings.

The Breastpiece

28:15–28pp — Ex 39:8–21

15"Fashion a breastpiece[y] for making decisions—the work of a skilled craftsman. Make it like the ephod: of gold, and of blue, purple and scarlet yarn, and of finely twisted linen. 16It is to be square—a span[f] long and a span wide—and folded double. 17Then mount four rows of precious stones[z] on it. In the first row there shall be a ruby, a topaz and a beryl; 18in the second row a turquoise, a sapphire[g] and an emerald; 19in the third row a jacinth, an agate and an amethyst; 20in the fourth row a chrysolite,[a] an onyx and a jasper.[h] Mount them in gold filigree settings. 21There are to be twelve stones, one for each of the names of the sons of Israel,[b] each engraved like a seal with the name of one of the twelve tribes.[c]

22"For the breastpiece make braided chains of pure gold, like a rope. 23Make two gold rings for it and fasten them to two corners of the breastpiece. 24Fasten the two gold chains to the rings at the corners of the breastpiece, 25and the other ends of the chains to the two settings, attaching them to the shoulder pieces of the ephod at the front. 26Make two gold rings and attach them to the other two corners of the breastpiece on the inside edge next to the ephod. 27Make two more gold rings and attach them to the bottom of the shoulder pieces on the front of the ephod, close to the seam just above the waistband of the ephod. 28The rings of the breastpiece are to be tied to the rings of the ephod with blue cord, connecting it to the waistband, so that the breast-

[c] *16* That is, about 30 feet (about 9 meters)
[d] *18* That is, about 150 feet (about 46 meters) long and 75 feet (about 23 meters) wide
[e] *18* That is, about 7 1/2 feet (about 2.3 meters)
[f] *16* That is, about 9 inches (about 22 centimeters)
[g] *18* Or *lapis lazuli*
[h] *20* The precise identification of some of these precious stones is uncertain.

piece will not swing out from the ephod.
29“Whenever Aaron enters the Holy
Place,[d] he will bear the names of the
sons of Israel over his heart on the breastpiece of decision as a continuing memorial before the LORD. 30Also put the Urim
and the Thummim[e] in the breastpiece,
so they may be over Aaron’s heart whenever he enters the presence of the LORD.
Thus Aaron will always bear the means of
making decisions for the Israelites over
his heart before the LORD.

Other Priestly Garments

28:31–43pp — Ex 39:22–31

31“Make the robe of the ephod entirely
of blue cloth, 32with an opening for the
head in its center. There shall be a woven
edge like a collar[i] around this opening,
so that it will not tear. 33Make pomegranates[f] of blue, purple and scarlet yarn
around the hem of the robe, with gold
bells between them. 34The gold bells and
the pomegranates are to alternate around
the hem of the robe. 35Aaron must wear
it when he ministers. The sound of the
bells will be heard when he enters the
Holy Place before the LORD and when he
comes out, so that he will not die.
36“Make a plate[g] of pure gold and engrave on it as on a seal: HOLY TO THE
LORD.[h] 37Fasten a blue cord to it to attach
it to the turban; it is to be on the front of
the turban. 38It will be on Aaron’s forehead, and he will bear the guilt[i] involved
in the sacred gifts the Israelites consecrate, whatever their gifts may be. It will
be on Aaron’s forehead continually so
that they will be acceptable[j] to the LORD.
39“Weave the tunic[k] of fine linen and
make the turban[l] of fine linen. The sash
is to be the work of an embroiderer.
40Make tunics, sashes and headbands for
Aaron’s sons,[m] to give them dignity and
honor.[n] 41After you put these clothes[o]
on your brother Aaron and his sons,
anoint[p] and ordain them. Consecrate
them so they may serve me as priests.[q]
42“Make linen undergarments[r] as a
covering for the body, reaching from the
waist to the thigh. 43Aaron and his sons
must wear them whenever they enter the
Tent of Meeting[s] or approach the altar to
minister in the Holy Place,[t] so that they
will not incur guilt and die.[u]
“This is to be a lasting ordinance[v] for
Aaron and his descendants.

Chapter 29

Consecration of the Priests

29:1–37pp — Lev 8:1–36

“THIS is what you are to do to consecrate[w] them, so they may serve
me as priests: Take a young bull and two
rams without defect.[x] 2And from fine
wheat flour, without yeast, make bread,
and cakes mixed with oil, and wafers
spread with oil.[y] 3Put them in a basket
and present them in it—along with the
bull and the two rams.[z] 4Then bring Aaron and his sons to the entrance to the
Tent of Meeting and wash them with water.[a] 5Take the garments[b] and dress Aaron with the tunic, the robe of the ephod,
the ephod itself and the breastpiece. Fasten the ephod on him by its skillfully woven waistband.[c] 6Put the turban[d] on his
head and attach the sacred diadem[e] to
the turban. 7Take the anointing oil[f] and
anoint him by pouring it on his head.
8Bring his sons and dress them in tunics[g]
9and put headbands on them. Then tie
sashes on Aaron and his sons.[j][h] The
priesthood is theirs by a lasting ordinance.[i] In this way you shall ordain Aaron and his sons.
10“Bring the bull to the front of the
Tent of Meeting, and Aaron and his sons
shall lay their hands on its head.[j]
11Slaughter it in the LORD’s presence[k] at
the entrance to the Tent of Meeting.
12Take some of the bull’s blood and put it

28:29 [d]ver 43 **28:30** [e]Lev 8:8; Nu 27:21; Dt 33:8; 1Sa 28:6; Ezr 2:63; Ne 7:65 **28:33** [f]Nu 13:23; 1Sa 14:2; 1Ki 7:18; SS 4:3; Jer 52:22; Joel 1:12; Hag 2:19 **28:36** [g]ver 37; Ex 29:6; Lev 8:9 [h]Zec 14:20 **28:38** [i]Lev 5:1; 10:17; 16:22; 22:9, 16; Nu 18:1; Isa 53:5,6,11; Eze 4:4-6; Heb 9:28; 1Pe 2:24 [j]S Ge 32:20; Lev 22:20,27; 23:11; Isa 56:7 **28:39** [k]ver 4 [l]Ex 29:6; Lev 16:4; Eze 24:17,23; 44:18 **28:40** [m]ver 4; Ex 29:8-9; 39:41; 40:14; Lev 8:13 [n]ver 2 **28:41** [o]Ex 40:13 [p]Ex 29:7; Lev 6:20; 10:7; 21:12; Nu 35:25 [q]Ex 29:7-9; 30:30; 40:15; Lev 4:3; 6:22; 8:1-36; Nu 3:3; Heb 7:28 **28:42** [r]Lev 6:10; 16:4,23; Eze 44:18 **28:43** [s]S Ex 27:21 [t]ver 29 [u]Ex 30:20, 21; Lev 16:13; 22:9; Nu 1:51; 4:15,20; 18:22 [v]S Ex 27:21 **29:1** [w]ver 21,44; Lev 20:7; Jos 3:5; 1Ch 15:12 [x]Eze 43:23 **29:2** [y]ver 23; Lev 2:1,4; 6:19-23; Nu 6:15 **29:3** [z]ver 15,19 **29:4** [a]Ex 40:12; Lev 14:8; 16:4; Heb 10:22 **29:5** [b]S Ex 28:2 [c]Ex 28:8 **29:6** [d]Ex 28:39; Isa 3:23; Zec 3:5 [e]S Ex 28:36 **29:7** [f]ver 21; S Ex 28:41; 30:25, 30,31; 37:29; 40:9; Lev 21:10; 1Sa 10:1; 1Ki 1:39; Ps 89:20; 133:2; 141:5 **29:8** [g]S Ex 28:4; Lev 16:4 **29:9** [h]Ex 28:40 [i]S Ex 27:21; 40:15; Nu 3:10; 18:7; 25:13; Dt 18:5; Jdg 17:5; 1Sa 2:30; 1Ki 12:31 **29:10** [j]ver 19; Lev 1:4; 4:15; 16:21; Nu 8:12 **29:11** [k]Lev 1:5,11; 4:24; 6:16,25; 14:13

[i]*32* The meaning of the Hebrew for this word is uncertain. [j]*9* Hebrew; Septuagint *on them*

28:29–30 DISCIPLESHIP, Spiritual Leaders—Priests functioned in making God’s will known. It cannot be determined with certainty what the Urim and Thummin really were. They enabled the priest to obtain yes or no answers or select between two choices. Compare Lev 8:8; Nu 27:21; Dt 33:8; 1 Sa *28:6*; Ezr 2:63; Ne 7:65. When the priest entered the holy place with the Urim and Thummin in his breastplate, he appeared before God as the people’s advocate seeking the illumination necessary to protect and uphold the people’s rights. The Urim and Thummin were God’s certain medium for receiving divine direction necessary to guide the actions of Israel in carrying out God’s will. For many centuries no other class possessed such great influence as the priests. No medium such as the Urim and Thummin is needed today. We have the Holy Spirit as our Guide and the Bible as our guidebook.

28:30 PRAYER, Will of God—The Urim and the Thummim were for the high priest, indicating the sacredness of their office. Their use indicated dependence on God and desire to know His will.

28:38 SALVATION, Atonement—Atonement is one of the great biblical words used to describe the taking away of sin. God provided the high priest a symbol to wear reminding him of his duty to bear the guilt of the people so God would accept them. God has always taken the initiative to cover our sins and guilt. He provides a way to make us at one with Him. See note on Lev 1:4.

29:7 PRAYER, Holiness of God—Anointing set aside the priests for sacred duty in God’s place of worship. The symbolic action represented the community’s prayer to God to accept the work of the anointed ones as they represented the community before God.

on the horns[l] of the altar with your finger, and pour out the rest of it at the base of the altar.[m] 13Then take all the fat[n] around the inner parts,[o] the covering of the liver, and both kidneys with the fat on them, and burn them on the altar. 14But burn the bull's flesh and its hide and its offal[p] outside the camp.[q] It is a sin offering.

15"Take one of the rams,[r] and Aaron and his sons shall lay their hands on its head.[s] 16Slaughter it and take the blood and sprinkle it against the altar on all sides. 17Cut the ram into pieces and wash[t] the inner parts and the legs, putting them with the head and the other pieces. 18Then burn the entire ram on the altar. It is a burnt offering to the LORD, a pleasing aroma,[u] an offering made to the LORD by fire.

19"Take the other ram,[v] and Aaron and his sons shall lay their hands on its head.[w] 20Slaughter it, take some of its blood and put it on the lobes of the right ears of Aaron and his sons, on the thumbs of their right hands, and on the big toes of their right feet.[x] Then sprinkle blood against the altar on all sides.[y] 21And take some of the blood[z] on the altar and some of the anointing oil[a] and sprinkle it on Aaron and his garments and on his sons and their garments. Then he and his sons and their garments will be consecrated.[b]

22"Take from this ram the fat,[c] the fat tail, the fat around the inner parts, the covering of the liver, both kidneys with the fat on them, and the right thigh. (This is the ram for the ordination.) 23From the basket of bread made without yeast, which is before the LORD, take a loaf, and a cake made with oil, and a wafer. 24Put all these in the hands of Aaron and his sons and wave them before the LORD as a wave offering.[d] 25Then take them from their hands and burn them on the altar along with the burnt offering for a pleasing aroma to the LORD, an offering made to the LORD by fire.[e] 26After you take the breast of the ram for Aaron's ordination, wave it before the LORD as a wave offering, and it will be your share.[f]

27"Consecrate those parts of the ordination ram that belong to Aaron and his sons:[g] the breast that was waved and the thigh that was presented. 28This is always to be the regular share from the Israelites for Aaron and his sons. It is the contribution the Israelites are to make to the LORD from their fellowship offerings.[k] [h]

29"Aaron's sacred garments[i] will belong to his descendants so that they can be anointed and ordained in them.[j] 30The son[k] who succeeds him as priest and comes to the Tent of Meeting to minister in the Holy Place is to wear them seven days.

31"Take the ram[l] for the ordination and cook the meat in a sacred place.[m] 32At the entrance to the Tent of Meeting, Aaron and his sons are to eat the meat of the ram and the bread[n] that is in the basket. 33They are to eat these offerings by which atonement was made for their ordination and consecration. But no one else may eat[o] them, because they are sacred. 34And if any of the meat of the ordination ram or any bread is left over till morning,[p] burn it up. It must not be eaten, because it is sacred.

35"Do for Aaron and his sons everything I have commanded you, taking seven days to ordain them. 36Sacrifice a bull each day[q] as a sin offering to make atonement[r]. Purify the altar by making atonement for it, and anoint it to consecrate[s] it. 37For seven days make atonement for the altar and consecrate it. Then the altar will be most holy, and whatever touches it will be holy.[t]

38"This is what you are to offer on the altar regularly each day:[u] two lambs a year old. 39Offer one in the morning and the other at twilight.[v] 40With the first lamb offer a tenth of an ephah[l] of fine flour mixed with a quarter of a hin[m] of oil[w] from pressed olives, and a quarter of a hin of wine as a drink offering.[x] 41Sacrifice the other lamb at twilight[y] with the same grain offering[z] and its drink offering as in the morning—a pleasing aroma, an offering made to the LORD by fire.

42"For the generations to come[a] this burnt offering is to be made regularly[b] at the entrance to the Tent of Meeting[c] before the LORD. There I will meet you and speak to you;[d] 43there also I will meet with the Israelites, and the place will be consecrated by my glory.[e]

44"So I will consecrate the Tent of Meeting and the altar and will consecrate Aaron and his sons to serve me as

29:12 [l]S Ex 27:2 [m]Lev 4:7; 9:9 **29:13** [n]ver 22; Lev 1:8; 3:3,5,9; 4:10; 6:12; 7:3,5, 31; 9:10; Nu 18:17; 1Sa 2:15; 1Ki 8:64; 2Ch 7:7; 29:35; 35:14; Isa 43:24; Eze 44:15 [o]S Ex 12:9 **29:14** [p]Na 3:6; Mal 2:3 [q]Lev 4:12, 21; 16:27; Nu 19:3-5; Heb 13:11 **29:15** [r]S ver 3 [s]ver 10; Lev 3:2; 2Ch 29:23 **29:17** [t]Lev 1:9,13 **29:18** [u]S Ge 8:21; 2Co 2:15 **29:19** [v]S ver 3 [w]S ver 10 **29:20** [x]Lev 14:14, 25 [y]ver 16; Lev 1:5, 11; 3:2 **29:21** [z]Heb 9:22 [a]S ver 7 [b]S ver 1 **29:22** [c]S ver 13 **29:24** [d]Lev 7:30; 9:21; 10:15; 14:12; 23:11,20; Nu 6:20; 8:11,13,15 **29:25** [e]ver 18 **29:26** [f]Lev 7:31-34 **29:27** [g]Ex 22:29; Lev 7:31,34; Nu 18:11,12; Dt 18:3 **29:28** [h]ver 22-27; Lev 7:30,34; 10:15 **29:29** [i]S Ex 28:2; S Lev 16:4 [j]Nu 20:28 **29:30** [k]Lev 6:22; Nu 3:3; 20:28 **29:31** [l]Lev 7:37; 2Ch 13:9 [m]Lev 10:14; Nu 19:9; Eze 42:13 **29:32** [n]Mt 12:4 **29:33** [o]Lev 22:10, 13 **29:34** [p]S Ex 12:10 **29:36** [q]Heb 10:11 [r]ver 33,37; Ex 30:10; Lev 1:4; 4:20; 16:16; Nu 6:11; 8:12,19; 16:46; 25:13; 2Ch 29:24 [s]Ex 40:10; Nu 7:10 **29:37** [t]Ex 30:28-29; 40:10; Eze 43:25; Mt 23:19 **29:38** [u]Lev 23:2; Nu 28:3-8; 1Ch 16:40; 2Ch 8:13; Eze 46:13-15; Da 12:11 **29:39** [v]Nu 28:4,8; 1Ki 18:36; 2Ch 13:11; Ezr 3:3; Ps 141:2; Da 9:21 **29:40** [w]Ex 30:24; Nu 15:4; 28:5 [x]S Ge 35:14; Lev 23:37; 2Ki 16:13 **29:41** [y]1Ki 18:29, 36; 2Ki 3:20; 16:15; Ezr 9:4,5; Ps 141:2; Da 9:21 [z]Lev 2:1; 5:13; 10:12; Nu 4:16; 6:17; 1Ki 8:64; Isa 43:23 **29:42** [a]Ex 30:8,10,21,31; 31:13 [b]Eze 46:15 [c]S Ex 26:1; S 27:21 [d]ver 43; Ex 25:22; 33:9,11; Nu 7:89 **29:43** [e]Ex 33:18; 40:34; Lev 9:6; 1Ki 8:11; 2Ch 5:14; 7:2; Ps 26:8; 85:9; Eze 1:28; 43:5; Hag 1:8; 2:7

[k]*28* Traditionally *peace offerings* [l]*40* That is, probably about 2 quarts (about 2 liters) [m]*40* That is, probably about 1 quart (about 1 liter)

29:19–37 SALVATION, *Atonement*—*Atonement, in the Old Testament sacrificial system,* purified persons and things and made them holy to God (Lev 8:15,34). Removal of guilt is not included in the meaning of atonement as used here. These references are to the fellowship offering of a ram and bread, and the sin offering of seven bulls, by which atonement was made at the ordination of priests, setting the priests aside as holy and prepared to enter God's presence.

priests.[f] 45 Then I will dwell[g] among the
Israelites and be their God.[h] 46 They will
know that I am the LORD their God, who
brought them out of Egypt[i] so that I
might dwell among them. I am the LORD
their God.[j]

Chapter 30

The Altar of Incense

30:1–5pp — Ex 37:25–28

"MAKE an altar[k] of acacia wood for
burning incense.[l] 2 It is to be
square, a cubit long and a cubit wide, and
two cubits high[n]—its horns[m] of one
piece with it. 3 Overlay the top and all the
sides and the horns with pure gold, and
make a gold molding around it.[n] 4 Make
two gold rings[o] for the altar below the
molding—two on opposite sides—to
hold the poles used to carry it. 5 Make the
poles of acacia wood and overlay them
with gold.[p] 6 Put the altar in front of the
curtain that is before the ark of the Testimony—before the atonement cover[q]
that is over the Testimony—where I will
meet with you.
7 "Aaron must burn fragrant incense[r]
on the altar every morning when he
tends the lamps. 8 He must burn incense
again when he lights the lamps at twilight
so incense will burn regularly before the
LORD for the generations to come.[s] 9 Do
not offer on this altar any other incense[t]
or any burnt offering or grain offering,
and do not pour a drink offering on it.
10 Once a year[u] Aaron shall make atonement[v] on its horns. This annual atonement must be made with the blood of the
atoning sin offering[w] for the generations
to come.[x] It is most holy to the LORD."

Atonement Money

11 Then the LORD said to Moses,
12 "When you take a census[y] of the Israelites to count them, each one must pay the
LORD a ransom[z] for his life at the time he
is counted. Then no plague[a] will come
on them when you number them. 13 Each
one who crosses over to those already
counted is to give a half shekel,[o] according to the sanctuary shekel,[b] which
weighs twenty gerahs. This half shekel is
an offering to the LORD. 14 All who cross
over, those twenty years old or more,[c]
are to give an offering to the LORD. 15 The
rich are not to give more than a half shekel and the poor are not to give less[d]
when you make the offering to the LORD
to atone for your lives. 16 Receive the
atonement[e] money from the Israelites
and use it for the service of the Tent of
Meeting.[f] It will be a memorial[g] for the
Israelites before the LORD, making atonement for your lives."

Basin for Washing

17 Then the LORD said to Moses,
18 "Make a bronze basin,[h] with its bronze
stand, for washing. Place it between the
Tent of Meeting and the altar, and put
water in it. 19 Aaron and his sons are to
wash their hands and feet[i] with water[j]
from it. 20 Whenever they enter the Tent
of Meeting, they shall wash with water so
that they will not die.[k] Also, when they
approach the altar to minister by presenting an offering made to the LORD by fire,
21 they shall wash their hands and feet so
that they will not die. This is to be a lasting ordinance[l] for Aaron and his descendants for the generations to come."[m]

Anointing Oil

22 Then the LORD said to Moses,
23 "Take the following fine spices:[n] 500
shekels[p] of liquid myrrh,[o] half as much
(that is, 250 shekels) of fragrant cinnamon,[p] 250 shekels of fragrant cane,[q]
24 500 shekels[r] of cassia[s]—all according
to the sanctuary shekel—and a hin[q] of
olive oil. 25 Make these into a sacred

29:44 f S ver 1 **29:45** g S Ex 25:8; Nu 35:34; Jn 14:17; S Ro 8:10 h S Ge 17:7; 2Co 6:16 **29:46** i S Ex 6:6; 19:4-6; Dt 5:6; Ps 114:1; Hag 2:5 j S Ge 17:7 **30:1** k Ex 40:5,26; Nu 4:11; 1Ki 6:20; Eze 41:22 l S Ex 25:6; 37:29; Lk 1:11; Heb 9:4; Rev 8:3 **30:2** m S Ex 27:2; Rev 9:13 **30:3** n S Ex 25:11 **30:4** o S Ex 25:12 **30:5** p S Ex 25:13 **30:6** q Ex 25:22; S 26:34 **30:7** r S Ex 25:6; 40:27; Nu 3:10; Dt 33:10; 1Sa 2:28; 1Ch 6:49; 2Ch 2:4; 26:18; 29:7 **30:8** s S Ex 25:37; S 29:42 **30:9** t Lev 10:1; Nu 16:7,40 **30:10** u Lev 16:2 v Lev 9:7; 16:18-19, 30; 23:27,28; 25:9 w Ex 29:14; Lev 4:3; 6:25; 7:7; 8:2,14; Nu 6:11 x S Ex 29:42 **30:12** y Ex 38:25; Nu 1:2,49; 4:2,29; 14:29; 26:2; 31:26; 2Sa 24:1; 2Ki 12:4 z Ex 38:26; Nu 31:50; S Mt 20:28 a Nu 14:12; Dt 28:58-61; 2Sa 24:13; 1Ki 8:37 **30:13** b ver 24; Ex 38:24,26; Lev 5:15; 27:3,25; Nu 3:47; 7:13; 18:16; Eze 4:10; 45:12; Mt 17:24 **30:14** c Ex 38:26; Nu 1:3,18; 14:29; 26:2; 32:11; 2Ch 25:5 **30:15** d Pr 22:2; Eph 6:9 **30:16** e ver 12 f Ex 38:25-28; 2Ch 24:5 g Nu 31:54 **30:18** h Ex 31:9; 35:16; 38:8; 39:39; 40:7,30; 1Ki 7:38; 2Ch 4:6 **30:19** i Ex 40:31-32; Jn 13:10 j Ex 29:4; 40:12; Lev 8:6; Ps 26:6; Heb 10:22 **30:20** k S Ex 28:43 **30:21** l S Ex 27:21 m Ex 29:42 **30:23** n S Ge 43:11 o S Ge 37:25 p Pr 7:17; SS 4:14 q SS 4:14; Isa 43:24; Jer 6:20 **30:24** r S ver 13 s Ps 45:8; Eze 27:19

n *2* That is, about 1 1/2 feet (about 0.5 meter) long and wide and about 3 feet (about 0.9 meter) high
o *13* That is, about 1/5 ounce (about 6 grams); also in verse 15
p *23* That is, about 12 1/2 pounds (about 6 kilograms)
q *24* That is, probably about 4 quarts (about 4 liters)

29:44–46 HISTORY, Worship—Worship is offered to a God present with His people. Israel became aware of the powerful presence of God through their deliverance from Egypt. God delivered them from Egypt so He could live among them in the worship place and be their God.

29:45–46 ELECTION, Presence—The Tent of Meeting gave concrete evidence of God's presence with His elect people. As they traveled to the land promised to God's elect, the Israelites could be sure of a safe conduct. The God who had kept His promises to liberate them was with them. God's presence reminded them who God was and what He had done. The presence of God is the sign of God's election. See note on Ge 26:2–33.

30:1,7 PRAYER, Worship—Incense came to be a symbol of prayer and indicated the delight God feels in receiving our prayers (Ps 141:2; Rev 5:8). The continual burning of incense (Ex 30:8) represented Israel's prayers constantly before God. The Levitical whole burnt offering was an "aroma pleasing to the LORD" (Lev 1:17). In the New Testament, Christ is a "fragrant offering" to God (Eph 5:2), and Christians are "the aroma of Christ" to God (2 Co 2:15). Compare Mal 1:11; Rev 8:3–4.

30:10–16 SALVATION, Atonement—The atonement for sin offered by the high priest of Israel was to be made annually and on a continuing basis. All Jews had to pay a half-shekel to atone for their lives. Death was the alternative to atonement. Compare Mt 17:24–27. Under the new covenant, Christ atoned for sins once for all time (Heb 9:12–15, 25–28; 10:1–18).

30:10 WORSHIP, Calendar—See note on 16:23–30.

anointing oil, a fragrant blend, the work
of a perfumer.[t] It will be the sacred
anointing oil.[u] 26Then use it to anoint[v]
the Tent of Meeting, the ark of the Testimony, 27the table and all its articles, the
lampstand and its accessories, the altar of
incense, 28the altar of burnt offering and
all its utensils, and the basin with its
stand. 29You shall consecrate them[w] so
they will be most holy, and whatever
touches them will be holy.[x]
30"Anoint Aaron and his sons and consecrate[y] them so they may serve me as
priests.[z] 31Say to the Israelites, 'This is to
be my sacred anointing oil[a] for the generations to come.[b] 32Do not pour it on
men's bodies and do not make any oil
with the same formula. It is sacred, and
you are to consider it sacred.[c] 33Whoever
makes perfume like it and whoever puts
it on anyone other than a priest must be
cut off[d] from his people.' "

Incense

34Then the LORD said to Moses, "Take
fragrant spices[e]—gum resin, onycha and
galbanum—and pure frankincense, all in
equal amounts, 35and make a fragrant
blend of incense,[f] the work of a perfumer.[g] It is to be salted and pure and sacred. 36Grind some of it to powder and
place it in front of the Testimony in the
Tent of Meeting, where I will meet[h] with
you. It shall be most holy[i] to you. 37Do
not make any incense with this formula
for yourselves; consider it holy[j] to the
LORD. 38Whoever makes any like it to enjoy its fragrance must be cut off[k] from his
people."

Chapter 31

Bezalel and Oholiab

31:2–6pp — Ex 35:30–35

THEN the LORD said to Moses, 2"See, I
have chosen Bezalel[l] son of Uri, the
son of Hur,[m] of the tribe of Judah, 3and I
have filled him with the Spirit of God,
with skill, ability and knowledge[n] in all
kinds of crafts[o]— 4to make artistic designs for work in gold, silver and bronze,
5to cut and set stones, to work in wood,
and to engage in all kinds of craftsmanship. 6Moreover, I have appointed Oholiab[p] son of Ahisamach, of the tribe of
Dan,[q] to help him. Also I have given skill
to all the craftsmen[r] to make everything
I have commanded you: 7the Tent of
Meeting,[s] the ark of the Testimony[t]
with the atonement cover[u] on it, and all
the other furnishings of the tent— 8the
table[v] and its articles, the pure gold
lampstand[w] and all its accessories, the altar of incense,[x] 9the altar of burnt offering[y] and all its utensils, the basin[z] with
its stand— 10and also the woven garments[a], both the sacred garments for
Aaron the priest and the garments for his
sons when they serve as priests, 11and
the anointing oil[b] and fragrant incense[c]
for the Holy Place. They are to make
them just as I commanded[d] you."

The Sabbath

12Then the LORD said to Moses, 13"Say
to the Israelites, 'You must observe my
Sabbaths.[e] This will be a sign[f] between
me and you for the generations to come,[g]
so you may know that I am the LORD,
who makes you holy.[r][h]
14" 'Observe the Sabbath, because it is
holy to you. Anyone who desecrates it
must be put to death;[i] whoever does any
work on that day must be cut off from his
people. 15For six days, work[j] is to be
done, but the seventh day is a Sabbath of
rest,[k] holy to the LORD. Whoever does
any work on the Sabbath day must be put
to death. 16The Israelites are to observe
the Sabbath,[l] celebrating it for the generations to come as a lasting covenant. 17It
will be a sign[m] between me and the Israelites forever, for in six days the LORD
made the heavens and the earth, and on
the seventh day he abstained from work
and rested.[n] ' "[o]
18When the LORD finished speaking to

30:25 [t]ver 35; Ex 37:29; 1Ch 9:30 [u]S Ex 29:7; S 1Sa 9:16
30:26 [v]Ex 40:9; Lev 8:10; Nu 7:1
30:29 [w]Lev 8:10-11 [x]Ex 29:37; Lev 6:18,27; Mt 23:17
30:30 [y]Ex 29:7; Lev 8:2,12,30; 10:7; 16:32; 21:10, 12; 1Ch 15:12; Ps 133:2 [z]S Ex 28:41
30:31 [a]S Ex 29:7 [b]S Ex 29:42
30:32 [c]ver 25,37
30:33 [d]ver 38; S Ge 17:14
30:34 [e]SS 3:6
30:35 [f]S Ex 25:6 [g]S ver 25
30:36 [h]S Ex 25:22 [i]ver 32; Ex 29:37; Lev 2:3
30:37 [j]S ver 32
30:38 [k]S ver 33
31:2 [l]Ex 36:1,2; 37:1; 38:22; 1Ch 2:20; 2Ch 1:5 [m]S Ex 17:10
31:3 [n]S Ex 28:3 [o]1Ki 7:14; 1Co 12:4
31:6 [p]Ex 36:1,2; 38:23 [q]1Ki 7:14; 2Ch 2:14 [r]S Ex 28:3
31:7 [s]Ex 36:8-38 [t]Ex 37:1-5 [u]Ex 37:6; 40:20
31:8 [v]Ex 37:10-16 [w]Ex 37:17-24; Lev 24:4 [x]Ex 37:25-28
31:9 [y]Ex 38:3; Nu 4:14 [z]S Ex 30:18
31:10 [a]S Ex 28:2
31:11 [b]Ex 30:22-32; 37:29 [c]S Ex 25:6 [d]S Ex 25:9
31:13 [e]S Ex 20:8 [f]ver 17; Isa 56:4; Eze 20:12,20 [g]S Ex 29:42 [h]Lev 11:44; 20:8; 21:8; Eze 37:28
31:14 [i]Ex 35:2; Nu 15:32-36
31:15 [j]S Ex 20:8-11; 35:2; Lev 16:29; 23:3; Nu 29:7 [k]S Ge 2:3
31:16 [l]S Ex 20:8
31:17 [m]S ver 13 [n]S Ge 2:2-3 [o]S Ge 2:2; S Ex 20:9; Isa 56:2; 58:13; 66:23; Jer 17:21-22; Eze 20:12,20

[r]13 Or *who sanctifies you*; or *who sets you apart as holy*

30:34–36 PRAYER, Worship—See note on vv 1,7.
31:1–11 HOLY SPIRIT, Gifts—Skills to do God's work come from God. For Bezalel, to be "filled" with the Spirit meant to have artistic skills to decorate God's dwelling place. Such skill was not limited to one person but was given to all the craftsmen. God gives gifts according to His purposes and His people's needs. Our responsibility is to use gifts God gives us to fulfill His purposes rather than to enhance our image and satisfy our desires. The time sequence for giving the gift is not described here.
31:12–17 HISTORY, Time—See note on 12:1–28. Once each week a significant day called Israel *to remember God* in *His holiness. They were to fill* the seventh day with significance through rest while they filled the other six with meaningful work. In so doing they imitated God's first acts in universal history (Ge 1:1—2:4).
31:16–17 THE CHURCH, Covenant People—Covenant people have responsibilities and privileges. See note on 19:4–8. God intended for the people of Israel to obey Him. Obedience included keeping the Sabbath as an everlasting observance. The Sabbath reminded the people of Israel that the Lord owns every day. By setting aside one day a week, the covenant people showed their acceptance of the Lord as Master of all aspects of their lives. By obeying God's commands concerning worship, we demonstrate our commitment of every area of our lives to Him. Weekly worship indicates our recognition of the Lord as Lord of creation. The church celebrates the Lord's Day on the day of His resurrection—the first day. The church incorporates the Sabbath meaning in our celebration.

Moses on Mount Sinai,[p] he gave him the
two tablets of the Testimony, the tablets
of stone[q] inscribed by the finger of
God.[r]

Chapter 32

The Golden Calf

WHEN the people saw that Moses was
so long in coming down from the
mountain,[s] they gathered around Aaron
and said, "Come, make us gods[s] who
will go before[t] us. As for this fellow Moses who brought us up out of Egypt, we
don't know what has happened to
him."[u]
2Aaron answered them, "Take off the
gold earrings[v] that your wives, your sons
and your daughters are wearing, and
bring them to me." 3So all the people
took off their earrings and brought them
to Aaron. 4He took what they handed him
and made it into an idol[w] cast in the
shape of a calf,[x] fashioning it with a tool.
Then they said, "These are your gods,[t][y]
O Israel, who brought you up out of
Egypt."[z]
5When Aaron saw this, he built an altar
in front of the calf and announced, "Tomorrow there will be a festival[a] to the
LORD." 6So the next day the people rose
early and sacrificed burnt offerings and
presented fellowship offerings.[u][b] Afterward they sat down to eat and drink[c] and
got up to indulge in revelry.[d]
7Then the LORD said to Moses, "Go
down, because your people, whom you
brought up out of Egypt,[e] have become
corrupt.[f] 8They have been quick to turn
away[g] from what I commanded them
and have made themselves an idol[h] cast
in the shape of a calf.[i] They have bowed
down to it and sacrificed[j] to it and have
said, 'These are your gods, O Israel, who
brought you up out of Egypt.'[k]
9"I have seen these people," the LORD
said to Moses, "and they are a stiff-
necked[l] people. 10Now leave me alone[m]
so that my anger may burn against them
and that I may destroy[n] them. Then I will
make you into a great nation."[o]
11But Moses sought the favor[p] of the
LORD his God. "O LORD," he said, "why
should your anger burn against your people, whom you brought out of Egypt with
great power and a mighty hand?[q] 12Why
should the Egyptians say, 'It was with evil
intent that he brought them out, to kill
them in the mountains and to wipe them
off the face of the earth'?[r] Turn from
your fierce anger; relent and do not bring
disaster[s] on your people. 13Remember[t]
your servants Abraham, Isaac and Israel,
to whom you swore by your own self:[u] 'I
will make your descendants as numerous

31:18 [p]S Ex 19:11 [q]S Ex 24:12; 2Co 3:3; Heb 9:4 [r]Ex 32:15-16; 34:1, 28; Dt 4:13; 9:10 **32:1** [s]S Ge 7:4; Dt 9:9-12 [t]S Ex 13:21 [u]ver 23; Ac 7:40* **32:2** [v]Jdg 8:24-27 **32:4** [w]S Ex 20:23; Jdg 17:3-4; Isa 30:22 [x]ver 8,24, 35; Dt 9:16; Ne 9:18; Ps 106:19; Ac 7:41 [y]Ex 20:23; Isa 42:17 [z]1Ki 12:28; 14:9; 2Ki 10:29; 17:16; 2Ch 13:8; Hos 8:6; 10:5 **32:5** [a]Lev 23:2,37; 2Ki 10:20; Joel 2:15 **32:6** [b]Ex 20:24; 34:15; Lev 3:1; 4:10; 6:12; 9:4; 22:21; Nu 6:14; 25:2; Dt 27:7; Jdg 20:26; Eze 43:27; Ac 7:41 [c]Jdg 19:4; Ru 3:3; 1Sa 1:9; 2Sa 11:11; 1Ki 13:23; 18:42; Ne 8:12; Job 1:4; Ecc 5:18; 8:15; Jer 16:8 [d]ver 17-19; 1Co 10:7* **32:7** [e]ver 4,11; Ex 33:1 [f]S Ge 6:11-12; Eze 20:8 **32:8** [g]Jer 7:26; 16:12; Mal 2:8; 3:7 [h]S Ex 20:4 [i]S ver 4 [j]Ex 22:20 [k]1Ki 12:28; Eze 23:8 **32:9** [l]Ex 33:3,5; 34:9; Dt 9:6,13; 10:16; 31:27; Jdg 2:19; 2Ki 17:14; 2Ch 30:8; 36:13; Ne 9:16; Ps 78:8; Pr 29:1; Isa 46:12; 48:4; Jer 7:26; Eze 2:4; Hos 4:16; Ac 7:51 **32:10** [m]1Sa 2:25; Jer 7:16; 11:14; 14:11 [n]Ex 22:24; 33:3,5; Nu 16:21,45; Dt 9:14,19; Ps 106:23; Jer 14:12; Eze 20:13 [o]Nu 14:12; Dt 9:14 **32:11** [p]Dt 9:18; 2Sa 21:1; 2Ch 15:2; Ps 9:10; 34:4; 106:23; Isa 9:13; Jer 15:1 [q]ver 13; Dt 9:26; 1Sa 7:9; Ne 1:10; Ps 136:12 **32:12** [r]Nu 14:13-16; Dt 9:28 [s]ver 14; Ex 33:13 **32:13** [t]S Ex 2:24; 33:13 [u]S Ge 22:16; Heb 6:13

[s] *1* Or *a god*; also in verses 23 and 31 [t] *4* Or *This is your god*; also in verse 8 [u] *6* Traditionally *peace offerings*

31:18 HOLY SCRIPTURE, Writing—See note on 24:4. The tablets reminded Israel that God's Law led them and gave them identity. The stones confirmed that God spoke to them, directed them through their leader, and had purposes for them as they walked on a journey to the land of promise. Writing gave a permanent, unchangeable form to God's fundamental teachings for His people. Compare 34:28.

32:1 GOD, One God—Despite the dramatic events of their delivery from the Egyptian captivity, the Israelites soon turned to other gods. This is not an ancient problem alone. We, too, are often quick to substitute something for God. How often we are prone to treasure, or depend upon, something to the extent it takes the place in our minds and hearts that ought to be reserved for God alone as sovereign Lord. Our idols and false gods can be much more subtle but nonetheless damaging to our spiritual relationship with the one true God.

32:1 HUMANITY, Spiritual Nature—The spiritual nature of people leads them to search for or to create something to worship and serve.

32:2–8 HISTORY, Worship—Worship with the right *statements* can be directed to the wrong god. Worship of the God of history *must not be directed* to historical gods made with human hands. In no way can such gods represent the true God. God is seen by what He has done in history and not by what humans create.

32:7–9 SIN, Disobeying—During Moses' absence, the people turned to idolatry and constructed a golden calf. Their sin was disobedience, crossing the line drawn by God's commands. Their example serves as a warning that even the chosen people of God can easily attribute their welfare to someone or something other than God. Human impatience does not justify disobedience.

32:10,12,34–35 GOD, Wrath—While Moses was on the mountain with God, the anger of God was kindled against the Israelites who had made a golden calf as an idol. God would have been justified to have destroyed or abandoned the nation immediately. Instead God tempered His wrath in response to Moses' plea. Love, compassion, and mercy are God's dominant characteristics. Therefore God tempered the deserved judgment in a way that would still be a solemn warning to the people for the future. To have overlooked their sin entirely would have been neither just nor loving.

32:11–14 PRAYER, Intercession—Intercessory prayer is effective. Moses based his prayer on God's faithfulness to the covenant He had made. See note on Ge 15:2–3. God relented (Hebrew *nicham*, "be sorry, have compassion") from the disaster (Hebrew *ra'ah*, "evil") He had announced. Prayer shows God the attitude and faith of the person praying and leads Him to act in accordance with His righteous will. See note on v 32.

32:13–14,34–35 HISTORY, Promise—God is committed to His promises even in face of a rebellious people. God is free to fulfill promises as He chooses. He fulfills them to build His reputation among the nations. He is free to punish a disobedient people, for the possession of the promise does not guarantee obedience. He is free to relent or turn from His announced punishment in answer to prayer and in light of His purposes.

32:13–14 ELECTION, Prayer—Moses asked God to turn away from His anger with His people by appealing to God's covenant with Abraham, Isaac, and Israel. Election gives God's elect courage to pray in crisis times. Election leaves God the freedom to punish or relent from punishing His people.

as the stars[v] in the sky and I will give
your descendants all this land[w] I promised them, and it will be their inheritance
forever.' " 14Then the LORD relented[x]
and did not bring on his people the disaster he had threatened.
15Moses turned and went down the
mountain with the two tablets of the Testimony[y] in his hands.[z] They were inscribed[a] on both sides, front and back.
16The tablets were the work of God; the
writing was the writing of God, engraved
on the tablets.[b]
17When Joshua[c] heard the noise of the
people shouting, he said to Moses,
"There is the sound of war in the camp."
18Moses replied:

"It is not the sound of victory,
it is not the sound of defeat;
it is the sound of singing that I
hear."

19When Moses approached the camp
and saw the calf[d] and the dancing,[e] his
anger burned[f] and he threw the tablets
out of his hands, breaking them to
pieces[g] at the foot of the mountain.
20And he took the calf they had made and
burned[h] it in the fire; then he ground it
to powder,[i] scattered it on the water[j]
and made the Israelites drink it.
21He said to Aaron, "What did these
people do to you, that you led them into
such great sin?"
22"Do not be angry,[k] my lord," Aaron
answered. "You know how prone these
people are to evil.[l] 23They said to me,
'Make us gods who will go before us. As
for this fellow Moses who brought us up
out of Egypt, we don't know what has
happened to him.'[m] 24So I told them,
'Whoever has any gold jewelry, take it
off.' Then they gave me the gold, and I
threw it into the fire, and out came this
calf!"[n]

25Moses saw that the people were running wild and that Aaron had let them get
out of control and so become a laughingstock[o] to their enemies. 26So he stood at
the entrance to the camp and said, "Whoever is for the LORD, come to me." And
all the Levites rallied to him.
27Then he said to them, "This is what
the LORD, the God of Israel, says: 'Each
man strap a sword to his side. Go back
and forth through the camp from one end
to the other, each killing his brother and
friend and neighbor.' "[p] 28The Levites
did as Moses commanded, and that day
about three thousand of the people died.
29Then Moses said, "You have been set
apart to the LORD today, for you were
against your own sons and brothers, and
he has blessed you this day."
30The next day Moses said to the people, "You have committed a great sin.[q]
But now I will go up to the LORD; perhaps
I can make atonement[r] for your sin."
31So Moses went back to the LORD and
said, "Oh, what a great sin these people
have committed![s] They have made themselves gods of gold.[t] 32But now, please
forgive their sin[u]—but if not, then blot
me[v] out of the book[w] you have written."
33The LORD replied to Moses, "Whoever has sinned against me I will blot out[x]
of my book. 34Now go, lead[y] the people
to the place[z] I spoke of, and my angel[a]
will go before you. However, when the
time comes for me to punish,[b] I will punish them for their sin."
35And the LORD struck the people with
a plague because of what they did with
the calf[c] Aaron had made.

Chapter 33

THEN the LORD said to Moses, "Leave
this place, you and the people you
brought up out of Egypt, and go up to the
land I promised on oath[d] to Abraham,

32:13 [v]Ge 15:5; 22:17 [w]S Ge 12:7
32:14 [x]Dt 9:19; 1Sa 15:11; 2Sa 24:16; 1Ki 21:29; 1Ch 21:15; Ps 106:45; Jer 18:8; 26:3,19; Am 7:3,6; Jnh 3:10
32:15 [y]Ex 31:18; Heb 9:4 [z]S Ex 19:18; 34:4, 29; Dt 9:15 [a]2Co 3:3
32:16 [b]S Ex 24:12
32:17 [c]S Ex 17:9
32:19 [d]Dt 9:16 [e]ver 6; 1Co 10:7 [f]Ezr 9:3; Ps 119:53, 158 [g]Ex 34:1; Dt 9:17
32:20 [h]Dt 7:25; 12:3; Jos 7:1; 2Ki 23:6; 1Ch 14:12 [i]2Ch 34:7; Mic 1:7 [j]Dt 9:21
32:22 [k]S Ge 18:30 [l]Dt 9:24; 28:20; 2Ki 21:15; Ezr 9:13; Ne 9:28; Jer 4:4; 44:3; Eze 6:9
32:23 [m]S ver 1; Ac 7:40
32:24 [n]S ver 4
32:25 [o]S Ge 38:23
32:27 [p]Nu 25:3,5; Dt 33:9; Eze 9:5
32:30 [q]1Sa 12:20; Ps 25:11; 85:2 [r]Lev 1:4; 4:20,26; 5:6,10,13; 6:7
32:31 [s]Ex 34:9; Dt 9:18 [t]S Ex 20:23
32:32 [u]Nu 14:19 [v]Ro 9:3 [w]Ps 69:28; Eze 13:9; Da 7:10; 12:1; Mal 3:16; S Lk 10:20
32:33 [x]S Ex 17:14; S Job 21:20; Rev 3:5
32:34 [y]S Ex 15:17 [z]Ex 3:17 [a]S Ex 14:19 [b]S Ge 50:19; Dt 32:35; Ps 89:32; 94:23; 99:8; 109:20; Isa 27:1; Jer 5:9; 11:22; 23:2; 44:13,29; Hos 12:2; Ro 2:5-6
32:35 [c]S ver 4
33:1 [d]S Ex 13:11; S Nu 14:23; Heb 6:13

32:21–24 SIN, Responsibility—Aaron refused to accept responsibility for his sin. His story obviously contradicts that of vv 1–6. Blaming other people is not an escape from responsibility for sin. Joining the sin of others remains a personal choice for which we are individually responsible.

32:30–32 SALVATION, Atonement—Atonement by personal intercession was the only way Moses saw to restore relationships between God and Israel, who had chosen an idol rather than God. No other way of atonement could deal with rejection of God. Moses was willing to sacrifice His relationship with God to restore the relationship with the people. This foreshadows the once-for-all atonement Jesus made by sacrificing His own sinless life on the cross. See Guide to Intercession (pp. 1800–1801).

32:30–34 DISCIPLESHIP, Spiritual Leaders—God rejected Moses' offer of self-sacrifice for the sins of the people and told him to continue to do as he was commanded. Moses learned his intercession for his people could *not avert God's* judgment. *He had accomplished much* for the people through *his leadership*, but his self-sacrificing love could not provide full atonement for the sins of the people. Spiritual leaders must put the welfare of the people they lead above their own welfare and self-interests. Leaders must be willing to abide by God's decisions and continue to follow God's leadership.

32:32 PRAYER, Intercession—Moses' request was not an attempt to bargain with God. Rather, it demonstrated his strong identity with the people for whom he was praying—a very important principle in prayer. Even self-sacrificing intercession is not effective for an unrepentant people. See note on vv 11–14. See Guide to Intercession, pp. 1800–1801.

33:1–17 REVELATION, Divine Presence—Revelation centers on God's presence with His people. Moses had the law (31:18) and the promise of an angel (33:2), but God refused to go with the people Himself because they were not holy. Without God's presence the people mourned. In the Tent of Meeting God's presence was with Moses to answer the people's questions. Moses pleaded with God for understanding of His ways. God maintains enough mystery in His revelation that we *are left* wanting more. God promised His presence with Moses. Moses asked for more—God's presence with the people. His presence with His people, not just with selected leaders, distinguishes the true God from all other gods. His presence (literally

Isaac and Jacob, saying, 'I will give it to
your descendants.'[e] 2I will send an angel[f] before you and drive out the Canaanites, Amorites, Hittites, Perizzites,
Hivites and Jebusites.[g] 3Go up to the land
flowing with milk and honey.[h] But I will
not go with you, because you are a stiff-
necked[i] people and I might destroy[j] you
on the way."

4When the people heard these distress-
ing words, they began to mourn[k] and no
one put on any ornaments. 5For the LORD
had said to Moses, "Tell the Israelites,
'You are a stiff-necked people.[l] If I were
to go with you even for a moment, I
might destroy[m] you. Now take off your
ornaments and I will decide what to do
with you.' " 6So the Israelites stripped off
their ornaments at Mount Horeb.[n]

The Tent of Meeting

7Now Moses used to take a tent and
pitch it outside the camp some distance
away, calling it the "tent of meeting."[o]
Anyone inquiring[p] of the LORD would go
to the tent of meeting outside the camp.
8And whenever Moses went out to the
tent, all the people rose and stood at the
entrances to their tents,[q] watching Moses until he entered the tent. 9As Moses
went into the tent, the pillar of cloud[r]
would come down and stay at the entrance, while the LORD spoke[s] with Moses. 10Whenever the people saw the pillar
of cloud standing at the entrance to the
tent, they all stood and worshiped, each
at the entrance to his tent.[t] 11The LORD
would speak to Moses face to face,[u] as a
man speaks with his friend. Then Moses
would return to the camp, but his young
aide Joshua[v] son of Nun did not leave the
tent.

Moses and the Glory of the LORD

12Moses said to the LORD, "You have
been telling me, 'Lead these people,'[w]
but you have not let me know whom you
will send with me. You have said, 'I know
you by name[x] and you have found favor[y]
with me.' 13If you are pleased with me,
teach me your ways[z] so I may know you
and continue to find favor with you. Remember that this nation is your people."[a]

14The LORD replied, "My Presence[b]
will go with you, and I will give you
rest."[c]

15Then Moses said to him, "If your
Presence[d] does not go with us, do not
send us up from here. 16How will anyone
know that you are pleased with me and
with your people unless you go with us?[e]
What else will distinguish me and your
people from all the other people on the
face of the earth?"[f]

17And the LORD said to Moses, "I will
do the very thing you have asked,[g] because I am pleased with you and I know
you by name."[h]

18Then Moses said, "Now show me
your glory."[i]

33:1 [e]S Ge 12:7 **33:2** [f]S Ex 14:19 [g]S Ex 23:28 **33:3** [h]S Ex 3:8 [i]Ex 32:9; Ac 7:51 [j]S Ex 32:10 **33:4** [k]Nu 14:39; Ezr 9:3; Est 4:1; Ps 119:53 **33:5** [l]S Ex 32:9 [m]S Ex 32:10 **33:6** [n]S Ex 3:1 **33:7** [o]S Ex 27:21 [p]S Ge 25:22; S 1Ki 22:5 **33:8** [q]ver 10; Nu 16:27 **33:9** [r]Ex 13:21; S 19:9; Dt 31:15; 1Co 10:1 [s]S Ex 29:42; 31:18; Ps 99:7 **33:10** [t]S ver 8 **33:11** [u]Nu 12:8; Dt 5:4; 34:10 [v]S Ex 17:9 **33:12** [w]Ex 3:10; S 15:17 [x]ver 17; Isa 43:1; 45:3; 49:1; Jn 10:14-15; 2Ti 2:19 [y]S Ge 6:8 **33:13** [z]Ps 25:4; 27:11; 51:13; 86:11; 103:7; 143:8 [a]Ex 3:7; Dt 9:26,29; Ps 77:15 **33:14** [b]S Ex 13:21; Dt 4:37; Isa 63:9; Hag 1:13; 2:4 [c]Dt 12:9,10; 25:19; Jos 1:13; 11:23; 21:44; 22:4; 23:1; 1Ki 8:56; Isa 63:14; Jer 31:2; Mt 11:28; Heb 4:1-11 **33:15** [d]ver 3; Ex 34:9; 2Ki 13:23; 17:18; 23:27; 24:20; Ps 51:11; 80:3,7,19; Jer 7:15; 52:3 **33:16** [e]Ex 34:5; 40:34,35; Nu 9:15; 14:14 [f]Ex 34:10; Lev 20:24,26; Nu 23:9; Dt 4:7,32,34; 32:9; 33:28 **33:17** [g]Ex 34:28; Dt 9:18,25; 10:10; Jas 5:16 [h]S Ge 6:8 **33:18** [i]S Ex 16:7; Jn 1:14; 12:41; 1Ti 6:16; Rev 15:8

"My face") is promised to people who please Him. That presence shows God's faithfulness to His own character. His early promise of the angel's leadership showed His faithfulness to His revealed promises. His response to Moses showed He is a person who responds to people, changing His plan of action when they commit themselves to Him and His way of life. God's people need to seek to know God's ways and be sure of His presence.

33:1–6,12–17 HISTORY, Promise—Israel learned that God's promises do not always guarantee Gods' presence. Intercessory prayer by God's faithful leader may lead God "to decide" (v 5) to be present to guide His people. God's presence in the history of His people shows His pleasure with His people, showing they are different from all other groups on earth.

33:1–16 ELECTION, Presence—See note on 29:45–46. Divine presence marks the elect. The holy God cannot be present with an unholy people. Intercessory prayer restored the relationship between God and His elect, but stubborn, people. Restoration was possible because God is free to show mercy and love to whom He chooses. This mercy and God's gracious choice are the distinguishing marks of the elect, whose stiff-necked behavior shows they do not deserve election. Such a people stand in danger of destruction (v 3).

33:3 GOD, Wrath—Our sins make us liable to the judgment of God. We must not presume upon His grace to save us from His wrath every time we sin. The longer we resist the will of God in our lives, the more liable we are to feel the heat of His anger. Israel had tempted God to extreme action. His holiness could not abide their sin.

33:7 SALVATION, Grace—The "tent of meeting" was a temporary place of worship prior to the tabernacle. It was a meeting place for God and Moses as another expression of God's grace. The tabernacle came to be identified as the tent of meeting (Lev 1:3).

33:9–11 WORSHIP, Individual—Worship is intensely private and individual. We need to worship together with others, but such meetings are worthless if we do not have our private and personal worship of the Lord. The Old Testament begins with individual worship (Ge 4:3–4). Compare Ge 24:26; Ex 34:8; 1 Ki 1:47–48; Mt 17:1–8; Jn 9:36–38. Individual worship is needed to prepare us for corporate worship with the congregation.

33:11–17 PRAYER, Personal—Prayer is a conversation between friends. Moses was intimate with God, "face to face" (Dt 34:10). The seeing was spiritual, not literal (33:20,23). Abraham was also called the friend of God (2 Ch 20:7; Isa 41:8; Jas 2:23). Prayer involves human search for direction, instruction, and confidence of God's presence. It brings identity to God's people. God responds to the personal requests of His friends.

33:12–16 DISCIPLESHIP, Spiritual Leaders—God often makes His presence known to His people through His leaders. Spiritual leadership is possible only when the human leader experiences and follows the presence of the Lord. The Lord's leaders should walk in faith and constantly learn God's ways, for no leader ever attains sufficient strength and wisdom to lead without new directions from God.

33:14 CHRISTIAN ETHICS, War and Peace—God's presence provides protection for His people, but the goal is rest from war, not domination through war. See note on Ge 13:7–12.

33:18–22 REVELATION, Divine Presence—Having

19And the LORD said, "I will cause all
my goodness to pass[j] in front of you, and
I will proclaim my name,[k] the LORD, in
your presence. I will have mercy on
whom I will have mercy, and I will have
compassion on whom I will have compassion.[l] 20But," he said, "you cannot see
my face, for no one may see[m] me and
live."
21Then the LORD said, "There is a place
near me where you may stand on a rock.
22When my glory passes by, I will put you
in a cleft in the rock[n] and cover you with
my hand[o] until I have passed by. 23Then
I will remove my hand and you will
see my back; but my face must not be
seen."

Chapter 34

The New Stone Tablets

THE LORD said to Moses, "Chisel out
two stone tablets like the first ones,[p]
and I will write on them the words that
were on the first tablets,[q] which you
broke.[r] 2Be ready in the morning, and
then come up on Mount Sinai.[s] Present
yourself to me there on top of the mountain. 3No one is to come with you or be
seen anywhere on the mountain;[t] not
even the flocks and herds may graze in
front of the mountain."
4So Moses chiseled[u] out two stone tablets like the first ones and went up Mount
Sinai early in the morning, as the LORD
had commanded him; and he carried the
two stone tablets in his hands.[v] 5Then
the LORD came down in the cloud[w] and
stood there with him and proclaimed his
name, the LORD.[x] 6And he passed in
front of Moses, proclaiming, "The LORD,
the LORD, the compassionate[y] and gracious God, slow to anger,[z] abounding in
love[a] and faithfulness,[b] 7maintaining
love to thousands,[c] and forgiving wickedness, rebellion and sin.[d] Yet he does not
leave the guilty unpunished;[e] he punishes the children and their children for
the sin of the fathers to the third and
fourth generation."[f]
8Moses bowed to the ground at once
and worshiped. 9"O Lord, if I have found
favor[g] in your eyes," he said, "then
let the Lord go with us.[h] Although this
is a stiff-necked[i] people, forgive our

33:19 [j]1Ki 19:11 [k]Ex 6:3; 34:5-7 [l]Ro 9:15* **33:20** [m]S Ge 16:13; S Ex 3:6; S Dt 5:26; S Jn 1:18 **33:22** [n]Ge 49:24; 1Ki 19:9; Ps 27:5; 31:20; 62:7; 91:1; Isa 2:21; Jer 4:29 [o]Ps 91:4; Isa 49:2; 51:16 **34:1** [p]S Ex 24:12 [q]Dt 10:2,4 [r]S Ex 32:19 **34:2** [s]S Ex 19:11 **34:3** [t]S Ex 19:13 **34:4** [u]Dt 10:3 [v]S Ex 32:15 **34:5** [w]S Ex 13:21; S 19:9 [x]Ex 6:3; 33:19 **34:6** [y]S Ex 22:27; S Nu 14:20; S Ps 86:15 [z]Nu 14:18; Ps 78:38; Jer 15:15; Ro 2:4 [a]S Ge 19:16 [b]Ps 61:7; 108:4; 115:1; 138:2; 143:1; La 3:23; Jas 5:11 **34:7** [c]S Ex 20:6; Dt 5:10 [d]1Ki 8:30; Ps 86:5; 103:3; 130:4,8; Isa 43:25; Da 9:9; 1Jn 1:9 [e]Ex 23:7; Jos 24:19; Job 7:20-21; 9:28; 10:14; Mic 6:1-16; Na 1:3 [f]S Ex 20:5 **34:9** [g]Ex 33:13; Nu 11:15 [h]S Ex 33:15 [i]Ex 32:9

secured the presence of God for the completion of the desert journey, Moses requested what most human beings want at some point in their lives: to see God (24:1–17). To see the glory of God is to see a visible manifestation of His presence. Glory (Hebrew *kabod*) means the weight and honor of something; in the case of God, it refers to His character and fullness. Because of his fidelity to God, Moses was allowed to see a moving presence, though not face to face (33:20). The reality of God can never be fully captured by human senses. Even Moses could not handle the fullness of God's presence. Even to witness the passing impact of the Creator, however, is to be affected in a dramatic way (34:29–30). Moses encountered God in a manner no one else had encountered Him. God was closer to Moses than anyone. Moses came as close to seeing the full majesty of God as possible for humans. The God of Moses made Himself known more clearly than ever as a God of love, forgiveness, and fidelity, and a God of great purposes for small people. God could not be seen in physical form. Human beings were the only image of God permitted on earth. God revealed Himself not in images but through His characteristics and actions.

33:18–23 PRAYER, Personal—Prayer is a deep search for God's personal presence. Moses thirsted and yearned for God. God satisfied that human yearning here and in a fuller way in Lk 9:30–32.

33:19 GOD, Sovereignty—Because He is sovereign Lord, it is God's prerogative to dispense mercy or judgment as He pleases. He answers to no one. He makes these awesome decisions in a way that is true to His own holy nature and in keeping with both His love and His righteousness.

34:4–12 REVELATION, Divine Presence—The God whom Moses sought to know better expressed Himself not just by allowing Moses to "see" more of Him. He came in the cloud (13:21; 19:9,16; 20:21; 24:15–16; 33:9–10) to reveal His character and heart deeply. The cloud gave concrete expression of the God whose features cannot be chiseled in concrete. God told the one who interpreted Him to Israel what kind of a God leads them into their promise. Faith matures all human beings in moments like this when we come "face to face" with the good news about who our Guide is and thus less concerned about where we are going with Him or how we are going to get there.

34:4–9 ELECTION, Forgiveness—God punished the elect children of Israel until the third and fourth generation for their wickedness, rebellion, and sin; but His compassion, grace, love, and covenant of faithfulness provided forgiveness for Israel. Election is based on the holy, loving God forgiving the sins of His sinful people.

34:5–7 GOD, Love—Some have said that the God of the Old Testament is only a God of strict justice. God can be stern in meting out justice, but He would rather be known for His love, compassion, and mercy.

34:5–9 PRAYER, Repentance—In reverent preparation for the second receiving of the Ten Commandments, Moses humbly represented the people, confessing the congregation's sins and seeking forgiveness so the Lord's presence would be with them. Prayer involves humble repentance. Each individual has to seek repentance for personal sin, but this may be done in community worship with a worship leader voicing the desires of the whole people. God renewed His covenant with Israel in response to the prayer of repentance.

34:6–9 SALVATION, Forgiveness—God is in the sin-forgiving business. Although He punishes sin, He loves sinners. Compare Nu 14:18–20. In God's new covenant each person is punished for his or her own sins (Jer 31:29–30; Eze 18:1–3).

34:8–16 HISTORY, Promise—God made the promise and His expectations more definite as time for fulfillment neared. Forgiveness rather than perfection is the identifying characteristic of the people of promise. God's historical acts fulfilling His promises seek to reveal the awesome, fearful power of God. The acts also call God's people to absolute allegiance to Him.

34:8–9 WORSHIP, Prayer—Moses worshiped the Lord with a prayer confessing sins and asking for forgiveness. Individual worship keeps community needs in focus. See notes on 33:9–11; Ge 12:6–8.

34:9 SIN, Responsibility—In asking God's guidance, Moses acknowledged the responsibility of the Israelites for their sins of rebellion. One of the biblical principles related to forgiveness is that we must acknowledge responsibility for sin before we can receive forgiveness.

wickedness and our sin,[j] and take us as
your inheritance."[k]
10 Then the LORD said: "I am making a
covenant[l] with you. Before all your people I will do wonders[m] never before done
in any nation in all the world.[n] The people you live among will see how awesome
is the work that I, the LORD, will do for
you. 11 Obey what I command[o] you today.
I will drive out before you the Amorites,
Canaanites, Hittites, Perizzites, Hivites
and Jebusites.[p] 12 Be careful not to make a
treaty[q] with those who live in the land
where you are going, or they will be a
snare[r] among you. 13 Break down their
altars, smash their sacred stones and cut
down their Asherah poles.[v][s] 14 Do not
worship any other god,[t] for the LORD,
whose name[u] is Jealous, is a jealous
God.[v]
15 "Be careful not to make a treaty[w]
with those who live in the land; for when
they prostitute[x] themselves to their gods
and sacrifice to them, they will invite you
and you will eat their sacrifices.[y] 16 And
when you choose some of their daughters
as wives[z] for your sons and those daughters prostitute themselves to their gods,[a]
they will lead your sons to do the same.
17 "Do not make cast idols.[b]
18 "Celebrate the Feast of Unleavened
Bread.[c] For seven days eat bread made
without yeast,[d] as I commanded you. Do
this at the appointed time in the month of
Abib,[e] for in that month you came out of
Egypt.
19 "The first offspring[f] of every womb
belongs to me, including all the firstborn
males of your livestock, whether from
herd or flock. 20 Redeem the firstborn
donkey with a lamb, but if you do not

34:9 [j]Nu 14:19; 1Ki 8:30; 2Ch 6:21; Ps 19:12; 25:11; Jer 33:8; Hos 14:2 [k]S Ex 6:7; 19:5; Dt 4:20; 7:6; 9:26, 29; 14:2; 26:18; 32:9; 1Sa 10:1; 2Sa 14:16; 1Ki 8:51,53; Ps 28:9; 33:12; 74:2; 79:1; 94:14; 106:5,40; Isa 19:25; 63:17; Jer 10:16; 51:19; Mic 7:18; Zec 2:12 34:10 [l]S Ge 6:18; S 9:15; S 15:18; Dt 5:2-3 [m]S Ex 3:20 [n]S Ex 33:16 34:11 [o]Dt 6:25; Jos 11:15 [p]S Ex 23:28 34:12 [q]Jdg 2:2 [r]S Ex 10:7 34:13 [s]S Ex 23:24; Nu 33:52; Dt 7:5; 12:3; Jdg 6:26; 1Ki 15:13; 2Ch 15:16; 17:6; 34:3-4; Mic 5:14 34:14 [t]S Ex 20:3 [u]Isa 9:6 [v]S Ex 20:5 34:15 [w]ver 12; Dt 23:6; Ezr 9:12 [x]Ex 22:20; 32:8; Dt 31:16; Jdg 2:17; 2Ki 17:8; 1Ch 5:25; 2Ch 11:15; Am 2:4 [y]S Ex 32:6; 1Co 8:4 34:16 [z]Dt 7:3; 17:17; Jos 23:12; Jdg 3:6; 14:3; 1Ki 11:1,2; 16:31; Ezr 9:2; 10:3; Ne 10:30; 13:25,26 [a]Dt 7:4; 12:31; 20:18; 1Ki 11:4; 2Ki 21:3-15; Ps 106:34-41; Mal 2:11 34:17 [b]S Ex 20:4 34:18 [c]S Ex 12:17; Mt 26:17; Lk 22:1; Ac 12:3 [d]S Ex 12:15 [e]S Ex 12:2 34:19 [f]Ex 13:2 34:20 [g]S Ex 13:13 [h]S Ex 13:2 [i]S Ex 22:29; Dt 16:16; Eze 46:9

redeem it, break its neck.[g] Redeem all
your firstborn sons.[h]
"No one is to appear before me empty-handed.[i]
21 "Six days you shall labor, but on the
seventh day you shall rest;[j] even during
the plowing season and harvest[k] you
must rest.
22 "Celebrate the Feast of Weeks with
the firstfruits[l] of the wheat harvest, and
the Feast of Ingathering[m] at the turn of
the year.[w] 23 Three times[n] a year all your
men are to appear before the Sovereign
LORD, the God of Israel. 24 I will drive out
nations[o] before you and enlarge your territory,[p] and no one will covet your land
when you go up three times each year to
appear before the LORD your God.
25 "Do not offer the blood of a sacrifice
to me along with anything containing
yeast,[q] and do not let any of the sacrifice
from the Passover Feast remain until
morning.[r]
26 "Bring the best of the firstfruits[s] of
your soil to the house of the LORD your
God.
"Do not cook a young goat in its mother's milk."[t]
27 Then the LORD said to Moses,
"Write[u] down these words, for in accordance with these words I have made a
covenant[v] with you and with Israel."
28 Moses was there with the LORD forty
days and forty nights[w] without eating

34:21 [j]Ge 2:2-3 [k]Ne 13:15; Isa 56:2; 58:13 34:22 [l]ver 26; Ex 23:19; Lev 2:12,14; 7:13; 23:10,17; Nu 28:26 [m]S Ex 23:16 34:23 [n]S Ex 23:14 34:24 [o]S Ex 23:28 [p]Dt 12:20; 19:8; Job 12:23 34:25 [q]S Ex 23:18 [r]S Ex 12:8 34:26 [s]S Ex 22:29; S Nu 18:12 [t]S Ex 23:19 34:27 [u]S Ex 17:14 [v]S Ge 6:18; S 15:18 34:28 [w]S Ge 7:4; Mt 4:2; Lk 4:2

[v] *13* That is, symbols of the goddess Asherah
[w] *22* That is, in the fall

34:10–28 THE CHURCH, Covenant People—The Lord reveals Himself to His covenant people. Although humans cannot know the fullness of the infinite God, God desires that we know Him. After Israel rebelled and broke the covenant (ch 32), God graciously restored the people. God allowed Moses to enter His presence in a unique way. God revealed Himself to Moses as merciful, righteous, and forgiving. Moses pleaded for God to lead the rebellious people to the land which He had promised. Commandments and laws remain for the people of God. If we are to be the covenant people of God, we must serve Him and obey His commands. He restores returning sinners but judges the obstinate. God gives instructions for meaningful living. He is willing to forgive and to lead His people in difficult times. Those who obey God's commands will live better lives because they have taken instructions from the Giver and Creator of life. Moses wrote the words to remind the people of their *relationship with God* and their responsibility to Him.

34:11–26,32 CHRISTIAN ETHICS, Moral Imperatives—Total allegiance is the basic demand of God. God requests the Christian to identify potential idolatrous practices and practitioners of those practices. The believer must find godly alternatives to an idolatrous life-style. We need the encouragement of other Christians, not the temptations of unbelievers, as we seek to follow God.

34:14 GOD, Jealous—To underscore His prohibition of idolatry, God named Himself *Jealous.* This name did not refer to a somewhat shallow and childish human emotion. It was intended to emphasize that God will not tolerate a divided loyalty from us. We ought to honor Him as the one true God and give Him something more than lip service.

34:18–28 HISTORY, Worship—God's grace and power in delivering His people in their historical need is the basis for worship. Israel's festivals represented response to the God who delivered from Egypt, conquered Canaan, and made a covenant with His people.

34:18–26 WORSHIP, Calendar—See note on 16:23–30.

34:19–24 STEWARDSHIP, Giving in Worship—"Firstfruits" of animals and grain crops were given in worship as required in Old Testament law. They taught people to give proportionately and purposefully. Firstfruit giving practices varied through the years. Such offerings were considered a worship act that acknowledged God's blessings. The worshipful spirit of giving is a vital element for Christians. Offerings need to be of the first and best, not of the leftovers. See note on Mt 5:23–24.

34:27–28 HOLY SCRIPTURE, Writing—On this occasion, Moses wrote the Ten Commandments, the central teachings God had for Israel. The entire Law or Pentateuch was not written down at once. God directed Moses clearly as He inspired him to write down His laws. See notes on 24:4; 31:18; Lev 1:1.

34:28 PRAYER, Humility—Prayer may involve prolonged

bread or drinking water.[x] And he wrote
on the tablets[y] the words of the covenant—the Ten Commandments.[z]

The Radiant Face of Moses

29When Moses came down from
Mount Sinai[a] with the two tablets of the
Testimony in his hands,[b] he was not
aware that his face was radiant[c] because
he had spoken with the LORD. 30When
Aaron and all the Israelites saw Moses,
his face was radiant, and they were afraid
to come near him. 31But Moses called to
them; so Aaron and all the leaders of the
community[d] came back to him, and he
spoke to them. 32Afterward all the Israelites came near him, and he gave them all
the commands[e] the LORD had given him
on Mount Sinai.
33When Moses finished speaking to
them, he put a veil[f] over his face. 34But
whenever he entered the LORD's presence to speak with him, he removed the
veil until he came out. And when he
came out and told the Israelites what he
had been commanded, 35they saw that
his face was radiant.[g] Then Moses would
put the veil back over his face until he
went in to speak with the LORD.

Chapter 35

Sabbath Regulations

MOSES assembled the whole Israelite
community and said to them,
"These are the things the LORD has commanded[h] you to do: 2For six days, work
is to be done, but the seventh day shall be
your holy day, a Sabbath[i] of rest to the
LORD. Whoever does any work on it must
be put to death.[j] 3Do not light a fire in
any of your dwellings on the Sabbath
day.[k]"

Materials for the Tabernacle

35:4–9pp — Ex 25:1–7
35:10–19pp — Ex 39:32–41

4Moses said to the whole Israelite community, "This is what the LORD has commanded: 5From what you have, take an
offering for the LORD. Everyone who is
willing is to bring to the LORD an offering
of gold, silver and bronze; 6blue, purple
and scarlet yarn and fine linen; goat hair;
7ram skins dyed red and hides of sea
cows[x]; acacia wood; 8olive oil[l] for the
light; spices for the anointing oil and for
the fragrant incense; 9and onyx stones
and other gems to be mounted on the
ephod and breastpiece.
10"All who are skilled among you are to
come and make everything the LORD has
commanded:[m] 11the tabernacle[n] with its
tent and its covering, clasps, frames,
crossbars, posts and bases; 12the ark[o]
with its poles and the atonement cover
and the curtain[p] that shields it; 13the table[q] with its poles and all its articles and
the bread of the Presence; 14the lampstand[r] that is for light with its accessories, lamps and oil for the light; 15the altar[s] of incense with its poles, the anointing oil[t] and the fragrant incense;[u] the
curtain for the doorway at the entrance to
the tabernacle;[v] 16the altar[w] of burnt offering with its bronze grating, its poles
and all its utensils; the bronze basin[x]
with its stand; 17the curtains of the courtyard with its posts and bases, and the curtain for the entrance to the courtyard;[y]
18the tent pegs[z] for the tabernacle and
for the courtyard, and their ropes; 19the
woven garments worn for ministering in
the sanctuary—both the sacred garments[a] for Aaron the priest and the garments for his sons when they serve as
priests."
20Then the whole Israelite community
withdrew from Moses' presence, 21and
everyone who was willing and whose
heart moved him came and brought an
offering to the LORD for the work on the
Tent of Meeting, for all its service, and for
the sacred garments. 22All who were willing, men and women alike, came and
brought gold jewelry of all kinds:
brooches, earrings, rings and ornaments.
They all presented their gold as a wave
offering to the LORD. 23Everyone who had
blue, purple or scarlet yarn[b] or fine lin-
en, or goat hair, ram skins dyed red or
hides of sea cows brought them. 24Those
presenting an offering of silver or bronze
brought it as an offering to the LORD, and
everyone who had acacia wood for any
part of the work brought it. 25Every

34:28 [x]Dt 9:9,18; Ezr 10:6 [y]ver 1; Ex 31:18 [z]Dt 4:13; 10:4
34:29 [a]S Ex 19:11 [b]S Ex 32:15 [c]ver 35; Ps 34:5; Isa 60:5; Mt 17:2; 2Co 3:7,13
34:31 [d]Ex 16:22
34:32 [e]S Ex 21:1; 35:1,4
34:33 [f]2Co 3:13
34:35 [g]S ver 29
35:1 [h]S Ex 34:32
35:2 [i]S Ge 2:3; Ex 34:21; Dt 5:13-14 [j]S Ex 31:14
35:3 [k]Ex 16:23
35:8 [l]S Ex 25:6
35:10 [m]Ex 31:6; 39:43
35:11 [n]Ex 26:1-37; 36:8-38
35:12 [o]Ex 25:10-22; 37:1-9 [p]S Ex 26:33
35:13 [q]Ex 25:23-30; 37:10-16
35:14 [r]S Ex 25:31
35:15 [s]Ex 30:1-6; 37:25-28 [t]Ex 30:25 [u]Ex 30:34-38 [v]S Ex 26:36
35:16 [w]Ex 27:1-8; 38:1-7 [x]S Ex 30:18
35:17 [y]S Ex 27:9; 38:9-20
35:18 [z]Ex 27:19; 38:20
35:19 [a]S Ex 28:2
35:23 [b]Ex 39:1

[x]7 That is, dugongs; also in verse 23

periods of self-denial. Moses fasted forty days, identifying with God in His sorrow over Israel's sin (Dt 9:18). See note on 2 Sa 1:12.

34:29–35 REVELATION, Divine Presence—God used Moses as a constant messenger who traveled between the people and God's presence in the mountain. Each of the commands that God uttered were passed on to the people, who waited anxiously to hear the word of the Lord. Whenever Moses *was in the presence of God, he* unveiled himself. Both servant and Master revealed themselves in an act of trust and closeness. Revelation changed Moses' appearance but not his humanity. The recipient of revelation and mediator of God's word did not become divine. The written divine word was not all the people needed. They needed a mediator to interpret the divine word in the new situations that passing time brought.

34:34–35 PRAYER, God's Presence—Prayer brings us into God's presence and changes our lives. Moses' closeness to God (33:11) brought a radiance the people could not bear. Nothing should veil us when we are in God's presence.

35:1–3 HISTORY, Time—See note on 31:12–17.

35:5,21–29 STEWARDSHIP, House of God—See note on 25:1–8.

skilled woman[c] spun with her hands and
brought what she had spun—blue, purple or scarlet yarn or fine linen. 26And all
the women who were willing and had the
skill spun the goat hair. 27The leaders[d]
brought onyx stones and other gems[e] to
be mounted on the ephod and breastpiece. 28They also brought spices and olive oil for the light and for the anointing
oil and for the fragrant incense.[f] 29All
the Israelite men and women who were
willing[g] brought to the LORD freewill offerings[h] for all the work the LORD
through Moses had commanded them
to do.

Bezalel and Oholiab

35:30–35pp — Ex 31:2–6

30Then Moses said to the Israelites,
"See, the LORD has chosen Bezalel son of
Uri, the son of Hur, of the tribe of Judah,
31and he has filled him with the Spirit of
God, with skill, ability and knowledge in
all kinds of crafts[i]— 32to make artistic
designs for work in gold, silver and
bronze, 33to cut and set stones, to work in
wood and to engage in all kinds of artistic
craftsmanship. 34And he has given both
him and Oholiab[j] son of Ahisamach, of
the tribe of Dan, the ability to teach[k] others. 35He has filled them with skill to do
all kinds of work[l] as craftsmen, design-
ers, embroiderers in blue, purple and
scarlet yarn and fine linen, and weavers
—all of them master craftsmen and de-
signers. 1So Bezalel, Oholiab and every
skilled person[m] to whom the LORD has
given skill and ability to know how to carry out all the work of constructing the
sanctuary[n] are to do the work just as the
LORD has commanded."

Chapter 36

2THEN Moses summoned Bezalel[o] and
Oholiab[p] and every skilled person to
whom the LORD had given ability and who
was willing[q] to come and do the work.
3They received from Moses all the offerings[r] the Israelites had brought to carry
out the work of constructing the sanctuary. And the people continued to bring
freewill offerings morning after morning.
4So all the skilled craftsmen who were
doing all the work on the sanctuary left
their work 5and said to Moses, "The people are bringing more than enough[s] for

35:25 [c]S Ex 28:3
35:27 [d]S Ex 25:2; 1Ch 29:6 [e]1Ch 29:8
35:28 [f]S Ex 25:6
35:29 [g]S Ex 25:2 [h]ver 4-9; Ex 25:1-7; 36:3; 2Ki 12:4
35:31 [i]ver 35; 2Ch 2:7,14
35:34 [j]S Ex 31:6 [k]2Ch 2:14
35:35 [l]ver 31
36:1 [m]S Ex 28:3 [n]Ex 25:8
36:2 [o]S Ex 31:2 [p]S Ex 31:6 [q]S Ex 25:2
36:3 [r]S Ex 35:29
36:5 [s]2Ch 24:14; 31:10; 2Co 8:2-3
36:7 [t]1Ki 7:47
36:13 [u]ver 18
36:18 [v]ver 13

doing the work the LORD commanded to
be done."

6Then Moses gave an order and they
sent this word throughout the camp: "No
man or woman is to make anything else
as an offering for the sanctuary." And so
the people were restrained from bringing
more, 7because what they already had
was more[t] than enough to do all the
work.

The Tabernacle

36:8–38pp — Ex 26:1–37

8All the skilled men among the workmen made the tabernacle with ten curtains of finely twisted linen and blue, purple and scarlet yarn, with cherubim
worked into them by a skilled craftsman.
9All the curtains were the same size—
twenty-eight cubits long and four cubits
wide.[y] 10They joined five of the curtains
together and did the same with the other
five. 11Then they made loops of blue material along the edge of the end curtain in
one set, and the same was done with the
end curtain in the other set. 12They also
made fifty loops on one curtain and fifty
loops on the end curtain of the other set,
with the loops opposite each other.
13Then they made fifty gold clasps and
used them to fasten the two sets of curtains together so that the tabernacle was
a unit.[u]

14They made curtains of goat hair for
the tent over the tabernacle—eleven altogether. 15All eleven curtains were the
same size—thirty cubits long and four cubits wide.[z] 16They joined five of the curtains into one set and the other six into
another set. 17Then they made fifty loops
along the edge of the end curtain in one
set and also along the edge of the end
curtain in the other set. 18They made fifty
bronze clasps to fasten the tent together
as a unit.[v] 19Then they made for the tent
a covering of ram skins dyed red, and
over that a covering of hides of sea
cows.[a]

20They made upright frames of acacia
wood for the tabernacle. 21Each frame
was ten cubits long and a cubit and a half
wide,[b] 22with two projections set parallel
to each other. They made all the frames

[y] *9* That is, about 42 feet (about 12.5 meters) long and 6 feet (about 1.8 meters) wide [z] *15* That is, about 45 feet (about 13.5 meters) long and 6 feet (about 1.8 meters) wide [a] *19* That is, dugongs [b] *21* That is, about 15 feet (about 4.5 meters) long and 2 1/4 feet (about 0.7 meter) wide

36:1–2 HUMANITY, Potentiality—The skills and abilities which people possess are the gifts of God. Such gifts are ultimately fruitless unless those who have them are willing to use them in His service. See note on Ge 4:17–22.

36:3–7 STEWARDSHIP, House of God—The people cheerfully provided more than enough for the tabernacle through freewill offerings. Giving pleases God when it is voluntary and cheerful. Properly motivated giving provides sufficient funds for God's purposes. See note on 25:1–8.

of the tabernacle in this way. 23They
made twenty frames for the south side of
the tabernacle 24and made forty silver
bases to go under them—two bases for
each frame, one under each projection.
25For the other side, the north side of the
tabernacle, they made twenty frames
26and forty silver bases—two under each
frame. 27They made six frames for the far
end, that is, the west end of the tabernacle, 28and two frames were made for the
corners of the tabernacle at the far end.
29At these two corners the frames were
double from the bottom all the way to the
top and fitted into a single ring; both
were made alike. 30So there were eight
frames and sixteen silver bases—two under each frame.

31They also made crossbars of acacia
wood: five for the frames on one side of
the tabernacle, 32five for those on the other side, and five for the frames on the
west, at the far end of the tabernacle.
33They made the center crossbar so that it
extended from end to end at the middle
of the frames. 34They overlaid the frames
with gold and made gold rings to hold the
crossbars. They also overlaid the crossbars with gold.

35They made the curtain[w] of blue, purple and scarlet yarn and finely twisted lin-
en, with cherubim worked into it by a
skilled craftsman. 36They made four posts
of acacia wood for it and overlaid them
with gold. They made gold hooks for
them and cast their four silver bases.
37For the entrance to the tent they made
a curtain of blue, purple and scarlet yarn
and finely twisted linen—the work of an
embroiderer;[x] 38and they made five
posts with hooks for them. They overlaid
the tops of the posts and their bands with
gold and made their five bases of bronze.

Chapter 37

The Ark

37:1–9pp — Ex 25:10–20

BEZALEL[y] made the ark[z] of acacia
wood—two and a half cubits long, a
cubit and a half wide, and a cubit and a
half high.[c] 2He overlaid it with pure
gold,[a] both inside and out, and made a
gold molding around it. 3He cast four gold
rings for it and fastened them to its four
feet, with two rings on one side and two
rings on the other. 4Then he made poles
of acacia wood and overlaid them with
gold. 5And he inserted the poles into the
rings on the sides of the ark to carry it.

6He made the atonement cover[b] of
pure gold—two and a half cubits long and
a cubit and a half wide.[d] 7Then he made
two cherubim[c] out of hammered gold at
the ends of the cover. 8He made one
cherub on one end and the second cherub on the other; at the two ends he made
them of one piece with the cover. 9The
cherubim had their wings spread upward,
overshadowing[d] the cover with them.
The cherubim faced each other, looking
toward the cover.[e]

The Table

37:10–16pp — Ex 25:23–29

10They[e] made the table[f] of acacia
wood—two cubits long, a cubit wide, and
a cubit and a half high.[f] 11Then they
overlaid it with pure gold[g] and made a
gold molding around it. 12They also made
around it a rim a handbreadth[g] wide and
put a gold molding on the rim. 13They
cast four gold rings for the table and fastened them to the four corners, where
the four legs were. 14The rings[h] were put
close to the rim to hold the poles used in
carrying the table. 15The poles for carrying the table were made of acacia wood
and were overlaid with gold. 16And they
made from pure gold the articles for the
table—its plates and dishes and bowls
and its pitchers for the pouring out of
drink offerings.

The Lampstand

37:17–24pp — Ex 25:31–39

17They made the lampstand[i] of pure
gold and hammered it out, base and shaft;
its flowerlike cups, buds and blossoms
were of one piece with it. 18Six branches
extended from the sides of the lampstand—three on one side and three on
the other. 19Three cups shaped like almond flowers with buds and blossoms
were on one branch, three on the next
branch and the same for all six branches
extending from the lampstand. 20And on
the lampstand were four cups shaped like
almond flowers with buds and blossoms.
21One bud was under the first pair of
branches extending from the lampstand,
a second bud under the second pair, and
a third bud under the third pair—six
branches in all. 22The buds and the
branches were all of one piece with the
lampstand, hammered out of pure gold.[j]

23They made its seven lamps,[k] as well
as its wick trimmers and trays, of pure
gold. 24They made the lampstand and all

36:35 [w]Ex
36:37 [x]Ex 27:16
37:1 [y]S Ex 31:2 [z]Ex 30:6; 39:35; Dt 10:3
37:2 [a]ver 11,26
37:6 [b]S Ex 26:34; S 31:7; Heb 9:5
37:7 [c]Eze 41:18
37:9 [d]Heb 9:5 [e]Dt 10:3
37:10 [f]Heb 9:2
37:11 [g]S ver 2
37:14 [h]ver 27
37:17 [i]Heb 9:2; Rev 1:12
37:22 [j]ver 17; Nu 8:4
37:23 [k]Ex 40:4,25

[c]*1* That is, about 3 3/4 feet (about 1.1 meters) long and 2 1/4 feet (about 0.7 meter) wide and high
[d]*6* That is, about 3 3/4 feet (about 1.1 meters) long and 2 1/4 feet (about 0.7 meter) wide
[e]*10* Or *He;* also in verses 11-29
[f]*10* That is, about 3 feet (about 0.9 meter) long, 1 1/2 feet (about 0.5 meter) wide, and 2 1/4 feet (about 0.7 meter) high
[g]*12* That is, about 3 inches (about 8 centimeters)

its accessories from one talent[h] of pure
gold.

The Altar of Incense

37:25–28pp — Ex 30:1–5

25They made the altar of incense[l] out
of acacia wood. It was square, a cubit long
and a cubit wide, and two cubits high[i]
—its horns[m] of one piece with it. 26They
overlaid the top and all the sides and the
horns with pure gold, and made a gold
molding around it. 27They made two gold
rings[n] below the molding—two on opposite sides—to hold the poles used to carry
it. 28They made the poles of acacia wood
and overlaid them with gold.[o]
29They also made the sacred anointing
oil[p] and the pure, fragrant incense[q]—
the work of a perfumer.

Chapter 38

The Altar of Burnt Offering

38:1–7pp — Ex 27:1–8

THEY[j] built the altar of burnt offering
of acacia wood, three cubits[k] high; it
was square, five cubits long and five cubits wide.[l] 2They made a horn at each of
the four corners, so that the horns and
the altar were of one piece, and they
overlaid the altar with bronze.[r] 3They
made all its utensils[s] of bronze—its pots,
shovels, sprinkling bowls, meat forks and
firepans. 4They made a grating for the altar, a bronze network, to be under its
ledge, halfway up the altar. 5They cast
bronze rings to hold the poles for the four
corners of the bronze grating. 6They
made the poles of acacia wood and overlaid them with bronze. 7They inserted
the poles into the rings so they would be
on the sides of the altar for carrying it.
They made it hollow, out of boards.

Basin for Washing

8They made the bronze basin[t] and its
bronze stand from the mirrors of the
women[u] who served at the entrance to
the Tent of Meeting.

The Courtyard

38:9–20pp — Ex 27:9–19

9Next they made the courtyard. The
south side was a hundred cubits[m] long
and had curtains of finely twisted linen,
10with twenty posts and twenty bronze
bases, and with silver hooks and bands on
the posts. 11The north side was also a
hundred cubits long and had twenty posts
and twenty bronze bases, with silver
hooks and bands on the posts.
12The west end was fifty cubits[n] wide
and had curtains, with ten posts and ten
bases, with silver hooks and bands on the
posts. 13The east end, toward the sunrise,
was also fifty cubits wide. 14Curtains fifteen cubits[o] long were on one side of the
entrance, with three posts and three bases, 15and curtains fifteen cubits long were
on the other side of the entrance to the
courtyard, with three posts and three bases. 16All the curtains around the courtyard were of finely twisted linen. 17The
bases for the posts were bronze. The
hooks and bands on the posts were silver,
and their tops were overlaid with silver;
so all the posts of the courtyard had silver
bands.
18The curtain for the entrance to the
courtyard was of blue, purple and scarlet
yarn and finely twisted linen—the work
of an embroiderer. It was twenty cubits[p]
long and, like the curtains of the courtyard, five cubits[q] high, 19with four posts
and four bronze bases. Their hooks and
bands were silver, and their tops were
overlaid with silver. 20All the tent pegs[v]
of the tabernacle and of the surrounding
courtyard were bronze.

The Materials Used

21These are the amounts of the materials used for the tabernacle, the tabernacle
of the Testimony,[w] which were recorded
at Moses' command by the Levites under
the direction of Ithamar[x] son of Aaron,
the priest. 22(Bezalel[y] son of Uri, the son
of Hur, of the tribe of Judah, made everything the LORD commanded Moses;
23with him was Oholiab[z] son of Ahisamach, of the tribe of Dan—a craftsman
and designer, and an embroiderer in
blue, purple and scarlet yarn and fine lin-
en.) 24The total amount of the gold from
the wave offering used for all the work on
the sanctuary[a] was 29 talents and 730
shekels,[r] according to the sanctuary
shekel.[b]
25The silver obtained from those of the
community who were counted in the
census[c] was 100 talents and 1,775 shekels,[s] according to the sanctuary shekel—
26one beka per person,[d] that is, half a
shekel,[t] according to the sanctuary shekel,[e] from everyone who had crossed over

37:25 [l]Ex 30:34-36; Lk 1:11; Heb 9:4; Rev 8:3 [m]S Ex 27:2; Rev 9:13
37:27 [n]ver 14
37:28 [o]S Ex 25:13
37:29 [p]S Ex 31:11 [q]Ex 30:1,25; 39:38
38:2 [r]2Ch 1:5
38:3 [s]S Ex 31:9
38:8 [t]S Ex 30:18; S 40:7 [u]Dt 23:17; 1Sa 2:22; 1Ki 14:24
38:20 [v]S Ex 35:18
38:21 [w]Nu 1:50, 53; 8:24; 9:15; 10:11; 17:7; 1Ch 23:32; 2Ch 24:6; Ac 7:44; Rev 15:5 [x]Nu 4:28, 33
38:22 [y]S Ex 31:2
38:23 [z]S Ex 31:6
38:24 [a]S Ex 30:16 [b]S Ex 30:13
38:25 [c]S Ex 30:12
38:26 [d]S Ex 30:12 [e]S Ex 30:13

[h]*24* That is, about 75 pounds (about 34 kilograms)
[i]*25* That is, about 1 1/2 feet (about 0.5 meter) long and wide, and about 3 feet (about 0.9 meter) high
[j]*1* Or *He*; also in verses 2-9
[k]*1* That is, about 4 1/2 feet (about 1.3 meters)
[l]*1* That is, about 7 1/2 feet (about 2.3 meters) long and wide
[m]*9* That is, about 150 feet (about 46 meters)
[n]*12* That is, about 75 feet (about 23 meters)
[o]*14* That is, about 22 1/2 feet (about 6.9 meters)
[p]*18* That is, about 30 feet (about 9 meters)
[q]*18* That is, about 7 1/2 feet (about 2.3 meters)
[r]*24* The weight of the gold was a little over one ton (about 1 metric ton).
[s]*25* The weight of the silver was a little over 3 3/4 tons (about 3.4 metric tons).
[t]*26* That is, about 1/5 ounce (about 5.5 grams)

to those counted, twenty years old or
more,[f] a total of 603,550 men.[g] 27 The
100 talents[u] of silver were used to cast
the bases[h] for the sanctuary and for the
curtain—100 bases from the 100 talents,
one talent for each base. 28 They used the
1,775 shekels[v] to make the hooks for the
posts, to overlay the tops of the posts, and
to make their bands.
29 The bronze from the wave offering
was 70 talents and 2,400 shekels.[w]
30 They used it to make the bases for the
entrance to the Tent of Meeting, the
bronze altar with its bronze grating and
all its utensils, 31 the bases for the surrounding courtyard and those for its entrance and all the tent pegs for the tabernacle and those for the surrounding
courtyard.

Chapter 39

The Priestly Garments

FROM the blue, purple and scarlet
yarn[i] they made woven garments for
ministering in the sanctuary.[j] They also
made sacred garments[k] for Aaron, as the
LORD commanded Moses.

The Ephod

39:2–7pp — Ex 28:6–14

2 They[x] made the ephod of gold, and of
blue, purple and scarlet yarn, and of finely twisted linen. 3 They hammered out
thin sheets of gold and cut strands to be
worked into the blue, purple and scarlet
yarn and fine linen—the work of a skilled
craftsman. 4 They made shoulder pieces
for the ephod, which were attached to
two of its corners, so it could be fastened.
5 Its skillfully woven waistband was like
it—of one piece with the ephod and
made with gold, and with blue, purple
and scarlet yarn, and with finely twisted
linen, as the LORD commanded Moses.
6 They mounted the onyx stones in gold
filigree settings and engraved them like a
seal with the names of the sons of Israel.
7 Then they fastened them on the shoulder pieces of the ephod as memorial[l]
stones for the sons of Israel, as the LORD
commanded Moses.

The Breastpiece

39:8–21pp — Ex 28:15–28

8 They fashioned the breastpiece[m]—
the work of a skilled craftsman. They
made it like the ephod: of gold, and of
blue, purple and scarlet yarn, and of finely twisted linen. 9 It was square—a span[y]
long and a span wide—and folded double. 10 Then they mounted four rows of
precious stones on it. In the first row
there was a ruby, a topaz and a beryl; 11 in
the second row a turquoise, a sapphire[z]
and an emerald; 12 in the third row a jacinth, an agate and an amethyst; 13 in the
fourth row a chrysolite, an onyx and a
jasper.[a] They were mounted in gold filigree settings. 14 There were twelve
stones, one for each of the names of the
sons of Israel, each engraved like a seal
with the name of one of the twelve
tribes.[n]
15 For the breastpiece they made braided chains of pure gold, like a rope. 16 They
made two gold filigree settings and two
gold rings, and fastened the rings to two
of the corners of the breastpiece. 17 They
fastened the two gold chains to the rings
at the corners of the breastpiece, 18 and
the other ends of the chains to the two
settings, attaching them to the shoulder
pieces of the ephod at the front. 19 They
made two gold rings and attached them to
the other two corners of the breastpiece
on the inside edge next to the ephod.
20 Then they made two more gold rings
and attached them to the bottom of the
shoulder pieces on the front of the ephod,
close to the seam just above the waistband of the ephod. 21 They tied the rings
of the breastpiece to the rings of the
ephod with blue cord, connecting it to
the waistband so that the breastpiece
would not swing out from the ephod—as
the LORD commanded Moses.

Other Priestly Garments

39:22–31pp — Ex 28:31–43

22 They made the robe of the ephod entirely of blue cloth—the work of a weaver— 23 with an opening in the center of
the robe like the opening of a collar,[b] and
a band around this opening, so that it
would not tear. 24 They made pomegranates of blue, purple and scarlet yarn and
finely twisted linen around the hem of
the robe. 25 And they made bells of pure
gold and attached them around the hem
between the pomegranates. 26 The bells
and pomegranates alternated around the
hem of the robe to be worn for ministering, as the LORD commanded Moses.
27 For Aaron and his sons, they made
tunics of fine linen[o]—the work of a
weaver— 28 and the turban[p] of fine lin-
en, the linen headbands and the undergarments of finely twisted linen. 29 The
sash was of finely twisted linen and blue,

38:26 [f] S Ex 30:14 [g] S Ex 12:37
38:27 [h] S Ex 26:19
39:1 [i] Ex 35:23 [j] Ex 35:19 [k] ver 41; Ex 28:2
39:7 [l] Lev 24:7; Jos 4:7
39:8 [m] Lev 8:8
39:14 [n] Rev 21:12
39:27 [o] Lev 6:10; 8:2
39:28 [p] ver 31; S Ex 28:4; Lev 8:9; Isa 61:10

[u] *27* That is, about 3 3/4 tons (about 3.4 metric tons)
[v] *28* That is, about 45 pounds (about 20 kilograms)
[w] *29* The weight of the bronze was about 2 1/2 tons (about 2.4 metric tons).
[x] *2* Or *He*; also in verses 7, 8 and 22
[y] *9* That is, about 9 inches (about 22 centimeters)
[z] *11* Or *lapis lazuli*
[a] *13* The precise identification of some of these precious stones is uncertain.
[b] *23* The meaning of the Hebrew for this word is uncertain.

purple and scarlet yarn—the work of an embroiderer—as the LORD commanded Moses.

30 They made the plate, the sacred diadem, out of pure gold and engraved on it, like an inscription on a seal: HOLY TO THE LORD.[q] 31 Then they fastened a blue cord to it to attach it to the turban,[r] as the LORD commanded Moses.

Moses Inspects the Tabernacle

39:32–41pp — Ex 35:10–19

32 So all the work on the tabernacle, the Tent of Meeting, was completed. The Israelites did everything just as the LORD commanded Moses.[s] 33 Then they brought the tabernacle[t] to Moses: the tent and all its furnishings, its clasps, frames, crossbars, posts and bases; 34 the covering of ram skins dyed red, the covering of hides of sea cows[c] and the shielding curtain; 35 the ark of the Testimony[u] with its poles and the atonement cover; 36 the table[v] with all its articles and the bread of the Presence;[w] 37 the pure gold lampstand[x] with its row of lamps and all its accessories,[y] and the oil[z] for the light; 38 the gold altar,[a] the anointing oil,[b] the fragrant incense,[c] and the curtain[d] for the entrance to the tent; 39 the bronze altar[e] with its bronze grating, its poles and all its utensils; the basin[f] with its stand; 40 the curtains of the courtyard with its posts and bases, and the curtain for the entrance to the courtyard;[g] the ropes and tent pegs for the courtyard; all the furnishings for the tabernacle, the Tent of Meeting; 41 and the woven garments[h] worn for ministering in the sanctuary, both the sacred garments for Aaron the priest and the garments for his sons when serving as priests.

42 The Israelites had done all the work just as the LORD had commanded Moses.[i] 43 Moses inspected the work and saw that they had done it just as the LORD had commanded.[j] So Moses blessed[k] them.

Chapter 40

Setting Up the Tabernacle

THEN the LORD said to Moses: 2 "Set up[l] the tabernacle, the Tent of Meeting,[m] on the first day of the first month.[n] 3 Place the ark[o] of the Testimony in it and shield the ark with the curtain. 4 Bring in the table[p] and set out what belongs on it.[q] Then bring in the lampstand[r] and set up its lamps. 5 Place the gold altar[s] of incense in front of the ark of the Testimony and put the curtain at the entrance to the tabernacle.

6 "Place the altar[t] of burnt offering in front of the entrance to the tabernacle, the Tent of Meeting; 7 place the basin[u] between the Tent of Meeting and the altar and put water in it. 8 Set up the courtyard[v] around it and put the curtain at the entrance to the courtyard.

9 "Take the anointing oil and anoint[w] the tabernacle and everything in it; consecrate it and all its furnishings,[x] and it will be holy. 10 Then anoint the altar of burnt offering and all its utensils; consecrate[y] the altar, and it will be most holy. 11 Anoint the basin and its stand and consecrate them.

12 "Bring Aaron and his sons to the entrance to the Tent of Meeting[z] and wash them with water.[a] 13 Then dress Aaron in the sacred garments,[b] anoint him and consecrate[c] him so he may serve me as priest. 14 Bring his sons and dress them in tunics.[d] 15 Anoint them just as you anointed their father, so they may serve me as priests. Their anointing will be to a priesthood that will continue for all generations to come.[e]" 16 Moses did everything just as the LORD commanded[f] him.

17 So the tabernacle[g] was set up on the first day of the first month[h] in the second year. 18 When Moses[i] set up the tabernacle, he put the bases in place, erected the frames,[j] inserted the crossbars and set up the posts. 19 Then he spread the tent over the tabernacle and put the covering[k] over the tent, as the LORD commanded[l] him.

20 He took the Testimony[m] and placed it in the ark,[n] attached the poles to the ark and put the atonement cover[o] over it. 21 Then he brought the ark into the tabernacle and hung the shielding curtain[p] and shielded the ark of the Testimony, as the LORD commanded[q] him.

22 Moses placed the table[r] in the Tent of Meeting on the north side of the tabernacle outside the curtain 23 and set out the bread[s] on it before the LORD, as the LORD commanded[t] him.

24 He placed the lampstand[u] in the Tent of Meeting opposite the table on the south side of the tabernacle 25 and set up the lamps[v] before the LORD, as the LORD commanded[w] him.

26 Moses placed the gold altar[x] in the Tent of Meeting in front of the curtain 27 and burned fragrant incense on it, as

[c] *34* That is, dugongs

39:30 [q]Isa 23:18; Zec 14:20
39:31 [r]S ver 28
39:32 [s]S Ex 25:9
39:33 [t]Ex 25:8-40; 36:8-38
39:35 [u]S Ex 37:1
39:36 [v]Ex 25:23-30; 37:10-16 [w]S Ex 25:30
39:37 [x]S Ex 25:31 [y]Ex 25:31-39 [z]S Ex 25:6
39:38 [a]Ex 30:1-10 [b]Ex 30:22-32; 37:29 [c]Ex 30:34-38; S 37:29 [d]S Ex 36:35
39:39 [e]Ex 27:1-8; 38:1-7 [f]S Ex 30:18
39:40 [g]Ex 27:9-19; 38:9-20
39:41 [h]S ver 1
39:42 [i]S Ex 25:9
39:43 [j]S Ex 25:9; S 35:10 [k]Ge 31:55; Lev 9:22,23; Nu 6:23-27; Dt 21:5; 26:15; 2Sa 6:18; 1Ki 8:14, 55; 1Ch 16:2; 2Ch 30:27
40:2 [l]S Ex 26:30 [m]ver 34,35; Lev 1:1; 3:2; 6:26; 9:23; 16:16; Nu 1:1; 7:89; 11:16; 17:4; 20:6; Jos 18:1; 19:51; Jer 7:12 [n]ver 17; S Ex 12:2; Nu 9:1
40:3 [o]S Ex 26:33
40:4 [p]S Ex 25:23 [q]S Ex 25:30 [r]S Ex 25:31
40:5 [s]S Ex 30:1
40:6 [t]S Ex 27:1; 2Ki 16:14; 2Ch 4:1
40:7 [u]Ex 30:18
40:8 [v]S Ex 27:9
40:9 [w]S Ex 30:26 [x]Nu 7:1
40:10 [y]S Ex 29:36
40:12 [z]Nu 8:9 [a]S Ex 29:4; S 30:19
40:13 [b]S Ex 28:41 [c]Lev 8:12
40:14 [d]S Ex 28:40; Lev 10:5
40:15 [e]S Ex 29:9
40:16 [f]S Ge 6:22
40:17 [g]Nu 7:1 [h]S ver 2
40:18 [i]2Ch 1:3 [j]Ex 36:20-34
40:19 [k]Ex 36:19 [l]S Ge 6:22
40:20 [m]S Ex 16:34; Heb 9:4 [n]S Ex 25:21 [o]Ex 25:17-22; S 26:34; S 31:7
40:21 [p]S Ex 26:33 [q]S Ge 6:22
40:22 [r]S Ex 25:23
40:23 [s]S Ex 25:30; Lev 24:5-8 [t]S Ge 6:22
40:24 [u]S Ex 25:31
40:25 [v]S Ex 37:23 [w]S Ge 6:22
40:26 [x]S Ex 30:1

40:9–16 GOD, Holy—God required that the tabernacle, all its furnishings, and Aaron and his sons be ceremonially consecrated and declared holy to the service of the Lord. The profane could not be used in worshiping God. The holy things shared in the holiness which was derived from the holiness of God. See notes on 3:5–6; 19:10–24.

the LORD commanded[y] him. 28 Then he
put up the curtain[z] at the entrance to the
tabernacle.

29 He set the altar[a] of burnt offering
near the entrance to the tabernacle, the
Tent of Meeting, and offered on it burnt
offerings and grain offerings,[b] as the
LORD commanded[c] him.

30 He placed the basin[d] between the
Tent of Meeting and the altar and put water in it for washing, 31 and Moses and
Aaron and his sons used it to wash[e] their
hands and feet. 32 They washed whenever
they entered the Tent of Meeting or approached the altar,[f] as the LORD commanded[g] Moses.

33 Then Moses set up the courtyard[h]
around the tabernacle and altar and put
up the curtain[i] at the entrance to the
courtyard. And so Moses finished the
work.

The Glory of the LORD

34 Then the cloud[j] covered the Tent of
Meeting, and the glory[k] of the LORD
filled the tabernacle. 35 Moses could not
enter the Tent of Meeting because the
cloud had settled upon it, and the glory[l]
of the LORD filled the tabernacle.[m]

36 In all the travels of the Israelites,
whenever the cloud lifted from above the
tabernacle, they would set out;[n] 37 but if
the cloud did not lift, they did not set
out—until the day it lifted. 38 So the
cloud[o] of the LORD was over the tabernacle by day, and fire was in the cloud by
night, in the sight of all the house of
Israel during all their travels.

40:27 [y]S Ge 6:22
40:28 [z]S Ex 26:36
40:29 [a]S Ex 20:24 [b]Ex 29:38-42 [c]S Ge 6:22
40:30 [d]S ver 7; S Ex 30:18
40:31 [e]Ex 30:19-21
40:32 [f]Ex 30:20 [g]S Ge 6:22
40:33 [h]S Ex 27:9; 38:9-20 [i]Ex 27:16
40:34 [j]Ex 19:16; Lev 16:2; Nu 9:15-23; 1Ki 8:12; 2Ch 5:13; Isa 6:4; Eze 10:4 [k]S Ex 16:7; Jn 1:14; 12:41; Rev 15:8
40:35 [l]S Ex 16:10 [m]1Ki 8:11; 2Ch 5:13-14; 7:2
40:36 [n]Nu 9:17-23; 10:13
40:38 [o]S Ex 13:21; 1Co 10:1

40:34–38 GOD, Glory—After the tabernacle had been duly consecrated to the Lord, His glory filled it in the form of a cloud that was visible both night and day. God gave a visible perception of His presence with them throughout their journeys. In the New Testament God gave His people an inner assurance of His presence with them in the form of the Holy Spirit. God is glorified when His people perceive His presence and greatness.

40:34–38 REVELATION, Events—God gave the children of Israel a cloud and fire to indicate His wishes (13:21). They could watch carefully for the revelation of God's will as the cloud and pillar signaled them to move on or wait. The Tent of Meeting was a specific place to which they could come to see that God was with them (33:7–11). God's presence confirmed His acceptance of the Tabernacle and His willingness to live with His people there. The overwhelming Presence appeared in all His glory so even Moses could not approach. Compare 33:20.

Leviticus

Theological Setting

How can sinful people know God and enter into the presence of the holy One? The people of Israel lived in a sinful world. They knew themselves to be a people tainted by sin and removed from the presence of God. How could they reenter God's presence?

Israel sought to respond in faith to God. They desired to live in proper relationship to God's covenant. Leviticus helped define the way in which sinful people might relate to the holy God. Leviticus gives this definition in the overall framework of Israel's history with God.

The larger biblical canon gives Leviticus its greatest meaning. Leviticus forms the centerpiece of the Pentateuch, the first five books of the Old Testament. In the background stand God's perfect creation and human rebellion (Ge 1—11); God's process of redemption and election and the human mission to bring blessing to the whole earth (Ge 12—50); God's demonstration of His lordship over nature and over the Egyptian gods and His covenant guidelines for His people (Ex 1—33); and God's provision for a place of worship and renewal (Ex 34—40).

The theological background of Genesis and Exodus raised new questions for God's people. They knew this God was different from the "gods" of other nations. They knew He had provided a place for their worship and guidelines for their lives of service to Him, but they also knew they did not live up to God's expectations. They were sinners. How did they deal with their sin? Since they had only one God, they had to depend on Him for leadership and blessing in all areas of life—military, agriculture, health, politics. How did they gain His favor in each of these areas? What type of worship was appropriate response to His leadership? Were prostitution and sexual immorality proper forms of worship for Yahweh as they were for the gods of their neighbors? Should they sacrifice their childen as did some of their neighbors? What is proper worship for a sinful people in the presence of the unique God of Israel?

In Leviticus, God encouraged the people to center their lives around His presence. He showed them how to respond to the divine presence in the tabernacle in the midst of their camp. He gave instructions for living and for worship in order that His people might experience His continued presence in the community.

Modern day readers may look upon the book of Leviticus as ancient ritual devoid of relevance. Actually, the book provided answers to many of the difficult theological problems of its day. Leviticus continues to point the modern reader to God's answer to the problem of sin.

Theological Outline

Leviticus: Directions for Knowing God

I. Offer Yourself in Praise and Adoration to God. (1:1—7:38)
   A. Offer pleasing sacrifices. (1:1—6:7)
      1. Offer burnt offerings. (1:1-17)
      2. Offer cereal offerings. (2:1-16)
      3. Offer peace offerings. (3:1-17)
      4. Offer sin offerings. (4:1-35)
      5. Offer guilt offerings. (5:1—6:7)
   B. Give instructions to the priests who offer pleasing sacrifices. (6:8—7:38)
      1. Give priestly instructions for burnt offerings. (6:8-13)
      2. Give priestly instructions for cereal offerings. (6:14-23)
      3. Give priestly instructions for sin offerings. (6:24-30)
      4. Give priestly instructions for guilt offerings. (7:1-10)
      5. Give priestly instructions for peace offerings. (7:11-38)

II. Consecrate Priests to Mediate Between God and Man. (8:1—10:20)
   A. Set apart priests who mediate. (8:1-36)

B. Sacrifice for the priests who mediate. (9:1-24)
C. Warn the priests who mediate. (10:1-20)

III. Purify Yourself Before God. (11:1—16:34)
A. Eat clean animals; reject unclean animals. (11:1-47)
B. Purify mother and child after childbirth. (12:1-8)
1. Purify the mother of a male infant. (12:1-4)
2. Purify the mother of a female infant. (12:5)
3. Worship the Lord who gives life. (12:6-8)
C. Test for an infectious skin disease and remove the infected one from the camp. (13:1-59)
1. Examine the inhabitant who appears with an infection. (13:1-8)
2. Examine the infected inhabitant for progress toward wholeness. (13:9-17)
3. Examine the inhabitant who appears with a boil. (13:18-23)
4. Examine the inhabitant who appears with a burn. (13:24-28)
5. Examine the inhabitant who appears with an infection on the head or beard. (13:29-37)
6. Examine the inhabitant who appears with bright spots on the skin. (13:38-39)
7. Examine the inhabitant who appears with hair loss. (13:40-44)
8. Remove the infection from the camp. (13:45-59)
D. Restore the cleansed inhabitant to the community. (14:1-32)
E. Remove the threat of infection from the house. (14:33-57)
F. Cleanse unhealthiness within the community. (15:1-33)
G. Make atonement for the community. (16:1-34)
1. Remove sin from the congregation. (16:1-10, 20-22)
2. Atone for the sins of the mediators. (16:11-14)
3. Atone for the sins of the people, and make purification for the tent and its articles. (16:15-19,23-28)
4. Deal with the sin problem yearly. (16:29-34)

IV. Present Yourself in Holiness Before God. (17:1—26:46)
A. Give attention to acceptable slaughter of beasts. (17:1-16)
1. Make proper sacrifices before the Lord. (17:1-9)
2. Sanctify life by refusing to eat blood. (17:10-16)
B. Follow the commandments of the Lord. (18:1—20:27)
1. Reject abominable sexual practices. (18:1-23; 20:10-21)
2. Warn concerning the danger of abominable practices. (18:24-30)
3. Reverence God in worship. (19:1-8)
4. Show love for your neighbor by righteous living. (19:9-18)
5. Observe proper practices in agriculture, slavery, sacrifices, and the body. (19:19-29)
6. Honor God through worship. (19:30-31)
7. Honor God through life. (19:32-37)
8. Worship God alone; forsake other gods. (20:1-8)
9. Honor father and mother. (20:9)
10. Give diligence to obeying God. (20:22-27)
C. Charge mediators to follow regulations which allow presence before God. (21:1—24:23)
1. Present themselves holy before God. (21:1-24)
2. Present holy gifts to God. (22:1-33)
3. Lead worship at holy times. (23:1-44)
4. Prepare the holy place. (24:1-9)
5. Keep the congregation holy before God. (24:10-23)
D. Present both land and people holy before God. (25:1-55)
1. Observe the sabbath year. (25:1-7)
2. Observe the jubilee year. (25:8-22)
3. Care for the poor brother and his land. (25:23-55)
E. Remember the blessings and curses concerning the covenant people. (26:1-46)
1. Remember the blessings associated with holy living. (26:1-13)
2. Remember the penalties associated with disobedience. (26:14-39)
3. *Remember the faithfulness* of God. (26:40-46)

V. Offer Proper Vows Before God. (27:1-34)
A. Offer proper vows related to people. (27:1-13)

B. Offer proper vows related to a house. (27:14-15)
C. Offer proper vows related to fields. (27:16-25)
D. Offer proper vows related to firstborn animals. (27:26-27)
E. Keep your vows. (27:28-34)

Theological Conclusions

The Book of Leviticus reveals the holy God and allows humans to know Him and to enter into His presence. The Book of Leviticus offers these theological teachings:

1. the grace of God,
2. the importance of preparation for meeting God,
3. the presence of God,
4. the necessity of righteous living.

God's grace fills the Book of Leviticus. Israel's existence depended on God's acts in history. God chose a group of slaves on whom to bestow His love. God's love and initiative created Israel and delivered the people from Egypt. Leviticus contains the requirements of the covenant which God made with Israel at Sinai. Because God wanted to be known, He gave directions for the people in the wilderness and for the day they would inhabit Palestine. In His grace He showed Israel how to approach His presence.

People who stand before God must prepare themselves for such a sacred event. The Book of Leviticus reminds worshipers of the holiness of God and of the necessity for cleansed lives. The emphasis in Leviticus on purity, holiness, and cleansing indicates the importance of preparation for worship. Standing before God is not a mundane ritualistic event; it is the greatest opportunity for a human being. Entering into the presence of the holy One requires proper preparation of life.

God appeared to the people at Sinai, making the covenant and directing the people to live holy lives. Leviticus strongly indicates that God wanted to dwell among His people and to be known by them. The sacrificial system allowed ways for sinful people to approach the holy God. As the people of Israel offered sacrifices, they indicated their desire to know God. God accepted the sacrifices and offerings. These sacrifices removed the barriers between God and His people.

The various laws in the Book of Leviticus indicate God's desire for righteous living. People who appear before Him must cleanse their lives and actions. Some people think of Leviticus only as a book of ritual, but the book also calls for ethical living. When Jesus spoke of the second great commandment to love your neighbor as yourself, He quoted from Leviticus (19:18). Leviticus shows God's concern for the poor and helpless of society.

Leviticus teaches the importance of worship. Worship calls for people's best and highest. Lives prepared by confession of sin, by reconciliation with neighbors, and by gratitude before God will be rewarded with the opportunity to know God and to dwell in His presence.

Contemporary Teaching

The Book of Leviticus reminds us of the eternal realities of life—the presence of God and our need to know Him. The book teaches that people may enter into His presence and serve Him.

1. God asks human beings to walk humbly with Him. Obedience to God must be a primary concern in our lives. Leviticus 1—16 may be summarized by the words of Jesus: "Love the Lord your God" (Mk 12:30).
2. Relationship to God involves right living with others. Leviticus 17—27 points toward correct behavior toward others. These chapters could be summarized by Leviticus 19:18: "Love your neighbor as yourself."
3. God pursues the sinner, seeking to forgive and to restore the rebellious one to fellowship. The Old Testament, as well as the New Testament, stands on the grace of God. He cares for His people. God desires forgiveness for them and fellowship with them.
4. God loves His people so deeply that He is willing to do His costly work (sacrifice). The costliness of sacrifice emphasizes the importance of forgiveness and the depth of God's love.
5. *Contemporary* worshipers must approach God with the same reverence and purity as those in the wilderness. Rituals and sacrifices have *been removed*, but the need for preparation and purity remain.
6. Jesus completely fulfilled the sacrificial system. In Jesus, God worked His perfect work of bringing His people unto Him. Jesus is the once and for all sacrifice for all sin. In Him we experience forgiveness and wholeness and understand the great opportunity to stand humbly but joyfully and boldly before the holy God.

Chapter 1

The Burnt Offering

THE LORD called to Moses[a] and spoke to him from the Tent of Meeting.[b] He said, 2"Speak to the Israelites and say to them: 'When any of you brings an offering to the LORD,[c] bring as your offering an animal from either the herd or the flock.[d]

3" 'If the offering is a burnt offering[e] from the herd,[f] he is to offer a male without defect.[g] He must present it at the entrance to the Tent[h] of Meeting so that it[a] will be acceptable[i] to the LORD. 4He is to lay his hand on the head[j] of the burnt offering,[k] and it will be accepted[l] on his behalf to make atonement[m] for him. 5He is to slaughter[n] the young bull[o] before the LORD, and then Aaron's sons[p] the priests shall bring the blood and sprinkle it against the altar on all sides[q] at the entrance to the Tent of Meeting. 6He is to skin[r] the burnt offering and cut it into pieces.[s] 7The sons of Aaron the priest are to put fire on the altar and arrange wood[t] on the fire. 8Then Aaron's sons the priests shall arrange the pieces, including the head and the fat,[u] on the burning wood[v] that is on the altar. 9He is to wash the inner parts and the legs with water,[w] and the priest is to burn all of it[x] on the altar.[y] It is a burnt offering,[z] an offering made by fire,[a] an aroma pleasing to the LORD.[b]

10" 'If the offering is a burnt offering from the flock, from either the sheep[c] or the goats,[d] he is to offer a male without defect. 11He is to slaughter it at the north side of the altar[e] before the LORD, and Aaron's sons the priests shall sprinkle its blood against the altar on all sides.[f] 12He is to cut it into pieces, and the priest shall arrange them, including the head and the fat,[g] on the burning wood that is on the altar. 13He is to wash the inner parts and the legs with water,[h] and the priest is to bring all of it and burn it[i] on the altar.[j] It is a burnt offering,[k] an offering made by fire, an aroma pleasing to the LORD.

14" 'If the offering to the LORD is a burnt offering of birds, he is to offer a dove or a young pigeon.[l] 15The priest shall bring it to the altar, wring off the head[m] and burn it on the altar; its blood shall be drained out on the side of the altar.[n] 16He is to remove the crop with its contents[b] and throw it to the east side of the altar, where the ashes[o] are. 17He shall tear it open by the wings, not severing it completely,[p] and then the priest shall burn it on the wood[q] that is on the fire on the altar. It is a burnt offering, an offering made by fire, an aroma pleasing to the LORD.

Chapter 2

The Grain Offering

" 'WHEN someone brings a grain offering[r] to the LORD, his offering is to be of fine flour.[s] He is to pour oil[t] on it,[u] put incense on it[v] 2and take

1:1 [a]S Ex 3:4; S 25:22 [b]S Ex 27:21; S 40:2 **1:2** [c]Lev 7:16,38; 22:21; 23:38; 27:9 [d]Lev 22:18-19; Nu 15:3 **1:3** [e]S Ge 8:20 [f]ver 10; Lev 22:27; Ezr 8:35; Mal 1:8 [g]S ver 5; S Ex 12:5; S Lev 22:19,20; Heb 9:14; 1Pe 1:19 [h]Lev 6:25; 17:9; Nu 6:16; Dt 12:5-6, 11 [i]Isa 58:5 **1:4** [j]S Ex 29:10,15 [k]ver 3; Lev 4:29; 6:25; Eze 45:15 [l]S Ge 32:20 [m]S Ex 29:36; S 32:30 **1:5** [n]Ex 29:11; Lev 3:2,8 [o]S ver 3; Ex 29:1; Nu 15:8; Dt 18:3; Ps 50:9; 69:31 [p]Lev 8:2; 10:6; 21:1 [q]S Ex 29:20; Heb 12:24; 1Pe 1:2 **1:6** [r]Lev 7:8 [s]Ex 29:17 **1:7** [t]ver 17; S Ge 22:9; Lev 3:5; 6:12 **1:8** [u]ver 12; S Ex 29:13; Lev 8:20 [v]Lev 9:13 **1:9** [w]S Ex 29:17 [x]Lev 6:22 [y]ver 13; Ex 29:18; Lev 9:14 [z]ver 3 [a]Lev 23:8, 25,36; Nu 28:6,19 [b]ver 13; Ge 8:21; Lev 2:2; 3:5,16; 17:6; Nu 18:17; 28:11-13; Eph 5:2 **1:10** [c]S Ge 22:7 [d]S ver 3; Ex 12:5; Lev 3:12; 4:23,28; 5:6; Nu 15:11 **1:11** [e]S Ex 29:11 [f]S Ex 29:20 **1:12** [g]S ver 8 **1:13** [h]S Ex 29:17 [i]Lev 6:22 [j]S ver 9 [k]Dt 12:27 **1:14** [l]S Ge 15:9; Lk 2:24

1:15 [m]Lev 5:8 [n]Lev 5:9 **1:16** [o]Lev 4:12; 6:10; Nu 4:13 **1:17** [p]S Ge 15:10 [q]S ver 7 **2:1** [r]S Ex 29:41; Lev 6:14-18 [s]Ex 29:2,40; Lev 5:11 [t]Nu 15:4; 28:5 [u]S Ex 29:2; Lev 7:12 [v]ver 2,15,16; Lev 24:7; Ne 13:9; Isa 43:23

[a]3 Or *he* [b]16 Or *crop and the feathers*; the meaning of the Hebrew for this word is uncertain.

1:1 GOD, Righteous—The Book of Leviticus records laws concerning worship, forgiveness of sin and guilt, and various aspects of daily life. Because the bulk of the material contains so many regulations, it may leave the impression that the religion of Israel was a vast legalistic system. God was not, however, merely imposing upon the people an arbitrary legal system to be slavishly followed. God had a gracious intent. God was seeking to bring a fledgling people to responsible maturity. Seen in this way, there is as much grace as there is law in the Book of Leviticus and the way of life and worship prescribed in it. The legalism which later grew out of the law through pharisaic interpretation was not God's original intent.

1:1 HOLY SCRIPTURE, Writing—God used the Tent of Meeting as the place in which He met Moses to deliver the laws and regulations by which His people were to live. The Book of Leviticus is a collection of these revelations made in speeches from God to Moses (11:1; 12:1; 13:1; 14:1; 15:1). Revelation includes both the personal revelation spoken to Moses and the inspiration to put the laws into written form. See note on Ex 31:18.

1:2 STEWARDSHIP, Sacrifice Giving—Sacrifices to God were an important part of the Old Testament people's giving and worship. God revealed the pattern of giving was pleasing to Him. Persons devoted to the Levitical law sacrificed animals and grain products as a *way to seek God's forgiveness in accordance with His revelation*. The giving spirit intended in these acts continues among Christians but with the recognition that Christ made the eternal atonement sacrifice for us.

1:4 SALVATION, Atonement—The Israelites were to offer an animal to the Lord as a burnt offering to make atonement for their sins. Worshipers laid a hand on the head of the offering, therein identifying themselves with their gift. The meaning of salvation as atonement (Hebrew *kipper*, "cover over") grows out of the Hebrew system of atonement. Its essential meaning is at-one-ment. Persons are by the will of God made at one, accepted or reconciled with God. Their sins are covered over out of God's sight. Thus, the relationship between the worshiper and God is restored, made right.

1:9 PRAYER, Worship—The offerings are discussed in chs 1—7. The burnt offering, the grain offering, and the fellowship offering are voluntary and present "an aroma pleasing to the LORD" (2:2; 3:5), suggesting prayer and dedication. These words are absent in the cases of the sin offering (4:1—5:13) and the guilt offering (5:14—6:7), which are mandatory. See note on Ex 30:1,7. Special stress is laid on the fact that the burnt offering was to be consumed in its entirety, except for the skin (1:6,9,13). Directions for the daily burnt offerings are given in Ex 29:35–42; 38:1–7. Jesus emphasized the prophets' stress on obedience and mercy in preference to sacrifice (1 Sa 15:22; Isa 1:11; Hos 6:6; Mic 6:6–8; Mt 9:13). The imperfection of all Old Testament sacrifice is contrasted with the perfection of Christ's sacrifice in Heb 10:10–14. Through Christ's sacrifice we are free to offer our prayers without need of prior ritual.

2:2 PRAYER, Worship—See note on Ex 30:1,7.

it to Aaron's sons the priests. The priest
shall take a handful of the fine flour[w] and
oil, together with all the incense,[x] and
burn this as a memorial portion[y] on the
altar, an offering made by fire,[z] an aroma
pleasing to the LORD.[a] 3The rest of the
grain offering belongs to Aaron and his
sons;[b] it is a most holy[c] part of the offerings made to the LORD by fire.
4" 'If you bring a grain offering baked
in an oven,[d] it is to consist of fine flour:
cakes made without yeast and mixed
with oil, or[c] wafers[e] made without yeast
and spread with oil.[f] 5If your grain offering is prepared on a griddle,[g] it is to be
made of fine flour mixed with oil, and
without yeast. 6Crumble it and pour oil
on it; it is a grain offering. 7If your grain
offering is cooked in a pan,[h] it is to be
made of fine flour and oil. 8Bring the
grain offering made of these things to the
LORD; present it to the priest, who shall
take it to the altar. 9He shall take out the
memorial portion[i] from the grain offering and burn it on the altar as an offering
made by fire, an aroma pleasing to the
LORD.[j] 10The rest of the grain offering
belongs to Aaron and his sons;[k] it is a
most holy part of the offerings made to
the LORD by fire.[l]
11" 'Every grain offering you bring to
the LORD must be made without yeast,[m]
for you are not to burn any yeast or honey
in an offering made to the LORD by fire.
12You may bring them to the LORD as an
offering of the firstfruits,[n] but they are
not to be offered on the altar as a pleasing
aroma. 13Season all your grain offerings
with salt.[o] Do not leave the salt of the
covenant[p] of your God out of your grain
offerings; add salt to all your offerings.
14" 'If you bring a grain offering of firstfruits[q] to the LORD, offer crushed heads
of new grain roasted in the fire. 15Put oil
and incense[r] on it; it is a grain offering.
16The priest shall burn the memorial portion[s] of the crushed grain and the oil,
together with all the incense,[t] as an offering made to the LORD by fire.[u]

Chapter 3

The Fellowship Offering

" 'IF someone's offering is a fellowship offering,[d][v] and he offers an
animal from the herd, whether male or
female, he is to present before the LORD
an animal without defect.[w] 2He is to lay
his hand on the head[x] of his offering and
slaughter it[y] at the entrance to the Tent
of Meeting.[z] Then Aaron's sons the
priests shall sprinkle[a] the blood against
the altar[b] on all sides.[c] 3From the fellowship offering he is to bring a sacrifice
made to the LORD by fire: all the fat[d] that
covers the inner parts[e] or is connected to
them, 4both kidneys[f] with the fat on
them near the loins, and the covering of
the liver, which he will remove with the
kidneys. 5Then Aaron's sons[g] are to burn
it on the altar[h] on top of the burnt offering[i] that is on the burning wood,[j] as an
offering made by fire, an aroma pleasing
to the LORD.[k]
6" 'If he offers an animal from the flock
as a fellowship offering[l] to the LORD, he
is to offer a male or female without defect. 7If he offers a lamb,[m] he is to present
it before the LORD.[n] 8He is to lay his hand
on the head of his offering and slaughter
it[o] in front of the Tent of Meeting. Then
Aaron's sons shall sprinkle its blood
against the altar on all sides. 9From the
fellowship offering he is to bring a sacrifice[p] made to the LORD by fire: its fat, the
entire fat tail cut off close to the back-
bone, all the fat that covers the inner
parts or is connected to them, 10both kidneys with the fat on them near the loins,
and the covering of the liver, which he
will remove with the kidneys. 11The
priest shall burn them on the altar[q] as
food,[r] an offering made to the LORD by
fire.[s]
12" 'If his offering is a goat,[t] he is to
present it before the LORD. 13He is to lay
his hand on its head and slaughter it in
front of the Tent of Meeting. Then Aaron's sons shall sprinkle[u] its blood against
the altar on all sides.[v] 14From what he
offers he is to make this offering to the
LORD by fire: all the fat that covers the
inner parts or is connected to them,
15both kidneys with the fat on them near
the loins, and the covering of the liver,
which he will remove with the kidneys.[w]
16The priest shall burn them on the altar[x] as food,[y] an offering made by fire, a

[c] *4* Or *and* [d] *1* Traditionally *peace offering*; also in verses 3, 6 and 9

2:2 [w]Lev 5:11 [x]Lev 6:15; Isa 1:13; 65:3; 66:3 [y]ver 9, 16; Lev 5:12; 6:15; 24:7; Nu 5:26; 18:8; Ps 16:5; 73:26; Isa 53:12 [z]ver 16 [a]S Lev 1:9
2:3 [b]ver 10; Lev 6:16; 10:12,13 [c]S Ex 30:36
2:4 [d]Lev 7:9; 26:26 [e]Lev 7:12; 8:26 [f]S Ex 29:2
2:5 [g]Lev 6:21; 7:9; Eze 4:3
2:7 [h]Lev 7:9
2:9 [i]S ver 2 [j]S Ge 8:21
2:10 [k]ver 3 [l]Ezr 2:63
2:11 [m]S Ex 23:18; Lev 6:16
2:12 [n]S Ex 34:22
2:13 [o]Mk 9:49 [p]Nu 18:19; 2Ch 13:5; Eze 43:24
2:14 [q]S Ex 34:22; Nu 15:20; Dt 16:13; 26:2; Ru 3:2
2:15 [r]S ver 1
2:16 [s]S ver 2 [t]S ver 1 [u]Nu 4:16; Jer 14:12
3:1 [v]S ver 6; S Ex 32:6; Lev 7:11-34; S 17:5 [w]S Ex 12:5
3:2 [x]S Ex 29:15; Nu 8:10 [y]S Lev 1:5 [z]S Ex 40:2 [a]S Ex 24:6 [b]Lev 17:6; Nu 18:17 [c]S Ex 29:20
3:3 [d]S Ex 29:13 [e]S Ex 12:9
3:4 [f]ver 10; Ex 29:13; Lev 4:9
3:5 [g]Lev 7:29-34 [h]ver 11,16 [i]Ex 29:13,38-42; Nu 28:3-10 [j]S Lev 1:7 [k]S Lev 1:9
3:6 [l]S ver 1; Lev 22:21; Nu 15:3, 8
3:7 [m]Lev 17:3; Nu 15:5; 28:5,7,8 [n]Lev 17:8-9; 1Ki 8:62
3:8 [o]S Lev 1:5
3:9 [p]Isa 34:6; Jer 46:10; Eze 39:19; Zep 1:7
3:11 [q]S ver 5 [r]ver 16; Lev 21:6, 17; Nu 28:2 [s]Lev 9:18
3:12 [t]S Lev 1:10; S 4:3
3:13 [u]S Ex 24:6 [v]Lev 1:5
3:15 [w]Lev 7:4
3:16 [x]S ver 5; Lev 7:31 [y]S ver 11

2:11 STEWARDSHIP, Sacrifice Giving—Grain offerings, like fellowship offerings, sin offerings, guilt offerings, peace offerings, and burnt offerings involve both giving something of material importance and the desire to be right with God through worship. See note on 1:2.

2:13 THE CHURCH, Covenant People—All of life relates to the commitment we make to God. For Israel, certain regulations were necessary when the people came before God with an offering. These regulations were a part of the covenant, along with other provisions. Putting valuable salt on offerings signified costly sacrifice and commitment to God's covenant as well as freedom from impurity.

3:1 STEWARDSHIP, Sacrifice Giving—See note on 1:2.

3:1–5 PRAYER, Worship—The fellowship offering, like the grain offering, was gratuitous, a voluntary act of worship. It was offered in addition to the burnt offerings and could indicate thanksgiving (7:12). See notes on 1:9; Ex 30:1,7.

pleasing aroma.[z] All the fat[a] is the
LORD's.[b]
17" 'This is a lasting ordinance[c] for the
generations to come,[d] wherever you
live:[e] You must not eat any fat or any
blood.[f]' "

Chapter 4

The Sin Offering

THE LORD said to Moses, 2"Say to the
Israelites: 'When anyone sins unintentionally[g] and does what is forbidden
in any of the LORD's commands[h]—

3" 'If the anointed priest[i] sins,[j] bringing guilt on the people, he must bring to
the LORD a young bull[k] without defect[l]
as a sin offering[m] for the sin he has committed.[n] 4He is to present the bull at the
entrance to the Tent of Meeting before
the LORD.[o] He is to lay his hand on its
head and slaughter it before the LORD.
5Then the anointed priest shall take some
of the bull's blood[p] and carry it into the
Tent of Meeting. 6He is to dip his finger
into the blood and sprinkle[q] some of it
seven times before the LORD,[r] in front of
the curtain of the sanctuary.[s] 7The priest
shall then put some of the blood on the
horns[t] of the altar of fragrant incense
that is before the LORD in the Tent of
Meeting. The rest of the bull's blood he
shall pour out at the base of the altar[u] of
burnt offering[v] at the entrance to the
Tent of Meeting. 8He shall remove all the
fat[w] from the bull of the sin offering—the
fat that covers the inner parts or is connected to them, 9both kidneys with the
fat on them near the loins, and the covering of the liver, which he will remove
with the kidneys[x]— 10just as the fat is
removed from the ox[e][y] sacrificed as a
fellowship offering.[f][z] Then the priest
shall burn them on the altar of burnt offering.[a] 11But the hide of the bull and all
its flesh, as well as the head and legs, the
inner parts and offal[b]— 12that is, all the
rest of the bull—he must take outside the
camp[c] to a place ceremonially clean,[d]
where the ashes[e] are thrown, and burn
it[f] in a wood fire on the ash heap.[g]

13" 'If the whole Israelite community
sins unintentionally[h] and does what is
forbidden in any of the LORD's commands, even though the community is
unaware of the matter, they are guilty.
14When they become aware of the sin
they committed, the assembly must bring
a young bull[i] as a sin offering[j] and
present it before the Tent of Meeting.
15The elders[k] of the community are to lay
their hands[l] on the bull's head[m] before
the LORD, and the bull shall be slaughtered before the LORD.[n] 16Then the
anointed priest is to take some of the
bull's blood[o] into the Tent of Meeting.
17He shall dip his finger into the blood
and sprinkle[p] it before the LORD[q] seven
times in front of the curtain. 18He is to
put some of the blood[r] on the horns of
the altar that is before the LORD[s] in the
Tent of Meeting. The rest of the blood he
shall pour out at the base of the altar[t] of
burnt offering at the entrance to the Tent
of Meeting. 19He shall remove all the fat[u]
from it and burn it on the altar,[v] 20and do
with this bull just as he did with the bull
for the sin offering. In this way the priest
will make atonement[w] for them, and they
will be forgiven.[x] 21Then he shall take
the bull outside the camp[y] and burn it as
he burned the first bull. This is the sin
offering for the community.[z]

22" 'When a leader[a] sins unintentionally[b] and does what is forbidden in any of
the commands of the LORD his God, he is
guilty. 23When he is made aware of the
sin he committed, he must bring as his

3:16 [z]S Lev 1:9 [a]S Ge 4:4 [b]1Sa 2:16 **3:17** [c]S Ex 12:14; S 27:21 [d]S Ge 9:12 [e]S Ex 12:20 [f]Ge 9:4; Lev 7:25-26; 17:10-16; Dt 12:16; Ac 15:20 **4:2** [g]ver 13,27; Lev 5:15-18; 22:14; Nu 15:24-29; 35:11-15; Jos 20:3, 9; Heb 9:7 [h]ver 22; Nu 15:22 **4:3** [i]S Ex 28:41 [j]S Ge 18:23 [k]ver 14; Lev 3:12; 8:14; 10:16; 16:3, 5; Nu 15:27; Ps 66:15; Eze 43:19,23 [l]S Ex 12:5 [m]S ver 24; S Ex 30:10; Lev 5:6-13; 9:2-22; Heb 9:13-14 [n]ver 32 **4:4** [o]ver 15,24; Lev 1:3; Nu 8:12 **4:5** [p]ver 16; Lev 16:14 **4:6** [q]Ex 24:8 [r]ver 17; Lev 16:14, 19 [s]S Ex 25:8 **4:7** [t]S Ex 27:2 [u]ver 34; S Ex 29:12; Lev 8:15 [v]ver 18, 30; Lev 5:9; 9:9; 16:18 **4:8** [w]ver 19 **4:9** [x]S Lev 3:4 **4:10** [y]Lev 9:4 [z]S Ex 32:6 [a]S Ex 29:13 **4:11** [b]Ex 29:14; Lev 8:17; 9:11; Nu 19:5 **4:12** [c]S Ex 29:14; Lev 8:17; 9:11; Heb 13:11 [d]Lev 6:11; 10:14; Nu 19:9 [e]S Lev 1:16 [f]Lev 6:30 [g]Lev 16:3 **4:13** [h]S ver 2 **4:14** [i]S ver 3 [j]Nu 15:24 **4:15** [k]S Ex 3:16; S 19:7 [l]2Ch 29:23 [m]S Ex 29:10; Lev 8:14,22; Nu 8:10 [n]S ver 4 **4:16** [o]S ver 5 **4:17** [p]Nu 19:4,18 [q]S ver 6 **4:18** [r]Lev 8:15; 17:6; 2Ch 29:22 [s]ver 7; Lev 6:30; 10:18 [t]Lev 5:9 **4:19** [u]ver 8 [v]ver 26

4:20 [w]S Ex 29:36; S 32:30; S Ro 3:25; Heb 10:10-12 [x]ver 26, 31,35; Nu 15:25 **4:21** [y]S ver 12 [z]Lev 16:5,15; 2Ch 29:21 **4:22** [a]Nu 31:13 [b]ver 2

[e] *10* The Hebrew word can include both male and female. [f] *10* Traditionally *peace offering*; also in verses 26, 31 and 35

4:1—5:19 SIN, Responsibility—This text reminds us of our sinful nature. We often sin without knowing it or intending to. The text relates to the covenant law and its details. We should be mindful of both our inclination to sin, even unwittingly, and of the atonement of Christ for our sin. Even though the transgression of the covenant law was unintentional, guilt was imputed either to the individual or the group. Such sin could be through negligence or ignorance. See 5:1–19. Specified steps had to be taken to eradicate the sin problem once there was an awareness of the problem. The Old Testament sacrificial system stipulated procedures to deal with unintentional sin; but defiant, high-handed sin (Nu 15:30) could not be atoned for by sacrifices. Violation of God's will is sin whether it is intentional or unintentional. Responsibility must be accepted by every person for every sin. The good news of God's Word, though, is that God in Christ has dealt with the power of sin. The blood of Christ atones for all sins for which we repent and ask forgiveness (Heb 9:7–15).

4:1–35 PRAYER, Holiness of God—The sin offerings in this chapter were mandatory. The higher the office of the one bringing the sacrifice, the more specific are the instructions and the more costly the sacrifice (vv 3,23,28). The offerer identified with the animal being slain by laying hands on the head of the animal (vv 4,15,24,29,33). In each case, all the blood of the animal had to be shed. Forgiveness was assured (5:13). Forgiveness has been assured for us by Christ's sacrifice. Our prayer of repentance asking for forgiveness appropriates Christ's sacrifice in our lives.

4:13–35 SALVATION, Forgiveness—God provided, in the Old Testament sacrificial system, a means through which His people could receive forgiveness of their sins. Compare 5:10,13,16,18; 6:7. Characteristically, God took the initiative in forgiveness by providing rites that symbolized and assured Israel of His forgiveness. The sinner had to initiate action to gain forgiveness. It was never automatic.

offering a male goat[c] without defect.
24He is to lay his hand on the goat's head
and slaughter it at the place where the
burnt offering is slaughtered before the
LORD.[d] It is a sin offering.[e] 25Then the
priest shall take some of the blood of the
sin offering with his finger and put it on
the horns of the altar[f] of burnt offering
and pour out the rest of the blood at the
base of the altar.[g] 26He shall burn all the
fat on the altar as he burned the fat of the
fellowship offering. In this way the priest
will make atonement[h] for the man's sin,
and he will be forgiven.[i]

27" 'If a member of the community sins
unintentionally[j] and does what is forbidden in any of the LORD's commands, he is
guilty. 28When he is made aware of the
sin he committed, he must bring as his
offering[k] for the sin he committed a female goat[l] without defect. 29He is to lay
his hand on the head[m] of the sin offering[n] and slaughter it at the place of the
burnt offering.[o] 30Then the priest is to
take some of the blood with his finger
and put it on the horns of the altar of
burnt offering[p] and pour out the rest of
the blood at the base of the altar. 31He
shall remove all the fat, just as the fat is
removed from the fellowship offering,
and the priest shall burn it on the altar[q]
as an aroma pleasing to the LORD.[r] In
this way the priest will make atonement[s]
for him, and he will be forgiven.[t]
32" 'If he brings a lamb[u] as his sin offering, he is to bring a female without
defect.[v] 33He is to lay his hand on its
head and slaughter it[w] for a sin offering[x]
at the place where the burnt offering is
slaughtered.[y] 34Then the priest shall take
some of the blood of the sin offering with
his finger and put it on the horns of the
altar of burnt offering and pour out the
rest of the blood at the base of the altar.[z]
35He shall remove all the fat, just as the
fat is removed from the lamb of the fellowship offering, and the priest shall burn
it on the altar[a] on top of the offerings
made to the LORD by fire. In this way the
priest will make atonement for him for
the sin he has committed, and he will be
forgiven.

Chapter 5

" 'IF a person sins because he does
not speak up when he hears a
public charge to testify[b] regarding something he has seen or learned about, he
will be held responsible.[c]
2" 'Or if a person touches anything ceremonially unclean—whether the carcasses of unclean wild animals or of unclean livestock or of unclean creatures
that move along the ground[d]—even
though he is unaware of it, he has become unclean[e] and is guilty.
3" 'Or if he touches human uncleanness[f]—anything that would make him
unclean[g]—even though he is unaware of
it, when he learns of it he will be guilty.
4" 'Or if a person thoughtlessly takes
an oath[h] to do anything, whether good or
evil[i]—in any matter one might carelessly swear about—even though he is unaware of it, in any case when he learns of
it he will be guilty.
5" 'When anyone is guilty in any of
these ways, he must confess[j] in what
way he has sinned 6and, as a penalty for
the sin he has committed, he must bring
to the LORD a female lamb or goat[k] from
the flock as a sin offering;[l] and the priest
shall make atonement[m] for him for his
sin.
7" 'If he cannot afford[n] a lamb,[o] he is
to bring two doves or two young pigeons[p] to the LORD as a penalty for his
sin—one for a sin offering and the other
for a burnt offering. 8He is to bring them
to the priest, who shall first offer the one
for the sin offering. He is to wring its
head from its neck,[q] not severing it completely,[r] 9and is to sprinkle[s] some of the
blood of the sin offering against the side
of the altar;[t] the rest of the blood must
be drained out at the base of the altar.[u] It
is a sin offering. 10The priest shall then
offer the other as a burnt offering in the
prescribed way[v] and make atonement[w]
for him for the sin he has committed, and
he will be forgiven.[x]
11" 'If, however, he cannot afford[y] two
doves or two young pigeons,[z] he is to
bring as an offering for his sin a tenth of
an ephah[g][a] of fine flour[b] for a sin offering. He must not put oil or incense on it,
because it is a sin offering. 12He is to
bring it to the priest, who shall take a
handful of it as a memorial portion[c] and
burn it on the altar[d] on top of the offerings made to the LORD by fire. It is a sin
offering. 13In this way the priest will
make atonement[e] for him for any of
these sins he has committed, and he will
be forgiven. The rest of the offering will
belong to the priest,[f] as in the case of the
grain offering.[g]' "

The Guilt Offering

14The LORD said to Moses: 15"When a

[g]*11* That is, probably about 2 quarts (about 2 liters)

4:23 [c]S ver 3; S Lev 1:10
4:24 [d]S ver 4 [e]S ver 3; Lev 6:25
4:25 [f]Lev 16:18; Eze 43:20,22 [g]Lev 9:9
4:26 [h]S Ex 32:30 [i]Lev 5:10; 12:8
4:27 [j]S ver 2
4:28 [k]Lev 5:6; Eze 40:39; 44:27 [l]S ver 3; S Lev 1:10
4:29 [m]ver 4,24 [n]S Lev 1:4 [o]S Ge 8:20
4:30 [p]S ver 7
4:31 [q]ver 35 [r]S Ge 8:21 [s]Lev 1:4 [t]S ver 20
4:32 [u]Ex 29:38; Lev 9:3; 14:10 [v]Lev 1:3
4:33 [w]Lev 1:5 [x]Lev 1:4 [y]ver 29
4:34 [z]S ver 7
4:35 [a]ver 31
5:1 [b]Pr 29:24; Mt 26:63 [c]ver 17; S Ex 28:38; Lev 7:18; 17:16; 19:8; 20:17; 24:15; Nu 5:31; 9:13; 15:31; 19:20; 30:15
5:2 [d]Lev 11:11, 24-40; Dt 14:8; Isa 52:11 [e]ver 3; Lev 7:21; 11:8,24; 13:45; Nu 19:22; Job 15:16; Ps 51:5; Isa 6:5; 64:6; Eze 36:17; Hag 2:13
5:3 [f]Nu 19:11-16 [g]Lev 7:20; 11:25; 14:19; 21:1; Nu 5:2; 9:6; 19:7; Eze 44:25
5:4 [h]Nu 30:6,8 [i]Isa 41:23
5:5 [j]Lev 16:21; 26:40; Nu 5:7; Jos 7:19; 1Ki 8:47; Pr 28:13
5:6 [k]S Lev 1:10; S 4:3 [l]S Lev 4:28 [m]S Ex 32:30
5:7 [n]ver 11; Lev 12:8; 14:21; 27:8 [o]Lev 12:8; 14:22,30 [p]S Ge 15:9; Nu 6:10
5:8 [q]Lev 1:15 [r]Lev 1:17
5:9 [s]S Ex 24:6 [t]Lev 1:15 [u]S Lev 4:7
5:10 [v]Lev 1:14-17; 1Ch 15:13 [w]S Ex 32:30 [x]S Lev 4:26
5:11 [y]S ver 7 [z]S Ge 15:9 [a]S Ex 16:36 [b]S Lev 2:1
5:12 [c]S Lev 2:2 [d]Lev 2:9
5:13 [e]S Ex 32:30 [f]Lev 2:3 [g]S Ex 29:41

5:5–18 SALVATION, Atonement—Atonement for sin in Israel was not automatic. The sinner had to confess his or her sin, pay the prescribed penalty offering, and make restitution. God never treats sin lightly. Compare 1 Jn 1:6–10.

person commits a violation and sins unintentionally[h] in regard to any of the LORD's holy things, he is to bring to the LORD as a penalty[i] a ram[j] from the flock, one without defect and of the proper value in silver, according to the sanctuary shekel.[h][k] It is a guilt offering.[l] 16 He must make restitution[m] for what he has failed to do in regard to the holy things, add a fifth of the value[n] to that and give it all to the priest, who will make atonement for him with the ram as a guilt offering, and he will be forgiven.

17 "If a person sins and does what is forbidden in any of the LORD's commands, even though he does not know it,[o] he is guilty and will be held responsible.[p] 18 He is to bring to the priest as a guilt offering[q] a ram from the flock, one without defect and of the proper value. In this way the priest will make atonement for him for the wrong he has committed unintentionally, and he will be forgiven.[r] 19 It is a guilt offering; he has been guilty of[i] wrongdoing against the LORD."[s]

Chapter 6

THE LORD said to Moses: 2 "If anyone sins and is unfaithful to the LORD[t] by deceiving his neighbor[u] about something entrusted to him or left in his care[v] or stolen, or if he cheats[w] him, 3 or if he finds lost property and lies about it,[x] or if he swears falsely,[y] or if he commits any such sin that people may do— 4 when he thus sins and becomes guilty, he must return[z] what he has stolen or taken by extortion, or what was entrusted to him, or the lost property he found, 5 or whatever it was he swore falsely about. He must make restitution[a] in full, add a fifth of the value to it and give it all to the owner on the day he presents his guilt offering.[b] 6 And as a penalty he must bring to the priest, that is, to the LORD, his guilt offering,[c] a ram from the flock, one without defect and of the proper value.[d] 7 In this way the priest will make atonement[e] for him before the LORD, and he will be forgiven for any of these things he did that made him guilty."

The Burnt Offering

8 The LORD said to Moses: 9 "Give Aaron and his sons this command: 'These are the regulations for the burnt offering[f]: The burnt offering is to remain on the altar hearth throughout the night, till morning, and the fire must be kept burning on the altar.[g] 10 The priest shall then put on his linen clothes,[h] with linen undergarments next to his body,[i] and shall remove the ashes[j] of the burnt offering that the fire has consumed on the altar and place them beside the altar. 11 Then he is to take off these clothes and put on others, and carry the ashes outside the camp to a place that is ceremonially clean.[k] 12 The fire on the altar must be kept burning; it must not go out. Every morning the priest is to add firewood[l] and arrange the burnt offering on the fire and burn the fat[m] of the fellowship offerings[j][n] on it. 13 The fire must be kept burning on the altar continuously; it must not go out.

The Grain Offering

14 " 'These are the regulations for the grain offering:[o] Aaron's sons are to bring it before the LORD, in front of the altar. 15 The priest is to take a handful of fine flour and oil, together with all the incense[p] on the grain offering,[q] and burn the memorial portion[r] on the altar as an aroma pleasing to the LORD. 16 Aaron and his sons[s] shall eat the rest[t] of it, but it is to be eaten without yeast[u] in a holy place;[v] they are to eat it in the courtyard[w] of the Tent of Meeting.[x] 17 It must not be baked with yeast; I have given it as their share[y] of the offerings made to me by fire.[z] Like the sin offering and the guilt offering, it is most holy.[a] 18 Any male descendant of Aaron may eat it.[b] It is his regular share[c] of the offerings made to the LORD by fire for the generations to come.[d] Whatever touches them will become holy.[k][e] ' "

19 The LORD also said to Moses, 20 "This

[h] *15* That is, about 2/5 ounce (about 11.5 grams)
[i] *19* Or *has made full expiation for his*
[j] *12* Traditionally *peace offerings*
[k] *18* Or *Whoever touches them must be holy*; similarly in verse 27

5:15 [h]S Lev 4:2 [i]Lev 22:14 [j]S Ex 29:3; Lev 6:6; Nu 5:8; 6:14; 15:6; 28:11 [k]S Ex 30:13 [l]ver 16,18; Lev 6:5, 6; 7:1,6-10,7; 14:12-17; 19:21, 22; Nu 6:12; 18:9; 1Sa 6:3; Ezr 10:19; Isa 53:10
5:16 [m]Lev 6:4 [n]ver 15; Lev 27:13; Nu 5:7
5:17 [o]ver 15 [p]S ver 1
5:18 [q]Lev 6:6; 14:12 [r]S ver 15
5:19 [s]2Ki 12:16
6:2 [t]Nu 5:6; Ps 73:27; Ac 5:4; Col 3:9 [u]Lev 19:11; Jer 9:4,5 [v]S Ex 22:7 [w]S Ge 31:7
6:3 [x]S Ex 23:4 [y]S Ex 22:11
6:4 [z]Lev 5:16; Eze 33:15; S Lk 19:8
6:5 [a]Nu 5:7 [b]S Lev 5:15
6:6 [c]S Lev 5:15 [d]Nu 5:8
6:7 [e]S Ex 32:30
6:9 [f]Lev 7:37 [g]ver 12
6:10 [h]S Ex 39:27 [i]Ex 28:39-42,43; 39:28 [j]S Lev 1:16
6:11 [k]S Lev 4:12
6:12 [l]S Lev 1:7 [m]S Ex 29:13 [n]S Ex 32:6
6:14 [o]S Lev 2:1; Nu 6:15; 15:4; 28:13
6:15 [p]S Lev 2:1 [q]Lev 2:9 [r]S Lev 2:2
6:16 [s]S Lev 2:3 [t]Eze 44:29 [u]S Lev 2:11 [v]ver 26; S Ex 29:11; Lev 10:13; 16:24; 24:9; Nu 18:10 [w]S Ex 27:9 [x]Ex 29:31; Lev 8:31
6:17 [y]Nu 5:9 [z]Ex 29:28; Lev 7:7; 10:16-18 [a]ver 29; Ex 40:10; Lev 10:12; 21:22; 24:9; Nu 18:9,10
6:18 [b]ver 29; Lev 2:3; 7:6; Nu 18:9-10 [c]Nu 5:9 [d]S Ge 9:12 [e]S Ex 30:29

5:14–19 PRAYER, Holiness of God—The guilt offering indicated the nature of sin. It is "against the LORD." Like the sin offering, the guilt offering required the shedding of blood (7:2). See note on 4:1–35.

6:1–3 SIN, Responsibility—A person must bear full responsibility for personal acts of unfaithfulness. The sinful act against another person is a sin against God. Such a sin demands renewing the relationship with the other person as well as renewing the relationship with God. Christians can go directly to God through Christ and His sacrificial death, so we do not employ the sacrificial system. We do need to remember that dealing with our sins involves dealing with the person(s) against whom we sinned.

6:1–5 CHRISTIAN ETHICS, Theft—Thieves must make things right with the offended human party and with God. Theft is both a crime and a sin. Part of society's justice involves restitution plus penalties for lost income and emotional distress. See note on Ex 20:15.

6:2–5 CHRISTIAN ETHICS, Justice—Lying, stealing, or any other dishonesty has no place among God's people. Believers should be instrumental in leading society to deal with crimes of dishonesty.

6:3 CHRISTIAN ETHICS, Language—Failure to admit we have found lost property makes us guilty of lying and theft. See note on Ex 20:16.

is the offering Aaron and his sons are to
bring to the LORD on the day he[l] is
anointed:[f] a tenth of an ephah[m][g] of fine
flour[h] as a regular grain offering,[i] half of
it in the morning and half in the evening.
21Prepare it with oil on a griddle;[j] bring
it well-mixed and present the grain offering broken[n] in pieces as an aroma pleasing to the LORD. 22The son who is to succeed him as anointed priest[k] shall prepare it. It is the LORD's regular share and
is to be burned completely.[l] 23Every
grain offering of a priest shall be burned
completely; it must not be eaten."

The Sin Offering

24The LORD said to Moses, 25"Say to
Aaron and his sons: 'These are the regulations for the sin offering:[m] The sin offering is to be slaughtered before the LORD[n]
in the place[o] the burnt offering is slaughtered; it is most holy. 26The priest who
offers it shall eat it; it is to be eaten in a
holy place,[p] in the courtyard[q] of the
Tent of Meeting.[r] 27Whatever touches
any of the flesh will become holy,[s] and if
any of the blood is spattered on a garment, you must wash it in a holy place.
28The clay pot[t] the meat is cooked in
must be broken; but if it is cooked in a
bronze pot, the pot is to be scoured and
rinsed with water. 29Any male in a
priest's family may eat it;[u] it is most
holy.[v] 30But any sin offering whose blood
is brought into the Tent of Meeting to
make atonement[w] in the Holy Place[x]
must not be eaten; it must be burned.[y]

Chapter 7

The Guilt Offering

" 'THESE are the regulations for the
guilt offering,[z] which is most
holy: 2The guilt offering is to be slaughtered in the place where the burnt offering is slaughtered, and its blood is to be
sprinkled against the altar on all sides.
3All its fat[a] shall be offered: the fat tail
and the fat that covers the inner parts,
4both kidneys with the fat on them near
the loins, and the covering of the liver,
which is to be removed with the kidneys.[b] 5The priest shall burn them on the
altar[c] as an offering made to the LORD by
fire. It is a guilt offering. 6Any male in a
priest's family may eat it,[d] but it must be
eaten in a holy place; it is most holy.[e]
7" 'The same law applies to both the
sin offering[f] and the guilt offering:[g]
They belong to the priest[h] who makes
atonement with them.[i] 8The priest who
offers a burnt offering for anyone may
keep its hide[j] for himself. 9Every grain
offering baked in an oven[k] or cooked in a
pan[l] or on a griddle[m] belongs to the
priest who offers it, 10and every grain offering, whether mixed with oil or dry, belongs equally to all the sons of Aaron.

The Fellowship Offering

11" 'These are the regulations for the
fellowship offering[o] a person may
present to the LORD:
12" 'If he offers it as an expression of
thankfulness, then along with this thank
offering[n] he is to offer cakes[o] of bread
made without yeast[p] and mixed with oil,
wafers[q] made without yeast and spread
with oil,[r] and cakes of fine flour well-
kneaded and mixed with oil. 13Along
with his fellowship offering of thanksgiving[s] he is to present an offering with
cakes of bread made with yeast.[t] 14He is
to bring one of each kind as an offering, a
contribution to the LORD; it belongs to
the priest who sprinkles the blood of the
fellowship offerings. 15The meat of his fellowship offering of thanksgiving must be
eaten on the day it is offered; he must
leave none of it till morning.[u]
16" 'If, however, his offering is the result of a vow[v] or is a freewill offering,[w]
the sacrifice shall be eaten on the day he
offers it, but anything left over may be
eaten on the next day.[x] 17Any meat of
the sacrifice left over till the third day
must be burned up.[y] 18If any meat of the
fellowship offering[z] is eaten on the third
day, it will not be accepted.[a] It will not
be credited[b] to the one who offered it,
for it is impure; the person who eats any
of it will be held responsible.[c]
19" 'Meat that touches anything ceremonially unclean must not be eaten; it
must be burned up. As for other meat,
anyone ceremonially clean may eat it.
20But if anyone who is unclean[d] eats any
meat of the fellowship offering belonging
to the LORD, that person must be cut off
from his people.[e] 21If anyone touches
something unclean[f]—whether human
uncleanness or an unclean animal or any
unclean, detestable thing—and then eats
any of the meat of the fellowship offering

6:20 [f]S Ex 28:41 [g]S Ex 16:36 [h]Nu 5:15; 28:5 [i]Ex 29:2; Lev 23:13; Nu 4:16
6:21 [j]Lev 2:5
6:22 [k]S Ex 28:41; S 29:30 [l]S Lev 1:9
6:25 [m]S Ex 30:10; S Lev 4:24 [n]S Lev 1:3 [o]S Ex 29:11
6:26 [p]S ver 16 [q]S Ex 27:9 [r]S Ex 27:21; S 40:2
6:27 [s]S Ex 29:37; Lev 10:10; Eze 44:19; 46:20; Hag 2:12
6:28 [t]Lev 11:33; 15:12; Nu 19:15
6:29 [u]S ver 18 [v]S ver 17; Eze 42:13
6:30 [w]Eze 45:15 [x]S Lev 4:18 [y]Lev 4:12
7:1 [z]S Lev 5:15; Eze 40:39
7:3 [a]S Ex 29:13
7:4 [b]Lev 3:15
7:5 [c]S Ex 29:13
7:6 [d]S Lev 6:18 [e]Eze 42:13
7:7 [f]S Ex 30:10 [g]S Lev 5:15 [h]ver 6; Lev 2:3; 6:17,26; 14:13; 2Ki 12:16; 1Co 9:13; 10:18 [i]Nu 5:8
7:8 [j]Lev 1:6
7:9 [k]S Lev 2:4 [l]Lev 2:7 [m]S Lev 2:5
7:12 [n]ver 13,15; Lev 22:29; Ps 50:14; 54:6; 107:22; 116:17; Jer 33:11 [o]Jer 44:19 [p]Nu 6:19 [q]S Lev 2:4 [r]S Lev 2:1
7:13 [s]S ver 12; S Ex 34:22 [t]Lev 23:17; Am 4:5
7:15 [u]S Ex 12:10
7:16 [v]S Ge 28:20; S Lev 1:2; Dt 23:21-23 [w]Ex 35:29; Lev 22:18,21; 23:38; Nu 15:3; 29:39; Dt 12:6; Ps 54:6; Eze 46:12 [x]Lev 19:5-8
7:17 [y]Ex 12:10; Lev 19:6
7:18 [z]2Ch 33:16 [a]Lev 19:7 [b]Nu 18:27 [c]S Lev 5:1
7:20 [d]S Lev 5:3 [e]S Ge 17:14; Lev 22:3-7
7:21 [f]S Lev 5:2

[l]20 Or *each* [m]20 That is, probably about 2 quarts (about 2 liters) [n]*21* The meaning of the Hebrew for this word is uncertain. [o]*11* Traditionally *peace offering*; also in verses 13-37

7:20,21,25,26,27 GOD, Wrath—Persons not ceremonially prepared to eat the offerings or participate in the rituals would suffer the wrath of God. This ought not be understood as petty, retributive justice of an angry God. God taught His people that they had to relate to Him responsibly, obediently, and according to His own terms. Mankind must not usurp God's authority, especially where God has given explicit instructions. Therefore, the elaborate instructions concerning the various offerings and rituals taught the people obedience as well as worship.

belonging to the LORD, that person must
be cut off from his people.' "

Eating Fat and Blood Forbidden

22The LORD said to Moses, 23"Say to
the Israelites: 'Do not eat any of the fat of
cattle, sheep or goats.[g] 24The fat of an
animal found dead or torn by wild animals[h] may be used for any other purpose,
but you must not eat it. 25Anyone who
eats the fat of an animal from which an
offering by fire may be[p] made to the
LORD must be cut off from his people.
26And wherever you live, you must not
eat the blood[i] of any bird or animal. 27If
anyone eats blood,[j] that person must be
cut off from his people.' "

The Priests' Share

28The LORD said to Moses, 29"Say to
the Israelites: 'Anyone who brings a fellowship offering to the LORD is to bring
part of it as his sacrifice to the LORD.
30With his own hands he is to bring the
offering made to the LORD by fire; he is to
bring the fat, together with the breast,
and wave the breast before the LORD as a
wave offering.[k] 31The priest shall burn
the fat on the altar,[l] but the breast belongs to Aaron and his sons.[m] 32You are
to give the right thigh of your fellowship
offerings to the priest as a contribution.[n]
33The son of Aaron who offers the blood
and the fat of the fellowship offering shall
have the right thigh as his share. 34From
the fellowship offerings of the Israelites, I
have taken the breast that is waved and
the thigh[o] that is presented and have giv-
en them to Aaron the priest and his
sons[p] as their regular share from the Israelites.' "

35This is the portion of the offerings
made to the LORD by fire that were allotted to Aaron and his sons on the day they
were presented to serve the LORD as
priests. 36On the day they were anointed,[q] the LORD commanded that the Israelites give this to them as their regular
share for the generations to come.

7:23 [g]Lev 17:13-14; Dt 14:4
7:24 [h]S Ex 22:31
7:26 [i]S Ge 9:4
7:27 [j]S Ge 9:4
7:30 [k]S Ex 29:24
7:31 [l]S Ex 29:13 [m]S Ex 29:27
7:32 [n]Ex 29:27; Lev 10:14,15; Nu 5:9; 6:20; 18:18
7:34 [o]Ex 29:22; Lev 10:15; Nu 6:20; 1Sa 9:24 [p]S Ex 29:27
7:36 [q]Lev 8:12,30
7:37 [r]Lev 6:9 [s]Lev 6:14 [t]S Ex 29:31
7:38 [u]Lev 26:46; Nu 36:13; Dt 4:5; 29:1 [v]S Ex 19:11 [w]S Lev 1:2
8:2 [x]S Ex 28:1; S Lev 1:5 [y]Ex 28:2, 4,43; S 39:27 [z]Ex 30:23-25,30 [a]S Ex 30:10 [b]ver 18,22 [c]Ex 29:2-3
8:3 [d]Nu 8:9
8:5 [e]Ex 29:1
8:6 [f]S Ex 29:4; S 30:19; S Ac 22:16
8:7 [g]Ex 28:4
8:8 [h]S Ex 25:7 [i]S Ex 28:30
8:9 [j]S Ex 39:28 [k]S Ex 28:36 [l]S Ex 28:2; Lev 21:10
8:10 [m]ver 2 [n]S Ex 30:26 [o]S Ex 26:1
8:11 [p]S Ex 30:29
8:12 [q]S Lev 7:36 [r]S Ex 30:30
8:13 [s]S Ex 28:40

37These, then, are the regulations for
the burnt offering,[r] the grain offering,[s]
the sin offering, the guilt offering, the ordination offering[t] and the fellowship offering, 38which the LORD gave Moses[u] on
Mount Sinai[v] on the day he commanded
the Israelites to bring their offerings to
the LORD,[w] in the Desert of Sinai.

Chapter 8

The Ordination of Aaron and His Sons

8:1–36pp — Ex 29:1–37

THE LORD said to Moses, 2"Bring Aaron
and his sons,[x] their garments,[y] the
anointing oil,[z] the bull for the sin offering,[a] the two rams[b] and the basket containing bread made without yeast,[c] 3and
gather the entire assembly[d] at the entrance to the Tent of Meeting." 4Moses
did as the LORD commanded him, and the
assembly gathered at the entrance to the
Tent of Meeting.

5Moses said to the assembly, "This is
what the LORD has commanded to be
done.[e]" 6Then Moses brought Aaron and
his sons forward and washed them with
water.[f] 7He put the tunic on Aaron, tied
the sash around him, clothed him with
the robe and put the ephod on him. He
also tied the ephod to him by its skillfully
woven waistband; so it was fastened on
him.[g] 8He placed the breastpiece[h] on
him and put the Urim and Thummim[i] in
the breastpiece. 9Then he placed the turban[j] on Aaron's head and set the gold
plate, the sacred diadem,[k] on the front of
it, as the LORD commanded Moses.[l]

10Then Moses took the anointing oil[m]
and anointed[n] the tabernacle[o] and everything in it, and so consecrated them.
11He sprinkled some of the oil on the altar
seven times, anointing the altar and all its
utensils and the basin with its stand, to
consecrate them.[p] 12He poured some of
the anointing oil on Aaron's head and
anointed[q] him to consecrate him.[r]
13Then he brought Aaron's sons[s] for-

[p]25 Or *fire is*

7:35–38 WORSHIP, Sacrifice—From the very beginning worship included giving an offering to the Lord (Ge 4:1–5). Offerings should be given on a regular schedule. Israel's worship included daily morning and evening sacrifices, as well as other special days and seasons of special offerings. Offerings and sacrifices represented the product of human labor as a symbol of gratitude to God (Dt 26:1–15). True sacrifice involves personal cost. King David insisted on purchasing land to sacrifice to the Lord, refusing to let the owner give him the land and offering (2 Sa 24:21–25). Old Testament animal sacrifice culminated in the New Testament in the once-for-all sacrifice of Christ (Heb 9). Because of the Lord's atoning death, the apostle Paul called on Christians *to offer our lives and our possessions to the Lord (Ro 12:1–2; 2 Co 8:1–9).*

8:1–36 PRAYER, Holiness of God—This chapter presents the separation of Aaron and his sons for the priesthood. The priests served the Lord on behalf of the entire assembly. Their consecration had to be carried out in the presence of all. See note on Nu 8:5–22.

8:6 ORDINANCES, Background of Baptism—This "Levitical washing" or symbolic cleansing of the priests (Aaron and his sons) for religious service is the background of all religious ceremonies of cleansing in the Bible. It was practiced in the Dead Sea Scrolls community of Qumran, and it probably influenced the popular understanding of John's baptism and Jewish proselyte baptism. Christian baptism differed from these washings in these ways: it was performed only once, pictured the death and resurrection of the believer with Christ, and pointed forward to the final resurrection unto eternal life. Because all Christians are priests and ministers unto God, Christian baptism became the sign of their dedication to Christ and their new life in Him. See note on Heb 10:22.

ward, put tunics[t] on them, tied sashes around them and put headbands on them, as the LORD commanded Moses.[u]

14He then presented the bull[v] for the sin offering,[w] and Aaron and his sons laid their hands on its head.[x] 15Moses slaughtered the bull and took some of the blood,[y] and with his finger he put it on all the horns of the altar[z] to purify the altar.[a] He poured out the rest of the blood at the base of the altar. So he consecrated it to make atonement for it.[b] 16Moses also took all the fat around the inner parts, the covering of the liver, and both kidneys and their fat, and burned it on the altar. 17But the bull with its hide and its flesh and its offal[c] he burned up outside the camp,[d] as the LORD commanded Moses.

18He then presented the ram[e] for the burnt offering, and Aaron and his sons laid their hands on its head. 19Then Moses slaughtered the ram and sprinkled the blood against the altar on all sides. 20He cut the ram into pieces and burned the head, the pieces and the fat.[f] 21He washed the inner parts and the legs with water and burned the whole ram on the altar as a burnt offering, a pleasing aroma, an offering made to the LORD by fire, as the LORD commanded Moses.

22He then presented the other ram, the ram for the ordination,[g] and Aaron and his sons laid their hands on its head.[h] 23Moses slaughtered the ram and took some of its blood and put it on the lobe of Aaron's right ear, on the thumb of his right hand and on the big toe of his right foot.[i] 24Moses also brought Aaron's sons forward and put some of the blood on the lobes of their right ears, on the thumbs of their right hands and on the big toes of their right feet. Then he sprinkled blood against the altar on all sides.[j] 25He took the fat[k], the fat tail, all the fat around the inner parts, the covering of the liver, both kidneys and their fat and the right thigh. 26Then from the basket of bread made without yeast, which was before the LORD, he took a cake of bread, and one made with oil, and a wafer;[l] he put these on the fat portions and on the right thigh. 27He put all these in the hands of Aaron and his sons and waved them before the LORD[m] as a wave offering. 28Then Moses took them from their hands and burned them on the altar on top of the burnt offering as an ordination offering, a pleasing aroma, an offering made to the LORD by fire. 29He also took the breast—Moses' share of the ordination ram[n]—and waved it before the LORD as a wave offering, as the LORD commanded Moses.

30Then Moses[o] took some of the anointing oil and some of the blood from the altar and sprinkled them on Aaron and his garments[p] and on his sons and their garments. So he consecrated[q] Aaron and his garments and his sons and their garments.

31Moses then said to Aaron and his sons, "Cook the meat at the entrance to the Tent of Meeting[r] and eat it there with the bread from the basket of ordination offerings, as I commanded, saying,[q] 'Aaron and his sons are to eat it.' 32Then burn up the rest of the meat and the bread. 33Do not leave the entrance to the Tent of Meeting for seven days, until the days of your ordination are completed, for your ordination will last seven days.[s] 34What has been done today was commanded by the LORD[t] to make atonement for you. 35You must stay at the entrance to the Tent of Meeting day and night for seven days and do what the LORD requires,[u] so you will not die; for that is what I have been commanded." 36So Aaron and his sons did everything the LORD commanded through Moses.

Chapter 9

The Priests Begin Their Ministry

ON the eighth day[v] Moses summoned Aaron and his sons and the elders[w] of Israel. 2He said to Aaron, "Take a bull calf for your sin offering and a ram for your burnt offering, both without defect, and present them before the LORD. 3Then say to the Israelites: 'Take a male goat[x] for a sin offering,[y] a calf[z] and a lamb[a]—both a year old and without defect—for a burnt offering, 4and an ox[r][b] and a ram for a fellowship offering[s][c] to sacrifice before the LORD, together with a grain offering mixed with oil. For today the LORD will appear to you.[d]' "

5They took the things Moses commanded to the front of the Tent of Meeting, and the entire assembly came near and stood before the LORD. 6Then Moses

8:13 [t]S Ex 28:4,39; 39:27 [u]Lev 21:10
8:14 [v]S Lev 4:3 [w]S Ex 30:10 [x]S Lev 4:15
8:15 [y]S Lev 4:18 [z]S Lev 4:7 [a]Heb 9:22 [b]Eze 43:20
8:17 [c]S Lev 4:11 [d]S Lev 4:12
8:18 [e]S ver 2
8:20 [f]S Lev 1:8
8:22 [g]S ver 2 [h]S Lev 4:15
8:23 [i]Lev 14:14,25
8:24 [j]Heb 9:18-22
8:25 [k]Lev 3:3-5
8:26 [l]S Lev 2:4
8:27 [m]Nu 5:25
8:29 [n]Lev 7:31-34
8:30 [o]S Ex 28:1 [p]S Ex 28:2 [q]S Lev 7:36
8:31 [r]S Lev 6:16
8:33 [s]Lev 14:8; 15:13,28; Nu 19:11; Eze 43:25
8:34 [t]Heb 7:16
8:35 [u]Lev 18:30; 22:9; Nu 3:7; 9:19; Dt 11:1; 1Ki 2:3; Eze 48:11; Zec 3:7
9:1 [v]Eze 43:27 [w]S Lev 4:15
9:3 [x]S Lev 4:3 [y]ver 15; Lev 10:16 [z]ver 8 [a]S Lev 4:32
9:4 [b]Lev 4:10 [c]S Ex 32:6 [d]Ex 29:43

[q]31 Or *I was commanded:* [r]4 The Hebrew word can include both male and female; also in verses 18 and 19. [s]4 Traditionally *peace offering*; also in verses 18 and 22

9:6,23–24 REVELATION, Author of Grace—Moses interpreted God's commands in regard to sacrifice for sin. The entire procedure of offerings and sacrifices in this book is a way of revealing God's requirements for those who worship Him. Israel was to bring an offering as a concrete reminder that they were sinners before God and accountable for their sins. Their gifts symbolized their gratitude and repentance. Obedience brought the opportunity for revelation. Thus the worshipers who assembled participated more fully in the presence and nature of God. Revelation brought joy to the people and sent them to their knees in reverent submission.

said, "This is what the LORD has commanded you to do, so that the glory of the LORD[e] may appear to you."

7Moses said to Aaron, "Come to the altar and sacrifice your sin offering and your burnt offering and make atonement for yourself and the people;[f] sacrifice the offering that is for the people and make atonement for them, as the LORD has commanded.[g]"

8So Aaron came to the altar and slaughtered the calf as a sin offering[h] for himself. 9His sons brought the blood to him,[i] and he dipped his finger into the blood and put it on the horns of the altar; the rest of the blood he poured out at the base of the altar.[j][k] 10On the altar he burned the fat, the kidneys and the covering of the liver from the sin offering, as the LORD commanded Moses; 11the flesh and the hide[l] he burned up outside the camp.[m]

12Then he slaughtered the burnt offering.[n] His sons handed him the blood,[o] and he sprinkled it against the altar on all sides. 13They handed him the burnt offering piece by piece, including the head, and he burned them on the altar.[p] 14He washed the inner parts and the legs and burned them on top of the burnt offering on the altar.[q]

15Aaron then brought the offering that was for the people.[r] He took the goat for the people's sin offering and slaughtered it and offered it for a sin offering as he did with the first one.

16He brought the burnt offering and offered it in the prescribed way.[s] 17He also brought the grain offering, took a handful of it and burned it on the altar in addition to the morning's burnt offering.[t]

18He slaughtered the ox and the ram as the fellowship offering for the people.[u] His sons handed him the blood, and he sprinkled it against the altar on all sides. 19But the fat portions of the ox and the ram—the fat tail, the layer of fat, the kidneys and the covering of the liver—20these they laid on the breasts, and then Aaron burned the fat on the altar. 21Aaron waved the breasts and the right thigh before the LORD as a wave offering,[v] as Moses commanded.

22Then Aaron lifted his hands toward the people and blessed them.[w] And having sacrificed the sin offering, the burnt offering and the fellowship offering, he stepped down.

23Moses and Aaron then went into the Tent of Meeting.[x] When they came out, they blessed the people; and the glory of the LORD[y] appeared to all the people. 24Fire[z] came out from the presence of the LORD and consumed the burnt offering and the fat portions on the altar. And when all the people saw it, they shouted for joy and fell facedown.[a]

Chapter 10

The Death of Nadab and Abihu

AARON'S sons Nadab and Abihu[b] took their censers,[c] put fire in them[d] and added incense;[e] and they offered unauthorized fire before the LORD,[f] contrary to his command.[g] 2So fire came out[h] from the presence of the LORD and consumed them,[i] and they died before the LORD.[j] 3Moses then said to Aaron, "This is what the LORD spoke of when he said:

" 'Among those who approach me[k]
  I will show myself holy;[l]
in the sight of all the people
  I will be honored.[m]' "

Aaron remained silent.

4Moses summoned Mishael and Elzaphan,[n] sons of Aaron's uncle Uzziel,[o] and said to them, "Come here; carry your cousins outside the camp,[p] away from the front of the sanctuary.[q]" 5So they

9:6 [e]S Ex 16:7
9:7 [f]Lev 16:6 [g]S Ex 30:10; Heb 5:1,3; 7:27
9:8 [h]Lev 4:1-12; 10:19
9:9 [i]ver 12,18 [j]S Ex 29:12 [k]Eze 43:20
9:11 [l]S Lev 4:11 [m]S Lev 4:12
9:12 [n]Lev 10:19 [o]S ver 9
9:13 [p]S Lev 1:8
9:14 [q]S Lev 1:9
9:15 [r]Lev 4:27-31
9:16 [s]Lev 1:1-13
9:17 [t]Lev 3:5
9:18 [u]Lev 3:1-11
9:21 [v]S Ex 29:24, 26
9:22 [w]S Ge 48:20; S Ex 39:43; Lk 24:50
9:23 [x]S Ex 40:2 [y]S Ex 24:16
9:24 [z]S Ex 19:18; Jdg 6:21; 13:20 [a]1Ki 18:39
10:1 [b]Ex 6:23; 24:1; 28:1; Nu 3:2-4; 26:61; 1Ch 6:3 [c]Nu 16:46; 1Ki 7:50; 2Ki 25:15; 2Ch 4:22; Jer 52:19; Eze 8:11 [d]Lev 16:12; Nu 16:7,18; Isa 6:6 [e]S Ex 30:9 [f]ver 2; Lev 16:1 [g]Ex 30:9
10:2 [h]Ps 106:18 [i]Nu 11:1; 16:35; Ps 2:12; 50:3; Isa 29:6 [j]S Ge 19:24; S 38:7; Nu 16:35; 1Ch 24:2; Job 1:16
10:3 [k]Ex 19:22 [l]Ex 30:29; Lev 21:6; 22:32; Nu 16:5; 20:13; Isa 5:16; Eze 28:22; 38:16 [m]Ex 14:4; Isa 44:23; 49:3; 55:5; 60:21
10:4 [n]S Ex 6:22 [o]Ex 6:18 [p]Ac 5:6,9,10 [q]S Ex 25:8

9:7 SALVATION, Atonement—Both high priest and people had to be atoned for in the Old Testament sacrificial system. Not even the officer who officiated at the altar was exempt. Compare Heb 9:11–14.

9:22 PRAYER, Vow—A priest had special and direct access to God. Priestly blessing utilized this access on behalf of others. In Christ, all believers are priests (1 Pe 2:9). See note on Nu 6:22–27.

9:23–24 WORSHIP, Reverence—The people responded immediately to the presence of the Lord. With deep reverence they rejoiced and fell flat on their faces before the Lord. True worship grows out of this sense of reverence and awe for God. Notice the same reaction by Manoah and his wife (Jdg 13:19–23) and of King Jehoshaphat and the people (2 Ch 20:18). Reverence is a prerequisite to true worship (Ps 5:7; 96:9; Isa 6:1–7; Mt 9:8; Lk 7:16; Heb 12:28–29; Rev 14:7).

9:24 HISTORY, Worship—*Israel's worship* rested on *God's historical* commands outlining the way to build a place of worship and how to worship. An historical act demonstrated God's acceptance of Israel's form of worship.

10:1–3 EVIL AND SUFFERING, Punishment—Human sin is evil. When God's chosen leaders sin, the evil is intensified. Aaron's two sons disobeyed God. God's punishing response was not evil. It was the way the holy God deals with sin. Sin is the evil, not God's response to it.

10:1–2 HUMANITY, Death and Sin—Death is consistently associated with disobedience to God. See notes on Ge 2:17; 15:15.

10:1–2 SIN, Transgression—Worship practices in God's house can be sinful. Leaders of worship must be careful to lead people to God rather than try innovative practices which fulfill personal desires and needs. Nadab and Abihu clearly transgressed God's law (Ex 30:7–8,34–38). Punishment was swift and severe. Though we may not always be able to see God's retribution for sin today, we can rest assured that eventually God deals with all injustice and impiety.

10:1–2 HISTORY, Worship—See note on 9:24. An historical act demonstrated the seriousness with which God takes worship. Improper worship brings God's judgment.

came and carried them, still in their tunics,[r] outside the camp, as Moses ordered.
6Then Moses said to Aaron and his
sons Eleazar and Ithamar,[s] "Do not let
your hair become unkempt,[t][t] and do
not tear your clothes,[u] or you will die
and the LORD will be angry with the
whole community.[v] But your relatives,
all the house of Israel, may mourn[w] for
those the LORD has destroyed by fire. 7Do
not leave the entrance to the Tent of
Meeting[x] or you will die, because the
LORD's anointing oil[y] is on you." So they
did as Moses said.
8Then the LORD said to Aaron, 9"You
and your sons are not to drink wine[z] or
other fermented drink[a] whenever you go
into the Tent of Meeting, or you will die.
This is a lasting ordinance[b] for the generations to come. 10You must distinguish
between the holy and the common, between the unclean and the clean,[c] 11and
you must teach[d] the Israelites all the decrees the LORD has given them through
Moses.[e]"
12Moses said to Aaron and his remaining sons, Eleazar and Ithamar, "Take the
grain offering[f] left over from the offerings made to the LORD by fire and eat it
prepared without yeast beside the altar,[g]
for it is most holy. 13Eat it in a holy
place,[h] because it is your share and your
sons' share of the offerings made to the
LORD by fire; for so I have been commanded.[i] 14But you and your sons and
your daughters may eat the breast[j] that
was waved and the thigh that was presented. Eat them in a ceremonially clean
place;[k] they have been given to you and
your children as your share of the Israelites' fellowship offerings.[u] 15The thigh[l]
that was presented and the breast that
was waved must be brought with the fat
portions of the offerings made by fire, to
be waved before the LORD as a wave offering.[m] This will be the regular share for
you and your children, as the LORD has
commanded."

10:5 [r]S Lev 8:13
10:6 [s]S Ex 6:23 [t]Lev 13:45; 21:10; Nu 5:18 [u]Jer 41:5; S Mk 14:63 [v]Nu 1:53; 16:22; Jos 7:1; 22:18 [w]Ge 50:3,10; Nu 20:29; 1Sa 25:1
10:7 [x]S Ex 25:8 [y]S Ex 28:41
10:9 [z]Ge 9:21; Ex 29:40; Lev 23:13; Nu 15:5; Dt 28:39; Isa 5:22; 22:13; 28:1; 29:9; 56:12; Jer 35:6; Hos 4:11; Hab 2:15-16 [a]Nu 6:3; 28:7; Dt 14:26; 29:6; Jdg 13:4; Pr 20:1; 23:29-35; 31:4-7; Isa 28:7; Eze 44:21; Mic 2:11; Lk 1:15; S Eph 5:18; 1Ti 3:3; Tit 1:7 [b]S Ex 12:14
10:10 [c]S Ge 7:2; S Lev 6:27; 14:57; 20:25; Eze 22:26
10:11 [d]2Ch 15:3; 17:7; Ezr 7:25; Ne 8:7; Mal 2:7 [e]Dt 17:10,11; 24:8; 25:1; 33:10; Pr 4:27; Hag 2:11; Mal 2:7
10:12 [f]S Ex 29:41 [g]Lev 6:14-18
10:13 [h]S Lev 6:16 [i]Eze 42:13
10:14 [j]Nu 5:9 [k]S Ex 29:31; S Lev 4:12
10:15 [l]S Lev 7:34 [m]S Ex 29:28
10:16 [n]S Lev 9:3
10:17 [o]Lev 6:24-30; Eze 42:13 [p]S Ex 28:38
10:18 [q]S Lev 4:18; 6:26 [r]S Lev 6:17
10:19 [s]Lev 9:12
11:2 [t]Ac 10:12-14
11:4 [u]Ac 10:14
11:7 [v]Isa 65:4; 66:3,17

16When Moses inquired about the goat
of the sin offering[n] and found that it had
been burned up, he was angry with Eleazar and Ithamar, Aaron's remaining sons,
and asked, 17"Why didn't you eat the sin
offering[o] in the sanctuary area? It is most
holy; it was given to you to take away the
guilt[p] of the community by making
atonement for them before the LORD.
18Since its blood was not taken into the
Holy Place,[q] you should have eaten the
goat in the sanctuary area, as I commanded.[r]"
19Aaron replied to Moses, "Today they
sacrificed their sin offering and their
burnt offering[s] before the LORD, but such
things as this have happened to me.
Would the LORD have been pleased if I
had eaten the sin offering today?"
20When Moses heard this, he was satisfied.

Chapter 11

Clean and Unclean Food

11:1–23pp — Dt 14:3–20

THE LORD said to Moses and Aaron,
2"Say to the Israelites: 'Of all the animals that live on land, these are the ones
you may eat:[t] 3You may eat any animal
that has a split hoof completely divided
and that chews the cud.
4" 'There are some that only chew the
cud or only have a split hoof, but you
must not eat them.[u] The camel, though it
chews the cud, does not have a split hoof;
it is ceremonially unclean for you. 5The
coney,[v] though it chews the cud, does
not have a split hoof; it is unclean for you.
6The rabbit, though it chews the cud,
does not have a split hoof; it is unclean
for you. 7And the pig,[v] though it has a
split hoof completely divided, does not
chew the cud; it is unclean for you. 8You

[t]6 Or *Do not uncover your heads* [u]14 Traditionally *peace offerings* [v]5 That is, the hyrax or rock badger

10:9 CHRISTIAN ETHICS, Alcohol—Alcohol robs people of the capacity to make decisions and judgments. Priests had to determine for the people what was holy and permitted in worship and what was common or unclean and forbidden in worship. The priests were required to retain all their mental capacities while serving in God's place of worship. Thus, they could not drink alcoholic beverages before or during their period of service. See note on Ge 9:21.

10:10–11 DISCIPLESHIP, Spiritual Leaders—Priests were to make God's will known through the teaching of the laws God had spoken through Moses. Aaron and his sons were told not to drink wine or strong drink when they were to enter the tabernacle to perform their priestly services, in order to be able to discern between the holy and the common, between the clean and the unclean. This also is an obvious word of moral guidance for all who serve God today. Those who serve God always should be at their best. See note on Ex 28:29–30.

10:11 GOD, Grace—A basic purpose of the priesthood was to teach the people the word of God. Making offerings and leading worship were not the priests' sole functions. God's grace is seen not only in the forgiveness of their sins but also in providing for the spiritual and intellectual growth of the people.

10:11 CHRISTIAN ETHICS, Moral Imperatives—Worship leaders must do more than lead God's people through traditional rituals. They must teach God's moral demands to the people. See note on Ex 18:20.

10:11 EDUCATION, Priests—The priests and Levites of Israel have generally been considered the custodians of the sacrificial system. From the beginning, God commanded priests to teach the people. Today, as in Old Testament times, religious instruction goes hand in hand with worship. People can worship God in spirit and in truth only if they know the truth concerning His nature and purpose. See note on 2 Ch 17:7–9.

must not eat their meat or touch their
carcasses; they are unclean for you.[w]
9“ ‘Of all the creatures living in the water of the seas and the streams, you may
eat any that have fins and scales. 10But all
creatures in the seas or streams that do
not have fins and scales—whether
among all the swarming things or among
all the other living creatures in the water
—you are to detest.[x] 11And since you are
to detest them, you must not eat their
meat and you must detest their carcasses.[y] 12Anything living in the water
that does not have fins and scales is to be
detestable to you.[z]
13“ ‘These are the birds you are to detest and not eat because they are detestable: the eagle, the vulture, the black vulture, 14the red kite, any kind[a] of black
kite, 15any kind of raven,[b] 16the horned
owl, the screech owl, the gull, any kind of
hawk, 17the little owl, the cormorant, the
great owl, 18the white owl,[c] the desert
owl, the osprey, 19the stork,[d] any kind[e]
of heron, the hoopoe and the bat.[w][f]
20“ ‘All flying insects that walk on all
fours are to be detestable to you.[g]
21There are, however, some winged creatures that walk on all fours that you may
eat: those that have jointed legs for hop-
ping on the ground. 22Of these you may
eat any kind of locust,[h] katydid, cricket
or grasshopper. 23But all other winged
creatures that have four legs you are to
detest.
24“ ‘You will make yourselves unclean
by these;[i] whoever touches their carcasses will be unclean till evening.[j]
25Whoever picks up one of their carcasses
must wash his clothes,[k] and he will be
unclean till evening.[l]
26“ ‘Every animal that has a split hoof
not completely divided or that does not
chew the cud is unclean for you; whoever
touches ⌊the carcass of⌋ any of them will
be unclean. 27Of all the animals that walk
on all fours, those that walk on their paws
are unclean for you; whoever touches
their carcasses will be unclean till evening. 28Anyone who picks up their carcasses must wash his clothes, and he will
be unclean till evening.[m] They are unclean for you.
29“ ‘Of the animals that move about on
the ground, these are unclean for you:[n]
the weasel, the rat,[o] any kind of great
lizard, 30the gecko, the monitor lizard,
the wall lizard, the skink and the chame-
leon. 31Of all those that move along the
ground, these are unclean for you. Whoever touches them when they are dead
will be unclean till evening. 32When one
of them dies and falls on something, that
article, whatever its use, will be unclean,
whether it is made of wood, cloth, hide
or sackcloth.[p] Put it in water; it will be
unclean till evening, and then it will be
clean. 33If one of them falls into a clay
pot, everything in it will be unclean, and
you must break the pot.[q] 34Any food that
could be eaten but has water on it from
such a pot is unclean, and any liquid that
could be drunk from it is unclean. 35Any-
thing that one of their carcasses falls on
becomes unclean; an oven or cooking pot
must be broken up. They are unclean,
and you are to regard them as unclean.
36A spring, however, or a cistern for collecting water remains clean, but anyone
who touches one of these carcasses is unclean. 37If a carcass falls on any seeds that
are to be planted, they remain clean.
38But if water has been put on the seed
and a carcass falls on it, it is unclean for
you.
39“ ‘If an animal that you are allowed
to eat dies,[r] anyone who touches the carcass[s] will be unclean till evening. 40Any-
one who eats some of the carcass[t] must
wash his clothes, and he will be unclean
till evening.[u] Anyone who picks up the
carcass must wash his clothes, and he
will be unclean till evening.
41“ ‘Every creature that moves about
on the ground is detestable; it is not to be
eaten. 42You are not to eat any creature
that moves about on the ground, whether
it moves on its belly or walks on all fours
or on many feet; it is detestable. 43Do not
defile yourselves by any of these creatures.[v] Do not make yourselves unclean
by means of them or be made unclean by
them. 44I am the LORD your God;[w] consecrate yourselves[x] and be holy,[y] because
I am holy.[z] Do not make yourselves unclean by any creature that moves about
on the ground.[a] 45I am the LORD who
brought you up out of Egypt[b] to be your
God;[c] therefore be holy, because I am
holy.[d]
46“ ‘These are the regulations concerning animals, birds, every living thing that
moves in the water and every creature

11:8 [w]S Lev 5:2; Heb 9:10
11:10 [x]ver 12
11:11 [y]S Lev 5:2
11:12 [z]ver 10
11:14 [a]S Ge 1:11
11:15 [b]S Ge 8:7
11:18 [c]Isa 13:21; 14:23; 34:11,13; Zep 2:14
11:19 [d]Zec 5:9 [e]S Ge 1:11 [f]Isa 2:20
11:20 [g]Ac 10:14
11:22 [h]Mt 3:4; Mk 1:6
11:24 [i]S Lev 5:2 [j]ver 27-40; Lev 13:3; 14:46; 15:5; 22:6; Nu 19:7,19
11:25 [k]ver 28; S Ex 19:10; Lev 13:6; 14:8,47; 15:5; 16:26; Nu 8:7; 19:7 [l]Lev 13:34; Nu 19:8; 31:24
11:28 [m]Heb 9:10
11:29 [n]ver 41 [o]Isa 66:17
11:32 [p]Lev 15:12; Nu 19:18; 31:20
11:33 [q]S Lev 6:28
11:39 [r]Lev 17:15; 22:8; Dt 14:21; Eze 4:14; 44:31 [s]ver 40; Lev 22:4; Nu 19:11
11:40 [t]S ver 39 [u]ver 25; Lev 14:8; 17:15; 22:8; Eze 44:31; Heb 9:10
11:43 [v]ver 44; Lev 20:25; 22:5
11:44 [w]S Ex 6:2,7; 20:2; Isa 43:3; 51:15; Eze 20:5 [x]S Ex 19:10; Lev 20:7; Nu 15:40; Jos 3:5; 7:13; 1Ch 15:12; 2Ch 29:5; 35:6 [y]S Ex 22:31; S Dt 14:2 [z]S Ex 31:13; Lev 19:2; 20:7; Jos 24:19; 1Sa 2:2; Job 6:10; Ps 99:3; Eph 1:4; 1Th 4:7; 1Pe 1:15,16* [a]S ver 43
11:45 [b]Lev 25:38, 55 [c]S Ge 17:7 [d]S Ex 19:6; 1Pe 1:16*

[w]*19* The precise identification of some of the birds, insects and animals in this chapter is uncertain.

11:44–45 GOD, Holy—God desires for His people to become like Him in holiness. The path to holiness is in consecration, that is, cleansing from sin and dedication to God. By drawing near to God in this way, the holiness that characterizes God's nature will also characterize His people. Just as temple implements derived holiness from being dedicated to God's service, so people can have a holiness derived from God.

11:45 HISTORY, Moral—Historical deliverance shows God's grace and power. It also reveals the moral uniqueness, the holiness of God. The holy God's self-revelation in history gives a moral base to history and calls people with historical existence to imitate the divine holiness.

that moves about on the ground. 47You must distinguish between the unclean and the clean, between living creatures that may be eaten and those that may not be eaten.[e] ' "

Chapter 12

Purification After Childbirth

THE LORD said to Moses, 2"Say to the Israelites: 'A woman who becomes pregnant and gives birth to a son will be ceremonially unclean for seven days, just as she is unclean during her monthly period.[f] 3On the eighth day[g] the boy is to be circumcised.[h] 4Then the woman must wait thirty-three days to be purified from her bleeding. She must not touch anything sacred or go to the sanctuary until the days of her purification are over. 5If she gives birth to a daughter, for two weeks the woman will be unclean, as during her period. Then she must wait sixty-six days to be purified from her bleeding.

6" 'When the days of her purification for a son or daughter are over,[i] she is to bring to the priest at the entrance to the Tent of Meeting a year-old lamb[j] for a burnt offering and a young pigeon or a dove for a sin offering.[k] 7He shall offer them before the LORD to make atonement for her, and then she will be ceremonially clean from her flow of blood.

" 'These are the regulations for the woman who gives birth to a boy or a girl. 8If she cannot afford a lamb, she is to bring two doves or two young pigeons,[l] one for a burnt offering and the other for a sin offering.[m] In this way the priest will make atonement for her, and she will be clean.[n] ' "

Chapter 13

Regulations About Infectious Skin Diseases

THE LORD said to Moses and Aaron, 2"When anyone has a swelling[o] or a rash or a bright spot[p] on his skin that may become an infectious skin disease,[x][q] he must be brought to Aaron the priest[r] or to one of his sons[y] who is a priest. 3The priest is to examine the sore on his skin, and if the hair in the sore has turned white and the sore appears to be more than skin deep,[z] it is an infectious skin disease. When the priest examines him, he shall pronounce him ceremonially unclean.[s] 4If the spot[t] on his skin is white but does not appear to be more than skin deep and the hair in it has not turned white, the priest is to put the infected person in isolation for seven days.[u] 5On the seventh day[v] the priest is to examine him,[w] and if he sees that the sore is unchanged and has not spread in the skin, he is to keep him in isolation another seven days. 6On the seventh day the priest is to examine him again, and if the sore has faded and has not spread in the skin, the priest shall pronounce him clean;[x] it is only a rash. The man must wash his clothes,[y] and he will be clean.[z] 7But if the rash does spread in his skin after he has shown himself to the priest to be pronounced clean, he must appear before the priest again.[a] 8The priest is to examine him, and if the rash has spread in the skin, he shall pronounce him unclean; it is an infectious disease.

9"When anyone has an infectious skin disease, he must be brought to the priest. 10The priest is to examine him, and if there is a white swelling in the skin that has turned the hair white and if there is raw flesh in the swelling, 11it is a chronic skin disease[b] and the priest shall pronounce him unclean. He is not to put him in isolation, because he is already unclean.

12"If the disease breaks out all over his skin and, so far as the priest can see, it covers all the skin of the infected person from head to foot, 13the priest is to examine him, and if the disease has covered his whole body, he shall pronounce that person clean. Since it has all turned white, he is clean. 14But whenever raw flesh appears on him, he will be unclean. 15When the priest sees the raw flesh, he shall pronounce him unclean. The raw flesh is unclean; he has an infectious disease.[c] 16Should the raw flesh change and turn white, he must go to the priest. 17The priest is to examine him, and if the sores have turned white, the priest shall pronounce the infected person clean;[d] then he will be clean.

18"When someone has a boil[e] on his skin and it heals, 19and in the place where the boil was, a white swelling or reddish-white[f] spot[g] appears, he must present himself to the priest. 20The priest is to examine it, and if it appears to be more than skin deep and the hair in it has turned white, the priest shall pronounce him unclean. It is an infectious skin disease[h] that has broken out where the boil was. 21But if, when the priest examines it, there is no white hair in it and it is not more than skin deep and has faded, then the priest is to put him in isolation for

11:47 [e]Lev 10:10
12:2 [f]Lev 15:19; 18:19; Isa 64:6; Eze 18:6; 22:10; 36:17
12:3 [g]S Ex 22:30 [h]S Ge 17:10; S Lk 1:59
12:6 [i]Lk 2:22 [j]Ex 29:38; Lev 23:12; Nu 6:12, 14; 7:15 [k]Lev 5:7
12:8 [l]S Ge 15:9; Lev 14:22 [m]Lev 5:7; Lk 2:22-24* [n]S Lev 4:26
13:2 [o]ver 10,19,28, 43 [p]ver 4,38,39; Lev 14:56 [q]ver 3,9, 15; S Ex 4:6; Lev 14:3,32; Nu 5:2; Dt 24:8 [r]Dt 24:8
13:3 [s]ver 8,11,20, 30; Lev 21:1; Nu 9:6
13:4 [t]S ver 2 [u]ver 5,21,26,33,46; Lev 14:38; Nu 12:14,15; Dt 24:9
13:5 [v]Lev 14:9 [w]ver 27,32,34,51
13:6 [x]ver 13,17,23, 28,34; Mt 8:3; Lk 5:12-14 [y]S Lev 11:25 [z]Lev 11:25; 14:8,9, 20,48; 15:8; Nu 8:7
13:7 [a]Lk 5:14
13:11 [b]S Ex 4:6; S Lev 14:8; S Nu 12:10; Mt 8:2
13:15 [c]S ver 2
13:17 [d]S ver 6
13:18 [e]S Ex 9:9
13:19 [f]ver 24,42; Lev 14:37 [g]S ver 2
13:20 [h]ver 2

[x]2 Traditionally *leprosy*; the Hebrew word was used for various diseases affecting the skin—not necessarily leprosy; also elsewhere in this chapter. [y]2 Or *descendants* [z]3 Or *be lower than the rest of the skin*; also elsewhere in this chapter

seven days. 22If it is spreading in the skin,
the priest shall pronounce him unclean;
it is infectious. 23But if the spot is unchanged and has not spread, it is only a
scar from the boil, and the priest shall
pronounce him clean.[i]
24"When someone has a burn on his
skin and a reddish-white or white spot
appears in the raw flesh of the burn, 25the
priest is to examine the spot, and if the
hair in it has turned white, and it appears
to be more than skin deep, it is an infectious disease that has broken out in the
burn. The priest shall pronounce him unclean; it is an infectious skin disease.[j]
26But if the priest examines it and there is
no white hair in the spot and if it is not
more than skin deep and has faded, then
the priest is to put him in isolation for
seven days.[k] 27On the seventh day the
priest is to examine him,[l] and if it is
spreading in the skin, the priest shall pronounce him unclean; it is an infectious
skin disease. 28If, however, the spot is unchanged and has not spread in the skin
but has faded, it is a swelling from the
burn, and the priest shall pronounce him
clean; it is only a scar from the burn.[m]
29"If a man or woman has a sore on the
head[n] or on the chin, 30the priest is to
examine the sore, and if it appears to be
more than skin deep and the hair in it is
yellow and thin, the priest shall pronounce that person unclean; it is an itch,
an infectious disease of the head or chin.
31But if, when the priest examines this
kind of sore, it does not seem to be more
than skin deep and there is no black hair
in it, then the priest is to put the infected
person in isolation for seven days.[o] 32On
the seventh day the priest is to examine
the sore,[p] and if the itch has not spread
and there is no yellow hair in it and it
does not appear to be more than skin
deep, 33he must be shaved except for the
diseased area, and the priest is to keep
him in isolation another seven days. 34On
the seventh day the priest is to examine
the itch,[q] and if it has not spread in the
skin and appears to be no more than skin
deep, the priest shall pronounce him
clean. He must wash his clothes, and he
will be clean.[r] 35But if the itch does
spread in the skin after he is pronounced
clean, 36the priest is to examine him, and
if the itch has spread in the skin, the
priest does not need to look for yellow
hair; the person is unclean.[s] 37If, however, in his judgment it is unchanged and
black hair has grown in it, the itch is
healed. He is clean, and the priest shall
pronounce him clean.
38"When a man or woman has white
spots on the skin, 39the priest is to examine them, and if the spots are dull white,
it is a harmless rash that has broken out
on the skin; that person is clean.
40"When a man has lost his hair and is
bald,[t] he is clean. 41If he has lost his hair
from the front of his scalp and has a bald
forehead, he is clean. 42But if he has a
reddish-white sore on his bald head or
forehead, it is an infectious disease breaking out on his head or forehead. 43The
priest is to examine him, and if the swollen sore on his head or forehead is reddish-white like an infectious skin disease,
44the man is diseased and is unclean. The
priest shall pronounce him unclean because of the sore on his head.
45"The person with such an infectious
disease must wear torn clothes,[u] let his
hair be unkempt,[a] cover the lower part
of his face[v] and cry out, 'Unclean! Unclean!'[w] 46As long as he has the infection
he remains unclean. He must live alone;
he must live outside the camp.[x]

Regulations About Mildew

47"If any clothing is contaminated with
mildew—any woolen or linen clothing,
48any woven or knitted material of linen
or wool, any leather or anything made of
leather— 49and if the contamination in
the clothing, or leather, or woven or knitted material, or any leather article, is
greenish or reddish, it is a spreading mildew and must be shown to the priest.[y]
50The priest is to examine the mildew[z]
and isolate the affected article for seven
days. 51On the seventh day he is to examine it,[a] and if the mildew has spread in
the clothing, or the woven or knitted material, or the leather, whatever its use, it
is a destructive mildew; the article is unclean.[b] 52He must burn up the clothing,
or the woven or knitted material of wool
or linen, or any leather article that has
the contamination in it, because the mildew is destructive; the article must be
burned up.[c]
53"But if, when the priest examines it,
the mildew has not spread in the clothing, or the woven or knitted material, or
the leather article, 54he shall order that
the contaminated article be washed.
Then he is to isolate it for another seven
days. 55After the affected article has been
washed, the priest is to examine it, and if
the mildew has not changed its appearance, even though it has not spread, it is
unclean. Burn it with fire, whether the
mildew has affected one side or the other. 56If, when the priest examines it, the
mildew has faded after the article has
been washed, he is to tear the contami-

13:23 [i]S ver 6
13:25 [j]ver 11
13:26 [k]S ver 4
13:27 [l]S ver 5
13:28 [m]S ver 2
13:29 [n]ver 43,44
13:31 [o]ver 4
13:32 [p]S ver 5
13:34 [q]S ver 5 [r]S Lev 11:25
13:36 [s]ver 30
13:40 [t]Lev 21:5; 2Ki 2:23; Isa 3:24; 15:2; 22:12; Eze 27:31; 29:18; Am 8:10; Mic 1:16
13:45 [u]S Lev 10:6 [v]Eze 24:17,22; Mic 3:7 [w]S Lev 5:2; La 4:15; Lk 17:12
13:46 [x]Nu 5:1-4; 12:14; 2Ki 7:3; 15:5
13:49 [y]Mk 1:44
13:50 [z]Eze 44:23
13:51 [a]S ver 5 [b]Lev 14:44
13:52 [c]ver 55,57

[a]*45* Or *clothes, uncover his head*

nated part out of the clothing, or the
leather, or the woven or knitted material.
57But if it reappears in the clothing, or in
the woven or knitted material, or in the
leather article, it is spreading, and whatever has the mildew must be burned with
fire. 58The clothing, or the woven or knitted material, or any leather article that
has been washed and is rid of the mildew, must be washed again, and it will be
clean."
59These are the regulations concerning
contamination by mildew in woolen or
linen clothing, woven or knitted material,
or any leather article, for pronouncing
them clean or unclean.

Chapter 14

Cleansing From Infectious Skin Diseases

THE LORD said to Moses, 2"These are
the regulations for the diseased person at the time of his ceremonial cleansing, when he is brought to the priest:[d]
3The priest is to go outside the camp and
examine him.[e] If the person has been
healed of his infectious skin disease,[b] [f]
4the priest shall order that two live clean
birds and some cedar wood, scarlet yarn
and hyssop[g] be brought for the one to be
cleansed.[h] 5Then the priest shall order
that one of the birds be killed over fresh
water in a clay pot.[i] 6He is then to take
the live bird and dip it, together with the
cedar wood, the scarlet yarn and the hyssop, into the blood of the bird that was
killed over the fresh water.[j] 7Seven
times[k] he shall sprinkle[l] the one to be
cleansed of the infectious disease and
pronounce him clean. Then he is to release the live bird in the open fields.[m]
8"The person to be cleansed must
wash his clothes,[n] shave off all his hair
and bathe with water;[o] then he will be
ceremonially clean.[p] After this he may
come into the camp,[q] but he must stay
outside his tent for seven days. 9On the
seventh day[r] he must shave off all his
hair;[s] he must shave his head, his beard,
his eyebrows and the rest of his hair. He
must wash his clothes and bathe himself
with water, and he will be clean.[t]
10"On the eighth day[u] he must bring
two male lambs and one ewe lamb[v] a
year old, each without defect, along with
three-tenths of an ephah[c] [w] of fine flour
mixed with oil for a grain offering,[x] and
one log[d] of oil.[y] 11The priest who pronounces him clean shall present[z] both
the one to be cleansed and his offerings
before the LORD at the entrance to the
Tent of Meeting.[a]
12"Then the priest is to take one of the
male lambs and offer it as a guilt offering,[b] along with the log of oil; he shall
wave them before the LORD as a wave
offering.[c] 13He is to slaughter the lamb in
the holy place[d] where the sin offering
and the burnt offering are slaughtered.
Like the sin offering, the guilt offering belongs to the priest;[e] it is most holy. 14The
priest is to take some of the blood of the
guilt offering and put it on the lobe of the
right ear of the one to be cleansed, on the
thumb of his right hand and on the big
toe of his right foot.[f] 15The priest shall
then take some of the log of oil, pour it in
the palm of his own left hand,[g] 16dip his
right forefinger into the oil in his palm,
and with his finger sprinkle some of it
before the LORD seven times.[h] 17The
priest is to put some of the oil remaining
in his palm on the lobe of the right ear of
the one to be cleansed, on the thumb of
his right hand and on the big toe of his
right foot, on top of the blood of the guilt
offering.[i] 18The rest of the oil in his palm
the priest shall put on the head of the one
to be cleansed[j] and make atonement for
him before the LORD.
19"Then the priest is to sacrifice the sin
offering and make atonement for the one
to be cleansed from his uncleanness.[k] After that, the priest shall slaughter the
burnt offering 20and offer it on the altar,
together with the grain offering, and
make atonement for him,[l] and he will be
clean.[m]
21"If, however, he is poor[n] and cannot
afford these,[o] he must take one male
lamb as a guilt offering to be waved to
make atonement for him, together with a
tenth of an ephah[e] of fine flour mixed
with oil for a grain offering, a log of oil,
22and two doves or two young pigeons,[p]
which he can afford, one for a sin offering
and the other for a burnt offering.[q]
23"On the eighth day he must bring
them for his cleansing to the priest at the
entrance to the Tent of Meeting,[r] before
the LORD.[s] 24The priest is to take the
lamb for the guilt offering,[t] together
with the log of oil,[u] and wave them before the LORD as a wave offering.[v] 25He
shall slaughter the lamb for the guilt offering and take some of its blood and put it
on the lobe of the right ear of the one to
be cleansed, on the thumb of his right
hand and on the big toe of his right foot.[w]
26The priest is to pour some of the oil into
the palm of his own left hand,[x] 27and

14:2 [d]Lev 13:57; Dt 24:8; Mt 8:2-4; Mk 1:40-44; Lk 5:12-14; 17:14
14:3 [e]Lev 13:46 [f]S Lev 13:2
14:4 [g]S Ex 12:22 [h]ver 6,49,51,52; Nu 19:6; Ps 51:7
14:5 [i]ver 50
14:6 [j]S ver 4
14:7 [k]ver 51 [l]2Ki 5:10,14; Isa 52:15; Eze 36:25 [m]ver 53
14:8 [n]S Lev 11:25 [o]ver 9; S Ex 29:4; Lev 15:5; 17:15; 22:6; Nu 19:7,8 [p]ver 20 [q]S Lev 13:11; Nu 5:2,3; 12:14,15; 19:20; 31:24; 2Ch 26:21
14:9 [r]S Lev 13:5 [s]Nu 6:9; Dt 21:12 [t]S Lev 13:6
14:10 [u]Nu 6:10; Mt 8:4; Mk 1:44; Lk 5:14 [v]S Lev 4:32 [w]Nu 15:9; 28:20 [x]Lev 2:1 [y]ver 12, 15,21,24
14:11 [z]Nu 6:16 [a]Nu 6:10
14:12 [b]S Lev 5:18 [c]S Ex 29:24
14:13 [d]S Ex 29:11 [e]Lev 6:24-30; S 7:7
14:14 [f]S Ex 29:20
14:15 [g]ver 26
14:16 [h]ver 27
14:17 [i]ver 28
14:18 [j]ver 31; Lev 15:15
14:19 [k]ver 31; S Lev 5:3; 15:15
14:20 [l]Lev 15:30 [m]ver 8
14:21 [n]S Lev 5:7 [o]ver 22,32
14:22 [p]S Lev 5:7 [q]Lev 15:30
14:23 [r]Lev 15:14, 29 [s]S ver 10,11
14:24 [t]Nu 6:14 [u]S ver 10 [v]ver 12
14:25 [w]S Ex 29:20
14:26 [x]ver 15

[b]*3* Traditionally *leprosy*; the Hebrew word was used for various diseases affecting the skin—not necessarily leprosy; also elsewhere in this chapter. [c]*10* That is, probably about 6 quarts (about 6.5 liters) [d]*10* That is, probably about 2/3 pint (about 0.3 liter); also in verses 12, 15, 21 and 24 [e]*21* That is, probably about 2 quarts (about 2 liters)

with his right forefinger sprinkle some of
the oil from his palm seven times before
the LORD. 28Some of the oil in his palm he
is to put on the same places he put the
blood of the guilt offering—on the lobe of
the right ear of the one to be cleansed, on
the thumb of his right hand and on the
big toe of his right foot. 29The rest of the
oil in his palm the priest shall put on the
head of the one to be cleansed, to make
atonement for him before the LORD.[y]
30Then he shall sacrifice the doves or the
young pigeons, which the person can afford,[z] 31one[f] as a sin offering and the
other as a burnt offering,[a] together with
the grain offering. In this way the priest
will make atonement before the LORD on
behalf of the one to be cleansed.[b]"

32These are the regulations for anyone
who has an infectious skin disease[c] and
who cannot afford the regular offerings[d]
for his cleansing.

Cleansing From Mildew

33The LORD said to Moses and Aaron,
34"When you enter the land of Canaan,[e]
which I am giving you as your possession,[f] and I put a spreading mildew in a
house in that land, 35the owner of the
house must go and tell the priest, 'I have
seen something that looks like mildew in
my house.' 36The priest is to order the
house to be emptied before he goes in to
examine the mildew, so that nothing in
the house will be pronounced unclean.
After this the priest is to go in and inspect
the house. 37He is to examine the mildew
on the walls, and if it has greenish or reddish[g] depressions that appear to be deeper than the surface of the wall, 38the
priest shall go out the doorway of the
house and close it up for seven days.[h]
39On the seventh day[i] the priest shall
return to inspect the house. If the mildew
has spread on the walls, 40he is to order
that the contaminated stones be torn out
and thrown into an unclean place outside
the town.[j] 41He must have all the inside
walls of the house scraped and the material that is scraped off dumped into an
unclean place outside the town. 42Then
they are to take other stones to replace
these and take new clay and plaster the
house.

43"If the mildew reappears in the
house after the stones have been torn out
and the house scraped and plastered,
44the priest is to go and examine it and, if
the mildew has spread in the house, it is
a destructive mildew; the house is unclean.[k] 45It must be torn down—its
stones, timbers and all the plaster—and
taken out of the town to an unclean
place.

46"Anyone who goes into the house
while it is closed up will be unclean till
evening.[l] 47Anyone who sleeps or eats in
the house must wash his clothes.[m]

48"But if the priest comes to examine it
and the mildew has not spread after the
house has been plastered, he shall pronounce the house clean,[n] because the
mildew is gone. 49To purify the house he
is to take two birds and some cedar wood,
scarlet yarn and hyssop.[o] 50He shall kill
one of the birds over fresh water in a clay
pot.[p] 51Then he is to take the cedar
wood, the hyssop,[q] the scarlet yarn and
the live bird, dip them into the blood of
the dead bird and the fresh water, and
sprinkle the house seven times.[r] 52He
shall purify the house with the bird's
blood, the fresh water, the live bird, the
cedar wood, the hyssop and the scarlet
yarn. 53Then he is to release the live bird
in the open fields[s] outside the town. In
this way he will make atonement for the
house, and it will be clean.[t]"

54These are the regulations for any infectious skin disease,[u] for an itch, 55for
mildew[v] in clothing or in a house, 56and
for a swelling, a rash or a bright spot,[w]
57to determine when something is clean
or unclean.

These are the regulations for infectious
skin diseases and mildew.[x]

Chapter 15

Discharges Causing Uncleanness

THE LORD said to Moses and Aaron,
2"Speak to the Israelites and say to
them: 'When any man has a bodily discharge,[y] the discharge is unclean.
3Whether it continues flowing from his
body or is blocked, it will make him unclean. This is how his discharge will bring
about uncleanness:

4" 'Any bed the man with a discharge
lies on will be unclean, and anything he
sits on will be unclean. 5Anyone who
touches his bed must wash his clothes[z]
and bathe with water,[a] and he will be
unclean till evening.[b] 6Whoever sits on
anything that the man with a discharge
sat on must wash his clothes and bathe
with water, and he will be unclean till
evening.

[f]31 Septuagint and Syriac; Hebrew *31such as the person can afford, one*

14:29 [y]ver 18
14:30 [z]S Lev 5:7
14:31 [a]ver 22; Lev 5:7; 15:15,30 [b]S ver 18,19
14:32 [c]S Lev 13:2 [d]S ver 21
14:34 [e]Ge 12:5; Ex 6:4; Nu 13:2 [f]Ge 17:8; 48:4; Nu 27:12; 32:22; Dt 3:27; 7:1; 32:49
14:37 [g]S Lev 13:19
14:38 [h]S Lev 13:4
14:39 [i]Lev 13:5
14:40 [j]ver 45
14:44 [k]Lev 13:51
14:46 [l]S Lev 11:24
14:47 [m]S Lev 11:25
14:48 [n]S Lev 13:6
14:49 [o]ver 4; 1Ki 4:33
14:50 [p]ver 5
14:51 [q]ver 6; Ps 51:7 [r]S ver 4,7
14:53 [s]S ver 7 [t]ver 20
14:54 [u]Lev 13:2
14:55 [v]Lev 13:47-52
14:56 [w]Lev 13:2
14:57 [x]S Lev 10:10
15:2 [y]ver 16,32; Lev 22:4; Nu 5:2; 2Sa 3:29; Mt 9:20
15:5 [z]S Lev 11:25 [a]Lev 14:8 [b]S Lev 11:24

14:33–57 HISTORY, Moral—*God's historical* gift of the *land placed* a moral demand on Israel to protect the land from anything which might infect it. The God of history is interested in the common problems of daily personal history as well as the unique problems of national history.

7" 'Whoever touches the man[c] who
has a discharge[d] must wash his clothes
and bathe with water, and he will be unclean till evening.
8" 'If the man with the discharge
spits[e] on someone who is clean, that person must wash his clothes and bathe with
water, and he will be unclean till evening.
9" 'Everything the man sits on when
riding will be unclean, 10and whoever
touches any of the things that were under
him will be unclean till evening; whoever
picks up those things[f] must wash his
clothes and bathe with water, and he will
be unclean till evening.
11" 'Anyone the man with a discharge
touches without rinsing his hands with
water must wash his clothes and bathe
with water, and he will be unclean till
evening.
12" 'A clay pot[g] that the man touches
must be broken, and any wooden article[h]
is to be rinsed with water.
13" 'When a man is cleansed from his
discharge, he is to count off seven days[i]
for his ceremonial cleansing; he must
wash his clothes and bathe himself with
fresh water, and he will be clean.[j] 14On
the eighth day he must take two doves or
two young pigeons[k] and come before the
LORD to the entrance to the Tent of Meeting and give them to the priest. 15The
priest is to sacrifice them, the one for a
sin offering[l] and the other for a burnt
offering.[m] In this way he will make atonement before the LORD for the man because of his discharge.[n]
16" 'When a man has an emission of
semen,[o] he must bathe his whole body
with water, and he will be unclean till
evening.[p] 17Any clothing or leather that
has semen on it must be washed with
water, and it will be unclean till evening.
18When a man lies with a woman and
there is an emission of semen,[q] both
must bathe with water, and they will be
unclean till evening.
19" 'When a woman has her regular
flow of blood, the impurity of her monthly period[r] will last seven days, and anyone who touches her will be unclean till
evening.
20" 'Anything she lies on during her
period will be unclean, and anything she
sits on will be unclean. 21Whoever
touches her bed must wash his clothes
and bathe with water, and he will be unclean till evening.[s] 22Whoever touches
anything she sits on must wash his
clothes and bathe with water, and he will
be unclean till evening. 23Whether it is
the bed or anything she was sitting on,
when anyone touches it, he will be unclean till evening.
24" 'If a man lies with her and her
monthly flow[t] touches him, he will be
unclean for seven days; any bed he lies
on will be unclean.
25" 'When a woman has a discharge of
blood for many days at a time other than
her monthly period[u] or has a discharge
that continues beyond her period, she
will be unclean as long as she has the
discharge, just as in the days of her period. 26Any bed she lies on while her discharge continues will be unclean, as is
her bed during her monthly period, and
anything she sits on will be unclean, as
during her period. 27Whoever touches
them will be unclean; he must wash his
clothes and bathe with water, and he will
be unclean till evening.
28" 'When she is cleansed from her discharge, she must count off seven days,
and after that she will be ceremonially
clean. 29On the eighth day she must take
two doves or two young pigeons[v] and
bring them to the priest at the entrance
to the Tent of Meeting. 30The priest is to
sacrifice one for a sin offering and the
other for a burnt offering. In this way he
will make atonement for her before the
LORD for the uncleanness of her discharge.[w]
31" 'You must keep the Israelites separate from things that make them unclean,
so they will not die in their uncleanness
for defiling my dwelling place,[g][x] which
is among them.' "
32These are the regulations for a man
with a discharge, for anyone made unclean by an emission of semen,[y] 33for a
woman in her monthly period, for a man
or a woman with a discharge, and for a
man who lies with a woman who is ceremonially unclean.[z]

Chapter 16

The Day of Atonement

16:2–34pp — Lev 23:26–32; Nu 29:7–11

THE LORD spoke to Moses after the
death of the two sons of Aaron who
died when they approached the LORD.[a]
2The LORD said to Moses: "Tell your

15:7 [c]ver 19; Lev 22:5 [d]ver 16; Lev 22:4
15:8 [e]Nu 12:14
15:10 [f]Nu 19:10
15:12 [g]S Lev 6:28 [h]S Lev 11:32
15:13 [i]S Lev 8:33 [j]ver 5
15:14 [k]Lev 14:22
15:15 [l]Lev 5:7 [m]Lev 14:31 [n]S Lev 14:18,19
15:16 [o]S ver 2; Dt 23:10 [p]ver 5; Dt 23:11
15:18 [q]1Sa 21:4
15:19 [r]S ver 24
15:21 [s]ver 27
15:24 [t]ver 19; Lev 12:2; 18:19; 20:18; Eze 18:6
15:25 [u]Mt 9:20; Mk 5:25; Lk 8:43
15:29 [v]Lev 14:22
15:30 [w]Lev 5:10; 14:20,31; 18:19; 2Sa 11:4; Mk 5:25; Lk 8:43
15:31 [x]Lev 20:3; Nu 5:3; 19:13,20; 2Sa 15:25; 2Ki 21:7; Ps 33:14; 74:7; 76:2; Eze 5:11; 23:38
15:32 [y]S ver 2
15:33 [z]ver 19,24, 25
16:1 [a]S Lev 10:1

[g]31 Or *my tabernacle*

16:1–34 EVIL AND SUFFERING, Redemptive—God uses suffering to deal with sin. On the Day of Atonement animals suffered the penalty for the people's sins. Jesus Christ suffered and died as the ultimate sacrifice for sins.

16:1–34 WORSHIP, Calendar—See note on Ex 16:23–30.

16:2 HISTORY, Worship—Worship for God's people rests on historical divine commands not on individual or institution-

brother Aaron not to come whenever he
chooses[b] into the Most Holy Place[c] behind the curtain[d] in front of the atonement cover[e] on the ark, or else he will
die, because I appear[f] in the cloud[g] over
the atonement cover.
3"This is how Aaron is to enter the
sanctuary area:[h] with a young bull[i] for a
sin offering and a ram for a burnt offering.[j] 4He is to put on the sacred linen
tunic,[k] with linen undergarments next to
his body; he is to tie the linen sash
around him and put on the linen turban.[l] These are sacred garments;[m] so he
must bathe himself with water[n] before
he puts them on.[o] 5From the Israelite
community[p] he is to take two male
goats[q] for a sin offering and a ram for a
burnt offering.
6"Aaron is to offer the bull for his own
sin offering to make atonement for himself and his household.[r] 7Then he is to
take the two goats and present them before the LORD at the entrance to the Tent
of Meeting. 8He is to cast lots[s] for the
two goats—one lot for the LORD and the
other for the scapegoat.[h][t] 9Aaron shall
bring the goat whose lot falls to the LORD
and sacrifice it for a sin offering. 10But the
goat chosen by lot as the scapegoat shall
be presented alive before the LORD to be
used for making atonement[u] by sending
it into the desert as a scapegoat.
11"Aaron shall bring the bull for his
own sin offering to make atonement for
himself and his household,[v] and he is to
slaughter the bull for his own sin offering.
12He is to take a censer full of burning
coals[w] from the altar before the LORD and
two handfuls of finely ground fragrant incense[x] and take them behind the curtain. 13He is to put the incense on the fire
before the LORD, and the smoke of the
incense will conceal the atonement cover[y] above the Testimony, so that he will
not die.[z] 14He is to take some of the
bull's blood[a] and with his finger sprinkle
it on the front of the atonement cover;
then he shall sprinkle some of it with his
finger seven times before the atonement
cover.[b]
15"He shall then slaughter the goat for
the sin offering for the people[c] and take
its blood behind the curtain[d] and do with
it as he did with the bull's blood: He shall
sprinkle[e] it on the atonement cover and
in front of it. 16In this way he will make
atonement[f] for the Most Holy Place[g] because of the uncleanness and rebellion of
the Israelites, whatever their sins have
been. He is to do the same for the Tent of
Meeting,[h] which is among them in the
midst of their uncleanness. 17No one is to
be in the Tent of Meeting from the time
Aaron goes in to make atonement in the
Most Holy Place until he comes out, having made atonement for himself, his
household and the whole community of
Israel.
18"Then he shall come out to the altar[i] that is before the LORD and make
atonement for it. He shall take some of
the bull's blood and some of the goat's
blood and put it on all the horns of the
altar.[j] 19He shall sprinkle some of the
blood on it with his finger seven times to
cleanse it and to consecrate it from the
uncleanness of the Israelites.[k]
20"When Aaron has finished making
atonement for the Most Holy Place, the
Tent of Meeting and the altar, he shall
bring forward the live goat.[l] 21He is to
lay both hands on the head of the live
goat[m] and confess[n] over it all the wickedness and rebellion of the Israelites—all
their sins—and put them on the goat's
head. He shall send the goat away into
the desert in the care of a man appointed
for the task. 22The goat will carry on itself
all their sins[o] to a solitary place; and the
man shall release it in the desert.
23"Then Aaron is to go into the Tent of
Meeting and take off the linen garments[p]
he put on before he entered the Most
Holy Place, and he is to leave them
there.[q] 24He shall bathe himself with water in a holy place[r] and put on his regular
garments.[s] Then he shall come out and
sacrifice the burnt offering for himself
and the burnt offering for the people,[t] to
make atonement for himself and for the
people.[u] 25He shall also burn the fat of
the sin offering on the altar.
26"The man who releases the goat as a
scapegoat[v] must wash his clothes[w] and
bathe himself with water;[x] afterward he
may come into the camp. 27The bull and
the goat for the sin offerings, whose blood
was brought into the Most Holy Place to
make atonement, must be taken outside
the camp;[y] their hides, flesh and offal are
to be burned up. 28The man who burns
them must wash his clothes and bathe

16:2 [b]Ex 30:10; Heb 9:7 [c]S Ex 26:33; Heb 9:25; 10:19 [d]S Ex 26:33; Heb 6:19 [e]S Ex 26:34 [f]S Ex 25:22 [g]S Ex 40:34; S 2Sa 22:10
16:3 [h]ver 6; Lev 4:1-12; Heb 9:24,25 [i]S Lev 4:3 [j]ver 5
16:4 [k]S Lev 8:13 [l]S Ex 28:39 [m]ver 32; S Ex 28:42; 29:29, 30; Lev 21:10; Nu 20:26,28 [n]S Ex 29:4; Heb 10:22 [o]Eze 9:2; 44:17-18
16:5 [p]S Lev 4:13-21 [q]ver 20; S Lev 4:3; 2Ch 29:23; Ps 50:9
16:6 [r]Lev 9:7; Heb 7:27; 9:7,12
16:8 [s]Nu 26:55,56; 33:54; 34:13; Jos 14:2; 18:6; Jdg 20:9; Ne 10:34; Est 3:7; 9:24; Ps 22:18; Pr 16:33 [t]ver 10,26
16:10 [u]Isa 53:4-10; S Ro 3:25
16:11 [v]S ver 6,24, 33
16:12 [w]S Lev 10:1; Rev 8:5 [x]S Ex 25:6; 30:34-38
16:13 [y]S Ex 25:17 [z]S Ex 28:43
16:14 [a]S Lev 4:5; Heb 9:7,13,25 [b]S Lev 4:6
16:15 [c]S Lev 4:13-21; Heb 7:27; 9:7,12; 13:11 [d]Heb 9:3 [e]S Lev 4:17; Nu 19:19; Isa 52:15; Eze 36:25
16:16 [f]S Ex 29:36; S Ro 3:25 [g]S Ex 26:33; Heb 9:25 [h]Ex 29:4; S 40:2
16:18 [i]S Lev 4:7 [j]S Lev 4:25
16:19 [k]Eze 43:20
16:20 [l]S ver 5
16:21 [m]S Ex 29:10 [n]S Lev 5:5
16:22 [o]S Ex 28:38; Isa 53:12
16:23 [p]S Ex 28:42 [q]Eze 42:14
16:24 [r]S Lev 6:16 [s]ver 3-5 [t]Lev 1:3 [u]S ver 11
16:26 [v]S ver 8 [w]S Lev 11:25 [x]Lev 14:8
16:27 [y]S Ex 29:14

[h]8 That is, the goat of removal; Hebrew *azazel*; also in verses 10 and 26

---

al sovereignty. God has set up the way of atonement. To be set right with God, humans must follow His revealed way.

16:6–34 SALVATION, Atonement—The Israelites were to set aside one day *each year as the Day of Atonement (Hebrew Yom Kippurim,* "the day of coverings"; 23:28; 25:9). This was the single most important day in the Hebrew calendar. On that day the high priest entered into the Most Holy Place behind the curtain and made atonement for his sins, *those of his household,* and of the whole community. These verses describe God's regulations regarding the Day of Atonement, showing His taking the initiative to deal with His people's sin and separation from Him.

himself with water; afterward he may come into the camp.[z]

29"This is to be a lasting ordinance[a] for you: On the tenth day of the seventh month[b] you must deny yourselves[i] [c] and not do any work[d]—whether native-born[e] or an alien living among you—30because on this day atonement will be made[f] for you, to cleanse you. Then, before the LORD, you will be clean from all your sins.[g] 31It is a sabbath of rest, and you must deny yourselves;[h] it is a lasting ordinance.[i] 32The priest who is anointed and ordained[j] to succeed his father as high priest is to make atonement. He is to put on the sacred linen garments[k] 33and make atonement for the Most Holy Place, for the Tent of Meeting and the altar, and for the priests and all the people of the community.[l]

34"This is to be a lasting ordinance[m] for you: Atonement is to be made once a year[n] for all the sins of the Israelites."

And it was done, as the LORD commanded Moses.

Chapter 17

Eating Blood Forbidden

THE LORD said to Moses, 2"Speak to Aaron and his sons[o] and to all the Israelites and say to them: 'This is what the LORD has commanded: 3Any Israelite who sacrifices an ox,[j] a lamb[p] or a goat[q] in the camp or outside of it 4instead of bringing it to the entrance to the Tent of Meeting[r] to present it as an offering to the LORD in front of the tabernacle of the LORD[s]—that man shall be considered guilty of bloodshed; he has shed blood and must be cut off from his people.[t] 5This is so the Israelites will bring to the LORD the sacrifices they are now making in the open fields. They must bring them to the priest, that is, to the LORD, at the entrance to the Tent of Meeting and sacrifice them as fellowship offerings.[k] [u] 6The priest is to sprinkle the blood against the altar[v] of the LORD[w] at the entrance to the Tent of Meeting and burn the fat as an aroma pleasing to the LORD.[x] 7They must no longer offer any of their sacrifices to the goat idols[l] [y] to whom they prostitute themselves.[z] This is to be a lasting ordinance[a] for them and for the generations to come.'[b]

8"Say to them: 'Any Israelite or any alien living among them who offers a burnt offering or sacrifice 9and does not bring it to the entrance to the Tent[c] of Meeting[d] to sacrifice it to the LORD[e]—that man must be cut off from his people.

10" 'Any Israelite or any alien living among them who eats any blood—I will set my face against that person who eats blood[f] and will cut him off from his people. 11For the life of a creature is in the blood,[g] and I have given it to you to make atonement for yourselves on the altar; it is the blood that makes atonement for one's life.[h] 12Therefore I say to the Israelites, "None of you may eat blood, nor may an alien living among you eat blood."

13" 'Any Israelite or any alien living among you who hunts any animal or bird that may be eaten must drain out the blood and cover it with earth,[i] 14because the life of every creature is its blood. That is why I have said to the Israelites, "You must not eat the blood of any creature, because the life of every creature is its blood; anyone who eats it must be cut off."[j]

15" 'Anyone, whether native-born or alien, who eats anything[k] found dead or torn by wild animals[l] must wash his clothes and bathe with water,[m] and he will be ceremonially unclean till evening;[n] then he will be clean. 16But if he does not wash his clothes and bathe himself, he will be held responsible.[o] ' "

Chapter 18

Unlawful Sexual Relations

THE LORD said to Moses, 2"Speak to the Israelites and say to them: 'I am the LORD your God.[p] 3You must not do as

16:28 [z]Nu 19:8,10
16:29 [a]S Ex 12:14 [b]Lev 25:9 [c]ver 31; Lev 23:27,32; Nu 29:7; Isa 58:3 [d]S Ex 31:15; S Lev 23:28 [e]Ex 12:19
16:30 [f]S Ex 30:10 [g]Ps 51:2; Jer 33:8; Eze 36:33; Zec 13:1; Eph 5:26
16:31 [h]Ezr 8:21; Isa 58:3,5; Da 10:12 [i]Ac 27:9
16:32 [j]S Ex 30:30 [k]S ver 4; S Ex 28:2
16:33 [l]S ver 11, 16-18; Eze 45:18
16:34 [m]S Ex 27:21 [n]Heb 9:7,25
17:2 [o]Lev 10:6,12
17:3 [p]S Lev 3:7 [q]S Lev 7:23
17:4 [r]ver 9; 1Ki 8:4; 2Ch 1:3 [s]Dt 12:5-21 [t]S Ge 17:14
17:5 [u]S Lev 3:1; Eze 43:27
17:6 [v]S Lev 4:18 [w]S Lev 3:2 [x]S Lev 1:9
17:7 [y]S Ex 22:20 [z]S Ex 34:15; Jer 3:6,9; Eze 23:3; 1Co 10:20 [a]S Ex 12:14 [b]S Ge 9:12
17:9 [c]S Lev 1:3 [d]S ver 4 [e]S Lev 3:7
17:10 [f]S Ge 9:4
17:11 [g]ver 14 [h]Heb 9:22
17:13 [i]Lev 7:26; Eze 24:7; 33:25; Ac 15:20
17:14 [j]S Ge 9:4
17:15 [k]S Lev 7:24 [l]S Ex 22:31 [m]S Lev 14:8 [n]S Lev 11:40
17:16 [o]S Lev 5:1
18:2 [p]S Ge 17:7

[i]29 Or *must fast*; also in verse 31 [j]3 The Hebrew word can include both male and female. [k]5 Traditionally *peace offerings* [l]7 Or *demons*

16:29–34 SIN, Serious—So serious was sin under the old covenant that a special day was appointed annually to make atonement for the sins of the people. Under the new covenant, Jesus died once for all sin. His death is the new covenant's answer to the Day of Atonement under the old covenant. See Heb 10:11–18. Still, God's people need to be aware of our sins, confess them to God regularly, and find His forgiveness. We can never ignore the serious nature of sin in our lives.

16:30 SALVATION, Forgiveness—Forgiveness of sin is cleansing from sin. This is what atonement accomplishes.

17:6 PRAYER, Worship—See notes on 1:9; Ex 30:1,7.

17:11 HUMANITY, Life—Observation illustrates what revelation declares, that blood carries the gift of life. Without blood, people and animals die. As the carrier of life, which God alone can give, blood is especially sacred. It had to be handled in a sacred manner in Old Testament rituals and became a central part of the gospel message, as Christ shed His blood for our sins. See Mt 26:28.

17:11 SALVATION, Atonement—Blood was used to make atonement because the life was in the blood. This should help us to understand the emphasis on blood in the doctrine of salvation. Sin brings death (Ge 2:17) and can be dealt with in God's plan only through that which represents life.

18:3 HISTORY, Moral—God is aware of the individual differences history brings to people. Historical differences do not change God's moral foundations. Living in Egypt or Canaan did not justify Israel's acceptance of their morality even though their cultural and educational systems had much older

they do in Egypt, where you used to live,
and you must not do as they do in the
land of Canaan, where I am bringing you.
Do not follow their practices.[q] 4You must
obey my laws[r] and be careful to follow
my decrees.[s] I am the LORD your God.[t]
5Keep my decrees and laws,[u] for the man
who obeys them will live by them.[v] I am
the LORD.

6" 'No one is to approach any close relative to have sexual relations. I am the
LORD.

7" 'Do not dishonor your father[w] by
having sexual relations with your mother.[x] She is your mother; do not have relations with her.

8" 'Do not have sexual relations with
your father's wife;[y] that would dishonor
your father.[z]

9" 'Do not have sexual relations with
your sister,[a] either your father's daughter or your mother's daughter, whether
she was born in the same home or elsewhere.[b]

10" 'Do not have sexual relations with
your son's daughter or your daughter's
daughter; that would dishonor you.

11" 'Do not have sexual relations with
the daughter of your father's wife, born to
your father; she is your sister.

12" 'Do not have sexual relations with
your father's sister;[c] she is your father's
close relative.

13" 'Do not have sexual relations with
your mother's sister,[d] because she is
your mother's close relative.

14" 'Do not dishonor your father's
brother by approaching his wife to have
sexual relations; she is your aunt.[e]

15" 'Do not have sexual relations with
your daughter-in-law.[f] She is your son's
wife; do not have relations with her.[g]

16" 'Do not have sexual relations with
your brother's wife;[h] that would dishon-
or your brother.

17" 'Do not have sexual relations with
both a woman and her daughter.[i] Do not
have sexual relations with either her
son's daughter or her daughter's daughter; they are her close relatives. That is
wickedness.

18" 'Do not take your wife's sister[j] as a
rival wife and have sexual relations with
her while your wife is living.

19" 'Do not approach a woman to have
sexual relations during the uncleanness[k]
of her monthly period.[l]

20" 'Do not have sexual relations with
your neighbor's wife[m] and defile yourself
with her.

21" 'Do not give any of your children[n]
to be sacrificed[m] to Molech,[o] for you
must not profane the name of your God.[p]
I am the LORD.[q]

22" 'Do not lie with a man as one lies
with a woman;[r] that is detestable.[s]

23" 'Do not have sexual relations with
an animal and defile yourself with it. A
woman must not present herself to an animal to have sexual relations with it; that
is a perversion.[t]

24" 'Do not defile yourselves in any of
these ways, because this is how the nations that I am going to drive out before
you[u] became defiled.[v] 25Even the land
was defiled;[w] so I punished it for its sin,[x]
and the land vomited out its inhabitants.[y] 26But you must keep my decrees
and my laws.[z] The native-born and the
aliens living among you must not do any
of these detestable things, 27for all these
things were done by the people who lived
in the land before you, and the land became defiled. 28And if you defile the
land,[a] it will vomit you out[b] as it vomited out the nations that were before you.

29" 'Everyone who does any of these
detestable things—such persons must be
cut off from their people. 30Keep my requirements[c] and do not follow any of the
detestable customs that were practiced
before you came and do not defile yourselves with them. I am the LORD your
God.[d]' "

18:3 [q]ver 24-30; S Ex 23:24; Dt 18:9; 2Ki 16:3; 17:8; 1Ch 5:25 **18:4** [r]S Ge 26:5 [s]Dt 4:1; 1Ki 11:11; Jer 44:10,23; Eze 11:12 [t]ver 2 **18:5** [u]S Ge 26:5 [v]Dt 4:1; Ne 9:29; Isa 55:3; Eze 18:9; 20:11; Am 5:4-6; Mt 19:17; S Ro 10:5*; Gal 3:12* **18:7** [w]ver 8; Lev 20:11; Dt 27:20 [x]Eze 22:10 **18:8** [y]1Co 5:1 [z]Ge 35:22; Lev 20:11; Dt 22:30; 27:20 **18:9** [a]ver 11; Lev 20:17; Dt 27:22 [b]Lev 20:17; Dt 27:22; 2Sa 13:13; Eze 22:11 **18:12** [c]ver 13; Lev 20:19 **18:13** [d]S ver 12,14; Lev 20:20 **18:14** [e]S ver 13 **18:15** [f]S Ge 11:31; S 38:16 [g]Eze 22:11 **18:16** [h]Lev 20:21; Mt 14:4; Mk 6:18 **18:17** [i]Lev 20:14; Dt 27:23 **18:18** [j]S Ge 30:1 **18:19** [k]S Lev 15:25-30 [l]S Lev 15:24 **18:20** [m]S Ex 20:14; Mt 5:27,28; 1Co 6:9; Heb 13:4 **18:21** [n]Dt 12:31; 18:10; 2Ki 16:3; 17:17; 21:6; 23:10; 2Ch 28:1-4; 33:6; Ps 106:37,38; Isa 57:5; Jer 7:30, 31; 19:5; 32:35; Eze 16:20; Mic 6:7 [o]Lev 20:2-5; Dt 9:4; 1Ki 11:5,7, 33; Isa 57:9; Jer 32:35; 49:1; Zep 1:5 [p]Lev 19:12; 21:6; Isa 48:11; Eze 22:26; 36:20; Am 2:7; Mal 1:12 [q]S Ex 6:2 **18:22** [r]Lev 20:13; Dt 23:18; Ro 1:27; 1Co 6:9 [s]S Ge 19:5 **18:23** [t]Ex 22:19; Lev 20:15; Dt 27:21 **18:24** [u]ver 3,27,30; Lev 20:23 [v]Dt 9:4; 18:12 **18:25** [w]Nu 35:34; Dt 21:23 [x]Lev 20:23; Dt 9:5; 12:31; 18:12 [y]ver 28; Lev 20:22; Job 20:15; Jer 51:34 **18:26** [z]S Ge 26:5 **18:28** [a]Lev 20:22; Ezr 9:11; La 1:17 [b]S ver 25 **18:30** [c]S Lev 8:35 [d]ver 2

[m]21 Or *to be passed through* ⌊*the fire*⌋

roots than did the young nation Israel's.

18:3–30 CHRISTIAN ETHICS, Moral Limits—Each person is free to make moral choices. Those choices should be made within the responsible boundaries of what God has declared as moral and immoral. Persons and societies outside God's people offer choices which may entice, but such choices are not options if we trust and follow God. Ungodly society tempts God's people with immoral sexual practices. No human logic can make it right for us to go beyond God's limits in our sexual behavior.

18:6–20 FAMILY, Sexual Sin—Sexual relations with members of both the primary and extended family were practiced by *the inhabitants of the land* that the Israelites were to possess. God instructed His covenant people not to do them. Engaging in such sexual activities is not only destructive to family relationships but also destructive to one's relationship to God. The Bible affirms that even the land becomes polluted by such sexual misbehavior among the people. Contemporary sexuality studies support the destructive effects of interfamily sexual involvements by adults as well as with children. See 20:10–20.

18:24–29 ELECTION, Righteousness—The God of election is the God of holiness who requires holy living from those whom He elects to be His people. Election does not relieve the elect of moral responsibility. It intensifies the demand for righteousness.

18:24–28 CHRISTIAN ETHICS, Moral Limits—Moral limits have enforcement mechanisms in God's relationship with His people. He punishes appropriately those who refuse to trust Him and abide by His limits. See note on Dt 28:25.

Chapter 19

Various Laws

THE LORD said to Moses, 2"Speak to
the entire assembly of Israel[e] and
say to them: 'Be holy because I, the LORD
your God,[f] am holy.[g]
3" 'Each of you must respect his mother and father,[h] and you must observe my
Sabbaths.[i] I am the LORD your God.[j]
4" 'Do not turn to idols or make gods of
cast metal for yourselves.[k] I am the LORD
your God.[l]
5" 'When you sacrifice a fellowship offering[n] to the LORD, sacrifice it in such a
way that it will be accepted on your behalf. 6It shall be eaten on the day you
sacrifice it or on the next day; anything
left over until the third day must be
burned up.[m] 7If any of it is eaten on the
third day, it is impure and will not be
accepted.[n] 8Whoever eats it will be held
responsible[o] because he has desecrated
what is holy[p] to the LORD; that person
must be cut off from his people.[q]
9" 'When you reap the harvest of your
land, do not reap to the very edges[r] of
your field or gather the gleanings of your
harvest.[s] 10Do not go over your vineyard
a second time[t] or pick up the grapes that
have fallen.[u] Leave them for the poor
and the alien.[v] I am the LORD your God.
11" 'Do not steal.[w]
" 'Do not lie.[x]
" 'Do not deceive one another.[y]
12" 'Do not swear falsely[z] by my
name[a] and so profane[b] the name of your
God. I am the LORD.
13" 'Do not defraud your neighbor[c] or
rob[d] him.[e]
" 'Do not hold back the wages of a
hired man[f] overnight.[g]
14" 'Do not curse the deaf or put a
stumbling block in front of the blind,[h]
but fear your God.[i] I am the LORD.
15" 'Do not pervert justice;[j] do not
show partiality[k] to the poor or favoritism
to the great,[l] but judge your neighbor
fairly.[m]
16" 'Do not go about spreading slander[n] among your people.
" 'Do not do anything that endangers
your neighbor's life.[o] I am the LORD.
17" 'Do not hate your brother in your
heart.[p] Rebuke your neighbor frankly[q]
so you will not share in his guilt.
18" 'Do not seek revenge[r] or bear a
grudge[s] against one of your people,[t] but
love your neighbor[u] as yourself.[v] I am
the LORD.

19:2 [e]Nu 14:5; Ps 68:26 [f]S Ex 20:2 [g]S Ex 15:11; 1Pe 1:16*; S Lev 11:44; S 20:26 **19:3** [h]Ex 20:12 [i]S Ex 20:8 [j]Lev 11:44 **19:4** [k]S Ex 20:4; Jdg 17:3; Ps 96:5; 115:4-7; 135:15 [l]Lev 11:44 **19:6** [m]Lev 7:16-17 **19:7** [n]Lev 7:18 **19:8** [o]S Lev 5:1 [p]Lev 22:2,15,16; Nu 18:32 [q]S Ge 17:14 **19:9** [r]Ru 2:2,3,7, 16,17 [s]Lev 23:10, 22; Dt 24:19-22; Job 24:10 **19:10** [t]Dt 24:20 [u]ver 9 [v]Dt 24:19,21 **19:11** [w]Ex 20:15; S 23:4; Lk 3:14 [x]S Ex 20:16; S Eph 4:25 [y]S Lev 6:2 **19:12** [z]Jer 5:2; 7:9; Mal 3:5 [a]Ex 3:13; 20:7; Dt 18:19; Pr 18:10; Isa 42:8; Jer 44:16, 26; S Mt 5:33 [b]Jer 34:16 **19:13** [c]Lev 25:14, 17 [d]S Ex 20:15 [e]S Ex 22:15,25-27 [f]Job 7:2; 24:12; 31:39; Isa 16:14; Mal 3:5 [g]Dt 24:15; Jer 22:13; Mt 20:8; 1Ti 5:18; Jas 5:4 **19:14** [h]S Ex 4:11; Lev 21:18; Dt 27:18 [i]ver 32; Lev 25:17, 36 **19:15** [j]S Ex 23:2; Ex 23:2,6 [k]Dt 24:17; Job 13:8,10; 32:21; Pr 28:21 [l]Job 34:19 [m]S Ex 23:8; Pr 24:23; Mal 2:9; Jas 2:1-4 **19:16** [n]Ps 15:3; 31:13; 41:6; 101:5; Jer 6:28; 9:4; Eze 22:9 [o]Ex 23:7; Dt 10:17; 27:25; Ps 15:5; Eze 22:12 **19:17** [p]S 1Jn 2:9 [q]S Mt 18:15 **19:18** [r]S Ge 4:23; Ro 12:19; Heb 10:30 [s]Ps 103:9 [t]S Ex 12:48 [u]S Ex 20:16 [v]ver 34; S Mt 5:43*; 19:16*; 22:39*; Mk 12:31*; Lk 10:27*; Jn 13:34; Ro 13:9*; Gal 5:14*; Jas 2:8*

[n]5 Traditionally *peace offering*

19:1–2 REVELATION, Actions—Revelation has a direct purpose. God ordered Moses to assemble the chosen people so He might restate to them what He hoped they would become—a holy people reflecting God's pure character. A listing of commands much like the ten known in Ex 20 and Dt 5 follows. God's commands are a revelation of who He is and who the people are who follow Him.

19:1–2,9–19 DISCIPLESHIP, Persons—One principle stands behind all biblical ethical teachings: be holy like the holy God. God's people want to be like Him. Striving to be like God is strong motivation to serve His purposes by respecting and helping other persons. Meeting the needs of others demonstrates being holy as God is holy. Holiness means being cut off or separated *from* all that is evil. It also means being separated *to* all that is good. Being holy as God is holy is very much like being perfect as God is perfect. See Mt 5:48. Being holy means concrete actions, not simply an unattainable goal. These include: (1) making provision for the poor and the homeless (vv 9–10), (2) practicing honesty toward all others (vv 11–12), (3) not taking or keeping anything that belongs to another person (v 13), (4) not taking advantage of handicapped persons (v 14), (5) being just in dealing with both the rich and the poor (vv 13,15), (6) not using gossip or lies to get what we desire (vv 11–13), and (7) not doing anything that would endanger a neighbor's life (vv 13–16). God's people are to seek corrective changes in the lives of their neighbors through the application of redemptive love (vv 17–18). From verse 18 Jesus drew the love-for-neighbor commandment that He combined with the love-for-God commandment from Dt 6:5. See Mt 22:37–39. See Guide to Service in Christ's Name, pp. 1823–1826.

19:1–18 CHRISTIAN ETHICS, Social Relationships—As a portion of the holiness code (chs 17—26), these ethical expectations are based on God's holiness. God's people are to be holy like God, not sinful like the nations. Horizontal relationships with our fellow human beings must reflect our vertical relationship with God.

19:9–10 HUMANITY, Community Relationships—A responsible society has concern for and seeks to meet the needs of its weak, impoverished, and disenfranchised members.

19:11 CHRISTIAN ETHICS, Theft—See note on Ex 20:15.

19:11 CHRISTIAN ETHICS, Language—See note on Ex 20:16.

19:13–18 HUMANITY, Community Relationships—A society needs a firm foundation of justice. The weaker and poorer members must be able to find justice within a society if it is to endure. Further, justice must not only be evenhanded, it must also be based upon loving others rather than rejecting them. No place exists in a society for vengeance as a basis for dealing with people. Justice tempered with mercy must be the rule.

19:14 DISCIPLESHIP, Handicapped—Motivated by unselfish love, the people of God will not do anything to harm a handicapped person. For example, we will not ridicule deaf persons who cannot hear and, therefore, cannot defend themselves. Nor will we put any kind of hindrance in the way of a blind person. We will not take advantage of any handicapped person. We remember that God sees and hears. He punishes those who mistreat the handicapped.

19:15 CHRISTIAN ETHICS, Justice—Fairness is a primary element of justice. Thus, a certain objectivity must be maintained whether one is poor or rich. Social standing, or lack of it, should not decide whether a person gets fair treatment. Economic and political power must not control the legal system. Neither can judges allow pity and personal relationships to influence decisions. A justice system begins on the local level with neighbors who are just and fair with their neighbors. Israel's system centered on elders handling cases in the city gate.

19" 'Keep my decrees.[w]
" 'Do not mate different kinds of animals.
" 'Do not plant your field with two
kinds of seed.[x]
" 'Do not wear clothing woven of two
kinds of material.[y]
20" 'If a man sleeps with a woman who
is a slave girl promised to another man[z]
but who has not been ransomed or given
her freedom, there must be due punishment. Yet they are not to be put to death,
because she had not been freed. 21The
man, however, must bring a ram to the
entrance to the Tent of Meeting for a
guilt offering to the LORD.[a] 22With the
ram of the guilt offering the priest is to
make atonement for him before the LORD
for the sin he has committed, and his sin
will be forgiven.[b]
23" 'When you enter the land and plant
any kind of fruit tree, regard its fruit as
forbidden.[o] For three years you are to
consider it forbidden[o]; it must not be
eaten. 24In the fourth year all its fruit will
be holy,[c] an offering of praise to the
LORD. 25But in the fifth year you may eat
its fruit. In this way your harvest will be
increased. I am the LORD your God.
26" 'Do not eat any meat with the
blood still in it.[d]
" 'Do not practice divination[e] or sorcery.[f]
27" 'Do not cut the hair at the sides of
your head or clip off the edges of your
beard.[g]
28" 'Do not cut[h] your bodies for the
dead or put tattoo marks on yourselves. I
am the LORD.
29" 'Do not degrade your daughter by
making her a prostitute,[i] or the land will
turn to prostitution and be filled with
wickedness.[j]
30" 'Observe my Sabbaths[k] and have
reverence for my sanctuary. I am the
LORD.[l]
31" 'Do not turn to mediums[m] or seek
out spiritists,[n] for you will be defiled by
them. I am the LORD your God.
32" 'Rise in the presence of the aged,
show respect[o] for the elderly[p] and revere your God.[q] I am the LORD.[r]
33" 'When an alien lives with you in
your land, do not mistreat him. 34The
alien living with you must be treated as
one of your native-born.[s] Love him as
yourself,[t] for you were aliens[u] in
Egypt.[v] I am the LORD your God.
35" 'Do not use dishonest standards
when measuring length, weight or quantity.[w] 36Use honest scales[x] and honest
weights, an honest ephah[p][y] and an honest hin.[q][z] I am the LORD your God, who
brought you out of Egypt.[a]
37" 'Keep all my decrees[b] and all my
laws[c] and follow them. I am the LORD.' "

Chapter 20

Punishments for Sin

THE LORD said to Moses, 2"Say to the
Israelites: 'Any Israelite or any alien
living in Israel who gives[r] any of his children to Molech must be put to death.[d]
The people of the community are to stone
him.[e] 3I will set my face against that man
and I will cut him off from his people;[f]
for by giving his children to Molech, he
has defiled[g] my sanctuary[h] and profaned
my holy name.[i] 4If the people of the
community close their eyes when that
man gives one of his children to Molech
and they fail to put him to death,[j] 5I will
set my face against that man and his family and will cut off from their people both
him and all who follow him in prostituting themselves to Molech.
6" 'I will set my face against the person
who turns to mediums and spiritists to
prostitute himself by following them, and
I will cut him off from his people.[k]
7" 'Consecrate yourselves[l] and be
holy,[m] because I am the LORD your God.[n]
8Keep my decrees[o] and follow them. I
am the LORD, who makes you holy.[s][p]

19:19 [w]S Ge 26:5 [x]Dt 22:9 [y]Dt 22:11 **19:20** [z]Dt 22:23-27 **19:21** [a]S Lev 5:15 **19:22** [b]S Lev 5:15 **19:24** [c]S Ex 22:29 **19:26** [d]S Ge 9:4 [e]S Ge 30:27; S Isa 44:25 [f]S Ex 22:18; 2Ki 17:17 **19:27** [g]Lev 21:5; Dt 14:1; 2Sa 10:4-5; Jer 41:5; 48:37; Eze 5:1-5 **19:28** [h]Lev 21:5; Dt 14:1; 1Ki 18:28; Jer 16:6; 41:5; 47:5 **19:29** [i]Lev 21:9; Dt 23:18 [j]Ge 34:7; Lev 21:9 **19:30** [k]S Ex 20:8 [l]Lev 26:2 **19:31** [m]S Ex 22:18; 1Sa 28:7-20; 1Ch 10:13 [n]Lev 20:6; 2Ki 21:6; 23:24; Isa 8:19; 19:3; 29:4; 47:12; 65:4 **19:32** [o]1Ki 12:8 [p]Job 32:4; Pr 23:22; La 5:12; 1Ti 5:1 [q]S ver 14; Job 29:8 [r]Lev 11:44; 25:17 **19:34** [s]S Ex 12:48 [t]S ver 18 [u]S Ex 22:21 [v]Ex 23:9; Dt 10:19; 23:7; Ps 146:9 **19:35** [w]Dt 25:13-16 **19:36** [x]Job 31:6; Pr 11:1; Hos 12:7; Mic 6:11 [y]Jdg 6:19; Ru 2:17; 1Sa 1:24; 17:17; Eze 45:10 [z]Dt 25:13-15; Pr 20:10; Eze 45:11 [a]S Ex 12:17 **19:37** [b]2Ki 17:37; 2Ch 7:17; Ps 119:5; Eze 18:9 [c]S Ge 26:5 **20:2** [d]ver 10; Ge 26:11; Ex 19:12 [e]ver 27; Lev 24:14; Nu 15:35,36; Dt 21:21; Jos 7:25 **20:3** [f]ver 5,6; Lev 23:30 [g]Ps 74:7; 79:1; Jer 7:30; Eze 5:11 [h]S Lev 15:31 [i]S Lev 18:21 **20:4** [j]Dt 17:2-5 **20:6** [k]S ver 3; S Lev 19:31 **20:7** [l]S Lev 11:44 [m]S Ex 29:1; 31:13; Lev 11:45; Eph 1:4; 1Pe 1:16* [n]S Ex 6:2; S 20:2 **20:8** [o]S Ge 26:5 [p]S Ex 31:13; Eze 20:12

[o]*23* Hebrew *uncircumcised* [p]*36* An ephah was a dry measure. [q]*36* A hin was a liquid measure. [r]*2* Or *sacrifices*; also in verses 3 and 4 [s]*8* Or *who sanctifies you*; or *who sets you apart as holy*

19:31 REVELATION, Oracles—See note on 20:6,27.

19:33–34 DISCIPLESHIP, Homeless—Foreigners in the midst of God's people are to be included in the scope of the caring neighbor love that characterizes the lives of those who serve God faithfully. God's disciples are to love such homeless foreigners as we do ourselves. See note on Mt 22:37–40.

19:35–36 CHRISTIAN ETHICS, Honesty—God's expectations include business practices. A merchant controls the scales and must use them honestly in charging customers. God our Savior is interested in how we measure what we sell. See notes on 6:1–5; Dt 27:17.

19:37 CHRISTIAN ETHICS, Social Relationships—Picking and choosing is not an alternative for God's people as we make moral choices. We must obey all God's commands and remain within all the limits He sets. The criterion is not what we like or agree with, but what He says. Such a system is not a tyrannical legalism for two reasons: (1) God has shown Himself to be good and trustworthy, and (2) we choose to enter the covenant relationship with God and pledge ourselves to obey His commands. See note on 19:1–18.

20:1–27 CHRISTIAN ETHICS, Social Order—See notes on 18:3–30; 19:1–18. Lower moral standards give cause for rejection from society and from God's people. We are different from all other parts of society. We are God's holy people.

20:6,27 REVELATION, Oracles—Certain ways of obtaining revelation are wrong. Seeking to consult the dead or spirits *for revelation* is wrong. Only the living God gives revelation. Among ways He revealed Himself are priests, prophets, prayer, sacred lot, dreams, angels, and His Spirit. Compare Dt 18:9–14.

9"'If anyone curses his father[q] or
mother,[r] he must be put to death.[s] He
has cursed his father or his mother, and
his blood will be on his own head.[t]
10"'If a man commits adultery with another man's wife[u]—with the wife of his
neighbor—both the adulterer and the
adulteress must be put to death.[v]
11"'If a man sleeps with his father's
wife, he has dishonored his father.[w] Both
the man and the woman must be put to
death; their blood will be on their own
heads.[x]
12"'If a man sleeps with his daughter-
in-law,[y] both of them must be put to
death. What they have done is a perversion; their blood will be on their own
heads.
13"'If a man lies with a man as one lies
with a woman, both of them have done
what is detestable.[z] They must be put to
death; their blood will be on their own
heads.
14"'If a man marries both a woman
and her mother,[a] it is wicked. Both he
and they must be burned in the fire,[b] so
that no wickedness will be among you.[c]
15"'If a man has sexual relations with
an animal,[d] he must be put to death,[e]
and you must kill the animal.
16"'If a woman approaches an animal
to have sexual relations with it, kill both
the woman and the animal. They must be
put to death; their blood will be on their
own heads.
17"'If a man marries his sister[f], the
daughter of either his father or his mother, and they have sexual relations, it is a
disgrace. They must be cut off before the
eyes[g] of their people. He has dishonored
his sister and will be held responsible.[h]
18"'If a man lies with a woman during
her monthly period[i] and has sexual relations with her, he has exposed the source
of her flow, and she has also uncovered
it. Both of them must be cut off from their
people.[j]
19"'Do not have sexual relations with
the sister of either your mother or your
father,[k] for that would dishonor a close
relative; both of you would be held responsible.
20"'If a man sleeps with his aunt,[l] he
has dishonored his uncle. They will be
held responsible; they will die childless.[m]
21"'If a man marries his brother's
wife,[n] it is an act of impurity; he has dishonored his brother. They will be childless.[o]
22"'Keep all my decrees and laws[p] and
follow them, so that the land[q] where I
am bringing you to live may not vomit
you out. 23You must not live according to
the customs of the nations[r] I am going to
drive out before you.[s] Because they did
all these things, I abhorred them.[t] 24But
I said to you, "You will possess their land;
I will give it to you as an inheritance, a
land flowing with milk and honey."[u] I
am the LORD your God, who has set you
apart from the nations.[v]
25"'You must therefore make a distinction between clean and unclean animals
and between unclean and clean birds.[w]
Do not defile yourselves by any animal or
bird or anything that moves along the
ground—those which I have set apart as
unclean for you. 26You are to be holy to
me[t][x] because I, the LORD, am holy,[y]
and I have set you apart from the nations[z] to be my own.
27"'A man or woman who is a medium[a] or spiritist among you must be put
to death.[b] You are to stone them;[c] their
blood will be on their own heads.'"

Chapter 21

Rules for Priests

THE LORD said to Moses, "Speak to the
priests, the sons of Aaron,[d] and say
to them: 'A priest must not make himself
ceremonially unclean[e] for any of his people who die,[f] 2except for a close relative,
such as his mother or father,[g] his son or
daughter, his brother, 3or an unmarried
sister who is dependent on him since she
has no husband—for her he may make
himself unclean.[h] 4He must not make
himself unclean for people related to him
by marriage,[u] and so defile himself.
5"'Priests must not shave[i] their heads
or shave off the edges of their beards[j] or
cut their bodies.[k] 6They must be holy to
their God[l] and must not profane the
name of their God.[m] Because they

[t]26 Or *be my holy ones* [u]4 Or *unclean as a leader among his people*

20:9 [q]Ex 20:12; Jer 35:16; Mal 1:6; 2:10 [r]S Ex 20:12; Dt 27:16; Eze 22:7 [s]Ex 21:17; Dt 21:20-21; Mt 15:4*; Mk 7:10* [t]ver 11; Dt 22:30; Jos 2:19; 2Sa 1:16; 3:29; 1Ki 2:37; Eze 18:13; 33:4,5
20:10 [u]Ex 20:14; Dt 5:18; 22:22; Jn 8:5 [v]S Ge 38:24; S Ex 21:12
20:11 [w]S Lev 18:7 [x]S ver 9; S Lev 18:8
20:12 [y]S Ge 11:31; S 38:16
20:13 [z]Lev 18:22
20:14 [a]S Lev 18:17 [b]Lev 21:9; Nu 16:39; Jdg 14:15; 15:6 [c]S Lev 18:8; Dt 27:23
20:15 [d]S Ex 22:19 [e]ver 10
20:17 [f]S Lev 18:9 [g]S Ge 17:14 [h]S Lev 5:1
20:18 [i]S Lev 15:24 [j]Eze 18:6
20:19 [k]S Lev 18:12
20:20 [l]S Lev 18:13 [m]ver 21; Ge 15:2
20:21 [n]S Lev 18:16; Mt 14:4; Mk 6:18 [o]S ver 20
20:22 [p]S Ge 26:5 [q]S Lev 18:25-28
20:23 [r]S Lev 18:3 [s]S Lev 18:24 [t]S Lev 18:25
20:24 [u]S Ex 3:8; Nu 14:8; 16:14 [v]S Ex 33:16
20:25 [w]Lev 10:10; Dt 14:3-21; Ac 10:14
20:26 [x]Dt 14:2 [y]ver 8; Lev 19:2; Jos 24:19; 2Ki 19:22; Ps 99:3 [z]S Ex 33:16
20:27 [a]S Ex 22:18 [b]S Lev 19:31 [c]S ver 2; S Lev 24:14
21:1 [d]S Ex 28:1; S Lev 1:5 [e]S Lev 5:3; S 13:3 [f]ver 11; Nu 5:2; 6:6; 19:11; 31:19
21:2 [g]ver 11
21:3 [h]Nu 6:6
21:5 [i]S Lev 13:40; Jer 7:29; 16:6 [j]Eze 5:1; 44:20 [k]S Lev 19:28
21:6 [l]ver 8; Ezr 8:28 [m]Lev 18:21

20:22–26 REVELATION, Fellowship—The God of promises repeated His purposes to His people, declaring His plans for a land of much abundance and hope. He also reminded Israel He had selected them to be a separate and unique nation (holy), totally distinct from their neighbors. See note on 19:1–2.

20:24,26 ELECTION, Righteousness—The elect of God cannot live by the values and life-styles of other nations. God elected Israel to be a people set apart from other nations, holy unto the holy God, who provides a rich inheritance to His elect. See note on 18:24–29.

21:1–4 HUMANITY, Moral Consciousness—Anyone who touched a dead person was considered unclean. Thus a priest who touched a dead person was unclean and was prohibited from serving in the Temple until he had been ritually purified. Having been set aside for the service of God, the priest was not supposed to allow the death of anyone other than a close relative to preclude his higher commitment. In a similar manner, life's commitments are to be built upon the basis of divine priorities.

present the offerings made to the LORD by
fire,[n] the food of their God,[o] they are to
be holy.[p]
7" 'They must not marry women defiled by prostitution or divorced from
their husbands,[q] because priests are holy
to their God.[r] 8Regard them as holy,[s]
because they offer up the food of your
God.[t] Consider them holy, because I the
LORD am holy—I who make you holy.[v] [u]
9" 'If a priest's daughter defiles herself
by becoming a prostitute, she disgraces
her father; she must be burned in the
fire.[v]
10" 'The high priest, the one among his
brothers who has had the anointing oil
poured on his head[w] and who has been
ordained to wear the priestly garments,[x]
must not let his hair become unkempt[w]
or tear his clothes.[y] 11He must not enter
a place where there is a dead body.[z] He
must not make himself unclean,[a] even
for his father or mother,[b] 12nor leave the
sanctuary[c] of his God or desecrate it, because he has been dedicated by the
anointing oil[d] of his God. I am the LORD.
13" 'The woman he marries must be a
virgin.[e] 14He must not marry a widow, a
divorced woman, or a woman defiled by
prostitution, but only a virgin from his
own people, 15so he will not defile his
offspring among his people. I am the
LORD, who makes him holy.[x] ' "
16The LORD said to Moses, 17"Say to
Aaron: 'For the generations to come none
of your descendants who has a defect[f]
may come near to offer the food of his
God.[g] 18No man who has any defect[h]
may come near: no man who is blind[i] or
lame,[j] disfigured or deformed; 19no man
with a crippled foot or hand, 20or who is
hunchbacked or dwarfed, or who has any
eye defect, or who has festering or running sores or damaged testicles.[k] 21No
descendant of Aaron the priest who has
any defect[l] is to come near to present
the offerings made to the LORD by fire.[m]
He has a defect; he must not come near
to offer the food of his God.[n] 22He may
eat the most holy food of his God,[o] as
well as the holy food; 23yet because of his
defect,[p] he must not go near the curtain
or approach the altar, and so desecrate
my sanctuary.[q] I am the LORD, who
makes them holy.[y] [r] ' "
24So Moses told this to Aaron and his
sons and to all the Israelites.

Chapter 22

THE LORD said to Moses, 2"Tell Aaron
and his sons to treat with respect the
sacred offerings[s] the Israelites consecrate to me, so they will not profane my
holy name.[t] I am the LORD.[u]
3"Say to them: 'For the generations to
come, if any of your descendants is ceremonially unclean and yet comes near the
sacred offerings that the Israelites consecrate to the LORD,[v] that person must be
cut off from my presence.[w] I am the
LORD.
4" 'If a descendant of Aaron has an infectious skin disease[z] or a bodily discharge,[x] he may not eat the sacred offerings until he is cleansed. He will also be
unclean if he touches something defiled
by a corpse[y] or by anyone who has an
emission of semen, 5or if he touches any
crawling thing[z] that makes him unclean,
or any person[a] who makes him unclean,
whatever the uncleanness may be. 6The
one who touches any such thing will be
unclean[b] till evening.[c] He must not eat
any of the sacred offerings unless he has
bathed himself with water.[d] 7When the
sun goes down, he will be clean, and after
that he may eat the sacred offerings, for
they are his food.[e] 8He must not eat anything found dead[f] or torn by wild animals,[g] and so become unclean[h] through
it. I am the LORD.[i]
9" 'The priests are to keep my requirements[j] so that they do not become
guilty[k] and die[l] for treating them with
contempt. I am the LORD, who makes
them holy.[a] [m]
10" 'No one outside a priest's family
may eat the sacred offering, nor may the
guest of a priest or his hired worker eat
it.[n] 11But if a priest buys a slave with
money, or if a slave is born in his household, that slave may eat his food.[o] 12If a
priest's daughter marries anyone other
than a priest, she may not eat any of the
sacred contributions. 13But if a priest's
daughter becomes a widow or is divorced, yet has no children, and she returns to live in her father's house as in
her youth, she may eat of her father's
food. No unauthorized person, however,
may eat any of it.
14" 'If anyone eats a sacred offering by
mistake,[p] he must make restitution to
the priest for the offering and add a fifth
of the value[q] to it. 15The priests must not

21:6 [n]S Lev 3:11 [o]ver 17,22; Lev 22:25 [p]S Ex 19:22; S Lev 10:3
21:7 [q]ver 13,14 [r]Eze 44:22
21:8 [s]ver 6 [t]Lev 3:11 [u]S Ex 31:13
21:9 [v]S Ge 38:24; S Lev 19:29
21:10 [w]S Ex 29:7 [x]S Lev 8:7-9,13; S 16:4 [y]S Lev 10:6
21:11 [z]Nu 5:2; 6:6; 9:6; 19:11,13, 14; 31:19 [a]Lev 19:28 [b]ver 2
21:12 [c]S Ex 25:8 [d]S Ex 28:41
21:13 [e]Eze 44:22
21:17 [f]ver 18,21,23 [g]S ver 6
21:18 [h]Lev 22:19-25 [i]S Lev 19:14 [j]2Sa 4:4; 9:3; 19:26
21:20 [k]Lev 22:24; Dt 23:1; Isa 56:3
21:21 [l]S ver 17 [m]S Lev 3:11 [n]Lev 22:19
21:22 [o]1Co 9:13
21:23 [p]S ver 17 [q]S Ex 25:8 [r]Lev 20:8
22:2 [s]S Lev 19:8 [t]S Ex 20:7; S Mt 5:33 [u]Eze 44:8
22:3 [v]Ezr 8:28 [w]Lev 7:20,21; Nu 19:13
22:4 [x]Lev 15:2-15 [y]Lev 11:24-28,39
22:5 [z]Lev 11:24-28,43 [a]S Lev 15:7
22:6 [b]Hag 2:13 [c]S Lev 11:24 [d]S Lev 14:8
22:7 [e]Nu 18:11
22:8 [f]S Lev 11:39 [g]S Ex 22:31 [h]S Lev 11:40 [i]Lev 11:44
22:9 [j]S Lev 8:35 [k]S Ex 28:38 [l]ver 16; S Ex 28:43 [m]Lev 20:8
22:10 [n]ver 13; Ex 12:45; 29:33
22:11 [o]Ge 17:13; Ex 12:44
22:14 [p]S Lev 4:2 [q]Lev 5:15

[v]8 Or *who sanctify you*; or *who set you apart as holy* [w]10 Or *not uncover his head* [x]15 Or *who sanctifies him*; or *who sets him apart as holy* [y]23 Or *who sanctifies them*; or *who sets them apart as holy* [z]4 Traditionally *leprosy*; the Hebrew word was used for various diseases affecting the skin—not necessarily leprosy. [a]9 Or *who sanctifies them*; or *who sets them apart as holy*; also in verse 16

22:9 CHRISTIAN ETHICS, Moral Limits—Moral limits apply to all God's people. Religious leaders have special responsibilities, not free exemptions. See note on Dt 28:25.

desecrate the sacred offerings[r] the Israelites present to the LORD[s] 16by allowing
them to eat[t] the sacred offerings and so
bring upon them guilt[u] requiring payment.[v] I am the LORD, who makes them
holy.[w]' "

Unacceptable Sacrifices

17The LORD said to Moses, 18"Speak to
Aaron and his sons and to all the Israelites and say to them: 'If any of you—either an Israelite or an alien living in Israel[x]—presents a gift[y] for a burnt offering
to the LORD, either to fulfill a vow[z] or as
a freewill offering,[a] 19you must present a
male without defect[b] from the cattle,
sheep or goats in order that it may be
accepted on your behalf.[c] 20Do not bring
anything with a defect,[d] because it will
not be accepted on your behalf.[e] 21When
anyone brings from the herd or flock[f] a
fellowship offering[b][g] to the LORD to fulfill a special vow or as a freewill offering,[h] it must be without defect or blemish[i] to be acceptable.[j] 22Do not offer to
the LORD the blind, the injured or the
maimed, or anything with warts or festering or running sores. Do not place any of
these on the altar as an offering made to
the LORD by fire. 23You may, however,
present as a freewill offering an ox[c] or a
sheep that is deformed or stunted, but it
will not be accepted in fulfillment of a
vow. 24You must not offer to the LORD an
animal whose testicles are bruised,
crushed, torn or cut.[k] You must not do
this in your own land, 25and you must not
accept such animals from the hand of a
foreigner and offer them as the food of
your God.[l] They will not be accepted on
your behalf, because they are deformed
and have defects.[m]' "

26The LORD said to Moses, 27"When a
calf, a lamb or a goat[n] is born, it is to
remain with its mother for seven days.[o]
From the eighth day[p] on, it will be acceptable[q] as an offering made to the
LORD by fire. 28Do not slaughter a cow or
a sheep and its young on the same day.[r]

29"When you sacrifice a thank offering[s] to the LORD, sacrifice it in such a
way that it will be accepted on your behalf. 30It must be eaten that same day;
leave none of it till morning.[t] I am the
LORD.[u]

31"Keep[v] my commands and follow
them.[w] I am the LORD. 32Do not profane
my holy name.[x] I must be acknowledged
as holy by the Israelites.[y] I am the LORD,
who makes[d] you holy[e][z] 33and who
brought you out of Egypt[a] to be your
God.[b] I am the LORD."

Chapter 23

THE LORD said to Moses, 2"Speak to
the Israelites and say to them: 'These
are my appointed feasts,[c] the appointed
feasts of the LORD, which you are to proclaim as sacred assemblies.[d]

The Sabbath

3" 'There are six days when you may
work,[e] but the seventh day is a Sabbath
of rest,[f] a day of sacred assembly. You
are not to do any work;[g] wherever you
live, it is a Sabbath to the LORD.

The Passover and Unleavened Bread

23:4–8pp — Ex 12:14–20; Nu 28:16–25; Dt 16:1–8

4" 'These are the LORD's appointed
feasts, the sacred assemblies you are to
proclaim at their appointed times:[h] 5The
LORD's Passover[i] begins at twilight on
the fourteenth day of the first month.[j]
6On the fifteenth day of that month the
LORD's Feast of Unleavened Bread[k] begins; for seven days[l] you must eat bread
made without yeast. 7On the first day
hold a sacred assembly[m] and do no regular work. 8For seven days present an offering made to the LORD by fire.[n] And on
the seventh day hold a sacred assembly
and do no regular work.' "

Firstfruits

9The LORD said to Moses, 10"Speak to
the Israelites and say to them: 'When you
enter the land I am going to give you[o]
and you reap its harvest,[p] bring to the
priest a sheaf[q] of the first grain you harvest.[r] 11He is to wave the sheaf before
the LORD[s] so it will be accepted[t] on
your behalf; the priest is to wave it on the

22:15 [r]S Lev 19:8 [s]Nu 18:32
22:16 [t]Nu 18:11 [u]S Ex 28:38 [v]S ver 9 [w]Lev 20:8
22:18 [x]Nu 15:16; 19:10; Jos 8:33 [y]S Lev 1:2 [z]ver 21; S Ge 28:20; Nu 15:8; Ps 22:25; 76:11; 116:18 [a]S Lev 7:16
22:19 [b]S Lev 1:3; 21:18-21; Nu 28:11; Dt 15:21 [c]S Lev 1:2
22:20 [d]S Lev 1:3; Dt 15:21; 17:1; Eze 43:23; 45:18; 46:6; Mal 1:8; Heb 9:14; 1Pe 1:19 [e]S Ex 28:38
22:21 [f]S Lev 1:2 [g]S Ex 32:6; S Lev 3:6 [h]S Lev 7:16 [i]S Ex 12:5; Mal 1:14 [j]Am 4:5
22:24 [k]S Lev 21:20
22:25 [l]S Lev 21:6 [m]S Lev 1:3; S 3:1; Nu 19:2
22:27 [n]S Lev 1:3 [o]S Ex 22:30 [p]S Ex 22:30 [q]S Ex 28:38
22:28 [r]Dt 22:6,7
22:29 [s]S Lev 7:12
22:30 [t]Lev 7:15 [u]Lev 11:44
22:31 [v]Dt 4:2,40; Ps 105:45 [w]S Ex 22:31
22:32 [x]Lev 18:21 [y]S Lev 10:3 [z]Lev 20:8
22:33 [a]S Ex 6:6 [b]S Ge 17:7
23:2 [c]ver 4,37,44; Nu 29:39; Eze 44:24; Col 2:16 [d]ver 21,27
23:3 [e]Ex 20:9 [f]S Ex 20:10; Heb 4:9,10 [g]ver 7, 21,35; Nu 28:26
23:4 [h]Na 1:15
23:5 [i]S Ex 12:11 [j]S Ex 12:6
23:6 [k]Ex 12:17 [l]S Ex 12:19
23:7 [m]ver 3,8
23:8 [n]S Lev 1:9
23:10 [o]Nu 15:2,18 [p]S Lev 19:9 [q]S Lev 19:9 [r]S Ex 22:29; S 34:22; Ro 11:16
23:11 [s]S Ex 29:24 [t]S Ex 28:38

[b]*21* Traditionally *peace offering* [c]*23* The Hebrew word can include both male and female. [d]*32* Or *made* [e]*32* Or *who sanctifies you*; or *who sets you apart as holy*

22:18–19,30 STEWARDSHIP, Sacrifice Giving—The quality of our gift reflects our reverence for God, who deserves only the best. This was true in Old Testament sacrificial offerings and continues to be true for Christians. See note on 1:2.
22:31–33 REVELATION, Divine Presence—See note on 20:22–26.
22:31–33 CHRISTIAN ETHICS, Social Relationships—The conclusion of chs 21—22 reminds religious leaders of their special responsibilities before God. Any misconduct on their part brings dishonor on God's name and leads God's people to ignore God's holiness. Religious leaders serve only because God has set them apart to obey Him in all aspects of life. See note on 19:1–18.
23:3 HISTORY, Time—See note on Ex 31:12–17.
23:4–43 HISTORY, Time—Worship patterns revealed by God and related to His saving history determined Israel's calendar. See note on Ex 12:1–28.
23:4–38 WORSHIP, Calendar—See note on Ex 16:23–30.
23:10–11 STEWARDSHIP, Giving in Worship—See note on Mt 5:23–24.

day after the Sabbath. 12On the day you
wave the sheaf, you must sacrifice as a
burnt offering to the LORD a lamb a year
old[u] without defect,[v] 13together with its
grain offering[w] of two-tenths of an
ephah[f][x] of fine flour mixed with oil—an
offering made to the LORD by fire, a pleasing aroma—and its drink offering[y] of a
quarter of a hin[g] of wine.[z] 14You must
not eat any bread, or roasted or new
grain,[a] until the very day you bring this
offering to your God.[b] This is to be a lasting ordinance for the generations to
come,[c] wherever you live.[d]

Feast of Weeks

23:15–22pp — Nu 28:26–31; Dt 16:9–12

15" 'From the day after the Sabbath,
the day you brought the sheaf of the wave
offering, count off seven full weeks.
16Count off fifty days up to the day after
the seventh Sabbath,[e] and then present
an offering of new grain to the LORD.
17From wherever you live, bring two
loaves made of two-tenths of an ephah[f]
of fine flour, baked with yeast, as a wave
offering of firstfruits[g] to the LORD.
18Present with this bread seven male
lambs, each a year old and without defect, one young bull and two rams. They
will be a burnt offering to the LORD, together with their grain offerings and
drink offerings[h]—an offering made by
fire, an aroma pleasing to the LORD.
19Then sacrifice one male goat for a sin
offering and two lambs, each a year old,
for a fellowship offering.[h] 20The priest is
to wave the two lambs before the LORD as
a wave offering,[i] together with the bread
of the firstfruits. They are a sacred offering to the LORD for the priest. 21On that
same day you are to proclaim a sacred
assembly[j] and do no regular work.[k] This
is to be a lasting ordinance for the gene-ra-
tions to come, wherever you live.

22" 'When you reap the harvest[l] of
your land, do not reap to the very edges
of your field or gather the gleanings of
your harvest.[m] Leave them for the poor
and the alien.[n] I am the LORD your
God.' "

Feast of Trumpets

23:23–25pp — Nu 29:1–6

23The LORD said to Moses, 24"Say to
the Israelites: 'On the first day of the seventh month you are to have a day of rest,
a sacred assembly[o] commemorated with
trumpet blasts.[p] 25Do no regular work,[q]
but present an offering made to the LORD
by fire.[r] ' "

Day of Atonement

23:26–32pp — Lev 16:2–34; Nu 29:7–11

26The LORD said to Moses, 27"The
tenth day of this seventh month[s] is the
Day of Atonement.[t] Hold a sacred assembly[u] and deny yourselves,[i] and present
an offering made to the LORD by fire. 28Do
no work[v] on that day, because it is the
Day of Atonement, when atonement is
made for you before the LORD your God.
29Anyone who does not deny himself on
that day must be cut off from his people.[w]
30I will destroy from among his people[x]
anyone who does any work on that day.
31You shall do no work at all. This is to be
a lasting ordinance[y] for the generations
to come, wherever you live. 32It is a sabbath of rest[z] for you, and you must deny
yourselves. From the evening of the ninth
day of the month until the following evening you are to observe your sabbath."[a]

Feast of Tabernacles

23:33–43pp — Nu 29:12–39; Dt 16:13–17

33The LORD said to Moses, 34"Say to
the Israelites: 'On the fifteenth day of the
seventh[b] month the LORD's Feast of Tabernacles[c] begins, and it lasts for seven

23:12 [u]S Lev 12:6 [v]S Ex 12:5
23:13 [w]Lev 2:14-16; S 6:20 [x]ver 17; Lev 24:5; Nu 15:6; 28:9 [y]S Ge 35:14 [z]S Lev 10:9
23:14 [a]Jos 5:11; Ru 2:14; 1Sa 17:17; 25:18; 2Sa 17:28 [b]Ex 34:26 [c]Lev 3:17; Nu 10:8; 15:21 [d]Jer 2:3
23:16 [e]Ac 2:1; 20:16
23:17 [f]S ver 13 [g]S Ex 34:22
23:18 [h]ver 13; Ex 29:41; 30:9; 37:16; Jer 19:13; 44:18
23:20 [i]S Ex 29:24
23:21 [j]S ver 2; Ex 32:5 [k]S ver 3
23:22 [l]S Lev 19:9 [m]S Lev 19:10; Dt 24:19-21; Ru 2:15 [n]Ru 2:2
23:24 [o]ver 27,36; Ezr 3:1 [p]Lev 25:9; Nu 10:9,10; 29:1; 31:6; 2Ki 11:14; 2Ch 13:12; Ps 98:6
23:25 [q]ver 21 [r]S Lev 1:9
23:27 [s]S Lev 16:29 [t]S Ex 30:10 [u]S ver 2,S 24
23:28 [v]ver 31
23:29 [w]Ge 17:14; Lev 7:20; Nu 5:2
23:30 [x]S Lev 20:3
23:31 [y]Lev 3:17
23:32 [z]S Lev 16:31 [a]Ne 13:19
23:34 [b]1Ki 8:2; Hag 2:1 [c]S Ex 23:16; Jn 7:2

[f] *13* That is, probably about 4 quarts (about 4.5 liters); also in verse 17 [g] *13* That is, probably about 1 quart (about 1 liter) [h] *19* Traditionally *peace offering* [i] *27* Or *and fast*; also in verses 29 and 32

23:14 CHRISTIAN ETHICS, Moral Limits—See note on Ex 20:6.

23:21 CHRISTIAN ETHICS, Social Order—Society must have guidelines for ongoing order. God's people provide a continuing witness through their ongoing practices. The rhythm of the calendar must provide time to work and time to celebrate the fruits of our labor which God provides.

23:22 GOD, Grace—The requirement of the Israelites not to glean their fields, that is, to leave a portion of the harvest in the field, was a gracious act of God on behalf of the poor and foreigners who happened to be in the vicinity. God is very much concerned for those who cannot help themselves. Perhaps this commandment is the justification for the church to help develop a modern welfare system. Not many today have farms where they can leave part of the harvest in the field. We do leave part of our paychecks behind in the form of taxes, some of which provide support for those who cannot support themselves. God's requirement of a compassionate act towards the poor is based upon His solemn declaration that He is the Lord. Since we are dependent upon God for life itself and are His people by redemption, God certainly can make a demand upon us to share our blessings in life with those who are less fortunate than ourselves.

23:22 DISCIPLESHIP, Poor—This verse follows the law for observance of the Feast of Harvest. See v 21; Ex 23:16. A feast was not sufficient to thank God for the harvest. God's people express gratitude to God by the way they harvest crops. They do not forget the poor and the distressed as they gather the harvest. They follow specific instructions to ensure the poor have reason for thanksgiving (Ru 2:14–20). Love not greed motivates God's people. See note on 19:1–2,9–19.

23:26–32 CHRISTIAN ETHICS, Moral Limits—Humans overstep God's good moral limits. We must have ways to repent of our sins and experience renewal through God's atonement and forgiveness. The Easter season is the Christian parallel to the Day of Atonement. Worship celebration at this season needs to be marked by signs of penitence and renewed relationship with God. See note on Ex 20:6.

days. 35The first day is a sacred assembly;[d] do no regular work.[e] 36For seven
days present offerings made to the LORD
by fire, and on the eighth day hold a sacred assembly[f] and present an offering
made to the LORD by fire.[g] It is the closing assembly; do no regular work.
37(" 'These are the LORD's appointed
feasts, which you are to proclaim as sacred assemblies for bringing offerings
made to the LORD by fire—the burnt offerings and grain offerings, sacrifices and
drink offerings[h] required for each day.
38These offerings[i] are in addition to
those for the LORD's Sabbaths[j] and[i] in
addition to your gifts and whatever you
have vowed and all the freewill offerings[k] you give to the LORD.)
39" 'So beginning with the fifteenth
day of the seventh month, after you have
gathered the crops of the land, celebrate
the festival[l] to the LORD for seven days;[m]
the first day is a day of rest, and the
eighth day also is a day of rest. 40On the
first day you are to take choice fruit from
the trees, and palm fronds, leafy
branches[n] and poplars,[o] and rejoice[p] before the LORD your God for seven days.
41Celebrate this as a festival to the LORD
for seven days each year. This is to be a
lasting ordinance for the generations to
come; celebrate it in the seventh month.
42Live in booths[q] for seven days: All native-born Israelites are to live in booths
43so your descendants will know[r] that I
had the Israelites live in booths when I
brought them out of Egypt. I am the LORD
your God.' "
44So Moses announced to the Israelites
the appointed feasts of the LORD.

Chapter 24

Oil and Bread Set Before the LORD

24:1–3pp — Ex 27:20–21

THE LORD said to Moses, 2"Command
the Israelites to bring you clear oil of
pressed olives for the light so that the
lamps may be kept burning continually.
3Outside the curtain of the Testimony in
the Tent of Meeting, Aaron is to tend the
lamps before the LORD from evening till
morning, continually. This is to be a lasting ordinance[s] for the generations to
come. 4The lamps on the pure gold lampstand[t] before the LORD must be tended
continually.
5"Take fine flour and bake twelve
loaves of bread,[u] using two-tenths of an
ephah[k][v] for each loaf. 6Set them in two
rows, six in each row, on the table of
pure gold[w] before the LORD. 7Along each
row put some pure incense[x] as a memorial portion[y] to represent the bread and
to be an offering made to the LORD by
fire. 8This bread is to be set out before
the LORD regularly,[z] Sabbath after Sabbath,[a] on behalf of the Israelites, as a
lasting covenant. 9It belongs to Aaron and
his sons,[b] who are to eat it in a holy
place,[c] because it is a most holy[d] part of
their regular share of the offerings made
to the LORD by fire."

A Blasphemer Stoned

10Now the son of an Israelite mother
and an Egyptian father went out among
the Israelites, and a fight broke out in the
camp between him and an Israelite.
11The son of the Israelite woman blasphemed the Name[e] with a curse;[f] so
they brought him to Moses.[g] (His mother's name was Shelomith, the daughter of
Dibri the Danite.)[h] 12They put him in
custody until the will of the LORD should
be made clear to them.[i]
13Then the LORD said to Moses:
14"Take the blasphemer outside the
camp. All those who heard him are to lay
their hands on his head, and the entire
assembly is to stone him.[j] 15Say to the
Israelites: 'If anyone curses his God,[k] he
will be held responsible;[l] 16anyone who
blasphemes[m] the name of the LORD must
be put to death.[n] The entire assembly
must stone him. Whether an alien or native-born, when he blasphemes the
Name, he must be put to death.
17" 'If anyone takes the life of a human

23:35 [d]ver 2 [e]ver 3
23:36 [f]S ver 24; 1Ki 8:2; 2Ch 7:9; Ne 8:18; Jn 7:37 [g]S Lev 1:9
23:37 [h]ver 13
23:38 [i]S Lev 1:2 [j]S Ex 20:10; 2Ch 2:4; Eze 45:17 [k]S Lev 7:16
23:39 [l]Isa 62:9 [m]S Ex 23:16
23:40 [n]Ps 118:27 [o]Ne 8:14-17; Ps 137:2; Isa 44:4 [p]Dt 12:7; 14:26; 28:47; Ne 8:10; Ps 9:2; 66:6; 105:43; Joel 2:26
23:42 [q]S Ex 23:16
23:43 [r]Ps 78:5
24:3 [s]S Ex 12:14
24:4 [t]S Ex 25:31
24:5 [u]S Ex 25:30; Heb 9:2 [v]S Lev 23:13
24:6 [w]Ex 25:23-30; Nu 4:7
24:7 [x]S Lev 2:1 [y]S Lev 2:2
24:8 [z]Ex 25:30; Nu 4:7; 1Ch 9:32; 2Ch 2:4 [a]Mt 12:5
24:9 [b]Mt 12:4; Mk 2:26; Lk 6:4 [c]S Lev 6:16 [d]S Lev 6:17
24:11 [e]S Ex 3:15 [f]S Ex 20:7; S 2Ki 6:33; S Job 1:11 [g]S Ex 18:22 [h]Ex 31:2; Nu 1:4; 7:2; 10:15; 13:2; 17:2; Jos 7:18; 1Ki 7:14
24:12 [i]S Ex 18:16
24:14 [j]ver 23; S Lev 20:2; Dt 13:9; 17:5,7; Ac 7:58
24:15 [k]S Ex 22:28 [l]S Lev 5:1
24:16 [m]S Ex 22:28 [n]S Ex 21:12; 1Ki 21:10,13; Mt 26:66; Mk 14:64; Jn 10:33; 19:7; Ac 7:58

[i]38 Or *These feasts are in addition to the LORD's Sabbaths, and these offerings are* [k]5 That is, probably about 4 quarts (about 4.5 liters)

23:40 PRAYER, Worship—The Feast of Booths (or Tabernacles or Ingathering) was a time of high rejoicing. The expression "before the LORD" is a reminder that we live in full knowledge of God's watchful eye. See note on Ge 19:27. Prayer expresses our joy and celebration in God's presence.

23:41 CHRISTIAN ETHICS, Social Order—See note on 23:21.

24:3 CHRISTIAN ETHICS, Social Order—See note on 23:21.

24:8 THE CHURCH, Covenant People—Commitments are to be remembered and observed. As Aaron and his successors placed bread regularly before the Lord as a sign of the covenant, we are to give ourselves continually to the Lord. We need symbolic reminders which call us to covenant obedience.

24:10–16,23 CHRISTIAN ETHICS, Language—Language used to refer to God is the most serious and important communication we make. God does not want us to use His holy name to bring a curse on our enemies. To use God's name improperly deserves death. Christ's atonement for our sins does not free us to use God's name to curse Him or our enemies. Compare Mt 5:33–36. See notes on Ex 20:7; 22:28.

24:13–16 SIN, Responsibility—The reprehensible act of cursing God brings alienation between the person and God. No circumstance justifies taking God's holy name and using it in a slanderous, blasphemous manner. God's name must be used only in highest respect. No way of shifting blame for such a sin exists. You are responsible for what your mouth utters in every moment of life.

being, he must be put to death.[o] 18Any-
one who takes the life of someone's animal must make restitution[p]—life for life.
19If anyone injures his neighbor, whatever he has done must be done to him:
20fracture for fracture, eye for eye, tooth
for tooth.[q] As he has injured the other,
so he is to be injured. 21Whoever kills an
animal must make restitution,[r] but whoever kills a man must be put to death.[s]
22You are to have the same law for the
alien[t] and the native-born.[u] I am the
LORD your God.' "

23Then Moses spoke to the Israelites,
and they took the blasphemer outside the
camp and stoned him.[v] The Israelites did
as the LORD commanded Moses.

Chapter 25

The Sabbath Year

THE LORD said to Moses on Mount Sinai,[w] 2"Speak to the Israelites and
say to them: 'When you enter the land I
am going to give you, the land itself must
observe a sabbath to the LORD. 3For six
years sow your fields, and for six years
prune your vineyards and gather their
crops.[x] 4But in the seventh year the land
is to have a sabbath of rest,[y] a sabbath to
the LORD. Do not sow your fields or prune
your vineyards.[z] 5Do not reap what
grows of itself[a] or harvest the grapes[b] of
your untended vines.[c] The land is to
have a year of rest. 6Whatever the land
yields during the sabbath year[d] will be
food for you—for yourself, your manservant and maidservant, and the hired
worker and temporary resident who live
among you, 7as well as for your livestock
and the wild animals[e] in your land.
Whatever the land produces may be
eaten.

The Year of Jubilee

25:8–38Ref — Dt 15:1–11
25:39–55Ref — Ex 21:2–11; Dt 15:12–18

8" 'Count off seven sabbaths of years
—seven times seven years—so that the
seven sabbaths of years amount to a period of forty-nine years. 9Then have the
trumpet[f] sounded everywhere on the
tenth day of the seventh month;[g] on the
Day of Atonement[h] sound the trumpet
throughout your land. 10Consecrate the
fiftieth year and proclaim liberty[i]
throughout the land to all its inhabitants.
It shall be a jubilee[j] for you; each one of
you is to return to his family property[k]
and each to his own clan. 11The fiftieth
year shall be a jubilee[l] for you; do not
sow and do not reap what grows of itself
or harvest the untended vines.[m] 12For it
is a jubilee and is to be holy for you; eat
only what is taken directly from the
fields.

13" 'In this Year of Jubilee[n] everyone is
to return to his own property.

14" 'If you sell land to one of your countrymen or buy any from him, do not take
advantage of each other.[o] 15You are to
buy from your countryman on the basis of
the number of years[p] since the Jubilee.
And he is to sell to you on the basis of the
number of years left for harvesting crops.
16When the years are many, you are to
increase the price, and when the years
are few, you are to decrease the price,[q]
because what he is really selling you is
the number of crops. 17Do not take advantage of each other,[r] but fear your
God.[s] I am the LORD your God.[t]

18" 'Follow my decrees and be careful
to obey my laws,[u] and you will live safely
in the land.[v] 19Then the land will yield
its fruit,[w] and you will eat your fill and
live there in safety.[x] 20You may ask,
"What will we eat in the seventh year[y] if
we do not plant or harvest our crops?"

24:17 [o]ver 21; Ge 9:6; S Ex 21:12; Dt 27:24 **24:18** [p]ver 21 **24:20** [q]S Ex 21:24; Mt 5:38* **24:21** [r]S ver 18 [s]S ver 17 **24:22** [t]S Ex 12:49; S 22:21; Eze 47:22 [u]Nu 9:14 **24:23** [v]S ver 14 **25:1** [w]Ex 19:11 **25:3** [x]Ex 23:10 **25:4** [y]ver 5,6,20; Lev 26:35; 2Ch 36:21 [z]Isa 36:16; 37:30 **25:5** [a]2Ki 19:29 [b]Ge 40:10; Nu 6:3; 13:20; Dt 23:24; Ne 13:15; Isa 5:2 [c]ver 4,11 **25:6** [d]S ver 4 **25:7** [e]Ex 23:11 **25:9** [f]Lev 23:24; Nu 10:8; Jos 6:4; Jdg 3:27; 7:16; 1Sa 13:3; Isa 27:13; Zec 9:14 [g]S Lev 16:29 [h]S Ex 30:10 **25:10** [i]Isa 61:1; Jer 34:8,15,17; S Lk 4:19 [j]ver 11, 28,50; Lev 27:17, 21; Nu 36:4; Eze 46:17 [k]ver 27 **25:11** [l]S ver 10 [m]S ver 5 **25:13** [n]ver 10 **25:14** [o]S Lev 19:13; 1Sa 12:3,4; 1Co 6:8 **25:15** [p]ver 27; Lev 27:18,23 **25:16** [q]ver 27,51, 52 **25:17** [r]S Lev 19:13; Job 31:16; Pr 22:22; Jer 7:5,6; 21:12; 22:3,15; Zec 7:9-10; 1Th 4:6 [s]S Lev 19:14 [t]S Lev 19:32 **25:18** [u]S Ge 26:5 [v]ver 19; Lev 26:4,5; Dt 12:10; 33:28; Job 5:22; Ps 4:8; Jer 23:6; 30:10; 32:37; 33:16; Eze 28:26; 34:25; 38:14 **25:19** [w]Lev 26:4; Dt 11:14; 28:12; Isa 55:10 [x]S ver 18 **25:20** [y]S ver 4

24:17–22 CHRISTIAN ETHICS, Justice—Justice demands a system of punishment for criminals. Such punishment must not be more cruel than the crime. The legal system must protect all people living under its jurisdiction. Jesus taught that retaliation must not become a law dominating our lives so that we seek reasons to punish other persons. Rather, we must seek to show God's love to all people. This law of revenge sets guidelines for public justice, not demands for private relationships. It leads society to bring the least harm to the most innocent of society.

25:1–55 HISTORY, Time—See note on Ex 31:12–17. The sabbath rest concept gave Israel's calendar larger sacred units of time than the week. It dominated Israel's relationship to the agricultural land, showing Israel had to care for the gift God had given. It also dominated Israel's social make-up providing permanent, long-term land ownership for Israel's families beyond short-term financial hardships. God is interested in the ongoing history of His people in all areas of *their historical* existence.

25:1–55 STEWARDSHIP, Management—Property is a trust from God. Its ownership and use is to be handled responsibly considering that God is the primary Owner. The seventh year of rest for land protected its productivity. The fiftieth or Jubilee Year protected personal liberty and equality and gave lasting strength to family ties in a social structure linked to land ownership. Biblical faith values the use of property in sustaining a family. See note on Ge 39:2–6.

25:8–13 DISCIPLESHIP, Poor—God has shown His concern for the less fortunate in many different ways. God set up the fiftieth year at the Year of Jubilee.God would not permit land to be accumulated to the detriment of the poor. Hebrew slaves were liberated, and all foreclosed mortgaged property was returned. Attention should be given today to finding ways for people to work through their problems and escape the heavy indebtedness that enslaves so many. God's people should be both merciful and just in dealing with heavily indebted poor people today. See notes on Isa 58:6–7; Lk 4:18–21.

25:9 WORSHIP, Calendar—See note on Ex 16:23–30.

25:18–19 CHRISTIAN ETHICS, Social Order—One who lives a godly life can expect generally a peaceable life. One goal of God's commands and moral limits is to establish a safe, peaceful social order.

21 I will send you such a blessing[z] in the
sixth year that the land will yield enough
for three years.[a] 22 While you plant during the eighth year, you will eat from the
old crop and will continue to eat from it
until the harvest of the ninth year comes
in.[b]
23 " 'The land[c] must not be sold permanently, because the land is mine[d] and
you are but aliens[e] and my tenants.
24 Throughout the country that you hold
as a possession, you must provide for the
redemption[f] of the land.
25 " 'If one of your countrymen becomes poor and sells some of his property, his nearest relative[g] is to come and
redeem[h] what his countryman has sold.
26 If, however, a man has no one to redeem it for him but he himself prospers[i]
and acquires sufficient means to redeem
it, 27 he is to determine the value for the
years[j] since he sold it and refund the
balance to the man to whom he sold it;
he can then go back to his own property.[k] 28 But if he does not acquire the
means to repay him, what he sold will
remain in the possession of the buyer until the Year of Jubilee. It will be returned[l] in the Jubilee, and he can then
go back to his property.[m]
29 " 'If a man sells a house in a walled
city, he retains the right of redemption a
full year after its sale. During that time he
may redeem it. 30 If it is not redeemed
before a full year has passed, the house in
the walled city shall belong permanently
to the buyer and his descendants. It is not
to be returned in the Jubilee. 31 But
houses in villages without walls around
them are to be considered as open country. They can be redeemed, and they are
to be returned in the Jubilee.
32 " 'The Levites always have the right
to redeem their houses in the Levitical
towns,[n] which they possess. 33 So the
property of the Levites is redeemable—
that is, a house sold in any town they
hold—and is to be returned in the Jubilee, because the houses in the towns of
the Levites are their property among the
Israelites. 34 But the pastureland belonging to their towns must not be sold; it is
their permanent possession.[o]
35 " 'If one of your countrymen becomes poor[p] and is unable to support
himself among you, help him[q] as you
would an alien or a temporary resident,
so he can continue to live among you.
36 Do not take interest[r] of any kind[1] from
him, but fear your God,[s] so that your
countryman may continue to live among
you. 37 You must not lend him money at
interest[t] or sell him food at a profit. 38 I
am the LORD your God, who brought you
out of Egypt to give you the land of Canaan[u] and to be your God.[v]
39 " 'If one of your countrymen becomes poor among you and sells himself
to you, do not make him work as a
slave.[w] 40 He is to be treated as a hired
worker[x] or a temporary resident among
you; he is to work for you until the Year
of Jubilee. 41 Then he and his children are
to be released, and he will go back to his
own clan and to the property[y] of his forefathers.[z] 42 Because the Israelites are my
servants, whom I brought out of Egypt,[a]
they must not be sold as slaves. 43 Do not
rule over them ruthlessly,[b] but fear your
God.[c]
44 " 'Your male and female slaves are to
come from the nations around you; from
them you may buy slaves. 45 You may also
buy some of the temporary residents living among you and members of their
clans born in your country, and they will
become your property. 46 You can will
them to your children as inherited property and can make them slaves for life,
but you must not rule over your fellow
Israelites ruthlessly.
47 " 'If an alien or a temporary resident
among you becomes rich and one of your
countrymen becomes poor and sells

25:21 [z]Dt 28:8,12; Ps 133:3; 134:3; 147:13; Eze 44:30; Hag 2:19; Mal 3:10 [a]S Ex 16:5
25:22 [b]Lev 26:10
25:23 [c]Nu 36:7; 1Ki 21:3; Eze 46:18 [d]Ex 19:5 [e]S Ge 23:4; S Heb 11:13
25:24 [f]ver 29,48; Ru 4:7
25:25 [g]ver 48; Ru 2:20; Jer 32:7 [h]Lev 27:13,19,31; Ru 4:4
25:26 [i]ver 49
25:27 [j]S ver 15 [k]ver 10
25:28 [l]Lev 27:24 [m]S ver 10
25:32 [n]Nu 35:1-8; Jos 21:2
25:34 [o]Nu 35:2-5; Eze 48:14
25:35 [p]Dt 24:14, 15 [q]Dt 15:8; Ps 37:21,26; Pr 21:26; Lk 6:35
25:36 [r]S Ex 22:25; Jer 15:10 [s]S Lev 19:32
25:37 [t]S Ex 22:25
25:38 [u]S Ge 10:19 [v]S Ge 17:7
25:39 [w]1Ki 5:13; 9:22; Jer 34:14
25:40 [x]ver 53
25:41 [y]ver 28 [z]Jer 34:8
25:42 [a]ver 38
25:43 [b]S Ex 1:13; Eze 34:4; Col 4:1 [c]S Ge 42:18

[1]36 Or *take excessive interest*; similarly in verse 37

25:21 SALVATION, Blessing—God promised to bless Israel for keeping the Sabbath Year and the Year of Jubilee so much that in the sixth year the land would yield enough to last for three years. The God of our salvation is the Lord over land and nature. His salvation includes caring for our physical needs.

25:24–55 SALVATION, Redemption—The Year of Jubilee played a special role in God's regulations regarding redemption. Every seventh year was a Sabbath Year, but the Year of Jubilee was the fiftieth year, or the year following seven sabbaths of years. Land and people in slavery were redeemed. God provided for economic failures to be redeemed, His ownership of all creation to be recognized, and His redemption of the nation from slavery to be remembered. Jesus' inaugural sermon in Lk 4:16–30 was likely a declaration that the Year of Jubilee had arrived in His own life and ministry.

25:35–37,39–43 DISCIPLESHIP, Poor—Disciples fight poverty by helping those who become poor. Such help may involve bad personal economic practices but good godly ethics. We are to give special economic benefits to a person who becomes poor. Our aim is for the poor to receive support for daily needs and for economic recovery. Specifically, no interest is to be charged for any reason, and no profit is to be made on food purchases. Under no circumstances may we treat a poor person like a slave. We are to hire the poor and pay proper wages, looking to make the poor financially independent. We must not exploit the poor for our own gain. Positive assistance is needed today to assist the growing number of poor people to gain respect and to increase economic power. See note on 23:22.

25:42,55 REVELATION, Author of Grace—God revealed His compassion through the historical act of the Exodus (Ex 14:1—15:18) and through His laws calling His people to be compassionate. Having freed His people from Egyptian slavery, God commanded that no Israelite would return to slavery at the hand of a fellow Israelite.

himself[d] to the alien living among you or
to a member of the alien's clan, 48he retains the right of redemption[e] after he has
sold himself. One of his relatives[f] may redeem him: 49An uncle or a cousin or any
blood relative in his clan may redeem
him. Or if he prospers,[g] he may redeem
himself. 50He and his buyer are to count
the time from the year he sold himself up
to the Year of Jubilee.[h] The price for his
release is to be based on the rate paid to a
hired man[i] for that number of years. 51If
many years remain, he must pay for his
redemption a larger share of the price
paid for him. 52If only a few years remain
until the Year of Jubilee, he is to compute
that and pay for his redemption accordingly.[j] 53He is to be treated as a man
hired from year to year; you must see to it
that his owner does not rule over him
ruthlessly.[k]

54" 'Even if he is not redeemed in any
of these ways, he and his children are to
be released in the Year of Jubilee, 55for
the Israelites belong to me as servants.
They are my servants, whom I brought
out of Egypt.[l] I am the LORD your God.[m]

Chapter 26

Reward for Obedience

" 'DO not make idols[n] or set up an
image[o] or a sacred stone[p] for
yourselves, and do not place a carved
stone[q] in your land to bow down before
it. I am the LORD your God.

2" 'Observe my Sabbaths[r] and have
reverence for my sanctuary.[s] I am the
LORD.

3" 'If you follow my decrees and are
careful to obey[t] my commands, 4I will
send you rain[u] in its season,[v] and the
ground will yield its crops and the trees of
the field their fruit.[w] 5Your threshing will
continue until grape harvest and the
grape harvest will continue until planting, and you will eat all the food you
want[x] and live in safety in your land.[y]

6" 'I will grant peace in the land,[z] and
you will lie down[a] and no one will make
you afraid.[b] I will remove savage beasts[c]
from the land, and the sword will not
pass through your country. 7You will pursue your enemies,[d] and they will fall by
the sword before you. 8Five[e] of you will
chase a hundred, and a hundred of you
will chase ten thousand, and your enemies will fall by the sword before you.[f]

9" 'I will look on you with favor and
make you fruitful and increase your numbers,[g] and I will keep my covenant[h]
with you. 10You will still be eating last
year's harvest when you will have to
move it out to make room for the new.[i]

25:47 [d]Ne 5:5; Job 24:9 **25:48** [e]S ver 24 [f]S ver 25 **25:49** [g]ver 26 **25:50** [h]S ver 10 [i]Job 7:1; 14:6; Isa 16:14; 21:16 **25:52** [j]S ver 16 **25:53** [k]Col 4:1 **25:55** [l]S Lev 11:45 [m]Lev 11:44 **26:1** [n]S Ex 20:4 [o]Ps 97:7; Isa 48:5; Jer 44:19; Hab 2:18 [p]S Ex 23:24 [q]Nu 33:52 **26:2** [r]S Ex 20:8 [s]Lev 19:30 **26:3** [t]S Ge 26:5; S Ex 24:8; Dt 6:17; 7:12; 11:13,22; 28:1,9 **26:4** [u]Dt 11:14; 28:12; Ps 68:9; Jer 5:24; Hos 6:3; Joel 2:23; Zec 10:1 [v]Job 5:10; Ps 65:9; 104:13; 147:8; Jer 5:24 [w]S Ex 23:26; S Lev 25:19; S Job 14:9; Ps 67:6 **26:5** [x]Dt 6:11; 11:15; Eze 36:29-30; Joel 2:19,26 [y]S Lev 25:18 **26:6** [z]Ps 29:11; 37:11; 85:8; 147:14; Isa 26:3; 54:13; 60:18; Hag 2:9 [a]Ps 3:5; 4:8; Pr 3:24 [b]Job 11:18,19; Isa 17:2; Jer 30:10; Mic 4:4; Zep 3:13 [c]S ver 22; S Ge 37:20 **26:7** [d]Ps 18:37; 44:5 **26:8** [e]Isa 30:17 [f]Dt 28:7; 32:30; Jos 23:10; Jdg 15:15; 1Ch 12:14 **26:9** [g]S Ge 1:22; S 17:6; Ne 9:23 [h]S Ge 17:7 **26:10** [i]Lev 25:22

25:55 ELECTION, God's Servants—Election is a call to serve God, not a mandate to rule others. The holy God sets His people apart for holy and ethical living. See note on 20:24,26. He owns those He has chosen. Israel was to be no longer slaves of death for Pharaoh in Egypt. They were servants of the electing God, who rescued them for life.

26:1–45 EVIL AND SUFFERING, Deserved—God presented two ways or directions for life to the Hebrews. If they obeyed Him, they would prosper. Good crops, peace, military success, and population increases illustrated this prosperity. If the Hebrews disobeyed God, He would punish them. The suffering had a clearly redemptive purpose—God wanted His people to repent and return to Him. God sent suffering both as punishment for sin and as a discipline that might guide the Hebrews back to Him. Today our suffering may be deserved and, depending on our response, can be redemptive. See note on Dt 28:1–68.

26:1–45 HISTORY, Judgment—See note on Ge 19:1–29. Relationship to God determines historical fortunes for God's people. This is not a rule which can be proved to work on the short-term for every individual. It is a rule which functions as God works out His purposes with and through His people over the long haul of history. Judgment in history does not mean eternal rejection. God is faithful to His covenant and to His people. Compare Dt 27:9—28:68.

26:3–13 GOD, Grace—God promised His blessing in the basic needs of economic well-being (good crops), stable social conditions, peace and political security, and most of all, fellowship with God as He dwelled among them. God promised all this and more to a faithful people of God. God, the sovereign Lord, is gracious.

26:3–8 HUMANITY, Relationship to Nature—A direct relation exists between people's obedience to God and their relation with the natural world around them. The world is hurt by human sinfulness and helped by obedience. People are a vital part of their natural world.

26:3–13 ELECTION, Blessing—Election includes promises of divine blessings (Ge 12:1–7). Blessings come to His servants as God chooses. The electing God who chose Israel for freedom from the slavery of Egypt enabled Israel to walk in holy servanthood with the dignity of heads held high. See note on 25:55.

26:3–45 CHRISTIAN ETHICS, Social Order—God's covenant regulations set up a way of life leading to security and peace. God wanted the best life for His people. Such blessings (vv 3–13) could come only to an obedient people. Refusing God's moral limits invited cursings (vv 14–45), disrupting the social order. Moral relationships involve personal communication and response between God and His people. When God acts in response to disobedience, He seeks to lead us back to obedience. He calls us to maintain social order.

26:6–13 CREATION, Hope—God wanted the best for Israel, as He wants the best for His people in all generations. Even the natural elements are subject to His control. He not only has the power to remove any contingencies on earth that threaten the peace and security of His faithful people; He can also create situations and guide events to work for our benefit. Most of all, He wishes for us to live in fellowship with Him. This is the greatest security and the greatest happiness that His people can enjoy. With a God who possesses such creative resources, we can face any discouraging situation with confidence and hope.

26:9 THE CHURCH, Covenant People—God promises blessings to those who follow Him. The people who followed God received blessings confirming the covenant which God made with the people of Israel. God continues to keep His covenant with us and calls us to commitment to Him and His covenant life-style.

11 I will put my dwelling place[m] [j] among
you, and I will not abhor you.[k] 12 I will
walk[l] among you and be your God,[m] and
you will be my people.[n] 13 I am the LORD
your God,[o] who brought you out of
Egypt[p] so that you would no longer be
slaves to the Egyptians; I broke the bars
of your yoke[q] and enabled you to walk
with heads held high.

Punishment for Disobedience

14 " 'But if you will not listen to me and
carry out all these commands,[r] 15 and if
you reject my decrees and abhor my
laws[s] and fail to carry out all my commands and so violate my covenant,[t]
16 then I will do this to you: I will bring
upon you sudden terror, wasting diseases
and fever[u] that will destroy your sight
and drain away your life.[v] You will plant
seed in vain, because your enemies will
eat it.[w] 17 I will set my face[x] against you
so that you will be defeated[y] by your enemies;[z] those who hate you will rule over
you,[a] and you will flee even when no
one is pursuing you.[b]
18 " 'If after all this you will not listen to
me,[c] I will punish[d] you for your sins sev-
en times over.[e] 19 I will break down your
stubborn pride[f] and make the sky above
you like iron and the ground beneath you
like bronze.[g] 20 Your strength will be
spent in vain,[h] because your soil will not
yield its crops, nor will the trees of the
land yield their fruit.[i]
21 " 'If you remain hostile[j] toward me
and refuse to listen to me, I will multiply
your afflictions seven times over,[k] as
your sins deserve. 22 I will send wild animals[l] against you, and they will rob you
of your children, destroy your cattle and
make you so few[m] in number that your
roads will be deserted.[n]
23 " 'If in spite of these things you do
not accept my correction[o] but continue
to be hostile toward me, 24 I myself will be
hostile[p] toward you and will afflict you
for your sins seven times over. 25 And I
will bring the sword[q] upon you to
avenge[r] the breaking of the covenant.
When you withdraw into your cities, I
will send a plague[s] among you, and you
will be given into enemy hands. 26 When I
cut off your supply of bread,[t] ten women
will be able to bake your bread in one
oven, and they will dole out the bread by
weight. You will eat, but you will not be
satisfied.
27 " 'If in spite of this you still do not
listen to me[u] but continue to be hostile
toward me, 28 then in my anger[v] I will be
hostile[w] toward you, and I myself will
punish you for your sins seven times
over.[x] 29 You will eat[y] the flesh of your
sons and the flesh of your daughters.[z] 30 I
will destroy your high places,[a] cut down
your incense altars[b] and pile your dead
bodies on the lifeless forms of your
idols,[c] and I will abhor[d] you. 31 I will
turn your cities into ruins[e] and lay
waste[f] your sanctuaries,[g] and I will take
no delight in the pleasing aroma of your
offerings.[h] 32 I will lay waste the land,[i]
so that your enemies who live there will
be appalled.[j] 33 I will scatter[k] you among

26:11 [j]Ex 25:8; Ps 74:7; 76:2; Eze 37:27 [k]ver 15, 43,44; Dt 31:6; 1Sa 12:22; 1Ki 6:13; 2Ki 17:15 **26:12** [l]S Ge 3:8 [m]S Ge 17:7 [n]Ex 6:7; Jer 7:23; 11:4; 24:7; 30:22; 31:1; Zec 13:9; 2Co 6:16* **26:13** [o]Lev 11:44 [p]S Ex 6:6; S 13:3 [q]Isa 10:27; Jer 2:20; 27:2; 28:10; 30:8; Eze 30:18; 34:27; Hos 11:4 **26:14** [r]Dt 28:15-68; Mal 2:2 **26:15** [s]S ver 11 [t]S Ge 17:7 **26:16** [u]Dt 28:22, 35; Ps 78:33 [v]ver 39; 1Sa 2:33; Ps 107:17; Eze 4:17; 24:23; 33:10 [w]Jdg 6:3-6; Job 31:8 **26:17** [x]Lev 17:10; Eze 15:7 [y]Dt 28:48; Jos 7:12; Jdg 2:15; 1Ki 8:33; 2Ch 6:24 [z]Jos 7:4; Jer 19:7; 21:7 [a]Ps 106:41 [b]ver 36,37; Dt 28:7,25; Ps 53:5; Pr 28:1; Isa 30:17 **26:18** [c]ver 14 [d]Ps 99:8; Jer 21:14; Am 3:14 [e]ver 21 **26:19** [f]Ps 10:4; 73:6; Isa 16:6; 25:11; 28:1-3; Jer 13:9; 48:29; Eze 24:21; Am 6:8; Zep 3:11 [g]Dt 28:23; Job 38:38 **26:20** [h]Dt 28:38; Ps 127:1; Isa 17:11; 49:4; Jer 12:13; Mic 6:15; Hag 1:6 [i]Dt 11:17; 28:24 **26:21** [j]ver 41 [k]ver 18; S Ge 4:15 **26:22** [l]S Ge 37:20 [m]Dt 28:62; Jer 42:2 [n]Jer 5:6; 14:16; 15:3; 16:4; Eze 14:15 **26:23** [o]Jer 2:30; 5:3; 7:28; 17:23; 32:33; Zep 3:2 **26:24** [p]2Sa 22:27 **26:25** [q]Jer 5:17; 15:3; 47:6; Eze 11:8; 14:17; 21:4; 33:2 [r]Jer 50:28; 51:6,11 [s]S Ex 5:3; S 9:3; Nu 16:46; 1Ki 8:37; Hab 3:5 **26:26** [t]1Ki 8:37; 18:2; 2Ki 4:38; 6:25; 8:1; 25:3; Ps 105:16; Isa 3:1; 9:20; Jer 37:21; 52:6; Eze 4:16,17; 5:16; 14:13; Hos 4:10; Mic 6:14 **26:27** [u]ver 14 **26:28** [v]Dt 32:19; Jdg 2:14; Ps 78:59; 106:40 [w]Dt 7:10; Job 34:11; Isa 59:18; 65:6-7; 66:6; Jer 17:10; 25:29; Joel 3:4 [x]ver 18 **26:29** [y]2Ki 6:29; Jer 19:9; La 4:10; Eze 5:10 [z]Dt 28:53 **26:30** [a]Dt 12:2; 1Sa 9:12; 10:5; 1Ki 3:2,4; 12:31; 13:2,32; 2Ki 17:29; 23:20; 2Ch 34:3; Ps 78:58; Eze 6:3; 16:16; Am 7:9 [b]2Ch 34:4; Isa 17:8; 27:9; Eze 6:6 [c]Isa 21:9; Jer 50:2; Eze 6:13 [d]Ps 106:40; Am 6:8 **26:31** [e]Ne 1:3; Isa 1:7; 3:8,26; 6:11; 24:12; 61:4; Jer 4:7; 9:11; 25:11; 34:22; 44:2,6,22; Eze 36:33; Mic 2:4; 3:12; Zep 2:5; 3:6 [f]2Ki 22:19 [g]Ps 74:3-7; Isa 63:18; 64:11; La 2:7; Eze 24:21; Am 7:9 [h]Am 5:21,22; 8:10 **26:32** [i]Isa 5:6; Jer 9:11; 12:11; 25:11; 26:9; 33:10; 34:22; 44:22 [j]1Ki 9:8; 2Ch 29:8; Isa 52:14; Jer 18:16; 19:8; 48:39; Eze 5:14; 26:16; 27:35; 28:19 **26:33** [k]Jer 40:15; 50:17; Eze 34:6; Joel 3:2

[m] *11* Or *my tabernacle*

26:11–13 REVELATION, Divine Presence—God closed the Levitical law with a series of covenant blessings and curses. Compare Dt 27:11—28:68. The greatest blessing was the continued presence of God with the people after they settled in the land. His presence shows His love as opposed to hatred. Walking among His people indicates He is not limited to the worship place. He is an active participant in His created world as He was in Eden (Ge 3:8). He reveals Himself to His people to protect them (Dt 23:14). God's revelation is often a call to remember His actions in our past to free us to act in the present and to lead us to commitment to His greater purposes for us in the future.

26:14–45 GOD, Wrath—God does not view sin lightly. If God's people do not take Him seriously, if they do not honor Him as Lord, if they do not follow His commandments, then they can expect to suffer His wrath poured out in judgment upon them. Although God much prefers to be gracious to His people in blessing, He is nevertheless a righteous God who will not let the unfaithfulness and gross sinfulness of His people go unpunished. As sovereign Lord, He can either bless or chastise His people, according to the circumstances of the people before Him. God pours out His wrath not simply to punish, but to bring people to responsible obedience. God will be faithful to His people when they are faithful to Him. But God will also be faithful to Himself in not letting His righteous will for individuals and their society be flagrantly disregarded by human sinfulness.

26:14–15 SIN, Rebellion—We are not free under God to pick and choose among His commands. God, not we, decides what is right and what is wrong, what is good for us and what is bad. Any violation of God's covenant is considered to be an act of rebellion against Him and, therefore, a sin. See note on Ge 11:4.

26:15–17 THE CHURCH, Covenant People—Obedience produces a full and meaningful life; disobedience produces an empty and meaningless existence. Breaking God's commands brings deserved divine judgment. God desires full and meaningful life for everyone.

26:25 THE CHURCH, Covenant People—See note on v 15.

the nations[l] and will draw out my
sword[m] and pursue you. Your land will be
laid waste,[n] and your cities will lie in ruins.[o] 34Then the land will enjoy its sabbath years all the time that it lies desolate[p] and you are in the country of your
enemies;[q] then the land will rest and enjoy its sabbaths. 35All the time that it lies
desolate, the land will have the rest[r] it
did not have during the sabbaths you
lived in it.
36" 'As for those of you who are left, I
will make their hearts so fearful in the
lands of their enemies that the sound of a
windblown leaf[s] will put them to flight.[t]
They will run as though fleeing from the
sword, and they will fall, even though no
one is pursuing them.[u] 37They will stumble over one another[v] as though fleeing
from the sword, even though no one is
pursuing them. So you will not be able to
stand before your enemies.[w] 38You will
perish[x] among the nations; the land of
your enemies will devour you.[y] 39Those
of you who are left will waste away in the
lands of their enemies because of their
sins; also because of their fathers'[z] sins
they will waste away.[a]
40" 'But if they will confess[b] their
sins[c] and the sins of their fathers[d]—
their treachery against me and their hostility toward me, 41which made me hostile[e] toward them so that I sent them
into the land of their enemies—then
when their uncircumcised hearts[f] are
humbled[g] and they pay[h] for their sin, 42I
will remember my covenant with Jacob[i]
and my covenant with Isaac[j] and my
covenant with Abraham,[k] and I will remember the land. 43For the land will be
deserted[l] by them and will enjoy its sabbaths while it lies desolate without them.
They will pay for their sins because they
rejected[m] my laws and abhorred my decrees.[n] 44Yet in spite of this, when they
are in the land of their enemies,[o] I will
not reject them or abhor[p] them so as to
destroy them completely,[q] breaking my
covenant[r] with them. I am the LORD
their God. 45But for their sake I will remember[s] the covenant with their ancestors whom I brought out of Egypt[t] in the
sight of the nations to be their God. I am
the LORD.' "
46These are the decrees, the laws and
the regulations that the LORD established
on Mount Sinai[u] between himself and
the Israelites through Moses.[v]

26:33 [l]Dt 4:27; 28:64; Ne 1:8; Ps 44:11; 106:27; Jer 4:11; 9:16; 13:24; 31:10; Eze 5:10; 12:15; 17:21; 20:23; 22:15; Zec 7:14 [m]Jer 42:16; Am 9:4 [n]Isa 49:19; Jer 7:34 [o]ver 31; 1Sa 15:22; Job 36:11; Jer 40:3 **26:34** [p]Isa 1:7; Jer 7:34; 25:11; 44:6; Eze 33:29 [q]ver 43; 2Ch 36:21 **26:35** [r]S Lev 25:4 **26:36** [s]Job 13:25 [t]2Ki 25:5; Ps 58:7; La 1:3,6; 4:19; Eze 21:7 [u]S ver 17 **26:37** [v]Jer 6:21; 13:16; 46:16; Eze 3:20; Na 3:3 [w]Jos 7:12 **26:38** [x]Job 4:9; 36:12; Ps 1:6; Isa 1:28; Jer 16:4; 44:27 [y]Dt 4:26 **26:39** [z]Ex 20:5; Isa 14:21 [a]S ver 16; Isa 24:16 **26:40** [b]S Lev 5:5 [c]Ps 32:5; 38:18 [d]Ne 9:2; Ps 106:6; Jer 3:12-15; 14:20; Hos 5:15; Lk 15:18; 1Jn 1:9 **26:41** [e]S ver 21 [f]Dt 10:16; 30:6; Jer 4:4; 9:25,26; Eze 44:7,9; Ac 7:51 [g]2Ch 7:14; 12:6; Eze 20:43 [h]Isa 6:7; 33:24; 40:2; 53:5, 6,11 **26:42** [i]Ge 28:15; 35:11-12 [j]S Ge 26:5 [k]S Ex 2:24 **26:43** [l]Ps 69:25; Isa 6:11; 32:14; 62:4; Jer 2:15; 44:2; La 1:1; Eze 36:4 [m]Nu 11:20; 14:31; 1Sa 8:7; Ps 106:24 [n]S ver 11; Eze 20:13 **26:44** [o]S ver 33; 2Ki 17:20; 25:11; 2Ch 6:36; 36:20 [p]S ver 11; Ro 11:2 [q]Dt 4:31; Jer 4:27; 5:10; 30:11 [r]Jdg 2:1; Jer 31:37; 33:26; 51:5 **26:45** [s]Dt 4:31 [t]Ex 6:8; Lev 25:38 **26:46** [u]S Ex 19:11 [v]S Lev 7:38; 27:34 **27:2** [w]S Ge 28:20 **27:3** [x]S Ex 30:13 **27:5** [y]S Ge 37:28 **27:6** [z]Nu 3:47; 18:16 **27:8** [a]S Lev 5:11 [b]ver 12,14 **27:9** [c]S Ge 28:20; S Lev 1:2 [d]ver 21, 26,28; Ex 40:9; Nu 6:20; 18:17; Dt 15:19 **27:10** [e]ver 33 **27:11** [f]ver 27; S Ex 13:13; Nu 18:15 **27:13** [g]S Lev 25:25 [h]S Lev 5:16

Chapter 27

Redeeming What Is the LORD's

THE LORD said to Moses, 2"Speak to
the Israelites and say to them: 'If anyone makes a special vow[w] to dedicate
persons to the LORD by giving equivalent
values, 3set the value of a male between
the ages of twenty and sixty at fifty shekels[n] of silver, according to the sanctuary
shekel[o];[x] 4and if it is a female, set her
value at thirty shekels.[p] 5If it is a person
between the ages of five and twenty, set
the value of a male at twenty shekels[q][y]
and of a female at ten shekels.[r] 6If it is a
person between one month and five
years, set the value of a male at five shekels[s][z] of silver and that of a female at
three shekels[t] of silver. 7If it is a person
sixty years old or more, set the value of a
male at fifteen shekels[u] and of a female at
ten shekels. 8If anyone making the vow is
too poor to pay[a] the specified amount, he
is to present the person to the priest, who
will set the value[b] for him according to
what the man making the vow can afford.
9" 'If what he vowed is an animal that
is acceptable as an offering to the LORD,[c]
such an animal given to the LORD becomes holy.[d] 10He must not exchange it
or substitute a good one for a bad one, or
a bad one for a good one;[e] if he should
substitute one animal for another, both it
and the substitute become holy. 11If what
he vowed is a ceremonially unclean animal[f]—one that is not acceptable as an
offering to the LORD—the animal must be
presented to the priest, 12who will judge
its quality as good or bad. Whatever value
the priest then sets, that is what it will
be. 13If the owner wishes to redeem[g] the
animal, he must add a fifth to its value.[h]
14" 'If a man dedicates his house as
something holy to the LORD, the priest

[n]*3* That is, about 1 1/4 pounds (about 0.6 kilogram); also in verse 16 [o]*3* That is, about 2/5 ounce (about 11.5 grams); also in verse 25 [p]*4* That is, about 12 ounces (about 0.3 kilogram) [q]*5* That is, about 8 ounces (about 0.2 kilogram) [r]*5* That is, about 4 ounces (about 110 grams); also in verse 7 [s]*6* That is, about 2 ounces (about 55 grams) [t]*6* That is, about 1 1/4 ounces (about 35 grams) [u]*7* That is, about 6 ounces (about 170 grams)

26:40–45 THE CHURCH, Covenant People—God establishes eternal relationships. He does not turn His back when we make mistakes. Judgment on sin is a part of God's covenant. God promised to punish the sinner but forgive those who returned to Him. Although judgment in the form of exile from the land would *occur, God promised to continue* in *covenant relationship* with His people and return them to the land, revealing His sovereign mercy.

27:1–8 HUMANITY, Worth—Monetary values for different persons were established in an ancient society despite the general attitude that life was cheap and some persons were thought to have little or no value at all. Every individual has worth. A person's ultimate worth is clearly shown in the teachings of the New Testament. See Mk 8:36; Jn 3:16; Ro 5:8.

27:14–33 SALVATION, Redemption—See note on

will judge its quality as good or bad.
Whatever value the priest then sets, so it
will remain. 15If the man who dedicates
his house redeems it,[i] he must add a
fifth to its value, and the house will again
become his.

16“ ‘If a man dedicates to the LORD part
of his family land, its value is to be set
according to the amount of seed required
for it—fifty shekels of silver to a homer[v]
of barley seed. 17If he dedicates his field
during the Year of Jubilee, the value that
has been set remains. 18But if he dedicates his field after the Jubilee,[j] the
priest will determine the value according
to the number of years that remain[k] until
the next Year of Jubilee, and its set value
will be reduced. 19If the man who dedicates the field wishes to redeem it,[l] he
must add a fifth to its value, and the field
will again become his. 20If, however, he
does not redeem the field, or if he has
sold it to someone else, it can never be
redeemed. 21When the field is released in
the Jubilee,[m] it will become holy,[n] like a
field devoted to the LORD;[o] it will become the property of the priests.[w]

22“ ‘If a man dedicates to the LORD a
field he has bought, which is not part of
his family land, 23the priest will determine its value up to the Year of Jubilee,[p]
and the man must pay its value on that
day as something holy to the LORD. 24In
the Year of Jubilee the field will revert to
the person from whom he bought it,[q] the
one whose land it was. 25Every value is to
be set according to the sanctuary shekel,[r] twenty gerahs[s] to the shekel.

26“ ‘No one, however, may dedicate
the firstborn of an animal, since the firstborn already belongs to the LORD;[t]
whether an ox[x] or a sheep, it is the
LORD’s. 27If it is one of the unclean animals,[u] he may buy it back at its set value,
adding a fifth of the value to it. If he does
not redeem it, it is to be sold at its set
value.

28“ ‘But nothing that a man owns and
devotes[y][v] to the LORD—whether man or
animal or family land—may be sold or
redeemed; everything so devoted is most
holy[w] to the LORD.

29“ ‘No person devoted to destruction[z]
may be ransomed; he must be put to
death.[x]

30“ ‘A tithe[y] of everything from the
land, whether grain from the soil or fruit
from the trees, belongs to the LORD; it is
holy[z] to the LORD. 31If a man redeems[a]
any of his tithe, he must add a fifth of the
value[b] to it. 32The entire tithe of the herd
and flock—every tenth animal that
passes under the shepherd’s rod[c]—will
be holy to the LORD. 33He must not pick
out the good from the bad or make any
substitution.[d] If he does make a substitution, both the animal and its substitute
become holy and cannot be redeemed.[e] ’ ”

34These are the commands the LORD
gave Moses on Mount Sinai[f] for the Israelites.[g]

27:15 [i]ver 13,20
27:18 [j]Lev 25:10 [k]Lev 25:15
27:19 [l]S Lev 25:25
27:21 [m]S Lev 25:10 [n]S ver 9 [o]ver 28; Nu 18:14; Eze 44:29
27:23 [p]S Lev 25:15
27:24 [q]Lev 25:28
27:25 [r]S Ex 30:13 [s]Nu 3:47; Eze 45:12
27:26 [t]S Ex 13:12
27:27 [u]S ver 11
27:28 [v]Nu 18:14; Jos 6:17-19 [w]S ver 9
27:29 [x]Dt 7:26
27:30 [y]Nu 18:26; Dt 12:6,17; 14:22,28; 2Ch 31:6; Ne 10:37; 12:44; 13:5; Mal 3:8 [z]Dt 7:6; Ezr 9:2; Isa 6:13
27:31 [a]S Lev 25:25 [b]Lev 5:16
27:32 [c]Ps 89:32; Jer 33:13; Eze 20:37
27:33 [d]ver 10 [e]Nu 18:21
27:34 [f]S Ex 19:11 [g]S Lev 7:38; Ac 7:38

[v]*16* That is, probably about 6 bushels (about 220 liters) [w]*21* Or *priest* [x]*26* The Hebrew word can include both male and female. [y]*28* The Hebrew term refers to the irrevocable giving over of things or persons to the LORD. [z]*29* The Hebrew term refers to the irrevocable giving over of things or persons to the LORD, often by totally destroying them.

25:24–55. Redemption included buying back from the priests or Temple those objects dedicated to God. Such redemption was costly, involving a twenty percent penalty. That which had been irrevocably given over (“devoted,” vv 28,29) to the Lord could not be redeemed. Examples were the booty taken at Jericho (Jos 6:19) and later Achan himself (Jos 7:1,13). These regulations were necessary for God’s people to know His will and protect their economic system. They foreshadowed the perfect redemption which is in the Lord Jesus Christ.

27:30–33 STEWARDSHIP, Tithe—The tithe of the produce of land belonged to God according to the tithe law. For one to redeem that which was to be tithed (such as an animal), a person had to give its value plus twenty percent. The Old Testament tithe law provides a valuable heritage for the Christian in giving to God for His work. See note on Nu 18:21–32.

27:34 HOLY SCRIPTURE, Inspired—Israel did not look on their religious law as the accumulated wisdom of the generations or as the secret learning of the priests. All law—religious, moral, and civil—had its basis in a historical event when God spoke to Moses on Sinai. Law was inspired commandment received directly from God for all God’s people. Law was God’s way of teaching His people the way they should live all phases of life in relationship to Him. See note on 1:1.

Numbers

Theological Setting

How does God lead a rebellious people? The fourth book of Moses carries on the record of God's redemptive dealings with His covenant people from the time of their departure from the southern end of the Sinai peninsula to their triumphal subjugation of the Transjordan and the marshaling of their troops at the east side of the Jordan River for the conquest of Canaan. It is a remarkable story of repeated failure in faith on the part of these erstwhile slaves, delivered by the miracle-working power of God, constantly accompanied by the glory-cloud symbolic of divine presence, and yet given to repeated relapse into distrust, self-pity, and rebellion in the face of any problem or crisis.

Numbers thus addressed a people who were a sorry excuse for an army of the Lord. Indeed, they were materialistic, self-centered warriors who lost courage at almost every challenge to faith and complained bitterly in the face of any testing that came their way. They lamented that God had drawn them into destruction in the desert and that their innocent, helpless children would die with them in the wilderness or be slaughtered by their pagan foes unless they returned in disgrace to the land of their oppressors. God had condemned them to wander the rest of their days in the wilderness until every last one of the rebellious adults had died in the desert. He promised to grant victory and complete conquest to those very children whose death they had dolefully predicted. The difference in their military effectiveness would result not from their increase in numbers but in the increase in their faith and the quality of their obedience to the commands of God and to the leadership of Joshua, Moses' chosen successor.

A new generation of promise facing the challenge of settling the land of promise after the history of rebellion and favor first received Numbers as its marching orders. Basic decisions faced them. Important options lay before them.

1. They could accept the status quo and try to establish life without accepting the risk of entering the unknown Promised Land.
2. They could retreat to the security of the past even though it meant eternal subjugation to foreign powers and forfeiture of God's promises.
3. They could continue complaining and fighting among themselves for leadership positions, power, and prestige without facing the task God had given them.
4. They could try to set up their own isolated religious community, following leaders, rituals, and worship patterns they invented rather than what God had commanded. This way they could avoid the contamination of the world and the challenge of obeying God.
5. They could find the faith to cut themselves off from the pattern of their fathers, search out God's will as revealed in His inspired Word, and cross into the Promised Land, depending on God to fulfill His promises and committed to becoming the people God always had wanted them to be despite their rebellious spirit.

Theological Outline

Numbers: Renewing a Rebellious People

I. God Prepares His People for the Task Ahead. (1:1—10:36)
   A. God prepares a people for conflict. (1:1-46)
   B. God calls a people to prepare for worship. (1:47-54)
   C. God organizes His people around His presence. (2:1-34)
   D. God separates religious leaders as His special representatives among the people. (3:1—4:49)
   E. God provides ways to deal with disobedient people and to ensure the faithful purity of His community. (5:1-31)
   F. God defines *procedures for holy volunteers.* (6:1-21)
   G. God provides a way of blessing His people and making them aware of their need for His presence among them. (6:22-27)

Chapter 1

The Census

THE LORD spoke to Moses in the Tent
of Meeting[a] in the Desert of Sinai[b]
on the first day of the second month[c] of
the second year after the Israelites came
out of Egypt.[d] He said: 2"Take a census[e]
of the whole Israelite community by their
clans and families,[f] listing every man by
name,[g] one by one. 3You and Aaron[h] are
to number by their divisions all the men
in Israel twenty years old or more[i] who
are able to serve in the army.[j] 4One man
from each tribe,[k] each the head of his
family,[l] is to help you.[m] 5These are the
names[n] of the men who are to assist you:

from Reuben,[o] Elizur son of Shedeur;[p]
6from Simeon,[q] Shelumiel son of Zurishaddai;[r]
7from Judah,[s] Nahshon son of Amminadab;[t]
8from Issachar,[u] Nethanel son of Zuar;[v]
9from Zebulun,[w] Eliab son of Helon;[x]
10from the sons of Joseph:
from Ephraim,[y] Elishama son of Ammihud;[z]
from Manasseh,[a] Gamaliel son of Pedahzur;[b]
11from Benjamin,[c] Abidan son of Gideoni;[d]
12from Dan,[e] Ahiezer son of Ammishaddai;[f]
13from Asher,[g] Pagiel son of Ocran;[h]
14from Gad,[i] Eliasaph son of Deuel;[j]
15from Naphtali,[k] Ahira son of Enan.[l]"

16These were the men appointed from
the community, the leaders[m] of their ancestral tribes.[n] They were the heads of
the clans of Israel.[o]
17Moses and Aaron took these men
whose names had been given, 18and they
called the whole community together on
the first day of the second month.[p] The
people indicated their ancestry[q] by their
clans and families,[r] and the men twenty
years old or more[s] were listed by name,
one by one, 19as the LORD commanded
Moses. And so he counted[t] them in the
Desert of Sinai:

20From the descendants of Reuben[u] the
firstborn son[v] of Israel:

All the men twenty years old or
more who were able to serve in
the army were listed by name,
one by one, according to the
records of their clans and families.
21The number from the tribe of
Reuben[w] was 46,500.

22From the descendants of Simeon:[x]

All the men twenty years old or
more who were able to serve in
the army were counted and listed
by name, one by one, according to
the records of their clans and families. 23The number from the tribe
of Simeon was 59,300.[y]

24From the descendants of Gad:[z]

All the men twenty years old or
more who were able to serve in
the army were listed by name, according to the records of their
clans and families. 25The number
from the tribe of Gad[a] was 45,
650.

26From the descendants of Judah:[b]

All the men twenty years old or
more who were able to serve in
the army were listed by name, according to the records of their
clans and families. 27The number
from the tribe of Judah[c] was 74,
600.

28From the descendants of Issachar:[d]

All the men twenty years old or
more who were able to serve in
the army were listed by name, according to the records of their
clans and families. 29The number
from the tribe of Issachar[e] was
54,400.[f]

30From the descendants of Zebulun:[g]

All the men twenty years old or
more who were able to serve in
the army were listed by name, according to the records of their
clans and families. 31The number
from the tribe of Zebulun was 57,
400.[h]

32From the sons of Joseph:[i]

1:1 [a]S Ex 27:21; S 40:2 [b]S Ex 19:1 [c]ver 18 [d]S Ex 6:14 **1:2** [e]Ex 30:11-16 [f]ver 18 [g]Nu 3:40 **1:3** [h]Ex 4:14; Nu 17:3 [i]S Ex 30:14 [j]ver 20; Nu 26:2; Jos 5:4; 1Ch 5:18 **1:4** [k]S Lev 24:11; S Jos 7:1 [l]ver 16; Nu 7:2; 30:1; 31:26 [m]Ex 18:21; Nu 34:18; Dt 1:15; Jos 22:14 **1:5** [n]Nu 17:2 [o]S Ge 29:32; Rev 7:5 [p]Nu 2:10; 7:30; 10:18 **1:6** [q]ver 22; Nu 25:14 [r]Nu 2:12; 7:36,41; 10:19 **1:7** [s]ver 26; S Ge 29:35; Ps 78:68 [t]Ex 6:23; Nu 7:12; Ru 4:20; 1Ch 2:10; Mt 1:4; Lk 3:32 **1:8** [u]S Ge 30:18; Nu 10:15 [v]Nu 2:5; 7:18 **1:9** [w]ver 30; Nu 10:16 [x]Nu 2:7; 7:24 **1:10** [y]ver 32 [z]Nu 2:18; 7:48,53; 10:22 [a]ver 34; Nu 10:23 [b]Nu 2:20; 7:54 **1:11** [c]Nu 10:24 [d]Nu 2:22; 7:60; Ps 68:27 **1:12** [e]ver 38 [f]Nu 2:25; 7:66; 10:25 **1:13** [g]ver 40; Nu 10:26 [h]Nu 2:27; 7:72 **1:14** [i]ver 24; Nu 10:20 [j]Nu 2:14; 7:42 **1:15** [k]ver 42; Nu 10:27 [l]Nu 2:29; 7:78 **1:16** [m]S Ex 18:25 [n]Nu 32:28 [o]S ver 4 **1:18** [p]ver 1 [q]Ezr 2:59; Heb 7:3 [r]ver 2 [s]S Ex 30:14 **1:19** [t]Ex 30:12; Nu 26:63; 31:49 **1:20** [u]S Ge 29:32; S 46:9; Rev 7:5 [v]S Ge 10:15 **1:21** [w]Nu 26:7 **1:22** [x]S Ge 29:33; Rev 7:7 **1:23** [y]Nu 26:14 **1:24** [z]S Ge 30:11; S Jos 13:24-28; Rev 7:5 **1:25** [a]Ge 46:16; Nu 26:18; 1Ch 5:11 **1:26** [b]S ver 7; Mt 1:2; Rev 7:5 **1:27** [c]Nu 26:22 **1:28** [d]S Ge 30:18; Rev 7:7 **1:29** [e]S Ge 30:18 [f]Nu 26:25 **1:30** [g]S Ge 30:20; Rev 7:8 **1:31** [h]Nu 26:27 **1:32** [i]Ge 49:26

1:1–2 REVELATION, Author of Life—God's request for a count had several caring purposes: He wanted Israel to take careful stock of every child of God, for provision and protection. He wanted Israel to realize how many in number they were so they could see God fulfilled His promise of offspring and strength (Ge 12:2). He wanted the people to assess their strength in relationship to warring nations they must face. The detailed numbering of Israelites also organized them for labor and distribution in the Promised Land. The God of order (Ge 1:1–2) reveals His care and administration of those to whom He is committed.

1:1–46 HISTORY, Politics—Being part of God's people does not eliminate political participation. God protected and fought for His people in the wilderness. Still they needed to be prepared for army duty. Only Levites were exempt from military duty because they had to attend to religious duties for the entire congregation of Israel.

1:3 HUMANITY, Community Relationships—Because persons are part of a community, they have responsibilities to serve the community in response to its needs.

From the descendants of Ephraim:[j]
All the men twenty years old or
more who were able to serve in
the army were listed by name, according to the records of their
clans and families. 33The number
from the tribe of Ephraim[k] was
40,500.
34From the descendants of Manasseh:[l]
All the men twenty years old or
more who were able to serve in
the army were listed by name, according to the records of their
clans and families. 35The number
from the tribe of Manasseh was
32,200.
36From the descendants of Benjamin:[m]
All the men twenty years old or
more who were able to serve in
the army were listed by name, according to the records of their
clans and families. 37The number
from the tribe of Benjamin[n] was
35,400.
38From the descendants of Dan:[o]
All the men twenty years old or
more who were able to serve in
the army were listed by name, according to the records of their
clans and families. 39The number
from the tribe of Dan was 62,
700.[p]
40From the descendants of Asher:[q]
All the men twenty years old or
more who were able to serve in
the army were listed by name, according to the records of their
clans and families. 41The number
from the tribe of Asher[r] was 41,
500.
42From the descendants of Naphtali:[s]
All the men twenty years old or
more who were able to serve in
the army were listed by name, according to the records of their
clans and families. 43The number
from the tribe of Naphtali[t] was
53,400.[u]

44These were the men counted by Moses and Aaron[v] and the twelve leaders of
Israel, each one representing his family.
45All the Israelites twenty years old or
more[w] who were able to serve in Israel's
army were counted according to their
families.[x] 46The total number was 603,
550.[y]
47The families of the tribe of Levi,[z]
however, were not counted[a] along with
the others. 48The LORD had said to Moses: 49"You must not count the tribe of
Levi or include them in the census of the
other Israelites. 50Instead, appoint the Levites to be in charge of the tabernacle[b] of
the Testimony[c]—over all its furnishings[d] and everything belonging to it.
They are to carry the tabernacle and all its
furnishings; they are to take care of it and
encamp around it. 51Whenever the tabernacle[e] is to move,[f] the Levites are to
take it down, and whenever the tabernacle is to be set up, the Levites shall do
it.[g] Anyone else who goes near it shall be
put to death.[h] 52The Israelites are to set
up their tents by divisions, each man in
his own camp under his own standard.[i]
53The Levites, however, are to set up
their tents around the tabernacle[j] of the
Testimony so that wrath will not fall[k] on
the Israelite community. The Levites are
to be responsible for the care of the tabernacle of the Testimony.[l]"
54The Israelites did all this just as the
LORD commanded Moses.

Chapter 2

The Arrangement of the Tribal Camps

THE LORD said to Moses and Aaron:
2"The Israelites are to camp around
the Tent of Meeting some distance from
it, each man under his standard[m] with
the banners of his family."
3On the east, toward the sunrise,
the divisions of the camp of Judah are
to encamp under their standard. The
leader of the people of Judah is Nahshon son of Amminadab.[n] 4His division numbers 74,600.
5The tribe of Issachar[o] will camp
next to them. The leader of the people of Issachar is Nethanel son of
Zuar.[p] 6His division numbers 54,
400.
7The tribe of Zebulun will be next.
The leader of the people of Zebulun
is Eliab son of Helon.[q] 8His division
numbers 57,400.
9All the men assigned to the camp
of Judah, according to their divisions,
number 186,400. They will set out
first.[r]

1:32 [j]S Ge 41:52
1:33 [k]Nu 26:37; 1Ch 7:20
1:34 [l]S Ge 41:51; Rev 7:6
1:36 [m]S Ge 35:18; 2Ch 17:17; Jer 32:44; Ob 1:19; Rev 7:8
1:37 [n]Nu 26:41
1:38 [o]Ge 30:6; Dt 33:22
1:39 [p]Nu 26:43
1:40 [q]S Ge 30:13; Nu 26:44; Rev 7:6
1:41 [r]Nu 26:47
1:42 [s]S Ge 30:8; Rev 7:6
1:43 [t]Nu 26:50 [u]S Ex 1:1-4
1:44 [v]Nu 26:64
1:45 [w]ver 3; Nu 14:29 [x]Nu 2:32
1:46 [y]S Ex 12:37; 2Sa 24:9
1:47 [z]S Nu 3:17-20 [a]Nu 4:3,49
1:50 [b]Ex 25:9; S 26:1 [c]S 16:34; Ac 7:44; Rev 15:5 [d]Nu 3:31
1:51 [e]S Ex 26:1 [f]Nu 4:5 [g]Nu 3:38; 4:15 [h]S Ex 21:12
1:52 [i]Nu 10:14; Ps 20:5; SS 2:4; 6:4
1:53 [j]Nu 2:10; 3:23,29,38 [k]Lev 10:6; Nu 16:46; 18:5; Dt 9:22 [l]S Ex 38:21; Nu 18:2-4
2:2 [m]Ps 74:4; Isa 31:9; Jer 4:21
2:3 [n]S Ex 6:23
2:5 [o]Nu 10:15 [p]S Nu 1:8
2:7 [q]Nu 1:9; 10:16
2:9 [r]Nu 10:14; Jdg 1:1

1:51 GOD, Holy—God was not making arbitrary and harsh regulations for the people. There was a serious educational purpose in this matter. The people had to learn that God is holy and they are sinful; they had to learn that they cannot approach God in any way they choose. They approach God only on God's own terms. We belong to God. He does not belong to us. We must respect the holiness, the complete otherness of God.

1:54 CHRISTIAN ETHICS, Moral Imperatives—Obedience is possible. God does not set up imperatives we cannot follow. Human weakness is not an acceptable excuse. God calls us to full-time obedience (Dt 30:11). See note on Ex 12:1—13:16.

10On the south[s] will be the divisions of the camp of Reuben under
their standard. The leader of the people of Reuben is Elizur son of Shedeur.[t] 11His division numbers 46,500.
12The tribe of Simeon[u] will camp
next to them. The leader of the people of Simeon is Shelumiel son of Zurishaddai.[v] 13His division numbers
59,300.
14The tribe of Gad[w] will be next.
The leader of the people of Gad is
Eliasaph son of Deuel.[a][x] 15His division numbers 45,650.
16All the men assigned to the camp
of Reuben,[y] according to their divisions, number 151,450. They will
set out second.

17Then the Tent of Meeting and
the camp of the Levites[z] will set out
in the middle of the camps. They will
set out in the same order as they encamp, each in his own place under
his standard.

18On the west[a] will be the divisions of the camp of Ephraim[b] under
their standard. The leader of the people of Ephraim is Elishama son of
Ammihud.[c] 19His division numbers
40,500.
20The tribe of Manasseh[d] will be
next to them. The leader of the people of Manasseh is Gamaliel son of
Pedahzur.[e] 21His division numbers
32,200.
22The tribe of Benjamin[f] will be
next. The leader of the people of Benjamin is Abidan son of Gideoni.[g]
23His division numbers 35,400.
24All the men assigned to the camp
of Ephraim,[h] according to their divisions, number 108,100. They will
set out third.[i]

25On the north[j] will be the divisions of the camp of Dan, under their
standard.[k] The leader of the people
of Dan is Ahiezer son of Ammishaddai.[l] 26His division numbers 62,700.
27The tribe of Asher will camp
next to them. The leader of the people of Asher is Pagiel son of Ocran.[m]
28His division numbers 41,500.
29The tribe of Naphtali[n] will be
next. The leader of the people of
Naphtali is Ahira son of Enan.[o] 30His
division numbers 53,400.
31All the men assigned to the camp
of Dan number 157,600. They will
set out last,[p] under their standards.

32These are the Israelites, counted
according to their families.[q] All
those in the camps, by their divisions, number 603,550.[r] 33The Levites, however, were not counted[s]
along with the other Israelites, as the
LORD commanded Moses.

34So the Israelites did everything the
LORD commanded Moses; that is the way
they encamped under their standards,
and that is the way they set out, each
with his clan and family.

Chapter 3

The Levites

THIS is the account of the family of Aaron and Moses[t] at the time the LORD
talked with Moses on Mount Sinai.[u]
2The names of the sons of Aaron were
Nadab the firstborn[v] and Abihu, Eleazar
and Ithamar.[w] 3Those were the names of
Aaron's sons, the anointed priests,[x] who
were ordained to serve as priests. 4Nadab
and Abihu, however, fell dead before the
LORD[y] when they made an offering with
unauthorized fire before him in the
Desert of Sinai.[z] They had no sons; so
only Eleazar and Ithamar[a] served as
priests during the lifetime of their father
Aaron.[b]
5The LORD said to Moses, 6"Bring the
tribe of Levi[c] and present them to Aaron
the priest to assist him.[d] 7They are to
perform duties for him and for the whole
community[e] at the Tent of Meeting by
doing the work[f] of the tabernacle. 8They
are to take care of all the furnishings of
the Tent of Meeting, fulfilling the obligations of the Israelites by doing the work
of the tabernacle. 9Give the Levites to
Aaron and his sons;[g] they are the Israelites who are to be given wholly to him.[b]
10Appoint Aaron[h] and his sons to serve
as priests;[i] anyone else who approaches
the sanctuary must be put to death."[j]
11The LORD also said to Moses, 12"I
have taken the Levites[k] from among the
Israelites in place of the first male offspring[l] of every Israelite woman. The Levites are mine,[m] 13for all the firstborn are
mine.[n] When I struck down all the firstborn in Egypt, I set apart for myself every
firstborn in Israel, whether man or animal. They are to be mine. I am the
LORD."[o]
14The LORD said to Moses in the Desert
of Sinai,[p] 15"Count[q] the Levites by their
families and clans. Count every male a
month old or more."[r] 16So Moses count-

2:10 [s]S Nu 1:53 [t]Nu 1:5
2:12 [u]Nu 10:19 [v]S Nu 1:6
2:14 [w]Nu 10:20 [x]Nu 1:14; 10:20
2:16 [y]Nu 10:18
2:17 [z]Nu 1:50; 10:21
2:18 [a]S Nu 1:53 [b]S Ge 48:20; Jer 31:18-20 [c]Nu 1:10
2:20 [d]S Ge 48:20 [e]S Nu 1:10
2:22 [f]Nu 10:24 [g]S Nu 1:11
2:24 [h]Nu 10:22 [i]Ps 80:2
2:25 [j]S Nu 1:53 [k]Nu 10:25 [l]S Nu 1:12
2:27 [m]Nu 1:13; 10:26
2:29 [n]Nu 10:27 [o]Nu 1:15; 10:27
2:31 [p]Nu 10:25; Jos 6:9
2:32 [q]Nu 1:45 [r]S Ex 12:37
2:33 [s]Nu 1:47; 26:57-62
3:1 [t]S Ex 6:27 [u]S Ex 19:11
3:2 [v]Nu 1:20 [w]S Ex 6:23
3:3 [x]S Ex 28:41; S 29:30
3:4 [y]S Lev 10:2 [z]S Lev 10:1 [a]Lev 10:6,12; Nu 4:28 [b]1Ch 24:1
3:6 [c]Dt 10:8; 31:9; 1Ch 15:2 [d]Nu 8:6-22; 18:1-7; 2Ch 29:11
3:7 [e]Nu 1:53; 8:19 [f]S Lev 8:35; Nu 1:50
3:9 [g]ver 12,45; Nu 8:19; 18:6
3:10 [h]S Ex 30:7 [i]S Ex 29:9 [j]Nu 1:51
3:12 [k]Ne 13:29; Mal 2:4 [l]ver 41; Nu 8:16,18 [m]S ver 9; Ex 13:2; Nu 8:14; 16:9
3:13 [n]S Ex 13:12 [o]Lev 11:44
3:14 [p]S Ex 19:1
3:15 [q]ver 39; S Nu 1:19 [r]ver 22; Nu 18:16; 26:62

a *14* Many manuscripts of the Masoretic Text, Samaritan Pentateuch and Vulgate (see also Num. 1:14); most manuscripts of the Masoretic Text *Reuel*
b *9* Most manuscripts of the Masoretic Text; some manuscripts of the Masoretic Text, Samaritan Pentateuch and Septuagint (see also Num. 8:16) *to me*

ed them, as he was commanded by the word of the LORD.

17These were the names of the sons of Levi:[s]

Gershon,[t] Kohath[u] and Merari.[v]

18These were the names of the Gershonite clans:

Libni and Shimei.[w]

19The Kohathite clans:

Amram, Izhar, Hebron and Uzziel.[x]

20The Merarite clans:[y]

Mahli and Mushi.[z]

These were the Levite clans, according to their families.

21To Gershon[a] belonged the clans of the Libnites and Shimeites;[b] these were the Gershonite clans. 22The number of all the males a month old or more who were counted was 7,500. 23The Gershonite clans were to camp on the west, behind the tabernacle.[c] 24The leader of the families of the Gershonites was Eliasaph son of Lael. 25At the Tent of Meeting the Gershonites were responsible for the care of the tabernacle[d] and tent, its coverings,[e] the curtain at the entrance[f] to the Tent of Meeting,[g] 26the curtains of the courtyard[h], the curtain at the entrance to the courtyard surrounding the tabernacle and altar,[i] and the ropes[j]—and everything[k] related to their use.

27To Kohath[l] belonged the clans of the Amramites, Izharites, Hebronites and Uzzielites;[m] these were the Kohathite[n] clans. 28The number of all the males a month old or more[o] was 8,600.[c] The Kohathites were responsible[p] for the care of the sanctuary.[q] 29The Kohathite clans were to camp on the south side[r] of the tabernacle. 30The leader of the families of the Kohathite clans was Elizaphan[s] son of Uzziel. 31They were responsible for the care of the ark,[t] the table,[u] the lampstand,[v] the altars,[w] the articles[x] of the sanctuary used in ministering, the curtain,[y] and everything related to their use.[z] 32The chief leader of the Levites was Eleazar[a] son of Aaron, the priest. He was appointed over those who were responsible[b] for the care of the sanctuary.[c]

33To Merari belonged the clans of the Mahlites and the Mushites;[d] these were the Merarite clans.[e] 34The number of all the males a month old or more[f] who were counted was 6,200. 35The leader of the families of the Merarite clans was Zuriel son of Abihail; they were to camp on the north side of the tabernacle.[g] 36The Merarites were appointed[h] to take care of the frames of the tabernacle,[i] its crossbars,[j] posts,[k] bases, all its equipment, and everything related to their use,[l] 37as well as the posts of the surrounding courtyard[m] with their bases, tent pegs[n] and ropes.

38Moses and Aaron and his sons were to camp to the east[o] of the tabernacle, toward the sunrise, in front of the Tent of Meeting.[p] They were responsible for the care of the sanctuary[q] on behalf of the Israelites. Anyone else who approached the sanctuary was to be put to death.[r]

39The total number of Levites counted[s] at the LORD's command by Moses and Aaron according to their clans, including every male a month old or more, was 22,000.[t]

40The LORD said to Moses, "Count all the firstborn Israelite males who are a month old or more[u] and make a list of their names.[v] 41Take the Levites for me in place of all the firstborn of the Israelites,[w] and the livestock of the Levites in place of all the firstborn of the livestock of the Israelites. I am the LORD."[x]

42So Moses counted all the firstborn of the Israelites, as the LORD commanded him. 43The total number of firstborn males a month old or more,[y] listed by name, was 22,273.[z]

44The LORD also said to Moses, 45"Take the Levites in place of all the firstborn of Israel, and the livestock of the Levites in place of their livestock. The Levites are to be mine.[a] I am the LORD.[b] 46To redeem[c] the 273 firstborn Israelites who exceed the number of the Levites, 47collect five shekels[d][d] for each one, according to the sanctuary shekel,[e] which weighs twenty gerahs.[f] 48Give the money for the redemption[g] of the additional Israelites to Aaron and his sons."[h]

49So Moses collected the redemption money[i] from those who exceeded the number redeemed by the Levites. 50From the firstborn of the Israelites[j] he collected silver weighing 1,365 shekels,[e][k] according to the sanctuary shekel. 51Moses gave the redemption money to Aaron and his sons, as he was commanded by the word of the LORD.

Chapter 4

The Kohathites

THE LORD said to Moses and Aaron: 2"Take a census[l] of the Kohathite branch of the Levites by their clans and

3:17 sS Ge 29:34; S 46:11; Nu 1:47; 1Ch 15:4; 23:6; 2Ch 29:12 tJos 21:6 uJos 21:4 vS Ex 6:16
3:18 wEx 6:17
3:19 xS Ex 6:18
3:20 yS Ge 46:11 zS Ex 6:19
3:21 aS Ge 46:11 bEx 6:17
3:23 cS Nu 2:18
3:25 dEx 25:9; Nu 7:1 eEx 26:14 fEx 26:36; Nu 4:25 gEx 40:2
3:26 hEx 27:9 iver 31 jEx 35:18 kNu 4:26
3:27 lS Ge 46:11; S Ex 6:18 mEx 6:18; 1Ch 26:23 nNu 4:15,37
3:28 over 15 pNu 4:4,15 qS Ex 25:8; 30:13; 2Ch 30:19; Ps 15:1; 20:2; Eze 44:27
3:29 rS Nu 1:53
3:30 sS Ex 6:22
3:31 tS Ex 25:10-22; Dt 10:1-8; 2Ch 5:2; Jer 3:16 uS Ex 25:23 vS Ex 25:31; 1Ch 28:15; Jer 52:19 wver 26 xNu 1:50 yS Ex 26:33; Nu 4:5 zNu 4:15; 18:3
3:32 aS Ex 6:23 bver 28 cNu 4:19; 18:3
3:33 dS Ex 6:19 eS Ge 46:11
3:34 fver 15
3:35 gS Nu 2:25
3:36 hNu 4:32 iEx 26:15-25; 35:20-29 jEx 26:26-29 kEx 36:36 lNu 18:3
3:37 mEx 27:10-17 nEx 27:19
3:38 oNu 2:3 pS Nu 1:53; 1Ch 9:27; 23:32 qver 7; Nu 18:5 rver 10; Nu 1:51
3:39 sS ver 15 tNu 26:62
3:40 uver 15 vNu 1:2
3:41 wver 12 xLev 11:44
3:43 yver 15 zver 39
3:45 aS ver 9 bLev 11:44
3:46 cEx 13:13; Nu 18:15
3:47 dS Lev 27:6 eS Ex 30:13 fS Lev 27:25
3:48 gver 51 hver 50
3:49 iver 48
3:50 jver 41,45 kS ver 46-48
4:2 lS Ex 30:12

c*28* Hebrew; some Septuagint manuscripts *8,300*
d*47* That is, about 2 ounces (about 55 grams)
e*50* That is, about 35 pounds (about 15.5 kilograms)

families. [3]Count[m] all the men from thirty
to fifty years of age[n] who come to serve
in the work in the Tent of Meeting.
[4]"This is the work[o] of the Kohathites[p]
in the Tent of Meeting: the care of the
most holy things.[q] [5]When the camp is to
move,[r] Aaron and his sons are to go in
and take down the shielding curtain[s] and
cover the ark of the Testimony with it.[t]
[6]Then they are to cover this with hides of
sea cows,[f][u] spread a cloth of solid blue
over that and put the poles[v] in place.
[7]"Over the table of the Presence[w] they
are to spread a blue cloth and put on it
the plates, dishes and bowls, and the jars
for drink offerings;[x] the bread that is
continually there[y] is to remain on it.
[8]Over these they are to spread a scarlet
cloth, cover that with hides of sea cows
and put its poles[z] in place.
[9]"They are to take a blue cloth and cover the lampstand that is for light, together
with its lamps, its wick trimmers and
trays,[a] and all its jars for the oil used to
supply it. [10]Then they are to wrap it and
all its accessories in a covering of hides of
sea cows and put it on a carrying frame.[b]
[11]"Over the gold altar[c] they are to
spread a blue cloth and cover that with
hides of sea cows and put its poles[d] in
place.
[12]"They are to take all the articles[e]
used for ministering in the sanctuary,
wrap them in a blue cloth, cover that
with hides of sea cows and put them on a
carrying frame.[f]
[13]"They are to remove the ashes[g] from
the bronze altar[h] and spread a purple
cloth over it. [14]Then they are to place on
it all the utensils[i] used for ministering at
the altar, including the firepans,[j] meat
forks,[k] shovels[l] and sprinkling bowls.[m]
Over it they are to spread a covering of
hides of sea cows and put its poles[n] in
place.
[15]"After Aaron and his sons have finished covering the holy furnishings and
all the holy articles, and when the camp
is ready to move,[o] the Kohathites[p] are to
come to do the carrying.[q] But they must
not touch the holy things[r] or they will
die.[s][t] The Kohathites are to carry those
things that are in the Tent of Meeting.
[16]"Eleazar[u] son of Aaron, the priest, is
to have charge of the oil for the light,[v]
the fragrant incense,[w] the regular grain
offering[x] and the anointing oil. He is to
be in charge of the entire tabernacle and
everything in it, including its holy furnishings and articles."
[17]The LORD said to Moses and Aaron,
[18]"See that the Kohathite tribal clans are
not cut off from the Levites. [19]So that
they may live and not die when they
come near the most holy things,[y] do this
for them: Aaron and his sons[z] are to go
into the sanctuary and assign to each man
his work and what he is to carry.[a] [20]But
the Kohathites must not go in to look[b] at
the holy things, even for a moment, or
they will die."

The Gershonites

[21]The LORD said to Moses, [22]"Take a
census also of the Gershonites by their
families and clans. [23]Count all the men
from thirty to fifty years of age[c] who
come to serve in the work at the Tent of
Meeting.
[24]"This is the service of the Gershonite
clans as they work and carry burdens:
[25]They are to carry the curtains of the
tabernacle,[d] the Tent of Meeting,[e] its
covering[f] and the outer covering of hides
of sea cows, the curtains for the entrance
to the Tent of Meeting, [26]the curtains of
the courtyard surrounding the tabernacle
and altar,[g] the curtain for the entrance,[h]
the ropes and all the equipment[i] used in
its service. The Gershonites are to do all
that needs to be done with these things.
[27]All their service, whether carrying or
doing other work, is to be done under the
direction of Aaron and his sons.[j] You
shall assign to them as their responsibility[k] all they are to carry. [28]This is the service of the Gershonite clans[l] at the Tent
of Meeting. Their duties are to be under
the direction of Ithamar[m] son of Aaron,
the priest.

The Merarites

[29]"Count[n] the Merarites by their clans
and families.[o] [30]Count all the men from
thirty to fifty years of age who come to
serve in the work at the Tent of Meeting.
[31]This is their duty as they perform service at the Tent of Meeting: to carry the

[f]6 That is, dugongs; also in verses 8, 10, 11, 12, 14 and 25

4:3 [m]S Nu 1:47 [n]ver 23; Nu 8:25; 1Ch 23:3,24,27; Ezr 3:8
4:4 [o]S Nu 3:28 [p]Nu 7:9 [q]ver 19
4:5 [r]Nu 1:51 [s]S Ex 26:31,33 [t]1Ch 23:26
4:6 [u]S Ex 25:5 [v]S Ex 25:13-15; 1Ki 8:7; 2Ch 5:8
4:7 [w]S Lev 24:6 [x]Ex 39:36; Jer 52:19 [y]S Ex 25:30
4:8 [z]Ex 26:26-28
4:9 [a]S Ex 25:38
4:10 [b]ver 12
4:11 [c]S Ex 30:1 [d]Ex 30:4
4:12 [e]Nu 3:31 [f]ver 10
4:13 [g]S Lev 1:16 [h]Ex 27:1-8; Nu 3:31
4:14 [i]S Ex 31:9 [j]S Ex 27:3 [k]1Ch 28:17; 2Ch 4:16 [l]2Ch 4:11 [m]Ex 27:3; Nu 7:84; 2Ch 4:8; Jer 52:18 [n]Ex 27:6
4:15 [o]ver 5 [p]S Nu 3:27 [q]Nu 7:9 [r]ver 4 [s]S Ex 28:43 [t]Nu 1:51; 2Sa 6:6,7
4:16 [u]Lev 10:6; Nu 3:32 [v]S Ex 25:6 [w]S Ex 25:6 [x]S Ex 29:41; Lev 6:14-23
4:19 [y]S ver 15 [z]ver 27 [a]S Nu 3:32
4:20 [b]S Ex 19:21
4:23 [c]S ver 3
4:25 [d]Ex 27:10-18 [e]Nu 3:25 [f]Ex 26:14
4:26 [g]Ex 27:9 [h]Ex 27:16 [i]Nu 3:26
4:27 [j]ver 19 [k]Nu 3:25,26
4:28 [l]Nu 7:7 [m]S Ex 6:23
4:29 [n]S Ex 30:12 [o]S Ge 46:11

4:7 REVELATION, Divine Presence—Preparing a table for feeding in the worship place was God's way of declaring that He always set before Israel enough provision for the day and that God was always present for them in the daily gift of bread (Ex 25:30). The symbolic importance of receiving sustenance from God is an important theme throughout the Scripture, from the manna as "bread from heaven" given to Israel (Ex 16), to the food of the Promised Land (flowing with milk and honey), to the divine Presence regularly set before them anywhere they camped, to the greatest gift of bread, Christ in the New Testament declaring in the breaking of the bread He was giving Himself to His followers. God is a faithful and present Deity, who cares enough to be involved in the daily lives of His children. These regulations give rise to the familiar comment that there is an unseen Guest present at every table. The Lord of life is always present where the gifts that sustain life are shared. Bread represented also Israel's continual offering to God from the provisions He supplied (Ex 25:30).

frames of the tabernacle, its crossbars,
posts and bases,[p] 32as well as the posts of
the surrounding courtyard with their bases, tent pegs, ropes,[q] all their equipment
and everything related to their use. Assign to each man the specific things he is
to carry. 33This is the service of the Merarite clans as they work at the Tent of
Meeting under the direction of Ithamar[r]
son of Aaron, the priest."

The Numbering of the Levite Clans

34Moses, Aaron and the leaders of the
community counted the Kohathites[s] by
their clans and families. 35All the men
from thirty to fifty years of age[t] who
came to serve in the work in the Tent of
Meeting, 36counted by clans, were 2,750.
37This was the total of all those in the
Kohathite clans[u] who served in the Tent
of Meeting. Moses and Aaron counted
them according to the LORD's command
through Moses.

38The Gershonites[v] were counted by
their clans and families. 39All the men
from thirty to fifty years of age who came
to serve in the work at the Tent of Meeting, 40counted by their clans and families,
were 2,630. 41This was the total of those
in the Gershonite clans who served at the
Tent of Meeting. Moses and Aaron counted them according to the LORD's command.

42The Merarites were counted by their
clans and families. 43All the men from
thirty to fifty years of age[w] who came to
serve in the work at the Tent of Meeting,
44counted by their clans, were 3,200.
45This was the total of those in the Merarite clans.[x] Moses and Aaron counted
them according to the LORD's command
through Moses.

46So Moses, Aaron and the leaders of
Israel counted[y] all the Levites by their
clans and families. 47All the men from
thirty to fifty years of age[z] who came to
do the work of serving and carrying the
Tent of Meeting 48numbered 8,580.[a]
49At the LORD's command through Moses, each was assigned his work and told
what to carry.

Thus they were counted,[b] as the LORD
commanded Moses.

Chapter 5

The Purity of the Camp

THE LORD said to Moses, 2"Command
the Israelites to send away from the
camp anyone who has an infectious skin
disease[g][c] or a discharge[d] of any kind, or
who is ceremonially unclean[e] because of
a dead body.[f] 3Send away male and female alike; send them outside the camp
so they will not defile their camp, where I
dwell among them.[g]" 4The Israelites did
this; they sent them outside the camp.
They did just as the LORD had instructed
Moses.

Restitution for Wrongs

5The LORD said to Moses, 6"Say to the
Israelites: 'When a man or woman
wrongs another in any way[h] and so is
unfaithful[h] to the LORD, that person is
guilty[i] 7and must confess[j] the sin he has
committed. He must make full restitution[k] for his wrong, add one fifth to it
and give it all to the person he has
wronged. 8But if that person has no close
relative to whom restitution can be made
for the wrong, the restitution belongs to
the LORD and must be given to the priest,
along with the ram[l] with which atonement is made for him.[m] 9All the sacred
contributions the Israelites bring to a
priest will belong to him.[n] 10Each man's
sacred gifts are his own, but what he
gives to the priest will belong to the
priest.[o] ' "

The Test for an Unfaithful Wife

11Then the LORD said to Moses,
12"Speak to the Israelites and say to
them: 'If a man's wife goes astray[p] and is
unfaithful to him 13by sleeping with another man,[q] and this is hidden from her
husband and her impurity is undetected
(since there is no witness against her and
she has not been caught in the act), 14and
if feelings of jealousy[r] come over her
husband and he suspects his wife and she
is impure—or if he is jealous and suspects her even though she is not impure— 15then he is to take his wife to the
priest. He must also take an offering of a
tenth of an ephah[i][s] of barley flour[t] on
her behalf. He must not pour oil on it or
put incense on it, because it is a grain
offering for jealousy,[u] a reminder[v] offering to draw attention to guilt.

16" 'The priest shall bring her and have
her stand before the LORD. 17Then he
shall take some holy water in a clay jar
and put some dust from the tabernacle
floor into the water. 18After the priest has

4:31 [p]Nu 3:36
4:32 [q]Nu 3:37
4:33 [r]S Ex 38:21
4:34 [s]ver 2
4:35 [t]ver 3
4:37 [u]S Nu 3:27
4:38 [v]S Ge 46:11
4:43 [w]ver 3
4:45 [x]ver 29
4:46 [y]Nu 1:19
4:47 [z]ver 3
4:48 [a]Nu 3:39
4:49 [b]S Nu 1:47
5:2 [c]S Lev 13:2 [d]S Lev 15:2; Mt 9:20 [e]Lev 13:3; Nu 9:6-10 [f]S Lev 21:11
5:3 [g]S Ex 29:45; Lev 26:12; 2Co 6:16
5:6 [h]S Lev 6:2 [i]Lev 5:14-6:7
5:7 [j]S Lev 5:5; S Lk 19:8 [k]S Lev 5:16
5:8 [l]S Lev 5:15 [m]Lev 6:6,7
5:9 [n]Lev 6:17
5:10 [o]Lev 7:29-34
5:12 [p]ver 19-21; S Ex 20:14
5:13 [q]S Ex 20:14
5:14 [r]ver 30; Pr 6:34; 27:4; SS 8:6
5:15 [s]S Ex 16:36 [t]S Lev 6:20 [u]ver 18, 25 [v]Eze 21:23; 29:16

[g]2 Traditionally *leprosy*; the Hebrew word was used for various diseases affecting the skin—not necessarily leprosy. [h]6 Or *woman commits any wrong common to mankind* [i]15 That is, probably about 2 quarts (about 2 liters)

5:6 SIN, Responsibility—Sin against another person must be confessed to God and made right with the person wronged. See notes on Ge 39:9; Lev 6:1–3. Wronging another person is sin against God.

had the woman stand before the LORD, he
shall loosen her hair[w] and place in her
hands the reminder offering, the grain offering for jealousy,[x] while he himself
holds the bitter water that brings a
curse.[y] 19Then the priest shall put the
woman under oath and say to her, "If no
other man has slept with you and you
have not gone astray[z] and become impure while married to your husband, may
this bitter water that brings a curse[a] not
harm you. 20But if you have gone astray[b]
while married to your husband and you
have defiled yourself by sleeping with a
man other than your husband"— 21here
the priest is to put the woman under this
curse of the oath[c]—"may the LORD
cause your people to curse and denounce
you when he causes your thigh to waste
away and your abdomen to swell.[j] 22May
this water[d] that brings a curse[e] enter
your body so that your abdomen swells
and your thigh wastes away.[k] "
" 'Then the woman is to say, "Amen.
So be it.[f] "

23" 'The priest is to write these curses
on a scroll[g] and then wash them off into
the bitter water. 24He shall have the
woman drink the bitter water that brings
a curse, and this water will enter her and
cause bitter suffering. 25The priest is to
take from her hands the grain offering for
jealousy, wave it before the LORD[h] and
bring it to the altar. 26The priest is then to
take a handful of the grain offering as a
memorial offering[i] and burn it on the
altar; after that, he is to have the woman
drink the water. 27If she has defiled herself and been unfaithful to her husband,
then when she is made to drink the water
that brings a curse, it will go into her and
cause bitter suffering; her abdomen will
swell and her thigh waste away,[l] and she
will become accursed[j] among her people. 28If, however, the woman has not defiled herself and is free from impurity,
she will be cleared of guilt and will be
able to have children.

29" 'This, then, is the law of jealousy
when a woman goes astray[k] and defiles
herself while married to her husband,
30or when feelings of jealousy[l] come
over a man because he suspects his wife.
The priest is to have her stand before the
LORD and is to apply this entire law to
her. 31The husband will be innocent of
any wrongdoing, but the woman will bear
the consequences[m] of her sin.' "

5:18 [w]S Lev 10:6; 1Co 11:6
5:18 [x]ver 15 [y]ver 19
5:19 [z]ver 12,29 [a]ver 18
5:20 [b]ver 12
5:21 [c]Jos 6:26; 1Sa 14:24; Ne 10:29
5:22 [d]Ps 109:18 [e]ver 18 [f]Dt 27:15
5:23 [g]Jer 45:1
5:25 [h]Lev 8:27
5:26 [i]S Lev 2:2
5:27 [j]Isa 43:28; 65:15; Jer 26:6; 29:18; 42:18; 44:12,22; Zec 8:13
5:29 [k]S ver 19
5:30 [l]S ver 14
5:31 [m]S Lev 5:1
6:2 [n]ver 5; S Ge 28:20; Ac 21:23 [o]ver 6 [p]Jdg 13:5; 16:17
6:3 [q]S Lev 10:9; S Lk 1:15 [r]Ru 2:14; Ps 69:21; Pr 10:26 [s]S Lev 25:5
6:5 [t]Ps 52:2; 57:4; 59:7; Isa 7:20; Eze 5:1 [u]1Sa 1:11
6:6 [v]S Lev 21:1-3; Nu 19:11-22
6:7 [w]Nu 9:6
6:9 [x]ver 18 [y]S Lev 14:9
6:10 [z]S Lev 14:10 [a]S Lev 5:7 [b]Lev 14:11
6:11 [c]S Ex 30:10 [d]S Ge 8:20 [e]S Ex 29:36
6:12 [f]S Lev 12:6 [g]S Lev 5:15
6:13 [h]Ac 21:26 [i]Lev 14:11
6:14 [j]S Ex 12:5

Chapter 6

The Nazirite

THE LORD said to Moses, 2"Speak to
the Israelites and say to them: 'If a
man or woman wants to make a special
vow[n], a vow of separation[o] to the LORD
as a Nazirite,[p] 3he must abstain from
wine[q] and other fermented drink and
must not drink vinegar[r] made from wine
or from other fermented drink. He must
not drink grape juice or eat grapes[s] or
raisins. 4As long as he is a Nazirite, he
must not eat anything that comes from
the grapevine, not even the seeds or
skins.

5" 'During the entire period of his vow
of separation no razor[t] may be used on
his head.[u] He must be holy until the period of his separation to the LORD is over;
he must let the hair of his head grow
long. 6Throughout the period of his separation to the LORD he must not go near a
dead body.[v] 7Even if his own father or
mother or brother or sister dies, he must
not make himself ceremonially unclean[w]
on account of them, because the symbol
of his separation to God is on his head.
8Throughout the period of his separation
he is consecrated to the LORD.

9" 'If someone dies suddenly in his
presence, thus defiling the hair he has
dedicated,[x] he must shave his head on
the day of his cleansing[y]—the seventh
day. 10Then on the eighth day[z] he must
bring two doves or two young pigeons[a]
to the priest at the entrance to the Tent of
Meeting.[b] 11The priest is to offer one as a
sin offering[c] and the other as a burnt offering[d] to make atonement[e] for him because he sinned by being in the presence
of the dead body. That same day he is to
consecrate his head. 12He must dedicate
himself to the LORD for the period of his
separation and must bring a year-old male
lamb[f] as a guilt offering.[g] The previous
days do not count, because he became
defiled during his separation.

13" 'Now this is the law for the Nazirite
when the period of his separation is
over.[h] He is to be brought to the entrance to the Tent of Meeting.[i] 14There
he is to present his offerings to the LORD:
a year-old male lamb without defect[j] for

[j]21 Or *causes you to have a miscarrying womb and barrenness* [k]22 Or *body and cause you to be barren and have a miscarrying womb* [l]27 Or *suffering; she will have barrenness and a miscarrying womb*

6:3–4,20 CHRISTIAN ETHICS, Alcohol—Abstaining from alcohol is a way of showing total commitment to God. The Nazirite vow was a way for lay people to dedicate themselves to serve God for a shorter or longer period (Jdg 13:4–5; Am 2:12). After the period of the vow, the Nazirite returned to the normal habits of Israelite life. Nazirites refused to practice anything which might be perceived as borrowed from Canaanite cultic practice. Their lives symbolized before the community a loyalty to Yahweh, the God of Israel.

a burnt offering, a year-old ewe lamb
without defect for a sin offering,[k] a ram[l]
without defect for a fellowship offering,[m][m] 15together with their grain offerings[n] and drink offerings,[o] and a basket
of bread made without yeast—cakes
made of fine flour mixed with oil, and
wafers spread with oil.[p]
16" 'The priest is to present them[q] before the LORD[r] and make the sin offering
and the burnt offering.[s] 17He is to
present the basket of unleavened bread
and is to sacrifice the ram as a fellowship
offering[t] to the LORD, together with its
grain offering[u] and drink offering.[v]
18" 'Then at the entrance to the Tent of
Meeting, the Nazirite must shave off the
hair that he dedicated.[w] He is to take the
hair and put it in the fire that is under the
sacrifice of the fellowship offering.
19" 'After the Nazirite has shaved off
the hair of his dedication, the priest is to
place in his hands a boiled shoulder of the
ram, and a cake and a wafer from the
basket, both made without yeast.[x] 20The
priest shall then wave them before the
LORD as a wave offering;[y] they are holy[z]
and belong to the priest, together with
the breast that was waved and the thigh
that was presented.[a] After that, the Nazirite may drink wine.[b]
21" 'This is the law of the Nazirite[c]
who vows his offering to the LORD in accordance with his separation, in addition
to whatever else he can afford. He must
fulfill the vow[d] he has made, according
to the law of the Nazirite.' "

The Priestly Blessing

22The LORD said to Moses, 23"Tell Aaron and his sons, 'This is how you are to
bless[e] the Israelites. Say to them:

24" ' "The LORD bless you[f]
and keep you;[g]
25the LORD make his face shine upon
you[h]
and be gracious to you;[i]
26the LORD turn his face[j] toward you
and give you peace.[k]" '

27"So they will put my name[l] on the
Israelites, and I will bless them."

6:14 [k]ver 11; Lev 4:3; 14:10 [l]S Lev 5:15 [m]Lev 3:1
6:15 [n]Lev 2:1; S 6:14 [o]S Ge 35:14 [p]S Ex 29:2
6:16 [q]Lev 1:3 [r]ver 10 [s]ver 11
6:17 [t]Lev 3:1 [u]S Ex 29:41 [v]Lev 23:13
6:18 [w]ver 9; Ac 21:24
6:19 [x]Lev 7:12
6:20 [y]Lev 7:30 [z]S Lev 27:9 [a]S Lev 7:34 [b]Ecc 9:7
6:21 [c]ver 13 [d]ver 2
6:23 [e]Dt 21:5; 1Ch 23:13
6:24 [f]S Ge 28:3; Dt 28:3-6; Ps 28:9; 128:5 [g]1Sa 2:9; Ps 17:8
6:25 [h]Job 29:24; Ps 4:6; 31:16; 80:3; 119:135 [i]Ge 43:29; Ps 25:16; 86:16; 119:29
6:26 [j]Ps 4:6; 44:3 [k]Ps 4:8; 29:11; 37:11,37; 127:2; Isa 14:7; Jer 33:6; Jn 14:27
6:27 [l]Dt 28:10; 2Sa 7:23; 2Ch 7:14; Ne 9:10; Jer 25:29; Eze 36:23
7:1 [m]Ex 40:17 [n]S Ex 30:26 [o]S Ex 40:9 [p]ver 84, 88; Ex 40:10; 2Ch 7:9
7:2 [q]Nu 1:5-16 [r]Nu 1:19
7:3 [s]Ge 45:19; 1Sa 6:7-14; 1Ch 13:7
7:7 [t]Nu 4:24-26,28
7:8 [u]Nu 4:31-33
7:9 [v]Nu 4:4 [w]Nu 4:15
7:10 [x]ver 1; S Ex 29:36 [y]2Ch 7:9
7:12 [z]S Nu 1:7
7:13 [a]S Ex 27:3 [b]ver 85 [c]S Ex 30:13; Lev 27:3-7

Chapter 7

Offerings at the Dedication of the Tabernacle

WHEN Moses finished setting up the
tabernacle,[m] he anointed[n] it and
consecrated it and all its furnishings.[o] He
also anointed and consecrated the altar
and all its utensils.[p] 2Then the leaders of
Israel,[q] the heads of families who were
the tribal leaders in charge of those who
were counted,[r] made offerings. 3They
brought as their gifts before the LORD six
covered carts[s] and twelve oxen—an ox
from each leader and a cart from every
two. These they presented before the tabernacle.
4The LORD said to Moses, 5"Accept
these from them, that they may be used
in the work at the Tent of Meeting. Give
them to the Levites as each man's work
requires."
6So Moses took the carts and oxen and
gave them to the Levites. 7He gave two
carts and four oxen to the Gershonites,[t]
as their work required, 8and he gave four
carts and eight oxen to the Merarites,[u] as
their work required. They were all under
the direction of Ithamar son of Aaron, the
priest. 9But Moses did not give any to the
Kohathites,[v] because they were to carry
on their shoulders[w] the holy things, for
which they were responsible.
10When the altar was anointed,[x] the
leaders brought their offerings for its dedication[y] and presented them before the
altar. 11For the LORD had said to Moses,
"Each day one leader is to bring his offering for the dedication of the altar."
12The one who brought his offering on
the first day was Nahshon[z] son of Amminadab of the tribe of Judah.
13His offering was one silver plate
weighing a hundred and thirty shekels,[n] and one silver sprinkling bowl[a]
weighing seventy shekels,[o][b] both
according to the sanctuary shekel,[c]
each filled with fine flour mixed with

[m]14 Traditionally *peace offering*; also in verses 17 and 18 [n]13 That is, about 3 1/4 pounds (about 1.5 kilograms); also elsewhere in this chapter [o]13 That is, about 1 3/4 pounds (about 0.8 kilogram); also elsewhere in this chapter

6:22–27 SALVATION, Blessing—God promised to bless the Israelites when Aaron and his sons put His name on them. Blessing is almost synonymous with the Lord's name. Those who confess God as their Savior are blessed with His keeping, grace, and peace. A ritual act by priests did not guarantee well-being apart from the dedication of God's people to His covenant. Compare Lev 9:23; Dt 10:8; 21:5.

6:22–27 PRAYER, Blessing—See notes on Ge 14:18–20; Lev 9:22. The "Aaronic blessing" in Numbers is effective because it originated at God's initiative. This invocation does not invoke an outward blessing of material goods or circumstances, but inward blessings. The blessing was God Himself. The prayer of blessing in formal worship assures the people of God's involvement in daily life, work, and family.

7:1–89 STEWARDSHIP, House of God—The sacred dedication of the house built for God renews the people's commitment to serve God. This Old Testament practice serves as a model for churches. God's people need to celebrate their accomplishments in His service and to use such celebrations to commit themselves to new tasks and continued faithfulness. See note on Ex 25:1–8.

oil as a grain offering;[d] 14one gold dish[e] weighing ten shekels,[p][f] filled with incense;[g] 15one young bull,[h] one ram and one male lamb a year old, for a burnt offering;[i] 16one male goat for a sin offering;[j] 17and two oxen, five rams, five male goats and five male lambs a year old, to be sacrificed as a fellowship offering.[q][k] This was the offering of Nahshon son of Amminadab.[l]

18On the second day Nethanel son of Zuar,[m] the leader of Issachar, brought his offering.

19The offering he brought was one silver plate weighing a hundred and thirty shekels, and one silver sprinkling bowl weighing seventy shekels, both according to the sanctuary shekel, each filled with fine flour mixed with oil as a grain offering; 20one gold dish[n] weighing ten shekels, filled with incense; 21one young bull, one ram and one male lamb a year old, for a burnt offering; 22one male goat for a sin offering; 23and two oxen, five rams, five male goats and five male lambs a year old, to be sacrificed as a fellowship offering. This was the offering of Nethanel son of Zuar.

24On the third day, Eliab son of Helon,[o] the leader of the people of Zebulun, brought his offering.

25His offering was one silver plate weighing a hundred and thirty shekels, and one silver sprinkling bowl weighing seventy shekels, both according to the sanctuary shekel, each filled with fine flour mixed with oil as a grain offering; 26one gold dish weighing ten shekels, filled with incense; 27one young bull, one ram and one male lamb a year old, for a burnt offering; 28one male goat for a sin offering; 29and two oxen, five rams, five male goats and five male lambs a year old, to be sacrificed as a fellowship offering. This was the offering of Eliab son of Helon.

30On the fourth day Elizur son of Shedeur,[p] the leader of the people of Reuben, brought his offering.

31His offering was one silver plate weighing a hundred and thirty shekels, and one silver sprinkling bowl weighing seventy shekels, both according to the sanctuary shekel, each filled with fine flour mixed with oil as a grain offering; 32one gold dish weighing ten shekels, filled with incense; 33one young bull, one ram and one male lamb a year old, for a burnt offering; 34one male goat for a sin offering; 35and two oxen, five rams, five male goats and five male lambs a year old, to be sacrificed as a fellowship offering. This was the offering of Elizur son of Shedeur.

36On the fifth day Shelumiel son of Zurishaddai,[q] the leader of the people of Simeon, brought his offering.

37His offering was one silver plate weighing a hundred and thirty shekels, and one silver sprinkling bowl weighing seventy shekels, both according to the sanctuary shekel, each filled with fine flour mixed with oil as a grain offering; 38one gold dish weighing ten shekels, filled with incense; 39one young bull, one ram and one male lamb a year old, for a burnt offering; 40one male goat for a sin offering; 41and two oxen, five rams, five male goats and five male lambs a year old, to be sacrificed as a fellowship offering. This was the offering of Shelumiel son of Zurishaddai.

42On the sixth day Eliasaph son of Deuel,[r] the leader of the people of Gad, brought his offering.

43His offering was one silver plate weighing a hundred and thirty shekels, and one silver sprinkling bowl weighing seventy shekels, both according to the sanctuary shekel, each filled with fine flour mixed with oil as a grain offering; 44one gold dish weighing ten shekels, filled with incense; 45one young bull, one ram and one male lamb a year old, for a burnt offering; 46one male goat for a sin offering; 47and two oxen, five rams, five male goats and five male lambs a year old, to be sacrificed as a fellowship offering. This was the offering of Eliasaph son of Deuel.

48On the seventh day Elishama son of Ammihud,[s] the leader of the people of Ephraim, brought his offering.

49His offering was one silver plate weighing a hundred and thirty shekels, and one silver sprinkling bowl weighing seventy shekels, both according to the sanctuary shekel, each filled with fine flour mixed with oil as a grain offering; 50one gold dish weighing ten shekels, filled with incense; 51one young bull, one ram and one male lamb a year old, for a burnt offering; 52one male goat for a sin

7:13 [d]Lev 2:1; Nu 6:15; 15:4
7:14 [e]ver 20; 1Ki 7:50; 2Ki 25:14; 2Ch 4:22; 24:14 [f]ver 86 [g]S Ex 25:6
7:15 [h]Ex 24:5; 29:3; Nu 28:11 [i]Lev 1:3
7:16 [j]Lev 4:3
7:17 [k]Lev 3:1 [l]Nu 1:7
7:18 [m]S Nu 1:8
7:20 [n]S ver 14
7:24 [o]S Nu 1:9
7:30 [p]S Nu 1:5
7:36 [q]S Nu 1:6
7:42 [r]S Nu 1:14
7:48 [s]S Nu 1:10

p *14* That is, about 4 ounces (about 110 grams); also elsewhere in this chapter q *17* Traditionally *peace offering*; also elsewhere in this chapter

offering; 53and two oxen, five rams, five male goats and five male lambs a year old, to be sacrificed as a fellowship offering. This was the offering of Elishama son of Ammihud.[t]

54On the eighth day Gamaliel son of Pedahzur,[u] the leader of the people of Manasseh, brought his offering.

55His offering was one silver plate weighing a hundred and thirty shekels, and one silver sprinkling bowl weighing seventy shekels, both according to the sanctuary shekel, each filled with fine flour mixed with oil as a grain offering; 56one gold dish weighing ten shekels, filled with incense; 57one young bull, one ram and one male lamb a year old, for a burnt offering; 58one male goat for a sin offering; 59and two oxen, five rams, five male goats and five male lambs a year old, to be sacrificed as a fellowship offering. This was the offering of Gamaliel son of Pedahzur.

60On the ninth day Abidan son of Gideoni,[v] the leader of the people of Benjamin, brought his offering.

61His offering was one silver plate weighing a hundred and thirty shekels, and one silver sprinkling bowl weighing seventy shekels, both according to the sanctuary shekel, each filled with fine flour mixed with oil as a grain offering; 62one gold dish weighing ten shekels, filled with incense; 63one young bull, one ram and one male lamb a year old, for a burnt offering; 64one male goat for a sin offering; 65and two oxen, five rams, five male goats and five male lambs a year old, to be sacrificed as a fellowship offering. This was the offering of Abidan son of Gideoni.

66On the tenth day Ahiezer son of Ammishaddai,[w] the leader of the people of Dan, brought his offering.

67His offering was one silver plate weighing a hundred and thirty shekels, and one silver sprinkling bowl weighing seventy shekels, both according to the sanctuary shekel, each filled with fine flour mixed with oil as a grain offering; 68one gold dish weighing ten shekels, filled with incense; 69one young bull, one ram and one male lamb a year old, for a burnt offering; 70one male goat for a sin offering; 71and two oxen, five rams, five male goats and five male lambs a year old, to be sacrificed as a fellowship offering. This was the offering of Ahiezer son of Ammishaddai.

72On the eleventh day Pagiel son of Ocran,[x] the leader of the people of Asher, brought his offering.

73His offering was one silver plate weighing a hundred and thirty shekels, and one silver sprinkling bowl weighing seventy shekels, both according to the sanctuary shekel, each filled with fine flour mixed with oil as a grain offering; 74one gold dish weighing ten shekels, filled with incense; 75one young bull, one ram and one male lamb a year old, for a burnt offering; 76one male goat for a sin offering; 77and two oxen, five rams, five male goats and five male lambs a year old, to be sacrificed as a fellowship offering. This was the offering of Pagiel son of Ocran.

78On the twelfth day Ahira son of Enan,[y] the leader of the people of Naphtali, brought his offering.

79His offering was one silver plate weighing a hundred and thirty shekels, and one silver sprinkling bowl weighing seventy shekels, both according to the sanctuary shekel, each filled with fine flour mixed with oil as a grain offering; 80one gold dish weighing ten shekels, filled with incense; 81one young bull, one ram and one male lamb a year old, for a burnt offering; 82one male goat for a sin offering; 83and two oxen, five rams, five male goats and five male lambs a year old, to be sacrificed as a fellowship offering. This was the offering of Ahira son of Enan.

84These were the offerings of the Israelite leaders for the dedication of the altar when it was anointed:[z] twelve silver plates, twelve silver sprinkling bowls[a] and twelve gold dishes.[b] 85Each silver plate weighed a hundred and thirty shekels, and each sprinkling bowl seventy shekels. Altogether, the silver dishes weighed two thousand four hundred shekels,[r] according to the sanctuary shekel.[c] 86The twelve gold dishes filled with incense weighed ten shekels each, according to the sanctuary shekel.[d] Altogether, the gold dishes weighed a hundred and twenty shekels.[s] 87The total number of animals for the burnt offering[e] came to twelve young bulls, twelve rams and twelve male lambs a year old, together with their grain offering.[f] Twelve male goats were used for the sin offering.[g] 88The total number of animals

7:53 [t]S Nu 1:10
7:54 [u]S Nu 1:10
7:60 [v]S Nu 1:11
7:66 [w]S Nu 1:12
7:72 [x]S Nu 1:13
7:78 [y]S Nu 1:15
7:84 [z]ver 1,10 [a]S Nu 4:14 [b]ver 14
7:85 [c]ver 13
7:86 [d]ver 13
7:87 [e]ver 15 [f]ver 13 [g]ver 16

[r]85 That is, about 60 pounds (about 28 kilograms)
[s]86 That is, about 3 pounds (about 1.4 kilograms)

for the sacrifice of the fellowship offering[h] came to twenty-four oxen, sixty
rams, sixty male goats and sixty male
lambs[i] a year old. These were the offerings for the dedication of the altar after it
was anointed.[j]
89 When Moses entered the Tent of
Meeting[k] to speak with the LORD,[l] he
heard the voice speaking to him from between the two cherubim above the atonement cover[m] on the ark of the Testimony.[n] And he spoke with him.

Chapter 8

Setting Up the Lamps

THE LORD said to Moses, 2 "Speak to
Aaron and say to him, 'When you set
up the seven lamps, they are to light the
area in front of the lampstand.[o]' "
3 Aaron did so; he set up the lamps so
that they faced forward on the lampstand,
just as the LORD commanded Moses.
4 This is how the lampstand was made: It
was made of hammered gold[p]—from its
base to its blossoms. The lampstand was
made exactly like the pattern[q] the LORD
had shown Moses.

The Setting Apart of the Levites

5 The LORD said to Moses: 6 "Take the
Levites from among the other Israelites
and make them ceremonially clean.[r] 7 To
purify them, do this: Sprinkle the water
of cleansing[s] on them; then have them
shave their whole bodies[t] and wash
their clothes,[u] and so purify themselves.[v] 8 Have them take a young bull
with its grain offering of fine flour mixed
with oil;[w] then you are to take a second
young bull for a sin offering.[x] 9 Bring the
Levites to the front of the Tent of Meeting[y] and assemble the whole Israelite
community.[z] 10 You are to bring the Levites before the LORD, and the Israelites
are to lay their hands on them.[a] 11 Aaron
is to present the Levites before the LORD
as a wave offering[b] from the Israelites, so
that they may be ready to do the work of
the LORD.
12 "After the Levites lay their hands on
the heads of the bulls,[c] use the one for a
sin offering[d] to the LORD and the other
for a burnt offering,[e] to make atonement[f] for the Levites. 13 Have the Levites
stand in front of Aaron and his sons and
then present them as a wave offering[g] to
the LORD. 14 In this way you are to set the
Levites apart from the other Israelites,
and the Levites will be mine.[h]
15 "After you have purified the Levites
and presented them as a wave offering,[i]
they are to come to do their work at the
Tent of Meeting.[j] 16 They are the Israelites who are to be given wholly to me. I
have taken them as my own in place of
the firstborn,[k] the first male offspring[l]
from every Israelite woman. 17 Every firstborn male in Israel, whether man or animal,[m] is mine. When I struck down all
the firstborn in Egypt, I set them apart for
myself.[n][o] 18 And I have taken the Levites
in place of all the firstborn sons in Israel.[p] 19 Of all the Israelites, I have given
the Levites as gifts to Aaron and his
sons[q] to do the work at the Tent of Meeting on behalf of the Israelites[r] and to
make atonement for them[s] so that no
plague will strike the Israelites when they
go near the sanctuary."
20 Moses, Aaron and the whole Israelite
community did with the Levites just as
the LORD commanded Moses. 21 The Levites purified themselves and washed
their clothes.[t] Then Aaron presented
them as a wave offering before the LORD
and made atonement[u] for them to purify
them.[v] 22 After that, the Levites came to
do their work[w] at the Tent of Meeting
under the supervision of Aaron and his

7:88 [h]ver 17 [i]Ge 32:14 [j]S ver 1, 10
7:89 [k]S Ex 40:2 [l]S Ex 29:42 [m]S Ex 16:34; Ps 80:1; 99:1 [n]Nu 3:31
8:2 [o]Ex 25:37
8:4 [p]S Ex 25:18,36 [q]S Ex 25:9
8:6 [r]Lev 22:2; Isa 1:16; 52:11
8:7 [s]Nu 19:9,17; 31:23 [t]S Lev 14:9; Nu 6:9; Dt 21:12 [u]S Ge 35:2; Lev 14:8 [v]S Ge 35:2
8:8 [w]Lev 2:1; Nu 15:8-10 [x]Lev 4:3
8:9 [y]Ex 40:12 [z]Lev 8:3
8:10 [a]S Lev 3:2; Ac 6:6
8:11 [b]S Ex 29:24
8:12 [c]S Ex 29:10 [d]Lev 4:3; Nu 6:11 [e]Lev 1:3 [f]S Ex 29:36
8:13 [g]S Ex 29:24
8:14 [h]S Nu 3:12
8:15 [i]S Ex 29:24 [j]Ex 40:2
8:16 [k]Nu 1:20 [l]S Nu 3:12
8:17 [m]S Ex 4:23 [n]S Ex 22:29 [o]S Ex 13:2
8:18 [p]S Nu 3:12
8:19 [q]S Nu 3:9 [r]S Nu 3:7 [s]Nu 16:46
8:21 [t]ver 7; S Ge 35:2 [u]Nu 16:47 [v]ver 12
8:22 [w]ver 11

7:89 REVELATION, Word—Tent of Meeting is an appropriate name for the place God designated to encounter Moses. The tent stood at the center of Israel's camping tents (2:17). It declared visually that God also was "tabernacling" with them. Here we have, as clearly as a human can explain, the mystery of how God revealed Himself to Moses: a voice "in between" objects which represent His divine messengers (Ex 25:22). The mystery of God, even when He reveals Himself, always leaves something of the unknown for the imagination and faith of the believer. Like Moses, even the most faithful never see or know all there is to know about God. See note on Ex 34:4–12.

7:89 PRAYER, Will of God—God met with Moses at the place He appointed. God has given all instructions and done everything necessary to save us. He is ready to speak to His people when we are ready to follow His instructions and speak with Him.

8:5–22 PRAYER, Corporate—Prayer and worship are private experiences of fellowship between one person and God. They are also opportunities for the people of God as a body to gather in God's presence. Corporate worship makes worship leaders necessary. God set aside the Levites in a special dedication ceremony to help the sons of Aaron lead in public worship. God continues to set aside certain members of His people as leaders of His people. Such leaders cannot substitute for the individual in worship and prayer. Leaders can help make worship and prayer more understandable and meaningful for the individual. The entire assembly laid hands on the Levites, setting them aside to represent the firstborn of each family. See note on Lev 8:1–36.

8:12,21 SALVATION, Atonement—Atonement had to be made for the Levites. The priests and singers of Israel came from the tribe of Levi. Those who work full-time in God's work have to get their sins forgiven just like everybody else.

8:17 REVELATION, Actions—The God who freed Israel from Egypt reminded the children He had set aside the firstborn as an offering of special service. In this regulation God explained that each firstborn had a special mission in God's purposes. God is in charge of that life as a gift human beings return to Him. Such a recurring theme in Israelite faith later made the gift of God's firstborn, Jesus Christ, an act of love and compassion by the God who offers His Son for the release of all enslaved.

sons. They did with the Levites just as the
LORD commanded Moses.
23The LORD said to Moses, 24"This applies to the Levites: Men twenty-five
years old or more[x] shall come to take
part in the work at the Tent of Meeting,[y]
25but at the age of fifty,[z] they must retire
from their regular service and work no
longer. 26They may assist their brothers
in performing their duties at the Tent of
Meeting, but they themselves must not
do the work.[a] This, then, is how you are
to assign the responsibilities of the Levites."

Chapter 9

The Passover

THE LORD spoke to Moses in the Desert
of Sinai in the first month[b] of the
second year after they came out of
Egypt.[c] He said, 2"Have the Israelites
celebrate the Passover[d] at the appointed
time.[e] 3Celebrate it at the appointed
time, at twilight on the fourteenth day of
this month,[f] in accordance with all its
rules and regulations.[g]"
4So Moses told the Israelites to celebrate the Passover,[h] 5and they did so in
the Desert of Sinai[i] at twilight on the
fourteenth day of the first month.[j] The
Israelites did everything just as the LORD
commanded Moses.[k]
6But some of them could not celebrate
the Passover on that day because they
were ceremonially unclean[l] on account
of a dead body.[m] So they came to Moses
and Aaron[n] that same day 7and said to
Moses, "We have become unclean because of a dead body, but why should we
be kept from presenting the LORD's offering with the other Israelites at the appointed time?[o]"
8Moses answered them, "Wait until I
find out what the LORD commands concerning you."[p]
9Then the LORD said to Moses, 10"Tell
the Israelites: 'When any of you or your
descendants are unclean because of a
dead body[q] or are away on a journey,
they may still celebrate[r] the LORD's Passover. 11They are to celebrate it on the
fourteenth day of the second month[s] at
twilight. They are to eat the lamb, together with unleavened bread and bitter
herbs.[t] 12They must not leave any of it
till morning[u] or break any of its bones.[v]
When they celebrate the Passover, they
must follow all the regulations.[w] 13But if a
man who is ceremonially clean and not
on a journey fails to celebrate the Passover, that person must be cut off from his
people[x] because he did not present the
LORD's offering at the appointed time.
That man will bear the consequences of
his sin.
14" 'An alien[y] living among you who
wants to celebrate the LORD's Passover
must do so in accordance with its rules
and regulations. You must have the same
regulations for the alien and the native-
born.' "

The Cloud Above the Tabernacle

15On the day the tabernacle, the Tent
of the Testimony,[z] was set up,[a] the
cloud[b] covered it. From evening till
morning the cloud above the tabernacle
looked like fire.[c] 16That is how it continued to be; the cloud covered it, and at
night it looked like fire.[d] 17Whenever the
cloud lifted from above the Tent, the Israelites set out;[e] wherever the cloud settled, the Israelites encamped.[f] 18At the
LORD's command the Israelites set out,
and at his command they encamped. As
long as the cloud stayed over the tabernacle, they remained[g] in camp. 19When the
cloud remained over the tabernacle a
long time, the Israelites obeyed the
LORD's order[h] and did not set out.[i]
20Sometimes the cloud was over the tabernacle only a few days; at the LORD's
command they would encamp, and then
at his command they would set out.
21Sometimes the cloud stayed only from

8:24 [x]1Ch 23:3 [y]S Ex 38:21
8:25 [z]S Nu 4:3
8:26 [a]ver 11
9:1 [b]S Ex 40:2 [c]Nu 1:1
9:2 [d]S Ex 12:11 [e]ver 7
9:3 [f]S Ex 12:6,42 [g]Ex 12:2-11,43-49; Lev 23:5-8; Dt 16:1-8
9:4 [h]ver 2; S Ex 12:11
9:5 [i]ver 1 [j]S Ex 12:6 [k]ver 3
9:6 [l]S Lev 5:3; S 13:3 [m]S Lev 21:11 [n]Ex 18:15; Nu 27:2
9:7 [o]ver 2
9:8 [p]Ex 18:15; Lev 24:12; Nu 15:34; 27:5,21; Ps 85:8
9:10 [q]ver 6 [r]2Ch 30:2
9:11 [s]S Ex 12:6 [t]Ex 12:8
9:12 [u]S Ex 12:8 [v]S Ex 12:46; Jn 19:36* [w]ver 3
9:13 [x]S Ge 17:14
9:14 [y]S Ex 12:19, 43
9:15 [z]S Ex 38:21 [a]S Ex 26:30 [b]S Ex 33:16 [c]Ex 13:21
9:16 [d]S Ex 40:38
9:17 [e]ver 21 [f]1Co 10:1
9:18 [g]Ex 40:37
9:19 [h]S Lev 8:35 [i]Ex 40:37

9:1–14 HISTORY, Time—See note on Ex 12:1–28. The day of the month was not the most significant factor in Israel's calendar of worship. The proper conduct, content, and attitude were important. All Israelites needed opportunity to celebrate God's saving acts in their history.

9:13 SIN, Responsibility—Worship is a serious matter. Individuals dare not take this lightly and fit worship of God into their schedules when it is convenient. God expects His people to celebrate His saving acts, teach these to another generation, and bring offerings signifying gratitude and dedication. Life not centered in worship is sinful and leads to death. See note on Ge 39:9.

9:14 CHRISTIAN ETHICS, Justice—Citizenship should carry equal responsibilities and rewards, whether one is a native or naturalized.

9:15–23 HISTORY, Presence—God's presence was not limited to a specific place, specific ceremonies, or specific dates. Israel learned to expect God's presence in their history. They knew God's presence was intended to direct their history. Experience of God's presence is a call to obey and follow.

9:15–23 DISCIPLESHIP, God's Leadership—For the march from the desert of Sinai to the Promised Land of Canaan, God chose to make His presence visible and guide His people by a cloud. The cloud had come down and covered the Tent of the Testimony on the day the tabernacle was completed. When the cloud rose from the dwelling of the tabernacle, it was a sign to move. It soared above the ark of the covenant as they moved, and a sign for encamping was given when it came down. The cloud "looked like fire" during the night. Whenever the cloud lifted, day or night, they would set out on the journey. God used Moses to make His will known, and the people obeyed His commands. God was with them all the time providing the leadership on which they were depending. Obedience and dependence still are required to enjoy God's leadership, no matter how He chooses to provide leadership.

evening till morning, and when it lifted in the morning, they set out. Whether by day or by night, whenever the cloud lifted, they set out. 22Whether the cloud stayed over the tabernacle for two days or a month or a year, the Israelites would remain in camp and not set out; but when it lifted, they would set out. 23At the LORD's command they encamped, and at the LORD's command they set out. They obeyed the LORD's order, in accordance with his command through Moses.

Chapter 10

The Silver Trumpets

THE LORD said to Moses: 2"Make two trumpets[j] of hammered silver, and use them for calling the community[k] together and for having the camps set out.[l] 3When both are sounded, the whole community is to assemble before you at the entrance to the Tent of Meeting. 4If only one is sounded, the leaders[m]—the heads of the clans of Israel—are to assemble before you. 5When a trumpet blast is sounded, the tribes camping on the east are to set out.[n] 6At the sounding of a second blast, the camps on the south are to set out.[o] The blast will be the signal for setting out. 7To gather the assembly, blow the trumpets,[p] but not with the same signal.[q]

8"The sons of Aaron, the priests, are to blow the trumpets. This is to be a lasting ordinance for you and the generations to come.[r] 9When you go into battle in your own land against an enemy who is oppressing you,[s] sound a blast on the trumpets.[t] Then you will be remembered[u] by the LORD your God and rescued from your enemies.[v] 10Also at your times of rejoicing—your appointed feasts and New Moon festivals[w]—you are to sound the trumpets[x] over your burnt offerings[y] and fellowship offerings,[t][z] and they will be a memorial for you before your God. I am the LORD your God.[a]"

The Israelites Leave Sinai

11On the twentieth day of the second month of the second year,[b] the cloud lifted[c] from above the tabernacle of the Testimony.[d] 12Then the Israelites set out from the Desert of Sinai and traveled from place to place until the cloud came to rest in the Desert of Paran.[e] 13They set out, this first time, at the LORD's command through Moses.[f]

14The divisions of the camp of Judah went first, under their standard.[g] Nahshon son of Amminadab[h] was in command. 15Nethanel son of Zuar was over the division of the tribe[i] of Issachar,[j] 16and Eliab son of Helon[k] was over the division of the tribe of Zebulun.[l] 17Then the tabernacle was taken down, and the Gershonites and Merarites, who carried it, set out.[m]

18The divisions of the camp of Reuben[n] went next, under their standard.[o] Elizur son of Shedeur[p] was in command. 19Shelumiel son of Zurishaddai was over the division of the tribe of Simeon,[q] 20and Eliasaph son of Deuel was over the division of the tribe of Gad.[r] 21Then the Kohathites[s] set out, carrying the holy things.[t] The tabernacle was to be set up before they arrived.[u]

22The divisions of the camp of Ephraim[v] went next, under their standard. Elishama son of Ammihud[w] was in command. 23Gamaliel son of Pedahzur was over the division of the tribe of Manasseh,[x] 24and Abidan son of Gideoni was over the division of the tribe of Benjamin.[y]

25Finally, as the rear guard[z] for all the units, the divisions of the camp of Dan set out, under their standard. Ahiezer son of Ammishaddai[a] was in command. 26Pagiel son of Ocran was over the division of the tribe of Asher,[b] 27and Ahira son of Enan was over the division of the tribe of Naphtali.[c] 28This was the order of march for the Israelite divisions as they set out.

29Now Moses said to Hobab[d] son of Reuel[e] the Midianite, Moses' father-in-law,[f] "We are setting out for the place about which the LORD said, 'I will give it to you.'[g] Come with us and we will treat you well, for the LORD has promised good things to Israel."

30He answered, "No, I will not go;[h] I am going back to my own land and my own people.[i]"

[t]*10* Traditionally *peace offerings*

10:2 [j]ver 8,9; Nu 31:6; Ne 12:35; Ps 47:5; 98:6; 150:3 [k]Ne 4:18; Jer 4:5,19; 6:1; Hos 5:8; 8:1; Joel 2:1,15; Am 3:6 [l]Nu 33:3
10:4 [m]S Ex 18:21
10:5 [n]ver 14
10:6 [o]ver 18
10:7 [p]Jer 4:5; 6:1; Eze 33:3; Joel 2:1 [q]1Co 14:8
10:8 [r]S Ge 9:12; Nu 15:14; 35:29
10:9 [s]Ex 3:9; Jdg 2:18; 6:9; 1Sa 10:18; 2Ki 13:4; Ps 106:42 [t]S Lev 23:24 [u]S Ge 8:1 [v]2Ch 13:12; Ps 106:4
10:10 [w]Nu 28:11; 1Sa 20:5,24; 2Ki 4:23; 2Ch 8:13; Ps 81:3; Isa 1:13; Eze 45:17; 46:6; Am 8:5 [x]S Lev 23:24 [y]Lev 1:3 [z]Lev 3:1; Nu 6:14 [a]Lev 11:44
10:11 [b]Ex 40:17 [c]Nu 9:17 [d]S Ex 38:21
10:12 [e]S Ge 14:6; Dt 1:1; 33:2
10:13 [f]Dt 1:6
10:14 [g]S Nu 1:52; S 2:3-9 [h]Nu 1:7
10:15 [i]S Lev 24:11 [j]S Nu 1:8
10:16 [k]S Nu 2:7 [l]S Nu 1:9
10:17 [m]ver 21; Nu 4:21-32
10:18 [n]Nu 2:16 [o]Nu 2:10-16 [p]S Nu 1:5
10:19 [q]Nu 1:6
10:20 [r]S Nu 1:14
10:21 [s]S Nu 2:17 [t]Nu 4:20 [u]S ver 17
10:22 [v]Nu 2:24 [w]S Nu 1:10
10:23 [x]S Nu 1:10
10:24 [y]Nu 1:11
10:25 [z]S Nu 2:31 [a]S Nu 1:12
10:26 [b]S Nu 1:13
10:27 [c]S Nu 1:15
10:29 [d]Jdg 4:11 [e]S Ex 2:18 [f]S Ex 3:1 [g]S Ge 12:7; S 15:14
10:30 [h]Mt 21:29 [i]S Ex 18:27

10:1–7 DISCIPLESHIP, Spiritual Leaders—Moses repeatedly received direct commands from God and relayed them to the people. Spiritual leaders must always work on God's initiative to accomplish His purposes. The New Testament clearly opens the door for all believers to have direct access to God through Christ to find God's will for our individual lives. Still, we need spiritual leaders to guide the community to seek and follow God's will.

10:9 CHRISTIAN ETHICS, War and Peace—See note on Ex 14:1—15:18.

10:11–32 HISTORY, Freedom—God's leadership in history was not a compelling force which humans were forced to follow. Moses issued an invitation for his father-in-law to join as God led and to receive God's "good things." To confess God's revealing leadership in history is to celebrate human freedom and to accept responsibility for free human choices.

10:29 ELECTION, Free Will—Without coercion but with persuasion, Hobab overcame his reluctance and exercised his free will to join those God had elected for the journey to the Promised Land. Free will is the human response to the electing invitation of God to become His people in pursuit of His promises.

31But Moses said, "Please do not leave
us. You know where we should camp in
the desert, and you can be our eyes.[j] 32If
you come with us, we will share with
you[k] whatever good things the LORD
gives us.[l]"

33So they set out[m] from the mountain
of the LORD and traveled for three days.
The ark of the covenant of the LORD[n]
went before them during those three days
to find them a place to rest.[o] 34The cloud
of the LORD was over them by day when
they set out from the camp.[p]

35Whenever the ark set out, Moses
said,

"Rise up,[q] O LORD!
May your enemies be scattered;[r]
may your foes flee before you.[s]"[t]

36Whenever it came to rest, he said,

"Return,[u] O LORD,
to the countless thousands of
Israel.[v]"

Chapter 11

Fire From the LORD

NOW the people complained[w] about
their hardships in the hearing of the
LORD,[x] and when he heard them his anger was aroused.[y] Then fire from the
LORD burned among them[z] and consumed[a] some of the outskirts of the
camp. 2When the people cried out to Moses, he prayed[b] to the LORD[c] and the fire
died down. 3So that place was called Taberah,[u][d] because fire from the LORD had
burned among them.[e]

Quail From the LORD

4The rabble with them began to crave
other food,[f] and again the Israelites started wailing[g] and said, "If only we had
meat to eat! 5We remember the fish we
ate in Egypt at no cost—also the cucum-
bers, melons, leeks, onions and garlic.[h]
6But now we have lost our appetite; we
never see anything but this manna![i]"

7The manna was like coriander seed[j]
and looked like resin.[k] 8The people went
around gathering it,[l] and then ground it
in a handmill or crushed it in a mortar.
They cooked it in a pot or made it into
cakes. And it tasted like something made
with olive oil. 9When the dew[m] settled
on the camp at night, the manna also
came down.

10Moses heard the people of every family wailing,[n] each at the entrance to his
tent. The LORD became exceedingly angry, and Moses was troubled. 11He asked
the LORD, "Why have you brought this
trouble[o] on your servant? What have I
done to displease you that you put the
burden of all these people on me?[p] 12Did
I conceive all these people? Did I give
them birth? Why do you tell me to carry
them in my arms, as a nurse carries an
infant,[q] to the land you promised on
oath[r] to their forefathers?[s] 13Where can
I get meat for all these people?[t] They
keep wailing to me, 'Give us meat to eat!'
14I cannot carry all these people by myself; the burden is too heavy for me.[u] 15If
this is how you are going to treat me, put
me to death[v] right now[w]—if I have
found favor in your eyes—and do not let
me face my own ruin."

16The LORD said to Moses: "Bring me

10:31 [j]Job 29:15 **10:32** [k]S Ex 12:48; Dt 10:18 [l]Ps 22:27-31; 67:5-7 **10:33** [m]ver 12; Dt 1:33 [n]Dt 10:8; 31:9; Jos 3:3; Jdg 20:27; 2Sa 15:24 [o]Jer 31:2 **10:34** [p]Nu 9:15-23 **10:35** [q]2Ch 6:41; Ps 17:13; 44:26; 94:2; 132:8 [r]Jdg 5:31; 1Sa 2:1; Ps 68:1; 92:9 [s]Dt 5:9; 7:10; 32:41; Ps 68:2; Isa 17:12-14 [t]Isa 59:18 **10:36** [u]Isa 52:8; 63:17 [v]Ge 15:5; 26:4; Dt 1:10; 10:22; Ne 9:23 **11:1** [w]S Ex 14:11; S 16:7; La 3:39 [x]Nu 12:2; Dt 1:34 [y]S Ex 4:14 [z]S Lev 10:2 [a]Nu 21:28; Ps 78:63; Isa 26:11 **11:2** [b]Dt 9:19; 1Sa 2:25; 12:23; Ps 106:23 [c]S Ge 20:7; Nu 21:7; Dt 9:20; Jnh 2:1 **11:3** [d]Dt 9:22 [e]Nu 16:35; Job 1:16; Isa 10:17 **11:4** [f]S Ex 16:3 [g]ver 18 **11:5** [h]S Ex 16:3; Nu 21:5 **11:6** [i]Ex 16:14 **11:7** [j]S Ex 16:31 [k]Ge 2:12 **11:8** [l]Ex 16:16 **11:9** [m]Ex 16:13 **11:10** [n]ver 4 **11:11** [o]S Ge 34:30 [p]S Ex 5:22; S 18:18 **11:12** [q]Isa 40:11; 49:23; 66:11,12 [r]Nu 14:16 [s]S Ge 12:7; Ex 13:5 **11:13** [t]S Ex 12:37; Jn 6:5-9 **11:14** [u]S Ex 18:18 **11:15** [v]Ex 32:32 [w]1Ki 19:4; Job 6:9; 7:15-16; 9:21; 10:1; Isa 38:12; Jnh 4:3

[u]3 *Taberah* means *burning.*

10:35–36 PRAYER, Fellowship with God—The Israelites were ready to leave Sinai under God's leadership. This prayer presents Moses' understanding of God. With the presence of God radiating outward from the camp, His enemies would flee; with the manifestation of His presence among His people, they would enjoy Him. Prayer expresses our desire for God's leadership, protection, and fellowship.

11:1 SIN, Alienation—The people's complaint against God's leadership alienated them from God. They refused to remember in gratitude what He had done or trust Him in present hardship. Sin always produces alienation between a person and God. We never have sufficient reason to lose trust in God. He has shown in Jesus that He cares supremely for us.

11:2 PRAYER, Intercession—Moses' prayer demonstrated that we need an intercessor. Sin and dissatisfaction invite God's anger. Prayer expresses desire for renewal and reconciliation. Intercessory prayer is most effective when people ask for it. See note on Ex 32:32.

11:4–17 EVIL AND SUFFERING, God's Present Help—A leader often suffers stress. God listens to His leaders and provides help to relieve their stress. He provided assistance for Moses when a complaining people became too much for him. See note on Ex 18:17–26.

11:10–15 PRAYER, Hindrances—Moses was discouraged with the complainers; they had forgotten God's promise to be with them (Ex 33:14–15). The prayer to die is dominated by personal pronouns. God's answer was to relieve Moses of some of the responsibility by appointing seventy elders to help carry the burden and to punish the complainers (11:16–20). God listens and responds to legitimate prayer even when it expresses personal anger and frustration.

11:12 ELECTION, God's Initiative—Moses heard the people of every Israelite family wailing at his tent. Deeply troubled, Moses reminded God of his almost unbearable burdens and overwhelming leadership responsibilities, asking, "Did I conceive all these people?" God's election, not Moses' leadership, brought Israel into being. God responded by advising Moses to bring seventy of Israel's leaders to the Tent of Meeting, where He would bestow His Spirit on them so that they could assist him in the responsibilities of leadership.

11:16–17 HOLY SPIRIT, Leaders—The Spirit supplies necessary administrative skills to lead His people. God had given His Spirit to Moses to lead Israel. When the administrative task became too great for one person, God gave the Spirit to proven leaders to assist Moses. This passage is one of the few in the Old Testament which speaks of the Spirit being given to a group of people rather than to an individual. The Spirit enabled the elders to carry the burden of the people. Thus, they received an ongoing spiritual gift. See vv 25–29. It might be called the gift of leadership or administration. Some of the first Christians received similar gifts. See Ro 12:8.

11:16–30 REVELATION, Spirit—One person cannot

seventy of Israel's elders[x] who are
known to you as leaders and officials
among the people.[y] Have them come to
the Tent of Meeting,[z] that they may
stand there with you. 17I will come down
and speak with you[a] there, and I will
take of the Spirit that is on you and put
the Spirit on them.[b] They will help you
carry the burden of the people so that you
will not have to carry it alone.[c]

18"Tell the people: 'Consecrate yourselves[d] in preparation for tomorrow,
when you will eat meat. The LORD heard
you when you wailed,[e] "If only we had
meat to eat! We were better off in
Egypt!"[f] Now the LORD will give you
meat,[g] and you will eat it. 19You will not
eat it for just one day, or two days, or five,
ten or twenty days, 20but for a whole
month—until it comes out of your nostrils and you loathe it[h]—because you
have rejected the LORD,[i] who is among
you, and have wailed before him, saying,
"Why did we ever leave Egypt?"' "[j]

21But Moses said, "Here I am among
six hundred thousand men[k] on foot, and
you say, 'I will give them meat to eat for a
whole month!' 22Would they have
enough if flocks and herds were slaughtered for them? Would they have enough
if all the fish in the sea were caught for
them?"[l]

23The LORD answered Moses, "Is the
LORD's arm too short?[m] You will now see
whether or not what I say will come true
for you.[n]"

24So Moses went out and told the people what the LORD had said. He brought
together seventy of their elders and had
them stand around the Tent. 25Then the
LORD came down in the cloud[o] and
spoke with him,[p] and he took of the Spirit[q] that was on him and put the Spirit on
the seventy elders.[r] When the Spirit rested on them, they prophesied,[s] but they
did not do so again.[v]

26However, two men, whose names
were Eldad and Medad, had remained in
the camp. They were listed among the
elders, but did not go out to the Tent. Yet
the Spirit also rested on them,[t] and they
prophesied in the camp. 27A young man
ran and told Moses, "Eldad and Medad
are prophesying in the camp."

28Joshua son of Nun,[u] who had been
Moses' aide[v] since youth, spoke up and
said, "Moses, my lord, stop them!"[w]

29But Moses replied, "Are you jealous
for my sake? I wish that all the LORD's
people were prophets[x] and that the LORD
would put his Spirit[y] on them!"[z] 30Then
Moses and the elders of Israel returned to
the camp.

31Now a wind went out from the LORD
and drove quail[a] in from the sea. It
brought them[w] down all around the camp
to about three feet[x] above the ground, as
far as a day's walk in any direction. 32All
that day and night and all the next day
the people went out and gathered quail.
No one gathered less than ten homers.[y]
Then they spread them out all around the
camp. 33But while the meat was still between their teeth[b] and before it could be
consumed, the anger[c] of the LORD
burned against the people, and he struck
them with a severe plague.[d] 34Therefore
the place was named Kibroth Hattaavah,[z][e] because there they buried the
people who had craved other food.

35From Kibroth Hattaavah the people
traveled to Hazeroth[f] and stayed there.

Chapter 12

Miriam and Aaron Oppose Moses

MIRIAM[g] and Aaron began to talk
against Moses because of his

[v]*25* Or *prophesied and continued to do so* [w]*31* Or *They flew* [x]*31* Hebrew *two cubits* (about 1 meter) [y]*32* That is, probably about 60 bushels (about 2.2 kiloliters) [z]*34* *Kibroth Hattaavah* means *graves of craving.*

11:16 [x]S Ex 3:16 [y]S Ex 18:25 [z]S Ex 40:2
11:17 [a]Ex 19:20 [b]ver 25,29; 1Sa 10:6; 2Ki 2:9, 15; 3:12; Isa 32:15; 40:5; 63:11; Joel 2:28; Hag 2:5 [c]S Ex 18:18; Jer 19:1
11:18 [d]S Ex 19:10 [e]S Ex 16:7 [f]ver 5; Ac 7:39 [g]Ps 78:20
11:20 [h]Ps 78:29; 106:14,15 [i]S Lev 26:43; Jos 24:27; Jdg 8:23; 1Sa 10:19; Job 31:28; Isa 59:13; Hos 13:11 [j]ver 33; Job 20:13,23
11:21 [k]S Ex 12:37
11:22 [l]Mt 15:33
11:23 [m]Isa 50:2; 59:1 [n]Nu 23:19; 1Sa 15:29; Eze 12:25; 24:14
11:25 [o]S Ex 19:9; Nu 12:5 [p]ver 17 [q]ver 29; 1Sa 10:6; 19:23 [r]S Ac 2:17 [s]ver 26; Nu 24:2; Jdg 3:10; 1Sa 10:10; 19:20; 2Ch 15:1
11:26 [t]S ver 25; 1Ch 12:18; Rev 1:10
11:28 [u]Ex 17:9; Nu 13:8; 26:65; Jos 14:10 [v]Ex 33:11; Jos 1:1 [w]Mk 9:38-40
11:29 [x]1Sa 10:5; 19:20; 2Ch 24:19; Jer 7:25; 44:4; 1Co 14:5 [y]S ver 17 [z]Nu 27:18
11:31 [a]S Ex 16:13; Ps 78:26-28
11:33 [b]Ps 78:30 [c]Nu 14:18; Dt 9:7; Jdg 2:12; 2Ki 22:17; Ps 106:29; Jer 44:3; Eze 8:17 [d]S ver 18-20; Ps 106:15; Isa 10:16
11:34 [e]Nu 33:16; Dt 9:22
11:35 [f]Nu 33:17
12:1 [g]S Ex 15:20

bear the burden of revelation for all God's people. God gives His Spirit to chosen leaders who can minister to His people. An ecstatic experience confirmed the Spirit's presence with the new leaders, but ecstacy was not a repeated experience for them. They did continue to have the Spirit's leadership in revealing God's will to the people. Institutional rites are not necessary to give a person the Spirit, who is free to act as He chooses. God's ultimate purpose is to let all His people be instruments of His revelation. See note on 1 Ki 22:6–28.

11:23 GOD, Power—In the face of impossible circumstances, God reassured Moses that His power was sufficient to meet Israel's needs. Although God works for us in many ordinary ways that we do not recognize, sometimes God uses extraordinary means to bless His people. As sovereign Lord, God has all the power needed to accomplish His will.

11:25–29 HOLY SPIRIT, Revelation—God's Spirit confirms God's call to people. The confirming Spirit enabled the seventy elders to prophesy, probably in an obvious state of ecstasy. This revelation showed God's choice clearly for the whole congregation. The confirming experience produced a one-time visible revelation. The Spirit remained with the elders to enable them to lead God's people (v 17). God repeated the experience for two elders absent the first time. Joshua jealously and zealously guarded his master's unique position. Moses taught him God's goal was for all His people to receive the prophetic gift, so all would know and be dedicated to His will. See notes on Joel 2:28–32; Ac 2:1–4, 14–22. God's Spirit and His gifts have never been confined to a few leaders. God wants each of us to exercise spiritual gifts. None should be jealous of another's gift. All should be ready to recognize the Spirit when God reveals Himself.

12:1–15 EVIL AND SUFFERING, Deserved—Rebellion against God's chosen leaders is just cause for divine punishment. Proud demand for prominence does not characterize God's leaders. Humility does. God's leader does not rejoice over such punishment. Rather, intercession for restoration is the action of God's leader. See note on 16:1–50.

12:1–8 REVELATION, Word—Revelation has often caused controversy among God's people. Humble Moses' unique position as the authoritative mediator of God's revela-

Cushite wife,[h] for he had married a
Cushite. 2"Has the LORD spoken only
through Moses?" they asked. "Hasn't he
also spoken through us?"[i] And the LORD
heard this.[j]
3(Now Moses was a very humble
man,[k] more humble than anyone else on
the face of the earth.)
4At once the LORD said to Moses, Aaron and Miriam, "Come out to the Tent of
Meeting, all three of you." So the three of
them came out. 5Then the LORD came
down in a pillar of cloud;[l] he stood at the
entrance to the Tent and summoned Aaron and Miriam. When both of them
stepped forward, 6he said, "Listen to my
words:

"When a prophet of the LORD is among
you,
I reveal[m] myself to him in visions,[n]
I speak to him in dreams.[o]
7But this is not true of my servant
Moses;[p]
he is faithful in all my house.[q]
8With him I speak face to face,
clearly and not in riddles;[r]
he sees the form of the LORD.[s]
Why then were you not afraid
to speak against my servant
Moses?"[t]

9The anger of the LORD burned against
them,[u] and he left them.[v]
10When the cloud lifted from above the
Tent,[w] there stood Miriam—leprous,[a]
like snow.[x] Aaron turned toward her and
saw that she had leprosy;[y] 11and he said
to Moses, "Please, my lord, do not hold
against us the sin we have so foolishly
committed.[z] 12Do not let her be like a
stillborn infant coming from its mother's
womb with its flesh half eaten away."
13So Moses cried out to the LORD, "O
God, please heal her![a] "
14The LORD replied to Moses, "If her
father had spit in her face,[b] would she
not have been in disgrace for seven days?

12:1 [h]S Ex 2:21
12:2 [i]Nu 16:3 [j]S Nu 11:1
12:3 [k]Mt 11:29
12:5 [l]S Ex 13:21; S Nu 11:25
12:6 [m]1Sa 3:7,21 [n]S Ge 15:1 [o]S Ge 20:3; S Mt 27:19; Heb 1:1
12:7 [p]Dt 34:5; Jos 1:1-2; Ps 105:26 [q]Heb 3:2,5
12:8 [r]Jdg 14:12; 1Ki 10:1; Ps 49:4; Pr 1:6; Da 5:12 [s]Ex 20:4; Job 19:26; Ps 17:15; 140:13; Isa 6:1 [t]Ex 24:2
12:9 [u]S Ex 4:14 [v]S Ge 17:22
12:10 [w]Ex 40:2 [x]S Ex 4:6; Dt 24:9 [y]S Lev 13:11; 2Ki 5:1,27; 2Ch 16:12; 21:12-15; 26:19
12:11 [z]2Sa 19:19; 24:10
12:13 [a]Ex 15:26; Ps 6:2; 147:3; Isa 1:6; 30:26; 53:5; Jer 17:14; Hos 6:1
12:14 [b]Dt 25:9; Job 17:6; 30:9-10; Isa 50:6 [c]S Lev 13:46
12:15 [d]S Lev 14:8 [e]S Lev 13:4
12:16 [f]Nu 11:35 [g]Ge 21:21; Nu 10:12; 15:32
13:2 [h]ver 16; Dt 1:22 [i]S Lev 14:34 [j]Jos 1:3 [k]S Lev 24:11
13:3 [l]Nu 1:16
13:6 [m]ver 30; Nu 14:6,24; 34:19; Dt 1:36; Jdg 1:12-15
13:8 [n]S Nu 11:28

Confine her outside the camp[c] for seven
days; after that she can be brought back."
15So Miriam was confined outside the
camp[d] for seven days,[e] and the people
did not move on till she was brought
back.
16After that, the people left Hazeroth[f]
and encamped in the Desert of Paran.[g]

Chapter 13

Exploring Canaan

THE LORD said to Moses, 2"Send some
men to explore[h] the land of Canaan,[i] which I am giving to the Israelites.[j] From each ancestral tribe[k] send
one of its leaders."
3So at the LORD's command Moses sent
them out from the Desert of Paran. All of
them were leaders of the Israelites.[l]
4These are their names:

from the tribe of Reuben, Shammua
son of Zaccur;
5from the tribe of Simeon, Shaphat
son of Hori;
6from the tribe of Judah, Caleb son of
Jephunneh;[m]
7from the tribe of Issachar, Igal son of
Joseph;
8from the tribe of Ephraim, Hoshea
son of Nun;[n]
9from the tribe of Benjamin, Palti son
of Raphu;
10from the tribe of Zebulun, Gaddiel
son of Sodi;
11from the tribe of Manasseh (a tribe
of Joseph), Gaddi son of Susi;
12from the tribe of Dan, Ammiel son of
Gemalli;
13from the tribe of Asher, Sethur son
of Michael;
14from the tribe of Naphtali, Nahbi son
of Vophsi;

[a] *10* The Hebrew word was used for various diseases affecting the skin—not necessarily leprosy.

---

tion aroused jealousy in his own family. God told them He did reveal Himself to other prophets (Ex 15:20) through dreams and visions, but only Moses was permitted direct access to God. Thus God confirmed the authority of Moses' teaching over that of anyone who dared oppose him. The New Testament reveals Jesus Christ as the perfect Mediator (1 Ti 2:5; Heb 8:6; 9:15; 12:24) through whom all believers have direct access to God (Heb 10:19–23). See note on Ex 34:4–12.

12:2 ELECTION, Leadership—Jealousy led Miriam and Aaron to talk against Moses. God intervened, stating that Moses had been elected as a special leader with unique gifts which allowed him to speak face to face with God instead of through visions and dreams, the normal manner in which God spoke to prophets. Human jealousy and desire for power do not characterize God's leaders. God elects leaders for His elect community, gives them gifts to exercise leadership, and calls them to humble service. Humility and faithfulness characterize God's elected leaders.

12:10–14 PRAYER, Intercession—Miriam, like Job's friends (Job 42:7–9), was dependent on the prayer of the one she criticized (v 1). God's servant is called to intercede even for enemies, particularly when they admit their sin and ask for our prayers (Mt 5:43–48).

12:11 SIN, Pride—Racial pride and prejudice is sin. Combining it with personal envy, greed, and ambition only compounds the sin. Such attitudes are foolish. When they find expression in public gossip, they become dangerous to God's community of people. God is free to choose His leaders and to use people from all nationalities, races, and skin colors. We need to follow His way, not complain and seek to gain our way which enhances our reputation. See note on Ex 14:11–12.

13:1—14:12 HISTORY, Faith—God's acts in history should lead to faith in God's continued guidance. Humans too often exercise freedom to rebel against God. Historical situations confront God's people with the decision to trust God's presence or to fear the perceived strength of human enemies. Individuals can act in faith even when no one else does.

15from the tribe of Gad, Geuel son of
Maki.

16These are the names of the men Moses
sent to explore[o] the land. (Moses gave
Hoshea son of Nun[p] the name Joshua.)[q]

17When Moses sent them to explore
Canaan,[r] he said, "Go up through the
Negev[s] and on into the hill country.[t]
18See what the land is like and whether
the people who live there are strong or
weak, few or many. 19What kind of land
do they live in? Is it good or bad? What
kind of towns do they live in? Are they
unwalled or fortified? 20How is the soil? Is
it fertile or poor? Are there trees on it or
not? Do your best to bring back some of
the fruit of the land.[u]" (It was the season
for the first ripe grapes.)[v]

21So they went up and explored the
land from the Desert of Zin[w] as far as
Rehob,[x] toward Lebo[b] Hamath.[y] 22They
went up through the Negev and came to
Hebron,[z] where Ahiman, Sheshai and
Talmai,[a] the descendants of Anak,[b]
lived. (Hebron had been built seven years
before Zoan in Egypt.)[c] 23When they
reached the Valley of Eshcol,[c][d] they cut
off a branch bearing a single cluster of
grapes. Two of them carried it on a pole
between them, along with some pomegranates[e] and figs.[f] 24That place was
called the Valley of Eshcol because of the
cluster of grapes the Israelites cut off
there. 25At the end of forty days[g] they
returned from exploring the land.[h]

Report on the Exploration

26They came back to Moses and Aaron
and the whole Israelite community at Kadesh[i] in the Desert of Paran.[j] There
they reported to them[k] and to the whole
assembly and showed them the fruit of
the land.[l] 27They gave Moses this account: "We went into the land to which
you sent us, and it does flow with milk
and honey![m] Here is its fruit.[n] 28But the
people who live there are powerful, and
the cities are fortified and very large.[o]
We even saw descendants of Anak[p]
there.[q] 29The Amalekites[r] live in the
Negev; the Hittites,[s] Jebusites[t] and Am-

13:16 [o]S ver 2 [p]ver 8 [q]Dt 32:44 **13:17** [r]ver 2; Jos 14:7 [s]S Ge 12:9 [t]Dt 1:7; Jos 9:1; Jdg 1:9 **13:20** [u]Dt 1:25 [v]S Lev 25:5 **13:21** [w]Nu 20:1; 27:14; 33:36; Dt 32:51; Jos 15:1 [x]Jos 19:28; Jdg 1:31; 18:28; 2Sa 10:6; 1Ch 6:75 [y]Nu 34:8; Jos 13:5; Jdg 3:3; 1Ki 8:65; 2Ki 14:25; 1Ch 13:5; 2Ch 7:8; Jer 52:9; Eze 47:16, 20; Am 6:14 **13:22** [z]S Ge 13:18; S 23:19 [a]Jos 15:14; Jdg 1:10 [b]ver 28; Dt 2:10; 9:2; Jos 11:21; 15:13; Jdg 1:20 [c]Ps 78:12, 43; Isa 19:11,13; 30:4; Eze 30:14 **13:23** [d]S Ge 14:13 [e]S Ex 28:33 [f]Ge 3:7; Nu 20:5; Dt 8:8; 2Ki 18:31; Ne 13:15 **13:25** [g]S Ge 7:4 [h]Nu 14:34 **13:26** [i]S Ge 14:7 [j]S Ge 14:6 [k]Nu 32:8 [l]Dt 1:25 **13:27** [m]S Ex 3:8 [n]Dt 1:25; Jer 2:7 **13:28** [o]Dt 1:28; 9:1,2 [p]S ver 22 [q]Jos 14:12 **13:29** [r]S Ge 14:7 [s]S Ge 10:15; Dt 7:1; 20:17; 1Ki 9:20; 10:29; 2Ki 7:6 [t]S Ex 3:8 [u]S Ge 10:16 [v]ver 17 [w]Ge 10:18 [x]S Ge 13:10; Nu 22:1; 32:5; Dt 1:1; Jos 1:2; Jdg 3:28; Ps 42:6 **13:30** [y]S ver 6 **13:31** [z]Dt 9:1; Jos 14:8 **13:32** [a]Nu 14:36, 37 [b]Eze 36:13,14 [c]Dt 1:28; Am 2:9 **13:33** [d]Ge 6:4 [e]ver 28; Dt 1:28; Jos 11:22; 14:12 [f]Ecc 12:5; Isa 40:22 **14:1** [g]S Ge 27:38; Ex 33:4; Nu 25:6; Dt 1:45; Jdg 20:23, 26; 2Sa 3:32; Job 31:29 **14:2** [h]S Ex 15:24; Heb 3:16 [i]S Ex 16:3 [j]S Nu 11:1; 16:13; 20:4; 21:5 **14:3** [k]S Ex 5:21 [l]ver 31 [m]S Ge 34:29; Dt 1:39; Ps 109:11; Isa 33:4; Eze 7:21;

orites[u] live in the hill country;[v] and the
Canaanites[w] live near the sea and along
the Jordan.[x]"

30Then Caleb[y] silenced the people before Moses and said, "We should go up
and take possession of the land, for we
can certainly do it."

31But the men who had gone up with
him said, "We can't attack those people;
they are stronger than we are."[z] 32And
they spread among the Israelites a bad report[a] about the land they had explored.
They said, "The land we explored devours[b] those living in it. All the people
we saw there are of great size.[c] 33We
saw the Nephilim[d] there (the descendants of Anak[e] come from the Nephilim).
We seemed like grasshoppers[f] in our
own eyes, and we looked the same to
them."

Chapter 14

The People Rebel

THAT night all the people of the community raised their voices and wept
aloud.[g] 2All the Israelites grumbled[h]
against Moses and Aaron, and the whole
assembly said to them, "If only we had
died in Egypt![i] Or in this desert![j] 3Why
is the LORD bringing us to this land only
to let us fall by the sword?[k] Our wives
and children[l] will be taken as plunder.[m]
Wouldn't it be better for us to go back to
Egypt?[n]" 4And they said to each other,
"We should choose a leader and go back
to Egypt.[o]"

5Then Moses and Aaron fell facedown[p] in front of the whole Israelite assembly[q] gathered there. 6Joshua son of
Nun[r] and Caleb son of Jephunneh, who
were among those who had explored the
land, tore their clothes[s] 7and said to the
entire Israelite assembly, "The land we
passed through and explored is exceed-

25:7; 26:5 [n]Ac 7:39 **14:4** [o]Ne 9:17 **14:5** [p]S Lev 9:24; Nu 16:4,22,45; 20:6; Jos 5:14; 2Sa 14:4; 1Ch 21:16; Eze 1:28 [q]S Lev 19:2 **14:6** [r]Nu 11:28 [s]S Ge 37:29,34; Jdg 11:35; 2Sa 13:31; 2Ki 19:1; Ezr 9:3; Est 4:1; S Mk 14:63

[b]*21* Or *toward the entrance to* [c]*23* *Eshcol* means *cluster*; also in verse 24.

14:1–4 HUMANITY, Relationship to God—God allows His human creatures the freedom to obey or rebel. Only so can humans be responsible for our actions and attitudes.

14:1–38 SIN, Rebellion—God can fulfill His announced plans and promises for His people. To refuse to follow Him is rebellion. We need fear no human opponent. We have God's protection when we walk in the path where He leads. When we do not believe His word, we treat Him with contempt and invite His wrath on us. See notes on Ex 14:11–12; 2 Ki 24:1–4.

14:1–44 DISCIPLESHIP, Spiritual Leaders—God's people and His chosen leaders do not always agree. Too often disciples want to take the easy way out and get rid of leaders. In troubled times of controversy, spiritual leaders must pray to ensure they know God's will, trust God to lead even amidst the controversy, fear God and not the people, love the people and intercede for them before God even when they rebel. Disciples must face controversy seeking God's will rather than personal security. They must work confidently with their leaders to find solutions rather than complaining and plotting. Disciples should not play on God's mercy. Rather they should take God's wrath seriously. Disciples should not try to ignore their sins and the resulting consequences. Sin prevents us from accomplishing some things for God. Forgiveness does not mean we can always accomplish what we at first refused to do.

ingly good.[t] 8If the LORD is pleased with
us,[u] he will lead us into that land, a land
flowing with milk and honey,[v] and will
give it to us.[w] 9Only do not rebel[x]
against the LORD. And do not be afraid[y]
of the people of the land,[z] because we
will swallow them up. Their protection is
gone, but the LORD is with[a] us.[b] Do not
be afraid of them."[c]

10But the whole assembly talked about
stoning[d] them. Then the glory of the
LORD[e] appeared at the Tent of Meeting
to all the Israelites. 11The LORD said to
Moses, "How long will these people treat
me with contempt?[f] How long will they
refuse to believe in me,[g] in spite of all
the miraculous signs[h] I have performed
among them? 12I will strike them down
with a plague[i] and destroy them, but I
will make you into a nation[j] greater and
stronger than they."[k]

13Moses said to the LORD, "Then the
Egyptians will hear about it! By your power you brought these people up from
among them.[l] 14And they will tell the
inhabitants of this land about it. They
have already heard[m] that you, O LORD,
are with these people[n] and that you, O
LORD, have been seen face to face,[o] that
your cloud stays over them,[p] and that
you go before them in a pillar of cloud by
day and a pillar of fire by night.[q] 15If you
put these people to death all at one time,
the nations who have heard this report
about you will say, 16'The LORD was not
able to bring these people into the land
he promised them on oath;[r] so he
slaughtered them in the desert.'[s]

17"Now may the Lord's strength be dis-

14:7 [t]Nu 13:27; Dt 1:25 **14:8** [u]Dt 7:8; 10:15; Ps 18:19; 22:8; 37:23; 41:11; 56:9; 147:11; Pr 11:20; Isa 62:4; Mal 2:17 [v]Nu 13:27 [w]Dt 1:21 **14:9** [x]Dt 1:26; 9:7, 23,24 [y]Ge 26:24; 2Ch 32:7; Ps 118:6; Jer 41:18; 42:11 [z]Dt 1:21; 7:18; 20:1 [a]Hag 2:4 [b]S Ge 21:22; Dt 1:30; 2Ch 13:12; Jer 15:20; 46:28; Hag 1:13 [c]ver 24 **14:10** [d]S Ex 17:4 [e]S Ex 24:16 **14:11** [f]Ex 23:21; Nu 15:31; 16:30; 1Sa 2:17; Eze 31:14; Mal 1:13 [g]Dt 1:32; Ps 78:22; 106:24; Jn 3:15 [h]S Ex 3:20; S 4:17; S 10:1 **14:12** [i]S Ex 5:3; S 30:12 [j]S Ex 32:10 [k]Dt 9:14; 29:20; 32:26; Ps 109:13 **14:13** [l]Ex 32:11-14; Ps 106:23 **14:14** [m]Ex 15:14 [n]Nu 5:3; 16:3; Jos 2:9 [o]Dt 5:4; 34:10 [p]S Ex 33:16 [q]S Ex 13:21 **14:16** [r]Nu 11:12 [s]Ex 32:12; Jos 7:7 **14:18** [t]S Ex 20:6; 34:6; Ps 145:8; Jnh 4:2; Jas 5:11 [u]Ex 20:5 **14:19** [v]S Ex 34:9; 1Ki 8:34; Ps 85:2; 103:3 [w]Ps 106:45 [x]Ps 78:38 **14:20** [y]Ex 34:6; Ps 99:8; 106:23; Mic 7:18-20 **14:21** [z]ver 28; Dt 32:40; Jdg 8:19; Ru 3:13; 1Sa 14:39; 19:6; Isa 49:18;

played, just as you have declared: 18'The
LORD is slow to anger, abounding in love
and forgiving sin and rebellion.[t] Yet he
does not leave the guilty unpunished; he
punishes the children for the sin of the
fathers to the third and fourth generation.'[u] 19In accordance with your great
love, forgive[v] the sin of these people,[w]
just as you have pardoned them from the
time they left Egypt until now."[x]

20The LORD replied, "I have forgiven
them,[y] as you asked. 21Nevertheless, as
surely as I live[z] and as surely as the glory
of the LORD[a] fills the whole earth,[b] 22not
one of the men who saw my glory and the
miraculous signs[c] I performed in Egypt
and in the desert but who disobeyed me
and tested me ten times[d]— 23not one of
them will ever see the land I promised on
oath[e] to their forefathers. No one who
has treated me with contempt[f] will ever
see it.[g] 24But because my servant Caleb[h]
has a different spirit and follows me
wholeheartedly,[i] I will bring him into
the land he went to, and his descendants
will inherit it.[j] 25Since the Amalekites[k]
and Canaanites[l] are living in the valleys,
turn[m] back tomorrow and set out toward
the desert along the route to the Red
Sea.[d] [n]"

26The LORD said to Moses and Aaron:
27"How long will this wicked community

Jer 4:2; Eze 5:11; Zep 2:9 [a]Lev 9:6 [b]Ps 72:19; Isa 6:3; 40:5; Hab 2:14 **14:22** [c]ver 11 [d]S Ex 14:11; 17:7; 32:1; Ps 81:7; 1Co 10:5 **14:23** [e]ver 16; S Ex 33:1; Nu 32:11; Dt 1:34; Ps 95:11; 106:26 [f]ver 11 [g]Heb 3:18 **14:24** [h]Nu 13:6 [i]ver 6-9; Dt 1:36; Jos 14:8,14 [j]Nu 26:65; 32:12; Ps 25:13; 37:9,11 **14:25** [k]S Ge 14:7 [l]S Ge 10:18 [m]Dt 1:40 [n]Ex 23:31; Nu 21:4; 1Ki 9:26

[d]25 Hebrew *Yam Suph*; that is, Sea of Reeds

14:8 ELECTION, Presence—It was the pleasure and goodness of God toward His elect that would lead them into the Land of Promise. His presence would determine their achievements. God's elect depend on His presence and thus can live without fear.

14:13–16 HISTORY, Universal—God's saving acts display His power to nations who oppose Him. Unbelieving people use every excuse of history to belittle God and cast doubt on His sovereign powers. God's concern for His reputation among the nations does not prevent Him from exercising deserved judgment against His people.

14:13–24 PRAYER, Forgiveness—Moses prayed for the Lord to protect His honor and reputation in the world. He sought forgiveness for an undeserving people. Prayer for forgiveness is not based on our merits but on God's purpose of salvation and mission. Even forgiveness does not exempt a people from divine discipline (vv 20–23). See note on Ex 32:32.

14:17–38 HISTORY, Judgment—God at times chooses to use history as the arena to display His power and justice in judging His disobedient people. Judgment for sin can come even to a people God forgives.

14:20–40 ELECTION, Condemnation—God's election did not mean that God would arbitrarily bring the chosen into the Land of Promise. God's elect are called to obedience. Because Caleb possessed a loving spirit that obeyed God wholeheartedly, he would be brought by God into the Land of Promise. God's elect may be forgiven of their sin, but this does not protect them from God's discipline. Election works through promise, deliverance, and discipline to create an obedient people according to God's purposes.

14:21,28 GOD, Living—All of God's dealings with His people up to this point should have conveyed the idea that He was a living God. Here it is explicitly stated. He is not like dead images that cannot speak, see, or move. By contrast, God is a living God with all of the characteristics of life: awareness, presence, purposiveness, power, wisdom, love, anger, and compassion. He is a personal, living God who communicates with us and is involved in the events of His world.

14:23 SIN, Discipline—The rebellion of the Israelites had been so consistent and so blatant that God threatened to destroy the whole nation and start over with Moses. Moses' intercession led God to forgive the nation but still punish the guilty generation, delaying the fulfillment of His promise. Thus, God intervened to keep that generation from entering the Land of Promise. God was not compelled to intervene in this matter, but He chose to do so because of Israel's lack of faith in His leadership. God always reacts to the sin of His people. He also listens and responds to the prayers of His faithful people. He remains free to choose to intervene in the lives of individuals or in the affairs of nations when circumstances warrant and in ways He considers appropriate.

14:26–35 EVIL AND SUFFERING, Punishment—God's punishment for sin is the cause of some suffering. God punished the rebellious Hebrews for refusing to enter the Promised Land. Caleb and Joshua were preserved because they were the

grumble against me? I have heard the
complaints of these grumbling Israelites.[o] 28So tell them, 'As surely as I live,[p]
declares the LORD, I will do to you[q] the
very things I heard you say: 29In this
desert your bodies will fall[r]—every one
of you twenty years old or more[s] who
was counted in the census[t] and who has
grumbled against me. 30Not one of you
will enter the land[u] I swore with uplifted
hand[v] to make your home, except Caleb
son of Jephunneh[w] and Joshua son of
Nun.[x] 31As for your children that you
said would be taken as plunder, I will
bring them in to enjoy the land you have
rejected.[y] 32But you—your bodies will
fall[z] in this desert. 33Your children will
be shepherds here for forty years,[a] suffering for your unfaithfulness, until the
last of your bodies lies in the desert. 34For
forty years[b]—one year for each of the
forty days you explored the land[c]—you
will suffer for your sins and know what it
is like to have me against you.' 35I, the
LORD, have spoken, and I will surely do
these things[d] to this whole wicked community, which has banded together
against me. They will meet their end in
this desert; here they will die.[e]"

36So the men Moses had sent[f] to explore the land, who returned and made
the whole community grumble[g] against
him by spreading a bad report[h] about
it— 37these men responsible for spreading the bad report[i] about the land were
struck down and died of a plague[j] before
the LORD. 38Of the men who went to explore the land,[k] only Joshua son of Nun
and Caleb son of Jephunneh survived.[l]

39When Moses reported this[m] to all the
Israelites, they mourned[n] bitterly. 40Early
the next morning they went up toward
the high hill country.[o] "We have
sinned[p]," they said. "We will go up to
the place the LORD promised."

41But Moses said, "Why are you disobeying the LORD's command? This will
not succeed![q] 42Do not go up, because
the LORD is not with you. You will be
defeated by your enemies,[r] 43for the Amalekites[s] and Canaanites[t] will face you

14:27 [o]Ex 16:12; Dt 1:34,35
14:28 [p]S ver 21 [q]Nu 33:56
14:29 [r]ver 23,30, 32; Nu 26:65; 32:13; 1Co 10:5; Heb 3:17; Jude 1:5 [s]S Nu 1:45 [t]S Ex 30:12
14:30 [u]S ver 29 [v]Ex 6:8; Dt 32:40; Ne 9:15; Ps 106:26; Eze 20:5; 36:7 [w]Nu 13:6 [x]Nu 11:28
14:31 [y]S Lev 26:43
14:32 [z]S ver 29,35
14:33 [a]ver 34; S Ex 16:35; Ac 13:18; Heb 3:9
14:34 [b]S ver 33 [c]Nu 13:25
14:35 [d]Nu 23:19 [e]S ver 32
14:36 [f]Nu 13:4-16 [g]ver 2 [h]S Nu 13:32
14:37 [i]S Nu 13:32; 1Co 10:10; Heb 3:17 [j]Nu 16:49; 5:9; 26:1; 31:16; Dt 4:3
14:38 [k]ver 30; Nu 13:4-16 [l]ver 24; Jos 14:6
14:39 [m]ver 28-35 [n]S Ex 33:4
14:40 [o]ver 45; Nu 13:17 [p]S Ex 9:27
14:41 [q]2Ch 24:20
14:42 [r]Dt 1:42
14:43 [s]Jdg 3:13 [t]ver 45; Nu 13:29 [u]S Ge 39:23; Dt 31:8; Jos 6:27; Jdg 1:19; 6:16; 1Sa 3:19; 18:14; 2Ch 1:1
14:44 [v]Dt 1:43 [w]Nu 31:6
14:45 [x]S ver 43 [y]S ver 40 [z]Nu 21:3; Dt 1:44; Jos 12:14; 15:30; 19:4; Jdg 1:17; 1Sa 30:30; 1Ch 4:30
15:2 [a]S Lev 23:10
15:3 [b]S Lev 1:2 [c]ver 24; S Lev 1:9 [d]Lev 1:3; Nu 28:13 [e]S Lev 7:16; S Ezr 1:4 [f]Lev 23:1-44
15:4 [g]S Lev 6:14 [h]S Ex 16:36
15:5 [i]S Lev 3:7 [j]S Lev 10:9 [k]S Ge 35:14
15:6 [l]S Lev 5:15 [m]Nu 28:12; 29:14 [n]S Lev 23:13 [o]Eze 46:14
15:7 [p]ver 5 [q]Lev 23:13; Nu 28:14; 29:18

there. Because you have turned away
from the LORD, he will not be with you[u]
and you will fall by the sword."

44Nevertheless, in their presumption
they went up[v] toward the high hill country, though neither Moses nor the ark of
the LORD's covenant moved from the
camp.[w] 45Then the Amalekites and Canaanites[x] who lived in that hill country[y]
came down and attacked them and beat
them down all the way to Hormah.[z]

Chapter 15

Supplementary Offerings

THE LORD said to Moses, 2"Speak to
the Israelites and say to them: 'After
you enter the land I am giving you[a] as a
home 3and you present to the LORD offerings made by fire, from the herd or the
flock,[b] as an aroma pleasing to the
LORD[c]—whether burnt offerings[d] or
sacrifices, for special vows or freewill offerings[e] or festival offerings[f]— 4then
the one who brings his offering shall
present to the LORD a grain offering[g] of a
tenth of an ephah[e] of fine flour[h] mixed
with a quarter of a hin[f] of oil. 5With each
lamb[i] for the burnt offering or the sacrifice, prepare a quarter of a hin of wine[j]
as a drink offering.[k]

6" 'With a ram[l] prepare a grain offering[m] of two-tenths of an ephah[g][n] of fine
flour mixed with a third of a hin[h] of oil,[o]
7and a third of a hin of wine[p] as a drink
offering.[q] Offer it as an aroma pleasing to
the LORD.[r]

8" 'When you prepare a young bull[s] as
a burnt offering or sacrifice, for a special
vow[t] or a fellowship offering[i][u] to the
LORD, 9bring with the bull a grain offering[v] of three-tenths of an ephah[j][w] of

[r]S Lev 1:9 15:8 [s]S Ex 12:5; S Lev 1:5 [t]S Lev 22:18 [u]S Lev 3:6 15:9 [v]Lev 2:1 [w]S Lev 14:10

[e]4 That is, probably about 2 quarts (about 2 liters)
[f]4 That is, probably about 1 quart (about 1 liter); also in verse 5 [g]6 That is, probably about 4 quarts (about 4.5 liters) [h]6 That is, probably about 1 1/4 quarts (about 1.2 liters); also in verse 7
[i]8 Traditionally *peace offering* [j]9 That is, probably about 6 quarts (about 6.5 liters)

only spies to give the proper report (14:30; 13:30). Faithful obedience and service, not constant complaint, is the proper response when things do not turn out as we want.

14:40 SIN, Guilt—Sin interrupts our history with God. Life is not the same. We cannot repent on our schedule and go on as if nothing happened. Sin produced a sense of guilt in the lives of the Israelites. Unfortunately, they recognized too late the error of their actions. God's judgment had been announced. No amount of sorrow could change their fate. Trying to live as if sin had not occurred added to their sin. They needed to acknowledge God's justified discipline and follow where He led under the new circumstances.

14:43 SIN, Alienation—Sin robs us of God's presence. See note on 11:1.

14:44 SIN, Blindness—Though Moses warned the people of the futility of their actions, they would not heed his warning. Because of their sins they had become morally and spiritually blind to the consequences of their actions. Continual sin makes a person morally blind.

15:1–31 ELECTION, Worship—In response to the love and mercy of the God of election, the elect were told to present various sacrifices at the specific feasts and festivals of worship. The priest was mandated to make atonement so the elect could be forgiven for their sins. Worship is the natural response to election. Defiance and rebellion as shown in ch 14 result only in radical judgment. Such attitudes are not tolerable among God's elect.

fine flour mixed with half a hin[k] of oil.
10Also bring half a hin of wine[x] as a drink
offering.[y] It will be an offering made by
fire, an aroma pleasing to the LORD.[z]
11Each bull or ram, each lamb or young
goat, is to be prepared in this manner.
12Do this for each one, for as many as you
prepare.[a]

13" 'Everyone who is native-born[b]
must do these things in this way when he
brings an offering made by fire as an aroma pleasing to the LORD.[c] 14For the generations to come,[d] whenever an alien[e]
or anyone else living among you presents
an offering[f] made by fire[g] as an aroma
pleasing to the LORD, he must do exactly
as you do. 15The community is to have
the same rules for you and for the alien
living among you; this is a lasting ordinance for the generations to come.[h] You
and the alien shall be the same before the
LORD: 16The same laws and regulations
will apply both to you and to the alien
living among you.[i] ' "

17The LORD said to Moses, 18"Speak to
the Israelites and say to them: 'When you
enter the land to which I am taking you[j]
19and you eat the food of the land,[k]
present a portion as an offering to the
LORD.[l] 20Present a cake from the first of
your ground meal[m] and present it as an
offering from the threshing floor.[n o]
21Throughout the generations to come[p]
you are to give this offering to the LORD
from the first of your ground meal.[q]

Offerings for Unintentional Sins

22" 'Now if you unintentionally fail to
keep any of these commands the LORD
gave Moses[r]— 23any of the LORD's commands to you through him, from the day
the LORD gave them and continuing
through the generations to come[s]—
24and if this is done unintentionally[t]
without the community being aware of
it,[u] then the whole community is to offer
a young bull for a burnt offering[v] as an
aroma pleasing to the LORD,[w] along with
its prescribed grain offering[x] and drink
offering,[y] and a male goat for a sin offering.[z] 25The priest is to make atonement
for the whole Israelite community, and
they will be forgiven,[a] for it was not intentional[b] and they have brought to the
LORD for their wrong an offering made by
fire[c] and a sin offering.[d] 26The whole Israelite community and the aliens living
among them will be forgiven, because all
the people were involved in the unintentional wrong.[e]

27" 'But if just one person sins unintentionally,[f] he must bring a year-old female
goat for a sin offering.[g] 28The priest is to
make atonement[h] before the LORD for
the one who erred by sinning unintentionally, and when atonement has been
made for him, he will be forgiven.[i]
29One and the same law applies to everyone who sins unintentionally, whether
he is a native-born Israelite or an alien.[j]

30" 'But anyone who sins defiantly,[k]
whether native-born or alien,[l] blasphemes the LORD,[m] and that person must
be cut off from his people.[n] 31Because he
has despised[o] the LORD's word and broken his commands,[p] that person must
surely be cut off; his guilt remains on
him.[q] ' "

The Sabbath-Breaker Put to Death

32While the Israelites were in the
desert,[r] a man was found gathering
wood on the Sabbath day.[s] 33Those who
found him gathering wood brought him
to Moses and Aaron and the whole assembly, 34and they kept him in custody,
because it was not clear what should be
done to him.[t] 35Then the LORD said to
Moses, "The man must die.[u] The whole
assembly must stone him outside the
camp.[v]" 36So the assembly took him
outside the camp and stoned him[w]
to death,[x] as the LORD commanded
Moses.[y]

Tassels on Garments

37The LORD said to Moses, 38"Speak to
the Israelites and say to them: 'Through-

15:10 [x]Nu 28:14 [y]Lev 23:13 [z]Lev 1:9
15:12 [a]Ezr 7:17
15:13 [b]S Lev 16:29 [c]Lev 1:9
15:14 [d]Lev 3:17; Nu 10:8 [e]S Ex 12:19,43; S 22:21 [f]S Lev 22:18 [g]ver 25
15:15 [h]ver 14,21
15:16 [i]Ex 12:49; S Lev 22:18; Nu 9:14
15:18 [j]S Lev 23:10
15:19 [k]Jos 5:11,12 [l]Nu 18:8
15:20 [m]S Lev 23:14 [n]S Lev 2:14; S Nu 18:27 [o]S Ge 50:10
15:21 [p]S Lev 23:14 [q]Eze 44:30; Ro 11:16
15:22 [r]S Lev 4:2
15:23 [s]ver 21
15:24 [t]ver 25,26 [u]S Lev 5:15 [v]Lev 4:14 [w]S ver 3 [x]Lev 2:1 [y]Lev 23:13; Nu 6:15 [z]Lev 4:3
15:25 [a]Lev 4:20; S Ro 3:25 [b]ver 22, S 24 [c]ver 14 [d]Lev 4:3
15:26 [e]S ver 24
15:27 [f]Lev 4:27 [g]Lev 4:3; Nu 6:14
15:28 [h]Nu 8:12; 28:22 [i]Lev 4:20
15:29 [j]S Ex 12:49
15:30 [k]Nu 14:40-44; Dt 1:43; 17:13; Ps 19:13 [l]ver 14 [m]2Ki 19:6,20; Isa 37:6,23; Eze 20:27 [n]S Ge 17:14; S Job 31:22
15:31 [o]S Nu 14:11 [p]1Sa 15:23,26; 2Sa 11:27; 12:9; Ps 119:126; Pr 13:13 [q]S Lev 5:1; Eze 18:20
15:32 [r]S Nu 12:16 [s]Ex 31:14,15; 35:2, 3
15:34 [t]Nu 9:8
15:35 [u]Ex 31:14, 15 [v]S Lev 20:2; Lk 4:29; Ac 7:58
15:36 [w]S Lev 20:2 [x]S Ex 31:14 [y]Jer 17:21

[k]9 That is, probably about 2 quarts (about 2 liters); also in verse 10

15:15–16,29 DISCIPLESHIP, Homeless—God's law is the same for homeless foreigners as for His chosen people. God views the sins of both the same. To treat the wrongdoing of homeless foreigners in a different way is to mistreat them. See note on Ex 22:21.

15:15,29 CHRISTIAN ETHICS, Justice—See note on 9:14.

15:22–31 SIN, Responsibility—Both the community and the individual may sin negligently. The group and the individual need to deal with their sins before God as God directs. Note the law includes "aliens," persons not born as Israelites but living among them and accepting their religious faith and practices. Sin applies to all people. So does the way to find atonement and salvation. See notes on Ge 39:9; Lev 4:1—5:19.

15:37–41 REVELATION, Actions—God understands the human need for tangible reminders. Wanting to be understood as the only God for Israel, the One who rescued them from Egypt, and the God who gave them a specific set of commands by which to live, He instructed the children to sew tassels on their clothes as constant reminders of all these interventions of God (Dt 22:12). Symbols can prod our memory and lead us to worship, but they can also lose their meaning and become objects of human pride (Mt 23:5). Jesus left baptism and the Lord's Supper as the only symbols necessary to call the church to worship and service.

15:37–41 CHRISTIAN ETHICS, Moral Limits—Reminders of God's moral limits help the child of God remember God's expectations and personal promises to obey. Such physical reminders may take various forms. Making and using such

out the generations to come[z] you are to
make tassels on the corners of your garments,[a] with a blue cord on each tassel.
39You will have these tassels to look at
and so you will remember[b] all the commands of the LORD, that you may obey
them and not prostitute yourselves[c] by
going after the lusts of your own hearts[d]
and eyes. 40Then you will remember to
obey all my commands[e] and will be consecrated to your God.[f] 41I am the LORD
your God, who brought you out of Egypt
to be your God.[g] I am the LORD your
God.[h]' "

Chapter 16

Korah, Dathan and Abiram

KORAH[i] son of Izhar, the son of Kohath, the son of Levi, and certain
Reubenites—Dathan and Abiram[j], sons
of Eliab,[k] and On son of Peleth—became
insolent[1] 2and rose up against Moses.[l]
With them were 250 Israelite men, well-
known community leaders who had been
appointed members of the council.[m]
3They came as a group to oppose Moses
and Aaron[n] and said to them, "You have
gone too far! The whole community is
holy,[o] every one of them, and the LORD
is with them.[p] Why then do you set yourselves above the LORD's assembly?"[q]
4When Moses heard this, he fell facedown.[r] 5Then he said to Korah and all
his followers: "In the morning the LORD
will show who belongs to him and who is
holy,[s] and he will have that person come
near him.[t] The man he chooses[u] he will
cause to come near him. 6You, Korah,
and all your followers[v] are to do this:
Take censers[w] 7and tomorrow put fire[x]
and incense[y] in them before the LORD.
The man the LORD chooses[z] will be the
one who is holy.[a] You Levites have gone
too far!"
8Moses also said to Korah, "Now listen, you Levites! 9Isn't it enough[b] for you
that the God of Israel has separated you
from the rest of the Israelite community
and brought you near himself to do the
work at the LORD's tabernacle and to
stand before the community and minister
to them?[c] 10He has brought you and all
your fellow Levites near himself, but now
you are trying to get the priesthood too.[d]
11It is against the LORD that you and all
your followers have banded together.
Who is Aaron that you should grumble[e]
against him?[f]"
12Then Moses summoned Dathan and
Abiram,[g] the sons of Eliab. But they said,
"We will not come![h] 13Isn't it enough
that you have brought us up out of a land
flowing with milk and honey[i] to kill us
in the desert?[j] And now you also want to
lord it over us?[k] 14Moreover, you haven't
brought us into a land flowing with milk
and honey[l] or given us an inheritance of
fields and vineyards.[m] Will you gouge out
the eyes of[m] these men?[n] No, we will
not come![o]"
15Then Moses became very angry[p] and
said to the LORD, "Do not accept their
offering. I have not taken so much as a
donkey[q] from them, nor have I wronged
any of them."
16Moses said to Korah, "You and all
your followers are to appear before the
LORD tomorrow—you and they and Aaron.[r] 17Each man is to take his censer and
put incense in it—250 censers in all—
and present it before the LORD. You and
Aaron are to present your censers also.[s]"
18So each man took his censer,[t] put fire
and incense in it, and stood with Moses
and Aaron at the entrance to the Tent of
Meeting. 19When Korah had gathered all
his followers in opposition to them[u] at

15:38 [z]Lev 3:17; Nu 10:8 [a]Dt 22:12; Mt 23:5
15:39 [b]Dt 4:23; 6:12; Ps 73:27 [c]S Lev 17:7; Jdg 2:17; Ps 106:39; Jer 3:2; Hos 4:12 [d]Ps 78:37; Jer 7:24; Eze 20:16
15:40 [e]S Ge 26:5; Dt 11:13; Ps 103:18; 119:56 [f]S Lev 11:44; Ro 12:1; Col 1:22; 1Pe 1:15
15:41 [g]S Ge 17:7 [h]S Ex 20:2
16:1 [i]S Ex 6:24; Jude 1:11 [j]ver 24; Ps 106:17 [k]Nu 26:8; Dt 11:6
16:2 [l]Nu 27:3 [m]Nu 1:16; 26:9
16:3 [n]ver 7; Ps 106:16 [o]Ex 19:6 [p]S Nu 14:14 [q]Nu 12:2
16:4 [r]Nu 14:5
16:5 [s]S Lev 10:3; 2Ti 2:19* [t]Jer 30:21 [u]Nu 17:5; Ps 65:4; 105:26; Jer 50:44
16:6 [v]ver 7,16 [w]S Lev 10:1; Rev 8:3
16:7 [x]S Lev 10:1 [y]S Ex 30:9 [z]S ver 6 [a]ver 5
16:9 [b]S Ge 30:15 [c]Nu 3:6; Dt 10:8; 17:12; 21:5; 1Sa 2:11; Ps 134:1; Eze 44:11
16:10 [d]Nu 3:10; 18:7; Jdg 17:5,12
16:11 [e]ver 41; 1Co 10:10 [f]S Ex 16:7
16:12 [g]S ver 1,27 [h]ver 14
16:13 [i]Nu 13:27 [j]Nu 14:2 [k]S Ge 13:8; Ac 7:27,35
16:14 [l]S Lev 20:24 [m]Ex 22:5; 23:11; Nu 20:5; 1Ki 4:25; Ne 13:15; Ps 105:33; Jer 5:17; Hos 2:12; Joel 2:22; Hag 2:19; Zec 3:10 [n]Jdg 16:21; 1Sa 11:2; Jer 39:7 [o]ver 12
16:15 [p]S Ex 4:14 [q]1Sa 12:3
16:16 [r]S ver 6 16:17 [s]Eze 8:11 16:18 [t]Lev 10:1 16:19 [u]ver 42; Nu 20:2

[1] *1* Or *Peleth—took* ⌊*men*⌋ [m] *14* Or *you make slaves of*; or *you deceive*

reminders should not become laws people impose on others or use to judge others (Mt 23:5).

16:1–50 EVIL AND SUFFERING, Deserved—Failure to accept God's leadership may bring suffering. God calls persons to various leadership roles. We are to accept the role God gives, fulfill it as best we can, and not envy those chosen for different roles. Rebellion against God's way deserves punishment. See note on 12:1–15.

16:1–50 REVELATION, Events—God is present with all His people but chooses certain people as instruments of His revelation for His people. Jealousy makes some people seek to be instruments of revelation. God used a dramatic event to reveal His wrath to Korah, Dathan, and Abijah. In a test of priests God revealed His glory, apparently a shining light. An earthquake with volcanic fire or lightning killed the guilty. God used the guilty men's censers, or pans with hot coals to burn incense, to provide Israel a memorial or continual revelation of God's anger against persons who would presume to take over tasks God had not given them. The cloud and glory (v 42) again revealed God's presence. See note on Ex 25:1—30:38; 34:4–12.

16:7 ELECTION, Leadership—See note on 12:2. Divine leadership, not human ambition, determines the leaders of God's people. A severe and bitter controversy rose against Moses and Aaron over the issue of the status of the priesthood. Levites desired to serve with equal authority and status of the priests. Moses informed them that God's election determined who would be priests. God sets persons apart for service as worship leaders of His people. God's choosing (Hebrew *bachar*) is central to an understanding of election. When people seek to choose leadership without God, they have gone too far.

16:15 PRAYER, Hindrances—Korah, the leader of this rebellion, wanted to usurp the priesthood for the Levites (v 10); he was jealous of Moses' leadership. God had appointed Moses. God did not honor Korah's prayer and worship because it was not aligned with God's purposes. Moses' prayer appealed to the integrity of God's history. God does not honor prayer which seeks to get Him to contradict His previous work with His people.

the entrance to the Tent of Meeting, the glory of the LORD[v] appeared to the entire assembly. 20The LORD said to Moses and Aaron, 21"Separate yourselves[w] from this assembly so I can put an end to them at once."[x]

22But Moses and Aaron fell facedown[y] and cried out, "O God, God of the spirits of all mankind,[z] will you be angry with the entire assembly[a] when only one man sins?"[b]

23Then the LORD said to Moses, 24"Say to the assembly, 'Move away from the tents of Korah, Dathan and Abiram.' "

25Moses got up and went to Dathan and Abiram, and the elders of Israel[c] followed him. 26He warned the assembly, "Move back from the tents of these wicked men![d] Do not touch anything belonging to them, or you will be swept away[e] because of all their sins.[f]" 27So they moved away from the tents of Korah, Dathan and Abiram.[g] Dathan and Abiram had come out and were standing with their wives, children[h] and little ones at the entrances to their tents.[i]

28Then Moses said, "This is how you will know[j] that the LORD has sent me[k] to do all these things and that it was not my idea: 29If these men die a natural death and experience only what usually happens to men, then the LORD has not sent me.[l] 30But if the LORD brings about something totally new, and the earth opens its mouth[m] and swallows them, with everything that belongs to them, and they go down alive into the grave,[n] [n] then you will know that these men have treated the LORD with contempt.[o]"

31As soon as he finished saying all this, the ground under them split apart[p] 32and the earth opened its mouth and swallowed them,[q] with their households and all Korah's men and all their possessions. 33They went down alive into the grave,[r] with everything they owned; the earth closed over them, and they perished and were gone from the community. 34At their cries, all the Israelites around them fled, shouting, "The earth is going to swallow us too!"

35And fire came out from the LORD[s] and consumed[t] the 250 men who were offering the incense.

36The LORD said to Moses, 37"Tell Eleazar[u] son of Aaron, the priest, to take the censers[v] out of the smoldering remains and scatter the coals some distance away, for the censers are holy— 38the censers of the men who sinned at the cost of their lives.[w] Hammer the censers into sheets to overlay the altar,[x] for they were presented before the LORD and have become holy. Let them be a sign[y] to the Israelites."

39So Eleazar the priest[z] collected the bronze censers brought by those who had been burned up,[a] and he had them hammered out to overlay the altar, 40as the LORD directed him through Moses. This was to remind the Israelites that no one except a descendant of Aaron should come to burn incense[b] before the LORD,[c] or he would become like Korah and his followers.[d]

41The next day the whole Israelite community grumbled against Moses and Aaron. "You have killed the LORD's people," they said.

42But when the assembly gathered in opposition[e] to Moses and Aaron and turned toward the Tent of Meeting, suddenly the cloud covered it and the glory of the LORD[f] appeared. 43Then Moses and Aaron went to the front of the Tent of Meeting, 44and the LORD said to Moses, 45"Get away from this assembly so I can put an end[g] to them at once." And they fell facedown.

46Then Moses said to Aaron, "Take your censer[h] and put incense in it, along with fire from the altar, and hurry to the assembly[i] to make atonement[j] for them. Wrath has come out from the LORD;[k] the plague[l] has started."

16:19 vS Ex 16:7; Nu 14:10; 20:6
16:21 wver 24 xS Ge 19:14; S Ex 32:10
16:22 yS Nu 14:5 zNu 27:16; Job 12:10; 27:8; 33:4; 34:14; Jer 32:27; Eze 18:4; Heb 12:9 aS Lev 10:6 bS Ge 18:23; S Job 21:20
16:25 cS Ex 19:7
16:26 dIsa 52:11 eS Ge 19:15 fJer 51:6
16:27 gS ver 12 hver 32; Jos 7:24; Isa 13:16; 14:21 iS Ex 33:8
16:28 j1Ki 18:36 kEx 3:12; Jn 5:36; 6:38
16:29 lNu 24:13; Job 31:2; Ecc 3:19
16:30 mPs 141:7; Isa 5:14 nver 33; S Ge 37:35; 1Sa 2:6; Job 5:26; 21:13; Ps 9:17; 16:10; 55:15; Isa 14:11; 38:18 oS Nu 14:11; S Eze 26:20
16:31 pIsa 64:1-2; Eze 47:1-12; Mic 1:3-4; Zec 14:4
16:32 qS Ex 15:12
16:33 rS ver 30; S Ecc 9:10
16:35 sS Nu 11:1-3; 26:10; Rev 11:5 tS Lev 10:2
16:37 uS Ex 6:23 vver 6
16:38 wLev 10:1; Pr 20:2 xS Ex 20:24; 38:1-7 yNu 26:10; Dt 28:46; Jer 44:29; Eze 14:8; 2Pe 2:6
16:39 z2Ch 26:18 aS Lev 20:14
16:40 bS Ex 30:1; 2Ki 12:3; Isa 1:13; 66:3; Jer 41:5; 44:3 cS Ex 30:9; 2Ch 26:18 dS Nu 3:10
16:42 eS ver 19 fEx 16:7; Nu 14:10
16:45 gS Ex 32:10
16:46 hS Lev 10:1 iLev 10:6 jS Ex 29:36 kS Nu 1:53 lS Lev 26:25; Nu 8:19; Ps 106:29

n30 Hebrew *Sheol*; also in verse 33

16:22 SIN, Individual Choice—Moses and Aaron pleaded with God on behalf of the entire assembly that He not hold all of them accountable for the sin of one person. A recurring theme throughout the Bible is that of individual accountability for sin. Since God created persons as responsible moral agents, we are each accountable for our own choices in this matter. We are not guilty of someone else's sin. We cannot blame someone else for our sins. See notes on Ge 39:9; Eze 18:1–32.

16:22 PRAYER, Mercy of God—Moses' prayer is the opposite of Abraham's appeal in Ge 18:23–32. Abraham prayed that God would spare the city for the sake of a few righteous. Moses prayed that God would not punish the many for the sins of a few. God responds in justice and mercy to the prayers of faithful people.

16:26 SIN, Punishment—God was about to punish Dathan and Abiram for their rebellion. He warned all others to remove themselves from the arena of action or they would also be destroyed. One should not conclude from this incident that being among sinners is cause enough for God to destroy a person. In this case, since physical destruction was about to be brought on Dathan and Abiram, those who were in that physical proximity would share their fate. Refusing to obey God's warnings or refusing to believe God will punish sinners is sin.

16:28–35 HISTORY, God's Will—God's will in a situation may be revealed through His historical acts. In punishing the rebels against Moses and Aaron, God revealed His will to work through Moses and Aaron as His chosen leaders.

16:30 LAST THINGS, Intermediate State—See note on Isa 14:9.

16:41 SIN, Lack of Faith—Sin brings punishment which we often do not understand. We seek to find human scapegoats to blame. To refuse to acknowledge the justice of God's punishment of sin is sin. See note on Ex 15:24.

47So Aaron did as Moses said, and ran into
the midst of the assembly. The plague had
already started among the people,[m] but
Aaron offered the incense and made
atonement for them. 48He stood between
the living and the dead, and the plague
stopped.[n] 49But 14,700 people died from
the plague, in addition to those who had
died because of Korah.[o] 50Then Aaron returned to Moses at the entrance to the
Tent of Meeting, for the plague had
stopped.

Chapter 17

The Budding of Aaron's Staff

THE LORD said to Moses, 2"Speak to
the Israelites and get twelve staffs[p]
from them, one from the leader of each of
their ancestral tribes.[q] Write the name of
each man on his staff. 3On the staff of
Levi write Aaron's name,[r] for there must
be one staff for the head of each ancestral
tribe. 4Place them in the Tent of Meeting[s] in front of the Testimony,[t] where I
meet with you.[u] 5The staff belonging to
the man I choose[v] will sprout,[w] and I
will rid myself of this constant grumbling[x] against you by the Israelites."
6So Moses spoke to the Israelites, and
their leaders gave him twelve staffs, one
for the leader of each of their ancestral
tribes, and Aaron's staff was among them.
7Moses placed the staffs before the LORD
in the Tent of the Testimony.[y]
8The next day Moses entered the Tent
of the Testimony[z] and saw that Aaron's
staff,[a] which represented the house of
Levi, had not only sprouted but had budded, blossomed and produced almonds.[b]
9Then Moses brought out all the staffs[c]
from the LORD's presence to all the Israelites. They looked at them, and each man
took his own staff.
10The LORD said to Moses, "Put back
Aaron's staff[d] in front of the Testimony,
to be kept as a sign to the rebellious.[e]
This will put an end to their grumbling
against me, so that they will not die."
11Moses did just as the LORD commanded
him.
12The Israelites said to Moses, "We
will die! We are lost, we are all lost![f]
13Anyone who even comes near the tabernacle of the LORD will die.[g] Are we all
going to die?"

Chapter 18

Duties of Priests and Levites

THE LORD said to Aaron, "You, your
sons and your father's family are to
bear the responsibility for offenses
against the sanctuary,[h] and you and your
sons alone are to bear the responsibility
for offenses against the priesthood. 2Bring
your fellow Levites from your ancestral
tribe to join you and assist you when you
and your sons minister[i] before the Tent
of the Testimony. 3They are to be responsible to you[j] and are to perform all the
duties of the Tent,[k] but they must not go
near the furnishings of the sanctuary or
the altar, or both they and you will die.[l]
4They are to join you and be responsible
for the care of the Tent of Meeting—all
the work at the Tent—and no one else
may come near where you are.[m]
5"You are to be responsible for the care
of the sanctuary and the altar,[n] so that
wrath will not fall on the Israelites again.
6I myself have selected your fellow Levites from among the Israelites as a gift to
you,[o] dedicated to the LORD to do the
work at the Tent of Meeting.[p] 7But only
you and your sons may serve as priests in
connection with everything at the altar
and inside the curtain.[q] I am giving you
the service of the priesthood as a gift.[r]
Anyone else who comes near the sanctuary must be put to death.[s]"

Offerings for Priests and Levites

8Then the LORD said to Aaron, "I myself have put you in charge of the offerings presented to me; all the holy offerings the Israelites give me I give to you
and your sons as your portion[t] and regular share.[u] 9You are to have the part of
the most holy offerings[v] that is kept from
the fire. From all the gifts they bring me
as most holy offerings, whether grain[w] or
sin[x] or guilt offerings,[y] that part belongs
to you and your sons. 10Eat it as some-

16:47 [m]Nu 25:6-8
16:48 [n]Nu 25:8; Ps 106:30
16:49 [o]ver 32
17:2 [p]S Ge 32:10; S Ex 4:2 [q]Nu 1:4
17:3 [r]S Nu 1:3
17:4 [s]S Ex 40:2 [t]ver 7; Ex 16:34 [u]Ex 25:22
17:5 [v]S Nu 16:5 [w]ver 8 [x]S Ex 16:7
17:7 [y]S Ex 38:21
17:8 [z]ver 7; Nu 1:50 [a]ver 2,10 [b]Eze 17:24; Heb 9:4
17:9 [c]ver 2
17:10 [d]S ver 8 [e]S Ex 23:21; Dt 9:24; Ps 66:7; 68:18; Pr 24:21
17:12 [f]Jdg 13:22; Isa 6:5; 15:1
17:13 [g]Nu 1:51
18:1 [h]S Ex 28:38
18:2 [i]Nu 3:10
18:3 [j]S Nu 3:32 [k]Nu 1:51 [l]ver 7
18:4 [m]S Nu 3:38
18:5 [n]ver 3; Lev 6:12
18:6 [o]S Nu 3:9 [p]Nu 3:8
18:7 [q]Heb 9:3,6 [r]ver 20; Ex 29:9; 40:13; Heb 5:4 [s]ver 3; Nu 3:10
18:8 [t]S Lev 2:2 [u]Lev 6:16; 7:6, 31-34,36; Dt 18:1; 2Ch 31:4
18:9 [v]S Lev 6:17 [w]Lev 2:1 [x]Lev 6:25 [y]S Lev 5:15

17:5 SIN, Rebellion—The constant grumbling of the Israelites against Moses and his leadership was a source of irritation to God. Continuous wrong action and attitudes as well as a single wrong act is sin. God punishes as sinful the constant complaints against His chosen leaders.

17:5 ELECTION, Leadership—See note on 16:7. The community had problems in coming to terms with the way leaders were selected. Moses had spoken in clear terms that the election of leaders was God's doing. A plague destroyed those who continued to reject the way God elected to choose leaders. Still unrest and grumbling persisted over the issue of leadership. God intervened by advising Moses to write the names of the leaders of the twelve tribes on the staff of each of the tribes. The twelve staffs were to be placed in the Tent of Meeting in front of the Testimony where God always met with Moses. The staff belonging to the leader God chose would sprout. God does not always give such a clear sign of His choice, but He does let His people know His chosen leader as they look to Him for guidance.

18:6 ELECTION, Leadership—See note on 17:5. God elected those to serve as priests and Levites. He also defined their duties and determined how they were to be provided for and protected. These God-chosen positions were a gift from God to the community. Leaders of God's people need to see leadership as a gift for which they are responsible to God and to His people, not as a right they deserve.

thing most holy; every male shall eat it.[z]
You must regard it as holy.[a]
11"This also is yours: whatever is set
aside from the gifts of all the wave offerings[b] of the Israelites. I give this to you
and your sons and daughters as your regular share.[c] Everyone in your household
who is ceremonially clean[d] may eat it.
12"I give you all the finest olive oil and
all the finest new wine and grain[e] they
give the LORD[f] as the firstfruits of their
harvest.[g] 13All the land's firstfruits that
they bring to the LORD will be yours.[h]
Everyone in your household who is ceremonially clean may eat it.[i]
14"Everything in Israel that is devoted[o] to the LORD[j] is yours. 15The first offspring of every womb, both man and animal, that is offered to the LORD is yours.[k]
But you must redeem[l] every firstborn[m]
son and every firstborn male of unclean
animals.[n] 16When they are a month
old,[o] you must redeem them at the redemption price set at five shekels[p][p] of
silver, according to the sanctuary shekel,[q] which weighs twenty gerahs.[r]
17"But you must not redeem the firstborn of an ox, a sheep or a goat; they are
holy.[s] Sprinkle their blood[t] on the altar
and burn their fat[u] as an offering made
by fire, an aroma pleasing to the LORD.[v]
18Their meat is to be yours, just as the
breast of the wave offering[w] and the right
thigh are yours.[x] 19Whatever is set aside
from the holy[y] offerings the Israelites
present to the LORD I give to you and your
sons and daughters as your regular share.
It is an everlasting covenant of salt[z] before the LORD for both you and your offspring."
20The LORD said to Aaron, "You will
have no inheritance in their land, nor will
you have any share among them;[a] I am
your share and your inheritance[b] among
the Israelites.
21"I give to the Levites all the tithes[c]
in Israel as their inheritance[d] in return
for the work they do while serving at the
Tent of Meeting.[e] 22From now on the Israelites must not go near the Tent of
Meeting, or they will bear the consequences of their sin and will die.[f] 23It is
the Levites who are to do the work at the
Tent of Meeting and bear the responsibility for offenses against it. This is a lasting
ordinance[g] for the generations to
come.[h] They will receive no inheritance[i] among the Israelites.[j] 24Instead, I
give to the Levites as their inheritance
the tithes that the Israelites present as an
offering to the LORD.[k] That is why I said
concerning them: 'They will have no inheritance among the Israelites.' "
25The LORD said to Moses, 26"Speak to
the Levites and say to them: 'When you
receive from the Israelites the tithe I give
you[l] as your inheritance, you must
present a tenth of that tithe as the LORD's
offering.[m] 27Your offering will be reckoned[n] to you as grain from the threshing
floor[o] or juice from the winepress.[p] 28In
this way you also will present an offering
to the LORD from all the tithes[q] you receive from the Israelites. From these
tithes you must give the LORD's portion to
Aaron the priest. 29You must present as
the LORD's portion the best and holiest
part of everything given to you.'
30"Say to the Levites: 'When you
present the best part, it will be reckoned
to you as the product of the threshing
floor or the winepress.[r] 31You and your
households may eat the rest of it anywhere, for it is your wages for your work
at the Tent of Meeting.[s] 32By presenting
the best part[t] of it you will not be guilty
in this matter;[u] then you will not defile
the holy offerings[v] of the Israelites, and
you will not die.' "

Chapter 19

The Water of Cleansing

THE LORD said to Moses and Aaron:
2"This is a requirement of the law
that the LORD has commanded: Tell the
Israelites to bring you a red heifer[w] without defect or blemish[x] and that has never
been under a yoke.[y] 3Give it to Eleazar[z]
the priest; it is to be taken outside the
camp[a] and slaughtered in his presence.

o *14* The Hebrew term refers to the irrevocable giving over of things or persons to the LORD. p *16* That is, about 2 ounces (about 55 grams)

18:10 [z]S Lev 6:16 [a]Lev 6:17,18
18:11 [b]Ex 29:26; Lev 7:30; Nu 6:20 [c]Lev 7:31-34 [d]Lev 13:3; 22:1-16
18:12 [e]Dt 7:13; 11:14; 12:17; 28:51; 2Ki 18:32; 2Ch 31:5; Ne 10:37; Jer 31:12; Eze 23:41; Hos 2:8; Joel 1:10; Hag 1:11 [f]S Ge 4:3 [g]Ex 23:19; 34:26; Ne 10:35
18:13 [h]S Ex 29:27 [i]ver 11
18:14 [j]S Lev 27:21; Jos 6:17-19
18:15 [k]Ex 13:2 [l]S Nu 3:46 [m]S Ge 10:15 [n]S Ex 13:13
18:16 [o]S Nu 3:15 [p]S Lev 27:6 [q]S Ex 30:13 [r]Nu 3:47
18:17 [s]S Lev 27:9 [t]S Lev 3:2 [u]S Ex 29:13 [v]S Lev 1:9
18:18 [w]Lev 7:30 [x]ver 11
18:19 [y]2Ki 12:4 [z]S Lev 2:13
18:20 [a]Nu 26:62; Dt 12:12 [b]ver 24; Dt 10:9; 14:27; 18:1-2; Jos 13:33; Eze 44:28
18:21 [c]ver 24; S Ge 28:22; Nu 31:28; Dt 14:22; Ne 10:37; 13:5; Mal 3:8 [d]Lev 27:30-33; Heb 7:5 [e]Nu 1:53
18:22 [f]S Ex 28:43
18:23 [g]S Ex 12:14; S 27:21 [h]Nu 10:8 [i]ver 20; Nu 26:62; Dt 10:9 [j]Eze 44:10
18:24 [k]Lev 27:30; Dt 26:12
18:26 [l]ver 21 [m]ver 28; Ne 10:38
18:27 [n]Lev 7:18 [o]Ge 50:10; Dt 15:14; Jdg 6:37; Ru 3:3,6,14; 1Sa 23:1 [p]ver 12,30
18:28 [q]Mal 3:8
18:30 [r]S ver 27
18:31 [s]ver 23
18:32 [t]Lev 22:15 [u]ver 29 [v]S Lev 19:8
19:2 [w]S Ge 15:9; Heb 9:13 [x]S Lev 22:19-25 [y]Dt 21:3; 1Sa 6:7
19:3 [z]Nu 3:4 [a]S Ex 29:14

18:19 THE CHURCH, Covenant People—See note on Lev 2:13.

18:21–32 STEWARDSHIP, Tithe—The Levites received no land through inheritance but were supported by the people's tithes for their service as God's chosen priests. The tithe required ten percent of the produce of the land—grain, oil, fruits, and animals. Many believe the Temple tithe is one of the three required in the Old Testament. The celebration tithe (see note on Dt 12:6–18) is the second, and the charity tithe (Dt *14:28–29*) is the third. Old Testament Scriptures are not clear; therefore, it is difficult to know whether the tithing requirements began with the celebration tithe, changed to the charity tithe, and finally became the Temple tithe—or included all three. Many accept the three-tithe view because strong Jewish tradition affirms it. Whichever view is correct, tithing was important in Old Testament religious life and is part of the religious heritage that guides the Christian in giving. Our gifts should foster the church's worship and celebration, the ministry of God's called-out servants, and the charitable ministries of the church.

18:22 SIN, Death—God separated the Levites for the priestly work in the tabernacle and before the altar. He forbade all others to enter the symbol of His holy presence. Death was the consequence for disobedience. The New Testament clearly says death is the consequence of all sin. See note on Ro 6:23.

4Then Eleazar the priest is to take some
of its blood on his finger and sprinkle[b] it
seven times toward the front of the Tent
of Meeting. 5While he watches, the heifer
is to be burned—its hide, flesh, blood
and offal.[c] 6The priest is to take some
cedar wood, hyssop[d] and scarlet wool[e]
and throw them onto the burning heifer.
7After that, the priest must wash his
clothes and bathe himself with water.[f]
He may then come into the camp, but he
will be ceremonially unclean till evening.
8The man who burns it must also wash
his clothes and bathe with water, and he
too will be unclean till evening.

9"A man who is clean shall gather up
the ashes of the heifer[g] and put them in
a ceremonially clean place[h] outside the
camp. They shall be kept by the Israelite
community for use in the water of cleansing;[i] it is for purification from sin.[j]
10The man who gathers up[k] the ashes of
the heifer must also wash his clothes, and
he too will be unclean till evening.[l] This
will be a lasting ordinance[m] both for the
Israelites and for the aliens living among
them.[n]

11"Whoever touches the dead body[o] of
anyone will be unclean for seven days.[p]
12He must purify himself with the water
on the third day and on the seventh
day;[q] then he will be clean. But if he
does not purify himself on the third and
seventh days, he will not be clean.[r]
13Whoever touches the dead body[s] of
anyone and fails to purify himself defiles
the LORD's tabernacle.[t] That person
must be cut off from Israel.[u] Because the
water of cleansing has not been sprinkled
on him, he is unclean;[v] his uncleanness
remains on him.

14"This is the law that applies when a
person dies in a tent: Anyone who enters
the tent and anyone who is in it will be
unclean for seven days, 15and every open
container[w] without a lid fastened on it
will be unclean.

16"Anyone out in the open who
touches someone who has been killed
with a sword or someone who has died a
natural death,[x] or anyone who touches a
human bone[y] or a grave,[z] will be unclean for seven days.[a]

17"For the unclean person, put some
ashes[b] from the burned purification offering into a jar and pour fresh water[c]
over them. 18Then a man who is ceremonially clean is to take some hyssop,[d]
dip it in the water and sprinkle[e] the tent
and all the furnishings and the people
who were there. He must also sprinkle
anyone who has touched a human bone
or a grave[f] or someone who has been
killed or someone who has died a natural
death. 19The man who is clean is to sprinkle[g] the unclean person on the third and
seventh days, and on the seventh day he
is to purify him.[h] The person being
cleansed must wash his clothes[i] and
bathe with water, and that evening he
will be clean. 20But if a person who is
unclean does not purify himself, he must
be cut off from the community, because
he has defiled[j] the sanctuary of the
LORD.[k] The water of cleansing has not
been sprinkled on him, and he is unclean.[l] 21This is a lasting ordinance[m] for
them.

"The man who sprinkles the water of
cleansing must also wash his clothes, and
anyone who touches the water of cleansing will be unclean till evening. 22Any-
thing that an unclean[n] person touches
becomes unclean, and anyone who
touches it becomes unclean till evening."

Chapter 20

Water From the Rock

IN the first month the whole Israelite
community arrived at the Desert of
Zin,[o] and they stayed at Kadesh.[p] There
Miriam[q] died and was buried.

2Now there was no water[r] for the
community,[s] and the people gathered in
opposition[t] to Moses and Aaron. 3They
quarreled[u] with Moses and said, "If only
we had died when our brothers fell
dead[v] before the LORD![w] 4Why did you
bring the LORD's community into this
desert,[x] that we and our livestock should
die here?[y] 5Why did you bring us up out
of Egypt to this terrible place? It has no
grain or figs, grapevines or pomegranates.[z] And there is no water to drink![a]"

6Moses and Aaron went from the assembly to the entrance to the Tent of
Meeting[b] and fell facedown,[c] and the

19:4 [b]S Lev 4:17
19:5 [c]S Ex 29:14
19:6 [d]ver 18; Ps 51:7 [e]S Lev 14:4
19:7 [f]S Lev 11:25; S 14:8
19:9 [g]Heb 9:13 [h]S Ex 29:31; S Lev 4:12 [i]ver 13; Nu 8:7 [j]S Ge 35:2
19:10 [k]Lev 15:10 [l]Lev 14:46 [m]Lev 3:17 [n]S Lev 22:18
19:11 [o]S Lev 21:1 [p]S Lev 8:33; Nu 31:19
19:12 [q]ver 19; Nu 31:19 [r]ver 20; 2Ch 26:21
19:13 [s]S Lev 21:11 [t]S Lev 15:31; 2Ch 36:14; Ps 79:1 [u]Lev 7:20; 22:3 [v]ver 22; Hag 2:13
19:15 [w]S Lev 6:28
19:16 [x]Nu 31:19 [y]1Ki 13:2; 2Ki 23:14; Eze 6:5 [z]2Ki 23:6; Mt 23:27 [a]S Lev 5:3
19:17 [b]ver 9 [c]S Nu 8:7
19:18 [d]S ver 6; S Ex 12:22 [e]S Lev 4:17 [f]ver 16
19:19 [g]S Lev 16:14-15 [h]Nu 31:19; Eze 36:25; Heb 10:22 [i]S Ge 35:2
19:20 [j]Ps 74:7 [k]S Lev 15:31 [l]S ver 12; S Lev 14:8
19:21 [m]S Ex 27:21
19:22 [n]S Lev 5:2; 15:4-12
20:1 [o]Nu 13:21 [p]ver 14; Nu 13:26; 33:36; Dt 1:46; Jdg 11:17; Ps 29:8 [q]S Ex 15:20
20:2 [r]S Ex 15:22 [s]Ex 17:1 [t]S Nu 16:19
20:3 [u]ver 13; S Ge 13:7; Ex 17:2; 21:18 [v]S Ex 5:21 [w]S Nu 14:2; 16:31-35
20:4 [x]S Nu 14:2 [y]S Ex 14:11; Nu 14:3; 16:13
20:5 [z]Nu 13:23; 16:14 [a]S Ex 17:1
20:6 [b]S Ex 40:2 [c]Nu 14:5

19:11–22 HUMANITY, Death and Sin—See note on Lev 10:1–2. As a consequence of sin, death was viewed as a kind of uncleanness. As a class of sin, all uncleanness is contaminating. Persons must be purified before they can again be clean and, thus, be properly related to God and to His people. The New Testament gospel proclaims that Christ has provided the way to wash away our sins (Heb 9:11–28).

20:2–5 SIN, Rebellion—See note on Ex 14:11–12.

20:6–13 GOD, Holy—Here the holiness and the sovereign authority of the Lord are virtually identical. When Moses failed to follow exactly the instructions given to him by God, he had violated the holiness of God. As a result, God deprived Him of the privilege of entering the Promised Land. At first this seems to be a harsh judgment, but remember the prominent position Moses occupied in leading Israel and representing God to them. Those who lead bear tremendous responsibility and have great influence. See Jas 3:1. Disregarding God's sovereignty violates His holiness and His very being at the deepest level.

glory of the LORD[d] appeared to them.
7The LORD said to Moses, 8"Take the
staff,[e] and you and your brother Aaron
gather the assembly together. Speak to
that rock before their eyes and it will
pour out its water.[f] You will bring water
out of the rock for the community so they
and their livestock can drink."
9So Moses took the staff[g] from the
LORD's presence,[h] just as he commanded
him. 10He and Aaron gathered the assembly together[i] in front of the rock and Moses said to them, "Listen, you rebels,
must we bring you water out of this
rock?"[j] 11Then Moses raised his arm and
struck the rock twice with his staff. Water[k] gushed out, and the community and
their livestock drank.
12But the LORD said to Moses and Aaron, "Because you did not trust in me
enough to honor me as holy[l] in the sight
of the Israelites, you will not bring this
community into the land I give them."[m]
13These were the waters of Meri-
bah,[q][n] where the Israelites quarreled[o]
with the LORD and where he showed
himself holy among them.[p]

Edom Denies Israel Passage

14Moses sent messengers from Kadesh[q] to the king of Edom,[r] saying:

"This is what your brother Israel
says: You know[s] about all the hardships[t] that have come upon us.
15Our forefathers went down into
Egypt,[u] and we lived there many
years.[v] The Egyptians mistreated[w]
us and our fathers, 16but when we
cried out to the LORD, he heard our
cry[x] and sent an angel[y] and brought
us out of Egypt.[z]
"Now we are here at Kadesh, a
town on the edge of your territory.[a]
17Please let us pass through your
country. We will not go through any
field or vineyard, or drink water from
any well. We will travel along the
king's highway and not turn to the
right or to the left until we have
passed through your territory.[b]"
18But Edom[c] answered:

"You may not pass through here; if
you try, we will march out and attack
you with the sword.[d]"

19The Israelites replied:

"We will go along the main road,
and if we or our livestock[e] drink any
of your water, we will pay for it.[f] We
only want to pass through on foot—
nothing else."

20Again they answered:

"You may not pass through.[g]"

Then Edom[h] came out against them
with a large and powerful army. 21Since
Edom refused to let them go through
their territory,[i] Israel turned away from
them.[j]

The Death of Aaron

22The whole Israelite community set
out from Kadesh[k] and came to Mount
Hor.[l] 23At Mount Hor, near the border of
Edom,[m] the LORD said to Moses and Aaron, 24"Aaron will be gathered to his people.[n] He will not enter the land I give the
Israelites, because both of you rebelled
against my command[o] at the waters of
Meribah.[p] 25Get Aaron and his son Eleazar and take them up Mount Hor.[q] 26Re-
move Aaron's garments[r] and put them
on his son Eleazar, for Aaron will be gathered to his people;[s] he will die there."
27Moses did as the LORD commanded:
They went up Mount Hor[t] in the sight of
the whole community. 28Moses removed
Aaron's garments and put them on his
son Eleazar.[u] And Aaron died there[v] on
top of the mountain. Then Moses and Eleazar came down from the mountain,
29and when the whole community

20:6 [d]S Nu 16:19
20:8 [e]S Ex 4:2; S 10:12-13 [f]Ex 17:6; Isa 41:18; 43:20; Jer 31:9
20:9 [g]Nu 17:2 [h]Nu 17:10
20:10 [i]ver 8 [j]Ps 106:32,33
20:11 [k]S Ex 17:6; S Isa 33:21
20:12 [l]Nu 27:14; Dt 32:51; Isa 5:16; 8:13 [m]ver 24; Dt 1:37; 3:27
20:13 [n]S Ex 17:7 [o]S ver 3 [p]S Lev 10:3
20:14 [q]S ver 1 [r]S ver 16; S Ge 25:30; S 36:16 [s]Ge 24:3; Dt 4:39; Jos 2:11; 9:9 [t]S Ex 18:8
20:15 [u]S Ge 46:6 [v]S Ge 15:13 [w]S Ex 1:14
20:16 [x]S Ge 16:11; S 21:17; S Ex 2:23 [y]Ex 14:19 [z]Ex 12:42; Dt 26:8 [a]ver 14,23; Nu 33:37
20:17 [b]ver 20; Nu 21:22; Dt 2:27; Jdg 11:17
20:18 [c]ver 14 [d]Nu 21:23
20:19 [e]Ex 12:38 [f]Dt 2:6,28
20:20 [g]S ver 17,18 [h]ver 14
20:21 [i]Nu 21:23 [j]Nu 21:4; Dt 2:8; Jdg 11:18
20:22 [k]Dt 1:46 [l]Nu 33:37; 34:7; Dt 32:50
20:23 [m]S ver 16
20:24 [n]S Ge 25:8 [o]S ver 10 [p]S Ex 17:7
20:25 [q]Nu 33:38
20:26 [r]Ex 28:1-4; 40:13; S Lev 16:4 [s]ver 24; Nu 27:13; 31:2
20:27 [t]Nu 33:38
20:28 [u]S Ex 29:29 [v]ver 26; Nu 33:38; Dt 10:6; 32:50

[q]*13 Meribah* means *quarreling.*

20:11–12 SIN, Unbelief—Moses was a great leader of God's people; but because he demonstrated unbelief in God's command, he was not allowed to lead the Israelites into the Land of Promise. The promises of God are thwarted when we attempt to supplement them with our own plans or carry out His plans through our ways and for our purposes. We must trust God's way of doing things rather than our own.

20:12 EVIL AND SUFFERING, Punishment—Did God act in an evil way when He punished Moses for striking the rock rather than speaking to it? A first response might quickly accuse God. The Bible shows God's righteousness in punishing Moses. Moses rebelled against God. He did not trust God's way of communicating with and helping His people. Thus, Moses did not respect God's holy purity. Acting for God, Moses did not show the trusting, respectful obedience of God's chosen leader. He deserved punishment. A leader cannot take God's place and make God's decisions for Him. A leader points people to God and His way. See notes on 16:1–50; Dt 32:51.

20:12 HISTORY, Faith—Faith is not a spiritual or intellectual reality distinct from history. Trusting faith reveals itself in obedient historical acts. To fail to act in our history in accord with God's known will is to demonstrate lack of faith and to deserve God's historical judgment. Moses and Aaron were heroes of faith who endured heart-breaking discipline and judgment for misusing positions of leadership among God's people.

20:16 PRAYER, Mercy of God—See note on Ex 2:23–24.

20:20–21 HISTORY, Politics—God's actions in history do not follow a set pattern which humans can predict. He did not automatically defeat all nations facing Israel. Edom refused to cooperate with Israel, but God did not call Israel to military action.

20:28–29 HUMANITY, Attitudes to Death—All death brings grief. The death of national leaders brings sorrow to entire communities.

learned that Aaron had died,[w] the entire
house of Israel mourned for him[x] thirty
days.

Chapter 21

Arad Destroyed

WHEN the Canaanite king of Arad,[y]
who lived in the Negev,[z] heard
that Israel was coming along the road to
Atharim, he attacked the Israelites and
captured some of them. 2Then Israel
made this vow[a] to the LORD: "If you will
deliver these people into our hands, we
will totally destroy[r][b] their cities." 3The
LORD listened to Israel's plea and gave the
Canaanites[c] over to them. They completely destroyed them[d] and their towns;
so the place was named Hormah.[s][e]

The Bronze Snake

4They traveled from Mount Hor[f] along
the route to the Red Sea,[t][g] to go around
Edom.[h] But the people grew impatient
on the way;[i] 5they spoke against God[j]
and against Moses, and said, "Why have
you brought us up out of Egypt[k] to die in
the desert?[l] There is no bread! There is
no water![m] And we detest this miserable
food!"[n]

6Then the LORD sent venomous
snakes[o] among them; they bit the people
and many Israelites died.[p] 7The people
came to Moses[q] and said, "We sinned[r]
when we spoke against the LORD and
against you. Pray that the LORD[s] will take
the snakes away from us." So Moses
prayed[t] for the people.

8The LORD said to Moses, "Make a
snake and put it up on a pole;[u] anyone
who is bitten can look at it and live." 9So
Moses made a bronze snake[v] and put it
up on a pole. Then when anyone was bitten by a snake and looked at the bronze
snake, he lived.[w]

The Journey to Moab

10The Israelites moved on and camped
at Oboth.[x] 11Then they set out from
Oboth and camped in Iye Abarim, in the
desert that faces Moab[y] toward the sunrise. 12From there they moved on and
camped in the Zered Valley.[z] 13They set
out from there and camped alongside the
Arnon[a], which is in the desert extending
into Amorite territory. The Arnon is the
border of Moab, between Moab and the
Amorites.[b] 14That is why the Book of the
Wars[c] of the LORD says:

"... Waheb in Suphah[u] and the
ravines,
the Arnon 15and[v] the slopes of the
ravines
that lead to the site of Ar[d]
and lie along the border of Moab."

16From there they continued on to Beer,[e]
the well where the LORD said to Moses,
"Gather the people together and I will
give them water."

17Then Israel sang this song:[f]

"Spring up, O well!
Sing about it,
18about the well that the princes dug,
that the nobles of the people sank—
the nobles with scepters and staffs."

Then they went from the desert to Mattanah, 19from Mattanah to Nahaliel, from
Nahaliel to Bamoth, 20and from Bamoth
to the valley in Moab where the top of
Pisgah[g] overlooks the wasteland.

Defeat of Sihon and Og

21Israel sent messengers[h] to say to Sihon[i] king of the Amorites:[j]

22"Let us pass through your country. We will not turn aside into any
field or vineyard, or drink water from

20:29 [w]Dt 32:50 [x]S Ge 27:41; S Lev 10:6; S Dt 34:8
21:1 [y]Nu 33:40; Jos 12:14 [z]S Ge 12:9; Nu 13:17; Dt 1:7; Jdg 1:9,16
21:2 [a]Lev 7:16 [b]ver 3; Ex 22:20; Dt 2:34; Jos 2:10; 8:26; Jer 25:9; 50:21
21:3 [c]S Ge 10:18 [d]S ver 2 [e]S Nu 14:45
21:4 [f]Nu 20:22 [g]Nu 14:25; Dt 2:1; 11:4 [h]S Nu 20:21 [i]Dt 2:8; Jdg 11:18
21:5 [j]Ps 78:19 [k]Nu 11:20 [l]S Ex 14:11; Nu 14:2,3 [m]Nu 20:5 [n]S Nu 11:5
21:6 [o]ver 7; Dt 8:15; 32:33; Job 20:14; Ps 58:4; 140:3; Jer 8:17 [p]1Co 10:9
21:7 [q]Ps 78:34; Hos 5:15 [r]Nu 14:40 [s]Ex 8:8; 1Sa 7:8; Jer 27:18; 37:3; Ac 8:24 [t]S Nu 11:2
21:8 [u]Jn 3:14
21:9 [v]2Ki 18:4 [w]Jn 3:14-15
21:10 [x]Nu 33:43
21:11 [y]S Ge 36:35; Nu 33:44; Dt 34:8; Jer 40:11
21:12 [z]Dt 2:13,14
21:13 [a]Nu 22:36; Dt 2:24; Jos 12:1; Jdg 11:13,18; 2Ki 10:33; Isa 16:2; Jer 48:20 [b]S Ge 10:16
21:14 [c]1Sa 17:47; 18:17; 25:28
21:15 [d]ver 28; Dt 2:9,18; Isa 15:1
21:16 [e]Nu 25:1; 33:49; Jdg 9:21; Isa 15:8
21:17 [f]S Ex 15:1
21:20 [g]Nu 23:14; Dt 3:17,27; 34:1; Jos 12:3; 13:20
21:21 [h]S Ge 32:3 [i]Nu 32:33; Dt 1:4; Jos 2:10; 12:2,4; 13:10; Jdg 11:19-21; 1Ki 4:19; Ne 9:22; Ps 135:11; 136:19; Jer 48:45 [j]S Ex 23:23

[r]*2* The Hebrew term refers to the irrevocable giving over of things or persons to the LORD, often by totally destroying them; also in verse 3. [s]*3* *Hormah* means *destruction.* [t]*4* Hebrew *Yam Suph*; that is, Sea of Reeds [u]*14* The meaning of the Hebrew for this phrase is uncertain. [v]*14,15* Or *"I have been given from Suphah and the ravines / of the Arnon 15to*

21:1–3 HISTORY, Deliverance—God acted to save His people when they obediently dedicated themselves to Him and His will. Each historical action was a separate test of the faithfulness of God's people.

21:1–3 CHRISTIAN ETHICS, War and Peace—Israel, in certain battles, dedicated the enemy "to the ban" (Hebrew *cherem*) or total destruction. The practice illustrated Israel's conviction that victory spoils belonged to God, who provided victory. This practice demonstrated Israel's total obedience to God. The ban was not carried out the same in all battles and was not a rule for battles fought outside Israel's cultural setting. See notes on Ex 14:1—15:18; 23:22–33; Jos 6:1–27.

21:4–9 EVIL AND SUFFERING, Repentance—Suffering can be a call to repent. Repeated complaints from the people brought God's just punishment. Repentance brought God's way for relief. Trust in God's chosen symbol lifted over the people brought healing. Today trust in God's lifted-up Son brings salvation (Jn 3:14–15).

21:4–5 SIN, Rebellion—See note on Ex 14:11–12.

21:7 PRAYER, Confession—The people confessed their sin against the Lord and against Moses. Moses' important prayer resulted not in the removal of the snakes, but in a method of healing from their venom. Compare Jn 3:14–15. In times of trouble, God listens when His people confess their sins together. A representative worship leader may present before God the confession of all the people.

21:8–9 JESUS CHRIST, Foretold—This remarkable experience of Israel is used as a prefiguring of the cross of Jesus and its saving power (Jn 3:14–15).

21:17–18,27–30 PRAYER, Praise—Prayer can be sung to consecrate the results of human labor to God and to remember special events in God's history with His people. Israel sang to God about wells they dug successfully and battles they won under God's leadership.

21:21–35 HISTORY, Politics—See note on 20:20–21. Israel sought peaceful solutions to political relationships but

any well. We will travel along the
king's highway until we have passed
through your territory.[k]"

23But Sihon would not let Israel pass
through his territory.[l] He mustered his
entire army and marched out into the
desert against Israel. When he reached
Jahaz,[m] he fought with Israel.[n] 24Israel,
however, put him to the sword[o] and took
over his land[p] from the Arnon to the Jabbok,[q] but only as far as the Ammonites,[r]
because their border was fortified. 25Isra-
el captured all the cities of the Amorites[s]
and occupied them,[t] including Heshbon[u] and all its surrounding settlements.
26Heshbon was the city of Sihon[v] king of
the Amorites,[w] who had fought against
the former king of Moab[x] and had taken
from him all his land as far as the Arnon.[y]
27That is why the poets say:

"Come to Heshbon and let it be
rebuilt;
let Sihon's city be restored.

28"Fire went out from Heshbon,
a blaze from the city of Sihon.[z]
It consumed[a] Ar[b] of Moab,
the citizens of Arnon's heights.[c]
29Woe to you, O Moab![d]
You are destroyed, O people of
Chemosh![e]
He has given up his sons as fugitives[f]
and his daughters as captives[g]
to Sihon king of the Amorites.

30"But we have overthrown them;
Heshbon is destroyed all the way to
Dibon.[h]
We have demolished them as far as
Nophah,
which extends to Medeba.[i]"

31So Israel settled in the land of the
Amorites.[j]
32After Moses had sent spies[k] to Jazer,[l] the Israelites captured its surrounding settlements and drove out the Amorites who were there. 33Then they turned
and went up along the road toward Bashan[m],[n] and Og king of Bashan and his
whole army marched out to meet them in
battle at Edrei.[o]
34The LORD said to Moses, "Do not be
afraid of him, for I have handed him over
to you, with his whole army and his land.
Do to him what you did to Sihon king of

21:22 [k]S Nu 20:17 **21:23** [l]Nu 20:21 [m]Dt 2:32; Jos 13:18; 21:36; Jdg 11:20; Isa 15:4; Jer 48:21,34 [n]Nu 20:18 **21:24** [o]Dt 2:33; 3:3; 29:7; Ps 135:10-11; Am 2:9 [p]ver 35; Dt 3:4 [q]S Ge 32:22; Nu 32:33; Jdg 11:13,22 [r]S Ge 19:38; Dt 2:37; Jos 13:10 **21:25** [s]Nu 13:29; Jdg 10:11; Am 2:10 [t]Jdg 11:26 [u]ver 30; Nu 32:3; Dt 1:4; 29:7; Jos 9:10; 12:2; Isa 15:4; 16:8; Jer 48:2,34 **21:26** [v]ver 21; Dt 29:7; Ps 135:11 [w]Nu 13:29 [x]ver 11 [y]ver 13 **21:28** [z]Jer 48:45 [a]S Nu 11:1 [b]S ver 15 [c]Nu 22:41; Dt 12:2; Jos 13:17; Isa 15:2; Jer 19:5 **21:29** [d]Nu 24:17; 2Sa 8:2; 1Ch 18:2; Ps 60:8; Isa 25:10; Jer 48:46 [e]Jdg 10:6; 11:24; Ru 1:15; 1Ki 11:7,33; 2Ki 23:13; Jer 48:7,46 [f]Isa 15:5 [g]Isa 16:2 **21:30** [h]Nu 32:3; Jos 13:9,17; Ne 11:25; Isa 15:2; Jer 48:18,22 [i]Jos 13:16; 1Ch 19:7 **21:31** [j]Nu 13:29 **21:32** [k]Jos 2:1; 6:22; 7:2; Jdg 18:2; 2Sa 10:3; 1Ch 19:3 [l]Nu 32:1,3,35; Jos 13:25; 2Sa 24:5; 1Ch 6:81; Isa 16:8; Jer 48:32 **21:33** [m]Nu 32:33; Dt 3:3; 31:4; Jos 2:10; 12:4; 13:30; 1Ki 4:19; Ne 9:22; Ps 135:11; 136:20 [n]Dt 3:4; 32:14; Jos 9:10; 1Ki 4:13 [o]Dt 1:4; 3:1,10; Jos 12:4; 13:12,31; 19:37 **21:34** [p]Dt 3:2 **21:35** [q]Jos 9:10 [r]S ver 24 **22:1** [s]S Nu 21:11 [t]S Nu 13:29; S Jos 2:7 [u]Nu 31:12; 33:48; Dt 32:49; Jos 2:1 **22:2** [v]Nu 23:1-3; Jos 24:9; Jdg 11:25; Mic 6:5; Rev 2:14 **22:3** [w]S Ex 15:15 **22:4** [x]S Ge 19:37 [y]S Ge 25:2 [z]Nu 32:17,18,29 [a]Job 5:25; Ps 72:16 **22:5** [b]ver 7; Nu 24:25; 31:8,16; Dt 23:4; Jos 13:22;

the Amorites, who reigned in Heshbon.[p]"
35So they struck him down, together
with his sons and his whole army, leaving
them no survivors.[q] And they took possession of his land.[r]

Chapter 22

Balak Summons Balaam

THEN the Israelites traveled to the
plains of Moab[s] and camped along
the Jordan[t] across from Jericho.[w][u]
2Now Balak son of Zippor[v] saw all that
Israel had done to the Amorites, 3and
Moab was terrified because there were so
many people. Indeed, Moab was filled
with dread[w] because of the Israelites.
4The Moabites[x] said to the elders of
Midian,[y] "This horde is going to lick up
everything[z] around us, as an ox licks up
the grass of the field.[a]"
So Balak son of Zippor, who was king of
Moab at that time, 5sent messengers to
summon Balaam son of Beor,[b] who was
at Pethor, near the River,[x][c] in his native
land. Balak said:

"A people has come out of Egypt;[d]
they cover the face of the land and
have settled next to me. 6Now come
and put a curse[e] on these people, because they are too powerful for me.
Perhaps then I will be able to defeat
them and drive them out of the country.[f] For I know that those you bless
are blessed, and those you curse are
cursed."

7The elders of Moab and Midian left,
taking with them the fee for divination.[g]
When they came to Balaam, they told him
what Balak had said.
8"Spend the night here," Balaam said
to them, "and I will bring you back the
answer the LORD gives me.[h]" So the Moabite princes stayed with him.
9God came to Balaam[i] and asked,[j]
"Who are these men with you?"
10Balaam said to God, "Balak son of
Zippor, king of Moab, sent me this message: 11'A people that has come out of

Ne 13:2; Mic 6:5; S 2Pe 2:15 [c]S Ge 2:14 [d]S Ex 13:3 **22:6** [e]ver 12,17; Nu 23:7,11,13; 24:9,10 [f]ver 11 **22:7** [g]S Ge 30:27 **22:8** [h]ver 19 **22:9** [i]S Ge 20:3 [j]ver 20; Nu 23:5; 24:4,16

[w]*1* Hebrew *Jordan of Jericho*; possibly an ancient name for the Jordan River [x]*5* That is, the Euphrates

responded with force when threatened by force. In His freedom God led them not to confront some nations such as the Ammonites. God's historical actions are always at His initiative for His purposes.

21:23–35 CHRISTIAN ETHICS, War and Peace—See notes on Ex 14:1—15:18; 23:22–33.

22:1—24:25 HISTORY, Universal—At times God's historical acts were evident far beyond Israel. Balak recognized his powerlessness before Israel's God, so he tried to gain spiritual power against Israel. God's historical acts cannot be commanded by an earthly king, determined by a human prophet, or paid for by materialistic means. God alone determines history for all nations.

22:1—24:25 PRAYER, Will of God—In this long and

Egypt covers the face of the land. Now
come and put a curse on them for me.
Perhaps then I will be able to fight them
and drive them away.' "
12But God said to Balaam, "Do not go
with them. You must not put a curse on
those people, because they are
blessed.[k]"
13The next morning Balaam got up and
said to Balak's princes, "Go back to your
own country, for the LORD has refused to
let me go with you."
14So the Moabite princes returned to
Balak and said, "Balaam refused to come
with us."
15Then Balak sent other princes, more
numerous and more distinguished than
the first. 16They came to Balaam and said:

"This is what Balak son of Zippor
says: Do not let anything keep you
from coming to me, 17because I will
reward you handsomely[l] and do
whatever you say. Come and put a
curse[m] on these people for me."

18But Balaam answered them, "Even if
Balak gave me his palace filled with silver
and gold, I could not do anything great or
small to go beyond the command of the
LORD my God.[n] 19Now stay here tonight
as the others did, and I will find out what
else the LORD will tell me.[o]"
20That night God came to Balaam[p] and
said, "Since these men have come to
summon you, go with them, but do only
what I tell you."[q]

Balaam's Donkey

21Balaam got up in the morning, saddled his donkey and went with the
princes of Moab. 22But God was very angry[r] when he went, and the angel of the
LORD[s] stood in the road to oppose him.
Balaam was riding on his donkey, and his
two servants were with him. 23When the
donkey saw the angel of the LORD standing in the road with a drawn sword[t] in
his hand, she turned off the road into a
field. Balaam beat her[u] to get her back on
the road.
24Then the angel of the LORD stood in a
narrow path between two vineyards,
with walls on both sides. 25When the
donkey saw the angel of the LORD, she
pressed close to the wall, crushing Balaam's foot against it. So he beat her
again.
26Then the angel of the LORD moved on
ahead and stood in a narrow place where
there was no room to turn, either to the
right or to the left. 27When the donkey
saw the angel of the LORD, she lay down
under Balaam, and he was angry[v] and
beat her with his staff. 28Then the LORD
opened the donkey's mouth,[w] and she
said to Balaam, "What have I done to you
to make you beat me these three
times?[x]"
29Balaam answered the donkey, "You
have made a fool of me! If I had a sword
in my hand, I would kill you right
now.[y]"
30The donkey said to Balaam, "Am I
not your own donkey, which you have
always ridden, to this day? Have I been in
the habit of doing this to you?"
"No," he said.
31Then the LORD opened Balaam's
eyes,[z] and he saw the angel of the LORD
standing in the road with his sword
drawn. So he bowed low and fell facedown.
32The angel of the LORD asked him,
"Why have you beaten your donkey these
three times? I have come here to oppose
you because your path is a reckless one
before me.[y] 33The donkey saw me and
turned away from me these three times.
If she had not turned away, I would certainly have killed you by now,[a] but I
would have spared her."
34Balaam said to the angel of the LORD,
"I have sinned.[b] I did not realize you
were standing in the road to oppose me.
Now if you are displeased, I will go
back."
35The angel of the LORD said to Balaam,
"Go with the men, but speak only what I
tell you." So Balaam went with the
princes of Balak.
36When Balak[c] heard that Balaam was
coming, he went out to meet him at the

22:12 [k]S Ge 12:2
22:17 [l]ver 37; Nu 24:11 [m]S ver 6
22:18 [n]ver 38; Nu 23:12,26; 24:13; 1Ki 22:14; 2Ch 18:13; Jer 42:4
22:19 [o]ver 8
22:20 [p]S Ge 20:3 [q]ver 35,38; Nu 23:5,12,16,26; 24:13; 2Ch 18:13
22:22 [r]S Ex 4:14 [s]S Ge 16:7; Jdg 13:3,6,13
22:23 [t]Jos 5:13 [u]ver 25,27
22:27 [v]Nu 11:1; Jas 1:19
22:28 [w]2Pe 2:16 [x]ver 32
22:29 [y]ver 33; Dt 25:4; Pr 12:10; 27:23-27; Mt 15:19
22:31 [z]Ge 21:19
22:33 [a]S ver 29
22:34 [b]Ge 39:9; Nu 14:40; 1Sa 15:24,30; 2Sa 12:13; 24:10; Job 33:27; Ps 51:4
22:36 [c]ver 2

[y]32 The meaning of the Hebrew for this clause is uncertain.

---

curious episode a mysterious diviner, Baalam, discovered that the purposes of God cannot be frustrated (22:38; 23:8) and that sorcery does not influence God (24:1). The King of Moab believed a professional prophet could utter words of blessing and curse which automatically affected the course of historical events. In prayer Baalam learned that blessing and cursing are reserved for God alone and that God can prevent a person from carrying out a mission in the wrong way. Even religious leaders must humble themselves and pray in repentant confession.

22:18–20 REVELATION, Divine Presence—God has control over revelation. Humans cannot expect revelation on command or manipulate its content to fit our plans. A foreign prophet was asked by God to be alert to His revelation and to be careful not to counter God's purposes for Israel. This "seer" unlike many others refused all manner of bribes in order to speak the truth he heard from God. He participated in the plans of the princes of Edom while he waited for God's next disclosure. God rarely reveals all He has in mind for those who follow. All who follow wait and learn as they follow. Note that foreigners knew of prophets and sought their inspired guidance. Balaam apparently was not an Israelite. His name also appears in an Aramaic text found at Deir Allah in the Jordan Valley dating from about 700 BC. God could use foreign prophets to accomplish His will. Compare 2 Pe 2:15–16; Jude 11; Rev 2:14.

Moabite town on the Arnon[d] border, at
the edge of his territory. 37Balak said to
Balaam, "Did I not send you an urgent
summons? Why didn't you come to me?
Am I really not able to reward you?"
38"Well, I have come to you now," Balaam replied. "But can I say just anything? I must speak only what God puts
in my mouth."[e]
39Then Balaam went with Balak to Kiriath Huzoth. 40Balak sacrificed cattle and
sheep,[f] and gave some to Balaam and the
princes who were with him. 41The next
morning Balak took Balaam up to Bamoth
Baal,[g] and from there he saw part of the
people.[h]

Chapter 23

Balaam's First Oracle

BALAAM said, "Build me seven altars
here, and prepare seven bulls and
seven rams[i] for me." 2Balak did as Balaam said, and the two of them offered a
bull and a ram on each altar.[j]
3Then Balaam said to Balak, "Stay here
beside your offering while I go aside. Perhaps the LORD will come to meet with
me.[k] Whatever he reveals to me I will
tell you." Then he went off to a barren
height.
4God met with him,[l] and Balaam said,
"I have prepared seven altars, and on
each altar I have offered a bull and a
ram."
5The LORD put a message in Balaam's
mouth[m n] and said, "Go back to Balak
and give him this message."[o]
6So he went back to him and found
him standing beside his offering, with all
the princes of Moab.[p] 7Then Balaam[q] uttered his oracle:[r]

"Balak brought me from Aram,[s]
the king of Moab from the eastern
mountains.[t]
'Come,' he said, 'curse Jacob for me;
come, denounce Israel.'[u]
8How can I curse
those whom God has not cursed?[v]
How can I denounce
those whom the LORD has not
denounced?[w]
9From the rocky peaks I see them,
from the heights I view them.[x]
I see a people who live apart
and do not consider themselves one
of the nations.[y]
10Who can count the dust of Jacob[z]
or number the fourth part of Israel?
Let me die the death of the
righteous,[a]
and may my end be like theirs![b]"

11Balak said to Balaam, "What have
you done to me? I brought you to curse
my enemies,[c] but you have done nothing
but bless them!"[d]
12He answered, "Must I not speak
what the LORD puts in my mouth?"[e]

Balaam's Second Oracle

13Then Balak said to him, "Come with
me to another place[f] where you can see
them; you will see only a part but not all
of them.[g] And from there, curse them for
me.[h]" 14So he took him to the field of
Zophim on the top of Pisgah,[i] and there
he built seven altars and offered a bull
and a ram on each altar.[j]
15Balaam said to Balak, "Stay here beside your offering while I meet with him
over there."
16The LORD met with Balaam and put a
message in his mouth[k] and said, "Go
back to Balak and give him this message."
17So he went to him and found him
standing beside his offering, with the
princes of Moab.[l] Balak asked him,
"What did the LORD say?"
18Then he uttered his oracle:[m]

"Arise, Balak, and listen;
hear me, son of Zippor.[n]
19God is not a man,[o] that he should
lie,[p]
nor a son of man, that he should
change his mind.[q]
Does he speak and then not act?
Does he promise[r] and not fulfill?
20I have received a command to bless;[s]
he has blessed,[t] and I cannot
change it.[u]

22:36 [d]S Nu 21:13
22:38 [e]Nu 23:5,16, 26
22:40 [f]Nu 23:1,14, 29; Eze 45:23
22:41 [g]S Nu 21:28 [h]Nu 23:13
23:1 [i]S Nu 22:40
23:2 [j]ver 14,30
23:3 [k]ver 15
23:4 [l]ver 16
23:5 [m]S Ex 4:12; Isa 59:21 [n]S Ex 4:15 [o]S Nu 22:20
23:6 [p]ver 17
23:7 [q]Nu 22:5; Jos 24:9 [r]ver 18; Nu 24:3,21; 2Sa 23:1 [s]2Ki 5:1 [t]S Ge 24:10 [u]S Nu 22:6; Ne 13:2
23:8 [v]Nu 22:12 [w]ver 20; Isa 43:13
23:9 [x]Nu 22:41 [y]S Ex 33:16; S Dt 32:8
23:10 [z]S Ge 13:16 [a]Ps 16:3; 116:15; Isa 57:1 [b]Ps 37:37
23:11 [c]S Nu 22:6 [d]Nu 24:10; Jos 24:10; Ne 13:2
23:12 [e]S Nu 22:18, 20
23:13 [f]ver 27 [g]Nu 22:41 [h]S Nu 22:6
23:14 [i]S Nu 21:20; 27:12 [j]S ver 2
23:16 [k]S Ex 4:15; S Nu 22:38
23:17 [l]ver 6
23:18 [m]S ver 7 [n]Nu 22:2
23:19 [o]Job 9:32; Isa 55:9; Hos 11:9 [p]S Nu 11:23 [q]1Sa 15:29; Job 12:13; 36:5; Ps 33:11; 89:34; 102:27; 110:4; Jer 4:28; 7:16; Mal 3:6; Tit 1:2; Heb 6:18; 7:21; Jas 1:17 [r]2Sa 7:25; Ps 119:38
23:20 [s]ver 5,16; Nu 24:1 [t]Ge 22:17; Nu 22:12 [u]S ver 8; S Job 9:12

23:1–12 REVELATION, Word—The prophet here indicated that he would deliver whatever he heard from God. The preceding chapter explains how God had been preparing Balaam to be the carrier of His message. The prophet sought God's message but could only say, "Perhaps the LORD will come to meet with me." One task expected of the prophet was advice for battle. The king expected encouragement for victory. He learned he could not stage a prophetic voice to promote his own strategy. The prophet answered to God, not to human authorities.

23:9–10 ELECTION, Israel—Elders of Moab and Midian sought the services of Balaam, hoping he would curse the traveling Israelites. God advised Balaam to refrain from cursing Israel because they were blessed. No human has power to curse a people chosen and blessed by God. Israel was a people who lived apart from other nations as the elect of God.

23:19 GOD, Nature—The nature of God is steadfast, unchanging, and faithful. What He was yesterday, He will be today and tomorrow. God's constant nature stands in sharp contrast to the changing and unpredictable nature of humans. See Jas 1:17. The constancy of God's nature also stands in sharp contrast to the gods of the ancient world. One could never be sure of the mood of his god. Often the gods were pictured as capricious and changeable; they had to be humored or persuaded or bribed and somehow rendered favorable. However Israel's God was constant, unchanging, and always faithful to Himself and to His people.

21"No misfortune is seen in Jacob,[v]
no misery observed in Israel.[z] [w]
The LORD their God is with them;[x]
the shout of the King[y] is among
them.
22God brought them out of Egypt;[z]
they have the strength of a wild
ox.[a]
23There is no sorcery against Jacob,
no divination[b] against Israel.
It will now be said of Jacob
and of Israel, 'See what God has
done!'
24The people rise like a lioness;[c]
they rouse themselves like a lion[d]
that does not rest till he devours his
prey
and drinks the blood[e] of his
victims."
25Then Balak said to Balaam, "Neither
curse them at all nor bless them at all!"
26Balaam answered, "Did I not tell you
I must do whatever the LORD says?"[f]

Balaam's Third Oracle

27Then Balak said to Balaam, "Come,
let me take you to another place.[g] Perhaps it will please God to let you curse
them for me[h] from there." 28And Balak
took Balaam to the top of Peor,[i] overlooking the wasteland.
29Balaam said, "Build me seven altars
here, and prepare seven bulls and seven
rams for me." 30Balak did as Balaam had
said, and offered a bull and a ram on each
altar.[j]

Chapter 24

NOW when Balaam saw that it pleased
the LORD to bless Israel,[k] he did not
resort to sorcery[l] as at other times, but
turned his face toward the desert.[m]
2When Balaam looked out and saw Israel
encamped tribe by tribe, the Spirit of God
came upon him[n] 3and he uttered his oracle:

"The oracle of Balaam son of Beor,
the oracle of one whose eye sees
clearly,[o]
4the oracle of one who hears the words
of God,[p]
who sees a vision from the
Almighty,[a] [q]
who falls prostrate, and whose eyes
are opened:

5"How beautiful are your tents,[r]
O Jacob,
your dwelling places, O Israel!

6"Like valleys they spread out,
like gardens beside a river,[s]
like aloes[t] planted by the LORD,
like cedars beside the waters.[u]
7Water will flow from their buckets;
their seed will have abundant water.

"Their king will be greater than
Agag;[v]
their kingdom will be exalted.[w]

8"God brought them out of Egypt;
they have the strength of a wild ox.
They devour hostile nations
and break their bones in pieces;[x]
with their arrows they pierce
them.[y]
9Like a lion they crouch and lie down,
like a lioness[z]—who dares to rouse
them?

"May those who bless you be blessed[a]
and those who curse you be
cursed!"[b]

10Then Balak's anger burned[c] against
Balaam. He struck his hands together[d]
and said to him, "I summoned you to
curse my enemies,[e] but you have blessed
them[f] these three times.[g] 11Now leave
at once and go home![h] I said I would
reward you handsomely,[i] but the LORD
has kept you from being rewarded."
12Balaam answered Balak, "Did I not
tell the messengers you sent me,[j]
13'Even if Balak gave me his palace filled
with silver and gold, I could not do anything of my own accord, good or bad, to
go beyond the command of the LORD[k]—
and I must say only what the LORD
says'?[l] 14Now I am going back to my people, but come, let me warn you of what
this people will do to your people in days
to come."[m]

23:21 [v]Ps 32:2,5; 85:2; Ro 4:7-8 [w]Isa 33:24; 40:2; Jer 50:20 [x]S Ge 26:3; Ex 29:45,46; Dt 4:7; Ps 34:17-18; 145:18; Zec 2:10 [y]Dt 32:15; 33:5; Ps 89:15-18; Isa 44:2
23:22 [z]Nu 24:8; Jos 2:10; 9:9 [a]Dt 33:17; Job 39:9; Ps 22:21; 29:6; 92:10; Isa 34:7
23:23 [b]ver 3; S Ge 30:27; Nu 24:1
23:24 [c]Nu 24:9; Eze 19:2; Na 2:11 [d]S Ge 49:9 [e]Isa 49:26
23:26 [f]S Nu 22:18, 20
23:27 [g]ver 13 [h]Nu 24:10
23:28 [i]Nu 25:3,18; 31:16; Dt 3:29; 4:3; Jos 22:17; Ps 106:28; Hos 9:10
23:30 [j]S ver 2
24:1 [k]S Nu 23:20 [l]S Nu 23:23 [m]Nu 23:28
24:2 [n]S Nu 11:25, 26
24:3 [o]ver 15
24:4 [p]S Nu 22:9 [q]S Ge 15:1
24:5 [r]Jer 4:20; 30:18; Mal 2:12
24:6 [s]S Ge 2:10 [t]Ps 45:8; SS 4:14 [u]Job 29:19; Ps 1:3; 104:16; Eze 31:5
24:7 [v]S Ex 17:8-16, 14 [w]Dt 28:1; 2Sa 5:12; 1Ch 14:2; Ps 89:27; 145:11-13
24:8 [x]S Ex 15:6; Jer 50: 17 [y]2Sa 18:14; Ps 45:5
24:9 [z]S Nu 23:24 [a]S Ge 12:2 [b]S Ge 12:3
24:10 [c]S Ex 4:14 [d]Job 27:23; 34:37; La 2:15; Eze 21:14; 22:13; 25:6 [e]S Nu 22:6 [f]S Nu 23:11; S Dt 23:5 [g]ver 3-9; Nu 23:7-10,18-24
24:11 [h]ver 14,25 [i]S Nu 22:17
24:12 [j]Nu 22:18
24:13 [k]S Nu 22:18 [l]S Nu 22:20
24:14 [m]S Ge 49:1; Nu 31:8,16; Mic 6:5

[z]21 Or *He has not looked on Jacob's offenses / or on the wrongs found in Israel.* [a]4 Hebrew *Shaddai*; also in verse 16

24:1–25 REVELATION, Visions—God reveals Himself in the spoken word. Balaam explained the nature and manner of God's revelation to him and proceeded to speak about each of the nations affected. Apparently Balaam was accustomed to using sorcery or divination (23:23) to obtain the divine will. This would include casting lots or examining livers, hearts, or other interior parts of sacrificial animals. God did not allow such means to gain His will. God gave His prophets clear visions. They came only as God willed and could not be bought for a price.

24:2 HOLY SPIRIT, Leaders—God's Spirit works with imperfect people to accomplish His purpose. Balaam had used the tools of pagan prophets to ply his trade (23:23; 24:1), reading signs in the skies, dreams, or livers and other parts of sacrificed animals. God gave even this covetous man (2 Pe 2:15; Jude v 11; Rev 2:14) the Spirit for the time of crisis. God's Spirit is not bound by human rules to persons of human choosing. God's Spirit remains free to choose persons to proclaim His Word. See Php 1:15–18.

24:7 ELECTION, God's Promise—An attempt to curse Israel only brought a renewal of God's promise to them. Election is based on God's promise, not on human power.

Balaam's Fourth Oracle

15 Then he uttered his oracle:

"The oracle of Balaam son of Beor,
the oracle of one whose eye sees clearly,
16 the oracle of one who hears the words[n] of God,
who has knowledge from the Most High,[o]
who sees a vision from the Almighty,
who falls prostrate, and whose eyes are opened:

17 "I see him, but not now;
I behold him, but not near.[p]
A star will come out of Jacob;[q]
a scepter will rise out of Israel.[r]
He will crush the foreheads of Moab,[s]
the skulls[b][t] of[c] all the sons of Sheth.[d]
18 Edom[u] will be conquered;
Seir,[v] his enemy, will be conquered,[w]
but Israel[x] will grow strong.
19 A ruler will come out of Jacob[y]
and destroy the survivors of the city."

Balaam's Final Oracles

20 Then Balaam saw Amalek[z] and uttered his oracle:

"Amalek was first among the nations,
but he will come to ruin at last."[a]

21 Then he saw the Kenites[b] and uttered his oracle:

"Your dwelling place is secure,[c]
your nest is set in a rock;
22 yet you Kenites will be destroyed
when Asshur[d] takes you captive."

23 Then he uttered his oracle:

"Ah, who can live when God does this?[e]
24 Ships will come from the shores of Kittim;[e]
they will subdue Asshur[f] and Eber,[g]
but they too will come to ruin."[h]

24:16 [n]S Nu 22:9 [o]Ge 14:18; Isa 14:14 **24:17** [p]Rev 1:7 [q]Mt 2:2 [r]S Ge 49:10 [s]S Ge 19:37; S Nu 21:29; S Dt 23:6; Isa 15:1-16:14 [t]Jer 48:45 **24:18** [u]2Sa 8:12; 1Ch 18:11; Ps 60:8; Isa 11:14; Am 9:12 [v]S Ge 14:6; Dt 1:44; Jos 12:7; 15:10; Jdg 5:4 [w]Ob 1:2 [x]S Ge 9:25 **24:19** [y]S Ge 49:10; Mic 5:2 **24:20** [z]S Ge 14:7; S Ex 17:14 [a]Dt 25:19; 1Sa 15:20; 30:17-20; 2Sa 8:12; 1Ch 18:11 **24:21** [b]S Ge 15:19 [c]Ps 37:27; Pr 1:33; Isa 32:18; Eze 34:27 **24:22** [d]S Ge 10:22 **24:24** [e]S Ge 10:4 [f]ver 22 [g]S Ge 10:21 [h]ver 20 **24:25** [i]S Nu 22:5 **25:1** [j]S Nu 21:16; Jos 2:1; Isa 66:11; Joel 3:18; Mic 6:5 [k]Jer 5:7; 7:9; 9:2; 1Co 10:8; Rev 2:14 [l]S Ge 19:37 [m]Nu 31:16 **25:2** [n]S Ex 32:6 [o]Ex 20:5; Dt 32:38; 1Co 10:20 **25:3** [p]Dt 4:19; Jdg 2:19; 1Ki 9:9; Jer 1:16; 44:3 [q]S Nu 23:28 **25:4** [r]Nu 7:2; 13:3 [s]2Sa 21:6 [t]Dt 4:3 [u]Ex 32:12; Dt 13:17; Jos 7:26; 2Ki 23:26; 2Ch 28:11; 29:10; 30:8; Ezr 10:14; Jer 44:3 **25:5** [v]S Ex 32:27 [w]Hos 9:10 **25:6** [x]S Ge 25:2 [y]S Nu 14:1; Jdg 2:4; Ru 1:9; 1Sa 11:4; 2Sa 15:30; Ezr 10:1; Ps 126:6; Jer 41:6 **25:7** [z]S Ex 6:25; Jos 22:13; Jdg 20:28 [a]Jdg 5:8; 1Sa 13:19, 22; 1Ki 18:28; Ps 35:3; 46:9; Joel 3:10; Mic 4:3 **25:8** [b]Ps 106:30 **25:9** [c]S Nu 14:37; 1Co 10:8 [d]Nu 31:16 **25:11** [e]Ps 106:30 [f]Ex 20:5; Dt 32:16, 21; Ps 78:58 **25:12** [g]Isa 11:9; 54:10; Eze 34:25; 37:26; Mal 2:4,5 **25:13** [h]S Ex 29:9

25 Then Balaam[i] got up and returned
home and Balak went his own way.

Chapter 25

Moab Seduces Israel

WHILE Israel was staying in Shittim,[j]
the men began to indulge in sexual
immorality[k] with Moabite[l] women,[m]
2 who invited them to the sacrifices[n] to
their gods.[o] The people ate and bowed
down before these gods. 3 So Israel joined
in worshiping[p] the Baal of Peor.[q] And
the LORD's anger burned against them.
4 The LORD said to Moses, "Take all the
leaders[r] of these people, kill them and
expose[s] them in broad daylight before
the LORD,[t] so that the LORD's fierce anger[u]
may turn away from Israel."
5 So Moses said to Israel's judges, "Each
of you must put to death[v] those of your
men who have joined in worshiping the
Baal of Peor."[w]
6 Then an Israelite man brought to his
family a Midianite[x] woman right before
the eyes of Moses and the whole assembly
of Israel while they were weeping[y] at
the entrance to the Tent of Meeting.
7 When Phinehas[z] son of Eleazar, the son
of Aaron, the priest, saw this, he left the
assembly, took a spear[a] in his hand 8 and
followed the Israelite into the tent. He
drove the spear through both of them—
through the Israelite and into the woman's
body. Then the plague against the
Israelites was stopped;[b] 9 but those who
died in the plague[c] numbered 24,000.[d]
10 The LORD said to Moses, 11 "Phinehas
son of Eleazar, the son of Aaron, the
priest, has turned my anger away from
the Israelites;[e] for he was as zealous as I
am for my honor[f] among them, so that in
my zeal I did not put an end to them.
12 Therefore tell him I am making my covenant
of peace[g] with him. 13 He and his
descendants will have a covenant of a
lasting priesthood,[h] because he was zeal-

[b] *17* Samaritan Pentateuch (see also Jer. 48:45); the meaning of the word in the Masoretic Text is uncertain. [c] *17* Or possibly *Moab, / batter* [d] *17* Or *all the noisy boasters* [e] *23* Masoretic Text; with a different word division of the Hebrew *A people will gather from the north.*

24:17–19 JESUS CHRIST, Foretold—The first part of v 17 foretells joyful good news for Jacob and Israel. Jesus is the ultimate Good News for all the world. This messianic promise was first a historical prediction of the downfall of a wicked nation (Moab) and their allies effected by David (2 Sa 8:2). The final ruler rising out of Israel was Jesus.

25:1–3 SIN, Punishment—Israel's sexual sin probably involved participation in immoral religious fertility rites dedicated to the Moabite god. Because of the serious nature of their sin, God intervened and punished them. God can and does intervene in human life to punish sin. See note on 14:23.

25:1–18 HISTORY, Moral—A moral foundation underlies history. At times immorality brings immediate historical judgment. Such judgment may be in the form of sickness or death. God is free to exercise judgment as He chooses. His judgment is not always as immediate as in this case.

25:10–13 THE CHURCH, Covenant People—Obedience results in more intimate fellowship with God. God established His covenant of peace with Phinehas because he desired to serve the Lord. God works through those who allow themselves to be used in His service.

ous[i] for the honor[j] of his God and made
atonement[k] for the Israelites."[l]
14The name of the Israelite who was
killed with the Midianite woman[m] was
Zimri son of Salu, the leader of a Simeon-
ite family.[n] 15And the name of the Midianite woman who was put to death was
Cozbi[o] daughter of Zur, a tribal chief of a
Midianite family.[p]
16The LORD said to Moses,[q] 17"Treat
the Midianites[r] as enemies[s] and kill
them,[t] 18because they treated you as enemies when they deceived you in the affair of Peor[u] and their sister Cozbi, the
daughter of a Midianite leader, the woman who was killed when the plague came
as a result of Peor."

Chapter 26

The Second Census

AFTER the plague[v] the LORD said to
Moses and Eleazar son of Aaron, the
priest, 2"Take a census[w] of the whole Israelite community by families—all those
twenty years old or more who are able to
serve in the army[x] of Israel." 3So on the
plains of Moab[y] by the Jordan across
from Jericho,[f][z] Moses and Eleazar the
priest spoke with them and said, 4"Take a
census of the men twenty years old or
more, as the LORD commanded Moses."

These were the Israelites who came
out of Egypt:[a]
5The descendants of Reuben,[b] the firstborn son of Israel, were:
through Hanoch,[c] the Hanochite clan;
through Pallu,[d] the Palluite clan;
6through Hezron,[e] the Hezronite clan;
through Carmi,[f] the Carmite clan.
7These were the clans of Reuben; those
numbered were 43,730.
8The son of Pallu was Eliab, 9and the
sons of Eliab[g] were Nemuel, Dathan and
Abiram. The same Dathan and Abiram
were the community[h] officials who rebelled against Moses and Aaron and were
among Korah's followers when they rebelled against the LORD.[i] 10The earth
opened its mouth and swallowed them[j]
along with Korah, whose followers died
when the fire devoured the 250 men.[k]
And they served as a warning sign.[l]
11The line of Korah,[m] however, did not
die out.[n]

12The descendants of Simeon by their
clans were:
through Nemuel,[o] the Nemuelite clan;
through Jamin,[p] the Jaminite clan;
through Jakin, the Jakinite clan;
13through Zerah,[q] the Zerahite clan;
through Shaul, the Shaulite clan.
14These were the clans of Simeon;[r] there
were 22,200 men.[s]
15The descendants of Gad by their clans
were:
through Zephon,[t] the Zephonite clan;
through Haggi, the Haggite clan;
through Shuni, the Shunite clan;
16through Ozni, the Oznite clan;
through Eri, the Erite clan;
17through Arodi,[g] the Arodite clan;
through Areli, the Arelite clan.
18These were the clans of Gad;[u] those
numbered were 40,500.
19Er[v] and Onan[w] were sons of Judah, but
they died[x] in Canaan.
20The descendants of Judah by their clans
were:
through Shelah,[y] the Shelanite clan;
through Perez,[z] the Perezite clan;
through Zerah, the Zerahite clan.[a]
21The descendants of Perez[b] were:
through Hezron,[c] the Hezronite clan;
through Hamul, the Hamulite clan.
22These were the clans of Judah;[d] those
numbered were 76,500.
23The descendants of Issachar by their
clans were:
through Tola,[e] the Tolaite clan;
through Puah, the Puite[h] clan;
24through Jashub,[f] the Jashubite clan;
through Shimron, the Shimronite clan.
25These were the clans of Issachar;[g]
those numbered were 64,300.
26The descendants of Zebulun[h] by their
clans were:
through Sered, the Seredite clan;
through Elon, the Elonite clan;
through Jahleel, the Jahleelite clan.
27These were the clans of Zebulun;[i]
those numbered were 60,500.

25:13 [i]1Ki 19:10; 2Ki 10:16 [j]ver 11 [k]S Ex 29:36; S Ro 3:25 [l]Ps 106:31; Jer 33:18
25:14 [m]ver 6 [n]S Nu 1:6
25:15 [o]ver 18 [p]Nu 31:8; Jos 13:21; Hab 3:7
25:16 [q]Nu 31:7
25:17 [r]Nu 31:1-3 [s]Ex 23:22; Jdg 2:16-18; Ne 9:27; Ps 8:2; 21:8; 74:23 [t]Dt 21:1; 1Sa 17:9, 35; 2Ki 9:27; 10:25
25:18 [u]S Nu 23:28
26:1 [v]S Nu 14:37; 25:8
26:2 [w]Ex 30:11-16 [x]S Nu 1:3
26:3 [y]ver 63; Nu 33:48; Jos 13:32 [z]Nu 22:1
26:4 [a]S Ex 6:14; S 13:3
26:5 [b]Nu 1:20 [c]S Ge 46:9 [d]1Ch 5:3
26:6 [e]1Ch 5:3 [f]Ge 46:9
26:9 [g]Nu 16:1 [h]Nu 1:16 [i]S Nu 16:2
26:10 [j]S Ex 15:12 [k]S Nu 16:35 [l]S Ex 3:12; S Nu 16:38
26:11 [m]Ex 6:24 [n]Nu 16:33; Dt 5:9; 24:16; 2Ki 14:6; 2Ch 25:4; Eze 18:20
26:12 [o]S Ge 46:10 [p]1Ch 4:24
26:13 [q]S Ge 46:10
26:14 [r]S Ge 46:10 [s]Nu 1:23
26:15 [t]Ge 46:16
26:18 [u]S Ge 30:11; S Nu 1:25; S Jos 13:24-28
26:19 [v]S Ge 38:3 [w]S Ge 38:4 [x]Ge 38:7
26:20 [y]S Ge 38:5 [z]S Ge 38:29 [a]Jos 7:17
26:21 [b]S Ge 38:29 [c]Ru 4:19; 1Ch 2:9
26:22 [d]Nu 1:27
26:23 [e]S Ge 46:13
26:24 [f]Ge 46:13
26:25 [g]S Ge 30:18
26:26 [h]Nu 1:30
26:27 [i]S Ge 30:20

[f]3 Hebrew *Jordan of Jericho*; possibly an ancient name for the Jordan River; also in verse 63 [g]17 Samaritan Pentateuch and Syriac (see also Gen. 46:16); Masoretic Text *Arod* [h]23 Samaritan Pentateuch, Septuagint, Vulgate and Syriac (see also 1 Chron. 7:1); Masoretic Text *through Puvah, the Punite*

26:1–65 HISTORY, Promise—See note on 1:1–46. The second census prepared Israel's new generation for action in conquering the land, showed the promise of judgment against an unbelieving generation was fulfilled (14:26–38), and established the framework for distributing the land. The promise of inheritance was fulfilled by Joshua (Jos 13—19). Even an historical act as simple as a census can play a role in the fulfillment of God's promises.

28 The descendants of Joseph[j] by their
clans through Manasseh and Ephraim[k]
were:

29 The descendants of Manasseh:[l]
through Makir,[m] the Makirite clan
(Makir was the father of Gilead[n]);
through Gilead, the Gileadite clan.
30 These were the descendants of Gilead:[o]
through Iezer,[p] the Iezerite clan;
through Helek, the Helekite clan;
31 through Asriel, the Asrielite clan;
through Shechem, the Shechem-
ite clan;
32 through Shemida, the Shemidaite
clan;
through Hepher, the Hepherite
clan.
33 (Zelophehad[q] son of Hepher had
no sons;[r] he had only daughters,
whose names were Mahlah,
Noah, Hoglah, Milcah and Tirzah.)[s]
34 These were the clans of Manasseh;
those numbered were 52,700.[t]

35 These were the descendants of Ephraim[u] by their clans:
through Shuthelah, the Shuthelahite
clan;
through Beker, the Bekerite clan;
through Tahan, the Tahanite clan.
36 These were the descendants of Shuthelah:
through Eran, the Eranite clan.
37 These were the clans of Ephraim;[v]
those numbered were 32,500.

These were the descendants of Joseph by
their clans.

38 The descendants of Benjamin[w] by their
clans were:
through Bela, the Belaite clan;
through Ashbel, the Ashbelite clan;
through Ahiram, the Ahiramite clan;
39 through Shupham,[i] the Shuphamite
clan;
through Hupham, the Huphamite
clan.
40 The descendants of Bela through
Ard[x] and Naaman were:
through Ard,[j] the Ardite clan;
through Naaman, the Naamite
clan.
41 These were the clans of Benjamin;[y]
those numbered were 45,600.

42 These were the descendants of Dan[z] by
their clans:[a]
through Shuham,[b] the Shuhamite
clan.
These were the clans of Dan: 43 All of
them were Shuhamite clans; and those
numbered were 64,400.

44 The descendants of Asher[c] by their
clans were:
through Imnah, the Imnite clan;
through Ishvi, the Ishvite clan;
through Beriah, the Beriite clan;
45 and through the descendants of Beriah:
through Heber, the Heberite clan;
through Malkiel, the Malkielite
clan.
46 (Asher had a daughter named Serah.)
47 These were the clans of Asher;[d] those
numbered were 53,400.

48 The descendants of Naphtali[e] by their
clans were:
through Jahzeel, the Jahzeelite clan;
through Guni, the Gunite clan;
49 through Jezer, the Jezerite clan;
through Shillem, the Shillemite clan.
50 These were the clans of Naphtali;[f]
those numbered were 45,400.[g]

51 The total number of the men of Israel
was 601,730.[h]

52 The LORD said to Moses, 53 "The land
is to be allotted to them as an inheritance
based on the number of names.[i] 54 To a
larger group give a larger inheritance, and
to a smaller group a smaller one; each is
to receive its inheritance according to the
number[j] of those listed.[k] 55 Be sure that
the land is distributed by lot.[l] What each
group inherits will be according to the
names for its ancestral tribe. 56 Each inheritance is to be distributed by lot
among the larger and smaller groups."

57 These were the Levites[m] who were
counted by their clans:
through Gershon, the Gershonite
clan;
through Kohath, the Kohathite clan;
through Merari, the Merarite clan.
58 These also were Levite clans:
the Libnite clan,
the Hebronite clan,
the Mahlite clan,
the Mushite clan,
the Korahite clan.

i39 A few manuscripts of the Masoretic Text, Samaritan Pentateuch, Vulgate and Syriac (see also Septuagint); most manuscripts of the Masoretic Text *Shephupham* j40 Samaritan Pentateuch and Vulgate (see also Septuagint); Masoretic Text does not have *through Ard.*

26:28 [j]Nu 1:32; 36:1 [k]S Ge 41:52
26:29 [l]Nu 1:34 [m]S Ge 50:23 [n]Jdg 11:1
26:30 [o]Nu 27:1; 36:1; 1Ch 7:14,17 [p]Jos 17:2; Jdg 6:11; 8:2
26:33 [q]Nu 27:1; 36:2; Jos 17:3; 1Ch 7:15 [r]Nu 27:3 [s]Nu 36:11
26:34 [t]Nu 1:35
26:35 [u]Nu 1:32
26:37 [v]S Nu 1:33
26:38 [w]Ge 46:21; Nu 1:36; 1Ch 8:40
26:40 [x]S Ge 46:21
26:41 [y]Nu 1:37
26:42 [z]Nu 1:38 [a]Jdg 18:19 [b]Ge 46:23
26:44 [c]S Nu 1:40
26:47 [d]Nu 1:41
26:48 [e]S Ge 30:8
26:50 [f]Nu 1:43 [g]Nu 1:42
26:51 [h]S Ex 12:37
26:53 [i]ver 55; Jos 11:23; 14:1; Eze 45:8
26:54 [j]Nu 33:54 [k]Nu 35:8
26:55 [l]S Lev 16:8
26:57 [m]S Ge 46:11

26:52–56 ELECTION, Divine Justice—"To a larger group give a larger inheritance; and to a smaller group, a smaller one" was God's way of providing justice for those whom He elected to receive the Land of Promise. Humans may not see it, but justice underlies all God does in establishing His elect people.

(Kohath was the forefather of Amram;[n] 59 the name of Amram's wife
was Jochebed,[o] a descendant of Levi,
who was born to the Levites[k] in
Egypt. To Amram she bore Aaron,
Moses[p] and their sister[q] Miriam.[r]
60 Aaron was the father of Nadab and
Abihu, Eleazar and Ithamar.[s] 61 But
Nadab and Abihu[t] died when they
made an offering before the LORD
with unauthorized fire.)[u]

62 All the male Levites a month old or
more numbered 23,000.[v] They were not
counted[w] along with the other Israelites
because they received no inheritance[x]
among them.[y]

63 These are the ones counted[z] by Moses and Eleazar the priest when they
counted the Israelites on the plains of
Moab[a] by the Jordan across from Jericho.[b] 64 Not one of them was among
those counted[c] by Moses and Aaron[d]
the priest when they counted the Israelites in the Desert of Sinai. 65 For the LORD
had told those Israelites they would surely die in the desert,[e] and not one of them
was left except Caleb[f] son of Jephunneh
and Joshua son of Nun.[g]

Chapter 27

Zelophehad's Daughters

27:1–11pp — Nu 36:1–12

THE daughters of Zelophehad[h] son of
Hepher,[i] the son of Gilead,[j] the son
of Makir,[k] the son of Manasseh, belonged to the clans of Manasseh son of
Joseph. The names of the daughters were
Mahlah, Noah, Hoglah, Milcah and Tirzah. They approached 2 the entrance to
the Tent of Meeting[l] and stood before
Moses,[m] Eleazar the priest, the leaders[n]
and the whole assembly, and said, 3 "Our
father died in the desert.[o] He was not
among Korah's followers, who banded together against the LORD,[p] but he died for
his own sin and left no sons.[q] 4 Why
should our father's name disappear from
his clan because he had no son? Give us
property among our father's relatives."
5 So Moses brought their case[r] before
the LORD[s] 6 and the LORD said to him,
7 "What Zelophehad's daughters are saying is right. You must certainly give them
property as an inheritance[t] among their
father's relatives and turn their father's
inheritance over to them.[u]
8 "Say to the Israelites, 'If a man dies
and leaves no son, turn his inheritance
over to his daughter. 9 If he has no daughter, give his inheritance to his brothers.
10 If he has no brothers, give his inheritance to his father's brothers. 11 If his father had no brothers, give his inheritance
to the nearest relative in his clan, that he
may possess it. This is to be a legal requirement[v] for the Israelites, as the LORD
commanded Moses.' "

Joshua to Succeed Moses

12 Then the LORD said to Moses, "Go up
this mountain[w] in the Abarim range[x]
and see the land[y] I have given the Israelites.[z] 13 After you have seen it, you too
will be gathered to your people,[a] as your
brother Aaron[b] was, 14 for when the community rebelled at the waters in the
Desert of Zin,[c] both of you disobeyed my
command to honor me as holy[d] before
their eyes." (These were the waters of
Meribah[e] Kadesh, in the Desert of Zin.)
15 Moses said to the LORD, 16 "May the
LORD, the God of the spirits of all man-

[k]59 Or *Jochebed, a daughter of Levi, who was born to Levi*

26:58 [n]Ex 6:20
26:59 [o]S Ex 2:1 [p]S Ex 6:20 [q]S Ex 2:4 [r]S Ex 15:20
26:60 [s]Ex 6:23
26:61 [t]S Lev 10:1-2 [u]Nu 3:4
26:62 [v]Nu 3:39 [w]Nu 1:47 [x]S Nu 18:23 [y]S Nu 2:33
26:63 [z]S Nu 1:19 [a]S ver 3 [b]Nu 22:1
26:64 [c]S Nu 14:29 [d]Nu 1:44
26:65 [e]Nu 14:28; 1Co 10:5 [f]Nu 13:6 [g]S Nu 11:28
27:1 [h]S Nu 26:33 [i]Jos 17:2,3 [j]S Nu 26:30 [k]S Ge 50:23; 1Ch 2:21
27:2 [l]Ex 40:2,17 [m]S Nu 9:6 [n]Nu 1:16; 31:13; 32:2; 36:1
27:3 [o]Nu 26:65 [p]Nu 16:2 [q]Nu 26:33
27:5 [r]S Ge 25:22; S Ex 18:19 [s]S Nu 9:8
27:7 [t]Job 42:15 [u]ver 8; Jos 17:4
27:11 [v]Nu 35:29
27:12 [w]Nu 23:14 [x]Nu 33:47; Jer 22:20 [y]Dt 3:23-27; 32:48-52 [z]S Lev 14:34
27:13 [a]Nu 20:12; 31:2; Dt 4:22; 31:14; 32:50; 1Ki 2:1 [b]Nu 20:28
27:14 [c]S Nu 20:1, 2-5 [d]S Nu 20:12 [e]S Ex 17:7

26:65 GOD, Faithfulness—God was true to His word. All of the faithless had perished, and a new generation had arisen. They would have the blessings and privileges of going into the Promised Land.

27:1–11 DISCIPLESHIP, Spiritual Leaders—Exceptional cases test spiritual leadership. Moses sought, found, and communicated God's will in a case without written law or precedence. It is significant that a daughter could receive the inheritance if the father had no son. God used Moses to set forth a legal requirement for the Israelites. God may use chosen leaders in establishing legal requirements through the processes of government today. Leaders who influence legal decisions must constantly seek God's will in making decisions. Spiritual leaders must be willing to go against cultural tendencies when God leads them. God's people have a right to expect decisive actions from spiritual leaders in difficult situations.

27:1–11 CHRISTIAN ETHICS, Justice—Society must carefully observe individual rights. Individuals should have the freedom to press for what they justly deserve within society. We cannot categorize people by race, color, bank account, sex, or cultural background and, thus, eliminate some from sharing legal rights. The daughters of Zelophehad gained inheritance rights normally reserved for males by persevering through Israel's legal system. Their victory set up a legal precedent for all future generations.

27:3–4 HUMANITY, Family Relationships—In Old Testament times the family line was thought to be transmitted only through sons. Justice suggests that surviving daughters of a sonless family should not be penalized for their father's sin and death.

27:3 SIN, Responsibility—Zelophehad had not participated in the infamous rebellion of Korah and his followers (ch 16). Innocence in one case did not release him from responsibility. He died as a result of his own sins. All deserve to die because of each individual's sin. Sin is shameful rebellion against God's holiness. He will punish whoever or whatever is responsible.

27:5–7 PRAYER, Petition—Prayer can help God's people make decisions. Moses took the complaint before God on behalf of His people. God showed the complaint was justified.

27:14 SIN, Unbelief—See note on 20:11–12.

27:15–16 GOD, One God—God is not just the tribal deity of the Israelites but the universal Lord over all mankind. It would be a long while before the Israelites recognized the larger implications of this. They had yet to understand that Israel was called to be a kingdom of priests to the nations and to be a channel of God's blessings to all of humanity. Somehow Israel always thought of herself as something special in the eyes of God and that God was uniquely her own. Even Christians,

kind,[f] appoint a man over this community 17to go out and come in before them,
one who will lead them out and bring
them in, so the LORD's people will not be
like sheep without a shepherd."[g]
18So the LORD said to Moses, "Take
Joshua son of Nun, a man in whom is the
spirit,[1][h] and lay your hand on him.[i]
19Have him stand before Eleazar the
priest and the entire assembly and commission him[j] in their presence.[k] 20Give
him some of your authority so the whole
Israelite community will obey him.[l] 21He
is to stand before Eleazar the priest, who
will obtain decisions for him by inquiring[m] of the Urim[n] before the LORD. At
his command he and the entire community of the Israelites will go out, and at his
command they will come in."
22Moses did as the LORD commanded
him. He took Joshua and had him stand
before Eleazar the priest and the whole
assembly. 23Then he laid his hands on
him and commissioned him,[o] as the
LORD instructed through Moses.

Chapter 28

Daily Offerings

THE LORD said to Moses, 2"Give this
command to the Israelites and say to
them: 'See that you present to me at the
appointed time[p] the food[q] for my offerings made by fire, as an aroma pleasing to
me.'[r] 3Say to them: 'This is the offering
made by fire that you are to present to the
LORD: two lambs a year old without defect,[s] as a regular burnt offering each
day.[t] 4Prepare one lamb in the morning
and the other at twilight,[u] 5together with
a grain offering[v] of a tenth of an ephah[m]
of fine flour[w] mixed with a quarter of a
hin[n] of oil[x] from pressed olives. 6This is
the regular burnt offering[y] instituted at

27:16 [f]S Nu 16:22; S Job 21:20
27:17 [g]1Ki 22:17; 2Ch 18:16; Eze 34:5; Zec 10:2; S Mt 9:36
27:18 [h]S Ge 41:38; Nu 11:25-29 [i]ver 23; Dt 34:9; Ac 6:6
27:19 [j]ver 23; Dt 3:28; 31:14,23 [k]Dt 31:7
27:20 [l]Jos 1:16,17
27:21 [m]S Ge 25:22; Jos 9:14; Ps 106:13; Isa 8:19; Hag 1:13; Mal 2:7; 3:1 [n]S Ex 28:30
27:23 [o]S ver 19
28:2 [p]Lev 23:1-44 [q]S Lev 3:11 [r]Lev 1:9
28:3 [s]S Ex 12:5 [t]Ex 29:38; Am 4:4
28:4 [u]S Ex 29:39
28:5 [v]Nu 29:6 [w]Lev 6:20 [x]S Lev 2:1
28:6 [y]Lev 1:3 [z]Ex 19:3 [a]S Lev 1:9
28:7 [b]Nu 6:15 [c]S Lev 10:9; S 23:13 [d]S Lev 3:7; Nu 3:28
28:8 [e]S Ex 29:39 [f]S Lev 3:7 [g]ver 2; Lev 1:9
28:9 [h]S Ex 20:10; Mt 12:5 [i]ver 3 [j]S Lev 23:13 [k]ver 5
28:10 [l]S Lev 23:38 [m]ver 3
28:11 [n]S Nu 10:10 [o]S Nu 7:15 [p]S Lev 5:15 [q]Lev 1:3
28:12 [r]S Nu 15:6; S 29:3 [s]Nu 15:9 [t]ver 20
28:13 [u]S Lev 6:14 [v]ver 21 [w]S Nu 15:3

Mount Sinai[z] as a pleasing aroma, an offering made to the LORD by fire.[a] 7The
accompanying drink offering[b] is to be a
quarter of a hin of fermented drink[c] with
each lamb. Pour out the drink offering to
the LORD at the sanctuary.[d] 8Prepare the
second lamb at twilight,[e] along with the
same kind of grain offering and drink offering that you prepare in the morning.[f]
This is an offering made by fire, an aroma
pleasing to the LORD.[g]

Sabbath Offerings

9" 'On the Sabbath[h] day, make an offering of two lambs a year old without
defect,[i] together with its drink offering
and a grain offering of two-tenths of an
ephah[o][j] of fine flour mixed with oil.[k]
10This is the burnt offering for every Sabbath,[l] in addition to the regular burnt
offering[m] and its drink offering.

Monthly Offerings

11" 'On the first of every month,[n]
present to the LORD a burnt offering of
two young bulls,[o] one ram[p] and seven
male lambs a year old, all without defect.[q] 12With each bull there is to be a
grain offering[r] of three-tenths of an
ephah[p][s] of fine flour mixed with oil;
with the ram, a grain offering of two-
tenths[t] of an ephah of fine flour mixed
with oil; 13and with each lamb, a grain
offering[u] of a tenth[v] of an ephah of fine
flour mixed with oil. This is for a burnt
offering,[w] a pleasing aroma, an offering

[1]*18* Or *Spirit* [m]*5* That is, probably about 2 quarts (about 2 liters); also in verses 13, 21 and 29
[n]*5* That is, probably about 1 quart (about 1 liter); also in verses 7 and 14 [o]*9* That is, probably about 4 quarts (about 4.5 liters); also in verses 12, 20 and 28
[p]*12* That is, probably about 6 quarts (about 6.5 liters); also in verses 20 and 28

---

who at least profess that God is the God of all people and that our mission is to all the peoples of the earth, too easily think of ourselves as somehow special and forget that God is just as interested in the rest of the world. One's sinful and selfish heart only gradually comes to understand the full meaning of God's universal lordship. Truths are embedded in Scripture that only the passage of time finally will make clear, and then we will wonder how we ever missed them.

27:15–21 HOLY SPIRIT, Leaders—God's Spirit often divides leadership gifts among His people. God gave His Spirit to Joshua to equip him to lead His people. The military commander's basic task was defined as shepherd, caring for the needs of the people. Moses laid his hand on Joshua, not to give the Spirit to Joshua but to symbolize for the people that Joshua would be their new leader. The association of laying on of hands with the Spirit continued in the early church (Ac 8:17). Joshua's assignment was clearly distinguished from that of Eleazar the priest. Eleazar was to seek God's will by the use of *Urim. Joshua was to carry out God's will. His gift was leadership, not prophecy.* Leadership is a gift of the Spirit of God, as are service (Ex 35:30–33) and prophecy (Nu 11:16–30).

27:15–19 PRAYER, Holy Spirit Guides—God selects leaders for His people in response to their prayers.

27:18–21 REVELATION, Oracles—Moses was the unique recipient of revelation. His successor had only "some" of his authority. Joshua had to turn to Eleazar, the priest, to gain God's decisions. Urim and Thummim (Ex 28:30) were two stones used to determine yes and no answers (1 Sa 14:40–42; 28:6). Revelation thus came through a consecrated priest's use of material objects as well as through dreams and prophetic words. These material objects were not magical things with mysterious power of their own or controlled by human sleight of hand. They were objects chosen and controlled by God to reveal His personal will in specific historical situations. See note on Jos 3:7–17.

27:18–23 CHURCH LEADERS, Ordination—Moses obeyed God's command and ordained Joshua to be his successor. By laying hands on him, Moses conferred his honor and authority on Joshua who was filled already with the Spirit. Jewish and Christian practices of ordination have been influenced by this account.

made to the LORD[x] by fire. 14With each
bull there is to be a drink offering[y] of half
a hin[q] of wine; with the ram, a third of a
hin[r]; and with each lamb, a quarter of a
hin. This is the monthly burnt offering to
be made at each new moon[z] during the
year. 15Besides the regular burnt offering[a] with its drink offering, one male
goat[b] is to be presented to the LORD as a
sin offering.[c]

The Passover

28:16–25pp — Ex 12:14–20; Lev 23:4–8; Dt 16:1–8

16" 'On the fourteenth day of the first
month the LORD's Passover[d] is to be
held. 17On the fifteenth day of this month
there is to be a festival; for seven days[e]
eat bread made without yeast.[f] 18On the
first day hold a sacred assembly and do no
regular work.[g] 19Present to the LORD an
offering made by fire,[h] a burnt offering of
two young bulls, one ram and seven male
lambs a year old, all without defect.[i]
20With each bull prepare a grain offering
of three-tenths of an ephah[j] of fine flour
mixed with oil; with the ram, two-
tenths;[k] 21and with each of the seven
lambs, one-tenth.[l] 22Include one male
goat as a sin offering[m] to make atonement
for you.[n] 23Prepare these in addition to
the regular morning burnt offering. 24In
this way prepare the food for the offering
made by fire every day for seven days as
an aroma pleasing to the LORD;[o] it is to
be prepared in addition to the regular
burnt offering and its drink offering. 25On
the seventh day hold a sacred assembly
and do no regular work.

Feast of Weeks

28:26–31pp — Lev 23:15–22; Dt 16:9–12

26" 'On the day of firstfruits,[p] when
you present to the LORD an offering of
new grain during the Feast of Weeks,[q]
hold a sacred assembly and do no regular
work.[r] 27Present a burnt offering of two
young bulls, one ram and seven male
lambs a year old as an aroma pleasing to
the LORD.[s] 28With each bull there is to
be a grain offering of three-tenths of an
ephah of fine flour mixed with oil; with
the ram, two-tenths;[t] 29and with each of
the seven lambs, one-tenth.[u] 30Include
one male goat[v] to make atonement
for you. 31Prepare these together with
their drink offerings, in addition to the
regular burnt offering[w] and its grain
offering. Be sure the animals are without
defect.

28:13 [x]Lev 1:9
28:14 [y]S Nu 15:7 [z]ver 11; 2Ch 2:4; Ezr 3:5
28:15 [a]ver 3,23,24 [b]ver 30 [c]Lev 4:3; Nu 29:16,19
28:16 [d]S Ex 12:11; 2Ch 30:13; 35:1
28:17 [e]S Ex 12:19 [f]S Ex 12:15
28:18 [g]S Ex 12:16
28:19 [h]S Lev 1:9 [i]ver 11
28:20 [j]S Lev 14:10 [k]ver 12
28:21 [l]ver 13
28:22 [m]Lev 4:3; Ro 8:3 [n]S Nu 15:28
28:24 [o]Lev 1:9
28:26 [p]S Ex 34:22 [q]S Ex 23:16 [r]ver 18
28:27 [s]ver 19
28:28 [t]ver 12
28:29 [u]ver 13
28:30 [v]ver 15
28:31 [w]ver 3,19
29:1 [x]Nu 28:18
29:2 [y]Nu 28:2 [z]Lev 1:9; Nu 28:11 [a]ver 36 [b]Lev 1:3; Nu 28:3
29:3 [c]ver 14; Nu 28:12
29:4 [d]Nu 28:13
29:5 [e]Nu 28:15
29:6 [f]Nu 28:11 [g]Nu 28:3 [h]Nu 28:5 [i]Nu 28:7 [j]Lev 1:9; Nu 28:2
29:7 [k]Ac 27:9 [l]S Ex 31:15
29:8 [m]ver 2
29:9 [n]S ver 3,18 [o]Nu 28:12
29:10 [p]Nu 28:13
29:11 [q]ver 5; Nu 28:15 [r]S Lev 16:3 [s]S ver 6
29:12 [t]1Ki 8:2; 12:32 [u]S Lev 23:24
29:13 [v]ver 2; Nu 28:2 [w]Nu 28:3
29:14 [x]S ver 3; S Nu 15:6

Chapter 29

Feast of Trumpets

29:1–6pp — Lev 23:23–25

" 'ON the first day of the seventh
month hold a sacred assembly
and do no regular work.[x] It is a day for
you to sound the trumpets. 2As an aroma
pleasing to the LORD,[y] prepare a burnt
offering[z] of one young bull, one ram and
seven male lambs a year old,[a] all without
defect.[b] 3With the bull prepare a grain
offering[c] of three-tenths of an ephah[s] of
fine flour mixed with oil; with the ram,
two-tenths[t]; 4and with each of the seven
lambs, one-tenth.[u][d] 5Include one male
goat[e] as a sin offering to make atonement
for you. 6These are in addition to the
monthly[f] and daily burnt offerings[g] with
their grain offerings[h] and drink offerings[i] as specified. They are offerings
made to the LORD by fire—a pleasing aroma.[j]

Day of Atonement

29:7–11pp — Lev 16:2–34; 23:26–32

7" 'On the tenth day of this seventh
month hold a sacred assembly. You must
deny yourselves[v][k] and do no work.[l]
8Present as an aroma pleasing to the LORD
a burnt offering of one young bull, one
ram and seven male lambs a year old, all
without defect.[m] 9With the bull prepare a
grain offering[n] of three-tenths of an
ephah of fine flour mixed with oil; with
the ram, two-tenths;[o] 10and with each of
the seven lambs, one-tenth.[p] 11Include
one male goat[q] as a sin offering, in addition to the sin offering for atonement and
the regular burnt offering[r] with its grain
offering, and their drink offerings.[s]

Feast of Tabernacles

29:12–39pp — Lev 23:33–43; Dt 16:13–17

12" 'On the fifteenth day of the seventh[t] month,[u] hold a sacred assembly
and do no regular work. Celebrate a festival to the LORD for seven days. 13Present
an offering made by fire as an aroma
pleasing to the LORD,[v] a burnt offering of
thirteen young bulls, two rams and fourteen male lambs a year old, all without
defect.[w] 14With each of the thirteen bulls
prepare a grain offering[x] of three-tenths
of an ephah of fine flour mixed with oil;

[q] *14* That is, probably about 2 quarts (about 2 liters) [r] *14* That is, probably about 1 1/4 quarts (about 1.2 liters) [s] *3* That is, probably about 6 quarts (about 6.5 liters); also in verses 9 and 14 [t] *3* That is, probably about 4 quarts (about 4.5 liters); also in verses 9 and 14 [u] *4* That is, probably about 2 quarts (about 2 liters); also in verses 10 and 15 [v] *7* Or *must fast*

28:16—29:39 HISTORY, Time—See note on 9:1–14.
28:16—29:39 WORSHIP, Calendar—See note on Ex 16:23–30. Special worship days enrich the life of God's people.

with each of the two rams, two-tenths;
15and with each of the fourteen lambs,
one-tenth.[y] 16Include one male goat as a
sin offering,[z] in addition to the regular
burnt offering with its grain offering and
drink offering.[a]
17" 'On the second day[b] prepare
twelve young bulls, two rams and fourteen male lambs a year old, all without
defect.[c] 18With the bulls, rams and
lambs, prepare their grain offerings[d] and
drink offerings[e] according to the number
specified.[f] 19Include one male goat as a
sin offering,[g] in addition to the regular
burnt offering[h] with its grain offering,
and their drink offerings.[i]
20" 'On the third day prepare eleven
bulls, two rams and fourteen male lambs
a year old, all without defect.[j] 21With the
bulls, rams and lambs, prepare their grain
offerings and drink offerings according to
the number specified.[k] 22Include one
male goat as a sin offering, in addition to
the regular burnt offering with its grain
offering and drink offering.
23" 'On the fourth day prepare ten
bulls, two rams and fourteen male lambs
a year old, all without defect. 24With the
bulls, rams and lambs, prepare their grain
offerings and drink offerings according to
the number specified. 25Include one male
goat as a sin offering, in addition to the
regular burnt offering with its grain offering and drink offering.
26" 'On the fifth day prepare nine bulls,
two rams and fourteen male lambs a year
old, all without defect. 27With the bulls,
rams and lambs, prepare their grain offerings and drink offerings according to the
number specified. 28Include one male
goat as a sin offering, in addition to the
regular burnt offering with its grain offering and drink offering.
29" 'On the sixth day prepare eight
bulls, two rams and fourteen male lambs
a year old, all without defect. 30With the
bulls, rams and lambs, prepare their grain
offerings and drink offerings according to
the number specified. 31Include one male
goat as a sin offering, in addition to the
regular burnt offering with its grain offering and drink offering.
32" 'On the seventh day prepare seven
bulls, two rams and fourteen male lambs
a year old, all without defect. 33With the
bulls, rams and lambs, prepare their grain
offerings and drink offerings according to
the number specified. 34Include one male
goat as a sin offering, in addition to the
regular burnt offering with its grain offering and drink offering.
35" 'On the eighth day hold an assembly[l] and do no regular work. 36Present
an offering made by fire as an aroma
pleasing to the LORD,[m] a burnt offering of
one bull, one ram and seven male lambs a
year old,[n] all without defect. 37With the
bull, the ram and the lambs, prepare their
grain offerings and drink offerings according to the number specified. 38Include
one male goat as a sin offering, in addition to the regular burnt offering with its
grain offering and drink offering.
39" 'In addition to what you vow[o] and
your freewill offerings,[p] prepare these for
the LORD at your appointed feasts:[q] your
burnt offerings,[r] grain offerings, drink offerings and fellowship offerings.[w] [s] ' "
40Moses told the Israelites all that the
LORD commanded him.

Chapter 30

Vows

MOSES said to the heads of the tribes
of Israel:[t] "This is what the LORD
commands: 2When a man makes a vow to
the LORD or takes an oath to obligate himself by a pledge, he must not break his
word but must do everything he said.[u]
3"When a young woman still living in
her father's house makes a vow to the
LORD or obligates herself by a pledge 4and
her father hears about her vow or pledge
but says nothing to her, then all her vows
and every pledge by which she obligated
herself will stand.[v] 5But if her father forbids her[w] when he hears about it, none
of her vows or the pledges by which she

29:15 [y]ver 4; Nu 28:13
29:16 [z]ver 5; S Nu 28:15 [a]ver 6
29:17 [b]Lev 23:36 [c]ver 2; Nu 28:3
29:18 [d]S ver 9 [e]Nu 28:7 [f]Nu 15:4-12
29:19 [g]S Nu 28:15 [h]Nu 28:3 [i]ver 6
29:20 [j]S ver 17
29:21 [k]S ver 18
29:35 [l]S Lev 23:36
29:36 [m]Lev 1:9 [n]ver 2
29:39 [o]Nu 6:2 [p]S Lev 7:16 [q]S Lev 23:2 [r]Lev 1:3; 1Ch 23:31; 2Ch 31:3 [s]Lev 3:1
30:1 [t]S Nu 1:4
30:2 [u]Dt 23:21-23; Jdg 11:35; Job 22:27; Ps 22:25; 50:14; 61:5,8; 76:11; 116:14; Pr 20:25; Ecc 5:4,5; Isa 19:21; Jnh 1:16; 2:9
30:4 [v]ver 7
30:5 [w]ver 8,12,15

[w]39 Traditionally *peace offerings*

30:1–16 CHRISTIAN ETHICS, Social Order—Responsibility is the keystone of social order. We must be able to trust a person to carry out commitments. On the other hand, the social order must protect members from rash vows they feel forced to make or which they make without proper understanding of circumstances. The laws protected women without financial or legal resources to fulfill commitments. At the same time, laws gave them freedom to make vows in consultation with persons legally responsible and financially able to fill them. Such laws applied to society as it was at the time. They did not mandate a social structure that should never change. See note on Mt 5:33–36.

30:1–15 FAMILY, Role Relationships—Vows are commitments to God to perform some duty or abstain from some activity. Instruction is given concerning an unmarried daughter living at home and a married woman living with her husband. In each case the final authority of the male is affirmed here. He had legal responsibility for the home and could either agree with or set aside the vow made by his daughter or wife. However, he had to do it as soon as he heard about it, or his silence was considered to be consent. Only if a woman was living alone as a widow or divorcee could she be the final legal authority in her own household as a woman. Men were the source of income for the household and, therefore, had to give approval for any commitments made by a daughter or wife whether or not they involved financial considerations. The New Testament gospel does not diminish the man's responsibility for the home though it does offer new attitudes toward the husband/wife relationship. See note on Eph 5:21.

obligated herself will stand; the LORD will
release her because her father has forbidden her.
6"If she marries after she makes a
vow[x] or after her lips utter a rash promise by which she obligates herself 7and
her husband hears about it but says nothing to her, then her vows or the pledges
by which she obligated herself will stand.
8But if her husband[y] forbids her when he
hears about it, he nullifies the vow that
obligates her or the rash promise by
which she obligates herself, and the LORD
will release her.[z]
9"Any vow or obligation taken by a
widow or divorced woman will be binding on her.
10"If a woman living with her husband
makes a vow or obligates herself by a
pledge under oath 11and her husband
hears about it but says nothing to her and
does not forbid her, then all her vows or
the pledges by which she obligated herself will stand. 12But if her husband nullifies them when he hears about them,
then none of the vows or pledges that
came from her lips will stand.[a] Her husband has nullified them, and the LORD
will release her. 13Her husband may confirm or nullify any vow she makes or any
sworn pledge to deny herself. 14But if her
husband says nothing to her about it from
day to day, then he confirms all her vows
or the pledges binding on her. He confirms them by saying nothing to her
when he hears about them. 15If, however, he nullifies them[b] some time after he
hears about them, then he is responsible
for her guilt."
16These are the regulations the LORD
gave Moses concerning relationships between a man and his wife, and between a
father and his young daughter still living
in his house.

Chapter 31

Vengeance on the Midianites

THE LORD said to Moses, 2"Take vengeance on the Midianites[c] for the Israelites. After that, you will be gathered
to your people.[d]"
3So Moses said to the people, "Arm
some of your men to go to war against the
Midianites and to carry out the LORD's
vengeance[e] on them. 4Send into battle a
thousand men from each of the tribes of
Israel." 5So twelve thousand men armed
for battle,[f] a thousand from each tribe,
were supplied from the clans of Israel.
6Moses sent them into battle,[g] a thousand from each tribe, along with Phinehas[h] son of Eleazar, the priest, who took
with him articles from the sanctuary[i]
and the trumpets[j] for signaling.
7They fought against Midian, as the
LORD commanded Moses,[k] and killed every man.[l] 8Among their victims were
Evi, Rekem, Zur, Hur and Reba[m]—the
five kings of Midian.[n] They also killed
Balaam son of Beor[o] with the sword.[p]
9The Israelites captured the Midianite
women[q] and children and took all the
Midianite herds, flocks and goods as plunder.[r] 10They burned[s] all the towns
where the Midianites had settled, as well
as all their camps.[t] 11They took all the
plunder and spoils, including the people
and animals,[u] 12and brought the captives, spoils[v] and plunder to Moses and
Eleazar the priest and the Israelite assembly[w] at their camp on the plains of Moab,
by the Jordan across from Jericho.[x] [x]
13Moses, Eleazar the priest and all the
leaders of the community went to meet
them outside the camp. 14Moses was angry with the officers of the army[y]—the
commanders of thousands and commanders of hundreds—who returned from the
battle.
15"Have you allowed all the women to
live?" he asked them. 16"They were the
ones who followed Balaam's advice[z] and
were the means of turning the Israelites
away from the LORD in what happened at
Peor,[a] so that a plague[b] struck the
LORD's people. 17Now kill all the boys.
And kill every woman who has slept with
a man,[c] 18but save for yourselves every
girl who has never slept with a man.
19"All of you who have killed anyone
or touched anyone who was killed[d] must
stay outside the camp seven days.[e] On

30:6 [x]S Lev 5:4
30:8 [y]S Ge 3:16 [z]ver 5
30:12 [a]Eph 5:22; Col 3:18
30:15 [b]S ver 5
31:2 [c]S Ge 25:2 [d]S Nu 20:26
31:3 [e]Jdg 11:36; 1Sa 24:12; 2Sa 4:8; 22:48; Ps 94:1; 149:7; Isa 34:8; Jer 11:20; 46:10; Eze 25:17
31:5 [f]ver 6,21
31:6 [g]S ver 5 [h]S Ex 6:25 [i]Nu 14:44 [j]S Nu 10:2
31:7 [k]Nu 25:16 [l]Dt 20:13; Jdg 21:11; 1Ki 11:15,16
31:8 [m]Jos 13:21 [n]S Nu 25:15 [o]S Nu 22:5; S 24:14 [p]Jos 13:22
31:9 [q]ver 15 [r]S Ge 34:29
31:10 [s]Jos 6:24; 8:28; 11:11; Jdg 18:27 [t]Ge 25:16; 1Ch 6:54; Ps 69:25; Eze 25:4
31:11 [u]ver 26; Dt 20:14; 2Ch 28:8
31:12 [v]ver 32,53; Ge 49:27; Ex 15:9 [w]S Nu 27:2 [x]Nu 22:1
31:14 [y]ver 48; Ex 18:21; Dt 1:15; 2Sa 18:1
31:16 [z]S Nu 22:5; S 24:14; S 2Pe 2:15 [a]S Nu 23:28; 25:1-9 [b]S Nu 14:37
31:17 [c]Dt 7:2; 20:16-18; Jdg 21:11
31:19 [d]Nu 19:16 [e]S Lev 21:1

[x] *12* Hebrew *Jordan of Jericho*; possibly an ancient name for the Jordan River

31:1–24 HISTORY, Judgment—Historical acts may bring God's vengeance on specific sinful acts. The agents who executed God's vengeance were not free to follow their own plans and desires. They, too, faced judgment when they disobeyed God. Acting for God calls for action in obedience to God.

31:1–54 CHRISTIAN ETHICS, War and Peace—God directed Israel to wage war to punish Midianites for leading Israel to sin (25:6–18). Explicit obedience to God's leadership and instructions was expected. Purity allowing all participants to remain qualified for worship was emphasized. God's dedicated religious leaders shared in the spoils of victory. Directions for God's nation Israel in a special time of gaining identity and space must not be taken over naively by a nation which was not directly chosen by God. The most we can learn theologically here about war would be that at special moments in history God allows human wars, uses them to accomplish His purposes, and expects obedience from His people in carrying them out. See notes on 21:1–3; Ex 23:22–33.

31:5–18 SIN, Serious—Killing women and their sons may seem brutal. It underscores how seriously God takes sin. People who turn God's people away from Him and to other gods must face the seriousness of their sin against the one true God. To resist God's purposes and lead people away from Him is an invitation for God's judgment.

the third and seventh days you must purify yourselves[f] and your captives. 20Purify
every garment[g] as well as everything
made of leather, goat hair or wood.[h]"
21Then Eleazar the priest said to the
soldiers who had gone into battle,[i] "This
is the requirement of the law that the
LORD gave Moses: 22Gold, silver, bronze,
iron,[j] tin, lead 23and anything else that
can withstand fire must be put through
the fire,[k] and then it will be clean. But it
must also be purified with the water of
cleansing.[l] And whatever cannot withstand fire must be put through that water.
24On the seventh day wash your clothes
and you will be clean.[m] Then you may
come into the camp.[n]"

Dividing the Spoils

25The LORD said to Moses, 26"You and
Eleazar the priest and the family heads[o]
of the community are to count all the people[p] and animals that were captured.[q]
27Divide[r] the spoils between the soldiers
who took part in the battle and the rest of
the community. 28From the soldiers who
fought in the battle, set apart as tribute
for the LORD[s] one out of every five hundred, whether persons, cattle, donkeys,
sheep or goats. 29Take this tribute from
their half share and give it to Eleazar the
priest as the LORD's part. 30From the Israelites' half, select one out of every fifty,
whether persons, cattle, donkeys, sheep,
goats or other animals. Give them to the
Levites, who are responsible for the care
of the LORD's tabernacle.[t]" 31So Moses
and Eleazar the priest did as the LORD
commanded Moses.
32The plunder remaining from the
spoils[u] that the soldiers took was 675,
000 sheep, 3372,000 cattle, 3461,000
donkeys 35and 32,000 women who had
never slept with a man.
36The half share of those who fought in
the battle was:

> 337,500 sheep, 37of which the trib-
> ute for the LORD[v] was 675;
> 3836,000 cattle, of which the tribute
> for the LORD was 72;
> 3930,500 donkeys, of which the trib-
> ute for the LORD was 61;
> 4016,000 people, of which the tribute
> for the LORD was 32.

31:19 [f]Nu 19:12
31:20 [g]Nu 19:19 [h]S Lev 11:32
31:21 [i]S ver 5
31:22 [j]Jos 6:19; 22:8
31:23 [k]S 1Co 3:13 [l]S Nu 8:7
31:24 [m]S Lev 11:25 [n]S Lev 14:8
31:26 [o]S Nu 1:4 [p]S Nu 1:19 [q]S ver 11,12
31:27 [r]Jos 22:8; 1Sa 25:13; 30:24
31:28 [s]ver 37-41; S Nu 18:21
31:30 [t]Nu 3:7; 18:3
31:32 [u]S ver 12
31:37 [v]ver 38-41
31:41 [w]Nu 5:9; 18:8 [x]ver 21,28
31:48 [y]S ver 14
31:49 [z]S Nu 1:19 [a]Jer 23:4
31:50 [b]S Ex 30:16
31:53 [c]S Ge 34:29; Dt 20:14
31:54 [d]S Ex 27:21; 40:2 [e]S Ex 28:12
32:1 [f]ver 24,36; Jdg 5:16 [g]S Nu 21:32 [h]S Ge 31:21 [i]Ex 12:38
32:2 [j]Lev 4:22; Nu 27:2
32:3 [k]ver 34; Jos 16:2,7; 18:13 [l]ver 34; S Nu 21:30 [m]ver 1 [n]ver 36; Jos 13:27 [o]Nu 21:25 [p]ver 37; Isa 15:4; 16:9; Jer 48:34 [q]Jos 13:19; Isa 16:8,9; Jer 48:32 [r]Nu 33:47; Dt 32:49; 34:1; 1Ch 5:8 [s]ver 38; Jos 13:17; Eze 25:9
32:4 [t]Nu 21:34

41Moses gave the tribute to Eleazar the
priest as the LORD's part,[w] as the LORD
commanded Moses.[x]
42The half belonging to the Israelites,
which Moses set apart from that of the
fighting men— 43the community's half
—was 337,500 sheep, 4436,000 cattle,
4530,500 donkeys 46and 16,000 people.
47From the Israelites' half, Moses selected
one out of every fifty persons and animals, as the LORD commanded him, and
gave them to the Levites, who were responsible for the care of the LORD's tabernacle.
48Then the officers[y] who were over
the units of the army—the commanders
of thousands and commanders of hundreds—went to Moses 49and said to him,
"Your servants have counted[z] the soldiers under our command, and not one is
missing.[a] 50So we have brought as an offering to the LORD the gold articles each
of us acquired—armlets, bracelets, signet
rings, earrings and necklaces—to make
atonement for ourselves[b] before the
LORD."
51Moses and Eleazar the priest accepted from them the gold—all the crafted
articles. 52All the gold from the commanders of thousands and commanders
of hundreds that Moses and Eleazar presented as a gift to the LORD weighed 16,
750 shekels.[y] 53Each soldier had taken
plunder[c] for himself. 54Moses and Eleazar the priest accepted the gold from the
commanders of thousands and commanders of hundreds and brought it into the
Tent of Meeting[d] as a memorial[e] for the
Israelites before the LORD.

Chapter 32

The Transjordan Tribes

THE Reubenites and Gadites, who had
very large herds and flocks,[f] saw
that the lands of Jazer[g] and Gilead[h] were
suitable for livestock.[i] 2So they came to
Moses and Eleazar the priest and to the
leaders of the community,[j] and said,
3"Ataroth,[k] Dibon,[l] Jazer,[m] Nimrah,[n]
Heshbon,[o] Elealeh,[p] Sebam,[q] Nebo[r]
and Beon[s]— 4the land the LORD subdued[t] before the people of Israel—are

[y] *52* That is, about 420 pounds (about 190 kilograms)

31:48–54 PRAYER, Thanksgiving—An offering made in gratitude for safety and for victory over the Midianites was a symbolic prayer to God.
32:1–42 HUMANITY, Community Relationships—Freedom allows choices which may separate one segment of a community from the rest. Despite such a situation, responsibility demands that community obligations must still be fulfilled.
32:1–13 SIN, Lack of Faith—Like the pessimistic spies sent to reconnoiter the Promised Land, a spiritual leadership can discourage its following if God's command is not believed. God's people are to encourage one another in His work. To do otherwise is sin.
32:1–42 HISTORY, God's People—God acts in history to form a people for Himself. He expects that people to maintain the unity of His people. He gives them freedom to form and express that unity in different ways. He allowed two and a half tribes to choose to live beyond the Jordan River if they promised to cooperate with and maintain identity with His people. Compare Jos 22.

suitable for livestock,[u] and your servants
have livestock. 5If we have found favor in
your eyes," they said, "let this land be
given to your servants as our possession.
Do not make us cross the Jordan.[v]"

6Moses said to the Gadites and Reubenites, "Shall your countrymen go to war
while you sit here? 7Why do you discourage the Israelites from going over into the
land the LORD has given them?[w] 8This is
what your fathers did when I sent them
from Kadesh Barnea to look over the
land.[x] 9After they went up to the Valley
of Eshcol[y] and viewed the land, they discouraged the Israelites from entering the
land the LORD had given them. 10The
LORD's anger was aroused[z] that day and
he swore this oath:[a] 11'Because they
have not followed me wholeheartedly,
not one of the men twenty years old or
more[b] who came up out of Egypt[c] will
see the land I promised on oath[d] to Abraham, Isaac and Jacob[e]— 12not one except Caleb son of Jephunneh the Kenizzite and Joshua son of Nun, for they followed the LORD wholeheartedly.'[f] 13The
LORD's anger burned against Israel[g] and
he made them wander in the desert forty
years, until the whole generation of those
who had done evil in his sight was
gone.[h]

14"And here you are, a brood of sinners, standing in the place of your fathers
and making the LORD even more angry
with Israel.[i] 15If you turn away from following him, he will again leave all this
people in the desert, and you will be the
cause of their destruction.[j]"

16Then they came up to him and said,
"We would like to build pens[k] here for
our livestock[l] and cities for our women
and children. 17But we are ready to arm
ourselves and go ahead of the Israelites[m]
until we have brought them to their
place.[n] Meanwhile our women and children will live in fortified cities, for protection from the inhabitants of the land.
18We will not return to our homes until
every Israelite has received his inheritance.[o] 19We will not receive any inheritance with them on the other side of the
Jordan, because our inheritance[p] has
come to us on the east side of the Jordan."[q]

20Then Moses said to them, "If you will
do this—if you will arm yourselves before
the LORD for battle,[r] 21and if all of you
will go armed over the Jordan before the
LORD until he has driven his enemies out
before him[s]— 22then when the land is
subdued before the LORD, you may return[t] and be free from your obligation to
the LORD and to Israel. And this land will
be your possession[u] before the LORD.[v]

23"But if you fail to do this, you will be
sinning against the LORD; and you may be
sure that your sin will find you out.[w]
24Build cities for your women and children, and pens for your flocks,[x] but do
what you have promised.[y]"

25The Gadites and Reubenites said to
Moses, "We your servants will do as our
lord commands.[z] 26Our children and
wives, our flocks and herds will remain
here in the cities of Gilead.[a] 27But your
servants, every man armed for battle, will
cross over to fight[b] before the LORD, just
as our lord says."

28Then Moses gave orders about
them[c] to Eleazar the priest and Joshua
son of Nun[d] and to the family heads of
the Israelite tribes.[e] 29He said to them,
"If the Gadites and Reubenites, every
man armed for battle, cross over the Jordan with you before the LORD, then when
the land is subdued before you,[f] give
them the land of Gilead as their possession.[g] 30But if they do not cross over[h]
with you armed, they must accept their
possession with you in Canaan.[i]"

31The Gadites and Reubenites answered, "Your servants will do what the
LORD has said.[j] 32We will cross over before the LORD into Canaan armed,[k] but
the property we inherit will be on this
side of the Jordan.[l]"

33Then Moses gave to the Gadites,[m]
the Reubenites and the half-tribe of Manasseh[n] son of Joseph the kingdom of Sihon king of the Amorites[o] and the kingdom of Og king of Bashan[p]—the whole
land with its cities and the territory
around them.[q]

34The Gadites built up Dibon, Ataroth,
Aroer,[r] 35Atroth Shophan, Jazer,[s] Jogbehah,[t] 36Beth Nimrah[u] and Beth Haran as
fortified cities, and built pens for their
flocks.[v] 37And the Reubenites rebuilt
Heshbon,[w] Elealeh[x] and Kiriathaim,[y]
38as well as Nebo[z] and Baal Meon (these
names were changed) and Sibmah.[a]
They gave names to the cities they rebuilt.

39The descendants of Makir[b] son of

32:4 [u]Ex 12:38 **32:5** [v]S Nu 13:29 **32:7** [w]Nu 13:27-14:4 **32:8** [x]Nu 13:3,26; Dt 1:19-25 **32:9** [y]Nu 13:23; Dt 1:24 **32:10** [z]Nu 11:1 [a]S Nu 14:20-23 **32:11** [b]S Ex 30:14 [c]Nu 1:1 [d]S Nu 14:23 [e]Nu 14:28-30 **32:12** [f]Nu 14:24, 30 **32:13** [g]S Ex 4:14 [h]Nu 14:28-35; 26:64,65 **32:14** [i]S ver 10; Dt 1:34; Ps 78:59 **32:15** [j]Dt 30:17-18; 2Ch 7:20 **32:16** [k]ver 24,36; 1Sa 24:3; Ps 50:9; 78:70 [l]Ex 12:38; Dt 3:19 **32:17** [m]Dt 3:18; Jos 4:12,13 [n]S Nu 22:4; Dt 3:20 **32:18** [o]Jos 22:1-4 **32:19** [p]ver 22,29 [q]Nu 21:33; Jos 12:1; 22:7 **32:20** [r]ver 17 **32:21** [s]ver 17 **32:22** [t]Jos 22:4 [u]S Lev 14:34 [v]Dt 3:18-20 **32:23** [w]S Ge 4:7; S Isa 3:9 **32:24** [x]S ver 1,16 [y]Nu 30:2 **32:25** [z]ver 29; Jos 1:16,18; 22:2 **32:26** [a]ver 16,24; Jos 1:14; 12:2; 22:9; 2Sa 2:9; 1Ch 5:9 **32:27** [b]ver 17,21 **32:28** [c]ver 29; Dt 3:18-20; Jos 1:13 [d]Nu 11:28 [e]Nu 1:16 **32:29** [f]S Nu 22:4 [g]S ver 19 **32:30** [h]ver 23 [i]ver 29,32 **32:31** [j]ver 29 **32:32** [k]ver 17 [l]S ver 30; Jos 12:6 **32:33** [m]Jos 13:24-28; 1Sa 13:7 [n]Jos 1:12 [o]Nu 21:21; Dt 2:26 [p]S ver 19; S Jos 12:5 [q]S Nu 21:24; 34:14; Dt 2:36; Jos 12:6 **32:34** [r]Dt 2:36; 3:12; 4:48; Jos 12:2; 13:9; Jdg 11:26; 1Sa 30:28; 1Ch 5:8; Jer 48:19 **32:35** [s]ver 3 [t]Jdg 8:11 **32:36** [u]S ver 3 [v]S ver 1 **32:37** [w]Nu 21:25 [x]S ver 3 [y]Jos 13:19; 1Ch 6:76; Jer 48:1, 23; Eze 25:9 **32:38** [z]S ver 3; Isa 15:2; Jer 48:1,22 [a]S ver 3 **32:39** [b]S Ge 50:23

32:11–33 ELECTION, Responsibility—The Gadites and Reubenites learned they were a part of the community. They could not seek their self-interest without engaging in the collective battle to possess Canaan. Wholehearted commitment in the common conquest was the requirement of the God of election. Election is not an individualistic doctrine isolating people from each other. It is a community-building teaching involving a community in achieving God's purposes.

32:23 SIN, Responsibility—To refuse to do what God wants is just as sinful as to do what He has forbidden. See note on 27:3.

Manasseh went to Gilead,[c] captured it
and drove out the Amorites[d] who were
there. 40So Moses gave Gilead to the Makirites,[e] the descendants of Manasseh,
and they settled there. 41Jair,[f] a descendant of Manasseh, captured their settlements and called them Havvoth Jair.[z] [g]
42And Nobah captured Kenath[h] and its
surrounding settlements and called it Nobah[i] after himself.[j]

Chapter 33

Stages in Israel's Journey

HERE are the stages in the journey[k] of
the Israelites when they came out of
Egypt[l] by divisions under the leadership
of Moses and Aaron.[m] 2At the LORD's
command Moses recorded[n] the stages in
their journey[o]. This is their journey by
stages:

3The Israelites set out[p] from Rameses[q] on the fifteenth day of the first
month, the day after the Passover.[r]
They marched out boldly[s] in full
view of all the Egyptians, 4who were
burying all their firstborn,[t] whom
the LORD had struck down among
them; for the LORD had brought judgment[u] on their gods.[v]
5The Israelites left Rameses and
camped at Succoth.[w]
6They left Succoth and camped at
Etham, on the edge of the desert.[x]
7They left Etham, turned back to Pi
Hahiroth, to the east of Baal Zephon,[y] and camped near Migdol.[z]
8They left Pi Hahiroth[a] [a] and
passed through the sea[b] into the
desert, and when they had traveled
for three days in the Desert of Etham,
they camped at Marah.[c]
9They left Marah and went to Elim,
where there were twelve springs and
seventy palm trees, and they
camped[d] there.
10They left Elim[e] and camped by
the Red Sea.[b]
11They left the Red Sea and
camped in the Desert of Sin.[f]
12They left the Desert of Sin and
camped at Dophkah.
13They left Dophkah and camped
at Alush.
14They left Alush and camped at
Rephidim, where there was no water
for the people to drink.[g]
15They left Rephidim[h] and camped
in the Desert of Sinai.[i]
16They left the Desert of Sinai and
camped at Kibroth Hattaavah.[j]
17They left Kibroth Hattaavah and
camped at Hazeroth.[k]
18They left Hazeroth and camped
at Rithmah.
19They left Rithmah and camped at
Rimmon Perez.
20They left Rimmon Perez and
camped at Libnah.[l]
21They left Libnah and camped at
Rissah.
22They left Rissah and camped at
Kehelathah.
23They left Kehelathah and
camped at Mount Shepher.
24They left Mount Shepher and
camped at Haradah.
25They left Haradah and camped at
Makheloth.
26They left Makheloth and camped
at Tahath.
27They left Tahath and camped at
Terah.
28They left Terah and camped at
Mithcah.
29They left Mithcah and camped at
Hashmonah.
30They left Hashmonah and
camped at Moseroth.[m]
31They left Moseroth and camped
at Bene Jaakan.[n]
32They left Bene Jaakan and
camped at Hor Haggidgad.
33They left Hor Haggidgad and
camped at Jotbathah.[o]
34They left Jotbathah and camped
at Abronah.
35They left Abronah and camped at
Ezion Geber.[p]
36They left Ezion Geber and
camped at Kadesh, in the Desert of
Zin.[q]
37They left Kadesh and camped at
Mount Hor,[r] on the border of
Edom.[s] 38At the LORD's command
Aaron the priest went up Mount Hor,
where he died[t] on the first day of

32:39 [c]Nu 26:29; Dt 2:36 [d]S Ge 10:16
32:40 [e]S Ge 50:23; Dt 3:15
32:41 [f]1Ki 4:13 [g]Dt 3:14; Jos 13:30; Jdg 10:4; 1Ch 2:23
32:42 [h]1Ch 2:23 [i]Jdg 8:11 [j]1Sa 15:12; 2Sa 18:18; Ps 49:11; Isa 22:16; 56:5
33:1 [k]Ex 17:1; 40:36 [l]Nu 1:1 [m]S Ex 4:16; 6:26
33:2 [n]S Ex 17:14 [o]S ver 1
33:3 [p]Nu 10:2 [q]S Ge 47:11 [r]Jos 5:10 [s]S Ex 14:8
33:4 [t]S Ex 4:23 [u]2Ch 24:24; Jer 15:3; Eze 14:21 [v]S Ex 12:12
33:5 [w]Ex 12:37
33:6 [x]Ex 13:20
33:7 [y]Ex 14:9 [z]S Ex 14:2
33:8 [a]Ex 14:2 [b]S Ex 14:22 [c]S Ex 15:23
33:9 [d]Ex 15:27
33:10 [e]Ex 16:1
33:11 [f]S Ex 16:1
33:14 [g]S Ex 15:22; S 17:2
33:15 [h]S Ex 17:1 [i]S Ex 19:1
33:16 [j]S Nu 11:34
33:17 [k]Nu 11:35
33:20 [l]Jos 10:29; 12:15; 15:42; 21:13; 2Ki 8:22; 19:8; 23:31; 1Ch 6:57; 2Ch 21:10; Isa 37:8; Jer 52:1
33:30 [m]Dt 10:6
33:31 [n]Dt 10:6
33:33 [o]Dt 10:7
33:35 [p]Dt 2:8; 1Ki 9:26; 22:48
33:36 [q]S Nu 13:21
33:37 [r]S Nu 20:22 [s]S Ge 36:16; S Nu 20:16
33:38 [t]S Nu 27:13

[z]*41* Or *them the settlements of Jair* [a]*8* Many manuscripts of the Masoretic Text, Samaritan Pentateuch and Vulgate; most manuscripts of the Masoretic Text *left from before Hahiroth*
[b]*10* Hebrew *Yam Suph*; that is, Sea of Reeds; also in verse 11

33:1–50 HISTORY, Linear—Not every moment or stage in history produces memorable events. A list of camping places can seem meaningless, but each camping place marked a new stage in God's daily direction of His people. God used each stage to create the whole in His history of delivering His people. The stages without exciting narratives to remember were just as important in God's plan of redemption as were the stages with memorable events. Looking back, God's people confess God's leadership through every part of our collective and individual history.

the fifth month of the fortieth year[u]
after the Israelites came out of
Egypt.[v] 39Aaron was a hundred and
twenty-three years old when he died
on Mount Hor.
40The Canaanite king[w] of Arad,[x]
who lived in the Negev[y] of Canaan,
heard that the Israelites were coming.
41They left Mount Hor and camped
at Zalmonah.
42They left Zalmonah and camped
at Punon.
43They left Punon and camped at
Oboth.[z]
44They left Oboth and camped at
Iye Abarim, on the border of Moab.[a]
45They left Iyim[c] and camped at
Dibon Gad.
46They left Dibon Gad and camped
at Almon Diblathaim.
47They left Almon Diblathaim and
camped in the mountains of Abarim,[b] near Nebo.[c]
48They left the mountains of Abarim[d] and camped on the plains of
Moab[e] by the Jordan[f] across from
Jericho.[d][g] 49There on the plains of
Moab they camped along the Jordan
from Beth Jeshimoth[h] to Abel
Shittim.[i]
50On the plains of Moab by the Jordan
across from Jericho[j] the LORD said to
Moses, 51"Speak to the Israelites and say
to them: 'When you cross the Jordan into
Canaan,[k] 52drive out all the inhabitants
of the land before you. Destroy all their
carved images and their cast idols, and
demolish all their high places.[l] 53Take
possession of the land and settle in it, for
I have given you the land to possess.[m]
54Distribute the land by lot,[n] according to
your clans.[o] To a larger group give a larger inheritance, and to a smaller group a
smaller one.[p] Whatever falls to them by
lot will be theirs. Distribute it according
to your ancestral tribes.[q]
55" 'But if you do not drive out the inhabitants of the land, those you allow to
remain will become barbs in your eyes
and thorns[r] in your sides. They will give
you trouble in the land where you will
live. 56And then I will do to you what I
plan to do to them.[s]' "

33:38 [u]S Ex 16:35 [v]Nu 20:25-28
33:40 [w]S Ge 10:18 [x]S Nu 21:1 [y]S Ge 12:9
33:43 [z]Nu 21:10
33:44 [a]S Nu 21:11
33:47 [b]Nu 27:12 [c]Nu 32:3
33:48 [d]Nu 27:12 [e]S Nu 26:3 [f]S Ge 13:10 [g]Nu 22:1; Jos 12:9
33:49 [h]Jos 12:3; 13:20; Eze 25:9 [i]S Nu 21:16
33:50 [j]ver 48
33:51 [k]Nu 34:2; Jos 3:17
33:52 [l]S Lev 26:1; Ps 106:34-36
33:53 [m]Dt 11:31; 17:14; Jos 1:11; 21:43
33:54 [n]S Lev 16:8; Nu 36:2 [o]Nu 26:54 [p]Nu 35:8 [q]Jos 18:10
33:55 [r]Jos 23:13; Jdg 2:3; Ps 106:36; Isa 55:13; Eze 2:6; 28:24; Mic 7:4; 2Co 12:7
33:56 [s]Nu 14:28
34:2 [t]S Nu 33:51 [u]Ge 17:8; Dt 1:7-8; Jos 23:4; Ps 78:54-55; 105:11 [v]Eze 47:15
34:3 [w]Nu 13:21; Jos 15:1-3 [x]S Ge 14:3
34:4 [y]Jos 15:3; Jdg 1:36 [z]Nu 32:8 [a]Jos 15:4
34:5 [b]Ge 15:18
34:6 [c]Jos 1:4; 9:1; 15:12,47; 23:4; Eze 47:10,15; 48:28 [d]Eze 47:19-20
34:7 [e]Eze 47:15-17 [f]S Nu 20:22
34:8 [g]Nu 13:21; Jos 13:5
34:10 [h]Jos 15:5
34:11 [i]2Ki 23:33; 25:6,21; Jer 39:5; 52:9,27 [j]Jos 15:32; 21:16; 1Ch 4:32 [k]Dt 3:17; Jos 11:2; 13:27
34:13 [l]S Lev 16:8; Jos 18:10; Mic 2:5 [m]Jos 13:6; 14:1-5; Isa 49:8; 65:9; Eze 45:1
34:14 [n]Nu 32:19; Dt 33:21; Jos 14:3

Chapter 34

Boundaries of Canaan

THE LORD said to Moses, 2"Command
the Israelites and say to them: 'When
you enter Canaan,[t] the land that will be
allotted to you as an inheritance[u] will
have these boundaries:[v]
3" 'Your southern side will include
some of the Desert of Zin[w] along the border of Edom. On the east, your southern
boundary will start from the end of the
Salt Sea,[e][x] 4cross south of Scorpion[f]
Pass,[y] continue on to Zin and go south of
Kadesh Barnea.[z] Then it will go to Hazar
Addar and over to Azmon,[a] 5where it
will turn, join the Wadi of Egypt[b] and
end at the Sea.[g]
6" 'Your western boundary will be the
coast of the Great Sea.[c] This will be your
boundary on the west.[d]
7" 'For your northern boundary,[e] run
a line from the Great Sea to Mount Hor[f]
8and from Mount Hor to Lebo[h] Hamath.[g] Then the boundary will go to Zedad, 9continue to Ziphron and end at Hazar Enan. This will be your boundary on
the north.
10" 'For your eastern boundary,[h] run a
line from Hazar Enan to Shepham. 11The
boundary will go down from Shepham to
Riblah[i] on the east side of Ain[j] and continue along the slopes east of the Sea of
Kinnereth.[i][k] 12Then the boundary will
go down along the Jordan and end at the
Salt Sea.
" 'This will be your land, with its boundaries on every side.' "
13Moses commanded the Israelites:
"Assign this land by lot[l] as an inheritance.[m] The LORD has ordered that it be
given to the nine and a half tribes, 14be-
cause the families of the tribe of Reuben,
the tribe of Gad and the half-tribe of Manasseh have received their inheritance.[n]
15These two and a half tribes have received their inheritance on the east side

[c]45 That is, Iye Abarim [d]48 Hebrew *Jordan of Jericho*; possibly an ancient name for the Jordan River; also in verse 50 [e]3 That is, the Dead Sea; also in verse 12 [f]4 Hebrew *Akrabbim* [g]5 That is, the Mediterranean; also in verses 6 and 7 [h]8 Or *to the entrance to* [i]11 That is, Galilee

33:50–56 HISTORY, Freedom—God's history of deliverance calls His people to cooperate with Him and with one another to achieve His purposes. God showed Israel clearly His plan for their life in the Promised Land. He spelled out the consequences of failure to cooperate in His plan. History is not a preset course people have to follow. History is a conversation between God and His people as He seeks to lead us to achieve His perfect purposes.

34:1–29 HISTORY, Geography—God made Himself known in concrete geographical places. The land of promise formed a goal for God's people. There they would know full, free human existence. There they would receive the fulfillment of God's promise (Ge 12:7). The biblical themes of land and geography show the historical nature of God's salvation and revelation.

34:1–29 ELECTION, Sovereignty—The God who elects determines boundaries for the elect. Election shows God to be sovereign ruler over every area of His people's lives.

of the Jordan of Jericho,[j] toward the sunrise."

16 The LORD said to Moses, 17 "These
are the names of the men who are to assign the land for you as an inheritance:
Eleazar the priest and Joshua[o] son of
Nun. 18 And appoint one leader from each
tribe to help[p] assign the land.[q] 19 These
are their names:[r]

Caleb[s] son of Jephunneh,
from the tribe of Judah;[t]
20 Shemuel son of Ammihud,
from the tribe of Simeon;[u]
21 Elidad son of Kislon,
from the tribe of Benjamin;[v]
22 Bukki son of Jogli,
the leader from the tribe of Dan;
23 Hanniel son of Ephod,
the leader from the tribe of Manasseh[w] son of Joseph;
24 Kemuel son of Shiphtan,
the leader from the tribe of Ephraim[x] son of Joseph;
25 Elizaphan son of Parnach,
the leader from the tribe of Zebulun;[y]
26 Paltiel son of Azzan,
the leader from the tribe of Issachar;
27 Ahihud son of Shelomi,
the leader from the tribe of Asher;[z]
28 Pedahel son of Ammihud,
the leader from the tribe of Naphtali."

29 These are the men the LORD commanded to assign the inheritance to the
Israelites in the land of Canaan.[a]

Chapter 35

Towns for the Levites

ON the plains of Moab by the Jordan
across from Jericho,[k][b] the LORD
said to Moses, 2 "Command the Israelites
to give the Levites towns to live in[c] from
the inheritance the Israelites will possess.
And give them pasturelands[d] around the
towns. 3 Then they will have towns to live
in and pasturelands for their cattle, flocks
and all their other livestock.[e]

4 "The pasturelands around the towns
that you give the Levites will extend out
fifteen hundred feet[l] from the town wall.
5 Outside the town, measure three thousand feet[m][f] on the east side, three thousand on the south side, three thousand on
the west and three thousand on the
north, with the town in the center. They
will have this area as pastureland for the
towns.[g]

Cities of Refuge

35:6–34Ref — Dt 4:41–43; 19:1–14; Jos 20:1–9

6 "Six of the towns you give the Levites
will be cities of refuge, to which a person
who has killed someone may flee.[h] In addition, give them forty-two other towns.
7 In all you must give the Levites forty-
eight towns, together with their pasturelands. 8 The towns you give the Levites
from the land the Israelites possess are to
be given in proportion to the inheritance
of each tribe: Take many towns from a
tribe that has many, but few from one
that has few."[i]

9 Then the LORD said to Moses:
10 "Speak to the Israelites and say to
them: 'When you cross the Jordan into
Canaan,[j] 11 select some towns to be your
cities of refuge, to which a person who
has killed someone[k] accidentally[l] may
flee. 12 They will be places of refuge from
the avenger,[m] so that a person accused of
murder[n] may not die before he stands
trial before the assembly.[o] 13 These six
towns you give will be your cities of refuge.[p] 14 Give three on this side of the Jordan and three in Canaan as cities of refuge. 15 These six towns will be a place of
refuge for Israelites, aliens and any other
people living among them, so that anyone
who has killed another accidentally can
flee there.

16 " 'If a man strikes someone with an
iron object so that he dies, he is a murderer; the murderer shall be put to
death.[q] 17 Or if anyone has a stone in his
hand that could kill, and he strikes someone so that he dies, he is a murderer; the
murderer shall be put to death. 18 Or if
anyone has a wooden object in his hand
that could kill, and he hits someone so
that he dies, he is a murderer; the murderer shall be put to death. 19 The avenger
of blood[r] shall put the murderer to
death; when he meets him, he shall put
him to death.[s] 20 If anyone with malice

34:17 [o]Nu 11:28; Dt 1:38
34:18 [p]S Nu 1:4 [q]Jos 14:1
34:19 [r]ver 29 [s]S Nu 26:65 [t]Ge 29:35; Dt 33:7; Ps 60:7
34:20 [u]S Ge 29:33
34:21 [v]Ge 49:27; Jdg 5:14; Ps 68:27
34:23 [w]Nu 1:34
34:24 [x]Nu 1:32
34:25 [y]S Ge 30:20
34:27 [z]Nu 1:40
34:29 [a]ver 19
35:1 [b]Nu 22:1
35:2 [c]Lev 25:32-34; Jos 14:3,4 [d]Jos 21:1-42
35:3 [e]Dt 18:6; Jos 14:4; 21:2
35:5 [f]Jos 3:4 [g]Lev 25:34; 2Ch 11:14; 13:9; 23:2; 31:19
35:6 [h]ver 11; Jos 21:13
35:8 [i]Nu 26:54; 33:54
35:10 [j]Nu 33:51; Dt 9:1; Jos 1:2,11
35:11 [k]ver 22-25 [l]S Ex 21:13
35:12 [m]ver 19; Dt 19:6; Jos 20:3; 2Sa 14:11 [n]ver 26, 27,28 [o]ver 24,25
35:13 [p]ver 6,14
35:16 [q]S Ex 21:12
35:19 [r]S ver 12 [s]ver 21

[j]*15 Jordan of Jericho* was possibly an ancient name for the Jordan River. [k]*1* Hebrew *Jordan of Jericho*; possibly an ancient name for the Jordan River
[l]*4* Hebrew *a thousand cubits* (about 450 meters)
[m]*5* Hebrew *two thousand cubits* (about 900 meters)

35:4 ELECTION, Leadership—God's servant leaders could not live as a normal tribal group controlling and administering a political territory. They did need homes. Election provided homes throughout Israel, so all people would have access to religious leadership.

35:6–34 CHRISTIAN ETHICS, Justice—Justice involves protection for the accused until their cases can be fairly judged. Israel's culture encouraged immediate blood vengeance by relatives of the victim. God set up a system of cities of refuge to protect falsely accused and accidental killers. Every society must define murder and set up a just system to determine innocence and guilt and to set punishment for the guilty. See note on Lev 24:17–22.

aforethought shoves another or throws something at him intentionally[t] so that he dies 21or if in hostility he hits him with his fist so that he dies, that person shall be put to death;[u] he is a murderer. The avenger of blood[v] shall put the murderer to death when he meets him.

22" 'But if without hostility someone suddenly shoves another or throws something at him unintentionally[w] 23or, without seeing him, drops a stone on him that could kill him, and he dies, then since he was not his enemy and he did not intend to harm him, 24the assembly[x] must judge between him and the avenger of blood according to these regulations. 25The assembly must protect the one accused of murder from the avenger of blood and send him back to the city of refuge to which he fled. He must stay there until the death of the high priest,[y] who was anointed[z] with the holy oil.[a]

26" 'But if the accused ever goes outside the limits of the city of refuge to which he has fled 27and the avenger of blood finds him outside the city, the avenger of blood may kill the accused without being guilty of murder. 28The accused must stay in his city of refuge until the death of the high priest; only after the death of the high priest may he return to his own property.

29" 'These are to be legal requirements[b] for you throughout the generations to come,[c] wherever you live.[d]

30" 'Anyone who kills a person is to be put to death as a murderer only on the testimony of witnesses. But no one is to be put to death on the testimony of only one witness.[e]

31" 'Do not accept a ransom[f] for the life of a murderer, who deserves to die. He must surely be put to death.

32" 'Do not accept a ransom for anyone who has fled to a city of refuge and so allow him to go back and live on his own land before the death of the high priest.

33" 'Do not pollute the land where you are. Bloodshed pollutes the land,[g] and atonement cannot be made for the land on which blood has been shed, except by the blood of the one who shed it. 34Do not defile the land[h] where you live and where I dwell,[i] for I, the LORD, dwell among the Israelites.' "

35:20 [t]S Ex 21:14
35:21 [u]Ex 21:14 [v]ver 19
35:22 [w]S Ex 21:13
35:24 [x]S ver 12
35:25 [y]ver 32 [z]S Ex 28:41 [a]S Ex 29:7
35:29 [b]Nu 27:11 [c]Nu 10:8 [d]S Ex 12:20
35:30 [e]Dt 17:6; 19:15; S Mt 18:16; Jn 7:51
35:31 [f]Ex 21:30; Job 6:22; Ps 49:8; Pr 13:8
35:33 [g]S Ge 4:10
35:34 [h]Lev 18:24, 25 [i]S Ex 29:45
36:1 [j]S Nu 26:30 [k]S Ge 50:23 [l]S Nu 26:28 [m]S Nu 27:2
36:2 [n]S Nu 33:54 [o]S Nu 26:33
36:4 [p]S Lev 25:10
36:7 [q]S Lev 25:23
36:8 [r]1Ch 23:22
36:11 [s]Nu 26:33
36:12 [t]1Ch 7:15

Chapter 36

Inheritance of Zelophehad's Daughters

36:1–12pp — Nu 27:1–11

THE family heads of the clan of Gilead[j] son of Makir,[k] the son of Manasseh, who were from the clans of the descendants of Joseph,[l] came and spoke before Moses and the leaders,[m] the heads of the Israelite families. 2They said, "When the LORD commanded my lord to give the land as an inheritance to the Israelites by lot,[n] he ordered you to give the inheritance of our brother Zelophehad[o] to his daughters. 3Now suppose they marry men from other Israelite tribes; then their inheritance will be taken from our ancestral inheritance and added to that of the tribe they marry into. And so part of the inheritance allotted to us will be taken away. 4When the Year of Jubilee[p] for the Israelites comes, their inheritance will be added to that of the tribe into which they marry, and their property will be taken from the tribal inheritance of our forefathers."

5Then at the LORD's command Moses gave this order to the Israelites: "What the tribe of the descendants of Joseph is saying is right. 6This is what the LORD commands for Zelophehad's daughters: They may marry anyone they please as long as they marry within the tribal clan of their father. 7No inheritance[q] in Israel is to pass from tribe to tribe, for every Israelite shall keep the tribal land inherited from his forefathers. 8Every daughter who inherits land in any Israelite tribe must marry someone in her father's tribal clan,[r] so that every Israelite will possess the inheritance of his fathers. 9No inheritance may pass from tribe to tribe, for each Israelite tribe is to keep the land it inherits."

10So Zelophehad's daughters did as the LORD commanded Moses. 11Zelophehad's daughters—Mahlah, Tirzah, Hoglah, Milcah and Noah[s]—married their cousins on their father's side. 12They married within the clans of the descendants of Manasseh son of Joseph, and their inheritance remained in their father's clan and tribe.[t]

35:20–25 CHRISTIAN ETHICS, Murder—Intention plays a strong role in biblical ethics. Justice is decided on a person's attitudes and purposes, not only on our judgment of specific actions.

35:30–32 CHRISTIAN ETHICS, Justice—A system of justice depends on proper use of evidence and ethical judges. More than one witness is needed to provide convicting evidence. Accepting ransom payments has no place in proper systems of justice.

[13]These are the commands and regulations the LORD gave through Moses[u] to the Israelites on the plains of Moab by the Jordan across from Jericho.[n v]

36:13 [u]S Lev 7:38; S 27:34 [v]Nu 22:1

[n]13 Hebrew *Jordan of Jericho*; possibly an ancient name for the Jordan River

35:34 REVELATION, Divine Presence—By His divine nature God is present throughout the universe. He chooses to make His presence available to human beings more intensely at certain times and in certain places. He chose to be present in a special way with Israel in her land. This special awareness of His presence gave Israel special responsibility to live holy lives in the holy presence. The Tent of Meeting was a definite sign that He dwelled in the land with them, but it did not mean He was confined to the tent.

36:1–13 CHRISTIAN ETHICS, Justice—Justice is created through a legal system, not through individual laws. Each new law must be integrated into the system to provide justice for all parties involved and for the national interest. This system may cause some people to give up self-interest for the national good. See note on 27:1–11.

Deuteronomy

Theological Setting

How do the people of God respond when God fulfills His promises? A new generation faced a new stage of God's history with His people. The people had wandered in the wilderness for thirty-eight years (2:14) because of their sin of unbelief. God raised up a new generation and had them poised to enter the Promised Land, but they had to enter without their leader Moses. What would God do with them? How should they respond? What did it mean to be people of God's covenant in the land of Canaan? Was life with God there different from life in the wilderness?

Moses performed one last task for God. He preached three sermons seeking to answer the people's questions. In the first (1:6—4:43) he recounted the wondrous acts the Lord had performed on behalf of His people. In the second (4:44—28:68) he reiterated and expanded upon the Law of Yahweh (God). In the third (29:1—30:20) he led the new generation to renew the covenant which had been enacted earlier at Horeb. The covenant was that formal agreement that reflected the intimate relationship between God and His people. This covenant relationship was as vital for a people entering a new land as it was for the nation wandering in the wilderness. Deuteronomy defines that covenant relationship between God and His people.

In the Book of Deuteronomy, the major issues facing the people of God are addressed by Moses:

1. In light of their recent history of idolatry, would the people continue to rebel against God and His appointed leaders? Would they truly trust Yahweh as the only God?

2. The people of God could have remained in the plains of Moab and been assimilated into the existent culture, adopting its religion, mores, and life-style. Did they have faith to follow God's new leader and depend on God's promise to give them the new land?

3. If and when the people moved toward the land of promise, would they cower against their enemies, be conquered by them, or be assimilated into them? Would they become as the Canaanites and engage in the decadent worship practices of the land? Or would they recognize the greatness of the God of the Exodus and Conquest and be faithful to Him?

4. The people could renew their relationship to the Lord, appropriate God's gift of the land by faith, and live in the land in the way God intended. Would they accept the teachings of Deuteronomy as God's gracious gift of a guide to life in the land under God?

Theological Outline

Deuteronomy: God's Design for His People Living in the Promised Land

- I. Introduction: God Protects His People. (1:1-5)
- II. First Sermon: Learn from God's Mighty Acts. (1:6—4:43)
  - A. God's people are to remember His works and then move out in faith. (1:6—3:29)
    1. God's people are to appropriate those gifts He has promised. (1:6-8)
    2. God calls out wise and experienced leaders for His people. (1:9-18)
    3. Unbelief and presumption bring loss of God's gifts and punishment. (1:19-46)
    4. God's people are to honor what He has granted to other peoples. (2:1-25)
    5. God's people must obey and trust Him to give victory over opposition. (2:26—3:11)
    6. God's people need unity to face opposition and claim victory. (3:12-22)
    7. God's servants should train disciples to carry on in the ministry. (3:23-29)
  - B. God's Word is the foundation for the life of His people. (4:1-43)
    1. God's law distinguishes its adherents as the unique people of God. (4:1-8)
    2. God's people are to remember His great acts and keep His words. (4:9-24)
    3. Idolatry brings judgment. (4:25-31)
    4. The chosen of God acknowledge His works and obey His commands. (4:32-40)
    5. God provides justice against vengeance. (4:41-43)

III. Second Sermon: God Has Given His Law to Guide and Set Apart His People. (4:44—28:68)

- A. Covenant faith demands total allegiance to the Lord. (4:44—11:32)
  1. The Ten Commandments are the basis of the covenant relationship. (4:44—5:21)
  2. God's glory can be accessed only with fear and devotion. (5:22-33)
  3. To love God is the principal commandment and motive for faith. (6:1-9)
     - a. Loving God is lifelong. (6:1-3)
     - b. Loving God involves totality of commitment. (6:4-5)
     - c. Loving God involves self, family, and neighbor. (6:6-9)
  4. God blesses those who fear Him and serve Him. (6:10-25)
  5. Devotion to God implies a war against sin and God's enemies. (7:1-26)
  6. Prosperity can threaten faith. (8:1-20)
  7. History provides a lesson of God's grace and justice regarding sin. (9:1—10:11)
  8. Love of God requires total love and total commitment. (10:12—11:25)
  9. God's people live under the promise of blessing and the threat of curse. (11:25-32)

- B. The people of God know His covenant expectations. (12:1—28:68)
  1. Proper worship of God should accord with what He demands. (12:1-28)
  2. Those leading God's people astray will suffer severe punishment. (12:29—13:18)
  3. God's people are distinguished by the laws which govern them. (14:1—16:17)
     - a. God's people avoid pagan practices. (14:1-2)
     - b. God's people are distinguished by what they consume. (14:3-21)
     - c. God's people are distinguished by economic practices such as tithing. (14:22—15:23)
     - d. God's people celebrate God's acts in history and in nature. (16:1-17)
  4. The leaders of God's people shall be just, righteous, and holy. (16:18—18:22)
     - a. Judicial leaders shall seek justice, but hate partiality and idolatry. (16:18—17:13)
     - b. Political leaders shall seek God and not wealth. (17:14-20)
     - c. Religious leaders shall be supported by the people. (18:1-8)
     - d. Divination is prohibited. (18:9-14)
     - e. Prophets shall be found true and faithful in proclaiming God's will. (18:15-22)
  5. God's Law sanctifies life. (19:1—22:4)
     - a. Protection is given for manslaughterers. (19:1-13; see 4:41-43)
     - b. Provision is made regarding criminal witnesses. (19:14-21)
     - c. Defeat of God's enemies keeps His people holy. (20:1-9)
     - d. Peace is to be offered before war. (20:10-20)
     - e. God's laws provide for the maintenance of community responsibility. (21:1—22:4)
  6. Purity is to be maintained in all aspects of life. (22:5—23:19)
  7. God's laws provide justice for all aspects of community life. (23:20—25:19)
     - a. Economics (23:20-25; 25:13-16)
     - b. Marriage (24:1-5; 25:11-12)
     - c. The poor (24:6-16)
     - d. The alien, orphan, and widow (24:17-22; 25:4-10)
     - e. Defendants (25:1-3)
     - f. An external threat (25:17-19)
  8. Offerings and tithes demonstrate the devotion of His people. (26:1-19)
  9. God's people need renewal of obedience and commitment. (27:1—28:68)

IV. Third Sermon: God Seeks to Renew the Covenant Relationship. (29:1—30:20)

- A. God's deliverance in the past is the foundation of the covenant relationship. (29:1-9)
- B. Rebellion and idolatry will bring destruction. (29:10-29)
- C. God restores His people when they repent. (30:1-10)
- D. God's covenant gives His people the choice of faith/life or rebellion/death. (30:11-20)

V. God's Design Is for Continuity of Leadership for His People. (31:1—34:12)

- A. God is the true Leader for His people. (31:1-8)
- B. God's Word is to be read regularly before the people. (31:9-13)
- C. God calls and commissions His people's leaders. (31:14-29)
- D. God is faithful and good in spite of His people's unfaithfulness. (31:30—33:29)
- E. God's servants are to be wise, faithful, and bold. (34:1-12)

Theological Conclusions

The Book of Deuteronomy gave the foundation and motivation for the new generation of God's people to appropriate and live in the land of promise by focusing on these themes:

1. the nature and character of God,
2. the covenant relationship,
3. the response of God's people in faith,
4. the concept of sin and its effects.

Deuteronomy centers on the loyal love of God for His people by recounting His wondrous, mighty acts. God's loving and purposeful direction of history for His people is one of the unique aspects of Israelite religion. The most startling aspect of Israel's faith appears in the "creed" or "Shema" (6:4). God is unique, the sole God of the universe. All the gods of the nations are fakes. Only Yahweh, the God of Israel, is God. The one true, invisible God does not allow physical representations to be made of Him. He demands the total devotion of His people—they shall have no other gods but Him. God's holiness and righteousness are reflected in the moral order set forth in the Law.

God's grace is seen in His "choosing" Israel as His own. As His elect people, Israel was to reflect His character. God elected His people by establishing the covenant relationship. God initiated the covenant out of His love (7:8). Election, the gift of the land, and the response of the people are the major elements of the covenant. God is the sovereign Lord of the covenant, and the people are His servants. He will not share His sovereignty with any other god, creature, or person. A human ruler may be called sovereign; but such human, earthly sovereignty can in no way compare to or imitate God's sovereign kingship.

Human response to the covenant is summed up in 6:5-9, "Love the LORD your God with all your heart and with all your soul and with all your strength . . . " (6:5). Devotion to God is to be total and unequivocal. Jesus proclaimed this the greatest command of the Bible (Mt 22:37-38). The command to love is based on the prior demonstration of God's love for people. Love for God comes as a heart response which is evidenced by the hearing and doing of His Word. God's way of life should be taught to family and neighbor and should characterize the totality of an individual's life-style.

The extensive range of the covenant regulations shows that no area of human living stands outside the perspective of God's concern. God expects the highest moral and ethical standards from His people. No distinction between the religious and secular is made; all of life comes under the sphere of a personal relationship to God.

Obedience to God's way of life is necessary for the community of God to maintain unity, purity, and effectual witness. Disobedience disrupts the relationship to God, to the community of faith, and to the world. God realizes the human tendency toward unfaithfulness. Sin in Deuteronomy was set against the background of the covenant. Obedience to the Lord would result in covenant blessing for His people. Disobedience would lead to cursing. Chapters 27 and 28 are weighted heavily toward the curses of the covenant, which included the final step of exile and destruction. The gift of the land, which the people were about to inherit, could be taken away by Yahweh if the people continued in sin. The ultimate sin was the worship of other gods. The penalty for idolatry within Israel was severe—death. The nation would also pay a severe penalty. Apostasy would breach the relationship between people and God. The history of the nation showed God carried out the threats of the covenant curses. The people's apostasy led to exile under Assyria (721 BC) and Babylon (586 BC). God freely gave His people the choice of allegiance or apostasy, and they reaped the results of their choice.

Contemporary Teaching

The Book of Deuteronomy draws us to a deeper understanding of our relationship to the Lord and His Word. We learn what God is like, what He has done for His people, and what He requires of His servants.

Deuteronomy shows us that: (1) God is a sovereign Lord over history, nature, and our lives. We must not place any thing, any institution, or any person in a position to compare with or imitate His lordship. (2) God loves us enough to show us how to enter into a relationship with Him by faith. (3) God gives abundantly to provide the needs of His people. (4) God wants and requires His people to be solely and totally devoted to Him. Nothing should hinder the relationship between God and us. Anything that does is idolatry. (5) We should love God with the totality of our being and share that love with others—family and neighbors. (6) God has chosen us by His grace to be a special and unique people who are to reflect His nature to the world. (7) God has given us guidance (His Word) as to how to fulfill the purpose of being witnesses of His character. (8) God blesses those who obey Him and judges those who rebel against Him.

Chapter 1

The Command to Leave Horeb

THESE are the words Moses spoke to all Israel in the desert east of the Jordan[a]—that is, in the Arabah[b]—opposite Suph, between Paran[c] and Tophel, Laban, Hazeroth and Dizahab. 2(It takes eleven days to go from Horeb[d] to Kadesh Barnea[e] by the Mount Seir[f] road.)[g]

3In the fortieth year,[h] on the first day of the eleventh month,[i] Moses proclaimed[j] to the Israelites all that the LORD had commanded him concerning them. 4This was after he had defeated Sihon[k] king of the Amorites,[l] who reigned in Heshbon,[m] and at Edrei had defeated Og[n] king of Bashan, who reigned in Ashtaroth.[o]

5East of the Jordan in the territory of Moab,[p] Moses began to expound this law, saying:

6The LORD our God said to us[q] at Horeb,[r] "You have stayed long enough[s] at this mountain. 7Break camp and advance into the hill country of the Amorites;[t] go to all the neighboring peoples in the Arabah,[u] in the mountains, in the western foothills, in the Negev[v] and along the coast, to the land of the Canaanites[w] and to Lebanon,[x] as far as the great river, the Euphrates.[y] 8See, I have given you this land.[z,a] Go in and take possession of the land that the LORD swore[b] he would give to your fathers—to Abraham, Isaac and Jacob—and to their descendants after them."

The Appointment of Leaders

9At that time I said to you, "You are too heavy a burden[c] for me to carry alone.[d] 10The LORD your God has increased[e] your numbers[f] so that today you are as many[g] as the stars in the sky.[h] 11May the LORD, the God of your fathers, increase[i] you a thousand times and bless you as he has promised![j] 12But how can I bear your problems and your burdens and your disputes all by myself?[k] 13Choose some wise, understanding and respected men[l] from each of your tribes, and I will set them over you."

14You answered me, "What you propose to do is good."

15So I took[m] the leading men of your tribes,[n] wise and respected men,[o] and appointed them to have authority over you—as commanders[p] of thousands, of hundreds, of fifties and of tens and as tribal officials.[q] 16And I charged your judges at that time: Hear the disputes between your brothers and judge[r] fairly,[s] whether the case is between brother Israelites or between one of them and an alien.[t] 17Do not show partiality[u] in judging; hear both small and great alike. Do not be afraid of any man,[v] for judgment belongs to God. Bring me any case too hard for you, and I will hear it.[w] 18And at that time I told you everything you were to do.[x]

Spies Sent Out

19Then, as the LORD our God commanded us, we set out from Horeb and went toward the hill country of the Amorites[y] through all that vast and dreadful desert[z] that you have seen, and so we reached Kadesh Barnea.[a] 20Then I said to you, "You have reached the hill country of the Amorites, which the LORD our God is giving us. 21See, the LORD your God has given you the land. Go up and take possession[b] of it as the LORD, the God of your fathers, told you. Do not be afraid;[c] do not be discouraged."[d]

22Then all of you came to me and said, "Let us send men ahead to spy[e] out the land[f] for us and bring back a report

1:1 [a]S Nu 13:29; Dt 4:46 [b]ver 7; Dt 2:8; 3:17; Jos 3:16; 8:14; 11:2; Eze 47:8 [c]S Nu 10:12 **1:2** [d]S Ex 3:1 [e]S Ge 14:7; Dt 2:14; 9:23; Jos 15:3 [f]S Nu 24:18 [g]ver 19 **1:3** [h]Nu 14:33; 32:13; Dt 8:2; Heb 3:7-9 [i]Ge 50:3; Dt 34:8; Jos 4:19 [j]Dt 4:1-2 **1:4** [k]Nu 21:21-26 [l]S Ge 10:16; S 14:7 [m]S Nu 21:25 [n]Nu 21:33-35; Dt 3:10 [o]Jos 9:10; 12:4; 1Ch 11:44 **1:5** [p]S Nu 21:11 **1:6** [q]Nu 10:13 [r]S Ex 3:1 [s]Dt 2:3 **1:7** [t]ver 19; Dt 2:24; 7:1; Jos 10:5 [u]S ver 1 [v]S Nu 21:1; Jos 11:16; 12:8; 2Sa 24:7 [w]S Ge 10:18 [x]Dt 11:24 [y]S Ge 2:14 **1:8** [z]S Jos 23:13 [a]S Nu 34:2 [b]S Ex 13:11; S Nu 14:23; Heb 6:13-14 **1:9** [c]S Nu 11:14; Ps 38:4 [d]S Ex 18:18 **1:10** [e]ver 11; Eze 16:7 [f]S Dt 7:13 [g]S Ge 15:5; Isa 51:2; 60:22; Eze 33:24 [h]S Ge 22:17; S Nu 10:36 **1:11** [i]S ver 10 [j]ver 8; Ex 32:13; 2Sa 24:3; 1Ch 21:3 **1:12** [k]S Ex 5:22; S 18:18 **1:13** [l]S Ge 47:6 **1:15** [m]Ex 18:25 [n]Ex 5:14; Nu 11:16; Jos 1:10; 3:2 [o]S Ge 47:6 [p]Nu 31:14; 1Sa 8:12; 22:7; 1Ki 14:27 [q]S Nu 1:4 **1:16** [r]1Ki 3:9; Ps 72:1; Pr 2:9 [s]S Ge 31:37; Jn 7:24 [t]S Ex 12:19, 49; S 22:21 **1:17** [u]S Ex 18:16; S Lev 19:15; Ac 10:34; Jas 2:1 [v]Pr 29:25 [w]Ex 18:26 **1:18** [x]S Ge 39:11 **1:19** [y]S ver 7 [z]Dt 2:7; 8:15; 32:10; Ps 136:16; Jer 2:2,6; Hos 13:5 [a]ver 2; Nu 13:26 **1:21** [b]Dt 9:23 [c]S Nu 14:9; Jos 1:6,9,18; 2Sa 10:12; Ps 27:14 [d]Dt 7:18; Jos 8:1; 10:8 **1:22** [e]Nu 13:1-3 [f]S Ge 42:9

1:3—3:29 HISTORY, Narrative—God's people need to hear their story with God. We need to remember what God has done for us and how we have responded. We need to learn the lessons history will teach us. The Bible repeatedly narrates God's history with His people to call for renewal and recommitment.

1:3 HISTORY, Time—Israel's salvation was dateable. God's commands and saving acts gave meaning to time. God's warnings had time conditions which He took seriously and fulfilled. The disobedient people had to spend forty years in the wilderness before hearing the command to conquer (Nu 14:33–34).

1:5—3:29 REVELATION, History—Moses described God's saving acts, employing "we" throughout the narration. Moses was speaking to a new generation, survivors of the wilderness wanderings, to tell them that God had been personally present on their journey as a caring and directing God. God blessed and watched over His people all the way. Israel's was a special history of salvation in which God revealed Himself as Savior and Guide of His people.

1:8–36 ELECTION, God's Promise—Promise preceded possession of the land. Election was God's plan long before it began to become reality. Courageous and inspired members of God's elect are obedient and industrious in possessing God's promises. The rebellious and disobedient miss attaining the promises of God.

1:10 GOD, Sovereignty—Moses attributed the substantial growth of the Hebrew people to the blessing of God. We do not want to take a deterministic viewpoint holding that every event is the direct result of God's intervention, but we ought to see God's hand in human affairs more than we do. Is there any good thing in life for which we are not indebted to God? We should be careful not to trace cause-effect relationships between God and everything that happens to us. We should also be careful to praise and thank God for all the good things that do come to us.

1:16–17 CHRISTIAN ETHICS, Justice—See note on Lev 19:15.

about the route we are to take and the
towns we will come to."
23The idea seemed good to me; so I
selected[g] twelve of you, one man from
each tribe. 24They left and went up into
the hill country, and came to the Valley of
Eshcol[h] and explored it. 25Taking with
them some of the fruit of the land, they
brought it down to us and reported,[i] "It
is a good land[j] that the LORD our God is
giving us."[k]

Rebellion Against the LORD

26But you were unwilling to go up;[l]
you rebelled[m] against the command of
the LORD your God. 27You grumbled[n] in
your tents and said, "The LORD hates us;
so he brought us out of Egypt to deliver us
into the hands of the Amorites to destroy
us. 28Where can we go? Our brothers
have made us lose heart. They say, 'The
people are stronger and taller[o] than we
are; the cities are large, with walls up to
the sky. We even saw the Anakites[p]
there.' "
29Then I said to you, "Do not be terrified; do not be afraid[q] of them.[r] 30The
LORD your God, who is going before you,
will fight[s] for you, as he did for you in
Egypt, before your very eyes, 31and in the
desert. There you saw how the LORD your
God carried[t] you, as a father carries his
son, all the way you went until you
reached this place."[u]
32In spite of this,[v] you did not trust[w]
in the LORD your God, 33who went ahead
of you on your journey, in fire by night
and in a cloud by day,[x] to search[y] out
places for you to camp and to show you
the way you should go.
34When the LORD heard[z] what you
said, he was angry[a] and solemnly
swore:[b] 35"Not a man of this evil generation shall see the good land[c] I swore to
give your forefathers, 36except Caleb[d]
son of Jephunneh. He will see it, and I
will give him and his descendants the
land he set his feet on, because he followed the LORD wholeheartedly.[e] "
37Because of you the LORD became angry[f] with me also and said, "You shall
not enter[g] it, either. 38But your assistant,
Joshua[h] son of Nun, will enter it. Encourage[i] him, because he will lead[j] Israel to
inherit[k] it. 39And the little ones that you
said would be taken captive,[l] your children who do not yet know[m] good from
bad—they will enter the land. I will give
it to them and they will take possession of
it. 40But as for you, turn around and set
out toward the desert along the route to
the Red Sea.[a] [n]"
41Then you replied, "We have sinned
against the LORD. We will go up and fight,
as the LORD our God commanded us." So
every one of you put on his weapons,
thinking it easy to go up into the hill
country.
42But the LORD said to me, "Tell them,
'Do not go up and fight, because I will not
be with you. You will be defeated by your
enemies.' "[o]
43So I told you, but you would not listen. You rebelled against the LORD's command and in your arrogance you marched
up into the hill country. 44The Amorites
who lived in those hills came out against
you; they chased you like a swarm of
bees[p] and beat you down from Seir[q] all
the way to Hormah.[r] 45You came back
and wept before the LORD,[s] but he paid
no attention[t] to your weeping and
turned a deaf ear[u] to you. 46And so you
stayed in Kadesh[v] many days—all the
time you spent there.

Chapter 2

Wanderings in the Desert

THEN we turned back and set out toward the desert along the route to
the Red Sea,[a] [w] as the LORD had directed
me. For a long time we made our way
around the hill country of Seir.[x]
2Then the LORD said to me, 3"You have
made your way around this hill country

[a] *40,1* Hebrew *Yam Suph*; that is, Sea of Reeds

1:23 [g]Nu 13:1-3
1:24 [h]Nu 13:21-25; S 32:9
1:25 [i]S Nu 13:27 [j]S Nu 14:7 [k]Jos 1:2
1:26 [l]Nu 14:1-4 [m]S Nu 14:9
1:27 [n]Dt 9:28; Ps 106:25
1:28 [o]S Nu 13:32 [p]S Nu 13:33; Dt 9:1-3
1:29 [q]Dt 3:22; 20:3; Ne 4:14 [r]Dt 7:18; 20:1; 31:6
1:30 [s]S Ex 14:14
1:31 [t]Ex 19:4; Dt 32:10-12; Ps 28:9; Isa 46:3-4; 63:9; Hos 11:3; Ac 13:18 [u]Jer 31:32
1:32 [v]S Nu 14:11 [w]Dt 9:23; Ps 78:22; 106:24; Zep 3:2; Heb 3:19; Jude 1:5
1:33 [x]Ex 13:21; Nu 9:15-23; Ne 9:12; Ps 78:14 [y]S Nu 10:33
1:34 [z]S Nu 11:1 [a]S Nu 32:14 [b]S Nu 14:23,28-30; Eze 20:15; Heb 3:11
1:35 [c]S Nu 14:29
1:36 [d]S Nu 13:6 [e]S Nu 14:24
1:37 [f]Ps 106:32 [g]S Nu 27:13
1:38 [h]S Nu 11:28 [i]Dt 31:7 [j]Dt 3:28 [k]Jos 11:23; Ps 78:55; 136:21
1:39 [l]S Nu 14:3 [m]Isa 7:15-16
1:40 [n]S Ex 14:27; Jdg 11:16
1:42 [o]S Nu 14:41-43
1:44 [p]Ps 118:12 [q]S Nu 24:18 [r]S Nu 14:45
1:45 [s]S Nu 14:1 [t]Job 27:9; 35:13; Ps 18:41; 66:18; Pr 1:28; Isa 1:15; Jer 14:12; La 3:8; Mic 3:4; S Jn 9:31 [u]Ps 28:1; 39:12; Pr 28:9
1:46 [v]S Nu 20:1
2:1 [w]S Ex 14:27; S Nu 21:4 [x]S Nu 24:18

1:26–43 SIN, Rebellion—Faith looks at God's possibilities, not human impossibilities. To say, "God cannot do it" is sin. See notes on Ex 14:11–12; Nu 32:23.

1:30 CHRISTIAN ETHICS, War and Peace—See note on Ex 14:1—15:18.

1:31 GOD, Father—The dominant idea of God in the Old Testament was God as sovereign Lord, but the idea of God as sovereign was warmly colored by many allusions to the love and grace of God. In a few instances the Old Testament pictures God with special tenderness as a loving Father. God's people learn this aspect of God's character when they experience His saving acts for them as Israel did in the Exodus and wilderness. See note on Hos 11:1–11.

1:33 DISCIPLESHIP, God's Leadership—See note on Nu 9:15–23.

1:34–40 EVIL AND SUFFERING, Endurance—Human evil may have lasting consequences which we can respond to only by endurance. Israel and Moses spent long years under God's leadership in the wilderness after their rebellion. Their only task was preparing a new generation to expect and receive the fulfillment of God's promise. See note on Nu 14:26–35.

1:42 REVELATION, Events—God's presence cannot be manipulated. He does not guarantee it for a disobedient people. God led His people to the border of the Promised Land, but they refused again to believe in His power and presence. He therefore declared that if they fought, they would fight without His presence. Because they lacked faith and chose to wander from His plans, He would allow that generation to wander in the desert. The God of good purposes never forces His plans on His people but will leave them to the consequences of their choices. Still He planned to bring them to the promised goal. God's purposes can be delayed by our disobedience but not defeated.

long enough;[y] now turn north. [4]Give the people these orders:[z] 'You are about to pass through the territory of your brothers the descendants of Esau,[a] who live in Seir.[b] They will be afraid[c] of you, but be very careful. [5]Do not provoke them to war, for I will not give you any of their land, not even enough to put your foot on. I have given Esau the hill country of Seir as his own.[d] [6]You are to pay them in silver for the food you eat and the water you drink.' "

[7]The LORD your God has blessed you in all the work of your hands. He has watched[e] over your journey through this vast desert.[f] These forty years[g] the LORD your God has been with you, and you have not lacked anything.[h]

[8]So we went on past our brothers the descendants of Esau, who live in Seir. We turned from[i] the Arabah[j] road, which comes up from Elath and Ezion Geber,[k] and traveled along the desert road of Moab.[l]

[9]Then the LORD said to me, "Do not harass the Moabites or provoke them to war, for I will not give you any part of their land. I have given Ar[m] to the descendants of Lot[n] as a possession."

[10](The Emites[o] used to live there—a people strong and numerous, and as tall as the Anakites.[p] [11]Like the Anakites, they too were considered Rephaites,[q] but the Moabites called them Emites. [12]Horites[r] used to live in Seir, but the descendants of Esau drove them out. They destroyed the Horites from before them and settled in their place, just as Israel did[s] in the land the LORD gave them as their possession.)

[13]And the LORD said, "Now get up and cross the Zered Valley.[t]" So we crossed the valley.

[14]Thirty-eight years[u] passed from the time we left Kadesh Barnea[v] until we crossed the Zered Valley. By then, that entire generation[w] of fighting men had perished from the camp, as the LORD had sworn to them.[x] [15]The LORD's hand was against them until he had completely eliminated[y] them from the camp.

[16]Now when the last of these fighting men among the people had died, [17]the LORD said to me, [18]"Today you are to pass by the region of Moab at Ar.[z] [19]When you come to the Ammonites,[a] do not harass them or provoke them to war,[b] for I will not give you possession of any land belonging to the Ammonites. I have given it as a possession to the descendants of Lot.[c]"

[20](That too was considered a land of the Rephaites,[d] who used to live there; but the Ammonites called them Zamzummites. [21]They were a people strong and numerous, and as tall as the Anakites.[e] The LORD destroyed them from before the Ammonites, who drove them out and settled in their place. [22]The LORD had done the same for the descendants of Esau, who lived in Seir,[f] when he destroyed the Horites from before them. They drove them out and have lived in their place to this day. [23]And as for the Avvites[g] who lived in villages as far as Gaza,[h] the Caphtorites[i] coming out from Caphtor[b][j] destroyed them and settled in their place.)

Defeat of Sihon King of Heshbon

[24]"Set out now and cross the Arnon Gorge.[k] See, I have given into your hand Sihon the Amorite,[l] king of Heshbon, and his country. Begin to take possession of it and engage[m] him in battle. [25]This very day I will begin to put the terror[n] and fear[o] of you on all the nations under heaven. They will hear reports of you and will tremble[p] and be in anguish because of you."

[26]From the desert of Kedemoth[q] I sent messengers to Sihon[r] king of Heshbon offering peace[s] and saying, [27]"Let us pass through your country. We will stay on the main road; we will not turn aside to the right or to the left.[t] [28]Sell us food to eat[u] and water to drink for their price in silver. Only let us pass through on foot[v]— [29]as the descendants of Esau, who live in Seir, and the Moabites, who live in Ar, did for us—until we cross the

2:3 [y]Dt 1:6
2:4 [z]Nu 20:14-21 [a]Ge 36:8 [b]ver 1 [c]Ex 15:16
2:5 [d]Jos 24:4
2:7 [e]Dt 8:2-4 [f]S Ex 13:21; S Dt 1:19 [g]ver 14; S Nu 14:33; 32:13; Jos 5:6 [h]Ne 9:21; Am 2:10
2:8 [i]S Nu 20:21 [j]S Dt 1:1 [k]Nu 33:35; 1Ki 9:26 [l]S Nu 21:4
2:9 [m]S Nu 21:15 [n]Ge 19:38; Ps 83:8
2:10 [o]Ge 14:5 [p]S Nu 13:22,33
2:11 [q]S Ge 14:5
2:12 [r]S Ge 14:6 [s]Nu 21:25,35
2:13 [t]S Nu 21:12
2:14 [u]S ver 7 [v]S Dt 1:2 [w]Nu 14:29-35 [x]Dt 1:34-35; Jos 5:6
2:15 [y]Ps 106:26; Jude 1:5
2:18 [z]S Nu 21:15
2:19 [a]S Ge 19:38 [b]2Ch 20:10 [c]S ver 9
2:20 [d]S Ge 14:5
2:21 [e]ver 10
2:22 [f]S Ge 14:6
2:23 [g]Jos 13:3; 18:23; 2Ki 17:31 [h]S Ge 10:19 [i]S Ge 10:14 [j]Jer 47:4; Am 9:7
2:24 [k]Nu 21:13-14; Jdg 11:13,18 [l]S Dt 1:7 [m]Dt 3:6
2:25 [n]S Ge 35:5; Dt 11:25 [o]Jos 2:9, 11; 1Ch 14:17; 2Ch 14:14; 17:10; 20:29; Isa 2:19; 13:13; 19:16 [p]Ex 15:14-16
2:26 [q]Jos 13:18; 1Ch 6:79 [r]Dt 1:4; Jdg 11:21-22 [s]Dt 20:10; Jdg 21:13; 2Sa 20:19
2:27 [t]Nu 21:21-22
2:28 [u]Dt 23:4 [v]S Nu 20:19

[b]*23* That is, Crete

2:5,9,24–25,30,36 GOD, Sovereignty—Frequently Moses attributed the outcome of the events in Israel's life to the hand of God guiding and winning victories for His people. God's sovereignty extends to all nations. The eye of faith sees the hand of God in charge of life. See note on 1:10.

2:5–25 ELECTION, Other Nations—God's elect are to travel as peacefully as possible in pursuit of God's promises. Deuteronomy emphasizes non-provocation and harmonious relationships in spite of living in the face of hostile settings. Election is not a license to control and/or destroy other peoples. Election involves plans for peoples other than the elect.

2:7 HUMANITY, Relationship to God—The blessings of God, not necessarily physical blessings, are bestowed upon people to whom He has related Himself through His gracious love. A look backward reminds us God has brought us to where we are. We have no reason for selfish pride.

2:7 SALVATION, Blessing—For forty years, God blessed Israel with all she needed to exist in a vast desert. In His wisdom God at times chooses to bless His people with all they need, even when they have been unfaithful to Him. Such blessing is part of God's salvation for which we give thanks. It is not a demand we place on and expect from God.

2:9–23 CHRISTIAN ETHICS, War and Peace—War is not a godly goal. We must not use self-interest to provoke others to war. See notes on Ge 13:7–12; Ex 23:22–33.

2:19—3:11 CHRISTIAN ETHICS, War and Peace—See notes on Nu 21:1–3; 31:1–54.

Jordan into the land the LORD our God is
giving us." 30But Sihon king of Heshbon
refused to let us pass through. For the
LORD[w] your God had made his spirit stubborn[x] and his heart obstinate[y] in order
to give him into your hands,[z] as he has
now done.

31The LORD said to me, "See, I have
begun to deliver Sihon and his country
over to you. Now begin to conquer and
possess his land."[a]

32When Sihon and all his army came
out to meet us in battle[b] at Jahaz, 33the
LORD our God delivered[c] him over to us
and we struck him down,[d] together with
his sons and his whole army. 34At that
time we took all his towns and completely destroyed[c e] them—men, women and
children. We left no survivors. 35But the
livestock[f] and the plunder[g] from the
towns we had captured we carried off for
ourselves. 36From Aroer[h] on the rim of
the Arnon Gorge, and from the town in
the gorge, even as far as Gilead,[i] not one
town was too strong for us. The LORD our
God gave[j] us all of them. 37But in accordance with the command of the LORD our
God,[k] you did not encroach on any of the
land of the Ammonites,[l] neither the land
along the course of the Jabbok[m] nor that
around the towns in the hills.

Chapter 3

Defeat of Og King of Bashan

NEXT we turned and went up along
the road toward Bashan, and Og
king of Bashan[n] with his whole army
marched out to meet us in battle at Edrei.[o] 2The LORD said to me, "Do not be
afraid[p] of him, for I have handed him
over to you with his whole army and his
land. Do to him what you did to Sihon
king of the Amorites, who reigned in
Heshbon."

3So the LORD our God also gave into
our hands Og king of Bashan and all his
army. We struck them down,[q] leaving no
survivors.[r] 4At that time we took all his
cities.[s] There was not one of the sixty
cities that we did not take from them—
the whole region of Argob, Og's kingdom[t] in Bashan.[u] 5All these cities were
fortified with high walls and with gates
and bars, and there were also a great
many unwalled villages. 6We completely
destroyed[c] them, as we had done with
Sihon king of Heshbon, destroying[c v] every city—men, women and children.
7But all the livestock[w] and the plunder
from their cities we carried off for ourselves.

8So at that time we took from these
two kings of the Amorites[x] the territory
east of the Jordan, from the Arnon Gorge
as far as Mount Hermon.[y] 9(Hermon is
called Sirion[z] by the Sidonians; the Amorites call it Senir.)[a] 10We took all the
towns on the plateau, and all Gilead, and
all Bashan as far as Salecah[b] and Edrei,
towns of Og's kingdom in Bashan.
11(Only Og king of Bashan was left of the
remnant of the Rephaites.[c] His bed[d] was
made of iron and was more than thirteen
feet long and six feet wide.[e] It is still in
Rabbah[d] of the Ammonites.)

Division of the Land

12Of the land that we took over at that
time, I gave the Reubenites and the Gadites the territory north of Aroer[e] by the
Arnon Gorge, including half the hill country of Gilead, together with its towns.
13The rest of Gilead and also all of Bashan, the kingdom of Og, I gave to the
half tribe of Manasseh.[f] (The whole region of Argob in Bashan used to be
known as a land of the Rephaites.[g]
14Jair,[h] a descendant of Manasseh, took
the whole region of Argob as far as the
border of the Geshurites and the Maaca-
thites;[i] it was named[j] after him, so that
to this day Bashan is called Havvoth
Jair.[f]) 15And I gave Gilead to Makir.[k]
16But to the Reubenites and the Gadites I
gave the territory extending from Gilead
down to the Arnon Gorge (the middle of
the gorge being the border) and out to the
Jabbok River,[l] which is the border of the
Ammonites. 17Its western border was the
Jordan in the Arabah,[m] from Kinnereth[n]
to the Sea of the Arabah[o] (the Salt
Sea[g p]), below the slopes of Pisgah.

18I commanded you at that time: "The
LORD your God has given[q] you this land
to take possession of it. But all your able-

2:30 [w]Jdg 14:4; 1Ki 12:15 [x]S Ex 4:21; Ro 9:18 [y]S Ex 14:17 [z]La 3:65
2:31 [a]S Ge 12:7
2:32 [b]S Nu 21:23
2:33 [c]Ex 23:31; Dt 7:2; 31:5 [d]S Nu 21:24
2:34 [e]S Nu 21:2; Dt 3:6; 7:2; Ps 106:34
2:35 [f]Dt 3:7 [g]S Ge 34:29; S 49:27
2:36 [h]S Nu 32:34 [i]S Nu 32:39 [j]Ps 44:3
2:37 [k]ver 18-19 [l]S Nu 21:24 [m]S Ge 32:22
3:1 [n]S Nu 32:19 [o]S Nu 21:33
3:2 [p]Jos 10:8; 2Ki 19:6; Isa 7:4
3:3 [q]S Nu 21:24 [r]Nu 21:35
3:4 [s]S Nu 21:24 [t]ver 13 [u]S Nu 21:33
3:6 [v]Dt 2:24
3:7 [w]Dt 2:35
3:8 [x]Nu 32:33; Jos 13:8-12 [y]Dt 4:48; Jos 11:3, 17; 12:1; 13:5; Jdg 3:3; 1Ch 5:23; Ps 42:6; 89:12; 133:3; SS 4:8
3:9 [z]Ps 29:6 [a]1Ch 5:23; SS 4:8; Eze 27:5
3:10 [b]Jos 12:5; 1Ch 5:11
3:11 [c]Ge 14:5 [d]Jos 13:25; 15:60; 2Sa 11:1; 12:26; 17:27; 1Ch 20:1; Jer 49:2; Eze 21:20; 25:5; Am 1:14
3:12 [e]Dt 2:36
3:13 [f]Dt 29:8 [g]S Ge 14:5
3:14 [h]S Nu 32:41 [i]Jos 12:5; 13:11,13; 2Sa 10:6; 23:34; 2Ki 25:23; 1Ch 4:19; Jer 40:8 [j]Jos 19:47; Ps 49:11
3:15 [k]S Ge 50:23; Nu 32:39-40
3:16 [l]S Nu 21:24
3:17 [m]2Sa 2:29; 4:7; Eze 47:8 [n]S Nu 34:11 [o]S Dt 1:1 [p]S Ge 14:3
3:18 [q]Jos 1:13

[c]*34,6* The Hebrew term refers to the irrevocable giving over of things or persons to the LORD, often by totally destroying them. [d]*11* Or *sarcophagus*
[e]*11* Hebrew *nine cubits long and four cubits wide* (about 4 meters long and 1.8 meters wide) [f]*14* Or *called the settlements of Jair* [g]*17* That is, the Dead Sea

3:1–11,21–22 GOD, Sovereignty—Moses traced here the remarkable blessing upon Israel as she overcame formidable foes. To have such notable military success was remarkable for a wandering people without anywhere they could call home. Because God was guiding and blessing them, Moses encouraged Joshua and the Israelites to continue trusting and following God. This is the story of God accomplishing His purposes in human history, developing a servant people for Himself from one man, Abraham. Christians can see the perspective of what God did in the life of the Israelites better than we can see what He is doing now. We are too much a small part of the picture for us to see the larger design under the hand of God. We can know, however, that the sovereign God who created this world and called to Himself a servant people is still working out His purposes and will bring His plan to a fitting completion.

bodied men, armed for battle, must cross
over ahead of your brother Israelites.[r]
19However, your wives,[s] your children
and your livestock[t] (I know you have
much livestock) may stay in the towns I
have given you, 20until the LORD gives
rest to your brothers as he has to you, and
they too have taken over the land that the
LORD your God is giving them, across the
Jordan. After that, each of you may go
back to the possession I have given you."

Moses Forbidden to Cross the Jordan

21At that time I commanded Joshua:
"You have seen with your own eyes all
that the LORD your God has done to these
two kings. The LORD will do the same to
all the kingdoms over there where you
are going. 22Do not be afraid[u] of them;[v]
the LORD your God himself will fight[w] for
you."
23At that time I pleaded[x] with the
LORD: 24"O Sovereign LORD, you have begun to show to your servant your greatness[y] and your strong hand. For what
god[z] is there in heaven or on earth who
can do the deeds and mighty works[a] you
do?[b] 25Let me go over and see the good
land[c] beyond the Jordan—that fine hill
country and Lebanon.[d]"
26But because of you the LORD was angry[e] with me and would not listen to me.
"That is enough," the LORD said. "Do not
speak to me anymore about this matter.
27Go up to the top of Pisgah[f] and look
west and north and south and east.[g]
Look at the land with your own eyes,
since you are not going to cross[h] this Jordan.[i] 28But commission[j] Joshua, and encourage[k] and strengthen him, for he will
lead this people across[l] and will cause
them to inherit the land that you will
see." 29So we stayed in the valley near
Beth Peor.[m]

Chapter 4

Obedience Commanded

HEAR now, O Israel, the decrees[n] and
laws I am about to teach[o] you. Follow them so that you may live[p] and may
go in and take possession of the land that
the LORD, the God of your fathers, is giving you. 2Do not add[q] to what I command you and do not subtract[r] from it,
but keep[s] the commands[t] of the LORD
your God that I give you.
3You saw with your own eyes what the
LORD did at Baal Peor.[u] The LORD your
God destroyed from among you everyone
who followed the Baal of Peor, 4but all of
you who held fast to the LORD your God
are still alive today.
5See, I have taught[v] you decrees and
laws[w] as the LORD my God commanded[x]
me, so that you may follow them in the
land you are entering[y] to take possession
of it. 6Observe[z] them carefully, for this
will show your wisdom[a] and understanding to the nations, who will hear about all
these decrees and say, "Surely this great
nation is a wise and understanding people."[b] 7What other nation is so great[c] as

3:18 [r]S Nu 32:17 **3:19** [s]Jos 1:14 [t]S Nu 32:16 **3:22** [u]S Dt 1:29 [v]Dt 7:18; 20:1; 31:6; 2Ch 32:8; Ps 23:4; Isa 41:10 [w]S Ex 14:14 **3:23** [x]Dt 1:37; 31:2; 32:52; 34:4 **3:24** [y]Dt 5:24; 11:2; 32:3 [z]S Ex 8:10 [a]Ps 71:16; 106:2; 145:12; 150:2 [b]2Sa 7:22 **3:25** [c]Dt 4:22 [d]Dt 1:7; Jos 1:4; 9:1; 11:17; 12:7; 13:5; Jdg 3:3; 9:15; 1Ki 4:33 **3:26** [e]ver 27; Dt 1:37; 31:2 **3:27** [f]S Nu 21:20 [g]S Ge 13:14 [h]S ver 26; S Nu 20:12; Dt 32:52 [i]S Nu 27:12 **3:28** [j]Nu 27:18-23 [k]Dt 31:7 [l]Dt 1:38; 31:3,23 **3:29** [m]S Nu 23:28; Dt 4:46; 34:6; Jos 13:20 **4:1** [n]S Lev 18:4 [o]Dt 1:3 [p]S Lev 18:5; Dt 30:15-20; S Ro 10:5 **4:2** [q]Dt 12:32; Jos 1:7; Pr 30:6; Rev 22:18-19 [r]Jer 26:2 [s]S Lev 22:31 [t]Dt 10:12-13; Ecc 12:13 **4:3** [u]Nu 25:1-9; Ps 106:28 **4:5** [v]Ps 71:17; 119:102; Jer 32:33 [w]S Ex 18:20 [x]S Lev 27:34 [y]Ezr 9:11 **4:6** [z]Dt 29:9; 1Ki 2:3 [a]Dt 30:19-20; 32:46-47; Ps 19:7; 119:98; Pr 1:7; 2Ti 3:15 [b]Job 1:1; 28:28; Ps 111:10; Pr 2:5; 3:7; 9:10; Ecc 12:13; Eze 5:5 **4:7** [c]ver 32-34; 2Sa 7:23

3:21–24 HISTORY, God—History shows people of faith the incomparable nature of God and relieves fears brought by historical crises.

3:22 CHRISTIAN ETHICS, War and Peace—See note on Ex 14:1—15:18.

3:23–27 PRAYER, Hindrances—God says, "No," to some of our petitions. Moses' request had been blocked by sin (Nu 20:6–12). Once God speaks, His word remains unalterable. See Dt 32:48–52. God's "No" to a prayer request does not mean He does not forgive us or accept us as His saved people. It means we must accept some earthly consequences of sin even when the sin no longer separates us from God. A divine, "No," does not end our prayer life. It does call us to accept His answer and continue our fellowship with Him.

3:24 GOD, One God—No human can do the things God does, and clearly no other god can match His power. The gods are no more than blocks of stone or wood or molten images created by human hands. The Lord has demonstrated His sovereign power by creating all things and calling a servant people for Himself.

3:26–28 ELECTION, Leadership—God calls leaders to commission, encourage, and strengthen others to inherit their leadership mantle. He commanded Moses to prepare Joshua to succeed him as the leader of God's chosen people. No leader is indispensable for the elect. Elect leaders are needed by the elect.

4:1–8 CHRISTIAN ETHICS, Social Order—See notes on Lev 25:18–19; 26:3–45. God's laws establish an order most outsiders recognize as wise and desirable. They meet all standards of righteousness. Humans have no reason to criticize or change God's social order.

4:2 HOLY SCRIPTURE, Canonization—God's statutes and judgments were consciously revealed Scripture given by God and not to be changed. Human attempts to modify God's expectations are sinful and doomed to failure. The order not to change God's Word established the writing as an authoritative canon by which human conduct could be measured. In a lengthy historical process God led His people to recognize and use the writings He inspired as the authoritative, written standard or measure for their lives. This process of establishing the canon of Scripture is called canonization.

4:3 HISTORY, God—God's people see Him at work in history bringing deliverance, discipline, and judgment.

4:7 GOD, Presence—God is accessible for His people. Israel's neighbors thought of their gods as fickle, asleep, or travelling on a journey. Only the one true God is near and available when we need Him. The teaching here, however, stands in contrast to the feeling noted in Ps 137:2 that they could not sing the Lord's songs in a foreign land. The principle that God is accessible everywhere was one thing, while the experience that God is near in adverse circumstances was quite another matter. Sometimes we do not trust in our hearts what we understand in our minds.

4:7 REVELATION, Divine Presence—God made Himself available to Israel as a continuous presence in visible signs (cloud, pillar of fire) and in the spoken word. This presence became real as the individuals prayed and God answered. Prayer makes God's presence real for the individual.

4:7 PRAYER, Love of God—God is near and hears our prayer no matter where we are when we pray. The nearness of

to have their gods near[d] them the way the LORD our God is near us whenever we pray to him? 8And what other nation is so great as to have such righteous decrees and laws[e] as this body of laws I am setting before you today?

9Only be careful,[f] and watch yourselves closely so that you do not forget the things your eyes have seen or let them slip from your heart as long as you live. Teach[g] them to your children[h] and to their children after them. 10Remember the day you stood before the LORD your God at Horeb,[i] when he said to me, "Assemble the people before me to hear my words so that they may learn[j] to revere[k] me as long as they live in the land[l] and may teach[m] them to their children." 11You came near and stood at the foot of the mountain[n] while it blazed with fire[o] to the very heavens, with black clouds and deep darkness.[p] 12Then the LORD spoke[q] to you out of the fire. You heard the sound of words but saw no form;[r] there was only a voice.[s] 13He declared to you his covenant,[t] the Ten Commandments,[u] which he commanded you to follow and then wrote them on two stone tablets. 14And the LORD directed me at that time to teach you the decrees and laws[v] you are to follow in the land that you are crossing the Jordan to possess.

4:7 [d]S Nu 23:21; S Ps 46:1; Ac 17:27 **4:8** [e]Ps 89:14; 97:2; 119:7,62,144, 160,172; Ro 3:2 **4:9** [f]S Ex 23:13 [g]S Ge 14:14; 18:19; Dt 6:20-25; Eph 6:4 [h]S Ex 10:2 **4:10** [i]S Ex 3:1 [j]Dt 14:23; 17:19; 31:12-13; Ps 2:11; 111:10; 147:11; Isa 8:13; Jer 32:40 [k]S Ex 20:20 [l]Dt 12:1 [m]ver 9 **4:11** [n]S Ex 3:1; S 19:17 [o]S Ex 19:18 [p]S Ex 19:9; Ps 18:11; 97:2 **4:12** [q]Ex 20:22; Dt 5:4,22; S Mt 3:17; Heb 12:19 [r]Jn 5:37 [s]S Ex 19:9 **4:13** [t]Dt 9:9; Ro 9:4 [u]S Ex 24:12 **4:14** [v]S Ex 21:1 **4:15** [w]Isa 40:18; 41:22-24 [x]S Ex 3:1 [y]Jos 23:11; Mal 2:15 **4:16** [z]S Ge 6:11-12; Dt 9:12; 31:29; 32:5; Jdg 2:19 [a]Ex 20:4-5; Ro 1:23 **4:17** [b]Ro 1:23 **4:19** [c]Dt 17:3; 2Ki 23:11; Job 31:26; Jer 8:2; 43:13; Eze 8:16 [d]S Ge 1:16 [e]S Ge 2:1; S 37:9; Ro 1:25 [f]Dt 13:5 [g]S Nu 25:3 **4:20** [h]S Ex 1:13 [i]S Ex 3:10 [j]S Ge 17:7; S Ex 8:22; S 34:9; Tit 2:14 **4:21** [k]Nu 20:12; Dt 1:37 **4:22** [l]Nu 27:13-14 [m]Dt 3:25 **4:23** [n]ver 9

Idolatry Forbidden

15You saw no form[w] of any kind the day the LORD spoke to you at Horeb[x] out of the fire. Therefore watch yourselves very carefully,[y] 16so that you do not become corrupt[z] and make for yourselves an idol,[a] an image of any shape, whether formed like a man or a woman, 17or like any animal on earth or any bird that flies in the air,[b] 18or like any creature that moves along the ground or any fish in the waters below. 19And when you look up to the sky and see the sun,[c] the moon and the stars[d]—all the heavenly array[e]—do not be enticed[f] into bowing down to them and worshiping[g] things the LORD your God has apportioned to all the nations under heaven. 20But as for you, the LORD took you and brought you out of the iron-smelting furnace,[h] out of Egypt,[i] to be the people of his inheritance,[j] as you now are.

21The LORD was angry with me[k] because of you, and he solemnly swore that I would not cross the Jordan and enter the good land the LORD your God is giving you as your inheritance. 22I will die in this land;[l] I will not cross the Jordan; but you are about to cross over and take possession of that good land.[m] 23Be careful not to forget the covenant[n] of the LORD

God is a promise for those who call on Him. See note on Ge 4:26. Christ is a "better hope" through whom we draw near to God (Heb 7:19).

4:9–10,14 EDUCATION, Commanded—Teaching is imperative, not optional, for the people of God. "Remembering" what God has done is of primary importance. Religious instruction preserves the memory of the community of faith from one generation to another. Where teaching is neglected, spiritual amnesia sets in. Parents (see note on 6:1–10) and spiritual leaders play essential roles in this educational process.

4:13 THE CHURCH, Covenant People—Covenant people must remember the blessings of the past and the possibilities for the future. The greatest possibilities exist when we obey God's commands, for they bring life and hope. God's Ten Commandments (in Hebrew—ten words) give directives for living in relationship with God and with other people. These commands are permanent and universal. Jesus Christ called His people to salvation through grace and promised power to fulfill all righteousness. He did not nullify the commandments. He called to a higher righteousness through the power of the Spirit (Mt 5:17—6:4).

4:15–19 SIN, Against God—Moses warned the people here against idolatry, which is a sin directly against God. There always is the danger of substituting the false for the true. This especially is true in one's religious experience. We must remember idols are made in the heart and do not necessarily need stone. What we love most becomes our god.

4:16–19 CREATION, Sovereignty—Though Moses had to give up the reins of leadership before Israel entered the Promised Land, he gave some final words to the people as they stood at its edge. Concerned about their religious faith in the new country Canaan, he pointed out the nature of God's created world. God made material things to be used, not worshiped. Since we become like whatever we constantly admire and worship, we must refrain from putting too much attention on things that can be seen and touched. Our worship must be spiritually oriented in order that our actions can be spiritually motivated. Nature is the realm we rule for God (Ge 1:26). Natural things are never to become an object of worship or the center of life.

4:20–38 ELECTION, Love—From the "iron smelting furnace of Egypt" to the Land of Promise, God led Israel. This action of identity and deliverance resulted from the unconditional love of God. God chooses us today, not because of human merit, but because of His matchless love. Election love seeks to lead the elect to obedience. Jealous love disciplines the elect until they obey. Faithful love never abandons the elect.

4:23–26 SIN, Covenant Breach—Moses reminded the people that idolatry is a breach of their covenant relationship with God. Any breach of the covenant is viewed as sin. A covenant relationship is not a mechanical relationship. The nation committed to it voluntarily and renewed the covenant relationship each year on the Day of Atonement. Thus, each person had a sacred responsibility to live within the stipulations of the covenant. This, then, is one of the standards by which sin was determined in the Old Testament. Under the new covenant sin still can be characterized as a breach of the new covenant relationship, for sin is a violation of God's love, grace, and mercy upon which the new covenant is predicated.

4:23 THE CHURCH, Covenant People—Covenants are commitments and need constant care lest they be neglected. Failing to give proper attention to that which is important is easy. Like the early Israelites, believers today must guard against falling into the trap of making idols or graven images which take the place of the Lord. We may feel we are too sophisticated to carve or mold an idol with our hands and then bow down to it. However, we often let the world mold an image for us that we must be like to be popular or successful. We need to remember we are created in God's image and represent Him to the world. See note on 4:13.

your God that he made with you; do not
make for yourselves an idol[o] in the form
of anything the LORD your God has forbidden. 24For the LORD your God is a consuming fire,[p] a jealous God.[q]
25After you have had children and
grandchildren and have lived in the land
a long time—if you then become corrupt[r] and make any kind of idol,[s] doing
evil[t] in the eyes of the LORD your God
and provoking him to anger, 26I call heav-
en and earth as witnesses[u] against you[v]
this day that you will quickly perish[w]
from the land that you are crossing the
Jordan to possess. You will not live there
long but will certainly be destroyed.
27The LORD will scatter[x] you among the
peoples, and only a few of you will survive[y] among the nations to which the
LORD will drive you. 28There you will
worship man-made gods[z] of wood and
stone,[a] which cannot see or hear or eat
or smell.[b] 29But if from there you seek[c]
the LORD your God, you will find him if
you look for him with all your heart[d] and
with all your soul.[e] 30When you are in
distress[f] and all these things have happened to you, then in later days[g] you will
return[h] to the LORD your God and obey
him. 31For the LORD your God is a merciful[i] God; he will not abandon[j] or destroy[k] you or forget[l] the covenant with
your forefathers, which he confirmed to
them by oath.

The LORD Is God

32Ask[m] now about the former days,
long before your time, from the day God
created man on the earth;[n] ask from one
end of the heavens to the other.[o] Has
anything so great[p] as this ever happened,
or has anything like it ever been heard of?
33Has any other people heard the voice of
God[h] speaking out of fire, as you have,
and lived?[q] 34Has any god ever tried to
take for himself one nation out of another
nation,[r] by testings,[s] by miraculous

4:23 [o]S Ex 20:4 **4:24** [p]S Ex 15:7; S 19:18; Heb 12:29 [q]S Ex 20:5 **4:25** [r]ver 16 [s]ver 23 [t]1Ki 11:6; 15:26; 16:25,30; 2Ki 17:2,17; 21:2 **4:26** [u]Ge 31:50; Pr 14:5 [v]Dt 30:18-19; 31:28; 32:1; Ps 50:4; Isa 1:2; 34:1; Jer 6:19; Mic 6:2 [w]Dt 6:15; 7:4 **4:27** [x]S Lev 26:33; Dt 28:36,64; 29:28; 1Ki 8:46; 2Ki 17:6; Ps 44:11; 106:27; Jer 3:8; Mic 1:16 [y]Isa 17:6; 21:17; Ob 1:5 **4:28** [z]Dt 13:2; 28:36,64; 1Sa 26:19; Jer 5:19; 16:13; Ac 19:26 [a]Dt 29:17 [b]Ps 115:4-8; 135:15-18; Isa 8:19; 26:14; 44:17-20; Rev 9:20 **4:29** [c]1Sa 13:12; 2Ki 13:4; 2Ch 7:14; 15:4; 33:12; Ps 78:34; 119:58; Isa 45:19,22; 55:6; Jer 26:19; Da 9:13; Hos 3:5; Am 5:4 [d]1Sa 7:3; 1Ki 8:48; Jer 29:13 [e]Dt 6:5; 30:1-3,10 **4:30** [f]Lev 26:41; Dt 31:17,21; Ps 4:1; 18:6; 46:1; 59:16; 107:6 [g]Dt 31:29; Jer 23:20; Hos 3:5; Heb 1:2 [h]Dt 30:2; 1Ki 8:48; Ne 1:9; Jer 3:1,12,22; 4:1; 18:11; Joel 2:12 **4:31** [i]Ex 34:6; Ne 9:31; Ps 111:4 [j]Dt 31:6,8; Jos 1:5; 1Ki 8:57; 1Ch 28:9, 20; Ps 9:10; 27:9; 71:9; Isa 42:16; Heb 13:5 [k]S Lev 26:44 [l]Lev 26:45 **4:32** [m]Dt 32:7 [n]S Ge 1:27; Isa 45:12 [o]Dt 28:64; 30:1; Jer 9:16; Mt 24:31 [p]ver 7; 2Sa 7:23 **4:33** [q]Ex 20:22; Dt 5:24-26 **4:34** [r]Ex 14:30

signs[t] and wonders,[u] by war, by a
mighty hand and an outstretched arm,[v]
or by great and awesome deeds,[w] like all
the things the LORD your God did for you
in Egypt before your very eyes?
35You were shown these things so that
you might know that the LORD is God;
besides him there is no other.[x] 36From
heaven he made you hear his voice[y] to
discipline[z] you. On earth he showed you
his great fire, and you heard his words
from out of the fire. 37Because he loved[a]
your forefathers and chose their descendants after them, he brought you out of
Egypt by his Presence and his great
strength,[b] 38to drive out before you nations greater and stronger than you and to
bring you into their land to give it to you
for your inheritance,[c] as it is today.
39Acknowledge[d] and take to heart this
day that the LORD is God in heaven above
and on the earth below. There is no other.[e] 40Keep[f] his decrees and commands,[g] which I am giving you today, so
that it may go well[h] with you and your
children after you and that you may live
long[i] in the land the LORD your God
gives you for all time.

Cities of Refuge

4:41–43Ref — Nu 35:6–34; Dt 19:1–14; Jos 20:1–9

41Then Moses set aside three cities east
of the Jordan, 42to which anyone who had
killed a person could flee if he had unintentionally[j] killed his neighbor without
malice aforethought. He could flee into
one of these cities and save his life. 43The

[s]Isa 7:12 [t]S Ex 4:17 [u]Dt 7:19; 26:8; 29:3; 1Ch 16:12; Ps 9:1; 40:5; Jer 32:20 [v]S Ex 3:20; Dt 5:15; 6:21; 15:15 [w]Ex 15:11; Dt 34:12; Ps 45:4; 65:5 **4:35** [x]ver 39; Ex 8:10; Dt 7:9; 32:4, 12; 1Sa 2:2; 1Ki 8:60; 2Ki 19:19; Isa 43:10; Mk 12:32 **4:36** [y]S Ex 19:19; Heb 12:25 [z]Dt 8:5 **4:37** [a]Dt 7:8; 10:15; 23:5; 33:3; Ps 44:3; Jer 31:3; Hos 11:1; Mal 1:2; 2:11 [b]S Ex 3:20; S 33:14 **4:38** [c]Nu 34:14-15; Dt 7:1; 9:5 **4:39** [d]Ex 8:10 [e]S ver 35; Ex 15:11 **4:40** [f]S Lev 22:31 [g]ver 1; S Ge 26:5; Dt 5:29; 11:1; Ps 105:45; Isa 48:18 [h]Dt 5:16; 12:25; Isa 3:10 [i]S Ex 23:26; Eph 6:2-3 **4:42** [j]S Ex 21:13

h33 Or *of a god*

4:25–31 EVIL AND SUFFERING, Deserved—Moses presented the Hebrews with two options. If they became idolatrous, God would punish them (4:25–28). If they turned to God, He would help them (4:29–31).

4:27–40 GOD, One God—Moses warned Israel of the captivity which awaited an unfaithful people. They would worship worthless, man-made gods. Still Moses held out hope. They could still break through to the one true God if they sought Him with all their hearts. The one and only God is always ready to hear and receive those who sincerely seek to know Him. The God who allows His people to suffer in their faithlessness is still a merciful God who remains faithful to His covenant promises. Israel had difficulty giving sole allegiance to an unseen God. Their neighbors had visible gods. Such "visible gods" could not see, hear, or speak. The only true God can do all this and more. Faithfulness to Him will bring His blessing; unfaithfulness to Him will bring His judgment.

4:31 THE CHURCH, Covenant People—God's covenant mercy will endure forever. His people should not fear we might one day be forsaken and so prepare an emergency plan. The eternal God will not abandon us. His love is too strong. He will punish and correct His people but always to renew us. He wants us to keep our commitments faithfully as He keeps His.

4:32 CREATION, Miracles—To deliver His people from Egypt and sustain them through the wilderness wanderings, God had acted with mighty power. He had created situations where He could reveal through miraculous events both His love and His strength. Miracles show that the creative power and sovereign control of the Creator are still at work in His world. One who accepts the fact of God's creative power that brought the world into existence from nothing should have no problem accepting His other strong acts. They played a major part in Israel's salvation.

4:32–40 HISTORY, God—See notes on 3:21–24; 4:3. Historical revelation is one unique feature proving God's claim to be the only God.

4:41–43 CHRISTIAN ETHICS, Justice—See note on Nu 35:6–34.

cities were these: Bezer in the desert plateau, for the Reubenites; Ramoth[k] in Gilead, for the Gadites; and Golan in Bashan, for the Manassites.

Introduction to the Law

44This is the law Moses set before the
Israelites. 45These are the stipulations,
decrees and laws Moses gave them when
they came out of Egypt 46and were in the
valley near Beth Peor east of the Jordan,
in the land of Sihon[l] king of the Amorites, who reigned in Heshbon and was
defeated by Moses and the Israelites as
they came out of Egypt. 47They took possession of his land and the land of Og
king of Bashan, the two Amorite kings
east of the Jordan. 48This land extended
from Aroer[m] on the rim of the Arnon
Gorge to Mount Siyon[i][n] (that is, Hermon[o]), 49and included all the Arabah
east of the Jordan, as far as the Sea of the
Arabah,[j] below the slopes of Pisgah.

Chapter 5

The Ten Commandments

5:6–21pp — Ex 20:1–17

MOSES summoned all Israel and said:
Hear, O Israel, the decrees and
laws[p] I declare in your hearing today.
Learn them and be sure to follow them.
2The LORD our God made a covenant[q]
with us at Horeb.[r] 3It was not with our
fathers that the LORD made this covenant,
but with us,[s] with all of us who are alive
here today.[t] 4The LORD spoke[u] to you
face to face[v] out of the fire[w] on the
mountain. 5(At that time I stood between[x] the LORD and you to declare to
you the word of the LORD, because you
were afraid[y] of the fire and did not go up
the mountain.) And he said:

6"I am the LORD your God, who
brought you out of Egypt,[z] out
of the land of slavery.[a]

7"You shall have no other gods before[k] me.

8"You shall not make for yourself an
idol in the form of anything in
heaven above or on the earth
beneath or in the waters below.[b] 9You shall not bow down
to them or worship them; for I,
the LORD your God, am a jealous God, punishing the children
for the sin of the fathers[c] to the
third and fourth generation of
those who hate me,[d] 10but
showing love to a thousand[e]
⌊generations⌋ of those who love
me and keep my command-
ments.[f]

11"You shall not misuse the name[g] of
the LORD your God, for the
LORD will not hold anyone guiltless who misuses his name.[h]

12"Observe the Sabbath day by keeping it holy,[i] as the LORD your
God has commanded you. 13Six
days you shall labor and do all
your work, 14but the seventh
day[j] is a Sabbath to the LORD
your God. On it you shall not do
any work, neither you, nor your
son or daughter, nor your manservant or maidservant,[k] nor
your ox, your donkey or any of
your animals, nor the alien
within your gates, so that your
manservant and maidservant
may rest, as you do.[l] 15Remem-
ber that you were slaves[m] in
Egypt and that the LORD your
God brought you out of there
with a mighty hand[n] and an
outstretched arm.[o] Therefore
the LORD your God has commanded you to observe the Sabbath day.

16"Honor your father[p] and your mother,[q] as the LORD your God has
commanded you, so that you
may live long[r] and that it may
go well with you in the land the
LORD your God is giving you.

4:43 [k]Jos 21:38; 1Ki 22:3; 2Ki 8:28; 9:14
4:46 [l]Nu 21:26
4:48 [m]Dt 2:36 [n]Dt 3:9 [o]S Dt 3:8
5:1 [p]S Ex 18:20
5:2 [q]Ex 19:5; Jer 11:2; Heb 9:15; 10:15-17 [r]S Ge 17:9; S Ex 3:1
5:3 [s]Dt 11:2-7 [t]Nu 26:63-65; Heb 8:9
5:4 [u]S Dt 4:12 [v]S Nu 14:14 [w]S Ex 19:18
5:5 [x]Gal 3:19 [y]S Ge 3:10; Heb 12:18-21
5:6 [z]S Ex 13:3; S 29:46 [a]Lev 26:1; Dt 6:4; Ps 81:10
5:8 [b]Lev 26:1; Dt 4:15-18; Ps 78:58; 97:7
5:9 [c]S Nu 26:11 [d]Ex 34:7; S Nu 10:35; 14:18
5:10 [e]S Ex 34:7 [f]Nu 14:18; Dt 7:9; Ne 1:5; Jer 32:18; Da 9:4
5:11 [g]Ps 139:20 [h]Lev 19:12; Dt 10:20; Mt 5:33-37
5:12 [i]Ex 16:23-30; 31:13-17; Mk 2:27-28
5:14 [j]S Ge 2:2; Mt 12:2; Mk 2:27; Heb 4:4 [k]Job 31:13; Jer 34:9-11 [l]Jer 17:21,24
5:15 [m]S Ge 15:13 [n]Ex 6:1; Ps 108:6; Jer 32:21 [o]S Dt 4:34
5:16 [p]Mal 1:6 [q]Ex 21:17; Lev 19:3; Eze 22:7; Mt 15:4*; 19:19*; Mk 7:10*; 10:9*; Lk 18:20*; Eph 6:2-3* [r]S Dt 4:40; 11:9; Pr 3:1-2

[i]48 Hebrew; Syriac (see also Deut. 3:9) *Sirion*
[j]49 That is, the Dead Sea [k]7 Or *besides*

5:1 CHRISTIAN ETHICS, Moral Imperatives—See note on 4:1–8. The imperative to hear carries the implicit and explicit note of doing or acting upon what is heard. Listening and learning is not enough. God's people must do what they know, act on what they believe.

5:2–3 THE CHURCH, Covenant People—Relationships are either growing or regressing, never static. Each generation must make its own commitment to God and His covenant. When we acknowledge our faith in God, the Bible's story of salvation becomes more than the history of a past generation. It becomes the story of our faith and the call for our obedience. A covenant is not a one-time historical act of God. It is an ongoing relationship God continually renews with His people.

5:4,23–27 REVELATION, Word—God was made visible in the fire on the mountain (Ex 19:18), one of the mysterious wonders of the ancient world. The God who spoke to Israel did so in a specific way, so that He would be identified, yet always with a certain degree of mystery, so that people would never entertain the illusion they controlled God or fully understood Him. The awesome presence frightened the Israelites, so they requested a mediator. Thus Moses became the spokesperson to and for God. Israel pledged to accept his words as revelation and to obey them. God uses different means to get His Word to His people. He always expects His people to obey the revealed word.

5:6–21 HUMANITY, Relationships—See notes on Ex 20:2–11, 12, 13–17.

5:7–15 GOD, One God—See comments on Ex 20:1–7.

5:9–10 EVIL AND SUFFERING, Deserved—See note on Ex 20:5–6.

5:11 CHRISTIAN ETHICS, Language—See note on Ex 20:7.

17“You shall not murder.[s]
18“You shall not commit adultery.[t]
19“You shall not steal.[u]
20“You shall not give false testimony
against your neighbor.[v]
21“You shall not covet your neighbor's
wife. You shall not set your desire on your neighbor's house
or land, his manservant or
maidservant, his ox or donkey,
or anything that belongs to your
neighbor.”[w]

22These are the commandments the
LORD proclaimed in a loud voice to your
whole assembly there on the mountain
from out of the fire, the cloud and the
deep darkness;[x] and he added nothing
more. Then he wrote them on two stone
tablets[y] and gave them to me.
23When you heard the voice out of the
darkness, while the mountain was ablaze
with fire, all the leading men of your
tribes and your elders[z] came to me.
24And you said, “The LORD our God has
shown us[a] his glory and his majesty,[b]
and we have heard his voice from the
fire. Today we have seen that a man can
live even if God speaks with him.[c] 25But
now, why should we die? This great fire
will consume us, and we will die if we
hear the voice of the LORD our God any
longer.[d] 26For what mortal man has ever
heard the voice of the living God speaking out of fire, as we have, and survived?[e] 27Go near and listen to all that
the LORD our God says.[f] Then tell us
whatever the LORD our God tells you. We
will listen and obey.”[g]
28The LORD heard you when you spoke
to me and the LORD said to me, “I have
heard what this people said to you. Everything they said was good.[h] 29Oh, that
their hearts would be inclined to fear
me[i] and keep all my commands[j] always,
so that it might go well with them and
their children forever![k]
30“Go, tell them to return to their
tents. 31But you stay here[l] with me so
that I may give you all the commands,
decrees and laws you are to teach them to
follow in the land I am giving them to
possess.”
32So be careful to do what the LORD
your God has commanded you;[m] do not
turn aside to the right or to the left.[n]
33Walk in all the way that the LORD your
God has commanded you,[o] so that you
may live and prosper and prolong your
days[p] in the land that you will possess.

Chapter 6

Love the LORD Your God

THESE are the commands, decrees and
laws the LORD your God directed me
to teach you to observe in the land that
you are crossing the Jordan to possess, 2so
that you, your children and their children
after them may fear[q] the LORD your God
as long as you live[r] by keeping all his
decrees and commands[s] that I give you,
and so that you may enjoy long life.[t]
3Hear, O Israel, and be careful to obey[u]
so that it may go well with you and that
you may increase greatly[v] in a land flowing with milk and honey,[w] just as the
LORD, the God of your fathers, promised[x]
you.
4Hear, O Israel: The LORD our God, the

5:17 [s]Ge 9:6; Lev 24:17; Ecc 3:3; Jer 40:15; 41:3; Mt 5:21-22*; 19:19*; Mk 10:19*; Lk 18:20*; Ro 13:9*; Jas 2:11* **5:18** [t]Lev 20:10; Mt 5:27-30; 19:18*; Mk 10:19*; Lk 18:20*; Ro 13:9*; Jas 2:11* **5:19** [u]Lev 19:11; Mt 19:19*; Mk 10:19*; Lk 18:20*; Ro 13:9* **5:20** [v]S Ex 23:1; Mt 19:18*; Mk 10:19*; Lk 18:20* **5:21** [w]Ro 7:7*; 13:9* **5:22** [x]S Ex 20:21 [y]S Ex 24:12 **5:23** [z]S Ex 3:16 **5:24** [a]Dt 4:34; 8:5; 11:2; Isa 53:4 [b]S Dt 3:24 [c]Ex 19:19 **5:25** [d]Ex 20:18-19; Dt 18:16; Heb 12:19 **5:26** [e]S Ex 33:20; Dt 4:33; Jdg 6:22-23; 13:22; Isa 6:5 **5:27** [f]S Ex 19:8 [g]S Ex 24:7 **5:28** [h]Dt 18:17 **5:29** [i]Ps 81:8,13 [j]Jos 22:5; Ps 78:7 [k]ver 33; S Dt 4:1, 40; 12:25; 22:7 **5:31** [l]Ex 24:12 **5:32** [m]S Dt 4:29; 10:12 [n]Dt 17:11, 20; 28:14; Jos 1:7; 1Ki 15:5; 2Ki 22:2; Pr 4:27 **5:33** [o]Isa 3:10; Jer 7:23; 38:20; S Lk 1:6 [p]S ver 29 **6:2** [q]S Ex 20:20; S 1Sa 12:24 [r]Dt 4:9 [s]S Ge 26:5 [t]S Ex 20:12 **6:3** [u]S Ex 19:5 [v]Ge 15:5; Dt 5:33 [w]S Ex 3:8; Dt 32:13-14 [x]Ex 13:5

5:17 CHRISTIAN ETHICS, Murder—See note on Ex 20:13.
5:19 CHRISTIAN ETHICS, Theft—See note on Ex 20:15.
5:20 CHRISTIAN ETHICS, Language—See note on Ex 20:16.
5:32–33 GOD, Sovereignty—God, and God's commandments, must be treated seriously. God will bless those who take the commandments seriously and order their lives by them. Prosperity did not necessarily mean gaining economic wealth. It encompassed all of the interests of life. In other words, one who honors God will do well in his life and have the blessing of God. To the Hebrews, long life was a clear sign of the blessing of God. This is the positive statement of the truth often stated negatively: God's hand of judgment will fall on the disobedient. Note the restatement of these verses in 6:1–3.
5:32–33 CHRISTIAN ETHICS, Moral Limits—See note on Lev 18:3–30.
6:1–10 EDUCATION, Parents—Nurturing the faith of children through God-centered teaching is one of the greatest privileges of parenthood. It is also a sacred obligation. The task cannot be done on an occasional basis. It must be a continuous process—morning, noon, and night. See 11:18–20. The subject matter emphasized in this passage is the *Shema* (6:4–9), probably the most quoted Scripture in Judaism. The methodology used in this parental teaching is varied. The Word of God is to be quoted, explained, discussed, symbolized, and written down. Most important, it is to be “written upon the heart” and incorporated into the parent's way of life so the children may have a daily example of godly living. See note on Pr 1:8–9.
6:2,13,24 SALVATION, Fear of God—God's commandments were given to us for our good, to teach us proper reverence for Him, and to bring us long and abundant life. We are to fear God only and to prove our reverence for Him by obeying His commandments.
6:4–9 GOD, One God—For Judaism 6:4–9 became the confession of faith, known as the *Shema*, that should be recited daily. Jesus cited this commandment as preeminent over all of the law (Mt 22:37). The people of God need to know, from their innermost being, that there is truly only one God. Faith in God is meant to be a living relationship involving the totality of life; faith is not an isolated item of intellectual belief stored in the recesses of the mind. Nor is faith in God performing certain rituals or adopting an uncommitted style of life. He wants us to organize our entire lives around His sovereign Lordship and love Him with the totality of our being.
6:4–9 FAMILY, Bible Study—This passage is one part of the *Shema*, a confession of faith read in contemporary Jewish synagogue worship in the Friday and Saturday services as the Torah is taken from its ark. Faithful Jews in Israel were required to read it twice daily to remind them of their faith in one God and their dependence on His Word. The central theme of having God's commandments in the heart and teaching them in the home is as relevant to modern Christian homes as it was to Jewish homes in the biblical world. See Ps 1; 119; 2 Ti

LORD is one.[1][y] 5Love[z] the LORD your
God with all your heart[a] and with all
your soul and with all your strength.[b]
6These commandments that I give you today are to be upon your hearts.[c] 7Im-
press them on your children. Talk about
them when you sit at home and when
you walk along the road, when you lie
down and when you get up.[d] 8Tie them
as symbols on your hands and bind them
on your foreheads.[e] 9Write them on the
doorframes of your houses and on your
gates.[f]

10When the LORD your God brings you
into the land he swore to your fathers, to
Abraham, Isaac and Jacob, to give you—a
land with large, flourishing cities you did
not build,[g] 11houses filled with all kinds
of good things you did not provide, wells
you did not dig,[h] and vineyards and olive
groves you did not plant—then when you
eat and are satisfied,[i] 12be careful that
you do not forget[j] the LORD, who
brought you out of Egypt, out of the land
of slavery.

13Fear the LORD[k] your God, serve him
only[l] and take your oaths[m] in his
name.[n] 14Do not follow other gods, the
gods of the peoples around you; 15for the
LORD your God[o], who is among you, is a
jealous God and his anger will burn
against you, and he will destroy you from
the face of the land. 16Do not test the
LORD your God[p] as you did at Massah.
17Be sure to keep[q] the commands of the
LORD your God and the stipulations and
decrees he has given you.[r] 18Do what is
right and good in the LORD's sight,[s] so
that it may go well[t] with you and you
may go in and take over the good land
that the LORD promised on oath to your
forefathers, 19thrusting out all your enemies[u] before you, as the LORD said.

20In the future, when your son asks
you,[v] "What is the meaning of the stipulations, decrees and laws the LORD our
God has commanded you?" 21tell him:
"We were slaves of Pharaoh in Egypt, but
the LORD brought us out of Egypt with a
mighty hand.[w] 22Before our eyes the
LORD sent miraculous signs and wonders
—great and terrible—upon Egypt and
Pharaoh and his whole household. 23But
he brought us out from there to bring us
in and give us the land that he promised
on oath to our forefathers. 24The LORD
commanded us to obey all these decrees
and to fear the LORD our God,[x] so that
we might always prosper and be kept
alive, as is the case today.[y] 25And if we
are careful to obey all this law[z] before
the LORD our God, as he has commanded
us, that will be our righteousness.[a]"

Chapter 7

Driving Out the Nations

WHEN the LORD your God brings you
into the land you are entering to

6:4 [y]Dt 4:35,39; Ne 9:6; Ps 86:10; Isa 44:6; Zec 14:9; Mk 12:29*; Jn 10:30; 1Co 8:4; Eph 4:6; Jas 2:19 **6:5** [z]Dt 11:1,22; Mt 22:37*; Mk 12:30*; Lk 10:27* [a]1Sa 12:24 [b]Dt 4:29; 10:12; Jos 22:5 **6:6** [c]ver 8; Dt 11:18; 30:14; 32:46; Ps 26:2; 37:31; 40:8; 119:11; Pr 3:3; Isa 51:7; Jer 17:1; 31:33; Eze 40:4 **6:7** [d]Dt 4:9; 11:19; Pr 22:6; Eph 6:4 **6:8** [e]S ver 6; S Ex 13:9; Mt 23:5 **6:9** [f]Dt 11:20 **6:10** [g]S Ge 11:4; Dt 12:29; 19:1; Jos 24:13; Ps 105:44 **6:11** [h]Jer 2:13 [i]S Lev 26:5; Dt 8:10; 14:29; 31:20 **6:12** [j]Dt 4:9,23; 2Ki 17:38; Ps 44:17; 78:7; 103:2 **6:13** [k]Ps 33:8; 34:9 [l]Dt 13:4; 1Sa 7:3; Jer 44:10; Mt 4:10*; Lk 4:4*; 4:8 [m]1Sa 20:3 [n]S Ex 20:7; S Mt 5:33 **6:15** [o]Dt 4:24; 5:9 **6:16** [p]S Ex 17:2; Mt 4:7*; Lk 4:12* **6:17** [q]S Lev 26:3 [r]Dt 11:22; Ps 119:4,56,100, 134,168 **6:18** [s]2Ki 18:6; Isa 36:7; 38:3 [t]Dt 4:40 **6:19** [u]Ex 23:27; Jos 21:44; Ps 78:53; 107:2; 136:24

6:20 [v]S Ex 10:2 **6:21** [w]S Dt 4:34 **6:24** [x]Dt 10:12; 30:6; Ps 86:11; Jer 32:39 [y]Ps 27:12; 41:2; S Ro 10:5 **6:25** [z]Ps 103:18; 119:34,55 [a]Dt 24:13; S Ro 9:31; Ro 10:3,5

[1]4 Or *The LORD our God is one LORD;* or *The LORD is our God, the LORD is one;* or *The LORD is our God, the LORD alone*

3:14–17; Heb 5:11—6:3. Reading and talking about the Word of God is intended to be a normal part of everyday life in the home rather than some formal time that is distinct from other home activities. Parents should share their own faith in God in times of crisis and joy to influence children to understand the reality of God's presence. Families reading the Bible together in response to questions and problems will help make it real for life in the minds of parents and children alike.

6:10–25 GOD, Jealous—God's jealousy means that He does not want His people to be disloyal to Him, or even lukewarm in their devotion to Him. He wants their undivided loyalty, expressed in full and meaningful commitment and obedience to Him. God recognized that His people might have a short memory and would quickly forget all He did for them. God reminded His people that we are to keep alive the memory of the blessings that have come from God. We are to teach our children and all our descendants what God has meant to His people. Obedience and reverence before God are the keys to the continued blessings of God (v 24).

6:10–23 ELECTION, Responsibility—God's chosen people are to love God completely and to teach that love to their offspring. They are to inform their children of God's history of salvation. Election by the loving God (4:37) is a call to love God and live responsibly before Him.

6:17–18 CHRISTIAN ETHICS, Social Order—See note on 4:1–8.

6:20–25 HISTORY, Confession—Personal confession of God's history with us is the basis for teaching the next generation. God's historical acts give content to our confession of faith.

6:24–25 CHRISTIAN ETHICS, Character—See note on 4:1–8. Acts of obeying God in and of themselves serve to reflect our true character. Righteousness (Hebrew *tsedaqah*) is the comprehensive term describing proper relationships. Living in the social order created by God's commands brings a person in proper relationship with God and the community of God's people. Obedience is not a legalism carefully maintained in fear, but a relationship properly nurtured in trust, gratitude, and love.

7:1–6 GOD, Jealous—God's commandment to Israel to show no mercy to captured peoples and to adopt an isolationist stance towards outsiders seems at variance with what we know of God elsewhere, especially in the light of Israel's calling to be a kingdom of priests to the nations (Ex 19:6). This passage must be interpreted in light of its particular setting. Vv 4–5 give the underlying rationale. In the infancy of Israel's faith, God knew that it was in the best interests of His people to have little contact with foreign worship. Experience had proved that Israel's weakest point was her susceptibility to going astray after other gods. See 7:16. Israel's worship of pagan gods made it necessary for God to send Israel back into captivity to learn once and for all that there is only one true God and that He demands an undivided allegiance. Circumstances required that God take a position of judgment rather than the preferred position of love for all mankind. God had to first establish His uniqueness in the minds and hearts of His people before He could clarify the basic nature of the loving, unique God. The destruction brought upon the Canaanites was a judgment they deserved because of their sins (9:4–5).

7:1–26 CHRISTIAN ETHICS, War and Peace—Israel's

possess[b] and drives out before you many
nations[c]—the Hittites,[d] Girgashites,[e]
Amorites,[f] Canaanites, Perizzites,[g] Hivites[h] and Jebusites,[i] seven nations larger and stronger than you— 2and when
the LORD your God has delivered[j] them
over to you and you have defeated them,
then you must destroy[k] them totally.[m][l]
Make no treaty[m] with them, and show
them no mercy.[n] 3Do not intermarry
with them.[o] Do not give your daughters
to their sons or take their daughters for
your sons, 4for they will turn your sons
away from following me to serve other
gods,[p] and the LORD's anger will burn
against you and will quickly destroy[q]
you. 5This is what you are to do to them:
Break down their altars, smash their sacred stones, cut down their Asherah
poles[n][r] and burn their idols in the fire.[s]
6For you are a people holy[t] to the LORD
your God.[u] The LORD your God has chosen[v] you out of all the peoples on the
face of the earth to be his people, his treasured possession.[w]

7The LORD did not set his affection on
you and choose you because you were
more numerous[x] than other peoples, for
you were the fewest[y] of all peoples.[z]
8But it was because the LORD loved[a] you
and kept the oath he swore[b] to your forefathers that he brought you out with a
mighty hand[c] and redeemed[d] you from
the land of slavery,[e] from the power of
Pharaoh king of Egypt. 9Know therefore
that the LORD your God is God;[f] he is the
faithful God,[g] keeping his covenant of
love[h] to a thousand generations[i] of
those who love him and keep his commands.[j] 10But

those who hate him he will repay to
their face by destruction;
he will not be slow to repay to their
face those who hate him.[k]

11Therefore, take care to follow the commands, decrees and laws I give you today.
12If you pay attention to these laws and
are careful to follow them, then the LORD
your God will keep his covenant of love
with you, as he swore to your forefathers.[l] 13He will love you and bless you[m]
and increase your numbers.[n] He will
bless the fruit of your womb,[o] the crops
of your land—your grain, new wine[p] and
oil[q]—the calves of your herds and the
lambs of your flocks in the land that he

7:1 [b]S Lev 14:34; S Dt 4:38 [c]Dt 20:16-18; 31:3 [d]Ge 15:20 [e]S Ge 10:16 [f]S Dt 1:7 [g]Ge 13:7 [h]S Ge 10:17 [i]Jos 3:10 7:2 [j]S Dt 2:33 [k]S Dt 2:34 [l]Nu 31:17; Dt 33:27; Jos 11:11 [m]S Ex 23:32 [n]ver 16; Dt 13:8; 19:13; 25:12 7:3 [o]Ex 34:15-16; Jos 22:16; Da 9:7 7:4 [p]Jdg 3:6 [q]S Dt 4:26 7:5 [r]S Ex 34:13; Dt 16:21 [s]S Ex 23:24 7:6 [t]Ex 19:6; S Lev 27:30 [u]Dt 26:19; Ps 30:4; 37:28; 50:5; 52:9 [v]Dt 14:2; 1Ki 3:8; Isa 41:9; Eze 20:5 [w]S Ge 17:7; S Ex 8:22; S 34:9; Isa 43:1; Ro 9:4; Tit 2:14 7:7 [x]S Ge 22:17 [y]Ge 34:30 [z]Dt 4:37; 10:22 7:8 [a]S Dt 4:37; 1Ki 10:9; 2Ch 2:11; Ps 44:3 [b]Ex 32:13; S Nu 14:8; Ro 11:28 [c]S Ex 3:20 [d]S Ex 6:6 [e]S Ex 13:14 7:9 [f]S Dt 4:35 [g]Ps 18:25; 33:4; 108:4; 145:13; 146:6; Isa 49:7; Jer 42:5; Hos 11:12; S 1Co 1:9 [h]ver 12; 1Ki 8:23; 2Ch 6:14; Ne 1:5; 9:32 [i]S Ex 20:6 [j]S Dt 5:10 7:10 [k]S Lev 26:28; S Nu 10:35; Na 1:2 7:12 [l]Lev 26:3-13; Dt 28:1-14; Ps 105:8-9; Mic 7:20 7:13 [m]Ps 11:5; 146:8; Pr 15:9; Isa 51:1; Jn 14:21 [n]S Ge 17:6; Ex 1:7; Dt 1:10; 13:17; 30:5; Ps 107:38 [o]S Ge 49:25 [p]S Ge 27:28 [q]S Nu 18:12

m2 The Hebrew term refers to the irrevocable giving over of things or persons to the LORD, often by totally destroying them; also in verse 26. n5 That is, symbols of the goddess Asherah; here and elsewhere in Deuteronomy

warfare was governed by rules to protect the young nation from the temptations to follow older cultures and thus reject God. Such rules do not apply to modern warfare conducted under entirely different cultural settings and relationships to God. See notes on 12:9–10; Nu 21:1–3.

7:3–4 FAMILY, Intermarriage—Intermarriage with followers of other religions is universally condemned in the Old Testament because of the temptation of idolatry within the family relationship (13:6–11). This prohibition of intermarriage is not based upon differences of race or culture but upon differences in religion. No marriage can be entered into with eyes closed to the possible harm of conflicting faiths. See Ezr 9:1—10:84; notes on Ne 10:28–30; 13:23–27; 1 Co 7:12–16; 2 Co 6:14–18.

7:6–15 ELECTION, Love—God's choice of His people is based on the unconditional love He has for us and not because of our merit. Election involves God's separation of His people from all other people so we will be different from all other people. Human qualifications do not come under consideration in election. God's love and expectations are the focal points of the doctrine. God's total faithfulness to His covenant promises is the foundation on which election rests.

7:6–8 THE CHURCH, Covenant People—God chooses people for service and responsibility. Blessings occur when we serve God and attempt to do His will. Blessings are secondary to the work God calls each believer to do. God's love called and sustained Israel. His love is always with us as we serve Him. When God calls people to Christian service, He does not choose people according to their fame or abilities, but according to availability to do His work and His sovereign will. See note on Ex 19:4–8.

7:7–8,12–13 GOD, Love—In a context that seems to set forth a picture of an unloving God (see the note on 7:1–6), Moses stressed God's loving action in calling Israel to be His people. He poured out His love to Israel, not because of some quality or value Israel possessed, but because His nature is to love (v 9) and He is faithful in keeping His covenant. The depth and breadth of that love became clearer in the New Testament revelation in Jesus Christ. In Deuteronomy God told His people that although He is stern and strict in meting out justice in some circumstances, He nevertheless is a God who loves and is faithful. To neglect either view of God is to miss something that is vitally important to our overall understanding of His character.

7:8 SALVATION, Redemption—The redemption of God's people is an expression of His love and faithfulness. Compare Ps 49:7. See note on Ex 13:13–15.

7:9–10 THE CHURCH, Covenant People—Others often disappoint us; God never fails. He remains faithful and constant through the storms of life. God has bound Himself to His people. His covenant relationship keeps Him faithful in doing good for His people. God responds through His covenant love to those who love and serve Him, but He judges those who rebel against Him (Ex 34:6–7).

7:11 CHRISTIAN ETHICS, Social Order—See note on 4:1–8.

7:12–16 EVIL AND SUFFERING, Deserved—Human evil brings deserved punishment. Is the reverse true? Does human goodness bring deserved rewards? The Bible gives complex answers to this question. No one passage provides the full answer. The problem begins with human sinfulness. As sinners, we can never claim to be good enough to deserve or demand rewards from God. Still God promises His faithful people blessings in the form of material goods to meet material needs. Such blessings result from God's love not from human merits.

7:12–13 THE CHURCH, Covenant People—The Lord is faithful. See note on 7:9–10. He abides with His people, blessing us with every good thing. God keeps the covenant relationship with His people. He calls His covenant people to be obedient to Him.

swore to your forefathers to give you.[r]
14 You will be blessed more than any other
people; none of your men or women will
be childless, nor any of your livestock
without young.[s] 15 The LORD will keep
you free from every disease.[t] He will not
inflict on you the horrible diseases you
knew in Egypt,[u] but he will inflict them
on all who hate you.[v] 16 You must destroy
all the peoples the LORD your God gives
over to you.[w] Do not look on them with
pity[x] and do not serve their gods,[y] for
that will be a snare[z] to you.

17 You may say to yourselves, "These
nations are stronger than we are. How
can we drive them out?[a]" 18 But do not
be afraid[b] of them; remember well what
the LORD your God did to Pharaoh and to
all Egypt.[c] 19 You saw with your own eyes
the great trials, the miraculous signs and
wonders, the mighty hand[d] and outstretched arm, with which the LORD your
God brought you out. The LORD your God
will do the same to all the peoples you
now fear.[e] 20 Moreover, the LORD your
God will send the hornet[f] among them
until even the survivors who hide from
you have perished. 21 Do not be terrified
by them, for the LORD your God, who is
among you,[g] is a great and awesome
God.[h] 22 The LORD your God will drive
out those nations before you, little by little.[i] You will not be allowed to eliminate
them all at once, or the wild animals will
multiply around you. 23 But the LORD your
God will deliver them over to you, throwing them into great confusion until they
are destroyed.[j] 24 He will give their
kings[k] into your hand,[l] and you will
wipe out their names from under heaven.
No one will be able to stand up against
you;[m] you will destroy them.[n] 25 The images of their gods you are to burn[o] in the
fire. Do not covet[p] the silver and gold on
them, and do not take it for yourselves, or
you will be ensnared[q] by it, for it is detestable[r] to the LORD your God. 26 Do not
bring a detestable thing into your house
or you, like it, will be set apart for destruction.[s] Utterly abhor and detest it,
for it is set apart for destruction.

Chapter 8

Do Not Forget the LORD

BE careful to follow every command I
am giving you today, so that you may
live[t] and increase and may enter and
possess the land that the LORD promised
on oath to your forefathers.[u] 2 Remember
how the LORD your God led[v] you all the
way in the desert these forty years, to
humble you and to test[w] you in order to
know what was in your heart, whether or
not you would keep his commands. 3 He
humbled[x] you, causing you to hunger
and then feeding you with manna,[y]
which neither you nor your fathers had
known, to teach[z] you that man does not
live on bread[a] alone but on every word
that comes from the mouth[b] of the
LORD.[c] 4 Your clothes did not wear out
and your feet did not swell during these
forty years.[d] 5 Know then in your heart
that as a man disciplines his son, so the
LORD your God disciplines you.[e]

6 Observe the commands of the LORD
your God, walking in his ways[f] and revering him.[g] 7 For the LORD your God is
bringing you into a good land[h]—a land
with streams and pools of water, with
springs flowing in the valleys and hills;[i]

7:13 [r]Dt 28:4 **7:14** [s]Ex 23:26 **7:15** [t]S Ex 15:26 [u]S Ex 9:9 [v]S Ex 23:25; Dt 30:8-10 **7:16** [w]ver 24; Jos 6:2; 10:26 [x]S ver 2 [y]Jdg 3:6; Ezr 9:1; Ps 106:36 [z]ver 25; S Ex 10:7 **7:17** [a]Nu 33:53 **7:18** [b]S Nu 14:9; S Dt 1:21,29 [c]Ps 105:5; 119:52 **7:19** [d]Ps 136:12 [e]Dt 4:34 **7:20** [f]S Ex 23:28 **7:21** [g]S Ge 17:7; Jos 3:10 [h]Dt 10:17; Ne 1:5; 9:32; Ps 47:2; 66:3; 68:35; Isa 9:6; Da 9:4 **7:22** [i]Ex 23:28-30 **7:23** [j]Ex 23:27; Jos 10:10 **7:24** [k]Jos 10:24; Ps 110:5 [l]S ver 16 [m]S Ex 23:31; Dt 11:25; Jos 1:5; 10:8; 23:9 [n]Jos 21:44 **7:25** [o]S Ex 4:14; S 32:20 [p]Ex 20:17; Jos 7:21 [q]S ver 16 [r]Dt 17:1 **7:26** [s]Lev 27:28-29 **8:1** [t]Dt 4:1 [u]S Ex 19:5; Job 36:11; Ps 16:11; Eze 20:19 **8:2** [v]Dt 29:5; Ps 136:16; Am 2:10 [w]S Ge 22:1 **8:3** [x]2Ch 36:12; Ps 44:9; Pr 18:12; Isa 2:11; Jer 44:10 [y]S Ex 16:4 [z]1Ki 8:36; Ps 25:5; 94:12; 119:171 [a]ver 9; S Ge 3:19; Job 23:12; Ps 104:15; Pr 28:21; Isa 51:14; Jer 42:14 [b]Job 22:22; Ps 119:13; 138:4 [c]S Ex 16:2-3; Mt 4:4*; Lk 4:4* **8:4** [d]Dt 29:5; Ne 9:21 **8:5** [e]Dt 4:36; 2Sa 7:14; Job 5:17; 33:19; Pr 3:11-12; Heb 12:5-11; Rev 3:19 **8:6** [f]S Ex 33:13; 1Ki 3:14; Ps 81:13; 95:10 [g]Dt 5:33 **8:7** [h]Ps 106:24; Jer 3:19; Eze 20:6 [i]Dt 11:9-12; Jer 2:7

7:17–24 REVELATION, Events—Past experiences with God should give confidence God will reveal Himself in future needs. The Exodus experience encouraged Israel as they looked to the conquest. They knew how awesome and fearful God was. God even revealed a gradual plan of conquest which protected His people. Memories which lead to courage do not come automatically. People need God's chosen leader to remind them.

8:1–5 GOD, Father—Like a father, God lovingly provided for the needs of His people and also disciplined them. A father who loves his children will both provide for their needs and discipline them when the need arises. This was God's way with Israel in Old Testament times and is God's way with us today.

8:1–5 EVIL AND SUFFERING, Testing—What we may call evil or suffering may be God's way of testing our faithfulness. The Hebrews' forty years in the wilderness was a time of testing and teaching. God related to the Hebrews as a father disciplines a son. God continues to give His children opportunities to grow in faith and to learn from experiences with Him. See note on Heb 12:1–11.

8:1–18 ELECTION, Responsibility—The chosen of God are never to forget the loving and redemptive acts of God for them. They are to be disciplined persons who remain loyal to the commands and teachings of God. Election produces humility, not pride, in God's people.

8:1–2,6 CHRISTIAN ETHICS, Social Order—See note on 4:1–8.

8:2–5 REVELATION, History—God's history lessons are not always obvious. We need God's inspired interpreter. Moses interpreted God's reasons for the long wilderness journey as a testing period for a fickle and inconsistent people (Ex 16:2; 32:1). Life's tough times may contain God's revelation if we are ready to learn from them. History tests the commitment of the heart not the knowledge of the head.

8:2–5 HISTORY, Judgment—History is the arena in which God disciplines His people. Remembering past discipline and its causes should help us avoid future discipline.

8:7–9,10–14,18 STEWARDSHIP, Purpose of Possessions—Material items that God intends to be good can be misused by people and lead us away from God. Remembering God in times of prosperity can be difficult. Abundance is truly a blessing when one remembers who gives it and when we use it to achieve God's purposes. God made material things to serve human needs and to bring glory to God. Both purposes are achieved when Christians use their God-given possessions for care of family (see note on 1 Ti 5:4,8), giving to needy (see note on 1 Jn 3:17), service to God (see note on Mt 25:31–46), and support of the ministry (see note on 2 Co 11:8–16).

[8]a land with wheat and barley,[j] vines[k]
and fig trees,[l] pomegranates, olive oil
and honey;[m] [9]a land where bread[n] will
not be scarce and you will lack nothing;[o]
a land where the rocks are iron and you
can dig copper out of the hills.[p]
[10]When you have eaten and are satisfied,[q] praise the LORD your God for the
good land he has given you. [11]Be careful
that you do not forget[r] the LORD your
God, failing to observe his commands, his
laws and his decrees that I am giving you
this day. [12]Otherwise, when you eat and
are satisfied, when you build fine houses
and settle down,[s] [13]and when your herds
and flocks grow large and your silver and
gold increase and all you have is multiplied, [14]then your heart will become
proud and you will forget[t] the LORD your
God, who brought you out of Egypt, out
of the land of slavery. [15]He led you
through the vast and dreadful desert,[u]
that thirsty and waterless land, with its
venomous snakes[v] and scorpions. He
brought you water out of hard rock.[w]
[16]He gave you manna[x] to eat in the
desert, something your fathers had never
known,[y] to humble and to test[z] you so
that in the end it might go well with you.
[17]You may say to yourself,[a] "My power
and the strength of my hands[b] have produced this wealth for me." [18]But remember the LORD your God, for it is he who
gives you the ability to produce wealth,[c]

8:8 [j]S Ex 9:31 [k]S Ge 49:11 [l]S Nu 13:23; S 1Ki 4:25 [m]Dt 32:13; Ps 81:16
8:9 [n]S ver 3 [o]Jdg 18:10 [p]Job 28:2
8:10 [q]Dt 6:10-12
8:11 [r]Dt 4:9
8:12 [s]Pr 30:9; Hos 13:6
8:14 [t]ver 11; Ps 78:7; 106:21
8:15 [u]S Dt 1:19; S 32:10 [v]Nu 21:6; Isa 14:29; 30:6 [w]Ex 17:6; Dt 32:13; Job 28:9; Ps 78:15; 114:8
8:16 [x]S Ex 16:14 [y]Ex 16:15 [z]S Ge 22:1
8:17 [a]Dt 9:4,7,24; 31:27 [b]Jdg 7:2; Ps 44:3; Isa 10:13
8:18 [c]Ge 26:13; Dt 26:10; 28:4; 1Sa 2:7; Ps 25:13; 112:3; Pr 8:18; 10:22; Ecc 9:11; Hos 2:8
8:19 [d]Dt 6:14; Ps 16:4; Jer 7:6; 13:10; 25:6 [e]Dt 4:26; 30:18
8:20 [f]2Ki 21:2; Ps 10:16 [g]Eze 5:5-17
9:1 [h]S Nu 35:10 [i]Dt 4:38 [j]S Nu 13:28 [k]S Ge 11:4
9:2 [l]Nu 13:22; Jos 11:22
9:3 [m]Dt 31:3; Jos 3:11 [n]S Ex 15:7; S 19:18; Heb 12:29 [o]S Ex 23:31
9:4 [p]S Dt 8:17

and so confirms his covenant, which he
swore to your forefathers, as it is today.
[19]If you ever forget the LORD your God
and follow other gods[d] and worship and
bow down to them, I testify against you
today that you will surely be destroyed.[e]
[20]Like the nations[f] the LORD destroyed
before you, so you will be destroyed for
not obeying the LORD your God.[g]

Chapter 9

Not Because of Israel's Righteousness

HEAR, O Israel. You are now about to
cross the Jordan[h] to go in and dispossess nations greater and stronger than
you,[i] with large cities[j] that have walls
up to the sky.[k] [2]The people are strong
and tall—Anakites! You know about
them and have heard it said: "Who can
stand up against the Anakites?"[l] [3]But be
assured today that the LORD your God is
the one who goes across ahead of you[m]
like a devouring fire.[n] He will destroy
them; he will subdue them before you.
And you will drive them out and annihilate them quickly,[o] as the LORD has
promised you.
[4]After the LORD your God has driven
them out before you, do not say to yourself,[p] "The LORD has brought me here to
take possession of this land because of my
righteousness." No, it is on account of

8:10–20 SIN, Rebellion—Moses warned future generations of Israelites of several potential sins, primarily forgetfulness and rebellion. When they forgot what God had done for them, they would be prone to rebel against Him. Sin will destroy a seemingly secure people who forget to recall the past.
8:10 PRAYER, Praise—Blessings from God should result in praise.
8:11–20 EVIL AND SUFFERING, Punishment—Prosperity is no guarantee against suffering. Prosperity may be a temptation to trust self instead of God. Security built on trust in self is short-lived, being based on the sin of selfishness and pride. Such sin invites God's punishment. Obedience and the worship of God alone are the only sure sources of security.
8:17–18 HUMANITY, Relationship to God—Pride causes a person to take credit for all human achievements. People are to remember that the skills and abilities which lie behind their achievements are God's gifts. These gifts are empowered through a committed relationship to Him. See note on Ex 36:1–2.
8:18 THE CHURCH, Covenant People—In times of prosperity, believers should remember God is the source of all blessings. We receive gifts because of God's goodness, not because of our education, intellect, or hard work. Education and hard work can develop the gifts God gives. The blessings of life confirm the covenant relationship God has established and kept.
8:19–20 GOD, Wrath—God wants all His people to know that forgetting Him brings dire consequences. Being God's people brings great responsibilities. Neglect of that great responsibility can only bring punishment. Forgetting to obey, forgetting to love, forgetting to serve will bring the wrath of God. God chastises those whom He loves (8:5).
9:1–3 HISTORY, Promise—The history of salvation does not rest on human power and evaluations. God's purposes and promises lead His people in their decisions. By themselves, Israel had no possibility of conquering the land. With God's leadership, conquest was certain.
9:4–6 GOD, Wrath—See note on 7:1–6. The destruction that God poured out on the Canaanites as Israel entered the Promised Land was just because of their sinfulness. They deserved their fate. Israel did not deserve the favor she received from God. Israel was no better than the other nations. In divine love and wisdom God chose Israel to be His people despite their sinfulness. That is equally true of our calling as Christians. He did not choose us to be saved because of our righteousness or merit or because we were less sinful than others. God simply chose to save and bless us. We always need to see the larger context of what God is doing. In His sovereignty God calls one people to serve Him and molds them for His own purposes. At the same time, He destroys another people in their sinfulness. All this is in keeping with God's purposes in human history. See note on Jer 18:6–17.
9:4–6 SIN, Unrighteousness—No human can claim to be righteous before God. No one deserves one single blessing from God. God does not punish anyone who does not deserve it. We all have sinned and deserve punishment. Israel was sinful and did not deserve the land. The Canaanites sinned and deserved to lose their land. God, in grace, chose to bless Israel at this time and to give deserved punishment to the Canaanites. See note on 8:10–20.
9:4–6 ELECTION, God's Purpose—God's purpose in election is not to honor and reward human righteousness and integrity. Compare 10:14–15. God's purpose is to separate out from the wickedness of the world a people who will become true to Him. Israel did not earn the Promised Land. The wicked nations forfeited their right to it, a path Israel later followed. Election seeks to create righteousness rather than reward an already existing righteousness.

the wickedness[q] of these nations[r] that
the LORD is going to drive them out before you. 5It is not because of your righteousness or your integrity[s] that you are
going in to take possession of their land;
but on account of the wickedness[t] of
these nations,[u] the LORD your God will
drive them out[v] before you, to accomplish what he swore[w] to your fathers, to
Abraham, Isaac and Jacob.[x] 6Understand,
then, that it is not because of your righteousness that the LORD your God is giving
you this good land to possess, for you are
a stiff-necked people.[y]

The Golden Calf

7Remember this and never forget how
you provoked[z] the LORD your God to anger in the desert. From the day you left
Egypt until you arrived here, you have
been rebellious[a] against the LORD.[b] 8At
Horeb you aroused the LORD's wrath[c] so
that he was angry enough to destroy
you.[d] 9When I went up on the mountain
to receive the tablets of stone, the tablets
of the covenant[e] that the LORD had made
with you, I stayed on the mountain forty
days[f] and forty nights; I ate no bread and
drank no water.[g] 10The LORD gave me
two stone tablets inscribed by the finger
of God.[h] On them were all the commandments the LORD proclaimed to you
on the mountain out of the fire, on the
day of the assembly.[i]

11At the end of the forty days and forty
nights,[j] the LORD gave me the two stone
tablets,[k] the tablets of the covenant.
12Then the LORD told me, "Go down from
here at once, because your people whom
you brought out of Egypt have become
corrupt.[l] They have turned away quickly[m] from what I commanded them and
have made a cast idol for themselves."

13And the LORD said to me, "I have
seen this people[n], and they are a stiff-
necked people indeed! 14Let me alone,[o]
so that I may destroy them and blot out[p]
their name from under heaven.[q] And I
will make you into a nation stronger and
more numerous than they."

15So I turned and went down from the
mountain while it was ablaze with fire.
And the two tablets of the covenant were
in my hands.[o][r] 16When I looked, I saw
that you had sinned against the LORD
your God; you had made for yourselves
an idol cast in the shape of a calf.[s] You
had turned aside quickly from the way
that the LORD had commanded you. 17So I
took the two tablets and threw them out
of my hands, breaking them to pieces before your eyes.

18Then once again I fell[t] prostrate before the LORD for forty days and forty
nights; I ate no bread and drank no water,[u] because of all the sin you had committed,[v] doing what was evil in the
LORD's sight and so provoking him to anger. 19I feared the anger and wrath of the
LORD, for he was angry enough with you
to destroy you.[w] But again the LORD listened to me.[x] 20And the LORD was angry
enough with Aaron to destroy him, but at
that time I prayed for Aaron too. 21Also I
took that sinful thing of yours, the calf
you had made, and burned it in the fire.
Then I crushed it and ground it to powder
as fine as dust[y] and threw the dust into a
stream that flowed down the mountain.[z]

22You also made the LORD angry[a] at
Taberah,[b] at Massah[c] and at Kibroth
Hattaavah.[d]

23And when the LORD sent you out
from Kadesh Barnea,[e] he said, "Go up
and take possession[f] of the land I have
given you." But you rebelled[g] against the
command of the LORD your God. You did
not trust[h] him or obey him. 24You have
been rebellious against the LORD ever
since I have known you.[i]

25I lay prostrate before the LORD those
forty days and forty nights[j] because the
LORD had said he would destroy you.[k] 26I
prayed to the LORD and said, "O Sovereign LORD, do not destroy your people,[l]

[o]15 Or *And I had the two tablets of the covenant with me, one in each hand*

9:4 [q]2Ki 16:3; 17:8; 21:2; Ezr 9:11 [r]S Ex 23:24; S Lev 18:21,24-30; Dt 18:9-14
9:5 [s]S Eph 2:9 [t]Dt 18:9 [u]S Lev 18:25 [v]Dt 4:38; 11:23 [w]S Ge 12:7 [x]Eze 36:32
9:6 [y]S Ex 32:9; Ac 7:51
9:7 [z]S Nu 11:33 [a]S Ex 23:21 [b]S Ex 14:11
9:8 [c]Nu 16:46; 1Sa 28:18; Job 20:28; Ps 2:12; 7:11; 69:24; 110:5; Isa 9:19; Eze 20:13 [d]Ex 32:7-10; Ezr 9:14; Ps 106:19
9:9 [e]S Dt 4:13 [f]S Ge 7:4 [g]S Ex 24:12
9:10 [h]S Ex 31:18 [i]Dt 10:4; 18:16
9:11 [j]S Ge 7:4 [k]S Ex 24:12
9:12 [l]S Dt 4:16 [m]Jdg 2:17
9:13 [n]ver 6; Dt 10:16
9:14 [o]Ex 32:10 [p]S Nu 14:12 [q]Jer 7:16
9:15 [r]S Ex 32:15
9:16 [s]S Ex 32:4
9:18 [t]S Ex 34:28 [u]ver 9 [v]S Ex 32:31
9:19 [w]S Ex 32:14; Heb 12:21* [x]ver 26; Ex 34:10; S Nu 11:2; 1Sa 7:9; Jer 15:1
9:21 [y]Ps 18:42; Isa 29:5; 40:15 [z]Ex 32:20; Isa 2:18; Mic 1:7
9:22 [a]S Nu 1:53 [b]Nu 11:3 [c]S Ex 17:7 [d]Nu 11:34
9:23 [e]S Dt 1:2 [f]Dt 1:21 [g]S Nu 14:9 [h]S Dt 1:32; Ps 106:24
9:24 [i]S Dt 8:17
9:25 [j]S Ge 7:4 [k]ver 18; S Ex 33:17
9:26 [l]S Ex 33:13

9:7–29 EVIL AND SUFFERING, Deserved—The people of God must be so more than in name only. Israel proudly claimed to be God's people, but their history could be retold as a history of sin. They expected blessing. God promised only punishment for a rebellious people. Moses' intercession led to another chance. Deserved punishment does not always come.
9:7—10:11 SIN, Rebellion—Israel might describe its history as one of God's grace and salvation. It could also be described as the history of God's judgment and anger. Compare Ps 105 and 106. Moses described it as a history of rebellion. God punished the rebellious sinners, then proceeded with His plan for His people. See note on Ex 14:11–12.
9:9–15 THE CHURCH, Covenant People—The tables of stone listed the basic responsibilities of the covenant relationship. Any relationship, whether in marriage, business, or religion, involves responsibility. Relationships are not easily made or cheaply maintained. God fulfills His covenant obligations and desires that His people obey the covenant's commands. The covenant God expresses anger against a disobedient people.
9:18–19 PRAYER, Humility—The sin of Israel caused her leader to fall prostrate and to fast. See note on Ex 34:28. We need to confess the sins of our worship community and seek His blessings on our service for Him.
9:25–29 ELECTION, Prayer—See note on Ex 32:13–14. When the Israelites failed to trust and honor God, Moses interceded, reminding God that He had chosen Israel to be His inheritance. Intercessory prayer is a necessary form of prayer for those elected of God to lead God's chosen ones. Such prayer grows out of the love that elect ones have for God and for each other. Such prayer seeks God's honor in the world rather than deserved justice for the elect.

your own inheritance[m] that you redeemed[n] by your great power and
brought out of Egypt with a mighty
hand.[o] 27Remember your servants Abraham, Isaac and Jacob. Overlook the stubbornness[p] of this people, their wickedness and their sin. 28Otherwise, the country[q] from which you brought us will say,
'Because the LORD was not able to take
them into the land he had promised
them, and because he hated them,[r] he
brought them out to put them to death in
the desert.'[s] 29But they are your people,[t] your inheritance[u] that you brought
out by your great power and your outstretched arm.[v]"

Chapter 10

Tablets Like the First Ones

At that time the LORD said to me,
"Chisel out two stone tablets[w] like
the first ones and come up to me on the
mountain. Also make a wooden chest.[p] 2I
will write on the tablets the words that
were on the first tablets, which you
broke. Then you are to put them in the
chest."[x]
3So I made the ark out of acacia wood[y]
and chiseled[z] out two stone tablets like
the first ones, and I went up on the
mountain with the two tablets in my
hands. 4The LORD wrote on these tablets
what he had written before, the Ten
Commandments[a] he had proclaimed[b] to
you on the mountain, out of the fire, on
the day of the assembly.[c] And the LORD
gave them to me. 5Then I came back
down the mountain[d] and put the tablets

9:26 mS Ex 34:9 nS Ex 6:6; Dt 15:15; 2Sa 7:23; Ps 78:35 oS ver 19; S Ex 32:11
9:27 pver 6; S Ex 32:9
9:28 qDt 32:27 rS Dt 1:27 sS Ex 32:12; Jos 7:9
9:29 tS Ex 33:13 uS Ex 34:9; Dt 32:9 vDt 4:34; Ne 1:10; Jer 27:5; 32:17
10:1 wEx 34:1-2
10:2 xEx 25:16,21; 2Ch 5:10; 6:11
10:3 yEx 37:1-9 zEx 34:4
10:4 aS Ex 24:12; S 34:28 bEx 20:1 cS Dt 9:10
10:5 dS Ex 19:11 eS Ex 25:10; S 1Sa 3:3 fS Ex 25:21 g1Ki 8:9
10:6 hNu 33:30 iS Nu 27:13 jS Ex 6:23 kS Nu 20:25-28
10:7 lNu 33:32-34; Ps 42:1; SS 5:12; Isa 32:2
10:8 mS Nu 3:6 nS Nu 10:33 oS Nu 16:9 pS Ge 48:20 q1Ch 23:26
10:9 rS Nu 18:20
10:10 sS Ex 33:17
10:12 tMic 6:8 uS Ex 20:20 v1Ki 2:3; 3:3; 9:4 wDt 5:33; 6:13; Mt 22:37; 1Ti 1:5 xDt 11:13; 28:47; Ps 100:2 yS Dt 6:5; Ps 119:2 zS Dt 5:32
10:13 aS Dt 4:2 bDt 5:33; 6:24
10:14 cPs 148:4; Isa 19:1; Hab 3:8 dNe 9:6; Job 35:5; Ps 8:3; 89:11; 104:3 eDt 33:26

in the ark[e] I had made,[f] as the LORD
commanded me, and they are there
now.[g]
6(The Israelites traveled from the wells
of the Jaakanites to Moserah.[h] There Aaron died[i] and was buried, and Eleazar[j]
his son succeeded him as priest.[k] 7From
there they traveled to Gudgodah and on
to Jotbathah, a land with streams of water.[l] 8At that time the LORD set apart the
tribe of Levi[m] to carry the ark of the covenant[n] of the LORD, to stand before the
LORD to minister[o] and to pronounce
blessings[p] in his name, as they still do
today.[q] 9That is why the Levites have no
share or inheritance among their brothers; the LORD is their inheritance,[r] as the
LORD your God told them.)
10Now I had stayed on the mountain
forty days and nights, as I did the first
time, and the LORD listened to me at this
time also. It was not his will to destroy
you.[s] 11"Go," the LORD said to me, "and
lead the people on their way, so that they
may enter and possess the land that I
swore to their fathers to give them."

Fear the LORD

12And now, O Israel, what does the
LORD your God ask of you[t] but to fear[u]
the LORD your God, to walk[v] in all his
ways, to love him,[w] to serve the LORD[x]
your God with all your heart[y] and with
all your soul,[z] 13and to observe the
LORD's commands[a] and decrees that I am
giving you today for your own good?[b]
14To the LORD your God belong
the heavens,[cde] even the highest

p1 That is, an ark

10:10–11 PRAYER, Petition—The lengthy fast became a powerful prayer bringing deliverance for God's people. God listens to humble people.

10:11,22 GOD, Faithfulness—God continually reminded His people He was faithful to His covenant with them. The little handful—seventy persons who went into Egypt—became a nation seemingly more numerous than the stars in the heavens. God still fulfills His promises far beyond what we could ask. Many times the people provoked God and failed to trust Him. Nevertheless, God continued to bless them, despite what they might have deserved. God is not a God whose will changes back and forth, nor is He easily discouraged. In His long-suffering with us, He continues to keep His eye on His long-term plans for us and often overlooks our short-term faults. That is the nature of the graciousness and faithfulness of God.

10:12–13 HUMANITY, Relationship to God—The demands of God are placed upon His chosen people. Such demands are neither arbitrary nor capricious, but are intended to make life both livable and satisfying.

10:12,20 SALVATION, Fear of God—Fearing God comes close to summing up what He requires of all persons. Those who fear God will walk along the paths He has laid out. They will obey Him and stand in reverence before Him. Loving God and serving Him are fruits of fearing Him. Compare Mic 6:8.

10:12–13 CHRISTIAN ETHICS, Worship—God's commands to heed and imitate His revealed character give rise to our reverential awe, or worship, from which springs our life-style. One's total being should be dedicated to having a personal character reflecting God's nature.

10:12–13 CHRISTIAN ETHICS, Social Order—See note on 4:1–8.

10:14–21 GOD, Sovereignty—Israel needed to learn the profound truth that God is the sovereign Lord of this universe. As Creator, He brought it all into existence; as sovereign Lord, it continues to belong to Him. There are enormous implications of this truth. We are not in this world by our own choice. The life we live has come to us from God. Our best interests in this world will be served by living lives that conform to the will of the one God who is the sovereign Lord over us all. He is a just and faithful God who has no favorites. He is not like other gods who can be bribed and bought off. God is just and loving in all His dealings with human beings. Although God had shown His loving favor to His chosen people, Israel, He was also concerned for those outside the chosen nation. He commanded the Israelites to love the foreigners and reminded His people that they had once been aliens themselves in the land of Egypt. He revealed Himself as the defender of widows and orphans, the stranger and the outcast, the ones so often overlooked by the more fortunate. As sovereign Lord, God owns, loves, and is concerned for all people, and wants His specially-called people to love Him and share His concern for all of humankind.

10:14–22 ELECTION, Worship—Blessings are given to those who fear God. The justice of God turns against those who ignore God's holy requirements on the grounds that they may do what they choose because they are elected. The elect

heavens,[f][g] the earth and everything in
it.[h] 15Yet the LORD set his affection on
your forefathers and loved[i] them, and
he chose you,[j] their descendants, above
all the nations, as it is today.[k] 16Circum-
cise[l] your hearts,[m] therefore, and do not
be stiff-necked[n] any longer. 17For the
LORD your God is God of gods[o] and Lord
of lords,[p] the great God, mighty and awesome,[q] who shows no partiality[r] and accepts no bribes.[s] 18He defends the cause
of the fatherless and the widow,[t] and
loves the alien, giving him food and clothing.[u] 19And you are to love[v] those who
are aliens,[w] for you yourselves were
aliens in Egypt.[x] 20Fear the LORD your
God and serve him.[y] Hold fast[z] to him
and take your oaths in his name.[a] 21He is
your praise;[b] he is your God, who performed for you those great[c] and awesome wonders[d] you saw with your own
eyes. 22Your forefathers who went down
into Egypt were seventy in all,[e] and now
the LORD your God has made you as numerous as the stars in the sky.[f]

Chapter 11

Love and Obey the LORD

LOVE[g] the LORD your God and keep his
requirements, his decrees, his laws
and his commands always.[h] 2Remember
today that your children[i] were not the
ones who saw and experienced the discipline of the LORD your God:[j] his majesty,[k] his mighty hand, his outstretched
arm;[l] 3the signs he performed and the
things he did in the heart of Egypt, both
to Pharaoh king of Egypt and to his whole
country;[m] 4what he did to the Egyptian
army, to its horses and chariots,[n] how he

10:14 [f]Ps 115:16 [g]1Ki 8:27 [h]Ex 19:5; Ps 24:1; Ac 17:24 **10:15** [i]S Dt 4:37 [j]Ps 105:6; 135:4 [k]S Nu 14:8; Ro 11:28; 1Pe 2:9 **10:16** [l]S Ge 17:11 [m]S Lev 26:41; Dt 30:6; Jer 32:39 [n]S Ex 32:9; S Dt 9:13 **10:17** [o]Jos 22:22; Ps 135:5; 136:2; Da 2:47; 11:36 [p]Ps 136:3; S 1Ti 6:15 [q]S Dt 7:21 [r]Dt 1:17; Mal 2:9 [s]S Ex 23:8; S Lev 19:16 **10:18** [t]Ex 22:21, 22-24; 23:9; Lev 19:33; Dt 27:19; Job 29:13; Ps 94:6; Isa 10:2; Jer 49:11 [u]S Nu 10:32 **10:19** [v]Dt 7:12 [w]S Ex 22:21; S Dt 24:19 [x]S Lev 19:34; Eze 47:22-23 **10:20** [y]Mt 4:10 [z]Dt 11:22; 13:4; 30:20; Jos 23:8; Ru 1:14; 2Ki 18:6; Ps 119:31; Isa 38:3 [a]S Ex 20:7 **10:21** [b]S Ex 15:2 [c]1Sa 12:24; Ps 126:2 [d]2Sa 7:23 **10:22** [e]S Ge 34:30; S 46:26; Ac 7:14 [f]S Ge 12:2; S Nu 10:36 **11:1** [g]S Dt 6:5 [h]S Lev 8:35 **11:2** [i]Dt 31:13; Ps 78:6 [j]S Dt 5:24 [k]S Dt 3:24 [l]Ps 136:12 **11:3** [m]Ex 7:8-21 **11:4** [n]S Ex 15:1 [o]S Ex 14:27; S Nu 21:4 **11:6** [p]Nu 16:1-35; Ps 106:16-18 [q]Isa 24:19 **11:7** [r]Dt 5:3 **11:8** [s]Ezr 9:10

overwhelmed them with the waters of
the Red Sea[q][o] as they were pursuing
you, and how the LORD brought lasting
ruin on them. 5It was not your children
who saw what he did for you in the
desert until you arrived at this place, 6and
what he did[p] to Dathan and Abiram, sons
of Eliab the Reubenite, when the earth
opened[q] its mouth right in the middle of
all Israel and swallowed them up with
their households, their tents and every
living thing that belonged to them. 7But it
was your own eyes that saw all these
great things the LORD has done.[r]

8Observe therefore all the commands[s]
I am giving you today, so that you may
have the strength to go in and take over
the land that you are crossing the Jordan
to possess,[t] 9and so that you may live
long[u] in the land that the LORD swore[v]
to your forefathers to give to them and
their descendants, a land flowing with
milk and honey.[w] 10The land you are entering to take over is not like the land of
Egypt,[x] from which you have come,
where you planted your seed and irrigat-
ed it by foot as in a vegetable garden.
11But the land you are crossing the Jordan
to take possession of is a land of mountains and valleys[y] that drinks rain from
heaven.[z] 12It is a land the LORD your God
cares for; the eyes[a] of the LORD your God
are continually on it from the beginning
of the year to its end.

13So if you faithfully obey[b] the commands I am giving you today—to love[c]
the LORD your God and to serve him with

[t]Dt 31:6-7,23; Jos 1:7 **11:9** [u]S Dt 5:16 [v]Dt 9:5 [w]S Ex 3:8 **11:10** [x]Isa 11:15; 37:25 **11:11** [y]Eze 36:4 [z]Dt 8:7; Ne 9:25 **11:12** [a]1Ki 8:29; 9:3 **11:13** [b]S Dt 6:17 [c]S Dt 10:12

[q]4 Hebrew *Yam Suph*; that is, Sea of Reeds

---

reverence and worship God, depending on His merciful love, not on human achievement. Such worship expresses itself in care for the needy.

10:17–19 DISCIPLESHIP, Homeless—God shows no partiality and accepts no bribes, nor should His people. God loves and defends the rights of those whom others oppress and mistreat. He leads His people to do the same thing. Homeless foreigners are of special concern to Him. See note on Ex 22:21.

10:21–22 HISTORY, Worship—History leads us to praise God for His miraculous deliverance in our times of need and for His faithful fulfillment of His promises (Ge 15:5).

11:1 CHRISTIAN ETHICS, Moral Limits—Love for God leads His people to accept gladly and obey the moral limits He sets for us. Such obedience is never a temporary means of gaining something from God, but a continuing, permanent response of love to God.

11:2–7 HISTORY, God's Will—God lets us see evidence of His power in history to lead us to love and obey Him.

11:8–9 CHRISTIAN ETHICS, Social Order—See note on 4:1–8.

11:9–21 ELECTION, Blessing—Election led Israel to a land where they had to depend on God for fertility. Dependence includes obedience to the Creator. Obedience does not seek to earn blessing. Rather obedience is the natural response to election, and blessing is one of the parts of election.

11:10–15 GOD, Love—God told the Israelites of His fatherly concern for their every need as they entered the Promised Land. The land He was giving them would be a much easier home for them, for they would not have to irrigate as they had done in Egypt. God declared that He would send the sun and the rain upon the land and give them good crops. See Mt 5:45. The promise of prosperity was linked to the continued faithfulness and obedience of the people. God blesses those who honor Him faithfully. Those who do not honor God have no right to expect His blessings. They may have the good fortune to receive some of the blessings that God pours out on His faithful people (as in the neighboring fields when it rains). God is a faithful and loving God who watches over His people providing for their needs. We ought not misunderstand this truth. God is not necessarily concerned for our luxuries, but He is concerned for our needs. As sovereign Lord, He has the power to supply our needs. As loving heavenly Father, He has the grace to do it.

11:13 WORSHIP, Service—Worship has at least two distinct aspects: adoration or praise, and obedience or service. To worship God is to "serve" (Hebrew *'abad*), that is to do the work of a slave (Hebrew *'ebed*). Such worship or service is done in reverential fear and the wonder of adoring awe, not grudgingly in face of threatened punishment. Service grows out of love and devotion. Worship is not outward actions as much as inner devotion (Eph 5:19; Col 3:16). See note on Mt 4:10.

all your heart and with all your soul[d] —
14then I will send rain[e] on your land in
its season, both autumn and spring
rains,[f] so that you may gather in your
grain, new wine and oil. 15I will provide
grass[g] in the fields for your cattle, and
you will eat and be satisfied.[h]

16Be careful, or you will be enticed to
turn away and worship other gods and
bow down to them.[i] 17Then the LORD's
anger[j] will burn against you, and he will
shut[k] the heavens so that it will not rain
and the ground will yield no produce,[l]
and you will soon perish[m] from the good
land the LORD is giving you. 18Fix these
words of mine in your hearts and minds;
tie them as symbols on your hands and
bind them on your foreheads.[n] 19Teach
them to your children,[o] talking about
them when you sit at home and when
you walk along the road, when you lie
down and when you get up.[p] 20Write
them on the doorframes of your houses
and on your gates,[q] 21so that your days
and the days of your children may be
many[r] in the land that the LORD swore to
give your forefathers, as many as the days
that the heavens are above the earth.[s]

22If you carefully observe[t] all these
commands I am giving you to follow—to
love[u] the LORD your God, to walk in all
his ways and to hold fast[v] to him—
23then the LORD will drive out[w] all these
nations[x] before you, and you will dispossess nations larger and stronger than
you.[y] 24Every place where you set your
foot will be yours:[z] Your territory will
extend from the desert to Lebanon, and
from the Euphrates River[a] to the western
sea.[r] 25No man will be able to stand
against you. The LORD your God, as he
promised you, will put the terror[b] and
fear of you on the whole land, wherever
you go.[c]

26See, I am setting before you today a
blessing[d] and a curse[e]— 27the blessing[f]
if you obey the commands of the LORD
your God that I am giving you today;
28the curse if you disobey[g] the commands of the LORD your God and turn
from the way that I command you today
by following other gods,[h] which you
have not known. 29When the LORD your
God has brought you into the land you
are entering to possess, you are to proclaim on Mount Gerizim[i] the blessings,
and on Mount Ebal[j] the curses.[k] 30As
you know, these mountains are across the
Jordan, west of the road,[s] toward the setting sun, near the great trees of Moreh,[l]
in the territory of those Canaanites living
in the Arabah in the vicinity of Gilgal.[m]
31You are about to cross the Jordan to enter and take possession[n] of the land the
LORD your God is giving[o] you. When you
have taken it over and are living there,
32be sure that you obey all the decrees
and laws I am setting before you today.

Chapter 12

The One Place of Worship

THESE are the decrees[p] and laws you
must be careful to follow in the land
that the LORD, the God of your fathers,
has given you to possess—as long as you
live in the land.[q] 2Destroy completely all
the places on the high mountains[r] and
on the hills and under every spreading
tree[s] where the nations you are dispossessing worship their gods. 3Break down
their altars, smash[t] their sacred stones
and burn[u] their Asherah[v] poles in the
fire; cut down the idols of their gods and
wipe out their names[w] from those places.

11:13 [d]Dt 4:29; Jer 17:24 **11:14** [e]S Lev 26:4; Ac 14:17 [f]Ps 147:8; Jer 3:3; 5:24; Joel 2:23; Jas 5:7 **11:15** [g]Ps 104:14 [h]S Lev 26:5 **11:16** [i]Dt 4:19; 8:19; 29:18; Job 31:9,27 **11:17** [j]Dt 6:15; 9:19 [k]1Ki 17:1; 2Ch 6:26; 7:13 [l]S Lev 26:20 [m]Dt 4:26; 28:12,24 **11:18** [n]S Ex 13:9; Dt 6:6-8 **11:19** [o]S Ex 12:26; Dt 6:7; Ps 145:4; Isa 38:19; Jer 32:39 [p]Dt 4:9-10 **11:20** [q]Dt 6:9 **11:21** [r]Job 5:26; Pr 3:2; 4:10; 9:11 [s]Ps 72:5 **11:22** [t]S Dt 6:17 [u]S Dt 6:5 [v]S Dt 10:20 **11:23** [w]S Dt 9:5 [x]S Ex 23:28 [y]Dt 9:1 **11:24** [z]Ge 15:18; Dt 1:36; 12:20; 19:8; Jos 1:3; 14:9 [a]S Ge 2:14 **11:25** [b]S Dt 2:25 [c]Ex 23:27; Dt 7:24 **11:26** [d]Ps 24:5 [e]Lev 26:14-17; Dt 27:13-26; 30:1, 15,19; La 2:17; Da 9:11; Hag 1:11; Mal 2:2; 3:9; 4:6 **11:27** [f]Dt 28:1-14; Ps 24:5 **11:28** [g]2Ch 24:20; Jer 42:13; 44:16 [h]S Dt 4:28; 13:6, 13; 29:26; 1Sa 26:19 **11:29** [i]Jdg 9:7 [j]Dt 27:4; Jos 8:30 [k]Dt 27:12-13; Jos 8:33; Jn 4:20 **11:30** [l]S Ge 12:6 [m]Jos 4:19; 5:9; 9:6; 10:6; 14:6; 15:7; Jdg 2:1; 2Ki 2:1; Mic 6:5 **11:31** [n]S Nu 33:53 [o]Dt 12:10; Jos 11:23 **12:1** [p]Ps 119:5 [q]Dt 4:9-10; 6:15; 1Ki 8:40; Eze 20:19 **12:2** [r]S Nu 21:28 [s]1Ki 14:23; 2Ki 17:10; Isa 57:5; Jer 2:20; 3:6,13 **12:3** [t]2Ki 11:18 [u]S Ex 32:20 [v]Ex 34:13; 1Ki 14:15,23 [w]S Ex 23:13

[r]*24* That is, the Mediterranean [s]*30* Or *Jordan, westward*

11:16–21 GOD, Wrath—These words of admonition and warning are in sharp contrast to the verses immediately preceding. Here, God warns that if we forget Him, if we compromise our loyalty to Him, His wrath will be exercised against us. God's provision for daily necessities can be changed so that we do not enjoy plenty but suffer deprivation instead. This is repeated in the New Testament by Paul in Gal 5:7–8. God is serious about Himself and His will for our lives, and He wants us to be serious about Him too. Not only does He warn us to be faithful to Him as a jealous God, but He also encourages—commands—that we teach our children about Him. We are responsible for passing our faith to them and leading them to grow in that faith. This is God's minimum expectation of us. See 6:10–25.

11:26–27 EVIL AND SUFFERING, Deserved—Life under the God of the covenant has two options. Loyal obedience leads to covenant blessing. Disobedience leads to covenant curses which involves suffering. God's people cannot blame suffering on Him. Our sin deserves punishment. See note on 28:1–68.

11:32 CHRISTIAN ETHICS, Social Order—See note on 4:1–8.

12:1 CHRISTIAN ETHICS, Social Order—See note on 4:1–8.

12:2–7 GOD, One God—Any culture that does not conform to the will of God is pagan, that is, foreign to God. Paying token lip service to God does not mean that our culture is Christian. Today we are hardly prone to lapse into the idol worship of ancient Israel, but we must be on guard lest our worship of God and life-style before Him become compromised with godless forms of modern culture. Keeping Christian faith and practice pure in a pagan setting is always difficult.

12:4–7 REVELATION, Fellowship—The God who made His people for community spoke clearly to them about His plans and designs for them. God intended to live in the Promised Land with them. They could not find God where pagan neighbors expected to. They must go to God's chosen place. There the human family of God would sit and break bread, sharing in God's presence and purpose.

12:4–14 WORSHIP, Buildings—See note on Ge 28:16–22.

4You must not worship the LORD your
God in their way.[x] 5But you are to seek
the place the LORD your God will choose
from among all your tribes to put his
Name[y] there for his dwelling.[z] To that
place you must go; 6there bring your
burnt offerings and sacrifices, your
tithes[a] and special gifts, what you have
vowed[b] to give and your freewill offerings, and the firstborn of your herds and
flocks.[c] 7There, in the presence[d] of the
LORD your God, you and your families
shall eat and shall rejoice[e] in everything
you have put your hand to, because the
LORD your God has blessed you.

8You are not to do as we do here today,
everyone as he sees fit,[f] 9since you have
not yet reached the resting place[g] and
the inheritance[h] the LORD your God is
giving you. 10But you will cross the Jordan
and settle in the land the LORD your God
is giving[i] you as an inheritance, and he
will give you rest[j] from all your enemies
around you so that you will live in safety.
11Then to the place the LORD your God
will choose as a dwelling for his Name[k]
—there you are to bring everything I
command you: your burnt offerings and
sacrifices, your tithes and special gifts,
and all the choice possessions you have
vowed to the LORD.[l] 12And there rejoice[m] before the LORD your God, you,
your sons and daughters, your menservants and maidservants, and the Levites[n]
from your towns, who have no allotment
or inheritance[o] of their own. 13Be careful
not to sacrifice your burnt offerings anywhere you please.[p] 14Offer them only at
the place the LORD will choose[q] in one of
your tribes, and there observe everything
I command you.

15Nevertheless, you may slaughter your
animals in any of your towns and eat as
much of the meat as you want, as if it
were gazelle or deer,[r] according to the
blessing the LORD your God gives you.
Both the ceremonially unclean and the
clean may eat it. 16But you must not eat
the blood;[s] pour[t] it out on the ground
like water.[u] 17You must not eat in your
own towns the tithe[v] of your grain and
new wine and oil,[w] or the firstborn of
your herds and flocks, or whatever you
have vowed to give,[x] or your freewill offerings or special gifts.[y] 18Instead, you
are to eat[z] them in the presence of the
LORD your God at the place the LORD your
God will choose[a]—you, your sons and
daughters, your menservants and maidservants, and the Levites from your
towns—and you are to rejoice[b] before
the LORD your God in everything you put
your hand to. 19Be careful not to neglect
the Levites[c] as long as you live in your
land.[d]

20When the LORD your God has enlarged your territory[e] as he promised[f]
you, and you crave meat[g] and say, "I
would like some meat," then you may eat
as much of it as you want. 21If the place
where the LORD your God chooses to put
his Name[h] is too far away from you, you
may slaughter animals from the herds and
flocks the LORD has given you, as I have
commanded you, and in your own towns
you may eat as much of them as you

12:4 [x]ver 30; 2Ki 17:15; Jer 10:2 **12:5** [y]S Ex 20:24; S 2Sa 7:13 [z]ver 11, 13; Dt 14:23; 15:20; 16:2,11; 18:6; 26:2; 1Sa 2:29; 1Ki 5:5; 8:16; 9:3; 2Ch 2:4; 6:6; 7:12,16; Ezr 6:12; 7:15; Ps 26:8; 78:68; Zec 2:12 **12:6** [a]S Lev 27:30 [b]S Ge 28:20 [c]Jos 22:27; Isa 66:20 **12:7** [d]S Ex 18:12 [e]S Lev 23:40; Ecc 3:12-13; 5:18-20; S Isa 62:9 **12:8** [f]Jdg 17:6; 21:25 **12:9** [g]S Ex 33:14; Dt 3:20; Ps 95:11; Mic 2:10 [h]Dt 4:21 **12:10** [i]S Dt 11:31 [j]S Ex 33:14 **12:11** [k]S ver 5 [l]S Lev 1:3; Jos 22:23 **12:12** [m]ver 7 [n]Dt 26:11-13 [o]S Nu 18:20 **12:13** [p]S ver 5 **12:14** [q]ver 11 **12:15** [r]ver 22; Dt 14:5; 15:22 **12:16** [s]S Ge 9:4; Ac 15:20 [t]ver 23-24; S Ge 35:14; 1Ch 11:18; Jer 7:18 [u]S Lev 17:13; S Dt 15:23; Jn 19:34 **12:17** [v]S Lev 27:30 [w]S Nu 18:12 [x]ver 26; Nu 18:19 [y]Dt 14:23; 15:20 **12:18** [z]Dt 14:23; 15:20 [a]ver 5 [b]ver 7, 12; Dt 14:26; Ne 8:10; Ecc 3:12-13; 5:18-20 **12:19** [c]ver 12; Dt 14:27; Ne 13:10 [d]Mal 3:8

12:20 [e]S Ex 34:24 [f]S Ge 15:8; S Dt 11:24 [g]S Ex 16:3 **12:21** [h]Dt 14:24

12:5–14 ELECTION, Worship—Proper worship does not deserve or earn election. God elects a people and a place and manner of worship. Election leads people to worship where and how God chooses. "The place . . . God will choose" (Hebrew *bachar*) punctuates the laws in Dt 12—26. The choice of only one worship center for an entire people is without parallel in Israel's environment. The one worship place with the one elect priesthood made sure a unity of worship, a way to know God's will, a sign of the one God's presence and blessing among His people, and memory of God's election of His people to be their God.

12:5 PRAYER, Worship—A praying community needs a central place for prayer and worship. Canaan was polytheistic with many worship places. At this point in the divine history, the one true God required one place of worship.

12:6–18 STEWARDSHIP, Tithe—The celebration tithe was shared in worship in a ceremony of thanksgiving and praise. A tenth of grain produce was to be carried to a worship place where the family joined in a celebration meal. In this case the tithe was consumed by the giver, after sharing it with the Levites in an act of worship. See note on Nu 18:21–32.

12:7,12 PRAYER, Worship—The injunction to rejoice is repeated numerous times in Scripture (3:12,18; 14:26; 16:11; 26:11; 27:7; Php 4:4,6), sometimes specifically "before the LORD." Prayer is a time to reflect joyfully on all the experiences God has given us. Rejoicing is a vital part of community worship. See note on Lev 23:40.

12:7 FAMILY, Worship—God established a place of worship for the new nation. Normally, the people celebrated their faith through home worship, but on designated holy days they were to go as households to the Temple and worship joyfully together (12:11–14,18; 15:20; 16:11,14). Worship was a family experience. Shared worship is considered so important to the development of faith that believers are warned against neglecting it (Heb 10:25). As in biblical times, families today need to know the Word of God by hearing it taught and by worshiping God through family worship in the church (Dt 31:12–13). See Ac 11:13–17; 16:14–15,31–34; Ro 16:3–5; 1 Co 1:16; Gal 6:10; Eph 2:19; 1 Ti 3:15.

12:9–10 CHRISTIAN ETHICS, War and Peace—Peace, not war, is the ideal of God for His people.

12:19 DISCIPLESHIP, Homeless—In making provision for the families and servants, God cautioned against neglecting the landless Levites who had no allotment or inheritance of their own. See Nu 14:27–29. Levites were charged with caring for the tabernacle and its furniture. These special servants transported the tabernacle when the camp moved, erected the tent when they rested, and assisted the priests in their services. See Nu 9:15–23. Levites began serving at the age of twenty and retired from active service at fifty. See Nu 4:3; 8:23–26; 1 Ch 23:24. Some continued to assist those who succeeded them after retirement. Not all homeless people are necessarily poor. Some serve in ways that make purchasing a home unwise, and some live in public housing. Some live in church property. God's people should be careful not to neglect such persons as they make provision for others.

want.[i] 22Eat them as you would gazelle
or deer.[j] Both the ceremonially unclean
and the clean may eat. 23But be sure you
do not eat the blood,[k] because the blood
is the life, and you must not eat the life
with the meat.[l] 24You must not eat the
blood; pour it out on the ground like water.[m] 25Do not eat it, so that it may go
well[n] with you and your children after
you, because you will be doing what is
right[o] in the eyes of the LORD.

26But take your consecrated things and
whatever you have vowed to give,[p] and
go to the place the LORD will choose.
27Present your burnt offerings[q] on the altar of the LORD your God, both the meat
and the blood. The blood of your sacrifices must be poured beside the altar of
the LORD your God, but you may eat[r] the
meat. 28Be careful to obey all these regulations I am giving you, so that it may
always go well[s] with you and your children after you, because you will be doing
what is good and right in the eyes of the
LORD your God.

29The LORD your God will cut off[t] before you the nations you are about to invade and dispossess. But when you have
driven them out and settled in their
land,[u] 30and after they have been destroyed before you, be careful not to be
ensnared[v] by inquiring about their gods,
saying, "How do these nations serve their
gods? We will do the same."[w] 31You must
not worship the LORD your God in their
way, because in worshiping their gods,
they do all kinds of detestable things the
LORD hates.[x] They even burn their sons[y]
and daughters in the fire as sacrifices to
their gods.[z]

32See that you do all I command you;
do not add[a] to it or take away from it.

Chapter 13

Worshiping Other Gods

If a prophet,[b] or one who foretells by
dreams,[c] appears among you and announces to you a miraculous sign or wonder, 2and if the sign[d] or wonder of which
he has spoken takes place, and he says,
"Let us follow other gods"[e] (gods you
have not known) "and let us worship
them," 3you must not listen to the words
of that prophet[f] or dreamer.[g] The LORD
your God is testing[h] you to find out
whether you love[i] him with all your
heart and with all your soul. 4It is the
LORD your God you must follow,[j] and
him you must revere.[k] Keep his commands and obey him; serve him and hold
fast[l] to him. 5That prophet or dreamer
must be put to death,[m] because he
preached rebellion against the LORD your
God, who brought you out of Egypt and
redeemed you from the land of slavery;
he has tried to turn[n] you from the way
the LORD your God commanded you to
follow. You must purge the evil[o] from
among you.

6If your very own brother, or your son
or daughter, or the wife you love, or your
closest friend secretly entices[p] you, saying, "Let us go and worship other gods"[q]
(gods that neither you nor your fathers
have known, 7gods of the peoples around
you, whether near or far, from one end of
the land to the other), 8do not yield[r] to
him or listen to him. Show him no pity.[s]
Do not spare him or shield him. 9You
must certainly put him to death.[t] Your
hand[u] must be the first in putting him to
death, and then the hands of all the people. 10Stone him to death, because he
tried to turn you away[v] from the LORD
your God, who brought you out of Egypt,
out of the land of slavery. 11Then all Israel
will hear and be afraid,[w] and no one
among you will do such an evil thing
again.

12If you hear it said about one of the
towns the LORD your God is giving you to
live in 13that wicked men[x] have arisen
among you and have led the people of
their town astray, saying, "Let us go and
worship other gods" (gods you have not
known), 14then you must inquire, probe
and investigate it thoroughly.[y] And if it is
true and it has been proved that this detestable thing has been done among
you,[z] 15you must certainly put to the
sword all who live in that town. Destroy

12:21 [i]Lev 17:4
12:22 [j]S ver 15
12:23 [k]S Lev 7:26 [l]Eze 33:25
12:24 [m]ver 16
12:25 [n]S Dt 4:40 [o]ver 28; Ex 15:26; Dt 13:18; 1Ki 11:38; 2Ki 12:2
12:26 [p]S ver 17; Nu 5:9-10
12:27 [q]S Lev 1:13 [r]Lev 3:1-17
12:28 [s]Dt 4:40; Ecc 8:12
12:29 [t]Jos 23:4 [u]S Dt 6:10
12:30 [v]S Ex 10:7 [w]S ver 4
12:31 [x]S Lev 18:25 [y]S Lev 18:21 [z]S 2Ki 3:27
12:32 [a]S Dt 4:2; Rev 22:18-19
13:1 [b]Mt 24:24; Mk 13:22; 2Th 2:9 [c]S Ge 20:3; Jer 23:25; 27:9; 29:8
13:2 [d]Dt 18:22; 1Sa 2:34; 10:9; 2Ki 19:29; 20:9; Isa 7:11 [e]S Dt 11:28
13:3 [f]2Pe 2:1 [g]1Sa 28:6,15 [h]S Ge 22:1; 1Ki 13:18; 22:22-23; Jer 29:31; 43:2; Eze 13:9; 1Co 11:19 [i]Dt 6:5
13:4 [j]2Ki 23:3; 2Ch 34:31; 2Jn 1:6 [k]S Dt 6:13; S Ps 5:7 [l]S Dt 10:20
13:5 [m]S Ex 21:12; S 22:20 [n]ver 10; Dt 4:19 [o]Dt 17:7, 12; 19:19; 24:7; Jdg 20:13; S 1Co 5:13
13:6 [p]Dt 17:2-7; 29:18 [q]S Dt 11:28
13:8 [r]Pr 1:10 [s]S Dt 7:2
13:9 [t]ver 5 [u]S Lev 24:14
13:10 [v]S Ex 20:3
13:11 [w]Dt 17:13; 19:20; 21:21; 1Ti 5:20
13:13 [x]ver 2,6; Jdg 19:22; 20:13; 1Sa 2:12; 10:27; 11:12; 25:17; 1Ki 21:10
13:14 [y]Jdg 20:12 [z]Dt 17:4

12:23–25 CHRISTIAN ETHICS, Moral Limits—Symbolically and literally, blood is a lifeline. Respect for life must be maintained. Israel had specific diet rules which forced them to remember the value of all living creatures. Christian freedom from such regulations must not cause us to forget to honor and to protect life.

12:28 CHRISTIAN ETHICS, Moral Imperatives—See notes on 4:1–8; Ge 18:19.

13:1–5 EVIL AND SUFFERING, Testing—Evil can be defined as anything which leads to worship of anything or anyone but the one true God. God cannot tolerate such evil. God's people are called on to take drastic steps to eliminate evil and its cause. The existence of such evil tests the loyalty of God's people. At times God calls for drastic measures to eliminate evil. This shows the power of evil which God's people must never underestimate.

13:1–11 HISTORY, God—Historical evidence should lead us to obey God without reservation and to go to any lengths to avoid following anyone who would lead us away from the one God.

13:4 CHRISTIAN ETHICS, Character—Inherent in God's moral imperative is the expectancy of human response. This expectancy is based on the human creature's characteristic of being a choice maker. We can reject or adopt the imperative, thus reflecting our true character. The decision to do what God says is not a judgment on the nature of the command. It is a personal response of trust in a personal God. See notes on 4:1–8; 6:24–25.

it completely,[t][a] both its people and its
livestock.[b] 16Gather all the plunder of the
town into the middle of the public square
and completely burn the town[c] and all its
plunder as a whole burnt offering to the
LORD your God.[d] It is to remain a ruin[e]
forever, never to be rebuilt. 17None of
those condemned things[t] shall be found
in your hands, so that the LORD will turn
from his fierce anger;[f] he will show you
mercy,[g] have compassion[h] on you, and
increase your numbers,[i] as he promised[j] on oath to your forefathers, 18be-
cause you obey the LORD your God, keeping all his commands that I am giving you
today and doing what is right[k] in his
eyes.

Chapter 14

Clean and Unclean Food

14:3-20pp — Lev 11:1-23

YOU are the children[l] of the LORD
your God. Do not cut yourselves or
shave the front of your heads for the
dead, 2for you are a people holy[m] to the
LORD your God.[n] Out of all the peoples
on the face of the earth, the LORD has
chosen you to be his treasured possession.[o]
3Do not eat any detestable thing.[p]
4These are the animals you may eat:[q] the
ox, the sheep, the goat,[r] 5the deer,[s] the
gazelle, the roe deer, the wild goat,[t] the
ibex, the antelope and the mountain
sheep.[u] 6You may eat any animal that has
a split hoof divided in two and that chews
the cud. 7However, of those that chew
the cud or that have a split hoof completely divided you may not eat the camel, the rabbit or the coney.[v] Although
they chew the cud, they do not have a
split hoof; they are ceremonially unclean
for you. 8The pig is also unclean; although it has a split hoof, it does not
chew the cud. You are not to eat their
meat or touch their carcasses.[u]
9Of all the creatures living in the water, you may eat any that has fins and
scales. 10But anything that does not have
fins and scales you may not eat; for you it
is unclean.

13:15 [a]Isa 24:6; 34:5; 43:28; 47:6; La 2:6; Da 9:11; Zec 8:13; Mal 4:6 [b]Ex 22:20
13:16 [c]2Ki 25:9; Jer 39:8; 52:13; Eze 16:41 [d]Dt 7:25, 26; Jos 6:24 [e]Jos 8:28; Isa 7:16; 17:1; 24:10; 25:2; 27:10; 32:14,19; 37:26; Jer 49:2; Mic 1:6
13:17 [f]Ex 32:12; Nu 25:4 [g]S Ge 43:14 [h]Dt 30:3 [i]S Dt 7:13 [j]S Ge 12:2; S 13:14; S 26:24
13:18 [k]S Dt 12:25
14:1 [l]S Jn 1:12; S Ro 8:14; 9:8
14:2 [m]S Ge 28:14; Ex 22:31; Isa 6:13; Mal 2:15 [n]S Lev 20:26; Ro 12:1 [o]S Ex 8:22; S Dt 7:6
14:3 [p]Eze 4:14
14:4 [q]Ac 10:14 [r]S Lev 7:23
14:5 [s]S Dt 12:15 [t]Job 39:1; Ps 104:18
14:8 [u]S Lev 5:2
14:13 [v]S Ge 1:11 [w]Isa 34:15
14:14 [x]S Ge 8:7
14:17 [y]Ps 102:6; Isa 13:21; 14:23; 34:11; Zep 2:14
14:20 [z]S Lev 20:25
14:21 [a]S Lev 11:39 [b]ver 2 [c]S Ex 23:19
14:22 [d]S Ge 14:20; S Lev 27:30; S Nu 18:21
14:23 [e]S Dt 12:17, 18 [f]Ps 4:7 [g]S Dt 12:5; 1Ki 3:2 [h]S Dt 4:10 [i]Ps 22:23; 33:8; Mal 2:5
14:25 [j]Mt 21:12; Jn 2:14
14:26 [k]S Lev 10:9; Ecc 10:16-17 [l]S Lev 23:40; S Dt 12:18
14:27 [m]S Dt 12:19 [n]S Nu 18:20; 26:62; Dt 18:1-2

11You may eat any clean bird. 12But
these you may not eat: the eagle, the vulture, the black vulture, 13the red kite, the
black kite, any kind[v] of falcon,[w] 14any
kind of raven,[x] 15the horned owl, the
screech owl, the gull, any kind of hawk,
16the little owl, the great owl, the white
owl, 17the desert owl,[y] the osprey, the
cormorant, 18the stork, any kind of heron,
the hoopoe and the bat.
19All flying insects that swarm are unclean to you; do not eat them. 20But any
winged creature that is clean you may
eat.[z]
21Do not eat anything you find already
dead.[a] You may give it to an alien living
in any of your towns, and he may eat it,
or you may sell it to a foreigner. But you
are a people holy to the LORD your God.[b]
Do not cook a young goat in its mother's milk.[c]

Tithes

22Be sure to set aside a tenth[d] of all
that your fields produce each year. 23Eat[e]
the tithe of your grain, new wine[f] and
oil, and the firstborn of your herds and
flocks in the presence of the LORD your
God at the place he will choose as a
dwelling for his Name,[g] so that you may
learn[h] to revere[i] the LORD your God always. 24But if that place is too distant and
you have been blessed by the LORD your
God and cannot carry your tithe (because
the place where the LORD will choose to
put his Name is so far away), 25then exchange[j] your tithe for silver, and take
the silver with you and go to the place the
LORD your God will choose. 26Use the silver to buy whatever you like: cattle,
sheep, wine or other fermented drink,[k]
or anything you wish. Then you and your
household shall eat there in the presence
of the LORD your God and rejoice.[l] 27And
do not neglect the Levites[m] living in your
towns, for they have no allotment or inheritance of their own.[n]

[t] *15,17* The Hebrew term refers to the irrevocable giving over of things or persons to the LORD, often by totally destroying them. [u] *5* The precise identification of some of the birds and animals in this chapter is uncertain. [v] *7* That is, the hyrax or rock badger

14:1–29 GOD, Father—The picture of God developed in the Old Testament featured two sides. The stern side is often associated with the justice and wrath of the sovereign God. The loving side speaks of the compassion and gentleness of a father. This passage combines the two, calling on the beloved children to be holy and obedient.

14:2 ELECTION, Israel—There is a mystery about God's election. God chooses whom He will. Of all the nations of the world, God chose Israel to be His treasured possession. God's loving election is the foundation of Israel's identity and faith. The doctrine of national election served as the basis for God's demands on His people to be visibly different, holy as compared to all other people. God's choice (Hebrew *bachar*) included Israel's people (7:6), their worship place (12:5), their priesthood (18:5), and their king (17:15).

14:22–29 STEWARDSHIP, Tithe—Tithing provided the worshiper a means of spiritual celebration, supporting the priests, and caring for the needy. God required His people to tithe of their grain and animal products. When the distance was great to the designated place for giving the tithe, they were permitted to exchange their gifts for money and take it instead. God's people in all ages and in all kinds of economic circumstances are responsible for worshipful giving of their resources to serve God's purposes of justice and righteousness. See note on Nu 18:21–32.

14:26 PRAYER, Worship—See note on 12:7,12.

28At the end of every three years, bring
all the tithes[o] of that year's produce and
store it in your towns,[p] 29so that the Levites (who have no allotment[q] or inheritance[r] of their own) and the aliens,[s] the
fatherless and the widows who live in
your towns may come and eat and be satisfied,[t] and so that the LORD your God
may bless[u] you in all the work of your
hands.

Chapter 15

The Year for Canceling Debts

15:1–11Ref — Lev 25:8–38

AT the end of every seven years you
must cancel debts.[v] 2This is how it
is to be done: Every creditor shall cancel
the loan he has made to his fellow Israelite. He shall not require payment from his
fellow Israelite or brother, because the
LORD's time for canceling debts has been
proclaimed. 3You may require payment
from a foreigner,[w] but you must cancel
any debt your brother owes you. 4Howev-
er, there should be no poor among you,
for in the land the LORD your God is giving you to possess as your inheritance, he
will richly bless[x] you, 5if only you fully
obey the LORD your God and are careful
to follow[y] all these commands I am giving you today. 6For the LORD your God
will bless you as he has promised, and
you will lend to many nations but will
borrow from none. You will rule over
many nations but none will rule over
you.[z]

7If there is a poor man[a] among your
brothers in any of the towns of the land
that the LORD your God is giving you, do
not be hardhearted or tightfisted[b] toward
your poor brother. 8Rather be openhanded[c] and freely lend him whatever he
needs. 9Be careful not to harbor this
wicked thought: "The seventh year, the
year for canceling debts,[d] is near," so
that you do not show ill will[e] toward
your needy brother and give him nothing.
He may then appeal to the LORD against
you, and you will be found guilty of sin.[f]
10Give generously to him and do so without a grudging heart;[g] then because of
this the LORD your God will bless[h] you in
all your work and in everything you put
your hand to. 11There will always be poor
people[i] in the land. Therefore I command you to be openhanded toward your
brothers and toward the poor and needy
in your land.[j]

Freeing Servants

15:12–18pp — Ex 21:2–6
15:12–18Ref — Lev 25:38–55

12If a fellow Hebrew, a man or a woman, sells himself to you and serves you six
years, in the seventh year you must let
him go free.[k] 13And when you release
him, do not send him away empty-handed. 14Supply him liberally from your flock,
your threshing floor[l] and your winepress. Give to him as the LORD your God
has blessed you. 15Remember that you
were slaves[m] in Egypt and the LORD your
God redeemed you.[n] That is why I give
you this command today.

16But if your servant says to you, "I do
not want to leave you," because he loves
you and your family and is well off with
you, 17then take an awl and push it
through his ear lobe into the door, and he
will become your servant for life. Do the
same for your maidservant.

18Do not consider it a hardship to set
your servant free, because his service to
you these six years has been worth twice
as much as that of a hired hand. And the
LORD your God will bless you in everything you do.

The Firstborn Animals

19Set apart for the LORD[o] your God every firstborn male[p] of your herds and
flocks.[q] Do not put the firstborn of your
oxen to work, and do not shear the firstborn of your sheep.[r] 20Each year you and
your family are to eat them in the presence of the LORD your God at the place he
will choose.[s] 21If an animal has a defect,[t] is lame or blind, or has any serious
flaw, you must not sacrifice it to the LORD
your God.[u] 22You are to eat it in your
own towns. Both the ceremonially

14:28 [o]S Lev 27:30 [p]Dt 26:12
14:29 [q]Ge 47:22 [r]Nu 26:62 [s]Dt 16:11; 24:19-21; Ps 94:6; Isa 1:17; 58:6 [t]S Dt 6:11 [u]Dt 15:10; Ps 41:1; Pr 22:9; Mal 3:10
15:1 [v]Dt 31:10; Ne 10:31
15:3 [w]S Ge 31:15; Dt 23:20; 28:12; Ru 2:10
15:4 [x]Dt 28:8
15:5 [y]S Ex 15:26; Dt 7:12; 28:1
15:6 [z]Dt 28:12-13, 44
15:7 [a]ver 11; Mt 26:11 [b]1Jn 3:17
15:8 [c]Mt 5:42; Lk 6:34; S Ac 24:17
15:9 [d]ver 1 [e]Mt 20:15 [f]S Ex 22:23; S Job 5:15; Jas 5:4
15:10 [g]2Co 9:5 [h]S Dt 14:29
15:11 [i]S ver 7 [j]Mt 26:11; Mk 14:7; Jn 12:8
15:12 [k]Jer 34:14
15:14 [l]S Nu 18:27
15:15 [m]Ex 13:3; Jer 34:13 [n]Ex 20:2; S Dt 4:34; S 9:26; 16:12; 24:18; Jer 16:14; 23:7
15:19 [o]S Lev 27:9 [p]S Ex 13:2 [q]S Ge 4:4 [r]S Ex 22:30
15:20 [s]S Lev 7:15-18; Dt 12:5-7,17,18
15:21 [t]S Ex 12:5 [u]S Lev 22:19-25; Dt 17:1; Mal 1:8,13

14:28–29 EVIL AND SUFFERING, Comfort—The Hebrews were to use their tithes to help the poor, needy, aliens, widows, orphans, and the Levites. Poverty causes suffering. God leads us to eliminate this and all other causes of suffering. We must be willing to share our resources to provide the needs of people suffering in poverty.

15:4–11 DISCIPLESHIP, Poor—None of God's people should be poor. We will have God's blessing if we obey Him, but we refuse to obey Him. Neither obedience nor absence of poverty is the reality in our world. Poor people are always among our number. God's will is communicated clearly concerning our relationship to the poor. God's people are to be openhanded and generous in assisting the poor. We are to lend freely whatever is needed and give cheerfully, not grudgingly. See notes on 24:6,10–15; Lev 25:35–37,39–43. Refusing to help the poor is sin.

15:5–6 CHRISTIAN ETHICS, Social Order—See note on 4:1–8. God's social order is set up to prevent want and need among His people. Full obedience by His people should lead to divine blessing which would eliminate poverty. People who do not fully obey cannot demand or expect such blessings.

15:7–11 EVIL AND SUFFERING, Comfort—The Bible faces reality head-on. Poverty is a continuing part of human life. Selfish interest is also. Only when we overcome selfish interest and quit seeking excuses and escapes can we effectively fight poverty. When we get our hearts right, we will act right with pocketbooks and checkbooks. The "always" of poverty is no reason to ignore or accept it. See note on 14:28–29.

unclean and the clean may eat it, as if it were gazelle or deer.[v] 23But you must not eat the blood; pour it out on the ground like water.[w]

Chapter 16

Passover

16:1–8pp — Ex 12:14–20; Lev 23:4–8; Nu 28:16–25

OBSERVE the month of Abib[x] and celebrate the Passover[y] of the LORD your God, because in the month of Abib he brought you out of Egypt by night. 2Sacrifice as the Passover to the LORD your God an animal from your flock or herd at the place the LORD will choose as a dwelling for his Name.[z] 3Do not eat it with bread made with yeast, but for seven days eat unleavened bread, the bread of affliction,[a] because you left Egypt in haste[b]—so that all the days of your life you may remember the time of your departure from Egypt.[c] 4Let no yeast be found in your possession in all your land for seven days. Do not let any of the meat you sacrifice on the evening[d] of the first day remain until morning.[e]

5You must not sacrifice the Passover in any town the LORD your God gives you 6except in the place he will choose as a dwelling for his Name. There you must sacrifice the Passover in the evening, when the sun goes down, on the anniversary[w][f] of your departure from Egypt. 7Roast[g] it and eat it at the place the LORD your God will choose. Then in the morning return to your tents. 8For six days eat unleavened bread and on the seventh day hold an assembly[h] to the LORD your God and do no work.[i]

Feast of Weeks

16:9–12pp — Lev 23:15–22; Nu 28:26–31

9Count off seven weeks[j] from the time you begin to put the sickle to the standing grain.[k] 10Then celebrate the Feast of Weeks to the LORD your God by giving a freewill offering in proportion to the blessings the LORD your God has given you. 11And rejoice[l] before the LORD your God at the place he will choose as a dwelling for his Name[m]—you, your sons and daughters, your menservants and maidservants, the Levites[n] in your towns, and the aliens,[o] the fatherless and the widows living among you.[p] 12Remember that you were slaves in Egypt,[q] and follow carefully these decrees.

Feast of Tabernacles

16:13–17pp — Lev 23:33–43; Nu 29:12–39

13Celebrate the Feast of Tabernacles for seven days after you have gathered the produce of your threshing floor[r] and your winepress.[s] 14Be joyful[t] at your Feast—you, your sons and daughters, your menservants and maidservants, and the Levites, the aliens, the fatherless and the widows who live in your towns. 15For seven days celebrate the Feast to the LORD your God at the place the LORD will choose. For the LORD your God will bless you in all your harvest and in all the work of your hands, and your joy[u] will be complete.

16Three times a year all your men must appear[v] before the LORD your God at the place he will choose: at the Feast of Unleavened Bread,[w] the Feast of Weeks and the Feast of Tabernacles.[x] No man should appear before the LORD empty-handed:[y] 17Each of you must bring a gift in proportion to the way the LORD your God has blessed you.

Judges

18Appoint judges[z] and officials for each of your tribes in every town the LORD your God is giving you, and they shall judge the people fairly.[a] 19Do not pervert justice[b] or show partiality.[c] Do not accept a bribe,[d] for a bribe blinds the eyes of the wise and twists the words of the righteous. 20Follow justice and justice alone, so that you may live and possess the land the LORD your God is giving you.

Worshiping Other Gods

21Do not set up any wooden Asherah pole[x][e] beside the altar you build to the

15:22 [v]S Dt 12:15
15:23 [w]S Ge 9:4; Dt 12:16; Eze 33:25
16:1 [x]S Ex 12:2 [y]S Ex 12:11; 2Ki 23:21; Mt 26:17-29
16:2 [z]Dt 12:5,26
16:3 [a]Ex 12:8,39; 34:18; 1Co 5:8 [b]S Ex 12:11 [c]Dt 4:9
16:4 [d]S Ex 12:6 [e]S Ex 12:8; Mk 14:12
16:6 [f]S Ex 12:42
16:7 [g]S Ex 12:8
16:8 [h]S Lev 23:8 [i]Mt 26:17; Lk 2:41; 22:7; Jn 2:13
16:9 [j]Ac 2:1 [k]S Ex 23:16
16:11 [l]Dt 12:7 [m]S Ex 20:24; S 2Sa 7:13 [n]Dt 12:12 [o]S Dt 14:29 [p]Ne 8:10
16:12 [q]S Dt 15:15
16:13 [r]S Lev 2:14 [s]S Ge 27:37; S Ex 23:16
16:14 [t]ver 11
16:15 [u]Job 38:7; Ps 4:7; 28:7; 30:11
16:16 [v]Dt 31:11; Ps 84:7 [w]S Ex 12:17 [x]S Ex 23:14,16; Ezr 3:4 [y]S Ex 34:20
16:18 [z]S Ex 18:21, 26 [a]S Ge 31:37
16:19 [b]S Ex 23:2 [c]S Lev 19:15 [d]S Ex 18:21; S 1Sa 8:3
16:21 [e]S Dt 7:5

[w]6 Or *down, at the time of day* [x]21 Or *Do not plant any tree dedicated to Asherah*

16:1–17 HISTORY, Worship—See note on Ex 13:1–16.
16:1–17 WORSHIP, Calendar—See note on Ex 16:23–30.
16:10,16–17 STEWARDSHIP, Giving in Worship—Harvest is a time for celebration and for special days of worship. No one should appear "empty-handed" before the Lord. We should show reverence for God with gifts in proportion to our prosperity. Generous giving honors God. See note on Mt 5:23–24.
16:11 PRAYER, Worship—See note on 12:7,12.
16:12 CHRISTIAN ETHICS, Moral Imperatives—The paradox of following God's moral imperatives is that what looks like it will be so confining is actually liberating to one's spirit. God reminded Israel they knew what physical slavery was like. If they failed to live by His ethical expectations, they would know of a worse slavery—the slavery of the spirit.
16:16–17 PRAYER, Worship—Compare Ex 34:20. Offerings expressing gratitude play an important role in congregational worship and prayer.
16:17 HUMANITY, Work—Work done faithfully will be blessed by God and will result in a fullness of joy in the life of the worker. See note on 2 Ch 1:14–17.
16:18–20 CHRISTIAN ETHICS, Justice—Justice is the basis for most legal systems. A legal system carried out for money instead of fairness is not just and destroys the entire system. Laws must be carried out according to their intentions, not according to twisted interpretations based on self-interest. See notes on Ex 23:1–2; Lev 19:15.

LORD your God,[f] 22and do not erect a sacred stone,[g] for these the LORD your God hates.

Chapter 17

DO not sacrifice to the LORD your God an ox or a sheep that has any defect[h] or flaw in it, for that would be detestable[i] to him.[j]

2If a man or woman living among you in one of the towns the LORD gives you is found doing evil in the eyes of the LORD your God in violation of his covenant,[k] 3and contrary to my command[l] has worshiped other gods,[m] bowing down to them or to the sun[n] or the moon or the stars of the sky,[o] 4and this has been brought to your attention, then you must investigate it thoroughly. If it is true[p] and it has been proved that this detestable thing has been done in Israel,[q] 5take the man or woman who has done this evil deed to your city gate and stone that person to death.[r] 6On the testimony of two or three witnesses a man shall be put to death, but no one shall be put to death on the testimony of only one witness.[s] 7The hands of the witnesses must be the first in putting him to death,[t] and then the hands of all the people.[u] You must purge the evil[v] from among you.

Law Courts

8If cases come before your courts that are too difficult for you to judge[w]—whether bloodshed, lawsuits or assaults[x]—take them to the place the LORD your God will choose.[y] 9Go to the priests, who are Levites,[z] and to the judge[a] who is in office at that time. Inquire of them and they will give you the verdict.[b] 10You must act according to the decisions they give you at the place the LORD will choose. Be careful to do everything they direct you to do. 11Act according to the law they teach you and the decisions they give you. Do not turn aside from what they tell you, to the right or to the left.[c] 12The man who shows contempt[d] for the judge or for the priest who stands ministering[e] there to the LORD your God must be put to death.[f] You must purge the evil from Israel.[g] 13All the people will hear and be afraid, and will not be contemptuous again.[h]

The King

14When you enter the land the LORD your God is giving you and have taken possession[i] of it and settled in it,[j] and you say, "Let us set a king over us like all the nations around us,"[k] 15be sure to appoint[l] over you the king the LORD your God chooses. He must be from among your own brothers.[m] Do not place a foreigner over you, one who is not a brother Israelite. 16The king, moreover, must not acquire great numbers of horses[n] for himself[o] or make the people return to Egypt[p] to get more of them,[q] for the LORD has told you, "You are not to go back that way again."[r] 17He must not take many wives,[s] or his heart will be led astray.[t] He must not accumulate[u] large amounts of silver and gold.[v]

18When he takes the throne[w] of his kingdom, he is to write[x] for himself on a scroll a copy[y] of this law, taken from that of the priests, who are Levites. 19It is to be with him, and he is to read it all the days of his life[z] so that he may learn to revere the LORD his God and follow carefully all the words of this law and these decrees[a] 20and not consider himself better than his brothers and turn from the law[b] to the right or to the left.[c] Then he and his descendants will reign a long time over his kingdom in Israel.[d]

Chapter 18

Offerings for Priests and Levites

THE priests, who are Levites[e]—indeed the whole tribe of Levi—are to have no allotment or inheritance with Israel. They shall live on the offerings[f] made to

16:21 fEx 34:13; 1Ki 14:15; 2Ki 17:16; 21:3; 2Ch 33:3 **16:22** gS Ex 23:24 **17:1** hS Ex 12:5; S Lev 22:20 iDt 7:25 jS Dt 15:21 **17:2** kDt 13:6-11 **17:3** lJer 7:31 mEx 22:20 nS Ge 1:16 oS Ge 2:1; S 37:9 **17:4** pDt 22:20 qDt 13:12-14 **17:5** rS Lev 24:14 **17:6** sNu 35:30; Dt 19:15; S Mt 18:16 **17:7** tJn 8:7 uS Lev 24:14; Ac 7:58 vS Dt 13:5; 1Co 5:13* **17:8** wEx 21:6 x2Ch 19:10 yDt 12:5; Ps 122:3-5 **17:9** zDt 24:8; 27:9 aS Ex 21:6 bS Ge 25:22; Dt 19:17; Eze 44:24; Hag 2:11 **17:11** cS Lev 10:11; S Dt 5:32 **17:12** dNu 15:30 eS Nu 16:9 fver 13; S Ge 17:14; Dt 13:11; 18:20; 19:20; 1Ki 18:40; Jer 14:14; Hos 4:4; Zec 13:3 gS Dt 13:5 **17:13** hS ver 12 **17:14** iS Nu 33:53 jJos 21:43 k1Sa 8:5, 19-20; 10:19 **17:15** l1Sa 16:3; 2Sa 5:3 mJer 30:21 **17:16** nIsa 2:7; 30:16 o1Sa 8:11; 1Ki 4:26; 9:19; 10:26; 2Ch 1:14; Ps 20:7 p1Ki 10:29; Isa 31:1; Jer 42:14 q1Ki 10:28; Isa 31:1; Eze 17:15 rS Ex 13:17 **17:17** sS Ex 34:16; 2Sa 5:13; 12:11; 1Ki 11:3; 2Ch 11:21 t1Ki 11:2; Pr 31:3 u1Ki 10:27 v2Ch 1:11; Isa 2:7 **17:18** w1Ki 1:46; 1Ch 29:23 xDt 31:22,24; Jos 24:26; 1Sa 10:25 y2Ch 23:11 **17:19** zDt 4:9-10; Jos 1:8 aDt 11:13; 1Ki 3:3; 11:38; 2Ki 22:2 **17:20** bJos 23:6; Job 23:12; Ps 119:102 cS Dt 5:32; S 1Ki 9:4 d1Sa 8:5; 10:25; 1Ki 2:3; 1Ch 28:8 **18:1** eJer 33:18,21 fS Nu 18:8

17:1–7,12 GOD, Wrath—The instructions here must be interpreted in the light of God's need to develop His people to an uncompromising, spiritual maturity if they were to be effective as His servant people. The wrath of God is not arbitrary. See note on 7:1–6.

17:2 THE CHURCH, Covenant People—Each believer bears the responsibility of keeping God's covenant which He graciously established with His people. Refusal to obey God shows a person's rejection of God. Such a person faces God's chastening.

17:8–13 CHRISTIAN ETHICS, Justice—Israel's system of justice centered around a national place of worship with priests and a national judge. However, no human judge is capable of deciding every case. Since complicated cases may not have clear answers from the law, society becomes responsible to establish a just system for helping local judges. Even complex cases must be resolved, and the resolution must be accepted and followed. A system leaving cases unresolved or allowing people to ignore decisions is unjust. Contempt for law destroys society. See note on Ro 13:1–7.

17:15 ELECTION, Leadership—Ethical behavior steers the elected of God away from behavior considered evil. The leader bears special responsibility in economics, family, and piety. The elected leader's actions can lead the entire people to disobey God and serve other gods.

17:18–20 HOLY SCRIPTURE, Purpose—God provided Scripture so people could know Him and His will. No person, not even the most powerful ruler, stands above His Word. To live effectively, people need to read Scripture daily, worship the God who gave us His Word, learn humility from God's Word, and obey Scripture. Praise of Scripture without obedience is worthless.

the LORD by fire, for that is their inheritance.[g] 2They shall have no inheritance
among their brothers; the LORD is their
inheritance,[h] as he promised them.[i]
3This is the share due the priests[j]
from the people who sacrifice a bull[k] or a
sheep: the shoulder, the jowls and the
inner parts.[l] 4You are to give them the
firstfruits of your grain, new wine and oil,
and the first wool from the shearing of
your sheep,[m] 5for the LORD your God has
chosen them[n] and their descendants out
of all your tribes to stand and minister[o]
in the LORD's name always.[p]
6If a Levite moves from one of your
towns anywhere in Israel where he is living, and comes in all earnestness to the
place the LORD will choose,[q] 7he may
minister in the name[r] of the LORD his
God like all his fellow Levites who serve
there in the presence of the LORD. 8He is
to share equally in their benefits, even
though he has received money from the
sale of family possessions.[s]

Detestable Practices

9When you enter the land the LORD
your God is giving you, do not learn to
imitate[t] the detestable ways[u] of the nations there. 10Let no one be found among
you who sacrifices his son or daughter
in[y] the fire,[v] who practices divination[w]
or sorcery,[x] interprets omens, engages in
witchcraft,[y] 11or casts spells,[z] or who is
a medium or spiritist[a] or who consults
the dead. 12Anyone who does these
things is detestable to the LORD, and because of these detestable practices the
LORD your God will drive out those nations before you.[b] 13You must be blameless[c] before the LORD your God.[d]

The Prophet

14The nations you will dispossess listen
to those who practice sorcery or divination.[e] But as for you, the LORD your God
has not permitted you to do so. 15The
LORD your God will raise up for you a
prophet like me from among your own
brothers.[f] You must listen to him. 16For
this is what you asked of the LORD your
God at Horeb on the day of the assembly
when you said, "Let us not hear the voice
of the LORD our God nor see this great
fire anymore, or we will die."[g]
17The LORD said to me: "What they say
is good. 18I will raise up for them a prophet[h] like you from among their brothers; I
will put my words[i] in his mouth,[j] and
he will tell them everything I command
him.[k] 19If anyone does not listen[l] to my
words that the prophet speaks in my
name,[m] I myself will call him to account.[n] 20But a prophet who presumes to
speak in my name anything I have not
commanded him to say, or a prophet who
speaks in the name of other gods,[o] must
be put to death."[p]
21You may say to yourselves, "How can
we know when a message has not been
spoken by the LORD?" 22If what a prophet
proclaims in the name of the LORD does
not take place or come true,[q] that is a
message the LORD has not spoken.[r] That
prophet has spoken presumptuously.[s] Do
not be afraid of him.

Chapter 19

Cities of Refuge

19:1–14Ref — Nu 35:6–34; Dt 4:41–43; Jos 20:1–9

WHEN the LORD your God has destroyed the nations whose land he
is giving you, and when you have driven
them out and settled in their towns and
houses,[t] 2then set aside for yourselves
three cities centrally located in the land
the LORD your God is giving you to possess. 3Build roads to them and divide into

18:1 gS Nu 18:20; 1Co 9:13
18:2 hNu 18:20 iJos 13:14
18:3 jS Ex 29:27 kS Lev 1:5 lLev 7:28-34; Nu 18:12
18:4 mEx 22:29; Nu 18:12
18:5 nS Ex 28:1 oDt 10:8 pS Ex 29:9
18:6 qS Nu 35:2-3; S Dt 12:5
18:7 rver 19; 1Ki 18:32; 22:16; Ps 118:26
18:8 sNu 18:24; 2Ch 31:4; Ne 12:44,47; 13:12
18:9 tDt 9:5; 12:29-31 uS Lev 18:3; 2Ki 21:2; 2Ch 28:3; 33:2; 34:33; Ezr 6:21; 9:11; Jer 44:4
18:10 vS Lev 18:21 w1Sa 15:23 xS Ex 7:11 yS Lev 19:31
18:11 zIsa 47:9 aS Ex 22:18; S 1Sa 28:13
18:12 bS Lev 18:24
18:13 cS Ge 6:9; Ps 119:1 dMt 5:48
18:14 e2Ki 21:6
18:15 fS Mt 21:11; Lk 2:25-35; Jn 1:21; Ac 3:22*; 7:37*
18:16 gS Ex 20:19; Dt 5:23-27
18:18 hS Ge 20:7 iIsa 2:3; 26:8; 51:4; Mic 4:2 jS Ex 4:12 kJn 4:25-26; S 14:24; Ac 3:22*
18:19 lS Ex 23:21 mS ver 7; S Lev 19:12; 2Ki 2:24 nJos 22:23; Ac 3:23*; Heb 12:25
18:20 oS Ex 23:13 pDt 13:1-5; S 17:12
18:22 qS Dt 13:2; 1Sa 3:20 r1Ki 22:28; Jer 28:9 sver 20
19:1 tDt 6:10-11

[y]10 Or *who makes his son or daughter pass through*

18:5 ELECTION, Responsibility—The chosen of God are required to support the elected priests, since priests are without land and related material assets. Stewardship is a basic responsibility to God, who is Lord of all creation and the Source of all blessings.

18:9–14 REVELATION, Oracles—Every religion has ways to gain contact with the gods. God's people cannot use ways common in pagan religions. See note on Lev 20:6,27.

18:9–22 PROCLAMATION, Authoritative—See note on Jer 19:14–15.

18:15–19 JESUS CHRIST, Foretold—God has always had His spokespersons. Moses was a primary prophet of God. God promised another great prophet whom Christians see as Jesus, the great, final Prophet of God (Jn 6:14; 7:40; Ac 3:17–26). He both is and speaks God's final message to us.

18:15–19 REVELATION, Word—God reveals His chosen spiritual leaders for His people. He chose priests and prophets for Israel so they could worship and hear God's word. Like He had done with Moses, God would choose another human being who would speak His words and record His will for the people. Humans try to go around God's revealed choice, so false prophets speak words that are not His. The people and their Lord agreed that God's people are held accountable for God's commands through His spoken revelation. The promise of God's prophets climaxed in Jesus (Jn 1:21).

18:15 DISCIPLESHIP, Spiritual Leaders—God promised through Moses that He would continue to make His will known through prophets. God has always been faithful to give His people spiritual leaders who help His people know, interpret, and follow His will. The ultimate Prophet like Moses is Jesus Christ (Jn 1:21,45; 6:14; 7:40; Ac 3:22; 7:37). The Lord continues to make God's will known to Christian disciples through the full ministry of the Holy Spirit.

18:21–22 REVELATION, Word—False prophets confused God's people. They needed a way to distinguish true and false prophets. God had one answer: see if the message comes true in history. God's people have no objective test of people's sermons. Only growing spiritual discernment and patience can discover the true prophet. See note on 1 Ki 22:6–28.

19:1–13 CHRISTIAN ETHICS, Justice—See note on Nu 35:6–34.

three parts the land the LORD your God is
giving you as an inheritance, so that anyone who kills a man may flee there.
4 This is the rule concerning the man
who kills another and flees there to save
his life—one who kills his neighbor unintentionally, without malice aforethought.
5 For instance, a man may go into the forest with his neighbor to cut wood, and as
he swings his ax to fell a tree, the head
may fly off and hit his neighbor and kill
him. That man may flee to one of these
cities and save his life. 6 Otherwise, the
avenger of blood[u] might pursue him in a
rage, overtake him if the distance is too
great, and kill him even though he is not
deserving of death, since he did it to his
neighbor without malice aforethought.
7 This is why I command you to set aside
for yourselves three cities.
8 If the LORD your God enlarges your
territory,[v] as he promised[w] on oath to
your forefathers, and gives you the whole
land he promised them, 9 because you
carefully follow all these laws I command
you today—to love the LORD your God
and to walk always in his ways[x]—then
you are to set aside three more cities.
10 Do this so that innocent blood[y] will not
be shed in your land, which the LORD
your God is giving you as your inheritance, and so that you will not be guilty of
bloodshed.[z]
11 But if a man hates his neighbor and
lies in wait for him, assaults and kills
him,[a] and then flees to one of these cities, 12 the elders of his town shall send for
him, bring him back from the city, and
hand him over to the avenger of blood to
die. 13 Show him no pity.[b] You must
purge from Israel the guilt of shedding
innocent blood,[c] so that it may go well
with you.
14 Do not move your neighbor's boundary stone set up by your predecessors
in the inheritance you receive in the
land the LORD your God is giving you to
possess.[d]

Witnesses

15 One witness is not enough to convict
a man accused of any crime or offense he
may have committed. A matter must be
established by the testimony of two or
three witnesses.[e]
16 If a malicious witness[f] takes the
stand to accuse a man of a crime, 17 the
two men involved in the dispute must
stand in the presence of the LORD before
the priests and the judges[g] who are in
office at the time. 18 The judges must
make a thorough investigation,[h] and if
the witness proves to be a liar, giving
false testimony against his brother, 19 then
do to him as he intended to do to his
brother.[i] You must purge the evil from
among you. 20 The rest of the people will
hear of this and be afraid,[j] and never
again will such an evil thing be done
among you. 21 Show no pity:[k] life for life,
eye for eye, tooth for tooth, hand for
hand, foot for foot.[l]

Chapter 20

Going to War

WHEN you go to war against your enemies and see horses and chariots
and an army greater than yours,[m] do not
be afraid[n] of them,[o] because the LORD
your God, who brought you up out of
Egypt, will be with[p] you. 2 When you are
about to go into battle, the priest shall
come forward and address the army. 3 He
shall say: "Hear, O Israel, today you are
going into battle against your enemies.
Do not be fainthearted[q] or afraid; do not
be terrified or give way to panic before
them. 4 For the LORD your God is the one
who goes with you[r] to fight[s] for you
against your enemies to give you victory.[t]"
5 The officers shall say to the army:
"Has anyone built a new house and not
dedicated[u] it? Let him go home, or he
may die in battle and someone else may
dedicate it. 6 Has anyone planted[v] a vineyard and not begun to enjoy it?[w] Let him
go home, or he may die in battle and
someone else enjoy it. 7 Has anyone become pledged to a woman and not married her? Let him go home, or he may die
in battle and someone else marry her.[x]"
8 Then the officers shall add, "Is any man
afraid or fainthearted? Let him go home
so that his brothers will not become disheartened too."[y] 9 When the officers

19:6 [u]S Nu 35:12
19:8 [v]S Ex 34:24 [w]S Ge 15:8; S Dt 11:24
19:9 [x]Dt 6:5
19:10 [y]Pr 6:17; Jer 7:6; 26:15 [z]Dt 21:1-9
19:11 [a]S Ex 21:12; 1Jn 3:15
19:13 [b]Dt 7:2 [c]Dt 21:9; 1Ki 2:31
19:14 [d]Dt 27:17; Job 24:2; Ps 16:6; Pr 15:25; 22:28; 23:10; Isa 1:23; Hos 5:10
19:15 [e]S Dt 17:6; S Mt 18:16*; 26:60; 2Co 13:1*
19:16 [f]Ex 23:1; Pr 6:19
19:17 [g]S Ex 21:6
19:18 [h]S Ex 23:7
19:19 [i]Pr 19:5,9; 1Co 5:13*
19:20 [j]S Dt 13:11
19:21 [k]ver 13 [l]S Ex 21:24; Mt 5:38*
20:1 [m]Ps 20:7; Isa 31:1 [n]S Nu 14:9 [o]S Dt 3:22; S 1Sa 17:45 [p]Isa 41:10
20:3 [q]1Sa 17:32; Job 23:16; Ps 22:14; Isa 7:4; 35:4; Jer 51:46
20:4 [r]2Ch 20:14-22 [s]S Ex 14:14; 1Ch 5:22; Ne 4:20 [t]Jdg 12:3; 15:18; Ps 44:7; 144:10
20:5 [u]Ne 12:27
20:6 [v]Jer 31:5; Eze 28:26; Mic 1:6 [w]1Co 9:7
20:7 [x]Dt 24:5; Pr 5:18
20:8 [y]Jdg 7:3

19:14 CHRISTIAN ETHICS, Justice—See note on 27:17.
19:15–21 CHRISTIAN ETHICS, Justice—The Hebrews were reminded in the Ten Commandments not to bear false witness or testimony about another (Ex 20:16). That commandment is necessary because people often ruin the reputations of others by what they say. Our tendency to become more involved in hearsay or outright lying means we need more than one perspective to find where truth lies. Truth and justice go hand in hand. Justice for the accused and for the community makes it mandatory that more than one witness testify.
20:1–20 HISTORY, Politics—Israel's adventures in international politics had religious significance. God provided for ways to prepare for and carry out military operations. Peace was the objective except in instances where God's purposes called for more drastic action. God's past actions and contemporary presence give new perspectives on political decisions, attitudes, and actions. God is interested in special individual cases as well as the collective whole.
20:1–20 CHRISTIAN ETHICS, War and Peace—Some limits must be imposed upon war efforts; otherwise, the results will be so barbaric as to render society worse after the war than before. See notes on Ex 14:1—15:18; Nu 21:1-3.

have finished speaking to the army, they
shall appoint commanders over it.
10When you march up to attack a city,
make its people an offer of peace.[z] 11If
they accept and open their gates, all the
people in it shall be subject[a] to forced
labor[b] and shall work for you. 12If they
refuse to make peace and they engage
you in battle, lay siege to that city.
13When the LORD your God delivers it
into your hand, put to the sword all the
men in it.[c] 14As for the women, the children, the livestock[d] and everything else
in the city,[e] you may take these as plunder[f] for yourselves. And you may use the
plunder the LORD your God gives you
from your enemies. 15This is how you are
to treat all the cities that are at a distance[g] from you and do not belong to the
nations nearby.
16However, in the cities of the nations
the LORD your God is giving you as an
inheritance, do not leave alive anything
that breathes.[h] 17Completely destroy[z]
them—the Hittites, Amorites, Canaanites, Perizzites, Hivites and Jebusites—as
the LORD your God has commanded you.
18Otherwise, they will teach you to follow
all the detestable things they do in worshiping their gods,[i] and you will sin[j]
against the LORD your God.
19When you lay siege to a city for a long
time, fighting against it to capture it, do
not destroy its trees by putting an ax to
them, because you can eat their fruit. Do
not cut them down. Are the trees of the
field people, that you should besiege
them?[a] 20However, you may cut down
trees that you know are not fruit trees[k]
and use them to build siege works until
the city at war with you falls.

Chapter 21

Atonement for an Unsolved Murder

IF a man is found slain, lying in a field in
the land the LORD your God is giving
you to possess, and it is not known who
killed him,[l] 2your elders and judges shall
go out and measure the distance from the
body to the neighboring towns. 3Then the
elders of the town nearest the body shall
take a heifer that has never been worked
and has never worn a yoke[m] 4and lead
her down to a valley that has not been
plowed or planted and where there is a
flowing stream. There in the valley they
are to break the heifer's neck. 5The
priests, the sons of Levi, shall step forward, for the LORD your God has chosen
them to minister and to pronounce blessings[n] in the name of the LORD and to
decide all cases of dispute and assault.[o]
6Then all the elders of the town nearest
the body shall wash their hands[p] over
the heifer whose neck was broken in the
valley, 7and they shall declare: "Our
hands did not shed this blood, nor did our
eyes see it done. 8Accept this atonement
for your people Israel, whom you have
redeemed, O LORD, and do not hold your
people guilty of the blood of an innocent
man." And the bloodshed will be atoned
for.[q] 9So you will purge[r] from yourselves
the guilt of shedding innocent blood,
since you have done what is right in the
eyes of the LORD.

Marrying a Captive Woman

10When you go to war against your enemies and the LORD your God delivers
them into your hands[s] and you take captives,[t] 11if you notice among the captives
a beautiful[u] woman and are attracted to
her,[v] you may take her as your wife.
12Bring her into your home and have her
shave her head,[w] trim her nails 13and put
aside the clothes she was wearing when
captured. After she has lived in your
house and mourned her father and mother for a full month,[x] then you may go to
her and be her husband and she shall be
your wife. 14If you are not pleased with
her, let her go wherever she wishes. You
must not sell her or treat her as a slave,
since you have dishonored her.[y]

The Right of the Firstborn

15If a man has two wives,[z] and he
loves one but not the other, and both

20:10 [z]S Dt 2:26; Lk 14:31-32
20:11 [a]ver 15; 2Ki 6:22 [b]1Ki 9:21; 1Ch 22:2; Isa 31:8
20:13 [c]Nu 31:7
20:14 [d]Jos 8:2; 22:8 [e]S Nu 31:11 [f]S Nu 31:53
20:15 [g]S ver 11; Jos 9:9
20:16 [h]Ex 23:31-33; Nu 21:2-3; S Dt 7:2; Jos 6:21; 10:1; 11:14
20:18 [i]S Ex 34:16 [j]S Ex 10:7
20:20 [k]Jer 6:6
21:1 [l]S Nu 25:17
21:3 [m]S Nu 19:2
21:5 [n]S Ge 48:20; S Ex 39:43 [o]Dt 17:8-11
21:6 [p]Mt 27:24
21:8 [q]Nu 35:33-34
21:9 [r]Dt 19:13
21:10 [s]Jos 21:44 [t]1Ki 8:46; 1Ch 9:1; Ezr 5:12; Jer 40:1; Eze 1:1; 17:12; Da 2:25; Mic 4:10
21:11 [u]Ge 6:2 [v]S Ge 34:8
21:12 [w]S Lev 14:9; S Nu 8:7; 1Co 11:5
21:13 [x]Ps 45:10
21:14 [y]S Ge 34:2
21:15 [z]S Ge 4:19

[z]*17* The Hebrew term refers to the irrevocable giving over of things or persons to the LORD, often by totally destroying them. [a]*19* Or *down to use in the siege, for the fruit trees are for the benefit of man.*

20:16–20 SIN, Alienation—God seeks to prevent temptation and sin. He knew when the Israelites conquered the land, they had to clear it of all who practiced idolatry lest they be deceived. If they were influenced too quickly by their neighbors, they would learn foreign worship practices and become alienated from the true God. The heart was made for one God only. To accomodate more than one is to leave no room for the true God.

21:1–9 SALVATION, Redemption—Israel's redemption in the Exodus required her to make an atonement for the shedding of innocent blood. We see here the corporateness of sin and redemption. Murder is no private matter. God's salvation provides for freedom from corporate sin and guilt as well as from individual sin and guilt.

21:1–9 CHRISTIAN ETHICS, Justice—The search for justice can present us with unresolved questions. Obtaining as many resolutions as possible maintains community integrity. The church needs to help its larger community deal with guilt caused by injustice or by unsolved crimes.

21:10–14 CHRISTIAN ETHICS, War and Peace—See note on 20:1–20. Prisoners of war offer a victorious army temptations for manipulation and cruelty. Society must provide just treatment for prisoners and others displaced by war.

21:15–17 CHRISTIAN ETHICS, Justice—Inheritance involves deep emotions and can leave long lasting scars in families. God's people must follow procedures and regulations

bear him sons but the firstborn is the son
of the wife he does not love,[a] 16when he
wills his property to his sons, he must not
give the rights of the firstborn to the son
of the wife he loves in preference to his
actual firstborn, the son of the wife he
does not love.[b] 17He must acknowledge
the son of his unloved wife as the firstborn by giving him a double[c] share of all
he has. That son is the first sign of his
father's strength.[d] The right of the firstborn belongs to him.[e]

A Rebellious Son

18If a man has a stubborn and rebellious[f] son[g] who does not obey his father
and mother[h] and will not listen to them
when they discipline him, 19his father
and mother shall take hold of him and
bring him to the elders at the gate of his
town. 20They shall say to the elders,
"This son of ours is stubborn and rebellious. He will not obey us. He is a profli-
gate and a drunkard." 21Then all the men
of his town shall stone him to death.[i]
You must purge the evil[j] from among
you. All Israel will hear of it and be
afraid.[k]

Various Laws

22If a man guilty of a capital offense[l] is
put to death and his body is hung on a
tree, 23you must not leave his body on the
tree overnight.[m] Be sure to bury[n] him
that same day, because anyone who is
hung on a tree is under God's curse.[o]
You must not desecrate[p] the land the
LORD your God is giving you as an inheritance.

Chapter 22

IF you see your brother's ox or sheep
straying, do not ignore it but be sure to
take it back to him.[q] 2If the brother does
not live near you or if you do not know
who he is, take it home with you and
keep it until he comes looking for it.
Then give it back to him. 3Do the same if
you find your brother's donkey or his
cloak or anything he loses. Do not ignore
it.

4If you see your brother's donkey[r] or
his ox fallen on the road, do not ignore it.
Help him get it to its feet.[s]

5A woman must not wear men's clothing, nor a man wear women's clothing,
for the LORD your God detests anyone
who does this.

6If you come across a bird's nest beside
the road, either in a tree or on the
ground, and the mother is sitting on the
young or on the eggs, do not take the
mother with the young.[t] 7You may take
the young, but be sure to let the mother
go,[u] so that it may go well with you and
you may have a long life.[v]

8When you build a new house, make a
parapet around your roof so that you may
not bring the guilt of bloodshed on your
house if someone falls from the roof.[w]

9Do not plant two kinds of seed in your
vineyard;[x] if you do, not only the crops
you plant but also the fruit of the vineyard
will be defiled.[b]

10Do not plow with an ox and a donkey
yoked together.[y]

11Do not wear clothes of wool and lin-
en woven together.[z]

12Make tassels on the four corners of
the cloak you wear.[a]

Marriage Violations

13If a man takes a wife and, after lying
with her[b], dislikes her 14and slanders her

21:15 [a]Ge 29:33
21:16 [b]1Ch 26:10
21:17 [c]2Ki 2:9; Isa 40:2; 61:7; Zec 9:12 [d]S Ge 49:3 [e]Ge 25:31; Lk 15:12
21:18 [f]Ps 78:8; Jer 5:23; Zep 3:1 [g]Pr 30:17 [h]S Ge 31:35; Pr 1:8; Isa 30:1; Eph 6:1-3
21:21 [i]S Lev 20:9 [j]Dt 19:19 [k]S Dt 13:11
21:22 [l]Dt 22:26; Mt 26:66; Mk 14:64; Ac 23:29
21:23 [m]Jos 8:29; 10:27; Jn 19:31 [n]Eze 39:12 [o]Ezr 6:11; Est 2:23; 7:9; 8:7; 9:13,25; Isa 50:11; Gal 3:13* [p]S Lev 18:25
22:1 [q]Ex 23:4-5; Pr 27:10; Zec 7:9
22:4 [r]Ex 23:5 [s]1Co 9:9
22:6 [t]Lev 22:28
22:7 [u]S Lev 22:28 [v]S Dt 5:29
22:8 [w]Jos 2:8; 1Sa 9:25; 2Sa 11:2
22:9 [x]Lev 19:19
22:10 [y]2Co 6:14
22:11 [z]Lev 19:19
22:12 [a]Nu 15:37-41; Mt 23:5
22:13 [b]Dt 24:1

[b]9 Or *be forfeited to the sanctuary*

which seek to avoid such scars and to protect all family members. Israel faced the problem particularly when polygamy was practiced. Modern equivalents occur in cases of divorce and remarriage. See note on Nu 27:1–11.

21:18–21 FAMILY, Rejecting Parents—Parents symbolically represent God to the children. Therefore, rejecting parents is not only disobedience to them but also rejects God's established order for family life. When a son consistently rejected parental discipline and lived a life contrary to God's will for Israel, the law prescribed the death penalty (Ex 21:15,17; Lev 20:9). The penalty was on the sin of disobedience to God as much as rejection of parents. It was also a public testimony to the seriousness of God's claim upon the people of Israel. Although the conditions of God's covenant have changed, the seriousness of His claim has not.

21:20 CHRISTIAN ETHICS, Alcohol—Biblical law does not tolerate drunken behavior, but society often condones or even affirms drunkenness. When this occurs, society sets up examples for new generations to follow which eventually may lead the society to ruin. Christians should work to discourage drunkenness in every way. See note on Ge 9:21.

21:23 JESUS CHRIST, Foretold—John saw an ancient Jewish curse as the reason Jesus was taken from the cross before sundown (Jn 19:31). Paul saw that by taking a curse of the law upon Himself Jesus removed the curse of the law from us (Gal 3:13).

22:1–4 CHRISTIAN ETHICS, Social Order—The ethical cohesiveness of a community depends upon mutual respect and care of property. Finder's keepers is not a biblical attitude. We must respect and restore property belonging to others.

22:13–28 FAMILY, Sexual Sin—Sexual sins cannot be lightly regarded. Hebrew faith placed great emphasis on women remaining virgins until marriage. Consequently, parents made every effort to guard daughters against premarital sexual activities. In addition, marital faithfulness was expected (Ex 20:14). The Bible condemns sex outside marriage for both men and women (1 Th 4:1–8). Three principles are central to this passage: (1) sexual relations are intended for marriage; (2) parents have rights and responsibilities for a married daughter; and (3) women have God-given rights and cannot be easily disposed of as property by ill-tempered men. This text underscores the moral, legal, and social responsibilities of Christian parents toward their children as they prepare for marriage and adulthood. It also underscores the sacred place of sexuality within marriage.

and gives her a bad name, saying, "I married this woman, but when I approached
her, I did not find proof of her virginity,"
15then the girl's father and mother shall
bring proof that she was a virgin to the
town elders at the gate.[c] 16The girl's father will say to the elders, "I gave my
daughter in marriage to this man, but he
dislikes her. 17Now he has slandered her
and said, 'I did not find your daughter to
be a virgin.' But here is the proof of my
daughter's virginity." Then her parents
shall display the cloth before the elders of
the town, 18and the elders[d] shall take the
man and punish him. 19They shall fine
him a hundred shekels of silver[c] and give
them to the girl's father, because this
man has given an Israelite virgin a bad
name. She shall continue to be his wife;
he must not divorce her as long as he
lives.
20If, however, the charge is true[e] and
no proof of the girl's virginity can be
found, 21she shall be brought to the door
of her father's house and there the men
of her town shall stone her to death. She
has done a disgraceful thing[f] in Israel by
being promiscuous while still in her father's house. You must purge the evil
from among you.
22If a man is found sleeping with another man's wife, both the man who slept[g]
with her and the woman must die.[h] You
must purge the evil from Israel.
23If a man happens to meet in a town a
virgin pledged to be married and he
sleeps with her, 24you shall take both of
them to the gate of that town and stone
them to death—the girl because she was
in a town and did not scream for help,
and the man because he violated another
man's wife. You must purge the evil from
among you.[i]
25But if out in the country a man happens to meet a girl pledged to be married
and rapes her, only the man who has
done this shall die. 26Do nothing to the
girl; she has committed no sin deserving
death. This case is like that of someone
who attacks and murders his neighbor,
27for the man found the girl out in the
country, and though the betrothed girl
screamed,[j] there was no one to rescue
her.

22:15 [c]S Ge 23:10
22:18 [d]Ex 18:21; Dt 1:9-18
22:20 [e]Dt 17:4
22:21 [f]S Ge 34:7; S 38:24; S Lev 19:29; Dt 23:17-18; 1Co 5:13*
22:22 [g]2Sa 11:4 [h]S Ge 38:24; S Ex 21:12; Mt 5:27-28; Jn 8:5; 1Co 6:9; Heb 13:4
22:24 [i]1Co 5:13*
22:27 [j]S Ge 39:14
22:28 [k]Ex 22:16
22:30 [l]S Ge 29:29; S Lev 18:8; S 20:9; 1Co 5:1
23:1 [m]S Lev 21:20
23:3 [n]S Ge 19:38 [o]ver 4; Ne 13:2
23:4 [p]Dt 2:28 [q]S Nu 23:7; S 2Pe 2:15 [r]S Ge 24:10 [s]S ver 3
23:5 [t]Nu 24:10; Jos 24:10; Pr 26:2 [u]S Dt 4:37
23:6 [v]S Nu 24:17; Isa 15:1; 25:10; Jer 25:21; 27:3; 48:1; Eze 25:8; Zep 2:9 [w]Ezr 9:12; Mt 5:43
23:7 [x]S Ge 25:30 [y]S Ge 25:26 [z]S Lev 19:34
23:9 [a]Lev 15:1-33
23:10 [b]Lev 15:16

28If a man happens to meet a virgin
who is not pledged to be married and
rapes her and they are discovered,[k] 29he
shall pay the girl's father fifty shekels of
silver.[d] He must marry the girl, for he
has violated her. He can never divorce
her as long as he lives.
30A man is not to marry his father's
wife; he must not dishonor his father's
bed.[l]

Chapter 23

Exclusion From the Assembly

No one who has been emasculated[m]
by crushing or cutting may enter the
assembly of the LORD.
2No one born of a forbidden marriage[e]
nor any of his descendants may enter the
assembly of the LORD, even down to the
tenth generation.
3No Ammonite[n] or Moabite or any of
his descendants may enter the assembly
of the LORD, even down to the tenth generation.[o] 4For they did not come to meet
you with bread and water[p] on your way
when you came out of Egypt, and they
hired Balaam[q] son of Beor from Pethor in
Aram Naharaim[f][r] to pronounce a curse
on you.[s] 5However, the LORD your God
would not listen to Balaam but turned the
curse[t] into a blessing for you, because
the LORD your God loves[u] you. 6Do not
seek a treaty[v] of friendship with them as
long as you live.[w]
7Do not abhor an Edomite,[x] for he is
your brother.[y] Do not abhor an Egyptian,
because you lived as an alien in his country.[z] 8The third generation of children
born to them may enter the assembly of
the LORD.

Uncleanness in the Camp

9When you are encamped against your
enemies, keep away from everything impure.[a] 10If one of your men is unclean
because of a nocturnal emission, he is to
go outside the camp and stay there.[b]
11But as evening approaches he is to wash

[c] *19* That is, about 2 1/2 pounds (about 1 kilogram)
[d] *29* That is, about 1 1/4 pounds (about 0.6 kilogram)
[e] *2* Or *one of illegitimate birth*
[f] *4* That is, Northwest Mesopotamia

23:3–8 HISTORY, Universal—Historical relationships with God's people determined religious possibilities for other nations. Such prohibitions did not exclude all individuals as seen in the case of Ruth and the teaching of Isa 56:3–7.

23:3–8 CHRISTIAN ETHICS, War and Peace—The wrong use of international politics too often leads to war and fosters enemies. Biblical law regulated how Israel's worshiping community should relate to foreigners who sought to join their worship. Those who had tempted Israel to be unfaithful to God were excluded. Such laws must be seen in light of Israel's larger mission to bless other nations (Ge 12:1–3) and to be a "kingdom of priests" (Ex 19:6). Jesus taught love of enemies (Lk 6:27). War experiences and traditions may make us wary of accepting foreigners. The Master leads us to love them.

23:9–14 CHRISTIAN ETHICS, Health—Because personal hygiene is important, certain basic practices leading to and maintaining good individual and corporate health should be implemented. Attention to positive physical and emotional health are marks of Christian character. History shows those societies which gave little credence to either also reflected low ethical standards. Even war must not lead a people to ignore good hygiene or religious practices.

himself, and at sunset[c] he may return to
the camp.[d]
12Designate a place outside the camp
where you can go to relieve yourself. 13As
part of your equipment have something
to dig with, and when you relieve yourself, dig a hole and cover up your excrement. 14For the LORD your God moves[e]
about in your camp to protect you and to
deliver your enemies to you. Your camp
must be holy,[f] so that he will not see
among you anything indecent and turn
away from you.

Miscellaneous Laws

15If a slave has taken refuge[g] with you,
do not hand him over to his master.[h]
16Let him live among you wherever he
likes and in whatever town he chooses.
Do not oppress[i] him.
17No Israelite man[j] or woman is to become a shrine prostitute.[k] 18You must
not bring the earnings of a female prostitute or of a male prostitute[g] into the
house of the LORD your God to pay any
vow, because the LORD your God detests
them both.[l]
19Do not charge your brother interest,
whether on money or food or anything
else that may earn interest.[m] 20You may
charge a foreigner[n] interest, but not a
brother Israelite, so that the LORD your
God may bless[o] you in everything you
put your hand to in the land you are entering to possess.
21If you make a vow to the LORD your
God, do not be slow to pay it,[p] for the
LORD your God will certainly demand it of
you and you will be guilty of sin.[q] 22But if
you refrain from making a vow, you will
not be guilty.[r] 23Whatever your lips utter
you must be sure to do, because you
made your vow freely to the LORD your
God with your own mouth.
24If you enter your neighbor's vineyard, you may eat all the grapes you want,
but do not put any in your basket. 25If you
enter your neighbor's grainfield, you may
pick kernels with your hands, but you
must not put a sickle to his standing
grain.[s]

Chapter 24

If a man marries a woman who becomes
displeasing to him[t] because he finds
something indecent about her, and he
writes her a certificate of divorce,[u] gives
it to her and sends her from his house,
2and if after she leaves his house she becomes the wife of another man, 3and her
second husband dislikes her and writes
her a certificate of divorce, gives it to her
and sends her from his house, or if he
dies, 4then her first husband, who divorced her, is not allowed to marry her
again after she has been defiled. That
would be detestable in the eyes of the
LORD. Do not bring sin upon the land the
LORD[v] your God is giving you as an inheritance.
5If a man has recently married, he must
not be sent to war or have any other duty
laid on him. For one year he is to be free
to stay at home and bring happiness to
the wife he has married.[w]
6Do not take a pair of millstones—not

23:11 [c]S Lev 15:16 [d]1Sa 21:5
23:14 [e]S Ge 3:8 [f]Ex 3:5
23:15 [g]2Sa 22:3; Ps 2:12; 71:1 [h]1Sa 30:15
23:16 [i]Ex 22:21; S 23:6
23:17 [j]1Ki 14:24; 15:12; 22:46; 2Ki 23:7; Job 36:14 [k]S Ge 38:21
23:18 [l]S Ge 19:5; S Lev 20:13; Rev 22:15
23:19 [m]S Lev 25:35-37; Ne 5:2-7
23:20 [n]S Ge 31:15; S Dt 15:3 [o]Dt 15:10
23:21 [p]S Nu 6:21; Jdg 11:35; Ps 15:4 [q]Nu 30:1-2; Job 22:27; Ps 61:8; 65:1; 76:11; Isa 19:21; S Mt 5:33; Ac 5:3
23:22 [r]Ac 5:4
23:25 [s]Mt 12:1; Mk 2:23; Lk 6:1
24:1 [t]Dt 22:13 [u]ver 3; 2Ki 17:6; Isa 50:1; Jer 3:8; Mal 2:16; Mt 1:19; 5:31*; 19:7-9; Mk 10:4-5
24:4 [v]Jer 3:1
24:5 [w]S Dt 20:7

[g]18 Hebrew *of a dog*

23:14 REVELATION, Divine Presence—The constant presence of the Lord is a source of comfort and challenge for His people. Our protecting, loving God reveals Himself as holy so His people are to be holy in manner and attitude.
23:15–16 CHRISTIAN ETHICS, Justice—God's people should be special sources of refuge from oppression.
23:18 GOD, Holy—The holy God does not wish to be worshiped through the proceeds of prostitution. He is righteous, holy, and wishes to separate Himself, in every way, from the foul sins of the people. Similarly, we should not worship God through the gift of money gotten through any foul, illegitimate means. There are at least two good reasons for this. One, God does not want His holy name associated with sinful practices. He does not condone sin in any way. Second, God does not want His people to engage in sinful practices for monetary gain. God wants His people to be marked by holiness that comes to them through a right relationship to Him. See note on Lev 11:44–45.
23:19–20 CHRISTIAN ETHICS, Justice—Economic justice sets the tone for much of the rest of society's structures for justice. God's people must help one another economically instead of taking advantage of another's need.
23:21–22 SIN, Responsibility—A vow to God commits one to a particular course of action. This course then becomes a criterion by which a life is judged and held accountable.
23:21–23 STEWARDSHIP, Vows—Vows are voluntarily made, but once made become a sacred obligation. Vows may include promises to make sacrificial offerings to God. Failure to fulfill a vow is lying to God.
24:1–4 FAMILY, Divorce—The Bible does not record when divorce first began. This passage neither institutes divorce nor forbids it but does specify two things: (1) the man divorcing his wife must give her a written statement intended to protect the woman, and (2) a divorced woman who remarries cannot return to her first husband if her second husband dies or divorces her. The process of divorce was between families rather than being a legal matter at this time. If the woman was guilty of misconduct, her father would have to forfeit her dowry. If she was divorced without blame, he could demand the return of some of it. This passage is central to the discussion between Jesus and the Pharisees about grounds for divorce. See notes on Mt 19:3–9; Mk 10:2–12.
24:4 SIN, Alienation—Any action opposed to the righteous law of God is detestable to Him and will produce alienation. We do not justify God's commands. We follow them.
24:5 CHRISTIAN ETHICS, War and Peace—Some concession for family life over national loyalty was considered in Israel. Society has claims on its citizens but must make those claims in a spirit of care for individual circumstances. See note on 20:1–20.
24:5 FAMILY, Priorities—Neither military service nor business responsibilities were to take a man away from his wife during the first year of marriage. Instead he was to remain home and "bring happiness" to his wife. See 20:7. Contemporary marriage studies illustrate the importance of the first months of marriage as a time of getting acquainted and establishing marital patterns. Giving a young marriage high priority helps insure its success.

even the upper one—as security for a
debt, because that would be taking a
man's livelihood as security.[x]
7If a man is caught kidnapping one of
his brother Israelites and treats him as a
slave or sells him, the kidnapper must
die.[y] You must purge the evil from
among you.[z]
8In cases of leprous[h] diseases be very
careful to do exactly as the priests, who
are Levites,[a] instruct you. You must follow carefully what I have commanded
them.[b] 9Remember what the LORD your
God did to Miriam along the way after
you came out of Egypt.[c]
10When you make a loan of any kind to
your neighbor, do not go into his house to
get what he is offering as a pledge.[d]
11Stay outside and let the man to whom
you are making the loan bring the pledge
out to you. 12If the man is poor, do not go
to sleep with his pledge[e] in your possession. 13Return his cloak to him by sunset[f] so that he may sleep in it.[g] Then he
will thank you, and it will be regarded as
a righteous act in the sight of the LORD
your God.[h]
14Do not take advantage of a hired man
who is poor and needy, whether he is a
brother Israelite or an alien living in one
of your towns.[i] 15Pay him his wages each
day before sunset, because he is poor[j]
and is counting on it.[k] Otherwise he may
cry to the LORD against you, and you will
be guilty of sin.[l]
16Fathers shall not be put to death for
their children, nor children put to death
for their fathers; each is to die for his
own sin.[m]

24:6 [x]S Ex 22:22
24:7 [y]S Ex 21:16 [z]1Co 5:13*
24:8 [a]S Dt 17:9 [b]Lev 13:1-46; S 14:2
24:9 [c]S Nu 12:10
24:10 [d]Ex 22:25-27
24:12 [e]S Ex 22:26
24:13 [f]Ex 22:26 [g]S Ex 22:27 [h]Dt 6:25; Ps 106:31; Da 4:27
24:14 [i]Lev 19:13; 25:35-43; Dt 15:12-18; Job 24:4; Pr 14:31; 19:17; Am 4:1; 1Ti 5:18
24:15 [j]S Lev 25:35 [k]S Lev 19:13; Mt 20:8 [l]S Ex 22:23; S Job 12:19; Jas 5:4
24:16 [m]S Nu 26:11; Jer 31:29-30
24:17 [n]Ex 22:22; Job 6:27; 24:9; 29:12; Ps 10:18; 82:3; Pr 23:10; Eze 22:7 [o]S Ex 22:21; S 23:2; S Dt 10:18
24:18 [p]S Dt 15:15
24:19 [q]S Lev 19:9 [r]Dt 10:19; 27:19; Eze 47:22; Zec 7:10; Mal 3:5 [s]ver 20; Dt 14:29 [t]S Dt 14:29; Pr 19:17; 28:27; Ecc 11:1
24:20 [u]Lev 19:10
24:22 [v]ver 18
25:1 [w]S Ex 21:6 [x]Dt 17:8-13; 19:17; Ac 23:3 [y]1Ki 8:32 [z]S Ex 23:7; Dt 1:16-17
25:2 [a]Pr 10:13; 19:29; Lk 12:47-48
25:3 [b]Mt 27:26; Jn 19:1; 2Co 11:24 [c]Jer 20:2

17Do not deprive the alien or the fatherless[n] of justice,[o] or take the cloak of
the widow as a pledge. 18Remember that
you were slaves in Egypt[p] and the LORD
your God redeemed you from there. That
is why I command you to do this.
19When you are harvesting in your
field and you overlook a sheaf, do not go
back to get it.[q] Leave it for the alien,[r]
the fatherless and the widow,[s] so that
the LORD your God may bless[t] you in all
the work of your hands. 20When you beat
the olives from your trees, do not go over
the branches a second time.[u] Leave what
remains for the alien, the fatherless and
the widow. 21When you harvest the
grapes in your vineyard, do not go over
the vines again. Leave what remains for
the alien, the fatherless and the widow.
22Remember that you were slaves in
Egypt. That is why I command you to do
this.[v]

Chapter 25

WHEN men have a dispute, they are
to take it to court and the judges[w]
will decide the case,[x] acquitting[y] the innocent and condemning the guilty.[z] 2If
the guilty man deserves to be beaten,[a]
the judge shall make him lie down and
have him flogged in his presence with the
number of lashes his crime deserves, 3but
he must not give him more than forty
lashes.[b] If he is flogged more than that,
your brother will be degraded in your
eyes.[c]

[h]*8* The Hebrew word was used for various diseases affecting the skin—not necessarily leprosy.

24:6,10–15 DISCIPLESHIP, Poor—God's people are not to take and hold as collateral anything needed in making a living. The millstones mentioned are just a representative specimen of things indispensable in the preservation of life. The poor are to be treated with courtesy and respect. God's people are never to oppress a poor person in distress. Concern for the poor is more important than concern for my rights, my property, or my demand for justice.

24:9,18 HISTORY, Judgment—History calls for special obedience to God's directions in light of past discipline (Nu 12:10) and past suffering (Ex 1—5).

24:10–22 CHRISTIAN ETHICS, Justice—Respect for human dignity must be shown to all people even when we have legal claims against them. See notes on 23:19–20; Lev 19:15.

24:16 EVIL AND SUFFERING, Deserved—God holds each person accountable for his or her actions. The courts are not to punish a family for the crime of one family member. Courts must not carry on the tradition of clan revenge. Every person must be encouraged to act responsibly. Still the Bible realistically shows that sin's results reach far beyond the individual. See notes on Ex 20:5–6; Eze 18:1–32.

24:16 HUMANITY, Death and Sin—Sin is penalized by death. We cannot blame a previous generation nor expect someone else to endure our punishment. God made this part of Israel's civil code. It is also true in the spiritual realm. See notes on Jer 31:29–30; Eze 18:1–32.

24:16 SIN, Responsibility—My sin makes neither my father nor my son guilty. I alone bear responsibility. See note on Ge 39:9.

24:16 CHRISTIAN ETHICS, Justice—Individual responsibility is the central assumption of a society that seeks justice. Tradition may dictate punishment for an entire family or household for a crime. However, justice calls for punishment only for the guilty. At the same time, the effects of the crime have lasting effects on the family (5:9). See Jer 31:29–30; Eze 18:2–3.

24:17–22 DISCIPLESHIP, Persons—God supports people in need. God warns against unjust treatment of strangers, orphans, and widows. God's concern for defenseless and underprivileged persons is clear. He is concerned that we protect and provide for them. See 26:12; Lev 19:9,10.

24:18 SALVATION, Redemption—See note on 21:1–9. Redemption leads to concern for people in need. Israel's treatment of aliens, the fatherless, and widows was based on her treatment by God in the Exodus. Compare 15:15; Eph 4:32—5:2.

24:19 HUMANITY, Community Relationships—The technique of gleaning was intended to provide for the needs of the weaker persons of society. Communities are still to exercise compassionate care for those who are helpless or outcast.

24:19 SALVATION, Blessing—God blesses those who are mindful of the alien, the fatherless, and the widow.

25:1–3 CHRISTIAN ETHICS, Justice—Punishment should fit the crime, with the human dignity of the criminal kept in mind.

4Do not muzzle an ox while it is treading out the grain.[d]
5If brothers are living together and one
of them dies without a son, his widow
must not marry outside the family. Her
husband's brother shall take her and marry her and fulfill the duty of a brother-in-
law to her.[e] 6The first son she bears shall
carry on the name of the dead brother so
that his name will not be blotted out from
Israel.[f]
7However, if a man does not want to
marry his brother's wife,[g] she shall go to
the elders at the town gate[h] and say,
"My husband's brother refuses to carry
on his brother's name in Israel. He will
not fulfill the duty of a brother-in-law to
me."[i] 8Then the elders of his town shall
summon him and talk to him. If he persists in saying, "I do not want to marry
her," 9his brother's widow shall go up to
him in the presence of the elders, take off
one of his sandals,[j] spit in his face[k] and
say, "This is what is done to the man
who will not build up his brother's family
line." 10That man's line shall be known
in Israel as The Family of the Unsandaled.
11If two men are fighting and the wife
of one of them comes to rescue her husband from his assailant, and she reaches
out and seizes him by his private parts,
12you shall cut off her hand. Show her no
pity.[l]
13Do not have two differing weights in
your bag—one heavy, one light.[m] 14Do
not have two differing measures in your
house—one large, one small. 15You must
have accurate and honest weights and
measures, so that you may live long[n] in
the land the LORD your God is giving you.
16For the LORD your God detests anyone
who does these things, anyone who deals
dishonestly.[o]
17Remember what the Amalekites[p] did
to you along the way when you came out
of Egypt. 18When you were weary and
worn out, they met you on your journey
and cut off all who were lagging behind;
they had no fear of God.[q] 19When the
LORD your God gives you rest[r] from all
the enemies[s] around you in the land he
is giving you to possess as an inheritance,
you shall blot out the memory of Amalek[t] from under heaven. Do not forget!

Chapter 26

Firstfruits and Tithes

WHEN you have entered the land the
LORD your God is giving you as an
inheritance and have taken possession of
it and settled in it, 2take some of the firstfruits[u] of all that you produce from the
soil of the land the LORD your God is giving you and put them in a basket. Then
go to the place the LORD your God will
choose as a dwelling for his Name[v] 3and
say to the priest in office at the time, "I
declare today to the LORD your God that I
have come to the land the LORD swore to
our forefathers to give us." 4The priest
shall take the basket from your hands and
set it down in front of the altar of the
LORD your God. 5Then you shall declare
before the LORD your God: "My father
was a wandering[w] Aramean,[x] and he
went down into Egypt with a few people[y] and lived there and became a great
nation,[z] powerful and numerous. 6But
the Egyptians mistreated us and made us
suffer,[a] putting us to hard labor.[b] 7Then
we cried out to the LORD, the God of our
fathers, and the LORD heard our voice[c]
and saw[d] our misery,[e] toil and oppression.[f] 8So the LORD brought us out of
Egypt[g] with a mighty hand and an outstretched arm,[h] with great terror and
with miraculous signs and wonders.[i]
9He brought us to this place and gave us
this land, a land flowing with milk and
honey;[j] 10and now I bring the firstfruits
of the soil that you, O LORD, have given

25:4 [d]S Nu 22:29; 1Co 9:9*; 1Ti 5:18*
25:5 [e]Ru 4:10,13; Mt 22:24; Mk 12:19; Lk 20:28
25:6 [f]Ge 38:9; Ru 4:5,10
25:7 [g]Ru 1:15 [h]S Ge 23:10 [i]Ru 4:1-2,5-6
25:9 [j]Jos 24:22; Ru 4:7-8,11 [k]Nu 12:14; Job 17:6; 30:10; Isa 50:6
25:12 [l]S Dt 7:2
25:13 [m]Pr 11:1; 20:23; Mic 6:11
25:15 [n]S Ex 20:12
25:16 [o]Pr 11:1
25:17 [p]S Ge 36:12
25:18 [q]Ps 36:1; Ro 3:18
25:19 [r]S Ex 33:14; Heb 3:18-19 [s]Est 9:16 [t]S Ge 36:12
26:2 [u]S Ex 22:29 [v]S Ex 20:24; S Dt 12:5
26:5 [w]S Ge 20:13 [x]S Ge 25:20 [y]S Ge 34:30; 43:14 [z]S Ge 12:2
26:6 [a]S Nu 20:15 [b]S Ex 1:13
26:7 [c]S Ge 21:17 [d]Ex 3:9; 2Ki 13:4; 14:26 [e]S Ge 16:11 [f]Ps 42:9; 44:24; 72:14
26:8 [g]S Nu 20:16 [h]S Ex 3:20 [i]S Dt 4:34; 34:11-12
26:9 [j]S Ex 3:8

25:13–16 CHRISTIAN ETHICS, Justice—See note on Lev 19:35–36.
25:19 CHRISTIAN ETHICS, War and Peace—See note on 23:3–8.
26:1–11 HISTORY, Confession—Israel's worship centered on reciting her history of salvation with God. The precise events recited were not always the same, but Israel's faithful knew their relationship with God had concrete foundations in historical experiences of salvation. The Exodus from Egypt was the central experience of salvation for Israel. God's acts not human theological formulations are central to biblical confessions of faith. See note on 6:20–25.
26:1–15 STEWARDSHIP, Tithe—Tithing and firstfruits showed faithfulness and gratitude to God. Firstfruits given from the harvest expressed gratitude to God for His providence in providing the land and the harvest. This same spirit was expressed in the giving of the tithe and in declaring to the priests that God's law had been honored. Economic conditions change, but the spirit of gratitude and faithfulness to God in giving is expected of God's people in all ages.
26:1–15 WORSHIP, Sacrifice—At the heart of true worship is sacrificial giving to the Lord. See note on Lev 7:35–38.
26:2 PRAYER, Worship—See note on Ex 23:19.
26:5–11 EVIL AND SUFFERING, God's Present Help—God's people confess that they exist because God has helped them out of trouble. Both individually and collectively as God's people, we express thanks to God for being present when we suffer. God uses the crisis times of His people to reveal His grace, power, and love.
26:5–11 REVELATION, History—Israel summarized their belief by reciting God's saving actions in their history during the thanksgiving celebration for their first crops. Thus in the worship ceremony God revealed anew His actions for Israel and His continuing role in their lives. All they received came from His gracious hand.
26:5–10 PRAYER, Thanksgiving—A favorite type of praise and thanksgiving was the recounting of God's role in history. Confessions of faith such as this help God's people express thanks for God's history of salvation.

me.[k]" Place the basket before the LORD
your God and bow down before him.
11And you and the Levites[l] and the
aliens among you shall rejoice[m] in all the
good things the LORD your God has given
to you and your household.
12When you have finished setting aside
a tenth[n] of all your produce in the third
year, the year of the tithe,[o] you shall give
it to the Levite, the alien, the fatherless
and the widow, so that they may eat in
your towns and be satisfied. 13Then say to
the LORD your God: "I have removed
from my house the sacred portion and
have given it to the Levite, the alien, the
fatherless and the widow, according to all
you commanded. I have not turned aside
from your commands nor have I forgotten
any of them.[p] 14I have not eaten any of
the sacred portion while I was in mourning, nor have I removed any of it while I
was unclean,[q] nor have I offered any of it
to the dead. I have obeyed the LORD my
God; I have done everything you commanded me. 15Look down from heaven,[r]
your holy dwelling place, and bless[s] your
people Israel and the land you have given
us as you promised on oath to our forefathers, a land flowing with milk and
honey."

Follow the LORD's Commands

16The LORD your God commands you
this day to follow these decrees and laws;
carefully observe them with all your heart
and with all your soul.[t] 17You have declared this day that the LORD is your God
and that you will walk in his ways, that
you will keep his decrees, commands and
laws, and that you will obey him.[u] 18And
the LORD has declared this day that you
are his people, his treasured possession[v]
as he promised, and that you are to keep
all his commands. 19He has declared that
he will set you in praise,[w] fame and hon-
or high above all the nations[x] he has
made and that you will be a people holy[y]
to the LORD your God, as he promised.

Chapter 27

The Altar on Mount Ebal

MOSES and the elders of Israel commanded the people: "Keep all
these commands[z] that I give you today.
2When you have crossed the Jordan[a] into
the land the LORD your God is giving you,
set up some large stones[b] and coat them
with plaster.[c] 3Write on them all the
words of this law when you have crossed
over to enter the land the LORD your God
is giving you, a land flowing with milk
and honey,[d] just as the LORD, the God of
your fathers, promised you. 4And when
you have crossed the Jordan, set up these
stones on Mount Ebal,[e] as I command
you today, and coat them with plaster.
5Build there an altar[f] to the LORD your
God, an altar of stones. Do not use any
iron tool[g] upon them. 6Build the altar of
the LORD your God with fieldstones and
offer burnt offerings on it to the LORD
your God. 7Sacrifice fellowship offerings[i][h] there, eating them and rejoicing[i]
in the presence of the LORD your God.[j]
8And you shall write very clearly all the
words of this law on these stones[k] you
have set up."[l]

Curses From Mount Ebal

9Then Moses and the priests, who are
Levites,[m] said to all Israel, "Be silent, O
Israel, and listen! You have now become
the people of the LORD your God.[n]
10Obey the LORD your God and follow his
commands and decrees that I give you today."
11On the same day Moses commanded
the people:
12When you have crossed the Jordan,
these tribes shall stand on Mount Gerizim[o] to bless the people: Simeon, Levi,
Judah, Issachar,[p] Joseph and Benjamin.[q]

26:10 [k]S Dt 8:18
26:11 [l]Dt 12:12 [m]S Dt 16:11
26:12 [n]S Ge 14:20 [o]S Nu 18:24; Dt 14:28-29; Heb 7:5,9
26:13 [p]Ps 119:141,153,176
26:14 [q]Lev 7:20; Hos 9:4
26:15 [r]Ps 68:5; 80:14; 102:19; Isa 63:15; Zec 2:13 [s]S Ex 39:43
26:16 [t]Dt 4:29
26:17 [u]Ex 19:8; Ps 48:14
26:18 [v]Ex 6:7; Dt 7:6
26:19 [w]Isa 62:7; Zep 3:20 [x]Dt 4:7-8; 28:1,13,44; 1Ch 14:2; Ps 148:14; Isa 40:11 [y]S Dt 7:6
27:1 [z]Ps 78:7
27:2 [a]Jos 4:1 [b]Ex 24:4; Jos 24:26; 1Sa 7:12 [c]Jos 8:31
27:3 [d]S Ex 3:8
27:4 [e]S Dt 11:29
27:5 [f]S Ex 20:24 [g]Ex 20:25
27:7 [h]S Ex 32:6 [i]S Dt 16:11 [j]Jos 8:31
27:8 [k]Isa 8:1; 30:8; Hab 2:2 [l]Jos 8:32
27:9 [m]S Dt 17:9 [n]Dt 26:18
27:12 [o]S Dt 11:29 [p]S Ge 30:18 [q]Jos 8:35

[i]7 Traditionally *peace offerings*

26:11 PRAYER, Worship—See note on 12:7,12.
26:12–15 EVIL AND SUFFERING, Comfort—See note on 15:7–11.
26:13 CHRISTIAN ETHICS, Justice—A mark of obedience to God is doing justice for those who cannot care for themselves.
26:14 HUMANITY, Relationship to God—God's people are expected to remain faithful and obedient to Him. Part of that obedience is caring for the needs of the poor.
26:16 GOD, Sovereignty—The sovereignty of God comes to us as a demand that we honor Him, obeying His commandments. This demand is justified because He created us and blessed us in His redemptive love. Because we belong to God both by creation and by redemption, we must obey His will.
26:16 CHRISTIAN ETHICS, Character—Obedience to God is not halfhearted but requires investment of one's self.
26:18–19 ELECTION, Blessing—Those chosen ones who are faithful to God in their covenant relationships are promised recognition, honor, and the necessities which are conducive for holy living.
27:1—28:68 ELECTION, Righteousness—Blessings come to those who honor God with obedience, and curses are upon those who disregard the covenant God makes with His elect. By entering God's covenant and accepting His demand for righteousness, Israel was accepted as God's chosen people. Such acceptance was not an eternal guarantee of blessing. Disobedient people face discipline. Loss of blessing will be seen in loss of numbers, prosperity, fertile land, freedom, and rest —the blessings marking the covenant people.
27:7 PRAYER, Worship—See note on 12:7,12.
27:10 CHRISTIAN ETHICS, Social Order—See note on 4:1–8.
27:12–26 PRAYER, Corporate—Israel used public ceremonies to instruct people in God's expectations for His people. The priests pronounced curses on disobedient people. This would set all areas of life under constant failure until life was utterly destroyed (28:20–68). Prayer in worship can help us remember God's expectations and punishment.

13And these tribes shall stand on Mount
Ebal[r] to pronounce curses: Reuben, Gad,
Asher, Zebulun, Dan and Naphtali.
14The Levites shall recite to all the people of Israel in a loud voice:

15"Cursed is the man who carves
an image or casts an idol[s]—a thing
detestable[t] to the LORD, the work of
the craftsman's hands—and sets it
up in secret."
Then all the people shall say,
"Amen!"[u]
16"Cursed is the man who dishonors his father or his mother."[v]
Then all the people shall say,
"Amen!"
17"Cursed is the man who moves
his neighbor's boundary stone."[w]
Then all the people shall say,
"Amen!"
18"Cursed is the man who leads
the blind astray on the road."[x]
Then all the people shall say,
"Amen!"
19"Cursed is the man who withholds justice from the alien,[y] the fatherless or the widow."[z]
Then all the people shall say,
"Amen!"
20"Cursed is the man who sleeps
with his father's wife, for he dishonors his father's bed."[a]
Then all the people shall say,
"Amen!"
21"Cursed is the man who has sexual relations with any animal."[b]
Then all the people shall say,
"Amen!"
22"Cursed is the man who sleeps
with his sister, the daughter of
his father or the daughter of his
mother."[c]
Then all the people shall say,
"Amen!"
23"Cursed is the man who sleeps
with his mother-in-law."[d]
Then all the people shall say,
"Amen!"
24"Cursed is the man who kills[e]
his neighbor secretly."[f]
Then all the people shall say,
"Amen!"
25"Cursed is the man who accepts
a bribe to kill an innocent person."[g]
Then all the people shall say,
"Amen!"
26"Cursed is the man who does
not uphold the words of this law by
carrying them out."[h]
Then all the people shall say,
"Amen!"[i]

Chapter 28

Blessings for Obedience

If you fully obey the LORD your God and
carefully follow[j] all his commands[k] I
give you today, the LORD your God will
set you high above all the nations on
earth.[l] 2All these blessings will come
upon you[m] and accompany you if you
obey the LORD your God:

3You will be blessed[n] in the city
and blessed in the country.[o]
4The fruit of your womb will be
blessed, and the crops of your land
and the young of your livestock—the
calves of your herds and the lambs of
your flocks.[p]
5Your basket and your kneading
trough will be blessed.
6You will be blessed when you
come in and blessed when you go
out.[q]

27:13 [r]S Dt 11:29
27:15 [s]S Ex 20:4 [t]1Ki 11:5,7; 2Ki 23:13; Isa 44:19; 66:3 [u]Nu 5:22; S 1Co 14:16
27:16 [v]S Ge 31:35; S Ex 21:12; S Dt 5:16
27:17 [w]S Dt 19:14
27:18 [x]S Lev 19:14
27:19 [y]S Ex 22:21; S Dt 24:19 [z]S Ex 23:2; S Dt 10:18
27:20 [a]S Ge 34:5; S Lev 18:7
27:21 [b]S Ex 22:19
27:22 [c]S Lev 18:9
27:23 [d]S Lev 20:14
27:24 [e]S Ge 4:23 [f]Ex 21:12
27:25 [g]Ex 23:7-8; S Lev 19:16
27:26 [h]S Lev 26:14; Dt 28:15; Ps 119:21; Jer 11:3; Gal 3:10* [i]Jer 11:5
28:1 [j]S Dt 15:5 [k]S Lev 26:3 [l]S Nu 24:7; S Dt 26:19
28:2 [m]Jer 32:24; Zec 1:6
28:3 [n]Ps 144:15 [o]S Ge 39:5
28:4 [p]S Ge 49:25; S Dt 8:18
28:6 [q]Ps 121:8

27:15–26 CHRISTIAN ETHICS, Moral Limits—Irresponsibility to moral limits does not have isolated results. Rather, all relationships are affected. The Israelites agreed that anyone who committed any of the acts described was a detriment to the social and spiritual well-being of the society. See notes on Ex 12:1—13:16; Lev 26:3–45.

27:17 CHRISTIAN ETHICS, Property Rights—God disdains any act of dishonesty which infringes upon a neighbor's property rights (19:4).

27:18 DISCIPLESHIP, Handicapped—See note on Lev 19:14.

27:24–25 CHRISTIAN ETHICS, Murder—See note on Ex 20:13.

28:1–68 GOD, Sovereignty—This whole chapter is a forceful statement of a universal principle: those who are faithful to God will receive His blessings, and those who are not faithful can expect to receive His judgment. God is faithful to His people and expects us to be faithful to Him in return. God does not exist for people's pleasure, but people exist for God's service. God shows in His actions that He prefers to bless His people. When His people through their disobedience will not allow Him to bless them, then God will punish instead. He punishes the disobedient to develop responsibility and obedience in them. God's wrath is not blind rage, but purposeful action that seeks a positive result in those being punished.

28:1–68 EVIL AND SUFFERING, Deserved—Moses described two ways open to the people: obedience (vv 1–14) and disobedience (vv 15–68). Obedience would lead to blessings such as military success, good crops, and healthy children. Disobedience would lead to suffering such as disease, famine, and military defeat. At this point in Hebrew thought the rewards and punishments mentioned were almost exclusively material. See note on Lev 26:1–45. Other books emphasize rewards in the future. See note on Rev 21:1–8. The rewards and punishments mentioned here are the direct result of God's action. See notes on Job 42:1–15; Pr 1:10–19. Both the old and new covenants call for God's people to obey and point to deserved punishment for those who do not.

28:1–68 CHRISTIAN ETHICS, Social Order—See note on Lev 26:3–45. God wants to bless His people. Blessings take many forms as God works personally with us. Curses replace blessings when we forsake God and refuse to repent.

28:1 CHRISTIAN ETHICS, Social Order—See note on 4:1–8.

28:1–14 PRAYER, Blessing—See notes on Ge 14:18–20; Nu 6:22–27. Blessing is not the automatic result of public prayer. Blessing involves obedience.

7 The LORD will grant that the enemies[r] who rise up against you will be
defeated before you. They will come at
you from one direction but flee from you
in seven.[s]
8 The LORD will send a blessing on your
barns and on everything you put your
hand to. The LORD your God will bless[t]
you in the land he is giving you.
9 The LORD will establish you as his holy
people,[u] as he promised you on oath, if
you keep the commands[v] of the LORD
your God and walk in his ways. 10 Then all
the peoples on earth will see that you are
called by the name[w] of the LORD, and
they will fear you. 11 The LORD will grant
you abundant prosperity—in the fruit of
your womb, the young of your livestock[x]
and the crops of your ground—in the
land he swore to your forefathers to give
you.[y]
12 The LORD will open the heavens, the
storehouse[z] of his bounty,[a] to send
rain[b] on your land in season and to
bless[c] all the work of your hands. You
will lend to many nations but will borrow
from none.[d] 13 The LORD will make you
the head, not the tail. If you pay attention
to the commands of the LORD your God
that I give you this day and carefully follow[e] them, you will always be at the top,
never at the bottom.[f] 14 Do not turn aside
from any of the commands I give you today, to the right or to the left,[g] following
other gods and serving them.

Curses for Disobedience

15 However, if you do not obey[h] the
LORD your God and do not carefully follow all his commands and decrees I am
giving you today,[i] all these curses will
come upon you and overtake you:[j]

16 You will be cursed in the city and
cursed in the country.[k]
17 Your basket and your kneading
trough will be cursed.[l]
18 The fruit of your womb will be
cursed, and the crops of your land,
and the calves of your herds and the
lambs of your flocks.[m]
19 You will be cursed when you
come in and cursed when you go
out.[n]

20 The LORD will send on you curses,[o]
confusion and rebuke[p] in everything you
put your hand to, until you are destroyed
and come to sudden ruin[q] because of the
evil[r] you have done in forsaking him.[1]
21 The LORD will plague you with diseases
until he has destroyed you from the land
you are entering to possess.[s] 22 The LORD
will strike you with wasting disease,[t]
with fever and inflammation, with
scorching heat and drought,[u] with
blight[v] and mildew, which will plague[w]
you until you perish.[x] 23 The sky over
your head will be bronze, the ground beneath you iron.[y] 24 The LORD will turn
the rain[z] of your country into dust and
powder; it will come down from the skies
until you are destroyed.
25 The LORD will cause you to be defeated[a] before your enemies. You will come
at them from one direction but flee from
them in seven,[b] and you will become a
thing of horror[c] to all the kingdoms on
earth.[d] 26 Your carcasses will be food for
all the birds of the air[e] and the beasts of
the earth, and there will be no one to
frighten them away.[f] 27 The LORD will afflict you with the boils of Egypt[g] and
with tumors, festering sores and the itch,
from which you cannot be cured. 28 The
LORD will afflict you with madness, blindness and confusion of mind. 29 At midday
you will grope[h] about like a blind man in
the dark. You will be unsuccessful in everything you do; day after day you will be
oppressed and robbed, with no one to
rescue[i] you.
30 You will be pledged to be married to
a woman, but another will take her and
ravish her.[j] You will build a house, but
you will not live in it.[k] You will plant a
vineyard, but you will not even begin to
enjoy its fruit.[l] 31 Your ox will be slaughtered before your eyes, but you will eat
none of it. Your donkey will be forcibly
taken from you and will not be returned.
Your sheep will be given to your enemies,
and no one will rescue them. 32 Your sons
and daughters will be given to another
nation,[m] and you will wear out your eyes
watching for them day after day, powerless to lift a hand. 33 A people that you do
not know will eat what your land and labor produce, and you will have nothing

28:7 r2Ch 6:34 sS Lev 26:8,17 **28:8** tDt 15:4 **28:9** uS Ex 19:6 vS Lev 26:3 **28:10** wS Nu 6:27; 1Ki 8:43; Jer 25:29; Da 9:18 **28:11** xS Ge 30:27 yver 4; Dt 30:9 **28:12** zJob 38:22; Ps 135:7; Jer 10:13; 51:16 aPs 65:11; 68:10; Jer 31:12 bS Lev 26:4; 1Ki 8:35-36; 18:1; Ps 104:13; Isa 5:6; 30:23; 32:20 cIsa 61:9; 65:23; Jer 32:38-41; Mal 3:12 dver 44; S Lev 25:19; S Dt 15:3,6; Eze 34:26 **28:13** eJer 11:6 fS Dt 26:19 **28:14** gS Dt 5:32; Jos 1:7 **28:15** h1Ki 9:6; 2Ch 7:19 iS Dt 27:26 jDt 29:27; Jos 23:15; 2Ch 12:5; Da 9:11; Mal 2:2 **28:16** kver 3 **28:17** lver 5 **28:18** mver 4 **28:19** nver 6 **28:20** over 8,15; Lev 26:16; Jer 42:18; Mal 2:2; 3:9; 4:6 pPs 39:11; 76:6; 80:16; Isa 17:13; 51:20; 54:9; 66:15; Eze 5:15 qDt 4:26 rS Ex 32:22 **28:21** sLev 26:25; Nu 14:12; Jer 24:10; Am 4:10 **28:22** tver 48; Dt 32:24 uLev 26:16; 2Ki 8:1; Job 12:15; Ps 105:16; Jer 14:1; Hag 1:11; Mal 3:9 vHag 2:17 wS Lev 26:25 xDt 4:26; Am 4:9 **28:23** yS Lev 26:19 **28:24** zLev 26:19; Dt 11:17; 1Ki 8:35; 17:1; Isa 5:6; Jer 14:1; Hag 1:10 **28:25** a1Sa 4:10; Ps 78:62 bS Lev 26:17 cver 37 d2Ch 29:8; 30:7; Jer 15:4; 24:9; 26:6; 29:18; 44:12; Eze 23:46 **28:26** eS Ge 40:19 fPs 79:2; Isa 18:6; Jer 7:33; 12:9; 15:2; 16:4; 19:7; 34:20 **28:27** gDt 7:15 **28:29** hGe 19:11; Ex 10:21; Job 5:14; 12:25; 24:13; 38:15; Isa 59:10 iJdg 3:9; 2Ki 13:5; Est 4:14; Isa 19:20; 43:11; Hos 13:4; Ob 1:21 **28:30** jJob 31:10 kIsa 65:22; Am 5:11 lJer 12:13 **28:32** mver 41

[1] 20 Hebrew *me*

28:7 CHRISTIAN ETHICS, Moral Imperatives—A part of the blessing of obedience to God is that enemies, concrete or abstract, flee.

28:13 CHRISTIAN ETHICS, Social Order—See note on 4:1–8.

28:25 CHRISTIAN ETHICS, Moral Imperatives—Consequences are to be expected when disobedience to God's ethical expectations becomes a way of life. The cause and effect relationship of obedience and blessing contrasts vividly with the disobedience and judgment pattern in the Old Testament. Here the judgment is expressed in terms of military defeat. Thus, God expressed His displeasure with the Hebrews' disobedience in such a way that they knew there were bounds beyond which their unethical conduct could not go without reprisal. Sin always exacts a price.

but cruel oppression[n] all your days.[o]
34The sights you see will drive you mad.[p]
35The LORD will afflict your knees and
legs with painful boils[q] that cannot be
cured, spreading from the soles of your
feet to the top of your head.[r]
36The LORD will drive you and the
king[s] you set over you to a nation unknown to you or your fathers.[t] There
you will worship other gods, gods of
wood and stone.[u] 37You will become a
thing of horror[v] and an object of scorn[w]
and ridicule[x] to all the nations where the
LORD will drive you.[y]
38You will sow much seed in the field
but you will harvest little,[z] because locusts[a] will devour[b] it. 39You will plant
vineyards and cultivate them but you will
not drink the wine[c] or gather the grapes,
because worms will eat[d] them.[e] 40You
will have olive trees throughout your
country but you will not use the oil, because the olives will drop off.[f] 41You will
have sons and daughters but you will not
keep them, because they will go into captivity.[g] 42Swarms of locusts[h] will take
over all your trees and the crops of your
land.
43The alien who lives among you will
rise above you higher and higher, but you
will sink lower and lower.[i] 44He will
lend to you, but you will not lend to
him.[j] He will be the head, but you will
be the tail.[k]
45All these curses will come upon you.
They will pursue you and overtake you[l]
until you are destroyed,[m] because you did
not obey the LORD your God and observe
the commands and decrees he gave you.
46They will be a sign and a wonder to you
and your descendants forever.[n] 47Be-
cause you did not serve[o] the LORD your
God joyfully and gladly[p] in the time of
prosperity, 48therefore in hunger and
thirst,[q] in nakedness and dire poverty,
you will serve the enemies the LORD
sends against you. He will put an iron
yoke[r] on your neck[s] until he has destroyed you.
49The LORD will bring a nation against
you[t] from far away, from the ends of the
earth,[u] like an eagle[v] swooping down, a
nation whose language you will not understand,[w] 50a fierce-looking nation without respect for the old[x] or pity for the
young. 51They will devour the young of
your livestock and the crops of your land
until you are destroyed. They will leave
you no grain, new wine[y] or oil,[z] nor any
calves of your herds or lambs of your
flocks until you are ruined.[a] 52They will
lay siege[b] to all the cities throughout
your land until the high fortified walls in
which you trust fall down. They will besiege all the cities throughout the land
the LORD your God is giving you.[c]
53Because of the suffering that your enemy will inflict on you during the siege,
you will eat the fruit of the womb, the
flesh of the sons and daughters the LORD
your God has given you.[d] 54Even the
most gentle and sensitive man among you
will have no compassion on his own
brother or the wife he loves or his surviving children, 55and he will not give to one
of them any of the flesh of his children
that he is eating. It will be all he has left
because of the suffering your enemy will
inflict on you during the siege of all your
cities.[e] 56The most gentle and sensitive[f]
woman among you—so sensitive and
gentle that she would not venture to
touch the ground with the sole of her
foot—will begrudge the husband she
loves and her own son or daughter[g] 57the
afterbirth from her womb and the children she bears. For she intends to eat
them[h] secretly during the siege and in
the distress that your enemy will inflict
on you in your cities.
58If you do not carefully follow all the
words of this law,[i] which are written in
this book, and do not revere[j] this glorious and awesome name[k]—the LORD
your God— 59the LORD will send fearful
plagues on you and your descendants,
harsh and prolonged disasters, and severe
and lingering illnesses. 60He will bring
upon you all the diseases of Egypt[l] that
you dreaded, and they will cling to you.
61The LORD will also bring on you every
kind of sickness and disaster not recorded
in this Book of the Law,[m] until you are
destroyed.[n] 62You who were as numerous as the stars in the sky[o] will be left
but few[p] in number, because you did not
obey the LORD your God. 63Just as it
pleased[q] the LORD to make you prosper
and increase in number, so it will please[r]
him to ruin and destroy you.[s] You will be
uprooted[t] from the land you are entering
to possess.
64Then the LORD will scatter[u] you
among all nations,[v] from one end of the
earth to the other.[w] There you will worship other gods—gods of wood and
stone, which neither you nor your fathers
have known.[x] 65Among those nations
you will find no repose, no resting place[y]
for the sole of your foot. There the LORD
will give you an anxious mind, eyes[z]
weary with longing, and a despairing

28:33 [n]Jer 6:6; 22:17 [o]Jer 5:15-17; Eze 25:4
28:34 [p]ver 67
28:35 [q]Dt 7:15; Rev 16:2 [r]Job 2:7; 7:5; 13:28; 30:17, 30; Isa 1:6
28:36 [s]1Sa 12:25 [t]S Dt 4:27; 2Ki 24:14; 25:7,11; 2Ch 33:11; 36:21; Ezr 5:12; Jer 15:14; 16:13; 27:20; 39:1-9; 52:28; La 1:3 [u]S Dt 4:28
28:37 [v]ver 25; Jer 42:18; Eze 5:15 [w]Ps 22:7; 39:8; 44:13; 64:8; Jer 18:16; 48:27; Mic 6:16 [x]2Ch 7:20; Ezr 9:7; Jer 44:8 [y]1Ki 9:7; Ps 44:14; Jer 19:8; 24:9; 25:9,18; 29:18; La 2:15
28:38 [z]Lev 26:20; Ps 129:7; Isa 5:10; Jer 12:13; Hos 8:7; Mic 6:15; Hag 1:6, 9; 2:16 [a]S Ex 10:4 [b]S Ex 10:15
28:39 [c]S Lev 10:9 [d]Joel 1:4; 2:25; Mal 3:11 [e]Isa 5:10; 17:10-11; Zep 1:13
28:40 [f]Jer 11:16; Mic 6:15
28:41 [g]ver 32
28:42 [h]ver 38; Jdg 6:5; 7:12; Jer 46:23
28:43 [i]ver 13
28:44 [j]S ver 12 [k]S Dt 26:19
28:45 [l]S Ex 15:9 [m]ver 15; Dt 4:25-26
28:46 [n]S Nu 16:38; Ps 71:7; Isa 8:18; 20:3; Eze 5:15; Zec 3:8
28:47 [o]S Dt 10:12 [p]S Lev 23:40; Ne 9:35
28:48 [q]Jer 14:3; La 4:4 [r]Jer 28:13-14; La 1:14 [s]Ge 49:8
28:49 [t]S Lev 26:44 [u]Isa 5:26-30,26; 7:18-20; 39:3; Jer 4:16; 5:15; 6:22; 25:32; 31:8; Hab 1:6 [v]2Sa 1:23; Jer 4:13; 48:40; 49:22; La 4:19; Eze 17:3 [w]S Ge 11:7; 1Co 14:21*
28:50 [x]Isa 47:6
28:51 [y]Ps 4:7; Isa 36:17; Hag 1:11 [z]S Nu 18:12 [a]ver 33; Jdg 6:4
28:52 [b]2Ki 6:24 [c]Jer 10:18; Eze 6:10; Zep 1:14-16,17
28:53 [d]ver 57; Lev 26:29; 2Ki 6:28-29; La 2:20
28:55 [e]2Ki 6:29
28:56 [f]Isa 47:1 [g]La 4:10
28:57 [h]S ver 53
28:58 [i]Dt 31:24 [j]Ps 96:4; Jer 5:22; Mal 1:14; 2:5; 3:5, 16; 4:2 [k]S Ex 3:15; S Jos 7:9
28:60 [l]Ex 15:26
28:61 [m]Dt 29:21; 30:10; 31:26; Jos 1:8; 8:34; 23:6; 24:26; 2Ki 14:6; 22:8; 2Ch 17:9; 25:4; Ne 8:1,18; Mal 4:4 [n]Dt 4:25-26
28:62 [o]S Ge 22:17; Dt 4:27; 10:22 [p]S Lev 26:22
28:63 [q]Dt 30:9; Isa 62:5; 65:19; Jer 32:41; Zep 3:17 [r]Pr 1:26 [s]S Ge 6:7 [t]Ps 52:5; Jer 12:14; 31:28; 45:4
28:64 [u]S Dt 4:27; Ezr 9:7; Isa 6:12; Jer 32:23; 43:11; 52:27 [v]Ne 1:8; Ps 44:11; Jer 13:24; 18:17; 22:22 [w]S Dt 4:32; S Jer 8:19 [x]Dt 11:28; 32:17
28:65 [y]La 1:3 [z]Job 11:20

heart.[a] 66You will live in constant suspense, filled with dread both night and
day, never sure of your life. 67In the
morning you will say, "If only it were
evening!" and in the evening, "If only it
were morning!"—because of the terror
that will fill your hearts and the sights
that your eyes will see.[b] 68The LORD will
send you back in ships to Egypt on a journey I said you should never make again.[c]
There you will offer yourselves for sale to
your enemies as male and female slaves,
but no one will buy you.

Chapter 29

Renewal of the Covenant

THESE are the terms of the covenant
the LORD commanded Moses to make
with the Israelites in Moab,[d] in addition
to the covenant he had made with them
at Horeb.[e]

2Moses summoned all the Israelites
and said to them:

Your eyes have seen all that the LORD
did in Egypt to Pharaoh, to all his officials
and to all his land.[f] 3With your own eyes
you saw those great trials, those miraculous signs and great wonders.[g] 4But to
this day the LORD has not given you a
mind that understands or eyes that see or
ears that hear.[h] 5During the forty years
that I led[i] you through the desert, your
clothes did not wear out, nor did the sandals on your feet.[j] 6You ate no bread and
drank no wine or other fermented
drink.[k] I did this so that you might know
that I am the LORD your God.[l]

7When you reached this place, Sihon[m]
king of Heshbon[n] and Og king of Bashan
came out to fight against us, but we defeated them.[o] 8We took their land and
gave it as an inheritance[p] to the Reubenites, the Gadites and the half-tribe of Manasseh.[q]

9Carefully follow[r] the terms of this
covenant,[s] so that you may prosper in
everything you do.[t] 10All of you are
standing today in the presence of the
LORD your God—your leaders and chief
men, your elders and officials, and all the
other men of Israel, 11together with your
children and your wives, and the aliens
living in your camps who chop your wood
and carry your water.[u] 12You are standing here in order to enter into a covenant
with the LORD your God, a covenant the
LORD is making with you this day and
sealing with an oath, 13to confirm you
this day as his people,[v] that he may be
your God[w] as he promised you and as he
swore to your fathers, Abraham, Isaac
and Jacob. 14I am making this covenant,[x]
with its oath, not only with you 15who are
standing here with us today in the presence of the LORD our God but also with
those who are not here today.[y]

16You yourselves know how we lived
in Egypt and how we passed through the
countries on the way here. 17You saw
among them their detestable images and
idols of wood and stone, of silver and
gold.[z] 18Make sure there is no man or
woman, clan or tribe among you today

28:65 [a]Lev 26:16, 36; Hos 9:17
28:67 [b]ver 34
28:68 [c]S Ex 13:14
29:1 [d]S Lev 7:38 [e]S Ex 3:1
29:2 [f]Ex 19:4
29:3 [g]S Dt 4:34
29:4 [h]Isa 6:10; 32:3; 48:8; Jer 5:21; Eze 12:2; S Mt 13:15; Eph 4:18
29:5 [i]S Dt 8:2 [j]S Dt 8:4
29:6 [k]S Lev 10:9 [l]Dt 8:3
29:7 [m]S Nu 21:26 [n]S Nu 21:25 [o]Nu 21:21-24, 33-35; Dt 2:26-3:11
29:8 [p]Ps 78:55; 135:12; 136:22 [q]Nu 32:33; Dt 3:12-13
29:9 [r]S Dt 4:6; S Jos 1:7 [s]Ex 19:5; Ps 25:10; 103:18 [t]Jos 1:8; 2Ch 31:21
29:11 [u]Jos 9:21,23, 27; 1Ch 20:3
29:13 [v]S Ge 6:18; S Ex 19:6 [w]S Ge 17:7
29:14 [x]Ex 19:5; Isa 59:21; Jer 31:31; 32:40; 50:5; Eze 16:62; 37:26; Heb 8:7-8
29:15 [y]S Ge 6:18; Ac 2:39
29:17 [z]Ex 20:23; Dt 4:28

29:1—30:20 ELECTION, Israel—Those who are God's elect are persons who have a covenant relationship with God. Each generation must renew its covenant with God. The covenant of God with parents and predecessors requires confirmation and renewal by a new generation of elected ones who enjoy the blessings of the legacy of the past. Covenant membership is not automatic. People must enter the covenant, understanding God's expectations of His covenant people. God is not an individual's God until the individual identifies personally with God's people, accepting their heritage, acknowledging God's right to discipline, and living on the basis of God's promises and teaching. Election of Israel was not a political action. It was a spiritual strategy to gain a people who would self-consciously be the covenant people serving God's holy purposes.

29:1–15 THE CHURCH, Covenant People—Relationships require constant attention. Recommitments are necessary to keep our relationship with God meaningful and fresh. Remembering previous commitments and making new commitments emphasizes the importance of our relationship with God. See note on Lev 26:9.

29:2–29 HISTORY, Judgment—God's historical acts do not automatically bring revelation or salvation. God must enable a person to recognize historical events as His actions and to accept Him as Lord because of those acts. God acts so people may know Him. Constant repetition of and meditation on such acts should lead to faith and understanding. The person of faith with such understanding does not take credit for understanding, knowing that even the ability to understand came from God. Persons who do not learn from God's acts and respond in obedience to His will know they deserve the judgment that comes upon them. Participating in a service of dedication and covenant renewal does not guarantee salvation. Only obedient faith commitment brings salvation. History past shows God's revelation and invites to salvation. History future is God's secret. History present is our opportunity to accept and obey God's revelation.

29:3–4 HUMANITY, Intellectual Nature—Seeing what God has done and understanding its meaning are two different things. Perception is not only intellectual but also spiritual. We must be properly related to God to receive spiritual insight. Such insight leads us to see that the greatest knowledge is the knowledge and will to obey God.

29:16–28 THE CHURCH, Covenant People—See note on 29:1–15. We serve God individually and as part of a community. What each believer says or does affects other believers. The poisons of hypocrisy, selfishness, and idolatry infect the entire covenant community. Violating God's will does not go unpunished. People cannot be safe when they consistently go their own way instead of God's.

29:18–21 GOD, One God—Worshiping anyone or anything other than the one God separates us from God's forgiveness and blessing. We can become so set in our determination to worship a false god that we are no longer sensitive to the call of the one true God. God does not overrule the freedom of the individual. God will not forgive one who will not repent and turn to Him. Compare Mk 3:28–29. We can become so determined in our sinful alienation from God that we place ourselves beyond the reach of God's forgiveness.

29:18 WORSHIP, False—See note on Ex 22:20.

whose heart turns[a] away from the LORD
our God to go and worship the gods of
those nations; make sure there is no root
among you that produces such bitter poison.[b]
19When such a person hears the words
of this oath, he invokes a blessing[c] on
himself and therefore thinks, "I will be
safe, even though I persist in going my
own way."[d] This will bring disaster on
the watered land as well as the dry.[k]
20The LORD will never be willing to forgive[e] him; his wrath and zeal[f] will
burn[g] against that man. All the curses
written in this book will fall upon him,
and the LORD will blot[h] out his name
from under heaven. 21The LORD will single him out from all the tribes of Israel for
disaster,[i] according to all the curses of
the covenant written in this Book of the
Law.[j]
22Your children who follow you in later
generations and foreigners who come
from distant lands will see the calamities
that have fallen on the land and the diseases with which the LORD has afflicted
it.[k] 23The whole land will be a burning
waste[l] of salt[m] and sulfur—nothing
planted, nothing sprouting, no vegetation
growing on it. It will be like the destruction of Sodom and Gomorrah,[n] Admah
and Zeboiim, which the LORD overthrew
in fierce anger.[o] 24All the nations will
ask: "Why has the LORD done this to this
land?[p] Why this fierce, burning anger?"
25And the answer will be: "It is because this people abandoned the covenant of the LORD, the God of their fathers, the covenant he made with them
when he brought them out of Egypt.[q]
26They went off and worshiped other
gods and bowed down to them, gods they
did not know, gods he had not given
them. 27Therefore the LORD's anger
burned against this land, so that he
brought on it all the curses written in this
book.[r] 28In furious anger and in great
wrath[s] the LORD uprooted[t] them from
their land and thrust them into another
land, as it is now."
29The secret things belong to the LORD
our God,[u] but the things revealed belong
to us and to our children forever, that we
may follow all the words of this law.[v]

Chapter 30

Prosperity After Turning to the LORD

WHEN all these blessings and curses[w]
I have set before you come upon
you and you take them to heart wherever
the LORD your God disperses you among
the nations,[x] 2and when you and your
children return[y] to the LORD your God
and obey him with all your heart[z] and
with all your soul according to everything
I command you today, 3then the LORD
your God will restore your fortunes[1] [a]
and have compassion[b] on you and gather[c] you again from all the nations where
he scattered[d] you.[e] 4Even if you have
been banished to the most distant land
under the heavens,[f] from there the LORD
your God will gather[g] you and bring you
back.[h] 5He will bring[i] you to the land
that belonged to your fathers, and you
will take possession of it. He will make
you more prosperous and numerous[j]
than your fathers. 6The LORD your God
will circumcise your hearts and the hearts
of your descendants,[k] so that you may
love[l] him with all your heart and with all
your soul, and live. 7The LORD your God
will put all these curses[m] on your enemies who hate and persecute you.[n] 8You
will again obey the LORD and follow all
his commands I am giving you today.
9Then the LORD your God will make you

29:18 [a]S Dt 13:6 [b]S Dt 11:16; Heb 12:15 **29:19** [c]Ps 72:17; Isa 65:16 [d]Ps 36:2 **29:20** [e]S Ex 23:21 [f]Ex 34:14; Eze 23:25; Zep 1:18 [g]Ps 74:1; 79:5; 80:4; Eze 36:5 [h]2Ki 13:23; 14:27; Rev 3:5 **29:21** [i]Dt 32:23; Eze 7:26 [j]S Dt 28:61 **29:22** [k]Jer 19:8; 49:17; 50:13 **29:23** [l]Isa 1:7; 6:11; 9:18; 64:10; Jer 12:11; 44:2,6; Mic 5:11 [m]S Ge 13:10; Eze 47:11 [n]S Ge 19:24,25; Zep 2:9; S Mt 10:15; Ro 9:29 [o]S Ge 14:8 **29:24** [p]1Ki 9:8; 2Ch 36:19; Jer 16:10; 22:8-9; 52:13 **29:25** [q]2Ki 17:23; 2Ch 36:21 **29:27** [r]S Dt 28:15 **29:28** [s]Ps 7:11 [t]1Ki 14:15; 2Ch 7:20; Ps 9:6; 52:5; Pr 2:22; Jer 12:14; 31:28; 42:10; Eze 19:12 **29:29** [u]Ac 1:7 [v]Jn 5:39; Ac 17:11; 2Ti 3:16 **30:1** [w]S Dt 11:26 [x]Lev 26:40-45; S Dt 4:32; 29:28 **30:2** [y]S Dt 4:30 [z]Dt 4:29; Ps 119:2 **30:3** [a]Ps 14:7; 53:6; 85:1; 126:4; Jer 30:18; 33:11; Eze 16:53; Joel 3:1; Zep 2:7 [b]Dt 13:17 [c]S Ge 48:21 [d]S Ge 11:4; Dt 4:27 [e]Isa 11:11; Jer 12:15; 16:15; 24:6; 29:14; 48:47; 49:6 **30:4** [f]Ps 19:6 [g]Isa 17:6; 24:13; 27:12; 40:11; 49:5; 56:8; Eze 20:34,41; 34:13 [h]Ne 1:8-9; Isa 11:12; 41:5; 42:10; 43:6; 48:20; 62:11; Jer 31:8,10; 50:2 **30:5** [i]Jer 29:14 [j]S Dt 7:13 **30:6** [k]S Dt 6:24; S 10:16 [l]Dt 6:5 **30:7** [m]S Ge 12:3 [n]Dt 7:15

[k]*19* Or *way, in order to add drunkenness to thirst."*
[1]*3* Or *will bring you back from captivity*

29:20–28 ELECTION, Condemnation—The anger of God comes upon the elect who abandon God's covenant. Election is an invitation to be God's people. Failure to accept the invitation leads to judgment.

30:1–4 GOD, Power—God's sovereign power at work in the world is such that He can provide for the needs of His people anywhere, anytime. Though His people may have been banished to the ends of the earth, God knows where His people are. He can reach out to them with the blessing they need. They may go far from God, but God is never far from them. He may have to let people endure hardship and suffering for a short time in order for them to turn to Him again in their hearts, but God is ready and able to extricate them from their suffering any time they are ready to turn to Him. God's power always goes beyond our understanding, just as His love is always beyond our expectation.

30:1–10 GOD, Love—God's heart would far rather pour itself out in love than in wrath. Although He may have to chastise His people, God will continue to show loving concern for them. He stands ready to pour out renewed blessings upon them when they learn their lesson and return to Him in faith.

30:1–20 EVIL AND SUFFERING, Deserved—God's people may rebel and receive the punishment they deserve. Grace, however, not punishment, is God's last word. Punishment should lead to repentance. Repentance leads to restored relationship and blessings. Even the unfaithful can repent and enjoy the rewards of communion with God. See note on 28:1–68.

30:1–10 ELECTION, Blessing—When the elect of God turn away from disobedience to obey God, prosperity is assured. Prosperity is defined in the terms of those who love God, not in terms of the secular world's greed.

30:1–10 SALVATION, Repentance—Discipline is not God's last word. God seeks through discipline to lead us to repentance. To repent (Hebrew *shub*, "turn, return") is to change life's directions, trust God, and obey Him. Repentance leads to salvation.

30:9–10 STEWARDSHIP, Rewards—God punishes His people when they are unfaithful. He seeks to restore and renew the people. A sign of His restoration is renewed blessings

most prosperous in all the work of your
hands and in the fruit of your womb, the
young of your livestock and the crops of
your land.[o] The LORD will again delight[p]
in you and make you prosperous, just as
he delighted in your fathers, 10if you obey
the LORD your God and keep his commands and decrees that are written in
this Book of the Law[q] and turn to the
LORD your God with all your heart and
with all your soul.[r]

The Offer of Life or Death

11Now what I am commanding you today is not too difficult for you or beyond
your reach.[s] 12It is not up in heaven, so
that you have to ask, "Who will ascend
into heaven[t] to get it and proclaim it to
us so we may obey it?"[u] 13Nor is it beyond the sea,[v] so that you have to ask,
"Who will cross the sea to get it and proclaim it to us so we may obey it?"[w] 14No,
the word is very near you; it is in your
mouth and in your heart so you may obey
it.[x]
15See, I set before you today life[y] and
prosperity,[z] death[a] and destruction.[b]
16For I command you today to love[c] the
LORD your God, to walk in his ways, and
to keep his commands, decrees and laws;
then you will live[d] and increase, and the
LORD your God will bless you in the land
you are entering to possess.
17But if your heart turns away and you
are not obedient, and if you are drawn
away to bow down to other gods and worship them, 18I declare to you this day that
you will certainly be destroyed.[e] You will
not live long in the land you are crossing
the Jordan to enter and possess.
19This day I call heaven and earth as
witnesses against you[f] that I have set before you life and death, blessings and
curses.[g] Now choose life, so that you and
your children may live 20and that you
may love[h] the LORD your God, listen to
his voice, and hold fast to him. For the
LORD is your life,[i] and he will give[j] you
many years in the land[k] he swore to

30:9 [o]Jer 1:10; 24:6; 31:28; 32:41; 42:10; 45:4 [p]S Dt 28:63
30:10 [q]S Dt 28:61 [r]S Dt 4:29
30:11 [s]Ps 19:8; Isa 45:19,23; 63:1
30:12 [t]Pr 30:4 [u]Ro 10:6*
30:13 [v]Job 28:14 [w]Ro 10:7*
30:14 [x]S Dt 6:6; Ro 10:8*
30:15 [y]Pr 10:16; 11:19; 12:28; Jer 21:8 [z]Dt 28:11; Job 36:11; Ps 25:13; 106:5; Pr 3:1-2 [a]S Ge 2:17 [b]S Dt 11:26
30:16 [c]Dt 6:5 [d]ver 19; Dt 4:1; 32:47; Ne 9:29
30:18 [e]S Dt 8:19
30:19 [f]Dt 4:26 [g]S Dt 11:26
30:20 [h]Dt 6:5 [i]Dt 4:1; S 8:3; 32:47; Ps 27:1; Pr 3:22; S Jn 5:26; Ac 17:28 [j]Ge 12:7 [k]Ps 37:3
31:2 [l]S Ex 7:7 [m]Nu 27:17; 1Ki 3:7 [n]S Dt 3:23,26
31:3 [o]Nu 27:18 [p]S Dt 9:3 [q]S Dt 7:1 [r]S Dt 3:28
31:4 [s]S Nu 21:33
31:5 [t]S Dt 2:33
31:6 [u]ver 7,23; Jos 1:6,9,18; 10:25; 1Ch 22:13; 28:20; 2Ch 32:7 [v]Jer 1:8, 17; Eze 2:6 [w]S Ge 28:15; S Dt 1:29; 20:4; S Mt 28:20 [x]Ps 56:9; 118:6 [y]S Dt 4:31; 1Sa 12:22; 1Ki 6:13; Ps 94:14; Isa 41:17; Heb 13:5*
31:7 [z]ver 23; Nu 27:23 [a]Jos 1:6
31:8 [b]S Ex 13:21 [c]S Ge 28:15; S Dt 4:31
31:9 [d]S Ex 17:14 [e]ver 25; 1Ch 15:2
31:10 [f]S Dt 15:1 [g]S Ex 23:16; Dt 16:13
31:11 [h]S Dt 16:16 [i]Dt 12:5

give to your fathers, Abraham, Isaac and
Jacob.

Chapter 31

Joshua to Succeed Moses

THEN Moses went out and spoke these
words to all Israel: 2"I am now a hundred and twenty years old[l] and I am no
longer able to lead you.[m] The LORD has
said to me, 'You shall not cross the Jordan.'[n] 3The LORD your God himself will
cross[o] over ahead of you.[p] He will destroy these nations[q] before you, and you
will take possession of their land. Joshua
also will cross[r] over ahead of you, as the
LORD said. 4And the LORD will do to them
what he did to Sihon and Og,[s] the kings
of the Amorites, whom he destroyed
along with their land. 5The LORD will deliver[t] them to you, and you must do to
them all that I have commanded you. 6Be
strong and courageous.[u] Do not be afraid
or terrified[v] because of them, for the
LORD your God goes with you;[w] he will
never leave you[x] nor forsake[y] you."
7Then Moses summoned Joshua and
said[z] to him in the presence of all Israel,
"Be strong and courageous, for you must
go with this people into the land that the
LORD swore to their forefathers to give
them,[a] and you must divide it among
them as their inheritance. 8The LORD
himself goes before you and will be with
you;[b] he will never leave you nor forsake
you.[c] Do not be afraid; do not be discouraged."

The Reading of the Law

9So Moses wrote[d] down this law and
gave it to the priests, the sons of Levi,
who carried[e] the ark of the covenant of
the LORD, and to all the elders of Israel.
10Then Moses commanded them: "At the
end of every seven years, in the year for
canceling debts,[f] during the Feast of Tabernacles,[g] 11when all Israel comes to appear[h] before the LORD your God at the
place he will choose,[i] you shall read this

---

for His people.

30:11–16 GOD, Love—What God expects of us is not something beyond our capabilities. He is not arbitrary and unrealistic in His expectations of us. He is a loving heavenly Father who has reasonable expectations that His children will respond to Him in faithfulness and loving obedience. When we understand that we live in God's world, and that He wants us to have a full and meaningful life in His world, then we understand that His commands are not foreign to our best interests. That is how any thoughtful parent shapes demands of children.

30:11 CHRISTIAN ETHICS, Social Order—See note on Nu 1:54.

30:12–13 PROCLAMATION, Divine Source—The source of proclamation is not a heavenly secret persons have to search all the way to heaven to find. God has revealed His word to His people. Moses wrote the "Book of the Law" (v 10) to help people learn God's word by memory. The Bible continues to give us an accessible source to the Word to be proclaimed. God's inspired Scriptures are our source for proclamation. See note on Jer 19:14–15.

30:15–20 SALVATION, Human Freedom—Moses set before Israel the choice between God's salvation and their own destruction. The same choice is set before all.

31:1–8 DISCIPLESHIP, Spiritual Leaders—The time had come for a successor to be designated for the aging Moses. The passing of the mantle of leadership to Joshua was made in the presence of all Israel. The aged Moses called for courage and for continuing confidence in God's leadership. Such public challenges still are appropriate when aging leaders are succeeded by new leaders. Aging leaders should make the process as beneficial to all as possible. Human leaders cannot maintain control forever. A major leadership role is to train and prepare the way for a new generation of leaders.

law[j] before them in their hearing. 12As-
semble the people—men, women and
children, and the aliens living in your
towns—so they can listen and learn[k] to
fear[l] the LORD your God and follow carefully all the words of this law. 13Their
children,[m] who do not know this law,
must hear it and learn to fear the LORD
your God as long as you live in the land
you are crossing the Jordan to possess."

Israel's Rebellion Predicted

14The LORD said to Moses, "Now the
day of your death[n] is near. Call Joshua[o]
and present yourselves at the Tent of
Meeting, where I will commission
him.[p]" So Moses and Joshua came and
presented themselves at the Tent of
Meeting.[q]
15Then the LORD appeared at the Tent
in a pillar of cloud, and the cloud stood
over the entrance to the Tent.[r] 16And
the LORD said to Moses: "You are going
to rest with your fathers,[s] and these people will soon prostitute[t] themselves to
the foreign gods of the land they are entering. They will forsake[u] me and break
the covenant I made with them. 17On
that day I will become angry[v] with them
and forsake[w] them; I will hide[x] my face[y]
from them, and they will be destroyed.
Many disasters[z] and difficulties will
come upon them, and on that day they
will ask, 'Have not these disasters come
upon us because our God is not with
us?'[a] 18And I will certainly hide my face
on that day because of all their wickedness in turning to other gods.
19"Now write[b] down for yourselves
this song and teach it to the Israelites and
have them sing it, so that it may be a
witness[c] for me against them. 20When I
have brought them into the land flowing
with milk and honey, the land I promised
on oath to their forefathers,[d] and when
they eat their fill and thrive, they will
turn to other gods[e] and worship them,[f]
rejecting me and breaking my covenant.[g]
21And when many disasters and difficulties come upon them,[h] this song will testify against them, because it will not be
forgotten by their descendants. I know
what they are disposed to do,[i] even before I bring them into the land I promised
them on oath." 22So Moses wrote[j] down
this song that day and taught it to the
Israelites.
23The LORD gave this command[k] to
Joshua son of Nun: "Be strong and courageous,[l] for you will bring the Israelites
into the land I promised them on oath,
and I myself will be with you."
24After Moses finished writing[m] in a
book the words of this law[n] from beginning to end, 25he gave this command to
the Levites who carried[o] the ark of the
covenant of the LORD: 26"Take this Book
of the Law and place it beside the ark of
the covenant of the LORD your God.
There it will remain as a witness against
you.[p] 27For I know how rebellious[q] and
stiff-necked[r] you are. If you have been
rebellious against the LORD while I am
still alive and with you, how much more
will you rebel after I die! 28Assemble before me all the elders of your tribes and

31:11 [j]Jos 8:34-35; 2Ki 23:2; Ne 8:2
31:12 [k]Dt 4:10 [l]Hag 1:12; Mal 1:6; 3:5,16
31:13 [m]S Dt 11:2
31:14 [n]S Ge 25:8; S Nu 27:13 [o]Nu 27:23; Dt 34:9; Jos 1:1-9 [p]S Nu 27:19 [q]Ex 33:9-11
31:15 [r]S Ex 33:9
31:16 [s]S Ge 15:15 [t]S Ex 34:15; Dt 4:25-28; Jdg 2:12 [u]Jdg 10:6, 13; 1Ki 9:9; 18:18; 19:10; Jer 2:13; 5:19; 19:4
31:17 [v]Dt 32:16; Jdg 2:14,20; 10:7; 2Ki 13:3; 22:13; Ps 106:29,40; Jer 7:18; 21:5; 36:7 [w]Jdg 6:13; 2Ch 15:2; 24:20; Ezr 8:22; Ps 44:9; Isa 2:6 [x]Dt 32:20; Isa 1:15; 45:15; 53:3; 54:8 [y]Job 13:24; Ps 13:1; 27:9; 30:7; 104:29; Isa 50:6; Jer 33:5; Eze 39:29; Mic 3:4 [z]Jer 4:20; Eze 7:26 [a]Nu 14:42; Hos 9:12
31:19 [b]ver 22 [c]S Ge 31:50
31:20 [d]Dt 6:10-12 [e]Ps 4:2; 16:4; 40:4; Jer 13:25; Da 3:28; Am 2:4 [f]Dt 8:19; 11:16-17 [g]ver 16
31:21 [h]S Dt 4:30 [i]1Ch 28:9; Hos 5:3; Jn 2:24-25
31:22 [j]ver 19
31:23 [k]S ver 7 [l]Jos 1:6
31:24 [m]Dt 17:18; 2Ki 22:8 [n]Dt 28:58
31:25 [o]S ver 9
31:26 [p]ver 19 **31:27** [q]S Ex 23:21 [r]S Dt 9:27

31:12–15 HOLY SCRIPTURE, Writing—The assembled people heard the Word of God as it was read from a written document. God revealed Himself and His will, giving the commands a holy people are to follow. The worship leader recited the words so the people would remember and practice God's laws. Since very few people could read or had a copy of the word, religious teaching took place in open assemblies where the prophet or priest interpreted God's will. The written Word was taught orally for God's people to learn and practice it.
31:12–13 EDUCATION, Commanded—Moses commanded the people—regardless of age, sex, or social status—to come together at designated times for instruction in the Law. See note on Ne 8:1–9. Even though it is extremely important to meditate upon the Word of God in private (see Pr 3:1) and to teach it in the home (see note on Dt 6:1–10), neither takes the place of gathering with others to share understandings of the revealed will of God.
31:14—32:49 EVIL AND SUFFERING, Deserved—God prepares us to expect His punishment for sin and provides His teaching to lead us back to Him. God told Moses to write a song so His people would eventually realize their suffering was His punishment for their sins. Nations sometimes suffer because God punishes them for their sins. Often God's judgment is preparation to show compassion and love to the remnant of His people.
31:16–19 THE CHURCH, Covenant People—God's people always stand in danger of rebelling against Him. Believers must guard against any lapse into sin. Falling into old patterns of sin are tempting when circumstances are easy and material possessions are plentiful. Our lapses arouse God's anger.
31:20 THE CHURCH, Covenant People—See note on v 16.
31:21 GOD, Wisdom—Only a living, personal God can *know* what is happening. Only a God whose wisdom is unlimited can *foreknow* with perfect clarity what will happen in the future. The fact that God can foreknow, however, does not mean that He causes to happen what He foreknows. That would eliminate human freedom. Then everything would be predetermined. History would be simply the unchangeable unfolding of what God had already programmed. Our lives and the decisions that we make would then be meaningless, for we would not really be making decisions and carrying out actions. We would only be doing what God programmed into us like mindless robots. God knows us so intimately that He knows what each of us will do in any given set of circumstances. As parents, we sometimes know our children so well that we are fairly well assured what they will do in certain circumstances. If we as limited human beings can know with a fair degree of accuracy what our children will do, how much more can God with His perfect wisdom know what will happen in the lives of His children?
31:27 SIN, Rebellion—If strong, faithful, humble leaders cannot keep people faithful to God, what will happen when such leadership vanishes. Leaders cannot prevent sin or ensure faithfulness. Leaders do, however, play a strong role in determining the loyalty of a people to God. See note on Ex 14:11–12.

all your officials, so that I can speak these
words in their hearing and call heaven
and earth to testify against them.[s] 29For I
know that after my death you are sure to
become utterly corrupt[t] and to turn from
the way I have commanded you. In days
to come, disaster[u] will fall upon you because you will do evil in the sight of the
LORD and provoke him to anger by what
your hands have made."

The Song of Moses

30And Moses recited the words of this
song from beginning to end in the hearing of the whole assembly of Israel:

Chapter 32

LISTEN,[v] O heavens,[w] and I will speak;
hear, O earth, the words of my
mouth.[x]
2Let my teaching fall like rain[y]
and my words descend like dew,[z] [a]
like showers[b] on new grass,
like abundant rain on tender plants.
3I will proclaim[c] the name of the
LORD.[d]
Oh, praise the greatness[e] of our
God!
4He is the Rock,[f] his works are
perfect,[g]
and all his ways are just.
A faithful God[h] who does no wrong,
upright[i] and just is he.[j]
5They have acted corruptly toward him;
to their shame they are no longer
his children,
but a warped and crooked
generation.[m] [k]
6Is this the way you repay[l] the LORD,
O foolish[m] and unwise people?[n]
Is he not your Father,[o] your Creator,[n]
who made you and formed you?[p]
7Remember the days of old;[q]
consider the generations long past.[r]
Ask your father and he will tell you,
your elders, and they will explain to
you.[s]
8When the Most High[t] gave the
nations their inheritance,
when he divided all mankind,[u]
he set up boundaries[v] for the peoples
according to the number of the sons
of Israel.[o] [w]
9For the LORD's portion[x] is his people,
Jacob his allotted inheritance.[y]
10In a desert[z] land he found him,

31:28 [s]Dt 4:26; 30:19; 32:1; Job 20:27; Isa 26:21 **31:29** [t]S Dt 4:16; Rev 9:20 [u]1Ki 9:9; 22:23; 2Ki 22:16 **32:1** [v]Ps 49:1; Mic 1:2 [w]Jer 2:12 [x]S Dt 4:26 **32:2** [y]2Sa 23:4 [z]Ps 107:20; Isa 9:8; 55:11 [a]Mic 5:7 [b]Ps 65:10; 68:9; 72:6; 147:8 **32:3** [c]Ps 118:17; 145:6 [d]Ex 33:19; 34:5-6 [e]S Dt 3:24 **32:4** [f]S Ge 49:24 [g]2Sa 22:31; Ps 18:30; 19:7 [h]S Dt 4:35 [i]Ps 92:15 [j]S Ge 18:25 **32:5** [k]ver 20; Mt 17:17; Lk 9:41; Ac 2:40 **32:6** [l]Ps 116:12 [m]Ps 94:8; Jer 5:21 [n]ver 28 [o]S Ex 4:22; 2Sa 7:24 [p]ver 15 **32:7** [q]Ps 44:1; 74:2; 77:5; Isa 51:9; 63:9 [r]Dt 4:32; Job 8:8; 20:4; Ps 78:4; Isa 46:9 [s]S Ex 10:2; Job 15:18 **32:8** [t]Ps 7:8 [u]S Ge 11:8; Ac 8:1 [v]Ps 74:17 [w]Nu 23:9; Dt 33:12,28; Jer 23:6 **32:9** [x]Ps 16:5; 73:26; 119:57; 142:5; Jer 10:16 [y]S Dt 9:29; S 1Sa 26:19 **32:10** [z]S Dt 1:19

[m]5 Or *Corrupt are they and not his children, / a generation warped and twisted to their shame*
[n]6 Or *Father, who bought you*
[o]8 Masoretic Text; Dead Sea Scrolls (see also Septuagint) *sons of God*

32:2 EDUCATION, Moses—As the great interpreter of the Law, Moses was regarded as the teacher *par excellence* in Israel. "My teaching" ("my doctrine") means literally, "my taking." That is to say, the teachings of Moses were first "taken" from God on Mount Sinai. See Ex 19:2–3. These God-breathed teachings renewed the Israelites just as showers from heaven refresh the parched earth. As Israel's great teacher, Moses set an example not only for the Old Testament prophets, but for every person called to be a minister of the Word today. He took from God and gave vital, refreshing words to the people.

32:3 GOD, Nature—God is righteous, loving, wise, and powerful. He is patient, on the one hand, but on the other hand can be quick to oppose His adversaries. The God of Israel is so far above all other gods that He is in a class all by Himself: the one true God. This is the greatness of God, revealed in all His ways, in all His dealings with Israel. He is a loving heavenly Father to His people, without comparison. He does no wrong and is always faithful to His people.

32:5 SIN, Rebellion—A people blessed by God is not necessarily His people. When they rebel against Him, as did the children in the wilderness, they become shameful and crooked. Such people must bear responsibility for their rebellion. See note on Ex 14:11–12.

32:6 GOD, Father—This is one of the strongest declarations of the fatherhood of God in the Old Testament. Both here and in 32:18, it is suggested that since God created Israel, He is Israel's Father. This suggests to us, therefore, that God has a fatherly interest in all people inasmuch as He is Creator of all people. The idea of God as Creator tells us something about the wisdom, power, and authority of God. The idea of God as Father tells us something about the love and compassion of God for those whom He has created. Each idea logically leads to the other. Because God is Creator, He is Father to us. Because God is Father, He creates. See note on Mal 2:10.

32:6 CREATION, Redemption—The Creator created a people for Himself by purchasing or redeeming them from Egyptian slavery (Ex 15:16). Redemption is thus a new creation and leads to special titles for God. He is Creator (Hebrew *qanah*), a word with a wide range of meaning—give birth (Ge 4:1); buy (Ge 33:19); ransom, redeem, or buy back (Ne 5:8; Isa 11:11); get or acquire (Pr 4:5); create (Ge 14:19,22; Ps 139:13); or take over (Ps 78:54). He made Israel (Hebrew *'asah*) just as God made (Hebrew *'asah*) the expanse of the firmament (Ge 1:7), the heavenly bodies (Ge 1:16), and the animals (Ge 1:25). Similarly, God decided to make humans in the divine image (Ge 1:26). God also formed Israel (Hebrew *kun*) in the same way He formed a sanctuary or holy place of worship (Ex 15:17), David's dynasty (2 Sa 7:13), the authority and fame of Jerusalem (Isa 62:7), and as He founded the earth (Isa 45:18) and the heavens (Pr 3:19). People of God, as His chosen community, are a unique creation of God just as is the universe. We show our praise and gratitude to Him in worship.

32:8–9 ELECTION, Other Nations—The sovereign God is concerned with and guides the destiny of all nations and peoples. This shows the awesome nature of being selected out as God's elect inheritance chosen to represent Him among the nations.

32:10–12,36 GOD, Love—God found Israel in a barren, desert land with no one to care for her and called Israel to be His own chosen people. His blessings came to the nation in a remarkable and unlimited way. He was patient with His people. When everyone else abandoned her, God still cared for Israel and provided for her. He had a father's undying love for his children. He did not always approve of what His children did, but He always loved His children and stood ready to receive them when they turned back in repentance. Perhaps the deepest and most comprehensive word that can be said about God is that He is love, and that all of His actions are loving actions. God's love for His people does not mean that He is blind to their sins when they turn aside from Him. Nor does God's love mean that He never brings suffering to His people. The love of God means that God must chastise His people, on occasion, *because* He loves them. When God's love is

in a barren and howling waste.[a]
He shielded[b] him and cared for him;
he guarded him as the apple of his
eye,[c]
11like an eagle that stirs up its nest
and hovers over its young,[d]
that spreads its wings to catch them
and carries them on its pinions.[e]
12The LORD alone led[f] him;[g]
no foreign god was with him.[h]

13He made him ride on the heights[i] of
the land
and fed him with the fruit of the
fields.
He nourished him with honey from
the rock,[j]
and with oil[k] from the flinty crag,
14with curds and milk from herd and
flock
and with fattened lambs and goats,
with choice rams of Bashan[l]
and the finest kernels of wheat.[m]
You drank the foaming blood of the
grape.[n]

15Jeshurun[p][o] grew fat[p] and kicked;
filled with food, he became heavy
and sleek.
He abandoned[q] the God who made
him
and rejected the Rock[r] his Savior.
16They made him jealous[s] with their
foreign gods
and angered[t] him with their
detestable idols.
17They sacrificed[u] to demons,[v] which
are not God—
gods they had not known,[w]
gods that recently appeared,[x]
gods your fathers did not fear.
18You deserted the Rock, who fathered
you;
you forgot[y] the God who gave you
birth.

19The LORD saw this and rejected them[z]
because he was angered by his sons
and daughters.[a]
20"I will hide my face[b] from them," he
said,
"and see what their end will be;
for they are a perverse generation,[c]
children who are unfaithful.[d]
21They made me jealous[e] by what is no
god
and angered me with their worthless
idols.[f]
I will make them envious by those
who are not a people;
I will make them angry by a nation
that has no understanding.[g]

22For a fire has been kindled by my
wrath,[h]
one that burns to the realm of
death[q] below.[i]
It will devour[j] the earth and its
harvests[k]
and set afire the foundations of the
mountains.[l]

23"I will heap calamities[m] upon them
and spend my arrows[n] against
them.
24I will send wasting famine[o] against
them,
consuming pestilence[p] and deadly
plague;[q]
I will send against them the fangs of
wild beasts,[r]
the venom of vipers[s] that glide in
the dust.[t]
25In the street the sword will make them
childless;
in their homes terror[u] will reign.[v]
Young men and young women will
perish,
infants and gray-haired men.[w]
26I said I would scatter[x] them
and blot out their memory from
mankind,[y]
27but I dreaded the taunt of the enemy,
lest the adversary misunderstand[z]
and say, 'Our hand has triumphed;
the LORD has not done all this.'"[a]

28They are a nation without sense,
there is no discernment[b] in them.
29If only they were wise and would
understand this[c]
and discern what their end will be![d]
30How could one man chase a thousand,
or two put ten thousand to flight,[e]
unless their Rock had sold them,[f]
unless the LORD had given them
up?[g]
31For their rock is not like our Rock,[h]
as even our enemies concede.[i]
32Their vine comes from the vine of
Sodom[j]
and from the fields of Gomorrah.
Their grapes are filled with poison,[k]
and their clusters with bitterness.[l]
33Their wine is the venom of serpents,
the deadly poison of cobras.[m]

34"Have I not kept this in reserve

32:10 [a]Dt 8:15; Job 12:24; Ps 107:40 [b]Ps 32:10; Jer 31:22 [c]Ps 17:8; Pr 7:2; Hos 13:5; Zec 2:8 **32:11** [d]S Ex 19:4 [e]Ps 17:8; 18:10-19; 61:4 **32:12** [f]Ps 106:9; Isa 63:13; Jer 31:32 [g]Dt 4:35 [h]ver 39; Jdg 2:12; Ps 18:31; 81:9; Isa 43:12; 45:5 **32:13** [i]Dt 33:29; 2Sa 22:34; Ps 18:33; Isa 33:16; 58:14; Eze 36:2; Hab 3:19 [j]S Dt 8:8 [k]Dt 33:24; Job 29:6 **32:14** [l]S Nu 21:33 [m]Ps 65:9; 81:16; 147:14 [n]S Ge 49:11 **32:15** [o]Dt 33:5,26; Isa 44:2 [p]Dt 31:20; Jer 5:28 [q]Dt 31:16; Isa 1:4,28; 58:2; 65:11; Jer 15:6; Eze 14:5 [r]S Ge 49:24 **32:16** [s]S Nu 25:11; S 1Co 10:22 [t]S Dt 31:17; S 1Ki 14:9 **32:17** [u]S Ex 32:8 [v]S Ex 22:20; 1Co 10:20 [w]S Dt 28:64 [x]Jdg 5:8 **32:18** [y]Jdg 3:7; 1Sa 12:9; Ps 44:17, 20; 106:21; Jer 2:32; Eze 23:35; Hos 8:14; 13:6 **32:19** [z]Lev 26:30; Ps 78:59 [a]Am 6:8 **32:20** [b]Dt 31:17, 29; Ps 4:6; 44:24 [c]S ver 5 [d]Dt 9:23 **32:21** [e]S Nu 25:11; S 1Co 10:22 [f]ver 17; 1Ki 16:13, 26; 2Ki 17:15; Ps 31:6; Jer 2:5; 8:19; 10:8; 16:19; Jnh 2:8 [g]Ro 10:19* **32:22** [h]Ps 7:11 [i]Nu 16:31-35; Ps 18:7-8; Jer 15:14; La 4:11 [j]Am 7:4 [k]Lev 26:20 [l]Ps 83:14 **32:23** [m]S Dt 29:21 [n]ver 42; 2Sa 22:15; Job 6:4; Ps 7:13; 18:14; 45:5; 77:17; 120:4; Isa 5:28; 49:2; Eze 5:16; Hab 3:9,11 **32:24** [o]Ge 26:1; S 41:55; 42:5; 2Sa 24:13; 1Ch 21:12 [p]S Dt 28:22 [q]Ps 91:6 [r]S Ge 37:20 [s]ver 33; Job 20:16; Ps 58:4; Jer 8:17; Am 5:18-19; Mic 7:17 [t]Job 20:16 **32:25** [u]Isa 24:17 [v]Jer 14:18; La 1:20; Eze 7:15; 2Co 7:5 [w]2Ch 36:17; Isa 13:18; Jer 4:31; La 2:21 **32:26** [x]Dt 4:27 [y]S Nu 14:12; Job 18:17; Ps 34:16; 37:28; 109:15; Isa 14:20 **32:27** [z]Dt 9:26-28 [a]Ps 140:8; Isa 10:13; Jer 40:2-3 **32:28** [b]Isa 1:3; 5:13; 27:11; Jer 8:7 **32:29** [c]Dt 5:29; Ps 81:13 [d]Isa 47:7; La 1:9 **32:30** [e]S Lev 26:8 [f]Jdg 2:14; 3:8; 4:2; 10:7; 1Sa 12:9 [g]Nu 21:34; 1Sa 23:7; Ps 31:8; 44:12; 106:41; Isa 50:1; 54:6 **32:31** [h]S Ge 49:24 [i]S Ex 14:25 **32:32** [j]Jer 23:14 [k]Job 6:4; 20:16 [l]Dt 29:18 **32:33** [m]S ver 24

[p]*15 Jeshurun* means *the upright one*, that is, Israel.
[q]22 Hebrew to *Sheol*

expressed in wrath or judgment, it is always wrath from a broken heart of love and with a purpose of bringing His people to obedience and maturity.

32:20 SIN, Alienation—See notes on Nu 11:1; Dt 32:5.

and sealed it in my vaults?[n]
35 It is mine to avenge;[o] I will repay.[p]
In due time their foot will slip;[q]
their day of disaster is near
and their doom rushes upon
them.[r]"

36 The LORD will judge his people[s]
and have compassion[t] on his
servants[u]
when he sees their strength is gone
and no one is left, slave[v] or free.
37 He will say: "Now where are their
gods,
the rock they took refuge in,[w]
38 the gods who ate the fat of their
sacrifices
and drank the wine of their drink
offerings?[x]
Let them rise up to help you!
Let them give you shelter!

39 "See now that I myself am He![y]
There is no god besides me.[z]
I put to death[a] and I bring to life,[b]
I have wounded and I will heal,[c]
and no one can deliver out of my
hand.[d]
40 I lift my hand[e] to heaven and declare:
As surely as I live forever,[f]
41 when I sharpen my flashing sword[g]
and my hand grasps it in judgment,
I will take vengeance[h] on my
adversaries
and repay those who hate me.[i]
42 I will make my arrows drunk with
blood,[j]
while my sword devours flesh:[k]
the blood of the slain and the captives,
the heads of the enemy leaders."

43 Rejoice,[l] O nations, with his
people,[r],[s]
for he will avenge the blood of his
servants;[m]
he will take vengeance on his
enemies[n]
and make atonement for his land
and people.[o]

44 Moses came with Joshua[t][p] son of
Nun and spoke all the words of this song
in the hearing of the people. 45 When Moses finished reciting all these words to all
Israel, 46 he said to them, "Take to heart
all the words I have solemnly declared to
you this day,[q] so that you may command[r] your children to obey carefully all
the words of this law. 47 They are not just
idle words for you—they are your life.[s]
By them you will live long[t] in the land
you are crossing the Jordan to possess."

Moses to Die on Mount Nebo

48 On that same day the LORD told Moses,[u] 49 "Go up into the Abarim[v] Range
to Mount Nebo[w] in Moab, across from
Jericho,[x] and view Canaan,[y] the land I
am giving the Israelites as their own possession. 50 There on the mountain that
you have climbed you will die[z] and be
gathered to your people, just as your
brother Aaron died[a] on Mount Hor[b] and
was gathered to his people. 51 This is because both of you broke faith with me in
the presence of the Israelites at the waters of Meribah Kadesh[c] in the Desert of
Zin[d] and because you did not uphold my
holiness among the Israelites.[e] 52 Therefore, you will see the land only from a
distance;[f] you will not enter[g] the land I
am giving to the people of Israel."

Chapter 33

Moses Blesses the Tribes

33:1–29Ref — Ge 49:1–28

THIS is the blessing[h] that Moses the man of God[i] pronounced on the Israelites before his death. 2 He said:

"The LORD came from Sinai[j]
and dawned over them from Seir;[k]
he shone forth[l] from Mount
Paran.[m]
He came with[u] myriads of holy ones[n]
from the south, from his mountain
slopes.[v]

32:34 [n]Job 14:17; Jer 2:22; Hos 13:12 **32:35** [o]S ver 41; S Ge 4:24; S Jer 51:6 [p]S Ge 30:2; S Ex 32:34; S Ps 54:5; S Ro 12:19*; Heb 10:30* [q]Ps 17:5; 35:6; 37:31; 38:16; 66:9; 73:2,18; 94:18; 121:3; Pr 4:19; Jer 23:12 [r]Eze 7:8-9 **32:36** [s]Heb 10:30* [t]Am 7:3 [u]Lev 26:43-45; Dt 30:1-3; Jdg 2:18; Ps 90:13; 102:13; 103:13; 106:45; 135:14; Joel 2:14 [v]1Ki 14:10; 21:21; 2Ki 9:8 **32:37** [w]Jdg 10:14; Jer 2:28; 11:12 **32:38** [x]Nu 25:1-2; Jer 11:12; 44:8,25 **32:39** [y]Isa 41:4; 43:10; 44:7; 46:4; 48:12 [z]S ver 12 [a]1Sa 2:6 [b]1Sa 2:6; 2Ki 5:7; Ps 68:20; Jn 11:25-26 [c]Ex 15:26; Job 5:18; 15:11; Ps 147:3; Isa 6:10; 19:22; 30:26; 53:5; 57:18; Jer 33:6; Hos 6:1; Mal 4:2; 1Pe 2:24 [d]Job 9:12; 10:7; Ps 7:2; 50:22; Isa 43:13; Da 4:35; Hos 5:14 **32:40** [e]S Ge 14:22 [f]S Ge 21:33; Rev 1:18 **32:41** [g]Jdg 7:20; Ps 7:12; 45:3; Isa 27:1; 34:6; 66:16; Jer 12:12; Eze 21:9-10 [h]ver 35; Ps 149:7; Jer 46:10; Na 1:2 [i]Ps 137:8; Jer 25:14; 50:29; 51:24,56 **32:42** [j]S ver 23 [k]2Sa 2:26; Jer 12:12; 44:1; 46:10,14 **32:43** [l]Ps 137:6; Isa 25:9; 65:18; 66:10; Ro 15:10* [m]2Ki 9:7; S Rev 6:10 [n]Isa 1:24; Jer 9:9 [o]Ps 65:3; 79:9 **32:44** [p]Nu 13:8,16 **32:46** [q]S Dt 6:6; Jn 1:17; 7:19 [r]Dt 6:7 **32:47** [s]S Dt 30:20 [t]S Ex 23:26; Dt 33:25; Isa 65:22 **32:48** [u]Nu 27:12 **32:49** [v]Nu 27:12 [w]S Nu 32:3 [x]S Nu 22:1 [y]S Lev 14:34

32:50 [z]S Ge 25:8; S Nu 27:13 [a]Nu 20:29 [b]S Nu 20:22 **32:51** [c]Eze 47:19 [d]S Nu 13:21; 20:11-13 [e]Nu 27:14 **32:52** [f]Dt 34:1-3 [g]S Dt 3:27 **33:1** [h]S Ge 27:4 [i]Jos 14:6; 1Sa 2:27; 9:6; 1Ki 12:22; 13:1; 2Ki 1:9-13; 5:8; Jer 35:4 **33:2** [j]Ex 19:18; Ps 68:8 [k]Jos 11:17; Jdg 5:4 [l]Ps 50:2; 80:1; 94:1 [m]S Nu 10:12 [n]Ps 89:7; Da 4:13; 7:10; 8:13; Zec 14:5; Ac 7:53; Gal 3:19; Heb 2:2; Rev 5:11

[r] *43* Or *Make his people rejoice, O nations*
[s] *43* Masoretic Text; Dead Sea Scrolls (see also Septuagint) *people, / and let all the angels worship him /*
[t] *44* Hebrew *Hoshea*, a variant of *Joshua*
[u] *2* Or *from*
[v] *2* The meaning of the Hebrew for this phrase is uncertain.

32:48–52 HUMANITY, Relationship to God—The consequences of sin are not necessarily experienced immediately. Long-term consequences follow disobedience to God.

32:51 EVIL AND SUFFERING, Punishment—God has high expectations of His chosen leaders. They must face His punishment when they are unfaithful. Moses' sin involved discontent with God and publicly putting Him to the test. See note on Nu 20:12.

33:1–29 PRAYER, Blessing—Moses spoke like a patriarch. See note on Ge 49:1–28. As Jacob prepared a family to become a nation, so Moses prepared a nomadic nation to become a settled people and an international power. Such new identity had to come through God's blessing and direction. It called for application of old traditions and commitments to a new historical and sociological situation. Prayer prepares people to meet the future with God.

33:2 HISTORY, Presence—God's presence is an historical action. He comes to His people. God takes the initiative to be with His people. His people cannot passively find security in a place or time when we expect God to be present. God's coming signified His historical rule over His people and His right to determine their future.

3Surely it is you who love[o] the people;
all the holy ones are in your hand.[p]
At your feet they all bow down,[q]
and from you receive instruction,
4the law that Moses gave us,[r]
the possession of the assembly of
Jacob.[s]
5He was king[t] over Jeshurun[w][u]
when the leaders of the people
assembled,
along with the tribes of Israel.

6"Let Reuben live and not die,
nor[x] his men be few."[v]

7And this he said about Judah:[w]

"Hear, O LORD, the cry of Judah;
bring him to his people.
With his own hands he defends his
cause.
Oh, be his help against his foes!"

8About Levi[x] he said:

"Your Thummim and Urim[y] belong
to the man you favored.[z]
You tested[a] him at Massah;
you contended with him at the
waters of Meribah.[b]
9He said of his father and mother,[c]
'I have no regard for them.'
He did not recognize his brothers
or acknowledge his own children,
but he watched over your word
and guarded your covenant.[d]
10He teaches[e] your precepts to Jacob
and your law to Israel.[f]
He offers incense before you[g]
and whole burnt offerings on your
altar.[h]
11Bless all his skills, O LORD,
and be pleased with the work of his
hands.[i]
Smite the loins of those who rise up
against him;
strike his foes till they rise no
more."

12About Benjamin[j] he said:

"Let the beloved of the LORD rest
secure in him,[k]
for he shields him all day long,[l]
and the one the LORD loves[m] rests
between his shoulders."[n]

13About Joseph[o] he said:

"May the LORD bless his land
with the precious dew from heaven
above
and with the deep waters that lie
below;[p]

33:3 [o]S Dt 4:37 [p]Dt 7:6 [q]Lk 10:39; Rev 4:10
33:4 [r]Dt 4:2; Jn 1:17; 7:19 [s]Ps 119:111
33:5 [t]S Ex 16:8; 1Sa 10:19; Ps 10:16; 149:2 [u]S Nu 23:21; S Dt 32:15
33:6 [v]S Ge 34:5
33:7 [w]S Ge 49:10
33:8 [x]S Ge 29:34 [y]Ex 28:30 [z]Ps 106:16 [a]S Nu 14:22 [b]S Ex 17:7
33:9 [c]Ex 32:26-29 [d]Ps 61:5; Mal 2:5
33:10 [e]Ezr 7:10; Ne 8:18; Ps 119:151; Jer 23:22; Mal 2:6 [f]S Lev 10:11; Dt 17:8-11; 31:9-13 [g]S Ex 30:7; Lev 16:12-13 [h]Ps 51:19
33:11 [i]2Sa 24:23; Ps 20:3; 51:19
33:12 [j]S Ge 35:18 [k]Dt 4:37-38; 12:10; S 32:8 [l]S Ex 19:4 [m]Ps 60:5; 127:2; Isa 5:1 [n]S Ex 28:12
33:13 [o]S Ge 30:24 [p]Ge 27:28; Ps 148:7
33:15 [q]Hab 3:6
33:16 [r]S Ex 3:2 [s]S Ge 37:8
33:17 [t]1Sa 2:10; 2Sa 22:3; Eze 34:21 [u]S Nu 23:22 [v]1Ki 22:11; Ps 44:5 [w]S Ge 41:52 [x]S Ge 41:51
33:18 [y]S Ge 30:20 [z]S Ge 30:18
33:19 [a]S Ex 15:17; Ps 48:1; Isa 2:3; 65:11; 66:20; Jer 31:6 [b]Ps 4:5; 51:19 [c]Isa 18:7; 23:18; 45:14; 60:5, 11; 61:6; Hag 2:7; Zec 14:14
33:20 [d]Ge 30:11 [e]Dt 3:12-17
33:21 [f]Nu 32:1-5, 31-32 [g]S Nu 34:14 [h]Jos 22:1-3
33:22 [i]Ge 49:16; S Nu 1:38
33:23 [j]S Ge 30:8

14with the best the sun brings forth
and the finest the moon can yield;
15with the choicest gifts of the ancient
mountains[q]
and the fruitfulness of the
everlasting hills;
16with the best gifts of the earth and its
fullness
and the favor of him who dwelt in
the burning bush.[r]
Let all these rest on the head of
Joseph,
on the brow of the prince among[y]
his brothers.[s]
17In majesty he is like a firstborn bull;
his horns[t] are the horns of a wild
ox.[u]
With them he will gore[v] the nations,
even those at the ends of the earth.
Such are the ten thousands of
Ephraim;[w]
such are the thousands of
Manasseh."[x]

18About Zebulun[y] he said:

"Rejoice, Zebulun, in your going out,
and you, Issachar,[z] in your tents.
19They will summon peoples to the
mountain[a]
and there offer sacrifices of
righteousness;[b]
they will feast on the abundance of the
seas,[c]
on the treasures hidden in the
sand."

20About Gad[d] he said:

"Blessed is he who enlarges Gad's
domain![e]
Gad lives there like a lion,
tearing at arm or head.
21He chose the best land for himself;[f]
the leader's portion was kept for
him.[g]
When the heads of the people
assembled,
he carried out the LORD's righteous
will,[h]
and his judgments concerning
Israel."

22About Dan[i] he said:

"Dan is a lion's cub,
springing out of Bashan."

23About Naphtali[j] he said:

[w]5 *Jeshurun* means *the upright one,* that is, Israel; also in verse 26. [x]6 Or *but let* [y]16 Or *of the one separated from*

33:9 THE CHURCH, Covenant People—Like Levi, believers must keep the covenant relationship faithfully and serve God supremely. If family wishes conflict with our commitment to God, we must obey God for the ultimate good of the family.

33:10 EDUCATION, Priests—The priestly family of Levi served as leader of both worship and instruction. See note on Lev 10:11.

"Naphtali is abounding with the favor of the LORD
and is full of his blessing;
he will inherit southward to the lake."

24About Asher[k] he said:

"Most blessed of sons is Asher;
let him be favored by his brothers,
and let him bathe his feet in oil.[l]
25The bolts of your gates will be iron and bronze,[m]
and your strength will equal your days.[n]

26"There is no one like the God of Jeshurun,[o]
who rides[p] on the heavens to help you[q]
and on the clouds[r] in his majesty.[s]
27The eternal[t] God is your refuge,[u]
and underneath are the everlasting[v] arms.
He will drive out your enemy before you,[w]
saying, 'Destroy him!'[x]
28So Israel will live in safety alone;[y]
Jacob's spring is secure
in a land of grain and new wine,
where the heavens drop dew.[z]
29Blessed are you, O Israel![a]
Who is like you,[b]
a people saved by the LORD?[c]
He is your shield and helper[d]
and your glorious sword.
Your enemies will cower before you,
and you will trample down their high places.[z][e]"

Chapter 34

The Death of Moses

THEN Moses climbed Mount Nebo[f]
from the plains of Moab to the top of
Pisgah,[g] across from Jericho.[h] There the
LORD showed[i] him the whole land—
from Gilead to Dan,[j] 2all of Naphtali, the
territory of Ephraim and Manasseh, all
the land of Judah as far as the western
sea,[a][k] 3the Negev[l] and the whole region from the Valley of Jericho, the City
of Palms,[m] as far as Zoar.[n] 4Then the
LORD said to him, "This is the land I
promised on oath[o] to Abraham, Isaac and
Jacob[p] when I said, 'I will give it[q] to
your descendants.' I have let you see it
with your eyes, but you will not cross[r]
over into it."
5And Moses the servant of the LORD[s]
died[t] there in Moab, as the LORD had
said. 6He buried him[b] in Moab, in the
valley opposite Beth Peor,[u] but to this
day no one knows where his grave is.[v]
7Moses was a hundred and twenty years
old[w] when he died, yet his eyes were not
weak[x] nor his strength gone.[y] 8The Israelites grieved for Moses in the plains of
Moab[z] thirty days,[a] until the time of
weeping and mourning[b] was over.
9Now Joshua son of Nun was filled
with the spirit[c] of wisdom[c] because Moses had laid his hands on him.[d] So the
Israelites listened to him and did what
the LORD had commanded Moses.
10Since then, no prophet[e] has risen in
Israel like Moses,[f] whom the LORD knew
face to face,[g] 11who did all those miraculous signs and wonders[h] the LORD sent
him to do in Egypt—to Pharaoh and to all
his officials[i] and to his whole land. 12For
no one has[j] ever shown the mighty power or performed the awesome deeds[k]
that Moses did in the sight of all Israel.

33:24 [k]S Ge 30:13 [l]S Ge 49:20; S Dt 32:13 **33:25** [m]Ne 3:3; 7:3; Ps 147:13 [n]S Dt 32:47 **33:26** [o]S Dt 32:15 [p]Ps 18:10; 68:33 [q]S Dt 10:14; S Ps 104:3 [r]2Sa 22:10; Ps 18:9; 68:4; Da 7:13 [s]S Ex 15:7 **33:27** [t]Ex 15:18; Isa 40:28; 57:15 [u]Ps 9:9; 84:1; 90:1; 91:9 [v]S Ge 21:33 [w]Ex 34:11; Jos 24:18 [x]S Dt 7:2 **33:28** [y]S Ex 33:16; S Lev 25:18; S Dt 32:8; Ps 16:9; Pr 1:33; Isa 14:30 [z]ver 13; Ge 27:28 **33:29** [a]Ps 1:1; 32:1-2; 144:15 [b]2Sa 22:45; Ps 18:44; 66:3; 81:15 [c]Dt 4:7 [d]Ge 15:1; Ex 18:4; Ps 10:14; 18:1; 27:1,9; 30:10; 54:4; 70:5; 115:9-11; 118:7; Isa 45:24; Hos 13:9; Hab 3:19 [e]S Nu 33:52; S Dt 32:13 **34:1** [f]S Nu 32:3 [g]S Nu 21:20 [h]Dt 32:49 [i]Dt 32:52 [j]S Ge 14:14 **34:2** [k]S Ex 23:31 **34:3** [l]S Ge 12:9 [m]Jdg 1:16; 3:13; 2Ch 28:15 [n]S Ge 13:10 **34:4** [o]Ge 28:13 [p]Jos 21:43 [q]Ge 12:7 [r]S Dt 3:23 **34:5** [s]S Nu 12:7 [t]S Ge 25:8 **34:6** [u]S Dt 3:29 [v]Jude 1:9 **34:7** [w]S Ex 7:7 [x]S Ge 27:1 [y]S Ge 15:15 **34:8** [z]S Nu 21:11 [a]S Ge 37:34; S Dt 1:3 [b]2Sa 11:27 **34:9** [c]S Ge 41:38; S Ex 28:3; Isa 11:2 [d]S Dt 31:14; Ac 6:6 **34:10** [e]S Ge 20:7 [f]Dt 18:15,18 [g]S Ex 33:11 **34:11** [h]Dt 4:34 [i]S Ex 11:3 **34:12** [j]Heb 3:1-6 [k]S Dt 4:34

[z]*29* Or *will tread upon their bodies* [a]*2* That is, the Mediterranean [b]*6* Or *He was buried* [c]*9* Or *Spirit*

33:26–29 HISTORY, God—God's unique character becomes apparent as His people find refuge and hope in Him. God's saving acts give a unique identity to His people. History shows that God is the only reliable source of security.

33:29 ELECTION, Israel—God's saving work for Israel in Egypt distinguished them from all other people. The Exodus (Ex 14) showed Israel was the undeserving, elect people of God. The original act of election gave Israel confidence as she confronted other enemies. God's salvation is one of the unique identifying marks of His elect people.

34:9 HOLY SPIRIT, Leaders—The Spirit gave Joshua the gift of wisdom. This did not mean knowledge in the abstract, but the understanding, judgment, and insight which equipped Joshua to lead Israel. The Spirit is often associated with power which can sometimes be understood impersonally. He is the personal Spirit who shares wisdom with His people. Laying on hands was a way of giving a blessing (Ge 48:15–19) and was a sign that God had chosen Joshua to be Moses' successor. See note on Nu 27:15–21.

34:10–12 HISTORY, God's Leaders—To make Himself known to His people, God empowered human leaders to lead in historical acts and to interpret those acts as God's acts. God entrusted His revelation to human agents so other humans could identify with it, trust it, and witness to it. The greatest example of an historical agent of revelation for Israel was Moses, leader of the central event of Old Testament revelation—the Exodus.

34:10 PRAYER, Personal—See note on Ex 33:11–17. As the prophet like Moses, Jesus knew God in intimate prayer (Ac 3:22). Jesus as Son of God showed us God's face.

Joshua

Theological Setting

What should God's people learn from prosperity?

When the book of Joshua was written, the Israelites were living in Canaan, the country God gave them in fulfillment of the promises to Abraham, Isaac, and Jacob. Canaan was called the place of Israel's "rest" (Dt 12:9-10; Jos 1:13,15; Ps 95:11). God gave Israel a period of success and prosperity. As Israel enjoyed its rest and inheritance in fellowship with God in Canaan, God wanted to keep alive the memories of what He had done for His people in the past and to direct their hopes toward greater things yet to come. Past events in Israel had made it clear the people were prone to forget God's saving acts on their behalf. God wanted to prevent future generations from forgetting (Ex 17:14; Dt 31:9-13; Jer 30:1-3). The Book of Joshua itself enjoined parents to keep the memories alive among their children (Jos 4:21-24). The same concern prompted Joshua to write the details of the ceremony described in Jos 24:1-27.

Israel's history after Joshua proved how much the people needed a constant reminder of what God had done on their behalf. Again and again Israel disobeyed God and suffered punishment, invasion, and deprivation at the hands of its enemies because of its wrongdoings. At such desperate moments Israel could remember the past, plead for God's honor (7:9; Ps 79:5-10), and remind Him of past favors (Ps 89:49). Recalling God's deeds in the past gave Israel confidence that He would act on their behalf (Ps 60:6-12). In better times the believing community would use the events of the past as a theme of thanksgiving and praise (Ps 105:42-45).

Stories of success and prosperity also served as the foundation for warning and admonition. God used the lengthy story of Achan's transgression and his subsequent punishment (Jos 7) to teach that the Holy Land in which God let them live required allegiance on the part of the people (23:12-13).

Final aspects of the book's theological setting are its view toward the future for God's people and its eschatological dimension. The future orientation is best perceived in light of God's promise to Abraham that in him all the nations of the earth would be blessed (Ge 12:3). This promise pointed forward to Jesus Christ (Ac 3:25; cf. Ge 22:18; 26:4). It also looked backward to the first promise God ever gave to sinful humankind concerning the woman's "offspring" who would crush the serpent's head (Ge 3:15). For these reasons it was necessary for Israel to keep its eyes trained on the future. The initial enjoyment of the "inheritance" in Canaan should not blind them to the still greater glory that was to come. The "already" of the initial fulfillment of God's promise should be coupled with the "not yet" of future blessings. This is why the book, while stressing on the one hand the complete fulfillment of God's promises (Jos 21:43-45), also speaks of land not yet possessed (13:1). It is also the reason why the land's boundaries are given in their widest possible extent (1:4), an extent to which the kingdom hardly ever attained. Joshua is in some ways a programmatic book, a book that calls for further fulfillment. At a future time the inheritance would be even more fully possessed (Eze 45:1; 47:21,23; Eph 1:11; Col 1:12; 1 Pe 1:3-5; Rev 21:7). Aliens as well as the native Israelites would have a part in it (Eze 47:21-23).

Theological Outline

Joshua: Lessons for a Prosperous People

I. God Brought Victory to a People of the Book. (1:1—12:24)
   - A. To possess the promise, God's people must be faithful to the book. (1:1-18)
   - B. God uses unexpected persons to fulfill His promises. (2:1-24)
   - C. God exalts His leaders and proves His presence so all people may know Him. (3:1—4:24)
   - D. God's people must worship Him to prepare for the victories He promises. (5:1-15)
   - E. Divine power, not human might, provides victory for God's people. (6:1-27)
   - F. A disobedient people cannot expect God's victories. (7:1-26)
   - G. A repentant people receive a strategy for victory from God. (8:1-35)
   - H. Human cunning and disobedience cannot overcome the purposes of God. (9:1-27)

Chapter 1

The LORD Commands Joshua

AFTER the death of Moses the servant of
the LORD,[a] the LORD said to Joshua[b]
son of Nun, Moses' aide: 2"Moses my servant is dead. Now then, you and all these
people, get ready to cross the Jordan River[c][d] into the land[e] I am about to give to
them[f]—to the Israelites. 3I will give you
every place where you set your foot,[g] as I
promised Moses.[h] 4Your territory will extend from the desert to Lebanon,[i] and
from the great river, the Euphrates[j] —all
the Hittite[k] country—to the Great Sea[a]
on the west.[l] 5No one will be able to
stand up against you[m] all the days of your
life. As I was with[n] Moses, so I will be
with you; I will never leave you nor forsake[o] you.
6"Be strong[p] and courageous,[q] because you will lead these people to inherit the land I swore to their forefathers[r] to
give them. 7Be strong and very courageous. Be careful to obey[s] all the law[t]
my servant Moses[u] gave you; do not turn
from it to the right or to the left,[v] that
you may be successful wherever you go.[w]
8Do not let this Book of the Law[x] depart
from your mouth;[y] meditate[z] on it day
and night, so that you may be careful to
do everything written in it. Then you will
be prosperous and successful.[a] 9Have I
not commanded you? Be strong and courageous. Do not be terrified;[b] do not be
discouraged,[c] for the LORD your God will
be with you wherever you go."[d]
10So Joshua ordered the officers of the
people:[e] 11"Go through the camp[f] and
tell the people, 'Get your supplies[g]
ready. Three days[h] from now you will
cross the Jordan[i] here to go in and take
possession[j] of the land the LORD your
God is giving you for your own.' "
12But to the Reubenites, the Gadites
and the half-tribe of Manasseh,[k] Joshua
said, 13"Remember the command that
Moses the servant of the LORD gave you:
'The LORD your God is giving you rest[l]
and has granted you this land.' 14Your
wives,[m] your children and your livestock
may stay in the land[n] that Moses gave
you east of the Jordan, but all your fighting men, fully armed,[o] must cross over
ahead of your brothers.[p] You are to help
your brothers 15until the LORD gives them
rest, as he has done for you, and until
they too have taken possession of the
land that the LORD your God is giving
them. After that, you may go back and
occupy your own land, which Moses the
servant of the LORD gave you east of the
Jordan toward the sunrise."[q]
16Then they answered Joshua, "Whatever you have commanded us we will do,
and wherever you send us we will go.[r]
17Just as we fully obeyed Moses, so we
will obey you.[s] Only may the LORD your
God be with you as he was with Moses.
18Whoever rebels against your word and
does not obey[t] your words, whatever
you may command them, will be put to
death. Only be strong and courageous![u]"

Chapter 2

Rahab and the Spies

THEN Joshua son of Nun secretly sent
two spies[v] from Shittim.[w] "Go, look
over[x] the land," he said, "especially Jericho.[y]" So they went and entered the

1:1 [a]Ex 14:31; Dt 34:5; Rev 15:3 [b]S Ex 17:9 **1:2** [c]S Nu 13:29 [d]S Nu 35:10 [e]S Ge 15:14 [f]Ge 12:7; Dt 1:25 **1:3** [g]S Dt 11:24 [h]Ge 50:24; Nu 13:2; Dt 1:8 **1:4** [i]S Dt 3:25 [j]S Ge 2:14 [k]S Ge 10:15; 23:10; Ex 3:8 [l]Nu 34:2-12; Ezr 4:20 **1:5** [m]S Dt 7:24 [n]ver 17; S Ge 26:3; S 39:2; Jdg 6:12; 1Sa 10:7; Jer 1:8; 30:11 [o]S Ge 28:15; S Dt 4:31 **1:6** [p]2Sa 2:7; 1Ki 2:2; Isa 41:6; Joel 3:9-10 [q]S Dt 1:21; S 31:6; S Jdg 5:21 [r]Jer 3:18; 7:7 **1:7** [s]Dt 29:9; 1Ki 2:3; 3:3 [t]Ezr 7:26; Ps 78:10; 119:136; Isa 42:24; Jer 26:4-6; 32:23; 44:10 [u]ver 2,15; S Nu 12:7; Job 1:8; 42:7 [v]S Dt 5:32; Jos 23:6 [w]ver 9; S Dt 4:2; 5:33; S 11:8; Jos 11:15 **1:8** [x]S Dt 28:61; S Ps 147:19 [y]S Ex 4:15; Isa 59:21 [z]S Ge 24:63 [a]Dt 29:9; 1Sa 18:14; Ps 1:1-3; Isa 52:13; 53:10; Jer 23:5 **1:9** [b]S Dt 31:6; Jos 10:8; 2Ki 19:6; Isa 35:4; 37:6 [c]S Dt 1:21; Job 4:5 [d]S ver 7; Dt 31:7-8; Jer 1:8 **1:10** [e]S Dt 1:15 **1:11** [f]Jos 3:2 [g]1Sa 17:22; Isa 10:28 [h]S Ge 40:13 [i]S Nu 35:10 [j]S Nu 33:53 **1:12** [k]Nu 32:33 **1:13** [l]S Ex 33:14; Ps 55:6; Isa 11:10; 28:12; 30:15; 32:18; 40:31; Jer 6:16; 45:3; La 5:5 **1:14** [m]Dt 3:19 [n]S Nu 32:26 [o]S Ex 13:18 [p]Jos 4:12 **1:15** [q]Nu 32:20-22; Jos 22:1-4 **1:16** [r]S Nu 27:20; S 32:25 **1:17** [s]S Nu 27:20 **1:18** [t]S Nu 32:25 [u]S Dt 1:21; S 31:6 **2:1** [v]S ver 4; S Ge 42:9 [w]S Nu 25:1; Jos 3:1; Joel 3:18 [x]S Nu 21:32; Jdg 18:2 [y]S Nu 33:48

[a]4 That is, the Mediterranean

1:1–11 HISTORY, God's Leaders—After Moses, historical leadership for Israel acted in the shadow of Moses and the written "Book of the Law." God's presence was described in terms of His presence with Moses. Moses' leadership, however, was not the end of revelation in history. Great tasks faced Joshua and succeeding leaders as they led Israel to occupy the land and adjust to life in it. To accomplish the tasks, leaders needed God's presence and knowledge of God's written Word. These continue to be the sources of revelation as God's people face historical existence.

1:2–3 SALVATION, Grace—The gift of the Promised Land of Palestine to Israel was an indication of God's grace. So was His provision of Joshua to succeed Moses.

1:3 ELECTION, Leadership—See note on Dt 3:26–28. The election of Joshua to succeed Moses carried the assurance of God's presence and the promise of victory. No enemy would be able to resist Joshua and Israel. Compare Dt 11:24–25.

1:5–9 HOLY SCRIPTURE, Obedience—Each generation needs God's revelation, but each cannot experience the unique events and teachings firsthand. The written form of revelation enables new generations to learn God's revelation and gain strength and courage from it. To know God's revealed Word requires reading it daily and relying on the strength of God's presence to practice the Word.

1:6 GOD, Faithfulness—As Joshua assumed leadership, God renewed His promise. God would demonstrate His faithfulness to His promises by bringing His people into their long awaited homeland. Whereas New Testament people look forward to a heavenly home, as promised by Jesus, these Old Testament people saw the ultimate blessing from God to be an earthly home. God faithfully provided this for them. That is His nature—a God overflowing with faithfulness and love.

1:7–9 HUMANITY, Relationship to God—People are expected to obey the commands of God as a basis for living a successful life. God's commandments establish the basis for doing with confidence the tasks to which He has called us. The strength both to obey and to live comes from God Himself.

1:7 CHRISTIAN ETHICS, Character—Following God's guidelines for character includes acting with resolve and courage. Courage as a biblical virtue has parallels in perseverance, consistency, and forthrightness. God's inspired Word is the source for building godly character. See note on Dt 6:24–25.

1:12–18 HISTORY, God's People—See note on Nu 32:1–42.

house of a prostitute[b] named Rahab[z]
and stayed there.
2The king of Jericho was told, "Look!
Some of the Israelites have come here tonight to spy out the land." 3So the king of
Jericho sent this message to Rahab:[a]
"Bring out the men who came to you and
entered your house, because they have
come to spy out the whole land."
4But the woman had taken the two
men[b] and hidden them.[c] She said, "Yes,
the men came to me, but I did not know
where they had come from. 5At dusk,
when it was time to close the city gate,[d]
the men left. I don't know which way
they went. Go after them quickly. You
may catch up with them."[e] 6(But she had
taken them up to the roof and hidden
them under the stalks of flax[f] she had
laid out on the roof.)[g] 7So the men set
out in pursuit of the spies on the road
that leads to the fords of the Jordan,[h] and
as soon as the pursuers[i] had gone out,
the gate was shut.
8Before the spies lay down for the
night, she went up on the roof[j] 9and said
to them, "I know that the LORD has given
this land to you and that a great fear[k] of
you has fallen on us, so that all who live
in this country are melting in fear because of you. 10We have heard how the
LORD dried up[l] the water of the Red
Sea[c] for you when you came out of
Egypt,[m] and what you did to Sihon and
Og,[n] the two kings of the Amorites[o] east
of the Jordan,[p] whom you completely destroyed.[d][q] 11When we heard of it, our
hearts melted[r] and everyone's courage
failed[s] because of you,[t] for the LORD
your God[u] is God in heaven above and
on the earth[v] below. 12Now then, please
swear to me[w] by the LORD that you will
show kindness[x] to my family, because I
have shown kindness to you. Give me a
sure sign[y] 13that you will spare the lives
of my father and mother, my brothers and
sisters, and all who belong to them,[z] and
that you will save us from death."
14"Our lives for your lives!"[a] the men
assured her. "If you don't tell what we
are doing, we will treat you kindly and

2:1 [z]Jos 6:17,25; S Heb 11:31 **2:3** [a]Jos 6:23 **2:4** [b]ver 1; Jos 6:22 [c]Jos 6:17 **2:5** [d]Jdg 5:8; 9:35; 16:2 [e]S Heb 11:31 **2:6** [f]Jdg 15:14; Pr 31:13; Isa 19:9 [g]S Ex 1:17,19; Jos 6:25; 2Sa 17:19 **2:7** [h]Nu 22:1; Jdg 3:28; 7:24; 12:5,6; Isa 16:2 [i]ver 16,22 **2:8** [j]S Dt 22:8; Jdg 16:27; 2Sa 16:22; Ne 8:16; Isa 15:3; 22:1; Jer 32:29 **2:9** [k]S Ge 35:5; S Ex 15:14 **2:10** [l]S Ge 8:1; Ex 14:21; Jos 3:17; Ps 74:15 [m]S Nu 23:22 [n]S Nu 21:21 [o]S Ge 10:16; S 14:7 [p]Jos 9:10 [q]S Nu 21:2 **2:11** [r]S Ge 42:28 [s]S Dt 2:25; Ps 107:26; Jnh 1:5 [t]Ex 15:14; Jos 5:1; 7:5; 2Sa 4:1; Ps 22:14; Isa 13:7; 19:1; Jer 51:30; Na 2:10 [u]2Ki 5:15; 19:15; Da 6:26 [v]S Ge 14:19; S Nu 20:14 **2:12** [w]S Ge 24:8; S 47:31 [x]S Ge 24:12; Ru 3:10 [y]S Ge 24:14; S Ex 3:12; Jos 4:6; 1Sa 2:34; 2Ki 19:29 **2:13** [z]ver 18; Jos 6:23 **2:14** [a]1Ki 20:39, 42; 2Ki 10:24 [b]S Ge 47:29 **2:15** [c]Jer 38:6,11 [d]ver 18,21; Ge 26:8; Jdg 5:28; 1Sa 19:12 **2:16** [e]S Ge 14:10 [f]S ver 7 [g]ver 22 [h]S Heb 11:31 **2:17** [i]S Ge 24:8 **2:18** [j]ver 21 [k]S ver 15 [l]S ver 13 **2:19** [m]S Lev 20:9 [n]Mt 27:25 **2:20** [o]S Ge 24:8; S 47:31 **2:21** [p]ver 18 [q]S ver 15 **2:22** [r]ver 16 [s]S ver 7 **2:24** [t]Jos 10:8; 11:6; Jdg 3:28; 7:9, 14; 20:28; 1Sa 14:10 [u]S Ex 15:15 **3:1** [v]S Jos 2:1

faithfully[b] when the LORD gives us the
land."
15So she let them down by a rope[c]
through the window,[d] for the house she
lived in was part of the city wall. 16Now
she had said to them, "Go to the hills[e] so
the pursuers[f] will not find you. Hide
yourselves there three days[g] until they
return, and then go on your way."[h]
17The men said to her, "This oath[i]
you made us swear will not be binding on
us 18unless, when we enter the land, you
have tied this scarlet cord[j] in the window[k] through which you let us down,
and unless you have brought your father
and mother, your brothers and all your
family[l] into your house. 19If anyone goes
outside your house into the street, his
blood will be on his own head;[m] we will
not be responsible. As for anyone who is
in the house with you, his blood will be
on our head[n] if a hand is laid on him.
20But if you tell what we are doing, we
will be released from the oath you made
us swear.[o]"
21"Agreed," she replied. "Let it be as
you say." So she sent them away and they
departed. And she tied the scarlet cord[p]
in the window.[q]
22When they left, they went into the
hills and stayed there three days,[r] until
the pursuers[s] had searched all along the
road and returned without finding them.
23Then the two men started back. They
went down out of the hills, forded the
river and came to Joshua son of Nun and
told him everything that had happened to
them. 24They said to Joshua, "The LORD
has surely given the whole land into our
hands;[t] all the people are melting in
fear[u] because of us."

Chapter 3

Crossing the Jordan

EARLY in the morning Joshua and all
the Israelites set out from Shittim[v]

[b]*1* Or possibly *an innkeeper* [c]*10* Hebrew *Yam Suph*; that is, Sea of Reeds [d]*10* The Hebrew term refers to the irrevocable giving over of things or persons to the LORD, often by totally destroying them.

2:9 ELECTION, Other Nations—Fear had come to Jericho. Not only were the people of Jericho aware of the military might of Israel, but also they knew that Israel's God was fighting for them. Even Rahab could testify that Israel was a people who enjoyed the election of God, Lord of heaven and earth. The world will recognize the moral and spiritual authority of persons chosen by God for witness and work on God's agenda.

2:10–11 HISTORY, Universal—The revelation in God's historical acts was not confined to Israel. Canaanites heard the news and reacted in fear. Some, like Rahab, became true believers. Compare Heb 11:31; Jas 2:25. Historical revelation allows knowledge of God to be accessible to people far beyond a select group with secret information.

2:11 GOD, Power—The mighty actions of God in delivering His people from captivity convinced pagan inhabitants as well as the Israelites of the power of God. Even foreigners learned that Yahweh, the God of Israel, is a God above all other gods. Yahweh could do something the gods of the people could not do. How much Rahab and others around her really understood Yahweh as the only true God, and the utter emptiness and vanity of the other gods, we cannot tell. At least, they clearly recognized that no other god could compare in might with the God of the Israelites. The inspired Word of God clearly teaches that other gods are no more than false ideas of the mind or creations of the hands. Neither heavenly bodies nor earthly materials or objects can claim any divine power.

3:1–17 MIRACLE, Revelation—Miracles let God's people

and went to the Jordan,[w] where they
camped before crossing over. 2After three
days[x] the officers[y] went throughout the
camp,[z] 3giving orders to the people:
"When you see the ark of the covenant[a]
of the LORD your God, and the priests,[b]
who are Levites,[c] carrying it, you are to
move out from your positions and follow
it. 4Then you will know which way to go,
since you have never been this way before. But keep a distance of about a thousand yards[e][d] between you and the ark;
do not go near it."

5Joshua told the people, "Consecrate
yourselves,[e] for tomorrow the LORD will
do amazing things[f] among you."

6Joshua said to the priests, "Take up
the ark of the covenant and pass on ahead
of the people." So they took it up and
went ahead of them.

7And the LORD said to Joshua, "Today I
will begin to exalt you[g] in the eyes of all
Israel, so they may know that I am with
you as I was with Moses.[h] 8Tell the
priests[i] who carry the ark of the covenant: 'When you reach the edge of the
Jordan's waters, go and stand in the
river.' "

9Joshua said to the Israelites, "Come
here and listen to the words of the LORD
your God. 10This is how you will know
that the living God[j] is among you[k] and
that he will certainly drive out before
you the Canaanites, Hittites,[l] Hivites,
Perizzites,[m] Girgashites, Amorites and
Jebusites.[n] 11See, the ark of the covenant
of the Lord of all the earth[o] will go into
the Jordan ahead of you.[p] 12Now then,
choose twelve men[q] from the tribes of
Israel, one from each tribe. 13And as soon
as the priests who carry the ark of the
LORD—the Lord of all the earth[r]—set
foot in the Jordan, its waters flowing
downstream[s] will be cut off[t] and stand
up in a heap.[u]"

14So when the people broke camp to
cross the Jordan, the priests carrying the
ark of the covenant[v] went ahead[w] of
them. 15Now the Jordan[x] is at flood
stage[y] all during harvest.[z] Yet as soon as
the priests who carried the ark reached
the Jordan and their feet touched the water's edge, 16the water from upstream
stopped flowing.[a] It piled up in a heap[b] a
great distance away, at a town called
Adam in the vicinity of Zarethan,[c] while
the water flowing down[d] to the Sea of
the Arabah[e] (the Salt Sea[f][f]) was completely cut off.[g] So the people crossed
over opposite Jericho.[h] 17The priests[i]
who carried the ark of the covenant of
the LORD stood firm on dry ground in the
middle of the Jordan,[j] while all Israel
passed by until the whole nation had
completed the crossing on dry ground.[k]

3:1 [w]S Ge 13:10; Job 40:23 **3:2** [x]S Ge 40:13; Jos 2:16 [y]S Dt 1:15 [z]Jos 1:11 **3:3** [a]S Nu 10:33 [b]ver 8,17; Nu 4:15; Dt 31:9; 1Ki 8:3 [c]1Sa 6:15 **3:4** [d]Nu 35:5 **3:5** [e]S Ex 29:1; S Lev 11:44 [f]Jdg 6:13; 1Ch 16:9,24; Ps 26:7; 75:1 **3:7** [g]Jos 4:14; 1Ch 29:25 [h]Jos 1:5 **3:8** [i]S ver 3 **3:10** [j]Dt 5:26; 1Sa 17:26,36; 2Ki 19:4,16; Ps 18:46; 42:2; 84:2; Isa 37:4,17; Jer 10:10; 23:36; Da 6:26; Hos 1:10; S Mt 16:16 [k]S Dt 7:21 [l]S Ge 26:34 [m]Jos 17:15; 24:11; Jdg 1:4; 3:5 [n]S Ex 3:8; S 23:23; S Dt 7:1; Jos 9:1; 11:3; 12:8; Jdg 19:11; 1Ch 11:4 **3:11** [o]ver 13; Ex 19:5; Dt 10:14; Job 9:10; 28:24; 41:11; Ps 50:12; 97:5; Zec 6:5 [p]S Dt 9:3 **3:12** [q]Jos 4:2,4 **3:13** [r]S ver 11 [s]ver 16 [t]Jos 4:7 [u]S Ex 14:22; S Isa 11:15 **3:14** [v]Ps 132:8 [w]Ac 7:44-45 **3:15** [x]2Ki 2:6 [y]Jos 4:18; 1Ch 12:15; Isa 8:7 [z]S Ge 8:22 **3:16** [a]Ps 66:6; 74:15; 114:3 [b]Job 38:37; Ps 33:7 [c]1Ki 4:12; 7:46 [d]ver 13 [e]S Dt 1:1 [f]S Ge 14:3 [g]S Ge 8:1; S Ex 14:22 [h]2Ki 2:4 **3:17** [i]S ver 3 [j]Jos 4:3,5,8,9,10 [k]S Ex 14:22; S Jos 2:10

[e]*4* Hebrew *about two thousand cubits* (about 900 meters) [f]*16* That is, the Dead Sea

---

know God is present with us. They show the spiritual leader is God's choice. They give God's people courage to face the task God has set out. The miracle at the Jordan reassured a people facing the monumental task of conquering enemy land that the "living God" was present with them and would lead them to victory. The huge Jordan flow was a seasonal occurrence caused by the melting snows of Mount Hermon. In more normal seasons, the Jordan would have been more easily fordable. God chose this season to act to impress His people with His power. At other times in history, the flooding Jordan has been blocked by landslides produced by earthquakes. God may have used such an event to produce this miracle. The Bible does not try to describe the details of how God acted. It testifies that in the hour of great need God acted miraculously to lead His people and to encourage and empower them. He showed He can use the forces of nature to reveal Himself and to bring His salvation.

3:1–17 HISTORY, Deliverance—Historical deliverance extended beyond Moses and the Exodus. The Jordan crossing gave a new generation concrete evidence of God's presence and a basis for trust that God would lead them to conquer the land.

3:4 GOD, Holy—The Israelites were not to try to erase the qualitative difference between themselves as sinful human beings and the holy God who occupies a unique category of existence. God would be with them in the ark. They were not to take God or His presence for granted. They must not think that God was simply their possession, like the gods possessed by the foreigners around them. The Israelites could not simply pack God in their luggage and move Him with them when they decided to move. They, instead, had to follow God obediently as He chose to lead. They must follow at a respectful distance. They must not seek to relate to God in a presumptuous manner. These ancient instructions ought to remind us of the vast difference between God and ourselves. We too must approach God with fear and respect, seeking to obey and honor Him. He is no more our private possession than He was the good luck charm of the ancient Israelites. He is the holy God who towers above His people.

3:7–17 REVELATION, Events—A new generation needs new God-chosen leadership. God installed Joshua in the office (Nu 27:12–23; Dt 1:38; 3:28; 31:1–8,14–15,23; 34:9; Jos 1:1–9). God confirmed Joshua's calling through a private promise of His presence and through the divine action allowing Israel to cross the Jordan. God's words and acts combined to validate Joshua's office and to reveal God's power as the only "living God" (v 10). History often reveals God's message through specific meaningful events. Such events must be interpreted in character with God's nature and purposes (2 Ti 2:16–19).

3:10–13 GOD, Living—Joshua reminded Israel that their God is a living God, in contrast to the idols of the nations. God leads His people and demonstrates His power for all to see. When the ark of the covenant, the symbol of the presence of God, was carried into the waters of the Jordan River, the waters parted and the people crossed on dry ground. This served as a vivid reminder of the miraculous crossing of the Red Sea in the Exodus from Egypt. God's people need to remember that He is a living God, actively involved in providing for the needs of His people when they are faithful to Him. He is not just an idea created in the human mind and given expression through an artisan's handiwork. Nor is He simply an underlying principle or force in the world, like gravity. He is alive and personal with awareness of what is going on and with the power to work in His world.

Chapter 4

WHEN the whole nation had finished
crossing the Jordan,[l] the LORD
said to Joshua, 2“Choose twelve men[m]
from among the people, one from each
tribe, 3and tell them to take up twelve
stones[n] from the middle of the Jordan[o]
from right where the priests stood and to
carry them over with you and put them
down at the place where you stay tonight.[p]”
4So Joshua called together the twelve
men[q] he had appointed from the Israelites, one from each tribe, 5and said to
them, “Go over before the ark of the
LORD your God into the middle of the Jordan.[r] Each of you is to take up a stone on
his shoulder, according to the number of
the tribes of the Israelites, 6to serve as a
sign[s] among you. In the future, when
your children[t] ask you, ‘What do these
stones mean?’[u] 7tell them that the flow
of the Jordan was cut off[v] before the ark
of the covenant of the LORD. When it
crossed the Jordan, the waters of the Jordan were cut off. These stones are to
be a memorial[w] to the people of Israel
forever.”
8So the Israelites did as Joshua commanded them. They took twelve stones[x]
from the middle of the Jordan,[y] according to the number of the tribes of the
Israelites, as the LORD had told Joshua;[z]
and they carried them over with them to
their camp, where they put them down.
9Joshua set up the twelve stones[a] that
had been[g] in the middle of the Jordan at
the spot where the priests who carried
the ark of the covenant had stood. And
they are there to this day.[b]
10Now the priests who carried the ark
remained standing in the middle of the
Jordan until everything the LORD had
commanded Joshua was done by the people, just as Moses had directed Joshua.
The people hurried over, 11and as soon as
all of them had crossed, the ark of the
LORD and the priests came to the other
side while the people watched. 12The
men of Reuben,[c] Gad[d] and the half-tribe
of Manasseh[e] crossed over, armed, in
front of the Israelites,[f] as Moses had directed them.[g] 13About forty thousand
armed for battle[h] crossed over[i] before
the LORD to the plains of Jericho for war.
14That day the LORD exalted[j] Joshua in
the sight of all Israel; and they revered
him all the days of his life, just as they
had revered Moses.
15Then the LORD said to Joshua,
16“Command the priests carrying the ark
of the Testimony[k] to come up out of the
Jordan.”
17So Joshua commanded the priests,
“Come up out of the Jordan.”
18And the priests came up out of the
river carrying the ark of the covenant of
the LORD. No sooner had they set their
feet on the dry ground than the waters of
the Jordan returned to their place[l] and
ran at flood stage[m] as before.
19On the tenth day of the first month
the people went up from the Jordan and
camped at Gilgal[n] on the eastern border
of Jericho. 20And Joshua set up at Gilgal
the twelve stones[o] they had taken out of
the Jordan. 21He said to the Israelites, “In
the future when your descendants ask
their fathers, ‘What do these stones
mean?’[p] 22tell them, ‘Israel crossed the
Jordan on dry ground.’[q] 23For the LORD
your God dried up the Jordan before you
until you had crossed over. The LORD
your God did to the Jordan just what he
had done to the Red Sea[h] when he dried
it up before us until we had crossed
over.[r] 24He did this so that all the peoples of the earth might know[s] that the
hand of the LORD is powerful[t] and so that
you might always fear the LORD your
God.[u]”

4:1 [l]Dt 27:2
4:2 [m]S Jos 3:12
4:3 [n]ver 20 [o]S Jos 3:17 [p]ver 19
4:4 [q]S Jos 3:12
4:5 [r]S Jos 3:17
4:6 [s]S Jos 2:12 [t]S Ex 10:2 [u]ver 21; Ex 12:26; S 13:14
4:7 [v]Jos 3:13 [w]S Ex 28:12
4:8 [x]Ex 28:21 [y]S Jos 3:17 [z]ver 20
4:9 [a]S Ge 28:18; Jos 24:26; 1Sa 7:12 [b]S Ge 35:20
4:12 [c]S Ge 29:32 [d]S Ge 30:11 [e]S Ge 41:51 [f]S Nu 32:27 [g]Nu 32:29
4:13 [h]S Ex 13:18 [i]S Nu 32:17
4:14 [j]S Jos 3:7
4:16 [k]Ex 25:22
4:18 [l]Ex 14:27 [m]S Jos 3:15
4:19 [n]S Dt 11:30
4:20 [o]ver 3,8
4:21 [p]S ver 6
4:22 [q]S Ex 14:22
4:23 [r]Ex 14:19-22
4:24 [s]1Ki 8:60; 18:36; 2Ki 5:15; Ps 67:2; 83:18; 106:8; Isa 37:20; 52:10 [t]Ex 15:16; 1Ch 29:12; Ps 44:3; 89:13; 98:1; 118:15-16 [u]S Ex 14:31

[g]9 Or *Joshua also set up twelve stones*
[h]23 Hebrew *Yam Suph;* that is, Sea of Reeds

4:1–24 HISTORY, Confession—Historical revelation has meaning beyond the generation which experiences the divine act of deliverance. Israel established memorials to cause them to remember and meditate on God's acts. They formulated teaching confessions to pass on through the generations and keep the memory and meaning of God's acts alive.

4:4–7 EDUCATION, Object Lessons—Even a mound of stones, used as an object lesson, can serve as an effective aid to learning the lessons of faith. The stones taken from the bed of the Jordan River to commemorate Israel's crossing over into the Land of Promise became a powerful teaching tool for future generations. In every age, the people of God have tangible reminders of the Lord's guidance and deliverance—a family homestead, a much-used place of prayer, a tattered Bible, a pocket-sized New Testament carried through a war, a country church house, a hospital where God's healing mercy was experienced. Such memorials can provide vivid lessons in the providential work of a living Lord. See 22:26–28.

4:20–24 REVELATION, Events—A physical monument can be God's instrument of revelation. God had a stone memorial set up so Israelite parents and teachers could instruct new generations about the great event by which God brought Israel into the Promised Land. Twelve stones on dry ground were constant reminders that God keeps His promises and purposes faithfully. This event was not limited in its significance to Israel. It showed God's ultimate goal of making Himself known to all peoples of the earth.

4:24 GOD, One God—God sometimes acts dramatically in His world so that others who look with a degree of sensitivity and perceptiveness will recognize Him as Lord. His actions as Israel entered the Promised Land were a mighty reminder of His previous actions at the Red Sea. If one looks about for evidence of God, it is not hard to see God's hand in many things. God does not wish to remain a mystery. Rather, He wishes to reveal Himself as the one true God to all people.

4:24 HISTORY, Universal—See note on 2:10–11.

Chapter 5

Circumcision at Gilgal

NOW when all the Amorite kings west
of the Jordan and all the Canaanite
kings along the coast[v] heard how the
LORD had dried up the Jordan before the
Israelites until we had crossed over, their
hearts melted[w] and they no longer had
the courage to face the Israelites.
2At that time the LORD said to Joshua,
"Make flint knives[x] and circumcise[y] the
Israelites again." 3So Joshua made flint
knives and circumcised the Israelites at
Gibeath Haaraloth.[1]
4Now this is why he did so: All those
who came out of Egypt—all the men of
military age[z]—died in the desert on the
way after leaving Egypt.[a] 5All the people
that came out had been circumcised, but
all the people born in the desert during
the journey from Egypt had not. 6The Israelites had moved about in the desert[b]
forty years[c] until all the men who were
of military age when they left Egypt had
died, since they had not obeyed the LORD.
For the LORD had sworn to them that they
would not see the land that he had solemnly promised their fathers to give us,[d]
a land flowing with milk and honey.[e] 7So
he raised up their sons in their place, and
these were the ones Joshua circumcised.
They were still uncircumcised because
they had not been circumcised on the
way. 8And after the whole nation had
been circumcised, they remained where
they were in camp until they were
healed.[f]
9Then the LORD said to Joshua, "Today
I have rolled away the reproach of Egypt
from you." So the place has been called
Gilgal[1][g] to this day.
10On the evening of the fourteenth day
of the month,[h] while camped at Gilgal on
the plains of Jericho, the Israelites celebrated the Passover.[i] 11The day after the
Passover, that very day, they ate some of
the produce of the land:[j] unleavened
bread[k] and roasted grain.[l] 12The manna
stopped the day after[k] they ate this food
from the land; there was no longer any
manna for the Israelites, but that year
they ate of the produce of Canaan.[m]

The Fall of Jericho

13Now when Joshua was near Jericho,
he looked up and saw a man[n] standing in
front of him with a drawn sword[o] in his
hand. Joshua went up to him and asked,
"Are you for us or for our enemies?"
14"Neither," he replied, "but as commander of the army of the LORD I have
now come." Then Joshua fell facedown[p]
to the ground[q] in reverence, and asked
him, "What message does my Lord[1] have
for his servant?"
15The commander of the LORD's army
replied, "Take off your sandals, for the
place where you are standing is holy."[r]
And Joshua did so.

Chapter 6

NOW Jericho[s] was tightly shut up because of the Israelites. No one went
out and no one came in.
2Then the LORD said to Joshua, "See, I
have delivered[t] Jericho into your hands,
along with its king and its fighting men.

5:1 [v]S Nu 13:29 [w]S Ge 42:28
5:2 [x]S Ex 4:25 [y]S Ge 17:10,12,14
5:4 [z]S Nu 1:3 [a]Dt 2:14
5:6 [b]Nu 32:13; Jos 14:10; Ps 107:4 [c]S Ex 16:35 [d]Nu 14:23,29-35; Dt 2:14 [e]S Ex 3:8
5:8 [f]Ge 34:25
5:9 [g]S Dt 11:30
5:10 [h]S Ex 12:6 [i]S Ex 12:11
5:11 [j]S Nu 15:19 [k]Ex 12:15 [l]S Lev 23:14
5:12 [m]Ex 16:35
5:13 [n]S Ge 18:2 [o]Nu 22:23
5:14 [p]S Ge 17:3 [q]S Ge 19:1
5:15 [r]S Ge 28:17; Ex 3:5; Ac 7:33
6:1 [s]Jos 24:11
6:2 [t]ver 16; Dt 7:24; Jos 8:1

[1]3 *Gibeath Haaraloth* means *hill of foreskins.*
[1]9 *Gilgal* sounds like the Hebrew for *roll.* [k]12 Or *the day* [1]14 Or *lord*

5:1 HISTORY, Politics—God's historical acts made further political actions easier for God's people by causing other political leaders to fear and retreat.

5:2–9 THE CHURCH, Covenant People—Joshua, like Abraham, circumcised male members of the covenant community. See note on Ge 17:1–21. This provided a constant reminder of their commitment to God. While no outward physical signs remain for believers today, the Spirit of God bears witness to our relationship with God. In a sense, baptism sets Christians apart as dedicated to the Lord.

5:13–15 REVELATION, Messengers—God presented Himself in Joshua's path as a messenger who, on being recognized, was worshiped by Joshua. The sacred encounter paralleled Moses' encounter and call (Ex 3) and reaffirmed God's choice of Joshua. The revealing messenger was referred to as a man, yet led the heavenly armies and brought Joshua to his knees. See note on Ge 18:1—19:29.

5:15 GOD, Holy—Joshua had a similar experience to that of Moses before the burning bush (Ex 3). God told him that he was standing on holy ground and should take off his sandals. Persons ought to humble themselves in the presence of God. Holiness is a line of demarcation between God and us. God's holiness reminds us of the infinite difference between God and human beings and should always remind us that we are to respect and honor God with reverence. We have nothing to fear when we come before Him properly, reverently, respecting His holiness.

5:15 PRAYER, Holiness of God—God's holiness demanded reverent prostration from His people. Compare Ex 3:5.

6:1–27 CHRISTIAN ETHICS, War and Peace—The element of *cherem,* or devotion of conquered people and material to God, is vividly portrayed in the fall of Jericho. See note on Nu 21:1–3. Such a practice stood as a reminder to the Hebrews of the total devotion they were to extend to God as their Sovereign. In such cases the victory was seen as God's. The scene is the evidence of the judgment of God toward those who had a sense of His sovereignty but failed to worship Him. Contemporary Christians should be careful not to consider the invasion of Canaan and its ensuing "Holy War" as an example for the way war should be waged. At that time, God's people were only one group of people seeking a place in which to establish a nation. In addition, it would seem likely that God made His purposes fit the level of moral understanding and practice out of which the Hebrews could operate to combat the people and ideologies of false gods. God's special work with Israel at that period of history did not set a precedent for suceeding generations to follow. Seldom did following generations of Israelites employ *cherem.* See note on 2 Ch 20:1–30.

6:2 SALVATION, As Deliverance—God's deliverance of Jericho to Israel was a sign of His power to fulfill His promises (Ex 6:8).

3March around the city once with all the
armed men. Do this for six days. 4Have
seven priests carry trumpets of rams'
horns[u] in front of the ark. On the seventh day, march around the city seven
times, with the priests blowing the trumpets.[v] 5When you hear them sound a
long blast[w] on the trumpets, have all the
people give a loud shout;[x] then the wall
of the city will collapse and the people
will go up, every man straight in."

6So Joshua son of Nun called the priests
and said to them, "Take up the ark of the
covenant of the LORD and have seven
priests carry trumpets in front of it."[y]
7And he ordered the people, "Advance[z]!
March around the city, with the armed
guard going ahead of the ark[a] of the
LORD."

8When Joshua had spoken to the people, the seven priests carrying the seven
trumpets before the LORD went forward,
blowing their trumpets, and the ark of
the LORD's covenant followed them. 9The
armed guard marched ahead of the
priests who blew the trumpets, and the
rear guard[b] followed the ark. All this
time the trumpets were sounding. 10But
Joshua had commanded the people, "Do
not give a war cry, do not raise your
voices, do not say a word until the day I
tell you to shout. Then shout![c]" 11So he
had the ark of the LORD carried around
the city, circling it once. Then the people
returned to camp and spent the night
there.

12Joshua got up early the next morning
and the priests took up the ark of the
LORD. 13The seven priests carrying the
seven trumpets went forward, marching
before the ark of the LORD and blowing
the trumpets. The armed men went
ahead of them and the rear guard followed the ark of the LORD, while the
trumpets kept sounding. 14So on the second day they marched around the city
once and returned to the camp. They did
this for six days.

15On the seventh day, they got up at
daybreak and marched around the city
seven times in the same manner, except
that on that day they circled the city sev-
en times.[d] 16The seventh time around,
when the priests sounded the trumpet
blast, Joshua commanded the people,
"Shout! For the LORD has given you the
city![e] 17The city and all that is in it are to
be devoted[m][f] to the LORD. Only Rahab
the prostitute[n][g] and all who are with her
in her house shall be spared, because she
hid[h] the spies we sent. 18But keep away
from the devoted things,[i] so that you
will not bring about your own destruction
by taking any of them. Otherwise you will
make the camp of Israel liable to destruction[j] and bring trouble[k] on it. 19All the
silver and gold and the articles of bronze
and iron[l] are sacred to the LORD and
must go into his treasury."

20When the trumpets sounded,[m] the
people shouted, and at the sound of the
trumpet, when the people gave a loud
shout,[n] the wall collapsed; so every man
charged straight in, and they took the
city.[o] 21They devoted[p] the city to the
LORD and destroyed[q] with the sword every living thing in it—men and women,
young and old, cattle, sheep and donkeys.

22Joshua said to the two men[r] who
had spied out[s] the land, "Go into the
prostitute's house and bring her out and
all who belong to her, in accordance with
your oath to her.[t]" 23So the young men
who had done the spying went in and
brought out Rahab, her father and mother
and brothers and all who belonged to
her.[u] They brought out her entire family
and put them in a place outside the camp
of Israel.

24Then they burned the whole city[v]
and everything in it, but they put the silver and gold and the articles of bronze
and iron[w] into the treasury of the LORD's
house.[x] 25But Joshua spared[y] Rahab the
prostitute,[z] with her family and all who
belonged to her, because she hid the men
Joshua had sent as spies to Jericho[a]—
and she lives among the Israelites to this
day.

26At that time Joshua pronounced this
solemn oath:[b] "Cursed[c] before the LORD
is the man who undertakes to rebuild this
city, Jericho:

"At the cost of his firstborn son
  will he lay its foundations;

6:4 [u]S Ex 19:13 [v]S Lev 25:9
6:5 [w]Ex 19:13 [x]ver 20; 1Sa 4:5; 2Sa 6:15; Ezr 3:11; 10:12; Ps 42:4; 95:1; Isa 8:9; 42:13
6:6 [y]ver 4
6:7 [z]Ex 14:15 [a]Nu 10:35; 1Sa 4:3; 7:1
6:9 [b]ver 13; S Nu 2:31; Isa 52:12
6:10 [c]ver 20; 1Sa 4:5; Ezr 3:11
6:15 [d]1Ki 18:44; 2Ki 4:35; 5:14
6:16 [e]S ver 2
6:17 [f]ver 21; Lev 27:28; Dt 20:17; Isa 13:5; 24:1; 34:2,5; Mal 4:6 [g]S Jos 2:1 [h]ver 25; Jos 2:4
6:18 [i]Jos 7:1; 1Ch 2:7 [j]Jos 7:12 [k]Jos 7:25,26
6:19 [l]ver 24; Nu 31:22
6:20 [m]Lev 25:9; Jdg 6:34; 7:22; 1Ki 1:41; Isa 18:3; 27:13; Jer 4:21; 42:14; Am 2:2 [n]S ver 5; S 10 [o]Heb 11:30
6:21 [p]S ver 17 [q]S Dt 20:16
6:22 [r]S Ge 42:9; S Jos 2:4 [s]S Nu 21:32 [t]Jos 2:14; Heb 11:31
6:23 [u]S Jos 2:13
6:24 [v]S Nu 31:10 [w]S ver 19 [x]S Dt 13:16
6:25 [y]Jdg 1:25 [z]S Jos 2:1 [a]S ver 17; S Jos 2:6
6:26 [b]1Sa 14:24 [c]S Nu 5:21

[m]*17* The Hebrew term refers to the irrevocable giving over of things or persons to the LORD, often by totally destroying them; also in verses 18 and 21. [n]*17* Or possibly *innkeeper*; also in verses 22 and 25

6:20 MIRACLE, Power—God works miraculously to master military might. The Jericho fortress stood in the way of God's purpose for Israel. An act of God removed it. Israel learned that human defenses cannot stand before God's power. Various Bible students have tried to determine if God used the natural order to produce His miracle at Jericho. Did He use the same earthquake many think He used to dam up the Jordan to weaken the walls of Jericho? Did the tramping and vibrations of the marching Israelites finally bring the weakened walls tumbling down? Such speculation may be interesting. Its ideas can never be proved. Whatever the secondary cause, if there were one, the primary action was God's. The Bible is concerned only with this. The powers of nature and the insecurity of foundations are both subject to the will and purpose of God. God's power is supreme in His universe. He uses that power to help His people accomplish His mission. God's evidence of His power sent His fame throughout the land of Canaan. Our task is to let that fame and power be known throughout our world.

at the cost of his youngest
will he set up its gates."[d]
27So the LORD was with Joshua,[e] and
his fame spread[f] throughout the land.

Chapter 7

Achan's Sin

BUT the Israelites acted unfaithfully in
regard to the devoted things[o];[g]
Achan[h] son of Carmi, the son of Zimri,[p]
the son of Zerah,[i] of the tribe of Judah,[j]
took some of them. So the LORD's anger
burned[k] against Israel.[l]
2Now Joshua sent men from Jericho to
Ai,[m] which is near Beth Aven[n] to the
east of Bethel,[o] and told them, "Go up
and spy out[p] the region." So the men
went up and spied out Ai.
3When they returned to Joshua, they
said, "Not all the people will have to go
up against Ai. Send two or three thousand
men to take it and do not weary all the
people, for only a few men are there."
4So about three thousand men went up;
but they were routed by the men of Ai,[q]
5who killed about thirty-six[r] of them.
They chased the Israelites from the city
gate as far as the stone quarries[q] and
struck them down on the slopes. At this
the hearts of the people melted[s] and became like water.
6Then Joshua tore his clothes[t] and fell
facedown[u] to the ground before the ark
of the LORD, remaining there till evening.[v] The elders of Israel[w] did the
same, and sprinkled dust[x] on their
heads. 7And Joshua said, "Ah, Sovereign
LORD, why[y] did you ever bring this people across the Jordan to deliver us into
the hands of the Amorites to destroy us?[z]
If only we had been content to stay on the
other side of the Jordan! 8O Lord, what
can I say, now that Israel has been routed
by its enemies? 9The Canaanites and the
other people of the country will hear
about this and they will surround us and
wipe out our name from the earth.[a]
What then will you do for your own great
name?[b]"
10The LORD said to Joshua, "Stand up!
What are you doing down on your face?

6:26 [d]1Ki 16:34 **6:27** [e]S Ge 39:2; S Nu 14:43 [f]Jos 9:1; 1Ch 14:17 **7:1** [g]S Jos 6:18 [h]ver 26; 1Ch 2:7 [i]Jos 22:20 [j]ver 18; Nu 1:4 [k]S Ex 4:14; S 32:20 [l]S Lev 10:6 **7:2** [m]S Ge 12:8; S Jos 8:1,28 [n]Jos 18:12; 1Sa 13:5; 14:23; Hos 4:15; 5:8; 10:5 [o]Ge 12:8; Jos 12:16; 16:1; Jdg 1:22; 1Sa 30:27; 2Ki 23:15; Jer 48:13; Am 3:14; 4:4; 5:5-6; 7:10,13 [p]S Nu 21:32 **7:4** [q]S Lev 26:17; S Dt 28:25 **7:5** [r]Jos 22:20 [s]S Ge 42:28; Ps 22:14; Isa 13:7; Eze 21:7; Na 2:10 **7:6** [t]S Ge 37:29 [u]S Ge 17:3; 1Ch 21:16; Eze 9:8 [v]Jdg 20:23 [w]Jos 8:10; 9:11; 20:4; 23:2 [x]1Sa 4:12; 2Sa 13:19; 15:32; Ne 9:1; Job 2:12; La 2:10; Eze 27:30; Rev 18:19 **7:7** [y]1Sa 4:3 [z]S Ex 5:22; S Nu 14:16 **7:9** [a]Ex 32:12; S Dt 9:28 [b]Dt 28:58; 1Sa 12:22; Ps 48:10; 106:8; Jer 14:21

[o] *1* The Hebrew term refers to the irrevocable giving over of things or persons to the LORD, often by totally destroying them; also in verses 11, 12, 13 and 15. [p] *1* See Septuagint and 1 Chron. 2:6; Hebrew *Zabdi*; also in verses 17 and 18. [q] *5* Or *as far as Shebarim*

7:1,25–26 GOD, Wrath—God's wrath does not mean His righteousness and justice overrule His love and mercy. He had clearly revealed that He is a God who would rather show love and mercy than punishment and judgment (Ex 20:5–6), but He also wanted His people to know that He could and would express Himself in wrath when necessary. In this early stage of His dealings with the young Israelite people, God needed to establish clearly in their minds and hearts that He is a God who takes Himself and His relationship with His people very seriously. His people must take Him very seriously also. Their well-being, their salvation as a people of God, depended upon their honoring Him as Lord. When we interpret the wrath of God, or the love of God, we must remember that we are dealing with God as described in very human terms. Human terms are the only terms that we have for describing God. They give us our highest and most intimate form of understanding God. These human terms give us much more insight into the nature and character of God than do abstract terms that are divorced from personality and human experience. However, we must be careful that we do not let the use of the very real human experiences of anger or love give us ideas about God that are inappropriate. God's anger is not a fit of wrath, a momentary loss of control over a fiery temper. God's love is not a sentimentality that makes God more a doting grandfather than a truly loving Father. God must be respected and obeyed, for He will punish our sins in judgment when the occasion makes it necessary; but God is not a vindictive God, who severely punishes every sin. The stern picture of God here must be set in the context of what God was doing in this instance and why. It must also be set in the larger context of what and who God is shown to be in other passages as well. See Guide to Interpreting the Bible, pp. 1769–1772.

7:1 HUMANITY, Community Relationships—A strong sense of corporate relationship exists throughout the Bible, although it is far stronger in the Old Testament than it is in the New. No person ever acts wholly in isolation. Individual actions always have effects upon the larger community.

7:1 SIN, Violation—To willfully disobey the divine commandment is not a transgression of some impersonal code, but an arrogant rejection of God's rightful claim. Selfishly appropriating what belongs to God shows lack of trust and failure to obey. It is sin. God called for war booty to be dedicated to Him. Normally such devoted things were destroyed. Some were placed in God's house (6:24). Achan selfishly took some booty for himself, calling God's wrath on the entire nation. God provided a way to determine the guilty party and punished only the guilty.

7:1–26 HISTORY, Judgment—God acted in history to give Israel the land He had promised. In acting He expected Israel to do their part in faith and obedience. When they disobeyed, anger and judgment followed. Thus in His historical acts God remained free to punish a disobedient people. His promises and their expectations of victory did not prevent God from disciplining disobedient people. Such judgment called forth praise and confession not retreat and abandonment of the mission.

7:1—8:29 CHRISTIAN ETHICS, War and Peace—The occasion of Achan's death and his family is difficult for a highly individualistic society to understand. As a general rule at this point in Israel's life, God acted toward this nation as a corporate personality. In no way does this imply that individuals were not important. In fact, the very opposite shows up here in that Achan's individual responsibility to the larger community broke down. Since they were such a tightly knit society, the moral lapses of one individual (especially with regard to devoted goods) affected the moral relationship of all with God. See note on 6:1–27. Thus, Achan (and those called by his name) had to suffer the consequences of disobedience to the covenant with his people. Their example led Joshua and Israel to repentance and obedience. Contemporary Christians can learn the same lessons.

7:7–9 PRAYER, Honor of God—Joshua based his plea on the honor of God's name. The basic purpose of prayer is to honor God and find ways to let His name be honored around the world. Our sin takes away from the honor of God's name as unbelievers watch us to know what our God is like.

7:10–26 EVIL AND SUFFERING, Punishment—A large group may suffer from one member's sin. The covenant relationship with God binds members together in mutual responsibility, sharing victory and defeat, joy and shame together. The community is responsible to discipline itself and its individual members so no sin disrupts the community and separates it

11Israel has sinned;[c] they have violated
my covenant,[d] which I commanded
them to keep. They have taken some of
the devoted things; they have stolen,
they have lied,[e] they have put them with
their own possessions.[f] 12That is why
the Israelites cannot stand against their
enemies;[g] they turn their backs[h] and
run[i] because they have been made liable
to destruction.[j] I will not be with you
anymore[k] unless you destroy whatever
among you is devoted to destruction.

13"Go, consecrate the people. Tell
them, 'Consecrate yourselves[l] in preparation for tomorrow; for this is what the
LORD, the God of Israel, says: That which
is devoted is among you, O Israel. You
cannot stand against your enemies until
you remove it.

14" 'In the morning, present[m] yourselves tribe by tribe. The tribe that the
LORD takes[n] shall come forward clan by
clan; the clan that the LORD takes shall
come forward family by family; and the
family that the LORD takes shall come forward man by man. 15He who is caught
with the devoted things[o] shall be destroyed by fire,[p] along with all that belongs to him.[q] He has violated the covenant[r] of the LORD and has done a disgraceful thing in Israel!' "[s]

16Early the next morning Joshua had
Israel come forward by tribes, and Judah
was taken. 17The clans of Judah came forward, and he took the Zerahites.[t] He had
the clan of the Zerahites come forward by
families, and Zimri was taken. 18Joshua
had his family come forward man by man,
and Achan son of Carmi, the son of Zimri,
the son of Zerah, of the tribe of Judah,[u]
was taken.[v]

19Then Joshua said to Achan, "My son,
give glory[w] to the LORD,[r] the God of Israel, and give him the praise.[s] Tell[x] me
what you have done; do not hide it from
me."

20Achan replied, "It is true! I have
sinned against the LORD, the God of Israel. This is what I have done: 21When I
saw in the plunder[y] a beautiful robe from
Babylonia,[t] two hundred shekels[u] of silver and a wedge of gold weighing fifty
shekels,[v] I coveted[z] them and took
them. They are hidden in the ground inside my tent, with the silver underneath."

22So Joshua sent messengers, and they
ran to the tent, and there it was, hidden
in his tent, with the silver underneath.
23They took the things from the tent,
brought them to Joshua and all the Israelites and spread them out before the LORD.

24Then Joshua, together with all Israel,
took Achan son of Zerah, the silver, the
robe, the gold wedge, his sons[a] and
daughters, his cattle, donkeys and sheep,
his tent and all that he had, to the Valley
of Achor.[b] 25Joshua said, "Why have you
brought this trouble[c] on us? The LORD
will bring trouble on you today."

Then all Israel stoned him,[d] and after
they had stoned the rest, they burned
them.[e] 26Over Achan they heaped[f] up a
large pile of rocks, which remains to this
day.[g] Then the LORD turned from his
fierce anger.[h] Therefore that place has
been called the Valley of Achor[w][i] ever
since.

Chapter 8

Ai Destroyed

THEN the LORD said to Joshua, "Do not
be afraid;[j] do not be discouraged.[k]

7:11 [c]S Ex 9:27; Dt 29:27; Jos 24:16-27; 2Ki 17:7; Hos 10:9 [d]ver 15; Jos 6:17-19; 23:16; Jdg 2:20; 1Sa 15:24; Ps 78:10 [e]Ac 5:1-2 [f]ver 21
7:12 [g]Lev 26:37 [h]Ps 18:40; 21:12 [i]S Lev 26:17 [j]Jos 6:18 [k]Ps 44:9; 60:10
7:13 [l]S Lev 11:44
7:14 [m]1Sa 10:19 [n]Pr 16:33
7:15 [o]Jos 6:18 [p]Dt 7:25; 2Ki 25:9; 1Ch 14:12; Isa 37:19; Jer 43:12; Eze 30:16 [q]1Sa 14:39 [r]S ver 11 [s]Ge 34:7
7:17 [t]Nu 26:20
7:18 [u]S ver 1; S Lev 24:11 [v]Jnh 1:7
7:19 [w]Ex 14:17; 1Sa 6:5; Ps 96:8; Isa 42:12; Jer 13:16; Jn 9:24* [x]S Lev 5:5; 1Sa 14:43
7:21 [y]S Ge 34:29; S 49:27 [z]S Dt 7:25; Eph 5:5; 1Ti 6:10
7:24 [a]S Nu 16:27 [b]ver 26; Jos 15:7; Isa 65:10; Hos 2:15
7:25 [c]S Jos 6:18 [d]S Lev 20:2; Dt 17:5; 1Ki 12:18; 2Ch 10:18; 24:21; Ne 9:26 [e]S Ge 38:24
7:26 [f]2Sa 18:17 [g]S Ge 35:20 [h]S Nu 25:4 [i]S ver 24
8:1 [j]Ge 26:24; Dt 31:6 [k]S Nu 14:9; S Dt 1:21

[r]*19* A solemn charge to tell the truth [s]*19* Or *and confess to him* [t]*21* Hebrew *Shinar* [u]*21* That is, about 5 pounds (about 2.3 kilograms) [v]*21* That is, about 1 1/4 pounds (about 0.6 kilogram) [w]*26* *Achor* means *trouble.*

from God. Eventually Achan had to pay the supreme price along with his family, who had been corrupted in his sin. The community suffered momentary defeat until it exercised discipline. See notes on Dt 24:16; Eze 18:1–32.

7:11 SIN, Covenant Breach—Sin is not simply an individual matter. Individual sin affects those with whom we live. Sin can be serious enough to destroy a whole congregation of God's people. Sin disrupts not only an individual relationship with God but fellowship with the covenant community. See note on 7:1.

7:11–12 REVELATION, Divine Presence—Revealing Himself as the God of constructive purposes, God reminded Joshua and Israel that He does not associate with anything outside His nature or will. He therefore left Israel when Israel left His will and returned only when they returned to His will. Those who leave God's plans to pursue their own poor choices cannot expect God's presence in their lives.

7:11–15 THE CHURCH, Covenant People—See notes on Dt 31:16–19; Jer 31:31–34. An unfaithful people must expect God's punishment instead of His blessings. A covenant establishes a relationship based on commitment and obedience. When this commitment is broken, serious consequences result.

7:20–25 HUMANITY, Family Relationships—Contemporary western cultures have moved to emphasize individualism, the importance and rights of each person. We have neglected the deep strain, within both the Old and the New Testaments, emphasizing the close ties and corporate solidarity of the family (as well as the community). The sins of any one person seriously affects and can have serious consequences for each member of a person's family. While the Bible clearly shows that I suffer for my own sins (Jer 31:29–30; Eze 18:2–4), it also reveals that my sins seriously affect those closest to me.

7:20 SIN, Against God—Achan recognized that his sin had been directed against God. He had stolen from enemy soldiers. He had disrupted the fellowship within God's people. He had broken the common rules of war conduct in Israel. His sin may be described in many ways. Ultimately, it and all sin is disobedience against God and His will.

8:1–29 HISTORY, Deliverance—God called on human cooperation to accomplish His historical deliverance. Battle tactics on the human level were part of God's method of deliverance. God expected all His people to participate, not just

Take the whole army[l] with you, and go
up and attack Ai.[m] For I have delivered[n]
into your hands the king of Ai, his people,
his city and his land. 2You shall do to Ai
and its king as you did to Jericho and its
king, except that you may carry off their
plunder[o] and livestock for yourselves.[p]
Set an ambush[q] behind the city."
3So Joshua and the whole army moved
out to attack Ai. He chose thirty thousand
of his best fighting men and sent them
out at night 4with these orders: "Listen
carefully. You are to set an ambush behind the city. Don't go very far from it.
All of you be on the alert. 5I and all those
with me will advance on the city, and
when the men come out against us, as
they did before, we will flee from them.
6They will pursue us until we have lured
them away from the city, for they will
say, 'They are running away from us as
they did before.' So when we flee from
them, 7you are to rise up from ambush
and take the city. The LORD your God will
give it into your hand.[r] 8When you have
taken the city, set it on fire.[s] Do what
the LORD has commanded.[t] See to it; you
have my orders."
9Then Joshua sent them off, and they
went to the place of ambush[u] and lay in
wait between Bethel and Ai, to the west
of Ai—but Joshua spent that night with
the people.
10Early the next morning[v] Joshua mustered his men, and he and the leaders of
Israel[w] marched before them to Ai. 11The
entire force that was with him marched
up and approached the city and arrived in
front of it. They set up camp north of Ai,
with the valley between them and
the city. 12Joshua had taken out five
thousand men and set them in ambush
between Bethel and Ai, to the west of the
city. 13They had the soldiers take up their
positions—all those in the camp to the
north of the city and the ambush to the
west of it. That night Joshua went into
the valley.
14When the king of Ai saw this, he and
all the men of the city hurried out early in
the morning to meet Israel in battle at a
certain place overlooking the Arabah.[x]
But he did not know[y] that an ambush
had been set against him behind the city.
15Joshua and all Israel let themselves be
driven back[z] before them, and they fled
toward the desert.[a] 16All the men of Ai
were called to pursue them, and they pursued Joshua and were lured away[b] from
the city. 17Not a man remained in Ai or
Bethel who did not go after Israel. They
left the city open and went in pursuit of
Israel.
18Then the LORD said to Joshua, "Hold
out toward Ai the javelin[c] that is in your
hand,[d] for into your hand I will deliver
the city." So Joshua held out his javelin[e]
toward Ai. 19As soon as he did this, the
men in the ambush rose quickly[f] from
their position and rushed forward. They
entered the city and captured it and
quickly set it on fire.[g]
20The men of Ai looked back and saw
the smoke of the city rising against the
sky,[h] but they had no chance to escape in
any direction, for the Israelites who had
been fleeing toward the desert had
turned back against their pursuers. 21For
when Joshua and all Israel saw that the
ambush had taken the city and that
smoke was going up from the city, they
turned around[i] and attacked the men of
Ai. 22The men of the ambush also came
out of the city against them, so that they
were caught in the middle, with Israelites
on both sides. Israel cut them down, leaving them neither survivors nor fugitives.[j] 23But they took the king of Ai
alive[k] and brought him to Joshua.
24When Israel had finished killing all
the men of Ai in the fields and in the
desert where they had chased them, and
when every one of them had been put to
the sword, all the Israelites returned to Ai
and killed those who were in it. 25Twelve
thousand men and women fell that day
—all the people of Ai.[l] 26For Joshua did
not draw back the hand that held out his
javelin[m] until he had destroyed[x][n] all
who lived in Ai.[o] 27But Israel did carry
off for themselves the livestock and plunder of this city, as the LORD had instructed Joshua.[p]
28So Joshua burned[q] Ai[r] and made it a
permanent heap of ruins,[s] a desolate
place to this day.[t] 29He hung the king of
Ai on a tree and left him there until evening. At sunset,[u] Joshua ordered them to
take his body from the tree and throw it

8:1 [l]Jos 10:7 [m]Jos 7:2; 9:3; 10:1; 12:9 [n]S Jos 6:2
8:2 [o]S Ge 49:27 [p]ver 27; Dt 20:14 [q]ver 4,12; Jdg 9:43; 20:29
8:7 [r]Jdg 7:7; 1Sa 23:4
8:8 [s]Jdg 20:29-38 [t]ver 19
8:9 [u]2Ch 13:13
8:10 [v]Ge 22:3 [w]S Jos 7:6
8:14 [x]S Dt 1:1 [y]Jdg 20:34
8:15 [z]Jdg 20:36 [a]Jos 15:61; 16:1; 18:12
8:16 [b]Jdg 20:31
8:18 [c]Job 41:26; Ps 35:3 [d]S Ex 4:2; 17:9-12 [e]ver 26
8:19 [f]Jdg 20:33 [g]S ver 8
8:20 [h]Jdg 20:40
8:21 [i]Jdg 20:41
8:22 [j]Dt 7:2; Jos 10:1
8:23 [k]1Sa 15:8
8:25 [l]Dt 20:16-18
8:26 [m]ver 18 [n]S Nu 21:2 [o]Ex 17:12
8:27 [p]S ver 2
8:28 [q]S Nu 31:10 [r]Jos 7:2; Jer 49:3 [s]S Dt 13:16; Jos 10:1 [t]S Ge 35:20
8:29 [u]S Dt 21:23; Jn 19:31

[x]26 The Hebrew term refers to the irrevocable giving over of things or persons to the LORD, often by totally destroying them.

a small portion (7:3–5).

8:10–23 MIRACLE, Faith—Miracles are for the obedient. God may choose to bless rebellious people with a miracle to accomplish His purposes (Nu 17:6–7), but ordinarily miracles honor the faith of God's people. Achan's deception (Jos 7:1) proved the temporary undoing of Israel's conquest attempt. Only when the deception was exposed and faith expressed in obedience could Ai be assaulted successfully. Israel finally conquered the city after losing their self-confidence and relying on God to supply a miraculous strategy to defeat the enemy. Joshua's obedient faith (8:18) provided the context for God's victory. God's people sin when they overconfidently expect miracles even for a disobedient people. We sin just as greatly when we do not believe God can provide miraculous help for an obedient people.

down at the entrance of the city gate. And they raised a large pile of rocks[v] over it, which remains to this day.

The Covenant Renewed at Mount Ebal

30Then Joshua built on Mount Ebal[w] an altar[x] to the LORD, the God of Israel, 31as Moses the servant of the LORD had commanded the Israelites. He built it according to what is written in the Book of the Law of Moses—an altar of uncut stones, on which no iron tool[y] had been used. On it they offered to the LORD burnt offerings and sacrificed fellowship offerings.[y][z] 32There, in the presence of the Israelites, Joshua copied on stones the law of Moses, which he had written.[a] 33All Israel, aliens and citizens[b] alike, with their elders, officials and judges, were standing on both sides of the ark of the covenant of the LORD, facing those who carried it—the priests, who were Levites.[c] Half of the people stood in front of Mount Gerizim and half of them in front of Mount Ebal,[d] as Moses the servant of the LORD had formerly commanded when he gave instructions to bless the people of Israel.

34Afterward, Joshua read all the words of the law—the blessings and the curses—just as it is written in the Book of the Law.[e] 35There was not a word of all that Moses had commanded that Joshua did not read to the whole assembly of Israel, including the women and children, and the aliens who lived among them.[f]

Chapter 9

The Gibeonite Deception

NOW when all the kings west of the Jordan heard about these things—those in the hill country,[g] in the western foothills, and along the entire coast of the Great Sea[z][h] as far as Lebanon[i] (the kings of the Hittites, Amorites, Canaanites, Perizzites,[j] Hivites[k] and Jebusites)[l]— 2they came together to make war against Joshua and Israel.

3However, when the people of Gibeon[m] heard what Joshua had done to Jericho and Ai,[n] 4they resorted to a ruse: They went as a delegation whose donkeys were loaded[a] with worn-out sacks and old wineskins, cracked and mended. 5The men put worn and patched sandals on their feet and wore old clothes. All the bread of their food supply was dry and moldy. 6Then they went to Joshua in the camp at Gilgal[o] and said to him and the men of Israel, "We have come from a distant country;[p] make a treaty[q] with us."

7The men of Israel said to the Hivites,[r] "But perhaps you live near us. How then can we make a treaty[s] with you?"

8"We are your servants,[t]" they said to Joshua.

But Joshua asked, "Who are you and where do you come from?"

9They answered: "Your servants have come from a very distant country[u] because of the fame of the LORD your God. For we have heard reports[v] of him: all that he did in Egypt,[w] 10and all that he did to the two kings of the Amorites east of the Jordan—Sihon king of Heshbon,[x] and Og king of Bashan,[y] who reigned in Ashtaroth.[z] 11And our elders and all those living in our country said to us, 'Take provisions for your journey; go and meet them and say to them, "We are your servants; make a treaty with us."' 12This bread of ours was warm when we packed it at home on the day we left to come to you. But now see how dry and moldy it is. 13And these wineskins that we filled were new, but see how cracked they are. And our clothes and sandals are worn out by the very long journey."

14The men of Israel sampled their provisions but did not inquire[a] of the LORD. 15Then Joshua made a treaty of peace[b] with them to let them live,[c] and the leaders of the assembly ratified it by oath.

16Three days after they made the treaty with the Gibeonites, the Israelites heard that they were neighbors, living near[d]

8:29 [v]2Sa 18:17
8:30 [w]ver 33; S Dt 11:29 [x]S Ex 20:24
8:31 [y]S Ex 20:25 [z]Dt 27:6-7
8:32 [a]Dt 27:8
8:33 [b]S Lev 16:29 [c]Dt 31:12 [d]Dt 11:29; Jn 4:20
8:34 [e]S Dt 28:61; 31:11
8:35 [f]S Ex 12:38; Dt 31:12
9:1 [g]S Nu 13:17 [h]S Nu 34:6 [i]S Dt 3:25 [j]Ge 13:7; S Jos 3:10 [k]ver 7; Jos 11:19 [l]S Jos 3:10
9:3 [m]ver 17; Jos 10:10; 11:19; 18:25; 21:17; 2Sa 2:12; 5:25; 20:8; 1Ki 3:4; 9:2; 1Ch 8:29; 14:16; 16:39; 21:29; 2Ch 1:3; Ne 3:7; Isa 28:21; Jer 28:1; 41:12 [n]Ge 12:8; S Jos 8:1
9:6 [o]S Dt 11:30 [p]ver 22 [q]S Ge 26:28
9:7 [r]S ver 1 [s]S Ex 23:32; S 1Ki 5:12
9:8 [t]2Ki 10:5
9:9 [u]S Dt 20:15 [v]ver 24 [w]S Nu 23:22
9:10 [x]S Nu 21:25 [y]S Nu 21:33 [z]S Nu 21:24,35; Jos 2:10
9:14 [a]S Ex 16:28; S Nu 27:21
9:15 [b]S ver 3,7; Jos 10:1,4; 11:19; 2Sa 21:2; 24:1 [c]ver 21; Jdg 1:21; Ps 106:34
9:16 [d]ver 22

[y]31 Traditionally *peace offerings* [z]1 That is, the Mediterranean [a]4 Most Hebrew manuscripts; some Hebrew manuscripts, Vulgate and Syriac (see also Septuagint) *They prepared provisions and loaded their donkeys*

8:30–35 HOLY SCRIPTURE, Writing—The people of His promise stood symbolically between two important mountains to worship and give thanks, to hear the law read, and to affirm that they would follow God's revealed words and purposes. The written Word revealed God's will to His people from Moses' time forward. God's people listened to all the Word, not just part of it. Joshua copied God's law on the public altar to make it more accessible to the people. Even the law-reading ceremony was based on God's revelation (Dt 27:12–14).

8:30–31 PRAYER, Thanksgiving—This altar was built in gratitude for the defeat of Ai. Humbly setting up a place of worship as a memorial to God's actions is a way of expressing a prayer of gratitude.

8:33–34 PRAYER, Corporate—See notes on Lev 9:22; Dt 27:12–26. Blessing ensured a new nation in a new land that the God who brought victory could and would guide successfully through the repeating processes of daily life. God's people need reassurance they stand under His daily care. Public prayer can provide such assurance.

9:1–27 HISTORY, Universal—See note on 5:1. Israel came to include people without Israelite blood. The Gibeonites became Temple servants because they tricked Israel into an unbreakable covenant. God used even human trickery and disobedience to provide personnel for His house of worship.

9:14 PRAYER, Hindrances—This is one of the few cases in the Bible where failure to pray is pointed out. Not inquiring of God's will leads to wrong decisions which have lasting effects in our lives and in the lives of others.

them. 17So the Israelites set out and on
the third day came to their cities: Gibeon,
Kephirah, Beeroth[e] and Kiriath Jearim.[f]
18But the Israelites did not attack them,
because the leaders of the assembly had
sworn an oath[g] to them by the LORD, the
God of Israel.
The whole assembly grumbled[h]
against the leaders, 19but all the leaders
answered, "We have given them our oath
by the LORD, the God of Israel, and we
cannot touch them now. 20This is what
we will do to them: We will let them live,
so that wrath will not fall on us for breaking the oath[i] we swore to them." 21They
continued, "Let them live,[j] but let them
be woodcutters and water carriers[k] for
the entire community." So the leaders'
promise to them was kept.
22Then Joshua summoned the Gibeonites and said, "Why did you deceive us by
saying, 'We live a long way[l] from you,'
while actually you live near[m] us? 23You
are now under a curse:[n] You will never
cease to serve as woodcutters and water
carriers for the house of my God."
24They answered Joshua, "Your servants were clearly told[o] how the LORD
your God had commanded his servant
Moses to give you the whole land and to
wipe out all its inhabitants from before
you. So we feared for our lives because of
you, and that is why we did this. 25We
are now in your hands.[p] Do to us whatever seems good and right[q] to you."
26So Joshua saved them from the Israelites, and they did not kill them. 27That
day he made the Gibeonites[r] woodcutters and water carriers[s] for the community and for the altar of the LORD at the
place the LORD would choose.[t] And that
is what they are to this day.

Chapter 10

The Sun Stands Still

NOW Adoni-Zedek[u] king of Jerusalem[v] heard that Joshua had taken
Ai[w] and totally destroyed[b][x] it, doing to
Ai and its king as he had done to Jericho
and its king, and that the people of Gibeon[y] had made a treaty of peace[z] with
Israel and were living near them. 2He and
his people were very much alarmed at
this, because Gibeon was an important
city, like one of the royal cities; it was
larger than Ai, and all its men were good
fighters. 3So Adoni-Zedek king of Jerusalem appealed to Hoham king of Hebron,[a]
Piram king of Jarmuth,[b] Japhia king of
Lachish[c] and Debir[d] king of Eglon.[e]
4"Come up and help me attack Gibeon,"
he said, "because it has made peace[f]
with Joshua and the Israelites."
5Then the five kings[g] of the Amorites[h]—the kings of Jerusalem, Hebron,
Jarmuth, Lachish and Eglon—joined
forces. They moved up with all their
troops and took up positions against Gibeon and attacked it.
6The Gibeonites then sent word to
Joshua in the camp at Gilgal:[i] "Do not
abandon your servants. Come up to us
quickly and save us! Help us, because all
the Amorite kings from the hill country
have joined forces against us."
7So Joshua marched up from Gilgal
with his entire army,[j] including all the
best fighting men. 8The LORD said to Joshua, "Do not be afraid[k] of them; I have
given them into your hand.[l] Not one of
them will be able to withstand you."[m]
9After an all-night march from Gilgal,
Joshua took them by surprise. 10The LORD
threw them into confusion[n] before Israel,[o] who defeated them in a great victory
at Gibeon.[p] Israel pursued them along
the road going up to Beth Horon[q] and cut
them down all the way to Azekah[r] and
Makkedah.[s] 11As they fled before Israel
on the road down from Beth Horon to
Azekah, the LORD hurled large hailstones[t] down on them from the sky,[u]
and more of them died from the hailstones than were killed by the swords of
the Israelites.
12On the day the LORD gave the Amorites[v] over to Israel, Joshua said to the
LORD in the presence of Israel:

[b] *1* The Hebrew term refers to the irrevocable giving over of things or persons to the LORD, often by totally destroying them; also in verses 28, 35, 37, 39 and 40.

9:17 [e]Jos 18:25; 2Sa 4:2; 23:37 [f]Jos 15:9,60; 18:14, 15; Jdg 18:12; 1Sa 6:21; 7:2; Ps 132:6; Jer 26:20
9:18 [g]ver 15; Jdg 21:1,7,18; 1Sa 20:17; Ps 15:4 [h]S Ex 15:24
9:20 [i]S Ge 24:8
9:21 [j]S ver 15 [k]S Dt 29:11
9:22 [l]ver 6 [m]ver 16
9:23 [n]S Ge 9:25
9:24 [o]ver 9
9:25 [p]Ge 16:6 [q]Jer 26:14
9:27 [r]S Ex 1:11 [s]S Dt 29:11 [t]Dt 12:5
10:1 [u]ver 3 [v]Jos 12:10; 15:8, 63; 18:28; Jdg 1:7 [w]S Jos 8:1 [x]S Dt 20:16; S Jos 8:22 [y]Jos 9:3 [z]S Jos 9:15
10:3 [a]S Ge 13:18 [b]ver 5; Jos 12:11; 15:35; 21:29; Ne 11:29 [c]ver 5,31; Jos 12:11; 15:39; 2Ki 14:19; 2Ch 11:9; 25:27; 32:9; Ne 11:30; Isa 36:2; 37:8; Jer 34:7; Mic 1:13 [d]ver 38; Jos 11:21; 12:13; 13:26; 15:7, 49; 21:15; Jdg 1:11; 1Ch 6:58 [e]ver 23,34,36; Jos 12:12; 15:39
10:4 [f]S Jos 9:15
10:5 [g]ver 16 [h]Nu 13:29; S Dt 1:7
10:6 [i]S Dt 11:30
10:7 [j]Jos 8:1
10:8 [k]S Dt 3:2; S Jos 1:9 [l]S Jos 2:24 [m]S Dt 7:24
10:10 [n]S Ex 14:24 [o]S Dt 7:23 [p]S Jos 9:3 [q]Jos 16:3,5; 18:13, 14; 21:22; 1Sa 13:18; 1Ki 9:17; 1Ch 6:68; 7:24; 2Ch 8:5; 25:13 [r]Jos 15:35; 1Sa 17:1; 2Ch 11:9; Ne 11:30; Jer 34:7 [s]ver 16,17,21; Jos 12:16; 15:41
10:11 [t]S Ex 9:18; Ps 18:12; Isa 28:2, 17; 32:19; Eze 13:11,13 [u]Jdg 5:20
10:12 [v]Am 2:9

10:1–43 HISTORY, Politics—God used the news of His acts of deliverance to cause Israel's enemies to gather together against His people. Thus the task of conquest was simpler and quicker than having to face each army separately. God in His mysterious ways can use human political maneuvering to achieve His purposes.

10:1–43 CHRISTIAN ETHICS, War and Peace—Joshua's wars were unique. God was directly involved in fighting for His people (Ex 15:3–10). God's military involvement in the Exodus and conquest established His chosen people and displayed His unique divine power before the nations. Contemporary war does not involve this onetime divine purpose or direct divine involvement. God remains the soverign Lord of history who can accomplish His will through the political and military actions of the nations. See note on 6:1–27.

10:12–13 HOLY SCRIPTURE, Writing—God led the inspired author to a written source for poetic language to describe Joshua's miraculous act. The same book is mentioned in 2 Sa 1:18 as the source for David's lament. The "Book of Jashar" has not been preserved complete, as it was not a writing God inspired for inclusion in the Scriptures. The book did serve God's purposes to provide language and information for His inspired writers. See note on 1 Ki 14:19,29.

10:12–14 PRAYER, Petition—Prayer helps us meet life's impossible tasks. Joshua sought and received a miracle as he led God's people to accomplish His mission. Faith brings great accomplishments. See note on Ge 18:14. Compare Nu 11:23.

"O sun, stand still over Gibeon,
O moon, over the Valley of
Aijalon.[w]"
13So the sun stood still,[x]
and the moon stopped,
till the nation avenged itself on[c] its
enemies,

as it is written in the Book of Jashar.[y]
The sun stopped[z] in the middle of the sky and delayed going down about a full day.
14There has never been a day like it before or since, a day when the LORD listened to a man. Surely the LORD was fighting[a] for Israel!

15Then Joshua returned with all Israel to the camp at Gilgal.[b]

Five Amorite Kings Killed

16Now the five kings had fled[c] and hidden in the cave at Makkedah.
17When Joshua was told that the five kings had been found hiding in the cave at Makkedah,
18he said, "Roll large rocks up to the mouth of the cave, and post some men there to guard it.
19But don't stop! Pursue your enemies, attack them from the rear and don't let them reach their cities, for the LORD your God has given them into your hand."

20So Joshua and the Israelites destroyed them completely[d]—almost to a man—but the few who were left reached their fortified cities.[e]
21The whole army then returned safely to Joshua in the camp at Makkedah, and no one uttered a word against the Israelites.

22Joshua said, "Open the mouth of the cave and bring those five kings out to me."
23So they brought the five kings out of the cave—the kings of Jerusalem, Hebron, Jarmuth, Lachish and Eglon.
24When they had brought these kings[f] to Joshua, he summoned all the men of Israel and said to the army commanders who had come with him, "Come here and put your feet[g] on the necks of these kings." So they came forward and placed their feet[h] on their necks.

25Joshua said to them, "Do not be afraid; do not be discouraged. Be strong and courageous.[i] This is what the LORD will do to all the enemies you are going to fight."
26Then Joshua struck and killed the kings and hung them on five trees, and they were left hanging on the trees until evening.

27At sunset[j] Joshua gave the order and they took them down from the trees and threw them into the cave where they had been hiding. At the mouth of the cave they placed large rocks, which are there to this day.[k]

28That day Joshua took Makkedah. He put the city and its king to the sword and totally destroyed everyone in it. He left no survivors.[l] And he did to the king of Makkedah as he had done to the king of Jericho.[m]

Southern Cities Conquered

29Then Joshua and all Israel with him moved on from Makkedah to Libnah[n] and attacked it.
30The LORD also gave that city and its king into Israel's hand. The city and everyone in it Joshua put to the sword. He left no survivors there. And he did to its king as he had done to the king of Jericho.

31Then Joshua and all Israel with him moved on from Libnah to Lachish;[o] he took up positions against it and attacked it.
32The LORD handed Lachish over to Israel, and Joshua took it on the second day. The city and everyone in it he put to the sword, just as he had done to Libnah.
33Meanwhile, Horam king of Gezer[p] had come up to help Lachish, but Joshua defeated him and his army—until no survivors were left.

34Then Joshua and all Israel with him moved on from Lachish to Eglon;[q] they took up positions against it and attacked it.
35They captured it that same day and put it to the sword and totally destroyed everyone in it, just as they had done to Lachish.

36Then Joshua and all Israel with him went up from Eglon to Hebron[r] and attacked it.
37They took the city and put it to the sword, together with its king, its villages and everyone[s] in it. They left no survivors. Just as at Eglon, they totally destroyed it and everyone in it.

38Then Joshua and all Israel with him turned around and attacked Debir.[t]
39They took the city, its king and its villages, and put them to the sword. Everyone in it they totally destroyed. They left no survivors. They did to Debir and its king as they had done to Libnah and its king and to Hebron.[u]

40So Joshua subdued the whole region, including the hill country, the Negev,[v] the western foothills and the mountain slopes,[w] together with all their kings.[x] He left no survivors. He totally destroyed all who breathed, just as the LORD, the

10:12 [w]Jos 19:42; 21:24; Jdg 1:35; 12:12; 1Sa 14:31; 1Ch 6:69; 8:13; 2Ch 11:10; 28:18
10:13 [x]Hab 3:11 [y]2Sa 1:18 [z]Isa 38:8
10:14 [a]ver 42; S Ex 14:14; Ps 106:43; 136:24; Isa 63:10; Jer 21:5
10:15 [b]ver 43
10:16 [c]Ps 68:12
10:20 [d]Dt 20:16 [e]2Ch 11:10; Jer 4:5; 5:17; 8:14; 35:11
10:24 [f]S Dt 7:24 [g]Mal 4:3 [h]2Sa 22:40; Ps 110:1; Isa 51:23
10:25 [i]S Dt 31:6
10:27 [j]S Dt 21:23 [k]S Ge 35:20
10:28 [l]Dt 20:16 [m]ver 30,32,35,39; Jos 6:21
10:29 [n]S Nu 33:20
10:31 [o]S ver 3
10:33 [p]Jos 12:12; 16:3,10; 21:21; Jdg 1:29; 2Sa 5:25; 1Ki 9:15; 1Ch 6:67
10:34 [q]S ver 3
10:36 [r]S Ge 13:18; Jos 14:13; 15:13; 20:7; 21:11; Jdg 16:3
10:37 [s]S ver 28
10:38 [t]S ver 3
10:39 [u]S ver 28
10:40 [v]S Ge 12:9; Jos 12:8; 15:19,21; 18:25; 19:8; 1Sa 30:27 [w]S Dt 1:7 [x]Dt 7:24

[c]13 Or *nation triumphed over*

10:14,42 ELECTION, Israel—The God of election fights to preserve and protect those elected to carry out His purposes. Only God could command the sun so that Joshua and the Israelites could defeat the Amorites. In so doing He confirmed the power He had shown and the salvation He provided in the Exodus. Israel knew election as the continuing experience of God's deliverance rather than as a doctrine to be learned and defended.

God of Israel, had commanded.[y] 41Joshua
subdued them from Kadesh Barnea[z] to
Gaza[a] and from the whole region of Goshen[b] to Gibeon. 42All these kings and
their lands Joshua conquered in one campaign, because the LORD, the God of Israel, fought[c] for Israel.
43Then Joshua returned with all Israel
to the camp at Gilgal.[d]

Chapter 11

Northern Kings Defeated

WHEN Jabin[e] king of Hazor[f] heard of
this, he sent word to Jobab king of
Madon, to the kings of Shimron[g] and Acshaph,[h] 2and to the northern kings who
were in the mountains, in the Arabah[i]
south of Kinnereth,[j] in the western foothills and in Naphoth Dor[d][k] on the west;
3to the Canaanites in the east and west;
to the Amorites, Hittites, Perizzites[l] and
Jebusites in the hill country;[m] and to the
Hivites[n] below Hermon[o] in the region of
Mizpah.[p] 4They came out with all their
troops and a large number of horses and
chariots—a huge army, as numerous as
the sand on the seashore.[q] 5All these
kings joined forces[r] and made camp together at the Waters of Merom,[s] to fight
against Israel.
6The LORD said to Joshua, "Do not be
afraid of them, because by this time tomorrow I will hand all of them over[t] to
Israel, slain. You are to hamstring[u] their
horses and burn their chariots."[v]
7So Joshua and his whole army came
against them suddenly at the Waters of
Merom and attacked them, 8and the LORD
gave them into the hand of Israel. They
defeated them and pursued them all the
way to Greater Sidon,[w] to Misrephoth
Maim,[x] and to the Valley of Mizpah on
the east, until no survivors were left.
9Joshua did to them as the LORD had directed: He hamstrung their horses and
burned their chariots.
10At that time Joshua turned back and
captured Hazor and put its king to the
sword.[y] (Hazor had been the head of all
these kingdoms.) 11Everyone in it they
put to the sword. They totally destroyed[e]
them,[z] not sparing anything that
breathed,[a] and he burned up[b] Hazor
itself.
12Joshua took all these royal cities and
their kings and put them to the sword. He
totally destroyed them, as Moses the servant of the LORD had commanded.[c] 13Yet
Israel did not burn any of the cities built
on their mounds—except Hazor, which
Joshua burned. 14The Israelites carried off
for themselves all the plunder and livestock of these cities, but all the people
they put to the sword until they completely destroyed them, not sparing anyone that breathed.[d] 15As the LORD commanded his servant Moses, so Moses
commanded Joshua, and Joshua did it; he
left nothing undone of all that the LORD
commanded Moses.[e]
16So Joshua took this entire land: the
hill country,[f] all the Negev,[g] the whole
region of Goshen, the western foothills,[h]
the Arabah and the mountains of Israel
with their foothills, 17from Mount Halak,
which rises toward Seir,[i] to Baal Gad[j]
in the Valley of Lebanon[k] below Mount
Hermon.[l] He captured all their kings and
struck them down, putting them to
death.[m] 18Joshua waged war against all
these kings for a long time. 19Except for
the Hivites[n] living in Gibeon,[o] not one
city made a treaty of peace[p] with the Israelites, who took them all in battle. 20For
it was the LORD himself who hardened
their hearts[q] to wage war against Israel,
so that he might destroy them totally, ex-
terminating them without mercy, as the
LORD had commanded Moses.[r]
21At that time Joshua went and de-

10:40 [y]Dt 20:16-17
10:41 [z]S Ge 14:7 [a]S Ge 10:19 [b]Jos 11:16; 15:51
10:42 [c]S ver 14
10:43 [d]ver 15; Jos 5:9; 1Sa 7:16; 10:8; 11:14; 13:12
11:1 [e]Jdg 4:2,7,23; Ps 83:9 [f]ver 10; Jos 12:19; 15:23, 25; 19:36; Jdg 4:2, 17; 1Sa 12:9; 1Ki 9:15; 2Ki 15:29; Ne 11:33; Jer 49:28,33 [g]Jos 19:15 [h]Jos 12:20; 19:25
11:2 [i]ver 16; S Dt 1:1; Jos 12:1; 18:18 [j]S Nu 34:11; Dt 3:17; Jos 19:35; 1Ki 15:20 [k]Jos 12:23; 17:11; Jdg 1:27; 1Ki 4:11; 1Ch 7:29
11:3 [l]S Jos 3:10 [m]Nu 13:17 [n]S Ex 3:8; Dt 7:1; Jdg 3:3,5; 1Ki 9:20 [o]S Dt 3:8 [p]ver 8; S Ge 31:49; Jos 15:38; 18:26; Jdg 11:11; 20:1; 21:1; 1Sa 7:5,6; 1Ki 15:22; 2Ki 25:23
11:4 [q]S Ge 12:2; Jdg 7:12; 1Sa 13:5
11:5 [r]Jdg 5:19 [s]ver 7
11:6 [t]S Jos 2:24 [u]S Ge 49:6 [v]ver 9
11:8 [w]S Ge 10:15; S Jdg 18:7 [x]Jos 13:6
11:10 [y]Isa 3:25; Jer 41:2; 44:18
11:11 [z]S Dt 7:2 [a]Dt 20:16-17 [b]S Nu 31:10
11:12 [c]Nu 33:50-52; Dt 7:2
11:14 [d]S Dt 20:16
11:15 [e]Ex 34:11; Dt 7:2; S Jos 1:7
11:16 [f]Nu 13:17 [g]S Dt 1:7 [h]S Jos 10:41
11:17 [i]S Ge 14:6; S Nu 24:18; S Dt 33:2 [j]Jos 13:5 [k]S Dt 3:25; Jos 12:7 [l]Dt 3:9; Jos 12:8 [m]Dt 7:24
11:19 [n]S Jos 9:1 [o]S Jos 9:3 [p]S Jos 9:15
11:20 [q]S Ex 4:21; S 14:17; Ro 9:18 [r]Dt 7:16; Jdg 14:4

[d] *2* Or *in the heights of Dor* [e] *11* The Hebrew term refers to the irrevocable giving over of things or persons to the LORD, often by totally destroying them; also in verses 12, 20 and 21.

11:1 HISTORY, Politics—See notes on 5:1; 10:1–43.

11:1–23 CHRISTIAN ETHICS, War and Peace—Obedience was the key for Joshua's wars. Israel won because Joshua obeyed God perfectly. The call to warfare no longer rings out from God to us. The call to obedience does. See note on 6:1–27.

11:8 MIRACLE, Instruments—God's miracles involve human leaders and actions. The simple statement of the Lord's deliverance must not be understood as occurring apart from Joshua and his people. A unified hostile force provoked this last major battle of conquest. God assured Joshua that He would make victory possible, and Joshua led his forces to the waters of Merom. God used Joshua and his whole army to produce a miraculous victory. Only eyes of faith can see God's miracle in some of His acts for His people.

11:20 GOD, Wrath—See note on Dt 7:1–6. God does what is necessary to carry out His will in any given set of circumstances. Here God was creating a homeland for His chosen people. Hostile peoples who did not welcome the migrating Israelites had to be eliminated for God to establish and develop His chosen people. The Israelite nation was chosen for the special task of being God's servant community in the world. Wrath was the necessary action that God had to take in carrying out His purpose. From our modern perspective, we may raise questions about the justice of God displacing one people with another, but we must also respect the sovereignty of God. This is God's earth, and all of the peoples of the earth are His to do with as He pleases. If one tribe or nation will not hospitably welcome God's chosen servant community, they only bring a just condemnation on themselves. We must be careful that we do not allow such a passage as this to lead us into understanding God as harsh and arbitrary rather than just and loving. Wrath was exercised consistent with God's sovereignty and righteousness, as He pursued His ultimate goals of love and mercy. His wrath for some people was the necessary step towards love and blessing for more people later.

stroyed the Anakites[s] from the hill country: from Hebron, Debir[t] and Anab,[u]
from all the hill country of Judah, and
from all the hill country of Israel. Joshua
totally destroyed them and their towns.
22No Anakites were left in Israelite territory; only in Gaza,[v] Gath[w] and Ashdod[x]
did any survive. 23So Joshua took the entire land,[y] just as the LORD had directed
Moses, and he gave it as an inheritance[z]
to Israel according to their tribal divisions.[a] [b]

Then the land had rest[c] from war.[d]

Chapter 12

List of Defeated Kings

THESE are the kings of the land whom the Israelites had defeated and whose territory they took[e] over east of the Jordan,[f] from the Arnon[g] Gorge to Mount Hermon,[h] including all the eastern side of the Arabah:[i]

2Sihon king of the Amorites,
who reigned in Heshbon.[j] He ruled
from Aroer[k] on the rim of the Arnon
Gorge—from the middle of the
gorge—to the Jabbok River,[l] which
is the border of the Ammonites.[m]
This included half of Gilead.[n] 3He
also ruled over the eastern Arabah
from the Sea of Kinnereth[f][o] to the
Sea of the Arabah (the Salt Sea[g][p]), to
Beth Jeshimoth,[q] and then southward below the slopes of Pisgah.[r]

4And the territory of Og king of Bashan,[s]
one of the last of the Rephaites,[t]
who reigned in Ashtaroth[u] and Edrei. 5He ruled over Mount Hermon,
Salecah,[v] all of Bashan[w] to the border of the people of Geshur[x] and Maacah,[y] and half of Gilead[z] to the border of Sihon king of Heshbon.

6Moses, the servant of the LORD, and
the Israelites conquered them.[a] And Moses the servant of the LORD gave their
land to the Reubenites, the Gadites and
the half-tribe of Manasseh to be their possession.[b]

7These are the kings of the land that
Joshua and the Israelites conquered on
the west side of the Jordan, from Baal Gad
in the Valley of Lebanon[c] to Mount Halak, which rises toward Seir (their lands
Joshua gave as an inheritance to the
tribes of Israel according to their tribal
divisions— 8the hill country, the western
foothills, the Arabah, the mountain
slopes, the desert and the Negev[d]—the
lands of the Hittites, Amorites, Canaanites, Perizzites, Hivites and Jebusites):[e]

9the king of Jericho[f] one
the king of Ai[g] (near Bethel[h]) one
10the king of Jerusalem[i] one
the king of Hebron one
11the king of Jarmuth one
the king of Lachish[j] one
12the king of Eglon[k] one
the king of Gezer[l] one
13the king of Debir[m] one
the king of Geder one
14the king of Hormah[n] one
the king of Arad[o] one
15the king of Libnah[p] one
the king of Adullam[q] one
16the king of Makkedah[r] one
the king of Bethel[s] one
17the king of Tappuah[t] one
the king of Hepher[u] one
18the king of Aphek[v] one
the king of Lasharon one
19the king of Madon one
the king of Hazor[w] one
20the king of Shimron Meron one
the king of Acshaph[x] one
21the king of Taanach[y] one
the king of Megiddo[z] one
22the king of Kedesh[a] one
the king of Jokneam[b] in Carmel[c] one
23the king of Dor (in Naphoth Dor[h][d]) one
the king of Goyim in Gilgal one
24the king of Tirzah[e] one
thirty-one kings in all.[f]

Chapter 13

Land Still to Be Taken

WHEN Joshua was old and well advanced in years,[g] the LORD said to

11:21 [s]S Nu 13:22, 33 [t]S Jos 10:3 [u]Jos 15:50 **11:22** [v]S Ge 10:19 [w]Jos 12:17; 19:13; 1Sa 5:8; 17:4; 1Ki 2:39; 2Ki 14:25; 1Ch 8:13; Am 6:2 [x]Jos 15:47; 1Sa 5:1; Isa 20:1 **11:23** [y]Jos 21:43-45; Ne 9:24 [z]S Dt 1:38; 12:9-10; S 25:19; S Jos 13:7 [a]S Nu 26:53 [b]Ps 105:44 [c]S Ex 33:14 [d]Jos 14:15 **12:1** [e]Ps 136:21 [f]S Nu 32:19 [g]S Nu 21:13 [h]S Dt 3:8 [i]S Jos 11:2 **12:2** [j]ver 5; S Nu 21:21,25; Jos 13:10; Jdg 11:19 [k]S Nu 32:34; S Jos 13:16 [l]S Ge 32:22 [m]S Ge 19:38 [n]S Ge 31:21; S Nu 32:26; Dt 2:36; S 3:15; Jos 13:11,25; 17:1; 20:8; 21:38; Jdg 5:17; 7:3; 10:8 **12:3** [o]Jos 11:2 [p]S Ge 14:3 [q]S Nu 33:49; Jos 13:20 [r]S Nu 21:20 **12:4** [s]S Nu 21:21, 33; Jos 13:30 [t]S Ge 14:5 [u]S Dt 1:4 **12:5** [v]S Dt 3:10 [w]Nu 32:33; Jos 17:1; 20:8; 21:27; 22:7 [x]Jos 13:2,13; 1Sa 27:8 [y]S Dt 3:14 [z]ver 2 **12:6** [a]S Dt 3:8 [b]Nu 32:29,33; Jos 13:8 **12:7** [c]S Jos 11:17 **12:8** [d]S Dt 1:7 [e]S Jos 3:10; S 11:17; Ezr 9:1 **12:9** [f]S Nu 33:48 [g]S Ge 12:8; S Jos 8:1 [h]S Jos 7:2; 8:9; 18:13; Jdg 1:23; 4:5; 20:18; 21:2; Ne 11:31 **12:10** [i]S Jos 10:1 **12:11** [j]S Jos 10:3 **12:12** [k]S Jos 10:3 [l]S Jos 10:33 **12:13** [m]S Jos 10:3 **12:14** [n]S Nu 14:45 [o]S Nu 21:1 **12:15** [p]S Nu 33:20 [q]S Ge 38:1; Jos 15:35; Mic 1:15 **12:16** [r]S Jos 10:10 [s]S Jos 7:2 **12:17** [t]Jos 15:34; 16:8; 17:8 [u]S Jos 11:22; 1Ki 4:10 **12:18** [v]Jos 13:4; 19:30; Jdg 1:31; 1Sa 4:1; 29:1 **12:19** [w]S Jos 11:1 **12:20** [x]S Jos 11:1 **12:21** [y]Jos 17:11; 21:25 [z]Jdg 1:27; 5:19; 1Ki 4:12 **12:22** [a]Jos 15:23; 19:37; 20:7; 21:32; Jdg 4:6,9 [b]Jos 19:11; 21:34 [c]Jos 15:55; 19:26; 1Sa 15:12; 2Sa 23:35 **12:23** [d]S Jos 11:2 **12:24** [e]1Ki 14:17; 15:33; 16:8,23; SS 6:4 [f]Ps 135:11; 136:18 **13:1** [g]Ge 24:1; Jos 14:10; 23:1,2; 1Ki 1:1

[f]3 That is, Galilee [g]3 That is, the Dead Sea
[h]23 Or *in the heights of Dor*

11:23 HISTORY, Promise—God fulfilled His promise to Abraham (Ge 12:7) and to Moses (Ex 3:8). Historical acts thus showed God's faithfulness. God's ultimate objective was rest, not war (Jos 1:13; Ex 33:14; Dt 12:9–10; 25:19). Political and military actions were practical ways God in His wisdom chose to accomplish His purposes in the human situations.

13:1—19:51 HISTORY, Geography—See note on Nu 34:1–29. God's interest in concrete human history rather than an isolated spiritual world is shown by the extended attention the Bible gives to geography. God provided specific places for the different parts of His people to live out their lives. Even the division of the land contained an element of hope and promise, for not all the land was "taken over" (13:1).

13:1–7 HUMANITY, Age—Old age is the natural end of the life process. Age alters the way people are expected to fulfill their responsibilities to God, but it does not end such responsibility. All physical and mental capacities are to be dedicated to God as long as He gives us life.

him, "You are very old, and there are still
very large areas of land to be taken over.

2"This is the land that remains: all
the regions of the Philistines[h] and
Geshurites:[i] 3from the Shihor River[j] on the east of Egypt to the territory of Ekron[k] on the north, all of it
counted as Canaanite (the territory of
the five Philistine rulers[l] in Gaza,
Ashdod,[m] Ashkelon,[n] Gath and Ekron—that of the Avvites);[o] 4from
the south, all the land of the Canaanites, from Arah of the Sidonians as far
as Aphek,[p] the region of the Amorites,[q] 5the area of the Gebalites[i];[r]
and all Lebanon[s] to the east, from
Baal Gad below Mount Hermon[t] to
Lebo[j] Hamath.[u]

6"As for all the inhabitants of the
mountain regions from Lebanon to Misrephoth Maim,[v] that is, all the Sidonians, I
myself will drive them out[w] before the
Israelites. Be sure to allocate this land to
Israel for an inheritance, as I have instructed you,[x] 7and divide it as an inheritance[y] among the nine tribes and half of
the tribe of Manasseh."

Division of the Land East of the Jordan

8The other half of Manasseh,[k] the Reubenites and the Gadites had received the
inheritance that Moses had given them
east of the Jordan, as he, the servant of
the LORD, had assigned[z] it to them.[a]

9It extended from Aroer[b] on the rim
of the Arnon Gorge, and from the
town in the middle of the gorge, and
included the whole plateau[c] of Medeba as far as Dibon,[d] 10and all the
towns of Sihon king of the Amorites,
who ruled in Heshbon,[e] out to the
border of the Ammonites.[f] 11It also
included Gilead,[g] the territory of the
people of Geshur and Maacah, all of
Mount Hermon and all Bashan as far
as Salecah[h]— 12that is, the whole
kingdom of Og in Bashan,[i] who had
reigned in Ashtaroth[j] and Edrei[k]
and had survived as one of the last of
the Rephaites.[l] Moses had defeated
them and taken over their land.[m]
13But the Israelites did not drive out
the people of Geshur[n] and Maacah,[o]
so they continue to live among the
Israelites to this day.[p]

14But to the tribe of Levi he gave no
inheritance, since the offerings made by
fire to the LORD, the God of Israel, are
their inheritance, as he promised them.[q]

15This is what Moses had given to the
tribe of Reuben, clan by clan:

16The territory from Aroer[r] on the
rim of the Arnon Gorge, and from the
town in the middle of the gorge, and
the whole plateau past Medeba[s] 17to
Heshbon and all its towns on the plateau,[t] including Dibon,[u] Bamoth
Baal,[v] Beth Baal Meon,[w] 18Jahaz,[x]
Kedemoth,[y] Mephaath,[z] 19Kiriatha-
im,[a] Sibmah,[b] Zereth Shahar on the
hill in the valley, 20Beth Peor,[c] the
slopes of Pisgah, and Beth Jeshimoth
21—all the towns on the plateau[d]
and the entire realm of Sihon king of
the Amorites, who ruled at Heshbon.
Moses had defeated him and the
Midianite chiefs,[e] Evi, Rekem, Zur,
Hur and Reba[f]—princes allied with
Sihon—who lived in that country.
22In addition to those slain in battle,
the Israelites had put to the sword
Balaam son of Beor,[g] who practiced
divination.[h] 23The boundary of the
Reubenites was the bank of the Jordan. These towns and their villages
were the inheritance of the Reubenites, clan by clan.[i]

24This is what Moses had given to the
tribe of Gad, clan by clan:

25The territory of Jazer,[j] all the
towns of Gilead[k] and half the Ammonite country as far as Aroer, near
Rabbah;[l] 26and from Heshbon[m] to
Ramath Mizpah and Betonim, and
from Mahanaim[n] to the territory of
Debir;[o] 27and in the valley, Beth Ha-
ram, Beth Nimrah,[p] Succoth[q] and
Zaphon[r] with the rest of the realm of
Sihon king of Heshbon (the east side
of the Jordan, the territory up to the
end of the Sea of Kinnereth[l][s]).
28These towns and their villages
were the inheritance of the Gadites,[t] clan by clan.

29This is what Moses had given to the
half-tribe of Manasseh, that is, to half the

13:2 [h]S Ge 10:14; S Jdg 3:31 [i]S Jos 12:5 **13:3** [j]1Ch 13:5; Isa 23:3; Jer 2:18 [k]Jos 15:11,45; 19:43; Jdg 1:18; 1Sa 5:10; 7:14 [l]Jdg 3:3; 16:5,18; 1Sa 6:4,17; Isa 14:29; Jer 25:20; Eze 25:15 [m]S Jos 11:22; Am 3:9 [n]Jdg 1:18; 14:19; 2Sa 1:20 [o]S Dt 2:23 **13:4** [p]S Jos 12:18 [q]S Ge 14:7; S 15:16; Am 2:10 **13:5** [r]1Ki 5:18; Ps 83:7; Eze 27:9 [s]S Jos 11:17 [t]S Dt 3:8 [u]S Nu 13:21; 34:8; Jdg 3:3 **13:6** [v]Jos 11:8 [w]Ps 80:8 [x]Nu 33:54; S 34:13 **13:7** [y]S Jos 11:23; Ps 78:55 **13:8** [z]S Jos 12:6 [a]Jos 18:7 **13:9** [b]ver 16; S Nu 32:34; Dt 2:36; Jdg 11:26; 2Sa 24:5 [c]ver 17, 21; Jer 48:8,21 [d]S Nu 21:30; S 32:3; Isa 15:2; Jer 48:18,22 **13:10** [e]S Jos 12:2 [f]S Nu 21:24 **13:11** [g]S Jos 12:2 [h]Jos 12:5 **13:12** [i]S Dt 1:4 [j]Jos 12:4 [k]S Nu 21:33 [l]S Ge 14:5 [m]S Dt 3:8 **13:13** [n]S Jos 12:5 [o]S Dt 3:14 [p]Dt 3:12 **13:14** [q]ver 33; Dt 18:1-2; Jos 14:3 **13:16** [r]S ver 9; Jos 12:2; 1Sa 30:28 [s]S Nu 21:30; Isa 15:2 **13:17** [t]S ver 9 [u]S Nu 32:3 [v]Nu 22:41 [w]1Ch 5:8; Jer 48:23; Eze 25:9 **13:18** [x]S Nu 21:23 [y]S Dt 2:26 [z]Jos 21:37; Jer 48:21 **13:19** [a]S Nu 32:37 [b]S Nu 32:3 **13:20** [c]S Dt 3:29 **13:21** [d]S ver 9 [e]S Ge 25:2; S Nu 25:15 [f]Nu 31:8 **13:22** [g]S Nu 22:5 [h]S Ge 30:27; S Nu 23:23 **13:23** [i]1Ch 5:7 **13:25** [j]S Nu 21:32; Jos 21:39 [k]S Jos 12:2 [l]S Dt 3:11 **13:26** [m]S Nu 21:25; Jer 49:3 [n]S Ge 32:2 [o]S Jos 10:3 **13:27** [p]S Nu 32:3 [q]S Ge 33:17 [r]Jdg 12:1; Ps 48:2 [s]S Nu 34:11 **13:28** [t]Ge 46:16; S Nu 32:33; Eze 48:27

[i]5 That is, the area of Byblos [j]5 Or *to the entrance to* [k]8 Hebrew *With it* (that is, with the other half of Manasseh) [l]27 That is, Galilee

13:6–7 ELECTION, Mission—Israel was called upon to occupy that portion of the land available to them while trusting God to assist them in possessing the remainder of the land held by their enemies. Joshua, because of old age, would not complete the mission. The land that remained had three sections: the land of the Philistines, the Phoenician coast, and the northern mountain country of Lebanon. David and Solomon helped to conquer the Philistines and to control Phoenicia (2 Sa 5:17–25; 8:1; 21:15–22; 23:8–17; 24:6–7). Solomon controlled Lebanon (1 Ki 9:19). Election leads God's people to God's mission, a task to be undertaken if never fully accomplished.

family of the descendants of Manasseh, clan by clan:

30The territory extending from Mahanaim[u] and including all of Bashan,[v] the entire realm of Og king of Bashan[w]—all the settlements of Jair[x] in Bashan, sixty towns, 31half of Gilead, and Ashtaroth and Edrei (the royal cities of Og in Bashan).[y] This was for the descendants of Makir[z] son of Manasseh—for half of the sons of Makir, clan by clan.[a]

32This is the inheritance Moses had given when he was in the plains of Moab[b] across the Jordan east of Jericho.[c] 33But to the tribe of Levi, Moses had given no inheritance;[d] the LORD, the God of Israel, is their inheritance,[e] as he promised them.[f]

Chapter 14

Division of the Land West of the Jordan

NOW these are the areas the Israelites received as an inheritance[g] in the land of Canaan, which Eleazar[h] the priest, Joshua son of Nun and the heads of the tribal clans of Israel[i] allotted[j] to them.[k] 2Their inheritances were assigned by lot[l] to the nine-and-a-half tribes,[m] as the LORD had commanded through Moses. 3Moses had granted the two-and-a-half tribes their inheritance east of the Jordan[n] but had not granted the Levites an inheritance among the rest,[o] 4for the sons of Joseph had become two tribes—Manasseh and Ephraim.[p] The Levites received no share of the land but only towns to live in, with pasturelands for their flocks and herds.[q] 5So the Israelites divided the land, just as the LORD had commanded Moses.[r]

Hebron Given to Caleb

6Now the men of Judah approached Joshua at Gilgal,[s] and Caleb son of Jephunneh[t] the Kenizzite said to him, "You know what the LORD said to Moses the man of God[u] at Kadesh Barnea[v] about you and me.[w] 7I was forty years old when Moses the servant of the LORD sent me from Kadesh Barnea[x] to explore the land.[y] And I brought him back a report according to my convictions,[z] 8but my brothers who went up with me made the hearts of the people melt with fear.[a] I, however, followed the LORD my God wholeheartedly.[b] 9So on that day Moses swore to me, 'The land on which your feet have walked will be your inheritance[c] and that of your children[d] forever, because you have followed the LORD my God wholeheartedly.'[m]

10"Now then, just as the LORD promised,[e] he has kept me alive for forty-five years since the time he said this to Moses, while Israel moved[f] about in the desert. So here I am today, eighty-five years old![g] 11I am still as strong[h] today as the day Moses sent me out; I'm just as vigorous[i] to go out to battle now as I was then. 12Now give me this hill country that the LORD promised me that day.[j] You yourself heard then that the Anakites[k] were there and their cities were large and fortified,[l] but, the LORD helping me, I will drive them out just as he said."

13Then Joshua blessed[m] Caleb son of Jephunneh[n] and gave him Hebron[o] as his inheritance.[p] 14So Hebron has belonged to Caleb son of Jephunneh the Kenizzite ever since, because he followed the LORD, the God of Israel, wholeheartedly.[q] 15(Hebron used to be called Kiriath Arba[r] after Arba,[s] who was the greatest man among the Anakites.)

Then the land had rest[t] from war.

Chapter 15

Allotment for Judah

15:15–19pp — Jdg 1:11–15

THE allotment for the tribe of Judah, clan by clan, extended down to the territory of Edom,[u] to the Desert of Zin[v] in the extreme south.[w]

2Their southern boundary started from the bay at the southern end of the Salt Sea,[n][x] 3crossed south of Scorpion[o] Pass,[y] continued on to Zin and went over to the south of Kadesh Barnea.[z] Then it ran past Hezron up to Addar and curved around to Karka. 4It then passed along to Azmon[a] and joined the Wadi of Egypt,[b] ending at the sea. This is their[p] southern boundary.

5The eastern boundary[c] is the Salt

13:30 [u]S Ge 32:2 [v]S Nu 21:33 [w]S Jos 12:4 [x]S Nu 32:41
13:31 [y]Nu 21:33 [z]S Ge 50:23 [a]Jos 17:5
13:32 [b]S Nu 26:3 [c]S Nu 22:1
13:33 [d]Nu 26:62 [e]S Nu 18:20 [f]S ver 14; Jos 18:7; Eze 44:28
14:1 [g]S Jos 11:23; Ps 16:6; 136:21 [h]S Ex 6:23 [i]Jos 21:1 [j]S Nu 26:53 [k]Nu 34:17-18; Jos 19:51
14:2 [l]S Lev 16:8 [m]Nu 34:13
14:3 [n]S Nu 32:33; S 34:14 [o]S Nu 35:2; S Jos 13:14
14:4 [p]S Ge 41:52; S Jdg 1:29 [q]S Nu 35:2-3; Jos 21:2
14:5 [r]S Nu 34:13
14:6 [s]S Dt 11:30 [t]Nu 13:6; 14:30 [u]S Dt 33:1 [v]Nu 13:26 [w]S Nu 14:38
14:7 [x]Jos 15:3 [y]S Nu 13:17 [z]Nu 13:30; S 14:6-9
14:8 [a]S Nu 13:31 [b]S Nu 14:24; S 32:12
14:9 [c]S Dt 11:24 [d]S Nu 14:24
14:10 [e]S Nu 11:28; 14:30 [f]S Jos 5:6 [g]S Jos 13:1
14:11 [h]S Dt 34:7 [i]S Ge 15:15
14:12 [j]S Nu 14:24 [k]S Nu 13:33 [l]Nu 13:28
14:13 [m]Jos 22:6,7 [n]1Sa 25:3; 30:14 [o]S Ge 23:19; S Jos 10:36 [p]Jdg 1:20; 1Ch 6:56
14:14 [q]S Nu 14:24
14:15 [r]S Ge 23:2 [s]Jos 15:13 [t]Jos 11:23; Jdg 3:11; 1Ki 4:24; 5:4; 1Ch 22:9
15:1 [u]Nu 34:3 [v]S Nu 13:21 [w]Jos 18:5
15:2 [x]S Ge 14:3
15:3 [y]S Nu 34:4 [z]S Dt 1:2
15:4 [a]Nu 34:4 [b]S Ge 15:18
15:5 [c]Nu 34:10

[m]9 Deut. 1:36 [n]2 That is, the Dead Sea; also in verse 5 [o]3 Hebrew *Akrabbim* [p]4 Hebrew *your*

14:6–15 GOD, Faithfulness—God has a long memory and is always faithful to those faithful to Him. He is faithful, dependable, unchanging. He is not like the gods of the nations—or like human beings—who are always changing, acting upon whim rather than reason, unpredictable, moody, erratic. See 21:45.

14:6–14 HUMANITY, Age—Growing old in the service of God does not diminish a person's enthusiasm for that service. Further, a life which has long been lived in an obedient and faithful relationship to God gives one confidence to seek additional opportunities and face new challenges.

14:6–15 HISTORY, Promise—God's historical promises proved true for individuals as well as the nation. God is interested in every individual's history as well as the history of His people. Fulfilled promises give faith for larger tasks.

Sea[d] as far as the mouth of the
Jordan.

The northern boundary[e] started
from the bay of the sea at the mouth
of the Jordan, 6went up to Beth Hoglah[f] and continued north of Beth Arabah[g] to the Stone of Bohan[h] son of
Reuben. 7The boundary then went
up to Debir[i] from the Valley of
Achor[j] and turned north to Gilgal,[k]
which faces the Pass of Adummim
south of the gorge. It continued along
to the waters of En Shemesh[l] and
came out at En Rogel.[m] 8Then it ran
up the Valley of Ben Hinnom[n] along
the southern slope of the Jebusite[o]
city (that is, Jerusalem[p]). From there
it climbed to the top of the hill west
of the Hinnom Valley[q] at the northern end of the Valley of Rephaim.[r]
9From the hilltop the boundary headed toward the spring of the waters of
Nephtoah,[s] came out at the towns of
Mount Ephron and went down toward Baalah[t] (that is, Kiriath Jearim).[u] 10Then it curved westward
from Baalah[v] to Mount Seir,[w] ran
along the northern slope of Mount Jearim (that is, Kesalon), continued
down to Beth Shemesh[x] and crossed
to Timnah.[y] 11It went to the northern slope of Ekron,[z] turned toward
Shikkeron, passed along to Mount Baalah[a] and reached Jabneel.[b] The
boundary ended at the sea.

12The western boundary is the
coastline of the Great Sea.[q] [c]
These are the boundaries around the people of Judah by their clans.

13In accordance with the LORD's command to him, Joshua gave to Caleb[d] son
of Jephunneh a portion in Judah—Kiriath
Arba[e], that is, Hebron.[f] (Arba was the
forefather of Anak.)[g] 14From Hebron Caleb drove out the three Anakites[h]—Sheshai, Ahiman and Talmai[i]—descendants
of Anak.[j] 15From there he marched
against the people living in Debir (formerly called Kiriath Sepher). 16And Caleb
said, "I will give my daughter Acsah[k] in
marriage to the man who attacks and captures Kiriath Sepher." 17Othniel[l] son of
Kenaz, Caleb's brother, took it; so Caleb
gave his daughter Acsah to him in marriage.

18One day when she came to Othniel,
she urged him[r] to ask her father for a
field. When she got off her donkey, Caleb
asked her, "What can I do for you?"

19She replied, "Do me a special favor.
Since you have given me land in the Negev,[m] give me also springs of water." So
Caleb gave her the upper and lower
springs.[n]

20This is the inheritance of the tribe of
Judah, clan by clan:

21The southernmost towns of the tribe of
Judah in the Negev[o] toward the boundary of Edom were:

Kabzeel,[p] Eder,[q] Jagur, 22Kinah,
Dimonah, Adadah, 23Kedesh,[r] Hazor,[s] Ithnan, 24Ziph,[t] Telem, Bea-
loth, 25Hazor Hadattah, Kerioth Hezron (that is, Hazor),[u] 26Amam, Shema, Moladah,[v] 27Hazar Gaddah,
Heshmon, Beth Pelet, 28Hazar Shual,[w] Beersheba,[x] Biziothiah, 29Baal-
ah,[y] Iim, Ezem,[z] 30Eltolad,[a] Kesil,
Hormah,[b] 31Ziklag,[c] Madmannah,[d]
Sansannah, 32Lebaoth, Shilhim, Ain[e]
and Rimmon[f]—a total of twenty-
nine towns and their villages.

33In the western foothills:

Eshtaol,[g] Zorah,[h] Ashnah,[i] 34Za-
noah,[j] En Gannim,[k] Tappuah,[l]
Enam, 35Jarmuth,[m] Adullam,[n] Socoh,[o] Azekah,[p] 36Shaaraim,[q] Adi-
thaim and Gederah[r] (or Gederothaim)[s]—fourteen towns and their
villages.

37Zenan, Hadashah, Migdal Gad,
38Dilean, Mizpah,[s] Joktheel,[t] 39La-
chish,[u] Bozkath,[v] Eglon,[w] 40Cab-
bon, Lahmas, Kitlish, 41Gederoth,[x]
Beth Dagon,[y] Naamah and Makkedah[z]—sixteen towns and their villages.

42Libnah,[a] Ether, Ashan,[b] 43Iph-
tah, Ashnah,[c] Nezib, 44Keilah,[d] Aczib[e] and Mareshah[f]—nine towns
and their villages.

45Ekron,[g] with its surrounding settlements and villages; 46west of Ekron, all that were in the vicinity of
Ashdod,[h] together with their villages; 47Ashdod,[i] its surrounding
settlements and villages; and Gaza,
its settlements and villages, as far as
the Wadi of Egypt[j] and the coastline
of the Great Sea.[k]

48In the hill country:

Shamir,[l] Jattir,[m] Socoh,[n] 49Dan-
nah, Kiriath Sannah (that is, Debir[o]),

15:5 [d]S Ge 14:3 [e]Jos 18:15-19 **15:6** [f]Jos 18:19,21 [g]ver 61; Jos 18:18 [h]Jos 18:17 **15:7** [i]S Jos 10:3 [j]S Jos 7:24 [k]S Dt 11:30 [l]Jos 18:17 [m]Jos 18:16; 2Sa 17:17; 1Ki 1:9 **15:8** [n]2Ch 28:3; Jer 19:6 [o]ver 63; Jos 18:16,28; Jdg 1:21; 19:10; 2Sa 5:6; 1Ch 11:4; Ezr 9:1 [p]S Jos 10:1 [q]2Ki 23:10; Jer 7:31; 19:2 [r]2Sa 5:18,22; 1Ch 14:9; Isa 17:5 **15:9** [s]Jos 18:15 [t]ver 10,11,29; 2Sa 6:2; 1Ch 13:6 [u]S Jos 9:17 **15:10** [v]S ver 9 [w]S Nu 24:18 [x]Jos 19:22,38; 21:16; Jdg 1:33; 1Sa 6:9; 1Ki 4:9; 2Ki 14:11 [y]S Ge 38:12 **15:11** [z]S Jos 13:3 [a]S ver 9 [b]Jos 19:33 **15:12** [c]S Nu 34:6 **15:13** [d]1Sa 25:3; 30:14 [e]S Ge 23:2 [f]S Jos 10:36; 21:12; 1Ch 6:56 [g]S Nu 13:22 **15:14** [h]S Nu 13:33 [i]S Nu 13:22 [j]Jdg 1:10,20 **15:16** [k]1Ch 2:49 **15:17** [l]Jdg 3:9,11; 1Ch 4:13; 27:15 **15:19** [m]S Jos 10:40 [n]Ge 36:24 **15:21** [o]S Jos 10:40 [p]2Sa 23:20; 1Ch 11:22 [q]Ge 35:21 **15:23** [r]S Jos 12:22 [s]S Jos 11:1 **15:24** [t]ver 55; 1Sa 23:14; 2Ch 11:8 **15:25** [u]S Jos 11:1 **15:26** [v]Jos 19:2; 1Ch 4:28; Ne 11:26 **15:28** [w]Jos 19:3; 1Ch 4:28 [x]S Ge 21:14 **15:29** [y]S ver 9 [z]Jos 19:3; 1Ch 4:29 **15:30** [a]Jos 19:4 [b]S Nu 14:45 **15:31** [c]Jos 19:5; 1Sa 27:6; 1Ch 4:30; 12:1; Ne 11:28 [d]1Ch 2:49 **15:32** [e]S Nu 34:11 [f]Jos 19:7; Jdg 20:45; 21:13; Zec 14:10 **15:33** [g]Jos 19:41; Jdg 13:25; 16:31; 18:2 [h]Jdg 13:2; 18:11; 2Ch 11:10; Ne 11:29 [i]ver 43 **15:34** [j]ver 56; 1Ch 4:18; Ne 3:13; 11:30 [k]Jos 19:21; 21:29 [l]S Jos 12:17 **15:35** [m]S Jos 10:3 [n]S Ge 38:1 [o]ver 48; 1Ki 4:10 [p]S Jos 10:10 **15:36** [q]1Sa 17:52; 1Ch 4:31 [r]1Ch 12:4 **15:38** [s]S Jos 11:3 [t]2Ki 14:7 **15:39** [u]S Jos 10:3 [v]2Ki 22:1 [w]S Jos 10:3 **15:41** [x]2Ch 28:18 [y]Jos 19:27 [z]S Jos 10:10 **15:42** [a]S Nu 33:20 [b]Jos 19:7; 1Sa 30:30; 1Ch 4:32; 6:59 **15:43** [c]ver 33 **15:44** [d]1Sa 23:1-2,1; 1Ch 4:19; Ne 3:17,18 [e]Jos 19:29; Jdg 1:31; Mic 1:14 [f]Mic 1:15 **15:45** [g]S Jos 13:3 **15:46** [h]Jos 11:22 **15:47** [i]S Jos 11:22 [j]S Ge 15:18 [k]S Nu 34:6 **15:48** [l]Jdg 10:1 [m]Jos 21:14; 1Sa 30:27; 1Ch 6:57 [n]S ver 35 **15:49** [o]S Jos 10:3

[q] *12* That is, the Mediterranean; also in verse 47
[r] *18* Hebrew and some Septuagint manuscripts; other Septuagint manuscripts (see also note at Judges 1:14) *Othniel, he urged her*
[s] *36* Or *Gederah and Gederothaim*

50Anab,[p] Eshtemoh,[q] Anim, 51Go-
shen,[r] Holon[s] and Giloh[t]—eleven
towns and their villages.
52Arab, Dumah,[u] Eshan, 53Janim,
Beth Tappuah, Aphekah, 54Humtah,
Kiriath Arba[v] (that is, Hebron) and
Zior—nine towns and their villages.
55Maon,[w] Carmel,[x] Ziph,[y] Juttah,[z] 56Jezreel,[a] Jokdeam, Zanoah,[b]
57Kain, Gibeah[c] and Timnah[d]—ten
towns and their villages.
58Halhul, Beth Zur,[e] Gedor,[f]
59Maarath, Beth Anoth and Eltekon
—six towns and their villages.
60Kiriath Baal[g] (that is, Kiriath Jearim[h]) and Rabbah[i]—two towns and
their villages.

61In the desert:[j]
Beth Arabah,[k] Middin, Secacah,
62Nibshan, the City of Salt and En
Gedi[l]—six towns and their villages.
63Judah could not[m] dislodge the Jebusites[n], who were living in Jerusalem;[o] to
this day the Jebusites live there with the
people of Judah.[p]

Chapter 16

Allotment for Ephraim and Manasseh

1THE allotment for Joseph began at
the Jordan of Jericho,[t] east of
the waters of Jericho, and went up
from there through the desert[q] into
the hill country of Bethel.[r] 2It went
on from Bethel (that is, Luz[s]),[u]
crossed over to the territory of the
Arkites[t] in Ataroth,[u] 3descended
westward to the territory of the Japh-
letites as far as the region of Lower
Beth Horon[v] and on to Gezer,[w] ending at the sea.
4So Manasseh and Ephraim, the descendants of Joseph, received their inheritance.[x]

5This was the territory of Ephraim, clan
by clan:
The boundary of their inheritance
went from Ataroth Addar[y] in the
east to Upper Beth Horon[z] 6and continued to the sea. From Micmethath[a] on the north it curved eastward to Taanath Shiloh, passing by it
to Janoah[b] on the east. 7Then it went
down from Janoah[c] to Ataroth[d] and
Naarah, touched Jericho and came
out at the Jordan. 8From Tappuah[e]
the border went west to the Kanah
Ravine[f] and ended at the sea. This
was the inheritance of the tribe of
the Ephraimites, clan by clan. 9It also
included all the towns and their villages that were set aside for the
Ephraimites within the inheritance
of the Manassites.[g]
10They did not dislodge the Canaanites
living in Gezer; to this day the Canaanites live among the people of Ephraim but
are required to do forced labor.[h]

Chapter 17

1THIS was the allotment for the tribe of
Manasseh[i] as Joseph's firstborn,[j]
that is, for Makir,[k] Manasseh's firstborn.
Makir was the ancestor of the Gileadites,
who had received Gilead[l] and Bashan[m]
because the Makirites were great soldiers. 2So this allotment was for the rest
of the people of Manasseh[n]—the clans of
Abiezer,[o] Helek, Asriel,[p] Shechem, Hepher[q] and Shemida.[r] These are the other male descendants of Manasseh son of
Joseph by their clans.
3Now Zelophehad son of Hepher,[s] the
son of Gilead, the son of Makir, the son of
Manasseh, had no sons but only daughters,[t] whose names were Mahlah, Noah,
Hoglah, Milcah and Tirzah. 4They went
to Eleazar the priest, Joshua son of Nun,
and the leaders and said, "The LORD commanded Moses to give us an inheritance
among our brothers." So Joshua gave
them an inheritance along with the
brothers of their father, according to the
LORD's command.[u] 5Manasseh's share
consisted of ten tracts of land besides Gilead and Bashan east of the Jordan,[v] 6be-
cause the daughters of the tribe of Manasseh received an inheritance among the
sons. The land of Gilead belonged to the
rest of the descendants of Manasseh.
7The territory of Manasseh extended from Asher[w] to Micmethath[x] east
of Shechem.[y] The boundary ran
southward from there to include the
people living at En Tappuah. 8(Manasseh had the land of Tappuah, but
Tappuah[z] itself, on the boundary of
Manasseh, belonged to the Ephraimites.) 9Then the boundary continued
south to the Kanah Ravine.[a] There
were towns belonging to Ephraim lying among the towns of Manasseh,
but the boundary of Manasseh was
the northern side of the ravine and
ended at the sea. 10On the south the
land belonged to Ephraim, on the
north to Manasseh. The territory of
Manasseh reached the sea and bor-

[t] *1 Jordan of Jericho* was possibly an ancient name for the Jordan River. [u] *2* Septuagint; Hebrew *Bethel to Luz*

15:50 [p]Jos 11:21 [q]Jos 21:14; 1Sa 30:28
15:51 [r]S Jos 10:41 [s]Jos 21:15; Jer 48:21 [t]2Sa 15:12
15:52 [u]S Ge 25:14
15:54 [v]S Ge 35:27
15:55 [w]Jdg 10:12; 1Sa 23:24,25; 25:1, 2; 1Ch 2:45 [x]S Jos 12:22 [y]S ver 24 [z]Jos 21:16
15:56 [a]Jos 17:16; 19:18; Jdg 6:33; 1Sa 25:43; 1Ki 18:45; 1Ch 3:1; Hos 1:5 [b]S ver 34
15:57 [c]Jos 18:28; 24:33; Jdg 19:12; 20:4; 2Sa 23:29; 1Ch 11:31 [d]S Ge 38:12
15:58 [e]1Ch 2:45; 2Ch 11:7; Ne 3:16 [f]1Ch 4:39; 12:7
15:60 [g]ver 9 [h]S Jos 9:17 [i]S Dt 3:11
15:61 [j]S Jos 8:15 [k]S ver 6
15:62 [l]1Sa 23:29; 24:1; Eze 47:10
15:63 [m]Jos 16:10; 17:12; Jdg 1:21; 1Ki 9:21 [n]S ver 8 [o]S Jos 10:1 [p]Eze 48:7
16:1 [q]S Jos 8:15 [r]S Jos 12:9
16:2 [s]S Ge 28:19 [t]2Sa 15:32 [u]S ver 5; S Nu 32:3
16:3 [v]S Jos 10:10 [w]S Jos 10:33
16:4 [x]Jos 18:5
16:5 [y]ver 2; Jos 18:13 [z]S Jos 10:10
16:6 [a]Jos 17:7 [b]ver 7; 2Ki 15:29
16:7 [c]S ver 6 [d]S Nu 32:3
16:8 [e]S Jos 12:17 [f]Jos 17:9; 19:28
16:9 [g]Eze 48:5
16:10 [h]S Jos 15:63; 17:13; Jdg 1:28-29; 1Ki 9:16
17:1 [i]S Nu 1:34; 1Ch 7:14 [j]S Ge 41:51 [k]S Ge 50:23 [l]S Jos 12:2 [m]S Jos 12:5
17:2 [n]Jos 22:7 [o]S Nu 26:30; Jdg 6:11,34; 8:2; 1Ch 7:18 [p]1Ch 7:14 [q]S Nu 27:1 [r]1Ch 7:19
17:3 [s]S Nu 27:1 [t]S Nu 26:33
17:4 [u]Nu 27:5-7
17:5 [v]Jos 13:30-31
17:7 [w]ver 10; Jos 19:24,31; 21:6, 30; Jdg 1:31; 5:17; 6:35; 7:23 [x]Jos 16:6 [y]S Ge 12:6; Jos 21:21; 24:25; Jdg 9:1
17:8 [z]S Jos 12:17
17:9 [a]S Jos 16:8

15:63 ELECTION, Mission—See note on 13:6–7.
15:63 HISTORY, Freedom—See note on 19:47.
16:10 ELECTION, Mission—See note on 13:6–7.

dered Asher[b] on the north and Issachar[c] on the east.[d]
11Within Issachar[e] and Asher, Manasseh also had Beth Shan,[f] Ibleam[g]
and the people of Dor,[h] Endor,[i] Taanach[j] and Megiddo,[k] together with
their surrounding settlements (the
third in the list is Naphoth[v]).[l]
12Yet the Manassites were not able[m] to
occupy these towns, for the Canaanites
were determined to live in that region.
13However, when the Israelites grew
stronger, they subjected the Canaanites
to forced labor but did not drive them out
completely.[n]
14The people of Joseph said to Joshua,
"Why have you given us only one allotment and one portion for an inheritance?
We are a numerous people and the LORD
has blessed us abundantly."[o]
15"If you are so numerous," Joshua answered, "and if the hill country of Ephraim is too small for you, go up into the
forest[p] and clear land for yourselves
there in the land of the Perizzites[q] and
Rephaites.[r]"
16The people of Joseph replied, "The
hill country is not enough for us, and all
the Canaanites who live in the plain have
iron chariots,[s] both those in Beth Shan[t]
and its settlements and those in the Valley of Jezreel."[u]
17But Joshua said to the house of Joseph—to Ephraim and Manasseh—"You
are numerous and very powerful. You
will have not only one allotment[v] 18but
the forested hill country[w] as well. Clear
it, and its farthest limits will be yours;
though the Canaanites have iron chariots[x] and though they are strong, you can
drive them out."

Chapter 18

Division of the Rest of the Land

THE whole assembly of the Israelites
gathered at Shiloh[y] and set up the
Tent of Meeting[z] there. The country was
brought under their control, 2but there
were still seven Israelite tribes who had
not yet received their inheritance.
3So Joshua said to the Israelites: "How
long will you wait before you begin to
take possession of the land that the LORD,
the God of your fathers, has given you?
4Appoint three men from each tribe. I
will send them out to make a survey of
the land and to write a description of it,[a]
according to the inheritance of each.[b]
Then they will return to me. 5You are to
divide the land into seven parts. Judah is
to remain in its territory on the south[c]
and the house of Joseph in its territory on
the north.[d] 6After you have written descriptions of the seven parts of the land,
bring them here to me and I will cast
lots[e] for you in the presence of the LORD
our God. 7The Levites, however, do not
get a portion among you, because the
priestly service of the LORD is their inheritance.[f] And Gad, Reuben and the half-
tribe of Manasseh have already received
their inheritance on the east side of the
Jordan. Moses the servant of the LORD
gave it to them.[g]"
8As the men started on their way to
map out the land, Joshua instructed
them, "Go and make a survey of the land
and write a description of it.[h] Then return to me, and I will cast lots for you
here at Shiloh[i] in the presence of the
LORD." 9So the men left and went
through the land. They wrote its description on a scroll, town by town, in seven
parts, and returned to Joshua in the camp
at Shiloh. 10Joshua then cast lots[j] for
them in Shiloh in the presence[k] of the
LORD, and there he distributed the land to
the Israelites according to their tribal divisions.[l]

Allotment for Benjamin

11The lot came up for the tribe of Benjamin, clan by clan. Their allotted territory

[v] *11* That is, Naphoth Dor

17:10 [b]S ver 7 [c]S Ge 30:18 [d]Eze 48:5
17:11 [e]ver 10 [f]ver 16; Jdg 1:27; 1Sa 31:10; 2Sa 21:12; 1Ki 4:12; 1Ch 7:29 [g]2Ki 9:27 [h]S Jos 11:2 [i]1Sa 28:7; Ps 83:10 [j]S Jos 12:21 [k]1Ki 9:15 [l]Eze 48:4
17:12 [m]S Jos 15:63
17:13 [n]Jdg 1:27-28
17:14 [o]Nu 26:28-37
17:15 [p]2Sa 18:6 [q]S Jos 3:10 [r]S Ge 14:5; Jos 15:8; 18:16; 2Sa 5:18; 23:13; Isa 17:5
17:16 [s]ver 18; Jdg 1:19; 4:3,13 [t]S ver 11 [u]S Jos 15:56; S 1Sa 29:1
17:17 [v]Eze 48:5
17:18 [w]1Sa 1:1 [x]S ver 16
18:1 [y]ver 8; Jos 19:51; 21:2; Jdg 18:31; 21:12, 19; 1Sa 1:3; 3:21; 4:3; 1Ki 14:2; Ps 78:60; Jer 7:12; 26:6; 41:5 [z]S ver 10; S Ex 27:21; S 40:2; Ac 7:45
18:4 [a]ver 8 [b]Mic 2:5
18:5 [c]Jos 15:1 [d]Jos 16:1-4
18:6 [e]S Lev 16:8
18:7 [f]S Jos 13:33 [g]Jos 13:8
18:8 [h]ver 4 [i]S ver 1
18:10 [j]S Nu 34:13 [k]S ver 1; Jer 7:12 [l]Nu 33:54; Jos 19:51

17:12–13 ELECTION, Mission—See note on 13:6–7.
17:14–18 HUMANITY, Work—Life's circumstances frequently make people believe they deserve a bigger and better share of God's gifts. Further, they also make people believe such gifts should be provided without any personal labor or commitment. To the contrary, God's provision more often *offers the opportunity* for success while placing upon His people the need to work to achieve the full fruition of His purposes. Personal energy must be expended to take advantage of the opportunities He provides.
17:14–18 HISTORY, Freedom—The Joseph tribes wanted more land. God gave them greater work responsibilities to get it. Being God's people seeking His purposes involves freedom to work and achieve. God honors such labor with achievement.
18:6–8 REVELATION, Oracles—God frequently revealed His will on a matter by casting lots. These were stones or other material objects with words inscribed on them. They could be thrown on the ground or drawn from a pile to determine the answer to specific questions (Lev 16:8; 1 Ch 24:31; 25:8; 26:13–14; Ne 10:34; 11:1; Ps 22:18; Jnh 1:7; Mt 27:35; Ac 1:26). See note on Nu 27:18–21.
18:6 PRAYER, Petition—This would be an unusual request for guidance today, but in view of the priestly use of the Urim and Thummim it was a prayer of faith. See note on Ex 28:30. The casting was "in the presence of the LORD," and the decision would be from the Lord (Pr 16:33).
18:8–9 HISTORY, Geography—Receiving God's Promised Land involved the labor of mapping it out and describing it in writing. God's historical gift included safeguards against human greed leading one people to claim another's land. The gift of land was carefully located in Palestine's physical geography with its various natural boundary markers and settlements.

lay between the tribes of Judah and Joseph:
12On the north side their boundary
began at the Jordan, passed the
northern slope of Jericho and headed
west into the hill country, coming
out at the desert[m] of Beth Aven.[n]
13From there it crossed to the south
slope of Luz[o] (that is, Bethel[p]) and
went down to Ataroth Addar[q]
on the hill south of Lower Beth
Horon.
14From the hill facing Beth Horon[r]
on the south the boundary turned
south along the western side and
came out at Kiriath Baal (that is,
Kiriath Jearim),[s] a town of the people
of Judah. This was the western
side.
15The southern side began at the
outskirts of Kiriath Jearim on the
west, and the boundary came out at
the spring of the waters of Nephtoah.[t] 16The boundary went down to
the foot of the hill facing the Valley of
Ben Hinnom, north of the Valley of
Rephaim.[u] It continued down the
Hinnom Valley[v] along the southern
slope of the Jebusite city and so to En
Rogel.[w] 17It then curved north, went
to En Shemesh, continued to Geliloth,[x] which faces the Pass of Adummim,[y] and ran down to the Stone of
Bohan[z] son of Reuben. 18It continued to the northern slope of Beth Arabah[w][a] and on down into the Arabah.[b] 19It then went to the northern
slope of Beth Hoglah[c] and came out
at the northern bay of the Salt
Sea,[x][d] at the mouth of the Jordan in
the south. This was the southern
boundary.
20The Jordan formed the boundary
on the eastern side.
These were the boundaries that marked
out the inheritance of the clans of Benjamin on all sides.[e]

21The tribe of Benjamin, clan by clan, had
the following cities:
Jericho, Beth Hoglah,[f] Emek Ke-
ziz, 22Beth Arabah,[g] Zemaraim,[h]
Bethel,[i] 23Avvim,[j] Parah, Ophrah,[k]
24Kephar Ammoni, Ophni and
Geba[l]—twelve towns and their villages.
25Gibeon,[m] Ramah,[n] Beeroth,[o]
26Mizpah,[p] Kephirah,[q] Mozah, 27Re-
kem, Irpeel, Taralah, 28Zelah,[r] Hae-
leph, the Jebusite city[s] (that is,
Jerusalem[t]), Gibeah[u] and Kiriath—
fourteen towns and their villages.[v]
This was the inheritance of Benjamin for
its clans.[w]

18:12 [m]S Jos 8:15 [n]S Jos 7:2
18:13 [o]S Ge 28:19 [p]S Jos 12:9 [q]S Nu 32:3; S Jos 16:5
18:14 [r]Jos 10:10 [s]S Jos 9:17
18:15 [t]Jos 15:9
18:16 [u]S Jos 17:15 [v]Jos 15:8 [w]S Jos 15:7
18:17 [x]Jos 22:10 [y]Jos 15:7 [z]Jos 15:6
18:18 [a]S Jos 15:6 [b]S Jos 11:2
18:19 [c]S Jos 15:6 [d]S Ge 14:3
18:20 [e]1Sa 9:1
18:21 [f]S Jos 15:6
18:22 [g]Jos 15:6 [h]2Ch 13:4 [i]Jos 16:1
18:23 [j]S Dt 2:23 [k]Jdg 6:11,24; 8:27, 32; 9:5; 1Sa 13:17
18:24 [l]Jos 21:17; 1Sa 13:3,16; 14:5; 1Ki 15:22; 2Ki 23:8; Isa 10:29
18:25 [m]Jos 9:3 [n]S Jos 10:40; Jdg 4:5; 19:13; Isa 10:29; Jer 31:15; 40:1 [o]S Jos 9:17; Ezr 2:25; Ne 7:29
18:26 [p]S Jos 11:3 [q]Jos 9:17; Ezr 2:25; Ne 7:29
18:28 [r]2Sa 21:14 [s]S Jos 15:8 [t]S Jos 10:1 [u]S Jos 15:57 [v]S Jos 9:17 [w]Eze 48:23
19:1 [x]S Ge 49:7
19:2 [y]S Ge 21:14; 1Ki 19:3 [z]S Jos 15:26
19:3 [a]S Jos 15:28 [b]S Jos 15:29
19:4 [c]Jos 15:30 [d]S Nu 14:45
19:5 [e]S Jos 15:31
19:7 [f]S Jos 15:32 [g]S Jos 15:42
19:8 [h]S Jos 10:40
19:9 [i]S Ge 49:7 [j]Eze 48:24
19:10 [k]ver 16,27, 34; Jos 21:7,34 [l]ver 12
19:11 [m]S Jos 12:22
19:12 [n]ver 10 [o]Jos 21:28; 1Ch 6:72
19:13 [p]S Jos 11:22 [q]Jos 15:32
19:14 [r]ver 27
19:15 [s]Jos 21:35 [t]Jos 11:1 [u]S Ge 35:19
19:16 [v]S ver 10 [w]Eze 48:26
19:17 [x]S Ge 30:18
19:18 [y]S Jos 15:56 [z]1Sa 28:4; 1Ki 1:3; 2Ki 4:8
19:20 [a]Jos 21:28
19:21 [b]S Jos 15:34
19:22 [c]Jdg 4:6,12; 8:18; Ps 89:12; Jer 46:18 [d]S Jos 15:10

Chapter 19

Allotment for Simeon

19:2–10pp — 1Ch 4:28–33

THE second lot came out for the tribe of
Simeon, clan by clan. Their inheritance lay within the territory of Judah.[x]
2It included:
Beersheba[y] (or Sheba),[y] Moladah,[z] 3Hazar Shual,[a] Balah, Ezem,[b]
4Eltolad,[c] Bethul, Hormah,[d] 5Zik-
lag,[e] Beth Marcaboth, Hazar Susah,
6Beth Lebaoth and Sharuhen—thirteen towns and their villages;
7Ain, Rimmon,[f] Ether and
Ashan[g]—four towns and their villages— 8and all the villages around
these towns as far as Baalath Beer
(Ramah in the Negev).[h]
This was the inheritance of the tribe of
the Simeonites, clan by clan. 9The inheritance of the Simeonites was taken from
the share of Judah,[i] because Judah's portion was more than they needed. So the
Simeonites received their inheritance
within the territory of Judah.[j]

Allotment for Zebulun

10The third lot came up for Zebulun,[k]
clan by clan:
The boundary of their inheritance
went as far as Sarid.[l] 11Going west it
ran to Maralah, touched Dabbesheth,
and extended to the ravine near Jokneam.[m] 12It turned east from Sarid[n]
toward the sunrise to the territory of
Kisloth Tabor and went on to Daberath[o] and up to Japhia. 13Then it continued eastward to Gath Hepher[p]
and Eth Kazin; it came out at Rimmon[q] and turned toward Neah.
14There the boundary went around
on the north to Hannathon and ended at the Valley of Iphtah El.[r] 15In-
cluded were Kattath, Nahalal,[s]
Shimron,[t] Idalah and Bethlehem.[u]
There were twelve towns and their
villages.
16These towns and their villages were the
inheritance of Zebulun,[v] clan by clan.[w]

Allotment for Issachar

17The fourth lot came out for Issachar,[x]
clan by clan. 18Their territory included:
Jezreel,[y] Kesulloth, Shunem,[z]
19Hapharaim, Shion, Anaharath,
20Rabbith, Kishion,[a] Ebez, 21Re-
meth, En Gannim,[b] En Haddah and
Beth Pazzez. 22The boundary
touched Tabor,[c] Shahazumah and
Beth Shemesh,[d] and ended at the

[w] *18* Septuagint; Hebrew *slope facing the Arabah*
[x] *19* That is, the Dead Sea [y] *2* Or *Beersheba, Sheba;* 1 Chron. 4:28 does not have *Sheba.*

Jordan. There were sixteen towns
and their villages.
23 These towns and their villages were the
inheritance of the tribe of Issachar,[e] clan
by clan.[f]

Allotment for Asher

24 The fifth lot came out for the tribe of
Asher,[g] clan by clan. 25 Their territory included:

Helkath, Hali, Beten, Acshaph,[h]
26 Allammelech, Amad and Mishal.[i]
On the west the boundary touched
Carmel[j] and Shihor Libnath. 27 It
then turned east toward Beth Dagon,[k] touched Zebulun[l] and the
Valley of Iphtah El,[m] and went north
to Beth Emek and Neiel, passing Cabul[n] on the left. 28 It went to Abdon,[z o] Rehob,[p] Hammon[q] and Kanah,[r] as far as Greater Sidon.[s] 29 The
boundary then turned back toward
Ramah[t] and went to the fortified city
of Tyre,[u] turned toward Hosah and
came out at the sea[v] in the region of
Aczib,[w] 30 Ummah, Aphek[x] and Rehob.[y] There were twenty-two towns
and their villages.

31 These towns and their villages were the
inheritance of the tribe of Asher,[z] clan
by clan.

Allotment for Naphtali

32 The sixth lot came out for Naphtali,
clan by clan:

33 Their boundary went from He-
leph and the large tree in Zaanannim,[a] passing Adami Nekeb and Jabneel[b] to Lakkum and ending at the
Jordan. 34 The boundary ran west
through Aznoth Tabor and came out
at Hukkok.[c] It touched Zebulun[d] on
the south, Asher on the west and the
Jordan[a] on the east. 35 The fortified
cities were Ziddim, Zer, Hammath,[e]
Rakkath, Kinnereth,[f] 36 Adamah, Ramah,[g] Hazor,[h] 37 Kedesh,[i] Edrei,[j]
En Hazor, 38 Iron, Migdal El, Horem,
Beth Anath[k] and Beth Shemesh.[l]
There were nineteen towns and their
villages.

39 These towns and their villages were the

19:23 [e]Jos 17:10 [f]Ge 49:15; Eze 48:25
19:24 [g]S Jos 17:7
19:25 [h]S Jos 11:1
19:26 [i]Jos 21:30 [j]S Jos 12:22; 1Ki 18:19; 2Ki 2:25
19:27 [k]Jos 15:41 [l]S ver 10 [m]ver 14 [n]1Ki 9:13
19:28 [o]Jos 21:30; 1Ch 6:74 [p]ver 30; Nu 13:21; Jos 21:31; Jdg 1:31 [q]1Ch 6:76 [r]S Jos 16:8 [s]S Ge 10:19
19:29 [t]Jos 18:25 [u]2Sa 5:11; 24:7; Ezr 3:7; Ps 45:12; Isa 23:1; Jer 25:22; Eze 26:2 [v]Jdg 5:17 [w]S Jos 15:44
19:30 [x]S Jos 12:18 [y]S ver 28
19:31 [z]S Ge 30:13; S Jos 17:7; Eze 48:2
19:33 [a]Jdg 4:11 [b]Jos 15:11
19:34 [c]1Ch 6:75 [d]S ver 10
19:35 [e]1Ch 2:55 [f]S Jos 11:2
19:36 [g]Jos 18:25 [h]S Jos 11:1
19:37 [i]S Jos 12:22 [j]S Nu 21:33
19:38 [k]Jdg 1:33 [l]S Jos 15:10
19:39 [m]Eze 48:3
19:41 [n]S Jos 15:33
19:42 [o]S Jos 10:12
19:43 [p]S Ge 38:12 [q]S Jos 13:3
19:44 [r]Jos 21:23; 1Ki 15:27; 16:15 [s]1Ki 9:18; 2Ch 8:6
19:45 [t]Jos 21:24; 1Ch 6:69
19:46 [u]2Ch 2:16; Ezr 3:7; Jnh 1:3; Ac 9:36
19:47 [v]Jdg 18:1 [w]Jdg 18:7,14 [x]S Dt 3:14 [y]Jdg 18:27,29
19:48 [z]S Ge 30:6
19:50 [a]Jos 24:30; Jdg 2:9
19:51 [b]Jos 23:4 [c]S Jos 14:1; S 18:10; Ac 13:19

inheritance of the tribe of Naphtali, clan
by clan.[m]

Allotment for Dan

40 The seventh lot came out for the tribe
of Dan, clan by clan. 41 The territory of
their inheritance included:

Zorah, Eshtaol,[n] Ir Shemesh,
42 Shaalabbin, Aijalon,[o] Ithlah,
43 Elon, Timnah,[p] Ekron,[q] 44 Eltekeh,
Gibbethon,[r] Baalath,[s] 45 Jehud,
Bene Berak, Gath Rimmon,[t] 46 Me
Jarkon and Rakkon, with the area facing Joppa.[u]

47 (But the Danites had difficulty taking
possession of their territory,[v] so they
went up and attacked Leshem[w], took it,
put it to the sword and occupied it. They
settled in Leshem and named[x] it Dan after their forefather.)[y]

48 These towns and their villages were the
inheritance of the tribe of Dan,[z] clan by
clan.

Allotment for Joshua

49 When they had finished dividing the
land into its allotted portions, the Israelites gave Joshua son of Nun an inheritance among them, 50 as the LORD had
commanded. They gave him the town he
asked for—Timnath Serah[b a] in the hill
country of Ephraim. And he built up the
town and settled there.

51 These are the territories that Eleazar
the priest, Joshua son of Nun and the
heads of the tribal clans of Israel assigned
by lot at Shiloh in the presence of the
LORD at the entrance to the Tent of Meeting. And so they finished dividing[b] the
land.[c]

Chapter 20

Cities of Refuge

20:1-9Ref — Nu 35:9-34; Dt 4:41-43; 19:1-14

THEN the LORD said to Joshua: 2 "Tell
the Israelites to designate the cities
of refuge, as I instructed you through Moses, 3 so that anyone who kills a person

[z] *28* Some Hebrew manuscripts (see also Joshua 21:30); most Hebrew manuscripts *Ebron*
[a] *34* Septuagint; Hebrew *west, and Judah, the Jordan,*
[b] *50* Also known as *Timnath Heres* (see Judges 2:9)

19:47 HISTORY, Freedom—God's historical act of giving the land involved the possibility of human failure. Dan could not gain control of the western inheritance and retreated to the northeast to gain a territory. Compare 15:63; 16:10; 17:12–13,15–18; Jdg 1:34–36. God's history is not a continuous series of successes for His people. He allows freedom to fail but remains present to direct through and beyond failure.

19:47 ELECTION, God's Promise—Even when the promised property was lost or not gained, God was able to fulfill His promise to provide His people with an inheritance. When Dan could not possess its original lot, God replaced it with a place called Leshem, which was renamed Dan. Election points to divine faithfulness, not guaranteed human achievement.

19:51 PRAYER, Petition—See note on 18:6.

20:1–9 CHRISTIAN ETHICS, Justice—The cities named are priestly or Levitical cities. They provided a place of refuge for those who had killed a fellow human being unintentionally. Little contemporary parallel exists to the cities of refuge. Its implementation in the ancient world, however, serves to remind us that an individual deserves societal protection until the matter of guilt or innocence is proven. See note on Nu 35:6–34.

accidentally and unintentionally[d] may
flee there and find protection from the
avenger of blood.[e]
4"When he flees to one of these cities,
he is to stand in the entrance of the city
gate[f] and state his case before the elders[g] of that city. Then they are to admit
him into their city and give him a place to
live with them. 5If the avenger of blood
pursues him, they must not surrender the
one accused, because he killed his neighbor unintentionally and without malice
aforethought. 6He is to stay in that city
until he has stood trial before the assembly[h] and until the death of the high priest
who is serving at that time. Then he may
go back to his own home in the town
from which he fled."
7So they set apart Kedesh[i] in Galilee
in the hill country of Naphtali, Shechem[j]
in the hill country of Ephraim, and Kiriath Arba[k] (that is, Hebron[l]) in the hill
country of Judah.[m] 8On the east side of
the Jordan of Jericho[c] they designated
Bezer[n] in the desert on the plateau in the
tribe of Reuben, Ramoth in Gilead[o][p] in
the tribe of Gad, and Golan in Bashan[q] in
the tribe of Manasseh. 9Any of the Israelites or any alien living among them who
killed someone accidentally[r] could flee
to these designated cities and not be
killed by the avenger of blood prior to
standing trial before the assembly.[s]

Chapter 21

Towns for the Levites

21:4–39pp — 1Ch 6:54–80

NOW the family heads of the Levites
approached Eleazar the priest, Joshua son of Nun, and the heads of the other
tribal families of Israel[t] 2at Shiloh[u] in
Canaan and said to them, "The LORD
commanded through Moses that you give
us towns[v] to live in, with pasturelands
for our livestock."[w] 3So, as the LORD had
commanded, the Israelites gave the Levites the following towns and pasturelands out of their own inheritance:
4The first lot came out for the Kohathites,[x] clan by clan. The Levites who were
descendants of Aaron the priest were allotted thirteen towns from the tribes of
Judah, Simeon and Benjamin.[y] 5The rest
of Kohath's descendants were allotted ten
towns from the clans of the tribes of
Ephraim, Dan and half of Manasseh.[z]
6The descendants of Gershon[a] were allotted thirteen towns from the clans of
the tribes of Issachar,[b] Asher,[c] Naphtali
and the half-tribe of Manasseh in Bashan.
7The descendants of Merari,[d] clan by
clan, received twelve[e] towns from the
tribes of Reuben, Gad and Zebulun.[f]

8So the Israelites allotted to the Levites
these towns and their pasturelands, as
the LORD had commanded through Moses.
9From the tribes of Judah and Simeon
they allotted the following towns by
name 10(these towns were assigned to the
descendants of Aaron who were from the
Kohathite clans of the Levites, because
the first lot fell to them):
11They gave them Kiriath Arba[g]
(that is, Hebron[h]), with its surrounding pastureland, in the hill country of
Judah. (Arba was the forefather of
Anak.) 12But the fields and villages
around the city they had given to Caleb son of Jephunneh as his possession.[i]
13So to the descendants of Aaron
the priest they gave Hebron (a city of
refuge[j] for one accused of murder),
Libnah,[k] 14Jattir,[l] Eshtemoa,[m] 15Ho-
lon,[n] Debir,[o] 16Ain,[p] Juttah[q] and
Beth Shemesh,[r] together with their
pasturelands—nine towns from
these two tribes.
17And from the tribe of Benjamin
they gave them Gibeon,[s] Geba,[t]
18Anathoth[u] and Almon, together
with their pasturelands—four towns.
19All the towns[v] for the priests, the descendants of Aaron, were thirteen, together with their pasturelands.[w]
20The rest of the Kohathite clans of the
Levites were allotted towns from the
tribe of Ephraim:
21In the hill country of Ephraim
they were given Shechem[x] (a city of
refuge for one accused of murder)
and Gezer,[y] 22Kibzaim and Beth Horon,[z] together with their pasturelands—four towns.[a]
23Also from the tribe of Dan they
received Eltekeh, Gibbethon,[b] 24Ai-
jalon[c] and Gath Rimmon,[d] together
with their pasturelands—four towns.
25From half the tribe of Manasseh
they received Taanach[e] and Gath
Rimmon, together with their pasturelands—two towns.
26All these ten towns and their pasturelands were given to the rest of the Kohathite clans.[f]
27The Levite clans of the Gershonites
were given:
from the half-tribe of Manasseh,
Golan in Bashan[g] (a city of refuge for
one accused of murder[h]) and Be Esh-
tarah, together with their pasturelands—two towns;

20:3 dS Lev 4:2 eS Nu 35:12
20:4 fS Ge 23:10; Jer 38:7 gS Jos 7:6
20:6 hS Nu 35:12
20:7 iS Jos 12:22 jS Ge 12:6 kS Ge 35:27 lS Jos 10:36 mLk 1:39
20:8 nJos 21:36; 1Ch 6:78 o1Ch 6:80 pS Jos 12:2 qS Jos 12:5; 1Ch 6:71
20:9 rS Lev 4:2 sS Ex 21:13
21:1 tJos 14:1
21:2 uS Jos 18:1 vS Lev 25:32 wS Nu 35:2-3; S Jos 14:4
21:4 xNu 3:17 yver 19
21:5 zver 26
21:6 aNu 3:17 bS Ge 30:18 cS Jos 17:7
21:7 dS Ex 6:16 ever 40 fS Jos 19:10
21:11 gS Ge 23:2 hS Jos 10:36
21:12 iS Jos 15:13
21:13 jNu 35:6 kS Nu 33:20
21:14 lS Jos 15:48 mS Jos 15:50
21:15 nS Jos 15:51 oS Jos 10:3
21:16 pS Nu 34:11 qJos 15:55 rS Jos 15:10
21:17 sS Jos 9:3 tS Jos 18:24; S Ne 11:31
21:18 u2Sa 23:27; 1Ki 2:26; Ezr 2:23; Ne 7:27; 11:32; Isa 10:30; Jer 1:1; 11:21; 32:7
21:19 v2Ch 31:15 wver 4
21:21 xS Jos 17:7 yS Jos 10:33
21:22 zS Jos 10:10 a1Sa 1:1
21:23 bS Jos 19:44
21:24 cS Jos 10:12 dS Jos 19:45
21:25 eS Jos 12:21
21:26 fver 5
21:27 gS Jos 12:5 hNu 35:6

c8 *Jordan of Jericho* was possibly an ancient name for the Jordan River.

28from the tribe of Issachar,[i]
Kishion,[j] Daberath,[k] 29Jarmuth[l]
and En Gannim,[m] together with their
pasturelands—four towns;
30from the tribe of Asher,[n]
Mishal,[o] Abdon,[p] 31Helkath and Rehob,[q] together with their pasturelands—four towns;
32from the tribe of Naphtali,
Kedesh[r] in Galilee (a city of refuge
for one accused of murder[s]), Ham-
moth Dor and Kartan, together with
their pasturelands—three towns.
33All the towns of the Gershonite[t] clans
were thirteen, together with their pasturelands.

34The Merarite clans (the rest of the Levites) were given:
from the tribe of Zebulun,[u]
Jokneam,[v] Kartah, 35Dimnah and
Nahalal,[w] together with their pasturelands—four towns;
36from the tribe of Reuben,
Bezer,[x] Jahaz,[y] 37Kedemoth and
Mephaath,[z] together with their pasturelands—four towns;
38from the tribe of Gad,
Ramoth[a] in Gilead[b] (a city of refuge
for one accused of murder), Mahanaim,[c] 39Heshbon and Jazer,[d] together
with their pasturelands—four towns
in all.
40All the towns allotted to the Merarite
clans, who were the rest of the Levites,
were twelve.[e]

41The towns of the Levites in the territory held by the Israelites were forty-eight
in all, together with their pasturelands.[f]
42Each of these towns had pasturelands
surrounding it; this was true for all these
towns.

43So the LORD gave Israel all the land
he had sworn to give their forefathers,[g]
and they took possession[h] of it and settled there.[i] 44The LORD gave them rest[j]
on every side, just as he had sworn to
their forefathers. Not one of their enemies[k] withstood them; the LORD handed
all their enemies[l] over to them.[m] 45Not
one of all the LORD's good promises[n] to
the house of Israel failed; every one was
fulfilled.

Chapter 22

Eastern Tribes Return Home

THEN Joshua summoned the Reubenites, the Gadites and the half-tribe of
Manasseh 2and said to them, "You have
done all that Moses the servant of the
LORD commanded,[o] and you have obeyed
me in everything I commanded. 3For a
long time now—to this very day—you
have not deserted your brothers but have
carried out the mission the LORD your
God gave you. 4Now that the LORD your
God has given your brothers rest[p] as he
promised, return to your homes[q] in the
land that Moses the servant of the LORD
gave you on the other side of the Jordan.[r] 5But be very careful to keep the
commandment[s] and the law that Moses
the servant of the LORD gave you: to love
the LORD[t] your God, to walk in all his
ways, to obey his commands,[u] to hold
fast to him and to serve him with all your
heart and all your soul.[v]"

6Then Joshua blessed[w] them and sent
them away, and they went to their
homes. 7(To the half-tribe of Manasseh
Moses had given land in Bashan,[x] and to
the other half of the tribe Joshua gave
land on the west side[y] of the Jordan with
their brothers.) When Joshua sent them
home, he blessed them,[z] 8saying, "Return to your homes with your great
wealth—with large herds of livestock,[a]
with silver, gold, bronze and iron,[b] and a
great quantity of clothing—and divide[c]
with your brothers the plunder[d] from
your enemies."

9So the Reubenites, the Gadites and
the half-tribe of Manasseh left the Israelites at Shiloh[e] in Canaan to return to Gilead,[f] their own land, which they had

21:28 [i]S Ge 30:18 [j]Jos 19:20 [k]S Jos 19:12
21:29 [l]S Jos 10:3 [m]S Jos 15:34
21:30 [n]S Jos 17:7 [o]Jos 19:26 [p]S Jos 19:28
21:31 [q]S Jos 19:28
21:32 [r]S Jos 12:22 [s]Nu 35:6
21:33 [t]ver 6
21:34 [u]S Jos 19:10 [v]S Jos 12:22
21:35 [w]Jos 19:15
21:36 [x]S Jos 20:8 [y]S Nu 21:23; Dt 2:32; Jdg 11:20
21:37 [z]S Jos 13:18
21:38 [a]S Dt 4:43 [b]S Jos 12:2 [c]S Ge 32:2
21:39 [d]S Jos 13:25
21:40 [e]ver 7
21:41 [f]Nu 35:7
21:43 [g]Dt 34:4 [h]Dt 11:31 [i]S Dt 17:14
21:44 [j]S Ex 33:14 [k]S Dt 6:19 [l]S Ex 23:31 [m]Dt 21:10
21:45 [n]Jos 23:14; Ne 9:8
22:2 [o]S Nu 32:25
22:4 [p]S Ex 33:14 [q]Nu 32:22; Dt 3:20 [r]Nu 32:18; S Jos 1:13-15
22:5 [s]Isa 43:22; Mal 3:14 [t]Jos 23:11 [u]S Dt 5:29 [v]S Dt 6:5
22:6 [w]S Ge 24:60; S Ex 39:43
22:7 [x]S Nu 32:19; S Jos 12:5 [y]Jos 17:2 [z]S Jos 14:13; Lk 24:50
22:8 [a]S Dt 20:14 [b]S Nu 31:22 [c]S Nu 31:27 [d]S Ge 49:27; 1Sa 30:16; 2Sa 1:1; Isa 9:3
22:9 [e]Jos 18:1 [f]S Nu 32:26

21:43–45 HISTORY, Promise—In their history God's people can count on God to fulfill His promises and lead them to a life of fulfilling peace and rest. See note on 11:23. No historical opposition can gain victory against God and His purposes.

21:43–44 ELECTION, Faithfulness—Present-day secular history has no thought of God directing the events. The theology of Joshua is that God is involved in directing human history. God fulfills His promises. God can be trusted by His people. Election theology has its roots in God's faithfulness.

21:43–45 SALVATION, Grace—In His grace, God gave Israel the land and fulfilled all His promises even when Israel did not fulfill their commitments (15:63; 16:10; 17:12–13,15–16,18). Salvation is sure because of God's grace and faithfulness to His promises.

21:43–45 CHRISTIAN ETHICS, War and Peace—Peace, not war, is the climax of Joshua. Rest from war, not continued involvement in fighting, is God's continuing will for His people. His people can enjoy peace because God fulfills His promises. See note on 6:1–27.

22:1–34 HISTORY, God's People—See note on Nu 32:1–42. Geography may divide God's people. Misunderstandings may cause one part of God's people to criticize or be suspicious of another group. Even religious practices may raise questions. God leads through human processes to maintain unity and to lead His people to carry out His mission. God's guiding Word stands as the basic guiding and unifying factor.

22:5 CHRISTIAN ETHICS, Moral Imperatives—God's written Word reveals His expectations of His people. We are called to follow biblical teachings. Obeying the Word in total devotion to God is the essence of biblical ethics.

22:8 HUMANITY, Community Relationships—People have a responsibility to share their God-given blessings with others. Selfish hoarding or prideful spending on self is never God's way.

acquired in accordance with the command of the LORD through Moses.
10When they came to Geliloth[g] near
the Jordan in the land of Canaan, the Reubenites, the Gadites and the half-tribe of
Manasseh built an imposing altar[h] there
by the Jordan. 11And when the Israelites
heard that they had built the altar on the
border of Canaan at Geliloth near the Jordan on the Israelite side, 12the whole assembly of Israel gathered at Shiloh[i] to go
to war against them.
13So the Israelites sent Phinehas[j] son
of Eleazar,[k] the priest, to the land of Gilead—to Reuben, Gad and the half-tribe of
Manasseh. 14With him they sent ten of
the chief men, one for each of the tribes
of Israel, each the head of a family division among the Israelite clans.[l]
15When they went to Gilead—to Reuben, Gad and the half-tribe of Manasseh
—they said to them: 16"The whole assembly of the LORD says: 'How could you
break faith[m] with the God of Israel like
this? How could you turn away from the
LORD and build yourselves an altar in rebellion[n] against him now? 17Was not the
sin of Peor[o] enough for us? Up to this
very day we have not cleansed ourselves
from that sin, even though a plague fell
on the community of the LORD! 18And are
you now turning away from the LORD?
" 'If you rebel against the LORD today,
tomorrow he will be angry with the
whole community[p] of Israel. 19If the land
you possess is defiled, come over to the
LORD's land, where the LORD's tabernacle[q] stands, and share the land with us.
But do not rebel against the LORD or
against us by building an altar[r] for yourselves, other than the altar of the LORD
our God. 20When Achan son of Zerah acted unfaithfully regarding the devoted
things,[d][s] did not wrath[t] come upon the
whole community[u] of Israel? He was not
the only one who died for his sin.' "[v]
21Then Reuben, Gad and the half-tribe
of Manasseh replied to the heads of the
clans of Israel: 22"The Mighty One, God,
the LORD! The Mighty One, God,[w] the
LORD![x] He knows![y] And let Israel know!
If this has been in rebellion or disobedience to the LORD, do not spare us this
day. 23If we have built our own altar to
turn away from the LORD and to offer
burnt offerings and grain offerings,[z] or to
sacrifice fellowship offerings[e] on it, may
the LORD himself call us to account.[a]
24"No! We did it for fear that some day
your descendants might say to ours,
'What do you have to do with the LORD,
the God of Israel? 25The LORD has made
the Jordan a boundary between us and
you—you Reubenites and Gadites! You
have no share in the LORD.' So your descendants might cause ours to stop fearing the LORD.
26"That is why we said, 'Let us get
ready and build an altar—but not for
burnt offerings or sacrifices.' 27On the
contrary, it is to be a witness[b] between
us and you and the generations that follow, that we will worship the LORD at his
sanctuary with our burnt offerings, sacrifices and fellowship offerings.[c] Then in
the future your descendants will not be
able to say to ours, 'You have no share in
the LORD.'
28"And we said, 'If they ever say this to
us, or to our descendants, we will answer: Look at the replica of the LORD's
altar, which our fathers built, not for
burnt offerings and sacrifices, but as a
witness[d] between us and you.'
29"Far be it from us to rebel[e] against
the LORD and turn away from him today
by building an altar for burnt offerings,
grain offerings and sacrifices, other than
the altar of the LORD our God that stands
before his tabernacle.[f]"
30When Phinehas the priest and the
leaders of the community—the heads of
the clans of the Israelites—heard what
Reuben, Gad and Manasseh had to say,
they were pleased. 31And Phinehas son of
Eleazar, the priest, said to Reuben, Gad
and Manasseh, "Today we know that the
LORD is with us,[g] because you have not
acted unfaithfully toward the LORD in this
matter. Now you have rescued the Israelites from the LORD's hand."
32Then Phinehas son of Eleazar, the

22:10 [g]Jos 18:17 [h]ver 19,26-27; Isa 19:19; 56:7
22:12 [i]Jos 18:1
22:13 [j]S Nu 25:7 [k]Nu 3:32; Jos 24:33
22:14 [l]ver 32; S Nu 1:4
22:16 [m]S Dt 7:3; 1Sa 13:13; 15:11 [n]Dt 12:13-14
22:17 [o]S Nu 23:28; 25:1-9
22:18 [p]S Lev 10:6
22:19 [q]S Ex 26:1 [r]S ver 10
22:20 [s]Jos 7:1 [t]Ps 7:11 [u]Lev 10:6 [v]Jos 7:5
22:22 [w]S Dt 10:17 [x]Ps 50:1 [y]1Sa 2:3; 16:7; 1Ki 8:39; 1Ch 28:9; Ps 11:4; 40:9; 44:21; 139:4; Jer 17:10
22:23 [z]Jer 41:5 [a]S Dt 12:11; S 18:19; 1Sa 20:16
22:27 [b]S Ge 21:30; Jos 24:27; Isa 19:20 [c]S Dt 12:6
22:28 [d]S Ge 21:30
22:29 [e]Jos 24:16 [f]S Ex 26:1
22:31 [g]2Ch 15:2

[d]*20* The Hebrew term refers to the irrevocable giving over of things or persons to the LORD, often by totally destroying them. [e]*23* Traditionally *peace offerings*; also in verse 27

22:10–34 GOD, One God—The worship of the one God was restricted to the one altar in the tabernacle setting. There, and only there, was formal worship to be celebrated. The two and one-half tribes who settled east of the Jordan, however, made for themselves a solemn reminder of the altar of the Lord. They wanted all to know they were part of the people of the God of Israel. The Israelites were careful to make it clear that they worshiped only one God according to the commandment of God Himself.

22:16–31 SIN, Rebellion—Humans cannot always clearly judge the actions of others. Tribes west of Jordan considered the eastern tribes' altar a symbol of rebellion against God's expressed will for one central, unifying worship place. A committee investigated the matter and cleared the accused (vv 30–31). God alone defines rebellion. We too quickly accuse. We must learn to trust and communicate with each other to determine real motives rather than suspected motives. Sin is not disobeying my desires. It is rebellion against God's will.

22:26–28 PRAYER, Worship—The offensive altar was not to be used for prescribed ordinances of worship, but only as a symbol of their faith in the one God of the central altar and their unity with the people of God. The altars prior to the occupation of Canaan had been, like incense, symbols. See notes on Ge 12:7–8; Ex 30:1,7.

priest, and the leaders returned to Canaan from their meeting with the Reubenites and Gadites in Gilead and reported to the Israelites.[h] 33They were glad to
hear the report and praised God.[i] And
they talked no more about going to war
against them to devastate the country
where the Reubenites and the Gadites
lived.
34And the Reubenites and the Gadites
gave the altar this name: A Witness[j] Between Us that the LORD is God.

Chapter 23

Joshua's Farewell to the Leaders

AFTER a long time had passed and the
LORD had given Israel rest[k] from all
their enemies around them, Joshua, by
then old and well advanced in years,[l]
2summoned all Israel—their elders,[m]
leaders, judges and officials[n]—and said
to them: "I am old and well advanced in
years.[o] 3You yourselves have seen everything the LORD your God has done to all
these nations for your sake; it was the
LORD your God who fought for you.[p] 4Re-
member how I have allotted[q] as an inheritance[r] for your tribes all the land of
the nations that remain—the nations I
conquered—between the Jordan and the
Great Sea[f][s] in the west. 5The LORD your
God himself will drive them out[t] of your
way. He will push them out[u] before you,
and you will take possession of their land,
as the LORD your God promised you.[v]
6"Be very strong; be careful to obey all
that is written in the Book of the Law[w] of
Moses, without turning aside[x] to the
right or to the left.[y] 7Do not associate
with these nations that remain among
you; do not invoke the names of their
gods or swear[z] by them. You must not
serve them or bow down[a] to them. 8But
you are to hold fast to the LORD[b] your
God, as you have until now.
9"The LORD has driven out before you
great and powerful nations;[c] to this day
no one has been able to withstand you.[d]
10One of you routs a thousand,[e] because
the LORD your God fights for you,[f] just as
he promised. 11So be very careful[g] to
love the LORD[h] your God.
12"But if you turn away and ally yourselves with the survivors of these nations
that remain among you and if you intermarry with them[i] and associate with
them,[j] 13then you may be sure that the
LORD your God will no longer drive out[k]
these nations before you. Instead, they
will become snares[l] and traps for you,
whips on your backs and thorns in your
eyes,[m] until you perish from this good
land,[n] which the LORD your God has giv-
en you.
14"Now I am about to go the way of all
the earth.[o] You know with all your heart
and soul that not one of all the good
promises the LORD your God gave you has
failed. Every promise[p] has been fulfilled;
not one has failed.[q] 15But just as every
good promise[r] of the LORD your God has
come true, so the LORD will bring on you
all the evil[s] he has threatened, until he
has destroyed you[t] from this good land
he has given you.[u] 16If you violate the
covenant of the LORD your God, which he
commanded you, and go and serve other
gods and bow down to them, the LORD's
anger will burn against you, and you will
quickly perish from the good land he has
given you.[v]"

Chapter 24

The Covenant Renewed at Shechem

THEN Joshua assembled[w] all the
tribes of Israel at Shechem.[x] He

22:32 [h]S ver 14
22:33 [i]1Ch 29:20; Da 2:19; Lk 2:28
22:34 [j]S Ge 21:30
23:1 [k]S Dt 12:9; Jos 21:44 [l]S Jos 13:1
23:2 [m]S Jos 7:6 [n]Jos 24:1 [o]S Jos 13:1
23:3 [p]S Ex 14:14; S Dt 20:4
23:4 [q]Jos 19:51 [r]S Nu 34:2; Ps 78:55 [s]S Nu 34:6
23:5 [t]ver 13; Jdg 2:21 [u]Ps 44:5; Jer 46:15 [v]Ex 23:30
23:6 [w]S Dt 28:61 [x]S Dt 17:20 [y]Jos 1:7
23:7 [z]Ex 23:13; Jer 5:7; 12:16 [a]S Ex 20:5
23:8 [b]S Dt 10:20
23:9 [c]Dt 11:23 [d]Dt 7:24
23:10 [e]Lev 26:8; Jdg 3:31 [f]S Ex 14:14
23:11 [g]S Dt 4:15 [h]Jos 22:5
23:12 [i]S Ge 34:9 [j]S Ex 34:16; Ps 106:34-35
23:13 [k]S ver 5 [l]S Ex 10:7 [m]S Nu 33:55 [n]Dt 1:8; 1Ki 9:7; 2Ki 25:21
23:14 [o]1Ki 2:2 [p]Ps 119:140; 145:13 [q]S Jos 21:45
23:15 [r]1Ki 8:56; Jer 33:14 [s]1Ki 14:10; 2Ki 22:16; Isa 24:6; 34:5; 43:28; Jer 6:19; 11:8; 35:17; 39:16; Mal 4:6 [t]Jos 24:20 [u]Lev 26:17; Dt 28:15; Jer 40:2
23:16 [v]Dt 4:25-26
24:1 [w]Ge 49:2 [x]S Ge 12:6

[f]4 That is, the Mediterranean

23:1–16 GOD, Righteous—While God is primarily a God of faithfulness and love to His people, He is also a God of righteousness who will not treat lightly the unfaithfulness and disobedience of His people. He is slow to anger (Ne 9:17) and does not respond to every sin with harsh judgment. Neither does He withhold His judgment forever. When His love is spurned and rejected or is carelessly taken for granted, God will chastise His people with deserved judgment.
23:1–16 HISTORY, Moral—Success is not an eternal possession of God's people. Loss of faith in and allegiance to God brings moral consequences and political judgment. God is as true to His historical threats as He is to His promises of deliverance.
23:1 HISTORY, Promise—See note on 21:43–45.
23:3 ELECTION, Israel—See note on 10:14,42.
23:6–16 EVIL AND SUFFERING, Deserved—God promised suffering for Israel as a consequence for disobedience. See note on Dt 13:1–5.
23:6 HOLY SCRIPTURE, Canonization—Moses' instructions or Law (Hebrew *torah*) gave Israel identity, separating them from all other peoples. Moses' inspired teachings formed the first canon or collection of authoritative Scriptures. God led in gradual additions to the canon until it included all the books of our Bible. Having a canon was not enough—Joshua called Israel to obey it.
23:6 CHRISTIAN ETHICS, Moral Imperatives—See note on 22:5.
23:13–16 ELECTION, Condemnation—Blessings are for God's elect as long as they are faithful to God. Doom or curses mean destruction and death for the disobedient people.
23:14 HUMANITY, Death—Death is the normal experience of all life and can be faced with peace and confidence when life has been built upon trust in God's promises. See note on Nu 19:11–22.
23:14 ELECTION, Faithfulness—See note on 21:43–44.
23:16 THE CHURCH, Covenant People—God has one basic expectation—absolute loyalty to Him above all other commitments. Less than this brings the threat of divine judgment. See notes on Dt 31:16–19; Jos 7:11–15.
24:1–27 HISTORY, Worship—Worship of God involves identifying with the history of God's people and committing oneself to serve God obediently and faithfully. God's historical

summoned[y] the elders,[z] leaders, judges
and officials of Israel,[a] and they presented
themselves before God.
2Joshua said to all the people, "This is
what the LORD, the God of Israel, says:
'Long ago your forefathers, including Terah the father of Abraham and Nahor,[b]
lived beyond the River[g] and worshiped
other gods.[c] 3But I took your father Abraham from the land beyond the River and
led him throughout Canaan[d] and gave
him many descendants.[e] I gave him
Isaac,[f] 4and to Isaac I gave Jacob and
Esau.[g] I assigned the hill country of Seir[h]
to Esau, but Jacob and his sons went
down to Egypt.[i]
5" 'Then I sent Moses and Aaron,[j] and
I afflicted the Egyptians by what I did
there, and I brought you out.[k] 6When I
brought your fathers out of Egypt, you
came to the sea,[l] and the Egyptians pursued them with chariots and horsemen[h][m] as far as the Red Sea.[i][n] 7But
they cried[o] to the LORD for help, and he
put darkness[p] between you and the
Egyptians; he brought the sea over them
and covered them.[q] You saw with your
own eyes what I did to the Egyptians.[r]
Then you lived in the desert for a long
time.[s]
8" 'I brought you to the land of the Amorites[t] who lived east of the Jordan. They
fought against you, but I gave them into
your hands. I destroyed them from before
you, and you took possession of their
land.[u] 9When Balak son of Zippor,[v] the
king of Moab, prepared to fight against
Israel, he sent for Balaam son of Beor[w] to
put a curse on you.[x] 10But I would not
listen to Balaam, so he blessed you[y]
again and again, and I delivered you out
of his hand.
11" 'Then you crossed the Jordan[z] and
came to Jericho.[a] The citizens of Jericho
fought against you, as did also the Amorites, Perizzites,[b] Canaanites, Hittites,
Girgashites, Hivites and Jebusites,[c] but I
gave them into your hands.[d] 12I sent the
hornet[e] ahead of you, which drove them
out[f] before you—also the two Amorite
kings. You did not do it with your own
sword and bow.[g] 13So I gave you a land[h]
on which you did not toil and cities you
did not build; and you live in them and
eat from vineyards and olive groves that
you did not plant.'[i]
14"Now fear the LORD[j] and serve him
with all faithfulness.[k] Throw away the
gods[l] your forefathers worshiped beyond
the River and in Egypt,[m] and serve the
LORD. 15But if serving the LORD seems un-
desirable to you, then choose for yourselves this day whom you will serve,
whether the gods your forefathers served
beyond the River, or the gods of the Amorites,[n] in whose land you are living. But
as for me and my household,[o] we will
serve the LORD."[p]
16Then the people answered, "Far be it
from us to forsake[q] the LORD to serve
other gods! 17It was the LORD our God

24:1 [y]1Sa 12:7; 1Ki 8:14 [z]Jos 7:6 [a]Jos 23:2
24:2 [b]Ge 11:26 [c]Ge 11:32
24:3 [d]S Ge 12:1 [e]S Ge 1:28; S 12:2 [f]S Ge 21:3
24:4 [g]S Ge 25:26 [h]S Ge 14:6; S Nu 24:18 [i]Ge 46:5-6
24:5 [j]S Ex 3:10 [k]Ex 12:51
24:6 [l]S Ex 14:22 [m]S Ex 14:9 [n]Ex 14:23
24:7 [o]S Ex 14:10 [p]Ex 14:20 [q]S Ex 14:28 [r]S Ex 19:4 [s]Dt 1:46
24:8 [t]S Ex 23:23 [u]S Nu 21:31
24:9 [v]Nu 22:2 [w]S Nu 23:7 [x]S Nu 22:6
24:10 [y]S Nu 23:11; S Dt 23:5
24:11 [z]S Ex 14:29 [a]Jos 6:1 [b]S Jos 3:10 [c]S Ge 15:18-21 [d]Ex 23:23; Dt 7:1
24:12 [e]S Ex 23:28; Ps 44:3,6-7 [f]S Ex 23:31 [g]Ps 135:11
24:13 [h]Ex 6:8 [i]Dt 6:10-11
24:14 [j]1Sa 12:14; Job 23:15; Ps 19:9; 119:120 [k]Dt 10:12; 18:13; 1Sa 12:24; 2Co 1:12 [l]ver 23; S Ge 31:19; Ex 12:12; 18:11; 20:3; Nu 25:2; Dt 11:28; Jdg 10:16; Ru 1:15; Isa 55:7 [m]Eze 23:3
24:15 [n]Jdg 6:10; Ru 1:15 [o]S Ge 35:2 [p]Ru 1:16; 2:12; 1Ki 18:21; Da 3:18
24:16 [q]Jos 22:29

[g]2 That is, the Euphrates; also in verses 3, 14 and 15
[h]6 Or *charioteers* [i]6 Hebrew *Yam Suph*; that is, Sea of Reeds

deliverance gives His people reason to trust and serve Him.

24:1,16–18,21–25 PRAYER, Corporate—Public congregational prayer includes recommitment to God and confession of God's saving acts. See note on Ex 34:5–9.

24:2–24 ELECTION, Israel—See note on Dt 29:1—30:20. Joshua led Israel in affirming her allegiance to the God of Israel rather than to the gods of her environment. After Joshua, the history of Israel moved downward. Jos 24 is a high point in Israel's history. Here Israel made total commitment to God in face of God's holy jealousy. Election takes seriously God's holy expectations. Election is to be God's servants, not to be freeloaders demanding blessing without obedience.

24:12–15 HUMANITY, Relationship to God—God's gifts to and provision for people place upon them the demand to decide what or whom they will serve with their lives. Responsible leaders not only press this choice upon their people, but they also furnish leadership by demonstrating their own choices openly.

24:14–24 GOD, One God—After Israel's many years of following God and hearing the frequent reminders that He is the only true God, Joshua was still greatly concerned to establish in the hearts of the people uncompromising loyalty to their God. God and Joshua both knew that Israel remained weak, immature, and uncertain in its devotion to God. The following centuries have shown that Israel's greatest vulnerability was at the point of truly understanding that there is only one God, and that He is a holy God who wants unqualified devotion from His people. Israel apparently did not completely understand the uniqueness of God and did not appreciate His holiness or His jealousy. Despite constant reminders by their leaders, priests, and prophets, the nation did not learn this lesson until Israel went through an additional period of captivity, the Exile. There their faith was refined in the crucible of suffering. See Jer 9:7; Zec 13:9.

24:14 SALVATION, Fear of God—We freely choose to fear the Lord. Fearing Him requires us to serve Him in sincerity and truth and to forsake all idols. God is not another tribal or national deity whom we can add to our collection of gods.

24:14–15 CHRISTIAN ETHICS, Moral Imperatives—Every person faces ethical choices. The main choice is to serve God or serve something less than God. Ethical examples like Joshua encourage and strengthen us as we choose. Choosing to serve God means eliminating certain practices from our lives.

24:14–15 FAMILY, Accepting Covenant—Faced with the challenge of settling the land God had given to Israel, Joshua confronted the people with an unwavering choice of loyalty in their worship. The God who described Himself as a "jealous God" (Ex 20:5) could have no rivals in their affection. As households in Israel, they must choose whom they would serve. In vv 16–27 the people joined Joshua in declaring their allegiance to the covenant with the Lord and committed themselves to Him. God still desires families to make that commitment of home and shared life to Him.

24:15,19 SALVATION, Human Freedom—See note on Dt 30:15–20. God's people cannot serve Him and worship idols at the same time. Serving God is a conscious choice and an absolute commitment. Anyone who wavers in choosing cannot serve the holy, jealous God. Insincere commitments separate us from His forgiveness. Forgiveness always rests on God's grace, not on what we deserve.

himself who brought us and our fathers
up out of Egypt, from that land of slavery,[r] and performed those great signs[s]
before our eyes. He protected us on our
entire journey and among all the nations
through which we traveled. 18And the
LORD drove out[t] before us all the nations,[u] including the Amorites, who lived
in the land.[v] We too will serve the LORD,
because he is our God.[w]"
19Joshua said to the people, "You are
not able to serve the LORD. He is a holy
God;[x] he is a jealous God.[y] He will not
forgive[z] your rebellion[a] and your sins.
20If you forsake the LORD[b] and serve foreign gods, he will turn[c] and bring disaster[d] on you and make an end of you,[e]
after he has been good to you."
21But the people said to Joshua, "No!
We will serve the LORD."
22Then Joshua said, "You are witnesses[f] against yourselves that you have
chosen[g] to serve the LORD."
"Yes, we are witnesses,[h]" they replied.
23"Now then," said Joshua, "throw
away the foreign gods[i] that are among
you and yield your hearts[j] to the LORD,
the God of Israel."
24And the people said to Joshua, "We
will serve the LORD our God and obey
him."[k]
25On that day Joshua made a covenant[l] for the people, and there at Shechem[m] he drew up for them decrees and
laws.[n] 26And Joshua recorded[o] these
things in the Book of the Law of God.[p]
Then he took a large stone[q] and set it up
there under the oak[r] near the holy place
of the LORD.

24:17 [r]Jdg 6:8 [s]S Ex 10:1 **24:18** [t]S Ex 23:31 [u]S Dt 33:27 [v]Ac 7:45 [w]S Ge 28:21 **24:19** [x]S Lev 11:44; S 20:26 [y]S Ex 20:5 [z]S Ex 34:7 [a]S Ex 23:21 **24:20** [b]1Ch 28:9, 20; 2Ch 24:18 [c]Ac 7:42 [d]1Sa 12:25; Hos 13:11 [e]Jos 23:15 **24:22** [f]ver 27; Ru 4:10; Isa 8:2; 43:10; 44:8; Jer 42:5; Mal 2:14 [g]Ps 119:30,173 [h]S Dt 25:9 **24:23** [i]S ver 14 [j]1Ki 8:58; Ps 119:36; 141:4; Jer 31:33 **24:24** [k]Ex 19:8; Jer 42:6 **24:25** [l]S Ex 24:8 [m]S Jos 17:7 [n]Ex 15:25 **24:26** [o]S Dt 17:18 [p]S Dt 28:61; S 31:24 [q]S Ge 28:18; S Dt 27:2 [r]S Ge 12:6; S Jdg 4:11 **24:27** [s]S Ge 28:18; Hab 2:11 [t]S ver 22; S Ge 21:30; S Jos 22:27 [u]S Jos 7:11 [v]S Nu 11:20; S Pr 30:9 **24:28** [w]Jdg 21:23, 24 **24:29** [x]Jdg 1:1 [y]S Ge 50:22 **24:30** [z]S Jos 19:50 [a]2Sa 23:30 **24:31** [b]Jos 7:6 **24:32** [c]Heb 11:22 [d]S Ge 47:29-30 [e]Ge 33:19; Jn 4:5; Ac 7:16

27"See!" he said to all the people.
"This stone[s] will be a witness[t] against
us. It has heard all the words the LORD
has said to us. It will be a witness against
you if you are untrue[u] to your God."[v]

Buried in the Promised Land

24:29–31pp — Jdg 2:6–9

28Then Joshua sent the people away,
each to his own inheritance.[w]
29After these things, Joshua son of
Nun, the servant of the LORD, died[x] at
the age of a hundred and ten.[y] 30And
they buried him in the land of his inheritance, at Timnath Serah[i][z] in the hill
country of Ephraim, north of Mount Gaash.[a]
31Israel served the LORD throughout
the lifetime of Joshua and of the elders[b]
who outlived him and who had experienced everything the LORD had done for
Israel.
32And Joseph's bones,[c] which the Israelites had brought up from Egypt,[d] were
buried at Shechem in the tract of land[e]
that Jacob bought for a hundred pieces of
silver[k] from the sons of Hamor, the father of Shechem. This became the inheritance of Joseph's descendants.
33And Eleazar son of Aaron[f] died and
was buried at Gibeah,[g] which had been
allotted to his son Phinehas[h] in the hill
country[i] of Ephraim.

24:33 [f]S Jos 22:13 [g]S Jos 15:57 [h]S Ex 6:25 [i]1Sa 9:4; 1Ki 4:8

[i]30 Also known as *Timnath Heres* (see Judges 2:9)
[k]32 Hebrew *hundred kesitahs*; a kesitah was a unit of money of unknown weight and value.

24:19–20 SIN, Rebellion—Promises do not make us innocent of sin. Obedience to the holy God does. No one of us is completely innocent. Before making rash promises, we need to understand the nature of God with whom we make the promises. Failure to keep a commitment with the holy, jealous God is sin.

24:19 SALVATION, Forgiveness—Joshua sought to discourage the people from a hasty and shallow commitment to follow the Lord. Our sins will not be forgiven unless we forsake our idols. Forgiveness of sin accompanies worship of the one holy God.

24:25–26 HOLY SCRIPTURE, Writing—Knowing God's people needed constant reminders, Joshua set up a holy memorial, to be a constant reminder of God's promises and the people's commitment to God. Compare 4:4–9,20–24. He drew up the covenant for the people, as Moses had done and declared that the stone upon which it was inscribed would be a witness for or against them. This became part of the "Book of the Law of God," a phrase which may refer to joining the Book of Joshua to the Book of the Law of Moses (8:34; 23:6). It may refer to a covenant document preserved at Shechem but no longer in existence, or it may refer to a finalizing of the Law of Moses as an authoritative teaching for Israel. It shows that Israel quite early was concerned about putting their commitment to God in writing.

24:25–27 THE CHURCH, Covenant People—Facing new events and horizons in life allows our faith to grow. The people of Israel faced the joys and trials of the Promised Land. Joshua called the people to renew their commitment to the Lord. In every new experience in life, we must commit to obey the Lord's commands and follow His statutes. See note on Dt 29:1–15. Events and places remind us of God's work in our lives. These reminders call us to rededicate our lives to God.

24:29 HUMANITY, Burial—Natural death capped the victorious life of Joshua. He was buried on the land the tribes gave him (19:50), having lived to an honorable age (Ge 50:22). The biblical text says nothing of mourning for Joshua, preferring to underline the honorable burial in the Promised Land.

24:31–33 DISCIPLESHIP, Spiritual Leaders—Leaders who have experienced God's saving work direct a people to obey God. Without such leadership, a people strays from God (Jdg 2:10). Leaders help a people remember what God has done for His people and teach them how to respond obediently.

Judges

Theological Setting

In the Exodus God fulfilled His promises to Abram, both the promise of a people and of a land. At Sinai He established His covenant. That covenant held these tribes together during the time of the judges. Israel made the difficult transition from wandering, displaced persons to a settled people with structured organizations and institutions. Still Israel remained a loosely-organized group of tribes. On feast days the tribes would gather at Shiloh to seek Yahweh's presence and renew their covenant allegiance to Him. Serious military threats from Israel's enemies were the only stimuli sufficient to break down this fierce independence. In times of danger a judge would appear led by "the Spirit of the Lord" (3:10). The inspired leader would rally the clans, lead the warriors into battle, and repel the foe. This leader's authority was temporary and rested entirely in the personal charismatic qualities bestowed by the presence of Yahweh's Spirit. As soon as the danger passed, the warriors returned to their tribes. The tribes returned to normal daily life, including worship of Canaanite gods in place of or alongside the worship of Yahweh, the God of Israel.

The days of the judges brought only a litany of apostasy, failure, and defeat. What went wrong? That is the question the author raised and then answered. God's promised blessings carried a condition. If Israel remained faithful in obedience to the covenant given at Sinai, God would give them victory. Israel disobeyed and thereby forfeited victory. Israel tried to worship Yahweh and the gods of the Canaanites. In attempting this she violated the basic premise of the covenant. Yahweh alone was responsible for Israel's existence; therefore, He alone deserved Israel's worship, adoration, and obedience. When Israel repented and returned to Yahweh with obedience, He forgave their disobedience and raised up a deliverer.

Writing for an Israel no longer under judges but now under kings, the inspired writer found the situation not significantly different. Israel still tried to accommodate worship of Yahweh and worship of the gods of the peoples. Chaos and failure to experience the promised blessings of God were again the results. If Israel and her kings had any hope of deliverance from chaos and destruction, they must confess disobedience and return to Yahweh in faithfulness to the covenant. Then Yahweh would forgive them, endow the king with His Spirit, and deliver them from their enemies. Otherwise destruction of the land, ejection from the land, and captivity in a foreign land would be the result.

Theological Outline

Judges: Serving God in Changing Times.

I. Disobedience Causes Chaos. (1:1—3:6)
   A. Partial obedience is disobedience. (1:1-36)
   B. Disobedience exposes people to further temptation. (2:1-5)
   C. Leaders who neglect God's covenant lead the people into punishment. (2:6-15)
   D. Failure to heed God's leaders leads to defeat. (2:16-23)
   E. God tests His people to see if they will obey. (3:1-6)

II. Repentance Is the Only Hope of Deliverance. (3:7—16:31)
   A. God listens to the agonized cries of His people. (3:7-31)
   B. God uses women leaders to achieve His purpose for His people. (4:1-24)
   C. A delivered people praised God for His gift of victory. (5:1-31)
   D. God provided a prophet to correct His people. (6:1-10)
   E. God called people even from insignificant families to deliver His people. (6:11-24)
   F. God proved more powerful than Baal. (6:25-32)
   G. God's Spirit gives power to God-called leaders. (6:33-40)
   H. Divine power, not human numbers, provides victory for God's people. (7:1-25)
   I. God is King and can rule His people without power groups, institutions, or symbols. (8:1-35)
   J. God does not honor self-seeking leaders of His people. (9:1-57)

K. God's deliverance comes only to a confessing, repenting people. (10:1-16)
L. God uses leaders considered unworthy in human eyes. (10:17—11:11)
M. God honors leaders who learn the lessons of history. (11:12-40)
N. God does not honor power-seekers. (12:1-15)
O. God blesses families who honor Him. (13:1-25)
P. God can turn human trickery, treachery, and hatred to accomplish His purposes. (14:1—15:20)
Q. Unfaithful leaders cannot follow selfish lusts and expect God's blessing. (16:1-21)
R. God delivers His people by the prayers and efforts of His leader. (16:22-31)

III. Chaos Is the Moral and Social Result of Disobedience. (17:1—21:25)
A. Leaderless people use unscrupulous means even in religion. (17:1—18:31)
B. Sexual crimes can lead to civil war. (19:1—20:48)
C. Worship can become a ruse. (21:1-25)

Theological Conclusions

Judges uses a critical transition period in Israel's history to make the following points:

1. Being part of God's people means letting God rule life.
2. Election is a gift not a deserved award.
3. God is the only God, and no one else deserves worship.
4. Sin is destructive to God's people.
5. Confession and petition lead to renewal.

Judges adds new insights to the nature of Israel's covenant obligations to Yahweh. Accepting the covenant, Israel voluntarily accepted Yahweh's rule, His lordship, His sovereignty. Here the Bible introduces a central theological concept: God's kingdom is God's rule over His chosen people.

The covenant was not an agreement between equals. Rather it was an inferior (Israel) accepting the terms of a superior (Yahweh). Israel's election was not deserved. Israel was a helpless people who had been delivered by an act of unmerited grace. The covenant relationship with Yahweh could only be maintained if Israel kept the stipulated terms. Primary among those terms was the demand that Israel worship Yahweh exclusively and recognize no other thing or person as divine.

Disobedience prevented Israel from receiving the blessings promised by God in the covenant. But the God who made the covenant is a God who is characterized by covenant-keeping love. When Israel recognized disobedience as the cause of their difficulties, they turned to God and confessed their rebellion. Then God acted again with unmerited grace, provided a deliverer, and led Israel to the promised blessings. The covenant people learned they needed a God-directed leader to ensure their loyalty to God. Without such leadership, "everyone did as he saw fit" (17:6; 18:1; 19:1; 21:25). God's people set themselves on the road to self-destruction.

Contemporary Teaching

Judges presents a graphic demonstration of the nature and character of Yahweh. He is personal, transcendent, righteous, purposeful, faithful. He is the Creator of the universe and of the people of faith. He alone is God, and therefore, demands and expects exclusive worship and service from us, His creatures.

Yahweh is the Lord of history. What He has promised He will perform. We are to believe in Him, accept the conditions of obedience to His covenant, and become like Him in character and attitude. This is righteousness. Anything else is disobedience, unrighteousness, sin. Sin cuts us off from God's promised blessings and plunges us into confusion and chaos. Confession of sin results in forgiveness by God and His provision of a deliverer. Old and New Testaments present a God who is able to provide what we truly need in this life, "a righteous God and a Savior" (Isa 45:21).

Something of how God's Spirit works may also be learned from Judges. The prime mover in God's deliverance is God's Spirit. This role is first presented in the period of the Judges but becomes a major motif throughout the Bible. Gospel narratives of Jesus' life also attribute this role to the Spirit of God. When God's power is acting on our behalf, it is God's Spirit in action. The Spirit empowers individuals with the necessary skills to accomplish God's assigned task. This endowment enhances the personality of its recipient, but it does not displace that personality.

The author also provided significant insight about the nature of God's kingdom. The rule of God over His people is the only way for God's people to accomplish God's will. Whatever political system believers live under, the kingdom of God will come in their lives only if they submit to the rule of God.

Jesus strongly argued the same position. "You call me 'Teacher' and 'Lord,' and rightly so, for that is what I am" (Jn 13:13). It is the goal and purpose of the body, the church, to do the will of its Head, Christ. When the will of God controls the life and mind of the believer, the kingdom of heaven is at hand.

Chapter 1

Israel Fights the Remaining Canaanites

1:11–15pp — Jos 15:15–19

AFTER the death[a] of Joshua, the Israelites asked the LORD, "Who will be
the first[b] to go up and fight for us against
the Canaanites?[c]"
2The LORD answered, "Judah[d] is to go;
I have given the land into their hands.[e]"
3Then the men of Judah said to the
Simeonites their brothers, "Come up
with us into the territory allotted to us, to
fight against the Canaanites. We in turn
will go with you into yours." So the Simeonites[f] went with them.
4When Judah attacked, the LORD gave
the Canaanites and Perizzites[g] into their
hands and they struck down ten thousand
men at Bezek.[h] 5It was there that they
found Adoni-Bezek[i] and fought against
him, putting to rout the Canaanites and
Perizzites. 6Adoni-Bezek fled, but they
chased him and caught him, and cut off
his thumbs and big toes.
7Then Adoni-Bezek said, "Seventy
kings with their thumbs and big toes cut
off have picked up scraps under my table.
Now God has paid me back[j] for what I
did to them." They brought him to Jerusalem,[k] and he died there.
8The men of Judah attacked Jerusalem[l] also and took it. They put the city to
the sword and set it on fire.
9After that, the men of Judah went
down to fight against the Canaanites living in the hill country,[m] the Negev[n] and
the western foothills. 10They advanced
against the Canaanites living in Hebron[o]
(formerly called Kiriath Arba[p]) and defeated Sheshai, Ahiman and Talmai.[q]
11From there they advanced against the
people living in Debir[r] (formerly called
Kiriath Sepher). 12And Caleb said, "I will
give my daughter Acsah in marriage to
the man who attacks and captures Kiriath
Sepher." 13Othniel son of Kenaz, Caleb's
younger brother, took it; so Caleb gave
his daughter Acsah to him in marriage.
14One day when she came to Othniel,
she urged him[a] to ask her father for a
field. When she got off her donkey, Caleb
asked her, "What can I do for you?"
15She replied, "Do me a special favor.
Since you have given me land in the Negev, give me also springs of water." Then
Caleb gave her the upper and lower
springs.[s]
16The descendants of Moses' father-in-
law,[t] the Kenite,[u] went up from the City
of Palms[b][v] with the men of Judah to live
among the people of the Desert of Judah
in the Negev near Arad.[w]
17Then the men of Judah went with the
Simeonites[x] their brothers and attacked
the Canaanites living in Zephath, and
they totally destroyed[c] the city. Therefore it was called Hormah.[d][y] 18The men
of Judah also took[e] Gaza,[z] Ashkelon[a]
and Ekron—each city with its territory.
19The LORD was with[b] the men of Judah. They took possession of the hill
country,[c] but they were unable to drive
the people from the plains, because they
had iron chariots.[d] 20As Moses had promised, Hebron[e] was given to Caleb, who
drove from it the three sons of Anak.[f]
21The Benjamites, however, failed[g] to
dislodge the Jebusites, who were living in

1:1 [a]Jos 24:29 [b]S Nu 2:3-9; Jdg 20:18; 1Ki 20:14 [c]ver 27; S Ge 10:18; Jdg 3:1-6
1:2 [d]S Ge 49:10 [e]ver 4; Jdg 3:28; 4:7,14; 7:9
1:3 [f]ver 17
1:4 [g]S Ge 13:7; S Jos 3:10 [h]1Sa 11:8
1:5 [i]ver 6,7
1:7 [j]Lev 24:19; Jer 25:12 [k]S Jos 10:1
1:8 [l]ver 21; Jos 15:63; 2Sa 5:6
1:9 [m]S Nu 13:17 [n]S Ge 12:9; S Nu 21:1; Isa 30:6
1:10 [o]S Ge 13:18 [p]S Ge 35:27 [q]ver 20; S Nu 13:22; Jos 15:14
1:11 [r]Jos 10:38
1:15 [s]S Nu 13:6
1:16 [t]Nu 10:29 [u]S Ge 15:19 [v]Dt 34:3; Jdg 3:13; 2Ch 28:15 [w]Nu 21:1; Jos 12:14
1:17 [x]ver 3 [y]S Nu 14:45
1:18 [z]Jos 11:22 [a]S Jos 13:3
1:19 [b]S Nu 14:43 [c]Nu 13:17 [d]S Jos 17:16
1:20 [e]Jos 10:36 [f]S ver 10; S Jos 14:13
1:21 [g]S Jos 9:15; S 15:63

[a]*14* Hebrew; Septuagint and Vulgate *Othniel, he urged her* [b]*16* That is, Jericho [c]*17* The Hebrew term refers to the irrevocable giving over of things or persons to the LORD, often by totally destroying them. [d]*17 Hormah* means *destruction.* [e]*18* Hebrew; Septuagint *Judah did not take*

1:1–2 REVELATION, Oracles—The mystery of God's revelation was at times clear to Israel. God was understood when a prophet was consulted and spoke, or when lots were cast, as probably took place here. The Israelites possessed sacred stones, given to them during the Exodus (Ex 27:30; Lev 8:8; Nu 27:21; 1 Sa 28:6; Ezr 2:63), and specifically designed to give the user a means of making a decision. The high priest, wearing them over his heart, was in a proper attitude to consult them and receive an answer, which was understood as God's answer. See note on Jos 18:6–8. The most important issue in the consultation of these stones was the seeker's attitude, that is, coming to God and to God's representative searching for God's will on a matter. Decisions covered many areas of life, including warfare.

1:1–36 CHRISTIAN ETHICS, War and Peace—Israel did not enjoy rest long. See note on Jos 21:43–45. Occupation of the land was not complete. Continuing fights brought judgment against violent enemies. It brought further evidence of God's presence with His people. It also showed the failure of God's people. They did not occupy some of the territory.

1:1 PRAYER, Petition*—The success of these campaigns* was due to Israel's dependence on the Lord. Prayer expresses dependence on God and seeks God's leadership in specific actions.

1:7 GOD, Wrath—The law of an eye for an eye, a tooth for a tooth, was a common practice not only in Israel but in other ancient cultures as well. It set a limit to punishment, prohibiting even harsher vengeance. See Mt 5:38–42. Jesus replaced the law of strict retribution with the law of a loving response to all people, regardless of the circumstances. In this ancient setting Adoni-Bezek recognized that what happened was only fitting after he had done the same to others. Both the principle and the practice of such cruel treatment of persons seems harsh and unjust to us today. But that was probably all that an ancient, developing culture was ready for, and from their perspective represented a step of progress in the development of civilization. What God reveals of Himself and what God expects of a people depend, in part, on where people are in their development and what they are capable of understanding at that point. God works with them at that level and proceeds to lead them to the level of understanding He wants them to have. It is part of God's graciousness towards us that He accommodates Himself to us in this way. God may work with us in a provisional, temporary way until He can work with us in the way that manifests His ultimate will for us. See Ac 17:30–31; 1 Pe 1:14.

1:21,27–36 ELECTION, Mission—See note on Jos 13:6–7. Failure to carry out the policy of conquest as laid out

has violated the covenant[m] that I laid
down for their forefathers and has not listened to me, 21I will no longer drive out[n]
before them any of the nations Joshua left
when he died. 22I will use them to test[o]
Israel and see whether they will keep the
way of the LORD and walk in it as their
forefathers did." 23The LORD had allowed
those nations to remain; he did not drive
them out at once by giving them into the
hands of Joshua.[p]

Chapter 3

THESE are the nations the LORD left to
test[q] all those Israelites who had not
experienced any of the wars in Canaan
2(he did this only to teach warfare to the
descendants of the Israelites who had not
had previous battle experience): 3the
five[r] rulers of the Philistines,[s] all the
Canaanites, the Sidonians, and the Hivites[t] living in the Lebanon mountains
from Mount Baal Hermon[u] to Lebo[j] Hamath.[v] 4They were left to test[w] the Israelites to see whether they would obey the
LORD's commands, which he had given
their forefathers through Moses.
5The Israelites lived[x] among the Canaanites, Hittites, Amorites, Perizzites,[y]
Hivites and Jebusites.[z] 6They took their
daughters[a] in marriage and gave their
own daughters to their sons, and served
their gods.[b c]

Othniel

7The Israelites did evil in the eyes of
the LORD; they forgot the LORD[d] their
God and served the Baals and the Ashe-
rahs.[e] 8The anger of the LORD burned
against Israel so that he sold[f] them into
the hands of Cushan-Rishathaim[g] king of
Aram Naharaim,[k h] to whom the Israelites were subject for eight years. 9But
when they cried out[i] to the LORD, he
raised up for them a deliverer,[j] Othniel[k]
son of Kenaz, Caleb's younger brother,
who saved them. 10The Spirit of the LORD
came upon him,[l] so that he became Israel's judge[l] and went to war. The LORD
gave Cushan-Rishathaim[m] king of Aram[n]
into the hands of Othniel, who overpowered him. 11So the land had peace[o] for
forty years,[p] until Othniel son of Kenaz[q]
died.

Ehud

12Once again the Israelites did evil in
the eyes of the LORD,[r] and because they
did this evil the LORD gave Eglon king of
Moab[s] power over Israel. 13Getting the
Ammonites[t] and Amalekites[u] to join
him, Eglon came and attacked Israel, and
they took possession of the City of
Palms.[m v] 14The Israelites were subject to
Eglon king of Moab[w] for eighteen years.
15Again the Israelites cried out to the
LORD, and he gave them a deliverer[x]—
Ehud[y], a left-handed[z] man, the son of
Gera the Benjamite. The Israelites sent
him with tribute[a] to Eglon king of Moab.
16Now Ehud[b] had made a double-edged
sword about a foot and a half[n] long,
which he strapped to his right thigh under his clothing. 17He presented the

2:20 [m]S Jos 7:11; S 2Ki 17:15
2:21 [n]S Jos 23:5
2:22 [o]S Ge 22:1; S Ex 15:25
2:23 [p]Jdg 1:1
3:1 [q]S Ex 15:25
3:3 [r]S Jos 13:3 [s]S Ge 10:14 [t]S Ge 10:17; S Ex 3:8 [u]S Dt 3:8 [v]S Nu 13:21
3:4 [w]S Ex 15:25
3:5 [x]Ps 106:35 [y]S Jos 3:10 [z]S Jos 11:3; Ezr 9:1
3:6 [a]Ezr 10:18; Ne 13:23; Mal 2:11 [b]S Ex 34:16; Dt 7:3-4 [c]S Dt 7:16
3:7 [d]Dt 4:9; S 32:18; Jdg 8:34; Ps 78:11,42; 106:7; Jer 23:27 [e]S Ex 34:13; S Jdg 2:11,13; 1Ki 16:33; 2Ch 34:7; Isa 17:8
3:8 [f]Jdg 2:14; Ps 44:12; Isa 50:1; 52:3 [g]ver 10 [h]S Ge 24:10
3:9 [i]ver 15; Jdg 6:6, 7; 10:10; 1Sa 12:10; Ps 106:44; 107:13 [j]S Dt 28:29; Ne 9:27 [k]S Jos 15:17
3:10 [l]S Nu 11:25, 29; Jdg 6:34; 11:29; 13:25; 14:6, 19; 15:14; 1Sa 11:6; 16:13; 1Ki 18:46; 1Ch 12:18; 2Ch 24:20; Isa 11:2 [m]ver 8 [n]S Ge 10:22
3:11 [o]ver 30; S Jos 14:15; Jdg 5:31; 8:28 [p]S Ex 16:35 [q]S Jos 15:17
3:12 [r]S Jdg 2:11,14 [s]1Sa 12:9
3:13 [t]S Ge 19:38; Jdg 10:11 [u]S Ge 14:7 [v]S Jdg 1:16
3:14 [w]Jer 48:1
3:15 [x]S ver 9 [y]ver 16; Jdg 4:1 [z]Jdg 20:16; 1Ch 12:2 [a]ver 17,18; 2Sa 8:2,6; 1Ki 4:21; 2Ki 17:3; Est 10:1; Ps 68:29; 72:10; 89:22; Ecc 2:8; Isa 60:5; Hos 10:6
3:16 [b]S ver 15

[j]3 Or *to the entrance to* [k]8 That is, Northwest Mesopotamia [l]10 Or *leader* [m]13 That is, Jericho [n]16 Hebrew *a cubit* (about 0.5 meter)

2:20–21 THE CHURCH, Covenant People—See note on 2:1–3.

2:21–22 ELECTION, Testing—The entrance of Israel into the Land of Promise did not result in total occupancy and complete victory. Their partial victories allowed them space and time to mature and develop national consciousness. To realize the election purposes of Israel, they had to endure testing. Those elected to carry out God's mission in the world need a period and place of testing. Testing ensures the free will side of election, giving God's people opportunity to choose to follow God rather than making the choice so easy no real choice exists.

2:22 SALVATION, Human Freedom—See note on Dt 30:15–20.

3:5–6 FAMILY, Intermarriage—See note on Dt 7:3–4.

3:7 SIN, Covenant Breach—A cycle of breaking the covenant can be observed in the Judges materials. God raised up a deliverer or judge, and for a while the Israelites served God. When the deliverer died, the nation lapsed into idolatry, a breach of the covenant. They forgot the Lord and began to worship the idols around them. Repetition does not improve sin. God judges each person and each generation no matter how often the sin has been repeated.

3:7—16:31 CHRISTIAN ETHICS, War and Peace—Human warfare remained one method God used to help His people. God gave judges victories in war to show His power and His commitment to His people. On a short-term basis, some learned the lesson; long-term they never learned.

3:9–10 HOLY SPIRIT, Leaders—God empowers the right people for the needed tasks at crucial junctures in His history with His people. The Spirit equipped Othniel to lead Israel's army and judge or decide disputes among Israel's people and tribes. The gift of military and political leadership was necessary for the survival of the people as they established themselves in the land.

3:9,15 SALVATION, As Deliverance—God gave Israel the deliverers Othniel and Ehud, who saved her from her enemies. Verse 9 points clearly to the connection between these deliverers and the doctrine of salvation. Salvation for Israel included earthly acts wrought by God.

3:9 SALVATION, Definition—God's salvation is His deliverance or rescue from our enemies. Judges such as Othniel saved Israel in the sense of delivering her from her enemies (3:31; 6:14,15,36; 7:7; 8:22; 10:1,11–12; 12:2).

3:9 PRAYER, Petition—As Israel established themselves in Canaan and faced temptations and enemies, they developed a pattern of repeated apostasy. Sin separates the sinner from the protective hand of God (Isa 59:2), so that oppression of the Canaanite enemy was inevitable. When they cried to the Lord each time, He delivered (3:15; 4:3; 6:6–8; 10:10–16). God responds to the desperate cries of a penitent people.

3:12 SIN, Covenant Breach—See note on 3:7.

tribute[c] to Eglon king of Moab, who was
a very fat man.[d] 18After Ehud had
presented the tribute, he sent on their
way the men who had carried it. 19At the
idols[o] near Gilgal he himself turned back
and said, "I have a secret message for you,
O king."

The king said, "Quiet!" And all his attendants left him.

20Ehud then approached him while he
was sitting alone in the upper room of his
summer palace[p] [e] and said, "I have a
message from God for you." As the king
rose[f] from his seat, 21Ehud reached with
his left hand, drew the sword[g] from his
right thigh and plunged it into the king's
belly. 22Even the handle sank in after the
blade, which came out his back. Ehud did
not pull the sword out, and the fat
closed in over it. 23Then Ehud went out
to the porch[q]; he shut the doors of
the upper room behind him and locked
them.

24After he had gone, the servants came
and found the doors of the upper room
locked. They said, "He must be relieving
himself[h] in the inner room of the
house." 25They waited to the point of embarrassment,[i] but when he did not open
the doors of the room, they took a key
and unlocked them. There they saw their
lord fallen to the floor, dead.

26While they waited, Ehud got away.
He passed by the idols and escaped to Sei-
rah. 27When he arrived there, he blew a
trumpet[j] in the hill country of Ephraim,
and the Israelites went down with
him from the hills, with him leading
them.

28"Follow me," he ordered, "for the
LORD has given Moab,[k] your enemy, into
your hands.[l]" So they followed him
down and, taking possession of the fords
of the Jordan[m] that led to Moab, they
allowed no one to cross over. 29At that
time they struck down about ten thousand
Moabites, all vigorous and strong; not a
man escaped. 30That day Moab[n] was
made subject to Israel, and the land had
peace[o] for eighty years.

Shamgar

31After Ehud came Shamgar son of
Anath,[p] who struck down six hundred[q]
Philistines[r] with an oxgoad. He too
saved Israel.

3:17 [c]S ver 15 [d]Job 15:27; Ps 73:4
3:20 [e]Am 3:15 [f]Ne 8:5
3:21 [g]2Sa 2:16; 3:27; 20:10
3:24 [h]1Sa 24:3
3:25 [i]2Ki 2:17; 8:11
3:27 [j]S Lev 25:9; Jdg 6:34; 7:18; 2Sa 2:28; Isa 18:3; Jer 42:14
3:28 [k]S Ge 19:37 [l]S Jos 2:24; S Jdg 1:2 [m]S Nu 13:29; S Jos 2:7
3:30 [n]S Ge 36:35 [o]S ver 11
3:31 [p]Jdg 5:6 [q]S Jos 23:10 [r]Jos 13:2; Jdg 10:11; 13:1; 1Sa 5:1; 31:1; 2Sa 8:1; Jer 25:20; 47:1
4:1 [s]S Jdg 3:15 [t]S Jdg 2:19 [u]S Jdg 2:11
4:2 [v]S Dt 32:30 [w]S Jos 11:1 [x]1Sa 12:9; Ps 83:9
4:3 [y]S Jos 17:16 [z]Jdg 10:12; Ps 106:42
4:4 [a]Jdg 5:1,7,12,15 [b]S Ex 15:20
4:5 [c]1Sa 14:2; 22:6 [d]S Jos 18:25 [e]S Jos 12:9
4:6 [f]Jdg 5:1,12,15; 1Sa 12:11; Heb 11:32 [g]S Jos 12:22 [h]S Ge 30:8 [i]Jdg 5:18; 6:35 [j]S Jos 19:22
4:7 [k]S Jos 11:1 [l]ver 13; Jdg 5:21; 1Ki 18:40; Ps 83:9 [m]S Jdg 1:2
4:9 [n]S Jos 12:22
4:10 [o]2Ch 36:23; Ezr 1:2; Isa 41:2; 42:6; 45:3; 46:11; 48:15
4:11 [p]S Ge 15:19 [q]Nu 10:29 [r]Jos 24:26; Jdg 9:6 [s]Jos 19:33

Chapter 4

Deborah

AFTER Ehud[s] died, the Israelites once
again did evil[t] in the eyes of the
LORD.[u] 2So the LORD sold them[v] into the
hands of Jabin, a king of Canaan, who
reigned in Hazor.[w] The commander of
his army was Sisera,[x] who lived in Harosheth Haggoyim. 3Because he had nine
hundred iron chariots[y] and had cruelly
oppressed[z] the Israelites for twenty
years, they cried to the LORD for help.

4Deborah,[a] a prophetess,[b] the wife of
Lappidoth, was leading[r] Israel at that
time. 5She held court[c] under the Palm of
Deborah between Ramah[d] and Bethel[e]
in the hill country of Ephraim, and the
Israelites came to her to have their disputes decided. 6She sent for Barak son of
Abinoam[f] from Kedesh[g] in Naphtali and
said to him, "The LORD, the God of Israel,
commands you: 'Go, take with you ten
thousand men of Naphtali[h] and Zebulun[i] and lead the way to Mount Tabor.[j]
7I will lure Sisera, the commander of Jabin's[k] army, with his chariots and his
troops to the Kishon River[l] and give him
into your hands.[m]' "

8Barak said to her, "If you go with me,
I will go; but if you don't go with me, I
won't go."

9"Very well," Deborah said, "I will go
with you. But because of the way you are
going about this,[s] the honor will not be
yours, for the LORD will hand Sisera over
to a woman." So Deborah went with Barak to Kedesh,[n] 10where he summoned[o]
Zebulun and Naphtali. Ten thousand men
followed him, and Deborah also went
with him.

11Now Heber the Kenite had left the
other Kenites,[p] the descendants of Hobab,[q] Moses' brother-in-law,[t] and
pitched his tent by the great tree[r] in
Zaanannim[s] near Kedesh.

12When they told Sisera that Barak son
of Abinoam had gone up to Mount

[o] *19* Or *the stone quarries*; also in verse 26
[p] *20* The meaning of the Hebrew for this phrase is uncertain. [q] *23* The meaning of the Hebrew for this word is uncertain. [r] *4* Traditionally *judging*
[s] *9* Or *But on the expedition you are undertaking*
[t] *11* Or *father-in-law*

4:1 SIN, Covenant Breach—See note on 3:7.
4:3 PRAYER, Petition—See note on 3:9.
4:4–10 HUMANITY, Work—Success in completing the tasks which God has assigned depends not upon one's sex but upon faithful obedience. People, both men and women, are called to accomplish what God has set before them.
4:4 DISCIPLESHIP, Women—Women functioned as prophets in the Bible Deborah was such a spiritual leader. Miriam, sister of Moses, is represented as speaking by divine inspiration (Ex 15:20). Huldah (2 Ki 22:14), Noadiah (Ne 6:14), Isaiah's wife (Isa 8:3), and Anna (Lk 2:36) are called prophetesses. Deborah also judged the people, settling their disputes (Jdg 4:5) and leading in political decisions (4:6–9). God inspired her to sing the song preserved in our Bibles as Jdg 5. God continues to use women to minister to His people.

Tabor,[t] 13Sisera gathered together his nine
hundred iron chariots[u] and all the men
with him, from Harosheth Haggoyim to
the Kishon River.[v]
14Then Deborah said to Barak, "Go!
This is the day the LORD has given Sisera
into your hands.[w] Has not the LORD gone
ahead[x] of you?" So Barak went down
Mount Tabor, followed by ten thousand
men. 15At Barak's advance, the LORD
routed[y] Sisera and all his chariots and
army by the sword, and Sisera abandoned
his chariot and fled on foot. 16But Barak
pursued the chariots and army as far as
Harosheth Haggoyim. All the troops of
Sisera fell by the sword; not a man was
left.[z]
17Sisera, however, fled on foot to the
tent of Jael,[a] the wife of Heber the Kenite,[b] because there were friendly relations between Jabin king of Hazor[c] and
the clan of Heber the Kenite.
18Jael[d] went out to meet Sisera and
said to him, "Come, my lord, come right
in. Don't be afraid." So he entered
her tent, and she put a covering over
him.
19"I'm thirsty," he said. "Please give
me some water." She opened a skin of
milk,[e] gave him a drink, and covered
him up.
20"Stand in the doorway of the tent,"
he told her. "If someone comes by and
asks you, 'Is anyone here?' say 'No.' "
21But Jael,[f] Heber's wife, picked up a
tent peg and a hammer and went quietly
to him while he lay fast asleep,[g] exhausted. She drove the peg through his temple
into the ground, and he died.[h]
22Barak came by in pursuit of Sisera,
and Jael[i] went out to meet him.
"Come," she said, "I will show you the
man you're looking for." So he went in
with her, and there lay Sisera with the
tent peg through his temple—dead.[j]
23On that day God subdued[k] Jabin,[l]
the Canaanite king, before the Israelites.
24And the hand of the Israelites grew
stronger and stronger against Jabin, the
Canaanite king, until they destroyed
him.[m]

4:12 [t]S Jos 19:22
4:13 [u]S Jos 17:16 [v]S ver 7; Jdg 5:19
4:14 [w]S Jdg 1:2 [x]Dt 9:3; 1Sa 8:20; 2Sa 5:24; Ps 68:7
4:15 [y]S
4:16 [z]S Ex 14:28; Ps 83:9
4:17 [a]ver 18,21,22; Jdg 5:6,24 [b]S Ge 15:19 [c]S Jos 11:1
4:18 [d]S ver 17
4:19 [e]S Ge 18:8
4:21 [f]S ver 17 [g]Ge 2:21; 15:12; 1Sa 26:12; Isa 29:10; Jnh 1:5 [h]Jdg 5:26
4:22 [i]S ver 17 [j]Jdg 5:27
4:23 [k]Ne 9:24; Ps 18:47; 44:2; 47:3; 144:2 [l]S Jos 11:1
4:24 [m]Ps 83:9; 106:43
5:1 [n]S Jdg 4:4 [o]S Jdg 4:6 [p]S Ex 15:1; Ps 32:7
5:2 [q]2Ch 17:16; Ps 110:3 [r]ver 9
5:3 [s]S Ex 15:1 [t]Ps 27:6
5:4 [u]S Ex 13:21 [v]S Nu 24:18; S Dt 33:2 [w]2Sa 22:8; Ps 18:7; 77:18; 82:5; Isa 2:19,21; 13:13; 24:18; 64:3; Jer 10:10; 50:46; 51:29; Joel 3:16; Na 1:5; Hab 3:6 [x]Ps 68:8; 77:17
5:5 [y]S Ex 19:18; Ps 29:6; 46:3; 77:18; 114:4; Isa 64:3
5:6 [z]Jdg 3:31 [a]S Jdg 4:17 [b]Lev 26:22; Isa 33:8 [c]Ps 125:5; Isa 59:8
5:7 [d]S Jdg 4:4
5:8 [e]Dt 32:17; S Jdg 2:13 [f]ver 11; S Jos 2:5 [g]S Nu 25:7
5:9 [h]S ver 2
5:10 [i]S Ge 49:11; Jdg

Chapter 5

The Song of Deborah

On that day Deborah[n] and Barak son
of Abinoam[o] sang this song:[p]

2"When the princes in Israel take the lead,
when the people willingly offer[q] themselves—
praise the LORD![r]

3"Hear this, you kings! Listen, you rulers!
I will sing to[u] the LORD, I will sing;[s]
I will make music to[v] the LORD, the God of Israel.[t]

4"O LORD, when you went out[u] from Seir,[v]
when you marched from the land of Edom,
the earth shook,[w] the heavens poured,
the clouds poured down water.[x]
5The mountains quaked[y] before the LORD, the One of Sinai,
before the LORD, the God of Israel.

6"In the days of Shamgar son of Anath,[z]
in the days of Jael,[a] the roads[b] were abandoned;
travelers took to winding paths.[c]
7Village life[w] in Israel ceased,
ceased until I,[x] Deborah,[d] arose,
arose a mother in Israel.
8When they chose new gods,[e]
war came to the city gates,[f]
and not a shield or spear[g] was seen
among forty thousand in Israel.
9My heart is with Israel's princes,
with the willing volunteers[h] among the people.
Praise the LORD!

10"You who ride on white donkeys,[i]
sitting on your saddle blankets,
and you who walk along the road,

[u]3 Or *of* [v]3 Or / *with song I will praise* [w]7 Or *Warriors* [x]7 Or *you*

5:1–31 HISTORY, Presence—See note on Dt 33:2. God's people praise Him because He shows His presence through specific historical acts. Such praise may occur in worship places and at daily "watering places" (v 11). God's people are expected to participate when He calls them to action.

5:1–31 WORSHIP, Music—Israel used music in worship to celebrate what God had done for them. Both men and women led out in such praise. See notes on Ex 15:1–21; 1 Ch 6:31–32.

5:1–31 PRAYER, Praise—This great song of praise is in psalm form. It celebrated the victory of Deborah and Barak over the Canaanites. Some of the greatest musical prayers were written after a mighty deliverance by the Lord. See notes on Ex 15:1–18; 2 Sa 22:1–51. This prayer acknowledged God's coming to help, described the helpless situation, recalled the people's praise of God and calling of leaders, listed the faithful members of God's people and those who refused to join the fight, described God's participation for His people, cursed nonparticipants, blessed dedicated volunteers, and described the moment of victory. Prayers of praise often refer in detail to events in which God brings victory for His people.

5:8 CHRISTIAN ETHICS, War and Peace—The Hebrews had lost the spiritual warfare taking place as they accepted other gods. The moral erosion that followed could not be combated because no strength—spritual or physical—was available. Biblical warfare was always tied to God's redemptive plans and His people's spiritual faithfulness.

consider 11the voice of the singers[y] at
the watering places.
They recite the righteous acts[j] of
the LORD,
the righteous acts of his warriors[z]
in Israel.

"Then the people of the LORD
went down to the city gates.[k]
12'Wake up,[l] wake up, Deborah![m]
Wake up, wake up, break out in
song!
Arise, O Barak![n]
Take captive your captives,[o] O son
of Abinoam.'

13"Then the men who were left
came down to the nobles;
the people of the LORD
came to me with the mighty.
14Some came from Ephraim,[p] whose
roots were in Amalek;[q]
Benjamin[r] was with the people who
followed you.
From Makir[s] captains came down,
from Zebulun those who bear a
commander's staff.
15The princes of Issachar[t] were with
Deborah;[u]
yes, Issachar was with Barak,[v]
rushing after him into the valley.
In the districts of Reuben
there was much searching of heart.
16Why did you stay among the
campfires[a] [w]
to hear the whistling for the
flocks?[x]
In the districts of Reuben
there was much searching of heart.
17Gilead[y] stayed beyond the Jordan.
And Dan, why did he linger by the
ships?
Asher[z] remained on the coast[a]
and stayed in his coves.
18The people of Zebulun[b] risked their
very lives;
so did Naphtali[c] on the heights of
the field.[d]

19"Kings came[e], they fought;
the kings of Canaan fought
at Taanach by the waters of Megiddo,[f]
but they carried off no silver, no
plunder.[g]
20From the heavens[h] the stars fought,
from their courses they fought
against Sisera.
21The river Kishon[i] swept them away,
the age-old river, the river Kishon.
March on, my soul; be strong!
22Then thundered the horses' hoofs—
galloping, galloping go his mighty
steeds.[k]

5:11 [j]1Sa 12:7; Da 9:16; Mic 6:5 [k]S ver 8
5:12 [l]Ps 44:23; 57:8; Isa 51:9,17 [m]S Jdg 4:4 [n]S Jdg 4:6 [o]Ps 68:18; Eph 4:8
5:14 [p]S Ge 41:52; S Jdg 1:29 [q]Jdg 3:13 [r]S Nu 34:21 [s]S Ge 50:23
5:15 [t]S Ge 30:18 [u]S Jdg 4:4 [v]S Jdg 4:6
5:16 [w]S Ge 49:14 [x]S Nu 32:1
5:17 [y]S Jos 12:2 [z]S Jos 17:7 [a]Jos 19:29
5:18 [b]S Ge 30:20 [c]S Ge 30:8; Ps 68:27 [d]S Jdg 4:6, 10
5:19 [e]Jos 11:5; S Jdg 4:13; Rev 16:16 [f]S Jos 12:21 [g]ver 30
5:20 [h]S Jos 10:11
5:21 [i]S Jdg 4:7 [j]Jos 1:6
5:22 [k]Jer 8:16
5:24 [l]Lk 1:42 [m]S Jdg 4:17 [n]S Ge 15:19
5:25 [o]S Ge 18:8
5:26 [p]Jdg 4:21
5:27 [q]Jdg 4:22
5:28 [r]S Jos 2:15 [s]Pr 7:6
5:30 [t]Ex 15:9; 1Sa 30:24; Ps 68:12 [u]Ps 45:14; Eze 16:10 [v]ver 19; 2Sa 1:24
5:31 [w]S Nu 10:35 [x]2Sa 23:4; Job 37:21; Ps 19:4; 89:36; Isa 18:4 [y]2Sa 18:32 [z]S Jdg 3:11
6:1 [a]S Jdg 2:11

23'Curse Meroz,' said the angel of the
LORD.
'Curse its people bitterly,
because they did not come to help the
LORD,
to help the LORD against the
mighty.'

24"Most blessed of women[l] be Jael,[m]
the wife of Heber the Kenite,[n]
most blessed of tent-dwelling
women.
25He asked for water, and she gave him
milk;[o]
in a bowl fit for nobles she brought
him curdled milk.
26Her hand reached for the tent peg,
her right hand for the workman's
hammer.
She struck Sisera, she crushed his
head,
she shattered and pierced his
temple.[p]
27At her feet he sank,
he fell; there he lay.
At her feet he sank, he fell;
where he sank, there he
fell—dead[q].

28"Through the window[r] peered
Sisera's mother;
behind the lattice she cried out,[s]
'Why is his chariot so long in coming?
Why is the clatter of his chariots
delayed?'
29The wisest of her ladies answer her;
indeed, she keeps saying to herself,
30'Are they not finding and dividing the
spoils:[t]
a girl or two for each man,
colorful garments as plunder for
Sisera,
colorful garments embroidered,
highly embroidered garments[u] for
my neck—
all this as plunder?[v]'

31"So may all your enemies perish,[w]
O LORD!
But may they who love you be like
the sun[x]
when it rises in its strength."[y]

Then the land had peace[z] forty years.

Chapter 6

Gideon

AGAIN the Israelites did evil in the eyes of the LORD,[a] and for seven years he

[y]*11* Or *archers;* the meaning of the Hebrew for this word is uncertain. [z]*11* Or *villagers* [a]*16* Or *saddlebags*

5:11 HISTORY, Worship—See note on Ex 15:1–21.

6:1 SIN, Covenant Breach—See note on 3:7.

gave them into the hands of the Midianites.[b] 2Because the power of Midian was
so oppressive,[c] the Israelites prepared
shelters for themselves in mountain
clefts, caves[d] and strongholds.[e] 3When-
ever the Israelites planted their crops, the
Midianites, Amalekites[f] and other eastern peoples[g] invaded the country. 4They
camped on the land and ruined the
crops[h] all the way to Gaza[i] and did not
spare a living thing for Israel, neither
sheep nor cattle nor donkeys. 5They came
up with their livestock and their tents
like swarms of locusts.[j] It was impossible
to count the men and their camels;[k] they
invaded the land to ravage it. 6Midian so
impoverished the Israelites that they
cried out[l] to the LORD for help.

7When the Israelites cried[m] to the
LORD because of Midian, 8he sent them a
prophet,[n] who said, "This is what the
LORD, the God of Israel, says: I brought
you up out of Egypt,[o] out of the land of
slavery.[p] 9I snatched you from the power
of Egypt and from the hand of all your
oppressors.[q] I drove them from before
you and gave you their land.[r] 10I said to
you, 'I am the LORD your God; do not
worship[s] the gods of the Amorites,[t] in
whose land you live.' But you have not
listened to me."

11The angel of the LORD[u] came and sat
down under the oak in Ophrah[v] that belonged to Joash[w] the Abiezrite,[x] where
his son Gideon[y] was threshing[z] wheat
in a winepress[a] to keep it from the Midianites. 12When the angel of the LORD appeared to Gideon, he said, "The LORD is
with you,[b] mighty warrior.[c]"

13"But sir," Gideon replied, "if the
LORD is with us, why has all this happened to us? Where are all his wonders[d]
that our fathers told[e] us about when they
said, 'Did not the LORD bring us up out of
Egypt?' But now the LORD has abandoned[f] us and put us into the hand of
Midian."

14The LORD turned to him and said,
"Go in the strength you have[g] and save[h]
Israel out of Midian's hand. Am I not
sending you?"

15"But Lord,[b]" Gideon asked, "how
can I save Israel? My clan[i] is the weakest
in Manasseh, and I am the least in my
family.[j]"

16The LORD answered, "I will be with
you[k], and you will strike down all the
Midianites together."

17Gideon replied, "If now I have found
favor in your eyes, give me a sign[l] that it
is really you talking to me. 18Please do not
go away until I come back and bring my
offering and set it before you."

And the LORD said, "I will wait until
you return."

19Gideon went in, prepared a young
goat,[m] and from an ephah[c][n] of flour he
made bread without yeast. Putting the
meat in a basket and its broth in a pot, he
brought them out and offered them to
him under the oak.[o]

20The angel of God said to him, "Take
the meat and the unleavened bread, place
them on this rock,[p] and pour out the

6:1 [b]S Ge 25:2 **6:2** [c]1Sa 13:6; Isa 5:30; 8:21; 26:16; 37:3 [d]Isa 2:19; Jer 48:28; 49:8,30 [e]Job 24:8; Jer 41:9; Heb 11:38 **6:3** [f]Nu 13:29 [g]S Ge 25:6; Isa 11:14; Jer 49:28 **6:4** [h]Lev 26:16; Dt 28:30,51; Isa 10:6; 39:6; 42:22 [i]S Ge 10:19 **6:5** [j]S Dt 28:42 [k]Jdg 8:10; Isa 21:7; 60:6; Jer 49:32 **6:6** [l]S Jdg 3:9 **6:7** [m]S Jdg 3:9 **6:8** [n]Dt 18:15; 1Ki 20:13,22; 2Ki 17:13,23; Ne 9:29; Job 36:10; Jer 25:5; Eze 18:30-31 [o]S Jdg 2:1 [p]Jos 24:17 **6:9** [q]S Nu 10:9; Ps 136:24 [r]Ps 44:2 **6:10** [s]S Ex 20:5 [t]S Jos 24:15 **6:11** [u]S Ge 16:7 [v]S Jos 18:23 [w]ver 29; Jdg 7:14; 8:13,29 [x]S Nu 26:30 [y]Jdg 7:1; 8:1; Heb 11:32 [z]Ru 2:17; 3:2; 1Sa 23:1; 1Ch 21:20 [a]Ne 13:15; Isa 16:10; 63:3; La 1:15; Joel 3:13 **6:12** [b]S Jos 1:5; Ru 2:4; 1Sa 10:7; Ps 129:8 [c]Jdg 11:1 **6:13** [d]S Jos 3:5 [e]2Sa 7:22; Ps 44:1; 78:3 [f]S Dt 31:17 **6:14** [g]Heb 11:34 [h]ver 36; Jdg 10:1; 2Ki 14:27 **6:15** [i]Isa 60:22 [j]1Sa 9:21 **6:16** [k]Ex 3:12; S Nu 14:43; Jos 1:5 **6:17** [l]ver 36-37; S Ge 24:14; S Ex 3:12; S 4:8 **6:19** [m]Jdg 13:15 [n]S Lev 19:36 [o]Ge 18:7-8 **6:20** [p]Jdg 13:19

[b]*15* Or *sir* [c]*19* That is, probably about 3/5 bushel (about 22 liters)

6:6–8 PRAYER, Petition—See note on 3:9.

6:11–40 EVIL AND SUFFERING, God's Present Help—God alleviated the Hebrews' suffering by calling Gideon to be a judge. Gideon expected God to intervene miraculously, but God chose to work through Gideon's leadership (6:14). God's people cannot always depend on miracles to lead us out of trouble. We must be ready to answer God's call to obedient action. Only so do we express our faith. God seeks a committed people, not an opportunity to show off His amazing power. He can help through miracle but often chooses to work His miracles through committed people. See note on Ex 3:7–10.

6:11–24 REVELATION, Messengers—The messenger from God appeared at unpredictable places to surprised people. Gideon was discouraged and confused about God's action in the face of Israel's plight. Like most young and impetuous believers, he had only heard of God's power from parents and teachers. He had not yet had a personal experience and felt that God had abandoned His people because his generation had not seen God's saving acts in history. Gideon reacted to the messenger as if he considered the messenger to be God. Gideon feared for his life after having seen the messenger face to face. Compare Ex 33:20. See note on Jdg 2:1–3.

6:11–24 PRAYER, Will of God—God's usual answer when His people cried to Him was to send a deliverer. Gideon's call came in a dialogue prayer with God. Gideon honestly voiced his sense of frustration and abandonment. Then he claimed to be unqualified to help. God provided a visible sign to reassure Gideon and then called Gideon to action. Gideon does not provide an example of how we should always pray. He does show us God will listen to our complaints, our frustrations, and our sense of inadequacy.

6:17 MIRACLE, God's Working—Miracles show God is working among His people. Gideon lacked confidence to believe God would actually appear to him and use him for divine purposes. He asked for a sign. See note on 1 Sa 10:9. God's angelic messenger lit a fire under Gideon's sacrifice. The action was outside the expectations of the natural order of things. God's miracles may be in the timing of natural events or the extraordinary use of natural laws. They may also, as here, be the work of special angelic messengers miraculously producing actions which occur in nature but do not follow the normal laws of nature. Some people narrow God's miraculous powers by insisting all miracles must overthrow natural law. Others limit the miraculous by saying all history must be explained within natural laws. The Bible testifies to God working miraculously to reveal Himself both through miraculous timing of natural events and through miracles which defy any natural explanation. The greatest of the latter include the virgin birth of Christ and His resurrection.

6:20–23 GOD, Holy—Gideon was fearful because He had great respect for the holiness of God. He apparently knew that sinners cannot look upon the holiness of God and live. Even to have seen an angel sent from the holy God seemed a dangerous position for a sinful person in the midst of a sinful people. See Isa 6:5. God was preparing Gideon for a special task. Perhaps any servant of God needs first to be awestruck with the holi-

broth." And Gideon did so. 21 With the tip
of the staff[q] that was in his hand, the
angel of the LORD touched the meat and
the unleavened bread.[r] Fire flared from
the rock, consuming the meat and the
bread. And the angel of the LORD disappeared. 22 When Gideon realized[s] that it
was the angel of the LORD, he exclaimed,
"Ah, Sovereign LORD! I have seen the angel of the LORD face to face!"[t]
23 But the LORD said to him, "Peace! Do
not be afraid.[u] You are not going to
die."[v]
24 So Gideon built an altar to the LORD
there and called[w] it The LORD is Peace.
To this day it stands in Ophrah[x] of the
Abiezrites.
25 That same night the LORD said to
him, "Take the second bull from your father's herd, the one seven years old.[d]
Tear down your father's altar to Baal and
cut down the Asherah pole[e][y] beside it.
26 Then build a proper kind of[f] altar to
the LORD your God on the top of this
height. Using the wood of the Asherah
pole that you cut down, offer the second[g]
bull as a burnt offering.[z]"
27 So Gideon took ten of his servants
and did as the LORD told him. But because
he was afraid of his family and the men of
the town, he did it at night rather than in
the daytime.
28 In the morning when the men of the
town got up, there was Baal's altar,[a] demolished, with the Asherah pole beside it
cut down and the second bull sacrificed
on the newly built altar!
29 They asked each other, "Who did
this?"
When they carefully investigated, they
were told, "Gideon son of Joash[b] did it."
30 The men of the town demanded of
Joash, "Bring out your son. He must die,
because he has broken down Baal's altar[c]
and cut down the Asherah pole beside
it."
31 But Joash replied to the hostile crowd
around him, "Are you going to plead
Baal's cause?[d] Are you trying to save
him? Whoever fights for him shall be put
to death by morning! If Baal really is a
god, he can defend himself when someone breaks down his altar." 32 So that day
they called Gideon "Jerub-Baal,[h][e]" saying, "Let Baal contend with him," because he broke down Baal's altar.
33 Now all the Midianites, Amalekites[f]
and other eastern peoples[g] joined forces
and crossed over the Jordan and camped
in the Valley of Jezreel.[h] 34 Then the Spirit of the LORD came upon[i] Gideon, and
he blew a trumpet,[j] summoning the Abiezrites[k] to follow him. 35 He sent messengers throughout Manasseh, calling them
to arms, and also into Asher,[l] Zebulun
and Naphtali,[m] so that they too went up
to meet them.[n]
36 Gideon said to God, "If you will
save[o] Israel by my hand as you have
promised— 37 look, I will place a wool
fleece[p] on the threshing floor.[q] If there
is dew only on the fleece and all the
ground is dry, then I will know[r] that you
will save Israel by my hand, as you said."
38 And that is what happened. Gideon
rose early the next day; he squeezed the
fleece and wrung out the dew—a bowlful
of water.
39 Then Gideon said to God, "Do not be
angry with me. Let me make just one
more request.[s] Allow me one more test
with the fleece. This time make the
fleece dry and the ground covered with
dew." 40 That night God did so. Only the
fleece was dry; all the ground was covered with dew.[t]

Chapter 7

Gideon Defeats the Midianites

EARLY in the morning, Jerub-Baal[u]
(that is, Gideon[v]) and all his men

6:21 [q]S Ex 4:2 [r]S Lev 9:24
6:22 [s]Jdg 13:16,21 [t]Ge 32:30; Jdg 13:22
6:23 [u]Da 10:19 [v]S Ge 16:13; S Dt 5:26
6:24 [w]S Ge 22:14 [x]S Jos 18:23
6:25 [y]ver 26,28,30; Ex 34:13; S Jdg 2:13
6:26 [z]S Ge 8:20
6:28 [a]ver 30; 1Ki 16:32; 2Ki 21:3
6:29 [b]S ver 11
6:30 [c]S ver 28
6:31 [d]1Sa 24:15; Ps 43:1; Jer 30:13
6:32 [e]Jdg 7:1; 8:29,35; 9:1; 1Sa 12:11
6:33 [f]Nu 13:29 [g]S Ge 25:6 [h]S Jos 15:56; Eze 25:4; Hos 1:5
6:34 [i]S Jdg 3:10 [j]S Jos 6:20; S Jdg 3:27 [k]S Jos 17:2
6:35 [l]S Jos 17:7 [m]S Jdg 4:6 [n]Jdg 7:23
6:36 [o]S ver 14
6:37 [p]Job 31:20 [q]S Nu 18:27; 2Sa 6:6; 24:16 [r]S Ge 24:14
6:39 [s]Ge 18:32
6:40 [t]Ex 4:3-7; Isa 38:7
7:1 [u]S Jdg 6:32 [v]S Jdg 6:11

[d]25 Or *Take a full-grown, mature bull from your father's herd* [e]25 That is, a symbol of the goddess Asherah; here and elsewhere in Judges [f]26 Or *build with layers of stone an* [g]26 Or *full-grown*; also in verse 28 [h]32 *Jerub-Baal* means *let Baal contend.*

ness of God and the sinfulness of his own being. Moses sensed the awesome presence of the holy God with whom he was confronted at the burning bush in the desert (Ex 3:1–6). Isaiah was confronted with the awesome presence of God in the Temple on the occasion of his call from God (Isa 6:1–8); Paul was stricken with blindness by the bright light and voice from heaven when he was confronted by Jesus on the Damascus Road (Ac 9:1–20). Every other description of God grows out of His holiness.

6:34–35 HOLY SPIRIT, Leaders—The Spirit's gift of leadership attracts followers. Literally, the text says, "The Spirit of Yahweh dressed (Himself) with Gideon." The human agent became the outer appearance through which the Spirit worked. See notes on 1 Ch 12:18; 2 Ch 24:20. The Spirit enabled Gideon to gather followers for his God-given task. God is always as concerned with followers as with leaders. Each role is necessary and important for God.

6:36–40 REVELATION, Signs—God uses signs in the material world to bolster His people's faith (Ex 4:1–9). Such signs joined to prayerful conversation with God reveal God's power and presence with His people. For Gideon the signs also signified divine patience with a young believer facing an awesome task.

6:36–40 PRAYER, Will of God—Prayer seeks to be sure of God's will. God can make us sure of His will for our lives as we talk to Him. His assurance may not take the dramatic form Gideon's did, but He responds to our need for confirmation of His call. Compare Isa 7:11.

7:1–25 CHRISTIAN ETHICS, War and Peace—Gideon's victory stirs every generation of believers to realize that their ultimate strength for life comes from God. A people using their resources to their limits and being steadfast in the application of them can find victory in all of life's fights. Courage and perseverance mixed with faith in God led to the demise of the

camped at the spring of Harod.[w] The
camp of Midian[x] was north of them in
the valley near the hill of Moreh.[y] 2The
LORD said to Gideon, "You have too many
men for me to deliver Midian into their
hands. In order that Israel may not boast
against me that her own strength[z] has
saved her, 3announce now to the people,
'Anyone who trembles with fear may
turn back and leave Mount Gilead.[a]' " So
twenty-two thousand men left, while ten
thousand remained.
4But the LORD said to Gideon, "There
are still too many[b] men. Take them
down to the water, and I will sift them for
you there. If I say, 'This one shall go with
you,' he shall go; but if I say, 'This one
shall not go with you,' he shall not go."
5So Gideon took the men down to the
water. There the LORD told him, "Separate those who lap the water with their
tongues like a dog from those who kneel
down to drink." 6Three hundred men[c]
lapped with their hands to their mouths.
All the rest got down on their knees to
drink.
7The LORD said to Gideon, "With the
three hundred men that lapped I will save
you and give the Midianites into your
hands.[d] Let all the other men go, each to
his own place."[e] 8So Gideon sent the
rest of the Israelites to their tents but
kept the three hundred, who took over
the provisions and trumpets of the others.
Now the camp of Midian lay below him
in the valley. 9During that night the LORD
said to Gideon, "Get up, go down against
the camp, because I am going to give it
into your hands.[f] 10If you are afraid to
attack, go down to the camp with your
servant Purah 11and listen to what they
are saying. Afterward, you will be encouraged to attack the camp." So he and Purah his servant went down to the outposts of the camp. 12The Midianites, the
Amalekites[g] and all the other eastern
peoples had settled in the valley, thick as
locusts.[h] Their camels[i] could no more
be counted than the sand on the seashore.[j]
13Gideon arrived just as a man was telling a friend his dream. "I had a dream,"
he was saying. "A round loaf of barley
bread came tumbling into the Midianite
camp. It struck the tent with such force
that the tent overturned and collapsed."
14His friend responded, "This can be
nothing other than the sword of Gideon
son of Joash,[k] the Israelite. God has giv-
en the Midianites and the whole camp
into his hands."
15When Gideon heard the dream and
its interpretation, he worshiped God.[l]
He returned to the camp of Israel and
called out, "Get up! The LORD has given
the Midianite camp into your hands."[m]
16Dividing the three hundred men[n] into
three companies,[o] he placed trumpets[p]
and empty jars[q] in the hands of all of
them, with torches[r] inside.
17"Watch me," he told them. "Follow
my lead. When I get to the edge of the
camp, do exactly as I do. 18When I and all
who are with me blow our trumpets,[s]
then from all around the camp blow
yours and shout, 'For the LORD and for
Gideon.' "
19Gideon and the hundred men with
him reached the edge of the camp at the
beginning of the middle watch, just after
they had changed the guard. They blew
their trumpets and broke the jars[t] that
were in their hands. 20The three companies blew the trumpets and smashed the
jars. Grasping the torches[u] in their left
hands and holding in their right hands
the trumpets they were to blow, they
shouted, "A sword[v] for the LORD and for
Gideon!" 21While each man held his position around the camp, all the Midianites
ran, crying out as they fled.[w]
22When the three hundred trumpets
sounded,[x] the LORD caused the men
throughout the camp to turn on each other[y] with their swords.[z] The army fled to
Beth Shittah toward Zererah as far as the
border of Abel Meholah[a] near Tabbath.
23Israelites from Naphtali, Asher[b] and all
Manasseh were called out,[c] and they
pursued the Midianites.[d] 24Gideon sent
messengers throughout the hill country of
Ephraim, saying, "Come down against
the Midianites and seize the waters of the
Jordan[e] ahead of them as far as Beth
Barah."
So all the men of Ephraim were called

7:1 [w]2Sa 23:25 [x]S Ge 25:2 [y]S Ge 12:6
7:2 [z]S Dt 8:17; 2Co 4:7
7:3 [a]Dt 20:8; S Jos 12:2
7:4 [b]1Sa 14:6
7:6 [c]Ge 14:14
7:7 [d]S Jos 8:7 [e]1Sa 14:6
7:9 [f]ver 13-15; S Jos 2:24; S Jdg 1:2
7:12 [g]Nu 13:29 [h]S Dt 28:42; Jer 46:23 [i]Jer 49:29 [j]S Jos 11:4
7:14 [k]S Jdg 6:11
7:15 [l]1Sa 15:31 [m]S ver 9
7:16 [n]Ge 14:15 [o]Jdg 9:43; 1Sa 11:11; 2Sa 18:2 [p]S Lev 25:9 [q]ver 19; Ge 24:14 [r]S Ge 15:17
7:18 [s]S Jdg 3:27
7:19 [t]S ver 16
7:20 [u]S Ge 15:17 [v]S Dt 32:41
7:21 [w]2Ki 7:7
7:22 [x]S Jos 6:20 [y]1Sa 14:20; 2Ch 20:23; Isa 9:21; 19:2; Eze 38:21; Hag 2:22; Zec 14:13 [z]Hab 3:14 [a]1Sa 18:19; 1Ki 4:12; 19:16
7:23 [b]S Jos 17:7 [c]Jdg 6:35 [d]Ps 83:9
7:24 [e]S Jos 2:7

Midianites. The victory was ultimately God's doing in that neither Gideon nor his men ever had to strike a blow. See note on Jos 10:1–43.

7:13 REVELATION, Dreams—Those who follow God seek particular signs of His presence and action in their lives. Gideon found assurance of that presence by overhearing the dream of an enemy soldier. Dreams are one of God's favorite means to speak to His people (Ge 20:3,6; 31:10; 37:6; 41:11; 42:9; Nu 12:6; 1 Sa 28:6). Here we see He can speak to His people through the dream of an unbeliever. Hearing the dream gave Gideon and his army courage to carry out their mission.

7:15 PRAYER, Worship—"Worshiped" (Hebrew *hishtachawah*) here implies that Gideon bowed in humility and reverence. Learning God's presence and will leads us to prayer and worship.

7:22 GOD, Power—God made His sovereign power very clear here. By His instructions to Gideon to pare down his followers to what may have been a ridiculous little handful of people, God emphasized to Gideon, and to all Israel, that it is not human strength or human ingenuity that would give them victory. Only the power of God's hand could bring them victory. Compare 1 Sa 17:4–8,38–39; Zec 4:6; Jn 6:1–13. See note on Jos 2:11. God's power often takes the seemingly insignificant resources at hand to perform His mighty works.

out and they took the waters of the Jordan as far as Beth Barah. 25They also captured two of the Midianite leaders, Oreb
and Zeeb[f]. They killed Oreb at the rock
of Oreb,[g] and Zeeb at the winepress of
Zeeb. They pursued the Midianites[h] and
brought the heads of Oreb and Zeeb to
Gideon, who was by the Jordan.[i]

Chapter 8

Zebah and Zalmunna

NOW the Ephraimites asked Gideon,[j]
"Why have you treated us like this?
Why didn't you call us when you went to
fight Midian?[k]"[l] And they criticized
him sharply.[m]
2But he answered them, "What have I
accomplished compared to you? Aren't
the gleanings of Ephraim's grapes better
than the full grape harvest of Abiezer?[n]
3God gave Oreb and Zeeb,[o] the Midianite leaders, into your hands. What was I
able to do compared to you?" At this,
their resentment against him subsided.
4Gideon and his three hundred men,
exhausted yet keeping up the pursuit,
came to the Jordan[p] and crossed it. 5He
said to the men of Succoth,[q] "Give my
troops some bread; they are worn out,[r]
and I am still pursuing Zebah and Zalmunna,[s] the kings of Midian."
6But the officials of Succoth[t] said, "Do
you already have the hands of Zebah and
Zalmunna in your possession? Why
should we give bread[u] to your troops?"[v]
7Then Gideon replied, "Just for that,
when the LORD has given Zebah and Zalmunna[w] into my hand, I will tear your
flesh with desert thorns and briers."
8From there he went up to Peniel[1] [x]
and made the same request of them, but
they answered as the men of Succoth
had. 9So he said to the men of Peniel,
"When I return in triumph, I will tear
down this tower."[y]
10Now Zebah and Zalmunna were in
Karkor with a force of about fifteen thousand men, all that were left of the armies
of the eastern peoples; a hundred and
twenty thousand swordsmen had fallen.[z]
11Gideon went up by the route of the nomads east of Nobah[a] and Jogbehah[b] and
fell upon the unsuspecting army. 12Zebah
and Zalmunna, the two kings of Midian,
fled, but he pursued them and captured
them, routing their entire army.
13Gideon son of Joash[c] then returned
from the battle by the Pass of Heres.[d]
14He caught a young man of Succoth and
questioned him, and the young man
wrote down for him the names of the seventy-seven officials of Succoth,[e] the elders[f] of the town. 15Then Gideon came
and said to the men of Succoth, "Here are
Zebah and Zalmunna, about whom you
taunted me by saying, 'Do you already
have the hands of Zebah and Zalmunna in
your possession? Why should we give
bread to your exhausted men?[g]' " 16He
took the elders of the town and taught
the men of Succoth a lesson[h] by punishing them with desert thorns and briers.
17He also pulled down the tower of Peniel[i] and killed the men of the town.[j]
18Then he asked Zebah and Zalmunna,
"What kind of men did you kill at Tabor?[k]"
"Men like you," they answered, "each
one with the bearing of a prince."
19Gideon replied, "Those were my
brothers, the sons of my own mother. As
surely as the LORD lives,[l] if you had
spared their lives, I would not kill you."
20Turning to Jether, his oldest son, he
said, "Kill them!" But Jether did not draw
his sword, because he was only a boy and
was afraid.
21Zebah and Zalmunna said, "Come,
do it yourself. 'As is the man, so is his
strength.' " So Gideon stepped forward
and killed them, and took the ornaments[m] off their camels' necks.

Gideon's Ephod

22The Israelites said to Gideon, "Rule

7:25 [f]Jdg 8:3; Ps 83:11 [g]Isa 10:26 [h]Isa 9:4 [i]Jdg 8:4; Ps 106:43
8:1 [j]S Jdg 6:11 [k]S Ge 25:2 [l]Jdg 12:1 [m]2Sa 19:41
8:2 [n]S Nu 26:30
8:3 [o]S Jdg 7:25
8:4 [p]Jdg 7:25
8:5 [q]S Ge 33:17 [r]Job 16:7; Ps 6:6; Jer 45:3 [s]ver 7,12; Ps 83:11
8:6 [t]ver 14 [u]1Sa 25:11 [v]ver 15
8:7 [w]S ver 5
8:8 [x]ver 9,17; Ge 32:30; 1Ki 12:25
8:9 [y]ver 17
8:10 [z]S Jdg 6:5; Isa 9:4
8:11 [a]Nu 32:42 [b]S Nu 32:35
8:13 [c]S Jdg 6:11 [d]Jdg 1:35
8:14 [e]ver 6 [f]S Ex 3:16
8:15 [g]ver 6
8:16 [h]1Sa 14:12
8:17 [i]S ver 8 [j]ver 9
8:18 [k]S Jos 19:22
8:19 [l]S Nu 14:21
8:21 [m]ver 26; Isa 3:18

[1]*8* Hebrew *Penuel,* a variant of *Peniel;* also in verses 9 and 17

8:10–21 CHRISTIAN ETHICS, Murder—Today's readers are often surprised how many murders are described in the Old Testament. Accounts such as this one are more descriptive than prescriptive in nature. They major on the "what" and "how" of an incident but do not develop the "why" of an incident beyond the matter of revenge. In a world dominated by cause and effect values, little time was given to reconciliation or rehabilitation. Thus, often the murders associated with political intrigue, war, and interpersonal conflict do not reflect normative, timeless principles for dealing with injustice. Caution must be applied before making quick jumps of application to contemporary time based on such incidents. Such caution asks from where the initiative comes for any acts of killing. For example, to say even "but God is on our side" must bear the proof when matters of life and death are raised. In Gideon's case the biblical emphasis is on punishment of murderers rather than justifying Gideon's attitude of vengeance. A helpful consideration is to read these passages through the light of Jesus' actions, words, and attitudes. See note on Ex 20:13. See Guide to Applying the Word, pp. 1811–1812.

8:22–27 SIN, Blindness—Sin produces spiritual blindness. We easily turn good things to bad purposes. The ephod was apparently a garment for the high priest (Ex 28—29; 39). Gideon may have tried to use the ephod to say he wanted to be God's priest rather than the nation's king. Gideon may not have intended for Israel to worship this ephod, but it became a monument to the memory of his leadership in Israel. Because of their great respect for Gideon, the Israelites venerated his ephod. Similar to idolatry, veneration of objects tends to divert the love and trust in what the object represents to the object itself. We become blind, thinking we are worshiping properly when we have become idol worshipers.

over us—you, your son and your grandson—because you have saved us out of
the hand of Midian."
23But Gideon told them, "I will not
rule over you, nor will my son rule over
you. The LORD will rule[n] over you."
24And he said, "I do have one request,
that each of you give me an earring[o]
from your share of the plunder.[p]" (It was
the custom of the Ishmaelites[q] to wear
gold earrings.)
25They answered, "We'll be glad to
give them." So they spread out a garment, and each man threw a ring from
his plunder onto it. 26The weight of the
gold rings he asked for came to seventeen
hundred shekels,[j] not counting the ornaments, the pendants and the purple garments worn by the kings of Midian or the
chains[r] that were on their camels' necks.
27Gideon made the gold into an ephod,[s]
which he placed in Ophrah,[t] his town.
All Israel prostituted themselves by worshiping it there, and it became a snare[u]
to Gideon and his family.[v]

Gideon's Death

28Thus Midian was subdued before the
Israelites and did not raise its head[w]
again. During Gideon's lifetime, the land
enjoyed peace[x] forty years.
29Jerub-Baal[y] son of Joash[z] went back
home to live. 30He had seventy sons[a] of
his own, for he had many wives. 31His
concubine,[b] who lived in Shechem, also
bore him a son, whom he named Abimelech.[c] 32Gideon son of Joash died at a
good old age[d] and was buried in the
tomb of his father Joash in Ophrah of the
Abiezrites.
33No sooner had Gideon died than the
Israelites again prostituted themselves to
the Baals.[e] They set up Baal-Berith[f] as
their god[g] and 34did not remember[h] the
LORD their God, who had rescued them
from the hands of all their enemies on
every side. 35They also failed to show
kindness to the family of Jerub-Baal[i]
(that is, Gideon) for all the good things he
had done for them.[j]

Chapter 9

Abimelech

ABIMELECH[k] son of Jerub-Baal[l] went
to his mother's brothers in Shechem
and said to them and to all his mother's
clan, 2"Ask all the citizens of Shechem,
'Which is better for you: to have all seventy of Jerub-Baal's sons rule over you, or
just one man?' Remember, I am your
flesh and blood.[m]"
3When the brothers repeated all this to
the citizens of Shechem, they were inclined to follow Abimelech, for they said,
"He is our brother." 4They gave him seventy shekels[k] of silver from the temple of
Baal-Berith,[n] and Abimelech used it to
hire reckless adventurers,[o] who became
his followers. 5He went to his father's
home in Ophrah and on one stone murdered his seventy brothers,[p] the sons of
Jerub-Baal. But Jotham,[q] the youngest
son of Jerub-Baal, escaped by hiding.[r]
6Then all the citizens of Shechem and
Beth Millo[s] gathered beside the great
tree[t] at the pillar in Shechem to crown
Abimelech king.
7When Jotham[u] was told about this, he
climbed up on the top of Mount Gerizim[v] and shouted to them, "Listen to
me, citizens of Shechem, so that God may
listen to you. 8One day the trees went out
to anoint a king for themselves. They said
to the olive tree, 'Be our king.'
9"But the olive tree answered, 'Should
I give up my oil, by which both gods and
men are honored, to hold sway over the
trees?'
10"Next, the trees said to the fig tree,
'Come and be our king.'
11"But the fig tree replied, 'Should I
give up my fruit, so good and sweet, to
hold sway over the trees?'
12"Then the trees said to the vine,
'Come and be our king.'
13"But the vine answered, 'Should I
give up my wine,[w] which cheers both

[j]*26* That is, about 43 pounds (about 19.5 kilograms)
[k]*4* That is, about 1 3/4 pounds (about 0.8 kilogram)

8:23 [n]S Ex 16:8; S Nu 11:20; 1Sa 12:12
8:24 [o]S Ge 35:4 [p]S Ge 49:27 [q]S Ge 16:11
8:26 [r]S ver 21
8:27 [s]S Ex 25:7; Jdg 17:5; 18:14 [t]S Jos 18:23 [u]S Ex 10:7 [v]S Ex 32:2
8:28 [w]Ps 83:2 [x]S Jdg 3:11
8:29 [y]S Jdg 6:32 [z]S Jdg 6:11
8:30 [a]Jdg 9:2,5,18, 24; 12:14; 2Ki 10:1
8:31 [b]S Ge 22:24 [c]Jdg 9:1; 10:1; 2Sa 11:21
8:32 [d]S Ge 15:15
8:33 [e]S Jdg 2:11, 13,19 [f]Jdg 9:4 [g]Jdg 9:27,46
8:34 [h]S Jdg 3:7; S Ne 9:17
8:35 [i]S Jdg 6:32 [j]Jdg 9:16
9:1 [k]S Jdg 8:31 [l]S Jdg 6:32
9:2 [m]S Ge 29:14
9:4 [n]S Jdg 8:33 [o]Jdg 11:3; 1Sa 25:25; 2Ch 13:7; Job 30:8
9:5 [p]S Jdg 8:30 [q]ver 7,21,57 [r]2Ki 11:2; 2Ch 22:9
9:6 [s]ver 20; 2Ki 12:20 [t]S Ge 12:6; S Jdg 4:11
9:7 [u]S ver 5 [v]S Dt 11:29; Jn 4:20
9:13 [w]S Ge 14:18; Ecc 2:3; SS 4:10

8:27,33 GOD, One God—The Israelites are said to be prostituting themselves in worshiping other gods. Perhaps this is the most base description that can be given for spiritual compromise. It is a vivid picture of an ugly practice of substituting a false god for the one true God. Any people who have placed the world's goods above their allegiance to God have prostituted themselves.

8:33–35 SIN, Covenant Breach—Yahweh, the God of Israel, had set up His covenant with His people. They used covenant worship to worship Baal-Berith, literally translated the Baal or lord of the Berith or covenant. See 9:4,46. Right language and ritual used to serve the wrong god is sin. See note on 3:7.

8:33–35 HISTORY, Faith—History is a call to see God in action and depend totally on Him. Israel was too often tempted to see history in Canaanite terms as a cycle of recurring agricultural seasons. They wanted to depend on Yahweh, the God of Israel, for political leadership and on Baal, the god of Canaanite agriculture and fertility, for crop protection. Even a leader like Gideon had received a name honoring Baal from his parents. God controls all aspects of history—military, political, economic, social, and agricultural. He expects His people to depend on Him in each new season because He has proved His power and care through history, not because they go through proper rituals to cause the seasons to repeat themselves.

9:5 CHRISTIAN ETHICS, Murder—Abimelech is not described as a hero here. His murderous acts are not justified or approved by Scripture. See notes on 8:10–21; Ex 20:13; Mt 5:21–22.

gods and men, to hold sway over the trees?'

14"Finally all the trees said to the thornbush, 'Come and be our king.'

15"The thornbush said to the trees, 'If you really want to anoint me king over you, come and take refuge in my shade;[x] but if not, then let fire come out[y] of the thornbush and consume the cedars of Lebanon!'[z]

16"Now if you have acted honorably and in good faith when you made Abimelech king, and if you have been fair to Jerub-Baal and his family, and if you have treated him as he deserves— 17and to think that my father fought for you, risked[a] his life to rescue you from the hand of Midian 18(but today you have revolted against my father's family, murdered his seventy sons[b] on a single stone, and made Abimelech, the son of his slave girl, king over the citizens of Shechem because he is your brother)— 19if then you have acted honorably and in good faith toward Jerub-Baal and his family today,[c] may Abimelech be your joy, and may you be his, too! 20But if you have not, let fire come out[d] from Abimelech and consume you, citizens of Shechem[e] and Beth Millo,[f] and let fire come out from you, citizens of Shechem and Beth Millo, and consume Abimelech!"

21Then Jotham[g] fled, escaping to Beer,[h] and he lived there because he was afraid of his brother Abimelech.

22After Abimelech had governed Israel three years, 23God sent an evil spirit[i] between Abimelech and the citizens of Shechem, who acted treacherously against Abimelech. 24God did this in order that the crime against Jerub-Baal's seventy sons,[j] the shedding[k] of their blood, might be avenged[l] on their brother Abimelech and on the citizens of Shechem, who had helped him[m] murder his brothers. 25In opposition to him these citizens of Shechem set men on the hilltops to ambush and rob everyone who passed by, and this was reported to Abimelech.

26Now Gaal son of Ebed[n] moved with his brothers into Shechem, and its citizens put their confidence in him. 27After they had gone out into the fields and gathered the grapes and trodden[o] them, they held a festival in the temple of their god.[p] While they were eating and drinking, they cursed Abimelech. 28Then Gaal son of Ebed[q] said, "Who[r] is Abimelech, and who is Shechem, that we should be subject to him? Isn't he Jerub-Baal's son, and isn't Zebul his deputy? Serve the men of Hamor,[s] Shechem's father! Why should we serve Abimelech? 29If only this people were under my command![t] Then I would get rid of him. I would say to Abimelech, 'Call out your whole army!' "[1] [u]

30When Zebul the governor of the city heard what Gaal son of Ebed said, he was very angry. 31Under cover he sent messengers to Abimelech, saying, "Gaal son of Ebed and his brothers have come to Shechem and are stirring up the city against you. 32Now then, during the night you and your men should come and lie in wait[v] in the fields. 33In the morning at sunrise, advance against the city. When Gaal and his men come out against you, do whatever your hand finds to do.[w]"

34So Abimelech and all his troops set out by night and took up concealed positions near Shechem in four companies. 35Now Gaal son of Ebed had gone out and was standing at the entrance to the city gate[x] just as Abimelech and his soldiers came out from their hiding place.[y]

36When Gaal saw them, he said to Zebul, "Look, people are coming down from the tops of the mountains!"

Zebul replied, "You mistake the shadows of the mountains for men."

37But Gaal spoke up again: "Look, people are coming down from the center of the land, and a company is coming from the direction of the soothsayers' tree."

38Then Zebul said to him, "Where is your big talk now, you who said, 'Who is Abimelech that we should be subject to him?' Aren't these the men you ridiculed?[z] Go out and fight them!"

39So Gaal led out[m] the citizens of Shechem and fought Abimelech. 40Abimelech chased him, and many fell wounded in the flight—all the way to the entrance to the gate. 41Abimelech stayed in Arumah, and Zebul drove Gaal and his brothers out of Shechem.

42The next day the people of Shechem

9:15 [x]Isa 30:2 [y]ver 20 [z]S Dt 3:25; 1Ki 5:6; Ps 29:5; 92:12; Isa 2:13
9:17 [a]Jdg 12:3; 1Sa 19:5; 28:21; Job 13:14; Ps 119:109
9:18 [b]S Jdg 8:30
9:19 [c]ver 16
9:20 [d]ver 15 [e]ver 45 [f]S ver 6
9:21 [g]S ver 5 [h]Nu 21:16
9:23 [i]1Sa 16:14,23; 18:10; 19:9; 1Ki 22:22
9:24 [j]S Jdg 8:30 [k]S Ge 9:6; Nu 35:33; 1Ki 2:32 [l]ver 56-57 [m]Dt 27:25
9:26 [n]ver 28,31,41
9:27 [o]Isa 16:10; Am 5:11; 9:13 [p]S Jdg 8:33
9:28 [q]S ver 26 [r]1Sa 25:10 [s]S Ge 33:19
9:29 [t]2Sa 15:4 [u]ver 38
9:32 [v]Jos 8:2
9:33 [w]1Sa 10:7
9:35 [x]S Jos 2:5 [y]Ps 32:7; Isa 28:15, 17; Jer 49:10
9:38 [z]ver 28-29

[1]*29 Septuagint; Hebrew him." Then he said to Abimelech, "Call out your whole army!"* [m]*39 Or Gaal went out in the sight of*

9:23–24,56–57 GOD, Sovereignty—The belief in monotheism—the existence of one and only one God—means that ultimately all actions can be traced to the one God, either by His active intervention, His passive permission, or His choice not to act. We know from Jas 1:13–15 that God has absolutely nothing to do with evil temptations for people. God took advantage of a developing political split to punish both sides because each had committed atrocious crimes (v 24). Because we know God is just, we can affirm that God's actions in this incident were just. He did not act in a morally dubious or arbitrary manner to accomplish His purposes. God may use other people's evil to accomplish His righteous purposes, but He does not cause their evil actions.

9:23 EVIL AND SUFFERING, Punishment—The "evil spirit" was a spirit controlled by God, who sent it to punish Abimelech for his violent actions. See note on 1 Sa 16:13–23.

went out to the fields, and this was reported to Abimelech. 43So he took his
men, divided them into three companies[a] and set an ambush[b] in the fields.
When he saw the people coming out of
the city, he rose to attack them. 44Abime-
lech and the companies with him rushed
forward to a position at the entrance to
the city gate. Then two companies rushed
upon those in the fields and struck them
down. 45All that day Abimelech pressed
his attack against the city until he had
captured it and killed its people. Then he
destroyed the city[c] and scattered salt[d]
over it.

46On hearing this, the citizens in the
tower of Shechem went into the stronghold of the temple[e] of El-Berith. 47When
Abimelech heard that they had assembled
there, 48he and all his men went up
Mount Zalmon.[f] He took an ax and cut
off some branches, which he lifted to his
shoulders. He ordered the men with him,
"Quick! Do what you have seen me do!"
49So all the men cut branches and followed Abimelech. They piled them
against the stronghold and set it on fire
over the people inside. So all the people
in the tower of Shechem, about a thousand men and women, also died.

50Next Abimelech went to Thebez[g]
and besieged it and captured it. 51Inside
the city, however, was a strong tower, to
which all the men and women—all the
people of the city—fled. They locked
themselves in and climbed up on the tower roof. 52Abimelech went to the tower
and stormed it. But as he approached the
entrance to the tower to set it on fire, 53a
woman dropped an upper millstone on
his head and cracked his skull.[h]

54Hurriedly he called to his armor-bearer, "Draw your sword and kill me,[i] so
that they can't say, 'A woman killed
him.'" So his servant ran him through,
and he died. 55When the Israelites saw
that Abimelech was dead, they went
home.

56Thus God repaid the wickedness that
Abimelech had done to his father by murdering his seventy brothers. 57God also
made the men of Shechem pay for all

9:43 [a]S Jdg 7:16 [b]Jos 8:2
9:45 [c]ver 20 [d]Jer 48:9
9:46 [e]S Jdg 8:33
9:48 [f]Ps 68:14
9:50 [g]2Sa 11:21
9:53 [h]2Sa 11:21
9:54 [i]1Sa 31:4; 2Sa 1:9
9:57 [j]ver 24; Ps 94:23 [k]S ver 5
10:1 [l]S Jdg 8:31 [m]S Ge 30:18 [n]S Ge 46:13 [o]S Jdg 6:14 [p]Jos 15:48
10:3 [q]S Nu 32:41
10:4 [r]S Ge 49:11; S 1Ki 1:33 [s]S Nu 32:41
10:5 [t]S Nu 32:41
10:6 [u]S Jdg 2:11 [v]S Jdg 2:13 [w]Eze 27:16 [x]S Ge 10:15 [y]S Ge 19:38 [z]S Nu 21:29 [a]S Ge 26:1; S Jdg 2:12 [b]S Dt 32:15
10:7 [c]S Dt 31:17 [d]S Dt 32:30
10:8 [e]S Jos 12:2
10:9 [f]ver 17; Jdg 11:4 [g]Jdg 1:22
10:10 [h]S Jdg 3:9 [i]S Ex 9:27; Ps 32:5; Jer 3:25; 8:14; 14:20 [j]Jer 2:27
10:11 [k]Ex 14:30 [l]S Ge 14:7 [m]S Jdg 3:13 [n]S Jdg 3:31
10:12 [o]S Ge 14:7 [p]S Jos 15:55

their wickedness.[j] The curse of Jotham[k]
son of Jerub-Baal came on them.

Chapter 10

Tola

AFTER the time of Abimelech[l] a man of
Issachar,[m] Tola son of Puah,[n] the
son of Dodo, rose to save[o] Israel. He
lived in Shamir,[p] in the hill country of
Ephraim. 2He led[n] Israel twenty-three
years; then he died, and was buried in
Shamir.

Jair

3He was followed by Jair[q] of Gilead,
who led Israel twenty-two years. 4He had
thirty sons, who rode thirty donkeys.[r]
They controlled thirty towns in Gilead,
which to this day are called Havvoth
Jair.[o][s] 5When Jair[t] died, he was buried
in Kamon.

Jephthah

6Again the Israelites did evil in the eyes
of the LORD.[u] They served the Baals and
the Ashtoreths,[v] and the gods of Aram,[w]
the gods of Sidon,[x] the gods of Moab, the
gods of the Ammonites[y][z] and the gods of
the Philistines.[a] And because the Israelites forsook the LORD[b] and no longer
served him, 7he became angry[c] with
them. He sold them[d] into the hands of
the Philistines and the Ammonites, 8who
that year shattered and crushed them. For
eighteen years they oppressed all the Israelites on the east side of the Jordan in
Gilead,[e] the land of the Amorites. 9The
Ammonites also crossed the Jordan to
fight against Judah,[f] Benjamin and the
house of Ephraim;[g] and Israel was in
great distress. 10Then the Israelites
cried[h] out to the LORD, "We have
sinned[i] against you, forsaking our God
and serving the Baals."[j]

11The LORD replied, "When the Egyptians,[k] the Amorites,[l] the Ammonites,[m]
the Philistines,[n] 12the Sidonians, the Amalekites[o] and the Maonites[p][p] oppressed

[n]2 Traditionally *judged*; also in verse 3 [o]4 Or *called the settlements of Jair* [p]12 Hebrew; some Septuagint manuscripts *Midianites*

10:6–9 GOD, One God—The one true God, the Lord who is sovereign over all the earth, makes a strong demand upon us. God, who has both created and redeemed us, wants to be honored as Lord in our lives. He will not tolerate our worship of other gods, no matter what form that worship might take. Repeatedly Israel turned aside from God and compromised her loyalty to God. The natural result was that God withdrew His blessing, at least temporarily. This is the loving heavenly Father's way of chastising His children to bring them to repentance and responsibility.

10:10–16 PRAYER, Petition—See note on 3:9. God expects calls for help to be based on genuine repentance and commitment to God's will. Prayer with improper attitudes to God are meaningless.

10:11–14 SIN, Alienation—God repeatedly answered His sinful people's prayers for deliverance. Finally, He quit answering them, telling them to let the gods they served save them. Repeated sin eventually alienates people from God.

10:11–16 HISTORY, Judgment—See note on 2:1–15. Neither deliverance nor judgment is God's automatic historical response to His people. History does not bind God to a certain action. God responds to the relationship with His people and what He knows is best for them at the specific historical moment. A praying people gains God's ear and learns that mercy is His dominant characteristic.

you[q] and you cried to me for help, did I
not save you from their hands? 13But you
have forsaken[r] me and served other
gods,[s] so I will no longer save you. 14Go
and cry out to the gods you have chosen.
Let them save[t] you when you are in trouble![u]"

15But the Israelites said to the LORD,
"We have sinned. Do with us whatever
you think best,[v] but please rescue us
now." 16Then they got rid of the foreign
gods among them and served the LORD.[w]
And he could bear Israel's misery[x] no
longer.[y]

17When the Ammonites were called to
arms and camped in Gilead, the Israelites
assembled and camped at Mizpah.[z]
18The leaders of the people of Gilead said
to each other, "Whoever will launch the
attack against the Ammonites will be the
head[a] of all those living in Gilead."

Chapter 11

JEPHTHAH[b] the Gileadite was a mighty
warrior.[c] His father was Gilead;[d] his
mother was a prostitute.[e] 2Gilead's wife
also bore him sons, and when they were
grown up, they drove Jephthah away.
"You are not going to get any inheritance
in our family," they said, "because you
are the son of another woman." 3So Jephthah fled from his brothers and settled in
the land of Tob,[f] where a group of adventurers[g] gathered around him and followed him.

4Some time later, when the Ammonites[h] made war on Israel, 5the elders of
Gilead went to get Jephthah from the
land of Tob. 6"Come," they said, "be our
commander, so we can fight the Ammonites."

7Jephthah said to them, "Didn't you
hate me and drive me from my father's
house?[i] Why do you come to me now,
when you're in trouble?"

8The elders of Gilead said to him,
"Nevertheless, we are turning to you
now; come with us to fight the Ammonites, and you will be our head[j] over all
who live in Gilead."

9Jephthah answered, "Suppose you
take me back to fight the Ammonites and
the LORD gives them to me—will I really
be your head?"

10:12 [q]S Jdg 4:3
10:13 [r]S Dt 32:15 [s]Jer 11:10; 13:10
10:14 [t]Isa 44:17; 57:13 [u]Dt 32:37; Jer 2:28; 11:12; Hab 2:18
10:15 [v]1Sa 3:18; 2Sa 10:12; 15:26; Job 1:21; Isa 39:8
10:16 [w]Jos 24:23; Jer 18:8 [x]Isa 63:9 [y]S Dt 32:36
10:17 [z]S Ge 31:49; Jdg 11:29
10:18 [a]Jdg 11:8,9
11:1 [b]Jdg 12:1; 1Sa 12:11; Heb 11:32 [c]Jdg 6:12 [d]Nu 26:29 [e]S Ge 38:15
11:3 [f]ver 5; 2Sa 10:6,8 [g]S Jdg 9:4
11:4 [h]S Jdg 10:9
11:7 [i]S Ge 26:16
11:8 [j]S Jdg 10:18
11:10 [k]S Ge 31:50; S Isa 1:2
11:11 [l]1Sa 8:4; 2Sa 3:17 [m]Ex 19:9; 1Sa 8:21 [n]S Jos 11:3
11:13 [o]S Nu 21:13 [p]S Nu 21:24
11:15 [q]Dt 2:9 [r]Dt 2:19
11:16 [s]Nu 14:25; S Dt 1:40 [t]S Ge 14:7
11:17 [u]ver 19; S Ge 32:3; Nu 20:14 [v]S Nu 20:17 [w]Jer 48:1 [x]S Jos 24:9
11:18 [y]S Nu 20:21 [z]Dt 2:8 [a]S Nu 21:13
11:19 [b]S ver 17 [c]S Jos 12:2 [d]Nu 21:21-22
11:20 [e]Nu 21:23

10The elders of Gilead replied, "The
LORD is our witness;[k] we will certainly
do as you say." 11So Jephthah went with
the elders[l] of Gilead, and the people
made him head and commander over
them. And he repeated[m] all his words before the LORD in Mizpah.[n]

12Then Jephthah sent messengers to
the Ammonite king with the question:
"What do you have against us that you
have attacked our country?"

13The king of the Ammonites answered
Jephthah's messengers, "When Israel
came up out of Egypt, they took away my
land from the Arnon[o] to the Jabbok,[p] all
the way to the Jordan. Now give it back
peaceably."

14Jephthah sent back messengers to the
Ammonite king, 15saying:

"This is what Jephthah says: Israel
did not take the land of Moab[q] or the
land of the Ammonites.[r] 16But when
they came up out of Egypt, Israel
went through the desert to the Red
Sea[q][s] and on to Kadesh.[t] 17Then Israel sent messengers[u] to the king of
Edom, saying, 'Give us permission to
go through your country,'[v] but the
king of Edom would not listen. They
sent also to the king of Moab,[w] and
he refused.[x] So Israel stayed at Kadesh.

18"Next they traveled through the
desert, skirted the lands of Edom[y]
and Moab, passed along the eastern
side[z] of the country of Moab, and
camped on the other side of the Arnon.[a] They did not enter the territory of Moab, for the Arnon was its border.

19"Then Israel sent messengers[b]
to Sihon king of the Amorites, who
ruled in Heshbon,[c] and said to him,
'Let us pass through your country to
our own place.'[d] 20Sihon, however,
did not trust Israel[r] to pass through
his territory. He mustered all his men
and encamped at Jahaz and fought
with Israel.[e]

21"Then the LORD, the God of Israel, gave Sihon and all his men into

[q] *16* Hebrew *Yam Suph*; that is, Sea of Reeds
[r] *20* Or *however, would not make an agreement for Israel*

10:17—11:32 CHRISTIAN ETHICS, War and Peace—War has certain conventions. Often war seeks to undo centuries of history and restore former conditions. Such is no reason for war. A generation of people who have tried to live peaceably and fairly with their neighbors should not face attack. God is the final Judge and in His own way settles international disputes. He does not honor land-hungry military machines. See note on 1:1–36.

11:1–7 HUMANITY, Human Nature—This Hebrew term for "hate" has a root meaning of rejection. Prejudice causes people to reject others for wrong reasons. Such rejection then deprives the community of the contributions and strength which come from the proper assimilation of each person's talents into the whole.

11:11 PRAYER, Corporate—God chose a social outcast to lead His people. His essential character is seen in his ensuing actions. God listened to Jephthah as he made a covenant of leadership with the people before God. Public ceremonies can be symbolic prayers of commitment.

Israel's hands, and they defeated
them. Israel took over all the land of
the Amorites who lived in that country, 22capturing all of it from the Arnon to the Jabbok and from the
desert to the Jordan.[f]
23"Now since the LORD, the God of
Israel, has driven the Amorites out
before his people Israel, what right
have you to take it over? 24Will you
not take what your god Chemosh[g]
gives you? Likewise, whatever the
LORD our God has given us,[h] we will
possess. 25Are you better than Balak
son of Zippor,[i] king of Moab? Did he
ever quarrel with Israel or fight with
them?[j] 26For three hundred years Israel occupied[k] Heshbon, Aroer,[l] the
surrounding settlements and all the
towns along the Arnon. Why didn't
you retake them during that time? 27I
have not wronged you, but you are
doing me wrong by waging war
against me. Let the LORD, the
Judge,[s][m] decide[n] the dispute this
day between the Israelites and the
Ammonites.[o]"

28The king of Ammon, however, paid no
attention to the message Jephthah sent
him.
29Then the Spirit[p] of the LORD came
upon Jephthah. He crossed Gilead and
Manasseh, passed through Mizpah[q] of
Gilead, and from there he advanced
against the Ammonites.[r] 30And Jephthah
made a vow[s] to the LORD: "If you give
the Ammonites into my hands, 31whatev-
er comes out of the door of my house to
meet me when I return in triumph[t] from
the Ammonites will be the LORD's, and I
will sacrifice it as a burnt offering.[u]"
32Then Jephthah went over to fight the
Ammonites, and the LORD gave them into
his hands. 33He devastated twenty towns
from Aroer to the vicinity of Minnith,[v] as
far as Abel Keramim. Thus Israel subdued
Ammon.

11:22 [f]Nu 21:21-26; S Dt 2:26
11:24 [g]S Nu 21:29; S Jos 3:10 [h]Dt 2:36
11:25 [i]Nu 22:2 [j]S Jos 24:9
11:26 [k]Nu 21:25 [l]S Nu 32:34; S Jos 13:9
11:27 [m]S Ge 18:25 [n]S Ge 16:5 [o]2Ch 20:12
11:29 [p]S Jdg 3:10 [q]S Ge 31:49 [r]S Jdg 10:17
11:30 [s]S Ge 28:20; Nu 30:10; 1Sa 1:11; Pr 31:2
11:31 [t]Ge 28:21 [u]S Ge 8:20; Lev 1:3; Jdg 13:16
11:33 [v]Eze 27:17
11:34 [w]S Ex 15:20 [x]S Ge 31:27; S Ex 15:20 [y]Zec 12:10
11:35 [z]S Nu 14:6 [a]Nu 30:2; S Dt 23:21; Ecc 5:2, 4,5
11:36 [b]Lk 1:38 [c]S Nu 31:3 [d]2Sa 18:19
12:1 [e]S Jos 13:27 [f]S Jdg 11:1 [g]Jdg 8:1
12:3 [h]S Jdg 9:17

34When Jephthah returned to his home
in Mizpah, who should come out to meet
him but his daughter, dancing[w] to the
sound of tambourines![x] She was an only
child.[y] Except for her he had neither son
nor daughter. 35When he saw her, he
tore his clothes[z] and cried, "Oh! My
daughter! You have made me miserable
and wretched, because I have made a
vow to the LORD that I cannot break.[a]"
36"My father," she replied, "you have
given your word to the LORD. Do to me
just as you promised,[b] now that the LORD
has avenged you[c] of your enemies,[d] the
Ammonites. 37But grant me this one request," she said. "Give me two months
to roam the hills and weep with my
friends, because I will never marry."
38"You may go," he said. And he let
her go for two months. She and the girls
went into the hills and wept because she
would never marry. 39After the two
months, she returned to her father and
he did to her as he had vowed. And she
was a virgin.
From this comes the Israelite custom
40that each year the young women of Israel go out for four days to commemorate
the daughter of Jephthah the Gileadite.

Chapter 12

Jephthah and Ephraim

THE men of Ephraim called out their
forces, crossed over to Zaphon[e] and
said to Jephthah,[f] "Why did you go to
fight the Ammonites without calling us to
go with you?[g] We're going to burn down
your house over your head."
2Jephthah answered, "I and my people
were engaged in a great struggle with the
Ammonites, and although I called, you
didn't save me out of their hands. 3When
I saw that you wouldn't help, I took my
life in my hands[h] and crossed over to
fight the Ammonites, and the LORD gave

[s]27 Or *Ruler*

11:27 PRAYER, Faith—Jephthah included a prayer in a political message. Jephthah gave God a name; God vindicated that name (v 32).

11:29 HOLY SPIRIT, Leaders—God's Spirit does not prevent a person from acting rashly and wrongly. God gave His Spirit to Jephthah, providing needed military skills. See notes on 3:9–10; 6:34–35. This gift may have included courage, military knowledge and cunning, the ability to inspire Israel's soldiers, and even extraordinary knowledge about when to fight or how to win a particular battle. The gift did not prevent Jephthah from making a foolhardy vow (vv 30–39).

11:30 PRAYER, Vow—See notes on Ge 28:20–21; 1 Sa 14:41–45. A vow commits a person to action before God. Jephthah made a foolish vow. He should have sought God's forgiveness for the foolish vow rather than compounding the sin by sacrificing his daughter.

11:30–40 FAMILY, Role Relationships—Two factors underlie this tragic story of Jepthah and his daughter: the absolute authority of father over daughter and the sanctity of vows. See note on Nu 30:1–15. Even though the vow was rashly made, it had invoked God's name. Jepthah's daughter knowingly agreed to her own death. Part of the tragedy of this situation is the essential nobility of the persons involved. Jepthah was committed to the Lord, and his daughter was committed to her father and her God. Sadly their commitment was not joined with moral judgment. The experience of Saul and his son Jonathan turned out differently (1 Sa 14:24–45). Saul committed his army to a vow that they would not eat until victory over the Philistines was accomplished. Unaware of the vow, Jonathan did eat some honey, and Saul was determined to put him to death. However, the army refused to permit this to happen and rescued Jonathan from his father's intention. Saul expressed no remorse for his intended action. In this way the circumstances are very different from that of Jepthah and his daughter. The Bible consistently values human life over legalistic obedience to rules.

me the victory[i] over them. Now why
have you come up today to fight me?"
4Jephthah then called together the men
of Gilead[j] and fought against Ephraim.
The Gileadites struck them down because
the Ephraimites had said, "You Gileadites
are renegades from Ephraim and Manasseh.[k]" 5The Gileadites captured the fords
of the Jordan[l] leading to Ephraim, and
whenever a survivor of Ephraim said,
"Let me cross over," the men of Gilead
asked him, "Are you an Ephraimite?" If
he replied, "No," 6they said, "All right,
say 'Shibboleth.'" If he said, "Sibbo-
leth," because he could not pronounce
the word correctly, they seized him and
killed him at the fords of the Jordan. Forty-two thousand Ephraimites were killed
at that time.
7Jephthah led[t] Israel six years. Then
Jephthah the Gileadite died, and was buried in a town in Gilead.

Ibzan, Elon and Abdon

8After him, Ibzan of Bethlehem[m] led
Israel. 9He had thirty sons and thirty
daughters. He gave his daughters away in
marriage to those outside his clan, and for
his sons he brought in thirty young wom-
en as wives from outside his clan. Ibzan
led Israel seven years. 10Then Ibzan died,
and was buried in Bethlehem.
11After him, Elon the Zebulunite led Israel ten years. 12Then Elon died, and was
buried in Aijalon[n] in the land of Zebulun.
13After him, Abdon son of Hillel, from
Pirathon,[o] led Israel. 14He had forty sons
and thirty grandsons,[p] who rode on seventy donkeys.[q] He led Israel eight years.
15Then Abdon son of Hillel died, and was
buried at Pirathon in Ephraim, in the hill
country of the Amalekites.[r]

12:3 [i]S Dt 20:4
12:4 [j]1Ki 17:1 [k]S Ge 46:20; Isa 9:21; 19:2
12:5 [l]S Jos 2:7
12:8 [m]S Ge 35:19
12:12 [n]S Jos 10:12
12:13 [o]ver 15; 2Sa 23:30; 1Ch 11:31; 27:14
12:14 [p]S Jdg 8:30 [q]S Jdg 5:10
12:15 [r]Jdg 5:14
13:1 [s]S Jdg 3:31 [t]Jdg 14:4
13:2 [u]S Jos 15:33 [v]ver 8; Jdg 16:31 [w]S Ge 30:6 [x]S Ge 11:30
13:3 [y]S Ge 16:7 [z]ver 10 [a]Isa 7:14; Lk 1:13
13:4 [b]S Lev 10:9 [c]ver 14; Nu 6:2-4; S Lk 1:15
13:5 [d]S Ge 3:15 [e]1Sa 1:11 [f]S Nu 6:2,13; Am 2:11,12 [g]1Sa 7:13
13:6 [h]ver 8; 1Sa 2:27; 9:6; 1Ki 13:1; 17:18 [i]S Nu 22:22 [j]Ps 66:5
13:7 [k]Jer 35:6 [l]Lev 10:9 [m]1Sa 1:11,28
13:8 [n]S ver 2 [o]S ver 6

Chapter 13

The Birth of Samson

AGAIN the Israelites did evil in the eyes
of the LORD, so the LORD delivered
them into the hands of the Philistines[s]
for forty years.[t]
2A certain man of Zorah,[u] named Manoah,[v] from the clan of the Danites,[w]
had a wife who was sterile and remained
childless.[x] 3The angel of the LORD[y] appeared to her[z] and said, "You are sterile
and childless, but you are going to conceive and have a son.[a] 4Now see to it
that you drink no wine or other fermented drink[b] and that you do not eat anything unclean,[c] 5because you will conceive and give birth to a son.[d] No razor[e]
may be used on his head, because the boy
is to be a Nazirite,[f] set apart to God from
birth, and he will begin[g] the deliverance
of Israel from the hands of the Philistines."
6Then the woman went to her husband
and told him, "A man of God[h] came to
me. He looked like an angel of God,[i]
very awesome.[j] I didn't ask him where
he came from, and he didn't tell me his
name. 7But he said to me, 'You will conceive and give birth to a son. Now then,
drink no wine[k] or other fermented
drink[l] and do not eat anything unclean,
because the boy will be a Nazirite of God
from birth until the day of his death.[m]'"
8Then Manoah[n] prayed to the LORD:
"O Lord, I beg you, let the man of God[o]
you sent to us come again to teach us
how to bring up the boy who is to be
born."
9God heard Manoah, and the angel of
God came again to the woman while she
was out in the field; but her husband

[t]7 Traditionally *judged*; also in verses 8-14

13:1 SIN, Covenant Breach—See note on 3:7.

13:1–7 EVANGELISM, Holy Life—The power of evangelism, and all Christian service, rests in a holy life. Manoah and his wife were to see that the son who would be miraculously born to them should be holy and separated to the Lord. He was to be given the Nazirite vow from his birth (Nu 6:1–21). That ancient Hebrew vow required one to drink no wine, never cut the hair, and abstain from any contact with the dead. It speaks of holiness of life and consecration to God. It tended to be a limited time vow (as illustrated in Ac 21:20–26), but for Samson it was a life commitment. For God to use us powerfully, we too must make a lifelong vow to holy, consecrated living. There is great power in witnessing when it comes out of our holy lives.

13:3–23 REVELATION, Angels—A simple man experienced the revelation of God through a messenger from God, who explained to Manoah and his wife that God planned to redeem Israel with the son to be born to them. The angel's appearance confused the woman. Was he man of God, that is a prophet, or angel of God? Manoah asked the nature of the angel, who kept the mystery of God's identity by refusing to reveal more than can be grasped. As with Moses (Ex 33:18–23), human beings seek to see and know as much as we can of God. Fire (Ex 3:2; 13:21; 19:18; 24:17; Nu 9:15; Dt 4:15,24; 5:23–24; 9:3) symbolized God's revelation and presence. The messenger left no doubt he was an angel by ascending in the flame. The proper response to such a messenger is falling to the ground in reverent fear (Jos 5:13–15). See note on Jdg 2:1–3.

13:4 CHRISTIAN ETHICS, Alcohol—See note on Nu 6:3–4,20.

13:6–14 HUMANITY, Parenthood—Both the physical and spiritual actions of parents before and after the birth of their children have ultimate consequences for those children. Dedicated parents lead to dedicated children.

13:8–25 PRAYER, Personal—Personal concerns such as how to parent can be shared with God in prayer. God gives leadership to people who ask Him for it. An offering to God is an appropriate response when He answers our personal concerns.

13:8 FAMILY, Education—The prayer of Manoah models for all Christian parents the need for God's guidance in the nurture and education of children. Even though Samson did not fulfill in his personal life the desires of his parents, the commitment of Manoah and his wife to the Lord is exemplary.

Manoah was not with her. 10The woman
hurried to tell her husband, "He's here!
The man who appeared to me[p] the other
day!"
11Manoah got up and followed his wife.
When he came to the man, he said, "Are
you the one who talked to my wife?"

"I am," he said.

12So Manoah asked him, "When your
words are fulfilled, what is to be the rule
for the boy's life and work?"
13The angel of the LORD answered,
"Your wife must do all that I have told
her. 14She must not eat anything that
comes from the grapevine, nor drink any
wine or other fermented drink[q] nor eat
anything unclean.[r] She must do everything I have commanded her."
15Manoah said to the angel of the
LORD, "We would like you to stay until
we prepare a young goat[s] for you."
16The angel of the LORD replied, "Even
though you detain me, I will not eat any
of your food. But if you prepare a burnt
offering,[t] offer it to the LORD." (Manoah
did not realize[u] that it was the angel of
the LORD.)
17Then Manoah inquired of the angel
of the LORD, "What is your name,[v] so
that we may honor you when your word
comes true?"
18He replied, "Why do you ask my
name?[w] It is beyond understanding.[u]"
19Then Manoah took a young goat, together with the grain offering, and sacrificed it on a rock[x] to the LORD. And the
LORD did an amazing thing while Manoah
and his wife watched: 20As the flame[y]
blazed up from the altar toward heaven,
the angel of the LORD ascended in the
flame. Seeing this, Manoah and his wife
fell with their faces to the ground.[z]
21When the angel of the LORD did not
show himself again to Manoah and his
wife, Manoah realized[a] that it was the
angel of the LORD.
22"We are doomed[b] to die!" he said to
his wife. "We have seen[c] God!"
23But his wife answered, "If the LORD
had meant to kill us, he would not have
accepted a burnt offering and grain offering from our hands, nor shown us all
these things or now told us this."[d]
24The woman gave birth to a boy and
named him Samson.[e] He grew[f] and the
LORD blessed him,[g] 25and the Spirit of
the LORD began to stir[h] him while he was
in Mahaneh Dan,[i] between Zorah and
Eshtaol.

Chapter 14

Samson's Marriage

SAMSON[j] went down to Timnah[k] and
saw there a young Philistine woman.
2When he returned, he said to his father
and mother, "I have seen a Philistine
woman in Timnah; now get her for me as
my wife."[l]
3His father and mother replied, "Isn't
there an acceptable woman among your
relatives or among all our people?[m] Must
you go to the uncircumcised[n] Philistines
to get a wife?[o]"
But Samson said to his father, "Get her
for me. She's the right one for me." 4(His
parents did not know that this was from
the LORD,[p] who was seeking an occasion
to confront the Philistines;[q] for at that
time they were ruling over Israel.)[r]
5Samson went down to Timnah together
with his father and mother. As they approached the vineyards of Timnah, suddenly a young lion came roaring toward
him. 6The Spirit of the LORD came upon
him in power[s] so that he tore the lion
apart[t] with his bare hands as he might
have torn a young goat. But he told nei-

[u] 18 Or *is wonderful*

13:10 [p]ver 3
13:14 [q]Lev 10:9 [r]S ver 4
13:15 [s]Jdg 6:19
13:16 [t]S Jdg 11:31 [u]S Jdg 6:22
13:17 [v]S Ge 32:29
13:18 [w]S Ge 32:29
13:19 [x]Jdg 6:20
13:20 [y]S Lev 9:24 [z]S Ge 17:3
13:21 [a]S Jdg 6:22
13:22 [b]S Nu 17:12; S Dt 5:26 [c]S Ge 16:13; S Ex 3:6; S 24:10; S Jdg 6:22
13:23 [d]Ps 25:14
13:24 [e]Jdg 14:1; 15:1; 16:1; Heb 11:32 [f]1Sa 2:21,26; 3:19 [g]Lk 1:80
13:25 [h]S Jdg 3:10 [i]Jdg 18:12
14:1 [j]S Jdg 13:24 [k]S Ge 38:12
14:2 [l]S Ge 21:21
14:3 [m]S Ge 24:4 [n]S Ge 34:14; S 1Sa 14:6 [o]S Ex 34:16
14:4 [p]S Dt 2:30 [q]S Jos 11:20 [r]Jdg 13:1; 15:11
14:6 [s]S Jdg 3:10 [t]1Sa 17:35

13:19–23 WORSHIP, Reverence—This worshiping couple responded to the Lord's presence with reverence and awe. See note on Lev 9:23–24.

13:22 GOD, Holy—Manoah recognized the holiness of God as an absolute boundary between humans and God. We are finite and sinful; God is infinite, pure, righteous, transcendent—He is holy, and stands above all else. The holiness of God is that constant reminder to humans that God is the Almighty. Sinners cannot look on God and live.

13:24–25 HOLY SPIRIT, Leaders—Youth does not limit the Spirit. Apparently Samson was still a young man when the Spirit began to stir him. God often works with young people to prepare them for tasks He has for their adult years. The expression here may mean the Spirit gave Samson a sense of God's mission.

14:6,19 HOLY SPIRIT, Leaders—The Spirit gave Samson supernatural physical strength. This gift helped confirm God's call for young Samson. Since Samson used his physical strength for purposes such as killing a lion, it is sometimes suggested that this gift was not used for a great moral purpose. Certainly Samson does not provide a prime moral example for us. In ways he wasted his gift. However, Samson's general purposes were to defeat the Philistines and to protect the people of Israel. Samson used his physical strength to help his nation survive, certainly a high moral purpose. The gifts the Spirit brings are always for the benefit of God's people. That fact was just as true of Samson's physical strength as it was of Bezalel's craftsmanship (Ex 35:30–31), Balaam's prophecy (see note on Nu 24:2), or Joshua's leadership (see note on Dt 34:9).

14:6 MIRACLE, Nature—God's miracle-workers may not be our best examples in other areas of life. From conception (13:3) onward, Samson's story is marked by miracle. His superhuman strength might be explained as the result of proper diet (13:5–7; Nu 6:1–4), but the inspired writer knew strength came through the power of the Lord's Spirit. Young, foolish, easily-allured, easily-deceived Samson did not set a moral standard for us to follow. God still used him to deliver His people from their enemies. Despite disobedience and failure (Jos 16:19), he was allowed one final mighty deed to defeat the enemy (16:30). God chooses who does miracles and when. We cannot limit Him as He carries out His purpose.

ther his father nor his mother what he
had done. 7Then he went down and
talked with the woman, and he liked her.
8Some time later, when he went back
to marry her, he turned aside to look at
the lion's carcass. In it was a swarm of
bees and some honey, 9which he scooped
out with his hands and ate as he went
along. When he rejoined his parents, he
gave them some, and they too ate it. But
he did not tell them that he had taken the
honey from the lion's carcass.
10Now his father went down to see the
woman. And Samson made a feast[u]
there, as was customary for bridegrooms.
11When he appeared, he was given thirty
companions.
12"Let me tell you a riddle,[v]" Samson
said to them. "If you can give me the
answer within the seven days of the
feast,[w] I will give you thirty linen garments and thirty sets of clothes.[x] 13If you
can't tell me the answer, you must give
me thirty linen garments and thirty sets
of clothes."
"Tell us your riddle," they said. "Let's
hear it."
14He replied,

"Out of the eater, something to eat;
out of the strong, something
sweet."[y]

For three days they could not give the
answer.
15On the fourth[v] day, they said to Samson's wife, "Coax[z] your husband into explaining the riddle for us, or we will burn
you and your father's household to
death.[a] Did you invite us here to rob
us?"
16Then Samson's wife threw herself on
him, sobbing, "You hate me! You don't
really love me.[b] You've given my people
a riddle, but you haven't told me the answer."
"I haven't even explained it to my father or mother," he replied, "so why
should I explain it to you?" 17She cried
the whole seven days[c] of the feast. So on
the seventh day he finally told her, because she continued to press him. She in
turn explained the riddle to her people.
18Before sunset on the seventh day the
men of the town said to him,

"What is sweeter than honey?
What is stronger than a lion?"[d]

Samson said to them,

"If you had not plowed with my heifer,
you would not have solved my
riddle."

19Then the Spirit of the LORD came
upon him in power.[e] He went down to
Ashkelon,[f] struck down thirty of their
men, stripped them of their belongings
and gave their clothes to those who had
explained the riddle. Burning with anger,[g] he went up to his father's house.
20And Samson's wife was given to the
friend[h] who had attended him at his
wedding.

Chapter 15

Samson's Vengeance on the Philistines

LATER on, at the time of wheat harvest,[i] Samson[j] took a young goat[k]
and went to visit his wife. He said, "I'm
going to my wife's room."[l] But her father would not let him go in.
2"I was so sure you thoroughly hated
her," he said, "that I gave her to your
friend.[m] Isn't her younger sister more attractive? Take her instead."
3Samson said to them, "This time I
have a right to get even with the Philistines; I will really harm them." 4So he
went out and caught three hundred foxes[n] and tied them tail to tail in pairs. He
then fastened a torch[o] to every pair of
tails, 5lit the torches[p] and let the foxes
loose in the standing grain of the Philistines. He burned up the shocks[q] and
standing grain, together with the vineyards and olive groves.
6When the Philistines asked, "Who did
this?" they were told, "Samson, the Tim-
nite's son-in-law, because his wife was
given to his friend.[r]"
So the Philistines went up and burned
her[s] and her father to death.[t] 7Samson
said to them, "Since you've acted like
this, I won't stop until I get my revenge
on you." 8He attacked them viciously and
slaughtered many of them. Then he went
down and stayed in a cave in the rock[u] of
Etam.[v]
9The Philistines went up and camped
in Judah, spreading out near Lehi.[w] 10The
men of Judah asked, "Why have you
come to fight us?"
"We have come to take Samson prisoner," they answered, "to do to him as he
did to us."
11Then three thousand men from Judah
went down to the cave in the rock of
Etam and said to Samson, "Don't you realize that the Philistines are rulers over
us?[x] What have you done to us?"
He answered, "I merely did to them
what they did to me."
12They said to him, "We've come to tie
you up and hand you over to the Philistines."

14:10 [u]S Ge 29:22
14:12 [v]S Nu 12:8; Eze 17:2; 20:49; 24:3; Hos 12:10 [w]Ge 29:27 [x]S Ge 45:22; S 2Ki 5:5
14:14 [y]ver 18
14:15 [z]Jdg 16:5; Ecc 7:26 [a]S Lev 20:14; Jdg 15:6
14:16 [b]Jdg 16:15
14:17 [c]Est 1:5
14:18 [d]ver 14
14:19 [e]S Jdg 3:10 [f]S Jos 13:3 [g]1Sa 11:6
14:20 [h]Jdg 15:2,6; Jn 3:29
15:1 [i]S Ge 30:14 [j]S Jdg 13:24 [k]S Ge 38:17 [l]Ge 29:21
15:2 [m]S Jdg 14:20
15:4 [n]SS 2:15 [o]S Ge 15:17
15:5 [p]S Ge 15:17 [q]Ex 22:6; 2Sa 14:30-31
15:6 [r]S Jdg 14:20 [s]S Ge 38:24 [t]S Jdg 14:15
15:8 [u]Isa 2:21 [v]ver 11
15:9 [w]ver 14,17,19
15:11 [x]S Jdg 14:4; Ps 106:40-42

[v]15 Some Septuagint manuscripts and Syriac; Hebrew *seventh*

Samson said, "Swear to me[y] that you
won't kill me yourselves."
13"Agreed," they answered. "We will
only tie you up and hand you over to
them. We will not kill you." So they
bound him with two new ropes[z] and led
him up from the rock. 14As he approached Lehi,[a] the Philistines came toward him shouting. The Spirit of the
LORD came upon him in power.[b] The
ropes on his arms became like charred
flax,[c] and the bindings dropped from his
hands. 15Finding a fresh jawbone of a
donkey, he grabbed it and struck down a
thousand men.[d]
16Then Samson said,

"With a donkey's jawbone
I have made donkeys of them.[w] [e]
With a donkey's jawbone
I have killed a thousand men."

17When he finished speaking, he threw
away the jawbone; and the place was
called Ramath Lehi.[x] [f]
18Because he was very thirsty, he cried
out to the LORD,[g] "You have given your
servant this great victory.[h] Must I now
die of thirst and fall into the hands of the
uncircumcised?" 19Then God opened up
the hollow place in Lehi, and water came
out of it. When Samson drank, his
strength returned and he revived.[i] So
the spring[j] was called En Hakkore,[y] and
it is still there in Lehi.
20Samson led[z] Israel for twenty years[k]
in the days of the Philistines.

Chapter 16

Samson and Delilah

ONE day Samson[l] went to Gaza,[m]
where he saw a prostitute.[n] He
went in to spend the night with her. 2The
people of Gaza were told, "Samson is
here!" So they surrounded the place and
lay in wait for him all night at the city
gate.[o] They made no move during the
night, saying, "At dawn[p] we'll kill him."
3But Samson lay there only until the
middle of the night. Then he got up and
took hold of the doors of the city gate,
together with the two posts, and tore
them loose, bar and all. He lifted them to
his shoulders and carried them to the top
of the hill that faces Hebron.[q]
4Some time later, he fell in love[r] with
a woman in the Valley of Sorek whose
name was Delilah.[s] 5The rulers of the
Philistines[t] went to her and said, "See if
you can lure[u] him into showing you the
secret of his great strength[v] and how we
can overpower him so we may tie him up
and subdue him. Each one of us will give
you eleven hundred shekels[a] of silver."[w]
6So Delilah[x] said to Samson, "Tell me
the secret of your great strength and how
you can be tied up and subdued."
7Samson answered her, "If anyone ties
me with seven fresh thongs[b] that have
not been dried, I'll become as weak as
any other man."
8Then the rulers of the Philistines
brought her seven fresh thongs that had
not been dried, and she tied him with
them. 9With men hidden in the room,[y]
she called to him, "Samson, the Philistines are upon you!"[z] But he snapped
the thongs as easily as a piece of string
snaps when it comes close to a flame. So
the secret of his strength was not discovered.
10Then Delilah said to Samson, "You
have made a fool of me;[a] you lied to me.
Come now, tell me how you can be tied."
11He said, "If anyone ties me securely
with new ropes[b] that have never been
used, I'll become as weak as any other
man."
12So Delilah took new ropes and tied
him with them. Then, with men hidden
in the room, she called to him, "Samson,
the Philistines are upon you!"[c] But he
snapped the ropes off his arms as if they
were threads.
13Delilah then said to Samson, "Until
now, you have been making a fool of me
and lying to me. Tell me how you can be
tied."
He replied, "If you weave the seven
braids of my head into the fabric ⌊on the

15:12 [y]S Ge 47:31
15:13 [z]Jdg 16:11, 12
15:14 [a]S ver 9 [b]S Jdg 3:10 [c]S Jos 2:6
15:15 [d]S Lev 26:8
15:16 [e]Jer 22:19
15:17 [f]S ver 9
15:18 [g]Jdg 16:28 [h]S Dt 20:4
15:19 [i]Ge 45:27; 1Sa 30:12; Isa 40:29 [j]S Ex 17:6
15:20 [k]Jdg 16:31
16:1 [l]S Jdg 13:24 [m]S Ge 10:19 [n]S Ge 38:15
16:2 [o]S Jos 2:5 [p]1Sa 19:11
16:3 [q]S Jos 10:36
16:4 [r]S Ge 24:67; S 34:3 [s]ver 6
16:5 [t]S Jos 13:3 [u]S Ex 10:7; S Jdg 14:15 [v]ver 6, 15 [w]ver 18
16:6 [x]ver 4
16:9 [y]ver 12 [z]ver 14
16:10 [a]ver 13
16:11 [b]S Jdg 15:13
16:12 [c]ver 14

[w]16 Or *made a heap or two*; the Hebrew for *donkey* sounds like the Hebrew for *heap*. [x]17 *Ramath Lehi* means *jawbone hill.* [y]19 *En Hakkore* means *caller's spring.* [z]20 Traditionally *judged* [a]5 That is, about 28 pounds (about 13 kilograms) [b]7 Or *bowstrings*; also in verses 8 and 9

15:14 HOLY SPIRIT, Leaders—Natural attributes alone do not explain the Spirit's gifts. The Spirit gave Samson physical strength. He needed more. The Spirit came to Samson with special strength in crisis situations, as in this battle with a group of Philistines. The gift was a supernatural one. Samson did not become strong through natural means such as proper diet and exercise but through an extraordinary gift from God. He used this gift to defend his people and to help them in their struggle to survive in the land which God had promised them. See note on 14:6,19.

15:18 PRAYER, Petition—In spite of his spiritual and moral weaknesses, Samson was dependent on the Lord. God listened to his prayers just as He will to ours even in our imperfection. A person does not have to be perfect to pray.

16:4–22 FAMILY, Conflict—The destructive effects of deceit and quarreling on personal relationships is exemplified tragically in the story of Delilah and Samson. It also demonstrates graphically how the word "love" can be used in a relationship which reveals no indication that love exists at all. Samson was apparently drawn primarily by sexual attraction, and Delilah showed no concern for his welfare when offered money to betray him. Relationships based on feelings such as these have little chance for survival. Only faithful commitment can overcome conflicts and competing loyalties.

loom, and tighten it with the pin, I'll become as weak as any other man." So
while he was sleeping, Delilah took the
seven braids of his head, wove them into
the fabric 14and[c] tightened it with the
pin.

Again she called to him, "Samson, the
Philistines are upon you!"[d] He awoke
from his sleep and pulled up the pin and
the loom, with the fabric.

15Then she said to him, "How can you
say, 'I love you,'[e] when you won't confide in me? This is the third time[f] you
have made a fool of me and haven't told
me the secret of your great strength.[g]"
16With such nagging she prodded him day
after day until he was tired to death.

17So he told her everything.[h] "No razor has ever been used on my head," he
said, "because I have been a Nazirite[i]
set apart to God since birth. If my head
were shaved, my strength would leave
me, and I would become as weak as any
other man."

18When Delilah saw that he had told
her everything, she sent word to the rulers of the Philistines[j], "Come back once
more; he has told me everything." So the
rulers of the Philistines returned with the
silver in their hands.[k] 19Having put him
to sleep on her lap, she called a man to
shave off the seven braids of his hair, and
so began to subdue him.[d] And his
strength left him.[l]

20Then she called, "Samson, the Philistines are upon you!"[m]

He awoke from his sleep and thought,
"I'll go out as before and shake myself
free." But he did not know that the LORD
had left him.[n]

21Then the Philistines[o] seized him,
gouged out his eyes[p] and took him down
to Gaza.[q] Binding him with bronze
shackles, they set him to grinding[r] in the
prison. 22But the hair on his head began
to grow again after it had been shaved.

The Death of Samson

23Now the rulers of the Philistines assembled to offer a great sacrifice to Dagon[s] their god and to celebrate, saying,
"Our god has delivered Samson, our enemy, into our hands."

24When the people saw him, they
praised their god,[t] saying,

"Our god has delivered our enemy
into our hands,[u]
the one who laid waste our land
and multiplied our slain."

25While they were in high spirits,[v]
they shouted, "Bring out Samson to entertain us." So they called Samson out of
the prison, and he performed for them.

When they stood him among the pillars, 26Samson said to the servant who
held his hand, "Put me where I can feel
the pillars that support the temple, so
that I may lean against them." 27Now the
temple was crowded with men and wom-
en; all the rulers of the Philistines were
there, and on the roof[w] were about three
thousand men and women watching Samson perform. 28Then Samson prayed to
the LORD,[x] "O Sovereign LORD, remember me. O God, please strengthen me just
once more, and let me with one blow get
revenge[y] on the Philistines for my two
eyes." 29Then Samson reached toward
the two central pillars on which the temple stood. Bracing himself against them,
his right hand on the one and his left
hand on the other, 30Samson said, "Let
me die with the Philistines!" Then he
pushed with all his might, and down
came the temple on the rulers and all the
people in it. Thus he killed many more
when he died than while he lived.

31Then his brothers and his father's
whole family went down to get him. They
brought him back and buried him between Zorah and Eshtaol in the tomb of
Manoah[z] his father. He had led[e][a] Israel
twenty years.[b]

Chapter 17

Micah's Idols

NOW a man named Micah[c] from the
hill country of Ephraim 2said to his
mother, "The eleven hundred shekels[f]
of silver that were taken from you and
about which I heard you utter a curse—I
have that silver with me; I took it."

Then his mother said, "The LORD bless
you,[d] my son!"

3When he returned the eleven hun-

16:14 [d]ver 9,20
16:15 [e]Jdg 14:16 [f]Nu 24:10 [g]S ver 5
16:17 [h]ver 18; Mic 7:5 [i]S Nu 6:2
16:18 [j]S Jos 13:3; 1Sa 5:8 [k]ver 5
16:19 [l]Pr 7:26-27
16:20 [m]S ver 14 [n]Nu 14:42; Jos 7:12; 1Sa 16:14; 18:12; 28:15
16:21 [o]Jer 47:1 [p]S Nu 16:14 [q]S Ge 10:19 [r]Job 31:10; Isa 47:2
16:23 [s]1Sa 5:2; 1Ch 10:10
16:24 [t]Da 5:4 [u]1Sa 31:9; 1Ch 10:9
16:25 [v]Jdg 9:27; 19:6,9,22; Ru 3:7; Est 1:10
16:27 [w]S Jos 2:8
16:28 [x]Jdg 15:18 [y]Jer 15:15
16:31 [z]S Jdg 13:2 [a]Ru 1:1; 1Sa 4:18; 7:6 [b]Jdg 15:20
17:1 [c]Jdg 18:2,13
17:2 [d]Ru 2:20; 3:10; 1Sa 15:13; 23:21; 2Sa 2:5

[c]*13,14* Some Septuagint manuscripts; Hebrew *"I can, if you weave the seven braids of my head into the fabric on the loom." 14So she* [d]*19* Hebrew; some Septuagint manuscripts *and he began to weaken* [e]*31* Traditionally *judged* [f]*2* That is, about 28 pounds (about 13 kilograms)

16:23–24 HISTORY, God—God's actions in history may not be evident. Other people may claim control of history for their god(s). The long run of history shows that only the one true God controls history.

16:28 PRAYER, Petition—Samson returned to the Lord after breaking his vows and losing his strength. God heard his self-sacrificing prayer and restored his strength. See note on 15:18. God listens to the prayers of repentant people.

17:1—21:25 SIN, Blindness—Repeated breach of God's covenant led Israel to forsake all moral and spiritual values to become completely self-centered. "In those days Israel had no king; everyone did as he saw fit" (17:6; 18:1; 19:1; 21:25). Self blinds us to spiritual reality. We need strong leadership to show us the way back to God. Israel soon learned, though, that strong leaders can become self-centered false leaders.

dred shekels of silver to his mother, she
said, "I solemnly consecrate my silver to
the LORD for my son to make a carved
image and a cast idol.[e] I will give it back
to you."
4So he returned the silver to his mother, and she took two hundred shekels[g] of
silver and gave them to a silversmith,
who made them into the image and the
idol.[f] And they were put in Micah's
house.
5Now this man Micah had a shrine,[g]
and he made an ephod[h] and some idols[i]
and installed[j] one of his sons as his
priest.[k] 6In those days Israel had no
king;[l] everyone did as he saw fit.[m]
7A young Levite[n] from Bethlehem in
Judah,[o] who had been living within the
clan of Judah, 8left that town in search of
some other place to stay. On his way[h] he
came to Micah's house in the hill country
of Ephraim.
9Micah asked him, "Where are you
from?"
"I'm a Levite from Bethlehem in Judah,[p]" he said, "and I'm looking for a
place to stay."
10Then Micah said to him, "Live with
me and be my father[q] and priest,[r] and
I'll give you ten shekels[i] of silver a year,
your clothes and your food." 11So the Levite agreed to live with him, and the
young man was to him like one of his
sons. 12Then Micah installed[s] the Levite,
and the young man became his priest[t]
and lived in his house. 13And Micah said,
"Now I know that the LORD will be good
to me, since this Levite has become my
priest."[u]

Chapter 18

Danites Settle in Laish

IN those days Israel had no king.[v]
1And in those days the tribe of the Danites was seeking a place of their own
where they might settle, because they
had not yet come into an inheritance
among the tribes of Israel.[w] 2So the Danites[x] sent five warriors[y] from Zorah and
Eshtaol to spy out[z] the land and explore
it. These men represented all their clans.
They told them, "Go, explore the
land."[a]
The men entered the hill country of
Ephraim and came to the house of Micah,[b] where they spent the night. 3When
they were near Micah's house, they recognized the voice of the young Levite;[c]
so they turned in there and asked him,
"Who brought you here? What are you
doing in this place? Why are you here?"
4He told them what Micah had done
for him, and said, "He has hired me and I
am his priest.[d]"
5Then they said to him, "Please inquire
of God[e] to learn whether our journey
will be successful."
6The priest answered them, "Go in
peace[f]. Your journey has the LORD's approval."
7So the five men[g] left and came to Laish,[h] where they saw that the people
were living in safety, like the Sidonians,
unsuspecting and secure.[i] And since
their land lacked nothing, they were prosperous.[j] Also, they lived a long way from
the Sidonians[j] and had no relationship
with anyone else.[k]
8When they returned to Zorah and Eshtaol, their brothers asked them, "How
did you find things?"
9They answered, "Come on, let's attack them! We have seen that the land is
very good. Aren't you going to do something? Don't hesitate to go there and take
it over.[k] 10When you get there, you will
find an unsuspecting people and a spacious land that God has put into your
hands, a land that lacks nothing[l] whatever.[m]"
11Then six hundred men[n] from the
clan of the Danites,[o] armed for battle, set
out from Zorah and Eshtaol. 12On their
way they set up camp near Kiriath Jearim[p] in Judah. This is why the place west
of Kiriath Jearim is called Mahaneh
Dan[l][q] to this day. 13From there they
went on to the hill country of Ephraim
and came to Micah's house.[r]
14Then the five men who had spied out
the land of Laish[s] said to their brothers,
"Do you know that one of these houses
has an ephod,[t] other household gods, a
carved image and a cast idol?[u] Now you
know what to do." 15So they turned in
there and went to the house of the young
Levite at Micah's place and greeted him.
16The six hundred Danites,[v] armed for
battle, stood at the entrance to the gate.

17:3 [e]S Ex 20:4
17:4 [f]S Ex 32:4; S Isa 17:8
17:5 [g]Isa 44:13; Eze 8:10 [h]S Jdg 8:27 [i]S Ge 31:19 [j]S Nu 16:10 [k]S Ex 29:9
17:6 [l]Jdg 18:1; 19:1; 21:25 [m]S Dt 12:8
17:7 [n]Jdg 18:3 [o]S Ge 35:19; Mt 2:1
17:9 [p]Ru 1:1
17:10 [q]S Ge 45:8 [r]Jdg 18:19
17:12 [s]S Nu 16:10 [t]Jdg 18:4
17:13 [u]Nu 18:7
18:1 [v]S Jdg 17:6 [w]Jos 19:47; Jdg 1:34
18:2 [x]S Ge 30:6 [y]ver 17 [z]S Nu 21:32 [a]S Jos 2:1 [b]S Jdg 17:1
18:3 [c]Jdg 17:7
18:4 [d]Jdg 17:12
18:5 [e]S Ge 25:22; Jdg 20:18,23,27; 1Sa 14:18; 2Sa 5:19; 2Ki 1:2; 8:8
18:6 [f]1Ki 22:6
18:7 [g]ver 17 [h]S Jos 19:47 [i]S Ge 34:25 [j]ver 28; Jos 11:8
18:9 [k]Nu 13:30; 1Ki 22:3
18:10 [l]Dt 8:9 [m]1Ch 4:40
18:11 [n]ver 16,17 [o]Jdg 13:2
18:12 [p]S Jos 9:17 [q]Jdg 13:25
18:13 [r]S Jdg 17:1
18:14 [s]S Jos 19:47 [t]S Jdg 8:27 [u]S Ge 31:19
18:16 [v]S ver 11

[g]4 That is, about 5 pounds (about 2.3 kilograms)
[h]8 Or *To carry on his profession* [i]10 That is, about 4 ounces (about 110 grams) [j]7 The meaning of the Hebrew for this clause is uncertain. [k]7 Hebrew; some Septuagint manuscripts *with the Arameans*
[l]12 *Mahaneh Dan* means *Dan's camp.*

17:6 HISTORY, God's Leaders—God's people need role models and spiritual leaders. Without them the past history of God's acts and the future hope based on those acts can be easily forgotten. Lack of leadership and forgetting of history lead to self-centered life. Israel ignored God's moral and religious demands when no one led them to remember His historical deliverance. Compare 18:1; 19:1; 21:25.

18:1–31 HISTORY, Freedom—See note on Jos 19:47. Isolated geographically from the religious centers of Israel, the tribe of Dan finally established a geographical inheritance. They gave succeeding generations a false religious heritage, gods made with human hands.

17The five men who had spied out the
land went inside and took the carved image, the ephod, the other household
gods[w] and the cast idol while the priest
and the six hundred armed men[x] stood
at the entrance to the gate.
18When these men went into Micah's
house and took[y] the carved image, the
ephod, the other household gods[z] and
the cast idol, the priest said to them,
"What are you doing?"
19They answered him, "Be quiet![a]
Don't say a word. Come with us, and be
our father and priest.[b] Isn't it better that
you serve a tribe and clan[c] in Israel as
priest rather than just one man's household?" 20Then the priest was glad. He
took the ephod, the other household gods
and the carved image and went along
with the people. 21Putting their little children, their livestock and their possessions in front of them, they turned away
and left.
22When they had gone some distance
from Micah's house, the men who lived
near Micah were called together and
overtook the Danites. 23As they shouted
after them, the Danites turned and said to
Micah, "What's the matter with you that
you called out your men to fight?"
24He replied, "You took[d] the gods I
made, and my priest, and went away.
What else do I have? How can you ask,
'What's the matter with you?' "
25The Danites answered, "Don't argue
with us, or some hot-tempered men will
attack you, and you and your family will
lose your lives." 26So the Danites went
their way, and Micah, seeing that they
were too strong for him,[e] turned around
and went back home.
27Then they took what Micah had
made, and his priest, and went on to Laish, against a peaceful and unsuspecting
people.[f] They attacked them with the
sword and burned[g] down their city.[h]
28There was no one to rescue them because they lived a long way from Sidon[i]
and had no relationship with anyone else.
The city was in a valley near Beth Rehob.[j]
The Danites rebuilt the city and settled
there. 29They named it Dan[k] after their
forefather Dan, who was born to Israel—
though the city used to be called Laish.[l]
30There the Danites set up for themselves
the idols, and Jonathan son of Gershom,[m]
the son of Moses,[m] and his sons were
priests for the tribe of Dan until the time
of the captivity of the land. 31They continued to use the idols Micah had made,[n] all
the time the house of God[o] was in Shiloh.[p]

Chapter 19

A Levite and His Concubine

IN those days Israel had no king.
Now a Levite who lived in a remote
area in the hill country of Ephraim[q] took
a concubine from Bethlehem in Judah.[r]
2But she was unfaithful to him. She left
him and went back to her father's house
in Bethlehem, Judah. After she had been
there four months, 3her husband went to
her to persuade her to return. He had
with him his servant and two donkeys.
She took him into her father's house, and
when her father saw him, he gladly welcomed him. 4His father-in-law, the girl's
father, prevailed upon him to stay; so he
remained with him three days, eating and
drinking,[s] and sleeping there.
5On the fourth day they got up early
and he prepared to leave, but the girl's
father said to his son-in-law, "Refresh
yourself[t] with something to eat; then
you can go." 6So the two of them sat
down to eat and drink together. Afterward the girl's father said, "Please stay
tonight and enjoy yourself.[u]" 7And when
the man got up to go, his father-in-law
persuaded him, so he stayed there that
night. 8On the morning of the fifth day,
when he rose to go, the girl's father said,
"Refresh yourself. Wait till afternoon!"
So the two of them ate together.
9Then when the man, with his concubine and his servant, got up to leave, his
father-in-law, the girl's father, said, "Now
look, it's almost evening. Spend the night
here; the day is nearly over. Stay and enjoy yourself. Early tomorrow morning you
can get up and be on your way home."
10But, unwilling to stay another night, the
man left and went toward Jebus[v] (that is,
Jerusalem), with his two saddled donkeys
and his concubine.
11When they were near Jebus and the
day was almost gone, the servant said to
his master, "Come, let's stop at this city
of the Jebusites[w] and spend the night."
12His master replied, "No. We won't
go into an alien city, whose people are
not Israelites. We will go on to Gibeah."
13He added, "Come, let's try to reach
Gibeah or Ramah[x] and spend the night

18:17 [w]S Ge 31:19; Mic 5:13 [x]ver 11
18:18 [y]ver 24; Isa 46:2; Jer 43:11; 48:7; 49:3; Hos 10:5 [z]S Ge 31:19
18:19 [a]Job 13:5; 21:5; 29:9; 40:4; Isa 52:15; Mic 7:16 [b]Jdg 17:10 [c]Nu 26:42
18:24 [d]S ver 17-18
18:26 [e]2Sa 3:39; Ps 18:17; 35:10
18:27 [f]S Ge 34:25 [g]S Nu 31:10 [h]Ge 49:17; S Jos 19:47
18:28 [i]S ver 7; S Ge 10:19 [j]S Nu 13:21
18:29 [k]S Ge 14:14 [l]S Jos 19:47; 1Ki 15:20
18:30 [m]Ex 2:22
18:31 [n]ver 17 [o]Jdg 19:18; 20:18 [p]S Jos 18:1; Jer 7:14
19:1 [q]ver 16,18 [r]Ru 1:1
19:4 [s]ver 6,8; S Ex 32:6
19:5 [t]ver 8; Ge 18:5
19:6 [u]S Jdg 16:25
19:10 [v]S Ge 10:16; S Jos 15:8
19:11 [w]S Ge 10:16; S Jos 3:10
19:13 [x]S Jos 18:25

[m]*30* An ancient Hebrew scribal tradition, some Septuagint manuscripts and Vulgate; Masoretic Text *Manasseh*

19:1—21:25 HISTORY, Moral—See note on 18:1,47. Lack of leadership led Israel to civil war and internal bloodshed. Immorality was a root cause of the troubles. God does not give historical deliverance to a people involved in immorality and dissension. Eventually God raised up Israel's first king from the disgraced tribe of Benjamin (1 Sa 9—10).

in one of those places." 14So they went
on, and the sun set as they neared Gibeah
in Benjamin.[y] 15There they stopped to
spend the night.[z] They went and sat in
the city square,[a] but no one took them
into his home for the night.
16That evening[b] an old man from the
hill country of Ephraim,[c] who was living
in Gibeah (the men of the place were
Benjamites), came in from his work in
the fields. 17When he looked and saw the
traveler in the city square, the old man
asked, "Where are you going? Where did
you come from?"[d]
18He answered, "We are on our way
from Bethlehem in Judah to a remote area
in the hill country of Ephraim where I
live. I have been to Bethlehem in Judah
and now I am going to the house of the
LORD.[e] No one has taken me into his
house. 19We have both straw and fodder[f]
for our donkeys[g] and bread and wine[h]
for ourselves your servants—me, your
maidservant, and the young man with us.
We don't need anything."
20"You are welcome at my house," the
old man said. "Let me supply whatever
you need. Only don't spend the night in
the square." 21So he took him into his
house and fed his donkeys. After they had
washed their feet, they had something to
eat and drink.[i]
22While they were enjoying themselves,[j] some of the wicked men[k] of the
city surrounded the house. Pounding on
the door, they shouted to the old man
who owned the house, "Bring out the
man who came to your house so we can
have sex with him.[l]"
23The owner of the house went outside[m] and said to them, "No, my friends,
don't be so vile. Since this man is my
guest, don't do this disgraceful thing.[n]
24Look, here is my virgin daughter,[o] and
his concubine. I will bring them out to
you now, and you can use them and do to
them whatever you wish. But to this
man, don't do such a disgraceful thing."
25But the men would not listen to him.
So the man took his concubine and sent
her outside to them, and they raped her[p]
and abused her[q] throughout the night,
and at dawn they let her go. 26At daybreak the woman went back to the house
where her master was staying, fell down
at the door and lay there until daylight.
27When her master got up in the morning and opened the door of the house and
stepped out to continue on his way, there
lay his concubine, fallen in the doorway
of the house, with her hands on the
threshold. 28He said to her, "Get up; let's
go." But there was no answer. Then the
man put her on his donkey and set out for
home.
29When he reached home, he took a
knife[r] and cut up his concubine, limb by
limb, into twelve parts and sent them
into all the areas of Israel.[s] 30Everyone
who saw it said, "Such a thing has never
been seen or done, not since the day the
Israelites came up out of Egypt.[t] Think
about it! Consider it! Tell us what to
do![u]"

Chapter 20

Israelites Fight the Benjamites

THEN all the Israelites[v] from Dan to
Beersheba[w] and from the land of Gilead came out as one man[x] and assembled[y] before the LORD in Mizpah.[z] 2The
leaders of all the people of the tribes of
Israel took their places in the assembly of
the people of God, four hundred thousand soldiers[a] armed with swords. 3(The
Benjamites heard that the Israelites had
gone up to Mizpah.) Then the Israelites
said, "Tell us how this awful thing happened."
4So the Levite, the husband of the murdered woman, said, "I and my concubine
came to Gibeah[b] in Benjamin to spend
the night.[c] 5During the night the men of
Gibeah came after me and surrounded
the house, intending to kill me.[d] They
raped my concubine, and she died.[e] 6I
took my concubine, cut her into pieces
and sent one piece to each region of Israel's inheritance,[f] because they committed this lewd and disgraceful act[g] in Israel. 7Now, all you Israelites, speak up and
give your verdict.[h]"
8All the people rose as one man, saying, "None of us will go home. No, not
one of us will return to his house. 9But
now this is what we'll do to Gibeah:
We'll go up against it as the lot directs.[i]
10We'll take ten men out of every hundred from all the tribes of Israel, and a
hundred from a thousand, and a thousand
from ten thousand, to get provisions for
the army. Then, when the army arrives at

19:14 [y]Jos 15:57; 1Sa 10:26; 11:4; 13:2; 15:34; Isa 10:29
19:15 [z]S Ge 24:23 [a]S Ge 19:2
19:16 [b]Ps 104:23 [c]S ver 1
19:17 [d]S Ge 29:4
19:18 [e]S Jdg 18:31
19:19 [f]Ge 24:25 [g]S Ge 42:27 [h]S Ge 14:18
19:21 [i]Ge 24:32-33; Lk 7:44
19:22 [j]S Jdg 16:25 [k]S Dt 13:13 [l]Ge 19:4-5; Jdg 20:5; Ro 1:26-27
19:23 [m]Ge 19:6 [n]S Ge 34:7; S Lev 19:29; S Jos 7:15; S Jdg 20:6; Ro 1:27
19:24 [o]Ge 19:8
19:25 [p]Jdg 20:5 [q]1Sa 31:4
19:29 [r]S Ge 22:6 [s]Jdg 20:6; 1Sa 11:7
19:30 [t]Hos 9:9 [u]Jdg 20:7; Pr 13:10
20:1 [v]Jdg 21:5 [w]S Ge 21:14; 1Sa 3:20; 2Sa 3:10; 17:11; 24:15; 1Ki 4:25; 2Ch 30:5 [x]ver 11; 1Sa 11:7 [y]1Sa 7:5 [z]S Jos 11:3
20:2 [a]1Sa 11:8
20:4 [b]S Jos 15:57 [c]S Ge 24:23
20:5 [d]S Jdg 19:22 [e]Jdg 19:25-26
20:6 [f]S Jdg 19:29 [g]S Jdg 19:23; 2Sa 13:12
20:7 [h]S Jdg 19:30
20:9 [i]S Lev 16:8

20:1 PRAYER, Petition—Israel took her political problems to God. The worship center was the starting point for political action. The state and the people of God can no longer be seen as identical, but God's people can still carry the problems of state before the Lord.

20:8–48 CHRISTIAN ETHICS, War and Peace—War is not limited to international conflict. Too often civil war divides a nation. Internal immorality and selfishness are often the root causes of war. Such a people desperately need leadership that will work for reconciliation, renewal, and peace (17:6; 18:1; 19:1; 21:25). Too often the result is alienation and destruction for one part of a nation. This weakens the whole nation (21:15).

20:9 PRAYER, Will of God—See note on Ex 28:30.

Gibeah[n] in Benjamin, it can give them
what they deserve for all this vileness
done in Israel." 11So all the men of Israel
got together and united as one man[j]
against the city.
12The tribes of Israel sent men throughout the tribe of Benjamin, saying, "What
about this awful crime that was committed among you?[k] 13Now surrender those
wicked men[l] of Gibeah so that we may
put them to death and purge the evil from
Israel.[m]"
But the Benjamites would not listen to
their fellow Israelites. 14From their towns
they came together at Gibeah to fight
against the Israelites. 15At once the Benjamites mobilized twenty-six thousand
swordsmen from their towns, in addition
to seven hundred chosen men from those
living in Gibeah. 16Among all these soldiers there were seven hundred chosen
men who were left-handed,[n] each of
whom could sling a stone at a hair and
not miss.
17Israel, apart from Benjamin, mustered four hundred thousand swordsmen,
all of them fighting men.
18The Israelites went up to Bethel[o] [o]
and inquired of God.[p] They said, "Who
of us shall go first[q] to fight[r] against the
Benjamites?"
The LORD replied, "Judah[s] shall go
first."
19The next morning the Israelites got
up and pitched camp near Gibeah. 20The
men of Israel went out to fight the Benjamites and took up battle positions against
them at Gibeah. 21The Benjamites came
out of Gibeah and cut down twenty-two
thousand Israelites[t] on the battlefield
that day. 22But the men of Israel encouraged one another and again took up their
positions where they had stationed themselves the first day. 23The Israelites went
up and wept before the LORD[u] until evening,[v] and they inquired of the LORD.[w]
They said, "Shall we go up again to battle[x] against the Benjamites, our brothers?"
The LORD answered, "Go up against
them."
24Then the Israelites drew near to Benjamin the second day. 25This time, when
the Benjamites came out from Gibeah to
oppose them, they cut down another
eighteen thousand Israelites,[y] all of them
armed with swords.
26Then the Israelites, all the people,
went up to Bethel, and there they sat
weeping before the LORD.[z] They fasted[a]
that day until evening and presented
burnt offerings[b] and fellowship offerings[p] [c] to the LORD.[d] 27And the Israelites
inquired of the LORD.[e] (In those days the
ark of the covenant of God[f] was there,
28with Phinehas son of Eleazar,[g] the son
of Aaron, ministering before it.)[h] They
asked, "Shall we go up again to battle
with Benjamin our brother, or not?"
The LORD responded, "Go, for tomorrow I will give them into your hands.[i]"
29Then Israel set an ambush[j] around
Gibeah. 30They went up against the Benjamites on the third day and took up positions against Gibeah as they had done before. 31The Benjamites came out to meet
them and were drawn away[k] from the
city. They began to inflict casualties on
the Israelites as before, so that about thirty men fell in the open field and on the
roads—the one leading to Bethel[l] and
the other to Gibeah.
32While the Benjamites were saying,
"We are defeating them as before,"[m] the
Israelites were saying, "Let's retreat and
draw them away from the city to the
roads."
33All the men of Israel moved from
their places and took up positions at Baal
Tamar, and the Israelite ambush charged
out of its place[n] on the west[q] of Gibeah.[r] 34Then ten thousand of Israel's finest men made a frontal attack on Gibeah.
The fighting was so heavy that the Benjamites did not realize[o] how near disaster
was.[p] 35The LORD defeated Benjamin[q]
before Israel, and on that day the Israelites struck down 25,100 Benjamites, all
armed with swords. 36Then the Benjamites saw that they were beaten.

20:11 [j]S ver 1
20:12 [k]Dt 13:14
20:13 [l]S Dt 13:13 [m]S Dt 13:5; S 1Co 5:13
20:16 [n]S Jdg 3:15
20:18 [o]S Jos 12:9; S Jdg 18:31 [p]S Jdg 18:5 [q]S Jdg 1:1 [r]ver 23, 28 [s]S Ge 49:10
20:21 [t]ver 25
20:23 [u]S Nu 14:1 [v]Jos 7:6 [w]S Jdg 18:5 [x]S ver 18
20:25 [y]ver 21
20:26 [z]S Nu 14:1 [a]2Sa 12:21 [b]Lev 1:3 [c]S Ex 32:6 [d]Jdg 21:4
20:27 [e]S Jdg 18:5 [f]S Nu 10:33
20:28 [g]Nu 25:7 [h]Dt 18:5 [i]S Jos 2:24
20:29 [j]S Jos 8:2,4
20:31 [k]Jos 8:16 [l]Jos 16:1
20:32 [m]ver 39
20:33 [n]Jos 8:19
20:34 [o]Jos 8:14 [p]ver 41
20:35 [q]1Sa 9:21

[n]*10* One Hebrew manuscript; most Hebrew manuscripts *Geba*, a variant of *Gibeah* [o]*18* Or *to the house of God*; also in verse 26 [p]*26* Traditionally *peace offerings* [q]*33* Some Septuagint manuscripts and Vulgate; the meaning of the Hebrew for this word is uncertain. [r]*33* Hebrew *Geba*, a variant of *Gibeah*

20:18 REVELATION, Oracles—Holy places are associated with God's revelation. Bethel was significant because of Abraham and Jacob and their encounters there with God (Ge 12:8; 13:3–4; 28:10–19; 35:1–15). God's direction was probably gained by using the sacred stones, Urim and Thummim. See notes on Jdg 1:1–2; Nu 27:18–21.

20:23 PRAYER, Sincerity—The tragic situation called for earnest prayer. Desperate situations call God's people to weeping and prolonged prayer as we seek God's will.

20:26 WORSHIP, Humility—An attitude of humility is absolutely required for true worship. This attitude found expression here as the people wept, fasted, and presented offerings to the Lord. True humility involves a complete yielding of oneself to the Lord. This expression often involves repentance. Weeping, fasting, and repentance is part of the worship experience of God's people. No evidence appears in Scripture that God ever accepts an arrogant spirit in worship. Compare Joel 1:13–14; Ac 13:2–3.

20:26–27 PRAYER, Sincerity—To weeping the people added fasting and offerings. See note on v 23. Prayer does not guarantee an endeavor will be successful. Prayer does give us a sense of God's direction and a will to try again.

Now the men of Israel had given way[r] before Benjamin, because they relied on the ambush[s] they had set near Gibeah. 37The men who had been in ambush made a sudden dash into Gibeah, spread out and put the whole city to the sword.[t] 38The men of Israel had arranged with the ambush that they should send up a great cloud of smoke[u] from the city,[v] 39and then the men of Israel would turn in the battle.

The Benjamites had begun to inflict casualties on the men of Israel (about thirty), and they said, "We are defeating them as in the first battle."[w] 40But when the column of smoke began to rise from the city, the Benjamites turned and saw the smoke of the whole city going up into the sky.[x] 41Then the men of Israel turned on them,[y] and the men of Benjamin were terrified, because they realized that disaster had come[z] upon them. 42So they fled before the Israelites in the direction of the desert, but they could not escape the battle. And the men of Israel who came out of the towns cut them down there. 43They surrounded the Benjamites, chased them and easily[s] overran them in the vicinity of Gibeah on the east. 44Eighteen thousand Benjamites fell, all of them valiant fighters.[a] 45As they turned and fled toward the desert to the rock of Rimmon,[b] the Israelites cut down five thousand men along the roads. They kept pressing after the Benjamites as far as Gidom and struck down two thousand more.

46On that day twenty-five thousand Benjamite[c] swordsmen fell, all of them valiant fighters. 47But six hundred men turned and fled into the desert to the rock of Rimmon, where they stayed four months. 48The men of Israel went back to Benjamin and put all the towns to the sword, including the animals and everything else they found. All the towns they came across they set on fire.[d]

Chapter 21

Wives for the Benjamites

THE men of Israel had taken an oath[e] at Mizpah:[f] "Not one of us will give[g] his daughter in marriage to a Benjamite."

2The people went to Bethel,[t] where they sat before God until evening, raising their voices and weeping bitterly. 3"O LORD, the God of Israel," they cried, "why has this happened to Israel? Why should one tribe be missing[h] from Israel today?"

4Early the next day the people built an altar and presented burnt offerings and fellowship offerings.[u] [i]

5Then the Israelites asked, "Who from all the tribes of Israel[j] has failed to assemble before the LORD?" For they had taken a solemn oath that anyone who failed to assemble before the LORD at Mizpah should certainly be put to death.

6Now the Israelites grieved for their brothers, the Benjamites. "Today one tribe is cut off from Israel," they said. 7"How can we provide wives for those who are left, since we have taken an oath[k] by the LORD not to give them any of our daughters in marriage?" 8Then they asked, "Which one of the tribes of Israel failed to assemble before the LORD at Mizpah?" They discovered that no one from Jabesh Gilead[l] had come to the camp for the assembly. 9For when they counted the people, they found that none of the people of Jabesh Gilead were there.

10So the assembly sent twelve thousand fighting men with instructions to go to Jabesh Gilead and put to the sword those living there, including the women and children. 11"This is what you are to do," they said. "Kill every male[m] and every woman who is not a virgin."[n] 12They found among the people living in Jabesh Gilead four hundred young women who had never slept with a man, and they took them to the camp at Shiloh[o] in Canaan.

13Then the whole assembly sent an offer of peace[p] to the Benjamites at the rock of Rimmon.[q] 14So the Benjamites returned at that time and were given the women of Jabesh Gilead who had been spared. But there were not enough for all of them.

15The people grieved for Benjamin,[r] because the LORD had made a gap in the tribes of Israel. 16And the elders of the assembly said, "With the women of Benjamin destroyed, how shall we provide wives for the men who are left? 17The Benjamite survivors must have heirs," they said, "so that a tribe of Israel will not be wiped out.[s] 18We can't give them our daughters as wives, since we Israelites have taken this oath:[t] 'Cursed be anyone who gives[u] a wife to a Benjamite.' 19But look, there is the annual festival of the

20:36 [r]Jos 8:15 [s]Jos 8:2
20:37 [t]Jos 8:19
20:38 [u]Jos 8:20 [v]Jos 8:4-8
20:39 [w]ver 32; Ps 78:9
20:40 [x]Jos 8:20
20:41 [y]Jos 8:21 [z]ver 34
20:44 [a]1Sa 10:26; Ps 76:5
20:45 [b]S Jos 15:32
20:46 [c]1Sa 9:21
20:48 [d]Jdg 21:23
21:1 [e]S Jos 9:18 [f]S Jos 11:3 [g]ver 18, 22
21:3 [h]ver 6,17
21:4 [i]Jdg 20:26
21:5 [j]Jdg 20:1
21:7 [k]S Jos 9:18
21:8 [l]1Sa 11:1; 31:11; 2Sa 2:4; 21:12; 1Ch 10:11
21:11 [m]S Nu 31:7 [n]Nu 31:17-18
21:12 [o]S Jos 18:1
21:13 [p]S Dt 2:26 [q]S Jos 15:32
21:15 [r]ver 6
21:17 [s]S ver 3
21:18 [t]S Jos 9:18 [u]S ver 1

[s]*43* The meaning of the Hebrew for this word is uncertain. [t]*2* Or *to the house of God* [u]*4* Traditionally *peace offerings*

21:2–4 PRAYER, Corporate—The close bond of Israel as a nation had been broken. Prayer was needed to restore that bond. Corporate prayer is the force that brings unity when God's people are divided.

LORD in Shiloh,[v] to the north of Bethel[w],
and east of the road that goes from Bethel
to Shechem,[x] and to the south of Lebo-
nah."
20So they instructed the Benjamites,
saying, "Go and hide in the vineyards
21and watch. When the girls of Shiloh
come out to join in the dancing,[y] then
rush from the vineyards and each of you
seize a wife from the girls of Shiloh and
go to the land of Benjamin. 22When their
fathers or brothers complain to us, we
will say to them, 'Do us a kindness by
helping them, because we did not get
wives for them during the war, and you
are innocent, since you did not give[z]
your daughters to them.'"
23So that is what the Benjamites did.
While the girls were dancing,[a] each man
caught one and carried her off to be his
wife. Then they returned to their inheritance[b] and rebuilt the towns and settled
in them.[c]
24At that time the Israelites left that
place and went home to their tribes and
clans, each to his own inheritance.
25In those days Israel had no king; everyone did as he saw fit.[d]

21:19 [v]S Jos 18:1 [w]Jos 16:1 [x]S Jos 17:7
21:21 [y]S Ex 15:20
21:22 [z]S ver 1; ver 1,18
21:23 [a]ver 21 [b]S Jos 24:28 [c]Jdg 20:48
21:25 [d]S Dt 12:8

21:25 HUMANITY, Community Relationships—God is the ultimate King. A community that is not obedient to His authority and which has no human authority faces catastrophic problems. Human government becomes a basic need for such a society. See 1 Sa 8:1–22.

Ruth

Theological Setting

Where is God in the time of crisis and great pain? Is there any affirmation of God's presence and power in the lives of His people when they are wracked by the tragedies of life?

The beautiful story of Ruth is God's response to such questions. Though the story of Ruth likely emerges from the early period of Israel's monarchy, its message is as timely as a daily newspaper. The skill of the inspired writer and the inspired/inspiring character of his message sweep the reader along until the story makes its impact.

The key element in the subtle, yet powerful, way the story unfolds its message is the character Naomi. Ruth and Boaz are important, but Naomi is the story's key figure with whose experiences readers are invited to identify. What happened to her in her family crisis portrays the faith which can be awakened in our own struggles.

The book begins by introducing the family of Naomi and the tragedy which befell them. Naomi was understandably bitter—bitter at God, bitter at life itself. God's presence seemed far from her, especially because she had to move to foreign territory, the land of the enemy. Her parting words to her daughters-in-law made clear that, for Naomi, God's blessings were in the past. No hint of God's presence or of His blessing could be found in her tragic circumstance.

Thus, the Book of Ruth raises important theological issues for God's people.

1. Where is God at the moment of tragedy?
2. Is any response other than bitterness appropriate in the tragic hour?
3. Can God work for His people in a foreign land?
4. Will God fulfill His promises for His people?
5. Does God work through ordinary, even foreign, people?

Theological Outline

Ruth: God's Grace in a Surprising Vessel

I. Trial and Tragedy Seemed to Offer Little Hope for God's Redeeming Grace. (1:1-22)
   - A. The trial of famine gave way to the tragedy of death for Naomi. (1:1-5)
   - B. The hint of blessing was seen in the tearful parting of Naomi from Orpah and the determined love of Ruth for her mother-in-law. (1:6-14)
   - C. In spite of Naomi's urging, Ruth resisted the injunction of her mother-in-law to remain in Moab and accompanied Naomi as she returned to Judah. (1:15-18)
   - D. The "emptiness" of Naomi's return to Judah provided the transition to God's grace by means of Ruth. (1:19-22)

II. In the Ordinary Actions of a Foreigner, God Began to Prepare the Way of Blessing. (2:1-23)
   - A. Ruth's initiative provided not only food for the present, but a foundation for the future welfare of her family. (2:1-7)
   - B. Ruth demonstrated that inclusion into the people of God is not predicated on birth alone. (2:8-13)
   - C. The encounter of Boaz and Ruth opened the way for God to bless in an unexpected manner. (2:14-23)

III. In More Ways Than One, God Took a Potential Scandal and Made It the Way of Grace. (3:1-18)
   - A. Naomi proposed a daring strategy in her match-making effort. (3:1-5)
   - B. The character of both Boaz and Ruth was demonstrated in the encounter at the threshing floor. (3:6-13)
   - C. The blessing of God began to be given to Ruth and Naomi through Boaz. (3:14-18)

IV. Through Boaz, the "Kinsman Redeemer," God "Filled" the "Emptiness" of Naomi and Demonstrated His Presence Through the Blessing of His People. (4:1-22)

A. Boaz became "kinsman redeemer." (4:1-6)
B. Before the assembled witnesses, Boaz fulfilled the custom of levirate marriage and received the blessing of witnesses. (4:7-12)
C. God "filled" the "emptiness" of Naomi through a son born to Ruth and Boaz, a son who was none other than the grandfather of the great King David. (4:13-22)

Theological Conclusions

The surprising providence of God is the equally surprising theological theme of the Book of Ruth. Biblical narratives often use the element of surprise to emphasize the unfathomable mystery of God. We cannot program God. His Word always seems to break through to call His people further on the way to Himself. The theological surprises of Ruth include:

1. Trial and tragedy bring surprising responses—from God's people and from God. Naomi's family sought escape from the Promised Land. God moved mysteriously with them. Trial and tragedy may lead people to lose faith at the moment. It cannot move God away from His people.

2. God can use surprising people to accomplish His purposes. Moabites epitomized pagan worship. They serve as Old Testament models for wrong, tempting worship. Yet, the Moabitess Ruth became the heroine of the story and the ancestress of the Messiah. Human categories and boundaries do not limit God as He works out His purpose.

3. Personal loyalty leads to surprising sacrifice. Ruth left her nation, her land, her blood kin, and her god to follow her mother-in-law back to a foreign land. God used such loyalty to accomplish His saving will for the family and through them for the world.

4. The greatest surprise comes with God's presence. God relieved Naomi's bitterness by working through the kindness of Boaz, her relative, to the foreign widow Ruth. Through Boaz's actions, God suddenly becomes the main hero of the story as He is of all of life. God is truly present in crisis, need, tragedy, and pain to redeem us in earthly trials and to provide an eternal Redeemer.

Contemporary Teaching

Ruth gives us a realistic portrait of life with its tragedies and frustrations. Most of us can readily identify with it. We identify especially with Naomi, the bitter one. Some identify with Ruth, the lonely foreigner. We all can learn:

1. Loving loyalty may separate us from heritage and family. It may also lead us to God's will for our life. In the moment of tragedy God is present even if we are not aware of His presence.

2. No person or people should be ignored or condemned. God may use the hated enemy to bring about His purpose for us. We need to be good neighbors to all people regardless of race, heritage, or culture. God may surprise us by the way He works through us to help others.

3. God can be trusted in the darkest hour. We need not seek escape from tragedy to a new place of opportunity. We need rather to see God's presence and wait for Him to reveal His grace and fulfill His promises.

4. Despair may be the only response we can give in the hour of tragedy. Despair is not the end of faith. Naomi became bitter, but God continued to work to bless her. He will do the same for us, helping us work our way through despair to faith in His redemption.

Chapter 1

Naomi and Ruth

IN the days when the judges ruled,[a] [a]
there was a famine in the land,[b] and a
man from Bethlehem in Judah,[c] together
with his wife and two sons, went to live
for a while[d] in the country of Moab.[e]
2The man's name was Elimelech,[f] his
wife's name Naomi, and the names of his
two sons were Mahlon and Kilion.[g] They
were Ephrathites[h] from Bethlehem,[i] Judah. And they went to Moab and lived
there.
3Now Elimelech, Naomi's husband,
died, and she was left with her two sons.
4They married Moabite women,[j] one
named Orpah and the other Ruth.[k] After
they had lived there about ten years,
5both Mahlon and Kilion[l] also died,[m]
and Naomi was left without her two sons
and her husband.
6When she heard in Moab[n] that the
LORD had come to the aid of his people[o]
by providing food[p] for them, Naomi and
her daughters-in-law[q] prepared to return
home from there. 7With her two daughters-in-law she left the place where she
had been living and set out on the road
that would take them back to the land of
Judah.
8Then Naomi said to her two daughters-in-law, "Go back, each of you, to
your mother's home.[r] May the LORD
show kindness[s] to you, as you have
shown to your dead[t] and to me. 9May
the LORD grant that each of you will find
rest[u] in the home of another husband."
Then she kissed[v] them and they wept
aloud[w] 10and said to her, "We will go
back with you to your people."
11But Naomi said, "Return home, my
daughters. Why would you come with
me? Am I going to have any more sons,
who could become your husbands?[x]
12Return home, my daughters; I am too
old to have another husband. Even if I
thought there was still hope for me—
even if I had a husband tonight and then
gave birth to sons— 13would you wait until they grew up?[y] Would you remain unmarried for them? No, my daughters. It is
more bitter[z] for me than for you, because
the LORD's hand has gone out against
me![a]"
14At this they wept[b] again. Then Orpah kissed her mother-in-law[c] good-by,[d]
but Ruth clung to her.[e]
15"Look," said Naomi, "your sister-in-
law[f] is going back to her people and her
gods.[g] Go back with her."
16But Ruth replied, "Don't urge me to
leave you[h] or to turn back from you.
Where you go I will go,[i] and where you
stay I will stay. Your people will be my
people[j] and your God my God.[k]
17Where you die I will die, and there I
will be buried. May the LORD deal with
me, be it ever so severely,[l] if anything

1:1 [a]Jdg 2:16-18 [b]S Ge 12:10; 2Ki 6:25; Ps 105:16; Hag 1:11 [c]S Ge 35:19 [d]Ge 47:4 [e]S Ge 36:35 **1:2** [f]ver 3; Ru 2:1; 4:3 [g]ver 5; Ru 4:9 [h]S Ge 35:16 [i]Ge 35:19; 1Sa 16:18 **1:4** [j]1Ki 11:1; 2Ch 24:26; Ezr 9:2; Ne 13:23 [k]ver 14; Ru 4:13; Mt 1:5 **1:5** [l]S ver 2 [m]ver 8; Ru 2:11 **1:6** [n]S Ge 36:35 [o]S Ge 50:24; Ex 4:31; Jer 29:10; Zep 2:7 [p]Ps 132:15; Mt 6:11 [q]S Ge 11:31; S 38:16 **1:8** [r]Ge 38:11 [s]S Ge 19:19; 2Ti 1:16 [t]S ver 5 **1:9** [u]Ru 3:1 [v]S Ge 27:27; S 29:11 [w]S Ge 27:38; S Nu 25:6 **1:11** [x]Ge 38:11; Dt 25:5 **1:13** [y]Ge 38:11 [z]ver 20; Ex 1:14; 15:23; 1Sa 30:6 [a]S Jdg 2:15; S Job 4:5 **1:14** [b]ver 9 [c]Ru 2:11; 3:1; Mic 7:6 [d]S Ge 31:28 [e]S Dt 10:20 **1:15** [f]Dt 25:7 [g]S Jos 24:14 **1:16** [h]2Ki 2:2 [i]Ge 24:58 [j]Ps 45:10 [k]S Jos 24:15 **1:17** [l]1Sa 3:17; 14:44; 20:13; 25:22; 2Sa 3:9,35; 2Sa 19:13; 1Ki 2:23; 19:2; 20:10; 2Ki 6:31

[a]*1* Traditionally *judged*

1:1—4:22 EVANGELISM, In the Home—The entire Book of Ruth is a testimony of doing effectual evangelism in the home. Ruth was a Moabite woman. She did not worship the Lord. The testimony and godly life of her mother-in-law, Naomi, so impacted the young widow that she vowed Naomi's God would be her God (1:16). A Christ-honoring home and family life make a deep and lasting impression on all the members and can be used by the Holy Spirit to lead those members to saving faith in Christ. Ruth stands as a classic example of that vital principle of the practicalities of evangelism. See Guide to Relational Evangelism, pp. 1784–1786.

1:6 REVELATION, Author of Creation—God reveals Himself by providing human needs such as food. God's people confess that God is active through the natural orders of creation to reveal His loving care.

1:8–9 PRAYER, Petition—In Moab, Naomi prayed to the one true God, the God of Israel. Geography is no barrier to prayer. She expressed the prayer in conversation with her daughters-in-law. Prayer can be included in daily conversation.

1:11–21 EVIL AND SUFFERING, Divine Origin—God controls all life and history. See note on Jdg 9:23. He uses even human suffering and misfortune to accomplish His purposes. At times we cannot say such misfortune is divine punishment for personal sin. We have no explanation for it. Instead, we have to accept our situation as being under God's control, weigh our alternatives prayerfully and reasonably, and act. In time we may discover how God is working even through our afflictions. In the midst of trouble we can only confess that God is at work in our lives and that we do not understand what is happening. Having passed through suffering, we may find other explanations for this dark side of life. We will at least confess that God is good and what He does cannot ultimately be called evil.

1:13,20–21 GOD, Sovereignty—Naomi believed God is the cause of everything that happens. See note on Jdg 9:23–24,56–57. As we read the Bible, we must distinguish between what is presented as eternal truth and what is a record of a person's viewpoint. Job's friends, for example, stated wrong viewpoints. Here Naomi stated her idea, but the text does not indicate it is God's. In Naomi's time Satan's activity was not fully understood. Later God revealed more concerning the nature and work of the evil tempter. The New Testament gives us the fuller picture. In the depths of despair, as Naomi was, it is easy to feel forsaken by God. A judgment wrought out of deep despair and anguish is not necessarily true. For a deeper understanding of God, see Ro 8:28. Paul teaches that God does not cause everything to happen, but He can work even in the tragedies of life to bring good out of them. See Guide to Interpreting the Bible, pp. 1769–1772.

1:15–18 FAMILY, Authentic Love—Ruth's fervent speech to her mother-in-law Naomi is one of the most beautiful declarations of authentic family love in the Bible. Even though not addressed to husband-wife relationships, it is often used in wedding ceremonies to describe what marital love should be. It affirms the desire to be together, to face life's challenges together, to be a family, and to worship the same God. All of these elements are central to a healthy Christian marriage when Christ becomes the Lord who makes the Father's presence known to the family.

1:17 PRAYER, Commitment—Ruth, a Moabitess, claimed Israel's God as her own and committed her life to God and to the one who had introduced her to God. Commitment to God often comes through commitment to His people. A solemn prayer of commitment is the first step to God.

but death separates you and me."[m]
18 When Naomi realized that Ruth was determined to go with her, she stopped
urging her.[n]
19 So the two women went on until
they came to Bethlehem.[o] When they arrived in Bethlehem, the whole town was
stirred[p] because of them, and the women
exclaimed, "Can this be Naomi?"
20 "Don't call me Naomi,[b]" she told
them. "Call me Mara,[c] because the Almighty[d][q] has made my life very bitter.[r]
21 I went away full, but the LORD has
brought me back empty.[s] Why call me
Naomi? The LORD has afflicted[e] me;[t]
the Almighty has brought misfortune
upon me."
22 So Naomi returned from Moab accompanied by Ruth the Moabitess,[u] her
daughter-in-law,[v] arriving in Bethlehem
as the barley harvest[w] was beginning.[x]

Chapter 2

Ruth Meets Boaz

NOW Naomi had a relative[y] on her
husband's side, from the clan of
Elimelech,[z] a man of standing,[a] whose
name was Boaz.[b]
2 And Ruth the Moabitess[c] said to Naomi, "Let me go to the fields and pick up
the leftover grain[d] behind anyone in
whose eyes I find favor.[e]"
Naomi said to her, "Go ahead, my
daughter." 3 So she went out and began to
glean in the fields behind the harvesters.[f] As it turned out, she found herself
working in a field belonging to Boaz, who
was from the clan of Elimelech.[g]
4 Just then Boaz arrived from Bethlehem and greeted the harvesters, "The
LORD be with you![h]"
"The LORD bless you![i]" they called
back.
5 Boaz asked the foreman of his harvesters, "Whose young woman is that?"
6 The foreman replied, "She is the Moabitess[j] who came back from Moab with
Naomi. 7 She said, 'Please let me glean
and gather among the sheaves[k] behind
the harvesters.' She went into the field
and has worked steadily from morning till
now, except for a short rest[l] in the shelter."

1:17 [m]2Sa 15:21
1:18 [n]Ac 21:14
1:19 [o]S Jdg 17:7 [p]Mt 21:10
1:20 [q]S Ge 15:1; S 17:1; Ps 91:1 [r]S ver 13
1:21 [s]Job 1:21 [t]Job 30:11; Ps 88:7; Isa 53:4
1:22 [u]Ru 2:2,6,21; 4:5,10 [v]S Ge 11:31 [w]S Ex 9:31; S Lev 19:9 [x]2Sa 21:9
2:1 [y]Ru 3:2; Pr 7:4 [z]S Ru 1:2 [a]1Sa 9:1; 1Ki 11:28 [b]Ru 4:21; 1Ch 2:12; Mt 1:5; Lk 3:32
2:2 [c]S Ru 1:22 [d]S Lev 19:9; S 23:22 [e]S Ge 6:8; S 18:3
2:3 [f]ver 14; 2Ki 4:18; Jer 9:22; Am 9:13 [g]ver 1
2:4 [h]S Jdg 6:12; Lk 1:28; 2Th 3:16 [i]S Ge 28:3; S Nu 6:24
2:6 [j]S Ru 1:22
2:7 [k]S Ge 37:7; S Lev 19:9 [l]2Sa 4:5
2:10 [m]S Ge 19:1; S 1Sa 20:41 [n]ver 19; Ps 41:1 [o]S Ge 31:15; S Dt 15:3
2:11 [p]S Ru 1:14 [q]S Ru 1:5 [r]Isa 55:5 [s]Ru 1:16-17
2:12 [t]1Sa 24:19; 26:23,25; Ps 18:20; Pr 25:22; Jer 31:16 [u]S Jos 24:15 [v]Ps 17:8; 36:7; 57:1; 61:4; 63:7; 91:4 [w]Ps 71:1
2:13 [x]S Ge 18:3
2:14 [y]S Ge 3:19 [z]S ver 3 [a]S Lev 23:14 [b]ver 18
2:15 [c]S Ge 37:7; S Lev 19:9
2:16 [d]S Ge 37:10
2:17 [e]S Jdg 6:11 [f]S Lev 19:36
2:18 [g]ver 14

8 So Boaz said to Ruth, "My daughter,
listen to me. Don't go and glean in another field and don't go away from here. Stay
here with my servant girls. 9 Watch the
field where the men are harvesting, and
follow along after the girls. I have told the
men not to touch you. And whenever you
are thirsty, go and get a drink from the
water jars the men have filled."
10 At this, she bowed down with her
face to the ground.[m] She exclaimed,
"Why have I found such favor in your
eyes that you notice me[n]—a foreigner?[o]"
11 Boaz replied, "I've been told all
about what you have done for your mother-in-law[p] since the death of your husband[q]—how you left your father and
mother and your homeland and came to
live with a people you did not know[r] before.[s] 12 May the LORD repay you for what
you have done. May you be richly rewarded by the LORD,[t] the God of Israel,[u]
under whose wings[v] you have come to
take refuge.[w]"
13 "May I continue to find favor in your
eyes,[x] my lord," she said. "You have giv-
en me comfort and have spoken kindly to
your servant—though I do not have the
standing of one of your servant girls."
14 At mealtime Boaz said to her, "Come
over here. Have some bread[y] and dip it
in the wine vinegar."
When she sat down with the harvesters,[z] he offered her some roasted grain.[a]
She ate all she wanted and had some left
over.[b] 15 As she got up to glean, Boaz
gave orders to his men, "Even if she gathers among the sheaves,[c] don't embarrass
her. 16 Rather, pull out some stalks for her
from the bundles and leave them for her
to pick up, and don't rebuke[d] her."
17 So Ruth gleaned in the field until evening. Then she threshed[e] the barley she
had gathered, and it amounted to about
an ephah.[f][f] 18 She carried it back to
town, and her mother-in-law saw how
much she had gathered. Ruth also
brought out and gave her what she had
left over[g] after she had eaten enough.
19 Her mother-in-law asked her,

[b] *20 Naomi* means *pleasant*; also in verse 21.
[c] *20 Mara* means *bitter.* [d] *20* Hebrew *Shaddai*; also in verse 21 [e] *21* Or *has testified against*
[f] *17* That is, probably about 3/5 bushel (about 22 liters)

2:4 PRAYER, Personal—Boaz brought the Lord into his daily life. His greeting to his employees took the form of prayer. Such personal prayer habits will be a witness to other people.

2:12 SALVATION, Blessing—Boaz expressed his desire for the God of Israel to richly bless Ruth the Moabitess. God does bless those who take refuge under His wings. His salvation goes beyond all national and political boundaries. Ruth is included in the genealogy of Jesus (Mt 1:5).

2:12 PRAYER, Intercession—Ruth had chosen God. Boaz invoked His blessing on her. Intercession is not limited to desperate situations. It includes seeking God's blessing on His faithful people.

2:17–18 HUMANITY, Community Relationships—Communities must provide for the weak and unfortunate members of their society. See note on Dt 24:19. The weak and poor also have a responsibility to share with their aging parents and others.

2:19–20 REVELATION, Author of Hope—The loving protection of the helpless, deeply ingrained in the Old Testament, is attractively portrayed in the care Boaz extended to

“Where did you glean today? Where did
you work? Blessed be the man who took
notice of you![h]”
Then Ruth told her mother-in-law
about the one at whose place she had
been working. “The name of the man I
worked with today is Boaz,” she said.
20“The LORD bless him![i]” Naomi said
to her daughter-in-law.[j] “He has not
stopped showing his kindness[k] to the living and the dead.” She added, “That man
is our close relative;[l] he is one of our
kinsman-redeemers.[m]”
21Then Ruth the Moabitess[n] said, “He
even said to me, ‘Stay with my workers
until they finish harvesting all my
grain.’ ”
22Naomi said to Ruth her daughter-in-
law, “It will be good for you, my daughter, to go with his girls, because in someone else’s field you might be harmed.”
23So Ruth stayed close to the servant
girls of Boaz to glean until the barley[o]
and wheat harvests[p] were finished. And
she lived with her mother-in-law.

Chapter 3

Ruth and Boaz at the Threshing Floor

ONE day Naomi her mother-in-law[q]
said to her, “My daughter, should I
not try to find a home[g][r] for you, where
you will be well provided for? 2Is not
Boaz, with whose servant girls you have
been, a kinsman[s] of ours? Tonight he
will be winnowing barley on the threshing floor.[t] 3Wash[u] and perfume yourself,[v] and put on your best clothes.[w]
Then go down to the threshing floor, but
don’t let him know you are there until he
has finished eating and drinking.[x] 4When
he lies down, note the place where he is
lying. Then go and uncover his feet and
lie down. He will tell you what to do.”
5“I will do whatever you say,”[y] Ruth
answered. 6So she went down to the
threshing floor[z] and did everything her
mother-in-law told her to do.
7When Boaz had finished eating and
drinking and was in good spirits,[a] he
went over to lie down at the far end of
the grain pile.[b] Ruth approached quietly,
uncovered his feet and lay down. 8In the
middle of the night something startled
the man, and he turned and discovered a
woman lying at his feet.
9“Who are you?” he asked.
“I am your servant Ruth,” she said.
“Spread the corner of your garment[c]
over me, since you are a kinsman-redeemer.[d]”
10“The LORD bless you,[e] my daughter,” he replied. “This kindness is greater
than that which you showed earlier:[f]
You have not run after the younger men,
whether rich or poor. 11And now, my
daughter, don’t be afraid. I will do for you
all you ask. All my fellow townsmen
know that you are a woman of noble
character.[g] 12Although it is true that I am
near of kin, there is a kinsman-redeemer[h] nearer than[i] I. 13Stay here for the
night, and in the morning if he wants to
redeem,[j] good; let him redeem. But if he
is not willing, as surely as the LORD lives[k]
I will do it.[l] Lie here until morning.”
14So she lay at his feet until morning,
but got up before anyone could be recognized; and he said, “Don’t let it be
known that a woman came to the threshing floor.[m]”[n]
15He also said, “Bring me the shawl[o]
you are wearing and hold it out.” When
she did so, he poured into it six measures
of barley and put it on her. Then he[h]
went back to town.
16When Ruth came to her mother-in-
law, Naomi asked, “How did it go, my
daughter?”
Then she told her everything Boaz had
done for her 17and added, “He gave me
these six measures of barley, saying,
‘Don’t go back to your mother-in-law
empty-handed.’ ”

[g] 1 Hebrew *find rest* (see Ruth 1:9) [h] 15 Most Hebrew manuscripts; many Hebrew manuscripts, Vulgate and Syriac *she*

2:19 [h]S ver 10
2:20 [i]S Jdg 17:2; S 1Sa 23:21 [j]S Ge 11:31 [k]S Ge 19:19 [l]S Lev 25:25 [m]Ru 3:9,12; 4:1,14
2:21 [n]S Ru 1:22
2:23 [o]S Ex 9:31 [p]S Ge 30:14; S 1Sa 6:13
3:1 [q]Ru 1:14 [r]Ru 1:9
3:2 [s]S Ru 2:1 [t]S Lev 2:14; S Nu 18:27; S Jdg 6:11
3:3 [u]2Sa 12:20; 2Ki 5:10; Ps 26:6; 51:2; Isa 1:16; Jer 4:14; Eze 16:9 [v]2Sa 14:2; Isa 61:3 [w]S Ge 41:14 [x]S Ex 32:6; S Ecc 2:3; S Jer 15:17
3:5 [y]Eph 6:1; Col 3:20
3:6 [z]S Nu 18:27
3:7 [a]Jdg 19:6,9,22; 1Sa 25:36; 2Sa 13:28; 1Ki 21:7; Est 1:10 [b]2Ch 31:6; SS 7:2; Jer 50:26; Hag 2:16
3:9 [c]Eze 16:8 [d]S Ru 2:20
3:10 [e]S Jdg 17:2 [f]S Jos 2:12
3:11 [g]Pr 12:4; 14:1; 31:10
3:12 [h]S Ru 2:20 [i]Ru 4:1
3:13 [j]Dt 25:5; Ru 4:5; Mt 22:24 [k]S Nu 14:21; Hos 4:15 [l]Ru 4:6
3:14 [m]S Nu 18:27 [n]Ro 14:16; 2Co 8:21
3:15 [o]Isa 3:22

Naomi and Ruth. The law provided that responsibility for property and offspring of deceased relatives were to be assumed by next of kin, so that no family member was left dispossessed or without name and kinship family (Lev 25:25–34; Dt 25:5–10). In such laws God has clearly revealed His compassionate nature.

2:20 GOD, Grace—Naomi praised the kindness, the grace of God. This joyous recognition of God's goodness to His people in their distress stands in stark contrast to the darker sentiments voiced in 1:13,20–21. God will bless His people in the midst of their needs. He is slow to bring suffering upon His people, even if they deserve it. The suffering He does cause His people is for the purpose of helping His people grow. The righteousness of God would not let Him bring evil and suffering upon His people without just cause. The righteousness of God prompts Him to aid and bless His people when they are in distress. That is the nature of God as a God of grace.

2:20 SALVATION, Redemption—Israel had laws relating to kinsman-redeemers (Hebrew *go'el*; Lev 25:25–27, 48–49; Nu 5:8; 35:12,19,24; Dt 19:12; Jos 20:3). The redeemer avenged wrong, redeemed from slavery and debt, and provided family continuity for widows. Boaz was acting in that capacity when he redeemed Ruth, the daughter-in-law of Naomi. That is why Ruth the Moabitess was included in the genealogy of Jesus (Mt 1:5). Compare Ru 3:9,12–13; 4:1,3–11,14.

2:20 PRAYER, Intercession—Naomi, Boaz, and Ruth constantly referred to Yahweh, Israel's God. See note on v 12.

3:1—4:12 FAMILY, Accepting Covenant—Marriage to a widow of an Israelite involved intricate covenant regulations. See Dt 25:7–10; note on Ge 38:1–10. Boaz showed loyalty to God's covenant, respect and love for Ruth, and concern for the near kinsman as he worked through the legal process to gain his wife. Such commitment is necessary in marriage.

3:10 PRAYER, Intercession—See note on 2:20.

18 Then Naomi said, "Wait, my daughter, until you find out what happens. For
the man will not rest until the matter is
settled today."[p]

Chapter 4

Boaz Marries Ruth

MEANWHILE Boaz went up to the
town gate[q] and sat there. When
the kinsman-redeemer[r] he had mentioned[s] came along, Boaz said, "Come
over here, my friend, and sit down." So
he went over and sat down.
2 Boaz took ten of the elders[t] of the
town and said, "Sit here," and they did
so.[u] 3 Then he said to the kinsman-redeemer, "Naomi, who has come back
from Moab, is selling the piece of land
that belonged to our brother Elimelech.[v]
4 I thought I should bring the matter to
your attention and suggest that you buy it
in the presence of these seated here and
in the presence of the elders of my people. If you will redeem it, do so. But if
you[i] will not, tell me, so I will know. For
no one has the right to do it except you,[w]
and I am next in line."
"I will redeem it," he said.
5 Then Boaz said, "On the day you buy
the land from Naomi and from Ruth the
Moabitess,[x] you acquire[j] the dead
man's widow, in order to maintain the
name of the dead with his property."[y]
6 At this, the kinsman-redeemer said,
"Then I cannot redeem[z] it because I
might endanger my own estate. You redeem it yourself. I cannot do it."[a]
7 (Now in earlier times in Israel, for the
redemption[b] and transfer of property to
become final, one party took off his sandal[c] and gave it to the other. This was
the method of legalizing transactions[d] in
Israel.)[e]
8 So the kinsman-redeemer said to
Boaz, "Buy it yourself." And he removed
his sandal.[f]
9 Then Boaz announced to the elders
and all the people, "Today you are witnesses[g] that I have bought from Naomi
all the property of Elimelech, Kilion and
Mahlon. 10 I have also acquired Ruth the
Moabitess,[h] Mahlon's widow, as my
wife,[i] in order to maintain the name of
the dead with his property, so that his
name will not disappear from among his
family or from the town records.[j] Today
you are witnesses![k]"
11 Then the elders and all those at the
gate[l] said, "We are witnesses.[m] May the
LORD make the woman who is coming
into your home like Rachel and Leah,[n]
who together built up the house of Israel.
May you have standing in Ephrathah[o]
and be famous in Bethlehem.[p] 12 Through
the offspring the LORD gives you by this
young woman, may your family be like
that of Perez,[q] whom Tamar[r] bore to Judah."

The Genealogy of David

4:18–22pp — 1Ch 2:5–15; Mt 1:3–6; Lk 3:31–33

13 So Boaz took Ruth and she became
his wife. Then he went to her, and the
LORD enabled her to conceive,[s] and she
gave birth to a son.[t] 14 The women[u] said
to Naomi: "Praise be to the LORD,[v] who
this day has not left you without a kinsman-redeemer.[w] May he become famous
throughout Israel! 15 He will renew your
life and sustain you in your old age. For
your daughter-in-law,[x] who loves you
and who is better to you than seven
sons,[y] has given him birth."
16 Then Naomi took the child, laid him
in her lap and cared for him. 17 The wom-
en living there said, "Naomi has a son."
And they named him Obed. He was the
father of Jesse,[z] the father of David.[a]
18 This, then, is the family line of
Perez[b]:

Perez was the father of Hezron,[c]
19 Hezron the father of Ram,
Ram the father of Amminadab,[d]

[i]4 Many Hebrew manuscripts, Septuagint, Vulgate and Syriac; most Hebrew manuscripts *he* [j]5 Hebrew; Vulgate and Syriac *Naomi, you acquire Ruth the Moabitess,*

3:18 [p]Ps 37:3-5
4:1 [q]S Ge 18:1; S 23:10 [r]S Ru 2:20 [s]Ru 3:12
4:2 [t]S Ex 3:16 [u]S Dt 25:7
4:3 [v]S Lev 25:25; S Ru 1:2
4:4 [w]S Lev 25:25; Jer 32:7-8
4:5 [x]S Ru 1:22 [y]S Ge 38:8; S Ru 3:13
4:6 [z]Lev 25:25; Ru 3:13 [a]S Dt 25:7
4:7 [b]S Lev 25:24 [c]ver 8 [d]Isa 8:1-2, 16,20 [e]Dt 25:7-9
4:8 [f]Dt 25:9
4:9 [g]Isa 8:2; Jer 32:10,44
4:10 [h]S Ru 1:22 [i]S Dt 25:5 [j]S Dt 25:6 [k]S Jos 24:22
4:11 [l]S Ge 23:10 [m]S Dt 25:9 [n]S Ge 4:19; S 29:16 [o]S Ge 35:16 [p]Ru 1:19
4:12 [q]S Ge 38:29 [r]Ge 38:6,24
4:13 [s]S Ge 8:1; S 29:31 [t]S Ge 29:32; S 30:6; Lk 1:57
4:14 [u]Lk 1:58 [v]S Ge 24:27 [w]S Ru 2:20
4:15 [x]S Ge 11:31 [y]1Sa 1:8; 2:5; Job 1:2
4:17 [z]ver 22; 1Sa 16:1,18; 17:12, 17,58; 1Ch 2:12, 13; Ps 72:20 [a]1Sa 16:13; 1Ch 2:15
4:18 [b]S Ge 38:29 [c]Nu 26:21
4:19 [d]S Ex 6:23

4:11 PRAYER, Intercession—See note on 2:20. The Obed-Jesse line is even more crucial than the original tribal lines. God used this prayer to direct the messianic genealogy (vv 18–22). Intercession may be directed to family matters.
4:13 GOD, Sovereignty—God's sovereign hand is at work even in the natural processes of life. Conception is a very human act, ordained as God's way of continuing the human life He created in the beginning. The eye of faith sees something of the miraculous power of God working within this otherwise human, natural process. Something does not have to defy explanation for the eye of faith to see God's sovereign power at work. The heart of faith thanks God for all of the good things of life, for they are indirectly, if not directly, blessings from God.
4:13–22 HUMANITY, Relationships—The ongoing processes of life are used by God to produce His great leaders and servants. He worked through Naomi's despair to prepare for David.
4:13–22 HISTORY, God's Leaders—See note on Dt 23:3–8. God raised His anointed leader from the unlikely union of a Moabite widow and a respected Israelite farmer. In the normal processes of birth and the passing of generations, God works to direct the history of His people and supply the needed leadership. See Mt 1:5.
4:14–15 PRAYER, Praise—Naomi's friends praised the Lord for fulfilling the law of the kinsman-redeemer (Lev 25:25–28). Boaz was related to Naomi through Naomi's dead husband Elimelech (2:3; 4:3) and was second in line for the role of kinsman-redeemer. He obtained the right of purchase when the first in line refused (4:6). A complex set of circumstances was closely intertwined with the working of prayer. Praise is the proper response to blessings God gives our friends.

20Amminadab the father of Nahshon,[e]
Nahshon the father of Salmon,[k]
21Salmon the father of Boaz,[f]
Boaz the father of Obed,
22Obed the father of Jesse,
and Jesse the father of David.

4:20 [e]S Nu 7:12
4:21 [f]S Ru 2:1

[k]*20* A few Hebrew manuscripts, some Septuagint manuscripts and Vulgate (see also verse 21 and Septuagint of 1 Chron. 2:11); most Hebrew manuscripts *Salma*

4:22 ELECTION, Other Nations—Moabites represented temptation and trouble for Israel (Ex 15:15; Nu 25:1; Ju 3:12–30). That fact of history did not prevent God from using a dedicated Moabite woman to carry out His saving purposes for the world. God works with people from all nations and races to accomplish His will in ways that often surprise His people.

1 Samuel

Theological Setting

Did God choose David and his descendants to lead Israel and Judah? To Christians who know the "rest of the story," it may seem absurd for anyone to question whether David was really God's chosen leader for his people. But for those people who had to give up lands, pay taxes, serve in armies, choose sides in civil wars, and live under a new system of kingship, the question could neither be escaped nor taken lightly. It became literally a matter of life and death as challengers to David's throne forced the people to take sides.

During the period of the judges the Hebrew tribal groups had settled in their territories. Life revolved around the groups. Everyone shared in the land's resources. No central government imposed restrictions on the tribes or made demands on them. But, likewise, no king and his army stood ready to defend them. As other peoples, such as the Philistines, threatened to drive the Israelites out of their homeland, the Israelites were forced to ask whether their system of loose tribal organization was divinely ordained. Would it be ungodly to have an earthly king help them meet the threat of invasion? For many Israelites, the answer to this question was yes. To have an earthly king was to abandon faith in the Lord (1 Sa 8:7). Others, however, came to believe that God could and would act through a king, and they asked Samuel to appoint a king to become the nation's leader (1 Sa 8:5). The difficult process of moving from an old, established form of government to a new government headed by a king brought anguish and confusion to a leader like Samuel (1 Sa 8:6). Samuel described for the people what the new form of government would cost them (1 Sa 8:10-18). But ultimately the people chose to have a king to provide military protection, and God instructed a reluctant Samuel to "give them a king" (1 Sa 8:22).

In unforgettable scenes drawn by an inspired master of the Hebrew language, the books of Samuel describe this transition to kingship under Saul and the emergence of David's dynasty.

But even after David succeeded Saul, the country remained sharply divided over whether David was God's chosen ruler. David's kingdom was made up of two major groups: Judah (southerners) and Israel (northerners). Saul had been identified closely with the northern group of tribes. When the northern people elected David as their king, they affirmed that "the Lord said to you, 'You will shepherd my people Israel' " (2 Sa 5:2). But a number of events caused these northern people to question David's leadership after he became their king: the death of Saul's son, Ishbosheth; the execution of seven of Saul's sons by the Gibeonites with David's approval; and the murder of Saul's commander, Abner, while traveling under David's pledge of safe conduct. After these events, many devout people wondered if they had been wrong.

The writer of 1 and 2 Samuel demonstrated that God, indeed, called David and used him. The writer confronted every issue that caused people to question David and dealt with each forthrightly, describing David as guilty when he was guilty, but defending him brilliantly when he knew David to be guiltless.

Obviously these events lie at the very foundation of the messianic hope in Israel. In them God's everlasting covenant with David emerges as the basis for a hope that yet lives.

Theological Outline

1 Samuel: Looking for a Leader

I. God Gives His People an Example of Dedicated Leadership. (1:1—7:17)
   - A. A dedicated leader is the answer to parental prayers. (1:1-28)
   - B. A dedicated leader comes from grateful, sacrificial parents who worship the incomparable God. (2:1-10)
   - C. A dedicated leader is a priest who faithfully serves God rather than seeking selfish interests. (2:11-36)
   - D. A dedicated leader is a prophet who is called by the Word of God and who faithfully delivers the Word of God. (3:1—4:15)
   - E. Superstitious use of religious relics is not a substitute for dedicated leadership. (4:16-22)

F. Only a dedicated priest, not foreign gods nor disobedient persons, can stand before God. (5:1—7:2)
G. A dedicated political leader is a man of prayer. (7:3-17)

II. Human Kingship Represents a Compromise with God by a People Who Have Rejected the Kingship of God. (8:1—15:35)
A. Hereditary kingship is a rejection of God which hurts His people and separates them from God. (8:1-22; compare Jdg 8:22—9:57)
B. A dedicated king is a humble person from a humble family who knows he owes his position to God's choice. (9:1—10:27)
C. The dedicated king is a Spirit-filled deliverer. (11:1-15)
D. The dedicated leader is morally pure and uses the history of God's people to call them to obedience. (12:1-25)
E. Kingship depends on obedience to God, not human wisdom. (13:1-23)
F. A dedicated leader is used by God to unify and deliver His people. (14:1-23)
G. God delivers His dedicated leader from inadvertent sins. (14:24-46)
H. The king is responsible to defeat the enemies of the people of God. (14:47-52)
I. A disobedient king is rejected by God. (15:1-35)

III. God Raises Up New Leadership for His People. (16:1—31:13)
A. God gives His Spirit to the chosen person meeting His leadership qualifications. (16:1-13)
B. God provides unexpected opportunities of service for His chosen king. (16:14-23)
C. God uses the skills and faith of His leader to defeat those who would defy God. (17:1-58)
D. God provides His presence and the loyalty of friends to protect His chosen one from the jealous plots of an evil leader. (18:1—20:42)
E. God's priests affirm the special position of God's chosen leader. (21:1-9)
F. God protects His benevolent and faithful leader from the vengeance of evil enemies. (21:10—22:23)
G. God heeds the prayer of His chosen and delivers him from treacherous enemies. (23:1-29)
H. God honors the righteousness of His chosen leader. (24:1-22)
I. God avenges His chosen against the insults of foolish enemies. (25:1-39*a*)
J. God provides family for His chosen. (25:39*b*-44)
K. God rewards the righteousness and faithfulness of His chosen leader. (26:1-25)
L. The chosen leader cunningly begins building his kingdom even under adverse circumstances. (27:1-12)
M. God fulfills His prophecy and destroys disobedient leaders. (28:1-25)
N. God protects His chosen leader from compromising situations. (29:1-11)
O. God restores the property taken from His chosen leader. (30:1-20)
P. God's chosen leader shares His goods with the needy and with colleagues. (30:21-31)
Q. God destroys disobedient leaders. (31:1-7)
R. God honors people who express loyalty to their chosen leaders. (31:8-13)

Theological Conclusions

The Books of 1 and 2 Samuel deal with the central themes of the Bible:
1. the activity of God in our history;
2. the consequences of human sin; and
3. the grace of God that is greater than all our sin.

The Books of 1 and 2 Samuel may at first glance seem as if they simply recount human events as they happened. Actually, they do that, but they also do much more. The writer chose just those accounts he needed to show God's work in Israel's history. Each account was intended to show us how God was working.

These books deal with human characters and events that would have made the daily newspapers if there had been any. But make no mistake about it, the writer intended us to see God's hand at work in all of this. Note, for example, the large amount of space given to the very human affairs of Elkanah and his family (1 Sa 1:1-28). In this story of a jealous wife, a frustrated husband, and a miserable, barren woman there are only a few phrases describing something God did (1 Sa 1:5*b*,6*a*,19*b*). But who can doubt that the writer wanted us to understand that even in the midst of this terrible personal situation God was at work bringing into being a Samuel. Or later, almost as if by accident, a David, whom God had just anointed as Saul's eventual successor, suddenly became the obvious choice of Saul's advisors for a musician in Saul's court (1 Sa 16:14-23). Was it mere chance? Nowhere does it say that God sent David to Saul's court, but surely the writer meant us to hear clearly that God was at work bringing about His purpose in the world. The great theme of the Bible is that God incarnates His word, supremely in Jesus of Nazareth, but in some degree in all those who will be used by Him. And how magnificently did this writer show it to be so in the lives of Samuel and David, and, yes, even Saul.

These books also show us so clearly that sin brings its ultimate consequences. There is no mathematics of sin that produces the same results every time one sins, obviously. But sin does have its effect on the individual and the world. Surely, none will forget the lesson that Job's friends taught us in this regard: it is dangerous to try to tie sin to specific human circumstances. Doing so can cause great suffering. And yet, just as a person's positive acts have an effect, so, too, do one's negative acts. Take for example the lurid account of Amnon's sin and its effects (2 Sa 13). As David's oldest son, Amnon would normally have been in line to succeed his father. Instead, his act led to his assassination and the exile of his brother, Absalom. Apparently, this episode also played a part in Absalom's attempt to kill his father and take the throne by force, a revolution that must have caused terrible wounds for the nation. Who knows what might have been?

Thankfully, the Books of 1 and 2 Samuel also magnify the grace of God that is greater than all our sin. Sinners are not simply discarded. There is no clearer demonstration in the Old Testament that we are valued by God "while we were still sinners" (Ro 5:8) than the account of David. Is it not a testimony to God's grace that David overcame his sin to become the model for all kings to come (1 Ki 15:5; 2 Ki 18:3)? In the Books of 1 and 2 Samuel, human sin is set clearly within the context of God's everlasting love and grace. God made an everlasting covenant with David that was not dependent on perfect righteousness (2 Sa 7:14-16). This affirmation of God's continuing love even to those who sin (2 Sa 7:15) became the foundation block of the messianic hope that God would not leave His people without a savior. It runs from beginning to end of these great works, appearing in Hannah's praise of the Lord, who "raises the poor from the dust . . . he seats them with princes and has them inherit a throne of honor" (1 Sa 2:8) and again at the end in David's testimony that He has "made with me an everlasting covenant" (2 Sa 23:5).

Contemporary Teaching

The Books of 1 and 2 Samuel are complex and many-faceted works. No simple listing of applications of their teachings could begin to do them justice. But clearly, these works can help us focus our attention especially on some major issues.

These books remind us that God is not tied to political systems. They help us see that God is supreme over systems and can be worshiped—or abandoned—in any one of them.

The note of apology for David that runs throughout these books points vividly to the truth that events can never be separated from the perspectives of those who witness and interpret them. Many, like Shimei (2 Sa 16:7), held David personally responsible for their losses and pain. The writer of these books saw another side of David, a repentant side, a David who kept promises and grieved when he could not prevent suffering caused by others under him. Thus these books call us to examine our biases and our motives when we are prone to be critical of others. They also remind us to look for the hand of God at work even in the lives of those we distrust.

The Books of 1 and 2 Samuel challenge us to confess that God is in our everyday world. Remember that God was using a family some of whose members hated each other (the Hannah account), that God was involved in a change of government, in revolutions, in dealing with human beings such as David and Bathsheba, and in the affairs of a king who had to make life and death decisions about people (2 Sa 19:21-23). First and Second Samuel suggest that the world of everyday life needs to be made central in our thinking about God. We need to see God in our daily lives so we can properly enter into His holy places to praise His name as Hannah did (1 Sa 2).

Chapter 1

The Birth of Samuel

THERE was a certain man from Ramathaim,[a] a Zuphite[a][b] from the hill
country[c] of Ephraim,[d] whose name was
Elkanah[e] son of Jeroham, the son of Elihu, the son of Tohu, the son of Zuph, an
Ephraimite. 2 He had two wives;[f] one
was called Hannah and the other Peninnah. Peninnah had children, but Hannah
had none.
3 Year after year[g] this man went up
from his town to worship[h] and sacrifice
to the LORD Almighty at Shiloh,[i] where
Hophni and Phinehas, the two sons of
Eli,[j] were priests of the LORD. 4 Whenever the day came for Elkanah to sacrifice,[k]
he would give portions of the meat to his
wife Peninnah and to all her sons and
daughters.[l] 5 But to Hannah he gave a
double portion[m] because he loved her,
and the LORD had closed her womb.[n]
6 And because the LORD had closed her
womb, her rival kept provoking her in
order to irritate her.[o] 7 This went on year
after year. Whenever Hannah went up to
the house of the LORD, her rival provoked
her till she wept and would not eat.[p] 8 Elkanah her husband would say to her,
"Hannah, why are you weeping? Why
don't you eat? Why are you downheart-
ed? Don't I mean more to you than ten
sons?[q]"

9 Once when they had finished eating
and drinking in Shiloh, Hannah stood up.
Now Eli the priest was sitting on a chair
by the doorpost of the LORD's temple.[b][r]
10 In bitterness of soul[s] Hannah wept
much and prayed to the LORD. 11 And she
made a vow,[t] saying, "O LORD Almighty[u], if you will only look upon your
servant's misery and remember[v] me, and
not forget your servant but give her a son,
then I will give him to the LORD for all the
days of his life,[w] and no razor[x] will ever
be used on his head."
12 As she kept on praying to the LORD,
Eli observed her mouth. 13 Hannah was
praying in her heart, and her lips were
moving but her voice was not heard. Eli
thought she was drunk 14 and said to her,
"How long will you keep on getting
drunk? Get rid of your wine."
15 "Not so, my lord," Hannah replied,
"I am a woman who is deeply troubled.[y]
I have not been drinking wine or beer; I
was pouring[z] out my soul to the LORD.
16 Do not take your servant for a wicked
woman; I have been praying here out of
my great anguish and grief."[a]
17 Eli answered, "Go in peace,[b] and
may the God of Israel grant you what you
have asked of him.[c]"
18 She said, "May your servant find

1:1 [a]S Jos 18:25 [b]1Sa 9:5 [c]Jos 17:17-18 [d]Jos 21:20-22 [e]1Ch 6:27,34
1:2 [f]S Ge 4:19
1:3 [g]ver 21; Ex 23:14; 1Sa 2:19; 20:6,29; Lk 2:41 [h]Dt 12:5-7 [i]S Jos 18:1 [j]1Sa 2:31; 14:3
1:4 [k]Lev 7:15-18; Dt 12:17-18 [l]S Ge 29:34
1:5 [m]S Ge 37:3 [n]S Ge 11:30; S 29:31
1:6 [o]S Ge 16:4
1:7 [p]2Sa 12:17; Ps 102:4
1:8 [q]S Ru 4:15
1:9 [r]1Sa 3:3
1:10 [s]Job 3:20; 7:11; 10:1; 21:25; 23:2; 27:2; Isa 38:15; Jer 20:18
1:11 [t]S Jdg 11:30 [u]S Ge 17:1; Ps 24:10; 46:7; Isa 1:9 [v]S Ge 8:1 [w]S Jdg 13:7 [x]Nu 6:1-21; Jdg 13:5; Lk 1:15
1:15 [y]2Ki 4:27 [z]Ps 42:4; 62:8; La 2:19
1:16 [a]Ps 55:2
1:17 [b]Nu 6:26; 1Sa 20:42; 2Ki 5:19; S Ac 15:33 [c]S Ge 25:21; Ps 20:3-5

[a] *1* Or *from Ramathaim Zuphim* [b] *9* That is, tabernacle

---

1:5,19–20 GOD, Grace—God works His grace in our lives in mysterious ways. He prepared a leader in Israel's great moment of crisis by working in the life of a barren woman. He graciously heard Hannah's prayer and came to the aid of the anguished woman. In His grace God has the power to direct circumstances in our lives to accomplish His purposes. We may not always understand, as Hannah did not understand her barren state. We can trust God to work out what is best for us and His people as a whole. See notes on Jdg 9:23–24,56–57; Ru 4:13.

1:5 EVIL AND SUFFERING, Divine Origin—Humans may formulate scientific explanations for life's processes, but science can never provide ultimate answers. Hannah could not become pregnant and have children. Whatever the physical or psychological causes, she knew the ultimate explanation. God had not blessed her with children. Such an explanation is a theological confession of faith. It does not lead to determinism, saying God has absolute control over every occurrence of life overriding human freedom and natural law. Rather the person of faith recognizes God's sovereign rule over life and acknowledges His working in our lives to accomplish His purposes.

1:8 HUMANITY, Commitment—The loving commitment of husband and wife should be the most precious experience in life.

1:9–28 WORSHIP, Obedience—Hannah's obedience to God revealed the depth and the genuineness of her worship. Her humble worship included weeping, praying, and making a vow. Her prayer was silent and internal, pouring her anguished, grieving soul out to God. See notes on 15:22–23; Jdg 20:26.

1:9–28; 2:18–21,26 FAMILY, Worship—Elkanah and his two wives Hannah and Peninnah were devout in their worship of the Lord even though Peninnah made fun of Hannah because she had borne no children. Hannah's devotion is clearly set forth in her fervent prayer life which received God's answer in the birth of Samuel. The depth of her devotion and that of her husband is demonstrated in their willingness to give Samuel to Eli, the priest, to grow up serving God in the Temple. She was fulfilling literally the consecration of the firstborn son commanded in Ex 13:1–2 in remembrance of the deliverance of the people from Egyptian bondage rather than redeeming the son (Ex 13:14; Nu 3:40–51; 18:14–16). Abraham showed such committed religious devotion in his willingness to sacrifice his only son (Ge 22:1–14). The supreme example is the sacrifice of Jesus Christ, God's only Son, on the cross. Christian families today express the depth of their religious devotion in giving sons and daughters to the ministry of missions and witness throughout the world as well as in encouraging Christian growth while at home.

1:10–17 PRAYER, Personal—Hannah's prayer is one of the most effective prayers in the Bible. She began with an appeal to the mighty power of God. She prayed with earnestness, reverence, and humility. Her prayer for a son went beyond the Nazirite vow (Nu 6:1–21), for she relinquished her parental rights. She prayed silently. See note on Ge 28:20–21. Elkanah affirmed her vow (Nu 30:10–15), for she was allowed to carry it out fully (1:28). Any matter we care enough to cry about, we should care enough to pray about. At times only the heart can pray. Words do not truly express our feelings and desires (Ro 8:26). We can trust God with the deepest feelings of our soul. Eli eventually added his prayer to Hannah's. In times of need, the prayers of other people encourage and strengthen us.

1:14–15 CHRISTIAN ETHICS, Alcohol—An interesting survey can be made of passages like Ac 2:13–15 and Eph 5:18, in which behavior is confused between one who is filled with spirits and one who is filled with the Spirit. A conclusion to be reached is that a euphoric level of life brought on by the use of alcohol pales in comparison to the sustaining euphoria brought by the Spirit of God.

favor in your eyes.[d]" Then she went her
way and ate something, and her face was
no longer downcast.[e]
19 Early the next morning they arose
and worshiped before the LORD and then
went back to their home at Ramah.[f] Elkanah lay with Hannah his wife, and the
LORD remembered[g] her. 20 So in the
course of time Hannah conceived and
gave birth to a son.[h] She named[i] him
Samuel,[c][j] saying, "Because I asked the
LORD for him."

Hannah Dedicates Samuel

21 When the man Elkanah went up with
all his family to offer the annual[k] sacrifice to the LORD and to fulfill his vow,[l]
22 Hannah did not go. She said to her husband, "After the boy is weaned, I will
take him and present[m] him before the
LORD, and he will live there always."
23 "Do what seems best to you," Elkanah her husband told her. "Stay here until you have weaned him; only may the
LORD make good[n] his[d] word." So the
woman stayed at home and nursed her
son until she had weaned[o] him.
24 After he was weaned, she took the
boy with her, young as he was, along
with a three-year-old bull,[e][p] an ephah[f]
of flour and a skin of wine, and brought
him to the house of the LORD at Shiloh.
25 When they had slaughtered the bull,
they brought the boy to Eli, 26 and she said
to him, "As surely as you live, my lord, I
am the woman who stood here beside
you praying to the LORD. 27 I prayed[q] for
this child, and the LORD has granted me
what I asked of him. 28 So now I give him
to the LORD. For his whole life[r] he will
be given over to the LORD." And he worshiped the LORD there.

1:18 [d]S Ge 18:3; Ru 2:13 [e]Ro 15:13
1:19 [f]S Jos 18:25 [g]S Ge 8:1; S 29:31
1:20 [h]S Ge 17:19; S 29:32; S 30:6 [i]Ex 2:10; Mt 1:21 [j]1Sa 7:5; 12:23; 1Ch 6:27; Jer 15:1; Heb 11:32
1:21 [k]S ver 3 [l]S Ge 28:20; Nu 30:2; Dt 12:11
1:22 [m]Ex 13:2; Lk 2:22
1:23 [n]S Ge 25:21 [o]Ge 21:8
1:24 [p]Nu 15:8-10
1:27 [q]1Sa 2:20; Ps 66:19-20
1:28 [r]S Jdg 13:7
2:1 [s]Lk 1:46-55 [t]Ps 13:5; 33:21; Zec 10:7 [u]Ps 18:2; 89:17,24; 148:14 [v]Ps 6:8 [w]S Nu 10:35; Ps 6:10
2:2 [x]S Ex 15:11; S Lev 11:44 [y]S Ex 8:10; Isa 40:25; 46:5 [z]S Ge 49:24; S Ex 33:22; Dt 32:37; 2Sa 22:2, 32; 23:3; Ps 31:3; 71:3
2:3 [a]Ps 17:10; 31:18; 73:8; 75:4; 94:4 [b]S Jos 22:22 [c]1Sa 16:7; 1Ki 8:39; 1Ch 28:9; 2Ch 6:30; Pr 15:11; Jer 11:20; 17:10 [d]Pr 16:2; 24:11-12
2:4 [e]2Sa 1:27; Ps 37:15; 46:9; 76:3 [f]Job 17:9; Isa 40:31; 41:1; 52:1; 57:10
2:5 [g]Lk 1:53 [h]Ps 113:9; Isa 54:1; Jer 15:9
2:6 [i]Dt 32:39

Chapter 2

Hannah's Prayer

THEN Hannah prayed and said:[s]
"My heart rejoices[t] in the LORD;
in the LORD my horn[g][u] is lifted high.
My mouth boasts[v] over my enemies,[w]
for I delight in your deliverance.

2 "There is no one holy[h][x] like[y] the LORD;
there is no one besides you;
there is no Rock[z] like our God.

3 "Do not keep talking so proudly
or let your mouth speak such arrogance,[a]
for the LORD is a God who knows,[b]
and by him deeds[c] are weighed.[d]

4 "The bows of the warriors are broken,[e]
but those who stumbled are armed with strength.[f]
5 Those who were full hire themselves out for food,
but those who were hungry[g] hunger no more.
She who was barren[h] has borne seven children,
but she who has had many sons pines away.

6 "The LORD brings death and makes alive;[i]

[c] *20 Samuel* sounds like the Hebrew for *heard of God.*
[d] *23* Masoretic Text; Dead Sea Scrolls, Septuagint and Syriac *your*
[e] *24* Dead Sea Scrolls, Septuagint and Syriac; Masoretic Text *with three bulls*
[f] *24* That is, probably about 3/5 bushel (about 22 liters)
[g] *1 Horn* here symbolizes strength; also in verse 10.
[h] *2* Or *no Holy One*

1:19–20 HUMANITY, Birth—Birth, a normal and natural life process, is also a gift of life which only God can give. Particularly in the Old Testament, names given to children expressed the hope and faith of parents.

1:20 PRAYER, Will of God—Samuel's birth was a clear answer to prayer. We need to recognize God's work in our lives in answer to our prayers and praise Him for it. Petition is not complete until praise has been given for God's response.

1:21–28 HUMANITY, Childhood and Youth—Parents are responsible for dedicating their children to the Lord. While contemporary society would not carry this out in such a drastic form as did ancient Israel, the need is no less real. Children should grow up with the awareness of devotion by parents to the purposes of God.

1:23 PRAYER, Personal—Elkanah affirmed Hannah's vow. See note on 1:10–17. He prayed for God to act as He said. Such a prayer is an affirmation of God's fidelity more than a petition. What God promises, He will do.

1:26–28 PRAYER, Worship—An answer to prayer should call forth worship. A vow should be fulfilled. See note on v 20.

2:1–10 EVIL AND SUFFERING, God's Present Help—Just as faith acknowledges God's working in the sorrows of life (1:5), so it expresses gratitude to God for providing help and bringing joy to replace sorrow. God exercises ultimate control over life and death, success and suffering. Eventually He will reward the faithful and punish the wicked. Only when He has completed His work in human history will we truly be able to see what is evil and what is good.

2:2–10 PRAYER, Praise—Psalm-like in form, this prayer is one of the most elevated praise-poems in the Bible. Hannah praised God's uniqueness, His justice, and His power and sovereignty. Previously afflicted by barrenness, she perceived clearly His dealing with the weak, the hungry, and the barren. She attached her prayer to hope for God's kingdom. Praise flows for God's nature, for specific actions, and for the signs of His kingdom coming on earth.

2:3 GOD, Wisdom—God is well aware of what is taking place in His world. Nothing escapes His attention. He is not a distant God, far removed from His people, unaware of their needs or their deeds. He is not like an idol, unable to know or respond. Nor is He isolated by time or space. He is living and knows what is happening. God's all-knowing wisdom warns us to be aware of what we say and do because God knows us and will hold us accountable.

2:6–10 GOD, Sovereignty—Hannah praised God for being in control of His world: His purposes will be achieved. We can rest assured that God is sovereign, in control, and will ultimately accomplish His will on earth. See note on Ge 15:13–16.

2:6–10 LAST THINGS, Unbelievers' Death—The con-

he brings down to the grave[i] and
raises up.[j]
7The LORD sends poverty and wealth;[k]
he humbles and he exalts.[l]
8He raises[m] the poor[n] from the dust[o]
and lifts the needy[p] from the ash heap;
he seats them with princes
and has them inherit a throne of honor.[q]

"For the foundations[r] of the earth are the LORD's;
upon them he has set the world.
9He will guard the feet[s] of his saints,[t]
but the wicked will be silenced in darkness.[u]

"It is not by strength[v] that one prevails;
10 those who oppose the LORD will be shattered.[w]
He will thunder[x] against them from heaven;
the LORD will judge[y] the ends of the earth.

"He will give strength[z] to his king
and exalt the horn[a] of his anointed."

11Then Elkanah went home to Ramah,[b] but the boy ministered[c] before
the LORD under Eli the priest.

Eli's Wicked Sons

12Eli's sons were wicked men; they
had no regard[d] for the LORD. 13Now it
was the practice[e] of the priests with the
people that whenever anyone offered a
sacrifice and while the meat[f] was being
boiled, the servant of the priest would
come with a three-pronged fork in his
hand. 14He would plunge it into the pan
or kettle or caldron or pot, and the priest
would take for himself whatever the fork
brought up. This is how they treated all
the Israelites who came to Shiloh. 15But
even before the fat was burned, the servant of the priest would come and say to
the man who was sacrificing, "Give the
priest some meat to roast; he won't accept boiled meat from you, but only
raw."

16If the man said to him, "Let the fat[g]
be burned up first, and then take whatever you want," the servant would then answer, "No, hand it over now; if you
don't, I'll take it by force."

17This sin of the young men was very
great in the LORD's sight, for they[j] were
treating the LORD's offering with contempt.[h]

18But Samuel was ministering[i] before
the LORD—a boy wearing a linen
ephod.[j] 19Each year his mother made
him a little robe and took it to him when
she went up with her husband to offer
the annual[k] sacrifice. 20Eli would bless
Elkanah and his wife, saying, "May the
LORD give you children by this woman to
take the place of the one she prayed[l] for
and gave to the LORD." Then they would
go home. 21And the LORD was gracious to
Hannah;[m] she conceived and gave birth
to three sons and two daughters. Meanwhile, the boy Samuel grew[n] up in the
presence of the LORD.

22Now Eli, who was very old, heard

2:6 [j]Isa 26:19; Eze 37:3,12 **2:7** [k]S Dt 8:18 [l]Job 5:11; 40:12; Ps 75:7; Isa 2:12; 13:11; 22:19; Da 4:37 **2:8** [m]Ps 113:7-8 [n]Jas 2:5 [o]1Ki 16:2 [p]Ps 72:12; 107:41; 145:14; 146:8; S Mt 23:12 [q]2Sa 7:8; Job 36:7; Isa 22:23; Eze 21:26 [r]Job 15:7; 38:4; Ps 104:5; Pr 8:29; Isa 40:12; Jer 10:12 **2:9** [s]Ps 91:12; 121:3; Pr 3:26 [t]Pr 2:8 [u]Job 10:22; Isa 5:30; 8:22; 59:9; 60:2; Jer 13:16; Am 5:18, 20; Zep 1:14-15; Mt 8:12 [v]1Sa 17:47; Ps 33:16-17; Zec 4:6 **2:10** [w]S Ex 15:6 [x]S Ex 19:16; 1Sa 7:10; 12:17; 2Sa 22:14; Job 37:4, 5; 38:1; Ps 18:13; 29:3; Isa 66:6 [y]Ps 96:13; 98:9; Mt 25:31-32 [z]Ps 18:1; 21:1; 59:16 [a]S Dt 33:17; Ps 89:24; S Lk 1:69 **2:11** [b]S Jos 18:25 [c]ver 18; S Nu 16:9; 1Sa 3:1 **2:12** [d]Jer 2:8; 9:6 **2:13** [e]Dt 18:3 [f]Lev 7:35-36 **2:16** [g]Lev 3:3, 14-16; 7:29-34 **2:17** [h]ver 22,29; S Nu 14:11; Jer 7:21; Eze 22:26; Mal 2:7-9 **2:18** [i]S ver 11 [j]ver 28; 1Sa 22:18; 23:9; 2Sa 6:14; 1Ch 15:27 **2:19** [k]S 1Sa 1:3 **2:20** [l]S 1Sa 1:27 **2:21** [m]Ge 21:1 [n]S Jdg 13:24; Lk 1:80; 2:40

[i]6 Hebrew *Sheol* [j]17 Or *men*

cept of death in the Old Testament is largely of something fearful and foreboding. The issues of life and death are in God's hands. This may be all this passage intended to say. Only a few Old Testament passages clearly set forth a resurrection hope. The language here is quite compatible with later biblical passages on death and resurrection for individuals. The death of the wicked was seen as a silencing in darkness.

2:12–36 EVIL AND SUFFERING, Punishment—Nothing can prevent God from punishing a wicked person when God determines to do so. Such punishment may bring sorrow and emotional suffering to others. When human sin, especially that of religious leaders, deserves punishment, God in His way and time punishes. No leader or group of leaders is indispensable to God. If they deserve punishment because of immoral deeds, they may expect God to discipline them.

2:12–17 SIN, Moral Insensitivity—Though Eli was himself a righteous man and a great leader of Israel, his sons were wicked. They filled important religious positions but were totally inept and unqualified. Their wickedness is demonstrated in their lack of regard for priestly customs regarding their portion of the sacrifices brought to the altar. Righteous parents are no guarantee of righteous children. Spiritual office is no guarantee of spiritual leaders.

2:12–17,22–25; 8:1–3 FAMILY, Parental Failure—Parenthood means devoting prime time to loving and training children even if other good works must be left undone. The children of two devout men, Eli and Samuel, violated the faith of the homes in which they grew by using the office of priest for personal gain through bribery. The Bible gives us little insight into the home life of these two families, but the disobedience of the sons to parents and to God is clearly evident. Parental responsibilities can be neglected by parents while doing important things for God in the church and community. To be sure that family life is not usurped so drastically by other concerns, mothers and fathers are faced with making the best choices for use of their time when children are young. Many things are valuable and important, but nothing is so important as to justify neglecting children.

2:20–21 GOD, Grace—God was exceedingly gracious to Hannah. He not only answered Hannah's anguished cry for a child, but blessed her with other children after her unselfish, faithful dedication of Samuel to the service of the Lord. God's grace usually comes to us far beyond what we could ask or deserve. See note on Ge 19:12–19,29.

2:20–21 PRAYER, Petition—Repeatedly the Bible records instances of prayer and answer. Petition is not a pious exercise seeking merit from God. It is a sincere conversation looking for action from God.

2:22–25 SIN, Punishment—Only God's punishing intervention can rescue God's people from some leaders of religious institutions. Eli's sons openly violated God's instructions. In love and grief their father warned them to give up their evil practices, but they would not. Thus, God intervened to punish them. Human mediation cannot avert punishment for flagrant

about everything[o] his sons were doing to
all Israel and how they slept with the
women[p] who served at the entrance to
the Tent of Meeting. 23So he said to
them, "Why do you do such things? I
hear from all the people about these
wicked deeds of yours. 24No, my sons; it
is not a good report that I hear spreading
among the LORD's people. 25If a man sins
against another man, God[k] may mediate
for him; but if a man sins against the
LORD, who will[q] intercede[r] for him?"
His sons, however, did not listen to their
father's rebuke, for it was the LORD's will
to put them to death.
26And the boy Samuel continued to
grow[s] in stature and in favor with the
LORD and with men.[t]

Prophecy Against the House of Eli

27Now a man of God[u] came to Eli and
said to him, "This is what the LORD says:
'Did I not clearly reveal myself to your
father's house when they were in Egypt
under Pharaoh? 28I chose[v] your father
out of all the tribes of Israel to be my
priest, to go up to my altar, to burn incense,[w] and to wear an ephod[x] in my
presence. I also gave your father's house
all the offerings[y] made with fire by the
Israelites. 29Why do you[1] scorn my sacrifice and offering[z] that I prescribed for my
dwelling?[a] Why do you honor your sons
more than me by fattening yourselves on
the choice parts of every offering made by
my people Israel?'
30"Therefore the LORD, the God of Israel, declares: 'I promised that your house
and your father's house would minister
before me forever.[b]' But now the LORD
declares: 'Far be it from me! Those who
honor me I will honor,[c] but those who
despise[d] me will be disdained.[e] 31The
time is coming when I will cut short your
strength and the strength of your father's
house, so that there will not be an old
man in your family line[f] 32and you will
see distress[g] in my dwelling. Although
good will be done to Israel, in your family
line there will never be an old man.[h]
33Every one of you that I do not cut off
from my altar will be spared only to blind
your eyes with tears and to grieve your
heart, and all your descendants[i] will die
in the prime of life.
34" 'And what happens to your two
sons, Hophni and Phinehas, will be a
sign[j] to you—they will both die[k] on the
same day.[l] 35I will raise up for myself a
faithful priest,[m] who will do according to
what is in my heart and mind. I will firmly establish his house, and he will minister before my anointed[n] one always.
36Then everyone left in your family line
will come and bow down before him for a
piece of silver and a crust of bread and
plead,[o] "Appoint me to some priestly office so I can have food to eat.[p]" ' "

Chapter 3

The LORD Calls Samuel

THE boy Samuel ministered[q] before
the LORD under Eli. In those days the
word of the LORD was rare;[r] there were
not many visions.[s]
2One night Eli, whose eyes[t] were becoming so weak that he could barely
see,[u] was lying down in his usual place.

2:22 [o]S ver 17 [p]S Ex 38:8
2:25 [q]Ex 4:21; Jos 11:20 [r]S Ex 32:10; S Nu 11:2; 1Sa 3:14; 1Ki 13:6; Job 9:33; Ps 106:30; Isa 1:18; 22:14; Jer 15:1; Heb 10:26
2:26 [s]S Jdg 13:24; Lk 2:52 [t]Pr 3:4
2:27 [u]S Dt 33:1; S Jdg 13:6
2:28 [v]S Ex 28:1 [w]S Ex 30:7 [x]1Sa 22:18; 23:6,9; 30:7 [y]Lev 7:35-36
2:29 [z]ver 12-17 [a]S Dt 12:5
2:30 [b]S Ex 29:9 [c]Ps 50:23; 91:15; Pr 8:17 [d]Isa 53:3; Na 3:6; Mal 2:9 [e]Jer 18:10
2:31 [f]1Sa 4:11-18; 22:16
2:32 [g]1Sa 4:3; 22:17-20; Jer 7:12, 14 [h]1Ki 2:26-27
2:33 [i]Jer 29:32; Mal 2:12
2:34 [j]S Dt 13:2 [k]1Sa 4:11 [l]1Ki 13:3
2:35 [m]2Sa 8:17; 20:25; 1Ki 1:8,32; 2:35; 4:4; 1Ch 16:39; 29:22; Eze 44:15-16 [n]1Sa 9:16; 10:1; 16:13; 2Sa 2:4; 12:7; 23:1; 1Ki 1:34; Ps 89:20
2:36 [o]Eze 44:10-14 [p]1Sa 3:12; 1Ki 2:27
3:1 [q]S 1Sa 2:11 [r]Ps 74:9; La 2:9; Eze 7:26 [s]Am 8:11
3:2 [t]1Sa 4:15 [u]S Ge 27:1

[k]25 Or *the judges* [1]29 The Hebrew is plural.

rebellion against God. Righteous parents cannot prevent their unrighteous offspring from receiving punishment for their sins.

2:26 SALVATION, Sanctification—God's salvation includes sanctification. Sanctification is growth in holiness, or becoming more like God in character and conduct. The child Samuel was being sanctified under Eli's direction. Compare Lk 1:80; 2:52.

2:27–36 HISTORY, God's Leaders—God's revelation in history should be sufficient motivation for His chosen leaders to remain faithful to Him. Leaders cannot expect to retain positions when they ignore God and His expectations. God is not bound to honor unfaithful leaders.

2:29 SIN, Against God—Religious leadership positions do not immunize a person from God's judgment. Eli's failure to control worship practices at God's house and to correct his sons' sinful behavior led God to find a different leader for His people's worship (v 35). God reacts strongly against those who openly defy Him.

2:30–34 ELECTION, Freedom—Election is no guarantee of blessings for all generations. Those who honor God are honored by God. Those who dishonor God are dishonored by God. Eli and his priestly sons were elected to honor God. The disobedient sons did not take God's covenant seriously. God retains freedom over His announcements so that humans cannot hold God hostage and force Him into actions contrary to His purposes. God will not force people to serve Him against their wills. A generation which will not take its identity in light of election promises does not have to enter the elect people of God. See note on Dt 29:1—30:20.

2:35 ELECTION, Leadership—Faithless leaders disciplined by God do not leave His people leaderless. God raises up faithful leaders for His elect. Compare 1 Ki 2:35.

3:1–10 REVELATION, Word—The personal call of Samuel is explained as coming during a time when God was revealing little to His people. God's revelation came in the last moments of the night in the place where He had many times declared His purposes. As a priest's apprentice and dedicated to God at birth (2:2–21), Samuel slept near the sacred tent. The combination of proximity to the sanctuary and time of sleep suggest a dream-revelaton from God. Three times the boy heard God's voice call him. Only with Eli's help did he understand that God was speaking to him. God can give His prophetic word to people of all ages. He may have to use an experienced teacher to help the person called out know that God is calling. Calling comes at God's decision and in His timing. Not every generation has the same number of revelations.

3:1–19 EVANGELISM, Obedience—God's call to speak His word comes, and those He calls are to obey. Obedience to the call of God is an essential motive in the task of evangelism. The doctrine of evangelism demands obeying God as He commits to us the task of witnessing. We are servants. That means obedience even if the message is a difficult one as in young Samuel's case. See Knowing and Experiencing the Will of God, pp. 1794–1796.

3The lamp[v] of God had not yet gone out,
and Samuel was lying down in the temple[m][w] of the LORD, where the ark[x] of
God was. 4Then the LORD called Samuel.

Samuel answered, "Here I am.[y]" 5And
he ran to Eli and said, "Here I am; you
called me."

But Eli said, "I did not call; go back and
lie down." So he went and lay down.

6Again the LORD called, "Samuel!" And
Samuel got up and went to Eli and said,
"Here I am; you called me."

"My son," Eli said, "I did not call; go
back and lie down."

7Now Samuel did not yet know[z] the
LORD: The word[a] of the LORD had not yet
been revealed[b] to him.

8The LORD called Samuel a third time,
and Samuel got up and went to Eli and
said, "Here I am; you called me."

Then Eli realized that the LORD was
calling the boy. 9So Eli told Samuel, "Go
and lie down, and if he calls you, say,
'Speak, LORD, for your servant is listening.' " So Samuel went and lay down in
his place.

10The LORD came and stood there, calling as at the other times, "Samuel! Samuel![c]"

Then Samuel said, "Speak, for your servant is listening."

11And the LORD said to Samuel: "See, I
am about to do something in Israel that
will make the ears of everyone who hears
of it tingle.[d] 12At that time I will carry
out against Eli everything[e] I spoke
against his family—from beginning to
end. 13For I told him that I would judge

3:3 [v]Ex 25:31-38; Lev 24:1-4 [w]1Sa 1:9 [x]Dt 10:1-5; 1Ki 6:19; 8:1
3:4 [y]S Ge 22:1; S Ex 3:4
3:7 [z]1Sa 2:12 [a]Jer 1:2 [b]S Nu 12:6; Am 3:7
3:10 [c]Ex 3:4
3:11 [d]2Ki 21:12; Job 15:21; Jer 19:3
3:12 [e]S 1Sa 2:27-36
3:13 [f]1Ki 1:6
3:14 [g]S 1Sa 2:25
3:17 [h]1Ki 22:14; Jer 23:28; 38:14; 42:4 [i]S Ru 1:17
3:18 [j]S Jdg 10:15
3:19 [k]S Ge 21:22; S Nu 14:43 [l]S Jdg 13:24 [m]1Sa 9:6
3:20 [n]S Jdg 20:1 [o]S Dt 18:22; Eze 33:33
3:21 [p]S Nu 12:6

his family forever because of the sin he
knew about; his sons made themselves
contemptible,[n] and he failed to restrain[f]
them. 14Therefore, I swore to the house
of Eli, 'The guilt of Eli's house will never
be atoned[g] for by sacrifice or offering.' "

15Samuel lay down until morning and
then opened the doors of the house of the
LORD. He was afraid to tell Eli the vision,
16but Eli called him and said, "Samuel,
my son."

Samuel answered, "Here I am."

17"What was it he said to you?" Eli
asked. "Do not hide[h] it from me. May
God deal with you, be it ever so severely,[i] if you hide from me anything he told
you." 18So Samuel told him everything,
hiding nothing from him. Then Eli said,
"He is the LORD; let him do what is good
in his eyes."[j]

19The LORD was with[k] Samuel as he
grew[l] up, and he let none[m] of his words
fall to the ground. 20And all Israel from
Dan to Beersheba[n] recognized that Samuel was attested as a prophet of the
LORD.[o] 21The LORD continued to appear
at Shiloh, and there he revealed[p] himself
to Samuel through his word.

Chapter 4

AND Samuel's word came to all Israel.

The Philistines Capture the Ark

Now the Israelites went out to fight
against the Philistines. The Israelites

[m]3 That is, tabernacle [n]13 Masoretic Text; an ancient Hebrew scribal tradition and Septuagint *sons blasphemed God*

3:7 SALVATION, Definition—Intimate knowledge of God is necessary for salvation. Saving knowledge is revealed by God Himself through His living and written Word. Such knowledge is based on personal experience and not on accumulation of facts. God takes the initiative in making Himself known to persons.

3:12–14 GOD, Wrath—God told Samuel that no atonement can cover continued, willful, deliberate sin. The sacrificial system was never meant to cover the sins of a high hand, that is, sins committed knowingly in flagrant disobedience to God. If such sins were ever to be forgiven, it could only be by the grace of God. All forgiveness of sins provided for in the offering of sacrifices ultimately came through the grace of God, not the sacrifices themselves. The sacrificial system was simply the method God provided for the people to follow in seeking forgiveness. Forgiveness of sins only comes from God, and only to those who are repentant, approaching God in a sincere quest for forgiveness. That was what the sons of Eli apparently lacked.

3:13 SIN, Punishment—See notes on 2:22–25, 29.

3:14 SALVATION, Atonement—Samuel's hard message from God to Eli was that his guilt would never be atoned for by sacrifice or offering. See notes on Lev 5:5–18; Nu 8:12,21. God is free to refuse to cover over the sins we try to cover up. When sin becomes a habit and a person refuses to repent, people cannot expect forgiveness. Compare Isa 22:14.

4:1–22 REVELATION, Divine Presence—The ark had long been associated with God's presence and favor (Ex 25:10–22; 40:3–21). It led their wilderness journeys, symbolizing God's direction (Nu 10:33–36; 14:44) and housing God's covenant tablets (Dt 10:1–5). In Joshua the ark led across Jordan (3—4) and into battle (ch 6). It came to represent God's presence in Israel's worship (1 Sa 3:3; Jos 8:33; Jdg 20:27). Israel's enemies saw the ark as a sure sign of the power of Israel's God. Israel tended to think the mere presence of the ark guaranteed God would reveal His power in battle. God punished such religious pride by allowing the ark to be captured. No physical symbol can guarantee God's presence. Symbols can become more precious to a people than the actual presence of God.

4:1–11 HISTORY, God—God's reputation based on previous historical experience may frighten the enemy, but His people cannot substitute rituals and symbols for His real presence. God chooses to lead and give victory to His people according to His plans and purposes. He is free to let an unfaithful people meet defeat and failure. Knowledge of the Exodus made the Philistines afraid. The ark of the covenant could not bring victory apart from the God of the covenant.

4:1–10 CHRISTIAN ETHICS, War and Peace—Israel used the ark in much the same way a good luck charm is used by some people. The people thought the symbol of God's presence guaranteed His presence and blessing. Apparently no one sought God's will in the matter. Thus, the Israelites went into battle without the blessing of God. No people can presume upon God and expect Him to do their bidding. God is in sovereign control of creation and history. He has the freedom and right to defeat a presumptuous people. See note on Jdg 2:1—3:6.

camped at Ebenezer,[q] and the Philistines at Aphek.[r] 2The Philistines deployed their forces to meet Israel, and as the battle spread, Israel was defeated by the Philistines, who killed about four thousand of them on the battlefield. 3When the soldiers returned to camp, the elders of Israel asked, "Why[s] did the LORD bring defeat upon us today before the Philistines? Let us bring the ark[t] of the LORD's covenant from Shiloh,[u] so that it[o] may go with us[v] and save us from the hand of our enemies."

4So the people sent men to Shiloh, and they brought back the ark of the covenant of the LORD Almighty, who is enthroned between the cherubim.[w] And Eli's two sons, Hophni and Phinehas, were there with the ark of the covenant of God.

5When the ark of the LORD's covenant came into the camp, all Israel raised such a great shout[x] that the ground shook. 6Hearing the uproar, the Philistines asked, "What's all this shouting in the Hebrew[y] camp?"

When they learned that the ark of the LORD had come into the camp, 7the Philistines were afraid.[z] "A god has come into the camp," they said. "We're in trouble! Nothing like this has happened before. 8Woe to us! Who will deliver us from the hand of these mighty gods? They are the gods who struck[a] the Egyptians with all kinds of plagues[b] in the desert. 9Be strong, Philistines! Be men, or you will be subject to the Hebrews, as they[c] have been to you. Be men, and fight!"

10So the Philistines fought, and the Israelites were defeated[d] and every man fled to his tent. The slaughter was very great; Israel lost thirty thousand foot soldiers. 11The ark of God was captured, and Eli's two sons, Hophni and Phinehas, died.[e]

Death of Eli

12That same day a Benjamite[f] ran from the battle line and went to Shiloh, his clothes torn and dust[g] on his head. 13When he arrived, there was Eli[h] sitting on his chair by the side of the road, watching, because his heart feared for the ark of God. When the man entered the town and told what had happened, the whole town sent up a cry.

14Eli heard the outcry and asked, "What is the meaning of this uproar?"

The man hurried over to Eli, 15who was ninety-eight years old and whose eyes[i] were set so that he could not see. 16He told Eli, "I have just come from the battle line; I fled from it this very day."

Eli asked, "What happened, my son?"

17The man who brought the news replied, "Israel fled before the Philistines, and the army has suffered heavy losses. Also your two sons, Hophni and Phinehas, are dead,[j] and the ark of God has been captured."[k]

18When he mentioned the ark of God, Eli fell backward off his chair by the side of the gate. His neck was broken and he died, for he was an old man and heavy. He had led[p][l] Israel forty years.[m]

19His daughter-in-law, the wife of Phinehas, was pregnant and near the time of delivery. When she heard the news that the ark of God had been captured and that her father-in-law and her husband were dead, she went into labor and gave birth, but was overcome by her labor pains. 20As she was dying, the women attending her said, "Don't despair; you have given birth to a son." But she did not respond or pay any attention.

21She named the boy Ichabod,[q][n] saying, "The glory[o] has departed from Israel"—because of the capture of the ark of God and the deaths of her father-in-law and her husband. 22She said, "The glory[p] has departed from Israel, for the ark of God has been captured."[q]

Chapter 5

The Ark in Ashdod and Ekron

AFTER the Philistines had captured the ark of God, they took it from Ebene-

4:1 q1Sa 5:1; 7:12 rJos 12:18; 1Sa 29:1; 1Ki 20:26
4:3 sJos 7:7 tS Jos 6:7 uS Jos 18:1; S 1Sa 2:32 v2Ch 13:8
4:4 wS Ge 3:24; S Ex 25:22
4:5 xS Jos 6:5,10
4:6 yS Ge 14:13
4:7 zS Ex 15:14
4:8 aEx 12:30; 1Sa 5:12 bRev 11:6
4:9 cS Jdg 13:1
4:10 dS Dt 28:25
4:11 ePs 78:64; Jer 7:12
4:12 fEze 24:26; 33:21 gS Jos 7:6; S 2Sa 1:2
4:13 hver 18
4:15 iS 1Sa 3:2
4:17 j1Sa 22:18; Ps 78:64 kPs 78:61
4:18 lS Jdg 2:16; S 16:31 m1Sa 2:31
4:21 nS Ge 35:18 oS Ex 24:16; Ps 106:20; Jer 2:11; Eze 1:28; 9:3; 10:18
4:22 pS Ex 24:16; Ps 78:61 qJer 7:12

o3 Or *he* p18 Traditionally *judged* q21 *Ichabod* means *no glory.*

4:3–11 PRAYER, Hindrances—The Israelites were tempted to regard the ark as a good luck piece or magic charm. They had seen the Jordan part at its presence, but had incorrectly interpreted the divine promise that the presence of God would drive out the heathen tribes (Jos 3:10). God's presence cannot be divorced from His character. The priests, Hophni and Phinehas, had continually acted contrary to the nature of God. To act contrary to God's nature is to demonstrate hostility to God Himself. Neither the presence of the ark nor priests could cause God to violate His character (Isa 59:2). Petition is hindered if not prevented by human arrogance and sin.

4:5–7,21–22 GOD, Glory—The ark of the covenant was extremely important to the Israelites because it was the visible reminder of the covenant between Israel and God. The covenant was the expression of God's grace towards Israel and a reminder of the responsibilities of Israel to God. For the Israelites, the ark of the covenant represented the presence of God Himself. When the ark was captured and taken from Israel, the glory of the Lord departed along with it. Sinful Israel could no longer look to the divine King for leadership. The glory of God in these ancient times was understood as a visible manifestation of the power and wonder of God's presence. See Ex 16:7. The loss of God's powerful presence did not mean God no longer ruled His world. It meant God would not work among a disobedient, rebellious people. God moved to another camp to show His power. See note on Ex 40:34–38.

4:8 SALVATION, As Deliverance—Israel was defeated, and the ark of the covenant was captured in this battle. Deliverance comes through divine decision and action, not human ritual and symbols.

zer[r] to Ashdod.[s] 2Then they carried the
ark into Dagon's temple and set it beside
Dagon.[t] 3When the people of Ashdod
rose early the next day, there was Dagon,
fallen[u] on his face on the ground before
the ark of the LORD! They took Dagon and
put him back in his place. 4But the following morning when they rose, there was
Dagon, fallen on his face on the ground
before the ark of the LORD! His head and
hands had been broken[v] off and were lying on the threshold; only his body remained. 5That is why to this day neither
the priests of Dagon nor any others who
enter Dagon's temple at Ashdod step on
the threshold.[w]

6The LORD's hand[x] was heavy upon
the people of Ashdod and its vicinity; he
brought devastation[y] upon them and afflicted them with tumors.[r][z] 7When the
men of Ashdod saw what was happening,
they said, "The ark of the god of Israel
must not stay here with us, because his
hand is heavy upon us and upon Dagon
our god." 8So they called together all the
rulers[a] of the Philistines and asked them,
"What shall we do with the ark of the god
of Israel?"

They answered, "Have the ark of the
god of Israel moved to Gath.[b]" So they
moved the ark of the God of Israel.

9But after they had moved it, the
LORD's hand was against that city, throwing it into a great panic.[c] He afflicted the
people of the city, both young and old,
with an outbreak of tumors.[s] 10So they
sent the ark of God to Ekron.[d]

As the ark of God was entering Ekron,
the people of Ekron cried out, "They
have brought the ark of the god of Israel
around to us to kill us and our people."
11So they called together all the rulers[e] of
the Philistines and said, "Send the ark of
the god of Israel away; let it go back to its
own place, or it[t] will kill us and our people." For death had filled the city with
panic; God's hand was very heavy upon
it. 12Those who did not die[f] were afflicted with tumors, and the outcry of the city
went up to heaven.

5:1 [r]S 1Sa 4:1 [s]S Jos 11:22; S 13:3
5:2 [t]S Jdg 16:23; Isa 2:18; 19:1; 46:1
5:3 [u]Isa 40:20; 41:7; 46:7; Jer 10:4
5:4 [v]Eze 6:6; Mic 1:7
5:5 [w]Zep 1:9
5:6 [x]S Ex 9:3; Ac 13:11 [y]2Sa 6:7; Ps 78:66 [z]S Ex 15:26; 1Sa 6:5
5:8 [a]S Jdg 16:18 [b]S Jos 11:22
5:9 [c]S Ex 14:24
5:10 [d]S Jos 13:3
5:11 [e]ver 8
5:12 [f]S 1Sa 4:8
6:2 [g]S Ex 7:11; S Isa 44:25
6:3 [h]S Ex 22:29; S 34:20 [i]S Lev 5:15 [j]ver 9
6:4 [k]S Jos 13:3 [l]2Sa 24:25
6:5 [m]S 1Sa 5:6-11 [n]S Jos 7:19; Rev 14:7
6:6 [o]S Ex 4:21 [p]Ex 10:2 [q]S Ex 12:33
6:7 [r]2Sa 6:3; 1Ch 13:7 [s]S Nu 19:2
6:9 [t]S Jos 15:10; 21:16

Chapter 6

The Ark Returned to Israel

WHEN the ark of the LORD had been
in Philistine territory seven
months, 2the Philistines called for the
priests and the diviners[g] and said, "What
shall we do with the ark of the LORD? Tell
us how we should send it back to its
place."

3They answered, "If you return the ark
of the god of Israel, do not send it away
empty,[h] but by all means send a guilt offering[i] to him. Then you will be healed,
and you will know why his hand[j] has not
been lifted from you."

4The Philistines asked, "What guilt offering should we send to him?"

They replied, "Five gold tumors and
five gold rats, according to the number[k]
of the Philistine rulers, because the same
plague[l] has struck both you and your rulers. 5Make models of the tumors[m] and of
the rats that are destroying the country,
and pay honor[n] to Israel's god. Perhaps
he will lift his hand from you and your
gods and your land. 6Why do you hard-
en[o] your hearts as the Egyptians and
Pharaoh did? When he[u] treated them
harshly,[p] did they[q] not send the Israelites out so they could go on their way?

7"Now then, get a new cart[r] ready,
with two cows that have calved and have
never been yoked.[s] Hitch the cows to
the cart, but take their calves away and
pen them up. 8Take the ark of the LORD
and put it on the cart, and in a chest beside it put the gold objects you are sending back to him as a guilt offering. Send it
on its way, 9but keep watching it. If it
goes up to its own territory, toward Beth
Shemesh,[t] then the LORD has brought
this great disaster on us. But if it does not,
then we will know that it was not his
hand that struck us and that it happened
to us by chance."

[r]*6* Hebrew; Septuagint and Vulgate *tumors. And rats appeared in their land, and death and destruction were throughout the city* [s]*9* Or *with tumors in the groin* (see Septuagint) [t]*11* Or *he* [u]*6* That is, God

5:1–5 GOD, One God—No false god can survive in the powerful presence of the one true God. God is concerned to teach all people that He is the only God. Such a dramatic lesson did not reach the Philistines. They tried to ignore God and go about their religion and life as usual. Accepting God's power is not enough. We must commit our lives to worship and serve Him.

5:1–3,9,10 REVELATION, Events—The ark did not guarantee God's presence for a proud people (4:1–22). It represented His powerful presence when His honor was at stake. The Philistines had to reckon with a God whose power was not bound by territories and who was stronger than all their gods. In every town to which the ark was taken, calamities occurred. The God of Israel was unhappy with His people, who had forsaken Him; but He would not be controlled or bound by any nation. God's power was not available for Philistine or Israelite use. God has His own purposes and will use His power only for His will. He reveals that power through specific events in His people's history.

6:1–20 HISTORY, Judgment—God's presence symbolized by the ark brought judgment on the unbelieving Philistines and on irreverent Israelites. News of details of the Exodus were known by the Philistines and motivated their action. They knew some events were directly caused by God, while others were chance happenings according to the natural rules of human and international relationships. God showed He had caused judgment on the Philistines.

10So they did this. They took two such
cows and hitched them to the cart and
penned up their calves. 11They placed the
ark of the LORD on the cart and along
with it the chest containing the gold rats
and the models of the tumors. 12Then the
cows went straight up toward Beth Shemesh, keeping on the road and lowing all
the way; they did not turn to the right or
to the left. The rulers of the Philistines
followed them as far as the border of Beth
Shemesh.
13Now the people of Beth Shemesh
were harvesting their wheat[u] in the valley, and when they looked up and saw
the ark, they rejoiced at the sight. 14The
cart came to the field of Joshua of Beth
Shemesh, and there it stopped beside a
large rock. The people chopped up the
wood of the cart and sacrificed the cows
as a burnt offering[v] to the LORD. 15The
Levites[w] took down the ark of the LORD,
together with the chest containing the
gold objects, and placed them on the
large rock.[x] On that day the people of
Beth Shemesh[y] offered burnt offerings
and made sacrifices to the LORD. 16The
five rulers of the Philistines saw all this
and then returned that same day to
Ekron.
17These are the gold tumors the Philistines sent as a guilt offering to the LORD
—one each[z] for Ashdod, Gaza, Ashkelon, Gath and Ekron. 18And the number
of the gold rats was according to the number of Philistine towns belonging to the
five rulers—the fortified towns with their
country villages. The large rock, on
which[v] they set the ark of the LORD, is a
witness to this day in the field of Joshua
of Beth Shemesh.
19But God struck down[a] some of the
men of Beth Shemesh, putting seventy[w]
of them to death because they had
looked[b] into the ark of the LORD. The
people mourned because of the heavy
blow the LORD had dealt them, 20and the
men of Beth Shemesh asked, "Who can
stand[c] in the presence of the LORD, this
holy[d] God? To whom will the ark go up
from here?"
21Then they sent messengers to the
people of Kiriath Jearim,[e] saying, "The
Philistines have returned the ark of the
LORD. Come down and take it up to your
place." 1So the men of Kiriath Jearim
came and took up the ark[f] of the LORD.
They took it to Abinadab's[g] house on the
hill and consecrated Eleazar his son to
guard the ark of the LORD.

Chapter 7

Samuel Subdues the Philistines at Mizpah

2IT was a long time, twenty years in all,
that the ark remained at Kiriath
Jearim,[h] and all the people of Israel
mourned and sought after the LORD.[i] 3And
Samuel said to the whole house of Israel,
"If you are returning[j] to the LORD with
all your hearts, then rid[k] yourselves of
the foreign gods and the Ashtoreths[l] and
commit[m] yourselves to the LORD and serve
him only,[n] and he will deliver[o] you out of
the hand of the Philistines." 4So the Israelites put away their Baals and Ashtoreths,
and served the LORD only.
5Then Samuel[p] said, "Assemble all Israel at Mizpah[q] and I will intercede[r]
with the LORD for you." 6When they had
assembled at Mizpah,[s] they drew water
and poured[t] it out before the LORD. On
that day they fasted and there they confessed, "We have sinned against the
LORD." And Samuel was leader[x u] of Israel at Mizpah.
7When the Philistines heard that Israel
had assembled at Mizpah, the rulers of
the Philistines came up to attack them.
And when the Israelites heard of it, they
were afraid[v] because of the Philistines.
8They said to Samuel, "Do not stop crying[w] out to the LORD our God for us, that
he may rescue us from the hand of the
Philistines." 9Then Samuel[x] took a suck-
ling lamb and offered it up as a whole
burnt offering to the LORD. He cried out

6:13 [u]S Ge 30:14; Ru 2:23; 1Sa 12:17
6:14 [v]1Sa 11:7; 2Sa 24:22; 1Ki 19:21
6:15 [w]Jos 3:3 [x]ver 18 [y]Jos 21:16
6:17 [z]S Jos 13:3
6:19 [a]2Sa 6:7 [b]S Ex 19:21
6:20 [c]2Sa 6:9; Ps 130:3; Mal 3:2; Rev 6:17 [d]S Lev 11:45
6:21 [e]S Jos 9:17
7:1 [f]S Jos 6:7 [g]2Sa 6:3; 1Ch 13:7
7:2 [h]1Ch 13:5; Ps 132:6 [i]1Ch 13:3
7:3 [j]Dt 30:10; 2Ki 18:5; 23:25; Jer 24:7 [k]S Ge 31:19; S Jos 24:14 [l]S Jdg 2:12-13; 1Sa 12:10; 31:10 [m]Joel 2:12 [n]S Dt 6:13; Mt 4:10; Lk 4:8 [o]S Jdg 2:18
7:5 [p]S 1Sa 1:20; Ps 99:6; Jer 15:1 [q]S Jos 11:3; Jdg 21:5; 1Sa 10:17 [r]S ver 8; S Ge 20:7; S Dt 9:19
7:6 [s]S Jos 11:3 [t]La 2:19 [u]S Jdg 2:16; S 16:31
7:7 [v]1Sa 17:11
7:8 [w]ver 5; S Ex 32:30; S Nu 21:7; 1Sa 12:19,23; 1Ki 18:24; Isa 37:4; Jer 15:1; 27:18
7:9 [x]Ps 99:6

[v]18 A few Hebrew manuscripts (see also Septuagint); most Hebrew manuscripts *villages as far as Greater Abel, where* [w]19 A few Hebrew manuscripts; most Hebrew manuscripts and Septuagint *50,070* [x]6 Traditionally *judge*

6:15 PRAYER, Worship—According to Jos 21:16, Beth Shemesh was a priestly city. The presence of the ark legalized the offerings, and priests were there to present them.

6:19–20 GOD, Holy—Humans in their sinfulness cannot look upon the holy God and live. We cannot take personal liberties with God and the holy places which symbolize His holy presence with His people. We must learn respect and obedience in the presence of the holiness of God. See notes on Ex 3:5–6; 19:10–24; Nu 1:51.

7:3–4 GOD, One God—God wants it clearly understood that He will accept no compromises of loyalty. His people must put away any semblance of worship of other gods if they want His blessing. Compare Ex 20:1–7; Dt 6:4–9; Mt 6:24.

7:3 SALVATION, As Deliverance—Those who expect God to deliver them have to get rid of their idols and serve Him only. See note on Jos 24:15,19.

7:5–11 PRAYER, Intercession—Prayer was the vital factor in Israel's fortunes during the period of the judges. Samuel, the last of the judges, interceded for Israel and led the people to confess sins. As throughout this period, God responded to His people's prayer. Contrite prayer, not military might, brought Israel's deliverance. See note on Jdg 3:9.

7:7–14 CHRISTIAN ETHICS, War and Peace—Israel saw her victory in battle as God's action assuring His people of His presence. They had learned not to presume upon God. See notes on 4:1–10; Jos 10:1–43.

to the LORD on Israel's behalf, and the
LORD answered him.[y]
10While Samuel was sacrificing the
burnt offering, the Philistines drew near
to engage Israel in battle. But that day the
LORD thundered[z] with loud thunder
against the Philistines and threw them
into such a panic[a] that they were routed
before the Israelites. 11The men of Israel
rushed out of Mizpah and pursued the
Philistines, slaughtering them along the
way to a point below Beth Car.
12Then Samuel took a stone[b] and set it
up between Mizpah and Shen. He named
it Ebenezer,[y][c] saying, "Thus far has the
LORD helped us." 13So the Philistines
were subdued[d] and did not invade Israelite territory again.
Throughout Samuel's lifetime, the
hand of the LORD was against the Philistines. 14The towns from Ekron[e] to Gath
that the Philistines had captured from Israel were restored to her, and Israel delivered the neighboring territory from the
power of the Philistines. And there was
peace between Israel and the Amorites.[f]
15Samuel[g] continued as judge[h] over
Israel all[i] the days of his life. 16From year
to year he went on a circuit from Bethel[j]
to Gilgal[k] to Mizpah, judging[l] Israel in
all those places. 17But he always went
back to Ramah,[m] where his home was,
and there he also judged[n] Israel. And he
built an altar[o] there to the LORD.

Chapter 8

Israel Asks for a King

WHEN Samuel grew old, he appointed[p] his sons as judges for Israel.
2The name of his firstborn was Joel and
the name of his second was Abijah,[q] and
they served at Beersheba.[r] 3But his
sons[s] did not walk in his ways. They
turned aside[t] after dishonest gain and accepted bribes[u] and perverted[v] justice.
4So all the elders[w] of Israel gathered
together and came to Samuel at Ramah.[x]
5They said to him, "You are old, and your
sons do not walk in your ways; now appoint a king[y] to lead[z][z] us, such as all
the other nations[a] have."
6But when they said, "Give us a king[b]
to lead us," this displeased[c] Samuel; so
he prayed to the LORD. 7And the LORD
told him: "Listen[d] to all that the people
are saying to you; it is not you they have
rejected,[e] but they have rejected me as
their king.[f] 8As they have done from the
day I brought them up out of Egypt until
this day, forsaking[g] me and serving other
gods, so they are doing to you. 9Now listen to them; but warn them solemnly and
let them know[h] what the king who will
reign over them will do."
10Samuel told[i] all the words of the
LORD to the people who were asking him
for a king. 11He said, "This is what the
king who will reign over you will do: He
will take[j] your sons and make them
serve[k] with his chariots and horses, and
they will run in front of his chariots.[l]
12Some he will assign to be commanders[m] of thousands and commanders of fifties, and others to plow his ground and
reap his harvest, and still others to make
weapons of war and equipment for his
chariots. 13He will take your daughters to

7:9 [y]S Ex 32:11; S Dt 9:19 **7:10** [z]S Ex 9:23; S 1Sa 2:10 [a]S Ge 35:5; S Ex 14:24 **7:12** [b]S Ge 28:22; S Dt 27:2; Jos 4:9 [c]S 1Sa 4:1 **7:13** [d]Jdg 13:1,5 **7:14** [e]S Jos 13:3 [f]S Jdg 1:34 **7:15** [g]ver 6; 1Sa 12:11 [h]S Jdg 2:16 [i]Jdg 2:18 **7:16** [j]S Ge 12:8 [k]S Jos 10:43; S 1Sa 10:8; Am 5:5 [l]ver 6; Ac 13:20 **7:17** [m]S Jos 18:25; 1Sa 8:4; 15:34; 19:18; 25:1; 28:3 [n]ver 6 [o]1Sa 9:12; 14:35; 20:6; 2Sa 24:25 **8:1** [p]Dt 16:18-19 **8:2** [q]1Ch 6:28 [r]Ge 22:19; 1Ki 19:3; Am 5:4-5 **8:3** [s]1Sa 2:12 [t]Ne 9:29; Job 34:27; Ps 14:3; 58:3; Isa 53:6 [u]Ex 23:8; 1Sa 12:3; Job 8:22; Pr 17:23 [v]S Ex 23:2 **8:4** [w]S Jdg 11:11; 1Sa 11:3 [x]S 1Sa 7:17 **8:5** [y]ver 19; S Dt 17:14-20; 1Sa 10:19; 12:12, 13; Hos 13:11 [z]1Sa 3:20; 12:2 [a]ver 20 **8:6** [b]Hos 13:10 [c]1Sa 12:17; 15:11; 16:1 **8:7** [d]ver 22; 1Sa 12:1 [e]S Nu 11:20 [f]S Ex 16:8 **8:8** [g]1Sa 12:10; 2Ki 21:22; Jer 2:17 **8:9** [h]ver 11-18; S Dt 17:14-20; 1Sa 10:25 **8:10** [i]S Ex 19:7 **8:11** [j]1Sa 14:52 [k]S Ge 41:46 [l]S Dt 17:16; 2Sa 15:1; 1Ki 1:5; 2Ch 1:14; 9:25; SS 3:7 **8:12** [m]S Dt 1:15

[y]12 *Ebenezer* means *stone of help.*
[z]5 Traditionally *judge;* also in verses 6 and 20

7:10 MIRACLE, Nature—As Samuel, the Lord's prophet, offered a sacrifice and prayed for deliverance, God "thundered with loud thunder," and the Philistines were defeated. More details are not provided, but a man of faith was there to interpret the event as God's handiwork. The God-inspired interpreter consistently appears in miracle narratives. Apart from the presence and ministry of the prophet, a miracle may be ignored or mistaken for magic.

7:10–12 EVIL AND SUFFERING, God's Present Help—War is a part of human existence caused by human sins of greed and selfishness. War causes human suffering and death. As such, war is evil. God is holy and pure but willing to involve Himself in the evil of human existence. He can use the evil of war to help His people. This does not say God causes the evil of war. God's people need to establish markers that lead us to remember what He has done to help us. God's goal for us is not victory in war but eternal peace (Isa 2:1–5; 11:1–9).

7:15–17 WORSHIP, Buildings—See note on Ge 28:16–22.

7:17 PRAYER, Worship—See note on Ge 12:7–8.

8:3 SIN, Moral Insensitivity—Religious office brings overwhelming temptation to unqualified, inept religious leaders. Having a father in a high office does not qualify a son for office. See note on 2:12–17.

8:6–7 LAST THINGS, Coming Kingdom—The idea of God's divine kingship is deeply rooted in the Old Testament. The rule of God over Israel in a theocratic nation was the ideal. In historical crisis, the people rejected God's ideal and demanded an earthly king. The event of establishing a king over Israel was a crucial one in terms of kingdom history. The Sinai covenant established God and no one else as king over Israel (v 7). Israel's demand for a king was a clear rejection of that covenant condition. So serious was this development that God made a new covenant with Israel, expressed in the promise later to David that a king of his lineage would reign forever. The two covenants were fulfilled in Jesus Christ, who is not only divine but also a descendant of David. No other person who has ever lived or ever will live can fulfill these two covenants and bring them together into one new covenant. In God's providence the less than ideal monarchy functioned as the earthly expression of God's rule over His people. See notes on 2 Ch 13:8; Da 2:44.

8:6–22 PRAYER, Petition—God allowed Israel to have a king even when the peoples' choice signified rejection of God. Samuel prayed for direction in the confusing situation. Prayer involves petitioning God to relieve our confusion.

8:7–8 SIN, Against God—God assured Samuel that Israel's rejection was not directed against Samuel but against God. In asking for a king, Israel was rejecting God as ruler in every affair of Israelite life. All sin is, directly or indirectly, an affront against God's holy character.

be perfumers and cooks and bakers. 14He
will take the best of your[n] fields and
vineyards[o] and olive groves and give
them to his attendants.[p] 15He will take a
tenth[q] of your grain and of your vintage
and give it to his officials and attendants.
16Your menservants and maidservants
and the best of your cattle[a] and donkeys
he will take for his own use. 17He will
take a tenth of your flocks, and you yourselves will become his slaves. 18When
that day comes, you will cry out for relief
from the king you have chosen, and the
LORD will not answer[r] you in that day.[s]"
19But the people refused[t] to listen to
Samuel. "No!" they said. "We want[u] a
king[v] over us. 20Then we will be like all
the other nations,[w] with a king to lead us
and to go out before us and fight our battles."
21When Samuel heard all that the people said, he repeated[x] it before the LORD.
22The LORD answered, "Listen[y] to them
and give them a king."
Then Samuel said to the men of Israel,
"Everyone go back to his town."

Chapter 9

Samuel Anoints Saul

THERE was a Benjamite,[z] a man of
standing,[a] whose name was Kish[b]
son of Abiel, the son of Zeror, the son of
Becorath, the son of Aphiah of Benjamin.
2He had a son named Saul, an impressive[c] young man without equal[d] among
the Israelites—a head taller[e] than any of
the others.
3Now the donkeys[f] belonging to Saul's
father Kish were lost, and Kish said to his
son Saul, "Take one of the servants with
you and go and look for the donkeys." 4So
he passed through the hill[g] country of
Ephraim and through the area around
Shalisha,[h] but they did not find them.
They went on into the district of Shaalim,
but the donkeys[i] were not there. Then
he passed through the territory of Benjamin, but they did not find them.
5When they reached the district of
Zuph,[j] Saul said to the servant who was
with him, "Come, let's go back, or my
father will stop thinking about the
donkeys and start worrying[k] about us."
6But the servant replied, "Look, in this
town there is a man of God;[l] he is highly
respected, and everything[m] he says
comes true. Let's go there now. Perhaps
he will tell us what way to take."
7Saul said to his servant, "If we go,
what can we give the man? The food in
our sacks is gone. We have no gift[n] to
take to the man of God. What do we
have?"
8The servant answered him again.
"Look," he said, "I have a quarter of a
shekel[b] of silver. I will give it to the man
of God so that he will tell us what way to
take." 9(Formerly in Israel, if a man went
to inquire[o] of God, he would say,
"Come, let us go to the seer," because
the prophet of today used to be called a
seer.)[p]
10"Good," Saul said to his servant.
"Come, let's go." So they set out for the
town where the man of God was.
11As they were going up the hill to the
town, they met some girls coming out to
draw[q] water, and they asked them, "Is
the seer here?"
12"He is," they answered. "He's ahead
of you. Hurry now; he has just come to
our town today, for the people have a sacrifice[r] at the high place.[s] 13As soon as
you enter the town, you will find him before he goes up to the high place to eat.
The people will not begin eating until he
comes, because he must bless[t] the sacrifice; afterward, those who are invited will
eat. Go up now; you should find him
about this time."
14They went up to the town, and as
they were entering it, there was Samuel,
coming toward them on his way up to the
high place.
15Now the day before Saul came, the
LORD had revealed this to Samuel:
16"About this time tomorrow I will send
you a man from the land of Benjamin.
Anoint[u] him leader[v] over my people

8:14 [n]Eze 46:18 [o]1Ki 21:7,15; Mic 2:2 [p]2Ki 22:12
8:15 [q]S Ge 41:34; 1Sa 17:25
8:18 [r]1Sa 28:6; Job 27:9; 35:12,13; Ps 18:41; 66:18; Pr 1:28; Isa 1:15; 58:4; 59:2; Jer 14:12; Eze 8:18; Mic 3:4 [s]1Sa 10:25; 1Ki 12:4
8:19 [t]Pr 1:24; Isa 50:2; 66:4; Jer 7:13; 8:12; 13:10; 44:16 [u]Ac 13:21 [v]S ver 5
8:20 [w]S ver 5
8:21 [x]S Jdg 11:11
8:22 [y]S ver 7
9:1 [z]Jos 18:11-20 [a]S Ru 2:1 [b]1Sa 14:51; 1Ch 8:33; 9:39; Est 2:5; Ac 13:21
9:2 [c]S Ge 39:6 [d]1Sa 10:24 [e]1Sa 10:23
9:3 [f]ver 20; 1Sa 10:14,16
9:4 [g]S Jos 24:33 [h]2Ki 4:42 [i]1Sa 10:2
9:5 [j]1Sa 1:1 [k]1Sa 10:2
9:6 [l]S Dt 33:1; S Jdg 13:6 [m]1Sa 3:19
9:7 [n]S Ge 32:20; 1Ki 13:7; 14:3; 2Ki 4:42; 5:5,15; Jer 40:5
9:9 [o]S Ge 25:22 [p]2Sa 15:27; 24:11; 2Ki 17:13; 1Ch 9:22; 21:9; 26:28; 29:29; 2Ch 19:2; Isa 29:10; 30:10; Am 7:12
9:11 [q]S Ge 24:11, 13
9:12 [r]Nu 28:11-15; S 1Sa 7:17 [s]S Lev 26:30
9:13 [t]S Mt 14:19; 1Co 10:16; 1Ti 4:3-5
9:16 [u]Ex 30:25; S 1Sa 2:35; 12:3; 15:1; 26:9; 2Ki 11:12; Ps 2:2 [v]2Sa 7:8; 1Ki 8:16; 1Ch 5:2

[a] *16* Septuagint; Hebrew *young men* [b] *8* That is, about 1/10 ounce (about 3 grams)

8:19–20 HUMANITY, Human Nature—The desire to be like others is a great motivator. For Israel, government was perceived as being necessary for defense against enemies. The acts of government are still perceived as being a people's greatest defense. God's people need to accept the fact that government cannot replace God.

9:12 WORSHIP, Buildings—See note on Ge 28:16–22.

9:13–25 DISCIPLESHIP, Spiritual Leaders—Samuel usually is considered a prophet, but he also exercised the functions of a priest. God uses His spiritual leaders in ways that suit His purposes and the time in which they serve.

9:13 PRAYER, Thanksgiving—Samuel led sacrificial celebrations ending in a community meal. He led in prayer prior to the sacrificial meal. Prayer before eating is a proper way to express gratitude to God for providing life's necessary resources.

9:15–16 REVELATION, Events—God revealed to prophets both words to preach and specific acts to do to carry out His will. Samuel received instruction from God to meet His chosen leader and anoint him the first king of Israel. God revealed His compassion for His oppressed children by answering their cry for help.

9:16 PRAYER, Mercy of God—The cry of the people for a king was second-best and willful. God Himself had always delivered them (Jdg 8:34), but they demanded a deliverer in permanent office. God responded in mercy to the cry of His oppressed people. See notes on Ex 2:23–24; Jdg 3:9.

Israel; he will deliver[w] my people from
the hand of the Philistines.[x] I have looked
upon my people, for their cry[y] has
reached me."
17When Samuel caught sight of Saul,
the LORD said to him, "This[z] is the man I
spoke to you about; he will govern my
people."
18Saul approached Samuel in the gateway and asked, "Would you please tell
me where the seer's house is?"
19"I am the seer," Samuel replied. "Go
up ahead of me to the high place, for today you are to eat with me, and in the
morning I will let you go and will tell you
all that is in your heart. 20As for the donkeys[a] you lost three days ago, do not
worry about them; they have been found.
And to whom is all the desire[b] of Israel
turned, if not to you and all your father's
family?"
21Saul answered, "But am I not a Benjamite, from the smallest tribe[c] of Israel,
and is not my clan the least[d] of all the
clans of the tribe of Benjamin?[e] Why do
you say such a thing to me?"
22Then Samuel brought Saul and his
servant into the hall and seated them at
the head of those who were invited—
about thirty in number. 23Samuel said to
the cook, "Bring the piece of meat I gave
you, the one I told you to lay aside."
24So the cook took up the leg[f] with
what was on it and set it in front of Saul.
Samuel said, "Here is what has been kept
for you. Eat, because it was set aside for
you for this occasion, from the time I
said, 'I have invited guests.' " And Saul
dined with Samuel that day.
25After they came down from the high
place to the town, Samuel talked with
Saul on the roof[g] of his house. 26They
rose about daybreak and Samuel called to
Saul on the roof, "Get ready, and I will
send you on your way." When Saul got
ready, he and Samuel went outside together. 27As they were going down to the
edge of the town, Samuel said to Saul,
"Tell the servant to go on ahead of us"
—and the servant did so—"but you stay
here awhile, so that I may give you a
message from God."

Chapter 10

THEN Samuel took a flask[h] of oil and
poured it on Saul's head and kissed
him, saying, "Has not the LORD anointed[i] you leader over his inheritance?[c] [j]
2When you leave me today, you will meet
two men near Rachel's tomb,[k] at Zelzah
on the border of Benjamin. They will say
to you, 'The donkeys[l] you set out to look
for have been found. And now your father has stopped thinking about them and
is worried[m] about you. He is asking,
"What shall I do about my son?" '
3"Then you will go on from there until
you reach the great tree of Tabor. Three
men going up to God at Bethel[n] will
meet you there. One will be carrying
three young goats, another three loaves of
bread, and another a skin of wine. 4They
will greet you and offer you two loaves of
bread,[o] which you will accept from
them.
5"After that you will go to Gibeah[p] of
God, where there is a Philistine outpost.[q] As you approach the town, you
will meet a procession of prophets[r] coming down from the high place[s] with
lyres, tambourines,[t] flutes[u] and harps[v]
being played before them, and they will
be prophesying.[w] 6The Spirit[x] of the
LORD will come upon you in power, and
you will prophesy with them; and you
will be changed[y] into a different person.
7Once these signs are fulfilled, do whatever[z] your hand[a] finds to do, for God is
with[b] you.
8"Go down ahead of me to Gilgal.[c] I
will surely come down to you to sacrifice
burnt offerings and fellowship offerings,[d]
but you must wait seven[d] days until I
come to you and tell you what you are to
do."

Saul Made King

9As Saul turned to leave Samuel, God
changed[e] Saul's heart, and all these

9:16 [w]Ex 3:7-9 [x]1Sa 23:4; 2Sa 3:18 [y]S Ge 16:11; Ps 102:1
9:17 [z]1Sa 16:12
9:20 [a]S ver 3 [b]1Sa 12:13; Ezr 6:8; Isa 60:4-9; Da 2:44; Hag 2:7; Mal 3:1
9:21 [c]Ps 68:27 [d]S Ex 3:11; Mt 2:6; 1Co 15:9 [e]Jdg 6:15; 20:35,46; 1Sa 18:18
9:24 [f]S Lev 7:32-34
9:25 [g]S Dt 22:8; S Jos 2:8; S Mt 24:17; Lk 5:19
10:1 [h]1Sa 16:1; 2Ki 9:1,3,6 [i]S Ex 29:7; S 1Sa 9:16; S 1Ki 1:39 [j]S Ex 34:9; 2Sa 20:19; Ps 78:62,71
10:2 [k]Ge 35:20 [l]1Sa 9:4 [m]1Sa 9:5
10:3 [n]S Ge 35:7-8
10:4 [o]ver 27; 1Sa 16:20; Pr 18:16
10:5 [p]ver 26; 1Sa 11:4; 15:34 [q]1Sa 13:3 [r]S Nu 11:29; 1Ki 20:35; 2Ki 2:3, 15; 4:1; 6:1; 9:1; Am 7:14 [s]S Lev 26:30 [t]S Ge 31:27; Jer 31:4 [u]1Ki 1:40; Isa 30:29 [v]1Sa 16:16; 18:10; 19:9; 2Ki 3:15; Ps 92:3 [w]ver 10; 1Sa 19:20; 1Ch 25:1; 1Co 14:1
10:6 [x]S Nu 11:25 [y]ver 9
10:7 [z]2Sa 7:3; 1Ki 8:17; 1Ch 22:7; 28:2; 2Ch 6:7; Ecc 9:10 [a]Jdg 9:33 [b]S Jos 1:5; Lk 1:28; Heb 13:5
10:8 [c]Jos 4:20; S 10:43; 1Sa 7:16; 11:14-15 [d]1Sa 13:8
10:9 [e]ver 6

[c] *1* Hebrew; Septuagint and Vulgate *over his people Israel? You will reign over the LORD's people and save them from the power of their enemies round about. And this will be a sign to you that the LORD has anointed you leader over his inheritance:*
[d] *8* Traditionally *peace offerings*

10:3–17 WORSHIP, Buildings—See note on Ge 28:16–22.

10:5–13 HOLY SPIRIT, Revelation—Leaders need revelation from God confirming His call to leadership. God gave Saul an unforgettable ecstatic experience in which Saul acted like a different person. The prophetic experience confirmed Saul's call to be king both for himself and for the people, but it was only temporary. His call was to political leadership, not prophecy. God's people must distinguish a temporary experience from a permanent call and responsibility. See note on Nu 11:25–29.

10:6–13 REVELATION, Messengers—God used prophetic messengers to reveal His word to His people. Some prophets worked together in groups and used music to create the mood in which they could receive and proclaim God's word to the people (1 Sa 19:20; 2 Ki 2—4; 3:15–16; 6:1; 9:1). The Spirit of God was the source of prophetic inspiration. The text does not give us the substance or nature of the prophecy.

10:8 PRAYER, Worship—The sacrifices were in preparation for Saul's public presentation as king. Prayer and worship are appropriate responses by God's people to significant political events. God and His people, not the politicians, maintain control of religious observances. A political leader who tries to control God and His work is doomed to failure.

10:9 MIRACLE, Instruments—God uses miracles to mark

signs[f] were fulfilled[g] that day. 10When
they arrived at Gibeah, a procession of
prophets met him; the Spirit[h] of God
came upon him in power, and he joined
in their prophesying.[i] 11When all those
who had formerly known him saw him
prophesying with the prophets, they
asked each other, "What is this[j] that has
happened to the son of Kish? Is Saul also
among the prophets?"[k]
12A man who lived there answered,
"And who is their father?" So it became a
saying: "Is Saul also among the prophets?"[l] 13After Saul stopped prophesying,[m] he went to the high place.
14Now Saul's uncle[n] asked him and his
servant, "Where have you been?"
"Looking for the donkeys,[o]" he said.
"But when we saw they were not to be
found, we went to Samuel."
15Saul's uncle said, "Tell me what Samuel said to you."
16Saul replied, "He assured us that the
donkeys[p] had been found." But he did
not tell his uncle what Samuel had said
about the kingship.
17Samuel summoned the people of Israel to the LORD at Mizpah[q] 18and said to
them, "This is what the LORD, the God of
Israel, says: 'I brought Israel up out of
Egypt, and I delivered you from the power of Egypt and all the kingdoms that oppressed[r] you.' 19But you have now rejected[s] your God, who saves[t] you out of
all your calamities and distresses. And
you have said, 'No, set a king[u] over us.'[v]
So now present[w] yourselves before the
LORD by your tribes and clans."
20When Samuel brought all the tribes
of Israel near, the tribe of Benjamin was
chosen. 21Then he brought forward the
tribe of Benjamin, clan by clan, and Ma-
tri's clan was chosen.[x] Finally Saul son of
Kish was chosen. But when they looked
for him, he was not to be found. 22So they
inquired[y] further of the LORD, "Has the
man come here yet?"
And the LORD said, "Yes, he has hidden himself among the baggage."
23They ran and brought him out, and as
he stood among the people he was a
head taller[z] than any of the others.
24Samuel said to all the people, "Do you
see the man the LORD has chosen?[a]
There is no one like[b] him among all
the people."
Then the people shouted, "Long live[c]
the king!"
25Samuel explained[d] to the people the
regulations[e] of the kingship.[f] He wrote
them down on a scroll and deposited it
before the LORD. Then Samuel dismissed
the people, each to his own home.
26Saul also went to his home in Gibeah,[g] accompanied by valiant men[h]
whose hearts God had touched. 27But
some troublemakers[i] said, "How can
this fellow save us?" They despised him

10:9 [f]S Dt 13:2 [g]ver 7
10:10 [h]S Nu 11:25; 1Sa 11:6 [i]S ver 5-6
10:11 [j]Mt 13:54; Jn 7:15 [k]ver 12; 1Sa 19:24; 2Ki 9:11; Jer 29:26; Hos 9:7
10:12 [l]S ver 11
10:13 [m]1Sa 19:23
10:14 [n]1Sa 14:50 [o]S 1Sa 9:3
10:16 [p]S 1Sa 9:3
10:17 [q]S 1Sa 7:5
10:18 [r]S Ex 1:14; S Nu 10:9
10:19 [s]S Nu 11:20; S Dt 33:5 [t]Ps 7:10; 18:48; 68:20; 145:19 [u]S 1Sa 8:5-7 [v]S Dt 17:14 [w]Jos 7:14
10:21 [x]Est 3:7; Pr 16:33
10:22 [y]S Ge 25:22; S Jdg 18:5
10:23 [z]1Sa 9:2
10:24 [a]Dt 17:15; 2Sa 21:6 [b]1Sa 9:2 [c]1Ki 1:25,34,39; 2Ki 11:12
10:25 [d]S 1Sa 8:9 [e]S Dt 17:14-20; S 1Sa 8:11-18; 2Ki 11:12 [f]1Sa 11:14
10:26 [g]S ver 5; S Jdg 19:14 [h]S Jdg 20:44
10:27 [i]S Dt 13:13; S 1Sa 20:7

turning points in history. A series of miraculous signs marked Samuel's reluctant search for a king to rule Israel. His preparation of Saul led Israel to accept the young Benjamite (10:24). The prophet interpreted the "signs" (10:9) as proof God was leading. Only Saul's disobedience (13:14) undid the divine choice. Later (16:13), Samuel obeyed God by anointing David as king. Uniting the selfish, independent Israelites (Jdg 21:25) under a political leader was a miracle. God used a prophet and two young, unsuspecting men to accomplish His purpose. "Signs" (Hebrew *'oth*) is a common word used for tribal identity standards (Nu 2:2), a special mark on a person's body (Ge 4:15), testimony accounts of travelers (Job 21:29), a box of verses worn on the body (Ex 14:16; Dt 6:8), heavenly bodies marking the seasons (Ge 1:14; compare Jer 10:2). False prophets can point out meaningless "signs" (Isa 44:25). Theologically, "signs" are God's ways of showing His power and presence to His people. He uses various acts and objects as signs: a rainbow (Ge 9:12–13), circumcision (Ge 17:11), Sabbath observance (Ex 31:12), Aaron's staff (Nu 17:10), stones in the Jordan (Jos 4:5–6), priestly censers (Nu 16:38), a historical act proving a prophetic word (Dt 13:1; Jer 44:29), restored fertility (Isa 55:13), the Egyptian plagues (Ex 4:8; 7:3), peaceful conditions allowing normal agricultural activity (2 Ki 19:29). Such signs should lead God's people to faith (Nu 14:11; Jos 24:17). The Bible, thus, reveals God's hand at work giving miraculous signs in many different ways. See note on Jdg 6:17.

10:17–25 REVELATION, Oracles—People gathered at the worship center at Mizpah to receive God's word delivered through the prophet Samuel. The revealed word showed they had rejected God's revealed will. God remained faithful to His purposes and promises. He revealed His chosen king to the people, probably through the sacred lot. See note on Jdg 20:18.

10:17–19 HISTORY, God's Leaders—God showed in the Exodus He was Israel's King. They were not satisfied and wanted a government like their neighbors. God let them have their way and directed in the selection of leaders. He did not surrender His place of leadership. Whatever form of government may be in place, God is the ultimate Ruler of all nations.

10:18 SALVATION, As Deliverance—Like Israel, at the beginning of Saul's reign, God's people need to be reminded of His great acts of deliverance. This is where the church ordinances of baptism and the Lord's Supper can especially help us in the doctrine of salvation. They picture what God has done for us and call us to renewed dedication to Him.

10:19 SIN, Against God—God had proved His ability to lead and rule His people. In moments of crisis they looked to their neighbors for a "better idea." Following "successful" world patterns rather than trusting God's grace and power is sin against God. See note on 8:7–8.

10:19–22 PRAYER, Petition—The public presentation was to be "before the LORD" acknowledging His sovereignty. God worked patiently with a people even when they chose the second best course of action. God does not bar a people from His presence when they fail Him. He is the God of second chances. God showed the people His chosen leader when they inquired of Him.

10:23–24 HUMANITY, Physical Nature—Outstanding physical attributes attract more attention than their actual importance. We need to stand to our full height spiritually regardless of our physical size.

10:24 ELECTION, Leadership—The neighbors of Israel always referred to their kings as elect persons. Some even claimed the kings were divine. An elect king in Israel could also be rejected. God's designation of Saul was by anointing, lot casting, and the consecration of the Spirit. Saul's acts did not please God, so God rejected his family. God's election is always a call to obedience. See note on 2:30–34.

and brought him no gifts.[j] But Saul kept
silent.

Chapter 11

Saul Rescues the City of Jabesh

NAHASH[k] the Ammonite went up and
besieged Jabesh Gilead.[l] And all
the men of Jabesh said to him, "Make a
treaty[m] with us, and we will be subject to
you."
2But Nahash the Ammonite replied, "I
will make a treaty with you only on the
condition[n] that I gouge[o] out the right
eye of every one of you and so bring disgrace[p] on all Israel."
3The elders[q] of Jabesh said to him,
"Give us seven days so we can send messengers throughout Israel; if no one
comes to rescue[r] us, we will surrender[s]
to you."
4When the messengers came to Gibeah[t] of Saul and reported these terms to
the people, they all wept[u] aloud. 5Just
then Saul was returning from the fields,
behind his oxen, and he asked, "What is
wrong with the people? Why are they
weeping?" Then they repeated to him
what the men of Jabesh had said.
6When Saul heard their words, the
Spirit[v] of God came upon him in power,
and he burned with anger. 7He took a
pair of oxen,[w] cut them into pieces, and
sent the pieces by messengers throughout
Israel,[x] proclaiming, "This is what will
be done to the oxen of anyone[y] who
does not follow Saul and Samuel." Then
the terror of the LORD fell on the people,
and they turned out as one man.[z] 8When
Saul mustered[a] them at Bezek,[b] the
men of Israel numbered three hundred
thousand and the men of Judah thirty
thousand.
9They told the messengers who had
come, "Say to the men of Jabesh Gilead,
'By the time the sun is hot tomorrow, you
will be delivered.'" When the messengers went and reported this to the men of
Jabesh, they were elated. 10They said
to the Ammonites, "Tomorrow we will
surrender[c] to you, and you can do to us
whatever seems good to you."
11The next day Saul separated his men
into three divisions;[d] during the last
watch of the night they broke into the
camp of the Ammonites[e] and slaughtered them until the heat of the day.
Those who survived were scattered, so
that no two of them were left together.

Saul Confirmed as King

12The people then said to Samuel,
"Who[f] was it that asked, 'Shall Saul
reign over us?' Bring these men to us and
we will put them to death."
13But Saul said, "No one shall be put to
death today,[g] for this day the LORD has
rescued[h] Israel."
14Then Samuel said to the people,
"Come, let us go to Gilgal[i] and there
reaffirm the kingship.[j]" 15So all the people went to Gilgal[k] and confirmed Saul as
king[l] in the presence of the LORD. There
they sacrificed fellowship offerings[e] before the LORD, and Saul and all the Israelites held a great celebration.

Chapter 12

Samuel's Farewell Speech

SAMUEL said to all Israel, "I have listened[m] to everything you said to me
and have set a king[n] over you. 2Now you
have a king as your leader.[o] As for me, I
am old and gray, and my sons[p] are here
with you. I have been your leader from
my youth until this day. 3Here I stand.
Testify against me in the presence of the
LORD and his anointed.[q] Whose ox have I
taken? Whose donkey[r] have I taken?
Whom have I cheated? Whom have I oppressed? From whose hand have I accepted a bribe[s] to make me shut my eyes? If I
have done[t] any of these, I will make it
right."[u]
4"You have not cheated or oppressed
us," they replied. "You have not taken
anything from anyone's hand."
5Samuel said to them, "The LORD is

[e]*15* Traditionally *peace offerings*

10:27 [j]S ver 4; 1Ki 10:25; 2Ch 17:5; 32:23; Ps 68:29
11:1 [k]S Ge 19:38; 1Sa 12:12; 2Sa 10:2; 17:27; 1Ch 19:1 [l]Jdg 21:8; 1Sa 31:11; 2Sa 2:4, 5; 21:12 [m]S Ex 23:32; S Jer 37:1
11:2 [n]Ge 34:15 [o]S Nu 16:14 [p]1Sa 17:26
11:3 [q]S 1Sa 8:4 [r]S Jdg 2:16 [s]ver 10
11:4 [t]S 1Sa 10:5,26 [u]S Ge 27:38; S Nu 25:6
11:6 [v]S Jdg 3:10
11:7 [w]S 1Sa 6:14 [x]S Jdg 19:29 [y]Jdg 21:5 [z]S Jdg 20:1
11:8 [a]Jdg 20:2 [b]Jdg 1:4
11:10 [c]ver 3
11:11 [d]S Jdg 7:16 [e]S Ge 19:38
11:12 [f]S Dt 13:13; Lk 19:27
11:13 [g]2Sa 19:22 [h]1Sa 19:5; 1Ch 11:14
11:14 [i]S Jos 10:43; S 1Sa 10:8 [j]1Sa 10:25
11:15 [k]S Jos 5:9; 2Sa 19:15 [l]1Sa 12:1
12:1 [m]S 1Sa 8:7 [n]1Sa 11:15
12:2 [o]S 1Sa 8:5 [p]1Sa 8:3
12:3 [q]S 1Sa 9:16; 24:6; 26:9,11; 2Sa 1:14; 19:21; Ps 105:15 [r]Nu 16:15 [s]S Ex 18:21; S 1Sa 8:3 [t]Ex 20:17; Ac 20:33 [u]S Lev 25:14

11:1–11 CHRISTIAN ETHICS, War and Peace—Treaties are the proper way to solve conflicts. War is not. Treaties must be fair to both sides. Unjust treaties do not settle conflicts. They create more. God is on the side of persons suffering injustice (Dt 10:17–18).

11:6–7 HOLY SPIRIT, Leaders—Passion and innovative leadership come to Spirit-driven leaders. The Spirit gave Saul righteous anger at the blasphemous and proud actions of the Ammonites. He used a symbolic act similar to prophetic acts to arouse the nation to defend itself and its friends.

11:6–7 DISCIPLESHIP, Spiritual Leaders—Saul was anointed king, but he also was regarded by the people as the man of God upon whom the Spirit of God had come. Israel would not follow anyone not considered to be the man of God. At Saul's death, David ascended to the throne, but David would never have become king if he had not been regarded as the man of God. The people sensed that the Spirit had passed from Saul to David even before the death of Saul. Persons today may claim to have authority for leadership but find that the people will not follow. The presence of the Holy Spirit in leadership is essential if good followship is to be expected among the people of God. Christian disciples can sense authentic leadership of the Spirit, and they can recognize those posing as spiritual leaders without the Spirit's presence. See note on Heb 13:7,17.

12:1–3 CHRISTIAN ETHICS, Character—Personal character is not a secret. Those we associate with daily know our character. We need to hear their testimony and be ready to make necessary changes.

witness[v] against you, and also his anointed is witness this day, that you have not
found anything[w] in my hand.[x]"

"He is witness," they said.

6Then Samuel said to the people, "It is
the LORD who appointed Moses and Aaron and brought[y] your forefathers up out
of Egypt. 7Now then, stand[z] here, because I am going to confront[a] you with
evidence before the LORD as to all the
righteous acts[b] performed by the LORD
for you and your fathers.

8"After Jacob[c] entered Egypt, they
cried[d] to the LORD for help, and the LORD
sent[e] Moses and Aaron, who brought
your forefathers out of Egypt and settled
them in this place.

9"But they forgot[f] the LORD their God;
so he sold them[g] into the hand of
Sisera,[h] the commander of the army of
Hazor,[i] and into the hands of Philistines[j] and the king of Moab,[k] who
fought against them. 10They cried[l] out to
the LORD and said, 'We have sinned; we
have forsaken[m] the LORD and served the
Baals and the Ashtoreths.[n] But now deliver us from the hands of our enemies,
and we will serve you.' 11Then the LORD
sent Jerub-Baal,[f][o] Barak,[g][p] Jephthah[q]
and Samuel,[h][r] and he delivered you
from the hands of your enemies on every
side, so that you lived securely.

12"But when you saw that Nahash[s]
king[t] of the Ammonites was moving
against you, you said to me, 'No, we want
a king to rule[u] over us'—even though
the LORD your God was your king. 13Now
here is the king[v] you have chosen, the
one you asked[w] for; see, the LORD has set
a king over you. 14If you fear[x] the LORD
and serve and obey him and do not rebel[y] against his commands, and if both
you and the king who reigns over you
follow the LORD your God—good! 15But if
you do not obey the LORD, and if you rebel against[z] his commands, his hand will
be against you, as it was against your
fathers.

16"Now then, stand still[a] and see[b]
this great thing the LORD is about to do
before your eyes! 17Is it not wheat harvest[c] now? I will call[d] upon the LORD to
send thunder[e] and rain.[f] And you will
realize what an evil[g] thing you did in the
eyes of the LORD when you asked for a
king."

18Then Samuel called upon the LORD,[h]
and that same day the LORD sent thunder
and rain. So all the people stood in awe[i]
of the LORD and of Samuel.

19The people all said to Samuel, "Pray[j]
to the LORD your God for your servants so
that we will not die,[k] for we have added
to all our other sins the evil of asking for a
king."

20"Do not be afraid," Samuel replied.
"You have done all this evil;[l] yet do not

12:5 [v]S Ge 31:50 [w]Ac 23:9; 24:20 [x]Ex 22:4 **12:6** [y]S Ex 3:10; Mic 6:4 **12:7** [z]S Jos 24:1 [a]Isa 1:18; 3:14; Jer 2:9; 25:31; Eze 17:20; 20:35; Mic 6:1-5 [b]S Jdg 5:11 **12:8** [c]S Ge 46:6 [d]S Ex 2:23 [e]S Ex 3:10; 4:16 **12:9** [f]S Dt 32:18; S Jdg 3:7 [g]S Dt 32:30 [h]Jdg 4:2 [i]S Jos 11:1 [j]Jdg 10:7 [k]Jdg 3:12 **12:10** [l]S Jdg 3:9 [m]S 1Sa 8:8 [n]S 1Sa 7:3 **12:11** [o]Jdg 6:32 [p]S Jdg 4:6 [q]S Jdg 11:1 [r]S 1Sa 7:15 **12:12** [s]S 1Sa 11:1 [t]S 1Sa 8:5 [u]1Sa 25:30; 2Sa 5:2; 1Ch 5:2 **12:13** [v]S 1Sa 8:5 [w]S 1Sa 9:20 **12:14** [x]S Jos 24:14 [y]Jer 4:17; La 1:18 **12:15** [z]Lev 26:16; Jos 24:20; Isa 1:20; Jer 4:17; 26:4 **12:16** [a]S Ex 14:14 [b]S Ex 14:13 **12:17** [c]S Ge 30:14; S 1Sa 6:13 [d]1Ki 18:42; Jas 5:18 [e]S Ex 9:23; S 1Sa 2:10 [f]Ge 7:12; Ex 9:18; Job 37:13; Pr 26:1 [g]S 1Sa 8:6-7 **12:18** [h]Ps 99:6 [i]S Ge 3:10; S Ex 14:31 **12:19** [j]S Ex 8:8; S 1Sa 7:8; S Jer 37:3; Jas 5:18; 1Jn 5:16 [k]S Dt 9:19 **12:20** [l]S Ex 32:30

[f]*11* Also called *Gideon* [g]*11* Some Septuagint manuscripts and Syriac; Hebrew *Bedan* [h]*11* Hebrew; some Septuagint manuscripts and Syriac *Samson*

12:6–25 HISTORY, Intentions—See note on 10:17–19. Wrong human choices do not thwart God's eternal purposes. He chooses to work through human choices to accomplish His purposes. He retains power and freedom to overthrow human choices to accomplish His will and to discipline His people. History shows God's acts are righteous, while humans have repeatedly made wrong choices. Wrong choices do not isolate people from God. They must live with the consequences of their choices, but they can be faithful to God and enjoy fellowship with Him. Choosing a king did not separate Israel from the covenant relationship with God. It joined the rest of Israel's history as a reminder of the goodness of God and the need to repent.
12:9–18 SIN, Against God—See notes on 8:7–8; 10:19.
12:10 PRAYER, Petition—See note on 7:5–11.
12:11 SALVATION, As Deliverance—See note on Jdg 3:9,15. God chose to bring His salvation to Israel in the midst of her history, through very human leaders. Salvation in the Bible is about deliverance in this world as well as the next.
12:13–25 EVIL AND SUFFERING, Human Origin—Political systems can introduce evil into the world. We tend to rely on the human system and give it the authority and devotion due only to God. Some political leaders take over the system and corrupt it to satisfy personal ego needs and amass personal fame and fortune. No system is immune to such corruption. God warned Israel of the dangers of their wanting a political system and leaders like the nations. All political systems and leaders are ultimately accountable to God.
12:14–15,20–24 CHRISTIAN ETHICS, Moral Imperatives—See notes on Ex 34:11–26,32; Dt 28:25; Jos 24:14–15.
12:16–25 GOD, Sovereignty—Samuel recognized that placing a king over Israel provided one more temptation to Israel to compromise her loyalty to God. He called forth a dramatic reminder that God is sovereign Lord and that both the people and their king must be humble and obedient before Him. God wants to bless His people, but He will not be blind to their unfaithfulness and disobedience.
12:17 SIN, Against God—Rejection of God is not unforgivable. In freedom God responded to the people's demands for a king. The king, however, injected a new opportunity for temptation and sin into Israel's life. See note on 8:7–8.
12:17–23 PRAYER, Petition—Samuel asked the Lord for evidence his charges of rebellion against the people were true. In crisis times, we can petition God to increase our confidence in Him. God's sovereign acts in nature led the people to prayer, confessing their sins. They asked Samuel to mediate their prayer to God. To fail to pray for people who request prayer is sin.
12:20–25 SIN, Against God—Failure to pray for sinful people is a sin. God gives His people new opportunities to worship and obey Him. Leaders who judge and condemn the people rather than pray for them sin against God's grace.
12:20–22 ELECTION, God's Purpose—Life under an earthly king can bring blessing or cursing. The people had to decide whether to be obedient to the righteous demands of the King of the universe or to be rebellious and disobedient. God's relationship to His people, irrespective of the form of earthly government under which the people live, is always based on righteousness. Election is a permanent part of God's plan to form a people for Himself. Even the evil of choosing an earthly king to imitate the nations, thus rejecting God's leadership, did not turn God away from His plan of election for Israel. Election aimed at establishing God's name, His reputation in the world.

turn away from the LORD, but serve the
LORD with all your heart. 21Do not turn
away after useless[m] idols.[n] They can do
you no good, nor can they rescue you,
because they are useless. 22For the sake[o]
of his great name[p] the LORD will not reject[q] his people, because the LORD was
pleased to make[r] you his own. 23As for
me, far be it from me that I should sin
against the LORD by failing to pray[s] for
you. And I will teach[t] you the way that is
good and right. 24But be sure to fear[u] the
LORD and serve him faithfully with all
your heart;[v] consider[w] what great[x]
things he has done for you. 25Yet if you
persist[y] in doing evil, both you and your
king[z] will be swept[a] away."

Chapter 13

Samuel Rebukes Saul

SAUL was ⌊thirty⌋[i] years old when he
became king, and he reigned over Israel ⌊forty-⌋[j] two years.
2Saul[k] chose three thousand men from
Israel; two thousand[b] were with him at
Micmash[c] and in the hill country of
Bethel, and a thousand were with Jonathan at Gibeah[d] in Benjamin. The rest of
the men he sent back to their homes.
3Jonathan attacked the Philistine outpost[e] at Geba,[f] and the Philistines heard
about it. Then Saul had the trumpet[g]
blown throughout the land and said, "Let
the Hebrews hear!" 4So all Israel heard
the news: "Saul has attacked the Philistine outpost, and now Israel has become a
stench[h] to the Philistines." And the people were summoned to join Saul at Gilgal.
5The Philistines assembled[i] to fight Israel, with three thousand[l] chariots, six
thousand charioteers, and soldiers as numerous as the sand[j] on the seashore.
They went up and camped at Micmash,[k]
east of Beth Aven.[l] 6When the men of
Israel saw that their situation was critical
and that their army was hard pressed,
they hid[m] in caves and thickets, among
the rocks, and in pits and cisterns.[n]
7Some Hebrews even crossed the Jordan
to the land of Gad[o] and Gilead.
Saul remained at Gilgal, and all the
troops with him were quaking[p] with
fear. 8He waited seven[q] days, the time
set by Samuel; but Samuel did not come
to Gilgal, and Saul's men began to scatter.
9So he said, "Bring me the burnt offering
and the fellowship offerings.[m]" And Saul
offered[r] up the burnt offering. 10Just as
he finished making the offering, Samuel[s]
arrived, and Saul went out to greet[t] him.
11"What have you done?" asked
Samuel.
Saul replied, "When I saw that the
men were scattering, and that you did not
come at the set time, and that the Philistines were assembling at Micmash,[u] 12I
thought, 'Now the Philistines will come
down against me at Gilgal,[v] and I have
not sought the LORD's favor.[w] So I felt
compelled to offer the burnt offering."
13"You acted foolishly,[x]" Samuel said.
"You have not kept[y] the command the
LORD your God gave you; if you had, he
would have established your kingdom
over Israel for all time.[z] 14But now your
kingdom[a] will not endure; the LORD has
sought out a man after his own heart[b]
and appointed[c] him leader[d] of his people, because you have not kept[e] the
LORD's command."
15Then Samuel left Gilgal[n] and went
up to Gibeah[f] in Benjamin, and Saul
counted the men who were with him.
They numbered about six hundred.[g]

Israel Without Weapons

16Saul and his son Jonathan and the
men with them were staying in Gibeah[o][h] in Benjamin, while the Philistines
camped at Micmash. 17Raiding[i] parties
went out from the Philistine camp in
three detachments. One turned toward
Ophrah[j] in the vicinity of Shual, 18anoth-
er toward Beth Horon,[k] and the third

12:21 [m]Isa 40:20; 41:24,29; 44:9; Jer 2:5,11; 14:22; 16:19; Jnh 2:8; Hab 2:18; Ac 14:15 [n]Dt 11:16
12:22 [o]Ps 25:11; 106:8; Isa 48:9,11; Jer 14:7; Da 9:19 [p]S Jos 7:9; 2Sa 7:23; Jn 17:12 [q]S Lev 26:11; S Dt 31:6 [r]Dt 7:7; 1Pe 2:9
12:23 [s]S Nu 11:2; S 1Sa 1:20; S 7:8; Ro 1:9-10 [t]1Ki 8:36; Ps 25:4; 34:11; 86:11; 94:12; Pr 4:11
12:24 [u]Dt 6:2; Ecc 12:13 [v]Dt 6:5; S Jos 24:14 [w]Job 34:27; Isa 5:12; 22:11; 26:10 [x]S Dt 10:21
12:25 [y]1Sa 31:1-5 [z]Dt 28:36 [a]S Jos 24:20; S 1Ki 14:10
13:2 [b]ver 15 [c]ver 5,11,23; Ne 11:31; Isa 10:28 [d]S Jdg 19:14
13:3 [e]S 1Sa 10:5 [f]S Jos 18:24 [g]S Lev 25:9; S Jdg 3:27
13:4 [h]S Ge 34:30
13:5 [i]1Sa 17:1 [j]S Jos 11:4; Rev 20:8 [k]S ver 2 [l]S Jos 7:2
13:6 [m]1Sa 14:11, 22 [n]S Jdg 6:2; Eze 33:27
13:7 [o]S Nu 32:33 [p]S Ge 35:5; S Ex 19:16
13:8 [q]1Sa 10:8
13:9 [r]Dt 12:5-14; 2Sa 24:25; 1Ki 3:4
13:10 [s]1Sa 15:13 [t]1Sa 25:14
13:11 [u]S ver 2
13:12 [v]S Jos 10:43 [w]S Dt 4:29; Ps 119:58; Jer 26:19
13:13 [x]2Ch 16:9 [y]ver 14; S Jos 22:16; 1Sa 15:23,24; 2Sa 7:15; 1Ch 10:13 [z]Ps 72:5
13:14 [a]1Sa 15:28; 18:8; 24:20; 1Ch 10:14 [b]Ac 7:46; 13:22 [c]2Sa 6:21 [d]1Sa 25:30; 2Sa 5:2; Ps 18:43; Isa 16:5; 55:4; Jer 30:9; Eze 34:23-24; 37:24; Da 9:25; Hos 3:5; Mic 5:2 [e]1Sa 15:26; 16:1; 2Sa 12:9; 1Ki 13:21; Hos 13:11
13:15 [f]1Sa 14:2 [g]ver 2
13:16 [h]S Jos 18:24
13:17 [i]1Sa 14:15 [j]S Jos 18:23
13:18 [k]S Jos 10:10

[i] *1* A few late manuscripts of the Septuagint; Hebrew does not have *thirty.* [j] *1* See the round number in Acts 13:21; Hebrew does not have *forty-.* [k] *1,2* Or *and when he had reigned over Israel two years, 2he* [l] *5* Some Septuagint manuscripts and Syriac; Hebrew *thirty thousand* [m] *9* Traditionally *peace offerings* [n] *15* Hebrew; Septuagint *Gilgal and went his way; the rest of the people went after Saul to meet the army, and they went out of Gilgal* [o] *16* Two Hebrew manuscripts; most Hebrew manuscripts *Geba,* a variant of *Gibeah*

God will accomplish that purpose through election despite human sin. He will discipline those who turn away to "useless idols" (Hebrew *tohu*; Ge 1:2, "formless" chaos). Only the God of election does good for and rescues His people.

12:25 SIN, Punishment—Sin leads to God's intervention in human affairs whether in the life of an individual or in the life of a nation. God never ignores sin. He forgives the repentant sinner and either waits patiently on or brings judgment against the unrepentant sinner.

13:9–13 WORSHIP, False—See note on Ex 22:20.

13:9,13 PRAYER, Will of God—Saul had been anointed king, but kingly anointing was not priestly anointing. Samuel had explained the "regulations of the kingship" and had solemnly placed them "before the LORD" (10:25). Prayer and worship must be done in the will of God, not at the whim of a ruler.

13:13–14 EVIL AND SUFFERING, Punishment—Political leaders are not and must not presume to be God. All human power structures stand under God's control and judgment. God expects leaders to seek and obey His will. When they do not, they face His punishment. Saul's disobedience of God's command led to the loss of his kingdom (15:10–29).

toward the borderland overlooking the
Valley of Zeboim[l] facing the desert.
19Not a blacksmith[m] could be found in
the whole land of Israel, because the Philistines had said, "Otherwise the Hebrews
will make swords or spears![n]" 20So all
Israel went down to the Philistines to
have their plowshares, mattocks, axes
and sickles[p] sharpened. 21The price was
two thirds of a shekel[q] for sharpening
plowshares and mattocks, and a third of a
shekel[r] for sharpening forks and axes
and for repointing goads.
22So on the day of the battle not a soldier with Saul and Jonathan[o] had a sword
or spear[p] in his hand; only Saul and his
son Jonathan had them.

Chapter 14

Jonathan Attacks the Philistines

23NOW a detachment of Philistines had
gone out to the pass[q] at Micmash.[r]
1One day Jonathan son of Saul said to the
young man bearing his armor, "Come,
let's go over to the Philistine outpost on
the other side." But he did not tell his
father.
2Saul was staying[s] on the outskirts of
Gibeah[t] under a pomegranate tree[u] in
Migron.[v] With him were about six hundred men, 3among whom was Ahijah,
who was wearing an ephod. He was a son
of Ichabod's[w] brother Ahitub[x] son of
Phinehas, the son of Eli,[y] the LORD's
priest in Shiloh.[z] No one was aware that
Jonathan had left.
4On each side of the pass[a] that Jonathan intended to cross to reach the Philistine outpost was a cliff; one was called
Bozez, and the other Seneh. 5One cliff
stood to the north toward Micmash, the
other to the south toward Geba.[b]
6Jonathan said to his young armor-bearer, "Come, let's go over to the outpost of
those uncircumcised[c] fellows. Perhaps
the LORD will act in our behalf. Nothing[d]
can hinder the LORD from saving, whether by many[e] or by few.[f]"
7"Do all that you have in mind," his
armor-bearer said. "Go ahead; I am with
you heart and soul."
8Jonathan said, "Come, then; we will
cross over toward the men and let them
see us. 9If they say to us, 'Wait there until
we come to you,' we will stay where we
are and not go up to them. 10But if they
say, 'Come up to us,' we will climb up,
because that will be our sign[g] that the
LORD has given them into our hands.[h]"
11So both of them showed themselves
to the Philistine outpost. "Look!" said the
Philistines. "The Hebrews[i] are crawling
out of the holes they were hiding[j] in."
12The men of the outpost shouted to Jonathan and his armor-bearer, "Come up to
us and we'll teach you a lesson.[k]"
So Jonathan said to his armor-bearer,
"Climb up after me; the LORD has given
them into the hand[l] of Israel."
13Jonathan climbed up, using his hands
and feet, with his armor-bearer right behind him. The Philistines fell before Jonathan, and his armor-bearer followed and
killed behind him. 14In that first attack
Jonathan and his armor-bearer killed
some twenty men in an area of about half
an acre.[s]

Israel Routs the Philistines

15Then panic[m] struck the whole army
—those in the camp and field, and those
in the outposts and raiding[n] parties—
and the ground shook. It was a panic sent
by God.[t]
16Saul's lookouts[o] at Gibeah in Benjamin saw the army melting away in all directions. 17Then Saul said to the men
who were with him, "Muster the forces
and see who has left us." When they did,
it was Jonathan and his armor-bearer who
were not there.
18Saul said to Ahijah, "Bring[p] the ark[q]
of God." (At that time it was with the
Israelites.)[u] 19While Saul was talking to
the priest, the tumult in the Philistine
camp increased more and more. So Saul
said to the priest,[r] "Withdraw your
hand."
20Then Saul and all his men assembled
and went to the battle. They found the
Philistines in total confusion, striking[s]
each other with their swords. 21Those
Hebrews who had previously been with
the Philistines and had gone up with
them to their camp went[t] over to the
Israelites who were with Saul and Jona-

13:18 [l]Ne 11:34
13:19 [m]S Ge 4:22 [n]S Nu 25:7
13:22 [o]1Ch 9:39 [p]S Nu 25:7; 1Sa 14:6; 17:47; Zec 4:6
13:23 [q]1Sa 14:4 [r]S ver 2
14:2 [s]S Jdg 4:5 [t]1Sa 13:15 [u]S Ex 28:33 [v]Isa 10:28
14:3 [w]S Ge 35:18 [x]1Sa 22:11,20 [y]S 1Sa 1:3 [z]Ps 78:60
14:4 [a]1Sa 13:23
14:5 [b]S Jos 18:24
14:6 [c]Jdg 14:3; 1Sa 17:26,36; 31:4; Jer 9:26; Eze 28:10 [d]S 1Sa 13:22; S 1Ki 19:12; S Mt 19:26; Heb 11:34 [e]Jdg 7:4 [f]Ps 33:16
14:10 [g]S Ge 24:14 [h]S Jos 2:24
14:11 [i]S Ge 14:13 [j]S 1Sa 13:6
14:12 [k]Jdg 8:16 [l]1Sa 17:46; 2Sa 5:24
14:15 [m]S Ge 35:5; S Ex 14:24; S 19:16; 2Ki 7:5-7 [n]1Sa 13:17
14:16 [o]2Sa 18:24; 2Ki 9:17; Isa 52:8; Eze 33:2
14:18 [p]1Sa 30:7 [q]S Jdg 18:5
14:19 [r]Nu 27:21
14:20 [s]S Jdg 7:22; Eze 38:21; Zec 14:13
14:21 [t]1Sa 29:4

[p] *20* Septuagint; Hebrew *plowshares* [q] *21* Hebrew *pim*; that is, about 1/4 ounce (about 8 grams) [r] *21* That is, about 1/8 ounce (about 4 grams) [s] *14* Hebrew *half a yoke*; a "yoke" was the land plowed by a yoke of oxen in one day. [t] *15* Or *a terrible panic* [u] *18* Hebrew; Septuagint *"Bring the ephod." (At that time he wore the ephod before the Israelites.)*

14:6–23 HISTORY, Deliverance—Human rules do not limit God. He can use a few people to gain victory if He chooses. No human can compel God to deliver. God acts as He chooses. Whatever human factors were involved in Israel's victory over the Philistines, the inspired writer confessed that God had "rescued Israel that day."

14:6 SALVATION, Definition—God rescues His people against all odds and foes when they completely rely on His power (vv 23,45).

14:8–10 PRAYER, Will of God—Jonathan recognized that the disposition of the battle was not in his hands but the Lord's. His conversation with his servant indicated he was asking God for a sign. See note on Jdg 6:36–40.

than. 22When all the Israelites who had
hidden[u] in the hill country of Ephraim
heard that the Philistines were on the
run, they joined the battle in hot pursuit.
23So the LORD rescued[v] Israel that day,
and the battle moved on beyond Beth
Aven.[w]

Jonathan Eats Honey

24Now the men of Israel were in distress that day, because Saul had bound
the people under an oath,[x] saying,
"Cursed be any man who eats food before evening comes, before I have
avenged myself on my enemies!" So none
of the troops tasted food.
25The entire army[v] entered the woods,
and there was honey on the ground.
26When they went into the woods, they
saw the honey oozing out, yet no one put
his hand to his mouth, because they
feared the oath. 27But Jonathan had not
heard that his father had bound the people with the oath, so he reached out the
end of the staff that was in his hand and
dipped it into the honeycomb.[y] He raised
his hand to his mouth, and his eyes
brightened.[w] 28Then one of the soldiers
told him, "Your father bound the army
under a strict oath, saying, 'Cursed be
any man who eats food today!' That is
why the men are faint."
29Jonathan said, "My father has made
trouble[z] for the country. See how my
eyes brightened[x] when I tasted a little of
this honey. 30How much better it would
have been if the men had eaten today
some of the plunder they took from their
enemies. Would not the slaughter of the
Philistines have been even greater?"
31That day, after the Israelites had
struck down the Philistines from Micmash[a] to Aijalon,[b] they were exhausted.
32They pounced on the plunder[c] and,
taking sheep, cattle and calves, they
butchered them on the ground and ate
them, together with the blood.[d] 33Then
someone said to Saul, "Look, the men are
sinning against the LORD by eating meat
that has blood[e] in it."
"You have broken faith," he said. "Roll
a large stone over here at once." 34Then
he said, "Go out among the men and tell
them, 'Each of you bring me your cattle
and sheep, and slaughter them here and
eat them. Do not sin against the LORD by
eating meat with blood still[f] in it.' "
So everyone brought his ox that night
and slaughtered it there. 35Then Saul
built an altar[g] to the LORD; it was the
first time he had done this.
36Saul said, "Let us go down after the
Philistines by night and plunder them till
dawn, and let us not leave one of them
alive."
"Do whatever seems best to you," they
replied.
But the priest said, "Let us inquire[h] of
God here."
37So Saul asked God, "Shall I go down
after the Philistines? Will you give them
into Israel's hand?" But God did not answer[i] him that day.
38Saul therefore said, "Come here, all
you who are leaders of the army, and let
us find out what sin has been committed[j] today. 39As surely as the LORD who
rescues Israel lives,[k] even if it lies with
my son Jonathan,[l] he must die."[m] But
not one of the men said a word.
40Saul then said to all the Israelites,
"You stand over there; I and Jonathan my
son will stand over here."
"Do what seems best to you," the men
replied.
41Then Saul prayed to the LORD, the
God of Israel, "Give[n] me the right[o] answer."[y] And Jonathan and Saul were tak-
en by lot, and the men were cleared.
42Saul said, "Cast the lot[p] between me
and Jonathan my son." And Jonathan was
taken.
43Then Saul said to Jonathan, "Tell me
what you have done."[q]
So Jonathan told him, "I merely tasted
a little honey[r] with the end of my staff.
And now must I die?"
44Saul said, "May God deal with me, be
it ever so severely,[s] if you do not die,
Jonathan.[t] "
45But the men said to Saul, "Should
Jonathan die—he who has brought about
this great deliverance in Israel? Never! As
surely as the LORD lives, not a hair[u] of his
head will fall to the ground, for he did

14:22 [u]S 1Sa 13:6
14:23 [v]S Ex 14:30 [w]S Jos 7:2
14:24 [x]Jos 6:26
14:27 [y]ver 43; Ps 19:10; Pr 16:24; 24:13
14:29 [z]Jos 7:25; 1Ki 18:18
14:31 [a]ver 5 [b]S Jos 10:12
14:32 [c]1Sa 15:19; Est 9:10 [d]S Ge 9:4
14:33 [e]S Ge 9:4
14:34 [f]Lev 19:26
14:35 [g]S 1Sa 7:17
14:36 [h]S Ge 25:22; S Jdg 18:5
14:37 [i]1Sa 28:6, 15; 2Sa 22:42; Ps 18:41
14:38 [j]Jos 7:11
14:39 [k]S Nu 14:21; 2Sa 12:5; Job 19:25; Ps 18:46; 42:2 [l]ver 44 [m]Jos 7:15
14:41 [n]Ac 1:24 [o]Pr 16:33
14:42 [p]Jnh 1:7
14:43 [q]S Jos 7:19 [r]S ver 27
14:44 [s]S Ru 1:17 [t]ver 39
14:45 [u]1Ki 1:52; S Mt 10:30

[v]25 Or *Now all the people of the land* [w]27 Or *his strength was renewed* [x]29 Or *my strength was renewed* [y]41 Hebrew; Septuagint *"Why have you not answered your servant today? If the fault is in me or my son Jonathan, respond with Urim, but if the men of Israel are at fault, respond with Thummim."*

14:27–45 FAMILY, Role Relationships—See note on Jdg 11:30–40.

14:32–34 SIN, Transgression—In crisis and physical need, Saul's men disobeyed God's instructions (Lev 17:10–11). They learned obedience to God is more important than meeting personal need. Emergencies do not justify any sin.

14:41–45 PRAYER, Hindrances—Saul had made a foolish vow that his men would fast (v 24). Jonathan had broken that vow in ignorance of it. That God considered the vow seriously is seen in His speaking through the lots. That the vow was itself sinful is seen in God's refusal to answer Saul (v 37) and His vindication of Jonathan by giving him victory. The men recognized that Jonathan's victory was accomplished "with God's help." Jonathan's death would have been an additional and unnecessary consequence of Saul's foolishness. See note on Jdg 11:30. Rash actions even involving prayer can hinder us from communicating with God.

this today with God's help." So the men
rescued[v] Jonathan, and he was not put to
death.
46Then Saul stopped pursuing the Philistines, and they withdrew to their own
land.
47After Saul had assumed rule over Israel, he fought against their enemies on
every side: Moab,[w] the Ammonites,[x]
Edom,[y] the kings[z] of Zobah,[z] and the
Philistines. Wherever he turned, he inflicted punishment on them.[a] 48He
fought valiantly and defeated the Amalekites,[a] delivering Israel from the hands of
those who had plundered them.

Saul's Family

49Saul's sons were Jonathan, Ishvi and
Malki-Shua.[b] The name of his older
daughter was Merab, and that of the
younger was Michal.[c] 50His wife's name
was Ahinoam daughter of Ahimaaz. The
name of the commander of Saul's army
was Abner[d] son of Ner, and Ner was
Saul's uncle.[e] 51Saul's father Kish[f] and
Abner's father Ner were sons of Abiel.
52All the days of Saul there was bitter
war with the Philistines, and whenever
Saul saw a mighty or brave man, he
took[g] him into his service.

Chapter 15

The LORD Rejects Saul as King

SAMUEL said to Saul, "I am the one the
LORD sent to anoint[h] you king over
his people Israel; so listen now to the
message from the LORD. 2This is what the
LORD Almighty says: 'I will punish the
Amalekites[i] for what they did to Israel
when they waylaid them as they came up
from Egypt. 3Now go, attack the Amalekites and totally[j] destroy[b] everything that
belongs to them. Do not spare them; put
to death men and women, children and
infants, cattle and sheep, camels and donkeys.' "
4So Saul summoned the men and mustered them at Telaim—two hundred
thousand foot soldiers and ten thousand
men from Judah. 5Saul went to the city of
Amalek and set an ambush in the ravine.
6Then he said to the Kenites,[k] "Go away,
leave the Amalekites so that I do not destroy you along with them; for you
showed kindness to all the Israelites
when they came up out of Egypt." So the
Kenites moved away from the Amalekites.
7Then Saul attacked the Amalekites[l]
all the way from Havilah to Shur,[m] to the
east of Egypt. 8He took Agag[n] king of the
Amalekites alive,[o] and all his people he
totally destroyed with the sword. 9But
Saul and the army spared[p] Agag and the
best of the sheep and cattle, the fat
calves[c] and lambs—everything that was
good. These they were unwilling to destroy completely, but everything that was
despised and weak they totally destroyed.
10Then the word of the LORD came to
Samuel: 11"I am grieved[q] that I have
made Saul king, because he has turned[r]
away from me and has not carried out my
instructions."[s] Samuel was troubled,[t]
and he cried out to the LORD all that
night.
12Early in the morning Samuel got up
and went to meet Saul, but he was told,
"Saul has gone to Carmel.[u] There he has
set up a monument[v] in his own honor
and has turned and gone on down to Gilgal."
13When Samuel reached him, Saul said,

14:45 [v]2Sa 14:11
14:47 [w]S Ge 19:37 [x]S Ge 19:38; 2Sa 12:31 [y]1Sa 21:7 [z]2Sa 8:3; 10:6; 23:36
14:48 [a]S Ge 36:12; Nu 13:29; Jdg 3:13; 1Sa 15:2,7; 27:8; 28:18; 30:13; 2Sa 1:13; 1Ch 4:43
14:49 [b]1Sa 31:2; 1Ch 8:33 [c]S Ge 29:26
14:50 [d]2Sa 2:8; 3:6; 1Ki 2:5 [e]1Sa 10:14
14:51 [f]S 1Sa 9:1
14:52 [g]1Sa 8:11
15:1 [h]S 1Sa 9:16
15:2 [i]S Ge 14:7; S 1Sa 14:48; S 2Sa 1:8
15:3 [j]ver 9,19; S Ge 14:23; Jos 6:17; 1Sa 22:19; 27:9; 28:18; Est 3:13; 9:5
15:6 [k]S Ge 15:19; Nu 24:22; Jdg 1:16; 1Sa 30:29
15:7 [l]S 1Sa 14:48 [m]S Ge 16:7
15:8 [n]Ex 17:8-16; S Nu 24:7 [o]S Jos 8:23
15:9 [p]S ver 3
15:11 [q]S Ge 6:6; S Ex 32:14 [r]S Jos 22:16 [s]Job 21:14; 34:27; Ps 28:5; Isa 5:12; 53:6; Jer 48:10; Eze 18:24 [t]S ver 35; S 1Sa 8:6
15:12 [u]Jos 15:55 [v]S Nu 32:42

[z]47 Masoretic Text; Dead Sea Scrolls and Septuagint *king*
[a]47 Hebrew; Septuagint *he was victorious*
[b]3 The Hebrew term refers to the irrevocable giving over of things or persons to the LORD, often by totally destroying them; also in verses 8, 9, 15, 18, 20 and 21.
[c]9 Or *the grown bulls*; the meaning of the Hebrew for this phrase is uncertain.

15:1–3 GOD, Wrath—See note on Ex 32:10,12,34–35. The wrath of God does not always come immediately. In God's own time and in His own way, He will punish those who oppose Him or try to defeat His actions in His world. God is not vindictive, seeking every opportunity to pour out harsh judgment.

15:1–35 SIN, Alienation—Political power and God-appointed office do not exempt a person from obeying God. Saul wanted to pick and choose among God's teachings. His sinful disobedience alienated him from God. No amount of human reasoning or pious language could justify his actions. We cannot justify sin. We must confess it or face alienation.

15:1–26 REVELATION, Faithfulness—Saul's attitudes and practices grew increasingly motivated by self-gain. He forgot who the real Leader was and what God intended to do with Israel. Revelation is given to God's people to lead us to *obey. When we do not, God reveals His judgment.*

15:7–35 CHRISTIAN ETHICS, War and Peace—God seeks righteousness and not ritual; He seeks obedience to Himself and not to stale, static traditions. Warfare does not relieve a people from the responsibility to obey God. No human power has the right to disobey God. God can turn victory into defeat for a disobedient people.

15:10–29 EVIL AND SUFFERING, Punishment—See note on 13:13–14.

15:10–29 HISTORY, God's Leaders—Faithful obedience is God's expectation of His leaders. Repeated disobedience and lack of faith eventually brings God's rejection. Partial obedience and desperation repentance cannot force God to change His mind and reinstate a rejected leader. God steadfastly announces and faithfully carries out His purposes.

15:11–35 PRAYER, Will of God—God's anger led Samuel to pray. The prayer did not lead to renewed favor for Saul. Both Samuel and God continued to be angry with him. Prayer did lead Samuel to the proper actions in a difficult situation. Prayer is the only source of guidance when humiliation, defeat, and ruptured relationships are at stake. Separated from Samuel and God, Saul was still permitted to confess his sins and worship. See note on Ge 19:27.

"The LORD bless you! I have carried out
the LORD's instructions."
14 But Samuel said, "What then is this
bleating of sheep in my ears? What is this
lowing of cattle that I hear?"
15 Saul answered, "The soldiers brought
them from the Amalekites; they spared
the best of the sheep and cattle to sacrifice to the LORD your God, but we totally
destroyed the rest."
16 "Stop!" Samuel said to Saul. "Let me
tell you what the LORD said to me last
night."
"Tell me," Saul replied.
17 Samuel said, "Although you were
once small[w] in your own eyes, did you
not become the head of the tribes of Israel? The LORD anointed you king over Israel. 18 And he sent you on a mission, saying, 'Go and completely destroy those
wicked people, the Amalekites; make war
on them until you have wiped them out.'
19 Why did you not obey the LORD? Why
did you pounce on the plunder[x] and do
evil in the eyes of the LORD?"
20 "But I did obey[y] the LORD," Saul
said. "I went on the mission the LORD
assigned me. I completely destroyed the
Amalekites and brought back Agag their
king. 21 The soldiers took sheep and cattle
from the plunder, the best of what was
devoted to God, in order to sacrifice them
to the LORD your God at Gilgal."
22 But Samuel replied:

"Does the LORD delight in burnt
offerings and sacrifices
as much as in obeying the voice of
the LORD?
To obey is better than sacrifice,[z]
and to heed is better than the fat of
rams.
23 For rebellion is like the sin of
divination,[a]
and arrogance like the evil of
idolatry.
Because you have rejected[b] the word
of the LORD,
he has rejected you as king."

24 Then Saul said to Samuel, "I have
sinned.[c] I violated[d] the LORD's command and your instructions. I was afraid[e]
of the people and so I gave in to them.

15:17 [w]S Ex 3:11
15:19 [x]S Ge 14:23; S 1Sa 14:32
15:20 [y]1Sa 28:18
15:22 [z]Ps 40:6-8; 51:16; Pr 21:3; Isa 1:11-15; Jer 7:22; Hos 6:6; Am 5:25; Mic 6:6-8; S Mk 12:33
15:23 [a]Dt 18:10 [b]S 1Sa 13:13
15:24 [c]S Ex 9:27; S Nu 22:34; Ps 51:4 [d]S 1Sa 13:13 [e]Pr 29:25; Isa 51:12-13; Jer 42:11
15:25 [f]Ex 10:17
15:26 [g]S Nu 15:31; S 1Sa 13:14; S 1Ki 14:10
15:27 [h]1Sa 28:14 [i]1Ki 11:11,31; 14:8; 2Ki 17:21
15:28 [j]1Sa 28:17 [k]S 1Sa 13:14 [l]2Sa 6:21; 7:15
15:29 [m]Tit 1:2 [n]S Nu 23:19; Heb 7:21
15:30 [o]S Nu 22:34 [p]Isa 29:13; Jn 12:43
15:33 [q]Est 9:7-10; Jer 18:21
15:34 [r]S 1Sa 7:17 [s]S Jdg 19:14; S 1Sa 10:5
15:35 [t]1Sa 19:24 [u]ver 11; 1Sa 16:1 [v]S Ge 6:6
16:1 [w]S 1Sa 8:6; S 15:35 [x]S 1Sa 13:14 [y]S 1Sa 10:1

25 Now I beg you, forgive[f] my sin and
come back with me, so that I may worship the LORD."
26 But Samuel said to him, "I will not go
back with you. You have rejected[g] the
word of the LORD, and the LORD has rejected you as king over Israel!"
27 As Samuel turned to leave, Saul
caught hold of the hem of his robe,[h] and
it tore.[i] 28 Samuel said to him, "The LORD
has torn[j] the kingdom[k] of Israel from
you today and has given it to one of your
neighbors—to one better than you.[l]
29 He who is the Glory of Israel does not
lie[m] or change[n] his mind; for he is not a
man, that he should change his mind."
30 Saul replied, "I have sinned.[o] But
please honor[p] me before the elders of my
people and before Israel; come back with
me, so that I may worship the LORD your
God." 31 So Samuel went back with Saul,
and Saul worshiped the LORD.
32 Then Samuel said, "Bring me Agag
king of the Amalekites."
Agag came to him confidently,[d] thinking, "Surely the bitterness of death is
past."
33 But Samuel said,

"As your sword has made women
childless,
so will your mother be childless
among women."[q]

And Samuel put Agag to death before the
LORD at Gilgal.
34 Then Samuel left for Ramah,[r] but
Saul went up to his home in Gibeah[s] of
Saul. 35 Until the day Samuel[t] died, he
did not go to see Saul again, though Samuel mourned[u] for him. And the LORD was
grieved[v] that he had made Saul king over
Israel.

Chapter 16

Samuel Anoints David

16 THE LORD said to Samuel, "How long
will you mourn[w] for Saul, since I
have rejected[x] him as king over Israel?
Fill your horn with oil[y] and be on your

[d]*32* Or *him trembling, yet*

15:22–23 WORSHIP, Obedience—Any apparent worship ritual that is not accompanied by obedience is worthless to the individual and an insult to God. It is nothing more than rebellion and arrogance. Obedience to God is an indispensable part of true worship. Ceremony is necessary and important but must be accompanied by service for God, by obedience to His will. True worship is adoring and obedient love for Him and loving service to others at God's direction. Compare Ps 61:8; Isa 6:8–9; Hos 6:6; Ro 12:1. See notes on 1 Sa 1:9–28; Dt 11:13.

15:29 GOD, Faithfulness—Our God is not a God who constantly changes, leaving His people to wonder what He is like at any given moment. He is constant, ever true to Himself, His principles and His people. We can trust Him and His Word. Compare Heb 13:8. See note on Ex 13:5,11.

16:1–13 ELECTION, Leadership—The anointings of Saul and David involved two young men who had not achieved royal standing. Their anointings took place in secret, but they happened because of God's election. Rejection of the disobedient Saul did not mean abandonment of kingship. David's older brothers were impressive and attractive as candidates for the office of king, but human beings can only judge a candidate by outward appearances. God is the only one qualified to do the electing, because God looks at the heart.

way; I am sending you to Jesse[z] of Bethlehem. I have chosen[a] one of his sons to
be king."
2But Samuel said, "How can I go? Saul
will hear about it and kill me."
The LORD said, "Take a heifer with you
and say, 'I have come to sacrifice to the
LORD.' 3Invite Jesse to the sacrifice, and I
will show[b] you what to do. You are to
anoint[c] for me the one I indicate."
4Samuel did what the LORD said. When
he arrived at Bethlehem,[d] the elders of
the town trembled[e] when they met him.
They asked, "Do you come in peace?[f]"
5Samuel replied, "Yes, in peace; I have
come to sacrifice to the LORD. Consecrate[g] yourselves and come to the sacrifice with me." Then he consecrated Jesse
and his sons and invited them to the sacrifice.
6When they arrived, Samuel saw Eliab[h] and thought, "Surely the LORD's
anointed stands here before the LORD."
7But the LORD said to Samuel, "Do not
consider his appearance or his height, for
I have rejected him. The LORD does not
look at the things man looks at. Man
looks at the outward appearance,[i] but
the LORD looks at the heart."[j]
8Then Jesse called Abinadab[k] and had
him pass in front of Samuel. But Samuel
said, "The LORD has not chosen this one
either." 9Jesse then had Shammah[l] pass
by, but Samuel said, "Nor has the LORD
chosen this one." 10Jesse had seven of his
sons pass before Samuel, but Samuel said
to him, "The LORD has not chosen
these." 11So he asked Jesse, "Are these
all[m] the sons you have?"
"There is still the youngest," Jesse answered, "but he is tending the sheep."[n]
Samuel said, "Send for him; we will
not sit down[e] until he arrives."
12So he[o] sent and had him brought in.
He was ruddy, with a fine appearance and
handsome[p] features.
Then the LORD said, "Rise and anoint
him; he is the one."
13So Samuel took the horn of oil and
anointed[q] him in the presence of his
brothers, and from that day on the Spirit
of the LORD[r] came upon David in power.[s] Samuel then went to Ramah.

David in Saul's Service

14Now the Spirit of the LORD had departed[t] from Saul, and an evil[f] spirit[u]
from the LORD tormented him.[v]
15Saul's attendants said to him, "See,
an evil spirit from God is tormenting you.
16Let our lord command his servants here
to search for someone who can play the
harp.[w] He will play when the evil spirit
from God comes upon you, and you will
feel better."
17So Saul said to his attendants, "Find
someone who plays well and bring him to
me."
18One of the servants answered, "I
have seen a son of Jesse[x] of Bethlehem
who knows how to play the harp. He is a
brave man and a warrior.[y] He speaks
well and is a fine-looking man. And the
LORD is with[z] him."
19Then Saul sent messengers to Jesse
and said, "Send me your son David, who
is with the sheep.[a]" 20So Jesse took a
donkey loaded with bread,[b] a skin of
wine and a young goat and sent them
with his son David to Saul.
21David came to Saul and entered his
service.[c] Saul liked him very much, and
David became one of his armor-bearers.
22Then Saul sent word to Jesse, saying,
"Allow David to remain in my service, for
I am pleased with him."
23Whenever the spirit from God came
upon Saul, David would take his harp and
play. Then relief would come to Saul; he
would feel better, and the evil spirit[d]
would leave him.

16:1 zS Ru 4:17 a2Sa 5:2; 7:8; 1Ki 8:16; 1Ch 12:23; Ps 78:70; Ac 13:22
16:3 bEx 4:15 cS Dt 17:15
16:4 dS Ge 48:7; Lk 2:4 e1Sa 21:1 f1Ki 2:13; 2Ki 9:17
16:5 gS Ex 19:10, 22
16:6 h1Sa 17:13; 1Ch 2:13
16:7 iPs 147:10 jS 1Sa 2:3; 2Sa 7:20; S Ps 44:21; S 139:23; S Rev 2:23
16:8 k1Sa 17:13
16:9 l1Sa 17:13; 2Sa 13:3; 21:21
16:11 m1Sa 17:12 nS Ge 37:2; 2Sa 7:8
16:12 o1Sa 9:17 pS Ge 39:6
16:13 qS 1Sa 2:35; S 2Sa 22:51 r1Sa 18:12 sS 1Sa 11:6
16:14 tS Jdg 16:20 uver 23; S Jdg 9:23; 1Sa 18:10 v2Sa 7:15
16:16 wver 23; S 1Sa 10:5,6; 2Ch 29:26-27; Ps 49:4
16:18 xS Ru 4:17 y2Sa 17:8 zS Ge 39:2; 1Sa 17:32-37; 20:13; 1Ch 22:11; Mt 1:23
16:19 a1Sa 17:15
16:20 bS Ge 32:13; S 1Sa 10:4
16:21 cS Ge 41:46
16:23 dS ver 14; S Jdg 9:23

e *11* Some Septuagint manuscripts; Hebrew *not gather around* f *14* Or *injurious*; also in verses 15, 16 and 23

16:2 PRAYER, Will of God—Prayer can bring God's answer out of personal danger and lead to doing God's will.
16:7 HUMANITY, Physical Nature—While outstanding physical attributes attract attention, the more important qualities of people are those within.
16:13–14 HOLY SPIRIT, Resisted—God's Spirit does not violate our freedom. The inspired writer dramatically made the point that Saul's repeated disobedience led the Spirit to depart, to quit working in Saul's life. Where Saul would not let the Spirit work, God let an evil spirit take charge. See vv 15,16,23; 18:10; 19:9; 1 Ki 22:22; 2 Th 2:11. God's leaders follow God, or they follow evil. David represented the contrast to Saul. The Spirit took charge of his life from that day on. Saul had political office and power. David had the Spirit's call and power. Holding a position does not make a person a leader. Obeying God's Spirit does.
16:13–23 EVIL AND SUFFERING, Divine Origin—The Bible tenaciously holds to monotheism—the belief in the existence of only one God. This distinguished the people of Israel radically from their neighbors. It also forces God's people to explain the evil we encounter in light of the sovereign rule of one God over all His creation. This means God is responsible for permitting evil to exist. The spirit is the power which drives a person's will and emotions. When a person allows God's Spirit to control life, true life under God results. Otherwise, evil controls the person. Ultimately in a world of only one God, this controlling evil spirit must also be part of God's creation. God used the evil spirit to punish a disobedient, unfaithful member of His people. To speak of an evil spirit from God does not lessen human responsibility for sin or place moral blame on God. The evil spirit was seen in Saul's depression, jealousy, and violent irrational threats. Even such an evil spirit remains under God's control. See notes on Jdg 9:23; 1 Ki 22:19–28.

Chapter 17

David and Goliath

NOW the Philistines gathered their forces for war and assembled[e] at Socoh in Judah. They pitched camp at Ephes Dammim, between Socoh[f] and Azekah.[g] 2Saul and the Israelites assembled and camped in the Valley of Elah[h] and drew up their battle line to meet the Philistines. 3The Philistines occupied one hill and the Israelites another, with the valley between them.

4A champion named Goliath,[i] who was from Gath, came out of the Philistine camp. He was over nine feet[g] tall. 5He had a bronze helmet on his head and wore a coat of scale armor of bronze weighing five thousand shekels[h]; 6on his legs he wore bronze greaves, and a bronze javelin[j] was slung on his back. 7His spear shaft was like a weaver's rod,[k] and its iron point weighed six hundred shekels.[i] His shield bearer[l] went ahead of him.

8Goliath stood and shouted to the ranks of Israel, "Why do you come out and line up for battle? Am I not a Philistine, and are you not the servants of Saul? Choose[m] a man and have him come down to me. 9If he is able to fight and kill me, we will become your subjects; but if I overcome him and kill him, you will become our subjects and serve us." 10Then the Philistine said, "This day I defy[n] the ranks of Israel! Give me a man and let us fight each other.[o]" 11On hearing the Philistine's words, Saul and all the Israelites were dismayed and terrified.

12Now David was the son of an Ephrathite[p] named Jesse,[q] who was from Bethlehem[r] in Judah. Jesse had eight[s] sons, and in Saul's time he was old and well advanced in years. 13Jesse's three oldest sons had followed Saul to the war: The firstborn was Eliab;[t] the second, Abinadab;[u] and the third, Shammah.[v] 14David was the youngest. The three oldest followed Saul, 15but David went back and forth from Saul to tend[w] his father's sheep[x] at Bethlehem.

16For forty days the Philistine came forward every morning and evening and took his stand.

17:1 [e]1Sa 13:5 [f]Jos 15:35; 2Ch 28:18 [g]S Jos 10:10,11
17:2 [h]1Sa 21:9
17:4 [i]1Sa 21:9; 2Sa 21:19
17:6 [j]ver 45; 1Sa 18:10
17:7 [k]2Sa 21:19; 1Ch 11:23; 20:5 [l]ver 41
17:8 [m]2Sa 2:12-17
17:10 [n]ver 26,45; 2Sa 21:21 [o]ver 23
17:12 [p]S Ge 35:16; S 48:7; Ps 132:6 [q]S Ru 4:17 [r]S Ge 35:19 [s]1Sa 16:11
17:13 [t]S 1Sa 16:6 [u]1Sa 16:8 [v]S 1Sa 16:9
17:15 [w]S Ge 37:2 [x]1Sa 16:19
17:17 [y]S Lev 19:36 [z]S Lev 23:14; 1Sa 25:18
17:18 [a]Ge 37:14
17:22 [b]S Jos 1:11
17:23 [c]ver 8-10
17:25 [d]1Sa 18:17 [e]S 1Sa 8:15
17:26 [f]1Sa 11:2 [g]S 1Sa 14:6 [h]S ver 10 [i]Dt 5:26; S Jos 3:10; 2Ki 18:35
17:28 [j]S Ge 27:41; Pr 18:19

17Now Jesse said to his son David, "Take this ephah[j][y] of roasted grain[z] and these ten loaves of bread for your brothers and hurry to their camp. 18Take along these ten cheeses to the commander of their unit.[k] See how your brothers[a] are and bring back some assurance[l] from them. 19They are with Saul and all the men of Israel in the Valley of Elah, fighting against the Philistines."

20Early in the morning David left the flock with a shepherd, loaded up and set out, as Jesse had directed. He reached the camp as the army was going out to its battle positions, shouting the war cry. 21Israel and the Philistines were drawing up their lines facing each other. 22David left his things with the keeper of supplies,[b] ran to the battle lines and greeted his brothers. 23As he was talking with them, Goliath, the Philistine champion from Gath, stepped out from his lines and shouted his usual[c] defiance, and David heard it. 24When the Israelites saw the man, they all ran from him in great fear.

25Now the Israelites had been saying, "Do you see how this man keeps coming out? He comes out to defy Israel. The king will give great wealth to the man who kills him. He will also give him his daughter[d] in marriage and will exempt his father's family from taxes[e] in Israel."

26David asked the men standing near him, "What will be done for the man who kills this Philistine and removes this disgrace[f] from Israel? Who is this uncircumcised[g] Philistine that he should defy[h] the armies of the living[i] God?"

27They repeated to him what they had been saying and told him, "This is what will be done for the man who kills him."

28When Eliab, David's oldest brother, heard him speaking with the men, he burned with anger[j] at him and asked, "Why have you come down here? And with whom did you leave those few sheep in the desert? I know how conceited you are and how wicked your heart is; you came down only to watch the battle."

[g]4 Hebrew *was six cubits and a span* (about 3 meters)
[h]5 That is, about 125 pounds (about 57 kilograms)
[i]7 That is, about 15 pounds (about 7 kilograms)
[j]17 That is, probably about 3/5 bushel (about 22 liters)
[k]18 Hebrew *thousand* [l]18 Or *some token*; or *some pledge of spoils*

17:1–58 CHRISTIAN ETHICS, War and Peace—A young, virtually unquestioning, faith in the power of God has extraordinary results. People and nations which defy God face His judgment. When God had only one nation, He revealed His power and exercised punishment through the means of human warfare. Even in warfare He worked through dedicated persons who trusted Him completely to make His sovereign power clear to Israel and to other nations.

17:26,36 GOD, Living—The God of Israel stands in the sharpest contrast to all other gods. The God of Israel is a living God—all of the other gods are the products of human hands and human imaginations. Only the living God is able to accomplish His purposes both in Israel and in the destiny of all the world's peoples. See note on Nu 14:21,28.

17:26 SIN, Against God—Human strength and military power cannot win the right to defy God. People may cringe in fear. God does not. He finds resources to punish the defiant sinner. God's people must learn to trust His power rather than human might.

29"Now what have I done?" said David. "Can't I even speak?" 30He then
turned away to someone else and brought
up the same matter, and the men answered him as before. 31What David said
was overheard and reported to Saul, and
Saul sent for him.
32David said to Saul, "Let no one lose
heart[k] on account of this Philistine; your
servant will go and fight him."
33Saul replied,[l] "You are not able to go
out against this Philistine and fight him;
you are only a boy, and he has been a
fighting man from his youth."
34But David said to Saul, "Your servant
has been keeping his father's sheep.
When a lion[m] or a bear came and carried
off a sheep from the flock, 35I went after
it, struck it and rescued the sheep from
its mouth. When it turned on me, I
seized[n] it by its hair, struck it and killed
it. 36Your servant has killed both the
lion[o] and the bear; this uncircumcised
Philistine will be like one of them, because he has defied the armies of the living God. 37The LORD who delivered[p] me
from the paw of the lion[q] and the paw of
the bear will deliver me from the hand of
this Philistine."
Saul said to David, "Go, and the LORD
be with[r] you."
38Then Saul dressed David in his own[s]
tunic. He put a coat of armor on him and
a bronze helmet on his head. 39David fastened on his sword over the tunic and
tried walking around, because he was not
used to them.
"I cannot go in these," he said to Saul,
"because I am not used to them." So he
took them off. 40Then he took his staff in
his hand, chose five smooth stones from
the stream, put them in the pouch of his
shepherd's bag and, with his sling in his
hand, approached the Philistine.
41Meanwhile, the Philistine, with his
shield bearer[t] in front of him, kept coming closer to David. 42He looked David
over and saw that he was only a boy, ruddy and handsome,[u] and he despised[v]
him. 43He said to David, "Am I a dog,[w]
that you come at me with sticks?" And
the Philistine cursed David by his gods.
44"Come here," he said, "and I'll give
your flesh to the birds of the air[x] and the
beasts of the field![y]"
45David said to the Philistine, "You
come against me with sword and spear
and javelin,[z] but I come against you in
the name[a] of the LORD Almighty, the
God of the armies of Israel, whom you
have defied.[b] 46This day the LORD will
hand[c] you over to me, and I'll strike you
down and cut off your head. Today I will
give the carcasses[d] of the Philistine army
to the birds of the air and the beasts of
the earth, and the whole world[e] will
know that there is a God in Israel.[f] 47All
those gathered here will know that it is
not by sword[g] or spear that the LORD
saves;[h] for the battle[i] is the LORD's, and
he will give all of you into our hands."
48As the Philistine moved closer to attack him, David ran quickly toward the
battle line to meet him. 49Reaching into
his bag and taking out a stone, he slung it
and struck the Philistine on the forehead.
The stone sank into his forehead, and he
fell facedown on the ground.
50So David triumphed over the Philistine with a sling[j] and a stone; without a
sword in his hand he struck down the
Philistine and killed him.
51David ran and stood over him. He
took hold of the Philistine's sword and
drew it from the scabbard. After he killed
him, he cut[k] off his head with the
sword.[l]
When the Philistines saw that their
hero was dead, they turned and ran.
52Then the men of Israel and Judah
surged forward with a shout and pursued
the Philistines to the entrance of Gath[m]
and to the gates of Ekron.[m] Their dead
were strewn along the Shaaraim[n] road to
Gath and Ekron. 53When the Israelites returned from chasing the Philistines, they
plundered their camp. 54David took the
Philistine's head and brought it to Jerusalem, and he put the Philistine's weapons
in his own tent.
55As Saul watched David[o] going out to
meet the Philistine, he said to Abner,
commander of the army, "Abner,[p]
whose son is that young man?"
Abner replied, "As surely as you live,
O king, I don't know."
56The king said, "Find out whose son
this young man is."
57As soon as David returned from killing the Philistine, Abner took him and

17:32 [k]S Dt 20:3; Ps 18:45; Isa 7:4; Jer 4:9; 38:4; Da 11:30
17:33 [l]Nu 13:31
17:34 [m]Job 10:16; Isa 31:4; Jer 49:19; Hos 13:8; Am 3:12
17:35 [n]Jdg 14:6
17:36 [o]1Ch 11:22
17:37 [p]2Co 1:10 [q]2Ti 4:17 [r]S 1Sa 16:18; S 18:12
17:38 [s]S Ge 41:42
17:41 [t]ver 7
17:42 [u]1Sa 16:12 [v]Ps 123:3-4; Pr 16:18
17:43 [w]1Sa 24:14; 2Sa 3:8; 9:8; 2Ki 8:13
17:44 [x]S Ge 40:19; Rev 19:17 [y]2Sa 21:10; Jer 34:20
17:45 [z]S ver 6 [a]Dt 20:1; 2Ch 13:12; 14:11; 32:8; Ps 20:7-8; 124:8; Heb 11:32-34 [b]S ver 10
17:46 [c]S 1Sa 14:12 [d]S Dt 28:26 [e]S Jos 4:24; S Isa 11:9 [f]1Ki 18:36; 2Ki 5:8; 19:19; Isa 37:20
17:47 [g]Hos 1:7 [h]1Sa 14:6; 2Ch 14:11; Jer 39:18 [i]S Ex 14:14; S Nu 21:14; S 1Sa 2:9; 2Ch 20:15; Ps 44:6-7
17:50 [j]1Sa 25:29
17:51 [k]Heb 11:34 [l]1Sa 21:9; 22:10
17:52 [m]Jos 15:11 [n]S Jos 15:36
17:55 [o]1Sa 16:21 [p]1Sa 26:5

[m]*52* Some Septuagint manuscripts; Hebrew *a valley*

17:37–54 HISTORY, Deliverance—See note on 14:6–23. The Lord's presence not human strength determines the outcome for God's people.

17:37 SALVATION, As Deliverance—The same Lord *who delivered David from the paw of the lion and the bear* and from the hands of Goliath can deliver us from every foe.

17:45–47 GOD, Sovereignty—A small boy, David, armed only with a simple slingshot, killed Goliath, a giant who was heavily armed. Throughout the unfolding story of the Bible, God moved in dramatic ways to make His sovereign power known both to Israel and to the nations involved with Israel.

17:45–47 ELECTION, Israel—See note on Jos 10:14,42. David gave God the credit for his victory over Goliath. David's victory verified his election as king. It also witnessed to God's reputation among the nations, a major purpose of election.

brought him before Saul, with David still
holding the Philistine's head.
58"Whose son are you, young man?"
Saul asked him.
David said, "I am the son of your servant Jesse[q] of Bethlehem."

Chapter 18

Saul's Jealousy of David

AFTER David had finished talking with
Saul, Jonathan[r] became one in spirit
with David, and he loved[s] him as himself.[t] 2From that day Saul kept David
with him and did not let him return to his
father's house. 3And Jonathan made a
covenant[u] with David because he loved
him as himself. 4Jonathan took off the
robe[v] he was wearing and gave it to David, along with his tunic, and even his
sword, his bow and his belt.[w]
5Whatever Saul sent him to do, David
did it so successfully[n][x] that Saul gave
him a high rank in the army.[y] This
pleased all the people, and Saul's officers
as well.
6When the men were returning home
after David had killed the Philistine, the
women came out from all the towns of
Israel to meet King Saul with singing and
dancing,[z] with joyful songs and with
tambourines[a] and lutes. 7As they danced,
they sang:[b]

"Saul has slain his thousands,
and David his tens[c] of thousands."

8Saul was very angry; this refrain galled
him. "They have credited David with
tens of thousands," he thought, "but me
with only thousands. What more can he
get but the kingdom?[d]" 9And from that
time on Saul kept a jealous[e] eye on David.
10The next day an evil[o] spirit[f] from
God came forcefully upon Saul. He was
prophesying in his house, while David
was playing the harp,[g] as he usually[h]
did. Saul had a spear[i] in his hand 11and
he hurled it, saying to himself,[j] "I'll pin
David to the wall." But David eluded[k]
him twice.[l]
12Saul was afraid[m] of David, because
the LORD[n] was with[o] David but had left[p]
Saul. 13So he sent David away from him
and gave him command over a thousand
men, and David led[q] the troops in their
campaigns.[r] 14In everything he did he
had great success,[p][s] because the LORD
was with[t] him. 15When Saul saw how
successful[q] he was, he was afraid of him.
16But all Israel and Judah loved David, because he led them in their campaigns.[u]
17Saul said to David, "Here is my older
daughter[v] Merab. I will give her to you
in marriage;[w] only serve me bravely and
fight the battles[x] of the LORD." For Saul
said to himself,[y] "I will not raise a hand
against him. Let the Philistines do that!"
18But David said to Saul, "Who am I,[z]
and what is my family or my father's clan
in Israel, that I should become the king's
son-in-law?[a]" 19So[r] when the time came
for Merab,[b] Saul's daughter, to be given
to David, she was given in marriage to
Adriel of Meholah.[c]
20Now Saul's daughter Michal[d] was in
love with David, and when they told Saul
about it, he was pleased.[e] 21"I will give
her to him," he thought, "so that she
may be a snare[f] to him and so that the
hand of the Philistines may be against
him." So Saul said to David, "Now you
have a second opportunity to become my
son-in-law."
22Then Saul ordered his attendants:
"Speak to David privately and say, 'Look,
the king is pleased with you, and his attendants all like you; now become his
son-in-law.' "
23They repeated these words to David.
But David said, "Do you think it is a small
matter to become the king's son-in-law?[g]

[n]5 Or *wisely* [o]10 Or *injurious* [p]14 Or *he was very wise* [q]15 Or *wise* [r]19 Or *However,*

17:58 [q]S Ru 4:17
18:1 [r]1Sa 19:1; 20:16; 31:2; 2Sa 4:4 [s]2Sa 1:26 [t]S Ge 44:30
18:3 [u]1Sa 20:8,16, 17,42; 22:8; 23:18; 24:21; 2Sa 21:7
18:4 [v]S Ge 41:42 [w]2Sa 18:11
18:5 [x]ver 30 [y]2Sa 5:2
18:6 [z]S Ex 15:20; 2Sa 1:20 [a]Ps 68:25
18:7 [b]Ex 15:21 [c]1Sa 21:11; 29:5; 2Sa 18:3
18:8 [d]S 1Sa 13:14; 1Sa 15:8
18:9 [e]1Sa 19:1
18:10 [f]S Jdg 9:23; S 1Sa 16:14 [g]S 1Sa 10:5 [h]1Sa 16:21; 19:7 [i]S 1Sa 17:6
18:11 [j]ver 25; 1Sa 20:7,33 [k]1Sa 19:10 [l]Ps 132:1
18:12 [m]ver 29 [n]1Sa 16:13 [o]Jos 1:5; 1Sa 17:37; 20:13; 1Ch 22:11 [p]S Jdg 16:20
18:13 [q]Nu 27:17 [r]2Sa 5:2
18:14 [s]S Ge 39:3 [t]S Ge 39:2; S Nu 14:43; 2Sa 7:9
18:16 [u]2Sa 5:2
18:17 [v]1Sa 17:25 [w]S Ge 29:26 [x]S Nu 21:14 [y]ver 25; 1Sa 20:33
18:18 [z]S Ex 3:11; S 1Sa 9:21 [a]ver 23
18:19 [b]2Sa 21:8 [c]S Jdg 7:22
18:20 [d]ver 28; S Ge 29:26 [e]ver 29
18:21 [f]S Ex 10:7; S Dt 7:16
18:23 [g]ver 18

18:1–4 HUMANITY, Relationships—Among the more precious human relationships are those where two people commit themselves one to another in the bonds and obligations of friendship.

18:1–4 FAMILY, Friendships—Family ties should give members freedom and encouragement to develop strong relationships outside the family. In spite of his father's jealousy of David, Jonathan loved David as though he were a brother and *was willing to defend David against his father's anger.* This fact illustrates the depth of commitment in true friendship and Saul's personal weakness in not freeing his son to enter the relationship openly. Family therapists indicate that families who have such friendships are generally happier in their own relationships. In so doing they simply underline ancient biblical truth.

18:5 HUMANITY, Work—The Hebrew word describing success here more properly refers to acting wisely rather than achieving success. Achievement in a person's work is founded upon pursuing that labor with wisdom. God, of course, is the source of true wisdom.

18:9 HUMANITY, Relationships—Our motives often determine how we evaluate the actions of another. Jealous anger says more about me than about the person of whom I am jealous. We need to devote energies to doing our job well rather than worrying about the other person's success.

18:10 EVIL AND SUFFERING, Divine Origin—See note on 16:13–23.

18:12–14 REVELATION, Divine Presence—The appearance and success of David were in direct proportion to his obedience to God's intentions. God's presence provided success. As Saul continued to move away from God's direction, he sensed God's absence. We know God's presence as we obey Him.

18:14–16 HUMANITY, Community Relationships—Differing opinions about the same person are often determined by the inner attitudes of those expressing them. See note on 18:9.

18:14 HISTORY, Presence—See note on 17:37–54.

I'm only a poor man and little known."

24When Saul's servants told him what David had said, 25Saul replied, "Say to David, 'The king wants no other price[h] for the bride than a hundred Philistine foreskins, to take revenge[i] on his enemies.'" Saul's plan[j] was to have David fall by the hands of the Philistines.

26When the attendants told David these things, he was pleased to become the king's son-in-law. So before the allotted time elapsed, 27David and his men went out and killed two hundred Philistines. He brought their foreskins and presented the full number to the king so that he might become the king's son-in-law. Then Saul gave him his daughter Michal[k] in marriage.

28When Saul realized that the LORD was with David and that his daughter Michal[l] loved David, 29Saul became still more afraid[m] of him, and he remained his enemy the rest of his days.

30The Philistine commanders continued to go out to battle, and as often as they did, David met with more success[s][n] than the rest of Saul's officers, and his name became well known.

Chapter 19

Saul Tries to Kill David

SAUL told his son Jonathan[o] and all the attendants to kill[p] David. But Jonathan was very fond of David 2and warned him, "My father Saul is looking for a chance to kill you. Be on your guard tomorrow morning; go into hiding[q] and stay there. 3I will go out and stand with my father in the field where you are. I'll speak[r] to him about you and will tell you what I find out."

4Jonathan spoke[s] well of David to Saul his father and said to him, "Let not the king do wrong[t] to his servant David; he has not wronged you, and what he has done has benefited you greatly. 5He took his life[u] in his hands when he killed the Philistine. The LORD won a great victory[v] for all Israel, and you saw it and were glad. Why then would you do wrong to an innocent[w] man like David by killing him for no reason?"

6Saul listened to Jonathan and took this oath: "As surely as the LORD lives, David will not be put to death."

7So Jonathan called David and told him the whole conversation. He brought him to Saul, and David was with Saul as before.[x]

8Once more war broke out, and David went out and fought the Philistines. He struck them with such force that they fled before him.

9But an evil[t] spirit[y] from the LORD came upon Saul as he was sitting in his house with his spear in his hand. While David was playing the harp,[z] 10Saul tried to pin him to the wall with his spear, but David eluded[a] him as Saul drove the spear into the wall. That night David made good his escape.

11Saul sent men to David's house to watch[b] it and to kill him in the morning.[c] But Michal, David's wife, warned him, "If you don't run for your life tonight, tomorrow you'll be killed." 12So Michal let David down through a window,[d] and he fled and escaped. 13Then Michal took an idol[u][e] and laid it on the bed, covering it with a garment and putting some goats' hair at the head.

14When Saul sent the men to capture David, Michal said,[f] "He is ill."

15Then Saul sent the men back to see David and told them, "Bring him up to me in his bed so that I may kill him." 16But when the men entered, there was the idol in the bed, and at the head was some goats' hair.

17Saul said to Michal, "Why did you deceive me like this and send my enemy away so that he escaped?"

Michal told him, "He said to me, 'Let me get away. Why should I kill you?'"

18When David had fled and made his escape, he went to Samuel at Ramah[g] and told him all that Saul had done to him. Then he and Samuel went to Naioth and stayed there. 19Word came to Saul: "David is in Naioth at Ramah"; 20so he

18:25 [h]S Ge 34:12 [i]Ps 8:2; 44:16; Jer 20:10 [j]S ver 11, S 17; ver 17
18:27 [k]2Sa 3:14; 6:16
18:28 [l]S ver 20
18:29 [m]ver 12
18:30 [n]ver 5
19:1 [o]S 1Sa 18:1 [p]1Sa 18:9
19:2 [q]1Sa 20:5,19
19:3 [r]1Sa 20:12
19:4 [s]1Sa 20:32; 22:14; Pr 31:8,9; Jer 18:20 [t]1Sa 25:21; Pr 17:13
19:5 [u]S Jdg 9:17; S 12:3 [v]S 1Sa 11:13 [w]S Ge 31:36; Dt 19:10-13
19:7 [x]S 1Sa 18:2,13
19:9 [y]S Jdg 9:23 [z]S 1Sa 10:5
19:10 [a]1Sa 18:11
19:11 [b]Ps 59 Title [c]Jdg 16:2
19:12 [d]S Jos 2:15; Ac 9:25; 2Co 11:33
19:13 [e]S Ge 31:19
19:14 [f]S Ex 1:19; Jos 2:4
19:18 [g]S 1Sa 7:17

[s]*30* Or *David acted more wisely* [t]*9* Or *injurious*
[u]*13* Hebrew *teraphim*; also in verse 16

18:28–29 HUMANITY, Relationships—Fear destroys many human relationships. Fear makes enemies of people who should love and help one another.

18:30 HUMANITY, Work—See note on 18:5. Acting wisely is a proper basis for being well-known.

19:1—20:42 HUMANITY, Relationships—One of the more difficult human situations is that of being torn because two people closely related to us make opposing demands. When obedience to parents becomes opposed to the bonds of love and friendship with others, one relationship must be sacrificed for the other. Ultimately we must base such decisions on our commitment to God.

19:9 EVIL AND SUFFERING, Punishment—The evil spirit (Hebrew *ruach Yahweh ra'ah*) is described in language paralleling references to the Spirit of the Lord (Hebrew *ruach Yahweh*). See note on 16:13–23.

19:18–24 HOLY SPIRIT, Protects—God's Spirit protects His endangered people, at times in almost bizarre ways. The Spirit made Saul a prophet instead of a killer. In prophetic ecstasy Saul behaved strangely (v 24; 10:6). He could not seek out and kill David, on whom the Spirit rested (16:13). God's Spirit could momentarily drive out the evil spirit (16:14) to accomplish God's purpose. The prophetic work in Saul's life at this stage contrasted to the confirming call to be king. See note on 10:5–13. The same activity of the Spirit may serve different purposes for God.

sent men to capture him. But when they
saw a group of prophets[h] prophesying,
with Samuel standing there as their leader, the Spirit of God came upon[i] Saul's
men and they also prophesied.[j] 21Saul
was told about it, and he sent more men,
and they prophesied too. Saul sent men a
third time, and they also prophesied. 22Fi-
nally, he himself left for Ramah and went
to the great cistern at Secu. And he
asked, "Where are Samuel and David?"
"Over in Naioth at Ramah," they said.
23So Saul went to Naioth at Ramah. But
the Spirit of God came even upon him,
and he walked along prophesying[k] until
he came to Naioth. 24He stripped[l] off his
robes and also prophesied in Samuel's[m]
presence. He lay that way all that day and
night. This is why people say, "Is Saul
also among the prophets?"[n]

Chapter 20

David and Jonathan

THEN David fled from Naioth at Ramah
and went to Jonathan and asked,
"What have I done? What is my crime?
How have I wronged[o] your father, that
he is trying to take my life?"[p]
2"Never!" Jonathan replied. "You are
not going to die! Look, my father doesn't
do anything, great or small, without con-
fiding in me. Why would he hide this
from me? It's not so!"
3But David took an oath[q] and said,
"Your father knows very well that I have
found favor in your eyes, and he has said
to himself, 'Jonathan must not know this
or he will be grieved.' Yet as surely as the
LORD lives and as you live, there is only a
step between me and death."
4Jonathan said to David, "Whatever
you want me to do, I'll do for you."
5So David said, "Look, tomorrow is the
New Moon festival,[r] and I am supposed
to dine with the king; but let me go and
hide[s] in the field until the evening of the
day after tomorrow. 6If your father misses
me at all, tell him, 'David earnestly asked
my permission[t] to hurry to Bethlehem,[u]
his hometown, because an annual[v] sacrifice is being made there for his whole
clan.' 7If he says, 'Very well,' then your
servant is safe. But if he loses his temper,[w] you can be sure that he is determined[x] to harm me. 8As for you, show
kindness to your servant, for you have
brought him into a covenant[y] with you
before the LORD. If I am guilty, then kill[z]
me yourself! Why hand me over to your
father?"
9"Never!" Jonathan said. "If I had the
least inkling that my father was determined to harm you, wouldn't I tell you?"
10David asked, "Who will tell me if
your father answers you harshly?"
11"Come," Jonathan said, "let's go out
into the field." So they went there together.
12Then Jonathan said to David: "By the
LORD, the God of Israel, I will surely
sound[a] out my father by this time the
day after tomorrow! If he is favorably disposed toward you, will I not send you
word and let you know? 13But if my father
is inclined to harm you, may the LORD
deal with me, be it ever so severely,[b] if I
do not let you know and send you away
safely. May the LORD be with[c] you as he
has been with my father. 14But show me
unfailing kindness[d] like that of the LORD
as long as I live, so that I may not be
killed, 15and do not ever cut off your kindness from my family[e]—not even when
the LORD has cut off every one of
David's enemies from the face of the
earth."
16So Jonathan[f] made a covenant[g] with
the house of David, saying, "May the
LORD call David's enemies to account.[h]"
17And Jonathan had David reaffirm his
oath[i] out of love for him, because he
loved him as he loved himself.
18Then Jonathan said to David: "Tomorrow is the New Moon festival. You
will be missed, because your seat will be
empty.[j] 19The day after tomorrow, toward evening, go to the place where you
hid[k] when this trouble began, and wait
by the stone Ezel. 20I will shoot three arrows[l] to the side of it, as though I were
shooting at a target. 21Then I will send a
boy and say, 'Go, find the arrows.' If I say
to him, 'Look, the arrows are on this side
of you; bring them here,' then come, because, as surely as the LORD lives, you are
safe; there is no danger. 22But if I say to
the boy, 'Look, the arrows are beyond[m]
you,' then you must go, because the LORD
has sent you away. 23And about the matter you and I discussed—remember, the
LORD is witness[n] between you and me
forever."
24So David hid in the field, and when
the New Moon festival[o] came, the king
sat down to eat. 25He sat in his customary
place by the wall, opposite Jonathan,[v]
and Abner sat next to Saul, but David's
place was empty.[p] 26Saul said nothing
that day, for he thought, "Something
must have happened to David to make
him ceremonially unclean—surely he is
unclean.[q]" 27But the next day, the second day of the month, David's place was

19:20 [h]S Nu 11:29 [i]S Nu 11:25 [j]S 1Sa 10:5
19:23 [k]1Sa 10:13
19:24 [l]2Sa 6:20; Isa 20:2 [m]1Sa 15:35 [n]S 1Sa 10:11
20:1 [o]1Sa 24:9 [p]1Sa 22:23; 23:15; 24:11; 25:29; Ps 40:14; 54:3; 63:9; 70:2
20:3 [q]Dt 6:13
20:5 [r]S Nu 10:10 [s]S 1Sa 19:2
20:6 [t]ver 28 [u]1Sa 17:58 [v]S 1Sa 1:3
20:7 [w]1Sa 10:27; 25:17 [x]S 1Sa 18:11
20:8 [y]S 1Sa 18:3 [z]2Sa 14:32
20:12 [a]1Sa 19:3
20:13 [b]S Ru 1:17 [c]S 1Sa 16:18; S 18:12
20:14 [d]S Ge 40:14
20:15 [e]1Sa 24:21; 2Sa 9:7
20:16 [f]S 1Sa 18:1 [g]S 1Sa 18:3 [h]S Jos 22:23
20:17 [i]S Jos 9:18; S 1Sa 18:3
20:18 [j]ver 25
20:19 [k]S 1Sa 19:2
20:20 [l]2Ki 13:15
20:22 [m]ver 37
20:23 [n]S Ge 31:50
20:24 [o]S Nu 10:10
20:25 [p]ver 18
20:26 [q]Lev 7:20-21

[v]*25* Septuagint; Hebrew *wall. Jonathan arose*

empty again. Then Saul said to his son
Jonathan, "Why hasn't the son of Jesse
come to the meal, either yesterday or today?"

28Jonathan answered, "David earnestly
asked me for permission[r] to go to Bethlehem. 29He said, 'Let me go, because our
family is observing a sacrifice[s] in the
town and my brother has ordered me to
be there. If I have found favor in your
eyes, let me get away to see my brothers.'
That is why he has not come to the king's
table."

30Saul's anger flared up at Jonathan and
he said to him, "You son of a perverse
and rebellious woman! Don't I know that
you have sided with the son of Jesse to
your own shame and to the shame of the
mother who bore you? 31As long as the
son of Jesse lives on this earth, neither
you nor your kingdom[t] will be established. Now send and bring him to me,
for he must die!"

32"Why[u] should he be put to death?
What[v] has he done?" Jonathan asked his
father. 33But Saul hurled his spear at him
to kill him. Then Jonathan knew that his
father intended[w] to kill David.

34Jonathan got up from the table in
fierce anger; on that second day of the
month he did not eat, because he was
grieved at his father's shameful treatment
of David.

35In the morning Jonathan went out to
the field for his meeting with David. He
had a small boy with him, 36and he said
to the boy, "Run and find the arrows I
shoot." As the boy ran, he shot an arrow
beyond him. 37When the boy came to the
place where Jonathan's arrow had fallen,
Jonathan called out after him, "Isn't the
arrow beyond[x] you?" 38Then he shouted,
"Hurry! Go quickly! Don't stop!" The boy
picked up the arrow and returned to his
master. 39(The boy knew nothing of all
this; only Jonathan and David knew.)
40Then Jonathan gave his weapons to the
boy and said, "Go, carry them back to
town."

41After the boy had gone, David got up
from the south side ⌞of the stone⌟ and
bowed down before Jonathan three
times, with his face to the ground.[y] Then
they kissed each other and wept together—but David wept the most.

42Jonathan said to David, "Go in
peace,[z] for we have sworn friendship[a]
with each other in the name of the
LORD,[b] saying, 'The LORD is witness[c] between you and me, and between your descendants and my descendants forever.[d]'" Then David left, and Jonathan
went back to the town.

Chapter 21

David at Nob

DAVID went to Nob,[e] to Ahimelech
the priest. Ahimelech trembled[f]
when he met him, and asked, "Why are
you alone? Why is no one with you?"

2David answered Ahimelech the priest,
"The king charged me with a certain matter and said to me, 'No one is to know
anything about your mission and your instructions.' As for my men, I have told
them to meet me at a certain place. 3Now
then, what do you have on hand? Give
me five loaves of bread, or whatever you
can find."

4But the priest answered David, "I
don't have any ordinary bread[g] on hand;
however, there is some consecrated[h]
bread here—provided the men have
kept[i] themselves from women."

5David replied, "Indeed women have
been kept from us, as usual[j] whenever[w]
I set out. The men's things[x] are holy[k]
even on missions that are not holy. How
much more so today!" 6So the priest gave
him the consecrated bread,[l] since there
was no bread there except the bread
of the Presence that had been removed
from before the LORD and replaced
by hot bread on the day it was taken
away.

7Now one of Saul's servants was there
that day, detained before the LORD; he
was Doeg[m] the Edomite,[n] Saul's head
shepherd.

8David asked Ahimelech, "Don't you
have a spear or a sword here? I haven't
brought my sword or any other weapon,
because the king's business was urgent."

9The priest replied, "The sword[o] of
Goliath[p] the Philistine, whom you killed
in the Valley of Elah,[q] is here; it is
wrapped in a cloth behind the ephod. If
you want it, take it; there is no sword
here but that one."

David said, "There is none like it; give
it to me."

David at Gath

10That day David fled from Saul and
went[r] to Achish king of Gath. 11But
the servants of Achish said to him, "Isn't
this David, the king of the land? Isn't
he the one they sing about in their
dances:

"'Saul has slain his thousands,
and David his tens of thousands'?"[s]

20:28 [r]ver 6
20:29 [s]S Ge 8:20
20:31 [t]1Sa 23:17; 24:20
20:32 [u]S 1Sa 19:4; Mt 27:23 [v]S Ge 31:36
20:33 [w]S 1Sa 18:11,17
20:37 [x]ver 22
20:41 [y]S Ge 33:3; Ru 2:10; 1Sa 24:8; 25:23; 2Sa 1:2
20:42 [z]S 1Sa 1:17; S Ac 15:33 [a]S Ge 40:14; 2Sa 1:26; Pr 18:24 [b]Isa 48:1 [c]S Ge 31:50; S 1Sa 18:3 [d]2Sa 9:1
21:1 [e]1Sa 22:9,19; Ne 11:32; Isa 10:32 [f]1Sa 16:4
21:4 [g]Lev 24:8-9 [h]Mt 12:4 [i]S Ex 19:15; S Lev 15:18
21:5 [j]Dt 23:9-11; Jos 3:5; 2Sa 11:11 [k]1Th 4:4
21:6 [l]S Ex 25:30; 1Sa 22:10; Mt 12:3-4; Mk 2:25-28; Lk 6:1-5
21:7 [m]1Sa 22:9,22 [n]1Sa 14:47; Ps 52 Title
21:9 [o]S 1Sa 17:51 [p]S 1Sa 17:4 [q]1Sa 17:2
21:10 [r]1Sa 25:13; 27:2
21:11 [s]S 1Sa 18:7

[w]5 Or *from us in the past few days since* [x]5 Or *bodies*

are raiding the land." 28Then Saul broke
off his pursuit of David and went to meet
the Philistines. That is why they call this
place Sela Hammahlekoth.[z] 29And David
went up from there and lived in the
strongholds[g] of En Gedi.[h]

Chapter 24

David Spares Saul's Life

AFTER Saul returned from pursuing the
Philistines, he was told, "David is in
the Desert of En Gedi.[i]" 2So Saul took
three thousand chosen men from all Israel and set out to look[j] for David and his
men near the Crags of the Wild Goats.
3He came to the sheep pens along the
way; a cave[k] was there, and Saul went in
to relieve[l] himself. David and his men
were far back in the cave. 4The men said,
"This is the day the LORD spoke[m] of
when he said[a] to you, 'I will give your
enemy into your hands for you to deal
with as you wish.'"[n] Then David crept
up unnoticed and cut[o] off a corner of
Saul's robe.
5Afterward, David was conscience-
stricken[p] for having cut off a corner of
his robe. 6He said to his men, "The LORD
forbid that I should do such a thing to my
master, the LORD's anointed,[q] or lift my
hand against him; for he is the anointed
of the LORD." 7With these words David
rebuked his men and did not allow them
to attack Saul. And Saul left the cave and
went his way.
8Then David went out of the cave and
called out to Saul, "My lord the king!"
When Saul looked behind him, David
bowed down and prostrated himself with
his face to the ground.[r] 9He said to Saul,
"Why do you listen[s] when men say, 'David is bent on harming[t] you'? 10This day
you have seen with your own eyes how
the LORD delivered you into my hands in
the cave. Some urged me to kill you, but I
spared[u] you; I said, 'I will not lift my
hand against my master, because he is
the LORD's anointed.' 11See, my father,
look at this piece of your robe in my
hand! I cut[v] off the corner of your robe
but did not kill you. Now understand and
recognize that I am not guilty[w] of wrongdoing[x] or rebellion. I have not wronged[y]
you, but you are hunting[z] me down to
take my life.[a] 12May the LORD judge[b] between you and me. And may the LORD
avenge[c] the wrongs you have done to
me, but my hand will not touch you. 13As
the old saying goes, 'From evildoers come
evil deeds,[d]' so my hand will not touch
you.
14"Against whom has the king of Israel
come out? Whom are you pursuing? A
dead dog?[e] A flea?[f] 15May the LORD be
our judge[g] and decide[h] between us. May
he consider my cause and uphold[i] it;
may he vindicate[j] me by delivering[k] me
from your hand."
16When David finished saying this,
Saul asked, "Is that your voice,[l] David
my son?" And he wept aloud. 17"You are
more righteous than I,"[m] he said. "You
have treated me well,[n] but I have treated
you badly.[o] 18You have just now told me
of the good you did to me; the LORD delivered[p] me into your hands, but you did
not kill me. 19When a man finds his enemy, does he let him get away unharmed?
May the LORD reward[q] you well for the
way you treated me today. 20I know that
you will surely be king[r] and that the
kingdom[s] of Israel will be established in
your hands. 21Now swear[t] to me by the
LORD that you will not cut off my descendants or wipe out my name from my
father's family.[u]"
22So David gave his oath to Saul. Then
Saul returned home, but David and his
men went up to the stronghold.[v]

Chapter 25

David, Nabal and Abigail

NOW Samuel died,[w] and all Israel assembled and mourned[x] for him;
and they buried him at his home in Ramah.[y]
Then David moved down into the
Desert of Maon.[b] 2A certain man in
Maon,[z] who had property there at Carmel, was very wealthy.[a] He had a thousand goats and three thousand sheep,
which he was shearing[b] in Carmel. 3His

[z]28 Sela Hammahlekoth means *rock of parting.*
[a]4 Or *"Today the LORD is saying*
[b]1 Some Septuagint manuscripts; Hebrew *Paran*

23:29 [g]1Sa 24:22 [h]S Jos 15:62; 2Ch 20:2; SS 1:14
24:1 [i]S Jos 15:62
24:2 [j]1Sa 26:2
24:3 [k]Ps 57 Title; 142 Title [l]Jdg 3:24
24:4 [m]1Sa 25:28-30 [n]2Sa 4:8 [o]ver 10,11
24:5 [p]1Sa 26:9; 2Sa 24:10
24:6 [q]S Ge 26:11; S 1Sa 12:3
24:8 [r]S 1Sa 20:41
24:9 [s]1Sa 26:19 [t]1Sa 20:1
24:10 [u]S ver 4
24:11 [v]S ver 4 [w]Ps 7:3 [x]1Sa 25:28 [y]Ps 35:7 [z]S Ge 31:36; 1Sa 26:20 [a]S 1Sa 20:1
24:12 [b]S Ge 16:5; S 1Sa 25:38; S Job 9:15 [c]S Nu 31:3
24:13 [d]Mt 7:20
24:14 [e]S 1Sa 17:43 [f]1Sa 26:20
24:15 [g]ver 12 [h]S Ge 16:5 [i]Ps 35:1,23; Isa 49:25 [j]Ps 26:1; 35:24; 43:1; 50:4; 54:1; 135:14 [k]Ps 119:134,154
24:16 [l]1Sa 26:17
24:17 [m]Ge 38:26 [n]Mt 5:44 [o]S Ex 9:27
24:18 [p]1Sa 26:23
24:19 [q]S Ru 2:12; S 2Ch 15:7
24:20 [r]S 1Sa 20:31 [s]S 1Sa 13:14
24:21 [t]Ge 21:23; S 47:31; S 1Sa 18:3; 2Sa 21:1-9 [u]S 1Sa 20:14-15
24:22 [v]1Sa 23:29
25:1 [w]1Sa 28:3 [x]S Lev 10:6; Dt 34:8 [y]S 1Sa 7:17
25:2 [z]S Jos 15:55 [a]2Sa 19:32 [b]S Ge 31:19

24:1–22 EVIL AND SUFFERING, Endurance—Having suffered from Saul's violent jealousy, David exemplified an attitude of non-retaliation against an enemy. David did not take advantage of the opportunity to kill Saul even though Saul had tried to kill him. Compare 26:1–25. God's people should not harbor vengeance and hatred. We should respond to evil acts of others in enduring love as Jesus taught and did. See note on Mt 5:38–48.

24:8–21 HISTORY, Deliverance—Opportunity to defeat enemies is not permission to do so. God had chosen David to succeed Saul. God delivered Saul into David's hands, but David knew that judgment, vengeance, and vindication were under God's control. This foreshadowed Jesus' teaching of love for enemies (Mt 5:44).

24:12–15 PRAYER, Petition—Prayer reveals a person's character. David anticipated the spirit and teaching of Christ (Mt 7:1–6). Allowing God to take vengeance requires faith. Compare Dt 32:35.

24:21–22 PRAYER, Vow—David made a vow to the Lord and kept it. Human agreements become instruments of prayer when made in God's name.

name was Nabal and his wife's name was Abigail.[c] She was an intelligent and beautiful woman, but her husband, a Calebite,[d] was surly and mean in his dealings.

4While David was in the desert, he heard that Nabal was shearing sheep. 5So he sent ten young men and said to them, "Go up to Nabal at Carmel and greet him in my name. 6Say to him: 'Long life to you! Good health[e] to you and your household! And good health to all that is yours![f]

7" 'Now I hear that it is sheep-shearing time. When your shepherds were with us, we did not mistreat[g] them, and the whole time they were at Carmel nothing of theirs was missing. 8Ask your own servants and they will tell you. Therefore be favorable toward my young men, since we come at a festive time. Please give your servants and your son David whatever[h] you can find for them.' "

9When David's men arrived, they gave Nabal this message in David's name. Then they waited.

10Nabal answered David's servants, "Who[i] is this David? Who is this son of Jesse? Many servants are breaking away from their masters these days. 11Why should I take my bread[j] and water, and the meat I have slaughtered for my shearers, and give it to men coming from who knows where?"

12David's men turned around and went back. When they arrived, they reported every word. 13David said to his men[k], "Put on your swords!" So they put on their swords, and David put on his. About four hundred men went[l] up with David, while two hundred stayed with the supplies.[m]

14One of the servants told Nabal's wife Abigail: "David sent messengers from the desert to give our master his greetings,[n] but he hurled insults at them. 15Yet these men were very good to us. They did not mistreat[o] us, and the whole time we were out in the fields near them nothing was missing.[p] 16Night and day they were a wall[q] around us all the time we were herding our sheep near them. 17Now think it over and see what you can do, because disaster is hanging over our master and his whole household. He is such a wicked[r] man that no one can talk to him."

18Abigail lost no time. She took two hundred loaves of bread, two skins of wine, five dressed sheep, five seahs[c] of roasted grain,[s] a hundred cakes of raisins[t] and two hundred cakes of pressed figs, and loaded them on donkeys.[u] 19Then she told her servants, "Go on ahead;[v] I'll follow you." But she did not tell[w] her husband Nabal.

20As she came riding her donkey into a mountain ravine, there were David and his men descending toward her, and she met them. 21David had just said, "It's been useless—all my watching over this fellow's property in the desert so that nothing of his was missing.[x] He has paid[y] me back evil[z] for good. 22May God deal with David,[d] be it ever so severely,[a] if by morning I leave alive one male[b] of all who belong to him!"

23When Abigail saw David, she quickly got off her donkey and bowed down before David with her face to the ground.[c] 24She fell at his feet and said: "My lord, let the blame[d] be on me alone. Please let your servant speak to you; hear what your servant has to say. 25May my lord pay no attention to that wicked man Nabal. He is just like his name—his name is Fool[e],[f] and folly goes with him. But as for me, your servant, I did not see the men my master sent.

26"Now since the LORD has kept you, my master, from bloodshed[g] and from avenging[h] yourself with your own hands, as surely as the LORD lives and as you live, may your enemies and all who intend to harm my master be like Nabal.[i] 27And let this gift,[j] which your servant has brought to my master, be given to the men who follow you. 28Please forgive[k] your servant's offense, for the LORD will certainly make a lasting[l] dynasty for my master, because he fights the LORD's battles.[m] Let no wrongdoing[n] be found in you as long as you live. 29Even though someone is pursuing you to take your life,[o] the life of my master will be bound securely in the bundle of the living by the LORD your God. But the lives of your enemies he will hurl[p] away as from the pocket of a sling.[q] 30When the LORD has done for my master every good thing he promised concerning him and has appointed him leader[r] over Israel, 31my master will not have on his conscience the staggering burden of needless bloodshed or of having avenged himself. And when the LORD has brought my master success, remember[s] your servant."[t]

32David said to Abigail, "Praise[u] be to the LORD, the God of Israel, who has sent

[c]*18* That is, probably about a bushel (about 37 liters)
[d]*22* Some Septuagint manuscripts; Hebrew *with David's enemies*

25:3 [c]Pr 31:10 [d]S Jos 14:13; S 15:13
25:6 [e]Ps 122:7; Mt 10:12 [f]1Ch 12:18
25:7 [g]ver 15
25:8 [h]Ne 8:10
25:10 [i]Jdg 9:28
25:11 [j]Jdg 8:6
25:13 [k]S 1Sa 22:2 [l]S 1Sa 21:10 [m]S Nu 31:27
25:14 [n]1Sa 13:10
25:15 [o]ver 7 [p]ver 21
25:16 [q]Ex 14:22; Job 1:10; Ps 139:5
25:17 [r]S Dt 13:13; S 1Sa 20:7
25:18 [s]S Lev 23:14; S 1Sa 17:17 [t]1Ch 12:40 [u]S Ge 42:26; 2Sa 16:1; Isa 30:6
25:19 [v]Ge 32:20 [w]ver 36
25:21 [x]ver 15 [y]Ps 109:5 [z]S 1Sa 19:4
25:22 [a]S Ru 1:17 [b]1Ki 14:10; 21:21; 2Ki 9:8
25:23 [c]S Ge 19:1; S 1Sa 20:41
25:24 [d]2Sa 14:9
25:25 [e]Pr 17:12 [f]Pr 12:16; 14:16; 20:3; Isa 32:5
25:26 [g]ver 33 [h]Heb 10:30 [i]ver 34; 2Sa 18:32
25:27 [j]S Ge 33:11
25:28 [k]ver 24; 2Sa 14:9 [l]2Sa 7:11, 26 [m]1Sa 18:17 [n]1Sa 24:11
25:29 [o]S 1Sa 20:1 [p]Jer 10:18; 22:26 [q]1Sa 17:50; 2Sa 4:8
25:30 [r]S 1Sa 12:12; S 13:14
25:31 [s]S Ge 40:14 [t]2Sa 3:10
25:32 [u]S Ge 24:27

25:32 HISTORY, God's Leaders—God uses unexpected individuals to reveal His will. Abigail revealed God's will to David and prevented national disaster.

25:32–34 PRAYER, Praise—David's resolve to wreak ven-

you today to meet me. 33May you be
blessed for your good judgment and for
keeping me from bloodshed[v] this day
and from avenging myself with my own
hands. 34Otherwise, as surely as the
LORD, the God of Israel, lives, who has
kept me from harming you, if you had not
come quickly to meet me, not one male
belonging to Nabal[w] would have been left
alive by daybreak."
35Then David accepted from her hand
what she had brought him and said, "Go
home in peace. I have heard your words
and granted[x] your request."
36When Abigail went to Nabal, he was
in the house holding a banquet like that
of a king. He was in high[y] spirits and
very drunk.[z] So she told[a] him nothing
until daybreak. 37Then in the morning,
when Nabal was sober, his wife told him
all these things, and his heart failed him
and he became like a stone.[b] 38About ten
days later, the LORD struck[c] Nabal and he
died.
39When David heard that Nabal was
dead, he said, "Praise be to the LORD,
who has upheld my cause against Nabal
for treating me with contempt. He has
kept his servant from doing wrong and
has brought Nabal's wrongdoing down on
his own head."
Then David sent word to Abigail, asking her to become his wife. 40His servants
went to Carmel and said to Abigail, "David has sent us to you to take you to become his wife."
41She bowed down with her face to the
ground and said, "Here is your maidservant, ready to serve you and wash the
feet of my master's servants." 42Abigail[d]
quickly got on a donkey and, attended by
her five maids, went with David's messengers and became his wife. 43David had
also married Ahinoam[e] of Jezreel, and
they both were his wives.[f] 44But Saul
had given his daughter Michal, David's
wife, to Paltiel[e][g] son of Laish, who was
from Gallim.[h]

Chapter 26

David Again Spares Saul's Life

THE Ziphites[i] went to Saul at Gibeah
and said, "Is not David hiding[j] on
the hill of Hakilah, which faces Jeshimon?[k]"
2So Saul went down to the Desert of
Ziph, with his three thousand chosen
men of Israel, to search[l] there for David.
3Saul made his camp beside the road on
the hill of Hakilah[m] facing Jeshimon, but
David stayed in the desert. When he saw
that Saul had followed him there, 4he
sent out scouts and learned that Saul had
definitely arrived.[f]
5Then David set out and went to the
place where Saul had camped. He saw
where Saul and Abner[n] son of Ner, the
commander of the army, had lain down.
Saul was lying inside the camp, with the
army encamped around him.
6David then asked Ahimelech the Hittite[o] and Abishai[p] son of Zeruiah,[q]
Joab's brother, "Who will go down into
the camp with me to Saul?"
"I'll go with you," said Abishai.
7So David and Abishai went to the
army by night, and there was Saul, lying
asleep inside the camp with his spear
stuck in the ground near his head. Abner
and the soldiers were lying around him.
8Abishai said to David, "Today God has
delivered your enemy into your hands.
Now let me pin him to the ground with
one thrust of my spear; I won't strike him
twice."
9But David said to Abishai, "Don't destroy him! Who can lay a hand on the
LORD's anointed[r] and be guiltless?[s] 10As
surely as the LORD lives," he said, "the
LORD himself will strike[t] him; either his
time[u] will come and he will die,[v] or he
will go into battle and perish. 11But the
LORD forbid that I should lay a hand on
the LORD's anointed. Now get the spear
and water jug that are near his head, and
let's go."
12So David took the spear and water jug
near Saul's head, and they left. No one
saw or knew about it, nor did anyone
wake up. They were all sleeping, because
the LORD had put them into a deep
sleep.[w]
13Then David crossed over to the other
side and stood on top of the hill some
distance away; there was a wide space

25:33 [v]ver 26
25:34 [w]S ver 26
25:35 [x]S Ge 19:21
25:36 [y]S Ru 3:7 [z]Pr 20:1; Ecc 10:17; Isa 5:11, 22; 22:13; 28:7; 56:12; Hos 4:11 [a]ver 19
25:37 [b]Ex 15:16
25:38 [c]Dt 32:35; 1Sa 24:12; 26:10; 2Sa 6:7; 12:15
25:42 [d]2Sa 2:2; 3:3; 1Ch 3:1
25:43 [e]2Sa 3:2; 1Ch 3:1 [f]1Sa 27:3; 30:5; 2Sa 2:2
25:44 [g]2Sa 3:15 [h]Isa 10:30
26:1 [i]1Sa 23:19 [j]Ps 54 Title [k]1Sa 23:24
26:2 [l]1Sa 24:2
26:3 [m]1Sa 23:19
26:5 [n]1Sa 17:55
26:6 [o]S Ge 10:15 [p]2Sa 2:18; 10:10; 16:9; 18:2; 19:21; 23:18; 1Ch 11:20; 19:11 [q]1Ch 2:16
26:9 [r]ver 16; S Ge 26:11; S 1Sa 9:16; 2Sa 1:14; 19:21; La 4:20 [s]S 1Sa 24:5
26:10 [t]S Ge 16:5; S 1Sa 25:38; S Ro 12:19 [u]Dt 31:14; Ps 37:13 [v]1Sa 31:6; 2Sa 1:1
26:12 [w]S Jdg 4:21

[e]44 Hebrew *Palti*, a variant of *Paltiel* [f]4 Or *had come to Nacon*

geance on Nabal was out of character for him. See note on 24:12–15. Abigail confronted him with the importance of his own honor. The realization of God's actions in human relationships leads to praise.

25:39 GOD, Sovereignty—Some things are best left in God's hands. God will accomplish His righteous judgment without our intervention. Although God does indeed work through humans, He also chooses, on occasion, to work directly in accomplishing His will. We need to be certain that God, not our own passions and reactions, directs us when we take serious steps with grave consequences. Compare 26:8–11. See note on 15:1–3.

25:39 PRAYER, Praise—David's faith in God's willingness to take His own vengeance was justified. Seeing God bring justice should lead to praise. Gloating over an enemy's defeat and death is not proper praise.

25:43–44 FAMILY, Multiple Wives—See note on Ge 16:1–16.

26:1–25 EVIL AND SUFFERING, Endurance—See note on 24:1–22.

between them. 14He called out to the army and to Abner son of Ner, "Aren't you going to answer me, Abner?"

Abner replied, "Who are you who calls to the king?"

15David said, "You're a man, aren't you? And who is like you in Israel? Why didn't you guard your lord the king? Someone came to destroy your lord the king. 16What you have done is not good. As surely as the LORD lives, you and your men deserve to die, because you did not guard your master, the LORD's anointed. Look around you. Where are the king's spear and water jug that were near his head?"

17Saul recognized David's voice and said, "Is that your voice,[x] David my son?"

David replied, "Yes it is, my lord the king." 18And he added, "Why is my lord pursuing his servant? What have I done, and what wrong[y] am I guilty of? 19Now let my lord the king listen[z] to his servant's words. If the LORD has incited you against me, then may he accept an offering.[a] If, however, men have done it, may they be cursed before the LORD! They have now driven me from my share in the LORD's inheritance[b] and have said, 'Go, serve other gods.'[c] 20Now do not let my blood[d] fall to the ground far from the presence of the LORD. The king of Israel has come out to look for a flea[e]—as one hunts a partridge in the mountains.[f]"

21Then Saul said, "I have sinned.[g] Come back, David my son. Because you considered my life precious[h] today, I will not try to harm you again. Surely I have acted like a fool and have erred greatly."

22"Here is the king's spear," David answered. "Let one of your young men come over and get it. 23The LORD rewards[i] every man for his righteousness[j] and faithfulness. The LORD delivered[k] you into my hands today, but I would not lay a hand on the LORD's anointed. 24As surely as I valued your life today, so may the LORD value my life and deliver[l] me from all trouble."

25Then Saul said to David, "May you be blessed,[m] my son David; you will do great things and surely triumph."

So David went on his way, and Saul returned home.

26:17 [x]1Sa 24:16
26:18 [y]Job 13:23; Jer 37:18
26:19 [z]1Sa 24:9 [a]2Sa 16:11 [b]Dt 20:16; 32:9; 2Sa 14:16; 20:19; 21:3 [c]S Dt 4:28; S 11:28
26:20 [d]S 1Sa 24:11 [e]1Sa 24:14 [f]Jer 4:29; 16:16; Am 9:3
26:21 [g]S Ex 9:27 [h]Ps 72:14
26:23 [i]S Ge 16:5; S Ru 2:12; Ps 62:12 [j]2Sa 22:21,25; Ps 7:8; 18:20,24 [k]1Sa 24:18
26:24 [l]Ps 54:7
26:25 [m]S Ru 2:12
27:2 [n]1Sa 30:9; 2Sa 2:3 [o]S 1Sa 21:10 [p]1Ki 2:39
27:3 [q]S 1Sa 25:43
27:6 [r]Jos 15:31; 19:5; 1Sa 30:1; 1Ch 12:20; Ne 11:28
27:7 [s]1Sa 29:3
27:8 [t]S Jos 12:5 [u]S Ex 17:14; S 1Sa 14:48; 30:1; 2Sa 1:8; 8:12 [v]S Ge 16:7
27:9 [w]S 1Sa 15:3
27:10 [x]1Sa 30:29 [y]Jdg 1:16
27:12 [z]S Ge 34:30 [a]1Sa 29:6

Chapter 27

David Among the Philistines

BUT David thought to himself, "One of these days I will be destroyed by the hand of Saul. The best thing I can do is to escape to the land of the Philistines. Then Saul will give up searching for me anywhere in Israel, and I will slip out of his hand."

2So David and the six hundred men[n] with him left and went[o] over to Achish[p] son of Maoch king of Gath. 3David and his men settled in Gath with Achish. Each man had his family with him, and David had his two wives:[q] Ahinoam of Jezreel and Abigail of Carmel, the widow of Nabal. 4When Saul was told that David had fled to Gath, he no longer searched for him.

5Then David said to Achish, "If I have found favor in your eyes, let a place be assigned to me in one of the country towns, that I may live there. Why should your servant live in the royal city with you?"

6So on that day Achish gave him Ziklag,[r] and it has belonged to the kings of Judah ever since. 7David lived[s] in Philistine territory a year and four months.

8Now David and his men went up and raided the Geshurites,[t] the Girzites and the Amalekites.[u] (From ancient times these peoples had lived in the land extending to Shur[v] and Egypt.) 9Whenever David attacked an area, he did not leave a man or woman alive,[w] but took sheep and cattle, donkeys and camels, and clothes. Then he returned to Achish.

10When Achish asked, "Where did you go raiding today?" David would say, "Against the Negev of Judah" or "Against the Negev of Jerahmeel[x]" or "Against the Negev of the Kenites.[y]" 11He did not leave a man or woman alive to be brought to Gath, for he thought, "They might inform on us and say, 'This is what David did.'" And such was his practice as long as he lived in Philistine territory. 12Achish trusted David and said to himself, "He has become so odious[z] to his people, the Israelites, that he will be my servant forever.[a]"

26:21 SIN, Estrangement—Saul recognized his jealousy and hatred for David were sins. His sin produced estrangement between two people God could use and who could help each other. David's merciful act led Saul to recognize his sin. Human mercy can overcome sin's estrangement on the human level. Only God's mercy can overcome spiritual estrangement.

26:23–24 HUMANITY, Relationship to God—Commitment to God serves as the basis for a commitment to those whom God has anointed as His servants. Carrying out the human desire for vengeance has no place in the life of a person devoted to God.

26:23 HISTORY, Deliverance—See note on 24:8–21.

27:1–12 HISTORY, God's Leaders—David was forced to flee Israelite territory and could be charged with aiding the enemy, but the inspired writer showed God protected the future king, who was able to defeat Israel's enemies and make the Philistine ruler appear foolish.

Chapter 28

Saul and the Witch of Endor

IN those days the Philistines gathered[b]
their forces to fight against Israel.
Achish said to David, "You must understand that you and your men will accompany me in the army."
2David said, "Then you will see for
yourself what your servant can do."
Achish replied, "Very well, I will make
you my bodyguard[c] for life."
3Now Samuel was dead,[d] and all Israel
had mourned for him and buried him in
his own town of Ramah.[e] Saul had expelled[f] the mediums and spiritists[g] from
the land.
4The Philistines assembled and came
and set up camp at Shunem,[h] while Saul
gathered all the Israelites and set up camp
at Gilboa.[i] 5When Saul saw the Philistine
army, he was afraid; terror[j] filled his
heart. 6He inquired[k] of the LORD, but the
LORD did not answer him by dreams[l] or
Urim[m] or prophets.[n] 7Saul then said to
his attendants, "Find me a woman who is
a medium,[o] so I may go and inquire of
her."
"There is one in Endor,[p]" they said.
8So Saul disguised[q] himself, putting on
other clothes, and at night he and two
men went to the woman. "Consult[r] a
spirit for me," he said, "and bring up for
me the one I name."
9But the woman said to him, "Surely
you know what Saul has done. He has cut
off[s] the mediums and spiritists from the
land. Why have you set a trap[t] for my life
to bring about my death?"
10Saul swore to her by the LORD, "As
surely as the LORD lives, you will not be
punished for this."
11Then the woman asked, "Whom
shall I bring up for you?"
"Bring up Samuel," he said.
12When the woman saw Samuel, she
cried out at the top of her voice and said
to Saul, "Why have you deceived me?[u]
You are Saul!"
13The king said to her, "Don't be
afraid. What do you see?"
The woman said, "I see a spirit[g] coming up out of the ground."[v]
14"What does he look like?" he asked.
"An old man wearing a robe[w] is coming up," she said.
Then Saul knew it was Samuel, and he
bowed down and prostrated himself with
his face to the ground.
15Samuel said to Saul, "Why have you
disturbed me by bringing me up?"
"I am in great distress," Saul said.
"The Philistines are fighting against me,
and God has turned[x] away from me. He
no longer answers[y] me, either by prophets or by dreams.[z] So I have called on
you to tell me what to do."
16Samuel said, "Why do you consult
me, now that the LORD has turned away
from you and become your enemy? 17The
LORD has done what he predicted
through me. The LORD has torn[a] the
kingdom out of your hands and given it to
one of your neighbors—to David. 18Be-
cause you did not obey[b] the LORD or carry out his fierce wrath[c] against the Amalekites,[d] the LORD has done this to you
today. 19The LORD will hand over both
Israel and you to the Philistines, and

[g]13 Or *see spirits*; or *see gods*

28:1 [b]1Sa 29:1
28:2 [c]1Sa 29:2
28:3 [d]1Sa 25:1 [e]S 1Sa 7:17 [f]ver 9 [g]S Ex 22:18
28:4 [h]S Jos 19:18 [i]1Sa 31:1,3; 2Sa 1:6,21; 21:12
28:5 [j]S Ex 19:16
28:6 [k]S 1Sa 8:18; 14:37 [l]S Dt 13:3 [m]S Ex 28:30; S Lev 8:8 [n]Eze 20:3; Am 8:11; Mic 3:7
28:7 [o]1Ch 10:13; Ac 16:16 [p]Jos 17:11; Ps 83:10
28:8 [q]1Ki 22:30; 2Ch 18:29; 35:22 [r]2Ki 1:3; Isa 8:19
28:9 [s]ver 3 [t]Job 18:10; Ps 31:4; 69:22; Isa 8:14
28:12 [u]S Ge 27:36; 1Ki 14:6
28:13 [v]ver 15; S Lev 19:31; 2Ch 33:6
28:14 [w]1Sa 15:27
28:15 [x]S Jdg 16:20 [y]S 1Sa 14:37 [z]S Dt 13:3
28:17 [a]1Sa 15:28
28:18 [b]1Sa 15:20 [c]S Dt 9:8; S 1Sa 15:3 [d]S Ge 14:7; S 1Sa 14:48

28:3 HUMANITY, Death—National grief over the death of a great leader is both natural and expected.

28:5–25 HUMANITY, Human Nature—When people have exhausted all normal means of trying to find God's will for themselves, they occasionally turn to means normally associated with the occult. God does not approve such desperate efforts. We cannot force or coerce God to give us a favorable answer.

28:6–25 REVELATION, Oracles—When His people fail to follow and fellowship with Him, God also withdraws from communication and revelation. Saul could find no word from God, regardless of the ways in which he sought God's will. God's will cannot be used for selfish purposes. It does not come automatically no matter what methods we use to find it. Seeking God's will through pagan means such as asking a medium to contact the dead brings only God's wrath. Israel apparently believed contact with dead spirits might be possible, but it was absolutely wrong. See note on Lev 20:6,27; Dt 18:9–14.

28:6 PRAYER, Hindrances—Saul had forsaken God until God left him. Constant disobedience eventually cuts us off from God and closes the channel for petitions (15:10; Isa 59:2).

28:15 GOD, Wrath—The blessings of God can be withdrawn when we disobey Him. The sense of God's leadership Saul once enjoyed was withdrawn from him. Saul felt very alone and vulnerable. God was not answering Saul's cries for help (v 18). God is faithful to bless those who honor Him, and He is faithful to chastise those who are unfaithful to Him. His apparent absence may express His wrath.

28:15–19 EVIL AND SUFFERING, Punishment—Necromancy—the consultation with spirits of the dead—was an evil practice of Israel's neighbors. God forbid the practice among His people (Lev 19:31; 20:6,27; Dt 18:10–12). How the practice was thought to work or why God allowed it to work in this instance the text does not tell us. God used an evil practice to accomplish His purpose of notifying Saul of the punishment he faced. Saul remained responsible for his actions even when an evil spirit worked in his life. See notes on 13:13–14; 16:13–23.

28:16–19 HISTORY, Judgment—God can become the enemy of His people and His leaders when they do not obey. Historical revelation comes through His judgment as well as through His salvation.

28:16–19 CHRISTIAN ETHICS, War and Peace—War is not a place to build a personal reputation, consolidate personal power, and then oppose God. All of us are vulnerable to rising quickly and then allowing that fame to displace our sense of obedience to God. God can become the enemy of His onetime hero. We can never gain enough power to oppose God.

28:18 CHRISTIAN ETHICS, Moral Imperatives—See notes on Lev 26:3–45; Dt 28:1–68.

tomorrow you and your sons[e] will be with
me. The LORD will also hand over the
army of Israel to the Philistines."
20 Immediately Saul fell full length on
the ground, filled with fear because of
Samuel's words. His strength was gone,
for he had eaten nothing all that day and
night.
21 When the woman came to Saul and
saw that he was greatly shaken, she said,
"Look, your maidservant has obeyed you.
I took my life[f] in my hands and did what
you told me to do. 22 Now please listen to
your servant and let me give you some
food so you may eat and have the
strength to go on your way."
23 He refused[g] and said, "I will not
eat."
But his men joined the woman in
urging him, and he listened to them. He
got up from the ground and sat on the
couch.
24 The woman had a fattened calf[h] at
the house, which she butchered at once.
She took some flour, kneaded it and
baked bread without yeast. 25 Then she
set it before Saul and his men, and they
ate. That same night they got up and left.

Chapter 29

Achish Sends David Back to Ziklag

THE Philistines gathered[i] all their
forces at Aphek,[j] and Israel camped
by the spring in Jezreel.[k] 2 As the Philistine rulers marched with their units of
hundreds and thousands, David and his
men were marching at the rear[l] with
Achish. 3 The commanders of the Philistines asked, "What about these Hebrews?"
Achish replied, "Is this not David,[m]
who was an officer of Saul king of Israel?
He has already been with me for over a
year,[n] and from the day he left Saul until
now, I have found no fault in him."
4 But the Philistine commanders were
angry with him and said, "Send[o] the
man back, that he may return to the place
you assigned him. He must not go with us
into battle, or he will turn[p] against us
during the fighting. How better could he
regain his master's favor than by taking
the heads of our own men? 5 Isn't this the
David they sang about in their dances:

" 'Saul has slain his thousands,
and David his tens of thousands'?"[q]

6 So Achish called David and said to
him, "As surely as the LORD lives, you
have been reliable, and I would be
pleased to have you serve with me in the
army. From the day[r] you came to me until now, I have found no fault in you, but
the rulers[s] don't approve of you. 7 Turn
back and go in peace; do nothing to displease the Philistine rulers."
8 "But what have I done?" asked David.
"What have you found against your servant from the day I came to you until
now? Why can't I go and fight against the
enemies of my lord the king?"
9 Achish answered, "I know that you
have been as pleasing in my eyes as an
angel[t] of God; nevertheless, the Philistine commanders[u] have said, 'He must
not go up with us into battle.' 10 Now get
up early, along with your master's servants who have come with you, and
leave[v] in the morning as soon as it is
light."
11 So David and his men got up early in
the morning to go back to the land of the
Philistines, and the Philistines went up to
Jezreel.

Chapter 30

David Destroys the Amalekites

DAVID and his men reached Ziklag[w]
on the third day. Now the Amalekites[x] had raided the Negev and Ziklag.
They had attacked Ziklag and burned[y] it,
2 and had taken captive the women and all
who were in it, both young and old. They
killed none of them, but carried them off
as they went on their way.
3 When David and his men came to Ziklag, they found it destroyed by fire and
their wives and sons and daughters taken
captive.[z] 4 So David and his men wept[a]
aloud until they had no strength left to
weep. 5 David's two wives[b] had been captured—Ahinoam of Jezreel and Abigail,
the widow of Nabal of Carmel. 6 David
was greatly distressed because the men
were talking of stoning[c] him; each one
was bitter[d] in spirit because of his sons

28:19 [e]1Sa 31:2; 1Ch 8:33
28:21 [f]S Jdg 9:17; S 12:3
28:23 [g]1Ki 21:4
28:24 [h]S Ge 18:7
29:1 [i]1Sa 28:1 [j]S 1Sa 4:1 [k]Jos 17:16; 1Ki 18:45; 21:1,23; 2Ki 9:30; Jer 50:5; Hos 1:4,5,11; 2:22
29:2 [l]1Sa 28:2
29:3 [m]1Ch 12:19 [n]1Sa 27:7
29:4 [o]1Ch 12:19 [p]1Sa 14:21
29:5 [q]S 1Sa 18:7
29:6 [r]1Sa 27:8-12 [s]ver 3
29:9 [t]2Sa 14:17, 20; 19:27 [u]ver 4
29:10 [v]1Ch 12:19
30:1 [w]S 1Sa 27:6 [x]S 1Sa 27:8 [y]ver 14
30:3 [z]S Ge 31:26
30:4 [a]S Ge 27:38
30:5 [b]S 1Sa 25:43
30:6 [c]S Ex 17:4; Jn 8:59 [d]S Ru 1:13

30:1–25 CHRISTIAN ETHICS, Justice—Those who appear to have insignificant, behind-the-scenes jobs could be fulfilling as heavy a responsibility as those more prominent. Compare Mt 20:1–16. Grace and generosity are facets of justice.

30:3–8 DISCIPLESHIP, Enabling Power—The circumstances David and his men faced at Ziklag were so devastating the men considered turning on David. He was left with the loneliness that often accompanies leadership. In his distress he turned to the God he served and found strength to go on leading. God gave David instructions and assured him of success. God always provides the power that enables His people to go on serving Him. Discipleship depends on God's power, not on human manipulation.

30:6 HISTORY, Presence—Disaster does not mean God is absent. In the midst of personal distress we can gain strength through God's presence.

30:6 PRAYER, Growth—At a time when weakness might have seemed excusable, David grew strong through prayer. Compare Ne 8:10. God's strength is available for the darkest hours through prayer.

and daughters. But David found
strength[e] in the LORD his God.
7Then David said to Abiathar[f] the
priest, the son of Ahimelech, "Bring me
the ephod.[g]" Abiathar brought it to him,
8and David inquired[h] of the LORD, "Shall
I pursue this raiding party? Will I overtake them?"
"Pursue them," he answered. "You
will certainly overtake them and succeed[i] in the rescue.[j]"
9David and the six hundred men[k] with
him came to the Besor Ravine, where
some stayed behind, 10for two hundred
men were too exhausted[l] to cross the
ravine. But David and four hundred men
continued the pursuit.
11They found an Egyptian in a field and
brought him to David. They gave him water to drink and food to eat— 12part of a
cake of pressed figs and two cakes of raisins. He ate and was revived,[m] for he had
not eaten any food or drunk any water for
three days and three nights.
13David asked him, "To whom do you
belong, and where do you come from?"
He said, "I am an Egyptian, the slave of
an Amalekite.[n] My master abandoned
me when I became ill three days ago.
14We raided the Negev of the Kerethites[o]
and the territory belonging to Judah and
the Negev of Caleb.[p] And we burned[q]
Ziklag."
15David asked him, "Can you lead me
down to this raiding party?"
He answered, "Swear to me before
God that you will not kill me or hand me
over to my master,[r] and I will take you
down to them."
16He led David down, and there they
were, scattered over the countryside, eating, drinking and reveling[s] because of
the great amount of plunder[t] they had
taken from the land of the Philistines and
from Judah. 17David fought[u] them from
dusk until the evening of the next day,
and none of them got away, except four
hundred young men who rode off on
camels and fled.[v] 18David recovered[w] everything the Amalekites had taken, including his two wives. 19Nothing was
missing: young or old, boy or girl, plunder or anything else they had taken. David brought everything back. 20He took all
the flocks and herds, and his men drove
them ahead of the other livestock, saying,
"This is David's plunder."
21Then David came to the two hundred
men who had been too exhausted[x] to follow him and who were left behind at the
Besor Ravine. They came out to meet David and the people with him. As David
and his men approached, he greeted
them. 22But all the evil men and troublemakers among David's followers said,
"Because they did not go out with us, we
will not share with them the plunder we
recovered. However, each man may take
his wife and children and go."
23David replied, "No, my brothers, you
must not do that with what the LORD has
given us. He has protected us and handed
over to us the forces that came against us.
24Who will listen to what you say? The
share of the man who stayed with the
supplies is to be the same as that of him
who went down to the battle. All will
share alike.[y]" 25David made this a statute and ordinance for Israel from that day
to this.
26When David arrived in Ziklag, he
sent some of the plunder to the elders of
Judah, who were his friends, saying,
"Here is a present[z] for you from the
plunder of the LORD's enemies."
27He sent it to those who were in Bethel,[a] Ramoth[b] Negev and Jattir;[c] 28to
those in Aroer,[d] Siphmoth,[e] Eshtemoa[f]
29and Racal; to those in the towns of the
Jerahmeelites[g] and the Kenites;[h] 30to
those in Hormah,[i] Bor Ashan,[j] Athach
31and Hebron;[k] and to those in all the
other places where David and his men
had roamed.

Chapter 31

Saul Takes His Life

31:1–13pp — 2Sa 1:4–12; 1Ch 10:1–12

NOW the Philistines fought against Israel; the Israelites fled before them,
and many fell slain on Mount Gilboa.[l]
2The Philistines pressed hard after Saul
and his sons,[m] and they killed his sons
Jonathan,[n] Abinadab and Malki-Shua.[o]
3The fighting grew fierce around Saul,
and when the archers overtook him, they
wounded[p] him critically.
4Saul said to his armor-bearer, "Draw
your sword and run me through,[q] or
these uncircumcised[r] fellows will come
and run me through and abuse me."
But his armor-bearer was terrified and
would not do it; so Saul took his own
sword and fell on it. 5When the armor-
bearer saw that Saul was dead, he too fell
on his sword and died with him. 6So Saul
and his three sons and his armor-bearer
and all his men died[s] together that same
day.
7When the Israelites along the valley

30:6 [e]S 1Sa 23:16; Ro 4:20
30:7 [f]S 1Sa 22:20 [g]S 1Sa 2:28
30:8 [h]S 1Sa 23:2 [i]S Ge 14:16 [j]S Ex 2:17
30:9 [k]S 1Sa 27:2
30:10 [l]ver 21
30:12 [m]S Jdg 15:19
30:13 [n]S 1Sa 14:48
30:14 [o]2Sa 8:18; 15:18; 20:7,23; 1Ki 1:38,44; 1Ch 18:17; Eze 25:16; Zep 2:5 [p]S Jos 14:13; S 15:13 [q]ver 1
30:15 [r]Dt 23:15
30:16 [s]Lk 12:19 [t]S ver 17; S Jos 22:8
30:17 [u]ver 16; 1Sa 11:11; 2Sa 1:1 [v]2Sa 1:8
30:18 [w]S Ge 14:16
30:21 [x]ver 10
30:24 [y]S Nu 31:27; S Jdg 5:30
30:26 [z]S Ge 33:11
30:27 [a]S Jos 7:2 [b]S Jos 10:40 [c]S Jos 15:48
30:28 [d]S Nu 32:34; S Jos 13:16 [e]1Ch 27:27 [f]S Jos 15:50
30:29 [g]1Sa 27:10 [h]S 1Sa 15:6
30:30 [i]S Nu 14:45; S 21:3 [j]S Jos 15:42
30:31 [k]Nu 13:22; S Jos 10:36; 2Sa 2:1,4
31:1 [l]S 1Sa 28:4
31:2 [m]S 1Sa 28:19 [n]S 1Sa 18:1 [o]S 1Sa 14:49
31:3 [p]S 1Sa 28:4
31:4 [q]S Jdg 9:54 [r]S Ge 34:14; S 1Sa 14:6
31:6 [s]S 1Sa 26:10

30:7 PRAYER, Petition—See note on 22:10. The ephod was closely associated with the breastplate, which contained the Urim and Thummim. See Ex. 28:30; Lev 8:8.

and those across the Jordan saw that the
Israelite army had fled and that Saul and
his sons had died, they abandoned their
towns and fled. And the Philistines came
and occupied them.
8The next day, when the Philistines[t]
came to strip the dead, they found Saul
and his three sons fallen on Mount Gilboa. 9They cut off his head and stripped
off his armor, and they sent messengers
throughout the land of the Philistines to
proclaim the news[u] in the temple of
their idols and among their people.[v]

31:8 [t]2Sa 1:20
31:9 [u]2Sa 1:20; 4:4 [v]S Jdg 16:24
31:10 [w]S Jdg 2:12-13; S 1Sa 7:3 [x]S Jos 17:11
31:11 [y]S Jdg 21:8; S 1Sa 11:1
31:12 [z]Ps 76:5 [a]S Ge 38:24; Am 6:10
31:13 [b]2Sa 21:12-14 [c]S Ge 21:33 [d]2Sa 3:35; 12:19-23 [e]S Ge 50:10

10They put his armor in the temple of the
Ashtoreths[w] and fastened his body to the
wall of Beth Shan.[x]
11When the people of Jabesh Gilead[y]
heard of what the Philistines had done to
Saul, 12all their valiant men[z] journeyed
through the night to Beth Shan. They
took down the bodies of Saul and his sons
from the wall of Beth Shan and went to
Jabesh, where they burned[a] them.
13Then they took their bones[b] and buried
them under a tamarisk[c] tree at Jabesh,
and they fasted[d] seven days.[e]

31:10–12 HUMANITY, Attitudes to Death—The citizens of Jabesh-Gilead remembered how Saul had rescued them from disaster (11:1–11). They refused to let the Philistines use Saul's dead remains as a trophy of victory and as a sign warning Israel of further opposition to the Philistines. Rather the people of Jabesh-Gilead acted heroically to provide proper honor for Saul through proper burial. Even the person who had rebelled so against God deserved to be remembered for the good he had done and deserved proper burial.

2 Samuel

See Introduction to 1 Samuel.

Theological Outline

2 Samuel: Discerning God's Hand at Work

I. To Achieve His Purposes, God Honors Obedience Not Treachery. (1:1—6:23)
   A. Those who dishonor God's chosen leaders are punished. (1:1-16)
   B. God's leader honors the memory of his predecessors. (1:17-27)
   C. God leads people to honor His obedient leader. (2:1-4*a*)
   D. God honors loyal, obedient people. (2:4*b*-7)
   E. God blesses efforts for peace. (2:8-28)
   F. God strengthens His obedient leader. (2:29—3:19)
   G. God's leader refuses to honor treachery and revenge. (3:20—4:12)
   H. God fulfills His promises to His patient servant. (5:1-16)
   I. God provides victory for His people. (5:17-25)
   J. God's people must honor His holy presence. (6:1-23)

II. God Establishes His Purposes Through His Faithful Yet Fallible Servant. (7:1—12:31)
   A. God promises to bless the house of David forever. (7:1-17)
   B. God's servant praises the incomparable God. (7:18-29)
   C. God gives victory to His faithful servant. (8:1-18)
   D. God's servant shows kindness in memory of his departed friends. (9:1-13)
   E. Enemy coalitions cannot prevent God from taking vengeance. (10:1-19)
   F. Disobedience from God's leader displeases the Lord and brings judgment but also mercy. (11:1—12:14*a*)
   G. God brings honor to His penitent servant. (12:14*b*-31)

III. Lack of Attention to Family Relations Leads to National Problems for God's Leader. (13:1—20:26)
   A. The inattention of a godly father can lead to family feuds, shame, and vengeance. (13:1-39)
   B. Reconciliation, not anger and judgments, should mark the family life of God's servants. (14:1-33)
   C. Unhealed family wounds lead to revolt. (15:1-37)
   D. Leaders need advisors whom God can use to accomplish His purposes. (16:1—17:29)
   E. The time of sorrow is too late to set family relationships right. (18:1-33)
   F. God's victorious servant deals kindly with those who helped and those who opposed him. (19:1-40)
   G. Victory cannot remove rivalries among God's people. (19:41—20:26)

IV. God's People Learn from the Experience and Example of God's Leader. (21:1—24:25)
   A. God blesses the leader who is faithful to the tradition of His people. (21:1-22)
   B. God's leader praises God for His deliverance. (22:1-51; compare Ps 18)
   C. God's leader teaches what he has learned—his experiences with God. (23:1-7)
   D. God's leader depends on brave, faithful associates. (23:8-39)
   E. The leader's foolish decisions bring punishment even on a repentant leader. (24:1-17)
   F. Proper worship brings God's mercy for His people. (24:18-25)

Chapter 1

David Hears of Saul's Death

1:4–12pp — 1Sa 31:1–13; 1Ch 10:1–12

AFTER the death[a] of Saul, David returned from defeating[b] the Amalekites[c] and stayed in Ziklag two days. 2On
the third day a man[d] arrived from Saul's
camp, with his clothes torn and with dust
on his head.[e] When he came to David,
he fell[f] to the ground to pay him honor.[g]
3"Where have you come from?" David
asked him.
He answered, "I have escaped from the
Israelite camp."
4"What happened?" David asked. "Tell
me."
He said, "The men fled from the battle.
Many of them fell and died. And Saul and
his son Jonathan are dead."
5Then David said to the young man
who brought him the report, "How do
you know that Saul and his son Jonathan
are dead?"
6"I happened to be on Mount Gilboa,[h]" the young man said, "and there
was Saul, leaning on his spear, with the
chariots and riders almost upon him.
7When he turned around and saw me, he
called out to me, and I said, 'What can I
do?'
8"He asked me, 'Who are you?'
" 'An Amalekite,[i]' I answered.
9"Then he said to me, 'Stand over me
and kill me![j] I am in the throes of death,
but I'm still alive.'
10"So I stood over him and killed him,
because I knew that after he had fallen he
could not survive. And I took the crown[k]
that was on his head and the band on his
arm and have brought them here to my
lord."
11Then David and all the men with him
took hold of their clothes and tore[l]
them. 12They mourned and wept and fasted till evening for Saul and his son Jonathan, and for the army of the LORD and
the house of Israel, because they had fall-
en by the sword.
13David said to the young man who
brought him the report, "Where are you
from?"
"I am the son of an alien, an Amalekite,[m]" he answered.
14David asked him, "Why were you not
afraid to lift your hand to destroy the
LORD's anointed?[n]"
15Then David called one of his men and
said, "Go, strike him down!"[o] So he
struck him down, and he died.[p] 16For David had said to him, "Your blood be on
your own head.[q] Your own mouth testified against you when you said, 'I killed
the LORD's anointed.' "

David's Lament for Saul and Jonathan

17David took up this lament[r] concerning Saul and his son Jonathan,[s] 18and ordered that the men of Judah be taught
this lament of the bow (it is written in the
Book of Jashar):[t]

19"Your glory, O Israel, lies slain on your
heights.
How the mighty[u] have fallen![v]
20"Tell it not in Gath,[w]
proclaim it not in the streets of
Ashkelon,[x]
lest the daughters of the Philistines[y]
be glad,
lest the daughters of the
uncircumcised rejoice.[z]
21"O mountains of Gilboa,[a]
may you have neither dew[b] nor
rain,[c]
nor fields that yield offerings[d] ⌊of
grain⌋.
For there the shield of the mighty was
defiled,
the shield of Saul—no longer rubbed
with oil.[e]
22From the blood[f] of the slain,
from the flesh of the mighty,
the bow[g] of Jonathan did not turn
back,
the sword of Saul did not return
unsatisfied.
23"Saul and Jonathan—
in life they were loved and gracious,
and in death they were not parted.
They were swifter than eagles,[h]
they were stronger than lions.[i]
24"O daughters of Israel,
weep for Saul,
who clothed you in scarlet and finery,
who adorned your garments with
ornaments of gold.[j]
25"How the mighty have fallen in battle!
Jonathan lies slain on your heights.

1:1 [a]S 1Sa 26:10; 1Ch 10:13 [b]S Jos 22:8; S 1Sa 30:17 [c]S Ge 14:7; Nu 13:29
1:2 [d]2Sa 4:10 [e]S 1Sa 4:12; Job 2:12; Eze 27:30 [f]S 1Sa 20:41 [g]S Ge 37:7
1:6 [h]ver 21; S 1Sa 28:4
1:8 [i]ver 13; S 1Sa 15:2; S 27:8; 30:13,17
1:9 [j]S Jdg 9:54
1:10 [k]2Ki 11:12
1:11 [l]S Ge 37:29; S Nu 14:6
1:13 [m]S ver 8; S 1Sa 14:48
1:14 [n]S 1Sa 12:3; S 26:9
1:15 [o]2Sa 4:12 [p]2Sa 4:10
1:16 [q]S Lev 20:9; Mt 27:24-25; Ac 18:6
1:17 [r]S Ge 50:10; S Eze 32:2 [s]ver 26
1:18 [t]Jos 10:13
1:19 [u]2Sa 23:8; Ps 29:1; 45:3 [v]2Sa 3:38
1:20 [w]Mic 1:10 [x]S Jos 13:3 [y]1Sa 31:8 [z]S 1Sa 18:6
1:21 [a]S ver 6 [b]S Ge 27:28; S Isa 18:4 [c]Dt 11:17; 1Ki 8:35; 17:1; 18:1; 2Ch 6:26; Job 36:27; 38:28; Ps 65:10; 147:8; Isa 5:6; Jer 5:24; 14:4; Am 1:2 [d]Jer 12:4; Eze 31:15 [e]Isa 21:5
1:22 [f]Isa 34:3,7; 49:26 [g]Dt 32:42
1:23 [h]S Dt 28:49 [i]Jdg 14:18
1:24 [j]S Jdg 5:30

1:12 PRAYER, Humility—Fasting was commanded only in connection with the Day of Atonement (Lev 23:27–29). It later became customary (Zec 7:5). The fast expressed humility and dependence before God. Fasts were often associated with occasions of repentance or mourning. Fasting was normally avoided on festive occasions and sabbaths, except for prolonged fasts which would involve sabbaths. Mourning should be more than a time of personal sorrow. It should represent prayer for strength and renewal before God.

1:15–16 HISTORY, Deliverance—See note on 1 Sa 24:8–21. Taking God's judgment into one's own hands shows total disrespect for God and His historical actions.

1:19–27 HUMANITY, Attitudes to Death—Grieving over the death of friends and enemies is admirable in human beings. Expressing grief openly in love and respect is proper. See note om 1 Sa 31:10–13.

26I grieve[k] for you, Jonathan[l] my
brother;[m]
you were very dear to me.
Your love for me was wonderful,[n]
more wonderful than that of
women.

27"How the mighty have fallen!
The weapons of war have
perished!"[o]

Chapter 2

David Anointed King Over Judah

IN the course of time, David inquired[p]
of the LORD. "Shall I go up to one of
the towns of Judah?" he asked.
The LORD said, "Go up."
David asked, "Where shall I go?"
"To Hebron,"[q] the LORD answered.
2So David went up there with his two
wives,[r] Ahinoam of Jezreel and Abigail,[s]
the widow of Nabal of Carmel. 3David
also took the men who were with him,[t]
each with his family, and they settled in
Hebron[u] and its towns. 4Then the men of
Judah came to Hebron[v] and there they
anointed[w] David king over the house of
Judah.
When David was told that it was the
men of Jabesh Gilead[x] who had buried
Saul, 5he sent messengers to the men of
Jabesh Gilead to say to them, "The LORD
bless[y] you for showing this kindness to
Saul your master by burying him. 6May
the LORD now show you kindness and
faithfulness,[z] and I too will show you the
same favor because you have done this.
7Now then, be strong[a] and brave, for
Saul your master is dead, and the house
of Judah has anointed me king over
them."

War Between the Houses of David and Saul

3:2–5pp — 1Ch 3:1–4

8Meanwhile, Abner[b] son of Ner, the
commander of Saul's army, had taken
Ish-Bosheth[c] son of Saul and brought
him over to Mahanaim.[d] 9He made him
king over Gilead,[e] Ashuri[a][f] and Jezreel,
and also over Ephraim, Benjamin and all
Israel.[g]
10Ish-Bosheth son of Saul was forty
years old when he became king over Israel, and he reigned two years. The house
of Judah, however, followed David. 11The
length of time David was king in Hebron
over the house of Judah was seven years
and six months.[h]
12Abner son of Ner, together with the
men of Ish-Bosheth son of Saul, left Mahanaim and went to Gibeon.[i] 13Joab[j]
son of Zeruiah and David's men went out
and met them at the pool of Gibeon. One
group sat down on one side of the pool
and one group on the other side.
14Then Abner said to Joab, "Let's have
some of the young men get up and fight
hand to hand in front of us."
"All right, let them do it," Joab said.
15So they stood up and were counted
off—twelve men for Benjamin and Ish-
Bosheth son of Saul, and twelve for David. 16Then each man grabbed his opponent by the head and thrust his dagger[k]
into his opponent's side, and they fell
down together. So that place in Gibeon
was called Helkath Hazzurim.[b]
17The battle that day was very fierce,
and Abner and the men of Israel were
defeated[l] by David's men.[m]
18The three sons of Zeruiah[n] were
there: Joab,[o] Abishai[p] and Asahel.[q]
Now Asahel was as fleet-footed as a wild
gazelle.[r] 19He chased Abner, turning neither to the right nor to the left as he pursued him. 20Abner looked behind him
and asked, "Is that you, Asahel?"
"It is," he answered.
21Then Abner said to him, "Turn aside
to the right or to the left; take on one of
the young men and strip him of his
weapons." But Asahel would not stop
chasing him.
22Again Abner warned Asahel, "Stop
chasing me! Why should I strike you
down? How could I look your brother
Joab in the face?"[s]
23But Asahel refused to give up the pursuit; so Abner thrust the butt of his spear
into Asahel's stomach,[t] and the spear
came out through his back. He fell there
and died on the spot. And every man
stopped when he came to the place
where Asahel had fallen and died.[u]
24But Joab and Abishai pursued Abner,

1:26 [k]Jer 22:18; 34:5 [l]ver 17 [m]S 1Sa 20:42 [n]S 1Sa 18:1
1:27 [o]S 1Sa 2:4
2:1 [p]S 1Sa 23:2, 11-12 [q]S Ge 13:18; S 23:19
2:2 [r]S 1Sa 25:43 [s]S 1Sa 25:42
2:3 [t]S 1Sa 27:2; 1Ch 12:22 [u]S Ge 13:18; 23:2; 37:14
2:4 [v]S 1Sa 30:31 [w]S 1Sa 2:35; 2Sa 5:3-5; 1Ch 12:23-40 [x]S Jdg 21:8; S 1Sa 11:1
2:5 [y]S Jdg 17:2; S 1Sa 23:21; 2Ti 1:16
2:6 [z]Ex 34:6
2:7 [a]S Jos 1:6; S Jdg 5:21
2:8 [b]S 1Sa 14:50; S 2Sa 3:27 [c]2Sa 4:5; 1Ch 8:33; 9:39 [d]S Ge 32:2
2:9 [e]S Nu 32:26 [f]S Jos 19:24-31 [g]1Ch 12:29
2:11 [h]2Sa 5:5
2:12 [i]S Jos 9:3
2:13 [j]2Sa 8:16; 19:13; 1Ki 1:7; 1Ch 2:16; 11:6; 27:34
2:16 [k]S Jdg 3:21
2:17 [l]2Sa 3:1 [m]S 1Sa 17:8
2:18 [n]2Sa 3:39; 16:10; 19:22 [o]2Sa 3:30; 10:7; 11:1; 14:1; 18:14; 20:8; 24:3; 1Ki 1:7; 2:5,34 [p]S 1Sa 26:6 [q]2Sa 23:24; 1Ch 2:16; 11:26; 27:7 [r]1Ch 12:8; Pr 6:5; SS 2:9
2:22 [s]2Sa 3:27
2:23 [t]2Sa 3:27; 4:6 [u]2Sa 20:12

[a]9 Or *Asher* [b]16 *Helkath Hazzurim* means *field of daggers* or *field of hostilities.*

2:1 PRAYER, Will of God—See note on 1 Sa 23:2. This prayer was especially important, since Samuel had already anointed David king. David did not seize what was his but sought the direction of the Lord.

2:4–7 HUMANITY, Community Relationships—Community choices establish basic relationships. Dealing with others in a generous spirit, as David had with Hebron and as he did with Jabesh Gilead, cements such relationships. God's people are encouraged to create good relationships to accomplish God's purposes.

2:5–6 PRAYER, Humility—David blessed those who had shown proper favor to his enemy. See note on 1 Sa 24:12–15. Concern and admiration for others are legitimate reasons for asking God to bless them. Seeking to gain political advantage is not. See note on 1 Sa 23:21.

2:8—4:12 CHRISTIAN ETHICS, Murder—Political intrigue and personal vengeance lead to war and murder. Neither is approved by the inspired writer. See notes on Ex 20:13; Jdg 8:10–21; Mt 5:21–22.

and as the sun was setting, they came to
the hill of Ammah, near Giah on the way
to the wasteland of Gibeon. 25Then the
men of Benjamin rallied behind Abner.
They formed themselves into a group and
took their stand on top of a hill.

26Abner called out to Joab, "Must the
sword devour[v] forever? Don't you realize
that this will end in bitterness? How long
before you order your men to stop pursuing their brothers?"

27Joab answered, "As surely as God
lives, if you had not spoken, the men
would have continued the pursuit of their
brothers until morning.[c]"

28So Joab[w] blew the trumpet,[x] and all
the men came to a halt; they no longer
pursued Israel, nor did they fight anymore.

29All that night Abner and his men
marched through the Arabah.[y] They
crossed the Jordan, continued through
the whole Bithron[d] and came to Mahanaim.[z]

30Then Joab returned from pursuing
Abner and assembled all his men. Besides
Asahel, nineteen of David's men were
found missing. 31But David's men had
killed three hundred and sixty Benjamites
who were with Abner. 32They took Asahel and buried him in his father's tomb[a]
at Bethlehem. Then Joab and his men
marched all night and arrived at Hebron
by daybreak.

Chapter 3

THE war between the house of Saul and
the house of David lasted a long
time.[b] David grew stronger and stronger,[c] while the house of Saul grew weaker and weaker.[d]

2Sons were born to David in Hebron:
His firstborn was Amnon[e] the
son of Ahinoam[f] of Jezreel;
3his second, Kileab the son of Abigail[g] the widow of Nabal of Carmel;
the third, Absalom[h] the son of
Maacah daughter of Talmai king
of Geshur;[i]
4the fourth, Adonijah[j] the son of
Haggith;
the fifth, Shephatiah the son of
Abital;
5and the sixth, Ithream the son of
David's wife Eglah.
These were born to David in Hebron.

Abner Goes Over to David

6During the war between the house of
Saul and the house of David, Abner[k] had
been strengthening his own position in
the house of Saul. 7Now Saul had had a
concubine[l] named Rizpah[m] daughter of
Aiah. And Ish-Bosheth said to Abner,
"Why did you sleep with my father's concubine?"

8Abner was very angry because of what
Ish-Bosheth said and he answered, "Am I
a dog's head[n]—on Judah's side? This
very day I am loyal to the house of your
father Saul and to his family and friends. I
haven't handed you over to David. Yet
now you accuse me of an offense involving this woman! 9May God deal with Abner, be it ever so severely, if I do not do
for David what the LORD promised[o] him
on oath 10and transfer the kingdom from
the house of Saul and establish David's
throne over Israel and Judah from Dan to
Beersheba."[p] 11Ish-Bosheth did not dare
to say another word to Abner, because he
was afraid of him.

12Then Abner sent messengers on his
behalf to say to David, "Whose land is it?
Make an agreement with me, and I will
help you bring all Israel over to you."

13"Good," said David. "I will make an
agreement with you. But I demand one
thing of you: Do not come into my presence unless you bring Michal daughter of
Saul when you come to see me."[q]
14Then David sent messengers to Ish-Bosheth son of Saul, demanding, "Give me
my wife Michal,[r] whom I betrothed to
myself for the price of a hundred Philistine foreskins."

15So Ish-Bosheth gave orders and had
her taken away from her husband[s] Paltiel[t] son of Laish. 16Her husband, however, went with her, weeping behind her all
the way to Bahurim.[u] Then Abner said to
him, "Go back home!" So he went back.

17Abner conferred with the elders[v] of
Israel and said, "For some time you have
wanted to make David your king. 18Now
do it! For the LORD promised David, 'By
my servant David I will rescue my people
Israel from the hand of the Philistines[w]
and from the hand of all their enemies.[x]' "

19Abner also spoke to the Benjamites in
person. Then he went to Hebron to tell
David everything that Israel and the
whole house of Benjamin[y] wanted to do.
20When Abner, who had twenty men

2:26 [v]S Dt 32:42; Jer 46:10,14; Na 2:13; 3:15
2:28 [w]2Sa 18:16; 20:23 [x]S Jdg 3:27
2:29 [y]S Dt 3:17 [z]S Ge 32:2
2:32 [a]S Ge 49:29
3:1 [b]1Ki 14:30 [c]2Sa 5:10 [d]2Sa 2:17; 22:44; Est 9:4
3:2 [e]2Sa 13:1 [f]S 1Sa 25:43
3:3 [g]S 1Sa 25:42 [h]2Sa 13:1,28 [i]2Sa 13:37; 14:32; 15:8
3:4 [j]1Ki 1:5,11; 2:13,22
3:6 [k]S 1Sa 14:50
3:7 [l]S Ge 22:24; 2Sa 16:21-22; S 1Ki 1:3 [m]2Sa 21:8-11
3:8 [n]S 1Sa 17:43; 2Sa 9:8; 16:9; 2Ki 8:13
3:9 [o]S 1Sa 15:28
3:10 [p]S Jdg 20:1; 1Sa 25:28-31; 2Sa 24:2
3:13 [q]S Ge 43:5
3:14 [r]S 1Sa 18:27
3:15 [s]Dt 24:1-4 [t]1Sa 25:44
3:16 [u]2Sa 16:5; 17:18
3:17 [v]S Jdg 11:11
3:18 [w]S 1Sa 9:16 [x]2Sa 8:6
3:19 [y]1Ch 12:2,16, 29

c27 Or *spoken this morning, the men would not have taken up the pursuit of their brothers*; or *spoken, the men would have given up the pursuit of their brothers by morning* d29 Or *morning*; or *ravine*; the meaning of the Hebrew for this word is uncertain.

3:9–10 PRAYER, Personal—This is a vow that Abner attempted to carry out (vv 12–21). A vow made to accomplish God's will is admirable. A vow made in anger and jealousy can be sinful. See note on 1 Sa 23:21.

with him, came to David at Hebron, David prepared a feast[z] for him and his
men. 21Then Abner said to David, "Let
me go at once and assemble all Israel for
my lord the king, so that they may make a
compact[a] with you, and that you may
rule over all that your heart desires."[b] So
David sent Abner away, and he went in
peace.

Joab Murders Abner

22Just then David's men and Joab returned from a raid and brought with them
a great deal of plunder. But Abner was no
longer with David in Hebron, because
David had sent him away, and he had
gone in peace. 23When Joab and all the
soldiers with him arrived, he was told
that Abner son of Ner had come to the
king and that the king had sent him away
and that he had gone in peace.
24So Joab went to the king and said,
"What have you done? Look, Abner came
to you. Why did you let him go? Now he
is gone! 25You know Abner son of Ner; he
came to deceive you and observe your
movements and find out everything you
are doing."
26Joab then left David and sent messengers after Abner, and they brought him
back from the well of Sirah. But David did
not know it. 27Now when Abner[c] returned to Hebron, Joab took him aside
into the gateway, as though to speak with
him privately. And there, to avenge the
blood of his brother Asahel, Joab stabbed
him[d] in the stomach, and he died.[e]
28Later, when David heard about this,
he said, "I and my kingdom are forever
innocent[f] before the LORD concerning
the blood of Abner son of Ner. 29May his
blood[g] fall upon the head of Joab and
upon all his father's house![h] May Joab's
house never be without someone who
has a running sore[i] or leprosy[e] or who
leans on a crutch or who falls by the
sword or who lacks food."
30(Joab and his brother Abishai murdered Abner because he had killed their
brother Asahel in the battle at Gibeon.)
31Then David said to Joab and all the
people with him, "Tear your clothes and
put on sackcloth[j] and walk in mourning[k] in front of Abner." King David himself walked behind the bier. 32They buried Abner in Hebron, and the king wept[l]
aloud at Abner's tomb. All the people
wept also.
33The king sang this lament[m] for Abner:

"Should Abner have died as the
lawless die?
34 Your hands were not bound,
your feet were not fettered.[n]
You fell as one falls before wicked
men."

And all the people wept over him
again.
35Then they all came and urged David
to eat something while it was still day;
but David took an oath, saying, "May God
deal with me, be it ever so severely,[o] if I
taste bread[p] or anything else before the
sun sets!"
36All the people took note and were
pleased; indeed, everything the king did
pleased them. 37So on that day all the
people and all Israel knew that the king
had no part[q] in the murder of Abner son
of Ner.
38Then the king said to his men, "Do
you not realize that a prince and a great
man has fallen[r] in Israel this day? 39And
today, though I am the anointed king, I
am weak, and these sons of Zeruiah[s] are
too strong[t] for me.[u] May the LORD repay[v] the evildoer according to his evil
deeds!"

Chapter 4

Ish-Bosheth Murdered

WHEN Ish-Bosheth son of Saul heard
that Abner[w] had died in Hebron,
he lost courage, and all Israel became
alarmed. 2Now Saul's son had two men
who were leaders of raiding bands. One
was named Baanah and the other Recab;
they were sons of Rimmon the Beerothite
from the tribe of Benjamin—Beeroth[x] is
considered part of Benjamin, 3because
the people of Beeroth fled to Gittaim[y]
and have lived there as aliens to this day.
4(Jonathan[z] son of Saul had a son who

3:20 [z]1Ch 12:39
3:21 [a]2Sa 5:3 [b]1Ki 11:37
3:27 [c]2Sa 2:8; 4:1; 1Ki 2:5,32 [d]S Ex 21:14; S Jdg 3:21; S 2Sa 2:23 [e]2Sa 2:22
3:28 [f]ver 37; Dt 21:9
3:29 [g]S Lev 20:9 [h]1Ki 2:31-33 [i]S Lev 15:2
3:31 [j]Ps 30:11; 35:13; 69:11; Isa 20:2 [k]S Ge 37:34
3:32 [l]S Nu 14:1; Pr 24:17
3:33 [m]S Ge 50:10
3:34 [n]Job 36:8; Ps 2:3; 149:8; Isa 45:14; Na 3:10
3:35 [o]S Ru 1:17 [p]S 1Sa 31:13; 2Sa 12:17; Jer 16:7
3:37 [q]S ver 28
3:38 [r]2Sa 1:19
3:39 [s]S 2Sa 2:18 [t]2Sa 16:9; 18:11 [u]S Jdg 18:26 [v]1Ki 2:32; Ps 41:10; 101:8
4:1 [w]S 2Sa 3:27
4:2 [x]S Jos 9:17
4:3 [y]Ne 11:33
4:4 [z]S 1Sa 18:1

[e]29 The Hebrew word was used for various diseases affecting the skin—not necessarily leprosy.

3:22–39 HUMANITY, Relationships—Acts of vengeance destroy relationships which have been worked out among people who disagree. However, by rising above such acts, leaders can still salvage the destroyed relationship. Oftentimes allegiance to one relationship keeps people from acting decisively when other relationships are destroyed. Such confused entanglements seldom offer solid foundations for the future.

3:29 PRAYER, Curse—God is the Judge. Biblical curses acknowledge His rights and human limitations. David uttered this curse in view of the seriousness of Joab's crime. Murder was punishable by death (Ex 21:12), and even the cities of refuge provided no protection for a murderer (Nu 35:16).

3:33–35 PRAYER, Lament—Lamentation is basically a funeral song expressing sorrow. David joined a vow to fast with his musical lament. See note on 1:12.

3:39 PRAYER, Vow—See note on v 29. This vow is not so praiseworthy if human weakness was the only reason David did not kill his enemies.

4:4 EVIL AND SUFFERING, Human Origin—Mephibosheth was crippled as a child in an accident. Apparently he was not crippled because of some sin. His suffering was caused by human haste and misfortune. The child was innocent. The

was lame in both feet. He was five years
old when the news[a] about Saul and Jonathan came from Jezreel. His nurse picked
him up and fled, but as she hurried to
leave, he fell and became crippled.[b] His
name was Mephibosheth.)[c]
5Now Recab and Baanah, the sons of
Rimmon the Beerothite, set out for the
house of Ish-Bosheth,[d] and they arrived
there in the heat of the day while he was
taking his noonday rest.[e] 6They went
into the inner part of the house as if to
get some wheat, and they stabbed[f] him
in the stomach. Then Recab and his
brother Baanah slipped away.
7They had gone into the house while
he was lying on the bed in his bedroom.
After they stabbed and killed him, they
cut off his head. Taking it with them,
they traveled all night by way of the Arabah.[g] 8They brought the head[h] of Ish-Bosheth to David at Hebron and said to the
king, "Here is the head of Ish-Bosheth
son of Saul,[i] your enemy, who tried to
take your life. This day the LORD has
avenged[j] my lord the king against Saul
and his offspring."
9David answered Recab and his brother
Baanah, the sons of Rimmon the Beerothite, "As surely as the LORD lives, who has
delivered[k] me out of all trouble, 10when
a man told me, 'Saul is dead,' and thought
he was bringing good news, I seized him
and put him to death in Ziklag.[l] That was
the reward I gave him for his news!
11How much more—when wicked men
have killed an innocent man in his own
house and on his own bed—should I not
now demand his blood[m] from your hand
and rid the earth of you!"
12So David gave an order to his men,
and they killed them.[n] They cut off their
hands and feet and hung the bodies by
the pool in Hebron. But they took the
head of Ish-Bosheth and buried it in Abner's tomb at Hebron.

Chapter 5

David Becomes King Over Israel

5:1–3pp — 1Ch 11:1–3

ALL the tribes of Israel[o] came to David
at Hebron and said, "We are your
own flesh and blood.[p] 2In the past, while
Saul was king over us, you were the one
who led Israel on their military campaigns.[q] And the LORD said[r] to you, 'You
will shepherd[s] my people Israel, and you
will become their ruler.[t]' "
3When all the elders of Israel had come
to King David at Hebron, the king made a
compact[u] with them at Hebron before
the LORD, and they anointed[v] David king
over Israel.
4David was thirty years old[w] when he
became king, and he reigned[x] forty[y]
years. 5In Hebron he reigned over Judah
seven years and six months,[z] and in Jerusalem he reigned over all Israel and Judah
thirty-three years.

David Conquers Jerusalem

5:6–10pp — 1Ch 11:4–9
5:11–16pp — 1Ch 3:5–9; 14:1–7

6The king and his men marched to Jerusalem[a] to attack the Jebusites,[b] who
lived there. The Jebusites said to David,
"You will not get in here; even the blind
and the lame can ward you off." They
thought, "David cannot get in here."
7Nevertheless, David captured the fortress of Zion,[c] the City of David.[d e]
8On that day, David said, "Anyone
who conquers the Jebusites will have to
use the water shaft[f][f] to reach those
'lame and blind'[g] who are David's enemies.[g]" That is why they say, "The
'blind and lame' will not enter the palace."
9David then took up residence in the
fortress and called it the City of David. He
built up the area around it, from the supporting terraces[h][h] inward. 10And he became more and more powerful,[i] because
the LORD God Almighty[j] was with him.[k]
11Now Hiram[l] king of Tyre sent messengers to David, along with cedar logs
and carpenters and stonemasons, and
they built a palace for David. 12And David
knew that the LORD had established him
as king over Israel and had exalted his
kingdom[m] for the sake of his people Israel.
13After he left Hebron, David took

4:4 aS 1Sa 31:9 bS Lev 21:18 c2Sa 9:8,12; 16:1-4; 19:24; 21:7-8; 1Ch 8:34; 9:40
4:5 dS 2Sa 2:8 eRu 2:7
4:6 fS 2Sa 2:23
4:7 gS Dt 3:17
4:8 h2Sa 20:21; 2Ki 10:7 i1Sa 24:4; 25:29 jS Nu 31:3
4:9 kS Ge 48:16; 1Ki 1:29
4:10 l2Sa 1:2-16
4:11 mS Ge 4:10; 9:5; Ps 9:12; 72:14
4:12 n2Sa 1:15
5:1 o2Sa 19:43 pS Ge 29:14; 35:26
5:2 q1Sa 18:5,13, 16 rS 1Sa 11:6 sS Ge 48:15; S 1Sa 16:1; 2Sa 7:7; Mt 2:6; Jn 21:16 tS 1Sa 12:12; S 13:14; S 2Sa 6:21
5:3 u2Sa 3:21 vS Dt 17:15; 2Sa 2:4
5:4 wS Ge 37:2; Lk 3:23 x1Ki 2:11; 1Ch 3:4 y1Ch 26:31
5:5 z2Sa 2:11; 1Ki 2:11; 1Ch 3:4
5:6 aS Jdg 1:8 bS Jos 15:8
5:7 cPs 76:2 dJer 21:13 e2Sa 6:12,16; 1Ki 2:10; 8:1; Isa 29:1; Jer 25:29
5:8 f2Ki 20:20; 2Ch 32:30 gMt 21:14
5:9 h1Ki 9:15,24
5:10 i2Sa 3:1 jPs 24:10 k2Sa 7:9
5:11 l1Ki 5:1,18; 2Ch 2:3
5:12 mS Nu 24:7

f8 Or *use scaling hooks* g8 Or *are hated by David*
h9 Or *the Millo*

suffering was not deserved. Suffering has a mysterious side. Sometimes the innocent suffer because they live in a world infiltrated by sin and controlled by humans who make mental miscalculations or act carelessly. Such human accidents cannot be called sinful, nor can the resulting suffering be linked to sin as its cause. Some suffering will always defy human explanation or understanding.

5:1–5 HISTORY, God's Leaders—God chooses historical leaders for His people. His choice does not automatically install them in office. Humans must recognize God's choice and install the leader in office. David waited years between the anointing by Samuel (1 Sa 16:13) and the coronation in Hebron.

5:3 PRAYER, Commitment—The covenant was made "before the LORD" as a commitment in prayer. See notes on Ge 19:27; 1 Sa 10:8.

5:10 HUMANITY, Relationship to God—The Hebrew word describing David's power refers not so much to power as to greatness. The ultimate basis for true human greatness is being rightly related to God.

5:10 REVELATION, Actions—See note on 1 Sa 18:12–14.

more concubines and wives[n] in Jerusalem, and more sons and daughters were
born to him. 14These are the names of the
children born to him there:[o] Shammua,
Shobab, Nathan,[p] Solomon, 15Ibhar, Eli-
shua, Nepheg, Japhia, 16Elishama, Eliada
and Eliphelet.

David Defeats the Philistines

5:17–25pp — 1Ch 14:8–17

17When the Philistines heard that David had been anointed king over Israel,
they went up in full force to search for
him, but David heard about it and went
down to the stronghold.[q] 18Now the Philistines had come and spread out in the
Valley of Rephaim;[r] 19so David inquired[s] of the LORD, "Shall I go and attack the Philistines? Will you hand them
over to me?"

The LORD answered him, "Go, for I
will surely hand the Philistines over to
you."

20So David went to Baal Perazim, and
there he defeated them. He said, "As waters break out, the LORD has broken out
against my enemies before me." So that
place was called Baal Perazim.[i][t] 21The
Philistines abandoned their idols there,
and David and his men carried them off.[u]

22Once more the Philistines came up
and spread out in the Valley of Rephaim;
23so David inquired of the LORD, and he
answered, "Do not go straight up, but circle around behind them and attack them
in front of the balsam trees. 24As soon as
you hear the sound[v] of marching in the
tops of the balsam trees, move quickly,
because that will mean the LORD has gone
out in front[w] of you to strike the Philistine army." 25So David did as the LORD
commanded him, and he struck down the
Philistines[x] all the way from Gibeon[j][y]
to Gezer.[z]

5:13 [n]S Dt 17:17
5:14 [o]1Ch 3:5 [p]Lk 3:31
5:17 [q]2Sa 23:14; 1Ch 11:16
5:18 [r]S Jos 15:8; S 17:15
5:19 [s]S Jdg 18:5; S 1Sa 23:2
5:20 [t]S Ge 38:29
5:21 [u]Dt 7:5; Isa 46:2
5:24 [v]S Ex 14:24 [w]Jdg 4:14
5:25 [x]2Sa 8:12; 21:15 [y]Isa 28:21 [z]S Jos 10:33
6:2 [a]S Jos 15:9 [b]1Sa 4:4; 7:1 [c]Lev 24:16; Dt 28:10; Isa 63:14 [d]Ps 99:1; 132:14 [e]S Ge 3:24; S Ex 25:22
6:3 [f]ver 7; Nu 7:4-9; S 1Sa 6:7 [g]2Sa 7:1
6:5 [h]S Ex 15:20 [i]Ezr 3:10; Ne 12:27; Ps 150:5
6:6 [j]S Nu 4:15, 19-20
6:7 [k]1Ch 15:13-15 [l]S Ex 19:22; S 1Sa 5:6; 6:19; S 25:38
6:8 [m]Ps 7:11 [n]S Ge 38:29

Chapter 6

The Ark Brought to Jerusalem

6:1–11pp — 1Ch 13:1–14
6:12–19pp — 1Ch 15:25–16:3

DAVID again brought together out of
Israel chosen men, thirty thousand
in all. 2He and all his men set out from
Baalah[a] of Judah[k] to bring up from there
the ark[b] of God, which is called by the
Name,[l][c] the name of the LORD Almighty, who is enthroned[d] between the
cherubim[e] that are on the ark. 3They set
the ark of God on a new cart[f] and
brought it from the house of Abinadab,
which was on the hill.[g] Uzzah and Ahio,
sons of Abinadab, were guiding the new
cart 4with the ark of God on it,[m] and Ahio
was walking in front of it. 5David and the
whole house of Israel were celebrating[h]
with all their might before the LORD, with
songs[n] and with harps, lyres, tambourines, sistrums and cymbals.[i]

6When they came to the threshing
floor of Nacon, Uzzah reached out and
took hold of[j] the ark of God, because the
oxen stumbled. 7The LORD's anger
burned against Uzzah because of his
irreverent act;[k] therefore God struck him
down[l] and he died there beside the ark
of God.

8Then David was angry because the
LORD's wrath[m] had broken out against
Uzzah, and to this day that place is called
Perez Uzzah.[o][n]

[i]20 *Baal Perazim* means *the lord who breaks out.* [j]25 Septuagint (see also 1 Chron. 14:16); Hebrew *Geba* [k]2 That is, Kiriath Jearim; Hebrew *Baale Judah*, a variant of *Baalah of Judah* [l]2 Hebrew; Septuagint and Vulgate do not have *the Name.* [m]3,4 Dead Sea Scrolls and some Septuagint manuscripts; Masoretic Text *cart 4and they brought it with the ark of God from the house of Abinadab, which was on the hill* [n]5 See Dead Sea Scrolls, Septuagint and 1 Chronicles 13:8; Masoretic Text *celebrating before the LORD with all kinds of instruments made of pine.* [o]8 *Perez Uzzah* means *outbreak against Uzzah.*

5:17–25 HISTORY, Deliverance—See note on Jos 8:1–29.
5:17–25 CHRISTIAN ETHICS, War and Peace—See notes on Jos 6:1–27; Jdg 1:1–36.
5:19 PRAYER, Petition—See note on 1 Sa 23:2.
5:23 PRAYER, Petition—See note on 1 Sa 23:2. Even the details were directed by the Lord when David relied on Him.
6:1–7 GOD, Holy—See note on 1 Sa 4:5–7,21–22. The Israelites had no tangible object of worship, like the idol worshipers among their neighbors. God had very carefully instructed Israel not to make any image or representation of Him (Ex 20:4–5). Since the ark of the covenant identified the presence of God, it was considered holy just as God was known to be holy and was to be treated with the utmost reverance. See notes on Ex 19:10–24; Nu 1:51; 1 Sa 6:19–20. God towers over us in His holiness, His righteousness, His pure love, His supreme, sovereign power. Uzzah knew God's commands and His nature when he was stricken for having touched the ark. This may seem harsh and arbitrary to our modern mind. In the context of the great difficulty God had in teaching His people that He alone is the holy God, adamantly opposed to our sinfulness, this drastic act of punishment became a necessary step in establishing His sovereign Lordship over His people.
6:2–19 REVELATION, Divine Presence—The ark, a visible symbol of God's reigning presence in Israel, was transported toward Jerusalem. Accounts of the move suggest that God's symbol was sacred enough that those who hosted the ark actually hosted God Himself. The holy God was revealed in the ark. Humans cannot irreverently and unthinkingly touch the symbol of God's presence and not be punished. Properly attended to, the ark brought prosperity and welfare. Reverent joy is the mood of God's people in His presence. See note on 1 Sa 5:1–3,9,10.
6:5 WORSHIP, Music—See note on 1 Ch 6:31–32. Music helps God's people celebrate His actions for us.
6:5 PRAYER, Worship—Worship is not casual or incidental. It involves the whole being—here, "with all their might." Stringed and percussion instruments were used. Musical celebration is one way of expressing thanksgiving and joy to God.

9David was afraid of the LORD that day
and said, "How[o] can the ark of the LORD
ever come to me?" 10He was not willing
to take the ark of the LORD to be with him
in the City of David. Instead, he took it
aside to the house of Obed-Edom[p] the
Gittite. 11The ark of the LORD remained
in the house of Obed-Edom the Gittite for
three months, and the LORD blessed him
and his entire household.[q]

12Now King David[r] was told, "The
LORD has blessed the household of Obed-
Edom and everything he has, because of
the ark of God." So David went down and
brought up the ark of God from the house
of Obed-Edom to the City of David with
rejoicing. 13When those who were carrying the ark of the LORD had taken six
steps, he sacrificed[s] a bull and a fattened
calf. 14David, wearing a linen ephod,[t]
danced[u] before the LORD with all his
might, 15while he and the entire house of
Israel brought up the ark of the LORD with
shouts[v] and the sound of trumpets.[w]

16As the ark of the LORD was entering
the City of David,[x] Michal[y] daughter of
Saul watched from a window. And when
she saw King David leaping and dancing
before the LORD, she despised him in her
heart.

17They brought the ark of the LORD and
set it in its place inside the tent that David had pitched for it,[z] and David sacrificed burnt offerings[a] and fellowship offerings[p] before the LORD. 18After he had
finished sacrificing[b] the burnt offerings
and fellowship offerings, he blessed[c] the
people in the name of the LORD Almighty.
19Then he gave a loaf of bread, a cake of
dates and a cake of raisins[d] to each person in the whole crowd of Israelites, both
men and women.[e] And all the people
went to their homes.

20When David returned home to bless
his household, Michal daughter of Saul
came out to meet him and said, "How the
king of Israel has distinguished himself
today, disrobing[f] in the sight of the slave
girls of his servants as any vulgar fellow
would!"

21David said to Michal, "It was before
the LORD, who chose me rather than your
father or anyone from his house when he
appointed[g] me ruler[h] over the LORD's
people Israel—I will celebrate before the
LORD. 22I will become even more undigni-
fied than this, and I will be humiliated in
my own eyes. But by these slave girls you
spoke of, I will be held in honor."

23And Michal daughter of Saul had no
children to the day of her death.

Chapter 7

God's Promise to David

7:1–17pp — 1Ch 17:1–15

AFTER the king was settled in his palace[i] and the LORD had given him

6:9 [o]S 1Sa 6:20
6:10 [p]1Ch 15:18; 26:4-5
6:11 [q]S Ge 30:27; 39:5
6:12 [r]1Ki 8:1
6:13 [s]1Ki 8:5,62; Ezr 6:17
6:14 [t]Ex 19:6; S 1Sa 2:18 [u]S Ex 15:20
6:15 [v]S Jos 6:5 [w]Ps 47:5; 98:6
6:16 [x]S 2Sa 5:7 [y]S 1Sa 18:27
6:17 [z]1Ki 8:6; 1Ch 15:1; 2Ch 1:4 [a]Lev 1:1-17; 1Ki 8:62-64
6:18 [b]1Ki 8:22 [c]S Ex 39:43
6:19 [d]Hos 3:1 [e]Dt 26:13; Ne 8:10
6:20 [f]S 1Sa 19:24
6:21 [g]1Sa 13:14; S 15:28 [h]2Sa 5:2; 7:8; 1Ch 5:2; 17:7; Mic 5:2
7:1 [i]2Sa 6:3

[p]*17* Traditionally *peace offerings*; also in verse 18

6:12–18 DISCIPLESHIP, Spiritual Leaders—The normal function of the Hebrew king was in the secular realm, but occasionally he was identified with priestly costumes and customs (1 Ki 2:26–28; 8:1–65). The Book of Kings is full of accusations of prophets against rulers. The dominant accusation was that the kings were not faithful to God. Prophets viewed the king as just another person subject to the moral law of God. Leaders of God's people must be spiritual and must never set themselves above the critique of God's Word.

6:14–23 PRAYER, Worship—See note on v 5. In the first stage, stringed and percussion instruments were used. To enter David's own city, trumpets were used. Trumpets were normally used in the Old Testament for announcement. The burnt offerings were required. The fellowship offerings were voluntary. Blessing the people was originally a function of the priest (Nu 6:23); David blessed as the Lord's anointed. Michal's reaction indicated the extravagance of David's dance. The opposite intentions of Michal and David are seen in vv 20–21. Michal saw the display as "in the sight of the slave girls"; David saw it as "before the LORD." See note on Ge 19:27.

6:16,20–23 FAMILY, Conflict—Devotion to God should unite marriage partners in inseparable commitment. Too often religion becomes a source of marital conflict. David and Michal had entered marriage because of their love for each other (3:13–16; 1 Sa 18:20–21), but this did not keep them from having interpersonal problems. Michal was disgusted with David's behavior while he was accompanying the ark of the Lord on its return to Jerusalem. She felt it inappropriate for the king to be dancing and singing in the streets. David justified his behavior on the basis of his devotion to the Lord. Marriage partners in a conflict situation often use religion to justify actions the mate dislikes. Unequal religious devotion can also cause marital conflict. See note on 1 Co 7:12–16.

6:21 ELECTION, Worship—Without inhibition, David joyously danced before the Lord. His action expressed grateful response to God for choosing him as Israel's leader in preference to the household of Saul. Joyous worship is the proper response of God's elect.

7:1 HISTORY, Deliverance—Rest is the Old Testament term for deliverance from enemies resulting in life without attack or war. God honors His obedient leaders with rest. See note on Jos 11:23.

7:1,11 CHRISTIAN ETHICS, War and Peace—We can draw both temporal hope and hope for life hereafter from David's experience of giving himself to the battle with God's enemies and then receiving a sense of peace for his work. After the warring work of David, God honored his efforts and particularly his sense of obedience to God with a time of peace. See note on Jos 21:43–45.

7:1–17 THE CHURCH, Covenant People—God's work with His people is one continuous work expressed in various ways in different time periods in order to meet the needs of His people. God gave the covenants of the Old Testament to testify of His faithfulness to His people. While the covenants are different, they all testify of God's love for His covenant people. The covenant with Noah demonstrates God's love for sinful people. See note on Ge 9:8–17. Though judgment came by means of a flood, God promised to provide stability for Noah and his descendants. God provided hope for the future by means of the covenant. As with Noah's covenant, God initiated the covenant with Abraham, promising him an heir. See notes on Ge 15:18; 17:1–21. Ge 3—11 depicts the sin of the human family. God's call to Abraham showed God's response to the human sin problem. With Noah and Abraham, the covenant had worldwide implications. God made the covenant of Ge 9:8–17 with the whole earth. Abraham's covenant

rest from all his enemies[j] around him,[k]
2he said to Nathan[l] the prophet, "Here I
am, living in a palace[m] of cedar, while the
ark of God remains in a tent."[n]

3Nathan replied to the king, "Whatever you have in mind,[o] go ahead and do it,
for the LORD is with you."

4That night the word of the LORD came
to Nathan, saying:

5"Go and tell my servant David,
'This is what the LORD says: Are
you[p] the one to build me a house to
dwell in?[q] 6I have not dwelt in a
house from the day I brought the Israelites up out of Egypt to this day.[r] I
have been moving from place to
place with a tent[s] as my dwelling.[t]
7Wherever I have moved with all the
Israelites,[u] did I ever say to any of
their rulers whom I commanded to
shepherd[v] my people Israel, "Why
have you not built me a house[w] of
cedar?[x]" '

8"Now then, tell my servant David, 'This is what the LORD Almighty
says: I took you from the pasture and
from following the flock[y] to be ruler[z] over my people Israel.[a] 9I have
been with you wherever you have
gone,[b] and I have cut off all your enemies from before you.[c] Now I will
make your name great, like the
names of the greatest men of the
earth.[d] 10And I will provide a place
for my people Israel and will plant[e]
them so that they can have a home of
their own and no longer be disturbed.[f] Wicked[g] people will not
oppress them anymore,[h] as they did
at the beginning 11and have done
ever since the time I appointed leaders[q][i] over my people Israel. I will
also give you rest from all your enemies.[j]

" 'The LORD declares[k] to you that
the LORD himself will establish[l] a
house[m] for you: 12When your days
are over and you rest[n] with your fathers, I will raise up your offspring to
succeed you, who will come from
your own body,[o] and I will establish
his kingdom.[p] 13He is the one who
will build a house[q] for my Name,[r]
and I will establish the throne of his
kingdom forever.[s] 14I will be his father, and he will be my son.[t] When
he does wrong, I will punish him[u]
with the rod[v] of men, with floggings
inflicted by men. 15But my love will
never be taken away from him,[w] as I
took it away from Saul,[x] whom I removed from before you. 16Your house
and your kingdom will endure forever before me[r]; your throne[y] will be
established[z] forever.[a]' "

17Nathan reported to David all the
words of this entire revelation.

David's Prayer

7:18–29pp — 1Ch 17:16–27

18Then King David went in and sat before the LORD, and he said:

7:1 [j]ver 11 [k]1Ch 22:18 **7:2** [l]2Sa 12:1; 1Ki 1:8,22; 1Ch 29:29; 2Ch 9:29 [m]2Sa 5:11; 1Ki 3:1; 7:1,2,7; 9:1; 2Ch 8:1; Jer 22:14; Hag 1:4 [n]S Ex 26:1; Ps 132:3; Ac 7:45-46 **7:3** [o]S 1Sa 10:7; Ps 132:1-5 **7:5** [p]1Ki 8:19; 1Ch 22:8 [q]1Ki 5:3-5; 1Ch 28:3 **7:6** [r]Ac 7:45 [s]Ex 40:18,34; Jos 18:1 [t]1Ki 8:16 **7:7** [u]Dt 23:14 [v]S 2Sa 5:2 [w]1Ki 8:27; Isa 66:1 [x]Lev 26:11-12 **7:8** [y]S 1Sa 16:11; 1Ch 21:17; Ps 74:1; Am 7:15 [z]S 1Sa 2:7-8; S 9:16; S 16:1; S 2Sa 6:21 [a]Ps 78:70-72; 2Co 6:18* **7:9** [b]S 1Sa 18:14; 2Sa 5:10 [c]Ps 18:37-42 [d]S Ex 11:3 **7:10** [e]S Ex 15:17; Isa 5:1-7 [f]2Ki 21:8; 2Ch 33:8 [g]Ps 89:22-23 [h]Ps 147:14; Isa 54:14; 60:18 **7:11** [i]S Jdg 2:16; 1Sa 12:9-11 [j]ver 1 [k]1Ki 2:24 [l]1Sa 25:28; Ps 89:35-37; S Mt 1:1; Lk 1:32-33; Ac 13:22-23; 2Ti 2:8 [m]S Ex 1:21; Isa 7:2 **7:12** [n]S Ge 15:15; 1Ki 2:1; Ac 13:36 [o]1Ki 8:20; Ps 132:11-12; Jer 30:21; 33:15 [p]2Ch 23:3 **7:13** [q]S Dt 12:5; 1Ki 6:12 [r]Dt 16:11; 1Ki 5:5; 8:19,29; 2Ki 21:4,7 [s]ver 16; S Ge 9:16; 2Sa 22:51; 1Ki 2:4,45; 1Ch 22:10; 28:6; 2Ch 6:16; 7:18; 13:5; 21:7; Ps 89:3-4,29,35-37; Pr 25:5; Isa 9:7; 16:5; Jer 17:25; 33:17,21; Da 7:27 **7:14** [t]Ps 2:7; 89:26; Jer 3:19; S Mt 3:17; Jn 1:49; 2Co 6:18*; Heb 1:5*; Rev 21:7 [u]S Dt 8:5; 1Ki 11:34; 1Ch 22:10; Heb 12:7 [v]Ps 89:30-33; Pr 13:24 **7:15** [w]ver 25; 1Ki 2:4; 6:12; 8:25; 9:5; 11:13,32; 2Ki 19:34; 2Ch 6:16; 7:18; 21:7; Ps 89:24,33; Jer 33:17 [x]S 1Sa 13:13; S 15:28; 16:14 **7:16** [y]Ps 89:36-37; S Lk 1:33 [z]Ps 9:7; 93:2; 103:19 [a]S ver 13

[q] *11* Traditionally *judges* [r] *16* Some Hebrew manuscripts and Septuagint; most Hebrew manuscripts *you*

---

extended to all his descendants, not just to the Hebrews. However, the covenant with Israel at Sinai singled out Israel as God's unique people who were called to proclaim Him to the world. 2 Sa 7 indicates that God intended to continue the covenant community and to provide it with stable leadership through the line of David.

7:4–11 REVELATION, Divine Presence—God's revelation challenged David's concern to build God a dwelling place at least as comfortable as his own. God does not need a beautiful house to be with His people and produce all the wonders Israel witnessed. God dwells in the sumptuous temple He made—the universe. Even that can not contain Him.

7:8–24 ELECTION, Faithfulness—God promised to establish the throne of David forever. Love formed the basis of David's election as it did Israel's (Dt 7:7–8). Election of David came to show God's faithfulness in fulfilling His word and to carry out His will or purpose. Election showed God's uniqueness. His unique saving acts made Israel unique, established His name or reputation among the nations, and created the covenant bond between Israel and Himself. God kept His promises to David. The promises of God to David find their fulfillment in Jesus Christ, who came from the house and lineage of David (Lk 2:1–12).

7:9,29 SALVATION, Blessing—God promised to bless David and his house forever, to make his name great like the greatest men of the earth. Jesus Christ, the Savior of the world, came through the lineage of David (Mt 1:1). God's salvation blessings lead to the accomplishment of His plans for the world and may go beyond human expectations. Compare 1 Ch 17:27.

7:12–28 JESUS CHRIST, Foretold—See note on 1 Ch 17:23–27.

7:14 GOD, Father—The Old Testament uses the term Father for God, sometimes in reference to single individuals, sometimes in reference to all Israel, or even all people by virtue of His being Creator. This shows the intimate, loving relationship God desires with His people. It also shows the obedience and respect His people should show to Him. See notes on Dt 8:1–5; 32:6.

7:18–29 PRAYER, Sovereignty of God—That David sat indicates that any posture is appropriate for prayer, if the attitude is one of humility. The parts of this important prayer cannot be understood apart from its climactic and central sentence in v 24. David began with humble acknowledgment of God's selection of his house for divine purposes. In that light, the humility of his acknowledgment was enhanced by his refusal to question God's dictum that he could not build the Temple. David submitted to the absolute authority of God's will. He then praised God in His uniqueness and attributed the uniqueness of Israel to God's gracious choice. Israel's greatness

"Who am I,[b] O Sovereign LORD,
and what is my family, that you have
brought me this far? 19And as if this
were not enough in your sight, O
Sovereign LORD, you have also spoken about the future of the house of
your servant. Is this your usual way
of dealing with man,[c] O Sovereign
LORD?

20"What more can David say[d] to
you? For you know[e] your servant,[f]
O Sovereign LORD. 21For the sake of
your word and according to your will,
you have done this great thing and
made it known to your servant.

22"How great[g] you are,[h] O Sovereign LORD! There is no one like[i]
you, and there is no God[j] but you, as
we have heard with our own ears.[k]
23And who is like your people Israel[l]—the one nation on earth that
God went out to redeem as a people
for himself, and to make a name[m] for
himself, and to perform great and
awesome wonders[n] by driving out
nations and their gods from before
your people, whom you redeemed[o]
from Egypt?[s] 24You have established
your people Israel as your very own[p]
forever, and you, O LORD, have become their God.[q]

25"And now, LORD God, keep forever the promise[r] you have made
concerning your servant and his
house. Do as you promised, 26so that
your name[s] will be great forever.
Then men will say, 'The LORD Almighty is God over Israel!' And the
house of your servant David will be
established[t] before you.

27"O LORD Almighty, God of Israel,
you have revealed this to your servant, saying, 'I will build a house for
you.' So your servant has found courage to offer you this prayer. 28O Sovereign LORD, you are God! Your
words are trustworthy,[u] and you
have promised these good things to
your servant. 29Now be pleased to
bless the house of your servant, that
it may continue forever in your sight;
for you, O Sovereign LORD, have spoken, and with your blessing[v] the
house of your servant will be blessed
forever."

7:18 [b]S Ex 3:11
7:19 [c]Isa 55:8-9
7:20 [d]Isa 38:15 [e]Jn 21:17 [f]S 1Sa 16:7
7:22 [g]Ps 48:1; 77:13; 86:10; Jer 10:6 [h]Dt 3:24 [i]S Ex 9:14 [j]S Ex 8:10; S 20:4 [k]Ex 10:2; S Jdg 6:13; Ps 44:1
7:23 [l]Dt 4:32-38; S 33:29; S 1Sa 12:22 [m]S Nu 6:27 [n]Dt 10:21 [o]Dt 7:7-8; S 9:26
7:24 [p]Dt 26:18 [q]Ex 6:6-7; Ps 48:14
7:25 [r]S ver 15; S Nu 23:19; 2Ch 1:9
7:26 [s]S Ex 6:3; Ne 9:5; Ps 72:19; 96:8; Mt 6:9 [t]S 1Sa 25:28
7:28 [u]Ex 34:6; Jn 17:17
7:29 [v]Nu 6:23-27
8:1 [w]Ps 60:8; 87:4; 108:9 [x]Heb 11:32-33
8:2 [y]S Ge 19:37; S Nu 21:29 [z]S Jdg 3:15; S Isa 45:14
8:3 [a]2Sa 10:16,19; 1Ki 11:23 [b]S 1Sa 14:47 [c]S Ge 2:14
8:4 [d]S Ge 49:6; Jos 11:9
8:5 [e]S Ge 14:15; 2Sa 10:6; 1Ki 11:24; 2Ki 8:7; 14:28
8:6 [f]1Ki 20:34 [g]2Sa 10:19 [h]2Sa 3:18
8:7 [i]1Ki 10:16; 14:26; 2Ki 11:10
8:8 [j]Eze 47:16
8:9 [k]1Ki 8:65; 2Ki 14:28; 2Ch 8:4 [l]Lk 14:31-32

Chapter 8

David's Victories

8:1-14pp — 1Ch 18:1-13

IN the course of time, David defeated
the Philistines[w] and subdued[x] them,
and he took Metheg Ammah from the
control of the Philistines.

2David also defeated the Moabites.[y]
He made them lie down on the ground
and measured them off with a length of
cord. Every two lengths of them were put
to death, and the third length was allowed to live. So the Moabites became
subject to David and brought tribute.[z]

3Moreover, David fought Hadadezer[a]
son of Rehob, king of Zobah,[b] when he
went to restore his control along the
Euphrates[c] River. 4David captured a
thousand of his chariots, seven thousand
charioteers[t] and twenty thousand foot soldiers. He hamstrung[d] all but a hundred
of the chariot horses.

5When the Arameans of Damascus[e]
came to help Hadadezer king of Zobah,
David struck down twenty-two thousand
of them. 6He put garrisons[f] in the
Aramean kingdom of Damascus, and the
Arameans became subject[g] to him and
brought tribute. The LORD gave David victory wherever he went.[h]

7David took the gold shields[i] that belonged to the officers of Hadadezer and
brought them to Jerusalem. 8From Tebah[u] and Berothai,[j] towns that belonged
to Hadadezer, King David took a great
quantity of bronze.

9When Tou[v] king of Hamath[k] heard
that David had defeated the entire army
of Hadadezer,[l] 10he sent his son Joram[w]
to King David to greet him and congratulate him on his victory in battle over Hadadezer, who had been at war with Tou.

[s] *23* See Septuagint and 1 Chron. 17:21; Hebrew *wonders for your land and before your people, whom you redeemed from Egypt, from the nations and their gods.* [t] *4* Septuagint (see also Dead Sea Scrolls and 1 Chron. 18:4); Masoretic Text *captured seventeen hundred of his charioteers* [u] *8* See some Septuagint manuscripts (see also 1 Chron. 18:8); Hebrew *Betah.* [v] *9* Hebrew *Toi,* a variant of *Tou;* also in verse 10 [w] *10* A variant of *Hadoram*

was not self-inherent but derived from its Source. The prayer demonstrates faith in one sovereign God and submission to His way even when we do not get our way.

7:22–28 GOD, Sovereignty—In an exalted moment of spiritual perception, David praised God's sovereign authority and His faithfulness to His promises and to His people. David was keenly conscious of God's abounding grace. God's greatness became evident as He acted to redeem His people. What God had been doing to establish His name in the minds and hearts of His oft rebellious people brought forth their praise and their trust in His sovereign faithfulness.

8:1–14 HISTORY, Politics—God directed David's military campaigns. David obediently gave credit to God. Political fame and power rest ultimately on God's deliverance, not on human abilities.

8:1–14 CHRISTIAN ETHICS, War and Peace—The key idea here is that God gave David his victories. These hinged upon David's faithfulness to a covenant relationship with God. The Bible does not picture war results as based on human greed or clever strategy. Biblical wars were used by God to carry out His purposes through His obedient leaders. See notes on Jos 6:1–27; 10:1–43, Jdg 1:1–36.

Joram brought with him articles of silver
and gold and bronze.
11 King David dedicated[m] these articles
to the LORD, as he had done with the silver and gold from all the nations he had
subdued: 12 Edom[x][n] and Moab,[o] the
Ammonites[p] and the Philistines,[q] and
Amalek.[r] He also dedicated the plunder
taken from Hadadezer son of Rehob, king
of Zobah.
13 And David became famous[s] after he
returned from striking down eighteen
thousand Edomites[y] in the Valley of
Salt.[t]
14 He put garrisons throughout Edom,
and all the Edomites[u] became subject to
David.[v] The LORD gave David victory[w]
wherever he went.[x]

David's Officials

8:15–18pp — 1Ch 18:14–17

15 David reigned over all Israel, doing
what was just and right[y] for all his people. 16 Joab[z] son of Zeruiah was over the
army; Jehoshaphat[a] son of Ahilud was
recorder;[b] 17 Zadok[c] son of Ahitub
and Ahimelech son of Abiathar[d]
were priests; Seraiah was secretary;[e]
18 Benaiah[f] son of Jehoiada was over the
Kerethites[g] and Pelethites; and David's
sons were royal advisers.[z]

Chapter 9

David and Mephibosheth

DAVID asked, "Is there anyone still left
of the house of Saul to whom I can
show kindness for Jonathan's sake?"[h]
2 Now there was a servant of Saul's
household named Ziba.[i] They called him
to appear before David, and the king said
to him, "Are you Ziba?"
"Your servant," he replied.
3 The king asked, "Is there no one still
left of the house of Saul to whom I can
show God's kindness?"
Ziba answered the king, "There is still
a son of Jonathan;[j] he is crippled[k] in
both feet."
4 "Where is he?" the king asked.
Ziba answered, "He is at the house of
Makir[l] son of Ammiel in Lo Debar."
5 So King David had him brought from

8:11 [m]ver 12; 1Ki 7:51; 15:15; 1Ch 26:26; 2Ch 5:1
8:12 [n]S Nu 24:18 [o]ver 2 [p]2Sa 10:14 [q]S 2Sa 5:25 [r]S Nu 24:20; S 1Sa 27:8
8:13 [s]2Sa 7:9 [t]2Ki 14:7; 1Ch 18:12; Ps 60 Title
8:14 [u]Nu 24:17-18; Ps 108:9; Isa 34:5; 63:1; Jer 49:7; Eze 25:12 [v]S Ge 27:29,37-40 [w]Ps 144:10 [x]2Sa 22:44; Ps 18:43
8:15 [y]S Ge 18:19; 1Ki 11:38; 14:8; 15:11; 22:43; 2Ki 12:2; Job 29:14; Ps 5:12; 119:121; Heb 11:33
8:16 [z]S 2Sa 2:13 [a]2Sa 20:24; 1Ki 4:3 [b]Isa 36:3,22
8:17 [c]S 1Sa 2:35; 2Sa 15:24,29; 20:25; 1Ki 1:8; 4:4; 1Ch 6:8,53; 16:39; 24:3; 27:17; 2Ch 31:10; Eze 40:46; 43:19; 44:15; 48:11 [d]Mk 2:26 [e]1Ki 4:3; 2Ki 12:10; 19:2; 22:3; Isa 36:3; Jer 36:12
8:18 [f]2Sa 20:23; 23:20; 1Ki 1:8,38; 2:25,35,46; 4:4 [g]S 1Sa 30:14
9:1 [h]S 1Sa 20:14-17,42; S 23:18
9:2 [i]2Sa 16:1-4; 19:17,26,29
9:3 [j]1Ch 8:34; 1Sa 20:14 [k]S Lev 21:18
9:4 [l]2Sa 17:27-29
9:6 [m]S Ge 37:7
9:7 [n]S 1Sa 20:14-15 [o]ver 13; 2Sa 19:28; 21:7; 1Ki 2:7; 2Ki 25:29; Jer 52:33
9:8 [p]S 2Sa 4:4 [q]S 2Sa 3:8
9:10 [r]2Sa 16:3
9:11 [s]Job 36:7; Ps 113:8
9:12 [t]S 2Sa 4:4
10:2 [u]S 1Sa 11:1

Lo Debar, from the house of Makir son of
Ammiel.
6 When Mephibosheth son of Jonathan,
the son of Saul, came to David, he bowed
down to pay him honor.[m]
David said, "Mephibosheth!"
"Your servant," he replied.
7 "Don't be afraid," David said to him,
"for I will surely show you kindness for
the sake of your father Jonathan.[n] I will
restore to you all the land that belonged
to your grandfather Saul, and you will
always eat at my table.[o]"
8 Mephibosheth[p] bowed down and
said, "What is your servant, that you
should notice a dead dog[q] like me?"
9 Then the king summoned Ziba, Saul's
servant, and said to him, "I have given
your master's grandson everything that
belonged to Saul and his family. 10 You
and your sons and your servants are to
farm the land for him and bring in the
crops, so that your master's grandson[r]
may be provided for. And Mephibosheth,
grandson of your master, will always eat
at my table." (Now Ziba had fifteen sons
and twenty servants.)
11 Then Ziba said to the king, "Your servant will do whatever my lord the king
commands his servant to do." So Mephibosheth ate at David's[a] table like one of
the king's sons.[s]
12 Mephibosheth had a young son
named Mica, and all the members of
Ziba's household were servants of Mephibosheth.[t] 13 And Mephibosheth lived
in Jerusalem, because he always ate at the
king's table, and he was crippled in both
feet.

Chapter 10

David Defeats the Ammonites

10:1–19pp — 1Ch 19:1–19

IN the course of time, the king of the
Ammonites died, and his son Hanun
succeeded him as king. 2 David thought,
"I will show kindness to Hanun son
of Nahash,[u] just as his father showed

[x] *12* Some Hebrew manuscripts, Septuagint and Syriac (see also 1 Chron. 18:11); most Hebrew manuscripts *Aram* [y] *13* A few Hebrew manuscripts, Septuagint and Syriac (see also 1 Chron. 18:12); most Hebrew manuscripts *Aram* (that is, Arameans) [z] *18* Or *were priests* [a] *11* Septuagint; Hebrew *my*

8:11 STEWARDSHIP, Purpose of Possessions—Possessions come from God and should be used to express gratitude to Him. David believed his victories resulted from God's care for him. He acknowledged his gratitude and his dependence on God by dedicating valuables taken in battle. See note on Dt 8:7–9,10–14,18.

8:11–12 PRAYER, Worship—Rather than assume the victor's right of property, David acknowledged the Source of the victory.

9:1—10:2 HUMANITY, Relationships—A measure of real human greatness is the evenhanded treatment of both friends and enemies.

9:3 GOD, Grace—David here recognized that his actions of kindness to others were rooted in God's own graciousness. God is the source of all goodness and kindness and love. As His grace flows through us, it motivates us to be gracious to others. This does not play down the human responsibility for acts of love. Rather, it points to the divine part in initiating these actions of kindness that may flow from us. See note on 1 Jn 4:7–21.

kindness to me." So David sent a delegation to express his sympathy to Hanun
concerning his father.

When David's men came to the land of
the Ammonites, 3the Ammonite nobles
said to Hanun their lord, "Do you think
David is honoring your father by sending
men to you to express sympathy? Hasn't
David sent them to you to explore the
city and spy it out[v] and overthrow it?"
4So Hanun seized David's men, shaved off
half of each man's beard,[w] cut off their
garments in the middle at the buttocks,[x]
and sent them away.

5When David was told about this, he
sent messengers to meet the men, for
they were greatly humiliated. The king
said, "Stay at Jericho till your beards have
grown, and then come back."

6When the Ammonites realized that
they had become a stench[y] in David's
nostrils, they hired twenty thousand
Aramean[z] foot soldiers from Beth Rehob[a]
and Zobah,[b] as well as the king of Maacah[c] with a thousand men, and also
twelve thousand men from Tob.[d]

7On hearing this, David sent Joab[e] out
with the entire army of fighting men.
8The Ammonites came out and drew up
in battle formation at the entrance to
their city gate, while the Arameans of Zobah and Rehob and the men of Tob and
Maacah were by themselves in the open
country.

9Joab saw that there were battle lines
in front of him and behind him; so he
selected some of the best troops in Israel
and deployed them against the Arameans.
10He put the rest of the men under the
command of Abishai[f] his brother and deployed them against the Ammonites.
11Joab said, "If the Arameans are too
strong for me, then you are to come to my
rescue; but if the Ammonites are too
strong for you, then I will come to rescue
you. 12Be strong[g] and let us fight bravely
for our people and the cities of our God.
The LORD will do what is good in his
sight."[h]

13Then Joab and the troops with him
advanced to fight the Arameans, and they
fled before him. 14When the Ammonites[i] saw that the Arameans were fleeing, they fled before Abishai and went inside the city. So Joab returned from fighting the Ammonites and came to
Jerusalem.

15After the Arameans saw that they had
been routed by Israel, they regrouped.
16Hadadezer had Arameans brought from
beyond the River[b]; they went to Helam,
with Shobach the commander of Hadadezer's army leading them.

17When David was told of this, he gathered all Israel, crossed the Jordan and
went to Helam. The Arameans formed
their battle lines to meet David and
fought against him. 18But they fled before
Israel, and David killed seven hundred of
their charioteers and forty thousand of
their foot soldiers.[c] He also struck down
Shobach the commander of their army,
and he died there. 19When all the kings
who were vassals of Hadadezer saw that
they had been defeated by Israel, they
made peace with the Israelites and became subject[j] to them.

So the Arameans[k] were afraid to help
the Ammonites anymore.

Chapter 11

David and Bathsheba

IN the spring,[l] at the time when kings
go off to war, David sent Joab[m] out
with the king's men and the whole Israelite army.[n] They destroyed the Ammonites and besieged Rabbah.[o] But David remained in Jerusalem.

2One evening David got up from his
bed and walked around on the roof[p] of
the palace. From the roof he saw[q] a
woman bathing. The woman was very
beautiful, 3and David sent someone to
find out about her. The man said, "Isn't
this Bathsheba,[r] the daughter of Eliam[s]
and the wife of Uriah[t] the Hittite?"

[b] *16* That is, the Euphrates [c] *18* Some Septuagint manuscripts (see also 1 Chron. 19:18); Hebrew *horsemen*

10:3 [v]S Nu 21:32
10:4 [w]S Lev 19:27; Isa 7:20; 15:2; 50:6; 52:14; Jer 48:37; Eze 5:1 [x]Isa 20:4
10:6 [y]S Ge 34:30 [z]S 2Sa 8:5 [a]S Nu 13:21 [b]S 1Sa 14:47 [c]S Dt 3:14 [d]Jdg 11:3-5
10:7 [e]S 2Sa 2:18
10:10 [f]S 1Sa 26:6
10:12 [g]S Dt 1:21; 31:6; S Eph 6:10 [h]S Jdg 10:15; Ne 4:14
10:14 [i]2Sa 8:12
10:19 [j]2Sa 8:6 [k]1Ki 11:25; 22:31; 2Ki 5:1
11:1 [l]1Ki 20:22,26 [m]S 2Sa 2:18 [n]1Ch 20:1 [o]S Dt 3:11
11:2 [p]S Dt 22:8; S Jos 2:8 [q]Mt 5:28
11:3 [r]1Ch 3:5 [s]2Sa 23:34 [t]2Sa 23:39

10:12 GOD, Righteous—We can count on God to be righteous in all circumstances. It is the very nature of God to do what is right, what is good in His eyes. This was the faith Joab expressed as he was confident that he was on the right side and that God would bless the right cause. Whether we happen to be on the right or wrong side of a question or a battle, we can count on God doing what is right. God is not necessarily on our side: *we must be sure to be on God's side.*

10:12 HISTORY, Politics—International politics stands under God's control. In the long run the results are what is good in God's sight.

***11:1—12:14* CHRISTIAN ETHICS, Murder**—Arranging another's death is murder as much as actually committing the crime. God condemns such action. A political ruler has no right to take another's life. See notes on Ex 20:13; Jdg 8:10–21; Mt 5:21–22.

11:2—12:13 FAMILY, Sexual Sin—Sexual relations outside marriage is sin. No office or position exempts a person. Adultery was forbidden by Hebrew law (Ex 20:14; Lev 20:10), but David's desire for Bathsheba caused him to ignore God's law. The web of sin enlarged to include further deceit and the planned murder of a faithful soldier. David's transgression is a classic example of the growth of sin (2 Sa 15:1—18:18; Jas 1:13–15). The story highlights the destructive effects of adultery and demonstrates the depths of God's grace. David, Bathsheba, and Solomon are included in the lineage of Jesus Christ (Mt 1:6–7). Sexual sin has its destructive effects, but it is not unforgivable when repentance is real and a new commitment to God is made.

4Then David sent messengers to get
her.[u] She came to him, and he slept[v]
with her. (She had purified herself from
her uncleanness.)[w] Then[d] she went back
home. 5The woman conceived and sent
word to David, saying, "I am pregnant."
6So David sent this word to Joab:
"Send me Uriah[x] the Hittite." And Joab
sent him to David. 7When Uriah came to
him, David asked him how Joab was, how
the soldiers were and how the war was
going. 8Then David said to Uriah, "Go
down to your house and wash your
feet."[y] So Uriah left the palace, and a gift
from the king was sent after him. 9But
Uriah slept at the entrance to the palace
with all his master's servants and did not
go down to his house.
10When David was told, "Uriah did not
go home," he asked him, "Haven't you
just come from a distance? Why didn't
you go home?"
11Uriah said to David, "The ark[z] and
Israel and Judah are staying in tents, and
my master Joab and my lord's men are
camped in the open fields. How could I
go to my house to eat and drink and lie[a]
with my wife? As surely as you live, I will
not do such a thing!"
12Then David said to him, "Stay here
one more day, and tomorrow I will send
you back." So Uriah remained in Jerusalem that day and the next. 13At David's
invitation, he ate and drank with him,
and David made him drunk. But in the
evening Uriah went out to sleep on his
mat among his master's servants; he did
not go home.
14In the morning David wrote a letter[b]
to Joab and sent it with Uriah. 15In it he
wrote, "Put Uriah in the front line where
the fighting is fiercest. Then withdraw
from him so he will be struck down[c] and
die.[d]"
16So while Joab had the city under
siege, he put Uriah at a place where he
knew the strongest defenders were.
17When the men of the city came out and
fought against Joab, some of the men in
David's army fell; moreover, Uriah the
Hittite died.
18Joab sent David a full account of the
battle. 19He instructed the messenger:
"When you have finished giving the king
this account of the battle, 20the king's anger may flare up, and he may ask you,
'Why did you get so close to the city to
fight? Didn't you know they would shoot
arrows from the wall? 21Who killed Abimelech[e] son of Jerub-Besheth[e]? Didn't a
woman throw an upper millstone on him
from the wall,[f] so that he died in Thebez? Why did you get so close to the
wall?' If he asks you this, then say to him,
'Also, your servant Uriah the Hittite is
dead.' "
22The messenger set out, and when he
arrived he told David everything Joab had
sent him to say. 23The messenger said to
David, "The men overpowered us and
came out against us in the open, but we
drove them back to the entrance to the
city gate. 24Then the archers shot arrows
at your servants from the wall, and some
of the king's men died. Moreover, your
servant Uriah the Hittite is dead."
25David told the messenger, "Say this
to Joab: 'Don't let this upset you; the
sword devours one as well as another.
Press the attack against the city and destroy it.' Say this to encourage Joab."
26When Uriah's wife heard that her
husband was dead, she mourned for him.
27After the time of mourning[g] was over,
David had her brought to his house, and
she became his wife and bore him a son.
But the thing David had done displeased[h]
the LORD.

Chapter 12

Nathan Rebukes David

11:1; 12:29–31pp — 1Ch 20:1–3

THE LORD sent Nathan[i] to David.[j]
When he came to him,[k] he said,

11:4 [u]S Lev 20:10; Ps 51 Title; Jas 1:14-15 [v]Dt 22:22 [w]S Lev 15:25-30
11:6 [x]1Ch 11:41
11:8 [y]S Ge 18:4
11:11 [z]2Sa 7:2 [a]S 1Sa 21:5
11:14 [b]1Ki 21:8
11:15 [c]ver 14-17; 2Sa 12:9 [d]2Sa 12:12
11:21 [e]S Jdg 8:31 [f]Jdg 9:50-54
11:27 [g]Dt 34:8 [h]2Sa 12:9; Ps 51:4-5
12:1 [i]S 2Sa 7:2 [j]Ps 51 Title [k]2Sa 14:4

[d]4 Or *with her. When she purified herself from her uncleanness,* [e]21 Also known as *Jerub-Baal* (that is, Gideon)

11:27—12:17 GOD, Wrath—It is dangerous to flaunt our moral irresponsibilities before God. God will not be mocked by our disregard for His will. David hid his sin, but he quickly learned his actions were not hidden from God or from other people. He brought the wrath of God down upon himself. No matter how close to God we may be in our hearts, not one of us is immune to sin. Still, we have hope. God can use us despite our sins and weaknesses. He is quick to respond with forgiveness when we confess our sins (v 13). Forgiveness of our sins does not, however, undo the tragic consequences, nor does it necessarily turn away God's punishment.

11:27 HISTORY, Moral—God does not give any leader a blank check to follow personal desires. A moral foundation underlies all God's historical acts. Immorality displeases God and brings His historical judgment.

12:1–14 EVIL AND SUFFERING, Punishment—Human actions defying God and harming other people are evil. Evil actions ultimately bring God's punishment. See note on Ps 51:1–19.

12:1–25 SIN, Discipline—David's sins of adultery and murder brought God's disciplining intervention. No matter what a person's status in this life, God can and will intervene when sin becomes so blatant. No one has the moral right to take something just because the power to do so is available. When humans cannot intervene against injustice, God will according to His purpose and schedule.

12:1–19 HISTORY, Individual—God's judgment may come in international affairs. It may also come in individual lives. Confession of sin does not automatically prevent divine judgment on sin. God controls and works in every area of historical existence.

12:1–15 DISCIPLESHIP, Spiritual Leaders—God used

"There were two men in a certain town,
one rich and the other poor. 2The rich
man had a very large number of sheep
and cattle, 3but the poor man had nothing
except one little ewe lamb he had
bought. He raised it, and it grew up with
him and his children. It shared his
food, drank from his cup and even slept
in his arms. It was like a daughter to
him.
4"Now a traveler came to the rich man,
but the rich man refrained from taking
one of his own sheep or cattle to prepare
a meal for the traveler who had come to
him. Instead, he took the ewe lamb that
belonged to the poor man and prepared it
for the one who had come to him."
5David[l] burned with anger[m] against
the man[n] and said to Nathan, "As surely
as the LORD lives,[o] the man who did this
deserves to die! 6He must pay for that
lamb four times over,[p] because he did
such a thing and had no pity."
7Then Nathan said to David, "You are
the man![q] This is what the LORD, the
God of Israel, says: 'I anointed[r] you[s]
king over Israel, and I delivered you from
the hand of Saul. 8I gave your master's
house to you,[t] and your master's wives
into your arms. I gave you the house of
Israel and Judah. And if all this had been
too little, I would have given you even
more. 9Why did you despise[u] the word of
the LORD by doing what is evil in his
eyes? You struck down[v] Uriah[w] the Hittite with the sword and took his wife to
be your own. You killed[x] him with the
sword of the Ammonites. 10Now, therefore, the sword[y] will never depart from
your house, because you despised me and
took the wife of Uriah the Hittite to be
your own.'
11"This is what the LORD says: 'Out of
your own household[z] I am going to bring
calamity upon you.[a] Before your very
eyes I will take your wives and give them
to one who is close to you, and he will lie
with your wives in broad daylight.[b]
12You did it in secret,[c] but I will do this
thing in broad daylight[d] before all Israel.'"
13Then David said to Nathan, "I have
sinned[e] against the LORD."
Nathan replied, "The LORD has taken
away[f] your sin.[g] You are not going to
die.[h] 14But because by doing this you
have made the enemies of the LORD show
utter contempt,[f] the son born to you
will die."
15After Nathan had gone home, the
LORD struck[j] the child that Uriah's wife
had borne to David, and he became ill.
16David pleaded with God for the child.
He fasted and went into his house and
spent the nights lying[k] on the ground.
17The elders of his household stood beside him to get him up from the ground,
but he refused,[l] and he would not eat
any food with them.[m]
18On the seventh day the child died.
David's servants were afraid to tell him
that the child was dead, for they thought,
"While the child was still living, we
spoke to David but he would not listen to
us. How can we tell him the child is
dead? He may do something desperate."
19David noticed that his servants were
whispering among themselves and he realized the child was dead. "Is the child
dead?" he asked.
"Yes," they replied, "he is dead."
20Then David got up from the ground.
After he had washed,[n] put on lotions and
changed his clothes,[o] he went into the
house of the LORD and worshiped. Then
he went to his own house, and at his request they served him food, and he ate.
21His servants asked him, "Why are
you acting this way? While the child was
alive, you fasted and wept,[p] but now that
the child is dead, you get up and eat!"
22He answered, "While the child was
still alive, I fasted and wept. I thought,
'Who knows?[q] The LORD may be gra-

12:5 [l]1Ki 20:40 [m]S Ge 34:7 [n]Ro 2:1 [o]S 1Sa 14:39
12:6 [p]Ex 22:1
12:7 [q]2Sa 14:13; Da 4:22 [r]S 1Sa 2:35 [s]1Ki 20:42
12:8 [t]S 2Sa 9:7
12:9 [u]S Nu 15:31; S 1Sa 13:14 [v]S 2Sa 11:15 [w]1Ki 15:5 [x]Ps 26:9; 51:14
12:10 [y]2Sa 13:28; 18:14-15; 1Ki 2:25
12:11 [z]2Sa 16:11 [a]Dt 28:30; 2Sa 16:21-22 [b]S Dt 17:17
12:12 [c]2Sa 11:4-15 [d]2Sa 16:22
12:13 [e]S Ge 13:13; S 20:6; S Nu 22:34 [f]Ps 32:1-5; 51:1,9; 103:12; Isa 43:25; 44:22; Zec 3:4,9 [g]Pr 28:13; Jer 2:35; Mic 7:18-19 [h]Lev 20:10; 24:17
12:14 [i]Isa 52:5; Ro 2:24
12:15 [j]S 1Sa 25:38
12:16 [k]Ps 5:7; 95:6
12:17 [l]S Ge 37:35; S 1Sa 1:7 [m]S 2Sa 3:35; Da 6:18
12:20 [n]Mt 6:17 [o]S Ge 41:14
12:21 [p]Jdg 20:26
12:22 [q]Jnh 3:9

[f]14 Masoretic Text; an ancient Hebrew scribal tradition *this you have shown utter contempt for the LORD*

prophets to speak bold rebukes to the courts of kings. As Nathan rebuked David, Jeremiah spoke to the princes of Judah (Jer 26:12–15). See note on Am 3:7.

12:7–14 CHRISTIAN ETHICS, Social Relationships—No one, no matter how powerful or prestigious, has the right to take another human for personal pleasure, especially when the action violates the sanctity of the marriage covenant (Ex 20:14). See notes on FAMILY, Sexual Sin.

12:13–14 SALVATION, Forgiveness—Death is the penalty for sin (Ge 2:17; Ro 6:23). Forgiveness is God taking away our sin and its ultimate penalty. David escaped death for his sins, but he still suffered certain consequences for his sins. Forgiveness does not relieve us of *responsibility for the consequences of sinful acts.*

12:13–16 PRAYER, Hindrances—David prayed as an humble sinner, but God had already spoken (v 14); the child of lust would have become a reminder of David's sin and a sign of contempt for God's commandments before the nations. This petition could not be granted.

12:18–23 HUMANITY, Attitudes to Death—Even the premature death of a loved one can be accepted ultimately as a natural part of life. Death, after all, cannot be reversed. The Christian has hope beyond death. See note on 1 Co 15:19. David's expressed hope for reunion may have been for little more than a reunion in the grave. On the other hand, it was clearly couched in terms that allow for the development of a hope of life after death and helps us affirm God's gift of resurrection so clearly revealed in Christ.

12:20 PRAYER, Worship—David's worship indicated that he went beyond mere resignation and acceptance. God's will is not only sovereign; it is good. In prayer we praise God for doing what is right and good even when we must suffer. See note on 7:18–29.

cious to me and let the child live.'[r] 23But now that he is dead, why should I fast? Can I bring him back again? I will go to him,[s] but he will not return to me."[t]

24Then David comforted his wife Bathsheba,[u] and he went to her and lay with her. She gave birth to a son, and they named him Solomon.[v] The LORD loved him; 25and because the LORD loved him, he sent word through Nathan the prophet to name him Jedidiah.[g] [w]

26Meanwhile Joab fought against Rabbah[x] of the Ammonites and captured the royal citadel. 27Joab then sent messengers to David, saying, "I have fought against Rabbah and taken its water supply. 28Now muster the rest of the troops and besiege the city and capture it. Otherwise I will take the city, and it will be named after me."

29So David mustered the entire army and went to Rabbah, and attacked and captured it. 30He took the crown[y] from the head of their king[h]—its weight was a talent[i] of gold, and it was set with precious stones—and it was placed on David's head. He took a great quantity of plunder from the city 31and brought out the people who were there, consigning them to labor with saws and with iron picks and axes, and he made them work at brickmaking.[j] He did this to all the Ammonite[z] towns. Then David and his entire army returned to Jerusalem.

Chapter 13

Amnon and Tamar

IN the course of time, Amnon[a] son of David fell in love with Tamar,[b] the beautiful sister of Absalom[c] son of David.

2Amnon became frustrated to the point of illness on account of his sister Tamar, for she was a virgin, and it seemed impossible for him to do anything to her.

3Now Amnon had a friend named Jonadab son of Shimeah,[d] David's brother. Jonadab was a very shrewd man. 4He asked Amnon, "Why do you, the king's son, look so haggard morning after morning? Won't you tell me?"

Amnon said to him, "I'm in love with Tamar, my brother Absalom's sister."

5"Go to bed and pretend to be ill," Jonadab said. "When your father comes to see you, say to him, 'I would like my sister Tamar to come and give me something to eat. Let her prepare the food in my sight so I may watch her and then eat it from her hand.' "

6So Amnon lay down and pretended to be ill. When the king came to see him, Amnon said to him, "I would like my sister Tamar to come and make some special bread in my sight, so I may eat from her hand."

7David sent word to Tamar at the palace: "Go to the house of your brother Amnon and prepare some food for him." 8So Tamar went to the house of her brother Amnon, who was lying down. She took some dough, kneaded it, made the bread in his sight and baked it. 9Then she took the pan and served him the bread, but he refused to eat.

"Send everyone out of here,"[e] Amnon said. So everyone left him. 10Then Amnon said to Tamar, "Bring the food here into my bedroom so I may eat from your hand." And Tamar took the bread she had prepared and brought it to her brother Amnon in his bedroom. 11But when she took it to him to eat, he grabbed[f] her and said, "Come to bed with me, my sister."[g]

12"Don't, my brother!" she said to him. "Don't force me. Such a thing should not be done in Israel![h] Don't do this wicked thing.[i] 13What about me?[j] Where could I get rid of my disgrace? And what about you? You would be like one of the wicked fools in Israel. Please speak to the king; he will not keep me from being married to you." 14But he refused to listen to her, and since he was stronger than she, he raped her.[k]

15Then Amnon hated her with intense hatred. In fact, he hated her more than

12:22 [r]Isa 38:1-5
12:23 [s]Ge 37:35 [t]S 1Sa 31:13; 2Sa 13:39; Job 7:10; 10:21
12:24 [u]1Ki 1:11 [v]1Ki 1:10; 1Ch 22:9; 28:5; Mt 1:6
12:25 [w]Ne 13:26
12:26 [x]S Dt 3:11
12:30 [y]Est 8:15; Ps 21:3; 132:18
12:31 [z]S 1Sa 14:47
13:1 [a]2Sa 3:2 [b]2Sa 14:27; 1Ch 3:9 [c]S 2Sa 3:3
13:3 [d]S 1Sa 16:9
13:9 [e]Ge 45:1
13:11 [f]S Ge 39:12 [g]S Ge 38:16
13:12 [h]Lev 20:17 [i]S Ge 34:7
13:13 [j]S Lev 18:9; S Dt 22:21,23-24
13:14 [k]S Ge 34:2; Eze 22:11

[g]*25 Jedidiah* means *loved by the LORD.* [h]*30* Or *of Milcom* (that is, Molech) [i]*30* That is, about 75 pounds (about 34 kilograms) [j]*31* The meaning of the Hebrew for this clause is uncertain.

12:23 LAST THINGS, Heaven—The idea of heaven or a blessed afterlife is not necessarily taught in this passage. However, the hope of joining a deceased child suggests such a possibility. David's expectation has come to express that of many other grieving parents in similar circumstances. David committed the child to God, clung to God's promises, and continued to seek God's will for his own life. He spoke out of great sorrow but out of an even greater faith in God's goodness even in the midst of sorrow.

12:24–25 GOD, Love—David and Bathsheba had both suffered the wrath of God in the death of the child born to their adulterous relationship. God in His infinite love and grace, gave them another child, Solomon. Among the many children of David, Solomon followed David to the throne and became one of the greatest kings of Israel. Solomon was appointed to build the temple for God, an accomplishment forbidden to David. Notice that the name of the child, meaning "loved by the Lord," was revealed to David and Bathsheba by Nathan, the prophet who had earlier exposed David's sin and pronounced God's judgment upon the guilty pair. The depth of God's love goes beyond our understanding. It works beyond human systems and reveals itself without human merit.

13:1—14:33 SIN, Estrangement—Sin produces an estrangement string. Absalom and Amnon's string involved lust, deceit, rape, hatred, drunkenness, murder, and estrangement. Even a king's use of royal power and mercy could not stop the string. When one person sins against another, estrangement results. Only genuine forgiveness can overcome this problem.

he had loved her. Amnon said to her,
"Get up and get out!"
16"No!" she said to him. "Sending me
away would be a greater wrong than what
you have already done to me."
But he refused to listen to her. 17He
called his personal servant and said, "Get
this woman out of here and bolt the door
after her." 18So his servant put her out
and bolted the door after her. She was
wearing a richly ornamented[k] robe,[l] for
this was the kind of garment the virgin
daughters of the king wore. 19Tamar put
ashes[m] on her head and tore the ornamented[l] robe she was wearing. She put
her hand on her head and went away,
weeping aloud as she went.
20Her brother Absalom said to her,
"Has that Amnon, your brother, been
with you? Be quiet now, my sister; he is
your brother. Don't take this thing to
heart." And Tamar lived in her brother
Absalom's house, a desolate woman.
21When King David heard all this, he
was furious.[n] 22Absalom never said a
word to Amnon, either good or bad;[o] he
hated[p] Amnon because he had disgraced
his sister Tamar.

Absalom Kills Amnon

23Two years later, when Absalom's
sheepshearers[q] were at Baal Hazor near
the border of Ephraim, he invited all the
king's sons to come there. 24Absalom
went to the king and said, "Your servant
has had shearers come. Will the king and
his officials please join me?"
25"No, my son," the king replied. "All
of us should not go; we would only be a
burden to you." Although Absalom urged
him, he still refused to go, but gave him
his blessing.
26Then Absalom said, "If not, please let
my brother Amnon come with us."
The king asked him, "Why should he
go with you?" 27But Absalom urged him,
so he sent with him Amnon and the rest
of the king's sons.
28Absalom[r] ordered his men, "Listen!
When Amnon is in high[s] spirits from
drinking wine and I say to you, 'Strike
Amnon down,' then kill him. Don't be
afraid. Have not I given you this order? Be
strong and brave.[t]" 29So Absalom's men
did to Amnon what Absalom had ordered.
Then all the king's sons got up, mounted
their mules and fled.
30While they were on their way, the
report came to David: "Absalom has
struck down all the king's sons; not one
of them is left." 31The king stood up,
tore[u] his clothes and lay down on the
ground; and all his servants stood by with
their clothes torn.
32But Jonadab son of Shimeah, David's
brother, said, "My lord should not think
that they killed all the princes; only Amnon is dead. This has been Absalom's expressed intention ever since the day Amnon raped his sister Tamar. 33My lord the
king should not be concerned about the
report that all the king's sons are dead.
Only Amnon is dead."
34Meanwhile, Absalom had fled.
Now the man standing watch looked
up and saw many people on the road west
of him, coming down the side of the hill.
The watchman went and told the king, "I
see men in the direction of Horonaim, on
the side of the hill."[m]
35Jonadab said to the king, "See, the
king's sons are here; it has happened just
as your servant said."
36As he finished speaking, the king's
sons came in, wailing loudly. The king,
too, and all his servants wept very
bitterly.
37Absalom fled and went to Talmai[v]
son of Ammihud, the king of Geshur. But
King David mourned for his son every
day.
38After Absalom fled and went to Geshur, he stayed there three years. 39And
the spirit of the king[n] longed to go to
Absalom,[w] for he was consoled[x] concerning Amnon's death.

Chapter 14

Absalom Returns to Jerusalem

JOAB[y] son of Zeruiah knew that the
king's heart longed for Absalom. 2So
Joab sent someone to Tekoa[z] and had a
wise woman[a] brought from there. He
said to her, "Pretend you are in mourning. Dress in mourning clothes, and don't
use any cosmetic lotions.[b] Act like a
woman who has spent many days grieving for the dead. 3Then go to the king and
speak these words to him." And Joab[c]
put the words in her mouth.

13:18 [l]S Ge 37:23
13:19 [m]S Jos 7:6; Est 4:1; Da 9:3
13:21 [n]S Ge 34:7
13:22 [o]Ge 31:24 [p]Lev 19:17-18; 1Jn 2:9-11
13:23 [q]1Sa 25:7
13:28 [r]S 2Sa 3:3 [s]S Ru 3:7 [t]S 2Sa 12:10
13:31 [u]S Nu 14:6
13:37 [v]S 2Sa 3:3
13:39 [w]2Sa 14:13 [x]S 2Sa 12:19-23
14:1 [y]S 2Sa 2:18
14:2 [z]Ne 3:5; Jer 6:1; Am 1:1 [a]2Sa 20:16 [b]S Ru 3:3; S Isa 1:6
14:3 [c]ver 19

[k]*18* The meaning of the Hebrew for this phrase is uncertain. [l]*19* The meaning of the Hebrew for this word is uncertain. [m]*34* Septuagint; Hebrew does not have this sentence. [n]*39* Dead Sea Scrolls and some Septuagint manuscripts; Masoretic Text *But* ⌊*the spirit of*⌋ *David the king*

13:23–33 CHRISTIAN ETHICS, Murder—Neither vengeance nor political ambition justify plotting and murdering another person. See notes on Ex 20:13; Jdg 8:10–21; Mt 5:21–22.

13:25 PRAYER, Blessing—The blessing was a form of prayer asking God's presence and guidance over the activities. David gave the blessing in naive innocence. We need to be careful about what and whom we ask God to bless. See note on Ge 14:18–20.

4When the woman from Tekoa went[o]
to the king, she fell with her face to the
ground to pay him honor, and she said,
"Help me, O king!"
5The king asked her, "What is troubling you?"
She said, "I am indeed a widow; my
husband is dead. 6I your servant had two
sons. They got into a fight with each other in the field, and no one was there to
separate them. One struck the other and
killed him. 7Now the whole clan has risen
up against your servant; they say, 'Hand
over the one who struck his brother
down, so that we may put him to death[d]
for the life of his brother whom he killed;
then we will get rid of the heir[e] as well.'
They would put out the only burning coal
I have left,[f] leaving my husband neither
name nor descendant on the face of the
earth."
8The king said to the woman, "Go
home,[g] and I will issue an order in your
behalf."
9But the woman from Tekoa said to
him, "My lord the king, let the blame[h]
rest on me and on my father's family,[i]
and let the king and his throne be without guilt.[j]"
10The king replied, "If anyone says anything to you, bring him to me, and he will
not bother you again."
11She said, "Then let the king invoke
the LORD his God to prevent the avenger[k] of blood from adding to the destruction, so that my son will not be destroyed."
"As surely as the LORD lives," he said,
"not one hair[l] of your son's head will fall
to the ground.[m]"
12Then the woman said, "Let your servant speak a word to my lord the king."
"Speak," he replied.
13The woman said, "Why then have
you devised a thing like this against the
people of God? When the king says this,
does he not convict himself,[n] for the king
has not brought back his banished son?[o]
14Like water[p] spilled on the ground,
which cannot be recovered, so we must
die.[q] But God does not take away life;
instead, he devises ways so that a banished person[r] may not remain estranged
from him.
15"And now I have come to say this to
my lord the king because the people have
made me afraid. Your servant thought, 'I
will speak to the king; perhaps he will do
what his servant asks. 16Perhaps the king
will agree to deliver his servant from the
hand of the man who is trying to cut off
both me and my son from the inheritance[s] God gave us.'
17"And now your servant says, 'May
the word of my lord the king bring me
rest, for my lord the king is like an angel[t]
of God in discerning[u] good and evil. May
the LORD your God be with you.' "
18Then the king said to the woman,
"Do not keep from me the answer to
what I am going to ask you."
"Let my lord the king speak," the
woman said.
19The king asked, "Isn't the hand of
Joab[v] with you in all this?"
The woman answered, "As surely as
you live, my lord the king, no one can
turn to the right or to the left from anything my lord the king says. Yes, it was
your servant Joab who instructed me to
do this and who put all these words into
the mouth of your servant. 20Your servant
Joab did this to change the present situation. My lord has wisdom[w] like that of an
angel of God—he knows everything that
happens in the land.[x]"
21The king said to Joab, "Very well, I
will do it. Go, bring back the young man
Absalom."
22Joab fell with his face to the ground
to pay him honor, and he blessed the
king.[y] Joab said, "Today your servant
knows that he has found favor in your
eyes, my lord the king, because the king
has granted his servant's request."
23Then Joab went to Geshur and
brought Absalom back to Jerusalem. 24But
the king said, "He must go to his own
house; he must not see my face." So Absalom went to his own house and did not
see the face of the king.
25In all Israel there was not a man so
highly praised for his handsome appearance as Absalom. From the top of his
head to the sole of his foot there was no
blemish in him. 26Whenever he cut the
hair of his head[z]—he used to cut his hair
from time to time when it became too

14:7 [d]Nu 35:19 [e]Mt 21:38 [f]Dt 19:10-13
14:8 [g]1Sa 25:35
14:9 [h]1Sa 25:24 [i]Mt 27:25 [j]1Sa 25:28
14:11 [k]S Nu 35:12, 21 [l]S Mt 10:30 [m]S 1Sa 14:45
14:13 [n]S 2Sa 12:7; 1Ki 20:40 [o]2Sa 13:38-39
14:14 [p]Job 14:11; Ps 58:7; Isa 19:5 [q]Job 10:8; 17:13; 30:23; Ps 22:15; Heb 9:27 [r]Nu 35:15,25-28
14:16 [s]S Ex 34:9; S 1Sa 26:19
14:17 [t]S 1Sa 29:9 [u]1Ki 3:9; Da 2:21
14:19 [v]ver 3
14:20 [w]1Ki 3:12, 28; 10:23-24; Isa 28:6 [x]2Sa 18:13
14:22 [y]S Ge 47:7
14:26 [z]2Sa 18:9

[o]*4* Many Hebrew manuscripts, Septuagint, Vulgate and Syriac; most Hebrew manuscripts *spoke*

14:11 PRAYER, Personal—The woman of Tekoa asked for and got an oath made in God's name and, thus, binding. See note on Ge 28:20–21.

14:14 GOD, Grace—God is primarily a God of grace rather than a God of harsh, unbending justice and wrath. This does not mean God is indifferent to justice. It does mean that He prefers mercy to strict justice. Wrath is employed only when grace cannot accomplish God's purposes in the lives of people over whom God reigns.

14:14 HUMANITY, Nature of Death—Death is as natural as water sinking into the ground when it has been spilled. Since the Garden of Eden, it has been viewed as the normal end of life and should be accepted as such.

14:17 PRAYER, Petition—The wise woman attributed supernatural discernment to David, attributes expected from a near eastern king recognized as God's adopted son (Ps 2:7). Still she asked for divine assistance for David. Only the presence of God could give him the wisdom he needed.

heavy for him—he would weigh it, and
its weight was two hundred shekels[p] by
the royal standard.
27Three sons[a] and a daughter were
born to Absalom. The daughter's name
was Tamar,[b] and she became a beautiful
woman.
28Absalom lived two years in Jerusalem
without seeing the king's face. 29Then
Absalom sent for Joab in order to send
him to the king, but Joab refused to come
to him. So he sent a second time, but he
refused to come. 30Then he said to his
servants, "Look, Joab's field is next to
mine, and he has barley[c] there. Go and
set it on fire." So Absalom's servants set
the field on fire.
31Then Joab did go to Absalom's house
and he said to him, "Why have your servants set my field on fire?[d]"
32Absalom said to Joab, "Look, I sent
word to you and said, 'Come here so I can
send you to the king to ask, "Why have I
come from Geshur?[e] It would be better
for me if I were still there!" ' Now then, I
want to see the king's face, and if I am
guilty of anything, let him put me to
death."[f]
33So Joab went to the king and told him
this. Then the king summoned Absalom,
and he came in and bowed down with his
face to the ground before the king. And
the king kissed[g] Absalom.

Chapter 15

Absalom's Conspiracy

IN the course of time,[h] Absalom provided himself with a chariot[i] and horses
and with fifty men to run ahead of him.
2He would get up early and stand by the
side of the road leading to the city gate.[j]
Whenever anyone came with a complaint
to be placed before the king for a decision, Absalom would call out to him,
"What town are you from?" He would
answer, "Your servant is from one of the
tribes of Israel." 3Then Absalom would
say to him, "Look, your claims are valid
and proper, but there is no representative
of the king to hear you."[k] 4And Absalom
would add, "If only I were appointed
judge in the land![l] Then everyone who
has a complaint or case could come to me
and I would see that he gets justice."
5Also, whenever anyone approached
him to bow down before him, Absalom
would reach out his hand, take hold of
him and kiss him. 6Absalom behaved in
this way toward all the Israelites who
came to the king asking for justice, and so
he stole the hearts[m] of the men of Israel.
7At the end of four[q] years, Absalom
said to the king, "Let me go to Hebron
and fulfill a vow I made to the LORD.
8While your servant was living at Geshur[n] in Aram, I made this vow:[o] 'If the
LORD takes me back to Jerusalem, I will
worship the LORD in Hebron.[r] ' "
9The king said to him, "Go in peace."
So he went to Hebron.
10Then Absalom sent secret messengers throughout the tribes of Israel to say,
"As soon as you hear the sound of the
trumpets,[p] then say, 'Absalom is king in
Hebron.' " 11Two hundred men from Jerusalem had accompanied Absalom. They
had been invited as guests and went quite
innocently, knowing nothing about the
matter. 12While Absalom was offering
sacrifices, he also sent for Ahithophel[q]
the Gilonite, David's counselor,[r] to come
from Giloh,[s] his hometown. And so the
conspiracy gained strength, and Absalom's following kept on increasing.[t]

David Flees

13A messenger came and told David,
"The hearts of the men of Israel are with
Absalom."
14Then David said to all his officials
who were with him in Jerusalem,
"Come! We must flee,[u] or none of us
will escape from Absalom.[v] We must
leave immediately, or he will move quickly to overtake us and bring ruin upon us
and put the city to the sword."
15The king's officials answered him,
"Your servants are ready to do whatever
our lord the king chooses."
16The king set out, with his entire
household following him; but he left ten
concubines[w] to take care of the palace.
17So the king set out, with all the people
following him, and they halted at a place
some distance away. 18All his men

p26 That is, about 5 pounds (about 2.3 kilograms)
q7 Some Septuagint manuscripts, Syriac and Josephus; Hebrew *forty* r8 Some Septuagint manuscripts; Hebrew does not have *in Hebron.*

14:27 a2Sa 18:18 bS 2Sa 13:1
14:30 cS Ex 9:31
14:31 dS Jdg 15:5
14:32 eS 2Sa 3:3 f1Sa 20:8
14:33 gLk 15:20
15:1 hS 2Sa 12:11 iS 1Sa 8:11
15:2 jS Ge 23:10; 2Sa 19:8
15:3 kPr 12:2
15:4 lJdg 9:29
15:6 mRo 16:18
15:8 nS 2Sa 3:3 oS Ge 28:20
15:10 p1Ki 1:34, 39; 2Ki 9:13
15:12 qver 31,34; 2Sa 16:15,23; 17:14; 23:34; 1Ch 27:33 rJob 19:14; Ps 41:9; 55:13; Jer 9:4 sJos 15:51 tPs 3:1
15:14 u1Ki 2:26; Ps 132:1; Ps 3 Title v2Sa 19:9
15:16 w2Sa 16:21-22; 20:3

15:2 DISCIPLESHIP, Spiritual Leaders—Judging in disputes was one of the responsibilities of the Hebrew king. He also led the armies in war with God's blessing (2 Ch 17:1–6). Christian disciples regard organized government as being ordained of God. They are expected to support the state in achieving the purposes God has established as the realm of civil authority (Ro 13:1–7). When serving as judicial or political releaders, God's people must seek to find His will and to exercise their positions in the best interests of the people as a whole.

15:3–6 CHRISTIAN ETHICS, Justice—Not every appearance of acting justly issues forth in justice as this account of Absalom demonstrates. A nation must not neglect setting up court systems for its people. The people must not too eagerly follow every voice calling for reform.

15:12 PRAYER, Hindrances—False worship, done under a false pretext, does not bring God's blessing and favorable response. Absalom used worship practices to conceal his evil plots against his own father.

marched past him, along with all the Kerethites[x] and Pelethites; and all the six
hundred Gittites who had accompanied
him from Gath marched before the king.
19 The king said to Ittai[y] the Gittite,
"Why should you come along with us?
Go back and stay with King Absalom. You
are a foreigner,[z] an exile from your
homeland. 20 You came only yesterday.
And today shall I make you wander[a]
about with us, when I do not know
where I am going? Go back, and take your
countrymen. May kindness and faithfulness[b] be with you."
21 But Ittai replied to the king, "As surely as the LORD lives, and as my lord the
king lives, wherever my lord the king
may be, whether it means life or death,
there will your servant be."[c]
22 David said to Ittai, "Go ahead, march
on." So Ittai the Gittite marched on with
all his men and the families that were
with him.
23 The whole countryside wept aloud[d]
as all the people passed by. The king also
crossed the Kidron Valley,[e,f] and all the
people moved on toward the desert.
24 Zadok[g] was there, too, and all the
Levites who were with him were carrying
the ark[h] of the covenant of God. They set
down the ark of God, and Abiathar[i] offered sacrifices[s] until all the people had
finished leaving the city.
25 Then the king said to Zadok, "Take
the ark of God back into the city. If I find
favor in the LORD's eyes, he will bring me
back and let me see it and his dwelling
place[j] again. 26 But if he says, 'I am not
pleased with you,' then I am ready; let
him do to me whatever seems good to
him.[k]"
27 The king also said to Zadok the
priest, "Aren't you a seer?[l] Go back to
the city in peace, with your son Ahimaaz
and Jonathan[m] son of Abiathar. You and
Abiathar take your two sons with you. 28 I
will wait at the fords[n] in the desert until
word comes from you to inform me."
29 So Zadok and Abiathar took the ark of
God back to Jerusalem and stayed there.
30 But David continued up the Mount of
Olives, weeping[o] as he went; his head[p]
was covered and he was barefoot. All the
people with him covered their heads too
and were weeping as they went up.
31 Now David had been told, "Ahithophel[q] is among the conspirators with Absalom." So David prayed, "O LORD, turn
Ahithophel's counsel into foolishness."
32 When David arrived at the summit,
where people used to worship God, Hushai[r] the Arkite[s] was there to meet him,
his robe torn and dust[t] on his head.
33 David said to him, "If you go with me,
you will be a burden[u] to me. 34 But if you
return to the city and say to Absalom, 'I
will be your servant, O king; I was your
father's servant in the past, but now I will
be your servant,'[v] then you can help me
by frustrating[w] Ahithophel's advice.
35 Won't the priests Zadok and Abiathar
be there with you? Tell them anything
you hear in the king's palace.[x] 36 Their
two sons, Ahimaaz[y] son of Zadok and
Jonathan[z] son of Abiathar, are there with
them. Send them to me with anything
you hear."
37 So David's friend Hushai[a] arrived at
Jerusalem as Absalom[b] was entering the
city.

Chapter 16

David and Ziba

WHEN David had gone a short distance beyond the summit, there
was Ziba,[c] the steward of Mephibosheth,
waiting to meet him. He had a string of
donkeys saddled and loaded with two
hundred loaves of bread, a hundred cakes
of raisins, a hundred cakes of figs and a
skin of wine.[d]
2 The king asked Ziba, "Why have you
brought these?"
Ziba answered, "The donkeys are for
the king's household to ride on, the bread
and fruit are for the men to eat, and the
wine is to refresh[e] those who become
exhausted in the desert."
3 The king then asked, "Where is your
master's grandson?"[f]
Ziba[g] said to him, "He is staying in
Jerusalem, because he thinks, 'Today the
house of Israel will give me back my
grandfather's kingdom.'"
4 Then the king said to Ziba, "All that
belonged to Mephibosheth[h] is now
yours."
"I humbly bow," Ziba said. "May I find
favor in your eyes, my lord the king."

Shimei Curses David

5 As King David approached Bahurim,[i]
a man from the same clan as Saul's family
came out from there. His name was Shimei[j] son of Gera, and he cursed[k] as he
came out. 6 He pelted David and all the
king's officials with stones, though all the
troops and the special guard were on David's right and left. 7 As he cursed, Shimei
said, "Get out, get out, you man of blood,
you scoundrel! 8 The LORD has repaid you
for all the blood you shed in the household of Saul, in whose place you have
reigned.[l] The LORD has handed the kingdom over to your son Absalom. You have

15:18 [x]S 1Sa 30:14; 2Sa 20:7,23; 1Ki 1:38,44; 1Ch 18:17
15:19 [y]2Sa 18:2 [z]S Ge 31:15
15:20 [a]S 1Sa 22:2 [b]2Sa 2:6
15:21 [c]Ru 1:16-17; Pr 17:17
15:23 [d]1Sa 11:4; Job 2:12 [e]1Ki 2:37; 2Ki 23:12; 2Ch 15:16; 29:16; 30:14; Jer 31:40 [f]Jn 18:1
15:24 [g]S 2Sa 8:17; 19:11 [h]Nu 4:15; S 10:33; 1Ki 2:26 [i]S 1Sa 22:20
15:25 [j]Ex 15:13; S Lev 15:31; Ps 43:3; 46:4; 84:1; 132:7
15:26 [k]S Jdg 10:15; 2Sa 22:20
15:27 [l]S 1Sa 9:9 [m]ver 36; 2Sa 17:17; 1Ki 1:42
15:28 [n]2Sa 17:16
15:30 [o]S Nu 25:6; S Ps 30:5 [p]Est 6:12
15:31 [q]S ver 12
15:32 [r]ver 37; 2Sa 16:16; 17:5; 1Ki 4:16 [s]Jos 16:2 [t]S Jos 7:6
15:33 [u]2Sa 19:35
15:34 [v]2Sa 16:19 [w]2Sa 17:14; Pr 11:14
15:35 [x]2Sa 17:15-16
15:36 [y]2Sa 18:19 [z]S ver 27; 2Sa 17:17; 1Ki 1:42
15:37 [a]1Ch 27:33 [b]2Sa 16:15
16:1 [c]2Sa 9:1-13 [d]S 1Sa 25:18; 1Ch 12:40
16:2 [e]2Sa 17:27-29
16:3 [f]2Sa 9:9-10 [g]S 2Sa 9:2
16:4 [h]S 2Sa 4:4
16:5 [i]S 2Sa 3:16 [j]2Sa 19:16-23; 1Ki 2:8-9,36,44 [k]S Ex 22:28
16:8 [l]2Sa 19:28; 21:9

[s]24 Or *Abiathar went up*

come to ruin because you are a man of
blood!"[m]
9Then Abishai[n] son of Zeruiah said to
the king, "Why should this dead dog[o]
curse my lord the king? Let me go over
and cut off his head."[p]
10But the king said, "What do you and I
have in common, you sons of Zeruiah?[q]
If he is cursing because the LORD said to
him, 'Curse David,' who can ask, 'Why
do you do this?' "[r]
11David then said to Abishai and all his
officials, "My son,[s] who is of my own
flesh, is trying to take my life. How much
more, then, this Benjamite! Leave him
alone; let him curse, for the LORD has told
him to.[t] 12It may be that the LORD will
see my distress[u] and repay me with
good[v] for the cursing I am receiving today.[w]"
13So David and his men continued
along the road while Shimei was going
along the hillside opposite him, cursing as
he went and throwing stones at him and
showering him with dirt. 14The king and
all the people with him arrived at their
destination exhausted.[x] And there he refreshed himself.

The Advice of Hushai and Ahithophel

15Meanwhile, Absalom[y] and all the
men of Israel came to Jerusalem, and
Ahithophel[z] was with him. 16Then Hushai[a] the Arkite, David's friend, went to
Absalom and said to him, "Long live the
king! Long live the king!"
17Absalom asked Hushai, "Is this the
love you show your friend? Why didn't
you go with your friend?"[b]
18Hushai said to Absalom, "No, the one
chosen by the LORD, by these people, and
by all the men of Israel—his I will be,
and I will remain with him. 19Further-
more, whom should I serve? Should I not
serve the son? Just as I served your father,
so I will serve you."[c]
20Absalom said to Ahithophel, "Give us
your advice. What should we do?"
21Ahithophel answered, "Lie with your
father's concubines whom he left to take
care of the palace. Then all Israel will
hear that you have made yourself a
stench in your father's nostrils, and the
hands of everyone with you will be
strengthened." 22So they pitched a tent
for Absalom on the roof, and he lay with
his father's concubines in the sight of all
Israel.[d]
23Now in those days the advice[e] Ahithophel gave was like that of one who inquires of God. That was how both David[f]
and Absalom regarded all of Ahithophel's
advice.

Chapter 17

AHITHOPHEL said to Absalom, "I
would[t] choose twelve thousand
men and set out tonight in pursuit of David. 2I would[u] attack him while he is
weary and weak.[g] I would[u] strike him
with terror, and then all the people with
him will flee. I would[u] strike down only
the king[h] 3and bring all the people back
to you. The death of the man you seek
will mean the return of all; all the people
will be unharmed." 4This plan seemed
good to Absalom and to all the elders of
Israel.
5But Absalom said, "Summon also Hushai[i] the Arkite, so we can hear what he
has to say." 6When Hushai came to him,
Absalom said, "Ahithophel has given this
advice. Should we do what he says? If
not, give us your opinion."
7Hushai replied to Absalom, "The advice Ahithophel has given is not good this
time. 8You know your father and his
men; they are fighters, and as fierce as a
wild bear robbed of her cubs.[j] Besides,
your father is an experienced fighter;[k] he
will not spend the night with the troops.
9Even now, he is hidden in a cave or
some other place.[l] If he should attack
your troops first,[v] whoever hears about it
will say, 'There has been a slaughter
among the troops who follow Absalom.'
10Then even the bravest soldier, whose
heart is like the heart of a lion,[m] will
melt[n] with fear, for all Israel knows that
your father is a fighter and that those
with him are brave.[o]
11"So I advise you: Let all Israel, from
Dan to Beersheba[p]—as numerous as the
sand[q] on the seashore—be gathered to
you, with you yourself leading them into
battle. 12Then we will attack him wherever he may be found, and we will fall on
him as dew settles on the ground. Neither he nor any of his men will be left
alive. 13If he withdraws into a city, then
all Israel will bring ropes to that city, and
we will drag it down to the valley[r] until
not even a piece of it can be found."

16:8 [m]2Sa 19:19; Ps 55:3
16:9 [n]S 1Sa 26:6 [o]S 2Sa 3:8 [p]S 2Sa 3:39; Lk 9:54
16:10 [q]S 2Sa 2:18; 19:22 [r]Ro 9:20
16:11 [s]2Sa 12:11 [t]S Ge 45:5; 1Sa 26:19
16:12 [u]Ps 4:1; 25:18 [v]Dt 23:5; Ro 8:28 [w]Ps 109:28
16:14 [x]2Sa 17:2
16:15 [y]S 2Sa 15:37 [z]S 2Sa 15:12
16:16 [a]S 2Sa 15:32
16:17 [b]2Sa 19:25
16:19 [c]2Sa 15:34
16:22 [d]S 2Sa 3:7; 12:11-12; S 15:16
16:23 [e]2Sa 17:14, 23 [f]S 2Sa 15:12
17:2 [g]2Sa 16:14 [h]1Ki 22:31; Zec 13:7
17:5 [i]S 2Sa 15:32
17:8 [j]Hos 13:8 [k]1Sa 16:18
17:9 [l]Jer 41:9
17:10 [m]1Ch 12:8 [n]Jos 2:9,11; Eze 21:15 [o]2Sa 23:8; 1Ch 11:11
17:11 [p]S Jdg 20:1 [q]S Ge 12:2; S Jos 11:4
17:13 [r]Mic 1:6

[t]1 Or *Let me* [u]2 Or *will* [v]9 Or *When some of the men fall at the first attack*

16:12 HISTORY, Deliverance—See note on 1 Sa 24:8–21.

16:18 ELECTION, Leadership—Hushai spoke to Absalom ironic words about the man whom God had chosen. This use of irony should have opened the eyes of Absalom so that he could see the futility of trying to snatch the kingdom from the hands of his father, David. No one can thwart God's purpose or dethrone anyone elected by God to perform a specific ministry. At all times, God is the sovereign Lord of history. The people's choice may be wrong. God is never wrong in electing a leader for His people.

[14]Absalom and all the men of Israel
said, "The advice[s] of Hushai the Arkite
is better than that of Ahithophel."[t] For
the LORD had determined to frustrate[u]
the good advice of Ahithophel in order to
bring disaster[v] on Absalom.[w]
[15]Hushai told Zadok and Abiathar, the
priests, "Ahithophel has advised Absalom
and the elders of Israel to do such and
such, but I have advised them to do so
and so. [16]Now send a message immediately and tell David, 'Do not spend the
night at the fords in the desert;[x] cross
over without fail, or the king and all the
people with him will be swallowed
up.[y]' "
[17]Jonathan[z] and Ahimaaz were staying
at En Rogel.[a] A servant girl was to go and
inform them, and they were to go and tell
King David, for they could not risk being
seen entering the city. [18]But a young man
saw them and told Absalom. So the two of
them left quickly and went to the house
of a man in Bahurim.[b] He had a well in
his courtyard, and they climbed down
into it. [19]His wife took a covering and
spread it out over the opening of the well
and scattered grain over it. No one knew
anything about it.[c]
[20]When Absalom's men came to the
woman[d] at the house, they asked,
"Where are Ahimaaz and Jonathan?"
The woman answered them, "They
crossed over the brook."[w] The men
searched but found no one, so they returned to Jerusalem.
[21]After the men had gone, the two
climbed out of the well and went to inform King David. They said to him, "Set
out and cross the river at once; Ahithophel has advised such and such against
you." [22]So David and all the people with
him set out and crossed the Jordan. By
daybreak, no one was left who had not
crossed the Jordan.
[23]When Ahithophel saw that his advice[e] had not been followed, he saddled
his donkey and set out for his house in
his hometown. He put his house in order[f] and then hanged himself. So he died
and was buried in his father's tomb.
[24]David went to Mahanaim,[g] and Absalom crossed the Jordan with all the men
of Israel. [25]Absalom had appointed Amasa[h] over the army in place of Joab. Amasa
was the son of a man named Jether,[x][i] an
Israelite[y] who had married Abigail,[z] the
daughter of Nahash and sister of Zeruiah
the mother of Joab. [26]The Israelites and
Absalom camped in the land of Gilead.
[27]When David came to Mahanaim,
Shobi son of Nahash[j] from Rabbah[k] of
the Ammonites, and Makir[l] son of Ammiel from Lo Debar, and Barzillai[m] the
Gileadite[n] from Rogelim [28]brought bed-
ding and bowls and articles of pottery.
They also brought wheat and barley, flour
and roasted grain, beans and lentils,[a]
[29]honey and curds, sheep, and cheese
from cows' milk for David and his people
to eat.[o] For they said, "The people have
become hungry and tired and thirsty in
the desert.[p]"

Chapter 18

Absalom's Death

DAVID mustered the men who were
with him and appointed over them
commanders of thousands and commanders of hundreds. [2]David sent the troops
out[q]—a third under the command of
Joab, a third under Joab's brother Abishai[r] son of Zeruiah, and a third under Ittai[s] the Gittite. The king told the troops,
"I myself will surely march out with
you."
[3]But the men said, "You must not go
out; if we are forced to flee, they won't
care about us. Even if half of us die, they
won't care; but you are worth ten[t] thousand of us.[b] It would be better now for
you to give us support from the city."[u]
[4]The king answered, "I will do whatever seems best to you."
So the king stood beside the gate while

17:14 [s]S 2Sa 16:23 [t]S 2Sa 15:12 [u]S 2Sa 15:34; Ne 4:15 [v]Ps 9:16 [w]2Ch 10:8
17:16 [x]2Sa 15:28 [y]2Sa 15:35
17:17 [z]S 2Sa 15:27,36 [a]Jos 15:7; 18:16; 1Ki 1:9
17:18 [b]S 2Sa 3:16
17:19 [c]S Jos 2:6
17:20 [d]S Ex 1:19
17:23 [e]2Sa S 2Sa 16:23 [f]2Ki 20:1
17:24 [g]S Ge 32:2
17:25 [h]2Sa 19:13; 20:4,9-12; 1Ki 2:5,32; 1Ch 12:18 [i]1Ch 2:13-17
17:27 [j]S 1Sa 11:1 [k]S Dt 3:11 [l]2Sa 9:4 [m]2Sa 19:31-39; 1Ki 2:7 [n]2Sa 19:31; Ezr 2:61
17:29 [o]1Ch 12:40 [p]2Sa 16:2; S Ro 12:13
18:2 [q]S Jdg 7:16; 1Sa 11:11 [r]S 1Sa 26:6 [s]2Sa 15:19
18:3 [t]S 1Sa 18:7 [u]2Sa 21:17

[w]*20* Or *"They passed by the sheep pen toward the water."* [x]*25* Hebrew *Ithra,* a variant of *Jether* [y]*25* Hebrew and some Septuagint manuscripts; other Septuagint manuscripts (see also 1 Chron. 2:17) *Ishmaelite* or *Jezreelite* [z]*25* Hebrew *Abigal,* a variant of *Abigail* [a]*28* Most Septuagint manuscripts and Syriac; Hebrew *lentils, and roasted grain* [b]*3* Two Hebrew manuscripts, some Septuagint manuscripts and Vulgate; most Hebrew manuscripts *care; for now there are ten thousand like us*

17:14 GOD, Sovereignty—This verse should not be read in the sense that God is unfaithful, changeable, arbitrary, or unpredictable. He is none of these. Neither should this verse be understood as meaning that God causes evil things to occur. See Guide to Interpreting a Bible Passage, pp. 1775–1776. This verse simply affirms the sovereignty of God working in the circumstances at hand to bring deserved judgment upon Absalom. God does not do or cause evil, but He may use what we judge to be evil circumstances that arise to accomplish His own good purposes. See notes on Ru 1:13,20–21; Ro 8:28; Jas 1:13–14.

17:14 HISTORY, Intentions—God works through the most complex human conspiracies to accomplish His purposes. He can lead people to disregard the best human advice and thus do that which brings about His will. Human opinion may see only human stupidity at work. Faith sees God's rule of history.

17:23 HUMANITY, Death—Suicide is not found often in the Bible as a means of death. No clear teaching is found in regard to its ultimate theological consequence, other than those teachings which reflect upon the taking of any life. See Ex 20:13; 21:12–14. Note that preparation for death is expected of those who are living. The natural progression of events following death was for the dead to be placed in the family burial place.

all the men marched out in units of hundreds and of thousands. 5 The king commanded Joab, Abishai and Ittai, "Be gentle with the young man Absalom for my
sake." And all the troops heard the king
giving orders concerning Absalom to each
of the commanders.

6 The army marched into the field to
fight Israel, and the battle took place in
the forest[v] of Ephraim. 7 There the army
of Israel was defeated by David's men,
and the casualties that day were great—
twenty thousand men. 8 The battle spread
out over the whole countryside, and the
forest claimed more lives that day than
the sword.

9 Now Absalom happened to meet David's men. He was riding his mule, and as
the mule went under the thick branches
of a large oak, Absalom's head[w] got
caught in the tree. He was left hanging in
midair, while the mule he was riding
kept on going.

10 When one of the men saw this, he
told Joab, "I just saw Absalom hanging in
an oak tree."

11 Joab said to the man who had told
him this, "What! You saw him? Why
didn't you strike[x] him to the ground
right there? Then I would have had to
give you ten shekels[c] of silver and a warrior's belt.[y]"

12 But the man replied, "Even if a thousand shekels[d] were weighed out into my
hands, I would not lift my hand against
the king's son. In our hearing the king
commanded you and Abishai and Ittai,
'Protect the young man Absalom for my
sake.[e]' 13 And if I had put my life in jeopardy[f]—and nothing is hidden from the
king[z]—you would have kept your distance from me."

14 Joab[a] said, "I'm not going to wait
like this for you." So he took three jave-
lins in his hand and plunged them into
Absalom's heart while Absalom was still
alive in the oak tree. 15 And ten of Joab's
armor-bearers surrounded Absalom,
struck him and killed him.[b]

16 Then Joab[c] sounded the trumpet,
and the troops stopped pursuing Israel,
for Joab halted them. 17 They took Absalom, threw him into a big pit in the forest
and piled up[d] a large heap of rocks[e] over
him. Meanwhile, all the Israelites fled to
their homes.

18 During his lifetime Absalom had tak-
en a pillar and erected it in the King's
Valley[f] as a monument[g] to himself, for
he thought, "I have no son[h] to carry on
the memory of my name." He named the
pillar after himself, and it is called Absalom's Monument to this day.

David Mourns

19 Now Ahimaaz[i] son of Zadok said,
"Let me run and take the news to the
king that the LORD has delivered him
from the hand of his enemies.[j]"

20 "You are not the one to take the
news today," Joab told him. "You may
take the news another time, but you must
not do so today, because the king's son is
dead."

21 Then Joab said to a Cushite, "Go, tell
the king what you have seen." The Cushite bowed down before Joab and ran off.

22 Ahimaaz son of Zadok again said to
Joab, "Come what may, please let me run
behind the Cushite."

But Joab replied, "My son, why do you
want to go? You don't have any news that
will bring you a reward."

23 He said, "Come what may, I want to
run."

So Joab said, "Run!" Then Ahimaaz ran
by way of the plain[g] and outran the
Cushite.

24 While David was sitting between the
inner and outer gates, the watchman[k]
went up to the roof of the gateway by the
wall. As he looked out, he saw a man
running alone. 25 The watchman called
out to the king and reported it.

The king said, "If he is alone, he must
have good news." And the man came
closer and closer.

26 Then the watchman saw another
man running, and he called down to the
gatekeeper, "Look, another man running
alone!"

The king said, "He must be bringing
good news,[l] too."

27 The watchman said, "It seems to me
that the first one runs like[m] Ahimaaz son
of Zadok."

"He's a good man," the king said. "He
comes with good news."

28 Then Ahimaaz called out to the king,
"All is well!" He bowed down before the
king with his face to the ground and said,
"Praise be to the LORD your God! He has
delivered up the men who lifted their
hands against my lord the king."

29 The king asked, "Is the young man
Absalom safe?"

Ahimaaz answered, "I saw great confusion just as Joab was about to send the
king's servant and me, your servant, but I
don't know what it was."

30 The king said, "Stand aside and wait

18:6 [v]S Jos 17:15
18:9 [w]2Sa 14:26
18:11 [x]S 2Sa 3:39 [y]1Sa 18:4
18:13 [z]2Sa 14:19-20
18:14 [a]S 2Sa 2:18
18:15 [b]S 2Sa 12:10
18:16 [c]S 2Sa 2:28
18:17 [d]Jos 7:26 [e]Jos 8:29
18:18 [f]Ge 14:17 [g]S Ge 50:5; S Nu 32:42 [h]2Sa 14:27
18:19 [i]S 2Sa 15:36 [j]Jdg 11:36
18:24 [k]S 1Sa 14:16; S Jer 51:12
18:26 [l]1Ki 1:42; Isa 52:7; 61:1
18:27 [m]2Ki 9:20

[c] *11* That is, about 4 ounces (about 115 grams)
[d] *12* That is, about 25 pounds (about 11 kilograms)
[e] *12* A few Hebrew manuscripts, Septuagint, Vulgate and Syriac; most Hebrew manuscripts may be translated *Absalom, whoever you may be.*
[f] *13* Or *Otherwise, if I had acted treacherously toward him*
[g] *23* That is, the plain of the Jordan

here." So he stepped aside and stood
there.
31Then the Cushite arrived and said,
"My lord the king, hear the good news!
The LORD has delivered you today from
all who rose up against you."
32The king asked the Cushite, "Is the
young man Absalom safe?"
The Cushite replied, "May the enemies of my lord the king and all who rise
up to harm you be like that young
man."[n]
33The king was shaken. He went up to
the room over the gateway and wept. As
he went, he said: "O my son Absalom!
My son, my son Absalom! If only I had
died[o] instead of you—O Absalom, my
son, my son!"[p]

Chapter 19

JOAB was told, "The king is weeping
and mourning for Absalom." 2And for
the whole army the victory that day was
turned into mourning, because on that
day the troops heard it said, "The king is
grieving for his son." 3The men stole into
the city that day as men steal in who are
ashamed when they flee from battle. 4The
king covered his face and cried aloud, "O
my son Absalom! O Absalom, my son, my
son!"
5Then Joab went into the house to the
king and said, "Today you have humiliated all your men, who have just saved your
life and the lives of your sons and daughters and the lives of your wives and concubines. 6You love those who hate you
and hate those who love you. You have
made it clear today that the commanders
and their men mean nothing to you. I see
that you would be pleased if Absalom
were alive today and all of us were dead.
7Now go out and encourage your men. I
swear by the LORD that if you don't go
out, not a man will be left with you by
nightfall. This will be worse for you than
all the calamities that have come upon
you from your youth till now."[q]
8So the king got up and took his seat in
the gateway. When the men were told,
"The king is sitting in the gateway,"[r]
they all came before him.

David Returns to Jerusalem

Meanwhile, the Israelites had fled to
their homes. 9Throughout the tribes of Israel, the people were all arguing with
each other, saying, "The king delivered
us from the hand of our enemies; he is
the one who rescued us from the hand of
the Philistines.[s] But now he has fled the
country because of Absalom;[t] 10and Absalom, whom we anointed to rule over
us, has died in battle. So why do you say
nothing about bringing the king back?"
11King David sent this message to Zadok[u] and Abiathar, the priests: "Ask the
elders of Judah, 'Why should you be the
last to bring the king back to his palace,
since what is being said throughout Israel
has reached the king at his quarters?
12You are my brothers, my own flesh and
blood. So why should you be the last to
bring back the king?' 13And say to Amasa,[v] 'Are you not my own flesh and
blood?[w] May God deal with me, be it
ever so severely,[x] if from now on you are
not the commander of my army in place
of Joab.[y]'"
14He won over the hearts of all the
men of Judah as though they were one
man. They sent word to the king, "Return, you and all your men." 15Then the
king returned and went as far as the Jordan.
Now the men of Judah had come to
Gilgal[z] to go out and meet the king and
bring him across the Jordan. 16Shimei[a]
son of Gera, the Benjamite from Bahurim,
hurried down with the men of Judah to
meet King David. 17With him were a
thousand Benjamites, along with Ziba,[b]
the steward of Saul's household,[c] and his
fifteen sons and twenty servants. They
rushed to the Jordan, where the king was.
18They crossed at the ford to take the
king's household over and to do whatever
he wished.
When Shimei son of Gera crossed the
Jordan, he fell prostrate before the king
19and said to him, "May my lord not hold
me guilty. Do not remember how your
servant did wrong on the day my lord the
king left Jerusalem.[d] May the king put it
out of his mind. 20For I your servant
know that I have sinned, but today I have
come here as the first of the whole house
of Joseph to come down and meet my
lord the king."
21Then Abishai[e] son of Zeruiah said,

18:32 [n]Jdg 5:31; S 1Sa 25:26
18:33 [o]Ex 32:32 [p]S Ge 43:14; 2Sa 19:4
19:7 [q]Pr 14:28
19:8 [r]S 2Sa 15:2
19:9 [s]2Sa 8:1-14 [t]2Sa 15:14
19:11 [u]S 2Sa 15:24
19:13 [v]S 2Sa 17:25 [w]S Ge 29:14 [x]S Ru 1:17 [y]S 2Sa 2:13
19:15 [z]S 1Sa 11:15
19:16 [a]2Sa 16:5-13
19:17 [b]S 2Sa 9:2 [c]S Ge 43:16
19:19 [d]S 2Sa 16:6-8
19:21 [e]S 1Sa 26:6

18:31 HISTORY, Deliverance—Deliverance from enemies is not the supreme good of life. David's troops won the battle, but David lost his son. Long before, he had lost Absalom's confidence, companionship, and emotional support. Still Absalom's death brought a sense of absolute loss which no news of victory could relieve. History shows us that final deliverance or salvation must involve more than military supremacy.

18:33 HUMANITY, Attitudes to Death—A normal human response to a loved one's death is the desire to have died in the place of the loved one. Few people actually take the step of sacrificing themselves for another, however.

19:7 PRAYER, Oath—Joab resorted to an oath to persuade David. The New Testament shows that such oaths should not be necessary for believers whose words should always be trustworthy (Mt 5:34).

19:13 PRAYER, Oath—David affirmed his commitment with an oath. See note on v 7.

"Shouldn't Shimei be put to death for
this? He cursed[f] the LORD's anointed."[g]
22David replied, "What do you and I
have in common, you sons of Zeruiah?[h]
This day you have become my adversaries! Should anyone be put to death in Israel today?[i] Do I not know that today I am
king over Israel?" 23So the king said to
Shimei, "You shall not die." And the king
promised him on oath.[j]
24Mephibosheth,[k] Saul's grandson,
also went down to meet the king. He had
not taken care of his feet or trimmed his
mustache or washed his clothes from the
day the king left until the day he returned
safely. 25When he came from Jerusalem
to meet the king, the king asked him,
"Why didn't you go with me,[l] Mephibosheth?"
26He said, "My lord the king, since I
your servant am lame,[m] I said, 'I will
have my donkey saddled and will ride on
it, so I can go with the king.' But Ziba[n]
my servant betrayed me. 27And he has
slandered your servant to my lord the
king. My lord the king is like an angel[o] of
God; so do whatever pleases you. 28All
my grandfather's descendants deserved
nothing but death[p] from my lord the
king, but you gave your servant a place
among those who eat at your table.[q] So
what right do I have to make any more
appeals to the king?"
29The king said to him, "Why say
more? I order you and Ziba to divide the
fields."
30Mephibosheth said to the king, "Let
him take everything, now that my lord
the king has arrived home safely."
31Barzillai[r] the Gileadite also came
down from Rogelim to cross the Jordan
with the king and to send him on his way
from there. 32Now Barzillai was a very old
man, eighty years of age. He had provided
for the king during his stay in Mahanaim,
for he was a very wealthy[s] man. 33The
king said to Barzillai, "Cross over with
me and stay with me in Jerusalem, and I
will provide for you."
34But Barzillai answered the king,
"How many more years will I live, that I
should go up to Jerusalem with the king?
35I am now eighty[t] years old. Can I tell
the difference between what is good and
what is not? Can your servant taste what
he eats and drinks? Can I still hear the
voices of men and women singers?[u] Why
should your servant be an added[v] burden
to my lord the king? 36Your servant will
cross over the Jordan with the king for a
short distance, but why should the king
reward me in this way? 37Let your servant
return, that I may die in my own town
near the tomb of my father[w] and mother.
But here is your servant Kimham.[x] Let
him cross over with my lord the king. Do
for him whatever pleases you."
38The king said, "Kimham shall cross
over with me, and I will do for him whatever pleases you. And anything you desire from me I will do for you."
39So all the people crossed the Jordan,
and then the king crossed over. The king
kissed Barzillai and gave him his blessing,[y] and Barzillai returned to his home.
40When the king crossed over to Gilgal,
Kimham crossed with him. All the troops
of Judah and half the troops of Israel had
taken the king over.
41Soon all the men of Israel were coming to the king and saying to him, "Why
did our brothers, the men of Judah, steal
the king away and bring him and his
household across the Jordan, together
with all his men?"[z]
42All the men of Judah answered the
men of Israel, "We did this because the
king is closely related to us. Why are you
angry about it? Have we eaten any of the
king's provisions? Have we taken anything for ourselves?"
43Then the men of Israel[a] answered
the men of Judah, "We have ten shares in
the king; and besides, we have a greater
claim on David than you have. So why do
you treat us with contempt? Were we not
the first to speak of bringing back our
king?"
But the men of Judah responded even
more harshly than the men of Israel.

Chapter 20

Sheba Rebels Against David

NOW a troublemaker named Sheba
son of Bicri, a Benjamite, happened
to be there. He sounded the trumpet and
shouted,

"We have no share[b] in David,[c]
no part in Jesse's son![d]
Every man to his tent, O Israel!"

2So all the men of Israel deserted David
to follow Sheba son of Bicri. But the men
of Judah stayed by their king all the way
from the Jordan to Jerusalem.

19:21 [f]S Ex 22:28 [g]S 1Sa 12:3; S 26:9
19:22 [h]S 2Sa 2:18; S 16:10 [i]1Sa 11:13
19:23 [j]1Ki 2:8,42
19:24 [k]S 2Sa 4:4
19:25 [l]2Sa 16:17
19:26 [m]S Lev 21:18 [n]S 2Sa 9:2
19:27 [o]S 1Sa 29:9
19:28 [p]S 2Sa 16:8 [q]S 2Sa 9:7,13
19:31 [r]S 2Sa 17:27-29,27; 1Ki 2:7
19:32 [s]1Sa 25:2
19:35 [t]Ps 90:10 [u]2Ch 35:25; Ezr 2:65; Ecc 2:8; 12:1 [v]2Sa 15:33
19:37 [w]S Ge 49:29 [x]Jer 41:17
19:39 [y]S Ge 47:7
19:41 [z]Jdg 8:1; 12:1
19:43 [a]S 2Sa 5:1
20:1 [b]S Ge 31:14 [c]S Ge 29:14; 1Ki 12:16 [d]1Sa 22:7-8

19:24–30 HUMANITY, Relationships—Genuine concern for someone else should be shown as much by deeds as by words.

19:32–37 HUMANITY, Age—David wanted to assist and honor his long-time supporter Barzillai, but the older man chose to stay in familiar surroundings. He did seek to help his young friend (or possibly his son) Kimham. It is a beautiful thing to see old people accept their limitations and seek to avoid forcing unnecessary burdens upon others. Loyalty to and love for hometown and familiar surroundings add richness to senior adult years. Desire to help younger friends and relatives is another admirable trait of senior adults.

3When David returned to his palace in
Jerusalem, he took the ten concubines[e]
he had left to take care of the palace and
put them in a house under guard. He provided for them, but did not lie with them.
They were kept in confinement till the
day of their death, living as widows.
4Then the king said to Amasa,[f] "Summon the men of Judah to come to me
within three days, and be here yourself."
5But when Amasa went to summon Judah, he took longer than the time the
king had set for him.
6David said to Abishai,[g] "Now Sheba
son of Bicri will do us more harm than
Absalom did. Take your master's men and
pursue him, or he will find fortified cities
and escape from us." 7So Joab's men and
the Kerethites[h] and Pelethites and all the
mighty warriors went out under the command of Abishai. They marched out from
Jerusalem to pursue Sheba son of Bicri.
8While they were at the great rock in
Gibeon,[i] Amasa came to meet them.
Joab[j] was wearing his military tunic, and
strapped over it at his waist was a belt
with a dagger in its sheath. As he stepped
forward, it dropped out of its sheath.
9Joab said to Amasa, "How are you, my
brother?" Then Joab took Amasa by the
beard with his right hand to kiss him.
10Amasa was not on his guard against the
dagger[k] in Joab[l]'s hand, and Joab
plunged it into his belly, and his intestines spilled out on the ground. Without
being stabbed again, Amasa died. Then
Joab and his brother Abishai pursued Sheba son of Bicri.
11One of Joab's men stood beside Amasa and said, "Whoever favors Joab, and
whoever is for David, let him follow
Joab!" 12Amasa lay wallowing in his blood
in the middle of the road, and the man
saw that all the troops came to a halt[m]
there. When he realized that everyone
who came up to Amasa stopped, he
dragged him from the road into a field
and threw a garment over him. 13After
Amasa had been removed from the road,
all the men went on with Joab to pursue
Sheba son of Bicri.
14Sheba passed through all the tribes of
Israel to Abel Beth Maacah[h] and through
the entire region of the Berites,[n] who
gathered together and followed him. 15All
the troops with Joab came and besieged
Sheba in Abel Beth Maacah.[o] They built
a siege ramp[p] up to the city, and it stood
against the outer fortifications. While
they were battering the wall to bring it
down, 16a wise woman[q] called from the
city, "Listen! Listen! Tell Joab to come
here so I can speak to him." 17He went
toward her, and she asked, "Are you
Joab?"

"I am," he answered.

She said, "Listen to what your servant
has to say."

"I'm listening," he said.

18She continued, "Long ago they used
to say, 'Get your answer at Abel,' and that
settled it. 19We are the peaceful[r] and
faithful in Israel. You are trying to destroy
a city that is a mother in Israel. Why do
you want to swallow up the LORD's inheritance?"[s]

20"Far be it from me!" Joab replied,
"Far be it from me to swallow up or destroy! 21That is not the case. A man
named Sheba son of Bicri, from the hill
country of Ephraim, has lifted up his hand
against the king, against David. Hand
over this one man, and I'll withdraw from
the city."

The woman said to Joab, "His head[t]
will be thrown to you from the wall."

22Then the woman went to all the people with her wise advice,[u] and they cut
off the head of Sheba son of Bicri and
threw it to Joab. So he sounded the trumpet, and his men dispersed from the city,
each returning to his home. And Joab
went back to the king in Jerusalem.

23Joab[v] was over Israel's entire army;
Benaiah son of Jehoiada was over the Kerethites and Pelethites; 24Adoniram[i][w]
was in charge of forced labor; Jehoshaphat[x] son of Ahilud was recorder; 25Sheva was secretary; Zadok[y] and Abiathar
were priests; 26and Ira the Jairite was David's priest.

Chapter 21

The Gibeonites Avenged

DURING the reign of David, there was
a famine[z] for three successive
years; so David sought[a] the face of the
LORD. The LORD said, "It is on account of
Saul and his blood-stained house; it is because he put the Gibeonites to death."

20:3 [e]S 2Sa 15:16
20:4 [f]S 2Sa 17:25
20:6 [g]2Sa 21:17
20:7 [h]S 1Sa 30:14; S 2Sa 15:18
20:8 [i]S Jos 9:3 [j]S 2Sa 2:18
20:10 [k]S Jdg 3:21 [l]1Ki 2:5
20:12 [m]S 2Sa 2:23
20:14 [n]Nu 21:16
20:15 [o]1Ki 15:20; 2Ki 15:29 [p]Isa 37:33; Jer 6:6; 32:24
20:16 [q]2Sa 14:2
20:19 [r]S Dt 2:26 [s]S 1Sa 26:19
20:21 [t]S 2Sa 4:8
20:22 [u]Ecc 9:13
20:23 [v]S 2Sa 2:28; 8:16-18; 24:2
20:24 [w]1Ki 4:6; 5:14; 12:18; 2Ch 10:18 [x]S 2Sa 8:16
20:25 [y]S 1Sa 2:35; S 2Sa 8:17
21:1 [z]S Ge 12:10; S Dt 32:24 [a]S Ex 32:11

[h]*14* Or *Abel, even Beth Maacah*; also in verse 15
[i]*24* Some Septuagint manuscripts (see also 1 Kings 4:6 and 5:14); Hebrew *Adoram*

20:8–10 CHRISTIAN ETHICS, Murder—Assassination is wrong. Done in the guise of friendship, it becomes even more abominable. Compare 17:25. See note on 13:23–33.
21:1–14 HISTORY, Nature—God's acts in history show His control of nature. Agricultural fertility is in His hands. He can withhold fertility to punish His people. He can restore fertility to show the relationship with His people has been restored. See note on Jdg 8:33–35.
21:1 PRAYER, Intercession—David interceded for his people in face of natural disaster. David looked first to the designs and purposes of the Lord. God honored David's prayer (v 14). Injustice not dealt with may bring God's judgment and His silence. God's people need to seek His direction in times of disaster.

[2]The king summoned the Gibeonites[b] and spoke to them. (Now the Gibeonites were not a part of Israel but were survivors of the Amorites; the Israelites had sworn to ˻spare˼ them, but Saul in his zeal for Israel and Judah had tried to annihilate them.) [3]David asked the Gibeonites, "What shall I do for you? How shall I make amends so that you will bless the LORD's inheritance?"[c]

[4]The Gibeonites answered him, "We have no right to demand silver or gold from Saul or his family, nor do we have the right to put anyone in Israel to death."[d]

"What do you want me to do for you?" David asked.

[5]They answered the king, "As for the man who destroyed us and plotted against us so that we have been decimated and have no place anywhere in Israel, [6]let seven of his male descendants be given to us to be killed and exposed[e] before the LORD at Gibeah of Saul—the Lord's chosen[f] one."

So the king said, "I will give them to you."

[7]The king spared Mephibosheth[g] son of Jonathan, the son of Saul, because of the oath[h] before the LORD between David and Jonathan son of Saul. [8]But the king took Armoni and Mephibosheth, the two sons of Aiah's daughter Rizpah,[i] whom she had borne to Saul, together with the five sons of Saul's daughter Merab,[j] whom she had borne to Adriel son of Barzillai the Meholathite.[l] [9]He handed them over to the Gibeonites, who killed and exposed them on a hill before the LORD. All seven of them fell together; they were put to death[k] during the first days of the harvest, just as the barley harvest was beginning.[l]

[10]Rizpah daughter of Aiah took sackcloth and spread it out for herself on a rock. From the beginning of the harvest till the rain poured down from the heavens on the bodies, she did not let the birds of the air touch them by day or the wild animals by night.[m] [11]When David was told what Aiah's daughter Rizpah, Saul's concubine, had done, [12]he went and took the bones of Saul[n] and his son Jonathan from the citizens of Jabesh Gilead.[o] (They had taken them secretly from the public square at Beth Shan,[p] where the Philistines had hung[q] them after they struck Saul down on Gilboa.)[r] [13]David brought the bones of Saul and his son Jonathan from there, and the bones of those who had been killed and exposed were gathered up.

[14]They buried the bones of Saul and his son Jonathan in the tomb of Saul's father Kish, at Zela[s] in Benjamin, and did everything the king commanded. After that,[t] God answered prayer[u] in behalf of the land.[v]

Wars Against the Philistines

21:15–22pp — 1Ch 20:4-8

[15]Once again there was a battle between the Philistines[w] and Israel. David went down with his men to fight against the Philistines, and he became exhausted. [16]And Ishbi-Benob, one of the descendants of Rapha, whose bronze spearhead weighed three hundred shekels[k] and who was armed with a new ˻sword˼, said he would kill David. [17]But Abishai[x] son of Zeruiah came to David's rescue; he struck the Philistine down and killed him. Then David's men swore to him, saying, "Never again will you go out with us to battle, so that the lamp[y] of Israel will not be extinguished.[z]"

[18]In the course of time, there was another battle with the Philistines, at Gob. At that time Sibbecai[a] the Hushathite killed Saph, one of the descendants of Rapha.

[19]In another battle with the Philistines at Gob, Elhanan son of Jaare-Oregim[l] the Bethlehemite killed Goliath[m] the Gittite,[b] who had a spear with a shaft like a weaver's rod.[c]

[20]In still another battle, which took place at Gath, there was a huge man with six fingers on each hand and six toes on each foot—twenty-four in all. He also was descended from Rapha. [21]When he taunted[d] Israel, Jonathan son of Shimeah,[e] David's brother, killed him.

[22]These four were descendants of Rapha in Gath, and they fell at the hands of David and his men.

Chapter 22

David's Song of Praise

22:1–51pp — Ps 18:1-50

DAVID sang[f] to the LORD the words of this song when the LORD delivered

21:2 [b]S Jos 9:15
21:3 [c]S 1Sa 26:19
21:4 [d]Nu 35:33-34
21:6 [e]Nu 25:4 [f]S 1Sa 10:24
21:7 [g]2Sa 4:4 [h]S 1Sa 18:3; S 2Sa 9:7
21:8 [i]2Sa 3:7 [j]1Sa 18:19
21:9 [k]S 2Sa 16:8 [l]S Ru 1:22
21:10 [m]S Ge 40:19; S 1Sa 17:44
21:12 [n]1Sa 31:11-13 [o]S Jdg 21:8; S 1Sa 11:1 [p]S Jos 17:11 [q]1Sa 31:10 [r]S 1Sa 28:4
21:14 [s]Jos 18:28 [t]Jos 7:26 [u]2Sa 24:25 [v]1Ch 8:34
21:15 [w]S 2Sa 5:25
21:17 [x]2Sa 20:6 [y]1Ki 11:36; 15:4; 2Ki 8:19; 2Ch 21:7; Ps 132:17 [z]2Sa 18:3
21:18 [a]1Ch 11:29; 27:11
21:19 [b]S 1Sa 17:4 [c]S 1Sa 17:7
21:21 [d]S 1Sa 17:10 [e]S 1Sa 16:9
22:1 [f]S Ex 15:1

[i]*8* Two Hebrew manuscripts, some Septuagint manuscripts and Syriac (see also 1 Samuel 18:19); most Hebrew and Septuagint manuscripts *Michal*
[k]*16* That is, about 7 1/2 pounds (about 3.5 kilograms)
[l]*19* Or *son of Jair the weaver* [m]*19* Hebrew and Septuagint; 1 Chron. 20:5 *son of Jair killed Lahmi the brother of Goliath*

22:1–51 GOD, Savior—This chapter is almost a commentary on David's understanding of the nature of God. David praised God as his Deliverer and Savior. David used strong poetic imagery to describe the righteous, sovereign power that God had displayed in coming to his rescue. Notice that David pictured God as Savior primarily from the perils of this life. As

him from the hand of all his enemies and
from the hand of Saul. 2He said:

"The LORD is my rock,[g] my fortress[h]
and my deliverer;[i]
3 my God is my rock, in whom I take
refuge,[j]
my shield[k] and the horn[n][l] of my
salvation.
He is my stronghold,[m] my refuge and
my savior—
from violent men you save me.
4I call to the LORD, who is worthy[n] of
praise,
and I am saved from my enemies.

5"The waves[o] of death swirled about
me;
the torrents of destruction
overwhelmed me.
6The cords of the grave[o][p] coiled
around me;
the snares of death confronted me.
7In my distress[q] I called[r] to the LORD;
I called out to my God.
From his temple he heard my voice;
my cry came to his ears.

8"The earth[s] trembled and quaked,[t]
the foundations[u] of the heavens[p]
shook;
they trembled because he was angry.
9Smoke rose from his nostrils;
consuming fire[v] came from his
mouth,
burning coals[w] blazed out of it.
10He parted the heavens and came
down;
dark clouds[x] were under his feet.
11He mounted the cherubim[y] and flew;
he soared[q] on the wings of the
wind.[z]
12He made darkness[a] his canopy around
him—
the dark[r] rain clouds of the sky.
13Out of the brightness of his presence
bolts of lightning[b] blazed forth.
14The LORD thundered[c] from heaven;
the voice of the Most High
resounded.
15He shot arrows[d] and scattered ⌊the
enemies⌋,
bolts of lightning and routed them.
16The valleys of the sea were exposed
and the foundations of the earth laid
bare
at the rebuke[e] of the LORD,
at the blast[f] of breath from his
nostrils.

17"He reached down from on high[g] and
took hold of me;
he drew[h] me out of deep waters.
18He rescued[i] me from my powerful
enemy,
from my foes, who were too strong
for me.
19They confronted me in the day of my
disaster,
but the LORD was my support.[j]
20He brought me out into a spacious[k]
place;

22:2 [g]S 1Sa 2:2 [h]Ps 31:3; 91:2 [i]Ps 144:2 **22:3** [j]S Dt 23:15; S 32:37; Ps 14:6; 31:2; 59:16; 71:7; 91:2; 94:22; Pr 10:29; Isa 25:4; Jer 16:19; Joel 3:16 [k]S Ge 15:1 [l]S Dt 33:17; S Lk 1:69 [m]Ps 9:9; 52:7 **22:4** [n]Ps 48:1; 96:4; 145:3 **22:5** [o]Ps 69:14-15; Jnh 2:3 **22:6** [p]Ps 116:3; Ac 2:24 **22:7** [q]Ge 35:3; S Jdg 2:15; 2Ch 15:4; Ps 4:1; 77:2; 120:1; Isa 26:16 [r]Ps 34:6, 15; 116:4 **22:8** [s]Jdg 5:4; Ps 97:4 [t]S Ex 19:18; S Jdg 5:4; Ps 68:8; 77:18; Jer 10:10 [u]Job 9:6; 26:11; Ps 75:3 **22:9** [v]Ps 50:3; 97:3; Heb 12:29; S Rev 11:5 [w]Isa 6:6; Eze 1:13; 10:2 **22:10** [x]S Ex 19:9; Lev 16:2; S Dt 33:26; 1Ki 8:12; Job 26:9; Ps 104:3; Isa 19:1; Jer 4:13; Na 1:3 **22:11** [y]S Ge 3:24; S Ex 25:22 [z]Ps 104:3 **22:12** [a]S Ex 19:9 **22:13** [b]Job 37:3; Ps 77:18 **22:14** [c]S 1Sa 2:10 **22:15** [d]S Dt 32:23 **22:16** [e]Ps 6:1; 50:8,21; 106:9; Na 1:4 [f]S Ex 14:21; Isa 30:33; 40:24 **22:17** [g]Ps 144:7 [h]Ex 2:10

22:18 [i]Lk 1:71 **22:19** [j]Ps 23:4 **22:20** [k]Job 36:16; Ps 31:8

[n]*3 Horn* here symbolizes strength. [o]*6* Hebrew *Sheol* [p]*8* Hebrew; Vulgate and Syriac (see also Psalm 18:7) *mountains* [q]*11* Many Hebrew manuscripts (see also Psalm 18:10); most Hebrew manuscripts *appeared* [r]*12* Septuagint and Vulgate (see also Psalm 18:11); Hebrew *massed*

---

yet, in Old Testament times, there was little understanding of life after death, a theme greatly developed in the New Testament. Accordingly in the New Testament, the idea of God as Savior takes on a vast new spiritual dimension largely unknown in the Old Testament. That should not lead us to miss the strong truth here that God's work as Savior includes delivering His people in time of danger and need.

22:1–51 EVIL AND SUFFERING, God's Present Help—David praised God for helping him in the midst of adversity. Even the best king of Israel had faced suffering. God does not lead us away from suffering. He helps us in it. We respond to His help in praise and thanks.

22:1–51 HOLY SCRIPTURE, Collection—This chapter appears also as Ps 18. Compare also Pss 14 and 53. God inspired authors. He also inspired the community of His people as they collected various inspired writings and placed them in the larger body of material, the Bible. His direction led to some words being included more than once.

22:1–51 HISTORY, Worship—Individual and national recognition of God's acts in history lead to praise of God. Such praise often describes the historical experiences with God.

22:1–51 WORSHIP, Reverence—See note on Ex 15:1–21. David's song of praise to God reveals the attitudes required for true worship: reverence (vv 1–4,8–20), humility (vv 26–30), submission (vv 22–25), thanksgiving (vv 31–43), and rejoicing (vv 44–51). Jesus declared that God seeks such worship (Jn 4:24). The second commandment specifically states that no one else should receive such worship (Ex 20:4–6). The attitudes which we bring to the experience of worship are vital for our Christian lives because worship is an essential part of each Christian's life. Compare Ro 12:1–2; Heb 12:28–29.

22:1–51 PRAYER, Praise—The historical books preserve songs from "Israel's singer of songs" (23:1). Compare 1:19–27; 3:33–34; 23:1–7; 1 Ch 16:8–36; 29:10–13. The psalms characteristically alternate between objective nouns or second person pronouns describing the greatness and glory of the Lord and subjective first person pronouns describing the psalmist's position and security in the Lord, or his feats under the Lord's hand and power. In this song, David opened with praise identifying the Lord with strength and using various military figures of the day. In v 7, he "called to the LORD," and the Lord heard. See note on Ge 4:26. Some of the figures in vv 8–16 may have been inspired by the Sinai experience. Vv 17–25 are David's personal experience of the Lord. In vv 26–37, David described God's ways, and in vv 38–51 he told of his exploits and position in the Lord. Praise centers on who God is, what He has done to save His people as a group and individually, and what He has empowered His servants to do. The *I* of prayer is always subordinated to the *You* of God.

22:6 LAST THINGS, Intermediate State—See note on Isa 14:9.

22:17–20 SALVATION, Initiative—Compare Ps 18:16–19. David gave God credit for rescue from his enemies. We do not have to stand on tiptoes and strain to have fellowship with God. God takes the initiative in saving us.

he rescued[l] me because he
delighted[m] in me.[n]
21"The LORD has dealt with me
according to my
righteousness;[o]
according to the cleanness[p] of my
hands[q] he has rewarded me.
22For I have kept[r] the ways of the LORD;
I have not done evil by turning from
my God.
23All his laws are before me;[s]
I have not turned[t] away from his
decrees.
24I have been blameless[u] before him
and have kept myself from sin.
25The LORD has rewarded me according
to my righteousness,[v]
according to my cleanness[s] in his
sight.

26"To the faithful you show yourself
faithful,
to the blameless you show yourself
blameless,
27to the pure[w] you show yourself pure,
but to the crooked you show
yourself shrewd.[x]
28You save the humble,[y]
but your eyes are on the haughty[z]
to bring them low.[a]
29You are my lamp,[b] O LORD;
the LORD turns my darkness into
light.
30With your help I can advance against a
troop[t];
with my God I can scale a wall.

31"As for God, his way is perfect;[c]
the word of the LORD is flawless.[d]
He is a shield[e]
for all who take refuge in him.
32For who is God besides the LORD?
And who is the Rock[f] except our
God?[g]
33It is God who arms me with strength[u]
and makes my way perfect.
34He makes my feet like the feet of a
deer;[h]
he enables me to stand on the
heights.[i]
35He trains my hands[j] for battle;
my arms can bend a bow[k] of
bronze.
36You give me your shield[l] of victory;
you stoop down to make me great.
37You broaden the path[m] beneath me,
so that my ankles do not turn.

38"I pursued my enemies and crushed
them;
I did not turn back till they were
destroyed.

22:20 [l]Ps 118:5 [m]Ps 22:8; Isa 42:1; Mt 12:18 [n]S 2Sa 15:26
22:21 [o]S 1Sa 26:23 [p]Ps 26:6 [q]Job 17:9; 22:30; 42:7-8; Ps 24:4
22:22 [r]Ge 18:19; Ps 128:1; Pr 8:32
22:23 [s]Dt 6:4-9; Ps 119:30-32 [t]Ps 119:102
22:24 [u]S Ge 6:9; Eph 1:4
22:25 [v]S 1Sa 26:23
22:27 [w]Mt 5:8 [x]Lev 26:23-24
22:28 [y]S Ex 3:8; 1Sa 2:8-9; Ps 72:12-13 [z]Ps 131:1; Pr 30:13; Da 4:31; Zep 3:11 [a]Isa 2:12, 17; 5:15; S Lk 1:51
22:29 [b]Ps 27:1; Isa 2:5; Mic 7:8; Rev 21:23; 22:5
22:31 [c]S Dt 32:4; Mt 5:48 [d]Ps 12:6; 119:140; Pr 30:5-6 [e]S Ge 15:1
22:32 [f]S 1Sa 2:2 [g]S 2Sa 7:22
22:34 [h]Isa 35:6; Hab 3:19 [i]S Dt 32:13
22:35 [j]Ps 144:1 [k]Ps 7:12; 11:2; Zec 9:13
22:36 [l]Eph 6:16
22:37 [m]Pr 4:11
22:39 [n]Ps 44:5; 110:6; Mal 4:3
22:40 [o]S Jos 10:24; S 1Ki 5:3
22:41 [p]S Ex 23:27
22:42 [q]Isa 1:15 [r]Ps 50:22 [s]S 1Sa 14:37
22:43 [t]1Ki 20:10; 2Ki 13:7; Isa 41:2; Am 1:3 [u]Ps 7:5; Isa 41:25; Mic 7:10; Zec 10:5 [v]Isa 5:25; 10:6; 22:5; Mic 7:10
22:44 [w]S Ex 11:3; S 2Sa 3:1 [x]Dt 28:13 [y]S 2Sa 8:1-14; Isa 55:3-5
22:45 [z]Ps 66:3; 81:15 [a]S Dt 33:29
22:46 [b]Mic 7:17
22:47 [c]S Ex 15:2 [d]Dt 32:15; Ps 18:31; 89:26; 95:1
22:48 [e]S Nu 31:3 [f]Ps 144:2
22:49 [g]Ps 140:1,4 [h]Ps 27:6
22:50 [i]Ps 9:11; 47:6; 68:4 [j]Ro 15:9*
22:51 [k]Ps 21:1; 144:9-10 [l]1Sa 16:13; Ps 89:20; Ac 13:23 [m]S 2Sa 7:13 [n]Ps 89:24,29

39I crushed[n] them completely, and they
could not rise;
they fell beneath my feet.
40You armed me with strength for battle;
you made my adversaries bow at my
feet.[o]
41You made my enemies turn their
backs[p] in flight,
and I destroyed my foes.
42They cried for help,[q] but there was no
one to save them—[r]
to the LORD, but he did not
answer.[s]
43I beat them as fine as the dust[t] of the
earth;
I pounded and trampled[u] them like
mud[v] in the streets.

44"You have delivered[w] me from the
attacks of my people;
you have preserved[x] me as the head
of nations.
People[y] I did not know are subject to
me,
45 and foreigners come cringing[z] to
me;
as soon as they hear me, they obey
me.[a]
46They all lose heart;
they come trembling[v][b] from their
strongholds.

47"The LORD lives! Praise be to my Rock!
Exalted[c] be God, the Rock, my
Savior![d]
48He is the God who avenges[e] me,[f]
who puts the nations under me,
49 who sets me free from my
enemies.[g]
You exalted me[h] above my foes;
from violent men you rescued me.
50Therefore I will praise you, O LORD,
among the nations;
I will sing praises[i] to your name.[j]
51He gives his king great victories;[k]
he shows unfailing kindness to his
anointed,[l]
to David[m] and his descendants
forever."[n]

Chapter 23

The Last Words of David

THESE are the last words of David:
"The oracle of David son of Jesse,

[s]*25* Hebrew; Septuagint and Vulgate (see also Psalm 18:24) *to the cleanness of my hands* [t]*30* Or *can run through a barricade* [u]*33* Dead Sea Scrolls, some Septuagint manuscripts, Vulgate and Syriac (see also Psalm 18:32); Masoretic Text *who is my strong refuge* [v]*46* Some Septuagint manuscripts and Vulgate (see also Psalm 18:45); Masoretic Text *they arm themselves.*

22:31 HOLY SCRIPTURE, Inspired—God's Word has no error mixed in.

23:1-4 HOLY SPIRIT, Revelation—Different gifts may come to the same person from the same Spirit. The Spirit's

the oracle of the man exalted[o] by
the Most High,
the man anointed[p] by the God of
Jacob,
Israel's singer of songs[w]:
2 "The Spirit[q] of the LORD spoke
through me;
his word was on my tongue.
3 The God of Israel spoke,
the Rock[r] of Israel said to me:
'When one rules over men in
righteousness,[s]
when he rules in the fear[t] of God,[u]
4 he is like the light[v] of morning[w] at
sunrise[x]
on a cloudless morning,
like the brightness after rain[y]
that brings the grass from the earth.'

5 "Is not my house right with God?
Has he not made with me an
everlasting covenant,[z]
arranged and secured in every part?
Will he not bring to fruition my
salvation
and grant me my every desire?
6 But evil men are all to be cast aside
like thorns,[a]
which are not gathered with the
hand.
7 Whoever touches thorns
uses a tool of iron or the shaft of a
spear;
they are burned up where they lie."

David's Mighty Men

23:8–39pp — 1Ch 11:10–41

8 These are the names of David's
mighty men:[b]
Josheb-Basshebeth,[x][c] a Tahkemo-
nite,[y] was chief of the Three; he raised
his spear against eight hundred men,
whom he killed[z] in one encounter.
9 Next to him was Eleazar son of Dodai[d] the Ahohite.[e] As one of the three
mighty men, he was with David when
they taunted the Philistines gathered ⌞at
Pas Dammim⌟[a] for battle. Then the men
of Israel retreated, 10 but he stood his
ground and struck down the Philistines
till his hand grew tired and froze to the
sword. The LORD brought about a great
victory that day. The troops returned to
Eleazar, but only to strip the dead.
11 Next to him was Shammah son of
Agee the Hararite. When the Philistines
banded together at a place where there
was a field full of lentils, Israel's troops
fled from them. 12 But Shammah took his
stand in the middle of the field. He defended it and struck the Philistines down,
and the LORD brought about a great victory.
13 During harvest time, three of the
thirty chief men came down to David at
the cave of Adullam,[f] while a band of
Philistines was encamped in the Valley of
Rephaim.[g] 14 At that time David was in
the stronghold,[h] and the Philistine garrison was at Bethlehem.[i] 15 David longed
for water and said, "Oh, that someone
would get me a drink of water from the
well near the gate of Bethlehem!" 16 So
the three mighty men broke through the
Philistine lines, drew water from the well
near the gate of Bethlehem and carried it
back to David. But he refused to drink it;
instead, he poured[j] it out before the
LORD. 17 "Far be it from me, O LORD, to do
this!" he said. "Is it not the blood[k] of
men who went at the risk of their lives?"
And David would not drink it.
Such were the exploits of the three
mighty men.
18 Abishai[l] the brother of Joab son of
Zeruiah was chief of the Three.[b] He

23:1 [o]S Ex 11:3; Ps 78:70-71; 89:27 [p]1Sa 2:10,35; Ps 18:50; 20:6; 84:9; Isa 45:1; Hab 3:13
23:2 [q]Mt 22:43; Mk 12:36; 2Pe 1:21
23:3 [r]Dt 32:4; S 1Sa 2:2; Ps 18:31 [s]Ps 72:3 [t]S Ge 42:18 [u]Isa 11:1-5
23:4 [v]Jn 1:5 [w]Ps 119:147; 130:6; Pr 4:18 [x]S Jdg 5:31; Mt 13:43 [y]S Dt 32:2
23:5 [z]S Ge 9:16; Ps 89:29
23:6 [a]Isa 5:6; 9:18; 10:17; 27:4; 33:12; Mic 7:4; Na 1:10; Mt 13:40-41
23:8 [b]S 2Sa 17:10 [c]1Ch 27:2
23:9 [d]1Ch 27:4 [e]1Ch 8:4
23:13 [f]S Ge 38:1; S Jos 12:15 [g]S Jos 17:15
23:14 [h]1Sa 22:4-5; S 2Sa 5:17 [i]Ru 1:19
23:16 [j]S Ge 35:14
23:17 [k]Lev 17:10-12
23:18 [l]S 1Sa 26:6

[w] *1* Or *Israel's beloved singer* [x] *8* Hebrew; some Septuagint manuscripts suggest *Ish-Bosheth,* that is, *Esh-Baal* (see also 1 Chron. 11:11 *Jashobeam*). [y] *8* Probably a variant of *Hacmonite* (see 1 Chron. 11:11) [z] *8* Some Septuagint manuscripts (see also 1 Chron. 11:11); Hebrew and other Septuagint manuscripts *Three; it was Adino the Eznite who killed eight hundred men* [a] *9* See 1 Chron. 11:13; Hebrew *gathered there.* [b] *18* Most Hebrew manuscripts (see also 1 Chron. 11:20); two Hebrew manuscripts and Syriac *Thirty*

continual presence enabled David to lead God's people (1 Sa 16:13). The Spirit's inspiring presence revealed to David the contents of his poetry. This poem is called an oracle (Hebrew *ne'um*), the word God gives a prophet (Nu 14:28; 2 Ki 9:26; Isa 30:1; Mal 1:2). Not all kings had the gift of inspired speech. See 1 Sa 10:13. This inspired speech pointed to the moral qualities of God's leader. Compare Gal 5:22.

23:1–3 HOLY SCRIPTURE, Inspired—David described his song as an oracle, a term normally used for prophetic words. His words were inspired by God's Spirit.

23:5 SALVATION, Initiative—See notes on 22:17–20; Ex 14:13,30.

23:5 THE CHURCH, Covenant People—God established an everlasting covenant with David (ch 7), promising that He would build David a house—an everlasting dynasty to occupy the throne of Israel. New Testament writers looked backward to David as they reflected on the coming of the Messiah. Just as David took comfort in the assurance of God's perpetual care and guidance, we can rejoice because God abides with us. God has promised never to forsake us. We can depend on God for help and guidance.

23:8–39 HISTORY, God's Leaders—God honors leaders of His people even when they do not occupy primary positions of responsibility. The faithful soldiers of David's army received an eternal place of honor in God's Word even though their exploits were not all enumerated.

23:16–17 PRAYER, Commitment—David's high-minded gesture was not a waste of the water; his pouring out of the water could only have suggested the drink offerings that accompanied the grain offerings, which in turn were to be made in connection with the burnt offerings (Nu 28:1–12). It is not unlike the figure of the drink offering which Paul used to describe the pouring out of his life (Php 2:17). David prayed a confession of commitment through his symbolic act. Such acts can speak more powerfully to God than do our words.

raised his spear against three hundred
men, whom he killed, and so he became
as famous as the Three. 19 Was he not
held in greater honor than the Three? He
became their commander, even though
he was not included among them.
20 Benaiah[m] son of Jehoiada was a valiant fighter from Kabzeel,[n] who performed great exploits. He struck down
two of Moab's best men. He also went
down into a pit on a snowy day and killed
a lion. 21 And he struck down a huge
Egyptian. Although the Egyptian had a
spear in his hand, Benaiah went against
him with a club. He snatched the spear
from the Egyptian's hand and killed him
with his own spear. 22 Such were the exploits of Benaiah son of Jehoiada; he too
was as famous as the three mighty men.
23 He was held in greater honor than any
of the Thirty, but he was not included
among the Three. And David put him in
charge of his bodyguard.

24 Among the Thirty were:
Asahel[o] the brother of Joab,
Elhanan son of Dodo from Bethlehem,
25 Shammah the Harodite,[p]
Elika the Harodite,
26 Helez[q] the Paltite,
Ira[r] son of Ikkesh from Tekoa,
27 Abiezer[s] from Anathoth,[t]
Mebunnai[c] the Hushathite,
28 Zalmon the Ahohite,
Maharai[u] the Netophathite,[v]
29 Heled[d][w] son of Baanah the Netophathite,
Ithai son of Ribai from Gibeah[x] in
Benjamin,
30 Benaiah the Pirathonite,[y]
Hiddai[e] from the ravines of Gaash,[z]
31 Abi-Albon the Arbathite,
Azmaveth the Barhumite,[a]
32 Eliahba the Shaalbonite,
the sons of Jashen,
Jonathan 33 son of[f] Shammah the
Hararite,
Ahiam son of Sharar[g] the Hararite,
34 Eliphelet son of Ahasbai the Maacathite,[b]
Eliam[c] son of Ahithophel[d] the
Gilonite,
35 Hezro the Carmelite,[e]
Paarai the Arbite,
36 Igal son of Nathan from Zobah,[f]
the son of Hagri,[h]
37 Zelek the Ammonite,
Naharai the Beerothite,[g] the armor-bearer of Joab son of Zeruiah,
38 Ira the Ithrite,[h]
Gareb the Ithrite
39 and Uriah[i] the Hittite.
There were thirty-seven in all.

Chapter 24

David Counts the Fighting Men

24:1–17pp — 1Ch 21:1–17

24 AGAIN[j] the anger of the LORD burned
against Israel,[k] and he incited David
against them, saying, "Go and take a census of[l] Israel and Judah."
2 So the king said to Joab[m] and the army
commanders[i] with him, "Go throughout
the tribes of Israel from Dan to Beersheba[n] and enroll[o] the fighting men, so that
I may know how many there are."

23:20 [m]S 2Sa 8:18; 1Ch 27:5 [n]Jos 15:21
23:24 [o]S 2Sa 2:18
23:25 [p]Jdg 7:1
23:26 [q]1Ch 27:10 [r]1Ch 27:9
23:27 [s]1Ch 27:12 [t]S Jos 21:18
23:28 [u]1Ch 27:13 [v]2Ki 25:23; Ezr 2:22; Ne 7:26; Jer 40:8
23:29 [w]1Ch 27:15 [x]S Jos 15:57
23:30 [y]S Jdg 12:13 [z]Jos 24:30
23:31 [a]2Sa 3:16
23:34 [b]S Dt 3:14 [c]S 2Sa 11:3 [d]S 2Sa 15:12
23:35 [e]S Jos 12:22
23:36 [f]S 1Sa 14:47
23:37 [g]S Jos 9:17
23:38 [h]1Ch 2:53
23:39 [i]2Sa 11:3
24:1 [j]S Jos 9:15 [k]Job 1:6; Zec 3:1 [l]S Ex 30:12; 1Ch 27:23
24:2 [m]S 2Sa 20:23 [n]S 2Sa 3:10 [o]2Ch 2:17; 17:14; 25:5

[c]27 Hebrew; some Septuagint manuscripts (see also 1 Chron. 11:29) *Sibbecai* [d]29 Some Hebrew manuscripts and Vulgate (see also 1 Chron. 11:30); most Hebrew manuscripts *Heleb* [e]30 Hebrew; some Septuagint manuscripts (see also 1 Chron. 11:32) *Hurai* [f]33 Some Septuagint manuscripts (see also 1 Chron. 11:34); Hebrew does not have *son of.* [g]33 Hebrew; some Septuagint manuscripts (see also 1 Chron. 11:35) *Sacar* [h]36 Some Septuagint manuscripts (see also 1 Chron. 11:38); Hebrew *Haggadi* [i]2 Septuagint (see also verse 4 and 1 Chron. 21:2); Hebrew *Joab the army commander*

24:1 EVIL AND SUFFERING, Satan—Why do humans devise and commit evil acts? This passage and its parallel in 1 Ch 21:1 shows the complex nature of the problem. David accepted personal responsibility for the census, confessing his sin (v 10) and accepting God's punishment as deserved (v 14). Yet God's anger at Israel's unspecified sins led Him to motivate David to act. God's punishment thus lay behind David's actions. The later account said Satan was the agent who led David to act (1 Ch 21:1). The personal Satan is mentioned only two other times in the Old Testament (Job 1:6—2:7; Zec 3:1–2), the understanding of Satan finding fuller development only in the New Testament. See note on Mt 4:1–11. The biblical theologian must ask how the concepts of human sin, divine anger and punishment, and Satan relate to one another. God the Creator and only God is ultimately responsible for all human history. See note on 1 Sa 16:13–23. He can use human agents and events to bring about His purposes. Sometimes His purpose is to punish. He may allow Satan to place wrong motivations in a person's heart, thus tempting the person. This does not mean Satan becomes a second god acting outside God's control. Ultimately, God allowed Satan to tempt people. God can use human response to Satan's actions to bring about His purposes. Even as God and Satan work, the human person remains responsible. Neither divine nor satanic acts remove human freedom. David had to decide to act contrary to God's will. His act was sin. Satan made me do it is no excuse. We can refuse to do Satan's bidding.

24:1–10 SIN, Against God—Business activities fall under God's judgment when they go against God's expressed will. The understanding in this text is quite complex. God's anger at an undescribed sin of the nation led Him to give David the idea of a military census to assess his power. Joab, the general, knew this was opposed to Israel's traditional reliance on God for military victory. 1 Ch 21:1 involves Satan in the activity. Apparently we learn here that God permits humans to face temptation. At times such temptation results not in isolation but from a string of sinful events which rouse God's anger and provide an opening for Satan. However sin rises, it results ultimately from personal decision to promote personal pride and refuse to trust God. Thus, military and business decisions can be sins against God.

3But Joab[p] replied to the king, "May
the LORD your God multiply the troops a
hundred times over,[q] and may the eyes
of my lord the king see it. But why does
my lord the king want to do such a
thing?"
4The king's word, however, overruled
Joab and the army commanders; so they
left the presence of the king to enroll the
fighting men of Israel.
5After crossing the Jordan, they
camped near Aroer,[r] south of the town
in the gorge, and then went through Gad
and on to Jazer.[s] 6They went to Gilead
and the region of Tahtim Hodshi, and on
to Dan Jaan and around toward Sidon.[t]
7Then they went toward the fortress of
Tyre[u] and all the towns of the Hivites[v]
and Canaanites. Finally, they went on to
Beersheba[w] in the Negev[x] of Judah.
8After they had gone through the entire land, they came back to Jerusalem at
the end of nine months and twenty days.
9Joab reported the number of the fighting men to the king: In Israel there were
eight hundred thousand able-bodied men
who could handle a sword, and in Judah
five hundred thousand.[y]
10David was conscience-stricken[z] after
he had counted the fighting men, and he
said to the LORD, "I have sinned[a] greatly
in what I have done. Now, O LORD, I beg
you, take away the guilt of your servant. I
have done a very foolish thing.[b]"
11Before David got up the next morning, the word of the LORD had come to
Gad[c] the prophet, David's seer:[d] 12"Go
and tell David, 'This is what the LORD
says: I am giving you three options.
Choose one of them for me to carry out
against you.'"
13So Gad went to David and said to
him, "Shall there come upon you three[j]
years of famine[e] in your land? Or three
months of fleeing from your enemies
while they pursue you? Or three days of
plague[f] in your land? Now then, think it
over and decide how I should answer the
one who sent me."
14David said to Gad, "I am in deep distress. Let us fall into the hands of the
LORD, for his mercy[g] is great; but do not
let me fall into the hands of men."
15So the LORD sent a plague on Israel
from that morning until the end of the
time designated, and seventy thousand of
the people from Dan to Beersheba died.[h]
16When the angel stretched out his hand
to destroy Jerusalem, the LORD was
grieved[i] because of the calamity and said
to the angel who was afflicting the people, "Enough! Withdraw your hand." The
angel of the LORD[j] was then at the
threshing floor of Araunah the Jebusite.
17When David saw the angel who was
striking down the people, he said to the
LORD, "I am the one who has sinned and
done wrong. These are but sheep.[k] What
have they done?[l] Let your hand fall upon
me and my family."[m]

David Builds an Altar

24:18–25pp — 1Ch 21:18–26

18On that day Gad went to David and
said to him, "Go up and build an altar to
the LORD on the threshing floor of Araunah[n] the Jebusite." 19So David went up,
as the LORD had commanded through
Gad. 20When Araunah looked and saw
the king and his men coming toward him,
he went out and bowed down before the
king with his face to the ground.
21Araunah said, "Why has my lord the
king come to his servant?"
"To buy your threshing floor," David
answered, "so I can build an altar to the
LORD, that the plague on the people may
be stopped."[o]
22Araunah said to David, "Let my lord
the king take whatever pleases him and
offer it up. Here are oxen[p] for the burnt
offering, and here are threshing sledges
and ox yokes for the wood. 23O king,
Araunah gives[q] all this to the king."
Araunah also said to him, "May the LORD
your God accept you."
24But the king replied to Araunah,
"No, I insist on paying you for it. I will
not sacrifice to the LORD my God burnt
offerings that cost me nothing."[r]
So David bought the threshing floor
and the oxen and paid fifty shekels[k][s] of

24:3 [p]S 2Sa 2:18 [q]S Dt 1:11
24:5 [r]S Jos 13:9 [s]S Nu 21:32
24:6 [t]S Ge 10:19; Jdg 1:31
24:7 [u]S Jos 19:29 [v]S Ex 3:8 [w]Ge 21:31 [x]S Dt 1:7
24:9 [y]S Nu 1:44-46
24:10 [z]S 1Sa 24:5 [a]S Nu 22:34 [b]S Nu 12:11
24:11 [c]S 1Sa 22:5 [d]1Sa 9:9
24:13 [e]Dt 28:38-42,48; S 32:24; Eze 14:21 [f]S Ex 5:3; S 30:12; S Lev 26:25; Dt 28:21-22,27-28, 35
24:14 [g]Ne 9:28; Ps 4:1; 51:1; 86:5; 103:8,13; 119:132; 130:4; Isa 54:7; 55:7; Jer 33:8; 42:12; Da 9:9
24:15 [h]1Ch 27:24
24:16 [i]S Ge 6:6 [j]S Ge 16:7; S 19:13; S Ex 12:23; Ac 12:23
24:17 [k]Ps 74:1; 100:3; Jer 49:20 [l]S Ge 18:23 [m]Jnh 1:12
24:18 [n]Ge 22:2; 2Ch 3:1
24:21 [o]Nu 16:44-50
24:22 [p]S 1Sa 6:14
24:23 [q]Ge 23:11
24:24 [r]Mal 1:13-14 [s]S Ge 23:16

[j]*13* Septuagint (see also 1 Chron. 21:12); Hebrew *seven* [k]*24* That is, about 1 1/4 pounds (about 0.6 kilogram)

24:10 PRAYER, Confession—David confessed his sin voluntarily before God confronted him. Compare ch 12. Confession brought forgiveness, but David still had to face the consequences of his actions.

24:11–13 REVELATION, Word—God's revealed word can change from blessing to judgment when His people follow selfish human goals rather than God's will. Apparently David lost trust in God's presence and power to control his enemies. God tested him even as He offered options for judgment.

24:17 PRAYER, Intercession—David had a kingly concern for his people afflicted through his sin. Intercession puts the needs of others before our own security.

24:21–25 WORSHIP, Sacrifice—King David revealed the classic attitude of true worship and sacrifice in these verses. Personal cost is always involved in making offerings to the Lord. See note on Lev 7:35–38.

24:24 PRAYER, Intercession—David's offering was a form of intercession for the people. To be a true sacrifice, it had to cost him something. See note on Dt 16:16–17.

24:25 PRAYER, Sovereignty of God—God's sovereignty had been offended in the prideful census. God's deliverance had never depended on numbers (Jdg 7:2–3). God put David to a test (v 13), and David correctly realized that it was to God's mercy that he must appeal. High and kingly sin required high

silver for them. 25David built an altar[t] to
the LORD there and sacrificed burnt offerings and fellowship offerings.[1] Then the
LORD answered prayer[u] in behalf of the
land, and the plague on Israel was
stopped.

24:25 [t]S 1Sa 7:17
24:25 [u]2Sa 21:14

[1]25 Traditionally *peace offerings*

and kingly restitution. God again answered prayer when David submitted obediently to Him.

24:25 EVIL AND SUFFERING, God's Compassion—God does not want His people to suffer. He has both the power and desire to relieve the suffering of His people. He wants to reveal His compassion by making all causes of suffering stop. His people can testify to many experiences in which God's people turn from sin, intercede with God for the good of the "land," and see God stop the cause of suffering. Such experiences cannot be turned into natural laws which guarantee God's compassionate response. Such experiences do encourage us to turn from sin and pray for relief from suffering.

24:25 PRAYER, Answer—God's answers to prayers sometimes take very concrete forms. The sin-punishing plague which killed 70,000 Israelites (v 15) ceased in answer to David's prayer. Prayer is not a people-pleasing ritual. It is a conversation in which the believer expects God to respond.

1 Kings

Theological Setting

The Books of Kings provide a prophetic interpretation of the history of Israel from the reign of Solomon (beginning approximately 1015 BC) to the thirty-seventh year of Jehoiachin in the Babylonian Captivity (approximately 560 BC). The reign of Solomon (1015 to 976 BC) was a time of unprecedented glory. However, Solomon's glory stemmed mainly from the blessings of God upon him for David's sake rather than for Solomon's own personal goodness. Although Solomon loved the Lord (3:3), his devotion was tainted by disobedience (14:21; 3:1,3). In his later life his disobedience led to his apostasy which caused the kingdom to be divided in the days of his son (11:1-13; 12:16-20). Solomon's sin cast a spell of doom across his wisdom, wealth, and building achievements.

The kingdom was divided into Judah and Israel from 974 B.C. until the fall of Israel in 722 B.C. Israel (the Northern Kingdom) was born in sin. Its first king, Jeroboam, led the people from the true worship of God into a false worship of God under the figure of the fertility calf that involved ritual prostitution (12:28-33). Israel never had a king that did right in the sight of the Lord and never experienced a revival of true religion. In contrast, many kings of Judah (the Southern Kingdom) were devoted to the Lord God of Israel, if not with a perfect heart. Moreover, Judah experienced revivals from time to time by which the people were brought back to God. One ruling house after another arose to fall in Israel. In contrast, throughout these turbulent years God maintained a son of David upon the throne of Judah in Jerusalem in faithfulness to His promise (2 Sa 7).

Judah stood alone from 721 BC until 587 BC when they were swept away into the Babylonian captivity. The godly reign of Hezekiah before the exile brought fleeting hope for Judah's salvation, but the unprecedented wickedness of Manasseh's reign led Judah to cross the line of God's mercy; thereafter, He marked Judah for destruction. Even the repentance of Manasseh in his later years and the godly reforms of Josiah could not avert Judah's plunge to destruction. After deportations in 605 BC and 597 BC, the end finally came in 587 BC with the fall of Jerusalem after the combined wicked reigns of four kings. The destruction of Jerusalem and the exile in Babylon did not mark the end of God's people, only His chastisement of them. Significantly, the Book of 2 Kings concluded with Evil-Merodach's gracious care of Jehoiachin. This event foreshadowed the good that God would yet bring upon His people in fulfillment of His promise to David to "establish the throne of his kingdom forever" (2 Sa 7:13).

Conditions during the more than four hundred years of history covered by 1 and 2 Kings were much like those today. God's people were plagued by such problems as false religion (3:3), rampant sex (11:1-8), wickedness in high places (16:30-31), poverty (2 Ki 4:1), death (2 Ki 4:20), and disease (2 Ki 5:1). God's people were constantly urged to forsake the Lord God of Israel to seek refuge in the fertility god Baal who was thought to have power to create new life among animals, crops, and people. Fertility religion was made more popular by its appeal to sensual desires and its easy access in the local high places. God's people were also pressed to adapt their worship to include the religious practices of their conquerors (2 Ki 16:9-18). With the fall of the nation, the destruction of the Temple, and the exile of the nation's leading citizens, despair threatened to conquer the people. The God of Israel appeared to be dead. The prophetic author(s) of Kings saw history from a different perspective. The inspired prophets called upon the people to worship with all their hearts the Lord God of Israel. Their national and individual problems were due to their disobedience to God and their compromise of true worship. God still ruled world history. He had exercised His power to punish His people, just as at other times He had punished foreign nations.

The prophets wrote 1 and 2 Kings to call their nation to God. Especially, they used the books to encourage the Israelites who would soon be brought back from captivity to establish themselves in the land in full obedience to God. The "modern" prophet finds in these books divinely interpreted historical experiences by which to call a nation back to God and encourage wholehearted obedience to God as the only way to build an enduring and blessed nation, society, church, family, and/or individual life.

Theological Outline

1 Kings: God Accomplishes Purposes Through Sinful People.

I. God Works Out His Purposes Even Through Human Revenge and Treachery. (1:1—2:46)

II. God Works Through the Wisdom He Gives His Humble Leader. (3:1—7:51)
   - A. God honors His humble leader's request and equips him with divine wisdom. (3:1-28)
   - B. God's leader administers his people wisely. (4:1-34)
   - C. God's leader wisely follows divine directives to build a house of worship. (5:1—7:51)

III. God Responds to the Worship and Sin of His People. (8:1—11:43)
   - A. God fulfills His promise to His people and their leaders. (8:1-21)
   - B. The incomparable God of heaven hears the prayers of His repentant people anywhere. (8:22-53)
   - C. The faithful God leads His people to faithfulness and calls the nations to recognize His uniqueness. (8:54-61)
   - D. God's people worship joyfully in His house. (8:62-66)
   - E. God's favor is related to His people's obedience. (9:1-9)
   - F. God blesses the efforts of His faithful leader. (9:10—10:29)
   - G. A leader's unfaithfulness brings divine discipline on His people. (11:1-43)

IV. Disobedience Brings Results. (12:1—16:34)
   - A. A leader who refuses to be a servant loses his subjects. (12:1-24)
   - B. False worship leads to doom for God's people and their leader. (12:25—13:10)
   - C. God's prophets must obey God's voice. (13:11-25)
   - D. Disobedience leads a nation to *eternal* ruin. (13:26—14:20)
   - E. God is faithful to His promises even when a people disobey. (14:21—15:8)
   - F. In the midst of disobedience God honors a faithful leader. (15:9-24)
   - G. God fulfills His threats against evil leaders. (15:25—16:34)

V. God Works in History Through His Prophetic Messengers. (17:1—22:53)
   - A. God blesses and brings recognition to His faithful prophet. (17:1-24)
   - B. Yahweh proves His claim to be the only God of Israel through His prophet. (18:1-46)
   - C. God revives His depressed prophet and provides for His purposes to be worked out. (19:1-21)
   - D. God uses a prophet to prove His lordship over history. (20:1-30*a*)
   - E. God sends prophets to condemn His disobedient leaders. (20:30*b*-43)
   - F. God uses His prophets to bring guilty leaders to repentance. (21:1-29)
   - G. God speaks through His chosen prophet, not through those depending on human appointment and provisions. (22:1-40)
   - H. God blesses the faithful but is angry at the disobedient. (22:41-53)

Theological Conclusions

The divinely inspired prophets wrote 1 and 2 Kings to underscore major truths concerning God's sovereign control of history. Here are seven of these truths:

1. God evaluates persons on the basis of their faithfulness to Him.
2. God blesses those who obey Him and honor His house.
3. God overthrows kingdoms because of sin.
4. God uses inspired spokesmen to rebuke sin and to inspire faith in God.
5. God controls daily life to work His kingdom purposes.
6. God hates sin and is determined to remove sin from His people.
7. God is faithful to His promise to establish forever David's house and throne.

The prophets used the introductory and concluding formula for each king to show God's evaluation of the king on the basis of their faithfulness to Him. Notice especially the synchronistic account of the kings of Northern Israel and of Judah. For the kings of Northern Israel, the author included the following information: (1) the date of the king's accession in terms of the year of the reign of each king of Judah; (2) the length of the king's reign; and (3) the condemnation of the king for his walking in the ways of Jeroboam the son of Nebat. The name of the capital from which the king reigned is listed at times.

For the kings of Judah, the introductory formula is expanded to include: (1) (often) the age of the king when he began to reign; (2) the name of the queen mother and sometimes that of her father; and (3) a comparison with David, his forebear, in doing right in the eyes of the Lord. Only Hezekiah and Josiah are given unqualified approval (2 Ki 18:3; 22:2). Six other kings are given modified praise (1 Ki 15:14; 22:43; 2 Ki 12:2-3; 14:3-4; 15:3-4,34-35). The remaining ten kings are condemned because they did evil in the sight of the Lord (1 Ki 15:3; 2 Ki 8:18,27; 16:2; 21:2,20; 23:32,37; 24:9,19).

The prophet(s) who wrote 1 and 2 Kings carefully showed how God blessed those kings who wholeheartedly obeyed Him and honored His house. A notable example is Hezekiah (2 Ki 18:7). A notable exception is the death of good King Josiah who was killed in battle by Neco, the king of Egypt (2 Ki 23:29). However, the later inspired historian explained that Josiah died because he ignored the word of God that came to him through Neco (2 Ch 35:20-23).

The main purpose of the prophets was to show God's overthrow of the Hebrew kingdom because of their sin. Those who reject God, He rejects. The prophets meticulously show how the kingdom was divided and taken away in fulfillment of prophetic condemnation of the sin of the kings and their people. Note the division of the kingdom in the days of Solomon's son (2 Ki 11:9-13,26-30; 12:21-33); the taking of the kingdom from the house of Jeroboam (2 Ki 14:7-17; 15:29); the taking of the kingdom from the house of Baasha (1 Ki 16:1-4,12); the taking of the kingdom from the house of Ahab (16:29-34; 20:42; 21:17-29; 22:37-38; 2 Ki 1:7; 9:24-26,36-37; 10:10-11,17); the taking of the kingdom from the house of Jehu (2 Ki 10:30-31; 15:12); the taking of the kingdom from all the seed of Israel (2 Ki 17:7-41, especially vv 20-23); and the taking of the kingdom from Judah (2 Ki 20:16-18; 21:10-15; 22:16-20; 23:26-27; 24:3-4,20; 25:21). The point is: God rejects and judges those who disobey Him.

The Books of 1 and 2 Kings magnify God's use of His spokesmen the prophets to rebuke sin and to inspire faith in God. Elijah's contest of gods on Mount Carmel is a case in point (1 Ki 18:1-40). The miracle of "the fire of the Lord" (v 38) convinced the people that the Lord God of Israel alone was the one true God, and they reverently followed Him (v 39).

An example of God's control of daily life to work His kingdom purposes is seen in His reassurance and commission of Elijah (19:9-18). Elijah's joy in his triumph over the prophets of Baal was turned to fear, flight, and despair by the wrath of Jezebel, who vowed to kill him as Elijah had killed the prophets of Baal (19:1-8). Elijah fled southward and finally came to Mount Sinai, where God revealed Himself once again. The meaning of God's revelation seems to be that God would not punish sinful Israel and destroy Baalism by spectacular methods such as tornado, earthquake, or fire, but by the seemingly quiet course of daily life (19:11-17). Accordingly, God would avenge Himself by the providentially controlled ministries of Hazael, King of Syria, Jehu, King of Israel, and of Elisha, the prophet, all of whom Elijah was to appoint to their respective offices.

God's use of Jehu to destroy the house of Omri (Ahab) and to purge Baalism from His people illustrates God's hatred of sin and His determination to remove sin from His people (2 Ki 9:1—10:36). Sin is whatever separates God's people from Himself. The prominent sin of the Kings' era was Baalism. Under the guise of serving Baal and honoring his devotees more than Ahab, Jehu assembled in Samaria and put to death all the worshipers of Baal. Jehu was praised for fulfilling his divine commission of destroying the wicked house of Ahab and of purging Baalism from Israel. However, he was condemned because he continued to follow calf worship as instituted by Jeroboam, the first king of the Northern Kingdom (2 Ki 10:28-31). The point is: God wants all sin removed from His people.

The prophets also carefully demonstrated God's faithfulness in fulfilling His promise to David to establish forever his house and his throne (2 Sa 7:12-17, especially v 16). God's covenant with David was both certain and conditional. Disobedience on the part of David's descendants would result in chastisement, but not forfeiture of the covenant. Accordingly, God is seen to have maintained the descendants and the throne of David throughout (1 Ki 2:1-4; 3:14; 9:1-9; 11:9-13,29-39; 12:20; 15:4-5; 2 Ki 8:16-19; 19:34; 20:6; 21:7-9). The division of the kingdom in the days of Solomon's son was an act of chastisement and not a permanent affliction (1 Ki 11:37-39). When wicked Athaliah sought to destroy all of David's descendants, God spared Joash and raised him to the throne of David (2 Ki 11:1-21). Even when the sin of Manasseh produced corruption in the people necessitating expulsion from the land, God maintained the light of David in exile (2 Ki 25:27-30). God's faithfulness led to the sending of the Christ and ultimately will lead to the fulfillment in Christ of all of His redemptive promises.

Contemporary Teaching

The Books of 1 and 2 Kings focus our attention upon God's sovereign control of history to fulfill His kingdom purposes. The inspired books call us: (1) to understand that God will indeed fulfill His kingdom purposes; (2) to obey and serve God with all of our hearts as the only basis for His blessings; (3) to turn from sin as that which separates us from God and hinders His purposes for us; (4) to fulfill our own role as spokespersons for God rebuking sin and inspiring faith in God; and (5) to utilize the divinely interpreted events of 1 and 2 Kings to call our nation to God as the way of perpetuity and blessing.

Chapter 1

Adonijah Sets Himself Up as King

WHEN King David was old and well advanced in years, he could not keep warm even when they put covers over him. 2So his servants said to him, "Let us look for a young virgin to attend the king and take care of him. She can lie beside him so that our lord the king may keep warm."

3Then they searched throughout Israel for a beautiful girl and found Abishag,[a] a Shunammite,[b] and brought her to the king. 4The girl was very beautiful; she took care of the king and waited on him, but the king had no intimate relations with her.

5Now Adonijah,[c] whose mother was Haggith, put himself forward and said, "I will be king." So he got chariots[d] and horses[a] ready, with fifty men to run ahead of him. 6(His father had never interfered[e] with him by asking, "Why do you behave as you do?" He was also very handsome and was born next after Absalom.)

7Adonijah conferred with Joab[f] son of Zeruiah and with Abiathar[g] the priest, and they gave him their support. 8But Zadok[h] the priest, Benaiah[i] son of Jehoiada, Nathan[j] the prophet, Shimei[k] and Rei[b] and David's special guard[l] did not join Adonijah.

9Adonijah then sacrificed sheep, cattle and fattened calves at the Stone of Zoheleth near En Rogel.[m] He invited all his brothers, the king's sons,[n] and all the men of Judah who were royal officials, 10but he did not invite[o] Nathan the prophet or Benaiah or the special guard or his brother Solomon.[p]

11Then Nathan asked Bathsheba,[q] Solomon's mother, "Have you not heard that Adonijah,[r] the son of Haggith, has become king without our lord David's knowing it? 12Now then, let me advise[s] you how you can save your own life and the life of your son Solomon. 13Go in to King David and say to him, 'My lord the king, did you not swear[t] to me your servant: "Surely Solomon your son shall be king after me, and he will sit on my throne"? Why then has Adonijah become king?' 14While you are still there talking to the king, I will come in and confirm what you have said."

15So Bathsheba went to see the aged king in his room, where Abishag[u] the Shunammite was attending him. 16Bathsheba bowed low and knelt before the king.

"What is it you want?" the king asked.

17She said to him, "My lord, you yourself swore[v] to me your servant by the LORD your God: 'Solomon your son shall be king after me, and he will sit on my throne.' 18But now Adonijah has become king, and you, my lord the king, do not know about it. 19He has sacrificed[w] great numbers of cattle, fattened calves, and sheep, and has invited all the king's sons, Abiathar the priest and Joab the commander of the army, but he has not invited Solomon your servant. 20My lord the king, the eyes of all Israel are on you, to learn from you who will sit on the throne of my lord the king after him. 21Otherwise, as soon as my lord the king is laid to rest[x] with his fathers, I and my son Solomon will be treated as criminals."

22While she was still speaking with the king, Nathan the prophet arrived. 23And they told the king, "Nathan the prophet is here." So he went before the king and bowed with his face to the ground.

24Nathan said, "Have you, my lord the king, declared that Adonijah shall be king after you, and that he will sit on your throne? 25Today he has gone down and sacrificed great numbers of cattle, fattened calves, and sheep. He has invited all the king's sons, the commanders of the army and Abiathar the priest. Right now they are eating and drinking with him and saying, 'Long live King Adonijah!' 26But me your servant, and Zadok the priest, and Benaiah son of Jehoiada, and your servant Solomon he did not invite.[y] 27Is this something my lord the king has done without letting his servants know who should sit on the throne of my lord the king after him?"

David Makes Solomon King

1:28–53pp — 1Ch 29:21–25

28Then King David said, "Call in Bath-

1:3 [a]ver 15; S 2Sa 3:7; 1Ki 2:17, 22 [b]S Jos 19:18
1:5 [c]S 2Sa 3:4 [d]S 1Sa 8:11
1:6 [e]1Sa 3:13
1:7 [f]S 2Sa 2:13,18 [g]S 1Sa 22:20
1:8 [h]S 1Sa 2:35; S 2Sa 8:17 [i]S 2Sa 8:18 [j]S 2Sa 7:2 [k]1Ki 4:18 [l]2Sa 23:8
1:9 [m]S 2Sa 17:17 [n]1Ch 29:24
1:10 [o]ver 26 [p]S 2Sa 12:24
1:11 [q]2Sa 12:24 [r]S 2Sa 3:4
1:12 [s]Pr 15:22
1:13 [t]ver 17,30
1:15 [u]S ver 3
1:17 [v]S ver 13
1:19 [w]ver 9
1:21 [x]S Ge 15:15; 1Ki 2:10
1:26 [y]ver 10

[a]5 Or *charioteers* [b]8 Or *and his friends*

1:1—2:46 CHRISTIAN ETHICS, Murder—Solomon established his throne through intrigue and regular use of the death penalty. The Bible reports the facts without giving any decision concerning the morality or justice of Solomon's acts. The larger biblical picture shows that murder for political reasons is wrong. See notes on Jdg 8:10–21; 2 Sa 20:8–10.

1:6 FAMILY, Parental Failure—Unwillingness to confront children when their actions are contrary to family expectations encourages them to continue those actions. David failed to exercise parental responsibility in this case. The long-range result was revolt and, ultimately, death for David's son.

1:9–10 PRAYER, Hindrances—Insincere worship for an ulterior motive cannot involve true prayer communication with God. Abiathar was the high priest and the proper one to anoint the next king. Samuel had offered sacrifices when Saul (1 Sa 10:8) and David (1 Sa 16:2) were anointed. It was Zadok who later anointed Solomon (v 39). Abiathar was banished (2:26–27).

1:13 PRAYER, Vow—David had made the vow (v 30) and would be bound to it.

sheba." So she came into the king's presence and stood before him.

29The king then took an oath: "As surely as the LORD lives, who has delivered me out of every trouble,[z] 30I will surely carry out today what I swore[a] to you by the LORD, the God of Israel: Solomon your son shall be king after me, and he will sit on my throne in my place."

31Then Bathsheba bowed low with her face to the ground and, kneeling before the king, said, "May my lord King David live forever!"

32King David said, "Call in Zadok[b] the priest, Nathan the prophet and Benaiah son of Jehoiada." When they came before the king, 33he said to them: "Take your lord's servants with you and set Solomon my son on my own mule[c] and take him down to Gihon.[d] 34There have Zadok the priest and Nathan the prophet anoint[e] him king over Israel. Blow the trumpet[f] and shout, 'Long live King Solomon!' 35Then you are to go up with him, and he is to come and sit on my throne and reign in my place. I have appointed him ruler over Israel and Judah."

36Benaiah son of Jehoiada answered the king, "Amen! May the LORD, the God of my lord the king, so declare it. 37As the LORD was with my lord the king, so may he be with[g] Solomon to make his throne even greater[h] than the throne of my lord King David!"

38So Zadok[i] the priest, Nathan the prophet, Benaiah son of Jehoiada, the Kerethites[j] and the Pelethites went down and put Solomon on King David's mule and escorted him to Gihon.[k] 39Zadok the priest took the horn of oil[l] from the sacred tent[m] and anointed Solomon. Then they sounded the trumpet[n] and all the people shouted,[o] "Long live King Solomon!" 40And all the people went up after him, playing flutes[p] and rejoicing greatly, so that the ground shook with the sound.

41Adonijah and all the guests who were with him heard it as they were finishing their feast. On hearing the sound of the trumpet, Joab asked, "What's the meaning of all the noise in the city?"[q]

42Even as he was speaking, Jonathan[r] son of Abiathar the priest arrived. Adonijah said, "Come in. A worthy man like you must be bringing good news."[s]

43"Not at all!" Jonathan answered. "Our lord King David has made Solomon king. 44The king has sent with him Zadok the priest, Nathan the prophet, Benaiah son of Jehoiada, the Kerethites and the Pelethites, and they have put him on the king's mule, 45and Zadok the priest and Nathan the prophet have anointed him king at Gihon. From there they have gone up cheering, and the city resounds[t] with it. That's the noise you hear. 46Moreover, Solomon has taken his seat[u] on the royal throne. 47Also, the royal officials have come to congratulate our lord King David, saying, 'May your God make Solomon's name more famous than yours and his throne greater[v] than yours!' And the king bowed in worship on his bed 48and said, 'Praise be to the LORD, the God of Israel, who has allowed my eyes to see a successor[w] on my throne today.' "

49At this, all Adonijah's guests rose in alarm and dispersed. 50But Adonijah, in fear of Solomon, went and took hold of the horns[x] of the altar. 51Then Solomon was told, "Adonijah is afraid of King Solomon and is clinging to the horns of the altar. He says, 'Let King Solomon swear to me today that he will not put his servant to death with the sword.' "

52Solomon replied, "If he shows himself to be a worthy man, not a hair[y] of his head will fall to the ground; but if evil is found in him, he will die." 53Then King Solomon sent men, and they brought him down from the altar. And Adonijah came and bowed down to King Solomon, and Solomon said, "Go to your home."

Chapter 2

David's Charge to Solomon

2:10–12pp — 1Ch 29:26–28

WHEN the time drew near for David to die,[z] he gave a charge to Solomon his son.

2"I am about to go the way of all the earth,"[a] he said. "So be strong,[b] show

1:29 [z]S 2Sa 4:9
1:30 [a]S ver 13; 1Ch 23:1
1:32 [b]S 1Sa 2:35
1:33 [c]Jdg 10:4; Zec 9:9 [d]ver 38; 2Ch 32:30; 33:14
1:34 [e]S 1Sa 2:35; 10:1 [f]S 2Sa 15:10
1:37 [g]Jos 1:5,17 [h]ver 47
1:38 [i]ver 8 [j]S 1Sa 30:14; S 2Sa 15:18 [k]S ver 33
1:39 [l]S Ex 29:7; S 1Sa 10:1; 2Ki 11:12; Ps 89:20 [m]S Ex 26:1; S 27:21 [n]S 2Sa 15:10; 2Ki 11:14 [o]ver 34; Nu 23:21; Ps 47:5; Zec 9:9
1:40 [p]S 1Sa 10:5
1:41 [q]2Ch 23:12-13
1:42 [r]S 2Sa 15:27, 36 [s]S 2Sa 18:26
1:45 [t]ver 40
1:46 [u]S Dt 17:18
1:47 [v]ver 37
1:48 [w]1Ki 3:6
1:50 [x]S Ex 27:2
1:52 [y]S 1Sa 14:45
2:1 [z]S Ge 27:2; S Nu 27:13
2:2 [a]Jos 23:14 [b]S Jos 1:6

1:36–37 PRAYER, Intercession—Palace politics may crown a ruler, but only God's presence can give success to his reign. The military leader of Solomon's followers (2:34–35; 2 Sa 23:20–23; 1 Ch 27:5) prayed for Solomon. If such a prayer is only polite, traditional language, it is ineffective. If it truly seeks God's leadership for a new regime, it is the appropriate response even for a military hero.

1:47–48 WORSHIP, Individual—See note on Ge 24:26.

1:47–48 PRAYER, Blessing—The royal servants congratulated (Hebrew *barak*, "bless") King David by wishing God's direction on Solomon. Such a blessing recognized David as the earthly source of the happy events and expressed appreciation to him as well as desire for God's blessing on Solomon. See note on vv 36–37.

2:1–9 HUMANITY, Age—"Gray head" is a synonym for age. To approach the grave in peace is to die naturally. "Bring his gray head down to the grave in blood" is to inflict a violent death. David prepared gracefully for his own approaching death, instructing his son how to make the necessary change of leadership. Some of his instructions involved brutal treatment of real or potential enemies. Such action appeared necessary in Solomon's situation, but they are not reported as examples for future generations to follow. Such vengeful acts fall short of Christ's call to love our enemies (Mt 5:44).

2:2–4 HUMANITY, Relationship to God—The expected way to live is in obedience to God. This is the basis for the good

yourself a man, 3and observe[c] what the
LORD your God requires: Walk in his
ways, and keep his decrees and commands, his laws and requirements, as
written in the Law of Moses, so that you
may prosper[d] in all you do and wherever
you go, 4and that the LORD may keep his
promise[e] to me: 'If your descendants
watch how they live, and if they walk
faithfully[f] before me with all their heart
and soul, you will never fail to have a
man on the throne of Israel.'
5"Now you yourself know what Joab[g]
son of Zeruiah did to me—what he did to
the two commanders of Israel's armies,
Abner[h] son of Ner and Amasa[i] son of
Jether. He killed them, shedding their
blood in peacetime as if in battle, and
with that blood stained the belt around
his waist and the sandals on his feet.
6Deal with him according to your wisdom,[j] but do not let his gray head go
down to the grave[c] in peace.
7"But show kindness[k] to the sons of
Barzillai[l] of Gilead and let them be
among those who eat at your table.[m]
They stood by me when I fled from your
brother Absalom.
8"And remember, you have with you
Shimei[n] son of Gera, the Benjamite from
Bahurim, who called down bitter curses
on me the day I went to Mahanaim.[o]
When he came down to meet me at the
Jordan, I swore[p] to him by the LORD: 'I
will not put you to death by the sword.'
9But now, do not consider him innocent.
You are a man of wisdom;[q] you will
know what to do to him. Bring his gray
head down to the grave in blood."
10Then David rested with his fathers
and was buried[r] in the City of David.[s]
11He had reigned[t] forty years over Israel
—seven years in Hebron and thirty-three
in Jerusalem. 12So Solomon sat on the
throne[u] of his father David, and his rule
was firmly established.[v]

Solomon's Throne Established

13Now Adonijah,[w] the son of Haggith,
went to Bathsheba, Solomon's mother.
Bathsheba asked him, "Do you come
peacefully?"[x]
He answered, "Yes, peacefully."
14Then he added, "I have something to
say to you."
"You may say it," she replied.
15"As you know," he said, "the kingdom was mine. All Israel looked to me as

2:3 [c]S Dt 4:6; S 10:12; S 17:14-20; S Jos 1:7 [d]1Ch 22:13
2:4 [e]S 2Sa 7:13,25; 2Ch 23:3 [f]2Ki 18:3-6; 20:3; Ps 26:1-3; 132:12
2:5 [g]S 2Sa 2:18 [h]S 1Sa 14:50; S 2Sa 3:27 [i]S 2Sa 17:25
2:6 [j]ver 9
2:7 [k]S Ge 40:14 [l]S 2Sa 17:27; 19:31-39 [m]S 2Sa 9:7
2:8 [n]ver 36-46; 2Sa 16:5-13 [o]S Ge 32:2 [p]2Sa 19:18-23
2:9 [q]ver 6
2:10 [r]Ac 2:29 [s]S 2Sa 5:7
2:11 [t]S 2Sa 5:4,5
2:12 [u]1Ch 17:14; 29:23; 2Ch 9:8 [v]ver 46; 2Ch 1:1; 12:13; 17:1; 21:4
2:13 [w]S 2Sa 3:4 [x]S 1Sa 16:4
2:17 [y]S 1Ki 1:3
2:19 [z]1Ki 15:13; 2Ki 10:13; 24:15; 2Ch 15:16; Jer 13:18; 22:26; 29:2 [a]Ps 45:9
2:21 [b]1Ki 1:3
2:22 [c]S Ge 22:24; S 1Ki 1:3 [d]1Ch 3:2 [e]S 1Sa 22:20
2:23 [f]S Ru 1:17
2:24 [g]2Sa 7:11
2:25 [h]S 2Sa 8:18 [i]S 2Sa 12:10
2:26 [j]S 1Sa 22:20 [k]S Jos 21:18 [l]S 2Sa 15:24 [m]S 2Sa 15:14
2:27 [n]S 1Sa 2:27-36

their king. But things changed, and the
kingdom has gone to my brother; for it
has come to him from the LORD. 16Now I
have one request to make of you. Do not
refuse me."
"You may make it," she said.
17So he continued, "Please ask King
Solomon—he will not refuse you—to
give me Abishag[y] the Shunammite as my
wife."
18"Very well," Bathsheba replied, "I
will speak to the king for you."
19When Bathsheba went to King Solomon to speak to him for Adonijah, the
king stood up to meet her, bowed down
to her and sat down on his throne. He
had a throne brought for the king's mother,[z] and she sat down at his right hand.[a]
20"I have one small request to make of
you," she said. "Do not refuse me."
The king replied, "Make it, my mother; I will not refuse you."
21So she said, "Let Abishag[b] the Shunammite be given in marriage to your
brother Adonijah."
22King Solomon answered his mother,
"Why do you request Abishag[c] the Shunammite for Adonijah? You might as well
request the kingdom for him—after all,
he is my older brother[d]—yes, for him
and for Abiathar[e] the priest and Joab son
of Zeruiah!"
23Then King Solomon swore by the
LORD: "May God deal with me, be it ever
so severely,[f] if Adonijah does not pay
with his life for this request! 24And now,
as surely as the LORD lives—he who has
established me securely on the throne of
my father David and has founded a dynasty for me as he promised[g]—Adonijah
shall be put to death today!" 25So King
Solomon gave orders to Benaiah[h] son of
Jehoiada, and he struck down Adonijah
and he died.[i]
26To Abiathar[j] the priest the king said,
"Go back to your fields in Anathoth.[k]
You deserve to die, but I will not put you
to death now, because you carried the
ark[l] of the Sovereign LORD before my father David and shared all my father's
hardships."[m] 27So Solomon removed Abiathar from the priesthood of the LORD,
fulfilling[n] the word the LORD had spoken
at Shiloh about the house of Eli.
28When the news reached Joab, who
had conspired with Adonijah though not

[c]6 Hebrew *Sheol*; also in verse 9

---

life, for receiving God's promises.

2:4,24,27 GOD, Faithfulness—God is true to His word; His promises are fulfilled. If His people are faithful to Him, God will bless them. See note on Ex 13:5,11.

2:23–24 PRAYER, Oath—Solomon confirmed his intention with an oath. The oath here is a curse against his enemy. It invokes God's action against the speaker if he does not carry out his announced intention. Compare Lk 6:28; Ro 12:14. Solomon followed near eastern practices of vengeance in securing his throne against competition. He saw himself as God's agent in securing justice and carefully avoided harming the priest (v 26).

with Absalom, he fled to the tent of the
LORD and took hold of the horns[o] of the
altar. 29King Solomon was told that Joab
had fled to the tent of the LORD and was
beside the altar.[p] Then Solomon ordered
Benaiah[q] son of Jehoiada, "Go, strike
him down!"
30So Benaiah entered the tent[r] of the
LORD and said to Joab, "The king says,
'Come out![s]'"
But he answered, "No, I will die
here."
Benaiah reported to the king, "This is
how Joab answered me."
31Then the king commanded Benaiah,
"Do as he says. Strike him down and bury
him, and so clear me and my father's
house of the guilt of the innocent blood[t]
that Joab shed. 32The LORD will repay[u]
him for the blood he shed,[v] because
without the knowledge of my father David he attacked two men and killed them
with the sword. Both of them—Abner
son of Ner, commander of Israel's army,
and Amasa[w] son of Jether, commander of
Judah's army—were better[x] men and
more upright than he. 33May the guilt of
their blood rest on the head of Joab and
his descendants forever. But on David
and his descendants, his house and his
throne, may there be the LORD's peace
forever."
34So Benaiah[y] son of Jehoiada went up
and struck down Joab[z] and killed him,
and he was buried on his own land[d] in
the desert. 35The king put Benaiah[a] son
of Jehoiada over the army in Joab's position and replaced Abiathar with Zadok[b]
the priest.
36Then the king sent for Shimei[c] and
said to him, "Build yourself a house in
Jerusalem and live there, but do not go
anywhere else. 37The day you leave and
cross the Kidron Valley,[d] you can be sure
you will die; your blood will be on your
own head."[e]
38Shimei answered the king, "What
you say is good. Your servant will do as
my lord the king has said." And Shimei
stayed in Jerusalem for a long time.
39But three years later, two of Shimei's
slaves ran off to Achish[f] son of Maacah,
king of Gath, and Shimei was told, "Your

2:28 [o]S Ex 27:2
2:29 [p]Ex 21:14 [q]ver 25
2:30 [r]2Ki 11:15 [s]Ex 21:14
2:31 [t]S Dt 19:13
2:32 [u]Jdg 9:57 [v]S Ge 4:14; S Jdg 9:24 [w]S 2Sa 17:25 [x]2Ch 21:13
2:34 [y]ver 25 [z]S 2Sa 2:18
2:35 [a]S 2Sa 8:18 [b]S 1Sa 2:35
2:36 [c]S 2Sa 16:5
2:37 [d]S 2Sa 15:23; Jn 18:1 [e]S Lev 20:9
2:39 [f]1Sa 27:2
2:42 [g]S 2Sa 19:23
2:44 [h]2Sa 16:5-13
2:45 [i]S 2Sa 7:13
2:46 [j]S 2Sa 8:18 [k]S ver 8 [l]S ver 12
3:1 [m]1Ki 7:8; 11:1-13 [n]1Ki 9:24; 2Ch 8:11 [o]2Sa 5:7; 1Ki 2:10 [p]S 2Sa 7:2; 1Ki 9:10
3:2 [q]Lev 17:3-5; S 26:30; Dt 12:14; 1Ki 15:14; 22:43 [r]S Dt 14:23
3:3 [s]Dt 6:5; Ps 31:23; 145:20 [t]S Dt 10:12; S Jos 1:7 [u]S Dt 17:19; S 1Ki 14:8 [v]S ver 2; Lev 17:3-5; 2Ki 12:3; 15:4,35; 16:4; 21:3
3:4 [w]S Jos 9:3
3:5 [x]1Ki 9:2; 11:9

slaves are in Gath." 40At this, he saddled
his donkey and went to Achish at Gath in
search of his slaves. So Shimei went away
and brought the slaves back from Gath.
41When Solomon was told that Shimei
had gone from Jerusalem to Gath and had
returned, 42the king summoned Shimei
and said to him, "Did I not make you
swear by the LORD and warn[g] you, 'On
the day you leave to go anywhere else,
you can be sure you will die'? At that
time you said to me, 'What you say is
good. I will obey.' 43Why then did you
not keep your oath to the LORD and obey
the command I gave you?"
44The king also said to Shimei, "You
know in your heart all the wrong[h] you
did to my father David. Now the LORD
will repay you for your wrongdoing. 45But
King Solomon will be blessed, and David's throne will remain secure[i] before
the LORD forever."
46Then the king gave the order to Benaiah[j] son of Jehoiada, and he went out
and struck Shimei[k] down and killed him.
The kingdom was now firmly established[l] in Solomon's hands.

Chapter 3

Solomon Asks for Wisdom

3:4–15pp — 2Ch 1:2–13

SOLOMON made an alliance with Pharaoh king of Egypt and married[m] his
daughter.[n] He brought her to the City of
David[o] until he finished building his palace[p] and the temple of the LORD, and the
wall around Jerusalem. 2The people, however, were still sacrificing at the high
places,[q] because a temple had not yet
been built for the Name[r] of the LORD.
3Solomon showed his love[s] for the LORD
by walking[t] according to the statutes[u] of
his father David, except that he offered
sacrifices and burned incense on the high
places.[v]
4The king went to Gibeon[w] to offer
sacrifices, for that was the most important high place, and Solomon offered a
thousand burnt offerings on that altar. 5At
Gibeon the LORD appeared[x] to Solomon

[d]34 Or *buried in his tomb*

2:42–43 PRAYER, Vow—Vows were binding since they were made in God's name. Compare Nu 30:2.

3:3,14 CHRISTIAN ETHICS, Moral Imperatives—See notes on Lev 26:3–45; Dt 28:1–68. God rewards obedience in unexpected ways. He does not release us from responsibility. A good family heritage should encourage us to follow God's commands.

3:3 PRAYER, Hindrances—High places were forbidden (Dt 12:2–4). See note on Dt 12:5. This weakness would ultimately lead Solomon into apostasy. Allowing allegiance to other gods weakens prayer life with the only God.

3:4–5 REVELATION, Dreams—God revealed Himself through a dream to the new leader and gave him an opportunity to request a special favor from God. Solomon had specifically gone to a place of worship to offer sacrifice and seek God's guidance. He probably spent the night, as did Jacob, seeking a word in a holy place (Ge 28:10–21).

3:5–14 PRAYER, Petition—The import of this prayer and answer suggest the pattern of Jesus' teaching in the Sermon on the Mount. God invited Solomon to ask; Jesus said, "Ask and it will be given to you" (Mt 7:7). God commended Solomon for not asking for long life, wealth, and victory. Jesus instructed the disciples not to worry about physical needs (Mt 6:25–32). Because Solomon's request was godly, God promised to grant

during the night in a dream,[y] and God said, "Ask[z] for whatever you want me to give you."

6Solomon answered, "You have shown great kindness to your servant, my father David, because he was faithful[a] to you and righteous and upright in heart. You have continued this great kindness to him and have given him a son[b] to sit on his throne this very day.

7"Now, O LORD my God, you have made your servant king in place of my father David. But I am only a little child[c] and do not know how to carry out my duties. 8Your servant is here among the people you have chosen,[d] a great people, too numerous to count or number.[e] 9So give your servant a discerning[f] heart to govern your people and to distinguish[g] between right and wrong. For who is able[h] to govern this great people of yours?"

10The Lord was pleased that Solomon had asked for this. 11So God said to him, "Since you have asked[i] for this and not for long life or wealth for yourself, nor have asked for the death of your enemies but for discernment[j] in administering justice, 12I will do what you have asked.[k] I will give you a wise[l] and discerning heart, so that there will never have been anyone like you, nor will there ever be. 13Moreover, I will give you what you have not[m] asked for—both riches and honor[n]—so that in your lifetime you will have no equal[o] among kings. 14And if you walk[p] in my ways and obey my statutes and commands as David your father did, I will give you a long life."[q] 15Then Solomon awoke[r]—and he realized it had been a dream.[s]

He returned to Jerusalem, stood before the ark of the Lord's covenant and sacrificed burnt offerings[t] and fellowship offerings.[e][u] Then he gave a feast[v] for all his court.

A Wise Ruling

16Now two prostitutes came to the king and stood before him. 17One of them said, "My lord, this woman and I live in the same house. I had a baby while she was there with me. 18The third day after my child was born, this woman also had a baby. We were alone; there was no one in the house but the two of us.

19"During the night this woman's son died because she lay on him. 20So she got up in the middle of the night and took my son from my side while I your servant was asleep. She put him by her breast and put her dead son by my breast. 21The next morning, I got up to nurse my son—and he was dead! But when I looked at him closely in the morning light, I saw that it wasn't the son I had borne."

22The other woman said, "No! The living one is my son; the dead one is yours."

But the first one insisted, "No! The dead one is yours; the living one is mine." And so they argued before the king.

23The king said, "This one says, 'My son is alive and your son is dead,' while that one says, 'No! Your son is dead and mine is alive.' "

24Then the king said, "Bring me a sword." So they brought a sword for the king. 25He then gave an order: "Cut the living child in two and give half to one and half to the other."

26The woman whose son was alive was filled with compassion[w] for her son and said to the king, "Please, my lord, give her the living baby! Don't kill him!"

But the other said, "Neither I nor you shall have him. Cut him in two!"

27Then the king gave his ruling: "Give the living baby to the first woman. Do not kill him; she is his mother."

28When all Israel heard the verdict the king had given, they held the king in awe, because they saw that he had wisdom[x] from God to administer justice.

Chapter 4

Solomon's Officials and Governors

SO King Solomon ruled over all Israel. 2And these were his chief officials:[y]

Azariah[z] son of Zadok—the priest;
3Elihoreph and Ahijah, sons of Shisha—secretaries;[a]
Jehoshaphat[b] son of Ahilud—recorder;

3:5 [y]S Mt 27:19 [z]S Mt 7:7
3:6 [a]S Ge 17:1 [b]1Ki 1:48
3:7 [c]Nu 27:17; 1Ch 22:5; 29:1; Jer 1:6
3:8 [d]S Dt 7:6 [e]S Ge 12:2; 15:5; S 1Ch 27:23
3:9 [f]S 2Sa 14:17; Jas 1:5 [g]S Dt 1:16 [h]2Co 2:16
3:11 [i]Jas 4:3 [j]1Ch 22:12
3:12 [k]1Jn 5:14-15 [l]S 2Sa 14:20; 1Ki 4:29,30,31; 5:12; 10:23; Ecc 1:16
3:13 [m]Mt 6:33; Eph 3:20 [n]Pr 3:1-2, 16; 8:18 [o]1Ki 10:23; 2Ch 9:22; Ne 13:26
3:14 [p]1Ki 9:4; Ps 25:13; 101:2; 128:1; Pr 3:1-2,16 [q]Ps 61:6
3:15 [r]S Ge 28:16 [s]ver 5 [t]Lev 6:8-13 [u]Lev 7:11-21 [v]Est 1:3,9; 2:18; 5:8; 6:14; 9:17; Da 5:1
3:26 [w]Ps 102:13; Isa 49:15; 63:15; Jer 3:12; 31:20; Hos 11:8
3:28 [x]S 2Sa 14:20; Col 2:3
4:2 [y]1Ki 12:6; Job 12:12 [z]1Ch 6:10; 2Ch 26:17
4:3 [a]S 2Sa 8:17 [b]S 2Sa 8:16

[e] *15* Traditionally *peace offerings*

---

the blessings he had not asked for. Jesus promised God would give life-needs to those who seek His kingdom and righteousness first (Mt 6:33).

3:6,10–14 GOD, Grace—See note on 2 Sa 14:14.

3:7–9 ELECTION, Prayer—As God had faithfully led David, He promised to be generous in taking care of Solomon, so Solomon could lead His elect people. God would grant Solomon all he needed to succeed his father as king. Our requests reveal whether we are the right kind of persons with hearts that seek those resources which will assist us in doing God's will.

3:7–9,16–28 CHRISTIAN ETHICS, Justice—Compassion and wisdom are bound up with justice as this ancient, provocative account illustrates. No human can rule wisely and justly without wisdom from God and humble dependence on God.

3:8,9 REVELATION, Author of Grace—Showing wisdom beyond his years, the new ruler asked for discernment in ruling, perhaps aware that his father had fluctuated from success to failure by making poor choices and poor judgments. The God who was present with Israel can also live in us and provide needed insight.

4 Benaiah[c] son of Jehoiada—commander in chief;
Zadok[d] and Abiathar—priests;
5 Azariah son of Nathan—in charge of the district officers;
Zabud son of Nathan—a priest and personal adviser to the king;
6 Ahishar—in charge of the palace;[e]
Adoniram[f] son of Abda—in charge of forced labor.[g]

7 Solomon also had twelve district governors[h] over all Israel, who supplied provisions for the king and the royal household. Each one had to provide supplies for one month in the year.
8 These are their names:

Ben-Hur—in the hill country[i] of Ephraim;
9 Ben-Deker—in Makaz, Shaalbim,[j] Beth Shemesh[k] and Elon Bethhanan;
10 Ben-Hesed—in Arubboth (Socoh[l] and all the land of Hepher[m] were his);
11 Ben-Abinadab—in Naphoth Dor[f] [n] (he was married to Taphath daughter of Solomon);
12 Baana son of Ahilud—in Taanach and Megiddo, and in all of Beth Shan[o] next to Zarethan[p] below Jezreel, from Beth Shan to Abel Meholah[q] across to Jokmeam;[r]
13 Ben-Geber—in Ramoth Gilead (the settlements of Jair[s] son of Manasseh in Gilead[t] were his, as well as the district of Argob in Bashan and its sixty large walled cities[u] with bronze gate bars);
14 Ahinadab son of Iddo—in Mahanaim;[v]
15 Ahimaaz[w]—in Naphtali (he had married Basemath daughter of Solomon);
16 Baana son of Hushai[x]—in Asher and in Aloth;
17 Jehoshaphat son of Paruah—in Issachar;
18 Shimei[y] son of Ela—in Benjamin;
19 Geber son of Uri—in Gilead (the country of Sihon[z] king of the Amorites and the country of Og[a] king of Bashan). He was the only governor over the district.

Solomon's Daily Provisions

20 The people of Judah and Israel were
as numerous as the sand[b] on the seashore; they ate, they drank and they were
happy.[c] 21 And Solomon ruled[d] over all
the kingdoms from the River[g] [e] to the
land of the Philistines, as far as the border
of Egypt.[f] These countries brought tribute[g] and were Solomon's subjects all his
life.
22 Solomon's daily provisions[h] were
thirty cors[h] of fine flour and sixty cors[i]
of meal, 23 ten head of stall-fed cattle,
twenty of pasture-fed cattle and a hundred sheep and goats, as well as deer, gazelles, roebucks and choice fowl.[i] 24 For
he ruled over all the kingdoms west of
the River, from Tiphsah[j] to Gaza, and
had peace[k] on all sides. 25 During Solomon's lifetime Judah and Israel, from Dan
to Beersheba,[l] lived in safety,[m] each
man under his own vine and fig tree.[n]
26 Solomon had four[j] thousand stalls
for chariot horses,[o] and twelve thousand
horses.[k]
27 The district officers,[p] each in his
month, supplied provisions for King Solomon and all who came to the king's table.
They saw to it that nothing was lacking.
28 They also brought to the proper place
their quotas of barley and straw for the
chariot horses and the other horses.

Solomon's Wisdom

29 God gave Solomon wisdom[q] and
very great insight, and a breadth of understanding as measureless as the sand[r] on
the seashore. 30 Solomon's wisdom was
greater than the wisdom of all the men of
the East,[s] and greater than all the wisdom of Egypt.[t] 31 He was wiser[u] than
any other man, including Ethan the Ezrahite—wiser than Heman, Calcol and Darda, the sons of Mahol. And his fame
spread to all the surrounding nations.
32 He spoke three thousand proverbs[v]
and his songs[w] numbered a thousand and
five. 33 He described plant life, from the
cedar of Lebanon to the hyssop[x] that
grows out of walls. He also taught about

[f] *11* Or *in the heights of Dor* [g] *21* That is, the Euphrates; also in verse 24 [h] *22* That is, probably about 185 bushels (about 6.6 kiloliters) [i] *22* That is, probably about 375 bushels (about 13.2 kiloliters) [j] *26* Some Septuagint manuscripts (see also 2 Chron. 9:25); Hebrew *forty* [k] *26* Or *charioteers*

4:4 [c]S 2Sa 8:18 [d]S 2Sa 8:17
4:6 [e]S Ge 41:40 [f]S 2Sa 20:24 [g]S Ge 49:15
4:7 [h]ver 27
4:8 [i]S Jos 24:33
4:9 [j]Jdg 1:35 [k]S Jos 15:10
4:10 [l]S Jos 15:35 [m]S Jos 12:17
4:11 [n]S Jos 11:2
4:12 [o]S Jos 17:11 [p]S Jos 3:16 [q]S Jdg 7:22 [r]1Ch 6:68
4:13 [s]S Nu 32:41 [t]Nu 32:40 [u]Dt 3:4
4:14 [v]Jos 13:26
4:15 [w]2Sa 15:27
4:16 [x]S 2Sa 15:32
4:18 [y]1Ki 1:8
4:19 [z]S Jos 12:2 [a]Dt 3:8-10; S Jos 12:4
4:20 [b]S Ge 12:2; S 32:12 [c]1Ch 22:9
4:21 [d]2Ch 9:26; Ezr 4:20; Ps 72:11; La 1:1 [e]S Ge 2:14; Ps 72:8 [f]S Ex 23:31 [g]S Jdg 3:15; Eze 16:13
4:22 [h]1Ki 10:5
4:23 [i]Ne 5:18
4:24 [j]2Ki 15:16 [k]S Jos 14:15
4:25 [l]S Jdg 20:1 [m]1Ch 22:9; Jer 23:6; Eze 28:26; 39:26 [n]Dt 8:8; 2Ki 18:31; Ps 105:33; Isa 36:16; Jer 5:17; Joel 2:22; Mic 4:4; Zec 3:10
4:26 [o]S Dt 17:16
4:27 [p]ver 7
4:29 [q]S 1Ki 3:12 [r]S Ge 32:12
4:30 [s]S Ge 25:6; S Jdg 6:3; Da 1:20; Mt 2:1 [t]Isa 19:11; Ac 7:22
4:31 [u]S 1Ki 3:12
4:32 [v]Pr 1:1; 10:1; 25:1; Ecc 12:9 [w]Ps 78:63; SS 1:1; Eze 33:32
4:33 [x]S Lev 14:49

4:20 GOD, Faithfulness—God is not mentioned in this verse but the passage nevertheless speaks of the faithfulness of God in fulfilling the promise made to Abraham and his descendents (Ge 12:2; 32:12).

4:21–28 HUMANITY, Community Relationships—Effective leadership of any community requires internal organization and administrative skills. Such organization should provide justice and opportunity for all members of the community.

4:29 GOD, Sovereignty—God's gracious gift of great wisdom to Solomon testified to the sovereignty and power of God. God works in His world in many ways that may escape our notice. The eye of faith sees the hand of God where unbelief misses it.

4:29–34 HUMANITY, Intellectual Nature—Wisdom is a gift from God. Wisdom involves literary and musical skills and factual knowledge. Its proper use attracts the attention of others.

animals and birds, reptiles and fish.
34Men of all nations came to listen to Solomon's wisdom, sent by all the kings[y] of
the world, who had heard of his wisdom.

Chapter 5

Preparations for Building the Temple

5:1–16pp — 2Ch 2:1–18

WHEN Hiram[z] king of Tyre heard
that Solomon had been anointed
king to succeed his father David, he sent
his envoys to Solomon, because he had
always been on friendly terms with David. 2Solomon sent back this message to
Hiram:

3"You know that because of the
wars[a] waged against my father David
from all sides, he could not build[b] a
temple for the Name of the LORD his
God until the LORD put his enemies
under his feet.[c] 4But now the LORD
my God has given me rest[d] on every
side, and there is no adversary[e] or
disaster. 5I intend, therefore, to build
a temple[f] for the Name of the LORD
my God, as the LORD told my father
David, when he said, 'Your son
whom I will put on the throne in
your place will build the temple for
my Name.'[g]
6"So give orders that cedars[h] of
Lebanon be cut for me. My men will
work with yours, and I will pay you
for your men whatever wages you
set. You know that we have no one
so skilled in felling timber as the Sidonians."

7When Hiram heard Solomon's message, he was greatly pleased and said,
"Praise be to the LORD[i] today, for he has
given David a wise son to rule over this
great nation."
8So Hiram sent word to Solomon:

"I have received the message you
sent me and will do all you want in
providing the cedar and pine logs.
9My men will haul them down from
Lebanon to the sea[j], and I will float
them in rafts by sea to the place you
specify. There I will separate them
and you can take them away. And
you are to grant my wish by providing food[k] for my royal household."

10In this way Hiram kept Solomon supplied with all the cedar and pine logs he
wanted, 11and Solomon gave Hiram twenty thousand cors[l] of wheat as food[l] for
his household, in addition to twenty
thousand baths[m,n] of pressed olive oil.
Solomon continued to do this for Hiram
year after year. 12The LORD gave Solomon
wisdom,[m] just as he had promised him.
There were peaceful relations between
Hiram and Solomon, and the two of them
made a treaty.[n]
13King Solomon conscripted laborers[o]
from all Israel—thirty thousand men.
14He sent them off to Lebanon in shifts of
ten thousand a month, so that they spent
one month in Lebanon and two months
at home. Adoniram[p] was in charge of the
forced labor. 15Solomon had seventy
thousand carriers and eighty thousand
stonecutters in the hills, 16as well as thirty-three hundred[o] foremen[q] who supervised the project and directed the workmen. 17At the king's command they removed from the quarry[r] large blocks of
quality stone[s] to provide a foundation of
dressed stone for the temple. 18The craftsmen of Solomon and Hiram[t] and the
men of Gebal[p u] cut and prepared the
timber and stone for the building of the
temple.

Chapter 6

Solomon Builds the Temple

6:1–29pp — 2Ch 3:1–14

IN the four hundred and eightieth[q] year
after the Israelites had come out of
Egypt, in the fourth year of Solomon's
reign over Israel, in the month of Ziv, the
second month,[v] he began to build the
temple of the LORD.[w]
2The temple[x] that King Solomon built
for the LORD was sixty cubits long, twenty
wide and thirty high.[r] 3The portico[y] at
the front of the main hall of the temple
extended the width of the temple, that is
twenty cubits,[s] and projected ten cubits[t] from the front of the temple. 4He

4:34 [y]2Ch 9:23
5:1 [z]S 2Sa 5:11
5:3 [a]1Ch 22:8; 28:3 [b]S 2Sa 7:5 [c]2Sa 22:40; Ps 8:6; 110:1; S Mt 22:44; 1Co 15:25
5:4 [d]S Jos 14:15; 1Ch 22:9; Lk 2:14 [e]1Ki 11:14,23
5:5 [f]S Dt 12:5; 1Ch 17:12; 1Co 3:16; Rev 21:22 [g]Dt 12:5; 2Sa 7:13
5:6 [h]1Ch 14:1; 22:4
5:7 [i]1Ki 10:9; Isa 60:6
5:9 [j]Ezr 3:7 [k]ver 11; Eze 27:17; Ac 12:20
5:11 [l]S ver 9
5:12 [m]S 1Ki 3:12 [n]Jos 9:7; 1Ki 15:19; Am 1:9
5:13 [o]S Ge 49:15; S Lev 25:39; 1Ki 9:15
5:14 [p]S 2Sa 20:24; 1Ki 4:6; 2Ch 10:18
5:16 [q]1Ki 9:23
5:17 [r]1Ki 6:7 [s]1Ch 22:2
5:18 [t]S 2Sa 5:11 [u]S Jos 13:5
6:1 [v]Ezr 3:8 [w]Ezr 5:11
6:2 [x]Ex 26:1
6:3 [y]Eze 40:49

[l] *11* That is, probably about 125,000 bushels (about 4,400 kiloliters) [m] *11* Septuagint (see also 2 Chron. 2:10); Hebrew *twenty cors* [n] *11* That is, about 115,000 gallons (about 440 kiloliters) [o] *16* Hebrew; some Septuagint manuscripts (see also 2 Chron. 2:2, 18) *thirty-six hundred* [p] *18* That is, Byblos
[q] *1* Hebrew; Septuagint *four hundred and fortieth*
[r] *2* That is, about 90 feet (about 27 meters) long and 30 feet (about 9 meters) wide and 45 feet (about 13.5 meters) high [s] *3* That is, about 30 feet (about 9 meters) [t] *3* That is, about 15 feet (about 4.5 meters)

5:3–4 REVELATION, Events—Events in history and faithfulness to past revelation can reveal God's present will. Solomon saw the time of peace as God's approval for Him to carry out the plans to build the *Temple which God had given David* (*2 Sa 7:4–11*).
5:4 CHRISTIAN ETHICS, War and Peace—One generation gets to reap the peaceful benefits of a preceding generation. Solomon's was a reign of peace because of David's relationship and obedience to God. See note on 2 Sa 7:1,11.
5:7 PRAYER, Universality of—Perhaps Hiram's praise was only a courtly courtesy, but Israel was to point the nations of the world to Yahweh. On other occasions a Gentile ruler praised Yahweh, the God of Israel (10:9; Da 3:28; 6:26–27). Compare 2 Ki 5:15.

made narrow clerestory windows[z] in the temple. 5Against the walls of the main hall and inner sanctuary he built a structure around the building, in which there were side rooms.[a] 6The lowest floor was five cubits[u] wide, the middle floor six cubits[v] and the third floor seven.[w] He made offset ledges around the outside of the temple so that nothing would be inserted into the temple walls.

7In building the temple, only blocks dressed[b] at the quarry were used, and no hammer, chisel or any other iron tool[c] was heard at the temple site while it was being built.

8The entrance to the lowest[x] floor was on the south side of the temple; a stairway led up to the middle level and from there to the third. 9So he built the temple and completed it, roofing it with beams and cedar[d] planks. 10And he built the side rooms all along the temple. The height of each was five cubits, and they were attached to the temple by beams of cedar.

11The word of the LORD came[e] to Solomon: 12"As for this temple you are building, if you follow my decrees, carry out my regulations and keep all my commands[f] and obey them, I will fulfill through you the promise[g] I gave to David your father. 13And I will live among the Israelites and will not abandon[h] my people Israel."

14So Solomon[i] built the temple and completed[j] it. 15He lined its interior walls with cedar boards, paneling them from the floor of the temple to the ceiling,[k] and covered the floor of the temple with planks of pine.[l] 16He partitioned off twenty cubits[y] at the rear of the temple with cedar boards from floor to ceiling to form within the temple an inner sanctuary, the Most Holy Place.[m] 17The main hall in front of this room was forty cubits[z] long. 18The inside of the temple was cedar,[n] carved with gourds and open flowers. Everything was cedar; no stone was to be seen.

19He prepared the inner sanctuary[o] within the temple to set the ark of the covenant[p] of the LORD there. 20The inner sanctuary[q] was twenty cubits long, twenty wide and twenty high.[a] He overlaid the inside with pure gold, and he also overlaid the altar of cedar.[r] 21Solomon covered the inside of the temple with pure gold, and he extended gold chains across the front of the inner sanctuary, which was overlaid with gold. 22So he overlaid the whole interior with gold. He also overlaid with gold the altar that belonged to the inner sanctuary.

23In the inner sanctuary he made a pair of cherubim[s] of olive wood, each ten cubits[b] high. 24One wing of the first cherub was five cubits long, and the other wing five cubits—ten cubits from wing tip to wing tip. 25The second cherub also measured ten cubits, for the two cherubim were identical in size and shape. 26The height of each cherub was ten cubits. 27He placed the cherubim[t] inside the innermost room of the temple, with their wings spread out. The wing of one cherub touched one wall, while the wing of the other touched the other wall, and their wings touched each other in the middle of the room. 28He overlaid the cherubim with gold.

29On the walls[u] all around the temple, in both the inner and outer rooms, he carved cherubim,[v] palm trees and open flowers. 30He also covered the floors of both the inner and outer rooms of the temple with gold.

31For the entrance of the inner sanctuary he made doors of olive wood with five-sided jambs. 32And on the two olive wood doors[w] he carved cherubim, palm trees and open flowers, and overlaid the cherubim and palm trees with beaten gold. 33In the same way he made four-sided jambs of olive wood for the entrance to the main hall. 34He also made two pine doors, each having two leaves that turned in sockets. 35He carved cherubim, palm trees and open flowers on them and overlaid them with gold hammered evenly over the carvings.

36And he built the inner courtyard[x] of three courses[y] of dressed stone and one course of trimmed cedar beams.

37The foundation of the temple of the LORD was laid in the fourth year, in the month of Ziv. 38In the eleventh year in the month of Bul, the eighth month, the temple was finished in all its details[z] according to its specifications.[a] He had spent seven years building it.

6:4 [z]Eze 41:16
6:5 [a]Jer 35:2; Eze 41:5-6
6:7 [b]S Ex 20:25 [c]S Dt 27:5
6:9 [d]SS 1:17
6:11 [e]1Ki 12:22; 13:20; 16:1,7; 17:2; 21:17; Jer 40:1
6:12 [f]1Ki 11:10 [g]2Sa 7:12-16; 1Ki 9:5
6:13 [h]S Lev 26:11; S Dt 31:6; Jn 14:18; Heb 13:5
6:14 [i]Ac 7:47 [j]1Ch 28:20; 2Ch 5:1
6:15 [k]1Ki 7:7 [l]Eze 41:15-16
6:16 [m]S Ex 26:33
6:18 [n]ver 29; Ps 74:6; Eze 41:18
6:19 [o]1Ki 8:6 [p]S Ex 25:10; S 1Sa 3:3
6:20 [q]Eze 41:3-4 [r]S Ex 30:1
6:23 [s]S Ex 37:1-9
6:27 [t]S Ge 3:24; S Ex 25:18
6:29 [u]S ver 18 [v]ver 32,35; Eze 41:18,25
6:32 [w]Eze 41:23
6:36 [x]2Ch 4:9 [y]1Ki 7:12; Ezr 6:4
6:38 [z]1Ch 28:19 [a]Ex 25:9; Heb 8:5

[u]*6* That is, about 7 1/2 feet (about 2.3 meters); also in verses 10 and 24 [v]*6* That is, about 9 feet (about 2.7 meters) [w]*6* That is, about 10 1/2 feet (about 3.1 meters) [x]*8* Septuagint; Hebrew *middle* [y]*16* That is, about 30 feet (about 9 meters) [z]*17* That is, about 60 feet (about 18 meters) [a]*20* That is, about 30 feet (about 9 meters) long, wide and high [b]*23* That is, about 15 feet (about 4.5 meters)

6:16 GOD, Holy—The Most Holy Place (also called the Holy of Holies) was a reminder that God Himself is holy, qualitatively above and apart from all else. People must respect the holiness, the unique otherness, of God. See notes on Ex 3:5–6; 19:10–24; Lev 11:44–45.

Chapter 7

Solomon Builds His Palace

IT took Solomon thirteen years, however, to complete the construction of his palace.[b] 2He built the Palace[c] of the Forest of Lebanon[d] a hundred cubits long, fifty wide and thirty high,[c] with four rows of cedar columns supporting trimmed cedar beams. 3It was roofed with cedar above the beams that rested on the columns—forty-five beams, fifteen to a row. 4Its windows were placed high in sets of three, facing each other. 5All the doorways had rectangular frames; they were in the front part in sets of three, facing each other.[d]

6He made a colonnade fifty cubits long and thirty wide.[e] In front of it was a portico, and in front of that were pillars and an overhanging roof.

7He built the throne hall, the Hall of Justice, where he was to judge,[e] and he covered it with cedar from floor to ceiling.[f][f] 8And the palace in which he was to live, set farther back, was similar in design. Solomon also made a palace like this hall for Pharaoh's daughter, whom he had married.[g]

9All these structures, from the outside to the great courtyard and from foundation to eaves, were made of blocks of high-grade stone cut to size and trimmed with a saw on their inner and outer faces. 10The foundations were laid with large stones of good quality, some measuring ten cubits[g] and some eight.[h] 11Above were high-grade stones, cut to size, and cedar beams. 12The great courtyard was surrounded by a wall of three courses[h] of dressed stone and one course of trimmed cedar beams, as was the inner courtyard of the temple of the LORD with its portico.

The Temple's Furnishings

7:23–26pp — 2Ch 4:2–5
7:38–51pp — 2Ch 4:6,10–5:1

13King Solomon sent to Tyre and brought Huram,[i][i] 14whose mother was a widow from the tribe of Naphtali and whose father was a man of Tyre and a craftsman in bronze. Huram was highly skilled[j] and experienced in all kinds of bronze work. He came to King Solomon and did all[k] the work assigned to him.

15He cast two bronze pillars,[l] each eighteen cubits high and twelve cubits around,[j] by line. 16He also made two capitals[m] of cast bronze to set on the tops of the pillars; each capital was five cubits[k] high. 17A network of interwoven chains festooned the capitals on top of the pillars, seven for each capital. 18He made pomegranates in two rows[l] encircling each network to decorate the capitals on top of the pillars.[m] He did the same for each capital. 19The capitals on top of the pillars in the portico were in the shape of lilies, four cubits[n] high. 20On the capitals of both pillars, above the bowl-shaped part next to the network, were the two hundred pomegranates[n] in rows all around. 21He erected the pillars at the portico of the temple. The pillar to the south he named Jakin[o] and the one to the north Boaz.[p][o] 22The capitals on top were in the shape of lilies. And so the work on the pillars[p] was completed.

23He made the Sea[q] of cast metal, circular in shape, measuring ten cubits[g] from rim to rim and five cubits high. It took a line[r] of thirty cubits[q] to measure around it. 24Below the rim, gourds encircled it—ten to a cubit. The gourds were cast in two rows in one piece with the Sea.

25The Sea stood on twelve bulls,[s] three facing north, three facing west, three facing south and three facing east. The Sea rested on top of them, and their hindquarters were toward the center. 26It was a handbreadth[r] in thickness, and its rim was like the rim of a cup, like a lily blossom. It held two thousand baths.[s]

27He also made ten movable stands[t] of bronze; each was four cubits long, four wide and three high.[t] 28This is how the stands were made: They had side panels attached to uprights. 29On the panels between the uprights were lions, bulls and cherubim—and on the uprights as well.

7:1 [b]S 2Sa 7:2
7:2 [c]S 2Sa 7:2 [d]1Ki 10:17; 2Ch 9:16; Isa 22:8; 37:24; Jer 22:6,23
7:7 [e]1Sa 7:15; Ps 122:5; Pr 20:8 [f]1Ki 6:15
7:8 [g]S 1Ki 3:1
7:12 [h]S 1Ki 6:36
7:13 [i]ver 45; 2Ch 2:13; 4:16
7:14 [j]Ex 31:2-5; S 35:31 [k]2Ch 4:11, 16
7:15 [l]2Ki 11:14; 23:3; 25:17; 2Ch 3:15; 23:13; 34:31; Jer 27:19; 52:17,21; Eze 40:49
7:16 [m]ver 20,42; 2Ki 25:17; Jer 52:22
7:20 [n]ver 18; 2Ch 3:16; 4:13
7:21 [o]2Ch 3:17
7:22 [p]2Ki 25:17
7:23 [q]ver 47; 2Ki 25:13; 1Ch 18:8; 2Ch 4:18; Jer 52:17; Rev 4:6 [r]Jer 31:39; Zec 2:1
7:25 [s]Jer 52:20
7:27 [t]2Ki 16:17

[c]*2* That is, about 150 feet (about 46 meters) long, 75 feet (about 23 meters) wide and 45 feet (about 13.5 meters) high [d]*5* The meaning of the Hebrew for this verse is uncertain. [e]*6* That is, about 75 feet (about 23 meters) long and 45 feet (about 13.5 meters) wide [f]*7* Vulgate and Syriac; Hebrew *floor* [g]*10,23* That is, about 15 feet (about 4.5 meters) [h]*10* That is, about 12 feet (about 3.6 meters) [i]*13* Hebrew *Hiram,* a variant of *Huram*; also in verses 40 and 45 [j]*15* That is, about 27 feet (about 8.1 meters) high and 18 feet (about 5.4 meters) around [k]*16* That is, about 7 1/2 feet (about 2.3 meters); also in verse 23 [l]*18* Two Hebrew manuscripts and Septuagint; most Hebrew manuscripts *made the pillars, and there were two rows* [m]*18* Many Hebrew manuscripts and Syriac; most Hebrew manuscripts *pomegranates* [n]*19* That is, about 6 feet (about 1.8 meters); also in verse 38 [o]*21* *Jakin* probably means *he establishes.* [p]*21* *Boaz* probably means *in him is strength.* [q]*23* That is, about 45 feet (about 13.5 meters) [r]*26* That is, about 3 inches (about 8 centimeters) [s]*26* That is, probably about 11,500 gallons (about 44 kiloliters); the Septuagint does not have this sentence. [t]*27* That is, about 6 feet (about 1.8 meters) long and wide and about 4 1/2 feet (about 1.3 meters) high

7:1–12 HUMANITY, Work—The dedication to developing an opulent life-style for oneself is a characteristic of many people but is ultimately destructive of national well-being.

Above and below the lions and bulls were
wreaths of hammered work. 30Each
stand[u] had four bronze wheels with
bronze axles, and each had a basin resting on four supports, cast with wreaths
on each side. 31On the inside of the stand
there was an opening that had a circular
frame one cubit[u] deep. This opening was
round, and with its basework it measured
a cubit and a half.[v] Around its opening
there was engraving. The panels of the
stands were square, not round. 32The four
wheels were under the panels, and the
axles of the wheels were attached to the
stand. The diameter of each wheel was a
cubit and a half. 33The wheels were made
like chariot wheels; the axles, rims,
spokes and hubs were all of cast metal.
34Each stand had four handles, one on
each corner, projecting from the stand.
35At the top of the stand there was a circular band half a cubit[w] deep. The supports and panels were attached to the top
of the stand. 36He engraved cherubim, lions and palm trees on the surfaces of the
supports and on the panels, in every
available space, with wreaths all around.
37This is the way he made the ten stands.
They were all cast in the same molds and
were identical in size and shape.
38He then made ten bronze basins,[v]
each holding forty baths[x] and measuring
four cubits across, one basin to go on
each of the ten stands. 39He placed five of
the stands on the south side of the temple
and five on the north. He placed the Sea
on the south side, at the southeast corner
of the temple. 40He also made the basins
and shovels and sprinkling bowls.[w]

So Huram finished all the work he had undertaken for King Solomon in the temple of the LORD:

41the two pillars;
the two bowl-shaped capitals on top of the pillars;
the two sets of network decorating the two bowl-shaped capitals on top of the pillars;
42the four hundred pomegranates for the two sets of network (two rows of pomegranates for each network, decorating the bowl-shaped capitals[x] on top of the pillars);
43the ten stands with their ten basins;
44the Sea and the twelve bulls under it;
45the pots, shovels and sprinkling bowls.[y]

All these objects that Huram[z] made for
King Solomon for the temple of the LORD
were of burnished bronze. 46The king had
them cast in clay molds in the plain[a] of
the Jordan between Succoth[b] and Zarethan.[c] 47Solomon left all these things un-
weighed,[d] because there were so
many;[e] the weight of the bronze[f] was
not determined.
48Solomon also made all[g] the furnishings that were in the LORD's temple:

the golden altar;
the golden table[h] on which was the bread of the Presence;[i]
49the lampstands[j] of pure gold (five on the right and five on the left, in front of the inner sanctuary);
the gold floral work and lamps and tongs;
50the pure gold basins, wick trimmers, sprinkling bowls, dishes[k] and censers;[l]
and the gold sockets for the doors of the innermost room, the Most Holy Place, and also for the doors of the main hall of the temple.

51When all the work King Solomon had
done for the temple of the LORD was finished, he brought in the things his father
David had dedicated[m]—the silver and
gold and the furnishings[n]—and he
placed them in the treasuries of the
LORD's temple.

Chapter 8

The Ark Brought to the Temple

8:1–21pp — 2Ch 5:2–6:11

THEN King Solomon summoned into
his presence at Jerusalem the elders
of Israel, all the heads of the tribes and
the chiefs[o] of the Israelite families, to
bring up the ark[p] of the LORD's covenant
from Zion, the City of David.[q] 2All the
men of Israel came together to King Solomon at the time of the festival[r] in the
month of Ethanim, the seventh month.[s]

[u]*31* That is, about 1 1/2 feet (about 0.5 meter) [v]*31* That is, about 2 1/4 feet (about 0.7 meter); also in verse 32 [w]*35* That is, about 3/4 foot (about 0.2 meter) [x]*38* That is, about 230 gallons (about 880 liters)

7:30 [u]2Ki 16:17
7:38 [v]S Ex 30:18
7:40 [w]S Ex 27:3; Jer 52:18
7:42 [x]S ver 16
7:45 [y]S Ex 27:3; Jer 52:18 [z]S ver 13
7:46 [a]S Ge 13:10 [b]S Ge 33:17 [c]Jos 3:16
7:47 [d]1Ch 22:3; Jer 52:20 [e]Ex 36:5-7 [f]S ver 23
7:48 [g]Ex 39:32-43 [h]S Ex 25:23 [i]S Ex 25:30
7:49 [j]S Ex 25:31-38
7:50 [k]S Nu 7:14 [l]2Ki 25:13; Jer 52:19
7:51 [m]S 2Sa 8:11 [n]2Ki 12:13; 24:13; Jer 27:19
8:1 [o]Nu 7:2 [p]S 1Sa 3:3; Rev 11:19 [q]S 2Sa 5:7
8:2 [r]ver 65; S Lev 23:36; Ne 8:17 [s]S Lev 23:34; S Nu 29:12

8:1–21 REVELATION, Divine Presence—The new Temple symbolized God's presence. Ancient symbols which had assured Israel that God was in their midst were brought to the inner room of the Temple. Symbolically God's presence is understood as hidden and accessible only through a veil. The stone tablets are a visible reminder that God speaks to His people and reveals His instructions for their lives. God was comfortable in the Tent of Meeting or Temple. The splendor of the structure was not significant. The Tent showed God could move with a people on the march. The Temple represented God's permanent dwelling with an established people. See note on 1 Sa 4:1–22.

8:1–66 WORSHIP, Buildings—See note on Ge 28:16–22.

3When all the elders of Israel had arrived, the priests[t] took up the ark, 4and
they brought up the ark of the LORD and
the Tent of Meeting[u] and all the sacred
furnishings in it. The priests and Levites[v]
carried them up, 5and King Solomon and
the entire assembly of Israel that had
gathered about him were before the ark,
sacrificing[w] so many sheep and cattle that
they could not be recorded or counted.
6The priests then brought the ark of
the LORD's covenant[x] to its place in the
inner sanctuary of the temple, the Most
Holy Place,[y] and put it beneath the
wings of the cherubim.[z] 7The cherubim
spread their wings over the place of the
ark and overshadowed[a] the ark and its
carrying poles. 8These poles were so long
that their ends could be seen from the
Holy Place in front of the inner sanctuary,
but not from outside the Holy Place; and
they are still there today.[b] 9There was
nothing in the ark except the two stone
tablets[c] that Moses had placed in it at
Horeb, where the LORD made a covenant
with the Israelites after they came out of
Egypt.
10When the priests withdrew from the
Holy Place, the cloud[d] filled the temple
of the LORD. 11And the priests could not
perform their service[e] because of the
cloud, for the glory[f] of the LORD filled his
temple.
12Then Solomon said, "The LORD has
said that he would dwell in a dark
cloud;[g] 13I have indeed built a magnificent temple for you, a place for you to
dwell[h] forever."
14While the whole assembly of Israel
was standing there, the king turned
around and blessed[i] them. 15Then he
said:

"Praise be to the LORD,[j] the God
of Israel, who with his own hand has
fulfilled what he promised with his
own mouth to my father David. For
he said, 16'Since the day I brought my
people Israel out of Egypt,[k] I have
not chosen a city in any tribe of Israel
to have a temple built for my Name[l]
to be there, but I have chosen[m] David[n] to rule my people Israel.'
17"My father David had it in his
heart[o] to build a temple[p] for the
Name of the LORD, the God of Israel.
18But the LORD said to my father David, 'Because it was in your heart to
build a temple for my Name, you did
well to have this in your heart.
19Nevertheless, you[q] are not the one
to build the temple, but your son,
who is your own flesh and blood—he
is the one who will build the temple
for my Name.'[r]
20"The LORD has kept the promise
he made: I have succeeded[s] David
my father and now I sit on the throne
of Israel, just as the LORD promised,
and I have built[t] the temple for the
Name of the LORD, the God of Israel.
21I have provided a place there for
the ark, in which is the covenant of
the LORD that he made with our fathers when he brought them out of
Egypt."

Solomon's Prayer of Dedication

8:22–53pp — 2Ch 6:12–40

22Then Solomon stood before the altar

8:3 [t]S Jos 3:3
8:4 [u]S Lev 17:4 [v]1Ch 15:13
8:5 [w]S 2Sa 6:13; S 2Ch 30:24
8:6 [x]S Ex 26:33; S 2Sa 6:17; Rev 11:19 [y]S Ex 26:33 [z]S Ge 3:24; S Ex 25:18
8:7 [a]S Ex 25:20
8:8 [b]Ex 25:13-15
8:9 [c]S Ex 16:34; S 25:16; Heb 9:4
8:10 [d]S Ex 16:10; S Lev 16:2; Rev 15:8
8:11 [e]2Ch 7:2; Rev 15:8 [f]S Ex 16:7; S 29:43
8:12 [g]S Ex 40:34; S 2Sa 22:10
8:13 [h]Ex 15:17; Ps 132:13; 135:21; Mt 23:21
8:14 [i]S Ex 39:43
8:15 [j]1Ch 16:36; Lk 1:68
8:16 [k]S Ex 3:10 [l]S Dt 12:5 [m]S 1Sa 9:16; S 16:1 [n]Ps 89:3-4
8:17 [o]S 1Sa 10:7; Ac 7:46 [p]2Sa 7:27; 1Ch 22:7; Ps 26:8; 132:5
8:19 [q]S 2Sa 7:5 [r]S 2Sa 7:13
8:20 [s]S 2Sa 7:12 [t]1Ch 28:6

8:9 THE CHURCH, Covenant People—See notes on Ex 19:4–8; Dt 4:13.

8:11 GOD, Glory—The glory of God is the revelation or manifestation of God Himself. Sometimes, the glory of God had a visible expression; sometimes it may only have been a mental perception. In either case the reality of God was made vivid. See notes on Ex 16:7,10; 40:34–38; Lk 2:9,14.

8:14–21 PRAYER, Blessing—As the Lord's anointed, Solomon could pronounce a blessing. The Temple dedication was an appropriate place to recognize the worshiping assembly as the human source of building the Temple. The blessing on the congregation is in the form of praise (Hebrew *barak*, "bless") to Yahweh. Whatever king or people had done, the ultimate Builder was God. The assembly deserved recognition and gratitude, but that gratitude was best expressed by praising God.

8:15,20,23–24,26,56 GOD, Faithfulness—The faithfulness of God was praised for His fulfilling His promises to His people. God's faithfulness allows us to trust His word and His actions. See notes on Ge 8:1; Nu 26:65; Dt 10:11,22; Jos 1:6.

8:15–21 HISTORY, Promise—God showed His faithfulness by keeping His promises of a Temple and a dynasty to David. Solomon recognized his achievements as based on God's faithfulness. The history of promise and fulfillment shows that God's relationship with His people is not static or unchanging. The relationship is a *dynamic one in which God prepares His people* for new cultural conditions and provides for their needs in those conditions.

8:16,51–53 ELECTION, Prayer—Solomon's prayer of dedication for the Temple was based on his awareness of God's choice of Israel as His heritage and treasure. This event marked a new stage in election history, the choice of a central worship place. See note on Dt 12:5–14. Solomon prayed that the Temple would be the place where Israel could seek reconciliation with God when they had broken their covenant. There they could be reminded of their responsibilities as a special people elected to show God's glory to foreigners who needed to know God as the one and only true God. Dedicated lives and dedicated buildings go hand in hand in the theology of those who enjoy God's election.

8:21 THE CHURCH, Covenant People—See note on Dt 4:13. The tables of the Ten Commandments represented the covenant God made with the people at Mount Sinai (Horeb). The tables were placed in the ark of the covenant to remind God's people of their responsibility and commitment to God.

8:22–53 PRAYER, Commitment—Solomon's prayer of dedication demonstrated the commitment inherent in covenant relationships. The prayer begins with a declaration of God's uniqueness (v 23) and ends with the uniqueness of Israel in relation to God (v 53). Solomon acknowledged that God is infinite (v 27) and yet chooses to respond personally to individual needs. Solomon named various violations and consequences and asked for mercy in each. He also asked for help for foreigners and for help in war. In each case, the help of the Lord is conditioned on prayer. The basis of the prayer is that "all the peoples of the earth may know" the name of the Lord and fear Him (v 43). This prayer of commitment seeks God's

of the LORD in front of the whole assembly of Israel, spread out his hands[u] toward heaven 23and said:

"O LORD, God of Israel, there is no
God like[v] you in heaven above or on
earth below—you who keep your
covenant of love[w] with your servants
who continue wholeheartedly in
your way. 24You have kept your
promise to your servant David my father; with your mouth you have
promised and with your hand you
have fulfilled it—as it is today.
25"Now LORD, God of Israel, keep
for your servant David my father the
promises[x] you made to him when
you said, 'You shall never fail to have
a man to sit before me on the throne
of Israel, if only your sons are careful
in all they do to walk before me as
you have done.' 26And now, O God of
Israel, let your word that you promised[y] your servant David my father
come true.
27"But will God really dwell[z] on
earth? The heavens, even the highest
heaven,[a] cannot contain[b] you. How
much less this temple I have built!
28Yet give attention to your servant's
prayer and his plea for mercy, O
LORD my God. Hear the cry and the
prayer that your servant is praying in
your presence this day. 29May your
eyes be open[c] toward[d] this temple
night and day, this place of which
you said, 'My Name[e] shall be there,'
so that you will hear the prayer your
servant prays toward this place.
30Hear the supplication of your servant and of your people Israel when
they pray[f] toward this place. Hear[g]
from heaven, your dwelling place,
and when you hear, forgive.[h]
31"When a man wrongs his neighbor and is required to take an oath
and he comes and swears the oath[i]
before your altar in this temple,
32then hear from heaven and act.
Judge between your servants, condemning the guilty and bringing
down on his own head what he has
done. Declare the innocent not
guilty, and so establish his innocence.[j]
33"When your people Israel have
been defeated[k] by an enemy because
they have sinned[l] against you, and
when they turn back to you and confess your name, praying and making
supplication to you in this temple,[m]
34then hear from heaven and forgive
the sin of your people Israel and
bring them back to the land you gave
to their fathers.
35"When the heavens are shut up
and there is no rain[n] because your
people have sinned[o] against you, and
when they pray toward this place and
confess your name and turn from
their sin because you have afflicted
them, 36then hear from heaven and
forgive the sin of your servants, your
people Israel. Teach[p] them the right
way[q] to live, and send rain[r] on the
land you gave your people for an inheritance.
37"When famine[s] or plague[t]
comes to the land, or blight[u] or

8:22 [u]S Ex 9:29
8:23 [v]S Ex 9:14 [w]S Dt 7:9,12; Ne 1:5; 9:32; Da 9:4
8:25 [x]S 2Sa 7:15; 1Ch 17:23; 2Ch 1:9
8:26 [y]S 2Sa 7:25
8:27 [z]Ac 7:48; 17:24 [a]S Dt 10:14 [b]2Ch 2:6; Ps 139:7-16; Isa 66:1; Jer 23:24
8:29 [c]ver 52; 2Ki 19:16; 2Ch 7:15; Ne 1:6; Ps 5:1; 31:2; 102:17; 130:2; Isa 37:17 [d]Ps 28:2; 138:2; Da 6:10 [e]S Dt 11:12; 12:11; S 2Sa 7:13
8:30 [f]ver 47; Lev 26:40; Ne 1:6; Jer 29:12; Da 9:4 [g]ver 39; Ps 34:6 [h]S Ex 34:7,9; Lev 26:40-42; Ps 85:2
8:31 [i]S Ex 22:11
8:32 [j]Dt 25:1; Eze 18:20
8:33 [k]S Lev 26:17 [l]Lev 26:39 [m]Isa 37:1,14,38
8:35 [n]S Dt 28:24; S 2Sa 1:21 [o]Jer 5:25
8:36 [p]S Dt 8:3; S 1Sa 12:23 [q]Ps 5:8; 27:11; 107:7; Pr 11:5; Isa 45:13; Jer 6:16; 7:23; 31:21 [r]ver 35; 1Ki 17:1; 18:1,45; Jer 5:24; 10:3; 14:22; Zec 10:1
8:37 [s]S Lev 26:26 [t]S Ex 30:12; S Lev 26:25 [u]S Dt 28:22

commitment to help and forgive His imperfect people.

8:23 GOD, Love—God's faithfulness to His covenant promises reveals His love for His people. See note on Dt 32:10–12,36.

8:23 THE CHURCH, Covenant People—No God exists but the Lord. Idols can never take credit for the work of the Lord. The Lord keeps the commitment He makes to His people. God's covenant love is steadfast and sure. By means of His covenant love God binds Himself to His people.

8:25,58 CHRISTIAN ETHICS, Prayer—Prayer is an exceedingly important ethical dynamic as it identifies pressing moral needs or issues before God. It solidifies resolve in the petitioner to address personal and social changes that should be made toward righteousness and is the beginning place for action for such changes to occur.

8:27,39,50 GOD, Sovereignty—God alone can forgive, and He alone is judge. He can declare one innocent (v 32), and He can pour out His wrath upon the guilty (v 46). The whole chapter is a passage of praise to the greatness of God. Neither human language nor human buildings can contain the greatness of God. This greatness beyond all human capacities qualifies Him and only Him to be the sovereign Ruler of the universe.

8:27–53 SIN, Universal Nature—God's place of worship is a place to deal with the human sin problem. That every individual sins is not a theory to be proved with evidence. It is a confession self-evident to any morally sensitive person (v 46). Sinful people may go to God's house to confess sins and to find assurance of forgiveness in God's merciful presence. Those who do not belong to God's people are welcome to pray for forgiveness of sin and to commit themselves to God in faith.

8:27–30 REVELATION, Divine Presence—God is not contained in a Temple. Even the heavens do not make an adequate dwelling place. God is present for His people. A visible place to encounter Him and worship Him is appropriate for His children.

8:33–40 EVIL AND SUFFERING, Human Origin—Some national and international events may be interpreted as results of human sin. Solomon knew Israel's sin would lead to God's punishment through military defeat. Similarly, disasters in nature may result from human sin and divine punishment. This does not mean all such disasters and suffering result directly as divine punishment for sin. Only the interpreter led by God can proclaim a particular disaster as related to a particular people's sin. Confession of sin and repentance may lead God to relieve the suffering brought on by sin. See note on vv 46–53.

8:33–49 CHRISTIAN ETHICS, War and Peace—At three points in his prayer of dedication before God, Solomon pled on behalf of the Hebrews before God that their confession and commitment be the same. For the Hebrews to be defeated in battle was a sign of being out of fellowship with God. From God's perspective these battles were not so much for territorial rights and loot as they were to establish the worship of the one true God in the land.

mildew, locusts or grasshoppers,[v] or
when an enemy besieges them in any
of their cities, whatever disaster or
disease may come, 38and when a
prayer or plea is made by any of your
people Israel—each one aware of the
afflictions of his own heart, and
spreading out his hands[w] toward this
temple— 39then hear[x] from heaven,
your dwelling place. Forgive[y] and
act; deal with each man according to
all he does, since you know[z] his
heart (for you alone know the hearts
of all men), 40so that they will fear[a]
you all the time they live in the
land[b] you gave our fathers.
41"As for the foreigner[c] who does
not belong to your people Israel but
has come from a distant land because
of your name— 42for men will hear[d]
of your great name and your mighty
hand[e] and your outstretched arm—
when he comes and prays toward
this temple, 43then hear from heav-
en, your dwelling place, and do whatever the foreigner asks of you, so that
all the peoples of the earth may
know[f] your name and fear[g] you, as
do your own people Israel, and may
know that this house I have built
bears your Name.[h]
44"When your people go to war
against their enemies, wherever you
send them, and when they pray[i] to
the LORD toward the city you have
chosen and the temple I have built
for your Name, 45then hear from
heaven their prayer and their plea,
and uphold their cause.[j]
46"When they sin against you—for
there is no one who does not sin[k]—
and you become angry with them
and give them over to the enemy,
who takes them captive[l] to his own
land, far away or near; 47and if they
have a change of heart in the land
where they are held captive, and repent and plead[m] with you in the land
of their conquerors and say, 'We
have sinned, we have done wrong,
we have acted wickedly';[n] 48and if
they turn back[o] to you with all their
heart[p] and soul in the land of their

8:37 [v]S Ex 10:13; Ps 105:34
8:38 [w]S Ex 9:29
8:39 [x]S ver 30 [y]Ps 130:4 [z]S Jos 22:22; S Ps 44:21; Jn 2:24; S Rev 2:23
8:40 [a]ver 39-40; Dt 6:13; Ps 103:11; 130:4 [b]S Dt 12:1
8:41 [c]S Ge 31:15; Isa 56:3,6; 61:5
8:42 [d]1Ki 10:1; Isa 60:3; Ac 8:27 [e]Dt 3:24
8:43 [f]S Jos 4:24; S 1Sa 17:46 [g]Ps 102:15 [h]S Dt 28:10
8:44 [i]1Ch 5:20; 2Ch 14:11
8:45 [j]Ps 9:4; 140:12
8:46 [k]Ps 130:3; 143:2; Pr 20:9; S Ro 3:9 [l]Lev 26:33-39; S Dt 4:27; S 21:10; S 28:64; 2Ki 25:21
8:47 [m]S ver 30; S Lev 5:5; Ezr 9:15; Ne 1:6; Jer 14:20 [n]Ezr 9:7; Ps 106:6; Jer 3:25
8:48 [o]S Dt 4:30 [p]S Dt 4:29 [q]1Jn 1:8-10 [r]Ps 5:7; 11:4; Jnh 2:4 [s]Dt 12:11-14; Ne 1:9; Jer 23:3; 31:8
8:50 [t]2Ki 25:28; 2Ch 30:9; Ps 106:46; Da 1:9
8:51 [u]S Ex 34:9; S Dt 9:29 [v]S Ex 1:13; Isa 48:10; Jer 11:4
8:52 [w]S ver 29 [x]Job 30:20; Ps 3:4; 22:2; 77:1; 142:1
8:53 [y]Ex 19:5; S 34:9
8:55 [z]S Ex 39:43; Nu 6:23
8:56 [a]S Ex 33:14; Dt 12:10; Heb 4:8 [b]S Jos 23:15; S Jer 29:10
8:57 [c]S Dt 4:31; S 31:6; S Mt 28:20; Heb 13:5
8:58 [d]S Jos 24:23
8:60 [e]S Jos 4:24

enemies who took them captive, and
pray[q] to you toward the land you
gave their fathers, toward the city
you have chosen and the temple[r] I
have built for your Name;[s] 49then
from heaven, your dwelling place,
hear their prayer and their plea, and
uphold their cause. 50And forgive
your people, who have sinned against
you; forgive all the offenses they
have committed against you, and
cause their conquerors to show them
mercy;[t] 51for they are your people
and your inheritance,[u] whom you
brought out of Egypt, out of that
iron-smelting furnace.[v]
52"May your eyes be open[w] to
your servant's plea and to the plea of
your people Israel, and may you listen to them whenever they cry out to
you.[x] 53For you singled them out
from all the nations of the world to
be your own inheritance,[y] just as
you declared through your servant
Moses when you, O Sovereign LORD,
brought our fathers out of Egypt."
54When Solomon had finished all these
prayers and supplications to the LORD, he
rose from before the altar of the LORD,
where he had been kneeling with his
hands spread out toward heaven. 55He
stood and blessed[z] the whole assembly of
Israel in a loud voice, saying:
56"Praise be to the LORD, who has
given rest[a] to his people Israel just as
he promised. Not one word has failed
of all the good promises[b] he gave
through his servant Moses. 57May
the LORD our God be with us as he
was with our fathers; may he never
leave us nor forsake[c] us. 58May he
turn our hearts[d] to him, to walk in
all his ways and to keep the commands, decrees and regulations he
gave our fathers. 59And may these
words of mine, which I have prayed
before the LORD, be near to the LORD
our God day and night, that he may
uphold the cause of his servant and
the cause of his people Israel according to each day's need, 60so that all
the peoples[e] of the earth may know

8:40,43 SALVATION, Fear of God—Solomon wanted all peoples to fear God as Israel feared Him when she built the Temple. Those who truly fear God should want to see others fear Him. See note on Ge 22:12.

8:46–53 EVIL AND SUFFERING, Redemptive—Suffering caused by sin should lead to repentance and confession and, thus, to a renewed relationship with God. Suffering can become redemptive for God's people, guiding us away from sin and back to God. See note on vv 33–40.

8:51 HISTORY, God's People—God's people are identified by what God has done for them in history. Those historical memories give promise of God's continuing concern for and relation with His people.

8:55–65 PRAYER, Blessing—See note on vv 14–21. Blessing here involves thanks, petition, and exhortation. Solomon began with a reminder of God's perfect faithfulness (v 56; Jos 23:14) and ended with a demand for Israel's full commitment (v 61). The purpose and the basis of the prayer is in v 60. Prayer seeks to fulfill God's missionary purposes.

8:56 CHRISTIAN ETHICS, War and Peace—See note on 5:4.

8:59–60 EVANGELISM, Glory to God—See note on Ex 7:5.

that the LORD is God and that there is
no other.[f] 61But your hearts[g] must
be fully committed[h] to the LORD our
God, to live by his decrees and obey
his commands, as at this time."

The Dedication of the Temple

8:62–66pp — 2Ch 7:1–10

62Then the king and all Israel with him
offered sacrifices[i] before the LORD. 63Sol-
omon offered a sacrifice of fellowship offerings[y] to the LORD: twenty-two thousand cattle and a hundred and twenty
thousand sheep and goats. So the king
and all the Israelites dedicated[j] the temple of the LORD.
64On that same day the king consecrated the middle part of the courtyard in
front of the temple of the LORD, and there
he offered burnt offerings, grain offerings
and the fat[k] of the fellowship offerings,
because the bronze altar[l] before the
LORD was too small to hold the burnt offerings, the grain offerings and the fat of
the fellowship offerings.[m]
65So Solomon observed the festival[n] at
that time, and all Israel with him—a vast
assembly, people from Lebo[z] Hamath[o]
to the Wadi of Egypt.[p] They celebrated it
before the LORD our God for seven days
and seven days more, fourteen days in all.
66On the following day he sent the people
away. They blessed the king and then
went home, joyful and glad in heart for all
the good[q] things the LORD had done for
his servant David and his people Israel.

Chapter 9

The LORD Appears to Solomon

9:1–9pp — 2Ch 7:11–22

WHEN Solomon had finished[r] building the temple of the LORD and the
royal palace, and had achieved all he had
desired to do, 2the LORD appeared[s] to
him a second time, as he had appeared to
him at Gibeon. 3The LORD said to him:
"I have heard[t] the prayer and plea
you have made before me; I have
consecrated this temple, which you
have built, by putting my Name[u]
there forever. My eyes[v] and my
heart will always be there.
4"As for you, if you walk before me
in integrity of heart[w] and uprightness, as David[x] your father did, and
do all I command and observe my decrees and laws,[y] 5I will establish[z]
your royal throne over Israel forever,
as I promised David your father when
I said, 'You shall never fail[a] to have a
man on the throne of Israel.'
6"But if you[a] or your sons turn
away[b] from me and do not observe
the commands and decrees I have
given you[a] and go off to serve other
gods[c] and worship them, 7then I will
cut off Israel from the land[d] I have
given them and will reject this temple I have consecrated for my
Name.[e] Israel will then become a byword[f] and an object of ridicule[g]
among all peoples. 8And though this
temple is now imposing, all who pass
by will be appalled[h] and will scoff
and say, 'Why has the LORD done
such a thing to this land and to this
temple?'[i] 9People will answer,[j] 'Because they have forsaken[k] the LORD
their God, who brought their fathers
out of Egypt, and have embraced other gods, worshiping and serving
them—that is why the LORD brought
all this disaster[l] on them.'"

8:60 [f]S Dt 4:35 **8:61** [g]Dt 6:5 [h]1Ki 9:4; 11:4; 15:3,14; 22:43; 2Ki 20:3; 1Ch 28:9; 29:19; 2Ch 16:9; 17:6; 25:2; Ps 119:80; Isa 38:3 **8:62** [i]S 2Sa 6:13; 1Ch 29:21; Eze 45:17 **8:63** [j]Ezr 6:16 **8:64** [k]S Ex 29:13 [l]S Ex 27:1; 2Ki 16:14; 2Ch 4:1; 8:12; 15:8; Eze 43:13-17 [m]S 2Sa 6:17 **8:65** [n]S ver 2 [o]S Nu 13:21 [p]S Ge 15:18 **8:66** [q]S Ex 18:9 **9:1** [r]S 2Sa 7:2 **9:2** [s]S 1Ki 3:5 **9:3** [t]S 1Sa 9:16; 2Ki 19:20; 20:5; Ps 10:17; 34:17 [u]S Ex 20:24; S Dt 12:5 [v]S Dt 11:12 **9:4** [w]S Ge 17:1 [x]Dt 17:20; 1Ki 14:8; 15:5 [y]S 1Ki 3:14; 1Ch 28:9; Pr 4:4 **9:5** [z]1Ch 22:10 [a]S 2Sa 7:15 **9:6** [b]Dt 28:15; 2Sa 7:14; 2Ki 18:12; Jer 17:27; 26:4; 32:23; 44:23 [c]1Ki 11:10 **9:7** [d]Lev 18:24-28; Dt 4:26; S Jos 23:13; 2Ki 17:23; Jer 24:10 [e]Dt 12:5; Jer 7:14 [f]Job 17:6; Ps 44:14; Jer 24:9; Joel 2:17 [g]S Dt 28:37; Eze 5:15 **9:8** [h]S Lev 26:32 [i]S Dt 29:24; Jer 7:4-15; Mt 23:38 **9:9** [j]Dt 29:25; 2Ki 22:17; Jer 5:19; 13:22; 16:11,13; 22:9 [k]S Nu 25:3; Jer 40:3; 44:23; La 4:12 [l]S Dt 31:29

[y]63 Traditionally *peace offerings;* also in verse 64 [z]65 Or *from the entrance to* [a]6 The Hebrew is plural.

9:2–3 REVELATION, Commitment—God revealed Himself in a dream (3:5), declaring His presence and blessing on the Temple and renewing the vows which He covenanted with David. The placing of the Name on the Temple (8:29) indicated that God's own character was stamped upon the structure. He owned the worship center. To place a name on anything was to exercise dominion and direction over it. God's promise of forever and always (literally, "all the days") points to the long distant future, not to eternity. The people remained free to reject God and have Him reject the Temple (v 7). God committed Himself to the Temple and expected the people to commit themselves to Him.

9:3–9 PRAYER, Answer—God promised to answer the petitions of Solomon's prayer but added warnings (vv 6–9) He had not included in His covenant with David (2 Sa 7:4–16). The covenant with David had included unconditional messianic promises, possible because of David's heart (2 Ki 11:4). God knew that Solomon needed very stringent warnings; these warnings hearken back to the reaffirmation of the covenant in Moses' final days (Dt 31:16–22,27–29). God's answer to prayer often makes demands as well as giving promises.

9:4–9 ELECTION, Responsibility—God wanted Solomon to behave as a member of the family of the elect. His father David strove to walk before the Lord in humble obedience to God's requirements for the people He elected. God expected nothing less of Solomon. A leader without commitment to God could not claim the election promises. The holy name could not and would not dwell among an unholy people. The Lord who elected a people through the saving Exodus could discipline them through the disastrous Exile.

9:4–5 CHRISTIAN ETHICS, Moral Imperatives—See note on 3:3,14.

9:5 GOD, Faithfulness—God will always bless His people and keep His promises to them if they will give Him the opportunity. See note on 2:4,24,27.

9:6–9 GOD, One God—God's people must not dilute or forget their loyalty to God as the one true God. He wants to be recognized and worshiped as the only God. If He is not, His wrath disciplines His people. Israel finally learned the lesson only when God sent them into exile. See note on Dt 4:27–40.

9:9 HISTORY, Judgment—God can bring disaster as well as deliverance. Past acts of deliverance show God's power to destroy and His expectations of faithfulness from His people. Even unbelieving peoples can interpret judgment as God's work on an unfaithful people.

Solomon's Other Activities

9:10–28pp — 2Ch 8:1–18

10At the end of twenty years, during which Solomon built these two buildings—the temple of the LORD and the royal palace— 11King Solomon gave twenty towns in Galilee to Hiram king of Tyre, because Hiram had supplied him with all the cedar and pine and gold[m] he wanted. 12But when Hiram went from Tyre to see the towns that Solomon had given him, he was not pleased with them. 13"What kind of towns are these you have given me, my brother?" he asked. And he called them the Land of Cabul,[b][n] a name they have to this day. 14Now Hiram had sent to the king 120 talents[c] of gold.[o]

15Here is the account of the forced labor King Solomon conscripted[p] to build the LORD's temple, his own palace, the supporting terraces,[d][q] the wall of Jerusalem, and Hazor,[r] Megiddo and Gezer.[s] 16(Pharaoh king of Egypt had attacked and captured Gezer. He had set it on fire. He killed its Canaanite inhabitants and then gave it as a wedding gift to his daughter,[t] Solomon's wife. 17And Solomon rebuilt Gezer.) He built up Lower Beth Horon,[u] 18Baalath,[v] and Tadmor[e] in the desert, within his land, 19as well as all his store cities[w] and the towns for his chariots[x] and for his horses[f]—whatever he desired to build in Jerusalem, in Lebanon and throughout all the territory he ruled.

20All the people left from the Amorites, Hittites,[y] Perizzites, Hivites and Jebusites[z] (these peoples were not Israelites), 21that is, their descendants[a] remaining in the land, whom the Israelites could not exterminate[g][b]—these Solomon conscripted for his slave labor force,[c] as it is to this day. 22But Solomon did not make slaves[d] of any of the Israelites; they were his fighting men, his government officials, his officers, his captains, and the commanders of his chariots and charioteers. 23They were also the chief officials[e] in charge of Solomon's projects—550 officials supervising the men who did the work.

24After Pharaoh's daughter[f] had come up from the City of David to the palace Solomon had built for her, he constructed the supporting terraces.[g]

25Three[h] times a year Solomon sacrificed burnt offerings and fellowship offerings[h] on the altar he had built for the LORD, burning incense before the LORD along with them, and so fulfilled the temple obligations.

26King Solomon also built ships[i] at Ezion Geber,[j] which is near Elath[k] in Edom, on the shore of the Red Sea.[i] 27And Hiram sent his men—sailors[l] who knew the sea—to serve in the fleet with Solomon's men. 28They sailed to Ophir[m] and brought back 420 talents[j] of gold,[n] which they delivered to King Solomon.

Chapter 10

The Queen of Sheba Visits Solomon

10:1–13pp — 2Ch 9:1–12

WHEN the queen of Sheba[o] heard about the fame[p] of Solomon and his relation to the name of the LORD, she came to test him with hard questions.[q] 2Arriving at Jerusalem with a very great caravan[r]—with camels carrying spices, large quantities of gold, and precious stones—she came to Solomon and talked with him about all that she had on her mind. 3Solomon answered all her questions; nothing was too hard for the king to explain to her. 4When the queen of Sheba saw all the wisdom of Solomon and the palace he had built, 5the food on his table,[s] the seating of his officials, the attending servants in their robes, his cupbearers, and the burnt offerings he made at[k] the temple of the LORD, she was overwhelmed.

6She said to the king, "The report I heard in my own country about your achievements and your wisdom is true. 7But I did not believe[t] these things until I came and saw with my own eyes. Indeed, not even half was told me; in wisdom and wealth[u] you have far exceeded the report I heard. 8How happy your men must be! How happy your officials, who continually stand before you and hear[v] your wisdom! 9Praise[w] be to the LORD

9:11 *m*ver 14
9:13 *n*Jos 19:27
9:14 *o*ver 11
9:15 *p*1Ki 5:13 *q*S 2Sa 5:9 *r*Jos 11:10-11 *s*S Jos 10:33
9:16 *t*1Ki 3:1; Ps 45:12; 68:29; 72:10
9:17 *u*S Jos 10:10
9:18 *v*S Jos 19:44
9:19 *w*S Ex 1:11 *x*S Dt 17:16; 1Ki 4:26; 2Ch 1:14; 9:25
9:20 *y*S Nu 13:29 *z*S Jos 11:3
9:21 *a*S Ge 9:25-26 *b*S Jos 15:63 *c*S Ge 49:15; S Ex 1:11; S Dt 20:11
9:22 *d*S Lev 25:39
9:23 *e*1Ki 5:16
9:24 *f*S 1Ki 3:1 *g*2Sa 5:9; 1Ki 11:27
9:25 *h*S Ex 23:14
9:26 *i*1Ki 10:22; 22:48; 2Ch 20:37; Isa 2:16 *j*S Nu 33:35 *k*2Ki 14:22; 16:6
9:27 *l*Eze 27:8
9:28 *m*S Ge 10:29 *n*ver 14; 1Ki 10:10, 11,14,21; 2Ch 1:15; Ecc 2:8
10:1 *o*S Ge 10:7, 28; S 25:3; Mt 12:42; Lk 11:31 *p*Eze 16:14 *q*S Nu 12:8; S Jdg 14:12
10:2 *r*S Ge 24:10
10:5 *s*1Ki 4:22
10:7 *t*S Ge 45:26 *u*1Ch 29:25
10:8 *v*Pr 8:34
10:9 *w*S 1Ki 5:7; S Isa 42:10

[b]*13 Cabul* sounds like the Hebrew for *good-for-nothing.* [c]*14* That is, about 4 1/2 tons (about 4 metric tons) [d]*15* Or *the Millo*; also in verse 24 [e]*18* The Hebrew may also be read *Tamar.* [f]*19* Or *charioteers* [g]*21* The Hebrew term refers to the irrevocable giving over of things or persons to the LORD, often by totally destroying them. [h]*25* Traditionally *peace offerings* [i]*26* Hebrew *Yam Suph*; that is, Sea of Reeds [j]*28* That is, about 16 tons (about 14.5 metric tons) [k]*5* Or *the ascent by which he went up to*

9:15—10:29 HUMANITY, Community Relationships—The oppression of others to accomplish personal or national goals is a pattern followed by many. It is also one which the prophets and the New Testament attacked with vehemence. *See Isa 5:8; Lk 12:13–21.*

9:25 PRAYER, Worship—All men were required to appear at the Feast of Unleavened Bread, the Feast of Harvest or Firstfruits, and the Feast of Ingathering or Tabernacles (Ex 23:14–17). Public worship represents commitment and gratitude to God.

10:1–9 PRAYER, Universality of—See note on 5:7.

10:9 GOD, Love—God's covenant with Israel is due to the love of God which is traced back into the eternal being of God. Such love was evident even to a foreign ruler who worshiped other gods. See notes on 8:23; Ex 3:7; 1 Jn 4:7–21.

10:9 ELECTION, Responsibility—The Queen of Sheba

your God, who has delighted in you and
placed you on the throne of Israel. Because of the LORD's eternal love[x] for Israel, he has made you king, to maintain justice[y] and righteousness."
10And she gave the king 120 talents[l]
of gold,[z] large quantities of spices, and
precious stones. Never again were so
many spices brought in as those the
queen of Sheba gave to King Solomon.
11(Hiram's ships brought gold from
Ophir;[a] and from there they brought
great cargoes of almugwood[m] and precious stones. 12The king used the almugwood to make supports for the temple of
the LORD and for the royal palace, and to
make harps and lyres for the musicians.
So much almugwood has never been imported or seen since that day.)
13King Solomon gave the queen of Sheba all she desired and asked for, besides
what he had given her out of his royal
bounty. Then she left and returned with
her retinue to her own country.

Solomon's Splendor

10:14–29pp — 2Ch 1:14–17; 9:13–28

14The weight of the gold[b] that Solomon received yearly was 666 talents,[n]
15not including the revenues from merchants and traders and from all the Arabi-
an kings and the governors of the land.
16King Solomon made two hundred
large shields[c] of hammered gold; six
hundred bekas[o] of gold went into each
shield. 17He also made three hundred
small shields of hammered gold, with
three minas[p] of gold in each shield. The
king put them in the Palace of the Forest
of Lebanon.[d]
18Then the king made a great throne
inlaid with ivory and overlaid with fine
gold. 19The throne had six steps, and its
back had a rounded top. On both sides of
the seat were armrests, with a lion standing beside each of them. 20Twelve lions
stood on the six steps, one at either end
of each step. Nothing like it had ever
been made for any other kingdom. 21All
King Solomon's goblets were gold, and all
the household articles in the Palace of the
Forest of Lebanon were pure gold.[e]
Nothing was made of silver, because silver was considered of little value in Solomon's days. 22The king had a fleet of trading ships[q][f] at sea along with the ships[g]
of Hiram. Once every three years it returned, carrying gold, silver and ivory,
and apes and baboons.
23King Solomon was greater in riches[h]
and wisdom[i] than all the other kings of
the earth. 24The whole world sought audience with Solomon to hear the wisdom[j] God had put in his heart. 25Year
after year, everyone who came brought a
gift[k]—articles of silver and gold, robes,
weapons and spices, and horses and
mules.
26Solomon accumulated chariots and
horses;[l] he had fourteen hundred chariots and twelve thousand horses,[r] which
he kept in the chariot cities and also with
him in Jerusalem. 27The king made silver
as common[m] in Jerusalem as stones,[n]
and cedar as plentiful as sycamore-fig[o]
trees in the foothills. 28Solomon's horses
were imported from Egypt[s] and from
Kue[t]—the royal merchants purchased
them from Kue. 29They imported a chariot from Egypt for six hundred shekels[u] of
silver, and a horse for a hundred and fifty.[v] They also exported them to all the
kings of the Hittites[p] and of the Arameans.

Chapter 11

Solomon's Wives

KING Solomon, however, loved many
foreign women[q] besides Pharaoh's

10:9 [x]S Dt 7:8 [y]Ps 11:7; 33:5; 72:2; 99:4; 103:6
10:10 [z]S 1Ki 9:28; Isa 60:6
10:11 [a]S Ge 10:29
10:14 [b]S 1Ki 9:28
10:16 [c]S 2Sa 8:7
10:17 [d]S 1Ki 7:2
10:21 [e]Isa 60:17
10:22 [f]S 1Ki 9:26 [g]1Ki 9:27; Ps 48:7; Isa 2:16; 23:1,14; 60:6,9
10:23 [h]1Ki 3:13; Mt 6:29 [i]S 1Ki 3:12; Mt 12:42
10:24 [j]S 2Sa 14:20
10:25 [k]S 1Sa 10:27
10:26 [l]S Dt 17:16
10:27 [m]Dt 17:17 [n]Job 27:16; Isa 60:17 [o]1Ch 27:28; Am 7:14
10:29 [p]S Nu 13:29
11:1 [q]S ver 3; S Ex 34:16

[l]*10* That is, about 4 1/2 tons (about 4 metric tons)
[m]*11* Probably a variant of *algumwood*; also in verse 12
[n]*14* That is, about 25 tons (about 23 metric tons)
[o]*16* That is, about 7 1/2 pounds (about 3.5 kilograms)
[p]*17* That is, about 3 3/4 pounds (about 1.7 kilograms)
[q]*22* Hebrew *of ships of Tarshish* [r]*26* Or *charioteers* [s]*28* Or possibly *Muzur*, a region in Cilicia; also in verse 29 [t]*28* Probably *Cilicia*
[u]*29* That is, about 15 pounds (about 7 kilograms)
[v]*29* That is, about 3 3/4 pounds (about 1.7 kilograms)

was aware of God's election of Israel based on His eternal, unconditional love. See note on Dt 7:6–15. She reminded Solomon that his election carried the responsibilities of ruling justly and righteously. God does not grant license for permissiveness when He makes a person or a people the object of election. *The election of* God is a call to obedience and responsibility.

11:1–13 SIN, Alienation—Marriage may alienate us from God. Even the wisest of God's leaders forgot to use wisdom in marriage. Solomon's involvement with foreign wives caused him to worship other gods. This is the basic sin which alienates a person from the true God. Marriage done to cement government or personal business alliances is sinful. Marriage must be based on a mutual commitment to God. Otherwise, it tends to lead away from God toward sin. Such sin in the personal realm of marriage may bring God's disciplining intervention in other areas of life.

11:1–39 HISTORY, God's Leaders—God faithfully fulfills His promises. He does not guarantee positions of leadership unconditionally. Disobedient leaders face His judgment. Solomon followed the political pattern of his day in making political alliances through marriage. In so doing he rebelled against God's pattern for His people. God raised opponents against him and pointed to the division of his empire. He promised to be faithful to His promise to David even as He punished Solomon.

11:1–9 FAMILY, Multiple Wives—Neither political strategy nor community acceptance justifies sinful behavior. Marriages cemented political alliances for Solomon. The community saw his actions as good politics. The marriages introduced false religions to Israel. God saw them as sin. See note on Ge 16:1–16.

daughter—Moabites, Ammonites,[r]
Edomites, Sidonians and Hittites. 2They
were from nations about which the LORD
had told the Israelites, "You must not intermarry[s] with them, because they will
surely turn your hearts after their gods."
Nevertheless, Solomon held fast to them
in love. 3He had seven hundred wives of
royal birth and three hundred concubines,[t] and his wives led him astray.[u]
4As Solomon grew old, his wives turned
his heart after other gods,[v] and his heart
was not fully devoted[w] to the LORD his
God, as the heart of David his father had
been. 5He followed Ashtoreth[x] the goddess of the Sidonians, and Molech[w][y] the
detestable god of the Ammonites. 6So Solomon did evil[z] in the eyes of the LORD;
he did not follow the LORD completely, as
David his father had done.
7On a hill east[a] of Jerusalem, Solomon
built a high place for Chemosh[b] the detestable god of Moab, and for Molech[c]
the detestable god of the Ammonites. 8He
did the same for all his foreign wives,
who burned incense and offered sacrifices to their gods.
9The LORD became angry with Solomon
because his heart had turned away from
the LORD, the God of Israel, who had appeared[d] to him twice. 10Although he had
forbidden Solomon to follow other gods,[e]
Solomon did not keep the LORD's command.[f] 11So the LORD said to Solomon,
"Since this is your attitude and you have
not kept my covenant and my decrees,[g]
which I commanded you, I will most certainly tear[h] the kingdom away from you
and give it to one of your subordinates.
12Nevertheless, for the sake of David[i]
your father, I will not do it during your
lifetime. I will tear it out of the hand of
your son. 13Yet I will not tear the whole
kingdom from him, but will give him one
tribe[j] for the sake[k] of David my servant
and for the sake of Jerusalem, which I
have chosen."[l]

Solomon's Adversaries

14Then the LORD raised up against Solomon an adversary,[m] Hadad the Edomite,

11:1 r1Ki 14:21,31
11:2 sS Ex 34:16; 1Ki 16:31
11:3 tS Ge 22:24; S Est 2:14 uver 1; Dt 17:17; Ne 13:26; Pr 31:3
11:4 vS Ex 34:16 wS 1Ki 8:61; S 1Ch 29:19
11:5 xS Jdg 2:13 yver 7; S Lev 18:21; Isa 57:9; Zep 1:5
11:6 zS Dt 4:25
11:7 a2Ki 23:13 bS Nu 21:29 cS Lev 18:21; 20:2-5; Ac 7:43
11:9 dS 1Ki 3:5
11:10 eS 1Ki 9:6 f1Ki 6:12
11:11 gS Lev 18:4 hver 31; S 1Sa 15:27; 2Ki 17:21; Mt 21:43
11:12 iPs 89:33
11:13 j1Ki 12:20 kS 2Sa 7:15 lDt 12:11
11:14 mS 1Ki 5:4
11:15 n1Ch 18:12
11:18 oNu 10:12
11:23 pS 1Ki 5:4 qS 2Sa 8:3
11:24 rS 2Sa 8:5
11:25 sS Ge 10:22; S 2Sa 10:19
11:26 t2Ch 13:6

from the royal line of Edom. 15Earlier
when David was fighting with Edom, Joab
the commander of the army, who had
gone up to bury the dead, had struck
down all the men in Edom.[n] 16Joab and
all the Israelites stayed there for six
months, until they had destroyed all the
men in Edom. 17But Hadad, still only a
boy, fled to Egypt with some Edomite officials who had served his father. 18They
set out from Midian and went to Paran.[o]
Then taking men from Paran with them,
they went to Egypt, to Pharaoh king of
Egypt, who gave Hadad a house and land
and provided him with food.
19Pharaoh was so pleased with Hadad
that he gave him a sister of his own wife,
Queen Tahpenes, in marriage. 20The sister of Tahpenes bore him a son named
Genubath, whom Tahpenes brought up
in the royal palace. There Genubath lived
with Pharaoh's own children.
21While he was in Egypt, Hadad heard
that David rested with his fathers and
that Joab the commander of the army was
also dead. Then Hadad said to Pharaoh,
"Let me go, that I may return to my own
country."
22"What have you lacked here that you
want to go back to your own country?"
Pharaoh asked.
"Nothing," Hadad replied, "but do let
me go!"
23And God raised up against Solomon
another adversary,[p] Rezon son of Eliada,
who had fled from his master, Hadadezer[q] king of Zobah. 24He gathered men
around him and became the leader of a
band of rebels when David destroyed the
forces[x] ⌊of Zobah⌋; the rebels went to Damascus,[r] where they settled and took
control. 25Rezon was Israel's adversary as
long as Solomon lived, adding to the trouble caused by Hadad. So Rezon ruled in
Aram[s] and was hostile toward Israel.

Jeroboam Rebels Against Solomon

26Also, Jeroboam son of Nebat rebelled[t] against the king. He was one of

w *5* Hebrew *Milcom*; also in verse 33 x *24* Hebrew *destroyed them*

11:9–13,29–39 GOD, One God—The wrath of God was expressed when Solomon compromised his loyalty to God with worship of other gods. See notes on Ge 6:5–8; 17:14; Mt 3:7–10; Ro 1:18.

11:9–13 REVELATION, Word—The Lord spoke to Solomon. As often, the Bible does not describe the process. A dream, a prophet, or direct word to Solomon may have been God's means of revelation. The Bible seldom emphasizes the how of revelation. It underlines God's message. See note on 2 Sa 24:11–13.

11:13–36 ELECTION, Condemnation—*When a leader or a people who enjoy God's election* flagrantly disobey and disrespect God, they face punishment. Because God was faithful to His election promises, chose to put His name in Jerusalem, and loved David, Solomon did not experience total punishment and the deeper embarrassment of losing the entire kingdom. Mercy can be found even in the judgment of God.

11:14–40 GOD, Sovereignty—The sovereignty of God, His ability to work in the ordinary affairs of the world to carry out His own purposes, does not mean that God simply manipulates people or nations like pawns on a chess board. It does mean that He works through them, respecting their own individual freedom of will, in such a way that He accomplishes His will.

***11:26–39* SIN, Punishment**—God's intervention to punish sinners is not a meaningless threat. God carries out His threats and punishes. He may use unexpected people, like Jeroboam, an employee promoted for good work, to put His

Solomon's officials, an Ephraimite from Zeredah, and his mother was a widow named Zeruah.

27Here is the account of how he rebelled against the king: Solomon had built the supporting terraces[y][u] and had filled in the gap in the wall of the city of David his father. 28Now Jeroboam was a man of standing,[v] and when Solomon saw how well[w] the young man did his work, he put him in charge of the whole labor force of the house of Joseph.

29About that time Jeroboam was going out of Jerusalem, and Ahijah[x] the prophet of Shiloh met him on the way, wearing a new cloak. The two of them were alone out in the country, 30and Ahijah took hold of the new cloak he was wearing and tore[y] it into twelve pieces. 31Then he said to Jeroboam, "Take ten pieces for yourself, for this is what the LORD, the God of Israel, says: 'See, I am going to tear[z] the kingdom out of Solomon's hand and give you ten tribes. 32But for the sake[a] of my servant David and the city of Jerusalem, which I have chosen out of all the tribes of Israel, he will have one tribe. 33I will do this because they have[z] forsaken me and worshiped[b] Ashtoreth the goddess of the Sidonians, Chemosh the god of the Moabites, and Molech the god of the Ammonites, and have not walked[c] in my ways, nor done what is right in my eyes, nor kept my statutes[d] and laws as David, Solomon's father, did.

34" 'But I will not take the whole kingdom out of Solomon's hand; I have made him ruler all the days of his life for the sake of David my servant, whom I chose and who observed my commands and statutes. 35I will take the kingdom from his son's hands and give you ten tribes. 36I will give one tribe[e] to his son so that David my servant may always have a lamp[f] before me in Jerusalem, the city where I chose to put my Name. 37However, as for you, I will take you, and you will rule[g] over all that your heart desires;[h] you will be king over Israel. 38If you do whatever I command you and walk in my ways and do what is right[i] in my eyes by keeping my statutes[j] and commands, as David my servant did, I will be with you. I will build you a dynasty[k] as enduring as the one I built for David and will give Israel to you. 39I will humble David's descendants because of this, but not forever.' "

40Solomon tried to kill Jeroboam, but Jeroboam fled[l] to Egypt, to Shishak[m] the king, and stayed there until Solomon's death.

Solomon's Death

11:41–43pp — 2Ch 9:29–31

41As for the other events of Solomon's reign—all he did and the wisdom he displayed—are they not written in the book of the annals of Solomon? 42Solomon reigned in Jerusalem over all Israel forty years. 43Then he rested with his fathers and was buried in the city of David his father. And Rehoboam[n] his son succeeded him as king.

Chapter 12

Israel Rebels Against Rehoboam

12:1–24pp — 2Ch 10:1–11:4

REHOBOAM went to Shechem,[o] for all the Israelites had gone there to make him king. 2When Jeroboam son of Nebat heard this (he was still in Egypt, where he had fled[p] from King Solomon), he returned from[a] Egypt. 3So they sent for Jeroboam, and he and the whole assembly of Israel went to Rehoboam and said to him: 4"Your father put a heavy yoke[q] on us, but now lighten the harsh labor and the heavy yoke he put on us, and we will serve you."

5Rehoboam answered, "Go away for three days and then come back to me." So the people went away.

6Then King Rehoboam consulted the elders[r] who had served his father Solomon during his lifetime. "How would you advise me to answer these people?" he asked.

7They replied, "If today you will be a servant to these people and serve them and give them a favorable answer,[s] they will always be your servants."

8But Rehoboam rejected[t] the advice the elders gave him and consulted the young men who had grown up with him and were serving him. 9He asked them, "What is your advice? How should we answer these people who say to me, 'Lighten the yoke your father put on us'?"

10The young men who had grown up with him replied, "Tell these people who have said to you, 'Your father put a heavy yoke on us, but make our yoke lighter'—tell them, 'My little finger is thicker than my father's waist. 11My father laid on you

11:27 [u]S 1Ki 9:24
11:28 [v]S Ru 2:1 [w]S Ge 39:4; Pr 22:29
11:29 [x]1Ki 12:15; 14:2; 2Ch 9:29; 10:15
11:30 [y]1Sa 15:27
11:31 [z]S ver 11; S 1Sa 15:27
11:32 [a]S 2Sa 7:15
11:33 [b]S Jdg 2:13 [c]2Ki 21:22 [d]1Ki 3:3
11:36 [e]1Ki 12:17 [f]S 2Sa 21:17
11:37 [g]1Ki 14:7 [h]2Sa 3:21
11:38 [i]S Dt 12:25; S 2Sa 8:15 [j]S Dt 17:19 [k]S Ex 1:21
11:40 [l]1Ki 12:2; 2Ch 10:2 [m]2Ch 12:2
11:43 [n]Mt 1:7
12:1 [o]ver 25; S Ge 12:6; Jos 24:32
12:2 [p]S 1Ki 11:40
12:4 [q]S 1Sa 8:11-18; 1Ki 4:20-28
12:6 [r]S 1Ki 4:2
12:7 [s]Pr 15:1
12:8 [t]Lev 19:32

[y]27 Or *the Millo* [z]33 Hebrew; Septuagint, Vulgate and Syriac *because he has* [a]2 Or *he remained in*

threats into reality.

11:29–40 CHRISTIAN ETHICS, Moral Imperatives—Refusal to follow God brings lost opportunities. God does not give up. He continues setting His moral imperatives before new generations. See note on 3:3,14.

11:41 HOLY SCRIPTURE, Writing—See note on 14:19, 29.

a heavy yoke; I will make it even heavier.
My father scourged you with whips; I will
scourge you with scorpions.' "
12Three days later Jeroboam and all the
people returned to Rehoboam, as the king
had said, "Come back to me in three
days." 13The king answered the people
harshly. Rejecting the advice given him
by the elders, 14he followed the advice of
the young men and said, "My father
made your yoke heavy; I will make it
even heavier. My father scourged[u] you
with whips; I will scourge you with scorpions." 15So the king did not listen to the
people, for this turn of events was from
the LORD,[v] to fulfill the word the LORD
had spoken to Jeroboam son of Nebat
through Ahijah[w] the Shilonite.
16When all Israel saw that the king refused to listen to them, they answered
the king:

"What share[x] do we have in David,
what part in Jesse's son?
To your tents, O Israel![y]
Look after your own house,
O David!"

So the Israelites went home.[z] 17But as for
the Israelites who were living in the
towns of Judah,[a] Rehoboam still ruled
over them.
18King Rehoboam sent out Adoni-
ram,[b][b] who was in charge of forced labor, but all Israel stoned him to death.[c]
King Rehoboam, however, managed to
get into his chariot and escape to Jerusalem. 19So Israel has been in rebellion
against the house of David[d] to this day.
20When all the Israelites heard that Jeroboam had returned, they sent and called
him to the assembly and made him king
over all Israel. Only the tribe of Judah remained loyal to the house of David.[e]
21When Rehoboam arrived in Jerusalem, he mustered the whole house of Judah and the tribe of Benjamin—a hundred and eighty thousand fighting men
—to make war[f] against the house of
Israel and to regain the kingdom for Rehoboam son of Solomon.
22But this word of God came to Shemaiah[g] the man of God:[h] 23"Say to Rehoboam son of Solomon king of Judah, to the
whole house of Judah and Benjamin, and
to the rest of the people, 24'This is what
the LORD says: Do not go up to fight
against your brothers, the Israelites. Go
home, every one of you, for this is my
doing.' " So they obeyed the word of the
LORD and went home again, as the LORD
had ordered.

Golden Calves at Bethel and Dan

25Then Jeroboam fortified Shechem[i]
in the hill country of Ephraim and lived
there. From there he went out and built
up Peniel.[c] [j]
26Jeroboam thought to himself, "The
kingdom will now likely revert to the
house of David. 27If these people go up to
offer sacrifices at the temple of the LORD
in Jerusalem,[k] they will again give their
allegiance to their lord, Rehoboam king of
Judah. They will kill me and return to
King Rehoboam."
28After seeking advice, the king made
two golden calves.[l] He said to the people, "It is too much for you to go up to
Jerusalem. Here are your gods, O Israel,
who brought you up out of Egypt."[m]
29One he set up in Bethel,[n] and the other
in Dan.[o] 30And this thing became a sin;[p]
the people went even as far as Dan to
worship the one there.
31Jeroboam built shrines[q] on high
places and appointed priests[r] from all
sorts of people, even though they were
not Levites. 32He instituted a festival on
the fifteenth day of the eighth[s] month,
like the festival held in Judah, and offered
sacrifices on the altar. This he did in
Bethel,[t] sacrificing to the calves he had
made. And at Bethel he also installed
priests at the high places he had made.
33On the fifteenth day of the eighth
month, a month of his own choosing, he
offered sacrifices on the altar he had built
at Bethel.[u] So he instituted the festival
for the Israelites and went up to the altar
to make offerings.

12:14 [u]Ex 1:14
12:15 [v]S Dt 2:30; 2Ch 25:20 [w]S 1Ki 11:29
12:16 [x]S Ge 31:14 [y]S 2Sa 20:1 [z]Isa 7:17
12:17 [a]1Ki 11:13, 36
12:18 [b]S 2Sa 20:24 [c]S Jos 7:25
12:19 [d]2Ki 17:21
12:20 [e]1Ki 11:13, 32; Eze 37:16
12:21 [f]1Ki 14:30; 15:6,16; 2Ch 11:1
12:22 [g]2Ch 12:5-7 [h]S Dt 33:1; 2Ki 4:7
12:25 [i]S ver 1 [j]S Jdg 8:8,17
12:27 [k]Dt 12:5-6
12:28 [l]S Ex 32:4; S 2Ch 11:15 [m]S Ex 32:8
12:29 [n]S Ge 12:8; S Jos 7:2 [o]Jdg 18:27-31; Am 8:14
12:30 [p]1Ki 13:34; 14:16; 15:26,30; 16:2; 2Ki 3:3; 10:29; 13:2; 17:21
12:31 [q]S Lev 26:30; 1Ki 13:32; 2Ki 17:29 [r]S Ex 29:9; 1Ki 13:33; 2Ki 17:32; 2Ch 11:14-15; 13:9
12:32 [s]S Nu 29:12 [t]2Ki 10:29
12:33 [u]2Ki 23:15; Am 7:13

[b]*18* Some Septuagint manuscripts and Syriac (see also 1 Kings 4:6 and 5:14); Hebrew *Adoram*
[c]*25* Hebrew *Penuel*, a variant of *Peniel*

12:15,24 GOD, Sovereignty—See note on 11:14–40.

12:26–33 SIN, Transgression—Sin is transgressing God's promises and His teachings. God set Jeroboam up and promised to bless him if he were faithful (11:37–38). Jeroboam sought to solidify his rebellion against Judah and decided to ensure the religious as well as political loyalty of his followers. He set up shrines in the northern section of the country for the people to worship. He fashioned his gods after the sacred bull of Egypt and the calves of Baal. He urged the people to worship at the shrines in Bethel and Dan. In doing this Jeroboam set a pattern of idolatry that became a standard for the later kings of the Northern Kingdom of Israel and soon spread throughout the people. Jeroboam's desire to solidify his kingdom became a national sin which ultimately led to the downfall of Israel. The actions of national leaders both reflect and determine the habits of the people they govern. Leaders who lead people to transgress God's promises and teachings bear added responsibility to God for their sins.

12:28–30 HISTORY, Confession—Confessing the right words in the wrong context is sinful. Jeroboam repeated Israel's basic confession of faith in God's deliverance in the Exodus. He suggested his calves represented the presence of the God of the Exodus. God punished his house for this grave sin because God explicitly prohibited images representing Him. See note on Jdg 18:1,47.

the book of the annals of the kings of Israel. 20He reigned for twenty-two years and then rested with his fathers. And Nadab his son succeeded him as king.

Rehoboam King of Judah

14:21,25–31pp — 2Ch 12:9–16

21Rehoboam son of Solomon was king in Judah. He was forty-one years old when he became king, and he reigned seventeen years in Jerusalem, the city the LORD had chosen out of all the tribes of Israel in which to put his Name. His mother's name was Naamah; she was an Ammonite.[r]

22Judah[s] did evil in the eyes of the LORD. By the sins they committed they stirred up his jealous anger[t] more than their fathers had done. 23They also set up for themselves high places, sacred stones[u] and Asherah poles[v] on every high hill and under every spreading tree.[w] 24There were even male shrine prostitutes[x] in the land; the people engaged in all the detestable[y] practices of the nations the LORD had driven out before the Israelites.

25In the fifth year of King Rehoboam, Shishak king of Egypt attacked[z] Jerusalem. 26He carried off the treasures of the temple[a] of the LORD and the treasures of the royal palace. He took everything, including all the gold shields[b] Solomon had made. 27So King Rehoboam made bronze shields to replace them and assigned these to the commanders of the guard on duty at the entrance to the royal palace.[c] 28Whenever the king went to the LORD's temple, the guards bore the shields, and afterward they returned them to the guardroom.

29As for the other events of Rehoboam's reign, and all he did, are they not written in the book of the annals of the kings of Judah? 30There was continual warfare[d] between Rehoboam and Jeroboam. 31And Rehoboam rested with his fathers and was buried with them in the City of David. His mother's name was Naamah; she was an Ammonite.[e] And Abijah[g] his son succeeded him as king.

Chapter 15

Abijah King of Judah

15:1–2,6–8pp —2Ch 13:1–2,22–14:1

IN the eighteenth year of the reign of Jeroboam son of Nebat, Abijah[h] became king of Judah, 2and he reigned in Jerusalem three years. His mother's name was Maacah[f] daughter of Abishalom.[i]

3He committed all the sins his father had done before him; his heart was not fully devoted[g] to the LORD his God, as the heart of David his forefather had been. 4Nevertheless, for David's sake the LORD his God gave him a lamp[h] in Jerusalem by raising up a son to succeed him and by making Jerusalem strong. 5For David had done what was right in the eyes of the LORD and had not failed to keep[i] any of the LORD's commands all the days of his life—except in the case of Uriah[j] the Hittite.

6There was war[k] between Rehoboam[j] and Jeroboam throughout ⌊Abijah's⌋ lifetime. 7As for the other events of Abijah's reign, and all he did, are they not written in the book of the annals of the kings of Judah? There was war between Abijah and Jeroboam. 8And Abijah rested with his fathers and was buried in the City of David. And Asa his son succeeded him as king.

Asa King of Judah

15:9–22pp — 2Ch 14:2–3; 15:16–16:6
15:23–24pp — 2Ch 16:11–17:1

9In the twentieth year of Jeroboam king of Israel, Asa became king of Judah,

14:21 [r]S 1Ki 11:1
14:22 [s]2Ki 17:19; 2Ch 12:1 [t]Dt 32:21; Ps 78:58; Jer 44:3; S 1Co 10:22
14:23 [u]S Ex 23:24; Dt 16:22; Hos 10:1 [v]S Dt 12:3 [w]S Dt 12:2; Eze 6:13
14:24 [x]S Dt 23:17 [y]1Ki 11:5-7; 2Ki 21:2; Ezr 9:11; Pr 21:27; Isa 1:13; Jer 16:18; 32:35; 44:4
14:25 [z]2Ch 12:2
14:26 [a]1Ki 15:15, 18 [b]S 2Sa 8:7
14:27 [c]2Ki 11:5
14:30 [d]2Sa 3:1; S 1Ki 12:21
14:31 [e]S 1Ki 11:1
15:2 [f]ver 10,13; 2Ch 11:20
15:3 [g]S 1Ki 8:61
15:4 [h]S 2Sa 21:17
15:5 [i]S Dt 5:32; S 1Ki 9:4 [j]2Sa 11:2-27; 12:9
15:6 [k]ver 16,32; S 1Ki 12:21; 2Ch 16:9

[g]*31* Some Hebrew manuscripts and Septuagint (see also 2 Chron. 12:16); most Hebrew manuscripts *Abijam* [h]*1* Some Hebrew manuscripts and Septuagint (see also 2 Chron. 12:16); most Hebrew manuscripts *Abijam*; also in verses 7 and 8 [i]*2* A variant of *Absalom*; also in verse 10 [j]*6* Most Hebrew manuscripts; some Hebrew manuscripts and Syriac *Abijam* (that is, Abijah)

lical author used written documents as sources for his writing (11:41; 15:7,23,31; 16:14,20,27; 22:39,45; 2 Ki 1:18; 8:23; 10:34; 12:19; 13:8,12; 14:15,18,28; 15:6,11, 15,21,26,31,36; 16:19; 20:20; 21:17,25; 23:28; 24:5). God led the writer to the documents to provide the needed historical information.

14:21 ELECTION, Responsibility—Like father, like son can be said of Rehoboam. A downward spiral of degeneracy manifested itself in the lives of Rehoboam and the people of Judah. They failed to remember their identity as a people elected by God to show forth the righteousness of God in their personal walk and national purpose. Bronze shields substituted for the gold shields used by the guard who watched the entrance of the Temple and the loss of the treasures of God's house to Egypt were outward symbols of the spiritual decay which occurs when God's people lose the meaning of election.

14:22–24 SIN, Transgression—Spiritual loyalty determines a nation's fate. Both the king and the people were responsible for this lapse into infidelity and idolatry. A people must share the blame with their political leaders for a moral environment that results in national sins and abuses of power. Military power cannot prevail against God's jealous anger. Not even strong religious tradition and trust in God's promise to David could save Judah. A sinful people meets God's judgment no matter who their ancestors were.

15:1–5 CHRISTIAN ETHICS, Moral Imperatives—See notes on 3:3,14; 11:29–40.

15:3 SIN, Transgression—See note on 14:22–24.

15:4 GOD, Faithfulness—God is faithful to His promises, even when we have acted irresponsibly toward Him and have no reason to expect Him to be faithful to us. See notes on Ge 8:1; Nu 26:65; Jos 1:6.

15:7,23,31 HOLY SCRIPTURE, Writing—See note on 14:19,29.

10and he reigned in Jerusalem forty-one
years. His grandmother's name was Maacah[l] daughter of Abishalom.

11Asa did what was right in the eyes of
the LORD, as his father David[m] had done.
12He expelled the male shrine prostitutes[n] from the land and got rid of all the
idols[o] his fathers had made. 13He even
deposed his grandmother Maacah[p] from
her position as queen mother,[q] because
she had made a repulsive Asherah pole.
Asa cut the pole down[r] and burned it in
the Kidron Valley. 14Although he did not
remove[s] the high places, Asa's heart was
fully committed[t] to the LORD all his life.
15He brought into the temple of the LORD
the silver and gold and the articles that he
and his father had dedicated.[u]

16There was war[v] between Asa and
Baasha king of Israel throughout their
reigns. 17Baasha king of Israel went up
against Judah and fortified Ramah[w] to
prevent anyone from leaving or entering
the territory of Asa king of Judah.

18Asa then took all the silver and gold
that was left in the treasuries of the
LORD's temple[x] and of his own palace.
He entrusted it to his officials and sent[y]
them to Ben-Hadad[z] son of Tabrimmon,
the son of Hezion, the king of Aram, who
was ruling in Damascus. 19"Let there be a
treaty[a] between me and you," he said,
"as there was between my father and
your father. See, I am sending you a gift
of silver and gold. Now break your treaty
with Baasha king of Israel so he will withdraw from me."

20Ben-Hadad agreed with King Asa and
sent the commanders of his forces against
the towns of Israel. He conquered[b] Ijon,
Dan, Abel Beth Maacah and all Kinnereth
in addition to Naphtali. 21When Baasha
heard this, he stopped building Ramah[c]
and withdrew to Tirzah.[d] 22Then King
Asa issued an order to all Judah—no one
was exempt—and they carried away
from Ramah[e] the stones and timber Baasha had been using there. With them
King Asa[f] built up Geba[g] in Benjamin,
and also Mizpah.[h]

23As for all the other events of Asa's
reign, all his achievements, all he did and
the cities he built, are they not written in
the book of the annals of the kings of Judah? In his old age, however, his feet became diseased. 24Then Asa rested with
his fathers and was buried with them in
the city of his father David. And Jehoshaphat[i] his son succeeded him as king.

Nadab King of Israel

25Nadab son of Jeroboam became king
of Israel in the second year of Asa king of
Judah, and he reigned over Israel two
years. 26He did evil[j] in the eyes of the
LORD, walking in the ways of his father[k]
and in his sin, which he had caused Israel
to commit.

27Baasha son of Ahijah of the house of
Issachar plotted against him, and he
struck him down[l] at Gibbethon,[m] a Philistine town, while Nadab and all Israel
were besieging it. 28Baasha killed Nadab
in the third year of Asa king of Judah and
succeeded him as king.

29As soon as he began to reign, he
killed Jeroboam's whole family.[n] He did
not leave Jeroboam anyone that breathed,
but destroyed them all, according to the
word of the LORD given through his servant Ahijah the Shilonite— 30because of
the sins[o] Jeroboam had committed and
had caused[p] Israel to commit, and because he provoked the LORD, the God of
Israel, to anger.

31As for the other events of Nadab's
reign, and all he did, are they not written
in the book of the annals[q] of the kings of
Israel? 32There was war[r] between Asa
and Baasha king of Israel throughout their
reigns.

Baasha King of Israel

33In the third year of Asa king of Judah,
Baasha son of Ahijah became king of all
Israel in Tirzah,[s] and he reigned twenty-
four years. 34He did evil[t] in the eyes of
the LORD, walking in the ways of Jeroboam and in his sin, which he had caused
Israel to commit.

Chapter 16

1THEN the word of the LORD came to
Jehu[u] son of Hanani[v] against Baasha: 2"I lifted you up from the dust[w] and
made you leader[x] of my people Israel,
but you walked in the ways of Jeroboam
and caused[y] my people Israel to sin and
to provoke me to anger by their sins. 3So I
am about to consume Baasha[z] and his
house,[a] and I will make your house like
that of Jeroboam son of Nebat. 4Dogs[b]
will eat those belonging to Baasha who
die in the city, and the birds of the air[c]

15:10 [l]S ver 2
15:11 [m]1Ki 9:4
15:12 [n]1Ki 14:24 [o]2Ch 15:8
15:13 [p]S ver 2 [q]S 1Ki 2:19 [r]S Ex 34:13
15:14 [s]2Ch 14:5; 17:6 [t]S 1Ki 8:61
15:15 [u]S 2Sa 8:11
15:16 [v]S ver 6; S 1Ki 12:21
15:17 [w]S Jos 18:25
15:18 [x]S 1Ki 14:26 [y]2Ki 12:18; 16:8; 18:14-16,15; Joel 3:5 [z]ver 18-20; 1Ki 20:1; 2Ki 6:24; 13:3; Jer 49:27
15:19 [a]S Ex 23:32; S 1Ki 5:12
15:20 [b]1Ki 20:34
15:21 [c]S Jos 18:25 [d]1Ki 16:15-17
15:22 [e]ver 17 [f]ver 9-24; Jer 41:9 [g]S Jos 18:24; 2Ki 23:8 [h]S Jos 11:3
15:24 [i]Mt 1:8
15:26 [j]S Dt 4:25 [k]S 1Ki 12:30
15:27 [l]1Ki 14:14 [m]S Jos 19:44
15:29 [n]S 1Ki 13:34
15:30 [o]S 1Ki 12:30 [p]1Ki 16:26; 2Ki 3:3; 14:24; 15:28; 21:16
15:31 [q]1Ki 11:41
15:32 [r]S ver 6
15:33 [s]1Ki 14:17; 16:6,23; 2Ki 15:14; SS 6:4
15:34 [t]ver 26
16:1 [u]ver 7; 2Ch 19:2; 20:34 [v]2Ch 16:7
16:2 [w]1Sa 2:8 [x]S 1Ki 14:7-9 [y]S 1Ki 12:30
16:3 [z]2Ki 9:9 [a]ver 11; 1Ki 21:22
16:4 [b]S 1Ki 14:11 [c]S Ge 40:19

15:12–13 GOD, One God—He is a jealous God. See note on 9:6–9.
15:26 SIN, Transgression—See note on 12:26–33.
15:27–30 GOD, Wrath—When people persist in their sin, they can expect to receive the wrath of God. See notes on Ge 6:5–8; 17:14; Mt 3:7–10; Gal 6:7–10.
15:29–30 SIN, Transgression—See note on 12:26–33.
15:34 SIN, Transgression—See note on 12:26–33.
16:1–7 SIN, Transgression—See note on 12:26–33.
16:2,7,13,26,33 GOD, Wrath—Continued sin brings the wrath of God in judgment. See note on 15:27–30.

will feed on those who die in the country."
5As for the other events of Baasha's
reign, what he did and his achievements,
are they not written in the book of the
annals[d] of the kings of Israel? 6Baasha
rested with his fathers and was buried in
Tirzah.[e] And Elah his son succeeded him
as king.
7Moreover, the word of the LORD
came[f] through the prophet Jehu[g] son of
Hanani to Baasha and his house, because
of all the evil he had done in the eyes of
the LORD, provoking him to anger by the
things he did, and becoming like the
house of Jeroboam—and also because he
destroyed it.

Elah King of Israel

8In the twenty-sixth year of Asa king of
Judah, Elah son of Baasha became king of
Israel, and he reigned in Tirzah two
years.
9Zimri, one of his officials, who had
command of half his chariots, plotted
against him. Elah was in Tirzah at the
time, getting drunk[h] in the home of
Arza, the man in charge[i] of the palace at
Tirzah. 10Zimri came in, struck him down
and killed him in the twenty-seventh year
of Asa king of Judah. Then he succeeded
him as king.[j]
11As soon as he began to reign and was
seated on the throne, he killed off Baasha's whole family.[k] He did not spare a
single male, whether relative or friend.
12So Zimri destroyed the whole family of
Baasha, in accordance with the word of
the LORD spoken against Baasha through
the prophet Jehu— 13because of all the
sins Baasha and his son Elah had committed and had caused Israel to commit, so
that they provoked the LORD, the God of
Israel, to anger by their worthless idols.[l]
14As for the other events of Elah's
reign, and all he did, are they not written
in the book of the annals of the kings of
Israel?

Zimri King of Israel

15In the twenty-seventh year of Asa
king of Judah, Zimri reigned in Tirzah
seven days. The army was encamped near
Gibbethon,[m] a Philistine town. 16When
the Israelites in the camp heard that Zimri had plotted against the king and murdered him, they proclaimed Omri, the
commander of the army, king over Israel
that very day there in the camp. 17Then
Omri and all the Israelites with him withdrew from Gibbethon and laid siege to
Tirzah. 18When Zimri saw that the city
was taken, he went into the citadel of the
royal palace and set the palace on fire
around him. So he died, 19because of the
sins he had committed, doing evil in the
eyes of the LORD and walking in the ways
of Jeroboam and in the sin he had committed and had caused Israel to commit.
20As for the other events of Zimri's
reign, and the rebellion he carried out,
are they not written in the book of the
annals of the kings of Israel?

Omri King of Israel

21Then the people of Israel were split
into two factions; half supported Tibni
son of Ginath for king, and the other half
supported Omri. 22But Omri's followers
proved stronger than those of Tibni son of
Ginath. So Tibni died and Omri became
king.
23In the thirty-first year of Asa king of
Judah, Omri became king of Israel, and
he reigned twelve years, six of them in
Tirzah.[n] 24He bought the hill of Samaria
from Shemer for two talents[k] of silver
and built a city on the hill, calling it Samaria,[o] after Shemer, the name of the
former owner of the hill.
25But Omri did evil[p] in the eyes of the
LORD and sinned more than all those before him. 26He walked in all the ways of
Jeroboam son of Nebat and in his sin,
which he had caused[q] Israel to commit,
so that they provoked the LORD, the God
of Israel, to anger by their worthless
idols.[r]
27As for the other events of Omri's
reign, what he did and the things he
achieved, are they not written in the
book of the annals of the kings of Israel?
28Omri rested with his fathers and was
buried in Samaria.[s] And Ahab his son
succeeded him as king.

Ahab Becomes King of Israel

29In the thirty-eighth year of Asa king
of Judah, Ahab son of Omri became king

16:5 [d] 1Ki 15:31
16:6 [e] S 1Ki 15:33
16:7 [f] S 1Ki 6:11 [g] S ver 1
16:9 [h] 1Ki 20:12, 16; Pr 31:4-5 [i] 1Ki 18:3
16:10 [j] 2Ki 9:31
16:11 [k] S ver 3
16:13 [l] S Dt 32:21
16:15 [m] S Jos 19:44
16:23 [n] S Jos 12:24; S 1Ki 15:33
16:24 [o] S 1Ki 13:32; S Mt 10:5
16:25 [p] ver 25-26; S Dt 4:25; Mic 6:16
16:26 [q] S 1Ki 15:30 [r] S Dt 32:21
16:28 [s] S 1Ki 13:32

[k] *24* That is, about 150 pounds (about 70 kilograms)

16:8–13 SIN, Transgression—See note on 12:26–33.
16:10–13 CHRISTIAN ETHICS, Murder—God punished evil actions through human agents. The historical action is not intended to set a theological precedent legitimating revolution, assassination, and murder. See note on 2 Sa 20:8–10.
16:13 GOD, Jealous—See note on 14:9–16,22. The anger of God was called forth by the failure to recognize Him as the one true God.
16:14,20,27 HOLY SCRIPTURE, Writing—See note on 14:19,29.
16:18–19 HUMANITY, Death and Sin—Zimri's death was self-inflicted (see note on 2 Sa 17:23) and was the ultimate consequence of his sinfulness. His personal sins not only destroyed the individual but also led to communal sins that led to civil war. Thus sin leads not just to spiritual death (Ro 6:23) but may lead to immediate physical death.
16:25–26 SIN, Transgression—See note on 12:26–33.

of Israel, and he reigned in Samaria over
Israel twenty-two years. 30Ahab son of
Omri did more[t] evil in the eyes of the
LORD than any of those before him. 31He
not only considered it trivial to commit
the sins of Jeroboam son of Nebat, but he
also married[u] Jezebel daughter[v] of Eth-
baal king of the Sidonians, and began to
serve Baal[w] and worship him. 32He set up
an altar[x] for Baal in the temple[y] of Baal
that he built in Samaria. 33Ahab also
made an Asherah pole[z] and did more[a] to
provoke the LORD, the God of Israel, to
anger than did all the kings of Israel before him.

34In Ahab's time, Hiel of Bethel rebuilt
Jericho. He laid its foundations at the cost
of his firstborn son Abiram, and he set up
its gates at the cost of his youngest son
Segub, in accordance with the word of
the LORD spoken by Joshua son of Nun.[b]

Chapter 17

Elijah Fed by Ravens

NOW Elijah[c] the Tishbite, from Tishbe[1] in Gilead,[d] said to Ahab, "As
the LORD, the God of Israel, lives, whom I
serve, there will be neither dew nor
rain[e] in the next few years except at my
word."

2Then the word of the LORD came to
Elijah: 3"Leave here, turn eastward and
hide[f] in the Kerith Ravine, east of the
Jordan. 4You will drink from the brook,
and I have ordered the ravens[g] to feed
you there."

5So he did what the LORD had told him.
He went to the Kerith Ravine, east of the
Jordan, and stayed there. 6The ravens
brought him bread and meat in the morning[h] and bread and meat in the evening,
and he drank from the brook.

The Widow at Zarephath

7Some time later the brook dried up
because there had been no rain in the
land. 8Then the word of the LORD came to
him: 9"Go at once to Zarephath[i] of Sidon and stay there. I have commanded a
widow[j] in that place to supply you with
food." 10So he went to Zarephath. When
he came to the town gate, a widow was
there gathering sticks. He called to her
and asked, "Would you bring me a little
water in a jar so I may have a drink?"[k]
11As she was going to get it, he called,
"And bring me, please, a piece of bread."

12"As surely as the LORD your God
lives," she replied, "I don't have any
bread—only a handful of flour in a jar and
a little oil[l] in a jug. I am gathering a few
sticks to take home and make a meal for
myself and my son, that we may eat it—
and die."

13Elijah said to her, "Don't be afraid.
Go home and do as you have said. But
first make a small cake of bread for me
from what you have and bring it to me,
and then make something for yourself
and your son. 14For this is what the LORD,
the God of Israel, says: 'The jar of flour
will not be used up and the jug of oil will

16:30 [t]S 1Ki 14:9
16:31 [u]S 1Ki 11:2 [v]S Jdg 3:6; 2Ki 9:34 [w]S Jdg 2:11
16:32 [x]S Jdg 6:28 [y]2Ki 10:21,27; 11:18; Jer 43:12
16:33 [z]S Jdg 3:7; 2Ki 13:6 [a]S 1Ki 14:9; 21:25
16:34 [b]Jos 6:26
17:1 [c]Mal 4:5; Mt 11:14; 17:3 [d]Jdg 12:4 [e]S Dt 11:17; S 28:24; S 2Sa 1:21; S 1Ki 8:36; Job 12:15; S Lk 4:25
17:3 [f]1Ki 18:4,10; Jer 36:19,26
17:4 [g]S Ge 8:7
17:6 [h]Ex 16:8
17:9 [i]Ob 1:20 [j]Lk 4:26
17:10 [k]S Ge 24:17; Jn 4:7
17:12 [l]2Ki 4:2

[1]1 Or *Tishbite, of the settlers*

16:30–33 SIN, Transgression—See note on 12:26–33.

16:34 SIN, Punishment—God's intervention in history to punish sin may seem long delayed according to human reckoning. God put a curse on Jericho and on anyone who would rebuild the city (Jos 6:26). Hiel rebuilt it and learned God takes His word seriously.

16:34 REVELATION, Word—God's warnings find fulfillment either in a repentant people or the predicted event happening. At times fulfillment lingers even for centuries as with the word through Joshua (Jos 6:26).

17:1,12 GOD, Living—God is a living, divine person with personal characteristics. He is not just a fixed principle or an inanimate object like the "gods" of the nations. See notes on Jos 3:10–13; 1 Sa 17:26,36.

17:1 EVIL AND SUFFERING, Divine Origin—The Creator remains in charge of His creation. He can use or alter nature's cycles for His purposes. When He chooses to do so, suffering may result. God does not cause evil. Evil is not that which causes temporary pain. Evil is that which seeks to thwart God's purposes. God used Elijah and nature to show that He, not Baal, controlled nature and history. Compare ch 18.

17:1–7 REVELATION, In Nature—God has established a universe with natural laws that determine its weather patterns. Natural law does not mean God has given up control of the weather. He can reveal coming weather patterns to His spokesperson and use the weather phenomena to reveal His power over the earth's fertility.

17:1 PRAYER, Sovereignty of God—Ahab had actively promoted Baal worship through the influence of his Sidonian wife Jezebel. One of the meanings of the word "Baal" was "possessor." Elijah began a long campaign to demonstrate the sovereignty of the God of Israel, who possessed heaven and earth. He swore an oath promising God would withhold the sources of fertility for the crops showing He, not Baal, controlled the land's productivity. See note on vv 7–16.

17:7–24 EVIL AND SUFFERING, Divine Origin—Does God cause personal tragedy? People of God continue to wrestle with the problem. A kind widow and Elijah the prophet both raised the question. The text does not give an answer. Rather, it shows that in tragedy, whatever the cause, God can work to show His love and power and to show the power of His chosen spokesperson. Often we have to live without answers to our questions. We can always be sure of God's willingness to help us. His help may come in miraculous form. It may come with strength and hope to face tragedy that remains.

17:7–16 PRAYER, Intercession—This begins a series of miracles which made the Elijah and Elisha period one of the high periods of miracles in biblical history. In many of these, prayer is not specifically mentioned, but Jas 5:17–18 makes it clear that prayer was the catalyst which moved God. Prayer characterized both prophets (1 Ki 18:36–37; 2 Ki 4:33). This miracle of the flour and oil supply occurred in Sidon, the source of Jezebel's Baal worship.

17:13–14 REVELATION, Actions—The widow's generosity inspired Elijah to bless her with the miracle of God's daily provision. The miraculous act revealed God's love for His faithful, loving people. His people are not confined to one race or nation.

not run dry until the day the LORD gives
rain[m] on the land.' "
15She went away and did as Elijah had
told her. So there was food every day for
Elijah and for the woman and her family.
16For the jar of flour was not used up and
the jug of oil did not run dry, in keeping
with the word of the LORD spoken by Elijah.
17Some time later the son of the woman who owned the house became ill. He
grew worse and worse, and finally
stopped breathing. 18She said to Elijah,
"What do you have against me, man of
God? Did you come to remind me of my
sin[n] and kill my son?"
19"Give me your son," Elijah replied.
He took him from her arms, carried him
to the upper room where he was staying,
and laid him on his bed. 20Then he
cried[o] out to the LORD, "O LORD my God,
have you brought tragedy also upon this
widow I am staying with, by causing her
son to die?" 21Then he stretched[p] himself out on the boy three times and cried
to the LORD, "O LORD my God, let this
boy's life return to him!"
22The LORD heard Elijah's cry, and the
boy's life returned to him, and he lived.
23Elijah picked up the child and carried
him down from the room into the house.
He gave him to his mother[q] and said,
"Look, your son is alive!"
24Then the woman said to Elijah,
"Now I know[r] that you are a man of
God[s] and that the word of the LORD from
your mouth is the truth."[t]

Chapter 18

Elijah and Obadiah

AFTER a long time, in the third[u] year,
the word of the LORD came to Elijah:
"Go and present[v] yourself to Ahab, and I
will send rain[w] on the land." 2So Elijah
went to present himself to Ahab.
Now the famine was severe[x] in Samaria, 3and Ahab had summoned Obadiah,
who was in charge[y] of his palace. (Obadiah was a devout believer[z] in the LORD.
4While Jezebel[a] was killing off the LORD's
prophets, Obadiah had taken a hundred
prophets and hidden[b] them in two caves,
fifty in each, and had supplied[c] them
with food and water.) 5Ahab had said to
Obadiah, "Go through the land to all the
springs[d] and valleys. Maybe we can find
some grass to keep the horses and mules
alive so we will not have to kill any of our
animals."[e] 6So they divided the land they
were to cover, Ahab going in one direction and Obadiah in another.
7As Obadiah was walking along, Elijah
met him. Obadiah recognized[f] him,
bowed down to the ground, and said, "Is
it really you, my lord Elijah?"
8"Yes," he replied. "Go tell your master, 'Elijah is here.' "
9"What have I done wrong," asked
Obadiah, "that you are handing your servant over to Ahab to be put to death? 10As
surely as the LORD your God lives, there
is not a nation or kingdom where my
master has not sent someone to look[g] for
you. And whenever a nation or kingdom
claimed you were not there, he made
them swear they could not find you. 11But
now you tell me to go to my master and
say, 'Elijah is here.' 12I don't know where
the Spirit[h] of the LORD may carry you
when I leave you. If I go and tell Ahab
and he doesn't find you, he will kill me.
Yet I your servant have worshiped the
LORD since my youth. 13Haven't you
heard, my lord, what I did while Jezebel
was killing the prophets of the LORD? I
hid a hundred of the LORD's prophets in
two caves, fifty in each, and supplied
them with food and water. 14And now
you tell me to go to my master and say,
'Elijah is here.' He will kill me!"
15Elijah said, "As the LORD Almighty
lives, whom I serve, I will surely
present[i] myself to Ahab today."

17:14 [m]ver 1
17:18 [n]Lk 5:8
17:20 [o]2Ki 4:33
17:21 [p]2Ki 4:34; Ac 20:10
17:23 [q]Heb 11:35
17:24 [r]Jn 16:30 [s]ver 18 [t]1Ki 22:16; Ps 119:43; Jn 17:17
18:1 [u]1Ki 17:1; Lk 4:25 [v]ver 15 [w]S Dt 28:12
18:2 [x]S Lev 26:26
18:3 [y]1Ki 16:9 [z]Ne 7:2
18:4 [a]1Ki 21:23; 2Ki 9:7 [b]S 1Ki 17:3; Isa 16:3; 25:4; 32:2; Ob 1:14 [c]Jer 26:24
18:5 [d]Jer 14:3 [e]S Ge 47:4
18:7 [f]2Ki 1:8; Zec 13:4
18:10 [g]S 1Ki 17:3
18:12 [h]2Ki 2:16; Eze 3:14; Ac 8:39
18:15 [i]ver 1

17:18 SIN, Universal Nature—In the presence of someone of exceptional holiness, one's consciousness of sin becomes particularly acute. The story mentions no specific sin the woman had committed. She, as all people, was aware of her own sinfulness. She concluded her son died to punish her sin. This was not the case. Sickness and death are not always punishment for sin. Rather, in this case, they allowed God to build the woman's faith in His word and in His messenger.
17:19–21 PRAYER, Petition—Elijah wanted to be in his own room where he had doubtless spent many hours in prayer before this miracle. Elisha also was in his own room (2 Ki 4:21,32–33) and shut others out when he prayed for the son of the Shunammite. Petition and intercession are private prayers between an individual and God. They are not public prayers for instruction.
17:22 MIRACLE, Instruments—Miracle is more than an act of charity. It confirms God's actions through His chosen human instruments. The widow of Zarephath had been kind to Elijah. He had assured her that God would not let her oil or her meal be used up (17:14). She trusted him. When her son became deathly ill, she angrily blamed the prophet. Elijah accepted the challenge. He prayed in lament and petition to God. His "life returned to him" after Elijah stretched himself out on him. This same action is described in 2 Ki 4:34–35 and Ac 20:10. God used a human instrument, a man of prayer, to give life. Prayer is an important instrument for God's believing miracle-worker. The miracle led the woman to trust Elijah and to know God spoke through him.
18:12 HOLY SPIRIT, Freedom—The Spirit surprises us with His free divine actions. We cannot predict what He will do. This is good for one God protects. It bewildered Obadiah, whose mission was to deliver God's protected prophet to a frustrated king. The Hebrew makes a subtle wordplay. The same word (*ruach*) means wind and spirit. God's Spirit made the prophet blow like the wind in unexpected places. See 2 Ki 2:16; Eze 3:14; Rev 21:10; notes on Ac 8:39; Rev 17:3. The Spirit is not limited to our ways of action or to our expectations.

Elijah on Mount Carmel

16So Obadiah went to meet Ahab and
told him, and Ahab went to meet Elijah.
17When he saw Elijah, he said to him, "Is
that you, you troubler[j] of Israel?"
18"I have not made trouble for Israel,"
Elijah replied. "But you[k] and your father's family have. You have abandoned[l]
the LORD's commands and have followed
the Baals. 19Now summon[m] the people
from all over Israel to meet me on Mount
Carmel.[n] And bring the four hundred
and fifty prophets of Baal and the four
hundred prophets of Asherah, who eat at
Jezebel's table."[o]
20So Ahab sent word throughout all Israel and assembled the prophets on
Mount Carmel.[p] 21Elijah went before the
people and said, "How long will you waver[q] between two opinions? If the LORD[r]
is God, follow him; but if Baal is God,
follow him."
But the people said nothing.
22Then Elijah said to them, "I am the
only one of the LORD's prophets left,[s] but
Baal has four hundred and fifty prophets.[t] 23Get two bulls for us. Let them
choose one for themselves, and let them
cut it into pieces and put it on the wood
but not set fire to it. I will prepare the
other bull and put it on the wood but not
set fire to it. 24Then you call[u] on the
name of your god, and I will call on the
name of the LORD.[v] The god who answers by fire[w]—he is God."
Then all the people said, "What you
say is good."
25Elijah said to the prophets of Baal,
"Choose one of the bulls and prepare it
first, since there are so many of you. Call
on the name of your god, but do not light
the fire." 26So they took the bull given
them and prepared it.
Then they called[x] on the name of Baal
from morning till noon. "O Baal, answer
us!" they shouted. But there was no response;[y] no one answered. And they
danced around the altar they had made.
27At noon Elijah began to taunt them.
"Shout louder!" he said. "Surely he is a
god! Perhaps he is deep in thought, or
busy, or traveling. Maybe he is sleeping
and must be awakened."[z] 28So they
shouted louder and slashed[a] themselves
with swords and spears, as was their custom, until their blood flowed. 29Midday
passed, and they continued their frantic
prophesying until the time for the evening sacrifice.[b] But there was no response, no one answered, no one paid
attention.[c]
30Then Elijah said to all the people,
"Come here to me." They came to him,
and he repaired the altar[d] of the LORD,
which was in ruins. 31Elijah took twelve
stones, one for each of the tribes descended from Jacob, to whom the word of the
LORD had come, saying, "Your name shall
be Israel."[e] 32With the stones he built an
altar in the name[f] of the LORD, and he
dug a trench around it large enough to
hold two seahs[m] of seed. 33He arranged[g]
the wood, cut the bull into pieces and laid
it on the wood. Then he said to them,
"Fill four large jars with water and pour it
on the offering and on the wood."
34"Do it again," he said, and they did it
again.
"Do it a third time," he ordered, and
they did it the third time. 35The water ran
down around the altar and even filled the
trench.
36At the time[h] of sacrifice, the prophet
Elijah stepped forward and prayed: "O
LORD, God of Abraham,[i] Isaac and Israel,

18:17 [j]Jos 7:25; 1Sa 14:29; 1Ki 21:20; Jer 38:4
18:18 [k]1Ki 16:31, 33; 21:25 [l]S Dt 31:16
18:19 [m]2Ki 10:19 [n]S Jos 19:26 [o]2Ki 9:22
18:20 [p]2Ki 2:25; 4:25
18:21 [q]Jos 24:15; 2Ki 17:41; Ps 119:113; Mt 6:24 [r]ver 39; Ps 100:3; 118:27
18:22 [s]1Ki 19:10 [t]Jer 2:8; 23:13
18:24 [u]S 1Sa 7:8 [v]S Ge 4:26 [w]S ver 38; S Ex 19:18; S Lev 9:24
18:26 [x]Isa 44:17; 45:20 [y]Ps 115:4-5; 135:16; Isa 41:26, 28; 46:7; Jer 10:5; 1Co 8:4; 12:2
18:27 [z]Hab 2:19
18:28 [a]S Lev 19:28
18:29 [b]S Ex 29:41 [c]2Ki 19:12; Isa 16:12; Jer 10:5
18:30 [d]1Ki 19:10
18:31 [e]S Ge 17:5; 2Ki 17:34
18:32 [f]S Dt 18:7; Col 3:17
18:33 [g]S Ge 22:9
18:36 [h]S Ex 29:39, 41 [i]S Ge 24:12; S Ex 4:5; Mt 22:32

m32 That is, probably about 13 quarts (about 15 liters)

18:16–39 MIRACLE, Nature—Miracle witnesses to God's power over all who would dispute His position as the only God. The dramatic setting of conflict between Baal and his prophets on one side and the Lord God and His prophet on the other came toward the end of a long drought. Agricultural people worshiped Baal because they considered him the source of natural fertility and blessing. Elijah prepared the altar and the sacrifice and called on the Lord to send fire to consume the sacrifice. Whether God's fire was a bolt of lightning or some other fiery power is not clear. The fire, whatever its source, came at a particular time and in a particular place. God did not send fire on Elijah's sacrifice to show off or to scare people. He proved His position of superiority over the false gods, leading people to acknowledge Him as God over all spheres of life. When we accept God as Creator, we expect Him to be Lord of creation.

18:16–46 REVELATION, In Nature—Revelation leads people to decision. Revelation verifies God's claim to be the only God and shows who God's true spokespersons are. Through the unexpected "fire of the Lord," God demonstrated His control of nature and thus His unique deity. Revelation came to Elijah through prayer. Prayer is a common way by which God makes Himself known to His people.

18:18 SIN, Transgression—Jeroboam set the pattern, but each king of Israel bore personal responsibility for leading the nation to transgress God's command and worship foreign gods. See note on 12:26–33.

18:21 SALVATION, Human Freedom—See note on Dt 30:15–20; Jos 24:15,19. Human freedom calls us to choose not to remain indecisive. God takes the initiative to provide salvation, here symbolized by lightning and rain. We are expected to accept actively salvation and commit our lives to the saving God.

18:24,27,36–39 GOD, One God—Ancient peoples had many man-made objects, heavenly or earthly bodies, and ideas called gods. The ancient problem was establishing that God is the only God, not one among many. Our modern problem is somewhat different: establishing the reality of the one God in the minds of people who seem to live without any idea of God, or else allow their personal interests to become a god in the priorities of their lives.

18:26–29 PRAYER, Hindrances—Frantic self-flagellation is foreign to the spirit and requirements of Israel's God.

18:36–39 GOD, Power—God acted in response to the prayer of His prophet to show His superiority to other gods. The people recognized His claim to their complete worship.

let it be known[j] today that you are God
in Israel and that I am your servant and
have done all these things at your command.[k] 37Answer me, O LORD, answer
me, so these people will know[l] that you,
O LORD, are God, and that you are turning their hearts back again."
38Then the fire[m] of the LORD fell and
burned up the sacrifice, the wood, the
stones and the soil, and also licked up the
water in the trench.
39When all the people saw this, they
fell prostrate[n] and cried, "The LORD—he
is God! The LORD—he is God!"[o]
40Then Elijah commanded them,
"Seize the prophets of Baal. Don't let anyone get away!" They seized them, and
Elijah had them brought down to the Kishon Valley[p] and slaughtered[q] there.
41And Elijah said to Ahab, "Go, eat and
drink, for there is the sound of a heavy
rain." 42So Ahab went off to eat and
drink, but Elijah climbed to the top of
Carmel, bent down to the ground and put
his face between his knees.[r]
43"Go and look toward the sea," he
told his servant. And he went up and
looked.
"There is nothing there," he said.
Seven times Elijah said, "Go back."
44The seventh time[s] the servant reported, "A cloud[t] as small as a man's
hand is rising from the sea."
So Elijah said, "Go and tell Ahab,
'Hitch up your chariot and go down before the rain stops you.' "
45Meanwhile, the sky grew black with
clouds, the wind rose, a heavy rain[u]
came on and Ahab rode off to Jezreel.[v]
46The power[w] of the LORD came upon Elijah and, tucking his cloak into his belt,[x]
he ran ahead of Ahab all the way to
Jezreel.

Chapter 19

Elijah Flees to Horeb

NOW Ahab told Jezebel[y] everything
Elijah had done and how he had
killed[z] all the prophets with the sword.
2So Jezebel sent a messenger to Elijah to
say, "May the gods deal with me, be it
ever so severely,[a] if by this time tomorrow I do not make your life like that of
one of them."[b]
3Elijah was afraid[n] and ran[c] for his
life.[d] When he came to Beersheba[e] in
Judah, he left his servant there, 4while he
himself went a day's journey into the
desert. He came to a broom tree,[f] sat
down under it and prayed that he might
die. "I have had enough, LORD," he said.
"Take my life;[g] I am no better than my
ancestors." 5Then he lay down under the
tree and fell asleep.[h]
All at once an angel[i] touched him and
said, "Get up and eat." 6He looked
around, and there by his head was a cake
of bread baked over hot coals, and a jar of
water. He ate and drank and then lay
down again.
7The angel of the LORD came back a
second time and touched him and said,
"Get up and eat, for the journey is too
much for you." 8So he got up and ate and
drank. Strengthened by that food, he traveled forty[j] days and forty nights until he
reached Horeb,[k] the mountain of God.
9There he went into a cave[l] and spent
the night.

[n]3 Or *Elijah saw*

18:36 [j]S Jos 4:24; S 1Sa 17:46; S Ps 46:10 [k]Nu 16:28
18:37 [l]S Jos 4:24
18:38 [m]ver 24; S Ex 19:18; S Lev 9:24; 2Ki 1:10; 1Ch 21:26; 2Ch 7:1; Job 1:16
18:39 [n]S Lev 9:24 [o]S ver 24; S Ps 46:10
18:40 [p]S Jdg 4:7 [q]S Ex 22:20; S Dt 17:12; S 2Ki 11:18
18:42 [r]S 1Sa 12:17; Jas 5:18
18:44 [s]S Jos 6:15 [t]Lk 12:54
18:45 [u]S 1Ki 8:36; Job 37:13 [v]S 1Sa 29:1; S Hos 1:4
18:46 [w]S Jdg 3:10; S 1Sa 11:6; Lk 1:35; 4:14 [x]2Ki 4:29; 9:1
19:1 [y]1Ki 16:31 [z]S Ex 22:20
19:2 [a]S Ru 1:17 [b]Ps 13:4; Jer 20:10; 26:21; 36:26
19:3 [c]S Ge 31:21 [d]S Ge 19:17 [e]S Jos 19:2
19:4 [f]Job 30:4 [g]S Nu 11:15; Job 6:9; 7:16; 10:1; Ps 69:19; Jer 20:18; Jnh 4:8
19:5 [h]Ge 28:11 [i]S Ge 16:7
19:8 [j]Ex 24:18; Mt 4:2 [k]S Ex 3:1
19:9 [l]S Ex 33:22

18:36–39 PRAYER, Sovereignty of God—Elijah did not mention the expected fire. Rather, his prayer was in three parts: (1) that God would make known that He is God; (2) that Elijah's campaign against Baalism was valid; and (3) that the hearts of Israel would be turned back to Him. God's answer came through the natural phenomenon of lightning at the right moment. Prayer seeks revelation of God's sovereign glory. God's answer led the people to a prayer of confession acknowledging God as the only God and as their God. Such confession is the basic prayer from which all other prayers arise.

18:41–46 PRAYER, Sovereignty of God—See note on 17:1. Prayer commanded the elements of nature. The prophet's prayer position showed his humble dependence on God.

19:4 PRAYER, Hindrances—This prayer was unlike and unworthy of Elijah. Three of the most righteous men in the Bible mistakenly prayed to die—Moses (Nu 11:11–15); Elijah; and Job (Job 6:8–9). God has the power to kill, but His loving character deafens Him to the prayer of the discouraged for death. Rather God uses the opportunity to introduce new depths of understanding about Himself.

19:5–8 REVELATION, Angels—God's messengers carry out whatever task God assigns. God sent His angel to supply Elijah's physical needs and send him on his way. See note on Ge 18:1—19:29.

19:8–18 PRAYER, Fellowship with God—This remarkable prayer indicates much that is basic in our fellowship with God. Elijah's frail humanity led him to typically human emotions. See note on Ge 4:26. He was afraid. Terror led him to overstate his aloneness. Obadiah had told him of at least one hundred other prophets loyal to the Lord (18:13). James pointed to our commonality with Elijah's frailty in urging us to pray (Jas 5:17). Elijah had seen tremendous divine power demonstrated on Mt. Carmel (18:38). The manifestations of terrifying power in the wind, earthquake, and fire were intended to remind him that the divine power and will were still available for him. God's voice for the discouraged prophet was a gentle whisper. Prayer fellowship brought new zeal and a new commission. The assurance of 7,000 who had remained faithful to the Lord would shortly be demonstrated. Elisha would have to enlarge the living quarters of his company of prophets (2 Ki 6:1–2).

19:9–18 REVELATION, Word—The prophet, having just won a battle with Jezebel's gods, feared for his safety. God sought him out, apparently while he slept. See note on 3:4–5. God did not reveal Himself in expected supernatural events, appearing instead in the quiet reflection of a silent whisper. Like Elijah, many expect God's manifestation in spectacular occurrences, while God seeks the private road of faith and openness of heart. God's whisper was heard again in the stable of a small village inn centuries later when Jesus was born. Coming out of the cave Elijah heard God's voice giving Him directions for personal action. God's revealing word may come

The LORD Appears to Elijah

And the word of the LORD came to
him: "What are you doing here, Elijah?"[m]
[10]He replied, "I have been very zealous[n] for the LORD God Almighty. The Israelites have rejected your covenant,[o]
broken down your altars,[p] and put your
prophets to death with the sword. I am
the only one left,[q] and now they are trying to kill me too."
[11]The LORD said, "Go out and stand on
the mountain[r] in the presence of the
LORD, for the LORD is about to pass by."[s]
Then a great and powerful wind[t] tore
the mountains apart and shattered[u] the
rocks before the LORD, but the LORD was
not in the wind. After the wind there was
an earthquake, but the LORD was not in
the earthquake. [12]After the earthquake
came a fire,[v] but the LORD was not in the
fire. And after the fire came a gentle
whisper.[w] [13]When Elijah heard it, he
pulled his cloak over his face[x] and went
out and stood at the mouth of the cave.
Then a voice said to him, "What are
you doing here, Elijah?"
[14]He replied, "I have been very zealous
for the LORD God Almighty. The Israelites
have rejected your covenant, broken
down your altars, and put your prophets
to death with the sword. I am the only
one left,[y] and now they are trying to kill
me too."
[15]The LORD said to him, "Go back the
way you came, and go to the Desert of
Damascus. When you get there, anoint
Hazael[z] king over Aram. [16]Also, anoint[a]
Jehu son of Nimshi king over Israel, and
anoint Elisha[b] son of Shaphat from Abel
Meholah[c] to succeed you as prophet.
[17]Jehu will put to death any who escape
the sword of Hazael,[d] and Elisha will put
to death any who escape the sword of
Jehu.[e] [18]Yet I reserve[f] seven thousand
in Israel—all whose knees have not
bowed down to Baal and all whose
mouths have not kissed[g] him."

The Call of Elisha

[19]So Elijah went from there and found
Elisha son of Shaphat. He was plowing
with twelve yoke of oxen, and he himself
was driving the twelfth pair. Elijah went
up to him and threw his cloak[h] around
him. [20]Elisha then left his oxen and ran
after Elijah. "Let me kiss my father and
mother good-by,"[i] he said, "and then I
will come with you."
"Go back," Elijah replied. "What have
I done to you?"
[21]So Elisha left him and went back. He
took his yoke of oxen[j] and slaughtered
them. He burned the plowing equipment
to cook the meat and gave it to the people, and they ate. Then he set out to follow Elijah and became his attendant.[k]

Chapter 20

Ben-Hadad Attacks Samaria

NOW Ben-Hadad[l] king of Aram mustered his entire army. Accompanied
by thirty-two kings with their horses and
chariots, he went up and besieged Samaria[m] and attacked it. [2]He sent messengers
into the city to Ahab king of Israel, saying, "This is what Ben-Hadad says: [3]'Your
silver and gold are mine, and the best of
your wives and children are mine.' "
[4]The king of Israel answered, "Just as
you say, my lord the king. I and all I have
are yours."
[5]The messengers came again and said,
"This is what Ben-Hadad says: 'I sent to
demand your silver and gold, your wives
and your children. [6]But about this time
tomorrow I am going to send my officials
to search your palace and the houses of
your officials. They will seize everything
you value and carry it away.' "
[7]The king of Israel summoned all the
elders[n] of the land and said to them,
"See how this man is looking for trouble![o] When he sent for my wives and my
children, my silver and my gold, I did not
refuse him."
[8]The elders and the people all answered, "Don't listen to him or agree to
his demands."
[9]So he replied to Ben-Hadad's messengers, "Tell my lord the king, 'Your servant will do all you demanded the first
time, but this demand I cannot meet.' "
They left and took the answer back to
Ben-Hadad.
[10]Then Ben-Hadad sent another message to Ahab: "May the gods deal with

19:9 [m]S Ge 3:9
19:10 [n]S Nu 25:13; Ac 22:3; Gal 4:18 [o]S Dt 31:16 [p]1Ki 18:30 [q]1Ki 18:4,22; Jer 5:11; 9:2; Ro 11:3*
19:11 [r]Ex 34:2; Mt 17:1-3 [s]Ex 33:19 [t]S Ex 14:21; S 2Ki 2:1 [u]Na 1:6
19:12 [v]S Ex 3:2 [w]ver 11; S 1Sa 14:6; Job 4:16; Zec 4:6; 2Co 12:9
19:13 [x]Ex 3:6
19:14 [y]1Ki 18:22; Ro 11:3*
19:15 [z]2Ki 8:7-15
19:16 [a]2Ki 9:1-3,6 [b]ver 21; 2Ki 2:1; 3:11 [c]S Jdg 7:22
19:17 [d]2Ki 8:12, 29; 10:32; 12:17; 13:3,7,22; Am 1:4 [e]Jer 48:44
19:18 [f]Ro 11:4* [g]Hos 13:2
19:19 [h]S Ge 41:42; 2Ki 2:8,14
19:20 [i]Lk 9:61
19:21 [j]S 1Sa 6:14 [k]S ver 16
20:1 [l]S 1Ki 15:18 [m]S 1Ki 13:32
20:7 [n]1Sa 11:3 [o]2Ki 5:7

---

in a dream or in speech to our inner ear. The word may be one to communicate to God's people or to direct one's personal life. See note on 11:9–13.

19:10,14 THE CHURCH, Covenant People—Individuals who rebel against God break the covenant relationship established between God and His people. In Christ we have an eternal covenant and are secure in Christ's hands (Jn 10:27–28). See note on Jer 31:31–34.

19:15–18 GOD, Sovereignty—God demonstrated His sovereignty here, both in the orders that He gave and in the fact that He had preserved many faithful servants in seemingly impossible circumstances.

19:19 SALVATION, As Deliverance—See note on Dt 30:15–20. Compare 2 Ch 32:8,11,22. God's deliverance has evangelistic and missionary implications, as Hezekiah's prayer reminds us. He delivers from physical dangers to lead us to spiritual trust and commitment to Him. He works in our lives to reveal Himself to all the world's population.

19:19–21 EVANGELISM, Obedience—See note on 1 Sa 3:1–19.

me, be it ever so severely, if enough dust[p] remains in Samaria to give each of my men a handful."

11 The king of Israel answered, "Tell him: 'One who puts on his armor should not boast[q] like one who takes it off.' "

12 Ben-Hadad heard this message while he and the kings were drinking[r] in their tents,[o] and he ordered his men: "Prepare to attack." So they prepared to attack the city.

Ahab Defeats Ben-Hadad

13 Meanwhile a prophet[s] came to Ahab king of Israel and announced, "This is what the LORD says: 'Do you see this vast army? I will give it into your hand today, and then you will know[t] that I am the LORD.' "

14 "But who will do this?" asked Ahab.

The prophet replied, "This is what the LORD says: 'The young officers of the provincial commanders will do it.' "

"And who will start[u] the battle?" he asked.

The prophet answered, "You will."

15 So Ahab summoned the young officers of the provincial commanders, 232 men. Then he assembled the rest of the Israelites, 7,000 in all. 16 They set out at noon while Ben-Hadad and the 32 kings allied with him were in their tents getting drunk.[v] 17 The young officers of the provincial commanders went out first.

Now Ben-Hadad had dispatched scouts, who reported, "Men are advancing from Samaria."

18 He said, "If they have come out for peace, take them alive; if they have come out for war, take them alive."

19 The young officers of the provincial commanders marched out of the city with the army behind them 20 and each one struck down his opponent. At that, the Arameans fled, with the Israelites in pursuit. But Ben-Hadad king of Aram escaped on horseback with some of his horsemen. 21 The king of Israel advanced and overpowered the horses and chariots and inflicted heavy losses on the Arameans.

22 Afterward, the prophet[w] came to the king of Israel and said, "Strengthen your position and see what must be done, because next spring[x] the king of Aram will attack you again."

23 Meanwhile, the officials of the king of Aram advised him, "Their gods are gods[y] of the hills. That is why they were too strong for us. But if we fight them on the plains, surely we will be stronger than they. 24 Do this: Remove all the kings from their commands and replace them with other officers. 25 You must also raise an army like the one you lost—horse for horse and chariot for chariot—so we can fight Israel on the plains. Then surely we will be stronger than they." He agreed with them and acted accordingly.

26 The next spring[z] Ben-Hadad mustered the Arameans and went up to Aphek[a] to fight against Israel. 27 When the Israelites were also mustered and given provisions, they marched out to meet them. The Israelites camped opposite them like two small flocks of goats, while the Arameans covered the countryside.[b]

28 The man of God came up and told the king of Israel, "This is what the LORD says: 'Because the Arameans think the LORD is a god of the hills and not a god[c] of the valleys, I will deliver this vast army into your hands, and you will know[d] that I am the LORD.' "

29 For seven days they camped opposite each other, and on the seventh day the battle was joined. The Israelites inflicted a hundred thousand casualties on the Aramean foot soldiers in one day. 30 The rest of them escaped to the city of Aphek,[e] where the wall collapsed[f] on twenty-seven thousand of them. And Ben-Hadad fled to the city and hid[g] in an inner room.

31 His officials said to him, "Look, we have heard that the kings of the house of Israel are merciful.[h] Let us go to the king of Israel with sackcloth[i] around our waists and ropes around our heads. Perhaps he will spare your life."

32 Wearing sackcloth around their waists and ropes around their heads, they went to the king of Israel and said, "Your servant Ben-Hadad says: 'Please let me live.' "

The king answered, "Is he still alive? He is my brother."

20:10 [p]S 2Sa 22:43
20:11 [q]Pr 27:1; Jer 9:23; Am 2:14
20:12 [r]S 1Ki 16:9
20:13 [s]S Jdg 6:8 [t]S Ex 6:7
20:14 [u]S Jdg 1:1
20:16 [v]S 1Ki 16:9
20:22 [w]S Jdg 6:8 [x]S 2Sa 11:1
20:23 [y]ver 28; Isa 36:20; Ro 1:21-23
20:26 [z]S 2Sa 11:1 [a]ver 30; S 1Sa 4:1; 2Ki 13:17
20:27 [b]Jdg 6:6; S 1Sa 13:6
20:28 [c]S ver 23 [d]S Ex 6:7; Jer 16:19-21
20:30 [e]S ver 26 [f]Ps 62:4; Isa 26:21; 30:13 [g]1Ki 22:25
20:31 [h]Job 41:3 [i]S Ge 37:34

[o]*12* Or *in Succoth*; also in verse 16

20:13–28 REVELATION, Divine Presence—The Aramean leadership assumed Israel's God was confined to certain localities. The God of no boundaries took the occasion to suprise Arameans and Israelites alike, for even His children suffered from this limited view of God's presence and activity. God is not contained in physical boundaries or within the small boundaries of the human imagination. God revealed His presence and will through a prophetic messenger using the messenger's standard formula, "This is what the LORD says."

20:13 HISTORY, Presence—God's continuing purpose was to introduce Himself in His personal name Yahweh (NIV LORD) as the only God. He gave victory in battle to make Himself known just as He gave deliverance in the Exodus. Compare Ex 3:13–15; 4:5; 6:2–8; 7:5; 10:1–2; 14:4,25,31; 16:12; 20:2; Lev 18:1–2; 19:1–37; Eze 20:5; 38:16; Hos 13:4.

20:28 HISTORY, Nature—God is a personal God who reveals Himself in historical actions. He cannot be identified with nor limited to one part of nature as were other gods of Israel's neighbors. By showing His power in all parts of nature, God showed His unique nature unrivalled by any other god. See note on v 13.

33The men took this as a good sign and were quick to pick up his word. "Yes, your brother Ben-Hadad!" they said.

"Go and get him," the king said. When Ben-Hadad came out, Ahab had him come up into his chariot.

34"I will return the cities[j] my father took from your father," Ben-Hadad[k] offered. "You may set up your own market areas[l] in Damascus,[m] as my father did in Samaria."

⌞Ahab said,⌟ "On the basis of a treaty[n] I will set you free." So he made a treaty with him, and let him go.

A Prophet Condemns Ahab

35By the word of the LORD one of the sons of the prophets[o] said to his companion, "Strike me with your weapon," but the man refused.[p]

36So the prophet said, "Because you have not obeyed the LORD, as soon as you leave me a lion[q] will kill you." And after the man went away, a lion found him and killed him.

37The prophet found another man and said, "Strike me, please." So the man struck him and wounded him. 38Then the prophet went and stood by the road waiting for the king. He disguised himself with his headband down over his eyes. 39As the king passed by, the prophet called out to him, "Your servant went into the thick of the battle, and someone came to me with a captive and said, 'Guard this man. If he is missing, it will be your life for his life,[r] or you must pay a talent[p] of silver.' 40While your servant was busy here and there, the man disappeared."

"That is your sentence,"[s] the king of Israel said. "You have pronounced it yourself."

41Then the prophet quickly removed the headband from his eyes, and the king of Israel recognized him as one of the prophets. 42He said to the king, "This is what the LORD says: 'You[t] have set free a man I had determined should die.[q] [u] Therefore it is your life for his life,[v] your people for his people.' " 43Sullen and angry,[w] the king of Israel went to his palace in Samaria.

Chapter 21

Naboth's Vineyard

SOME time later there was an incident involving a vineyard belonging to Naboth[x] the Jezreelite. The vineyard was in Jezreel,[y] close to the palace of Ahab king of Samaria. 2Ahab said to Naboth, "Let me have your vineyard to use for a vegetable garden, since it is close to my palace. In exchange I will give you a better vineyard or, if you prefer, I will pay you whatever it is worth."

3But Naboth replied, "The LORD forbid that I should give you the inheritance[z] of my fathers."

4So Ahab went home, sullen and angry[a] because Naboth the Jezreelite had said, "I will not give you the inheritance of my fathers." He lay on his bed sulking and refused[b] to eat.

5His wife Jezebel came in and asked him, "Why are you so sullen? Why won't you eat?"

6He answered her, "Because I said to Naboth the Jezreelite, 'Sell me your vineyard; or if you prefer, I will give you another vineyard in its place.' But he said, 'I will not give you my vineyard.' "

7Jezebel his wife said, "Is this how you act as king over Israel? Get up and eat! Cheer up. I'll get you the vineyard[c] of Naboth the Jezreelite."

8So she wrote letters[d] in Ahab's name, placed his seal[e] on them, and sent them to the elders and nobles who lived in Naboth's city with him. 9In those letters she wrote:

> "Proclaim a day of fasting and seat Naboth in a prominent place among the people. 10But seat two scoundrels[f] opposite him and have them testify that he has cursed[g] both God and the king. Then take him out and stone him to death."

11So the elders and nobles who lived in Naboth's city did as Jezebel directed in the letters she had written to them. 12They proclaimed a fast[h] and seated Naboth in a prominent place among the people. 13Then two scoundrels came and sat opposite him and brought charges against Naboth before the people, saying, "Naboth has cursed both God and the king." So they took him outside the city and stoned him to death.[i] 14Then they sent word to Jezebel: "Naboth has been stoned and is dead."

15As soon as Jezebel heard that Naboth had been stoned to death, she said to Ahab, "Get up and take possession of the vineyard[j] of Naboth the Jezreelite that he refused to sell you. He is no longer

20:34 [j]1Ki 15:20 [k]S Ge 10:22 [l]2Sa 8:6 [m]S Ge 14:15; Jer 49:23-27 [n]S Ex 23:32
20:35 [o]S 1Sa 10:5; Am 7:14 [p]S 1Ki 13:21
20:36 [q]1Ki 13:24
20:39 [r]S Jos 2:14
20:40 [s]2Sa 12:5; S 14:13
20:42 [t]S 2Sa 12:7 [u]Jer 48:10 [v]S Jos 2:14
20:43 [w]1Ki 21:4
21:1 [x]2Ki 9:21 [y]S 1Sa 29:1; 2Ki 10:1
21:3 [z]S Lev 25:23
21:4 [a]1Ki 20:43 [b]1Sa 28:23
21:7 [c]S 1Sa 8:14
21:8 [d]2Sa 11:14 [e]S Ge 38:18
21:10 [f]S Dt 13:13; Ac 6:11 [g]S Ex 22:28; Lev 24:15-16
21:12 [h]Isa 58:4
21:13 [i]S Lev 24:16
21:15 [j]S 1Sa 8:14

[p]*39* That is, about 75 pounds (about 34 kilograms)
[q]*42* The Hebrew term refers to the irrevocable giving over of things or persons to the LORD, often by totally destroying them.

21:1–19 CHRISTIAN ETHICS, Justice—Justice depends on the fair and wise use of power by political leaders. Leaders who manipulate and destroy others to satisfy personal greed stand under God's judgment. See note on Isa 5:7–8.

alive, but dead." 16When Ahab heard that
Naboth was dead, he got up and went
down to take possession of Naboth's vineyard.
17Then the word of the LORD came to
Elijah the Tishbite: 18"Go down to meet
Ahab king of Israel, who rules in Samaria.
He is now in Naboth's vineyard, where
he has gone to take possession of it. 19Say
to him, 'This is what the LORD says: Have
you not murdered a man and seized his
property?'[k] Then say to him, 'This is
what the LORD says: In the place where
dogs licked up Naboth's blood,[l] dogs[m]
will lick up your blood—yes, yours!'"
20Ahab said to Elijah, "So you have
found me, my enemy!"[n]
"I have found you," he answered, "because you have sold[o] yourself to do evil
in the eyes of the LORD. 21'I am going to
bring disaster on you. I will consume
your descendants and cut off from Ahab
every last male[p] in Israel—slave or
free.[q] 22I will make your house[r] like that
of Jeroboam son of Nebat and that of Baasha son of Ahijah, because you have provoked me to anger and have caused Israel
to sin.'[s]
23"And also concerning Jezebel the
LORD says: 'Dogs[t] will devour Jezebel by
the wall of[r] Jezreel.'
24"Dogs[u] will eat those belonging to
Ahab who die in the city, and the birds of
the air[v] will feed on those who die in the
country."
25(There was never[w] a man like Ahab,
who sold himself to do evil in the eyes of
the LORD, urged on by Jezebel his wife.
26He behaved in the vilest manner by going after idols, like the Amorites[x] the
LORD drove out before Israel.)
27When Ahab heard these words, he
tore his clothes, put on sackcloth[y] and
fasted. He lay in sackcloth and went
around meekly.[z]
28Then the word of the LORD came to
Elijah the Tishbite: 29"Have you noticed
how Ahab has humbled himself before
me? Because he has humbled[a] himself, I
will not bring this disaster in his day,[b]
but I will bring it on his house in the days
of his son."[c]

21:19 [k]Job 24:6; 31:39 [l]2Ki 9:26; Ps 9:12; Isa 14:20 [m]1Ki 22:38; Ps 68:23; Jer 15:3
21:20 [n]S 1Ki 18:17 [o]2Ki 17:17; Ro 7:14
21:21 [p]Jdg 9:5; 2Ki 10:7 [q]S Dt 32:36
21:22 [r]1Ki 16:3 [s]S 1Ki 12:30
21:23 [t]2Ki 9:10, 34-36
21:24 [u]1Ki 14:11 [v]S Ge 40:19; S Dt 28:26
21:25 [w]S 1Ki 14:9; S 16:33
21:26 [x]S Ge 15:16
21:27 [y]S Ge 37:34; S Jer 4:8 [z]Isa 38:15
21:29 [a]S Ex 10:3 [b]S Ex 32:14; 2Ki 22:20 [c]Ex 20:5; 2Ki 9:26; 10:6-10
22:3 [d]S Dt 4:43
22:4 [e]2Ki 3:7
22:5 [f]Ex 33:7; 2Ki 3:11; Job 38:2; Ps 32:8; 73:24; 107:11
22:6 [g]S Jdg 18:6 [h]S 1Ki 13:18
22:7 [i]Dt 18:15; 2Ki 3:11; 5:8 [j]S Nu 27:21; 2Ki 3:11
22:8 [k]Am 5:10 [l]ver 13; Isa 5:20; 30:10; Jer 23:17
22:10 [m]S Jdg 6:37
22:11 [n]ver 24 [o]Dt 33:17; Jer 27:2; 28:10; Zec 1:18-21

Chapter 22

Micaiah Prophesies Against Ahab

22:1-28pp — 2Ch 18:1-27

FOR three years there was no war between Aram and Israel. 2But in the
third year Jehoshaphat king of Judah went
down to see the king of Israel. 3The king
of Israel had said to his officials, "Don't
you know that Ramoth Gilead[d] belongs
to us and yet we are doing nothing to
retake it from the king of Aram?"
4So he asked Jehoshaphat, "Will you go
with me to fight[e] against Ramoth Gilead?"
Jehoshaphat replied to the king of Israel, "I am as you are, my people as your
people, my horses as your horses." 5But
Jehoshaphat also said to the king of Israel,
"First seek the counsel[f] of the LORD."
6So the king of Israel brought together
the prophets—about four hundred men
—and asked them, "Shall I go to war
against Ramoth Gilead, or shall I refrain?"
"Go,"[g] they answered, "for the Lord
will give it into the king's hand."[h]
7But Jehoshaphat asked, "Is there not a
prophet[i] of the LORD here whom we can
inquire[j] of?"
8The king of Israel answered Jehoshaphat, "There is still one man through
whom we can inquire of the LORD, but I
hate[k] him because he never prophesies
anything good[l] about me, but always
bad. He is Micaiah son of Imlah."
"The king should not say that," Jehoshaphat replied.
9So the king of Israel called one of his
officials and said, "Bring Micaiah son of
Imlah at once."
10Dressed in their royal robes, the king
of Israel and Jehoshaphat king of Judah
were sitting on their thrones at the
threshing floor[m] by the entrance of the
gate of Samaria, with all the prophets
prophesying before them. 11Now Zedekiah[n] son of Kenaanah had made iron
horns[o] and he declared, "This is what
the LORD says: 'With these you will gore

[r]*23* Most Hebrew manuscripts; a few Hebrew manuscripts, Vulgate and Syriac (see also 2 Kings 9:26) *the plot of ground at*

21:21–22 GOD, Wrath—The wrath of God is the inevitable result of man's continued refusal to bow to the will of God. See notes on Ge 6:5–8; 17:14; Mt 3:7–10; Ro 1:18.
21:21–28 SIN, Forgiveness—Humble repentance can turn away God's announced judgment from even the worst sinner. See notes on 12:26–33; 18:18.
22:6–28 REVELATION, Spirit—Prophetic revelation came from God's Spirit, though the Spirit is not always mentioned. God's people have problems when people falsely claim to speak through God's Spirit. The true word of God is not always easily determined. God's prophet often represents a minority opinion as did Micaiah. Only the continued life and history of God's people clearly show whose proclamation was inspired. Evil, lying spirits seek to use God's speakers to deceive God's people. God gives such spirits freedom to work among people who are committed more to self than to God. See note on Nu 11:16–30.
22:8–17 PRAYER, Petition—Inquiry of the Lord by the high priest came through the Urim and Thummim. See note on Ex 28:30. Because the Northern Kingdom was separated from the Temple, God spoke through prophets, whose only credentials were the accuracy of their prophecies (Dt 18:21–22). Jehoshaphat wanted to inquire of a true prophet of the Lord, but the true prophet was out of favor with Israel's king. Prayer indicates a willingness to hear God's truth.

the Arameans until they are destroyed.' "
12 All the other prophets were prophesying the same thing. "Attack Ramoth
Gilead and be victorious," they said, "for
the LORD will give it into the king's
hand."
13 The messenger who had gone to
summon Micaiah said to him, "Look, as
one man the other prophets are predicting success for the king. Let your word
agree with theirs, and speak favorably."[p]
14 But Micaiah said, "As surely as the
LORD lives, I can tell him only what the
LORD tells me."[q]
15 When he arrived, the king asked
him, "Micaiah, shall we go to war against
Ramoth Gilead, or shall I refrain?"
"Attack and be victorious," he answered, "for the LORD will give it into the
king's hand."
16 The king said to him, "How many
times must I make you swear to tell me
nothing but the truth in the name of the
LORD?"
17 Then Micaiah answered, "I saw all
Israel scattered[r] on the hills like sheep
without a shepherd,[s] and the LORD said,
'These people have no master. Let each
one go home in peace.' "
18 The king of Israel said to Jehoshaphat, "Didn't I tell you that he never
prophesies anything good about me, but
only bad?"
19 Micaiah continued, "Therefore hear
the word of the LORD: I saw the LORD
sitting on his throne[t] with all the host[u]
of heaven standing around him on his
right and on his left. 20 And the LORD said,
'Who will entice Ahab into attacking Ramoth Gilead and going to his death
there?'
"One suggested this, and another that.
21 Finally, a spirit came forward, stood before the LORD and said, 'I will entice
him.'
22 " 'By what means?' the LORD asked.
" 'I will go out and be a lying[v] spirit in
the mouths of all his prophets,' he said.
" 'You will succeed in enticing him,'
said the LORD. 'Go and do it.'
23 "So now the LORD has put a lying[w]
spirit in the mouths of all these prophets[x] of yours. The LORD has decreed disaster[y] for you."

24 Then Zedekiah[z] son of Kenaanah
went up and slapped[a] Micaiah in the
face. "Which way did the spirit from[s]
the LORD go when he went from me to
speak[b] to you?" he asked.
25 Micaiah replied, "You will find out
on the day you go to hide[c] in an inner
room."
26 The king of Israel then ordered,
"Take Micaiah and send him back to
Amon the ruler of the city and to Joash
the king's son 27 and say, 'This is what the
king says: Put this fellow in prison[d] and
give him nothing but bread and water until I return safely.' "
28 Micaiah declared, "If you ever return
safely, the LORD has not spoken[e] through
me." Then he added, "Mark my words,
all you people!"

Ahab Killed at Ramoth Gilead

22:29–36pp — 2Ch 18:28–34

29 So the king of Israel and Jehoshaphat
king of Judah went up to Ramoth Gilead.
30 The king of Israel said to Jehoshaphat,
"I will enter the battle in disguise,[f] but
you wear your royal robes." So the king
of Israel disguised himself and went into
battle.
31 Now the king of Aram[g] had ordered
his thirty-two chariot commanders, "Do
not fight with anyone, small or great, except the king[h] of Israel." 32 When the
chariot commanders saw Jehoshaphat,
they thought, "Surely this is the king of
Israel." So they turned to attack him, but
when Jehoshaphat cried out, 33 the chariot
commanders saw that he was not the
king of Israel and stopped pursuing him.
34 But someone drew his bow[i] at random and hit the king of Israel between
the sections of his armor. The king told
his chariot driver, "Wheel around and get
me out of the fighting. I've been wounded." 35 All day long the battle raged, and
the king was propped up in his chariot
facing the Arameans. The blood from his
wound ran onto the floor of the chariot,
and that evening he died. 36 As the sun
was setting, a cry spread through the
army: "Every man to his town; everyone
to his land!"[j]
37 So the king died and was brought to

22:13 [p]S ver 8
22:14 [q]S Nu 22:18; S 1Sa 3:17
22:17 [r]S Ge 11:4; Na 3:18 [s]Nu 27:17; Isa 13:14; S Mt 9:36
22:19 [t]Ps 47:8; Isa 6:1; 63:15; Eze 1:26; Da 7:9 [u]Job 1:6; 15:8; 38:7; Ps 103:20-21; 148:2; Jer 23:18, 22; Lk 2:13
22:22 [v]S Jdg 9:23; 2Th 2:11
22:23 [w]S Dt 13:3 [x]Eze 14:9 [y]S Dt 31:29
22:24 [z]ver 11 [a]Ac 23:2 [b]Job 26:4
22:25 [c]1Ki 20:30
22:27 [d]2Ch 16:10; Jer 20:2; 26:21; 37:15; Heb 11:36
22:28 [e]S Dt 18:22
22:30 [f]S 1Sa 28:8
22:31 [g]S Ge 10:22; S 2Sa 10:19 [h]S 2Sa 17:2
22:34 [i]2Ki 9:24; 2Ch 35:23
22:36 [j]2Ki 14:12

[s]24 Or *Spirit of*

22:19 GOD, Sovereignty—God is in control of His world and is working out His will in it. See notes on Ge 15:13–16; 18:14; 24:3,7,50.

22:19–28 EVIL AND SUFFERING, Divine Origin—How can we know God's truth when so many different interpretations are given? God's people have always faced this problem. Micaiah had to suffer imprisonment because he had an unpopular, minority interpretation. Both he and his prophetic opponents claimed to speak by the one Spirit of God. Micaiah agreed his opponents had a spirit given by God, but it was not the Holy Spirit. Their spirit was a member of the heavenly council of God commissioned to carry out punishment against the wicked King Ahab. We must raise the question of God's moral purity. Is He the Father of lies? Certainly not! He is Truth. God allowed the prophets to do what they had been doing and what Micaiah refused to do—tell the king lies that pleased him. They retained power not to follow the lying spirit. They retained responsibility. God remained in control and used their evil to accomplish His purpose. See note on 2 Sa 24:1.

Samaria, and they buried him there.
38They washed the chariot at a pool in
Samaria (where the prostitutes bathed),[t]
and the dogs[k] licked up his blood, as the
word of the LORD had declared.
39As for the other events of Ahab's
reign, including all he did, the palace he
built and inlaid with ivory,[l] and the cities
he fortified, are they not written in
the book of the annals of the kings of Israel?
40Ahab rested with his fathers. And
Ahaziah his son succeeded him as king.

Jehoshaphat King of Judah

22:41–50pp — 2Ch 20:31–21:1

41Jehoshaphat son of Asa became king
of Judah in the fourth year of Ahab king of
Israel. 42Jehoshaphat was thirty-five years
old when he became king, and he reigned
in Jerusalem twenty-five years. His
mother's name was Azubah daughter of
Shilhi. 43In everything he walked in the
ways of his father Asa[m] and did not stray
from them; he did what was right in the
eyes of the LORD. The high places,[n] however,
were not removed, and the people
continued to offer sacrifices and burn incense
there. 44Jehoshaphat was also at
peace with the king of Israel.
45As for the other events of Jehoshaphat's
reign, the things he achieved and
his military exploits, are they not written
in the book of the annals of the kings of
Judah? 46He rid the land of the rest of the
male shrine prostitutes[o] who remained
there even after the reign of his father
Asa. 47There was then no king[p] in Edom;
a deputy ruled.
48Now Jehoshaphat built a fleet of trading
ships[u][q] to go to Ophir for gold, but
they never set sail—they were wrecked
at Ezion Geber.[r] 49At that time Ahaziah
son of Ahab said to Jehoshaphat, "Let my
men sail with your men," but Jehoshaphat
refused.
50Then Jehoshaphat rested with his fathers
and was buried with them in the
city of David his father. And Jehoram his
son succeeded him.

Ahaziah King of Israel

51Ahaziah son of Ahab became king of
Israel in Samaria in the seventeenth year
of Jehoshaphat king of Judah, and he
reigned over Israel two years. 52He did
evil[s] in the eyes of the LORD, because he
walked in the ways of his father and
mother and in the ways of Jeroboam son
of Nebat, who caused Israel to sin. 53He
served and worshiped Baal[t] and provoked
the LORD, the God of Israel, to anger,
just as his father[u] had done.

22:38 [k]S 1Ki 21:19
22:39 [l]2Ch 9:17; Ps 45:8; Am 3:15
22:43 [m]S 1Ki 8:61; 2Ch 17:3 [n]S 1Ki 3:2
22:46 [o]S Dt 23:17
22:47 [p]1Ki 11:14-18; 2Ki 3:9; 8:20
22:48 [q]S 1Ki 9:26 [r]S Nu 33:35
22:52 [s]1Ki 15:26
22:53 [t]S Jdg 2:11 [u]1Ki 21:25

[t]38 Or *Samaria and cleaned the weapons*
[u]48 Hebrew *of ships of Tarshish*

22:39,45 HOLY SCRIPTURE, Writing—See note on 14:19,29.
22:52–53 SIN, Transgression—See note on 12:26–33.
22:53 HISTORY, Judgment—Historical human actions affect the relationship with God. Divine anger eventually finds expression in historical acts of judgment. History is thus the story of relationship between God and the people He created. Any way of explaining historical events that ignores God is a method dealing with secondary causes rather then primary causes. God called history into being and will ultimately bring it to an end. He never leaves history to its own interests and agents. He maintains interest in every moment of human history.

2 Kings

See Introduction to 1 Kings.

Theological Outline

2 Kings: Doom for Disobedient People

I. Through His Prophets God Guides History and Reveals His Will. (1:1—8:29)
   A. God alone controls the fortunes of His people. (1:1-18)
   B. God provides spiritual leadership for His people. (2:1-25)
   C. The prophetic word from God controls history. (3:1-27)
   D. God's minister helps God's faithful people in their time of need. (4:1-44)
   E. God's mercy reaches across international lines. (5:1-19*a*)
   F. Greedy ministers cannot deceive God. (5:19*b*-27)
   G. God defeats the enemies of His people. (6:1—7:20)
   H. God does not forget His faithful people. (8:1-6)
   I. God controls the destiny of all nations. (8:7-29)

II. God's Mercy Has Limits. (9:1—17:41)
   A. God keeps His threats against false worship but honors those who carry out His will. (9:1—10:36)
   B. God protects His chosen leader. (11:1-21)
   C. God's people support His house of worship. (12:1-16)
   D. God's offerings are not to be used for political purposes. (12:17-21)
   E. God's mercy and faithfulness protect even His disobedient people. (13:1—14:29)
   F. God works to punish a people who remain disobedient. (15:1—16:20)
   G. God brings an end to the nation that refuses to follow the prophetic word. (17:1-41)

III. God Honors Righteous Rulers but Punishes a Sinful People. (18:1—25:30)
   A. God rewards those who trust in Him but punishes those who mock Him. (18:1—19:37; compare to Isa 36:1—37:38)
   B. God hears the prayers of His faithful servant. (20:1-11; compare to Isa 38:1-22)
   C. God knows the future of His people. (20:12-21; compare to Isa 39:1-8)
   D. Rebellion against God brings divine rejection. (21:1-26)
   E. A righteous ruler can delay divine judgment. (22:1-20)
   F. A righteous ruler cannot avert judgment forever. (23:1-30)
   G. Deserved punishment comes to God's disobedient people. (23:31—25:26)
   H. God preserves hope for His people. (25:27-30)

Chapter 1

The LORD's Judgment on Ahaziah

AFTER Ahab's death, Moab[a] rebelled
against Israel. 2Now Ahaziah had
fallen through the lattice of his upper
room in Samaria and injured himself. So
he sent messengers,[b] saying to them,
"Go and consult Baal-Zebub,[c] the god of
Ekron,[d] to see if I will recover[e] from this
injury."
3But the angel[f] of the LORD said to Elijah[g] the Tishbite, "Go up and meet the
messengers of the king of Samaria and ask
them, 'Is it because there is no God in
Israel[h] that you are going off to consult
Baal-Zebub, the god of Ekron?' 4Therefore
this is what the LORD says: 'You will not
leave[i] the bed you are lying on. You will
certainly die!' " So Elijah went.
5When the messengers returned to the
king, he asked them, "Why have you
come back?"
6"A man came to meet us," they replied. "And he said to us, 'Go back to the
king who sent you and tell him, "This is
what the LORD says: Is it because there is
no God in Israel that you are sending men
to consult Baal-Zebub, the god of Ekron?
Therefore you will not leave[j] the bed
you are lying on. You will certainly
die!" ' "
7The king asked them, "What kind of
man was it who came to meet you and
told you this?"
8They replied, "He was a man with a
garment of hair[k] and with a leather belt
around his waist."
The king said, "That was Elijah the
Tishbite."
9Then he sent[l] to Elijah a captain[m]
with his company of fifty men. The captain went up to Elijah, who was sitting on
the top of a hill, and said to him, "Man of
God, the king says, 'Come down!' "
10Elijah answered the captain, "If I am
a man of God, may fire come down from
heaven and consume you and your fifty
men!" Then fire[n] fell from heaven and
consumed the captain and his men.
11At this the king sent to Elijah another
captain with his fifty men. The captain
said to him, "Man of God, this is what
the king says, 'Come down at once!' "
12"If I am a man of God," Elijah replied, "may fire come down from heaven
and consume you and your fifty men!"
Then the fire of God fell from heaven and
consumed him and his fifty men.
13So the king sent a third captain with
his fifty men. This third captain went up
and fell on his knees before Elijah. "Man
of God," he begged, "please have respect
for my life[o] and the lives of these fifty
men, your servants! 14See, fire has fallen
from heaven and consumed the first two
captains and all their men. But now have
respect for my life!"
15The angel[p] of the LORD said to Elijah,
"Go down with him; do not be afraid[q] of
him." So Elijah got up and went down
with him to the king.
16He told the king, "This is what the
LORD says: Is it because there is no God
in Israel for you to consult that you have
sent messengers[r] to consult Baal-Zebub,
the god of Ekron? Because you have done
this, you will never leave[s] the bed you
are lying on. You will certainly die!" 17So
he died,[t] according to the word of the
LORD that Elijah had spoken.
Because Ahaziah had no son, Joram[a] [u]
succeeded him as king in the second year
of Jehoram son of Jehoshaphat king of Judah. 18As for all the other events of Ahaziah's reign, and what he did, are they not
written in the book of the annals of the
kings of Israel?

Chapter 2

Elijah Taken Up to Heaven

WHEN the LORD was about to take[v]
Elijah up to heaven in a whirl-
wind,[w] Elijah and Elisha[x] were on their

[a] *17* Hebrew *Jehoram,* a variant of *Joram*

1:1 [a]S Ge 19:37; 2Ki 3:5
1:2 [b]ver 16 [c]S Mk 3:22 [d]1Sa 6:2; Isa 2:6; 14:29 [e]S Jdg 18:5
1:3 [f]ver 15 [g]1Ki 17:1 [h]S 1Sa 28:8
1:4 [i]ver 6,16; Ps 41:8
1:6 [j]S ver 4
1:8 [k]S 1Ki 18:7; Mt 3:4; Mk 1:6
1:9 [l]2Ki 6:14 [m]Ex 18:25; Isa 3:3
1:10 [n]S 1Ki 18:38; S Rev 11:5; S 13:13
1:13 [o]Ps 72:14
1:15 [p]ver 3 [q]Isa 51:12; 57:11; Jer 1:17; Eze 2:6
1:16 [r]S ver 2 [s]ver 4
1:17 [t]2Ki 8:15; Jer 20:6; 28:17 [u]2Ki 3:1; 8:16
2:1 [v]S Ge 5:24 [w]ver 11; 1Ki 19:11; Isa 5:28; 66:15; Jer 4:13; Na 1:3 [x]S 1Ki 19:16,21

1:1–17 HISTORY, God's Leaders—Political power cannot compete with divine power. God uses even drastic means to authenticate the authority of His leaders over against self-sufficient leaders who would ignore Him.

1:2–6 GOD, One God—God seeks to bring people to realize that He is the only true God. He is a jealous God, and He wants His people to give Him first place in their lives. We do not need to look for help to any other person or power. The one God will supply all our needs.

1:3–15 REVELATION, Angels—God sent His messenger to commission His prophetic messenger to confront the king's messengers. See notes on Ge 18:1—19:29; 1 Ki 20:13–28. Only God is able to give revelation to His people. All other sources of revelation are fakes. When He chooses, God can send miraculous signs to confirm His human instrument of revelation.

1:10,12 PRAYER, Curse—God had authenticated Elijah's ministry under Ahab by fire. For Ahaziah, following in Ahab's steps, God did the same. In the encounter on Mt. Carmel, God responded to the curses His prophets and leaders placed on other people when they fulfilled His purposes. The curse was not a weapon to be used indiscriminately against one's enemies. God's responses revealed God's power, not the prophet's.

1:16–18 HOLY SCRIPTURE, Writing—Inspired writers carefully recorded each king's reaction in faith or resistance to God's will. They used earlier written records of the kings of Israel. These earlier records were not preserved as part of the inspired Word. Being in written form did not automatically qualify a document for inclusion in the Bible. Only those records God inspired to teach His people were preserved and collected as Scriptures. See note on 1 Ki 14:19,29.

2:1–18 HOLY SPIRIT, Leaders—God's Spirit bridges the generation gap in His own free way. Elisha wanted the first-

way from Gilgal.[y] 2Elijah said to Elisha,
"Stay here;[z] the LORD has sent me to
Bethel."
But Elisha said, "As surely as the LORD
lives and as you live, I will not leave
you."[a] So they went down to Bethel.
3The company[b] of the prophets at
Bethel came out to Elisha and asked, "Do
you know that the LORD is going to take
your master from you today?"
"Yes, I know," Elisha replied, "but do
not speak of it."
4Then Elijah said to him, "Stay here,
Elisha; the LORD has sent me to Jericho.[c]"
And he replied, "As surely as the LORD
lives and as you live, I will not leave
you." So they went to Jericho.
5The company[d] of the prophets at Jericho went up to Elisha and asked him,
"Do you know that the LORD is going to
take your master from you today?"
"Yes, I know," he replied, "but do not
speak of it."
6Then Elijah said to him, "Stay here;[e]
the LORD has sent me to the Jordan."[f]
And he replied, "As surely as the LORD
lives and as you live, I will not leave
you."[g] So the two of them walked on.
7Fifty men of the company of the
prophets went and stood at a distance,
facing the place where Elijah and Elisha
had stopped at the Jordan. 8Elijah took his
cloak,[h] rolled it up and struck[i] the water
with it. The water divided[j] to the right
and to the left, and the two of them
crossed over on dry[k] ground.
9When they had crossed, Elijah said to
Elisha, "Tell me, what can I do for you
before I am taken from you?"
"Let me inherit a double[l] portion of
your spirit,"[m] Elisha replied.
10"You have asked a difficult thing,"
Elijah said, "yet if you see me when I am
taken from you, it will be yours—otherwise not."
11As they were walking along and talking together, suddenly a chariot of fire[n]
and horses of fire appeared and separated
the two of them, and Elijah went up to
heaven[o] in a whirlwind.[p] 12Elisha saw
this and cried out, "My father! My father!
The chariots[q] and horsemen of Israel!"
And Elisha saw him no more. Then he
took hold of his own clothes and tore[r]
them apart.
13He picked up the cloak that had fallen
from Elijah and went back and stood on
the bank of the Jordan. 14Then he took
the cloak[s] that had fallen from him and
struck[t] the water with it. "Where now is
the LORD, the God of Elijah?" he asked.
When he struck the water, it divided to
the right and to the left, and he crossed
over.
15The company[u] of the prophets from
Jericho, who were watching, said, "The
spirit[v] of Elijah is resting on Elisha." And
they went to meet him and bowed to the
ground before him. 16"Look," they said,
"we your servants have fifty able men.
Let them go and look for your master.
Perhaps the Spirit[w] of the LORD has
picked him up[x] and set him down on
some mountain or in some valley."
"No," Elisha replied, "do not send
them."
17But they persisted until he was too
ashamed[y] to refuse. So he said, "Send
them." And they sent fifty men, who
searched for three days but did not find
him. 18When they returned to Elisha,
who was staying in Jericho, he said to
them, "Didn't I tell you not to go?"

Healing of the Water

19The men of the city said to Elisha,

2:1 [y]S Dt 11:30; 2Ki 4:38
2:2 [z]ver 6 [a]Ru 1:16
2:3 [b]S 1Sa 10:5
2:4 [c]Jos 3:16
2:5 [d]ver 3
2:6 [e]ver 2 [f]Jos 3:15 [g]Ru 1:16
2:8 [h]S 1Ki 19:19 [i]ver 14 [j]S Ex 14:21 [k]Ex 14:22,29
2:9 [l]S Dt 21:17 [m]S Nu 11:17
2:11 [n]2Ki 6:17; Ps 68:17; 104:3,4; Isa 66:15; Hab 3:8; Zec 6:1 [o]S Ge 5:24 [p]S ver 1
2:12 [q]2Ki 6:17; 13:14 [r]S Ge 37:29
2:14 [s]S 1Ki 19:19 [t]ver 8
2:15 [u]S 1Sa 10:5 [v]S Nu 11:17
2:16 [w]S 1Ki 18:12 [x]Ac 8:39
2:17 [y]S Jdg 3:25

born son's double portion of the father's estate (Dt 21:17). Elijah's most valued possession was the Spirit of God. He could not will it to anyone. God maintains control of the Spirit. Yet God, in His desire to assure the new generation of His continued presence and to confirm Elisha's prophetic leadership, allowed Elijah to describe the conditions whereby Elisha would have the Spirit. However God chooses to work, He continues to provide Spirit-filled leaders for each new generation of His people. A leader's possessions are worthless without the Spirit.

2:4 PRAYER, Vow—Elisha had left home and family to follow Elijah (1 Ki 19:20–21). He now pledged his faithfulness with a vow. Vows in God's name commit a person to action.

2:11 MIRACLE, Instruments—Miracles spark hope in God's people. As Elijah neared the end of his earthly journey, Elisha followed more closely (vv 2,4,6). Elijah, the prophet of great faith, walked with God, as had Enoch. God took him. Later, search parties were unable to find his body (2:17). Little wonder then that the reappearance of Elijah remained a part of Israel's hope (Mal 4:5; Mt 17:10). His miraculous disappearance gave hope and courage for his young protege and successor—Elisha. He became the instrument for God's miracles after he witnessed this miracle.

2:14 MIRACLE, Faith—Miracles strengthen the faith of God's people. In rare instances God lets His people put Him to the test (Jdg 6:36–40). This first of Elisha's miracles appears to have been a test case for the prophet. It is almost as if Elisha thought some magic to be in Elijah's cloak. His question, "Where now is the LORD, the God of Elijah?", challenged God to action to verify his call as Elijah's successor. God strengthened His chosen prophet's faith by parting the waters, just as He had strengthened Israel's faith at the sea in Egypt (Ex 14:31). Through the miracle Elisha gained authority over the other prophets (v 15). God does not invite all of us to test Him, nor does He give such miraculous signs to all His called leaders. He displays His miraculous power when He knows it is needed to strengthen the faith of His people.

2:14 PRAYER, Faith—The outstanding characteristic of Elijah's prayers had been faith. Elisha identified himself with Elijah's God and Elijah's faith. God indicated His commitment to Elisha by letting him cross Jordan as had Joshua (Jos 3).

2:19–22 MIRACLE, Continual Creation—The Creator continues to care for the needs of His people. He miraculously provides the needs of life. Water was a precious commodity. Purification of Jericho's water supply provided life for crops, animals, and people. The prophet poured salt into the springs, and the water became usable. The use of a new dish may

"Look, our lord, this town is well situated, as you can see, but the water is bad
and the land is unproductive."
20"Bring me a new bowl," he said,
"and put salt in it." So they brought it to
him.
21Then he went out to the spring and
threw[z] the salt into it, saying, "This is
what the LORD says: 'I have healed this
water. Never again will it cause death or
make the land unproductive.' " 22And the
water has remained wholesome[a] to this
day, according to the word Elisha had
spoken.

Elisha Is Jeered

23From there Elisha went up to Bethel.
As he was walking along the road, some
youths came out of the town and jeered[b]
at him. "Go on up, you baldhead!" they
said. "Go on up, you baldhead!" 24He
turned around, looked at them and called
down a curse[c] on them in the name[d] of
the LORD. Then two bears came out of the
woods and mauled forty-two of the
youths. 25And he went on to Mount Carmel[e] and from there returned to Samaria.

Chapter 3

Moab Revolts

JORAM[b] [f] son of Ahab became king of
Israel in Samaria in the eighteenth
year of Jehoshaphat king of Judah, and he
reigned twelve years. 2He did evil[g] in the
eyes of the LORD, but not as his father[h]
and mother had done. He got rid of the
sacred stone[i] of Baal that his father had
made. 3Nevertheless he clung to the
sins[j] of Jeroboam son of Nebat, which he
had caused Israel to commit; he did not
turn away from them.
4Now Mesha king of Moab[k] raised
sheep, and he had to supply the king of
Israel with a hundred thousand lambs[l]
and with the wool of a hundred thousand
rams. 5But after Ahab died, the king of
Moab rebelled[m] against the king of Israel.
6So at that time King Joram set out from
Samaria and mobilized all Israel. 7He also
sent this message to Jehoshaphat king of
Judah: "The king of Moab has rebelled
against me. Will you go with me to fight[n]
against Moab?"
"I will go with you," he replied. "I am
as you are, my people as your people, my
horses as your horses."
8"By what route shall we attack?" he
asked.
"Through the Desert of Edom," he answered.
9So the king of Israel set out with the
king of Judah and the king of Edom.[o] After a roundabout march of seven days, the
army had no more water for themselves
or for the animals with them.
10"What!" exclaimed the king of Israel.
"Has the LORD called us three kings together only to hand us over to Moab?"
11But Jehoshaphat asked, "Is there no
prophet of the LORD here, that we may
inquire[p] of the LORD through him?"
An officer of the king of Israel answered, "Elisha[q] son of Shaphat is here.
He used to pour water on the hands of
Elijah.[c] [r] "
12Jehoshaphat said, "The word[s] of the
LORD is with him." So the king of Israel
and Jehoshaphat and the king of Edom
went down to him.

[b] *1* Hebrew *Jehoram,* a variant of *Joram*; also in verse 6
[c] *11* That is, he was Elijah's personal servant.

2:21 [z]S Ex 15:25; 2Ki 4:41; 6:6
2:22 [a]Ex 15:25
2:23 [b]S Ex 22:28; 2Ch 30:10; 36:16; Job 19:18; Ps 31:18
2:24 [c]S Ge 4:11 [d]S Dt 18:19
2:25 [e]S 1Ki 18:20
3:1 [f]S 2Ki 1:17
3:2 [g]1Ki 15:26 [h]1Ki 16:30-32 [i]S Ex 23:24
3:3 [j]S 1Ki 12:28-32
3:4 [k]S Ge 19:37; 2Ki 1:1 [l]Ezr 7:17; Isa 16:1
3:5 [m]S 2Ki 1:1
3:7 [n]1Ki 22:4
3:9 [o]S 1Ki 22:47
3:11 [p]S Ge 25:22; S 1Ki 22:5 [q]S Ge 20:7 [r]S 1Ki 19:16
3:12 [s]S Nu 11:17

reflect a new day for Jericho itself—cursed by Joshua at its fall in the conquest (Jos 6:26). The Creator continues to exercise His creative powers on our behalf.

2:21–22 PRAYER, Intercession—The miraculous act demonstrated the prophet's intercession with God for the people. See notes on Ex 15:25; 1 Ki 17:7–16.

2:23–25 MIRACLE, Judgment—This brief description of judgment on the disrespectful young lads appears unduly harsh. Perhaps there is more to the story than meets the eye. In any event the bears came out of the woods after Elisha had cursed the lads "in the name of the LORD." Most miracles are redemptive in nature.

2:24 PRAYER, Curse—See note on vv 1:10,12. All prayer must reflect the mind of God. If a blessing is possible, a curse must also be possible. God had said He would curse those who cursed Abraham (Ge 12:3). The outworking of God's kingdom depends on the strictures, guidance, and care He places around His chosen instruments. Apostasy in the Northern Kingdom had not been eliminated by Elijah's work. Elisha showed the strong hand of God in judgment. Curse was the outworking of the covenant against disobedience (Lev 26; Dt 26—28).

3:2–3 SIN, Transgression—A partial reformation does not encourage true repentance with the entire heart, mind, and soul. God encourages every step in the right direction, but His expectation is total loyalty. See note on 1 Ki 12:26–33.

3:4–27 CHRISTIAN ETHICS, War and Peace—Victory in battle is easy for God. It does not come easy to the people pretending to be God's people but not obeying Him. The prophet did not seek blessing for the disobedient king of Israel. Winning a battle does not always mean a group of people is right with God even though Israel and many of their religious descendants tend to interpret military victory as divine blessing. See note on Jdg 1:1–36.

3:10–27 REVELATION, Messengers—See note on 1 Sa 10:6–13. God revealed His historical plans to His people through prophetic messengers. Kings sought God's revelation in battle (1 Ki 22). Other gods also had prophets who claimed they could reveal the gods' direction in battle. True prophets refused to reveal God's word to idolatrous kings. Music helped place the prophet in the mood or attitude to receive God's word. The word to Elijah demanded obedient action from the kings to bring victory. The king of Moab resorted to child sacrifice to determine the gods' will and to placate the gods' anger. God prohibited such actions by His people (Ex 13:2,13,15; 22:29; Lev 18:21; 20:2–5; Dt 12:31; 18:10).

3:11 PRAYER, Petition—To inquire of God was to seek His will in a particular matter. See note on 1 Ki 22:8–17. Without Urim and Thummim or prophetic mediators, God's people can still seek His will in direct prayer.

13Elisha said to the king of Israel,
"What do we have to do with each other?
Go to the prophets of your father and the
prophets of your mother."
"No," the king of Israel answered, "because it was the LORD who called us three
kings together to hand us over to Moab."
14Elisha said, "As surely as the LORD
Almighty lives, whom I serve, if I did not
have respect for the presence of Jehoshaphat king of Judah, I would not look at
you or even notice you. 15But now bring
me a harpist."[t]
While the harpist was playing, the
hand[u] of the LORD came upon Elisha
16and he said, "This is what the LORD
says: Make this valley full of ditches.
17For this is what the LORD says: You will
see neither wind nor rain, yet this valley
will be filled with water,[v] and you, your
cattle and your other animals will drink.
18This is an easy[w] thing in the eyes of the
LORD; he will also hand Moab over to
you. 19You will overthrow every fortified
city and every major town. You will cut
down every good tree, stop up all the
springs, and ruin every good field with
stones."
20The next morning, about the time[x]
for offering the sacrifice, there it was—
water flowing from the direction of
Edom! And the land was filled with water.[y]
21Now all the Moabites had heard that
the kings had come to fight against them;
so every man, young and old, who could
bear arms was called up and stationed on
the border. 22When they got up early in
the morning, the sun was shining on the
water. To the Moabites across the way,
the water looked red—like blood.
23"That's blood!" they said. "Those kings
must have fought and slaughtered each
other. Now to the plunder, Moab!"
24But when the Moabites came to the
camp of Israel, the Israelites rose up and
fought them until they fled. And the Israelites invaded the land and slaughtered
the Moabites. 25They destroyed the
towns, and each man threw a stone on
every good field until it was covered.
They stopped up all the springs and cut
down every good tree. Only Kir Hareseth[z] was left with its stones in place,
but men armed with slings surrounded it
and attacked it as well.
26When the king of Moab saw that the
battle had gone against him, he took with
him seven hundred swordsmen to break
through to the king of Edom, but they
failed. 27Then he took his firstborn[a] son,
who was to succeed him as king, and offered him as a sacrifice on the city wall.
The fury against Israel was great; they
withdrew and returned to their own land.

Chapter 4

The Widow's Oil

THE wife of a man from the company[b]
of the prophets cried out to Elisha,
"Your servant my husband is dead, and
you know that he revered the LORD. But
now his creditor[c] is coming to take my
two boys as his slaves."
2Elisha replied to her, "How can I help
you? Tell me, what do you have in your
house?"
"Your servant has nothing there at
all," she said, "except a little oil."[d]
3Elisha said, "Go around and ask all
your neighbors for empty jars. Don't ask
for just a few. 4Then go inside and shut
the door behind you and your sons. Pour
oil into all the jars, and as each is filled,
put it to one side."
5She left him and afterward shut the
door behind her and her sons. They
brought the jars to her and she kept pouring. 6When all the jars were full, she said
to her son, "Bring me another one."
But he replied, "There is not a jar left."
Then the oil stopped flowing.
7She went and told the man of God,[e]
and he said, "Go, sell the oil and pay your
debts. You and your sons can live on what
is left."

The Shunammite's Son Restored to Life

8One day Elisha went to Shunem.[f]

3:15 [t]S 1Sa 10:5 [u]Jer 15:17; Eze 1:3
3:17 [v]Ps 107:35; Isa 12:3; 32:2; 35:6; 41:18; 65:13
3:18 [w]S Ge 18:14; 2Ki 20:10; Isa 49:6; Jer 32:17,27; Mk 10:27
3:20 [x]S Ex 29:41 [y]S Ex 17:6
3:25 [z]Isa 15:1; 16:7; Jer 48:31,36
3:27 [a]S Dt 12:31; 2Ki 16:3; 21:6; 2Ch 28:3; Ps 106:38; Jer 19:4-5; Mic 6:7
4:1 [b]S 1Sa 10:5 [c]S Ex 22:26; Lev 25:39-43; Ne 5:3-5; Job 22:6; 24:9
4:2 [d]S 1Ki 17:12
4:7 [e]S 1Ki 12:22
4:8 [f]S Jos 19:18

3:15–18 PRAYER, Music—The course of Israel and Judah was reversed when they turned to the Lord. Elisha used music in his prayer. The supply of water without rain demonstrated that it was God who was supplying it.

4:1–7 MIRACLE, Faith—Miracles restore justice to the faithful. Enslavement of sons for a father's debt might be justified by legal codes (Ex 21:7; Lev 25:39; Ne 5:5), but no widow would see justice in it (Lev 25:35–38,40–41; Dt 15:1–11). God used a miracle to meet a crisis and insure justice. Like the provision of oil and meal for the widow of Zarephath, this miracle challenged the faith of the needy person. In the earlier story concerning Elijah (1 Ki 17:8–16), the woman used her meager resources to feed the prophet and experienced continued provision. Here the blessing is limited only by her faith in providing containers for the oil. Miracles may assist people in need. They also call for faith to grow.

4:1–37 EVIL AND SUFFERING, God's Present Help—Poverty causes suffering and loss. God can help His faithful people escape poverty's dread clutches. He often uses leaders of His people to minister to people suffering in poverty.

4:8–37 MIRACLE, Instruments—Miracles dominate the ministry of some of God's chosen leaders. See the works of Samson (Jdg 13—16). Several chapters outline the compassionate ministry of Elisha, who performed a series of mighty works. The birth of a son to the Shunammite woman was God's response to her generous provision for the prophet. Like the birth of a son to Abraham and Sarah, to Elkanah and Hannah, and to Zechariah and Elizabeth, the son is described as God's gift to those who honor Him and long for a child—even in their old age. When the child became ill, the mother

And a well-to-do woman was there, who urged him to stay for a meal. So whenever he came by, he stopped there to eat. 9She said to her husband, "I know that this man who often comes our way is a holy man of God. 10Let's make a small room on the roof and put in it a bed and a table, a chair and a lamp for him. Then he can stay[g] there whenever he comes to us."

11One day when Elisha came, he went up to his room and lay down there. 12He said to his servant Gehazi, "Call the Shunammite."[h] So he called her, and she stood before him. 13Elisha said to him, "Tell her, 'You have gone to all this trouble for us. Now what can be done for you? Can we speak on your behalf to the king or the commander of the army?' "

She replied, "I have a home among my own people."

14"What can be done for her?" Elisha asked.

Gehazi said, "Well, she has no son and her husband is old."

15Then Elisha said, "Call her." So he called her, and she stood in the doorway. 16"About this time[i] next year," Elisha said, "you will hold a son in your arms."

"No, my lord," she objected. "Don't mislead your servant, O man of God!"

17But the woman became pregnant, and the next year about that same time she gave birth to a son, just as Elisha had told her.

18The child grew, and one day he went out to his father, who was with the reapers.[j] 19"My head! My head!" he said to his father.

His father told a servant, "Carry him to his mother." 20After the servant had lifted him up and carried him to his mother, the boy sat on her lap until noon, and then he died. 21She went up and laid him on the bed[k] of the man of God, then shut the door and went out.

22She called her husband and said, "Please send me one of the servants and a donkey so I can go to the man of God quickly and return."

23"Why go to him today?" he asked. "It's not the New Moon[l] or the Sabbath."

"It's all right," she said.

24She saddled the donkey and said to her servant, "Lead on; don't slow down for me unless I tell you." 25So she set out and came to the man of God at Mount Carmel.[m]

When he saw her in the distance, the man of God said to his servant Gehazi, "Look! There's the Shunammite! 26Run to meet her and ask her, 'Are you all right? Is your husband all right? Is your child all right?' "

"Everything is all right," she said.

27When she reached the man of God at the mountain, she took hold of his feet. Gehazi came over to push her away, but the man of God said, "Leave her alone! She is in bitter distress,[n] but the LORD has hidden it from me and has not told me why."

28"Did I ask you for a son, my lord?" she said. "Didn't I tell you, 'Don't raise my hopes'?"

29Elisha said to Gehazi, "Tuck your cloak into your belt,[o] take my staff[p] in your hand and run. If you meet anyone, do not greet him, and if anyone greets you, do not answer. Lay my staff on the boy's face."

30But the child's mother said, "As surely as the LORD lives and as you live, I will not leave you." So he got up and followed her.

31Gehazi went on ahead and laid the staff on the boy's face, but there was no sound or response. So Gehazi went back to meet Elisha and told him, "The boy has not awakened."

32When Elisha reached the house, there was the boy lying dead on his couch.[q] 33He went in, shut the door on the two of them and prayed[r] to the LORD. 34Then he got on the bed and lay upon the boy, mouth to mouth, eyes to eyes, hands to hands. As he stretched[s] himself out upon him, the boy's body grew warm. 35Elisha turned away and walked back and forth in the room and then got on the bed and stretched out upon him once more. The boy sneezed seven times[t] and opened his eyes.[u]

36Elisha summoned Gehazi and said, "Call the Shunammite." And he did. When she came, he said, "Take your son."[v] 37She came in, fell at his feet and bowed to the ground. Then she took her son and went out.

Death in the Pot

38Elisha returned to Gilgal[w] and there was a famine[x] in that region. While the

4:10 [g]Mt 10:41; S Ro 12:13
4:12 [h]2Ki 8:1
4:16 [i]S Ge 18:10
4:18 [j]S Ru 2:3
4:21 [k]ver 32
4:23 [l]S Nu 10:10; 1Ch 23:31; Ps 81:3
4:25 [m]S 1Ki 18:20
4:27 [n]1Sa 1:15
4:29 [o]S 1Ki 18:46 [p]S Ex 4:2
4:32 [q]ver 21
4:33 [r]1Ki 17:20; Mt 6:6
4:34 [s]1Ki 17:21; Ac 20:10
4:35 [t]S Jos 6:15 [u]2Ki 8:5
4:36 [v]Heb 11:35
4:38 [w]S 2Ki 2:1 [x]S Lev 26:26; 2Ki 8:1

went to Elisha for help (4:26). When Gehazi, Elisha's servant, laid the staff on the boy's face, nothing changed. Only the presence and touch of the prophet, who was God's instrument, could bring the boy back to life. The same emphasis upon the holy man of God as God's instrument may be seen in the briefer stories of the poisoned pottage (4:38–41) and the feeding of the hundred men (4:42–44). Humans cannot choose miracle-working as the center of their ministry. God chooses to use miracles when they help achieve His purposes.

4:18–37 HUMANITY, Death—Because the death of a child is premature and catastrophic, it is not accepted as easily as the death of an adult. The miraculous restoration of a young life joyfully reaffirms that God alone is the Giver of life.

company of the prophets was meeting
with him, he said to his servant, "Put on
the large pot and cook some stew for
these men."
39One of them went out into the fields
to gather herbs and found a wild vine. He
gathered some of its gourds and filled the
fold of his cloak. When he returned, he
cut them up into the pot of stew, though
no one knew what they were. 40The stew
was poured out for the men, but as they
began to eat it, they cried out, "O man of
God, there is death in the pot!" And they
could not eat it.
41Elisha said, "Get some flour." He put
it into the pot and said, "Serve it to the
people to eat." And there was nothing
harmful in the pot.[y]

Feeding of a Hundred

42A man came from Baal Shalishah,[z]
bringing the man of God twenty loaves[a]
of barley bread[b] baked from the first ripe
grain, along with some heads of new
grain. "Give it to the people to eat," Elisha said.
43"How can I set this before a hundred
men?" his servant asked.
But Elisha answered, "Give it to the
people to eat.[c] For this is what the LORD
says: 'They will eat and have some left
over.[d]'" 44Then he set it before them,
and they ate and had some left over, according to the word of the LORD.

Chapter 5

Naaman Healed of Leprosy

NOW Naaman was commander of the
army of the king of Aram.[e] He was
a great man in the sight of his master and
highly regarded, because through him the
LORD had given victory to Aram. He was a
valiant soldier, but he had leprosy.[d][f]
2Now bands[g] from Aram had gone out
and had taken captive a young girl from
Israel, and she served Naaman's wife.
3She said to her mistress, "If only my
master would see the prophet[h] who is in
Samaria! He would cure him of his leprosy."
4Naaman went to his master and told
him what the girl from Israel had said.
5"By all means, go," the king of Aram
replied. "I will send a letter to the king of
Israel." So Naaman left, taking with him
ten talents[e] of silver, six thousand shekels[f] of gold and ten sets of clothing.[i]
6The letter that he took to the king of
Israel read: "With this letter I am sending
my servant Naaman to you so that you
may cure him of his leprosy."
7As soon as the king of Israel read the
letter,[j] he tore his robes and said, "Am I
God?[k] Can I kill and bring back to life?[l]
Why does this fellow send someone to
me to be cured of his leprosy? See how he
is trying to pick a quarrel[m] with me!"
8When Elisha the man of God heard
that the king of Israel had torn his robes,
he sent him this message: "Why have
you torn your robes? Have the man come
to me and he will know that there is a
prophet[n] in Israel." 9So Naaman went
with his horses and chariots and stopped
at the door of Elisha's house. 10Elisha sent
a messenger to say to him, "Go, wash[o]
yourself seven times[p] in the Jordan, and

4:41 [y]S Ex 15:25; S 2Ki 2:21
4:42 [z]1Sa 9:4 [a]Mt 14:17; 15:36 [b]S 1Sa 9:7
4:43 [c]Lk 9:13 [d]Mt 14:20; Jn 6:12
5:1 [e]S Ge 10:22; S 2Sa 10:19 [f]S Ex 4:6; S Nu 12:10; Lk 4:27
5:2 [g]2Ki 6:23; 13:20; 24:2
5:3 [h]S Ge 20:7
5:5 [i]ver 22; S Ge 24:53; Jdg 14:12; S 1Sa 9:7
5:7 [j]2Ki 19:14 [k]S Ge 30:2 [l]S Dt 32:39 [m]1Ki 20:7
5:8 [n]S 1Ki 22:7
5:10 [o]Jn 9:7 [p]S Ge 33:3; S Lev 14:7

[d] *1* The Hebrew word was used for various diseases affecting the skin—not necessarily leprosy; also in verses 3, 6, 7, 11 and 27. [e] *5* That is, about 750 pounds (about 340 kilograms) [f] *5* That is, about 150 pounds (about 70 kilograms)

4:44 GOD, Faithfulness—God is faithful to perform His promises. We can always depend upon Him to be true to us when we honor Him. The Word of the Lord is always certain; He is never in doubt.

4:44 PRAYER, Faith—The words "according to the word of the LORD" indicate Elisha's reliance upon God. God's prodigality of supply was encouraging in view of the famine.

5:1–27 MIRACLE, Faith—Miracles help people in need no matter their race, position, or residence. Miracles do not satisfy human pride, prejudice, or greed. They respond to humble faith. The story of Naaman is a story of faith. The faith of the servant girl in his household (5:3) was matched by the faith of Naaman. Only the king of Israel is depicted as lacking in faith. Naaman's arrival at Elisha's house with his horses and chariots—and leprosy—was met with a strangely impersonal command. God was to provide the healing, and He was to be obeyed. After first resisting, Naaman was counseled to wash in the Jordan, and he was cleansed. Only God's chosen prophet, not the political ruler, could be God's instrument. Only God's chosen place could be the setting. Only obedience to God's command, not angry pride, made the person open to miraculous healing. Profession of faith in the only God, not payment for the prophet, was the intended result.

5:1–27 REVELATION, Events—The frustrated Syrian leader had already humbled himself by coming to a conquered land for help and rebelled at having to immerse himself in waters inferior to those of his native land. God's miracle required that the visitor be willing to humble himself, that he wait patiently, and that he trust the unspectacular as the means of God's grace and healing. The specific act revealed God's willingness to help a non-Israelite, the power of Israel's God over other gods, and the authority of Elisha as a prophet. Gehazi learned that greed and desire for material rewards are not proper motives for serving God.

5:1–8 EVANGELISM, In the Home—Declaring the power and grace of God should begin in the home, to those nearest and dearest to us. In this case, it was a little servant girl who spoke to her mistress of what a powerful God her Lord was. We may find it difficult to witness to those in our own family. Yet, it could not be more difficult for us than it was for a little slave girl to share with her mistress.

5:9–15 PRAYER, Intercession—Intercession is available for people of all races and nations, but it must be done in God's way. Jesus pointed out that God performed miracles for Gentiles through both Elijah (1 Ki 17:9–14) and Elisha (Lk 4:24–27). Naaman's rank led to a pride which had to be humbled. He expected Elisha to perform a ritual which was pagan in nature. Rather, Naaman was required to acknowledge the sovereignty of the God of Israel.

your flesh will be restored and you will be
cleansed."
11But Naaman went away angry and
said, "I thought that he would surely
come out to me and stand and call on the
name of the LORD his God, wave his
hand[q] over the spot and cure me of my
leprosy. 12Are not Abana and Pharpar, the
rivers of Damascus, better than any of the
waters[r] of Israel? Couldn't I wash in
them and be cleansed?" So he turned and
went off in a rage.[s]
13Naaman's servants went to him and
said, "My father,[t] if the prophet had told
you to do some great thing, would you
not have done it? How much more, then,
when he tells you, 'Wash and be
cleansed'!" 14So he went down and
dipped himself in the Jordan seven
times,[u] as the man of God had told him,
and his flesh was restored[v] and became
clean like that of a young boy.[w]
15Then Naaman and all his attendants
went back to the man of God[x]. He stood
before him and said, "Now I know[y] that
there is no God in all the world except in
Israel. Please accept now a gift[z] from
your servant."
16The prophet answered, "As surely as
the LORD lives, whom I serve, I will not
accept a thing." And even though Naaman urged him, he refused.[a]
17"If you will not," said Naaman,
"please let me, your servant, be given as
much earth[b] as a pair of mules can carry,
for your servant will never again make
burnt offerings and sacrifices to any other
god but the LORD. 18But may the LORD
forgive your servant for this one thing:
When my master enters the temple of
Rimmon to bow down and he is leaning[c]
on my arm and I bow there also—when I
bow down in the temple of Rimmon, may
the LORD forgive your servant for this."
19"Go in peace,"[d] Elisha said.
After Naaman had traveled some distance, 20Gehazi, the servant of Elisha the
man of God, said to himself, "My master
was too easy on Naaman, this Aramean,
by not accepting from him what he
brought. As surely as the LORD[e] lives, I
will run after him and get something from
him."
21So Gehazi hurried after Naaman.
When Naaman saw him running toward
him, he got down from the chariot to
meet him. "Is everything all right?" he
asked.
22"Everything is all right," Gehazi answered. "My master sent me to say, 'Two
young men from the company of the
prophets have just come to me from the
hill country of Ephraim. Please give them
a talent[g] of silver and two sets of clothing.' "[f]
23"By all means, take two talents," said
Naaman. He urged Gehazi to accept
them, and then tied up the two talents of
silver in two bags, with two sets of clothing. He gave them to two of his servants,
and they carried them ahead of Gehazi.
24When Gehazi came to the hill, he took
the things from the servants and put
them away in the house. He sent the men
away and they left. 25Then he went in
and stood before his master Elisha.
"Where have you been, Gehazi?" Elisha asked.
"Your servant didn't go anywhere,"
Gehazi answered.
26But Elisha said to him, "Was not my
spirit with you when the man got down
from his chariot to meet you? Is this the
time[g] to take money, or to accept
clothes, olive groves, vineyards, flocks,
herds, or menservants and maidservants?[h] 27Naaman's leprosy[i] will cling to
you and to your descendants forever."
Then Gehazi[j] went from Elisha's presence and he was leprous, as white as
snow.[k]

Chapter 6

An Axhead Floats

THE company[l] of the prophets said to
Elisha, "Look, the place where we
meet with you is too small for us. 2Let us
go to the Jordan, where each of us can get
a pole; and let us build a place there for
us to live."
And he said, "Go."

5:11 [q]S Ex 7:19
5:12 [r]Isa 8:6 [s]Pr 14:17,29; 19:11; 29:11
5:13 [t]2Ki 6:21; 13:14
5:14 [u]S Ge 33:3; S Lev 14:7; S Jos 6:15 [v]S Ex 4:7 [w]Job 33:25
5:15 [x]S Jos 2:11 [y]S Jos 4:24; S 1Sa 17:46 [z]S 1Sa 9:7
5:16 [a]ver 20,26; Ge 14:23; Da 5:17
5:17 [b]Ex 20:24
5:18 [c]2Ki 7:2
5:19 [d]1Sa 1:17; S Ac 15:33
5:20 [e]Ex 20:7
5:22 [f]S ver 5; S Ge 45:22
5:26 [g]S ver 16 [h]Jer 45:5
5:27 [i]S Nu 12:10 [j]Col 3:5 [k]S Ex 4:6
6:1 [l]S 1Sa 10:5

[g]22 That is, about 75 pounds (about 34 kilograms)

5:14 ORDINANCES, Form of Baptism—The Septuagint, which is the Greek translation of the Old Testament that came before the time of Christ, uses *baptizō* (baptize) for Naaman's dipping of himself in the Jordan. Throughout the Old Testament such dippings were associated with religious significance and, therefore, influenced the later practices of John the Baptist, Jewish proselyte baptism, and the Christian ordinance of baptism.

5:19–27 EVIL AND SUFFERING, Punishment—God may use suffering to punish sin. Gehazi's dramatic case shows how God hates human greed. This one case does not mean God punishes all sinners with disease. Nor does it say all illness is punishment for sin. We must seek to determine God's direction in each case.

6:1–6 MIRACLE, Power—Miracles may reward faithful service. When God's people do His work, He works to meet their needs. Unlike the demonsration of Naaman's personal faith, this story describes ancient magical powers. See note on Ex 7:8–13. God uses many methods to perform His miracles. A tree limb under His direction produced the miraculous. God's compassionate consideration of the prophet was involved. Loss of a precious borrowed ax meant financial problems. Miracle prevented this. Ultimately the story presented evidence of Elisha's great power.

6:1 REVELATION, Messengers—See note on 1 Sa 10:6–13.

3Then one of them said, "Won't you
please come with your servants?"
"I will," Elisha replied. 4And he went
with them.
They went to the Jordan and began to
cut down trees. 5As one of them was cutting down a tree, the iron axhead fell into
the water. "Oh, my lord," he cried out,
"it was borrowed!"
6The man of God asked, "Where did it
fall?" When he showed him the place,
Elisha cut a stick and threw[m] it there, and
made the iron float. 7"Lift it out," he
said. Then the man reached out his hand
and took it.

Elisha Traps Blinded Arameans

8Now the king of Aram was at war with
Israel. After conferring with his officers,
he said, "I will set up my camp in such
and such a place."
9The man of God sent word to the
king[n] of Israel: "Beware of passing that
place, because the Arameans are going
down there." 10So the king of Israel
checked on the place indicated by the
man of God. Time and again Elisha
warned[o] the king, so that he was on his
guard in such places.
11This enraged the king of Aram. He
summoned his officers and demanded of
them, "Will you not tell me which of us is
on the side of the king of Israel?"
12"None of us, my lord the king[p]."
said one of his officers, "but Elisha, the
prophet who is in Israel, tells the king of
Israel the very words you speak in your
bedroom."
13"Go, find out where he is," the king
ordered, "so I can send men and capture
him." The report came back: "He is in
Dothan."[q] 14Then he sent[r] horses and
chariots and a strong force there. They
went by night and surrounded the city.
15When the servant of the man of God
got up and went out early the next morning, an army with horses and chariots had
surrounded the city. "Oh, my lord, what
shall we do?" the servant asked.
16"Don't be afraid,"[s] the prophet answered. "Those who are with us are
more[t] than those who are with them."
17And Elisha prayed, "O LORD, open
his eyes so he may see." Then the LORD
opened the servant's eyes, and he looked
and saw the hills full of horses and chariots[u] of fire all around Elisha.
18As the enemy came down toward
him, Elisha prayed to the LORD, "Strike
these people with blindness."[v] So he
struck them with blindness, as Elisha had
asked.
19Elisha told them, "This is not the
road and this is not the city. Follow me,
and I will lead you to the man you are
looking for." And he led them to Samaria.
20After they entered the city, Elisha
said, "LORD, open the eyes of these men
so they can see." Then the LORD opened
their eyes and they looked, and there
they were, inside Samaria.
21When the king of Israel saw them, he
asked Elisha, "Shall I kill them, my father?[w] Shall I kill them?"
22"Do not kill them," he answered.
"Would you kill men you have captured[x]
with your own sword or bow? Set food
and water before them so that they may
eat and drink and then go back to their
master." 23So he prepared a great feast
for them, and after they had finished eating and drinking, he sent them away, and
they returned to their master. So the
bands[y] from Aram stopped raiding Israel's territory.

Famine in Besieged Samaria

24Some time later, Ben-Hadad[z] king of
Aram mobilized his entire army and
marched up and laid siege[a] to Samaria.
25There was a great famine[b] in the city;
the siege lasted so long that a donkey's
head sold for eighty shekels[h] of silver,
and a quarter of a cab[i] of seed pods[j][c]
for five shekels.[k]
26As the king of Israel was passing by
on the wall, a woman cried to him, "Help
me, my lord the king!"
27The king replied, "If the LORD does
not help you, where can I get help for
you? From the threshing floor? From the
winepress?" 28Then he asked her,
"What's the matter?"
She answered, "This woman said to
me, 'Give up your son so we may eat him

6:6 [m]S Ex 15:25; S 2Ki 2:21
6:9 [n]ver 12
6:10 [o]Jer 11:18
6:12 [p]ver 9
6:13 [q]Ge 37:17
6:14 [r]2Ki 1:9
6:16 [s]S Ge 15:1 [t]2Ch 32:7; Ps 55:18; Ro 8:31; 1Jn 4:4
6:17 [u]S 2Ki 2:11,12
6:18 [v]Ge 19:11; Ac 13:11
6:21 [w]S 2Ki 5:13
6:22 [x]S Dt 20:11; 2Ch 28:8-15
6:23 [y]S 2Ki 5:2
6:24 [z]S 1Ki 15:18; 2Ki 8:7 [a]Dt 28:52
6:25 [b]S Lev 26:26; S Ru 1:1 [c]Isa 36:12

[h]*25* That is, about 2 pounds (about 1 kilogram)
[i]*25* That is, probably about 1/2 pint (about 0.3 liter)
[j]*25* Or *of dove's dung* [k]*25* That is, about 2 ounces (about 55 grams)

6:8–17 REVELATION, Divine Presence—The danger for Israel was apparent to Elisha's servant, but God's strength and presence were not. Elisha revealed to his servant God's redemptive presence. We are frequently blinded by the seemingly overwhelming obstacles directly in front of the path and do not raise our sight to God's deliverance and presence just beyond the first horizon. Elisha's revelation was specific enough to warn the king of specific military maneuvers.

6:8–23 CHRISTIAN ETHICS, War and Peace—This account demonstrates the themes of mercy, peace, and reconciliation with one's enemies that were a part of the Hebrew theological tradition. Israel engaged in the political conflicts of the time, but Israel knew God's will was peace, rest, and mediation of conflict.

6:17 PRAYER, Intercession—Elisha, the man of prayer, was more sensitive than his servant, who required the intercession of the man of God to see the chariots of fire. Intercession for immature believers is one part of the prayer responsibility of mature disciples.

today, and tomorrow we'll eat my son.' [29]So we cooked my son and ate[d] him. The next day I said to her, 'Give up your son so we may eat him,' but she had hidden him."

[30]When the king heard the woman's words, he tore[e] his robes. As he went along the wall, the people looked, and there, underneath, he had sackcloth[f] on his body. [31]He said, "May God deal with me, be it ever so severely, if the head of Elisha son of Shaphat remains on his shoulders today!"

[32]Now Elisha was sitting in his house, and the elders[g] were sitting with him. The king sent a messenger ahead, but before he arrived, Elisha said to the elders, "Don't you see how this murderer[h] is sending someone to cut off my head?[i] Look, when the messenger comes, shut the door and hold it shut against him. Is not the sound of his master's footsteps behind him?"

[33]While he was still talking to them, the messenger came down to him. And ⌊the king⌋ said, "This disaster is from the LORD. Why should I wait[j] for the LORD any longer?"

Chapter 7

ELISHA said, "Hear the word of the LORD. This is what the LORD says: About this time tomorrow, a seah[l] of flour will sell for a shekel[m] and two seahs[n] of barley for a shekel[k] at the gate of Samaria."

[2]The officer on whose arm the king was leaning[l] said to the man of God, "Look, even if the LORD should open the floodgates[m] of the heavens, could this happen?"

"You will see it with your own eyes," answered Elisha, "but you will not eat[n] any of it!"

The Siege Lifted

[3]Now there were four men with leprosy[o][o] at the entrance of the city gate. They said to each other, "Why stay here until we die? [4]If we say, 'We'll go into the city'—the famine is there, and we will die. And if we stay here, we will die. So let's go over to the camp of the Arameans and surrender. If they spare us, we live; if they kill us, then we die."

[5]At dusk they got up and went to the camp of the Arameans. When they reached the edge of the camp, not a man was there, [6]for the Lord had caused the Arameans to hear the sound[p] of chariots and horses and a great army, so that they said to one another, "Look, the king of Israel has hired[q] the Hittite[r] and Egyptian kings to attack us!" [7]So they got up and fled[s] in the dusk and abandoned their tents and their horses and donkeys. They left the camp as it was and ran for their lives.

[8]The men who had leprosy[t] reached the edge of the camp and entered one of the tents. They ate and drank, and carried away silver, gold and clothes, and went off and hid them. They returned and entered another tent and took some things from it and hid them also.

[9]Then they said to each other, "We're not doing right. This is a day of good news and we are keeping it to ourselves. If we wait until daylight, punishment will overtake us. Let's go at once and report this to the royal palace."

[10]So they went and called out to the city gatekeepers and told them, "We went into the Aramean camp and not a man was there—not a sound of anyone—only tethered horses and donkeys, and the tents left just as they were." [11]The gatekeepers shouted the news, and it was reported within the palace.

[12]The king got up in the night and said to his officers, "I will tell you what the Arameans have done to us. They know we are starving; so they have left the camp to hide[u] in the countryside, thinking, 'They will surely come out, and then we will take them alive and get into the city.'"

[13]One of his officers answered, "Have some men take five of the horses that are left in the city. Their plight will be like that of all the Israelites left here—yes, they will only be like all these Israelites who are doomed. So let us send them to find out what happened."

[14]So they selected two chariots with their horses, and the king sent them after the Aramean army. He commanded the drivers, "Go and find out what has happened." [15]They followed them as far as the Jordan, and they found the whole

6:29 [d]S Lev 26:29; Dt 28:53-55
6:30 [e]2Ki 18:37; Isa 22:15 [f]S Ge 37:34
6:32 [g]Eze 8:1; 14:1; 20:1 [h]1Ki 18:4 [i]ver 31
6:33 [j]Lev 24:11; Job 2:9; 14:14; Isa 40:31
7:1 [k]ver 16
7:2 [l]2Ki 5:18 [m]ver 19; Ge 7:11; Ps 78:23; Mal 3:10 [n]ver 17
7:3 [o]Lev 13:45-46; Nu 5:1-4
7:6 [p]S Ex 14:24; Eze 1:24 [q]2Sa 10:6; Jer 46:21 [r]S Nu 13:29
7:7 [s]Jdg 7:21; Ps 48:4-6; Pr 28:1; Isa 30:17
7:8 [t]Isa 33:23; 35:6
7:12 [u]Jos 8:4

[l]*1* That is, probably about 7 quarts (about 7.3 liters); also in verses 16 and 18 [m]*1* That is, about 2/5 ounce (about 11 grams); also in verses 16 and 18 [n]*1* That is, probably about 13 quarts (about 15 liters); also in verses 16 and 18 [o]*3* The Hebrew word is used for various diseases affecting the skin—not necessarily leprosy; also in verse 8.

7:1–7 REVELATION, Events—The Israelites assumed defeat, but four sick beggars who went to surrender to the enemy discovered God's deliverance. From the most unexpected sources, at the most surprising moments, God transforms defeat into relief and victory.

7:1–20 HISTORY, Promise—God's historical promises may be short-term as well as long-term. Against all odds, He defeated the Assyrians. The man who refused to believe God's promises did not get to benefit from them. God's historical promises call for faith from His people.

road strewn with the clothing and equipment the Arameans had thrown away in their headlong flight.[v] So the messengers returned and reported to the king. 16Then the people went out and plundered[w] the camp of the Arameans. So a seah of flour sold for a shekel, and two seahs of barley sold for a shekel,[x] as the LORD had said.

17Now the king had put the officer on whose arm he leaned in charge of the gate, and the people trampled him in the gateway, and he died,[y] just as the man of God had foretold when the king came down to his house. 18It happened as the man of God had said to the king: "About this time tomorrow, a seah of flour will sell for a shekel and two seahs of barley for a shekel at the gate of Samaria."

19The officer had said to the man of God, "Look, even if the LORD should open the floodgates[z] of the heavens, could this happen?" The man of God had replied, "You will see it with your own eyes, but you will not eat any of it!" 20And that is exactly what happened to him, for the people trampled him in the gateway, and he died.

Chapter 8

The Shunammite's Land Restored

NOW Elisha had said to the woman[a] whose son he had restored to life, "Go away with your family and stay for a while wherever you can, because the LORD has decreed a famine[b] in the land that will last seven years."[c] 2The woman proceeded to do as the man of God said. She and her family went away and stayed in the land of the Philistines seven years.

3At the end of the seven years she came back from the land of the Philistines and went to the king to beg for her house and land. 4The king was talking to Gehazi, the servant of the man of God, and had said, "Tell me about all the great things Elisha has done." 5Just as Gehazi was telling the king how Elisha had restored[d] the dead to life, the woman whose son Elisha had brought back to life came to beg the king for her house and land.

Gehazi said, "This is the woman, my lord the king, and this is her son whom Elisha restored to life." 6The king asked the woman about it, and she told him.

Then he assigned an official to her case and said to him, "Give back everything that belonged to her, including all the income from her land from the day she left the country until now."

7:15 [v]Job 27:22
7:16 [w]Isa 33:4,23 [x]ver 1
7:17 [y]S ver 2
7:19 [z]S ver 2
8:1 [a]2Ki 4:8-37 [b]S Lev 26:26; S Dt 28:22; S Ru 1:1 [c]S Ge 12:10
8:5 [d]2Ki 4:35
8:7 [e]S 2Sa 8:5 [f]S 2Ki 6:24
8:8 [g]1Ki 19:15 [h]S Ge 32:20; S 1Sa 9:7 [i]S Jdg 18:5
8:10 [j]Isa 38:1
8:11 [k]S Jdg 3:25 [l]Lk 19:41
8:12 [m]S 1Ki 19:17 [n]Ps 137:9; Isa 13:16; Hos 13:16; Na 3:10; Lk 19:44 [o]S Ge 34:29 [p]2Ki 15:16; Am 1:13
8:13 [q]S 1Sa 17:43; S 2Sa 3:8 [r]1Ki 19:15
8:15 [s]S 2Ki 1:17
8:16 [t]S 2Ki 1:17 [u]2Ch 21:1-4
8:18 [v]ver 26; 2Ki 11:1

Hazael Murders Ben-Hadad

7Elisha went to Damascus,[e] and Ben-Hadad[f] king of Aram was ill. When the king was told, "The man of God has come all the way up here," 8he said to Hazael,[g] "Take a gift[h] with you and go to meet the man of God. Consult[i] the LORD through him; ask him, 'Will I recover from this illness?' "

9Hazael went to meet Elisha, taking with him as a gift forty camel-loads of all the finest wares of Damascus. He went in and stood before him, and said, "Your son Ben-Hadad king of Aram has sent me to ask, 'Will I recover from this illness?' "

10Elisha answered, "Go and say to him, 'You will certainly recover';[j] but[p] the LORD has revealed to me that he will in fact die." 11He stared at him with a fixed gaze until Hazael felt ashamed.[k] Then the man of God began to weep.[l]

12"Why is my lord weeping?" asked Hazael.

"Because I know the harm[m] you will do to the Israelites," he answered. "You will set fire to their fortified places, kill their young men with the sword, dash[n] their little children[o] to the ground, and rip open[p] their pregnant women."

13Hazael said, "How could your servant, a mere dog,[q] accomplish such a feat?"

"The LORD has shown me that you will become king[r] of Aram," answered Elisha.

14Then Hazael left Elisha and returned to his master. When Ben-Hadad asked, "What did Elisha say to you?" Hazael replied, "He told me that you would certainly recover." 15But the next day he took a thick cloth, soaked it in water and spread it over the king's face, so that he died.[s] Then Hazael succeeded him as king.

Jehoram King of Judah

8:16-24pp — 2Ch 21:5-10,20

16In the fifth year of Joram[t] son of Ahab king of Israel, when Jehoshaphat was king of Judah, Jehoram[u] son of Jehoshaphat began his reign as king of Judah. 17He was thirty-two years old when he became king, and he reigned in Jerusalem eight years. 18He walked in the ways of the kings of Israel, as the house of Ahab had done, for he married a daughter[v] of Ahab. He did evil in the eyes of the LORD. 19Nevertheless, for the sake of

[p] *10* The Hebrew may also be read *Go and say, 'You will certainly not recover,' for.*

8:15 CHRISTIAN ETHICS, Murder—See note on 1 Ki 16:10–13.

8:18 SIN, Transgression—See notes on 1 Ki 11:1–13; 14:22–24.

8:19 GOD, Faithfulness—God is faithful and unchanging. His purposes do not change with the changing character of the

his servant David, the LORD was not willing to destroy[w] Judah. He had promised
to maintain a lamp[x] for David and his
descendants forever.
20In the time of Jehoram, Edom rebelled against Judah and set up its own
king.[y] 21So Jehoram[q] went to Zair with
all his chariots. The Edomites surrounded
him and his chariot commanders, but he
rose up and broke through by night; his
army, however, fled back home. 22To this
day Edom has been in rebellion[z] against
Judah. Libnah[a] revolted at the same
time.
23As for the other events of Jehoram's
reign, and all he did, are they not written
in the book of the annals of the kings of
Judah? 24Jehoram rested with his fathers
and was buried with them in the City of
David. And Ahaziah his son succeeded
him as king.

Ahaziah King of Judah

8:25–29pp — 2Ch 22:1–6

25In the twelfth[b] year of Joram son of
Ahab king of Israel, Ahaziah son of Jehoram king of Judah began to reign. 26Ahazi-
ah was twenty-two years old when he became king, and he reigned in Jerusalem
one year. His mother's name was Athaliah,[c] a granddaughter of Omri[d] king of
Israel. 27He walked in the ways of the
house of Ahab[e] and did evil[f] in the eyes
of the LORD, as the house of Ahab had
done, for he was related by marriage to
Ahab's family.
28Ahaziah went with Joram son of
Ahab to war against Hazael king of Aram
at Ramoth Gilead.[g] The Arameans
wounded Joram; 29so King Joram returned to Jezreel[h] to recover from the
wounds the Arameans had inflicted on
him at Ramoth[r] in his battle with Hazael[i] king of Aram.
Then Ahaziah[j] son of Jehoram king of
Judah went down to Jezreel to see Joram
son of Ahab, because he had been
wounded.

Chapter 9

Jehu Anointed King of Israel

THE prophet Elisha summoned a man
from the company[k] of the prophets
and said to him, "Tuck your cloak into
your belt,[l] take this flask of oil[m] with
you and go to Ramoth Gilead.[n] 2When
you get there, look for Jehu son of Jehoshaphat, the son of Nimshi. Go to him, get
him away from his companions and take
him into an inner room. 3Then take the
flask and pour the oil[o] on his head and
declare, 'This is what the LORD says: I
anoint you king over Israel.' Then open
the door and run; don't delay!"
4So the young man, the prophet, went
to Ramoth Gilead. 5When he arrived, he
found the army officers sitting together.
"I have a message for you, commander,"
he said.
"For which of us?" asked Jehu.
"For you, commander," he replied.
6Jehu got up and went into the house.
Then the prophet poured the oil[p] on
Jehu's head and declared, "This is what
the LORD, the God of Israel, says: 'I anoint
you king over the LORD's people Israel.
7You are to destroy the house of Ahab
your master, and I will avenge[q] the blood
of my servants[r] the prophets and the
blood of all the LORD's servants shed by
Jezebel.[s] 8The whole house[t] of Ahab
will perish. I will cut off from Ahab every
last male[u] in Israel—slave or free. 9I will
make the house of Ahab like the house of
Jeroboam[v] son of Nebat and like the
house of Baasha[w] son of Ahijah. 10As for
Jezebel, dogs[x] will devour her on the plot
of ground at Jezreel, and no one will bury
her.' " Then he opened the door and ran.
11When Jehu went out to his fellow officers, one of them asked him, "Is everything all right? Why did this madman[y]
come to you?"
"You know the man and the sort of
things he says," Jehu replied.
12"That's not true!" they said. "Tell
us."
Jehu said, "Here is what he told me:
'This is what the LORD says: I anoint you
king over Israel.' "
13They hurried and took their cloaks
and spread[z] them under him on the bare
steps. Then they blew the trumpet[a] and
shouted, "Jehu is king!"

8:19 [w]S Ge 6:13 [x]S 2Sa 21:17; Rev 21:23
8:20 [y]S 1Ki 22:47
8:22 [z]Ge 27:40 [a]S Nu 33:20; Jos 21:13; 2Ki 19:8
8:25 [b]2Ki 9:29
8:26 [c]S ver 18 [d]1Ki 16:23
8:27 [e]1Ki 16:30 [f]1Ki 15:26
8:28 [g]S Dt 4:43; 2Ki 9:1,14
8:29 [h]1Ki 21:29; 2Ki 9:21 [i]1Ki 19:15,17 [j]2Ki 10:13
9:1 [k]S 1Sa 10:5 [l]S 1Ki 18:46 [m]S 1Sa 10:1 [n]S 2Ki 8:28
9:3 [o]1Ki 19:16
9:6 [p]1Ki 19:16
9:7 [q]S Ge 4:24; S Rev 6:10 [r]S Dt 32:43 [s]S 1Ki 18:4
9:8 [t]2Ki 10:17 [u]S 1Sa 25:22
9:9 [v]S 1Ki 13:34; S 14:10 [w]1Ki 16:3
9:10 [x]S 1Ki 21:23
9:11 [y]S 1Sa 10:11; S Jn 10:20
9:13 [z]Mt 21:8; Lk 19:36 [a]S 2Sa 15:10

[q]*21* Hebrew *Joram,* a variant of *Jehoram;* also in verses 23 and 24 [r]*29* Hebrew *Ramah,* a variant of *Ramoth*

times. He is faithful to His promises made in past times; and He continues to pursue the goals He set in the beginning. What God started, He will certainly finish.

8:23 HOLY SCRIPTURE, Writing—See note on 1:16–18.

8:27 SIN, Transgression—See notes on 1 Ki 11:1–13; 14:22–24.

9:1–37 HISTORY, God's Leaders—God chooses leaders to fulfill His purposes. They may be instruments to punish unfaithful leaders.

9:1—10:33 CHRISTIAN ETHICS, War and Peace—God used human warfare and violence to punish disobedient rulers. They died violently as they had lived. God's desired peace (see notes on Jos 21:43–45; 2 Sa 7:1,11) did not come because the people practiced false religion. See note on Jdg 2:1—3:6.

9:7–10 GOD, Wrath—The wrath of God is performed here, not as a fit of anger, but as the righteous judgment upon those who have flagrantly and obstinately opposed Him. See notes on Ge 6:5–8; 17:14; 19:13,24–26; Mt 3:7–10; Ro 1:18.

Jehu Kills Joram and Ahaziah

9:21–29pp — 2Ch 22:7–9

14So Jehu son of Jehoshaphat, the son
of Nimshi, conspired against Joram. (Now
Joram and all Israel had been defending
Ramoth Gilead[b] against Hazael king of
Aram, 15but King Joram[s] had returned to
Jezreel to recover[c] from the wounds the
Arameans had inflicted on him in the battle with Hazael king of Aram.) Jehu said,
"If this is the way you feel, don't let anyone slip out of the city to go and tell the
news in Jezreel." 16Then he got into his
chariot and rode to Jezreel, because Joram was resting there and Ahaziah[d] king
of Judah had gone down to see him.
17When the lookout[e] standing on the
tower in Jezreel saw Jehu's troops approaching, he called out, "I see some
troops coming."
"Get a horseman," Joram ordered.
"Send him to meet them and ask, 'Do
you come in peace?[f]' "
18The horseman rode off to meet Jehu
and said, "This is what the king says: 'Do
you come in peace?' "
"What do you have to do with peace?"
Jehu replied. "Fall in behind me."
The lookout reported, "The messenger
has reached them, but he isn't coming
back."
19So the king sent out a second horseman. When he came to them he said,
"This is what the king says: 'Do you
come in peace?' "
Jehu replied, "What do you have to do
with peace? Fall in behind me."
20The lookout reported, "He has
reached them, but he isn't coming back
either. The driving is like[g] that of Jehu
son of Nimshi—he drives like a madman."
21"Hitch up my chariot," Joram ordered. And when it was hitched up, Joram king of Israel and Ahaziah king of
Judah rode out, each in his own chariot,
to meet Jehu. They met him at the plot of
ground that had belonged to Naboth[h] the
Jezreelite. 22When Joram saw Jehu he
asked, "Have you come in peace, Jehu?"
"How can there be peace," Jehu replied, "as long as all the idolatry and
witchcraft of your mother Jezebel[i]
abound?"
23Joram turned about and fled, calling
out to Ahaziah, "Treachery,[j] Ahaziah!"
24Then Jehu drew his bow[k] and shot
Joram between the shoulders. The arrow
pierced his heart and he slumped down
in his chariot. 25Jehu said to Bidkar, his
chariot officer, "Pick him up and throw
him on the field that belonged to Naboth
the Jezreelite. Remember how you and I
were riding together in chariots behind
Ahab his father when the LORD made this
prophecy[l] about him: 26'Yesterday I saw
the blood of Naboth[m] and the blood of his
sons, declares the LORD, and I will surely
make you pay for it on this plot of ground,
declares the LORD.'[t] Now then, pick him
up and throw him on that plot, in accordance with the word of the LORD."[n]
27When Ahaziah king of Judah saw
what had happened, he fled up the road
to Beth Haggan.[u] Jehu chased him,
shouting, "Kill him too!" They wounded
him in his chariot on the way up to Gur
near Ibleam,[o] but he escaped to Megiddo[p] and died there. 28His servants took
him by chariot[q] to Jerusalem and buried
him with his fathers in his tomb in the
City of David. 29(In the eleventh[r] year of
Joram son of Ahab, Ahaziah had become
king of Judah.)

Jezebel Killed

30Then Jehu went to Jezreel. When Jezebel heard about it, she painted[s] her
eyes, arranged her hair and looked out of
a window. 31As Jehu entered the gate,
she asked, "Have you come in peace,
Zimri,[t] you murderer of your master?"[v]
32He looked up at the window and
called out, "Who is on my side? Who?"
Two or three eunuchs looked down at
him. 33"Throw her down!" Jehu said. So
they threw her down, and some of her
blood spattered the wall and the horses as
they trampled her underfoot.[u]
34Jehu went in and ate and drank.
"Take care of that cursed woman," he
said, "and bury her, for she was a king's
daughter."[v] 35But when they went out to
bury her, they found nothing except her
skull, her feet and her hands. 36They
went back and told Jehu, who said, "This
is the word of the LORD that he spoke
through his servant Elijah the Tishbite:
On the plot of ground at Jezreel dogs[w]
will devour Jezebel's flesh.[w][x] 37Jezebel's
body will be like refuse[y] on the ground

9:14 [b]S Dt 4:43; S 2Ki 8:28
9:15 [c]S 2Ki 8:29
9:16 [d]2Ch 22:7
9:17 [e]S 1Sa 14:16; Isa 21:6 [f]S 1Sa 16:4
9:20 [g]2Sa 18:27
9:21 [h]1Ki 21:1-7, 15-19
9:22 [i]1Ki 18:19; Rev 2:20
9:23 [j]2Ki 11:14
9:24 [k]S 1Ki 22:34
9:25 [l]1Ki 21:19-22, 24-29
9:26 [m]S 1Ki 21:19 [n]S 1Ki 21:29
9:27 [o]S Jdg 1:27 [p]2Ki 23:29
9:28 [q]2Ki 14:20; 23:30
9:29 [r]2Ki 8:25
9:30 [s]Jer 4:30; Eze 23:40
9:31 [t]1Ki 16:9-10
9:33 [u]Ps 7:5
9:34 [v]S 1Ki 16:31
9:36 [w]Ps 68:23; Jer 15:3 [x]S 1Ki 21:23
9:37 [y]Ps 83:10; Isa 5:25; Jer 8:2; 9:22; 16:4; 25:33; Zep 1:17

[s]*15* Hebrew *Jehoram,* a variant of *Joram;* also in verses 17 and 21-24 [t]*26* See 1 Kings 21:19. [u]*27* Or *fled by way of the garden house* [v]*31* Or *"Did Zimri have peace, who murdered his master?"* [w]*36* See 1 Kings 21:23.

9:22 SIN, Transgression—Even in times of political stability and economic prosperity, peace is not assured if God's law is ignored and the way is paved for future brutality. Peace is measured in spiritual terms, not in military terms.

9:25–26,36–37 GOD, Faithfulness—What God says, God will do. He is constant and unchanging in character and will faithfully carry out His promises.

9:30 HUMANITY, Physical Nature—Cosmetics make people more attractive but do not alter their inner nature. Even in a beautiful package, sin deserves death.

in the plot at Jezreel, so that no one will be able to say, 'This is Jezebel.' "

Chapter 10

Ahab's Family Killed

NOW there were in Samaria[z] seventy sons[a] of the house of Ahab. So Jehu wrote letters and sent them to Samaria: to the officials of Jezreel,[x b] to the elders and to the guardians[c] of Ahab's children. He said, [2]"As soon as this letter reaches you, since your master's sons are with you and you have chariots and horses, a fortified city and weapons, [3]choose the best and most worthy of your master's sons and set him on his father's throne. Then fight for your master's house."

[4]But they were terrified and said, "If two kings could not resist him, how can we?"

[5]So the palace administrator, the city governor, the elders and the guardians sent this message to Jehu: "We are your servants[d] and we will do anything you say. We will not appoint anyone as king; you do whatever you think best."

[6]Then Jehu wrote them a second letter, saying, "If you are on my side and will obey me, take the heads of your master's sons and come to me in Jezreel by this time tomorrow."

Now the royal princes, seventy of them, were with the leading men of the city, who were rearing them. [7]When the letter arrived, these men took the princes and slaughtered all seventy[e] of them. They put their heads[f] in baskets and sent them to Jehu in Jezreel. [8]When the messenger arrived, he told Jehu, "They have brought the heads of the princes."

Then Jehu ordered, "Put them in two piles at the entrance of the city gate until morning."

[9]The next morning Jehu went out. He stood before all the people and said, "You are innocent. It was I who conspired against my master and killed him, but who killed all these? [10]Know then, that not a word the LORD has spoken against the house of Ahab will fail. The LORD has done what he promised[g] through his servant Elijah."[h] [11]So Jehu[i] killed everyone in Jezreel who remained of the house of Ahab, as well as all his chief men, his close friends and his priests, leaving him no survivor.[j]

[12]Jehu then set out and went toward Samaria. At Beth Eked of the Shepherds, [13]he met some relatives of Ahaziah king of Judah and asked, "Who are you?"

They said, "We are relatives of Ahaziah,[k] and we have come down to greet the families of the king and of the queen mother.[l]"

[14]"Take them alive!" he ordered. So they took them alive and slaughtered them by the well of Beth Eked—forty-two men. He left no survivor.[m]

[15]After he left there, he came upon Jehonadab[n] son of Recab,[o] who was on his way to meet him. Jehu greeted him and said, "Are you in accord with me, as I am with you?"

"I am," Jehonadab answered.

"If so," said Jehu, "give me your hand."[p] So he did, and Jehu helped him up into the chariot. [16]Jehu said, "Come with me and see my zeal[q] for the LORD." Then he had him ride along in his chariot.

[17]When Jehu came to Samaria, he killed all who were left there of Ahab's family;[r] he destroyed them, according to the word of the LORD spoken to Elijah.

Ministers of Baal Killed

[18]Then Jehu brought all the people together and said to them, "Ahab served[s] Baal a little; Jehu will serve him much. [19]Now summon[t] all the prophets of Baal, all his ministers and all his priests. See that no one is missing, because I am going to hold a great sacrifice for Baal. Anyone who fails to come will no longer live." But Jehu was acting deceptively in order to destroy the ministers of Baal.

[20]Jehu said, "Call an assembly[u] in honor of Baal." So they proclaimed it. [21]Then he sent word throughout Israel, and all the ministers of Baal came; not one stayed away. They crowded into the temple of Baal until it was full from one end to the other. [22]And Jehu said to the keeper of the wardrobe, "Bring robes for all the ministers of Baal." So he brought out robes for them.

[23]Then Jehu and Jehonadab son of Recab went into the temple of Baal. Jehu said to the ministers of Baal, "Look around and see that no servants of the LORD are here with you—only ministers of Baal." [24]So they went in to make sacrifices and burnt offerings. Now Jehu had

[x] *1* Hebrew; some Septuagint manuscripts and Vulgate *of the city*

10:1 [z]S 1Ki 13:32 [a]S Jdg 8:30 [b]S 1Ki 21:1 [c]ver 5
10:5 [d]Jos 9:8
10:7 [e]S 1Ki 21:21 [f]S 2Sa 4:8
10:10 [g]2Ki 9:7-10 [h]S 1Ki 21:29
10:11 [i]Hos 1:4 [j]ver 14; Job 18:19; Mal 4:1
10:13 [k]2Ki 8:24, 29; 2Ch 22:8 [l]S 1Ki 2:19
10:14 [m]S ver 11
10:15 [n]Jer 35:6, 14-19 [o]1Ch 2:55; Jer 35:2 [p]Ezr 10:19; Eze 17:18
10:16 [q]S Nu 25:13
10:17 [r]2Ki 9:8
10:18 [s]S Jdg 2:11
10:19 [t]1Ki 18:19
10:20 [u]S Ex 32:5

10:10,17,30 GOD, Faithfulness—See notes on 9:25–26,36–37.

10:18–27 GOD, One God—This was a dramatic and drastic action on the part of Jehu to establish clearly the authority and sovereignty of the one true God. This was necessary in the light of the long struggle to purify the faith of Israel which was so often corrupted by worship of other gods. There was little that God could do in or through Israel until she learned that there is truly only one God.

10:18–36 SIN, Transgression—See notes on 3:2–3; 1 Ki 12:26–33.

posted eighty men outside with this
warning: "If one of you lets any of the
men I am placing in your hands escape, it
will be your life for his life."[v]
25As soon as Jehu had finished making
the burnt offering, he ordered the guards
and officers: "Go in and kill[w] them; let
no one escape."[x] So they cut them down
with the sword. The guards and officers
threw the bodies out and then entered
the inner shrine of the temple of Baal.
26They brought the sacred stone[y] out of
the temple of Baal and burned it. 27They
demolished the sacred stone of Baal and
tore down the temple[z] of Baal, and people have used it for a latrine to this day.
28So Jehu[a] destroyed Baal worship in
Israel. 29However, he did not turn away
from the sins[b] of Jeroboam son of Nebat,
which he had caused Israel to commit—
the worship of the golden calves[c] at
Bethel[d] and Dan.
30The LORD said to Jehu, "Because you
have done well in accomplishing what is
right in my eyes and have done to the
house of Ahab all I had in mind to do,
your descendants will sit on the throne of
Israel to the fourth generation."[e] 31Yet
Jehu was not careful[f] to keep the law of
the LORD, the God of Israel, with all his
heart. He did not turn away from the
sins[g] of Jeroboam, which he had caused
Israel to commit.
32In those days the LORD began to reduce[h] the size of Israel. Hazael[i] overpowered the Israelites throughout their
territory 33east of the Jordan in all the
land of Gilead (the region of Gad, Reuben
and Manasseh), from Aroer[j] by the Arnon[k] Gorge through Gilead to Bashan.
34As for the other events of Jehu's
reign, all he did, and all his achievements, are they not written in the book of
the annals[l] of the kings of Israel?
35Jehu rested with his fathers and was
buried in Samaria. And Jehoahaz his son
succeeded him as king. 36The time that
Jehu reigned over Israel in Samaria was
twenty-eight years.

Chapter 11

Athaliah and Joash

11:1-21pp — 2Ch 22:10-23:21

WHEN Athaliah[m] the mother of Ahaziah saw that her son was dead,
she proceeded to destroy the whole royal
family. 2But Jehosheba, the daughter of
King Jehoram[y] and sister of Ahaziah,
took Joash[n] son of Ahaziah and stole him
away from among the royal princes, who
were about to be murdered. She put him
and his nurse in a bedroom to hide him
from Athaliah; so he was not killed.[o] 3He
remained hidden with his nurse at the
temple of the LORD for six years while
Athaliah ruled the land.

4In the seventh year Jehoiada sent for
the commanders of units of a hundred,
the Carites[p] and the guards and had
them brought to him at the temple of the
LORD. He made a covenant with them
and put them under oath at the temple of
the LORD. Then he showed them the
king's son. 5He commanded them, saying, "This is what you are to do: You who
are in the three companies that are going
on duty on the Sabbath[q]—a third of you
guarding the royal palace,[r] 6a third at the
Sur Gate, and a third at the gate behind
the guard, who take turns guarding the
temple— 7and you who are in the other
two companies that normally go off Sabbath duty are all to guard the temple for
the king. 8Station yourselves around the
king, each man with his weapon in his
hand. Anyone who approaches your
ranks[z] must be put to death. Stay close to
the king wherever he goes."

9The commanders of units of a hundred did just as Jehoiada the priest ordered. Each one took his men—those
who were going on duty on the Sabbath
and those who were going off duty—and
came to Jehoiada the priest. 10Then he
gave the commanders the spears and
shields[s] that had belonged to King David
and that were in the temple of the LORD.
11The guards, each with his weapon in
his hand, stationed themselves around
the king—near the altar and the temple,
from the south side to the north side of
the temple.

12Jehoiada brought out the king's son
and put the crown on him; he presented
him with a copy of the covenant[t] and
proclaimed him king. They anointed[u]

10:24 [v]S Jos 2:14
10:25 [w]S Ex 22:20; S 2Ki 11:18 [x]S 1Ki 18:40
10:26 [y]S Ex 23:24
10:27 [z]S 1Ki 16:32
10:28 [a]1Ki 19:17
10:29 [b]S 1Ki 12:30 [c]S Ex 32:4 [d]1Ki 12:32
10:30 [e]2Ki 15:12
10:31 [f]Dt 4:9; Pr 4:23 [g]1Ki 12:30
10:32 [h]2Ki 13:25; Ps 107:39 [i]S 1Ki 19:17
10:33 [j]S Nu 32:34; Dt 2:36; Jdg 11:26; Isa 17:2 [k]S Nu 21:13
10:34 [l]1Ki 15:31
11:1 [m]S 2Ki 8:18
11:2 [n]2Ki 12:1 [o]S Jdg 9:5
11:4 [p]ver 19
11:5 [q]1Ch 9:25 [r]1Ki 14:27
11:10 [s]S 2Sa 8:7
11:12 [t]Ex 25:16; 2Ki 23:3 [u]S 1Sa 9:16; S 1Ki 1:39

[y]2 Hebrew *Joram,* a variant of *Jehoram* [z]8 Or *approaches the precincts*

10:28–31 HISTORY, Worship—See note on 1 Ki 12:28–30. Knowledge of God's acts in history leads to opposition to all other gods and ways of worship. Such knowledge should also lead us to proper worship of God, not to a continuation of a popular but improper type of worship.

10:34 HOLY SCRIPTURE, Writing—See note on 1:16–18.

11:12,17 THE CHURCH, Covenant People—Commitments include responsibilities. Covenant people must live according to the demands of the relationship with God. Israel's king had rights and responsibilities given by God. In contrast to rulers of surrounding nations, Israel's king did not possess absolute authority. The only right of Israel's king was to do right. Believers are not given unlimited authority. We cannot selfishly assert our rights. Our right is to do right before God. Our authority comes from doing the will of God. God's cov-

him, and the people clapped their
hands[v] and shouted, "Long live the
king!"[w]
13When Athaliah heard the noise made
by the guards and the people, she went to
the people at the temple of the LORD.
14She looked and there was the king,
standing by the pillar,[x] as the custom
was. The officers and the trumpeters
were beside the king, and all the people
of the land were rejoicing and blowing
trumpets.[y] Then Athaliah tore[z] her
robes and called out, "Treason! Treason!"[a]
15Jehoiada the priest ordered the commanders of units of a hundred, who were
in charge of the troops: "Bring her out
between the ranks[a] and put to the sword
anyone who follows her." For the priest
had said, "She must not be put to death
in the temple[b] of the LORD." 16So they
seized her as she reached the place
where the horses enter[c] the palace
grounds, and there she was put to
death.[d]
17Jehoiada then made a covenant[e] between the LORD and the king and people
that they would be the LORD's people.
He also made a covenant between the
king and the people.[f] 18All the people
of the land went to the temple[g] of Baal
and tore it down. They smashed[h] the
altars and idols to pieces and killed
Mattan the priest[i] of Baal in front of the
altars.

Then Jehoiada the priest posted guards
at the temple of the LORD. 19He took with
him the commanders of hundreds, the
Carites,[j] the guards and all the people of
the land, and together they brought the
king down from the temple of the LORD
and went into the palace, entering by way
of the gate of the guards. The king then
took his place on the royal throne, 20and
all the people of the land rejoiced.[k] And
the city was quiet, because Athaliah had
been slain with the sword at the palace.
21Joash[b] was seven years old when he
began to reign.

11:14 [x]S 1Ki 7:15 [y]S 1Ki 1:39 [z]S Ge 37:29 [a]2Ki 9:23
11:15 [b]1Ki 2:30
11:16 [c]Ne 3:28; Jer 31:40 [d]S Ge 4:14
11:17 [e]S Ex 24:8; 2Sa 5:3; 2Ch 15:12; 23:3; 29:10; 34:31; Ezr 10:3 [f]2Ki 23:3; Jer 34:8
11:18 [g]S 1Ki 16:32 [h]S Dt 12:3 [i]1Ki 18:40; 2Ki 10:25; 23:20
11:19 [j]ver 4
11:20 [k]Pr 11:10; 28:12; 29:2
12:1 [l]2Ki 11:2
12:2 [m]S Dt 12:25; S 2Sa 8:15
12:3 [n]S 1Ki 3:3; S 2Ki 18:4
12:4 [o]2Ki 22:4 [p]Nu 18:19 [q]S Ex 30:12 [r]S Ex 25:2; S 35:29
12:5 [s]2Ki 22:5
12:9 [t]2Ki 25:18; Jer 35:4; 52:24 [u]Mk 12:41; Lk 21:1
12:10 [v]S 2Sa 8:17

Chapter 12

Joash Repairs the Temple

12:1–21pp — 2Ch 24:1–14; 24:23–27

IN the seventh year of Jehu, Joash[c][l] became king, and he reigned in Jerusalem forty years. His mother's name was
Zibiah; she was from Beersheba. 2Joash
did what was right[m] in the eyes of the
LORD all the years Jehoiada the priest instructed him. 3The high places,[n] however, were not removed; the people continued to offer sacrifices and burn incense
there.
4Joash said to the priests, "Collect[o] all
the money that is brought as sacred offerings[p] to the temple of the LORD—the
money collected in the census,[q] the
money received from personal vows and
the money brought voluntarily[r] to the
temple. 5Let every priest receive the
money from one of the treasurers, and let
it be used to repair[s] whatever damage is
found in the temple."
6But by the twenty-third year of King
Joash the priests still had not repaired the
temple. 7Therefore King Joash summoned
Jehoiada the priest and the other priests
and asked them, "Why aren't you repairing the damage done to the temple? Take
no more money from your treasurers, but
hand it over for repairing the temple."
8The priests agreed that they would not
collect any more money from the people
and that they would not repair the temple
themselves.
9Jehoiada the priest took a chest and
bored a hole in its lid. He placed it beside
the altar, on the right side as one enters
the temple of the LORD. The priests who
guarded the entrance[t] put into the chest
all the money[u] that was brought to the
temple of the LORD. 10Whenever they saw
that there was a large amount of money
in the chest, the royal secretary[v] and the
high priest came, counted the money that

[a]*15* Or *out from the precincts* [b]*21* Hebrew *Jehoash,* a variant of *Joash* [c]*1* Hebrew *Jehoash,* a variant of *Joash*; also in verses 2, 4, 6, 7 and 18

enant directs our lives. See note on Jos 24:25–27.

11:15 GOD, Holy—God's holy presence in the Temple meant that violent acts could not be carried out there. Holiness is that special character of God that separates Him from all else. It is the qualitative difference between God and humans. God's holiness, His exalted otherness, always demands respect. See notes on Ex 3:5–6; 19:10–24; Lev 11:44–45.

11:15–16 CHRISTIAN ETHICS, Murder—See note on 1 Ki 16:10–13.

11:18 GOD, One God—The destruction of the temple of Baal was due to the realization that there is only one God and that He is a jealous God who will not tolerate divided loyalty on the part of His people. See notes on Ge 31:30–35; 35:2; Ex 20:1–7; 34:14.

12:1–3 SIN, Blindness—Even though Joash attempted to do right, the people continued in their sin of idolatry. Their continual sin had produced moral and spiritual blindness. Sinful habits are hard to give up. See note on 3:2–3.

12:2 EDUCATION, Guidance—A teacher-priest dramatically influenced an Israelite ruler. So long as the priest Jehoiada instructed him in the way of the Lord, King Joash remained in God's will. After the death of his teacher, Joash became very wicked. See 2 Ch 24:17–22. Kings and peasants alike need the corrective influence of godly teaching in their lives.

12:4–16 STEWARDSHIP, Management—Offerings from God's people must be properly used and accounted for. When priests did not use designated funds to repair God's house, Joash intervened to establish a new system. Any people responsible for using tithes and offerings given by God's people must not use them for personal gain but for the good of God's people and the furtherance of their ministry. See note on Ex 25:1–8.

had been brought into the temple of the
LORD and put it into bags. 11When the
amount had been determined, they gave
the money to the men appointed to supervise the work on the temple. With it
they paid those who worked on the temple of the LORD—the carpenters and
builders, 12the masons and stonecutters.[w]
They purchased timber and dressed stone
for the repair of the temple of the LORD,
and met all the other expenses of restoring the temple.

13The money brought into the temple
was not spent for making silver basins,
wick trimmers, sprinkling bowls, trumpets or any other articles of gold[x] or silver for the temple of the LORD; 14it was
paid to the workmen, who used it to repair the temple. 15They did not require an
accounting from those to whom they gave
the money to pay the workers, because
they acted with complete honesty.[y]
16The money from the guilt offerings[z]
and sin offerings[a] was not brought into
the temple of the LORD; it belonged[b] to
the priests.

17About this time Hazael[c] king of
Aram went up and attacked Gath and captured it. Then he turned to attack Jerusalem. 18But Joash king of Judah took all the
sacred objects dedicated by his fathers—
Jehoshaphat, Jehoram and Ahaziah, the
kings of Judah—and the gifts he himself
had dedicated and all the gold found in
the treasuries of the temple of the LORD
and of the royal palace, and he sent[d]
them to Hazael king of Aram, who then
withdrew[e] from Jerusalem.

19As for the other events of the reign of
Joash, and all he did, are they not written
in the book of the annals of the kings of
Judah? 20His officials[f] conspired against
him and assassinated[g] him at Beth Millo,[h] on the road down to Silla. 21The officials who murdered him were Jozabad
son of Shimeath and Jehozabad son of
Shomer. He died and was buried with his
fathers in the City of David. And Amaziah
his son succeeded him as king.

Chapter 13

Jehoahaz King of Israel

IN the twenty-third year of Joash son of
Ahaziah king of Judah, Jehoahaz son of
Jehu became king of Israel in Samaria,
and he reigned seventeen years. 2He did
evil[i] in the eyes of the LORD by following
the sins of Jeroboam son of Nebat, which
he had caused Israel to commit, and he
did not turn away from them. 3So the
LORD's anger[j] burned against Israel, and
for a long time he kept them under the
power[k] of Hazael king of Aram and Ben-
Hadad[l] his son.

4Then Jehoahaz sought[m] the LORD's favor, and the LORD listened to him, for he
saw[n] how severely the king of Aram was
oppressing[o] Israel. 5The LORD provided a
deliverer[p] for Israel, and they escaped
from the power of Aram. So the Israelites
lived in their own homes as they had before. 6But they did not turn away from the
sins[q] of the house of Jeroboam, which he
had caused Israel to commit; they continued in them. Also, the Asherah pole[d] [r]
remained standing in Samaria.

7Nothing had been left[s] of the army of
Jehoahaz except fifty horsemen, ten chariots and ten thousand foot soldiers, for
the king of Aram had destroyed the rest
and made them like the dust[t] at threshing time.

8As for the other events of the reign of
Jehoahaz, all he did and his achievements, are they not written in the book of
the annals of the kings of Israel? 9Jehoa-
haz rested with his fathers and was buried in Samaria. And Jehoash[e] his son succeeded him as king.

Jehoash King of Israel

10In the thirty-seventh year of Joash
king of Judah, Jehoash son of Jehoahaz
became king of Israel in Samaria, and he
reigned sixteen years. 11He did evil in the
eyes of the LORD and did not turn away
from any of the sins of Jeroboam son of
Nebat, which he had caused Israel to
commit; he continued in them.

12As for the other events of the reign of
Jehoash, all he did and his achievements,
including his war against Amaziah[u] king
of Judah, are they not written in the book
of the annals[v] of the kings of Israel? 13Je-
hoash rested with his fathers, and Jeroboam[w] succeeded him on the throne. Jeho-

[d]6 That is, a symbol of the goddess Asherah; here and elsewhere in 2 Kings [e]9 Hebrew *Joash,* a variant of *Jehoash;* also in verses 12-14 and 25

12:12 [w]2Ki 22:5-6
12:13 [x]S 1Ki 7:48-51
12:15 [y]2Ki 22:7; 1Co 4:2
12:16 [z]Lev 5:14-19 [a]Lev 4:1-35 [b]S Lev 7:7
12:17 [c]2Ki 8:12
12:18 [d]S 1Ki 15:18; S 2Ch 21:16-17 [e]1Ki 15:21; 2Ki 15:20; 19:36
12:20 [f]2Ki 14:5 [g]2Ki 14:19; 15:10, 14,25,30; 21:23; 25:25 [h]Jdg 9:6
13:2 [i]1Ki 12:26-33
13:3 [j]S Dt 31:17 [k]S 1Ki 19:17 [l]ver 24
13:4 [m]S Dt 4:29 [n]S Dt 26:7 [o]S Nu 10:9; 2Sa 7:10
13:5 [p]S Ge 45:7; S Dt 28:29; S Jdg 2:18
13:6 [q]1Ki 12:30 [r]S 1Ki 16:33
13:7 [s]2Ki 10:32-33 [t]S 2Sa 22:43
13:12 [u]2Ki 14:15 [v]1Ki 15:31
13:13 [w]2Ki 14:23; Hos 1:1

12:14,15,18,28 HOLY SCRIPTURE, Writing—See note on 1:16–18.
12:19 HOLY SCRIPTURE, Writing—See note on 1:16–18.
12:20–21 CHRISTIAN ETHICS, Murder—See note on *1 Ki 16:10–13.*
13:1–3 HISTORY, Judgment—See note on 1 Ki 22:53.
13:2 SIN, Transgression—See note on 1 Ki 12:26–33.
13:3 GOD, Wrath—See note on 9:7–10.
13:4 PRAYER, Petition—The Northern Kingdom of Israel had rebelled against God in setting up their places of worship (1 Ki 12:26–33). Still God listened in compassion to the sincere prayer of Israel's king. The past cannot completely separate us from communication with God in prayer.
13:6 SIN, Transgression—See note on 1 Ki 12:26–33.
13:8,12 HOLY SCRIPTURE, Writing—See note on 1:16–18.
13:11 SIN, Transgression—See note on 1 Ki 12:26–33.

ash was buried in Samaria with the kings
of Israel.
14 Now Elisha was suffering from the illness from which he died. Jehoash king of
Israel went down to see him and wept
over him. "My father! My father!" he
cried. "The chariots[x] and horsemen of
Israel!"
15 Elisha said, "Get a bow and some arrows,"[y] and he did so. 16 "Take the bow
in your hands," he said to the king of
Israel. When he had taken it, Elisha put
his hands on the king's hands.
17 "Open the east window," he said,
and he opened it. "Shoot!"[z] Elisha said,
and he shot. "The LORD's arrow of victory, the arrow of victory over Aram!" Elisha declared. "You will completely destroy the Arameans at Aphek."[a]
18 Then he said, "Take the arrows,"
and the king took them. Elisha told him,
"Strike the ground." He struck it three
times and stopped. 19 The man of God was
angry with him and said, "You should
have struck the ground five or six times;
then you would have defeated Aram and
completely destroyed it. But now you will
defeat it only three times."[b]
20 Elisha died and was buried.
Now Moabite raiders[c] used to enter
the country every spring. 21 Once while
some Israelites were burying a man, suddenly they saw a band of raiders; so they
threw the man's body into Elisha's tomb.
When the body touched Elisha's bones,
the man came to life[d] and stood up on
his feet.
22 Hazael king of Aram oppressed[e] Israel throughout the reign of Jehoahaz. 23 But
the LORD was gracious to them and had
compassion and showed concern for
them because of his covenant[f] with
Abraham, Isaac and Jacob. To this day he
has been unwilling to destroy[g] them or
banish them from his presence.[h]
24 Hazael king of Aram died, and Ben-
Hadad[i] his son succeeded him as king.
25 Then Jehoash son of Jehoahaz recap-
tured from Ben-Hadad son of Hazael the
towns he had taken in battle from his father Jehoahaz. Three times[j] Jehoash defeated him, and so he recovered[k] the Israelite towns.

13:14 [x]S 2Ki 2:12
13:15 [y]1Sa 20:20
13:17 [z]Jos 8:18 [a]S 1Ki 20:26
13:19 [b]ver 25
13:20 [c]S 2Ki 5:2
13:21 [d]Mt 27:52
13:22 [e]S 1Ki 19:17
13:23 [f]S Ex 2:24 [g]S Dt 29:20 [h]S Ex 33:15; 2Ki 17:18; 24:3,20
13:24 [i]ver 3
13:25 [j]ver 18,19 [k]S 2Ki 10:32
14:4 [l]2Ki 12:3
14:5 [m]2Ki 21:24 [n]2Ki 12:20
14:6 [o]S Dt 28:61 [p]S Nu 26:11; Job 21:20; Jer 31:30; 44:3; Eze 18:4,20
14:7 [q]S 2Sa 8:13 [r]S Jdg 1:36
14:9 [s]Jdg 9:8-15
14:10 [t]2Ch 26:16; 32:25

Chapter 14

Amaziah King of Judah

14:1–7pp — 2Ch 25:1–4,11–12
14:8–22pp — 2Ch 25:17–26:2

IN the second year of Jehoash[f] son of
Jehoahaz king of Israel, Amaziah son of
Joash king of Judah began to reign. 2 He
was twenty-five years old when he became king, and he reigned in Jerusalem
twenty-nine years. His mother's name
was Jehoaddin; she was from Jerusalem.
3 He did what was right in the eyes of the
LORD, but not as his father David had
done. In everything he followed the example of his father Joash. 4 The high
places,[l] however, were not removed;
the people continued to offer sacrifices
and burn incense there.
5 After the kingdom was firmly in his
grasp, he executed[m] the officials[n] who
had murdered his father the king. 6 Yet he
did not put the sons of the assassins to
death, in accordance with what is written
in the Book of the Law[o] of Moses where
the LORD commanded: "Fathers shall not
be put to death for their children, nor
children put to death for their fathers;
each is to die for his own sins."[g] [p]
7 He was the one who defeated ten
thousand Edomites in the Valley of Salt[q]
and captured Sela[r] in battle, calling it
Joktheel, the name it has to this day.
8 Then Amaziah sent messengers to Jehoash son of Jehoahaz, the son of Jehu,
king of Israel, with the challenge:
"Come, meet me face to face."
9 But Jehoash king of Israel replied to
Amaziah king of Judah: "A thistle[s] in
Lebanon sent a message to a cedar in Lebanon, 'Give your daughter to my son in
marriage.' Then a wild beast in Lebanon
came along and trampled the thistle underfoot. 10 You have indeed defeated
Edom and now you are arrogant.[t] Glory
in your victory, but stay at home! Why

[f]*1* Hebrew *Joash,* a variant of *Jehoash*; also in verses 13, 23 and 27 [g]*6* Deut. 24:16

13:23 GOD, Grace—The grace of God is the expression of God's love. His love finds concrete expression in the covenant promises He gives His people. At times God must show His wrath, but He prefers to move in grace and love. See notes on Ge 19:12–19,29; 39:21–23; 45:5–9; Mt 10:29–31; Lk 1:30; 2:14,40.

13:23 HISTORY, God—Historical existence depends on God's grace. He allows sinful people to continue in existence. We do not get what we deserve in history. We get what God's grace provides. Eventually God did banish and destroy the Northern Kingdom, giving historical evidence that His grace with sinners is not endless.

13:23 THE CHURCH, Covenant People—God will always be a loving, compassionate God. He ever turns toward His covenant community, remembering the promises He has made to His people. See note on Ge 17:1–21.

14:4 SIN, Blindness—See notes on 3:2–3; 12:1–3.

14:5–6 EVIL AND SUFFERING, Deserved—Scripture should guide God's people when they have responsibility for disciplining wrongdoers. The basic teaching is that only those who are guilty and deserve punishment should be punished for wrongdoing. See note on Dt 24:16; Jos 7:10–26.

14:5–6 CHRISTIAN ETHICS, Justice—Justice depends on fair execution of the law. Personal vengeance cannot be tolerated in a society seeking justice. See notes on Dt 17:8–13; 24:16.

ask for trouble and cause your own downfall and that of Judah also?"
11 Amaziah, however, would not listen,
so Jehoash king of Israel attacked. He and
Amaziah king of Judah faced each other at
Beth Shemesh[u] in Judah. 12 Judah was
routed by Israel, and every man fled to
his home.[v] 13 Jehoash king of Israel captured Amaziah king of Judah, the son of
Joash, the son of Ahaziah, at Beth Shemesh. Then Jehoash went to Jerusalem
and broke down the wall[w] of Jerusalem
from the Ephraim Gate[x] to the Corner
Gate[y]—a section about six hundred feet
long.[h] 14 He took all the gold and silver
and all the articles found in the temple of
the LORD and in the treasuries of the royal
palace. He also took hostages and returned to Samaria.
15 As for the other events of the reign of
Jehoash, what he did and his achievements, including his war[z] against Amaziah king of Judah, are they not written in
the book of the annals of the kings of Israel? 16 Jehoash rested with his fathers and
was buried in Samaria with the kings of
Israel. And Jeroboam his son succeeded
him as king.
17 Amaziah son of Joash king of Judah
lived for fifteen years after the death of
Jehoash son of Jehoahaz king of Israel.
18 As for the other events of Amaziah's
reign, are they not written in the book of
the annals of the kings of Judah?
19 They conspired[a] against him in Jerusalem, and he fled to Lachish,[b] but they
sent men after him to Lachish and killed
him there. 20 He was brought back by
horse[c] and was buried in Jerusalem with
his fathers, in the City of David.
21 Then all the people of Judah took Azariah,[i][d] who was sixteen years old, and
made him king in place of his father Amaziah. 22 He was the one who rebuilt
Elath[e] and restored it to Judah after Amaziah rested with his fathers.

Jeroboam II King of Israel

23 In the fifteenth year of Amaziah son
of Joash king of Judah, Jeroboam[f] son of
Jehoash king of Israel became king in Samaria, and he reigned forty-one years.
24 He did evil in the eyes of the LORD and
did not turn away from any of the sins of
Jeroboam son of Nebat, which he had
caused Israel to commit.[g] 25 He was the
one who restored the boundaries of Israel
from Lebo[j] Hamath[h] to the Sea of the
Arabah,[k][i] in accordance with the word
of the LORD, the God of Israel, spoken
through his servant Jonah[j] son of Amittai, the prophet from Gath Hepher.
26 The LORD had seen how bitterly everyone in Israel, whether slave or free,[k]
was suffering;[l] there was no one to help
them.[m] 27 And since the LORD had not
said he would blot out[n] the name of Israel from under heaven, he saved[o] them by
the hand of Jeroboam son of Jehoash.
28 As for the other events of Jeroboam's
reign, all he did, and his military achievements, including how he recovered for
Israel both Damascus[p] and Hamath,[q]
which had belonged to Yaudi,[l] are they
not written in the book of the annals[r] of
the kings of Israel? 29 Jeroboam rested
with his fathers, the kings of Israel. And
Zechariah his son succeeded him as king.

Chapter 15

Azariah King of Judah

15:1–7pp — 2Ch 26:3–4,21–23

IN the twenty-seventh year of Jeroboam
king of Israel, Azariah[s] son of Amaziah king of Judah began to reign. 2 He was
sixteen years old when he became king,
and he reigned in Jerusalem fifty-two
years. His mother's name was Jecoliah;
she was from Jerusalem. 3 He did what
was right[t] in the eyes of the LORD, just as
his father Amaziah had done. 4 The high
places, however, were not removed; the
people continued to offer sacrifices and
burn incense there.
5 The LORD afflicted[u] the king with leprosy[m] until the day he died, and he lived
in a separate house.[n][v] Jotham[w] the
king's son had charge of the palace[x] and
governed the people of the land.

14:11 [u]S Jos 15:10
14:12 [v]1Ki 22:36
14:13 [w]1Ki 3:1; 2Ch 33:14; 36:19; Jer 39:2 [x]Ne 8:16; 12:39 [y]2Ch 26:9; Jer 31:38; Zec 14:10
14:15 [z]2Ki 13:12
14:19 [a]S 2Ki 12:20 [b]S Jos 10:3
14:20 [c]S 2Ki 9:28
14:21 [d]2Ki 15:1; 2Ch 26:23; Isa 1:1; Hos 1:1; Am 1:1
14:22 [e]S 1Ki 9:26
14:23 [f]S 2Ki 13:13; 1Ch 5:17; Am 1:1; 7:10
14:24 [g]S 1Ki 15:30
14:25 [h]S Nu 13:21 [i]Dt 3:17 [j]Jnh 1:1; Mt 12:39
14:26 [k]Dt 32:36 [l]2Ki 13:4 [m]Ps 18:41; 22:11; 72:12; 107:12; Isa 63:5; La 1:7
14:27 [n]S Dt 29:20 [o]S Jdg 6:14
14:28 [p]S 2Sa 8:5 [q]S 2Sa 8:9 [r]1Ki 15:31
15:1 [s]S ver 32; S 2Ki 14:21
15:3 [t]S 1Ki 14:8
15:5 [u]S Ge 12:17 [v]Lev 13:46 [w]ver 7, 32; 2Ch 27:1; Mic 1:1 [x]S Ge 41:40

[h]*13* Hebrew *four hundred cubits* (about 180 meters)
[i]*21* Also called *Uzziah*
[j]*25* Or *from the entrance to*
[k]*25* That is, the Dead Sea
[l]*28* Or *Judah*
[m]*5* The Hebrew word was used for various diseases affecting the skin—not necessarily leprosy.
[n]*5* Or *in a house where he was relieved of responsibility*

14:23–29 SIN, Transgression—God can use sinful people to accomplish His purposes. Mercy for suffering people rules God's heart. See note on 1 Ki 12:26–33.

14:23–29 HISTORY, Narrative—Historical narrative dominates the inspired Old Testament. This narrative documents that which God wants to teach His people, not that which human historians need to reconstruct a political history of Israel. Political historians would provide extensive details of Jeroboam's forty-one years, particularly of his important military victories. The biblical historian simply summarized the reign briefly, emphasizing the king's serious spiritual errors and noting the goodness of God in fulfilling the prophetic word and in responding to the people's suffering. God's Word is interested in obedience more than political accomplishment.

14:25 HISTORY, Promise—See note on 7:1–20.

15:4 SIN, Blindness—See notes on 3:2–3; 12:1–3.

15:5 GOD, Sovereignty—Because God is sovereign, He controls this world and all its laws and systems. He can cause disease, when necessary, as punishment. That does not mean that every instance of disease is a judgment, or that it is caused by God.

15:5 EVIL AND SUFFERING, Punishment—See note on 5:19–27.

6As for the other events of Azariah's
reign, and all he did, are they not written
in the book of the annals of the kings of
Judah? 7Azariah rested[y] with his fathers
and was buried near them in the City of
David. And Jotham[z] his son succeeded
him as king.

Zechariah King of Israel

8In the thirty-eighth year of Azariah
king of Judah, Zechariah son of Jeroboam
became king of Israel in Samaria, and he
reigned six months. 9He did evil[a] in the
eyes of the LORD, as his fathers had done.
He did not turn away from the sins of
Jeroboam son of Nebat, which he had
caused Israel to commit.
10Shallum son of Jabesh conspired
against Zechariah. He attacked him in
front of the people,[o] assassinated[b] him
and succeeded him as king. 11The other
events of Zechariah's reign are written in
the book of the annals[c] of the kings of
Israel. 12So the word of the LORD spoken
to Jehu was fulfilled:[d] "Your descendants
will sit on the throne of Israel to the
fourth generation."[p]

Shallum King of Israel

13Shallum son of Jabesh became king in
the thirty-ninth year of Uzziah king of Judah, and he reigned in Samaria[e] one
month. 14Then Menahem son of Gadi
went from Tirzah[f] up to Samaria. He attacked Shallum son of Jabesh in Samaria,
assassinated[g] him and succeeded him as
king.
15The other events of Shallum's reign,
and the conspiracy he led, are written in
the book of the annals[h] of the kings of
Israel.
16At that time Menahem, starting out
from Tirzah, attacked Tiphsah[i] and everyone in the city and its vicinity, because they refused to open[j] their gates.
He sacked Tiphsah and ripped open all
the pregnant women.

Menahem King of Israel

17In the thirty-ninth year of Azariah
king of Judah, Menahem son of Gadi became king of Israel, and he reigned in
Samaria ten years. 18He did evil[k] in the
eyes of the LORD. During his entire reign
he did not turn away from the sins of Jeroboam son of Nebat, which he had
caused Israel to commit.
19Then Pul[q][l] king of Assyria invaded
the land, and Menahem gave him a thousand talents[r] of silver to gain his support
and strengthen his own hold on the kingdom. 20Menahem exacted this money
from Israel. Every wealthy man had to
contribute fifty shekels[s] of silver to be
given to the king of Assyria. So the king of
Assyria withdrew[m] and stayed in the land
no longer.
21As for the other events of Menahem's
reign, and all he did, are they not written
in the book of the annals of the kings of
Israel? 22Menahem rested with his fathers. And Pekahiah his son succeeded
him as king.

Pekahiah King of Israel

23In the fiftieth year of Azariah king of
Judah, Pekahiah son of Menahem became
king of Israel in Samaria, and he reigned
two years. 24Pekahiah did evil[n] in the
eyes of the LORD. He did not turn away
from the sins of Jeroboam son of Nebat,
which he had caused Israel to commit.
25One of his chief officers, Pekah[o] son of
Remaliah, conspired against him. Taking
fifty men of Gilead with him, he assassinated[p] Pekahiah, along with Argob and
Arieh, in the citadel of the royal palace at
Samaria. So Pekah killed Pekahiah and
succeeded him as king.
26The other events of Pekahiah's reign,
and all he did, are written in the book of
the annals of the kings of Israel.

Pekah King of Israel

27In the fifty-second year of Azariah
king of Judah, Pekah[q] son of Remaliah[r]
became king of Israel in Samaria, and he
reigned twenty years. 28He did evil in the
eyes of the LORD. He did not turn away
from the sins of Jeroboam son of Nebat,
which he had caused Israel to commit.
29In the time of Pekah king of Israel,
Tiglath-Pileser[s] king of Assyria came and
took Ijon,[t] Abel Beth Maacah, Janoah,
Kedesh and Hazor. He took Gilead and
Galilee, including all the land of Naphtali,[u] and deported[v] the people to Assyria.
30Then Hoshea[w] son of Elah conspired
against Pekah son of Remaliah. He attacked and assassinated[x] him, and then
succeeded him as king in the twentieth
year of Jotham son of Uzziah.
31As for the other events of Pekah's
reign, and all he did, are they not written
in the book of the annals[y] of the kings of
Israel?

[o] *10* Hebrew; some Septuagint manuscripts *in Ibleam*
[p] *12* 2 Kings 10:30 [q] *19* Also called *Tiglath-Pileser*
[r] *19* That is, about 37 tons (about 34 metric tons)
[s] *20* That is, about 1 1/4 pounds (about 0.6 kilogram)

15:7 [y]Isa 6:1; 14:28 [z]S ver 5
15:9 [a]1Ki 15:26
15:10 [b]S 2Ki 12:20
15:11 [c]1Ki 15:31
15:12 [d]2Ki 10:30
15:13 [e]S 1Ki 13:32
15:14 [f]S 1Ki 15:33 [g]S 2Ki 12:20
15:15 [h]1Ki 15:31
15:16 [i]1Ki 4:24 [j]S 2Ki 8:12; S Hos 13:16
15:18 [k]1Ki 15:26
15:19 [l]1Ch 5:6,26
15:20 [m]S 2Ki 12:18
15:24 [n]1Ki 15:26
15:25 [o]2Ch 28:6; Isa 7:1 [p]S 2Ki 12:20
15:27 [q]2Ch 28:6; Isa 7:1 [r]Isa 7:4
15:29 [s]2Ki 16:7; 17:6; 1Ch 5:26; 2Ch 28:20; Jer 50:17 [t]1Ki 15:20 [u]2Ki 16:9; 17:24; 2Ch 16:4; Isa 7:9; 9:1; 10:9,10; 28:1; 36:19; 37:18 [v]2Ki 24:14-16; 1Ch 5:22; Isa 14:6, 17; 36:17; 45:13
15:30 [w]2Ki 17:1 [x]S 2Ki 12:20
15:31 [y]1Ki 15:31

15:6,11,15,21,26,31,36 HOLY SCRIPTURE, Writing—See note on 1:16–18.
15:9 SIN, Transgression—See note on 1 Ki 12:26–33.
15:18 SIN, Transgression—See note on 1 Ki 12:26–33.
15:24 SIN, Transgression—See note on 1 Ki 12:26–33.
15:25,30 CHRISTIAN ETHICS, Murder—See note on 1 Ki 16:10–13.
15:28 SIN, Transgression—See note on 1 Ki 12:26–33.

Jotham King of Judah

15:33–38pp — 2Ch 27:1–4,7–9

32In the second year of Pekah son of
Remaliah king of Israel, Jotham[z] son of
Uzziah king of Judah began to reign. 33He
was twenty-five years old when he became king, and he reigned in Jerusalem
sixteen years. His mother's name was Jerusha daughter of Zadok. 34He did what
was right[a] in the eyes of the LORD, just as
his father Uzziah had done. 35The high
places,[b] however, were not removed;
the people continued to offer sacrifices
and burn incense there. Jotham rebuilt
the Upper Gate[c] of the temple of the
LORD.
36As for the other events of Jotham's
reign, and what he did, are they not written in the book of the annals of the kings
of Judah? 37(In those days the LORD began
to send Rezin[d] king of Aram and Pekah
son of Remaliah against Judah.) 38Jotham
rested with his fathers and was buried
with them in the City of David, the city of
his father. And Ahaz his son succeeded
him as king.

Chapter 16

Ahaz King of Judah

16:1–20pp — 2Ch 28:1–27

IN the seventeenth year of Pekah son of
Remaliah, Ahaz[e] son of Jotham king of
Judah began to reign. 2Ahaz was twenty
years old when he became king, and he
reigned in Jerusalem sixteen years. Unlike David his father, he did not do what
was right[f] in the eyes of the LORD his
God. 3He walked in the ways of the kings
of Israel[g] and even sacrificed his son[h]
in[t] the fire, following the detestable[i]
ways of the nations the LORD had driven
out before the Israelites. 4He offered sacrifices and burned incense[j] at the high
places, on the hilltops and under every
spreading tree.[k]
5Then Rezin[l] king of Aram and Pekah
son of Remaliah king of Israel marched up
to fight against Jerusalem and besieged
Ahaz, but they could not overpower him.
6At that time, Rezin[m] king of Aram recovered Elath[n] for Aram by driving out the
men of Judah. Edomites then moved into
Elath and have lived there to this day.
7Ahaz sent messengers to say to Tiglath-Pileser[o] king of Assyria, "I am your
servant and vassal. Come up and save[p]
me out of the hand of the king of Aram
and of the king of Israel, who are attacking me." 8And Ahaz took the silver and
gold found in the temple of the LORD and
in the treasuries of the royal palace and
sent it as a gift[q] to the king of Assyria.
9The king of Assyria complied by attacking Damascus[r] and capturing it. He deported its inhabitants to Kir[s] and put Rezin to death.
10Then King Ahaz went to Damascus to
meet Tiglath-Pileser king of Assyria. He
saw an altar in Damascus and sent to Uriah[t] the priest a sketch of the altar, with
detailed plans for its construction. 11So
Uriah the priest built an altar in accordance with all the plans that King Ahaz
had sent from Damascus and finished it
before King Ahaz returned. 12When the
king came back from Damascus and saw
the altar, he approached it and presented
offerings[u][u] on it. 13He offered up his
burnt offering[v] and grain offering,[w]
poured out his drink offering,[x] and sprinkled the blood of his fellowship offerings[v][y] on the altar. 14The bronze altar[z]
that stood before the LORD he brought
from the front of the temple—from between the new altar and the temple of
the LORD—and put it on the north side of
the new altar.
15King Ahaz then gave these orders to
Uriah the priest: "On the large new altar,
offer the morning[a] burnt offering and the
evening grain offering, the king's burnt
offering and his grain offering, and the
burnt offering of all the people of the
land, and their grain offering and their
drink offering. Sprinkle on the altar all
the blood of the burnt offerings and sacrifices. But I will use the bronze altar for
seeking guidance."[b] 16And Uriah the
priest did just as King Ahaz had ordered.
17King Ahaz took away the side panels
and removed the basins from the movable stands. He removed the Sea from the
bronze bulls that supported it and set it
on a stone base.[c] 18He took away the
Sabbath canopy[w] that had been built at
the temple and removed the royal entryway outside the temple of the LORD, in
deference to the king of Assyria.[d]
19As for the other events of the reign of

15:32 [z]ver 1,S 5; 1Ch 5:17; Isa 1:1; Hos 1:1
15:34 [a]S 1Ki 14:8
15:35 [b]2Ki 12:3 [c]S Ge 23:10; 2Ch 23:20
15:37 [d]2Ki 16:5; Isa 7:1; 8:6; 9:11
16:1 [e]Isa 1:1; 7:1; 14:28; Hos 1:1; Mic 1:1
16:2 [f]S 1Ki 14:8
16:3 [g]2Ki 17:19 [h]S Lev 18:21; S 2Ki 3:27 [i]S Lev 18:3; S Dt 9:4
16:4 [j]2Ki 22:17; 23:5 [k]Dt 12:2; Eze 6:13
16:5 [l]S 2Ki 15:37
16:6 [m]Isa 9:12 [n]S 1Ki 9:26
16:7 [o]S 2Ki 15:29 [p]Isa 2:6; 10:20; Jer 2:18; 3:1; Eze 16:28; 23:5; Hos 10:6
16:8 [q]S 1Ki 15:18; 2Ki 12:18
16:9 [r]S Ge 14:15; S 2Ki 15:29 [s]Isa 22:6; Am 1:5; 9:7
16:10 [t]ver 11,15, 16; Isa 8:2
16:12 [u]2Ch 26:16
16:13 [v]Lev 6:8-13 [w]Lev 6:14-23 [x]S Ex 29:40 [y]Lev 7:11-21
16:14 [z]S Ex 20:24; S 40:6; S 1Ki 8:64
16:15 [a]Ex 29:38-41 [b]1Sa 9:9
16:17 [c]1Ki 7:27
16:18 [d]Eze 16:28

[t]3 Or *even made his son pass through* [u]12 Or *and went up* [v]13 Traditionally *peace offerings* [w]18 Or *the dais of his throne* (see Septuagint)

15:35 SIN, Blindness—See note on 12:1–3.
15:37 HISTORY, Politics—Political reasons easily explain why Syria and Israel attacked Judah. They needed resources to defend themselves against Assyria. The inspired historian did not look to political causes. He knew God controlled history and was using enemy forces to punish the wicked king of Judah (v 28).
16:2–4 SIN, Transgression—See note on 1 Ki 14:22–24.
16:10–12 HUMANITY, Relationship to God—The desire to please others can become a hindrance in our obedient service of God. This is especially true when political motivations are involved.
16:19 HOLY SCRIPTURE, Writing—See note on 1:16–18.

Ahaz, and what he did, are they not written in the book of the annals of the kings
of Judah? 20 Ahaz rested[e] with his fathers
and was buried with them in the City of
David. And Hezekiah his son succeeded
him as king.

Chapter 17

Hoshea Last King of Israel

17:3–7pp — 2Ki 18:9–12

IN the twelfth year of Ahaz king of Judah, Hoshea[f] son of Elah became king
of Israel in Samaria, and he reigned nine
years. 2 He did evil[g] in the eyes of the
LORD, but not like the kings of Israel who
preceded him.
3 Shalmaneser[h] king of Assyria came up
to attack Hoshea, who had been Shalmaneser's vassal and had paid him tribute.[i]
4 But the king of Assyria discovered that
Hoshea was a traitor, for he had sent envoys to So[x] king of Egypt,[j] and he no
longer paid tribute to the king of Assyria,
as he had done year by year. Therefore
Shalmaneser seized him and put him in
prison.[k] 5 The king of Assyria invaded the
entire land, marched against Samaria and
laid siege[l] to it for three years. 6 In the
ninth year of Hoshea, the king of
Assyria[m] captured Samaria[n] and deported[o]
the Israelites to Assyria. He settled them
in Halah, in Gozan[p] on the Habor River
and in the towns of the Medes.

Israel Exiled Because of Sin

7 All this took place because the Israelites had sinned[q] against the LORD their
God, who had brought them up out of
Egypt[r] from under the power of Pharaoh
king of Egypt. They worshiped other gods
8 and followed the practices of the nations[s] the LORD had driven out before
them, as well as the practices that the
kings of Israel had introduced. 9 The Israelites secretly did things against the LORD
their God that were not right. From
watchtower to fortified city[t] they built
themselves high places in all their towns.
10 They set up sacred stones[u] and Asherah poles[v] on every high hill and under
every spreading tree.[w] 11 At every high
place they burned incense, as the nations
whom the LORD had driven out before
them had done. They did wicked things
that provoked the LORD to anger. 12 They
worshiped idols,[x] though the LORD had
said, "You shall not do this."[y] 13 The
LORD warned[y] Israel and Judah through
all his prophets and seers:[z] "Turn from
your evil ways.[a] Observe my commands
and decrees, in accordance with the entire Law that I commanded your fathers
to obey and that I delivered to you
through my servants the prophets."[b]
14 But they would not listen and were as
stiff-necked[c] as their fathers, who did not
trust in the LORD their God. 15 They rejected his decrees and the covenant[d] he had
made with their fathers and the warnings
he had given them. They followed worthless idols[e] and themselves became
worthless.[f] They imitated the nations[g]
around them although the LORD had ordered them, "Do not do as they do," and

16:20 [e]Isa 14:28
17:1 [f]2Ki 15:30
17:2 [g]S Dt 4:25
17:3 [h]Hos 10:14 [i]S Jdg 3:15
17:4 [j]Ps 146:3; Isa 30:1,7; 36:6; Jer 2:36; Hos 12:1 [k]Hos 13:10
17:5 [l]Hos 13:16
17:6 [m]ver 20; S 2Ki 15:29; Isa 42:24 [n]Isa 10:9 [o]S Dt 4:27; S 24:1; S 2Ki 15:29; Am 7:17 [p]1Ch 5:26
17:7 [q]S Jos 7:11 [r]Ex 14:15-31
17:8 [s]S Ex 34:15; S Lev 18:3; S Dt 9:4
17:9 [t]2Ki 18:8
17:10 [u]S Ex 23:24 [v]Ex 34:13; Isa 17:8; Mic 5:14 [w]S Dt 12:2
17:12 [x]S Ex 20:4
17:13 [y]S Jdg 6:8; S 2Ch 7:14; S Job 34:33; Eze 3:17-19 [z]S 1Sa 9:9 [a]Jer 4:1; 18:11; 23:22; 25:5; 35:15; 36:3; Zec 1:4 [b]Mt 23:34
17:14 [c]S Ex 32:9; Ac 7:51
17:15 [d]S Lev 26:11; Dt 29:25; Jdg 2:20; 1Ki 11:11; 2Ki 18:12; Ps 78:10; Eze 5:6; Mal 2:10 [e]S Dt 32:21; Hos 11:2; Ro 1:21-23 [f]Jer 2:5 [g]S Dt 12:4

[x]4 Or *to Sais, the*; *So* is possibly an abbreviation for *Osorkon.* [y]12 Exodus 20:4, 5

17:1–41 ELECTION, Condemnation—God's election is always a designation to single-minded devotion and full commitment to God. Israel's exile and failure can be traced to their lack of total commitment to the God who elected them. The penalty for refusing to be God's elect was loss of His presence.

17:1–6 CHRISTIAN ETHICS, War and Peace—The account of the very last king of Israel shows the ultimate consequences of a nation failing to follow its ethical vision. God's power had not failed, but His power on behalf of righteousness was stymied because of the hardheartedness of the Hebrews. A lesson to be learned is that no one and no nation ever rises above the possibility of judgment from God. See note on Jos 11:1–23.

17:2 SIN, Transgression—See note on 3:2–3.

17:3–23 HISTORY, Promise—The prophetic word controlled Israel's history. The rise and fall of international powers occurred as God announced them through His prophets. God promised judgment on a people who followed other gods, and after two centuries of enduring their false worship in mercy, He fulfilled His threats. Thus God's Word describes history as God's response to the sin of His people.

17:7–23 EVIL AND SUFFERING, Punishment—Evil political practices bring God's anger and eventually His punishment on a nation. God is free to determine when and how to punish a wicked nation. He may use an even more evil nation to punish His people. In 722 BC, God used the notoriously wicked Assyrians to put an end to the Northern Kingdom because they refused to be loyal to Him.

17:7–23 SIN, Discipline—The history of the Northern Kingdom teaches one major lesson: God will intervene in human history to punish His unfaithful people because He takes sin seriously. Israel followed neighbors and kings—everyone but God. They knew they were doing wrong. They tried to hide from God. They openly violated their covenant agreement with Him. They refused to listen to His chosen ministers sent to warn them. Everything they did showed they trusted their judgment instead of God's word. Thus they became a worthless people in God's eyes, incapable of carrying out His purposes. They had no justified complaint when God intervened to punish. See note on 24:1–4.

17:11–41 GOD, Jealous—See note on 1 Ki 14:9–16,22.

17:13–23 CHRISTIAN ETHICS, Moral Imperatives—God's people need teachers and role models to act as guides for our living together as God's people. God sent His prophets for this purpose. Israel and Judah suffered God's wrath because they chose foreign models instead of God's. We must wisely discern who the proper models are and follow them.

17:15–17 CHRISTIAN ETHICS, Moral Limits—The Israelites faced exile because of their determination to step over God's explicit moral boundaries. Their choices for worship and life-style values demonstrated poor judgment. Your life-style is shaped by whom and what you worship. Life is too important to waste it on idolatrous ways.

17:15 THE CHURCH, Covenant People—God expects His covenant people to be holy as He is holy. When we break our relationship with God, we become like those idols toward which we turn—worthless and useless. See note on Lev 26:15–17.

they did the things the LORD had forbidden them to do.
16They forsook all the commands of the
LORD their God and made for themselves
two idols cast in the shape of calves,[h]
and an Asherah[i] pole. They bowed down
to all the starry hosts,[j] and they worshiped Baal.[k] 17They sacrificed[l] their
sons and daughters in[z] the fire. They
practiced divination and sorcery[m] and
sold[n] themselves to do evil in the eyes of
the LORD, provoking him to anger.
18So the LORD was very angry with Israel and removed them from his presence.[o] Only the tribe of Judah was left,
19and even Judah did not keep the commands of the LORD their God. They followed the practices Israel had introduced.[p] 20Therefore the LORD rejected all
the people of Israel; he afflicted them and
gave them into the hands of plunderers,[q]
until he thrust them from his presence.[r]
21When he tore[s] Israel away from the
house of David, they made Jeroboam son
of Nebat their king.[t] Jeroboam enticed
Israel away from following the LORD and
caused them to commit a great sin.[u]
22The Israelites persisted in all the sins of
Jeroboam and did not turn away from
them 23until the LORD removed them
from his presence,[v] as he had warned[w]
through all his servants the prophets. So
the people of Israel were taken from their
homeland[x] into exile in Assyria, and they
are still there.

Samaria Resettled

24The king of Assyria[y] brought people
from Babylon, Cuthah, Avva, Hamath and
Sepharvaim[z] and settled them in the
towns of Samaria to replace the Israelites.
They took over Samaria and lived in its
towns. 25When they first lived there, they
did not worship the LORD; so he sent lions[a] among them and they killed some of
the people. 26It was reported to the king
of Assyria: "The people you deported and
resettled in the towns of Samaria do not
know what the god of that country requires. He has sent lions among them,
which are killing them off, because the
people do not know what he requires."
27Then the king of Assyria gave this order: "Have one of the priests you took
captive from Samaria go back to live there
and teach the people what the god of the
land requires." 28So one of the priests
who had been exiled from Samaria came
to live in Bethel and taught them how to
worship the LORD.
29Nevertheless, each national group
made its own gods in the several towns[b]
where they settled, and set them up in
the shrines[c] the people of Samaria had
made at the high places.[d] 30The men
from Babylon made Succoth Benoth, the
men from Cuthah made Nergal, and the
men from Hamath made Ashima; 31the
Avvites made Nibhaz and Tartak, and the
Sepharvites burned their children in the
fire as sacrifices to Adrammelech[e] and
Anammelech, the gods of Sepharvaim.[f]
32They worshiped the LORD, but they also
appointed all sorts[g] of their own people
to officiate for them as priests in the
shrines at the high places. 33They worshiped the LORD, but they also served
their own gods in accordance with the
customs of the nations from which they
had been brought.
34To this day they persist in their former practices. They neither worship the
LORD nor adhere to the decrees and ordinances, the laws and commands that the
LORD gave the descendants of Jacob,
whom he named Israel.[h] 35When the
LORD made a covenant with the Israelites,
he commanded them: "Do not worship[i]
any other gods or bow down to them,
serve them or sacrifice to them.[j] 36But

17:16 [h]S Ex 32:4 [i]S Dt 16:21 [j]S Ge 2:1; Isa 40:26; Jer 19:13 [k]S Jdg 2:11
17:17 [l]S Dt 12:31; 18:10-12; 2Ki 16:3; Eze 16:21 [m]S Lev 19:26 [n]S 1Ki 21:20; Ro 7:14
17:18 [o]S Ge 4:14; S Ex 33:15; S 2Ki 13:23; 2Th 1:9
17:19 [p]2Ki 16:3; Jer 3:6-10; Eze 23:13
17:20 [q]S ver 6 [r]Jer 7:15; 15:1
17:21 [s]S 1Sa 15:27; S 1Ki 11:11 [t]1Ki 12:20 [u]S 1Ki 12:30
17:23 [v]Eze 39:23-24 [w]S Jdg 6:8 [x]S 1Ki 9:7
17:24 [y]2Ki 19:37; Ezr 4:2,10; Isa 37:38 [z]ver 31; S 2Ki 15:29; 18:34; Isa 36:19; 37:13; Am 6:2
17:25 [a]S Ge 37:20; Isa 5:29; 15:9; Jer 50:17
17:29 [b]Jer 2:28; 11:13 [c]S Lev 26:30; S 1Ki 12:31 [d]Mic 4:5
17:31 [e]2Ki 19:37 [f]S ver 24
17:32 [g]S 1Ki 12:31
17:34 [h]S Ge 17:5; S 1Ki 18:31
17:35 [i]S Ex 20:5 [j]S Ex 20:3

[z]17 Or *They made their sons and daughters pass through*

17:19 SIN, Transgression—Not even an otherwise faithful community is immune from the presence and practice of sin. As with Judah, disaster beckons a people who take too lightly their special relationship with God.

17:24–41 SIN, Transgression—History teaches, but we do not learn. God exiled the Northern Kingdom. He punished the new inhabitants, who learned only half a lesson. They learned to hold worship services for the God of Israel. They did not learn to forsake all other gods. Israel entered the era of paganism, seeking to cover all religious bases. This set the stage for the Jews' hatred of Samaritans in Jesus' day. See Mt 10:5; Lk 9:51–56; 17:16; Jn 4:4–9,39–40; 8:48; Ac 8:1–25; 9:31; 15:3.

17:24–28 EVANGELISM, Mass—When a people do not know God and His will, sin and the inevitable judgment will fall (Pr 14:34). God desires the masses, all of society, to know His will and way. In the case of the resettlement of Samaria, the priest instructed the masses concerning God's purposes, and to some limited extent they responded positively. We must reach with the gospel as many of the masses of people as we can by all the means we can employ.

17:25–41 WORSHIP, False—See note on Ex 22:20.

17:27–28 EDUCATION, Social Order—A pagan king showed unusual insight when he recognized that the foreign colony living in Samaria needed to live in accordance with the will of the God of Israel. The law of God provides a basis for a stable and durable social order. Where love, justice, honesty, and reverence are woven into the fabric of society through the teaching of God's Word, the people will know how to live in right relationships with God and with one another. On the other hand, widespread ignorance of the will of God provides a fertile seedbed for injustice, crime, and social chaos.

17:34–40 REVELATION, Commitment—Revelation even in written form does not help a people who are not committed to obey it. See note on 1 Ki 11:9–13.

17:35–39 THE CHURCH, Covenant People—Keeping God's covenant requires obeying His commands and following His ways. We break the covenant when we reject God's ways and follow desires of our hearts. God's covenant people worship Him and Him alone. See note on 17:15.

the LORD, who brought you up out of
Egypt with mighty power and outstretched arm,[k] is the one you must worship. To him you shall bow down and to
him offer sacrifices. 37You must always be
careful[l] to keep the decrees[m] and ordinances, the laws and commands he wrote
for you. Do not worship other gods. 38Do
not forget[n] the covenant I have made
with you, and do not worship other gods.
39Rather, worship the LORD your God; it
is he who will deliver you from the hand
of all your enemies."
40They would not listen, however, but
persisted in their former practices.
41Even while these people were worshiping the LORD,[o] they were serving their
idols. To this day their children and
grandchildren continue to do as their fathers did.

Chapter 18

Hezekiah King of Judah

18:2–4pp — 2Ch 29:1–2; 31:1
18:5–7pp — 2Ch 31:20–21
18:9–12pp — 2Ki 17:3–7

IN the third year of Hoshea son of Elah
king of Israel, Hezekiah[p] son of Ahaz
king of Judah began to reign. 2He was
twenty-five years old when he became
king, and he reigned in Jerusalem twenty-nine years.[q] His mother's name was
Abijah[a] daughter of Zechariah. 3He did
what was right[r] in the eyes of the LORD,
just as his father David[s] had done. 4He
removed[t] the high places,[u] smashed the
sacred stones[v] and cut down the Asherah
poles. He broke into pieces the bronze
snake[w] Moses had made, for up to that
time the Israelites had been burning incense to it. (It was called[b] Nehushtan.[c])
5Hezekiah trusted[x] in the LORD, the
God of Israel. There was no one like him
among all the kings of Judah, either before him or after him. 6He held fast[y] to
the LORD and did not cease to follow him;
he kept the commands the LORD had giv-
en Moses. 7And the LORD was with him;
he was successful[z] in whatever he undertook. He rebelled[a] against the king of
Assyria and did not serve him. 8From
watchtower to fortified city,[b] he defeated
the Philistines, as far as Gaza and its territory.
9In King Hezekiah's fourth year,[c]
which was the seventh year of Hoshea
son of Elah king of Israel, Shalmaneser
king of Assyria marched against Samaria
and laid siege to it. 10At the end of three
years the Assyrians took it. So Samaria
was captured in Hezekiah's sixth year,
which was the ninth year of Hoshea king
of Israel. 11The king[d] of Assyria deported
Israel to Assyria and settled them in Halah, in Gozan on the Habor River and in
towns of the Medes.[e] 12This happened
because they had not obeyed the LORD
their God, but had violated his covenant[f]—all that Moses the servant of the
LORD commanded.[g] They neither listened to the commands[h] nor carried
them out.
13In the fourteenth year[i] of King Hezekiah's reign, Sennacherib king of Assyria
attacked all the fortified cities of Judah[j]
and captured them. 14So Hezekiah king of
Judah sent this message to the king of
Assyria at Lachish:[k] "I have done
wrong.[l] Withdraw from me, and I will
pay whatever you demand of me." The
king of Assyria exacted from Hezekiah
king of Judah three hundred talents[d] of
silver and thirty talents[e] of gold. 15So
Hezekiah gave[m] him all the silver that
was found in the temple of the LORD and
in the treasuries of the royal palace.
16At this time Hezekiah king of Judah
stripped off the gold with which he had

17:36 [k]S Ex 3:20; Ps 136:12
17:37 [l]Dt 5:32 [m]S Lev 19:37
17:38 [n]S Dt 6:12
17:41 [o]S 1Ki 18:21; Ezr 4:2; Mt 6:24
18:1 [p]Isa 1:1; Hos 1:1; Mic 1:1
18:2 [q]ver 13; Isa 38:5
18:3 [r]S 1Ki 14:8 [s]Isa 38:5
18:4 [t]2Ch 31:1; Isa 36:7 [u]2Ki 12:3; 21:3 [v]S Ex 23:24 [w]Nu 21:9
18:5 [x]ver 19; S 1Sa 7:3; 2Ki 19:10; Ps 21:7; 125:1; Pr 3:26
18:6 [y]Dt 10:20; S Dt 6:18
18:7 [z]S Ge 39:3; S Job 22:25 [a]2Ki 24:1; Ezr 4:19; Isa 36:5
18:8 [b]2Ki 17:9
18:9 [c]Isa 1:1; 36:1
18:11 [d]Isa 37:12 [e]Eze 16:39; 23:9
18:12 [f]S 2Ki 17:15 [g]2Ki 21:8; Da 9:6, 10 [h]S 1Ki 9:6
18:13 [i]S ver 2 [j]Isa 1:7; Mic 1:9
18:14 [k]2Ki 19:8 [l]Isa 24:5; 33:8
18:15 [m]S 1Ki 15:18; Isa 39:2

[a]2 Hebrew *Abi*, a variant of *Abijah* [b]4 Or *He called it* [c]4 *Nehushtan* sounds like the Hebrew for *bronze* and *snake* and *unclean thing.* [d]14 That is, about 11 tons (about 10 metric tons) [e]14 That is, about 1 ton (about 1 metric ton)

18:5–6 DISCIPLESHIP, God's Leadership—Hezekiah was unique in his trust in God. As a result of his faith, he obeyed the Mosaic Law and never ceased to follow God. Legalistic obedience without active faith in God will not be adequate in finding and following the will of God. Dynamic faith permits God to reveal His will to His followers. Each generation needs dedicated leaders who trust God and follow His directions.

18:7 HUMANITY, Relationship to God—A right relationship to God is the basis for success in human endeavors. Success is not always measured by the world's standards, as an examination of the lives of Isaiah, Jeremiah, Paul, and Jesus reveals. God does, however, grant material success for those endeavors which fulfill His purposes.

18:9–12 HISTORY, Politics—See note on 17:3–23.

18:9–12 ELECTION, Condemnation—The Assyrian deportation of Israel was due to Israel's violation of God's covenant. Israel learned God is as faithful to election requirements and threats as He is to election promises.

18:9—19:37 CHRISTIAN ETHICS, War and Peace—Jerusalem, the capital of the kingdom of Judah, was threatened by the leading military power of the time, Assyria. Through the intercession of Hezekiah on behalf of the Hebrews, they were spared the terror of the Assyrian war machine. This account helps us know one way to begin to address our present world arms race. Take it before God, and pray for peace.

18:9–12 CHRISTIAN ETHICS, Covenant— Violation of the covenant Israel freely chose to enter led to the covenant curses becoming reality. See note on Ex 24:3,7; Lev 26:3–45; Dt 28:25.

18:11–12 THE CHURCH, Covenant People—Rebellion against God keeps us from experiencing the highest possible good. The promise of the covenant does not overrule the consequences of sinning. By violating God's good way, we choose the way which leads to ruin and must turn to Him for forgiveness. When we follow the covenant stipulations, we choose life and the joys which come from serving God.

covered the doors[n] and doorposts of the
temple of the LORD, and gave it to the
king of Assyria.

Sennacherib Threatens Jerusalem

18:13, 17–37pp — Isa 36:1–22
18:17–35pp — 2Ch 32:9–19

17The king of Assyria sent his supreme
commander,[o] his chief officer and his
field commander with a large army, from
Lachish to King Hezekiah at Jerusalem.
They came up to Jerusalem and stopped
at the aqueduct of the Upper Pool,[p] on
the road to the Washerman's Field.
18They called for the king; and Eliakim[q]
son of Hilkiah the palace administrator,
Shebna[r] the secretary, and Joah son of
Asaph the recorder went out to them.
19The field commander said to them,
"Tell Hezekiah:

" 'This is what the great king, the
king of Assyria, says: On what are
you basing this confidence[s] of yours?
20You say you have strategy and military strength—but you speak only
empty words. On whom are you depending, that you rebel against me?
21Look now, you are depending on
Egypt,[t] that splintered reed of a
staff,[u] which pierces a man's hand
and wounds him if he leans on it!
Such is Pharaoh king of Egypt to all
who depend on him. 22And if you say
to me, "We are depending on the
LORD our God"—isn't he the one
whose high places and altars Hezekiah removed, saying to Judah and Jerusalem, "You must worship before
this altar in Jerusalem"?
23" 'Come now, make a bargain
with my master, the king of Assyria: I
will give you two thousand horses—
if you can put riders on them! 24How
can you repulse one officer[v] of the
least of my master's officials, even
though you are depending on Egypt
for chariots and horsemen[t]? 25Fur-
thermore, have I come to attack and
destroy this place without word from
the LORD?[w] The LORD himself told
me to march against this country and
destroy it.' "

26Then Eliakim son of Hilkiah, and
Shebna and Joah said to the field commander, "Please speak to your servants in
Aramaic,[x] since we understand it. Don't
speak to us in Hebrew in the hearing of
the people on the wall."
27But the commander replied, "Was it
only to your master and you that my master sent me to say these things, and not to
the men sitting on the wall—who, like
you, will have to eat their own filth and
drink their own urine?"
28Then the commander stood and
called out in Hebrew: "Hear the word of
the great king, the king of Assyria! 29This
is what the king says: Do not let Hezekiah deceive[y] you. He cannot deliver you
from my hand. 30Do not let Hezekiah persuade you to trust in the LORD when he
says, 'The LORD will surely deliver us;
this city will not be given into the hand of
the king of Assyria.'
31"Do not listen to Hezekiah. This is
what the king of Assyria says: Make
peace with me and come out to me. Then
every one of you will eat from his own
vine and fig tree[z] and drink water from
his own cistern,[a] 32until I come and take
you to a land like your own, a land of
grain and new wine, a land of bread and
vineyards, a land of olive trees and honey.
Choose life[b] and not death!
"Do not listen to Hezekiah, for he is
misleading you when he says, 'The LORD
will deliver us.' 33Has the god[c] of any
nation ever delivered his land from the
hand of the king of Assyria? 34Where are
the gods of Hamath[d] and Arpad?[e] Where
are the gods of Sepharvaim, Hena and Ivvah? Have they rescued Samaria from my
hand? 35Who of all the gods of these
countries has been able to save his land
from me? How then can the LORD deliver
Jerusalem from my hand?"[f]
36But the people remained silent and
said nothing in reply, because the king
had commanded, "Do not answer him."
37Then Eliakim[g] son of Hilkiah the palace administrator, Shebna the secretary
and Joah son of Asaph the recorder went
to Hezekiah, with their clothes torn,[h]
and told him what the field commander
had said.

Chapter 19

Jerusalem's Deliverance Foretold

19:1–13pp — Isa 37:1–13

WHEN King Hezekiah heard this, he
tore[i] his clothes and put on sack-

18:16 [n]2Ch 29:3
18:17 [o]Isa 20:1 [p]2Ki 20:20; 2Ch 32:4,30; Ne 2:14; Isa 22:9
18:18 [q]2Ki 19:2; Isa 22:20; 36:3,11, 22; 37:2 [r]ver 26, 37; Isa 22:15
18:19 [s]S ver 5; S Job 4:6
18:21 [t]Isa 20:5; 31:1; Eze 29:6 [u]2Ki 24:7; Isa 20:6; 30:5,7; Jer 25:19; 37:7; 46:2
18:24 [v]Isa 10:8
18:25 [w]2Ki 19:6, 22; 24:3; 2Ch 35:21
18:26 [x]Ezr 4:7
18:29 [y]2Ki 19:10
18:31 [z]S Nu 13:23; S 1Ki 4:25 [a]Jer 14:3; La 4:4
18:32 [b]Dt 30:19
18:33 [c]2Ki 19:12
18:34 [d]S 2Ki 17:24; S Jer 49:23 [e]Isa 10:9
18:35 [f]Ps 2:1-2
18:37 [g]S ver 18; Isa 33:7; 36:3,22 [h]S 2Ki 6:30
19:1 [i]S Ge 37:34; S Nu 14:6

[t]24 Or *charioteers*

18:25 HISTORY, Intentions—Assyria claimed revelation from Israel's God as the basis for calling Hezekiah to surrender. God does not honor false religious claims. He turns such evil human intentions to fulfill His own will.

18:31–35 HISTORY, God—The Assyrians mocked Israel's trust in God for historical help. They compared God to the powerless gods of other countries. God cannot be compared to anyone or anything in human experience. History shows His power over all other gods and over all human armies. No one mocks God and escapes.

19:1–37 HISTORY, Universal—Prayer, prophecy, and God's power brought deliverance from a situation human

cloth and went into the temple of the
LORD. 2He sent Eliakim[j] the palace administrator, Shebna the secretary and the
leading priests,[k] all wearing sackcloth,[l]
to the prophet Isaiah[m] son of Amoz.
3They told him, "This is what Hezekiah
says: This day is a day of distress and rebuke and disgrace, as when children
come to the point[n] of birth and there is
no strength to deliver them. 4It may be
that the LORD your God will hear all the
words of the field commander, whom his
master, the king of Assyria, has sent to
ridicule[o] the living God, and that he will
rebuke[p] him for the words the LORD your
God has heard. Therefore pray for the
remnant[q] that still survives."
5When King Hezekiah's officials came
to Isaiah, 6Isaiah said to them, "Tell your
master, 'This is what the LORD says: Do
not be afraid[r] of what you have heard—
those words with which the underlings of
the king of Assyria have blasphemed[s]
me. 7Listen! I am going to put such a spirit in him that when he hears a certain
report,[t] he will return to his own country, and there I will have him cut down
with the sword.[u]' "
8When the field commander heard that
the king of Assyria had left Lachish,[v] he
withdrew and found the king fighting
against Libnah.[w]
9Now Sennacherib received a report
that Tirhakah, the Cushite[g] king ⌞of
Egypt⌟, was marching out to fight against
him. So he again sent messengers to Hezekiah with this word: 10"Say to Hezekiah
king of Judah: Do not let the god you depend[x] on deceive[y] you when he says,
'Jerusalem will not be handed over to the
king of Assyria.' 11Surely you have heard
what the kings of Assyria have done to all
the countries, destroying them completely. And will you be delivered? 12Did the
gods of the nations that were destroyed
by my forefathers deliver[z] them: the
gods of Gozan,[a] Haran,[b] Rezeph and the
people of Eden who were in Tel Assar?
13Where is the king of Hamath, the king
of Arpad, the king of the city of Sepharvaim, or of Hena or Ivvah?"[c]

Hezekiah's Prayer

19:14–19pp — Isa 37:14–20

14Hezekiah received the letter[d] from
the messengers and read it. Then he
went up to the temple of the LORD and
spread it out before the LORD. 15And Hezekiah prayed to the LORD: "O LORD, God
of Israel, enthroned between the cherubim,[e] you alone[f] are God over all the
kingdoms of the earth. You have made
heaven and earth. 16Give ear,[g] O LORD,
and hear;[h] open your eyes,[i] O LORD,
and see; listen to the words Sennacherib
has sent to insult the living God.
17"It is true, O LORD, that the Assyrian
kings have laid waste these nations and
their lands. 18They have thrown their
gods into the fire and destroyed them, for
they were not gods[j] but only wood and
stone, fashioned by men's hands.[k]
19Now, O LORD our God, deliver[l] us
from his hand, so that all kingdoms[m] on
earth may know[n] that you alone, O
LORD, are God."

Isaiah Prophesies Sennacherib's Fall

19:20–37pp — Isa 37:21–38
19:35–37pp — 2Ch 32:20–21

20Then Isaiah son of Amoz sent a message to Hezekiah: "This is what the
LORD, the God of Israel, says: I have
heard[o] your prayer concerning Sennacherib king of Assyria. 21This is the word
that the LORD has spoken against[p] him:

" 'The Virgin Daughter[q] of Zion
despises[r] you and mocks[s] you.
The Daughter of Jerusalem
tosses her head[t] as you flee.
22Who is it you have insulted and
blasphemed?[u]
Against whom have you raised your
voice
and lifted your eyes in pride?

19:2 jS 2Ki 18:18 kJer 19:1 lS Ge 37:34 mIsa 1:1
19:3 nHos 13:13
19:4 oS 1Sa 17:26 p2Sa 16:12 qS Ge 45:7; S Jer 37:3
19:6 rS Dt 3:2; S Jos 1:9 sS 2Ki 18:25
19:7 tS Ex 14:24; Jer 51:46 uver 37; 2Ch 32:21; Isa 10:12
19:8 v2Ki 18:14 wS Nu 33:20; S 2Ki 8:22
19:10 xS 2Ki 18:5 y2Ki 18:29
19:12 z2Ki 18:33; 2Ch 32:17 a2Ki 17:6 bS Ge 11:31
19:13 cIsa 10:9-11; Jer 49:23
19:14 d2Ki 5:7
19:15 eS Ge 3:24; S Ex 25:22 fS Ge 1:1; S Jos 2:11
19:16 gPs 31:2; 71:2; 88:2; 102:2 hS 1Ki 8:29 iS Ex 3:16
19:18 jIsa 44:9-11; Jer 10:3-10 kDt 4:28; Ps 115:4; Ac 17:29
19:19 l1Sa 12:10; Job 6:23; Ps 3:7; 71:4 mS 1Ki 8:43; 1Ch 16:8 nS Jos 4:24; S 1Sa 17:46
19:20 oS 1Ki 9:3
19:21 pIsa 10:5; 33:1 qIsa 47:1; Jer 14:17; 18:13; 31:4; 46:11; La 2:13; Am 5:2 rPs 53:5 sPr 1:26; 3:34 tJob 16:4; Ps 44:14; 64:8; 109:25; Jer 18:16
19:22 uS 2Ki 18:25

g9 That is, from the upper Nile region

strategists would call impossible. God delivered His people to show all the nations His power as the only God. Assyria thought they were more powerful than all enemy gods. They did not realize they had not faced a God until they faced Israel.

19:4 PRAYER, Righteousness of God—The righteousness of God gave Hezekiah reason to pray. He called his people to pray for the remnant of the nation which had survived Assyrian attacks. He had faith a righteous God would punish Assyria for the scornful speech against God.

19:14–19 PRAYER, Sovereignty of God—Sennacherib's contempt had been for the gods of the nations he had conquered (v 12). Hezekiah based his prayer on the fact that God is unique and sovereign. He made the Temple a house of prayer and recognized God's universal rule and prayed His rule would be universally recognized.

19:19 EVANGELISM, Glory to God—See note on Ex 7:5.

19:20–36 GOD, Sovereignty—Isaiah used the themes of the sovereignty and the faithfulness of God to reassure Hezekiah that he need not fear. God is in control of His world and can defend His people. See notes on Ge 15:13–16; 18:14; 24:3,7, 50.

19:20–36 PRAYER, Answer—God answered Hezekiah's prayer through the prophet's oracle against Sennacherib, Assyria's proud and scornful king. The answer of captivity for Assyria meant productivity for Judah. God's answer was based on His covenant commitment to David (2 Sa 7).

19:22–23 CHRISTIAN ETHICS, Language—Using Sennacherib as an example, Isaiah articulated God's opinion against language which indicated a prideful spirit. Though we throw insults at other people, our attitude is ultimately one which insults God. God hates those attitudes of deceit and greediness which our language expresses as we ridicule and condemn others.

Against the Holy One[v] of Israel!
23By your messengers
you have heaped insults on the Lord.
And you have said,[w]
"With my many chariots[x]
I have ascended the heights of the mountains,
the utmost heights of Lebanon.
I have cut down[y] its tallest cedars,
the choicest of its pines.
I have reached its remotest parts,
the finest of its forests.
24I have dug wells in foreign lands
and drunk the water there.
With the soles of my feet
I have dried up all the streams of Egypt."

25" 'Have you not heard?[z]
Long ago I ordained it.
In days of old I planned[a] it;
now I have brought it to pass,
that you have turned fortified cities
into piles of stone.[b]
26Their people, drained of power,[c]
are dismayed[d] and put to shame.
They are like plants in the field,
like tender green shoots,[e]
like grass sprouting on the roof,
scorched[f] before it grows up.

27" 'But I know[g] where you stay
and when you come and go
and how you rage against me.
28Because you rage against me
and your insolence has reached my ears,
I will put my hook[h] in your nose
and my bit[i] in your mouth,
and I will make you return[j]
by the way you came.'

29"This will be the sign[k] for you, O
Hezekiah:

"This year you will eat what grows by itself,[l]
and the second year what springs from that.
But in the third year sow and reap,
plant vineyards[m] and eat their fruit.
30Once more a remnant[n] of the house of Judah
will take root[o] below and bear fruit above.
31For out of Jerusalem will come a remnant,[p]
and out of Mount Zion a band of survivors.[q]

The zeal[r] of the LORD Almighty will accomplish this.

32"Therefore this is what the LORD says
concerning the king of Assyria:

"He will not enter this city
or shoot an arrow here.
He will not come before it with shield
or build a siege ramp against it.
33By the way that he came he will return;[s]
he will not enter this city,
declares the LORD.
34I will defend[t] this city and save it,
for my sake and for the sake of David[u] my servant."

35That night the angel of the LORD[v]
went out and put to death a hundred and
eighty-five thousand men in the Assyrian
camp. When the people got up the next
morning—there were all the dead bodies![w] 36So Sennacherib king of Assyria
broke camp and withdrew.[x] He returned
to Nineveh[y] and stayed there.
37One day, while he was worshiping in
the temple of his god Nisroch, his sons
Adrammelech[z] and Sharezer cut him
down with the sword,[a] and they escaped
to the land of Ararat.[b] And Esarhaddon[c]
his son succeeded him as king.

19:22 [v]Lev 19:2; 1Sa 2:2; Job 6:10; Ps 16:10; 22:3; 71:22; 78:41; 89:18; Isa 1:4; 6:3; 57:15; Hos 11:9
19:23 [w]Isa 10:18; Jer 21:14; Eze 20:47 [x]Ps 20:7; Jer 50:37 [y]Isa 10:34; 14:8; 33:9; Eze 31:3
19:25 [z]Isa 40:21, 28 [a]Isa 22:11 [b]Mic 1:6
19:26 [c]Isa 13:7; Eze 7:17; Zep 3:16 [d]Ps 6:10; 71:24; 83:17; Isa 41:23; Jer 8:9 [e]Isa 4:2; 11:1; 53:2; Jer 23:5 [f]Job 8:12; Ps 37:2; 129:6
19:27 [g]Ps 139:1-4
19:28 [h]2Ch 33:11; Eze 19:9; 29:4; 38:4; Am 4:2 [i]Isa 30:28 [j]ver 33
19:29 [k]S Ex 7:9; S Dt 13:2; Lk 2:12 [l]Lev 25:5 [m]Ps 107:37; Isa 65:21; Am 9:14
19:30 [n]S Ge 45:7 [o]Isa 5:24; 11:1; 27:6; Eze 17:22; Am 2:9
19:31 [p]S Ge 45:7 [q]Isa 66:19; Zep 2:9; Zec 14:16 [r]Isa 9:7
19:33 [s]ver 28
19:34 [t]2Ki 20:6 [u]S 2Sa 7:15
19:35 [v]S Ge 19:13; S Ex 12:23 [w]Job 24:24; Isa 17:14; 41:12; Na 3:3
19:36 [x]S 2Ki 12:18 [y]S Ge 10:11
19:37 [z]2Ki 17:31 [a]S ver 7 [b]S Ge 8:4 [c]S 2Ki 17:24

Chapter 20

Hezekiah's Illness

20:1–11pp — 2Ch 32:24–26; Isa 38:1–8

IN those days Hezekiah became ill and
was at the point of death. The prophet
Isaiah son of Amoz went to him and said,

19:29–34 ELECTION, Remnant—Election is not a one-sided commitment. Election demands responsible commitment. Israel learned through historical experience that election included only the faithful remnant, not the mass of proud, self-satisfied but unfaithful members of the nation. The remnant idea taught Israel of God's wrath in destroying all but a small remnant and of God's faithfulness in preserving a remnant despite Israel's unfaithfulness. The elect Israel remained alive in the remnant. Compare Ge 7:23; 45:7; 1 Ki 19:10–18; Isa 1:8–9; 7:3; 17:3–6; 30:17; Am 5:3.

20:1–11 MIRACLE, Nature—Miracles can reverse a prophet's pronouncement. Miracles respond to the prayers of God's faithful people. They represent God's free personal response to the needs and faith of His people. God's prophet Isaiah said the sickness of Hezekiah was to end in death. The passionate prayer plea of the king changed the circumstances. God spoke to the prophet, and the prophet spoke to the king: you will recover and enjoy fifteen more years of life. The prophet called for a poultice of figs, and the festering sore was anointed and healed. So nature cooperated in the healing miracle. The king was confused by the abrupt change and asked for a "sign." The sign was a reversal of the sun dial's steps. Some have supposed that a partial eclipse of the sun was responsible for the moving shadow. Hezekiah and the Bible do not ask such questions. They testify to a sign of God's gift—fifteen more years of life—a sign strengthening a great leader's faith.

20:1–11 EVIL AND SUFFERING, God's Present Help—God can help overcome suffering even when it means replacing one prophetic word with another. God takes seriously the repentance and faithfulness of His suffering people. He responded to Hezekiah's prayer and added fifteen years to his life.

20:1–11 HUMANITY, Death—Illness, as the precursor of death, is often viewed as a form of death. God as the Author of life can prolong life by bringing healing from the illness. Death,

"This is what the LORD says: Put your
house in order, because you are going to
die; you will not recover."
2Hezekiah turned his face to the wall
and prayed to the LORD, 3"Remember,[d]
O LORD, how I have walked[e] before you
faithfully[f] and with wholehearted devotion and have done what is good in your
eyes." And Hezekiah wept bitterly.
4Before Isaiah had left the middle
court, the word of the LORD came to him:
5"Go back and tell Hezekiah, the leader
of my people, 'This is what the LORD, the
God of your father David, says: I have
heard[g] your prayer and seen your tears;[h]
I will heal you. On the third day from
now you will go up to the temple of the
LORD. 6I will add fifteen years to your life.
And I will deliver you and this city from
the hand of the king of Assyria. I will defend[i] this city for my sake and for the
sake of my servant David.' "
7Then Isaiah said, "Prepare a poultice
of figs." They did so and applied it to the
boil,[j] and he recovered.
8Hezekiah had asked Isaiah, "What
will be the sign that the LORD will heal
me and that I will go up to the temple of
the LORD on the third day from now?"
9Isaiah answered, "This is the LORD's
sign[k] to you that the LORD will do what
he has promised: Shall the shadow go forward ten steps, or shall it go back ten
steps?"
10"It is a simple[l] matter for the shadow to go forward ten steps," said Hezekiah. "Rather, have it go back ten steps."
11Then the prophet Isaiah called upon
the LORD, and the LORD made the shadow
go back[m] the ten steps it had gone down
on the stairway of Ahaz.

Envoys From Babylon

20:12–19pp — Isa 39:1–8
20:20–21pp — 2Ch 32:32–33

12At that time Merodach-Baladan son
of Baladan king of Babylon sent Hezekiah
letters and a gift, because he had heard of
Hezekiah's illness. 13Hezekiah received
the messengers and showed them all that
was in his storehouses—the silver, the
gold, the spices and the fine oil—his armory and everything found among his
treasures. There was nothing in his palace or in all his kingdom that Hezekiah
did not show them.
14Then Isaiah the prophet went to King
Hezekiah and asked, "What did those
men say, and where did they come
from?"
"From a distant land," Hezekiah replied. "They came from Babylon."
15The prophet asked, "What did they
see in your palace?"
"They saw everything in my palace,"
Hezekiah said. "There is nothing among
my treasures that I did not show them."
16Then Isaiah said to Hezekiah, "Hear
the word of the LORD: 17The time will
surely come when everything in your palace, and all that your fathers have stored
up until this day, will be carried off to
Babylon.[n] Nothing will be left, says the
LORD. 18And some of your descendants,[o]
your own flesh and blood, that will be
born to you, will be taken away, and they
will become eunuchs in the palace of the
king of Babylon."[p]
19"The word of the LORD you have spoken is good," Hezekiah replied. For he
thought, "Will there not be peace and security in my lifetime?"
20As for the other events of Hezekiah's
reign, all his achievements and how he
made the pool[q] and the tunnel[r] by
which he brought water into the city, are
they not written in the book of the annals
of the kings of Judah? 21Hezekiah rested
with his fathers. And Manasseh his son
succeeded him as king.

Chapter 21

Manasseh King of Judah

21:1–10pp — 2Ch 33:1–10
21:17–18pp — 2Ch 33:18–20

MANASSEH was twelve years old
when he became king, and he
reigned in Jerusalem fifty-five years. His
mother's name was Hephzibah.[s] 2He did

20:3 [d]S Ge 8:1; Ne 1:8; 5:19; 13:14 [e]S Ge 5:22 [f]S 1Ki 2:4; 2Ch 31:20
20:5 [g]S 1Ki 9:3 [h]Ps 6:6,8; 39:12; 56:8
20:6 [i]S 2Ki 19:34; S 1Ch 17:19
20:7 [j]S Ex 9:9
20:9 [k]S Dt 13:2; Jer 44:29
20:10 [l]S 2Ki 3:18
20:11 [m]Jos 10:13; 2Ch 32:31
20:17 [n]2Ki 24:13; 2Ch 36:10; Jer 20:5; 27:22; 52:17-23
20:18 [o]2Ki 24:15; Da 1:3 [p]Mic 4:10
20:20 [q]S 2Ki 18:17 [r]S 2Sa 5:8
21:1 [s]Isa 62:4

however, cannot be ultimately avoided.

20:3 PRAYER, Petition—Hezekiah's prayer had an unusual basis—his wholehearted devotion to the Lord. This was not an extravagant claim. He knew his own heart, and God confirmed the fact. Without the extension of life, Manasseh would not have been born. Hezekiah's petition preserved the messianic line. God answered through the prophet and showed His freedom to overrule His own prophetic announcement (v 1). God's knowledge of all things and His plan and purpose for the universe do not mean prayer has no effect. God is free to respond to a responsive people and let their history go in new directions. Prayer means the universe is not a closed, determined system.

20:9–11 PRAYER, Answer—See note on Jos 10:12–14. God sometimes confirmed His word with a sign.

20:16–19 ELECTION, Leadership—The promise to David (2 Sa 7) did not guarantee the nation's security. Idolatry and political strategies permitting worship of foreign gods meant Israel had forfeited their right to God's promise. God announced their punishment and led them to a transformed understanding of the promise as pointing to the Messiah.

20:20 HOLY SCRIPTURE, Writing—See note on 1:16–18.

21:1–15 HISTORY, Judgment—God's intention was to bless Judah and His Temple forever. He warned His people of the consequences of sin. Under Manasseh Judah became worse than the peoples Joshua destroyed (Jos 1—12). God exercised His freedom to announce judgment on such sin and to revoke His people's hold on the land. Sin by God's people has historical consequences.

21:1–9 CHRISTIAN ETHICS, Covenant—See note on 18:9–12.

evil[t] in the eyes of the LORD, following
the detestable practices[u] of the nations
the LORD had driven out before the Israelites. 3He rebuilt the high places[v] his father Hezekiah had destroyed; he also
erected altars to Baal[w] and made an Asherah pole,[x] as Ahab king of Israel had
done. He bowed down to all the starry
hosts[y] and worshiped them. 4He built altars[z] in the temple of the LORD, of which
the LORD had said, "In Jerusalem I will
put my Name."[a] 5In both courts[b] of the
temple of the LORD, he built altars to all
the starry hosts. 6He sacrificed his own
son[c] in[h] the fire, practiced sorcery and
divination,[d] and consulted mediums and
spiritists.[e] He did much evil in the eyes
of the LORD, provoking[f] him to anger.
7He took the carved Asherah pole[g] he
had made and put it in the temple,[h] of
which the LORD had said to David and to
his son Solomon, "In this temple and in
Jerusalem, which I have chosen out of all
the tribes of Israel, I will put my Name[i]
forever. 8I will not again[j] make the feet
of the Israelites wander from the land I
gave their forefathers, if only they will be
careful to do everything I commanded
them and will keep the whole Law that
my servant Moses[k] gave them." 9But the
people did not listen. Manasseh led them
astray, so that they did more evil[l] than
the nations[m] the LORD had destroyed before the Israelites.
10The LORD said through his servants
the prophets: 11"Manasseh king of Judah
has committed these detestable sins. He
has done more evil[n] than the Amorites[o]
who preceded him and has led Judah into
sin with his idols.[p] 12Therefore this is
what the LORD, the God of Israel, says: I
am going to bring such disaster[q] on Jerusalem and Judah that the ears of everyone
who hears of it will tingle.[r] 13I will
stretch out over Jerusalem the measuring
line used against Samaria and the plumb
line[s] used against the house of Ahab. I
will wipe[t] out Jerusalem as one wipes a
dish, wiping it and turning it upside
down. 14I will forsake[u] the remnant[v] of
my inheritance and hand them over to
their enemies. They will be looted and
plundered by all their foes, 15because
they have done evil[w] in my eyes and have
provoked[x] me to anger from the day
their forefathers came out of Egypt until
this day."
16Moreover, Manasseh also shed so
much innocent blood[y] that he filled Jerusalem from end to end—besides the sin
that he had caused Judah[z] to commit, so
that they did evil in the eyes of the LORD.
17As for the other events of Manasseh's
reign, and all he did, including the sin he
committed, are they not written in the
book of the annals of the kings of Judah?
18Manasseh rested with his fathers and
was buried in his palace garden,[a] the garden of Uzza. And Amon his son succeeded him as king.

Amon King of Judah

21:19–24pp — 2Ch 33:21–25

19Amon was twenty-two years old
when he became king, and he reigned in
Jerusalem two years. His mother's name
was Meshullemeth daughter of Haruz;
she was from Jotbah. 20He did evil[b] in
the eyes of the LORD, as his father Manasseh had done. 21He walked in all the ways
of his father; he worshiped the idols his
father had worshiped, and bowed down
to them. 22He forsook[c] the LORD, the
God of his fathers, and did not walk[d] in
the way of the LORD.
23Amon's officials conspired against
him and assassinated[e] the king in his palace. 24Then the people of the land killed[f]
all who had plotted against King Amon,
and they made Josiah[g] his son king in his
place.
25As for the other events of Amon's
reign, and what he did, are they not written in the book of the annals of the kings
of Judah? 26He was buried in his grave in
the garden[h] of Uzza. And Josiah his son
succeeded him as king.

Chapter 22

The Book of the Law Found

22:1–20pp — 2Ch 34:1–2,8–28

JOSIAH[i] was eight years old when he
became king, and he reigned in Jerusalem thirty-one years. His mother's name

h6 Or *He made his own son pass through*

21:2 tver 16; S Dt 4:25; Jer 15:4 uDt 9:4; S 18:9; S 1Ki 14:24; 2Ki 16:3
21:3 vS 1Ki 3:3; S 2Ki 18:4 wS Jdg 6:28 xS Dt 16:21 yS Ge 2:1; Dt 17:3; Jer 19:13
21:4 zIsa 66:4; Jer 4:1; 7:30; 23:11; 32:34; Eze 23:39 aS Ex 20:24; S 2Sa 7:13
21:5 b1Ki 7:12; 2Ki 23:12
21:6 cS Lev 18:21; S Dt 18:10; S 2Ki 3:27 dDt 18:14 eS Lev 19:31 f2Ki 23:26
21:7 gDt 16:21; 2Ki 23:4 hS Lev 15:31 iS Ex 20:24; S 2Sa 7:13
21:8 jS 2Sa 7:10 kS 2Ki 18:12
21:9 lS 1Ki 14:9; Eze 5:7 mDt 9:4
21:11 nS 1Ki 14:9 oS Ge 15:16 pEze 18:12
21:12 q2Ki 23:26; 24:3; Jer 15:4; Eze 7:5 rS 1Sa 3:11
21:13 sIsa 28:17; 34:11; La 2:8; Am 7:7-9 t2Ki 23:27
21:14 uPs 78:58-60; Jer 12:7; 23:33 v2Ki 19:4; Ezr 9:8; Ne 1:2; Isa 1:9; 10:21; Jer 6:9; 40:15; 42:2; 44:7, 28; 50:20; Mic 2:12
21:15 wS Ex 32:22 xJer 25:7
21:16 y2Ki 24:4; Job 22:14; Ps 10:11; 94:7; 106:38; Isa 29:15; 47:10; 59:3,7; Jer 2:34; 7:6; 19:4; 22:17; La 4:13; Eze 7:23; 8:12; 9:9; 22:3-4; Hos 4:2; Zep 1:12 zS ver 2,11
21:18 aver 26; Est 1:5; 7:7
21:20 b1Ki 15:26
21:22 cS 1Sa 8:8 d1Ki 11:33
21:23 eS 2Ki 12:20
21:24 f2Ki 14:5 g2Ch 33:21; Zep 1:1
21:26 hS ver 18
22:1 iJer 1:2; 25:3

21:2–17 SIN, Discipline—God's chosen people may become worse than pagans. A leader with political priorities rather than spiritual ones can lead a people astray. Such habitual sin can eventually rob a people of God's promises. Judah had to face the same devastating punishment as did the Northern Kingdom (17:7–23). Sin by God's people provokes His anger. Only faithfulness to Him and His way of life guarantee we are truly part of His chosen ones. Such faithfulness does not earn salvation, but it demonstrates we are saved. See note on 1 Ki 14:22–24.

21:8–15 ELECTION, Condemnation—Manasseh led Judah away from the salvation they had been elected to enjoy into the state of sinful disobedience. Sin must be punished, even if the sinners are persons elected to benefit from the blessings of covenant obedience.

21:17,25 HOLY SCRIPTURE, Writing—See note on 1:16–18.

21:20–22 SIN, Transgression—See note on 1 Ki 14:22–24.

21:23–24 CHRISTIAN ETHICS, Murder—See note on 1 Ki 16:10–13.

was Jedidah daughter of Adaiah; she was
from Bozkath.[j] 2He did what was right[k]
in the eyes of the LORD and walked in all
the ways of his father David, not turning
aside to the right[l] or to the left.
3In the eighteenth year of his reign,
King Josiah sent the secretary, Shaphan[m]
son of Azaliah, the son of Meshullam, to
the temple of the LORD. He said: 4"Go up
to Hilkiah[n] the high priest and have him
get ready the money that has been
brought into the temple of the LORD,
which the doorkeepers have collected[o]
from the people. 5Have them entrust it to
the men appointed to supervise the work
on the temple. And have these men pay
the workers who repair[p] the temple of
the LORD— 6the carpenters, the builders
and the masons. Also have them purchase timber and dressed stone to repair
the temple.[q] 7But they need not account
for the money entrusted to them, because
they are acting faithfully."[r]
8Hilkiah the high priest said to Shaphan the secretary, "I have found the
Book of the Law[s] in the temple of the
LORD." He gave it to Shaphan, who read
it. 9Then Shaphan the secretary went to
the king and reported to him: "Your officials have paid out the money that was in
the temple of the LORD and have entrusted it to the workers and supervisors at
the temple." 10Then Shaphan the secretary informed the king, "Hilkiah the
priest has given me a book." And Shaphan read from it in the presence of the
king.[t]
11When the king heard the words of
the Book of the Law,[u] he tore his robes.
12He gave these orders to Hilkiah the
priest, Ahikam[v] son of Shaphan, Acbor
son of Micaiah, Shaphan the secretary
and Asaiah the king's attendant:[w] 13"Go
and inquire[x] of the LORD for me and for
the people and for all Judah about what is
written in this book that has been found.
Great is the LORD's anger[y] that burns
against us because our fathers have not
obeyed the words of this book; they have
not acted in accordance with all that is
written there concerning us."
14Hilkiah the priest, Ahikam, Acbor,
Shaphan and Asaiah went to speak to the
prophetess[z] Huldah, who was the wife of
Shallum son of Tikvah, the son of Harhas,
keeper of the wardrobe. She lived in Jerusalem, in the Second District.
15She said to them, "This is what the
LORD, the God of Israel, says: Tell the
man who sent you to me, 16'This is what
the LORD says: I am going to bring disaster[a] on this place and its people, according to everything written in the book[b]
the king of Judah has read. 17Because
they have forsaken[c] me and burned incense to other gods and provoked me to
anger by all the idols their hands have
made,[1] my anger will burn against this
place and will not be quenched.' 18Tell
the king of Judah, who sent you to inquire[d] of the LORD, 'This is what the
LORD, the God of Israel, says concerning
the words you heard: 19Because your
heart was responsive and you humbled[e]
yourself before the LORD when you heard
what I have spoken against this place and
its people, that they would become accursed[f] and laid waste,[g] and because
you tore your robes and wept in my presence, I have heard you, declares the
LORD. 20Therefore I will gather you to
your fathers, and you will be buried in
peace.[h] Your eyes[i] will not see all the

22:1 jJos 15:39
22:2 kS Dt 17:19; S 1Ki 14:8 lS Dt 5:32
22:3 m2Ch 34:20; Jer 39:14
22:4 nEzr 7:1 o2Ki 12:4-5
22:5 p2Ki 12:5, 11-14
22:6 q2Ki 12:11-12
22:7 rS 2Ki 12:15
22:8 sS Dt 28:61; S 31:24; Gal 3:10
22:10 tJer 36:21
22:11 uver 8
22:12 v2Ki 25:22; Jer 26:24; 39:14 w1Sa 8:14
22:13 xS Ge 25:22; S 1Sa 9:9 yDt 29:24-28; S 31:17; Isa 5:25; 42:25; Am 2:4
22:14 zS Ex 15:20
22:16 aS Dt 31:29; S Jos 23:15; Jer 6:19; 11:11; 18:11; 35:17 bDa 9:11
22:17 cS 1Ki 9:9
22:18 dJer 21:2; 37:3,7
22:19 eS Ex 10:3; Isa 57:15; 61:1; Mic 6:8 fJer 24:9; 25:18; 26:6 gLev 26:31
22:20 hIsa 47:11; 57:1; Jer 18:11 iS 1Ki 21:29

1 17 Or *by everything they have done*

22:4–7 STEWARDSHIP, House of God—See note on Ex 25:1–8.

22:13–17 GOD, Wrath—The wrath of God was expressed against the people who had forgotten to follow the word of the Lord diligently. Wrath is God's punishment of those who will not yield to His loving will for them. It is not a fit of anger or a loss of temper. See notes on Ge 6:5–8; 17:14; 19:13,24–26; Mt 3:7–10; Ro 1:18.

22:13 SIN, Alienation—God's Word is the standard by which God's people can measure their obedience. God's people must preserve and learn God's Word to know what sin is. Josiah heard the Book of the Law found by the priests in the Temple and recognized that Judah had been unfaithful to God's standards. He knew God was angry and sin had alienated the people from God. Ignorance of God's Word did not exempt Judah from the Lord's anger. They were guilty because they had neglected God's Word. Whether rejection is expressed by neglect or by disobedience, it still makes a people guilty and alienates them from God.

22:13–14 PRAYER, Petition—See note on 1 Ki 22:8–17. Josiah sought to know the meaning of God's written Word for his day. He found it by inquiring of God. Bible study should always be accompanied by prayer.

22:15–20 HISTORY, Deliverance—God's response to righteousness is deliverance of the righteous even in face of His announced judgment. God remains free to act in history in personal response to people. He has not so determined the course of history that He cannot respond to sin and righteousness. God gladly gives peace to people like Josiah who hear and do His will.

22:16–20 HOLY SCRIPTURE, Canonization—God's written revelation can steer people from destruction to hope. Josiah had at least part of the Pentateuch (Genesis—Deuteronomy). Some scholars think the book the king of Judah read was the law code of Deuteronomy. Because Josiah promised to obey the Word, God promised protection. Josiah regarded the law book as God's authoritative Word for his life. This was another step towards developing a canon of authoritative Scripture.

22:17 SIN, Alienation—Neglect of God and His Word leads to worship of other gods. See note on 22:13.

22:19 PRAYER, Faithfulness of God—Josiah's repentance was couched in terms very similar to a divine promise made in the days of Solomon (2 Ch 7:14). This is an example of a precise fulfillment of a promise of God. He is faithful to answer our prayers. Prayer does play an important role in God's work in the lives of individuals and nations. See note on 2 Ki 20:3.

disaster I am going to bring on this place.' "

So they took her answer back to the king.

Chapter 23

Josiah Renews the Covenant

23:1-3pp — 2Ch 34:29-32
23:4-20Ref — 2Ch 34:3-7,33
23:21-23pp — 2Ch 35:1,18-19
23:28-30pp — 2Ch 35:20-36:1

THEN the king called together all the elders of Judah and Jerusalem. 2He went up to the temple of the LORD with the men of Judah, the people of Jerusalem, the priests and the prophets—all the people from the least to the greatest. He read[j] in their hearing all the words of the Book of the Covenant,[k] which had been found in the temple of the LORD. 3The king stood by the pillar[l] and renewed the covenant[m] in the presence of the LORD—to follow[n] the LORD and keep his commands, regulations and decrees with all his heart and all his soul, thus confirming the words of the covenant written in this book. Then all the people pledged themselves to the covenant.

4The king ordered Hilkiah the high priest, the priests next in rank and the doorkeepers[o] to remove[p] from the temple of the LORD all the articles made for Baal and Asherah and all the starry hosts. He burned them outside Jerusalem in the fields of the Kidron Valley and took the ashes to Bethel. 5He did away with the pagan priests appointed by the kings of Judah to burn incense on the high places of the towns of Judah and on those around Jerusalem—those who burned incense[q] to Baal, to the sun and moon, to the constellations and to all the starry hosts.[r][s] 6He took the Asherah pole from the temple of the LORD to the Kidron Valley[t] outside Jerusalem and burned it there. He ground it to powder[u] and scattered the dust over the graves[v] of the common people.[w] 7He also tore down the quarters of the male shrine prostitutes,[x] which were in the temple of the LORD and where women did weaving for Asherah.

8Josiah brought all the priests from the towns of Judah and desecrated the high places, from Geba[y] to Beersheba, where the priests had burned incense. He broke down the shrines[j] at the gates—at the entrance to the Gate of Joshua, the city governor, which is on the left of the city gate. 9Although the priests of the high places did not serve[z] at the altar of the LORD in Jerusalem, they ate unleavened bread with their fellow priests.

10He desecrated Topheth,[a] which was in the Valley of Ben Hinnom,[b] so no one could use it to sacrifice his son[c] or daughter in[k] the fire to Molech. 11He removed from the entrance to the temple of the LORD the horses that the kings of Judah[d] had dedicated to the sun. They were in the court near the room of an official named Nathan-Melech. Josiah then burned the chariots dedicated to the sun.[e]

12He pulled down[f] the altars the kings of Judah had erected on the roof[g] near the upper room of Ahaz, and the altars Manasseh had built in the two courts[h] of the temple of the LORD. He removed them from there, smashed them to pieces and threw the rubble into the Kidron Valley.[i] 13The king also desecrated the high places that were east of Jerusalem on the south of the Hill of Corruption—the ones Solomon[j] king of Israel had built for Ashtoreth the vile goddess of the Sidonians, for Chemosh the vile god of Moab, and for Molech[l] the detestable[k] god of the people of Ammon.[l] 14Josiah smashed[m] the sacred stones and cut down the Asherah poles and covered the sites with human bones.[n]

15Even the altar[o] at Bethel, the high place made by Jeroboam[p] son of Nebat, who had caused Israel to sin—even that altar and high place he demolished. He burned the high place and ground it to powder, and burned the Asherah pole also. 16Then Josiah[q] looked around, and

j8 Or *high places* k10 Or *to make his son or daughter pass through* l13 Hebrew *Milcom*

23:2 jS Dt 31:11 kS Ex 24:7
23:3 lS 1Ki 7:15 mS 2Ki 11:12 nS Dt 13:4
23:4 o2Ki 25:18; Jer 35:4 pS 2Ki 21:7
23:5 qS 2Ki 16:4 rJer 8:2 sJer 43:13
23:6 tJer 31:40 uS Ex 32:20 vS Nu 19:16 wJer 26:23
23:7 xS Ge 38:21; 1Ki 14:24; Eze 16:16
23:8 yS Jos 18:24; S 1Ki 15:22
23:9 zEze 44:10-14
23:10 aIsa 30:33; Jer 7:31,32; 19:6 bS Jos 15:8 cS Lev 18:21; S Dt 18:10
23:11 dver 5,19; Ne 9:34; Jer 44:9 eS Dt 4:19
23:12 f2Ch 33:15 gJer 19:13; Zep 1:5 hS 2Ki 21:5 iS 2Sa 15:23
23:13 j1Ki 11:7 kS Dt 27:15 lJer 11:13
23:14 mS Ex 23:24 nS Nu 19:16; S Ps 53:5
23:15 oS Jos 7:2; 1Ki 13:1-3 pS 1Ki 12:33
23:16 qS 1Ki 13:2

23:1–27 ELECTION, Israel—See note on Jos 24:2–24. Josiah demonstrated the responsible life and leadership expected of the elect. The renewal of covenant commitment under his leadership could not change the religious course of Israel. Israel's unfaithfulness led to removal of the elect people, rejection of the elect city, and destruction of the elect worship place. When people claim election but live rejection, they can move God to reject them just as He removed Judah from His sight.

23:2–3 THE CHURCH, Covenant People—See notes on Dt 29:1–15; 2 Ki 11:12,17.

23:3 CHRISTIAN ETHICS, Covenant—Josiah represents an example of one in a leadership role who took seriously the matter of high personal and community standards. Because of the intensity and seriousness of his commitment to renewed application of God's standards for his life, others followed his example. Our society, unlike Josiah's, is not one in which "as the king does, so goes the community." Yet, ours is like Josiah's in that authenticity of word and life-style can be strong communicators of God's truths.

23:3 PRAYER, Commitment—This renewal of the covenant is a vow of commitment by the nation. Reading or hearing God's Word should lead to prayers of commitment.

23:4–20 SIN, Alienation—Reform and revival, no matter how enthusiastic and thoroughgoing, do not save a people forever. Reform must be more than a one-time act. It must be more than a government-led campaign. Reform must take root in the life of the people and become an ongoing mission. God's people must be constantly experiencing reform and revival.

when he saw the tombs that were there
on the hillside, he had the bones removed from them and burned on the altar to defile it, in accordance[r] with the
word of the LORD proclaimed by the man
of God who foretold these things.
17 The king asked, "What is that tomb-
stone I see?"
The men of the city said, "It marks the
tomb of the man of God who came from
Judah and pronounced against the altar of
Bethel the very things you have done to
it."
18 "Leave it alone," he said. "Don't let
anyone disturb his bones[s]." So they
spared his bones and those of the prophet[t] who had come from Samaria.
19 Just as he had done at Bethel, Josiah
removed and defiled all the shrines at the
high places that the kings of Israel had
built in the towns of Samaria that had
provoked the LORD to anger. 20 Josiah
slaughtered[u] all the priests of those high
places on the altars and burned human
bones[v] on them. Then he went back to
Jerusalem.
21 The king gave this order to all the
people: "Celebrate the Passover[w] to the
LORD your God, as it is written in this
Book of the Covenant."[x] 22 Not since the
days of the judges who led Israel, nor
throughout the days of the kings of Israel
and the kings of Judah, had any such Passover been observed. 23 But in the eighteenth year of King Josiah, this Passover
was celebrated to the LORD in Jerusalem.[y]
24 Furthermore, Josiah got rid of the
mediums and spiritists,[z] the household
gods,[a] the idols and all the other detestable[b] things seen in Judah and Jerusalem.
This he did to fulfill the requirements of
the law written in the book that Hilkiah
the priest had discovered in the temple of
the LORD. 25 Neither before nor after Josiah was there a king like him who
turned[c] to the LORD as he did—with all
his heart and with all his soul and with all
his strength, in accordance with all the
Law of Moses.[d]
26 Nevertheless, the LORD did not turn
away from the heat of his fierce anger,[e]
which burned against Judah because of all
that Manasseh[f] had done to provoke him
to anger. 27 So the LORD said, "I will remove[g] Judah also from my presence[h] as
I removed Israel, and I will reject[i] Jerusalem, the city I chose, and this temple,
about which I said, 'There shall my Name
be.'[m]"
28 As for the other events of Josiah's
reign, and all he did, are they not written
in the book of the annals of the kings of
Judah?
29 While Josiah was king, Pharaoh
Neco[j] king of Egypt went up to the Euphrates River to help the king of Assyria.
King Josiah marched out to meet him in
battle, but Neco faced him and killed him
at Megiddo.[k] 30 Josiah's servants brought
his body in a chariot[l] from Megiddo to
Jerusalem and buried him in his own
tomb. And the people of the land took
Jehoahaz son of Josiah and anointed him
and made him king in place of his father.

Jehoahaz King of Judah

23:31–34pp — 2Ch 36:2–4

31 Jehoahaz[m] was twenty-three years
old when he became king, and he reigned
in Jerusalem three months. His mother's
name was Hamutal[n] daughter of Jeremiah; she was from Libnah. 32 He did evil[o]
in the eyes of the LORD, just as his fathers
had done. 33 Pharaoh Neco put him in
chains at Riblah[p] in the land of Hamath[n][q] so that he might not reign in Jerusalem, and he imposed on Judah a levy
of a hundred talents[o] of silver and a talent[p] of gold. 34 Pharaoh Neco made Eliakim[r] son of Josiah king in place of his
father Josiah and changed Eliakim's name
to Jehoiakim. But he took Jehoahaz and
carried him off to Egypt, and there he
died.[s] 35 Jehoiakim paid Pharaoh Neco
the silver and gold he demanded. In order
to do so, he taxed the land and exacted
the silver and gold from the people of the
land according to their assessments.[t]

Jehoiakim King of Judah

23:36–24:6pp — 2Ch 36:5–8

36 Jehoiakim[u] was twenty-five years old
when he became king, and he reigned in
Jerusalem eleven years. His mother's
name was Zebidah daughter of Pedaiah;
she was from Rumah. 37 And he did evil[v]

23:16 [r]1Ki 13:32
23:18 [s]1Ki 13:31 [t]1Ki 13:29
23:20 [u]S Ex 22:20; S 2Ki 11:18 [v]S 1Ki 13:2
23:21 [w]S Ex 12:11; Dt 16:1-8 [x]S Ex 24:7
23:23 [y]S Ex 12:11; S Nu 28:16
23:24 [z]S Lev 19:31; S Dt 18:11 [a]S Ge 31:19 [b]Dt 7:26; 2Ki 16:3
23:25 [c]S 1Sa 7:3 [d]Jer 22:15
23:26 [e]2Ki 21:6; Jer 23:20; 30:24 [f]S 2Ki 21:12
23:27 [g]2Ki 21:13 [h]S Ex 33:15; 2Ki 24:3 [i]Jer 27:10; 32:31
23:29 [j]ver 33-35; Jer 46:2 [k]2Ki 9:27
23:30 [l]S 2Ki 9:28
23:31 [m]1Ch 3:15; Jer 22:11 [n]2Ki 24:18
23:32 [o]1Ki 15:26
23:33 [p]S Nu 34:11 [q]1Ki 8:65
23:34 [r]2Ki 24:6; 1Ch 3:15; 2Ch 36:5-8; Jer 1:3 [s]Jer 22:12
23:35 [t]Jer 2:16
23:36 [u]Jer 26:1
23:37 [v]1Ki 15:26

[m]*27* 1 Kings 8:29 [n]*33* Hebrew; Septuagint (see also 2 Chron. 36:3) *Neco at Riblah in Hamath removed him* [o]*33* That is, about 3 3/4 tons (about 3.4 metric tons) [p]*33* That is, about 75 pounds (about 34 kilograms)

23:19–20 CHRISTIAN ETHICS, Murder—See note on Jdg 8:10–21.

23:21–25 HOLY SCRIPTURE, Redemption—The discovery of the book of God's covenant led to a sweeping return to former religious practices by a king who was committed to God. The Word of God leads people to condemn sin and commit themselves to God. See note on 22:16–20.

23:26–27 HISTORY, Judgment—God remains true to His word. He carries out judgment He has announced. While Josiah's obedience spared him, it did not turn God away from His announced intention to punish His wicked people.

23:28 HOLY SCRIPTURE, Writing—See note on 1:16–18.

23:32 SIN, Transgression—See notes on 21:2–17; 1 Ki 14:22–24.

23:37 SIN, Transgression—See notes on 23:4–20; 1 Ki

in the eyes of the LORD, just as his fathers
had done.

Chapter 24

DURING Jehoiakim's reign, Nebuchadnezzar[w] king of Babylon invaded[x]
the land, and Jehoiakim became his vassal
for three years. But then he changed his
mind and rebelled[y] against Nebuchadnezzar. 2The LORD sent Babylonian,[q] [z]
Aramean,[a] Moabite and Ammonite raiders[b] against him. He sent them to destroy[c] Judah, in accordance with the
word of the LORD proclaimed by his servants the prophets.[d] 3Surely these things
happened to Judah according to the
LORD's command,[e] in order to remove
them from his presence[f] because of the
sins of Manasseh[g] and all he had done,
4including the shedding of innocent
blood.[h] For he had filled Jerusalem with
innocent blood, and the LORD was not
willing to forgive.[i]
5As for the other events of Jehoiakim's
reign,[j] and all he did, are they not written in the book of the annals of the kings
of Judah? 6Jehoiakim rested[k] with his fathers. And Jehoiachin[l] his son succeeded
him as king.
7The king of Egypt[m] did not march out
from his own country again, because the
king of Babylon[n] had taken all his territory, from the Wadi of Egypt to the Euphrates River.

Jehoiachin King of Judah

24:8–17pp — 2Ch 36:9–10

8Jehoiachin[o] was eighteen years old
when he became king, and he reigned in
Jerusalem three months. His mother's
name was Nehushta[p] daughter of Elnathan; she was from Jerusalem. 9He did
evil[q] in the eyes of the LORD, just as his
father had done.
10At that time the officers of Nebuchadnezzar[r] king of Babylon advanced on Jerusalem and laid siege to it, 11and Nebuchadnezzar himself came up to the city
while his officers were besieging it. 12Je-
hoiachin king of Judah, his mother, his
attendants, his nobles and his officials all
surrendered[s] to him.
In the eighth year of the reign of the
king of Babylon, he took Jehoiachin prisoner. 13As the LORD had declared,[t] Nebuchadnezzar removed all the treasures[u]
from the temple of the LORD and from the
royal palace, and took away all the gold
articles[v] that Solomon[w] king of Israel
had made for the temple of the LORD.
14He carried into exile[x] all Jerusalem: all
the officers and fighting men,[y] and all
the craftsmen and artisans—a total of ten
thousand. Only the poorest[z] people of
the land were left.
15Nebuchadnezzar took Jehoiachin[a]
captive to Babylon. He also took from Jerusalem to Babylon the king's mother,[b]
his wives, his officials and the leading
men[c] of the land. 16The king of Babylon
also deported to Babylon the entire force
of seven thousand fighting men, strong
and fit for war, and a thousand craftsmen
and artisans.[d] 17He made Mattaniah, Jehoiachin's uncle, king in his place and
changed his name to Zedekiah.[e]

Zedekiah King of Judah

24:18–20pp — 2Ch 36:11–16; Jer 52:1–3

18Zedekiah[f] was twenty-one years old
when he became king, and he reigned in
Jerusalem eleven years. His mother's
name was Hamutal[g] daughter of Jeremiah; she was from Libnah. 19He did evil[h]
in the eyes of the LORD, just as Jehoiakim
had done. 20It was because of the LORD's
anger that all this happened to Jerusalem
and Judah, and in the end he thrust[i]
them from his presence.[j]

24:1 [w]ver 10; 2Ki 25:11; Ezr 5:12; Jer 4:7; 25:1,9; 39:1; 40:1; 50:17; 52:15; Eze 32:2; Da 1:1; 7:4 [x]Jer 35:11 [y]S 2Ki 18:7 **24:2** [z]Jer 5:15; Hab 1:6 [a]Jer 35:11 [b]S 2Ki 5:2 [c]Isa 28:18-19 [d]Jer 12:7-9; 25:1; 26:1; 36:1; Eze 23:23; Da 1:2 **24:3** [e]S 2Ki 18:25 [f]2Ki 13:23 [g]S 1Ki 14:9; S 2Ki 21:12; Jer 15:4 **24:4** [h]S 2Ki 21:16; Jer 22:3 [i]S Ex 23:21; La 3:42 **24:5** [j]Jer 22:18-19 **24:6** [k]Jer 22:19; 36:30 [l]1Ch 3:16; Jer 22:24,28; Eze 19:1 **24:7** [m]S Ge 15:18; S 2Ki 18:21; S Jer 46:25 [n]Jer 1:14; 25:9; 46:24 **24:8** [o]1Ch 3:16; Jer 22:24; 37:1 [p]ver 15; Jer 13:18; 22:26; 29:2 **24:9** [q]1Ki 15:26 **24:10** [r]S ver 1 **24:12** [s]2Ki 25:27; Jer 13:18; 22:24-30; 24:1; 29:2 **24:13** [t]2Ki 20:17 [u]2Ki 25:15; Isa 39:6; 42:22 [v]2Ki 25:14; Ezr 1:7; Isa 39:6; Jer 15:13; 17:3; 20:5; 27:16; 28:3; Eze 7:21; Da 1:2; 5:2,23; Zep 1:13 [w]S 1Ki 7:51 **24:14** [x]S Dt 28:36; S 2Ch 36:20; S Mt 1:11 [y]Isa 3:1-3 [z]Dt 15:11; 2Ki 25:12; Job 5:16; Ps 9:18; Jer 40:7; 52:16 **24:15** [a]S 2Ki 20:18; Eze 19:9 [b]S ver 8; S 1Ki 2:19 [c]Est 2:6; Isa 39:7; La 2:9; Eze 1:2; 17:12-14; Da 1:3 **24:16** [d]Ezr 2:1; Jer 24:1 **24:17** [e]1Ch 3:15; 2Ch 36:11; Jer 1:3; 37:1; 52:1; Eze 17:13 **24:18** [f]1Ch 3:16; Jer 39:1 [g]2Ki 23:31 **24:19** [h]1Ki 15:26; Jer 37:2 **24:20** [i]Dt 4:26; 29:27 [j]S Ex 33:15; S 2Ki 13:23

[q]2 Or *Chaldean*

14:22–24.

24:1–4 SIN, Alienation—To be people of God is an activity as well as a calling. The prophets called Israel and Judah to act like people of God relating to Yahweh, the God of Israel, and to no other gods. Israel heard only that they were people of God. They never got the message to change their way of living. They finally received God's judgment. It surprised many of them. God's judgment usually surprises a people alienated from Him by their sin. People sin when they refuse to listen to all of God's Word, its threats as well as its promises. See note on 23:4–20.

24:1–4 CHRISTIAN ETHICS, War and Peace—Ironically, because of the moral decadence of the people of Judah, God used the same kind of judgment (war from an invading army) *as He did to deal with the Canaanites centuries earlier.* God does not play favorites. He exercises His wrath in the way He chooses to get rid of idolatry and lead people to worship Him only. See note on Jdg 1:1–36.

24:2,13 GOD, Faithfulness—God does what He says He will do. He brought the promised judgment upon His own people because of their continued unfaithfulness to Him. We can never presume upon God's blessings. We can expect His blessings only as we are faithful to Him. He is faithful to the point that He will not let us manipulate Him, use Him for our own purposes, or neglect our duties to Him.

24:2–3 HISTORY, Judgment—See note on 23:26–27.

24:5 HOLY SCRIPTURE, Writing—See note on 1:16–18.

24:8–17 SIN, Discipline—See notes on 23:4–20; 1 Ki 14:22–24.

24:8–17 HISTORY, Judgment—See note on 23:26–27.

24:19–20 SIN, Alienation—Sin's final consequence leads us out of God's presence into judgment. We find ourselves totally alienated from our Creator and Savior. See notes on 23:4–20; 24:1–4; 1 Ki 14:22–24.

24:20 GOD, Wrath—God's wrath comes when His loving will is repeatedly rejected and His gracious purposes are thwarted. See notes on 22:13–17; Jn 3:36.

The Fall of Jerusalem

25:1–12pp — Jer 39:1–10
25:1–21pp — 2Ch 36:17–20; Jer 52:4–27
25:22–26pp — Jer 40:7–9; 41:1–3, 16–18

Now Zedekiah rebelled against the
king of Babylon.

Chapter 25

SO in the ninth[k] year of Zedekiah's
reign, on the tenth day of the tenth
month, Nebuchadnezzar[l] king of Babylon marched against Jerusalem with his
whole army. He encamped outside the
city and built siege works[m] all around it.
2The city was kept under siege until the
eleventh year of King Zedekiah. 3By the
ninth day of the ⌊fourth⌋[r] month the famine[n] in the city had become so severe
that there was no food for the people to
eat. 4Then the city wall was broken
through,[o] and the whole army fled at
night through the gate between the two
walls near the king's garden, though the
Babylonians[s] were surrounding[p] the
city. They fled toward the Arabah,[t] 5but
the Babylonian[u] army pursued the king
and overtook him in the plains of Jericho.
All his soldiers were separated from him
and scattered,[q] 6and he was captured.[r]
He was taken to the king of Babylon at
Riblah,[s] where sentence was pronounced on him. 7They killed the sons of
Zedekiah before his eyes. Then they put
out his eyes, bound him with bronze
shackles and took him to Babylon.[t]
8On the seventh day of the fifth month,
in the nineteenth year of Nebuchadnezzar king of Babylon, Nebuzaradan commander of the imperial guard, an official
of the king of Babylon, came to Jerusalem.
9He set fire[u] to the temple of the LORD,
the royal palace and all the houses of Jerusalem. Every important building he
burned down.[v] 10The whole Babylonian
army, under the commander of the imperial guard, broke down the walls[w] around
Jerusalem. 11Nebuzaradan the commander of the guard carried into exile[x] the
people who remained in the city, along
with the rest of the populace and those
who had gone over to the king of Babylon.[y] 12But the commander left behind
some of the poorest people[z] of the land
to work the vineyards and fields.
13The Babylonians broke[a] up the
bronze pillars, the movable stands and
the bronze Sea that were at the temple of
the LORD and they carried the bronze to
Babylon. 14They also took away the pots,
shovels, wick trimmers, dishes[b] and all
the bronze articles[c] used in the temple
service. 15The commander of the imperial
guard took away the censers and sprinkling bowls—all that were made of pure
gold or silver.[d]
16The bronze from the two pillars, the
Sea and the movable stands, which Solomon had made for the temple of the
LORD, was more than could be weighed.
17Each pillar[e] was twenty-seven feet[v]
high. The bronze capital on top of one
pillar was four and a half feet[w] high and
was decorated with a network and pomegranates of bronze all around. The other
pillar, with its network, was similar.
18The commander of the guard took as
prisoners Seraiah[f] the chief priest, Zephaniah[g] the priest next in rank and the
three doorkeepers.[h] 19Of those still in
the city, he took the officer in charge of
the fighting men and five royal advisers.
He also took the secretary who was chief
officer in charge of conscripting the people of the land and sixty of his men who
were found in the city. 20Nebuzaradan
the commander took them all and
brought them to the king of Babylon at
Riblah. 21There at Riblah,[i] in the land of
Hamath, the king had them executed.[j]
So Judah went into captivity,[k] away
from her land.[l]
22Nebuchadnezzar king of Babylon appointed Gedaliah[m] son of Ahikam,[n] the
son of Shaphan, to be over the people he
had left behind in Judah. 23When all the
army officers and their men heard that
the king of Babylon had appointed Gedali-

25:1 [k]Jer 32:1 [l]Jer 21:2; 34:1-7 [m]Isa 23:13; 29:3; Jer 4:16-17; 32:2; 33:4; Eze 21:22; 24:2
25:3 [n]S Lev 26:26; Isa 22:2; Jer 14:18; 37:21; La 2:20; 4:9
25:4 [o]Job 30:14; Ps 144:14; Jer 50:15; 51:44, 58; Eze 33:21 [p]Jer 4:17; 6:3
25:5 [q]S Lev 26:36; Eze 12:14; 17:21
25:6 [r]Isa 22:3; Jer 38:23 [s]S Nu 34:11
25:7 [t]S Dt 28:36; Jer 21:7; 32:4-5; 34:3,21; Eze 12:11; 19:9; 40:1
25:9 [u]Isa 60:7; 63:15,18; 64:11 [v]S Dt 13:16; Ne 1:3; Ps 74:3-8; 79:1; Jer 2:15; 17:27; 21:10; 26:6, 18; La 4:11; Am 2:5; Mic 3:12
25:10 [w]Ne 1:3; Jer 50:15
25:11 [x]S Lev 26:44; 2Ki 24:14 [y]S Dt 28:36; S 2Ki 24:1
25:12 [z]S 2Ki 24:14
25:13 [a]S 1Ki 7:50
25:14 [b]S Nu 7:14 [c]S 2Ki 24:13; Ezr 1:7
25:15 [d]S 2Ki 24:13; Jer 15:13; 20:5; 27:16-22
25:17 [e]1Ki 7:15-22
25:18 [f]ver 18-21; 1Ch 6:14; Ezr 7:1; Ne 11:11 [g]Jer 21:1; 29:25; 37:3 [h]S 2Ki 12:9; S 23:4
25:21 [i]S Nu 34:11 [j]Jer 34:21 [k]S 1Ki 8:46 [l]S Ge 12:7; S Jos 23:13
25:22 [m]Jer 39:14; 40:5,7; 41:18 [n]S 2Ki 22:12

[r]*3* See Jer. 52:6. [s]*4* Or *Chaldeans*; also in verses 13, 25 and 26 [t]*4* Or *the Jordan Valley* [u]*5* Or *Chaldean*; also in verses 10 and 24 [v]*17* Hebrew *eighteen cubits* (about 8.1 meters) [w]*17* Hebrew *three cubits* (about 1.3 meters)

25:1–21 SIN, Discipline—The saddest page of the Old Testament reports that God intervened in the history of His people and destroyed His Temple, the symbol of His presence with His people. Judah refused to learn the lesson of Israel. They refused to listen to God's prophets. They refused to abandon political solutions to their problems for spiritual solutions (21:1–16). Yet they continued to expect Yahweh, the God of Israel, to intervene in history to save them. Instead He intervened to destroy them. See notes on 17:7–23; 24:1–4, 19–20.

25:1–21 CHRISTIAN ETHICS, War and Peace—Judah did not escape the fate that had befallen the Northern Kingdom of Israel decades before. Ethical erosion had become so dominant that God's judgment was inevitable. Thus, they passed into captivity as their northern neighbors had. God used the uncontrolled violence of a wicked nation to accomplish His purposes. This does not show God's approval of war and violence. It shows His sovereignty over human history and His ability to direct even the most horrible of human actions to achieve His purposes for His people.

25:21 HISTORY, Judgment—The biblical narrative describes Jerusalem's fall without mentioning God. Reading this chapter alone might give the impression Babylon's military and political might were the sole causes of Jerusalem's fall. The chapter must be read in context. Jerusalem fell as a result of God's anger, the prophets' words, and the people's sin. See note on 23:26–27.

ah as governor, they came to Gedaliah at
Mizpah—Ishmael son of Nethaniah, Johanan son of Kareah, Seraiah son of Tanhumeth the Netophathite, Jaazaniah the son of the Maacathite, and their men.
24Gedaliah took an oath to reassure them and their men. "Do not be afraid of the Babylonian officials," he said. "Settle down in the land and serve the king of Babylon, and it will go well with you."
25In the seventh month, however, Ishmael son of Nethaniah, the son of Elishama, who was of royal blood, came with ten men and assassinated[o] Gedaliah and also the men of Judah and the Babylonians who were with him at Mizpah.[p] 26At
this, all the people from the least to the greatest, together with the army officers, fled to Egypt[q] for fear of the Babylonians.

25:25 [o]S 2Ki 12:20 [p]Zec 7:5
25:26 [q]Isa 30:2; Jer 43:7
25:27 [r]S 2Ki 24:12
25:28 [s]S 1Ki 8:50 [t]Ezr 5:5; 7:6,28; 9:9; Ne 2:1; Da 2:48
25:29 [u]S 2Sa 9:7
25:30 [v]Ge 43:34; Est 2:9; 9:22; Jer 28:4

Jehoiachin Released

25:27–30pp — Jer 52:31–34

27In the thirty-seventh year of the exile of Jehoiachin king of Judah, in the year Evil-Merodach[x] became king of Babylon, he released Jehoiachin[r] from prison on the twenty-seventh day of the twelfth month. 28He spoke kindly[s] to him and gave him a seat of honor[t] higher than those of the other kings who were with him in Babylon. 29So Jehoiachin put aside his prison clothes and for the rest of his life ate regularly at the king's table.[u]
30Day by day the king gave Jehoiachin a regular allowance as long as he lived.[v]

[x]27 Also called *Amel-Marduk*

25:24–30 HISTORY, Hope—Gedaliah echoed the message of Jeremiah (Jer 21:1–14; 24:1—25:14; 38:1–23). Judah's political hopes had vanished for the present. Hope lay in Babylon with the exiled community and in Judah with those ready to wait patiently and serve Babylon. Gedaliah paid for his "treasonous" loyalty to God with his life. History proved Gedaliah and Jeremiah right. The first sign of hope came when exiled king Jehoiachin received kindness and release in Babylon. On this faint note of hope the Books of Kings end. This was not the end for God's work in history. He continued working out His missionary, election purposes with an exiled and restored people even without restoring their political power. Thus He showed true hope lies in His historical direction not in human political systems.

1 Chronicles

Theological Setting

Does God forgive His people and restore them to usefulness? Writing in neither the best of times nor the worst of times for the Jews, the Chronicler sought to give hope to a people returning from exile and punishment. Adrift in a sea of transition, they were tempted to doubt God's promises and be disillusioned over past failures. They had gone from the military might of David and the material splendor of Solomon to the humiliation of the Babylonian captivity (586-538 BC). See introductions to Zephaniah, Haggai. Return from Exile and renewal of the Temple, marvelous as they were, had not fulfilled expectations of a renewed Israelite kingdom with a messianic ruler from the line of David. Thus the Jéws needed to understand their roots and hear a reaffirmation of God's covenant promise to Israel.

The setting of transition, unfulfilled hopes, and uncertainty presented several options for the people.

1. They could settle down to routine life and go through religious routines for Israel's God, Persia's gods, and the traditional Canaanite gods of Palestine. In so doing religion would be another means of seeking security in an insecure world without having real hope or expectations of change.

2. They could develop a religion of legalism in which they attempted to earn God's favor and demand His blessings because of their righteousness.

3. They could give up on God and surrender to the religions of the victors in battle, worshiping Persian gods and accommodating themselves to the Persian life-style and political demands.

4. They could develop cult-like sects of the religious pure, separating themselves from normal life-styles to form an isolated religious community undefiled by the world and waiting for God to act.

5. They could develop intricate apocalyptic theology, determining precisely God's times and expecting God's imminent apocalyptic actions to bring in the day of the Lord.

6. They could study the history of their people, learn anew the lessons of their decline as a nation and as a faithful people, and renew their commitment to covenant worship and obedience.

Chronicles was written to call Israel back to its covenant commitments. The author wrote not from the perspective of bitterness but from brokenness and from faith in God's continuing purpose for His people. The Chronicler depicts the ongoing plan of grace and redemption from Adam to the post-Exilic community. He wanted fifth-century Jews to see themselves as the true Israel of God. He emphasized the place of the Temple, true worship, and the continual validity of the promises to the Davidic line. The apostate Northern Kingdom could be excluded from the discussion because of its poor example (2 Ch 10:19). Chronicles thus used history to teach Israel the lesson of history and their own past failures. God will not tolerate disobedience even from the chosen people. He will hear the prayer of penitence, for His final word is one of grace and mercy.

Theological Outline

1 Chronicles: History Reminds Us of God's Holy and Gracious Work in the Lives of His People.

I. God Works Throughout History in the Lives of His People to Provide Continuity and to Fulfill His Ongoing Purpose of Redemption Through the Messiah. (1:1—9:44)

II. God Works Through His People During a Time of Unity. (10:1—29:30)

   A. God punishes an appointed leader who disobeys divine commands, involves himself in the occult, and refuses to pray. (10:1-14)

   B. God establishes His redemptive plan through His obedient leader. (11:1—29:30)

      1. God's leader must be recognized and received by His people. (11:1-3)
      2. God's presence and power give victory and greatness to His leader. (11:4-9)
      3. God uses and honors persons with courage, loyalty, faithfulness, skill, and perseverance. (11:10—12:22)
      4. God's people follow His leader and obey His commands. (12:23-40)
      5. God's people sometimes seek to achieve the right goals with wrong methods. (13:1-8)

6. God strictly and swiftly judges disobedience. (13:9-10)
7. God's leader may react wrongly to God's ways. (13:11-14)
8. God's leader gains assurance of God's election through success in all areas of life. (14:1-17)
9. God's leader follows God's commands and provides proper worship leaders and places for God's people. (15:1-29)
10. God's appointed leaders are to thank Him, call on His name, proclaim His deeds, sing praises to Him, seek Him, and maintain proper worship practices. (16:1-43)
11. God's leader must follow God's directions in preparing for a worship place, for God has eternal purposes to work through the Davidic line. (17:1-27)
12. God's leader reveals a godly heart by selflessly dedicating material things to the Lord. (18:1-13)
13. God's leader administers justice, righteousness, and kindness for all. (18:14—19:2)
14. God's leader may act in kindness and justice but be misunderstood by evil people. (19:3-5)
15. Aggressors may force God's people to protect themselves and their nation. (19:6—20:8)
16. God deals righteously with sin in the life of His leader through holy judgment, merciful forgiveness, and gracious restitution. (21:1-30)
17. God's leader learns God's way even in judgment and prepares the successor God elects to realize the leader's dreams. (22:1—23:1)
18. God's leader organizes worship leaders to praise Him in a variety of ways. (23:2—26:32)
19. God's leader manages military and civil leaders. (27:1-34)
20. God's leader brings the people to commit themselves to God. (28:1-8)
21. God's leader directs the successor God elects to acknowledge and serve God willingly by completing the work still unfinished. (28:9-21)
22. God's people contribute willingly, abundantly, and joyfully to His work. (29:1-9)
23. God's leader humbly recognizes the divine source of all human gifts and leads the people in worship. (29:10-21)
24. God's leader enjoys honor and long life. (29:22-30)

Theological Conclusions

1 and 2 Chronicles provided renewed identity for God's people in transition by reminding them of God's holy and gracious work in the lives of His leaders. Renewed identity is based on five doctrines:

(1) the nature of God;
(2) the necessity of covenant commitment by His people;
(3) the importance of worship;
(4) the imperative of godly leadership; and
(5) the redemptive plan God is working through His people.

God controls all greatness, power, glory, and victory, ruling above all and through all the events of history (1 Ch 29:10-12; compare 2 Ch 20:6). All idols are an abomination to Him and must be ruthlessly put away (2 Ch 34:2-5). He can move the heart of even the most powerful unbelieving ruler to accomplish His purpose (2 Ch 36:22). He can restore His people to prominence and fulfill His divine purpose for them. Such restoration may not come as soon as some people expect, but memories of God's victories based on His people's praise and obedience (2 Ch 20:22-29) should give confidence in God's ability to do what His prophets promised.

Hope based on God's power does not relieve a generation of responsibility. God is a holy God, so holy He could not allow even His first choice as king to rebel continually without rejection (1 Ch 10:13). He could not allow priests intent on returning the holy ark to handle it in the wrong fashion without extreme discipline (13:9-10). Because He is holy, God punishes sin and demands righteousness. At the same time, He is merciful and forgiving (2 Ch 7:14; 30:9). Accordingly, Rehoboam (2 Ch 12:5-8) and Manasseh (1 Ch 33:10-13) were forgiven after their sincere repentance. His love (Hebrew *chesed*) is everlasting (2 Ch 20:21).

God's people are called to respond to the holy yet loving God in covenant commitment. The Chronicler emphasized the importance of seeking God with a whole heart (1 Ch 28:8-9; 1 Ch 28:20; 2 Ch 34:31). Seeking God involves commitment to His covenant. God's covenant promises have not been annulled despite the centuries of unfaithfulness to the covenant by His people. The call is not to shame and despair for opportunities lost but to hope, remembrance, and renewal through humble commitment (16:15; 2 Ch 7:14). Sin is not the end of the road for God's people, but an occasion for confession and renewal of covenant vows (2 Ch 15:12; 29:10).

Covenant renewal led to devotion to covenant worship. The Temple, its personnel, and its worship occupy center stage through much of Chronicles. Sincerity is always more important, however, than proper ritual. In emergencies Levites could assume priestly functions (2 Ch 29:34). Laypersons who had not been ceremonially cleansed might observe the Passover (2 Ch 30:18). Worship moved beyond the precincts of the Temple to the field of battle (2 Ch 20:21-22). Worship was thus a way of life as well as specific ceremonies in the Temple.

Still, the worship place was important. The Lord manifested His glory and presence in the ark and later in the Temple resulting in praise and thanksgiving (1 Ch 13:3; 15:1-14; 15:25—16:36). Much of 1 Chronicles thus centers on David's elaborate and careful planning and preparation for the Temple along with the people's willing cooperation in its building (22:1—26:32; 28:1—29:20). Building the Temple represented giving to God what He had given the people (29:16).

The purpose of worship was to bring praise and thanksgiving to God. Some of the greatest prayers of praise and thanksgiving are found in Chronicles (16:8-36; 29:10-20; 2 Ch 5:13-14; 6:4-11,14-42). Worship is not for priests and kings alone but for all people (29:20). Kings were assessed according to their treatment of and loyalty to God's Temple. Their loyalty greatly influenced that of the people.

This made godly leadership imperative. During the post Exilic period the high priest tended to usurp the functions formerly reserved for the king. The Chronicler paid little attention to the high priest except in the execution of specific rituals and important historical acts (2 Ch 23:1—24:19; 26:16-21). Emphasis on the king's role in maintaining proper worship may reflect the Chronicler's skillful way of maintaining hopes in God's Messiah, a new David, without specifically stating such politically explosive doctrine.

God's leaders are to model sincere obedience and faithful worship, calling the people to covenant commitment. Their role as forerunners of the King of kings was so essential that the Chronicler did not want to besmirch that reputation by mentioning the well-known sins of David and Solomon. The son of David held the kingdom of the Lord in his hands (2 Ch 13:8). The king ruled for the Lord (2 Ch 9:8), who was still the true King.

Leadership was not placed wholly in the hands of one person. The king exercised great spiritual leadership, but he was not allowed to proudly usurp the role of God's priests (2 Ch 19:8-11; 26:16-21). Lesser priests also played important roles as worship leaders. The Chronicler focused special attention on Levites (1 Ch 9:14-34; 13:2; 15:2-27; 16:4; 23:2—24:31; 26:17,20; 27:17; 28:13-21; 2 Ch 5:4-12; 7:6; 8:14-15; 11:13-14; 13:9-10; 17:8; 19:8,11; 20:19; 23:2—24:11; 29:4—31:19; 34:9—35:18). Worship thus required strong leadership from many of God's chosen leaders. No one person could claim credit for the Temple worship.

Worship was possible because of God's redemptive plan for His people. Chronicles reviewed history to show that every event, even the darkest days of the tragedy of Exile were in God's plan. God revealed His person and plan through His chosen people, the Jews. The Jews were to be a faithful nucleus, not an exclusive clique. God's eternal plan to use Israel as His instrument of blessing remained in force. Isolation and separation from the world were not God's directions. He sought a newly committed people through whom He could continue to work out His plan of world redemption.

Contemporary Teaching

Chronicles reminds us of God's holy and gracious work among His people. God can use Chronicles to give new identity to modern Christians as He gave identity to the Jews in transition from Exile.

God calls us to understand His true nature. We must not confine God to our limited concepts or attempt to confine His power to our limited goals. We should look for His continued working in human affairs and cooperate with Him as He continues to carry out His plan of redemption. Seeing Him in His holiness, we can repent of our sins to receive His mercy. God still wants to bring revival to His people. He calls us to covenant commitment so we can see the continued fulfillment of His covenant promises.

The Temple as a building is gone. The need for worship is not. The physical bodies of Christians are now the temples of the Holy Spirit. We need to commit ourselves to moral purity and holy worship. We need to regain the sense of praise and thanksgiving in all elements of life. We need to revitalize those special occasions of worship in God's house. His miracles are not just past history. He is still working in His people. Believing prayer brings victory and true success in life.

God uniquely uses available and surrendered leaders to model His holiness and to call His people to covenant commitment. Leaders should know the history of God's people, as did the Chronicler, and teach its lessons to His people. God is working through His people continually. All of His saints are important to His plan. Every believer is called to pass on from generation to generation the good news of God's redemption.

Chapter 1

Historical Records From Adam to Abraham

To Noah's Sons

ADAM,[a] Seth, Enosh, 2Kenan,[b] Mahalalel,[c] Jared,[d] 3Enoch,[e] Methuselah,[f] Lamech,[g] Noah.[h]

4The sons of Noah:[a] [i]
Shem, Ham and Japheth.[j]

The Japhethites

1:5–7pp — Ge 10:2–5

5The sons[b] of Japheth:
Gomer, Magog, Madai, Javan, Tubal, Meshech and Tiras.
6The sons of Gomer:
Ashkenaz, Riphath[c] and Togarmah.
7The sons of Javan:
Elishah, Tarshish, the Kittim and the Rodanim.

The Hamites

1:8–16pp — Ge 10:6–20

8The sons of Ham:
Cush, Mizraim,[d] Put and Canaan.
9The sons of Cush:
Seba, Havilah, Sabta, Raamah and Sabteca.
The sons of Raamah:
Sheba and Dedan.
10Cush was the father[e] of
Nimrod, who grew to be a mighty warrior on earth.
11Mizraim was the father of
the Ludites, Anamites, Lehabites, Naphtuhites, 12Pathrusites, Casluhites (from whom the Philistines came) and Caphtorites.
13Canaan was the father of
Sidon his firstborn,[f] and of the Hittites, 14Jebusites, Amorites, Girgashites, 15Hivites, Arkites, Sinites, 16Arvadites, Zemarites and Hamathites.

The Semites

1:17–23pp — Ge 10:21–31; 11:10–27

17The sons of Shem:
Elam, Asshur, Arphaxad, Lud and Aram.
The sons of Aram[g]:
Uz, Hul, Gether and Meshech.
18Arphaxad was the father of Shelah, and Shelah the father of Eber.
19Two sons were born to Eber:
One was named Peleg,[h] because in his time the earth was divided; his brother was named Joktan.
20Joktan was the father of
Almodad, Sheleph, Hazarmaveth, Jerah, 21Hadoram, Uzal, Diklah, 22Obal,[i] Abimael, Sheba, 23Ophir, Havilah and Jobab. All these were sons of Joktan.

24Shem,[k] Arphaxad,[l] Shelah,
25Eber, Peleg, Reu,
26Serug, Nahor, Terah
27and Abram (that is, Abraham).

The Family of Abraham

28The sons of Abraham:
Isaac and Ishmael.

Descendants of Hagar

1:29–31pp — Ge 25:12–16

29These were their descendants:
Nebaioth the firstborn of Ishmael, Kedar, Adbeel, Mibsam, 30Mishma, Dumah, Massa, Hadad, Tema, 31Jetur, Naphish and Kedemah. These were the sons of Ishmael.

Descendants of Keturah

1:32–33pp — Ge 25:1–4

32The sons born to Keturah, Abraham's concubine:[l]

1:1 [a]Ge 5:1-32; Lk 3:36-38
1:2 [b]S Ge 5:9 [c]S Ge 5:12 [d]S Ge 5:15
1:3 [e]S Ge 5:18; Jude 1:14 [f]S Ge 5:21 [g]S Ge 5:25 [h]S Ge 5:29
1:4 [i]Ge 6:10; 10:1 [j]S Ge 5:32
1:24 [k]S Ge 10:21-25; Lk 3:34-36
1:32 [l]S Ge 22:24

[a]4 Septuagint; Hebrew does not have *The sons of Noah:* [b]5 *Sons* may mean *descendants* or *successors* or *nations;* also in verses 6-10, 17 and 20. [c]6 Many Hebrew manuscripts and Vulgate (see also Septuagint and Gen. 10:3); most Hebrew manuscripts *Diphath* [d]8 That is, Egypt; also in verse 11 [e]10 *Father* may mean *ancestor* or *predecessor* or *founder;* also in verses 11, 13, 18 and 20. [f]13 Or *of the Sidonians, the foremost* [g]17 One Hebrew manuscript and some Septuagint manuscripts (see also Gen. 10:23); most Hebrew manuscripts do not have this line. [h]19 *Peleg* means *division.* [i]22 Some Hebrew manuscripts and Syriac (see also Gen. 10:28); most Hebrew manuscripts *Ebal* [j]24 Hebrew; some Septuagint manuscripts *Arphaxad, Cainan* (see also note at Gen. 11:10)

1:1–54 HUMANITY, Relationships—Our identity comes in large measure from our roots. As humans, we understand ourselves as being like our family, our ancestors. This is not the totality of our identity. Biological genes do not imprison us. God's Spirit can give new motivation, new life, new birth. We can change our ways of living. Still family history shows us much about ourselves. It opens our world so we may see that ultimately we are kin to all people and have no claim to superiority over any other human. God's purposes have always been formed in a universal framework. So should ours.

1:1—2:17 HISTORY, Linear—Chronicles begins with a seemingly endless list of names. The list sets Israel in a universal context. It shows that all history is important to and directed by God. Significant history, even the history of salvation, is not limited to Israel's history. History began long before Israel or their patriarchs entered the scene. The implication is that history will continue leading to God's goals even though God's people have lost political power and identity. The Bible is thus interested in the long expanse of all universal history and the goal to which God is leading. No one group of people nor one small span of history can claim to be the center of interest for God. To understand history we must view the whole scope of God's activities from Adam to the end of history.

Zimran, Jokshan, Medan, Midian,
Ishbak and Shuah.
The sons of Jokshan:
Sheba and Dedan.[m]
33The sons of Midian:
Ephah, Epher, Hanoch, Abida and
Eldaah.
All these were descendants of Keturah.

Descendants of Sarah

1:35–37pp — Ge 36:10–14

34Abraham[n] was the father of Isaac.[o]
The sons of Isaac:
Esau and Israel.[p]

Esau's Sons

35The sons of Esau:[q]
Eliphaz, Reuel,[r] Jeush, Jalam and
Korah.
36The sons of Eliphaz:
Teman, Omar, Zepho,[k] Gatam
and Kenaz;
by Timna: Amalek.[l] [s]
37The sons of Reuel:[t]
Nahath, Zerah, Shammah and
Mizzah.

The People of Seir in Edom

1:38–42pp — Ge 36:20–28

38The sons of Seir:
Lotan, Shobal, Zibeon, Anah, Dishon, Ezer and Dishan.
39The sons of Lotan:
Hori and Homam. Timna was Lotan's sister.
40The sons of Shobal:
Alvan,[m] Manahath, Ebal, Shepho
and Onam.
The sons of Zibeon:
Aiah and Anah.[u]
41The son of Anah:
Dishon.
The sons of Dishon:
Hemdan,[n] Eshban, Ithran and Keran.
42The sons of Ezer:
Bilhan, Zaavan and Akan.[o]
The sons of Dishan[p]:
Uz and Aran.

The Rulers of Edom

1:43–54pp — Ge 36:31–43

43These were the kings who reigned
in Edom before any Israelite king
reigned[q]:
Bela son of Beor, whose city was
named Dinhabah.
44When Bela died, Jobab son of Zerah
from Bozrah succeeded him as
king.
45When Jobab died, Husham from the
land of the Temanites[v] succeeded
him as king.
46When Husham died, Hadad son of
Bedad, who defeated Midian in
the country of Moab, succeeded
him as king. His city was named
Avith.
47When Hadad died, Samlah from
Masrekah succeeded him as king.
48When Samlah died, Shaul from Rehoboth on the river[r] succeeded
him as king.
49When Shaul died, Baal-Hanan son of
Acbor succeeded him as king.
50When Baal-Hanan died, Hadad succeeded him as king. His city was
named Pau,[s] and his wife's name
was Mehetabel daughter of Matred, the daughter of Me-Zahab.
51Hadad also died.

The chiefs of Edom were:
Timna, Alvah, Jetheth, 52Oholibamah, Elah, Pinon, 53Kenaz, Teman, Mibzar, 54Magdiel and Iram.
These were the chiefs of Edom.

Chapter 2

Israel's Sons

2:1–2pp — Ge 35:23–26

THESE were the sons of Israel:
Reuben, Simeon, Levi, Judah, Issachar, Zebulun, 2Dan, Joseph,
Benjamin, Naphtali, Gad and
Asher.

Judah

2:5–15pp — Ru 4:18–22; Mt 1:3–6

To Hezron's Sons

3The sons of Judah:[w]
Er, Onan and Shelah.[x] These
three were born to him by a Canaanite woman, the daughter of
Shua.[y] Er, Judah's firstborn, was
wicked in the LORD's sight; so the
LORD put him to death.[z] 4Tamar,[a] Judah's daughter-in-law,[b]
bore him Perez[c] and Zerah. Judah had five sons in all.
5The sons of Perez:[d]

1:32 [m]S Ge 10:7
1:34 [n]Lk 3:34 [o]Mt 1:2; Ac 7:8 [p]S Ge 17:5
1:35 [q]Ge 36:19 [r]S Ge 36:4
1:36 [s]S Ex 17:14
1:37 [t]Ge 36:17
1:40 [u]S Ge 36:2
1:45 [v]S Ge 36:11
2:3 [w]S Ge 29:35; 38:2-10 [x]S Ge 38:5 [y]S Ge 38:2 [z]S Nu 26:19
2:4 [a]Ge 38:11-30 [b]S Ge 11:31 [c]S Ge 38:29
2:5 [d]S Ge 46:12

[k]*36* Many Hebrew manuscripts, some Septuagint manuscripts and Syriac (see also Gen. 36:11); most Hebrew manuscripts *Zephi* [l]*36* Some Septuagint manuscripts (see also Gen. 36:12); Hebrew *Gatam, Kenaz, Timna and Amalek* [m]*40* Many Hebrew manuscripts and some Septuagint manuscripts (see also Gen. 36:23); most Hebrew manuscripts *Alian* [n]*41* Many Hebrew manuscripts and some Septuagint manuscripts (see also Gen. 36:26); most Hebrew manuscripts *Hamran* [o]*42* Many Hebrew and Septuagint manuscripts (see also Gen. 36:27); most Hebrew manuscripts *Zaavan, Jaakan* [p]*42* Hebrew *Dishon,* a variant of *Dishan* [q]*43* Or *before an Israelite king reigned over them* [r]*48* Possibly the Euphrates [s]*50* Many Hebrew manuscripts, some Septuagint manuscripts, Vulgate and Syriac (see also Gen. 36:39); most Hebrew manuscripts *Pai*

Hezron[e] and Hamul.
6The sons of Zerah:
Zimri, Ethan, Heman, Calcol and
Darda[t]—five in all.
7The son of Carmi:
Achar,[u f] who brought trouble on
Israel by violating the ban on tak-
ing devoted things.[v g]
8The son of Ethan:
Azariah.
9The sons born to Hezron[h] were:
Jerahmeel, Ram and Caleb.[w]

From Ram Son of Hezron

10Ram[i] was the father of
Amminadab[j], and Amminadab
the father of Nahshon,[k] the leader of the people of Judah. 11Nah-
shon was the father of Salmon,[x]
Salmon the father of Boaz,
12Boaz[l] the father of Obed and
Obed the father of Jesse.[m]
13Jesse[n] was the father of
Eliab[o] his firstborn; the second
son was Abinadab, the third Shimea, 14the fourth Nethanel, the fifth
Raddai, 15the sixth Ozem and the
seventh David. 16Their sisters
were Zeruiah[p] and Abigail. Zeruiah's[q] three sons were Abishai,
Joab[r] and Asahel. 17Abigail was
the mother of Amasa,[s] whose father was Jether the Ishmaelite.

Caleb Son of Hezron

18Caleb son of Hezron had children by
his wife Azubah (and by Jerioth).
These were her sons: Jesher, Shobab and Ardon. 19When Azubah
died, Caleb[t] married Ephrath,
who bore him Hur. 20Hur was the
father of Uri, and Uri the father of
Bezalel.[u]
21Later, Hezron lay with the daughter
of Makir the father of Gilead[v] (he
had married her when he was sixty years old), and she bore him
Segub. 22Segub was the father of
Jair, who controlled twenty-three
towns in Gilead. 23(But Geshur
and Aram captured Havvoth
Jair,[y w] as well as Kenath[x] with
its surrounding settlements—sixty towns.) All these were descendants of Makir the father of Gilead.
24After Hezron died in Caleb Ephrathah, Abijah the wife of Hezron
bore him Ashhur[y] the father[z] of
Tekoa.

Jerahmeel Son of Hezron

25The sons of Jerahmeel the firstborn
of Hezron:
Ram his firstborn, Bunah, Oren,
Ozem and[a] Ahijah. 26Jerahmeel
had another wife, whose name
was Atarah; she was the mother
of Onam.
27The sons of Ram the firstborn of Jerahmeel:
Maaz, Jamin and Eker.
28The sons of Onam:
Shammai and Jada.
The sons of Shammai:
Nadab and Abishur.
29Abishur's wife was named Abihail,
who bore him Ahban and Molid.
30The sons of Nadab:
Seled and Appaim. Seled died
without children.
31The son of Appaim:
Ishi, who was the father of Sheshan.
Sheshan was the father of Ahlai.
32The sons of Jada, Shammai's brother:
Jether and Jonathan. Jether died
without children.
33The sons of Jonathan:
Peleth and Zaza.
These were the descendants of Jerahmeel.
34Sheshan had no sons—only daughters.
He had an Egyptian servant
named Jarha. 35Sheshan gave his
daughter in marriage to his servant Jarha, and she bore him Attai.
36Attai was the father of Nathan,
Nathan the father of Zabad,[z]
37Zabad the father of Ephlal,
Ephlal the father of Obed,
38Obed the father of Jehu,
Jehu the father of Azariah,
39Azariah the father of Helez,
Helez the father of Eleasah,
40Eleasah the father of Sismai,
Sismai the father of Shallum,
41Shallum the father of Jekamiah,
and Jekamiah the father of Elishama.

The Clans of Caleb

42The sons of Caleb[a] the brother of
Jerahmeel:
Mesha his firstborn, who was the

2:5 [e]Nu 26:21
2:7 [f]S Jos 7:1 [g]S Jos 6:18
2:9 [h]S Nu 26:21
2:10 [i]Lk 3:32-33 [j]S Ex 6:23 [k]S Nu 1:7
2:12 [l]S Ru 2:1 [m]S Ru 4:17
2:13 [n]S Ru 4:17 [o]S 1Sa 16:6
2:16 [p]1Sa 26:6 [q]2Sa 2:18 [r]S 2Sa 2:13
2:17 [s]2Sa 17:25
2:19 [t]ver 42,50
2:20 [u]S Ex 31:2
2:21 [v]S Nu 27:1
2:23 [w]S Nu 32:41; Dt 3:14 [x]Nu 32:42
2:24 [y]1Ch 4:5
2:36 [z]1Ch 11:41
2:42 [a]S ver 19

[t]*6* Many Hebrew manuscripts, some Septuagint manuscripts and Syriac (see also 1 Kings 4:31); most Hebrew manuscripts *Dara* [u]*7 Achar* means *trouble*; *Achar* is called *Achan* in Joshua. [v]*7* The Hebrew term refers to the irrevocable giving over of things or persons to the LORD, often by totally destroying them. [w]*9* Hebrew *Kelubai*, a variant of *Caleb*
[x]*11* Septuagint (see also Ruth 4:21); Hebrew *Salma*
[y]*23* Or *captured the settlements of Jair* [z]*24 Father* may mean *civic leader* or *military leader*; also in verses 42, 45, 49-52 and possibly elsewhere. [a]*25* Or *Oren and Ozem, by*

father of Ziph, and his son Mareshah,[b] who was the father of Hebron.
43 The sons of Hebron:
Korah, Tappuah, Rekem and Shema. 44 Shema was the father of Raham, and Raham the father of Jor-
keam. Rekem was the father of
Shammai. 45 The son of Shammai
was Maon[b], and Maon was the
father of Beth Zur.[c]
46 Caleb's concubine Ephah was the
mother of Haran, Moza and Ga-
zez. Haran was the father of Ga-
zez.
47 The sons of Jahdai:
Regem, Jotham, Geshan, Pelet,
Ephah and Shaaph.
48 Caleb's concubine Maacah was the
mother of Sheber and Tirhanah.
49 She also gave birth to Shaaph
the father of Madmannah[d] and to
Sheva the father of Macbenah and
Gibea. Caleb's daughter was Acsah.[e] 50 These were the descendants of Caleb.
The sons of Hur[f] the firstborn of
Ephrathah:
Shobal the father of Kiriath Jearim,[g] 51 Salma the father of Bethlehem, and Hareph the father of
Beth Gader.
52 The descendants of Shobal the father
of Kiriath Jearim were:
Haroeh, half the Manahathites,
53 and the clans of Kiriath Jearim:
the Ithrites,[h] Puthites, Shumath-
ites and Mishraites. From these
descended the Zorathites and Esh-
taolites.
54 The descendants of Salma:
Bethlehem, the Netophathites,[i]
Atroth Beth Joab, half the Manahathites, the Zorites, 55 and the
clans of scribes[c] who lived at Jabez: the Tirathites, Shimeathites
and Sucathites. These are the Kenites[j] who came from Hammath,[k] the father of the house of
Recab.[d] [l]

Chapter 3

The Sons of David

3:1–4pp — 2Sa 3:2–5
3:5–8pp — 2Sa 5:14–16; 1Ch 14:4–7

THESE were the sons of David[m] born to
him in Hebron:
The firstborn was Amnon the son
of Ahinoam[n] of Jezreel;[o]
the second, Daniel the son of Abigail[p] of Carmel;
2 the third, Absalom the son of Maacah daughter of Talmai king of
Geshur;
the fourth, Adonijah[q] the son of
Haggith;
3 the fifth, Shephatiah the son of
Abital;
and the sixth, Ithream, by his wife
Eglah.
4 These six were born to David in
Hebron,[r] where he reigned sev-
en years and six months.[s]
David reigned in Jerusalem thirty-three
years, 5 and these were the children born
to him there:
Shammua,[e] Shobab, Nathan and
Solomon. These four were by
Bathsheba[f] [t] daughter of Ammiel. 6 There were also Ibhar, Eli-
shua,[g] Eliphelet, 7 Nogah, Nepheg, Japhia, 8 Elishama, Eliada
and Eliphelet—nine in all. 9 All
these were the sons of David, besides his sons by his concubines.
And Tamar[u] was their sister.[v]

The Kings of Judah

10 Solomon's son was Rehoboam,[w]
Abijah[x] his son,
Asa[y] his son,
Jehoshaphat[z] his son,
11 Jehoram[h] [a] his son,
Ahaziah[b] his son,
Joash[c] his son,
12 Amaziah[d] his son,
Azariah[e] his son,
Jotham[f] his son,
13 Ahaz[g] his son,
Hezekiah[h] his son,
Manasseh[i] his son,
14 Amon[j] his son,
Josiah[k] his son.
15 The sons of Josiah:
Johanan the firstborn,
Jehoiakim[l] the second son,
Zedekiah[m] the third,
Shallum[n] the fourth.
16 The successors of Jehoiakim:

2:45 *b*S Jos 15:55 *c*S Jos 15:58
2:49 *d*Jos 15:31 *e*Jos 15:16
2:50 *f*1Ch 4:4 *g*S ver 19
2:53 *h*2Sa 23:38
2:54 *i*Ezr 2:22; Ne 7:26; 12:28
2:55 *j*S Ge 15:19; S Jdg 4:11 *k*Jos 19:35 *l*2Ki 10:15,23; Jer 35:2-19
3:1 *m*1Ch 14:3; 28:5 *n*S 1Sa 25:43 *o*S Jos 15:56 *p*S 1Sa 25:42
3:2 *q*1Ki 2:22
3:4 *r*S 2Sa 5:4; 1Ch 29:27 *s*S 2Sa 5:5
3:5 *t*2Sa 11:3
3:9 *u*S 2Sa 13:1 *v*1Ch 14:4
3:10 *w*1Ki 14:21-31; 2Ch 12:16 *x*1Ki 15:1-8; 2Ch 13:1 *y*1Ki 15:9-24 *z*2Ch 17:1-21:3
3:11 *a*2Ki 8:16-24; 2Ch 21:1 *b*2Ki 8:25-10:14; 2Ch 22:1-10 *c*2Ki 11:1-12:21; 2Ch 22:11-24:27
3:12 *d*2Ki 14:1-22; 2Ch 25:1-28 *e*2Ki 15:1-7; 2Ch 26:1-23 *f*2Ki 15:32-38; 2Ch 27:1; Isa 1:1; Hos 1:1; Mic 1:1
3:13 *g*2Ki 16:1-20; 2Ch 28:1; Isa 7:1 *h*2Ki 18:1-20:21; 2Ch 29:1; Isa 1:1; Jer 26:19; Hos 1:1; Mic 1:1 *i*2Ki 21:1-18; 2Ch 33:1
3:14 *j*2Ki 21:19-26; 2Ch 33:21; Zep 1:1 *k*2Ki 22:1; 2Ch 34:1; Jer 1:2; 3:6; 25:3
3:15 *l*S 2Ki 23:34 *m*Jer 37:1 *n*S 2Ki 23:31

b *42* The meaning of the Hebrew for this phrase is uncertain. **c** *55* Or *of the Sopherites* **d** *55* Or *father of Beth Recab* **e** *5* Hebrew *Shimea,* a variant of *Shammua* **f** *5* One Hebrew manuscript and Vulgate (see also Septuagint and 2 Samuel 11:3); most Hebrew manuscripts *Bathshua* **g** *6* Two Hebrew manuscripts (see also 2 Samuel 5:15 and 1 Chron. 14:5); most Hebrew manuscripts *Elishama* **h** *11* Hebrew *Joram,* a variant of *Jehoram*

3:1–24 HISTORY, Hope—The house of David received special attention. Descendants of David after the Exile occupy the climactic position in the list. Israel continued to look to the Davidic line for hope long after they lost political freedom and power. The entire work of the Chronicler centers on the house of David. Israel preserved their history even in genealogical form to maintain hope in God's promises (2 Sa 7).

Jehoiachin[i] [o] his son,
and Zedekiah.[p]

The Royal Line After the Exile

17The descendants of Jehoiachin the captive:
Shealtiel[q] his son, 18Malkiram, Pedaiah, Shenazzar,[r] Jekamiah, Hoshama and Nedabiah.[s]
19The sons of Pedaiah:
Zerubbabel[t] and Shimei.
The sons of Zerubbabel:
Meshullam and Hananiah.
Shelomith was their sister.
20There were also five others:
Hashubah, Ohel, Berekiah, Hasadiah and Jushab-Hesed.
21The descendants of Hananiah:
Pelatiah and Jeshaiah, and the sons of Rephaiah, of Arnan, of Obadiah and of Shecaniah.
22The descendants of Shecaniah:
Shemaiah and his sons:
Hattush,[u] Igal, Bariah, Neariah and Shaphat—six in all.
23The sons of Neariah:
Elioenai, Hizkiah and Azrikam—three in all.
24The sons of Elioenai:
Hodaviah, Eliashib, Pelaiah, Akkub, Johanan, Delaiah and Anani—seven in all.

Chapter 4

Other Clans of Judah

THE descendants of Judah:[v]
Perez, Hezron,[w] Carmi, Hur and Shobal.
2Reaiah son of Shobal was the father of Jahath, and Jahath the father of Ahumai and Lahad. These were the clans of the Zorathites.
3These were the sons[j] of Etam:
Jezreel, Ishma and Idbash. Their sister was named Hazzelelponi.
4Penuel was the father of Gedor, and Ezer the father of Hushah.
These were the descendants of Hur,[x] the firstborn of Ephrathah and father[k] of Bethlehem.[y]
5Ashhur[z] the father of Tekoa had two wives, Helah and Naarah.
6Naarah bore him Ahuzzam, Hepher, Temeni and Haahashtari. These were the descendants of Naarah.

3:16 [o]S 2Ki 24:6,8 [p]S 2Ki 24:18
3:17 [q]Ezr 3:2
3:18 [r]Ezr 1:8; 5:14 [s]Jer 22:30
3:19 [t]Ezr 2:2; 3:2; 5:2; Ne 7:7; 12:1; Hag 1:1; 2:2; Zec 4:6
3:22 [u]Ezr 8:2-3
4:1 [v]S Ge 29:35; S 1Ch 2:3 [w]Nu 26:21
4:4 [x]1Ch 2:50 [y]Ru 1:19
4:5 [z]1Ch 2:24
4:13 [a]S Jos 15:17
4:17 [b]S Ex 15:20
4:18 [c]S Jos 15:34

7The sons of Helah:
Zereth, Zohar, Ethnan, 8and Koz, who was the father of Anub and Hazzobebah and of the clans of Aharhel son of Harum.

9Jabez was more honorable than his
brothers. His mother had named him Jabez,[l] saying, "I gave birth to him in
pain." 10Jabez cried out to the God of Is-
rael, "Oh, that you would bless me and enlarge my territory! Let your hand be with me, and keep me from harm so that I will be free from pain." And God granted his request.

11Kelub, Shuhah's brother, was the father of Mehir, who was the father of Eshton. 12Eshton was the father of Beth Rapha, Paseah and Tehinnah the father of Ir Nahash.[m] These were the men of Recah.

13The sons of Kenaz:
Othniel[a] and Seraiah.
The sons of Othniel:
Hathath and Meonothai.[n] 14Meonothai was the father of Ophrah.
Seraiah was the father of Joab, the father of Ge Harashim.[o] It was called this because its people were craftsmen.
15The sons of Caleb son of Jephunneh:
Iru, Elah and Naam.
The son of Elah:
Kenaz.
16The sons of Jehallelel:
Ziph, Ziphah, Tiria and Asarel.
17The sons of Ezrah:
Jether, Mered, Epher and Jalon. One of Mered's wives gave birth to Miriam,[b] Shammai and Ishbah the father of Eshtemoa. 18(His Judean wife gave birth to Jered the father of Gedor, Heber the father of Soco, and Jekuthiel the father of Zanoah.[c]) These were the children of Pharaoh's daughter Bithiah, whom Mered had married.

[i] *16* Hebrew *Jeconiah,* a variant of *Jehoiachin*; also in verse 17 [j] *3* Some Septuagint manuscripts (see also Vulgate); Hebrew *father* [k] *4* *Father* may mean *civic leader* or *military leader*; also in verses 12, 14, 17, 18 and possibly elsewhere. [l] *9* *Jabez* sounds like the Hebrew for *pain.* [m] *12* Or *of the city of Nahash* [n] *13* Some Septuagint manuscripts and Vulgate; Hebrew does not have *and Meonothai.* [o] *14* *Ge Harashim* means *valley of craftsmen.*

4:9–10 REVELATION, Author of Hope—God visits individuals whose commitment to His principles and purposes make them recipients of His presence and care in special ways. Jabez is singled out as one whom God prospered for his faithfulness. His prayer led to God's actions giving him hope.

4:10 PRAYER, Answer—Through a popular wordplay, the name "Jabez" indicated sorrow or pain. Jabez prayed that the meaning of his name would be reversed. "Cried" (Hebrew *qara'*) does not indicate distress but a calling out to God. See note on Ge 4:26. God granted Jabez's petition. The Bible does not explicitly say why. It implies his honorable, faithful life brought God's response to him. God is not automatically bound to honor any person's request. He invites all people to call on Him and trust Him to respond in the way He knows is best. Faithful people do not call on personal merit to gain God's response. They trust in God's love and faithfulness.

19The sons of Hodiah's wife, the sister
of Naham:
the father of Keilah[d] the Garmite,
and Eshtemoa the Maacathite.[e]
20The sons of Shimon:
Amnon, Rinnah, Ben-Hanan and
Tilon.
The descendants of Ishi:
Zoheth and Ben-Zoheth.
21The sons of Shelah[f] son of Judah:
Er the father of Lecah, Laadah the
father of Mareshah and the clans
of the linen workers at Beth Ash-
bea, 22Jokim, the men of Cozeba,
and Joash and Saraph, who ruled
in Moab and Jashubi Lehem.
(These records are from ancient
times.) 23They were the potters
who lived at Netaim and Gederah; they stayed there and worked
for the king.

Simeon

4:28–33pp — Jos 19:2–10

24The descendants of Simeon:[g]
Nemuel, Jamin, Jarib,[h] Zerah and
Shaul;
25Shallum was Shaul's son, Mibsam
his son and Mishma his son.
26The descendants of Mishma:
Hammuel his son, Zaccur his son
and Shimei his son.
27Shimei had sixteen sons and six
daughters, but his brothers did not have
many children; so their entire clan did
not become as numerous as the people of
Judah. 28They lived in Beersheba,[i] Moladah,[j] Hazar Shual, 29Bilhah, Ezem,[k] To-
lad, 30Bethuel, Hormah,[l] Ziklag,[m] 31Beth
Marcaboth, Hazar Susim, Beth Biri and
Shaaraim.[n] These were their towns until
the reign of David. 32Their surrounding
villages were Etam, Ain,[o] Rimmon, Token and Ashan[p]—five towns— 33and all
the villages around these towns as far as
Baalath.[p] These were their settlements.
And they kept a genealogical record.
34Meshobab, Jamlech, Joshah son of
Amaziah, 35Joel, Jehu son of Joshibi-
ah, the son of Seraiah, the son of Asi-
el, 36also Elioenai, Jaakobah, Jeshoha-
iah, Asaiah, Adiel, Jesimiel, Benaiah,
37and Ziza son of Shiphi, the son of
Allon, the son of Jedaiah, the son of
Shimri, the son of Shemaiah.
38The men listed above by name were
leaders of their clans. Their families increased greatly, 39and they went to the
outskirts of Gedor[q] to the east of the valley in search of pasture for their flocks.
40They found rich, good pasture, and the
land was spacious, peaceful and quiet.[r]
Some Hamites had lived there formerly.
41The men whose names were listed
came in the days of Hezekiah king of Judah. They attacked the Hamites in their
dwellings and also the Meunites[s] who
were there and completely destroyed[q]
them, as is evident to this day. Then they
settled in their place, because there was
pasture for their flocks. 42And five hundred of these Simeonites, led by Pelatiah,
Neariah, Rephaiah and Uzziel, the sons of
Ishi, invaded the hill country of Seir.[t]
43They killed the remaining Amalekites[u]
who had escaped, and they have lived
there to this day.

Chapter 5

Reuben

THE sons of Reuben[v] the firstborn of
Israel (he was the firstborn, but
when he defiled his father's marriage
bed,[w] his rights as firstborn were given to
the sons of Joseph[x] son of Israel;[y] so he
could not be listed in the genealogical
record in accordance with his birthright,[z] 2and though Judah[a] was the
strongest of his brothers and a ruler[b]
came from him, the rights of the firstborn[c] belonged to Joseph)— 3the sons of
Reuben[d] the firstborn of Israel:
Hanoch, Pallu,[e] Hezron[f] and Carmi.
4The descendants of Joel:
Shemaiah his son, Gog his son,
Shimei his son, 5Micah his son,
Reaiah his son, Baal his son,
6and Beerah his son, whom Tiglath-Pileser[r][g] king of Assyria

4:19 [d]S Jos 15:44 [e]S Dt 3:14
4:21 [f]S Ge 38:5
4:24 [g]S Ge 29:33 [h]Nu 26:12
4:28 [i]S Ge 21:14 [j]S Jos 15:26
4:29 [k]S Jos 15:29
4:30 [l]S Nu 14:45 [m]S Jos 15:31
4:31 [n]S Jos 15:36
4:32 [o]S Nu 34:11 [p]S Jos 15:42
4:39 [q]S Jos 15:58
4:40 [r]Jdg 18:7-10
4:41 [s]2Ch 20:1; 26:7
4:42 [t]S Ge 14:6
4:43 [u]S Ge 14:7; Est 3:1; 9:16
5:1 [v]S Ge 29:32 [w]Ge 35:22; 49:4 [x]S Ge 48:16,22; S 49:26 [y]Ge 48:5 [z]1Ch 26:10
5:2 [a]S Ge 49:10,12 [b]S 1Sa 9:16; S 12:12; S 2Sa 6:21; 1Ch 11:2; S 2Ch 7:18; Mt 2:6 [c]S Ge 25:31
5:3 [d]S Ge 29:32; 46:9; Ex 6:14; Nu 26:5-11 [e]S Nu 26:5 [f]S Nu 26:6
5:6 [g]ver 26; S 2Ki 15:19; 16:10; 2Ch 28:20

[p]*33* Some Septuagint manuscripts (see also Joshua 19:8); Hebrew *Baal* [q]*41* The Hebrew term refers to the irrevocable giving over of things or persons to the LORD, often by totally destroying them. [r]*6* Hebrew *Tilgath-Pilneser,* a variant of *Tiglath-Pileser;* also in verse 26

5:1–2 HUMANITY, Community Relationships—The rights of the firstborn were initially a concern within family relationships. Later they became a matter of community and national concern as well. The firstborn son possessed the right of a double portion of the inheritance along with assuming the leadership of the family upon the death of the father. This right in Israel was lost by Reuben because of sin. See Ge 35:22; 48:5; 49:4*b*. Judah, as ancestor of the line of David, picked up the right of leadership, but the inheritance rights of the firstborn went to Ephraim and Manasseh, descendants of Joseph. Inheritance and family membership play extremely important roles in community relationships. They often determine our resources, our educational opportunities, our access to leadership positions. Humans often use standing gained by inheritance as criteria to judge other humans. God uses entirely different criteria to judge human worth. Sin makes us all guilty in His sight. Redemption provides us the opportunity to be His obedient servants. We cannot inherit redemption. We must individually trust Him for it. God's salvation is available to all people, regardless of our sociological class in society.

took into exile. Beerah was a leader of the Reubenites.
7Their relatives by clans,[h] listed according to their genealogical
records:
Jeiel the chief, Zechariah, 8and
Bela son of Azaz, the son of Shema, the son of Joel. They settled
in the area from Aroer[i] to Nebo[j]
and Baal Meon.[k] 9To the east
they occupied the land up to the
edge of the desert that extends to
the Euphrates[l] River, because
their livestock had increased in
Gilead.[m]
10During Saul's reign they waged
war against the Hagrites[n], who
were defeated at their hands; they
occupied the dwellings of the Hagrites throughout the entire region
east of Gilead.

Gad

11The Gadites[o] lived next to them in
Bashan, as far as Salecah:[p]
12Joel was the chief, Shapham the
second, then Janai and Shaphat,
in Bashan.
13Their relatives, by families, were:
Michael, Meshullam, Sheba, Jorai,
Jacan, Zia and Eber—seven in all.
14These were the sons of Abihail
son of Huri, the son of Jaroah, the
son of Gilead, the son of Michael,
the son of Jeshishai, the son of
Jahdo, the son of Buz.
15Ahi son of Abdiel, the son of
Guni, was head of their family.
16The Gadites lived in Gilead, in Bashan and its outlying villages, and
on all the pasturelands of Sharon
as far as they extended.
17All these were entered in the genealogical records during the reigns of Jotham[q] king of Judah and Jeroboam[r] king
of Israel.

18The Reubenites, the Gadites and the
half-tribe of Manasseh had 44,760 men
ready for military service[s] —able-bodied
men who could handle shield and sword,
who could use a bow, and who were
trained for battle. 19They waged war
against the Hagrites, Jetur,[t] Naphish and
Nodab. 20They were helped[u] in fighting
them, and God handed the Hagrites and
all their allies over to them, because they
cried[v] out to him during the battle. He
answered their prayers, because they
trusted[w] in him. 21They seized the livestock of the Hagrites—fifty thousand
camels, two hundred fifty thousand sheep
and two thousand donkeys. They also
took one hundred thousand people captive, 22and many others fell slain, because
the battle[x] was God's. And they occupied
the land until the exile.[y]

The Half-Tribe of Manasseh

23The people of the half-tribe of Manasseh[z] were numerous; they settled in the
land from Bashan to Baal Hermon, that is,
to Senir (Mount Hermon).[a]
24These were the heads of their families: Epher, Ishi, Eliel, Azriel, Jeremiah,
Hodaviah and Jahdiel. They were brave
warriors, famous men, and heads of their
families. 25But they were unfaithful[b] to
the God of their fathers and prostituted[c]
themselves to the gods of the peoples of
the land, whom God had destroyed before them. 26So the God of Israel stirred
up the spirit[d] of Pul[e] king of Assyria
(that is, Tiglath-Pileser[f] king of Assyria),
who took the Reubenites, the Gadites and
the half-tribe of Manasseh into exile. He
took them to Halah,[g] Habor, Hara and
the river of Gozan, where they are to this
day.

Chapter 6

Levi

THE sons of Levi:[h]
Gershon, Kohath and Merari.
2The sons of Kohath:
Amram, Izhar, Hebron and Uzziel.[i]
3The children of Amram:
Aaron, Moses and Miriam.[j]
The sons of Aaron:
Nadab, Abihu,[k] Eleazar[l] and Ithamar.[m]
4Eleazar was the father of Phinehas,[n]
Phinehas the father of Abishua,

5:7 [h]Jos 13:15-23
5:8 [i]S Nu 32:34; Jdg 11:26 [j]S Nu 32:3 [k]S
5:9 [l]S Ge 2:14 [m]S Nu 32:26
5:10 [n]ver 22; 1Ch 27:31
5:11 [o]S Ge 30:11; S Nu 1:25; S Jos 13:24-28 [p]S Dt 3:10
5:17 [q]S 2Ki 15:32 [r]S 2Ki 14:23
5:18 [s]S Nu 1:3
5:19 [t]Ge 25:15
5:20 [u]Ps 37:40; 46:5; 54:4 [v]1Ki 8:44; 2Ch 6:34; 13:14; 14:11; Ps 20:7-9; 22:5; 107:6 [w]Ps 26:1; Isa 26:3; Da 6:23
5:22 [x]S Dt 20:4; 2Ch 32:8 [y]S ver 10; S 2Ki 15:29
5:23 [z]1Ch 7:14 [a]S Dt 3:8,9; SS 4:8
5:25 [b]Dt 32:15-18; 1Ch 9:1; 10:13; 2Ch 12:2; 26:16; 28:19; 29:6; 30:7; 36:14 [c]S Ex 34:15; S Lev 18:3
5:26 [d]Isa 37:7 [e]S 2Ki 15:19 [f]S ver 6; S 2Ki 15:29 [g]2Ki 17:6
6:1 [h]S Ge 29:34; S Nu 3:17
6:2 [i]S Ex 6:18
6:3 [j]S Ex 15:20 [k]S Lev 10:1; S 10:1-20:2 [l]Lev 10:6 [m]S Ex 6:23
6:4 [n]Ezr 7:5

5:18–26 HISTORY, Faith—God acts in history to reward faith and to discipline unfaithfulness. The history of the tribes east of the Jordan River exemplifies this. They were victorious when they trusted God, but they went into exile when they were unfaithful.
5:18–22 CHRISTIAN ETHICS, War and Peace—God fought for His people in response to their prayers. Human power statistics are unimportant compared to God's sovereignty. See notes on Jos 10:1–43; Jdg 1:1–36.
5:20–22,25–26 REVELATION, Events—The children of God cried out to God, and He responded according to their fidelity and commitment to Him. Sometimes He rewarded them with immediate victory; at other times, His presence brought defeat by their enemies because they forsook Him. Specific historical events revealed God's relationship to the people.
5:20 PRAYER, Answer—God may answer prayer through the results of our endeavors. The tribes east of Jordan found God's answer in their military victory. God's answer honored the people's faith. Prayer is appropriate at any time, even in the midst of battle. In the midst of personal or community distress, prayer shows our hope and reliance on God.
5:25 SIN, Rebellion—See note on 1 Ki 15:29–30.

5Abishua the father of Bukki,
Bukki the father of Uzzi,
6Uzzi the father of Zerahiah,
Zerahiah the father of Meraioth,
7Meraioth the father of Amariah,
Amariah the father of Ahitub,
8Ahitub the father of Zadok,[o]
Zadok the father of Ahimaaz,
9Ahimaaz the father of Azariah,
Azariah the father of Johanan,
10Johanan the father of Azariah[p] (it was he who served as priest in the temple Solomon built in Jerusalem),
11Azariah the father of Amariah,
Amariah the father of Ahitub,
12Ahitub the father of Zadok,
Zadok the father of Shallum,
13Shallum the father of Hilkiah,[q]
Hilkiah the father of Azariah,
14Azariah the father of Seraiah,[r]
and Seraiah the father of Jehozadak.
15Jehozadak[s] was deported when the LORD sent Judah and Jerusalem into exile by the hand of Nebuchadnezzar.

16The sons of Levi:[t]
Gershon,[s] Kohath and Merari.[u]
17These are the names of the sons of Gershon:
Libni and Shimei.[v]
18The sons of Kohath:
Amram, Izhar, Hebron and Uzziel.[w]
19The sons of Merari:[x]
Mahli and Mushi.[y]
These are the clans of the Levites listed according to their fathers:
20Of Gershon:
Libni his son, Jehath his son,
Zimmah his son, 21Joah his son,
Iddo his son, Zerah his son
and Jeatherai his son.
22The descendants of Kohath:
Amminadab his son, Korah[z] his son,
Assir his son, 23Elkanah his son,
Ebiasaph his son, Assir his son,
24Tahath his son, Uriel[a] his son,
Uzziah his son and Shaul his son.
25The descendants of Elkanah:
Amasai, Ahimoth,
26Elkanah his son,[t] Zophai his son,
Nahath his son, 27Eliab his son,
Jeroham his son, Elkanah[b] his son
and Samuel[c] his son.[u]
28The sons of Samuel:
Joel[v][d] the firstborn
and Abijah the second son.
29The descendants of Merari:
Mahli, Libni his son,
Shimei his son, Uzzah his son,
30Shimea his son, Haggiah his son
and Asaiah his son.

The Temple Musicians

6:54–80pp — Jos 21:4–39

31These are the men[e] David put in charge of the music[f] in the house of the LORD after the ark came to rest there. 32They ministered with music before the tabernacle, the Tent of Meeting, until Solomon built the temple of the LORD in Jerusalem. They performed their duties according to the regulations laid down for them.

33Here are the men who served, together with their sons:
From the Kohathites:
Heman,[g] the musician,
the son of Joel,[h] the son of Samuel,
34the son of Elkanah,[i] the son of Jeroham,
the son of Eliel, the son of Toah,
35the son of Zuph, the son of Elkanah,
the son of Mahath, the son of Amasai,
36the son of Elkanah, the son of Joel,
the son of Azariah, the son of Zephaniah,
37the son of Tahath, the son of Assir,
the son of Ebiasaph, the son of Korah,[j]
38the son of Izhar,[k] the son of Kohath,

6:8 [o]S 2Sa 8:17; S 1Ch 12:28; S Ezr 7:2
6:10 [p]S 1Ki 4:2
6:13 [q]2Ki 22:1-20; 2Ch 34:9; 35:8
6:14 [r]S 2Ki 25:18; S Ezr 2:2
6:15 [s]Ne 12:1; Hag 1:1,14; 2:2,4; Zec 6:11
6:16 [t]S Ge 29:34; S Nu 3:17-20 [u]S Nu 26:57
6:17 [v]S Ex 6:17
6:18 [w]S Ex 6:18
6:19 [x]S Ge 46:11; 1Ch 23:21; 24:26 [y]S Ex 6:19
6:22 [z]S Ex 6:24
6:24 [a]1Ch 15:5
6:27 [b]S 1Sa 1:1 [c]S 1Sa 1:20
6:28 [d]ver 33; 1Sa 8:2
6:31 [e]1Ch 25:1; 2Ch 29:25-26; Ne 12:45 [f]1Ch 9:33; 15:19; Ezr 3:10; Ps 68:25
6:33 [g]1Ki 4:31; 1Ch 15:17; 25:1 [h]S ver 28
6:34 [i]S 1Sa 1:1
6:37 [j]S Ex 6:24
6:38 [k]Ex 6:21

[s]*16* Hebrew *Gershom,* a variant of *Gershon;* also in verses 17, 20, 43, 62 and 71 [t]*26* Some Hebrew manuscripts, Septuagint and Syriac; most Hebrew manuscripts *Ahimoth* [26]*and Elkanah. The sons of Elkanah:* [u]*27* Some Septuagint manuscripts (see also 1 Samuel 1:19,20 and 1 Chron. 6:33,34); Hebrew does not have *and Samuel his son.* [v]*28* Some Septuagint manuscripts and Syriac (see also 1 Samuel 8:2 and 1 Chron. 6:33); Hebrew does not have *Joel.*

6:31–32 WORSHIP, Music—See Ge 4:21. We do not know when music began to be used in worship. The record of elaborate musical arrangements in this chapter, led by King David himself, shows the prominent place given to music in Israel's worship. The Book of Psalms records much of the music of Jewish worship. Many songs were sung antiphonally (one group answering another group in song). Various types of musical instruments accompanied worship. No doubt music in worship has done much to guard the vitality of worship against the deadening effects of formalism. As early as Ex 15:1–21 Moses, Miriam, and the Israelites sang a song to the Lord. Deborah and Barak sang a song to the Lord (Jdg 5:1–31). Compare 2 Sa 6:5; 2 Ch 20:28; Ezr 3:10–11; Isa 38:20. Music expresses the emotions of God's people as they worship Him. Music was important in the worship of the early church (Eph 5:19; Col 3:16). When the disciples celebrated the first Lord's Supper, they concluded their worship with a hymn (Mt 26:30; Mk 14:26). Singing characterized the dramatic worship experience of Paul and Silas in the Philippian jail (Ac 16:25).

the son of Levi, the son of Israel;
39 and Heman's associate Asaph,[l] who
served at his right hand:
Asaph son of Berekiah, the son of
Shimea,[m]
40 the son of Michael, the son of Baa-
seiah,[w]
the son of Malkijah, 41 the son of
Ethni,
the son of Zerah, the son of Adaiah,
42 the son of Ethan, the son of Zimmah,
the son of Shimei, 43 the son of Jahath,
the son of Gershon, the son of
Levi;
44 and from their associates, the Merarites,[n] at his left hand:
Ethan son of Kishi, the son of
Abdi,
the son of Malluch, 45 the son of
Hashabiah,
the son of Amaziah, the son of
Hilkiah,
46 the son of Amzi, the son of Bani,
the son of Shemer, 47 the son of
Mahli,
the son of Mushi, the son of Merari,
the son of Levi.

48 Their fellow Levites[o] were assigned
to all the other duties of the tabernacle,
the house of God. 49 But Aaron and his
descendants were the ones who presented offerings on the altar[p] of burnt offering and on the altar of incense[q] in connection with all that was done in the
Most Holy Place, making atonement for
Israel, in accordance with all that Moses
the servant of God had commanded.

50 These were the descendants of Aaron:
Eleazar his son, Phinehas his son,
Abishua his son, 51 Bukki his son,
Uzzi his son, Zerahiah his son,
52 Meraioth his son, Amariah his
son,
Ahitub his son, 53 Zadok[r] his son
and Ahimaaz his son.

54 These were the locations of their settlements[s] allotted as their territory (they
were assigned to the descendants of Aaron who were from the Kohathite clan,
because the first lot was for them):
55 They were given Hebron in Judah with its surrounding pasturelands. 56 But the fields and villages
around the city were given to Caleb
son of Jephunneh.[t]
57 So the descendants of Aaron
were given Hebron (a city of refuge),
and Libnah,[x][u] Jattir,[v] Eshtemoa,
58 Hilen, Debir,[w] 59 Ashan,[x] Juttah[y]
and Beth Shemesh, together with
their pasturelands. 60 And from the
tribe of Benjamin they were given
Gibeon,[z] Geba, Alemeth and Anathoth,[y] together with their pasturelands.
These towns, which were distributed among the Kohathite clans,
were thirteen in all.
61 The rest of Kohath's descendants
were allotted ten towns from the clans of
half the tribe of Manasseh.
62 The descendants of Gershon, clan by
clan, were allotted thirteen towns from
the tribes of Issachar, Asher and Naphtali,
and from the part of the tribe of Manasseh that is in Bashan.
63 The descendants of Merari, clan by
clan, were allotted twelve towns from the
tribes of Reuben, Gad and Zebulun.
64 So the Israelites gave the Levites
these towns[z] and their pasturelands.
65 From the tribes of Judah, Simeon and
Benjamin they allotted the previously
named towns.
66 Some of the Kohathite clans were giv-
en as their territory towns from the tribe
of Ephraim.
67 In the hill country of Ephraim
they were given Shechem (a city of
refuge), and Gezer,[a][a] 68 Jokmeam,[b]
Beth Horon,[c] 69 Aijalon[d] and Gath
Rimmon,[e] together with their pasturelands.
70 And from half the tribe of Manasseh the Israelites gave Aner and Bile-
am, together with their pasturelands,
to the rest of the Kohathite clans.

6:39 [l]1Ch 25:1,9; 2Ch 29:13; Ne 11:17 [m]1Ch 15:17
6:44 [n]1Ch 15:17
6:48 [o]1Ch 23:32
6:49 [p]Ex 27:1-8 [q]S Ex 30:1-7,10; 2Ch 26:18
6:53 [r]S 2Sa 8:17
6:54 [s]S Nu 31:10
6:56 [t]S Jos 14:13; S 15:13
6:57 [u]S Nu 33:20 [v]S Jos 15:48
6:58 [w]S Jos 10:3
6:59 [x]S Jos 15:42
6:60 [y]Jer 1:1
6:64 [z]Nu 35:1-8
6:67 [a]S Jos 10:33
6:68 [b]1Ki 4:12 [c]S Jos 10:10
6:69 [d]S Jos 10:12 [e]S Jos 19:45

[w]*40* Most Hebrew manuscripts; some Hebrew manuscripts, one Septuagint manuscript and Syriac *Maaseiah* [x]*57* See Joshua 21:13; Hebrew *given the cities of refuge: Hebron, Libnah.* [y]*59* Syriac (see also Septuagint and Joshua 21:16); Hebrew does not have *Juttah.* [z]*60* See Joshua 21:17; Hebrew does not have *Gibeon.* [a]*67* See Joshua 21:21; Hebrew *given the cities of refuge: Shechem, Gezer.*

6:48–49 WORSHIP, Priesthood—Congregational worship requires preparation and leadership. God designated that certain individuals should preside over public worship. This order of priests carried out the ritual and ceremony of worship. Compare 15:25–28; 16:1–4; 2 Ch 8:12–16; 29:25–36. A tension developed between the spiritual and ritualistic aspects of worship. The prophets represented the spiritual, and the priests of the Temple represented the ritualistic. This very tension revealed that both aspects were needed. In the New Testament we see this position expressed in the person of the apostles, elders, bishops, and pastors of the early church. These New Testament leaders led in the "ritual" of the church and equipped each individual to be a "priest." Compare Eph 4:11–13; 1 Pe 2:9.

6:49 PRAYER, Worship—Israel's relation to Yahweh depended on prayer. See note on Ex 30:1,7.

71The Gershonites[f] received the following:
From the clan of the half-tribe of Manasseh
they received Golan in Bashan[g]
and also Ashtaroth, together with
their pasturelands;
72from the tribe of Issachar
they received Kedesh, Daberath,[h]
73Ramoth and Anem, together
with their pasturelands;
74from the tribe of Asher
they received Mashal, Abdon,[i]
75Hukok[j] and Rehob,[k] together
with their pasturelands;
76and from the tribe of Naphtali
they received Kedesh in Galilee,
Hammon[l] and Kiriathaim,[m] together with their pasturelands.

77The Merarites (the rest of the Levites) received the following:
From the tribe of Zebulun
they received Jokneam, Kartah,[b]
Rimmono and Tabor, together
with their pasturelands;
78from the tribe of Reuben across the
Jordan east of Jericho
they received Bezer[n] in the
desert, Jahzah, 79Kedemoth[o] and
Mephaath, together with their
pasturelands;
80and from the tribe of Gad
they received Ramoth in Gilead,[p]
Mahanaim,[q] 81Heshbon and Jazer,[r] together with their pasturelands.[s]

Chapter 7

Issachar

THE sons of Issachar:[t]
Tola, Puah,[u] Jashub and Shimron
—four in all.
2The sons of Tola:
Uzzi, Rephaiah, Jeriel, Jahmai, Ibsam and Samuel—heads of their
families. During the reign of David, the descendants of Tola listed
as fighting men in their genealogy
numbered 22,600.
3The son of Uzzi:
Izrahiah.
The sons of Izrahiah:
Michael, Obadiah, Joel and Isshiah. All five of them were chiefs.
4According to their family genealogy, they had 36,000 men ready
for battle, for they had many
wives and children.
5The relatives who were fighting men
belonging to all the clans of Issachar, as listed in their genealogy,
were 87,000 in all.

Benjamin

6Three sons of Benjamin:[v]
Bela, Beker and Jediael.
7The sons of Bela:
Ezbon, Uzzi, Uzziel, Jerimoth and
Iri, heads of families—five in all.
Their genealogical record listed
22,034 fighting men.
8The sons of Beker:
Zemirah, Joash, Eliezer, Elioenai,
Omri, Jeremoth, Abijah, Anathoth
and Alemeth. All these were the
sons of Beker. 9Their genealogical
record listed the heads of families
and 20,200 fighting men.
10The son of Jediael:
Bilhan.
The sons of Bilhan:
Jeush, Benjamin, Ehud, Kenaanah, Zethan, Tarshish and Ahishahar. 11All these sons of Jediael
were heads of families. There
were 17,200 fighting men ready
to go out to war.
12The Shuppites and Huppites were
the descendants of Ir, and the Hushites the descendants of Aher.

Naphtali

13The sons of Naphtali:[w]
Jahziel, Guni, Jezer and Shillem[c]
—the descendants of Bilhah.

Manasseh

14The descendants of Manasseh:[x]
Asriel was his descendant
through his Aramean concubine.
She gave birth to Makir the father
of Gilead.[y] 15Makir took a wife
from among the Huppites and
Shuppites. His sister's name was
Maacah.
Another descendant was named
Zelophehad,[z] who had only daughters.
16Makir's wife Maacah gave birth
to a son and named him Peresh. His
brother was named Sheresh, and
his sons were Ulam and Rakem.
17The son of Ulam:
Bedan.
These were the sons of Gilead[a] son
of Makir, the son of Manasseh.
18His sister Hammoleketh gave
birth to Ishhod, Abiezer[b] and
Mahlah.
19The sons of Shemida[c] were:
Ahian, Shechem, Likhi and Aniam.

6:71 [f]1Ch 23:7 [g]S Jos 20:8
6:72 [h]S Jos 19:12
6:74 [i]S Jos 19:28
6:75 [j]Jos 19:34 [k]S Nu 13:21
6:76 [l]Jos 19:28 [m]S Nu 32:37
6:78 [n]S Jos 20:8
6:79 [o]S Dt 2:26
6:80 [p]Jos 20:8 [q]S Ge 32:2
6:81 [r]S Nu 21:32 [s]2Ch 11:14
7:1 [t]S Ge 30:18 [u]S Ge 46:13
7:6 [v]S Nu 26:38
7:13 [w]S Ge 30:8
7:14 [x]S Ge 41:51; S Jos 17:1; 1Ch 5:23 [y]S Nu 26:30
7:15 [z]S Nu 26:33; 36:1-12
7:17 [a]S Nu 26:30
7:18 [b]S Jos 17:2
7:19 [c]Jos 17:2

[b]*77* See Septuagint and Joshua 21:34; Hebrew does not have *Jokneam, Kartah.* [c]*13* Some Hebrew and Septuagint manuscripts (see also Gen. 46:24 and Num. 26:49); most Hebrew manuscripts *Shallum*

Ephraim

20The descendants of Ephraim:[d]
Shuthelah, Bered his son,
Tahath his son, Eleadah his son,
Tahath his son, 21Zabad his son
and Shuthelah his son.
Ezer and Elead were killed by the
native-born men of Gath, when
they went down to seize their livestock. 22Their father Ephraim
mourned for them many days, and
his relatives came to comfort him.
23Then he lay with his wife again,
and she became pregnant and gave
birth to a son. He named him Beriah,[d] because there had been misfortune in his family. 24His daughter was Sheerah, who built Lower
and Upper Beth Horon[e] as well as
Uzzen Sheerah.
25Rephah was his son, Resheph his
son,[e]
Telah his son, Tahan his son,
26Ladan his son, Ammihud his son,
Elishama his son, 27Nun his son
and Joshua his son.
28Their lands and settlements included
Bethel and its surrounding villages, Naa-
ran to the east, Gezer[f] and its villages to
the west, and Shechem and its villages all
the way to Ayyah and its villages. 29Along
the borders of Manasseh were Beth
Shan,[g] Taanach, Megiddo and Dor,[h] together with their villages. The descendants of Joseph son of Israel lived in these
towns.

Asher

30The sons of Asher:[i]
Imnah, Ishvah, Ishvi and Beriah.
Their sister was Serah.
31The sons of Beriah:
Heber and Malkiel, who was the
father of Birzaith.
32Heber was the father of Japhlet, Shomer and Hotham and of their sister Shua.
33The sons of Japhlet:
Pasach, Bimhal and Ashvath.
These were Japhlet's sons.
34The sons of Shomer:
Ahi, Rohgah,[f] Hubbah and Aram.
35The sons of his brother Helem:
Zophah, Imna, Shelesh and Amal.
36The sons of Zophah:
Suah, Harnepher, Shual, Beri, Im-
rah, 37Bezer, Hod, Shamma, Shil-
shah, Ithran[g] and Beera.
38The sons of Jether:
Jephunneh, Pispah and Ara.
39The sons of Ulla:
Arah, Hanniel and Rizia.
40All these were descendants of Asher
—heads of families, choice men, brave
warriors and outstanding leaders. The
number of men ready for battle, as listed
in their genealogy, was 26,000.

Chapter 8

The Genealogy of Saul the Benjamite

8:28-38pp — 1Ch 9:34-44

BENJAMIN[j] was the father of Bela his
firstborn,
Ashbel the second son, Aharah
the third,
2Nohah the fourth and Rapha the
fifth.
3The sons of Bela were:
Addar,[k] Gera, Abihud,[h] 4Abish-
ua, Naaman, Ahoah,[l] 5Gera, She-
phuphan and Huram.
6These were the descendants of
Ehud,[m] who were heads of families of those living in Geba and
were deported to Manahath:
7Naaman, Ahijah, and Gera, who
deported them and who was the
father of Uzza and Ahihud.
8Sons were born to Shaharaim in
Moab after he had divorced his
wives Hushim and Baara. 9By his
wife Hodesh he had Jobab, Zibia,
Mesha, Malcam, 10Jeuz, Sakia and
Mirmah. These were his sons,
heads of families. 11By Hushim he
had Abitub and Elpaal.
12The sons of Elpaal:
Eber, Misham, Shemed (who built
Ono[n] and Lod with its surrounding villages), 13and Beriah and
Shema, who were heads of families of those living in Aijalon[o] and
who drove out the inhabitants of
Gath.[p]
14Ahio, Shashak, Jeremoth, 15Zeba-
diah, Arad, Eder, 16Michael, Ish-
pah and Joha were the sons of
Beriah,
17Zebadiah, Meshullam, Hizki, Heber,
18Ishmerai, Izliah and Jobab were
the sons of Elpaal.
19Jakim, Zicri, Zabdi, 20Elienai, Zillethai, Eliel, 21Adaiah, Beraiah and
Shimrath were the sons of
Shimei.
22Ishpan, Eber, Eliel, 23Abdon, Zicri,
Hanan, 24Hananiah, Elam, Antho-
thijah, 25Iphdeiah and Penuel
were the sons of Shashak.
26Shamsherai, Shehariah, Athaliah,

7:20 [d]S Ge 41:52; S Nu 1:33
7:24 [e]S Jos 10:10
7:28 [f]Jos 10:33
7:29 [g]S Jos 17:11 [h]S Jos 11:2
7:30 [i]S Nu 1:40
8:1 [j]S Ge 46:21
8:3 [k]S Ge 46:21
8:4 [l]2Sa 23:9
8:6 [m]Jdg 3:12-30
8:12 [n]Ezr 2:33; Ne 6:2; 7:37; 11:35
8:13 [o]S Jos 10:12 [p]S Jos 11:22

[d]*23* *Beriah* sounds like the Hebrew for *misfortune.* [e]*25* Some Septuagint manuscripts; Hebrew does not have *his son.* [f]*34* Or *of his brother Shomer: Rohgah* [g]*37* Possibly a variant of *Jether* [h]*3* Or *Gera the father of Ehud*

27 Jaareshiah, Elijah and Zicri were
the sons of Jeroham.
28 All these were heads of families,
chiefs as listed in their genealogy, and
they lived in Jerusalem.

29 Jeiel[i] the father[j] of Gibeon lived in
Gibeon.[q]
His wife's name was Maacah,
30 and his firstborn son was Abdon, followed by Zur, Kish, Baal,
Ner,[k] Nadab, 31 Gedor, Ahio, Ze-
ker 32 and Mikloth, who was the
father of Shimeah. They too lived
near their relatives in Jerusalem.
33 Ner[r] was the father of Kish,[s] Kish
the father of Saul[t], and Saul the
father of Jonathan, Malki-Shua,
Abinadab and Esh-Baal.[l] [u]
34 The son of Jonathan:[v]
Merib-Baal,[m] [w] who was the father of Micah.
35 The sons of Micah:
Pithon, Melech, Tarea and Ahaz.
36 Ahaz was the father of Jehoaddah,
Jehoaddah was the father of Alemeth, Azmaveth and Zimri, and
Zimri was the father of Moza.
37 Moza was the father of Binea;
Raphah was his son, Eleasah his
son and Azel his son.
38 Azel had six sons, and these were
their names:
Azrikam, Bokeru, Ishmael, Sheari-
ah, Obadiah and Hanan. All these
were the sons of Azel.
39 The sons of his brother Eshek:
Ulam his firstborn, Jeush the second son and Eliphelet the third.
40 The sons of Ulam were brave
warriors who could handle the
bow. They had many sons and
grandsons—150 in all.
All these were the descendants of
Benjamin.[x]

Chapter 9

ALL Israel[y] was listed in the genealogies recorded in the book of the
kings of Israel.

The People in Jerusalem

9:1–17pp — Ne 11:3–19

The people of Judah were taken captive
to Babylon[z] because of their unfaithfulness.[a] 2 Now the first to resettle on their
own property in their own towns[b] were
some Israelites, priests, Levites and temple servants.[c]
3 Those from Judah, from Benjamin,
and from Ephraim and Manasseh who
lived in Jerusalem were:
4 Uthai son of Ammihud, the son of
Omri, the son of Imri, the son of
Bani, a descendant of Perez son of
Judah.[d]
5 Of the Shilonites:
Asaiah the firstborn and his sons.
6 Of the Zerahites:
Jeuel.
The people from Judah numbered
690.
7 Of the Benjamites:
Sallu son of Meshullam, the son of
Hodaviah, the son of Hassenuah;
8 Ibneiah son of Jeroham; Elah son
of Uzzi, the son of Micri; and Meshullam son of Shephatiah, the
son of Reuel, the son of Ibnijah.
9 The people from Benjamin, as listed in their genealogy, numbered
956. All these men were heads of
their families.
10 Of the priests:
Jedaiah; Jehoiarib; Jakin;
11 Azariah son of Hilkiah, the son of
Meshullam, the son of Zadok, the
son of Meraioth, the son of Ahitub, the official in charge of the
house of God;
12 Adaiah son of Jeroham, the son of
Pashhur,[e] the son of Malkijah;
and Maasai son of Adiel, the son
of Jahzerah, the son of Meshullam, the son of Meshillemith, the
son of Immer.
13 The priests, who were heads of
families, numbered 1,760. They
were able men, responsible for
ministering in the house of God.
14 Of the Levites:
Shemaiah son of Hasshub, the son
of Azrikam, the son of Hashabiah,
a Merarite; 15 Bakbakkar, Heresh,
Galal and Mattaniah[f] son of
Mica, the son of Zicri, the son of
Asaph; 16 Obadiah son of Shemaiah, the son of Galal, the son of
Jeduthun; and Berekiah son of
Asa, the son of Elkanah, who lived
in the villages of the Netophathites.[g]
17 The gatekeepers:[h]
Shallum, Akkub, Talmon, Ahiman
and their brothers, Shallum their

8:29 [q]S Jos 9:3
8:33 [r]S 1Sa 28:19 [s]S 1Sa 9:1 [t]1Sa 14:49 [u]S 2Sa 2:8
8:34 [v]S 2Sa 9:12 [w]S 2Sa 4:4; S 21:7-14
8:40 [x]S Nu 26:38
9:1 [y]1Ch 11:1,10; 12:38; 14:8; 15:3, 28; 18:14; 19:17; 21:5; 28:4,8; 29:21,23; 2Ch 1:2; 5:3; 7:8; 10:3,16; 12:1; 13:4,15; 18:16; 24:5; 28:23; 29:24; 30:1 [z]S Dt 21:10 [a]S 1Ch 5:25
9:2 [b]Jos 9:27; Ezr 2:70 [c]Ezr 2:43, 58; 8:20; Ne 7:60
9:4 [d]S Ge 38:29; 46:12
9:12 [e]Ezr 2:38; 10:22; Ne 10:3; Jer 21:1; 38:1
9:15 [f]2Ch 20:14; Ne 11:22
9:16 [g]Ne 12:28
9:17 [h]ver 22; 1Ch 26:1; 2Ch 8:14; 31:14; Ezr 2:42; Ne 7:45

[i]*29* Some Septuagint manuscripts (see also 1 Chron. 9:35); Hebrew does not have *Jeiel.* [j]*29 Father* may mean *civic leader* or *military leader.* [k]*30* Some Septuagint manuscripts (see also 1 Chron. 9:36); Hebrew does not have *Ner.* [l]*33* Also known as *Ish-Bosheth* [m]*34* Also known as *Mephibosheth*

9:1 SIN, Rebellion—See notes on 1 Ki 14:22–24; 2 Ki 25:1–21.
9:3 HISTORY, God's People—After the Exile, Israel was concerned to emphasize the unity of the people of God. Elements from the major tribes of the south and the north lived together in Jerusalem.

chief 18being stationed at the
King's Gate[i] on the east, up to
the present time. These were the
gatekeepers belonging to the
camp of the Levites. 19Shallum[j]
son of Kore, the son of Ebiasaph,
the son of Korah, and his fellow
gatekeepers from his family (the
Korahites) were responsible for
guarding the thresholds of the
Tent[n] just as their fathers had
been responsible for guarding the
entrance to the dwelling of the
LORD. 20In earlier times Phinehas[k] son of Eleazar was in charge
of the gatekeepers, and the LORD
was with him. 21Zechariah[l] son
of Meshelemiah was the gatekeeper at the entrance to the Tent
of Meeting.

22Altogether, those chosen to be gatekeepers[m] at the thresholds numbered
212. They were registered by genealogy
in their villages. The gatekeepers had
been assigned to their positions of trust
by David and Samuel the seer.[n] 23They
and their descendants were in charge of
guarding the gates of the house of the
LORD—the house called the Tent. 24The
gatekeepers were on the four sides: east,
west, north and south. 25Their brothers
in their villages had to come from time to
time and share their duties for seven-
day[o] periods. 26But the four principal
gatekeepers, who were Levites, were entrusted with the responsibility for the
rooms and treasuries[p] in the house of
God. 27They would spend the night stationed around the house of God,[q] because they had to guard it; and they had
charge of the key[r] for opening it each
morning.

28Some of them were in charge of the
articles used in the temple service; they
counted them when they were brought in
and when they were taken out. 29Others
were assigned to take care of the furnishings and all the other articles of the sanctuary,[s] as well as the flour and wine, and
the oil, incense and spices. 30But some[t]
of the priests took care of mixing the
spices. 31A Levite named Mattithiah, the
firstborn son of Shallum the Korahite,
was entrusted with the responsibility for
baking the offering bread. 32Some of their
Kohathite brothers were in charge of preparing for every Sabbath the bread set out
on the table.[u]

33Those who were musicians,[v] heads
of Levite families, stayed in the rooms of
the temple and were exempt from other
duties because they were responsible for
the work day and night.[w]

34All these were heads of Levite families, chiefs as listed in their genealogy,
and they lived in Jerusalem.

The Genealogy of Saul

9:34–44pp — 1Ch 8:28–38

35Jeiel[x] the father[o] of Gibeon lived in
Gibeon.
His wife's name was Maacah,
36and his firstborn son was Abdon, followed by Zur, Kish, Baal,
Ner, Nadab, 37Gedor, Ahio, Zechariah and Mikloth. 38Mikloth was
the father of Shimeam. They too
lived near their relatives in
Jerusalem.

39Ner[y] was the father of Kish,[z] Kish
the father of Saul, and Saul the father of Jonathan,[a] Malki-Shua,
Abinadab and Esh-Baal.[p] [b]

40The son of Jonathan:
Merib-Baal,[q] [c] who was the father of Micah.

41The sons of Micah:
Pithon, Melech, Tahrea and
Ahaz.[r]

42Ahaz was the father of Jadah, Jadah[s] was the father of Alemeth,
Azmaveth and Zimri, and Zimri
was the father of Moza. 43Moza
was the father of Binea; Rephaiah
was his son, Eleasah his son and
Azel his son.

44Azel had six sons, and these were
their names:
Azrikam, Bokeru, Ishmael, Sheari-
ah, Obadiah and Hanan. These
were the sons of Azel.

Chapter 10

Saul Takes His Life

10:1–12pp — 1Sa 31:1–13; 2Sa 1:4–12

NOW the Philistines fought against Israel; the Israelites fled before them,

9:18 [i]1Ch 26:14; Eze 43:1; 46:1
9:19 [j]Jer 35:4
9:20 [k]Nu 25:7-13
9:21 [l]1Ch 26:2,14
9:22 [m]S ver 17 [n]S 1Sa 9:9
9:25 [o]2Ki 11:5
9:26 [p]1Ch 26:22
9:27 [q]S Nu 3:38 [r]Isa 22:22
9:29 [s]S Nu 3:28; 1Ch 23:29
9:30 [t]S Ex 30:23-25
9:32 [u]Lev 24:5-8; 1Ch 23:29; 2Ch 13:11
9:33 [v]S 1Ch 6:31; 25:1-31; S 2Ch 5:12 [w]Ps 134:1
9:35 [x]1Ch 8:29
9:39 [y]S 1Ch 8:33 [z]S 1Sa 9:1 [a]1Sa 13:22 [b]S 2Sa 2:8
9:40 [c]S 2Sa 4:4

[n] *19* That is, the temple; also in verses 21 and 23
[o] *35* *Father* may mean *civic leader* or *military leader.*
[p] *39* Also known as *Ish-Bosheth* [q] *40* Also known as *Mephibosheth* [r] *41* Vulgate and Syriac (see also Septuagint and 1 Chron. 8:35); Hebrew does not have *and Ahaz.* [s] *42* Some Hebrew manuscripts and Septuagint (see also 1 Chron. 8:36); most Hebrew manuscripts *Jarah, Jarah*

9:22 HISTORY, God's Leaders—History gives claim to inherited positions. Returning from the Exile, Israel's religious leaders used genealogical lists reaching back to David to show their right to serve in the new Temple. God's leaders need roots in the history and traditions of His people. The Chronicler used the genealogies of chs 1—9 to give such identifying roots to his post-Exilic audience before telling Israel's story. The center of history for Chronicles is the reign of David, so the writer began with Saul's death, introducing David's reign.

10:1–12 CHRISTIAN ETHICS, War and Peace—God used human war to punish unfaithful leaders. See note on 1 Sa 28:16–19.

and many fell slain on Mount Gilboa.
2The Philistines pressed hard after Saul
and his sons, and they killed his sons Jonathan, Abinadab and Malki-Shua. 3The
fighting grew fierce around Saul, and
when the archers overtook him, they
wounded him.
4Saul said to his armor-bearer, "Draw
your sword and run me through, or these
uncircumcised fellows will come and
abuse me."
But his armor-bearer was terrified and
would not do it; so Saul took his own
sword and fell on it. 5When the armor-
bearer saw that Saul was dead, he too fell
on his sword and died. 6So Saul and his
three sons died, and all his house died
together.
7When all the Israelites in the valley
saw that the army had fled and that Saul
and his sons had died, they abandoned
their towns and fled. And the Philistines
came and occupied them.
8The next day, when the Philistines
came to strip the dead, they found Saul
and his sons fallen on Mount Gilboa.
9They stripped him and took his head and
his armor, and sent messengers throughout the land of the Philistines to proclaim
the news among their idols and their people. 10They put his armor in the temple of
their gods and hung up his head in the
temple of Dagon.[d]
11When all the inhabitants of Jabesh
Gilead[e] heard of everything the Philistines had done to Saul, 12all their valiant
men went and took the bodies of Saul and
his sons and brought them to Jabesh.
Then they buried their bones under the
great tree in Jabesh, and they fasted sev-
en days.
13Saul died[f] because he was unfaithful[g] to the LORD; he did not keep[h] the
word of the LORD and even consulted a
medium[i] for guidance, 14and did not inquire of the LORD. So the LORD put him to
death and turned[j] the kingdom[k] over to
David son of Jesse.

Chapter 11

David Becomes King Over Israel

11:1–3pp — 2Sa 5:1–3

ALL Israel[l] came together to David at
Hebron[m] and said, "We are your
own flesh and blood. 2In the past, even
while Saul was king, you were the one
who led Israel on their military campaigns.[n] And the LORD your God said to
you, 'You will shepherd[o] my people Israel, and you will become their ruler.[p]' "
3When all the elders of Israel had come
to King David at Hebron, he made a compact with them at Hebron before the
LORD, and they anointed[q] David king
over Israel, as the LORD had promised
through Samuel.

David Conquers Jerusalem

11:4–9pp — 2Sa 5:6–10

4David and all the Israelites marched to
Jerusalem (that is, Jebus). The Jebusites[r]
who lived there 5said to David, "You will
not get in here." Nevertheless, David
captured the fortress of Zion, the City of
David.
6David had said, "Whoever leads the
attack on the Jebusites will become com-
mander-in-chief." Joab[s] son of Zeruiah
went up first, and so he received the
command.
7David then took up residence in the
fortress, and so it was called the City of
David. 8He built up the city around it,
from the supporting terraces[t][t] to the
surrounding wall, while Joab restored the
rest of the city. 9And David became more
and more powerful,[u] because the LORD
Almighty was with him.

10:10 [d]S Jdg 16:23
10:11 [e]S Jdg 21:8
10:13 [f]S 2Sa 1:1; [g]S 1Ch 5:25 [h]S 1Sa 13:13 [i]S Lev 19:31; S 20:6; Dt 18:9-14
10:14 [j]1Ch 12:23 [k]S 1Sa 13:14
11:1 [l]S 1Ch 9:1 [m]S Ge 13:18; S 23:19
11:2 [n]S 1Sa 18:5, 16 [o]Ps 78:71; Mt 2:6 [p]S 1Ch 5:2
11:3 [q]1Sa 16:1-13
11:4 [r]S Ge 10:16; S 15:18-21; S Jos 3:10; S 15:8
11:6 [s]S 2Sa 2:13
11:8 [t]S 2Sa 5:9; 2Ch 32:5
11:9 [u]Est 9:4

[t]8 Or *the Millo*

10:11–12 HUMANITY, Burial—The last act of service which can be rendered the dead is to give them proper burial. By rescuing the bodies of Saul and his sons from further desecration, the people of Jabesh Gilead demonstrated both compassionate love and bravery.

10:13–14 HUMANITY, Death and Sin—Death is consistently viewed as the end result of sin. See note on Lev 10:1–2. The visit to the medium is clearly described as an act of rebellion. See note on 1 Sa 28:5–25. God is the ultimate Revealer of truth and the One from whom guidance must be sought. When we seek life-preserving or life-enriching resources from any other source, we will discover we are on the road to death, not life.

10:13 SIN, Unfaithfulness—Unfaithfulness (Hebrew *ma'al*) is a conscious rebellion against a commitment to another person (Nu 5:12). God chose Saul to be His servant-ruler over Israel. Saul refused to fulfill His commitments to God, making rash decisions to act before God acted and to devise ways to find God's will before God was ready to reveal it. Thus, he even sought contact with the dead prophet through a medium (1 Sa 28). See Dt 18:9–14. God intervened dramatically, bringing defeat to Saul in battle, causing such shame and fear Saul killed himself. Unfaithful rebellion against God is the sin of people who are numbered among God's people but refuse to trust God and thus rebel against their commitments to Him.

10:13–14 REVELATION, Faithfulness—God's revelation seeks to develop a faithful people for the faithful God, who leaves the faithless to their own destructive end. God's Spirit withdrew from Saul, who sought divine guidance apart from God. See note on 1 Sa 28:6–25.

11:2 ELECTION, Leadership—The people followed God's leading and anointed David as king. The covenant David made with the elders of Israel fulfilled the promise God made through Samuel. God always keeps His word. People in tune to God and listening to His word can find His chosen leaders.

11:3 PRAYER, Commitment—See note on 2 Sa 5:3.

11:9 HUMANITY, Relationship to God—See note on 2 Sa 5:10.

David's Mighty Men

11:10–41pp — 2Sa 23:8–39

10These were the chiefs of David's
mighty men—they, together with all Israel,[v] gave his kingship strong support to
extend it over the whole land, as the
LORD had promised— 11this is the list of
David's mighty men:[w]
Jashobeam,[u] a Hacmonite, was chief of
the officers[v]; he raised his spear against
three hundred men, whom he killed in
one encounter.
12Next to him was Eleazar son of Dodai
the Ahohite, one of the three mighty
men. 13He was with David at Pas Dammim when the Philistines gathered there
for battle. At a place where there was a
field full of barley, the troops fled from
the Philistines. 14But they took their
stand in the middle of the field. They defended it and struck the Philistines down,
and the LORD brought about a great
victory.[x]
15Three of the thirty chiefs came down
to David to the rock at the cave of Adullam, while a band of Philistines was encamped in the Valley[y] of Rephaim. 16At
that time David was in the stronghold,[z]
and the Philistine garrison was at Bethlehem. 17David longed for water and said,
"Oh, that someone would get me a drink
of water from the well near the gate of
Bethlehem!" 18So the Three broke
through the Philistine lines, drew water
from the well near the gate of Bethlehem
and carried it back to David. But he refused to drink it; instead, he poured[a] it
out before the LORD. 19"God forbid that I
should do this!" he said. "Should I drink
the blood of these men who went at the
risk of their lives?" Because they risked
their lives to bring it back, David would
not drink it.
Such were the exploits of the three
mighty men.
20Abishai[b] the brother of Joab was
chief of the Three. He raised his spear
against three hundred men, whom he
killed, and so he became as famous as the
Three. 21He was doubly honored above
the Three and became their commander,
even though he was not included among
them.
22Benaiah son of Jehoiada was a valiant
fighter from Kabzeel,[c] who performed
great exploits. He struck down two of
Moab's best men. He also went down
into a pit on a snowy day and killed a
lion.[d] 23And he struck down an Egyptian
who was seven and a half feet[w] tall. Although the Egyptian had a spear like a
weaver's rod[e] in his hand, Benaiah went
against him with a club. He snatched the
spear from the Egyptian's hand and killed
him with his own spear. 24Such were the
exploits of Benaiah son of Jehoiada; he
too was as famous as the three mighty
men. 25He was held in greater honor than
any of the Thirty, but he was not included
among the Three. And David put him in
charge of his bodyguard.

26The mighty men were:
Asahel[f] the brother of Joab,
Elhanan son of Dodo from Bethlehem,
27Shammoth[g] the Harorite,
Helez the Pelonite,
28Ira son of Ikkesh from Tekoa,
Abiezer[h] from Anathoth,
29Sibbecai[i] the Hushathite,
Ilai the Ahohite,
30Maharai the Netophathite,
Heled son of Baanah the Netophathite,
31Ithai son of Ribai from Gibeah in
Benjamin,
Benaiah[j] the Pirathonite,[k]
32Hurai from the ravines of Gaash,
Abiel the Arbathite,
33Azmaveth the Baharumite,
Eliahba the Shaalbonite,
34the sons of Hashem the Gizonite,
Jonathan son of Shagee the Hararite,
35Ahiam son of Sacar the Hararite,
Eliphal son of Ur,
36Hepher the Mekerathite,
Ahijah the Pelonite,
37Hezro the Carmelite,
Naarai son of Ezbai,
38Joel the brother of Nathan,
Mibhar son of Hagri,
39Zelek the Ammonite,
Naharai the Berothite, the armor-
bearer of Joab son of Zeruiah,
40Ira the Ithrite,
Gareb the Ithrite,
41Uriah[l] the Hittite,
Zabad[m] son of Ahlai,
42Adina son of Shiza the Reubenite,
who was chief of the Reubenites,
and the thirty with him,
43Hanan son of Maacah,

[u]*11* Possibly a variant of *Jashob-Baal* [v]*11* Or *Thirty*; some Septuagint manuscripts *Three* (see also 2 Samuel 23:8) [w]*23* Hebrew *five cubits* (about 2.3 meters)

11:10 [v]ver 1
11:11 [w]S 2Sa 17:10
11:14 [x]S Ex 14:30; S 1Sa 11:13
11:15 [y]1Ch 14:9; Isa 17:5
11:16 [z]S 2Sa 5:17
11:18 [a]S Dt 12:16
11:20 [b]S 1Sa 26:6
11:22 [c]S Jos 15:21 [d]1Sa 17:36
11:23 [e]S 1Sa 17:7
11:26 [f]S 2Sa 2:18
11:27 [g]1Ch 27:8
11:28 [h]1Ch 27:12
11:29 [i]S 2Sa 21:18
11:31 [j]1Ch 27:14 [k]S Jdg 12:13
11:41 [l]2Sa 11:6 [m]1Ch 2:36

11:14 HISTORY, Deliverance—Deliverance comes from God's actions not human power. This theme echoes throughout Chronicles.
11:15–19 HUMANITY, Relationships—The ability to lead others brings from them acts of sacrificial dedication and loyalty. A leader who recognizes and acknowledges such acts on the part of followers further cements their loyalty.
11:18 PRAYER, Commitment—See note on 2 Sa 23:16–17.

Joshaphat the Mithnite,
44 Uzzia the Ashterathite,[n]
Shama and Jeiel the sons of Hotham the Aroerite,
45 Jediael son of Shimri,
his brother Joha the Tizite,
46 Eliel the Mahavite,
Jeribai and Joshaviah the sons of
Elnaam,
Ithmah the Moabite,
47 Eliel, Obed and Jaasiel the Mezo-
baite.

Chapter 12

Warriors Join David

1 THESE were the men who came to David at Ziklag,[o] while he was banished from the presence of Saul son of
Kish (they were among the warriors who
helped him in battle; 2 they were armed
with bows and were able to shoot arrows
or to sling stones right-handed or left-
handed;[p] they were kinsmen of Saul[q]
from the tribe of Benjamin):

3 Ahiezer their chief and Joash the
sons of Shemaah the Gibeathite; Jezi-
el and Pelet the sons of Azmaveth;
Beracah, Jehu the Anathothite, 4 and
Ishmaiah the Gibeonite, a mighty
man among the Thirty, who was a
leader of the Thirty; Jeremiah, Jahaziel, Johanan, Jozabad the Gedera-
thite,[r] 5 Eluzai, Jerimoth, Bealiah,
Shemariah and Shephatiah the Haru-
phite; 6 Elkanah, Isshiah, Azarel, Joe-
zer and Jashobeam the Korahites;
7 and Joelah and Zebadiah the sons of
Jeroham from Gedor.[s]

8 Some Gadites[t] defected to David at
his stronghold in the desert. They were
brave warriors, ready for battle and able
to handle the shield and spear. Their
faces were the faces of lions,[u] and they
were as swift as gazelles[v] in the mountains.

9 Ezer was the chief,
Obadiah the second in command,
Eliab the third,

11:44 [n]S Dt 1:4
12:1 [o]S Jos 15:31
12:2 [p]S Jdg 3:15 [q]S 2Sa 3:19
12:4 [r]Jos 15:36
12:7 [s]S Jos 15:58
12:8 [t]S Ge 30:11 [u]2Sa 17:10 [v]S 2Sa 2:18
12:14 [w]S Lev 26:8 [x]S Dt 32:30
12:15 [y]S Jos 3:15
12:16 [z]S 2Sa 3:19
12:18 [a]S Jdg 3:10; 1Ch 28:12; 2Ch 15:1; 20:14; 24:20 [b]S 2Sa 17:25 [c]1Sa 25:5-6
12:19 [d]1Sa 29:2-11
12:20 [e]S 1Sa 27:6

10 Mishmannah the fourth, Jeremiah
the fifth,
11 Attai the sixth, Eliel the seventh,
12 Johanan the eighth, Elzabad the
ninth,
13 Jeremiah the tenth and Macbannai
the eleventh.

14 These Gadites were army commanders; the least was a match for a hundred,[w] and the greatest for a thousand.[x]
15 It was they who crossed the Jordan in
the first month when it was overflowing
all its banks,[y] and they put to flight everyone living in the valleys, to the east
and to the west.

16 Other Benjamites[z] and some men
from Judah also came to David in his
stronghold. 17 David went out to meet
them and said to them, "If you have
come to me in peace, to help me, I am
ready to have you unite with me. But if
you have come to betray me to my enemies when my hands are free from violence, may the God of our fathers see it
and judge you."

18 Then the Spirit[a] came upon Amasai,[b] chief of the Thirty, and he said:

"We are yours, O David!
We are with you, O son of Jesse!
Success,[c] success to you,
and success to those who help you,
for your God will help you."

So David received them and made
them leaders of his raiding bands.

19 Some of the men of Manasseh defected to David when he went with the Philistines to fight against Saul. (He and his
men did not help the Philistines because,
after consultation, their rulers sent him
away. They said, "It will cost us our
heads if he deserts to his master Saul.")[d]
20 When David went to Ziklag,[e] these
were the men of Manasseh who defected
to him: Adnah, Jozabad, Jediael, Michael,
Jozabad, Elihu and Zillethai, leaders of
units of a thousand in Manasseh. 21 They
helped David against raiding bands, for all
of them were brave warriors, and they
were commanders in his army. 22 Day af-

12:2 HUMANITY, Physical Nature—The ability to use either hand effectively is a striking physical skill, and may be exploited in numerous ways. On the other hand, the ability to win the loyalty of relatives of one's enemies is equally important or more so. People cannot choose the skills they have. Much of this is determined by the gene structure implanted in us by our Creator. We do have the responsibility to discover the skills we possess and sharpen them through discipline and training so we can serve God and other humans to the best of our abilities.

12:8–15 HUMANITY, Physical Nature—The physical skills necessary for offensive battle were those of fighting and running, either to attack or escape. A good leader gathers followers with skills to accomplish his purposes.

12:17 GOD, Wisdom—David recognized that God is the Judge who holds all persons accountable to Himself and judges us out of His wisdom. See note on Ge 3:8–24.

12:17–18 HUMANITY, Relationships—Those who are properly related to God and who demonstrate that faithfulness in daily life are able to attract the loyalty of others. God helps such committed groups to achieve success in His purposes.

12:18 HOLY SPIRIT, Revelation—One moment in history may be the focal point to which the Spirit leads an individual. Amasai was given the Spirit, apparently for this one occasion, to help him recognize that God had chosen David to be king and to stir his band of men to follow David. To accomplish the task, the Spirit inspired Amasai to utter an oracle or prophetic poem. His inspired oracle was collected under God's direction as part of our Bible. See note on 2 Sa 23:1–4.

ter day men came to help David, until he
had a great army, like the army of God.[x]

Others Join David at Hebron

23These are the numbers of the men
armed for battle who came to David at
Hebron[f] to turn[g] Saul's kingdom over to
him, as the LORD had said:[h]
24men of Judah, carrying shield and
spear—6,800 armed for battle;
25men of Simeon, warriors ready for
battle—7,100;
26men of Levi—4,600, 27including Jehoiada, leader of the family of Aaron, with 3,700 men, 28and Zadok,[i] a brave young warrior, with
22 officers from his family;
29men of Benjamin,[j] Saul's kinsmen—3,000, most[k] of whom
had remained loyal to Saul's
house until then;
30men of Ephraim, brave warriors, famous in their own clans—
20,800;
31men of half the tribe of Manasseh,
designated by name to come and
make David king—18,000;
32men of Issachar, who understood the
times and knew what Israel
should do[l]—200 chiefs, with all
their relatives under their command;
33men of Zebulun, experienced soldiers prepared for battle with every type of weapon, to help David
with undivided loyalty—50,000;
34men of Naphtali—1,000 officers, together with 37,000 men carrying
shields and spears;
35men of Dan, ready for battle—
28,600;
36men of Asher, experienced soldiers
prepared for battle—40,000;
37and from east of the Jordan, men of
Reuben, Gad and the half-tribe of
Manasseh, armed with every type
of weapon—120,000.

38All these were fighting men who volunteered to serve in the ranks. They
came to Hebron fully determined to make
David king over all Israel.[m] All the rest of
the Israelites were also of one mind to
make David king. 39The men spent three
days there with David, eating and drinking,[n] for their families had supplied provisions for them. 40Also, their neighbors
from as far away as Issachar, Zebulun and
Naphtali came bringing food on donkeys,
camels, mules and oxen. There were
plentiful supplies[o] of flour, fig cakes, raisin[p] cakes, wine, oil, cattle and sheep,
for there was joy[q] in Israel.

Chapter 13

Bringing Back the Ark

13:1–14pp — 2Sa 6:1–11

DAVID conferred with each of his officers, the commanders of thousands
and commanders of hundreds. 2He then
said to the whole assembly of Israel, "If it
seems good to you and if it is the will of
the LORD our God, let us send word far
and wide to the rest of our brothers
throughout the territories of Israel, and
also to the priests and Levites who are
with them in their towns and pasturelands, to come and join us. 3Let us bring
the ark of our God back to us,[r] for we did
not inquire[s] of[y] it[z] during the reign of
Saul." 4The whole assembly agreed to do
this, because it seemed right to all the
people.

5So David assembled all the Israelites,[t]
from the Shihor River[u] in Egypt to Lebo[a]
Hamath,[v] to bring the ark of God from
Kiriath Jearim.[w] 6David and all the Israelites with him went to Baalah[x] of Judah
(Kiriath Jearim) to bring up from there
the ark of God the LORD, who is enthroned between the cherubim[y]—the
ark that is called by the Name.

7They moved the ark of God from Abinadab's[z] house on a new cart, with Uzzah
and Ahio guiding it. 8David and all the
Israelites were celebrating with all their
might before God, with songs and with
harps, lyres, tambourines, cymbals and
trumpets.[a]

9When they came to the threshing
floor of Kidon, Uzzah reached out his
hand to steady the ark, because the oxen
stumbled. 10The LORD's anger[b] burned
against Uzzah, and he struck him down[c]
because he had put his hand on the ark.
So he died there before God.

11Then David was angry because the
LORD's wrath had broken out against Uz-
zah, and to this day that place is called
Perez Uzzah.[b] [d]

12David was afraid of God that day and
asked, "How can I ever bring the ark of
God to me?" 13He did not take the ark to
be with him in the City of David. Instead,
he took it aside to the house of Obed-

12:23 [f]2Sa 2:3-4 [g]1Ch 10:14 [h]S 1Sa 16:1; 1Ch 11:10
12:28 [i]1Ch 6:8; 15:11; 16:39; 27:17
12:29 [j]S 2Sa 3:19 [k]2Sa 2:8-9
12:32 [l]Est 1:13
12:38 [m]S 1Ch 9:1
12:39 [n]2Sa 3:20; Isa 25:6-8
12:40 [o]S 2Sa 16:1; 17:29 [p]1Sa 25:18 [q]1Ch 29:22
13:3 [r]1Sa 7:1-2 [s]2Ch 1:5
13:5 [t]1Ch 11:1; 15:3 [u]S Jos 13:3 [v]S Nu 13:21 [w]S 1Sa 7:2
13:6 [x]S Jos 15:9 [y]S Ex 25:22; 2Ki 19:15
13:7 [z]S 1Sa 7:1
13:8 [a]1Ch 15:16, 19,24; 2Ch 5:12; Ps 92:3
13:10 [b]1Ch 15:13, 15 [c]S Lev 10:2
13:11 [d]1Ch 15:13; Ps 7:11

[x]22 Or *a great and mighty army* [y]3 Or *we neglected* [z]3 Or *him* [a]5 Or *to the entrance to* [b]11 *Perez Uzzah* means *outbreak against Uzzah.*

13:8 PRAYER, Worship—David often used music in his worship, expressing praise and thanksgiving to God.
13:10–12 GOD, Holy—God is holy and exalted above us in the purity of His existence. His holiness demands that we reverence Him. Even the ark of the covenant, which represented His presence to the Israelites, was considered to be holy and had to be carried strictly according to instructions. No one could touch it. It was very important for people to learn His instructions for coming into His presence. See note on 2 Sa 6:1–7.

Edom[e] the Gittite. 14The ark of God remained with the family of Obed-Edom in
his house for three months, and the LORD
blessed his household[f] and everything
he had.

Chapter 14

David's House and Family

14:1–7pp — 2Sa 5:11–16; 1Ch 3:5–8

NOW Hiram king of Tyre sent messengers to David, along with cedar
logs,[g] stonemasons and carpenters to
build a palace for him. 2And David knew
that the LORD had established him as king
over Israel and that his kingdom had been
highly exalted[h] for the sake of his people
Israel.
3In Jerusalem David took more wives
and became the father of more sons[i] and
daughters. 4These are the names of the
children born to him there:[j] Shammua,
Shobab, Nathan, Solomon, 5Ibhar, Eli-
shua, Elpelet, 6Nogah, Nepheg, Japhia,
7Elishama, Beeliada[c] and Eliphelet.

David Defeats the Philistines

14:8–17pp — 2Sa 5:17–25

8When the Philistines heard that David
had been anointed king over all Israel,[k]
they went up in full force to search for
him, but David heard about it and went
out to meet them. 9Now the Philistines
had come and raided the Valley[l] of Rephaim; 10so David inquired of God: "Shall I
go and attack the Philistines? Will you
hand them over to me?"
The LORD answered him, "Go, I will
hand them over to you."
11So David and his men went up to
Baal Perazim,[m] and there he defeated
them. He said, "As waters break out, God
has broken out against my enemies by my
hand." So that place was called Baal Perazim.[d] 12The Philistines had abandoned
their gods there, and David gave orders to
burn[n] them in the fire.[o]
13Once more the Philistines raided the
valley;[p] 14so David inquired of God
again, and God answered him, "Do not
go straight up, but circle around them
and attack them in front of the balsam
trees. 15As soon as you hear the sound of
marching in the tops of the balsam trees,
move out to battle, because that will
mean God has gone out in front of you to
strike the Philistine army." 16So David
did as God commanded him, and they
struck down the Philistine army, all the
way from Gibeon[q] to Gezer.[r]
17So David's fame[s] spread throughout
every land, and the LORD made all the
nations fear[t] him.

Chapter 15

The Ark Brought to Jerusalem

15:25–16:3pp — 2Sa 6:12–19

AFTER David had constructed buildings
for himself in the City of David, he
prepared[u] a place for the ark of God and
pitched[v] a tent for it. 2Then David said,
"No one but the Levites[w] may carry[x] the
ark of God, because the LORD chose them
to carry the ark of the LORD and to minister[y] before him forever."
3David assembled all Israel[z] in Jerusalem to bring up the ark of the LORD to the
place he had prepared for it. 4He called
together the descendants of Aaron and
the Levites:[a]
5From the descendants of Kohath,
Uriel[b] the leader and 120 relatives;
6from the descendants of Merari,
Asaiah the leader and 220 relatives;
7from the descendants of Gershon,[e]
Joel the leader and 130 relatives;
8from the descendants of Elizaphan,[c]
Shemaiah the leader and 200 relatives;
9from the descendants of Hebron,[d]
Eliel the leader and 80 relatives;
10from the descendants of Uzziel,
Amminadab the leader and 112 relatives.
11Then David summoned Zadok[e] and
Abiathar[f] the priests, and Uriel, Asaiah,
Joel, Shemaiah, Eliel and Amminadab the
Levites. 12He said to them, "You are the
heads of the Levitical families; you and
your fellow Levites are to consecrate[g]
yourselves and bring up the ark of the
LORD, the God of Israel, to the place I

[c]7 A variant of *Eliada* [d]11 *Baal Perazim* means *the lord who breaks out.* [e]7 Hebrew *Gershom,* a variant of *Gershon*

13:13 [e]1Ch 15:18, 24; 16:38; 26:4-5, 15
13:14 [f]S 2Sa 6:11
14:1 [g]S 1Ki 5:6; 1Ch 17:6; 22:4; 2Ch 2:3; Ezr 3:7; Hag 1:8
14:2 [h]S Nu 24:7; S Dt 26:19
14:3 [i]S 1Ch 3:1
14:4 [j]S 1Ch 3:9
14:8 [k]1Ch 11:1
14:9 [l]ver 13; S Jos 15:8; S 1Ch 11:15
14:11 [m]Ps 94:16; Isa 28:21
14:12 [n]S Ex 32:20 [o]S Jos 7:15
14:13 [p]S ver 9
14:16 [q]S Jos 9:3 [r]Jos 10:33
14:17 [s]S Jos 6:27 [t]Ex 15:14-16; S Dt 2:25; Ps 2:1-12
15:1 [u]Ps 132:1-18 [v]S 2Sa 6:17; 1Ch 16:1; 17:1
15:2 [w]S Nu 3:6; 4:15; Dt 10:8; 31:25; 2Ch 5:5 [x]S Dt 31:9 [y]1Ch 16:4; 23:13; 2Ch 29:11; 31:2; Ps 134:1; 135:2
15:3 [z]S 1Ch 13:5
15:4 [a]S Nu 3:17-20
15:5 [b]1Ch 6:24
15:8 [c]S Ex 6:22
15:9 [d]Ex 6:18
15:11 [e]S 1Ch 12:28 [f]S 1Sa 22:20
15:12 [g]S Ex 29:1; 30:19-21,30; 40:31-32; S Lev 11:44

14:10,14 PRAYER, Petition—See note on 1 Sa 23:2.
14:11–17 GOD, Sovereignty—The victories David won by the power of God made plain the sovereignty of God. God controls the fates of all nations. No nation can use military might or political strategy to defeat God's purpose. Eventually He will give every nation cause to fear Him.
15:2 ELECTION, Leadership—David was obedient to God's election in designating the Levites to carry the ark (Dt 10:8; 18:1–5). God's people should always seek God's chosen leaders.
15:11–15 GOD, Holy—The holiness of God is the reason that the priests and Levites were to move the ark of the covenant in a specific way. See note on 13:10–12.
15:12–14 PRAYER, Commitment—The first attempt to bring up the ark had failed. The people did not ask God how He wanted it done. They had not observed God's regulations for handling the holy ark (2 Sa 6:6–7). Consciousness of the presence of God should demand strictest reverence and lead us to submissive prayer.

have prepared for it. 13It was because
you, the Levites,[h] did not bring it up the
first time that the LORD our God broke
out in anger against us.[i] We did not inquire of him about how to do it in the
prescribed way.[j]" 14So the priests and
Levites consecrated themselves in order
to bring up the ark of the LORD, the God
of Israel. 15And the Levites carried the ark
of God with the poles on their shoulders,
as Moses had commanded[k] in accordance with the word of the LORD.[l]

16David[m] told the leaders of the Levites[n] to appoint their brothers as singers[o] to sing joyful songs, accompanied by
musical instruments: lyres, harps and
cymbals.[p]

17So the Levites appointed Heman[q]
son of Joel; from his brothers, Asaph[r]
son of Berekiah; and from their brothers
the Merarites,[s] Ethan son of Kushaiah;
18and with them their brothers next in
rank: Zechariah,[f] Jaaziel, Shemiramoth,
Jehiel, Unni, Eliab, Benaiah, Maaseiah,
Mattithiah, Eliphelehu, Mikneiah, Obed-
Edom[t] and Jeiel,[g] the gatekeepers.

19The musicians Heman,[u] Asaph and
Ethan were to sound the bronze cymbals;
20Zechariah, Aziel, Shemiramoth, Jehiel,
Unni, Eliab, Maaseiah and Benaiah were
to play the lyres according to *alamoth*,[h]
21and Mattithiah, Eliphelehu, Mikneiah,
Obed-Edom, Jeiel and Azaziah were to
play the harps, directing according to
sheminith.[h] 22Kenaniah the head Levite
was in charge of the singing; that was his
responsibility because he was skillful
at it.

23Berekiah and Elkanah were to be
doorkeepers for the ark. 24Shebaniah,
Joshaphat, Nethanel, Amasai, Zechariah,
Benaiah and Eliezer the priests were to
blow trumpets[v] before the ark of God.
Obed-Edom and Jehiah were also to be
doorkeepers for the ark.

15:13 [h]1Ki 8:4 [i]S 1Ch 13:7-10 [j]S Lev 5:10
15:15 [k]S Ex 25:14 [l]2Sa 6:7
15:16 [m]1Ch 6:31 [n]2Ch 7:6 [o]Ezr 2:41; Ne 11:23; Ps 68:25 [p]S 1Ch 13:8; 23:5; 2Ch 29:26; Ne 12:27,36; Job 21:12; Ps 150:5; Am 6:5
15:17 [q]S 1Ch 6:33 [r]1Ch 6:39 [s]1Ch 6:44
15:18 [t]S 2Sa 6:10; 1Ch 26:4-5
15:19 [u]1Ch 16:41; 25:6
15:24 [v]2Ch 5:12; 7:6; 29:26
15:25 [w]2Ch 1:4; 5:2; Jer 3:16
15:26 [x]Nu 23:1-4, 29
15:27 [y]S 1Sa 2:18
15:28 [z]S 1Ch 9:1 [a]S 1Ki 1:39; Zec 4:7 [b]S Ex 19:13
16:1 [c]S 1Ch 15:1
16:2 [d]S Ex 39:43; Nu 6:23-27
16:3 [e]Isa 16:7
16:4 [f]S 1Ch 15:2

25So David and the elders of Israel and
the commanders of units of a thousand
went to bring up the ark[w] of the covenant
of the LORD from the house of Obed-
Edom, with rejoicing. 26Because God had
helped the Levites who were carrying the
ark of the covenant of the LORD, seven
bulls and seven rams[x] were sacrificed.
27Now David was clothed in a robe of fine
linen, as were all the Levites who were
carrying the ark, and as were the singers,
and Kenaniah, who was in charge of the
singing of the choirs. David also wore a
linen ephod.[y] 28So all Israel[z] brought up
the ark of the covenant of the LORD with
shouts,[a] with the sounding of rams'
horns[b] and trumpets, and of cymbals,
and the playing of lyres and harps.

29As the ark of the covenant of the
LORD was entering the City of David, Michal daughter of Saul watched from a
window. And when she saw King David
dancing and celebrating, she despised
him in her heart.

Chapter 16

THEY brought the ark of God and set it
inside the tent that David had
pitched[c] for it, and they presented burnt
offerings and fellowship offerings[i] before
God. 2After David had finished sacrificing
the burnt offerings and fellowship offerings, he blessed[d] the people in the name
of the LORD. 3Then he gave a loaf of
bread, a cake of dates and a cake of raisins[e] to each Israelite man and woman.

4He appointed some of the Levites to
minister[f] before the ark of the LORD, to
make petition, to give thanks, and to

[f]*18* Three Hebrew manuscripts and most Septuagint manuscripts (see also verse 20 and 1 Chron. 16:5); most Hebrew manuscripts *Zechariah son and* or *Zechariah, Ben and* [g]*18* Hebrew; Septuagint (see also verse 21) *Jeiel and Azaziah* [h]*20,21* Probably a musical term [i]*1* Traditionally *peace offerings*; also in verse 2

15:16–28 PRAYER, Worship—David was himself a musician (1 Sa 16:18). He developed a high view of worship and of all expressions of it, especially music and poetry. Singing and music can often express our joy and thanks to God better than spoken words. See note on 2 Sa 6:14–23.

15:25–28 WORSHIP, Priesthood—See note on 6:48–49; 2 Sa 6:5.

15:29 FAMILY, Conflict—See note on 2 Sa 6:16,20–23.

16:1 PRAYER, Worship—These were voluntary offerings. See note on Lev 1:9.

16:2 PRAYER, Blessing—Previously, blessing was the responsibility of the priest (Lev 9:22). Both David and Solomon assumed this prerogative. See note on 1 Ki 8:55–65. Blessing the congregation was apparently a standard part of worship. The worship leader stood in front of the congregation (1 Ki 8:55), lifted his hands over the assembly (Lev 9:22), spoke with a loud voice (1 Ki 8:55), and pronounced the benediction over the people asking for God's blessing, protection, mercy, presence, and provision of wholeness for life (Nu 6:22–26). The worship leader pronounced Yahweh's name over the worshipers, giving the people a strong sense of belonging to God (Nu 6:27).

16:4 WORSHIP, Thanksgiving—See note on 6:48–49; Ge 12:6–8. King David appointed Levites to lead in prayer, thanksgiving, and praise. At the heart of this chapter is thanksgiving. Beginning in v 7 David recited his own "psalm of thanks to the LORD." The verses following reveal a beautiful song of gratitude to God. True worship of God issues forth from grateful hearts. Feelings such as bitterness, envy, hostility, and pride disqualify one from genuine worship. Thanksgiving opens up the door of the heart toward God in such a way that the individual is freed for true worship of God. Everywhere in Scripture this spirit of thanksgiving is revealed as vital to our worship experience. Compare 2 Ch 7:3; Ezr 3:10–11; Ps 100:4; Eph 5:19–20; Heb 12:28.

16:4–6 PRAYER, Worship—Worship ministers to the Lord. See note on 15:16–28. The orchestra for worship consisted of lyres, harps, and cymbals. Trumpets were used for announcement. These Temple ministers expressed the prayers of Israel to God through music. Prayers are of various types—petition, thanksgiving, and hymns of praise.

praise the LORD, the God of Israel: 5Asaph
was the chief, Zechariah second, then Jeiel, Shemiramoth, Jehiel, Mattithiah, Eliab, Benaiah, Obed-Edom and Jeiel. They
were to play the lyres and harps, Asaph
was to sound the cymbals, 6and Benaiah
and Jahaziel the priests were to blow the
trumpets regularly before the ark of the
covenant of God.

David's Psalm of Thanks

16:8–22pp — Ps 105:1–15
16:23–33pp — Ps 96:1–13
16:34–36pp — Ps 106:1,47–48

7That day David first committed to Asaph and his associates this psalm[g] of thanks to the LORD:

8Give thanks[h] to the LORD, call on his name;
make known among the nations[i] what he has done.
9Sing to him, sing praise[j] to him;
tell of all his wonderful acts.
10Glory in his holy name;[k]
let the hearts of those who seek the LORD rejoice.
11Look to the LORD and his strength;
seek[l] his face always.
12Remember[m] the wonders[n] he has done,
his miracles,[o] and the judgments he pronounced,
13O descendants of Israel his servant,
O sons of Jacob, his chosen ones.
14He is the LORD our God;
his judgments[p] are in all the earth.
15He remembers[j][q] his covenant forever,
the word he commanded, for a thousand generations,
16the covenant[r] he made with Abraham,
the oath he swore to Isaac.
17He confirmed it to Jacob[s] as a decree,
to Israel as an everlasting covenant:
18"To you I will give the land of Canaan[t]
as the portion you will inherit."
19When they were but few in number,[u]
few indeed, and strangers in it,
20they[k] wandered[v] from nation to nation,
from one kingdom to another.
21He allowed no man to oppress them;
for their sake he rebuked kings:[w]
22"Do not touch my anointed ones;
do my prophets[x] no harm."
23Sing to the LORD, all the earth;
proclaim his salvation day after day.
24Declare his glory[y] among the nations,
his marvelous deeds among all peoples.
25For great is the LORD and most worthy of praise;[z]
he is to be feared[a] above all gods.[b]
26For all the gods of the nations are idols,
but the LORD made the heavens.[c]
27Splendor and majesty are before him;
strength and joy in his dwelling place.
28Ascribe to the LORD, O families of nations,
ascribe to the LORD glory and strength,[d]
29 ascribe to the LORD the glory due his name.[e]
Bring an offering and come before him;
worship the LORD in the splendor of his[l] holiness.[f]
30Tremble[g] before him, all the earth!

16:7 [g]Ps 47:7
16:8 [h]ver 34; Ps 107:1; 118:1; 136:1 [i]S 2Ki 19:19
16:9 [j]S Ex 15:1; Ps 7:17
16:10 [k]Ps 8:1; 29:2; 66:2
16:11 [l]ver 10; 1Ch 28:9; 2Ch 7:14; 14:4; 15:2,12; 16:12; 18:4; 20:4; 34:3; Ps 24:6; 27:8; 105:4; 119:2,58; Pr 8:17
16:12 [m]Ps 77:11 [n]S Dt 4:34 [o]Ps 78:43
16:14 [p]Isa 4:4; 26:9
16:15 [q]S Ge 8:1; Ps 98:3; 111:5; 115:12; 136:23
16:16 [r]S Ge 12:7; S 15:18; 22:16-18
16:17 [s]Ge 35:9-12
16:18 [t]Ge 13:14-17
16:19 [u]Dt 7:7
16:20 [v]S Ge 20:13
16:21 [w]Ge 12:17; S 20:3; Ex 7:15-18; Ps 9:5
16:22 [x]S Ge 20:7
16:24 [y]Isa 42:12; 66:19
16:25 [z]Ps 18:3; 48:1 [a]Ps 76:7; 89:7 [b]Ex 18:11; Dt 32:39; 2Ch 2:5; Ps 135:5; Isa 40:25
16:26 [c]Ps 8:3; 102:25
16:28 [d]Ps 29:1-2
16:29 [e]Ps 8:1 [f]2Ch 20:21; Ps 29:1-2
16:30 [g]Ps 2:11; 33:8; 76:8; 99:1; 114:7

[j]*15* Some Septuagint manuscripts (see also Psalm 105:8); Hebrew *Remember* [k]*18-20* One Hebrew manuscript, Septuagint and Vulgate (see also Psalm 105:12); most Hebrew manuscripts *inherit, / 19though you are but few in number, / few indeed, and strangers in it." / 20They* [l]*29* Or *LORD with the splendor of*

16:8–36 GOD, One God—In this psalm of praise to God many of the basic ideas about God are emphasized. The dominant theme is the idea that the God of Israel is the only true God. Only He is mighty in His sovereign power over all the earth.

16:8–36 HISTORY, Confession—In community worship Israel expressed gratitude to God by reciting what He had done for them through their history. His actions gave comfort and help to His people and showed the nations His universal power. History proved all other gods to be worthless idols.

16:8–36 PRAYER, Thanksgiving—This psalm is a compilation from the Book of Psalms (vv 8–22 from Ps 105:1–15; vv 23–33 from the entirety of Ps 96; vv 34–36 from Ps 106:1, 47–48), forming a new thanksgiving psalm. The psalm praises God as sovereign over history and creation (vv 12,31–33), and as faithful to the covenant He chose to make with Israel. The compilation shows us authentic prayers can be formulated with words given by other people. Thanksgiving centers on God's actions and His attributes. Thanksgiving leads to renewed petition for God to act in the present situation as He has in the past. Thanksgiving sends thoughts beyond local, personal situations to the universal character of God and the universal call to worship Him. The congregation appropriated the worship leaders' prayer for themselves through public oral response: "Amen." "Praise the Lord."

16:10,29,35 GOD, Holy—See notes on Ex 3:5–6; 19:10–24; Lev 11:44–45.

16:13 ELECTION, Worship—As elect children of Jacob, Israel was to be faithful to the covenant God made with Jacob. They were to remember God's saving acts in worship, praise, and thanksgiving. They were to tell His reputation among the nations. They were to call to Him and trust Him when new deliverance was needed.

16:15–17 THE CHURCH, Covenant People—Remembering God's blessings calls us to reaffirm our commitment to the Lord. God blesses His people by His faithfulness and presence. As God promised Abraham, Isaac, and Jacob to be faithful, He promises to be available in every situation we face. God continually proves Himself faithful and reliable.

16:29 STEWARDSHIP, Giving in Worship—Worship and giving are linked together. The gifts of God's people express our reverence and awe before His glory. See notes on Dt 16:10,16–17; Mt 5:23–24.

16:30 CREATION, Confidence—David brought the ark of

The world is firmly established; it
cannot be moved.[h]
31Let the heavens rejoice, let the earth
be glad;[i]
let them say among the nations,
"The LORD reigns![j]"
32Let the sea resound, and all that is in
it;[k]
let the fields be jubilant, and
everything in them!
33Then the trees[l] of the forest will sing,
they will sing for joy before the
LORD,
for he comes to judge[m] the earth.

34Give thanks[n] to the LORD, for he is
good;[o]
his love endures forever.[p]
35Cry out, "Save us, O God our Savior;[q]
gather us and deliver us from the
nations,
that we may give thanks to your holy
name,
that we may glory in your praise."
36Praise be to the LORD, the God of
Israel,[r]
from everlasting to everlasting.

Then all the people said "Amen" and
"Praise the LORD."

37David left Asaph and his associates
before the ark of the covenant of the
LORD to minister there regularly, according to each day's requirements.[s] 38He
also left Obed-Edom[t] and his sixty-eight
associates to minister with them. Obed-
Edom son of Jeduthun, and also Hosah,[u]
were gatekeepers.
39David left Zadok[v] the priest and his
fellow priests before the tabernacle of the
LORD at the high place in Gibeon[w] 40to
present burnt offerings to the LORD on
the altar of burnt offering regularly, morning and evening, in accordance with everything written in the Law[x] of the
LORD, which he had given Israel. 41With
them were Heman[y] and Jeduthun and
the rest of those chosen and designated
by name to give thanks to the LORD, "for
his love endures forever." 42Heman and
Jeduthun were responsible for the sounding of the trumpets and cymbals and for
the playing of the other instruments for
sacred song.[z] The sons of Jeduthun[a]
were stationed at the gate.
43Then all the people left, each for his
own home, and David returned home to
bless his family.

16:30 [h]Ps 93:1
16:31 [i]Isa 44:23; 49:13 [j]Ps 9:7; 47:8; 93:1; 97:1; 99:1; 146:10; Isa 52:7; La 5:19
16:32 [k]Ex 20:11; Isa 42:10
16:33 [l]Isa 14:8; 55:12 [m]1Sa 2:10; Ps 7:8; 96:10; 98:9; 110:6; Isa 2:4
16:34 [n]S ver 8; Ps 105:1; Isa 12:4 [o]Ps 25:7; 34:8; 100:5; 135:3; 145:9; Na 1:7 [p]2Ch 5:13; 7:3; Ezr 3:11; Ps 136:1-26; Jer 33:11
16:35 [q]Dt 32:15; Ps 18:46; 38:22; Mic 7:7
16:36 [r]S 1Ki 8:15; Ps 72:18-19
16:37 [s]2Ch 8:14
16:38 [t]S 1Ch 13:13; 26:4-5 [u]1Ch 26:10
16:39 [v]S 1Sa 2:35; S 2Sa 8:17; S 1Ch 12:28 [w]S Jos 9:3; 2Ch 1:3
16:40 [x]S Ex 29:38; Nu 28:1-8
16:41 [y]S 1Ch 15:19
16:42 [z]2Ch 7:6 [a]1Ch 25:3
17:1 [b]S 1Ch 15:1
17:2 [c]1Ch 22:7; 28:2; 2Ch 6:7
17:4 [d]1Ch 22:10; 28:3
17:6 [e]S 1Ch 14:1
17:7 [f]S 2Sa 6:21

Chapter 17

God's Promise to David

17:1–15pp — 2Sa 7:1–17

AFTER David was settled in his palace,
he said to Nathan the prophet,
"Here I am, living in a palace of cedar,
while the ark of the covenant of the LORD
is under a tent.[b]"
2Nathan replied to David, "Whatever
you have in mind,[c] do it, for God is with
you."
3That night the word of God came to
Nathan, saying:
4"Go and tell my servant David,
'This is what the LORD says: You[d] are
not the one to build me a house to
dwell in. 5I have not dwelt in a house
from the day I brought Israel up out
of Egypt to this day. I have moved
from one tent site to another, from
one dwelling place to another.
6Wherever I have moved with all the
Israelites, did I ever say to any of
their leaders[m] whom I commanded
to shepherd my people, "Why have
you not built me a house of cedar?[e]" '
7"Now then, tell my servant David, 'This is what the LORD Almighty
says: I took you from the pasture and
from following the flock, to be ruler[f]
over my people Israel. 8I have been
with you wherever you have gone,
and I have cut off all your enemies
from before you. Now I will make
your name like the names of the
greatest men of the earth. 9And I will
provide a place for my people Israel
and will plant them so that they can
have a home of their own and no longer be disturbed. Wicked people will
not oppress them anymore, as they

[m]6 Traditionally *judges;* also in verse 10

the covenant to Jerusalem so that the people might feel secure in knowing that this symbol of God's presence was near. The song he wrote showed his confidence in the Creator who brought into being a world that is stable and trustworthy as a safe dwelling place.

16:34,41 GOD, Love—God is often pictured in the Old Testament as acting in wrath, but He also wishes to be known as a God of love. Love is His basic characteristic (1 Jn 4:8). Wrath only comes when His love is repeatedly rejected or neglected. God's people praise Him and express our thanks to Him not only for His actions on our behalf but also for His basic nature as a God of love. See notes on Ex 3:7; 20:1–7; Mt 10:29–31; Mk 1:11; Jn 3:16; Ro 5:5–8.

16:37–42 PRAYER, Worship—David established continuing worship in a period somewhat confused by two worship centers. The ark was in Jerusalem, but the holy tent or tabernacle remained at the high place in Gibeon with altars that continued to be important through the early reign of Solomon, who had his prayer-dream there (1 Ki 3:5–9). Worship included thanksgiving for God's enduring love and music to praise God.

17:7–8,24 GOD, Sovereignty—God expresses His sovereignty in the way He leads individuals as well as through His guiding of nations in world history. See notes on Ge 15:13–16; 18:14; 24:3,7,50.

did at the beginning 10and have done
ever since the time I appointed leaders[g] over my people Israel. I will also
subdue all your enemies.
"'I declare to you that the LORD
will build a house for you: 11When
your days are over and you go to be
with your fathers, I will raise up your
offspring to succeed you, one of your
own sons, and I will establish his
kingdom. 12He is the one who will
build[h] a house for me, and I will establish his throne forever.[i] 13I will
be his father,[j] and he will be my
son.[k] I will never take my love away
from him, as I took it away from your
predecessor. 14I will set him over my
house and my kingdom forever;
his throne[l] will be established
forever.[m]'"

15Nathan reported to David all the
words of this entire revelation.

David's Prayer

17:16–27pp — 2Sa 7:18–29

16Then King David went in and sat before the LORD, and he said:

"Who am I, O LORD God, and what
is my family, that you have brought
me this far? 17And as if this were not
enough in your sight, O God, you
have spoken about the future of the
house of your servant. You have
looked on me as though I were the
most exalted of men, O LORD God.
18"What more can David say to
you for honoring your servant? For
you know your servant, 19O LORD.
For the sake[n] of your servant and according to your will, you have done
this great thing and made known all
these great promises.[o]
20"There is no one like you, O
LORD, and there is no God but you,[p]
as we have heard with our own ears.

17:10 [g]S Jdg 2:16
17:12 [h]S 1Ki 5:5 [i]1Ch 22:10; 2Ch 7:18; 13:5
17:13 [j]2Co 6:18 [k]1Ch 28:6; Lk 1:32; Heb 1:5
17:14 [l]S 1Ki 2:12; 1Ch 28:5; 29:23; 2Ch 9:8 [m]Ps 132:11; Jer 33:17
17:19 [n]2Sa 7:16-17; 2Ki 20:6; Isa 9:7; 37:35; 55:3 [o]S 2Sa 7:25
17:20 [p]S Ex 8:10; S 9:14; S 15:11; Isa 44:6; 46:9
17:21 [q]S Ex 6:6
17:22 [r]Ex 19:5-6
17:23 [s]S 1Ki 8:25
17:27 [t]Ps 16:11; 21:6
18:2 [u]S Nu 21:29

21And who is like your people Israel
—the one nation on earth whose
God went out to redeem[q] a people
for himself, and to make a name for
yourself, and to perform great and
awesome wonders by driving out nations from before your people, whom
you redeemed from Egypt? 22You
made your people Israel your very
own forever,[r] and you, O LORD,
have become their God.
23"And now, LORD, let the promise[s] you have made concerning your
servant and his house be established
forever. Do as you promised, 24so
that it will be established and that
your name will be great forever.
Then men will say, 'The LORD Almighty, the God over Israel, is Israel's God!' And the house of your servant David will be established before
you.
25"You, my God, have revealed to
your servant that you will build a
house for him. So your servant has
found courage to pray to you. 26O
LORD, you are God! You have promised these good things to your servant. 27Now you have been pleased
to bless the house of your servant,
that it may continue forever in your
sight;[t] for you, O LORD, have blessed
it, and it will be blessed forever."

Chapter 18

David's Victories

18:1–13pp — 2Sa 8:1–14

IN the course of time, David defeated
the Philistines and subdued them,
and he took Gath and its surrounding
villages from the control of the
Philistines.
2David also defeated the Moabites,[u]

17:13 GOD, Father—See note on 2 Sa 7:14.
17:15 REVELATION, Dreams—The prophet was empowered to receive God's declaration and relay it to the king. The disclosure came to Nathan in a dream. See note on 1 Ki 3:4–5. History proved Nathan's prophecy true (2 Ch 6:15).
17:16–27 HOLY SCRIPTURE, Collection—David prayed, adoring and thanking God for His redemptive acts in the king's life and in the nation's history. Sung by worshipers and historians in the kingdom, the prayer became a written record of God's purposes and presence in the life of Israel and His servant David. Preserved in Scripture, the prayer teaches how God directed David's life. God directed the verbal formulation, preservation, inclusion in the written record, and canonizing in Scripture. God's revelation to His people was done in making promises, fulfilling them in historical acts, guiding His servants to respond in worship and obedience, and preserving that response until it became part of Scripture. He continues to use the written record to reveal Himself.
17:16–27 PRAYER, Sovereignty of God—See note on 2 Sa 7:18–29.
17:20–22 HISTORY, God's People—God's saving action in the Exodus showed His unique power as the only God. It also created a unique people redeemed by God to perform a unique mission, helping extend the reputation and fame of the world's only Redeemer. The Exodus created the unique eternal relationship between God and His people.
17:21–22,27 SALVATION, Preparation—God chose and redeemed Israel to be His own people forever and to be their God. He chose to bless the house of David forever. It was through both that Jesus the Messiah was born. God's work through Israel and the Davidic kingship were deliberate preparations for His work through Jesus.
17:23–27 JESUS CHRIST, Foretold—God's promise to David that there would be an heir forever to sit on David's throne (2 Sa 7:12–28; 1 Ch 17:11–27) was fulfilled in Jesus Christ (Mt 19:28; 21:4–5; 25:31; Mk 12:36–37; Lk 1:32; Ac 2:30; 13:22–23; Ro 1:2–3; Heb 1:8; Rev 22:1). The Old Testament and the New Testament are bound together by this spiritual and final fulfillment in Jesus of God's promise to David.

and they became subject to him and
brought tribute.
3 Moreover, David fought Hadadezer
king of Zobah,[v] as far as Hamath, when
he went to establish his control along the
Euphrates River.[w] 4 David captured a
thousand of his chariots, seven thousand
charioteers and twenty thousand foot soldiers. He hamstrung[x] all but a hundred
of the chariot horses.
5 When the Arameans of Damascus[y]
came to help Hadadezer king of Zobah,
David struck down twenty-two thousand
of them. 6 He put garrisons in the Aramean kingdom of Damascus, and the Arameans became subject to him and brought
tribute. The LORD gave David victory everywhere he went.
7 David took the gold shields carried by
the officers of Hadadezer and brought
them to Jerusalem. 8 From Tebah[n] and
Cun, towns that belonged to Hadadezer,
David took a great quantity of bronze,
which Solomon used to make the bronze
Sea,[z] the pillars and various bronze
articles.
9 When Tou king of Hamath heard that
David had defeated the entire army of
Hadadezer king of Zobah, 10 he sent his
son Hadoram to King David to greet him
and congratulate him on his victory in
battle over Hadadezer, who had been
at war with Tou. Hadoram brought all
kinds of articles of gold and silver and
bronze.
11 King David dedicated these articles to
the LORD, as he had done with the silver
and gold he had taken from all these
nations: Edom[a] and Moab, the Ammonites and the Philistines, and Amalek.[b]
12 Abishai son of Zeruiah struck down
eighteen thousand Edomites[c] in the Valley of Salt. 13 He put garrisons in Edom,
and all the Edomites became subject to
David. The LORD gave David victory everywhere he went.

David's Officials

18:14–17pp — 2Sa 8:15–18

14 David reigned[d] over all Israel,[e] doing what was just and right for all his people. 15 Joab[f] son of Zeruiah was over the
army; Jehoshaphat son of Ahilud was recorder; 16 Zadok[g] son of Ahitub and
Ahimelech[o][h] son of Abiathar were
priests; Shavsha was secretary; 17 Benaiah
son of Jehoiada was over the Kerethites
and Pelethites;[i] and David's sons were
chief officials at the king's side.

18:3 [v]1Ch 19:6 [w]S Ge 2:14
18:4 [x]S Ge 49:6
18:5 [y]2Ki 16:9
18:8 [z]S 1Ki 7:23; 2Ch 4:2-5
18:11 [a]S Nu 24:18 [b]Nu 24:20
18:12 [c]1Ki 11:15
18:14 [d]1Ch 29:26 [e]1Ch 11:1
18:15 [f]2Sa 5:6-8
18:16 [g]1Ch 6:8 [h]1Ch 24:6
18:17 [i]S 1Sa 30:14; S 2Sa 15:18
19:1 [j]S Ge 19:38; Jdg 10:17-11:33; 2Ch 20:1-2; Zep 2:8-11
19:3 [k]S Nu 21:32
19:6 [l]S Ge 34:30 [m]S 1Ch 18:3
19:7 [n]S Nu 21:30
19:11 [o]S 1Sa 26:6

Chapter 19

The Battle Against the Ammonites

19:1–19pp — 2Sa 10:1–19

IN the course of time, Nahash king of
the Ammonites[j] died, and his son
succeeded him as king. 2 David thought,
"I will show kindness to Hanun son of
Nahash, because his father showed kindness to me." So David sent a delegation
to express his sympathy to Hanun concerning his father.
When David's men came to Hanun in
the land of the Ammonites to express
sympathy to him, 3 the Ammonite nobles
said to Hanun, "Do you think David is
honoring your father by sending men to
you to express sympathy? Haven't his
men come to you to explore and spy out[k]
the country and overthrow it?" 4 So Hanun seized David's men, shaved them,
cut off their garments in the middle at the
buttocks, and sent them away.
5 When someone came and told David
about the men, he sent messengers to
meet them, for they were greatly humiliated. The king said, "Stay at Jericho till
your beards have grown, and then come
back."
6 When the Ammonites realized that
they had become a stench[l] in David's
nostrils, Hanun and the Ammonites sent
a thousand talents[p] of silver to hire chariots and charioteers from Aram Naharaim,[q] Aram Maacah and Zobah.[m] 7 They
hired thirty-two thousand chariots and
charioteers, as well as the king of Maacah
with his troops, who came and camped
near Medeba,[n] while the Ammonites
were mustered from their towns and
moved out for battle.
8 On hearing this, David sent Joab out
with the entire army of fighting men.
9 The Ammonites came out and drew up
in battle formation at the entrance to
their city, while the kings who had come
were by themselves in the open country.
10 Joab saw that there were battle lines
in front of him and behind him; so he
selected some of the best troops in Israel
and deployed them against the Arameans.
11 He put the rest of the men under the
command of Abishai[o] his brother, and
they were deployed against the Ammonites. 12 Joab said, "If the Arameans are too
strong for me, then you are to rescue me;

[n] *8* Hebrew *Tibhath,* a variant of *Tebah* [o] *16* Some Hebrew manuscripts, Vulgate and Syriac (see also 2 Samuel 8:17); most Hebrew manuscripts *Abimelech*
[p] *6* That is, about 37 tons (about 34 metric tons)
[q] *6* That is, Northwest Mesopotamia

18:6,13 GOD, Sovereignty—See note on 17:7–8,24.
18:11 STEWARDSHIP, Purpose of Possessions—See note on 2 Sa 8:11.
18:11 PRAYER, Commitment—See note on 2 Sa 8:11–12. Victory belonged to God, so David prayerfully gave Him the spoils.

but if the Ammonites are too strong for
you, then I will rescue you. [13]Be strong
and let us fight bravely for our people and
the cities of our God. The LORD will do
what is good in his sight."
[14]Then Joab and the troops with him
advanced to fight the Arameans, and they
fled before him. [15]When the Ammonites
saw that the Arameans were fleeing, they
too fled before his brother Abishai and
went inside the city. So Joab went back to
Jerusalem.
[16]After the Arameans saw that they had
been routed by Israel, they sent messengers and had Arameans brought from beyond the River,[r] with Shophach the commander of Hadadezer's army leading
them.
[17]When David was told of this, he gathered all Israel[p] and crossed the Jordan;
he advanced against them and formed his
battle lines opposite them. David formed
his lines to meet the Arameans in battle,
and they fought against him. [18]But they
fled before Israel, and David killed seven
thousand of their charioteers and forty
thousand of their foot soldiers. He also
killed Shophach the commander of their
army.
[19]When the vassals of Hadadezer saw
that they had been defeated by Israel,
they made peace with David and became
subject to him.
So the Arameans were not willing to
help the Ammonites anymore.

Chapter 20

The Capture of Rabbah

20:1–3pp — 2Sa 11:1; 12:29–31

IN the spring, at the time when kings go
off to war, Joab led out the armed
forces. He laid waste the land of the Ammonites and went to Rabbah[q] and besieged it, but David remained in Jerusalem. Joab attacked Rabbah and left it in
ruins.[r] [2]David took the crown from the
head of their king[s]—its weight was
found to be a talent[t] of gold, and it was
set with precious stones—and it was
placed on David's head. He took a great
quantity of plunder from the city [3]and
brought out the people who were there,
consigning them to labor with saws and
with iron picks and axes.[s] David did this
to all the Ammonite towns. Then David
and his entire army returned to Jerusalem.

War With the Philistines

20:4–8pp — 2Sa 21:15–22

[4]In the course of time, war broke out
with the Philistines, at Gezer.[t] At that
time Sibbecai the Hushathite killed Sip-
pai, one of the descendants of the Rephaites,[u] and the Philistines were subjugated.
[5]In another battle with the Philistines,
Elhanan son of Jair killed Lahmi the
brother of Goliath the Gittite, who had a
spear with a shaft like a weaver's rod.[v]
[6]In still another battle, which took
place at Gath, there was a huge man with
six fingers on each hand and six toes on
each foot—twenty-four in all. He also
was descended from Rapha. [7]When he
taunted Israel, Jonathan son of Shimea,
David's brother, killed him.
[8]These were descendants of Rapha in
Gath, and they fell at the hands of David
and his men.

Chapter 21

David Numbers the Fighting Men

21:1–26pp — 2Sa 24:1–25

SATAN[w] rose up against Israel and incited David to take a census[x] of Israel. [2]So David said to Joab and the commanders of the troops, "Go and count[y]
the Israelites from Beersheba to Dan.
Then report back to me so that I may
know how many there are."
[3]But Joab replied, "May the LORD multiply his troops a hundred times over.[z]
My lord the king, are they not all my
lord's subjects? Why does my lord want
to do this? Why should he bring guilt on
Israel?"
[4]The king's word, however, overruled
Joab; so Joab left and went throughout
Israel and then came back to Jerusalem.
[5]Joab reported the number of the fighting
men to David: In all Israel[a] there were
one million one hundred thousand men
who could handle a sword, including four
hundred and seventy thousand in Judah.
[6]But Joab did not include Levi and Benjamin in the numbering, because the

19:17 [p]S 1Ch 9:1
20:1 [q]S Dt 3:11 [r]Am 1:13-15
20:3 [s]S Dt 29:11
20:4 [t]Jos 10:33 [u]S Ge 14:5
20:5 [v]S 1Sa 17:7
21:1 [w]S 2Ch 18:21; S Ps 109:6 [x]2Ch 14:8; 25:5
21:2 [y]1Ch 27:23-24
21:3 [z]S Dt 1:11
21:5 [a]S 1Ch 9:1

[r]*16* That is, the Euphrates [s]*2* Or *of Milcom,* that is, Molech [t]*2* That is, about 75 pounds (about 34 kilograms)

19:13 GOD, Faithfulness—God is faithful to His own basic character. He is a righteous God who always does what is right, in all circumstances. Because He is righteous, He defines what is good. We do not always have sufficient information and wisdom to know what is right. See note on Mt 19:17.

19:13 HISTORY, God's Will—Historical acts ultimately reveal God's will for a people and for the world. Humans do their best but know God must bless their efforts if they are to succeed. God's will ultimately leads to good.

21:1 EVIL AND SUFFERING, Satan—See note on 2 Sa 24:1.

21:1–8 SIN, Discipline—David recognized his error, but God's judgment was still visited upon the people. The effects of sin in a person's life cannot be eradicated totally even by repentance and remorse. See note on 2 Sa 24:1–10.

king's command was repulsive to him.
7This command was also evil in the sight
of God; so he punished Israel.
8Then David said to God, "I have
sinned greatly by doing this. Now, I beg
you, take away the guilt of your servant. I
have done a very foolish thing."
9The LORD said to Gad,[b] David's
seer,[c] 10"Go and tell David, 'This is what
the LORD says: I am giving you three options. Choose one of them for me to carry
out against you.' "
11So Gad went to David and said to
him, "This is what the LORD says: 'Take
your choice: 12three years of famine,[d]
three months of being swept away[u] before your enemies, with their swords
overtaking you, or three days of the
sword[e] of the LORD[f]—days of plague in
the land, with the angel of the LORD rav-
aging every part of Israel.' Now then, decide how I should answer the one who
sent me."
13David said to Gad, "I am in deep distress. Let me fall into the hands of the
LORD, for his mercy[g] is very great; but do
not let me fall into the hands of men."
14So the LORD sent a plague on Israel,
and seventy thousand men of Israel fell
dead.[h] 15And God sent an angel[i] to destroy Jerusalem.[j] But as the angel was
doing so, the LORD saw it and was
grieved[k] because of the calamity and said
to the angel who was destroying[l] the
people, "Enough! Withdraw your hand."
The angel of the LORD was then standing
at the threshing floor of Araunah[v] the
Jebusite.
16David looked up and saw the angel of
the LORD standing between heaven and
earth, with a drawn sword in his hand
extended over Jerusalem. Then David
and the elders, clothed in sackcloth, fell
facedown.[m]
17David said to God, "Was it not I who
ordered the fighting men to be counted? I
am the one who has sinned and done
wrong. These are but sheep.[n] What have
they done? O LORD my God, let your
hand fall upon me and my family,[o] but do
not let this plague remain on your people."
18Then the angel of the LORD ordered
Gad to tell David to go up and build an
altar to the LORD on the threshing floor[p]
of Araunah the Jebusite. 19So David went
up in obedience to the word that Gad had
spoken in the name of the LORD.
20While Araunah was threshing
wheat,[q] he turned and saw the angel; his
four sons who were with him hid themselves. 21Then David approached, and
when Araunah looked and saw him, he
left the threshing floor and bowed down
before David with his face to the ground.
22David said to him, "Let me have the
site of your threshing floor so I can build
an altar to the LORD, that the plague on
the people may be stopped. Sell it to me
at the full price."
23Araunah said to David, "Take it! Let
my lord the king do whatever pleases
him. Look, I will give the oxen for the
burnt offerings, the threshing sledges for
the wood, and the wheat for the grain
offering. I will give all this."
24But King David replied to Araunah,
"No, I insist on paying the full price. I
will not take for the LORD what is yours,
or sacrifice a burnt offering that costs me
nothing."
25So David paid Araunah six hundred
shekels[w] of gold for the site. 26David built
an altar to the LORD there and sacrificed
burnt offerings and fellowship offerings.[x]
He called on the LORD, and the LORD answered him with fire[r] from heaven on
the altar of burnt offering.
27Then the LORD spoke to the angel,
and he put his sword back into its sheath.
28At that time, when David saw that the
LORD had answered him on the threshing

21:9 [b]S 1Sa 22:5 [c]S 1Sa 9:9
21:12 [d]S Dt 32:24 [e]Eze 30:25 [f]S Ge 19:13
21:13 [g]Ps 6:4; 86:15; 130:4,7
21:14 [h]1Ch 27:24
21:15 [i]S Ge 32:1 [j]Ps 125:2 [k]S Ge 6:6; S Ex 32:14 [l]S Ge 19:13
21:16 [m]S Nu 14:5; S Jos 7:6
21:17 [n]S 2Sa 7:8 [o]Jnh 1:12
21:18 [p]2Ch 3:1
21:20 [q]S Jdg 6:11
21:26 [r]S Ex 19:18; S Jdg 6:21

[u] *12* Hebrew; Septuagint and Vulgate (see also 2 Samuel 24:13) *of fleeing* [v] *15* Hebrew *Ornan,* a variant of *Araunah;* also in verses 18-28 [w] *25* That is, about 15 pounds (about 7 kilograms) [x] *26* Traditionally *peace offerings*

21:7–15 GOD, Wrath—This passage may seem to picture God as very harsh and vindictive. It was crucially important for Him to establish in the minds of His people the importance of following His will, not that of Satan or themselves. It is a serious matter to act against God's will in a flagrant manner. The destruction exacted here seems enormous—but if later generations profit from this lesson, it will have served its purpose. Even in exercising His wrath, God does what is right and just.

21:7 HISTORY, Judgment—The most faithful of God's people make mistakes. King David's command was evil and brought God's judgment. Even judgment brought evidence of God's mercy (v 15).

21:16–30 ELECTION, Worship—God revealed the threshing floor of Araunah as His chosen site for the Temple. The ark was now in Jerusalem. The Levites were chosen to minister before it. Solomon was designated as Temple builder. The Temple site was the final revelation for David to plan and prepare for worship at God's chosen place. See note on Dt 12:5–14.

21:24 STEWARDSHIP, Giving in Worship—Gifts to God that cost the giver little tend to have little significance. Giving to God should represent personal sacrifice. David's refusal to offer a sacrifice that cost him nothing reflected both his reverence for God and the significance of giving. See notes on Dt 16:10,16–17; Mt 5:23–24.

21:26 WORSHIP, Prayer—See note on Ge 12:6–8.

21:26 PRAYER, Answer—See note on 2 Sa 24:25. From 22:1 it is evident that David understood the fire as approval of this site for the future Temple. In times He chooses God responds with concrete signs to prayer. Here David received assurance God accepted him and would bless his Temple project even though he had sinned.

floor of Araunah the Jebusite, he offered
sacrifices there. 29 The tabernacle of the
LORD, which Moses had made in the
desert, and the altar of burnt offering
were at that time on the high place at
Gibeon.[s] 30 But David could not go before
it to inquire of God, because he was
afraid of the sword of the angel of the
LORD.

Chapter 22

THEN David said, "The house of the
LORD God[t] is to be here, and also
the altar of burnt offering for Israel."

Preparations for the Temple

2 So David gave orders to assemble the
aliens[u] living in Israel, and from among
them he appointed stonecutters[v] to prepare dressed stone for building the house
of God. 3 He provided a large amount of
iron to make nails for the doors of the
gateways and for the fittings, and more
bronze than could be weighed.[w] 4 He also
provided more cedar logs[x] than could be
counted, for the Sidonians and Tyrians
had brought large numbers of them to David.
5 David said, "My son Solomon is
young[y] and inexperienced, and the
house to be built for the LORD should be
of great magnificence and fame and splendor[z] in the sight of all the nations. Therefore I will make preparations for it." So
David made extensive preparations before his death.
6 Then he called for his son Solomon
and charged him to build[a] a house for
the LORD, the God of Israel. 7 David said to
Solomon: "My son, I had it in my heart[b]
to build[c] a house for the Name[d] of the
LORD my God. 8 But this word of the LORD
came to me: 'You have shed much blood
and have fought many wars.[e] You are not
to build a house for my Name,[f] because
you have shed much blood on the earth
in my sight. 9 But you will have a son who
will be a man of peace[g] and rest,[h] and I
will give him rest from all his enemies on
every side. His name will be Solomon,[y] [i]
and I will grant Israel peace and quiet[j]
during his reign. 10 He is the one who will
build a house for my Name.[k] He will be
my son,[l] and I will be his father. And I
will establish[m] the throne of his kingdom
over Israel forever.'[n]
11 "Now, my son, the LORD be with[o]
you, and may you have success and build
the house of the LORD your God, as he
said you would. 12 May the LORD give you
discretion and understanding[p] when he
puts you in command over Israel, so that
you may keep the law of the LORD your
God. 13 Then you will have success[q] if
you are careful to observe the decrees
and laws[r] that the LORD gave Moses for
Israel. Be strong and courageous.[s] Do not
be afraid or discouraged.
14 "I have taken great pains to provide
for the temple of the LORD a hundred
thousand talents[z] of gold, a million talents[a] of silver, quantities of bronze and
iron too great to be weighed, and wood
and stone. And you may add to them.[t]
15 You have many workmen: stonecutters,
masons and carpenters,[u] as well as men
skilled in every kind of work 16 in gold and
silver, bronze and iron—craftsmen[v] beyond number. Now begin the work, and
the LORD be with you."
17 Then David ordered[w] all the leaders
of Israel to help his son Solomon. 18 He
said to them, "Is not the LORD your God

21:29 [s]S Jos 9:3
22:1 [t]S Ge 28:17
22:2 [u]S Ex 1:11; S Dt 20:11; 2Ch 8:10; S Isa 56:6 [v]1Ki 5:17-18; Ezr 3:7
22:3 [w]S 1Ki 7:47; 1Ch 29:2-5
22:4 [x]S 1Ki 5:6
22:5 [y]S 1Ki 3:7; 1Ch 29:1 [z]2Ch 2:5
22:6 [a]Ac 7:47
22:7 [b]S 1Ch 17:2 [c]S 1Ki 8:17 [d]Dt 12:5,11
22:8 [e]S 1Ki 5:3 [f]1Ch 28:3
22:9 [g]S Jos 14:15; S 1Ki 5:4 [h]ver 18; 1Ch 23:25; 2Ch 14:6,7; 15:15; 20:30; 36:21 [i]S 2Sa 12:24; S 1Ch 23:1 [j]1Ki 4:20
22:10 [k]S 1Ch 17:12 [l]S 2Sa 7:13 [m]1Ki 9:5 [n]S 2Sa 7:14; S 1Ch 17:4; 2Ch 6:15
22:11 [o]S 1Sa 16:18; S 18:12
22:12 [p]1Ki 3:9-12
22:13 [q]1Ki 2:3 [r]1Ch 28:7 [s]S Dt 31:6
22:14 [t]1Ch 29:2-5, 19
22:15 [u]Ezr 3:7
22:16 [v]2Ch 2:7
22:17 [w]1Ch 28:1-6

[y]9 *Solomon* sounds like and may be derived from the Hebrew for *peace.* [z]14 That is, about 3,750 tons (about 3,450 metric tons) [a]14 That is, about 37,500 tons (about 34,500 metric tons)

22:1–19 REVELATION, History—God reveals Himself in personal and national history. He spoke to David through Nathan the prophet (2 Sa 7) preventing David from building the Temple. He led David to military victory and established peace in the land, making possible Solomon's building of the Temple. His presence made Solomon's building efforts successful. His written revelation gave guidance to Solomon's life. His gift of wisdom gave Solomon the leadership skills to accomplish the task. He was with the leaders of Israel, giving Solomon the necessary support. He placed His name in the Temple showing His presence with and lordship of His people. In all this God was revealing Himself to Israel.

22:1 HISTORY, Worship—Israel's neighbors often traced their centers of worship back to creation. Israel knew her place of worship came late in her history when God chose to reveal its place and allow its construction. History showed no sacred place is essential to the relationship between God and His people. The relationship was established long before the worship place was built.

22:1–19 WORSHIP, Buildings—See note on Ge 28:16–22.

22:5–10 EVIL AND SUFFERING, Punishment—Suffering may take the form of unfulfilled dreams and goals. At times God does not allow us to fulfill even goals designed for His glory and honor. God has His reasons. David wanted to build a Temple for God. He did not gain God's permission because he had spent his time in wars (1 Ki 5:3) and thus was not the proper person to build a house of worship. David responded by doing everything possible to make sure his successor would carry out his dream. We should follow his example when we must suffer unfulfilled dreams. Compare 28:3.

22:10 GOD, Father—See note on 2 Sa 7:14.

22:11–12 PRAYER, Petition—David's prayer for discretion and understanding became a part of Solomon's thinking and later prompted a remarkable dream in which Solomon prayed for discernment (1 Ki 3:9). Prayer was woven as a natural part into this conversation between father and son. Prayer can be a natural part of our communication with others, particularly with loved ones.

22:12–13 CHRISTIAN ETHICS, Moral Imperatives—See note on 1 Ki 3:3,14.

22:18–19 REVELATION, Events—An assembly of leaders was the teaching occasion for David's retelling of God's saving presence and guidance with Israel. The recorded comments became written witnesses of God's actions for Israel, confirmed over many years in their personal history.

with you? And has he not granted you
rest[x] on every side?[y] For he has handed
the inhabitants of the land over to me,
and the land is subject to the LORD and to
his people. 19Now devote your heart and
soul to seeking the LORD your God.[z] Begin to build the sanctuary of the LORD
God, so that you may bring the ark of the
covenant of the LORD and the sacred articles belonging to God into the temple
that will be built for the Name of the
LORD."

Chapter 23

The Levites

WHEN David was old and full of years,
he made his son Solomon[a] king
over Israel.[b]
2He also gathered together all the leaders of Israel, as well as the priests and
Levites. 3The Levites thirty years old or
more[c] were counted,[d] and the total
number of men was thirty-eight thousand.[e] 4David said, "Of these, twenty-
four thousand are to supervise[f] the
work[g] of the temple of the LORD and six
thousand are to be officials and judges.[h]
5Four thousand are to be gatekeepers and
four thousand are to praise the LORD with
the musical instruments[i] I have provided
for that purpose."[j]
6David divided[k] the Levites into
groups corresponding to the sons of
Levi:[l] Gershon, Kohath and Merari.

Gershonites

7Belonging to the Gershonites:[m]
Ladan and Shimei.
8The sons of Ladan:
Jehiel the first, Zetham and Joel
—three in all.
9The sons of Shimei:
Shelomoth, Haziel and Haran—
three in all.
These were the heads of the families of Ladan.
10And the sons of Shimei:
Jahath, Ziza,[b] Jeush and Beriah.
These were the sons of Shimei—
four in all.
11Jahath was the first and Ziza the
second, but Jeush and Beriah did
not have many sons; so they were

22:18 [x]S ver 9 [y]2Sa 7:1
22:19 [z]2Ch 7:14
23:1 [a]1Ch 22:9; 28:5; 2Ch 1:8 [b]S 1Ki 1:30; 1Ch 29:28
23:3 [c]Nu 8:24 [d]1Ch 21:7 [e]Nu 4:3-49
23:4 [f]Ezr 3:8 [g]2Ch 34:13; Ne 4:10 [h]1Ch 26:29; 2Ch 19:8; Eze 44:24
23:5 [i]S 1Ch 15:16; Ps 92:3 [j]Ne 12:45
23:6 [k]2Ch 8:14; 23:18; 29:25 [l]S Nu 3:17; 1Ch 24:20
23:7 [m]1Ch 6:71
23:12 [n]S Ge 46:11; S Ex 6:18
23:13 [o]Ex 6:20 [p]Ex 30:7-10 [q]S 1Ch 15:2 [r]S Nu 6:23
23:14 [s]Dt 33:1
23:15 [t]Ex 18:4
23:16 [u]1Ch 26:24-28
23:17 [v]1Ch 24:21
23:18 [w]1Ch 26:25
23:19 [x]1Ch 24:23; 26:31
23:21 [y]S 1Ch 6:19 [z]S Ex 6:19
23:22 [a]Nu 36:8

counted as one family with one
assignment.

Kohathites

12The sons of Kohath:[n]
Amram, Izhar, Hebron and Uzziel
—four in all.
13The sons of Amram:[o]
Aaron and Moses.
Aaron was set apart,[p] he and his
descendants forever, to consecrate the most holy things, to offer
sacrifices before the LORD, to minister[q] before him and to pronounce blessings[r] in his name
forever. 14The sons of Moses the
man[s] of God were counted as
part of the tribe of Levi.
15The sons of Moses:
Gershom and Eliezer.[t]
16The descendants of Gershom:[u]
Shubael was the first.
17The descendants of Eliezer:
Rehabiah[v] was the first.
Eliezer had no other sons, but the
sons of Rehabiah were very numerous.
18The sons of Izhar:
Shelomith[w] was the first.
19The sons of Hebron:[x]
Jeriah the first, Amariah the second, Jahaziel the third and Jekameam the fourth.
20The sons of Uzziel:
Micah the first and Isshiah the
second.

Merarites

21The sons of Merari:[y]
Mahli and Mushi.[z]
The sons of Mahli:
Eleazar and Kish.
22Eleazar died without having sons:
he had only daughters. Their
cousins, the sons of Kish, married
them.[a]
23The sons of Mushi:
Mahli, Eder and Jerimoth—three
in all.
24These were the descendants of Levi
by their families—the heads of families as
they were registered under their names

[b] *10* One Hebrew manuscript, Septuagint and Vulgate (see also verse 11); most Hebrew manuscripts *Zina*

22:18 HISTORY, Presence—God showed His presence by giving peace and rest from war just as by giving victory in battle. Rest provided opportunity to seek God and build His place of worship. See note on Jos 11:23.

23:5 PRAYER, Praise—See note on 15:16–28.

23:13 PRAYER, Command of God—God set up a system to ensure that worship and prayer continued among His people. Prayer is a part of God's eternal plan for His people. The Aaronic priests were to pronounce benedictions on Israel as well as offer sacrifice and prayer to God. See note on 16:2. To minister (Hebrew *sheret*) is to serve a person (Ex 24:13; 1 Ki 19:21) by free choice, not as a slave. In worship, to minister is to prepare for and lead in worship (1 Ch 6:17; 16:4,37; Nu 1:50; 3:31; 4:12; Eze 44:11,17,27). In essence, to minister is to serve God (Dt 10:8; 17:12). Prayer is part of that service. The danger is that to minister can come to mean to serve the worship house, the worship service, or the worship leaders. Ministry is to God and not to an institution. It is to bring God's blessing to the people, not to bless the institution with people as its servants. Compare 1 Ch 23:28–32.

and counted individually, that is, the
workers twenty years old or more[b] who
served in the temple of the LORD. 25For
David had said, "Since the LORD, the God
of Israel, has granted rest[c] to his people
and has come to dwell in Jerusalem forever, 26the Levites no longer need to carry
the tabernacle or any of the articles used
in its service."[d] 27According to the last
instructions of David, the Levites were
counted from those twenty years old or
more.
28The duty of the Levites was to help
Aaron's descendants in the service of the
temple of the LORD: to be in charge of the
courtyards, the side rooms, the purification[e] of all sacred things and the performance of other duties at the house of
God. 29They were in charge of the bread
set out on the table,[f] the flour for the
grain offerings,[g] the unleavened wafers,
the baking and the mixing, and all measurements of quantity and size.[h] 30They
were also to stand every morning to
thank and praise the LORD. They were to
do the same in the evening[i] 31and whenever burnt offerings were presented to
the LORD on Sabbaths and at New Moon[j]
festivals and at appointed feasts.[k] They
were to serve before the LORD regularly
in the proper number and in the way prescribed for them.
32And so the Levites[l] carried out their
responsibilities for the Tent of Meeting,[m]
for the Holy Place and, under their brothers the descendants of Aaron, for the service of the temple of the LORD.[n]

Chapter 24

The Divisions of Priests

THESE were the divisions[o] of the sons
of Aaron:[p]
The sons of Aaron were Nadab, Abihu,
Eleazar and Ithamar.[q] 2But Nadab and
Abihu died before their father did,[r] and
they had no sons; so Eleazar and Ithamar
served as the priests. 3With the help of
Zadok[s] a descendant of Eleazar and
Ahimelech a descendant of Ithamar, David separated them into divisions for their
appointed order of ministering. 4A larger
number of leaders were found among Eleazar's descendants than among Ithamar's,
and they were divided accordingly: sixteen heads of families from Eleazar's descendants and eight heads of families
from Ithamar's descendants. 5They divided them impartially by drawing lots,[t] for
there were officials of the sanctuary and
officials of God among the descendants of
both Eleazar and Ithamar.
6The scribe Shemaiah son of Nethanel,
a Levite, recorded their names in the
presence of the king and of the officials:
Zadok the priest, Ahimelech[u] son of Abiathar and the heads of families of the
priests and of the Levites—one family being taken from Eleazar and then one from
Ithamar.

7The first lot fell to Jehoiarib,
the second to Jedaiah,[v]
8the third to Harim,[w]
the fourth to Seorim,
9the fifth to Malkijah,
the sixth to Mijamin,
10the seventh to Hakkoz,
the eighth to Abijah,[x]
11the ninth to Jeshua,
the tenth to Shecaniah,
12the eleventh to Eliashib,
the twelfth to Jakim,
13the thirteenth to Huppah,
the fourteenth to Jeshebeab,
14the fifteenth to Bilgah,
the sixteenth to Immer,[y]
15the seventeenth to Hezir,[z]
the eighteenth to Happizzez,
16the nineteenth to Pethahiah,
the twentieth to Jehezkel,
17the twenty-first to Jakin,
the twenty-second to Gamul,
18the twenty-third to Delaiah
and the twenty-fourth to Maaziah.

19This was their appointed order of
ministering when they entered the temple of the LORD, according to the regulations prescribed for them by their forefather Aaron, as the LORD, the God of
Israel, had commanded him.

The Rest of the Levites

20As for the rest of the descendants of
Levi:[a]
from the sons of Amram: Shubael;
from the sons of Shubael: Jehdeiah.
21As for Rehabiah,[b] from his sons:
Isshiah was the first.
22From the Izharites: Shelomoth;
from the sons of Shelomoth: Jahath.
23The sons of Hebron:[c] Jeriah the
first,[c] Amariah the second,

c23 Two Hebrew manuscripts and some Septuagint manuscripts (see also 1 Chron. 23:19); most Hebrew manuscripts *The sons of Jeriah:*

23:24 bS Nu 4:3
23:25 cS 1Ch 22:9
23:26 dNu 4:5,15; 7:9; Dt 10:8
23:28 e2Ch 29:15; Ne 13:9; Mal 3:3
23:29 fS Ex 25:30 gLev 2:4-7; 6:20-23 hLev 19:35-36; S 1Ch 9:29,32
23:30 iS 1Ch 9:33; Ps 134:1
23:31 jS 2Ki 4:23 kNu 28:9-29:39; Isa 1:13-14; Col 2:16
23:32 l1Ch 6:48 mNu 3:6-8,38 n2Ch 23:18; 31:2; Eze 44:14
24:1 o1Ch 23:6; 28:13; 2Ch 5:11; 8:14; 23:8; 31:2; 35:4,5; Ezr 6:18 pNu 3:2-4 qS Ex 6:23
24:2 rLev 10:1-2
24:3 sS 2Sa 8:17
24:5 tver 31; 1Ch 25:8; 26:13
24:6 u1Ch 18:16
24:7 vEzr 2:36; Ne 12:6
24:8 wEzr 2:39; 10:21; Ne 10:5
24:10 xNe 12:4,17; Lk 1:5
24:14 yEzr 2:37; 10:20; Jer 20:1
24:15 zNe 10:20
24:20 aS 1Ch 23:6
24:21 b1Ch 23:17
24:23 cS 1Ch 23:19

23:25 REVELATION, Divine Presence—God's ongoing presence in the desert, symbolized by the ark and the Tent of Meeting was transferred and reaffirmed through God's permanent presence in the city of Jerusalem and His commitment to abide with His children.

23:30–31 PRAYER, Persistence—Prayer is a constant part of the congregation's life. True prayer cannot be discontinuous, for prayer is fellowship with God. See note on Ge 5:24. Morning and evening prayers surround our days in God's presence.

Jahaziel the third and Jekameam
the fourth.
24The son of Uzziel: Micah;
from the sons of Micah: Shamir.
25The brother of Micah: Isshiah;
from the sons of Isshiah: Zechariah.
26The sons of Merari:[d] Mahli and Mushi.
The son of Jaaziah: Beno.
27The sons of Merari:
from Jaaziah: Beno, Shoham, Zaccur and Ibri.
28From Mahli: Eleazar, who had no sons.
29From Kish: the son of Kish:
Jerahmeel.
30And the sons of Mushi: Mahli, Eder
and Jerimoth.

These were the Levites, according to
their families. 31They also cast lots,[e] just
as their brothers the descendants of Aaron did, in the presence of King David and
of Zadok, Ahimelech, and the heads of
families of the priests and of the Levites.
The families of the oldest brother were
treated the same as those of the youngest.

Chapter 25

The Singers

DAVID, together with the commanders
of the army, set apart some of the
sons of Asaph,[f] Heman[g] and Jeduthun[h]
for the ministry of prophesying,[i] accompanied by harps, lyres and cymbals.[j]
Here is the list of the men[k] who performed this service:[l]

2From the sons of Asaph:
Zaccur, Joseph, Nethaniah and Asarelah. The sons of Asaph were under
the supervision of Asaph, who prophesied under the king's supervision.
3As for Jeduthun, from his sons:[m]
Gedaliah, Zeri, Jeshaiah, Shimei,[d]
Hashabiah and Mattithiah, six in all,
under the supervision of their father
Jeduthun, who prophesied, using the
harp[n] in thanking and praising the
LORD.
4As for Heman, from his sons:
Bukkiah, Mattaniah, Uzziel, Shubael
and Jerimoth; Hananiah, Hanani, Eliathah, Giddalti and Romamti-Ezer;
Joshbekashah, Mallothi, Hothir and
Mahazioth. 5All these were sons of
Heman the king's seer. They were
given him through the promises of
God to exalt him.[e] God gave Heman
fourteen sons and three daughters.

6All these men were under the supervision of their fathers[o] for the music of the
temple of the LORD, with cymbals, lyres
and harps, for the ministry at the house of
God. Asaph, Jeduthun and Heman[p] were
under the supervision of the king.[q]
7Along with their relatives—all of them
trained and skilled in music for the LORD
—they numbered 288. 8Young and old
alike, teacher as well as student, cast
lots[r] for their duties.

9The first lot, which was for
Asaph,[s] fell to Joseph,
his sons and relatives,[f] 12[g]
the second to Gedaliah,
he and his relatives and sons, 12
10the third to Zaccur,
his sons and relatives, 12
11the fourth to Izri,[h]
his sons and relatives, 12
12the fifth to Nethaniah,
his sons and relatives, 12
13the sixth to Bukkiah,
his sons and relatives, 12
14the seventh to Jesarelah,[i]
his sons and relatives, 12
15the eighth to Jeshaiah,
his sons and relatives, 12
16the ninth to Mattaniah,
his sons and relatives, 12
17the tenth to Shimei,
his sons and relatives, 12
18the eleventh to Azarel,[j]
his sons and relatives, 12
19the twelfth to Hashabiah,
his sons and relatives, 12
20the thirteenth to Shubael,
his sons and relatives, 12
21the fourteenth to Mattithiah,
his sons and relatives, 12
22the fifteenth to Jerimoth,
his sons and relatives, 12
23the sixteenth to Hananiah,
his sons and relatives, 12
24the seventeenth to Joshbekashah,
his sons and relatives, 12
25the eighteenth to Hanani,
his sons and relatives, 12
26the nineteenth to Mallothi,
his sons and relatives, 12

24:26 [d]S 1Ch 6:19
24:31 [e]S ver 5
25:1 [f]S 1Ch 6:39 [g]S 1Ch 6:33 [h]1Ch 16:41,42; Ne 11:17 [i]S 1Sa 10:5; 2Ki 3:15 [j]S 1Ch 15:16 [k]S 1Ch 6:31 [l]2Ch 5:12; 8:14; 34:12; 35:15; Ezr 3:10
25:3 [m]1Ch 16:41-42 [n]S Ge 4:21; Ps 33:2
25:6 [o]S 1Ch 15:16 [p]S 1Ch 15:19 [q]2Ch 23:18; 29:25
25:8 [r]1Ch 26:13
25:9 [s]S 1Ch 6:39

[d]*3* One Hebrew manuscript and some Septuagint manuscripts (see also verse 17); most Hebrew manuscripts do not have *Shimei.* [e]*5* Hebrew *exalt the horn* [f]*9* See Septuagint; Hebrew does not have *his sons and relatives.* [g]*9* See the total in verse 7; Hebrew does not have *twelve.* [h]*11* A variant of *Zeri* [i]*14* A variant of *Asarelah* [j]*18* A variant of *Uzziel*

25:1–31 WORSHIP, Music—Organized music ministry was part of the prophetic task of revealing God's will to His people. See note on 6:31–32.
25:3 PRAYER, Praise—Music is a primary vehicle for praise. See note on 15:16–28.
25:8 HUMANITY, Work—In fulfilling community responsibilities, there are tasks for all ages and for all kinds of abilities and skills.

27the twentieth to Eliathah,
his sons and relatives, 12
28the twenty-first to Hothir,
his sons and relatives, 12
29the twenty-second to Giddalti,
his sons and relatives, 12
30the twenty-third to Mahazioth,
his sons and relatives, 12
31the twenty-fourth to Romamti-Ezer,
his sons and relatives, 12[t]

Chapter 26

The Gatekeepers

THE divisions of the gatekeepers:[u]
From the Korahites: Meshelemiah son of Kore, one of the sons of Asaph.
2Meshelemiah had sons:
Zechariah[v] the firstborn,
Jediael the second,
Zebadiah the third,
Jathniel the fourth,
3Elam the fifth,
Jehohanan the sixth
and Eliehoenai the seventh.
4Obed-Edom also had sons:
Shemaiah the firstborn,
Jehozabad the second,
Joah the third,
Sacar the fourth,
Nethanel the fifth,
5Ammiel the sixth,
Issachar the seventh
and Peullethai the eighth.
(For God had blessed Obed-Edom.[w])
6His son Shemaiah also had sons, who were leaders in their father's family because they were very capable men.
7The sons of Shemaiah: Othni, Rephael, Obed and Elzabad; his relatives Elihu and Semakiah were also able men.
8All these were descendants of Obed-Edom; they and their sons and their relatives were capable men with the strength to do the work—descendants of Obed-Edom, 62 in all.
9Meshelemiah had sons and relatives, who were able men—18 in all.
10Hosah the Merarite had sons: Shimri the first (although he was not the firstborn, his father had appointed him the first),[x]
11Hilkiah the second, Tabaliah the third and Zechariah the fourth. The sons and relatives of Hosah were 13 in all.

12These divisions of the gatekeepers, through their chief men, had duties for ministering[y] in the temple of the LORD, just as their relatives had.
13Lots[z] were cast for each gate, according to their families, young and old alike.
14The lot for the East Gate[a] fell to Shelemiah.[k] Then lots were cast for his son Zechariah,[b] a wise counselor, and the lot for the North Gate fell to him.
15The lot for the South Gate fell to Obed-Edom,[c] and the lot for the storehouse fell to his sons.
16The lots for the West Gate and the Shalleketh Gate on the upper road fell to Shuppim and Hosah.
Guard was alongside of guard:
17There were six Levites a day on the east, four a day on the north, four a day on the south and two at a time at the storehouse.
18As for the court to the west, there were four at the road and two at the court itself.
19These were the divisions of the gatekeepers who were descendants of Korah and Merari.[d]

The Treasurers and Other Officials

20Their fellow Levites[e] were[l] in charge of the treasuries of the house of God and the treasuries for the dedicated things.[f]
21The descendants of Ladan, who were Gershonites through Ladan and who were heads of families belonging to Ladan the Gershonite,[g] were Jehieli,
22the sons of Jehieli, Zetham and his brother Joel. They were in charge of the treasuries[h] of the temple of the LORD.
23From the Amramites, the Izharites, the Hebronites and the Uzzielites:[i]
24Shubael,[j] a descendant of Gershom son of Moses, was the officer in charge of the treasuries.
25His relatives through Eliezer: Rehabiah his son, Jeshaiah his son, Joram his son, Zicri his son and Shelomith[k] his son.
26Shelomith and his relatives were in charge of all the treasuries for the things dedicated[l] by King David, by the heads of families who were the commanders of thousands and commanders of hundreds, and by the other army commanders.
27Some of the plunder taken in battle they dedicated for the repair of the temple of the LORD.
28And everything dedicated by Samuel the seer[m] and by Saul son

25:31 [t]S 1Ch 9:33
26:1 [u]S 1Ch 9:17
26:2 [v]S 1Ch 9:21
26:5 [w]S 2Sa 6:10; S 1Ch 13:13; S 16:38
26:10 [x]Dt 21:16; 1Ch 5:1
26:12 [y]1Ch 9:22
26:13 [z]S 1Ch 24:5, 31; 25:8
26:14 [a]S 1Ch 9:18 [b]S 1Ch 9:21
26:15 [c]S 1Ch 13:13; 2Ch 25:24
26:19 [d]2Ch 35:15; Ne 7:1; Eze 44:11
26:20 [e]2Ch 24:5 [f]1Ch 28:12
26:21 [g]1Ch 23:7; 29:8
26:22 [h]1Ch 9:26
26:23 [i]S Nu 3:27
26:24 [j]1Ch 23:16
26:25 [k]1Ch 23:18
26:26 [l]S 2Sa 8:11
26:28 [m]S 1Sa 9:9

[k] *14* A variant of *Meshelemiah* [l] *20* Septuagint; Hebrew *As for the Levites, Ahijah was*

26:20–28 STEWARDSHIP, Management—Responsible handling of gifts dedicated to God is a sacred task. Those selected for the task are entrusted with an important ministry. The waste or misuse of gifts for God's work offends God and discourages the people in their spirit of giving. See notes on Ge 39:2–6; 2 Ki 12:4–16.

of Kish, Abner son of Ner and
Joab son of Zeruiah, and all the
other dedicated things were in
the care of Shelomith and his relatives.
29From the Izharites: Kenaniah and
his sons were assigned duties
away from the temple, as officials
and judges[n] over Israel.
30From the Hebronites: Hashabiah[o]
and his relatives—seventeen hundred able men—were responsible
in Israel west of the Jordan for all
the work of the LORD and for the
king's service. 31As for the Hebronites,[p] Jeriah was their chief
according to the genealogical
records of their families. In the
fortieth[q] year of David's reign a
search was made in the records,
and capable men among the Hebronites were found at Jazer in
Gilead. 32Jeriah had twenty-seven
hundred relatives, who were able
men and heads of families, and
King David put them in charge of
the Reubenites, the Gadites and
the half-tribe of Manasseh for every matter pertaining to God and
for the affairs of the king.

Chapter 27

Army Divisions

THIS is the list of the Israelites—heads
of families, commanders of thousands and commanders of hundreds, and
their officers, who served the king in all
that concerned the army divisions that
were on duty month by month throughout the year. Each division consisted of
24,000 men.

2In charge of the first division, for the
first month, was Jashobeam[r] son of
Zabdiel. There were 24,000 men in
his division. 3He was a descendant
of Perez and chief of all the army
officers for the first month.
4In charge of the division for the second
month was Dodai[s] the Ahohite;
Mikloth was the leader of his division. There were 24,000 men in
his division.
5The third army commander, for the
third month, was Benaiah[t] son of
Jehoiada the priest. He was chief
and there were 24,000 men in his
division. 6This was the Benaiah
who was a mighty man among the
Thirty and was over the Thirty. His
son Ammizabad was in charge of
his division.
7The fourth, for the fourth month, was
Asahel[u] the brother of Joab; his son
Zebadiah was his successor. There
were 24,000 men in his division.
8The fifth, for the fifth month, was the
commander Shamhuth[v] the Izra-
hite. There were 24,000 men in his
division.
9The sixth, for the sixth month, was
Ira[w] the son of Ikkesh the Tekoite.
There were 24,000 men in his division.
10The seventh, for the seventh month,
was Helez[x] the Pelonite, an Ephraimite. There were 24,000 men in
his division.
11The eighth, for the eighth month, was
Sibbecai[y] the Hushathite, a Zerahite. There were 24,000 men in his
division.
12The ninth, for the ninth month, was
Abiezer[z] the Anathothite, a Benjamite. There were 24,000 men in
his division.
13The tenth, for the tenth month, was
Maharai[a] the Netophathite, a Zerahite. There were 24,000 men in his
division.
14The eleventh, for the eleventh month,
was Benaiah[b] the Pirathonite, an
Ephraimite. There were 24,000
men in his division.
15The twelfth, for the twelfth month, was
Heldai[c] the Netophathite, from the
family of Othniel.[d] There were
24,000 men in his division.

Officers of the Tribes

16The officers over the tribes of Israel:
over the Reubenites: Eliezer son of
Zicri;
over the Simeonites: Shephatiah son
of Maacah;
17over Levi: Hashabiah[e] son of Kemuel;
over Aaron: Zadok;[f]
18over Judah: Elihu, a brother of David;
over Issachar: Omri son of Michael;
19over Zebulun: Ishmaiah son of Obadiah;
over Naphtali: Jerimoth son of
Azriel;
20over the Ephraimites: Hoshea son of
Azaziah;
over half the tribe of Manasseh:
Joel son of Pedaiah;
21over the half-tribe of Manasseh in
Gilead: Iddo son of Zechariah;
over Benjamin: Jaasiel son of Abner;
22over Dan: Azarel son of Jeroham.
These were the officers over the tribes
of Israel.
23David did not take the number of the

26:29 [n]Dt 17:8-13; S 1Ch 23:4
26:30 [o]1Ch 27:17
26:31 [p]S 1Ch 23:19 [q]S 2Sa 5:4
27:2 [r]2Sa 23:8
27:4 [s]S 2Sa 23:9
27:5 [t]S 2Sa 23:20
27:7 [u]S 2Sa 2:18
27:8 [v]1Ch 11:27
27:9 [w]2Sa 23:26
27:10 [x]2Sa 23:26
27:11 [y]S 2Sa 21:18
27:12 [z]2Sa 23:27
27:13 [a]2Sa 23:28
27:14 [b]S 1Ch 11:31
27:15 [c]2Sa 23:29 [d]S Jos 15:17
27:17 [e]1Ch 26:30 [f]S 2Sa 8:17; S 1Ch 12:28

men twenty years old or less,[g] because
the LORD had promised to make Israel as
numerous as the stars[h] in the sky. 24Joab
son of Zeruiah began to count the men
but did not finish. Wrath came on Israel
on account of this numbering,[i] and the
number was not entered in the book[m] of
the annals of King David.

The King's Overseers

25Azmaveth son of Adiel was in charge
of the royal storehouses.

Jonathan son of Uzziah was in charge
of the storehouses in the outlying districts, in the towns, the villages and the
watchtowers.

26Ezri son of Kelub was in charge of the
field workers who farmed the land.

27Shimei the Ramathite was in charge
of the vineyards.

Zabdi the Shiphmite was in charge of
the produce of the vineyards for the wine
vats.

28Baal-Hanan the Gederite was in
charge of the olive and sycamore-fig[j]
trees in the western foothills.

Joash was in charge of the supplies of
olive oil.

29Shitrai the Sharonite was in charge of
the herds grazing in Sharon.[k]

Shaphat son of Adlai was in charge of
the herds in the valleys.

30Obil the Ishmaelite was in charge of
the camels.

Jehdeiah the Meronothite was in
charge of the donkeys.

31Jaziz the Hagrite[l] was in charge of
the flocks.

All these were the officials in charge of
King David's property.

32Jonathan, David's uncle, was a counselor, a man of insight and a scribe. Jehiel
son of Hacmoni took care of the king's
sons.

33Ahithophel[m] was the king's counselor.

Hushai[n] the Arkite was the king's
friend. 34Ahithophel was succeeded by Jehoiada son of Benaiah and by Abiathar.[o]

Joab[p] was the commander of the royal
army.

27:23 [g]S 2Sa 24:1; 1Ch 21:2-5 [h]S Ge 12:2
27:24 [i]S 2Sa 24:15; 1Ch 21:14
27:28 [j]S 1Ki 10:27
27:29 [k]SS 2:1; Isa 33:9; 35:2; 65:10
27:31 [l]S 1Ch 5:10
27:33 [m]S 2Sa 15:12 [n]S 2Sa 15:37
27:34 [o]S 1Sa 22:20 [p]S 2Sa 2:13
28:1 [q]1Ch 22:17 [r]1Ch 27:1-31; 29:6
28:2 [s]S 1Sa 10:7; S 1Ch 17:2 [t]2Ch 6:41 [u]Ps 99:5; 132:7; Isa 60:13 [v]Ps 132:1-5
28:3 [w]S 2Sa 7:5 [x]1Ch 22:8 [y]S 1Ki 5:3; S 1Ch 17:4
28:4 [z]2Ch 6:6 [a]1Sa 16:1-13 [b]S Ge 49:10; Nu 24:17-19 [c]1Ch 11:1
28:5 [d]S 1Ch 3:1 [e]S 2Sa 12:24; S 1Ch 23:1 [f]S 1Ch 17:14
28:6 [g]1Ki 8:20 [h]S 2Sa 7:13; S 1Ch 17:13
28:7 [i]1Ch 22:13
28:8 [j]S 1Ch 9:1 [k]Dt 6:1 [l]Dt 4:1; S 17:14-20
28:9 [m]S 1Ch 29:19 [n]S 1Sa 2:3; 2Ch 6:30; Ps 7:9 [o]S 1Ch 16:11; S Ps 40:16 [p]S Dt 4:31; S Jos 24:20; S 2Ch 7:19; 15:2 [q]1Ki 9:7; Ps 44:23; 74:1; 77:7

Chapter 28

David's Plans for the Temple

DAVID summoned[q] all the officials[r]
of Israel to assemble at Jerusalem:
the officers over the tribes, the commanders of the divisions in the service of the
king, the commanders of thousands and
commanders of hundreds, and the officials in charge of all the property and livestock belonging to the king and his sons,
together with the palace officials, the
mighty men and all the brave warriors.
2King David rose to his feet and said:
"Listen to me, my brothers and my people. I had it in my heart[s] to build a house
as a place of rest[t] for the ark of the covenant of the LORD, for the footstool[u] of
our God, and I made plans to build it.[v]
3But God said to me,[w] 'You are not to
build a house for my Name,[x] because you
are a warrior and have shed blood.'[y]
4"Yet the LORD, the God of Israel,
chose me[z] from my whole family[a] to be
king over Israel forever. He chose Judah[b]
as leader, and from the house of Judah he
chose my family, and from my father's
sons he was pleased to make me king
over all Israel.[c] 5Of all my sons—and the
LORD has given me many[d]—he has chosen my son Solomon[e] to sit on the
throne[f] of the kingdom of the LORD over
Israel. 6He said to me: 'Solomon your son
is the one who will build[g] my house and
my courts, for I have chosen him to be
my son,[h] and I will be his father. 7I will
establish his kingdom forever if he is unswerving in carrying out my commands
and laws,[i] as is being done at this time.'
8"So now I charge you in the sight of
all Israel[j] and of the assembly of the
LORD, and in the hearing of our God: Be
careful to follow all the commands[k] of
the LORD your God, that you may possess
this good land and pass it on as an inheritance to your descendants forever.[l]
9"And you, my son Solomon, acknowledge the God of your father, and serve
him with wholehearted devotion[m] and
with a willing mind, for the LORD
searches every heart[n] and understands
every motive behind the thoughts. If you
seek him,[o] he will be found by you; but if
you forsake[p] him, he will reject[q] you forever. 10Consider now, for the LORD has

[m]24 Septuagint; Hebrew *number*

28:3 EVIL AND SUFFERING, Punishment—See note on 22:5–10.

28:4–10 ELECTION, Leadership—David reminded Solomon of the responsibilities of election to build God's Temple. Election for the task demanded commitment to God and the task. Rejection or acceptance of God's plans and purposes are choices which the elect must make.

28:6–10 CHRISTIAN ETHICS, Moral Imperatives—See note on 1 Ki 3:3,14.

28:9 GOD, Wisdom—God has intimate knowledge of all that happens on the earth, even to the thoughts and motives of our hearts. He blesses or chastises on the basis of this knowledge, exercising His sovereignty over us and the world. Such complete wisdom and knowledge enable Him to judge us in absolute righteousness. They do not eliminate our freedom of action and decision.

chosen you to build a temple as a sanctuary. Be strong and do the work."
11Then David gave his son Solomon the
plans[r] for the portico of the temple, its
buildings, its storerooms, its upper parts,
its inner rooms and the place of atonement. 12He gave him the plans of all that
the Spirit[s] had put in his mind for the
courts of the temple of the LORD and all
the surrounding rooms, for the treasuries
of the temple of God and for the treasuries for the dedicated things.[t] 13He gave
him instructions for the divisions[u] of the
priests and Levites, and for all the work of
serving in the temple of the LORD, as well
as for all the articles to be used in its
service. 14He designated the weight of
gold for all the gold articles to be used in
various kinds of service, and the weight
of silver for all the silver articles to be
used in various kinds of service: 15the
weight of gold for the gold lampstands[v]
and their lamps, with the weight for each
lampstand and its lamps; and the weight
of silver for each silver lampstand and its
lamps, according to the use of each lampstand; 16the weight of gold for each table[w] for consecrated bread; the weight of
silver for the silver tables; 17the weight of
pure gold for the forks, sprinkling bowls[x]
and pitchers; the weight of gold for each
gold dish; the weight of silver for each
silver dish; 18and the weight of the refined gold for the altar of incense.[y] He
also gave him the plan for the chariot,[z]
that is, the cherubim of gold that spread
their wings and shelter[a] the ark of the
covenant of the LORD.
19"All this," David said, "I have in
writing from the hand of the LORD upon
me, and he gave me understanding in all
the details[b] of the plan.[c]"
20David also said to Solomon his son,
"Be strong and courageous,[d] and do the
work. Do not be afraid or discouraged, for
the LORD God, my God, is with you. He
will not fail you or forsake[e] you until all
the work for the service of the temple of
the LORD is finished.[f] 21The divisions of
the priests and Levites are ready for all
the work on the temple of God, and every
willing man skilled[g] in any craft will help
you in all the work. The officials and all
the people will obey your every command."

Chapter 29

Gifts for Building the Temple

THEN King David said to the whole assembly: "My son Solomon, the one
whom God has chosen, is young and inexperienced.[h] The task is great, because
this palatial structure is not for man but
for the LORD God. 2With all my resources
I have provided for the temple of my
God—gold[i] for the gold work, silver for
the silver, bronze for the bronze, iron for
the iron and wood for the wood, as well
as onyx for the settings, turquoise,[n] [j]
stones of various colors, and all kinds of
fine stone and marble—all of these in
large quantities.[k] 3Besides, in my devotion to the temple of my God I now give
my personal treasures of gold and silver
for the temple of my God, over and above
everything I have provided[l] for this holy
temple: 4three thousand talents[o] of gold
(gold of Ophir)[m] and seven thousand talents[p] of refined silver,[n] for the overlay-
ing of the walls of the buildings, 5for the
gold work and the silver work, and for all
the work to be done by the craftsmen.
Now, who is willing to consecrate himself
today to the LORD?"
6Then the leaders of families, the officers of the tribes of Israel, the commanders of thousands and commanders of hun-

[n]2 The meaning of the Hebrew for this word is uncertain. [o]4 That is, about 110 tons (about 100 metric tons) [p]4 That is, about 260 tons (about 240 metric tons)

28:11 [r]S Ex 25:9; Ac 7:44; Heb 8:5
28:12 [s]S 1Ch 12:18 [t]1Ch 26:20
28:13 [u]S 1Ch 24:1
28:15 [v]Ex 25:31
28:16 [w]S Ex 25:23
28:17 [x]S Ex 27:3
28:18 [y]Ex 30:1-10 [z]S Ex 25:22 [a]S Ex 25:20
28:19 [b]1Ki 6:38 [c]S Ex 25:9
28:20 [d]S Dt 31:6; 1Ch 22:13; 2Ch 19:11; Hag 2:4 [e]S Dt 4:31; S Jos 24:20 [f]S 1Ki 6:14; 2Ch 7:11
28:21 [g]Ex 35:25-36:5
29:1 [h]1Ki 3:7; 1Ch 22:5; 2Ch 13:7
29:2 [i]ver 7,14,16; Ezr 1:4; 6:5; Hag 2:8 [j]Isa 54:11 [k]1Ch 22:2-5
29:3 [l]2Ch 24:10; 31:3; 35:8
29:4 [m]S Ge 10:29 [n]1Ch 22:14

28:11–19 HOLY SPIRIT, Leaders—The Spirit leads some to plan for others to act. God forbade David to build the Temple. The Spirit put plans for the Temple and its worship in David's mind (v 12) just as He did with Moses and the tabernacle (Ex 25:1—30:38). The instructions for Moses are preserved, but those for David do not appear unless they form the basis for 1 Ch 22—26 and 2 Ch 3:1—4:22. The Spirit inspired some writing which was not collected and preserved as part of Scripture. It was only for the writer's time. The Spirit leads each generation to plan how they can best worship and serve God. See note on Ge 41:38–39.

28:11–20 HOLY SCRIPTURE, Writing—God provided written plans to David for the Temple, its contents, and the organization of its personnel, just as He gave Moses directions for the tabernacle (Ex 25—31). Revelation included the written plans and understanding of those plans. The Word and the ability to understand the Word are both parts of God's revelation—as is the divine Presence, which enabled Solomon to carry out God's Word.

28:20 GOD, Faithfulness—God will fulfill His promises and will bless His people as they serve Him. He meets our needs and blesses our efforts when we are serving Him. He is not simply the Almighty One who rules the universe. He is the personal One whom I can call "my God."

29:1 ELECTION, Leadership—David prepared the people to accept Solomon as God's chosen to build the Temple. Unable to fulfill his cherished dream, he faithfully prepared the way for another to accomplish it. David is a reminder of our responsibility as role models in giving, praying, organizing, worshiping, and teaching. A chosen leader accomplishes God's assigned task and prepares the way for successors to accomplish even greater things.

29:2–5 STEWARDSHIP, Service to God—A leader's example and testimony influences the response of the people. David's appeal was made effective by his example of worthy and generous giving. See note on Ac 4:32—5:11.

29:6–9 PRAYER, Worship—Voluntary offerings are an indication of the heart which pleases God. Voluntary giving is a way of rejoicing in God and praising Him. See note on Lev 1:9.

dreds, and the officials[o] in charge of the
king's work gave willingly.[p] 7They[q] gave
toward the work on the temple of God
five thousand talents[q] and ten thousand
darics[r] of gold, ten thousand talents[s] of
silver, eighteen thousand talents[t] of
bronze and a hundred thousand talents[u]
of iron. 8Any who had precious stones[r]
gave them to the treasury of the temple of
the LORD in the custody of Jehiel the Gershonite.[s] 9The people rejoiced at the
willing response of their leaders, for they
had given freely and wholeheartedly[t] to
the LORD. David the king also rejoiced
greatly.

David's Prayer

10David praised the LORD in the presence of the whole assembly, saying,

"Praise be to you, O LORD,
God of our father Israel,
from everlasting to everlasting.
11Yours, O LORD, is the greatness and
the power[u]
and the glory and the majesty and
the splendor,
for everything in heaven and earth is
yours.[v]
Yours, O LORD, is the kingdom;
you are exalted as head over all.[w]
12Wealth and honor[x] come from you;
you are the ruler[y] of all things.
In your hands are strength and power
to exalt and give strength to all.
13Now, our God, we give you thanks,
and praise your glorious name.

14"But who am I, and who are my people, that we should be able to give as generously as this?[z] Everything comes from
you, and we have given you only what
comes from your hand.[a] 15We are aliens
and strangers[b] in your sight, as were all
our forefathers. Our days on earth are like
a shadow,[c] without hope. 16O LORD our
God, as for all this abundance that we
have provided for building you a temple
for your Holy Name, it comes from your
hand, and all of it belongs to you. 17I
know, my God, that you test the heart[d]
and are pleased with integrity. All these
things have I given willingly and with
honest intent. And now I have seen with
joy how willingly your people who are
here have given to you.[e] 18O LORD, God
of our fathers Abraham, Isaac and Israel,
keep this desire in the hearts of your people forever, and keep their hearts loyal to
you. 19And give my son Solomon the
wholehearted devotion[f] to keep your
commands, requirements and decrees[g]
and to do everything to build the palatial
structure for which I have provided."[h]
20Then David said to the whole assembly, "Praise the LORD your God." So they
all praised the LORD, the God of their fathers; they bowed low and fell prostrate
before the LORD and the king.

29:6 [o]1Ch 27:1; S 28:1 [p]ver 9; Ex 25:1-8; 35:20-29; 36:2; 2Ch 24:10; Ezr 7:15
29:7 [q]S Ex 25:2; Ne 7:70-71
29:8 [r]Ex 35:27 [s]S 1Ch 26:21
29:9 [t]1Ki 8:61
29:11 [u]Ps 24:8; 59:17; 62:11 [v]Ps 89:11 [w]Rev 5:12-13
29:12 [x]2Ch 1:12; 32:27; Ezr 7:27; Ecc 5:19 [y]2Ch 20:6
29:14 [z]Ps 8:4; 144:3 [a]S ver 2
29:15 [b]S Ge 17:8; S 23:4; Ps 39:12; S Heb 11:13 [c]Job 7:6; 8:9; 14:2; 32:7; Ps 102:11; 144:4; Ecc 6:12
29:17 [d]Ps 139:23; Pr 15:11; 17:3; Jer 11:20; 17:10 [e]1Ch 28:9; Ps 15:1-5; Pr 11:20
29:19 [f]S 1Ki 8:61; 11:4; 1Ch 28:9; Isa 38:3 [g]Ps 72:1 [h]S 1Ch 22:14

[q]7 That is, about 190 tons (about 170 metric tons)
[r]7 That is, about 185 pounds (about 84 kilograms)
[s]7 That is, about 375 tons (about 345 metric tons)
[t]7 That is, about 675 tons (about 610 metric tons)
[u]7 That is, about 3,750 tons (about 3,450 metric tons)

29:10 GOD, Eternal—God is eternal, without beginning and without ending. This is basic to our understanding of God. If He had a beginning, we should look for the one who brought about His beginning. And if He had an ending, we could not have full confidence in Him to watch over us in the future. Thus His eternal nature calls forth our praise. See notes on Ge 1:1; 21:33.

29:10–13 WORSHIP, Reverence—Worship centers on God in His holy, unique nature before it looks to His acts on behalf of His people. One great characteristic of worship is pure love for or adoration of the Lord. Focusing the mind and heart on the majesty of God, contemplating the glory of God, meditating upon all the glorious attributes of God are all vital to worship. The sovereignty of God is the basic reason for and focus of worship. These verses vividly illustrate such adoration. We have lost much of this sense of awe and adoration which ought to be at the heart of worship. See note on Ex 15:1–21.

29:10–22 PRAYER, Corporate—More prayers are recorded by David than of any other person in the Bible. He recognized God's uniqueness and sovereignty, the graciousness of His provision, and His desire that Israel honor the Lord. David's prayer in song led the congregation in prayer and worship. David spoke in first person plural ("we"), representing the congregation before God.

29:11–12 GOD, Sovereignty—God is praised as sovereign Ruler over all the earth. He is great in power and majesty and is the source of all good things. Such greatness and power could easily overwhelm us, causing us to cower in fear. His redeeming love leads us to praise Him even for such unequaled power.

29:11 GOD, Glory—The glory of God is the manifestation, or the recognition, of who and what He is. See note on Ex 16:7,10; 40:34–38; Lk 2:9,14.

29:11–19 STEWARDSHIP, God's Ownership—Stewardship rests on the fundamental belief that God owns everything that exists. People are His servants, serving Him as stewards of what He chooses to let us have. All earthly wealth comes from Him. So does human strength, power, and position. We do not deserve to have anything to give back to God. We give only what we have received. Stewardship is one test of our integrity to see if we act on our belief that God is Lord and Owner of all. David and his people passed the test as they provided for God's Temple. He prayed that God's people would continue to work with such loyalty, generosity, and faithfulness forever. He also prayed that Solomon would be faithful in using the resources David had given for God's purposes. A major part of stewardship involves God's people collecting and allocating financial resources in ways that will please God and fulfill His purposes.

29:14–16 GOD, Grace—The grace of God was praised here as the source of all the good blessings that have come to God's people. We must admit that we deserve to be only strangers in His sight. His love and power combine to bring us His gracious blessings that we do not deserve. God's people respond to such grace by bringing offerings to God.

29:15 HUMANITY, Life—Human beings are insignificant when compared with God. All that people can do in God's service still does not bring real hope. That ultimately comes solely from God. See Jn 10:10.

29:18–19 CHRISTIAN ETHICS, Prayer—Desire to do God's will comes through prayer. See note on 1 Ki 8:25,58.

29:20 WORSHIP, Corporate—See note on 2 Ch 7:3; Ps 42:1–4.

Solomon Acknowledged as King

29:21–25pp — 1Ki 1:28–53

21The next day they made sacrifices to
the LORD and presented burnt offerings to
him:[i] a thousand bulls, a thousand rams
and a thousand male lambs, together with
their drink offerings, and other sacrifices
in abundance for all Israel.[j] 22They ate
and drank with great joy[k] in the presence of the LORD that day.
Then they acknowledged Solomon son
of David as king a second time, anointing
him before the LORD to be ruler and Zadok[l] to be priest. 23So Solomon sat[m] on
the throne[n] of the LORD as king in place
of his father David. He prospered and all
Israel obeyed him. 24All the officers and
mighty men, as well as all of King David's
sons,[o] pledged their submission to King
Solomon.
25The LORD highly exalted[p] Solomon
in the sight of all Israel and bestowed on
him royal splendor[q] such as no king over
Israel ever had before.[r]

The Death of David

29:26–28pp — 1Ki 2:10–12

26David son of Jesse was king[s] over all
Israel.[t] 27He ruled over Israel forty years
—seven in Hebron[u] and thirty-three in
Jerusalem.[v] 28He died[w] at a good old age,
having enjoyed long life, wealth and hon-
or. His son Solomon succeeded him as
king.[x]
29As for the events of King David's
reign, from beginning to end, they are
written in the records of Samuel the
seer,[y] the records of Nathan[z] the prophet and the records of Gad[a] the seer, 30to-
gether with the details of his reign and
power, and the circumstances that surrounded him and Israel and the kingdoms
of all the other lands.

29:21 [i]S 1Ki 8:62 [j]1Ch 11:1
29:22 [k]1Ch 12:40 [l]S 1Sa 2:35
29:23 [m]S Dt 17:18 [n]S 1Ki 2:12; S 1Ch 17:14
29:24 [o]1Ki 1:9
29:25 [p]S Jos 3:7 [q]1Ki 10:7; 2Ch 1:1, 12 [r]Ecc 2:9
29:26 [s]1Ch 18:14 [t]1Ch 11:1
29:27 [u]S Ge 23:19 [v]2Sa 5:4-5; S 1Ch 3:4
29:28 [w]S Ge 15:15; Ac 13:36 [x]S 1Ch 23:1
29:29 [y]S 1Sa 9:9 [z]S 2Sa 7:2 [a]S 1Sa 22:5

29:28 HUMANITY, Death—Death is consistently viewed as the normal end of life. When it came at the end of a long and prosperous life, it was accepted with peace by ancient Israelites. In view of Christ's resurrection, Christians have even more reason to face death in peace.

29:29 HOLY SCRIPTURE, Writing—The prophets and their disciples provided one means by which the revealed word of God was transcribed and preserved. Here mentioned are three recording prophets whose accounts were not preserved in individual books but served as sources for the inspired author of Chronicles (2 Ch 9:29; 12:15; 26:22; 33:19). Close examination shows the Chronicler used the Books of Samuel and Kings for much of his work. Early chapters rely on the Pentateuch (Genesis—Deuteronomy). God's inspiration of His Word thus involved preparing sources for inspired writers and leading them as they used and interpreted the sources to present His inspired historical record. See note on 2 Ki 1:16–18.

29:29–30 HISTORY, Narrative—Biblical history is an inspired selection and presentation of God's direction of His people. Many details needed to reconstruct political history are omitted. The biblical historian's contemporaries were guided to other sources for such information. We do not possess those sources and thus cannot reconstruct the historical details as fully as we might like. We do have the trustworthy Word God gave us to learn His directions for us, His people. Our task is to study that Word to learn more about God's nature, our nature, and the nature of His relationship with us.

2 Chronicles

See Introduction to 1 Chronicles.

Theological Outline

2 Chronicles: The Road to Revival Is Open After Disaster.

I. Past Glory Was Based on a Wise, Humble Leader and Devotion to God's House. (1:1—9:31)
   A. Greatness was based on God's presence with His humble leader. (1:1-17)
   B. The great leader of the past made building a Temple for God first priority. (2:1—8:16)
      1. The Temple, built by people's and craftsmen's best efforts, represents a great God present everywhere and so not contained by any building. (2:1-18)
      2. God is interested in every detail of worship to insure His house symbolizes unity, beauty, simplicity, and divine mystery. (3:1—5:14)
      3. The Temple shows that God fulfills His promises and expects His people to fulfill their covenant promises. (6:1-17)
      4. The Temple represents the active presence of God with His people and the nations in judgment, forgiveness, teaching, blessing, and discipline. (6:18-42)
      5. Joyful worship is the proper response of God's people to God's presence. (7:1-10)
      6. Prayer is the central activity for God's people in His house of worship. (7:11-16)
      7. Royal sin can lead to exile and destruction of God's Temple, thus removing His presence from His people. (7:17-22)
      8. God blesses an obedient leader of a people worshiping as He has commanded. (8:1-16)
   E. Wealth, fame, and wisdom characterized God's glorious leader of the past. (8:17—9:31)

II. God Works Through His People Even in Time of Division. (10:1—36:21)
   A. Selfish leadership divides God's people. (10:1—12:16)
      1. Ignoring wise, experienced counsel for younger, self-seeking counselors paves the road to ruin. (10:1-19)
      2. Following God leads away from revenge. (11:1-12)
      3. Godly leaders remain loyal to God's house and defend God's people. (11:13-23)
      4. Judgment punishes the guilty and teaches the humble. (12:1-16)
   B. Fighting against God and His kingdom will never succeed, while faithful fulfillment of His requirements brings victory. (13:1-22)
   C. God blesses His leader as long as he does good in God's sight. (14:1—16:14)
      1. God gives rest and victory to those who seek Him. (14:1-8)
      2. God's leader obeys God's word and attracts committed followers. (15:1-9)
      3. God's leader brings His people to joyful renewal of God's covenant. (15:10-19)
      4. A leader faces defeat for trusting in human alliances rather than in God. (16:1-14)
   D. Trust in God brings peace, but helping God's enemies brings His wrath. (17:1—21:3)
      1. God is present with the leader who opposes false gods, ensures His people learn God's Word, and spreads reverence for God among other peoples. (17:1-19)
      2. The prophetic word controls history. (18:1-34)
      3. A righteous, just leader can influence a nation to turn back to God. (19:1-11)
      4. Humble worship, prayer, and remembrance of God's historical acts bring divine response, assuring the battle is His and leading nations to reverence. (20:1-30)
      5. A godly leader cannot remove completely an idolatrous and independent spirit from the people. (20:31-33)
      6. God judges leaders who make unholy alliances rather than trust in Him. (20:34—21:3)
   E. Ungodly marriage and role models can bring God's leader to sin and ruin but do not destroy God's messianic promises. (21:4-20)

F. An ungodly mother can lead a ruler and the nation to destruction. (22:1-9)
G. Ungodly leaders cannot wrest control of God's kingdom when God's faithful people cooperate to do His will. (22:10—23:15)
H. True religious leaders can bring a people to renew their covenant obligations to God. (23:16-21)
I. Political leaders need support and direction from religious leaders. (24:1-27)
J. Half-hearted devotion to God brings reliance on military alliances and on false gods, which leads to defeat, lack of obedience to God's word, and desecration of God's house. (25:1-28)
K. God's leaders must know the limits of their roles and not proudly usurp power from other leaders. (26:1-23)
L. Bad examples and judgment may lead a new generation to turn to God. (27:1-9)
M. Following pagan practices of other nations brought God's judgment, but God continued to protect His people. (28:1-27)
N. Following the way of history's heroes of faith leads to national revival. (29:1—32:33)
   1. Covenant renewal leads to worship renewal. (29:1-36)
   2. Faith seeks to reunite God's people in celebrating His historical acts of salvation. (30:1—31:21)
   3. The prayer and trust of God's leader brings God's deliverance to vindicate His name, save His people, and honor His leader. (32:20-23)
O. Rebellion against God brings judgment, but repentance brings restoration. (33:1-20)
P. A son found the father's bad example easier to follow than the good one. (33:21-25)
Q. A young leader can bring national revival to God's people. (34:1—35:27)
R. Stubborn refusal to listen to God's prophetic word brings final wrath and destruction on God's people. (36:1-21)

III. God Restored the Hope of His People Through an Unlikely Gentile Ruler Who Freed Exiles to Return Home and Restore God's House of Worship. (36:22-23)

Chapter 1

Solomon Asks for Wisdom

1:2–13pp — 1Ki 3:4–15
1:14–17pp — 1Ki 10:26–29; 2Ch 9:25–28

SOLOMON son of David established[a]
himself firmly over his kingdom, for
the LORD his God was with[b] him and
made him exceedingly great.[c]
2Then Solomon spoke to all Israel[d] —
to the commanders of thousands and
commanders of hundreds, to the judges
and to all the leaders in Israel, the heads
of families— 3and Solomon and the
whole assembly went to the high place at
Gibeon,[e] for God's Tent of Meeting[f]
was there, which Moses[g] the LORD's servant had made in the desert. 4Now David
had brought up the ark[h] of God from Kiriath Jearim to the place he had prepared
for it, because he had pitched a tent[i] for
it in Jerusalem. 5But the bronze altar[j]
that Bezalel[k] son of Uri, the son of Hur,
had made was in Gibeon in front of the
tabernacle of the LORD; so Solomon and
the assembly inquired[l] of him there.
6Solomon went up to the bronze altar before the LORD in the Tent of Meeting and
offered a thousand burnt offerings on it.
7That night God appeared[m] to Solomon
and said to him, "Ask for whatever you
want me to give you."
8Solomon answered God, "You have
shown great kindness to David my father
and have made me[n] king in his place.
9Now, LORD God, let your promise[o] to
my father David be confirmed, for you
have made me king over a people who
are as numerous as the dust of the
earth.[p] 10Give me wisdom and knowledge, that I may lead[q] this people, for
who is able to govern this great people of
yours?"
11God said to Solomon, "Since this is
your heart's desire and you have not
asked for wealth,[r] riches or honor, nor
for the death of your enemies, and since
you have not asked for a long life but for
wisdom and knowledge to govern my
people over whom I have made you king,
12therefore wisdom and knowledge will
be given you. And I will also give you
wealth, riches and honor,[s] such as no
king who was before you ever had and
none after you will have.[t] "
13Then Solomon went to Jerusalem
from the high place at Gibeon, from before the Tent of Meeting. And he reigned
over Israel.
14Solomon accumulated chariots[u] and
horses; he had fourteen hundred chariots
and twelve thousand horses,[a] which he
kept in the chariot cities and also with
him in Jerusalem. 15The king made silver
and gold[v] as common in Jerusalem as
stones, and cedar as plentiful as sycamore-fig trees in the foothills. 16Solo-
mon's horses were imported from Egypt[b]
and from Kue[c]—the royal merchants
purchased them from Kue. 17They imported a chariot[w] from Egypt for six hundred shekels[d] of silver, and a horse for a
hundred and fifty.[e] They also exported
them to all the kings of the Hittites and of
the Arameans.

Chapter 2

Preparations for Building the Temple

2:1–18pp — 1Ki 5:1–16

SOLOMON gave orders to build a temple[x] for the Name of the LORD and a
royal palace for himself.[y] 2He conscripted seventy thousand men as carriers and
eighty thousand as stonecutters in the
hills and thirty-six hundred as foremen
over them.[z]
3Solomon sent this message to Hiram[f][a] king of Tyre:

"Send me cedar logs[b] as you did
for my father David when you sent
him cedar to build a palace to live in.
4Now I am about to build a temple[c]

1:1 [a]S 1Ki 2:12,26; S 2Ch 12:1 [b]S Ge 21:22; S 39:2; S Nu 14:43 [c]S 1Ch 29:25
1:2 [d]S 1Ch 9:1
1:3 [e]S Jos 9:3 [f]S Lev 17:4 [g]Ex 40:18
1:4 [h]S 1Ch 15:25 [i]2Sa 6:17
1:5 [j]Ex 38:2 [k]S Ex 31:2 [l]1Ch 13:3
1:7 [m]2Ch 7:12
1:8 [n]S 1Ch 23:1
1:9 [o]S 2Sa 7:25; S 1Ki 8:25 [p]S Ge 12:2
1:10 [q]Nu 27:17; 2Sa 5:2; Pr 8:15-16
1:11 [r]S Dt 17:17
1:12 [s]S 1Ch 29:12 [t]S 1Ch 29:25; 2Ch 9:22; Ne 13:26
1:14 [u]S 1Sa 8:11; S 1Ki 9:19
1:15 [v]S 1Ki 9:28; Isa 60:5
1:17 [w]SS 1:9
2:1 [x]S Dt 12:5 [y]Ecc 2:4
2:2 [z]2Ch 10:4
2:3 [a]S 2Sa 5:11 [b]S 1Ch 14:1
2:4 [c]S Dt 12:5

[a]*14* Or *charioteers* [b]*16* Or possibly *Muzur,* a region in Cilicia; also in verse 17 [c]*16* Probably Cilicia [d]*17* That is, about 15 pounds (about 7 kilograms) [e]*17* That is, about 3 3/4 pounds (about 1.7 kilograms) [f]*3* Hebrew *Huram,* a variant of *Hiram*; also in verses 11 and 12

1:2–12 REVELATION, Faithfulness—God is faithful to carry out His revealed promises. Solomon and the people in worship actively sought God's revelation. Thanksgiving and offerings indicated their attitude was right. Solomon's prayer acknowledged God's revelation and guidance had made Him king and had fulfilled the promise to Abraham (Ge 12:2). God used a dream to answer Solomon. See note on 1 Ki 3:4–5.
1:8 GOD, Grace—Grace is the undeserved blessing or favor of God. Even an earthly ruler must attribute his personal power and authority to God's grace. See notes on Ge 19:12–19,29; 39:21–23; 45:5–9; Lk 1:30.
1:8–11 PRAYER, Petition—See notes on 1 Ki 3:5–14; 1 Ch 22:11–12. True political power comes only in submission to God in prayer.
1:12 HUMANITY, Intellectual Nature—Wisdom and knowledge are the basic skills needed by a ruler or a person who leads. Ultimately, every thing and every ability people possess comes from God.
1:14–17 HUMANITY, Work—The proper leadership of the king brought prosperity and economic well-being to his people. Hard work, properly directed and organized, brings results, though not always as readily measurable as here. Material success is not the major purpose of work. Contribution to the community's welfare is a much more important reason to work. Using work to glorify God is a still greater goal.
2:4 PRAYER, Commitment—The idea behind the word for "dedicate" was that the Temple would be a holy place devoted to the purposes Solomon named in this verse. All these purposes have to do with prayer. Incense is itself a symbol of prayer. See note on Ex 30:1,7. Later, Isaiah would call the Temple a "house of prayer" (Isa 56:7), and Jesus used this name of the Temple in cleansing it (Mt 21:13). Providing a

for the Name of the LORD my God
and to dedicate it to him for burning
fragrant incense[d] before him, for setting out the consecrated bread[e] regularly, and for making burnt offerings[f] every morning and evening
and on Sabbaths[g] and New Moons[h]
and at the appointed feasts of the
LORD our God. This is a lasting ordinance for Israel.
5"The temple I am going to build
will be great,[i] because our God is
greater than all other gods.[j] 6But
who is able to build a temple for him,
since the heavens, even the highest
heavens, cannot contain him?[k] Who
then am I[l] to build a temple for him,
except as a place to burn sacrifices
before him?
7"Send me, therefore, a man
skilled to work in gold and silver,
bronze and iron, and in purple, crimson and blue yarn, and experienced
in the art of engraving, to work in
Judah and Jerusalem with my skilled
craftsmen,[m] whom my father David
provided.
8"Send me also cedar, pine and al-
gum[g] logs from Lebanon, for I know
that your men are skilled in cutting
timber there. My men will work with
yours 9to provide me with plenty of
lumber, because the temple I build
must be large and magnificent. 10I
will give your servants, the woods-
men who cut the timber, twenty
thousand cors[h] of ground wheat,
twenty thousand cors of barley,
twenty thousand baths[i] of wine and
twenty thousand baths of olive oil.[n]"
11Hiram king of Tyre replied by letter
to Solomon:

"Because the LORD loves[o] his people, he has made you their king."

12And Hiram added:

"Praise be to the LORD, the God of
Israel, who made heaven and earth![p]
He has given King David a wise son,
endowed with intelligence and discernment, who will build a temple
for the LORD and a palace for himself.

2:4 [d]S Ex 30:7 [e]Ex 25:30 [f]Ex 29:42; 2Ch 13:11; 29:28 [g]S Lev 23:38 [h]S Nu 28:14
2:5 [i]1Ch 22:5 [j]S Ex 12:12; S 1Ch 16:25
2:6 [k]S 1Ki 8:27; Jer 23:24 [l]S Ex 3:11
2:7 [m]S Ex 35:31; 1Ch 22:16
2:10 [n]Ezr 3:7
2:11 [o]1Ki 10:9; 2Ch 9:8
2:12 [p]Ne 9:6; Ps 8:3; 33:6; 96:5; 102:25; 146:6
2:13 [q]S 1Ki 7:13
2:14 [r]S Ex 31:6 [s]S Ex 35:31 [t]Ex 35:35
2:15 [u]Ezr 3:7
2:16 [v]S Jos 19:46; Jnh 1:3
2:17 [w]1Ch 22:2 [x]S 2Sa 24:2
2:18 [y]1Ch 22:2; 2Ch 8:8
3:1 [z]Ac 7:47 [a]S Ge 28:17 [b]S 2Sa 24:18
3:2 [c]Ezr 5:11
3:3 [d]Eze 41:2

13"I am sending you Huram-Abi,[q]
a man of great skill, 14whose mother
was from Dan[r] and whose father
was from Tyre. He is trained[s] to
work in gold and silver, bronze and
iron, stone and wood, and with purple and blue[t] and crimson yarn and
fine linen. He is experienced in all
kinds of engraving and can execute
any design given to him. He will
work with your craftsmen and with
those of my lord, David your father.
15"Now let my lord send his servants the wheat and barley and the
olive oil[u] and wine he promised,
16and we will cut all the logs from
Lebanon that you need and will float
them in rafts by sea down to Joppa.[v]
You can then take them up to Jerusalem."

17Solomon took a census of all the
aliens[w] who were in Israel, after the census[x] his father David had taken; and they
were found to be 153,600. 18He assigned[y] 70,000 of them to be carriers
and 80,000 to be stonecutters in the
hills, with 3,600 foremen over them to
keep the people working.

Chapter 3

Solomon Builds the Temple

3:1–14pp — 1Ki 6:1–29

THEN Solomon began to build[z] the
temple of the LORD[a] in Jerusalem on
Mount Moriah, where the LORD had appeared to his father David. It was on the
threshing floor of Araunah[j][b] the Jebusite, the place provided by David. 2He began building on the second day of the second month in the fourth year of his
reign.[c]
3The foundation Solomon laid for building the temple of God was sixty cubits
long and twenty cubits wide[k][d] (using
the cubit of the old standard). 4The portico at the front of the temple was twenty

[g]*8* Probably a variant of *almug*; possibly juniper
[h]*10* That is, probably about 125,000 bushels (about 4,400 kiloliters)
[i]*10* That is, probably about 115,000 gallons (about 440 kiloliters)
[j]*1* Hebrew *Ornan*, a variant of *Araunah*
[k]*3* That is, about 90 feet (about 27 meters) long and 30 feet (about 9 meters) wide

place of prayer is the essential function of God's house.

2:5 GOD, One God—The Israelites saw many gods worshiped by other people and only slowly realized that these gods were no more than empty human ideas and worthless man-made objects. The one true God surpasses all the others who claim to be gods. This means His worshipers must do everything in our power to show forth His unsurpassed greatness. *See notes on Ge 31:30–35; 35:2; Dt 6:4–9.*

2:6 GOD, Nature—God is beyond comparison and understanding. We may say He is present in our place of worship, but we must never think He is confined to our building. Even the world's richest ruler cannot build a place worthy of Him. Our buildings do not meet God's needs. They provide us the necessary place to express our worship in light of His greatness.

2:6–7,13 HISTORY, Worship—See note on 1 Ch 22:1. Israel's sacred Temple was built under the leadership of a person with Gentile blood. Israel used the best-trained and experienced person available to ensure the construction was the best humans could do. The worship place provided humans a place to express devotion to God. It could not pretend to house the God of the heavens.

cubits[l] long across the width of the building and twenty cubits[m] high.

He overlaid the inside with pure gold. 5He paneled the main hall with pine and covered it with fine gold and decorated it with palm tree[e] and chain designs. 6He adorned the temple with precious stones. And the gold he used was gold of Parvaim. 7He overlaid the ceiling beams, doorframes, walls and doors of the temple with gold, and he carved cherubim[f] on the walls.

8He built the Most Holy Place,[g] its length corresponding to the width of the temple—twenty cubits long and twenty cubits wide. He overlaid the inside with six hundred talents[n] of fine gold. 9The gold nails[h] weighed fifty shekels.[o] He also overlaid the upper parts with gold.

10In the Most Holy Place he made a pair[i] of sculptured cherubim and overlaid them with gold. 11The total wingspan of the cherubim was twenty cubits. One wing of the first cherub was five cubits[p] long and touched the temple wall, while its other wing, also five cubits long, touched the wing of the other cherub. 12Similarly one wing of the second cherub was five cubits long and touched the other temple wall, and its other wing, also five cubits long, touched the wing of the first cherub. 13The wings of these cherubim[j] extended twenty cubits. They stood on their feet, facing the main hall.[q]

14He made the curtain[k] of blue, purple and crimson yarn and fine linen, with cherubim[l] worked into it.

15In the front of the temple he made two pillars,[m] which ⌞together⌟ were thirty-five cubits[r] long, each with a capital[n] on top measuring five cubits. 16He made interwoven chains[s][o] and put them on top of the pillars. He also made a hundred pomegranates[p] and attached them to the chains. 17He erected the pillars in the front of the temple, one to the south and one to the north. The one to the south he named Jakin[t] and the one to the north Boaz.[u]

Chapter 4

The Temple's Furnishings

4:2–6,10–5:1pp — 1Ki 7:23–26,38–51

HE made a bronze altar[q] twenty cubits long, twenty cubits wide and ten cubits high.[v] 2He made the Sea[r] of cast metal, circular in shape, measuring ten cubits from rim to rim and five cubits[w] high. It took a line of thirty cubits[x] to measure around it. 3Below the rim, figures of bulls encircled it—ten to a cubit.[y] The bulls were cast in two rows in one piece with the Sea.

4The Sea stood on twelve bulls, three facing north, three facing west, three facing south and three facing east.[s] The Sea rested on top of them, and their hindquarters were toward the center. 5It was a handbreadth[z] in thickness, and its rim was like the rim of a cup, like a lily blossom. It held three thousand baths.[a]

6He then made ten basins[t] for washing and placed five on the south side and five on the north. In them the things to be used for the burnt offerings[u] were rinsed, but the Sea was to be used by the priests for washing.

7He made ten gold lampstands[v] according to the specifications[w] for them and placed them in the temple, five on the south side and five on the north.

8He made ten tables[x] and placed them in the temple, five on the south side and five on the north. He also made a hundred gold sprinkling bowls.[y]

9He made the courtyard[z] of the priests, and the large court and the doors for the court, and overlaid the doors with bronze. 10He placed the Sea on the south side, at the southeast corner.

11He also made the pots and shovels and sprinkling bowls.

So Huram finished[a] the work he had undertaken for King Solomon in the temple of God:

12the two pillars;
the two bowl-shaped capitals on top of the pillars;
the two sets of network decorating the two bowl-shaped capitals on top of the pillars;

3:5 [e]Eze 40:16
3:7 [f]Ge 3:24; Eze 41:18
3:8 [g]S Ex 26:33
3:9 [h]Ex 26:32
3:10 [i]Ex 25:18
3:13 [j]S Ex 25:18
3:14 [k]S Ex 26:31, 33 [l]Ge 3:24
3:15 [m]S 1Ki 7:15; Rev 3:12 [n]1Ki 7:22
3:16 [o]1Ki 7:17 [p]S 1Ki 7:20
4:1 [q]S Ex 20:24; S 40:6; S 1Ki 8:64
4:2 [r]Rev 4:6; 15:2
4:4 [s]Nu 2:3-25; Eze 48:30-34; Rev 21:13
4:6 [t]S Ex 30:18 [u]Ne 13:5,9; Eze 40:38
4:7 [v]S Ex 25:31 [w]Ex 25:40
4:8 [x]S Ex 25:23 [y]S Nu 4:14
4:9 [z]1Ki 6:36; 2Ch 33:5
4:11 [a]1Ki 7:14

[l]*4* That is, about 30 feet (about 9 meters); also in verses 8, 11 and 13 [m]*4* Some Septuagint and Syriac manuscripts; Hebrew *and a hundred and twenty* [n]*8* That is, about 23 tons (about 21 metric tons) [o]*9* That is, about 1 1/4 pounds (about 0.6 kilogram) [p]*11* That is, about 7 1/2 feet (about 2.3 meters); also in verse 15 [q]*13* Or *facing inward* [r]*15* That is, about 52 feet (about 16 meters) [s]*16* Or possibly *made chains in the inner sanctuary*; the meaning of the Hebrew for this phrase is uncertain. [t]*17* *Jakin* probably means *he establishes.* [u]*17* *Boaz* probably means *in him is strength.* [v]*1* That is, about 30 feet (about 9 meters) long and wide, and about 15 feet (about 4.5 meters) high [w]*2* That is, about 7 1/2 feet (about 2.3 meters) [x]*2* That is, about 45 feet (about 13.5 meters) [y]*3* That is, about 1 1/2 feet (about 0.5 meter) [z]*5* That is, about 3 inches (about 8 centimeters) [a]*5* That is, about 17,500 gallons (about 66 kiloliters)

3:8,10 GOD, Holy—The Most Holy Place is a reminder of the holiness of God, which separates Him from all else. See notes on Ex 3:5–6; 19:10–24; Lev 11:44–45.

13 the four hundred pomegranates for
the two sets of network (two rows
of pomegranates for each network, decorating the bowl-shaped
capitals on top of the pillars);
14 the stands[b] with their basins;
15 the Sea and the twelve bulls under
it;
16 the pots, shovels, meat forks and all
related articles.

All the objects that Huram-Abi[c] made
for King Solomon for the temple of the
LORD were of polished bronze. 17 The king
had them cast in clay molds in the plain
of the Jordan between Succoth[d] and Zarethan.[b] 18 All these things that Solomon
made amounted to so much that the
weight of the bronze[e] was not determined.

19 Solomon also made all the furnishings that were in God's temple:

the golden altar;
the tables[f] on which was the bread
of the Presence;
20 the lampstands[g] of pure gold with
their lamps, to burn in front of the
inner sanctuary as prescribed;
21 the gold floral work and lamps and
tongs (they were solid gold);
22 the pure gold wick trimmers, sprinkling bowls, dishes[h] and censers;[i] and the gold doors of the
temple: the inner doors to the
Most Holy Place and the doors of
the main hall.

Chapter 5

WHEN all the work Solomon had done
for the temple of the LORD was finished,[j] he brought in the things his father David had dedicated[k]—the silver
and gold and all the furnishings—and he
placed them in the treasuries of God's
temple.

The Ark Brought to the Temple

5:2–6:11pp — 1Ki 8:1–21

2 Then Solomon summoned to Jerusalem the elders of Israel, all the heads of
the tribes and the chiefs of the Israelite
families, to bring up the ark[l] of the
LORD's covenant from Zion, the City of
David. 3 And all the men of Israel[m] came
together to the king at the time of the
festival in the seventh month.

4 When all the elders of Israel had arrived, the Levites took up the ark, 5 and
they brought up the ark and the Tent of
Meeting and all the sacred furnishings in
it. The priests, who were Levites,[n] carried them up; 6 and King Solomon and the
entire assembly of Israel that had gathered about him were before the ark,
sacrificing so many sheep and cattle
that they could not be recorded or
counted.

7 The priests then brought the ark[o] of
the LORD's covenant to its place in the
inner sanctuary of the temple, the Most
Holy Place, and put it beneath the wings
of the cherubim. 8 The cherubim[p] spread
their wings over the place of the ark and
covered the ark and its carrying poles.
9 These poles were so long that their ends,
extending from the ark, could be seen
from in front of the inner sanctuary, but
not from outside the Holy Place; and they
are still there today. 10 There was nothing
in the ark except[q] the two tablets[r]
that Moses had placed in it at Horeb,
where the LORD made a covenant with
the Israelites after they came out of
Egypt.

11 The priests then withdrew from the
Holy Place. All the priests who were
there had consecrated themselves, regardless of their divisions.[s] 12 All the Levites who were musicians[t]—Asaph, Heman, Jeduthun and their sons and relatives—stood on the east side of the altar,
dressed in fine linen and playing cymbals,
harps and lyres. They were accompanied
by 120 priests sounding trumpets.[u]
13 The trumpeters and singers joined in
unison, as with one voice, to give praise
and thanks to the LORD. Accompanied by
trumpets, cymbals and other instruments,
they raised their voices in praise to the
LORD and sang:

"He is good;
his love endures forever."[v]

Then the temple of the LORD was filled
with a cloud,[w] 14 and the priests could not
perform[x] their service because of the
cloud,[y] for the glory[z] of the LORD filled
the temple of God.

4:14 [b] 1Ki 7:27-30
4:16 [c] S 1Ki 7:13
4:17 [d] S Ge 33:17
4:18 [e] S 1Ki 7:23
4:19 [f] S Ex 25:23,30
4:20 [g] Ex 25:31
4:22 [h] S Nu 7:14 [i] S Lev 10:1
5:1 [j] S 1Ki 6:14 [k] S 2Sa 8:11
5:2 [l] S Nu 3:31; S 1Ch 15:25
5:3 [m] S 1Ch 9:1
5:5 [n] S Nu 3:31; S 1Ch 15:2
5:7 [o] Rev 11:19
5:8 [p] S Ge 3:24
5:10 [q] Heb 9:4 [r] S Ex 16:34; S Dt 10:2
5:11 [s] S 1Ch 24:1
5:12 [t] 1Ki 10:12; 1Ch 9:33; S 25:1; Ps 68:25 [u] S 1Ch 13:8
5:13 [v] S 1Ch 16:34, 41; 2Ch 7:3; 20:21; Ezr 3:11; Ps 100:5; 106:1; 107:1; 118:1; 136:1; Jer 33:11 [w] S Ex 40:34
5:14 [x] Ex 40:35; Rev 15:8 [y] Ex 19:16 [z] S Ex 29:43; S 40:35

[b] *17* Hebrew *Zeredatha,* a variant of *Zarethan*

5:7–9 GOD, Holy—The ark of the covenant reminded Israel of God's grace to her and her responsibilities to God. It represented God's holy presence with His people and was considered a holy object that must be treated with utmost respect in prescribed ways. See note on 2 Sa 6:1–7.

5:10 HISTORY, Worship—Israel's worship place did not contain an image of God. It contained the tablets received at the start of Israel's national history, creating the historical relationship of God and His people, and reminding the people of their obligations before God.

5:10 THE CHURCH, Covenant People—See note on 1 Ki 8:21.

5:12–14 PRAYER, Praise—God manifested His glory when there was common prayer in a united heart. In Ex 13:21–22, there was common need; here there is common praise; in Ac 2:1–2 there is common prayer. Musical prayer and praise are one way to God's presence.

5:13 GOD, Love—See notes on Ex 3:7; 20:1–7; 1 Ch 16:34,41.

5:14 GOD, Glory—See notes on Ex 16:7,10; 40:34–38.

Chapter 6

THEN Solomon said, "The LORD has
said that he would dwell in a dark
cloud;[a] 2I have built a magnificent temple for you, a place for you to dwell forever.[b]"
3While the whole assembly of Israel was standing there, the king
turned around and blessed them. 4Then
he said:

"Praise be to the LORD, the God of
Israel, who with his hands has fulfilled what he promised with his
mouth to my father David. For he
said, 5'Since the day I brought my
people out of Egypt, I have not chosen a city in any tribe of Israel to
have a temple built for my Name to
be there, nor have I chosen anyone
to be the leader over my people Israel. 6But now I have chosen Jerusalem[c] for my Name[d] to be there, and
I have chosen David[e] to rule my people Israel.'
7"My father David had it in his
heart[f] to build a temple for the
Name of the LORD, the God of Israel.
8But the LORD said to my father David, 'Because it was in your heart to
build a temple for my Name, you did
well to have this in your heart. 9Nev-
ertheless, you are not the one to
build the temple, but your son, who
is your own flesh and blood—he is
the one who will build the temple for
my Name.'
10"The LORD has kept the promise
he made. I have succeeded David my
father and now I sit on the throne of
Israel, just as the LORD promised, and
I have built the temple for the Name
of the LORD, the God of Israel.
11There I have placed the ark, in
which is the covenant[g] of the LORD
that he made with the people of Israel."

6:1 [a]S Ex 19:9
6:2 [b]Ezr 6:12; 7:15; Ps 135:21
6:6 [c]S Dt 12:5; S Isa 14:1 [d]S Ex 20:24 [e]S 1Ch 28:4
6:7 [f]S 1Sa 10:7; S 1Ch 17:2; Ac 7:46
6:11 [g]S Dt 10:2; Ps 25:10; 50:5
6:13 [h]Ne 8:4 [i]Ps 95:6
6:14 [j]S Ex 8:10; 15:11 [k]S Dt 7:9
6:15 [l]S 1Ch 22:10
6:16 [m]S 2Sa 7:13, 15; 2Ch 23:3 [n]Ps 132:12
6:18 [o]S Rev 21:3 [p]Ps 11:4; Isa 40:22; 66:1

Solomon's Prayer of Dedication

6:12–40pp — 1Ki 8:22–53
6:41–42pp — Ps 132:8–10

12Then Solomon stood before the altar
of the LORD in front of the whole assembly of Israel and spread out his hands.
13Now he had made a bronze platform,[h]
five cubits[c] long, five cubits wide and
three cubits[d] high, and had placed it in
the center of the outer court. He stood on
the platform and then knelt down[i] before the whole assembly of Israel and
spread out his hands toward heaven. 14He
said:

"O LORD, God of Israel, there is no
God like you[j] in heaven or on earth
—you who keep your covenant of
love[k] with your servants who continue wholeheartedly in your way.
15You have kept your promise to your
servant David my father; with your
mouth you have promised[l] and with
your hand you have fulfilled it—as it
is today.
16"Now LORD, God of Israel, keep
for your servant David my father the
promises you made to him when you
said, 'You shall never fail[m] to have a
man to sit before me on the throne of
Israel, if only your sons are careful in
all they do to walk before me according to my law,[n] as you have done.'
17And now, O LORD, God of Israel, let
your word that you promised your
servant David come true.
18"But will God really dwell[o] on
earth with men? The heavens,[p] even
the highest heavens, cannot contain
you. How much less this temple I
have built! 19Yet give attention to
your servant's prayer and his plea for
mercy, O LORD my God. Hear the cry

[c] *13* That is, about 7 1/2 feet (about 2.3 meters)
[d] *13* That is, about 4 1/2 feet (about 1.3 meters)

6:1–2,18–21 REVELATION, Divine Presence—See notes on 1 Ki 8:1–21, 27–30. God's presence with His people had a long history including different symbols—cloud, ark, tent, Temple. All encouraged God's people to worship, pray, and obey. None confined or contained all of God.

6:3 PRAYER, Blessing—See notes on 1 Ki 8:14–21; 1 Ch 16:2.

6:4,10,14–17,42 GOD, Faithfulness—The faithfulness of God in keeping His promises and being an unchanging God is a very important idea in the Old Testament. In important moments in life, we can call on God, asking Him to show us His faithfulness and to keep His promises. Such prayers do not express doubt. Rather they reaffirm our dependence on His faithfulness. See notes on Ge 8:1; Nu 26:65; Dt 10:11,22; Jos 1:6.

6:4–6,14–17 HISTORY, Promise—Israel was conscious of the changing history of their relationship with God. A people without a land, leader, or sanctuary became a people with territory, king, and Temple because God chose them as His people and fulfilled His promises to them.

6:5–16 ELECTION, Prayer—Solomon's dedication of the Temple rehearsed the theology of election, emphasized the practice of prayer, and articulated the request for forgiveness of sin. The elect of today should practice the prayer of commitment, dedication, and forgiveness.

6:11 THE CHURCH, Covenant People—See note on 1 Ki 8:21.

6:13–42 PRAYER, Faithfulness of God—See note on 1 Ki 8:22–53. The appeal for mercy is on the basis of God's covenant faithfulness. Solomon prayed in public kneeling before God with hands raised to heaven.

6:14 THE CHURCH, Covenant People—Even in times of distress and worry God is dependable. God shows steadfast love (Hebrew *chesed*) toward His followers. *Chesed* is translated in different contexts as steadfast love, kindness, mercy, loving-kindness, and covenant love. *Chesed* forms the bond between God and His people. God keeps the covenant because of His covenant love. God's love and care for His people is unique.

and the prayer that your servant is
praying in your presence. 20May your
eyes[q] be open toward this temple
day and night, this place of which
you said you would put your Name[r]
there. May you hear[s] the prayer
your servant prays toward this place.
21Hear the supplications of your servant and of your people Israel when
they pray toward this place. Hear
from heaven, your dwelling place;
and when you hear, forgive.[t]

22"When a man wrongs his neighbor and is required to take an oath[u]
and he comes and swears the oath
before your altar in this temple,
23then hear from heaven and act.
Judge between your servants, repaying[v] the guilty by bringing down on
his own head what he has done. Declare the innocent not guilty and so
establish his innocence.

24"When your people Israel have
been defeated[w] by an enemy because
they have sinned against you and
when they turn back and confess
your name, praying and making supplication before you in this temple,
25then hear from heaven and forgive
the sin of your people Israel and
bring them back to the land you gave
to them and their fathers.

26"When the heavens are shut up
and there is no rain[x] because your
people have sinned against you, and
when they pray toward this place and
confess your name and turn from
their sin because you have afflicted
them, 27then hear from heaven and
forgive[y] the sin of your servants,
your people Israel. Teach them the
right way to live, and send rain on
the land you gave your people for an
inheritance.

28"When famine[z] or plague comes
to the land, or blight or mildew, locusts or grasshoppers, or when enemies besiege them in any of their cities, whatever disaster or disease may
come, 29and when a prayer or plea is
made by any of your people Israel—
each one aware of his afflictions and
pains, and spreading out his hands toward this temple— 30then hear from
heaven, your dwelling place. Forgive,[a] and deal with each man according to all he does, since you
know his heart (for you alone know
the hearts of men),[b] 31so that they
will fear you[c] and walk in your ways
all the time they live in the land you
gave our fathers.

32"As for the foreigner who does
not belong to your people Israel but
has come[d] from a distant land because of your great name and your
mighty hand[e] and your outstretched
arm—when he comes and prays toward this temple, 33then hear from
heaven, your dwelling place, and do
whatever the foreigner[f] asks of you,
so that all the peoples of the earth
may know your name and fear you,
as do your own people Israel, and
may know that this house I have built
bears your Name.

34"When your people go to war
against their enemies,[g] wherever
you send them, and when they pray[h]
to you toward this city you have chosen and the temple I have built for
your Name, 35then hear from heaven
their prayer and their plea, and uphold their cause.

36"When they sin against you—for
there is no one who does not sin[i]—
and you become angry with them
and give them over to the enemy,
who takes them captive[j] to a land far

6:20 [q]S Ex 3:16; Ps 34:15 [r]Dt 12:11 [s]2Ch 7:14; 30:20
6:21 [t]Ps 51:1; Isa 33:24; 40:2; 43:25; 44:22; 55:7; Mic 7:18
6:22 [u]S Ex 22:11
6:23 [v]Isa 3:11; 65:6; S Mt 16:27
6:24 [w]S Lev 26:17
6:26 [x]Lev 26:19; S Dt 11:17; 28:24; S 2Sa 1:21
6:27 [y]ver 30,39; 2Ch 7:14
6:28 [z]2Ch 20:9
6:30 [a]S ver 27 [b]S 1Sa 2:3; Ps 7:9; 44:21; Pr 16:2; 17:3
6:31 [c]S Dt 6:13; Ps 34:7,9; 103:11, 13; Pr 8:13
6:32 [d]2Ch 9:6 [e]S Ex 3:19,20
6:33 [f]S Ex 12:43
6:34 [g]Dt 28:7 [h]S 1Ch 5:20
6:36 [i]S 1Ki 8:46; Job 11:12; 15:14; Ps 143:2; Ecc 7:20; Jer 9:5; 13:23; 17:9; S Ro 3:9; Eph 2:3 [j]S Lev 26:44

6:24–31 EVIL AND SUFFERING, Punishment—See note on 1 Ki 8:33–40.

6:32–33 REVELATION, Author of Hope—Revelation invites all people to hope in God. God's historical acts attracted foreigners. Solomon acknowledged God as the Lord of all, declaring that the foreigner was to be welcomed at this shrine of worship. Thus God discloses Himself as a God who includes all His children in His family, wishing them to know the good news that He is the Author of life and hope. The Samaritan woman heard the same message centuries later at the well (Jn 4:21–24).

6:32–33 HISTORY, Universal—God's mighty historical acts served as an invitation to foreigners to join Israel in the worship of the one true God.

6:32–33 EVANGELISM, Personal—Regardless of race, color, ethnic origin, or any human difference, all people are to hear our word of witness. God loves all and wants to include in His kingdom all who will turn to Him. They will hear of God's "great name" and be drawn to Him as we personally share Jesus Christ with them. Then we are to include them in the family of God and accept them as brothers and sisters. Personal witnessing to all is essential to vital evangelism. See Guide to Personal Testimony, pp. 1786–1788.

6:32–33 MISSIONS, Scope—Solomon's remarkable prayer pointed out that God's love for Israel was for the purpose of blessing other nations and peoples as well. God's Temple had been built by an Israelite king in the national capital, but its purpose was never restricted to Israelites alone. It was to be one of God's means of blessing all people. God's acts for Israel were intended to draw all people to Him. The central teaching is that God is Lord of the whole earth and of all peoples who come to Him. The New Testament records God's people reaching out and sharing the message (Ac 1:8; 5:42; 8:4).

6:33 ELECTION, Other Nations—Solomon asked that the foreigner's prayer be answered so that all the peoples of earth might know God and worship Him and that God's name be glorified among all nations. Today the Temple is no more, but Christians of many nations, languages, and races find answers to prayers through Jesus Christ. God looks on the heart, not the outer appearance (1 Sa 16:7; Ac 10:34–35).

6:36–39 EVIL AND SUFFERING, Punishment—See note on 1 Ki 8:46–53.

6:36 SIN, Universal Nature—See note on 1 Ki 8:27–53.

away or near; 37and if they have a
change of heart[k] in the land where
they are held captive, and repent and
plead with you in the land of their
captivity and say, 'We have sinned,
we have done wrong and acted wickedly'; 38and if they turn back to you
with all their heart and soul in the
land of their captivity where they
were taken, and pray toward the land
you gave their fathers, toward the
city you have chosen and toward the
temple I have built for your Name;
39then from heaven, your dwelling
place, hear their prayer and their
pleas, and uphold their cause. And
forgive[l] your people, who have
sinned against you.

40"Now, my God, may your eyes
be open and your ears attentive[m] to
the prayers offered in this place.

41"Now arise,[n] O LORD God, and
come to your resting
place,[o]
you and the ark of your might.
May your priests,[p] O LORD God,
be clothed with salvation,
may your saints rejoice in your
goodness.[q]
42O LORD God, do not reject your
anointed one.[r]
Remember the great love[s]
promised to David your
servant."

Chapter 7

The Dedication of the Temple

7:1–10pp — 1Ki 8:62–66

WHEN Solomon finished praying,
fire[t] came down from heaven and
consumed the burnt offering and the sacrifices, and the glory of the LORD filled[u]
the temple.[v] 2The priests could not enter[w] the temple of the LORD because the
glory[x] of the LORD filled it. 3When all the
Israelites saw the fire coming down and
the glory of the LORD above the temple,
they knelt on the pavement with their
faces to the ground, and they worshiped
and gave thanks to the LORD, saying,

"He is good;
his love endures forever."[y]

4Then the king and all the people offered
sacrifices before the LORD. 5And King Solomon offered a sacrifice of twenty-two
thousand head of cattle and a hundred
and twenty thousand sheep and goats. So
the king and all the people dedicated the
temple of God. 6The priests took their positions, as did the Levites[z] with the
LORD's musical instruments,[a] which
King David had made for praising the
LORD and which were used when he gave
thanks, saying, "His love endures forever." Opposite the Levites, the priests
blew their trumpets, and all the Israelites
were standing.

7Solomon consecrated the middle part
of the courtyard in front of the temple of
the LORD, and there he offered burnt offerings and the fat[b] of the fellowship offerings,[e] because the bronze altar he had
made could not hold the burnt offerings,
the grain offerings and the fat portions.

8So Solomon observed the festival[c] at
that time for seven days, and all Israel[d]
with him—a vast assembly, people from
Lebo[f] Hamath[e] to the Wadi of Egypt.[f]
9On the eighth day they held an assembly, for they had celebrated[g] the dedication of the altar for seven days and the
festival[h] for seven days more. 10On the
twenty-third day of the seventh month he
sent the people to their homes, joyful and
glad in heart for the good things the LORD
had done for David and Solomon and for
his people Israel.

The LORD Appears to Solomon

7:11–22pp — 1Ki 9:1–9

11When Solomon had finished[i] the
temple of the LORD and the royal palace,
and had succeeded in carrying out all he
had in mind to do in the temple of the
LORD and in his own palace, 12the LORD
appeared[j] to him at night and said:

"I have heard your prayer and

[e]7 Traditionally *peace offerings* [f]8 Or *from the entrance to*

6:37 [k]1Ki 8:48; 2Ch 7:14; 12:6,12; 30:11; 33:12,19, 23; 34:27; 36:12; Isa 58:3; Jer 24:7; 29:13
6:39 [l]S ver 27; 2Ch 30:9
6:40 [m]S 1Ki 8:29, 52; 2Ch 7:15; Ne 1:6,11; Ps 17:1, 6; 116:1; 130:2; Isa 37:17
6:41 [n]Ps 3:7; 7:6; 59:4; Isa 33:10 [o]1Ch 28:2 [p]Ps 132:16 [q]Ps 13:6; 27:13; 116:12; 142:7
6:42 [r]Ps 2:2 [s]Ps 89:24,28
7:1 [t]S Ex 19:18; S Lev 9:24; S 1Ki 18:38 [u]S Ex 16:10 [v]Ps 26:8
7:2 [w]S 1Ki 8:11 [x]S Ex 29:43; S 40:35
7:3 [y]S 1Ch 16:34; 2Ch 5:13; Ezr 3:11
7:6 [z]1Ch 15:16 [a]S 1Ch 15:24
7:7 [b]S Ex 29:13
7:8 [c]2Ch 30:26; Ne 8:17 [d]S 1Ch 9:1 [e]S Nu 13:21 [f]S Ge 15:18
7:9 [g]2Ch 30:23 [h]S Lev 23:36
7:11 [i]S 1Ch 28:20
7:12 [j]2Ch 1:7

7:3 WORSHIP, Thanksgiving—Thanksgiving and worship are inevitably bound together. Thanksgiving should be expressed from a position of humility and reverence. The worshipers here bowed their faces to the pavement leading to the Temple. Worship (Hebrew *hishtachawah*) means to bow down to pay homage or honor to a person with superior rank or position (2 Sa 14:4,22). The basic definition of worship includes giving homage to God because He is superior to us by nature.

7:5 PRAYER, Commitment—See note on 2:4.

7:10 REVELATION, Worship—Dedicating the Temple and celebrating the Feast of Tabernacles (Ex 23:16; 34:22; Lev 23:33–36,39–43; Nu 29:12–34; Dt 16:13–15) revealed God's continued presence in the history of His people and His love for them. The Creator who made a good world (Ge 1:31) continues to do good things for His people providing peace and joy, fulfilling His purposes for creation in fullness of life. Public worship is an opportunity to review the past history of God's revelation to His people and to experience in a renewing way God's powerful presence. In acceptable worship God is present with His people. His revealing presence can come to the congregation as well as to individuals.

7:11–22 REVELATION, Commitment—See note on 1 Ki 9:2–3. God invites us to seek His face, that is to ask for His presence and revealed will in our lives. To experience such revelation, God's people are called to repent. God's place of worship is the place of revelation where we encounter God and He reveals His will.

have chosen[k] this place for myself[l]
as a temple for sacrifices.

13"When I shut up the heavens so
that there is no rain,[m] or command
locusts to devour the land or send a
plague among my people, 14if my
people, who are called by my name,[n]
will humble[o] themselves and pray
and seek my face[p] and turn[q] from
their wicked ways, then will I hear[r]
from heaven and will forgive[s] their
sin and will heal[t] their land. 15Now
my eyes will be open and my ears
attentive to the prayers offered in
this place.[u] 16I have chosen[v] and
consecrated this temple so that my
Name may be there forever. My eyes
and my heart will always be there.

17"As for you, if you walk before
me[w] as David your father did, and do
all I command, and observe my decrees[x] and laws, 18I will establish
your royal throne, as I covenanted[y]
with David your father when I said,
'You shall never fail to have a man[z]
to rule over Israel.'[a]

19"But if you[g] turn away[b] and forsake[c] the decrees and commands I
have given you[g] and go off to serve
other gods and worship them, 20then
I will uproot[d] Israel from my land,[e]
which I have given them, and will
reject this temple I have consecrated
for my Name. I will make it a byword
and an object of ridicule[f] among all
peoples. 21And though this temple is
now so imposing, all who pass by will
be appalled[g] and say,[h] 'Why has the
LORD done such a thing to this land
and to this temple?' 22People will answer, 'Because they have forsaken
the LORD, the God of their fathers,
who brought them out of Egypt, and
have embraced other gods, worshiping and serving them[i]—that is why
he brought all this disaster on
them.' "

7:12 [k]Dt 12:11 [l]S Dt 12:5
7:13 [m]S Dt 11:17; Am 4:7
7:14 [n]S Nu 6:27 [o]S Ex 10:3; S Lev 26:41; S 2Ch 6:37 [p]S 1Ch 16:11 [q]S 2Ki 17:13; Isa 55:7; Eze 18:32; Zec 1:4 [r]S 2Ch 6:20 [s]S 2Ch 6:27 [t]S Ex 15:26; 2Ch 30:20; Ps 60:2; Isa 30:26; 53:5; 57:18; Jer 33:6; Mal 4:2
7:15 [u]S 1Ki 8:29; S 2Ch 6:40; Ne 1:6
7:16 [v]S Dt 12:5; 2Ch 33:7
7:17 [w]S 1Ki 9:4 [x]S Lev 19:37
7:18 [y]Isa 9:7; Jer 33:17,21 [z]S 1Ch 5:2; Isa 55:4; Mic 5:2 [a]S 2Sa 7:13; S 1Ch 17:12; 2Ch 13:5; 23:3
7:19 [b]S Dt 28:15 [c]S 1Ch 28:9; 2Ch 12:1; 24:18; Jer 9:13; 11:8
7:20 [d]S Dt 29:28 [e]1Ki 14:15; Jer 12:14; 16:13; 50:11 [f]S Dt 28:37
7:21 [g]Jer 19:8 [h]Dt 29:24
7:22 [i]Jer 16:11
8:1 [j]S 2Sa 7:2
8:4 [k]S 2Sa 8:9
8:5 [l]S Jos 10:10
8:6 [m]S Jos 19:44
8:7 [n]S Ge 10:16; S 15:18-21; Ezr 9:1
8:8 [o]S 2Ch 2:18
8:11 [p]S 1Ki 3:1

Chapter 8

Solomon's Other Activities

8:1-18pp — 1Ki 9:10-28

AT the end of twenty years, during
which Solomon built the temple of
the LORD and his own palace,[j] 2Solomon
rebuilt the villages that Hiram[h] had given
him, and settled Israelites in them. 3Solo-
mon then went to Hamath Zobah and
captured it. 4He also built up Tadmor in
the desert and all the store cities he had
built in Hamath.[k] 5He rebuilt Upper Beth
Horon[l] and Lower Beth Horon as fortified cities, with walls and with gates and
bars, 6as well as Baalath[m] and all his store
cities, and all the cities for his chariots
and for his horses[i]—whatever he desired to build in Jerusalem, in Lebanon
and throughout all the territory he ruled.

7All the people left from the Hittites,
Amorites, Perizzites, Hivites and Jebusites[n] (these peoples were not Israelites),
8that is, their descendants remaining in
the land, whom the Israelites had not destroyed—these Solomon conscripted[o] for
his slave labor force, as it is to this day.
9But Solomon did not make slaves of the
Israelites for his work; they were his
fighting men, commanders of his captains, and commanders of his chariots
and charioteers. 10They were also King
Solomon's chief officials—two hundred
and fifty officials supervising the men.

11Solomon brought Pharaoh's daughter[p] up from the City of David to the palace he had built for her, for he said, "My
wife must not live in the palace of David

[g]*19* The Hebrew is plural. [h]*2* Hebrew *Huram,* a variant of *Hiram;* also in verse 18 [i]*6* Or *charioteers*

7:13–16 PRAYER, Faithfulness of God—This prayer-promise is necessary for the continuation of the covenant. God's faithfulness is absolute. His fulfillment of the promise when conditions were met can be seen in 34:27. God hears prayer from an humble, repentant, and trusting people.

7:13–14 EVANGELISM, Power—Effective evangelism is possible only as God's own people live and witness humbly in the power of the Spirit. This passage lays out the conditions for so doing. Every condition must be met by believers for God to "heal their land." No passage in the Old Testament is more important to vital witnessing than this verse. It alone presents the principles of revival and spiritual reality.

7:14 SALVATION, Forgiveness—God has promised forgiveness of sin to His people who humble themselves, pray, seek His face, and turn from their wicked ways.

7:16 ELECTION, Prayer—God responds to the prayers of the elect. He provides a worship place as symbol of His hearing presence. He renews commitment to His promises.

7:17–22 ELECTION, Responsibility—See note on 1 Ki 9:4–9.

7:17 CHRISTIAN ETHICS, Moral Imperatives—See note on 1 Ki 3:3,14.

7:17–22 THE CHURCH, Covenant People—God's covenant with David assured that someone from the line of David would always reign over Israel. God's covenant promise did not leave Israel without responsibility. Refusal to obey God meant exile and discipline. The church and the New Testament writers interpreted this promise to be fulfilled in the coming of Christ, who will reign forever. See note on 2 Sa 23:5.

7:19–22 GOD, One God—See notes on 2 Ki 22:13–17; 24:20. To forsake the one God is to forsake covenant blessings.

7:22 HISTORY, Judgment—Loss of God's house of worship says nothing about God's weakness. It shows His strength of will to discipline His own people when they are unfaithful.

8:1–6 HUMANITY, Work—The work of a leader is carried on by the followers. The end results accomplish the leader's plans and bring honor and reputation to the leader.

8:11 GOD, Holy—Only God Himself is holy. God's holiness is the absolute difference or superiority of God over all else. However, things or persons brought into association with God may share in God's holiness, and must be given special respect. See notes on Ex 3:5–6; 19:10–24; Lev 11:44–45; 2 Sa 6:1–7.

king of Israel, because the places the ark
of the LORD has entered are holy."
12On the altar[q] of the LORD that he had
built in front of the portico, Solomon sacrificed burnt offerings to the LORD, 13ac-
cording to the daily requirement[r] for offerings commanded by Moses for Sabbaths,[s] New Moons[t] and the three[u]
annual feasts—the Feast of Unleavened
Bread,[v] the Feast of Weeks[w] and the
Feast of Tabernacles.[x] 14In keeping with
the ordinance of his father David, he appointed the divisions[y] of the priests for
their duties, and the Levites[z] to lead the
praise and to assist the priests according
to each day's requirement. He also appointed the gatekeepers[a] by divisions for
the various gates, because this was what
David the man of God[b] had ordered.[c]
15They did not deviate from the king's
commands to the priests or to the Levites
in any matter, including that of the treasuries.
16All Solomon's work was carried out,
from the day the foundation of the temple
of the LORD was laid until its completion.
So the temple of the LORD was finished.
17Then Solomon went to Ezion Geber
and Elath on the coast of Edom. 18And
Hiram sent him ships commanded by his
own officers, men who knew the sea.
These, with Solomon's men, sailed to
Ophir and brought back four hundred and
fifty talents[j] of gold,[d] which they delivered to King Solomon.

Chapter 9

The Queen of Sheba Visits Solomon

9:1–12pp — 1Ki 10:1–13

WHEN the queen of Sheba[e] heard of
Solomon's fame, she came to Jerusalem to test him with hard questions.
Arriving with a very great caravan—with
camels carrying spices, large quantities of
gold, and precious stones—she came to
Solomon and talked with him about all
she had on her mind. 2Solomon answered
all her questions; nothing was too hard
for him to explain to her. 3When the
queen of Sheba saw the wisdom of Solomon,[f] as well as the palace he had built,
4the food on his table, the seating of his
officials, the attending servants in their
robes, the cupbearers in their robes and
the burnt offerings he made at[k] the temple of the LORD, she was overwhelmed.
5She said to the king, "The report I
heard in my own country about your
achievements and your wisdom is true.
6But I did not believe what they said until
I came[g] and saw with my own eyes. Indeed, not even half the greatness of your
wisdom was told me; you have far exceeded the report I heard. 7How happy
your men must be! How happy your officials, who continually stand before you
and hear your wisdom! 8Praise be to the
LORD your God, who has delighted in you
and placed you on his throne[h] as king to
rule for the LORD your God. Because of
the love of your God for Israel and his
desire to uphold them forever, he has
made you king[i] over them, to maintain
justice and righteousness."
9Then she gave the king 120 talents[l]
of gold,[j] large quantities of spices, and
precious stones. There had never been
such spices as those the queen of Sheba
gave to King Solomon.
10(The men of Hiram and the men of
Solomon brought gold from Ophir;[k] they
also brought algumwood[m] and precious
stones. 11The king used the algumwood
to make steps for the temple of the LORD
and for the royal palace, and to make
harps and lyres for the musicians. Nothing like them had ever been seen in
Judah.)
12King Solomon gave the queen of Sheba all she desired and asked for; he gave
her more than she had brought to him.
Then she left and returned with her retinue to her own country.

Solomon's Splendor

9:13–28pp — 1Ki 10:14–29; 2Ch 1:14–17

13The weight of the gold that Solomon
received yearly was 666 talents,[n] 14not
including the revenues brought in by
merchants and traders. Also all the kings
of Arabia[l] and the governors of the land
brought gold and silver to Solomon.
15King Solomon made two hundred
large shields of hammered gold; six hundred bekas[o] of hammered gold went into
each shield. 16He also made three

8:12 [q]S 1Ki 8:64; 2Ch 15:8
8:13 [r]S Ex 29:38 [s]Nu 28:9 [t]S Nu 10:10 [u]S Ex 23:14 [v]S Ex 12:17; Nu 28:16-25 [w]S Ex 23:16 [x]Nu 29:12-38; Ne 8:17
8:14 [y]S 1Ch 24:1 [z]S 1Ch 25:1 [a]S 1Ch 9:17 [b]Ne 12:24,36 [c]S 1Ch 23:6; Ne 12:45
8:18 [d]2Ch 9:9
9:1 [e]S Ge 10:7; Eze 23:42; Mt 12:42; Lk 11:31
9:3 [f]1Ki 5:12
9:6 [g]2Ch 6:32
9:8 [h]S 1Ki 2:12; S 1Ch 17:14; 2Ch 13:8 [i]2Ch 2:11
9:9 [j]2Ch 8:18
9:10 [k]2Ch 8:18
9:14 [l]2Ch 17:11; Isa 21:13; Jer 25:24; Eze 27:21; 30:5

[j] *18* That is, about 17 tons (about 16 metric tons)
[k] *4* Or *the ascent by which he went up to*
[l] *9* That is, about 4 1/2 tons (about 4 metric tons)
[m] *10* Probably a variant of *almugwood*
[n] *13* That is, about 25 tons (about 23 metric tons)
[o] *15* That is, about 7 1/2 pounds (about 3.5 kilograms)

8:12–16 WORSHIP, Priesthood—See notes on Ex 16:23–30; 1 Ch 6:48–49.

9:1–28 HUMANITY, Relationships—The fame, prosperity, and success of leaders reflect on the community which they lead.

9:8 HISTORY, God's Leaders—God revealed His love for His people by providing good leaders for His people. The leader's responsibility was to reflect that love to the people by maintaining justice and righteousness.

9:8 ELECTION, Responsibility—See note on 1 Ki 10:9. God makes leaders because He loves His people. God provides resources needed to lead effectively. Election is a call to covenant loyalty, love, and faithfulness. At times voices outside the community of faith call the elect back to their responsibilities.

9:8 PRAYER, Universality of—See note on 1 Ki 5:7.

hundred small shields[m] of hammered
gold, with three hundred bekas[p] of gold in
each shield. The king put them in the Palace of the Forest of Lebanon.[n]
17Then the king made a great throne
inlaid with ivory[o] and overlaid with pure
gold. 18The throne had six steps, and a
footstool of gold was attached to it. On
both sides of the seat were armrests, with
a lion standing beside each of them.
19Twelve lions stood on the six steps, one
at either end of each step. Nothing like it
had ever been made for any other kingdom. 20All King Solomon's goblets were
gold, and all the household articles in the
Palace of the Forest of Lebanon were pure
gold. Nothing was made of silver, because
silver was considered of little value in Solomon's day. 21The king had a fleet of trading ships[q] manned by Hiram's[r] men.
Once every three years it returned, carrying gold, silver and ivory, and apes and
baboons.
22King Solomon was greater in riches
and wisdom than all the other kings of
the earth.[p] 23All the kings[q] of the earth
sought audience with Solomon to hear
the wisdom God had put in his heart.
24Year after year, everyone who came
brought a gift[r]—articles of silver and
gold, and robes, weapons and spices, and
horses and mules.
25Solomon had four thousand stalls for
horses and chariots,[s] and twelve thousand horses,[s] which he kept in the chariot cities and also with him in Jerusalem.
26He ruled[t] over all the kings from the
River[t][u] to the land of the Philistines, as
far as the border of Egypt.[v] 27The king
made silver as common in Jerusalem as
stones, and cedar as plentiful as sycamore-fig trees in the foothills. 28Solo-
mon's horses were imported from Egypt[u]
and from all other countries.

Solomon's Death

9:29–31pp — 1Ki 11:41–43

29As for the other events of Solomon's
reign, from beginning to end, are they
not written in the records of Nathan[w] the
prophet, in the prophecy of Ahijah[x] the
Shilonite and in the visions of Iddo the
seer concerning Jeroboam[y] son of Nebat?
30Solomon reigned in Jerusalem over all
Israel forty years. 31Then he rested with
his fathers and was buried in the city of

9:16 *m*2Ch 12:9 *n*S 1Ki 7:2
9:17 *o*S 1Ki 22:39
9:22 *p*S 1Ki 3:13; S 2Ch 1:12
9:23 *q*1Ki 4:34
9:24 *r*2Ch 32:23; Ps 45:12; 68:29; 72:10; Isa 18:7
9:25 *s*S 1Sa 8:11
9:26 *t*S 1Ki 4:21 *u*Ps 72:8-9 *v*Ge 15:18-21
9:29 *w*S 2Sa 7:2 *x*S 1Ki 11:29 *y*2Ch 10:2
9:31 *z*1Ki 2:10
10:2 *a*S 2Ch 9:29 *b*S 1Ki 11:40
10:3 *c*S 1Ch 9:1
10:4 *d*2Ch 2:2
10:6 *e*Job 8:8-9; 12:12; 15:10; 32:7
10:7 *f*Pr 15:1
10:8 *g*S 2Sa 17:14 *h*Pr 13:20

David[z] his father. And Rehoboam his son
succeeded him as king.

Chapter 10

Israel Rebels Against Rehoboam

10:1–11:4pp — 1Ki 12:1–24

REHOBOAM went to Shechem, for all
the Israelites had gone there to make
him king. 2When Jeroboam[a] son of Nebat heard this (he was in Egypt, where he
had fled[b] from King Solomon), he returned from Egypt. 3So they sent for Jeroboam, and he and all Israel[c] went to Rehoboam and said to him: 4"Your father
put a heavy yoke on us,[d] but now lighten
the harsh labor and the heavy yoke he put
on us, and we will serve you."
5Rehoboam answered, "Come back to
me in three days." So the people went
away.
6Then King Rehoboam consulted the
elders[e] who had served his father Solomon during his lifetime. "How would you
advise me to answer these people?" he
asked.
7They replied, "If you will be kind to
these people and please them and give
them a favorable answer,[f] they will always be your servants."
8But Rehoboam rejected[g] the advice
the elders[h] gave him and consulted the
young men who had grown up with him
and were serving him. 9He asked them,
"What is your advice? How should we
answer these people who say to me,
'Lighten the yoke your father put on us'?"
10The young men who had grown up
with him replied, "Tell the people who
have said to you, 'Your father put a heavy
yoke on us, but make our yoke lighter'—
tell them, 'My little finger is thicker than
my father's waist. 11My father laid on you
a heavy yoke; I will make it even heavier.
My father scourged you with whips; I will
scourge you with scorpions.' "
12Three days later Jeroboam and all the
people returned to Rehoboam, as the king
had said, "Come back to me in three
days." 13The king answered them harshly. Rejecting the advice of the elders, 14he

[p] *16* That is, about 3 3/4 pounds (about 1.7 kilograms)
[q] *21* Hebrew *of ships that could go to Tarshish*
[r] *21* Hebrew *Huram,* a variant of *Hiram* [s] *25* Or *charioteers* [t] *26* That is, the Euphrates [u] *28* Or possibly *Muzur,* a region in Cilicia

9:26 HISTORY, Promise—God fulfilled the promises given to the patriarchs (Ge 15:18–21) and to Joshua (Jos 13:1–7). History is the story of God's promises and their historical fulfillment.
9:29 *HISTORY, Narrative*—*See note on 1 Ch 29:29–30.*
9;29 HOLY SCRIPTURE, Writing—See note on 2 Ch 9:29.
9:31 HUMANITY, Death—The Hebrew expression here literally says that he "lay down" with his fathers, a beautiful description of death, clearly viewed as a process as natural as going to sleep at night.
10:1–19 CHRISTIAN ETHICS, Justice—Harshness and injustice may get expedient short-term results, but the long-term consequences will be the judgment of God against such treatment. Society needs to listen to the wise counsel of experience rather than the ambitious impatience of youth.

followed the advice of the young men and
said, "My father made your yoke heavy; I
will make it even heavier. My father
scourged you with whips; I will scourge
you with scorpions." 15So the king did
not listen to the people, for this turn of
events was from God,[i] to fulfill the word
the LORD had spoken to Jeroboam son of
Nebat through Ahijah the Shilonite.[j]
16When all Israel[k] saw that the king
refused to listen to them, they answered
the king:

"What share do we have in David,[l]
what part in Jesse's son?
To your tents, O Israel!
Look after your own house,
O David!"

So all the Israelites went home. 17But as
for the Israelites who were living in the
towns of Judah, Rehoboam still ruled over
them.
18King Rehoboam sent out Adoni-
ram,[v][m] who was in charge of forced labor, but the Israelites stoned him to
death. King Rehoboam, however, managed to get into his chariot and escape to
Jerusalem. 19So Israel has been in rebellion against the house of David to this
day.

Chapter 11

WHEN Rehoboam arrived in Jerusalem,[n] he mustered the house of Judah and Benjamin—a hundred and
eighty thousand fighting men—to make
war against Israel and to regain the kingdom for Rehoboam.
2But this word of the LORD came to
Shemaiah[o] the man of God: 3"Say to Rehoboam son of Solomon king of Judah and
to all the Israelites in Judah and Benjamin, 4'This is what the LORD says: Do not
go up to fight against your brothers.[p] Go
home, every one of you, for this is my
doing.'" So they obeyed the words of the
LORD and turned back from marching
against Jeroboam.

Rehoboam Fortifies Judah

5Rehoboam lived in Jerusalem and built
up towns for defense in Judah: 6Bethle-
hem, Etam, Tekoa, 7Beth Zur, Soco, Adullam, 8Gath, Mareshah, Ziph, 9Adoraim,
Lachish, Azekah, 10Zorah, Aijalon and Hebron. These were fortified cities[q] in Judah and Benjamin. 11He strengthened
their defenses and put commanders in
them, with supplies of food, olive oil and
wine. 12He put shields and spears in all
the cities, and made them very strong. So
Judah and Benjamin were his.
13The priests and Levites from all their
districts throughout Israel sided with
him. 14The Levites[r] even abandoned
their pasturelands and property,[s] and
came to Judah and Jerusalem because Jeroboam and his sons had rejected them as
priests of the LORD. 15And he appointed[t]
his own priests[u] for the high places and
for the goat[v] and calf[w] idols he had
made. 16Those from every tribe of Israel[x]
who set their hearts on seeking the LORD,
the God of Israel, followed the Levites to
Jerusalem to offer sacrifices to the LORD,
the God of their fathers. 17They strengthened[y] the kingdom of Judah and supported Rehoboam son of Solomon three years,
walking in the ways of David and Solomon during this time.

Rehoboam's Family

18Rehoboam married Mahalath, who
was the daughter of David's son Jerimoth
and of Abihail, the daughter of Jesse's son
Eliab. 19She bore him sons: Jeush, Shemariah and Zaham. 20Then he married Maacah[z] daughter of Absalom, who bore him
Abijah,[a] Attai, Ziza and Shelomith. 21Re-
hoboam loved Maacah daughter of Absalom more than any of his other wives and
concubines. In all, he had eighteen
wives[b] and sixty concubines, twenty-
eight sons and sixty daughters.
22Rehoboam appointed Abijah[c] son of
Maacah to be the chief prince among his
brothers, in order to make him king. 23He
acted wisely, dispersing some of his sons
throughout the districts of Judah and Benjamin, and to all the fortified cities. He
gave them abundant provisions[d] and
took many wives for them.

10:15 [i]2Ch 11:4; 25:16-20 [j]S 1Ki 11:29
10:16 [k]S 1Ch 9:1 [l]S 2Sa 20:1
10:18 [m]S 2Sa 20:24; S 1Ki 5:14
11:1 [n]S 1Ki 12:21
11:2 [o]S 1Ki 12:22; 2Ch 12:5-7,15
11:4 [p]2Ch 28:8-11
11:10 [q]S Jos 10:20; 2Ch 12:4; 17:2,19; 21:3
11:14 [r]S Nu 35:2-5 [s]1Ch 6:81
11:15 [t]S 1Ki 13:33 [u]S 1Ki 12:31 [v]Lev 17:7 [w]1Ki 12:28; 2Ch 13:8
11:16 [x]2Ch 15:9
11:17 [y]2Ch 12:1
11:20 [z]S 1Ki 15:2 [a]2Ch 12:16; 13:2
11:21 [b]S Dt 17:17
11:22 [c]Dt 21:15-17
11:23 [d]2Ch 21:3

[v]*18* Hebrew *Hadoram,* a variant of *Adoniram*

11:2–4 CHRISTIAN ETHICS, War and Peace—War is not always an option to settle differences. Even though war was a mechanism in the Old Testament for change, the qualification was that God was always in charge on behalf of the Hebrews. As long as their purposes and His agreed, victory came. God commanded and expected Israel to obey. See notes on Jos 7:1—8:29; 10:1–43; 11:1–23.

11:4 HISTORY, God's People—God protected His people from themselves. He ordered them not to fight one another. God's actions in history are seen in what He refuses to let happen as well as in what He does.

11:14–16 SIN, Rebellion—A leader's rebellion against God affects many innocent people. God's faithful ministers had to flee from Israel because of Jeroboam's idolatry. Faithful laypersons refused to join Jeroboam's spiritual rebellion. They worshiped with the faithful in Jerusalem. A leader's rebellion against God will not work if he finds no followers. See note on 1 Ki 14:22–24.

11:18–21 FAMILY, Multiple Wives—Imitating your father's sin does not excuse you from guilt. Compare Eze 18. See notes on Ge 16:1–16; 1 Ki 11:1–9.

Chapter 12

Shishak Attacks Jerusalem

12:9–16pp — 1Ki 14:21, 25–31

AFTER Rehoboam's position as king was
established[e] and he had become
strong,[f] he and all Israel[w g] with him
abandoned[h] the law of the LORD. 2Be-
cause they had been unfaithful[i] to the
LORD, Shishak[j] king of Egypt attacked Jerusalem in the fifth year of King Rehoboam. 3With twelve hundred chariots and
sixty thousand horsemen and the innumerable troops of Libyans,[k] Sukkites and
Cushites[x l] that came with him from
Egypt, 4he captured the fortified cities[m]
of Judah and came as far as Jerusalem.
5Then the prophet Shemaiah[n] came to
Rehoboam and to the leaders of Judah
who had assembled in Jerusalem for fear
of Shishak, and he said to them, "This is
what the LORD says, 'You have abandoned
me; therefore, I now abandon[o] you to
Shishak.' "
6The leaders of Israel and the king
humbled[p] themselves and said, "The
LORD is just."[q]
7When the LORD saw that they humbled themselves, this word of the LORD
came to Shemaiah: "Since they have
humbled themselves, I will not destroy
them but will soon give them deliverance.[r] My wrath[s] will not be poured out
on Jerusalem through Shishak. 8They
will, however, become subject[t] to him,
so that they may learn the difference between serving me and serving the kings
of other lands."
9When Shishak king of Egypt attacked
Jerusalem, he carried off the treasures of
the temple of the LORD and the treasures
of the royal palace. He took everything,
including the gold shields[u] Solomon had
made. 10So King Rehoboam made bronze
shields to replace them and assigned
these to the commanders of the guard on
duty at the entrance to the royal palace.
11Whenever the king went to the LORD's
temple, the guards went with him, bearing the shields, and afterward they returned them to the guardroom.
12Because Rehoboam humbled[v] himself, the LORD's anger turned from him,
and he was not totally destroyed. Indeed,
there was some good[w] in Judah.
13King Rehoboam established[x] himself
firmly in Jerusalem and continued as
king. He was forty-one years old when he
became king, and he reigned seventeen
years in Jerusalem, the city the LORD had
chosen out of all the tribes of Israel in
which to put his Name.[y] His mother's
name was Naamah; she was an Ammonite. 14He did evil because he had not set
his heart on seeking the LORD.
15As for the events of Rehoboam's
reign, from beginning to end, are they
not written in the records of Shemaiah[z]
the prophet and of Iddo the seer that deal
with genealogies? There was continual
warfare between Rehoboam and Jeroboam. 16Rehoboam[a] rested with his fathers
and was buried in the City of David. And
Abijah[b] his son succeeded him as king.

Chapter 13

Abijah King of Judah

13:1–2,22–14:1pp — 1Ki 15:1–2,6–8

IN the eighteenth year of the reign of
Jeroboam, Abijah became king of Ju-

[w] *1* That is, Judah, as frequently in 2 Chronicles
[x] *3* That is, people from the upper Nile region

12:1 [e]ver 13; 2Ch 1:1 [f]2Ch 11:17 [g]S 1Ch 9:1 [h]S 2Ch 7:19
12:2 [i]1Ki 14:22-24; S 1Ch 5:25 [j]1Ki 11:40
12:3 [k]Da 11:43 [l]S Ge 10:6; 2Ch 14:9; 16:8; Isa 18:2; Am 9:7; Na 3:9
12:4 [m]S 2Ch 11:10
12:5 [n]2Ch 11:2 [o]S Dt 28:15
12:6 [p]S Lev 26:41; S 2Ch 6:37 [q]Ex 9:27; Ezr 9:15; Ps 11:7; 116:5; Da 9:14
12:7 [r]Ps 78:38 [s]Dt 9:19; Ps 69:24; Jer 7:20; 42:18; Eze 5:13
12:8 [t]Dt 28:48
12:9 [u]2Ch 9:16
12:12 [v]S 2Ch 6:37 [w]S 1Ki 14:13; 2Ch 19:3
12:13 [x]S ver 1; S 1Ki 2:12 [y]S Ex 20:24; Dt 12:5
12:15 [z]S 2Ch 11:2
12:16 [a]S 1Ch 3:10 [b]S 2Ch 11:20

12:1–2 SIN, Transgression—A position of political power too often leads to spiritual weakness. No one, not even the heads of state, can live by their own laws and succeed. Eventually God will intervene to punish those who refuse to follow His will. See notes on 1 Ki 14:22–24; 1 Ch 10:13.

12:1–12 HISTORY, Judgment—In judging His people, God remained responsive to them. He retracted the announcement of total abandonment when the leaders of His people humbly returned to Him. He used judgment to show His people the privilege they had in serving Him.

12:5–12 GOD, Wrath—The wrath of God was announced against Judah for the worship of false gods as reported in the preceding chapter. Because they humbled themselves, this judgment was tempered with mercy. This shows us wrath is not an absolute decree made by God but is a personal response to the actions of His people. See notes on Ge 6:5–8; 17:14; 19:13,24–26.

12:6 GOD, Justice—God is just and righteous. Thus he can respond to a people who accept His discipline in humble repentance by limiting their punishment. See notes on Ge 18:20–33; 20:4–6; Lev 1:1; Jos 23:1–16; 2 Sa 10:12; Jn 17:25.

12:7,12 PRAYER, Faithfulness of God—Rehoboam met the conditions of 7:14. In answering prayer God exercised His freedom even over His own word. See note on 2 Ki 20:3.

12:13 ELECTION, Free Will—King Rehoboam was chosen by God. Those chosen do not automatically obey God. Rehoboam did not "set his heart" on God. Continual warfare and conflict arise in every person who is too busy to obey the commandments of the God of election.

12:14 SIN, Transgression—See note on 1 Ki 14:22–24.

12:15 HOLY SCRIPTURE, Writing—See note on 1 Ch 29:29.

13:1–20 SIN, Transgression—Military might in the hands of sinners has no chance when God fights for His people. Following "not gods" (v 9), Jeroboam lost. God's presence is the vital element of victory in all of life's battles. Sin drives us from that Presence. See note on 1 Ki 12:26–33.

13:1–18 HISTORY, Deliverance—Faithful worship practices and steadfast devotion to God are more important factors for God's people than overwhelming military might. Chronicles details the victories of God's faithful people against all human odds. See note on 1 Ch 11:14.

13:1–20 THE CHURCH, Covenant People—Using the title "people of God" does not make us God's people. King Abijah of Judah explained to the Northern Kingdom of Israel the difference between the Kingdoms, both of whom claimed to be people of the God of Abraham, Isaac, and Jacob. Being people of God includes having God-called leaders, participating in worship pleasing to God, serving God without images like

dah, 2and he reigned in Jerusalem three
years. His mother's name was Maa-
cah,[y][c] a daughter[z] of Uriel of Gibeah.
There was war between Abijah[d] and
Jeroboam.[e] 3Abijah went into battle with
a force of four hundred thousand able
fighting men, and Jeroboam drew up a
battle line against him with eight hundred thousand able troops.
4Abijah stood on Mount Zemaraim,[f] in
the hill country of Ephraim, and said,
"Jeroboam and all Israel,[g] listen to me!
5Don't you know that the LORD, the God
of Israel, has given the kingship of Israel
to David and his descendants forever[h] by
a covenant of salt?[i] 6Yet Jeroboam son of
Nebat, an official of Solomon son of David, rebelled[j] against his master. 7Some
worthless scoundrels[k] gathered around
him and opposed Rehoboam son of Solomon when he was young and indecisive[l]
and not strong enough to resist them.
8"And now you plan to resist the kingdom of the LORD, which is in the hands of
David's descendants.[m] You are indeed a
vast army and have with you[n] the golden
calves[o] that Jeroboam made to be your
gods. 9But didn't you drive out the
priests[p] of the LORD,[q] the sons of Aaron,
and the Levites, and make priests of your
own as the peoples of other lands do?
Whoever comes to consecrate himself
with a young bull[r] and seven rams[s] may
become a priest of what are not gods.[t]
10"As for us, the LORD is our God, and
we have not forsaken him. The priests
who serve the LORD are sons of Aaron,
and the Levites assist them. 11Every
morning and evening[u] they present
burnt offerings and fragrant incense[v] to
the LORD. They set out the bread on the
ceremonially clean table[w] and light the
lamps[x] on the gold lampstand every evening. We are observing the requirements
of the LORD our God. But you have forsak-
en him. 12God is with us; he is our leader. His priests with their trumpets will
sound the battle cry against you.[y] Men of
Israel, do not fight against the LORD,[z] the

13:2 [c]2Ch 15:16 [d]S 2Ch 11:20 [e]1Ki 15:6
13:4 [f]Jos 18:22 [g]1Ch 11:1
13:5 [h]S 2Sa 7:13; S 1Ch 17:12 [i]S Lev 2:13
13:6 [j]1Ki 11:26
13:7 [k]S Jdg 9:4 [l]S 1Ch 29:1
13:8 [m]S 2Ch 9:8 [n]1Sa 4:3 [o]S Ex 32:4; S 2Ch 11:15
13:9 [p]S 1Ki 12:31 [q]2Ch 11:14-15 [r]Ex 29:35-36 [s]S Ex 29:31 [t]Jer 2:11; Gal 4:8
13:11 [u]S Ex 29:39; S 2Ch 2:4 [v]S Ex 25:6 [w]S 1Ch 9:32 [x]S Ex 25:37
13:12 [y]S Nu 10:8-9 [z]S Jdg 2:15; Ac 5:39 [a]Job 9:4; Pr 21:30; 29:1
13:13 [b]Jos 8:9; 2Ch 20:22
13:14 [c]S 1Ch 5:20; 2Ch 14:11; 18:31
13:15 [d]S 1Ch 9:1
13:16 [e]2Ch 16:8
13:18 [f]2Ch 14:11; 16:7; Ps 22:5
14:2 [g]2Ch 21:12

God of your fathers, for you will not succeed."[a]
13Now Jeroboam had sent troops
around to the rear, so that while he was
in front of Judah the ambush[b] was behind them. 14Judah turned and saw that
they were being attacked at both front
and rear. Then they cried out[c] to the
LORD. The priests blew their trumpets
15and the men of Judah raised the battle
cry. At the sound of their battle cry, God
routed Jeroboam and all Israel[d] before
Abijah and Judah. 16The Israelites fled before Judah, and God delivered[e] them into
their hands. 17Abijah and his men inflicted heavy losses on them, so that there
were five hundred thousand casualties
among Israel's able men. 18The men of
Israel were subdued on that occasion, and
the men of Judah were victorious because
they relied[f] on the LORD, the God of
their fathers.
19Abijah pursued Jeroboam and took
from him the towns of Bethel, Jeshanah
and Ephron, with their surrounding villages. 20Jeroboam did not regain power
during the time of Abijah. And the LORD
struck him down and he died.
21But Abijah grew in strength. He married fourteen wives and had twenty-two
sons and sixteen daughters.
22The other events of Abijah's reign,
what he did and what he said, are written
in the annotations of the prophet Iddo.

Chapter 14

AND Abijah rested with his fathers and was buried in the City of David. Asa his son succeeded him as king, and in his days the country was at peace for ten years.

Asa King of Judah

14:2-3pp — 1Ki 15:11-12

2Asa did what was good and right in
the eyes of the LORD his God.[g] 3He re-

[y]2 Most Septuagint manuscripts and Syriac (see also 2 Chron. 11:20 and 1 Kings 15:2); Hebrew *Micaiah*
[z]2 Or *granddaughter*

the golden calves, and observing God's requirements. People of God live and worship differently than do other persons. See notes on 7:17–22; 2 Sa 23:5.

13:5–12 ELECTION, Leadership—God often elects a minority to win battles against the majority who disrespect His agenda and purpose. The Northern Kingdom refused to accept God's election of David's house. Election to leadership does not guarantee acceptance by the people. In free will people may choose to fight God.

13:8 LAST THINGS, Kingdom Established—The earthly kingdom of David was the earthly Old Testament expression of the kingdom of the Lord. David was the Lord's anointed, and his kingdom was God's design. The new covenant ushered in new dimensions of God's kingdom. His kingdom is eternal and one day will be established in its fullness. During Old Testament periods the earthly kingdom was resisted. Today people continue to resist the spiritual one. Nonetheless, God's kingdom is present and will come. See note on 1 Co 15:24–28.

13:9–10 GOD, One God—The human inclination is to create gods out of our material world. Whatever we can create is not worthy of our worship and thus not a god. Only one God deserves our worship. See note on 2:5.

13:14–18 PRAYER, Answer—See note on 1 Ch 5:20.

13:22 HOLY SCRIPTURE, Writing—See note on 1 Ch 29:29.

14:1—15:19 CHRISTIAN ETHICS, War and Peace—The military success of Asa was directly tied to his intentions of ridding the land of idolatry and to his prayerful dependence on God. These were battles to determine religious loyalty. Greater reward than victory in battle came for obedient Asa. He received peace—rest from war and fullness of life. See note on Ps 34:14.

moved the foreign altars[h] and the high
places, smashed the sacred stones[i] and
cut down the Asherah poles.[a][j] 4He commanded Judah to seek the LORD,[k] the
God of their fathers, and to obey his laws
and commands. 5He removed the high
places[l] and incense altars[m] in every
town in Judah, and the kingdom was at
peace under him. 6He built up the fortified cities of Judah, since the land was at
peace. No one was at war with him during those years, for the LORD gave him
rest.[n]
7"Let us build up these towns," he said
to Judah, "and put walls around them,
with towers, gates and bars. The land is
still ours, because we have sought the
LORD our God; we sought him and he has
given us rest[o] on every side." So they
built and prospered.
8Asa had an army of three hundred
thousand[p] men from Judah, equipped
with large shields and with spears, and
two hundred and eighty thousand from
Benjamin, armed with small shields and
with bows. All these were brave fighting
men.
9Zerah the Cushite[q] marched out
against them with a vast army[b] and three
hundred chariots, and came as far as Mareshah.[r] 10Asa went out to meet him,
and they took up battle positions in the
Valley of Zephathah near Mareshah.
11Then Asa called[s] to the LORD his
God and said, "LORD, there is no one like
you to help the powerless against the
mighty. Help us,[t] O LORD our God, for
we rely[u] on you, and in your name[v] we
have come against this vast army. O
LORD, you are our God; do not let man
prevail[w] against you."

14:3 [h]S Jdg 2:2 [i]S Ex 23:24 [j]S Ex 34:13
14:4 [k]S 1Ch 16:11
14:5 [l]S 1Ki 15:14 [m]Isa 27:9; Eze 6:4
14:6 [n]S 1Ch 22:9
14:7 [o]S 1Ch 22:9
14:8 [p]S 1Ch 21:1
14:9 [q]S 2Ch 12:3 [r]S Ge 10:8-9; 2Ch 11:8; 24:24
14:11 [s]S 1Ki 8:44; S 2Ch 13:14; 25:8 [t]Ps 60:11-12; 79:9 [u]S 2Ch 13:18 [v]S 1Sa 17:45 [w]Ps 9:19
14:12 [x]1Ki 8:45
14:13 [y]Ge 10:19 [z]2Sa 22:38; Ne 9:24; Ps 44:2, 19; 135:10 [a]2Ch 15:11,18
14:14 [b]S Ge 35:5; S Dt 2:25; 11:25
15:1 [c]S Nu 11:25, 26
15:2 [d]2Ch 20:17 [e]Jas 4:8 [f]2Ch 7:14; Ps 78:34; Isa 45:19; 55:6; Jer 29:13; Hos 3:5 [g]S Dt 31:17; S 1Ch 28:9
15:3 [h]S Lev 10:11 [i]La 2:9; Am 8:11
15:4 [j]S Dt 4:29
15:5 [k]S Jdg 5:6; 19:20; Zec 8:10

12The LORD struck down[x] the Cushites
before Asa and Judah. The Cushites fled,
13and Asa and his army pursued them as
far as Gerar.[y] Such a great number of
Cushites fell that they could not recover;
they were crushed[z] before the LORD and
his forces. The men of Judah carried off a
large amount of plunder.[a] 14They destroyed all the villages around Gerar, for
the terror[b] of the LORD had fallen upon
them. They plundered all these villages,
since there was much booty there. 15They
also attacked the camps of the herdsmen
and carried off droves of sheep and goats
and camels. Then they returned to Jerusalem.

Chapter 15

Asa's Reform

15:16–19pp — 1Ki 15:13–16

THE Spirit of God came upon[c] Azariah
son of Oded. 2He went out to meet
Asa and said to him, "Listen to me, Asa
and all Judah and Benjamin. The LORD is
with you[d] when you are with him.[e] If
you seek[f] him, he will be found by you,
but if you forsake him, he will forsake
you.[g] 3For a long time Israel was without
the true God, without a priest to teach[h]
and without the law.[i] 4But in their distress they turned to the LORD, the God of
Israel, and sought him,[j] and he was
found by them. 5In those days it was not
safe to travel about,[k] for all the inhabitants of the lands were in great turmoil.
6One nation was being crushed by anoth-

[a]3 That is, symbols of the goddess Asherah; here and elsewhere in 2 Chronicles [b]9 Hebrew *with an army of a thousand thousands* or *with an army of thousands upon thousands*

14:2–6 CHRISTIAN ETHICS, Moral Imperatives—God honored kings who honored Him. No matter what our predecessors or contemporaries do, God calls us to choose to follow Him. See note on 2 Ki 17:13–23.
14:6–7 HISTORY, Promise—See note on Jos 11:23.
14:8–17 HISTORY, Deliverance—See note on 13:1–18.
14:11–13 GOD, Power—Human power and destructive might stand no chance when lined up against God's power. See notes on Ge 15:13–16; 18:14; 24:3,7,50.
14:11 GOD, One God—God's people realize the uniqueness of God in time of need when He proves the only One able to help. See notes on Ex 20:1–7; Dt 6:4–9.
14:11 PRAYER, Sovereignty of God—Asa's prayer recognized the uniqueness of God. This is a prayer of total trust. At times the believer's only prayer is, "Help."
15:1–2 HOLY SPIRIT, Revelation—God's Spirit inspired Azariah to pronounce a prophetic oracle calling the nation to be faithful to the Lord. The Spirit assured them if they followed God, they would prevail, for He would help them. How the prophet's message was written down and preserved until the writing of Chronicles hundreds of years later is one of the marvelous mysteries of God's process of inspiring His written Word. Revelation often began as spoken word long before it became written Word. The Spirit started the oral process and guided the preservation of His word until it became part of the collection of inspired books we call the Bible.
15:1–4 REVELATION, Divine Presence—God is available to His people when we obediently seek Him. He responds to our rejection of Him by becoming distant Himself. Israel was without a genuine experience of and revelation from God for a period of time by their own choosing. When the people called on Him even without committed leaders, He was present. The loving God is still available, always prepared to forgive and renew the intimacy of a faith-relationship (Ps 73:23). A distressed and penitent child always receives God's attention. See note on 1 Ki 22:6–28.
15:2–7 GOD, Faithfulness—God is faithful to be present to help His needy people. Such faithfulness is not something humans can take advantage of according to our timetable. The faithful God expects His people to be faithful and responsible in seeking Him. See notes on Ge 18:20–33; Jos 23:1–16; Gal 6:7–10.
15:2 ELECTION, Freedom—Although the king was elected by God to lead, the king did not possess license to do what he willed. Such independent action prevented the king from having the blessings of God. God retains freedom to forsake people who forsake Him. King Asa, upon learning this truth from the prophet, Azariah, obeyed God and brought about reform in the kingdom.
15:2 PRAYER, Command of God—Reciprocity is an important prayer principle (Jas 4:8). God listens to persons who listen to Him.

er and one city by another,[l] because God
was troubling them with every kind of
distress. 7But as for you, be strong[m] and
do not give up, for your work will be rewarded."[n]

8When Asa heard these words and the
prophecy of Azariah son of[c] Oded the
prophet, he took courage. He removed
the detestable idols[o] from the whole land
of Judah and Benjamin and from the
towns he had captured[p] in the hills of
Ephraim. He repaired the altar[q] of the
LORD that was in front of the portico of
the LORD's temple.

9Then he assembled all Judah and Benjamin and the people from Ephraim, Manasseh and Simeon who had settled
among them, for large numbers[r] had
come over to him from Israel when they
saw that the LORD his God was with him.

10They assembled at Jerusalem in the
third month[s] of the fifteenth year of
Asa's reign. 11At that time they sacrificed
to the LORD seven hundred head of cattle
and seven thousand sheep and goats from
the plunder[t] they had brought back.
12They entered into a covenant[u] to seek
the LORD,[v] the God of their fathers, with
all their heart and soul. 13All who would
not seek the LORD, the God of Israel,
were to be put to death,[w] whether small
or great, man or woman. 14They took an
oath to the LORD with loud acclamation,
with shouting and with trumpets and
horns. 15All Judah rejoiced about the oath
because they had sworn it wholeheartedly. They sought God[x] eagerly, and he was
found by them. So the LORD gave them
rest[y] on every side.

16King Asa also deposed his grandmother Maacah[z] from her position as
queen mother,[a] because she had made a
repulsive Asherah pole.[b] Asa cut the pole
down, broke it up and burned it in the
Kidron Valley.[c] 17Although he did not remove the high places from Israel, Asa's
heart was fully committed ⌞to the LORD⌟ all
his life. 18He brought into the temple of
God the silver and gold and the articles
that he and his father had dedicated.[d]

19There was no more war until the
thirty-fifth year of Asa's reign.

Chapter 16

Asa's Last Years

16:1–6pp — 1Ki 15:17–22
16:11–17:1pp — 1Ki 15:23–24

1IN the thirty-sixth year of Asa's reign Baasha[e] king of Israel went up against
Judah and fortified Ramah to prevent anyone from leaving or entering the territory
of Asa king of Judah.

2Asa then took the silver and gold out
of the treasuries of the LORD's temple and
of his own palace and sent it to Ben-Hadad king of Aram, who was ruling in Damascus.[f] 3"Let there be a treaty[g] between me and you," he said, "as there
was between my father and your father.
See, I am sending you silver and gold.
Now break your treaty with Baasha king
of Israel so he will withdraw from me."

4Ben-Hadad agreed with King Asa and
sent the commanders of his forces against
the towns of Israel. They conquered Ijon,
Dan, Abel Maim[d] and all the store cities
of Naphtali.[h] 5When Baasha heard this,
he stopped building Ramah and abandoned his work. 6Then King Asa brought
all the men of Judah, and they carried
away from Ramah the stones and timber
Baasha had been using. With them he
built up Geba and Mizpah.[i]

7At that time Hanani[j] the seer came to
Asa king of Judah and said to him:

15:6 [l]Isa 19:2; Mt 24:7; Mk 13:8; Lk 21:10
15:7 [m]Jos 1:7,9 [n]1Sa 24:19; Ps 18:20; 58:11; Pr 14:14; Jer 31:16
15:8 [o]1Ki 15:12 [p]2Ch 17:2 [q]S 1Ki 8:64; S 2Ch 8:12
15:9 [r]2Ch 11:16-17
15:10 [s]S Lev 23:15-21
15:11 [t]S 2Ch 14:13
15:12 [u]S 2Ki 11:17 [v]S 1Ch 16:11
15:13 [w]S Ex 22:20; Dt 13:9-16
15:15 [x]Dt 4:29 [y]S 1Ch 22:9
15:16 [z]2Ch 13:2 [a]S 1Ki 2:19 [b]S Ex 34:13 [c]S 2Sa 15:23
15:18 [d]S 2Ch 14:13
16:1 [e]2Ki 9:9; Jer 41:9
16:2 [f]2Ch 19:1-20:37; 22:1-9
16:3 [g]2Ch 20:35; 25:7
16:4 [h]S 2Ki 15:29
16:6 [i]Jer 41:9
16:7 [j]1Ki 16:1

[c]8 Vulgate and Syriac (see also Septuagint and verse 1); Hebrew does not have *Azariah son of.* [d]4 Also known as *Abel Beth Maacah*

15:6 HISTORY, Judgment—A people unfaithful to God face turbulence and distress. God works through international crises to teach His people their need for faithfulness.

15:10–18 GOD, One God—A major problem of the Old Testament peoples was learning that there is truly only one God and that the worship of false gods must be strictly avoided. The discipline God exercises here shows how seriously He takes His demand for total allegiance. See notes on Ge 31:30–35; 35:2; Ex 20:1–7; Dt 6:4–9.

15:12 THE CHURCH, Covenant People—Being God's people is not a matter of birth and inheritance. Each generation must individually and collectively choose to be God's covenant people. Such a decision is not a ritual formality or simple intellectual agreement. It involves commitment of heart and soul—intellect and emotions. See note on Jos 24:25–27.

15:12–15 PRAYER, Faithfulness of God—Asa and Judah honored God's promise in v 2 wholeheartedly.

15:13 CHRISTIAN ETHICS, Murder—Refusal to worship Yahweh, the God of Israel, was a capital offense (Ex 22:20; Dt 13:1–18; 17:2–7). Such offenders became foreign enemies in Israel and were under the holy war ban. See note on Nu 21:1–3. Israel's inspired leaders sought to show the people how seriously God took the covenant and how seriously He expected them to take it. See notes on Jdg 8:10–21; 1 Ki 16:10–13.

15:15 HISTORY, Promise—See note on Jos 11:23.

16:1–10 CHRISTIAN ETHICS, War and Peace—After a brilliant career of devotion to God and social reform, Asa turned away from God. One can see the terrible consequences against Asa's own people which resulted from rejecting God's ways. God did not call on His people to use human ingenuity to defeat enemies. He did not lead to foreign alliances which robbed His worship place of its resources and subjected His people to worship obligations to foreign gods. War became God's agent of punishment (v 9), as peace had been the agent of blessing (14:6,7; 15:19). See notes on Jos 21:43–45; 1 Ki 5:4.

16:7–9 GOD, Wrath—Past history of reliance on God is not sufficient. The wrath of God was expressed against the failure to trust and follow God's leading in a new situation, even though God had proved sufficient and faithful in the past. See notes on Ge 6:5–8; 17:14; 19:13,24–26; Mt 3:7–10.

16:7–9 HISTORY, Faith—God used history to call His people to faith. They repeatedly sought security in international

"Because you relied[k] on the king of Aram
and not on the LORD your God, the army
of the king of Aram has escaped from
your hand. [8]Were not the Cushites[e] [l]
and Libyans a mighty army with great
numbers[m] of chariots and horsemen[f]?
Yet when you relied on the LORD, he delivered[n] them into your hand. [9]For the
eyes[o] of the LORD range throughout the
earth to strengthen those whose hearts
are fully committed to him. You have
done a foolish[p] thing, and from now on
you will be at war.[q]"
[10]Asa was angry with the seer because
of this; he was so enraged that he put him
in prison.[r] At the same time Asa brutally
oppressed some of the people.
[11]The events of Asa's reign, from beginning to end, are written in the book of
the kings of Judah and Israel. [12]In the
thirty-ninth year of his reign Asa was afflicted[s] with a disease in his feet. Though
his disease was severe, even in his illness
he did not seek[t] help from the LORD,[u]
but only from the physicians. [13]Then in
the forty-first year of his reign Asa died
and rested with his fathers. [14]They buried
him in the tomb that he had cut out for
himself[v] in the City of David. They laid
him on a bier covered with spices and
various blended perfumes,[w] and they
made a huge fire[x] in his honor.

Chapter 17

Jehoshaphat King of Judah

JEHOSHAPHAT his son succeeded him
as king and strengthened[y] himself
against Israel. [2]He stationed troops in all
the fortified cities[z] of Judah and put garrisons in Judah and in the towns of Ephraim that his father Asa had captured.[a]
[3]The LORD was with Jehoshaphat because in his early years he walked in the
ways his father David[b] had followed. He
did not consult the Baals [4]but sought[c]
the God of his father and followed his
commands rather than the practices of Israel. [5]The LORD established the kingdom
under his control; and all Judah brought
gifts[d] to Jehoshaphat, so that he had
great wealth and honor.[e] [6]His heart was
devoted[f] to the ways of the LORD; furthermore, he removed the high places[g]
and the Asherah poles[h] from Judah.[i]
[7]In the third year of his reign he sent
his officials Ben-Hail, Obadiah, Zechariah,
Nethanel and Micaiah to teach[j] in the
towns of Judah. [8]With them were certain
Levites[k]—Shemaiah, Nethaniah, Zebadiah, Asahel, Shemiramoth, Jehonathan,
Adonijah, Tobijah and Tob-Adonijah—
and the priests Elishama and Jehoram.
[9]They taught throughout Judah, taking
with them the Book of the Law[l] of the
LORD; they went around to all the towns
of Judah and taught the people.
[10]The fear[m] of the LORD fell on all the
kingdoms of the lands surrounding Judah,
so that they did not make war with Jehoshaphat. [11]Some Philistines brought Jehoshaphat gifts and silver as tribute, and
the Arabs[n] brought him flocks:[o] seven
thousand seven hundred rams and seven
thousand seven hundred goats.
[12]Jehoshaphat became more and more
powerful; he built forts and store cities in
Judah [13]and had large supplies in the
towns of Judah. He also kept experienced
fighting men in Jerusalem. [14]Their enrollment[p] by families was as follows:

From Judah, commanders of units of 1,000:
Adnah the commander, with 300,000 fighting men;
[15]next, Jehohanan the commander, with 280,000;
[16]next, Amasiah son of Zicri, who volunteered[q] himself for the service of the LORD, with 200,000.

[17]From Benjamin:[r]
Eliada, a valiant soldier, with 200,000 men armed with bows and shields;
[18]next, Jehozabad, with 180,000 men armed for battle.

[19]These were the men who served the
king, besides those he stationed in the
fortified cities[s] throughout Judah.[t]

[e]*8* That is, people from the upper Nile region [f]*8* Or *charioteers*

16:7 [k]S 2Ch 13:18
16:8 [l]S Ge 10:6, 8-9; S 2Ch 12:3 [m]2Ch 24:24 [n]2Ch 13:16
16:9 [o]Job 24:23; Ps 33:13-15; Pr 15:3; Jer 16:17; Zec 3:9; 4:10 [p]1Sa 13:13 [q]S 1Ki 15:6; 2Ch 19:2; 25:7; 28:16-21
16:10 [r]S 1Ki 22:27
16:12 [s]2Ch 21:18; 26:19; Ps 103:3 [t]2Ch 7:14 [u]Jer 17:5-6
16:14 [v]S Ge 50:5 [w]S Ge 50:2 [x]2Ch 21:19; Jer 34:5
17:1 [y]S 1Ki 2:12
17:2 [z]S 2Ch 11:10 [a]2Ch 15:8
17:3 [b]S 1Ki 22:43
17:4 [c]2Ch 22:9
17:5 [d]S 1Sa 10:27 [e]2Ch 18:1
17:6 [f]S 1Ki 8:61 [g]S 1Ki 15:14; 2Ch 19:3; 20:33 [h]S Ex 34:13 [i]2Ch 21:12
17:7 [j]S Lev 10:11; Dt 6:4-9; 2Ch 19:4-11; 35:3; Ne 8:7; Mal 2:7
17:8 [k]2Ch 19:8; Ne 8:7-8; Hos 4:6
17:9 [l]S Dt 28:61
17:10 [m]S Ge 35:5; S Dt 2:25
17:11 [n]S 2Ch 9:14 [o]2Ch 21:16
17:14 [p]S 2Sa 24:2
17:16 [q]S Jdg 5:9
17:17 [r]S Nu 1:36
17:19 [s]S 2Ch 11:10 [t]2Ch 25:5

---

alliances. He showed them their covenant alliance with Him was all they needed for true security.

16:7–9 PRAYER, Faithfulness of God—Asa's turning from the Lord late in his life led him to seek alliances that appeared strong to his eyes. He forgot the promise of 15:2. God's eyes perceive those who rely on Him. Reliance on Him cannot be mixed with reliance on human strength (Ps 20:7).

16:9 GOD, Wisdom—God actively follows what happens in His world, and He acts upon that knowledge. God's grace helps those who need Him. *See notes on 1:8; 1 Sa 2:3.*

16:12 PRAYER, Hindrances—In the latter part of his life, Asa sought help in military matters from Aram (v 2) and in medical matters from physicians but not from the Lord. See note on vv 7–9.

16:13–14 HUMANITY, Burial—This detailed description of the Hebrew burial practices is quite unusual. Although it may refer to cremation, as some have suggested, it does not appear to do so. Rather the lighting of a fire let the entire surrounding community know of the passing of a beloved and honored leader.

17:7–9 EDUCATION, Priests—In addition to presiding over Temple worship, the priests and Levites of Israel were religious instructors. See Dt 33:10; 2 Ch 35:3. Today, as in Old Testament times, teaching constitutes a significant part of a minister's work. Learning continues to be an important responsibility of the members of the community of faith.

Chapter 18

Micaiah Prophesies Against Ahab

18:1-27pp — 1Ki 22:1-28

NOW Jehoshaphat had great wealth
and honor,[u] and he allied[v] himself
with Ahab[w] by marriage. 2Some years later he went down to visit Ahab in Samaria. Ahab slaughtered many sheep and cattle for him and the people with him and
urged him to attack Ramoth Gilead.
3Ahab king of Israel asked Jehoshaphat
king of Judah, "Will you go with me
against Ramoth Gilead?"
Jehoshaphat replied, "I am as you are,
and my people as your people; we will
join you in the war." 4But Jehoshaphat
also said to the king of Israel, "First seek
the counsel of the LORD."
5So the king of Israel brought together
the prophets—four hundred men—and
asked them, "Shall we go to war against
Ramoth Gilead, or shall I refrain?"
"Go," they answered, "for God will
give it into the king's hand."
6But Jehoshaphat asked, "Is there not a
prophet of the LORD here whom we can
inquire of?"
7The king of Israel answered Jehoshaphat, "There is still one man through
whom we can inquire of the LORD, but I
hate him because he never prophesies
anything good about me, but always bad.
He is Micaiah son of Imlah."
"The king should not say that," Jehoshaphat replied.
8So the king of Israel called one of his
officials and said, "Bring Micaiah son of
Imlah at once."
9Dressed in their royal robes, the king
of Israel and Jehoshaphat king of Judah
were sitting on their thrones at the
threshing floor by the entrance to the
gate of Samaria, with all the prophets
prophesying before them. 10Now Zedekiah son of Kenaanah had made iron horns,
and he declared, "This is what the LORD
says: 'With these you will gore the Arameans until they are destroyed.' "
11All the other prophets were prophesying the same thing. "Attack Ramoth
Gilead[x] and be victorious," they said,
"for the LORD will give it into the king's
hand."
12The messenger who had gone to
summon Micaiah said to him, "Look, as
one man the other prophets are predicting success for the king. Let your word
agree with theirs, and speak favorably."
13But Micaiah said, "As surely as the
LORD lives, I can tell him only what my
God says."[y]
14When he arrived, the king asked
him, "Micaiah, shall we go to war against
Ramoth Gilead, or shall I refrain?"
"Attack and be victorious," he answered, "for they will be given into your
hand."
15The king said to him, "How many
times must I make you swear to tell me
nothing but the truth in the name of the
LORD?"
16Then Micaiah answered, "I saw all
Israel[z] scattered on the hills like sheep
without a shepherd,[a] and the LORD said,
'These people have no master. Let each
one go home in peace.' "
17The king of Israel said to Jehoshaphat, "Didn't I tell you that he never
prophesies anything good about me, but
only bad?"
18Micaiah continued, "Therefore hear
the word of the LORD: I saw the LORD
sitting on his throne[b] with all the host of
heaven standing on his right and on his
left. 19And the LORD said, 'Who will entice Ahab king of Israel into attacking Ramoth Gilead and going to his death
there?'
"One suggested this, and another that.
20Finally, a spirit came forward, stood before the LORD and said, 'I will entice
him.'
" 'By what means?' the LORD asked.
21" 'I will go and be a lying spirit[c] in
the mouths of all his prophets,' he said.
" 'You will succeed in enticing him,'
said the LORD. 'Go and do it.'
22"So now the LORD has put a lying
spirit in the mouths of these prophets of
yours.[d] The LORD has decreed disaster
for you."
23Then Zedekiah son of Kenaanah
went up and slapped[e] Micaiah in the
face. "Which way did the spirit from[g]
the LORD go when he went from me to
speak to you?" he asked.
24Micaiah replied, "You will find out
on the day you go to hide in an inner
room."
25The king of Israel then ordered,
"Take Micaiah and send him back to
Amon the ruler of the city and to Joash
the king's son, 26and say, 'This is what
the king says: Put this fellow in prison[f]
and give him nothing but bread and water until I return safely.' "
27Micaiah declared, "If you ever return
safely, the LORD has not spoken through

18:1 [u]2Ch 17:5 [v]2Ch 19:1-3; 22:3 [w]2Ch 21:6
18:11 [x]2Ch 22:5
18:13 [y]Nu 22:18, 20,35
18:16 [z]S 1Ch 9:1 [a]S Nu 27:17
18:18 [b]Da 7:9
18:21 [c]1Ch 21:1; Job 1:6; Zec 3:1; Jn 8:44
18:22 [d]Job 12:16; Eze 14:9
18:23 [e]Ac 23:2
18:26 [f]Heb 11:36

[g]23 Or *Spirit of*

18:5–7 REVELATION, Spirit—Many voices claim to represent God but often substitute their own desires over God's revelation. See note on 1 Ki 22:6–28.

18:6 PRAYER, Petition—See note on 1 Ki 22:8–17.

18:18–27 EVIL AND SUFFERING, Divine Origin—See note on 1 Ki 22:19–28.

me." Then he added, "Mark my words, all you people!"

Ahab Killed at Ramoth Gilead

18:28–34pp — 1Ki 22:29–36

28So the king of Israel and Jehoshaphat king of Judah went up to Ramoth Gilead. 29The king of Israel said to Jehoshaphat, "I will enter the battle in disguise, but you wear your royal robes." So the king of Israel disguised[g] himself and went into battle.

30Now the king of Aram had ordered his chariot commanders, "Do not fight with anyone, small or great, except the king of Israel." 31When the chariot commanders saw Jehoshaphat, they thought, "This is the king of Israel." So they turned to attack him, but Jehoshaphat cried out,[h] and the LORD helped him. God drew them away from him, 32for when the chariot commanders saw that he was not the king of Israel, they stopped pursuing him.

33But someone drew his bow at random and hit the king of Israel between the sections of his armor. The king told the chariot driver, "Wheel around and get me out of the fighting. I've been wounded." 34All day long the battle raged, and the king of Israel propped himself up in his chariot facing the Arameans until evening. Then at sunset he died.[i]

Chapter 19

WHEN Jehoshaphat king of Judah returned safely to his palace in Jerusalem, 2Jehu[j] the seer, the son of Hanani, went out to meet him and said to the king, "Should you help the wicked[k] and love[h] those who hate the LORD?[l] Because of this, the wrath[m] of the LORD is upon you. 3There is, however, some good[n] in you, for you have rid the land of the Asherah poles[o] and have set your heart on seeking God.[p]"

Jehoshaphat Appoints Judges

4Jehoshaphat lived in Jerusalem, and he went out again among the people from Beersheba to the hill country of Ephraim and turned them back to the LORD, the God of their fathers. 5He appointed judges[q] in the land, in each of the fortified cities of Judah. 6He told them, "Consider carefully what you do,[r] because you are not judging for man[s] but for the LORD, who is with you whenever you give a verdict. 7Now let the fear of the LORD be upon you. Judge carefully, for with the LORD our God there is no injustice[t] or partiality[u] or bribery."

8In Jerusalem also, Jehoshaphat appointed some of the Levites,[v] priests[w] and heads of Israelite families to administer[x] the law of the LORD and to settle disputes. And they lived in Jerusalem. 9He gave them these orders: "You must serve faithfully and wholeheartedly in the fear of the LORD. 10In every case that comes before you from your fellow countrymen who live in the cities—whether bloodshed or other concerns of the law, commands, decrees or ordinances—you are to warn them not to sin against the LORD;[y] otherwise his wrath will come on you and your brothers. Do this, and you will not sin.

11"Amariah the chief priest will be over you in any matter concerning the LORD, and Zebadiah son of Ishmael, the leader of the tribe of Judah, will be over you in any matter concerning the king, and the Levites will serve as officials before you. Act with courage,[z] and may the LORD be with those who do well."

Chapter 20

Jehoshaphat Defeats Moab and Ammon

AFTER this, the Moabites[a] and Ammonites with some of the Meunites[i] [b] came to make war on Jehoshaphat.

18:29 [g]S 1Sa 28:8
18:31 [h]S 2Ch 13:14
18:34 [i]2Ch 22:5
19:2 [j]S 1Ki 16:1 [k]S 2Ch 16:2-9 [l]Ps 139:21-22 [m]2Ch 24:18; 32:25; Ps 7:11
19:3 [n]S 1Ki 14:13 [o]S 2Ch 17:6 [p]S 2Ch 18:1; 20:35; 25:7
19:5 [q]S Ge 47:6; S Ex 18:26
19:6 [r]S Lev 19:15 [s]Dt 16:18-20; 17:8-13
19:7 [t]S Ge 18:25; S Job 8:3 [u]S Ex 18:16; Dt 10:17; Job 13:10; 32:21; 34:19
19:8 [v]S 1Ch 23:4 [w]Eze 44:24 [x]2Ch 17:8-9
19:10 [y]Dt 17:8-13
19:11 [z]S 1Ch 28:20
20:1 [a]Ps 83:6 [b]S 1Ch 4:41

[h]*2* Or *and make alliances with* [i]*1* Some Septuagint manuscripts; Hebrew *Ammonites*

18:31 PRAYER, Answer—Jehoshaphat had insisted on hearing from the prophet of the Lord. When he called to God in desperation, God helped him. God hears our most desperate cries and can help in the darkest situation. When we have sought Him in calmer hours, it is natural to call on Him in crisis moments.

19:2,10 GOD, Wrath—The wrath of God is His reaction to sin when one refuses to yield to the will of God. Wrath is expressed against those who oppose God's people as well as those who directly oppose God. See notes on Ge 6:5–8; 17:14; 19:13,24–26; Mt 3:7–10.

19:2–3 HISTORY, Faith—See note on 16:7–9. Evil alliances included alliances with unfaithful kings of Israel, the Northern Kingdom. Jehoshaphat followed Solomon's bad example (1 Ki 11) by using marriage to gain political advantage (1 Ch 18:1). God did not ignore the king's good side. The kings of Judah illustrate the complexity of sin-prone humans seeking to be faithful to God.

19:5–11 CHRISTIAN ETHICS, Justice—A particular concern of Jehoshaphat was the inequities, especially bribery, occurring among the people. In appointing judges as he did, Jehoshaphat articulated a continuing principle that judges must act to uphold impartiality. The judge must always be aware that God is the supreme Judge. Earthly judges should be His representatives seeking to decide cases as He would.

19:7 GOD, Righteous—God always does what is right. He never shows partiality or favoritism. He does not use unjust methods such as bribery to accomplish His purposes. See notes on Ge 18:20–33; 20:4–6; 2 Sa 10:12; Jn 17:25.

20:1–30 CHRISTIAN ETHICS, War and Peace—Most elements of the Old Testament conceptions of war appear clearly here. (1) Israel gained the land in a unique offensive war God led. (2) God was the chief Planner and Actor in wars defending a faithful people. (3) God's people must seek God's

2 Some men came and told Jehoshaphat,
"A vast army[c] is coming against you
from Edom,[j] from the other side of the
Sea.[k] It is already in Hazazon Tamar[d]"
(that is, En Gedi).[e] 3 Alarmed, Jehoshaphat resolved to inquire of the LORD, and
he proclaimed a fast[f] for all Judah. 4 The
people of Judah[g] came together to seek
help from the LORD; indeed, they came
from every town in Judah to seek him.
5 Then Jehoshaphat stood up in the assembly of Judah and Jerusalem at the temple of the LORD in the front of the new
courtyard 6 and said:

"O LORD, God of our fathers,[h] are
you not the God who is in heaven?[i]
You rule over all the kingdoms[j] of
the nations. Power and might are in
your hand, and no one can withstand
you.[k] 7 O our God, did you not drive
out the inhabitants of this land[l] before your people Israel and give it forever to the descendants of Abraham
your friend?[m] 8 They have lived in it
and have built in it a sanctuary[n] for
your Name, saying, 9 'If calamity
comes upon us, whether the sword
of judgment, or plague or famine,[o]
we will stand in your presence before
this temple that bears your Name and
will cry out to you in our distress,
and you will hear us and save us.'
10 "But now here are men from
Ammon, Moab and Mount Seir,
whose territory you would not allow
Israel to invade when they came
from Egypt;[p] so they turned away
from them and did not destroy them.
11 See how they are repaying us by
coming to drive us out of the possession[q] you gave us as an inheritance.
12 O our God, will you not judge
them?[r] For we have no power to
face this vast army that is attacking
us. We do not know what to do, but
our eyes are upon you.[s]"

13 All the men of Judah, with their
wives and children and little ones, stood
there before the LORD.
14 Then the Spirit[t] of the LORD came
upon Jahaziel son of Zechariah, the son of
Benaiah, the son of Jeiel, the son of Mattaniah,[u] a Levite and descendant of
Asaph, as he stood in the assembly.
15 He said: "Listen, King Jehoshaphat
and all who live in Judah and Jerusalem!
This is what the LORD says to you: 'Do
not be afraid or discouraged[v] because of
this vast army. For the battle[w] is not
yours, but God's. 16 Tomorrow march
down against them. They will be climb-
ing up by the Pass of Ziz, and you will
find them at the end of the gorge in the
Desert of Jeruel. 17 You will not have to
fight this battle. Take up your positions;
stand firm and see[x] the deliverance the
LORD will give you, O Judah and Jerusalem. Do not be afraid; do not be discouraged. Go out to face them tomorrow,
and the LORD will be with you.'"
18 Jehoshaphat bowed[y] with his face to
the ground, and all the people of Judah
and Jerusalem fell down in worship before the LORD. 19 Then some Levites from
the Kohathites and Korahites stood up
and praised the LORD, the God of Israel,
with very loud voice.
20 Early in the morning they left for the
Desert of Tekoa. As they set out, Jehoshaphat stood and said, "Listen to me, Judah
and people of Jerusalem! Have faith[z] in
the LORD your God and you will be upheld; have faith in his prophets and you
will be successful.[a]" 21 After consulting
the people, Jehoshaphat appointed men

20:2 [c]2Ch 24:24 [d]S Ge 14:7 [e]S 1Sa 23:29; SS 1:14
20:3 [f]1Sa 7:6; Ezr 8:23; Ne 1:4; Est 4:16; Isa 58:6; Jer 36:9; Da 9:3; Joel 1:14; 2:15; Jnh 3:5,7
20:4 [g]Jer 36:6
20:6 [h]Mt 6:9 [i]Dt 4:39 [j]1Ch 29:11-12 [k]2Ch 25:8; Job 25:2; 41:10; 42:2; Isa 14:27; Jer 32:27; 49:19
20:7 [l]S Ge 12:7 [m]Isa 41:8; Jas 2:23
20:8 [n]2Ch 6:20
20:9 [o]S 2Ch 6:28
20:10 [p]Nu 20:14-21; Dt 2:4-6,9,18-19
20:11 [q]Ps 83:1-12
20:12 [r]Jdg 11:27 [s]Ps 25:15; Isa 30:15; 45:22; Mic 7:7
20:14 [t]S 1Ch 12:18 [u]S 1Ch 9:15
20:15 [v]2Ch 32:7 [w]S 1Sa 17:47; Ps 91:8
20:17 [x]S Ex 14:13
20:18 [y]S Ge 24:26; 2Ch 29:29
20:20 [z]Isa 7:9 [a]S Ge 39:3; Pr 16:3

j2 One Hebrew manuscript; most Hebrew manuscripts, Septuagint and Vulgate *Aram* k2 That is, the Dead Sea

guidance before going to war. (4) Yahweh, the God of Israel, is sovereign Lord of all history and can defeat all nations no matter how powerful their armies. (5) The chosen worship place represented God's presence with His people where they could seek His deliverance from calamity through lamentation. (6) Nations which violate treaty conditions or return evil for good deserve punishment. (7) Victory does not depend on the military strength of God's people. (8) God reveals His will for the specific occasion to His people. (9) God is with His people in battle. (10) Faith in God is the chief weapon of God's people. (11) God's people respond in praise to God. (12) God rewards His people for their faith and obedience. (13) Victory causes other nations to be afraid and refrain from fighting Israel. (14) Peace, not war, is God's goal. See note on Jos 6:1–27.

20:1–12 PRAYER, Sincerity—Jehoshaphat fasted to show his sincere dependence on God in face of national crisis. See note on 2 Sa 1:12. The nation joined him in sincere pursuit of God's leadership. Jehoshaphat spoke for the people as he recalled God's sovereign faithfulness and power. He based his petition for help on God's history and promises with His people. Prayer finds strength from the past to have faith for the future.

20:5–13 HISTORY, Confession—Confession of God's past history with His people was the basis for petition. History taught that human power cannot win if divine power is not available.

20:6,15,17,29 GOD, Sovereignty—God is in charge of His world and is accomplishing His own purposes. In desperate situations, we have no cause for despair. He can win our victories against all human odds. His sovereign intention is to bring peace and rest to His people. See notes on Ge 15:13–16; 18:14; 24:3,7,50.

20:15–30 HISTORY, Deliverance—See notes on 13:1–18; Jos 11:23.

20:18 WORSHIP, Reverence—True worship of God is always evidenced by reverence for God. The response of King Jehoshaphat and the people is a vital one to true worship. See note on Lev 9:23–24.

20:18–22 PRAYER, Praise—The only weapon Judah used in this battle was praise.

20:21 GOD, Holy—Holiness is the most basic word that can be said about God. Holiness expresses the unique existence of God separate from and above all else. The proper human response to holiness is praise. See notes on Ex 3:5–6;

to sing to the LORD and to praise him for
the splendor of his[l] holiness[b] as they
went out at the head of the army, saying:

"Give thanks to the LORD,
for his love endures forever."[c]

22As they began to sing and praise, the
LORD set ambushes[d] against the men of
Ammon and Moab and Mount Seir who
were invading Judah, and they were defeated. 23The men of Ammon[e] and Moab
rose up against the men from Mount
Seir[f] to destroy and annihilate them. After they finished slaughtering the men
from Seir, they helped to destroy one another.[g]
24When the men of Judah came to the
place that overlooks the desert and
looked toward the vast army, they saw
only dead bodies lying on the ground; no
one had escaped. 25So Jehoshaphat and
his men went to carry off their plunder,
and they found among them a great
amount of equipment and clothing[m] and
also articles of value—more than they
could take away. There was so much
plunder that it took three days to collect
it. 26On the fourth day they assembled in
the Valley of Beracah, where they praised
the LORD. This is why it is called the Valley of Beracah[n] to this day.
27Then, led by Jehoshaphat, all the
men of Judah and Jerusalem returned joyfully to Jerusalem, for the LORD had given
them cause to rejoice over their enemies.
28They entered Jerusalem and went to the
temple of the LORD with harps and lutes
and trumpets.
29The fear[h] of God came upon all the
kingdoms of the countries when they
heard how the LORD had fought[i] against
the enemies of Israel. 30And the kingdom
of Jehoshaphat was at peace, for his God
had given him rest[j] on every side.

The End of Jehoshaphat's Reign

20:31–21:1pp — 1Ki 22:41–50

31So Jehoshaphat reigned over Judah.
He was thirty-five years old when he became king of Judah, and he reigned in
Jerusalem twenty-five years. His mother's
name was Azubah daughter of Shilhi.
32He walked in the ways of his father Asa
and did not stray from them; he did what
was right in the eyes of the LORD. 33The
high places,[k] however, were not removed, and the people still had not set
their hearts on the God of their fathers.
34The other events of Jehoshaphat's
reign, from beginning to end, are written
in the annals of Jehu[l] son of Hanani,
which are recorded in the book of the
kings of Israel.
35Later, Jehoshaphat king of Judah
made an alliance[m] with Ahaziah king of
Israel, who was guilty of wickedness.[n]
36He agreed with him to construct a fleet
of trading ships.[o] After these were built
at Ezion Geber, 37Eliezer son of Dodava-
hu of Mareshah prophesied against Jehoshaphat, saying, "Because you have
made an alliance with Ahaziah, the LORD
will destroy what you have made." The
ships[o] were wrecked and were not able
to set sail to trade.[p]

Chapter 21

THEN Jehoshaphat rested with his fathers and was buried with them in
the City of David. And Jehoram[p] his son
succeeded him as king. 2Jehoram's brothers, the sons of Jehoshaphat, were Azariah, Jehiel, Zechariah, Azariahu, Michael
and Shephatiah. All these were sons of
Jehoshaphat king of Israel.[q] 3Their father
had given them many gifts[q] of silver and
gold and articles of value, as well as fortified cities[r] in Judah, but he had given the
kingdom to Jehoram because he was his
firstborn son.

Jehoram King of Judah

21:5–10,20pp — 2Ki 8:16–24

4When Jehoram established[s] himself
firmly over his father's kingdom, he put
all his brothers[t] to the sword along with
some of the princes of Israel. 5Jehoram
was thirty-two years old when he became

20:21 [b]S 1Ch 16:29 [c]S 2Ch 5:13; Ps 136:1
20:22 [d]S 2Ch 13:13
20:23 [e]S Ge 19:38 [f]2Ch 21:8 [g]S Jdg 7:22; 1Sa 14:20; Eze 38:21
20:29 [h]S Ge 35:5; S Dt 2:25 [i]S Ex 14:14
20:30 [j]S 1Ch 22:9
20:33 [k]S 2Ch 17:6
20:34 [l]S 1Ki 16:1
20:35 [m]S 2Ch 16:3 [n]S 2Ch 19:1-3
20:37 [o]S 1Ki 9:26
21:1 [p]S 1Ch 3:11
21:3 [q]2Ch 11:23 [r]S 2Ch 11:10
21:4 [s]S 1Ki 2:12 [t]Jdg 9:5

[l]21 Or *him with the splendor of* [m]25 Some Hebrew manuscripts and Vulgate; most Hebrew manuscripts *corpses* [n]26 *Beracah* means *praise.* [o]36 Hebrew *of ships that could go to Tarshish* [p]37 Hebrew *sail for Tarshish* [q]2 That is, Judah, as frequently in 2 Chronicles

19:10–24; Lev 11:44–45; 2 Co 7:1.

20:21 GOD, Love—See notes on Ex 3:7; 1 Ch 16:34,41; Mt 10:29–31; Mk 1:11; Jn 3:16.

20:26–28 PRAYER, Praise—The battle was fought with praise, and the thanksgiving was expressed in praise. Thanksgiving is closely tied to petition as parts of a prayer sequence. Petition is the before. Thanks is the after.

20:28 WORSHIP, Music—See note on 2 Sa 6:5.

20:33 SIN, Transgression—See notes on 1 Ki 14:22–24; 2 Ki 3:2–3.

21:1–8 FAMILY, Violence—Jealousy among family members and the desire for power incited violent attacks upon other members of the family among the rulers in Israel and Judah. Jehoram, son of Jehoshaphat, slaughtered his brothers along with other princes of Israel to avert any threat to the throne. His sin brought God's judgment upon his family and upon himself (vv 12–20). The kings' family life does not describe that of the ordinary people in that day. Violence toward family members and sexual abuse of children were forbidden by law and were not characteristic of Hebrew families. Such historical descriptions certainly are not set up as examples to follow. They illustrate the extreme results of the sins of jealousy, pride, and the hunger for personal power.

21:4 CHRISTIAN ETHICS, Murder—See notes on Jdg 8:10–21; 1 Ki 16:10–13.

king, and he reigned in Jerusalem eight
years. 6He walked in the ways of the
kings of Israel,[u] as the house of Ahab had
done, for he married a daughter of
Ahab.[v] He did evil in the eyes of the
LORD. 7Nevertheless, because of the covenant the LORD had made with David,[w]
the LORD was not willing to destroy the
house of David.[x] He had promised to
maintain a lamp[y] for him and his descendants forever.

8In the time of Jehoram, Edom[z] rebelled against Judah and set up its own
king. 9So Jehoram went there with his
officers and all his chariots. The Edomites
surrounded him and his chariot commanders, but he rose up and broke
through by night. 10To this day Edom has
been in rebellion against Judah.

Libnah[a] revolted at the same time, because Jehoram had forsaken the LORD,
the God of his fathers. 11He had also built
high places on the hills of Judah and had
caused the people of Jerusalem to prostitute themselves and had led Judah astray.

12Jehoram received a letter from Elijah[b] the prophet, which said:

> "This is what the LORD, the God of
> your father[c] David, says: 'You have
> not walked in the ways of your father
> Jehoshaphat or of Asa[d] king of Judah.
> 13But you have walked in the ways of
> the kings of Israel, and you have led
> Judah and the people of Jerusalem to
> prostitute themselves, just as the
> house of Ahab did.[e] You have also
> murdered your own brothers, mem-
> bers of your father's house, men who
> were better[f] than you. 14So now the
> LORD is about to strike your people,
> your sons, your wives and everything
> that is yours, with a heavy blow.
> 15You yourself will be very ill with a
> lingering disease[g] of the bowels, un-
> til the disease causes your bowels to
> come out.' "

16The LORD aroused against Jehoram
the hostility of the Philistines and of the
Arabs[h] who lived near the Cushites.
17They attacked Judah, invaded it and carried off all the goods found in the king's
palace, together with his sons and wives.
Not a son was left to him except Ahaziah,[r] the youngest.[i]

18After all this, the LORD afflicted Jehoram with an incurable disease of the bowels. 19In the course of time, at the end of
the second year, his bowels came out because of the disease, and he died in great
pain. His people made no fire in his hon-
or,[j] as they had for his fathers.

20Jehoram was thirty-two years old
when he became king, and he reigned in
Jerusalem eight years. He passed away, to
no one's regret, and was buried[k] in the
City of David, but not in the tombs of the
kings.

21:6 [u]1Ki 12:28-30 [v]2Ch 18:1; 22:3
21:7 [w]S 2Sa 7:13 [x]S 2Sa 7:15; 2Ch 23:3 [y]S 2Sa 21:17
21:8 [z]2Ch 20:22-23
21:10 [a]S Nu 33:20
21:12 [b]2Ki 1:16-17 [c]2Ch 17:3-6 [d]2Ch 14:2
21:13 [e]1Ki 16:29-33 [f]1Ki 2:32
21:15 [g]S Nu 12:10
21:16 [h]2Ch 17:10-11; 22:1; 26:7
21:17 [i]2Ki 12:18; 2Ch 22:1; Joel 3:5
21:19 [j]S 2Ch 16:14
21:20 [k]2Ch 24:25; 28:27; 33:20
22:1 [l]2Ch 33:25; 36:1 [m]2Ch 23:20-21; 26:1 [n]S 2Ch 21:16-17
22:3 [o]S 2Ch 18:1 [p]S 2Ch 21:6

Chapter 22

Ahaziah King of Judah

22:1–6pp — 2Ki 8:25–29
22:7–9pp — 2Ki 9:21–29

THE people[l] of Jerusalem[m] made Ahaziah, Jehoram's youngest son, king in
his place, since the raiders,[n] who came
with the Arabs into the camp, had killed
all the older sons. So Ahaziah son of Jehoram king of Judah began to reign.

2Ahaziah was twenty-two[s] years old
when he became king, and he reigned in
Jerusalem one year. His mother's name
was Athaliah, a granddaughter of Omri.

3He too walked[o] in the ways of
the house of Ahab,[p] for his mother

[r] *17* Hebrew *Jehoahaz,* a variant of *Ahaziah*
[s] *2* Some Septuagint manuscripts and Syriac (see also 2 Kings 8:26); Hebrew *forty-two*

21:6–7 SIN, Transgression—Sin alienates us from God, but it cannot defeat God's purpose. He holds onto His promises even in the face of human rebellion. See note on 1 Ki 12:26–33.

21:7 HISTORY, Promise—God is faithful to His promises. He does not abandon His people at the first opportunity. In grace God endured the unfaithfulness and sin of His people long centuries before He took away their land and political power.

21:7 THE CHURCH, Covenant People—We as the covenant people center our confidence on God, who keeps His covenant promises. He is faithful even when we are not. See notes on 2 Sa 7:17–22; 23:5.

21:10 SIN, Transgression—Spiritual transgression can lead to earthly alienation. Jehoram's rebellion against God led God to let vassal nations rebel against Jehoram. See note on 1 Ki 14:22–24.

21:11 SIN, Transgression—See note on 1 Ki 14:22–24.

21:12–19 GOD, Wrath—See notes on Ge 6:5–8; 17:14; 19:13,24–26.

21:12–19 SIN, Judgment—God's intervention against the leader of His people may come on the community (v 10) or individual (v 14) level. Jehoram sinned by following the modern example of his neighbors instead of the old-fashioned faithfulness of his father. Insecurity and family jealousy led Jehoram to kill his own family to secure his power. Such selfish, immoral behavior brought God's intervening judgment. See note on 1 Ki 14:22–24.

21:12–19 HISTORY, Judgment—Judgment for sin can come immediately upon God's people when they disregard Him and His Word.

21:18–20 HUMANITY, Attitudes to Death—The very vivid description of the king's death is almost told with glee. The nation did not go into great mourning at the passing of this king. The fact that he was not buried in the royal tombs indicates their attitude toward his passing. Some deaths are welcomed by those who have been oppressed by the deceased.

22:3–6 SIN, Transgression—Parental need for power can lead to pressuring children to sin in order to "succeed." Parent and child must each bear responsibility for the resulting sin. No matter who encourages us in the wrong direction, we must decide for ourselves and accept God's judgment on our actions. See note on 1 Ki 14:22–24.

encouraged him in doing wrong. 4He did evil in the eyes of the LORD, as the house of Ahab had done, for after his father's death they became his advisers, to his undoing. 5He also followed their counsel when he went with Joram[t] son of Ahab king of Israel to war against Hazael king of Aram at Ramoth Gilead.[q] The Arameans wounded Joram; 6so he returned to Jezreel to recover from the wounds they had inflicted on him at Ramoth[u] in his battle with Hazael[r] king of Aram.

Then Ahaziah[v] son of Jehoram king of Judah went down to Jezreel to see Joram son of Ahab because he had been wounded.

7Through Ahaziah's[s] visit to Joram, God brought about Ahaziah's downfall. When Ahaziah arrived, he went out with Joram to meet Jehu son of Nimshi, whom the LORD had anointed to destroy the house of Ahab. 8While Jehu was executing judgment on the house of Ahab,[t] he found the princes of Judah and the sons of Ahaziah's relatives, who had been attending Ahaziah, and he killed them. 9He then went in search of Ahaziah, and his men captured him while he was hiding[u] in Samaria. He was brought to Jehu and put to death. They buried him, for they said, "He was a son of Jehoshaphat, who sought[v] the LORD with all his heart." So there was no one in the house of Ahaziah powerful enough to retain the kingdom.

Athaliah and Joash

22:10–23:21pp — 2Ki 11:1–21

10When Athaliah the mother of Ahaziah saw that her son was dead, she proceeded to destroy the whole royal family of the house of Judah. 11But Jehosheba,[w] the daughter of King Jehoram, took Joash son of Ahaziah and stole him away from among the royal princes who were about to be murdered and put him and his nurse in a bedroom. Because Jehosheba,[w] the daughter of King Jehoram and wife of the priest Jehoiada, was Ahaziah's sister, she hid the child from Athaliah so she could not kill him. 12He remained hidden with them at the temple of God for six years while Athaliah ruled the land.

Chapter 23

IN the seventh year Jehoiada showed his strength. He made a covenant with the commanders of units of a hundred: Azariah son of Jeroham, Ishmael son of Jehohanan, Azariah son of Obed, Maaseiah son of Adaiah, and Elishaphat son of Zicri. 2They went throughout Judah and gathered the Levites[w] and the heads of Israelite families from all the towns. When they came to Jerusalem, 3the whole assembly made a covenant[x] with the king at the temple of God.

Jehoiada said to them, "The king's son shall reign, as the LORD promised concerning the descendants of David.[y] 4Now this is what you are to do: A third of you priests and Levites who are going on duty on the Sabbath are to keep watch at the doors, 5a third of you at the royal palace and a third at the Foundation Gate, and all the other men are to be in the courtyards of the temple of the LORD. 6No one is to enter the temple of the LORD except the priests and Levites on duty; they may enter because they are consecrated, but all the other men are to guard[z] what the LORD has assigned to them.[x] 7The Levites are to station themselves around the king, each man with his weapons in his hand. Anyone who enters the temple must be put to death. Stay close to the king wherever he goes."

8The Levites and all the men of Judah did just as Jehoiada the priest ordered.[a] Each one took his men—those who were going on duty on the Sabbath and those who were going off duty—for Jehoiada the priest had not released any of the divisions.[b] 9Then he gave the commanders of units of a hundred the spears and the large and small shields that had belonged to King David and that were in the temple of God. 10He stationed all the men, each with his weapon in his hand, around the king—near the altar and the temple, from the south side to the north side of the temple.

11Jehoiada and his sons brought out the king's son and put the crown on him; they presented him with a copy[c] of the covenant and proclaimed him king. They

22:5 [q]2Ch 18:11, 34
22:6 [r]1Ki 19:15; 2Ki 8:13-15
22:7 [s]2Ki 9:16
22:8 [t]S 2Ki 10:13
22:9 [u]S Jdg 9:5 [v]2Ch 17:4
23:2 [w]S Nu 35:2-5
23:3 [x]S 2Ki 11:17 [y]S 2Sa 7:12; S 1Ki 2:4; S 2Ch 6:16; S 7:18; S 21:7
23:6 [z]Zec 3:7
23:8 [a]2Ki 11:9 [b]S 1Ch 24:1
23:11 [c]Dt 17:18

[t]5 Hebrew *Jehoram*, a variant of *Joram*; also in verses 6 and 7 [u]6 Hebrew *Ramah*, a variant of *Ramoth* [v]6 Some Hebrew manuscripts, Septuagint, Vulgate and Syriac (see also 2 Kings 8:29); most Hebrew manuscripts *Azariah* [w]11 Hebrew *Jehoshabeath*, a variant of *Jehosheba* [x]6 Or *to observe the LORD's command* ⌊*not to enter*⌋

22:7 GOD, Sovereignty—God is in control of the affairs of this world and can work His will in them. He can also bring His wrath to bear upon anyone in judgment. See notes on 19:2,10; 20:6,15,17,29.

23:11 THE CHURCH, Covenant People—See note on 2 Ki 11:12,17.

23:13–21 PRAYER, Praise—The priestly leadership of praise in Chronicles is given more prominence than in the

reigned in Jerusalem twenty-nine years.
His mother's name was Jehoaddin[d]; she
was from Jerusalem. 2He did what was
right in the eyes of the LORD, but not
wholeheartedly.[m] 3After the kingdom
was firmly in his control, he executed the
officials who had murdered his father the
king. 4Yet he did not put their sons to
death, but acted in accordance with what
is written in the Law, in the Book of Moses,[n] where the LORD commanded: "Fathers shall not be put to death for their
children, nor children put to death for
their fathers; each is to die for his own
sins."[e] [o]
5Amaziah called the people of Judah together and assigned them according to
their families to commanders of thousands and commanders of hundreds for
all Judah and Benjamin. He then mustered[p] those twenty years old[q] or more
and found that there were three hundred
thousand men ready for military service,[r] able to handle the spear and
shield. 6He also hired a hundred thousand fighting men from Israel for a hundred talents[f] of silver.
7But a man of God came to him and
said, "O king, these troops from Israel[s]
must not march with you, for the LORD is
not with Israel—not with any of the people of Ephraim. 8Even if you go and fight
courageously in battle, God will overthrow you before the enemy, for God has
the power to help or to overthrow."[t]
9Amaziah asked the man of God, "But
what about the hundred talents I paid for
these Israelite troops?"
The man of God replied, "The LORD
can give you much more than that."[u]
10So Amaziah dismissed the troops
who had come to him from Ephraim and
sent them home. They were furious with
Judah and left for home in a great rage.[v]
11Amaziah then marshaled his strength
and led his army to the Valley of Salt,
where he killed ten thousand men of
Seir. 12The army of Judah also captured
ten thousand men alive, took them to the
top of a cliff and threw them down so that
all were dashed to pieces.[w]
13Meanwhile the troops that Amaziah
had sent back and had not allowed to take
part in the war raided Judean towns from
Samaria to Beth Horon. They killed three
thousand people and carried off great
quantities of plunder.
14When Amaziah returned from
slaughtering the Edomites, he brought
back the gods of the people of Seir. He set
them up as his own gods,[x] bowed down
to them and burned sacrifices to them.
15The anger of the LORD burned against
Amaziah, and he sent a prophet to him,
who said, "Why do you consult this people's gods, which could not save[y] their
own people from your hand?"
16While he was still speaking, the king
said to him, "Have we appointed you an
adviser to the king? Stop! Why be struck
down?"
So the prophet stopped but said, "I
know that God has determined to destroy
you, because you have done this and have
not listened to my counsel."
17After Amaziah king of Judah consulted his advisers, he sent this challenge to
Jehoash[g] son of Jehoahaz, the son of
Jehu, king of Israel: "Come, meet me face
to face."
18But Jehoash king of Israel replied to
Amaziah king of Judah: "A thistle[z] in
Lebanon sent a message to a cedar in Lebanon, 'Give your daughter to my son in
marriage.' Then a wild beast in Lebanon
came along and trampled the thistle underfoot. 19You say to yourself that you
have defeated Edom, and now you are arrogant and proud. But stay at home! Why
ask for trouble and cause your own downfall and that of Judah also?"
20Amaziah, however, would not listen,
for God so worked that he might hand
them over to ⌊Jehoash⌋, because they
sought the gods of Edom.[a] 21So Jehoash
king of Israel attacked. He and Amaziah
king of Judah faced each other at Beth
Shemesh in Judah. 22Judah was routed by
Israel, and every man fled to his home.
23Jehoash king of Israel captured Amaziah
king of Judah, the son of Joash, the son of

25:2 [m]S 1Ki 8:61; S 2Ch 24:2
25:4 [n]S Dt 28:61 [o]S Nu 26:11
25:5 [p]S 2Sa 24:2 [q]S Ex 30:14 [r]S 1Ch 21:1; 2Ch 17:14-19
25:7 [s]S 2Ch 16:2-9; S 19:1-3
25:8 [t]S 2Ch 14:11; S 20:6
25:9 [u]Dt 8:18; Pr 10:22
25:10 [v]ver 13
25:12 [w]Ps 141:6; Ob 1:3
25:14 [x]Ex 20:3; 2Ch 28:23; Isa 44:15
25:15 [y]Isa 36:20
25:18 [z]Jdg 9:8-15
25:20 [a]S 2Ch 10:15

[d]*1* Hebrew *Jehoaddan,* a variant of *Jehoaddin*
[e]*4* Deut. 24:16 [f]*6* That is, about 3 3/4 tons (about 3.4 metric tons); also in verse 9 [g]*17* Hebrew *Joash,* a variant of *Jehoash*; also in verses 18, 21, 23 and 25

vengeance. Motivation and attitude are involved in sin as well as action.

25:4 HUMANITY, Death and Sin—While sin clearly has consequences for others, death as punishment for sin is ultimately a matter of personal responsibility. See Dt 24:16; note on Jos 7:20–25.

25:5–12 HISTORY, Faith—See note on 19:2–3. History should teach us God's ability to help or defeat according to our faith in Him.

25:8–9,20 GOD, Sovereignty—See notes at Ge 15:13–16; 18:14; 24:3,7,50.

25:13–24 HISTORY, Judgment—See note on 21:12–19.

25:14–15 SIN, Transgression—Sin is illogical. To worship a defeated nation's gods is nonsense. Their powerlessness to save has been demonstrated. The human mind justifies all kinds of sin rather than following God's directions. God leads His people in paths of righteousness. He even prepares them for military defeat by proclaiming it through His prophets. See note on 1 Ki 14:22–24.

25:19–20 SIN, Discipline—God uses human processes and relationships to intervene in history and discipline sinful people. He can deliver a prophetic message through an enemy king. He can lead a sinner to reject good advice. God works to punish human pride and rebellion. See note on 1 Ki 14:22–24.

Ahaziah,[h] at Beth Shemesh. Then Jehoash brought him to Jerusalem and broke
down the wall of Jerusalem from the
Ephraim Gate[b] to the Corner Gate[c]—a
section about six hundred feet[i] long.
24He took all the gold and silver and all
the articles found in the temple of God
that had been in the care of Obed-
Edom,[d] together with the palace treasures and the hostages, and returned to
Samaria.
25Amaziah son of Joash king of Judah
lived for fifteen years after the death of
Jehoash son of Jehoahaz king of Israel.
26As for the other events of Amaziah's
reign, from beginning to end, are they
not written in the book of the kings of
Judah and Israel? 27From the time that
Amaziah turned away from following the
LORD, they conspired against him in Jerusalem and he fled to Lachish[e], but they
sent men after him to Lachish and killed
him there. 28He was brought back by
horse and was buried with his fathers in
the City of Judah.

Chapter 26

Uzziah King of Judah

26:1–4pp — 2Ki 14:21–22; 15:1–3
26:21–23pp — 2Ki 15:5–7

THEN all the people of Judah[f] took Uzziah,[j] who was sixteen years old,
and made him king in place of his father
Amaziah. 2He was the one who rebuilt
Elath and restored it to Judah after Amaziah rested with his fathers.
3Uzziah was sixteen years old when he
became king, and he reigned in Jerusalem
fifty-two years. His mother's name was
Jecoliah; she was from Jerusalem. 4He did
what was right in the eyes of the LORD,
just as his father Amaziah had done. 5He
sought God during the days of Zechariah,
who instructed him in the fear[k] of God.[g]
As long as he sought the LORD, God gave
him success.[h]
6He went to war against the Philistines[i] and broke down the walls of Gath,
Jabneh and Ashdod.[j] He then rebuilt
towns near Ashdod and elsewhere among
the Philistines. 7God helped him against
the Philistines and against the Arabs[k]
who lived in Gur Baal and against the Meunites.[l] 8The Ammonites[m] brought tribute to Uzziah, and his fame spread as far
as the border of Egypt, because he had
become very powerful.
9Uzziah built towers in Jerusalem at
the Corner Gate,[n] at the Valley Gate[o]
and at the angle of the wall, and he fortified them. 10He also built towers in the
desert and dug many cisterns, because he
had much livestock in the foothills and in
the plain. He had people working his
fields and vineyards in the hills and in the
fertile lands, for he loved the soil.
11Uzziah had a well-trained army,
ready to go out by divisions according to
their numbers as mustered by Jeiel the
secretary and Maaseiah the officer under
the direction of Hananiah, one of the royal officials. 12The total number of family
leaders over the fighting men was 2,600.
13Under their command was an army of
307,500 men trained for war, a powerful
force to support the king against his enemies. 14Uzziah provided shields, spears,
helmets, coats of armor, bows and slingstones for the entire army.[p] 15In Jerusalem he made machines designed by skillful men for use on the towers and on the
corner defenses to shoot arrows and hurl
large stones. His fame spread far and
wide, for he was greatly helped until he
became powerful.
16But after Uzziah became powerful,
his pride[q] led to his downfall.[r] He was
unfaithful[s] to the LORD his God, and en-

25:23 [b]2Ki 14:13; Ne 8:16; 12:39 [c]2Ch 26:9; Jer 31:38
25:24 [d]S 1Ch 26:15
25:27 [e]S Jos 10:3
26:1 [f]S 2Ch 22:1
26:5 [g]S 2Ch 24:2 [h]2Ch 27:6
26:6 [i]Isa 2:6; 11:14; 14:29; Jer 25:20 [j]Am 1:8; 3:9
26:7 [k]S 2Ch 21:16 [l]2Ch 20:1
26:8 [m]S Ge 19:38
26:9 [n]S 2Ki 14:13; S 2Ch 25:23 [o]Ne 2:13; 3:13
26:14 [p]Jer 46:4
26:16 [q]S 2Ki 14:10 [r]Dt 32:15 [s]S 1Ch 5:25

[h]*23* Hebrew *Jehoahaz,* a variant of *Ahaziah*
[i]*23* Hebrew *four hundred cubits* (about 180 meters)
[j]*1* Also called *Azariah* [k]*5* Many Hebrew manuscripts, Septuagint and Syriac; other Hebrew manuscripts *vision*

26:5 HISTORY, Faith—God blesses His faithful people. History is the success story of faith, but success is measured in God's terms and not always in terms of material goods and political popularity.

26:6–22 CHRISTIAN ETHICS, War and Peace—Uzziah exhibited model behavior in his covenant with God until his pride got the best of him. He evidently determined he could rule without God's help. Making that situation worse, Uzziah tried to take over priestly functions, too. Such a swing of attitudes called forth the judgment of God. See notes on 1 Sa 4:1–10; 15:7–35.

26:15 HUMANITY, Work—One of a king's tasks was providing defense for his people. In any endeavor, a good worker should be able to use the skills of others to accomplish the tasks in his own responsibility.

26:16–21 EVIL AND SUFFERING, Punishment—Success does not give unlimited power and authority. A person who assumes such authority in the face of God's directions faces God's punishment. Success and power cannot protect one from suffering God's punishment. Humans may consider the suffering of a popular figure sad and evil. God sees such suffering as deserved through failure to be faithful to Him.

26:16–21 SIN, Pride—Human power structures do not provide entrance to divine power structures. Uzziah allowed his pride to grow as fast as his royal power. He decided he had the right to take over the duties of God's appointed priests. Thus, he did not respect God's holiness and the division of power set out in God's law. In so doing he was unfaithful to his commitment to honor God. See note on 1 Ch 10:13. Because he would not separate himself from the powers of God's priests, God intervened to separate him from all humanity. Trying to minister where God has neither called nor authorized you is sin.

26:16–21 HISTORY, Judgment—God's people find material success difficult to handle. Uzziah let pride blind him to the true Source of his success. He refused to accept the limits of his office and suffered God's judgment. See note on 21:12–19.

tered the temple of the LORD to burn incense[t] on the altar of incense. 17Azari-
ah[u] the priest with eighty other courageous priests of the LORD followed him
in. 18They confronted him and said, "It is
not right for you, Uzziah, to burn incense
to the LORD. That is for the priests,[v] the
descendants[w] of Aaron,[x] who have been
consecrated to burn incense.[y] Leave the
sanctuary, for you have been unfaithful;
and you will not be honored by the LORD
God."
19Uzziah, who had a censer in his hand
ready to burn incense, became angry.
While he was raging at the priests in their
presence before the incense altar in the
LORD's temple, leprosy[1][z] broke out on
his forehead. 20When Azariah the chief
priest and all the other priests looked at
him, they saw that he had leprosy on his
forehead, so they hurried him out. Indeed, he himself was eager to leave, because the LORD had afflicted him.
21King Uzziah had leprosy until the day
he died. He lived in a separate house[m][a]
—leprous, and excluded from the temple
of the LORD. Jotham his son had charge of
the palace and governed the people of the
land.
22The other events of Uzziah's reign,
from beginning to end, are recorded by
the prophet Isaiah[b] son of Amoz. 23Uzzi-
ah[c] rested with his fathers and was buried near them in a field for burial that
belonged to the kings, for people said,
"He had leprosy." And Jotham his son
succeeded him as king.[d]

Chapter 27

Jotham King of Judah

27:1–4,7–9pp — 2Ki 15:33–38

JOTHAM[e] was twenty-five years old
when he became king, and he reigned
in Jerusalem sixteen years. His mother's
name was Jerusha daughter of Zadok. 2He
did what was right in the eyes of the
LORD, just as his father Uzziah had done,
but unlike him he did not enter the temple of the LORD. The people, however,
continued their corrupt practices. 3Jo-
tham rebuilt the Upper Gate of the temple of the LORD and did extensive work
on the wall at the hill of Ophel.[f] 4He
built towns in the Judean hills and forts
and towers in the wooded areas.
5Jotham made war on the king of the
Ammonites[g] and conquered them. That
year the Ammonites paid him a hundred
talents[n] of silver, ten thousand cors[o] of
wheat and ten thousand cors of barley.
The Ammonites brought him the same
amount also in the second and third
years.
6Jotham grew powerful[h] because he
walked steadfastly before the LORD his
God.
7The other events in Jotham's reign, including all his wars and the other things
he did, are written in the book of the
kings of Israel and Judah. 8He was twenty-five years old when he became king,
and he reigned in Jerusalem sixteen
years. 9Jotham rested with his fathers and
was buried in the City of David. And
Ahaz his son succeeded him as king.

Chapter 28

Ahaz King of Judah

28:1–27pp — 2Ki 16:1–20

AHAZ[i] was twenty years old when he
became king, and he reigned in Jerusalem sixteen years. Unlike David his father, he did not do what was right in the
eyes of the LORD. 2He walked in the ways
of the kings of Israel and also made cast
idols[j] for worshiping the Baals. 3He
burned sacrifices in the Valley of Ben
Hinnom[k] and sacrificed his sons[l] in the
fire, following the detestable[m] ways of
the nations the LORD had driven out before the Israelites. 4He offered sacrifices
and burned incense at the high places, on
the hilltops and under every spreading
tree.
5Therefore the LORD his God handed
him over to the king of Aram.[n] The

26:16 [t]2Ki 16:12
26:17 [u]S 1Ki 4:2
26:18 [v]Nu 16:39 [w]Nu 18:1-7 [x]S Ex 30:7 [y]S 1Ch 6:49
26:19 [z]S Nu 12:10
26:21 [a]S Ex 4:6; Lev 13:46; S 14:8; Nu 5:2; S 19:12
26:22 [b]2Ki 15:1; Isa 1:1; 6:1
26:23 [c]Isa 1:1; 6:1 [d]S 2Ki 14:21; Am 1:1
27:1 [e]S 2Ki 15:5, 32; S 1Ch 3:12
27:3 [f]2Ch 33:14; Ne 3:26
27:5 [g]S Ge 19:38
27:6 [h]2Ch 26:5
28:1 [i]S 1Ch 3:13; Isa 1:1
28:2 [j]Ex 34:17
28:3 [k]S Jos 15:8 [l]S Lev 18:21; S 2Ki 3:27; Eze 20:26 [m]S Dt 18:9; 2Ch 33:2
28:5 [n]Isa 7:1

[1]*19* The Hebrew word was used for various diseases affecting the skin—not necessarily leprosy; also in verses 20, 21 and 23. [m]*21* Or *in a house where he was relieved of responsibilities* [n]*5* That is, about 3 3/4 tons (about 3.4 metric tons) [o]*5* That is, probably about 62,000 bushels (about 2,200 kiloliters)

26:20 GOD, Wrath—See note on 2 Ki 15:5.
26:22 HOLY SCRIPTURE, Writing—See note on 1 Ch 29:29.
26:23 HUMANITY, Burial—So contaminating was leprosy that a leper was not buried where the bodies of loved ones might be made unclean. Such care and respect for the memories of all the dead can be honored in all societies.
27:2 SIN, Blindness—After a pattern of sinfulness has been followed for generations, it is extremely difficult for one righteous leader to alter the pattern of transgression. Sinful habits develop into spiritual blindness. People can no longer recognize or practice righteousness.
27:6 HUMANITY, Relationship to God—Literally, the Hebrew says "He strengthened His ways" or "He established His ways." Life lived in an obedient relationship to God brings God's power to work within it.
28:1–4 SIN, Transgression—See note on 1 Ki 14:22–24.
28:1–8 HISTORY, Judgment—See note on 21:12–19.
28:4–10 ELECTION, Condemnation—Ahaz, unlike David, walked in the wicked ways of those who worshiped Baal. God punished him. Even those who enjoy the election of God must pay for their disobedience with punishment.
28:5–13,19,24–25 GOD, Wrath—The impartial wrath of God is expressed in these verses. Because He is righteous, God opposes all sin, no matter who is sinning. He can use part of His own people to punish another part of His people. He can also

Arameans defeated him and took many of
his people as prisoners and brought them
to Damascus.
He was also given into the hands of the
king of Israel, who inflicted heavy casualties on him. 6In one day Pekah[o] son of
Remaliah killed a hundred and twenty
thousand soldiers in Judah[p]—because Judah had forsaken the LORD, the God of
their fathers. 7Zicri, an Ephraimite warrior, killed Maaseiah the king's son, Azrikam the officer in charge of the palace,
and Elkanah, second to the king. 8The Israelites took captive from their kinsmen[q]
two hundred thousand wives, sons and
daughters. They also took a great deal of
plunder, which they carried back to Samaria.[r]
9But a prophet of the LORD named
Oded was there, and he went out to meet
the army when it returned to Samaria. He
said to them, "Because the LORD, the God
of your fathers, was angry[s] with Judah,
he gave them into your hand. But you
have slaughtered them in a rage that
reaches to heaven.[t] 10And now you intend to make the men and women of Judah and Jerusalem your slaves.[u] But
aren't you also guilty of sins against the
LORD your God? 11Now listen to me! Send
back your fellow countrymen you have
taken as prisoners, for the LORD's fierce
anger rests on you.[v]"
12Then some of the leaders in Ephraim
—Azariah son of Jehohanan, Berekiah
son of Meshillemoth, Jehizkiah son of
Shallum, and Amasa son of Hadlai—confronted those who were arriving from the
war. 13"You must not bring those prisoners here," they said, "or we will be guilty
before the LORD. Do you intend to add to
our sin and guilt? For our guilt is already
great, and his fierce anger rests on Israel."
14So the soldiers gave up the prisoners
and plunder in the presence of the officials and all the assembly. 15The men designated by name took the prisoners, and
from the plunder they clothed all who
were naked. They provided them with
clothes and sandals, food and drink,[w] and
healing balm. All those who were weak
they put on donkeys. So they took them
back to their fellow countrymen at Jericho, the City of Palms,[x] and returned to
Samaria.[y]
16At that time King Ahaz sent to the
king[p] of Assyria[z] for help. 17The Edomites[a] had again come and attacked Judah
and carried away prisoners,[b] 18while the
Philistines[c] had raided towns in the foothills and in the Negev of Judah. They captured and occupied Beth Shemesh, Aijalon[d] and Gederoth,[e] as well as Soco,[f]
Timnah[g] and Gimzo, with their surrounding villages. 19The LORD had humbled Judah because of Ahaz king of Israel,[q] for he had promoted wickedness in
Judah and had been most unfaithful[h] to
the LORD. 20Tiglath-Pileser[r][i] king of Assyria[j] came to him, but he gave him
trouble[k] instead of help.[l] 21Ahaz[m] took
some of the things from the temple of the
LORD and from the royal palace and from
the princes and presented them to the
king of Assyria, but that did not help
him.[n]
22In his time of trouble King Ahaz became even more unfaithful[o] to the LORD.
23He offered sacrifices to the gods[p] of Damascus, who had defeated him; for he
thought, "Since the gods of the kings of
Aram have helped them, I will sacrifice to
them so they will help me."[q] But they
were his downfall and the downfall of all
Israel.[r]
24Ahaz gathered together the furnishings[s] from the temple of God[t] and took
them away.[s] He shut the doors[u] of the
LORD's temple and set up altars[v] at every
street corner in Jerusalem. 25In every

28:6 [o]S 2Ki 15:25,27 [p]ver 8; Isa 9:21; 11:13
28:8 [q]Dt 28:25-41 [r]2Ch 29:9
28:9 [s]Isa 10:6; 47:6; Zec 1:15 [t]Ezr 9:6; Rev 18:5
28:10 [u]Lev 25:39-46
28:11 [v]2Ch 11:4
28:15 [w]2Ki 6:22; Pr 25:21-22 [x]S Dt 34:3; S Jdg 1:16 [y]Lk 10:25-37
28:16 [z]S 2Ki 16:7; Eze 23:12
28:17 [a]Ps 137:7; Isa 34:5; 63:1; Jer 25:21; Eze 16:57; 25:12; Am 1:11 [b]2Ch 29:9
28:18 [c]Isa 9:12; 11:14; Jer 25:20; Eze 16:27,57; 25:15 [d]S Jos 10:12 [e]Jos 15:41 [f]S 1Sa 17:1 [g]S Ge 38:12
28:19 [h]S 1Ch 5:25
28:20 [i]S 2Ki 15:29; S 1Ch 5:6 [j]Isa 7:17; 8:7; 10:5-6; 36:1 [k]Isa 10:20 [l]S 2Ki 16:7
28:21 [m]S 2Ch 16:2-9 [n]Jer 2:36
28:22 [o]Jer 5:3; 15:7; 17:23
28:23 [p]S 2Ch 25:14 [q]Isa 10:20; Jer 44:17-18 [r]1Ch 11:1; Jer 18:15
28:24 [s]2Ch 29:19 [t]S 2Ki 16:18 [u]Mal 1:10 [v]2Ch 30:14

[p]*16* One Hebrew manuscript, Septuagint and Vulgate (see also 2 Kings 16:7); most Hebrew manuscripts *kings* [q]*19* That is, Judah, as frequently in 2 Chronicles [r]*20* Hebrew *Tilgath-Pilneser,* a variant of *Tiglath-Pileser* [s]*24* Or *and cut them up*

announce punishment on the agents of His wrath when they overstep their bounds in dealing out punishment. See notes on Ge 6:5–8; 17:14; 19:13,24–26.

28:5–11 CHRISTIAN ETHICS, Murder—Even the violence of warfare should be controlled by concern for human welfare. God condemns persons who violate all common understandings of fair treatment to the enemies. See note on Jdg 8:10–21.

28:6 SIN, Transgression—See notes on 1 Ki 14:22–24; 2 Ch 24:17–26.

28:9–13 SIN, Guilt—God uses humans to carry out His punishment of other sinful humans. He holds the punishers responsible for the way they act toward the people God punishes. They must not overreact in their own rage and treat people inhumanely. Rather they must remember their own guilt before God. Guilt (Hebrew *'asham*) includes the sinful action, condition, and consequences. Sinful acts lead to a sense of guilt and alienation. The sin results in punishment. When this does not bring repentance and forgiveness, the state of guilt remains. We cannot isolate one stage of the sin process as guilt. The entire string from act to punishment and enduring sense of alienation are all guilt. Further sinful acts increase guilt. See note on 1 Ki 12:26–33.

28:9–15 HISTORY, Judgment—Being agents to inflict God's judgment does not give unlimited freedom to punish. Obedience to God's word can bring reprieve from punishment.

28:19 SIN, Forgiveness—See notes on 1 Sa 12:25; 1 Ch 10:13.

28:22–25 SIN, Transgression—Politics does not provide religious proof. Assyria gained political victory over Judah. King Ahaz decided this victory proved the superiority of Assyria's gods. He went further. He decreed the defeat of Yahweh, the God of Israel, and closed His Temple. He sought to please all gods but the true One to whom he had a commitment. This is utter unfaithfulness. See 25:14–15; 1 Ch 10:13. See note on 1 Ki 14:22–24.

town in Judah he built high places to
burn sacrifices to other gods and provoked the LORD, the God of his fathers, to
anger.
26The other events of his reign and all
his ways, from beginning to end, are written in the book of the kings of Judah and
Israel. 27Ahaz rested[w] with his fathers
and was buried[x] in the city of Jerusalem,
but he was not placed in the tombs of the
kings of Israel. And Hezekiah his son succeeded him as king.

Chapter 29

Hezekiah Purifies the Temple

29:1–2pp — 2Ki 18:2–3

HEZEKIAH[y] was twenty-five years old
when he became king, and he
reigned in Jerusalem twenty-nine years.
His mother's name was Abijah daughter
of Zechariah. 2He did what was right in
the eyes of the LORD, just as his father
David[z] had done.
3In the first month of the first year of
his reign, he opened the doors of the temple of the LORD and repaired[a] them. 4He
brought in the priests and the Levites, assembled them in the square on the east
side 5and said: "Listen to me, Levites!
Consecrate[b] yourselves now and consecrate the temple of the LORD, the God of
your fathers. Remove all defilement from
the sanctuary. 6Our fathers[c] were unfaithful;[d] they did evil in the eyes of the
LORD our God and forsook him. They
turned their faces away from the LORD's
dwelling place and turned their backs on
him. 7They also shut the doors of the portico and put out the lamps. They did not
burn incense[e] or present any burnt offerings at the sanctuary to the God of Israel.
8Therefore, the anger of the LORD has fall-
en on Judah and Jerusalem; he has made
them an object of dread and horror[f] and
scorn,[g] as you can see with your own
eyes. 9This is why our fathers have fallen
by the sword and why our sons and
daughters and our wives are in captivity.[h] 10Now I intend to make a covenant[i]
with the LORD, the God of Israel, so that
his fierce anger[j] will turn away from us.
11My sons, do not be negligent now, for
the LORD has chosen you to stand before
him and serve him,[k] to minister[l] before
him and to burn incense."
12Then these Levites[m] set to work:
from the Kohathites,
Mahath son of Amasai and
Joel son of Azariah;
from the Merarites,
Kish son of Abdi and Azariah son
of Jehallelel;
from the Gershonites,
Joah son of Zimmah and Eden[n]
son of Joah;
13from the descendants of Elizaphan,[o]
Shimri and Jeiel;
from the descendants of Asaph,[p]
Zechariah and Mattaniah;
14from the descendants of Heman,
Jehiel and Shimei;
from the descendants of Jeduthun,
Shemaiah and Uzziel.
15When they had assembled their
brothers and consecrated themselves,
they went in to purify[q] the temple of the
LORD, as the king had ordered, following
the word of the LORD. 16The priests went
into the sanctuary of the LORD to purify it.
They brought out to the courtyard of the
LORD's temple everything unclean that
they found in the temple of the LORD. The
Levites took it and carried it out to the
Kidron Valley.[r] 17They began the consecration on the first day of the first month,
and by the eighth day of the month they
reached the portico of the LORD. For eight

28:27 [w]Isa 14:28-32 [x]S 2Ch 21:20
29:1 [y]S 1Ch 3:13
29:2 [z]2Ch 34:2
29:3 [a]2Ki 18:16
29:5 [b]S Lev 11:44; Ne 13:9
29:6 [c]Ezr 9:7; Ps 106:6-47; Jer 2:27; 18:17; Eze 23:35; Da 9:5-6 [d]S 1Ch 5:25
29:7 [e]S Ex 30:7
29:8 [f]S Dt 28:25 [g]S Lev 26:32; Jer 18:16; 19:8; 25:9,18
29:9 [h]2Ch 28:5-8, 17
29:10 [i]S 2Ki 11:17; S 2Ch 23:16 [j]S Nu 25:4; 2Ch 30:8; Ezr 10:14
29:11 [k]S Nu 3:6; 8:6,14 [l]S 1Ch 15:2
29:12 [m]S Nu 3:17-20 [n]2Ch 31:15
29:13 [o]S Ex 6:22 [p]S 1Ch 6:39
29:15 [q]S 1Ch 23:28; S Isa 1:25
29:16 [r]S 2Sa 15:23

28:27 HUMANITY, Burial—Israel denied proper burial to persons who flagrantly disobeyed God. Such burial separated the wicked from those who had lived in a proper relationship to God. The full New Testament understanding of life after death carries this concept even further, pointing to the ultimate separation of the faithful from the unbelievers. See Mt 25:32.

29:3–10 GOD, Wrath—We cannot take the continued blessing of God for granted. Repeated sin will bring His wrath upon us. The intercession and spiritual leadership of a committed leader can restore a people so God will remove His anger. See notes on Ge 6:5–8; 17:14; 19:13,24–26.

29:5–36 PRAYER, Hindrances—Ahaz had defiled the sacred furnishings and closed the Temple (28:24). People who do not worship together properly do not pray in the right way. Recommitment and renewal of worship are the only solutions. Then prayer can rise again in the form of offerings, songs, music, and humble thanksgiving.

29:6–7 SIN, Alienation—An earlier generation's sins may have brought alienation and judgment to a people. See note on 28:22–25. This action does not close the doors on the present generation. They do not have to carry the guilt or follow the examples of their predecessors. They can renew their relationship to God and feel God's anger turn away. Forgiving sin is God's joy, not punishing it.

29:10 THE CHURCH, Covenant People—Covenant people of God cannot expect God to make all the commitments. When we realize we have not fulfilled our commitments, we need to make a new covenant commitment to God. God responds to our new commitments in forgiveness. When we have experienced His anger, our new commitment is often met with an experience of His anger withdrawing from us. The process of making a new commitment to God is not a bargaining process. We do not get a guarantee that He will turn from anger and bless us before we make our commitment. We do not commit ourselves to Him so His anger will go away. We make a commitment because we are sorry for our sins and are determined with God's help to turn from them. We make a commitment because our major desire in life is to be rightly related to God. God's free, gracious responses show His affirmation of our commitment. See notes on 23:16; Dt 29:1–15.

29:11 ELECTION, Leadership—Those who enjoy the election of God must be attentive, alert, and able as leaders in the assembly of God. Election is a call to service as well as to salvation.

more days they consecrated the temple of the LORD itself, finishing on the sixteenth day of the first month.

18Then they went in to King Hezekiah and reported: "We have purified the entire temple of the LORD, the altar of burnt offering with all its utensils, and the table for setting out the consecrated bread, with all its articles. 19We have prepared and consecrated all the articles[s] that King Ahaz removed in his unfaithfulness while he was king. They are now in front of the LORD's altar."

20Early the next morning King Hezekiah gathered the city officials together and went up to the temple of the LORD. 21They brought seven bulls, seven rams, seven male lambs and seven male goats[t] as a sin offering[u] for the kingdom, for the sanctuary and for Judah. The king commanded the priests, the descendants of Aaron, to offer these on the altar of the LORD. 22So they slaughtered the bulls, and the priests took the blood and sprinkled it on the altar; next they slaughtered the rams and sprinkled their blood on the altar; then they slaughtered the lambs and sprinkled their blood[v] on the altar. 23The goats[w] for the sin offering were brought before the king and the assembly, and they laid their hands[x] on them. 24The priests then slaughtered the goats and presented their blood on the altar for a sin offering to atone[y] for all Israel, because the king had ordered the burnt offering and the sin offering for all Israel.[z]

25He stationed the Levites in the temple of the LORD with cymbals, harps and lyres in the way prescribed by David[a] and Gad[b] the king's seer and Nathan the prophet; this was commanded by the LORD through his prophets. 26So the Levites stood ready with David's instruments,[c] and the priests with their trumpets.[d]

27Hezekiah gave the order to sacrifice the burnt offering on the altar. As the offering began, singing to the LORD began also, accompanied by trumpets and the instruments[e] of David king of Israel. 28The whole assembly bowed in worship, while the singers sang and the trumpeters played. All this continued until the sacrifice of the burnt offering[f] was completed.

29When the offerings were finished, the king and everyone present with him knelt down and worshiped.[g] 30King Hezekiah and his officials ordered the Levites to praise the LORD with the words of David and of Asaph the seer. So they sang praises with gladness and bowed their heads and worshiped.

31Then Hezekiah said, "You have now dedicated yourselves to the LORD. Come and bring sacrifices[h] and thank offerings to the temple of the LORD." So the assembly brought sacrifices and thank offerings, and all whose hearts were willing[i] brought burnt offerings.

32The number of burnt offerings[j] the assembly brought was seventy bulls, a hundred rams and two hundred male lambs—all of them for burnt offerings to the LORD. 33The animals consecrated as sacrifices amounted to six hundred bulls and three thousand sheep and goats. 34The priests, however, were too few to skin all the burnt offerings;[k] so their kinsmen the Levites helped them until the task was finished and until other priests had been consecrated,[l] for the Levites had been more conscientious in consecrating themselves than the priests had been. 35There were burnt offerings in abundance, together with the fat[m] of the fellowship offerings[t][n] and the drink offerings[o] that accompanied the burnt offerings.

So the service of the temple of the LORD was reestablished. 36Hezekiah and all the people rejoiced at what God had brought about for his people, because it was done so quickly.[p]

Chapter 30

Hezekiah Celebrates the Passover

HEZEKIAH sent word to all Israel[q] and Judah and also wrote letters to Ephraim and Manasseh,[r] inviting them to come to the temple of the LORD in Jerusalem and celebrate the Passover[s] to the LORD, the God of Israel. 2The king and his officials and the whole assembly in Jerusalem decided to celebrate[t] the Passover in the second month. 3They had not been able to celebrate it at the regular time because not enough priests had consecrated[u] themselves and the people had not assembled in Jerusalem. 4The plan

[t]35 Traditionally *peace offerings*

29:19 [s]2Ch 28:24
29:21 [t]Ezr 6:17; 8:35 [u]S Lev 4:13-14
29:22 [v]S Lev 4:18; Nu 18:17
29:23 [w]S Lev 16:5 [x]Lev 4:15
29:24 [y]S Ex 29:36; Lev 4:26 [z]1Ch 11:1; Ezr 8:35
29:25 [a]S 1Ch 25:6; 28:19 [b]S 1Sa 22:5
29:26 [c]S 1Ch 15:16 [d]S 1Ch 15:24
29:27 [e]S 1Sa 16:16
29:28 [f]S 2Ch 2:4
29:29 [g]S 2Ch 20:18
29:31 [h]Heb 13:15-16 [i]S Ex 25:2; 35:22
29:32 [j]Lev 1:1-17
29:34 [k]Eze 44:11 [l]2Ch 30:3,15
29:35 [m]S Ge 4:4; S Ex 29:13 [n]Lev 7:11-21 [o]S Ge 35:14
29:36 [p]2Ch 35:8
30:1 [q]S 1Ch 9:1 [r]S Ge 41:52 [s]S Ex 12:11; S Nu 28:16
30:2 [t]Nu 9:10
30:3 [u]Nu 9:6-13; S 2Ch 29:34

29:21–24 STEWARDSHIP, Sacrifice Giving—See note on Lev 1:2.

29:25–36 WORSHIP, Priesthood—See note on 1 Ch 6:48–49. Temple worship followed a prescribed pattern with an offering seeking forgiveness of sin, God's chosen worship leaders, offerings of praise and thanksgiving, music, reverent prayer and worship, personal dedication, and congregational participation. Renewed proper worship brought joy to the people.

29:36 GOD, Grace—God is quick to respond in grace to His people when they honor Him. God prefers to be known as a God of grace rather than a God of wrath. See note on Ex 20:1–7.

seemed right both to the king and to the
whole assembly. 5They decided to send a
proclamation throughout Israel, from Beersheba to Dan,[v] calling the people to
come to Jerusalem and celebrate the Passover to the LORD, the God of Israel. It had
not been celebrated in large numbers according to what was written.
6At the king's command, couriers went
throughout Israel and Judah with letters
from the king and from his officials,
which read:

"People of Israel, return to the
LORD, the God of Abraham, Isaac and
Israel, that he may return to you who
are left, who have escaped from the
hand of the kings of Assyria. 7Do not
be like your fathers[w] and brothers,
who were unfaithful[x] to the LORD,
the God of their fathers, so that he
made them an object of horror,[y] as
you see. 8Do not be stiff-necked,[z] as
your fathers were; submit to the
LORD. Come to the sanctuary, which
he has consecrated forever. Serve the
LORD your God, so that his fierce anger[a] will turn away from you. 9If you
return[b] to the LORD, then your
brothers and your children will be
shown compassion[c] by their captors
and will come back to this land, for
the LORD your God is gracious and
compassionate.[d] He will not turn his
face from you if you return to him."

10The couriers went from town to town
in Ephraim and Manasseh, as far as Zebulun, but the people scorned and ridiculed[e] them. 11Nevertheless, some men
of Asher, Manasseh and Zebulun humbled[f] themselves and went to Jerusalem.[g] 12Also in Judah the hand of God
was on the people to give them unity[h] of
mind to carry out what the king and his
officials had ordered, following the word
of the LORD.
13A very large crowd of people assembled in Jerusalem to celebrate the Feast of
Unleavened Bread[i] in the second month.
14They removed the altars[j] in Jerusalem
and cleared away the incense altars and
threw them into the Kidron Valley.[k]
15They slaughtered the Passover lamb
on the fourteenth day of the second
month. The priests and the Levites were
ashamed and consecrated[l] themselves
and brought burnt offerings to the temple
of the LORD. 16Then they took up their
regular positions[m] as prescribed in the
Law of Moses the man of God. The
priests sprinkled the blood handed to
them by the Levites. 17Since many in the
crowd had not consecrated themselves,
the Levites had to kill[n] the Passover
lambs for all those who were not ceremonially clean and could not consecrate
⌊their lambs⌋ to the LORD. 18Although most
of the many people who came from
Ephraim, Manasseh, Issachar and Zebulun had not purified themselves,[o] yet
they ate the Passover, contrary to what
was written. But Hezekiah prayed for
them, saying, "May the LORD, who is
good, pardon everyone 19who sets his
heart on seeking God—the LORD, the
God of his fathers—even if he is not
clean according to the rules of the sanctuary." 20And the LORD heard[p] Hezekiah
and healed[q] the people.[r]
21The Israelites who were present in
Jerusalem celebrated the Feast of Unleavened Bread[s] for seven days with great
rejoicing, while the Levites and priests
sang to the LORD every day, accompanied
by the LORD's instruments of praise.[u]

[u]21 Or *priests praised the LORD every day with resounding instruments belonging to the LORD*

30:5 [v]S Jdg 20:1
30:7 [w]Ps 78:8,57; 106:6; Jer 11:10; Eze 20:18 [x]S 1Ch 5:25 [y]S Dt 28:25
30:8 [z]S Ex 32:9 [a]S Nu 25:4; S 2Ch 29:10
30:9 [b]Dt 30:2-5; Isa 1:16; 55:7; Jer 25:5; Eze 33:11 [c]S Ex 3:21; S 1Ki 8:50 [d]S Ex 22:27; S Dt 4:31; S 2Ch 6:39; Mic 7:18
30:10 [e]2Ch 36:16
30:11 [f]S 2Ch 6:37 [g]ver 25
30:12 [h]Jer 32:39; Eze 11:19
30:13 [i]S Nu 28:16
30:14 [j]2Ch 28:24 [k]S 2Sa 15:23
30:15 [l]S 2Ch 29:34
30:16 [m]2Ch 35:10
30:17 [n]2Ch 35:11; Ezr 6:20
30:18 [o]Ex 12:43-49; Nu 9:6-10
30:20 [p]S 2Ch 6:20 [q]S 2Ch 7:14; Mal 4:2 [r]Jas 5:16
30:21 [s]Ex 12:15, 17; 13:6

30:6–9 HISTORY, Faith—History calls God's people to repentance and faith. The history of unfaithfulness and judgment experienced by ancestors should lead us to faithfulness and trust in God's grace.

30:6 SALVATION, Repentance—Repentance is a proper human response to God's salvation. Those who repent turn or return to the Lord. They have a change of mind and heart toward God and sin. This call to repentance by godly King Hezekiah came after the conquest of Samaria by the Assyrians.

30:6–9 EVANGELISM, Power—Evangelistic power comes to a repentant people who serve and obey God. See note on 2 Ch 7:13–14.

30:7–12 SIN, Depravity—Even though Hezekiah attempted to turn the people to God, there was no hope. Sin had produced such moral depravity in the people that they ridiculed the king's messengers. When people become so entrenched in sin because of years of sinful activity, they scarcely can see the need for a change. Each generation needs regular reminders of the past so that they may know the destructive effects of sinful actions. Depravity does not rob all individuals of hope before God. Those who respond to God's call to repent find grace.

30:9,18–20 GOD, Grace—God's grace, pouring from a heart of love, is much more characteristic of the true nature of God than is His wrath, the only response left when people refuse His love. When a repentant people turn to worship Him, He accepts their worship even though it does not conform precisely to the regulation of the community. God is free to bend rules to exercise His grace. See notes on Ge 19:13, 24–26; Ex 20:1–7.

30:18–27 PRAYER, Sincerity—One of the great revivals of the Bible illustrates the reward of sincerity, one of God's basic requirements for prayer (Jas 5:17). Israel had already made the mistake in Amos's day (and would make it again) of believing that mere ritual correctness would obligate God to them (Am 5:21–23). Here the legal requirements were not met. Passover was observed at the wrong time (v 2, the second month instead of the fourteenth day of the first month), and the people did not purify themselves (v 17). Hezekiah recognized this and asked God to accept the purpose of their hearts rather than mere technicalities of observance (Pr 23:26).

30:20 SALVATION, Definition—Healing is one way in which the Bible speaks of salvation (Ex 15:26; Ps 30:1–3). Above all He heals us of the cancer of sin. Here God suspended the rules about ceremonial cleansing for the sake of His people.

22Hezekiah spoke encouragingly to all
the Levites, who showed good understanding of the service of the LORD. For
the seven days they ate their assigned
portion and offered fellowship offerings[v]
and praised the LORD, the God of their
fathers.
23The whole assembly then agreed to
celebrate[t] the festival seven more days;
so for another seven days they celebrated
joyfully. 24Hezekiah king of Judah provided[u] a thousand bulls and seven thousand
sheep and goats for the assembly, and the
officials provided them with a thousand
bulls and ten thousand sheep and goats. A
great number of priests consecrated
themselves. 25The entire assembly of Judah rejoiced, along with the priests and
Levites and all who had assembled from
Israel[v], including the aliens who had
come from Israel and those who lived in
Judah. 26There was great joy in Jerusalem,
for since the days of Solomon[w] son of David king of Israel there had been nothing
like this in Jerusalem. 27The priests and
the Levites stood to bless[x] the people,
and God heard them, for their prayer
reached heaven, his holy dwelling place.

Chapter 31

WHEN all this had ended, the Israelites who were there went out to
the towns of Judah, smashed the sacred
stones and cut down[y] the Asherah poles.
They destroyed the high places and the
altars throughout Judah and Benjamin
and in Ephraim and Manasseh. After they
had destroyed all of them, the Israelites
returned to their own towns and to their
own property.

Contributions for Worship

31:20–21pp — 2Ki 18:5–7

2Hezekiah[z] assigned the priests and
Levites to divisions[a]—each of them according to their duties as priests or Levites—to offer burnt offerings and fellowship offerings,[v] to minister,[b] to give
thanks and to sing praises[c] at the gates of
the LORD's dwelling.[d] 3The king contributed[e] from his own possessions for the
morning and evening burnt offerings and
for the burnt offerings on the Sabbaths,
New Moons and appointed feasts as written in the Law of the LORD.[f] 4He ordered
the people living in Jerusalem to give the
portion[g] due the priests and Levites so
they could devote themselves to the Law
of the LORD. 5As soon as the order went
out, the Israelites generously gave the
firstfruits[h] of their grain, new wine,[i] oil
and honey and all that the fields produced. They brought a great amount, a
tithe of everything. 6The men of Israel
and Judah who lived in the towns of Judah also brought a tithe[j] of their herds
and flocks and a tithe of the holy things
dedicated to the LORD their God, and they
piled them in heaps.[k] 7They began doing
this in the third month and finished in
the seventh month.[l] 8When Hezekiah
and his officials came and saw the heaps,
they praised the LORD and blessed[m] his
people Israel.
9Hezekiah asked the priests and Levites about the heaps; 10and Azariah the
chief priest, from the family of Zadok,[n]
answered, "Since the people began to
bring their contributions to the temple of
the LORD, we have had enough to eat and
plenty to spare, because the LORD has
blessed his people, and this great amount
is left over."[o]
11Hezekiah gave orders to prepare
storerooms in the temple of the LORD,
and this was done. 12Then they faithfully
brought in the contributions, tithes and
dedicated gifts. Conaniah,[p] a Levite, was
in charge of these things, and his brother
Shimei was next in rank. 13Jehiel, Azaziah, Nahath, Asahel, Jerimoth, Jozabad,[q]
Eliel, Ismakiah, Mahath and Benaiah
were supervisors under Conaniah and
Shimei his brother, by appointment of
King Hezekiah and Azariah the official in
charge of the temple of God.
14Kore son of Imnah the Levite, keeper
of the East Gate, was in charge of the
freewill offerings given to God, distributing the contributions made to the LORD
and also the consecrated gifts. 15Eden,[r]
Miniamin, Jeshua, Shemaiah, Amariah
and Shecaniah assisted him faithfully in
the towns[s] of the priests, distributing to
their fellow priests according to their divisions, old and young alike.
16In addition, they distributed to the
males three years old or more whose
names were in the genealogical records[t]
—all who would enter the temple of the
LORD to perform the daily duties of their
various tasks, according to their responsibilities and their divisions. 17And they

30:23 [t]2Ch 7:9
30:24 [u]1Ki 8:5; 2Ch 35:7; Ezr 6:17; 8:35
30:25 [v]ver 11
30:26 [w]S 2Ch 7:8
30:27 [x]S Ex 39:43
31:1 [y]S 2Ki 18:4; 2Ch 32:12; Isa 36:7
31:2 [z]S 2Ch 29:9 [a]S 1Ch 24:1 [b]S 1Ch 15:2 [c]Ps 7:17; 9:2; 47:6; 71:22 [d]S 1Ch 23:28-32
31:3 [e]S 1Ch 29:3; 2Ch 35:7; Eze 45:17 [f]Nu 28:1-29:40
31:4 [g]S Nu 18:8; S Dt 18:8; Ne 13:10
31:5 [h]S Nu 18:12, 24; Ne 13:12; Eze 44:30 [i]Dt 12:17
31:6 [j]S Lev 27:30; Ne 13:10-12 [k]S Ru 3:7
31:7 [l]Ex 23:16
31:8 [m]Ps 144:13-15
31:10 [n]S 2Sa 8:17 [o]S Ex 36:5; Eze 44:30; Mal 3:10-12
31:12 [p]2Ch 35:9
31:13 [q]2Ch 35:9
31:15 [r]2Ch 29:12 [s]Jos 21:9-19
31:16 [t]1Ch 23:3

[v]22,2 Traditionally *peace offerings*

30:24 STEWARDSHIP, Sacrifice Giving—See notes on Lev 1:2; 1 Ch 29:2–5.

31:2–13 STEWARDSHIP, Storehouse—The people generously provided for the Levites' needs through tithes and first-fruit offerings. Temple storehouses had to be built to save the excess goods until they were needed. This marked the beginning of the "storehouse" idea upon which many appeals for support of the church are based. God's people do not have to spend offerings immediately. They may be saved and stored for later needs. Just because a church is storing funds for the future does not excuse members from continuing to bring tithes and offerings.

distributed to the priests enrolled by their
families in the genealogical records and
likewise to the Levites twenty years old
or more, according to their responsibilities and their divisions. 18They included
all the little ones, the wives, and the sons
and daughters of the whole community
listed in these genealogical records. For
they were faithful in consecrating themselves.
19As for the priests, the descendants of
Aaron, who lived on the farm lands
around their towns or in any other
towns,[u] men were designated by name
to distribute portions to every male
among them and to all who were recorded in the genealogies of the Levites.
20This is what Hezekiah did throughout
Judah, doing what was good and right and
faithful[v] before the LORD his God. 21In
everything that he undertook in the service of God's temple and in obedience to
the law and the commands, he sought his
God and worked wholeheartedly. And so
he prospered.[w]

Chapter 32

Sennacherib Threatens Jerusalem

32:9–19pp — 2Ki 18:17–35; Isa 36:2–20
32:20–21pp — 2Ki 19:35–37; Isa 37:36–38

AFTER all that Hezekiah had so faithfully done, Sennacherib[x] king of Assyria came and invaded Judah. He laid siege
to the fortified cities, thinking to conquer
them for himself. 2When Hezekiah saw
that Sennacherib had come and that he
intended to make war on Jerusalem,[y] 3he
consulted with his officials and military
staff about blocking off the water from the
springs outside the city, and they helped
him. 4A large force of men assembled,
and they blocked all the springs[z] and the
stream that flowed through the land.
"Why should the kings[w] of Assyria come
and find plenty of water?" they said.
5Then he worked hard repairing all the
broken sections of the wall[a] and building
towers on it. He built another wall outside that one and reinforced the supporting terraces[x][b] of the City of David. He
also made large numbers of weapons[c]
and shields.
6He appointed military officers over the
people and assembled them before him in
the square at the city gate and encouraged them with these words: 7"Be strong
and courageous.[d] Do not be afraid or discouraged[e] because of the king of Assyria
and the vast army with him, for there is a
greater power with us than with him.[f]
8With him is only the arm of flesh,[g] but
with us[h] is the LORD our God to help us
and to fight our battles."[i] And the people gained confidence from what Hezekiah the king of Judah said.
9Later, when Sennacherib king of Assyria and all his forces were laying siege
to Lachish,[j] he sent his officers to Jerusalem with this message for Hezekiah king
of Judah and for all the people of Judah
who were there:

10"This is what Sennacherib king
of Assyria says: On what are you basing your confidence,[k] that you remain in Jerusalem under siege?
11When Hezekiah says, 'The LORD
our God will save us from the hand of
the king of Assyria,' he is misleading[l] you, to let you die of hunger
and thirst. 12Did not Hezekiah himself remove this god's high places
and altars, saying to Judah and Jerusalem, 'You must worship before one
altar[m] and burn sacrifices on it'?
13"Do you not know what I and my
fathers have done to all the peoples
of the other lands? Were the gods of
those nations ever able to deliver
their land from my hand?[n] 14Who of
all the gods of these nations that my
fathers destroyed has been able to
save his people from me? How then
can your god deliver you from my
hand? 15Now do not let Hezekiah deceive[o] you and mislead you like this.
Do not believe him, for no god of any
nation or kingdom has been able to
deliver[p] his people from my hand or
the hand of my fathers.[q] How much
less will your god deliver you from
my hand!"

16Sennacherib's officers spoke further
against the LORD God and against his servant Hezekiah. 17The king also wrote letters[r] insulting[s] the LORD, the God of Israel, and saying this against him: "Just as
the gods[t] of the peoples of the other
lands did not rescue their people from my
hand, so the god of Hezekiah will not rescue his people from my hand." 18Then
they called out in Hebrew to the people
of Jerusalem who were on the wall, to

31:19 [u]S Nu 35:2-5
31:20 [v]S 2Ki 20:3
31:21 [w]S Dt 29:9
32:1 [x]Isa 36:1; 37:9,17,37
32:2 [y]Isa 22:7; Jer 1:15
32:4 [z]S 2Ki 18:17; Isa 22:9,11; Na 3:14
32:5 [a]Isa 22:10 [b]S 1Ch 11:8 [c]Isa 22:8
32:7 [d]S Dt 31:6 [e]2Ch 20:15 [f]S Nu 14:9; 2Ki 6:16
32:8 [g]Job 40:9; Isa 52:10; Jer 17:5; 32:21 [h]S Dt 3:22; S 1Sa 17:45 [i]S 1Ch 5:22; Ps 20:7; Isa 28:6
32:9 [j]S Jos 10:3,31
32:10 [k]Eze 29:16
32:11 [l]Isa 37:10
32:12 [m]S 2Ch 31:1
32:13 [n]ver 15
32:15 [o]Isa 37:10 [p]Da 3:15 [q]Ex 5:2
32:17 [r]Isa 37:14 [s]Ps 74:22; Isa 37:4,17 [t]S 2Ki 19:12

[w]*4* Hebrew; Septuagint and Syriac *king* [x]*5* Or *the Millo*

31:21 HISTORY, Faith—See note on 26:5.
32:13–21 GOD, One God—The gods of the nations are empty ideas, worthless man-made objects; but their supporters can use historical evidence to claim their god(s) is the most powerful one. God's people are called to take the long look throughout history and believe in the unique superiority of God even when current circumstances do not seem to support our claim. In the long run God will defeat all other claimants to His throne and prove Himself to be the only God.

terrify them and make them afraid in order to capture the city. 19They spoke
about the God of Jerusalem as they did
about the gods of the other peoples of the
world—the work of men's hands.[u]
20King Hezekiah and the prophet Isaiah
son of Amoz cried out in prayer[v] to heav-
en about this. 21And the LORD sent an
angel,[w] who annihilated all the fighting
men and the leaders and officers in the
camp of the Assyrian king. So he withdrew to his own land in disgrace. And
when he went into the temple of his god,
some of his sons cut him down with the
sword.[x]
22So the LORD saved Hezekiah and the
people of Jerusalem from the hand of Sennacherib king of Assyria and from the
hand of all others. He took care of them[y]
on every side. 23Many brought offerings
to Jerusalem for the LORD and valuable
gifts[y] for Hezekiah king of Judah. From
then on he was highly regarded by all the
nations.

Hezekiah's Pride, Success and Death

32:24–33pp — 2Ki 20:1–21; Isa 37:21–38; 38:1–8

24In those days Hezekiah became ill
and was at the point of death. He prayed
to the LORD, who answered him and gave
him a miraculous sign.[z] 25But Hezekiah's
heart was proud[a] and he did not respond
to the kindness shown him; therefore the
LORD's wrath[b] was on him and on Judah
and Jerusalem. 26Then Hezekiah repented[c] of the pride of his heart, as did the
people of Jerusalem; therefore the LORD's
wrath did not come upon them during
the days of Hezekiah.[d]
27Hezekiah had very great riches and
honor,[e] and he made treasuries for his
silver and gold and for his precious
stones, spices, shields and all kinds of
valuables. 28He also made buildings to
store the harvest of grain, new wine and
oil; and he made stalls for various kinds of
cattle, and pens for the flocks. 29He built
villages and acquired great numbers of
flocks and herds, for God had given him
very great riches.[f]
30It was Hezekiah who blocked[g] the
upper outlet of the Gihon[h] spring and
channeled[i] the water down to the west
side of the City of David. He succeeded in
everything he undertook. 31But when envoys were sent by the rulers of Babylon[j]
to ask him about the miraculous sign[k]
that had occurred in the land, God left
him to test[l] him and to know everything
that was in his heart.
32The other events of Hezekiah's reign
and his acts of devotion are written in the
vision of the prophet Isaiah son of Amoz
in the book of the kings of Judah and Israel. 33Hezekiah rested with his fathers and
was buried on the hill where the tombs of
David's descendants are. All Judah and
the people of Jerusalem honored him
when he died. And Manasseh his son succeeded him as king.

Chapter 33

Manasseh King of Judah

33:1–10pp — 2Ki 21:1–10
33:18–20pp — 2Ki 21:17–18

MANASSEH[m] was twelve years old
when he became king, and he
reigned in Jerusalem fifty-five years. 2He
did evil in the eyes of the LORD,[n] following the detestable[o] practices of the nations the LORD had driven out before the
Israelites. 3He rebuilt the high places his
father Hezekiah had demolished; he also
erected altars to the Baals and made
Asherah poles.[p] He bowed down[q] to all
the starry hosts and worshiped them. 4He
built altars in the temple of the LORD, of
which the LORD had said, "My Name[r]

[y]22 Hebrew; Septuagint and Vulgate *He gave them rest*

32:19 [u]Ps 115:4, 4-8; Isa 2:8; 17:8; 37:19; Jer 1:16
32:20 [v]Isa 1:15; 37:15
32:21 [w]S Ge 19:13 [x]S 2Ki 19:7; Isa 37:7,38; Jer 41:2
32:23 [y]S 1Sa 10:27; S 2Ch 9:24; Ps 68:18,29; 76:11; Isa 16:1; 18:7; 45:14; Zep 3:10; Zec 14:16-17
32:24 [z]ver 31
32:25 [a]S 2Ki 14:10 [b]S 2Ch 19:2
32:26 [c]Jer 26:18-19 [d]2Ch 34:27,28; Isa 39:8
32:27 [e]S 1Ch 29:12; S 2Ch 9:24
32:29 [f]Isa 39:2
32:30 [g]S 2Ki 18:17 [h]S 1Ki 1:33 [i]S 2Sa 5:8
32:31 [j]Isa 13:1; 39:1 [k]S ver 24; Isa 38:7 [l]S Ge 22:1; Dt 8:16
33:1 [m]S 1Ch 3:13
33:2 [n]Jer 15:4 [o]S Dt 18:9
33:3 [p]Dt 16:21-22; S 2Ch 24:18 [q]Dt 17:3
33:4 [r]2Ch 7:16

32:20–23 HISTORY, Deliverance—Prayer is the basic human action for deliverance. See note on 2 Ki 19:1–37.
32:20–21 PRAYER, Sovereignty of God—See note on 2 Ki 19:14–19. The Chronicler adds the note that Isaiah also prayed. United prayer is effective before God.
32:24–26 HISTORY, Judgment—See note on 26:16–21. God postponed judgment in response to the people's repentance.
32:24 PRAYER, Petition—See note on 2 Ki 20:3.
32:25 GOD, Wrath—Even God's miraculous intervention in our life may not drive out our pride. Failure to acknowledge God's goodness brings God's wrath even to one who has experienced God's miraculous power. See note on 29:3–10.
32:25 SIN, Pride—God's intervention in an individual's life may take several forms—miracle to encourage, wrath to discipline, or delay of intervention in response to repentance. Human pride can cause us to ignore God even when He miraculously intervenes. Such sinful pride need not be a permanent part of our character. We can repent of pride and find God's acceptance. See note on 1 Ki 11:26–39.
32:30 HUMANITY, Work—The Hebrew term carries the idea of finishing well, rather than mere success. The faithful worker seeks to finish well what God has given to do.
32:33 HUMANITY, Attitudes to Death—Leaders who have led well deserve honor at the time of their death.
33:2–17 SIN, Transgression—Even the most wicked of Judah's kings had not moved beyond the bounds of God's compassion. Humble repentance before God brings forgiveness of any sin though the consequences of sin are not removed. Repentance should be our response to God's discipline. See notes on 1 Ki 14:22–24; 2 Ki 21:2–17.
33:4–13 GOD, One God—Manasseh used religion as a political tool to please the rulers of stronger nations. In so doing he violated all God's expectations. God used drastic measures to teach him that allegiance to the one God must be top priority. Manasseh learned the lesson and received God's blessing. In all circumstances we are called to be faithful to the one true God. See notes on Ex 20:1–7; Dt 6:4–9.

will remain in Jerusalem forever." 5In
both courts of the temple of the LORD,[s]
he built altars to all the starry hosts. 6He
sacrificed his sons[t] in[z] the fire in the
Valley of Ben Hinnom, practiced sorcery,
divination and witchcraft, and consulted
mediums[u] and spiritists.[v] He did much
evil in the eyes of the LORD, provoking
him to anger.
7He took the carved image he had
made and put it in God's temple,[w] of
which God had said to David and to his
son Solomon, "In this temple and in Jerusalem, which I have chosen out of all the
tribes of Israel, I will put my Name forever. 8I will not again make the feet of the
Israelites leave the land[x] I assigned to
your forefathers, if only they will be careful to do everything I commanded them
concerning all the laws, decrees and ordinances given through Moses." 9But Manasseh led Judah and the people of Jerusalem astray, so that they did more evil
than the nations the LORD had destroyed
before the Israelites.[y]
10The LORD spoke to Manasseh and his
people, but they paid no attention. 11So
the LORD brought against them the army
commanders of the king of Assyria, who
took Manasseh prisoner,[z] put a hook[a] in
his nose, bound him with bronze shackles[b] and took him to Babylon. 12In his
distress he sought the favor of the LORD
his God and humbled[c] himself greatly
before the God of his fathers. 13And when
he prayed to him, the LORD was moved
by his entreaty and listened to his plea; so
he brought him back to Jerusalem and to
his kingdom. Then Manasseh knew that
the LORD is God.
14Afterward he rebuilt the outer wall of
the City of David, west of the Gihon[d]
spring in the valley, as far as the entrance
of the Fish Gate[e] and encircling the hill
of Ophel;[f] he also made it much higher.
He stationed military commanders in all
the fortified cities in Judah.
15He got rid of the foreign gods and removed[g] the image from the temple of the

33:5 [s]S 2Ch 4:9
33:6 [t]S Lev 18:21; S Dt 18:10 [u]S Ex 22:18; S Lev 19:31 [v]S 1Sa 28:13
33:7 [w]S 2Ch 7:16
33:8 [x]S 2Sa 7:10
33:9 [y]Jer 15:4; Eze 5:7
33:11 [z]S Dt 28:36 [a]S 2Ki 19:28; Isa 37:29; Eze 29:4; 38:4; Am 4:2 [b]Ps 149:8
33:12 [c]S 2Ch 6:37
33:14 [d]S 1Ki 1:33 [e]Ne 3:3; 12:39; Zep 1:10 [f]2Ch 27:3; Ne 3:26
33:15 [g]2Ki 23:12
33:16 [h]Lev 7:11-18
33:19 [i]S 2Ch 6:37 [j]2Ki 21:17
33:20 [k]2Ki 21:18; S 2Ch 21:20
33:21 [l]S 1Ch 3:14
33:23 [m]S Ex 10:3; 2Ch 7:14; Ps 18:27; 147:6; Pr 3:34
33:25 [n]S 2Ch 22:1

LORD, as well as all the altars he had built
on the temple hill and in Jerusalem; and
he threw them out of the city. 16Then he
restored the altar of the LORD and sacrificed fellowship offerings[a] and thank offerings[h] on it, and told Judah to serve the
LORD, the God of Israel. 17The people,
however, continued to sacrifice at the
high places, but only to the LORD their
God.
18The other events of Manasseh's
reign, including his prayer to his God and
the words the seers spoke to him in the
name of the LORD, the God of Israel, are
written in the annals of the kings of Israel.[b] 19His prayer and how God was
moved by his entreaty, as well as all his
sins and unfaithfulness, and the sites
where he built high places and set up
Asherah poles and idols before he humbled[i] himself—all are written in the
records of the seers.[c][j] 20Manasseh rested with his fathers and was buried[k] in
his palace. And Amon his son succeeded
him as king.

Amon King of Judah

33:21–25pp — 2Ki 21:19–24

21Amon[l] was twenty-two years old
when he became king, and he reigned in
Jerusalem two years. 22He did evil in the
eyes of the LORD, as his father Manasseh
had done. Amon worshiped and offered
sacrifices to all the idols Manasseh had
made. 23But unlike his father Manasseh,
he did not humble[m] himself before the
LORD; Amon increased his guilt.
24Amon's officials conspired against
him and assassinated him in his palace.
25Then the people[n] of the land killed all
who had plotted against King Amon, and
they made Josiah his son king in his
place.

[z]6 Or *He made his sons pass through*
[a]16 Traditionally *peace offerings* [b]18 That is, Judah, as frequently in 2 Chronicles [c]19 One Hebrew manuscript and Septuagint; most Hebrew manuscripts *of Hozai*

33:6 GOD, Wrath—See note on 29:3–10.
33:7–11 ELECTION, Leadership—The irresponsible activity of leading God's elect away from the commission, commands, and concerns of God invites divine judgment.
33:8 CHRISTIAN ETHICS, Moral Imperatives—See notes on Lev 26:3–45; Dt 28:1–68; 1 Ki 3:3,14.
33:9–13 HISTORY, Judgment—God's judgment is discipline seeking to turn His people back to Him. When people respond to judgment in repentance, God responds in grace. Both deliverance and judgment in history seek to lead people to confess God as the only God and to serve Him faithfully.
33:12–17 ELECTION, Forgiveness—The massive sins of Manasseh were forgiven when he sincerely turned back to God. Election founds a relationship with God in which forgiveness is possible.
33:12–13 PRAYER, Humility—In prosperity, Manasseh served false gods. Distress opened his eyes and brought humility, a quality essential in prayer. Answered prayer brought renewed faith in God. See note on 7:13–16.
33:16 PRAYER, Worship—Manasseh's return to the Lord was genuine. These were freewill offerings, not mandatory offerings. Obedience shows the sincerity of prayer.
33:16 EVANGELISM, Holy Life—The principle of "restoring the altar" means the restoration of holy living and worship. We cannot worship on a "strange altar" and expect God to honor our witness. Powerful evangelism grows out of a yielded life, lived wholly unto the Lord.
33:19 HOLY SCRIPTURE, Writing—See note on 1 Ch 29:29.
33:22–23 SIN, Transgression—See notes on 28:9–13; 1 Ki 14:22–24.
33:23–24 HISTORY, Judgment—See note on 21:12–19.
33:24–25 CHRISTIAN ETHICS, Murder—See note on 1 Ki 16:10–13.

Chapter 34

Josiah's Reforms

34:1–2pp — 2Ki 22:1–2
34:3–7Ref — 2Ki 23:4–20
34:8–13pp — 2Ki 22:3–7

JOSIAH[o] was eight years old when he
became king,[p] and he reigned in Jerusalem thirty-one years. 2He did what was
right in the eyes of the LORD and walked
in the ways of his father David,[q] not
turning aside to the right or to the left.
3In the eighth year of his reign, while
he was still young, he began to seek the
God[r] of his father David. In his twelfth
year he began to purge Judah and Jerusalem of high places, Asherah poles, carved
idols and cast images. 4Under his direction the altars of the Baals were torn
down; he cut to pieces the incense altars
that were above them, and smashed the
Asherah poles,[s] the idols and the images.
These he broke to pieces and scattered
over the graves of those who had sacrificed to them.[t] 5He burned[u] the bones
of the priests on their altars, and so he
purged Judah and Jerusalem. 6In the
towns of Manasseh, Ephraim and Simeon, as far as Naphtali, and in the ruins
around them, 7he tore down the altars
and the Asherah poles and crushed the
idols to powder[v] and cut to pieces all the
incense altars throughout Israel. Then he
went back to Jerusalem.
8In the eighteenth year of Josiah's
reign, to purify the land and the temple,
he sent Shaphan son of Azaliah and Maaseiah the ruler of the city, with Joah son
of Joahaz, the recorder, to repair the temple of the LORD his God.
9They went to Hilkiah[w] the high priest
and gave him the money that had been
brought into the temple of God, which
the Levites who were the doorkeepers
had collected from the people of Manasseh, Ephraim and the entire remnant of
Israel and from all the people of Judah
and Benjamin and the inhabitants of Jerusalem. 10Then they entrusted it to the
men appointed to supervise the work on
the LORD's temple. These men paid the
workers who repaired and restored the
temple. 11They also gave money[x] to the
carpenters and builders to purchase
dressed stone, and timber for joists and
beams for the buildings that the kings of
Judah had allowed to fall into ruin.[y]
12The men did the work faithfully.[z]
Over them to direct them were Jahath
and Obadiah, Levites descended from
Merari, and Zechariah and Meshullam,
descended from Kohath. The Levites—all
who were skilled in playing musical instruments—[a] 13had charge of the laborers[b] and supervised all the workers from
job to job. Some of the Levites were secretaries, scribes and doorkeepers.

The Book of the Law Found

34:14–28pp — 2Ki 22:8–20
34:29–32pp — 2Ki 23:1–3

14While they were bringing out the
money that had been taken into the temple of the LORD, Hilkiah the priest found
the Book of the Law of the LORD that had
been given through Moses. 15Hilkiah said
to Shaphan the secretary, "I have found
the Book of the Law[c] in the temple of the
LORD." He gave it to Shaphan.
16Then Shaphan took the book to the
king and reported to him: "Your officials
are doing everything that has been committed to them. 17They have paid out the
money that was in the temple of the LORD
and have entrusted it to the supervisors
and workers." 18Then Shaphan the secretary informed the king, "Hilkiah the
priest has given me a book." And Shaphan read from it in the presence of the
king.
19When the king heard the words of
the Law,[d] he tore[e] his robes. 20He gave
these orders to Hilkiah, Ahikam son of
Shaphan,[f] Abdon son of Micah,[d] Shaphan the secretary and Asaiah the king's
attendant: 21"Go and inquire of the LORD

34:1 [o]S 1Ch 3:14 [p]Zep 1:1
34:2 [q]2Ch 29:2
34:3 [r]S 1Ch 16:11
34:4 [s]S Ex 34:13 [t]Ex 32:20; S Lev 26:30; 2Ki 23:11; Mic 1:5
34:5 [u]S 1Ki 13:2
34:7 [v]S Ex 32:20
34:9 [w]S 1Ch 6:13
34:11 [x]2Ch 24:12 [y]2Ch 33:4-7
34:12 [z]2Ki 12:15 [a]S 1Ch 25:1
34:13 [b]S 1Ch 23:4
34:15 [c]S 2Ki 22:8; Ezr 7:6; Ne 8:1
34:19 [d]Dt 28:3-68 [e]Isa 36:22; 37:1
34:20 [f]S 2Ki 22:3

[d]20 Also called *Acbor son of Micaiah*

34:3–7,32 GOD, One God—See note on 32:13–21.
34:3 PRAYER, Command of God—See note on 15:2.
34:9 THE CHURCH, Remnant—God's people are not identified with a nation. Israel learned this slowly. Division of David's kingdom into Judah and Israel and exile for the Northern Kingdom to Assyria finally forced God's people to develop a theology of the remnant, the righteous, obedient group preserved by God to fulfill His plans and promises. One hundred years after the fall of Israel as a kingdom, a remnant maintained their faith and supported Josiah's reform. They faced the temptations and ridicule of foreigners brought in by Assyria to populate the northern territory (2 Ki 17:24–34). God's people are those who trust Him even under ridicule and persecution. This is a remnant of those who identify themselves as people of God.
34:19–28 SIN, Disobeying—God's Word reveals His will. Refusing to obey His Word brings His anger, alienation, and discipline. Humble repentance can delay God's punishing intervention. See note on 2 Ki 22:13.
34:21 GOD, Wrath—See note on 2 Ki 22:13–17.
34:21 HOLY SCRIPTURE, Purpose—The recorded history of God's will is also the written record of man's rejection of His revelation. Hilkiah's discovery (2 Ki 22:8–10) of the written law called God's people to remember what they had forgotten—God's revealed truth was to live in their hearts and wills. See note on 2 Ki 22:16–20.
34:21 THE CHURCH, Remnant—The remnant are not simply those left behind by political exile or the few faithful living among worshipers of other gods. The remnant are faithful, obedient worshipers. They live among those who, though they claim to be people of God, do not remain loyal to Him. Thus Josiah spoke of a remnant in Israel, the exiled Northern Kingdom, and a remnant in Judah, the remaining kingdom for God's people. See note on v 9.

for me and for the remnant in Israel and
Judah about what is written in this book
that has been found. Great is the LORD's
anger that is poured out[g] on us because
our fathers have not kept the word of the
LORD; they have not acted in accordance
with all that is written in this book."
22Hilkiah and those the king had sent
with him[e] went to speak to the prophetess[h] Huldah, who was the wife of Shallum son of Tokhath,[f] the son of Hasrah,[g]
keeper of the wardrobe. She lived in Jerusalem, in the Second District.
23She said to them, "This is what the
LORD, the God of Israel, says: Tell the
man who sent you to me, 24'This is what
the LORD says: I am going to bring disaster[i] on this place and its people[j]—all
the curses[k] written in the book that has
been read in the presence of the king of
Judah. 25Because they have forsaken me[l]
and burned incense to other gods and
provoked me to anger by all that their
hands have made,[h] my anger will be
poured out on this place and will not be
quenched.' 26Tell the king of Judah, who
sent you to inquire of the LORD, 'This is
what the LORD, the God of Israel, says
concerning the words you heard: 27Be-
cause your heart was responsive[m] and
you humbled[n] yourself before God when
you heard what he spoke against this
place and its people, and because you
humbled yourself before me and tore
your robes and wept in my presence, I
have heard you, declares the LORD.
28Now I will gather you to your fathers,[o]
and you will be buried in peace. Your
eyes will not see all the disaster I am going to bring on this place and on those
who live here.'"[p]
So they took her answer back to the
king.
29Then the king called together all the
elders of Judah and Jerusalem. 30He went
up to the temple of the LORD[q] with the
men of Judah, the people of Jerusalem,
the priests and the Levites—all the people from the least to the greatest. He read
in their hearing all the words of the Book
of the Covenant, which had been found
in the temple of the LORD. 31The king
stood by his pillar[r] and renewed the covenant[s] in the presence of the LORD—to
follow[t] the LORD and keep his commands, regulations and decrees with all
his heart and all his soul, and to obey the
words of the covenant written in this
book.
32Then he had everyone in Jerusalem
and Benjamin pledge themselves to it;
the people of Jerusalem did this in accordance with the covenant of God, the God
of their fathers.
33Josiah removed all the detestable[u]
idols from all the territory belonging to
the Israelites, and he had all who were
present in Israel serve the LORD their
God. As long as he lived, they did not fail
to follow the LORD, the God of their fathers.

Chapter 35

Josiah Celebrates the Passover

35:1,18–19pp — 2Ki 23:21–23

JOSIAH celebrated the Passover[v] to the
LORD in Jerusalem, and the Passover
lamb was slaughtered on the fourteenth
day of the first month. 2He appointed the
priests to their duties and encouraged
them in the service of the LORD's temple.
3He said to the Levites, who instructed[w]
all Israel and who had been consecrated
to the LORD: "Put the sacred ark in the
temple that Solomon son of David king of
Israel built. It is not to be carried about
on your shoulders. Now serve the LORD
your God and his people Israel. 4Prepare
yourselves by families in your divisions,[x]
according to the directions written by David king of Israel and by his son Solomon.
5"Stand in the holy place with a group
of Levites for each subdivision of the families of your fellow countrymen, the lay
people. 6Slaughter the Passover lambs,
consecrate yourselves[y] and prepare ⌞the
lambs⌟ for your fellow countrymen, doing
what the LORD commanded through Moses."
7Josiah provided for all the lay people
who were there a total of thirty thousand
sheep and goats for the Passover offerings,[z] and also three thousand cattle—all
from the king's own possessions.[a]
8His officials also contributed[b] voluntarily to the people and the priests and

34:21 [g]La 2:4; 4:11; Eze 36:18
34:22 [h]S Ex 15:20; Ne 6:14
34:24 [i]Pr 16:4; Isa 3:9; Jer 40:2; 42:10; 44:2,11 [j]2Ch 36:14-20 [k]Dt 28:15-68
34:25 [l]2Ch 33:3-6; Jer 22:9
34:27 [m]S 2Ch 32:26 [n]S Ex 10:3; S 2Ch 6:37
34:28 [o]2Ch 35:20-25 [p]S 2Ch 32:26
34:30 [q]S 2Ki 23:2
34:31 [r]S 1Ki 7:15 [s]S 2Ki 11:17; S 2Ch 23:16 [t]S Dt 13:4
34:33 [u]S Dt 18:9
35:1 [v]Ex 12:1-30; S Nu 28:16
35:3 [w]S 2Ch 17:7
35:4 [x]ver 10; S 1Ch 24:1; Ezr 6:18
35:6 [y]S Lev 11:44
35:7 [z]S 2Ch 30:24 [a]S 2Ch 31:3
35:8 [b]S 1Ch 29:3; 2Ch 29:31-36

[e] *22* One Hebrew manuscript, Vulgate and Syriac; most Hebrew manuscripts do not have *had sent with him.*
[f] *22* Also called *Tikvah* [g] *22* Also called *Harhas*
[h] *25* Or *by everything they have done*

34:21–22 PRAYER, Inquire—See note on 2 Ki 22:13–14.
34:26–28 HISTORY, Judgment—See notes on 32:24–26; 2 Ki 23:26–27.
34:27 PRAYER, Faithfulness of God—See note on 7:13–16.
34:28 HUMANITY, Death—One of the more beautiful images of death points to a reunion in the family burial ground. The New Testament fully developed this idea of reunion.
34:31–33 CHRISTIAN ETHICS, Covenant—See note on 2 Ki 23:3.
34:31–32 THE CHURCH, Covenant People—See notes on 23:16; 29:10; Dt 29:1–15.
35:3 EDUCATION, Priests—See note on 17:7–9.
35:7–9 STEWARDSHIP, Sacrifice Giving—See notes on Lev 1:2; 1 Ch 29:2–5.

Levites. Hilkiah,[c] Zechariah and Jehiel, the administrators of God's temple, gave the priests twenty-six hundred Passover offerings and three hundred cattle. 9 Also Conaniah[d] along with Shemaiah and Nethanel, his brothers, and Hashabiah, Jeiel and Jozabad,[e] the leaders of the Levites, provided five thousand Passover offerings and five hundred head of cattle for the Levites.

10 The service was arranged and the priests stood in their places with the Levites in their divisions[f] as the king had ordered.[g] 11 The Passover lambs were slaughtered,[h] and the priests sprinkled the blood handed to them, while the Levites skinned the animals. 12 They set aside the burnt offerings to give them to the subdivisions of the families of the people to offer to the LORD, as is written in the Book of Moses. They did the same with the cattle. 13 They roasted the Passover animals over the fire as prescribed,[i] and boiled the holy offerings in pots, caldrons and pans and served them quickly to all the people. 14 After this, they made preparations for themselves and for the priests, because the priests, the descendants of Aaron, were sacrificing the burnt offerings and the fat portions[j] until nightfall. So the Levites made preparations for themselves and for the Aaronic priests.

15 The musicians,[k] the descendants of Asaph, were in the places prescribed by David, Asaph, Heman and Jeduthun the king's seer. The gatekeepers at each gate did not need to leave their posts, because their fellow Levites made the preparations for them.

16 So at that time the entire service of the LORD was carried out for the celebration of the Passover and the offering of burnt offerings on the altar of the LORD, as King Josiah had ordered. 17 The Israelites who were present celebrated the Passover at that time and observed the Feast of Unleavened Bread for seven days. 18 The Passover had not been observed like this in Israel since the days of the prophet Samuel; and none of the kings of Israel had ever celebrated such a Passover as did Josiah, with the priests, the Levites and all Judah and Israel who were there with the people of Jerusalem. 19 This Passover was celebrated in the eighteenth year of Josiah's reign.

The Death of Josiah

35:20–36:1pp — 2Ki 23:28–30

20 After all this, when Josiah had set the temple in order, Neco king of Egypt went up to fight at Carchemish[l] on the Euphrates,[m] and Josiah marched out to meet him in battle. 21 But Neco sent messengers to him, saying, "What quarrel is there between you and me, O king of Judah? It is not you I am attacking at this time, but the house with which I am at war. God has told[n] me to hurry; so stop opposing God, who is with me, or he will destroy you."

22 Josiah, however, would not turn away from him, but disguised[o] himself to engage him in battle. He would not listen to what Neco had said at God's command but went to fight him on the plain of Megiddo.

23 Archers[p] shot King Josiah, and he told his officers, "Take me away; I am badly wounded." 24 So they took him out of his chariot, put him in the other chariot he had and brought him to Jerusalem, where he died. He was buried in the tombs of his fathers, and all Judah and Jerusalem mourned for him.

25 Jeremiah composed laments for Josiah, and to this day all the men and women singers commemorate Josiah in the laments.[q] These became a tradition in Israel and are written in the Laments.[r]

26 The other events of Josiah's reign and his acts of devotion, according to what is written in the Law of the LORD— 27 all the events, from beginning to end, are written in the book of the kings of Israel and Judah. 1 And the people[s] of the land took Jehoahaz son of Josiah and made him king in Jerusalem in place of his father.

Chapter 36

Jehoahaz King of Judah

36:2–4pp — 2Ki 23:31–34

2 JEHOAHAZ[i] was twenty-three years old when he became king, and he

[i]2 Hebrew *Joahaz*, a variant of *Jehoahaz*; also in verse 4

35:8 [c]S 1Ch 6:13
35:9 [d]2Ch 31:12 [e]2Ch 31:13
35:10 [f]S ver 4 [g]2Ch 30:16
35:11 [h]S 2Ch 30:17
35:13 [i]Ex 12:2-11
35:14 [j]S Ex 29:13
35:15 [k]S 1Ch 25:1; S 26:12-19; 2Ch 29:30; Ne 12:46; Ps 68:25
35:20 [l]Isa 10:9; Jer 46:2 [m]S Ge 2:14
35:21 [n]S 1Ki 13:18; S 2Ki 18:25
35:22 [o]S 1Sa 28:8
35:23 [p]S 1Ki 22:34
35:25 [q]S Ge 50:10; Jer 22:10,15-16 [r]2Ch 34:28
36:1 [s]S 2Ch 22:1

35:13 GOD, Holy—The offerings were considered holy because they were being offered to God. His holiness carries over to things or persons associated with Him. See notes on Ex 3:5–6; 19:10–24; Lev 11:44–45.

35:16–18 PRAYER, Worship—This Passover, unlike Hezekiah's, was characterized both by legal correctness and sincerity of heart. See note on 30:18–27.

35:20–24 SIN, Rebellion—Even the righteous are susceptible to grave moral errors. Though Josiah had followed God's will in reform, he rebelled against the word God delivered through King Neco. Because of this rebellion he was killed in battle on the plain of Meggido. Our rebellion against God's Word can bring dire consequences. We must be ready to hear God's Word from unexpected sources. See note on 2 Ki 24:1–4.

35:25 HISTORY, God's Leaders—Fallen faithful leaders should not be forgotten. Lament over their death helps God's people learn the needed lessons of history.

reigned in Jerusalem three months. 3The
king of Egypt dethroned him in Jerusalem
and imposed on Judah a levy of a hundred
talents[j] of silver and a talent[k] of gold. 4The
king of Egypt made Eliakim, a brother of
Jehoahaz, king over Judah and Jerusalem
and changed Eliakim's name to Jehoiakim.
But Neco[t] took Eliakim's brother Jehoahaz
and carried him off to Egypt.[u]

Jehoiakim King of Judah

36:5–8pp — 2Ki 23:36–24:6

5Jehoiakim[v] was twenty-five years old
when he became king, and he reigned in
Jerusalem eleven years. He did evil in the
eyes of the LORD his God. 6Nebuchadnez-
zar[w] king of Babylon attacked him and
bound him with bronze shackles to take
him to Babylon.[x] 7Nebuchadnezzar also
took to Babylon articles from the temple
of the LORD and put them in his temple[l]
there.[y]
8The other events of Jehoiakim's reign,
the detestable things he did and all that
was found against him, are written in the
book of the kings of Israel and Judah. And
Jehoiachin his son succeeded him as
king.

Jehoiachin King of Judah

36:9–10pp — 2Ki 24:8–17

9Jehoiachin[z] was eighteen[m] years old
when he became king, and he reigned in
Jerusalem three months and ten days. He
did evil in the eyes of the LORD. 10In the
spring, King Nebuchadnezzar sent for
him and brought him to Babylon,[a] together with articles of value from the
temple of the LORD, and he made Jehoiachin's uncle,[n] Zedekiah, king over Judah
and Jerusalem.

Zedekiah King of Judah

36:11–16pp — 2Ki 24:18–20; Jer 52:1–3

11Zedekiah[b] was twenty-one years old
when he became king, and he reigned in
Jerusalem eleven years. 12He did evil in
the eyes of the LORD[c] his God and did
not humble[d] himself before Jeremiah the
prophet, who spoke the word of the
LORD. 13He also rebelled against King
Nebuchadnezzar, who had made him
take an oath[e] in God's name. He became
stiff-necked[f] and hardened his heart and
would not turn to the LORD, the God of
Israel. 14Furthermore, all the leaders of
the priests and the people became more
and more unfaithful,[g] following all the
detestable practices of the nations and defiling the temple of the LORD, which he
had consecrated in Jerusalem.

The Fall of Jerusalem

36:17–20pp — 2Ki 25:1–21; Jer 52:4–27
36:22–23pp — Ezr 1:1–3

15The LORD, the God of their fathers,
sent word to them through his messengers[h] again and again,[i] because he had
pity on his people and on his dwelling
place. 16But they mocked God's messengers, despised his words and scoffed[j] at
his prophets until the wrath[k] of the LORD
was aroused against his people and there
was no remedy.[l] 17He brought up against
them the king of the Babylonians,[o][m] who
killed their young men with the sword in
the sanctuary, and spared neither young
man[n] nor young woman, old man or
aged.[o] God handed all of them over to
Nebuchadnezzar.[p] 18He carried to Babylon all the articles[q] from the temple of
God, both large and small, and the treasures of the LORD's temple and the treasures of the king and his officials. 19They
set fire[r] to God's temple[s] and broke
down the wall[t] of Jerusalem; they
burned all the palaces and destroyed[u] everything of value there.[v]

[j]3 That is, about 3 3/4 tons (about 3.4 metric tons) [k]3 That is, about 75 pounds (about 34 kilograms) [l]7 Or *palace* [m]9 One Hebrew manuscript, some Septuagint manuscripts and Syriac (see also 2 Kings 24:8); most Hebrew manuscripts *eight* [n]10 Hebrew *brother,* that is, relative (see 2 Kings 24:17) [o]17 Or *Chaldeans*

36:4 [t]Jer 22:10-12 [u]Eze 19:4
36:5 [v]Jer 22:18; 25:1; 26:1; 35:1; 36:1; 45:1; 46:2
36:6 [w]Jer 25:9; 27:6; Eze 29:18 [x]Eze 19:9; Da 1:1
36:7 [y]ver 18; Ezr 1:7; Jer 27:16; Da 1:2
36:9 [z]Jer 22:24-28; 24:1; 27:20; 29:21; 52:31
36:10 [a]ver 18; S 2Ki 20:17; Ezr 1:7; Isa 52:11; Jer 14:18; 21:7; 22:25; 24:1; 27:16, 20,22; 29:1; 34:21; 40:1; Eze 17:12; Da 5:2
36:11 [b]S 2Ki 24:17; Jer 27:1; 28:1; 34:2; 37:1; 39:1
36:12 [c]Jer 37:1-39:18 [d]S Dt 8:3; 2Ch 7:14; Jer 44:10
36:13 [e]Eze 17:13 [f]S Ex 32:9; S Dt 9:27
36:14 [g]S 1Ch 5:25
36:15 [h]Isa 5:4; 44:26; Jer 7:25; Hag 1:13; Zec 1:4; Mal 2:7; 3:1; S Mt 5:12 [i]Jer 7:13, 25; 11:7; 25:3-4; 35:14,15; 44:4-6
36:16 [j]S 2Ki 2:23; Job 8:2; Isa 28:14, 22; 29:20; 57:4; Jer 5:13; 43:2; Mic 2:11 [k]Ezr 5:12; Pr 1:30-31; Jer 44:3 [l]Ne 9:30; Pr 29:1; Jer 7:26; 20:8; 25:4; 30:12; Da 9:6; Zec 1:2
36:17 [m]S Ge 10:10 [n]Jer 6:11; 9:21; 18:21; 44:7 [o]S Dt 32:25; Jer 51:22 [p]Ezr 5:12; Jer 32:28; La 2:21; Eze 9:6; 23:47
36:18 [q]S ver 7; S ver 10; Jer 27:20
36:19 [r]Jer 11:16; 17:27; 21:10,14; 22:7; 32:29; 39:8; La 4:11; Eze 20:47; Am 2:5; Zec 11:1 [s]1Ki 9:8-9 [t]S 2Ki 14:13 [u]La 2:6 [v]Ps 79:1-3

36:5 SIN, Transgression—See notes on 1 Ki 14:22–24; 2 Ki 23:37; 24:1–4.

36:9 SIN, Transgression—See note on 1 Ki 14:22–24.

36:11–21 HISTORY, Judgment—In grace God calls His people to repent and be faithful. Eventually He exercises His wrath to bring historical judgment. Ignoring or mocking God's Word invites God's wrath.

36:12–14 SIN, Transgression—A leader's unfaithfulness can be compounded and exceeded by followers. Sin produces more of its kind. Sin explicitly carried out in the face of God's Word leads inevitably to downfall. Only a proud, stubborn heart can resist God's Word. See note on 1 Ki 14:22–24.

36:15 GOD, Grace—God is gracious because He is basically a God of love. He repeatedly warns His people and seeks to lead them back to Himself and His ways before exercising His judging wrath.

36:15–21 EVIL AND SUFFERING, Punishment—Political power based on opposition to God's Word cannot stand. Judah in 587 BC, as Israel in 522, fell to a wicked power as part of God's judgment on their rejection of His way of life. God was willing to let His people suffer the loss of all power and international visibility if they would not be His obedient people. See note on 2 Ki 17:7–23.

36:16 GOD, Wrath—God's wrath is the inevitable result of people's determined refusal to do the will of God when God has continually revealed His love and grace. Notice the contrast with the preceding verse. See notes on Ge 6:5–8; 17:14; 19:13,24–26.

36:16 SIN, Depravity—See notes on 30:7–12; 2 Ki 25:1–21.

36:17–23 GOD, Sovereignty—God can work in the world according to His will and carry out His purposes. He does not manipulate human beings; He works through them as He respects their individual freedom and responsibility. He uses even people who neither know nor acknowledge Him to work out His purposes for His people. See notes on Ge 15:13–16; 18:14; 24:3,7,50.

20He carried into exile[w] to Babylon the
remnant, who escaped from the sword,
and they became servants[x] to him and
his sons until the kingdom of Persia came
to power. 21The land enjoyed its sabbath
rests;[y] all the time of its desolation it
rested,[z] until the seventy years[a] were
completed in fulfillment of the word of
the LORD spoken by Jeremiah.
22In the first year of Cyrus[b] king of
Persia, in order to fulfill the word of the
LORD spoken by Jeremiah, the LORD
moved the heart of Cyrus king of Persia to
make a proclamation throughout his
realm and to put it in writing:
23"This is what Cyrus king of Persia
says:

"'The LORD, the God of heaven, has given me all the kingdoms of the earth and he has appointed[c] me to build a temple for him at Jerusalem in Judah. Anyone of his people among you—may the LORD his God be with him, and let him go up.'"

36:20 [w]S Lev 26:44; S 2Ki 24:14; Ezr 2:1; Ne 7:6 [x]Jer 27:7
36:21 [y]S Lev 25:4 [z]S 1Ch 22:9 [a]Jer 1:1; 25:11; 27:22; 29:10; 40:1; Da 9:2; Zec 1:12; 7:5
36:22 [b]Isa 44:28; 45:1,13; Da 1:21; 6:28; 10:1
36:23 [c]S Jdg 4:10

36:21–23 GOD, Faithfulness—Although God sent His people into captivity because they had forgotten Him, God had not forgotten His people, promises, or purposes. What He promised through His prophets, He brought to pass in history.
36:21–23 HISTORY, Promise—Promise not judgment is the dominant theme of God's history. He works faithfully even through judgment to fulfill His promises and establish a people for Himself.
36:22–23 ELECTION, Other Nations—Just as God elected Cyrus, King of Persia, to fulfill His word, spoken many years ago by Jeremiah (25:1–14; 51:1–14; Isa 41:2,25; 44:28; 45:1), so God selects those of any race or religion to accomplish the lofty goals of His purpose. Election does not restrict God from using any person or people to do His will.
36:22–23 HOLY SCRIPTURE, God's Initiative—Holy Scripture resulted from God's direction of His inspired speakers and writers. He gave Jeremiah words to describe His direction of history a generation later. He mysteriously worked in the heart of a pagan king to fulfill prophecy and to produce a written proclamation which became a part of written Scripture. Both the historical acts Scripture describes and the spoken and written words Scripture records came at God's initiative as He mysteriously worked within the free will of human agents, some dedicated to Him as was Jeremiah and others dedicated to other gods as was Cyrus. See note on Ezr 1:1.

Ezra

Theological Setting

God's people faced threats from two directions. Temptations to empty formalism and meaningless legalism threatened their worship life. Just plain disinterest and indifference nagged them constantly. The world's moral or immoral values threatened to replace God's standards. Racially and religiously mixed marriages were commonplace, described as "unfaithfulness" to God (Ezr 9:2). Both threats gnawed at the faith of the returning Jews. Their relation to God became as weak as water.

Ezra and Nehemiah preserve three major stories that illustrate and relate to these threats to God's people. They were written to counteract the threats and to strengthen the faith of a hopeless people. The first story is of rebuilding the Temple, which demonstrated the supreme importance of worship. Next is the account of a renewed emphasis on God's law by Ezra, which underscored the absolute necessity for rules and regulations if worship and life before God were to be acceptable. The third major story is of Nehemiah's restoring the walls of Jerusalem and of his reforms. These reforms magnified the need for a genuine concern for reputation, for public image. What can the world think of God's people with delapidated city walls? What would distinguish God's people who were guilty of intermarriage with those not in proper covenant relation with the one true God? Nehemiah's drastic actions reminded his people and us that it does matter what others think of us and our faith.

Thus Ezra and Nehemiah are a profound encouragement to God's people to magnify worship as supremely important, to emphasize the need for and use of God's Word as the only authoritative rule for living, and to be concerned about the image God's people give the world.

Theological Outline

Ezra: God's Worship, Word, Work, and Way

I. God's Worship Must Be Restored. (1:1—6:22)
   - A. God can use a pagan "to fulfill the word of the Lord." (1:1-4)
   - B. God's people respond to God's ways. (1:5-6)
   - C. God will recover and reclaim His possessions. (1:7-11)
   - D. God's people, by name and as individuals, are important. (2:1-67)
   - E. God's people are generous givers for a good cause. (2:68-70)
   - F. God's people worship, regardless of the circumstances. (3:1-6)
   - G. God's people will give and organize to get a job done. (3:7-9)
   - H. God's people praise Him in success or in disappointment. (3:10-13)
   - I. God's people must reject some offers of help. (4:1-3)
   - J. God's work can be opposed and stopped. (4:4-24)
   - K. God's work and workers must be encouraged. (5:1-2)
   - L. God's work and workers are in His watchcare. (5:3-5)
   - M. God's work may get pagan authorization and support. (5:6—6:12)
   - N. God's work must ultimately be completed. (6:13-15)
   - O. God's work must be dedicated publicly with joyful celebration. (6:16-22)

II. God's Word Must Be Followed. (7:1—10:44)
   - A. God's Word needs skilled teachers and helpers. (7:1-7)
   - B. God's Word elicits commitment. (7:8-10)
   - C. God's work accepts all the help it can get from many different sources. (7:11-26)
   - D. God blesses His workers and expects to be praised. (7:27-28)
   - E. God's work warrants good records. (8:1-14)
   - F. God's work must enlist trained workers. (8:15-20)
   - G. God's work calls for faith, prayer, and humility. (8:21-23)
   - H. God's work warrants division of responsibility. (8:24-30)

I. God's work necessitates good stewardship and generous sacrifice. (8:31-36)
J. Gross violations of God's Word must be acknowledged. (9:1-5)
K. Acknowledged sin leads to prayer and confession with deep theological insights. (9:6-15)
L. God's grace and human confession call for active commitment. (10:1-4)
M. God's people must act unitedly. (10:5-9)
N. God's call for the separated life must be made clear by God's leaders to God's people. (10:10-11)
O. God's way utilizes practical solutions for difficult problems. (10:12-17)
P. God's way expects "fruit in keeping with repentance" (Mt 3:8) from all who are guilty. (Ezr 10:18-44)

Theological Conclusions

Ezra and Nehemiah are historical books. They contain the last century of Israel's history that the Bible records. Ezra begins with the first group of Jews to return from Exile, 538 BC; Nehemiah concludes with the last group, 432 BC. This history centers on the books' three main characters: Zerubbabel, Ezra, and Nehemiah.

The two books will be treated as one for two main reasons. They were one in the ancient Hebrew and Greek Old Testament. Also, each is necessary to complete the other. Ezra's story is climaxed in Nehemiah (chs 8—10), and part of Nehemiah's story is in Ezra (4:6-23).

Not only are the books Ezra and Nehemiah historical, they are theological. They teach eloquently of God. Thirteen times He is described as "the God of heaven" (9 in Ezr, 4 in Ne), and the same number of times as "the God of Israel," but only in Ezra. Fifty-one times He is referred to as "our God" or "my God" (23 in Ezr, 28 in Ne). His proper name, Yahweh, is found fifty-three times (37 in Ezra, 16 in Nehemiah). Strangely, God is called Lord (Adonai, Master) only four times, exclusively in Nehemiah.

Theological themes abound. God's house gets much attention with at least sixty-four references (44 in Ezr, 20 in Ne). God's law is referred to directly no less than twenty-seven times (8 in Ezr, 19 in Ne), along with references to His commands, ordinances, regulations, decrees, and warnings. Worship of God is woven throughout both books. Much is said about the Temple, the Levites, sacrifices, prayer, music, feasts, and confessions.

These books inform us on these essential doctrines:

1. God's Word is trustworthy and essential for faith.
2. Worship is necessary for God's people.
3. God's disciples obey Him.
4. God gives His people leaders.
5. Opponents hinder God's work.
6. Prayer is our response to God's presence.
7. God is sovereign.

God's Word is important and essential. It must be greatly emphasized. It must be studied and heeded as the only authoritative rule for living. Ezra and Nehemiah make it transparently clear how important and essential God's truth is for God's people.

Scripture is to be trusted. Ezra and Nehemiah were written to "fulfill the word of the LORD" (1:1). God's words spoken by Jeremiah were literally fulfilled, as recorded in these two books. God's Temple was rebuilt, God's law was taught, and God's city was restored and repopulated, as predicted.

God is universally sovereign. He is not limited. He can use a Cyrus, polytheistic king of Persia, to make possible His people's release from captivity and return to their fatherland. He can use an Artaxerxes, another Persian king, to authorize and finance the trip of an Ezra to teach God's people God's law. This same king also helped Nehemiah restore some measure of respectability to God's holy city.

Worship of God is absolutely necessary. It is so necessary that the worship center simply must be built. Enthusiasm for restoring the worship center had died quickly. God raised up a Haggai and a Zechariah to encourage His people back on course to complete the worship center. Nothing must supersede worship of God by His people.

Obedience to God is not optional. It is obligatory. This sometimes comes at a very high price. God said His people should not marry those who are not His people. When they did, they had to pay a painful price to correct the problem. Spouses and offspring who were not the people of God were to be sent away. God's people must strive for godly uniqueness sometimes at a very high cost.

Hard work is necessary for obedience and worship. Resurrecting the worship center was no easy job. Though expensive and difficult, it had to be done. Rebuilding Jerusalem's walls was a demanding and exhausting task. It too had to be done.

Leadership is God's plan. He raises up leaders. Some of God's chosen leaders are unpopular and opposed at every hand. But God raised up a Zerubbabel; He chose an Ezra; and He used a Nehemiah. Important to notice is that only Ezra was a religious leader; Zerubbabel and Nehemiah were laymen.

Opposition is real. It must be expected and prepared for. Zerubbabel and Nehemiah were confronted with damaging opposition. But God's assigned tasks had to be done. Both stood their ground in their confidence in God. Opposition to God's people doing God's work cannot be a reason for God's people not doing God's work. When the Jews were opposed in building the worship center, "the eye of their God was watching over the elders of the Jews, and they were not stopped" (5:5).

Encouragement is always in order. Opposition causes discouragement; encouragement is needed. God raises up encouragers like Haggai and Zechariah. When the work on the worship center came to a halt, Haggai and Zechariah showed up on the scene. And God's people "continued to build and prosper under the preaching of Haggai the prophet and Zechariah" (6:14).

Godly uniqueness should characterize God's people. Intimate relations with those who are not God's people undermines godly character. Correcting worldly entanglements can be sad and very expensive. The Jews' sending away their spouses and children must be understood in the right context. They "separated themselves from the unclean practices of their Gentile neighbors in order to seek the Lord, the God of Israel" and "the LORD had filled them with joy" (6:21,22).

God is imminent. God is with us. He is intimately involved in our lives. Ezra and Nehemiah portray this in a very graphic sense. Ezra did the impossible, "for the hand of the LORD his God was on him" (Ezr 7:6; see 7:9,28; 8:18,22,31). Nehemiah got the unexpected "because the gracious hand of my God was upon me" (Ne 2:8; see 1:10; 2:18).

Prayer is fundamental and indispensable. Both books magnify this concept. Both men prayed. See Ezra's brief prayer (Ezr 7:27-28) and his long prayer (9:6-15). Nehemiah prayed a long prayer (1:5-11); he prayed a short one. He breathed a quick prayer in conversation with his boss, King Artaxerxes: "Then I prayed to the God of heaven, and I answered the king" (2:4-5).

Confession and covenant making are basic to the godly life. Ezra and Nehemiah teach much about the need and the how of confession and covenanting. Both practices indicate seriousness of intention and validate faith.

Contemporary Teaching

Ezra and Nehemiah are rich with lessons relevant to today's society. Ezra and Nehemiah are a real challenge for us: (1) to magnify the preeminent importance and supreme necessity of worship of God, of prayer to God, and of the Word of God, like the central theme in these two books; (2) to make some changes, to pull up stakes and move for God, like the Jews leaving Exile to return home; (3) to worship and live according to God's way and God's Word, regardless of the circumstances, like the Jews when opposed by Sanballat; (4) to be a separate, distinctive people for God, and yet avoid racism, isolationism, separatism, like the Jews in relation to the Samaritans; (5) to be willing to work hard, determined to complete jobs (or buildings) begun for God, like building the Temple and city walls; (6) to ensure God's Word is taught by skilled, trained teachers, like Ezra; (7) to be willing to confess our sins, openly at times, and to pay the price to make corrections, like the Jews in sending away their non-Jewish families; (8) to make God's Word and God's way the determining factors when dealing with sticky social, ethical issues, like Nehemiah dealing with sabbath breakers; and (9) to pray and work for some good, old-fashioned revivals, like Ezra's great revival.

Chapter 1

Cyrus Helps the Exiles to Return

1:1–3pp — 2Ch 36:22–23

IN the first year of Cyrus king of Persia,
in order to fulfill the word of the LORD
spoken by Jeremiah,[a] the LORD moved
the heart[b] of Cyrus king of Persia to
make a proclamation throughout his
realm and to put it in writing:

2"This is what Cyrus king of Persia
says:

" 'The LORD, the God of heaven,
has given me all the kingdoms of the
earth and he has appointed[c] me to
build[d] a temple for him at Jerusalem
in Judah. 3Anyone of his people
among you—may his God be with
him, and let him go up to Jerusalem
in Judah and build the temple of the
LORD, the God of Israel, the God who
is in Jerusalem. 4And the people of
any place where survivors[e] may now
be living are to provide him with silver and gold,[f] with goods and livestock, and with freewill offerings[g]
for the temple of God[h] in Jerusalem.' "[i]

5Then the family heads of Judah and
Benjamin,[j] and the priests and Levites
—everyone whose heart God had
moved[k]—prepared to go up and build
the house[l] of the LORD in Jerusalem. 6All
their neighbors assisted them with articles of silver and gold,[m] with goods and
livestock, and with valuable gifts, in addition to all the freewill offerings. 7More-
over, King Cyrus brought out the articles
belonging to the temple of the LORD,
which Nebuchadnezzar had carried away
from Jerusalem and had placed in the
temple of his god.[a][n] 8Cyrus king of Persia had them brought by Mithredath the
treasurer, who counted them out to
Sheshbazzar[o] the prince of Judah.
9This was the inventory:

gold dishes	30
silver dishes	1,000
silver pans[b]	29
10gold bowls	30
matching silver bowls	410
other articles	1,000

11In all, there were 5,400 articles of
gold and of silver. Sheshbazzar brought
all these along when the exiles came up
from Babylon to Jerusalem.

1:1 [a]Jer 25:11-12; 29:10-14; Zec 1:12-16 [b]Ezr 6:22; 7:27
1:2 [c]S Jdg 4:10; Ps 72:11; Isa 41:2, 25; 44:28; 45:13; 46:11; 49:7,23; 60:3,10 [d]Hag 1:2
1:4 [e]Isa 10:20-22 [f]S Ex 3:22 [g]Nu 15:3; Ps 50:14; 54:6; 116:17 [h]Ps 72:8-11; Rev 21:24 [i]Ezr 3:7; 4:3; 5:13; 6:3,14
1:5 [j]2Ch 11:1,3,10, 12,23; 15:2,8-9; 25:5; 31:1; 34:9; Ezr 4:1; 10:9; Ne 11:4; 12:34 [k]ver 1; Ex 35:20-22; 2Ch 36:22; Hag 1:14; S Php 2:13 [l]Ps 127:1
1:6 [m]S Ex 3:22
1:7 [n]S 2Ki 24:13; S 2Ch 36:7,10; Ezr 5:14; 6:5; Jer 52:17-19
1:8 [o]S 1Ch 3:18
2:1 [p]S 2Ch 36:20 [q]S 2Ki 24:16; 25:12 [r]ver 70; 1Ch 9:2; Ne 7:73; 11:3
2:2 [s]S 1Ch 3:19; Mt 1:12; Lk 3:27 [t]Ezr 3:2; 5:2; 10:18; Ne 12:1,8; Hag 1:1,12; 2:4; Zec 3:1-10; 6:9-15 [u]1Ch 6:14; Ne 10:2; 11:11; 12:1
2:3 [v]Ezr 8:3; 10:25; Ne 3:25

Chapter 2

The List of the Exiles Who Returned

2:1–70pp — Ne 7:6–73

NOW these are the people of the province who came up from the captivity
of the exiles,[p] whom Nebuchadnezzar
king of Babylon[q] had taken captive to
Babylon (they returned to Jerusalem and
Judah, each to his own town,[r] 2in company with Zerubbabel,[s] Jeshua,[t] Nehemiah, Seraiah,[u] Reelaiah, Mordecai, Bilshan, Mispar, Bigvai, Rehum and Baanah):

The list of the men of the people of
Israel:

3the descendants of Parosh[v]	2,172
4of Shephatiah	372
5of Arah	775
6of Pahath-Moab (through the line of Jeshua and Joab)	2,812
7of Elam	1,254
8of Zattu	945
9of Zaccai	760
10of Bani	642
11of Bebai	623

[a] *7* Or *gods* [b] *9* The meaning of the Hebrew for this word is uncertain.

1:1 GOD, Faithfulness—See note on 2 Ch 36:21–23.

1:1 HOLY SCRIPTURE, Writing—God searched His people out, having never forgotten their plight in Exile, and worked in the heart and attitude of a foreign ruler to realize His purposes for His people. Cyrus' edict released the Israelite children who felt God's Spirit leading them to return to their Promised Land and rebuild. The edict fulfilled Jeremiah's prophecy (25:11–12; 29:10), though certainly Cyrus did not issue it for that reason. The edict also became part of the inspired Scriptures, again independently of Cyrus' plans. God inspired His written Word in mysterious ways. The passage in 1:1–3 repeats almost word for word 2 Ch 36:22–23. Apparently, one author intentionally copied the end of a previous work to show the continuity and continuation of God's work with His people. See note on 2 Sa 22:1–51.

1:1 HISTORY, Universal—God's history has never been limited to one nation. He controls the world's destiny and can lead any ruler, even an unbelieving one, to accomplish His will.

1:2 ELECTION, Other Nations—God uses foreign leaders and nations to accomplish His intentions for His chosen ones. See note on 2 Ch 36:22–23.

1:4 STEWARDSHIP, House of God—Reclaiming and rebuilding the homeland as Israel returned from exile involved the spiritual duty of rebuilding the house of God. Special offerings from all members of the people of God were needed for the project. Special projects demand special sacrifices in giving. See note on Ex 25:1–8.

1:4 THE CHURCH, Remnant—God's people are not limited to one geographical location. In rebuilding after the Exile, Israel learned that people of God could live in many places—Egypt, Assyria, Babylon, Persia. Wherever they lived, God's survivors formed a remnant called on to support the rebuilding efforts in Jerusalem. Geographical distance should not hinder the cooperation of God's people to do His work. See note on 2 Ch 34:9.

1:5–11 HISTORY, Worship—Through the long years of judgment God preserved the Temple articles and prepared for the reestablishment of His worship.

2:1–70 HISTORY, Deliverance—God's deliverance from exile renewed the history of His people. They preserved family, geographical, and occupational traditions of God's people. In delivering His people God preserves historical continuity with His previous acts of deliverance.

[12]of Azgad 1,222
[13]of Adonikam[w] 666
[14]of Bigvai 2,056
[15]of Adin 454
[16]of Ater (through Hezekiah) 98
[17]of Bezai 323
[18]of Jorah 112
[19]of Hashum 223
[20]of Gibbar 95

[21]the men of Bethlehem[x] 123
[22]of Netophah 56
[23]of Anathoth 128
[24]of Azmaveth 42
[25]of Kiriath Jearim,[c] Kephirah and Beeroth 743
[26]of Ramah[y] and Geba 621
[27]of Micmash 122
[28]of Bethel and Ai[z] 223
[29]of Nebo 52
[30]of Magbish 156
[31]of the other Elam 1,254
[32]of Harim 320
[33]of Lod, Hadid and Ono 725
[34]of Jericho[a] 345
[35]of Senaah 3,630

[36]The priests:

the descendants of Jedaiah[b] (through the family of Jeshua) 973
[37]of Immer[c] 1,052
[38]of Pashhur[d] 1,247
[39]of Harim[e] 1,017

[40]The Levites:[f]

the descendants of Jeshua[g] and Kadmiel (through the line of Hodaviah) 74

[41]The singers:[h]

the descendants of Asaph 128

[42]The gatekeepers[i] of the temple:

the descendants of
Shallum, Ater, Talmon,
Akkub, Hatita and Shobai 139

[43]The temple servants:[j]

the descendants of
Ziha, Hasupha, Tabbaoth,
[44]Keros, Siaha, Padon,
[45]Lebanah, Hagabah, Akkub,
[46]Hagab, Shalmai, Hanan,
[47]Giddel, Gahar, Reaiah,
[48]Rezin, Nekoda, Gazzam,
[49]Uzza, Paseah, Besai,
[50]Asnah, Meunim, Nephussim,
[51]Bakbuk, Hakupha, Harhur,
[52]Bazluth, Mehida, Harsha,
[53]Barkos, Sisera, Temah,

2:13 [w]Ezr 8:13
2:21 [x]Mic 5:2
2:26 [y]S Jos 18:25
2:28 [z]S Ge 12:8
2:34 [a]1Ki 16:34; 2Ch 28:15
2:36 [b]S 1Ch 24:7
2:37 [c]S 1Ch 24:14
2:38 [d]S 1Ch 9:12
2:39 [e]S 1Ch 24:8
2:40 [f]Ge 29:34; Nu 3:9; Dt 18:6-7; 1Ch 16:4; Ezr 7:7; 8:15; Ne 12:24 [g]Ezr 3:9
2:41 [h]S 1Ch 15:16
2:42 [i]1Sa 3:15; S 1Ch 9:17
2:43 [j]S 1Ch 9:2; Ne 11:21
2:58 [k]S 1Ch 9:2
2:59 [l]S Nu 1:18
2:61 [m]S 2Sa 17:27
2:62 [n]Nu 3:10; 16:39-40
2:63 [o]Lev 2:3,10 [p]S Ex 28:30
2:65 [q]S 2Sa 19:35
2:66 [r]Isa 66:20
2:68 [s]S Ex 25:2

[54]Neziah and Hatipha

[55]The descendants of the servants of Solomon:

the descendants of
Sotai, Hassophereth, Peruda,
[56]Jaala, Darkon, Giddel,
[57]Shephatiah, Hattil,
Pokereth-Hazzebaim and Ami

[58]The temple servants[k] and the descendants of the servants of Solomon 392

[59]The following came up from the
towns of Tel Melah, Tel Harsha, Kerub, Addon and Immer, but they
could not show that their families
were descended[l] from Israel:

[60]The descendants of
Delaiah, Tobiah and Nekoda 652

[61]And from among the priests:

The descendants of
Hobaiah, Hakkoz and Barzillai (a man who had married a daughter of Barzillai the Gileadite[m] and was called by that name).

[62]These searched for their family
records, but they could not find them
and so were excluded from the
priesthood[n] as unclean. [63]The governor ordered them not to eat any of
the most sacred food[o] until there
was a priest ministering with the
Urim and Thummim.[p]

[64]The whole company numbered
42,360, [65]besides their 7,337 menservants and maidservants; and they
also had 200 men and women singers.[q] [66]They had 736 horses,[r] 245
mules, [67]435 camels and 6,720 donkeys.

[68]When they arrived at the house of
the LORD in Jerusalem, some of the heads
of the families[s] gave freewill offerings toward the rebuilding of the house of God
on its site. [69]According to their ability
they gave to the treasury for this work
61,000 drachmas[d] of gold, 5,000 minas[e] of silver and 100 priestly garments.
[70]The priests, the Levites, the singers,
the gatekeepers and the temple servants
settled in their own towns, along with

[c] *25* See Septuagint (see also Neh. 7:29); Hebrew *Kiriath Arim.* [d] *69* That is, about 1,100 pounds (about 500 kilograms) [e] *69* That is, about 3 tons (about 2.9 metric tons)

2:68–69 STEWARDSHIP, House of God—See note on 1:4.
2:68–69 PRAYER, Worship—God had given them their freedom; they freely gave to God. Joyful giving expresses gratitude to God and forms an integral part of worship.

some of the other people, and the rest of
the Israelites settled in their towns.[t]

Chapter 3

Rebuilding the Altar

WHEN the seventh month came and
the Israelites had settled in their
towns,[u] the people assembled[v] as one
man in Jerusalem. 2Then Jeshua[w] son of
Jozadak[x] and his fellow priests and Zerubbabel son of Shealtiel[y] and his associates began to build the altar of the God of
Israel to sacrifice burnt offerings on it, in
accordance with what is written in the
Law of Moses[z] the man of God. 3Despite
their fear[a] of the peoples around them,
they built the altar on its foundation and
sacrificed burnt offerings on it to the
LORD, both the morning and evening sacrifices.[b] 4Then in accordance with what
is written, they celebrated the Feast of
Tabernacles[c] with the required number
of burnt offerings prescribed for each day.
5After that, they presented the regular
burnt offerings, the New Moon[d] sacrifices and the sacrifices for all the appointed sacred feasts of the LORD,[e] as well as
those brought as freewill offerings to the
LORD. 6On the first day of the seventh
month they began to offer burnt offerings
to the LORD, though the foundation of the
LORD's temple had not yet been laid.

Rebuilding the Temple

7Then they gave money to the masons
and carpenters,[f] and gave food and drink
and oil to the people of Sidon and Tyre, so
that they would bring cedar logs[g] by sea
from Lebanon[h] to Joppa, as authorized by
Cyrus[i] king of Persia.
8In the second month[j] of the second
year after their arrival at the house of God
in Jerusalem, Zerubbabel[k] son of Shealtiel, Jeshua son of Jozadak and the rest of
their brothers (the priests and the Levites
and all who had returned from the captivity to Jerusalem) began the work, appointing Levites twenty[l] years of age and older to supervise the building of the house
of the LORD. 9Jeshua[m] and his sons and
brothers and Kadmiel and his sons (descendants of Hodaviah[f]) and the sons of
Henadad and their sons and brothers—all
Levites—joined together in supervising
those working on the house of God.
10When the builders laid[n] the foundation of the temple of the LORD, the priests
in their vestments and with trumpets,[o]
and the Levites (the sons of Asaph) with
cymbals, took their places to praise[p] the
LORD, as prescribed by David[q] king of Israel.[r] 11With praise and thanksgiving
they sang to the LORD:

"He is good;
his love to Israel endures forever."[s]

And all the people gave a great shout[t] of
praise to the LORD, because the foundation[u] of the house of the LORD was laid.
12But many of the older priests and Levites and family heads, who had seen the
former temple,[v] wept[w] aloud when they
saw the foundation of this temple being
laid, while many others shouted for joy.
13No one could distinguish the sound of
the shouts of joy[x] from the sound of
weeping, because the people made so
much noise. And the sound was heard far
away.

Chapter 4

Opposition to the Rebuilding

WHEN the enemies of Judah and Benjamin heard that the exiles were
building[y] a temple for the LORD, the God
of Israel, 2they came to Zerubbabel and to
the heads of the families and said, "Let us
help you build because, like you, we seek
your God and have been sacrificing to
him since the time of Esarhaddon[z] king
of Assyria, who brought us here."[a]
3But Zerubbabel, Jeshua and the rest of
the heads of the families of Israel answered, "You have no part with us in
building a temple to our God. We alone
will build it for the LORD, the God of Israel, as King Cyrus, the king of Persia, commanded us."[b]
4Then the peoples around them set out
to discourage the people of Judah and
make them afraid to go on building.[g] [c]
5They hired counselors to work against
them and frustrate their plans during the
entire reign of Cyrus king of Persia and
down to the reign of Darius king of Persia.

Later Opposition Under Xerxes and Artaxerxes

6At the beginning of the reign of Xer-

2:70 [t]S ver 1; S 1Ch 9:2; Ne 11:3-4
3:1 [u]Ne 7:73 [v]S Lev 23:24
3:2 [w]S Ezr 2:2 [x]Hag 1:1; Zec 6:11 [y]1Ch 3:17 [z]S Ex 20:24; Dt 12:5-6
3:3 [a]Ezr 4:4; Da 9:25 [b]S Ex 29:39; Nu 28:1-8
3:4 [c]S Ex 23:16; Nu 29:12-38; Ne 8:14-18; Zec 14:16-19
3:5 [d]S Nu 28:3,11, 14; Col 2:16 [e]Lev 23:1-44; S Nu 29:39
3:7 [f]1Ch 22:15 [g]S 1Ch 14:1 [h]Isa 35:2; 60:13 [i]S Ezr 1:2-4
3:8 [j]1Ki 6:1 [k]Zec 4:9 [l]S Nu 4:3
3:9 [m]Ezr 2:40
3:10 [n]Ezr 5:16; 6:3; Hag 2:15 [o]S Nu 10:2; S 2Sa 6:5; 1Ch 16:6; 2Ch 5:13; Ne 12:35 [p]S 1Ch 25:1 [q]S 1Ch 6:31 [r]Zec 6:12
3:11 [s]1Ch 16:34, 41; S 2Ch 7:3; Ps 30:5; 107:1; 118:1; 138:8 [t]S Jos 6:5,10 [u]Hag 2:18; Zec 4:9; 8:9
3:12 [v]Hag 2:3,9 [w]Jer 31:9; 50:4
3:13 [x]Job 8:21; 33:26; Ps 27:6; 42:4; Isa 16:9; Jer 48:33
4:1 [y]Ne 2:20
4:2 [z]S 2Ki 17:24 [a]S 2Ki 17:41
4:3 [b]Ezr 1:1-4
4:4 [c]S Ezr 3:3

[f]9 Hebrew *Yehudah,* probably a variant of *Hodaviah*
[g]4 Or *and troubled them as they built*

3:5–6 STEWARDSHIP, Sacrifice Giving—Giving to God's work should be done on a regular, continuing basis. Only ongoing cooperation in giving can provide the resources needed for God's work. See note on Lev 1:2.

3:10–11 WORSHIP, Rejoicing—See note on 1 Ch 6:31–32. Genuine worship involves rejoicing in the purposes and goodness of God. Here the cause of the rejoicing was the fulfillment of the plans of God in the rebuilding of the Temple. Both the rejoicing and the actual service of rebuilding were acts of worship. The spirit of rejoicing is seen especially in Paul's letter to the Philippians. Compare Php 4:4.

3:11 GOD, Goodness—Both the love and the goodness of God were praised here. See notes on 1 Ch 16:34,41; Mt 19:17.

xes,[h][d] they lodged an accusation against
the people of Judah and Jerusalem.[e]
7And in the days of Artaxerxes[f] king of
Persia, Bishlam, Mithredath, Tabeel and
the rest of his associates wrote a letter to
Artaxerxes. The letter was written in Aramaic script and in the Aramaic[g] language.[i,j]
8Rehum the commanding officer and
Shimshai the secretary wrote a letter
against Jerusalem to Artaxerxes the king
as follows:

9Rehum the commanding officer and
Shimshai the secretary, together with
the rest of their associates[h]—the
judges and officials over the men
from Tripolis, Persia,[k] Erech[i] and
Babylon, the Elamites of Susa,[j] 10and
the other people whom the great and
honorable Ashurbanipal[l][k] deported
and settled in the city of Samaria and
elsewhere in Trans-Euphrates.[l]

11(This is a copy of the letter they sent
him.)

To King Artaxerxes,

From your servants, the men of
Trans-Euphrates:

12The king should know that the
Jews who came up to us from you
have gone to Jerusalem and are rebuilding that rebellious and wicked
city. They are restoring the walls and
repairing the foundations.[m]
13Furthermore, the king should
know that if this city is built and its
walls are restored, no more taxes,
tribute or duty[n] will be paid, and the
royal revenues will suffer. 14Now
since we are under obligation to the
palace and it is not proper for us to
see the king dishonored, we are
sending this message to inform the
king, 15so that a search may be made
in the archives[o] of your predecessors. In these records you will find
that this city is a rebellious city, troublesome to kings and provinces, a
place of rebellion from ancient times.
That is why this city was destroyed.[p]
16We inform the king that if this city
is built and its walls are restored, you
will be left with nothing in Trans-Euphrates.

17The king sent this reply:

To Rehum the commanding officer,
Shimshai the secretary and the rest of
their associates living in Samaria and
elsewhere in Trans-Euphrates:[q]

Greetings.

18The letter you sent us has been
read and translated in my presence.
19I issued an order and a search was
made, and it was found that this city
has a long history of revolt[r] against
kings and has been a place of rebellion and sedition. 20Jerusalem has
had powerful kings ruling over the
whole of Trans-Euphrates,[s] and
taxes, tribute and duty were paid to
them. 21Now issue an order to these
men to stop work, so that this city
will not be rebuilt until I so order.
22Be careful not to neglect this matter. Why let this threat grow, to the
detriment of the royal interests?[t]

23As soon as the copy of the letter of
King Artaxerxes was read to Rehum and
Shimshai the secretary and their associates,[u] they went immediately to the Jews
in Jerusalem and compelled them by
force to stop.

24Thus the work on the house of God
in Jerusalem came to a standstill until the
second year of the reign of Darius[v] king
of Persia.

Chapter 5

Tattenai's Letter to Darius

NOW Haggai[w] the prophet and Zechariah[x] the prophet, a descendant of
Iddo, prophesied[y] to the Jews in Judah
and Jerusalem in the name of the God of
Israel, who was over them. 2Then Zerubbabel[z] son of Shealtiel and Jeshua[a] son
of Jozadak set to work[b] to rebuild the
house of God in Jerusalem. And the
prophets of God were with them, helping
them.
3At that time Tattenai,[c] governor of
Trans-Euphrates, and Shethar-Bozenai[d]
and their associates went to them and
asked, "Who authorized you to rebuild
this temple and restore this structure?"[e]
4They also asked, "What are the names of
the men constructing this building?"[m]
5But the eye of their God[f] was watching
over the elders of the Jews, and they

4:6 [d]Est 1:1; Da 9:1 [e]Est 3:13; 9:5
4:7 [f]Ezr 7:1; Ne 2:1 [g]2Ki 18:26; Isa 36:11; Da 1:4; 2:4
4:9 [h]ver 23; Ezr 5:6; 6:6,13 [i]Ge 10:10 [j]Ne 1:1; Est 1:2; Da 8:2
4:10 [k]S 2Ki 17:24 [l]ver 17; Ne 4:2
4:12 [m]Ezr 5:3,9
4:13 [n]Ezr 7:24; Ne 5:4
4:15 [o]Ezr 5:17; 6:1 [p]Est 3:8
4:17 [q]S ver 10
4:19 [r]S 2Ki 18:7
4:20 [s]Ge 15:18-21; S Ex 23:31; S Jos 1:4; S 1Ki 4:21; 1Ch 18:3; Ps 72:8-11
4:22 [t]Da 6:2
4:23 [u]S ver 9
4:24 [v]Ne 2:1-8; Da 9:25; Hag 1:1,15; Zec 1:1
5:1 [w]Ezr 6:14; Hag 1:1,3,12; 2:1,10,20 [x]Zec 1:1; 7:1 [y]Hag 1:14-2:9; Zec 4:9-10; 8:9
5:2 [z]S 1Ch 3:19; Hag 1:14; 2:21; Zec 4:6-10 [a]S Ezr 2:2 [b]ver 8; Hag 2:2-5
5:3 [c]Ezr 6:6 [d]Ezr 6:6 [e]S Ezr 4:12
5:5 [f]S 2Ki 25:28; Ezr 7:6,9,28; 8:18,22,31; Ne 2:8,18; Ps 33:18; Isa 66:14

[h]6 Hebrew *Ahasuerus*, a variant of Xerxes' Persian name [i]7 Or *written in Aramaic and translated* [j]7 The text of Ezra 4:8—6:18 is in Aramaic. [k]9 Or *officials, magistrates and governors over the men from* [l]10 Aramaic *Osnappar*, a variant of *Ashurbanipal* [m]4 See Septuagint; Aramaic [4]*We told them the names of the men constructing this building.*

5:4 HISTORY, God—God can work through hostile political actions and government red tape to accomplish His purposes.

5:5 GOD, Sovereignty—The enemies of God's people may use manipulation and political influence to discourage His people and defeat His purposes. They forget one thing. God

were not stopped until a report could go
to Darius and his written reply be received.

6This is a copy of the letter that Tattenai, governor of Trans-Euphrates, and
Shethar-Bozenai and their associates, the
officials of Trans-Euphrates, sent to King
Darius. 7The report they sent him read as
follows:

To King Darius:

Cordial greetings.

8The king should know that we
went to the district of Judah, to the
temple of the great God. The people
are building it with large stones and
placing the timbers in the walls. The
work[g] is being carried on with diligence and is making rapid progress
under their direction.

9We questioned the elders and
asked them, "Who authorized you to
rebuild this temple and restore this
structure?"[h] 10We also asked them
their names, so that we could write
down the names of their leaders for
your information.

11This is the answer they gave us:

"We are the servants of the God of
heaven and earth, and we are rebuilding the temple[i] that was built
many years ago, one that a great king
of Israel built and finished. 12But because our fathers angered[j] the God
of heaven, he handed them over to
Nebuchadnezzar the Chaldean, king
of Babylon, who destroyed this temple and deported the people to Babylon.[k]

13"However, in the first year of Cyrus king of Babylon, King Cyrus issued a decree[l] to rebuild this house
of God. 14He even removed from the
temple[n] of Babylon the gold and silver articles of the house of God,
which Nebuchadnezzar had taken
from the temple in Jerusalem and
brought to the temple[n] in Babylon.[m]

"Then King Cyrus gave them to a
man named Sheshbazzar,[n] whom he
had appointed governor, 15and he
told him, 'Take these articles and go
and deposit them in the temple in
Jerusalem. And rebuild the house of
God on its site.' 16So this Sheshbazzar came and laid the foundations of
the house of God[o] in Jerusalem.
From that day to the present it has
been under construction but is not
yet finished."

17Now if it pleases the king, let a
search be made in the royal archives[p] of Babylon to see if King Cyrus did in fact issue a decree to rebuild this house of God in Jerusalem.
Then let the king send us his decision in this matter.

Chapter 6

The Decree of Darius

KING Darius then issued an order, and
they searched in the archives[q]
stored in the treasury at Babylon. 2A
scroll was found in the citadel of Ecbatana
in the province of Media, and this was
written on it:

Memorandum:

3In the first year of King Cyrus, the
king issued a decree concerning the
temple of God in Jerusalem:

Let the temple be rebuilt as a place
to present sacrifices, and let its foundations be laid.[r] It is to be ninety
feet[o] high and ninety feet wide,
4with three courses[s] of large stones
and one of timbers. The costs are to
be paid by the royal treasury.[t] 5Also,
the gold[u] and silver articles of the
house of God, which Nebuchadnezzar took from the temple in Jerusalem and brought to Babylon, are to be
returned to their places in the temple
in Jerusalem; they are to be deposited in the house of God.[v]

6Now then, Tattenai,[w] governor of
Trans-Euphrates, and Shethar-Bozenai[x] and you, their fellow officials of
that province, stay away from there.
7Do not interfere with the work on
this temple of God. Let the governor
of the Jews and the Jewish elders rebuild this house of God on its site.

8Moreover, I hereby decree what
you are to do for these elders of the
Jews in the construction of this house
of God:

The expenses of these men are to
be fully paid out of the royal treasury,[y] from the revenues[z] of Trans-
Euphrates, so that the work will not
stop. 9Whatever is needed—young
bulls, rams, male lambs for burnt of-

5:8 [g]S ver 2
5:9 [h]S Ezr 4:12
5:11 [i]1Ki 6:1; 2Ch 3:1-2
5:12 [j]S 2Ch 36:16 [k]S Dt 21:10; S 28:36; S 2Ki 24:1; S Jer 1:3
5:13 [l]S Ezr 1:2-4
5:14 [m]Ezr 1:7 [n]S 1Ch 3:18
5:16 [o]S Ezr 3:10
5:17 [p]S Ezr 4:15
6:1 [q]S Ezr 4:15
6:3 [r]S Ezr 3:10; Hag 2:3
6:4 [s]S 1Ki 6:36 [t]ver 8; Ezr 7:20
6:5 [u]S 1Ch 29:2 [v]S Ezr 1:7
6:6 [w]Ezr 5:3 [x]Ezr 5:3
6:8 [y]S ver 4 [z]S 1Sa 9:20

[n] 14 Or *palace* [o] 3 Aramaic *sixty cubits* (about 27 meters)

always knows what is happening in His world and provides for His people accordingly.

5:11–17 GOD, Wrath—God's people learn from their experience of His wrath and gain new faith to carry out His will. See note on 2 Ch 36:16.

6:3–12 ELECTION, Other Nations—See note on 1:2.

ferings[a] to the God of heaven, and
wheat, salt, wine and oil, as requested by the priests in Jerusalem—must
be given them daily without fail, 10so
that they may offer sacrifices pleasing
to the God of heaven and pray for the
well-being of the king and his sons.[b]
11Furthermore, I decree that if anyone changes this edict, a beam is to
be pulled from his house and he is to
be lifted up and impaled[c] on it. And
for this crime his house is to be made
a pile of rubble.[d] 12May God, who
has caused his Name to dwell
there,[e] overthrow any king or people who lifts a hand to change this
decree or to destroy this temple in
Jerusalem.

I Darius[f] have decreed it. Let it be
carried out with diligence.

Completion and Dedication of the Temple

13Then, because of the decree King Darius had sent, Tattenai, governor of
Trans-Euphrates, and Shethar-Bozenai
and their associates[g] carried it out with
diligence. 14So the elders of the Jews continued to build and prosper under the
preaching[h] of Haggai the prophet and
Zechariah, a descendant of Iddo. They finished building the temple according to
the command of the God of Israel and the
decrees of Cyrus,[i] Darius[j] and Artaxerxes,[k] kings of Persia. 15The temple was
completed on the third day of the month
Adar, in the sixth year of the reign of
King Darius.[l]
16Then the people of Israel—the
priests, the Levites and the rest of the
exiles—celebrated the dedication[m] of the
house of God with joy. 17For the dedication of this house of God they offered[n] a
hundred bulls, two hundred rams, four
hundred male lambs and, as a sin offering
for all Israel, twelve male goats, one for
each of the tribes of Israel. 18And they
installed the priests in their divisions[o]
and the Levites in their groups[p] for the
service of God at Jerusalem, according to
what is written in the Book of Moses.[q]

The Passover

19On the fourteenth day of the first
month, the exiles celebrated the Passover.[r] 20The priests and Levites had purified themselves and were all ceremonially
clean. The Levites slaughtered[s] the Passover lamb for all the exiles, for their
brothers the priests and for themselves.
21So the Israelites who had returned from
the exile ate it, together with all who had
separated themselves[t] from the unclean
practices[u] of their Gentile neighbors in
order to seek the LORD,[v] the God of Israel. 22For seven days they celebrated with
joy the Feast of Unleavened Bread,[w] because the LORD had filled them with joy
by changing the attitude[x] of the king of
Assyria, so that he assisted them in the
work on the house of God, the God of
Israel.

Chapter 7

Ezra Comes to Jerusalem

AFTER these things, during the reign of
Artaxerxes[y] king of Persia, Ezra son
of Seraiah,[z] the son of Azariah, the son of
Hilkiah,[a] 2the son of Shallum, the son of
Zadok,[b] the son of Ahitub,[c] 3the son of
Amariah, the son of Azariah, the son of
Meraioth, 4the son of Zerahiah, the son of
Uzzi, the son of Bukki, 5the son of Abishua, the son of Phinehas,[d] the son of Eleazar, the son of Aaron the chief priest—
6this Ezra[e] came up from Babylon. He
was a teacher well versed in the Law of
Moses, which the LORD, the God of Israel, had given. The king had granted[f] him
everything he asked, for the hand of the
LORD his God was on him.[g] 7Some of the
Israelites, including priests, Levites, singers, gatekeepers and temple servants, also
came up to Jerusalem in the seventh year
of King Artaxerxes.[h]
8Ezra arrived in Jerusalem in the fifth
month of the seventh year of the king.
9He had begun his journey from Babylon
on the first day of the first month, and he
arrived in Jerusalem on the first day of
the fifth month, for the gracious hand of
his God was on him.[i] 10For Ezra had de-

6:9 [a]Lev 1:3,10
6:10 [b]Ezr 7:23; 1Ti 2:1-2
6:11 [c]S Dt 21:22-23; Est 2:23; 5:14; 9:14 [d]Ezr 7:26; Da 2:5; 3:29
6:12 [e]S Ex 20:24; S Dt 12:5; S 2Ch 6:2 [f]ver 14
6:13 [g]S Ezr 4:9
6:14 [h]S Ezr 5:1 [i]S Ezr 1:1-4 [j]ver 12 [k]Ezr 7:1; Ne 2:1
6:15 [l]Zec 1:1; 4:9
6:16 [m]S 1Ki 8:63
6:17 [n]S 2Sa 6:13; S 2Ch 29:21; S 30:24
6:18 [o]S 2Ch 35:4; Lk 1:5 [p]S 1Ch 24:1 [q]Nu 3:6-9; 8:9-11; 18:1-32
6:19 [r]S Ex 12:11; S Nu 28:16
6:20 [s]S 2Ch 30:15, 17; 35:11
6:21 [t]Ezr 9:1; Ne 9:2 [u]S Dt 18:9; Eze 36:25 [v]1Ch 22:19; Ps 14:2
6:22 [w]S Ex 12:17 [x]S Ezr 1:1
7:1 [y]S Ezr 4:7; S 6:14 [z]S 2Ki 25:18 [a]2Ki 22:4
7:2 [b]1Ki 1:8; 2:35; 1Ch 6:8; Eze 40:46; 43:19; 44:15 [c]Ne 11:11
7:5 [d]1Ch 6:4
7:6 [e]Ne 12:36 [f]S 2Ki 25:28 [g]S Ezr 5:5; S Isa 41:20
7:7 [h]Ezr 8:1
7:9 [i]ver 6

6:10,12 PRAYER, Universality of—History records that Darius and Cyrus deferred to the gods of the vassal nations of Persia. Darius realized the value of prayer to Israel's God. These foreign kings did not believe in the uniqueness of the God of Israel, but God makes even pagan rulers serve His purposes. See v 22. Compare 1:2–4.
6:14 HUMANITY, Responsibility—People have a responsibility to be faithful to God. This includes heeding His Word as proclaimed by His messengers. Lives so lived will bring to ultimate fruition the purposes which God has set before them.
6:16–17 STEWARDSHIP, House of God—See notes on Ex 25:1–8; Nu 7:1–89.
6:21–22 PRAYER, Worship—God demands separation and purity in worship (Isa 52:11). To seek God is to forsake all other deities. See note on 1 Ki 22:8–17.
6:22 HISTORY, Universal—See note on 1:1.
7:6 HOLY SCRIPTURE, Canonization—God had been preparing a servant even in the wilderness of Exile. Ezra had been a willing student of the recorded revelation of God. He followed the promptings of God's presence in events in his own life. God kept Ezra safe in each step of the preparation and return to Jerusalem as part of preparing His inspired revelation through the work and writing of Ezra. Ezra's use of the written Law is a major piece of evidence to see how the collected writings functioned as authoritative canon among God's people.

voted himself to the study and observance of the Law of the LORD, and to
teaching[j] its decrees and laws in Israel.

King Artaxerxes' Letter to Ezra

11 This is a copy of the letter King Artaxerxes had given to Ezra the priest and
teacher, a man learned in matters concerning the commands and decrees of the
LORD for Israel:

12 [p]Artaxerxes, king of kings,[k]

To Ezra the priest, a teacher of the
Law of the God of heaven:

Greetings.

13 Now I decree that any of the Israelites in my kingdom, including
priests and Levites, who wish to go to
Jerusalem with you, may go. 14 You
are sent by the king and his seven
advisers[l] to inquire about Judah and
Jerusalem with regard to the Law of
your God, which is in your hand.
15 Moreover, you are to take with you
the silver and gold that the king and
his advisers have freely given[m] to the
God of Israel, whose dwelling[n] is in
Jerusalem, 16 together with all the silver and gold[o] you may obtain from
the province of Babylon, as well as
the freewill offerings of the people
and priests for the temple of their
God in Jerusalem.[p] 17 With this money be sure to buy bulls, rams and
male lambs,[q] together with their
grain offerings and drink offerings,[r]
and sacrifice[s] them on the altar of
the temple of your God in Jerusalem.
18 You and your brother Jews may
then do whatever seems best with
the rest of the silver and gold, in accordance with the will of your God.
19 Deliver[t] to the God of Jerusalem
all the articles entrusted to you for
worship in the temple of your God.
20 And anything else needed for the
temple of your God that you may
have occasion to supply, you may
provide from the royal treasury.[u]

7:10 [j]S Dt 33:10
7:12 [k]Eze 26:7; Da 2:37
7:14 [l]Est 1:14
7:15 [m]S 1Ch 29:6 [n]S Dt 12:5; S 2Ch 6:2
7:16 [o]S Ex 3:22 [p]Zec 6:10
7:17 [q]S 2Ki 3:4 [r]Nu 15:5-12 [s]Dt 12:5-11
7:19 [t]Ezr 5:14; Jer 27:22
7:20 [u]S Ezr 6:4
7:23 [v]S Ezr 6:10
7:24 [w]S Ezr 4:13 [x]Ezr 8:36
7:25 [y]S Ex 18:21, 26 [z]S Lev 10:11
7:26 [a]S Ezr 6:11
7:27 [b]S Ezr 1:1 [c]S 1Ch 29:12
7:28 [d]S 2Ki 25:28 [e]S Ezr 5:5

21 Now I, King Artaxerxes, order all
the treasurers of Trans-Euphrates to
provide with diligence whatever Ezra
the priest, a teacher of the Law of the
God of heaven, may ask of you—
22 up to a hundred talents[q] of silver, a
hundred cors[r] of wheat, a hundred
baths[s] of wine, a hundred baths[s] of
olive oil, and salt without limit.
23 Whatever the God of heaven has
prescribed, let it be done with diligence for the temple of the God of
heaven. Why should there be wrath
against the realm of the king and of
his sons?[v] 24 You are also to know
that you have no authority to impose
taxes, tribute or duty[w] on any of the
priests, Levites, singers, gatekeepers,
temple servants or other workers at
this house of God.[x]

25 And you, Ezra, in accordance
with the wisdom of your God, which
you possess, appoint[y] magistrates
and judges to administer justice to all
the people of Trans-Euphrates—all
who know the laws of your God. And
you are to teach[z] any who do not
know them. 26 Whoever does not
obey the law of your God and the law
of the king must surely be punished
by death, banishment, confiscation of
property, or imprisonment.[a]

27 Praise be to the LORD, the God of
our fathers, who has put it into the
king's heart[b] to bring honor[c] to the
house of the LORD in Jerusalem in this
way 28 and who has extended his good
favor[d] to me before the king and his
advisers and all the king's powerful officials. Because the hand of the LORD my
God was on me,[e] I took courage and
gathered leading men from Israel to go up
with me.

[p]*12* The text of Ezra 7:12-26 is in Aramaic.
[q]*22* That is, about 3 3/4 tons (about 3.4 metric tons)
[r]*22* That is, probably about 600 bushels (about 22 kiloliters)
[s]*22* That is, probably about 600 gallons (about 2.2 kiloliters)

7:11–28 REVELATION, Divine Presence—Ezra explained God's multiple activity in the events which propelled his life. God intervened in the attitude of a nonbeliever king. He made possible the openness and support which the entire royal court provided Ezra as he began the plans. He gave Ezra constant encouragement and support as he made his way to the reconstruction site. Specific events combined with an awesome presence to communicate God's will in this historical occurrence. The sense of God's inspired leadership was so great that even the authorizing letter of the Persian king was preserved. The inspired author of Ezra incorporated this official document into his book, and thus a Persian document is part of God's authoritative Scripture.

7:24 CHRISTIAN ETHICS, Church and State—Exempting religious bodies from taxes is a government tradition with a long history. It is a way by which government honors religious bodies and the good work they do. It is not a God-given right churches should demand from the state. Religious institutions should always be careful to avoid any actions which tie them to the state for support. See note on 1 Sa 22:1–23.

7:27 HISTORY, Universal—See note on 1:1.

7:27–28 PRAYER, Sovereignty of God—Artaxerxes of Persia issued the decree, but Ezra acknowledged that the source of blessing was not Artaxerxes but God. Praise belongs to the sovereign God as we see His actions in the affairs of international politics.

7:28 GOD, Grace—Grace is God's good favor that meets our needs and is an expression of His love. His grace opens doors for His people and enables them to accomplish His will. See notes on Ge 19:12–19,29; 39:21–23; 45:5–9; Lk 1:30.

Chapter 8

List of the Family Heads Returning With Ezra

THESE are the family heads and those
registered with them who came up
with me from Babylon during the reign of
King Artaxerxes:[f]
2 of the descendants of Phinehas, Gershom;
of the descendants of Ithamar, Daniel;
of the descendants of David, Hattush
3 of the descendants of Shecaniah;[g]
of the descendants of Parosh,[h] Zechariah, and with him were registered 150 men;
4 of the descendants of Pahath-
Moab,[i] Eliehoenai son of Zerahiah, and with him 200 men;
5 of the descendants of Zattu,[t] Shecaniah son of Jahaziel, and with him
300 men;
6 of the descendants of Adin,[j] Ebed
son of Jonathan, and with him 50
men;
7 of the descendants of Elam, Jeshaiah
son of Athaliah, and with him 70
men;
8 of the descendants of Shephatiah,
Zebadiah son of Michael, and
with him 80 men;
9 of the descendants of Joab, Obadiah
son of Jehiel, and with him 218
men;
10 of the descendants of Bani,[u] Shelomith son of Josiphiah, and with
him 160 men;
11 of the descendants of Bebai, Zechariah son of Bebai, and with him 28
men;
12 of the descendants of Azgad, Johanan son of Hakkatan, and with
him 110 men;
13 of the descendants of Adonikam,[k]
the last ones, whose names were
Eliphelet, Jeuel and Shemaiah,
and with them 60 men;
14 of the descendants of Bigvai, Uthai
and Zaccur, and with them 70
men.

The Return to Jerusalem

15 I assembled them at the canal that
flows toward Ahava,[l] and we camped
there three days. When I checked among
the people and the priests, I found no Levites[m] there. 16 So I summoned Eliezer,
Ariel, Shemaiah, Elnathan, Jarib, Elnathan, Nathan, Zechariah and Meshullam,
who were leaders, and Joiarib and Elnathan, who were men of learning, 17 and I
sent them to Iddo, the leader in Casiphia.
I told them what to say to Iddo and his
kinsmen, the temple servants[n] in Casiphia, so that they might bring attendants to
us for the house of our God. 18 Because
the gracious hand of our God was on us,[o]
they brought us Sherebiah,[p] a capable
man, from the descendants of Mahli son
of Levi, the son of Israel, and Sherebiah's
sons and brothers, 18 men; 19 and Hashabiah, together with Jeshaiah from the descendants of Merari, and his brothers and
nephews, 20 men. 20 They also brought
220 of the temple servants[q]—a body
that David and the officials had established to assist the Levites. All were registered by name.
21 There, by the Ahava Canal,[r] I proclaimed a fast, so that we might humble
ourselves before our God and ask him for
a safe journey[s] for us and our children,
with all our possessions. 22 I was ashamed
to ask the king for soldiers[t] and horsemen to protect us from enemies on the
road, because we had told the king, "The
gracious hand of our God is on everyone[u]
who looks to him, but his great anger is
against all who forsake him.[v]" 23 So we
fasted[w] and petitioned our God about
this, and he answered our prayer.
24 Then I set apart twelve of the leading
priests, together with Sherebiah,[x] Hashabiah and ten of their brothers, 25 and I
weighed out[y] to them the offering of silver and gold and the articles that the

8:1 [f]Ezr 7:7
8:3 [g]1Ch 3:22 [h]S Ezr 2:3
8:4 [i]Ezr 2:6
8:6 [j]Ezr 2:15; Ne 7:20; 10:16
8:13 [k]Ezr 2:13
8:15 [l]ver 21,31 [m]S Ezr 2:40
8:17 [n]Ezr 2:43
8:18 [o]S Ezr 5:5 [p]ver 24
8:20 [q]S 1Ch 9:2
8:21 [r]S ver 15 [s]Ps 5:8; 27:11; 107:7
8:22 [t]Ne 2:9; Jer 41:16 [u]S Ezr 5:5 [v]S Dt 31:17
8:23 [w]S 2Ch 20:3; Ac 14:23
8:24 [x]ver 18
8:25 [y]ver 33

[t]*5* Some Septuagint manuscripts (also 1 Esdras 8:32); Hebrew does not have *Zattu*. [u]*10* Some Septuagint manuscripts (also 1 Esdras 8:36); Hebrew does not have *Bani*.

8:1–14 HISTORY, Deliverance—See note on 2:1–70.

8:21–23 REVELATION, Events—The saving acts of God were not limited to Moses, Joshua, and David, Israel's conquering heroes. The dangerous return to Jerusalem was also part of salvation history. Ezra candidly shared his embarrassment to ask the foreign king for human protection after he had assured Cyrus of his God's power to protect. Robbers and warring tribes separated him from his native land (v 22), and enemies of the plan were within the king's domain also (4:12). God provided safety all the way.

8:21–23 PRAYER, Answer—The Persian rulers generously allowed free religious practice to subject peoples. Ezra wanted to demonstrate his faith in the uniqueness of Israel's God. Travel in that day was unsafe, but Ezra declared that the hand of Israel's God was on all. Their safety depended not on military help but on God. Humble prayer and fasting prepared the people for the trip. God answered by providing safety during the trip. Answers to prayer often come through successful completion of actions for which we prayed.

8:22–23 GOD, Grace—God's grace calls forth our faith. He wants to provide for the needs of His people. Too often we are too confident of our ability to supply our needs. At times we need to be ashamed of our lack of reliance on God's grace. See notes on Ge 6:5–8; 17:14; 19:12–19,29; 19:13,24–26; 39:21–23.

king, his advisers, his officials and all Israel present there had donated for the
house of our God. 26 I weighed out to
them 650 talents[v] of silver, silver articles
weighing 100 talents,[w] 100 talents[w] of
gold, 27 20 bowls of gold valued at 1,000
darics,[x] and two fine articles of polished
bronze, as precious as gold.
28 I said to them, "You as well as these
articles are consecrated to the LORD.[z]
The silver and gold are a freewill offering
to the LORD, the God of your fathers.
29 Guard them carefully until you weigh
them out in the chambers of the house of
the LORD in Jerusalem before the leading
priests and the Levites and the family
heads of Israel." 30 Then the priests and
Levites received the silver and gold and
sacred articles that had been weighed out
to be taken to the house of our God in
Jerusalem.
31 On the twelfth day of the first month
we set out from the Ahava Canal[a] to go
to Jerusalem. The hand of our God was on
us,[b] and he protected us from enemies
and bandits along the way. 32 So we arrived in Jerusalem, where we rested
three days.[c]
33 On the fourth day, in the house of
our God, we weighed out[d] the silver and
gold and the sacred articles into the
hands of Meremoth[e] son of Uriah, the
priest. Eleazar son of Phinehas was with
him, and so were the Levites Jozabad[f]
son of Jeshua and Noadiah son of Binnui.[g] 34 Everything was accounted for by
number and weight, and the entire
weight was recorded at that time.

8:28 [z]S Lev 21:6; 22:2-3
8:31 [a]S ver 15 [b]S Ezr 5:5
8:32 [c]S Ge 40:13
8:33 [d]ver 25 [e]Ne 3:4,21 [f]Ne 11:16 [g]Ne 3:24
8:35 [h]S Lev 1:3 [i]S 2Ch 29:24 [j]S 2Ch 29:21; S 30:24
8:36 [k]Ezr 7:21-24 [l]Ne 2:7 [m]Est 9:3
9:1 [n]S Ezr 6:21 [o]S Ge 10:16; S Jos 15:8 [p]Ge 19:38 [q]S Ge 19:37 [r]Ex 13:5; 23:28; Dt 20:17; S Jos 3:10; S Jdg 3:5; 1Ki 9:20; S 2Ch 8:7; Ne 9:8
9:2 [s]S Ex 34:16; S Ru 1:4 [t]Ps 106:35 [u]S Ex 22:31; S Lev 27:30; S Dt 14:2 [v]Ezr 10:2
9:3 [w]S Nu 14:6 [x]S Ex 32:19; S 33:4
9:4 [y]Ezr 10:3; Ps 119:120; Isa 66:2,5

35 Then the exiles who had returned
from captivity sacrificed burnt offerings to
the God of Israel: twelve bulls[h] for all
Israel,[i] ninety-six rams, seventy-seven
male lambs and, as a sin offering, twelve
male goats.[j] All this was a burnt offering
to the LORD. 36 They also delivered the
king's orders[k] to the royal satraps and to
the governors of Trans-Euphrates,[l] who
then gave assistance to the people and to
the house of God.[m]

Chapter 9

Ezra's Prayer About Intermarriage

After these things had been done, the
leaders came to me and said, "The
people of Israel, including the priests and
the Levites, have not kept themselves
separate[n] from the neighboring peoples
with their detestable practices, like those
of the Canaanites, Hittites, Perizzites,
Jebusites,[o] Ammonites,[p] Moabites,[q]
Egyptians and Amorites.[r] 2 They have
taken some of their daughters[s] as wives
for themselves and their sons, and have
mingled[t] the holy race[u] with the peoples around them. And the leaders and
officials have led the way in this unfaithfulness."[v]
3 When I heard this, I tore[w] my tunic
and cloak, pulled hair from my head and
beard and sat down appalled.[x] 4 Then everyone who trembled[y] at the words of

[v]*26* That is, about 25 tons (about 22 metric tons)
[w]*26* That is, about 3 3/4 tons (about 3.4 metric tons)
[x]*27* That is, about 19 pounds (about 8.5 kilograms)

8:28,35 STEWARDSHIP, Management—Israel's return from captivity brought a spiritual renewal that resulted in new commitments to serve God and the generous use of resources for rebuilding the house of God. Exiles in Babylon gave generously to rebuild God's house. Ezra followed careful procedures in determining and reporting the amounts given. Everyone responsible for collecting, storing, and spending money given to God's work should follow Ezra's example of care and accountability. See note on Ex 25:1–8.

8:31–32 HISTORY, Deliverance—God's deliverance includes protection from attack as well as victory in battle.

9:1–15 EVIL AND SUFFERING, Repentance—Ezra led the people in repenting for marrying foreigners, a practice which threatened their religious loyalty. Ezra acknowledged they had not been punished as severely as they deserved. We must admit our evil practices to God, confess that our suffering under His punishment is justified, and commit ourselves anew to His way of life.

9:1–2 HUMANITY, Relationships—Being properly related to God demands that we not enter into some relationships. Improper relationships with others give a visible testimony that personal relationship with and commitment to God is considered unimportant. Such relationships can lead us away from God and into practices which God condemns.

9:1–2 SIN, Transgression—The returned exiles repeated Solomon's sin. See note on 1 Ki 11:1–13. Even the clergy joined in the sinful practice of bringing foreign gods into the community through marriage. When religious leaders open the door to sin, what better can be expected from their co-workers?

9:1–15 PRAYER, Confession—God demands radical separation from practices of the world. Ezra the priest identified with God's grief over sin inwardly and outwardly. In this prayer, Ezra made no petition to God. He identified with his sinful people and confessed their sinfulness. The confession implied the request for forgiveness and for new direction.

9:1—10:17 FAMILY, Intermarriage—Ezra made the most direct attack on intermarriage with unbelievers in the Bible. He demanded dissolution of marriages which threatened to guide the rebuilding Exile community away from God. The one-time crisis action is not meant to justify divorce as a practice. It does teach the importance of family life to the religious well-being of God's people and shows the danger of intermarriage with unbelievers. See notes on Dt 7:3–4; 1 Ki 11:1–9; 2 Co 6:14–18.

9:2 GOD, Holy—God's people form a holy race by virtue of God's choosing the people as His own servant nation. Only God is holy. Those persons or objects set aside for God's service may be called holy as a result of participating in God's holiness. An unfaithful people can no longer be called a holy people. Such unholiness comes not from marrying the wrong nationality but from disobeying God and joining oneself to a people who will lead you away from total allegiance to the Holy One. See notes on Ex 3:5–6; 19:10–24; Lev 11:44–45.

9:3–7 SALVATION, Repentance—Ezra's actions were signs of mourning over the sins of his people. He was horror-stricken over the news of vv 1–2. The prayer of vv 6–7 bears the marks of deep repentance. Repentance is the appropriate way to deal with sin and guilt. It is the path to salvation (10:2–3,6,13). See note on 2 Ch 30:6.

the God of Israel gathered around me because of this unfaithfulness of the exiles.
And I sat there appalled[z] until the evening sacrifice.
5Then, at the evening sacrifice,[a] I rose
from my self-abasement, with my tunic
and cloak torn, and fell on my knees with
my hands[b] spread out to the LORD my
God 6and prayed:

"O my God, I am too ashamed[c]
and disgraced to lift up my face to
you, my God, because our sins are
higher than our heads and our guilt
has reached to the heavens.[d] 7From
the days of our forefathers[e] until
now, our guilt has been great. Because of our sins, we and our kings
and our priests have been subjected
to the sword[f] and captivity,[g] to pillage and humiliation[h] at the hand of
foreign kings, as it is today.
8"But now, for a brief moment, the
LORD our God has been gracious[i] in
leaving us a remnant[j] and giving us
a firm place[k] in his sanctuary, and so
our God gives light to our eyes[l] and
a little relief in our bondage. 9Though
we are slaves,[m] our God has not deserted us in our bondage. He has
shown us kindness[n] in the sight of
the kings of Persia: He has granted us
new life to rebuild the house of our
God and repair its ruins,[o] and he has
given us a wall of protection in Judah
and Jerusalem.
10"But now, O our God, what can
we say after this? For we have disregarded the commands[p] 11you gave
through your servants the prophets
when you said: 'The land you are entering[q] to possess is a land polluted[r]
by the corruption of its peoples. By
their detestable practices[s] they have
filled it with their impurity from one
end to the other. 12Therefore, do not
give your daughters in marriage to
their sons or take their daughters for
your sons. Do not seek a treaty of
friendship with them[t] at any time,
that you may be strong[u] and eat the
good things[v] of the land and leave it
to your children as an everlasting inheritance.'[w]
13"What has happened to us is a
result of our evil[x] deeds and our
great guilt, and yet, our God, you
have punished us less than our sins
have deserved[y] and have given us a
remnant like this. 14Shall we again
break your commands and intermarry[z] with the peoples who commit
such detestable practices? Would you
not be angry enough with us to destroy us,[a] leaving us no remnant[b] or
survivor? 15O LORD, God of Israel,
you are righteous![c] We are left this
day as a remnant. Here we are before
you in our guilt, though because of it
not one of us can stand[d] in your
presence.[e]"

Chapter 10

The People's Confession of Sin

WHILE Ezra was praying and confessing,[f] weeping[g] and throwing himself down before the house of God, a

9:4 [z]Ne 1:4; Ps 119:136; Da 10:2
9:5 [a]S Ex 29:41 [b]Ne 8:6; Ps 28:2; 134:2
9:6 [c]Jer 31:19 [d]S 2Ch 28:9; Job 42:6; Ps 38:4; Isa 59:12; Jer 3:25; 14:20; Rev 18:5
9:7 [e]S 2Ch 29:6 [f]Eze 21:1-32 [g]S Dt 28:64 [h]S Dt 28:37
9:8 [i]Ps 25:16; 67:1; 119:58; Isa 33:2 [j]S Ge 45:7 [k]Ecc 12:11; Isa 22:23 [l]Ps 13:3; 19:8
9:9 [m]S Ex 1:14; Ne 9:36 [n]S 2Ki 25:28; Ps 106:46 [o]Ps 69:35; Isa 43:1; 44:26; 48:20; 52:9; 63:9; Jer 32:44; Zec 1:16-17
9:10 [p]Dt 11:8; Isa 1:19-20
9:11 [q]Dt 4:5 [r]S Lev 18:25-28 [s]S Dt 9:4; S 18:9; S 1Ki 14:24
9:12 [t]S Ex 34:15 [u]Dt 11:8 [v]S Ge 45:18 [w]Ps 103:17; Eze 37:25; Joel 3:20
9:13 [x]S Ex 32:22 [y]Job 11:6; 15:5; 22:5; 33:27; Ps 103:10
9:14 [z]Ne 13:27 [a]S Dt 9:8 [b]Dt 9:14
9:15 [c]S Ge 18:25; S 2Ch 12:6; Ne 9:8; Ps 51:4; 129:4; 145:17; Isa 24:16; Jer 12:1; 23:6; 33:16; La 1:18; Da 9:7; Zep 3:5 [d]Ps 76:7; 130:3; Mal 3:2 [e]S 1Ki 8:47
10:1 [f]2Ch 20:9; Da 9:20 [g]S Nu 25:6

9:5–15 WORSHIP, Prayer—See note on Ge 12:6–8.

9:6–7 SIN, Shame—Sin starts a chain of consequences in the life of an individual and of a community. Shame (Hebrew *bosh*) is a feeling of disgrace, a sense of being isolated from God and the community of faith because of failure. It destroys our trust in ourselves and in others. The emphasis appears to be on the loss of standing in the community rather than on the inner feelings. Sin causes us to lose our standing and confidence before God. For guilt, see note on 2 Ch 28:9–13. Shame receives objective expression in military defeat resulting in humiliating treatment as prisoners of war. All sin does not lead to such humiliation, but certainly it brings a sense of disgrace and alienation which we can overcome only by confessing our sins in prayer to God.

9:7,14 GOD, Wrath—Here is a frank recognition that God, a righteous God, expresses His wrath against sin. We need to recognize God's discipline and express renewed faith in Him. Then wrath has accomplished its purpose. See notes on Ge 6:5–8; 17:14; 19:13,24–26.

9:8–15 GOD, Grace—God shows His love and mercy to His people even when they are suffering justly for their sins. We must be able to recognize the moment of grace in the darkness and give thanks for it. God's grace means that even in our darkest hour He will not desert us. In response God's guilty people must forsake their sinful way of life. Notice the contrast with the expression of the wrath of God in v 7.

9:8 THE CHURCH, Remnant—God's remnant exists because of His grace, not because of human righteousness. The remnant should be grateful for what God has done rather than complaining about what might have been. The remnant should show gratitude in righteous living rather than imitating and becoming part of the unfaithful world.

9:11–13 SIN, Disobeying—Prophets also issued commandments (Hebrew *mitswoth*) which God's people had to obey. God works through His chosen ministers to show His people His expectations of them. To fall short of God's expectations is sin. One of God's expectations is that His people not imitate the popular practices of society. God's Word, not momentary fads, must direct our lives.

9:13–15 THE CHURCH, Remnant—The cause of justice would have required the total destruction of the people of Israel. In contrast, God in His grace left a remnant to repopulate the land and offer sacrifices of praise unto Him. See note on v 8.

9:15 GOD, Righteous—God did what was right for Israel, leaving a remnant to accomplish His purposes even though the remnant was also guilty. See notes on Lev 1:1; Jos 23:1–16; 2 Sa 10:12; Jn 17:25.

9:15 SIN, Alienation—The highest price we must pay for our sin is the loss of the right to stand in God's presence. His holiness is not compatible with human sin. We must confess our sin and accept His forgiveness to stand in His holy presence and enjoy fellowship with Him. See note on 9:6–7.

10:1–17 PRAYER, Confession—The priest's confession led to the people's contrition. Confession was expressed in humble actions as well as words. The words listed specific sins of which the people were guilty. Their repentance led to action. In three months, they achieved a radical separation.

large crowd of Israelites—men, women
and children—gathered around him.
They too wept bitterly. 2 Then Shecaniah
son of Jehiel, one of the descendants of
Elam,[h] said to Ezra, "We have been unfaithful[i] to our God by marrying foreign
women from the peoples around us. But
in spite of this, there is still hope for Israel.[j] 3 Now let us make a covenant[k] before our God to send away[l] all these
women and their children, in accordance
with the counsel of my lord and of those
who fear the commands of our God. Let it
be done according to the Law. 4 Rise up;
this matter is in your hands. We will support you, so take courage and do it."
5 So Ezra rose up and put the leading
priests and Levites and all Israel under
oath[m] to do what had been suggested.
And they took the oath. 6 Then Ezra withdrew from before the house of God and
went to the room of Jehohanan son of
Eliashib. While he was there, he ate no
food and drank no water,[n] because he
continued to mourn over the unfaithfulness of the exiles.
7 A proclamation was then issued
throughout Judah and Jerusalem for all
the exiles to assemble in Jerusalem. 8 Anyone who failed to appear within three
days would forfeit all his property, in accordance with the decision of the officials
and elders, and would himself be expelled from the assembly of the exiles.
9 Within the three days, all the men of
Judah and Benjamin[o] had gathered in Jerusalem. And on the twentieth day of the
ninth month, all the people were sitting
in the square before the house of God,
greatly distressed by the occasion and because of the rain. 10 Then Ezra[p] the priest
stood up and said to them, "You have
been unfaithful; you have married foreign
women, adding to Israel's guilt.[q] 11 Now
make confession to the LORD, the God of
your fathers, and do his will. Separate
yourselves from the peoples around you
and from your foreign wives."[r]
12 The whole assembly responded with
a loud voice:[s] "You are right! We must
do as you say. 13 But there are many people here and it is the rainy season; so we
cannot stand outside. Besides, this matter
cannot be taken care of in a day or two,
because we have sinned greatly in this
thing. 14 Let our officials act for the whole
assembly. Then let everyone in our towns
who has married a foreign woman come
at a set time, along with the elders and
judges[t] of each town, until the fierce anger[u] of our God in this matter is turned
away from us." 15 Only Jonathan son of
Asahel and Jahzeiah son of Tikvah, supported by Meshullam and Shabbethai[v]
the Levite, opposed this.
16 So the exiles did as was proposed.
Ezra the priest selected men who were
family heads, one from each family division, and all of them designated by name.
On the first day of the tenth month they
sat down to investigate the cases, 17 and
by the first day of the first month they
finished dealing with all the men who
had married foreign women.

Those Guilty of Intermarriage

18 Among the descendants of the
priests, the following had married
foreign women:[w]

From the descendants of Jeshua[x]
son of Jozadak, and his brothers:
Maaseiah, Eliezer, Jarib and Gedaliah. 19 (They all gave their hands[y]
in pledge to put away their wives,
and for their guilt they each presented a ram from the flock as a
guilt offering.)[z]
20 From the descendants of Immer:[a]
Hanani and Zebadiah.
21 From the descendants of Harim:[b]
Maaseiah, Elijah, Shemaiah, Jehiel
and Uzziah.
22 From the descendants of Pashhur:[c]
Elioenai, Maaseiah, Ishmael, Nethanel, Jozabad and Elasah.
23 Among the Levites:[d]
Jozabad, Shimei, Kelaiah (that is,
Kelita), Pethahiah, Judah and Eliezer.
24 From the singers:
Eliashib.[e]

10:2 [h]ver 26 [i]S Ezr 9:2 [j]Dt 30:8-10
10:3 [k]S 2Ki 11:17 [l]S Ex 34:16
10:5 [m]Ne 5:12; 13:25
10:6 [n]S Ex 34:28; Dt 9:18; Ps 102:4; Jnh 3:7
10:9 [o]S Ezr 1:5
10:10 [p]Ezr 7:21 [q]2Ch 28:13
10:11 [r]S Dt 24:1; Mal 2:10-16
10:12 [s]S Jos 6:5
10:14 [t]Dt 16:18 [u]S Nu 25:4; S 2Ch 29:10
10:15 [v]Ne 11:16
10:18 [w]S Jdg 3:6 [x]S Ezr 2:2
10:19 [y]S 2Ki 10:15 [z]S Lev 5:15; 6:6
10:20 [a]S 1Ch 24:14
10:21 [b]S 1Ch 24:8
10:22 [c]S 1Ch 9:12
10:23 [d]Ne 8:7; 9:4
10:24 [e]Ne 3:1; 12:10; 13:7,28

Confession without action accomplishes little. God does not want us to rehearse our sins but to repent from our sins.

10:2–5 THE CHURCH, Covenant People—Being God's covenant people, at times, requires drastic action to renew our commitment and to cleanse our lives from temptation and sin. See notes on Dt 29:1–15; 2 Ch 29:10.

10:7–17 THE CHURCH, Practice—Ezra called the returned exiles to renewed faith and encouraged the people to obey the Law of the Lord. The people gathered to hear God's word and to renew their faith. God's assembly (Hebrew *qahal*) and congregation (Hebrew *'edah*) served to bind the people in allegiance to God. The church serves a similar function, calling people to faith and encouraging obedience to God. When the church meets, believers are strengthened in their faith in Christ. The fellowship of the church reminds us of spiritual duties and encourages us to serve Christ faithfully.

10:9–17 DISCIPLESHIP, Spiritual Leaders—In times of trouble and crisis God's people must make crucial decisions and carry them out. The entire congregation should be informed of the problem and be given a voice in solving it. Often unanimous agreement cannot be reached. The congregation as a whole cannot work out all details of a problem. Spiritual leaders need to be given responsibility to carry out the congregation's decisions.

10:10 SIN, Transgression—See notes on 9:1–2; 1 Ch 10:13.

10:13–14 GOD, Wrath—See note on 9:7,14.

From the gatekeepers:
Shallum, Telem and Uri.

25And among the other Israelites:

From the descendants of Parosh:[f]
Ramiah, Izziah, Malkijah, Mijamin, Eleazar, Malkijah and Benaiah.
26From the descendants of Elam:[g]
Mattaniah, Zechariah, Jehiel, Abdi, Jeremoth and Elijah.
27From the descendants of Zattu:
Elioenai, Eliashib, Mattaniah, Jeremoth, Zabad and Aziza.
28From the descendants of Bebai:
Jehohanan, Hananiah, Zabbai and Athlai.
29From the descendants of Bani:
Meshullam, Malluch, Adaiah, Jashub, Sheal and Jeremoth.
30From the descendants of Pahath-Moab:
Adna, Kelal, Benaiah, Maaseiah, Mattaniah, Bezalel, Binnui and Manasseh.
31From the descendants of Harim:
Eliezer, Ishijah, Malkijah, Shemaiah, Shimeon, 32Benjamin, Malluch and Shemariah.
33From the descendants of Hashum:
Mattenai, Mattattah, Zabad, Eliphelet, Jeremai, Manasseh and Shimei.
34From the descendants of Bani:
Maadai, Amram, Uel, 35Benaiah, Bedeiah, Keluhi, 36Vaniah, Meremoth, Eliashib, 37Mattaniah, Mattenai and Jaasu.
38From the descendants of Binnui:[y]
Shimei, 39Shelemiah, Nathan, Adaiah, 40Macnadebai, Shashai, Sharai, 41Azarel, Shelemiah, Shemariah, 42Shallum, Amariah and Joseph.
43From the descendants of Nebo:
Jeiel, Mattithiah, Zabad, Zebina, Jaddai, Joel and Benaiah.

44All these had married foreign women, and some of them had children by these wives.[z]

10:25 [f]S Ezr 2:3
10:26 [g]S ver 2

[y]*37,38* See Septuagint (also 1 Esdras 9:34); Hebrew *Jaasu* [38]*and Bani and Binnui,* [z]*44* Or *and they sent them away with their children*

10:44 SIN, Results—Israel's sin of forsaking God because of the influence of foreign women brought disastrous results to the spiritual life of the nation. It also affected a new generation of children caught between the need for stable home life under strong fatherly influence and the necessity for the drastic divorce measures instituted by Ezra to save the nation from spiritual suicide. A sinful people may find measures to avoid future temptation. They cannot undo the life-breaking results of past sins.

Nehemiah

See Introduction to Ezra.

Theological Outline

Nehemiah: Rebuilding the Wall

I. God's Work Must Be Done. (1:1—7:73)
   A. God's leaders must be informed of needs in God's work. (1:1-3)
   B. God's leaders must be responsive spiritually to needs in God's work and must pray. (1:4-11)
   C. God's leaders must enlist the aid of others, sometimes outside the family of God. (2:1-9)
   D. God's leaders likely will encounter opposition. (2:10)
   E. God's leaders must exercise caution and discretion along with careful planning. (2:11-16)
   F. God's leaders must inform and challenge God's people to work. (2:17-20)
   G. God's work demands hard work, good organization, plenty of cooperation, and good records to give credit where credit is due. (3:1-32)
   H. God's leaders will pray in the face of ridicule and insult. (4:1-9)
   I. God's leaders may expect opposition from within as well as from without. (4:10-12)
   J. God's leaders must encourage weary workers with practical, prayerful faith. (4:13-15)
   K. God's work gets done by hard work and committed workers. (4:16-23)
   L. God's work is slowed by internal problems of unfairness. (5:1-5)
   M. God's leaders must confront profiteering problem causers. (5:6-13)
   N. God's leaders at times can be sacrificially generous to meet a pressing need. (5:14-19)
   O. God's leaders know opposition can be very personal and must deal with it head on. (6:1-14)
   P. God's help and the cooperation of many workers bring success. (6:15-16)
   Q. God's work can have traitors within. (6:17-19)
   R. God's leaders will enlist others and give them clear instructions. (7:1-5)
   S. God's leaders need to keep and use good records. (7:6-73)

II. God's Way Must Include Revival and Reformation. (8:1—13:31)
   A. God's people want to hear God's Word. (8:1-3)
   B. God's Word must be read and then interpreted. (8:4-8)
   C. God's way calls for joyous celebration. (8:9-12)
   D. God's way prescribes formal expressions of joyous worship. (8:13-18)
   E. God's way elicits confession. (9:1-5)
   F. God's people give practical expression to prayerful repentance. (9:6-37)
   G. God's people are willing to commit themselves. (9:38)
   H. God's people will sign pledges of commitment. (10:1-27)
   I. God's people must give practical expressions of commitment. (10:28-39)
   J. God's people must be willing to make some changes. (11:1-2)
   K. God's work requires good records. (11:3—12:26)
   L. God's work should be dedicated and celebrated. (12:27-47)
   M. God's people must be a separated people. (13:1-9)
   N. God's work, including His finance program, must not be neglected. (13:10-14)
   O. God's day must be respected. (13:15-22)
   P. God's way demands purity in marriage and in ministers. (13:23-31)

Chapter 1

Nehemiah's Prayer

THE words of Nehemiah son of Hacaliah:

In the month of Kislev[a] in the twentieth year, while I was in the citadel of
Susa,[b] 2Hanani,[c] one of my brothers,
came from Judah with some other men,
and I questioned them about the Jewish
remnant[d] that survived the exile, and
also about Jerusalem.
3They said to me, "Those who survived
the exile and are back in the province are
in great trouble and disgrace. The wall of
Jerusalem is broken down, and its gates
have been burned with fire.[e]"
4When I heard these things, I sat down
and wept.[f] For some days I mourned and
fasted[g] and prayed before the God of
heaven. 5Then I said:

"O LORD, God of heaven, the great
and awesome God,[h] who keeps his
covenant of love[i] with those who
love him and obey his commands,
6let your ear be attentive and your
eyes open to hear[j] the prayer[k] your
servant is praying before you day and
night for your servants, the people of
Israel. I confess[l] the sins we Israelites, including myself and my father's
house, have committed against you.
7We have acted very wickedly[m] toward you. We have not obeyed the

1:1 [a]Zec 7:1 [b]S Ezr 4:9; S Est 2:8
1:2 [c]Ne 7:2 [d]S 2Ki 21:14; Ne 7:6; Jer 52:28
1:3 [e]S Lev 26:31; 2Ki 25:10; Ne 2:3, 13,17; Isa 22:9; Jer 39:8; 52:14; La 2:9
1:4 [f]Ps 137:1 [g]S 2Ch 20:3; S Ezr 9:4; Da 9:3
1:5 [h]S Dt 7:21; Ne 4:14 [i]S Dt 7:9; S 1Ki 8:23; Da 9:4
1:6 [j]S 1Ki 8:29; S 2Ch 7:15 [k]S 1Ki 8:30 [l]S 1Ki 8:47
1:7 [m]Ps 106:6
1:8 [n]S Ge 8:1; S 2Ki 20:3; Ne 4:14; 5:19; 6:14; 13:22,29,31 [o]S Lev 26:33
1:9 [p]S Dt 30:4; Ps 106:47; 107:3; Isa 11:12; 56:8; Jer 42:12; Eze 11:17 [q]S 1Ki 8:48; Jer 29:14; Eze 11:17; 20:34-38; 36:24-38; Mic 2:12
1:10 [r]S Ex 32:11; Isa 51:9-11
1:11 [s]S 2Ch 6:40 [t]S Ex 3:21 [u]S Ge 40:1
2:1 [v]S Ezr 4:7; S 6:14

commands, decrees and laws you
gave your servant Moses.
8"Remember[n] the instruction you
gave your servant Moses, saying, 'If
you are unfaithful, I will scatter[o] you
among the nations, 9but if you return
to me and obey my commands, then
even if your exiled people are at the
farthest horizon, I will gather[p] them
from there and bring them to the
place I have chosen as a dwelling for
my Name.'[q]
10"They are your servants and your
people, whom you redeemed by your
great strength and your mighty
hand.[r] 11O Lord, let your ear be attentive[s] to the prayer of this your
servant and to the prayer of your servants who delight in revering your
name. Give your servant success today by granting him favor[t] in the
presence of this man."

I was cupbearer[u] to the king.

Chapter 2

Artaxerxes Sends Nehemiah to Jerusalem

IN the month of Nisan in the twentieth
year of King Artaxerxes,[v] when wine
was brought for him, I took the wine and
gave it to the king. I had not been sad in
his presence before; 2so the king asked
me, "Why does your face look so sad
when you are not ill? This can be nothing
but sadness of heart."
I was very much afraid, 3but I said to

1:2 THE CHURCH, Remnant—See note on Ezr 1:4.

1:4–11 WORSHIP, Prayer—See note on Ge 12:6–8.

1:4–11 PRAYER, Confession—Like Ezra, Nehemiah identified himself with sinful Israel and confessed Israel's sins to God. Nehemiah went a step beyond Ezra. He claimed the promises of Scripture and asked for success as he initiated a plan to help Israel. Ezra initiated his plan only in a second step. See note on Ezr 9:1–15; 10:1–17. Confession of sin is an appropriate prayer before one undertakes a challenging project for God and His people.

1:5 GOD, One God—Nehemiah addressed his prayer to God in a way that expressed faith in the one, unique God. Lack of clarity on this issue is what had sent the chosen people into captivity. They did not worship God alone. They did not trust God to keep His covenant. They refused to believe God would bring the covenant curses upon them. See notes on Ge 31:30–35; 35:2; Dt 6:4–9.

1:5 GOD, Love—The love of God and the faithfulness of God are related attributes. His love for His chosen people leads Him to exercise His faithfulness to His covenant promises. These attributes make it possible for His people to pray to Him with trust that He will be faithful to answer in love. See notes on Ge 8:1; Ex 3:7; Nu 26:65; Dt 10:11,22; Jos 1:6; Mt 10:29–31; Mk 1:11; Jn 3:16.

1:5–11 HISTORY, Deliverance—Deliverance includes helping an individual in a personal conference. Prayer is the preparation for such deliverance. Nehemiah's prayer claimed God's promises.

1:5 CHRISTIAN ETHICS, Covenant—The covenant demands grow out of God's love, not out of a tyrant's need to manipulate and exercise power.

1:5 THE CHURCH, Covenant People—See note on 2 Ch 6:14.

1:6–7 SIN, Missing the Mark—Sin (Hebrew *chatta'th*) is the failure to hit the target God has set for your life. See the literal use of the term in Jdg 20:16. This is the most comprehensive Old Testament understanding of sin. Sin is failure to be what God created us to be. Sin is thus wicked (Hebrew *chabal*). It is corrupt action which leads to ruin. It is offensive to God (Job 34:31), violating His commands. Sin, thus, is a concrete act against a known expectation of God, but it is also a general failure to be what we can be. All sin may be confessed to God, who forgives repentant sinners and renews their lives.

1:8–9 HOLY SCRIPTURE, Hope—Prayers are used as revelation to refresh the people's understanding of God's part in their history and purposes. For Nehemiah, the Law of Moses had become authoritative Scripture he could refer to and expect the people to recognize (Lev 26:27–45; Dt 30:1–10). See note on 2 Ch 34:21.

1:8–9 ELECTION, Responsibility—Nehemiah confessed the elect people's sins. He sought God's forgiveness of His chosen nation. He acknowledged the unfaithful past of his people and mourned, fasted, and prayed for an opportunity to be faithful and to influence his people to become faithful to the election stipulations of God. God is faithful to His promises in spite of His people's disobedience.

1:9 SALVATION, Repentance—See note on Dt 30:1–10. Persons who have turned to other gods, activities, or goals as life's center need to repent. Repentance is returning to God and obeying His commands. God promised to bless His exiled people when they repented.

1:10 SALVATION, Redemption—Compare Dt 9:29. God's people can count on His redemption in the present and the future, based on His redemption in the past.

the king, "May the king live forever![w]
Why should my face not look sad when
the city[x] where my fathers are buried
lies in ruins, and its gates have been destroyed by fire?[y]"
4 The king said to me, "What is it you
want?"
Then I prayed to the God of heaven,
5 and I answered the king, "If it pleases
the king and if your servant has found
favor in his sight, let him send me to the
city in Judah where my fathers are buried
so that I can rebuild it."
6 Then the king[z], with the queen sitting beside him, asked me, "How long
will your journey take, and when will you
get back?" It pleased the king to send me;
so I set a time.
7 I also said to him, "If it pleases the
king, may I have letters to the governors
of Trans-Euphrates,[a] so that they will
provide me safe-conduct until I arrive in
Judah? 8 And may I have a letter to Asaph,
keeper of the king's forest, so he will give
me timber to make beams for the gates of
the citadel[b] by the temple and for the
city wall and for the residence I will occupy?" And because the gracious hand of
my God was upon me,[c] the king granted
my requests.[d] 9 So I went to the governors of Trans-Euphrates and gave them
the king's letters. The king had also sent
army officers and cavalry[e] with me.
10 When Sanballat[f] the Horonite and
Tobiah[g] the Ammonite official heard
about this, they were very much disturbed that someone had come to promote the welfare of the Israelites.[h]

Nehemiah Inspects Jerusalem's Walls

11 I went to Jerusalem, and after staying
there three days[i] 12 I set out during the
night with a few men. I had not told anyone what my God had put in my heart to
do for Jerusalem. There were no mounts
with me except the one I was riding on.
13 By night I went out through the Valley Gate[j] toward the Jackal[a] Well and
the Dung Gate,[k] examining the walls[l] of
Jerusalem, which had been broken down,
and its gates, which had been destroyed
by fire. 14 Then I moved on toward the
Fountain Gate[m] and the King's Pool,[n] but
there was not enough room for my mount
to get through; 15 so I went up the valley
by night, examining the wall. Finally, I
turned back and reentered through the
Valley Gate. 16 The officials did not know
where I had gone or what I was doing,
because as yet I had said nothing to the
Jews or the priests or nobles or officials or
any others who would be doing the work.
17 Then I said to them, "You see the
trouble we are in: Jerusalem lies in ruins,
and its gates have been burned with
fire.[o] Come, let us rebuild the wall[p] of
Jerusalem, and we will no longer be in
disgrace.[q]" 18 I also told them about the
gracious hand of my God upon me[r] and
what the king had said to me.
They replied, "Let us start rebuilding."
So they began this good work.
19 But when Sanballat[s] the Horonite,
Tobiah the Ammonite official and Geshem[t] the Arab heard about it, they
mocked and ridiculed us.[u] "What is this
you are doing?" they asked. "Are you rebelling against the king?"
20 I answered them by saying, "The
God of heaven will give us success. We
his servants will start rebuilding,[v] but as
for you, you have no share[w] in Jerusalem
or any claim or historic right to it."

Chapter 3

Builders of the Wall

ELIASHIB[x] the high priest and his fellow priests went to work and rebuilt[y] the Sheep Gate.[z] They dedicated
it and set its doors in place, building as far
as the Tower of the Hundred, which they
dedicated, and as far as the Tower of Hananel.[a] 2 The men of Jericho[b] built the adjoining section, and Zaccur son of Imri
built next to them.
3 The Fish Gate[c] was rebuilt by the
sons of Hassenaah. They laid its beams
and put its doors and bolts and bars in
place. 4 Meremoth[d] son of Uriah, the son
of Hakkoz, repaired the next section.
Next to him Meshullam son of Berekiah,
the son of Meshezabel, made repairs, and
next to him Zadok son of Baana also made

[a] 13 Or *Serpent* or *Fig*

2:3 [w] 1Ki 1:31; Da 2:4; 3:9; 5:10; 6:6,21 [x] Ps 137:6 [y] S Ne 1:3
2:6 [z] Ne 5:14; 13:6
2:7 [a] S Ezr 8:36
2:8 [b] Ne 7:2 [c] S Ezr 5:5 [d] S Ezr 4:24
2:9 [e] S Ezr 8:22
2:10 [f] ver 19; Ne 4:1,7; 6:1-2,5, 12,14; 13:28 [g] Ne 4:3; 13:4-7 [h] Est 10:3
2:11 [i] S Ge 40:13
2:13 [j] S 2Ch 26:9 [k] Ne 3:13; 12:31 [l] S Ne 1:3
2:14 [m] Ne 3:15; 12:37 [n] S 2Ki 18:17
2:17 [o] S Ne 1:3 [p] Ps 102:16; Isa 30:13; 58:12 [q] Eze 5:14
2:18 [r] S Ezr 5:5
2:19 [s] S ver 10 [t] Ne 6:1,2,6 [u] Ps 44:13-16
2:20 [v] Ezr 4:1 [w] Ezr 4:3; Ac 8:21
3:1 [x] S Ezr 10:24 [y] Isa 58:12 [z] ver 32; Ne 12:39; Jn 5:2 [a] Ne 12:39; Ps 48:12; Jer 31:38; Zec 14:10
3:2 [b] Ne 7:36
3:3 [c] S 2Ch 33:14
3:4 [d] S Ezr 8:33

2:4,8 PRAYER, Persistence—Nehemiah constantly sought God. He had already prayed aloud. See note on 1:4–11. This brief, silent prayer was effective because of his habit of prayer. Business conversations like this one need to be saturated with prayer beforehand and sprinkled with silent prayer as they progress.

2:8,18 GOD, Grace—Faith recognizes that all of the good things in life are expressions of the *grace of God to us.* When *other people* graciously supply our needs, their actions can ultimately be traced to God's gracious leadership in our lives. See notes on Ge 19:12–19,29; 39:21–23; 45:5–9.

2:8,18 REVELATION, Events—The rebuilder of the walls explained the king's favorable reception of Nehemiah as God's blessing and presence on the plan. The unhindered occurrence of an event is often explained in the Old Testament as God's approval and support of the event. Seeing God working in their lives inspires His people to work for Him.

2:20 HUMANITY, Work—The Hebrew expression carries the idea that God will bring the work of His people to a proper conclusion. See note on 2 Ch 32:30. The end result of the labors of those committed to God is ultimately God's responsibility and not the worker's. The worker is responsible for being faithful to a commitment to God, leaving the results to God.

repairs. 5The next section was repaired by the men of Tekoa,[e] but their nobles would not put their shoulders to the work under their supervisors.[b]

6The Jeshanah[c] Gate[f] was repaired by Joiada son of Paseah and Meshullam son of Besodeiah. They laid its beams and put its doors and bolts and bars in place. 7Next to them, repairs were made by men from Gibeon[g] and Mizpah—Melatiah of Gibeon and Jadon of Meronoth—places under the authority of the governor of Trans-Euphrates. 8Uzziel son of Harhaiah, one of the goldsmiths, repaired the next section; and Hananiah, one of the perfume-makers, made repairs next to that. They restored[d] Jerusalem as far as the Broad Wall.[h] 9Rephaiah son of Hur, ruler of a half-district of Jerusalem, repaired the next section. 10Adjoining this, Jedaiah son of Harumaph made repairs opposite his house, and Hattush son of Hashabneiah made repairs next to him. 11Malkijah son of Harim and Hasshub son of Pahath-Moab repaired another section and the Tower of the Ovens.[i] 12Shallum son of Hallohesh, ruler of a half-district of Jerusalem, repaired the next section with the help of his daughters.

13The Valley Gate[j] was repaired by Hanun and the residents of Zanoah.[k] They rebuilt it and put its doors and bolts and bars in place. They also repaired five hundred yards[e] of the wall as far as the Dung Gate.[l]

14The Dung Gate was repaired by Malkijah son of Recab, ruler of the district of Beth Hakkerem.[m] He rebuilt it and put its doors and bolts and bars in place.

15The Fountain Gate was repaired by Shallun son of Col-Hozeh, ruler of the district of Mizpah. He rebuilt it, roofing it over and putting its doors and bolts and bars in place. He also repaired the wall of the Pool of Siloam,[f][n] by the King's Garden, as far as the steps going down from the City of David. 16Beyond him, Nehemiah son of Azbuk, ruler of a half-district of Beth Zur,[o] made repairs up to a point opposite the tombs[g][p] of David, as far as the artificial pool and the House of the Heroes.

17Next to him, the repairs were made by the Levites under Rehum son of Bani. Beside him, Hashabiah, ruler of half the district of Keilah,[q] carried out repairs for his district. 18Next to him, the repairs were made by their countrymen under Binnui[h] son of Henadad, ruler of the other half-district of Keilah. 19Next to him, Ezer son of Jeshua, ruler of Mizpah, repaired another section, from a point facing the ascent to the armory as far as the angle. 20Next to him, Baruch son of Zabbai zealously repaired another section, from the angle to the entrance of the house of Eliashib the high priest. 21Next to him, Meremoth[r] son of Uriah, the son of Hakkoz, repaired another section, from the entrance of Eliashib's house to the end of it.

22The repairs next to him were made by the priests from the surrounding region. 23Beyond them, Benjamin and Hasshub made repairs in front of their house; and next to them, Azariah son of Maaseiah, the son of Ananiah, made repairs beside his house. 24Next to him, Binnui[s] son of Henadad repaired another section, from Azariah's house to the angle and the corner, 25and Palal son of Uzai worked opposite the angle and the tower projecting from the upper palace near the court of the guard.[t] Next to him, Pedaiah son of Parosh[u] 26and the temple servants[v] living on the hill of Ophel[w] made repairs up to a point opposite the Water Gate[x] toward the east and the projecting tower. 27Next to them, the men of Tekoa[y] repaired another section, from the great projecting tower[z] to the wall of Ophel.

28Above the Horse Gate,[a] the priests made repairs, each in front of his own house. 29Next to them, Zadok son of Immer made repairs opposite his house. Next to him, Shemaiah son of Shecaniah, the guard at the East Gate, made repairs. 30Next to him, Hananiah son of Shelemiah, and Hanun, the sixth son of Zalaph, repaired another section. Next to them, Meshullam son of Berekiah made repairs opposite his living quarters. 31Next to him, Malkijah, one of the goldsmiths, made repairs as far as the house of the temple servants and the merchants, opposite the Inspection Gate, and as far as the room above the corner; 32and between the room above the corner and the Sheep Gate[b] the goldsmiths and merchants made repairs.

Chapter 4

Opposition to the Rebuilding

WHEN Sanballat[c] heard that we were rebuilding the wall, he became angry and was greatly incensed. He ridiculed the Jews, 2and in the presence of

3:5 [e]ver 27; S 2Sa 14:2
3:6 [f]Ne 12:39
3:7 [g]S Jos 9:3
3:8 [h]Ne 12:38
3:11 [i]Ne 12:38
3:13 [j]S 2Ch 26:9 [k]S Jos 15:34 [l]S Ne 2:13
3:14 [m]Jer 6:1
3:15 [n]Isa 8:6; Jn 9:7
3:16 [o]S Jos 15:58 [p]Ac 2:29
3:17 [q]S Jos 15:44
3:21 [r]S Ezr 8:33
3:24 [s]S Ezr 8:33
3:25 [t]Jer 32:2; 37:21; 39:14 [u]S Ezr 2:3
3:26 [v]Ne 7:46; 11:21 [w]S 2Ch 33:14 [x]Ne 8:1,3,16; 12:37
3:27 [y]S ver 5 [z]Ps 48:12
3:28 [a]S 2Ki 11:16
3:32 [b]S ver 1; Jn 5:2
4:1 [c]S Ne 2:10

[b]5 Or *their Lord* or *the governor* [c]6 Or *Old*
[d]8 Or *They left out part of* [e]13 Hebrew *a thousand cubits* (about 450 meters) [f]15 Hebrew *Shelah*, a variant of *Shiloah*, that is, Siloam [g]16 Hebrew; Septuagint, some Vulgate manuscripts and Syriac *tomb*
[h]18 Two Hebrew manuscripts and Syriac (see also Septuagint and verse 24); most Hebrew manuscripts *Bavvai*

his associates[d] and the army of Samaria,
he said, "What are those feeble Jews doing? Will they restore their wall? Will
they offer sacrifices? Will they finish in a
day? Can they bring the stones back to
life from those heaps of rubble[e]—burned
as they are?"
3Tobiah[f] the Ammonite, who was at
his side, said, "What they are building—
if even a fox climbed up on it, he would
break down their wall of stones!"[g]

4Hear us, O our God, for we are despised.[h] Turn their insults back on their
own heads. Give them over as plunder in
a land of captivity. 5Do not cover up their
guilt[i] or blot out their sins from your
sight,[j] for they have thrown insults in
the face of[1] the builders.

6So we rebuilt the wall till all of it
reached half its height, for the people
worked with all their heart.
7But when Sanballat, Tobiah,[k] the
Arabs, the Ammonites and the men of
Ashdod heard that the repairs to Jerusalem's walls had gone ahead and that the
gaps were being closed, they were very
angry. 8They all plotted together[l] to
come and fight against Jerusalem and stir
up trouble against it. 9But we prayed to
our God and posted a guard day and night
to meet this threat.
10Meanwhile, the people in Judah said,
"The strength of the laborers[m] is giving
out, and there is so much rubble that we
cannot rebuild the wall."
11Also our enemies said, "Before they
know it or see us, we will be right there
among them and will kill them and put an
end to the work."
12Then the Jews who lived near them
came and told us ten times over, "Wherever you turn, they will attack us."
13Therefore I stationed some of the
people behind the lowest points of the
wall at the exposed places, posting them
by families, with their swords, spears and
bows. 14After I looked things over, I stood
up and said to the nobles, the officials and
the rest of the people, "Don't be afraid[n]
of them. Remember[o] the Lord, who is
great and awesome,[p] and fight[q] for your
brothers, your sons and your daughters,
your wives and your homes."
15When our enemies heard that we
were aware of their plot and that God had
frustrated it,[r] we all returned to the wall,
each to his own work.
16From that day on, half of my men did
the work, while the other half were
equipped with spears, shields, bows and
armor. The officers posted themselves behind all the people of Judah 17who were
building the wall. Those who carried materials did their work with one hand and
held a weapon[s] in the other, 18and each
of the builders wore his sword at his side
as he worked. But the man who sounded
the trumpet[t] stayed with me.
19Then I said to the nobles, the officials
and the rest of the people, "The work is
extensive and spread out, and we are
widely separated from each other along
the wall. 20Wherever you hear the sound
of the trumpet,[u] join us there. Our God
will fight[v] for us!"
21So we continued the work with half
the men holding spears, from the first
light of dawn till the stars came out. 22At
that time I also said to the people, "Have
every man and his helper stay inside Jerusalem at night, so they can serve us as
guards by night and workmen by day."
23Neither I nor my brothers nor my men
nor the guards with me took off our
clothes; each had his weapon, even when
he went for water.[j]

Chapter 5

Nehemiah Helps the Poor

NOW the men and their wives raised a
great outcry against their Jewish
brothers. 2Some were saying, "We and

[1]5 Or *have provoked you to anger before* [j]23 The meaning of the Hebrew for this clause is uncertain.

4:2 [d]S Ezr 4:9-10 [e]Ps 79:1; Jer 26:18
4:3 [f]S Ne 2:10 [g]Job 13:12; 15:3
4:4 [h]Ps 44:13; 123:3-4; Jer 33:24
4:5 [i]Isa 2:9; La 1:22 [j]2Ki 14:27; Ps 51:1; 69:27-28; 109:14; Jer 18:23
4:7 [k]S Ne 2:10
4:8 [l]Ps 2:2; 83:1-18
4:10 [m]S 1Ch 23:4
4:14 [n]S Ge 28:15; S Dt 1:29 [o]S Ne 1:8 [p]S Ne 1:5 [q]S 2Sa 10:12
4:15 [r]S 2Sa 17:14; Job 5:12
4:17 [s]Ps 149:6
4:18 [t]S Nu 10:2
4:20 [u]Eze 33:3 [v]S Ex 14:14; S Dt 20:4; Jos 10:14

4:1–23 CHRISTIAN ETHICS, War and Peace—Prayer, preparation, and work go together for God's threatened people. Danger was imminent to the fulfillment of God's directives to rebuild the wall. In such circumstances an appropriate response is always to prepare to resist attack using sound principles of defense. Confidence is based on faith and prayer, not on military strength although sensible defensive precautions should be taken. See note on 2 Ch 20:1–30.

4:4–5 PRAYER, Curse—This prayer must be seen in the light of Nehemiah's other prayers. He had so totally identified himself with God and His will that he knew his enemies were God's enemies. God had promised Abraham that those who cursed him would be cursed (Ge 12:3). This prayer still allows vengeance to be the Lord's (Dt 32:35), for Nehemiah did not take revenge. See note on 2 Ki 1:10,12.

4:9 PRAYER, Commitment—Prayer must be coupled with commitment and action.

4:13–23 HISTORY, Deliverance—God led the people to rebuild the city fortifications. Their readiness to fight, willingness to work, and trust in God brought success. God's historical acts involve faithful human participation.

4:14 GOD, Sovereignty—The doctrine of God's sovereignty does not simply increase our knowledge. It increases our trust level. Because God is great, powerful, and in total control of our world, we can do what He calls us to in total confidence and trust. We need fear no human powers. See notes on Ge 15:13–16; 18:14; 24:3,7,50.

5:1–18 CHRISTIAN ETHICS, Citizenship—Believers in places of civil authority can witness to Christ by seeking and implementing justice for those who are weak and potentially vulnerable to a system. Overcharging and underserving are immoralities crying to be addressed. Christian citizens must impact the economic system of society if they are to fulfill Christ's calling. See note on Am 5:7–24.

our sons and daughters are numerous; in
order for us to eat and stay alive, we must
get grain."
3Others were saying, "We are mortgag-
ing our fields,[w] our vineyards and our
homes to get grain during the famine."[x]
4Still others were saying, "We have
had to borrow money to pay the king's
tax[y] on our fields and vineyards. 5Al-
though we are of the same flesh and
blood[z] as our countrymen and though
our sons are as good as theirs, yet we
have to subject our sons and daughters to
slavery.[a] Some of our daughters have already been enslaved, but we are powerless, because our fields and our vineyards
belong to others."[b]
6When I heard their outcry and these
charges, I was very angry. 7I pondered
them in my mind and then accused the
nobles and officials. I told them, "You are
exacting usury[c] from your own countrymen!" So I called together a large meeting to deal with them 8and said: "As far
as possible, we have bought[d] back our
Jewish brothers who were sold to the
Gentiles. Now you are selling your brothers, only for them to be sold back to us!"
They kept quiet, because they could find
nothing to say.[e]
9So I continued, "What you are doing
is not right. Shouldn't you walk in the
fear of our God to avoid the reproach[f] of
our Gentile enemies? 10I and my brothers
and my men are also lending the people
money and grain. But let the exacting of
usury stop![g] 11Give back to them immediately their fields, vineyards, olive
groves and houses, and also the usury[h]
you are charging them—the hundredth
part of the money, grain, new wine and
oil."
12"We will give it back," they said.
"And we will not demand anything more
from them. We will do as you say."
Then I summoned the priests and
made the nobles and officials take an
oath[i] to do what they had promised. 13I
also shook[j] out the folds of my robe and
said, "In this way may God shake out of
his house and possessions every man who
does not keep this promise. So may such
a man be shaken out and emptied!"
At this the whole assembly said,
"Amen,"[k] and praised the LORD. And
the people *did as they had promised*.
14Moreover, from the twentieth year of
King Artaxerxes,[l] when I was appointed
to be their governor[m] in the land of Judah, until his thirty-second year—twelve
years—neither I nor my brothers ate the
food allotted to the governor. 15But the
earlier governors—those preceding me
—placed a heavy burden on the people
and took forty shekels[k] of silver from
them in addition to food and wine. Their
assistants also lorded it over the people.
But out of reverence for God[n] I did not
act like that. 16Instead,[o] I devoted myself
to the work on this wall. All my men
were assembled there for the work; we[l]
did not acquire any land.
17Furthermore, a hundred and fifty
Jews and officials ate at my table, as well
as those who came to us from the surrounding nations. 18Each day one ox, six
choice sheep and some poultry[p] were
prepared for me, and every ten days an
abundant supply of wine of all kinds. In
spite of all this, I never demanded the
food allotted to the governor, because the
demands were heavy on these people.
19Remember[q] me with favor, O my
God, for all I have done for these people.

Chapter 6

Further Opposition to the Rebuilding

WHEN word came to Sanballat, Tobiah,[r] Geshem[s] the Arab and the
rest of our enemies that I had rebuilt the
wall and not a gap was left in it—though
up to that time I had not set the doors in
the gates— 2Sanballat and Geshem sent
me this message: "Come, let us meet together in one of the villages[m] on the plain
of Ono.[t]"
But they were scheming to harm me;
3so I sent messengers to them with this
reply: "I am carrying on a great project
and cannot go down. Why should the
work stop while I leave it and go down to
you?" 4Four times they sent me the same
message, and each time I gave them the
same answer.
5Then, the fifth time, Sanballat[u] sent
his aide to me with the same message,
and in his hand was an unsealed letter 6in
which was written:

"It is reported among the nations
—and Geshem[n][v] says it is true—

5:3 [w]Ps 109:11 [x]Ge 47:23
5:4 [y]S Ezr 4:13
5:5 [z]S Ge 29:14 [a]Lev 25:39-43,47; S 2Ki 4:1; Isa 50:1 [b]Dt 15:7-11; S 2Ki 4:1
5:7 [c]Ex 22:25-27; S Lev 25:35-37; Dt 23:19-20; 24:10-13
5:8 [d]Lev 25:47 [e]Jer 34:8
5:9 [f]Isa 52:5
5:10 [g]S Ex 22:25
5:11 [h]Isa 58:6
5:12 [i]S Ezr 10:5
5:13 [j]S Mt 10:14 [k]Dt 27:15-26
5:14 [l]S Ne 2:6 [m]Ge 42:6; Ezr 6:7; Jer 40:7; Hag 1:1
5:15 [n]S Ge 20:11
5:16 [o]2Th 3:7-10
5:18 [p]1Ki 4:23
5:19 [q]S Ge 8:1; S 2Ki 20:3; S Ne 1:8
6:1 [r]Ne 2:10 [s]S Ne 2:19
6:2 [t]S 1Ch 8:12
6:5 [u]S Ne 2:10
6:6 [v]S Ne 2:19

[k]*15* That is, about 1 pound (about 0.5 kilogram)
[l]*16* Most Hebrew manuscripts; some Hebrew manuscripts, Septuagint, Vulgate and Syriac *I*
[m]*2* Or *in Kephirim*
[n]*6* Hebrew *Gashmu,* a variant of *Geshem*

5:12–13 PRAYER, Commitment—Every part of Nehemiah's reform was accompanied by prayer. An oath was appropriate for this commitment. It signified a commitment to God as well as to Nehemiah to quit charging excess interest.

5:19 PRAYER, Petition—Legally, Nehemiah could have appropriated the food and tax allotted to the governor. He preferred to please God rather than self. He asked God to remember his work, since it was done to honor and please God. Prayer dedicates our work to God and calls for reassurance that our work gains His favor. Compare 6:14; 13:14,22, 31. The work that pleases God is work done for God's people.

that you and the Jews are plotting to
revolt, and therefore you are building
the wall. Moreover, according to
these reports you are about to become their king 7and have even appointed prophets to make this proclamation about you in Jerusalem:
'There is a king in Judah!' Now this
report will get back to the king; so
come, let us confer together."

8I sent him this reply: "Nothing like
what you are saying is happening; you are
just making it up out of your head."
9They were all trying to frighten us,
thinking, "Their hands will get too weak
for the work, and it will not be completed."
⌞But I prayed,⌟ "Now strengthen my
hands."
10One day I went to the house of Shemaiah son of Delaiah, the son of Mehetabel, who was shut in at his home. He
said, "Let us meet in the house of God,
inside the temple[w], and let us close the
temple doors, because men are coming to
kill you—by night they are coming to kill
you."
11But I said, "Should a man like me run
away? Or should one like me go into the
temple to save his life? I will not go!" 12I
realized that God had not sent him, but
that he had prophesied against me[x] because Tobiah and Sanballat[y] had hired
him. 13He had been hired to intimidate
me so that I would commit a sin by doing
this, and then they would give me a bad
name to discredit me.[z]

14Remember[a] Tobiah and Sanballat,[b]
O my God, because of what they have
done; remember also the prophetess[c]
Noadiah and the rest of the prophets[d]
who have been trying to intimidate me.

The Completion of the Wall

15So the wall was completed on the
twenty-fifth of Elul, in fifty-two days.
16When all our enemies heard about this,
all the surrounding nations were afraid
and lost their self-confidence, because
they realized that this work had been
done with the help of our God.
17Also, in those days the nobles of Judah were sending many letters to Tobiah,
and replies from Tobiah kept coming to
them. 18For many in Judah were under
oath to him, since he was son-in-law to
Shecaniah son of Arah, and his son Jehohanan had married the daughter of Meshullam son of Berekiah. 19Moreover,
they kept reporting to me his good deeds
and then telling him what I said. And Tobiah sent letters to intimidate me.

Chapter 7

AFTER the wall had been rebuilt and I
had set the doors in place, the gatekeepers[e] and the singers[f] and the Levites[g] were appointed. 2I put in charge of
Jerusalem my brother Hanani,[h] along
with° Hananiah[i] the commander of the
citadel,[j] because he was a man of integrity and feared[k] God more than most men
do. 3I said to them, "The gates of Jerusalem are not to be opened until the sun is
hot. While the gatekeepers are still on
duty, have them shut the doors and bar
them. Also appoint residents of Jerusalem
as guards, some at their posts and some
near their own houses."

The List of the Exiles Who Returned

7:6–73pp — Ezr 2:1–70

4Now the city was large and spacious,
but there were few people in it,[l] and the
houses had not yet been rebuilt. 5So my
God put it into my heart to assemble the
nobles, the officials and the common people for registration by families. I found
the genealogical record of those who had
been the first to return. This is what I
found written there:

6These are the people of the province who came up from the captivity
of the exiles[m] whom Nebuchadnezzar king of Babylon had taken captive
(they returned to Jerusalem and Judah, each to his own town, 7in company with Zerubbabel,[n] Jeshua, Nehemiah, Azariah, Raamiah, Nahama-
ni, Mordecai, Bilshan, Mispereth,
Bigvai, Nehum and Baanah):

The list of the men of Israel:

6:10 [w]Nu 18:7
6:12 [x]Eze 13:22-23 [y]S Ne 2:10
6:13 [z]Jer 20:10
6:14 [a]S Ne 1:8 [b]S Ne 2:10 [c]S Ex 15:20; Eze 13:17-23; S Ac 21:9; Rev 2:20 [d]Jer 23:9-40; Zec 13:2-3
7:1 [e]1Ch 9:27; S 26:12-19 [f]Ps 68:25 [g]Ne 8:9
7:2 [h]Ne 1:2 [i]Ne 10:23 [j]Ne 2:8 [k]1Ki 18:3
7:4 [l]Ne 11:1
7:6 [m]S 2Ch 36:20; S Ne 1:2
7:7 [n]S 1Ch 3:19

°2 Or *Hanani, that is,*

6:9 PRAYER, Petition—Circumstances could have discouraged Nehemiah. The joy of the Lord was his strength (8:10). Petition includes asking for skill, patience, and strength to complete the tasks God gives us.

6:14 PRAYER, Curse—See notes on 4:4–5; 5:19; 2 Ki 2:24. Nehemiah left final judgment to God on enemies who hindered his work on God's mission. A curse may be a healthy way to deal with anger while leaving action to God. Compare Ro 12:14; Eph 4:26.

***6:15–16* HISTORY, Universal**—God works for His people in history to establish His people and to let the nations know His power.

7:4–73 HISTORY, Deliverance—See note on Ezr 2:1–70.

7:5–73 REVELATION, Divine Presence—Nehemiah received a message in his heart to organize and assemble the leadership of Judah. The revelation came as a personal conviction after prayer and openness to God's communication. The emptiness of the city could have been the constraining fact that God used to impress Nehemiah with the need to register the population. Nehemiah used the same written source as did Ezra 2. In weakness and crisis the identity of God's people is important. God inspired His authors to duplicate material to emphasize the importance of this identity.

[8]the descendants of Parosh 2,172
[9]of Shephatiah 372
[10]of Arah 652
[11]of Pahath-Moab (through the line of Jeshua and Joab) 2,818
[12]of Elam 1,254
[13]of Zattu 845
[14]of Zaccai 760
[15]of Binnui 648
[16]of Bebai 628
[17]of Azgad 2,322
[18]of Adonikam 667
[19]of Bigvai 2,067
[20]of Adin[o] 655
[21]of Ater (through Hezekiah) 98
[22]of Hashum 328
[23]of Bezai 324
[24]of Hariph 112
[25]of Gibeon 95
[26]the men of Bethlehem and Netophah[p] 188
[27]of Anathoth[q] 128
[28]of Beth Azmaveth 42
[29]of Kiriath Jearim, Kephirah[r] and Beeroth[s] 743
[30]of Ramah and Geba 621
[31]of Micmash 122
[32]of Bethel and Ai[t] 123
[33]of the other Nebo 52
[34]of the other Elam 1,254
[35]of Harim 320
[36]of Jericho[u] 345
[37]of Lod, Hadid and Ono[v] 721
[38]of Senaah 3,930

[39]The priests:

the descendants of Jedaiah (through the family of Jeshua) 973
[40]of Immer 1,052
[41]of Pashhur 1,247
[42]of Harim 1,017

[43]The Levites:

the descendants of Jeshua (through Kadmiel through the line of Hodaviah) 74

[44]The singers:[w]

the descendants of Asaph 148

[45]The gatekeepers:[x]

the descendants of
Shallum, Ater, Talmon,
Akkub, Hatita and Shobai 138

[46]The temple servants:[y]

the descendants of
Ziha, Hasupha, Tabbaoth,
[47]Keros, Sia, Padon,

7:20 [o]S Ezr 8:6
7:26 [p]S 2Sa 23:28; S 1Ch 2:54
7:27 [q]S Jos 21:18
7:29 [r]S Jos 18:26 [s]S Jos 18:25
7:32 [t]S Ge 12:8
7:36 [u]Ne 3:2
7:37 [v]S 1Ch 8:12
7:44 [w]Ne 11:23
7:45 [x]S 1Ch 9:17
7:46 [y]S Ne 3:26
7:60 [z]S 1Ch 9:2
7:65 [a]S Ex 28:30

[48]Lebana, Hagaba, Shalmai,
[49]Hanan, Giddel, Gahar,
[50]Reaiah, Rezin, Nekoda,
[51]Gazzam, Uzza, Paseah,
[52]Besai, Meunim, Nephussim,
[53]Bakbuk, Hakupha, Harhur,
[54]Bazluth, Mehida, Harsha,
[55]Barkos, Sisera, Temah,
[56]Neziah and Hatipha

[57]The descendants of the servants of Solomon:

the descendants of
Sotai, Sophereth, Perida,
[58]Jaala, Darkon, Giddel,
[59]Shephatiah, Hattil,
Pokereth-Hazzebaim and Amon

[60]The temple servants and the descendants of the servants of Solomon[z] 392

[61]The following came up from the towns of Tel Melah, Tel Harsha, Kerub, Addon and Immer, but they could not show that their families were descended from Israel:

[62]the descendants of
Delaiah, Tobiah and Nekoda 642

[63]And from among the priests:

the descendants of
Hobaiah, Hakkoz and Barzillai (a man who had married a daughter of Barzillai the Gileadite and was called by that name).

[64]These searched for their family
records, but they could not find them
and so were excluded from the
priesthood as unclean. [65]The governor, therefore, ordered them not to
eat any of the most sacred food until
there should be a priest ministering
with the Urim and Thummim.[a]

[66]The whole company numbered
42,360, [67]besides their 7,337 menservants and maidservants; and they
also had 245 men and women singers. [68]There were 736 horses, 245
mules,[p] [69]435 camels and 6,720
donkeys.

[70]Some of the heads of the families
contributed to the work. The governor gave to the treasury 1,000 drachmas[q] of gold, 50 bowls and 530 garments for priests. [71]Some of the

[p] 68 Some Hebrew manuscripts (see also Ezra 2:66); most Hebrew manuscripts do not have this verse.
[q] 70 That is, about 19 pounds (about 8.5 kilograms)

7:70–72 STEWARDSHIP, House of God—See note on Ezr 8:28,35. Stewardship involves helping build houses of worship. Stewardship of life leads to worship in God's house.

heads of the families[b] gave to the
treasury for the work 20,000 drachmas[r] of gold and 2,200 minas[s] of
silver. 72The total given by the rest of
the people was 20,000 drachmas of
gold, 2,000 minas[t] of silver and 67
garments for priests.[c]
73The priests, the Levites, the gatekeepers, the singers and the temple
servants,[d] along with certain of the
people and the rest of the Israelites,
settled in their own towns.[e]

Chapter 8

Ezra Reads the Law

WHEN the seventh month came and
the Israelites had settled in their
towns,[f] 1all the people assembled as one
man in the square before the Water Gate.
[g] They told Ezra the scribe to bring out the
Book of the Law of Moses,[h] which the
LORD had commanded for Israel.
2So on the first day of the seventh
month[i] Ezra the priest brought the
Law[j] before the assembly, which was
made up of men and women and all who
were able to understand. 3He read it
aloud from daybreak till noon as he faced
the square before the Water Gate[k] in the
presence of the men, women and others
who could understand. And all the people
listened attentively to the Book of the
Law.
4Ezra the scribe stood on a high wood-
en platform[l] built for the occasion. Beside him on his right stood Mattithiah,
Shema, Anaiah, Uriah, Hilkiah and Maaseiah; and on his left were Pedaiah, Mishael, Malkijah, Hashum, Hashbaddanah,
Zechariah and Meshullam.
5Ezra opened the book. All the people
could see him because he was standing[m]
above them; and as he opened it, the people all stood up. 6Ezra praised the LORD,
the great God; and all the people lifted
their hands[n] and responded, "Amen!
Amen!" Then they bowed down and worshiped the LORD with their faces to the
ground.
7The Levites[o]—Jeshua, Bani, Sherebiah, Jamin, Akkub, Shabbethai, Hodiah,
Maaseiah, Kelita, Azariah, Jozabad, Hanan and Pelaiah—instructed[p] the people
in the Law while the people were standing there. 8They read from the Book of
the Law of God, making it clear[u] and giving the meaning so that the people could
understand what was being read.
9Then Nehemiah the governor, Ezra
the priest and scribe, and the Levites[q]
who were instructing the people said to
them all, "This day is sacred to the LORD
your God. Do not mourn or weep."[r] For
all the people had been weeping as they
listened to the words of the Law.
10Nehemiah said, "Go and enjoy
choice food and sweet drinks, and send
some to those who have nothing[s] prepared. This day is sacred to our Lord. Do
not grieve, for the joy[t] of the LORD is
your strength."
11The Levites calmed all the people,
saying, "Be still, for this is a sacred day.
Do not grieve."
12Then all the people went away to eat
and drink, to send portions of food and to
celebrate with great joy,[u] because they
now understood the words that had been
made known to them.
13On the second day of the month, the
heads of all the families, along with the
priests and the Levites, gathered around
Ezra the scribe to give attention to the
words of the Law. 14They found written
in the Law, which the LORD had commanded through Moses, that the Israelites were to live in booths[v] during the
feast of the seventh month 15and that
they should proclaim this word and
spread it throughout their towns and in
Jerusalem: "Go out into the hill country

7:71 [b]S 1Ch 29:7
7:72 [c]S Ex 25:2
7:73 [d]Ne 1:10; Ps 34:22; 103:21; 113:1; 135:1 [e]S Ezr 3:1; Ne 11:1 [f]Ezr 3:1
8:1 [g]S Ne 3:26 [h]S Dt 28:61; S 2Ch 34:15
8:2 [i]Lev 23:23-25; Nu 29:1-6 [j]S Dt 31:11
8:3 [k]S Ne 3:26
8:4 [l]2Ch 6:13
8:5 [m]Jdg 3:20
8:6 [n]S Ezr 9:5; 1Ti 2:8
8:7 [o]S Ezr 10:23 [p]S Lev 10:11; S 2Ch 17:7
8:9 [q]Ne 7:1,65,70 [r]Dt 12:7,12; 16:14-15
8:10 [s]1Sa 25:8; S 2Sa 6:19; Est 9:22; Lk 14:12-14 [t]S Lev 23:40; S Dt 12:18; 16:11, 14-15
8:12 [u]Est 9:22
8:14 [v]S Ex 23:16

[r] *71* That is, about 375 pounds (about 170 kilograms); also in verse 72 [s] *71* That is, about 1 1/3 tons (about 1.2 metric tons) [t] *72* That is, about 1 1/4 tons (about 1.1 metric tons) [u] *8* Or *God, translating it*

8:1–3 HOLY SCRIPTURE, Canonization—The assembled people saw and heard Ezra read aloud from the preserved and recovered book of the Law. Apparently two reasons lay behind the public reading. The people could not read the book themselves, and the assembly was often asked to be a witness against itself (Jos 24:22). God's scribe also acted as an interpreter of the holy words, explaining the meaning to a people reverently standing to hear. Clearly, Moses' Law was accepted as written, authoritative Scripture. Having the written Word and recognizing its authority are only part of the responsibility of God's people. We are called to understand and obey revelation. See note on Ezr 7:6.

8:1–6 WORSHIP, Proclamation—The reading of the Word of God was used to lead a great revival in worship. This revival was characterized by confession and repentance. Reading and proclaiming God's Word is a basic part of worship. Compare Col 3:16. See note on Jer 26:2–7.

8:1–9 EDUCATION, Spiritual Renewal—Education and worship are closely related. Knowledge of the Word of God can create the conditions for dramatic spiritual renewal. When Ezra read the Law to the assembled congregation, the people were moved to tears. Even to the present, instruction in the Word of God has frequently transformed lives, led to personal salvation, brought comfort and joy, produced tears of conviction, and reawakened commitment to God's purpose. See 2 Ki 23:1–3.

8:6 PRAYER, Worship—Ezra led a moment of high worship characterized by outward demonstration. The gestures indicated dependence on the Lord and humility. Ezra's praise was a traditional benediction (Hebrew *barak*, "bless") before reading Scripture. The people expressed their expectation that Scripture would bring praise to God and hope for their situation. Prayer is a central part of community worship.

and bring back branches from olive and
wild olive trees, and from myrtles, palms
and shade trees, to make booths"—as it
is written.[v]
16 So the people went out and brought
back branches and built themselves
booths on their own roofs, in their courtyards, in the courts of the house of God
and in the square by the Water Gate[w]
and the one by the Gate of Ephraim.[x]
17 The whole company that had returned
from exile built booths and lived in
them.[y] From the days of Joshua son of
Nun until that day, the Israelites had not
celebrated[z] it like this. And their joy was
very great.
18 Day after day, from the first day to
the last, Ezra read[a] from the Book of the
Law[b] of God. They celebrated the feast
for seven days, and on the eighth day, in
accordance with the regulation,[c] there
was an assembly.[d]

Chapter 9

The Israelites Confess Their Sins

1 On the twenty-fourth day of the same
month, the Israelites gathered together, fasting and wearing sackcloth and
having dust on their heads.[e] 2 Those of
Israelite descent had separated themselves from all foreigners.[f] They stood in
their places and confessed their sins and
the wickedness of their fathers.[g] 3 They
stood where they were and read from the
Book of the Law of the LORD their God for
a quarter of the day, and spent another
quarter in confession and in worshiping
the LORD their God. 4 Standing on the
stairs were the Levites[h]—Jeshua, Bani,
Kadmiel, Shebaniah, Bunni, Sherebiah,
Bani and Kenani—who called with loud
voices to the LORD their God. 5 And the
Levites—Jeshua, Kadmiel, Bani, Hashabneiah, Sherebiah, Hodiah, Shebaniah and
Pethahiah—said: "Stand up and praise
the LORD your God,[i] who is from everlasting to everlasting.[w]"

"Blessed be your glorious name,[j]
and may it be exalted above all blessing and praise. 6 You alone are the
LORD.[k] You made the heavens,[l]
even the highest heavens, and all
their starry host,[m] the earth[n] and all
that is on it, the seas[o] and all that is
in them.[p] You give life to everything,
and the multitudes of heaven[q] worship you.
7 "You are the LORD God, who
chose Abram[r] and brought him out
of Ur of the Chaldeans[s] and named
him Abraham.[t] 8 You found his heart
faithful to you, and you made a cov-

8:16 [w]S Ne 3:26 [x]S 2Ch 25:23
8:17 [y]Hos 12:9 [z]S 1Ki 8:2; S 2Ch 7:8; S 8:13
8:18 [a]Dt 31:11; S 33:10 [b]S Dt 28:61 [c]S Lev 23:36,40; S Ezr 3:4 [d]S Lev 23:36
9:1 [e]Lev 26:40-45; S Jos 7:6; 2Ch 7:14-16
9:2 [f]S Ezr 6:21; Ne 10:28; 13:3,30 [g]S Lev 26:40; S Ezr 10:11; Ps 106:6
9:4 [h]S Ezr 10:23
9:5 [i]Ps 78:4 [j]S 2Sa 7:26
9:6 [k]S Dt 6:4 [l]S Ex 8:19 [m]Isa 40:26; 45:12 [n]S Ge 1:1; Isa 37:16 [o]Ps 95:5; 146:6; Jnh 1:9 [p]Dt 10:14; Ac 4:24; Rev 10:6 [q]Ps 103:20; 148:2
9:7 [r]S Ge 16:11 [s]S Ge 11:28 [t]S Ge 17:5

[v]*15* See Lev. 23:37-40. [w]*5* Or *God for ever and ever*

9:1–37 EVIL AND SUFFERING, Punishment—From a human viewpoint, history may seem a series of hardships and suffering. God's people must see it as the story of God's compassion and justice in response to human evil. See note on Ezr 9:1–15.
9:1–38 WORSHIP, Prayer—The entire nation gathered to worship. At the heart of that worship was the confession of their sins in prayer and the adoration and exaltation of God. Meditation on the gracious acts of God is a major component of worship. See note on Ge 12:6–8.
9:1–37 PRAYER, Confession—Confession was marked outwardly by self-deprivation and rough clothing as well as through words admitting and expressing sorrow for sin. Such confession is necessary for the renewal of God's people. The long prayer involves both sides of confession—affirmation of belief in who God is and what He has done as well as admission of guilt. Israel recited history to contrast their disobedience with God's faithfulness. They admitted they deserved their current distress and threw themselves on God's covenant mercy and faithfulness. They implied but did not directly state a petition for deliverance.
9:2–3 SALVATION, Repentance—This is an example of repentance by the Israelites in the days of Ezra. Genuine repentance manifests itself in reading and hearing the Word of God, confession of sin, and worship.
9:5–37 GOD, Creator—We can confess that our God is the only God because He is the Creator worshiped in heaven, because in His election grace He chose us to be His people, because He has proved faithful to His covenant promises, because He delivered and redeemed His people, because He leads His people, because He provides His people with guidelines for living under His rulership, because He supplies the physical needs of His people, and because in compassion and love He forgives and restores His people. To such a God we can go freely confessing our sins and asking to be forgiven and restored. We can trust this God to save us from times of distress even when we have brought the distress on ourselves. See note on Dt 6:4–9.
9:5–37 SIN, Covenant Breach—Israel's history should be told as a growth in covenant obedience and blessing. Instead, it had to be recited as a history of covenant breach and curse. God takes seriously the commitments He makes to us and expects us to do the same. When we violate our commitments, He is prepared to discipline us. See note on Jdg 2:20.
9:5–37 HISTORY, God—Deliverance and judgment through history teach God's people His justice and faithfulness. History becomes the content of a prayer of confession and a prayer for new deliverance.
9:6 CREATION, Personal Creator—After Ezra read the Law, the people became convicted of their shortcomings. A prayer of confession followed, beginning with an affirmation of their God as a personal Creator of everything and everyone that existed. Such an attitude is prerequisite to all ethical standards. Because the world came into being through a personal Creator, morality has a unique claim on our lives. Monotheism destroys all claims to moral relativity. A holy Creator demands holiness from His creation.
9:6–37 REVELATION, History—God's saving acts in the history of His people formed the center of revelation for Israel. Rehearsed and repeated before the people often, such oral histories became a written record of God's saving activity in the lives of His children. See note on Ex 14:1—15:18. Interpreting and reviewing their history with God became a new source of revelation for Israel as they saw in it God's love, faithfulness, and care. Such history became the basis of prayer to God and a window to see the people's arrogance, rebellion, and sin.
9:7–8 THE CHURCH, Covenant People—See notes on Ge 17:1–21; 2 Ki 13:23.
9:8 GOD, Righteous—God's faithfulness is grounded in His righteousness. He is faithful because He does what is right. A sinful people learned this lesson after suffering God's just punishment. They trusted in God's faithfulness and righteousness

enant with him to give to his descendants the land of the Canaanites,
Hittites, Amorites, Perizzites, Jebusites and Girgashites.[u] You have kept
your promise[v] because you are righteous.[w]
9“You saw the suffering of our
forefathers in Egypt;[x] you heard
their cry at the Red Sea.[x][y] 10You
sent miraculous signs[z] and wonders[a] against Pharaoh, against all his
officials and all the people of his land,
for you knew how arrogantly the
Egyptians treated them. You made a
name[b] for yourself,[c] which remains
to this day. 11You divided the sea before them,[d] so that they passed
through it on dry ground, but you
hurled their pursuers into the
depths,[e] like a stone into mighty waters.[f] 12By day[g] you led[h] them with
a pillar of cloud,[i] and by night with a
pillar of fire to give them light on the
way they were to take.
13“You came down on Mount Si-
nai;[j] you spoke[k] to them from heav-
en.[l] You gave them regulations and
laws that are just[m] and right, and decrees and commands that are good.[n]
14You made known to them your holy
Sabbath[o] and gave them commands,
decrees and laws through your servant Moses. 15In their hunger you
gave them bread from heaven[p] and
in their thirst you brought them water from the rock;[q] you told them to
go in and take possession of the land
you had sworn with uplifted hand[r]
to give them.[s]
16“But they, our forefathers, became arrogant and stiff-necked,[t] and
did not obey your commands.[u]
17They refused to listen and failed to
remember[v] the miracles[w] you performed among them. They became
stiff-necked[x] and in their rebellion
appointed a leader in order to return
to their slavery.[y] But you are a forgiving God,[z] gracious and compassionate,[a] slow to anger[b] and
abounding in love.[c] Therefore you
did not desert them,[d] 18even when
they cast for themselves an image of
a calf[e] and said, ‘This is your god,
who brought you up out of Egypt,’ or
when they committed awful blasphemies.[f]
19“Because of your great compassion you did not abandon[g] them in
the desert. By day the pillar of cloud[h]
did not cease to guide them on their
path, nor the pillar of fire by night to
shine on the way they were to take.
20You gave your good Spirit[i] to instruct[j] them. You did not withhold
your manna[k] from their mouths, and
you gave them water[l] for their
thirst. 21For forty years[m] you sustained them in the desert; they
lacked nothing,[n] their clothes did
not wear out nor did their feet become swollen.[o]
22“You gave them kingdoms and
nations, allotting to them even the
remotest frontiers. They took over
the country of Sihon[y][p] king of Heshbon and the country of Og king of
Bashan.[q] 23You made their sons as
numerous as the stars in the sky,[r]
and you brought them into the land
that you told their fathers to enter
and possess. 24Their sons went in
and took possession of the land.[s]

9:8 [u]S Ge 15:18-21; S Ezr 9:1 [v]S Jos 21:45 [w]Ge 15:6; S Ezr 9:15 9:9 [x]Ex 2:23-25; 3:7 [y]Ex 14:10-30 9:10 [z]S Ex 10:1; Ps 74:9 [a]S Ex 3:20; S 6:6 [b]Jer 32:20; Da 9:15 [c]S Nu 6:27 9:11 [d]Ps 78:13 [e]S Ex 14:28 [f]Ex 15:4-5,10; Heb 11:29 9:12 [g]S Dt 1:33 [h]S Ex 15:13 [i]S Ex 13:21 9:13 [j]S Ex 19:11 [k]S Ex 19:19 [l]S Ex 20:22 [m]Ps 119:137 [n]S Ex 20:1; Dt 4:7-8 9:14 [o]S Ge 2:3; Ex 20:8-11 9:15 [p]S Ex 16:4; Ps 78:24-25; Jn 6:31 [q]Ex 17:6; Nu 20:7-13 [r]S Ge 14:22 [s]Dt 1:8,21 9:16 [t]S Ex 32:9; Jer 7:26; 17:23; 19:15 [u]Dt 1:26-33; 31:29 9:17 [v]Jdg 8:34; Ps 78:42 [w]Ps 77:11; 78:12; 105:5; 106:7 [x]Jer 7:26; 19:15 [y]Nu 14:1-4 [z]Ps 130:4; Da 9:9 [a]S Dt 4:31 [b]S Ex 34:6; Ps 103:8; Na 1:3 [c]S Ex 22:27; Nu 14:17-19; Ps 86:15 [d]Ps 78:11; Eze 5:6 9:18 [e]S Ex 32:4 [f]S Ex 20:23 9:19 [g]Ex 13:22 [h]S Ex 13:21 9:20 [i]Nu 9:17; 11:17; Isa 63:11, 14; Hag 2:5; Zec 4:6 [j]Ps 23:3; 143:10 [k]S Ex 16:15 [l]Ex 17:6 9:21 [m]S Ex 16:35 [n]S Dt 2:7 [o]S Dt 8:4 9:22 [p]S Nu 21:21 [q]S Nu 21:33; Dt 2:26-3:11 9:23 [r]S Ge 12:2; S Lev 26:9; S Nu 10:36 9:24 [s]S Jos 11:23

[x]9 Hebrew *Yam Suph*; that is, Sea of Reeds
[y]22 One Hebrew manuscript and Septuagint; most Hebrew manuscripts *Sihon, that is, the country of the*

as they confessed their sins.

9:10 GOD, Sovereignty—The sovereignty of God to work in His world, in any way He pleases, was shown in the signs and wonders that He performed in the Exodus (Ex 6—15).

9:10,17 MIRACLE, Vocabulary—Ezra described the Exodus event as signs and wonders. “Signs” (Hebrew *'oth*) covers a wide range of meanings from physical marks (Ge 4:15) and military standards (Nu 2:2) to season indicators (Ge 1:14) and physical indicators for spiritual realities (Ge 9:12–13; 17:11; Ex 31:13). Most often “signs” are miraculous divine actions pointing people to God. Such signs may seem quite ordinary occurrences to people not expecting divine signs (1 Sa 2:34; 14:10). Such signs should lead people to know and trust God (Ex 10:1–3; Nu 14:11). “Wonders” (Hebrew *mophet*) is used only in a theological meaning in the Old Testament. Most often wonders refer to God’s actions for Israel in Egypt during the Exodus (Ex 4:21; 7:9; 11:9; Dt 26:8). God’s curses destroying His own people are also wonders (Dt 28:45–46). See note on 1 Sa 10:9.

9:13,29 CHRISTIAN ETHICS, Moral Imperatives—We have no complaint against God. His commands are good and fair. They lead us to the life that is best for us, the life the Creator intends us to have. The problem is not the nature of God’s commands but our refusal to trust Him and obey. Even when another person’s or institution’s actions harm us, we do not have just cause to forsake our trust in God.

9:16–18 SIN, Rebellion—See note on Nu 17:5.

9:17–19 GOD, Love—The love of God is the primary expression of God’s nature. God exercised his forgiving love even when His people deliberately rejected his leadership and made for themselves an idol to be their god. God exercises His wrath only when His love cannot achieve its aim. See note on Ex 20:1–7.

9:17,25,28,31,35 GOD, Grace—God’s grace is a recurring theme running through this chapter. The grace of God appears in many ways: in forgiveness, in patience, in supplying needs of many kinds, in mercy, and in watching over His people. God’s people can rely on this grace. Thus we can confess our sins and plead for help in time of distress.

9:20,30 HOLY SPIRIT, Revelation—God’s Spirit seeks to interpret God’s will to His people throughout their history. He may teach the people through Moses or warn them through prophets. The Spirit continually guides God’s people to respond in faith and obedience.

You subdued[t] before them the Canaanites, who lived in the land; you
handed the Canaanites over to them,
along with their kings and the peoples of the land, to deal with them as
they pleased. 25They captured fortified cities and fertile land;[u] they
took possession of houses filled with
all kinds of good things,[v] wells already dug, vineyards, olive groves
and fruit trees in abundance. They
ate to the full and were well-nour-
ished;[w] they reveled in your great
goodness.[x]
26"But they were disobedient and
rebelled against you; they put your
law behind their backs.[y] They
killed[z] your prophets,[a] who had admonished them in order to turn them
back to you; they committed awful
blasphemies.[b] 27So you handed them
over to their enemies,[c] who oppressed them. But when they were
oppressed they cried out to you.
From heaven you heard them, and in
your great compassion[d] you gave
them deliverers,[e] who rescued them
from the hand of their enemies.
28"But as soon as they were at rest,
they again did what was evil in your
sight.[f] Then you abandoned them to
the hand of their enemies so that
they ruled over them. And when
they cried out to you again, you
heard from heaven, and in your compassion[g] you delivered them[h] time
after time.
29"You warned[i] them to return to
your law, but they became arrogant[j]
and disobeyed your commands. They
sinned against your ordinances, by
which a man will live if he obeys
them.[k] Stubbornly they turned their
backs[l] on you, became stiff-necked[m]
and refused to listen.[n] 30For many
years you were patient with them. By
your Spirit you admonished them
through your prophets.[o] Yet they
paid no attention, so you handed
them over to the neighboring peoples.[p] 31But in your great mercy you
did not put an end[q] to them or abandon them, for you are a gracious and
merciful[r] God.
32"Now therefore, O our God, the
great, mighty[s] and awesome God,[t]
who keeps his covenant of love,[u] do
not let all this hardship seem trifling
in your eyes—the hardship[v] that has
come upon us, upon our kings and
leaders, upon our priests and prophets, upon our fathers and all your
people, from the days of the kings of
Assyria until today. 33In all that has
happened to us, you have been just;[w]
you have acted faithfully, while we
did wrong.[x] 34Our kings,[y] our leaders, our priests and our fathers[z] did
not follow your law; they did not pay
attention to your commands or the
warnings you gave them. 35Even
while they were in their kingdom,
enjoying your great goodness[a] to
them in the spacious and fertile land
you gave them, they did not serve
you[b] or turn from their evil ways.
36"But see, we are slaves[c] today,
slaves in the land you gave our forefathers so they could eat its fruit and
the other good things it produces.
37Because of our sins, its abundant
harvest goes to the kings you have
placed over us. They rule over our
bodies and our cattle as they please.
We are in great distress.[d]

The Agreement of the People

38"In view of all this, we are making a
binding agreement,[e] putting it in writing,[f] and our leaders, our Levites and
our priests are affixing their seals to it."

Chapter 10

THOSE who sealed it were:
Nehemiah the governor, the son of
Hacaliah.
Zedekiah, 2Seraiah,[g] Azariah, Jeremiah,
3Pashhur,[h] Amariah, Malkijah,
4Hattush, Shebaniah, Malluch,
5Harim,[i] Meremoth, Obadiah,
6Daniel, Ginnethon, Baruch,
7Meshullam, Abijah, Mijamin,
8Maaziah, Bilgai and Shemaiah.
These were the priests.[j]
9The Levites:[k]
Jeshua son of Azaniah, Binnui of the
sons of Henadad, Kadmiel,
10and their associates: Shebaniah,
Hodiah, Kelita, Pelaiah, Hanan,

9:24 [t]S Jdg 4:23; S 2Ch 14:13
9:25 [u]S Dt 11:11 [v]S Ex 18:9 [w]Dt 6:10-12 [x]8:8-11; 32:12-15; Ps 23:6; 25:7; 69:16
9:26 [y]S 1Ki 14:9; Jer 44:10 [z]S Jos 7:25 [a]Jer 2:30; 26:8; Mt 21:35-36; 23:29-36; Ac 7:52 [b]S Jdg 2:12-13
9:27 [c]S Nu 25:17; S Jdg 2:14 [d]Ps 51:1; 103:8; 106:45; 119:156 [e]S Jdg 3:9
9:28 [f]S Ex 32:22; S Jdg 2:17 [g]S 2Sa 24:14 [h]Ps 22:4; 106:43; 136:24
9:29 [i]S Jdg 6:8 [j]ver 16-17; Ps 5:5; Isa 2:11; Jer 43:2 [k]S Dt 30:16 [l]S 1Sa 8:3 [m]Jer 19:15 [n]Zec 7:11-12
9:30 [o]2Ki 17:13-18; S 2Ch 36:16 [p]Jer 16:11; Zec 7:12
9:31 [q]Isa 48:9; 65:9 [r]S Dt 4:31
9:32 [s]Job 9:19; Ps 24:8; 89:8; 93:4 [t]S Dt 7:21 [u]S Dt 7:9; S 1Ki 8:23; Da 9:4 [v]S Ex 18:8
9:33 [w]S Ge 18:25 [x]Jer 44:3; Da 9:7-8, 14
9:34 [y]S 2Ki 23:11 [z]Jer 44:17
9:35 [a]Isa 63:7 [b]Dt 28:45-48
9:36 [c]S Ezr 9:9
9:37 [d]Dt 28:33; La 5:5
9:38 [e]S 2Ch 23:16 [f]Isa 44:5
10:2 [g]S Ezr 2:2
10:3 [h]S 1Ch 9:12
10:5 [i]S 1Ch 24:8
10:8 [j]Ne 12:1
10:9 [k]Ne 12:1

9:27,28 SALVATION, As Deliverance—Israel's story is our story, too. God's patience in bringing about salvation is very great. His deliverance comes from His compassion for His people and His devotion to His plan to create a people for Himself.

9:30 REVELATION, Spirit—See note on 1 Ki 22:6–28.

9:32–37 THE CHURCH, Covenant People—See notes on 2 Ch 6:14; 7:17–22.

9:38 THE CHURCH, Covenant People—Public worship ceremonies lead God's people to renew their covenant commitments to God. God's people often find it necessary to write down the characteristics that identify us as people of God and the commitments we make to our God which distinguish us from all other people. The Israelites in Nehemiah's day set a good example for all succeeding written covenants. See notes on Dt 29:1–15; Jos 24:25–27.

11Mica, Rehob, Hashabiah,
12Zaccur, Sherebiah, Shebaniah,
13Hodiah, Bani and Beninu.

14The leaders of the people:

Parosh, Pahath-Moab, Elam, Zattu, Bani,
15Bunni, Azgad, Bebai,
16Adonijah, Bigvai, Adin,[l]
17Ater, Hezekiah, Azzur,
18Hodiah, Hashum, Bezai,
19Hariph, Anathoth, Nebai,
20Magpiash, Meshullam, Hezir,[m]
21Meshezabel, Zadok, Jaddua,
22Pelatiah, Hanan, Anaiah,
23Hoshea, Hananiah,[n] Hasshub,
24Hallohesh, Pilha, Shobek,
25Rehum, Hashabnah, Maaseiah,
26Ahiah, Hanan, Anan,
27Malluch, Harim and Baanah.

28"The rest of the people—priests,
Levites, gatekeepers, singers, temple
servants[o] and all who separated
themselves from the neighboring
peoples[p] for the sake of the Law of
God, together with their wives and
all their sons and daughters who are
able to understand— 29all these now
join their brothers the nobles, and
bind themselves with a curse and an
oath[q] to follow the Law of God given
through Moses the servant of God
and to obey carefully all the commands, regulations and decrees of
the LORD our Lord.

30"We promise not to give our
daughters in marriage to the peoples
around us or take their daughters for
our sons.[r]

31"When the neighboring peoples
bring merchandise or grain to sell on
the Sabbath,[s] we will not buy from
them on the Sabbath or on any holy
day. Every seventh year we will forgo
working the land[t] and will cancel all
debts.[u]

32"We assume the responsibility
for carrying out the commands to
give a third of a shekel[z] each year for
the service of the house of our God:
33for the bread set out on the table;[v]
for the regular grain offerings and
burnt offerings; for the offerings on
the Sabbaths, New Moon[w] festivals
and appointed feasts; for the holy
offerings; for sin offerings to
make atonement for Israel; and for
all the duties of the house of our
God.[x]

34"We—the priests, the Levites
and the people—have cast lots[y] to
determine when each of our families
is to bring to the house of our God at
set times each year a contribution of
wood[z] to burn on the altar of the
LORD our God, as it is written in the
Law.

35"We also assume responsibility
for bringing to the house of the LORD
each year the firstfruits[a] of our crops
and of every fruit tree.[b]

36"As it is also written in the Law,
we will bring the firstborn[c] of our
sons and of our cattle, of our herds
and of our flocks to the house of our
God, to the priests ministering
there.[d]

37"Moreover, we will bring to the
storerooms of the house of our God,
to the priests, the first of our ground
meal, of our ⌊grain⌋ offerings, of the
fruit of all our trees and of our new
wine and oil.[e] And we will bring a
tithe[f] of our crops to the Levites,[g]
for it is the Levites who collect the
tithes in all the towns where we
work.[h] 38A priest descended from
Aaron is to accompany the Levites
when they receive the tithes, and the
Levites are to bring a tenth of the
tithes[i] up to the house of our God,
to the storerooms of the treasury.
39The people of Israel, including the
Levites, are to bring their contributions of grain, new wine and oil to
the storerooms where the articles for
the sanctuary are kept and where the
ministering priests, the gatekeepers
and the singers stay.

"We will not neglect the house of
our God."[j]

10:16 [l]S Ezr 8:6
10:20 [m]1Ch 24:15
10:23 [n]S Ne 7:2
10:28 [o]Ps 135:1 [p]2Ch 6:26; S Ne 9:2
10:29 [q]S Nu 5:21; Ps 119:106
10:30 [r]S Ex 34:16; Ne 13:23
10:31 [s]Ne 13:16, 18; Jer 17:27; Eze 23:38; Am 8:5 [t]S Ex 23:11; Lev 25:1-7 [u]S Dt 15:1
10:33 [v]Lev 24:6 [w]Nu 10:10; Ps 81:3; Isa 1:14 [x]S 2Ch 24:5
10:34 [y]S Lev 16:8 [z]Ne 13:31
10:35 [a]S Ex 22:29; S Nu 18:12 [b]Dt 26:1-11
10:36 [c]S Ex 13:2; S Nu 18:14-16 [d]Ne 13:31
10:37 [e]S Nu 18:12 [f]S Lev 27:30; S Nu 18:21 [g]Dt 14:22-29 [h]Eze 44:30
10:38 [i]Nu 18:26
10:39 [j]Ne 13:11,12

[z]*32* That is, about 1/8 ounce (about 4 grams)

10:28–29 PRAYER, Curse—The people renewed the covenant given Moses (Ex 24:1–11). The acknowledgment of the curse along with the oath by the people is unusual and indicates the strength of their commitment. The curse was the covenant curses for those who broke the covenant (Lev 26:14–46; Dt 26—28).

10:28–30; 13:23–27 FAMILY, Intermarriage—Faithfulness to family is subordinate to faithfulness to God. Nehemiah forcefully condemned Judean men who risked their allegiance to God by marrying women who worshiped other gods. Marriage should strengthen faith, not test it. See Ezr 9:1—10:17; notes on Dt 7:3–4; 1 Ki 11:1–9.

10:29 CHRISTIAN ETHICS, Worship—See note on Ex 24:3,7.

10:29 THE CHURCH, Covenant People—See note on 9:38.

10:32 STEWARDSHIP, Service to God—Offerings represent one way God's people can serve Him. A commitment to regular offerings is part of being God's people. Such offerings supply the materials used in worship and the physical needs of God's ministers. See note on Ac 4:32—5:11.

10:36 HOLY SCRIPTURE, Writing—See note on 8:1–3.

Chapter 11

The New Residents of Jerusalem

11:3–19pp — 1Ch 9:1–17

NOW the leaders of the people settled
in Jerusalem, and the rest of the
people cast lots to bring one out of every
ten to live in Jerusalem,[k] the holy city,[l]
while the remaining nine were to stay in
their own towns.[m] 2The people commended all the men who volunteered to
live in Jerusalem.

3These are the provincial leaders who
settled in Jerusalem (now some Israelites,
priests, Levites, temple servants and descendants of Solomon's servants lived in
the towns of Judah, each on his own
property in the various towns,[n] 4while
other people from both Judah and Benjamin[o] lived in Jerusalem):[p]

From the descendants of Judah:

Athaiah son of Uzziah, the son of
Zechariah, the son of Amariah, the
son of Shephatiah, the son of Mahalalel, a descendant of Perez; 5and Maaseiah son of Baruch, the son of Col-
Hozeh, the son of Hazaiah, the son of
Adaiah, the son of Joiarib, the son of
Zechariah, a descendant of Shelah.
6The descendants of Perez who lived
in Jerusalem totaled 468 able men.

7From the descendants of Benjamin:

Sallu son of Meshullam, the son of
Joed, the son of Pedaiah, the son of
Kolaiah, the son of Maaseiah, the son
of Ithiel, the son of Jeshaiah, 8and his
followers, Gabbai and Sallai—928
men. 9Joel son of Zicri was their chief
officer, and Judah son of Hassenuah
was over the Second District of the
city.

10From the priests:

Jedaiah; the son of Joiarib; Jakin;
11Seraiah[q] son of Hilkiah, the son of
Meshullam, the son of Zadok, the son
of Meraioth, the son of Ahitub,[r] supervisor in the house of God, 12and
their associates, who carried on work
for the temple—822 men; Adaiah
son of Jeroham, the son of Pelaliah,
the son of Amzi, the son of Zechariah, the son of Pashhur, the son of
Malkijah, 13and his associates, who
were heads of families—242 men;
Amashsai son of Azarel, the son of
Ahzai, the son of Meshillemoth, the
son of Immer, 14and his[a] associates,
who were able men—128. Their
chief officer was Zabdiel son of Hag-
gedolim.

15From the Levites:

Shemaiah son of Hasshub, the son of
Azrikam, the son of Hashabiah, the
son of Bunni; 16Shabbethai[s] and Jozabad,[t] two of the heads of the Levites, who had charge of the outside
work of the house of God; 17Mattani-
ah[u] son of Mica, the son of Zabdi,
the son of Asaph,[v] the director who
led in thanksgiving and prayer; Bakbukiah, second among his associates;
and Abda son of Shammua, the son of
Galal, the son of Jeduthun.[w] 18The
Levites in the holy city[x] totaled 284.

19The gatekeepers:

Akkub, Talmon and their associates,
who kept watch at the gates—172
men.

20The rest of the Israelites, with the
priests and Levites, were in all the towns
of Judah, each on his ancestral property.
21The temple servants[y] lived on the
hill of Ophel, and Ziha and Gishpa were
in charge of them.
22The chief officer of the Levites in Jerusalem was Uzzi son of Bani, the son of
Hashabiah, the son of Mattaniah,[z] the
son of Mica. Uzzi was one of Asaph's descendants, who were the singers responsible for the service of the house of God.
23The singers[a] were under the king's orders, which regulated their daily activity.
24Pethahiah son of Meshezabel, one of
the descendants of Zerah[b] son of Judah,
was the king's agent in all affairs relating
to the people.
25As for the villages with their fields,
some of the people of Judah lived in Kiriath Arba[c] and its surrounding settle-

11:1 [k]Ne 7:4 [l]Isa 48:2; 52:1; 64:10; Zec 14:20-21 [m]S Ne 7:73
11:3 [n]S Ezr 2:1
11:4 [o]S Ezr 1:5 [p]S Ezr 2:70
11:11 [q]S 2Ki 25:18; S Ezr 2:2 [r]S Ezr 7:2
11:16 [s]Ezr 10:15 [t]S Ezr 8:33
11:17 [u]S 1Ch 9:15; Ne 12:8 [v]2Ch 5:12 [w]S 1Ch 25:1
11:18 [x]S Rev 21:2
11:21 [y]S Ezr 2:43; S Ne 3:26
11:22 [z]S 1Ch 9:15
11:23 [a]S 1Ch 15:16; Ne 7:44
11:24 [b]S Ge 38:30
11:25 [c]S Ge 35:27

[a] *14* Most Septuagint manuscripts; Hebrew *their*

11:17 PRAYER, Worship—One division of the priests was assigned to lead in prayer. They were descendants of Asaph, the most prominent of the praise leaders assigned by David (1 Ch 16:7,37). Three important words for prayer appear here. The first (Hebrew *tehillah*) involves a very slight change of the transmitted Hebrew text. It means praise and is often used in the Psalms to call worshipers to praise God (100:4; 149:1). It represents the inner impulse of God's people that God's greatness must be recognized and proclaimed. It represents the great joy of God's worshipers in His presence. Not only humans but all parts of creation are invited to join in praise (Ps 150:6). Thanksgiving (Hebrew *hodah*) represents a person's reaction to an event. Thanksgiving is more intensively personal and individual in comparison to the community orientation of praise. Thanksgiving is an individual's decision to praise on the basis of an event or act of God. Thanksgiving is an individual reaction, but it is expressed in a group as a witness to and invitation before others to praise God for His actions. Prayer (Hebrew *tiphillah*) was closely related to intercessory prayer and petition for help in a crisis situation. Thus it became the technical term for lament as its use in the title of Ps 102 shows. Finally *tephillah* became generalized to represent all kinds of prayer to God. Praise, lament, and thanksgiving are all proper parts of public worship.

ments, in Dibon[d] and its settlements, in
Jekabzeel and its villages, 26 in Jeshua, in
Moladah,[e] in Beth Pelet,[f] 27 in Hazar
Shual,[g] in Beersheba[h] and its settlements, 28 in Ziklag,[i] in Meconah and its
settlements, 29 in En Rimmon, in Zorah,[j]
in Jarmuth,[k] 30 Zanoah,[l] Adullam[m] and
their villages, in Lachish[n] and its fields,
and in Azekah[o] and its settlements. So
they were living all the way from Beersheba[p] to the Valley of Hinnom.
31 The descendants of the Benjamites
from Geba[q] lived in Micmash,[r] Aija,
Bethel[s] and its settlements, 32 in Anathoth,[t] Nob[u] and Ananiah, 33 in Hazor,[v]
Ramah[w] and Gittaim,[x] 34 in Hadid, Zeboim[y] and Neballat, 35 in Lod and Ono,[z]
and in the Valley of the Craftsmen.
36 Some of the divisions of the Levites
of Judah settled in Benjamin.

Chapter 12

Priests and Levites

THESE were the priests[a] and Levites[b]
who returned with Zerubbabel[c] son
of Shealtiel[d] and with Jeshua:[e]
Seraiah,[f] Jeremiah, Ezra,
2 Amariah, Malluch, Hattush,
3 Shecaniah, Rehum, Meremoth,
4 Iddo,[g] Ginnethon,[b] Abijah,[h]
5 Mijamin,[c] Moadiah, Bilgah,
6 Shemaiah, Joiarib, Jedaiah,[i]
7 Sallu, Amok, Hilkiah and Jedaiah.
These were the leaders of the priests and
their associates in the days of Jeshua.
8 The Levites were Jeshua,[j] Binnui,
Kadmiel, Sherebiah, Judah, and also Mattaniah,[k] who, together with his associates, was in charge of the songs of thanksgiving. 9 Bakbukiah and Unni, their associates, stood opposite them in the services.
10 Jeshua was the father of Joiakim, Joiakim the father of Eliashib,[l] Eliashib the
father of Joiada, 11 Joiada the father of Jonathan, and Jonathan the father of Jaddua.
12 In the days of Joiakim, these were the
heads of the priestly families:
of Seraiah's family, Meraiah;
of Jeremiah's, Hananiah;
13 of Ezra's, Meshullam;
of Amariah's, Jehohanan;
14 of Malluch's, Jonathan;
of Shecaniah's,[d] Joseph;
15 of Harim's, Adna;
of Meremoth's,[e] Helkai;
16 of Iddo's,[m] Zechariah;
of Ginnethon's, Meshullam;
17 of Abijah's,[n] Zicri;
of Miniamin's and of Moadiah's, Pil-
tai;
18 of Bilgah's, Shammua;
of Shemaiah's, Jehonathan;
19 of Joiarib's, Mattenai;
of Jedaiah's, Uzzi;
20 of Sallu's, Kallai;
of Amok's, Eber;
21 of Hilkiah's, Hashabiah;
of Jedaiah's, Nethanel.
22 The family heads of the Levites in the
days of Eliashib, Joiada, Johanan and Jaddua, as well as those of the priests, were
recorded in the reign of Darius the Persian. 23 The family heads among the descendants of Levi up to the time of Johanan son of Eliashib were recorded in the
book of the annals. 24 And the leaders of
the Levites[o] were Hashabiah, Sherebiah,
Jeshua son of Kadmiel, and their associates, who stood opposite them to give
praise and thanksgiving, one section responding to the other, as prescribed by
David the man of God.[p]
25 Mattaniah, Bakbukiah, Obadiah, Meshullam, Talmon and Akkub were gatekeepers who guarded the storerooms at
the gates. 26 They served in the days of
Joiakim son of Jeshua, the son of Jozadak,
and in the days of Nehemiah the governor and of Ezra the priest and scribe.

Dedication of the Wall of Jerusalem

27 At the dedication[q] of the wall of Jerusalem, the Levites were sought out from
where they lived and were brought to Jerusalem to celebrate joyfully the dedication with songs of thanksgiving and with
the music of cymbals,[r] harps and lyres.[s]
28 The singers also were brought together
from the region around Jerusalem—from
the villages of the Netophathites,[t] 29 from
Beth Gilgal, and from the area of Geba
and Azmaveth, for the singers had built
villages for themselves around Jerusalem.
30 When the priests and Levites had purified themselves ceremonially, they purified the people,[u] the gates and the wall.
31 I had the leaders of Judah go up on
top[f] of the wall. I also assigned two large

11:25 [d]S Nu 21:30
11:26 [e]Jos 15:26 [f]Jos 15:27
11:27 [g]Jos 15:28 [h]S Ge 21:14
11:28 [i]S 1Sa 27:6
11:29 [j]Jos 15:33 [k]S Jos 10:3; S 15:35
11:30 [l]Jos 15:34 [m]Jos 15:35 [n]S Jos 10:3; 15:39 [o]S Jos 10:10 [p]Jos 15:28
11:31 [q]Jos 21:17; Isa 10:29 [r]S 1Sa 13:2 [s]S Jos 12:9
11:32 [t]Jos 21:18; Isa 10:30; Jer 1:1 [u]S 1Sa 21:1
11:33 [v]S Jos 11:1 [w]S Jos 18:25 [x]2Sa 4:3
11:34 [y]1Sa 13:18
11:35 [z]S 1Ch 8:12
12:1 [a]Ne 10:1-8 [b]Ne 10:9 [c]S 1Ch 3:19; Ezr 3:2; Zec 4:6-10 [d]Ezr 3:2 [e]S Ezr 2:2 [f]S Ezr 2:2
12:4 [g]ver 16; Zec 1:1 [h]S 1Ch 24:10; Lk 1:5
12:6 [i]S 1Ch 24:7
12:8 [j]S Ezr 2:2 [k]S Ne 11:17
12:10 [l]S Ezr 10:24; Ne 3:20
12:16 [m]S ver 4
12:17 [n]S 1Ch 24:10
12:24 [o]S Ezr 2:40 [p]S 2Ch 8:14
12:27 [q]Dt 20:5 [r]S 2Sa 6:5 [s]S 1Ch 15:16,28; 25:6; Ps 92:3
12:28 [t]S 1Ch 2:54; 9:16
12:30 [u]Ex 19:10; Job 1:5

[b] *4* Many Hebrew manuscripts and Vulgate (see also Neh. 12:16); most Hebrew manuscripts *Ginnethoi* [c] *5* A variant of *Miniamin* [d] *14* Very many Hebrew manuscripts, some Septuagint manuscripts and Syriac (see also Neh. 12:3); most Hebrew manuscripts *Shebaniah's* [e] *15* Some Septuagint manuscripts (see also Neh. 12:3); Hebrew *Meraioth's* [f] *31* Or *go alongside*

12:24 PRAYER, Worship—Worship was expressed in antiphonal singing. Such singing involved praise and thanksgiving, both types of prayer. *See note on 11:17.*

12:27–43 PRAYER, Worship—The dedication of the second Temple was characterized by elaborate sacrifice (Ezr 6:16–17) and involved mainly priests and Levites. The dedication of the wall was characterized by elaborate ceremony and involved priests, Levites, and the people. The division of the Levites into two massed choirs is unusual. The completion of the wall was a specific action led by God for which thanksgiving was appropriate. See note on 11:17.

choirs to give thanks. One was to proceed
on top[g] of the wall to the right, toward
the Dung Gate.[v] 32Hoshaiah and half the
leaders of Judah followed them, 33along
with Azariah, Ezra, Meshullam, 34Judah,
Benjamin,[w] Shemaiah, Jeremiah, 35as
well as some priests with trumpets,[x] and
also Zechariah son of Jonathan, the son of
Shemaiah, the son of Mattaniah, the son
of Micaiah, the son of Zaccur, the son of
Asaph, 36and his associates—Shemaiah,
Azarel, Milalai, Gilalai, Maai, Nethanel,
Judah and Hanani—with musical instruments[y] prescribed by David the man of
God.[z] Ezra[a] the scribe led the procession. 37At the Fountain Gate[b] they continued directly up the steps of the City of
David on the ascent to the wall and
passed above the house of David to the
Water Gate[c] on the east.

38The second choir proceeded in the
opposite direction. I followed them on
top[h] of the wall, together with half the
people—past the Tower of the Ovens[d] to
the Broad Wall,[e] 39over the Gate of
Ephraim,[f] the Jeshanah[i] Gate,[g] the
Fish Gate,[h] the Tower of Hananel[i] and
the Tower of the Hundred,[j] as far as the
Sheep Gate.[k] At the Gate of the Guard
they stopped.

40The two choirs that gave thanks then
took their places in the house of God; so
did I, together with half the officials, 41as
well as the priests—Eliakim, Maaseiah,
Miniamin, Micaiah, Elioenai, Zechariah
and Hananiah with their trumpets—
42and also Maaseiah, Shemaiah, Eleazar,
Uzzi, Jehohanan, Malkijah, Elam and
Ezer. The choirs sang under the direction
of Jezrahiah. 43And on that day they offered great sacrifices, rejoicing because
God had given them great joy. The wom-
en and children also rejoiced. The sound
of rejoicing in Jerusalem could be heard
far away.

44At that time men were appointed to
be in charge of the storerooms[l] for the
contributions, firstfruits and tithes.[m]
From the fields around the towns they
were to bring into the storerooms the
portions required by the Law for the
priests and the Levites, for Judah was
pleased with the ministering priests and
Levites.[n] 45They performed the service of
their God and the service of purification,
as did also the singers and gatekeepers,
according to the commands of David[o]
and his son Solomon.[p] 46For long ago, in
the days of David and Asaph,[q] there had
been directors for the singers and for the
songs of praise[r] and thanksgiving to God.
47So in the days of Zerubbabel and of Nehemiah, all Israel contributed the daily
portions for the singers and gatekeepers.
They also set aside the portion for the
other Levites, and the Levites set aside
the portion for the descendants of
Aaron.[s]

Chapter 13

Nehemiah's Final Reforms

On that day the Book of Moses was
read aloud in the hearing of the people and there it was found written that no
Ammonite or Moabite should ever be admitted into the assembly of God,[t] 2be-
cause they had not met the Israelites with
food and water but had hired Balaam[u] to
call a curse down on them.[v] (Our God,
however, turned the curse into a blessing.)[w] 3When the people heard this law,
they excluded from Israel all who were of
foreign descent.[x]

4Before this, Eliashib the priest had
been put in charge of the storerooms[y] of
the house of our God. He was closely associated with Tobiah,[z] 5and he had provided him with a large room formerly
used to store the grain offerings and incense and temple articles, and also the
tithes[a] of grain, new wine and oil prescribed for the Levites, singers and gatekeepers, as well as the contributions for
the priests.

6But while all this was going on, I was
not in Jerusalem, for in the thirty-second
year of Artaxerxes[b] king of Babylon I had
returned to the king. Some time later I
asked his permission 7and came back to
Jerusalem. Here I learned about the evil
thing Eliashib[c] had done in providing Tobiah[d] a room in the courts of the house
of God. 8I was greatly displeased and
threw all Tobiah's household goods out of
the room.[e] 9I gave orders to purify the
rooms,[f] and then I put back into them

12:31 [v]Ne 2:13
12:34 [w]S Ezr 1:5
12:35 [x]S Ezr 3:10
12:36 [y]S 1Ch 15:16 [z]S 2Ch 8:14 [a]Ezr 7:6
12:37 [b]S Ne 2:14 [c]S Ne 3:26
12:38 [d]Ne 3:11 [e]Ne 3:8
12:39 [f]S 2Ki 14:13 [g]Ne 3:6 [h]S 2Ch 33:14 [i]S Ne 3:1 [j]Ne 3:1 [k]S Ne 3:1
12:44 [l]Ne 13:4,13 [m]S Lev 27:30 [n]S Dt 18:8
12:45 [o]S 2Ch 8:14 [p]S 1Ch 6:31; 23:5
12:46 [q]S 2Ch 35:15 [r]2Ch 29:27; Ps 137:4
12:47 [s]S Dt 18:8
13:1 [t]ver 23; Dt 23:3
13:2 [u]Nu 22:3-11 [v]S Nu 23:7; S Dt 23:3 [w]S Nu 23:11; Dt 23:4-5
13:3 [x]ver 23; S Ne 9:2
13:4 [y]S Ne 12:44 [z]Ne 2:10
13:5 [a]S Lev 27:30; S Nu 18:21
13:6 [b]S Ne 2:6
13:7 [c]S Ezr 10:24 [d]S Ne 2:10
13:8 [e]Mt 21:12-13; Mk 11:15-17; Lk 19:45-46; Jn 2:13-16
13:9 [f]S 1Ch 23:28; S 2Ch 29:5

[g]31 Or *proceed alongside* [h]38 Or *them alongside* [i]39 Or *Old*

12:44–47 STEWARDSHIP, Storehouse—Offerings are stored in God's house to meet the needs of God's appointed worship leaders. The service of these people should please the people resulting in cheerful and generous giving. See note on 2 Ch 31:2–13.

13:1–3 HOLY SCRIPTURE, Canonization—Dt 23:1–6 served as authoritative Scripture for Nehemiah as he led in a renewal of God's people. Compare Isa 56:4–7. God's Word in the past remains authoritative for the present. God and His Word do not change with the times.

13:4–5 STEWARDSHIP, Management—Whenever people store and manage gifts negligently, both the ministries supported and the practice of giving suffer. The person who treasures or manages gifts performs a sacred responsibility. Offerings to God should be used only in ways directed by God and His people. Such gifts must not be used to buy influence from powerful leaders. See note on Ezr 8:28,35.

the equipment of the house of God, with
the grain offerings and the incense.[g]
10 I also learned that the portions assigned to the Levites had not been given
to them,[h] and that all the Levites and
singers responsible for the service had
gone back to their own fields.[i] 11 So I rebuked the officials and asked them, "Why
is the house of God neglected?"[j] Then I
called them together and stationed them
at their posts.

12 All Judah brought the tithes[k] of
grain, new wine and oil into the storerooms.[l] 13 I put Shelemiah the priest, Zadok the scribe, and a Levite named Pedaiah in charge of the storerooms and made
Hanan son of Zaccur, the son of Mattaniah, their assistant, because these men
were considered trustworthy. They were
made responsible for distributing the supplies to their brothers.[m]

14 Remember[n] me for this, O my God,
and do not blot out what I have so faithfully done for the house of my God and its
services.

15 In those days I saw men in Judah
treading winepresses on the Sabbath and
bringing in grain and loading it on donkeys, together with wine, grapes, figs and
all other kinds of loads. And they were
bringing all this into Jerusalem on the
Sabbath.[o] Therefore I warned them
against selling food on that day. 16 Men
from Tyre who lived in Jerusalem were
bringing in fish and all kinds of merchandise and selling them in Jerusalem on the
Sabbath[p] to the people of Judah. 17 I rebuked the nobles of Judah and said to
them, "What is this wicked thing you are
doing—desecrating the Sabbath day?
18 Didn't your forefathers do the same
things, so that our God brought all this
calamity upon us and upon this city?[q]
Now you are stirring up more wrath
against Israel by desecrating the Sabbath."[r]

19 When evening shadows fell on the
gates of Jerusalem before the Sabbath,[s] I
ordered the doors to be shut and not
opened until the Sabbath was over. I stationed some of my own men at the gates
so that no load could be brought in on the
Sabbath day. 20 Once or twice the merchants and sellers of all kinds of goods
spent the night outside Jerusalem. 21 But I
warned them and said, "Why do you
spend the night by the wall? If you do this
again, I will lay hands on you." From that
time on they no longer came on the Sabbath. 22 Then I commanded the Levites to
purify themselves and go and guard the
gates in order to keep the Sabbath day
holy.

Remember[t] me for this also, O my
God, and show mercy to me according to
your great love.

23 Moreover, in those days I saw men of
Judah who had married[u] women from
Ashdod, Ammon and Moab.[v] 24 Half of
their children spoke the language of Ashdod or the language of one of the other
peoples, and did not know how to speak
the language[w] of Judah. 25 I rebuked them
and called curses down on them. I beat
some of the men and pulled out their
hair. I made them take an oath[x] in God's
name and said: "You are not to give your
daughters in marriage to their sons, nor
are you to take their daughters in marriage for your sons or for yourselves.[y]
26 Was it not because of marriages like
these that Solomon king of Israel sinned?
Among the many nations there was no
king like him.[z] He was loved by his
God,[a] and God made him king over all
Israel, but even he was led into sin by
foreign women.[b] 27 Must we hear now
that you too are doing all this terrible
wickedness and are being unfaithful
to our God by marrying[c] foreign
women?"

28 One of the sons of Joiada son of Eliashib[d] the high priest was son-in-law to
Sanballat[e] the Horonite. And I drove him
away from me.

29 Remember[f] them, O my God, be-

13:9 g S Lev 2:1
13:10 h S Dt 12:19 i S 2Ch 31:4
13:11 j S Ne 10:37-39; Hag 1:1-9; Mal 3:8-9
13:12 k S 2Ch 31:6 l S Dt 18:8; 1Ki 7:51; S 2Ch 31:5; S Ne 10:37-39; Mal 3:10
13:13 m S Ne 12:44; Ac 6:1-5
13:14 n S Ge 8:1; S 2Ki 20:3
13:15 o Ex 20:8-11; S 34:21; Dt 5:12-15
13:16 p S Ne 10:31
13:18 q Jer 44:23 r S Ne 10:31
13:19 s Lev 23:32
13:22 t S Ge 8:1; S Ne 1:8
13:23 u Ezr 9:1-2; Mal 2:11 v ver 1; S ver 1,S 3; Ex 34:16; S Ru 1:4; S Ne 10:30
13:24 w Est 1:22; 3:12; 8:9
13:25 x S Ezr 10:5 y S Ex 34:16
13:26 z S 1Ki 3:13; S 2Ch 1:12 a 2Sa 12:25 b S Ex 34:16; S 1Ki 11:3
13:27 c Ezr 9:14
13:28 d S Ezr 10:24 e S Ne 2:10
13:29 f S Ne 1:8

13:14,22,29,30 PRAYER, Petition—Nehemiah frequently asked God to remember. Reminding God is a privilege of fellowship with God. Humans forget what we have done. God does not forget our service for Him.

13:15–18 SIN, Covenant Breach—Monetary gain does not determine moral values. God provided guidelines for life with Him in the covenant relationship (Ex 20:1–17). Following the guidelines brings the best possible life for humans. Disobeying them disrupts the whole foundation for community life. Keeping the Sabbath as a day of rest and worship is not an arbitrary, selfish rule God set up to test and judge us. It is a pattern of life needed for people enduring stress. When we refuse to set aside one day for God, we endanger our own lives. Convenience and money do not give sufficient reason for not following God's guidelines. Disobedience shows our lack of trust in God and is sinful. See notes on 9:5–37; Jdg 2:20.

13:18 GOD, Wrath—The wrath of God inevitably comes when we persist in sinning. Sadly, God's people can experience God's disciplining wrath and not learn their lesson. See notes on Ge 6:5–8; 17:14; 19:13,24–26.

13:23–27 FAMILY, Intermarriage—See note on 10:28–30.

13:26 SIN, Alienation—See note on 1 Ki 11:1–13.

13:26–27 HISTORY, God's Will—Historical examples teach us God's moral will. Nehemiah could show the sin of his people by pointing to Solomon's example.

13:29–30 THE CHURCH, Covenant People—Leadership of God's people does not come automatically because of God's calling in past generations. Each generation of God's leaders must follow His leadership and not make agreements for personal political gain. Nehemiah disciplined a member of the high priest's family for entering into agreements with the

cause they defiled the priestly office and the covenant of the priesthood and of the Levites.[g]

30So I purified the priests and the Levites of everything foreign,[h] and assigned them duties, each to his own task. 31I also made provision for contributions of wood[i] at designated times, and for the firstfruits.[j]

Remember[k] me with favor, O my God.

13:29 [g]S Nu 3:12
13:30 [h]S Ne 9:2
13:31 [i]Ne 10:34 [j]Ne 10:35-36 [k]S Ge 8:1; S Ne 1:8

enemy of God's people through a marriage alliance. God's people must ensure their leadership remains true to God and does not give in to selfish desires and ambitions. See note on Nu 25:10–13.

13:30 WORSHIP, Ordered—Worship requires a leadership team. Nehemiah organized Israel's worship leaders, giving each a specific task. He also ensured the people would provide proper support for the ministry team.

Esther

Theological Setting

How can a powerless people find reason to celebrate? The Book of Esther addressed God's people at one of the lowest points of their history. Persia had replaced Babylon as the dominant world power. Different groups of Jews had returned from Babylon to Palestine. The Temple had been rebuilt. Still, the great expectations for Jewish return to political power and for a major new redemptive act of God for His people remained dreams unrelated to reality. Jews lived scattered all over the known world. Each group began to develop their own ways of maintaining the religious traditions of their people. Political and social conditions threatened to destroy the unity of God's people. Geographical distance, ongoing generations without memories of Palestine, and social integration into the Persian culture lessened Jewish ties to Palestine and the new Temple in Jerusalem. For some Jews remaining in Babylon and Persia, economic prosperity made life there too comfortable to worry much about faithfulness to a homeland and religious traditions. The ancient festivals seemed far removed from life for some living so far from the Temple in Jerusalem. They wondered if the ancient faith had any meaning for modern living.

Original readers of Esther thus faced many options in their spiritual life. They could:

1. Ignore the religious tradition of the fathers and become integrated into the modern, progressive society of the Persian rulers.
2. Develop a special kind of Jewish religious practice suitable to life in Persia without regard to its continuity with traditional Israelite life.
3. Retreat into a sect of Judaism in Persia and avoid contact with Persian life as much as possible.
4. Turn religious practice into a constant act of self-pitying lament and wailing.
5. Pursue economic goals within the Persian international world of trade and ignore the consequences of religious teachings.
6. Center life on apocalyptic expectations of the day of the Lord, thus withdrawing from society and waiting on God's final acts of salvation.
7. Recognize God's continuing actions on their behalf even in the midst of Persian political control, develop appropriate ways to celebrate those actions, and maintain the continuity of relevant contemporary faith with the religious traditions of Scripture.

The writer of Esther, whose name we cannot know, skillfully formulated the story of Esther to provide Israelites living under Persian rule a model for faith and life and a way to celebrate God's work in their day. Writing about 400 BC the inspired writer used language and scenes that would remind biblically educated readers of God's work in the dark days of Joseph and Moses to describe God's work in the life of an orphaned Jewish teenager. The book of Esther described God's new deliverance of His people from the threat of foreign domination and extinction. The book gave God's people in Exile a special festival to celebrate God's actions for them and to let them remember annually the joy of living and serving the God who acted for His people no matter where they were living.

Theological Outline

Esther: Celebrating God's Deliverance

I. A Humble Jewish Girl Gained a Position of International Influence. (1:1—2:18)

A. Political power of ungodly rulers may be far-reaching with great material resources. (1:1-8)

B. Protection of personal rights may result in loss of position, prestige, and all personal rights. (1:9-15)

C. Family relationships and respect cannot be enforced by political means. (1:16-22)

D. Self-giving love and humble faithfulness to family and nation may require hiding one's national identity to gain opportunity to serve one's people. (2:1-11)

E. Humble obedience can lead to positions of influence and opportunities to serve the nation. (2:12-18)

II. Faithfulness to One's People Can Be Expressed Through Service of a Foreign Ruler. (2:19—3:15)
   A. Loyalty to one's people does not demand participation in conspiracy against foreign rulers. (2:19-23)
   B. Loyalty to the foreign ruler does not mean honoring and participating in immoral practices of the government. (3:1-2)
   C. Placing loyalty to traditions of the people of God before loyalty to the foreign ruler may bring personal and national persecution. (3:3-14)
   D. Even citizens of the ruling power may not understand the severity of actions against God's people. (3:15)

III. Positions of Influence Bring Responsibility to Act on Behalf of God's People. (4:1-17)
   A. Mourning ceremonies are appropriate when God's people actually face imminent danger. (4:1-4)
   B. God's help for His troubled people is certain, and people with opportunity to avert danger have responsibility under God to act even in face of personal harm and danger. (4:5-14)
   C. God's people are responsible to support and pray for persons who have opportunity to act to save the people of God from disaster. (4:15-17)

IV. Responsible Action for the People of God is Honored Through Providential Workings in History. (5:1—8:17)
   A. Brave, self-giving action on behalf of God's people is rewarded even against all traditions and expectations. (5:1-8)
   B. Human pride leads to rash actions. (5:9-14)
   C. Honor comes to God's faithful servants at the opportune moment. (6:1-3)
   D. Human pride most often leads to humiliation. (6:4-12)
   E. God's people will experience vindication eventually. (6:13-14)
   F. Brave action for God's people brings deliverance from enemies. (7:1-10)
   G. The providential course of history honors those who sacrifice themselves for God's people and bring joy to His people. (8:1-17)
      1. Heroes of faith find reward. (8:1-2)
      2. National delivery, not personal reward, is the ultimate goal of the hero of faith. (8:3-4)
      3. Long-term animosities finally are resolved for God's people in the providence of history. (8:5-14)
      4. History's providence brings others to join God's people in celebration. (8:15-17)

V. Celebration Through the Ages Helps God's People Remember the Lessons of History. (9:1-32)
   A. God's people are given victory against military odds. (9:1-10)
   B. The most powerful foreign ruler can be used to bring victory for God's people. (9:11-15)
   C. All God's people should celebrate His salvation even if in different ways. (9:16-32)

VI. Work for God's People Can Bring New Opportunities for Political Influence, Historical Greatness, and Personal Prestige. (10:1-3)

Theological Conclusions

The Book of Esther was inspired by God even though the name of God or even the word *God* does not appear in the book. This shows that God can teach His people through entertaining, historical literature as well as through strongly theological writings. Theological teaching is not limited to any one form of writing. God chose many forms of literature to ensure His people understood the many aspects of His working for them and of their proper responses to Him. Theological lessons to be learned from Esther include:

1. God works in all history even when His actions are not obvious and when He does not raise up a prophet to interpret His actions.
2. Positions of influence are opportunities to show loyalty to God and His purposes for His people.
3. Social station at birth does not determine one's potential for ministry.
4. God's people do not have to exercise political power to have reason for celebration.
5. Celebration of God's victories is not limited to one time, one location, or one race.
6. No age gives sufficient reason to forget or forsake the faith of our fathers.

History stands under God's control. Outward conditions may indicate God has suffered defeat and pagan powers serving pagan gods have gained total control. Such a view sees only a limited range of history. The historical festivals of God's people remind us of God's control of history under Egyptian, Persian, and Roman rule as well as under the political domination of God's people. Xerxes' banquets and his treatment of his first queen show his immoral side and his political and economic power. The triumphs of Esther and Mordecai show God's faithfulness to bring historical deliverance when His people prove faithful. Understanding God's working in history does not necessarily come through a prophetic leader like Moses or Isaiah announcing what God has done and the response God expects. Understanding can come through literature that consciously refers to God only in oblique language such as 4:12-14 and 6:1. God's people are expected to be wise enough to know such language is a confession of faith even without explicit religious references.

Positions of influence may come to God's people when they least expect them. Such positions may be in service of a pagan empire and bring moments of tension and crisis when one's loyalty to God is tested against loyalty to the ruler served. As long as service of the ruler does not contradict God's values, such service may bring righteous influence into an otherwise pagan environment. When the service of the empire makes God's servant violate God's teachings, then loyalty to God must come before loyalty to the empire. Service to the empire itself must be regarded as a gift from God with responsibility to look for opportunities to serve God's purposes and help His people.

Birth does not set limits a person can never overcome. Esther's opportunities seemed nil. She was young, orphaned, poor, female, and foreign in a society dominated by upper-class Persian males. Humble obedience to God and trust in her pious uncle Mordecai opened doors of opportunity for influence and service. Heroes of faith are often surprises to the world's value system. God does not work according to worldly values and expectations. He works through committed people willing to do His will, fulfill His purposes for His people, and give Him the praise and honor.

God's people do not have to have political power to celebrate God's power. Persian Jews who did not participate in the exiles' return to the Holy Land seemed the least likely people to find reason to celebrate God's historical deliverance. Mordecai sitting at the palace gate seemed to have little opportunity for honor over Haman, sitting at the king's right hand. The Jews without any military power seemed doomed under Haman's irrevocable decree. Still God used the unlikely Esther to open doors of opportunity. Faithful Jews under Mordecai's leadership did not credit human ingenuity with their victory. They celebrated God's festival, seeing their deliverance as a miniature Exodus. God's power to deliver is greater than any danger we will face. Our challenge is to depend on His power and to celebrate His deliverance.

Celebration of God's victories is open to every generation, everywhere, without exclusion of any person. God's deliverance brought non-Jews to celebrate His victory (8:17). Generations of Jews after Esther could not actively participate in God's miraculous deliverance. They did particpate in the Feast of Purim celebrating the victory in Esther's day. Such celebration kept alive hopes for new victories of God and strengthened faith to face daily situations without immediate victory. They could tell the story of Esther without mentioning the name of God, yet center attention on God's chosen people. In so doing they celebrated and worshiped God without religious language.

Persia offered the perfect opportunity for Jews to become part of the culture, pattern their lives by those things that made for material success, and ignore or give up their religious tradition or heritage. Through the skillful framing of the inspired Book of Esther, Persian Jews were reminded of God's great victories in their history and called to retain their religious tradition even while serving a foreign emperor and while not telling their story in such a way to offend and alienate the people in their host culture. Indeed, told in the literary art of Esther, the story of the Jews in Persia could become an evangelistic tool to invite other nationalities to join the Jewish people in maintaining their religious heritage and celebrating God's deliverance of His people.

Contemporary Teaching

Esther stands as a beacon to a people tempted to trade success in a secular society for the faith of the fathers. It calls our society to: (1) be aware of God's work in our day even though prophetic leaders do not point out specific events where God has delivered His people; (2) trust God even in the darkest moments of life; (3) not underestimate our own skills and opportunities for ministry nor those of other people because they are of the wrong race, class, sex, or educational level; (4) find ways to communicate God's news that will speak to people of our day rather than alienating them immediately; (5) make worship moments of celebration that attract the attention and participation of people outside our religious circle; and (6) maintain continuity with the traditions of our faith while we find ways to exercise that faith under new social conditions.

Trent C. Butler

Chapter 1

Queen Vashti Deposed

THIS is what happened during the time
of Xerxes,[a][a] the Xerxes who ruled
over 127 provinces[b] stretching from India to Cush[b]:[c] 2At that time King Xerxes
reigned from his royal throne in the citadel of Susa,[d] 3and in the third year of his
reign he gave a banquet[e] for all his nobles and officials. The military leaders of
Persia and Media, the princes, and the
nobles of the provinces were present.
4For a full 180 days he displayed the
vast wealth of his kingdom and the splendor and glory of his majesty. 5When these
days were over, the king gave a banquet,
lasting seven days,[f] in the enclosed garden[g] of the king's palace, for all the people from the least to the greatest, who
were in the citadel of Susa. 6The garden
had hangings of white and blue linen, fastened with cords of white linen and purple material to silver rings on marble pillars. There were couches[h] of gold and
silver on a mosaic pavement of porphyry,
marble, mother-of-pearl and other costly
stones. 7Wine was served in goblets of
gold, each one different from the other,
and the royal wine was abundant, in
keeping with the king's liberality.[i] 8By
the king's command each guest was allowed to drink in his own way, for the
king instructed all the wine stewards to
serve each man what he wished.
9Queen Vashti also gave a banquet[j] for
the women in the royal palace of King
Xerxes.
10On the seventh day, when King Xerxes was in high spirits[k] from wine,[l] he
commanded the seven eunuchs who
served him—Mehuman, Biztha, Harbona,[m] Bigtha, Abagtha, Zethar and Car-
cas— 11to bring[n] before him Queen
Vashti, wearing her royal crown, in order
to display her beauty[o] to the people and
nobles, for she was lovely to look at. 12But
when the attendants delivered the king's
command, Queen Vashti refused to
come. Then the king became furious and
burned with anger.[p]
13Since it was customary for the king to
consult experts in matters of law and justice, he spoke with the wise men who
understood the times[q] 14and were closest
to the king—Carshena, Shethar, Adma-
tha, Tarshish, Meres, Marsena and Memucan, the seven nobles[r] of Persia and
Media who had special access to the king
and were highest in the kingdom.
15"According to law, what must be
done to Queen Vashti?" he asked. "She
has not obeyed the command of King Xerxes that the eunuchs have taken to her."
16Then Memucan replied in the presence of the king and the nobles, "Queen
Vashti has done wrong, not only against
the king but also against all the nobles
and the peoples of all the provinces of
King Xerxes. 17For the queen's conduct
will become known to all the women,
and so they will despise their husbands
and say, 'King Xerxes commanded Queen
Vashti to be brought before him, but she
would not come.' 18This very day the Persian and Median women of the nobility
who have heard about the queen's conduct will respond to all the king's nobles
in the same way. There will be no end of
disrespect and discord.[s]
19"Therefore, if it pleases the king,[t]
let him issue a royal decree and let it be
written in the laws of Persia and Media,
which cannot be repealed,[u] that Vashti is
never again to enter the presence of King
Xerxes. Also let the king give her royal
position to someone else who is better
than she. 20Then when the king's edict is
proclaimed throughout all his vast realm,
all the women will respect their
husbands, from the least to the greatest."
21The king and his nobles were pleased
with this advice, so the king did as Memucan proposed. 22He sent dispatches to
all parts of the kingdom, to each province
in its own script and to each people in its
own language,[v] proclaiming in each people's tongue that every man should be
ruler over his own household.

1:1 [a]S Ezr 4:6 [b]Est 9:30; Da 3:2; 6:1 [c]Est 8:9
1:2 [d]S Ezr 4:9; S Est 2:8
1:3 [e]S 1Ki 3:15
1:5 [f]Jdg 14:17 [g]S 2Ki 21:18
1:6 [h]Est 7:8; Eze 23:41; Am 3:12; 6:4
1:7 [i]Est 2:18; Da 5:2
1:9 [j]S 1Ki 3:15
1:10 [k]S Jdg 16:25; S Ru 3:7 [l]S Ge 14:18; Est 3:15; 5:6; 7:2; Pr 31:4-7; Da 5:1-4 [m]Est 7:9
1:11 [n]SS 2:4 [o]Ps 45:11; Eze 16:14
1:12 [p]Ge 39:19; Est 2:21; 7:7; Pr 19:12
1:13 [q]1Ch 12:32
1:14 [r]Ezr 7:14
1:18 [s]Pr 19:13; 27:15
1:19 [t]Ecc 8:4 [u]Est 8:8; Da 6:8,12
1:22 [v]S Ne 13:24

[a] *1* Hebrew *Ahasuerus,* a variant of Xerxes' Persian name; here and throughout Esther [b] *1* That is, the upper Nile region

1:1—10:3 HISTORY, Narrative—Biblical history is not limited to the acts of Jewish rulers and religious leaders. It includes the unlikely story of an orphaned girl who became queen of Persia and delivered her people with the help of her faithful uncle. The narrative itself teaches the story without mentioning God or giving prophetic explanations. God's people see God's hand directing history in all nations even without explicit interpretation of history by divinely-inspired speakers. God's people of all classes of society should be available for use in God's historical actions.

1:10–22 FAMILY, Female Subordination—The fear of women gaining an upper hand over men if not forced into submission is clearly reflected in the text. It is apparent that the king was drunk and wanted to put Vashti on display when he sent servants to bring her into the banquet hall. Her refusal was not based upon stubbornness but upon propriety. She did not want to be a spectacle. The fact of her refusal, however, aroused the king's anger and created tension for his advisers. Fearful that other wives would follow her example, they decreed that every man should be the ruler in his household. The text suggests two principles: (1) a wife is not wrong to refuse her husband's will when it would make her do that which she believes is wrong for herself, and (2) fear of women becoming dominant may lead men to take actions that are ill-advised and inappropriate to the circumstances involved.

Chapter 2

Esther Made Queen

LATER when the anger of King Xerxes
had subsided,[w] he remembered
Vashti and what she had done and what
he had decreed about her. 2Then the
king's personal attendants proposed, "Let
a search be made for beautiful young virgins for the king. 3Let the king appoint
commissioners in every province of his
realm to bring all these beautiful girls into
the harem at the citadel of Susa. Let them
be placed under the care of Hegai, the
king's eunuch, who is in charge of the
women; and let beauty treatments be giv-
en to them. 4Then let the girl who pleases
the king be queen instead of Vashti."
This advice appealed to the king, and he
followed it.
5Now there was in the citadel of Susa a
Jew of the tribe of Benjamin, named Mordecai son of Jair, the son of Shimei, the
son of Kish,[x] 6who had been carried into
exile from Jerusalem by Nebuchadnezzar
king of Babylon, among those taken captive with Jehoiachin[c][y] king of Judah.[z]
7Mordecai had a cousin named Hadassah,
whom he had brought up because she
had neither father nor mother. This girl,
who was also known as Esther,[a] was
lovely[b] in form and features, and Mordecai had taken her as his own daughter
when her father and mother died.
8When the king's order and edict had
been proclaimed, many girls were
brought to the citadel of Susa[c] and put
under the care of Hegai. Esther also was
taken to the king's palace and entrusted
to Hegai, who had charge of the harem.
9The girl pleased him and won his favor.[d] Immediately he provided her with
her beauty treatments and special food.[e]
He assigned to her seven maids selected
from the king's palace and moved her and
her maids into the best place in the harem.
10Esther had not revealed her nationality and family background, because Mordecai had forbidden her to do so.[f] 11Ev-
ery day he walked back and forth near the
courtyard of the harem to find out how
Esther was and what was happening to
her.
12Before a girl's turn came to go in to
King Xerxes, she had to complete twelve
months of beauty treatments prescribed
for the women, six months with oil of
myrrh and six with perfumes[g] and cosmetics. 13And this is how she would go to
the king: Anything she wanted was given
her to take with her from the harem to
the king's palace. 14In the evening she

2:1 [w]Est 7:10
2:5 [x]S 1Sa 9:1
2:6 [y]S 2Ki 24:6,15 [z]Da 1:1-5; 5:13
2:7 [a]Ge 41:45 [b]S Ge 39:6
2:8 [c]Ne 1:1; Est 1:2; Da 8:2
2:9 [d]S Ge 39:21 [e]S Ge 37:3; 1Sa 9:22-24; S 2Ki 25:30; Est 9:19; Eze 16:9-13; Da 1:5
2:10 [f]ver 20
2:12 [g]Pr 27:9; SS 1:3; Isa 3:24
2:14 [h]1Ki 11:3; SS 6:8; Da 5:2 [i]Est 4:11
2:15 [j]Est 9:29 [k]Ps 45:14 [l]S Ge 18:3; S 30:27; Est 5:8; 7:3; 8:5
2:17 [m]Eze 16:9-13
2:18 [n]S 1Ki 3:15 [o]S Ge 40:20 [p]S Est 1:7
2:19 [q]Est 4:2; 5:13
2:20 [r]ver 10
2:21 [s]S Ge 40:2 [t]S Est 1:12; 3:5; 5:9; 7:7
2:23 [u]S Ge 40:19; S Dt 21:22-23; Ps 7:14-16; Pr 26:27; Ecc 10:8 [v]Est 6:1; 10:2 [w]Est 6:2
3:1 [x]S Ex 17:8-16; S Nu 24:7; Dt 25:17-19; 1Sa 14:48

would go there and in the morning return
to another part of the harem to the care of
Shaashgaz, the king's eunuch who was in
charge of the concubines.[h] She would
not return to the king unless he was
pleased with her and summoned her by
name.[i]
15When the turn came for Esther (the
girl Mordecai had adopted, the daughter
of his uncle Abihail[j]) to go to the king,[k]
she asked for nothing other than what
Hegai, the king's eunuch who was in
charge of the harem, suggested. And Esther won the favor[l] of everyone who saw
her. 16She was taken to King Xerxes in
the royal residence in the tenth month,
the month of Tebeth, in the seventh year
of his reign.
17Now the king was attracted to Esther
more than to any of the other women,
and she won his favor and approval more
than any of the other virgins. So he set a
royal crown on her head and made her
queen[m] instead of Vashti. 18And the king
gave a great banquet,[n] Esther's banquet,
for all his nobles and officials.[o] He proclaimed a holiday throughout the provinces and distributed gifts with royal liberality.[p]

Mordecai Uncovers a Conspiracy

19When the virgins were assembled a
second time, Mordecai was sitting at the
king's gate.[q] 20But Esther had kept secret
her family background and nationality
just as Mordecai had told her to do, for
she continued to follow Mordecai's instructions as she had done when he was
bringing her up.[r]
21During the time Mordecai was sitting
at the king's gate, Bigthana[d] and Teresh,
two of the king's officers[s] who guarded
the doorway, became angry[t] and conspired to assassinate King Xerxes. 22But
Mordecai found out about the plot and
told Queen Esther, who in turn reported
it to the king, giving credit to Mordecai.
23And when the report was investigated
and found to be true, the two officials
were hanged[u] on a gallows.[e] All this was
recorded in the book of the annals[v] in
the presence of the king.[w]

Chapter 3

Haman's Plot to Destroy the Jews

AFTER these events, King Xerxes honored Haman son of Hammedatha,
the Agagite,[x] elevating him and giving
him a seat of honor higher than that of all

[c]6 Hebrew *Jeconiah*, a variant of *Jehoiachin*
[d]21 Hebrew *Bigthan*, a variant of *Bigthana*
[e]23 Or *were hung* (or *impaled*) *on poles*; similarly elsewhere in Esther

the other nobles. 2All the royal officials at
the king's gate knelt down and paid hon-
or to Haman, for the king had commanded this concerning him. But Mordecai
would not kneel down or pay him honor.
3Then the royal officials at the king's
gate asked Mordecai, "Why do you disobey the king's command?"[y] 4Day after
day they spoke to him but he refused to
comply.[z] Therefore they told Haman
about it to see whether Mordecai's behavior would be tolerated, for he had told
them he was a Jew.
5When Haman saw that Mordecai
would not kneel down or pay him honor,
he was enraged.[a] 6Yet having learned
who Mordecai's people were, he scorned
the idea of killing only Mordecai. Instead
Haman looked for a way[b] to destroy[c] all
Mordecai's people, the Jews,[d] throughout the whole kingdom of Xerxes.
7In the twelfth year of King Xerxes, in
the first month, the month of Nisan, they
cast the *pur*[e] (that is, the lot[f]) in the
presence of Haman to select a day and
month. And the lot fell on[f] the twelfth
month, the month of Adar.[g]
8Then Haman said to King Xerxes,
"There is a certain people dispersed and
scattered among the peoples in all the
provinces of your kingdom whose customs[h] are different from those of all other people and who do not obey[i] the
king's laws; it is not in the king's best
interest to tolerate them.[j] 9If it pleases
the king, let a decree be issued to destroy
them, and I will put ten thousand talents[g] of silver into the royal treasury for
the men who carry out this business."[k]
10So the king took his signet ring[l]
from his finger and gave it to Haman son
of Hammedatha, the Agagite, the enemy
of the Jews. 11"Keep the money," the
king said to Haman, "and do with the
people as you please."
12Then on the thirteenth day of the
first month the royal secretaries were
summoned. They wrote out in the script
of each province and in the language[m] of
each people all Haman's orders to the
king's satraps, the governors of the various provinces and the nobles of the various peoples. These were written in the
name of King Xerxes himself and sealed[n]
with his own ring. 13Dispatches were
sent by couriers to all the king's provinces with the order to destroy, kill and
annihilate all the Jews[o]—young and old,
women and little children—on a single
day, the thirteenth day of the twelfth
month, the month of Adar,[p] and to plunder[q] their goods. 14A copy of the text of
the edict was to be issued as law in every
province and made known to the people
of every nationality so they would be
ready for that day.[r]
15Spurred on by the king's command,
the couriers went out, and the edict was
issued in the citadel of Susa.[s] The king
and Haman sat down to drink,[t] but the
city of Susa was bewildered.[u]

Chapter 4

Mordecai Persuades Esther to Help

WHEN Mordecai learned of all that
had been done, he tore his
clothes,[v] put on sackcloth and ashes,[w]
and went out into the city, wailing[x] loudly and bitterly. 2But he went only as far as
the king's gate,[y] because no one clothed
in sackcloth was allowed to enter it. 3In
every province to which the edict and order of the king came, there was great
mourning among the Jews, with fasting,
weeping and wailing. Many lay in sackcloth and ashes.
4When Esther's maids and eunuchs
came and told her about Mordecai, she
was in great distress. She sent clothes for
him to put on instead of his sackcloth, but
he would not accept them. 5Then Esther
summoned Hathach, one of the king's eunuchs assigned to attend her, and ordered
him to find out what was troubling Mordecai and why.
6So Hathach went out to Mordecai in
the open square of the city in front of the
king's gate. 7Mordecai told him everything that had happened to him, including the exact amount of money Haman
had promised to pay into the royal treasury for the destruction of the Jews.[z] 8He
also gave him a copy of the text of the

[f]7 Septuagint; Hebrew does not have *And the lot fell on.* [g]9 That is, about 375 tons (about 345 metric tons)

3:3 [y]Est 5:9; Da 3:12
3:4 [z]Ge 39:10
3:5 [a]S Est 2:21
3:6 [b]Pr 16:25 [c]Ps 74:8; 83:4 [d]Est 9:24
3:7 [e]Est 9:24,26 [f]S Lev 16:8; S 1Sa 10:21 [g]ver 13; Est 9:19
3:8 [h]Ac 16:20-21 [i]Jer 29:7; Da 6:13 [j]Ezr 4:15
3:9 [k]Est 7:4
3:10 [l]S Ge 41:42
3:12 [m]S Ne 13:24 [n]S Ge 38:18
3:13 [o]S 1Sa 15:3; S Ezr 4:6 [p]S ver 7 [q]Est 8:11; 9:10
3:14 [r]Est 8:8; 9:1
3:15 [s]Est 8:14 [t]S Est 1:10 [u]Est 8:15
4:1 [v]S Nu 14:6 [w]S 2Sa 13:19; Eze 27:30-31 [x]S Ex 11:6; Ps 30:11
4:2 [y]S Est 2:19
4:7 [z]Est 7:4

***3:2* GOD, One God**—The Book of Esther does not use the word God or any *name or title of God. Still* God and trust in Him form the central theme. Mordecai would not even appear to give the king the honor that he felt was due only to God. Belief in the uniqueness of God is not expressed as well in creeds or statements of faith as it is in action when temptations lead us to acknowledge the authority or power of an earthly sovereign who would substitute himself for God.

4:3 PRAYER, Humility—See note on 2 Sa 1:12. Prayer can be expressed symbolically as well as orally. Kneeling or lying on one's face before God represents humility. Outstretched hands represent dependence on God for our needs. Fasting represents total dedication and willingness to forego normal needs to concentrate on one particular need before God. Weeping shows sorrow and heartfelt emotional reaction to a need or crisis. Sackcloth represents the willingness to sacrifice life's luxuries and efforts to impress others in absolute concentration on finding God's solution to the problem at hand. Ashes placed on the head or face represent a sense of worthlessness, shame, humility, and penitence. Expression of these attitudes is proper when asking God for help in a desperate community or individual situation.

edict for their annihilation, which had
been published in Susa, to show to Esther
and explain it to her, and he told him to
urge her to go into the king's presence to
beg for mercy and plead with him for her
people.
9Hathach went back and reported to
Esther what Mordecai had said. 10Then
she instructed him to say to Mordecai,
11"All the king's officials and the people
of the royal provinces know that for any
man or woman who approaches the king
in the inner court without being summoned[a] the king has but one law:[b] that
he be put to death. The only exception to
this is for the king to extend the gold
scepter[c] to him and spare his life. But
thirty days have passed since I was called
to go to the king."
12When Esther's words were reported
to Mordecai, 13he sent back this answer:
"Do not think that because you are in the
king's house you alone of all the Jews will
escape. 14For if you remain silent[d] at this
time, relief[e] and deliverance[f] for the
Jews will arise from another place, but
you and your father's family will perish.
And who knows but that you have come
to royal position for such a time as
this?"[g]
15Then Esther sent this reply to Mordecai: 16"Go, gather together all the Jews
who are in Susa, and fast[h] for me. Do not
eat or drink for three days, night or day. I
and my maids will fast as you do. When
this is done, I will go to the king, even
though it is against the law. And if I perish, I perish."[i]
17So Mordecai went away and carried
out all of Esther's instructions.

Chapter 5

Esther's Request to the King

ON the third day Esther put on her royal robes[j] and stood in the inner
court of the palace, in front of the king's[k]
hall. The king was sitting on his royal
throne in the hall, facing the entrance.
2When he saw Queen Esther standing in
the court, he was pleased with her and
held out to her the gold scepter that was
in his hand. So Esther approached and
touched the tip of the scepter.[l]
3Then the king asked, "What is it,
Queen Esther? What is your request?
Even up to half the kingdom,[m] it will be
given you."
4"If it pleases the king," replied Esther, "let the king, together with Haman,
come today to a banquet I have prepared
for him."
5"Bring Haman at once," the king said,
"so that we may do what Esther asks."
So the king and Haman went to the
banquet Esther had prepared. 6As they
were drinking wine,[n] the king again
asked Esther, "Now what is your petition? It will be given you. And what is
your request? Even up to half the kingdom,[o] it will be granted."[p]
7Esther replied, "My petition and my
request is this: 8If the king regards me
with favor[q] and if it pleases the king to
grant my petition and fulfill my request,
let the king and Haman come tomorrow
to the banquet[r] I will prepare for them.
Then I will answer the king's question."

Haman's Rage Against Mordecai

9Haman went out that day happy and
in high spirits. But when he saw Mordecai at the king's gate and observed that he
neither rose nor showed fear in his presence, he was filled with rage[s] against
Mordecai.[t] 10Nevertheless, Haman restrained himself and went home.
Calling together his friends and Zeresh,[u] his wife, 11Haman boasted[v] to
them about his vast wealth, his many
sons,[w] and all the ways the king had honored him and how he had elevated him
above the other nobles and officials.
12"And that's not all," Haman added.
"I'm the only person[x] Queen Esther invited to accompany the king to the banquet she gave. And she has invited me
along with the king tomorrow. 13But all
this gives me no satisfaction as long as I
see that Jew Mordecai sitting at the king's
gate.[y]"
14His wife Zeresh and all his friends
said to him, "Have a gallows built, seven-

4:11 [a]Est 2:14 [b]Da 2:9 [c]Est 5:1,2; 8:4; Ps 125:3
4:14 [d]Job 34:29; Ps 28:1; 35:22; Ecc 3:7; Isa 42:14; 57:11; 62:1; 64:12; Am 5:13 [e]Est 9:16, 22 [f]S Ge 45:7; S Dt 28:29 [g]S Ge 50:20
4:16 [h]S 2Ch 20:3; Est 9:31 [i]S Ge 43:14
5:1 [j]Eze 16:13 [k]Pr 21:1
5:2 [l]S Est 4:11
5:3 [m]Est 7:2; Da 5:16; Mk 6:23
5:6 [n]S Est 1:10 [o]Da 5:16; Mk 6:23 [p]Est 9:12
5:8 [q]S Est 2:15 [r]S 1Ki 3:15
5:9 [s]S Est 2:21; Pr 14:17 [t]S Est 3:3, 5
5:10 [u]Est 6:13
5:11 [v]Pr 13:16 [w]Est 9:7-10,13
5:12 [x]Job 22:29; Pr 16:18; 29:23
5:13 [y]S Est 2:19

4:12–15 HISTORY, Freedom—Humans face decisions to be available for God's use or not. God leads people to places in life where they can be useful in His purposes. He forces no one to be so used. He can always accomplish His saving purposes through someone else.
4:14 EVIL AND SUFFERING, God's Present Help—God's help may prevent His people from suffering. He offers that help often through the courageous actions of His chosen leader. Esther and Mordecai acted in faith and courage to prevent the massacre of their people. Mordecai knew that no one leader is indispensable. God could raise someone else to deliver His people.
4:14 REVELATION, Author of Hope—God used Esther's work as queen to bring hope and deliverance for His people. Her story became the basis for the Book of Esther in which God is not explicitly mentioned. God's revelation at times involves working through His people in the secular world to achieve His purposes without the explicit religious language being involved. Revelation includes the placing of people in critical positions at the right time.
4:16 PRAYER, Sincerity—Fasting is usually associated with prayer. See notes on v 3; 2 Sa 1:12. Fasting in the sumptuous luxury of the palace (2:9) was an indication of unusual earnestness. Esther needed dedicated prayer as she prepared to risk her life for her people.

ty-five feet[h] high,[z] and ask the king in
the morning to have Mordecai hanged[a]
on it. Then go with the king to the dinner
and be happy." This suggestion delighted
Haman, and he had the gallows built.

Chapter 6

Mordecai Honored

THAT night the king could not sleep;[b]
so he ordered the book of the chronicles,[c] the record of his reign, to be
brought in and read to him. 2It was found
recorded there that Mordecai had exposed Bigthana and Teresh, two of the
king's officers who guarded the doorway,
who had conspired to assassinate King
Xerxes.[d]

3"What honor and recognition has
Mordecai received for this?" the king
asked.

"Nothing has been done for him,"[e]
his attendants answered.

4The king said, "Who is in the court?"
Now Haman had just entered the outer
court of the palace to speak to the king
about hanging Mordecai on the gallows
he had erected for him.

5His attendants answered, "Haman is
standing in the court."

"Bring him in," the king ordered.

6When Haman entered, the king asked
him, "What should be done for the man
the king delights to honor?"

Now Haman thought to himself, "Who
is there that the king would rather honor
than me?" 7So he answered the king,
"For the man the king delights to honor,
8have them bring a royal robe[f] the king
has worn and a horse[g] the king has ridden, one with a royal crest placed on its
head. 9Then let the robe and horse be
entrusted to one of the king's most noble
princes. Let them robe the man the king
delights to honor, and lead him on the
horse through the city streets, proclaiming before him, 'This is what is done for
the man the king delights to honor![h]' "

10"Go at once," the king commanded
Haman. "Get the robe and the horse and
do just as you have suggested for Mordecai the Jew, who sits at the king's gate.
Do not neglect anything you have recommended."

11So Haman got[i] the robe and the
horse. He robed Mordecai, and led him
on horseback through the city streets,
proclaiming before him, "This is what is
done for the man the king delights to
honor!"

12Afterward Mordecai returned to the
king's gate. But Haman rushed home,
with his head covered[j] in grief, 13and
told Zeresh[k] his wife and all his friends
everything that had happened to him.

His advisers and his wife Zeresh said to
him, "Since Mordecai, before whom your
downfall[l] has started, is of Jewish origin,
you cannot stand against him—you will
surely come to ruin!"[m] 14While they
were still talking with him, the king's eunuchs arrived and hurried Haman away
to the banquet[n] Esther had prepared.

Chapter 7

Haman Hanged

SO the king and Haman went to dine[o]
with Queen Esther, 2and as they were
drinking wine[p] on that second day, the
king again asked, "Queen Esther, what is
your petition? It will be given you. What
is your request? Even up to half the kingdom,[q] it will be granted.[r]"

3Then Queen Esther answered, "If I
have found favor[s] with you, O king, and
if it pleases your majesty, grant me my
life—this is my petition. And spare my
people—this is my request. 4For I and my
people have been sold for destruction and
slaughter and annihilation.[t] If we had
merely been sold as male and female
slaves, I would have kept quiet, because
no such distress would justify disturbing
the king.[i]"

5King Xerxes asked Queen Esther,
"Who is he? Where is the man who has
dared to do such a thing?"

6Esther said, "The adversary and enemy is this vile Haman."

Then Haman was terrified before the
king and queen. 7The king got up in a
rage,[u] left his wine and went out into the
palace garden.[v] But Haman, realizing
that the king had already decided his
fate,[w] stayed behind to beg Queen Esther
for his life.

8Just as the king returned from the palace garden to the banquet hall, Haman
was falling on the couch[x] where Esther
was reclining.[y]

The king exclaimed, "Will he even molest the queen while she is with me in
the house?"[z]

As soon as the word left the king's
mouth, they covered Haman's face.[a]
9Then Harbona,[b] one of the eunuchs attending the king, said, "A gallows seventy-five feet[h] high[c] stands by Haman's
house. He had it made for Mordecai, who
spoke up to help the king."

The king said, "Hang him on it!"[d] 10So
they hanged[e] Haman[f] on the gallows[g]

5:14 zEst 7:9 aS Ezr 6:11
6:1 bDa 2:1; 6:18 cS Est 2:23
6:2 dEst 2:21-23
6:3 eEcc 9:13-16
6:8 fS Ge 41:42; S Isa 52:1 g1Ki 1:33
6:9 hGe 41:43
6:11 iS Ge 41:42
6:12 j2Sa 15:30; Est 7:8; Jer 14:3,4; Mic 3:7
6:13 kEst 5:10 lPs 57:6; Pr 26:27; 28:18 mEst 7:7
6:14 nS 1Ki 3:15
7:1 oGe 40:20-22; Mt 22:1-14
7:2 pS Est 1:10 qS Est 5:3 rEst 9:12
7:3 sS Est 2:15
7:4 tEst 3:9; S 4:7
7:7 uS Ge 34:7; S Est 1:12; Pr 19:12; 20:1-2 vS 2Ki 21:18 wEst 6:13
7:8 xS Est 1:6 yGe 39:14; Jn 13:23 zS Ge 34:7 aS Est 6:12
7:9 bEst 1:10 cEst 5:14 dS Dt 21:22-23; Ps 7:14-16; 9:16; Pr 11:5-6; S 26:27; S Mt 7:2
7:10 eGe 40:22 fPr 10:28 gEst 9:25

h*14,9* Hebrew *fifty cubits* (about 23 meters) i*4* Or *quiet, but the compensation our adversary offers cannot be compared with the loss the king would suffer*

he had prepared for Mordecai.[h] Then the king's fury subsided.[i]

Chapter 8

The King's Edict in Behalf of the Jews

THAT same day King Xerxes gave Queen Esther the estate of Haman,[j] the enemy of the Jews. And Mordecai came into the presence of the king, for Esther had told how he was related to her. 2The king took off his signet ring,[k] which he had reclaimed from Haman, and presented it to Mordecai. And Esther appointed him over Haman's estate.[l]

3Esther again pleaded with the king, falling at his feet and weeping. She begged him to put an end to the evil plan of Haman the Agagite,[m] which he had devised against the Jews. 4Then the king extended the gold scepter[n] to Esther and she arose and stood before him.

5"If it pleases the king," she said, "and if he regards me with favor[o] and thinks it the right thing to do, and if he is pleased with me, let an order be written overruling the dispatches that Haman son of Hammedatha, the Agagite, devised and wrote to destroy the Jews in all the king's provinces. 6For how can I bear to see disaster fall on my people? How can I bear to see the destruction of my family?"[p]

7King Xerxes replied to Queen Esther and to Mordecai the Jew, "Because Haman attacked the Jews, I have given his estate to Esther, and they have hanged[q] him on the gallows. 8Now write another decree[r] in the king's name in behalf of the Jews as seems best to you, and seal[s] it with the king's signet ring[t]—for no document written in the king's name and sealed with his ring can be revoked."[u]

9At once the royal secretaries were summoned—on the twenty-third day of the third month, the month of Sivan. They wrote out all Mordecai's orders to the Jews, and to the satraps, governors and nobles of the 127 provinces stretching from India to Cush.[j][v] These orders were written in the script of each province and the language of each people and also to the Jews in their own script and language.[w] 10Mordecai wrote in the name of King Xerxes, sealed the dispatches with the king's signet ring, and sent them by mounted couriers, who rode fast horses especially bred for the king.

11The king's edict granted the Jews in every city the right to assemble and protect themselves; to destroy, kill and annihilate any armed force of any nationality or province that might attack them and their women and children; and to plunder[x] the property of their enemies. 12The day appointed for the Jews to do this in all the provinces of King Xerxes was the thirteenth day of the twelfth month, the month of Adar.[y] 13A copy of the text of the edict was to be issued as law in every province and made known to the people of every nationality so that the Jews would be ready on that day[z] to avenge themselves on their enemies.

14The couriers, riding the royal horses, raced out, spurred on by the king's command. And the edict was also issued in the citadel of Susa.[a]

15Mordecai[b] left the king's presence wearing royal garments of blue and white, a large crown of gold[c] and a purple robe of fine linen.[d] And the city of Susa held a joyous celebration.[e] 16For the Jews it was a time of happiness and joy,[f] gladness and honor.[g] 17In every province and in every city, wherever the edict of the king went, there was joy[h] and gladness among the Jews, with feasting and celebrating. And many people of other nationalities became Jews because fear[i] of the Jews had seized them.[j]

Chapter 9

Triumph of the Jews

ON the thirteenth day of the twelfth month, the month of Adar,[k] the edict commanded by the king was to be carried out. On this day the enemies of the Jews had hoped to overpower them, but now the tables were turned and the Jews got the upper hand[l] over those who hated them.[m] 2The Jews assembled in their cities[n] in all the provinces of King Xerxes to attack those seeking their destruction. No one could stand against them,[o] because the people of all the other nationalities were afraid of them. 3And all the nobles of the provinces, the satraps, the governors and the king's administrators helped the Jews,[p] because fear of Mordecai had seized them.[q] 4Mordecai[r] was prominent[s] in the palace; his reputation spread throughout the provinces, and he became more and more powerful.[t]

5The Jews struck down all their enemies with the sword, killing and destroy-

[j]9 That is, the upper Nile region

7:10 [h]Da 6:24 [i]Est 2:1
8:1 [j]Pr 22:22-23
8:2 [k]S Ge 24:22; S 41:42 [l]S Ge 41:41; Pr 13:22; 14:35; Da 2:48
8:3 [m]S Ex 17:8-16
8:4 [n]S Est 4:11
8:5 [o]S Est 2:15
8:6 [p]Ge 44:34
8:7 [q]S Dt 21:22-23
8:8 [r]S Est 3:12-14 [s]S Ge 38:18 [t]S Ge 41:42 [u]S Est 1:19; Da 6:15
8:9 [v]Est 1:1 [w]S Ne 13:24
8:11 [x]S Ge 14:23; S Est 3:13; 9:10,15,16
8:12 [y]Est 3:13; 9:1
8:13 [z]Est 3:14
8:14 [a]Est 3:15
8:15 [b]Est 9:4; 10:2 [c]S 2Sa 12:30 [d]S Ge 41:42 [e]Est 3:15
8:16 [f]Ps 97:10-12 [g]Est 4:1-3; Ps 112:4; Jer 29:4-7
8:17 [h]Ps 35:27; 45:15; 51:8; Pr 11:10 [i]S Ex 15:14,16; Dt 11:25; Da 6:26 [j]Est 9:3
9:1 [k]S Est 8:12 [l]Jer 29:4-7 [m]S Est 3:12-14; Pr 22:22-23
9:2 [n]S Ge 22:17 [o]Ps 35:26; 40:14; 70:2; 71:13,24
9:3 [p]S Ezr 8:36 [q]Est 8:17
9:4 [r]S Est 8:15 [s]S Ex 11:3 [t]S 2Sa 3:1; 1Ch 11:9

8:1—9:17 EVIL AND SUFFERING, Vindication—Without mentioning God, the inspired writer showed how He vindicated Himself and His people against evil plots worked out under governmental authority.

ing them,[u] and they did what they
pleased to those who hated them. 6In the
citadel of Susa, the Jews killed and destroyed five hundred men. 7They also
killed Parshandatha, Dalphon, Aspatha,
8Poratha, Adalia, Aridatha, 9Parmashta,
Arisai, Aridai and Vaizatha, 10the ten
sons[v] of Haman son of Hammedatha, the
enemy of the Jews.[w] But they did not lay
their hands on the plunder.[x]

11The number of those slain in the citadel of Susa was reported to the king that
same day. 12The king said to Queen Esther, "The Jews have killed and destroyed five hundred men and the ten
sons of Haman in the citadel of Susa.
What have they done in the rest of the
king's provinces? Now what is your petition? It will be given you. What is your
request? It will also be granted."[y]

13"If it pleases the king," Esther answered, "give the Jews in Susa permission to carry out this day's edict tomorrow also, and let Haman's ten sons[z] be
hanged[a] on gallows."

14So the king commanded that this be
done. An edict was issued in Susa, and
they hanged[b] the ten sons of Haman.
15The Jews in Susa came together on the
fourteenth day of the month of Adar, and
they put to death in Susa three hundred
men, but they did not lay their hands on
the plunder.[c]

16Meanwhile, the remainder of the
Jews who were in the king's provinces
also assembled to protect themselves and
get relief[d] from their enemies.[e] They
killed seventy-five thousand of them[f] but
did not lay their hands on the plunder.[g]
17This happened on the thirteenth day of
the month of Adar, and on the fourteenth
they rested and made it a day of feasting[h]
and joy.

Purim Celebrated

18The Jews in Susa, however, had assembled on the thirteenth and fourteenth, and then on the fifteenth they
rested and made it a day of feasting and
joy.

19That is why rural Jews—those living
in villages—observe the fourteenth of the
month of Adar[i] as a day of joy and feasting, a day for giving presents to each other.[j]

20Mordecai recorded these events, and
he sent letters to all the Jews throughout
the provinces of King Xerxes, near and
far, 21to have them celebrate annually the
fourteenth and fifteenth days of the
month of Adar 22as the time when the
Jews got relief[k] from their enemies, and
as the month when their sorrow was
turned into joy and their mourning into a
day of celebration.[l] He wrote them to
observe the days as days of feasting and
joy and giving presents of food[m] to one
another and gifts to the poor.[n]

23So the Jews agreed to continue the
celebration they had begun, doing what
Mordecai had written to them. 24For Haman son of Hammedatha, the Agagite,[o]
the enemy of all the Jews, had plotted
against the Jews to destroy them and had
cast the *pur*[p] (that is, the lot[q]) for their
ruin and destruction.[r] 25But when the
plot came to the king's attention,[k] he issued written orders that the evil scheme
Haman had devised against the Jews
should come back onto his own head,[s]
and that he and his sons should be
hanged[t] on the gallows.[u] 26(Therefore
these days were called Purim, from the
word *pur*.[v]) Because of everything written in this letter and because of what
they had seen and what had happened to
them, 27the Jews took it upon themselves
to establish the custom that they and
their descendants and all who join them
should without fail observe these two
days every year, in the way prescribed
and at the time appointed. 28These days
should be remembered and observed in
every generation by every family, and in
every province and in every city. And
these days of Purim should never cease to
be celebrated by the Jews, nor should the
memory of them die out among their descendants.

29So Queen Esther, daughter of Abihail,[w] along with Mordecai the Jew,
wrote with full authority to confirm this
second letter concerning Purim. 30And
Mordecai sent letters to all the Jews in
the 127 provinces[x] of the kingdom of
Xerxes—words of goodwill and assurance— 31to establish these days of Purim
at their designated times, as Mordecai the
Jew and Queen Esther had decreed for
them, and as they had established for
themselves and their descendants in regard to their times of fasting[y] and lamentation.[z] 32Esther's decree confirmed
these regulations about Purim, and it was
written down in the records.

9:5 [u]Dt 25:17-19; S 1Sa 15:3; S Ezr 4:6
9:10 [v]S Est 5:11; Ps 127:3-5 [w]S 1Sa 15:33 [x]S Ge 14:23; S 1Sa 14:32; S Est 3:13
9:12 [y]Est 5:6; 7:2
9:13 [z]S Est 5:11 [a]S Dt 21:22-23
9:14 [b]S Ezr 6:11
9:15 [c]S Ge 14:23; S Est 8:11
9:16 [d]S Est 4:14 [e]Dt 25:19 [f]S 1Ch 4:43 [g]S Est 8:11
9:17 [h]S 1Ki 3:15
9:19 [i]S Est 3:7 [j]S Est 2:9; Rev 11:10
9:22 [k]S Est 4:14 [l]Ne 8:12; Ps 30:11-12 [m]S 2Ki 25:30 [n]S Ne 8:10
9:24 [o]S Ex 17:8-16 [p]S Est 3:7 [q]S Lev 16:8 [r]Est 3:6
9:25 [s]Ps 7:16 [t]S Dt 21:22-23 [u]Est 7:10
9:26 [v]S Est 3:7
9:29 [w]Est 2:15
9:30 [x]S Est 1:1
9:31 [y]S Est 4:16 [z]Est 4:1-3

[k]25 Or *when Esther came before the king*

9:30–31 PRAYER, Corporate—The thirteenth day of the month of Adar (the twelfth month of the Hebrew year, corresponding to February-March) was established as a day of fasting and included prayers of repentance. The fourteenth and fifteenth are days of rejoicing (v 17). God's people appropriately celebrate His deliverance in annual national festivals or holidays representing a type of community prayer to God. These include times of repentance and rededication as well as days of celebration and joy.

Chapter 10

The Greatness of Mordecai

KING Xerxes imposed tribute throughout the empire, to its distant
shores.[a] 2And all his acts of power and
might, together with a full account of the
greatness of Mordecai[b] to which the king
had raised him,[c] are they not written in
the book of the annals[d] of the kings of
Media and Persia? 3Mordecai the Jew was
second[e] in rank[f] to King Xerxes,[g] preeminent among the Jews, and held in
high esteem by his many fellow Jews, because he worked for the good of his people and spoke up for the welfare of all the
Jews.[h]

10:1 [a]Ps 72:10; 97:1
10:2 [b]S Est 8:15 [c]S Ge 41:44 [d]S Est 2:23
10:3 [e]Da 5:7 [f]Ge 41:43 [g]Ge 41:40 [h]Ne 2:10; Jer 29:4-7; Da 6:3

10:1-3 ELECTION, Righteousness—See note on Ge 15:1-21. The Book of Esther is about the mystery of election. The elect people found deliverance from an impossible situation because they were faithful to their election calling. Faithful Mordecai gained prestige and power in both the Jewish and Persian communities because of His faithful commitment to His people and to His God. Israel learned from Esther and Mordecai that God can work silently through the affairs even of a foreign government to reward His righteous servants and to achieve His election purposes.

Job

Theological Setting

Why do bad things happen to good people? That was Job's question. Job was a good person. God said he was good (1:8; 2:3). Job claimed he was innocent and righteous (9:15,20; 31:1-40). At first his friends did not accuse him of evil (2:11-13). Only Satan doubted Job's sincerity. Satan's question was, "Does Job fear God for nothing?" (1:9).

Job's external circumstances indicated to some he was righteous. Traditional teaching showed from experience that God blesses the righteous and curses the wicked (Dt 28:1-35; Pr 3:15-18). Job had been blessed with an ideal family—seven sons and three daughters (1:2). He was rich in houses, land, servants, possessions, and social standing. He observed all the religious practices.

Outwardly, Job appeared to be righteous. But Satan claimed otherwise. In a meeting of the heavenly council (unattended by Job), he accused Job of being good only because goodness paid dividends. Indirectly, Satan accused God. He said God gave Job reason to practice religion simply to get material rewards. Satan claimed that God had placed a hedge around Job and had blessed him abundantly. Why should Job not be religious?

Satan proposed a test to see if Job would continue to serve God even if he lost everything and suffered personal anguish and pain. Satan was so sure of the shallowness of Job's faith he claimed Job would curse God to His face (1:11; 2:5). God had such confidence in Job He accepted Satan's challenge and agreed to the test. However, God retained ultimate control over everything Satan could do to Job.

Job's problem really began in heaven, but it was carried out in the world. Job lost his property, his family, his health, and his standing in the community. He was not consulted. He had no control over the test; yet he experienced all its trauma and fury.

What responses or options do righteous people have when bad things happen to them? Several such options might be considered.

1. One response remained closed for Job. He could not unlock the secrets of heaven and obtain perfect divine wisdom. God gives wisdom but only in limited amounts (26:14). Job had to deal with his problem with the limited wisdom God gave him.

2. He did acknowledge God's gifts and recognize that the God who gives good gifts has the right to take them away (1:21; 2:10).

3. Still, he lamented his fate bitterly (3:1-26). Job defended his innocence, debated his accusers, and questioned God's justice (3:23).

4. Job's three friends reacted differently. They considered his suffering evidence of his sinfulness.

5. Elihu argued that Job's suffering was primarily to discipline and teach Job (33:13-30).

All of these options may be legitimate in varying circumstances. No one of the opinions can be made into a general rule that covers every problem any person may have. Job finally humbled himself before God. He confessed that God can do all things and that none of His purposes will fail (42:2).

The Book of Job does not deal abstractly with the problem of evil in the world. It deals instead with a very practical problem: Why am I suffering? The book is about the sufferings of one righteous man in the Old Testament. Most of us have occasion to raise Job's question.

Theological Outline

Job: A Study in Providence and Faith

I. Prologue: A Righteous Man Can Endure Injustice Without Sinning. (1:1—2:10)

II. First Round: Will a Just God Answer a Righteous Sufferer's Questions? (2:11—14:22)
  - A. Job: Why must a person be born to a life of suffering? (2:11—3:26)
  - B. Eliphaz: Do not claim to be just, but seek the disciplining God, who is just. (4:1—5:27)
  - C. Job: Death is the only respite for a just person persecuted by God. (6:1—7:21)
  - D. Bildad: A just God does not punish the innocent. (8:1-22)

E. Job: Humans cannot win an argument in court against the Creator. (9:1—10:22)
F. Zophar: Feeble, ignorant humans must confess sins. (11:1-20)
G. Job: An intelligent person demands an answer from the all-powerful, all-knowing God, not from other humans. (12:1—14:22)

III. Second Round: Does the Fate of the Wicked Prove the Mercy and Justice of God? (15:1—21:34)
A. Eliphaz: Be quiet, admit your guilt, and accept your punishment. (15:1-35)
B. Job: Oh that an innocent person might plead my case with the merciless God. (16:1—17:16)
C. Bildad: Wise up and admit you are suffering the just fate of the wicked. (18:1-21)
D. Job: In a world without justice or friends, a just person must wait for a Redeemer to win his case. (19:1-29)
E. Zophar: Your short-lived prosperity shows you are a wicked oppressor. (20:1-29)
F. Job: Lying comforters do not help my struggle against the injustice of God. (21:1-34)

IV. Third Round: Can the Innocent Sufferer Ever Know God's Ways and Will? (22:1—28:28)
A. Eliphaz: You wicked sinner, return to Almighty God and be restored. (22:1-30)
B. Job: I cannot find God, but evidence shows He pays undue attention to me but gives no attention to the wicked. (23:1—24:25)
C. Bildad: No person can be righteous before the awesome God. (25:1-6)
D. Job: Neither your meaningless counsel nor God's faint word helps the innocent sufferer. (26:1—27:23)
E. Job: Humans cannot know wisdom; only God reveals its content: Fear the Lord. (28:1-28)

V. Job's Summary: Let God Restore the Good Old Days or Answer My Complaint. (29:1—31:40)
A. In the good old days I had respect and integrity. (29:1-25)
B. Now men and God are cruel to me. (30:1-31)
C. In my innocence, I cry out for a hearing before God. (31:1-40)
1. I have not looked with lust on a maiden. (31:1-4)
2. I am not guilty of lying or deceit. (31:5-8)
3. I have not committed adultery. (31:9-12)
4. I have treated my servants fairly. (31:13-15)
5. I have been generous and kind to the poor and the disadvantaged. (31:16-23)
6. I have not worshiped gold nor celestial bodies. (31:24-28)
7. I have not rejoiced in others' ruin. (31:29-30)
8. I have not refused hospitality to anyone. (31:31-32)
9. I have nothing to hide, but I wish God would give me a written statement of charges. (31:33-37)
10. I have not withheld payment for the laborers on my land. (31:38-40)

VI. Elihu: An Angry Young Man Defends God. (32:1—37:24)
A. Elihu is angry with Job and with the friends. (32:1-22)
B. Elihu speaks to Job as a man; God speaks through dreams, visions, pain, and deliverance. (33:1-33)
C. God is just; Job speaks without knowledge. (34:1-37)
D. Is there any advantage in serving God? Human sin is no threat to God; human righteousness is no gift to Him. (35:1-16)
E. God is just, all-wise, mysterious, and sovereign over humans and nature. (36:1—37:24)

VII. Dialogue: Prove Your Wisdom Is Sufficient to Contend with the Eternal Creator. (38:1—42:6)
A. God: Can you control the inanimate and animate creation? (38:1—39:30)
B. Job: I am overwhelmed and powerless to answer. (40:1-5)
C. God: Will you condemn God to justify yourself? (40:6-9)
D. God: Take charge of the universe. (40:10-14)
E. Two inexplicable creatures illustrate God's unfathomable ways. (40:15—41:34)
F. Job: Seeing God, I confess His power and repent of sin. (42:1-6)

VIII. Epilogue: Prayer Brings Reconciliation, Forgiveness, and Restoration. (42:7-17)

Theological Conclusions

The Book of Job is concerned primarily with undeserved suffering. That issue is raised in several other places in the Old Testament (Ps 26:1-12; 73:13-14; Jer 12:1,3; 20:12; Hab 1:13). At least five theological conclusions may be drawn from the Book of Job about God and undeserved suffering.

1. Suffering can come suddenly and inexplicably to anyone, even to a righteous person. On one day Job lost his oxen, donkeys, sheep, camels, and all his children. Later, he lost his health. Job knew the

immediate causes of his suffering and loss—thieves, storms, and disease; but he believed that behind these immediate causes God was in control of all things. God's apparent failure to control these disasters as Job had expected Him to disturbed Job.

2. Undeserved suffering raises the question of justice in the world and ultimately the justice of God. The Book of Job is not a theodicy (the justification of the ways of God to man). Solutions to the problem of suffering which lie outside biblical revelation (such as polytheism or reincarnation) are not considered in the Book of Job. Job pressed God for an explanation within his faith in one all-powerful God. He questioned the ways of God, and God agreed Job was justified in doing so (42:7-8). God encourages people to exercise their moral judgment, even to the point of questioning His conduct of history or nature. God does not, however, want us to justify ourselves by condemning Him.

3. Human wisdom is not adequate to solve the problem of undeserved suffering. The reader learns in this instance that Job was suffering because of a test of his faith. However, as readers, we can never be sure our suffering is only a test. We, like Job, must suffer "in the dark." Job and his friends used human wisdom to speculate, to argue, and to debate possible reasons for Job's sufferings; but they never discovered the real reason. In the process they said things that had no basis in fact (21:34). The friends were silenced, and Job confessed he spoke without knowledge about things he did not understand (42:3). Human wisdom is severely limited (26:14); only God has perfect wisdom (28:23).

4. The Book of Job provides us hints of possible explanations for human suffering. Suffering may be a test. In our struggles and suffering we can, without knowing it, struggle and suffer for God's honor. Again, suffering may be to discipline and to teach us (5:17; 33:16-18; Pr 3:11-12), but this is not a comforting explanation. Suffering may be due to known or unknown sin. The three friends thought all suffering was due to the sin of the sufferer. This is not always so. Jesus said of the man blind from birth, "no one sinned" (Jn 9:1-3). Hints of possible explanations may or may not help the sufferer.

5. Only God can meet our needs in a time of suffering. Humans are unitary beings. When our bodies suffer, our minds, emotions, and spiritual life are affected. The book aims to deliver a spiritual message to tortured people. Job's problem was not primarily physical. The account of his healing and restoration serves only to inform the reader the test is over. Job's problem was not primarily mental, because Job was never given an explanation of his suffering. Job's problem was mainly spiritual. Although he held on to his righteousness and faith, he felt his suffering had separated him from God. When God spoke to him while he was suffering, Job found relief but not *from* his sufferings. God assured him that innocent suffering is no proof of isolation from God. Job and Paul were sufferers in common (2 Co 6:10).

Contemporary Teaching

Suffering may come suddenly and inexplicably to anyone. Suffering does not necessarily mean God is angry with or separated from the sufferer. A mystery surrounds much suffering. Human wisdom is severely limited in its ability to explain the ultimate causes of suffering. God can relieve the distress and calm the fears of the sufferer. The sufferer, in turn, must have faith in God's goodness and sovereignty (Ro 8:28). God can transform evil into good as He did at the cross.

This theological statement will not meet our needs when we must suffer. Rather, the theological statement seeks to point us beyond wisdom and knowledge to faith and trust. Suffering calls us to renewed dialogue with God. In conversation with Him, we, like Job, can discover His personal presence with us. The joy and comfort of that presence may not still our pain. It will, however, provide our greater need of assurance that He still cares and accepts us even as we suffer. His presence reminds us that our Redeemer lives today even after suffering and dying for us. He understands what we are enduring and gives the ultimate answer—resurrection to life beyond pain.

Chapter 1

Prologue

IN the land of Uz[a] there lived a man
whose name was Job.[b] This man was
blameless[c] and upright;[d] he feared
God[e] and shunned evil.[f] 2He had seven
sons[g] and three daughters,[h] 3and he
owned seven thousand sheep, three thousand camels, five hundred yoke of oxen
and five hundred donkeys,[i] and had a
large number of servants.[j] He was the
greatest man[k] among all the people of
the East.[l]

4His sons used to take turns holding
feasts[m] in their homes, and they would
invite their three sisters to eat and drink
with them. 5When a period of feasting
had run its course, Job would send and
have them purified.[n] Early in the morning he would sacrifice a burnt offering[o]
for each of them, thinking, "Perhaps my
children have sinned[p] and cursed God[q]
in their hearts." This was Job's regular
custom.

Job's First Test

6One day the angels[a][r] came to
present themselves before the LORD, and
Satan[b][s] also came with them.[t] 7The
LORD said to Satan, "Where have you
come from?"

Satan answered the LORD, "From roaming through the earth and going back and
forth in it."[u]

8Then the LORD said to Satan, "Have
you considered my servant Job?[v] There is
no one on earth like him; he is blameless
and upright, a man who fears God[w] and
shuns evil."[x]

9"Does Job fear God for nothing?"[y] Satan replied. 10"Have you not put a
hedge[z] around him and his household
and everything he has?[a] You have
blessed the work of his hands, so that his
flocks and herds are spread throughout
the land.[b] 11But stretch out your hand
and strike everything he has,[c] and he
will surely curse you to your face."[d]

12The LORD said to Satan, "Very well,
then, everything he has[e] is in your
hands, but on the man himself do not lay
a finger."[f]

1:1 [a]S Ge 10:23 [b]Eze 14:14,20; Jas 5:11 [c]S Ge 6:9; S Job 23:10 [d]Job 23:7; Ps 11:7; 107:42; Pr 21:29; Mic 7:2 [e]S Ge 22:12 [f]ver 8; S Dt 4:6; Job 2:3; 1Th 5:22 **1:2** [g]S Ru 4:15 [h]ver 13,18; Job 42:13; Ps 127:3; 144:12 **1:3** [i]S Ge 13:2 [j]S Ge 12:16 [k]ver 8; Job 29:25 [l]S Ge 25:6; Job 42:10; Ps 103:10 **1:4** [m]ver 13,18 **1:5** [n]S Ne 12:30 [o]S Ge 8:20 [p]Job 8:4 [q]1Ki 21:10,13; Ps 10:3; 74:10 **1:6** [r]S 1Ki 22:19; fn Ge 6:2 [s]S 2Sa 24:1; S 2Ch 18:21; S Ps 109:6; Lk 22:31 [t]Job 2:1 **1:7** [u]S Ge 3:1; 1Pe 5:8 **1:8** [v]S Jos 1:7 [w]Ps 25:12; 112:1; 128:4 [x]S ver 1; S Ex 20:20 **1:9** [y]1Ti 6:5 **1:10** [z]S 1Sa 25:16 [a]ver 12; Job 2:4; Ps 34:7 [b]ver 3; Job 8:7; 29:6; 42:12,17

1:11 [c]Job 19:21; Lk 22:31 [d]Lev 24:11; Job 2:5; Isa 3:8; 65:3; Rev 12:9-10 **1:12** [e]S ver 10 [f]Job 2:6; 1Co 10:13

[a]6 Hebrew *the sons of God* [b]6 *Satan* means *accuser.*

1:1—42:17 REVELATION, Author of Hope—Job shows God's revelation can occur in unexpected situations—tragedy, suffering, debate with friends, and debate with God. Such revelation shows God is the author of hope and forgiveness not of evil, suffering, and legalistic religion.

1:1,8 SALVATION, Fear of God—Job's shunning of evil was proof he feared God. See note on Ge 22:12.

1:1—2:10 SALVATION, Obedience—God permitted Satan to test Job's faith. Would Job be obedient to God if he lost his great wealth, his family, and health? He was obedient and provided an example of obedience to all Christ's followers.

1:3,10 SALVATION, Blessing—God had greatly blessed Job and the work of his hands. He had not, however, put the kind of hedge around Job which Satan contended. God's blessing is not necessarily protection from all harm, temptation, and sorrow.

1:4 FAMILY, Shared Joy—Job's family shared joy together as his sons invited their sisters to celebrate feast days with them. Jealousy and rivalry seem absent as they took turns enjoying their times of fellowship together.

1:5 PRAYER, Intercession—See note on Lev 1:9. The Mosaic Law revealed that some sin is unintentional, but all sin requires atonement (Lev 4:2–35; 5:15–19; Nu 15:22–29). The sacrifices on the Day of Atonement covered all the sins of the people (Lev 16:16; Heb 9:7). Although the author did not specify whether Job's children were conscious of their sin, the crucial factor here was the mind of Job. Acting as priest for his family, his preoccupation was with pleasing God. He sought to intercede with God on behalf of his family. Prayer for sinners is a constant duty of God's people, but our prayers cannot bring forgiveness for another's sins. Each person must confess personal sin and seek personal forgiveness.

1:5 FAMILY, Worship—Job's persistent desire for his children to be acceptable to God is vividly expressed in this picture of his continual intercession for them. Christian families do not sacrifice burnt offerings but can continue to offer prayers for God's guidance and forgiveness on behalf of their children.

1:6–12 EVIL AND SUFFERING, *Testing*—*Job's suffering* was a test of his faith. Satan argued that Job was obedient to God only because God allowed him to prosper. Tradition taught that faithfulness to God led to prosperity and wickedness to suffering. The Book of Job argues against making this tradition into a dogma which could be used to judge individual cases. God allowed Satan to take away Job's prosperity through a series of tragic events. God intended to demonstrate and test Job's faith. See notes on 42:1–15; Isa 52:13—53:12. Satan, not God, was the direct cause of Job's suffering. God, however, remained in control of creation. Without His permission, Satan could not have acted. Satan appeared in God's presence along with the angels (literally, "sons of God"). The name "Satan" means the accuser or adversary. It occurs in only three contexts in the Old Testament. See notes on 1 Ch 21:1; Zec 3:1–2. The understanding of Satan as a demonic figure fully opposed to God did not come all at once to Israel. The fullest understanding came only in the New Testament. See note on Mt 4:1–11.

1:8 HUMANITY, Intellectual Nature—"Considered" literally means "set your heart upon." To the ancient Hebrews, the heart was the seat of thought and will. See note on 2:3.

1:8–10 SIN, Satan—The Bible does not contain a philosophical statement concerning the origin of sin. In Job, Satan accuses man before God. Satan, here, instigates sin. He must receive God's permission before he can carry out his devious plan, and even then God places limits on his activity. Human beings sin because an outside force (see Ge 3:1–15; 1 Ch 21:1) influences people to trust their own judgments and desires rather than trusting God and His good will towards us. Job shows it is possible for a person to withstand Satan's allurements and temptations (Job 2:10; 42:7).

1:8 THE CHURCH, Servants—God's servants designate people, like Job, who wish to do God's will. God's servants are ordinary people who allow God to use them according to His purposes. Job is a good example of a servant of God because he lived righteously before other people and God. Servants obey God, living uprightly in awe of the greatness of God.

1:9–22 CHRISTIAN ETHICS, Property Rights—One of the major lessons of Job is that in this life suffering is not limited by one's level of wealth, poverty, or level of integrity. Loss of property should not lead to loss of faith or integrity. Job's example helps us maintain proper perspective on material goods.

Then Satan went out from the presence of the LORD.
13One day when Job's sons and daughters[g] were feasting[h] and drinking wine
at the oldest brother's house, 14a messenger came to Job and said, "The oxen were
plowing and the donkeys were grazing[i]
nearby, 15and the Sabeans[j] attacked and
carried them off. They put the servants to
the sword, and I am the only one who has
escaped to tell you!"
16While he was still speaking, another
messenger came and said, "The fire of
God fell from the sky[k] and burned up the
sheep and the servants,[l] and I am the
only one who has escaped to tell you!"
17While he was still speaking, another
messenger came and said, "The Chaldeans[m] formed three raiding parties and
swept down on your camels and carried
them off. They put the servants to the
sword, and I am the only one who has
escaped to tell you!"
18While he was still speaking, yet another messenger came and said, "Your
sons and daughters[n] were feasting[o] and
drinking wine at the oldest brother's
house, 19when suddenly a mighty wind[p]
swept in from the desert and struck the
four corners of the house. It collapsed on
them and they are dead,[q] and I am the
only one who has escaped to tell you![r]"
20At this, Job got up and tore his robe[s]
and shaved his head.[t] Then he fell to the
ground in worship[u] 21and said:

"Naked I came from my mother's
womb,
and naked I will depart.[c] [v]
The LORD gave and the LORD has taken
away;[w]
may the name of the LORD be
praised."[x]

22In all this, Job did not sin by charging
God with wrongdoing.[y]

Chapter 2

Job's Second Test

On another day the angels[d] [z] came to
present themselves before the LORD,
and Satan also came with them[a] to
present himself before him. 2And the
LORD said to Satan, "Where have you
come from?"
Satan answered the LORD, "From roaming through the earth and going back and
forth in it."[b]
3Then the LORD said to Satan, "Have
you considered my servant Job? There is
no one on earth like him; he is blameless
and upright, a man who fears God and
shuns evil.[c] And he still maintains his
integrity,[d] though you incited me against
him to ruin him without any reason."[e]
4"Skin for skin!" Satan replied. "A
man will give all he has[f] for his own life.
5But stretch out your hand and strike his
flesh and bones,[g] and he will surely
curse you to your face."[h]
6The LORD said to Satan, "Very well,
then, he is in your hands;[i] but you must
spare his life."[j]
7So Satan went out from the presence
of the LORD and afflicted Job with painful
sores from the soles of his feet to the top
of his head.[k] 8Then Job took a piece of

1:13 [g]S ver 2 [h]S ver 4
1:14 [i]Ge 36:24
1:15 [j]S Ge 10:7; S Job 9:24
1:16 [k]S 1Ki 18:38; 2Ki 1:12; Job 20:26 [l]S Ge 18:17; S Lev 10:2; S Nu 11:1-3
1:17 [m]S Ge 11:28, 31; S Job 9:24
1:18 [n]S ver 2 [o]S ver 4
1:19 [p]Ps 11:6; Isa 5:28; 21:1; Jer 4:11; 13:24; 18:17; Eze 17:10; Hos 13:15; Mt 7:25 [q]Job 16:7; 19:13-15 [r]Eze 24:26
1:20 [s]S Ge 37:29; S Mk 14:63 [t]Isa 3:24; 15:2; 22:12; Jer 7:29; 16:6; Eze 27:31; 29:18; Mic 1:16 [u]1Pe 5:6
1:21 [v]Ecc 5:15; 1Ti 6:7 [w]Ru 1:21; 1Sa 2:7 [x]S Jdg 10:15; Job 2:10; Ecc 7:14; Jer 40:2; S Eph 5:20; 1Th 5:18; Jas 5:11
1:22 [y]Job 2:10; Ps 39:1; Pr 10:19; 13:3; Isa 53:7; Ro 9:20
2:1 [z]*fn* Ge 6:2 [a]S Job 1:6
2:2 [b]S Ge 3:1
2:3 [c]S Ex 20:20; S Job 1:1,8 [d]Job 6:29; 13:18; 27:6; 31:6; 32:1; 40:8 [e]Job 9:17; Ps 44:17
2:4 [f]S Job 1:10
2:5 [g]Job 16:8; 19:20; 33:21; Ps 102:5; La 4:8 [h]S Ex 20:7; S Job 1:11
2:6 [i]2Co 12:7 [j]S Job 1:12
2:7 [k]S Dt 28:35; S Job 16:16

[c]*21* Or *will return there* [d]*1* Hebrew *the sons of God*

1:16 CREATION, Judgment—The messenger interpreted lightning as God's judging fire. This paved the way for Job's friends to argue that all the problems Job endured originated with God as punishment for Job's sins. God allowed the evil to come on Job to test His faith and moral sincerity. Nature may prove destructive through storms and earthquakes. This does not mean the Creator is evil or that the Creator is judging a particular person for sin.

1:16–22 EVIL AND SUFFERING, Divine Origin—God permits life's tragedies but cannot be blamed for doing wrong. Human wisdom can never fully understand God's reasons. Human faith must accept God's goodness and love. Job was not aware of the conversation between God and Satan. The messengers attributed the tragedy to God's action because He was in control of their affairs. Job praised God for who He was. Suffering did not destroy His faith.

1:20–21 PRAYER, Worship—The praiseworthiness of God does not depend on our circumstances. Job praised God, not for his circumstances, but for God's unchanging and inherent worth.

1:21–22 GOD, Sovereignty—Job expressed profound faith in God. He followed the ancient custom of ascribing everything that happens to the work of God. In this, Job praised God and declared that He had done nothing wrong. Other biblical passages help us recognize that God is not the immediate cause of all things, for God only does that which is right or good. In the final analysis, however, God remains in control of the world and permits all things to happen whether the immediate cause is human free choice or Satanic powers. God had not taken away Job's wealth and family. God had only permitted the conditions in which Satan could bring evil and suffering upon Job. In allowing Satan to act, God knew that everything would eventually lead to the accomplishment of His purposes. See notes on Ru 1:13,20–21; Ro 8:28.

2:1–10 EVIL AND SUFFERING, Testing—Each time we suffer we face another test of our faith. Such suffering may be totally unrelated to our sin and without any reason other than testing. Satan claimed every person's faith has its price. Job showed Satan was wrong. Job's wife finally gave in; Job did not. His wife even presented a different type of test. Loyalty to and desire to please loved ones may tempt us to disobey or forsake God. Job shows we can pass Satan's test and maintain our trust in God no matter how much we suffer.

2:3 HUMANITY, Potentiality—"Blameless" actually refers more to completeness than to moral perfection. On the other hand, God's further evaluation of Job indicates his spiritual accomplishments. Only Jesus is sinless, but human potential for faithfulness and obedience should not be underestimated. The goal should be Christlikeness and nothing else. See note on 1:8.

2:3 THE CHURCH, Servants—Personal catastrophe does not lead God's servants away from faith in Him. See note on 1:8.

broken pottery and scraped himself with
it as he sat among the ashes.[l]
9His wife said to him, "Are you still
holding on to your integrity?[m] Curse God
and die!"[n]
10He replied, "You are talking like a
foolish[e] woman. Shall we accept good
from God, and not trouble?"[o]
In all this, Job did not sin in what he
said.[p]

Job's Three Friends

11When Job's three friends, Eliphaz the
Temanite,[q] Bildad the Shuhite[r] and Zophar the Naamathite,[s] heard about all
the troubles that had come upon him,
they set out from their homes and met
together by agreement to go and sympathize with him and comfort him.[t]
12When they saw him from a distance,
they could hardly recognize him;[u] they
began to weep aloud,[v] and they tore
their robes[w] and sprinkled dust on their
heads.[x] 13Then they sat on the ground[y]
with him for seven days and seven
nights.[z] No one said a word to him,[a]
because they saw how great his suffering
was.

Chapter 3

Job Speaks

AFTER this, Job opened his mouth and
cursed the day of his birth.[b] 2He
said:

3"May the day of my birth perish,
and the night it was said, 'A boy is
born!'[c]
4That day—may it turn to darkness;
may God above not care about it;
may no light shine upon it.
5May darkness and deep shadow[f] [d]
claim it once more;
may a cloud settle over it;
may blackness overwhelm its light.
6That night—may thick darkness[e] seize
it;

2:8 [l]Ge 18:27; Est 4:3; Job 16:15; 19:9; 30:19; 42:6; Ps 7:5; Isa 58:5; 61:3; Jer 6:26; La 3:29; Eze 26:16; Jnh 3:5-8,6; Mt 11:21
2:9 [m]Job 6:29; 13:15; 27:5; 33:9; 35:2; 1Th 5:8 [n]S Ex 20:7; S 2Ki 6:33
2:10 [o]S Job 1:21; S Ecc 2:24; La 3:38 [p]S Job 1:22; S 6:24; Jas 1:12; 5:11
2:11 [q]S Ge 36:11 [r]S Ge 25:2 [s]Job 11:1; 20:1 [t]S Ge 37:35; S Job 6:10; Jn 11:19
2:12 [u]Job 17:7; Isa 52:14 [v]S 2Sa 15:23 [w]S Ge 37:29; S Mk 14:63 [x]S Jos 7:6; S 2Sa 1:2
2:13 [y]Isa 3:26; 47:1; Jer 48:18; La 2:10; Eze 26:16; Jnh 3:6; Hag 2:22 [z]S Ge 50:10 [a]Pr 17:28; Isa 23:2; 47:5
3:1 [b]Jer 15:10; 20:14
3:3 [c]ver 11,16; Job 10:18-19; Ecc 4:2; 6:3; Jer 20:14-18; Mt 26:24
3:5 [d]Job 10:21,22; 34:22; 38:17; Ps 23:4; 44:19; 88:12; Jer 2:6; 13:16
3:6 [e]Job 23:17; 30:26
3:7 [f]Ps 20:5; 33:3; 65:13; Isa 26:19; Jer 51:48
3:8 [g]Job 10:18; Jer 20:14 [h]S Ge 1:21; Job 41:1,8,10,25; Ps 74:14; 104:26
3:9 [i]Job 41:18; Hab 3:4
3:11 [j]S ver 3
3:12 [k]S Ge 48:12; Isa 66:12
3:13 [l]Job 17:13; 30:23 [m]ver 17; Job 7:8-10,21; 10:22; 13:19; 14:10-12; 19:27; 21:13,23; 27:19; Ps 139:11; Isa 8:22
3:14 [n]Job 9:24; 12:17; Isa 14:9; Eze 32:28-32

may it not be included among the
days of the year
nor be entered in any of the months.
7May that night be barren;
may no shout of joy[f] be heard in it.
8May those who curse days[g] curse that
day,[g]
those who are ready to rouse
Leviathan.[h]
9May its morning stars become dark;
may it wait for daylight in vain
and not see the first rays of dawn,[i]
10for it did not shut the doors of the
womb on me
to hide trouble from my eyes.

11"Why did I not perish at birth,
and die as I came from the womb?[j]
12Why were there knees to receive me[k]
and breasts that I might be nursed?
13For now I would be lying down[l] in
peace;
I would be asleep and at rest[m]
14with kings and counselors of the
earth,[n]
who built for themselves places now
lying in ruins,[o]
15with rulers[p] who had gold,
who filled their houses with silver.[q]
16Or why was I not hidden in the
ground like a stillborn child,[r]
like an infant who never saw the
light of day?[s]
17There the wicked cease from turmoil,[t]
and there the weary are at rest.[u]
18Captives[v] also enjoy their ease;
they no longer hear the slave
driver's[w] shout.[x]
19The small and the great are there,[y]

[o]Job 15:28; Jer 51:37; Na 3:7 **3:15** [p]Job 12:21; Isa 45:1 [q]Job 15:29; 20:10; 27:17; Ps 49:16-17; Pr 13:22; 28:8; Ecc 2:26; Isa 2:7; Zep 1:11 **3:16** [r]Ps 58:8; Ecc 4:3; 6:3 [s]S ver 3; Ps 71:6 **3:17** [t]ver 26; Job 30:26; Ecc 4:2; Isa 14:3 [u]S ver 13 **3:18** [v]Isa 51:14 [w]S Ge 15:13 [x]Job 39:7 **3:19** [y]Job 9:22; 17:16; 21:33; 24:24; 30:23; Ecc 12:5

[e] *10* The Hebrew word rendered *foolish* denotes moral deficiency. [f] *5* Or *and the shadow of death* [g] *8* Or *the sea*

2:10 GOD, Sovereignty—If God's people truly believe in His control over our world, we must be willing to trust and praise Him in all circumstances of life. See note on 1:21–22.

2:11–13 EVIL AND SUFFERING, Comfort—Even people of faith suffer grief and need comfort. Job's friends comforted him by their physical presence and identification with his troubles. Their silence was more comforting than their later speeches. Words could not answer the questions Job faced. Only God's love could. Comforters symbolized that love.

2:11–13 HUMANITY, Community Relationships—The relationship of friends is one of the more precious among human relationships. Such friendship shares grief and heartache without having to say words. This kind of friendship recognizes the necessity and opportunity for sharing a ministry of silence.

3:1–26 EVIL AND SUFFERING, Endurance—At chapter 3 the book switches from prose to poetry. Here Job reacted strongly to his suffering, raising the doubts and problems that flooded His soul. He wondered why God let him be born if he had to face such misery. Rest, quietness, and peace became the great desires of life. Grief and suffering also cause us to face such questions. Uttering them among friends is natural and not to be condemned. Admitting our doubts may be necessary as we endure grief. See note on 26:12–13.

3:1–26 HUMANITY, Attitudes to Death—Human nature frequently leads those who are in the midst of deep grief or intense suffering to long for death as a release from their troubles. At such times, death is viewed as a welcomed friend rather than an enemy to be defeated. Proper working through the grief process leads to a renewed affirmation of life and its potential. See 42:1–17.

3:3–19 PRAYER, Curse—Job prayed that God would reverse creation itself—an impossible prayer, since it would contradict the nature of God. Later (6:8–9) he prayed to die. A curse on self may deal with anger before God, but its fulfillment should not be expected. Compare 42:7. See note on 1 Ki 19:4.

and the slave is freed from his
master.

20"Why is light given to those in misery,
and life to the bitter of soul,[z]
21to those who long for death that does
not come,[a]
who search for it more than for
hidden treasure,[b]
22who are filled with gladness
and rejoice when they reach the
grave?[c]
23Why is life given to a man
whose way is hidden,[d]
whom God has hedged in?[e]
24For sighing[f] comes to me instead of
food;[g]
my groans[h] pour out like water.[i]
25What I feared has come upon me;
what I dreaded[j] has happened to
me.[k]
26I have no peace,[l] no quietness;
I have no rest,[m] but only turmoil."[n]

Chapter 4

Eliphaz

THEN Eliphaz the Temanite[o] replied:
2"If someone ventures a word with
you, will you be impatient?
But who can keep from speaking?[p]
3Think how you have instructed
many,[q]
how you have strengthened feeble
hands.[r]
4Your words have supported those who
stumbled;[s]
you have strengthened faltering
knees.[t]
5But now trouble comes to you, and you
are discouraged;[u]
it strikes[v] you, and you are
dismayed.[w]
6Should not your piety be your
confidence[x]
and your blameless[y] ways your
hope?

7"Consider now: Who, being innocent,
has ever perished?[z]
Where were the upright ever
destroyed?[a]
8As I have observed,[b] those who plow
evil[c]
and those who sow trouble reap it.[d]
9At the breath of God[e] they are
destroyed;
at the blast of his anger they
perish.[f]
10The lions may roar[g] and growl,
yet the teeth of the great lions[h] are
broken.[i]
11The lion perishes for lack of prey,[j]
and the cubs of the lioness are
scattered.[k]

12"A word[l] was secretly brought to me,
my ears caught a whisper[m] of it.[n]
13Amid disquieting dreams in the night,
when deep sleep falls on men,[o]
14fear and trembling[p] seized me
and made all my bones shake.[q]
15A spirit glided past my face,
and the hair on my body stood on
end.[r]
16It stopped,
but I could not tell what it was.
A form stood before my eyes,
and I heard a hushed voice:[s]
17'Can a mortal be more righteous than
God?[t]
Can a man be more pure than his
Maker?[u]
18If God places no trust in his servants,[v]
if he charges his angels with error,[w]

3:20 [z]S 1Sa 1:10; Eze 27:30-31 **3:21** [a]Rev 9:6 [b]Ps 119:127; Pr 2:4 **3:22** [c]Job 7:16; Ecc 4:3; Jer 8:3 **3:23** [d]Pr 4:19; Isa 59:10; Jer 13:16; 23:12 [e]Job 6:4; 16:13; 19:6,8,12; Ps 88:8; La 2:4; 3:7; Hos 2:6 **3:24** [f]Ps 5:1; 38:9; Isa 35:10 [g]Job 6:7; 33:20; Ps 107:18 [h]Ps 22:1; 32:3; 38:8 [i]1Sa 1:15; Job 30:16; Ps 6:6; 22:14; 42:3,4; 80:5; Isa 53:12; La 2:12 **3:25** [j]Job 7:9; 9:28; 30:15; Hos 13:3 [k]S Ge 42:36 **3:26** [l]Isa 48:22; Jn 14:27 [m]Job 7:4, 14; Ps 6:6; Da 4:5; Mt 11:28 [n]S ver 17; S Job 10:18; S 19:8 **4:1** [o]S Ge 36:11; Job 15:1; 22:1 **4:2** [p]Job 32:20; Jer 4:19; 20:9 **4:3** [q]Dt 32:2; Job 29:23; Hos 6:3 [r]Job 26:2; Ps 71:9; Isa 13:7; 35:3; Zep 3:16; Heb 12:12 **4:4** [s]Job 16:5; 29:16,25; Isa 1:17 [t]Job 29:11,15; Isa 35:3; Jer 31:8; Heb 12:12 **4:5** [u]S Jos 1:9 [v]Ru 1:13; Job 1:11; 19:21; 30:21; Ps 38:2; Isa 53:4 [w]Job 6:14; Pr 24:10 **4:6** [x]2Ki 18:19; Ps 27:3; 71:5; Pr 3:26 [y]S Ge 6:9 **4:7** [z]Job 5:11; 36:7; Ps 41:12; 2Pe 2:9 [a]Job 8:20; Ps 37:25; 91:9-10; Pr 12:21; 19:23 **4:8** [b]Job 5:3; 15:17 [c]Jdg 14:18; Job 5:6; 15:35; Ps 7:14; Isa 59:4 [d]Ps 7:15; 9:15; Pr 11:18; 22:8; Isa 17:11; Hos 8:7; 10:13; Gal 6:7-8 **4:9** [e]S Ex 15:10; S Job 41:21; 2Th 2:8 [f]S Lev 26:38; Job 40:13; Isa 25:7 **4:10** [g]Ps 22:13 [h]Ps 17:12; 22:21; Pr 28:15 [i]Job 5:15; 29:17; 36:6; 38:15; Ps 35:10; 58:6 **4:11** [j]Dt 28:41; Job 27:14; 29:17; Ps 34:10; 58:6; Pr 30:14 [k]Job 5:4 **4:12** [l]ver 17-21; Job 32:13; Jer 9:23 [m]Job 26:14 [n]Job 33:14 **4:13** [o]Job 33:15 **4:14** [p]Job 21:6; Ps 48:6; 55:5; 119:120, 161; Jer 5:22; Hab 3:16; S 2Co 7:15 [q]Jer 23:9; Da 10:8; Hab 3:16 **4:15** [r]Da 5:6; 7:15,28; 10:8; Mt 14:26 **4:16** [s]S 1Ki 19:12 **4:17** [t]Job 9:2; 13:18; Ps 143:2 [u]Job 8:3; 10:3; 14:4; 15:14; 21:14; 25:4; 31:15; 32:22; 35:10; 36:3,13; 37:23; 40:19; Ps 18:26; 51:5; 119:73; Pr 20:9; Ecc 7:20; Isa 51:13; Mal 2:10; Ac 17:24 **4:18** [v]Heb 1:14 [w]Job 15:15; 21:22; 25:5

3:26 SALVATION, Definition—Rest is the absence of conflict (Ex 33:14; Dt 3:20; 12:10; Jos 1:13,15; 21:44; 22:4; 23:1; 2 Sam 7:1). It is more, for God's salvation is rest, the peace and quietness which He gives in the midst of turmoil and suffering (Ps 3:5–6). Job had to learn that truth, as do we.

4:7–8 EVIL AND SUFFERING, Punishment—Eliphaz presented a common opinion that the righteous prospered and the wicked suffered. Two assumptions shaped his view. First, Eliphaz assumed that Job's faith or lack of it could be determined by his material success. Prosperity was evidence of piety. Because Job suffered, he must be a sinner. Second, Eliphaz and the other friends also assumed the traditional view was a comprehensive, exhaustive explanation of suffering. All suffering was deserved. The Book of Job contradicts their view. Job was innocent and faithful to God. Job's suffering was actually a testing of his faith, not a punishment. Our suffering may be a punishment for some sin, but it may be a testing of our faith, like Job's. We must seek to see how our suffering fits into God's redemptive purpose. See note on Isa 52:13—53:12. We must be slow to judge people personally for their misfortunes.

4:17 GOD, Righteous—The Book of Job calls its readers to exercise theological caution. The theological arguments of Job's friends evoke theological thought and force Job to reply to theological statements taken to extreme positions. From the truth that God is the standard of righteousness by which all others are measured, Eliphaz drew the proper conclusion that all humans are sinners. Eliphaz, however, wanted to take his argument a step further and infer that Job was a sinner because he suffered. Then Eliphaz could defend God and say Job deserved all the suffering he was enduring, suffering Eliphaz believed God had placed on Job as punishment. This last step in the argument misunderstands the nature of God and of sin. The righteous God does not bring such punishment on a person for sins other people assume to have been committed. The Bible teaches the general truth that sin causes misfortune and suffering; it does not teach that a sufferer has sinned in proportion to the suffering.

19how much more those who live in
houses of clay,[x]
whose foundations[y] are in the
dust,[z]
who are crushed[a] more readily than
a moth![b]
20Between dawn and dusk they are
broken to pieces;
unnoticed, they perish forever.[c]
21Are not the cords of their tent pulled
up,[d]
so that they die[e] without
wisdom?'[h] [f]

Chapter 5

"CALL if you will, but who will
answer you?[g]
To which of the holy ones[h] will you
turn?
2Resentment[i] kills a fool,
and envy slays the simple.[j]
3I myself have seen[k] a fool taking
root,[l]
but suddenly[m] his house was
cursed.[n]
4His children[o] are far from safety,[p]
crushed in court[q] without a
defender.[r]
5The hungry consume his harvest,[s]
taking it even from among thorns,
and the thirsty pant after his wealth.
6For hardship does not spring from the
soil,
nor does trouble sprout from the
ground.[t]
7Yet man is born to trouble[u]
as surely as sparks fly upward.
8"But if it were I, I would appeal to
God;
I would lay my cause before him.[v]
9He performs wonders[w] that cannot be
fathomed,[x]
miracles that cannot be counted.[y]
10He bestows rain on the earth;[z]
he sends water upon the
countryside.[a]
11The lowly he sets on high,[b]
and those who mourn[c] are lifted[d]
to safety.
12He thwarts the plans[e] of the crafty,
so that their hands achieve no
success.[f]
13He catches the wise[g] in their
craftiness,[h]
and the schemes of the wily are
swept away.[i]
14Darkness[j] comes upon them in the
daytime;
at noon they grope as in the night.[k]

4:19 [x]Job 10:9; 33:6; Isa 64:8; Ro 9:21; 2Co 4:7; 5:1 [y]Job 22:16 [z]S Ge 2:7 [a]Job 5:4 [b]Job 7:17; 15:16; 17:14; 25:6; Ps 22:6; Isa 41:14 **4:20** [c]Job 14:2,20; 15:33; 20:7; 24:24; Ps 89:47; 90:5-6; Jas 4:14 **4:21** [d]Job 8:22; Isa 38:12 [e]Jn 8:24 [f]Job 18:21; 36:12; Pr 5:23; Jer 9:3 **5:1** [g]Hab 1:2 [h]Job 15:15; Ps 89:5,7 **5:2** [i]Job 21:15; 36:13 [j]Pr 12:16; Gal 5:26 **5:3** [k]S Job 4:8 [l]Ps 37:35; Isa 40:24; Jer 12:2; Eze 17:6 [m]Pr 6:15 [n]Job 24:18; Ps 37:22,35-36; 109:9-10; Pr 3:33 **5:4** [o]Job 20:10; 27:14 [p]S Job 4:11 [q]Job 4:19; Am 5:12 [r]Ps 109:12; Isa 9:17; 1Jn 2:1 **5:5** [s]Lev 26:16; S Jdg 2:15; Job 20:18; 31:8; Mic 6:15 **5:6** [t]S Job 4:8 **5:7** [u]S Ge 3:17; Job 10:17; 15:35; Ps 51:5; 58:3; 90:10; Pr 22:8 **5:8** [v]Job 8:5; 11:13; 13:3,15; 23:4; 40:1; Ps 35:23; 50:15; Jer 12:1; 1Co 4:4 **5:9** [w]Ps 78:4; 111:2 [x]Dt 29:29; Job 9:4,10; 11:7; 25:2; 26:14; 33:12; 36:5,22,26; 37:5, 14,16,23; 42:3; Ps 40:5; 71:17; 72:18; 86:10; 131:1; 139:6, 17; 145:3; Isa 40:28; Ro 11:33 [y]Ps 71:15 **5:10** [z]Mt 5:45 [a]S Lev 26:4; Job 36:28; 37:6,13; 38:28,34; Ps 135:7; Jer 14:22 **5:11** [b]S 1Sa 2:7-8; S Job 4:7; Ps 75:7; 113:7-8 [c]Isa 61:2; Mt 5:4; Ro 12:15 [d]S Mt 23:12; Jas 4:10 **5:12** [e]Ne 4:15; Ps 33:10; Isa 8:10; 19:3; Jer 19:7 [f]Job 12:23; Ps 78:59; 140:8 **5:13** [g]Job 37:24; Isa 29:14; 44:25; Jer 8:8; 18:18; 51:57 [h]Job 15:5; Ps 36:3; Lk 20:23; 1Co 3:19*; 2Co 11:3; Eph 4:14 [i]Job 9:4; 18:7; Pr 21:30; 29:6; Jer 8:9 **5:14** [j]Job 15:22,30; 18:6,18; 20:26; 22:11; 27:20; Isa 8:22; Jn 12:35 [k]S Dt 28:29; S Job 18:5; Am 8:9

[h]*21* Some interpreters end the quotation after verse 17.

4:18–21 HUMANITY, Human Nature—No basis for pride exists in human nature. The several images of human nature used here all point to human mortality and transcience.

5:1 PRAYER, Hindrances—Eliphaz challenged Job to seek a mediator between Job and God among the holy angels, assuming Job's sin would make finding a mediator impossible or that a mediator would bring confession of sin. Our sin hinders communication with God, but Jesus is always ready to intercede for us when we confess our sins.

5:3–7,16 CHRISTIAN ETHICS, Justice—In His sovereignty God is good. His justice will be done. Eliphaz was correct in His statement about God, who is the ultimate hope of the poor and oppressed. In using the theological truth to judge Job's case, Eliphaz erred. Every individual does not get immediate justice from God.

5:7 EVIL AND SUFFERING, Endurance—Eliphaz suggested that human life normally involves trouble. Here he was right. He drew the wrong consequences for Job's case. Job's friends show us traditional theology is neither wholly right nor wholly wrong. Such theology must always be tested by God's Word and by personal experience with God such as Job's. We also learn that proper theological statements may be applied in wrong ways to individual cases and lead to wrong conclusions. The formulation of theological doctrinal statements must be based on study of all of God's Word and on personal devotion to God.

5:8–16 GOD, Justice—God will do what is right, both in opposing evil and in defending what is right. He is righteous and just in providing for the needy. He hears the pleas of His people when they present their case to Him. Still Eliphaz was wrong in advising Job to go to God as a poor, sinful man seeking mercy. Job's sin was not the basic cause of his problems. He could not go to God with a dishonest plea. See notes on Ge 18:20–33; 20:4–6; Lev 1:1; Jos 23:1–16; 2 Sa 10:12; Jn 17:25. A just God does not want insincere confession.

5:8 PRAYER, Confession—Eliphaz demonstrated a fundamental misunderstanding of Job. He expected Job humbly to confess his sins and seek God's pardon. Confession was not an option for Job. He could not discover any sin deserving such horrible suffering. Nor could he discover God's presence. Job's honest confrontation with God, not false confession, was the proper mode of prayer in his situation. One person cannot tell another how to pray. No one type of prayer is proper in all situations. The one who claims to be an authority on prayer like Eliphaz may actually stand in need of prayer (42:8).

5:9 CREATION, Miracles—Eliphaz tried to convince Job of his sinfulness by arguing from God's creative acts. As the oldest and most traditional in religious thought, he appealed to God's miraculous power. God not only made the world but continues through marvelous deeds to sustain it. We are blessed only when we give in to Him and shape our lives by His precepts. Eliphaz was correct in a general sense, but he did not know the specific facts about Job's condition. General arguments based on God as Creator, Sustainer, and Performer of miracles do not prove the guilt of one individual. God's moral universe is much more complex.

5:9–16 MIRACLE, God's Working—Miracles are God's work in the world. They cover a wide range of actions: rain, social justice, intervention against evil people, rescue of the needy. Miracles work in both the natural and social orders. They show us the greatness of God and our inability to know and understand all He does. Notice that here Job's friend teaches correct, traditional theology but, as usual, then applies it incorrectly to Job's situation. Job uses similar language with a different application. See 9:10.

15He saves the needy[l] from the sword
in their mouth;
he saves them from the clutches of
the powerful.[m]
16So the poor[n] have hope,
and injustice shuts its mouth.[o]

17"Blessed is the man whom God
corrects;[p]
so do not despise the discipline[q] of
the Almighty.[i] [r]
18For he wounds, but he also binds
up;[s]
he injures, but his hands also
heal.[t]
19From six calamities he will rescue[u]
you;
in seven no harm will befall
you.[v]
20In famine[w] he will ransom you from
death,
and in battle from the stroke of the
sword.[x]
21You will be protected from the lash of
the tongue,[y]
and need not fear[z] when
destruction comes.[a]
22You will laugh[b] at destruction and
famine,[c]
and need not fear the beasts of the
earth.[d]
23For you will have a covenant[e] with
the stones[f] of the field,
and the wild animals will be at
peace with you.[g]
24You will know that your tent is
secure;[h]
you will take stock of your property
and find nothing missing.[i]
25You will know that your children will
be many,[j]
and your descendants like the grass
of the earth.[k]
26You will come to the grave in full
vigor,[l]
like sheaves gathered in season.[m]

27"We have examined this, and it is
true.
So hear it[n] and apply it to
yourself."[o]

5:15 [l]S Ex 22:23; Job 8:6; 22:27; 33:26; 36:15 [m]S Job 4:10; S 31:22 **5:16** [n]Job 20:19; 31:16; Pr 17:5; 22:22; Isa 11:4; 41:17; 61:1 [o]Ps 63:11; 107:42; Ro 3:19 **5:17** [p]Dt 8:5; Job 33:19; 36:10; Zep 3:7; Jas 1:12 [q]Ps 94:12; Pr 3:11; Jer 31:18 [r]S Ge 17:1; S Job 15:11; Heb 12:5-11 **5:18** [s]Ps 147:3; Isa 57:15; 61:1; Hos 6:1 [t]S Dt 32:39 **5:19** [u]Da 3:17; 6:16 [v]Ps 34:19; 91:10; Pr 3:25-26; 24:15-16 **5:20** [w]ver 22; Ps 33:19; 37:19 [x]Ps 22:20; 91:7; 140:7; 144:10; Jer 39:18 **5:21** [y]Ps 12:2-4; 31:20 [z]Ps 23:4; 27:1; 91:5 [a]ver 15 **5:22** [b]Job 8:21; 39:7,18,22; 41:29 [c]S ver 20 [d]S Lev 25:18; Ps 91:13; Hos 2:18; Mk 1:13 **5:23** [e]Isa 28:15; Hos 2:18 [f]2Ki 3:19, 25; Ps 91:12; Mt 13:8 [g]Job 40:20; Isa 11:6-9; 65:25; Eze 34:25 **5:24** [h]Job 12:6; 21:9 [i]Job 8:6; 22:23 **5:25** [j]Dt 28:4; Ps 112:2 [k]Ps 72:16; Isa 44:3-4; 48:19 **5:26** [l]S Ge 15:15; S Dt 11:21; S Ecc 8:13 [m]Pr 3:21-26 **5:27** [n]Job 32:10,17 [o]Job 8:5; 11:13; 22:27 **6:2** [p]Job 31:6; Pr 11:1; Da 5:27 **6:3** [q]1Ki 4:29; Pr 27:3 [r]ver 11,26; Job 7:11; 16:6; 21:4; 23:2 **6:4** [s]S Dt 32:23; Ps 38:2 [t]S Ge 17:1 [u]Job 7:20; 16:12, 13; 19:12; La 3:12 [v]Job 21:20 [w]S Dt 32:32; Job 30:21; 34:6; Jer 15:18; 30:12 [x]Job 9:34; 13:21; 18:11; 23:6; 27:20; 30:15; 33:16 [y]S Job 3:23;

Chapter 6

Job

THEN Job replied:

2"If only my anguish could be
weighed
and all my misery be placed on the
scales![p]
3It would surely outweigh the sand[q] of
the seas—
no wonder my words have been
impetuous.[r]
4The arrows[s] of the Almighty[t] are in
me,[u]
my spirit drinks[v] in their poison;[w]
God's terrors[x] are marshaled against
me.[y]
5Does a wild donkey[z] bray[a] when it
has grass,
or an ox bellow when it has
fodder?[b]
6Is tasteless food eaten without salt,
or is there flavor in the white of an
egg[j] ?[c]
7I refuse to touch it;
such food makes me ill.[d]
8"Oh, that I might have my request,
that God would grant what I hope
for,[e]
9that God would be willing to crush[f]
me,
to let loose his hand and cut me
off![g]
10Then I would still have this
consolation[h]—
my joy in unrelenting pain[i]—
that I had not denied the words[j] of
the Holy One.[k]
11"What strength do I have, that I
should still hope?
What prospects, that I should be
patient?[l]

Ps 88:15-18 **6:5** [z]S Ge 16:12 [a]Job 30:7 [b]Job 24:6; Isa 30:24 **6:6** [c]Job 33:20; Ps 107:18 **6:7** [d]S Job 3:24 **6:8** [e]Job 14:13 **6:9** [f]Job 19:2 [g]S Nu 11:15; S Ps 31:22 **6:10** [h]S Job 2:11; 15:11; Ps 94:19 [i]Ps 38:17; Jer 4:19; 45:3 [j]Job 22:22; 23:12; Ps 119:102; Mk 8:38 [k]S Lev 11:44; S 2Ki 19:22; S Isa 31:1 **6:11** [l]S ver 3

[i]17 Hebrew *Shaddai*; here and throughout Job
[j]6 The meaning of the Hebrew for this phrase is uncertain.

5:17–27 EVIL AND SUFFERING, Testing—Eliphaz knew that some suffering was disciplinary, designed by God to draw the sinner back to Him. He decided this explained Job's grief. If Job would listen to God, he could learn from this tragedy. His theology was correct. He applied it to the wrong case. Suffering has more than one purpose. Human wisdom cannot decide the purpose of suffering in another person's life. See note on v 7.

5:26 HUMANITY, Age—Since God was the Giver of life, those blessed by Him were expected to come to the end of a long life still filled with strength. Both the Bible and human experience indicate that this is an ideal. Sickness may plague God's most devoted servants as it did Job. Job's friends often reflect an idealized theology which does not hold true for individual cases.

6:1–30 EVIL AND SUFFERING, Endurance—In his anguish, Job perceived God as an archer shooting arrows at him. Job was not aware of Satan's involvement. He endured his pain by complaining to God and asking for death. His basic desire was to remain loyal to God. When we do not understand circumstances, we need to tell God our feelings while remaining steadfast in our faith. Even when we feel God is after us, we must keep our trust in Him. Searching for the truth is part of enduring pain in faith.

6:8–10 PRAYER, Curse—See note on 3:3–19.

12 Do I have the strength of stone?
Is my flesh bronze?[m]
13 Do I have any power to help myself,[n]
now that success has been driven from me?

14 "A despairing man[o] should have the devotion[p] of his friends,[q]
even though he forsakes the fear of the Almighty.[r]
15 But my brothers are as undependable as intermittent streams,[s]
as the streams that overflow
16 when darkened by thawing ice
and swollen with melting snow,[t]
17 but that cease to flow in the dry season,
and in the heat[u] vanish from their channels.
18 Caravans turn aside from their routes;
they go up into the wasteland and perish.
19 The caravans of Tema[v] look for water,
the traveling merchants of Sheba[w] look in hope.
20 They are distressed, because they had been confident;
they arrive there, only to be disappointed.[x]
21 Now you too have proved to be of no help;
you see something dreadful and are afraid.[y]
22 Have I ever said, 'Give something on my behalf,
pay a ransom[z] for me from your wealth,[a]
23 deliver me from the hand of the enemy,
ransom me from the clutches of the ruthless'?[b]

24 "Teach me, and I will be quiet;[c]
show me where I have been wrong.[d]
25 How painful are honest words![e]
But what do your arguments prove?
26 Do you mean to correct what I say,
and treat the words of a despairing man as wind?[f]
27 You would even cast lots[g] for the fatherless[h]
and barter away your friend.

28 "But now be so kind as to look at me.
Would I lie to your face?[i]
29 Relent, do not be unjust;[j]
reconsider, for my integrity[k] is at stake.[k l]
30 Is there any wickedness on my lips?[m]
Can my mouth not discern[n] malice?

Chapter 7

1 "DOES not man have hard service[o] on earth?[p]
Are not his days like those of a hired man?[q]
2 Like a slave longing for the evening shadows,[r]
or a hired man waiting eagerly for his wages,[s]
3 so I have been allotted months of futility,
and nights of misery have been assigned to me.[t]
4 When I lie down I think, 'How long before I get up?'[u]
The night drags on, and I toss till dawn.[v]
5 My body is clothed with worms[w] and scabs,
my skin is broken and festering.[x]

6 "My days are swifter than a weaver's shuttle,[y]
and they come to an end without hope.[z]
7 Remember, O God, that my life is but a breath;[a]
my eyes will never see happiness again.[b]

6:12 [m]Job 26:2 **6:13** [n]Job 26:2 **6:14** [o]S Job 4:5 [p]1Sa 20:42; Job 15:4 [q]Job 12:4; 17:2,6; 19:19,21; 21:3; 30:1,10; Ps 38:11; 69:20; 1Jn 3:17 [r]S Ge 17:1 **6:15** [s]Job 13:4; 16:2; 21:34; Ps 22:1; 38:11; Jer 15:18 **6:16** [t]Ps 147:18 **6:17** [u]Job 24:19 **6:19** [v]S Ge 25:15 [w]S Ge 10:7,28 **6:20** [x]Jer 14:3; Joel 1:11 **6:21** [y]Ps 38:11 **6:22** [z]S Nu 35:31; Job 33:24; Ps 49:7 [a]Jer 15:10 **6:23** [b]S 2Ki 19:19 **6:24** [c]S Job 2:10; 33:33; Ps 39:1; 141:3; Pr 10:19; 11:12; 17:27; Ecc 5:2 [d]Job 19:4 **6:25** [e]Ecc 12:11; Isa 22:23 **6:26** [f]S ver 3; S Ge 41:6; Job 8:2; 15:3; 16:3; Jer 5:13 **6:27** [g]Eze 24:6; Joel 3:3; Ob 1:11; Na 3:10 [h]S Ex 22:22,24; Job 31:17,21; Isa 10:2 **6:28** [i]Job 9:15; 24:25; 27:4; 32:10; 33:1,3; 34:6; 36:3,4 **6:29** [j]Job 19:6; 27:2; 40:8; Isa 40:27 [k]S Job 2:3 [l]Job 9:21; 10:7; 11:2; 12:4; 23:7,10; 33:9,32; 34:5,36; 35:2; 42:6; Ps 66:10; Zec 13:9 **6:30** [m]Job 27:4 [n]Job 12:11 **7:1** [o]Job 14:14; Isa 40:2 [p]S Job 5:7 [q]S Lev 25:50 **7:2** [r]Job 14:1; Ecc 2:23 [s]S Lev 19:13; S Job 14:6 **7:3** [t]Job 16:7; Ps 6:6; 42:3; 56:8; Ecc 4:1; Isa 16:9; Jer 9:1; La 1:2,16 **7:4** [u]Dt 28:67 [v]ver 13-14 **7:5** [w]Job 17:14; 21:26; 24:20; 25:6; Isa 14:11 [x]S Dt 28:35 **7:6** [y]Job 9:25; Ps 39:5; Isa 38:12 [z]Job 13:15; 14:19; 17:11,15; 19:10; Ps 37:4; 52:9 **7:7** [a]ver 16; Ge 27:46; Ps 39:4,5,11; 62:9; 78:39; 89:47; 144:4; Ecc 7:15; S Jas 4:14 [b]Job 10:20

[k]29 Or *my righteousness still stands*

6:14–16 HUMANITY, Community Relationships—Job protested when his friends became his judges. Friends are expected to be as close and as dependable as members of one's family. This should be true even if the friend has turned against or away from God. One of life's greatest tragedies comes when friends become undependable and turn away.

6:24 EDUCATION, Discipline—Job was willing to learn even from the criticisms of others. This is the mark of a wise man. See note on Pr 15:31–33. Only a fool assumes that his critics are always in the wrong. See Pr 17:10.

7:1–16 EVIL AND SUFFERING, Punishment—In anguish we cannot endure silently. We must consider all options. Job thought God was punishing him. He faced the reality of his own death honestly. Part of the agony of innocent suffering is the uncertainty that we are innocent. The humility of the innocent always raises the possibility of guilt that deserves punishment. The only solution is to seek answers from God.

7:1–6 HUMANITY, Life—For a person who has experienced tragedy and overwhelming pain, life becomes a burden which would be readily put aside. Like Job, the believer admits the feelings of frustration and despair, talks to God about them, and trusts God to bring patience, insight, and hope. See note on 3:1–26.

7:7–10 HUMANITY, Nature of Death—Death was viewed by many of the Old Testament peoples as the end of life. To those pondering it, it presented a kind of hopeless futility. It remained for the New Testament to offer a genuine hope beyond the grave. See note on 1 Co 15:19.

7:7–21 PRAYER, Lament—Job expressed the opposite of Ps 8, where God's attention on humans was seen as a marvel of His grace. Here, Job sees God's attentiveness as a scrutiny penetrating beyond purposes we can comprehend. Lament is an honest expression of the deepest personal frustration to God. Lament does not so much inform God of facts as it shares feelings with Him.

8The eye that now sees me will see me
no longer;
you will look for me, but I will be no
more.[c]
9As a cloud vanishes[d] and is gone,
so he who goes down to the
grave[l][e] does not return.[f]
10He will never come to his house again;
his place[g] will know him no more.[h]

11"Therefore I will not keep silent;[i]
I will speak out in the anguish[j] of
my spirit,
I will complain[k] in the bitterness of
my soul.[l]
12Am I the sea,[m] or the monster of the
deep,[n]
that you put me under guard?[o]
13When I think my bed will comfort me
and my couch will ease my
complaint,[p]
14even then you frighten me with
dreams
and terrify[q] me with visions,[r]
15so that I prefer strangling and death,[s]
rather than this body of mine.[t]
16I despise my life;[u] I would not live
forever.[v]
Let me alone;[w] my days have no
meaning.[x]

17"What is man that you make so much
of him,
that you give him so much
attention,[y]
18that you examine him every morning[z]
and test him[a] every moment?[b]
19Will you never look away from me,[c]
or let me alone even for an
instant?[d]
20If I have sinned, what have I done to
you,[e]
O watcher of men?
Why have you made me your target?[f]
Have I become a burden to you?[m][g]
21Why do you not pardon my offenses
and forgive my sins?[h]
For I will soon lie down in the dust;[i]
you will search for me, but I will be
no more."[j]

Chapter 8

Bildad

THEN Bildad the Shuhite[k] replied:
2"How long will you say such
things?[l]
Your words are a blustering wind.[m]
3Does God pervert justice?[n]
Does the Almighty pervert what is
right?[o]
4When your children sinned against
him,
he gave them over to the penalty of
their sin.[p]
5But if you will look to God
and plead[q] with the Almighty,[r]
6if you are pure and upright,
even now he will rouse himself on
your behalf[s]
and restore you to your rightful
place.[t]
7Your beginnings will seem humble,
so prosperous[u] will your future be.[v]

8"Ask the former generations[w]
and find out what their fathers
learned,
9for we were born only yesterday and
know nothing,[x]
and our days on earth are but a
shadow.[y]
10Will they not instruct[z] you and tell
you?
Will they not bring forth words from
their understanding?[a]

7:8 [c]S Job 3:13; 8:18; 15:29; 20:7, 9,21; 27:17; Ps 37:36; 103:16; Isa 41:12; Jn 16:16; Ac 20:25 **7:9** [d]S Job 3:25 [e]S Job 3:13; 11:8; 14:13; 17:16; 26:6; 38:17; Am 9:2 [f]2Sa 12:23 **7:10** [g]Job 18:21; 21:18; 27:21,23; Ps 58:9; Jer 18:17; 19:8 [h]S ver 8; Ps 37:10; 104:35 **7:11** [i]Job 9:35; 13:13; Ps 22:2; 40:9 [j]Job 10:1; Ps 6:3; Isa 38:15,17 [k]ver 13; Job 9:27; 21:4; 23:2 [l]S 1Sa 1:10; S Job 6:3 **7:12** [m]Job 38:8-11 [n]S Ge 1:21 [o]ver 20; Isa 1:14 **7:13** [p]S ver 11 **7:14** [q]Job 9:34 [r]S Ge 41:8; S Job 3:26 **7:15** [s]1Ki 19:4; Jnh 4:3 [t]Job 6:9; Rev 9:6 **7:16** [u]S 1Ki 19:4; Job 9:21 [v]S Job 3:22 [w]ver 19; Job 10:20; Ps 39:13 [x]S ver 7 **7:17** [y]S Job 4:19; 22:2; Ps 8:4; 144:3; Heb 2:6 **7:18** [z]Ps 73:14 [a]Job 23:10; Ps 139:23 [b]Job 14:3; Ps 17:3; 26:2; 66:10; 139:1-6; 143:2 **7:19** [c]S ver 16 [d]Job 9:18; 13:26; 14:6; 27:2; Ps 139:7 **7:20** [e]Job 35:6; Jer 7:19 [f]S Job 6:4 [g]S ver 12 **7:21** [h]Job 9:28; 10:14; 16:6; Ps 119:120; Isa 43:25; Jer 31:34; Heb 1:3 [i]S Ge 3:19; Job 10:9; 34:15; Ps 7:5; 22:15; 90:3; 104:29 [j]S ver 8; S Job 3:13 **8:1** [k]S Ge 25:2; Job 18:1; 25:1 **8:2** [l]Job 11:2; 18:2 [m]S 2Ch 36:16; S Job 6:26 **8:3** [n]S Job 4:17; 34:12; Isa 29:15; Ro 3:5 [o]S Ge 18:25; S Jer 12:1 **8:4** [p]Job 1:19 **8:5** [q]Job 9:15 [r]S Job 5:8,27 **8:6** [s]S Job 5:15; 22:27; 33:26; 34:28; Isa 58:9; 65:24 [t]S Job 5:24 **8:7** [u]Job 21:13; 22:21; 36:11; Ps 25:13 [v]S Job 1:10; Jer 29:11; 31:17 **8:8** [w]S Dt 32:7; S Ps 71:18 **8:9** [x]S Ge 47:9 [y]S 1Ch 29:15; S 2Ch 10:6; S Ps 39:6 **8:10** [z]Pr 1:8 [a]Pr 2:1-2; 4:1

[l]9 Hebrew *Sheol* [m]20 A few manuscripts of the Masoretic Text, an ancient Hebrew scribal tradition and Septuagint; most manuscripts of the Masoretic Text *I have become a burden to myself.*

7:9 LAST THINGS, Intermediate State—See note on Isa 14:9.

7:16 HUMANITY, Life—Life beyond the grave is not at issue here. Rather Job boldly complained that life had become so unbearable death would be a welcomed relief. Circumstances can become so oppressive that life simply does not appear to be worth living. See notes on 3:1–26; 7:1–6.

7:17–21 EVIL AND SUFFERING, Testing—Job realized that the purpose of his suffering could be a testing of his faith. He did not feel his sins merited this kind of suffering as punishment. Yet, he could not understand why God would pay so much attention to someone as unimportant as himself. He pleaded for God to ignore him or forgive him and let him die in peace. Amidst testing we must seek to find His purpose and His forgiveness.

7:17–21 HUMANITY, Relationship to God—Job complained that God was paying too much attention to him. He prayed for God to leave him alone. To a person who has enjoyed a good relationship with God, a sudden change of material circumstances may produce a feeling that God has become an enemy. Such circumstances arouse an intense desire for the restoration of the earlier relationship. This is particularly important for one without a strong hope for personal resurrection. Death can be seen as the ultimate injustice, the final separation from God. The New Testament promise of resurrection brought a new hope to humanity.

8:1–6 EVIL AND SUFFERING, Punishment—Job's second friend Bildad held to the traditional view that suffering was a punishment for sin. He defended his view by defining God in correct language. Argument from a definition of God does not always lead to a proper solution to a particular problem. Job agreed God was just. He just could not see the justice in his own case, so he sought more evidence to understand his situation. Bildad ignored evidence to defend his traditional theology.

8:3–20 GOD, Justice—See notes on 4:17; 5:8–16.

11Can papyrus grow tall where there is no marsh?[b]
Can reeds[c] thrive without water?
12While still growing and uncut,
they wither more quickly than grass.[d]
13Such is the destiny[e] of all who forget God;[f]
so perishes the hope of the godless.[g]
14What he trusts in is fragile[n];
what he relies on is a spider's web.[h]
15He leans on his web,[i] but it gives way;
he clings to it, but it does not hold.[j]
16He is like a well-watered plant in the sunshine,
spreading its shoots[k] over the garden;[l]
17it entwines its roots around a pile of rocks
and looks for a place among the stones.
18But when it is torn from its spot,
that place disowns[m] it and says, 'I never saw you.'[n]
19Surely its life withers[o] away,
and[o] from the soil other plants grow.[p]

20"Surely God does not reject a blameless[q] man
or strengthen the hands of evildoers.[r]
21He will yet fill your mouth with laughter[s]
and your lips with shouts of joy.[t]
22Your enemies will be clothed in shame,[u]
and the tents[v] of the wicked will be no more."[w]

8:11 [b]Job 40:21 [c]S Ex 2:3; Isa 19:6; 35:7 **8:12** [d]ver 19; S 2Ki 19:26; Job 18:16; 20:5; Ps 90:5-6; 102:11; Isa 34:4; 40:7,24 **8:13** [e]Ps 37:38; 73:17 [f]Ps 9:17; 50:22; Isa 51:13; Jer 17:6 [g]Job 6:9; 11:20; 13:16; 15:34; 20:5; 27:8; 34:30; Ps 37:1-2; 112:10; Pr 10:28; 11:7; Jer 15:9 **8:14** [h]ver 15; Job 27:18; Isa 59:5 **8:15** [i]S ver 14 [j]Ps 49:11; Mt 7:26-27 **8:16** [k]Ps 80:11; Isa 16:8 [l]Ps 37:35; Jer 11:16 **8:18** [m]Job 20:9; Ps 103:16 [n]S Job 7:8; S 14:20 **8:19** [o]S ver 12; S Job 15:30 [p]Ps 119:90; Ecc 1:4 **8:20** [q]Job 1:1 [r]S Ge 18:25 **8:21** [s]S Job 5:22 [t]S Ezr 3:13; Job 35:10; Ps 47:5; 107:22; 118:15; 126:2; 132:16; Isa 35:6 **8:22** [u]Job 27:7; Ps 6:10; 35:26; 44:7; 53:5; 71:13; 86:17; 109:29; 132:18; Eze 7:27; 26:16 [v]S Job 4:21 [w]S 1Sa 8:3; Job 18:6,14,21; 21:28; 27:8,18; 34:26; 36:6; 38:13; Ps 52:5; Pr 14:11 **9:2** [x]S Job 4:17; Ro 3:20 **9:3** [y]ver 32; Job 40:5 [z]ver 12,14, 29,32; Job 10:2; 12:14; 13:9,14; 22:4; 23:7,13; 37:19; 40:2; Ps 44:21; Isa 14:24 **9:4** [a]Job 11:6;

Chapter 9

Job

THEN Job replied:

2"Indeed, I know that this is true.
But how can a mortal be righteous before God?[x]
3Though one wished to dispute with him,[y]
he could not answer him one time out of a thousand.[z]
4His wisdom[a] is profound, his power is vast.[b]
Who has resisted[c] him and come out unscathed?[d]
5He moves mountains[e] without their knowing it
and overturns them in his anger.[f]
6He shakes the earth[g] from its place
and makes its pillars tremble.[h]
7He speaks to the sun and it does not shine;[i]
he seals off the light of the stars.[j]
8He alone stretches out the heavens[k]
and treads on the waves of the sea.[l]
9He is the Maker[m] of the Bear and Orion,
the Pleiades and the constellations of the south.[n]

28:12,20,23; 38:36; Ps 51:6; Pr 2:6; Ecc 2:26 [b]ver 19; S Job 5:9; 12:13,16; 23:6; 24:22; 26:12; 30:18; Ps 93:4; 95:3; Pr 8:14; Isa 40:26; 63:1; Da 2:20; 4:35 [c]Jer 50:24 [d]S 2Ch 13:12; S Job 5:13 **9:5** [e]Mt 17:20 [f]Ps 18:7; 46:2-3; Isa 13:13; Mic 1:4 **9:6** [g]S Ex 19:18; Isa 2:21; 13:13; 24:18-20; Am 8:8; Heb 12:26 [h]S 2Sa 22:8; Job 26:14; 36:29; 37:4-5; Ps 75:3; Hab 3:4 **9:7** [i]Isa 34:4; Jer 4:28; Joel 2:2,10, 31; 3:15; Zep 1:15; Zec 14:6 [j]Isa 13:10; Jer 4:23; Eze 32:8 **9:8** [k]S Ge 1:1,8; S Isa 48:13 [l]Job 38:16; Ps 77:19; Pr 8:28; Hab 3:15; Mt 14:25; Mk 6:48; Jn 6:19 **9:9** [m]Job 32:22; 40:15,19 [n]S Ge 1:16

[n]*14* The meaning of the Hebrew for this word is uncertain. [o]*19* Or *Surely all the joy it has / is that*

8:20 EVIL AND SUFFERING, Punishment—See note on vv 1–6.

9:1—10:22 PRAYER, Lament—Here Job did not address God directly but rather expressed a profound desire to address Him or to have a mediator who would address Him (9:32–33). Job cried out that God is invisible (9:11), seemingly unaddressable (9:12), and unanswerable (9:3,14–16). He understood God's greatness (9:4–10) but not His purpose in the situation at hand. In the two trials of Job which God had allowed in 1:13–19 and 2:7–8, Job had no blame for God. His frustration developed after the arguments of his friends. Personal relationships often bring frustrations. Lament offers a type of prayer to express such frustrations to God. See note on 7:7–21.

9:2–35 GOD, Sovereignty—This entire chapter preserves Job's view of the sovereignty of God. Job saw himself as insignificant before almighty God who towered over him. This sharp contrast between God's sovereignty and righteousness and Job's insignificance and sinfulness caused Job's problem. He wanted to argue his case with God and have a chance to be proven right. Humans do not have sufficient wisdom or knowledge to argue with God. The great insight here is that the sovereign God allows us to bring our complaints to Him in such strong language, even language based on true theological insights. The result of the argument here is that humans need a mediator who can effectively present our case to God. The New Testament shows us we have such a mediator in the person of Jesus (1 Ti 2:5; Heb 8:1–6). See notes on Ge 15:13–16; 18:14; 24:3,7,50; Dt 1:10.

9:2–3 HUMANITY, Human Nature—Human nature is clearly seen when contrasted with the divine nature. Human sinfulness is seen in stark reality when viewed against the background of God's righteousness. Human intellectual accomplishments are radically devalued when contrasted with the divine wisdom.

9:4–10 CREATION, Miracles—Job agreed with his friends concerning the power of God. He believed as strongly as they that the world with all its wonders came into being through the act of a personal Creator. He also knew this Creator is a miracle-working God in complete control of everything He has made. No one can understand the mighty deeds He performs, nor should they argue with Him concerning the way He orders human lives. He can intervene when He wishes to right any wrong that occurs in His world. Belief in an all-powerful Creator is only one part of biblical faith. Saving faith must go further, establishing personal trust in the Creator as Savior. Compare Ro 1.

9:9–11 REVELATION, Divine Presence—Revelation deals with the mystery of God. The Revealer is at the same time the unknown Mystery which is not fully understood. Biblical revelation repeatedly describes this tension between making things clear and keeping some mystery at the center of God's revelation to us. The purpose of the mystery is double: to make sure that we never assume we may control God by knowing Him fully and to remind us that we never can fully grasp all that

10He performs wonders[o] that cannot be
fathomed,
miracles that cannot be counted.[p]
11When he passes me, I cannot see him;
when he goes by, I cannot perceive
him.[q]
12If he snatches away, who can stop
him?[r]
Who can say to him, 'What are you
doing?'[s]
13God does not restrain his anger;[t]
even the cohorts of Rahab[u] cowered
at his feet.

14"How then can I dispute with him?
How can I find words to argue with
him?[v]
15Though I were innocent, I could not
answer him;[w]
I could only plead[x] with my Judge[y]
for mercy.[z]
16Even if I summoned him and he
responded,
I do not believe he would give me a
hearing.[a]
17He would crush me[b] with a storm[c]
and multiply[d] my wounds for no
reason.[e]
18He would not let me regain my breath
but would overwhelm me with
misery.[f]
19If it is a matter of strength, he is
mighty![g]
And if it is a matter of justice, who
will summon him[p]?[h]
20Even if I were innocent, my mouth
would condemn me;
if I were blameless, it would
pronounce me guilty.[i]

21"Although I am blameless,[j]
I have no concern for myself;[k]
I despise my own life.[l]
22It is all the same; that is why I say,
'He destroys both the blameless and
the wicked.'[m]
23When a scourge[n] brings sudden death,
he mocks the despair of the
innocent.[o]

9:10 [o]Dt 6:22; Ps 72:18; 136:4; Jer 32:20 [p]S Job 5:9 **9:11** [q]Job 23:8-9; 35:14 **9:12** [r]Nu 23:20; Job 11:10; Isa 14:27; 43:13 [s]S ver 3; S Dt 32:39; Isa 29:16; 45:9; Da 2:21; 4:32; Ro 9:20 **9:13** [t]Nu 14:18; Job 10:15; Ps 78:38; Isa 3:11; 6:5; 48:9 [u]Job 26:12; Ps 87:4; 89:10; Isa 30:7; 51:9 **9:14** [v]S ver 3 **9:15** [w]Job 10:15; 13:19; 34:5-6; 40:5; 42:7 [x]Job 8:5 [y]S Ge 18:25; 1Sa 24:12; Ps 50:6; 96:13 [z]ver 20,29; Job 15:6; 23:4; 40:2 **9:16** [a]Job 13:22; Ro 9:20-21 **9:17** [b]Job 16:12; 30:16; Ps 10:10; Isa 38:13 [c]Job 30:22; Ps 83:15; Jnh 1:4 [d]Job 16:14 [e]S Job 2:3 **9:18** [f]S Job 7:19; S 10:1 **9:19** [g]S ver 4; S Ne 9:32 [h]ver 33; Jer 49:19 **9:20** [i]S ver 15 **9:21** [j]S Ge 6:9; Job 34:6,7 [k]ver 14; S Job 6:29; 10:1; 13:13 [l]S Nu 11:15; S Job 7:16 **9:22** [m]S Job 3:19; 10:8; Ecc 9:2,3; Eze 21:3 **9:23** [n]Heb 11:36 [o]Job 24:1,12; Ps 64:4; Hab 1:3; 1Pe 1:7 **9:24** [p]Job 1:15,17; 10:3; 16:11; 21:16; 22:18; 27:2; 40:8; Ps 73:3 [q]S Job 3:14; 12:6; 19:7; 21:7; 24:23; 31:35; 35:15; Ps 73:12; Ecc 8:11; Jer 12:1; La 3:9 [r]Job 12:9; 13:1; 24:12; Isa 41:20 **9:25** [s]S Job 7:6 [t]Job 7:7; 10:20 **9:26** [u]Job 24:18; Ps 46:3 [v]Isa 18:2 [w]Job 39:29; Hab 1:8

24When a land falls into the hands of the
wicked,[p]
he blindfolds its judges.[q]
If it is not he, then who is it?[r]

25"My days are swifter than a runner;[s]
they fly away without a glimpse of
joy.[t]
26They skim past[u] like boats of
papyrus,[v]
like eagles swooping down on their
prey.[w]
27If I say, 'I will forget my complaint,[x]
I will change my expression, and
smile,'
28I still dread[y] all my sufferings,
for I know you will not hold me
innocent.[z]
29Since I am already found guilty,
why should I struggle in vain?[a]
30Even if I washed myself with soap[q][b]
and my hands[c] with washing soda,[d]
31you would plunge me into a slime pit[e]
so that even my clothes would
detest me.[f]

32"He is not a man[g] like me that I might
answer him,[h]
that we might confront each other
in court.[i]
33If only there were someone to arbitrate
between us,[j]
to lay his hand upon us both,[k]
34someone to remove God's rod from
me,[l]
so that his terror would frighten me
no more.[m]
35Then I would speak up without fear of
him,[n]
but as it now stands with me, I
cannot.[o]

9:27 [x]S Job 7:11 **9:28** [y]S Job 3:25 [z]S Ex 34:7; S Job 7:21 **9:29** [a]S ver 3,S 15; Ps 37:33 **9:30** [b]Mal 3:2 [c]Job 17:9; 31:7; Isa 1:15 [d]Job 14:4,17; 33:9; Isa 1:18; Jer 2:22; Hos 13:12 **9:31** [e]Ps 35:7; 40:2; 51:9; Jer 2:22; Na 3:6; Mal 2:3 [f]S Job 7:20; 34:9; 35:3; Ps 73:13 **9:32** [g]S Nu 23:19 [h]S ver 3; Ro 9:20 [i]Ps 143:2; Ecc 6:10 **9:33** [j]S 1Sa 2:25 [k]S ver 19 **9:34** [l]Job 21:9; Ps 39:10; 73:5 [m]S Job 6:4; 7:14; 33:7; Ps 32:4 **9:35** [n]S Job 7:11 [o]Job 7:15; 13:21

[p]*19* See Septuagint; Hebrew *me.* [q]*30* Or *snow*

God is (26:14).

9:10 MIRACLE, God's Working—God's miracles may confound His people. Miracles are based on God's profound wisdom (v 4). They occur without us expecting them, understanding them, or being able to list them all. They affect the earth's landscape and the heavens' lights. While He does all this, God Himself remains invisible. No human can prevent miracles. This shows how radically different God is from us humans. Such difference frustrated Job. He wanted to argue his case with God on an equal footing. Instead, he feared God would use an unexpected miracle to destroy him. In the end Job learned he had to trust the miracle-working God even though he could not understand God's ways at all times. Job had to repent of his attempts to be equal with God. He learned to praise the greatness which enables God to perform miracles. God's miracles may at times confound and mystify us. They should always lead us to faith and praise, not to doubt and fear.

9:13 EVIL AND SUFFERING, Divine Origin—God's power over the world includes Rahab, apparently a personification of evil destroyed by God during creation (26:12; Ps 89:10). The human sufferer cannot compete with or win a debate against God. Suffering will not be overcome by intellectual knowledge or theological debate. Only the work of the Creator can overcome our suffering and the world's evil.

9:14–35 EVIL AND SUFFERING, Punishment—Is God's punishment just? If not, evil rules our world. In his frustration and despair, Job complained that he could not prove his innocence to God, for God destroyed innocent and wicked alike. Thus, Job appealed to a mediator above God who would treat God and him as equals and decide the case fairly. The just God allowed the desperate Job to make such outrageous claims. The New Testament reveals that God sent His Son Jesus to be our Mediator (1 Ti 2:5; Heb 8:6; 9:15; 12:24). He showed that God is more than just in His punishment.

Chapter 10

"I loathe my very life;[p]
therefore I will give free rein to
my complaint
and speak out in the bitterness of
my soul.[q]
2I will say to God:[r] Do not condemn
me,
but tell me what charges[s] you have
against me.[t]
3Does it please you to oppress me,[u]
to spurn the work of your hands,[v]
while you smile on the schemes of
the wicked?[w]
4Do you have eyes of flesh?
Do you see as a mortal sees?[x]
5Are your days like those of a mortal
or your years like those of a man,[y]
6that you must search out my faults
and probe after my sin[z] —
7though you know that I am not guilty[a]
and that no one can rescue me from
your hand?[b]

8"Your hands shaped[c] me and made
me.
Will you now turn and destroy me?[d]
9Remember that you molded me like
clay.[e]
Will you now turn me to dust
again?[f]
10Did you not pour me out like milk
and curdle me like cheese,
11clothe me with skin and flesh
and knit me together[g] with bones
and sinews?
12You gave me life[h] and showed me
kindness,[i]
and in your providence[j] watched
over[k] my spirit.

13"But this is what you concealed in
your heart,
and I know that this was in your
mind:[l]
14If I sinned, you would be watching
me[m]
and would not let my offense go
unpunished.[n]
15If I am guilty[o]—woe to me![p]
Even if I am innocent, I cannot lift
my head,[q]
for I am full of shame
and drowned in[r] my affliction.[r]
16If I hold my head high, you stalk me
like a lion[s]
and again display your awesome
power against me.[t]
17You bring new witnesses against me[u]
and increase your anger toward
me;[v]
your forces come against me wave
upon wave.[w]

18"Why then did you bring me out of the
womb?[x]
I wish I had died before any eye saw
me.[y]
19If only I had never come into being,
or had been carried straight from the
womb to the grave![z]
20Are not my few days[a] almost over?[b]
Turn away from me[c] so I can have a
moment's joy[d]
21before I go to the place of no return,[e]
to the land of gloom and deep
shadow,[s] [f]
22to the land of deepest night,
of deep shadow[g] and disorder,
where even the light is like
darkness."[h]

Chapter 11

Zophar

THEN Zophar the Naamathite[i] replied:
2"Are all these words to go
unanswered?[j]

10:1 [p]S Nu 11:15; S 1Ki 19:4 [q]S 1Sa 1:10; S Job 7:11; 9:18,21 **10:2** [r]Job 13:3; 40:1 [s]Isa 3:13; Hos 4:1; 5:1; 12:2; Mic 6:2; Ro 8:33 [t]S Job 9:3 **10:3** [u]S Job 9:22; 16:9,14; 19:6,21; 22:10; 30:13,21; 31:23; 34:6 [v]ver 8; Ge 1:26; S Job 4:17; 14:15; 34:19; Ps 8:6; 95:6; 100:3; 138:8; 149:2; Isa 60:21; 64:8 [w]S Job 9:24 **10:4** [x]1Sa 16:7; Job 11:11; 14:16; 24:23; 28:24; 31:4; 34:21; 41:11; Ps 11:4; 33:15; 119:168; 139:12; Pr 5:21; 15:3; Jer 11:20-23; 16:17 **10:5** [y]Job 36:26; Ps 39:5; 90:2,4; 102:24; 2Pe 3:8 **10:6** [z]Job 14:16 **10:7** [a]ver 15; S Job 6:29; 11:4; 16:17; 27:5,6; 31:6; 32:1 [b]S Dt 32:39 **10:8** [c]Ge 2:7 [d]S ver 3; S 2Sa 14:14; S Job 30:15 **10:9** [e]S Job 4:19; Isa 29:16 [f]S Ge 2:7; S Job 7:21 **10:11** [g]Ps 139:13, 15 **10:12** [h]S Ge 2:7 [i]S Ge 24:12 [j]S Ge 45:5 [k]1Pe 2:25 **10:13** [l]Job 23:13; Ps 115:3 **10:14** [m]Job 13:27 [n]S Ex 34:7; S Job 7:21 **10:15** [o]S ver 7 [p]S Job 9:13 [q]S Job 9:15 [r]Ps 25:16 **10:16** [s]S 1Sa 17:34; Ps 7:2; Isa 38:13; Jer 5:6; 25:38; La 3:10; Hos 5:14; 13:7 [t]Job 5:9; Isa 28:21; 29:14; 65:7 **10:17** [u]1Ki 21:10; Job 16:8 [v]Ru 1:21 [w]S Job 5:7 **10:18** [x]S Job 3:8; S Ps 22:9 [y]Job 3:26; Ecc 4:2; 7:1

10:19 [z]S Job 3:3; Jer 15:10 **10:20** [a]Job 14:1; Ecc 6:12 [b]S Job 7:7 [c]S Job 7:16 [d]S Job 9:25 **10:21** [e]S 2Sa 12:23; S Job 3:13; 16:22; Ps 39:13; Ecc 12:5 [f]S Job 3:5 **10:22** [g]S Job 3:5 [h]S 1Sa 2:9; S Job 3:13 **11:1** [i]S Job 2:11 **11:2** [j]S Job 8:2; S 16:3

[r]*15* Or *and aware of* [s]*21* Or *and the shadow of death*; also in verse 22

10:5 HUMANITY, Human Nature—The very essence of being human is to be limited in time. No matter how old a person may become, we always face a limit to life as it is. We must die unless Christ returns. Humans must find meaning in the face of death. Relationship to God in Jesus Christ is the only foundation for such meaning, for it is the basis for all eternal hopes. Everything outside Christ will ultimately face eternal destruction.

10:8–12 HUMANITY, Physical Nature—We are dust, clay, and of the earth. The physical body is made of skin and flesh covering bones and sinews. Even this, however, is the gift of God. No matter how far back you trace the physical, biological processes that produce flesh and bone, you ultimately discover the Creator who planned and produced human beings. At times we may join Job in wishing we had never been born (vv 18–19), but the long-term relationship with God makes us grateful for the physical nature He gave us.

10:20–22 LAST THINGS, Intermediate State—See note on Isa 14:9.

10:21–22 HUMANITY, Nature of Death—To the Old Testament person death was often seen as the absolute end of life. With God being perceived as the Giver of light, the abode of the dead was understood as a place of utter darkness. When Jesus Christ was raised from the tomb He made the hope of eternal life clear.

11:1–20 EVIL AND SUFFERING, Humility—Can humble acceptance ever be the wrong response to suffering? Zophar, Job's third friend, used traditional theological teaching to say humble repentance was Job's only course of action. Job, however, did not believe his sin had produced his suffering. Humble repentance would have been a lie for Job. Honest dialogue with God was the course he chose. To claim suffering is undeserved is not to mock God, nor is it to claim one has not sinned. Zophar's theology was not suited to a world in which suffering can test faith rather than punish sin. Because we are not as wise or as powerful as God does not mean we cannot tell

Is this talker to be vindicated?[k]
3Will your idle talk[l] reduce men to silence?
Will no one rebuke you when you mock?[m]
4You say to God, 'My beliefs are flawless[n]
and I am pure[o] in your sight.'
5Oh, how I wish that God would speak,[p]
that he would open his lips against you
6and disclose to you the secrets of wisdom,[q]
for true wisdom has two sides.
Know this: God has even forgotten some of your sin.[r]

7"Can you fathom[s] the mysteries of God?
Can you probe the limits of the Almighty?
8They are higher[t] than the heavens[u]—what can you do?
They are deeper than the depths of the grave[t][v]—what can you know?[w]
9Their measure[x] is longer than the earth
and wider than the sea.[y]

10"If he comes along and confines you in prison
and convenes a court, who can oppose him?[z]
11Surely he recognizes deceitful men;
and when he sees evil, does he not take note?[a]
12But a witless man can no more become wise
than a wild donkey's colt[b] can be born a man.[u] [c]

13"Yet if you devote your heart[d] to him
and stretch out your hands[e] to him,[f]
14if you put away[g] the sin that is in your hand
and allow no evil[h] to dwell in your tent,[i]
15then you will lift up your face[j]
without shame;
you will stand firm[k] and without fear.[l]
16You will surely forget your trouble,[m]
recalling it only as waters gone by.[n]
17Life will be brighter than noonday,[o]
and darkness will become like morning.[p]
18You will be secure, because there is hope;
you will look about you and take your rest[q] in safety.[r]
19You will lie down, with no one to make you afraid,[s]
and many will court your favor.[t]
20But the eyes of the wicked will fail,[u]
and escape will elude them;[v]
their hope will become a dying gasp."[w]

Chapter 12

Job

THEN Job replied:

2"Doubtless you are the people,
and wisdom will die with you![x]
3But I have a mind as well as you;
I am not inferior to you.
Who does not know all these things?[y]

4"I have become a laughingstock[z] to my friends,[a]
though I called upon God and he answered[b]—
a mere laughingstock, though righteous and blameless![c]
5Men at ease have contempt[d] for misfortune
as the fate of those whose feet are slipping.[e]
6The tents of marauders are undisturbed,[f]
and those who provoke God are secure[g]—

11:2 [k]S Ge 41:6; S Job 6:29 **11:3** [l]Eph 4:29; 5:4 [m]Job 12:4; 16:10; 17:2; 21:3; 30:1; Ps 1:1 **11:4** [n]Job 9:21 [o]S Job 10:7 **11:5** [p]Ex 20:19; Job 23:5; 32:13; 38:1 **11:6** [q]S Job 9:4; 1Co 2:10 [r]S Ezr 9:13; S Job 15:5 **11:7** [s]S Job 5:9; Ecc 3:11 **11:8** [t]Eph 3:18 [u]S Ge 15:5; Job 22:12; 25:2; Ps 57:10; Isa 55:9 [v]S Job 7:9 [w]Job 15:13,25; 33:13; 40:2; Ps 139:8 **11:9** [x]Eph 3:19-20 [y]Job 22:12; 35:5; 36:26; 37:5,23; Isa 40:26 **11:10** [z]S Job 9:12; Rev 3:7 **11:11** [a]S Job 10:4; 31:37; 34:11,25; 36:7; Ps 10:14 **11:12** [b]S Ge 16:12 [c]S 2Ch 6:36 **11:13** [d]1Sa 7:3; Ps 78:8 [e]S Ex 9:29 [f]S Job 5:8,27 **11:14** [g]S Jos 24:14 [h]Ps 101:4 [i]Job 22:23 **11:15** [j]Job 22:26 [k]S 1Sa 2:9; Ps 20:8; 37:23; 40:2; 119:5; Eph 6:14 [l]S Ge 4:7; S Ps 3:6 **11:16** [m]Isa 26:16; 37:3; 65:16 [n]Jos 7:5; Job 22:11; Ps 58:7; 112:10; Eze 21:7 **11:17** [o]Job 22:28; Ps 37:6; Isa 58:8, 10; 62:1 [p]Job 17:12; 18:6; 29:3; Ps 18:28; 112:4; 119:105; Isa 5:20; Jn 8:12 **11:18** [q]Ps 3:5; 4:8; 127:2; Ecc 5:12 [r]S Lev 26:6; Pr 3:24; Isa 11:10; 14:3; 28:12; 30:15; 32:18; Zec 3:10 **11:19** [s]S Lev 26:6 [t]Isa 45:14 **11:20** [u]Dt 28:65; Job 17:5 [v]Job 12:10; 18:18; 27:22; 34:22; 36:6; Ps 139:11-12; Jer 11:11; 23:24; 25:35; Am 2:14; 9:2-3 [w]S Job 8:13

12:2 [x]Job 15:8; 17:10 **12:3** [y]Job 13:2; 15:9 **12:4** [z]S Ge 38:23 [a]S Job 6:14; S 11:3; S 16:10; S 19:14 [b]Ps 91:15 [c]S Ge 6:9; S Job 6:29; S 15:16 **12:5** [d]Ps 123:4 [e]Ps 17:5; 37:31; 38:16; 66:9; 73:2; 94:18 **12:6** [f]S Job 5:24 [g]S Job 9:24

[t]8 Hebrew *than Sheol* [u]12 Or *wild donkey can be born tame*

God the truth about our deepest feelings. False humility and repentance cannot purchase hope and security.

11:4–12 GOD, Wisdom—In these verses Zophar praised the sovereignty and wisdom of God in contrast to Job as a mere human. See notes on 4:17; 5:8–16; 9:2–35.

12:1—13:12 EVIL AND SUFFERING, Compassion—Knowledge and traditional theology may not provide needed answers for people who suffer. Job, the sufferer, knew the correct answers his friends so easily provided. He also felt the contempt they had for him. He needed compassion from persons willing to suffer with him. Right answers without compassion provoked God because theological systems had become a god controlled by the hands of humans. Relationship to the true God had been lost. Human wisdom with improper motives cannot defend a just and compassionate God.

12:3 HUMANITY, Physical Nature—The word used here is literally "heart," but it clearly refers to the place where people have wisdom and understanding. The ancient Hebrews normally perceived the heart to be the seat of the intellect, thought, and will. Too often we treat people we argue with as if we had the mind of God and they had no minds at all. Even in times of disagreement, we need to respect the abilities God has given other people.

12:4–5 HUMANITY, Community Relationships—One of life's greatest tragedies is when friends fail. Even worse is when they ridicule. Too often we ridicule because we do not understand the other person's physical and emotional agony. When we take time to understand the other person's sufferings, we often become supportive and helpful rather than ridiculing. Silence may be the best support we can give.

those who carry their god in their
hands.[v]

7"But ask the animals, and they will
teach you,[h]
or the birds of the air,[i] and they
will tell you;[j]
8or speak to the earth, and it will teach
you,
or let the fish of the sea inform
you.
9Which of all these does not know[k]
that the hand of the LORD has done
this?[l]
10In his hand is the life[m] of every
creature
and the breath of all mankind.[n]
11Does not the ear test words
as the tongue tastes food?[o]
12Is not wisdom found among the
aged?[p]
Does not long life bring
understanding?[q]

13"To God belong wisdom[r] and
power;[s]
counsel and understanding are his.[t]
14What he tears down[u] cannot be
rebuilt;[v]
the man he imprisons cannot be
released.[w]
15If he holds back the waters,[x] there is
drought;[y]
if he lets them loose, they devastate
the land.[z]
16To him belong strength and victory;[a]
both deceived and deceiver are
his.[b]
17He leads counselors away stripped[c]
and makes fools of judges.[d]
18He takes off the shackles[e] put on by
kings
and ties a loincloth[w] around their
waist.[f]
19He leads priests away stripped[g]
and overthrows men long
established.[h]
20He silences the lips of trusted advisers
and takes away the discernment of
elders.[i]
21He pours contempt on nobles[j]
and disarms the mighty.[k]
22He reveals the deep things of
darkness[l]
and brings deep shadows[m] into the
light.[n]
23He makes nations great, and destroys
them;[o]
he enlarges nations,[p] and disperses
them.[q]
24He deprives the leaders of the earth of
their reason;[r]
he sends them wandering through a
trackless waste.[s]
25They grope in darkness with no light;[t]
he makes them stagger like
drunkards.[u]

Chapter 13

"MY eyes have seen all this,[v]
my ears have heard and
understood it.
2What you know, I also know;
I am not inferior to you.[w]
3But I desire to speak to the Almighty[x]

12:7 [h]Job 35:11 *fn* [i]Mt 6:26 [j]Job 18:3; Ro 1:20 **12:9** [k]Isa 1:3 [l]S Job 9:24 **12:10** [m]Da 5:23 [n]S Ge 2:7; S Nu 16:22; S Job 11:20; Ac 17:28 **12:11** [o]Job 34:3 **12:12** [p]S 1Ki 4:2; Job 15:10 [q]ver 20; Job 17:4; 32:7,9; 34:4,10 **12:13** [r]Pr 21:30; Isa 45:9 [s]S Job 9:4; S Jer 32:19; 1Co 1:24 [t]S Nu 23:19; 1Ki 3:12; Job 32:8; 38:36; Pr 2:6; Isa 40:13-14; Da 1:17 **12:14** [u]Job 16:9; 19:10 [v]Dt 13:16; Ps 127:1; Isa 24:20; 25:2; Eze 26:14 [w]S Job 9:3; Isa 22:22; Rev 3:7 **12:15** [x]Job 28:25; Isa 40:12 [y]S Dt 28:22; S 1Ki 17:1 [z]S Ge 7:24 **12:16** [a]S Job 9:4 [b]2Ch 18:22; Job 13:7,9; 27:4; Ro 2:11 **12:17** [c]ver 19; Job 19:9; Isa 20:4 [d]S Job 3:14; 1Co 1:20 **12:18** [e]Ps 107:14; 116:16; Na 1:13 [f]ver 21; Job 34:18; Ps 107:40; Isa 5:27; 40:23 **12:19** [g]S ver 17 [h]S Dt 24:15; S Job 9:24; 14:20; 22:8; 24:12,22; 34:20,28; 35:9; Isa 2:22; 31:8; 40:17,23; Jer 25:18; Da 2:21, 34; Lk 1:52 **12:20** [i]S ver 12,24; Da 4:33-34 **12:21** [j]S ver 18; S Isa 34:12 [k]S Job 3:15

12:22 [l]1Co 4:5 [m]Job 3:5 [n]Ps 139:12; Da 2:22 **12:23** [o]Ps 2:1; 46:6; Isa 13:4; Jer 25:9 [p]S Ex 34:24; Ps 107:38; Isa 9:3; 26:15; 54:3 [q]S Job 5:12; Ac 17:26 **12:24** [r]S ver 20 [s]Ps 107:40 **12:25** [t]S Dt 28:29; Job 18:6; 21:17; 29:3 [u]Ps 107:27; Isa 24:20 **13:1** [v]S Job 9:24 **13:2** [w]S Job 12:3 **13:3** [x]Job 5:17; 40:2

[v]*6* Or *secure / in what God's hand brings them*
[w]*18* Or *shackles of kings / and ties a belt*

12:7–15 CREATION, Hope—In Job's reply to his third friend, Zophar, he began to become impatient with the supposed comforters. They had uttered profound statements about God's power and consistency. Job had stated forcefully that he believed as much as they in these divine traits. God created a good world. Its inhabitants, including the animals, evidence His creative power. Everything that happens is under His control. He is no absentee Creator. When problems come, we can be assured of God's caring presence. Because God did not intervene immediately and solve his problem, Job began to feel despair; however, we can remain optimistic. The world is created in such a way that God will not only eventually win the victory but will vindicate His people. Compare 42:7–17.

12:10—14:22 GOD, Sovereignty—Job knew his doctrinal statements were as good as those of his friends (13:2). He knew God is in full control of everything and does as He pleases. Powerful, influential human leaders stand no chance against Him. Such knowledge of doctrinal truth does not help the one who wishes to bring a complaint against God. In fact, it can be used in a wrong way as humans try to defend the sovereign God (13:7–12). God's sovereignty is actually a reason for the perplexed, complainer to place hope in God and to continue presenting the facts to God. The sovereign God, not the theologically wise friends, offered Job true hope. See notes on 1:21–22; 9:2–35.

12:10 HUMANITY, Life—God is the direct Source of all life. It is wholly His gift and not something natural. Neither science nor psychology, with all the help and insight they give us, can ultimately define or explain the dynamic vitality we call life. Only God knows and is responsible for this ultimate mystery.

12:13 GOD, Wisdom—This is a statement concerning the all-knowing wisdom of God, sometimes called God's omniscience, though that is not a biblical term. See notes on Ex 6:5; Dt 31:21; 1 Sa 2:3.

13:2 HUMANITY, Intellectual Nature—Knowledge is not the private preserve of any individual. It is open to all. No one has any basis for assuming knowledge is reserved for one person while another remains ignorant. However, granting the availability of knowledge does not mean that everyone will appropriate it in the same way. Job's friends could not understand and appreciate his tragic situation. Thus, he wanted to turn to the only One who could understand and help.

13:3—14:17 GOD, Justice—Job voiced strong confidence in the justice of God. If he could just present his case to God, he would be vindicated, for God always knows and does what is right. God cannot be deceived by the accusations of people like Job's friends. Job did not seek to be proven right so much as to understand the cause of his problems. He believed a just God knew that cause and would show it to him. See note on 5:8–16.

and to argue my case with God.[y]
4 You, however, smear me with lies;[z]
you are worthless physicians,[a] all of you![b]
5 If only you would be altogether silent![c]
For you, that would be wisdom.[d]
6 Hear now my argument;
listen to the plea of my lips.[e]
7 Will you speak wickedly on God's behalf?
Will you speak deceitfully for him?[f]
8 Will you show him partiality?[g]
Will you argue the case for God?
9 Would it turn out well if he examined you?[h]
Could you deceive him as you might deceive men?[i]
10 He would surely rebuke you
if you secretly showed partiality.[j]
11 Would not his splendor[k] terrify you?
Would not the dread of him fall on you?[l]
12 Your maxims are proverbs of ashes;
your defenses are defenses of clay.[m]
13 "Keep silent[n] and let me speak;[o]
then let come to me what may.[p]
14 Why do I put myself in jeopardy
and take my life in my hands?[q]
15 Though he slay me, yet will I hope[r] in him;[s]
I will surely[x] defend my ways to his face.[t]
16 Indeed, this will turn out for my deliverance,[u]
for no godless[v] man would dare come before him![w]
17 Listen carefully to my words;[x]
let your ears take in what I say.
18 Now that I have prepared my case,[y]
I know I will be vindicated.[z]
19 Can anyone bring charges against me?[a]
If so, I will be silent[b] and die.[c]
20 "Only grant me these two things, O God,
and then I will not hide from you:
21 Withdraw your hand[d] far from me,
and stop frightening me with your terrors.[e]
22 Then summon me and I will answer,[f]
or let me speak, and you reply.[g]
23 How many wrongs and sins have I committed?[h]
Show me my offense and my sin.[i]
24 Why do you hide your face[j]
and consider me your enemy?[k]
25 Will you torment[l] a windblown leaf?[m]
Will you chase[n] after dry chaff?[o]
26 For you write down bitter things against me
and make me inherit the sins of my youth.[p]
27 You fasten my feet in shackles;[q]
you keep close watch on all my paths[r]
by putting marks on the soles of my feet.
28 "So man wastes away like something rotten,
like a garment[s] eaten by moths.[t]

Chapter 14

"MAN born of woman[u]
is of few days[v] and full of trouble.[w]

13:3 [y]S Job 5:8; 9:14-20; S 10:2 **13:4** [z]Ps 119:69; Isa 9:15; Jer 23:32 [a]Jer 8:22 [b]S Job 6:15 **13:5** [c]ver 13; S Jdg 18:19 [d]Pr 17:28 **13:6** [e]Job 33:1; 36:4 **13:7** [f]S Job 12:16; S 16:17 **13:8** [g]S Lev 19:15 **13:9** [h]S Job 9:3 [i]S Job 12:16; Gal 6:7 **13:10** [j]S Lev 19:15; S 2Ch 19:7 **13:11** [k]Job 31:23 [l]S Ex 3:6 **13:12** [m]S Ne 4:2-3 **13:13** [n]S ver 5 [o]S Job 7:11 [p]S Job 9:21 **13:14** [q]S Jdg 9:17 **13:15** [r]S Job 7:6 [s]Ps 23:4; 27:1; Pr 14:32; Isa 12:2; Da 3:28 [t]S Job 5:8; 27:5 **13:16** [u]Ps 30:5; Isa 12:1; 54:7-8; Hos 14:4; Php 1:19 [v]S Job 8:13 [w]S Ge 3:8 **13:17** [x]Job 21:2 **13:18** [y]S ver 3; Job 23:4; 37:19 [z]S Job 2:3; S 9:21 **13:19** [a]Job 40:4; Isa 50:8; Ro 8:33 [b]S Job 9:15 [c]S Job 3:13; 10:8 **13:21** [d]S Ex 9:3; Heb 10:31 [e]S Job 6:4 **13:22** [f]Job 9:35; 14:15 [g]S Job 9:16 **13:23** [h]S 1Sa 26:18 [i]Job 7:21; 9:21; 14:17; 33:9 **13:24** [j]S Dt 32:20 [k]Job 16:9; 19:11; 33:10; Ps 88:14-15; Jer 30:14; La 2:5 **13:25** [l]Job 19:2 [m]Lev 26:36 [n]Job 19:22,28 [o]Job 21:18; Ps 1:4; 35:5; 83:13; Isa 17:13; 42:3; 43:17; Hos 13:3 **13:26** [p]Job 18:7; 20:11; 21:23; Ps 25:7 **13:27** [q]S Ge 40:15; Job 33:11; Jer 20:2; Ac 16:24 [r]Job 10:14 **13:28** [s]Ps 102:26; Mk 2:21 [t]S Dt 28:35; Ps 39:11; Isa 50:9; 51:8; Hos 5:12; Jas 5:2 **14:1** [u]Job 15:14; Mt 11:11 [v]S Job 10:20 [w]S Ge 3:17; S Job 7:2

[x] *15* Or *He will surely slay me; I have no hope— / yet I will*

13:13–27 EVIL AND SUFFERING, Punishment—Does God really forgive our sins, or does He just delay punishment? Job decided God had stored up the punishment due for sins of younger days and made Job suffer it all at once. Job wanted proof that his sins rightly led to such punishment. His apparently hopeless situation did not change. He continued to carry his case to God. In the end Job experienced again the merciful forgiveness of God and knew that God's forgiveness includes total forgetfulness.

13:15 LAST THINGS, Inspires Hope—The bright prospect of hope in the New Testament rests on the resurrection of Jesus. His resurrection gives us assurance that we will be raised from the dead. See note on 2 Co 4:14–18. For Job there was not such a firm basis of hope. As he argued with his friends, his hope waned at times (Job 6:11; 7:6). Occasionally, it seemed to rise up in confidence, as in this passage. It burned brightest in 19:25–27 and lowest in 14:7–12. Only the full revelation of the Redeemer's resurrection and final triumph brought in the full measure of hope for human hearts. See note on 19:25–27.

13:16 GOD, Holy—Job referred here to the holiness of God, though it is not specifically mentioned. A godless, wicked person could not stand before the holy, pure God. Job did not place himself in this category. He denied being as sinful as his friends claimed. He wanted his day in court when God would forgive his sin. See notes on Ex 3:5–6; 19:10–24; Lev 11:44–45.

13:23 SIN, Against God—Job pleaded innocent to the claims of his friends that he deserved the intense grief and suffering he was enduring. Job wanted to argue his case with the silent, withdrawn God. He called on God to show how He had been wronged by Job's actions (7:20–21; 9:28–29; 10:6–7,14–15). Job recognized that sin is ultimately a matter between an individual and God. He also realized that suffering did not automatically make a person a sinner. Sin is related to the cosmic powers, the powers of good and evil, of God and Satan. The struggle between these forces revolves around their desire to lead people to follow willingly their way of life. Ultimately God will win this struggle, do away with all Satan's power, and establish a world without sin.

14:1–22 EVIL AND SUFFERING, God's Future Help—Does the future offer hope to the sufferer? Job struggled to say yes, yet he did not have sufficient evidence to do so. He could only ask for God to hide him in the grave and bring him back for a second chance after God's anger had passed. He wanted God to be more concerned to have a relationship with him than to keep accurate records of his sins and their punishment. Job's understanding at this point was resignation to

[2]He springs up like a flower[x] and
withers away;[y]
like a fleeting shadow,[z] he does not
endure.[a]
[3]Do you fix your eye on such a one?[b]
Will you bring him[y] before you for
judgment?[c]
[4]Who can bring what is pure[d] from the
impure?[e]
No one![f]
[5]Man's days are determined;[g]
you have decreed the number of his
months[h]
and have set limits he cannot
exceed.[i]
[6]So look away from him and let him
alone,[j]
till he has put in his time like a
hired man.[k]

[7]"At least there is hope for a tree:[l]
If it is cut down, it will sprout again,
and its new shoots[m] will not fail.[n]
[8]Its roots may grow old in the ground
and its stump[o] die in the soil,
[9]yet at the scent of water[p] it will bud
and put forth shoots like a plant.[q]
[10]But man dies and is laid low;[r]
he breathes his last and is no
more.[s]
[11]As water disappears from the sea
or a riverbed becomes parched and
dry,[t]
[12]so man lies down and does not rise;[u]
till the heavens are no more,[v] men
will not awake
or be roused from their sleep.[w]

[13]"If only you would hide me in the
grave[z] [x]
and conceal me till your anger has
passed![y]
If only you would set me a time
and then remember[z] me![a]
[14]If a man dies, will he live again?
All the days of my hard service[b]
I will wait for my renewal[a] [c] to
come.
[15]You will call and I will answer you;[d]
you will long for the creature your
hands have made.[e]
[16]Surely then you will count my steps[f]
but not keep track of my sin.[g]
[17]My offenses will be sealed[h] up in a
bag;[i]
you will cover over my sin.[j]

[18]"But as a mountain erodes and
crumbles[k]
and as a rock is moved from its
place,[l]
[19]as water wears away stones
and torrents[m] wash away the soil,[n]
so you destroy man's hope.[o]
[20]You overpower him once for all, and
he is gone;[p]
you change his countenance and
send him away.[q]
[21]If his sons are honored, he does not
know it;
if they are brought low, he does not
see it.[r]
[22]He feels but the pain of his own body[s]
and mourns only for himself.[t]"

Chapter 15

Eliphaz

THEN Eliphaz the Temanite[u] replied:
[2]"Would a wise man answer with
empty notions

14:2 [x]Ps 103:15; S Jas 1:10 [y]Ps 37:2; 90:5-6; Isa 40:6-8 [z]Job 8:9; Ps 39:4; 102:11; 109:23; 144:4; Ecc 6:12 [a]S Job 4:20; Ps 49:12 **14:3** [b]Ps 8:4; 144:3 [c]S Job 7:18 **14:4** [d]Ps 51:10 [e]S Job 4:17; Eph 2:1-3 [f]S Job 9:30; Jn 3:6; Ro 5:12; 7:14 **14:5** [g]Job 24:1; Ps 31:15; 139:16 [h]Job 21:21; Ps 39:4; 90:12 [i]Ac 17:26 **14:6** [j]S Job 7:19 [k]Job 7:1,2; Ps 39:13; Isa 16:14; 21:16 **14:7** [l]Job 19:10; 24:20; Ps 52:5 [m]Isa 11:1; 53:2; 60:21 [n]Isa 6:13 **14:8** [o]Isa 6:13; 11:1; 53:2 **14:9** [p]Job 29:19; Ps 1:3; Jer 17:8; Eze 31:7 [q]Lev 26:4; Eze 34:27; Zec 10:1 **14:10** [r]ver 12 [s]S Job 10:21; 13:19 **14:11** [t]S 2Sa 14:14 **14:12** [u]ver 10 [v]Ps 102:26; Rev 20:11; 21:1 [w]Ac 3:21 **14:13** [x]S Job 7:9 [y]Ps 30:5; Isa 26:20; 54:7 [z]S Ge 8:1 [a]Job 6:8 **14:14** [b]S Job 7:1 [c]S 2Ki 6:33 **14:15** [d]S Job 13:22 [e]S Job 10:3 **14:16** [f]S Job 10:4; Ps 139:1-3; Pr 5:21; Jer 16:17; 32:19 [g]Job 10:6; 1Co 13:5 **14:17** [h]Jer 32:10 [i]S Dt 32:34 [j]S Job 9:30; S 13:23 **14:18** [k]Eze 38:20 [l]Job 18:4 **14:19** [m]Eze 13:13 [n]S Ge 7:23 [o]S Job 7:6 **14:20** [p]S Job 4:20 [q]S Job 7:10; 8:18; S 12:19; 27:19; Jas 1:10 **14:21** [r]Job 21:21; Ecc 9:5; Isa 63:16 **14:22** [s]Ps 38:7; Isa 21:3; Jer 4:19 [t]Job 21:21 **15:1** [u]S Job 4:1

[y]3 Septuagint, Vulgate and Syriac; Hebrew *me*
[z]13 Hebrew *Sheol*
[a]14 Or *release*

death and hopelessness. The New Testament shows Job had more hope than he realized. Death is not the last word. Resurrection with Christ is. Thus the future is the final answer to the problem of innocent suffering and ongoing evil.

14:1–2 HUMANITY, Physical Nature—Common characteristics can be found among all people. Everyone enters the world through the same process of human birth. For all, life is transient and fleeting. All face troubles and problems. No accomplishment of any kind can alter this basic nature of human existence. The mystery is that Almighty God would bother to notice such seemingly insignificant and short-lived creatures.

14:5 CREATION, Freedom—Job complained that God, his Creator, had established certain boundaries to his life. One with mature insight realizes this must always be a part of freedom. If we were granted unconditional license, we would ignore the disciplined life and indulge in unprofitable and unwholesome activities. Though God wants us to be free, He has wisely established limits to our liberty. Only in this way can we be truly free! Freedom is not the absence of God but the opportunity to work with the Creator responsibly to maintain His created order. Compare Ge 1:26.

14:5 HUMANITY, Physical Nature—No doubt exists as to the difference between God and humanity. The creature is always limited and subject to the sovereign control of God. It is possible that we have here a direct reference to specific foreknowledge of God in regard to an individual. It appears more likely that this refers to the general fact that any person's days are ultimately limited, no matter how long physical life goes on.

14:10–22 HUMANITY, Nature of Death—To the Old Testament saint, death was regularly perceived as the end of vital existence. A tree stump might live again. People did not. Death was sleep in which one had no awareness of any thing after death. Such a state of hopelessness was clearly altered by the resurrection of Jesus (1 Co 15:12–19).

14:1–22 LAST THINGS, Believers' Resurrection—Job's question (v 14) is one of life's ultimate questions which we all face. All evidence around Job pointed to a negative answer. Trees sprout again, but humans are no more (v 10). Job sought a chance to live without enduring God's anger (v 13) and to face the divine Judge with a hope for grace. Evidence pointed, however, to the destruction of his hopes (v 19). Thus Job had no clear, sure answer in the affirmative. Only at times dared he rise in hope to think one just might live again following death. See note on 19:25–27. The words of Jesus began to inform Job's question (Jn 14:19). His resurrection answers it. See note on 1 Co 15:20–23.

or fill his belly with the hot east
wind?[v]
3 Would he argue with useless words,
with speeches that have no value?[w]
4 But you even undermine piety
and hinder devotion to God.[x]
5 Your sin[y] prompts your mouth;[z]
you adopt the tongue of the crafty.[a]
6 Your own mouth condemns you, not
mine;
your own lips testify against you.[b]

7 "Are you the first man ever born?[c]
Were you brought forth before the
hills?[d]
8 Do you listen in on God's council?[e]
Do you limit wisdom to yourself?[f]
9 What do you know that we do not
know?
What insights do you have that we
do not have?[g]
10 The gray-haired and the aged[h] are on
our side,
men even older than your father.[i]
11 Are God's consolations[j] not enough
for you,
words[k] spoken gently to you?[l]
12 Why has your heart[m] carried you
away,
and why do your eyes flash,
13 so that you vent your rage[n] against
God
and pour out such words[o] from your
mouth?[p]

14 "What is man, that he could be pure,
or one born of woman,[q] that he
could be righteous?[r]
15 If God places no trust in his holy
ones,[s]
if even the heavens are not pure in
his eyes,[t]
16 how much less man, who is vile and
corrupt,[u]
who drinks up evil[v] like water![w]

17 "Listen to me and I will explain to
you;
let me tell you what I have seen,[x]
18 what wise men have declared,
hiding nothing received from their
fathers[y]
19 (to whom alone the land[z] was given
when no alien passed among them):
20 All his days the wicked man suffers
torment,[a]
the ruthless through all the years
stored up for him.[b]
21 Terrifying sounds fill his ears;[c]
when all seems well, marauders
attack him.[d]
22 He despairs of escaping the darkness;[e]
he is marked for the sword.[f]
23 He wanders about[g]—food for
vultures[b];[h]
he knows the day of darkness[i] is at
hand.[j]
24 Distress and anguish[k] fill him with
terror;[l]
they overwhelm him, like a king[m]
poised to attack,
25 because he shakes his fist[n] at God
and vaunts himself against the
Almighty,[o]
26 defiantly charging against him
with a thick, strong shield.[p]

27 "Though his face is covered with fat
and his waist bulges with flesh,[q]
28 he will inhabit ruined towns
and houses where no one lives,[r]
houses crumbling to rubble.[s]
29 He will no longer be rich and his
wealth will not endure,[t]
nor will his possessions spread over
the land.[u]
30 He will not escape the darkness;[v]
a flame[w] will wither his shoots,[x]
and the breath of God's mouth[y] will
carry him away.[z]
31 Let him not deceive[a] himself by
trusting what is worthless,[b]
for he will get nothing in return.[c]

15:2 [v]S Ge 41:6 **15:3** [w]S Ne 4:2-3; S Job 6:26 **15:4** [x]Job 25:6 **15:5** [y]Job 11:6; 22:5 [z]Pr 16:23 [a]S Job 5:13 **15:6** [b]S Job 9:15; 18:7; Ps 10:2; S Mt 12:37; Lk 19:22 **15:7** [c]Job 38:21 [d]S 1Sa 2:8; Ps 90:2; Pr 8:25 **15:8** [e]Job 29:4; Isa 9:6; 40:13; 41:28; Jer 23:18; Ro 11:34; 1Co 2:11 [f]S Job 12:2 **15:9** [g]S Job 12:3 **15:10** [h]S Job 12:12 [i]S 2Ch 10:6 **15:11** [j]S Ge 37:35; S Job 6:10; 2Co 1:3-4 [k]Zec 1:13 [l]S Dt 8:3; S 32:39; S Job 5:17; 22:22; 23:12; 36:16; Ps 119:11,72; Jer 15:16 **15:12** [m]Job 11:13; 36:13 **15:13** [n]Pr 29:11; Da 11:30 [o]Ps 94:4 [p]S Job 11:8; 22:5; 32:3 **15:14** [q]S Job 14:1 [r]S 2Ch 6:36; S Job 4:17 **15:15** [s]S Job 5:1 [t]S Job 4:18 **15:16** [u]S Lev 5:2; S Job 4:19; Ps 14:1 [v]Job 20:12 [w]Job 12:4; 34:7; Pr 19:28 **15:17** [x]S Job 4:8 **15:18** [y]S Dt 32:7 **15:19** [z]Ge 12:1; Job 22:8 **15:20** [a]ver 24; Isa 8:22; 50:11; 66:24 [b]Job 24:1; 27:13-23; Isa 2:12; Jer 46:10; Ob 1:15; Zep 1:7 **15:21** [c]ver 24; S 1Sa 3:11; Job 18:11; 20:25; Jer 6:25; 20:3 [d]Job 22:10; 27:20; Isa 13:3; Jer 51:25, 53,56; 1Th 5:3 **15:22** [e]ver 23; S Job 5:14; 24:17; 38:15; Ps 91:5; SS 3:8 [f]Job 16:13; 18:19; 19:29; 20:24; 27:14; 33:18; 36:12; Pr 7:23; Isa 1:20; Jer 44:27; Hos 9:13; Am 5:19 **15:23** [g]Ps 109:10 [h]Pr 30:17; Eze 39:17; Mt 24:28; Lk 17:37 [i]S ver 22 [j]Job 18:12 **15:24** [k]Isa 8:22; 9:1 [l]S ver 20 [m]Job 18:14 **15:25** [n]Ps 44:16; Isa 10:32; 37:23 [o]S Job 11:8; 35:12; 36:9; 40:8; Ps 2:2-3; 73:9; 75:5; Pr 21:30; Isa 3:16; 45:9 **15:26** [p]Jer 44:16 **15:27** [q]S Jdg 3:17 **15:28** [r]Isa 5:9 [s]S Job 3:14 **15:29** [t]S Job 3:15; S 7:8 [u]Isa 5:8 **15:30** [v]S Job 5:14 [w]ver 34; Job 16:7; 20:26; 22:20; 31:12 [x]ver 32; Job 8:19; 18:16; 29:19; Hos 9:1-16; Mal 4:1 [y]S Ex 15:10 [z]Isa 40:23-24 **15:31** [a]Job 31:5; Pr 1:16; 6:18; Isa 44:20; 59:7; Mic 2:11; S Mk 13:5; Jas 1:16 [b]Isa 30:12; 47:10; 59:4; Jer 7:4,8; S Mt 6:19 [c]Job 20:7; 22:13; 27:9; 35:13; Pr 15:29; Isa 1:15; Jer 11:11; Mic 3:4

[b]23 Or *about, looking for food*

15:1–35 EVIL AND SUFFERING, Humility—Is silent acceptance the proper response to suffering? Eliphaz used traditional teachings of the fathers to quiet Job. Tradition said all persons sin, sin is punished, and the wicked suffer. Eliphaz turned this around to say all sufferers are wicked and have no right to complain in anger to God. The inspired writer of Job could not accept such twisting of tradition. Some suffering is not deserved. In such cases emotional conversation with God is better than bitter silence. See notes on 5:7; 11:1–20.

15:7–9 HUMANITY, Life—All people share a commonness. As we relate to others, we must be careful to emphasize our common traits and shared humanity rather than attempting to demonstrate our superiority.

15:14–16 SIN, Universal Nature—Though Eliphaz accused Job falsely, he accurately described the universal nature of sin. The Bible writers leave no doubt that all persons are sinners. Each of us has chosen to follow our desires and not trust God's directions. We would not dare compare ourselves to the heavenly beings, yet even they do not come up to God's standards. Humans have no basis for pride in moral accomplishment. We thirst for evil, not righteousness, until we experience the new birth (Jn 3). Then we become a new creation, receiving a new heart and spirit (2 Co 5:17).

15:17–35 GOD, Justice—Eliphaz declared that God is just and no sinner will escape His judgment. Again, he had proper theology, but his application of a doctrine to the specific case of Job did not mean Job was the sinner who would not escape judgment. See notes on 4:17; 5:8–16.

[32]Before his time[d] he will be paid in
full,[e]
and his branches will not flourish.[f]
[33]He will be like a vine stripped of its
unripe grapes,[g]
like an olive tree shedding its
blossoms.[h]
[34]For the company of the godless[i] will
be barren,
and fire will consume[j] the tents of
those who love bribes.[k]
[35]They conceive trouble[l] and give birth
to evil;[m]
their womb fashions deceit."

Chapter 16

Job

THEN Job replied:
[2]"I have heard many things like
these;
miserable comforters[n] are you all![o]
[3]Will your long-winded speeches never
end?[p]
What ails you that you keep on
arguing?[q]
[4]I also could speak like you,
if you were in my place;
I could make fine speeches against you
and shake my head[r] at you.
[5]But my mouth would encourage you;
comfort[s] from my lips would bring
you relief.[t]

[6]"Yet if I speak, my pain is not relieved;
and if I refrain, it does not go
away.[u]
[7]Surely, O God, you have worn me
out;[v]
you have devastated my entire
household.[w]
[8]You have bound me—and it has
become a witness;
my gauntness[x] rises up and testifies
against me.[y]
[9]God assails me and tears[z] me in his
anger[a]
and gnashes his teeth at me;[b]
my opponent fastens on me his
piercing eyes.[c]
[10]Men open their mouths[d] to jeer at
me;[e]
they strike my cheek[f] in scorn
and unite together against me.[g]
[11]God has turned me over to evil men
and thrown me into the clutches of
the wicked.[h]
[12]All was well with me, but he shattered
me;
he seized me by the neck and
crushed me.[i]
He has made me his target;[j]
[13] his archers surround me.[k]
Without pity, he pierces[l] my kidneys
and spills my gall on the ground.
[14]Again and again[m] he bursts upon me;
he rushes at me like a warrior.[n]

[15]"I have sewed sackcloth[o] over my
skin
and buried my brow in the dust.[p]
[16]My face is red with weeping,[q]
deep shadows ring my eyes;[r]
[17]yet my hands have been free of
violence[s]
and my prayer is pure.[t]

[18]"O earth, do not cover my blood;[u]
may my cry[v] never be laid to rest![w]
[19]Even now my witness[x] is in heaven;[y]
my advocate is on high.[z]
[20]My intercessor[a] is my friend[c][b]
as my eyes pour out[c] tears[d] to God;
[21]on behalf of a man he pleads[e] with
God
as a man pleads for his friend.

[22]"Only a few years will pass
before I go on the journey of no
return.[f]

Chapter 17

[1]MY spirit[g] is broken,
my days are cut short,[h]
the grave awaits me.[i]
[2]Surely mockers[j] surround me;[k]

15:32 [d]Ecc 7:17 [e]Job 22:16; 36:14; Ps 55:23; 109:8; Pr 10:27 [f]S ver 30 **15:33** [g]Hab 3:17 [h]S Job 4:20 **15:34** [i]S Job 8:13 [j]S ver 30; Heb 10:27 [k]S Ex 23:8; S 1Sa 8:3 **15:35** [l]S Job 5:7 [m]S Job 4:8; S Isa 29:20; Gal 6:7; Jas 1:15 **16:2** [n]Ps 69:20 [o]S Job 6:15 **16:3** [p]Job 11:2; 18:2 [q]S Job 6:26 **16:4** [r]S 2Ki 19:21; Ps 22:7; Isa 37:22; Jer 48:27; La 2:15; Zep 2:15; S Mt 27:39 **16:5** [s]Job 29:25 [t]S Ge 37:35 **16:6** [u]S Job 6:3; S 7:21 **16:7** [v]S Jdg 8:5; S Job 7:3 [w]S Job 1:19 **16:8** [x]Job 17:7; 19:20; 33:21; Ps 6:7; 22:17; 88:9; 102:5; 109:24; La 5:17 [y]S Job 10:17 **16:9** [z]S Job 12:14; Hos 6:1 [a]S Job 9:5; 18:4; 19:11 [b]Job 30:21; Ps 35:16; 37:12; 112:10; La 2:16; Ac 7:54 [c]S Job 13:24 **16:10** [d]Ps 22:13; 35:21 [e]Job 12:4; 19:18; 21:3; 30:1, 9; Ps 22:13; 69:12; 119:51 [f]Isa 50:6; La 3:30; Mic 5:1; Ac 23:2 [g]ver 7; S Job 11:3; 19:12; 30:12; Ps 27:3; 35:15; Ac 7:57 **16:11** [h]S Job 9:24 **16:12** [i]S Job 9:17 [j]S Job 6:4; La 3:12 **16:13** [k]S Job 3:23 [l]Job 20:24; Pr 7:23; La 3:13 **16:14** [m]Job 9:17 [n]S Job 10:3; Joel 2:7 **16:15** [o]S Ge 37:34 [p]S Job 2:8 **16:16** [q]ver 20; Ps 6:6 [r]Job 2:7; 17:7; 30:17,30; 33:19; Isa 52:14 **16:17** [s]Isa 55:7; 59:6; Jer 18:11; Jnh 3:8 [t]S Job 6:28; S 10:7; 13:7; Isa 53:9; Zep 3:13 **16:18** [u]S Ge 4:10; Isa 26:21 [v]Ps 5:2; 18:6; 102:1; 119:169 [w]Job 19:24; Ps 66:18-19; Heb 11:4 **16:19** [x]S Ge 31:50; S Ro 1:9; 1Th 2:5 [y]Job 22:12; 42:2 [z]Job 19:27; 21:17; 25:2; 27:13; 31:2; Ps 113:5; Isa 33:5; 57:15; 58:4; 66:1; Mk 11:10 **16:20** [a]S Ro 8:34 [b]Jn 15:15 [c]La 2:19 [d]S ver 16 **16:21** [e]1Ki 8:45; Ps 9:4; 140:12 **16:22** [f]S Job 10:21 **17:1** [g]Ps 143:4 [h]Isa 38:12 [i]Ps 88:3-4; Ecc 12:1-7 **17:2** [j]S Job 11:3 [k]S Job 6:14; Ps 22:7; 119:51; Jer 20:7; La 3:14

[c]20 Or *My friends treat me with scorn*

16:1–5 EVIL AND SUFFERING, Comfort—Sufferers do not appreciate long-winded speeches condemning their conduct. They need encouragement, relief, and comfort from friends. The sufferer wants love, acceptance, and hope, not guilt. See note on 2:11–13.

16:6–14 EVIL AND SUFFERING, Divine Origin—In his agony Job perceived God as the cause of his suffering and, therefore, as his enemy. Suffering often gives us the wrong perspective on life. What we feel emotionally in our pain is not what we would state intellectually as our basic beliefs when we are free from agony. Later, Job discovered God was his only source of hope rather than his enemy.

16:17 SALVATION, Obedience—Compare 2:10; 6:10; 8:6; 11:14. Job's case contradicted the opinion that persons only serve God for what they can get out of Him. Bad things sometimes do happen to obedient followers of God. That does not indicate salvation is lost. Saved people may suffer.

16:18–21 EVIL AND SUFFERING, God's Future Help—Feeling alienated from God, Job expressed hope in an advocate or intercessor with God. He could not identify the figure concretely. He reached out in faith knowing the world was unjust if he were never vindicated. The New Testament shows us Jesus Christ as our heavenly Witness. Suffering may be our lot even to death, but hope does not end there. See note on 9:14–35.

my eyes must dwell on their
hostility.
[3]"Give me, O God, the pledge you
demand.[l]
Who else will put up security[m] for
me?[n]
[4]You have closed their minds to
understanding;[o]
therefore you will not let them
triumph.
[5]If a man denounces his friends for
reward,[p]
the eyes of his children will fail.[q]

[6]"God has made me a byword[r] to
everyone,[s]
a man in whose face people spit.[t]
[7]My eyes have grown dim with grief;[u]
my whole frame is but a shadow.[v]
[8]Upright men are appalled at this;
the innocent are aroused[w] against
the ungodly.
[9]Nevertheless, the righteous[x] will hold
to their ways,
and those with clean hands[y] will
grow stronger.[z]

[10]"But come on, all of you, try again!
I will not find a wise man among
you.[a]
[11]My days have passed,[b] my plans are
shattered,
and so are the desires of my heart.[c]
[12]These men turn night into day;[d]
in the face of darkness they say,
'Light is near.'[e]
[13]If the only home I hope for is the
grave,[d] [f]
if I spread out my bed[g] in
darkness,[h]
[14]if I say to corruption,[i] 'You are my
father,'
and to the worm,[j] 'My mother' or
'My sister,'
[15]where then is my hope?[k]
Who can see any hope for me?[l]
[16]Will it go down to the gates of
death[d]?[m]
Will we descend together into the
dust?"[n]

Chapter 18

Bildad

THEN Bildad the Shuhite[o] replied:
[2]"When will you end these
speeches?[p]
Be sensible, and then we can talk.
[3]Why are we regarded as cattle[q]
and considered stupid in your
sight?[r]
[4]You who tear yourself[s] to pieces in
your anger,[t]
is the earth to be abandoned for
your sake?
Or must the rocks be moved from
their place?[u]

[5]"The lamp of the wicked is snuffed
out;[v]
the flame of his fire stops burning.[w]
[6]The light in his tent[x] becomes dark;[y]
the lamp beside him goes out.[z]
[7]The vigor[a] of his step is weakened;[b]
his own schemes[c] throw him
down.[d]
[8]His feet thrust him into a net[e]
and he wanders into its mesh.
[9]A trap seizes him by the heel;
a snare[f] holds him fast.[g]
[10]A noose[h] is hidden for him on the
ground;
a trap[i] lies in his path.[j]
[11]Terrors[k] startle him on every side[l]
and dog[m] his every step.
[12]Calamity[n] is hungry[o] for him;
disaster[p] is ready for him when he
falls.[q]
[13]It eats away parts of his skin;[r]
death's firstborn devours his limbs.[s]
[14]He is torn from the security of his
tent[t]
and marched off to the king[u] of
terrors.[v]
[15]Fire resides[e] in his tent;[w]
burning sulfur[x] is scattered over his
dwelling.
[16]His roots dry up below[y]
and his branches wither above.[z]
[17]The memory of him perishes from the
earth;[a]
he has no name[b] in the land.[c]
[18]He is driven from light into darkness[d]
and is banished[e] from the world.[f]
[19]He has no offspring[g] or descendants[h]
among his people,
no survivor[i] where once he lived.[j]
[20]Men of the west are appalled[k] at his
fate;[l]

17:3 [l]Ps 35:27; 119:122 [m]Pr 6:1 [n]Ps 35:2; 40:17; Isa 38:14 **17:4** [o]S Job 12:12 **17:5** [p]S Ex 22:15 [q]S Job 11:20 **17:6** [r]S 1Ki 9:7; Job 30:9; Jer 15:4 [s]S ver 2 [t]S Nu 12:14 **17:7** [u]S Job 16:8 [v]S Job 2:12; S 16:16 **17:8** [w]S Ex 4:14 **17:9** [x]Pr 4:18 [y]S 2Sa 22:21; S Job 9:30 [z]S 1Sa 2:4; Ps 84:7 **17:10** [a]S Job 12:2 **17:11** [b]ver 15; Isa 38:10 [c]S Job 7:6 **17:12** [d]Isa 50:11 [e]Job 5:17-26; S 11:17 **17:13** [f]S 2Sa 14:14; S Job 3:13 [g]Ps 139:8 [h]Ps 88:18 **17:14** [i]Job 13:28; 30:28,30; Ps 16:10; 49:9 [j]S Job 4:19; S 7:5 **17:15** [k]S Job 7:6 [l]Ps 31:22; La 3:18; Eze 37:11 **17:16** [m]S Job 7:9; 33:28; Ps 9:13; 30:3; 107:18; Isa 38:10,17; Jnh 2:6 [n]S Ge 2:7; S Job 3:19; 20:11; 21:26 **18:1** [o]S Job 8:1 **18:2** [p]S Job 8:2; S 16:3 **18:3** [q]S Job 12:7 [r]Ps 73:22 **18:4** [s]Job 13:14 [t]S Job 16:9 [u]Job 14:18 **18:5** [v]Job 21:17; 35:15; Pr 13:9; 20:20; 24:20; Jer 25:10; Mt 25:8; Jn 8:12 [w]S Job 5:14; 12:25; 24:17; 38:15 **18:6** [x]S Job 8:22 [y]S Job 5:14 [z]S Job 11:17; S 12:25 **18:7** [a]S Job 13:26 [b]Ps 18:36; Pr 4:12 [c]S Job 5:13 [d]S Job 15:6 **18:8** [e]Job 19:6; Ps 9:15; 10:9; 35:7; 57:6; 66:11; 140:5; La 1:13; Mic 7:2; Hab 1:15 **18:9** [f]Job 22:10; 30:12; Isa 24:18; Jer 48:44; Am 5:19 [g]Pr 5:22 **18:10** [h]Pr 7:22; Isa 51:20 [i]S 1Sa 28:9 [j]Ps 140:5 **18:11** [k]ver 14; S Job 6:4; 20:25; 24:17; Ps 55:4; 88:15; Isa 28:19; Jer 15:8; La 2:22 [l]S Job 15:21; Ps 31:13 [m]ver 18; Job 20:8; Isa 22:18 **18:12** [n]Job 21:17 [o]Isa 8:21; 9:20; 65:13 [p]Job 31:3 [q]Job 15:23 **18:13** [r]Nu 12:12 [s]Zec 14:12 **18:14** [t]S Job 8:22 [u]Job 15:24 [v]S ver 11 **18:15** [w]ver 18; Job 20:26 [x]S Ge 19:24 **18:16** [y]Isa 5:24; Hos 5:12; Am 2:9 [z]S Ge 27:28; S Job 8:12; S 15:30 **18:17** [a]S Dt 32:26 [b]Dt 9:14; Ps 9:5; 69:28; Pr 10:7; Isa 14:22 [c]Job 24:20; Ps 34:16; Pr 2:22; 10:7; Isa 49:15 **18:18** [d]S Job 5:14 [e]S ver 11 [f]S Job 11:20; 30:8 **18:19** [g]Ps 37:28; Isa 1:4; 14:20; Jer 22:30 [h]Ps 21:10; 109:13; Isa 14:22 [i]S 2Ki 10:11; S Eze 17:8 [j]Job 27:14-15 **18:20** [k]Ps 22:6-7; Isa 52:14; 53:2-3; Eze 27:35 [l]Ps 37:13; Jer 46:21; 50:27,31; Eze 7:7

[d]*13,16* Hebrew *Sheol* [e]*15* Or *Nothing he had remains*

17:13–16 LAST THINGS, Intermediate State—See notes on Pr 15:24; Isa 14:9.
18:3–21 GOD, Justice—This is Bildad's tribute to the justice of God. No one can escape God's just judgment, for God is a God of justice. See notes on 5:8–16; 15:17–35.

men of the east are seized with
horror.
21Surely such is the dwelling[m] of an evil
man;[n]
such is the place[o] of one who
knows not God."[p]

Chapter 19

Job

THEN Job replied:
2"How long will you torment[q] me
and crush[r] me with words?
3Ten times[s] now you have
reproached[t] me;
shamelessly you attack me.
4If it is true that I have gone astray,
my error[u] remains my concern
alone.
5If indeed you would exalt yourselves
above me[v]
and use my humiliation against me,
6then know that God has wronged me[w]
and drawn his net[x] around me.[y]
7"Though I cry, 'I've been wronged!' I
get no response;[z]
though I call for help,[a] there is no
justice.[b]
8He has blocked my way so I cannot
pass;[c]
he has shrouded my paths in
darkness.[d]
9He has stripped[e] me of my honor[f]
and removed the crown from my
head.[g]
10He tears me down[h] on every side till I
am gone;
he uproots my hope[i] like a tree.[j]
11His anger[k] burns against me;
he counts me among his enemies.[l]

18:21 [m]Job 21:28 [n]Isa 57:20 [o]S Job 7:10 [p]S Job 4:21; 1Th 4:5 **19:2** [q]Job 13:25 [r]Job 6:9 **19:3** [s]S Ge 31:7 [t]Job 20:3 **19:4** [u]Job 6:24 **19:5** [v]Ps 35:26; 38:16; 55:12 **19:6** [w]S Job 6:29 [x]S Job 18:8 [y]S Job 10:3 **19:7** [z]Job 30:20; Ps 22:2 [a]Job 30:24, 28; 31:35; Ps 5:2 [b]S Job 9:24; Hab 1:2-4 **19:8** [c]La 3:7; Hos 2:6 [d]Job 3:26; 23:17; 30:26; Ecc 6:4; Isa 59:9; Jer 8:15; 14:19; La 3:2 **19:9** [e]S Job 12:17 [f]Ge 43:28; Ex 12:42; Ps 15:4; 50:23; Pr 14:31 [g]S Job 2:8; 29:14; Ps 89:39,44; La 5:16 **19:10** [h]S Job 12:14 [i]S Job 7:6 [j]S Job 14:7 **19:11** [k]Job 16:9 [l]S Job 13:24 **19:12** [m]S Job 16:13 [n]S Job 16:10 [o]S Job 3:23 **19:13** [p]Ps 69:8 [q]ver 19; Job 16:7; 42:11; Ps 31:11; 38:11; 88:8 **19:14** [r]ver 19; S 2Sa 15:12; Job 12:4; 16:20; Ps 88:18; Jer 20:10; 38:22 **19:15** [s]Ge 14:14 [t]Ecc 2:7 **19:17** [u]Ps 38:5 **19:18** [v]S 2Ki 2:23 [w]S Job 16:10 **19:19** [x]S ver 14; S Job 6:14; Ps 55:12-13 [y]Job 30:10 [z]S ver 13; Jn 13:18 **19:20** [a]S Job 2:5 **19:21** [b]S Job 6:14

12His troops advance in force;[m]
they build a siege ramp[n] against me
and encamp around my tent.[o]
13"He has alienated my brothers[p] from
me;
my acquaintances are completely
estranged from me.[q]
14My kinsmen have gone away;
my friends[r] have forgotten me.
15My guests[s] and my maidservants[t]
count me a stranger;
they look upon me as an alien.
16I summon my servant, but he does not
answer,
though I beg him with my own
mouth.
17My breath is offensive to my wife;
I am loathsome[u] to my own
brothers.
18Even the little boys[v] scorn me;
when I appear, they ridicule me.[w]
19All my intimate friends[x] detest me;[y]
those I love have turned against
me.[z]
20I am nothing but skin and bones;[a]
I have escaped with only the skin of
my teeth.[f]
21"Have pity on me, my friends,[b] have
pity,
for the hand of God has struck[c] me.
22Why do you pursue[d] me as God
does?[e]
Will you never get enough of my
flesh?[f]

23"Oh, that my words were recorded,

[c]S Jdg 2:15; S Job 4:5; S 10:3; La 3:1 **19:22** [d]S Job 13:25 [e]ver 6 [f]S 2Ch 28:9; Ps 14:4; 27:2; 69:26; Pr 30:14; Isa 53:4

[f]20 Or *only my gums*

19:1–22 EVIL AND SUFFERING, Divine Origin—Faith in God may lead us to make desperate accusations. Job knew God controlled His creation. No one was powerful enough to thwart God's purpose. Unable to understand his own unjust situation, Job complained about God's treatment, which appeared to be unjust, alienating, and unmerciful. Only after he met God personally did Job come to see again that God does not cause evil or treat us unjustly. He experienced God's mercy for the sinner anew. When people utter the bitter, almost blasphemous, complaints of Job, they still need comfort instead of the tormenting condemnation his friends supplied.

19:13–20 HUMANITY, Relationships—Loneliness may be life's greatest tragedy. Separation from loved ones and friends brings despair. When external circumstances cause others to forsake, the human spirit is overwhelmed. The sense of aloneness, of being alienated from loved ones, friends, and even the helpless, crush the spirit as nothing else can. In such circumstances we reach out desperately for help. God proves our great Redeemer in such times. With Him we are never alone.

19:21 GOD, Sovereignty—Job showed profound reverence for the sovereignty of God. He accepted all the calamities that befell him as sent to him by God. See note on 1:21–22 to get the context of Job's understanding. Remember that Job's troubles were sent to him by Satan to test Job's loyalty to God (1:11–12). See Guide to Studying a Bible Book, pp. 1773–1775.

19:23–29 EVIL AND SUFFERING, God's Future Help—Hope in the future will not die for the sufferer. Repeatedly Job grasped for a vision of vindication and hope (6:8–10; 7:21; 9:33–35; 13:15–23; 14:13–17; 16:18–22; 17:13–16). His vision reached its height with this call for a kinsman redeemer (Hebrew *go'el*; compare Lev 25:25; Dt 25:5–10; Ru 3:2, 12; 4:1–10). In an unspecified way Job hoped the Redeemer would use the eternally written record of his case, vindicate him after he died, and enable him to see God as only the justified can see Him. This text comes closer to a firm belief in rewards in a life after death than any other in Job. See note on 14:1–22; Da 12:2. How much Job knew about eternity and an eternal Redeemer is not known, but he uttered an inspired truth which pointed forward to Jesus Christ, the Redeemer, and to the certainty of eternal life. Any suffering God's people may endure will be insignificant compared to our future hope.

19:23–27 HUMANITY, Attitudes to Death—The passage in Hebrew is both difficult and ambigious. In desperate loneliness Job reached out for hope that his case would be settled in his favor even after his own death. Apparently Job looked to God as the only One able to take his case and prove him innocent of charges his friends made. Whatever glimmer of eternal hope Job showed, he looked in the right direction. God is the only Redeemer who can help us after we die. This hope of life beyond death, however unclear it may have been,

that they were written on a scroll,[g]
24that they were inscribed with an iron
tool[h] on[g] lead,
or engraved in rock forever![i]
25I know that my Redeemer[h][j] lives,[k]
and that in the end he will stand
upon the earth.[i]
26And after my skin has been destroyed,
yet[j] in[k] my flesh I will see God;[l]
27I myself will see him
with my own eyes[m]—I, and not
another.
How my heart yearns[n] within me!

28"If you say, 'How we will hound[o]
him,
since the root of the trouble lies in
him,[l]'
29you should fear the sword yourselves;
for wrath will bring punishment by
the sword,[p]
and then you will know that there is
judgment.[m]"[q]

Chapter 20

Zophar

THEN Zophar the Naamathite[r] replied:
2"My troubled thoughts prompt me
to answer
because I am greatly disturbed.[s]
3I hear a rebuke[t] that dishonors me,
and my understanding inspires me
to reply.

4"Surely you know how it has been
from of old,[u]
ever since man[n] was placed on the
earth,
5that the mirth of the wicked[v] is brief,
the joy of the godless[w] lasts but a
moment.[x]
6Though his pride[y] reaches to the
heavens[z]
and his head touches the clouds,[a]
7he will perish forever,[b] like his own
dung;
those who have seen him will say,
'Where is he?'[c]
8Like a dream[d] he flies away,[e] no
more to be found,
banished[f] like a vision of the
night.[g]
9The eye that saw him will not see him
again;
his place will look on him no
more.[h]
10His children[i] must make amends to
the poor;
his own hands must give back his
wealth.[j]
11The youthful vigor[k] that fills his
bones[l]
will lie with him in the dust.[m]
12"Though evil[n] is sweet in his mouth
and he hides it under his tongue,[o]
13though he cannot bear to let it go
and keeps it in his mouth,[p]
14yet his food will turn sour in his
stomach;[q]
it will become the venom of
serpents[r] within him.
15He will spit out the riches[s] he
swallowed;
God will make his stomach vomit[t]
them up.
16He will suck the poison[u] of serpents;
the fangs of an adder will kill him.[v]
17He will not enjoy the streams,
the rivers[w] flowing with honey[x]
and cream.[y]
18What he toiled for he must give back
uneaten;[z]
he will not enjoy the profit from his
trading.[a]

19:23 gS Ex 17:14; S Ps 40:7; S Isa 8:1 **19:24** hJer 17:1 iS Job 16:18 **19:25** jS Ex 6:6; S Lev 25:25; Ps 68:5; 78:35; Pr 23:11; Isa 41:14; 43:14; 44:6,24; 47:4; 48:17; 49:26; 54:5; 59:20; 60:16 kS 1Sa 14:39; Job 16:19 **19:26** lS Nu 12:8; S Mt 5:8; 1Co 13:12; 1Jn 3:2 **19:27** mLk 2:30 nPs 42:1; 63:1; 84:2 **19:28** oS Job 13:25 **19:29** pJob 15:22 qJob 27:13-23; Ps 1:5; 9:7; 58:11; Ecc 3:17; 11:9; 12:14 **20:1** rS Job 2:11 **20:2** sPs 42:5; La 1:20 **20:3** tJob 19:3 **20:4** uDt 4:32; S 32:7 **20:5** vPs 94:3 wS Job 8:13 xS Job 8:12; Ps 37:35-36; 73:19 **20:6** yJob 33:17; Isa 16:6 zS Ge 11:4 aIsa 14:13-14; Ob 1:3-4 **20:7** bS Job 4:20 cS Job 7:8; S 14:20 **20:8** dPs 73:20; Ecc 5:3 ePs 90:10; Ecc 6:12; 12:7 fS Job 18:11 gJob 27:20; 34:20; Ps 90:5; Isa 17:14; 29:7 **20:9** hS Job 7:8 **20:10** iS Job 5:4 jver 15,18,20; S Job 3:15; 31:8 **20:11** kS Job 13:26 lJob 21:24 mS Job 17:16 **20:12** nS Job 15:16 oPs 10:7; 140:3 **20:13** pS Nu 11:18-20 **20:14** qPr 20:17; Jer 2:19; 4:18; Rev 10:9 rS Nu 21:6 **20:15** sS ver 10 tS Lev 18:25 **20:16** uS Dt 32:32 vDt 32:24 **20:17** wPs 36:8 xDt 32:13 yDt 32:14; Job 29:6 **20:18** zS ver 10; S Job 5:5 aPs 109:11

g24 Or *and* h25 Or *defender* i25 Or *upon my grave* j26 Or *And after I awake, / though this* ⌞*body*⌟ *has been destroyed, / then* k26 Or */ apart from* l28 Many Hebrew manuscripts, Septuagint and Vulgate; most Hebrew manuscripts *me* m29 Or */ that you may come to know the Almighty* n4 Or *Adam*

offers an entirely new dimension to the human attitude to death. In His resurrection Christ provided full hope for mortal believers.

19:25 JESUS CHRIST, Foretold—Job desperately cried for a heavenly Redeemer (Hebrew *go'el*) to vindicate him in his arguments against his friends and God. Christians look to Jesus as the Redeemer God sent to set us free from slavery to sin and guilt (Eph 1:7,14; Col 1:14; Heb 9:12). Christians also have the Spirit to plead our cause and stand beside us (Jn 14:16–17). Compare 1 Jn 2:1.

19:25–27 LAST THINGS, Believers' Resurrection—The doctrine of the resurrection of believers is latent in the Old Testament in passages like this. This is one of the highest peaks in the Old Testament from which to view the New Testament revelation of believers' resurrection. Job groped for hope in face of suffering and loss. He decided justice had to come after death since it was not coming in this life. Thus he looked to see God beyond the grave. The Old Testament contains other peaks. See notes on Ps 16:7–11; Isa 26:19; Da 12:2; Hos 13:14. The height of Old Testament expectation was a resurrection of the body in which an individual could see God. Such hope grew out of a personal relationship with God in life so rich and real it must surely extend beyond the grave. Many scholars believe that even where God had not yet fully revealed His eternal purpose to raise believers from the dead, some people clung to a hope of continued existence and memory through their children or through contributions to the community. At other times, a shadowy afterlife as shades in *Sheol* (the region of the dead) was projected. These gropings toward light, made possible by God's progressive revelation of truth, ultimately broke through in the expectation of bodily existence beyond death. The resurrection of Jesus would affirm and authenticate this emerging hope. God's purpose has always been for humans to receive eternal life. Compare Ro 6:23. See note on Ge 2:9.

20:4–29 GOD, Justice—This whole passage is Zophar's commentary upon the justice of God prevailing over human sin. See notes on 5:8–16; 15:17–35.

19For he has oppressed the poor[b] and
left them destitute;[c]
he has seized houses[d] he did not
build.

20"Surely he will have no respite from
his craving;[e]
he cannot save himself by his
treasure.[f]
21Nothing is left for him to devour;
his prosperity will not endure.[g]
22In the midst of his plenty, distress will
overtake him;[h]
the full force of misery will come
upon him.[i]
23When he has filled his belly,[j]
God will vent his burning anger[k]
against him
and rain down his blows upon
him.[l]
24Though he flees[m] from an iron
weapon,
a bronze-tipped arrow pierces him.[n]
25He pulls it out of his back,
the gleaming point out of his liver.
Terrors[o] will come over him;[p]
26 total darkness[q] lies in wait for his
treasures.
A fire[r] unfanned will consume him[s]
and devour what is left in his tent.[t]
27The heavens will expose his guilt;
the earth will rise up against him.[u]
28A flood will carry off his house,[v]
rushing waters[o] on the day of God's
wrath.[w]
29Such is the fate God allots the wicked,
the heritage appointed for them by
God."[x]

Chapter 21

Job

THEN Job replied:

2"Listen carefully to my words;[y]
let this be the consolation you give
me.[z]
3Bear with me while I speak,
and after I have spoken, mock on.[a]

4"Is my complaint[b] directed to man?
Why should I not be impatient?[c]
5Look at me and be astonished;
clap your hand over your mouth.[d]
6When I think about this, I am
terrified;[e]
trembling seizes my body.[f]
7Why do the wicked live on,
growing old and increasing in
power?[g]
8They see their children established
around them,
their offspring before their eyes.[h]
9Their homes are safe and free from
fear;[i]
the rod of God is not upon them.[j]
10Their bulls never fail to breed;
their cows calve and do not
miscarry.[k]
11They send forth their children as a
flock;[l]
their little ones dance about.
12They sing to the music of tambourine
and harp;[m]
they make merry to the sound of the
flute.[n]
13They spend their years in prosperity[o]
and go down to the grave[p][p] in
peace.[q][q]
14Yet they say to God, 'Leave us alone![r]
We have no desire to know your
ways.[s]
15Who is the Almighty, that we should
serve him?
What would we gain by praying to
him?'[t]
16But their prosperity is not in their own
hands,
so I stand aloof from the counsel of
the wicked.[u]

17"Yet how often is the lamp of the
wicked snuffed out?[v]
How often does calamity[w] come
upon them,
the fate God allots in his anger?[x]
18How often are they like straw before
the wind,
like chaff[y] swept away[z][a] by a
gale?[b]
19⌊It is said,⌋ 'God stores up a man's
punishment for his sons.'[c]
Let him repay the man himself, so
that he will know it![d]
20Let his own eyes see his destruction;[e]
let him drink[f] of the wrath of the
Almighty.[r] [g]
21For what does he care about the family
he leaves behind[h]
when his allotted months[i] come to
an end?[j]

22"Can anyone teach knowledge to
God,[k]
since he judges even the highest?[l]

20:19 [b]S Job 5:16; Ps 10:2; 94:6; 109:16 [c]S Dt 15:11; 24:14; Job 24:4,14; 35:9; Pr 14:31; 28:28; Am 8:4 [d]Isa 5:8 **20:20** [e]Ecc 5:12-14 [f]S ver 10; Pr 11:4; Zep 1:18; Lk 12:15 **20:21** [g]S Job 7:8 **20:22** [h]S Jdg 2:15; Lk 12:16-20 [i]ver 29; Job 21:17, 30; 31:2-3 **20:23** [j]S Nu 11:18-20 [k]La 4:11; Eze 5:13; 6:12 [l]ver 14; Ps 78:30-31 **20:24** [m]Isa 24:18; Jer 46:21; 48:44 [n]S Job 15:22 **20:25** [o]S Job 18:11 [p]S Job 15:21; Ps 88:15-16 **20:26** [q]S Job 5:14 [r]S Job 1:16 [s]Job 15:34; 26:6; 28:22; 31:12; Ps 21:9 [t]S Job 18:15 **20:27** [u]S Dt 31:28 **20:28** [v]Dt 28:31; Mt 7:26-27 [w]ver 29; Nu 14:28-32; Job 21:17,20,30; 40:11; Ps 60:3; 75:8; Pr 16:4; Isa 24:18; 51:17; Am 5:18; Jn 3:36; Ro 1:18; Eph 5:6 **20:29** [x]S ver 22; S Job 15:20; 22:5; 31:2; 36:17; Jer 13:25; Rev 21:8 **21:2** [y]S Job 13:17 [z]ver 34 **21:3** [a]S Job 6:14; S 11:3; S 16:10 **21:4** [b]S Job 7:11 [c]S Job 6:3 **21:5** [d]S Jdg 18:19; Job **21:6** [e]S Ge 45:3 [f]S Job 4:14 **21:7** [g]ver 13; S Job 9:24; 12:19; Ps 37:1; 73:3; Ecc 7:15; 8:14; Hab 1:13; Mal 3:15 **21:8** [h]Ps 17:14; Mal 3:15 **21:9** [i]S Job 5:24 [j]S Job 9:34 **21:10** [k]Ex 23:26 **21:11** [l]Ps 78:52; 107:41 **21:12** [m]Ps 33:2 [n]S Ge 4:21; S 1Ch 15:16; Ps 71:22; 81:2; 108:2; Isa 5:12; Mt 11:17 **21:13** [o]S ver 7; S Job 8:7; Ps 10:1-12; 94:3 [p]Job 24:19; Ps 49:14; Isa 14:15 [q]S Job 3:13 **21:14** [r]S Job 4:17; 22:17; Isa 30:11 [s]S Dt 32:15; S 1Sa 15:11; Ps 95:10; Pr 1:29; Jer 2:20,31 **21:15** [t]S Job 5:2; 34:9; 35:3; Ps 73:13; 139:20; Isa 48:5; Jer 9:6; 44:17 **21:16** [u]Job 22:18; Ps 1:1; 26:5; 36:1

21:17 [v]S Job 18:5 [w]Job 18:12 [x]S Job 20:22,28 **21:18** [y]S Job 13:25 [z]S Ge 19:15 [a]S Job 7:10; Pr 10:25 [b]S Ge 7:23 **21:19** [c]Ex 20:5; Jer 31:29; Eze 18:2; Jn 9:2 [d]Jer 25:14; 50:29; 51:6,24,56 **21:20** [e]S Ex 32:33; Nu 16:22; S 2Ki 14:6; Jer 42:16 [f]Job 6:4 [g]S Job 20:28; Jer 25:15; Rev 14:10 **21:21** [h]Job 14:22 [i]S Job 14:5 [j]S Job 14:21; Ecc 9:5-6 **21:22** [k]Job 35:11; 36:22; 39:17; Ps 94:12; Isa 40:13-14; Jer 32:33; Ro 11:34 [l]S Job 4:18; Ps 82:1; 86:8; 135:5

[o]*28* Or *The possessions in his house will be carried off, / washed away* [p]*13* Hebrew *Sheol* [q]*13* Or *in an instant* [r]*17-20* Verses 17 and 18 may be taken as exclamations and 19 and 20 as declarations.

21:13 LAST THINGS, Intermediate State—See note on Isa 14:9.

23One man dies in full vigor,[m]
completely secure and at ease,[n]
24his body[s] well nourished,[o]
his bones[p] rich with marrow.[q]
25Another man dies in bitterness of soul,[r]
never having enjoyed anything good.
26Side by side they lie in the dust,[s]
and worms[t] cover them both.[u]
27"I know full well what you are thinking,
the schemes by which you would wrong me.
28You say, 'Where now is the great man's[v] house,
the tents where wicked men lived?'[w]
29Have you never questioned those who travel?
Have you paid no regard to their accounts—
30that the evil man is spared from the day of calamity,[x]
that he is delivered from[t] the day of wrath?[y]
31Who denounces his conduct to his face?
Who repays him for what he has done?[z]
32He is carried to the grave,
and watch is kept over his tomb.[a]
33The soil in the valley is sweet to him;[b]
all men follow after him,
and a countless throng goes[u] before him.[c]
34"So how can you console me[d] with your nonsense?
Nothing is left of your answers but falsehood!"[e]

Chapter 22

Eliphaz

THEN Eliphaz the Temanite[f] replied:
2"Can a man be of benefit to God?[g]
Can even a wise man benefit him?[h]
3What pleasure[i] would it give the Almighty if you were righteous?[j]
What would he gain if your ways were blameless?[k]
4"Is it for your piety that he rebukes you
and brings charges against you?[l]
5Is not your wickedness great?
Are not your sins[m] endless?[n]
6You demanded security[o] from your brothers for no reason;[p]
you stripped men of their clothing, leaving them naked.[q]
7You gave no water[r] to the weary
and you withheld food from the hungry,[s]
8though you were a powerful man, owning land[t]—
an honored man,[u] living on it.[v]
9And you sent widows[w] away empty-handed[x]
and broke the strength of the fatherless.[y]
10That is why snares[z] are all around you,[a]
why sudden peril terrifies you,[b]
11why it is so dark[c] you cannot see,
and why a flood of water covers you.[d]
12"Is not God in the heights of heaven?[e]
And see how lofty are the highest stars!
13Yet you say, 'What does God know?[f]
Does he judge through such darkness?[g]
14Thick clouds[h] veil him, so he does not see us[i]
as he goes about in the vaulted heavens.'[j]
15Will you keep to the old path
that evil men[k] have trod?[l]
16They were carried off before their time,[m]
their foundations[n] washed away by a flood.[o]
17They said to God, 'Leave us alone!
What can the Almighty do to us?'[p]
18Yet it was he who filled their houses with good things,[q]
so I stand aloof from the counsel of the wicked.[r]
19"The righteous see their ruin and rejoice;[s]
the innocent mock[t] them, saying,
20'Surely our foes are destroyed,[u]
and fire[v] devours their wealth.'
21"Submit to God and be at peace[w] with him;[x]

21:23 [m]S Ge 15:15; S Job 13:26 [n]S Job 3:13 **21:24** [o]Ps 73:4 [p]Job 20:11 [q]Pr 3:8 **21:25** [r]S Job 10:1 **21:26** [s]S Job 17:16 [t]S Job 7:5 [u]Job 24:20; Ecc 9:2-3; Isa 14:11 **21:28** [v]Job 1:3; 12:21; 29:25; 31:37 [w]S Job 8:22 **21:30** [x]Job 31:3 [y]S Job 20:22,28; S Isa 5:30; Ro 2:5; 2Pe 2:9 **21:31** [z]Job 34:11; Ps 62:12; Pr 24:11-12; Isa 59:18 **21:32** [a]Isa 14:18 **21:33** [b]Job 3:22 [c]S Job 3:19 **21:34** [d]ver 2 [e]S Job 6:15; 8:20 **22:1** [f]S Job 4:1 **22:2** [g]Lk 17:10 [h]S Job 7:17 **22:3** [i]Isa 1:11; Hag 1:8 [j]Ps 143:2 [k]Job 35:7; Pr 9:12 **22:4** [l]S Job 9:3; 19:29; Ps 143:2; Isa 3:14; Eze 20:35 **22:5** [m]S Ezr 9:13; S Job 15:5 [n]S Job 15:13; S 20:29; 29:17 **22:6** [o]S Ex 22:26 [p]S 2Ki 4:1 [q]S Ex 22:27; Dt 24:12-13 **22:7** [r]Mt 10:42 [s]ver 9; Job 29:12; 31:17,21,31; Isa 58:7,10; Eze 18:7; Mt 25:42 **22:8** [t]S Job 15:19 [u]Isa 3:3; 5:13; 9:15 [v]S Job 12:19 **22:9** [w]Job 29:13; 31:16; Ps 146:9 [x]Job 24:3,21; Isa 10:2; Lk 1:53 [y]S ver 7; S Job 6:27; S Isa 1:17 **22:10** [z]S Job 18:9 [a]S Job 10:3 [b]S Job 15:21 **22:11** [c]S Job 5:14 [d]S Ge 7:23; Job 36:28; 38:34, 37; Ps 69:1-2; 124:4-5; Isa 58:10-11; La 3:54 **22:12** [e]S Job 11:8; S 16:19 **22:13** [f]ver 14; Ps 10:11; 59:7; 64:5; 73:11; 94:7; Isa 29:15; Eze 9:9; Zep 1:12 [g]Ps 139:11; Eze 8:12; Eph 6:12 **22:14** [h]Job 26:9; Ps 97:2; 105:39 [i]S ver 13; S 2Ki 21:16 [j]Job 37:18; Ps 18:11; Pr 8:27; Isa 40:22; Jer 23:23-24 **22:15** [k]Job 23:10; 34:36 [l]Job 34:8; Ps 1:1; 50:18 **22:16** [m]S Job 15:32 [n]S Job 4:19 [o]S Ge 7:23; Mt 7:26-27 **22:17** [p]Job 21:15 **22:18** [q]S Job 12:6 [r]S Job 21:16 **22:19** [s]Ps 5:11; 9:2; 32:11; 58:10; 64:10; 97:12; 107:42 [t]Job 21:3; Ps 52:6 **22:20** [u]Ps 18:39 [v]S Job 15:30 **22:21** [w]Isa 26:3,12; 27:5; Ro 5:1 [x]S Ge 17:1; Jer 9:24

[s]*24* The meaning of the Hebrew for this word is uncertain. [t]*30* Or *man is reserved for the day of calamity, / that he is brought forth to* [u]*33* Or / *as a countless throng went*

21:23–26 HUMANITY, Death—Riches cannot buy life. Regardless of the circumstances of life, death is the unavoidable end for all people, for rich and poor alike.

21:27–33 HUMANITY, Attitudes to Death—Human injustice continues even to the grave. We often honor wicked people with elaborate tombs and burial ceremonies. Fame and honor may continue for these persons after they die. This fact illustrates that Job's friends were wrong in arguing that the wicked always suffer and the good do not.

22:21–26 SALVATION, Repentance—Eliphaz urged Job

in this way prosperity will come to
you.[y]
22Accept instruction from his mouth[z]
and lay up his words[a] in your
heart.[b]
23If you return[c] to the Almighty, you
will be restored:[d]
If you remove wickedness far from
your tent[e]
24and assign your nuggets[f] to the dust,
your gold[g] of Ophir[h] to the rocks in
the ravines,[i]
25then the Almighty will be your gold,[j]
the choicest silver for you.[k]
26Surely then you will find delight in the
Almighty[l]
and will lift up your face[m] to God.[n]
27You will pray to him,[o] and he will
hear you,[p]
and you will fulfill your vows.[q]
28What you decide on will be done,[r]
and light[s] will shine on your
ways.[t]
29When men are brought low[u] and you
say, 'Lift them up!'
then he will save the downcast.[v]
30He will deliver even one who is not
innocent,[w]
who will be delivered through the
cleanness of your hands."[x]

Chapter 23

Job

THEN Job replied:
2"Even today my complaint[y] is
bitter;[z]
his hand[v] is heavy in spite of[w] my
groaning.[a]
3If only I knew where to find him;
if only I could go to his dwelling![b]
4I would state my case[c] before him
and fill my mouth with arguments.[d]
5I would find out what he would
answer me,[e]
and consider what he would say.
6Would he oppose me with great
power?[f]
No, he would not press charges
against me.[g]
7There an upright man[h] could present
his case before him,[i]
and I would be delivered forever
from my judge.[j]

8"But if I go to the east, he is not there;
if I go to the west, I do not find him.
9When he is at work in the north, I do
not see him;
when he turns to the south, I catch
no glimpse of him.[k]
10But he knows the way that I take;[l]
when he has tested me,[m] I will
come forth as gold.[n]
11My feet have closely followed his
steps;[o]
I have kept to his way without
turning aside.[p]
12I have not departed from the
commands of his lips;[q]
I have treasured the words of his
mouth more than my daily
bread.[r]

13"But he stands alone, and who can
oppose him?[s]
He does whatever he pleases.[t]
14He carries out his decree against me,
and many such plans he still has in
store.[u]
15That is why I am terrified before
him;[v]
when I think of all this, I fear him.[w]
16God has made my heart faint;[x]
the Almighty[y] has terrified me.[z]
17Yet I am not silenced by the
darkness,[a]
by the thick darkness that covers my
face.

Chapter 24

"WHY does the Almighty not set
times[b] for judgment?[c]

22:21 [y]S Job 8:7; Ps 34:8-10; Pr 3:10; 1Pe 5:6 **22:22** [z]S Dt 8:3 [a]S Job 6:10 [b]S Job 15:11; 28:23; Ps 37:31; 40:8; Pr 2:6; Eze 3:10 **22:23** [c]Isa 31:6; 44:22; 55:7; 59:20; Jer 3:14,22; Eze 18:32; Zec 1:3; Mal 3:7 [d]S Job 5:24; Isa 19:22; Ac 20:32 [e]Job 11:14 **22:24** [f]Job 28:6 [g]Ps 19:10 [h]S Ge 10:29 [i]S Job 1:10; 31:25; Isa 2:20; 30:22; 31:7; 40:19-20; Mt 6:19 **22:25** [j]Job 31:24; Ps 49:6; 52:7; Pr 11:28 [k]2Ki 18:7; Isa 33:6; Mt 6:20-21 **22:26** [l]Job 27:10; Ps 2:8; 16:6; 37:4; Isa 58:14; 61:10 [m]Job 11:15 [n]Job 11:17; 33:26; Ps 27:6; 100:1 **22:27** [o]S Job 5:27 [p]S Job 5:15; S Ps 86:7; S Isa 30:19 [q]S Nu 30:2 **22:28** [r]Ps 103:11; 145:19 [s]Job 33:28; Ps 97:11; Pr 4:18 [t]S Job 11:17 **22:29** [u]S Est 5:12 [v]Ps 18:27; S Mt 23:12 **22:30** [w]Isa 1:18; Ro 4:5 [x]S 2Sa 22:21 **23:2** [y]S Job 7:11 [z]S 1Sa 1:10; S Job 6:3 [a]Ps 6:6; 32:4; Jer 45:3; Eze 21:7 **23:3** [b]Dt 4:29 **23:4** [c]S Job 13:18 [d]S Job 9:15 **23:5** [e]S Job 11:5 **23:6** [f]S Job 9:4 [g]S Job 6:4 **23:7** [h]S Job 1:1 [i]S Ge 3:8; S Job 9:3; 13:3 [j]S Job 6:29 **23:9** [k]S Job 9:11 **23:10** [l]Job 1:1; 27:6; 31:6; 36:7; Ps 7:9; 11:5; 34:15; 37:18; 94:11; 119:168; 146:8 [m]S Job 7:18; Ps 139:1-3 [n]S Job 6:29; S 22:15; S Ps 12:6; 1Pe 1:7 **23:11** [o]Ps 17:5 [p]Job 31:7; Ps 40:4; 44:18; 119:51,59, 157; 125:5; Jer 11:20 **23:12** [q]S Job 6:10 [r]S Job 15:11; Mt 4:4; Jn 4:32,34 **23:13** [s]S Job 9:3 [t]S Job 10:13; Isa 55:11 **23:14** [u]1Th 3:3; 1Pe 4:12 **23:15** [v]S Ge 45:3 [w]S Jos 24:14; Ps 34:9; 36:1; 111:10; Pr 1:7; Ecc 3:14; 12:13; 2Co 5:11 **23:16** [x]S Dt 20:3 [y]Job 27:2 [z]S Ex 3:6; Rev 6:16 **23:17** [a]S Job 3:6; S 19:8 **24:1** [b]S Job 14:5 [c]S Job 9:23; 2Pe 3:7

[v]2 Septuagint and Syriac; Hebrew / *the hand on me*
[w]2 Or *heavy on me in*

---

to return to God so his prosperity would be restored. He assumed mistakenly that physical and material prosperity would come from repentance. Compare 34:31–33; 36:10. Job's friend was mistaken. Salvation does not always bring material wealth. See note on 16:17.

23:12 CHRISTIAN ETHICS, Moral Imperatives—To identify God's commandments is not enough. The transition of character they can bring begins when one feeds upon them and finds sustenance for one's soul from them. They must become our greatest treasure even in dark days of suffering.

23:13–16 GOD, Justice—Job did not understand why his troubles had come upon him, but he trusted in the sovereignty and justice of God. He wanted his appointed time for a legal hearing with God so that divine justice could be established and understood. This highlights a major issue related to divine justice. Humans do not have sufficient knowledge or live long enough to see justice worked out in life. Only at the final judgment will we fully see God establish His justice in His world. Until then the power of Satan and the effects of human sin prevent us from enjoying justice. As with Job, people do suffer unjustly. See notes on 1:21–22; 9:2–35.

24:1,12 GOD, Justice—Job wondered why God did not move more swiftly in bringing judgment upon evildoers. Job was confident that God is just, but wondered why God sometimes delays His justice. This is an understandable question for one who was suffering as Job was, especially in the light of the accusations his "friends" were making against him. See note on 23:13–16.

Why must those who know him look
in vain for such days?[d]
2Men move boundary stones;[e]
they pasture flocks they have
stolen.[f]
3They drive away the orphan's donkey
and take the widow's ox in pledge.[g]
4They thrust the needy[h] from the path
and force all the poor[i] of the land
into hiding.[j]
5Like wild donkeys[k] in the desert,
the poor go about their labor[l] of
foraging food;
the wasteland[m] provides food for
their children.
6They gather fodder[n] in the fields
and glean in the vineyards[o] of the
wicked.[p]
7Lacking clothes, they spend the night
naked;
they have nothing to cover
themselves in the cold.[q]
8They are drenched[r] by mountain rains
and hug[s] the rocks for lack of
shelter.[t]
9The fatherless[u] child is snatched[v]
from the breast;
the infant of the poor is seized[w] for
a debt.[x]
10Lacking clothes, they go about naked;[y]
they carry the sheaves,[z] but still go
hungry.
11They crush olives among the
terraces[x];
they tread the winepresses,[a] yet
suffer thirst.[b]
12The groans of the dying rise from the
city,
and the souls of the wounded cry
out for help.[c]
But God charges no one with
wrongdoing.[d]

13"There are those who rebel against the
light,[e]
who do not know its ways
or stay in its paths.[f]
14When daylight is gone, the murderer
rises up
and kills[g] the poor and needy;[h]
in the night he steals forth like a
thief.[i]
15The eye of the adulterer[j] watches for
dusk;[k]
he thinks, 'No eye will see me,'[l]
and he keeps his face concealed.
16In the dark, men break into houses,[m]
but by day they shut themselves in;
they want nothing to do with the
light.[n]

24:1 [d]S Job 15:20; Ac 1:7 **24:2** [e]S Dt 19:14 [f]Ex 20:15; Dt 28:31 **24:3** [g]S Job 6:27; S 22:9 **24:4** [h]Job 29:16; 31:19 [i]Job 29:12; 30:25; Ps 12:5; 41:1; 82:3,4; Isa 11:4 [j]S Job 20:19; S Pr 28:12 **24:5** [k]S Ge 16:12 [l]Ps 104:23 [m]Job 30:3 **24:6** [n]S Job 6:5 [o]ver 18 [p]Ru 2:22; S 1Ki 21:19 **24:7** [q]S Ex 22:27 **24:8** [r]Da 4:25,33 [s]La 4:5 [t]S Jdg 6:2 **24:9** [u]S Dt 24:17 [v]Job 29:17 [w]Ps 14:4; Pr 30:14; Isa 3:14; 10:1-2; Eze 18:12 [x]S Lev 25:47; S 2Ki 4:1 **24:10** [y]Dt 24:12-13 [z]S Lev 19:9 **24:11** [a]Isa 5:2; 16:10; Hag 2:16 [b]Mic 6:15 **24:12** [c]S Job 12:19; 30:28; Ps 5:2; 22:24; 39:12; 119:147; Isa 30:19; Jer 50:46; 51:52, 54; Eze 26:15; Rev 6:10 [d]S Job 9:23 **24:13** [e]ver 16; Job 38:15; Jn 3:19-20; 1Th 5:4-5 [f]Job 17:12; 38:20; Ps 18:28; Isa 5:20; Eph 5:8-14 **24:14** [g]Isa 3:15; Mic 3:3 [h]S Job 20:19; Ps 37:32 [i]Ps 10:9 **24:15** [j]Job 31:9,27; Pr 1:10 [k]Pr 7:8-9 [l]Ps 10:11 **24:16** [m]S Ex 22:2; Mt 6:19 [n]S ver 13 **24:17** [o]S Job 18:11 [p]S Job 15:22; S 18:5 **24:18** [q]S Job 9:26; Jude 1:13 [r]Job 22:16; Isa 57:20 [s]S Job 5:3 [t]ver 6 **24:19** [u]Job 6:17 [v]S Job 21:13 **24:20** [w]S Job 7:5 [x]S Job 21:26 [y]S Job 18:17 [z]S Job 14:7; Ps 31:12; Da 4:14 **24:21** [a]S Job 22:9 **24:22** [b]S Job 9:4 [c]S Job 12:19 [d]Dt 28:66; Mt 6:27; Jas 4:14 **24:23** [e]S Job 9:24; Am 6:1 [f]S 2Ch 16:9 [g]S Job 10:4 **24:24** [h]S 2Ki 19:35; S Job 4:20; Ps 37:10; 83:13; Isa 5:24; 17:13; 40:24; 41:2,15 [i]S Job 3:19 [j]Isa 17:5 **24:25** [k]S Job 6:28;

17For all of them, deep darkness is their
morning[y];
they make friends with the terrors[o]
of darkness.[z] [p]
18"Yet they are foam[q] on the surface of
the water;[r]
their portion of the land is cursed,[s]
so that no one goes to the
vineyards.[t]
19As heat and drought snatch away the
melted snow,[u]
so the grave[a] [v] snatches away those
who have sinned.
20The womb forgets them,
the worm[w] feasts on them;[x]
evil men are no longer remembered[y]
but are broken like a tree.[z]
21They prey on the barren and childless
woman,
and to the widow show no
kindness.[a]
22But God drags away the mighty by his
power;[b]
though they become established,[c]
they have no assurance of
life.[d]
23He may let them rest in a feeling of
security,[e]
but his eyes[f] are on their ways.[g]
24For a little while they are exalted, and
then they are gone;[h]
they are brought low and gathered
up like all others;[i]
they are cut off like heads of grain.[j]

25"If this is not so, who can prove me
false
and reduce my words to nothing?"[k]

Chapter 25

Bildad

THEN Bildad the Shuhite[l] replied:
2"Dominion and awe belong to
God;[m]
he establishes order in the heights of
heaven.[n]
3Can his forces be numbered?
Upon whom does his light not
rise?[o]
4How then can a man be righteous
before God?

S 16:17 **25:1** [l]S Job 8:1 **25:2** [m]S Job 9:4; Ps 47:9; 89:18; Zec 9:7; Rev 1:6 [n]S 2Ch 20:6; S Job 11:8; S 16:19 **25:3** [o]Mt 5:45; Jas 1:17

[x]*11* Or *olives between the millstones*; the meaning of the Hebrew for this word is uncertain. [y]*17* Or *them, their morning is like the shadow of death* [z]*17* Or *of the shadow of death* [a]*19* Hebrew *Sheol*

25:1–6 GOD, Transcendent—God is so great, so high and lifted up, so holy that every human is but a worm by contrast. See note on 23:13–16.

25:4–6 HUMANITY, Human Nature—A basic contrast between people and God is human sinfulness. The difference between us and God can make us appear to be no more significant than a worm. God's love and grace give us significance. See Ps 8.

How can one born of woman be
pure?[p]
5If even the moon[q] is not bright
and the stars are not pure in his
eyes,[r]
6how much less man, who is but a
maggot—
a son of man,[s] who is only a
worm!"[t]

Chapter 26

Job

THEN Job replied:
2"How you have helped the
powerless![u]
How you have saved the arm that is
feeble![v]
3What advice you have offered to one
without wisdom!
And what great insight[w] you have
displayed!
4Who has helped you utter these
words?
And whose spirit spoke from your
mouth?[x]

5"The dead are in deep anguish,[y]
those beneath the waters and all
that live in them.
6Death[b][z] is naked before God;
Destruction[c][a] lies uncovered.[b]
7He spreads out the northern ⌊skies⌋[c]
over empty space;
he suspends the earth over
nothing.[d]
8He wraps up the waters[e] in his
clouds,[f]
yet the clouds do not burst under
their weight.
9He covers the face of the full moon,
spreading his clouds[g] over it.
10He marks out the horizon on the face
of the waters[h]
for a boundary between light and
darkness.[i]
11The pillars of the heavens quake,[j]
aghast at his rebuke.
12By his power he churned up the sea;[k]
by his wisdom[l] he cut Rahab[m] to
pieces.
13By his breath the skies[n] became fair;
his hand pierced the gliding
serpent.[o]
14And these are but the outer fringe of
his works;
how faint the whisper[p] we hear of
him![q]
Who then can understand the
thunder of his power?"[r]

Chapter 27

AND Job continued his discourse:[s]
2"As surely as God lives, who has
denied me justice,[t]
the Almighty,[u] who has made me
taste bitterness of soul,[v]
3as long as I have life within me,
the breath of God[w] in my nostrils,
4my lips will not speak wickedness,
and my tongue will utter no deceit.[x]
5I will never admit you are in the right;
till I die, I will not deny my
integrity.[y]
6I will maintain my righteousness[z] and
never let go of it;
my conscience[a] will not reproach
me as long as I live.[b]

7"May my enemies be like the
wicked,[c]
my adversaries[d] like the unjust!
8For what hope has the godless[e] when
he is cut off,
when God takes away his life?[f]

25:4 [p]S Job 4:17
25:5 [q]Job 31:26 [r]S Job 4:18
25:6 [s]Ps 80:17; 144:3; Eze 2:1 [t]S Job 4:19; S 7:5
26:2 [u]Job 6:12 [v]S Job 4:3
26:3 [w]Job 34:35
26:4 [x]1Ki 22:24
26:5 [y]Ps 88:10; Isa 14:9; 26:14
26:6 [z]Ps 139:8 [a]S Job 20:26; S Rev 9:11 [b]Job 10:22; 11:8; 38:17; 41:11; Ps 139:11-12; Pr 15:11; S Heb 4:13
26:7 [c]Job 9:8 [d]Job 38:6; Ps 104:5; Pr 3:19-20; 8:27; Isa 40:22
26:8 [e]Pr 30:4 [f]S Ge 1:2; Job 36:27; 37:11; Ps 147:8
26:9 [g]S 2Sa 22:10; S Job 22:14
26:10 [h]Pr 8:27,29; Isa 40:22 [i]S Ge 1:4; S Job 28:3; 38:8-11
26:11 [j]S 2Sa 22:8
26:12 [k]S Ex 14:21 [l]Job 12:13 [m]S Job 9:13
26:13 [n]Job 9:8 [o]Isa 27:1
26:14 [p]Job 4:12 [q]Job 42:5; Hab 3:2; 1Co 13:12 [r]S Job 9:6
27:1 [s]Job 29:1
27:2 [t]S Job 6:29; S 9:24; Isa 45:9; 49:4,14 [u]Job 23:16 [v]S 1Sa 1:10; S Job 7:19; S 10:1
27:3 [w]S Ge 2:7; Job 32:8; 33:4; 34:14; S Ps 144:4
27:4 [x]S Job 6:28; S 12:16; S 16:17
27:5 [y]S Job 2:9; S 10:7; S 32:2
27:6 [z]Job 29:14; Ps 119:121; 132:9; Isa 59:17; 61:10 [a]S Ac 23:1; Ro 2:15 [b]S Job 2:3; S 10:7; S 23:10; S 34:17
27:7 [c]S Job 8:22 [d]Job 31:35
27:8 [e]S Job 8:13 [f]S Nu 16:22; S Job 8:22; S 11:20; Lk 12:20

[b]6 Hebrew *Sheol* [c]6 Hebrew *Abaddon*

26:5 LAST THINGS, Intermediate State—See note on Isa 14:9.

26:6–14 GOD, Sovereignty—Job understood that God is sovereign and just, but he did not understand why God's justice was so slow in coming to him. Of course, Job did not know Satan was testing him with God's permission. God knew Job would remain faithful to Him no matter what happened. See notes on 1:21–22; 5:8–16; 23:13–16.

26:6 HUMANITY, Nature of Death—The Hebrew word here is *Sheol*, normally understood to refer to the grave, the abode of the dead. In human experience, a person who is dead is lost to human vision; no one sees such a person after burial. God is not so limited. He knows us before we are born (Jer 1:5) and after we die. In Jesus Christ He provides the way to life beyond the grave.

26:12–13 EVIL AND SUFFERING, Satan—The Bible uses many terms and names from different sources to describe evil powers who fight against God. Apparently Israel knew a story told by her neighbors in which Rahab was a monster representing and controlling the chaotic forces opposed to creation of the world. In creation the monster was cut in two to form heaven and earth. Job used the well-known understanding to picture God's power over all evil powers which oppose Him. Another name for the monster was the serpent or Leviathan. Compare 3:8; 9:13; 41:1; Ps 74:14; 89:10; 104:26; Isa 27:1; 51:9. Eventually Rahab became a symbol for the wicked pride of Egypt (Ps 87:4; Isa 30:7).

27:2,11–23 GOD, Justice—Job did not understand his sufferings and why God had not acted to defend him. Still he maintained great confidence in the justice of God. He refused to accept the conclusion of his "friends" that he was a horrible sinner getting his just deserts. Job decided he had only one course of action in face of divine silence. He would live with integrity so no one could actually point to specific sins in his life. God's justice may not always be self-evident in individual lives. The proper response is dialog with God and moral purity before people. See notes on 5:8–16; 23:13–16.

27:3 HUMANITY, Life—Life is always considered to be the gift of God. It comes through the breath of God within. See Ge 2:7.

27:4 CHRISTIAN ETHICS, Language—Job's discipline of his tongue exemplifies a profound test of character. We all need to be able to echo his testimony.

9 Does God listen to his cry
when distress comes upon him?[g]
10 Will he find delight in the Almighty?[h]
Will he call upon God at all times?

11 "I will teach you about the power of God;
the ways[i] of the Almighty I will not conceal.[j]
12 You have all seen this yourselves.
Why then this meaningless talk?

13 "Here is the fate God allots to the wicked,
the heritage a ruthless man receives from the Almighty:[k]
14 However many his children,[l] their fate is the sword;[m]
his offspring will never have enough to eat.[n]
15 The plague will bury those who survive him,
and their widows will not weep for them.[o]
16 Though he heaps up silver like dust[p]
and clothes like piles of clay,[q]
17 what he lays up[r] the righteous will wear,[s]
and the innocent will divide his silver.[t]
18 The house[u] he builds is like a moth's cocoon,[v]
like a hut[w] made by a watchman.
19 He lies down wealthy, but will do so no more;[x]
when he opens his eyes, all is gone.[y]
20 Terrors[z] overtake him like a flood;[a]
a tempest snatches him away in the night.[b]
21 The east wind[c] carries him off, and he is gone;[d]
it sweeps him out of his place.[e]
22 It hurls itself against him without mercy[f]
as he flees headlong[g] from its power.[h]
23 It claps its hands[i] in derision
and hisses him out of his place.[j]

Chapter 28

28 "THERE is a mine for silver
and a place where gold is refined.[k]
2 Iron is taken from the earth,
and copper is smelted from ore.[l]
3 Man puts an end to the darkness;[m]
he searches the farthest recesses
for ore in the blackest darkness.[n]
4 Far from where people dwell he cuts a shaft,[o]
in places forgotten by the foot of man;
far from men he dangles and sways.
5 The earth, from which food comes,[p]
is transformed below as by fire;
6 sapphires[d][q] come from its rocks,
and its dust contains nuggets of gold.[r]
7 No bird of prey knows that hidden path,
no falcon's eye has seen it.[s]
8 Proud beasts[t] do not set foot on it,
and no lion prowls there.[u]
9 Man's hand assaults the flinty rock[v]
and lays bare the roots of the mountains.[w]
10 He tunnels through the rock;[x]
his eyes see all its treasures.[y]
11 He searches[e] the sources of the rivers[z]
and brings hidden things[a] to light.

12 "But where can wisdom be found?[b]
Where does understanding dwell?[c]
13 Man does not comprehend its worth;[d]
it cannot be found in the land of the living.[e]
14 The deep[f] says, 'It is not in me';
the sea[g] says, 'It is not with me.'
15 It cannot be bought with the finest gold,
nor can its price be weighed in silver.[h]
16 It cannot be bought with the gold of Ophir,[i]
with precious onyx or sapphires.[j]
17 Neither gold nor crystal can compare with it,[k]
nor can it be had for jewels of gold.[l]
18 Coral[m] and jasper[n] are not worthy of mention;

27:9 [g]S Dt 1:45; S 1Sa 8:18; S Job 15:31 **27:10** [h]S Job 22:26 **27:11** [i]Job 36:23 [j]ver 13 **27:13** [k]S Job 16:19; S 20:29 **27:14** [l]S Job 5:4 [m]S Job 15:22; S La 2:22 [n]S Job 4:11 **27:15** [o]Ps 78:64 **27:16** [p]S 1Ki 10:27 [q]Zec 9:3 **27:17** [r]Ps 39:6; 49:10; Ecc 2:26 [s]S Job 7:8; Pr 13:22; 28:8; Ecc 2:26 [t]Ex 3:22; S Job 3:15 **27:18** [u]S Job 8:22 [v]S Job 8:14 [w]Isa 1:8; 24:20 **27:19** [x]S Job 3:13; S 7:8 [y]S Job 14:20 **27:20** [z]S Job 6:4 [a]S Job 15:21 [b]S Job 20:8 **27:21** [c]Job 38:24; Jer 13:24; 22:22 [d]Job 30:22 [e]S Job 7:10 **27:22** [f]Jer 13:14; Eze 5:11; 24:14 [g]2Ki 7:15 [h]S Job 11:20 **27:23** [i]S Nu 24:10; Na 3:19 [j]S Job 7:10 **28:1** [k]Ps 12:6; 66:10; Jer 9:7; Da 11:35; Mal 3:3 **28:2** [l]Dt 8:9 **28:3** [m]Ecc 1:13; 7:25; 8:17 [n]S Job 26:10; 38:19 **28:4** [o]ver 10; 2Sa 5:8 **28:5** [p]Ge 1:29; Ps 104:14; 145:15 **28:6** [q]ver 16; SS 5:14; Isa 54:11 [r]S Job 22:24 **28:7** [s]ver 21 **28:8** [t]Job 41:34 [u]Isa 35:9 **28:9** [v]S Dt 8:15 [w]Jnh 2:6 **28:10** [x]S ver 4 [y]Pr 2:4 **28:11** [z]S Ge 7:11 [a]Isa 48:6; Jer 33:3 **28:12** [b]ver 28; Pr 1:20; 3:13-20; 8:1; 9:1-3; Ecc 7:24 [c]ver 20,23 **28:13** [d]Pr 3:15; Mt 13:44-46 [e]Dt 29:29; Ps 27:13; 52:5; 116:9; 142:5; Isa 38:11; Jer 11:19; Eze 26:20; 32:24 **28:14** [f]Ps 42:7; Ro 10:7 [g]Dt 30:13 **28:15** [h]ver 17; Pr 3:13-14; 8:10-11; 16:16; Ac 8:20 **28:16** [i]S Ge 10:29 [j]S ver 6; S Ex 24:10 **28:17** [k]Ps 119:72; Pr 8:10 [l]S ver 15 **28:18** [m]Eze 27:16 [n]Rev 21:11

[d]6 Or *lapis lazuli*; also in verse 16 [e]11 Septuagint, Aquila and Vulgate; Hebrew *He dams up*

28:1–28 GOD, Wisdom—Job praised the wisdom of God, contrasting it to human achievements. God towers over humans in His infinite wisdom. We are unable to share His wisdom. Thus we cannot answer the deep questions Job raised concerning God's justice in individual cases such as Job's. Only God knows such answers. He knows what He is doing in His world. Our best wisdom is to fear and to reverence God. We must trust His wisdom when our search for answers fails. See note on 23:13–16.

28:1–28 HUMANITY, Potentiality—The catalog of human accomplishments staggers the imagination. Yet, thorough and sober examination clearly reveals that even with all our accomplishments, our basic lack is the wisdom which comes only from God. Using the wisdom He gives us, we expand the limits of human knowledge. As we do so, we need to offer Him praise for giving us the potential to accomplish what we have accomplished.

28:12–28 EVIL AND SUFFERING, Humility—Job testified to God's infinite wisdom and the need for human humility. Human wisdom appears as we learn to reverence God and to stay away from evil actions and attitudes. Only God in His unmatched wisdom can truly determine what is evil.

the price of wisdom is beyond
rubies.[o]
19The topaz[p] of Cush[q] cannot compare
with it;
it cannot be bought with pure
gold.[r]

20"Where then does wisdom come from?
Where does understanding dwell?[s]
21It is hidden from the eyes of every
living thing,
concealed even from the birds of the
air.[t]
22Destruction[f][u] and Death[v] say,
'Only a rumor of it has reached our
ears.'
23God understands the way to it
and he alone[w] knows where it
dwells,[x]
24for he views the ends of the earth[y]
and sees everything under the
heavens.[z]
25When he established the force of the
wind
and measured out the waters,[a]
26when he made a decree for the rain[b]
and a path for the thunderstorm,[c]
27then he looked at wisdom and
appraised it;
he confirmed it and tested it.[d]
28And he said to man,
'The fear of the Lord—that is
wisdom,
and to shun evil[e] is
understanding.[f]' "

Chapter 29

JOB continued his discourse:[g]

2"How I long for the months gone
by,[h]
for the days when God watched over
me,[i]
3when his lamp shone upon my head
and by his light I walked through
darkness![j]
4Oh, for the days when I was in my
prime,
when God's intimate friendship[k]
blessed my house,[l]
5when the Almighty was still with me
and my children[m] were around
me,[n]
6when my path was drenched with
cream[o]
and the rock[p] poured out for me
streams of olive oil.[q]

7"When I went to the gate[r] of the city
and took my seat in the public
square,
8the young men saw me and stepped
aside[s]
and the old men rose to their feet;[t]
9the chief men refrained from
speaking[u]
and covered their mouths with their
hands;[v]
10the voices of the nobles were
hushed,[w]
and their tongues stuck to the roof
of their mouths.[x]
11Whoever heard me spoke well of me,
and those who saw me commended
me,[y]
12because I rescued the poor[z] who cried
for help,
and the fatherless[a] who had none to
assist him.[b]
13The man who was dying blessed me;[c]
I made the widow's[d] heart sing.
14I put on righteousness[e] as my
clothing;
justice was my robe and my
turban.[f]
15I was eyes[g] to the blind
and feet to the lame.[h]
16I was a father to the needy;[i]
I took up the case[j] of the stranger.[k]
17I broke the fangs of the wicked
and snatched the victims[l] from
their teeth.[m]

18"I thought, 'I will die in my own
house,
my days as numerous as the grains
of sand.[n]
19My roots will reach to the water,[o]
and the dew will lie all night on my
branches.[p]
20My glory will remain fresh[q] in me,
the bow[r] ever new in my hand.'[s]

21"Men listened to me expectantly,
waiting in silence for my counsel.[t]
22After I had spoken, they spoke no
more;[u]
my words fell gently on their ears.[v]
23They waited for me as for showers
and drank in my words as the spring
rain.[w]
24When I smiled at them, they scarcely
believed it;

28:18 [o]Pr 3:15; 8:11 **28:19** [p]Ex 28:17 [q]Isa 11:11 [r]Pr 3:14-15; 8:10-11,19 **28:20** [s]S Job 9:4 **28:21** [t]ver 7 **28:22** [u]S Job 20:26; S Rev 9:11 [v]Pr 8:32-36 **28:23** [w]Ecc 3:11; 8:17 [x]S Job 9:4; S 22:22; Pr 8:22-31 **28:24** [y]Job 36:32; 37:3; 38:18,24,35; Ps 33:13-14; 66:7; Isa 11:12 [z]S Jos 3:11; S Job 10:4; S Heb 4:13 **28:25** [a]S Job 12:15; 38:8-11 **28:26** [b]Job 36:28; 37:6; Jer 51:16 [c]Job 36:33; 37:3,8, 11; 38:25,27; Ps 65:12; 104:14; 147:8; Isa 35:7 **28:27** [d]Pr 3:19; 8:22-31 **28:28** [e]Ps 11:5; 97:10; Pr 3:7; 8:13 [f]S Ex 20:20; S Dt 4:6; S Job 37:24 **29:1** [g]Job 27:1 **29:2** [h]S Ge 31:30 [i]Jer 1:12; 31:28; 44:27 **29:3** [j]S Job 11:17; S 12:25 **29:4** [k]S Job 15:8 [l]Ps 25:14; Pr 3:32 **29:5** [m]Ps 127:3-5; 128:3 [n]Ru 4:1 **29:6** [o]S Job 20:17 [p]Ps 81:16 [q]Ge 49:20; S Dt 32:13 **29:7** [r]ver 21; Job 5:4; 31:21; Jer 20:2; 38:7 **29:8** [s]1Ti 5:1 [t]S Lev 19:32 **29:9** [u]ver 21; Job 31:21 [v]S Jdg 18:19; Job 40:4; Pr 30:32 **29:10** [w]ver 22 [x]Ps 137:6 **29:11** [y]S Job 4:4; Heb 11:4 **29:12** [z]S Job 24:4 [a]S Dt 24:17; Job 31:17,21 [b]Ps 72:12; Pr 21:13 **29:13** [c]Job 31:20 [d]S Dt 10:18; S Job 22:9 **29:14** [e]S 2Sa 8:15; S Job 27:6; Eph 4:24; 6:14 [f]S Job 19:9 **29:15** [g]Nu 10:31 [h]S Job 4:4 **29:16** [i]S Job 24:4 [j]Ex 18:26 [k]S Job 4:4; Pr 22:22-23 **29:17** [l]Job 24:9 [m]S Job 4:10,11; S Ps 3:7 **29:18** [n]Ps 1:1-3; 15:5; 16:8; 30:6; 62:2; 139:18; Pr 3:1-2 **29:19** [o]S Nu 24:6; S Job 14:9 [p]S Ge 27:8; S Job 15:30; S Ps 133:3 **29:20** [q]Ps 92:14 [r]Job 30:11; Ps 18:34; Isa 38:12 [s]Ge 49:24 **29:21** [t]S ver 7,S 9 **29:22** [u]ver 10 [v]Dt 32:2 **29:23** [w]S Job 4:3

[f]22 Hebrew *Abaddon*

28:28 EDUCATION, Wisdom—Wisdom is more than accumulation of information or training in logical thinking. True wisdom is inseparable from knowledge of God, for He is Truth in its ultimate form. Genuine education goes back to the basic sources of knowledge, and the Lord is the fundamental source of all knowledge and wisdom. True wisdom produces a moral life not just an admired mind. See Ps 14:1.

29:12–17 CHRISTIAN ETHICS, Justice—Biblical justice exhibits a bias toward the weak and poor. One who acts upon it will take on the cause of those unable to defend themselves. Job's action challenges us to go beyond superficial compassion to action that attacks suffering and wrong.

the light of my face[x] was precious
to them.[g] [y]
25I chose the way for them and sat as
their chief;[z]
I dwelt as a king[a] among his troops;
I was like one who comforts
mourners.[b]

Chapter 30

"BUT now they mock me,[c]
men younger than I,
whose fathers I would have disdained
to put with my sheep dogs.[d]
2Of what use was the strength of their
hands to me,
since their vigor had gone from
them?
3Haggard from want and hunger,
they roamed[h] the parched land[e]
in desolate wastelands[f] at night.[g]
4In the brush they gathered salt herbs,[h]
and their food[i] was the root of the
broom tree.[i]
5They were banished from their fellow
men,
shouted at as if they were thieves.
6They were forced to live in the dry
stream beds,
among the rocks and in holes in the
ground.[j]
7They brayed[k] among the bushes[l]
and huddled in the undergrowth.
8A base and nameless brood,[m]
they were driven out of the land.[n]

9"And now their sons mock me[o] in
song;[p]
I have become a byword[q] among
them.
10They detest me[r] and keep their
distance;
they do not hesitate to spit in my
face.[s]
11Now that God has unstrung my bow[t]
and afflicted me,[u]
they throw off restraint[v] in my
presence.
12On my right[w] the tribe[j] attacks;
they lay snares[x] for my feet,[y]
they build their siege ramps against
me.[z]
13They break up my road;[a]
they succeed in destroying me[b]—
without anyone's helping them.[k]
14They advance as through a gaping
breach;[c]
amid the ruins they come rolling in.
15Terrors[d] overwhelm me;[e]
my dignity is driven away as by the
wind,
my safety vanishes like a cloud.[f]

16"And now my life ebbs away;[g]
days of suffering grip me.[h]
17Night pierces my bones;
my gnawing pains never rest.[i]
18In his great power[j] ⌞God⌟ becomes like
clothing to me[l];
he binds me like the neck of my
garment.
19He throws me into the mud,[k]
and I am reduced to dust and
ashes.[l]

20"I cry out to you,[m] O God, but you do
not answer;[n]
I stand up, but you merely look at
me.
21You turn on me ruthlessly;[o]
with the might of your hand[p] you
attack me.[q]
22You snatch me up and drive me before
the wind;[r]
you toss me about in the storm.[s]
23I know you will bring me down to
death,[t]
to the place appointed for all the
living.[u]

24"Surely no one lays a hand on a
broken man[v]
when he cries for help in his
distress.[w]
25Have I not wept for those in trouble?[x]
Has not my soul grieved for the
poor?[y]
26Yet when I hoped for good, evil came;
when I looked for light, then came
darkness.[z]
27The churning inside me never stops;[a]
days of suffering confront me.[b]
28I go about blackened,[c] but not by the
sun;
I stand up in the assembly and cry
for help.[d]
29I have become a brother of jackals,[e]
a companion of owls.[f]

29:24 [x]S Nu 6:25 [y]Pr 16:14,15 **29:25** [z]S Job 21:28 [a]S Job 1:3 [b]S Job 4:4 **30:1** [c]S Job 6:14; S 11:3; S Ps 119:21 [d]Isa 56:10 **30:3** [e]Isa 8:21 [f]Job 24:5 [g]Jer 17:6 **30:4** [h]Job 39:6 [i]S 1Ki 19:4 **30:6** [j]Isa 2:19; Hos 10:8 **30:7** [k]Job 6:5 [l]Job 39:5-6 **30:8** [m]S Jdg 9:4 [n]S Job 18:18 **30:9** [o]S Job 16:10; Ps 69:11 [p]Job 12:4; La 3:14,63 [q]S Job 17:6 **30:10** [r]Job 19:19 [s]S Dt 25:9; Mt 26:67 **30:11** [t]S Job 29:20 [u]S Ge 12:17; S Ru 1:21 [v]Job 41:13; Ps 32:9 **30:12** [w]Ps 109:6; Zec 3:1 [x]S Job 18:9 [y]Ps 140:4-5 [z]S Job 16:10 **30:13** [a]Isa 3:12 [b]S Job 10:3 **30:14** [c]S 2Ki 25:4 **30:15** [d]S Job 6:4 [e]S Ex 3:6; Job 10:8; 31:2-3,23; Ps 55:4-5 [f]S Job 3:25 **30:16** [g]S Job 3:24 [h]ver 27; S Job 9:17 **30:17** [i]S Dt 28:35; S Job 16:16 **30:18** [j]S Job 9:4 **30:19** [k]Ps 40:2; 69:2,14; 130:1; Jer 38:6,22 [l]S Ge 3:19; S Job 2:8 **30:20** [m]S 1Ki 8:52; Ps 34:17; Pr 2:3; Mic 4:9 [n]S Job 19:7; La 3:8 **30:21** [o]Jer 6:23; 30:14; 50:42 [p]Isa 9:12; 14:26; 31:3; Eze 6:14 [q]S Job 4:5; S 6:4; S 10:3 **30:22** [r]Job 27:21; Jude 1:12 [s]S Job 9:17 **30:23** [t]S 2Sa 14:14; S Job 3:13; S 10:3 [u]S Job 3:19 **30:24** [v]Ps 145:14; Isa 42:3; 57:15 [w]S Job 19:7 **30:25** [x]Lk 19:41; Php 3:18 [y]S Job 24:4; Ps 35:13-14; Ro 12:15 **30:26** [z]S Job 3:6, 17; S 19:8; S Ps 82:5; S Jer 4:23 **30:27** [a]Ps 38:8; La 2:11 [b]S ver 16 **30:28** [c]S Job 17:14; La 4:8 [d]S Job 19:7; S 24:12 **30:29** [e]Ps 44:19; Isa 34:13; Jer 9:11 [f]Ps 102:6; Mic 1:8

[g]*24* The meaning of the Hebrew for this clause is uncertain. [h]*3* Or *gnawed* [i]*4* Or *fuel* [j]*12* The meaning of the Hebrew for this word is uncertain. [k]*13* Or *me. / 'No one can help him,' ⌞they say⌟.* [l]*18* Hebrew; Septuagint *⌞God⌟ grasps my clothing*

30:11–31 EVIL AND SUFFERING, Divine Origin—Job knew that ultimately God was responsible for his troubles. Job's hopes were not enough. See note on 19:23–29. He still faced evil days in all their ugliness. The greatest pain came from God's refusal to answer. Still Job faithfully sought an answer. No theological or philosophical trickery can avoid the truth that God permits righteous people to suffer when He has the power to prevent it. We must endure suffering and seek God's purposes in it. We must maintain faith in God even when answers do not come.

30:23 HUMANITY, Nature of Death—Death is just as much in God's hands as life is. The difference in humans is in our attitude toward our death. Job was correct to affirm God's sovereign control over death. We need to learn to trust God through all life's experiences, even that of approaching death.

[30]My skin grows black[g] and peels;[h]
my body burns with fever.[i]
[31]My harp is tuned to mourning,[j]
and my flute[k] to the sound of
wailing.

Chapter 31

"I made a covenant with my eyes[l]
not to look lustfully at a girl.[m]
[2]For what is man's lot[n] from God
above,
his heritage from the Almighty on
high?[o]
[3]Is it not ruin[p] for the wicked,
disaster[q] for those who do wrong?[r]
[4]Does he not see my ways[s]
and count my every step?[t]
[5]"If I have walked in falsehood
or my foot has hurried after
deceit[u] —
[6]let God weigh me[v] in honest scales[w]
and he will know that I am
blameless[x] —
[7]if my steps have turned from the
path,[y]
if my heart has been led by my eyes,
or if my hands[z] have been defiled,[a]
[8]then may others eat what I have
sown,[b]
and may my crops be uprooted.[c]
[9]"If my heart has been enticed[d] by a
woman,[e]
or if I have lurked at my neighbor's
door,
[10]then may my wife grind[f] another
man's grain,
and may other men sleep with her.[g]
[11]For that would have been shameful,[h]
a sin to be judged.[i]
[12]It is a fire[j] that burns to
Destruction[m];[k]
it would have uprooted my
harvest.[l]
[13]"If I have denied justice to my
menservants and
maidservants[m]
when they had a grievance against
me,[n]
[14]what will I do when God confronts
me?[o]
What will I answer when called to
account?[p]
[15]Did not he who made me in the womb
make them?[q]
Did not the same one form us both
within our mothers?[r]
[16]"If I have denied the desires of the
poor[s]
or let the eyes of the widow[t] grow
weary,[u]
[17]if I have kept my bread to myself,
not sharing it with the fatherless[v] —
[18]but from my youth I reared him as
would a father,
and from my birth I guided the
widow[w] —
[19]if I have seen anyone perishing for lack
of clothing,[x]
or a needy[y] man without a garment,
[20]and his heart did not bless me[z]
for warming him with the fleece[a]
from my sheep,
[21]if I have raised my hand against the
fatherless,[b]
knowing that I had influence in
court,[c]
[22]then let my arm fall from the shoulder,
let it be broken off at the joint.[d]
[23]For I dreaded destruction from God,[e]
and for fear of his splendor[f] I could
not do such things.[g]
[24]"If I have put my trust in gold[h]
or said to pure gold, 'You are my
security,'[i]
[25]if I have rejoiced over my great
wealth,[j]
the fortune my hands had gained,[k]

30:30 [g]S Job 17:14 [h]La 3:4; 4:8 [i]S Dt 28:35; S Job 16:16; Ps 102:3; La 1:13; 5:10 **30:31** [j]S Ge 8:8; Ps 137:2; Isa 16:11; 24:8; Eze 26:13 [k]S Ge 4:21 **31:1** [l]Pr 4:25; 17:24; 2Pe 2:14 [m]Ex 20:14,17; Dt 5:18; Mt 5:28 **31:2** [n]Nu 26:55; Ps 11:6; 16:5; 50:18; Ecc 3:22; 5:19; 9:9 [o]S Job 16:19; S 20:29 **31:3** [p]S Job 21:30 [q]Job 18:12 [r]Job 34:22; Ro 2:9 **31:4** [s]2Ch 16:9; Ps 139:3; Da 4:37; 5:23 [t]S ver 14; S Job 10:4 **31:5** [u]S Job 15:31 **31:6** [v]Ps 139:23 [w]S Lev 19:36; S Job 6:2 [x]S Ge 6:9; S Job 2:3; S 23:10 **31:7** [y]S Job 23:11 [z]S Job 9:30 [a]Ps 7:3 **31:8** [b]S Job 5:5; S 20:10; Jn 4:37 [c]ver 12; Mic 6:15 **31:9** [d]S Dt 11:16; S Job 24:15; Jas 1:14 [e]Pr 5:3; 7:5 **31:10** [f]S Jdg 16:21 [g]Dt 28:30 **31:11** [h]Pr 6:32-33 [i]S Ge 38:24; S Ex 21:12; Jn 8:4-5 **31:12** [j]S Job 15:30 [k]S Job 26:6 [l]S ver 8 **31:13** [m]S Dt 5:14 [n]Ex 21:2-11; Lev 25:39-46; Dt 24:14-15 **31:14** [o]Job 33:5 [p]ver 4,37; Ps 10:13, 15; 94:7; Isa 10:3; Jer 5:31; Hos 9:7; Mic 7:4; Col 4:1 **31:15** [q]S Job 4:17; Pr 22:2 [r]S Job 10:3; Eph 6:9 **31:16** [s]S Lev 25:17; S Job 5:16 [t]S Job 22:9; Jas 1:27 [u]Job 22:7 **31:17** [v]S Job 6:27; S 22:7 **31:18** [w]Isa 51:18 **31:19** [x]Job 22:6; Isa 58:7 [y]S Job 24:4 **31:20** [z]Job 29:13 [a]Jdg 6:37

31:21 [b]S Job 22:7; Jas 1:27 [c]S Job 29:7,9 **31:22** [d]Nu 15:30; Job 5:15; 38:15; Ps 10:15; 37:17; 137:5 **31:23** [e]S Job 10:3; S 30:15 [f]Job 13:11 [g]S Ge 20:11 **31:24** [h]S Job 22:25 [i]Mt 6:24; Lk 12:15 **31:25** [j]S Ge 12:16; Ps 49:6; 52:7; 62:10; Isa 10:14 [k]S Job 22:24; Eze 28:5; Lk 12:20-21

[m]*12* Hebrew *Abaddon*

31:1–40 EVIL AND SUFFERING, Punishment—Suffering is no excuse for sin and immorality. Job defended his innocence by mentioning several sins he might have committed but did not. He invited deserved punishment, implying that what he was suffering was not deserved. Thus, he rejected tradition which taught suffering was always a punishment for sin.

31:1–40 CHRISTIAN ETHICS, Character—Integrity of personal character finds its roots in a relationship with God. Job's confession of integrity ranks with the expectations of character given in Ps 15; 24; Isa 1:11–17; Am 5:24; Mic 6:6–8. Job invited specific curses on his life from God if he had committed the sins surveyed. His statement covers virtually every aspect of personality and life: the sexual dimension; the sphere of economics (materialism and daily work); treatment of the needy; attitude toward enemies; responsibility as a steward of creation. The implicit understanding is that his relationship with God shaped his character as well as provided the grounding and energy for living life on such an ethical plane.

31:13–14,21–23 CHRISTIAN ETHICS, Justice—Job realized God would act on any injustice he might commit. It is wrong to oppress the weak or to use personal reputation and influence to manipulate the court system. Short-term gains are not worth the eventual judgment of God. See note on 5:3–7,16.

31:15 HUMANITY, Birth—Birth is the common entrance into life for all people. It comes as the response to the life-giving acts of God. Biologists can explain many of the physical aspects of birth. They cannot explain the miracle of life which God gives.

31:24–28 SIN, Against God—Temptation to false worship comes in two major forms: finding security in material possessions or worshiping part of the created order instead of God. Both are unfaithfulness to God, who is the only Object of worship and the only Source of security.

26 if I have regarded the sun[l] in its
radiance
or the moon[m] moving in splendor,
27 so that my heart was secretly enticed[n]
and my hand offered them a kiss of
homage,[o]
28 then these also would be sins to be
judged,[p]
for I would have been unfaithful to
God on high.[q]

29 "If I have rejoiced at my enemy's
misfortune[r]
or gloated over the trouble that
came to him[s] —
30 I have not allowed my mouth to sin
by invoking a curse against his
life[t] —
31 if the men of my household have never
said,
'Who has not had his fill of Job's
meat?'[u] —
32 but no stranger had to spend the night
in the street,
for my door was always open to the
traveler[v] —
33 if I have concealed[w] my sin as men
do,[n]
by hiding[x] my guilt in my heart
34 because I so feared the crowd[y]
and so dreaded the contempt of the
clans
that I kept silent[z] and would not go
outside

35 ("Oh, that I had someone to hear
me![a]
I sign now my defense—let the
Almighty answer me;
let my accuser[b] put his indictment
in writing.
36 Surely I would wear it on my
shoulder,[c]
I would put it on like a crown.[d]
37 I would give him an account of my
every step;[e]
like a prince[f] I would approach
him.)—

38 "if my land cries out against me[g]
and all its furrows are wet[h] with
tears,
39 if I have devoured its yield without
payment[i]
or broken the spirit of its tenants,[j]

31:26 [l]S Ge 1:16 [m]Job 25:5
31:27 [n]S Dt 11:16; S Job 24:15; Jas 1:14 [o]Jer 8:2; 16:11
31:28 [p]S Ge 38:24; Dt 17:2-7 [q]S Nu 11:20; Eze 8:16
31:29 [r]S Nu 14:1; Ps 35:15; Ob 1:12; Mt 5:44 [s]Pr 17:5; 24:17-18
31:30 [t]Job 5:3; Ro 12:14
31:31 [u]S Job 22:7
31:32 [v]Ge 19:2-3; Jdg 19:20; Mt 25:35; S Ro 12:13
31:33 [w]Ps 32:5; Pr 28:13 [x]S Ge 3:8
31:34 [y]Ex 23:2 [z]Ps 32:3; 39:2
31:35 [a]S Job 9:24; 30:28 [b]Job 27:7
31:36 [c]S Ex 28:12 [d]Job 29:14
31:37 [e]S ver 14; S Job 11:11 [f]S Job 21:28
31:38 [g]S Ge 4:10 [h]Ps 65:10
31:39 [i]S 1Ki 21:19 [j]S Lev 19:13; Jas 5:4
31:40 [k]S Ge 3:18; Mt 13:7 [l]Zep 2:9; Mt 13:26 [m]Ps 72:20; Jer 51:64
32:1 [n]ver 15 [o]S Job 2:3; S 10:7
32:2 [p]S Ge 22:21 [q]ver 1 [r]S Job 13:19; 27:5; 30:21; 35:2
32:3 [s]Job 42:7 [t]ver 12-13 [u]S Job 15:13
32:4 [v]S Lev 19:32
32:6 [w]Job 15:10
32:7 [x]S 1Ch 29:15; S 2Ch 10:6
32:8 [y]ver 18 [z]S Job 27:3 [a]S Job 12:13; S Ps 119:34; Jas 1:5
32:9 [b]1Co 1:26 [c]Ps 119:100 [d]S Job 12:12,20; Lk 2:47; 1Ti 4:12
32:10 [e]Job 33:1,31, 33; 34:2,16; 37:2, 14; Ps 34:11 [f]S Job 5:27
32:12 [g]ver 3
32:13 [h]S Job 4:12; S Ecc 9:11 [i]S Job 11:5

40 then let briers[k] come up instead of
wheat
and weeds[l] instead of barley."

The words of Job are ended.[m]

Chapter 32

Elihu

SO these three men stopped answering
Job,[n] because he was righteous in his
own eyes.[o] 2 But Elihu son of Barakel the
Buzite,[p] of the family of Ram, became
very angry with Job for justifying himself[q] rather than God.[r] 3 He was also angry with the three friends,[s] because they
had found no way to refute Job,[t] and yet
had condemned him.[o][u] 4 Now Elihu had
waited before speaking to Job because
they were older than he.[v] 5 But when he
saw that the three men had nothing more
to say, his anger was aroused.
6 So Elihu son of Barakel the Buzite
said:

"I am young in years,
and you are old;[w]
that is why I was fearful,
not daring to tell you what I know.
7 I thought, 'Age should speak;
advanced years should teach
wisdom.'[x]
8 But it is the spirit[p][y] in a man,
the breath of the Almighty,[z] that
gives him understanding.[a]
9 It is not only the old[q] who are wise,[b]
not only the aged[c] who understand
what is right.[d]

10 "Therefore I say: Listen to me;[e]
I too will tell you what I know.[f]
11 I waited while you spoke,
I listened to your reasoning;
while you were searching for words,
12 I gave you my full attention.
But not one of you has proved
Job wrong;
none of you has answered his
arguments.[g]
13 Do not say, 'We have found wisdom;[h]
let God refute[i] him, not man.'

[n]33 Or *as Adam did* [o]3 Masoretic Text; an ancient Hebrew scribal tradition *Job, and so had condemned God* [p]8 Or *Spirit*; also in verse 18 [q]9 Or *many*; or *great*

31:35–37 GOD, Justice—Job was confident God is just. He was just as confident he had not sinned in such a way as to deserve all his calamities, as his "friends" had claimed. He was prepared to sign an affadavit confirming his innocence. Job wanted an opportunity to present his case to God. He was confident that God in His justice would pronounce him innocent. God's justice, however, does not guarantee us proof for each individual case. Rather God calls on us to trust His justice and to continue to live according to His will. See notes on 5:8–16; 23:13–16; 28:1–28.

32:8 HUMANITY, Intellectual Nature—The same God who gives life also gives wisdom to His people. Biology can provide many insights into the nature of the human brain. Our distinct reasoning advantage over the animals can be explained only as God's creative gift. Just as much as life itself, intellectual attainments come from His grace. Elihu was correct in claiming God can give wisdom and understanding to all people no matter what age. His own claim to possess God's wisdom may be questioned. His implied disrespect for the intellectual maturity of the aged may also be questioned.

14But Job has not marshaled his words
against me,[j]
and I will not answer him with your
arguments.

15"They are dismayed and have no more
to say;
words have failed them.[k]
16Must I wait, now that they are silent,
now that they stand there with no
reply?
17I too will have my say;
I too will tell what I know.[l]
18For I am full of words,
and the spirit[m] within me compels
me;[n]
19inside I am like bottled-up wine,
like new wineskins ready to burst.[o]
20I must speak and find relief;
I must open my lips and reply.[p]
21I will show partiality[q] to no one,[r]
nor will I flatter any man;[s]
22for if I were skilled in flattery,
my Maker[t] would soon take me
away.[u]

Chapter 33

"BUT now, Job, listen[v] to my words;
pay attention to everything I
say.[w]
2I am about to open my mouth;
my words are on the tip of my
tongue.
3My words come from an upright
heart;[x]
my lips sincerely speak what I
know.[y]
4The Spirit[z] of God has made me;[a]
the breath of the Almighty[b] gives
me life.[c]
5Answer me[d] then, if you can;
prepare[e] yourself and confront
me.[f]
6I am just like you before God;[g]
I too have been taken from clay.[h]
7No fear of me should alarm you,
nor should my hand be heavy upon
you.[i]
8"But you have said in my hearing—
I heard the very words—
9'I am pure[j] and without sin;[k]
I am clean and free from guilt.[l]
10Yet God has found fault with me;
he considers me his enemy.[m]
11He fastens my feet in shackles;[n]
he keeps close watch on all my
paths.'[o]

12"But I tell you, in this you are not
right,
for God is greater than man.[p]
13Why do you complain to him[q]
that he answers none of man's
words[r]?[r]
14For God does speak[s]—now one way,
now another[t]—
though man may not perceive it.[u]
15In a dream,[v] in a vision[w] of the
night,[x]
when deep sleep[y] falls on men
as they slumber in their beds,
16he may speak[z] in their ears
and terrify them[a] with warnings,[b]
17to turn man from wrongdoing
and keep him from pride,[c]
18to preserve his soul from the pit,[s] [d]
his life from perishing by the
sword.[t] [e]
19Or a man may be chastened[f] on a bed
of pain[g]
with constant distress in his bones,[h]
20so that his very being finds food[i]
repulsive
and his soul loathes the choicest
meal.[j]
21His flesh wastes away to nothing,

32:14 [j]Job 23:4 **32:15** [k]ver 1 **32:17** [l]S Job 5:27; 33:3; 36:4 **32:18** [m]ver 8 [n]Ac 4:20; 1Co 9:16; 2Co 5:14 **32:19** [o]Jer 20:9; Am 3:8; Mt 9:17 **32:20** [p]S Job 4:2; S Jer 6:11 **32:21** [q]S Lev 19:15; S 2Ch 19:7; S Job 13:10 [r]Mt 22:16 [s]Pr 29:5; 1Th 2:5 **32:22** [t]S Job 4:17; S 9:9 [u]Ps 12:2-4 **33:1** [v]Job 32:10 [w]S Job 6:28; S 13:6 **33:3** [x]1Ki 3:6; Ps 7:10; 11:2; 64:10 [y]S Job 6:28 **33:4** [z]S Ge 1:2 [a]Job 10:3 [b]S Job 27:3 [c]S Nu 16:22; S Job 12:10 **33:5** [d]ver 32 [e]Job 13:18 [f]S Job 31:14 **33:6** [g]Ac 14:15; Jas 5:17 [h]S Job 4:19 **33:7** [i]S Job 9:34; 2Co 2:4 **33:9** [j]S Job 10:7 [k]S Job 9:30; S 13:23 [l]S Job 2:9 **33:10** [m]S Job 13:24 **33:11** [n]S Job 13:27 [o]Job 14:16; Pr 3:6; Isa 30:21 **33:12** [p]S Job 5:9; Ps 8:4; 50:21; Ecc 7:20; Isa 55:8-9 **33:13** [q]Job 40:2; Isa 45:9 [r]S Job 11:8 **33:14** [s]Ps 62:11 [t]ver 29 [u]Job 4:12 **33:15** [v]S Ge 20:3; Job 4:13; S Mt 27:19 [w]Ac 16:9 [x]S Ge 15:1; Da 2:19 [y]S Ge 2:21 **33:16** [z]Job 36:10, 15 [a]S Job 6:4 [b]Ps 88:15-16 **33:17** [c]S Job 20:6 **33:18** [d]ver 22,24, 28,30; Ps 28:1; 30:9; 69:15; 88:6; 103:4; Pr 1:12; Isa 14:15; 38:17; Jnh 2:6; Zec 9:11 [e]S Job 15:22; Mt 26:52 **33:19** [f]S Job 5:17 [g]S Ge 17:1; S Dt 8:5; 2Co 12:7-10; Jas 1:3 [h]S Job 16:16; Ps 6:2; 38:3; Isa 38:13 **33:20** [i]Ps 102:4; 107:18 [j]S Job 3:24; S 6:6

[r] 13 Or *that he does not answer for any of his actions*
[s] 18 Or *preserve him from the grave*
[t] 18 Or *from crossing the River*

33:1–4 HOLY SPIRIT, Creation—God's Spirit creates our life. Even the feisty, arrogant Elihu was correct at this point. Using language from Ge 2:7, he confessed that God's Spirit (Hebrew *ruach*) made him, and God's breath (Hebrew *neshamah*) gave him life. Here Hebrew poetic parallel structure shows God's Spirit is conceived as closely identified with His life-giving breath. Without the Spirit we would have no vitality, no dynamism, no life. This dynamic, divine element inhabiting us gives us our wisdom and understanding (32:8).
33:4–7 HUMANITY, Human Nature—Life depends on God's direct act of creation. No person can claim natural superiority to another. No person should stand in fear and awe of another. See notes on 31:15; 32:8; Ge 2:7.
33:6 HUMANITY, Human Nature—At the very best, everyone is still made from clay, leaving no basis for self-exaltation or pride. *See Ge 2.*
33:12–30 EVIL AND SUFFERING, Testing—Is an answer always immediately available for the sufferer? Job's fourth counselor, the unexpectedly brash, young Elihu insisted Job could have an answer if he listened. Suffering might be punishment for sin, a call for repentance, an opportunity for experience with an angelic mediator and God's redemption, or a call to testify to God's actions. Each of Elihu's suggestions are true in some situations. None fit Job, for they all assumed Job was guilty and deserved his suffering. Even Elihu's claim to divine inspiration did not make his words true. No pat answers fit every sufferer's case.
33:13–22 REVELATION, Actions—Elihu did not understand Job's situation. He did know the nature of revelation. God reveals Himself in many different ways: in dreams and visions, in warnings to the inner consciousness, through suffering, and by angels. The purpose of such disclosures are to warn, correct, redirect, preserve, and chasten or discipline. These were common views of God's communication. Job's friends had yet to deal with God employing events He had not directly caused as instruments of revelation. The Book of Job shows God can even use Satan's work as opportunity for revelation.

and his bones,[k] once hidden, now
stick out.[l]
22His soul draws near to the pit,[u] [m]
and his life to the messengers of
death.[v] [n]

23"Yet if there is an angel on his side
as a mediator,[o] one out of a
thousand,
to tell a man what is right for him,[p]
24to be gracious to him and say,
'Spare him from going down to the
pit[w];[q]
I have found a ransom for him'[r] —
25then his flesh is renewed[s] like a
child's;
it is restored as in the days of his
youth.[t]
26He prays to God and finds favor with
him,[u]
he sees God's face and shouts for
joy;[v]
he is restored by God to his
righteous state.[w]
27Then he comes to men and says,
'I sinned,[x] and perverted what was
right,[y]
but I did not get what I deserved.[z]
28He redeemed[a] my soul from going
down to the pit,[x] [b]
and I will live to enjoy the light.'[c]

29"God does all these things to a
man[d] —
twice, even three times[e] —
30to turn back[f] his soul from the pit,[y] [g]
that the light of life[h] may shine on
him.[i]

31"Pay attention, Job, and listen[j] to
me;[k]
be silent,[l] and I will speak.
32If you have anything to say, answer
me;[m]
speak up, for I want you to be
cleared.[n]
33But if not, then listen to me;[o]
be silent,[p] and I will teach you
wisdom.[q]"

Chapter 34

THEN Elihu said:

2"Hear my words, you wise men;
listen to me,[r] you men of learning.
3For the ear tests words
as the tongue tastes food.[s]
4Let us discern for ourselves what is
right;[t]
let us learn together what is good.[u]

5"Job says, 'I am innocent,[v]
but God denies me justice.[w]
6Although I am right,
I am considered a liar;[x]
although I am guiltless,[y]
his arrow inflicts an incurable
wound.'[z]
7What man is like Job,
who drinks scorn like water?[a]
8He keeps company with evildoers;
he associates with wicked men.[b]
9For he says, 'It profits a man nothing
when he tries to please God.'[c]

10"So listen to me,[d] you men of
understanding.[e]
Far be it from God to do evil,[f]
from the Almighty to do wrong.[g]
11He repays a man for what he has
done;[h]
he brings upon him what his
conduct deserves.[i]
12It is unthinkable that God would do
wrong,[j]
that the Almighty would pervert
justice.[k]
13Who appointed[l] him over the earth?
Who put him in charge of the whole
world?[m]
14If it were his intention
and he withdrew his spirit[z] [n] and
breath,[o]
15all mankind would perish[p] together
and man would return to the dust.[q]

16"If you have understanding,[r] hear
this;
listen to what I say.[s]

33:21 [k]S Job 2:5 [l]S Job 16:8 **33:22** [m]S ver 18 [n]Job 38:17; Ps 9:13; 88:3; 107:18; 116:3 **33:23** [o]Gal 3:19; Heb 8:6; 9:15 [p]Job 36:9-10; Mic 6:8 **33:24** [q]S ver 18 [r]S Job 6:22 **33:25** [s]Ps 103:5 [t]2Ki 5:14 **33:26** [u]S Job 5:15; Pr 8:35; 12:2; 18:22; Lk 2:52 [v]S Ezr 3:13; S Job 22:26 [w]Ps 13:5; 50:15; 51:12; 1Jn 1:9 **33:27** [x]S Nu 22:34 [y]Lk 15:21 [z]S Ezr 9:13; Ps 22:27; 51:13; Ro 6:21; Jas 2:13 **33:28** [a]S Ex 15:13; Ps 34:22; 107:20 [b]S ver 18; S Job 17:16 [c]S Job 22:28 **33:29** [d]Ps 139:16; Pr 16:9; 20:24; Jer 10:23; 1Co 12:6; Eph 1:11; Php 2:13 [e]ver 14 **33:30** [f]Jas 5:19 [g]S ver 18 [h]Ps 49:19; 56:13; 116:9; Isa 53:11 [i]Isa 60:1; Eph 5:14 **33:31** [j]Jer 23:18 [k]S Job 32:10 [l]ver 33 **33:32** [m]ver 5 [n]S Job 6:29; 35:2 **33:33** [o]S Job 32:10 [p]ver 31 [q]S Job 6:24; Pr 10:8,10,19 **34:2** [r]S Job 32:10 **34:3** [s]Job 12:11 **34:4** [t]S Job 12:12; Heb 5:14 [u]1Th 5:21 **34:5** [v]S Job 10:7 [w]S Job 6:29 **34:6** [x]S Job 6:28 [y]S Job 9:21 [z]S Job 6:4; S 10:3; S Jer 10:19 **34:7** [a]S Job 9:21; S 15:16 **34:8** [b]S Job 22:15 **34:9** [c]S Job 9:29-31; S 21:15 **34:10** [d]Job 32:10 [e]ver 16; S Job 12:12 [f]S Ge 18:25 [g]ver 12; Dt 32:4; Job 8:3; 36:23; Ps 92:15; Ro 3:5; 9:14 **34:11** [h]S Job 21:31; S Mt 16:27 [i]Jer 17:10; 32:19; Eze 33:20 **34:12** [j]S ver 10; Tit 1:2; Heb 6:18 [k]S Job 8:3; Ps 9:16; Col 3:25; 2Th 1:6 **34:13** [l]Heb 1:2 [m]Job 36:23; 38:4,6; Isa 40:14 **34:14** [n]S Ge 6:3 [o]S Nu 16:22; S Job 27:3 **34:15** [p]S Ge 6:13; La 3:22; Mal 3:6; Jn 3:16 [q]S Ge 2:7; S Job 7:21; 9:22; Ps 90:10 **34:16** [r]S ver 10 [s]S Job 32:10

[u]22 Or *He draws near to the grave* [v]22 Or *to the dead* [w]24 Or *grave* [x]28 Or *redeemed me from going down to the grave* [y]30 Or *turn him back from the grave* [z]14 Or *Spirit*

34:1–30 GOD, Sovereignty—Elihu praised the sovereignty and justice of God, while severely condemning Job. The inspired Book of Job wants us to accept the statements about God but to learn that such theological insight does not give us the right to condemn another human being because we do not have God's wisdom or sovereignty. God's justice is not the only answer to human suffering. See notes on 1:21–22; 9:2–35; 28:1–28.

34:10–17 GOD, Justice—Elihu appealed to the justice of God in trying to prove that Job had sinned some great sin to bring so much calamity upon himself. Both Job and his friends appealed to the justice of God. Their point of disagreement came not over God's justice but over Job's individual case. Does God's justice mean that all suffering can be traced back to specific sin? Does God's justice allow humans to judge other people as sinners by their material and physical prosperity? The friends said yes. The Book of Job says no. Some things remain known only to God. See notes on 5:8–16; 23:13–16; 28:1–28.

34:14–15 HUMANITY, Life—Human life is sustained by the direct will of God. He who gave breath can withdraw it at His will. We cannot explain the mystery of life, nor can we control it. We can destroy it.

17Can he who hates justice govern?[t]
Will you condemn the just and
mighty One?[u]
18Is he not the One who says to kings,
'You are worthless,'
and to nobles,[v] 'You are wicked,'[w]
19who shows no partiality[x] to princes
and does not favor the rich over the
poor,[y]
for they are all the work of his
hands?[z]
20They die in an instant, in the middle of
the night;[a]
the people are shaken and they pass
away;
the mighty are removed without
human hand.[b]

21"His eyes are on the ways of men;[c]
he sees their every step.[d]
22There is no dark place,[e] no deep
shadow,[f]
where evildoers can hide.[g]
23God has no need to examine men
further,[h]
that they should come before him
for judgment.[i]
24Without inquiry he shatters[j] the
mighty[k]
and sets up others in their place.[l]
25Because he takes note of their deeds,[m]
he overthrows them in the night[n]
and they are crushed.[o]
26He punishes them for their
wickedness[p]
where everyone can see them,
27because they turned from following
him[q]
and had no regard for any of his
ways.[r]
28They caused the cry of the poor to
come before him,
so that he heard the cry of the
needy.[s]
29But if he remains silent,[t] who can
condemn him?[u]
If he hides his face,[v] who can see
him?
Yet he is over man and nation alike,[w]
30 to keep a godless[x] man from
ruling,[y]
from laying snares for the people.[z]

31"Suppose a man says to God,
'I am guilty[a] but will offend no
more.
32Teach me what I cannot see;[b]
if I have done wrong, I will not do
so again.'[c]
33Should God then reward you on your
terms,
when you refuse to repent?[d]
You must decide, not I;
so tell me what you know.

34"Men of understanding declare,
wise men who hear me say to me,
35'Job speaks without knowledge;[e]
his words lack insight.'[f]
36Oh, that Job might be tested to the
utmost
for answering like a wicked man![g]
37To his sin he adds rebellion;
scornfully he claps his hands[h]
among us
and multiplies his words[i] against
God."[j]

Chapter 35

THEN Elihu said:

2"Do you think this is just?
You say, 'I will be cleared[k] by
God.[a]'[l]
3Yet you ask him, 'What profit is it to
me,[b]
and what do I gain by not sinning?'[m]

4"I would like to reply to you
and to your friends with you.
5Look up at the heavens[n] and see;
gaze at the clouds so high above
you.[o]
6If you sin, how does that affect him?
If your sins are many, what does
that do to him?[p]
7If you are righteous, what do you give
to him,[q]
or what does he receive[r] from your
hand?[s]
8Your wickedness affects only a man
like yourself,[t]
and your righteousness only the sons
of men.[u]

9"Men cry out[v] under a load of
oppression;[w]
they plead for relief from the arm of
the powerful.[x]
10But no one says, 'Where is God my
Maker,[y]
who gives songs[z] in the night,[a]
11who teaches[b] more to[c] us than to[c]
the beasts of the earth
and makes us wiser than[d] the birds
of the air?'
12He does not answer[d] when men cry
out
because of the arrogance[e] of the
wicked.[f]
13Indeed, God does not listen to their
empty plea;
the Almighty pays no attention to
it.[g]
14How much less, then, will he listen

34:17 [t]ver 30; 2Sa 23:3-4; Pr 20:8, 26; 24:23-25; 28:28 [u]ver 29; S Job 10:7; 40:8; Ro 3:5-6 **34:18** [v]S Job 12:18 [w]Ex 22:28; Isa 40:24 **34:19** [x]S Job 13:10; S Ac 10:34 [y]S Lev 19:15; Jas 2:5 [z]S Job 10:3 **34:20** [a]ver 25; S Ex 11:4; S Job 20:8 [b]S Job 12:19 **34:21** [c]Jer 32:19 [d]S Job 14:16; Pr 15:3; S Heb 4:13 **34:22** [e]Ps 74:20 [f]S Job 3:5 [g]S Ge 3:8; S Job 11:20 **34:23** [h]Ps 11:4 [i]Job 11:11 **34:24** [j]Isa 8:9; 9:4; Jer 51:20; Da 2:34 [k]Job 12:19 [l]Da 2:21 **34:25** [m]S Job 11:11 [n]S ver 20 [o]Pr 5:21-23 **34:26** [p]S Ge 6:5; S Job 8:22; S 28:24; Ps 9:5; Jer 44:5 **34:27** [q]Ps 14:3 [r]S 1Sa 15:11 **34:28** [s]S Ex 22:23; S Job 5:15; S 12:19 **34:29** [t]Ps 28:1; 83:1; 109:1 [u]S ver 17; Ro 8:34 [v]Ps 13:1 [w]Ps 83:18; 97:9 **34:30** [x]S Job 8:13 [y]S ver 17 [z]Ps 25:15; 31:4; 91:3; 124:7; 140:5; Pr 29:2-12 **34:31** [a]Ps 51:5; Lk 15:21; Ro 7:24; 1Jn 1:8,10 **34:32** [b]Ex 33:13; Job 35:11; 38:36; Ps 15:2; 25:4; 27:11; 51:6; 86:11; 139:23-24; 143:8 [c]Job 33:27; S Lk 19:8 **34:33** [d]S 2Ki 17:13; Job 33:23; 36:10, 15,18,21; 41:11; 42:6; Pr 17:23; Jnh 3:8 **34:35** [e]Job 35:16; 38:2; 42:3 [f]Job 26:3 **34:36** [g]S Job 6:29; S 22:15 **34:37** [h]S Job 27:23 [i]Job 35:16 [j]Job 23:2 **35:2** [k]S Job 33:32 [l]S Job 2:9; S 32:2 **35:3** [m]S Job 9:29-31; S 21:15 **35:5** [n]S Ge 15:5; S Dt 10:14 [o]S Job 11:7-9; Ps 19:1-4 **35:6** [p]S Job 7:20 **35:7** [q]Ro 11:35 [r]1Co 4:7 [s]S Job 22:2-3; Lk 17:10 **35:8** [t]Eze 18:24 [u]Eze 18:5-9; Zec 7:9-10 **35:9** [v]Ex 2:23 [w]S Job 20:19 [x]S Job 5:15; S 12:19 **35:10** [y]S Job 4:17 [z]S Job 8:21 [a]Ps 42:8; 77:6; 119:62; 149:5; Ac 16:25 **35:11** [b]S Job 21:22; Lk 12:24 [c]Job 12:7 **35:12** [d]S 1Sa 8:18 [e]S Job 15:25 [f]Ps 66:18 **35:13** [g]S Dt 1:45; S 1Sa 8:18; S Job 15:31; S Pr 15:8

[a]2 Or *My righteousness is more than God's* [b]3 Or *you* [c]11 Or *teaches us by* [d]11 Or *us wise by*

when you say that you do not see
him,[h]
that your case[i] is before him
and you must wait for him,[j]
15and further, that his anger never
punishes[k]
and he does not take the least notice
of wickedness.[e] [l]
16So Job opens his mouth with empty
talk;[m]
without knowledge he multiplies
words."[n]

Chapter 36

ELIHU continued:
2"Bear with me a little longer and I
will show you
that there is more to be said in
God's behalf.
3I get my knowledge from afar;[o]
I will ascribe justice to my Maker.[p]
4Be assured that my words are not
false;[q]
one perfect in knowledge[r] is with
you.[s]

5"God is mighty,[t] but does not despise
men;[u]
he is mighty, and firm in his
purpose.[v]
6He does not keep the wicked alive[w]
but gives the afflicted their rights.[x]
7He does not take his eyes off the
righteous;[y]
he enthrones them with kings[z]
and exalts them forever.[a]
8But if men are bound in chains,[b]
held fast by cords of affliction,[c]
9he tells them what they have done—
that they have sinned arrogantly.[d]
10He makes them listen[e] to correction[f]
and commands them to repent of
their evil.[g]
11If they obey and serve him,[h]
they will spend the rest of their days
in prosperity[i]
and their years in contentment.[j]
12But if they do not listen,
they will perish by the sword[f] [k]
and die without knowledge.[l]

13"The godless in heart[m] harbor
resentment;[n]
even when he fetters them, they do
not cry for help.[o]
14They die in their youth,[p]
among male prostitutes of the
shrines.[q]
15But those who suffer[r] he delivers in
their suffering;[s]
he speaks[t] to them in their
affliction.[u]

16"He is wooing[v] you from the jaws of
distress
to a spacious place[w] free from
restriction,[x]
to the comfort of your table[y] laden
with choice food.[z]
17But now you are laden with the
judgment due the wicked;[a]
judgment and justice have taken
hold of you.[b]
18Be careful that no one entices you by
riches;
do not let a large bribe[c] turn you
aside.[d]
19Would your wealth[e]
or even all your mighty efforts
sustain you so you would not be in
distress?
20Do not long for the night,[f]
to drag people away from their
homes.[g]
21Beware of turning to evil,[g]
which you seem to prefer to
affliction.[h]

22"God is exalted in his power.[i]
Who is a teacher like him?[j]
23Who has prescribed his ways[k] for
him,[l]
or said to him, 'You have done
wrong'?[m]
24Remember to extol his work,[n]

35:14 [h]S Job 9:11 [i]Ps 37:6 [j]Job 31:35 **35:15** [k]S Job 9:24 [l]S Job 18:5; Ps 10:11; Hos 7:2; Am 8:7 **35:16** [m]Tit 1:10 [n]S Job 34:35,37; 1Co 4:20; Jude 1:10 **36:3** [o]S Job 6:28 [p]S Job 4:17 **36:4** [q]S Job 6:28; S 13:6 [r]Job 37:5,16, 23 [s]S Job 32:17 **36:5** [t]S Job 9:4 [u]Ps 5:2; 22:24; 31:22; 69:33; 102:17; 103:10 [v]S Nu 23:19; Ro 11:29 **36:6** [w]S Job 34:26 [x]S Job 4:10 **36:7** [y]S Job 11:11; Ps 11:5; 33:18; 34:15; Mt 6:18 [z]Ps 113:8; Isa 22:23 [a]S 1Sa 2:7-8; S Job 4:7 **36:8** [b]S 2Sa 3:34; 2Ki 23:33; Ps 107:10,14 [c]ver 10,15,21; Ps 119:67,71 **36:9** [d]S Job 15:25 **36:10** [e]S Job 33:16 [f]S Job 5:17 [g]S ver 8; S Jdg 6:8; S Job 34:33; 1Th 5:22 **36:11** [h]S Lev 26:33; Dt 28:1; Isa 1:19; Hag 1:12 [i]S Dt 30:15; S Job 8:7 [j]S Ex 8:22; S Dt 8:1; Jn 14:21; 1Ti 4:8 **36:12** [k]S Lev 26:38; S Job 15:22 [l]S Job 4:21; Eph 4:18 **36:13** [m]S Job 15:12; Ro 2:5 [n]S Job 5:2 [o]S Job 4:17; Am 4:11 **36:14** [p]S Job 15:32 [q]S Dt 23:17 **36:15** [r]S Job 5:15 [s]2Co 12:10 [t]S Job 33:16 [u]S ver 8; S Job 34:33 **36:16** [v]Hos 2:14 [w]S 2Sa 22:20; Ps 18:19 [x]Ps 118:5 [y]Ps 23:5; 78:19 [z]S Ge 17:1; S Job 15:11 **36:17** [a]S Job 20:29 [b]Job 22:11 **36:18** [c]S Ex 23:8; Am 5:12 [d]S Job 34:33 **36:19** [e]Ps 49:6; Jer 9:23 **36:20** [f]Job 34:20,25 **36:21** [g]S Job 34:33; Ps 66:18 [h]S ver 8; Heb 11:25 **36:22** [i]S Job 5:9; S 9:4 [j]S Job 21:22; S Ro 11:34 **36:23** [k]Job 27:11 [l]S Job 34:13; Ro 11:33 [m]S Ge 18:25; S Job 34:10 **36:24** [n]1Ch 16:24; Ps 35:27; 92:5; 111:2; 138:5; 145:10

[e] *15* Symmachus, Theodotion and Vulgate; the meaning of the Hebrew for this word is uncertain. [f] *12* Or *will cross the River* [g] *20* The meaning of the Hebrew for verses 18-20 is uncertain.

36:1–26 EVIL AND SUFFERING, God's Compassion—Divine love is the basic reality of life, but even it cannot be placed in a theological system and controlled by human teachers. God knows and cares for the suffering, but God does not always speak to and deliver the afflicted. Job's extended arguments and experience show that only too well. God's compassion for the suffering is a personal emotion in a personal relationship which finds expression according to God's wisdom and freedom. No doctrine can tell God how He must act. As Job was tested, God refused to act in mercy to Job. He waited to accomplish His larger purpose. Absence of God's merciful action did not prove Job's wickedness.

36:3–12 GOD, Justice—See note on 34:10–17.

36:18 CHRISTIAN ETHICS, Property Rights—Temptations toward dishonesty are abundant. The believer must be alert to these and avoid them.

36:22–33 GOD, Power—God's way of recycling water to provide moisture for the crops of earth points to God's unique sovereignty and power. Again, Job would agree. This evidence did not help Job understand his personal circumstances. See notes on 1:21–22; 4:17; 9:2–35.

36:22 EDUCATION, God—The Bible presents God as the divine Educator. He reveals Himself to His people by instructing them in wisdom and knowledge. See Ps 94:10. He calls co-teachers into His service, but the Lord Himself is their exemplar as Teacher and the ultimate source of their subject matter. See Dt 4:1.

which men have praised in song.[o]
25 All mankind has seen it;[p]
men gaze on it from afar.
26 How great is God—beyond our
understanding![q]
The number of his years is past
finding out.[r]

27 "He draws up the drops of water,[s]
which distill as rain to the
streams[h];[t]
28 the clouds pour down their moisture
and abundant showers[u] fall on
mankind.[v]
29 Who can understand how he spreads
out the clouds,
how he thunders[w] from his
pavilion?[x]
30 See how he scatters his lightning[y]
about him,
bathing the depths of the sea.[z]
31 This is the way he governs[i] the
nations[a]
and provides food[b] in abundance.[c]
32 He fills his hands with lightning
and commands it to strike its
mark.[d]
33 His thunder announces the coming
storm;[e]
even the cattle make known its
approach.[j][f]

Chapter 37

"At this my heart pounds[g]
and leaps from its place.
2 Listen![h] Listen to the roar of his
voice,[i]
to the rumbling that comes from his
mouth.[j]
3 He unleashes his lightning[k] beneath
the whole heaven
and sends it to the ends of the
earth.[l]
4 After that comes the sound of his roar;
he thunders[m] with his majestic
voice.[n]
When his voice resounds,
he holds nothing back.
5 God's voice thunders[o] in marvelous
ways;[p]
he does great things beyond our
understanding.[q]
6 He says to the snow,[r] 'Fall on the
earth,'
and to the rain shower, 'Be a mighty
downpour.'[s]
7 So that all men he has made may know
his work,[t]
he stops every man from his
labor.[k][u]
8 The animals take cover;[v]
they remain in their dens.[w]
9 The tempest comes out from its
chamber,[x]
the cold from the driving winds.[y]
10 The breath of God produces ice,
and the broad waters become
frozen.[z]
11 He loads the clouds with moisture;[a]
he scatters his lightning[b] through
them.[c]
12 At his direction they swirl around
over the face of the whole earth
to do whatever he commands
them.[d]
13 He brings the clouds to punish men,[e]
or to water his earth[l] and show his
love.[f]

14 "Listen[g] to this, Job;
stop and consider God's wonders.[h]
15 Do you know how God controls the
clouds
and makes his lightning[i] flash?[j]
16 Do you know how the clouds hang
poised,[k]
those wonders of him who is perfect
in knowledge?[l]
17 You who swelter in your clothes
when the land lies hushed under the
south wind,[m]
18 can you join him in spreading out the
skies,[n]
hard as a mirror of cast bronze?[o]

19 "Tell us what we should say to him;[p]

36:24 [o]S Ex 15:1; Rev 15:3 **36:25** [p]Ro 1:20 **36:26** [q]S Job 5:9; 1Co 13:12 [r]S Ge 21:33; S Job 10:5; Heb 1:12 **36:27** [s]S Job 26:8 [t]S 2Sa 1:21; Job 28:26; 38:28; Isa 55:10 **36:28** [u]Ps 65:10; 72:6; Joel 2:23 [v]S Job 5:10; S 22:11; S 28:26; Mt 5:45 **36:29** [w]Ps 29:3; Jer 10:13 [x]S Job 9:6; 37:16; Ps 18:7-15; 19:4,5; 104:2; Pr 8:28; Isa 40:22 **36:30** [y]Ex 19:16; Job 37:11,15; Ps 18:12,14; 97:4; Jer 10:13; Hab 3:11 [z]Ps 68:22; Isa 51:10 **36:31** [a]Dt 28:23-24; 1Ki 17:1; Job 37:13; Am 4:7-8 [b]Ps 145:15 [c]Ps 104:14-15, 27-28; Isa 30:23; Ac 14:17 **36:32** [d]S Job 28:24; 37:12,15; Ps 18:14; 29:7-9 **36:33** [e]Job 37:5; 40:9 [f]S Job 28:26 **37:1** [g]Ps 38:10; Isa 15:5; Jer 4:19; Hab 3:16 **37:2** [h]S Job 32:10 [i]ver 5 [j]Ps 18:13; 29:3-9 **37:3** [k]S 2Sa 22:13; Ps 18:14 [l]S Job 36:32; Mt 24:27; Lk 17:24 **37:4** [m]S 1Sa 2:10 [n]S Ex 20:19 **37:5** [o]S 1Sa 2:10; Jn 12:29 [p]S Job 36:33 [q]S Job 5:9; S 11:7-9; S 36:4 **37:6** [r]Dt 28:12; Job 38:22 [s]S Ge 7:4; S Job 5:10; S 28:26 **37:7** [t]Ps 109:27 [u]Ps 104:19-23; 111:2 **37:8** [v]S Job 28:26 [w]Job 38:40; Ps 104:22 **37:9** [x]Ps 50:3 [y]Ps 147:17 **37:10** [z]Job 38:29-30; Ps 147:17 **37:11** [a]S Job 26:8 [b]S Job 36:30 [c]S Job 28:26 **37:12** [d]S ver 3; Ps 147:16; 148:8 **37:13** [e]S Ge 7:4; Ex 9:22-23; S 1Sa 12:17 [f]S 1Ki 18:45; S Job 5:10; S 36:31; 38:27 **37:14** [g]S Job 32:10 [h]S Job 5:9 **37:15** [i]S Job 36:30 [j]S Job 36:32 **37:16** [k]S Job 36:29 [l]S Job 5:9; S 36:4 **37:17** [m]Ac 27:13 **37:18** [n]S Ge 1:1,8; S Job 22:14 [o]Dt 28:23 **37:19** [p]Ro 8:26

[h]27 Or *distill from the mist as rain* [i]31 Or *nourishes* [j]33 Or *announces his coming— / the One zealous against evil* [k]7 Or / *he fills all men with fear by his power* [l]13 Or *to favor them*

37:1–24 GOD, Transcendent—All who have spoken in this book have emphasized the transcendence of God, His sovereignty, and His justice and righteousness. The vexing question was why Job was suffering. Job praised the sovereignty and justice of God even though he—a righteous man—was suffering. His friends were trying to use these theological doctrines concerning the nature of God to prove that Job was a gross sinner. They reasoned that God who was righteous was obviously punishing Job. They drew the conclusion that Job must be the world's worst sinner to be punished so horribly. Job's friends had not yet learned that suffering is not necessarily caused by God as a punishment for sin. They did not understand that theological argument does not prove another person is a sinner condemned by God.

37:14—39:30 REVELATION, Author of Creation—God's hurting servant learned from Elihu and God that we may learn the fact of creation but seldom can we know how God brought things together. Even God's purposes are obscure for His people at times. As God reveals Himself in creation, much remains mystery. See notes on 9:9–11; Ro 1:18–20. The important element for Job was God's willingness to break the silence and talk with Him. Hard questions revealing God's sovereign presence were better than silence which raised doubts.

we cannot draw up our case[q]
because of our darkness.[r]
20Should he be told that I want to speak?
Would any man ask to be swallowed up?
21Now no one can look at the sun,[s]
bright as it is in the skies
after the wind has swept them clean.
22Out of the north he comes in golden splendor;[t]
God comes in awesome majesty.[u]
23The Almighty is beyond our reach and exalted in power;[v]
in his justice[w] and great righteousness, he does not oppress.[x]
24Therefore, men revere him,[y]
for does he not have regard for all the wise[z] in heart?[m]"

Chapter 38

The LORD Speaks

THEN the LORD answered Job[a] out of the storm.[b] He said:

2"Who is this that darkens my counsel[c]
with words without knowledge?[d]
3Brace yourself like a man;
I will question you,
and you shall answer me.[e]

4"Where were you when I laid the earth's foundation?[f]
Tell me, if you understand.[g]
5Who marked off its dimensions?[h]
Surely you know!
Who stretched a measuring line[i] across it?
6On what were its footings set,[j]
or who laid its cornerstone[k] —
7while the morning stars[l] sang together[m]
and all the angels[n][n] shouted for joy?[o]

8"Who shut up the sea behind doors[p]
when it burst forth from the womb,[q]
9when I made the clouds its garment
and wrapped it in thick darkness,[r]
10when I fixed limits for it[s]
and set its doors and bars in place,[t]
11when I said, 'This far you may come and no farther;[u]
here is where your proud waves halt'?[v]

12"Have you ever given orders to the morning,[w]
or shown the dawn its place,[x]
13that it might take the earth by the edges
and shake the wicked[y] out of it?[z]
14The earth takes shape like clay under a seal;[a]
its features stand out like those of a garment.
15The wicked are denied their light,[b]
and their upraised arm is broken.[c]

16"Have you journeyed to the springs of the sea
or walked in the recesses of the deep?[d]
17Have the gates of death[e] been shown to you?

37:19 [q]S Job 13:18 [r]S Job 9:3 **37:21** [s]S Jdg 5:31; Ac 22:11; 26:13 **37:22** [t]Ps 19:5 [u]Ex 24:17 **37:23** [v]S Job 5:9; S 36:4; Ro 11:33; 1Ti 6:16 [w]S Job 8:3 [x]S Job 4:17; Ps 44:1; Isa 63:9; Jer 25:5; La 3:33; Eze 18:23,32 **37:24** [y]S Ge 22:12; Job 28:28; Ecc 12:13; Mic 6:8; Mt 10:28 [z]S Job 5:13; Eph 5:15 **38:1** [a]S Job 11:5 [b]S Ex 14:21; S 1Sa 2:10; Job 40:6; Isa 21:1; Eze 1:4 **38:2** [c]S 1Ki 22:5; Isa 40:13 [d]S Job 34:35; Mk 10:38; 1Ti 1:7 **38:3** [e]Job 40:7; 42:4; Mk 11:29 **38:4** [f]S ver 5; S Ge 1:1; S 1Sa 2:8 [g]ver 18; S Job 34:13; Pr 30:4 **38:5** [h]ver 4; Ps 102:25; Pr 8:29; Isa 40:12; 48:13; Jer 31:37 [i]Jer 31:39; Zec 1:16; 4:9-10 **38:6** [j]Pr 8:25 [k]S Job 26:7 **38:7** [l]S Ge 1:16 [m]Ps 19:1-4; 148:2-3 [n]S 1Ki 22:19 [o]S Dt 16:15 **38:8** [p]ver 11; Ps 33:7; Pr 8:29; Jer 5:22 [q]S Ge 1:9-10 **38:9** [r]S Ge 1:2 **38:10** [s]S Job 28:25; Ps 33:7; 104:9; Isa 40:12 [t]Ne 3:3; Job 7:12; 26:10 **38:11** [u]S ver 8 [v]Ps 65:7; 89:9; 104:6-9 **38:12** [w]Ps 57:8 [x]Ps 74:16; Am 5:8 **38:13** [y]Ps 104:35 [z]S Job 8:22 **38:14** [a]Ex 28:11 **38:15** [b]S Dt 28:29; S Job 15:22; S 18:5 [c]S Ge 17:14; S Job 4:10; S 31:22 **38:16** [d]S Ge 1:7; S Job 9:8 **38:17** [e]S Job 33:22; Mt 16:18; Rev 1:18

[m]24 Or *for he does not have regard for any who think they are wise.* [n]7 Hebrew *the sons of God*

38:1—39:30 GOD, Sovereignty—The Lord's answer to Job centered on the mysterious sovereignty and wisdom of God. Job had sought to understand why God who is righteous had allowed him to suffer. He had described God's sovereignty and wisdom in eloquent words (9:1–35; 28:1–28). In the ardor of debate, he lost touch with the personal relationship to the sovereign God. God's sovereignty is not only a doctrine for us to know with our mind. It is a personal reality which maintains our humility, stirs our worship, and destroys our pride.

38:1—41:34 EVIL AND SUFFERING, God's Present Help—The sufferer needs response not answers. God did not answer Job's questions. He did not mention Satan's role or Job's testing. Rather He showed Job he did not have or need answers which only God has. Job needed to trust God to do His work in His time. If God can control the wonders of creation and the powers of the natural world, surely He can take care of one individual's pains and frustrations. We do not need to try to change God's ways of doing things. God's greatest help is making His presence known to us. In His presence, we can humbly endure whatever comes knowing we are His.

38:2 HUMANITY, Intellectual Nature—A common human failing is talking about things of which we possess no knowledge, thus distorting the understanding of others as well as parading our own ignorance. Job's friends had engaged him in a debate about the nature of God and His sovereign control of the universe He created and rules. At last Job learned no one can become an expert on God. We can never describe what God must do.

38:4 CREATION, Purposeful—The climax of the Job narrative came when God spoke to the ailing and complaining patriarch. God did not defend Himself against the false accusations. He rather pointed to the great universe and asked Job how much he knew about its origin and nature. God bombarded Job with words about the creation of the earth and the things in it. The "foundation" means more than the structure upon which a building sits. God asked Job if he understood the fundamental nature of the universe. God made a world that has order and meaning even if creatures such as Job do not always see it. The human mind cannot understand the inequities of this world. God does not provide us with a formula concerning His activity. People who seek such a solution to religious matters are doomed to disappointment and frustration. We must trust God and believe that the One who created the wonders of this world will guide us if we make an honest effort to live in fellowship with Him. Faith in the Creator offers ultimate answers. Human reason does not. Human wisdom is in no way superior to the Creator's wisdom. Only One who is personally acquainted with all of creation in all of its history can understand all its riddles.

38:17–18 HUMANITY, Intellectual Nature—For all the great attainments of people, human ignorance of both life and

Have you seen the gates of the
shadow of death[o] ?[f]
18Have you comprehended the vast
expanses of the earth?[g]
Tell me, if you know all this.[h]

19"What is the way to the abode of light?
And where does darkness reside?[i]
20Can you take them to their places?
Do you know the paths[j] to their
dwellings?
21Surely you know, for you were already
born![k]
You have lived so many years!

22"Have you entered the storehouses of
the snow[l]
or seen the storehouses[m] of the
hail,[n]
23which I reserve for times of trouble,[o]
for days of war and battle?[p]
24What is the way to the place where
the lightning is dispersed,[q]
or the place where the east winds[r]
are scattered over the earth?[s]
25Who cuts a channel for the torrents of
rain,
and a path for the thunderstorm,[t]
26to water[u] a land where no man lives,
a desert with no one in it,[v]
27to satisfy a desolate wasteland
and make it sprout with grass?[w]
28Does the rain have a father?[x]
Who fathers the drops of dew?
29From whose womb comes the ice?
Who gives birth to the frost from the
heavens[y]
30when the waters become hard as
stone,
when the surface of the deep is
frozen?[z]

31"Can you bind the beautiful[p] Pleiades?
Can you loose the cords of Orion?[a]
32Can you bring forth the constellations[b]
in their seasons[q]
or lead out the Bear[r] with its
cubs?[c]
33Do you know the laws[d] of the
heavens?[e]
Can you set up ⌊God's[s]⌋ dominion
over the earth?

34"Can you raise your voice to the
clouds

38:17 [f]S Job 7:9
38:18 [g]S Job 28:24; Isa 40:12 [h]S ver 4
38:19 [i]S Ge 1:4; S Job 28:3; Ps 139:11-12
38:20 [j]S Job 24:13
38:21 [k]Job 15:7
38:22 [l]S Job 37:6 [m]S Dt 28:12 [n]Ps 105:32; 147:17
38:23 [o]Ps 27:5; Isa 28:17; 30:30; Eze 13:11 [p]Ex 9:26; Jos 10:11; Eze 13:13; Rev 16:21
38:24 [q]S Job 28:24 [r]S Job 27:21 [s]Jer 10:13; 51:16
38:25 [t]Job 28:26
38:26 [u]Job 36:27 [v]Ps 84:6; 107:35; Isa 41:18
38:27 [w]S Job 28:26; S 37:13; S Ps 104:14
38:28 [x]S 2Sa 1:21; S Job 5:10
38:29 [y]Ps 147:16-17
38:30 [z]Job 37:10
38:31 [a]Job 9:9; Am 5:8
38:32 [b]2Ki 23:5; Isa 13:10; 40:26; 45:12; Jer 19:13 [c]S Ge 1:16
38:33 [d]Ps 148:6; Jer 31:36 [e]S Ge 1:16
38:34 [f]S Job 5:10; S 22:11
38:35 [g]S Job 36:32
38:36 [h]S Job 9:4; S 34:32; Jas 1:5 [i]S Job 12:13
38:37 [j]S Jos 3:16 [k]S Job 22:11
38:38 [l]S Lev 26:19 [m]1Ki 18:45
38:39 [n]S Ge 49:9
38:40 [o]S Job 37:8 [p]S Ge 49:9
38:41 [q]S Ge 1:30 [r]S Ge 8:7; Lk 12:24 [s]Ps 147:9; S Mt 6:26
39:1 [t]S Dt 14:5 [u]Ge 49:21
39:2 [v]S Ge 31:7-9
39:5 [w]S Ge 16:12
39:6 [x]Job 24:5; Ps 107:34; Jer 2:24 [y]Job 30:4 [z]Job 30:7; Jer 14:6; 17:6
39:7 [a]S Job 5:22

and cover yourself with a flood of
water?[f]
35Do you send the lightning bolts on
their way?[g]
Do they report to you, 'Here we
are'?
36Who endowed the heart[t] with
wisdom[h]
or gave understanding[i] to the
mind[t] ?
37Who has the wisdom to count the
clouds?
Who can tip over the water jars[j] of
the heavens[k]
38when the dust becomes hard[l]
and the clods of earth stick
together?[m]

39"Do you hunt the prey for the lioness
and satisfy the hunger of the lions[n]
40when they crouch in their dens[o]
or lie in wait in a thicket?[p]
41Who provides food[q] for the raven[r]
when its young cry out to God
and wander about for lack of food?[s]

Chapter 39

"DO you know when the mountain
goats[t] give birth?
Do you watch when the doe bears
her fawn?[u]
2Do you count the months till they
bear?
Do you know the time they give
birth?[v]
3They crouch down and bring forth
their young;
their labor pains are ended.
4Their young thrive and grow strong in
the wilds;
they leave and do not return.

5"Who let the wild donkey[w] go free?
Who untied his ropes?
6I gave him the wasteland[x] as his
home,
the salt flats[y] as his habitat.[z]
7He laughs[a] at the commotion in the
town;

[o]17 Or *gates of deep shadows* [p]31 Or *the twinkling*; or *the chains of the* [q]32 Or *the morning star in its season* [r]32 Or *out Leo* [s]33 Or *his*; or *their* [t]36 The meaning of the Hebrew for this word is uncertain.

death far outstrips human knowledge. Until we know the secrets of life and death, we have no basis to challenge God's justice or His control of the universe.

38:31–33 CREATION, Purposeful—Creation is not an unordered accident. The universe is controlled by moral and physical laws which the Creator established. He made and directs earth (vv 4–7), sea (vv 8–11), sky (vv 12–15), and even the realm of death (vv 16–18) and of light and darkness (vv 19–21). Weather phenomena are not accidents of nature. They serve His purposes (vv 22–30), as do the heavenly constellations (vv 31–33).

38:39—39:30 CREATION, Purposeful—Creation includes a kingdom of wild animals which humans often fear and of which humans in general have little knowledge. The freedom and mysteries of animal life are part of God's plan in creation. Humans should rule over this kingdom (Ge 1:26) rather than fear it. This rule does not mean to dominate and destroy life but to live in harmony with it (Isa 11:6–8). God made and directs all of creation, even the mysterious parts we do not understand. Divine wisdom sees meaning in that which humans may scorn.

he does not hear a driver's shout.[b]
8He ranges the hills[c] for his pasture
and searches for any green thing.

9"Will the wild ox[d] consent to serve
you?[e]
Will he stay by your manger[f] at
night?
10Can you hold him to the furrow with a
harness?[g]
Will he till the valleys behind you?
11Will you rely on him for his great
strength?[h]
Will you leave your heavy work to
him?
12Can you trust him to bring in your
grain
and gather it to your threshing floor?

13"The wings of the ostrich flap joyfully,
but they cannot compare with the
pinions and feathers of the
stork.[i]
14She lays her eggs on the ground
and lets them warm in the sand,
15unmindful that a foot may crush them,
that some wild animal may trample
them.[j]
16She treats her young harshly,[k] as if
they were not hers;
she cares not that her labor was in
vain,
17for God did not endow her with
wisdom
or give her a share of good sense.[l]
18Yet when she spreads her feathers to
run,
she laughs[m] at horse and rider.

19"Do you give the horse his strength[n]
or clothe his neck with a flowing
mane?
20Do you make him leap like a locust,[o]
striking terror[p] with his proud
snorting?[q]
21He paws fiercely, rejoicing in his
strength,[r]
and charges into the fray.[s]
22He laughs[t] at fear, afraid of nothing;
he does not shy away from the
sword.
23The quiver[u] rattles against his side,
along with the flashing spear[v] and
lance.
24In frenzied excitement he eats up the
ground;
he cannot stand still when the
trumpet sounds.[w]
25At the blast of the trumpet[x] he snorts,
'Aha!'
He catches the scent of battle from
afar,
the shout of commanders and the
battle cry.[y]

26"Does the hawk take flight by your
wisdom
and spread his wings toward the
south?[z]
27Does the eagle soar at your command
and build his nest on high?[a]
28He dwells on a cliff and stays there at
night;
a rocky crag[b] is his stronghold.
29From there he seeks out his food;[c]
his eyes detect it from afar.
30His young ones feast on blood,
and where the slain are, there is
he."[d]

Chapter 40

THE LORD said to Job:[e]

2"Will the one who contends with
the Almighty[f] correct him?[g]
Let him who accuses God answer
him!"[h]

3Then Job answered the LORD:

4"I am unworthy[i]—how can I reply to
you?
I put my hand over my mouth.[j]
5I spoke once, but I have no answer[k]—
twice, but I will say no more."[l]

6Then the LORD spoke to Job out of the
storm:[m]

7"Brace yourself like a man;
I will question you,
and you shall answer me.[n]

8"Would you discredit my justice?[o]

39:7 [b]Job 3:18
39:8 [c]Isa 32:20
39:9 [d]S Nu 23:22 [e]S Ex 21:6 [f]S Ge 42:27
39:10 [g]Job 41:13; Ps 32:9
39:11 [h]ver 19; Job 40:16; 41:12, 22; Ps 147:10
39:13 [i]Zec 5:9
39:15 [j]2Ki 14:9
39:16 [k]ver 17; La 4:3
39:17 [l]S ver 16; S Job 21:22
39:18 [m]S Job 5:22
39:19 [n]S ver 11
39:20 [o]Joel 2:4-5; Rev 9:7 [p]Job 41:25 [q]Jer 8:16
39:21 [r]ver 11 [s]Jer 8:6
39:22 [t]S Job 5:22
39:23 [u]Isa 5:28; Jer 5:16 [v]Na 3:3
39:24 [w]Nu 10:9; Jer 4:5,19; Eze 7:14; Am 3:6
39:25 [x]Jos 6:5 [y]Jer 8:6; Am 1:14; 2:2
39:26 [z]Jer 8:7
39:27 [a]Jer 49:16; Ob 1:4; Hab 2:9
39:28 [b]Jer 49:16; Ob 1:3
39:29 [c]S Job 9:26
39:30 [d]Mt 24:28; Lk 17:37
40:1 [e]S Job 5:8; S 10:2
40:2 [f]S Job 13:3 [g]S Job 9:15; S 11:8; S 33:13; Ro 9:20 [h]S Job 9:3
40:4 [i]Job 42:6 [j]S Jdg 18:19; S Job 29:9
40:5 [k]S Job 9:3 [l]S Job 9:15
40:6 [m]S Ex 14:21; S Job 38:1
40:7 [n]S Job 38:3
40:8 [o]S Job 15:25; S 27:2; Ro 3:3

40:1—41:34 CREATION, Justice—Is the created order an unjust order? That had been Job's agonizing question. The question assumes the all-powerful Creator should destroy all *evil and establish justice by force.* The animal kingdom shows the false logic here. If strength were the only meaningful aspect of legitimate authority, then the strongest members of the animal kingdom, those most beyond human control, would be kings over all earthly pride and power (41:33–34). Just as we do not want to let uncontrollable beasts decide justice on earth, so God in His wisdom has chosen not to establish justice through power alone. He established humans in His image (Ge 1:26) with freedom to work for justice through wisdom, insight, and reason. Ultimately He will reveal fully His kingdom of justice.

40:1–14 SALVATION, Grace—Some things only God can do. They indicate God's matchless grace and power. We cannot save ourselves. Justification is by grace through faith. Limited humans cannot devise a better way of salvation than God has provided.

40:4–5 SALVATION, Repentance—Job did repent, not in order to be restored to his health and wealth, but because he realized his unworthiness before God (42:6).

40:7—42:3 HUMANITY, Life—At the very best, when we stand in God's presence, our own weakness and ignorance are clearly exposed. The stark contrast between divinity and humanity undercuts all basis for pride.

40:8 GOD, Justice—Job and his friends constantly defended God's justice. Job simply wanted to see it realized in his individual case. God turned the tables. He showed Job he, like his friends, was using theological argument in an improper

Would you condemn me to justify
yourself?[p]
9Do you have an arm like God's,[q]
and can your voice[r] thunder like
his?[s]
10Then adorn yourself with glory and
splendor,
and clothe yourself in honor and
majesty.[t]
11Unleash the fury of your wrath,[u]
look at every proud man and bring
him low,[v]
12look at every proud[w] man and humble
him,[x]
crush[y] the wicked where they
stand.
13Bury them all in the dust together;[z]
shroud their faces in the grave.[a]
14Then I myself will admit to you
that your own right hand can save
you.[b]

15"Look at the behemoth,[u]
which I made[c] along with you
and which feeds on grass like an
ox.[d]
16What strength[e] he has in his loins,
what power in the muscles of his
belly![f]
17His tail[v] sways like a cedar;
the sinews of his thighs are
close-knit.[g]
18His bones are tubes of bronze,
his limbs[h] like rods of iron.[i]
19He ranks first among the works of
God,[j]
yet his Maker[k] can approach him
with his sword.[l]
20The hills bring him their produce,[m]
and all the wild animals play[n]
nearby.[o]
21Under the lotus plants he lies,
hidden among the reeds[p] in the
marsh.[q]
22The lotuses conceal him in their
shadow;
the poplars by the stream[r] surround
him.
23When the river rages,[s] he is not
alarmed;
he is secure, though the Jordan[t]
should surge against his
mouth.
24Can anyone capture him by the eyes,[w]
or trap him and pierce his nose?[u]

40:8 [p]S Job 2:3; S 34:17 **40:9** [q]S 2Ch 32:8; S Ps 98:1 [r]Isa 6:8; Eze 10:5 [s]S Ex 20:19; S Job 36:33 **40:10** [t]Ps 29:1-2; 45:3; 93:1; 96:6; 104:1; 145:5 **40:11** [u]S Job 20:28; Ps 7:11; Isa 5:25; 9:12,19; 10:5; 13:3,5; 30:27; 42:25; 51:20; Jer 7:20; Na 1:6; Zep 1:18 [v]Ps 18:27; Isa 2:11,12,17; 23:9; 24:10; 25:12; 26:5; 32:19 **40:12** [w]Ps 10:4; Isa 25:11; Jer 48:29; 49:16; Zep 2:10 [x]S 1Sa 2:7; S Ps 52:5; 1Pe 5:5 [y]Ps 60:12; Isa 22:5; 28:3; 63:2-3,6; Da 5:20; Mic 5:8; 7:10; Zec 10:5; Mal 4:3 **40:13** [z]Nu 16:31-34 [a]S Job 4:9 **40:14** [b]Ex 15:6,12; Ps 18:35; 20:6; 48:10; 60:5; 108:6; Isa 41:10; 63:5 **40:15** [c]S Job 9:9 [d]Isa 11:7; 65:25 **40:16** [e]S Job 39:11 [f]Job 41:9 **40:17** [g]Job 41:15 **40:18** [h]Job 41:12 [i]Isa 11:4; 49:2 **40:19** [j]Job 41:33; Ps 40:5; 139:14; Isa 27:1 [k]S Job 4:17; S 9:9 [l]S Ge 3:24 **40:20** [m]Ps 104:14 [n]Ps 104:26 [o]S Job 5:23 **40:21** [p]S Ge 41:2; Ps 68:30; Isa 35:7 [q]Job 8:11 **40:22** [r]Ps 1:3; Isa 44:4 **40:23** [s]Isa 8:7; 11:15 [t]S Jos 3:1 **40:24** [u]2Ki 19:28; Job 41:2,7,26; Isa 37:29 **41:1** [v]S Job 3:8 [w]Am 4:2 **41:2** [x]S Job 40:24 [y]Eze 19:4 **41:3** [z]1Ki 20:31 **41:4** [a]S Ex 21:6 **41:7** [b]S Job 40:24 **41:8** [c]S Job 3:8 **41:9** [d]Job 40:16 **41:10** [e]S Job 3:8 [f]S 2Ch 20:6; S Isa 46:5; Jer 50:44; Rev 6:17 **41:11** [g]S Job 34:33; Ro 11:35 [h]S Jos 3:11; S Job 10:4; Ac 4:24; 1Co 10:26

Chapter 41

"CAN you pull in the leviathan[x] [v]
with a fishhook[w]
or tie down his tongue with a rope?
2Can you put a cord through his nose[x]
or pierce his jaw with a hook?[y]
3Will he keep begging you for mercy?[z]
Will he speak to you with gentle
words?
4Will he make an agreement with you
for you to take him as your slave for
life?[a]
5Can you make a pet of him like a bird
or put him on a leash for your girls?
6Will traders barter for him?
Will they divide him up among the
merchants?
7Can you fill his hide with harpoons
or his head with fishing spears?[b]
8If you lay a hand on him,
you will remember the struggle and
never do it again![c]
9Any hope of subduing him is false;
the mere sight of him is
overpowering.[d]
10No one is fierce enough to rouse
him.[e]
Who then is able to stand against
me?[f]
11Who has a claim against me that I
must pay?[g]
Everything under heaven belongs to
me.[h]

12"I will not fail to speak of his limbs,[i]
his strength[j] and his graceful form.
13Who can strip off his outer coat?
Who would approach him with a
bridle?[k]
14Who dares open the doors of his
mouth,[l]
ringed about with his fearsome
teeth?
15His back has[y] rows of shields
tightly sealed together;[m]
16each is so close to the next
that no air can pass between.
17They are joined fast to one another;

41:12 [i]Job 40:18 [j]S Job 39:11 **41:13** [k]S Job 30:11; S 39:10 **41:14** [l]Ps 22:13 **41:15** [m]Job 40:17

[u]*15* Possibly the hippopotamus or the elephant
[v]*17* Possibly trunk [w]*24* Or *by a water hole*
[x]*1* Possibly the crocodile [y]*15* Or *His pride is his*

fashion. He talked of the justice of God in order to prove the justice of Job. In so doing he actually ended up claiming God was not just. Such a claim was not necessary to prove Job's point. Certainly God is just. In His wisdom, however, He does not choose to let us know all the evidence to prove His justice. *We must trust Him even when we do not understand His just ways.*

41:1 EVIL AND SUFFERING, Divine Origin—God controlled the Leviathan, perhaps a sea monster, signifying evil or chaos. See note on 26:12–13.

41:11 GOD, Justice—Job and his friends agreed God was sovereign Ruler of all existence. God echoed the point with a surprising twist. God's sovereignty means no person can win an argument or a court case with God. Victory in doctrinal dispute is not the goal. The goal is to trust God to run the universe and to treat us with ultimate justice even when we do not understand present circumstances. God does not owe anyone anything, including answers to theological questions. We are the debtors to our Creator and Redeemer, the just Judge and Ruler of our universe. See note on 40:8.

they cling together and cannot be
parted.
18His snorting throws out flashes of
light;
his eyes are like the rays of dawn.[n]
19Firebrands[o] stream from his mouth;
sparks of fire shoot out.
20Smoke pours from his nostrils[p]
as from a boiling pot over a fire of
reeds.
21His breath[q] sets coals ablaze,
and flames dart from his mouth.[r]
22Strength[s] resides in his neck;
dismay goes before him.
23The folds of his flesh are tightly
joined;
they are firm and immovable.
24His chest is hard as rock,
hard as a lower millstone.[t]
25When he rises up, the mighty are
terrified;[u]
they retreat before his thrashing.[v]
26The sword that reaches him has no
effect,
nor does the spear or the dart or the
javelin.[w x]
27Iron he treats like straw[y]
and bronze like rotten wood.
28Arrows do not make him flee;[z]
slingstones are like chaff to him.
29A club seems to him but a piece of
straw;[a]
he laughs[b] at the rattling of the
lance.
30His undersides are jagged potsherds,
leaving a trail in the mud like a
threshing sledge.[c]
31He makes the depths churn like a
boiling caldron[d]
and stirs up the sea like a pot of
ointment.[e]
32Behind him he leaves a glistening
wake;
one would think the deep had white
hair.
33Nothing on earth is his equal[f] —
a creature without fear.
34He looks down on all that are
haughty;[g]
he is king over all that are proud.[h]"

Chapter 42

Job

THEN Job replied to the LORD:
2"I know that you can do all
things;[i]
no plan of yours can be thwarted.[j]
3⌞You asked,⌟ 'Who is this that obscures
my counsel without
knowledge?'[k]
Surely I spoke of things I did not
understand,
things too wonderful for me to
know.[l]

4⌞"You said,⌟ 'Listen now, and I will
speak;
I will question you,
and you shall answer me.'[m]
5My ears had heard of you[n]
but now my eyes have seen you.[o]
6Therefore I despise myself[p]
and repent[q] in dust and ashes."[r]

Epilogue

7After the LORD had said these things

41:18 [n]S Job 3:9
41:19 [o]Da 10:6
41:20 [p]Ps 18:8
41:21 [q]S Job 4:9; Isa 11:4; 40:7 [r]Ps 18:8; Isa 10:17; 30:27; 33:14; 66:14-16; Jer 4:4
41:22 [s]S Job 39:11
41:24 [t]Mt 18:6
41:25 [u]Job 39:20 [v]S Job 3:8
41:26 [w]S Jos 8:18 [x]S Job 40:24
41:27 [y]ver 29
41:28 [z]Ps 91:5
41:29 [a]ver 27 [b]S Job 5:22
41:30 [c]Isa 28:27; 41:15; Am 1:3
41:31 [d]1Sa 2:14 [e]Eze 32:2
41:33 [f]S Job 40:19
41:34 [g]Ps 18:27; 101:5; 131:1; Pr 6:17; 21:4; 30:13 [h]Job 28:8
42:2 [i]S Ge 18:14; S Mt 19:26 [j]S 2Ch 20:6; S Job 16:19; Ac 4:28; Eph 1:11
42:3 [k]S Job 34:35 [l]S Job 5:9
42:4 [m]S Job 38:3
42:5 [n]S Job 26:14; Ro 10:17 [o]Jdg 13:22; Isa 6:5; S Mt 5:8; Lk 2:30; Eph 1:17-18
42:6 [p]Job 40:4; Eze 6:9; Ro 12:3 [q]S Job 34:33 [r]S Ex 10:3; S Ezr 9:6; S Job 2:8; S 6:29

42:1–15 EVIL AND SUFFERING, Testing—Job's response to the appearance of God is reverence and the realization that he knows himself and God better than before. He repented not for some undisclosed sin but for his arrogant attitude toward God. Job's friends had been wrong in their understanding of Job's suffering. The Book of Job challenges the view that all suffering is due to sin. Job's suffering did not fit that explanation. Instead, Job's suffering was a testing of his faith. No one explanation fits all cases of suffering. As Job, so we may struggle long and hard to understand or even be able to endure with peace our suffering. Job assures us God will accept our protests. He knows and understands our situation and has a purpose and direction that far exceeds our ability to understand. As we endure and trust Him, we know we will finally experience His presence. We really need nothing more.

42:2–6 GOD, Sovereignty—Job had acknowleged the sovereignty of God, recognizing His authority and power to do as He pleases. Suddenly the presence of God speaking directly to him changed Job's attitude, not his doctrine. Job humbly bowed before the Lord, acknowledged His greatness, and admitted his own insignificance. Job had maintained his innocence before God all along. He could not understand why the righteous and just God had allowed him to suffer so severely. In this climactic scene, Job did not receive an answer to his question. Instead he discovered that the greatness of God and the privilege of trusting God made the search for answers insignificant and unnecessary. He could trust God even in his suffering. See notes on 1:21–22; 19:21.

42:4–6 HUMANITY, Moral Consciousness—Job's friends had set up rules they thought they could keep. According to their rules the just God was in their debt, owing them success, health, prosperity, and long life. Anyone who did not receive these blessings could be categorized among God's enemies. They had made a caricature of God, robbing Him of His sovereign freedom. Job confronted the real God in all His holiness. Such confrontation stirs the human conscience. We see we do not measure up to God morally. No longer do we demand "justified blessing." Instead, we ask for grace and forgiveness. When a person is confronted with God as He is instead of as He had been characterized, there is an awakening of a sense of human need for restoration.

42:5 REVELATION, Divine Presence—God's declaration of Himself brought Job to affirm His présence and action in his own life, indicating that he now saw God. Insight was added to the events of his life and to his conversation with friends, who, even when wrong, served God's revealing purposes by helping Job to see God as He really is. A conversation with friends and extended personal reflection are instruments of God's revelation. Yet God remained a mystery to Job and did not answer his questions completely. Job moved from knowledge of God learned from tradition to knowledge of God learned in personal experience and dialog.

42:7–9 GOD, Justice—Job earlier had wondered why God did not defend him in his troubles. Finally, God spoke up on Job's behalf, rebuking Job's three "friends" for their accusations against Job. In a note of irony, God had Job pray for Eliphaz, Bildad, and Zophar. Thus Job demonstrated his trust in and commitment to God. God truly is a God of justice, though

to Job[s], he said to Eliphaz the Temanite,
"I am angry with you and your two
friends,[t] because you have not spoken of
me what is right, as my servant Job has.[u]
8So now take seven bulls and seven
rams[v] and go to my servant Job[w] and sacrifice a burnt offering[x] for yourselves. My
servant Job will pray for you, and I will
accept his prayer[y] and not deal with you
according to your folly.[z] You have not
spoken of me what is right, as my servant
Job has."[a] 9So Eliphaz the Temanite, Bildad the Shuhite and Zophar the Naamathite[b] did what the LORD told them; and
the LORD accepted Job's prayer.[c]
10After Job had prayed for his friends,
the LORD made him prosperous again[d]
and gave him twice as much as he had
before.[e] 11All his brothers and sisters and
everyone who had known him before[f]
came and ate with him in his house. They
comforted and consoled him over all the
trouble the LORD had brought upon
him,[g] and each one gave him a piece of
silver[z] and a gold ring.
12The LORD blessed the latter part of
Job's life more than the first. He had fourteen thousand sheep, six thousand camels, a thousand yoke of oxen and a thousand donkeys. 13And he also had seven
sons and three daughters. 14The first
daughter he named Jemimah, the second
Keziah and the third Keren-Happuch.
15Nowhere in all the land were there
found women as beautiful as Job's daughters, and their father granted them an inheritance along with their brothers.
16After this, Job lived a hundred and
forty years; he saw his children and their
children to the fourth generation. 17And
so he died, old and full of years.[h]

[z] *11* Hebrew *him a kesitah*; a kesitah was a unit of money of unknown weight and value.

42:7 [s]S Jos 1:7 [t]Job 32:3 [u]ver 8; S Job 9:15
42:8 [v]Nu 23:1,29; Eze 45:23 [w]Job 1:8 [x]S Ge 8:20 [y]Jas 5:15-16; 1Jn 5:16 [z]Ge 20:7; Job 22:30 [a]S ver 7
42:9 [b]Job 2:11 [c]S Ge 19:21; S 20:17; Eze 14:14
42:10 [d]Dt 30:3; Ps 14:7 [e]S Job 1:3; Ps 85:1-3; 126:5-6; Php 2:8-9; Jas 5:11
42:11 [f]S Job 19:13 [g]S Ge 37:35
42:17 [h]S Ge 15:15

He does not always exercise His judgment according to our timetables.

42:8–10 PRAYER, Intercession—See note on 1 Ki 13:6. Job was a man of prayer, even taking his anger, uncertainty, doubt, hopelessness, and frustrations to God. A person faithful in prayer in all situations can make strong intercession for others.

42:10–17 GOD, Grace—The love and grace of God were poured out on Job after his faithful endurance of almost unbelievable tragedy and suffering. God in His time and way rewards those who are faithful to Him. He is not only just, as so often emphasized in this book, but He is also loving and gracious.

42:10,12 SALVATION, Blessing—After all of Job's trials and tribulations, God blessed him twice as much as He had before. This happened *after* Job had repented (v 6) and prayed (vv 8–9) for his erring friends. Ultimately, every person who trusts in God will have a happy ending for his or her story—if not in this world, then surely in the next.

42:11 HUMANITY, Relationships—Just as sorrow is more easily borne when others bring comfort, joy is also more meaningful when shared.

Psalms

Theological Setting

The faith of Israel set to music—that is what we find in Psalms, the hymnbook of the Bible. The 150 hymns provide a source of praise, prayer, and worship. They sound the notes of both celebration and lament. They allow God's people to speak to Him in every mood of life. Written over many centuries, the Psalms are a treasury of devotion, both personal and national. They were not written to be analyzed, but to be read, recited, and sung in the worship of God.

The Psalms mirror life and have as their central theme God Himself. Each psalm presents a new setting in which the faithful bring a special moment of life with all its hopes, needs, and frustrations before the Lord of life. The Psalms provide a way for the human creature to meet and converse with the Creator either in private devotion or in public worship.

Theological Outline

The Book of Psalms is divided into five sections just as the Pentateuch has five books. Each section of the Book of Psalms concludes with a doxology. See 41:13; 72:18-19; 89:52; 106:48; 150. Psalm 1 introduces the book by dividing people into two categories and describing the fate of each. Psalm 150 closes Psalms with a symphony of praise. Otherwise, a way to describe a theological structure for the book as a whole has not been found. What devoted students of God's Word have discovered is the limited number of types of prayer represented in the Psalms. A look at the major types helps us understand how many different functions prayer and praise can serve as we communicate with and worship God.

1. Psalms of lamentation or complaint cry out for help in a situation of distress or frustration. Psalmists protest their innocence or confess their sins. They vow to praise God and give thanks for deliverance. Such psalms show prayer as an honest communication with God in life's worst situations. The following psalms are laments: 3, 4, 5, 6, 7, 12, 13, 17, 22, 25, 26, 28, 35, 38, 39, 40, 41, 42-43, 44, 51, 54, 55, 56, 57, 59, 60, 61, 63, 64, 69, 70, 71, 74, 77, 79, 80, 83, 85, 86, 88, 90, 94, 102, 109, 123, 126, 130, 134, 137, 140, 141, 142, 143, 144.

2. Psalms of thanksgiving describe a situation of distress and how God delivered the psalmist. The psalmist promises to fulfill vows made to God during the distress and invites the congregation to join in thanksgiving and praise to God. These psalms show us our need to acknowledge God's work in our times of trouble and to witness to others of what God has done for us. Thanksgiving psalms are 9-10, 18, 30, 31, 32, 34, 66, 92, 107, 116, 118, 120, 124, 129, 138, 139.

3. Hymns lift the congregation's praise to God, describing God's greatness and majesty. In the hymn, worshipers invite one another to praise God and to provide reasons for such praise. These psalms are hymns: 8, 19, 29, 33, 65, 100, 103, 104, 105, 111, 113, 114, 117, 135, 136, 145, 146, 147, 148, 149, 150.

4. Wisdom psalms probe life's mysteries to teach the congregation about itself and God. These include psalms 1, 14, 36, 37, 49, 53, 73, 78, 112, 119, 127, 128, 133.

5. Kingship psalms detail the role of the human king in God's rule over His people. They also point ahead to the Messiah, who would inaugurate God's kingdom. From them we learn to pray for and respect the role of government officials as well as praise God's Messiah. These include psalms 2, 18, 20, 21, 28, 45, 61, 63, 72, 89, 101, 110, 132.

6. Entrance ceremonies provide questions and answers to teach the expectations God has of His worshipers. Psalms 15 and 24 are entrance ceremonies.

7. Enthronement psalms praise Yahweh as the King enthroned over His universe. They include psalms 47, 93, 96, 97, 98, 99.

8. Songs of Zion praise God indirectly by describing the Holy City where He has chosen to live among His people and be worshiped. They show God lives among His people to protect and direct their lives. These are psalms 46, 48, 76, 84, 87, 122, 132.

9. Psalms of confidence express trust in God's care for and leadership of His people. These appear in psalms 4, 11, 16, 23, 27, 62, 125, 131.

10. Prophetic psalms announce God's will to His worshiping people. These are 50, 52, 58, 81, 82, 91, 95.

11. Liturgical psalms describe activities and responses of God's worshiping congregation. These appear in psalms 67, 68, 75, 106, 108, 115, 121.

Theological Conclusions

The theology of the Psalms is not abstract and philosophical. Rather, it is "popular theology" which emerges from corporate worship. It is really more the theology of the people than the thoughtful formulations of systematic theologians.

These religious poems reflect faith in God. The theme of the Psalms is the presence of God and the continuing encounter of God and His people in worship. God is present in heaven, in His world, and in Israel's worship. This sense of the presence of the Divine is variously described: as the face of God; the name of God; and the glory of God. These terms all describe the nearness of God. The psalmists were certain God was near and would hear their prayers. The Psalms thus constitute a theology of worship and prayer.

Since God Himself is the focus of the Psalms, we will note what they teach about His character and His mighty acts on behalf of His people.

The focus of theology and doctrine in the Psalms is God. They teach that:

1. *God is One.* The Psalms clearly reflect the unique monotheism of the Old Testament. Israel did not worship many gods as did her neighbors. She gave all worship and praise to the one and only God. See Dt 6:4-5.

2. *God is Holy.* He is separate, in a category by Himself, by nature and in moral actions different from humans. He rightly expects His worshipers to be morally pure and the buildings and utensils used in worship to be ritually clean. God's mysterious holiness sets Him apart from all created beings and things.

3. *God is Spirit.* In the Old Testament, the Hebrew word *ruach* can be translated "wind, breath, or spirit." God is eternal Spirit and not a mortal creature. Spirit is more than a symbol of God. It describes His very being, His creative power, divine presence (139:7), and guidance. His Spirit represents His power in the world. It gives healing and health (104:29-30).

4. *God is steadfast Love.* This word describes both His nature and His activity, for they are one and the same. His love prompted His gracious and undeserved choice of Israel (47:4). God's steadfast love is also called His "covenant love." It describes how God deals with His people. God promised to be their God, and they promised to live in obedience to His revealed will in the Law. Divine love includes God's faithfulness (89:1-2,24,33-34) and His total dependability (25:10). God cares and can be counted on to keep His promises. Every verse of Psalm 136 reminds us, "His love endures forever." God's dependable love for His people calls for their corresponding faithfulness (37:27-28). We are under the demand of God's steadfast love. His is holy love and is not to be taken lightly. God's steadfast love is revealed toward all His creation and is not limited to Israel (33:4-6; 36:5-10).

The Psalms frequently praise the mighty acts of God on behalf of individuals and the nation. The historical acts of God became the basis of faith and trust. His actions reflect His character: God creates, saves, reigns, elects, judges, and, thus, reveals Himself to all persons.

1. *God creates.* Israel's faith stood on two mighty creative acts. The Psalms celebrate God's creation (136; 104). The Psalms also celebrated God's creation of the nation Israel by delivering a slave people from Egypt (77:16-20; 78:12-13; 95:7; 100:3; 106; 136). Creation faith led Israel away from pagan worship, for it called the nations to praise Israel's God (96). Such belief in God as Creator also led Israel to call upon the natural elements—sun, moon, stars—to worship the God of Israel, a remarkable claim in a world where such elements were worshiped as chief gods by Israel's neighbors (148). Even the feared sea monsters were viewed as frolicking creatures of Israel's God (104:24-26).

2. *God rules.* Because God is Creator of nature and director of human history, He controls nature and historical events. Free human sinners may thwart His purpose for the time being, but His ultimate goal for creation and His purpose of redemption shall be achieved. The will of God shall be done on earth, in history, as it is done in heaven. The Lord's ultimate goal for His creation is an age of peace, the realization of the kingdom of God on earth (46:8-11). To say God is sovereign King of the universe means He cannot be controlled or manipulated by men and women. He hears our laments and complaints but remains free to act how and when He chooses. He saves from destruction and dispenses justice. God's sovereignty extends over the whole of creation and all the nations (22:27-28). His kingdom, across all generations, is everlasting (145:10-13).

3. *God reveals Himself.* People do not discover God; He reveals Himself to them. In special events, such as the Exodus from Egypt and the coming of Christ, God disclosed Himself to those ready to receive Him. He raised prophets such as Moses to interpret His acts of revelation to His people.

4. *God chooses.* God chose to reveal Himself in a particular land to an elect nation. He elected Abraham (47:9; 105:6-7) and the nation of Israel (33:12; 105:6), but His purpose included all nations (117). Such election involves both privilege and the responsibility to obey God and share one's faith. Evangelism and mission result from the electing love of God (96:1-3). God's election is always of grace and always at the divine initiative. No human can ever deserve the electing love of God. As humans, we can only experience God's loving election and respond in praise and gratitude, obedience and worship. Election calls us to live in covenant relationship with the Creator and with one another.

5. *God forgives.* The Psalms take sin seriously. All sin is opposed to God, and all people are sinners. The Psalms divide people into two groups: the friends of God (forgiven sinners) and the enemies of God and His people (those who do not seek divine forgiveness). Psalm 1 sets forth this truth clearly. The psalmist depicts these two types of people and what happens to them. Many different words describe our separation and estrangement from our Maker. These expressions include missing the mark, evil, wickedness, transgression, and iniquity (51). Because the psalmists took sin seriously, they focused on the importance of divine forgiveness. "Create in me a pure heart, O God" (51:10). To experience divine forgiveness, people must turn from sin and return to the Lord (80:3,7,19).

6. *God saves.* Psalms couples divine forgiveness with salvation. This concept has several facets: God saves from pain and suffering to wellness and wholeness; He saves from sin to pardon; and He saves from the danger of death, giving life. Salvation in the Psalms is both material and spiritual. God saves us in the midst of suffering, with His presence and comfort, and simultaneously saves believers from suffering and from the penalty of our sins. God does not treat our sins fairly. Instead, God Himself atones for our sins, covering them over. He lifts the burden of guilt, cancels the sin debt, and no longer remembers our sin against us. Forgiveness, atonement, and salvation are rooted in the gracious nature and activity of God. He wants to be our Redeemer (103:2-14).

The Psalms teach that humans are endowed with the power of moral choice (1). They also show humans as the crown of God's creation (8). The psalmist stood in awe and wonder at our place in the panorama of creation. God was the source of human dignity and is the hope of our destiny. He made us "a little lower than the heavenly beings" (8:5) or than God (NIV footnote) and crowned us "with glory and honor." He gave us dominion over the created world of nature and animals. How can we respond? We praise our Creator God (8:9).

In the Psalms we find no complete doctrine of life after death. Usually the psalmists spoke of existence after death as Sheol. This was a shadowy existence of both the wicked and righteous dead with no remembrance or praise of God (6:5; 30:9). While God's presence might be in Sheol (139:8), they felt more certain of it "in the land of the living" (27:13). Apparently, as far as the ancient Hebrews knew, death was destruction (88:3-12). The truth of death as departure to be with the Lord awaited a fuller revelation (2 Ti 4:6-8; 1 Co 15:51-53). Only Christ's resurrection fully unlocked death's fearful mystery. The Psalms do reflect the human longing for eternal life (49:15; 73:23-26). However, at best, the psalmist had only a hint of what would be revealed in time by the resurrection of Jesus Christ. God had not yet "brought life and immortality to light through the gospel" (2 Ti 1:10).

Contemporary Teaching

The list of teachings we gain from Psalms has no end. Its 150 songs call us to pray, to praise, to confess, and to testify. The prayer path to God is open at all times for all people in all situations. At all times we should take our feelings to God. He hears and accepts us. In His own way He answers. He brings salvation to our lives. Sin plagues each of us. We rebel against God's way. God waits for us to confess our sins. He does not give us our deserts. He forgives, redeems, and renews our life. We may not be able to sing. We can praise God. We need to be aware of the great acts He is accomplishing in our lives and the great things He has accomplished for us in creation and in His saving actions through Jesus Christ. Knowing His acts for us, we can rejoice and praise Him at all times. We have no monopoly on God. He has chosen us to help all nations praise Him. We must daily testify to others what God has done for us.

BOOK I

Psalms 1–41

Psalm 1

BLESSED is the man[a]
who does not walk[b] in the counsel
of the wicked[c]
or stand in the way[d] of sinners[e]
or sit[f] in the seat of mockers.[g]
2 But his delight[h] is in the law of the
LORD,[i]
and on his law he meditates[j] day
and night.
3 He is like a tree[k] planted by streams[l]
of water,[m]
which yields its fruit[n] in season
and whose leaf[o] does not wither.
Whatever he does prospers.[p]

4 Not so the wicked!
They are like chaff[q]
that the wind blows away.
5 Therefore the wicked will not stand[r]
in the judgment,[s]
nor sinners in the assembly[t] of the
righteous.

6 For the LORD watches over[u] the way
of the righteous,
but the way of the wicked will
perish.[v]

Psalm 2

WHY do the nations conspire[a]
and the peoples plot[w] in vain?
2 The kings[x] of the earth take their
stand
and the rulers gather together
against the LORD
and against his Anointed[y] One.[b] [z]
3 "Let us break their chains,[a]" they say,
"and throw off their fetters."[b]

4 The One enthroned[c] in heaven
laughs;[d]
the Lord scoffs at them.
5 Then he rebukes them in his anger[e]
and terrifies them in his wrath,[f]
saying,
6 "I have installed my King[c] [g]
on Zion,[h] my holy hill.[i]"

7 I will proclaim the decree of the LORD:

1:1 [a]S Dt 33:29; Ps 40:4; 128:4 [b]Ps 89:15 [c]S Job 21:16; Ps 10:2-11 [d]S Ge 49:6 [e]Ps 26:9; 37:38; 51:13; 104:35 [f]Ps 26:4 [g]S Job 11:3; Pr 1:22; Isa 28:14; Hos 7:5 **1:2** [h]Ps 112:1; 119:16,35; Ro 7:22 [i]Ps 19:7; 119:1; Eze 11:20; 18:17 [j]S Ge 24:63 **1:3** [k]Ps 52:8; 92:12; 128:3; Jer 11:16; Zec 4:3 [l]Ps 46:4; 65:9; Isa 33:21; Jer 31:9 [m]S Nu 24:6; S Job 14:9; S Eze 17:5 [n]Ps 92:14; Eze 47:12 [o]Isa 1:30; 64:6 [p]S Ge 39:3 **1:4** [q]S Job 13:25; Isa 40:24; Jer 13:24 **1:5** [r]Ps 5:5 [s]S Job 19:29 [t]Ps 26:12; 35:18; 82:1; 89:5; 107:32; 111:1; 149:1 **1:6** [u]Ps 37:18; 121:5; 145:20; Na 1:7 [v]S Lev 26:38; Ps 9:6 **2:1** [w]Ps 21:11; 83:5; Pr 24:2 **2:2** [x]Ps 48:4 [y]S 1Sa 9:16; Jn 1:41 [z]Ac 4:25-26* **2:3** [a]S Job 36:8 [b]S 2Sa 3:34 **2:4** [c]Isa 37:16; 40:22; 66:1 [d]Ps 37:13; Pr 1:26 **2:5** [e]Ps 6:1; 27:9; 38:1 [f]Ps 21:9; 79:6; 90:7; 110:5 **2:6** [g]Ps 10:16; 24:10 [h]2Ki 19:31; Ps 9:11; 48:2,11; 78:68; 110:2; 133:3 [i]S Ex 15:17

[a] *1* Hebrew; Septuagint *rage* [b] *2* Or *anointed one* [c] *6* Or *king*

1:1—150:6 WORSHIP, Prayer—The individual psalms began for the most part as prayers. They have been annotated in that light. They were collected as components of the singing worship of Israel. As such, they provide a textbook for the study of worship. They show that all experiences and emotions of the individual and the community can be expressed to God as part of worship. Politics, warfare, travel, unjust treatment, illness, marriage—all events of life—can become the subject taken before God in worship. The incorporation of human prayers and hymns addressed to God within the inspired Word of God shows how hymns and prayers of worship express the theology and beliefs of the people as well as teach theology to the people. Worship is response of the human before God in all His glory and compassion. The worship response frees the person to bring all personal and community situations and feelings to God.

1:1–6 EVIL AND SUFFERING, Deserved—The writer of this wisdom psalm stressed the different consequences for two types of people—the person who follows God's law and the wicked. If you study and obey God's Word, you will be blessed. If your character and conduct are shaped by wicked people, you will be punished. Your actions have consequences. This is the generalization affirmed by God's people. The Book of Job teaches us that it is not a theological law which lets us judge the faithfulness of an individual. See note on Pr 1:10–19.

1:1 HUMANITY, Moral Consciousness—This Hebrew word for blessing carries the idea of happiness, indicating a state of pleasurable satisfaction. A life characterized by this emotion comes to those who avoid the path of sin. The Bible assumes everyone recognizes the path of descent into sinfulness through their own inner conscience. To avoid this path we must study God's teachings and fellowship with God's people.

1:1 SALVATION, Blessing—The man who does not walk, stand, or sit with the wicked is blessed. "Blessed" (Hebrew *'ashre*) here means happy. *The blessed person lives within the boundary God sets out for life* with Him and receives observable blessings, sometimes material and always spiritual, which bring happiness. Such blessings are not so much a reward for good acts as the natural product of life with God.

1:1–6 CHRISTIAN ETHICS, Character—God's people are marked by a consciousness of God which pervades all of life. God's ways are a source of guidance, encouragement, and moral strength for us. God's people portray patterns of integrity to their society and are known for their moral uprightness based on obedience to God's Word. Other people display opposite characteristics. They are wicked and face condemnation.

1:2–3 HUMANITY, Relationship to God—We experience delightful life when we are so closely related to God that we find pleasure in habitual, daily study of God's revelation, His Word. The life of those who truly immerse themselves in such study becomes fruitful and ultimately imperishable.

1:6 GOD, Judge—God is the righteous Judge to whom all must give answer. As Creator and sovereign Lord over all creation, God has the right and the authority to hold us accountable to Himself. It reassures us to know the righteous Judge keeps a watchful eye on the pathways of His faithful children.

1:6 HUMANITY, Death and Sin—Death is regularly connected with sin. See note on Ge 2:17.

2:1–12 JESUS CHRIST, Foretold—This is a psalm used when Judah enthroned her kings of David's line. It may also have been a ritual reading used on the anniversary of the king's coronation. Christians also see this as a messianic song referring to Jesus Christ as God's Anointed and His Son. Compare Mt 3:17; 17:5; Mk 1:11; Ac 4:25–28; 13:33; Heb 1:5; 5:5; Rev 1:5; 2:27; 12:5; 19:15. Modern Christians, who do not experience monarchy, must find ways to relate to God and Christ in service and reverence. Worship is an important way for Christians to affirm the truth of this messianic song.

2:4–6 GOD, Sovereignty—God's throne stands not in an earthly temple or palace controlled by humans. He rules from His heavenly throne. He has power and authority to work out *His will* in the world and rule over it. No human ruler may overrule God, but God does use human political authorities and institutions to achieve His purposes. See notes on Ge 15:13–16; 18:14; 24:3,7,50; Dt 1:10.

He said to me, "You are my Son[d];[j]
today I have become your Father.[e][k]
8Ask of me,
and I will make the nations[l] your inheritance,[m]
the ends of the earth[n] your possession.
9You will rule them with an iron scepter[f];[o]
you will dash them to pieces[p] like pottery.[q]"
10Therefore, you kings, be wise;[r]
be warned, you rulers[s] of the earth.
11Serve the LORD with fear[t]
and rejoice[u] with trembling.[v]
12Kiss the Son,[w] lest he be angry
and you be destroyed in your way,
for his wrath[x] can flare up in a moment.
Blessed[y] are all who take refuge[z] in him.

Psalm 3

A psalm of David. When he fled from his son Absalom.[a]

O LORD, how many are my foes!
How many rise up against me!
2Many are saying of me,
"God will not deliver him.[b]" *Selah*[g]
3But you are a shield[c] around me, O LORD;
you bestow glory on me and lift[h] up my head.[d]
4To the LORD I cry aloud,[e]
and he answers me from his holy hill.[f] *Selah*
5I lie down and sleep;[g]
I wake again,[h] because the LORD sustains me.
6I will not fear[i] the tens of thousands
drawn up against me on every side.[j]
7Arise,[k] O LORD!
Deliver me,[l] O my God!
Strike[m] all my enemies on the jaw;
break the teeth[n] of the wicked.
8From the LORD comes deliverance.[o]
May your blessing[p] be on your people. *Selah*

Psalm 4

For the director of music. With stringed instruments. A psalm of David.

ANSWER me[q] when I call to you,
O my righteous God.
Give me relief from my distress;[r]

2:7 [j]S Mt 3:17; S 4:3 [k]S 2Sa 7:14; Ac 13:33*; Heb 1:5*; 6:5 **2:8** [l]Rev 2:26 [m]S Job 22:26; Mt 21:38 [n]Ps 22:27; 67:7 **2:9** [o]S Ge 49:10; Rev 12:5 [p]S Ex 15:6 [q]Isa 30:14; Jer 19:10; Rev 2:27*; 19:15 **2:10** [r]Pr 27:11 [s]Ps 141:6; Pr 8:15; Am 2:3 **2:11** [t]Ps 103:11 [u]Ps 9:2; 35:9; 104:34; Isa 61:10 [v]S 1Ch 16:30 **2:12** [w]ver 7 [x]S Dt 9:8; Rev 6:16 [y]Ps 84:12 [z]Ps 5:11; 34:8; 64:10 **3:1** [a]**3: Title** 2Sa 15:14 **3:2** [b]Ps 22:8; 71:11; Isa 36:15; 37:20 **3:3** [c]S Ge 15:1 [d]Ps 27:6 **3:4** [e]S Job 30:20 [f]Ps 2:6 **3:5** [g]S Lev 26:6 [h]Ps 17:15; 139:18 **3:6** [i]Job 11:15; Ps 23:4; 27:3 [j]Ps 118:11 **3:7** [k]S 2Ch 6:41 [l]Ps 6:4; 7:1; 59:1; 109:21; 119:153; Isa 25:9; 33:22; 35:4; 36:15; 37:20; Jer 42:11; Mt 6:13 [m]Job 16:10 [n]Job 29:17; Ps 57:4; Pr 30:14; La 3:16 **3:8** [o]Ps 27:1; 37:39; 62:1; Isa 43:3,11; 44:6,8; 45:21; Hos 13:4; Jnh 2:9; Rev 7:10 [p]Nu 6:23; Ps 29:11; 129:8 **4:1** [q]Ps 13:3; 27:7; 69:16; 86:7; 102:2 [r]S Ge 32:7; S Jdg 2:15

[d]7 Or *son;* also in verse 12 [e]7 Or *have begotten you* [f]9 Or *will break them with a rod of iron* [g]2 A word of uncertain meaning, occurring frequently in the Psalms; possibly a musical term [h]3 Or *LORD, / my Glorious One, who lifts*

2:10 EVANGELISM, In the Marketplace—God's message must be shared everywhere. The gospel makes an impact in the marketplaces of life, even in the courts of government. Kings and rulers, along with all people, are to be warned so they may become wise unto salvation. That is the evangelistic responsibility of all who have been transformed by God's salvation.

2:12 SALVATION, Blessing—Those who trust in God for their refuge are blessed. See note on 1:1.

3:1–8 GOD, Grace—This whole psalm is a commentary on the grace of God: God's loving way of sustaining us in times of trouble and providing for our needs. In life's most trying times, when even our family deserts us, we can rely on God to hear our cries and help. See notes on Ge 19:12–19,29; 39:21–23; 45:5–9.

3:1–8 EVIL AND SUFFERING, Prayer—A typical lament, this psalm reflects a common response to suffering in the Bible. A lament is a psalm about suffering. There are more lament psalms than any other type. In a typical lament, the sufferer addressed God (v 1*a*), stated the complaint (vv 1*b*–2), expressed trust in God's help (vv 3–6), asked God for help in this situation (v 7*a*), and repeated his confidence in God's help (v 7*b*). Some laments were amazingly candid about the writer's fears and doubts, but the psalmist consistently turned to God for help. The psalmist often wondered why God did not intervene more quickly to alleviate the suffering, but he was confident of God's concern for him. The psalmist patiently waited for God's help and endured unjust suffering. Laments are basically protests of injustice and pleas to God for His justice to prevail. Christians can be equally honest with God in prayer. Taking our concerns about injustice and suffering to God is a basic part of the Christian response to evil and suffering. Like the Hebrews, we can be confident of God's help. If we experience an injustice, we can approach God, knowing that eventually He will correct the situation. We may never see God's correction in this life, but we still maintain hope and faith in God's final victory. See notes on 11:1–7; 35:1–28.

3:1–8 PRAYER, Lament—Ps 3 is a morning prayer; Ps 4, an evening prayer (3:5; 4:8). Both are laments calling on God during stress. The lament invokes God's name, describes the problem, condemns or complains about enemies, affirms confidence in God, petitions for help, and concludes in praise or blessing. A progression typical of laments appears here. David saw that many said God would not deliver him; yet he prayed confidently for deliverance. Finally he declared that deliverance is from God. Many of the "distress" psalms contain this contrast between a clouded opening in adversity with a confident close in faith. Lamentation is a private prayer, but v 8 indicates that it was intended for public use. Expression of laments to God can become occasions for encouraging, instructing, and blessing the worshiping community. See note on Job 7:7–21. See Guide to Petition, pp. 1765–1767.

3:4 REVELATION, Author of Hope—The despairing worshiper cried out to God, who revealed Himself as present and attentive to His hurting child. God revealed His care in the encounter of a night's sleep and sleeplessness. Revelation includes God's answer to the individual who expresses personal need to God.

4:1 GOD, Righteous—In distress, the psalmist called upon God as the righteous One. The ideas of mercy and grace are intimately connected to the idea of righteousness. Because God is righteous, He is asked to aid in times of distress. God's righteousness not only moves Him to oppose what is evil but also to uphold and aid the cause of right when people are in trouble. See note on Jn 17:25.

4:1–8 EVIL AND SUFFERING, Prayer—Suffering may bring anger. The sufferer must learn to express anger in correct ways rather than sinful ones. See note on 3:1–8.

be merciful[s] to me and hear my
prayer.[t]

2How long, O men, will you turn my
glory[u] into shame[i] ?[v]
How long will you love delusions
and seek false gods[j] ?[w] *Selah*
3Know that the LORD has set apart the
godly[x] for himself;
the LORD will hear[y] when I call to
him.

4In your anger do not sin;[z]
when you are on your beds,[a]
search your hearts and be silent.
Selah
5Offer right sacrifices
and trust in the LORD.[b]
6Many are asking, "Who can show us
any good?"
Let the light of your face shine upon
us,[c] O LORD.
7You have filled my heart[d] with greater
joy[e]
than when their grain and new
wine[f] abound.
8I will lie down and sleep[g] in peace,[h]
for you alone, O LORD,
make me dwell in safety.[i]

Psalm 5

For the director of music. For flutes.
A psalm of David.

GIVE ear[j] to my words, O LORD,
consider my sighing.[k]
2Listen to my cry for help,[l]
my King and my God,[m]
for to you I pray.
3In the morning,[n] O LORD, you hear my
voice;
in the morning I lay my requests
before you
and wait in expectation.[o]

4You are not a God who takes pleasure
in evil;
with you the wicked[p] cannot dwell.
5The arrogant[q] cannot stand[r] in your
presence;
you hate[s] all who do wrong.
6You destroy those who tell lies;[t]
bloodthirsty and deceitful men
the LORD abhors.
7But I, by your great mercy,
will come into your house;
in reverence[u] will I bow down[v]
toward your holy temple.[w]
8Lead me, O LORD, in your
righteousness[x]
because of my enemies—
make straight your way[y] before me.

9Not a word from their mouth can be
trusted;
their heart is filled with destruction.

4:1 [s]Ps 30:10 [t]Ps 17:6; 54:2; 84:8; 88:2 **4:2** [u]Ex 16:7; 1Sa 4:21 [v]2Ki 19:26; Job 8:22; Ps 35:26 [w]Jdg 2:17; Ps 31:6; 40:4; Jer 13:25; 16:19; Am 2:4 **4:3** [x]Ps 12:1; 30:4; 31:23; 79:2; Mic 7:2; 1Ti 4:7; 2Pe 3:11 [y]Ps 6:8; Mic 7:7 **4:4** [z]Eph 4:26* [a]Ps 63:6; Da 2:28 **4:5** [b]Ps 31:6; 115:9; Pr 3:5; 28:26; Isa 26:4; Jn 14:1 **4:6** [c]Nu 6:25 **4:7** [d]Ac 14:17 [e]Isa 9:3; 35:10; 65:14,18 [f]S Ge 27:28; S Dt 28:51 **4:8** [g]S Lev 26:6 [h]S Nu 6:26; S Job 11:18 [i]S Dt 33:28; S Jer 32:37 **5:1** [j]S 1Ki 8:29; Ps 17:1; 40:1; 116:2; Da 9:18 [k]Ps 38:9; Isa 35:10; 51:11 **5:2** [l]S Job 19:7; S 24:12; S 36:5 [m]Ps 44:4; 68:24; 84:3 **5:3** [n]Isa 28:19; 50:4; Jer 21:12; Eze 46:13; Zep 3:5 [o]Ps 62:1; 119:81; 130:5; Hab 2:1; Ro 8:19 **5:4** [p]Ps 1:5; 11:5; 104:35; Pr 2:22 **5:5** [q]2Ki 19:32; Ps 73:3; 75:4; Isa 33:19; 37:33 [r]Ps 1:5 [s]Ps 45:7; 101:3; 119:104; Pr 8:13 **5:6** [t]Pr 19:22; S Jn 8:44; Ac 5:3; Rev 21:8 **5:7** [u]Dt 13:4; Jer 44:10; Da 6:26 [v]S 2Sa 12:16; Ps 138:2 [w]S 1Ki 8:48 **5:8** [x]Ps 23:3; 31:1; 71:2; 85:13; 89:16; Pr 8:20 [y]S 1Ki 8:36; Jn 1:23

i2 Or *you dishonor my Glorious One* j2 Or *seek lies*

4:1 SALVATION, As Deliverance—God gives us relief in our distress and makes us stronger. Relief is literally "to make wide, extend, make room for." God gives us room to operate when life seems to restrict us.

4:1–8 PRAYER, Lament—See note on 3:1–8. This is a prayer of faith. When David called on the Lord to answer, he had confidence He would hear. The faith expressed itself in agonizing questions. "How long" frequently appears in laments, expressing impatience and suffering. These are appropriate feelings to take to God in prayer. Anger can be the subject of meditation with God but should be ultimately silenced. Compare Eph 4:26. Worship and faith help overcome anger. Compare Ps 51:17,19; Dt 33:19.

4:3 GOD, Faithfulness—God is faithful to His people. He can always be counted on to hear and to bless when His faithful people need Him. His actions may not suit our timetable, but the faithful God will act. See notes on Ge 8:1; Nu 26:65; Dt 10:11,22; Jos 1:6.

4:5 SALVATION, Belief—Trust (Hebrew *batach*) is belief, faith, and commitment. Trust involves a feeling of security without fear, depending for deliverance on the One with power to rescue. The saved are those who trust in God.

4:6–7 REVELATION, Author of Grace—The Revealer of forgiveness responds to one who prays even when the person is surrounded with doubt. God offers grace to the penitent heart and transforms the restless night of remorse into a peaceful slumber of gratitude and grace. The hour of sleep and meditation is very frequently the hour of revelation, when God can best be heard by the anxious petitioner. The light of God's face is the revealing of His forgiving nature.

4:7 SALVATION, Joy—Often the Bible defines salvation as joy—both in the Old and New Testaments. Joy is the direct response one has to salvation. God's joy is greater than the abundance of food and drink. Such joy leads us to spontaneous praise of God. See note on 9:14.

4:8 ELECTION, Faith—The elect of the God of righteousness need not fear. God vindicates the elect who trust in Him.

5:1–2 GOD, Sovereignty—Addressing prayer to God is a frank recognition of His sovereignty. By praying we confess God is the only One with power and authority to meet our needs and to receive our praise. See note on 2:4–6.

5:1–12 EVIL AND SUFFERING, Prayer—Whatever our situation, we can be sure God does not take pleasure in or ignore evil. See note on 3:1–8.

5:1–12 PRAYER, Ordered—This morning prayer clearly shows the need for daily devotions. Requests should be laid out in orderly fashion before the Lord, expecting God to respond to our needs. The prayer is based on God's holiness and mercy and uttered in reverent humility and faith. See note on 3:1–8.

5:3 GOD, Faithfulness—We can confidently wait for God's answer when we pray. He is always awake listening to us. He faithfully attends to the problems of His faithful people. See note on 4:3.

5:4–6 SIN, Alienation—Sin and God are opposite in meaning. God does not sin, and sin cannot enter God's holy presence. God does not react to sin with passive acceptance. He actively opposes sin. Sin against God is both in attitude and action. As sinners, we must approach God in repentance, humility, reverence, and worship. Only God's mercy allows us in His presence.

5:7–8 GOD, Grace—God's grace is His love and power reaching out to bless and help those who call upon Him. His grace provides an undeserved blessing. See notes on Ge 19:12–19,29; 39:21–23; 45:5–9; Lk 1:30.

5:7 WORSHIP, Reverence—See note on Lev 9:23–24.

5:8 GOD, Righteous—The righteousness of God not only

Their throat is an open grave;[z]
with their tongue they speak
deceit.[a]
10 Declare them guilty, O God!
Let their intrigues be their downfall.
Banish them for their many sins,[b]
for they have rebelled[c] against you.

11 But let all who take refuge in you be
glad;
let them ever sing for joy.[d]
Spread your protection over them,
that those who love your name[e]
may rejoice in you.[f]
12 For surely, O LORD, you bless the
righteous;[g]
you surround them[h] with your favor
as with a shield.[i]

Psalm 6

For the director of music. With stringed instruments. According to *sheminith*.[k]
A psalm of David.

O LORD, do not rebuke me in your
anger[j]
or discipline me in your wrath.
2 Be merciful to me,[k] LORD, for I am
faint;[l]
O LORD, heal me,[m] for my bones are
in agony.[n]
3 My soul is in anguish.[o]
How long,[p] O LORD, how long?

4 Turn,[q] O LORD, and deliver me;
save me because of your unfailing
love.[r]
5 No one remembers you when he is
dead.
Who praises you from the grave[l]?[s]

6 I am worn out[t] from groaning;[u]
all night long I flood my bed with
weeping[v]
and drench my couch with tears.[w]
7 My eyes grow weak[x] with sorrow;
they fail because of all my foes.

8 Away from me,[y] all you who do evil,[z]
for the LORD has heard my weeping.
9 The LORD has heard my cry for
mercy;[a]
the LORD accepts my prayer.
10 All my enemies will be ashamed and
dismayed;[b]
they will turn back in sudden
disgrace.[c]

Psalm 7

A *shiggaion*[m][d] of David, which he sang to the LORD concerning Cush, a Benjamite.

O LORD my God, I take refuge[e] in
you;

5:9 [z]Jer 5:16; Lk 11:44 [a]Ps 12:2; 28:3; 36:3; Pr 15:4; Jer 9:8; Ro 3:13* **5:10** [b]La 1:5 [c]Ps 78:40; 106:7; 107:11; La 3:42 **5:11** [d]Ps 33:1; 81:1; 90:14; 92:4; 95:1; 145:7 [e]Ps 69:36; 119:132 [f]S Job 22:19 **5:12** [g]Ps 112:2 [h]Ps 32:7 [i]S Ge 15:1 **6:1** [j]S Ps 2:5 **6:2** [k]Ps 4:1; 26:11; Jer 3:12; 12:15; 31:20 [l]Ps 61:2; 77:3; 142:3; Isa 40:31; Jer 8:18; Eze 21:7 [m]S Nu 12:13 [n]Ps 22:14; 31:10; 32:3; 38:3; 42:10; 102:3 **6:3** [o]S Job 7:11; Ps 31:7; 38:8; 55:4; S Jn 12:27; Ro 9:2; 2Co 2:4 [p]1Sa 1:14; 1Ki 18:21; Ps 4:2; 89:46; Isa 6:11; Jer 4:14; Hab 1:2; Zec 1:12 **6:4** [q]Ps 25:16; 31:2; 69:16; 71:2; 86:16; 88:2; 102:2; 119:132 [r]Ps 13:5; 31:16; 77:8; 85:7; 119:41; Isa 54:8,10 **6:5** [s]Ps 30:9; 88:10-12; 115:17; Ecc 9:10; Isa 38:18 **6:6** [t]S Jdg 8:5 [u]S Job 3:24; S 23:2; Ps 12:5; 77:3; 102:5; La 1:8,11, 21,22 [v]S Job 16:16 [w]S Job 7:3; Lk 7:38; Ac 20:19 **6:7** [x]S Job 16:8; Ps 31:9; 69:3; 119:82; Isa 38:14 **6:8** [y]Ps 119:115; 139:19 [z]Ps 5:5; S Mt 7:23 **6:9** [a]Ps 28:6; 116:1 **6:10** [b]S 2Ki 19:26 [c]Ps 40:14 **7:1** [d]**7 Title** Hab 3:1 [e]Ps 2:12; 11:1; 31:1

[k]Title: Probably a musical term [l]5 Hebrew *Sheol*
[m]Title: Probably a literary or musical term

opposes what is evil, but also seeks to establish what is right. Because God is righteous, He seeks to lead His people to grow in righteousness.

5:10 PRAYER, Curse—See notes on 3:1–8; 2 Ki 2:24. Commentaries on the imprecatory psalms have varied in their stance from justifying the psalmist's hostility to dismissing the imprecation as valueless for the Christian in view of Mt 5:44. The teaching of Christ is clear. The Christian's primary concern must be for the redemption of persecutors. Still, the imprecatory prayer asking evil for enemies must be valued as a part of holy Scripture. In our prayers, the following factors should be held in balance: (1) *God's* holiness must be uppermost; (2) that holiness must be ultimately vindicated in justice; (3) vindication is in the Lord's hands, not ours (Dt 32:35); and (4) prayer rises above pious language to express true feeling. Not even David could seek his own revenge. He appealed to God (1 Sa 24:1–15). For the Christian, the teaching of Jesus in Mt 5:38–48 is superior as instruction in prayer to the imprecatory psalms in the same way that the New Testament sacrifice is superior to the Old Testament sacrifice.

5:11 SALVATION, Joy—See note on 4:7. God's protection brings singing and rejoicing.

5:11 SALVATION, As Deliverance—God's deliverance is His protection, His defense.

6:1 GOD, Wrath—*The wrath* of God is His expression of opposition to sin. Wrath is not a fit of anger on God's part but is the inevitable expression of God's righteousness when love does not achieve God's purposes. Sickness and trouble may lead us to believe God's wrath is upon us. It may be. Still in the worst of situations, we can pray for His mercy and expect to receive it. See notes on Ge 6:5–8; 17:14; 19:13,24–26; Jos 7:1,25–26; Mt 3:7–10.

6:1–10 EVIL AND SUFFERING, Testing—Traditionally this psalm is known as one of seven "penitential psalms" (6,32,38,51,102,130,143), which express repentance for sins. Here the writer acknowledged that his suffering was a form of divine discipline (v 1). The psalm is in lament form. See note on 3:1–8.

6:1–10 PRAYER, Answer—See note on 3:1–8. Laments were expressed so openly because the psalmist had faith God would answer. A prophet in the Temple may have given an assuring word from God, or inward experience may have produced the confidence. David saw his outer and inner anguish as deserved discipline. He appealed not to his own change of heart but to God's unfailing love. "Agony" (v 2), "anguish" (v 3), and "dismayed" (v 10) represent the same Hebrew word. God's anger showed His enemies would suffer the same anguish they had caused Him. God's answers to our laments are sure and just.

6:2,9 GOD, Grace—God is a God of grace, full of mercy. He desires to save and bless because He is a God of love. In prayer we may find God's mercy already at work in our lives. See note on 5:7–8.

6:4 GOD, Faithfulness—God's love and faithfulness form the basis for prayer. We would not want to pray to a God who did not care for us and would not answer us. See note on 5:3.

6:4 SALVATION, As Deliverance—See note on Jdg 3:9, 15. God delivers us because of His unfailing love. In distress we can call on His love to help us.

6:5 HUMANITY, Nature of Death—The Hebrew word for grave is *Sheol*, the abode of the dead. The normal Old Testament understanding of death was that it was the final end of life. Only the shadowy existence of *Sheol* lay ahead. See Isa 14:9–21. The psalmist seeks the opportunity to continue worshiping God, knowing the dead had no opportunity to praise Him. See note on Job 14:10–22.

6:5 LAST THINGS, Intermediate State—See note on Isa 14:9.

7:1 GOD, Savior—God is the Savior, the refuge of the psalmist. Salvation is the most basic work that God does,

save and deliver me[f] from all who
pursue me,[g]
2 or they will tear me like a lion[h]
and rip me to pieces with no one to
rescue[i] me.

3 O LORD my God, if I have done this
and there is guilt on my hands[j]—
4 if I have done evil to him who is at
peace with me
or without cause[k] have robbed my
foe—
5 then let my enemy pursue and
overtake[l] me;
let him trample my life to the
ground[m]
and make me sleep in the dust.[n]
Selah

6 Arise,[o] O LORD, in your anger;
rise up against the rage of my
enemies.[p]
Awake,[q] my God; decree justice.
7 Let the assembled peoples gather
around you.
Rule over them from on high;[r]
8 let the LORD judge[s] the peoples.
Judge me, O LORD, according to my
righteousness,[t]
according to my integrity,[u] O Most
High.[v]
9 O righteous God,[w]
who searches minds and hearts,[x]
bring to an end the violence of the
wicked
and make the righteous secure.[y]

10 My shield[n][z] is God Most High,
who saves the upright in heart.[a]
11 God is a righteous judge,[b]
a God who expresses his wrath[c]
every day.
12 If he does not relent,[d]
he[o] will sharpen his sword;[e]
he will bend and string his bow.[f]
13 He has prepared his deadly weapons;
he makes ready his flaming arrows.[g]

14 He who is pregnant with evil
and conceives trouble gives birth[h]
to disillusionment.
15 He who digs a hole and scoops it out
falls into the pit[i] he has made.[j]
16 The trouble he causes recoils on
himself;
his violence comes down on his own
head.

17 I will give thanks to the LORD because
of his righteousness[k]
and will sing praise[l] to the name of
the LORD Most High.[m]

7:1 [f]S Ps 3:7 [g]Ps 31:15; 119:86, 157,161
7:2 [h]S Ge 49:9; Rev 4:7 [i]Ps 3:2; 71:11
7:3 [j]Isa 59:3
7:4 [k]Ps 35:7,19; Pr 24:28
7:5 [l]S Ex 15:9 [m]S 2Sa 22:43; 2Ki 9:33; Isa 10:6; La 3:16 [n]S Job 7:21
7:6 [o]S 2Ch 6:41 [p]Ps 138:7 [q]Ps 35:23; 44:23
7:7 [r]Ps 68:18
7:8 [s]S 1Ch 16:33 [t]S 1Sa 26:23; Ps 18:20 [u]S Ge 20:5 [v]S Ge 3:5; S Nu 24:16; S Mk 5:7
7:9 [w]Jer 11:20 [x]S 1Ch 28:9; Ps 26:2; Rev 2:23 [y]Ps 37:23; 40:2
7:10 [z]Ps 3:3 [a]S Job 33:3
7:11 [b]S Ge 18:25; Ps 9:8; 67:4; 75:2; 96:13; 98:9; Isa 11:4; Jer 11:20 [c]S Dt 9:8
7:12 [d]Eze 3:19; 33:9 [e]S Dt 32:41 [f]S 2Sa 22:35; Ps 21:12; Isa 5:28; 13:18
7:13 [g]Ps 11:2; 18:14; 64:3
7:14 [h]Isa 59:4; Jas 1:15
7:15 [i]Ps 35:7,8; 40:2; 94:13; Pr 26:27 [j]S Job 4:8
7:17 [k]Ps 5:8 [l]S 2Ch 31:2; Ro 15:11; Heb 2:12 [m]S Ge 14:18
8:1 [n]S 1Ch 16:10 [o]S Ex 15:11; Lk 2:9 [p]Ps 57:5; 108:5; 113:4; 148:13; Hab 3:3
8:2 [q]Mt 21:16* [r]Ps 143:12

Psalm 8

For the director of music. According to *gittith*.[p] A psalm of David.

1 O LORD, our Lord,
how majestic is your name[n] in all
the earth!

You have set your glory[o]
above the heavens.[p]
2 From the lips of children and infants
you have ordained praise[q][q]
because of your enemies,
to silence the foe[r] and the avenger.

[n]10 Or *sovereign* [o]12 Or *If a man does not repent, / God* [p]Title: Probably a musical term [q]2 Or *strength*

revealing more clearly to us what God is than anything else that God does. Salvation involves deliverance from momentary troubles as here, but it involves much more. See notes on 38:22; 62:1–2,6–8; Lk 1:47; 1 Ti 1:1.

7:1–17 EVIL AND SUFFERING, Deserved—See note on 3:1–8. Here the writer stressed that the wicked would be punished by a just God (vv 14–16). Such suffering is deserved.

7:1–17 PRAYER, God's Presence—Sin and guilt do not have to dominate our prayers. At times we can rightly pray because we are undeserving of the fate we face. David did so in this prayer for protection. He appealed to God as Refuge and as Judge. He affirmed his innocence with an oath and laid before the Lord his motives and those of his enemies with the assurance that God as righteous Judge knows the hidden motives of the heart. Trusting God to answer, he followed the normal Israelite pattern and promised to worship God with thanksgiving and praise when the prayer was answered. False accusations from enemies are no reason for accepting guilt, confessing wrong, or feeling afraid to pray. God can and will protect His faithful against all enemies. See note on 3:1–8.

7:3–5 HUMANITY, Relationship to God—Guilty people must relate to God as the accused with the Judge. If we are guilty of sin, we must expect justice from God. Its end is death. Only total trust in God and His Son Jesus for salvation can change this relationship.

***7:6,8,11* GOD, Justice**—God is a God of justice. He is the righteous Judge. Notice the close relationship between the idea of justice and salvation, for which the writer called in verse 1. Salvation is justice. God saves because He is righteous or just. The person who is right with God welcomes God's judgment as well as praying for Him to judge the enemies. See notes on Ge 3:8–24; 18:20–33; 20:4–6; Ro 2:2.

7:9,11,17 GOD, Righteous—The righteous God knows and examines the inner thoughts of individuals, judges and brings an end to wickedness, makes His righteous people secure, and is constantly at work against evil. Our response to the work of the righteous God is thanksgiving and praise, not fear and trembling. See notes on Lev 1:1; Jos 23:1–16; 2 Sa 10:12; Jn 17:25.

8:1,9 GOD, Glory—This whole psalm praises the glory and sovereignty of God. The God of such glory and power still expresses His concern for us as insignificant creatures. God shares glory and honor with us. See notes on Ex 16:7,10; 40:34–38; Lk 2:9,14.

8:1–9 CREATION, Purposeful—God's created world eloquently testifies to its Maker's grandeur. From the starry universe on high to the small children, everything speaks of the Creator's wisdom and resourcefulness. As we learn more about the universe, we can have the same confidence as the ancient Hebrew poet. Our world is so constructed that cooperation with its Creator and His revealed truth leads us to fulfillment in life. God continues to give seemingly insignificant humans unbelievable controlling powers over His creation.

8:1–9 PRAYER, Praise—Our function as humans is to glorify God. The prayer of praise or hymn does that. God's glory is above the heavens, seen in the heavens, and revealed in the exalted position of humanity. Compare Heb 2:6–8.

3When I consider your heavens,[s]
the work of your fingers,[t]
the moon and the stars,[u]
which you have set in place,
4what is man that you are mindful of him,
the son of man that you care for him?[v]
5You made him a little lower than the heavenly beings[r] [w]
and crowned him with glory and honor.[x]
6You made him ruler[y] over the works of your hands;[z]
you put everything under his feet:[a] [b]
7all flocks and herds,[c]
and the beasts of the field,[d]
8the birds of the air,
and the fish of the sea,[e]
all that swim the paths of the seas.

9O LORD, our Lord,
how majestic is your name in all the earth![f]

Psalm 9[s]

For the director of music. To ⌊the tune of⌋ "The Death of the Son." A psalm of David.

1I will praise you, O LORD, with all my heart;[g]
I will tell of all your wonders.[h]
2I will be glad and rejoice[i] in you;
I will sing praise[j] to your name,[k]
O Most High.

3My enemies turn back;
they stumble and perish before you.
4For you have upheld my right[l] and my cause;[m]
you have sat on your throne,[n]
judging righteously.[o]
5You have rebuked the nations[p] and destroyed the wicked;
you have blotted out their name[q]
for ever and ever.
6Endless ruin has overtaken the enemy,
you have uprooted their cities;[r]
even the memory of them[s] has perished.

7The LORD reigns forever;[t]
he has established his throne[u] for judgment.
8He will judge the world in righteousness;[v]
he will govern the peoples with justice.[w]
9The LORD is a refuge[x] for the oppressed,[y]
a stronghold in times of trouble.[z]
10Those who know your name[a] will trust in you,
for you, LORD, have never forsaken[b]
those who seek you.[c]

11Sing praises[d] to the LORD, enthroned in Zion;[e]

8:3 [s]S Ge 15:5; S Dt 10:14 [t]S Ex 8:19; S 1Ch 16:26; S 2Ch 2:12; Ps 102:25 [u]S Ge 1:16; 1Co 15:41 **8:4** [v]S 1Ch 29:14 **8:5** [w]S Ge 1:26 [x]Ps 21:5; 103:4 **8:6** [y]S Ge 1:28 [z]S Job 10:3; Ps 19:1; 102:25; 145:10; Isa 26:12; 29:23; 45:11; Heb 1:10 [a]Heb 2:6-8* [b]S 1Ki 5:3; 1Co 15:25,27; Eph 1:22 **8:7** [c]Ge 13:5; 26:14 [d]S Ge 2:19 **8:8** [e]Ge 1:26 **8:9** [f]ver 1 **9:1** [g]Ps 86:12; 111:1; 119:2,10, 145; 138:1 [h]S Dt 4:34 **9:2** [i]S Job 22:19; Ps 14:7; 31:7; 70:4; 97:8; 126:3; Pr 23:15; Isa 25:9; Jer 30:19; Joel 2:21; Zep 3:14; S Mt 5:12; Rev 19:7 [j]S 2Ch 31:2 [k]Ps 92:1 **9:4** [l]S 1Ki 8:45 [m]S Job 16:21 [n]Ps 11:4; 47:8; Isa 6:1 [o]Ps 7:11; 67:4; 98:9; 1Pe 2:23 **9:5** [p]Ge 20:7; S 37:10; S 1Ch 16:21; Ps 59:5; 105:14; Isa 26:14; 66:15 [q]S Job 18:17 **9:6** [r]S Dt 29:28; Jer 2:3; 46:1-51:58; Zep 2:8-10 [s]Ps 34:16; 109:15; Ecc 9:5; Isa 14:22; 26:14 **9:7** [t]S 1Ch 16:31; Rev 19:6 [u]Ps 11:4; 47:8; 93:2; Isa 6:1; 66:1 **9:8** [v]S ver 4; Ps 7:11 [w]Ps 11:7; 45:6; 72:2 **9:9** [x]S Dt 33:27; S 2Sa 22:3 [y]Ps 10:18; 74:21 [z]Ps 32:7; 121:7 **9:10** [a]Ps 91:14 [b]S Ge 28:15; S Dt 4:31; Ps 22:1; 37:25; 71:11; Isa 49:14; Jer 15:18; Heb 13:5 [c]Ps 70:4 **9:11** [d]Ps 7:17 [e]S Ps 2:6

[r]5 Or *than God* [s]Psalms 9 and 10 may have been originally a single acrostic poem, the stanzas of which begin with the successive letters of the Hebrew alphabet. In the Septuagint they constitute one psalm.

8:3–8 HUMANITY, Human Nature—In comparison with the heavenly bodies, a person appears to be inconsequential. On the other hand, people are the crown of God's creation. He has given us a responsible place in His created order which sets us just below Him in importance. We do not earn such importance. It is not ours through some evolutionary process which makes us the rulers of our fate and the world's. Human significance comes from the love and honor which God bestows. See note on Ge 1:26–29.

8:3–6 REVELATION, Author of Creation—Contemplating the nighttime sky, the psalmist gained new revelation concerning the smallness of human beings compared to His vast creation. Smallness does not mean lack of power or importance. The psalmist laid awake long enough to grasp the reality of God's purpose for people and creation. Such revelation is awe-inspiring.

9:1—10:18 EVIL AND SUFFERING, Prayer—These two psalms of lament were possibly one psalm originally (NIV text note). See note on 3:1–8. The writer reflected the impatience of the sufferer before God's acts (10:1) and the arrogance of the wicked before they are punished (10:3–13). The wicked are not atheists who deny the existence of God, but they doubt God will punish them. God's just punishment of the wicked is certain but at times is delayed and often is not apparent.

9:1 REVELATION, Worship—The worshiper realized his part in God's revelation. He was to declare and publicize the amazing experiences God produced. The psalmist, first a witness to God's revelation in history and nature, became a means of revelation, a carrier and interpreter of the revelation to others. Revelation begins as personal or community experience but is completed only as God's chosen people testify to, write about, and interpret the revelatory experience.

9:1–20 PRAYER, Praise—Pss 9—10 contrast the strength and justice of the Lord with the weakness and wickedness of man. In Ps 9 God is a Judge. The prayer is to let the enemies know their human limitations. In Ps 10 God is the King who hears the cry of the afflicted to stop terror brought by earthbound humans. The psalmist's identification with the Lord in His righteousness is the basis of appeal in both psalms. The psalmist was a helpless victim who relied on the justice of a powerful God. He contrasted the temporal nature of his enemies with the eternal nature of the Lord. Two gates are pictured in 9:13–14. David was confident God would lift him out of the gates of death so that he could declare the Lord's praises in the gates of Zion. Ps 9 is primarily concerned with the open might and justice of God; Ps 10, with the arrogance and stealthy lurking of people. See note on 34:1–22.

9:4–9 GOD, Judge—God is the righteous Judge. He defends the rights of His people and destroys His wicked enemies. He is determined to establish His justice on earth despite the powers of evil and human sin. The oppressed can trust Him for refuge. See notes on Ge 3:8–24; Ro 2:2.

9:10 GOD, Faithfulness—Human friends may desert us. The faithful God never does. See note on 4:3.

9:10 SALVATION, Belief—Knowing God's name and trusting in Him are the same thing, for to know His name means to be introduced to His basic nature. Those who trust God seek Him, knowing Him to be trustworthy. See note on 4:5.

proclaim among the nations[f] what
he has done.[g]
12For he who avenges blood[h]
remembers;
he does not ignore the cry of the
afflicted.[i]

13O LORD, see how my enemies[j]
persecute me!
Have mercy[k] and lift me up from
the gates of death,[l]
14that I may declare your praises[m]
in the gates of the Daughter of
Zion[n]
and there rejoice in your salvation.[o]
15The nations have fallen into the pit
they have dug;[p]
their feet are caught in the net they
have hidden.[q]
16The LORD is known by his justice;
the wicked are ensnared by the
work of their hands.[r]
Higgaion.[t] *Selah*
17The wicked return to the grave,[u] [s]
all the nations that forget God.[t]
18But the needy will not always be
forgotten,
nor the hope[u] of the afflicted[v] ever
perish.

19Arise,[w] O LORD, let not man
triumph;[x]
let the nations be judged[y] in your
presence.
20Strike them with terror,[z] O LORD;
let the nations know they are but
men.[a] *Selah*

Psalm 10[v]

WHY, O LORD, do you stand far
off?[b]
Why do you hide yourself[c] in times
of trouble?

9:11 [f]Ps 18:49; 44:11; 57:9; 106:27; Isa 24:13; Eze 20:23; 1Ti 3:16 [g]Ps 105:1 **9:12** [h]S 2Sa 4:11 [i]ver 18; Ps 10:17; 22:24; 72:4; Isa 49:13 **9:13** [j]Nu 10:9; Ps 3:7; 18:3 [k]Ps 6:2; 41:4; 51:1; 86:3,16; 119:132 [l]S Job 17:16; Mt 16:18 **9:14** [m]Ps 51:15; 1Pe 2:9 [n]2Ki 19:21; Isa 1:8; 10:32; 37:22; 62:11; Jer 4:31; 6:2; La 1:6; Mic 1:13; Zep 3:14; Zec 2:10; Mt 21:5; Jn 12:15 [o]Ps 13:5; 35:9; 50:23; 51:12 **9:15** [p]S Job 4:8; Ps 35:7 [q]Ps 35:8; 57:6 **9:16** [r]Pr 5:22 **9:17** [s]S Nu 16:30; Pr 5:5 [t]S Job 8:13 **9:18** [u]Ps 25:3; 39:7; 71:5; Pr 23:18; Jer 14:8 [v]ver 12; Ps 74:19 **9:19** [w]Ps 3:7 [x]2Ch 14:11 [y]Ps 110:6; Isa 2:4; Joel 3:12 **9:20** [z]S Ge 35:5; Ps 31:13; Isa 13:8; Lk 21:26 [a]Ps 62:9; Isa 31:3; Eze 28:2 **10:1** [b]Ps 22:1,11; 35:22; 38:21; 71:12 [c]Ps 13:1 **10:2** [d]ver 9; S Job 20:19 **10:3** [e]Ps 49:6; 94:4; Jer 48:30 [f]S Job 1:5 **10:4** [g]Ps 36:1 **10:5** [h]Ps 18:27; 101:5; Pr 6:17; Isa 13:11; Jer 48:29 **10:6** [i]Rev 18:7 **10:7** [j]Ro 3:14* [k]Ps 73:8; 119:134; Ecc 4:1; Isa 30:12 [l]S Job 20:12 **10:8** [m]Ps 37:32; 59:3; 71:10; Pr 1:11; Jer 5:26; Mic 7:2 [n]Hos 6:9

2In his arrogance the wicked man hunts
down the weak,[d]
who are caught in the schemes he
devises.
3He boasts[e] of the cravings of his heart;
he blesses the greedy and reviles the
LORD.[f]
4In his pride the wicked does not seek
him;
in all his thoughts there is no room
for God.[g]
5His ways are always prosperous;
he is haughty[h] and your laws are far
from him;
he sneers at all his enemies.
6He says to himself, "Nothing will
shake me;
I'll always be happy[i] and never
have trouble."
7His mouth is full of curses[j] and lies
and threats;[k]
trouble and evil are under his
tongue.[l]
8He lies in wait[m] near the villages;
from ambush he murders the
innocent,[n]
watching in secret for his victims.
9He lies in wait like a lion in cover;
he lies in wait to catch the
helpless;[o]
he catches the helpless and drags
them off in his net.[p]
10His victims are crushed,[q] they
collapse;
they fall under his strength.
11He says to himself, "God has
forgotten;[r]

10:9 [o]S ver 2 [p]S Job 18:8 **10:10** [q]S Job 9:17 **10:11** [r]Job 22:13; Ps 42:9; 77:9

[t]*16* Or *Meditation*; possibly a musical notation
[u]*17* Hebrew *Sheol* [v]Psalms 9 and 10 may have been originally a single acrostic poem, the stanzas of which begin with the successive letters of the Hebrew alphabet. In the Septuagint they constitute one psalm.

9:11 EVANGELISM, Worship—Although one can worship anywhere, worship reaches its highest level in the corporate worship of God's people. In that worship setting we are to "proclaim among the nations" God's wonderful deeds of salvation. Worship and evangelism go together and complement each other. See note on 48:9.

9:13 HUMANITY, Relationship to God—God, the Giver of life, is the only One who can grant a continuation of life by delivering people from those who oppress or persecute. In our deepest troubles we can cry out in frustration to Him and depend on Him to hear and help.

9:14 SALVATION, Definition—God's salvation causes His people to rejoice. See note on 4:7. Such salvation removes the fear of death.

9:20 HOLY SCRIPTURE, Collection—See note on 41:13. Pss 9—10 form an acrostic, the first letter of 9:1 being the first letter of the Hebrew alphabet and the first letter of 10:17 being the last letter of the Hebrew alphabet. The pattern is not complete. The Septuagint, *the earliest Greek translation,* combines the two psalms into one. Apparently in the process of collecting individual psalms into a literary whole, the psalm was divided to separate the two moods—praise (9) and lament (10), though the separation is not total. God worked through the human process of copying and transmitting biblical texts to preserve and provide His inspired Word.

10:1–18 SIN, Depravity—Psalms of lament graphically describe the plight of helpless righteous worshipers in face of wicked enemies. Sin alienates people from one another and from God. It separates humanity into two camps—depraved sinners and forgiven sinners. Depraved sinners have made sin lord of life. Pride describes God's majestic character (68:35; Ex 15:7). Sinful pride places self on the level with God. The wicked (Hebrew *rasha'*) are sinners who threaten the lives of other people in the community, especially the helpless. Such people praise and bless their own appetites when such praise or boasting belongs only to God. The sinful person has room only for self with no room for God, blithely ignorant that God calls all people to account. Ignorant self-confidence will not help when we face God. We will find God does not forget sin; nor does He neglect the needy. Only the redeemed have sins forgotten (Jer 31:34).

10:1–18 PRAYER, Lament—See note on 3:1–8; 9:1–20. When justice is not served, God's people may confidently carry the case to God. Even when we feel He is hidden in the distance, we can pray in faith.

he covers his face and never sees."[s]

12Arise,[t] LORD! Lift up your hand,[u]
O God.
Do not forget the helpless.[v]
13Why does the wicked man revile
God?[w]
Why does he say to himself,
"He won't call me to account"?[x]
14But you, O God, do see trouble[y] and
grief;
you consider it to take it in hand.
The victim commits himself to you;[z]
you are the helper[a] of the
fatherless.
15Break the arm of the wicked and evil
man;[b]
call him to account for his
wickedness
that would not be found out.

16The LORD is King for ever and ever;[c]
the nations[d] will perish from his
land.
17You hear, O LORD, the desire of the
afflicted;[e]
you encourage them, and you listen
to their cry,[f]
18defending the fatherless[g] and the
oppressed,[h]
in order that man, who is of the
earth, may terrify no more.

Psalm 11

For the director of music. Of David.

IN the LORD I take refuge.[i]
How then can you say to me:
"Flee[j] like a bird to your
mountain.[k]
2For look, the wicked bend their
bows;[l]
they set their arrows[m] against the
strings
to shoot from the shadows[n]
at the upright in heart.[o]
3When the foundations[p] are being
destroyed,
what can the righteous do[w]?"

4The LORD is in his holy temple;[q]
the LORD is on his heavenly
throne.[r]
He observes the sons of men;[s]
his eyes examine[t] them.
5The LORD examines the righteous,[u]
but the wicked[x] and those who love
violence
his soul hates.[v]
6On the wicked he will rain
fiery coals and burning sulfur;[w]
a scorching wind[x] will be their lot.

7For the LORD is righteous,[y]
he loves justice;[z]
upright men[a] will see his face.[b]

Psalm 12

For the director of music. According to *sheminith.*[y] A psalm of David.

HELP, LORD, for the godly are no
more;[c]
the faithful have vanished from
among men.
2Everyone lies[d] to his neighbor;
their flattering lips speak with
deception.[e]

3May the LORD cut off all flattering lips[f]

10:11 [s]S Job 22:14 **10:12** [t]Ps 3:7 [u]Ps 17:7; 20:6; 106:26; Isa 26:11; Mic 5:9 [v]Ps 9:12 **10:13** [w]ver 3 [x]S Job 31:14 **10:14** [y]ver 7; Ps 22:11 [z]S Ps 37:5 [a]S Dt 33:29 **10:15** [b]S Job 31:22 **10:16** [c]S Ex 15:18 [d]S Dt 8:20 **10:17** [e]S Ps 9:12 [f]S Ex 22:23 **10:18** [g]S Dt 24:17; Ps 146:9 [h]S Ps 9:9 **11:1** [i]S Ps 7:1 [j]S Ge 14:10 [k]Ps 50:11 **11:2** [l]S 2Sa 22:35 [m]S Ps 7:13; S 58:7 [n]Ps 10:8 [o]S Job 33:3; Ps 7:10 **11:3** [p]Ps 18:15; 82:5; Isa 24:18 **11:4** [q]S 1Ki 8:48; Ps 18:6; 27:4; Jnh 2:7; Mic 1:2; Hab 2:20 [r]S 2Ch 6:18; S Ps 9:7; Mt 5:34; 23:22; S Rev 4:2 [s]Pr 15:3 [t]Ps 33:18; 66:7 **11:5** [u]S Dt 7:13; S Job 23:10 [v]S Job 28:28; Ps 5:5; 45:7; Isa 1:14 **11:6** [w]S Ge 19:24; S Rev 9:17 [x]S Ge 41:6; S Job 1:19 **11:7** [y]S 2Ch 12:6; S Ezr 9:15; 2Ti 4:8 [z]S Ps 9:8; 33:5; 99:4; Isa 28:17; 30:18; 56:1; 61:8; Jer 9:24 [a]S Job 1:1; Lk 23:50 [b]Ps 17:15; 140:13 **12:1** [c]Isa 57:1; Mic 7:2 **12:2** [d]Ps 5:6; 34:13; 141:3; Pr 6:19; 12:17; 13:3; Isa 32:7 [e]S Ps 5:9; Ro 16:18 **12:3** [f]Pr 26:28; 28:23

[w]3 Or *what is the Righteous One doing* [x]5 Or *The LORD, the Righteous One, examines the wicked, /* [y]Title: Probably a musical term

10:16 GOD, Sovereignty—God is a righteous ruler who will both put down the wicked and lift up the downtrodden and helpless. No matter how powerful human rulers may appear to be, in His supreme authority God rules over all. One day the whole earth will recognize His rule.
10:18 HUMANITY, Physical Nature—The Bible has an exalted view of humanity. See note on 8:3–8. Still it always understands people as being of the earth with all of the physical and mortal limitations which that implies. See note on Ge 2:7. This includes all military and political rulers who exercise terrifying power. They soon return to earth to terrify no more. God continues to rule the world and protect the helpless from proud, power-mad rulers.
11:1,4 GOD, Sovereignty—Nothing can displace or overcome God in His world. We can depend upon Him when all else fails because of His power and authority. He brought this world into being and will guide it to its successful conclusion. The sovereignty of God is poured out in wrath upon the wicked to defend the helpless and the godly because God is righteous and loves justice. See notes on 2:4–6; 7:9,11,17.
11:1–7 EVIL AND SUFFERING, Prayer—This psalm of trust in God stresses that God will eventually punish the wicked (vv 5–7). Although we may be perplexed about the reason for our suffering, our basic confidence is in God's character. We may experience injustice, but God's justice will eventually prevail.
11:1–7 PRAYER, Faith—David's friends counseled safety in the seen, in the mountain. David trusted in the unseen God. His friends saw the lurking arrow. David trusted the searching eye of God. Times of trouble need not bring forth lamentation. They may give rise to statements of confidence in God.
11:4–7 REVELATION, Divine Presence—The place of worship is God's symbolic dwelling place, where people meet God and offer Him sacrifices as expressions of love and gratitude. The Temple revealed God's constant presence and watchful testing of His people (17:3). The writer linked upright behavior with closeness with God, revealing that God reveals Himself to those who follow His right living. To see God's face is to know and understand His nature (22:24; 24:6). See note on Ex 33:18–22.
12:1–8 EVIL AND SUFFERING, Endurance—Evil forces may appear to dominate the world and our life, but God's people can trust Him for protection and justice. See note on 3:1–8.
12:1–8 PRAYER, Lament—See note on 3:1–8. This lament appeals to the God of righteous words against the attacks of unrighteous words. David based his prayer on God's opposition to the specific wickedness of his enemies. Righteousness may bring loneliness. God is always there to hear and act. God's specific answer may have been spoken in private worship by a priest or prophet. See note on 6:1–10.

and every boastful tongue[g]
4that says, "We will triumph with our
tongues;[h]
we own our lips[z]—who is our
master?"

5"Because of the oppression[i] of the
weak
and the groaning[j] of the needy,
I will now arise,[k]" says the LORD.
"I will protect them[l] from those
who malign them."
6And the words of the LORD are
flawless,[m]
like silver refined[n] in a furnace[o] of
clay,
purified seven times.
7O LORD, you will keep us safe[p]
and protect us from such people
forever.[q]
8The wicked freely strut[r] about
when what is vile is honored among
men.

Psalm 13

For the director of music. A psalm of David.

1HOW long,[s] O LORD? Will you forget
me[t] forever?
How long will you hide your face[u]
from me?
2How long must I wrestle with my
thoughts[v]
and every day have sorrow in my
heart?
How long will my enemy triumph
over me?[w]

3Look on me[x] and answer,[y] O LORD
my God.
Give light to my eyes,[z] or I will
sleep in death;[a]
4my enemy will say, "I have overcome
him,[b]"
and my foes will rejoice when I
fall.[c]

5But I trust in your unfailing love;[d]
my heart rejoices in your salvation.[e]
6I will sing[f] to the LORD,
for he has been good to me.

Psalm 14

14:1–7pp — Ps 53:1–6

For the director of music. Of David.

1THE fool[a] says in his heart,
"There is no God."[g]
They are corrupt, their deeds are vile;
there is no one who does good.

2The LORD looks down from heaven[h]
on the sons of men
to see if there are any who
understand,[i]
any who seek God.[j]
3All have turned aside,[k]

12:3 [g]Ps 73:9; Da 7:8; Jas 3:5; Rev 13:5 **12:4** [h]Pr 18:21; Jas 3:6 **12:5** [i]Ps 44:24; 62:10; 72:14; 73:8; Ecc 4:1; 5:8; Isa 3:15; 5:7; 30:12; 59:13; Ac 7:34 [j]S Ps 6:6 [k]Ps 3:7 [l]Ps 34:6; 35:10 **12:6** [m]S 2Sa 22:31; Ps 18:30 [n]S Job 23:10; S 28:1; Isa 48:10; Zec 13:9 [o]Ps 119:140 **12:7** [p]Ps 16:1; 27:5 [q]Ps 37:28; Jn 17:12 **12:8** [r]Ps 55:10-11 **13:1** [s]Ps 6:3 [t]Ps 42:9; La 5:20 [u]S Dt 31:17; S Ps 22:24; S Isa 8:17; S 54:9 **13:2** [v]Ps 42:4; 55:2; 139:23; Isa 33:18; Da 7:28 [w]Ps 94:3 **13:3** [x]Ps 9:12; 25:18; 31:7; 35:23; 59:4; 80:14; 107:41; 119:50,153 [y]S Ps 4:1 [z]S Ezr 9:8 [a]Ps 76:5; 90:5; Jer 51:39 **13:4** [b]S 1Ki 19:2; Ps 25:2 [c]Ps 38:16; 118:13 **13:5** [d]S Ps 6:4 [e]S Job 33:26; Ps 9:14; Isa 25:9; 33:2 **13:6** [f]S Ex 15:1; Ps 7:17 **14:1** [g]Ps 10:4 **14:2** [h]Job 41:34; Ps 85:11; 102:19; La 3:50 [i]Ps 92:6 [j]S Ezr 6:21 **14:3** [k]S 1Sa 8:3; 1Ti 5:15

[z]*4* Or */ our lips are our plowshares* [a]*1* The Hebrew words rendered *fool* in Psalms denote one who is morally deficient.

12:6 HOLY SCRIPTURE, Word—God's declared words are revealed as without error, as pure as the product of the most complete refining method for silver known at the time: seven times fired in a furnace to remove any impurity. Word in the Hebrew refers to a verbal speech and is used many times in Scripture to refer to God's utterances. An inspired priest or prophet gave the worshiper a direct word from God. The words were preserved in writing for education and worship in the Temple.

12:7 SALVATION, Definition—God's salvation is refuge. It offers safety and protection from our enemies (27:5).

13:1–6 EVIL AND SUFFERING, Endurance—God's people experience moments when God seems to have vanished and to have forgotten us. Even then we can trust God's love and praise Him. He is good even to the sufferer. See note on 3:1–8.

13:1 REVELATION, Divine Presence—The distraught psalmist understood that to see God's face is to be right with Him and that the justice in this life is also a manifestation of God's face. Revelation of God is our basic need. Too often we realize this only in time of crisis.

13:1–6 PRAYER, Faith—See note on 3:1–8. Lamentation is a statement of faith in trusting God with our most serious questions. The prayer is in three parts: despair (vv 1–2), prayer (vv 3–4), and trust (vv 5–6). The despair is expressed in four "how long?" questions. The "how long" is balanced by David's trust in God's nontemporal "unfailing love." Trust is expressed in the promise to praise. See note on 7:1–17.

13:3 HUMANITY, Life—Human illness brings us to the brink of death, where we fear God has forsaken us. Our only hope is to cry out for the light of life. Death is viewed as bringing darkness, since the dead cannot see light. God, however, is the only One who can give life. As long as life endures, God has power to renew life and health.

13:5 GOD, Love—The psalmist praised the love of God, making it equivalent to the salvation of God. This expression of faith in the love of God was made when the writer was in the depths of despair or suffering. Even in the midst of difficulties we can trust the love and goodness of God. See notes on Ex 3:7; Dt 32:10–12,36; Mt 10:29–31; Jn 3:16.

13:5 SALVATION, Belief—Salvation and trust belong together. We can trust because we know God loves us. See note on 4:5.

14:1–7 EVIL AND SUFFERING, Endurance—Righteous suffering and the prosperity of the wicked do not prove God has lost interest and will not act to restore justice. See note on 9:1—10:18.

14:1 SIN, Depravity—Sin involves atheism. Such atheism does not argue philosophically that God does not exist. It argues practically with every action of life that God does not care and will not act. Such an approach to a particular moment of life lies behind a sinful act. Every person is guilty both of the attitude and the act. The only solution to our sin problem is to seek God consciously in every moment of life, in every decision of life, and through every act of life. See note on 10:1–18.

14:1–7 PRAYER, Instruction—Ps 14 contrasts the wickedness of scorn for God with a thoroughgoing righteousness of regard for God in Ps 15. The extreme evil derives from lack of faith. Unbelief is foolish because the skeptic never learns (v 4) or never experiences God's presence. The prayer is given in worship or instruction (v 7), showing that prayer not only speaks to God but also instructs the congregation. Compare Pss 1; 15; 37; 49; 73; 112; 127; 128; 133.

14:3–4 SIN, Universal Nature—In God's sight all people are sinners. We have each chosen to ignore God (v 1) and not to do what is good. Failure to do good is as sinful as choosing to

they have together become
corrupt;[l]
there is no one who does good,[m]
not even one.[n]

4Will evildoers never learn—[o]
those who devour my people[p] as
men eat bread
and who do not call on the LORD?[q]
5There they are, overwhelmed with
dread,
for God is present in the company of
the righteous.
6You evildoers frustrate the plans of the
poor,
but the LORD is their refuge.[r]

7Oh, that salvation for Israel would
come out of Zion![s]
When the LORD restores the
fortunes[t] of his people,
let Jacob rejoice and Israel be glad!

Psalm 15

A psalm of David.

LORD, who may dwell[u] in your
sanctuary?[v]
Who may live on your holy hill?[w]

2He whose walk is blameless[x]
and who does what is righteous,
who speaks the truth[y] from his heart
3 and has no slander[z] on his tongue,
who does his neighbor no wrong
and casts no slur on his fellowman,
4who despises a vile man
but honors[a] those who fear the
LORD,
who keeps his oath[b]
even when it hurts,
5who lends his money without usury[c]
and does not accept a bribe[d] against
the innocent.

He who does these things
will never be shaken.[e]

Psalm 16

A *miktam*[b] of David.

KEEP me safe,[f] O God,
for in you I take refuge.[g]

2I said to the LORD, "You are my Lord;[h]
apart from you I have no good
thing."[i]
3As for the saints[j] who are in the
land,[k]
they are the glorious ones in whom
is all my delight.[c]
4The sorrows[l] of those will increase
who run after other gods.[m]
I will not pour out their libations of
blood
or take up their names[n] on my lips.

5LORD, you have assigned me my
portion[o] and my cup;[p]
you have made my lot[q] secure.
6The boundary lines[r] have fallen for
me in pleasant places;
surely I have a delightful
inheritance.[s]

7I will praise the LORD, who counsels
me;[t]
even at night[u] my heart instructs
me.
8I have set the LORD always before me.

14:3 [l]2Pe 2:7 [m]1Ki 8:46; Ps 143:2; Ecc 7:20 [n]Ro 3:10-12* **14:4** [o]Ps 82:5; Jer 4:22 [p]Ps 27:2; Mic 3:3 [q]Ps 79:6; Isa 64:7; 65:1; Jer 10:25; Hos 7:7 **14:6** [r]S 2Sa 22:3 **14:7** [s]Ps 2:6 [t]S Dt 30:3; S Jer 48:47 **15:1** [u]Ex 29:46; Ps 23:6; 27:4; 61:4 [v]Ex 25:8; 1Ch 22:19; Ps 20:2; 78:69; 150:1 [w]S Ex 15:17 **15:2** [x]S Ge 6:9; S Ps 18:32; Eph 1:4; S 1Th 3:13; Tit 1:6 [y]Pr 16:13; Isa 45:19; Jer 7:28; 9:5; Zec 8:3,16; Ro 9:1; S Eph 4:25 **15:3** [z]S Lev 19:16 **15:4** [a]S Job 19:9; Ac 28:10 [b]S Dt 23:21; S Jos 9:18; Mt 5:33 **15:5** [c]S Ex 22:25 [d]S Ex 18:21; S 1Sa 8:3; Ac 24:26 [e]S Job 29:18; Ps 21:7; 112:6; Ac 2:25; Heb 12:28; 2Pe 1:10 **16:1** [f]S Ps 12:7 [g]Ps 2:12 **16:2** [h]Ps 31:14; 118:28; 140:6 [i]Ps 73:25 **16:3** [j]Dt 33:3; Ps 30:4; 85:8; Da 7:18; Ac 9:13; Ro 1:7 [k]Ps 101:6 **16:4** [l]Ps 32:10; Pr 23:29 [m]Ex 18:11; 20:3; S Dt 8:19; S 31:20 [n]S Ex 23:13 **16:5** [o]S Lev 2:2 [p]Ps 23:5; 75:8; 116:13; Isa 51:17; La 4:21; Eze 23:32-34; Hab 2:16 [q]S Job 31:2 **16:6** [r]S Dt 19:14; Ps 104:9; Pr 8:29; Jer 5:22 [s]S Job 22:26 **16:7** [t]Ps 73:24; Pr 15:22; Isa 11:2 [u]Job 35:10; Ps 42:8; 77:6

[b]Title: Probably a literary or musical term [c]3 Or *As for the pagan priests who are in the land / and the nobles in whom all delight, I said:*

---

do bad. The sinful life has turned sour, losing desire and ability to make proper moral choices. Only calling on the Lord can change such sinners. By calling on God they can find forgiveness and become part of the community He calls righteous as He looks down from heaven. See note on Job 15:14–16.

15:1–5 CHRISTIAN ETHICS, Worship—Who will truly worship God? The psalmist answers that with one of the many character portrayals of the Old Testament. Note the several references to treatment of other persons which are given as direct proofs of relationship to God. See note on 24:3–6.

15:1–5 PRAYER, Instruction—See note on 14:1–7. The psalmist asked God who may dwell as His guest. Vv 2–5 describe what God searched for in 14:2 and who are invited to worship. Public worship ceremonies include prayers which help God's people learn God's expectations of His worshipers.

15:4 SALVATION, Fear of God—God wants His people to honor those who fear and worship Him. God-fearers is another description of God's people. See note on Ge 22:12.

16:1–11 EVIL AND SUFFERING, God's Future Help—Worship of other gods leads to sorrow. Trust in God brings hope of healing in the face of death. This Old Testament step toward resurrection hope found fulfillment in Christ.

16:1–11 PRAYER, Fellowship with God—This prayer expresses a perfect relationship to the Lord. This includes total dependence on God for all that is good and true delight in the Lord's saints. Compare Mk 12:30–31. Joy in the Lord contrasts with the sorrow of those who choose other gods. Exclusive loyalty to the Lord brings contentment with whatever lot God gives us in our lives. Prayer is a time to express confidence in God. Compare Ac 2:25–28.

16:3 GOD, Holy—Saints are people touched by God's holiness. No one is saintly, or holy, apart from God. Only God is holy. Those who come into right relationship with Him may be said to share in His holiness. See notes on Ex 3:5–6; 19:10–24; Lev 11:44–45; 2 Co 7:1.

16:7–11 REVELATION, Word—God's word of counsel and hope can come to the individual in many forms. In worship the psalmist would have heard God's written word interpreted. At night God spoke through vision, dream, or personal meditation. Revelation led to awareness of God's continual presence and confidence God will not abandon His followers. Revelation of God's presence brings direction in life and hope for eternity.

16:7–11 LAST THINGS, Believers' Resurrection—The psalmist hoped for salvation from death and decay. The expectation was that God does not abandon the righteous to *Sheol.* See note on Isa 14:9. Rather, God makes for His own a path of life, fills them with joy in His presence, and bestows eternal pleasures at His own right hand. The embryonic hope of life beyond the grave reaches full revelation in the New Testament. See Ac 2:25–28.

16:8–10 JESUS CHRIST, Foretold—This ancient hymn of confidence in God was taken up by the early Christian commu-

Because he is at my right hand,[v]
I will not be shaken.[w]

9Therefore my heart is glad[x] and my tongue rejoices;
my body also will rest secure,[y]
10because you will not abandon me to the grave,[d] [z]
nor will you let your Holy One[e] [a] see decay.[b]
11You have made[f] known to me the path of life;[c]
you will fill me with joy in your presence,[d]
with eternal pleasures[e] at your right hand.[f]

Psalm 17

A prayer of David.

HEAR,[g] O LORD, my righteous plea;
listen to my cry.[h]
Give ear[i] to my prayer—
it does not rise from deceitful lips.[j]
2May my vindication[k] come from you;
may your eyes see what is right.[l]

3Though you probe my heart[m] and examine me at night,
though you test me,[n] you will find nothing;[o]
I have resolved that my mouth will not sin.[p]
4As for the deeds of men—
by the word of your lips
I have kept myself
from the ways of the violent.
5My steps have held to your paths;[q]
my feet have not slipped.[r]

6I call on you, O God, for you will answer me;[s]
give ear to me[t] and hear my prayer.[u]
7Show the wonder of your great love,[v]
you who save by your right hand[w]
those who take refuge[x] in you from their foes.
8Keep me[y] as the apple of your eye;[z]
hide me[a] in the shadow of your wings[b]
9from the wicked who assail me,
from my mortal enemies who surround me.[c]

10They close up their callous hearts,[d]
and their mouths speak with arrogance.[e]
11They have tracked me down, they now surround me,[f]
with eyes alert, to throw me to the ground.
12They are like a lion[g] hungry for prey,[h]
like a great lion crouching in cover.

13Rise up,[i] O LORD, confront them, bring them down;[j]
rescue me from the wicked by your sword.
14O LORD, by your hand save me from such men,
from men of this world[k] whose reward is in this life.[l]
You still the hunger of those you cherish;
their sons have plenty,
and they store up wealth[m] for their children.
15And I—in righteousness I will see your face;
when I awake,[n] I will be satisfied with seeing your likeness.[o]

16:8 [v]1Ki 2:19; 1Ch 6:39; Ps 73:23 [w]Ps 15:5
16:9 [x]Ps 4:7; 13:5; 28:7; 30:11 [y]S Dt 33:28
16:10 [z]S Nu 16:30; Ps 30:3; 31:17; 86:13; Hos 13:14 [a]S 2Ki 19:22 [b]S Job 17:14; Ac 2:31; 13:35*
16:11 [c]Ps 139:24; Mt 7:14 [d]Ac 2:25-28* [e]Ps 21:6 [f]Ps 80:17
17:1 [g]Ps 30:10; 64:1; 80:1; 140:6 [h]Ps 5:2; 39:12; 142:6; 143:1 [i]S Ps 5:1 [j]Isa 29:13
17:2 [k]Ps 24:5; 26:1; Isa 46:13; 50:8-9; 54:17 [l]Ps 99:4
17:3 [m]Ps 139:1; Jer 12:3 [n]S Job 7:18 [o]Job 23:10; Jer 50:20 [p]Ps 39:1
17:5 [q]Job 23:11; Ps 44:18; 119:133 [r]Dt 32:35; Ps 73:2; 121:3
17:6 [s]Ps 86:7 [t]Ps 116:2 [u]S Ps 4:1
17:7 [v]Ps 31:21; 69:13; 106:45; 107:43; 117:2 [w]S Ps 10:12 [x]Ps 2:12
17:8 [y]S Nu 6:24 [z]S Dt 32:10; Pr 7:2 [a]Ps 27:5; 31:20; 32:7 [b]Ru 2:12; Ps 36:7; 63:7; Isa 34:15
17:9 [c]Ps 109:3
17:10 [d]Ps 73:7; 119:70; Isa 6:10 [e]S 1Sa 2:3
17:11 [f]Ps 88:17
17:12 [g]Ps 7:2; Jer 5:6; 12:8; La 3:10 [h]S Ge 49:9
17:13 [i]S Nu 10:35 [j]Ps 35:8; 55:23; 73:18
17:14 [k]Lk 16:8 [l]Ps 49:17; Lk 16:25 [m]Isa 2:7; 57:17
17:15 [n]S Ps 3:5 [o]S Nu 12:8; S Mt 5:8; 1Jn 3:2

[d]10 Hebrew *Sheol* [e]10 Or *your faithful one* [f]11 Or *You will make*

nity and applied to the resurrection of Christ (Ac 2:27; 13:35). Contemporary Christians still sing the faith of resurrection, adding their voices to the anthem of praise for the eternal life God gives through Jesus Christ.

16:11 SALVATION, Joy—We experience joy in God's presence. The path of life is strewn with eternal pleasures. We catch a glimpse of salvation as eternal life in this text. See note on 4:7.

17:1–15 EVIL AND SUFFERING, Prayer—Evil people are arrogant, callous, and violent. They have no future hope. God's people must endure the distress caused by the wicked until God chooses to answer our prayers. See note on 3:1–8.

17:1–15 PRAYER, Lament—See note on 3:1–8. Prayer is seeking agreement with God, whether in confession, petition, or praise. Here, David aligned himself with God as righteous Judge. His plea was righteous (v 1); his steps were in God's path (v 5); *his desire was for the face of the Lord* (v 15). *Because of this* alignment, he expected an answer (v 6). See note on 6:1–10. This is one of six psalms actually designated a prayer (86; 90; 102; 142; Hab 3). See note on Ne 11:17.

17:7 GOD, Savior—Love and salvation are very closely related ideas. God shows His love by saving us from our enemies. His love becomes active in opposing evil. See notes on 7:1; 13:5.

17:15 LAST THINGS, Believers' Resurrection—In dire circumstances the psalmist prayed for God to hear his righteous plea (Hebrew *tsedeq*) and give him vindication (Hebrew *mishpat*). The prayer concludes in hope for the community (v 14) and individual (v 15). When he awoke, the psalmist was confident he would see righteousness (Hebrew *tsedeq*) granted. He would know God's presence. The language of waking from sleep to behold God's face came to be understood as hope in a life beyond death. This fits the use of similar language in the New Testament in which death for believers is called sleep. See note on Ac 7:60. Resurrection elsewhere also is called an awakening. See note on Da 12:2. The psalmist, in a high moment of inspiration, was able to rise above the usual fatalism about death to a hope of awakening from death in the presence of God. See notes on Ps 49:9–15; 2 Co 5:8.

Psalm 18

18:Title–50pp — 2Sa 22:1–51

For the director of music. Of David the servant of the LORD. He sang to the LORD the words of this song when the LORD delivered him from the hand of all his enemies and from the hand of Saul. He said:

I love you, O LORD, my strength.[p]
2The LORD is my rock,[q] my fortress[r]
and my deliverer;[s]
my God is my rock, in whom I take
refuge.[t]
He is my shield[u] and the horn[g] of
my salvation,[v] my stronghold.
3I call to the LORD, who is worthy of
praise,[w]
and I am saved from my enemies.[x]

4The cords of death[y] entangled me;
the torrents[z] of destruction
overwhelmed me.
5The cords of the grave[h] coiled around
me;
the snares of death[a] confronted me.
6In my distress[b] I called to the LORD;[c]
I cried to my God for help.
From his temple he heard my voice;[d]
my cry came[e] before him, into his
ears.
7The earth trembled[f] and quaked,[g]
and the foundations of the
mountains shook;[h]
they trembled because he was
angry.[i]
8Smoke rose from his nostrils;[j]
consuming fire[k] came from his
mouth,
burning coals[l] blazed out of it.
9He parted the heavens and came
down;[m]
dark clouds[n] were under his feet.
10He mounted the cherubim[o] and flew;
he soared[p] on the wings of the
wind.[q]
11He made darkness his covering,[r] his
canopy[s] around him—
the dark rain clouds of the sky.
12Out of the brightness of his presence[t]
clouds advanced,
with hailstones[u] and bolts of
lightning.[v]
13The LORD thundered[w] from heaven;
the voice of the Most High
resounded.[i]
14He shot his arrows[x] and scattered ⌞the
enemies⌟,
great bolts of lightning[y] and routed
them.[z]
15The valleys of the sea were exposed
and the foundations[a] of the earth
laid bare
at your rebuke,[b] O LORD,
at the blast of breath from your
nostrils.[c]

16He reached down from on high and
took hold of me;
he drew me out of deep waters.[d]
17He rescued me from my powerful
enemy,[e]
from my foes, who were too strong
for me.[f]
18They confronted me in the day of my
disaster,[g]
but the LORD was my support.[h]
19He brought me out into a spacious
place;[i]
he rescued me because he delighted
in me.[j]
20The LORD has dealt with me according
to my righteousness;[k]
according to the cleanness of my
hands[l] he has rewarded me.[m]

18:1 [p]S Ex 15:2; S Dt 33:29; S 1Sa 2:10; Ps 22:19; 28:7; 59:9; 81:1; Isa 12:2; 49:5; Jer 16:19 **18:2** [q]S Ex 33:22 [r]Ps 28:8; 31:2,3; Isa 17:10; Jer 16:19 [s]Ps 40:17 [t]Ps 2:12; 9:9; 94:22 [u]S Ge 15:1; Ps 28:7; 84:9; 119:114; 144:2 [v]S 1Sa 2:1; S Lk 1:69 **18:3** [w]S 1Ch 16:25 [x]S Ps 9:13 **18:4** [y]Ps 116:3 [z]Ps 93:4; 124:4; Isa 5:30; 17:12; Jer 6:23; 51:42,55; Eze 43:2 **18:5** [a]Pr 13:14 **18:6** [b]S Dt 4:30 [c]Ps 30:2; 99:6; 102:2; 120:1 [d]Ps 66:19; 116:1 [e]S Job 16:18 **18:7** [f]Ps 97:4; Isa 5:25; 64:3 [g]S Jdg 5:4 [h]S Jdg 5:5 [i]S Job 9:5; Jer 10:10 **18:8** [j]S Job 41:20 [k]S Ex 15:7; S 19:18; S Job 41:21; Ps 50:3; 97:3; Da 7:10 [l]Pr 25:22; Ro 12:20 **18:9** [m]S Ge 11:5; S Ps 57:3 [n]S Ex 20:21; S Dt 33:26; S Ps 104:3 **18:10** [o]S Ge 3:24; Eze 10:18 [p]S Dt 33:26 [q]Ps 104:3 **18:11** [r]S Ex 19:9; S Dt 4:11 [s]S Job 22:14; Isa 4:5; Jer 43:10 **18:12** [t]Ps 104:2 [u]S Jos 10:11 [v]S Job 36:30 **18:13** [w]S Ex 9:23; S 1Sa 2:10 **18:14** [x]S Dt 32:23 [y]S Job 36:30; Rev 4:5 [z]S Jdg 4:15 **18:15** [a]S Ps 11:3 [b]Ps 76:6; 104:7; 106:9; Isa 50:2 [c]S Ex 15:8 **18:16** [d]Ex 15:5; Ps 69:2; Pr 18:4; 20:5

18:17 [e]ver 48; Ps 38:19; 59:1; 143:9 [f]S Jdg 18:26 **18:18** [g]Pr 1:27; 16:4; Jer 17:17; 40:2; Ob 1:13 [h]Ps 20:2; Isa 3:1 **18:19** [i]Ps 31:8 [j]S Nu 14:8 **18:20** [k]S 1Sa 26:23 [l]Job 22:30; Ps 24:4 [m]S Ru 2:12; S 2Ch 15:7; 1Co 3:8

[g]*2 Horn* here symbolizes strength. [h]*5* Hebrew *Sheol* [i]*13* Some Hebrew manuscripts and Septuagint (see also 2 Samuel 22:14); most Hebrew manuscripts *resounded, / amid hailstones and bolts of lightning*

18:1–48 GOD, Savior—We praise God because He is our powerful Savior. Salvation includes both refuge and deliverance. God rescues and protects those who faithfully obey Him. Such rescue may involve equipping us to defend ourselves (vv 32–45). See notes on 17:7; Nu 11:23; Dt 30:1–4; Mt 19:16–26.

18:1–50 EVIL AND SUFFERING, God's Present Help—See note on 2 Sa 22:1–51.

18:1–50 *REVELATION, Faithfulness*—The anxious worshiper cried openly to God, who responded from His dwelling place to comfort. God is always present for His troubled child. Even though we do not understand all the actions of nature around us, we know that God is moving toward us out of the mystery to reveal Himself. Poetic language based on Israel's experience at Sinai (Ex 19—20) described the psalmist's overwhelming sense of God's appearance to rescue His worshiper. The experience of rescue taught the psalmist much about the nature of God.

18:1–50 PRAYER, Thanksgiving—See notes on 2 Sa 22:1–51; Ne 11:17. Thanksgiving prayers are a reaction to a special action of God—here His gift of victory in battle. Often the thanksgiving service fulfilled a promise made in the lament to give thanks. See note on 7:1–17. The prayer is in three sections. The opening section describes the heights of God in the depths of human adversity (vv 2–19). In the middle section, David expressed agreement with God and described God's righteous dealing with those whose lives reflect His character (vv 20–29). In the last section, David praised the greatness of God as the source of human greatness (vv 30–50).

18:4–5 HUMANITY, Nature of Death—Death is not God's ultimate intent for people. Rather, it is seen as a trap into which people fall or by which they are captured. God can rescue us from the trap. In Jesus Christ He wants to give us eternal life.

18:7–15 GOD, Wrath—The wrath of God leaps into action against oppressors. Note the close relationship of the wrath of God to the salvation, sovereignty, and power of God. See notes on 6:1.

21For I have kept the ways of the LORD;[n]
I have not done evil by turning[o]
from my God.
22All his laws are before me;[p]
I have not turned away from his
decrees.
23I have been blameless[q] before him
and have kept myself from sin.
24The LORD has rewarded me according
to my righteousness,[r]
according to the cleanness of my
hands in his sight.

25To the faithful[s] you show yourself
faithful,[t]
to the blameless you show yourself
blameless,
26to the pure[u] you show yourself pure,
but to the crooked you show
yourself shrewd.[v]
27You save the humble[w]
but bring low those whose eyes are
haughty.[x]
28You, O LORD, keep my lamp[y] burning;
my God turns my darkness into
light.[z]
29With your help[a] I can advance against
a troop[j];
with my God I can scale a wall.

30As for God, his way is perfect;[b]
the word of the LORD is flawless.[c]
He is a shield[d]
for all who take refuge[e] in him.
31For who is God besides the LORD?[f]
And who is the Rock[g] except our
God?
32It is God who arms me with strength[h]
and makes my way perfect.[i]
33He makes my feet like the feet of a
deer;[j]
he enables me to stand on the
heights.[k]
34He trains my hands for battle;[l]
my arms can bend a bow of bronze.
35You give me your shield of victory,
and your right hand sustains[m] me;
you stoop down to make me great.
36You broaden the path[n] beneath me,
so that my ankles do not turn.[o]

37I pursued my enemies[p] and overtook
them;
I did not turn back till they were
destroyed.
38I crushed them[q] so that they could not
rise;[r]
they fell beneath my feet.[s]
39You armed me with strength[t] for
battle;
you made my adversaries bow[u] at
my feet.
40You made my enemies turn their
backs[v] in flight,
and I destroyed[w] my foes.
41They cried for help, but there was no
one to save them[x]—
to the LORD, but he did not
answer.[y]
42I beat them as fine as dust[z] borne on
the wind;
I poured them out like mud in the
streets.
43You have delivered me from the
attacks of the people;
you have made me the head of
nations;[a]
people I did not know[b] are subject
to me.
44As soon as they hear me, they obey
me;
foreigners[c] cringe before me.
45They all lose heart;[d]
they come trembling[e] from their
strongholds.[f]

46The LORD lives![g] Praise be to my
Rock![h]
Exalted be God[i] my Savior![j]
47He is the God who avenges[k] me,
who subdues nations[l] under
me,
48 who saves[m] me from my enemies.[n]
You exalted me above my foes;
from violent men[o] you rescued
me.
49Therefore I will praise you among the
nations,[p] O LORD;
I will sing[q] praises to your name.[r]
50He gives his king great victories;
he shows unfailing kindness to his
anointed,[s]
to David[t] and his descendants
forever.[u]

18:21 [n]2Ch 34:33; Ps 37:34; 119:2; Pr 8:32; 23:26 [o]Ps 119:102 **18:22** [p]Ps 119:30 **18:23** [q]S Ge 6:9 **18:24** [r]S 1Sa 26:23 **18:25** [s]Ps 31:23; 37:28; 50:5; Pr 2:8 [t]Ps 25:10; 40:11; 89:24; 146:6 **18:26** [u]Pr 15:26; Mt 5:8; Php 1:10; 1Ti 5:22; Tit 1:15; 1Jn 3:3 [v]Pr 3:34; Mt 10:16; Lk 16:8 **18:27** [w]S 2Ch 33:23; S Mt 23:12 [x]S Job 41:34; S Ps 10:5; Pr 3:33-34 **18:28** [y]1Ki 11:36; Ps 132:17 [z]Job 29:3; Ps 97:11; 112:4; Jn 1:5; S Ac 26:18; 2Co 4:6; 2Pe 1:19 **18:29** [a]ver 32,39; Isa 45:5; Heb 11:34 **18:30** [b]S Dt 32:4 [c]S Ps 12:6; Pr 30:5 [d]Ps 3:3 [e]Ps 2:12 **18:31** [f]S Dt 4:35; 32:39; Ps 35:10; 86:8; 89:6; Isa 44:6,8; 45:5,6, 14,18,21; 46:9 [g]S Ge 49:24 **18:32** [h]S ver 29; 1Pe 5:10 [i]S Ps 15:2; 19:13; Heb 10:14; Jas 3:2 **18:33** [j]Ps 42:1; Pr 5:19; Isa 35:6; Hab 3:19 [k]S Dt 32:13 **18:34** [l]Ps 144:1 **18:35** [m]Ps 3:5; 37:5,17; 41:3; 51:12; 54:4; 55:22; 119:116; Isa 41:4, 10,13; 43:2; 46:4 **18:36** [n]Ps 31:8 [o]S Job 18:7; Ps 66:9 **18:37** [p]S Lev 26:7 **18:38** [q]Ps 68:21; 110:6 [r]Ps 36:12; 140:10; Isa 26:14 [s]Ps 47:3 **18:39** [t]ver 32; Isa 45:5,24 [u]ver 47; Ps 47:3; 144:2 **18:40** [v]S Jos 7:12 [w]ver 37 **18:41** [x]S 2Ki 14:26; Ps 50:22 [y]S 1Sa 8:18; S 14:37; Jer 11:11 **18:42** [z]S Dt 9:21; S Isa 2:22 **18:43** [a]2Sa 8:1-14 [b]Isa 55:5 **18:44** [c]Ps 54:3; 144:7,11; Isa 25:5 **18:45** [d]S 1Sa 17:32; 2Co 4:1; Heb 12:3 [e]Isa 66:2; Hos 3:5; 11:10 [f]Ps 9:9; Mic 7:17 **18:46** [g]S Jos 3:10; S 1Sa 14:39; 2Co 13:4 [h]ver 31; Ex 33:22 [i]Ps 21:13; 35:27; 40:16; 108:5 [j]S 1Ch 16:35; S Lk 1:47 **18:47** [k]S Ge 4:24 [l]S ver 39; S Jdg 4:23 **18:48** [m]Ps 7:10; 37:40; Da 3:17 [n]S ver 17 [o]Ps 140:1 **18:49** [p]S Ps 9:11 [q]Ps 7:17; 9:2; 101:1; 108:1; 146:2 [r]Ro 15:9* **18:50** [s]S 2Sa 23:1 [t]Ps 144:10 [u]Ps 89:4

[j]29 Or *can run through a barricade*

18:25–31 GOD, Nature—This whole psalm is a commentary on the nature of God. Our faithful, trustworthy God is holy. We recognize this characteristic unique to God by recognizing His moral purity, a purity that surpasses that of the most blameless human. The holy God still cares for humble, oppressed people and uses His wisdom to be their Savior. He uses His power to empower us in our daily struggles. Because of the way the powerful, holy God acts to save us, we gladly confess that He alone is God. No other acts for us as He does.

18:30–50 CHRISTIAN ETHICS, War and Peace—God is sovereign. He revealed this in Israel's victories. Israel's king and armies attributed their successes to Him. The appropriate response to such a God is praise. The passage also helps us realize that we are as vulnerable to come under the judgment of God for our sins as are our enemies. See notes on 44:5–16; 2 Ki 24:1–4; 2 Ch 20:1–30.

18:49 EVANGELISM, In the Marketplace—See notes on 2:10; 9:11.

Psalm 19

For the director of music. A psalm of David.

THE heavens[v] declare[w] the glory of
God;[x]
the skies[y] proclaim the work of his
hands.[z]
2Day after day they pour forth speech;
night after night they display
knowledge.[a]
3There is no speech or language
where their voice is not heard.[k]
4Their voice[l] goes out into all the
earth,
their words to the ends of the
world.[b]

In the heavens he has pitched a tent[c]
for the sun,[d]
5 which is like a bridegroom[e] coming
forth from his pavilion,[f]
like a champion[g] rejoicing to run
his course.
6It rises at one end of the heavens[h]
and makes its circuit to the other;[i]
nothing is hidden from its heat.

7The law of the LORD[j] is perfect,[k]
reviving the soul.[l]
The statutes of the LORD are
trustworthy,[m]
making wise the simple.[n]
8The precepts of the LORD are right,[o]
giving joy[p] to the heart.
The commands of the LORD are
radiant,
giving light to the eyes.[q]
9The fear of the LORD[r] is pure,
enduring forever.

19:1 [v]Ps 89:5; Isa 40:22 [w]Ps 50:6; 148:3; Ro 1:19 [x]Ps 4:2; 8:1; 97:6; Isa 6:3 [y]S Ge 1:8 [z]S Ps 8:6; S 103:22 **19:2** [a]Ps 74:16 **19:4** [b]Ro 10:18* [c]S Job 36:29; Ps 104:2 [d]S Jdg 5:31 **19:5** [e]Joel 2:16 [f]S Job 36:29 [g]1Sa 17:4 **19:6** [h]Dt 30:4 [i]Ps 113:3; Ecc 1:5 **19:7** [j]S Ps 1:2 [k]Ps 119:142; Jas 1:25 [l]Ps 23:3 [m]Ps 93:5; 111:7; 119:138,144 [n]S Dt 4:6; Ps 119:130 **19:8** [o]Ps 33:4; 119:128 [p]Ps 119:14 [q]S Ezr 9:8; Ps 38:10 **19:9** [r]Ps 34:11; 111:10; Pr 1:7; Ecc 12:13; Isa 33:6 [s]Ps 119:138,142 **19:10** [t]S Job 22:24; Ps 119:72; Pr 8:10 [u]Ps 119:103; SS 4:11; Eze 3:3 [v]S 1Sa 14:27 **19:12** [w]Ps 51:2; 90:8; Ecc 12:14 **19:13** [x]S Nu 15:30 [y]Ps 119:133 [z]S Ge 6:9; S Ps 18:32 **19:14** [a]Ps 104:34 [b]Ps 18:31 [c]S Ex 6:6; S Job 19:25 **20:1** [d]Ps 4:1 [e]Ex 3:6; Ps 46:7,11 [f]Ps 59:1; 69:29; 91:14 **20:2** [g]Ps 30:10; 33:20; 37:40; 40:17; 54:4; 118:7 [h]S Nu 3:28 [i]S Ps 18:18 [j]Ps 2:6; 128:5; 134:3; 135:21 **20:3** [k]Ac 10:4

The ordinances of the LORD are sure
and altogether righteous.[s]
10They are more precious than gold,[t]
than much pure gold;
they are sweeter than honey,[u]
than honey from the comb.[v]
11By them is your servant warned;
in keeping them there is great
reward.

12Who can discern his errors?
Forgive my hidden faults.[w]
13Keep your servant also from willful
sins;[x]
may they not rule over me.[y]
Then will I be blameless,[z]
innocent of great transgression.

14May the words of my mouth and the
meditation of my heart
be pleasing[a] in your sight,
O LORD, my Rock[b] and my
Redeemer.[c]

Psalm 20

For the director of music. A psalm of David.

MAY the LORD answer you when you
are in distress;[d]
may the name of the God of Jacob[e]
protect you.[f]
2May he send you help[g] from the
sanctuary[h]
and grant you support[i] from Zion.[j]
3May he remember[k] all your sacrifices

[k]3 Or *They have no speech, there are no words; / no sound is heard from them* [l]4 Septuagint, Jerome and Syriac; Hebrew *line*

19:1–4 GOD, Creator—God's world bears witness to its sovereign Lord and points to His glory. We can confess the abstract doctrine of God as Creator because we can see the concrete evidence of His creation. If we confess Him as Creator, we need to go the next step and confess Him as the Ruler, the Lord, who controls us and all His creation.

19:1–6 REVELATION, Author of Creation—The very sky and whole panorama of heaven reveal the enormous size of God's purposes and order to all people. Human response and witness to God's creation also becomes revelation by pointing other worshipers to the power and plan of God laid out for humans to see.

19:1–14 PRAYER, Repentance—Praise for the Creator and for the Source of divine law is the basis for repentance. V 11 turns the pronouncements about the Lord in third person to direct second person address. The basic prayer is that the outer and inner person in perfect conformity with one another will be pleasing in the Lord's sight. This will require forgiveness of hidden sins as well as presumptuous, willful sins. See note on Job 1:5.

19:1–4 EVANGELISM, Results—God's great deeds and judgments are known everywhere. There is an innate awareness in everyone that God is just and is to be sought (Ro 1:20). People can see the results of God's great redemptive deeds all around them. This fact forms a basis for appeal and creates an openness for people to receive God's salvation for themselves. In most instances, believers can assume this when they witness for Christ.

19:7–14 EVIL AND SUFFERING, Deserved—Obeying God brings rewards. See note on 1:1–6.

19:7–10 HOLY SCRIPTURE, Obedience—Trustworthy Scripture is God's perfect treasure for human life reviving the discouraged and sick, giving wisdom to the trusting, filling the believer with joy, enlightening the faithful student with truth and understanding, bringing eternal fear and reverence of God to the worshiper, leading the humble servant to righteousness, warning the disciple of needed moral and spiritual changes, and promising rewards to those who faithfully study and obey God's Word. Human words cannot sufficiently praise God's Word, but the best praise is doing what the Word teaches.

19:7–11 EDUCATION, Law—The psalmist regarded the Law of the Lord as a perfect curriculum and effective teacher. To know the Law is to know the mind of God, the true Teacher of Israel (see note on 25:4–9), since God Himself gave the Law to Israel through Moses. As we learn from the Law of the Lord, we will not only gain understanding and wisdom, but we will also experience gladness and fullness of life.

20:1–9 EVIL AND SUFFERING, God's Present Help—See note on 21:1–13.

20:1–9 PRAYER, Worship—Historical crises are appropriate times for special worship services. This psalm is a prayer of the king and his people prior to battle. A worship leader interceded for the king (vv 1–5), who responded in trust (vv 6–8). The congregation then petitioned God for the king. Trusting solely in the Lord is the way to endure crisis. Congregational worship strengthens faith. Compare Dt 2:7; 17:16.

20:3 STEWARDSHIP, Giving in Worship—In distress, people turn to God asking for help. A normal part of such

and accept your burnt offerings.[l]
Selah
4May he give you the desire of your
heart[m]
and make all your plans succeed.[n]
5We will shout for joy[o] when you are
victorious
and will lift up our banners[p] in the
name of our God.
May the LORD grant all your requests.[q]

6Now I know that the LORD saves his
anointed;[r]
he answers him from his holy
heaven
with the saving power of his right
hand.[s]
7Some trust in chariots[t] and some in
horses,[u]
but we trust in the name of the
LORD our God.[v]
8They are brought to their knees and
fall,[w]
but we rise up[x] and stand firm.[y]

9O LORD, save the king!
Answer[m] us[z] when we call!

Psalm 21

For the director of music. A psalm of David.

O LORD, the king rejoices in your
strength.[a]
How great is his joy in the victories
you give![b]
2You have granted him the desire of his
heart[c]
and have not withheld the request
of his lips. *Selah*
3You welcomed him with rich blessings
and placed a crown of pure gold[d] on
his head.[e]
4He asked you for life, and you gave it
to him—
length of days, for ever and ever.[f]
5Through the victories[g] you gave, his
glory is great;
you have bestowed on him splendor
and majesty.[h]
6Surely you have granted him eternal
blessings
and made him glad with the joy[i] of
your presence.[j]
7For the king trusts in the LORD;[k]
through the unfailing love[l] of the
Most High[m]
he will not be shaken.[n]

8Your hand will lay hold[o] on all your
enemies;
your right hand will seize your foes.
9At the time of your appearing
you will make them like a fiery
furnace.
In his wrath the LORD will swallow
them up,
and his fire will consume them.[p]
10You will destroy their descendants
from the earth,
their posterity from mankind.[q]
11Though they plot evil[r] against you
and devise wicked schemes,[s] they
cannot succeed;
12for you will make them turn their
backs[t]
when you aim at them with drawn
bow.

13Be exalted,[u] O LORD, in your
strength;[v]
we will sing and praise your might.

Psalm 22

For the director of music. To ⌞the tune of⌟ "The Doe of the Morning." A psalm of David.

My God, my God, why have you
forsaken me?[w]

20:3 [l]S Dt 33:11
20:4 [m]Ps 21:2; 37:4; 145:16,19; Isa 26:8; Eze 24:25; Ro 10:1 [n]Ps 140:8; Pr 16:3; Da 11:17
20:5 [o]S Job 3:7 [p]S Nu 1:52; Ps 60:4; Isa 5:26; 11:10,12; 13:2; 30:17; 49:22; 62:10; Jer 50:2; 51:12,27 [q]1Sa 1:17
20:6 [r]S 2Sa 23:1; Ps 28:8 [s]S Job 40:14; Hab 3:13
20:7 [t]S 2Ki 19:23 [u]S Dt 17:16; Ps 33:17; 147:10; Pr 21:31; Isa 31:1; 36:8,9 [v]S 2Ch 32:8
20:8 [w]Ps 27:2; Isa 40:30; Jer 46:6; 50:32 [x]Mic 7:8 [y]S Job 11:15; Ps 37:23; Pr 10:25; Isa 7:9
20:9 [z]Ps 17:6
21:1 [a]S 1Sa 2:10 [b]S 2Sa 22:51
21:2 [c]S Ps 20:4
21:3 [d]S 2Sa 12:30; Rev 14:14 [e]Zec 6:11
21:4 [f]Ps 10:16; 45:17; 48:14; 133:3
21:5 [g]ver 1; Ps 18:50; 44:4 [h]S Ps 8:5; 45:3; 93:1; 96:6; 104:1
21:6 [i]Ps 43:4; 126:3 [j]S 1Ch 17:27
21:7 [k]S 2Ki 18:5 [l]Ps 6:4 [m]Ge 14:18 [n]S Ps 15:5; S 55:22
21:8 [o]Isa 10:10
21:9 [p]S Dt 32:22; Ps 50:3; Jer 15:14
21:10 [q]Dt 28:18
21:11 [r]Ps 2:1 [s]Job 10:3; Ps 10:2; 26:10; 37:7
21:12 [t]S Ex 23:27
21:13 [u]S Ps 18:46 [v]Ps 18:1
22:1 [w]S Job 6:15; S Ps 9:10; Mt 27:46*; Mk 15:34*

[m]9 Or *save! / O King, answer*

worship is a sacrifice or offering. Such a gift is an expression of reverence, commitment, and obedience to God. God's remembrance and acceptance means that God has accepted the entire act of worship because He has recognized a proper attitude and commitment on the worshiper's part. God responds to the worshiper in the times of distress. The proper offering can be brought only by one who recognizes God's saving power and trusts God for help (vv 6–7).

20:7–8 CHRISTIAN ETHICS, War and Peace—Though the Hebrews often were warlike, they knew their ultimate source of power and might came from God. Any military advantage they might have had was not enough if their disposition toward God was improper. See note on 18:30–50.

21:1,13 GOD, Power—We praise God for His power, because He uses that power in love to give His people victory. His power is sometimes called His omnipotence, meaning that He has all power to do anything He desires. The loving faithfulness of God controls His power. Otherwise, He would simply be a tyrant whom we could neither trust nor praise. See notes on Nu 11:23; Dt 30:1–4; Mt 19:16–26.

21:1–13 EVIL AND SUFFERING, God's Present Help—God helped defeat the Hebrews' enemies (v 1). Although the psalmist often stressed the physical help of God and physical blessings, he sometimes stressed the companionship of God in the crisis (v 6). God's help in one battle is not a guarantee that God will always eliminate our enemies or remove our physical problems in this life. Many psalms reflect perplexity about the prevalence of injustice. See note on 37:1–40. The wicked may prosper for a long time before God's justice prevails, but God always helps the righteous by offering His presence.

21:1–13 PRAYER, Praise—See note on 20:1–9. Ps 20 represented the king and the people trusting in the Lord. The companion Ps 21 celebrated past victories and looked to future ones. It was probably used regularly in ceremonies celebrating the king's coronation. To rule God's people required repeated expression of trust in God. The trust of 20:7 was a choice of the will. The trust of 21:7 is unshakable fact. To celebrate the earthly king's accomplishments was to praise God for His accomplishments.

22:1,7–8,18 JESUS CHRIST, Foretold—Matthew drew out the correspondence between this sad psalm and Jesus' crucifixion. There was the roll of the dice for Jesus' few possessions (Mt 27:35), the great cry of abandonment (Mt 27:46),

Why are you so far[x] from saving
me,
so far from the words of my
groaning?[y]
2O my God, I cry out by day, but you do
not answer,[z]
by night,[a] and am not silent.

3Yet you are enthroned as the Holy
One;[b]
you are the praise[c] of Israel.[n]
4In you our fathers put their trust;
they trusted and you delivered
them.[d]
5They cried to you[e] and were saved;
in you they trusted[f] and were not
disappointed.[g]

6But I am a worm[h] and not a man,
scorned by men[i] and despised[j] by
the people.
7All who see me mock me;[k]
they hurl insults,[l] shaking their
heads:[m]
8"He trusts in the LORD;
let the LORD rescue him.[n]
Let him deliver him,[o]
since he delights[p] in him."

9Yet you brought me out of the womb;[q]
you made me trust[r] in you
even at my mother's breast.
10From birth[s] I was cast upon you;
from my mother's womb you have
been my God.
11Do not be far from me,[t]
for trouble is near[u]
and there is no one to help.[v]

12Many bulls[w] surround me;[x]
strong bulls of Bashan[y] encircle me.
13Roaring lions[z] tearing their prey[a]
open their mouths wide[b] against
me.
14I am poured out like water,
and all my bones are out of joint.[c]
My heart has turned to wax;[d]
it has melted away[e] within me.
15My strength is dried up like a
potsherd,[f]
and my tongue sticks to the roof of
my mouth;[g]
you lay me[o] in the dust[h] of death.
16Dogs[i] have surrounded me;
a band of evil men has encircled me,
they have pierced[p][j] my hands and
my feet.
17I can count all my bones;
people stare[k] and gloat over me.[l]
18They divide my garments among them
and cast lots[m] for my clothing.[n]

19But you, O LORD, be not far off;[o]

22:1 [x]Ps 10:1 [y]S Job 3:24 **22:2** [z]S Job 19:7 [a]Ps 42:3; 88:1 **22:3** [b]S 2Ki 19:22; Ps 71:22; S Mk 1:24 [c]S Ex 15:2; Ps 148:14 **22:4** [d]Ps 78:53; 107:6 **22:5** [e]S 1Ch 5:20 [f]Isa 8:17; 25:9; 26:3; 30:18 [g]S 2Ch 13:18; Ps 25:3; 31:17; 71:1; Isa 49:23; Ro 9:33 **22:6** [h]S Job 4:19 [i]S 2Sa 12:14; Ps 31:11; 64:8; 69:19; 109:25 [j]Ps 119:141; Isa 49:7; 53:3; 60:14; Mal 2:9; Mt 16:21 **22:7** [k]S Job 17:2; Ps 35:16; 69:12; 74:18; Mt 27:41; Mk 15:31; Lk 23:36 [l]Mt 27:39,44; Mk 15:32; Lk 23:39 [m]Mk 15:29 **22:8** [n]Ps 91:14 [o]S Ps 3:2 [p]S 2Sa 22:20; S Mt 3:17; 27:43 **22:9** [q]Job 10:18; Ps 71:6 [r]Ps 78:7; Na 1:7 **22:10** [s]Ps 71:6; Isa 46:3; 49:1 **22:11** [t]ver 19; S Ps 10:1 [u]S Ps 10:14 [v]S 2Ki 14:26; S Isa 41:28 **22:12** [w]Ps 68:30 [x]Ps 17:9; 27:6; 49:5; 109:3; 140:9 [y]Dt 32:14; Isa 2:13; Eze 27:6; 39:18; Am 4:1 **22:13** [z]ver 21; Eze 22:25; Zep 3:3 [a]S Ge 49:9 [b]La 3:46 **22:14** [c]S Ps 6:2 [d]Job 23:16; Ps 68:2; 97:5; Mic 1:4 [e]Jos 7:5; Ps 107:26; Da 5:6 **22:15** [f]Isa 45:9 [g]Ps 137:6; La 4:4; Eze 3:26; Jn 19:28 [h]S Job 7:21; Ps 104:29 **22:16** [i]Php 3:2 [j]Isa 51:9; 53:5; Zec 12:10; Jn 20:25 **22:17** [k]Lk 23:35 [l]Ps 25:2; 30:1; 35:19; 38:16; La 2:17; Mic 7:8 **22:18** [m]S Lev 16:8; Mt 27:35*; Mk 15:24; Lk 23:34; Jn 19:24* [n]Mk 9:12 **22:19** [o]S ver 11

[n]3 Or *Yet you are holy, / enthroned on the praises of Israel* [o]15 Or */ I am laid* [p]16 Some Hebrew manuscripts, Septuagint and Syriac; most Hebrew manuscripts */ like the lion,*

---

and the mockings and insults (Mt 27:39). Christians of today will recognize that following abandonment and despair (vv 1–21), there is confidence and hope (vv 22–31). Jesus experienced both. So should we.

22:1–31 EVIL AND SUFFERING, Prayer—See note on 3:1–8. On the cross Jesus quoted this psalm to express His sense of abandonment by God (Mk 15:34). Other descriptions of suffering in this psalm parallel Jesus' experiences: vv 7–8 (Mt 27:39); v 16 (Jn 19:34); v 18 (Mt 27:35). Feeling deserted by God is a typical experience of the sufferer. Some contemporary sufferers doubt the existence of God, but the Hebrews were more likely to doubt God's concern for them. In the midst of our suffering, we may feel totally alone. We may feel God does not hear us (vv 1–2) or wonder why God does not help us as He helped others (vv 4–5). Eventually God does help us, and we will realize He is present (vv 27–31). Jesus promised us that we would have divine companionship in the midst of our troubles (Jn 14:15).

22:1–31 PRAYER, Lament—See note on 3:1–8. This is one of the greatest prayers in the Bible, perhaps second in its cosmic scope and mighty faith only to the prayer of Jesus in Jn 17. It shows the strength of honesty and deep faith in lamentation. It shows a twin focus on divine greatness and human agony. The intensity of the suffering in vv 1–21 was poetic hyperbole from the mouth of David. The verses precisely picture Christ's suffering on the cross. The psalmist groaned (v 1); his body was weakened (v 14); he suffered extreme thirst (v 15); his hands and feet were pierced (v 16); and his clothing was divided out by lot (v 18). His enemies were as strong and vicious as animals encircling and tearing their prey. Even the relation of the sufferer to God is like that of Christ on the cross to God. He was separated from God (vv 1–2) yet belonged utterly to God (vv 9–10) and trusted the Lord (vv 4–5). The sufferer here, like Christ, uttered no words of recrimination. Vv 22–31 ascend to a vision of God's dominion which is worldwide and unending. If this section stood alone, it would be a paean of praise; coupled with the suffering of vv 1–21, it is a monument of noble trust and high praise. Compare Mt 27:27–51.

22:3 GOD, Holy—Everything else that is said about God is an outgrowth of His holiness. The remarkable mystery is that the holy God chooses to relate Himself to His people. His is a loving holiness which calls forth praise rather than fright, trust rather than terror. See note on 16:3.

22:4–8 SALVATION, As Deliverance—God delivers those who put their trust in Him. Impatient, unbelieving people often mock believers for their faith, but ridicule cannot destroy true faith. See note on Ex 18:8–10.

22:5,8 SALVATION, Belief—See note on 4:5. "Trusts" (v 8; Hebrew *galal*) means to roll (Ge 29:10), thus to roll burdens and worries onto God (Ps 37:5; Pr 16:3). Skeptics cannot change reality. God does deliver His people through salvation.

22:6 HUMANITY, Human Nature—Other creatures of the earth are of less significance than people. To feel like them is to feel less than God intended people to be. Ridicule and scorn by other people cause such feelings. Even more a sense of God's absence brings self-doubt and feelings of inferiority. Renewed trust in God and His answer to our prayer removes such feelings of inadequacy and self-pity.

22:15 HUMANITY, Nature of Death—A body in the grave returns to dust, thus death is viewed as dusty. Its approach is seen as the growing loss of strength and moisture, a vivid description of the onset of death.

O my Strength,[p] come quickly[q] to
help me.[r]
20Deliver my life from the sword,[s]
my precious life[t] from the power of
the dogs.[u]
21Rescue me from the mouth of the
lions;[v]
save[q] me from the horns of the wild
oxen.[w]

22I will declare your name to my
brothers;
in the congregation[x] I will praise
you.[y]
23You who fear the LORD, praise him![z]
All you descendants of Jacob, honor
him![a]
Revere him,[b] all you descendants of
Israel!
24For he has not despised[c] or disdained
the suffering of the afflicted one;[d]
he has not hidden his face[e] from him
but has listened to his cry for help.[f]

25From you comes the theme of my
praise in the great assembly;[g]
before those who fear you[r] will I
fulfill my vows.[h]
26The poor will eat[i] and be satisfied;
they who seek the LORD will praise
him—[j]
may your hearts live forever!
27All the ends of the earth[k]
will remember and turn to the LORD,
and all the families of the nations
will bow down before him,[l]
28for dominion belongs to the LORD[m]
and he rules over the nations.

29All the rich[n] of the earth will feast and
worship;[o]
all who go down to the dust[p] will
kneel before him—
those who cannot keep themselves
alive.[q]
30Posterity[r] will serve him;

22:19 [p]S Ps 18:1 [q]Ps 38:22; 70:5; 141:1 [r]Ps 40:13
22:20 [s]S Job 5:20; Ps 37:14 [t]Ps 35:17 [u]Php 3:2
22:21 [v]S ver 13; S Job 4:10 [w]ver 12; S Nu 23:22
22:22 [x]Ps 26:12; 40:9,10; 68:26 [y]Ps 35:18; Heb 2:12*
22:23 [z]Ps 33:2; 66:8; 86:12; 103:1; 106:1; 113:1; 117:1; 135:19 [a]Ps 50:15; Isa 24:15; 25:3; 49:23; 60:9; Jer 3:17 [b]S Dt 14:23; Ps 33:8
22:24 [c]Ps 102:17 [d]S Ps 9:12 [e]Ps 13:1; 27:9; 69:17; 102:2; 143:7 [f]S Job 24:12; S 36:5; Heb 5:7
22:25 [g]Ps 26:12; 35:18; 40:9; 82:1 [h]S Nu 30:2
22:26 [i]Ps 107:9 [j]Ps 40:16
22:27 [k]S Ps 2:8 [l]Ps 86:9; 102:22; Da 7:27; Mic 4:1
22:28 [m]Ps 47:7-8; Zec 14:9
22:29 [n]Ps 45:12 [o]Ps 95:6; 96:9; 99:5; Isa 27:13; 49:7; 66:23; Zec 14:16 [p]Isa 26:19 [q]Ps 89:48
22:30 [r]Isa 53:10; 54:3; 61:9; 66:22 [s]Ps 102:18
22:31 [t]S Ps 5:8; 40:9 [u]Ps 71:18; 78:6; 102:18 [v]Lk 18:31; 24:44
23:1 [w]S Ge 48:15; S Ps 28:9; S Jn 10:11 [x]Ps 34:9, 10; 84:11; 107:9; Php 4:19
23:2 [y]Ps 36:8; 46:4; Rev 7:17
23:3 [z]S Ps 19:7 [a]Ps 25:9; 73:24; Isa 42:16 [b]S Ps 5:8 [c]Ps 25:11; 31:3; 79:9; 106:8; 109:21; 143:11
23:4 [d]S Job 3:5; Ps 107:14 [e]Ps 3:6; 27:1 [f]Ps 16:8;

future generations[s] will be told
about the Lord.
31They will proclaim his righteousness[t]
to a people yet unborn[u]—
for he has done it.[v]

Psalm 23

A psalm of David.

THE LORD is my shepherd,[w] I shall not
be in want.[x]
2 He makes me lie down in green
pastures,
he leads me beside quiet waters,[y]
3 he restores my soul.[z]
He guides me[a] in paths of
righteousness[b]
for his name's sake.[c]
4Even though I walk
through the valley of the shadow of
death,[s] [d]
I will fear no evil,[e]
for you are with me;[f]
your rod and your staff,
they comfort me.

5You prepare a table[g] before me
in the presence of my enemies.
You anoint my head with oil;[h]
my cup[i] overflows.
6Surely goodness and love[j] will follow
me
all the days of my life,
and I will dwell in the house of the
LORD
forever.

Psalm 24

Of David. A psalm.

THE earth is the LORD's,[k] and
everything in it,

Isa 43:2 **23:5** [g]S Job 36:16 [h]Ps 45:7; 92:10; Lk 7:46 [i]S Ps 16:5 **23:6** [j]S Ne 9:25 **24:1** [k]S Ex 9:29; Job 41:11

[q]*21* Or / *you have heard* [r]*25* Hebrew *him*
[s]*4* Or *through the darkest valley*

22:26–31 GOD, Sovereignty—God has all power and authority and rules over the earth. No human ruler has power apart from God. One day all peoples will recognize that authority.

23:1–6 GOD, Grace—This psalm reveals the many ways God shows His loving-kindness and protecting power to those who need Him. Grace is God's unmerited blessing, freely bestowed on those who do not deserve it. See note on 5:7–8.

23:1–6 EVIL AND SUFFERING, God's Present Help—The psalm expresses confidence that God will help even in the worst of circumstances, including death and evil (v 4). See note on 11:1–7. God's concern for us is illustrated by His being the Good Shepherd (vv 1–4) and the gracious Host (vv 5–6). Although we will face evil, we will not fear it because of God's companionship. We can trust in God's goodness despite the problems of life, including *the dark valley of death.*

23:1–6 PRAYER, Love of God—God is the loving Shepherd and caring Host. At the beginning, the sheep looked to the Shepherd for leadership, guidance, and protection. In the end the guest, now situated securely in the safety of the Lord's sanctuary, described the abundance of eternal provision. Life faces us with dangers and enemies. We can face life with confidence in God. We gain confidence through prayers of confidence.

23:4 REVELATION, Divine Presence—The psalmist affirmed God's tender presence during some of the most painful events in life. Personal hardship revealed that God is a present help during very difficult times. God is revealed here not as one who changes bad times but as the One who remains with His children throughout the bad times.

24:1–2,7–10 GOD, Creator—God as Creator of the earth is its sovereign Lord, exercising control over all He created. Humans can worship only when they are in the presence of the glorious divine King. No one else deserves our worship.

24:1–5 CREATION, Sovereignty—As the pilgrims followed the ark of the covenant to Jerusalem singing this song, they reflected on the nature of their God. He is the sole Creator, having brought a world into being that reflects His character but is not a physical extension or emanation of Himself. He brought the universe into being without help from

the world, and all who live in it;[l]
2for he founded it upon the seas
and established it upon the waters.[m]

3Who may ascend the hill[n] of the LORD?
Who may stand in his holy place?[o]
4He who has clean hands[p] and a pure heart,[q]
who does not lift up his soul to an idol[r]
or swear by what is false.[t]
5He will receive blessing[s] from the LORD
and vindication[t] from God his Savior.
6Such is the generation of those who seek him,
who seek your face,[u] O God of Jacob.[u] *Selah*

7Lift up your heads, O you gates;[v]
be lifted up, you ancient doors,
that the King[w] of glory[x] may come in.[y]
8Who is this King of glory?
The LORD strong and mighty,[z]
the LORD mighty in battle.[a]
9Lift up your heads, O you gates;
lift them up, you ancient doors,
that the King of glory may come in.
10Who is he, this King of glory?
The LORD Almighty[b]—
he is the King of glory. *Selah*

24:1 [l]1Co 10:26* **24:2** [m]S Ge 1:6; Ps 104:3; 2Pe 3:5 **24:3** [n]Ps 2:6 [o]Ps 15:1; 65:4 **24:4** [p]S 2Sa 22:21 [q]Ps 51:10; 73:1; Mt 5:8 [r]Eze 18:15 **24:5** [s]Dt 11:26 [t]Ps 17:2 **24:6** [u]Ps 27:8; 105:4; 119:58; Hos 5:15 **24:7** [v]Ps 118:19, 20; Isa 26:2; 60:11, 18; 62:10 [w]Ps 44:4; 74:12 [x]Ps 29:3; Ac 7:2; 1Co 2:8 [y]Zec 9:9; Mt 21:5 **24:8** [z]S 1Ch 29:11; Ps 89:13; Jer 50:34; Eph 6:10 [a]Ex 15:3, 6; Dt 4:34 **24:10** [b]S 1Sa 1:11 **25:1** [c]Ps 86:4; 143:8 **25:2** [d]Ps 31:6; 143:8 **25:3** [e]S Ps 22:5; S Isa 29:22 [f]Isa 24:16; Hab 1:13; Zep 3:4; 2Ti 3:4 **25:4** [g]S Job 34:32 **25:5** [h]Ps 31:3; 43:3; Jn 16:13 [i]Ps 24:5 [j]ver 3; Ps 33:20; 39:7; 42:5; 71:5; 130:7; 131:3 **25:6** [k]Ps 5:7; 98:3; Isa 63:7,15; Jer 31:20; Hos 11:8 **25:7** [l]Job 13:26; Isa 54:4; Jer 3:25; 31:19; 32:30; Eze 16:22,60; 23:3; 2Ti 2:22 [m]S Ex 23:21; Ps 107:17 [n]Ps 6:4; 51:1; 69:16; 109:26; 119:124 [o]S 1Ch 16:34; Ps 34:8; 73:1 **25:8** [p]Ps 92:15; Isa 26:7

Psalm 25[v]

Of David.

1To you, O LORD, I lift up my soul;[c]
2 in you I trust,[d] O my God.
Do not let me be put to shame,
nor let my enemies triumph over me.
3No one whose hope is in you
will ever be put to shame,[e]
but they will be put to shame
who are treacherous[f] without excuse.

4Show me your ways, O LORD,
teach me your paths;[g]
5guide me in your truth[h] and teach me,
for you are God my Savior,[i]
and my hope is in you[j] all day long.
6Remember, O LORD, your great mercy and love,[k]
for they are from of old.
7Remember not the sins of my youth[l]
and my rebellious ways;[m]
according to your love[n] remember me,
for you are good,[o] O LORD.

8Good and upright[p] is the LORD;

[t]4 Or *swear falsely* [u]6 Two Hebrew manuscripts and Syriac (see also Septuagint); most Hebrew manuscripts *face, Jacob* [v]This psalm is an acrostic poem, the verses of which begin with the successive letters of the Hebrew alphabet.

anyone else. It, therefore, belongs to Him exclusively. He alone has the power to dictate the laws that govern it. Though we discover many marvelous truths about the created order through scientific research, only God's revealed Word gives us the basic moral standards to guide it.

24:1 STEWARDSHIP, God's Ownership—All stewardship begins with acknowledgment that God is the true Owner of everything. The material world is His by right of creation. All human beings are created in His likeness and are responsible to Him. God is the Owner. We possess only what He entrusts to us. We hold a secondary title of ownership, a delegated authority to use and enjoy responsibly what God gives us. As they sought entrance to God's house of worship, God's people acknowledged His ownership and control of all they had and were. They knew even their cherished Promised Land was a gift (Ge 12:1; Dt 8:1; 10:11; 34:4), received and held in faith (Dt 6:10,18; 31:7), to be used in faithfulness (Dt 7:11,13,21; 28:11; 30:20) without arrogant feelings of self-sufficiency (Dt 9:5), and to be preserved for family ownership. See Lev 27:17–24; note on Lev 25:1–55. God had a purpose for the land. God's people were stewards called to assure justice, care for their families, and meet the needs of others (Dt 15:4). For the Christian, this Old Testament heritage is enriched by *Christ's principle of living to serve*, an exciting purpose for ownership. Christian stewards use everything God has entrusted to serve His people, to proclaim His good news of salvation, and to demonstrate His love for the needy.

24:3–6 CHRISTIAN ETHICS, Worship—Israel took the opportunity to worship seriously. People wanting to enter the Temple were asked to confess basic character traits. See note on 15:1–5.

25:1–22 EVIL AND SUFFERING, Endurance—Enduring hope in God despite all circumstances will eventually be rewarded. See note on 3:1–8.

25:1–22 PRAYER, Lament—See notes on 3:1–8; 34:1–22. This psalmist depended entirely on the Lord and looked for a relationship based on His attributes. The psalmist was a humble (v 9), God-fearing (v 14), and God-seeking (v 15) sinner (vv 7–8) who appealed not on the basis of his performance but on the basis of the Lord's mercy and love (v 6) guaranteed by the covenant (v 10). Lamentation is possible because God is faithful to His covenant people. He shares our concerns.

25:4–9 EDUCATION, God—The Lord Himself was the true Teacher of Israel. All others—Moses, priests, prophets, and parents—were His "teaching assistants." All who teach in the name of God teach by His authority and share His purpose—to guide learners in His truth. This "truth" is not a set of abstract doctrines, but a way of life. To learn from this Teacher is to walk in the path which He shows us. See 27:11; 32:8.

25:5 GOD, Savior—We normally apply the term Savior to Jesus. In the Old Testament God is called Savior many times. As Savior, He teaches us how to live, gives hope in the face of trouble, and forgives our sins. See note on 18:1–48.

25:6–10 GOD, Love—Notice the many different ways the love of God is mentioned throughout this psalm. His love leads the faithful God to remember us in our needs. As His faithful people we confess that everything He does is loving even when we are in trouble and plead for His help. See note on 13:5.

25:7,11,18 SALVATION, Forgiveness—When God forgives our sins, He takes them away and forgets them. He forgives when we sincerely ask Him. Often, physical and emotional stress lead us to confession and repentance seeking forgiveness. No matter how great or how long-standing our sin, He will forgive it.

25:8–9 GOD, Righteous—Righteousness refers to more than God's work as judge. God is also the righteous Teacher. The righteous God works to develop righteousness in His sinful people. See note on 7:9,11,17.

therefore he instructs[q] sinners in
his ways.
9He guides[r] the humble in what is
right
and teaches them[s] his way.
10All the ways of the LORD are loving and
faithful[t]
for those who keep the demands of
his covenant.[u]
11For the sake of your name,[v] O LORD,
forgive[w] my iniquity,[x] though it is
great.
12Who, then, is the man that fears the
LORD?[y]
He will instruct him in the way[z]
chosen for him.
13He will spend his days in prosperity,[a]
and his descendants will inherit the
land.[b]
14The LORD confides[c] in those who fear
him;
he makes his covenant known[d] to
them.
15My eyes are ever on the LORD,[e]
for only he will release my feet from
the snare.[f]

16Turn to me[g] and be gracious to me,[h]
for I am lonely[i] and afflicted.
17The troubles[j] of my heart have
multiplied;
free me from my anguish.[k]
18Look upon my affliction[l] and my
distress[m]
and take away all my sins.[n]
19See how my enemies[o] have increased
and how fiercely they hate me![p]
20Guard my life[q] and rescue me;[r]
let me not be put to shame,[s]
for I take refuge[t] in you.
21May integrity[u] and uprightness[v]
protect me,
because my hope is in you.[w]

22Redeem Israel,[x] O God,
from all their troubles!

Psalm 26

Of David.

VINDICATE me,[y] O LORD,
for I have led a blameless life;[z]
I have trusted[a] in the LORD
without wavering.[b]
2Test me,[c] O LORD, and try me,
examine my heart and my mind;[d]
3for your love[e] is ever before me,
and I walk continually[f] in your
truth.[g]
4I do not sit[h] with deceitful men,
nor do I consort with hypocrites;[i]
5I abhor[j] the assembly of evildoers
and refuse to sit with the wicked.
6I wash my hands in innocence,[k]
and go about your altar, O LORD,
7proclaiming aloud your praise[l]
and telling of all your wonderful
deeds.[m]
8I love[n] the house where you live,
O LORD,
the place where your glory dwells.[o]

25:8 [q]Ps 32:8; Isa 28:26 **25:9** [r]S Ps 23:3 [s]ver 4; Ps 27:11 **25:10** [t]S Ps 18:25 [u]Ps 103:18; 132:12 **25:11** [v]S Ex 9:16; Ps 31:3; 79:9; Jer 14:7 [w]S Ex 34:9 [x]S Ex 32:30; S Ps 78:38 **25:12** [y]S Job 1:8 [z]ver 8 **25:13** [a]S Dt 30:15; S 1Ki 3:14; S Job 8:7 [b]S Nu 14:24; Mt 5:5 **25:14** [c]Pr 3:32 [d]Ge 17:2; Jn 7:17 **25:15** [e]S 2Ch 20:12; Ps 123:2; Heb 12:2 [f]S Job 34:30; S Ps 119:110 **25:16** [g]S Ps 6:4 [h]S Nu 6:25 [i]Ps 68:6 **25:17** [j]1Ki 1:29; Ps 34:6,17; 40:12; 54:7; 116:3 [k]Ps 6:3; 39:2 **25:18** [l]S Ps 13:3; Ro 12:12 [m]S 2Sa 16:12 [n]Ps 103:3 **25:19** [o]Ps 3:1; 9:13 [p]Ps 35:19; 38:19; 69:4 **25:20** [q]Ps 86:2 [r]Ps 17:13; 22:21; 43:1; 71:2; 116:4; 140:1; 142:6; 144:11 [s]ver 3 [t]Ps 2:12 **25:21** [u]S Ge 20:5; Pr 10:9 [v]1Ki 9:4; Ps 85:10; 111:8; Isa 60:17; Mal 2:6 [w]ver 3 **25:22** [x]Ps 130:8; Lk 24:21 **26:1** [y]S 1Sa 24:15 [z]Ps 15:2; Pr 20:7 [a]Ps 22:4; 40:4; Isa 12:2; 25:9; Jer 17:7; Da 3:28 [b]2Ki 20:3; Heb 10:23 **26:2** [c]Ps 66:10 [d]S Dt 6:6; S Ps 7:9; Jer 11:20; 20:12; Eze 11:5 **26:3** [e]Ps 6:4 [f]S 1Ki 2:4 [g]Ps 40:11; 43:3; 86:11; 119:30 **26:4** [h]Ps 1:1 [i]Ps 28:3; Mt 6:2 **26:5** [j]Ps 139:21 **26:6** [k]Ps 73:13; Mt 27:24 **26:7** [l]Isa 42:12; 60:6 [m]S Jos 3:5; Ps 9:1 **26:8** [n]Ps 122:6; Isa 66:10 [o]S Ex 29:43; 2Ch 7:1; Ps 96:6

25:10 THE CHURCH, Covenant People—Covenant (Hebrew *berith*) is associated with two words. *Chesed* (translated variously as loving, steadfast love, or loving-kindness) is God's love which binds Him to His people in covenant relationships. See note on 2 Ch 6:14. *'Emeth* (translated as faithful, truth, or faithfulness) indicates the Lord's loyalty to His people. God is the foundation of truth and faithfulness. In the Old Testament *chesed* and *'emeth* are found together only in reference to God. He supremely shows steadfast love and faithfulness. His love and loyalty are unique. The people God has chosen can take heart in knowing God always demonstrates love and loyalty. When things around us seem shaky, God's throne is sure. We can count on God in the most difficult times.

25:14 HUMANITY, Relationship to God—The Hebrew word for confides actually refers to the secret counsel of God which He ultimately intends for His people to have. This includes His offer of a covenant relationship to people. Even in time of deep trouble we can find new hope and confidence by knowing God's intention to confide His secrets and to bring us into covenant relationship with Him.

25:14 THE CHURCH, Covenant People—God's covenant is not a secret agreement for the few initiates. He lets all His people know His covenant commitments and expectations.

26:1–12 EVIL AND SUFFERING, Prayer—Like Job, the psalmist experienced innocent suffering and could not understand why. His only action was *prayer to God for vindication.* See note on 3:1–8.

26:1–12 CHRISTIAN ETHICS, Character—In desperate circumstances the psalmist pleaded that he did not deserve his suffering and gave evidence of his moral integrity. Love of God heads the list. Refusal to associate with persons who might lead him astray was emphasized.

26:1–12 PRAYER, Petition—See notes on 3:1–8; 7:1–17. The psalmist's appeal was based on his willful choice of the Lord and his willingness to have that choice tested by the Lord. His hope rested not on his merits but on God's justice. The blameless life David presented consists not in a perfect performance but in an inner life which loves the Lord's house and His glory. We can neither earn nor demand God's vindication. We can vigorously ask for it because of who He is and not because of who we are.

26:3 GOD, Love—Love is one of the most important characteristics of God. It distinguishes Him from the capricious gods of other religions. It lets us focus on God to gain strength in time of trouble. This leads us to God's house rather than the house of temptation. See note on 25:6–10.

26:7 HISTORY, Confession—Proclaiming God's saving acts is a central part of worship.

26:7 EVANGELISM, Mass—God wants believers to tell the masses the wondrous deeds of the Lord. The "joy of the LORD" is not only our strength (Ne 8:10); it is the motivation of our evangelization to all people.

26:8 GOD, Glory—Glory can describe God's magnificent presence with His people. See note on 8:1,9.

26:8 REVELATION, Divine Presence—The house where God lives is the place from which He reveals Himself to the worshiper. At the Temple, God "meets" His people and communicates His nature and will. Such experiences lead people to deep affection for God's house.

26:8 WORSHIP, Buildings—See note on Ge 28:16–22.

[9]Do not take away my soul along with sinners,
my life with bloodthirsty men,[p]
[10]in whose hands are wicked schemes,[q]
whose right hands are full of bribes.[r]
[11]But I lead a blameless life;
redeem me[s] and be merciful to me.

[12]My feet stand on level ground;[t]
in the great assembly[u] I will praise the LORD.

Psalm 27

Of David.

THE LORD is my light[v] and my salvation[w]—
whom shall I fear?
The LORD is the stronghold[x] of my life—
of whom shall I be afraid?[y]
[2]When evil men advance against me
to devour my flesh,[w]
when my enemies and my foes attack me,
they will stumble and fall.[z]
[3]Though an army besiege me,
my heart will not fear;[a]
though war break out against me,
even then will I be confident.[b]

[4]One thing[c] I ask of the LORD,
this is what I seek:
that I may dwell in the house of the LORD
all the days of my life,[d]
to gaze upon the beauty of the LORD
and to seek him in his temple.
[5]For in the day of trouble[e]
he will keep me safe[f] in his dwelling;
he will hide me[g] in the shelter of his tabernacle
and set me high upon a rock.[h]
[6]Then my head will be exalted[i]
above the enemies who surround me;[j]
at his tabernacle will I sacrifice[k] with shouts of joy;[l]
I will sing[m] and make music[n] to the LORD.

[7]Hear my voice[o] when I call,
O LORD;
be merciful to me and answer me.[p]
[8]My heart says of you, "Seek his[x] face![q]"
Your face, LORD, I will seek.
[9]Do not hide your face[r] from me,
do not turn your servant away in anger;[s]
you have been my helper.[t]
Do not reject me or forsake[u] me,
O God my Savior.[v]
[10]Though my father and mother forsake me,
the LORD will receive me.
[11]Teach me your way,[w] O LORD;
lead me in a straight path[x]
because of my oppressors.[y]
[12]Do not turn me over to the desire of my foes,
for false witnesses[z] rise up against me,
breathing out violence.

[13]I am still confident of this:
I will see the goodness of the LORD[a]
in the land of the living.[b]
[14]Wait[c] for the LORD;
be strong[d] and take heart
and wait for the LORD.

26:9 [p]Ps 5:6; 28:3; 55:23; 139:19; Pr 29:10 **26:10** [q]S Ps 21:11 [r]S Job 36:18; S Isa 1:23; S Eze 22:12 **26:11** [s]Ps 31:5; 69:18; 119:134; Tit 2:14 **26:12** [t]Ps 27:11; 40:2; 143:10; Isa 26:7; 40:3-4; 45:13; Zec 4:7; Lk 6:17 [u]S Ps 22:25 **27:1** [v]S 2Sa 22:29 [w]S Ex 15:2; S Ps 3:8 [x]Ps 9:9 [y]S Job 13:15; Ps 56:4,11; 118:6 **27:2** [z]Ps 9:3; S 20:8; 37:24; Da 11:19; Ro 11:11 **27:3** [a]S Ge 4:7; S Ps 3:6 [b]S Job 4:6 **27:4** [c]Lk 10:42 [d]Ps 23:6; 61:4 **27:5** [e]S Job 38:23 [f]S Ps 12:7 [g]S Ps 17:8 [h]Ps 40:2 **27:6** [i]2Sa 22:49; Ps 3:3; 18:48 [j]S Ps 22:12 [k]Ps 50:14; 54:6; 107:22; 116:17 [l]S Ezr 3:13; S Job 22:26 [m]S Ex 15:1 [n]Ps 33:2; 92:1; 147:7; S Eph 5:19 **27:7** [o]Ps 5:3; 18:6; 55:17; 119:149; 130:2; Isa 28:23 [p]S Ps 4:1 **27:8** [q]S 1Ch 16:11 **27:9** [r]S Dt 31:17; S Ps 22:24 [s]S Ps 2:5 [t]S Ge 49:25; S Dt 33:29 [u]S Dt 4:31; Ps 37:28; 119:8; Isa 41:17; 62:12; Jer 14:9 [v]Ps 18:46 **27:11** [w]S Ex 33:13 [x]S Ezr 8:21; Ps 5:8 [y]Ps 72:4; 78:42; 106:10; Jer 21:12 **27:12** [z]S Dt 19:16; S Mt 26:60; Ac 6:13; 1Co 15:15 **27:13** [a]Ex 33:19; S 2Ch 6:41; Ps 23:6; 31:19; 145:7 [b]S Job 28:13 **27:14** [c]Ps 33:20; 130:5,6; Isa 8:17; 30:18; Hab 2:3; Zep 3:8; Ac 1:4 [d]S Dt 1:21; S Jdg 5:21; S Eph 6:10

[w]2 Or *to slander me* [x]8 Or *To you, O my heart, he has said, "Seek my*

26:11 SALVATION, Grace—Frequently the psalmist sought God's mercy (27:7; 28:2; 30:8,10; 31:9,22; 41:4,10; 51:1; 57:1). God's mercy (Hebrew *chanan*) is His unmerited blessing and favor. It expresses His love and compassion, apart from which there would be no salvation. Mercy is a basic characteristic of God. He defines the word by who He is. No human analogies are sufficient to define it. Compare Ge 6:8; Ex 33:12,19; 34:6. God is not neutral or basically opposed to humans. He is partial to us and shows us undeserved mercy. God's mercy makes deliverance and forgiveness possible.
27:1,9 GOD, Savior—The basic role of God is that of Savior. Knowing this drives out all our fears and lets us call confidently on God in time of need or threat. See note on 25:5.
27:1–14 EVIL AND SUFFERING, Endurance—Fear causes as much distress as actual pain. Even the sufferer need not fear if hope is placed fully in God. Confidence in God's presence is the basic weapon against fear. See note on 3:1–8.
27:1–4 PRAYER, Petition—We can petition God for mercy and protection because we have confidence in Him and are willing to learn from Him. Confidence gives us patience to wait for God's timing and not demand immediate response to our petitions.
27:4–9 REVELATION, Fellowship—The request is for closeness with God, to live in companionship with His purpose and protection. The writer declared that to be in fellowship with God is to be exalted in one's position as a human being, to be protected by a strength beyond human nature, and to be forgiven and drawn close to the spirit and right way of living God provides.
27:9 GOD, Wrath—In trouble we fear God's wrath is upon us, but we turn in faith to our Savior for help. See notes on Ge 6:5–8; 17:14; 19:13,24–26; Jos 7:1,25–26; Mt 3:7–10.
27:9 THE CHURCH, Servants—God's servants obey Him and do His will. They also receive strength and help from the God whom they serve. God never forsakes His servants. In times of distress we can turn to Him and know He hears our problems. See notes on Job 1:8; 2:3.
27:11 EDUCATION, God—In persecution and hard times, God's people need His teaching to lead us to react properly. See note on 25:4–9.
27:12 JESUS CHRIST, Foretold—Matthew read Jesus' last days from the Psalms and the Psalms in the light of Jesus' last days. False witnesses (Mt 26:60–61) were responsible for the accusations against Jesus.

Psalm 28

Of David.

[1]TO you I call, O LORD my Rock;
do not turn a deaf ear[e] to me.
For if you remain silent,[f]
I will be like those who have gone down to the pit.[g]
[2]Hear my cry for mercy[h]
as I call to you for help,
as I lift up my hands[i]
toward your Most Holy Place.[j]

[3]Do not drag me away with the wicked,
with those who do evil,
who speak cordially with their neighbors
but harbor malice in their hearts.[k]
[4]Repay them for their deeds
and for their evil work;
repay them for what their hands have done[l]
and bring back upon them what they deserve.[m]
[5]Since they show no regard for the works of the LORD
and what his hands have done,[n]
he will tear them down
and never build them up again.

[6]Praise be to the LORD,[o]
for he has heard my cry for mercy.[p]
[7]The LORD is my strength[q] and my shield;
my heart trusts[r] in him, and I am helped.
My heart leaps for joy[s]
and I will give thanks to him in song.[t]

[8]The LORD is the strength[u] of his people,
a fortress of salvation[v] for his anointed one.[w]
[9]Save your people[x] and bless your inheritance;[y]
be their shepherd[z] and carry them[a] forever.

Psalm 29

A psalm of David.

[1]ASCRIBE to the LORD,[b] O mighty ones,[c]
ascribe to the LORD glory[d] and strength.
[2]Ascribe to the LORD the glory due his name;
worship the LORD in the splendor of his[y] holiness.[e]

[3]The voice[f] of the LORD is over the waters;
the God of glory[g] thunders,[h]
the LORD thunders over the mighty waters.[i]
[4]The voice of the LORD is powerful;[j]
the voice of the LORD is majestic.
[5]The voice of the LORD breaks the cedars;
the LORD breaks in pieces the cedars of Lebanon.[k]
[6]He makes Lebanon skip[l] like a calf,
Sirion[z][m] like a young wild ox.[n]
[7]The voice of the LORD strikes
with flashes of lightning.[o]
[8]The voice of the LORD shakes the desert;
the LORD shakes the Desert of Kadesh.[p]
[9]The voice of the LORD twists the oaks[a][q]
and strips the forests bare.

28:1 [e]S Dt 1:45 [f]S Est 4:14 [g]S Job 33:18 **28:2** [h]Ps 17:1; 61:1; 116:1; 130:2; 142:1; 143:1 [i]S Ezr 9:5; Ps 63:4; 141:2; La 2:19; 1Ti 2:8 [j]Ps 5:7; 11:4 **28:3** [k]Ps 12:2; S 26:4; 55:21; Jer 9:8 **28:4** [l]Ps 62:12; 2Ti 4:14; Rev 22:12 [m]La 3:64; Rev 18:6 **28:5** [n]Isa 5:12 **28:6** [o]S Ge 24:27; 2Co 1:3; Eph 1:3; 1Pe 1:3 [p]ver 2 **28:7** [q]S Ps 18:1 [r]Ps 13:5; 112:7; Isa 26:3 [s]S Dt 16:15; S Ps 16:9 [t]Ps 33:3; 40:3; 69:30; 144:9; 149:1 **28:8** [u]Ps 18:1 [v]S Ex 15:2; Ps 27:1; Hab 3:13 [w]S Ps 20:6 **28:9** [x]1Ch 16:35; Ps 106:47; 118:25 [y]S Ex 34:9 [z]1Ch 11:2; S Ps 23:1; 78:52, 71; 80:1; Isa 40:11; Jer 31:10; Eze 34:12-16,23,31; Mic 7:14 [a]S Dt 1:31; 32:11; Isa 46:3; 63:9 **29:1** [b]ver 2; 1Ch 16:28 [c]S 2Sa 1:19; Ps 103:20; Isa 10:13 [d]Ps 8:1 **29:2** [e]S 1Ch 16:29; Ps 96:7-9 **29:3** [f]Job 37:5 [g]S Ps 24:7; Ac 7:2 [h]S 1Sa 2:10; Ps 18:13; 46:6; 68:33; 77:17; Jer 10:13; 25:30; Joel 2:11; Am 1:2 [i]S Ex 15:10 **29:4** [j]Ps 68:33 **29:5** [k]S Jdg 9:15 **29:6** [l]Ps 114:4 [m]Dt 3:9 [n]S Nu 23:22; Job 39:9; Ps 92:10 **29:7** [o]Eze 1:14; Rev 8:5 **29:8** [p]Nu 13:26; S 20:1 **29:9** [q]Nu 13:32; Isa 2:13; Eze 27:6; Am 2:9

[y]2 Or *LORD with the splendor of* [z]6 That is, Mount Hermon [a]9 Or *LORD makes the deer give birth*

28:1–8 GOD, Power—Temptation and trouble drive us to confess God's power to save and protect His people. Notice how closely related the ideas of God's power, sovereignty, and saviorhood are here. See note on 21:1,13.

28:1–9 EVIL AND SUFFERING, Prayer—Attitudes and motives are more important than words and as important as actions in determining who is wicked. Vengeance against the wicked is the work of God and not of God's people. In trouble we call to God for mercy. See note on 3:1–8.

28:1–9 PRAYER, Lament—See notes on 3:1–8; 5:10; 6:1–10. This is a desperate prayer. If God would not answer, the psalmist might as well have been dead. This is the only place in the psalter where the Lord is addressed as being in His Holy of Holies. The call for strength and for tenderness can only be met by a shepherd who is simultaneously strong and gentle. Answered prayer led to a swift change in mood at v 6, leading to a promise to give thanks. The psalmist's experience contains a lesson of assurance for all the people of God (vv 8–9).

28:2 GOD, Holy—The perfect, *holy nature of God can be present only* amidst purity and righteousness. Thus the place of worship can be called holy because the holy God is there. See note on 22:3.

28:6–9 GOD, Savior—The grace of God and God as Savior are very closely related. God's people do not deserve mercy or salvation. We have not earned it. Because God is gracious, we call on Him and trust Him to save us. See notes on 38:22; Lk 1:30, 47; 1 Ti 1:1.

29:1–3,9 GOD, Glory—See note on 8:1,9.

29:1–11 PRAYER, Praise—God makes His presence known in many ways, leading us to praise Him. The psalmist saw and heard God in a powerful thunderstorm moving from north (Lebanon) to south (Desert of Kadesh). He called on the mighty angels (literally, "sons of God") to credit the Lord with glory and strength, described the sevenfold voice of God thundering over creation, and declared God's dominion over His people. God's people need to be aware of signs of God's glory and strength. Such signs should lift our hearts to praise.

29:3–9 REVELATION, Author of Creation—God has power to create and reshape the world He makes. His very speaking creates and alters existence. The worshiper, picturing a thunderstorm moving in from the Mediterranean, was astounded at God's use of nature to affect the created order. In Ge 1 when God spoke, creation occurred, and chaos was changed. Here creation is again affected. The word of God became flesh when He declared Himself in Bethlehem (Jn 1:14).

And in his temple all cry, "Glory!"[r]
10The LORD sits[b] enthroned over the
flood;[s]
the LORD is enthroned as King
forever.[t]
11The LORD gives strength to his
people;[u]
the LORD blesses his people with
peace.[v]

Psalm 30

A psalm. A song. For the dedication of the temple.[c] Of David.

I will exalt[w] you, O LORD,
for you lifted me out of the depths[x]
and did not let my enemies gloat
over me.[y]
2O LORD my God, I called to you for
help[z]
and you healed me.[a]
3O LORD, you brought me up from the
grave[d];[b]
you spared me from going down into
the pit.[c]

4Sing[d] to the LORD, you saints[e] of his;
praise his holy name.[f]
5For his anger[g] lasts only a moment,[h]
but his favor lasts a lifetime;[i]
weeping[j] may remain for a night,
but rejoicing comes in the
morning.[k]

6When I felt secure, I said,
"I will never be shaken."[l]
7O LORD, when you favored me,
you made my mountain[e] stand firm;
but when you hid your face,[m]
I was dismayed.

8To you, O LORD, I called;
to the Lord I cried for mercy:
9"What gain is there in my
destruction,[f]
in my going down into the pit?[n]
Will the dust praise you?
Will it proclaim your faithfulness?[o]
10Hear,[p] O LORD, and be merciful to
me;[q]
O LORD, be my help.[r]"

11You turned my wailing[s] into
dancing;[t]
you removed my sackcloth[u] and
clothed me with joy,[v]
12that my heart may sing to you and not
be silent.
O LORD my God, I will give you
thanks[w] forever.[x]

Psalm 31

31:1-4pp — Ps 71:1-3

For the director of music. A psalm of David.

IN you, O LORD, I have taken refuge;[y]
let me never be put to shame;
deliver me in your righteousness.[z]

29:9 [r]Ps 26:8
29:10 [s]Ge 6:17 [t]S Ex 15:18
29:11 [u]S Ps 18:1; 28:8; 68:35 [v]S Lev 26:6; S Nu 6:26
30:1 [w]S Ex 15:2 [x]Job 11:8; Ps 63:9; 107:26; Pr 9:18; Isa 14:15 [y]S Ps 22:17
30:2 [z]Ps 5:2; 88:13 [a]S Nu 12:13
30:3 [b]S Ps 16:10; S 56:13 [c]Ps 28:1; 55:23; 69:15; 86:13; 143:7; Pr 1:12; Isa 38:17; Jnh 2:6
30:4 [d]Ps 33:1; 47:7; 68:4 [e]S Ps 16:3 [f]Ex 3:15; Ps 33:21; 103:1; 145:21
30:5 [g]Ps 103:9 [h]S Job 14:13 [i]S Ezr 3:11 [j]2Sa 15:30; Ps 6:6; 126:6; Jer 31:16 [k]2Co 4:17
30:6 [l]S Job 29:18
30:7 [m]S Dt 31:17
30:9 [n]S Job 33:18; Isa 38:18 [o]S Ps 6:5; 88:11
30:10 [p]S Ps 17:1 [q]Ps 4:1 [r]S Ps 20:2
30:11 [s]S Est 4:1 [t]S Ex 15:20 [u]S 2Sa 3:31; S Ps 35:13 [v]S Dt 16:15; S Ps 16:9
30:12 [w]Ps 35:18; 75:1; 118:21; Rev 11:17 [x]Ps 44:8; 52:9
31:1 [y]S Ps 7:1 [z]Ps 5:8

[b]*10* Or *sat* [c]Title: Or *palace* [d]*3* Hebrew *Sheol* [e]*7* Or *hill country* [f]*9* Or *there if I am silenced*

29:10–11 GOD, Sovereignty—We confess God's sovereignty as we realize that He controls even the chaotic waters out of which the earth was formed (Ge 1:2). Certainly He has no rival as King of the universe. See note on 22:26–31.
30:1–12 EVIL AND SUFFERING, God's Present Help—The writer thanked God for healing from a life-threatening illness (vv 2–3, 8–10). Paul, however, did not experience relief from the thorn in the flesh, which may have been a physical illness. See note on 2 Co 12:1–10. Believers are not exempt from disease, but should be ready to acknowledge God's help when it comes and to thank Him for His help. In the long-term perspective of our relationship with God, suffering is a momentary inconvenience which will ultimately disappear.
30:1–12 PRAYER, Thanksgiving—See note on 18:1–50. This prayer of thanks makes no petition to the Lord. It describes the answer to a prayer for healing. David had asked if the dust to which his dead body would return would praise the Lord. Delivered from the point of death, he gave thanks to the Lord. Thanksgiving in the Psalms includes: (1) a call or resolve to give thanks directed to oneself or to fellow worshipers (v 1); (2) a reason for giving thanks (v 1); (3) a description of the troubles endured and God's salvation from them (vv 2–3,6–12); and (4) praise to God for His salvation (vv 4–5,12). Compare Pss 9; 18; 30; 34; 92; 116; 138. See Guide to Thanksgiving, p. 1763.
30:3 LAST THINGS, Intermediate State—See note on Isa 14:9.
30:5 GOD, Wrath—Here is an excellent contrast between the grace and the wrath of God. Both are valid expressions of God's nature. Grace is God's preferred expression. God exercises His wrath at a particular moment to accomplish a particular objective. God's ongoing attitude toward His world and its inhabitants is love. See note on 27:9.
30:6–7 ELECTION, Eternal Security—Security and stability are blessings which come to the elect from God. Experience of God's hiddenness may trouble us at times, but the door to prayer and security is always open, bringing renewed joy.
30:11 SALVATION, Joy—God's salvation removes our sackcloth and ashes and makes us want to dance. See note on 4:7.
31:1 GOD, Righteous—The righteousness of God is the basis of God's being Savior. His righteousness means that He protects those who cannot help themselves. He not only opposes what is evil but works to uphold what is right. He seeks to bring about justice. God's righteousness provided a basis for the psalmist to seek God as a refuge, a Savior (vv 1,5,16).
31:1–24 EVIL AND SUFFERING, Prayer—The sufferer must trust God and His love, aware that God knows and understands our troubles. We have no right to demand God's action but can confidently rely on His mercy. This trust may bring ridicule and forgetfulness on the part of human acquaintances because many people emotionally cannot handle suffering and physical weakness. God gives the isolated sufferer strength and protection. See note on 3:1–8.
31:1 SALVATION, As Deliverance—God's righteousness is behind our deliverance. Righteousness (Hebrew *tsedeqah*) refers to the righteous character of God which leads to right acts. The God of righteousness delivers the innocent sufferer and restores a right order to the universe.
31:1–24 PRAYER, Lament—See notes on 3:1–8; 5:10; 6:1–10. In no psalm is trust shown to be more serene than in this lament. The strength of God was a refuge for the psalmist, so he confidently committed his spirit to the Lord. Compare Lk 23:46. He based his confidence in God's strong love. His answer came, and he praised God in the traditional thanksgiving form (vv 21–24). See note on 30:1–12. All saints can gain confidence in prayer from this encouraging example.

2 Turn your ear to me,[a]
come quickly to my rescue;[b]
be my rock of refuge,[c]
a strong fortress to save me.
3 Since you are my rock and my fortress,[d]
for the sake of your name[e] lead and guide me.
4 Free me from the trap[f] that is set for me,
for you are my refuge.[g]
5 Into your hands I commit my spirit;[h]
redeem me, O LORD, the God of truth.[i]

6 I hate those who cling to worthless idols;[j]
I trust in the LORD.[k]
7 I will be glad and rejoice in your love,
for you saw my affliction[l]
and knew the anguish[m] of my soul.
8 You have not handed me over[n] to the enemy
but have set my feet in a spacious place.[o]

9 Be merciful to me, O LORD, for I am in distress;[p]
my eyes grow weak with sorrow,[q]
my soul and my body[r] with grief.
10 My life is consumed by anguish[s]
and my years by groaning;[t]
my strength fails[u] because of my affliction,[g][v]
and my bones grow weak.[w]
11 Because of all my enemies,[x]
I am the utter contempt[y] of my neighbors;[z]
I am a dread to my friends—
those who see me on the street flee from me.
12 I am forgotten by them as though I were dead;[a]
I have become like broken pottery.
13 For I hear the slander[b] of many;
there is terror on every side;[c]
they conspire against me[d]
and plot to take my life.[e]

14 But I trust[f] in you, O LORD;
I say, "You are my God."
15 My times[g] are in your hands;
deliver me from my enemies
and from those who pursue me.
16 Let your face shine[h] on your servant;
save me in your unfailing love.[i]
17 Let me not be put to shame,[j] O LORD,
for I have cried out to you;
but let the wicked be put to shame
and lie silent[k] in the grave.[h]
18 Let their lying lips[l] be silenced,
for with pride and contempt
they speak arrogantly[m] against the righteous.

19 How great is your goodness,[n]
which you have stored up for those who fear you,
which you bestow in the sight of men[o]
on those who take refuge[p] in you.
20 In the shelter[q] of your presence you hide[r] them
from the intrigues of men;[s]
in your dwelling you keep them safe
from accusing tongues.

21 Praise be to the LORD,[t]
for he showed his wonderful love[u] to me
when I was in a besieged city.[v]
22 In my alarm[w] I said,
"I am cut off[x] from your sight!"
Yet you heard my cry[y] for mercy
when I called to you for help.

23 Love the LORD, all his saints![z]
The LORD preserves the faithful,[a]
but the proud he pays back[b] in full.
24 Be strong and take heart,[c]
all you who hope in the LORD.

Psalm 32

Of David. A *maskil*.[i]

BLESSED is he
whose transgressions are forgiven,

[g] *10* Or *guilt* [h] *17* Hebrew *Sheol* [i] Title: Probably a literary or musical term

31:2 [a]S Ps 6:4 [b]S Ex 2:17 [c]S 2Sa 22:3; S Ps 18:2 **31:3** [d]S Ps 18:2 [e]S Ps 23:3 **31:4** [f]S 1Sa 28:9; S Job 18:10 [g]Ps 9:9 **31:5** [h]Lk 23:46; Ac 7:59 [i]Isa 45:19; 65:16 **31:6** [j]S Dt 32:21 [k]S Ps 4:5 **31:7** [l]S Ps 13:3 [m]S Ps 25:17; Lk 22:44 **31:8** [n]S Dt 32:30 [o]S 2Sa 22:20 **31:9** [p]Ps 4:1 [q]Ps 6:7 [r]Ps 63:1 **31:10** [s]ver 7 [t]Ps 6:6 [u]Ps 22:15; 32:4; 38:10; 73:26 [v]Ps 25:18 [w]S Ps 6:2 **31:11** [x]Dt 30:7; Ps 3:7; 25:19; 102:8 [y]S Ps 22:6 [z]Ps 38:11 **31:12** [a]Ps 28:1; 88:4 **31:13** [b]S Lev 19:16; Ps 50:20 [c]S Job 18:11; Isa 13:8; Jer 6:25; 20:3,10; 46:5; 49:5; La 2:22 [d]Ps 41:7; 56:6; 71:10; 83:3 [e]S Ge 37:18; S Mt 12:14 **31:14** [f]Ps 4:5 **31:15** [g]S Job 14:5 **31:16** [h]S Nu 6:25 [i]S Ps 6:4 **31:17** [j]S Ps 22:5 [k]1Sa 2:9; Ps 94:17; 115:17 **31:18** [l]Ps 120:2; Pr 10:18; 26:24 [m]S 1Sa 2:3; Jude 1:15 **31:19** [n]S Ps 27:13; Ro 11:22 [o]Ps 23:5 [p]Ps 2:12 **31:20** [q]Ps 55:8 [r]S Ps 17:8 [s]S Ge 37:18 **31:21** [t]Ps 28:6 [u]S Ps 17:7 [v]1Sa 23:7 **31:22** [w]Ps 116:11 [x]Job 6:9; 17:1; Ps 37:9; 88:5; Isa 38:12 [y]Ps 6:9; 66:19; 116:1; 145:19 **31:23** [z]S Ps 4:3 [a]S Ps 18:25; Rev 2:10 [b]Dt 32:41; Ps 94:2 **31:24** [c]Ps 27:14

31:5 JESUS CHRIST, Foretold—Luke 23:46 gives this cry from the cross. What was to the psalmist a commitment of life was for Jesus a committal in death. Paul gathered up both uses in his all-encompassing affirmation, "Whether we live or die, we belong to the Lord" (Ro 14:8).

31:5 SALVATION, Redemption—Redemption here is personal, rather than national as in the Exodus. God's redemption is individual as well as corporate. To redeem (Hebrew *padah*) had a concrete meaning in Israel's sacrificial system, referring to the setting free of the firstborn son from the command to sacrifice all firstborn to God (Ex 13:2,12–13; 34:19–20; Nu 18:16). Redemption can also mean deliverance from crisis situations—illness, *oppression, attack, false accusations (Ps 26:11; 44:26; 69:18; 119:134)*. See note on Ex 13:13–15.

31:7,16,19,21 GOD, Love—The love and grace of God are almost inseparable from the idea of God as Savior. Love and grace are not neutral, theoretical ideas, but are translated into practical action in saving and protecting God's people. His love is a sympathetic love which understands our afflictions and troubles. It is a love which calls forth our trust in the darkest moments, a love which never flickers, always available to His people.

31:11–12 HUMANITY, Nature of Death—The living quickly forget those who die. The worst crisis in life may be the feeling of total isolation comparable only to the forgotten dead.

31:15 HUMANITY, Life—God is sovereign over all life. No one ever gets beyond His ultimate authority. Humans may isolate, forsake, and forget us. God never does. He is our personal God. We can trust Him.

31:16 THE CHURCH, Servants—God's servants depend on Him to rescue us in times of danger and trial. See note on 27:9.

32:1–11 EVIL AND SUFFERING, Repentance—One of

whose sins are covered.[d]
2Blessed is the man
whose sin the LORD does not count against him[e]
and in whose spirit is no deceit.[f]

3When I kept silent,[g]
my bones wasted away[h]
through my groaning[i] all day long.
4For day and night
your hand was heavy[j] upon me;
my strength was sapped[k]
as in the heat of summer. *Selah*
5Then I acknowledged my sin to you
and did not cover up my iniquity.[l]
I said, "I will confess[m]
my transgressions[n] to the LORD"—
and you forgave
the guilt of my sin.[o] *Selah*

6Therefore let everyone who is godly
pray to you
while you may be found;[p]
surely when the mighty waters[q] rise,[r]
they will not reach him.[s]
7You are my hiding place;[t]
you will protect me from trouble[u]
and surround me with songs of deliverance.[v] *Selah*

8I will instruct[w] you and teach you[x] in the way you should go;
I will counsel you and watch over[y] you.
9Do not be like the horse or the mule,
which have no understanding
but must be controlled by bit and bridle[z]
or they will not come to you.
10Many are the woes of the wicked,[a]
but the LORD's unfailing love
surrounds the man who trusts[b] in him.

11Rejoice in the LORD[c] and be glad, you righteous;
sing, all you who are upright in heart!

Psalm 33

SING joyfully[d] to the LORD, you righteous;
it is fitting[e] for the upright[f] to praise him.
2Praise the LORD with the harp;[g]
make music to him on the ten-stringed lyre.[h]
3Sing to him a new song;[i]
play skillfully, and shout for joy.[j]
4For the word of the LORD is right[k] and true;[l]
he is faithful[m] in all he does.
5The LORD loves righteousness and justice;[n]
the earth is full of his unfailing love.[o]

6By the word[p] of the LORD were the heavens made,[q]
their starry host[r] by the breath of his mouth.

32:1 [d]Ps 85:2; 103:3 **32:2** [e]S Ro 4:7-8* [f]Jn 1:47; Rev 14:5 **32:3** [g]S Job 31:34 [h]Ps 31:10 [i]S Job 3:24; Ps 6:6 **32:4** [j]1Sa 5:6; S Job 9:34; Ps 38:2; 39:10 [k]Ps 22:15 **32:5** [l]Job 31:33 [m]Pr 28:13 [n]Ps 103:12 [o]S Lev 26:40; 1Jn 1:9 **32:6** [p]Ps 69:13; Isa 55:6 [q]S Ex 15:10 [r]Ps 69:1 [s]Isa 43:2 **32:7** [t]S Jdg 9:35 [u]S Ps 9:9 [v]S Jdg 5:1 **32:8** [w]S Ps 25:8 [x]Ps 34:11 [y]Ps 33:18 **32:9** [z]S Job 30:11; S 39:10; Jas 3:3 **32:10** [a]Ro 2:9 [b]Ps 4:5; Pr 16:20 **32:11** [c]Ps 64:10 **33:1** [d]S Ps 5:11; S 101:1 [e]Ps 147:1 [f]Ps 11:7 **33:2** [g]S Ge 4:21; 1Co 14:7; Rev 5:8 [h]Ps 92:3; 144:9 **33:3** [i]Ps 40:3; Isa 42:10; S Rev 5:9 [j]S Job 3:7; Ps 35:27; 47:1 **33:4** [k]S Ps 19:8 [l]Ps 119:142; Rev 19:9; 22:6 [m]Ps 18:25; 25:10 **33:5** [n]Ps 11:7 [o]Ps 6:4 **33:6** [p]S Ge 1:3; Heb 11:3 [q]S Ex 8:19; S 2Ch 2:12 [r]S Ge 1:16

the seven traditional penitential psalms (6,32,38,51, 102, 130,143), this psalm focuses on healing from disease. The disease was God's punishment for sin (vv 3–5), but other passages note that disease is not always a deserved suffering. For sin-related illness, repentance and confession restore the spiritual relationship with God and open the possibility of God's healing. See notes on Jn 9:1–4; 11:3.

32:1–5 HUMANITY, Spiritual Nature—People are created so that God's forgiveness brings us overwhelming happiness. The confession of sin and guilt to God opens the door to His forgiveness and to the establishment of a happy relationship with Him.

32:1–11 PRAYER, Confession—This prayer of gratitude for forgiveness of sins is almost Pauline in its theology. Forgiveness is a matter of the Lord's reckoning, or imputation, and is total. The relationship with the Lord is a matter of human trust in God's unfailing love. Guilt harbored in the heart rather than confessed openly to God is deadly. Guilt entrusted to God is dead, freeing the sinner to enjoy God's love. To fail to confess sin is to be stubborn. Confession fills the heart with a new song.

32:8 EDUCATION, God—In the worship setting, a priest delivered God's Word of assurance to His people. God's teaching is available if His people will listen and obey. See note on 25:4–9.

32:10 GOD, Faithfulness—Both the love and the faithfulness of God are praised here. They allow and invite us to confess our sins and accept God's forgiveness. See notes on 9:10; 26:3; 31:7,16,19,21.

32:10 SALVATION, Belief—Those who trust in God can count on His faithful love to surround them (143:8).

33:1–22 PRAYER, Praise—God's word, God's character, God's creation, and God's rule are compelling reasons to join the congregation in praise. Music and singing are ways to praise God. God's unfailing covenant love (Hebrew *chesed*) is the overriding basis for all human praise. Praise includes a call to the congregation to join in praise (vv 1–3,8), a list of reasons to praise (vv 4–7,9–19), and a concluding call to praise or a statement of trust (vv 20–22). See Guide to Praise, p. 1762.

33:4 GOD, Faithfulness—God's faithfulness is more than an abstract characteristic. Faithfulness finds expression in action. God's acts have a purpose. They carry out His dependable promises and threats. See notes on Ge 8:1; Nu 26:65; Dt 10:11,22; Jos 1:6.

33:5 GOD, Justice—God's righteousness and justice are closely related ideas. His justice grows out of His righteousness. God's strongest positive feeling, His love, goes out to everything which establishes what is right and just in this world. See notes on 7:6,8,11; 25:8–9; 31:1.

33:5,22 GOD, Love—God's love is basic to His character. No conflict exists between His love and righteousness. In v 5, they are virtually used as synonyms. Righteousness is the goal He loves to achieve in His world. His love is the goal His people seek in their distress. See note on 26:3.

33:5 CHRISTIAN ETHICS, Justice—The goal of society should be establishing right and justice because God loves and embodies these characteristics. The believer in praise and worship sees evidence of these divine qualities filling our world.

33:6–9 GOD, Creator—God is the Creator who spoke our world into existence. He has total control over the chaotic waters out of which He called forth the land. We need not fear any part of His creation. We need only fear the Lord, that is, reverence and worship Him. See notes on 19:1–4; 24:1–2,7–10; Ge 1:3—2:25; Ro 4:17.

7 He gathers the waters[s] of the sea into
jars[j] ;[t]
he puts the deep into storehouses.
8 Let all the earth fear the LORD;[u]
let all the people of the world[v]
revere him.[w]
9 For he spoke, and it came to be;
he commanded,[x] and it stood firm.
10 The LORD foils[y] the plans[z] of the
nations;[a]
he thwarts the purposes of the
peoples.
11 But the plans of the LORD stand firm[b]
forever,
the purposes[c] of his heart through
all generations.

12 Blessed is the nation whose God is the
LORD,[d]
the people he chose[e] for his
inheritance.[f]
13 From heaven the LORD looks down[g]
and sees all mankind;[h]
14 from his dwelling place[i] he watches
all who live on earth—
15 he who forms[j] the hearts of all,
who considers everything they do.[k]
16 No king is saved by the size of his
army;[l]
no warrior escapes by his great
strength.
17 A horse[m] is a vain hope for
deliverance;
despite all its great strength it
cannot save.
18 But the eyes[n] of the LORD are on those
who fear him,
on those whose hope is in his
unfailing love,[o]
19 to deliver them from death[p]
and keep them alive in famine.[q]

20 We wait[r] in hope for the LORD;
he is our help and our shield.
21 In him our hearts rejoice,[s]
for we trust in his holy name.[t]
22 May your unfailing love[u] rest upon us,
O LORD,
even as we put our hope in you.

Psalm 34[k]

Of David. When he pretended to be insane[v] before Abimelech, who drove him away, and he left.

I will extol the LORD at all times;[w]
his praise will always be on my lips.
2 My soul will boast[x] in the LORD;
let the afflicted hear and rejoice.[y]
3 Glorify the LORD[z] with me;
let us exalt[a] his name together.

4 I sought the LORD,[b] and he answered
me;
he delivered[c] me from all my fears.
5 Those who look to him are radiant;[d]
their faces are never covered with
shame.[e]
6 This poor man called, and the LORD
heard him;

33:7 [s]S Ge 1:10 [t]S Jos 3:16 **33:8** [u]S Dt 6:13; Ps 2:11 [v]Ps 49:1; Isa 18:3; Mic 1:2 [w]S Dt 14:23 **33:9** [x]Ps 148:5 **33:10** [y]Isa 44:25 [z]S Job 5:12 [a]Ps 2:1 **33:11** [b]S Nu 23:19 [c]Jer 51:12,29 **33:12** [d]Ps 144:15 [e]S Ex 8:22; Dt 7:6; Ps 4:3; 65:4; 84:4 [f]S Ex 34:9 **33:13** [g]Ps 53:2; 102:19 [h]Job 28:24; Ps 11:4; 14:2; S Heb 4:13 **33:14** [i]S Lev 15:31; 1Ki 8:39 **33:15** [j]Job 10:8; Ps 119:73 [k]S Job 10:4; Jer 32:19 **33:16** [l]1Sa 14:6 **33:17** [m]S Ps 20:7 **33:18** [n]S Ex 3:16; S Ps 11:4; 1Pe 3:12 [o]S Ps 6:4 **33:19** [p]Ps 56:13; Ac 12:11 [q]S Job 5:20 **33:20** [r]S Ps 27:14 **33:21** [s]S 1Sa 2:1; S Joel 2:23 [t]S Ps 30:4; S 99:3 **33:22** [u]Ps 6:4 **34:1** [v]**34 Title** 1Sa 21:13 [w]Ps 71:6; S Eph 5:20; 1Th 5:18 **34:2** [x]Ps 44:8; Jer 9:24; 1Co 1:31 [y]Ps 69:32; 107:42; 119:74 **34:3** [z]Ps 63:3; 86:12; Da 4:37; Jn 17:1; Ro 15:6 [a]S Ex 15:2 **34:4** [b]S Ex 32:11; Ps 77:2 [c]ver 17; Ps 18:43; 22:4; 56:13; 86:13 **34:5** [d]S Ex 34:29 [e]Ps 25:3; 44:15; 69:7; 83:16

[j]7 Or *sea as into a heap* [k]This psalm is an acrostic poem, the verses of which begin with the successive letters of the Hebrew alphabet.

33:10–21 GOD, Sovereignty—The sovereignty of God, His authority and power to rule over the world and achieve His purposes, empowers Him to cause human plans opposed to His to fail. He accomplishes His own plans for His creation. His sovereignty thus leads to salvation that He offers His people.

33:11–12 SALVATION, Blessing—God blesses the nation who owns Him as Lord. This is His eternal plan to which He steadfastly commits Himself. This does not mean a nation cannot sin and come under God's curses (Dt 28). It means God's basic work is to save a people for fellowship and worship with Him.

33:13–19 HUMANITY, Relationship to God—God, the Creator, is sovereign over all His creation, including every human. Any creature, whether great or small, is ultimately subservient to the Creator. Most remarkably, the sovereign God is defined by love, so He uses His sovereign knowledge and power for our good. He delivers us from all threatening forces.

33:16–18 CHRISTIAN ETHICS, War and Peace—See notes on 18:30–50; 20:7–8.

33:18–22 LAST THINGS, Believers' Resurrection—The psalmist confessed that God can deliver *from* death, that is, prevent one from encountering an untimely death. This furnished the language to express the idea of deliverance from the far side of death, that is, by means of resurrection. By means of resurrection God does redeem from death in the fullest and most final way.

34:1–22 EVIL AND SUFFERING, *God's Present Help*—*The* writer thanked God for helping him in his troubles. The righteous are not exempt from trouble, but God ultimately delivers the righteous and punishes the wicked. God's help sometimes takes the form of physical deliverance from trouble. The psalmist described God's help in the form of an angelic watchman but did not develop a doctrine of individual angels watching over each of God's people. Generalizing that the faithful will have no fears (v 4) or troubles (v 17) needs to be balanced by passages that indicate believers will endure suffering in this life. See note on Jn 15:18–27.

34:1–21 SALVATION, As Deliverance—God delivers us from our fears, foes, and troubles. His deliverance extends to those who fear Him and to the righteous. God uses even His heavenly messengers to protect and deliver His people (v 7). Such confessions of deliverance represent the experiences and testimonies of God's people. They do not form a law which means God's people will never suffer. If this were true, deliverance would not be necessary. Compare 54:7; 69:14.

34:1–22 PRAYER, Thanksgiving—See note on 30:1–12. Some of the psalms praise God for His glory in creation. This one praises Him because of the meaning of relationship with Him. He delivers, not merely from things feared but from fear itself, removing shame. He protects and provides. Above all, He is attentive and answers the prayer of the righteous. Artistic forms can be used to express thanks to God. This psalmist used an acrostic to thank God from *aleph* to *taw* (or for us from A to Z), beginning each verse with a succeeding letter of the Hebrew alphabet. Compare Pss 9—10; 25; 37; 111; 112; 119; 145; Pr 31:10–31; La 1;2;3;4.

34:6,17–18 SALVATION, Definition—God saves the poor, the brokenhearted, and those who cry out to Him. His salvation reaches out to include those whom the world would exclude. God wants to include in His kingdom whomever will come to Him.

he saved him out of all his
troubles.[f]
7The angel of the LORD[g] encamps
around those who fear him,
and he delivers[h] them.

8Taste and see that the LORD is good;[i]
blessed is the man who takes
refuge[j] in him.
9Fear the LORD,[k] you his saints,
for those who fear him lack
nothing.[l]
10The lions may grow weak and hungry,
but those who seek the LORD lack no
good thing.[m]

11Come, my children, listen[n] to me;
I will teach you[o] the fear of the
LORD.[p]
12Whoever of you loves life[q]
and desires to see many good days,
13keep your tongue[r] from evil
and your lips from speaking lies.[s]
14Turn from evil and do good;[t]
seek peace[u] and pursue it.

15The eyes of the LORD[v] are on the
righteous[w]
and his ears are attentive[x] to their
cry;
16the face of the LORD is against[y] those
who do evil,[z]
to cut off the memory[a] of them
from the earth.

17The righteous cry out, and the LORD
hears[b] them;
he delivers them from all their
troubles.
18The LORD is close[c] to the
brokenhearted[d]
and saves those who are crushed in
spirit.

19A righteous man may have many
troubles,[e]
but the LORD delivers him from
them all;[f]
20he protects all his bones,
not one of them will be broken.[g]

21Evil will slay the wicked;[h]
the foes of the righteous will be
condemned.
22The LORD redeems[i] his servants;
no one will be condemned who
takes refuge[j] in him.

Psalm 35

Of David.

CONTEND,[k] O LORD, with those who
contend with me;
fight[l] against those who fight
against me.
2Take up shield[m] and buckler;
arise[n] and come to my aid.[o]
3Brandish spear[p] and javelin[1][q]
against those who pursue me.

34:6 [f]S Ps 25:17 **34:7** [g]S Ge 32:1; S Da 3:28; S Mt 18:10 [h]Ps 22:4; 37:40; 41:1; 97:10; Isa 31:5; Ac 12:11 **34:8** [i]Heb 6:5; 1Pe 2:3 [j]S Ps 2:12 **34:9** [k]S Dt 6:13; Rev 14:7 [l]S Ps 23:1 **34:10** [m]S Ps 23:1 **34:11** [n]Ps 66:16 [o]S Ps 32:8 [p]S Ps 19:9 **34:12** [q]Ecc 3:13 **34:13** [r]Ps 39:1; 141:3; Pr 13:3; 21:23; Jas 1:26 [s]S Ps 12:2; 1Pe 2:22 **34:14** [t]Ps 37:27; Isa 1:17; 3Jn 1:11 [u]S Ro 14:19 **34:15** [v]Ps 33:18 [w]S Job 23:10; S 36:7 [x]Mal 3:16; S Jn 9:31 **34:16** [y]Lev 17:10; Jer 23:30 [z]1Pe 3:10-12* [a]S Ex 17:14; Ps 9:6 **34:17** [b]Ps 145:19 **34:18** [c]Dt 4:7; Ps 119:151; 145:18; Isa 50:8 [d]Ps 51:17; 109:16; 147:3; Isa 61:1 **34:19** [e]ver 17; Ps 25:17 [f]S Job 5:19; 2Ti 3:11 **34:20** [g]Jn 19:36* **34:21** [h]Ps 7:9; 9:16; 11:5; 37:20; 73:27; 94:23; 106:43; 112:10; 140:11; Pr 14:32; 24:16 **34:22** [i]S Ex 6:6; S 15:13; Lk 1:68; Rev 14:3 [j]Ps 2:12 **35:1** [k]S 1Sa 24:15 [l]S Ex 14:14 **35:2** [m]Ps 3:3 [n]Ps 3:7 [o]S Ge 50:24; S Job 17:3 **35:3** [p]S Nu 25:7 [q]S Jos 8:18

[1]3 Or *and block the way*

34:7–18 REVELATION, Events—God sees and hears. He is deeply attentive to His children's needs and actions. Unlike the uncaring gods of neighboring people, Israel's God was worshiped as an involved and concerned Creator. His actions in individual lives become revelatory events. The messenger of God represents God Himself camping near His children. See note on Jdg 13:3–23.
34:8–10 SALVATION, Fear of God—Those who fear God lack nothing good that they need. See note on Ge 22:12.
34:8 SALVATION, As Refuge—Refuge is a prominent meaning of salvation in the Old Testament. God is a safe refuge for all who will turn to Him. No source of security is as sure as our good Lord. See note on 22:5,8.
34:9–10 CHRISTIAN ETHICS, Property Rights—God cares for His children. He knows our material needs. Such a condition provides relief and a basis for hope in this life and the one to come.
34:11–14 CHRISTIAN ETHICS, Language—Our words indicate our goals. If we want to bring peace and good to the world, we must not speak evil or lie about other people. Such restraint demonstrates our reverence for and dedication to God.
34:14 CHRISTIAN ETHICS, Moral Imperatives—Biblical ethics begins *with two basic principles:* (1) negative, evil life-styles should be rejected; and (2) peace or wholeness is the goal of life. One must proceed from rejecting evil to choosing and acting upon virtues which are positive. Peace (Hebrew *shalom*) is the all-encompassing value. Peace represents a sufficiency in all areas of life so that satisfaction with the full life ensues. Peace is more than the absence of conflict. It is the presence of all components of meaningful life. Peace does not come by passive waiting. Peace must be pursued.
34:20 JESUS CHRIST, Foretold—See note on Ex 12:46.
34:22 ELECTION, Eternal Security—The elect are confident of the deliverance which comes from God. Faithful elect need not fear condemnation.
34:22 SALVATION, Redemption—God's redemption and freedom from condemnation are equated in the text. Redemption is available to those who take refuge in God. See note on 31:5.
34:22 THE CHURCH, Servants—God gives special blessings to those who follow Him. The life of the servant of God may require hardship and pain, but God cares for His own, providing abundant spiritual blessings. See note on 27:9.
35:1–28 EVIL AND SUFFERING, Vindication—See note on 3:1–8. The writer pleaded for the destruction of the wicked. To a Christian, this act may sound vindictive, but it is a plea for justice. The sufferer desperately wanted the God of justice to vindicate him. The psalmist did not intend to get revenge on his own. Christians can appreciate the honesty of the psalmist without imitating his vindictive attitude. We can see the many types of emotional suffering we must endure from God's enemies.
35:1–28 PRAYER, Curse—See note on 5:10. This imprecatory prayer shows the violent opposition between innocence and evil. The evil intentions of the psalmist's enemies were causeless, a theme frequent in the psalter (38:19; 69:4; 119:78,86,161) and mentioned by Jesus (Jn 15:25). God's punishment of unjust actions of His people's enemies shows He alone is God. When God delivers us, we are called to testify to others of His righteous salvation.
35:3 GOD, Savior—God is Savior for His faithful people. Salvation in the Old Testament was often experienced as deliverance from the perils of this life. In the New Testament salvation takes on the spiritualized meaning of eternal life, though it still maintains a sense of establishing well-being and

Say to my soul,
"I am your salvation.[r]"

4May those who seek my life[s]
be disgraced[t] and put to shame;[u]
may those who plot my ruin
be turned back[v] in dismay.
5May they be like chaff[w] before the wind,
with the angel of the LORD[x] driving them away;
6may their path be dark and slippery,
with the angel of the LORD pursuing them.
7Since they hid their net[y] for me without cause[z]
and without cause dug a pit[a] for me,
8may ruin overtake them by surprise—[b]
may the net they hid entangle them,
may they fall into the pit,[c] to their ruin.
9Then my soul will rejoice[d] in the LORD
and delight in his salvation.[e]
10My whole being will exclaim,
"Who is like you,[f] O LORD?
You rescue the poor from those too strong[g] for them,
the poor and needy[h] from those who rob them."

11Ruthless witnesses[i] come forward;
they question me on things I know nothing about.
12They repay me evil for good[j]
and leave my soul forlorn.
13Yet when they were ill, I put on sackcloth[k]
and humbled myself with fasting.[l]
When my prayers returned to me unanswered,
14 I went about mourning[m]
as though for my friend or brother.
I bowed my head in grief
as though weeping for my mother.
15But when I stumbled, they gathered in glee;[n]
attackers gathered against me when I was unaware.
They slandered[o] me without ceasing.
16Like the ungodly they maliciously mocked[m];[p]
they gnashed their teeth[q] at me.
17O Lord, how long[r] will you look on?
Rescue my life from their ravages,
my precious life[s] from these lions.[t]
18I will give you thanks in the great assembly;[u]
among throngs[v] of people I will praise you.[w]
19Let not those gloat over me
who are my enemies[x] without cause;
let not those who hate me without reason[y]
maliciously wink the eye.[z]
20They do not speak peaceably,
but devise false accusations[a]
against those who live quietly in the land.
21They gape[b] at me and say, "Aha! Aha![c]
With our own eyes we have seen it."
22O LORD, you have seen[d] this; be not silent.
Do not be far[e] from me, O Lord.
23Awake,[f] and rise[g] to my defense!
Contend[h] for me, my God and Lord.
24Vindicate me in your righteousness, O LORD my God;
do not let them gloat[i] over me.
25Do not let them think, "Aha,[j] just what we wanted!"
or say, "We have swallowed him up."[k]

26May all who gloat[l] over my distress[m]
be put to shame[n] and confusion;
may all who exalt themselves over me[o]
be clothed with shame and disgrace.
27May those who delight in my vindication[p]
shout for joy[q] and gladness;
may they always say, "The LORD be exalted,
who delights[r] in the well-being of his servant."[s]
28My tongue will speak of your righteousness[t]
and of your praises all day long.[u]

35:3 [r]Ps 27:1 **35:4** [s]Ps 38:12; 40:14; Jer 4:30 [t]Ps 69:6,19; 70:2; 83:17; Isa 45:16; Mal 2:9 [u]Ps 25:3 [v]Ps 129:5 **35:5** [w]S Job 13:25; Ps 1:4 [x]Ps 34:7 **35:7** [y]S Job 18:8 [z]S Ps 7:4 [a]S Job 9:31; S Ps 7:15; S 55:23 **35:8** [b]Isa 47:11; 1Th 5:3 [c]S Ps 7:15 **35:9** [d]S Ps 2:11; S Lk 1:47 [e]Ps 9:14; 13:5; 27:1 **35:10** [f]S Ex 9:14; S Ps 18:31; 113:5 [g]Ps 18:17 [h]Ps 12:5; 37:14; 74:21; 86:1; 109:16; 140:12; Isa 41:17 **35:11** [i]S Ex 23:1; S Mt 26:60 **35:12** [j]Ps 38:20; 109:5; Pr 17:13; Jer 18:20 **35:13** [k]S 2Sa 3:31; 1Ki 20:31; Ps 30:11; 69:11 [l]Job 30:25; Ps 69:10; 109:24 **35:14** [m]Ps 38:6; 42:9; 43:2 **35:15** [n]S Job 31:29 [o]S Job 16:10 **35:16** [p]S Ps 22:7; Mk 10:34 [q]S Job 16:9; Mk 9:18; Ac 7:54 **35:17** [r]Ps 6:3 [s]Ps 22:20 [t]Ps 22:21; 57:4; 58:6 **35:18** [u]S Ps 22:25 [v]Ps 42:4; 109:30 [w]S Ps 22:22 **35:19** [x]Ps 9:13 [y]ver 7; Ps 38:19; 69:4; Jn 15:25* [z]Pr 6:13; 10:10 **35:20** [a]Ps 38:12; 55:21; Jer 9:8; Mic 6:12 **35:21** [b]S Job 16:10 [c]Ps 40:15; 70:3; Eze 25:3 **35:22** [d]Ex 3:7; Ps 10:14 [e]S Ps 10:1 **35:23** [f]S Ps 7:6; 80:2 [g]Ps 17:13 [h]S 1Sa 24:15 **35:24** [i]Ps 22:17 **35:25** [j]ver 21 [k]Ps 124:3; Pr 1:12; La 2:16 **35:26** [l]Ps 22:17 [m]Ps 4:1 [n]S Job 8:22; Ps 109:29; Mic 7:10 [o]Job 19:5; Ps 38:16 **35:27** [p]Ps 9:4 [q]Ps 20:5; S 33:3 [r]Ps 147:11; 149:4 [s]S Job 17:3 **35:28** [t]Ps 5:8; 51:14 [u]Ps 71:15, 24; 72:15

[m]16 Septuagint; Hebrew may mean *ungodly circle of mockers.*

---

peace for God's people in this world.

35:10–16 CHRISTIAN ETHICS, Justice—The wise person knows that society often turns on us and denies us justice, but God still administers justice. We can call on Him to help when all earthly hope fails.

35:11 JESUS CHRIST, Foretold—*Where there is no truth, there is no justice.* This was demonstrated in the trial of Jesus (Mt 26:60–61; Mk 14:56–59; Ps 27:12).

35:24 GOD, Righteous—As righteous, God not only opposes what is evil. He upholds what is right, defends the defenseless, and works for justice. See note on 33:5.

35:28 EVANGELISM, Personal—We are to develop a life-style evangelism, telling of His righteousness "all day long." Personal witnessing comes from the overflow of our lives and is to be a daily exercise as we share Christ in the normal pursuits of our lives. See Guide to Life-style Evangelism, pp. 1831–1832.

Psalm 36

For the director of music. Of David the servant of the LORD.

AN oracle is within my heart
concerning the sinfulness of the wicked:[n] [v]
There is no fear[w] of God
before his eyes.[x]
2For in his own eyes he flatters himself
too much to detect or hate his sin.[y]
3The words of his mouth[z] are wicked
and deceitful;[a]
he has ceased to be wise[b] and to do good.[c]
4Even on his bed he plots evil;[d]
he commits himself to a sinful course[e]
and does not reject what is wrong.[f]

5Your love, O LORD, reaches to the heavens,
your faithfulness[g] to the skies.[h]
6Your righteousness[i] is like the mighty mountains,[j]
your justice like the great deep.[k]
O LORD, you preserve both man and beast.[l]
7 How priceless is your unfailing love![m]
Both high and low among men
find[o] refuge in the shadow of your wings.[n]
8They feast on the abundance of your house;[o]
you give them drink from your river[p] of delights.[q]
9For with you is the fountain of life;[r]
in your light[s] we see light.

10Continue your love[t] to those who know you,[u]
your righteousness to the upright in heart.[v]
11May the foot of the proud not come against me,
nor the hand of the wicked[w] drive me away.
12See how the evildoers lie fallen—
thrown down, not able to rise![x]

Psalm 37[p]

Of David.

DO not fret because of evil men
or be envious[y] of those who do wrong;[z]
2for like the grass they will soon wither,[a]
like green plants they will soon die away.[b]

3Trust in the LORD and do good;
dwell in the land[c] and enjoy safe pasture.[d]
4Delight[e] yourself in the LORD
and he will give you the desires of your heart.[f]

5Commit your way to the LORD;
trust in him[g] and he will do this:
6He will make your righteousness[h]
shine like the dawn,[i]

36:1 [v]S Job 21:16 [w]Jer 2:19; 36:16,24 [x]S Job 23:15; Ro 3:18* **36:2** [y]Dt 29:19 **36:3** [z]Ps 10:7 [a]S Job 5:13; Ps 5:6, 9; 43:1; 144:8,11; Isa 44:20 [b]Ps 94:8 [c]Jer 4:22; 13:23; Am 3:10 **36:4** [d]Pr 4:16 [e]Isa 65:2 [f]Ps 52:3; Ro 12:9 **36:5** [g]Ps 89:1; 119:90 [h]Ps 57:10; 71:19; 89:2; 103:11; 108:4 **36:6** [i]Ps 5:8 [j]Ps 68:15 [k]S Ge 1:2; S 7:11 [l]Ne 9:6; Ps 104:14; 145:16 **36:7** [m]Ps 6:4 [n]S Ru 2:12; S Ps 17:8; 57:1; 91:4 **36:8** [o]Ps 65:4; Isa 25:6; Jer 31:12, 14 [p]Job 20:17; Rev 22:1 [q]S Ps 23:2; 63:5 **36:9** [r]Ps 87:7; Pr 10:11; 16:22; Jer 2:13 [s]Ps 4:6; 27:1; 76:4; 104:2; Isa 2:5; 9:2; 60:1, 19; Jn 1:4; 1Pe 2:9 **36:10** [t]Jer 31:3 [u]Jer 9:24; 22:16 [v]Ps 7:10; 11:2; 94:15; 125:4 **36:11** [w]Ps 71:4; 140:4 **36:12** [x]S Ps 18:38 **37:1** [y]Pr 3:31; 23:17-18 [z]Ps 73:3; Pr 24:19 **37:2** [a]S 2Ki 19:26; Job 14:2; Ps 102:4; Isa 40:7 [b]ver 38; Ps 90:6; 92:7; Jas 1:10 **37:3** [c]Dt 30:20 [d]Eze 34:14; Jn 10:9 **37:4** [e]S Job 27:10 [f]S Job 7:6; Ps 21:2; 145:19; Mt 6:33 **37:5** [g]Ps 4:5 **37:6** [h]Ps 18:24; 103:17; 112:3 [i]S Job 11:17

[n]*1* Or *heart: / Sin proceeds from the wicked.* [o]*7* Or *love, O God! / Men find*; or *love! / Both heavenly beings and men / find* [p]This psalm is an acrostic poem, the stanzas of which begin with the successive letters of the Hebrew alphabet.

36:1–12 EVIL AND SUFFERING, Deserved—The psalmist describes the character of a wicked person and his ultimate rejection by God. The righteous person will enjoy the blessings of knowing a loving and just God.

36:1–4 SIN, Depravity—Sinners make sin a habit of attitude, thought, and action. They lose the ability to identify sin. They forfeit the will to hate and oppose sin. Life's plans and dreams become wicked rather than good. Even for such sinners, God's love reaches down. We must accept that love in repentance to become part of the righteous (v 10). See note on 10:1–18.

36:1–12 PRAYER, Instruction—Psalms uses language usually associated with prophets and wise men to address God but also to teach the listening congregation. See note on 15:1–5. Here the psalmist received a prophetic oracle and taught the fear of God (Pr 1:7). Prayer at times needs to meditate on sin and its consequences for the individual's life. This stands in contrast to God's faithfulness, righteousness, justice, and love, qualities which are also subjects for meditation and instruction.

36:5,7,10 GOD, Love—Love preserves God's people in the midst of problems. It is more precious than any gem. No one can buy it. God unceasingly offers His love to those who in faith will accept it. See note on 33:5,22.

36:6,10 GOD, Righteous—Righteousness is closely related to God's love, mentioned in v 10, and to justice in v 6, where righteousness and justice are virtually synonymous. God's people need both the favor of God's love and the security of His righteousness. See note on 35:24.

36:7–9 SALVATION, Definition—See notes on 9:14; 22:5,8. Salvation is the result of God's covenant love (Hebrew *chesed*) (Isa 55:3) and makes provision for physical and spiritual needs. These verses point us forward to Jesus Christ as the Water of life (Jn 4:13–14) and the Light of the world (Jn 1:9). Light and life are synonyms in the doctrine of salvation.

37:1–40 EVIL AND SUFFERING, God's Future Help—The apparent prosperity of the wicked often perplexes God's people. The psalmist learned that God would eventually punish the wicked. God's people should not be angry or envious of the wicked. We should trust God in His justice.

37:1–8 CHRISTIAN ETHICS, Character—Trust, faith, perseverance in the ways of God will be rewarded in due time. Only time and experience can validate the claim of this passage, but its advice is valuable in gaining perspective regarding those who have less integrity but apparently gain ground in this life.

37:2 HUMANITY, Life—Evil people often haunt our existence. We need not worry. Their life is always temporary. Mortality is a common human characteristic. Eternal life is not something we possess by nature. Eternal life is God's gift to us through Christ.

37:4 PRAYER, Instruction—See notes on 15:1–5; 34:1–22. Prayer is agreement with God; choose His pleasures, and He will choose yours. The psalmist showed this through a series of proverbs encouraging trust, commitment, and patience.

37:6,25,35–36 CHRISTIAN ETHICS, Justice—God honors justice and righteousness. The way of the wicked may seem

the justice of your cause like the
noonday sun.

7 Be still[j] before the LORD and wait
patiently[k] for him;
do not fret[l] when men succeed in
their ways,[m]
when they carry out their wicked
schemes.[n]

8 Refrain from anger[o] and turn from
wrath;
do not fret[p]—it leads only to evil.
9 For evil men will be cut off,[q]
but those who hope[r] in the LORD
will inherit the land.[s]

10 A little while, and the wicked will be
no more;[t]
though you look for them, they will
not be found.
11 But the meek will inherit the land[u]
and enjoy great peace.[v]

12 The wicked plot[w] against the righteous
and gnash their teeth[x] at them;
13 but the Lord laughs at the wicked,
for he knows their day is coming.[y]

14 The wicked draw the sword[z]
and bend the bow[a]
to bring down the poor and needy,[b]
to slay those whose ways are
upright.
15 But their swords will pierce their own
hearts,[c]
and their bows will be broken.[d]

16 Better the little that the righteous have
than the wealth[e] of many wicked;
17 for the power of the wicked will be
broken,[f]
but the LORD upholds[g] the
righteous.

18 The days of the blameless are known
to the LORD,[h]
and their inheritance will endure
forever.[i]
19 In times of disaster they will not
wither;
in days of famine they will enjoy
plenty.

20 But the wicked will perish:[j]
The LORD's enemies will be like the
beauty of the fields,
they will vanish—vanish like
smoke.[k]

21 The wicked borrow and do not repay,
but the righteous give generously;[l]
22 those the LORD blesses will inherit the
land,
but those he curses[m] will be cut
off.[n]

23 If the LORD delights[o] in a man's way,
he makes his steps firm;[p]
24 though he stumble, he will not fall,[q]
for the LORD upholds[r] him with his
hand.

25 I was young and now I am old,
yet I have never seen the righteous
forsaken[s]
or their children begging[t] bread.
26 They are always generous and lend
freely;[u]
their children will be blessed.[v]

27 Turn from evil and do good;[w]
then you will dwell in the land
forever.[x]
28 For the LORD loves the just
and will not forsake his faithful
ones.[y]

They will be protected forever,
but the offspring of the wicked will
be cut off;[z]
29 the righteous will inherit the land[a]
and dwell in it forever.[b]

30 The mouth of the righteous man utters
wisdom,[c]
and his tongue speaks what is just.
31 The law of his God is in his heart;[d]
his feet do not slip.[e]

32 The wicked lie in wait[f] for the
righteous,[g]
seeking their very lives;
33 but the LORD will not leave them in
their power

37:7 [j]S Ex 14:14; S Isa 41:1 [k]S Ps 27:14; 40:1; 130:5; Isa 38:13; Hab 3:16; Ro 8:25 [l]ver 1 [m]Jer 12:1 [n]Ps 21:11; 26:10; 119:150 **37:8** [o]Eph 4:31; Col 3:8 [p]ver 1 **37:9** [q]S Ps 31:22; 101:8; 118:10; Pr 2:22 [r]Isa 25:9; 26:8; 40:31; 49:23; 51:5 [s]ver 22; Ps 25:13; Isa 49:8; 57:13; Mt 5:5 **37:10** [t]S Job 7:10; Eze 27:36 **37:11** [u]S Nu 14:24; Mt 5:5 [v]S Lev 26:6; S Nu 6:26 **37:12** [w]Ps 2:1; 31:13 [x]S Job 16:9; Ps 35:16; 112:10 **37:13** [y]1Sa 26:10; Eze 12:23 **37:14** [z]S Ps 22:20 [a]Ps 11:2 [b]S Ps 35:10 **37:15** [c]S Ps 9:16 [d]S 1Sa 2:4; Ps 46:9; Jer 49:35 **37:16** [e]Pr 15:16; 16:8 **37:17** [f]Job 38:15; Ps 10:15 [g]Ps 41:12; 140:12; 145:14; 146:7 **37:18** [h]S Job 23:10; Ps 44:21 [i]ver 27,29 **37:20** [j]S Ps 34:21 [k]Ps 68:2; 102:3; Isa 51:6 **37:21** [l]S Lev 25:35; Ps 112:5 **37:22** [m]S Job 5:3 [n]ver 9 **37:23** [o]S Nu 14:8; Ps 147:11 [p]S Job 11:15; S Ps 7:9; 66:9 **37:24** [q]S Ps 13:4; 27:2; 38:17; 55:22; 119:165; Pr 3:23; 10:9 [r]2Ch 9:8; Ps 41:12; 145:14 **37:25** [s]ver 28; S Ge 15:1; Heb 13:5 [t]Ps 111:5; 145:15; Mk 10:46 **37:26** [u]S Lev 25:35 [v]Dt 28:4; Ps 112:2 **37:27** [w]Ps 34:14; 3Jn 1:11 [x]S Nu 24:21 **37:28** [y]S Dt 7:6; S Ps 18:25; S 97:10 [z]S Ge 17:14; S Dt 32:26; Pr 2:22 **37:29** [a]ver 9; Pr 2:21 [b]Isa 34:17 **37:30** [c]Ps 49:3; Pr 10:13 **37:31** [d]S Dt 6:6; S Job 22:22 [e]S Dt 32:35 **37:32** [f]S Ps 10:8 [g]Ps 11:5

profitable, but eventually fails.

37:9–13 LAST THINGS, Hell—The wicked are ultimately repaid by a just God. They will be cut off and will be no more because "their day is coming." The truth of recompense and retribution demands a future time of punishment. The scales do not balance this side of death. God was early preparing human thought to receive the revelation of a future state of punishment, as well as of rewards.

37:16–17 CHRISTIAN ETHICS, Property Rights—The wicked of this world may have more of its goods than the righteous, but in the perspective of eternity the righteous are better off. Being on God's side is better than being rich.

37:18–29 ELECTION, Blessing—Divine approval, support in trouble, provisions for material needs, and the faithful presence of God are blessings which come to the righteous committed to the leadership of the God of election.

37:21–26 STEWARDSHIP, Giving in Worship—Grasping things for self characterizes the wicked. The righteous give generously. Giving is the nature of persons who are close to God, for giving is God's nature. See note on Mt 5:23–24.

37:28 GOD, Love—God's faithful love motivates us to repent and act like He wants us to. See note on 36:5,7,10.

37:28 GOD, Wrath—God's love does not prevent Him from acting in judgment against the wicked who will not receive His love. See notes on Ge 6:5–8; 17:14; 19:13, 24–26; Jos 7:1,25–26.

37:33 GOD, Faithfulness—God's faithful love protects His faithful people in persecution. See notes on Ge 8:1; Nu 26:65; Dt 10:11,22; Jos 1:6.

or let them be condemned[h] when
brought to trial.[i]
34Wait for the LORD[j]
and keep his way.[k]
He will exalt you to inherit the land;
when the wicked are cut off,[l] you
will see[m] it.
35I have seen a wicked and ruthless man
flourishing[n] like a green tree in its
native soil,
36but he soon passed away and was no
more;
though I looked for him, he could
not be found.[o]
37Consider the blameless,[p] observe the
upright;[q]
there is a future[q] for the man of
peace.[r]
38But all sinners[s] will be destroyed;[t]
the future[r] of the wicked will be
cut off.[u]
39The salvation[v] of the righteous comes
from the LORD;
he is their stronghold in time of
trouble.[w]
40The LORD helps[x] them and delivers[y]
them;
he delivers them from the wicked
and saves[z] them,
because they take refuge[a] in him.

Psalm 38

A psalm of David. A petition.

O LORD, do not rebuke me in your
anger
or discipline me in your wrath.[b]
2For your arrows[c] have pierced me,
and your hand has come down upon
me.
3Because of your wrath there is no
health[d] in my body;
my bones[e] have no soundness
because of my sin.
4My guilt has overwhelmed[f] me
like a burden too heavy to bear.[g]
5My wounds[h] fester and are
loathsome[i]
because of my sinful folly.[j]
6I am bowed down[k] and brought very
low;
all day long I go about mourning.[l]
7My back is filled with searing pain;[m]
there is no health[n] in my body.
8I am feeble and utterly crushed;[o]
I groan[p] in anguish of heart.[q]
9All my longings[r] lie open before you,
O Lord;
my sighing[s] is not hidden from you.
10My heart pounds,[t] my strength fails[u]
me;
even the light has gone from my
eyes.[v]
11My friends and companions avoid me
because of my wounds;[w]
my neighbors stay far away.
12Those who seek my life set their
traps,[x]
those who would harm me talk of
my ruin;[y]
all day long they plot deception.[z]
13I am like a deaf man, who cannot
hear,[a]
like a mute, who cannot open his
mouth;
14I have become like a man who does
not hear,
whose mouth can offer no reply.
15I wait[b] for you, O LORD;
you will answer,[c] O Lord my God.
16For I said, "Do not let them gloat[d]
or exalt themselves over me when
my foot slips."[e]
17For I am about to fall,[f]
and my pain[g] is ever with me.
18I confess my iniquity;[h]
I am troubled by my sin.
19Many are those who are my vigorous
enemies;[i]
those who hate me[j] without
reason[k] are numerous.
20Those who repay my good with evil[l]
slander[m] me when I pursue what is
good.
21O LORD, do not forsake me;[n]

37:33 [h]Job 32:3; Ps 34:22; 79:11 [i]2Pe 2:9
37:34 [j]Ps 27:14 [k]S Ps 18:21 [l]ver 9 [m]Ps 52:6
37:35 [n]S Job 5:3
37:36 [o]ver 10; Pr 12:7; Isa 41:12; Da 11:19
37:37 [p]ver 18; S Ge 6:9; Ps 18:25 [q]Ps 11:7 [r]Isa 57:1-2
37:38 [s]S Ps 1:1 [t]S ver 2; Ps 73:19 [u]ver 9
37:39 [v]S Ps 3:8 [w]S Ps 9:9
37:40 [x]S 1Ch 5:20; S Ps 20:2 [y]S Ps 34:7 [z]S Ps 18:48 [a]Ps 2:12
38:1 [b]Ps 6:1
38:2 [c]S Job 6:4
38:3 [d]Pr 3:8; 4:22; Isa 66:14 [e]S Job 33:19
38:4 [f]Ps 40:12; 65:3 [g]S Nu 11:14; S Ezr 9:6; Lk 11:46
38:5 [h]ver 11; Ps 147:3 [i]Job 19:17 [j]Ps 69:5; Pr 5:23; 12:23; 13:16; Ecc 10:3
38:6 [k]Ps 57:6; 145:14; 146:8 [l]S Ps 35:14
38:7 [m]S Job 14:22 [n]ver 3
38:8 [o]Ps 34:18; Pr 17:22 [p]S Ps 6:6; 22:1; Pr 5:11 [q]S Ps 6:3
38:9 [r]Ps 119:20; 143:7 [s]S Job 3:24
38:10 [t]S Job 37:1 [u]S Ps 31:10 [v]S Ps 6:7; S 19:8; 88:9
38:11 [w]S ver 5
38:12 [x]Ps 31:4; 140:5; 141:9 [y]Ps 35:4; 41:5 [z]S Ps 35:20
38:13 [a]Ps 115:6; 135:17; Isa 43:8; Mk 7:37
38:15 [b]Ps 27:14 [c]Ps 17:6
38:16 [d]S Ps 22:17 [e]S Dt 32:35
38:17 [f]S Ps 37:24 [g]ver 7; S Job 6:10
38:18 [h]S Lev 26:40
38:19 [i]S Ps 18:17 [j]S Ps 25:19 [k]S Ps 35:19
38:20 [l]S Ge 44:4; 1Jn 3:12 [m]Ps 54:5; 59:10; 119:23
38:21 [n]Ps 27:9; 71:18; 119:8

[q]*37* Or *there will be posterity* [r]*38* Or *posterity*

38:1–3 GOD, Wrath—The guilty sinner experiences illness and weakness as God's punishing wrath, yet still pleads to God for forgiveness and healing. Wrath does not block the door of prayer for God's sinful people. See notes on Ge 6:5–8; 17:14; 19:13,24–26; Jos 7:1,25–26.

38:1–22 EVIL AND SUFFERING, Repentance—One of the traditional penitential psalms (6,32,38,51,102,130,143), the psalm includes the belief that some disease is punishment for sin. See note on 32:1–11. Repentance is the first step back to God for the sinful sufferer. Suffering may repel humans, but God will not forsake us.

38:1–22 PRAYER, Repentance—Repentance for sin is the escape route from divine punishment. David was sick and sought healing. He was not in grief for his circumstances but for his sin. The vivid description of physical suffering and oppression from without demonstrates that sin intensifies the pain of outer circumstances. David had removed himself from God's protective presence. Only he could pray for restoration to the Lord's presence. Sin produced anger in Cain (Ge 4:5) and terror in Saul (1 Sa 28:5–6) but repentance in David. True repentance leads to faith (v 15). See note on 39:1–13.

38:11 JESUS CHRIST, Foretold—This is one of the seven great penitential songs of the early Christians, in which desertion and loneliness are major themes. The Gospels stress this isolation of Jesus in His death (Lk 23:49).

38:18 SALVATION, Confession—Confession is admitting our sins to God because we are troubled by them. We agree with God that we are sinful and need forgiveness. This is the first step to repentance.

be not far[o] from me, O my God.
22 Come quickly[p] to help me,[q]
O Lord my Savior.[r]

Psalm 39

For the director of music. For Jeduthun.
A psalm of David.

I said, "I will watch my ways[s]
and keep my tongue from sin;[t]
I will put a muzzle on my mouth[u]
as long as the wicked are in my
presence."
2 But when I was silent[v] and still,
not even saying anything good,
my anguish[w] increased.
3 My heart grew hot[x] within me,
and as I meditated,[y] the fire[z]
burned;
then I spoke with my tongue:
4 "Show me, O LORD, my life's end
and the number of my days;[a]
let me know how fleeting[b] is my
life.[c]
5 You have made my days[d] a mere
handbreadth;
the span of my years is as nothing
before you.
Each man's life is but a breath.[e]
Selah
6 Man is a mere phantom[f] as he goes to
and fro:[g]
He bustles about, but only in vain;[h]
he heaps up wealth,[i] not knowing
who will get it.[j]

7 "But now, Lord, what do I look for?
My hope is in you.[k]
8 Save me[l] from all my transgressions;[m]
do not make me the scorn[n] of fools.
9 I was silent;[o] I would not open my
mouth,[p]
for you are the one who has done
this.[q]
10 Remove your scourge from me;
I am overcome by the blow[r] of your
hand.[s]
11 You rebuke[t] and discipline[u] men for
their sin;
you consume[v] their wealth like a
moth[w]—
each man is but a breath.[x] *Selah*

12 "Hear my prayer, O LORD,
listen to my cry for help;[y]
be not deaf[z] to my weeping.[a]
For I dwell with you as an alien,[b]
a stranger,[c] as all my fathers were.[d]
13 Look away from me, that I may rejoice
again
before I depart and am no more."[e]

Psalm 40

40:13–17pp — Ps 70:1–5

For the director of music. Of David.
A psalm.

I waited patiently[f] for the LORD;
he turned to me and heard my cry.[g]
2 He lifted me out of the slimy pit,[h]
out of the mud[i] and mire;[j]
he set my feet[k] on a rock[l]
and gave me a firm place to stand.
3 He put a new song[m] in my mouth,
a hymn of praise to our God.
Many will see and fear[n]
and put their trust[o] in the LORD.

4 Blessed is the man[p]
who makes the LORD his trust,[q]
who does not look to the proud,[r]

38:21 [o]S Ps 10:1; S 22:11; 35:22; 71:12 **38:22** [p]S Ps 22:19 [q]Ps 40:13 [r]S 1Ch 16:35 **39:1** [s]1Ki 2:4; Ps 119:9,59; Pr 20:11 [t]S Job 1:22; Ps 34:13; Jas 3:2 [u]S Job 6:24; Jas 1:26 **39:2** [v]ver 9; S Job 31:34; Ps 77:4 [w]Ps 6:3; S 25:17; 31:10 **39:3** [x]Lk 24:32 [y]Ps 1:2; 48:9; 77:12; 119:15 [z]Jer 5:14; 20:9; 23:29 **39:4** [a]S Job 14:5 [b]S Job 14:2 [c]S Ge 47:9; S Job 7:7 **39:5** [d]S Job 10:20; Ps 89:45; 102:23 [e]S Job 7:7; Ps 62:9 **39:6** [f]Job 8:9; Ps 102:11; Ecc 6:12; S Jas 4:14 [g]Jas 1:11 [h]Ps 127:2 [i]S Job 27:17 [j]Lk 12:20 **39:7** [k]S Ps 9:18; S 25:5 **39:8** [l]Ps 6:4; 51:14 [m]Ps 32:1; 51:1; Isa 53:5,8,10 [n]S Dt 28:37; Ps 69:7; 79:4; Isa 43:28; Da 9:16 **39:9** [o]S ver 2 [p]Ps 38:13 [q]Isa 38:15 **39:10** [r]2Ch 21:14; Eze 7:9; 24:16 [s]S Ex 9:3 **39:11** [t]S Dt 28:20; Isa 66:15; Eze 5:15; 2Pe 2:16 [u]Ps 94:10; Isa 26:16 [v]Ps 90:7 [w]S Job 13:28; S Isa 51:8; Lk 12:33; S Jas 5:2 [x]S Job 7:7 **39:12** [y]S Ps 17:1 [z]S Dt 1:45 [a]S 2Ki 20:5 [b]Lev 25:23 [c]S Ge 23:4; S Heb 11:13 [d]S Ge 47:9; S 1Ch 29:15 **39:13** [e]S Job 10:21 **40:1** [f]S Ps 37:7 [g]Ps 6:9; S 31:22; 34:15; 116:1; 145:19 **40:2** [h]S Job 9:31; S Ps 7:15 [i]S Job 30:19 [j]Ps 69:14 [k]Ps 31:8 [l]Ps 27:5 **40:3** [m]S Ps 28:7; S 96:1; Rev 5:9 [n]Ps 52:6; 64:9 [o]S Ex 14:31 **40:4** [p]Ps 34:8 [q]Ps 84:12 [r]Ps 101:5; 138:6; Pr 3:34; 16:5; Isa 65:5; 1Pe 5:5

38:22 GOD, Savior—Because He can heal, God is called Savior. See note at 25:5.

39:1–13 EVIL AND SUFFERING, Prayer—Sufferers cannot simply endure in silence. Anguish demands verbal expression. God's people can express all our pains to God, even when we feel God has sent our suffering as punishment for our sins. See note on 3:1–8.

39:1–13 PRAYER, Sincerity—The other side to Ps 38 appears here. David could repent freely from sin because his heart was inclined to avoid sin at all cost. Silence produced only anguish before God. He could not refrain from prayer. See note on 3:1–8.

39:4–6 HUMANITY, Life—God's people are all aware our life is wholly in His hands. He establishes the ultimate limits of human life. Illness increases our awareness of life's limits and our sins. By contrast with the stability of the earth, individual human existence is always seen as being quite temporary. Aware of our limits, we turn to God for renewed hope.

39:6 CHRISTIAN ETHICS, Property Rights—In our natural state, the God-created desire for order and creativity are perverted into covetousness and greed. Without the guidance of God's perspective regarding the reasons why we have material things and how we can use those, we are aimless wanderers. To collect wealth for no good purpose is meaningless.

40:1–17 EVIL AND SUFFERING, Prayer—The psalm combines thanksgiving for God's help in the past and a plea for more help. The suffering singer learned that religious rites and acts do not satisfy God. He wants us to determine to do His will and to share our experience of His righteous acts with others. We must be conscious of our own sins which separate us from God and His healing power. See note on 3:1–8.

40:1–17 PRAYER, Corporate—Many psalms were composed for congregational involvement in worship. Some show the movement of worship clearly. Compare 15; 24; 78; 84; 105; 106; 122. This psalm moves from thanksgiving (vv 1–10) to lament (vv 11–17). Prayer is not confined to one subject or mood. Worshipers need to express thanksgiving for God's action in their lives and sorrow for unwanted and even undeserved circumstances. Likewise, a psalm was not confined to one use. Vv 13–17 form an independent unit and appear as Ps 70 in our Bible. Petition can be based on thanksgiving as here, on God's covenant faithfulness (Ps 44), or God's greatness and election (Ps 89). Compare Heb 10:5–10.

40:3 EVANGELISM, Testimony—Our own redemption puts a new song in our mouths. Out of hearts of gratitude and love for God, we share our witness. The consequence is, many will "see and fear" and come to trust Jesus Christ. Our testimony shared in love is powerful in winning others.

to those who turn aside to false
gods.[s] [s]
5Many, O LORD my God,
are the wonders[t] you have done.
The things you planned for us
no one can recount[u] to you;
were I to speak and tell of them,
they would be too many[v] to declare.

6Sacrifice and offering you did not
desire,[w]
but my ears you have pierced[t,u];[x]
burnt offerings[y] and sin offerings
you did not require.
7Then I said, "Here I am, I have
come—
it is written about me in the
scroll.[v] [z]
8I desire to do your will,[a] O my God;[b]
your law is within my heart."[c]

9I proclaim righteousness[d] in the great
assembly;[e]
I do not seal my lips,
as you know,[f] O LORD.
10I do not hide your righteousness in my
heart;
I speak of your faithfulness[g] and
salvation.
I do not conceal your love and your
truth
from the great assembly.[h]

11Do not withhold your mercy[i] from
me, O LORD;
may your love[j] and your truth[k]
always protect[l] me.
12For troubles[m] without number
surround me;

40:4 [s]S Dt 31:20; S Ps 4:2; S 26:1
40:5 [t]S Dt 4:34; Ps 75:1; 105:5; 136:4 [u]Ps 139:18 [v]Ps 71:15; 139:17
40:6 [w]S 1Sa 15:22; Jer 6:20; Am 5:22 [x]Ex 21:6 [y]Ps 50:8; 51:16; Isa 1:11; Hos 6:6
40:7 [z]Job 19:23; Jer 36:2; 45:1; Eze 2:9; Zec 5:1
40:8 [a]S Mt 26:39 [b]Heb 10:5-7* [c]S Dt 6:6; S Job 22:22; Ro 7:22
40:9 [d]S Ps 22:31 [e]S Ps 22:25 [f]S Jos 22:22
40:10 [g]Ps 89:1 [h]S Ps 22:22
40:11 [i]Zec 1:12 [j]Pr 20:28 [k]S Ps 26:3 [l]Ps 61:7
40:12 [m]S Ps 25:17 [n]Ps 38:4; 65:3 [o]Ps 69:4 [p]Ps 73:26
40:13 [q]Ps 22:19; 38:22
40:14 [r]S 1Sa 20:1 [s]S Est 9:2; Ps 35:26 [t]S Ps 35:4
40:15 [u]S Ps 35:21
40:16 [v]Dt 4:29; 1Ch 28:9; Ps 9:10; 119:2 [w]Ps 9:2 [x]Ps 35:27
40:17 [y]Ps 86:1; 109:22 [z]Ps 144:3 [a]S Ps 20:2 [b]S Ps 18:2 [c]Ps 119:60
41:1 [d]S Dt 14:29 [e]S Job 24:4 [f]Ps 25:17
41:2 [g]Ps 12:5; 32:7 [h]Ezr 9:9; Ps 71:20; 119:88,159; 138:7; 143:11 [i]Ps 37:22

my sins have overtaken me, and I
cannot see.[n]
They are more than the hairs of my
head,[o]
and my heart fails[p] within me.

13Be pleased, O LORD, to save me;
O LORD, come quickly to help me.[q]
14May all who seek to take my life[r]
be put to shame and confusion;[s]
may all who desire my ruin[t]
be turned back in disgrace.
15May those who say to me, "Aha!
Aha!"[u]
be appalled at their own shame.
16But may all who seek you[v]
rejoice and be glad[w] in you;
may those who love your salvation
always say,
"The LORD be exalted!"[x]

17Yet I am poor and needy;[y]
may the Lord think[z] of me.
You are my help[a] and my deliverer;[b]
O my God, do not delay.[c]

Psalm 41

For the director of music. A psalm of David.

BLESSED[d] is he who has regard for
the weak;[e]
the LORD delivers him in times of
trouble.[f]
2The LORD will protect[g] him and
preserve his life;[h]
he will bless him in the land[i]

[s]4 Or *to falsehood* [t]6 Hebrew; Septuagint *but a body you have prepared for me* (see also Symmachus and Theodotion) [u]6 Or *opened* [v]7 Or *come / with the scroll written for me*

40:5 REVELATION, History—The writer extolled God's creative power and spoke of himself as an agent of revelation who declared God's work to all. God's wonders are too many to recount, yet the worship of God is the occasion for such celebration. In history God's acts for His people have revealed Him in love and power.

40:6–8 JESUS CHRIST, Foretold—The translation of 6b is very difficult. The Greek translation reads "a body you have prepared for me" (NIV footnote). The author of Heb 10:5–10 used this version. Early Christians used it as an expression of the incarnation. The idea is you have made me so that I can hear you and be obedient to you. This whole paragraph is about obedience and sacrifice. Some interpreters say this reference is against sacrifice. Others say it is setting forth the proper requirements and attitudes for sacrifice. Hebrews sees in Jesus Christ both the proper obedience and attitude for sacrifice and the final and conclusive sacrifice which makes further sacrifices unnecessary. The actions and attitude of Jesus expressed by the *words "I desire to do your will"* is the primary and appropriate way in which Christians should approach their worship and work for God.

40:6 STEWARDSHIP, Service to God—Gifts and sacrifices cannot earn God's forgiveness for sins. Giving is a practice to show love for God, not to achieve the love of God. Gifts must be validated by a life of obedient service. See note on Ac 4:32—5:11.

40:9–11 GOD, Righteous—God's love and righteousness are mentioned here coordinately, almost synonymously. The two ideas do not stand in conflict. God's love leads Him to righteous acts which punish the wicked but free and save His faithful people. See notes on 36:5,7,10; 36:6,10.

40:10 GOD, Nature—The joyous worshiper experiences God's deliverance and testifies of the experience to the congregation. Such experiences are personal lessons in God's righteous acts of salvation and His faithful love for His people. From testimonies of other worshipers we learn of the very personal meaning of God's nature for us.

41:1–13 EVIL AND SUFFERING, Vindication—See note on 3:1–8. Friends may forsake the sufferer, but God sustains the sick and sometimes heals them. Confession of sin is proper for one who suffers. Desire to repay evil for evil is a natural feeling properly expressed to God in prayer but not properly put into practice. Sickness must not cause us to lose our love and compassion for others. See note on 34:1–22.

41:1 SALVATION, As Deliverance—God delivers those who have regard for the weak. See note on 1:1.

41:1–12 PRAYER, Petition—Sickness apparently stands behind many psalms. It is most apparent here. Apparently Israel had special worship times for the ill. The priest would pronounce a blessing (vv 1–3). The sick person would ask for mercy, forgiveness, and healing, describing personal feelings in the crisis of sickness (vv 4–10). The priest would give a word of assurance from God, and the patient would express confidence in God's healing presence (vv 11–12). Such worship cannot guarantee healing for all people. It does help people deal with their mixed emotions about being sick and gain confidence of God's caring presence in their sickness. See notes on 5:10; 6:1–10. Compare Jn 13:18.

and not surrender him to the desire
of his foes.[j]
3The LORD will sustain him on his
sickbed[k]
and restore him from his bed of
illness.[l]

4I said, "O LORD, have mercy[m] on me;
heal[n] me, for I have sinned[o] against
you."
5My enemies say of me in malice,
"When will he die and his name
perish?[p]"
6Whenever one comes to see me,
he speaks falsely,[q] while his heart
gathers slander;[r]
then he goes out and spreads[s] it
abroad.

7All my enemies whisper together[t]
against me;
they imagine the worst for me,
saying,
8"A vile disease has beset him;
he will never get up[u] from the place
where he lies."
9Even my close friend,[v] whom I
trusted,
he who shared my bread,
has lifted up his heel against me.[w]

41:2 [j]S Dt 6:24 **41:3** [k]Ps 6:6 [l]2Sa 13:5; 2Ki 1:4 **41:4** [m]Ps 6:2; S 9:13 [n]S Dt 32:39 [o]Ps 51:4 **41:5** [p]S Ps 38:12 **41:6** [q]Ps 12:2; 101:7; Mt 5:11 [r]Pr 26:24 [s]S Lev 19:16 **41:7** [t]Ps 71:10 **41:8** [u]S 2Ki 1:4 **41:9** [v]S 2Sa 15:12; S Job 19:14 [w]Nu 30:2; Job 19:19; Ps 55:20; 89:34; Mt 26:23; Lk 22:21; Jn 13:18* **41:10** [x]ver 4 [y]Ps 3:3; 9:13 [z]S 2Sa 3:39 **41:11** [a]S Nu 14:8 [b]Ps 25:2 **41:12** [c]S Ps 25:21 [d]Ps 18:35; S 37:17; 63:8 [e]S Job 4:7; Ps 21:6; 61:7 **41:13** [f]S Ge 24:27 [g]Ps 72:18 [h]Ps 72:19; 89:52; 106:48 **42:1** [i]S Ps 18:33 [j]S Dt 10:7 [k]S Job 19:27; Ps 119:131; Joel 1:20

10But you, O LORD, have mercy[x] on me;
raise me up,[y] that I may repay[z]
them.
11I know that you are pleased with me,[a]
for my enemy does not triumph over
me.[b]
12In my integrity[c] you uphold me[d]
and set me in your presence
forever.[e]

13Praise[f] be to the LORD, the God of
Israel,[g]
from everlasting to everlasting.
Amen and Amen.[h]

BOOK II

Psalms 42–72

Psalm 42[w]

For the director of music. A *maskil*[x] of the Sons of Korah.

AS the deer[i] pants for streams of
water,[j]
so my soul pants[k] for you, O God.

[w]In many Hebrew manuscripts Psalms 42 and 43 constitute one psalm. [x]Title: Probably a literary or musical term

41:9 JESUS CHRIST, Foretold—This sad verse of betrayal is alluded to in Mt 26:23; Mk 14:20; Lk 22:21 and expressly applied to Judas' betrayal of Jesus in Jn 13:18. To lift up a heel against someone is to be violent toward one, to kick at one, to try to trample someone. The violence and treachery which lie behind the smiling face or greeting kiss of a friend are the worst kind of betrayal. Jesus suffered this from Judas.

41:11–12 ELECTION, Presence—The mercy of God brings consolation that God will raise up the elect from a sick bed and from the low place in which an enemy can triumph. The presence of God that brings healing and deliverance is the basis for praise.

41:13 HOLY SCRIPTURE, Collection—Psalms represent writing intended for singing. Many may well have been used orally long before being written. Psalms are individual units meaningful in isolation from preceding and following psalms. To become part of inspired Scripture, psalms had to be collected in writing and placed in order. Part of the ordering process is apparent in the division of Psalms into five parts or books by the addition of doxologies or verses of praise (41:13; 72:18–19; 89:52; 106:48; 150:1–6). Inspiration includes not only the writing of individual psalms but the process of collecting them. The inspired editor used doxologies to call readers to worship. Reading the psalms is a wise meditation on their meaning (1:2) but also a worship experience calling forth praise to God.

41:13 PRAYER, Corporate—The Psalms are obviously prayers which have been written down for use in worship and meditation. V 13 is apparently either a familiar choral refrain or a verse written specifically to close the first section of the Psalms with doxology. The medium in which a prayer is composed has nothing to do with its validity as prayer. Prayer may be oral or written, prose or poetry, private or congregational, monotone or musical. Borrowing of written prayers such as the Psalms or the Model Prayer (Mt 6:9–13) can provide meaningful prayer times for individuals or congregations if the people truly appropriate and apply the prayers for their own lives. Compare 72:18–19; 89:52; 106:48; 150:1–6.

42:1—43:5 EVIL AND SUFFERING, God's Present Help—A refrain stressing God's help in a time of discouragement links these two psalms: 42:5,11; 43:5. See notes on 3:1–8; 21:1–13. Feeling God is absent causes God's people to suffer. Such feelings come when we cannot join God's people in worship. Prayer, praise, and hopeful waiting on God can help us endure loneliness and rediscover God's presence and salvation.

42:1–2 HUMANITY, Spiritual Nature—The Hebrew word for soul is *nephesh*. This is not to be understood as we popularly talk about soul. This term sums up the totality of life. Even animals have a *nephesh* (Ge 1:20). The point here is that people are given a spiritual nature which leads them to seek God. Despite philosophical and atheistic claims to the contrary, the human being is by nature religious. Particularly in times of trouble we search for the higher Power who can deliver us. In Jesus Christ we find the fulfillment of our longing for God.

42:1–4 WORSHIP, Corporate—These verses describe part of Israel's pattern of worship. The multitudes came together at the sacred place to praise, to worship the Lord. This sense of the corporate nature of worship is seen in the institution of the Passover (Ex 12:1—13:16). Each individual household was responsible, but all the people were involved. They were all to act at the same time. The same pattern is seen when King David commanded all the people to worship (1 Ch 29:20). The New Testament begins with this same corporate responsibility to worship (Lk 1:10). The early church developed a strong sense of need to worship with other believers (Lk 19:37–38; Ac 16:25; 1 Co 14:26–27; Heb 10:24–25). The strong emphasis in both the Old and New Testament is on the corporate worship in the congregation. Corporate worship gives encouragement, strengthens faith, provides a sense of fellowship and identity, and gives instruction for the worshiper.

42:1—43:5 PRAYER, Lament—See note on 3:1–8. Both as poetry and as prayer, Ps 42—43 should be regarded as a unit with stanzas joined by a refrain (42:5,11; 43:5). Each stanza ascends in a higher, more plaintive call to God. The psalmist was in exile somewhere to the north of Mt. Hermon, longing to be on the mountain of God with God Himself. God's apparent absence gives the basic reason for lamentation. See note on 84:1–12.

2 My soul thirsts[l] for God, for the living
God.[m]
When can I go[n] and meet with
God?
3 My tears[o] have been my food
day and night,
while men say to me all day long,
"Where is your God?"[p]
4 These things I remember
as I pour out my soul:[q]
how I used to go with the multitude,
leading the procession to the house
of God,[r]
with shouts of joy[s] and thanksgiving[t]
among the festive throng.[u]

5 Why are you downcast,[v] O my soul?
Why so disturbed[w] within me?
Put your hope in God,[x]
for I will yet praise[y] him,
my Savior[z] and 6 my God.[a]

My[y] soul is downcast within me;
therefore I will remember[b] you
from the land of the Jordan,[c]
the heights of Hermon[d]—from
Mount Mizar.
7 Deep calls to deep[e]
in the roar of your waterfalls;
all your waves and breakers
have swept over me.[f]

8 By day the LORD directs his love,[g]
at night[h] his song[i] is with me—
a prayer to the God of my life.[j]

9 I say to God my Rock,[k]
"Why have you forgotten[l] me?
Why must I go about mourning,[m]
oppressed[n] by the enemy?"[o]
10 My bones suffer mortal agony[p]
as my foes taunt[q] me,
saying to me all day long,
"Where is your God?"[r]

11 Why are you downcast, O my soul?
Why so disturbed within me?
Put your hope in God,
for I will yet praise him,
my Savior and my God.[s]

Psalm 43[z]

VINDICATE me, O God,
and plead my cause[t] against an
ungodly nation;
rescue me[u] from deceitful and
wicked men.[v]
2 You are God my stronghold.
Why have you rejected[w] me?
Why must I go about mourning,[x]
oppressed by the enemy?[y]
3 Send forth your light[z] and your
truth,[a]
let them guide me;[b]
let them bring me to your holy
mountain,[c]
to the place where you dwell.[d]
4 Then will I go[e] to the altar[f] of God,
to God, my joy[g] and my delight.[h]
I will praise you with the harp,[i]
O God, my God.

5 Why are you downcast, O my soul?
Why so disturbed within me?
Put your hope in God,
for I will yet praise him,
my Savior and my God.[j]

Psalm 44

For the director of music. Of the Sons of Korah. A *maskil*.[a]

WE have heard with our ears,[k]
O God;

42:2 [l]Ps 63:1; 143:6 [m]S Jos 3:10; S 1Sa 14:39; S Mt 16:16; Ro 9:26 [n]Ps 43:4; 84:7 **42:3** [o]S Job 3:24 [p]ver 10; Ps 79:10; 115:2; Joel 2:17; Mic 7:10 **42:4** [q]S 1Sa 1:15 [r]Ps 55:14; 122:1; Isa 2:2; 30:29 [s]S Ezr 3:13 [t]S Jos 6:5; Ps 95:2; 100:4; 147:7; Jnh 2:9 [u]Ps 35:18; 109:30 **42:5** [v]Ps 38:6; 77:3; La 3:20; Mt 26:38 [w]S Job 20:2 [x]S Ps 25:5; S 71:14 [y]Ps 9:1 [z]Ps 18:46 **42:6** [a]ver 11; Ps 43:5 [b]Ps 63:6; 77:11 [c]Ge 13:10; S Nu 13:29 [d]S Dt 3:8; S 4:48 **42:7** [e]S Ge 1:2; S 7:11 [f]Ps 69:2; Jnh 2:3 **42:8** [g]Ps 57:3 [h]S Ps 16:7 [i]Ps 77:6 [j]Ps 133:3; Ecc 5:18; 8:15 **42:9** [k]Ps 18:31 [l]S Ps 10:11 [m]S Ps 35:14 [n]Job 20:19; Ps 43:2; 106:42 [o]Ps 9:13; 43:2 **42:10** [p]S Ps 6:2 [q]Dt 32:27; Ps 44:16; 89:51; 102:8; 119:42 [r]S ver 3 **42:11** [s]ver 5; Ps 43:5 **43:1** [t]S Jdg 6:31 [u]S Ps 25:20 [v]S Ps 36:3; 109:2 **43:2** [w]Ps 44:9; 74:1; 88:14; 89:38 [x]S Ps 35:14 [y]S Ps 42:9 **43:3** [z]Ps 27:1 [a]S Ps 26:3 [b]S Ps 25:5 [c]Ps 2:6 [d]S 2Sa 15:25 **43:4** [e]S Ps 42:2 [f]Ps 26:6; 84:3 [g]S Ps 21:6 [h]Ps 16:3 [i]S Ge 4:21

43:5 [j]S Ps 42:6 **44:1** [k]2Sa 7:22; 1Ch 17:20; Jer 26:11

[y]5,6 A few Hebrew manuscripts, Septuagint and Syriac; most Hebrew manuscripts *praise him for his saving help. / 6O my God, my* [z]In many Hebrew manuscripts Psalms 42 and 43 constitute one psalm. [a]Title: Probably a literary or musical term

42:2 GOD, Living—The idea of God as a living God was important to God's Old Testament people. The gods of the nations so often were wooden or stone idols without life. By contrast, the God of the Hebrews was alive and active for His people. Worshipers are eager to meet and praise a God who is alive even if the God has no image to make Him visible. See notes on Ex 3:12–16; Nu 14:21,28; Jn 6:57.

42:5–6,11 GOD, Savior—The living God (v 2) brings hope and salvation to the isolated worshiper. See note on 38:22.

42:5,11 LAST THINGS, Heaven—Twice in this psalm and once in the next (43:5), a person's soliloquy with his own soul called for hope. The hope looks beyond trouble and oppression to a future time when praise will replace grief. Such language also can express the fuller revelation of heaven and the endless praises made possible there. See note on Rev 21:1–5.

42:6 HUMANITY, Spiritual Nature—When the circumstances of life overwhelm the people of God, regardless of where they are, they instinctively turn to Him.

42:8–11 REVELATION, Author of Hope—The true feeling of abandonment by the believer was also the moment of faith, as he confessed the closeness of God, the kinship between Creator and creature, and the assurance that God would save again. The psalmist testified to God's presence even when he sensed His absence, for he knew God would appear to him and direct him.

43:3 GOD, Holy—Mountains where worship places are located are not holy of themselves. Only God is holy. Other persons or objects may acquire that holiness by virtue of being in relationship to God. See notes on Ex 3:5–6; 19:10–24; Lev 11:44–45; Ps 22:3; 28:2.

43:4 SALVATION, Joy—God's joy makes us want to praise Him with musical instruments. See note on 4:7.

44:1–26 EVIL AND SUFFERING, Prayer—History does not always repeat itself for God's people. We may not always experience the glorious victories of the past. Shame and disgrace may be our lot, even when we remain faithful to God. Prayer and faithful endurance are the only hope in such times. God's unfailing love gives us reason for hope.

44:1–8 REVELATION, History—The psalmist witnesses to God's revelation and at the same time receives revelation in the form of oral history passed on from one generation to another and eventually recorded. Early accounts of God's actions and words were passed on by retelling His revelation. Israel's personal history became a record of God's saving activity in the past and present. The psalmist gave God credit for every success, declaring Him the means of Israel's understand-

our fathers have told us[l]
what you did in their days,
in days long ago.[m]
2With your hand you drove out[n] the nations
and planted[o] our fathers;
you crushed[p] the peoples
and made our fathers flourish.[q]
3It was not by their sword[r] that they won the land,
nor did their arm bring them victory;
it was your right hand,[s] your arm,[t]
and the light[u] of your face, for you loved[v] them.

4You are my King[w] and my God,[x]
who decrees[b] victories[y] for Jacob.
5Through you we push back[z] our enemies;
through your name we trample[a] our foes.
6I do not trust in my bow,[b]
my sword does not bring me victory;
7but you give us victory[c] over our enemies,
you put our adversaries to shame.[d]
8In God we make our boast[e] all day long,[f]
and we will praise your name forever.[g] *Selah*

9But now you have rejected[h] and humbled us;[i]
you no longer go out with our armies.[j]
10You made us retreat[k] before the enemy,
and our adversaries have plundered[l] us.
11You gave us up to be devoured like sheep[m]
and have scattered us among the nations.[n]
12You sold your people for a pittance,[o]
gaining nothing from their sale.

13You have made us a reproach[p] to our neighbors,[q]
the scorn[r] and derision[s] of those around us.
14You have made us a byword[t] among the nations;
the peoples shake their heads[u] at us.
15My disgrace[v] is before me all day long,
and my face is covered with shame[w]
16at the taunts[x] of those who reproach and revile[y] me,
because of the enemy,[z] who is bent on revenge.

17All this happened to us,
though we had not forgotten[a] you
or been false to your covenant.
18Our hearts had not turned[b] back;
our feet had not strayed from your path.
19But you crushed[c] us and made us a haunt for jackals[d]
and covered us over with deep darkness.[e]

20If we had forgotten[f] the name of our God
or spread out our hands to a foreign god,[g]
21would not God have discovered it,
since he knows the secrets of the heart?[h]
22Yet for your sake we face death all day long;

44:1 [l]S Jdg 6:13 [m]S Dt 32:7; S Job 37:23 **44:2** [n]S Jos 3:10; Ac 7:45 [o]S Ex 15:17; S Isa 60:21 [p]S Jdg 4:23; S 2Ch 14:13 [q]Ps 80:9; Jer 32:23 **44:3** [r]Jos 24:12 [s]Ps 78:54 [t]Ex 15:16; Ps 77:15; 79:11; 89:10; 98:1; Isa 40:10; 52:10; 63:5 [u]Ps 89:15 [v]S Dt 4:37 **44:4** [w]S Ps 24:7 [x]Ps 5:2 [y]S Ps 21:5 **44:5** [z]S Jos 23:5 [a]Ps 60:12; 108:13 **44:6** [b]Ge 48:22; Hos 1:7 **44:7** [c]S Dt 20:4 [d]S Job 8:22 **44:8** [e]S Ps 34:2; 1Co 1:31; 2Co 10:17 [f]Ps 52:1 [g]S Ps 30:12 **44:9** [h]S Ps 43:2 [i]S Dt 8:3; S 31:17; Ps 107:39; Isa 5:15 [j]S Jos 7:12; Ps 108:11 **44:10** [k]S Lev 26:17 [l]S Jdg 2:14 **44:11** [m]ver 22; Jer 12:3 [n]S Lev 26:33; S Ps 9:11; Eze 6:8; Zec 2:6 **44:12** [o]S Dt 32:30; Isa 52:3; Jer 15:13; 50:1; 52:3; Jer 15:13 **44:13** [p]S 2Ch 29:8; Isa 30:3; Jer 25:9; 42:18; 44:8 [q]Ps 79:4; 80:6; 89:41 [r]S Dt 28:37; S Mic 2:6 [s]Eze 23:32 **44:14** [t]S 1Ki 9:7 [u]S 2Ki 19:21 **44:15** [v]Ge 30:23; 2Ch 32:21; Ps 35:26 [w]S Ps 34:5 **44:16** [x]S Ps 42:10 [y]Ps 10:13; 55:3; 74:10 [z]S 1Sa 18:25; S Jer 11:19; Ro 12:19 **44:17** [a]S Dt 6:12; S 32:18; Ps 119:16,61,153,176; Pr 3:1 **44:18** [b]Ps 119:51, 157 **44:19** [c]S 2Ch 14:13; Ps 51:8 [d]S Job 30:29; S Isa 34:13 [e]S Job 3:5 **44:20** [f]S Dt 32:18; S Jdg 3:7 [g]S Ex 20:3; Isa 43:12; Jer 5:19 **44:21** [h]S 1Sa 16:7; 1Ki 8:39; Pr 15:11; Jer 12:3; 17:10

[b]4 Septuagint, Aquila and Syriac; Hebrew *King, O God; / command*

ing of its own purpose. History experienced, interpreted, retold, and written convinced Israel her God was the only God.

44:1–8 HISTORY, Deliverance—Knowledge of God's past acts gives hope in new situations and leads us to confess Him as King and God. He is our only source of praise and hope.

44:1–26 PRAYER, Lament—See notes on 3:1–8; 40:1–17. Prayers such as this demonstrate an important biblical principle of, and practice in, prayer. Psalmists often plead their case with God. Vv 1–8 present the case—ultimate strength is with God alone. Vv 9–22 plead the case—the circumstances are desperate, but Israel remains faithful. The petition appears in vv 23–26. National history may be the basis on which lamentation is based. Rational argument is a basic part of prayer. Ultimately, however, prayer does not seek to convince a neutral or opposing God. Prayer seeks to restore fellowship with and confidence in a caring Father through open communication.

44:3,26 GOD, Love—God's people attribute their victories and achievements to God's love. When in need, we call on God's dependable covenant love. See note on 37:28.

44:4 GOD, Sovereignty—God's people do not depend on their own resources and strength. We look to the sovereign God who made and controls our world. See notes on Ge 15:13–16; 18:14; 24:3,7,50; Dt 1:10.

44:5–16 CHRISTIAN ETHICS, War and Peace—Victory in war did not come automatically even for an obedient Israel. God's help in war could appear to be past history which would never be repeated. Even such circumstances did not rob Israel of faith and of knowledge that God was Israel's only source of hope. In time of trouble it appeared God had forgotten and neglected His people, but Israel knew He would rouse to action at the proper time because of His dependable love.

44:17 THE CHURCH, Covenant—Keeping covenant commitments does not guarantee material prosperity and freedom from problems. It does give free access to God with whom we can share our problems. Keeping the covenant includes worshiping Him alone, doing righteousness, and shunning unrighteousness.

44:21 GOD, Wisdom—In time of desperation God's people proclaim their innocence before God. They have not deserved the calamities they suffer. They call on God in His all-knowing wisdom to testify to their innocence. We can be sure God knows our situation and what we deserve. See notes on Ex 6:5; Dt 31:21; 1 Sa 2:3.

44:22 HUMANITY, Relationships—Sin exercises a strong grip on our world. It disrupts human relationships. God's people can expect to be wrongly related to many forces within our sinful world. The forces of evil will not allow peace to the

we are considered as sheep[i] to be
slaughtered.[j]
23Awake,[k] O Lord! Why do you sleep?[l]
Rouse yourself![m] Do not reject us
forever.[n]
24Why do you hide your face[o]
and forget[p] our misery and
oppression?[q]
25We are brought down to the dust;[r]
our bodies cling to the ground.
26Rise up[s] and help us;
redeem[t] us because of your
unfailing love.[u]

Psalm 45

For the director of music. To ˻the tune of˼ "Lilies." Of the Sons of Korah. A *maskil.*[c] A wedding song.[v]

MY heart is stirred by a noble theme
as I recite my verses for the king;
my tongue is the pen of a skillful
writer.
2You are the most excellent of men
and your lips have been anointed
with grace,[w]
since God has blessed you forever.[x]
3Gird your sword[y] upon your side,
O mighty one;[z]
clothe yourself with splendor and
majesty.[a]
4In your majesty ride forth victoriously[b]
in behalf of truth, humility and
righteousness;[c]
let your right hand[d] display
awesome deeds.[e]
5Let your sharp arrows[f] pierce the
hearts[g] of the king's
enemies;[h]
let the nations fall beneath your feet.
6Your throne, O God, will last for ever
and ever;[i]
a scepter of justice will be the
scepter of your kingdom.

44:22 [i]S ver 11 [j]Isa 53:7; Jer 11:19; 12:3; Ro 8:36* **44:23** [k]S Ps 7:6 [l]Ps 78:65 [m]Ps 59:5 [n]Ps 74:1; 77:7 **44:24** [o]S Dt 32:20; Ps 13:1 [p]La 5:20 [q]S Dt 26:7 **44:25** [r]Ps 119:25 **44:26** [s]S Nu 10:35; S Ps 12:5; 102:13 [t]Ps 26:11 [u]Ps 6:4 **45:1** [v]45 Title SS 1:1 **45:2** [w]Lk 4:22 [x]Ps 21:6 **45:3** [y]S Dt 32:41; Ps 149:6; Rev 1:16 [z]S 2Sa 1:19 [a]S Job 40:10; S Ps 21:5 **45:4** [b]Rev 6:2 [c]Zep 2:3 [d]Ps 21:8 [e]S Dt 4:34; Ps 65:5; 66:3 **45:5** [f]S Dt 32:23 [g]S Nu 24:8 [h]Ps 9:13; 92:9 **45:6** [i]S Ge 21:33; La 5:19 **45:7** [j]Ps 33:5 [k]S Ps 11:5 [l]Ps 2:2; Isa 45:1; 61:1; Zec 4:14 [m]S Ps 23:5; Heb 1:8-9* **45:8** [n]Pr 27:9; SS 1:3; 4:10 [o]S Ge 37:25 [p]S Nu 24:6; Jn 19:39 [q]S Ex 30:24 [r]S 1Ki 22:39 [s]Ps 144:9; 150:4; Isa 38:20 **45:9** [t]SS 6:8 [u]1Ki 2:19 [v]Isa 62:5 [w]S Ge 10:29 **45:10** [x]Ru 1:11 [y]Jer 5:1 [z]Ru 1:16 **45:11** [a]S Est 1:11; S La 2:15 [b]Eph 5:33 [c]1Pe 3:6 **45:12** [d]S Jos 19:29 [e]S 1Ki 9:16; S 2Ch 9:24 **45:13** [f]Isa 61:10 [g]Ex 39:3 **45:14** [h]S Jdg 5:30 [i]Est 2:15 [j]SS 1:3 **45:15** [k]S Est 8:17 **45:16** [l]1Sa 2:8; Ps 68:27; 113:8

7You love righteousness[j] and hate
wickedness;[k]
therefore God, your God, has set you
above your companions
by anointing[l] you with the oil of
joy.[m]
8All your robes are fragrant[n] with
myrrh[o] and aloes[p] and
cassia;[q]
from palaces adorned with ivory[r]
the music of the strings[s] makes you
glad.
9Daughters of kings[t] are among your
honored women;
at your right hand[u] is the royal
bride[v] in gold of Ophir.[w]

10Listen, O daughter,[x] consider[y] and
give ear:
Forget your people[z] and your
father's house.
11The king is enthralled by your
beauty;[a]
honor[b] him, for he is your lord.[c]
12The Daughter of Tyre[d] will come with
a gift,[d][e]
men of wealth will seek your favor.

13All glorious[f] is the princess within
˻her chamber˼;
her gown is interwoven with gold.[g]
14In embroidered garments[h] she is led
to the king;[i]
her virgin companions[j] follow her
and are brought to you.
15They are led in with joy and
gladness;[k]
they enter the palace of the king.

16Your sons will take the place of your
fathers;
you will make them princes[l]
throughout the land.

[c]Title: Probably a literary or musical term [d]*12* Or *A Tyrian robe is among the gifts*

people of God.

44:23 GOD, Wrath—The Bible uses picturesque human language to express the feelings of God's people. The gods of other nations were actually thought to sleep like humans and thus to have times of unconcern for their worshipers. Israel knew the true God did not sleep (121:4). Troubled times awakened the feeling of isolation and helplessness leading to the poetic use of language to describe God's inactivity. God's wrath can be expressed by His doing nothing. In prayer the worshiper seeks to rouse Him to action (7:6; 78:65).

45:1–17 PRAYER, Intercession—Israel's psalms could be directed to as well as written by kings. Temple priests apparently composed this psalm to celebrate a king's wedding. As such, it represents involvement of institutional religion in the political arena. God's people can involve themselves in political celebration. The danger lies in making the religious institution dependent on the political establishment or identifying the political leader too closely with God. At his best, Israel's king was God's anointed representative on earth. Eventually Israel learned that no political ruler deserved such high praise. This psalm thus came to be interpreted in light of hopes for God's Messiah. Political hopes can be realized fully as Messiah establishes God's kingdom on earth. Prayer for political leaders should be spoken in this light, asking that political celebrations may be foretastes of and commitment to the celebration of God's coming kingdom.

45:2,6–7 JESUS CHRIST, Foretold—This psalm is a royal psalm used originally as praise for the reigning king of Israel. Heb 1:8–9 quotes these verses as a way of building up a case for the superiority of Jesus Christ, the King of kings. God exalted Jesus and granted Him the throne of David as its perpetual heir.

45:3–5 CHRISTIAN ETHICS, War and Peace—Israel praised the king on his wedding day. Within the formation of the inspired canon of Scripture, the song was applied to the Messiah. Thus it gives us both a description of the king's place in battle and of the Messiah's mission. King and Messiah fight to defend basic godly virtues—truth, humility, and righteousness—and to establish God's eternal kingdom. A quality of God's anointed warrior is opposition to wickedness combined with love for righteousness and justice.

17 I will perpetuate your memory through
all generations;[m]
therefore the nations will praise
you[n] for ever and ever.[o]

Psalm 46

For the director of music. Of the Sons of Korah. According to *alamoth*.[e] A song.

GOD is our refuge[p] and strength,[q]
an ever-present[r] help[s] in
trouble.[t]
2 Therefore we will not fear,[u] though
the earth give way[v]
and the mountains fall[w] into the
heart of the sea,[x]
3 though its waters roar[y] and foam[z]
and the mountains quake[a] with
their surging. *Selah*
4 There is a river[b] whose streams[c]
make glad the city of God,[d]
the holy place where the Most
High[e] dwells.[f]
5 God is within her,[g] she will not fall;[h]
God will help[i] her at break of day.
6 Nations[j] are in uproar,[k] kingdoms[l]
fall;
he lifts his voice,[m] the earth melts.[n]
7 The LORD Almighty[o] is with us;[p]
the God of Jacob[q] is our fortress.[r]
Selah
8 Come and see the works of the LORD,[s]
the desolations[t] he has brought on
the earth.
9 He makes wars[u] cease to the ends of
the earth;
he breaks the bow[v] and shatters the
spear,
he burns the shields[f] with fire.[w]
10 "Be still, and know that I am God;[x]
I will be exalted[y] among the
nations,
I will be exalted in the earth."
11 The LORD Almighty is with us;
the God of Jacob[z] is our fortress.[a]
Selah

Psalm 47

For the director of music. Of the Sons of Korah. A psalm.

CLAP your hands,[b] all you nations;
shout to God with cries of joy.[c]
2 How awesome[d] is the LORD Most
High,[e]
the great King[f] over all the earth!
3 He subdued[g] nations under us,
peoples under our feet.
4 He chose our inheritance[h] for us,
the pride of Jacob,[i] whom he loved.
Selah
5 God has ascended[j] amid shouts of
joy,[k]
the LORD amid the sounding of
trumpets.[l]

45:17 [m]S Ex 3:15; Ps 33:11; 119:90; 135:13 [n]Ps 138:4 [o]S Ps 21:4; Rev 22:5 **46:1** [p]Ps 9:9; 37:39; 61:3; 73:26; 91:2,9; 142:5; Isa 33:16; Jer 16:19; 17:17; Joel 3:16; Na 1:7 [q]Ps 18:1 [r]Ps 34:18; La 3:57 [s]Ps 18:6; Lk 1:54 [t]S Dt 4:30; Ps 25:17 **46:2** [u]S Ge 4:7; Ps 3:6 [v]Ps 82:5; Isa 13:13; 24:1,19, 20; Jer 4:23; Da 11:19; Am 8:14; S Rev 6:14 [w]ver 6; Ps 18:7; 97:5; Isa 54:10; Am 9:5; Mic 1:4; Na 1:5; Hab 3:6 [x]Ex 15:8 **46:3** [y]Ps 93:3; Isa 17:13; Jer 5:22; Eze 1:24; Rev 19:6 [z]S Job 9:26 [a]S Jdg 5:5 **46:4** [b]S Ge 2:10; Rev 22:1 [c]S Ps 1:3 [d]Ps 48:1,8; 87:3; 101:8; Rev 3:12 [e]Ge 14:18 [f]S 2Sa 15:25 **46:5** [g]Dt 23:14; S Ps 26:8; Isa 12:6; Zec 2:5 [h]Ps 125:1 [i]S 1Ch 5:20 **46:6** [j]S Job 12:23 [k]Ps 74:23; Isa 5:30; 17:12 [l]Ps 68:32; 102:22; Isa 13:4, 13; 23:11; Eze 26:18; Mt 4:8 [m]S Ps 29:3; Isa 33:3 [n]S ver 2 **46:7** [o]S 1Sa 1:11 [p]S Ge 21:22 [q]S Ps 20:1 [r]ver 11; Ps 18:2 **46:8** [s]Ps 66:5 [t]Isa 17:9; 64:10; Da 9:26; Lk 21:20 **46:9** [u]Isa 2:4 [v]S Ps 37:15; S Isa 22:6 [w]Isa 9:5; Eze 39:9; Hos 2:18 **46:10** [x]Dt 4:35; 1Ki 18:36,39; Ps 100:3; Isa 37:16,20; 43:11; 45:21; Eze 36:23 [y]Ps 18:46; Isa 2:11 **46:11** [z]S Ps 20:1 [a]S ver 7 **47:1** [b]S 2Ki 11:12 [c]S Ps 33:3 **47:2** [d]S Dt 7:21 [e]Ge 14:18 [f]Ps 2:6; 48:2; 95:3; Mt 5:35 **47:3** [g]Ps 18:39,47; Isa 14:6 **47:4** [h]Ps 2:8; 16:6; 78:55; 1Pe 1:4 [i]Am 6:8; 8:7 **47:5** [j]Ps 68:18; Eph 4:8 [k]S Job 8:21; S Ps 106:5 [l]S Nu 10:2; S 2Sa 6:15

[e]Title: Probably a musical term [f]9 Or *chariots*

46:1 GOD, Power—This verse is a striking statement of God's power and sovereignty, two intimately related ideas. Such lofty ideas have great practical application. God has power and authority to help us out of any trouble anytime, anywhere. See note on 28:1–8.

46:1 SALVATION, As Refuge—Compare 37:40. The Hebrew parallelism helps us to see what is meant by salvation as our refuge. God helps us when we are in trouble. A mighty fortress is our God. See note on 34:8.

46:1–11 PRAYER, Faith—Nature and nations threaten our security. Prayer expresses confidence in God's strength and protection for His people against all terrors. The cataclysmic events of nature and history cannot threaten God's people, for He is with us. He is invincible. Compare 4; 11; 16; 23; 27; 62; 125; 131.

46:4 GOD, Holy—See notes on 28:2; 43:3; Ex 3:5–6; 19:10–24; Lev 11:44–45; 2 Co 7:1.

46:4–11 REVELATION, Divine Presence—The Temple symbolized God's presence so strongly Israel gained confidence against all threats. In worship the acts of God in creating the world and the people Israel were portrayed and could be seen. Review of what God had done gives confidence in what He will do. Past acts of war do not form the pattern for God's subsequent acts. God's presence is to bring peace not war. In silent meditation people can experience God's presence and gain faith in His protecting power.

46:6,10* GOD, *Sovereignty—God is supreme, in control of His world, and will be victorious. One divine word destroys all our enemies. See notes on Ge 15:13–16; 18:14; 24:3,7,50; Dt 1:10.

46:8–10 HISTORY, Politics—God works in human events to destroy war, establish peace, and call all nations to worship Him.

46:8–10 CHRISTIAN ETHICS, War and Peace—The terror of war can be brought under God's control. The vision of God's people centers not so much on victory in battle as on peace with the eternal cessation of war. Such is possible when all nations are introduced to and recognize God as Lord of all the earth. See note on 34:14.

46:10 EVANGELISM, God's Provision—God is exalted. When people see the Lord for who He is, He will be exalted; and they will fall at His feet, accepting His wonderful salvation. Evangelism is telling people who God is and what He has provided for them in Jesus Christ.

47:1–9 PRAYER, Sovereignty of God—The psalmists delighted in describing God's sovereignty in its various expressions. His sovereignty is expressed: over Jerusalem (46; 48; 87; 122; 125; 147), over Israel (80; 81; 105; 136), over ages and generations (145), over nature (104), and over the cosmos (8; 19; 103). The favorite expression of sovereignty, however, is seen in His direction and control of the affairs and kingdoms of earth (2; 9; 24; 33; 47; 72; 95—100; 117). God is "King over all the earth," reigning on His throne over the nations. God's sovereignty is the basis for His people's joyful praise.

47:1 EVANGELISM, Mass—See note on 26:7.

47:2–9 GOD, Sovereignty—The whole psalm praises God's sovereignty. Israel learned this through their historical, personal experiences with God. That is the only way we can fully learn of God's sovereignty. He must control our lives. See notes on Ge 15:13–16; 18:14; 24:3,7,50; Dt 1:10.

6Sing praises[m] to God, sing praises;
sing praises to our King, sing praises.

7For God is the King of all the earth;[n]
sing to him a psalm[g][o] of praise.
8God reigns[p] over the nations;
God is seated on his holy throne.[q]
9The nobles of the nations assemble
as the people of the God of Abraham,
for the kings[h] of the earth belong to God;[r]
he is greatly exalted.[s]

Psalm 48

A song. A psalm of the Sons of Korah.

GREAT is the LORD,[t] and most worthy of praise,[u]
in the city of our God,[v] his holy mountain.[w]
2It is beautiful[x] in its loftiness,
the joy of the whole earth.
Like the utmost heights of Zaphon[i][y]
is Mount Zion,[z]
the[j] city of the Great King.[a]
3God is in her citadels;[b]
he has shown himself to be her fortress.[c]

4When the kings joined forces,
when they advanced together,[d]
5they saw ⌊her⌋ and were astounded;
they fled in terror.[e]
6Trembling seized[f] them there,
pain like that of a woman in labor.[g]
7You destroyed them like ships of Tarshish[h]
shattered by an east wind.[i]

8As we have heard,
so have we seen
in the city of the LORD Almighty,
in the city of our God:
God makes her secure forever.[j]
Selah

9Within your temple, O God,
we meditate[k] on your unfailing love.[l]
10Like your name,[m] O God,
your praise reaches to the ends of the earth;[n]
your right hand is filled with righteousness.
11Mount Zion rejoices,
the villages of Judah are glad
because of your judgments.[o]

12Walk about Zion, go around her,
count her towers,[p]
13consider well her ramparts,[q]
view her citadels,[r]
that you may tell of them to the next generation.[s]
14For this God is our God for ever and ever;
he will be our guide[t] even to the end.

Psalm 49

For the director of music. Of the Sons of Korah. A psalm.

HEAR[u] this, all you peoples;[v]
listen, all who live in this world,[w]
2both low and high,[x]
rich and poor alike:
3My mouth will speak words of wisdom;[y]
the utterance from my heart will give understanding.[z]
4I will turn my ear to a proverb;[a]
with the harp[b] I will expound my riddle:[c]

5Why should I fear[d] when evil days come,
when wicked deceivers surround me—
6those who trust in their wealth[e]
and boast[f] of their great riches?[g]
7No man can redeem the life of another
or give to God a ransom for him—
8the ransom[h] for a life is costly,
no payment is ever enough—[i]
9that he should live on[j] forever

47:6 [m]S 2Sa 22:50 **47:7** [n]Zec 14:9 [o]1Ch 16:7; Col 3:16 **47:8** [p]S 1Ch 16:31 [q]S 1Ki 22:19; S Ps 9:4; Rev 4:9 **47:9** [r]S Job 25:2 [s]Ps 46:10; 97:9 **48:1** [t]Ps 86:10; 96:4; 99:2; 135:5; 147:5; Jer 10:6 [u]S 2Sa 22:4; S 1Ch 16:25; Ps 18:3 [v]S Ps 46:4 [w]S Dt 33:19; Ps 2:6; 87:1; Isa 11:9; 32:16; Jer 31:23; Da 9:16; Mic 4:1; Zec 8:3 **48:2** [x]Ps 50:2; La 2:15; Eze 16:14 [y]S Jos 13:27 [z]S Ps 2:6 [a]Mt 5:35 **48:3** [b]ver 13; Ps 122:7 [c]Ps 18:2 **48:4** [d]2Sa 10:1-19 **48:5** [e]Ex 15:16; Isa 13:8; Jer 46:5; Da 5:9 **48:6** [f]S Job 4:14 [g]S Ge 3:16 **48:7** [h]S Ge 10:4; S 1Ki 10:22; 22:48 [i]S Ge 41:6 **48:8** [j]Jer 23:6; Zec 8:13; 14:11 **48:9** [k]S Ps 39:3 [l]Ps 6:4 **48:10** [m]S Ex 6:3; S Jos 7:9 [n]1Sa 2:10; Ps 22:27; 65:5; 98:3; 100:1; Isa 11:12; 24:16; 42:10; 49:6 **48:11** [o]Ps 97:8 **48:12** [p]S Ne 3:1 **48:13** [q]2Sa 20:15; Isa 26:1; La 2:8; Hab 2:1 [r]S ver 3 [s]Ps 71:18; 78:6; 109:13 **48:14** [t]Ps 25:5; 73:24; Pr 6:22; Isa 49:10; 57:18; 58:11 **49:1** [u]Isa 1:2 [v]Ps 78:1 [w]S Ps 33:8 **49:2** [x]Ps 62:9 **49:3** [y]S Ps 37:30 [z]Ps 119:130 **49:4** [a]Ps 78:2; Pr 1:6; Eze 12:22; 16:44; 18:2-3; Lk 4:23 [b]S 1Sa 16:16; Ps 33:2 [c]S Nu 12:8 **49:5** [d]Ps 23:4; 27:1 **49:6** [e]S Job 22:25; Ps 73:12; Jer 48:7 [f]S Ps 10:3 [g]S Job 36:19 **49:8** [h]S Nu 35:31 [i]Mt 16:26 **49:9** [j]Ps 22:29; 89:48

[g]7 Or *a maskil* (probably a literary or musical term)
[h]9 Or *shields*
[i]2 *Zaphon* can refer to a sacred mountain or the direction north.
[j]2 Or *earth, / Mount Zion, on the northern side / of the*

48:1–14 PRAYER, God's Presence—Delight in the Lord finds expression in what He is and what He does, in His choices, and in His dwelling place, Jerusalem. The city and its Temple symbolized God's presence with His people. Its glory derived from God's presence in it. Everything about it reminded the psalmist of God Himself. Praising the city in prayer was praising God. The presence of God among His people is a primary reason for prayer. Compare Pss 76; 84; 87; 122.

48:9 EVANGELISM, Worship—In the midst of the worship experience, it is fitting to praise God for who He is, His steadfast love, and His grace which brought salvation. Out of His great love and mercy, redemption springs. Worship and praise should always move us to share that glorious reality with others. True worship and praise result in the evangelization of others.

48:10 GOD, Righteous—The righteousness of God means both that He opposes evil and works to promote that which is right, especially for the fallen and helpless. See notes on Lev 1:1; Jos 23:1–16; 2 Sa 10:12; Ps 33:5; 35:24; Jn 17:25.

48:14 HUMANITY, Relationship to God—The Hebrew is literally "to death." The relationship to God is seen as being one which goes on and on, yet is somehow limited by death. The relationship generates hope, but the harsh reality of death also seems to put a limit to that hope within much of the Old Testament. Christ has conquered even death for us (1 Co 15:20–28,51–57).

49:7–10 HUMANITY, Worth—Human wealth cannot buy human life. Death shows us how valuable life is. God paid the price of His only Son to redeem us from death. See Mt 16:26; Jn 3:16.

and not see decay.[k]

10For all can see that wise men die;[l]
the foolish and the senseless[m] alike perish
and leave their wealth[n] to others.[o]
11Their tombs[p] will remain their houses[k] forever,
their dwellings for endless generations,[q]
though they had[l] named[r] lands after themselves.

12But man, despite his riches, does not endure;[s]
he is[m] like the beasts that perish.[t]

13This is the fate of those who trust in themselves,[u]
and of their followers, who approve their sayings. *Selah*
14Like sheep they are destined[v] for the grave,[n] [w]
and death will feed on them.
The upright will rule[x] over them in the morning;
their forms will decay in the grave,[n]
far from their princely mansions.
15But God will redeem my life[o] from the grave;[y]
he will surely take me to himself.[z] *Selah*

16Do not be overawed when a man grows rich,
when the splendor of his house increases;
17for he will take nothing[a] with him when he dies,
his splendor will not descend with him.[b]
18Though while he lived he counted himself blessed—[c]
and men praise you when you prosper—
19he will join the generation of his fathers,[d]
who will never see the light[e] ⌊of life⌋.

20A man who has riches without understanding[f]
is like the beasts that perish.[g]

Psalm 50

A psalm of Asaph.

THE Mighty One, God, the LORD,[h]
speaks and summons the earth
from the rising of the sun to the place where it sets.[i]
2From Zion,[j] perfect in beauty,[k]
God shines forth.[l]
3Our God comes[m] and will not be silent;[n]

49:9 [k]Ps 16:10
49:10 [l]Ecc 2:16 [m]Ps 92:6; 94:8 [n]S Job 27:17 [o]Ecc 2:18,21; Lk 12:20
49:11 [p]Mk 5:3; Lk 8:27 [q]Ps 106:31 [r]S Dt 3:14
49:12 [s]S Job 14:2 [t]ver 20; 2Pe 2:12
49:13 [u]Lk 12:20
49:14 [v]Jer 43:11; Eze 31:14 [w]Nu 16:30; S Job 21:13; Ps 9:17; 55:15 [x]Isa 14:2; Da 7:18; 1Co 6:2
49:15 [y]Ps 56:13; Hos 13:14 [z]S Ge 5:24
49:17 [a]1Ti 6:7 [b]S Ps 17:14
49:18 [c]Ps 10:6; Lk 12:19
49:19 [d]S Ge 15:15 [e]S Job 33:30
49:20 [f]Pr 16:16 [g]S ver 12
50:1 [h]Jos 22:22 [i]Ps 113:3
50:2 [j]Ps 2:6 [k]S Ps 48:2; S La 2:15 [l]S Dt 33:2
50:3 [m]Ps 96:13 [n]ver 21; Isa 42:14; 64:12; 65:6

[k]*11* Septuagint and Syriac; Hebrew *In their thoughts their houses will remain* [l]*11* Or */ for they have* [m]*12* Hebrew; Septuagint and Syriac read verse 12 the same as verse 20. [n]*14* Hebrew *Sheol*; also in verse 15 [o]*15* Or *soul*

49:9–15 LAST THINGS, Believers' Resurrection—The thoughts of death with nothing beyond are depressing thoughts. It is especially so for the wicked. Living without regard for God gives one no basis for hope from Him at death, but for the righteous there wells up hope beyond the grave. A right relationship with God leads naturally to the hope of eternal fellowship with Him. It is a reasonable step from knowing God in life to trusting Him in death. Faith says God will receive His own to Himself after death. See note on Isa 14:9.

49:10–17 HUMANITY, Nature of Death—Nothing which is possessed in this life can be carried beyond the grave. Ancient societies tried to let a person carry wealth to the next world by burying personal belongings in the grave. The goods perished with the corpse. Humans share this in common with the animal world. The human animal dies and perishes. This does not mean we are animals to be analyzed and explained by scientific observation. Our ability to relate to God and find hope in Him distinguishes us from animals. Hope in God will be rewarded. Accumulation of possessions leads only to a beastly hope.

49:10–19 CHRISTIAN ETHICS, Property Rights—See note on 39:6.

49:15 GOD, Savior—This verse expresses hope God will provide salvation beyond the grave, one of the few Old Testament references to life after death. This verse anticipates the clear New Testament teaching of life after death and eternal life and salvation from God. The Bible pictures God as the only Savior able to provide hope beyond the grave in fellowship with Him.

49:15 JESUS CHRIST, Foretold—The earliest Christians saw this as a reference to Christ's resurrection. What the psalmist saw as God's providential care in present danger Jesus knew was God's ultimate caring and power to bring life from death.

49:18–19 HUMANITY, Nature of Death—In the natural progression of life, each generation dies, bringing its life to an ultimate end. The praise of men gained by our wealth and position dies with us.

50:1 GOD, Power—God the all-powerful Ruler is not content to remain alone in His heavens. He comes to speak to His worshiping people. He seeks to correct their ways and renew their appreciation and praise for who He is and what He does. See note on 46:1.

50:1–23 EVIL AND SUFFERING, Deserved—The wicked will be punished by God. The emphasis in the Psalms is generally on divine judgment occurring in human history. Some psalms reflect the human desire for judgment to occur sooner. See note on 37:1–40. Later revelation stressed God's judgment at the end of time. See note on Da 12:2. The New Testament develops this emphasis. Religious ceremonies and promises do not protect a person from judgment. Obedience to and trust in God show proper relationship to Him.

50:1–23 REVELATION, Actions—God takes what He says and does seriously. Anyone who fails to do the same stands in vivid contrast to God's declared purposes and thus faces God's judgment. Judgment is God's revelation to those who refuse to commit themselves to Him. The psalm was apparently used in a covenant ceremony announcing God's judgment and calling people to covenant commitment.

50:1–23 PRAYER, Corporate—See note on 40:1–17. Israel had not failed to bring their offerings, but in bringing them they had failed to be genuinely grateful (v 14). This was reflected in their character (vv 16–20). Public prayer and worship should represent sincere praise and gratitude to God by a people who have been living obediently for God. Otherwise, a service of prayer to God may be turned to hear the word of judgment from God's spokesperson. See note on 6:1–10.

a fire devours[o] before him,[p]
and around him a tempest[q] rages.
4He summons the heavens above,
and the earth,[r] that he may judge
his people:[s]
5"Gather to me my consecrated ones,[t]
who made a covenant[u] with me by
sacrifice."
6And the heavens proclaim[v] his
righteousness,
for God himself is judge.[w] *Selah*
7"Hear, O my people, and I will speak,
O Israel, and I will testify[x] against
you:
I am God, your God.[y]
8I do not rebuke[z] you for your
sacrifices
or your burnt offerings,[a] which are
ever before me.
9I have no need of a bull[b] from your
stall
or of goats[c] from your pens,[d]
10for every animal of the forest[e] is mine,
and the cattle on a thousand hills.[f]
11I know every bird[g] in the mountains,
and the creatures of the field[h] are
mine.
12If I were hungry I would not tell you,
for the world[i] is mine, and all that
is in it.[j]
13Do I eat the flesh of bulls
or drink the blood of goats?
14Sacrifice thank offerings[k] to God,
fulfill your vows[l] to the Most
High,[m]
15and call[n] upon me in the day of
trouble;[o]
I will deliver[p] you, and you will
honor[q] me."

16But to the wicked, God says:
"What right have you to recite my
laws
or take my covenant[r] on your lips?[s]
17You hate[t] my instruction
and cast my words behind[u] you.
18When you see a thief, you join[v] with
him;
you throw in your lot with
adulterers.[w]
19You use your mouth for evil
and harness your tongue to deceit.[x]
20You speak continually against your
brother[y]
and slander your own mother's
son.
21These things you have done and I kept
silent;[z]
you thought I was altogether[p] like
you.
But I will rebuke[a] you
and accuse[b] you to your face.

22"Consider this, you who forget God,[c]
or I will tear you to pieces, with
none to rescue:[d]
23He who sacrifices thank offerings
honors me,
and he prepares the way[e]
so that I may show him[q] the
salvation of God.[f]"

Psalm 51

For the director of music. A psalm of David.
When the prophet Nathan came to him
after David had committed adultery with
Bathsheba.[g]

HAVE mercy[h] on me, O God,
according to your unfailing love;[i]

50:3 [o]S Lev 10:2 [p]S Ps 18:8 [q]Job 37:9; Ps 83:15; 107:25; 147:18; Isa 29:6; 30:28; Jnh 1:4; Na 1:3 **50:4** [r]Dt 4:26; 31:28; Isa 1:2 [s]Heb 10:30 **50:5** [t]S Dt 7:6; S Ps 18:25 [u]Ex 24:7; S 2Ch 6:11 **50:6** [v]S Ps 19:1 [w]S Ge 16:5; S Job 9:15 **50:7** [x]Heb 2:4 [y]Ex 20:2; Ps 48:14 **50:8** [z]S 2Sa 22:16 [a]S Ps 40:6 **50:9** [b]S Lev 1:5 [c]S Lev 16:5 [d]S Nu 32:16 **50:10** [e]Ps 104:20; Isa 56:9; Mic 5:8 [f]Ps 104:24 **50:11** [g]Mt 6:26 [h]Ps 8:7; 80:13 **50:12** [i]Ex 19:5 [j]Dt 10:14; S Jos 3:11; Ps 24:1; 1Co 10:26 **50:14** [k]S Ezr 1:4; S Ps 27:6 [l]S Nu 30:2; S Ps 66:13; 76:11 [m]Ps 7:8 **50:15** [n]Ps 4:1; 81:7; Isa 55:6; 58:9; Zec 13:9 [o]Ps 69:17; 86:7; 107:6; 142:2; Jas 5:13 [p]Ps 3:7 [q]S Ps 22:23 **50:16** [r]Ps 25:10 [s]Isa 29:13 **50:17** [t]Pr 1:22 [u]S 1Ki 14:9 **50:18** [v]Ro 1:32; 1Ti 5:22 [w]S Job 22:15 **50:19** [x]Ps 10:7; 36:3; 52:2; 101:7 **50:20** [y]Mt 10:21 **50:21** [z]Isa 42:14; 57:11; 62:1; 64:12 [a]Ps 6:1; S 18:15; 76:6; 104:7; Isa 50:2 [b]Ps 85:5; Isa 57:16 **50:22** [c]S Job 8:13; S Isa 17:10 [d]S Dt 32:39; Mic 5:8 **50:23** [e]Ps 85:13 [f]S Ps 9:14; 91:16; 98:3; Isa 52:10 **51:1** [g]**51 Title** 2Sa 11:4; 12:1 [h]S 2Sa 24:14; S Ps 9:13 [i]S Ps 25:7; S 119:88

[p]21 Or *thought the 'I AM' was* [q]23 Or *and to him who considers his way / I will show*

50:4,6,16–23 GOD, Judge—God is the supreme Judge of the world He has created. He has and takes the right to hold every person accountable unto Himself. His ultimate goal is not to judge but to give salvation (v 23). See notes on Ge 3:8–24; Ro 2:2.

50:5,16 THE CHURCH, Covenant People—Covenant people face God's judgment when we do not keep covenant commitments. God expects us to do more than go through worship ceremonies. He expects our total dedication to Him and His way of life. See note on 25:14.

50:7–15 HUMANITY, Spiritual Nature—People are so made that they need to worship. God does not need people in order to survive. It is people who need God for survival.

50:7–15 STEWARDSHIP, Giving in Worship—God owns all things, and His well-being does not depend on our gifts. Material things do provide us a means of serving God. The psalmist showed the distinction between Yahweh, the God of Israel, and other gods, as well as that between God and humans. People might think gods, like people, need food for daily sustenance. The true God can live without our offerings. Our gifts do not fill His needs. They provide us a means to show reverence, gratitude, and praise to God. They also let us have a way to make and fulfill vows or promises to God. See note on Mt 5:23–24.

50:15 SALVATION, As Deliverance—God wants those whom He delivers to honor Him.

50:16–21 CHRISTIAN ETHICS, Language—What and how we say things is an indicator of our true spirit. God's judgment is lodged against speech which does not exemplify love of neighbor. God's judgment rests on those who publicly profess religious faith in rituals and ceremonies but then do not do what they have committed themselves to. Our religious talk is only as good as our ethical actions.

50:22–23 HUMANITY, Spiritual Nature—Human worship opens the way for God to bring His blessings into human life to meet our needs. See note on vv 7–15. Forgetting God destroys human life.

51:1 GOD, Love—Salvation and all of the gracious blessings God gives to us are the result of His love. We can ask Him to forgive us and renew our relationship with Him only because we know He loves us. See note on 44:3,26.

51:1–19 EVIL AND SUFFERING, Repentance—This is the most famous of the penitential psalms (6,32,38, 51,102, 130,143). When suffering is the consequence of sin, the sufferer should repent. Reconciliation with God opens the way for God's saving actions. God remains free to determine when and how to act. Repentance is no guarantee of God's immediate healing, but without repentance, the way to God is blocked.

according to your great compassion[j]
blot out[k] my transgressions.[l]
2Wash away[m] all my iniquity
and cleanse[n] me from my sin.

3For I know my transgressions,
and my sin is always before me.[o]
4Against you, you only, have I sinned[p]
and done what is evil in your sight,[q]
so that you are proved right when you speak
and justified when you judge.[r]
5Surely I was sinful[s] at birth,[t]
sinful from the time my mother conceived me.
6Surely you desire truth in the inner parts[r];
you teach[s] me wisdom[u] in the inmost place.[v]

7Cleanse[w] me with hyssop,[x] and I will be clean;
wash me, and I will be whiter than snow.[y]
8Let me hear joy and gladness;[z]
let the bones[a] you have crushed rejoice.
9Hide your face from my sins[b]
and blot out[c] all my iniquity.

10Create in me a pure heart,[d] O God,
and renew a steadfast spirit within me.[e]
11Do not cast me[f] from your presence[g]
or take your Holy Spirit[h] from me.
12Restore to me the joy of your salvation[i]
and grant me a willing spirit,[j] to sustain me.[k]

51:1 [j]S Ne 9:27; Ps 86:15; Isa 63:7 [k]S 2Sa 12:13; S 2Ch 6:21; S Ne 4:5; Ac 3:19 [l]S Ps 39:8 **51:2** [m]S Ru 3:3; Jer 2:22; 13:27; Ac 22:16; 1Jn 1:9 [n]Pr 20:30; Isa 4:4; Eze 36:25; Zec 13:1; Mt 23:25-26; Heb 9:14 **51:3** [o]Isa 59:12 **51:4** [p]S 1Sa 15:24 [q]S Ge 20:6; Lk 15:21 [r]Ro 3:4* **51:5** [s]S Lev 5:2 [t]S Job 5:7 **51:6** [u]Ps 119:66; 143:10 [v]S Job 9:4; S 34:32 **51:7** [w]Isa 4:4; Eze 36:25; Zec 13:1 [x]S Ex 12:22; S Nu 19:6; Heb 9:19 [y]Isa 1:18; 43:25; 44:22 **51:8** [z]Isa 35:10; Jer 33:11; Joel 1:16 [a]S Ex 12:46 **51:9** [b]Jer 16:17; Zec 4:10 [c]S 2Sa 12:13 **51:10** [d]S Ps 24:4; 78:37; Mt 5:8; Ac 15:9 [e]Eze 18:31; 36:26 **51:11** [f]Ps 27:9; 71:9; 138:8 [g]S Ge 4:14; S Ex 33:15 [h]Ps 106:33; Isa 63:10; Eph 4:30 **51:12** [i]S Job 33:26 [j]Ps 110:3 [k]S Ps 18:35

[r]6 The meaning of the Hebrew for this phrase is uncertain. [s]6 Or *you desired . . . ; / you taught*

51:1–19 SIN, Guilt—Sin need not control a person's life. God's mercy is available. We can experience that mercy only when sin produces such a sense of guilt that we turn humbly with broken hearts asking for forgiveness. See note on 2 Ch 28:9–13. The proper function of guilt is to lead us to take full responsibility for our sin, to recognize that sin ultimately relates to God and alienates us from Him, and to confess God's justice rather than trying to justify ourselves. Guilt achieves its goal when we desire a clean heart from God rather than the evil dreams sin produces. See note on 36:1–4.

51:1–9 SALVATION, Forgiveness—Sin is terrible, but God's grace is greater than our guilt. In David's poignant plea for God's pardon, he asked God to blot out his revolt or rebellion against Him. He could ask for forgiveness because he trusted God's mercy.

51:1–9 SALVATION, Repentance—This is one of the best examples of individual repentance in the Old Testament. Such personal penitence is unparalleled even in the New Testament. Its nearest New Testament parallel is the tax collector in Lk 18:13. The words fit King David following his sin of adultery with Bathsheba and the murder of her husband Uriah (2 Sa 11:1–27). Compare Ps 32:5; 39:8; 41:4. Those who repent trust God's love, seek to get rid of sin and guilt, acknowledge that all sin is against God, do not try to justify themselves in any way, and ask for new dedication and a new start.

51:1–19 PRAYER, Confession—This is the most adequate confession of sin in the Bible. There is no attempt to justify the sin. Sin is stated for what it is, and God is perceived for what He is. David could not forget his transgression. Its magnitude consisted not in what he had done to Bathsheba and Uriah, but in what he had done against the Lord (2 Sa 11:1–27). Confession is agreement with God. Sin springs from the inherent perversity of human nature. It is not an accident. It sullies the sinner and separates from God. The stain must be cleansed and the relationship restored. Both are possible only through the unfailing love of God. God's cleansing is not a result of ritual sacrifice but of God's mercy when the yearning, broken heart returns to Him. See note on Lev 1:9. See Guide to Confession, pp. 1763–1765.

51:5 HUMANITY, Human Nature—People are born with a nature prone to sin, inherited from their parents. This line goes all the way back to Adam and Eve. No indication is here given that sex is wrong and, thus, the cause of our evil tendencies. Neither is it said that people are born already guilty. Sin is not what we inherit. We inherit the tendency to sin. Sin is the evil we do before God. The psalmist did not try to confess someone else's sin or blame someone for his own sin. Rather he confessed the enormity of sin before God. Sin has pervaded all of society and all of life. An individual is never aware of a time without sin. The remarkable thing is a person so aware of sin can go to God directly in prayer and find cleansing and forgiveness.

51:5 SIN, Universal Nature—The psalmist acknowledged that from his birth he was a sinful creature. He did not use this as an excuse. He did not claim he had no control over the fact of his sins. He simply confessed his sinfulness. In the deepest sense he recognized that his sinful nature encompassed his entire history as a person and that he shared with all people an affinity for sin. At no moment in his life had he acted righteously. He did not attempt to set forth a philosophical rationale for the origin of sin. He did not try to argue that babies are accountable for sinful actions and, thus, stand eternally condemned before God. He did recognize the seriousness of sin in his own life and tried to deal with it in face of a merciful God. We can join in his confession, his confidence in God's mercy, and his hope for forgiveness.

51:7–13 EVANGELISM, Love—Evangelists are forgiven sinners. We confess our sins before witnessing to others. Because we have been forgiven, gratitude and love fill our lives. The love of God flows through us to others. We show them they are sinners and can find the forgiveness God has given us. Evangelism is a forgiven sinner leading another sinner to God for forgiveness and salvation.

51:8,12 SALVATION, Joy—God can fill our whole personality with joy. Joy is a natural side effect of salvation.

51:10–12 HOLY SPIRIT, Indwells—The usual phrases for the Spirit in the Old Testament are: "The Spirit of God" and "The Spirit of the Lord." In two passages the Spirit is referred to as Holy Spirit. See note on Isa 63:10–14. The confession of personal sin caused the psalmist to recognize the great contrast between his guilt and God's holiness. The logical conclusion was that God in His holiness could no longer dwell in a sinful life. Without the Spirit, life would be meaningless. See Job 33:4. Proper prayer thus asks for God's forgiveness, cleansing the human heart so the Spirit with its holiness may remain.

51:10 CREATION, Redemption—Create (Hebrew *bara'*) is God's unique action. See note on Ge 1:1. David was horror-stricken because of his sin's gravity. He felt that for God to remove the curse of this terrible wrongdoing from his conscience would take a miracle comparable to bringing the world into existence from nothing. Spiritual miracles are far more amazing than those concerning the physical universe. Forgiving, renewing, and reforming the human personality is one of God's great creative acts. Human power and intelligence cannot produce morally and spiritually pure persons.

51:11 REVELATION, Author of Hope—The anxious worshiper feared the absence of God. Trouble and distress may

13Then I will teach transgressors your ways,[l]
and sinners[m] will turn back to you.[n]
14Save me[o] from bloodguilt,[p] O God,
the God who saves me,[q]
and my tongue will sing of your righteousness.[r]
15O Lord, open my lips,[s]
and my mouth will declare your praise.
16You do not delight in sacrifice,[t] or I would bring it;
you do not take pleasure in burnt offerings.
17The sacrifices[u] of God are[t] a broken spirit;
a broken and contrite heart,[v]
O God, you will not despise.

18In your good pleasure make Zion[w] prosper;
build up the walls of Jerusalem.[x]
19Then there will be righteous sacrifices,[y]
whole burnt offerings[z] to delight you;
then bulls[a] will be offered on your altar.

Psalm 52

For the director of music. A *maskil*[u] of David. When Doeg the Edomite[b] had gone to Saul and told him: "David has gone to the house of Ahimelech."

WHY do you boast of evil, you mighty man?
Why do you boast[c] all day long,[d]
you who are a disgrace in the eyes of God?
2Your tongue plots destruction;[e]
it is like a sharpened razor,[f]
you who practice deceit.[g]
3You love evil[h] rather than good,
falsehood[i] rather than speaking the truth. *Selah*
4You love every harmful word,
O you deceitful tongue![j]
5Surely God will bring you down to everlasting ruin:
He will snatch you up and tear[k] you from your tent;
he will uproot[l] you from the land of the living.[m] *Selah*
6The righteous will see and fear;
they will laugh[n] at him, saying,
7"Here now is the man
who did not make God his stronghold[o]
but trusted in his great wealth[p]
and grew strong by destroying others!"

8But I am like an olive tree[q]
flourishing in the house of God;
I trust[r] in God's unfailing love
for ever and ever.
9I will praise you forever[s] for what you have done;
in your name I will hope,[t] for your name is good.[u]
I will praise you in the presence of your saints.[v]

Psalm 53

53:1–6pp — Ps 14:1–7

For the director of music. According to *mahalath*.[v] A *maskil*[u] of David.

THE fool[w] says in his heart,
"There is no God."[x]
They are corrupt, and their ways are vile;
there is no one who does good.

2God looks down from heaven[y]
on the sons of men
to see if there are any who understand,[z]
any who seek God.[a]
3Everyone has turned away,
they have together become corrupt;
there is no one who does good,

51:13 [l]S Ex 33:13; Ac 9:21-22 [m]S Ps 1:1 [n]S Job 33:27
51:14 [o]S Ps 39:8 [p]S 2Sa 12:9 [q]Ps 25:5; 68:20; 88:1 [r]S Ps 5:8; 35:28; 71:15
51:15 [s]Ex 4:15
51:16 [t]S 1Sa 15:22
51:17 [u]Pr 15:8; Hag 2:14 [v]Mt 11:29
51:18 [w]Ps 102:16; 147:2; Isa 14:32; 51:3; Zec 1:16-17 [x]Ps 69:35; Isa 44:26
51:19 [y]Dt 33:19 [z]Ps 66:13; 96:8; Jer 17:26 [a]Ps 66:15
52:1 [b]52:1 Title 1Sa 21:7; 22:9 [c]Ps 10:3; 94:4 [d]Ps 44:8
52:2 [e]Ps 5:9 [f]S Nu 6:5 [g]S Ps 50:19
52:3 [h]Ex 10:10; 1Sa 12:25; Am 5:14-15; Jn 3:20 [i]Ps 58:3; Jer 9:5; Rev 21:8
52:4 [j]Ps 5:9; 10:7; 109:2; 120:2,3; Pr 10:31; 12:19
52:5 [k]S Dt 29:28; S Job 40:12; Isa 22:19; Eze 17:24 [l]S Dt 28:63 [m]S Job 28:13
52:6 [n]S Job 22:19
52:7 [o]S 2Sa 22:3 [p]S Ps 49:6; S Pr 11:28; Mk 10:23
52:8 [q]S Ps 1:3; S Rev 11:4 [r]Ps 6:4; 13:5
52:9 [s]S Ps 30:12 [t]S Job 7:6; Ps 25:3 [u]Ps 54:6 [v]S Dt 7:6; Ps 16:3
53:1 [w]Ps 74:22; 107:17; Pr 10:23 [x]Ps 10:4
53:2 [y]S Ps 33:13 [z]Ps 82:5; Jer 4:22; 8:8 [a]2Ch 15:2

[t]17 Or *My sacrifice, O God, is* [u]Title: Probably a literary or musical term [v]Title: Probably a musical term

lead us to perceive God's absence. This may be a revelation of God's displeasure and punishment and should lead to repentance. Israel regularly understood God as withdrawing and angry at His sinful people. Still they knew they could confess their sins and call on God for salvation.

51:14 GOD, Savior—Salvation can only come from God. When God saves us, we, in turn, praise Him and tell others what He has done for us. See note on 38:22.

51:16–17 STEWARDSHIP, Giving in Worship—Right attitude must precede proper offerings. See notes on 40:6; 50:7–15; Mt 5:23–24.

52:1–9 EVIL AND SUFFERING, Vindication—See note on 3:1–8. The destruction of the wicked is guaranteed. Wealth and earthly power are of no avail against God.

52:1–4 HUMANITY, Human Nature—In a vivid image, the human tongue is viewed as being a major source of evil in the human experience. That this is clearly a figure of speech is seen by the transition from the image of the tongue to that of a person. Words are the source of much evil and misery. Without regard for God, humans can become so wicked they boast of evil, loving it rather than good. No society or philosophy can point to the goodness or progress of human nature. We remain as people in biblical times prone to lies, deceit, and evil. Only God's grace and salvation can rescue us from becoming this type of person.

52:1–9 PRAYER, Curse—See note on 5:10. Expressing anger against enemies to God may calm the soul and bring trust. Expressing it to the enemies only deepens hatred.

52:8 GOD, Love—Wickedness and wealth may last a season. They are still too temporary to merit our trust and allegiance. Only the true God who loves us forever merits such trust. See note on 51:1.

53:1–6 EVIL AND SUFFERING, Endurance—See notes on 9:1—10:18; 14:1–7.

53:1 SIN, Depravity—See note on 14:1.

53:1–6 PRAYER, Instruction—See note on 14:1–7, which is very similar except for 14:5–6. Prayer may teach us lessons that restore our hope.

not even one.[b]

4Will the evildoers never learn—
those who devour my people as men eat bread
and who do not call on God?
5There they were, overwhelmed with dread,
where there was nothing to dread.[c]
God scattered the bones[d] of those who attacked you;[e]
you put them to shame,[f] for God despised them.[g]

6Oh, that salvation for Israel would come out of Zion!
When God restores the fortunes of his people,
let Jacob rejoice and Israel be glad!

Psalm 54

For the director of music. With stringed instruments. A *maskil*[w] of David. When the Ziphites[h] had gone to Saul and said, "Is not David hiding among us?"

SAVE me[i], O God, by your name;[j]
vindicate me by your might.[k]
2Hear my prayer, O God;[l]
listen to the words of my mouth.

3Strangers are attacking me;[m]
ruthless men[n] seek my life[o]—
men without regard for God.[p] *Selah*

4Surely God is my help;[q]
the Lord is the one who sustains me.[r]

5Let evil recoil[s] on those who slander me;
in your faithfulness[t] destroy them.

6I will sacrifice a freewill offering[u] to you;
I will praise[v] your name, O LORD,
for it is good.[w]

7For he has delivered me[x] from all my troubles,
and my eyes have looked in triumph on my foes.[y]

Psalm 55

For the director of music. With stringed instruments. A *maskil*[w] of David.

LISTEN to my prayer, O God,
do not ignore my plea;[z]
2 hear me and answer me.[a]
My thoughts trouble me and I am distraught[b]
3 at the voice of the enemy,
at the stares of the wicked;
for they bring down suffering upon me[c]
and revile[d] me in their anger.[e]

4My heart is in anguish[f] within me;
the terrors[g] of death assail me.
5Fear and trembling[h] have beset me;
horror[i] has overwhelmed me.
6I said, "Oh, that I had the wings of a dove!
I would fly away and be at rest—
7I would flee far away
and stay in the desert;[j] *Selah*
8I would hurry to my place of shelter,[k]
far from the tempest and storm.[l]"

9Confuse the wicked, O Lord, confound their speech,[m]
for I see violence and strife[n] in the city.[o]
10Day and night they prowl[p] about on its walls;
malice and abuse are within it.
11Destructive forces[q] are at work in the city;
threats and lies[r] never leave its streets.

53:3 [b]Ro 3:10-12* **53:5** [c]S Lev 26:17 [d]2Ki 23:14; Ps 141:7; Jer 8:1; Eze 6:5 [e]2Ki 17:20 [f]S Job 8:22 [g]Jer 6:30; 14:19; La 5:22 **54:1** [h]**54 Title** 1Sa 23:19; 26:1 [i]S 1Sa 24:15 [j]Ps 20:1 [k]2Ch 20:6 **54:2** [l]S Ps 4:1; 5:1; 55:1 **54:3** [m]Ps 86:14 [n]Ps 18:48; 140:1,4, 11 [o]S 1Sa 20:1 [p]Ps 36:1 **54:4** [q]S 1Ch 5:20; S Ps 20:2 [r]S Ps 18:35 **54:5** [s]S Dt 32:35; Ps 94:23; Pr 24:12 [t]Ps 89:49; Isa 42:3 **54:6** [u]S Lev 7:12, 16; S Ezr 1:4; S Ps 27:6 [v]Ps 44:8; 69:30; 138:2; 142:7; 145:1 [w]Ps 52:9 **54:7** [x]Ps 34:6 [y]Ps 59:10; 92:11; 112:8; 118:7 **55:1** [z]Ps 27:9; La 3:56 **55:2** [a]Ps 4:1 [b]1Sa 1:15-16; Ps 77:3; 86:6-7; 142:2 **55:3** [c]S 2Sa 16:6-8; Ps 17:9; 143:3 [d]S Ps 44:16 [e]Ps 71:11 **55:4** [f]S Ps 6:3 [g]S Job 18:11 **55:5** [h]S Job 4:14; S 2Co 7:15 [i]Dt 28:67; Isa 21:4; Jer 46:5; 49:5; Eze 7:18 **55:7** [j]1Sa 23:14 **55:8** [k]Ps 31:20 [l]Ps 77:18; Isa 4:6; 25:4; 28:2; 29:6; 32:2 **55:9** [m]Ge 11:9; Ac 2:4 [n]Ps 11:5; Isa 59:6; Jer 6:7; Eze 7:11; Hab 1:3 [o]Ge 4:17 **55:10** [p]1Pe 5:8 **55:11** [q]Ps 5:9 [r]Ps 10:7

[w]Title: Probably a literary or musical term

53:6 SALVATION, Definition—God's salvation is restoration and renewal. It produces joy. Zion is Mount Zion in Jerusalem where God's Temple was located. Salvation came from Zion because the God who saves His people revealed Himself to His people there and was worshiped there.
54:1,4 GOD, Judge—As a righteous Judge, God will use His power to save or defend those who call upon Him in faith when they face trouble. When God helps us, we worship and praise Him.
54:1–7 EVIL AND SUFFERING, Prayer—God's people often live under attack and must seek God's help. See note on 3:1–8.
54:1 SALVATION, Definition—God's salvation is His vindication of us through His all-powerful name. Vindication is literally "judge my case." The psalmist expected God to find him innocent and his enemy guilty. In salvation God declares us innocent. He acts to save us from injustice and persecution according to His purposes. We can only admit we have sinned and turn to God with the prayer of repentance.
54:1–7 PRAYER, Lament—See notes on 3:1–8; 5:10. Lamentation in personal crisis should lead to renewed commitment to worship and praise as it did for David.
55:1–23 EVIL AND SUFFERING, Prayer—Escape and flight may seem the only alternative when as God's people we live as the minority in a hostile environment. We find even our closest friends bowing to pressure and turning against us. Constant prayer and faith are the only course of action available. God will never turn against His faithful people. See notes on 3:1–8; 35:1–28.
55:1–23 PRAYER, Lament—See note on 3:1–8. This desperate call to God came in extreme circumstances which correspond to the period of Absalom's rebellion in David's life. The close friend who betrayed the psalmist could well be Ahithophel (2 Sa 17:1–4). David called on the Lord to "confound their speech" (v 9) as at Babel. This is, indeed, what happened to the counsel of Ahithophel (2 Sa 17:5–14). David's call to God was incessant (vv 16–17). See note on Ge 4:26. This prayer names burdens dreadful to bear but casts them on the Lord. That is the essence of lamentation.
55:4 HUMANITY, Attitudes to Death—Death is a natural part of life we normally face with resignation and/or acceptance. Crisis moments may cause us to react in fear of death. When trusted friends cause our crisis, the fear heightens even more. Death becomes a terror we want to escape. Trust in God provides escape from death's terror.

12If an enemy were insulting me,
I could endure it;
if a foe were raising himself against me,
I could hide from him.
13But it is you, a man like myself,
my companion, my close friend,[s]
14with whom I once enjoyed sweet
fellowship[t]
as we walked with the throng at the
house of God.[u]

15Let death take my enemies by
surprise;[v]
let them go down alive to the
grave,[x] [w]
for evil finds lodging among them.

16But I call to God,
and the LORD saves me.
17Evening,[x] morning[y] and noon[z]
I cry out in distress,
and he hears my voice.
18He ransoms me unharmed
from the battle waged against me,
even though many oppose me.
19God, who is enthroned forever,[a]
will hear[b] them and afflict them—
Selah
men who never change their ways
and have no fear of God.[c]

20My companion attacks his friends;[d]
he violates his covenant.[e]
21His speech is smooth as butter,[f]
yet war is in his heart;
his words are more soothing than oil,[g]
yet they are drawn swords.[h]

22Cast your cares on the LORD
and he will sustain you;[i]
he will never let the righteous fall.[j]
23But you, O God, will bring down the
wicked
into the pit[k] of corruption;
bloodthirsty and deceitful men[l]
will not live out half their days.[m]
But as for me, I trust in you.[n]

55:13 [s]S 2Sa 15:12
55:14 [t]Ac 1:16-17 [u]Ps 42:4
55:15 [v]Ps 64:7; Pr 6:15; Isa 29:5; 47:9,11; 1Th 5:3 [w]S Ps 49:14
55:17 [x]Ps 141:2; Ac 3:1; 10:3,30 [y]Ps 5:3; 88:13; 92:2 [z]Ac 10:9
55:19 [a]S Ex 15:18; Dt 33:27; Ps 29:10 [b]Ps 78:59 [c]Ps 36:1; 64:4
55:20 [d]Ps 7:4 [e]S Ps 41:9
55:21 [f]Ps 12:2 [g]Pr 5:3; 6:24 [h]Ps 57:4; 59:7; 64:3; Pr 12:18; Rev 1:16
55:22 [i]S Ps 18:35; Mt 6:25-34; 1Pe 5:7 [j]Ps 15:5; 21:7; 37:24; 112:6
55:23 [k]Ps 9:15; S 30:3; 73:18; 94:13; Isa 14:15; Eze 28:8; S Lk 8:31 [l]Ps 5:6 [m]S Job 15:32 [n]Ps 11:1; 25:2; 56:3
56:1 [o]Ps 6:2 [p]Ps 57:1-3 [q]Ps 17:9
56:2 [r]Ps 35:25; 124:3 [s]Ps 35:1
56:3 [t]Ps 55:4-5 [u]S Ps 55:23
56:4 [v]ver 10 [w]S Ps 27:1 [x]Ps 118:6; Mt 10:28; Heb 13:6
56:5 [y]Ps 41:7; 2Pe 3:16
56:6 [z]Ps 59:3; 94:21; Mk 3:6 [a]Ps 17:11 [b]Ps 71:10
56:7 [c]Pr 19:5; Eze 17:15; Ro 2:3; Heb 12:25 [d]Ps 36:12; 55:23
56:8 [e]S 2Ki 20:5 [f]Isa 4:3; Da 7:10; 12:1; Mal 3:16
56:9 [g]Ps 9:3 [h]Ps 102:2 [i]S Nu 14:8; S Dt 31:6; Ro 8:31
56:12 [j]Ps 50:14

Psalm 56

For the director of music. To ⌞the tune of⌟ "A Dove on Distant Oaks." Of David. A *miktam.*[y] When the Philistines had seized him in Gath.

Be merciful to me,[o] O God, for men
hotly pursue me;[p]
all day long they press their attack.[q]
2My slanderers pursue me all day
long;[r]
many are attacking me in their
pride.[s]

3When I am afraid,[t]
I will trust in you.[u]
4In God, whose word I praise,[v]
in God I trust; I will not be afraid.[w]
What can mortal man do to me?[x]

5All day long they twist my words;[y]
they are always plotting to harm me.
6They conspire,[z] they lurk,
they watch my steps,[a]
eager to take my life.[b]

7On no account let them escape;[c]
in your anger, O God, bring down
the nations.[d]
8Record my lament;
list my tears on your scroll[z] [e]—
are they not in your record?[f]

9Then my enemies will turn back[g]
when I call for help.[h]
By this I will know that God is for
me.[i]
10In God, whose word I praise,
in the LORD, whose word I praise—
11in God I trust; I will not be afraid.
What can man do to me?

12I am under vows[j] to you, O God;

[x]*15* Hebrew *Sheol* [y]Title: Probably a literary or musical term [z]*8* Or / *put my tears in your wineskin*

55:12–14 HUMANITY, Relationships—Friendship born of common, shared experiences is a most precious possession. When such a relationship is broken and betrayed, the resulting experience is utterly overwhelming. Love, shared in friendship, always carries the risk of betrayal.

55:15 HUMANITY, Nature of Death—Death is to be expected as the normal end of life, but under persecution and betrayal, we may wish it to come upon our enemies early, immediately, in the prime of life. We think their evil lives deserve such a fate. Admittedly this is a far cry from Jesus' teachings about love, but it is a very human response to unjust persecution.

55:19 GOD, Eternal—The eternity and the sovereignty of God are linked together here. Only an eternal God can truly claim to rule the universe. If He is not eternal, God must some day let another take control. The inspired Bible teaches us without doubt God is eternal and therefore is the supreme Ruler of all creation. See notes on 47:2–9; Ge 1:1; 21:33; Ro 16:25–27.

55:20–21 CHRISTIAN ETHICS, War and Peace—Those who are not at peace with themselves or with God will exhibit this warlikeness, however cleverly hidden, by actions and words to others. War can end only when it ends in human hearts. See note on 46:8–10.

55:22 ELECTION, Faith—God does not remove our burdens. God sustains and enables His elect to carry their burdens because God cares for His elect.

56:1–13 EVIL AND SUFFERING, Endurance—Trust in God is the only cure for fear of enemies. See note on 3:1–8.

56:1–13 PRAYER, Lament—See notes on 3:1–8; 5:10; 7:1–17. The psalmist carefully weighed the issues and confidently asserted his belief in the power and mercy of God. David could legitimately appeal to a record-keeping God to set the record straight. Lamentation includes a search for mercy and a renewal of trust in God.

56:3–4,11 SALVATION, Belief—Those who trust in God do not have to be afraid of other persons.

56:7 GOD, Wrath—Proper prayer depends on God's wrath, not human anger and power, to bring justice against the wicked. See notes on Ge 6:5–8; 17:14; 19:13,24–26; Jos 7:1, 25–26.

56:12 STEWARDSHIP, Vows—Israelite worship often

I will present my thank offerings to
you.
13For you have delivered me[a] from
death[k]
and my feet from stumbling,
that I may walk before God
in the light of life.[b] [l]

Psalm 57

57:7–11pp — Ps 108:1–5

For the director of music. ⌞To the tune of⌟ "Do Not Destroy." Of David. A *miktam*.[c] When he had fled from Saul into the cave.[m]

HAVE mercy on me, O God, have
mercy on me,
for in you my soul takes refuge.[n]
I will take refuge in the shadow of
your wings[o]
until the disaster has passed.[p]

2I cry out to God Most High,
to God, who fulfills ⌞his purpose⌟ for
me.[q]
3He sends from heaven and saves me,[r]
rebuking those who hotly pursue
me;[s] *Selah*
God sends his love and his
faithfulness.[t]

4I am in the midst of lions;[u]
I lie among ravenous beasts—
men whose teeth are spears and
arrows,
whose tongues are sharp swords.[v]

5Be exalted, O God, above the heavens;
let your glory be over all the earth.[w]

6They spread a net for my feet[x] —
I was bowed down[y] in distress.
They dug a pit[z] in my path—
but they have fallen into it
themselves.[a] *Selah*

7My heart is steadfast, O God,
my heart is steadfast;[b]
I will sing and make music.
8Awake, my soul!
Awake, harp and lyre![c]
I will awaken the dawn.

9I will praise you, O Lord, among the
nations;
I will sing of you among the peoples.
10For great is your love, reaching to the
heavens;
your faithfulness reaches to the
skies.[d]

11Be exalted, O God, above the
heavens;[e]
let your glory be over all the earth.[f]

Psalm 58

For the director of music. ⌞To the tune of⌟ "Do Not Destroy." Of David. A *miktam*.[c]

DO you rulers indeed speak justly?[g]
Do you judge uprightly among
men?
2No, in your heart you devise
injustice,[h]
and your hands mete out violence
on the earth.[i]
3Even from birth the wicked go astray;
from the womb they are wayward
and speak lies.
4Their venom is like the venom of a
snake,[j]
like that of a cobra that has stopped
its ears,
5that will not heed[k] the tune of the
charmer,[l]
however skillful the enchanter may
be.

6Break the teeth in their mouths,
O God;[m]

56:13 [k]Ps 30:3; 33:19; 49:15; 86:13; 107:20; 116:8 [l]S Job 33:30
57:1 [m]57 Title 1Sa 22:1; 24:3; Ps 142 Title [n]Ps 2:12; 9:9; 34:22 [o]S Ru 2:12; S Mt 23:37 [p]Isa 26:20
57:2 [q]Ps 138:8
57:3 [r]Ps 18:9,16; 69:14; 142:6; 144:5,7 [s]Ps 56:1 [t]Ps 25:10; 40:11; 115:1
57:4 [u]S Ps 35:17 [v]S Ps 55:21; Pr 30:14
57:5 [w]ver 11; Ps 108:5
57:6 [x]Ps 10:9; 31:4; 140:5 [y]S Ps 38:6; 145:14 [z]S Ps 9:15 [a]S Est 6:13; Ps 7:15; Pr 28:10; Ecc 10:8
57:7 [b]Ps 112:7
57:8 [c]Ps 33:2; 149:3; 150:3
57:10 [d]S Ps 36:5
57:11 [e]S Ps 8:1; 113:4 [f]S ver 5
58:1 [g]Ps 82:2
58:2 [h]Mt 15:19 [i]Ps 94:20; Isa 10:1; Lk 6:38
58:4 [j]S Nu 21:6
58:5 [k]Ps 81:11 [l]Ecc 10:11; Jer 8:17
58:6 [m]Ps 3:7

[a]13 Or *my soul* [b]13 Or *the land of the living*
[c]Title: Probably a literary or musical term

brought complaints and pleas for help to God. These concluded with a vow or promise to return to the houses of worship, give a thanksgiving offering, and sing thanks to God when He had answered the prayer for mercy (7:17; 54:6; 79:13; 80:18; 109:30). Special thanksgiving offerings are an appropriate way to acknowledge and testify to God's help in our lives. See note on Dt 23:21–23.

57:1 GOD, Grace—God's mercy and grace are our only hope in distress. See note on 23:1–6.

57:1–11 EVIL AND SUFFERING, Endurance—God has a purpose for His people. This assurance should comfort us in the midst of trouble and persecution. See note on 3:1–8.

57:1 SALVATION, As Refuge—God is our refuge for every disaster. See note on 34:8.

57:1–11 PRAYER, Lament—See note on 3:1–8. This prayer rises above circumstances. Amid lions and ravenous beasts the psalmist knew he was in the "refuge of the shadow of your wings." Lamentation often leads to a new dawn with new hopes and new praise. Recalling God's love calls us away from concentration on enemy weapons.

57:3,10 GOD, Faithfulness—Our salvation in time of trouble depends on God's love for us and His faithfulness to the covenant commitments He has made with us and to His own saving purpose. When we experience His salvation we praise His love and faithfulness. See notes on 37:33; 52:8.

57:5,11 GOD, Glory—In worship we express our deep desire for all the earth to see God's glorious presence. See notes on Ex 16:7,10; 40:34–38; Lk 2:9,14; Jn 11:4.

58:1–11 EVIL AND SUFFERING, Vindication—Powerful politicians may exercise power and influence for their own advantage. Such unjust leadership creates difficult times for obedient servants of God. We must remember that ultimately He rules the earth. The psalmist counted on the vengeance of God to vindicate a bad situation. See note on 35:1–28.

58:1–11 PRAYER, Sovereignty of God—See note on 5:10. This prayer contrasts the present power of wickedness with its ultimate weakness and the sovereignty of God as Judge with the sly intention of the wicked. Such violent prayer is appropriate in a desperate situation of injustice to restore the certainty that God will judge. Doubts expressed before God help us affirm His sovereignty.

tear out, O LORD, the fangs of the
lions![n]
7Let them vanish like water that flows
away;[o]
when they draw the bow, let their
arrows be blunted.[p]
8Like a slug melting away as it moves
along,[q]
like a stillborn child,[r] may they not
see the sun.

9Before your pots can feel ⌊the heat of⌋
the thorns[s] —
whether they be green or dry—the
wicked will be swept away.[d] [t]
10The righteous will be glad[u] when they
are avenged,[v]
when they bathe their feet in the
blood of the wicked.[w]
11Then men will say,
"Surely the righteous still are
rewarded;[x]
surely there is a God who judges the
earth."[y]

Psalm 59

For the director of music. ⌊To the tune of⌋ "Do Not Destroy." Of David. A *miktam*.[e] When Saul had sent men to watch David's house[z] in order to kill him.

DELIVER me from my enemies,
O God;[a]
protect me from those who rise up
against me.[b]
2Deliver me from evildoers[c]
and save me from bloodthirsty
men.[d]

3See how they lie in wait for me!
Fierce men conspire[e] against me
for no offense or sin of mine,
O LORD.
4I have done no wrong,[f] yet they are
ready to attack me.[g]
Arise to help me; look on my
plight![h]
5O LORD God Almighty, the God of
Israel,[i]
rouse yourself[j] to punish all the
nations;[k]
show no mercy to wicked traitors.[l]
Selah

58:6 [n]S Job 4:10
58:7 [o]S Lev 26:36; S Job 11:16 [p]Ps 11:2; 57:4; 64:3
58:8 [q]Isa 13:7 [r]S Job 3:16
58:9 [s]Ps 118:12; Ecc 7:6 [t]S Job 7:10; S 21:18
58:10 [u]S Job 22:19 [v]Dt 32:35; Ps 7:9; 91:8; Jer 11:20; Ro 12:17-21 [w]Ps 68:23
58:11 [x]S Ge 15:1; S Ps 128:2; Lk 6:23 [y]S Ge 18:25
59:1 [z]59 Title 1Sa 19:11 [a]Ps 143:9 [b]S Ps 20:1
59:2 [c]Ps 14:4; 36:12; 53:4; 92:7; 94:16 [d]S Ps 26:9; 139:19; Pr 29:10
59:3 [e]S Ps 56:6
59:4 [f]Ps 119:3 [g]Mt 5:11 [h]S Ps 13:3
59:5 [i]Ps 69:6; 80:4; 84:8 [j]S Ps 44:23 [k]S Ps 9:5; S Isa 10:3 [l]Jer 18:23
59:6 [m]ver 14; Ps 22:16
59:7 [n]Ps 94:4; Pr 10:32; 12:23; 15:2,28 [o]S Ps 55:21 [p]S Job 22:13
59:8 [q]Ps 37:13; Pr 1:26 [r]Ps 2:4
59:9 [s]S Ps 18:1 [t]Ps 9:9; 18:2; 62:2; 71:3
59:11 [u]Ps 3:3; 84:9 [v]Dt 4:9; 6:12 [w]Ps 89:10; 106:27; 144:6; Isa 33:3
59:12 [x]Ps 10:7 [y]Ps 64:8; Pr 10:14; 12:13 [z]Isa 2:12; 5:15; Zep 3:11
59:13 [a]Ps 104:35 [b]Ps 83:18
59:15 [c]Job 15:23
59:16 [d]Ps 108:1 [e]S 1Sa 2:10 [f]Ps 5:3; 88:13 [g]Ps 101:1 [h]S 2Sa 22:3 [i]S Dt 4:30
59:17 [j]ver 10

6They return at evening,
snarling like dogs,[m]
and prowl about the city.
7See what they spew from their
mouths[n] —
they spew out swords[o] from their
lips,
and they say, "Who can hear
us?"[p]
8But you, O LORD, laugh at them;[q]
you scoff at all those nations.[r]
9O my Strength,[s] I watch for you;
you, O God, are my fortress,[t] 10my
loving God.

God will go before me
and will let me gloat over those who
slander me.
11But do not kill them, O Lord our
shield,[f] [u]
or my people will forget.[v]
In your might make them wander
about,
and bring them down.[w]
12For the sins of their mouths,[x]
for the words of their lips,[y]
let them be caught in their
pride.[z]
For the curses and lies they utter,
13 consume them in wrath,
consume them till they are no
more.[a]
Then it will be known to the ends of
the earth
that God rules over Jacob.[b]
Selah
14They return at evening,
snarling like dogs,
and prowl about the city.
15They wander about for food[c]
and howl if not satisfied.
16But I will sing[d] of your strength,[e]
in the morning[f] I will sing of your
love;[g]
for you are my fortress,[h]
my refuge in times of trouble.[i]
17O my Strength, I sing praise to you;
you, O God, are my fortress, my
loving God.[j]

[d]9 The meaning of the Hebrew for this verse is uncertain. [e]Title: Probably a literary or musical term [f]11 Or *sovereign*

59:1–17 EVIL AND SUFFERING, God's Future Help—God's innocent people depend on Him for help from evil opponents. He acts to save His people and let the world know of His power. See note on 3:1–8.
59:1–17 PRAYER, Lament—See notes on 3:1–8; 5:10; 7:1–17. The one who watches for God's strength (v 9) will sing of God's strength (v 17). Relying on God's strength lets us not worry about the enemy's strength.
59:5,13 GOD, Sovereignty—God's sovereign control over His created world and all its people and nations brought the psalmist to depend on God for help against wicked enemies. God's actions in wrath express love for His people (v 9) and serve to let all people know His sovereign power (v 13). The sovereignty of God is expressed here as His authority and ability to rule in His world and exercise judgment over earth's people. See note on 47:2–9.
59:9,16–17 GOD, Power—God's power is closely associated with His grace and love. When God exercises His power to show grace to His people, we respond in praise. See notes on Nu 11:23; Dt 30:1–4; Mt 19:16–26.

Psalm 60

60:5–12pp — Ps 108:6–13

For the director of music. To ⌊the tune of⌋ "The Lily of the Covenant." A *miktam*[g] of David. For teaching. When he fought Aram Naharaim[h] and Aram Zobah,[i] and when Joab returned and struck down twelve thousand Edomites in the Valley of Salt.[k]

YOU have rejected us,[l] O God, and
burst forth upon us;
you have been angry[m]—now restore
us![n]
2You have shaken the land[o] and torn it
open;
mend its fractures,[p] for it is
quaking.
3You have shown your people desperate
times;[q]
you have given us wine that makes
us stagger.[r]
4But for those who fear you, you have
raised a banner[s]
to be unfurled against the bow.
Selah
5Save us and help us with your right
hand,[t]
that those you love[u] may be
delivered.
6God has spoken from his sanctuary:
"In triumph I will parcel out
Shechem[v]
and measure off the Valley of
Succoth.[w]
7Gilead[x] is mine, and Manasseh is
mine;
Ephraim[y] is my helmet,
Judah[z] my scepter.[a]
8Moab is my washbasin,
upon Edom I toss my sandal;
over Philistia I shout in triumph.[b]"
9Who will bring me to the fortified city?
Who will lead me to Edom?
10Is it not you, O God, you who have
rejected us
and no longer go out with our
armies?[c]
11Give us aid against the enemy,
for the help of man is worthless.[d]
12With God we will gain the victory,
and he will trample down our
enemies.[e]

Psalm 61

For the director of music. With stringed instruments. Of David.

HEAR my cry, O God;[f]
listen to my prayer.[g]
2From the ends of the earth I call to
you,
I call as my heart grows faint;[h]
lead me to the rock[i] that is higher
than I.
3For you have been my refuge,[j]
a strong tower against the foe.[k]
4I long to dwell[l] in your tent forever
and take refuge in the shelter of
your wings.[m] *Selah*
5For you have heard my vows,[n] O God;
you have given me the heritage of
those who fear your name.[o]
6Increase the days of the king's life,[p]
his years for many generations.[q]
7May he be enthroned in God's
presence forever;[r]
appoint your love and faithfulness to
protect him.[s]
8Then will I ever sing praise to your
name[t]
and fulfill my vows day after day.[u]

60:1 [k]60 Title 2Sa 8:13 [l]2Sa 5:20; Ps 44:9 [m]Ps 79:5 [n]Ps 80:3
60:2 [o]Ps 18:7 [p]S 2Ch 7:14
60:3 [q]Ps 71:20 [r]Ps 75:8; Isa 29:9; 51:17; 63:6; Jer 25:16; Zec 12:2; Rev 14:10
60:4 [s]Isa 5:26; 11:10,12; 18:3
60:5 [t]S Job 40:14 [u]S Dt 33:12
60:6 [v]S Ge 12:6 [w]S Ge 33:17
60:7 [x]Jos 13:31 [y]S Ge 41:52 [z]S Nu 34:19 [a]S Ge 49:10
60:8 [b]S 2Sa 8:1
60:10 [c]S Jos 7:12
60:11 [d]Ps 146:3; Pr 3:5
60:12 [e]S Job 40:12; Ps 44:5
61:1 [f]Ps 64:1 [g]Ps 4:1; 86:6
61:2 [h]S Ps 6:2 [i]Ps 18:2; 31:2; 94:22
61:3 [j]Ps 9:9; S 46:1; 62:7 [k]Ps 59:9; Pr 18:10
61:4 [l]S Ps 15:1 [m]S Dt 32:11; S Mt 23:37
61:5 [n]S Nu 30:2; Ps 56:12 [o]S Ex 6:3; S Dt 33:9; Ne 1:11; Ps 102:15; Isa 59:19; Mt 6:9
61:6 [p]1Ki 3:14 [q]S Ps 21:4
61:7 [r]S Ps 41:12; Lk 22:69; Eph 1:20; Col 3:1 [s]Ps 40:11
61:8 [t]S Ex 15:1; Ps 7:17; 30:4 [u]S Nu 30:2; S Dt 23:21

[g]Title: Probably a literary or musical term [h]Title: That is, Arameans of Northwest Mesopotamia [i]Title: That is, Arameans of central Syria

---

60:1–12 EVIL AND SUFFERING, Prayer—See note on 3:1–8. Troubles at times represent God's discipline of a disobedient people. In their suffering, God's people still prayed for restoration and depended on God's abiding love for those He punished. In worship God's people heard the proclamation of His intent to deliver His people.

60:1–12 PRAYER, Lament—See notes on 3:1–8; 6:1–10. Although the situation was desperate, the prayer was confident. God, who parceled out the allotment of the tribes, still speaks. Lamentation seeks a word of direction from a God who appears to be silent. Defeat and feeling of isolation from God are not occasions to stop praying. They call for honest communication and tough faith.

60:5–12 GOD, Savior—Notice the contrast between the dismal human efforts to save ourselves and the power of God's efforts in salvation. God's salvation comes to those He loves (v 5). It consisted in this instance of victory in battle.

60:6 REVELATION, Oracles—The symbolic place of worship is many times the setting for an inspired sense of God's presence and communication. The writer had probably gone to the religious site for a divine encounter. His alertness to God's revelation made him sensitive to God's leading. A priest or prophet may have spoken a word from God to answer the prayer. Renewed prayer was the response to the word of assurance.

61:1–8 EVIL AND SUFFERING, Endurance—See note on 3:1–8. Suffering may lead God's people to desire total security by escaping the world and living in God's house under His protection. God sends us out into His world to find His protection amid the world's problems. One responsibility there is to pray for political leaders.

61:1–8 PRAYER, Lament—See notes on 3:1–8; 7:1–17. The psalmist mixed the lowest possible desperation with the highest possible faith. It could have been written when David fled across the Jordan from Absalom (2 Sa 17:21–22). Geography does not limit lamentation. Prayer renews previous promises made to God and seeks life in God's presence as the ultimate good.

61:3–4 SALVATION, As Refuge—Making God our refuge means dwelling where He dwells and being covered by the shelter of His wings, much like chicks covered by a mother hen.

61:8 WORSHIP, Obedience—See note on 1 Sa 15:22–23. Worship often includes making promises to God and then fulfilling promises made.

Psalm 62

For the director of music. For Jeduthun.
A psalm of David.

MY soul finds rest[v] in God alone;[w]
my salvation comes from him.
2He alone is my rock[x] and my
salvation;[y]
he is my fortress,[z] I will never be
shaken.[a]

3How long will you assault a man?
Would all of you throw him down—
this leaning wall,[b] this tottering
fence?
4They fully intend to topple him
from his lofty place;
they take delight in lies.
With their mouths they bless,
but in their hearts they curse.[c]
Selah

5Find rest, O my soul, in God alone;[d]
my hope comes from him.
6He alone is my rock and my salvation;
he is my fortress, I will not be
shaken.
7My salvation and my honor depend on
God[j];
he is my mighty rock, my refuge.[e]
8Trust in him at all times, O people;[f]
pour out your hearts to him,[g]
for God is our refuge. *Selah*

9Lowborn men[h] are but a breath,[i]
the highborn are but a lie;
if weighed on a balance,[j] they are
nothing;
together they are only a breath.

10Do not trust in extortion[k]
or take pride in stolen goods;[l]
though your riches increase,
do not set your heart on them.[m]

11One thing God has spoken,
two things have I heard:
that you, O God, are strong,[n]
12 and that you, O Lord, are loving.[o]
Surely you will reward each person
according to what he has done.[p]

Psalm 63

A psalm of David. When he was in the
Desert of Judah.

O God, you are my God,
earnestly I seek you;
my soul thirsts for you,[q]
my body longs for you,
in a dry and weary land
where there is no water.[r]

2I have seen you in the sanctuary[s]
and beheld your power and your
glory.[t]
3Because your love is better than life,[u]
my lips will glorify you.
4I will praise you as long as I live,[v]
and in your name I will lift up my
hands.[w]
5My soul will be satisfied as with the
richest of foods;[x]
with singing lips my mouth will
praise you.
6On my bed I remember you;

j7 Or / *God Most High is my salvation and my honor*

62:1 vS Ps 5:3 wver 5
62:2 xPs 18:31; 89:26 yS Ex 15:2 zS Ps 59:9 aS Job 29:18
62:3 bIsa 30:13
62:4 cPs 28:3; 55:21
62:5 dver 1
62:7 eS Ps 61:3
62:8 fPs 37:5; Isa 26:4 g1Sa 1:15; Ps 42:4; Mt 26:36-46
62:9 hPs 49:2 iS Job 7:7 jIsa 40:15
62:10 kS Ps 12:5; 1Ti 6:17 lIsa 61:8; Eze 22:29; Na 3:1 mS Job 31:25; Mt 19:23-24; 1Ti 6:6-10
62:11 nS 1Ch 29:11; Rev 19:1
62:12 oPs 86:5; 103:8; 130:7 pS Job 21:31; Ps 28:4; S Mt 16:27; Ro 2:6*; 1Co 3:8; Col 3:25
63:1 qPs 42:2; 84:2 rPs 143:6
63:2 sS Ps 15:1; 27:4; 68:24 tS Ex 16:7
63:3 uPs 36:7; 69:16; 106:45; 109:21
63:4 vPs 104:33; 146:2; Isa 38:20 wS Ps 28:2; 1Ti 2:8
63:5 xS Ps 36:8; Mt 5:6

62:1–2,6–8 GOD, Savior—God the Savior provides rest for His people. In Old Testament times, salvation was largely thought of as deliverance from perils in this earthly life, but notice the personal intimacy pictured here in finding security in God. Salvation is not an objective event where I win and my enemy loses. It is a state of security and confidence in God no matter what the material circumstances. See note on 18:1–48.

62:1–12 EVIL AND SUFFERING, Endurance—See note on 3:1–8. Human power, authority, and wealth may impress us in our weakness and suffering. God calls us to faithful obedience to His way of life and trust in Him for deliverance from enemies.

62:1–12 PRAYER, Commitment—Caught in the swirl of human evil, the psalmist found rest in God alone. Prayer is resting in God amid all human evil. Prayer affirms God alone as the unswervable mighty rock and fortress in whom there can be no shaking. Commitment is based on assurance of God's love and strength.

62:2,8 SALVATION, As Refuge—Salvation as refuge means making God our rock and our fortress. The Lord is a refuge for the individual and the nation. We can unload all our troubles on Him.

62:9 HUMANITY, Life—Measured against eternity, human life is a short breath, empty and vain, weighing nothing on the scales. Social classes make no difference. None carry weight in eternity. Contrasted with God Himself, human life is insignificant. Material possessions add nothing. Only trust in God's power and love fills life's emptiness.

62:11–12 GOD, Love—The God who is Savior is characterized by love and power. Salvation is the product both of God's love and God's power. See note on 59:9,16–17.

62:11 REVELATION, God's Nature—The worshiper's inspiration caused him to reflect on two aspects of God: power and love. The writer, probably reflecting at the Temple or shrine in worship, struggled to understand God's power in relationship to His intervention in the lives of human beings. The proclamation of God's word brought assurance of God's love and strength. The psalmist was concerned to know God as revealed in His power to save and in His nature to love and not destroy.

63:1–11 EVIL AND SUFFERING, Prayer—See note on 3:1–8. Political rulers can depend on God for help in trouble. Worship can give kings and rulers new directions and renewed faith. Such worship fulfills their needs much more than the material goods. Private prayer, as well as public worship, is essential for a person in power.

63:1–11 PRAYER, Commitment—The psalmist found satisfaction in God alone. Satisfaction grew out of worship experiences in God's house and matured in personal experiences of God's love. Satisfaction led to commitment to praise and meditation and to confidence in God's deliverance. Prayer of commitment should be the product of satisfaction in God.

63:2–3 GOD, Glory—Worship experiences with God provide memories which encourage and empower God's people during times we cannot worship. In worship at God's sanctuary, God revealed Himself in all His power and glory. Such an experience assured the psalmist of God's love.

I think of you through the watches
of the night.[y]
7Because you are my help,[z]
I sing in the shadow of your wings.[a]
8My soul clings to you;[b]
your right hand upholds me.[c]
9They who seek my life will be
destroyed;[d]
they will go down to the depths of
the earth.[e]
10They will be given over to the sword[f]
and become food for jackals.[g]
11But the king will rejoice in God;
all who swear by God's name will
praise him,[h]
while the mouths of liars will be
silenced.[i]

Psalm 64

For the director of music. A psalm of David.

HEAR me, O God, as I voice my
complaint;[j]
protect my life from the threat of the
enemy.[k]
2Hide me from the conspiracy[l] of the
wicked,[m]
from that noisy crowd of evildoers.
3They sharpen their tongues like
swords[n]
and aim their words like deadly
arrows.[o]
4They shoot from ambush at the
innocent man;[p]
they shoot at him suddenly, without
fear.[q]
5They encourage each other in evil
plans,
they talk about hiding their snares;[r]
they say, "Who will see them[k]?"[s]
6They plot injustice and say,
"We have devised a perfect plan!"
Surely the mind and heart of man
are cunning.
7But God will shoot them with arrows;
suddenly they will be struck down.
8He will turn their own tongues against
them[t]
and bring them to ruin;
all who see them will shake their
heads[u] in scorn.[v]
9All mankind will fear;[w]
they will proclaim the works of God
and ponder what he has done.[x]
10Let the righteous rejoice in the LORD[y]
and take refuge in him;[z]
let all the upright in heart praise
him![a]

Psalm 65

For the director of music. A psalm of David.
A song.

PRAISE awaits[l] you, O God, in Zion;[b]
to you our vows will be fulfilled.[c]
2O you who hear prayer,
to you all men will come.[d]
3When we were overwhelmed by
sins,[e]
you forgave[m] our transgressions.[f]
4Blessed are those you choose[g]
and bring near[h] to live in your
courts!
We are filled with the good things of
your house,[i]
of your holy temple.
5You answer us with awesome deeds of
righteousness,[j]
O God our Savior,[k]

63:6 [y]Dt 6:4-9; Ps 16:7; 119:148; Mt 14:25
63:7 [z]Ps 27:9; 118:7 [a]S Ru 2:12
63:8 [b]S Nu 32:12; Hos 6:3 [c]S Ps 41:12
63:9 [d]Ps 40:14 [e]Ps 55:15; 71:20; 95:4; 139:15
63:10 [f]Jer 18:21; Eze 35:5; Am 1:11 [g]La 5:18
63:11 [h]Isa 19:18; 45:23; 65:16 [i]S Job 5:16; Ro 3:19
64:1 [j]Ps 142:2 [k]Ps 140:1
64:2 [l]S Ex 1:10 [m]Ps 56:6; 59:2
64:3 [n]S Ps 55:21; Isa 49:2 [o]S Ps 7:13; S 58:7
64:4 [p]S Job 9:23; Ps 10:8; 11:2 [q]S Ps 55:19
64:5 [r]Ps 91:3; 119:110; 140:5; 141:9 [s]S Job 22:13
64:8 [t]S Ps 59:12; Pr 18:7 [u]S 2Ki 19:21; Ps 109:25 [v]S Dt 28:37
64:9 [w]S Ps 40:3 [x]Jer 51:10
64:10 [y]S Job 22:19 [z]Ps 11:1; 25:20; 31:2 [a]Ps 32:11
65:1 [b]Ps 2:6 [c]S Dt 23:21; Ps 116:18
65:2 [d]Ps 86:9; Isa 66:23
65:3 [e]S Ps 40:12 [f]Ps 79:9; Ro 3:25; Heb 9:14
65:4 [g]S Ps 33:12 [h]S Nu 16:5 [i]S Ps 36:8
65:5 [j]S Dt 4:34; S Ps 45:4; 106:22; Isa 64:3 [k]Ps 18:46; 68:19; 85:4

[k]5 Or *us* [l]1 Or *befits*; the meaning of the Hebrew for this word is uncertain. [m]3 Or *made atonement for*

63:9 LAST THINGS, Intermediate State—See note on Isa 14:9.
64:1–10 EVIL AND SUFFERING, Endurance—See note on 3:1–8. Evil people feed on the encouragement of one another. Too often the sharpest human minds are devoted to wickedness. Such minds are no competition for God. His actions will show the world that God rules.
64:1–10 CHRISTIAN ETHICS, Justice—David portrayed a dark, but accurate, picture of our nature apart from God. Our bent is away from the working of justice and right. We think we can execute the perfect crime without getting caught. Ignoring God so completely is foolish. He protects His righteous people and punishes the criminal.
64:1–10 PRAYER, Lament—Lamentation may be complaint. Here the complaint is against the insidiousness of evil that springs from the deepest part of human wickedness. Expressing such complaint leads to assurance God knows evil and causes it to defeat its own purposes. See note on 3:1–8.
64:5–9 HISTORY, Deliverance—God delivers individuals as well as nations from enemies. Deliverance on each level is accomplished to reveal God's power and lead all people to reverence God.
64:9 REVELATION, Events—Proclamation of God's salvation is in reflective response to specific redeeming acts. God often reveals His purposes through redemptive actions for His people. The repetition and public celebration of those acts in worship leads others to proclaim God's salvation. Soon a written record of His revealed intentions throughout history develops and becomes revelation for a new generation. Historical event, reflection, worship celebration, public testimony, and written record are all part of God's revelation (66:5–6; 68:8–18; 71:16).
65:1–13 PRAYER, Thanksgiving—See notes on 30:1–12; Ne 11:17. Praise is God's due. It should and will be universal. Praise is one way to express thanks to the Creator, who is also our Savior. One way the Creator saves is by giving bountiful crops. Thus thanksgiving is our response to limitless giving from a limitless God.
65:5 GOD, Righteous—God's righteousness here refers to the historical acts He has used to restore an atmosphere of righteousness among His people. These acts serve as testimonies that God is our Savior. On Him all peoples can base their hopes.
65:5–13 CREATION, Hope—God's miraculous works in redemption and creation give confidence to His people. The power of creation is compared to the power of stilling international turmoil. When we see that God is in complete control of His created world, we relax with joy and confidence. His

the hope of all the ends of the earth[l]
and of the farthest seas,[m]
6 who formed the mountains[n] by your power,
having armed yourself with strength,[o]
7 who stilled the roaring of the seas,[p]
the roaring of their waves,
and the turmoil of the nations.[q]
8 Those living far away fear your wonders;
where morning dawns and evening fades
you call forth songs of joy.[r]

9 You care for the land and water it;[s]
you enrich it abundantly.[t]
The streams of God are filled with water
to provide the people with grain,[u]
for so you have ordained it.[n]
10 You drench its furrows
and level its ridges;
you soften it with showers[v]
and bless its crops.
11 You crown the year with your bounty,[w]
and your carts overflow with abundance.[x]
12 The grasslands of the desert overflow;[y]
the hills are clothed with gladness.[z]
13 The meadows are covered with flocks[a]
and the valleys are mantled with grain;[b]
they shout for joy and sing.[c]

Psalm 66

For the director of music. A song. A psalm.

SHOUT with joy to God, all the earth![d]
2 Sing the glory of his name;[e]
make his praise glorious![f]
3 Say to God, "How awesome are your deeds![g]
So great is your power
that your enemies cringe[h] before you.
4 All the earth bows down[i] to you;
they sing praise[j] to you,
they sing praise to your name." *Selah*
5 Come and see what God has done,
how awesome his works[k] in man's behalf!
6 He turned the sea into dry land,[l]
they passed through[m] the waters on foot—
come, let us rejoice[n] in him.
7 He rules forever[o] by his power,
his eyes watch[p] the nations—
let not the rebellious[q] rise up
against him. *Selah*

8 Praise[r] our God, O peoples,
let the sound of his praise be heard;
9 he has preserved our lives[s]
and kept our feet from slipping.[t]
10 For you, O God, tested[u] us;
you refined us like silver.[v]
11 You brought us into prison[w]
and laid burdens[x] on our backs.
12 You let men ride over our heads;[y]
we went through fire and water,
but you brought us to a place of abundance.[z]

13 I will come to your temple with burnt offerings[a]
and fulfill my vows[b] to you—
14 vows my lips promised and my mouth spoke
when I was in trouble.
15 I will sacrifice fat animals to you
and an offering of rams;
I will offer bulls and goats.[c] *Selah*

16 Come and listen,[d] all you who fear God;

65:5 [l]S Ps 48:10 [m]Ps 107:23 **65:6** [n]Am 4:13 [o]S Ps 18:1; 93:1; Isa 51:9 **65:7** [p]Ps 89:9; 93:3-4; 107:29; S Mt 8:26 [q]Dt 32:41; Ps 2:1; 74:23; 139:20; Isa 17:12-13 **65:8** [r]Ps 100:2; 107:22; 126:2; Isa 24:16; 52:9 **65:9** [s]S Lev 26:4 [t]Ps 104:24 [u]S Ge 27:28; S Dt 32:14; Ps 104:14 **65:10** [v]S Dt 32:2; S 2Sa 1:21; S Job 36:28; Ac 14:17 **65:11** [w]S Dt 28:12; Ps 104:28; Jn 10:10 [x]Job 36:28; Ps 147:14; Lk 6:38 **65:12** [y]S Job 28:26; Joel 2:22 [z]Ps 98:8 **65:13** [a]Ps 144:13; Isa 30:23; Zec 8:12 [b]Ps 72:16 [c]Ps 98:8; Isa 14:8; 44:23; 49:13; 55:12 **66:1** [d]Ps 81:1; 84:8; 95:1; 98:4; 100:1 **66:2** [e]Ps 79:9; 86:9 [f]Isa 42:8,12; 43:21 **66:3** [g]S Dt 7:21; S 10:21; Ps 65:5; 106:22; 111:6; 145:6 [h]S 2Sa 22:45 **66:4** [i]Ps 22:27 [j]Ps 7:17; 67:3 **66:5** [k]ver 3; Ps 106:22 **66:6** [l]S Ge 8:1; S Ex 14:22 [m]1Co 10:1 [n]S Lev 23:40 **66:7** [o]S Ex 15:18; Ps 145:13 [p]S Ex 3:16; S Ps 11:4 [q]S Nu 17:10; Ps 112:10; 140:8 **66:8** [r]S Ps 22:23 **66:9** [s]Ps 30:3 [t]S Dt 32:35; S Job 12:5 **66:10** [u]S Ex 15:25 [v]S Job 6:29; S 28:1; S Ps 12:6 **66:11** [w]Ps 142:7; 146:7; Isa 42:7,22; 61:1 [x]S Ge 3:17; S Ex 1:14; Ps 38:4; Isa 10:27 **66:12** [y]Isa 51:23 [z]Ps 18:19 **66:13** [a]S Ps 51:19 [b]Ps 22:25; 50:14; 116:14; Ecc 5:4; Jnh 2:9 **66:15** [c]S Lev 16:5; Ps 51:19 **66:16** [d]Ps 34:11

[n]9 Or *for that is how you prepare the land*

power, manifested in His watering the earth, enriches the lands He made. This enhances the fields, resulting in a continuous creation as vegetation abounds and the hills become fruitful.

65:6 GOD, Creator—Creation is a demonstration of the power of God and the basis for God's continuing care for the physical world He created and supplies.

65:8 MIRACLE, Nature—God works His wonders in numerous arenas of life—righteous acts in history, creation of the earth, stilling of chaotic waters and nations, supplying fertility for crops, decorating the hills in beauty and the pastures with flocks.

66:1–20 EVIL AND SUFFERING, Testing—The psalmist praised God for His care for His people. Our suffering may not be the deserved punishment for sin but a testing of our faith. God allows us to face situations where our faith in Him is challenged and can be strengthened. Looking back on such experiences, we praise God for them and use them as personal testimony to encourage others.

66:1–20 PRAYER, Praise—See note on 33:1–22. Although some psalms praise God as the peculiar God of Israel (114; 122; 124; 129; 136; 137), the majority extol Him as the God of all peoples. This one typifies the many expressions of praise for Him as universal Sovereign. God's actions against Israel's enemies formed the basis for praise. Praise is not uttered in words alone. Sacrificial gifts provide concrete signs of praise and fulfill vows made in lamentation. See note on 7:1–17. Such praise is not a private act but a public testimony. V 18 provides an important principle of prayer. Unconfessed, and thus unforgiven, sin blocks communication with God.

66:1 EVANGELISM, Worship—See note on 48:9.

66:2 GOD, Glory—See note on 57:5,11; 63:2–3.

66:3,7 GOD, Power—In His unlimited power God rules the world. He displays His power in historical acts which defeat the enemies of His people. These acts reveal God's power to all people.

66:5–7 HISTORY, Praise—Review of God's mighty acts calls God's people to praise.

let me tell[e] you what he has done
for me.
17I cried out to him with my mouth;
his praise was on my tongue.
18If I had cherished sin in my heart,
the Lord would not have listened;[f]
19but God has surely listened
and heard my voice[g] in prayer.
20Praise be to God,
who has not rejected[h] my prayer
or withheld his love from me!

Psalm 67

For the director of music. With stringed instruments. A psalm. A song.

MAY God be gracious to us and bless
us
and make his face shine upon us,[i]
Selah
2that your ways may be known on
earth,
your salvation[j] among all nations.[k]
3May the peoples praise you, O God;
may all the peoples praise you.[l]
4May the nations be glad and sing for
joy,[m]
for you rule the peoples justly[n]
and guide the nations of the earth.[o]
Selah
5May the peoples praise you, O God;
may all the peoples praise you.
6Then the land will yield its harvest,[p]
and God, our God, will bless us.[q]
7God will bless us,
and all the ends of the earth[r] will
fear him.[s]

Psalm 68

For the director of music. Of David. A psalm. A song.

MAY God arise,[t] may his enemies be
scattered;[u]
may his foes flee[v] before him.
2As smoke[w] is blown away by the wind,
may you blow them away;
as wax melts[x] before the fire,
may the wicked perish[y] before God.
3But may the righteous be glad
and rejoice[z] before God;
may they be happy and joyful.
4Sing to God, sing praise to his name,[a]
extol him who rides on the
clouds°[b] —
his name is the LORD[c] —
and rejoice before him.
5A father to the fatherless,[d] a defender
of widows,[e]
is God in his holy dwelling.[f]

66:16 [e]Ps 71:15,24 66:18 [f]S Dt 1:45; S 1Sa 8:18; Jas 4:3 66:19 [g]S Ps 18:6 66:20 [h]Ps 22:24 67:1 [i]Nu 6:24-26 67:2 [j]Isa 40:5; 52:10; 62:1 [k]Ps 98:2; Isa 62:2; Ac 10:35; Tit 2:11 67:3 [l]ver 5 67:4 [m]Ps 100:1-2 [n]S Ps 9:4; 96:10-13 [o]Ps 68:32 67:6 [p]S Ge 8:22; S Lev 26:4; Ps 85:12; Isa 55:10; Eze 34:27; Zec 8:12 [q]S Ge 12:2 67:7 [r]S Ps 2:8 [s]Ps 33:8 68:1 [t]Ps 12:5; 132:8 [u]Ps 18:14; 89:10; 92:9; 144:6 [v]Nu 10:35; Isa 17:13; 21:15; 33:3 68:2 [w]S Ps 37:20 [x]S Ps 22:14 [y]S Nu 10:35; Ps 9:3; 80:16 68:3 [z]Ps 64:10; 97:12 68:4 [a]S 2Sa 22:50; Ps 7:17; S 30:4; 66:2; 96:2; 100:4; 135:3 [b]ver 33; S Ex 20:21; S Dt 33:26 [c]S Ex 6:3; Ps 83:18 68:5 [d]Ps 10:14 [e]S Ex 22:22; S Dt 10:18 [f]S Dt 26:15; Jer 25:30

°4 Or / *prepare the way for him who rides through the deserts*

67:1 GOD, Grace—Our basic prayer is to live in God's grace, that undeserved kindness that God shows to us. We testify of that grace so that all other peoples may know God's salvation. See note on 57:1.

67:1–2,6–7 SALVATION, Blessing—God's blessing has a missionary dimension. He blesses Israel that His salvation might be known to the ends of the earth. See note on Nu 6:22–27.

67:1–7 PRAYER, Blessing—Blessing is God's constant action in supplying daily needs through an almost unnoticeable process. The slow but sure growth of crops is a major example of blessing, as are continued good health and availability of necessary resources for living. God promised to use His people as a source of blessing to all nations (Ge 12:3). This is a missionary prayer which recognizes the principle that the ends of the earth will fear God when He works through those He has chosen. When the nation has been a blessing, then it will receive blessing. Prayer involves the missionary purpose of God's people and the daily blessings needed for survival as well as deliverance from enemies and catastrophe.

67:1–2 EVANGELISM, Salvation—God's saving power is for all people. Redemption is universal, available to all who will respond to the gospel in repentance and faith. All nations should hear of God's way of salvation. He is gracious and makes His face shine on His people. Revived and blessed, His people then become the agents to carry the gospel to all. We need constant spiritual renewal to take the Word of redemption to all nations.

67:1–7 MISSIONS, Scope—This may well be the most missionary of all of the psalms. Beginning with a prayer for God's grace, presence, and blessing, it moves to seek His blessing for all the peoples of the earth. God has the right to invite and expect all peoples to praise Him because He rules the world fairly in justice. One way God extends His salvation to all the nations is through blessing the harvest. This act leads all peoples to reverence and worship Him. The Psalm uses a Hebrew style called parallelism by stating a great longing that God's ways be known to all peoples of the earth and then repeating it in a slightly different form, asking that God's salvation be made known among all nations. Even in modern times there is no more eloquent call to world evangelization.

67:2 GOD, Savior—God's grace in v 1 leads immediately to the idea of God as Savior. God is a saving kind of God because He is a gracious, loving God. See note on 62:1–2,6–8.

67:3–4 MISSIONS, Results—The final purpose of missions is to bring all nations to worship and praise God. Ultimately, the psalmist's prayer will be answered (7:9–10). God's sovereignty in our world makes it imperative that all nations and peoples have the opportunity to know Him. Not only nations on the map are to celebrate God's love and greatness but also peoples—tribes, extended families, and all ethnic and language groups. God blends the voices of languages altogether into harmonious praise of Him.

68:1–35 EVIL AND SUFFERING, God's Present Help—God's people celebrate His direction and protection of their nation. God's interest is not confined to individual believers. He works to establish His rule over all the earth. He uses human politicians and events to accomplish His purposes. He judges wicked rulers who oppose His will. God's protection extends from the poorest, most helpless individuals (vv 5–6) to the most powerful international rulers (vv 28–31). He has power over all that burdens us, even death (vv 19–20).

68:1–35 PRAYER, Worship—Prayer can be oral or written response to elaborate worship ceremonies. Ps 68 apparently describes the various parts of a ceremony celebrating God's victories for His people. Congregational petition (vv 1–3), praise (vv 4–6), recitation of historical tradition (vv 7–14), affirmation of His saving presence (vv 15–20), statement of confidence (vv 21–23), description of the ark of the covenant representing God's presence in a ceremonial procession (vv 24–27), prayer for victory (vv 28–31), and a concluding hymn (vv 31–35) are joined here to express worship for the sovereign God who shows compassion for His people. Compare Eph 4:8.

6God sets the lonely[g] in families,[p] [h]
he leads forth the prisoners[i] with
singing;
but the rebellious live in a
sun-scorched land.[j]

7When you went out[k] before your
people, O God,
when you marched through the
wasteland,[l] *Selah*
8the earth shook,[m]
the heavens poured down rain,[n]
before God, the One of Sinai,[o]
before God, the God of Israel.[p]
9You gave abundant showers,[q] O God;
you refreshed your weary
inheritance.
10Your people settled in it,
and from your bounty,[r] O God, you
provided[s] for the poor.

11The Lord announced the word,
and great was the company[t] of
those who proclaimed it:
12"Kings and armies flee[u] in haste;
in the camps men divide the
plunder.[v]
13Even while you sleep among the
campfires,[q] [w]
the wings of ⌊my⌋ dove are sheathed
with silver,
its feathers with shining gold."
14When the Almighty[r] scattered[x] the
kings in the land,
it was like snow fallen on Zalmon.[y]

15The mountains of Bashan[z] are
majestic mountains;[a]
rugged are the mountains of Bashan.
16Why gaze in envy, O rugged
mountains,
at the mountain where God
chooses[b] to reign,
where the LORD himself will dwell
forever?[c]
17The chariots[d] of God are tens of
thousands

68:6 [g]Ps 25:16 [h]Ps 113:9 [i]Ps 79:11; 102:20; 146:7; Isa 61:1; Lk 4:18 [j]Isa 35:7; 49:10; 58:11
68:7 [k]S Ex 13:21 [l]Ps 78:40; 106:14
68:8 [m]S 2Sa 22:8 [n]S Jdg 5:4; 2Sa 21:10; Ecc 11:3 [o]S Dt 33:2 [p]S Jdg 5:5
68:9 [q]S Dt 32:2; S Job 36:28; S Eze 34:26
68:10 [r]S Dt 28:12 [s]Ps 65:9
68:11 [t]Lk 2:13
68:12 [u]Jos 10:16 [v]S Jdg 5:30
68:13 [w]S Ge 49:14
68:14 [x]2Sa 22:15 [y]Jdg 9:48
68:15 [z]ver 22; Nu 21:33; Jer 22:20 [a]S Ps 36:6
68:16 [b]Dt 12:5; S Ps 2:6; 132:13 [c]Ps 132:14
68:17 [d]S 2Ki 2:11; Isa 66:15; Hab 3:8 [e]Da 7:10
68:18 [f]S Ps 47:5 [g]Ps 7:7 [h]Jdg 5:12 [i]Eph 4:8* [j]S Nu 17:10
68:19 [k]S Ps 65:5 [l]Ps 81:6
68:20 [m]S 1Sa 10:19 [n]Ps 56:13; Jer 45:5; Eze 6:8
68:21 [o]Ps 74:14; 110:5; Hab 3:13
68:22 [p]S Job 36:30; Mt 18:6
68:23 [q]Ps 58:10 [r]S 1Ki 21:19; S 2Ki 9:36
68:24 [s]S Ps 63:2
68:25 [t]S 1Ch 15:16 [u]S 1Ch 6:31; S 2Ch 5:12; Rev 18:22 [v]S Ge 31:27; S Isa 5:12
68:26 [w]S Ps 22:22; Heb 2:12 [x]S Lev 19:2
68:27 [y]S 1Sa 9:21 [z]S Nu 34:21

and thousands of thousands;[e]
the Lord ⌊has come⌋ from Sinai into
his sanctuary.
18When you ascended[f] on high,[g]
you led captives[h] in your train;
you received gifts from men,[i]
even from[s] the rebellious[j]—
that you,[t] O LORD God, might dwell
there.

19Praise be to the Lord, to God our
Savior,[k]
who daily bears our burdens.[l] *Selah*
20Our God is a God who saves;[m]
from the Sovereign LORD comes
escape from death.[n]

21Surely God will crush the heads[o] of
his enemies,
the hairy crowns of those who go on
in their sins.
22The Lord says, "I will bring them from
Bashan;
I will bring them from the depths of
the sea,[p]
23that you may plunge your feet in the
blood of your foes,[q]
while the tongues of your dogs[r]
have their share."

24Your procession has come into view,
O God,
the procession of my God and King
into the sanctuary.[s]
25In front are the singers,[t] after them
the musicians;[u]
with them are the maidens playing
tambourines.[v]
26Praise God in the great congregation;[w]
praise the LORD in the assembly of
Israel.[x]
27There is the little tribe[y] of Benjamin,[z]
leading them,

[p]6 Or *the desolate in a homeland* [q]13 Or *saddlebags* [r]14 Hebrew *Shaddai* [s]18 Or *gifts for men, / even* [t]18 Or *they*

68:5 GOD, Father—God is Father for the fatherless and needy. This is an idea rooted in the Old Testament and made prominent in the New Testament. Notice that the fatherhood of God is closely related to His sovereignty expressed in the preceding verse. See notes on 2 Sa 7:14; Mt 5:43–48; 6:1–34.

68:5 SALVATION, As Refuge—God is a protector of the needy and oppressed. He wants to be the refuge of those who have no hiding place.

68:6 HUMANITY, Family Relationships—This may refer to Ge 2:18. God intends people to live in families. Human nature has a deep need to be related to other people in a loving and secure relationship. God's people seek out the lonely and unrelated to incorporate them into God's family.

68:16 GOD, Immanent—The sovereign God does not remain aloof in the heavens. He chooses to live, to be present among His people. This is not a temporary decision. It is forever.

68:18 JESUS CHRIST, Foretold—This psalm used in the victory processionals of earthly rulers is quoted in Eph 4:8 to express the exaltation of Jesus Christ. The ascent/descent idea about Jesus—God's Son from heaven coming to earth, descending even to hell and rising above all creation to God's heaven—is a marvelous way of expressing in spatial terms the thoroughness of Christ's redemption.

68:19–20 GOD, Savior—As Savior, God helps with daily problems and needs. He also delivers from death-threatening enemies. By implication He promises escape from the final enemy—death. See notes on 38:22; Lk 1:47; 1 Ti 1:1.

68:20 HUMANITY, Death—God, the Author of life, is the only One who can deliver people from death. In the Psalm context this refers to escape from an enemy seeking the psalmist's life. In the context of the Bible it points to God's power to defeat death itself (1 Co 15:20–28).

68:21 SIN, Judgment—Reflection on history leads to one conclusion: God intervenes in history to defeat His enemies and protect His people. His people have the right to pray for God to intervene today in our history. As we pray, we must leave to God the how and when. See note on Nu 14:23.

68:21 HISTORY, Deliverance—God's delivering actions give His people confidence and form the content of praise.

there the great throng of Judah's
princes,
and there the princes of Zebulun
and of Naphtali.[a]

28Summon your power,[b] O God[u];
show us your strength,[c] O God, as
you have done[d] before.
29Because of your temple at Jerusalem
kings will bring you gifts.[e]
30Rebuke the beast[f] among the reeds,[g]
the herd of bulls[h] among the calves
of the nations.
Humbled, may it bring bars of silver.
Scatter the nations[i] who delight in
war.[j]
31Envoys will come from Egypt;[k]
Cush[v][l] will submit herself to God.

32Sing to God, O kingdoms of the
earth,[m]
sing praise[n] to the Lord, *Selah*
33to him who rides[o] the ancient skies
above,
who thunders[p] with mighty voice.[q]
34Proclaim the power[r] of God,
whose majesty[s] is over Israel,
whose power is in the skies.
35You are awesome,[t] O God, in your
sanctuary;[u]
the God of Israel gives power and
strength[v] to his people.[w]

Praise be to God![x]

Psalm 69

For the director of music. To ⌊the tune of⌋ "Lilies." Of David.

SAVE me, O God,
for the waters[y] have come up to my
neck.[z]
2I sink in the miry depths,[a]
where there is no foothold.
I have come into the deep waters;
the floods engulf me.
3I am worn out calling for help;[b]
my throat is parched.
My eyes fail,[c]
looking for my God.
4Those who hate me[d] without reason[e]
outnumber the hairs of my head;
many are my enemies without cause,[f]
those who seek to destroy me.[g]
I am forced to restore
what I did not steal.

5You know my folly,[h] O God;
my guilt is not hidden from you.[i]

6May those who hope in you
not be disgraced because of me,
O Lord, the LORD Almighty;
may those who seek you
not be put to shame because of me,
O God of Israel.
7For I endure scorn[j] for your sake,[k]
and shame covers my face.[l]
8I am a stranger to my brothers,
an alien to my own mother's sons;[m]
9for zeal for your house consumes me,[n]
and the insults of those who insult
you fall on me.[o]
10When I weep and fast,[p]
I must endure scorn;
11when I put on sackcloth,[q]
people make sport of me.
12Those who sit at the gate[r] mock me,
and I am the song of the
drunkards.[s]

13But I pray to you, O LORD,
in the time of your favor;[t]
in your great love,[u] O God,
answer me with your sure salvation.
14Rescue me from the mire,
do not let me sink;

68:27 [a]S Jdg 5:18 **68:28** [b]S Ex 9:16 [c]Ps 29:11 [d]Isa 26:12; 29:23; 45:11; 60:21; 64:8 **68:29** [e]S 2Ch 9:24; S 32:23 **68:30** [f]Isa 27:1; 51:9; Eze 29:3 [g]S Job 40:21 [h]Ps 22:12; Isa 34:7; Jer 50:27 [i]Ps 18:14; 89:10 [j]Ps 120:7; 140:2 **68:31** [k]Isa 19:19; 43:3; 45:14 [l]Isa 11:11; 18:1; Zep 3:10 **68:32** [m]S Ps 46:6; 67:4 [n]Ps 7:17 **68:33** [o]S Dt 33:26 [p]S Ex 9:23; S Ps 29:3 [q]Ps 29:4; Isa 30:30; 33:3; 66:6 **68:34** [r]ver 28 [s]Ps 45:3 **68:35** [t]S Dt 7:21 [u]S Ge 28:17 [v]Ps 18:1; Isa 40:29; 41:10; 50:2 [w]S Ps 29:11 [x]Ps 28:6; 66:20; 2Co 1:3 **69:1** [y]S Ps 42:7 [z]Ps 32:6; Jnh 2:5 **69:2** [a]S Job 30:19 **69:3** [b]Ps 6:6 [c]Ps 119:82 **69:4** [d]S Ps 25:19 [e]Jn 15:25* [f]S Ps 35:19; 38:19 [g]Ps 40:14; 119:95; Isa 32:7 **69:5** [h]Ps 38:5 [i]S Ps 44:21 **69:7** [j]S Ps 39:8 [k]Jer 15:15 [l]Ps 44:15 **69:8** [m]Job 19:13-15; Ps 31:11; 38:11; Isa 53:3; Jn 7:5 **69:9** [n]Jn 2:17* [o]Ps 89:50-51; Ro 15:3 **69:10** [p]S Ps 35:13 **69:11** [q]S 2Sa 3:31; S Ps 35:13 **69:12** [r]S Ge 18:1; S 23:10 [s]Job 30:9 **69:13** [t]Isa 49:8; 2Co 6:2 [u]S Ps 17:7; 51:1

[u]*28* Many Hebrew manuscripts, Septuagint and Syriac; most Hebrew manuscripts *Your God has summoned power for you* [v]*31* That is, the upper Nile region

68:28–35 GOD, Power—God showed His power to rule all nations when He delivered Israel from Egypt and led them into the Promised Land. Such past experiences lead God's people to ask that God again display His power in another time of great need. Such display of power should lead all people to worship God. See notes on 59:9,16–17; 66:3,7.

69:1–36 GOD, Savior—God as Savior prompts God's people to cry for salvation from desperate circumstances. Such desperation leads to the request that enemies be excluded from God's righteous acts of salvation (v 27). See notes on 38:22; Lk 1:47; 1 Ti 1:1.

69:1–36 EVIL AND SUFFERING, Endurance—See note on 3:1–8. Shame, disgrace, and failure do not separate us from God's love. An Israelite king could admit his defeat, confess his sins (v 5), and ask for God's help. See note on 51:1–19. He sought God's judgment on his enemies (vv 22–28). See note on 35:1–28. Christians will face suffering, some deserved and some undeserved. Like the psalmist, we should repent for our sins and trust in the goodness of God (vv 13,33).

69:1–36 PRAYER, Lament—See note on 3:1–8. This prayer of intense but innocent suffering is one of the two most often quoted psalms in the New Testament. The other is Ps 22. Together they describe the mental and physical anguish of a victim suffering from persecution inflicted for uncommitted crimes. Scorn, disgrace, and shame bring emotional agony, but God's love is a reason for hope and prayer. See notes on 5:10; 6:1–10; 46:1–11; Lev 1:9. Compare Mt 27:34; Mk 15:23; Jn 2:17; 19:28–29.

69:4 JESUS CHRIST, Foretold—The expression "hate me without reason" is a poignant and descriptive phrase expressed by Jesus in John's Gospel (15:25). Compare Ps 35:19. No one has legitimate reason to hate Jesus, who showed us God's love.

69:9 JESUS CHRIST, Foretold—The first part of this verse is quoted in Jn 2:17 and the second part in Ro 15:3. Jesus' cleansing of the Temple was one of the acts which led to the insults heaped upon Him at His death. Jesus extended the meaning when He suggested that whoever hates Him denies the Father; whoever hates the disciples, hates God's representative (Jesus) whom God sent; and whoever hates God's representative, hates God Himself (Jn 15:18–25). Christians need to be very careful not to bring on hatred and scorn to the cause of Christ. We also need to be very critical of our own interpretations, lest we nurse imaginary insults and engender hatred for the cause of Christ.

69:13,16 GOD, Love—God's love is the basis of His being Savior to those who call upon Him. See note on 62:11–12.

deliver me from those who hate me,
from the deep waters.[v]
15Do not let the floodwaters[w] engulf me
or the depths swallow me up[x]
or the pit close its mouth over me.[y]
16Answer me, O LORD, out of the
goodness of your love;[z]
in your great mercy turn to me.
17Do not hide your face[a] from your
servant;
answer me quickly,[b] for I am in
trouble.[c]
18Come near and rescue me;
redeem[d] me because of my foes.
19You know how I am scorned,[e]
disgraced and shamed;
all my enemies are before you.
20Scorn has broken my heart
and has left me helpless;
I looked for sympathy, but there was
none,
for comforters,[f] but I found none.[g]
21They put gall in my food
and gave me vinegar[h] for my
thirst.[i]
22May the table set before them become
a snare;
may it become retribution and[w] a
trap.[j]
23May their eyes be darkened so they
cannot see,
and their backs be bent forever.[k]
24Pour out your wrath[l] on them;
let your fierce anger overtake them.
25May their place be deserted;[m]
let there be no one to dwell in their
tents.[n]
26For they persecute those you wound
and talk about the pain of those you
hurt.[o]
27Charge them with crime upon crime;[p]
do not let them share in your
salvation.[q]
28May they be blotted out of the book of
life[r]
and not be listed with the
righteous.[s]
29I am in pain and distress;
may your salvation, O God, protect
me.[t]
30I will praise God's name in song[u]

69:14 [v]ver 2; Ps 144:7
69:15 [w]Ps 124:4-5 [x]Nu 16:33 [y]Ps 28:1
69:16 [z]S Ps 63:3
69:17 [a]S Ps 22:24 [b]Ps 143:7 [c]S Ps 50:15; 66:14
69:18 [d]Ps 49:15
69:19 [e]S Ps 22:6
69:20 [f]Job 16:2 [g]Ps 142:4; Isa 63:5
69:21 [h]S Nu 6:3; Mt 27:48; Mk 15:36; Lk 23:36 [i]Mt 27:34; Mk 15:23; Jn 19:28-30
69:22 [j]S 1Sa 28:9; S Job 18:10
69:23 [k]Ro 11:9-10*
69:24 [l]Ps 79:6; Jer 10:25
69:25 [m]S Lev 26:43; Mt 23:38 [n]Ac 1:20*
69:26 [o]S Job 19:22; Zec 1:15
69:27 [p]Ne 4:5 [q]Ps 109:14
69:28 [r]Ex 32:32-33; S Lk 10:20 [s]Eze 13:9
69:29 [t]S Ps 20:1
69:30 [u]Ps 28:7 [v]Ps 34:3
69:31 [w]Ps 50:9-13; 51:16
69:32 [x]S Ps 34:2 [y]Ps 22:26
69:33 [z]Ps 12:5
69:34 [a]Ps 96:11; 98:7; Isa 44:23
69:35 [b]Ob 1:17 [c]S Ezr 9:9; S Ps 51:18
69:36 [d]Ps 25:13 [e]S Ps 37:29
70:1 [f]Ps 22:19; 71:12
70:2 [g]Ps 35:4 [h]Ps 6:10; 35:26; 71:13; 109:29; 129:5
70:3 [i]S Ps 35:21
70:4 [j]Ps 9:10 [k]Ps 31:6-7; 32:11; 118:24 [l]Ps 35:27
70:5 [m]Ps 86:1; 109:22 [n]Ps 141:1 [o]Ps 30:10; 33:20 [p]Ps 18:2 [q]Ps 119:60
71:1 [r]S Dt 23:15; Ru 2:12 [s]S Ps 22:5

and glorify him[v] with thanksgiving.
31This will please the LORD more than an
ox,
more than a bull with its horns and
hoofs.[w]
32The poor will see and be glad[x] —
you who seek God, may your hearts
live![y]
33The LORD hears the needy[z]
and does not despise his captive
people.
34Let heaven and earth praise him,
the seas and all that move in them,[a]
35for God will save Zion[b]
and rebuild the cities of Judah.[c]
Then people will settle there and
possess it;
36 the children of his servants will
inherit it,[d]
and those who love his name will
dwell there.[e]

Psalm 70

70:1–5pp — Ps 40:13–17

For the director of music. Of David.
A petition.

HASTEN, O God, to save me;
O LORD, come quickly to help me.[f]
2May those who seek my life[g]
be put to shame and confusion;
may all who desire my ruin
be turned back in disgrace.[h]
3May those who say to me, "Aha!
Aha!"[i]
turn back because of their shame.
4But may all who seek you[j]
rejoice and be glad[k] in you;
may those who love your salvation
always say,
"Let God be exalted!"[l]
5Yet I am poor and needy;[m]
come quickly to me,[n] O God.
You are my help[o] and my deliverer;[p]
O LORD, do not delay.[q]

Psalm 71

71:1–3pp — Ps 31:1–4

IN you, O LORD, I have taken refuge;[r]
let me never be put to shame.[s]

[w]22 Or *snare / and their fellowship become*

69:22–28 CHRISTIAN ETHICS, Language—The same *words used in different* ways may represent different ethical problems and perspectives. These verses spoken to the enemy with the intention to bring the descriptions to pass would represent cursing, hatred, vengeance, anger, and the desire to kill. Taken to God in prayer, the verses represent a healthy way to deal with the anger and frustration that most humans at some time feel and express faith in God to deal with a bad situation. Compare Ps 137. See Guide to Petition, pp. 1765–1767.

69:24 GOD, Wrath—The wrath of God is just as real as His love, but the wrath of God needs to be understood properly. The psalmist asked for God's wrath to be displayed against personal enemies. Such requests are acceptable in prayer, but God chooses when, how, and whether to exercise wrath. See notes on Ge 6:5–8; 17:14; 19:13,24–26; Jos 7:1,25–26; Mt 3:7–10.

70:1–5 EVIL AND SUFFERING, Endurance—See note on 3:1–8.

70:1–5 PRAYER, Lament—See notes on 3:1–8; 40:1–17. The psalmist emphasized his need for quick action. An answer to prayer should result in other people praising God. Humility is a basic attitude for prayer.

71:1–24 EVIL AND SUFFERING, Endurance—In his

2Rescue me and deliver me in your
righteousness;
turn your ear[t] to me and save me.
3Be my rock of refuge,
to which I can always go;
give the command to save me,
for you are my rock and my
fortress.[u]
4Deliver[v] me, O my God, from the
hand of the wicked,[w]
from the grasp of evil and cruel
men.[x]

5For you have been my hope,[y]
O Sovereign LORD,
my confidence[z] since my youth.
6From birth[a] I have relied on you;
you brought me forth from my
mother's womb.[b]
I will ever praise[c] you.
7I have become like a portent[d] to
many,
but you are my strong refuge.[e]
8My mouth[f] is filled with your praise,
declaring your splendor[g] all day
long.

9Do not cast[h] me away when I am
old;[i]
do not forsake[j] me when my
strength is gone.
10For my enemies[k] speak against me;
those who wait to kill[l] me
conspire[m] together.
11They say, "God has forsaken[n] him;
pursue him and seize him,
for no one will rescue[o] him."
12Be not far[p] from me, O God;
come quickly, O my God, to help[q]
me.
13May my accusers[r] perish in shame;[s]
may those who want to harm me
be covered with scorn and
disgrace.[t]
14But as for me, I will always have
hope;[u]
I will praise you more and more.
15My mouth will tell[v] of your
righteousness,[w]
of your salvation all day long,
though I know not its measure.
16I will come and proclaim your mighty
acts,[x] O Sovereign LORD;
I will proclaim your righteousness,
yours alone.
17Since my youth, O God, you have
taught[y] me,
and to this day I declare your
marvelous deeds.[z]
18Even when I am old and gray,[a]
do not forsake me, O God,
till I declare your power[b] to the next
generation,
your might to all who are to come.[c]

19Your righteousness reaches to the
skies,[d] O God,
you who have done great things.[e]
Who, O God, is like you?[f]
20Though you have made me see
troubles,[g] many and bitter,
you will restore[h] my life again;
from the depths of the earth[i]
you will again bring me up.
21You will increase my honor[j]
and comfort[k] me once again.

22I will praise you with the harp[l]
for your faithfulness, O my God;
I will sing praise to you with the lyre,[m]
O Holy One of Israel.[n]
23My lips will shout for joy[o]

71:2 [t]S 2Ki 19:16 **71:3** [u]Ps 18:2 **71:4** [v]S 2Ki 19:19 [w]Ps 140:4 [x]S Ge 48:16 **71:5** [y]S Ps 9:18; S 25:5 [z]S Job 4:6; Jer 17:7 **71:6** [a]S Ps 22:10 [b]S Job 3:16; S Ps 22:9 [c]Ps 9:1; 34:1; 52:9; 119:164; 145:2 **71:7** [d]S Dt 28:46; Isa 8:18; 1Co 4:9 [e]S 2Sa 22:3; Ps 61:3 **71:8** [f]ver 15; Ps 51:15; 63:5 [g]Ps 96:6; 104:1 **71:9** [h]S Ps 51:11 [i]Ps 92:14; Isa 46:4 [j]S Dt 4:31; S 31:6 **71:10** [k]Ps 3:7 [l]S Ps 10:8; 59:3; Pr 1:18 [m]S Ex 1:10; S Ps 31:13; S Mt 12:14 **71:11** [n]S Ps 9:10; Isa 40:27; 54:7; La 5:20; Mt 27:46 [o]S Ps 7:2 **71:12** [p]S Ps 38:21 [q]Ps 22:19; 38:22 **71:13** [r]Jer 18:19 [s]S Job 8:22; Ps 25:3 [t]S Ps 70:2 **71:14** [u]Ps 25:3; 42:5; 130:7; 131:3 **71:15** [v]S ver 8; S Ps 66:16 [w]S Ps 51:14 **71:16** [x]Ps 9:1; 77:12; 106:2; 118:15; 145:4 **71:17** [y]S Dt 4:5; S Jer 7:13 [z]S Job 5:9; Ps 26:7; 86:10; 96:3 **71:18** [a]Isa 46:4 [b]S Ex 9:16 [c]Job 8:8; Ps 22:30, 31; 78:4; 145:4; Joel 1:3 **71:19** [d]S Ps 36:5 [e]Ps 126:2; Lk 1:49 [f]Ps 35:10; 77:13; 89:8 **71:20** [g]Ps 25:17 [h]Ps 80:3,19; 85:4; Hos 6:2 [i]S Ps 63:9 **71:21** [j]Ps 18:35 [k]Ps 23:4; 86:17; Isa 12:1; 40:1-2; 49:13; 54:10 **71:22** [l]Ps 33:2 [m]S Job 21:12; Ps 92:3; 144:9 [n]S 2Ki 19:22 **71:23** [o]Ps 20:5

old age the writer asked for God's help. God does not abandon us because we are old. He sustains us and cares for us throughout life. Becoming older may bring some special problems, but God continues to help us.

71:1,3,7 SALVATION, As Refuge—God is the refuge of His saints in their old age. Other people may look on our physical appearance and condition and think God has punished us in vengeance. We should still turn to Him in trusting prayer as our refuge and salvation.

71:1–24 PRAYER, Lament—See notes on 3:1–8; 7:1–17. The one praying was an old person looking back on a lifetime of trust in the Lord. He was familiar with earlier psalms and freely quoted them in formulating his prayer (vv 1–2 quote 31:1–2; v 6 quotes 22:10; v 24 quotes 35:28). He was under attack from enemies but confident in hope in the Lord. Like many psalms, the initial plea is stated in distress and the final strophe in praise and confidence. Prayer is a part of the believer's life in all situations and at all ages. The act of prayer puts one in closer touch with God and brings renewed confidence.

71:2–3,15–19 GOD, Righteous—In the Psalms, God is frequently called upon to save in His righteousness. This asks *God to act to help the individual or nation in trouble* so that an atmosphere of righteousness may be restored in God's world. Righteousness is as much a source of God's salvation as is His love. See note on 65:5.

71:5–6,15–22 GOD, Faithfulness—God's faithfulness throughout past experiences in life causes us to pray for salvation and deliverance in new circumstances. His faithfulness assures us He will act in righteousness to bring salvation. See note on 57:3,10.

71:14–18 HISTORY, Confession—See note on 26:7. History is the foundation of hope and the content of proclamation for a new generation.

71:14–18 EVANGELISM, Gospel—The gospel is good news that God has acted to meet our needs. In the Old Testament His acts included helping individuals escape their enemies' cruel plans. In the New Testament He acted in Jesus Christ to provide eternal salvation. In both Testaments God's people respond in hope and praise, testifying to all who will listen to God's mighty acts. Youth can share God's gracious acts. So can senior citizens. Our responsibility is to be sure that the next generation knows what God has done for us.

71:20 LAST THINGS, Believers' Resurrection—Deliverance by God from present troubles is like restoration to life if those troubles are many and bitter. God used such experiences of restoration in this life to lead Israelite believers to the belief that God can restore life even from the depths of the earth—the grave (86:13). God who has delivered will go on delivering, even from death. See notes on Hos 13:14; 1 Co 15:50–57.

when I sing praise to you—
I, whom you have redeemed.[p]
24My tongue will tell of your righteous acts
all day long,[q]
for those who wanted to harm me[r]
have been put to shame and confusion.[s]

Psalm 72

Of Solomon.

ENDOW the king with your justice,[t] O God,
the royal son with your righteousness.
2He will[x] judge your people in righteousness,[u]
your afflicted ones with justice.
3The mountains will bring prosperity to the people,
the hills the fruit of righteousness.
4He will defend the afflicted[v] among the people
and save the children of the needy;[w]
he will crush the oppressor.[x]

5He will endure[y][y] as long as the sun,
as long as the moon, through all generations.[z]
6He will be like rain[a] falling on a mown field,
like showers watering the earth.
7In his days the righteous will flourish;[b]
prosperity will abound till the moon is no more.

8He will rule from sea to sea
and from the River[z][c] to the ends of the earth.[a][d]
9The desert tribes will bow before him
and his enemies will lick the dust.
10The kings of Tarshish[e] and of distant shores[f]
will bring tribute to him;
the kings of Sheba[g] and Seba
will present him gifts.[h]
11All kings will bow down[i] to him
and all nations will serve[j] him.
12For he will deliver the needy who cry out,
the afflicted who have no one to help.
13He will take pity[k] on the weak and the needy
and save the needy from death.
14He will rescue[l] them from oppression and violence,
for precious[m] is their blood in his sight.

15Long may he live!
May gold from Sheba[n] be given him.
May people ever pray for him
and bless him all day long.[o]
16Let grain[p] abound throughout the land;
on the tops of the hills may it sway.
Let its fruit[q] flourish like Lebanon;[r]
let it thrive like the grass of the field.[s]
17May his name endure forever;[t]
may it continue as long as the sun.[u]

All nations will be blessed through him,
and they will call him blessed.[v]

18Praise be to the LORD God, the God of Israel,[w]
who alone does marvelous deeds.[x]
19Praise be to his glorious name[y] forever;
may the whole earth be filled with his glory.[z]
Amen and Amen.[a]

20This concludes the prayers of David son of Jesse.[b]

71:23 [p]S Ex 15:13
71:24 [q]S Ps 35:28 [r]ver 13 [s]S Est 9:2
72:1 [t]S Dt 1:16; S Ps 9:8
72:2 [u]Isa 9:7; 11:4-5; 16:5; 32:1; 59:17; 63:1; Jer 23:5; 33:15
72:4 [v]S Ps 9:12; 76:9; Isa 49:13 [w]ver 13; Isa 11:4; 29:19; 32:7 [x]S Ps 27:11
72:5 [y]1Sa 13:13 [z]Ps 33:11
72:6 [a]S Dt 32:2
72:7 [b]Ps 92:12; Pr 14:11
72:8 [c]S Ex 23:31; S 1Ki 4:21 [d]Zec 9:10
72:10 [e]S Ge 10:4 [f]S Est 10:1 [g]S Ge 10:7 [h]S 1Ki 9:16; S 2Ch 9:24
72:11 [i]S Ge 27:29 [j]S Ezr 1:2
72:13 [k]Isa 60:10; Joel 2:18; Lk 10:33
72:14 [l]Ps 69:18; Eze 13:23; 34:10 [m]1Sa 26:21
72:15 [n]S Ge 10:7 [o]S Ps 35:28
72:16 [p]S Ge 27:28; Ps 4:7 [q]Isa 4:2; 27:6; Eze 34:27 [r]Ps 92:12; 104:16 [s]S Nu 22:4; Isa 44:4; 58:11; 66:14
72:17 [t]S Ex 3:15 [u]Ps 89:36 [v]S Ge 12:3; Lk 1:48
72:18 [w]1Ch 29:10; Ps 41:13; 106:48; Lk 1:68 [x]S Job 5:9
72:19 [y]S 2Sa 7:26 [z]Nu 14:21 [a]S Ps 41:13
72:20 [b]S Ru 4:17

x2 Or *May he*; similarly in verses 3-11 and 17 **y**5 Septuagint; Hebrew *You will be feared* **z**8 That is, the Euphrates **a**8 Or *the end of the land*

72:1 GOD, Justice—The justice and the righteousness of God are virtually synonymous terms. God's righteousness is the basis of human righteousness and creates righteousness in others. God not only opposes evil, He seeks to create righteousness in those with whom He deals. Political rulers must rely on God for the qualities needed to rule and judge a people fairly.
72:1–19 JESUS CHRIST, Foretold—Both Jesus and early Christians understood this royal psalm messianically. Exact quotations of it do not appear in the New Testament, but great Christological passages such as Eph 1; Php 2; Col 1; and Hebrews draw out and apply to Christ the majesty and praise expressed in the psalm.
72:1–14 CHRISTIAN ETHICS, Justice—Inherent in the office of the civil leader is the responsibility for delivering the oppressed and using power for justice. God's people need to pray for political leaders to have courage to establish justice.
72:1–20 PRAYER, Politics—This prayer for the righteous reign of the king could well be prayed for a modern ruler or governor. God's people through the ages have seen the psalm as messianic. The hymn "Jesus Shall Reign" is based on this psalm. God's people should make their basic involvement in politics through prayer. Prayer in written form becomes a means of instruction and hope for the future.
72:12–14 SALVATION, Redemption—"Rescue" (Hebrew *ga'al*) may be translated "redeems." See note on Ru 2:20. God redeems the weak and needy from death. Their life is precious to Him.
72:17 EVANGELISM, Salvation—See note on 67:1–2.
72:18–19 HOLY SCRIPTURE, Collection—See note on 41:13.
72:18 HISTORY, God—Historical deliverance is the unique characteristic which establishes God as the only God.
72:18–20 PRAYER, Praise—See note on 41:13.

BOOK III

Psalms 73–89

Psalm 73

A psalm of Asaph.

SURELY God is good to Israel,
to those who are pure in heart.[c]
2But as for me, my feet had almost
slipped;[d]
I had nearly lost my foothold.[e]
3For I envied[f] the arrogant
when I saw the prosperity of the
wicked.[g]

4They have no struggles;
their bodies are healthy and
strong.[b]
5They are free[h] from the burdens
common to man;
they are not plagued by human ills.
6Therefore pride[i] is their necklace;[j]
they clothe themselves with
violence.[k]
7From their callous hearts[l] comes
iniquity[c];
the evil conceits of their minds
know no limits.
8They scoff, and speak with malice;[m]
in their arrogance[n] they threaten
oppression.[o]
9Their mouths lay claim to heaven,
and their tongues take possession of
the earth.
10Therefore their people turn to them
and drink up waters in abundance.[d]
11They say, "How can God know?
Does the Most High have
knowledge?"
12This is what the wicked are like—
always carefree,[p] they increase in
wealth.[q]

13Surely in vain[r] have I kept my heart
pure;
in vain have I washed my hands in
innocence.[s]
14All day long I have been plagued;[t]
I have been punished every
morning.

15If I had said, "I will speak thus,"
I would have betrayed your children.
16When I tried to understand[u] all this,
it was oppressive to me
17till I entered the sanctuary[v] of God;
then I understood their final
destiny.[w]

18Surely you place them on slippery
ground;[x]
you cast them down to ruin.[y]
19How suddenly[z] are they destroyed,
completely swept away[a] by terrors!
20As a dream[b] when one awakes,[c]
so when you arise, O Lord,
you will despise them as fantasies.[d]

21When my heart was grieved
and my spirit embittered,
22I was senseless[e] and ignorant;
I was a brute beast[f] before you.

73:1 [c]S Ps 24:4; Mt 5:8
73:2 [d]S Dt 32:35 [e]Ps 69:2; Eph 4:27
73:3 [f]Pr 3:31; 23:17; 24:1-2 [g]S Job 9:24; S 21:7; Jer 12:1; Mal 3:15
73:5 [h]ver 12; Eze 23:42
73:6 [i]S Lev 26:19 [j]S Ge 41:42; SS 4:9; Eze 16:11 [k]S Ge 6:11; S Pr 4:17
73:7 [l]S Ps 17:10
73:8 [m]Ps 41:5; Eze 25:15; Col 3:8 [n]Ps 17:10 [o]S Ps 10:7; S 12:5
73:12 [p]S ver 5 [q]S Ps 49:6
73:13 [r]S Job 9:29-31; S 21:15 [s]S Ge 44:16
73:14 [t]ver 5
73:16 [u]Ecc 8:17
73:17 [v]Ex 15:17; Ps 15:1 [w]S Job 8:13; Php 3:19
73:18 [x]S Dt 32:35; Ps 35:6 [y]S Ps 17:13
73:19 [z]Dt 28:20; Pr 24:22; Isa 47:11 [a]S Ge 19:15
73:20 [b]S Job 20:8 [c]Ps 78:65; Isa 29:8 [d]Pr 12:11; 28:19
73:22 [e]Ps 49:10; 92:6; 94:8 [f]Ps 49:12,20; Ecc 3:18; 9:12

[b]*4* With a different word division of the Hebrew; Masoretic Text *struggles at their death; / their bodies are healthy* [c]*7* Syriac (see also Septuagint); Hebrew *Their eyes bulge with fat* [d]*10* The meaning of the Hebrew for this verse is uncertain.

73:1 GOD, Goodness—God is good in relationship to His people. We can find nothing to criticize in His character or in His dealings with us. He delivers us from enemies and brings us into His glorious presence (v 24). See note on Mt 19:17.
73:1–28 EVIL AND SUFFERING, God's Future Help—See note on 37:1–40. The psalmist was disturbed by the prosperity of the wicked but learned that God would eventually punish them. We are often impatient with the injustices of life, but God's justice will prevail. We can discuss our frustrations with God candidly, knowing the prosperity of the wicked is only temporary. God knows the world's wickedness and injustice. He has plans to establish His kingdom and eliminate that which opposes Him. Only in worship do God's people learn of God's plans and gain assurance of His judgment on evil.
73:1–28 SIN, Depravity—Sin often begins with envy of another's success in earthly terms. The sinful thought is that God blesses the righteous, so the prosperous must be righteous. Thus, we justify our imitation of sinful actions to gain blessings. We forget our ignorance. We do not know another person's total experience. They may not see themselves as blessed. They may envy our situation. We do not have God's vision of the whole. Eventually He will ensure just reward and punishment for all even if He waits to eternity. When we confess that the Most High God has all knowledge, we will dismiss human envious thoughts and not take the first step to sin. We will know righteous action is not in vain. We will wait for the glory God has for us (v 24).
73:1–28 PRAYER, Thanksgiving—See note on 18:1–50. The psalmist did not understand the prosperity of the wicked until he entered God's sanctuary. He gave thanks by repeating his own experience. Fastening his eyes on appearances led to insensitivity and bitterness. As a Levite in Asaph's family (1 Ch 6:39), his inheritance was the Lord (Dt 10:9). He affirmed that God was his desire and his strength. In common with Abraham, God was the psalmist's very great reward (Ge 15:1). Experience taught him confidence in God's goodness despite outward appearances. Prayer can help us see our situation in a new light, the light of God's presence and goodness.
73:11 GOD, Wisdom—Unbelievers scoff at God, not realizing He knows everyone and everything. See note on 44:21.
73:16–28 HOLY SCRIPTURE, Inspiration—Lack of understanding is cleared when the worshiper receives God's revelation in the sanctuary. Seeking God is regularly expressed by going to God's Temple to be receptive to His inspiration (literally God breathing truth into a person's life). Unclear events begin to take on meaning and purpose to the one who seeks God's revelation. Awed by the presence of God, the psalmist affirmed that God was with him even when he left the sanctuary. Neither space nor time can separate us from the revelation of God's presence.
73:21–22 HUMANITY, Psychological Nature—"Spirit" may be literally translated as "kidneys." Even as the heart refers to the mind in the Old Testament, so kidneys refers to the seat of the emotions. A person who loses control of both the intellect and the emotions is acting no better than an animal. Human beings may operate on this animal level, but in so doing they miss the life of meaningful relationships God intends us to have. Living life in God's presence and under His direction lifts us above the animal level of existence.

23Yet I am always with you;
you hold me by my right hand.[g]
24You guide[h] me with your counsel,[i]
and afterward you will take me into glory.
25Whom have I in heaven but you?[j]
And earth has nothing I desire besides you.[k]
26My flesh and my heart[l] may fail,[m]
but God is the strength[n] of my heart
and my portion[o] forever.

27Those who are far from you will perish;[p]
you destroy all who are unfaithful[q] to you.
28But as for me, it is good to be near God.[r]
I have made the Sovereign LORD my refuge;[s]
I will tell of all your deeds.[t]

Psalm 74

A *maskil*[e] of Asaph.

WHY have you rejected[u] us forever,[v] O God?
Why does your anger smolder against the sheep of your pasture?[w]
2Remember the people you purchased[x] of old,[y]
the tribe of your inheritance,[z]
whom you redeemed[a]—
Mount Zion,[b] where you dwelt.[c]
3Turn your steps toward these everlasting ruins,[d]
all this destruction the enemy has brought on the sanctuary.

4Your foes roared[e] in the place where you met with us;
they set up their standards[f] as signs.
5They behaved like men wielding axes
to cut through a thicket of trees.[g]
6They smashed all the carved[h] paneling
with their axes and hatchets.
7They burned your sanctuary to the ground;
they defiled[i] the dwelling place[j] of your Name.[k]
8They said in their hearts, "We will crush[l] them completely!"
They burned[m] every place where God was worshiped in the land.

9We are given no miraculous signs;[n]
no prophets[o] are left,
and none of us knows how long this will be.
10How long[p] will the enemy mock[q] you, O God?
Will the foe revile[r] your name forever?
11Why do you hold back your hand, your right hand?[s]
Take it from the folds of your garment[t] and destroy them!

12But you, O God, are my king[u] from of old;
you bring salvation[v] upon the earth.
13It was you who split open the sea[w] by your power;
you broke the heads of the monster[x] in the waters.
14It was you who crushed the heads of Leviathan[y]
and gave him as food to the creatures of the desert.[z]
15It was you who opened up springs[a] and streams;
you dried up[b] the ever flowing rivers.

73:23 [g]S Ge 48:13 **73:24** [h]S Ps 48:14 [i]S 1Ki 22:5 **73:25** [j]Ps 16:2 [k]Php 3:8 **73:26** [l]Ps 84:2 [m]S Ps 31:10; 40:12 [n]Ps 18:1 [o]S Dt 32:9 **73:27** [p]S Ps 34:21 [q]S Lev 6:2; Jer 5:11; Hos 4:12; 9:1 **73:28** [r]Zep 3:2; Heb 10:22; Jas 4:8 [s]Ps 9:9 [t]Ps 26:7; 40:5 **74:1** [u]S Ps 43:2 [v]S Ps 44:23 [w]Ps 79:13; 95:7; 100:3 **74:2** [x]S Ex 15:16; S 1Co 6:20 [y]S Dt 32:7 [z]S Ex 34:9 [a]S Ex 15:13; S Isa 48:20 [b]Ps 2:6 [c]Ps 43:3; 68:16; Isa 46:13; Joel 3:17, 21; Ob 1:17 **74:3** [d]Isa 44:26; 52:9 **74:4** [e]La 2:7 [f]S Nu 2:2; S Jer 4:6 **74:5** [g]Jer 46:22 **74:6** [h]S 1Ki 6:18 **74:7** [i]S Lev 20:3; Ac 21:28 [j]S Lev 15:31 [k]Ps 75:1 **74:8** [l]Ps 94:5 [m]2Ki 25:9; 2Ch 36:19; Jer 21:10; 34:22; 52:13 **74:9** [n]S Ex 4:17; S 10:1 [o]S 1Sa 3:1 **74:10** [p]Ps 6:3; 79:5; 80:4 [q]ver 22 [r]S Ps 44:16 **74:11** [s]S Ex 15:6 [t]Ne 5:13; Eze 5:3 **74:12** [u]Ps 2:6; S 24:7; 68:24 [v]Ps 27:1 **74:13** [w]S Ex 14:21 [x]Isa 27:1; 51:9; Eze 29:3; 32:2 **74:14** [y]S Job 3:8 [z]Isa 13:21; 23:13; 34:14; Jer 50:39 **74:15** [a]S Ex 17:6; S Nu 20:11 [b]S Ex 14:29; S Jos 2:10

[e]Title: Probably a literary or musical term

73:27–28 HUMANITY, Relationship to God—Since God is the Source of life, those who separate themselves from God have separated themselves from life itself.
73:28 SALVATION, As Refuge—The psalmist made the Lord his refuge that he might tell of God's deeds. We speak of this as the inward and outward journey. The doctrine of salvation teaches us that we should go deeper with God in order to go out and tell others what He has done for us. Worship and witness belong together in the doctrine of salvation.
74:1 GOD, Wrath—See note on 69:24.
74:1–23 EVIL AND SUFFERING, Endurance—See note on 3:1–8. Can God be defeated? Do we suffer because God has lost control? Israel pondered such questions when Babylon conquered their land and destroyed the Temple in 587 BC. External circumstances indicated God was out of business. The people did not know where to turn to hear His word or see evidence of His presence. A look to past experiences with God helped. God's power over the forces of evil is illustrated by His control of Leviathan (v 14), who represents evil or chaos. Although evil and destructive natural forces are a threat to us, the ultimate power is God's. God created the world, controls it, and will not let His enemies be victorious. See note on Job 26:12–13.
74:1–23 PRAYER, Lament—Prayer helps a distressed nation. Judah suffered the savage destruction of its sanctuary. The appeal was based on Israel's identification with God. Seeing the signs of the oppressor, the psalmist, representing Israel, called for the signs of God. The mighty acts of the enemy were puny compared with those of the sovereign God, who hears the helpless and needy. All needs—personal, congregational, and national—can be addressed to God in prayer. Remembering what God has done gives us confidence to carry present needs to Him. Lament does not always end in immediate answer and confidence. See note on 6:1–10. It may continue with questions and petitions from beginning to end.
74:9 MIRACLE, Faith—Miracles give suffering, despairing people reason for faith and hope. During the exile with Jerusalem in ruins, the psalmist pleaded for God to act. A miracle would provide evidence of the Lord's presence and purpose. The absence of miracles was a source of great grief. In periods of grief we can call on God for miracles to encourage us. In His time He will give us what we need.
74:9–23 HISTORY, Hope—Some generations do not see marvelous historic deliverance. They suffer oppression. God's past acts give reason to pray for help with confidence God will ultimately establish His people and purposes.

16The day is yours, and yours also the
night;
you established the sun and moon.[c]
17It was you who set all the boundaries[d]
of the earth;
you made both summer and
winter.[e]

18Remember how the enemy has
mocked you, O LORD,
how foolish people[f] have reviled
your name.
19Do not hand over the life of your
dove[g] to wild beasts;
do not forget the lives of your
afflicted[h] people forever.
20Have regard for your covenant,[i]
because haunts of violence fill the
dark places[j] of the land.
21Do not let the oppressed[k] retreat in
disgrace;
may the poor and needy[l] praise
your name.

22Rise up,[m] O God, and defend your
cause;
remember how fools[n] mock you all
day long.
23Do not ignore the clamor[o] of your
adversaries,[p]
the uproar[q] of your enemies,[r]
which rises continually.

Psalm 75

For the director of music. ⌞To the tune of⌟ "Do Not Destroy." A psalm of Asaph. A song.

WE give thanks to you, O God,
we give thanks, for your Name is
near;[s]
men tell of your wonderful deeds.[t]

2You say, "I choose the appointed
time;[u]
it is I who judge uprightly.[v]

74:16 [c]S Ge 1:16; Ps 136:7-9
74:17 [d]Dt 32:8; Ac 17:26 [e]S Ge 8:22
74:18 [f]Dt 32:6
74:19 [g]S Ge 8:8; S Isa 59:11 [h]S Ps 9:18
74:20 [i]S Ge 6:18 [j]Job 34:22
74:21 [k]Ps 9:9; 10:18; 103:6; Isa 58:10 [l]S Ps 35:10
74:22 [m]Ps 17:13 [n]S Ps 53:1
74:23 [o]Isa 31:4 [p]S Ps 65:7 [q]S Ps 46:6 [r]S Nu 25:17
75:1 [s]Ps 145:18 [t]S Jos 3:5; Ps 44:1; S 71:16; 77:12; 105:2; 107:8,15; 145:5,12
75:2 [u]S Ex 13:10 [v]S Ps 7:11
75:3 [w]Isa 24:19 [x]1Sa 2:8; S 2Sa 22:8
75:4 [y]S Ps 5:5 [z]S 1Sa 2:3 [a]Zec 1:21
75:5 [b]S Job 15:25
75:7 [c]S Ge 16:5; Ps 50:6; 58:11; Rev 18:8 [d]1Sa 2:7; S Job 5:11; Ps 147:6; Eze 21:26; Da 2:21
75:8 [e]Pr 23:30 [f]Isa 51:17; Jer 25:15; Zec 12:2
75:9 [g]Ps 40:10 [h]Ps 108:1 [i]S Ge 24:12; Ps 76:6
75:10 [j]Ps 89:17; 92:10; 112:9; 148:14
76:1 [k]Ps 99:3
76:2 [l]S Ge 14:18; Heb 7:1 [m]S 2Sa 5:7; Ps 2:6
76:3 [n]Eze 39:9 [o]Ps 46:9
76:4 [p]S Ps 36:9

3When the earth and all its people
quake,[w]
it is I who hold its pillars[x] firm.
Selah
4To the arrogant[y] I say, 'Boast no
more,'[z]
and to the wicked, 'Do not lift up
your horns.[a]
5Do not lift your horns against heaven;
do not speak with outstretched
neck.[b]' "

6No one from the east or the west
or from the desert can exalt a man.
7But it is God who judges:[c]
He brings one down, he exalts
another.[d]
8In the hand of the LORD is a cup
full of foaming wine mixed[e] with
spices;
he pours it out, and all the wicked of
the earth
drink it down to its very dregs.[f]

9As for me, I will declare[g] this forever;
I will sing[h] praise to the God of
Jacob.[i]
10I will cut off the horns of all the
wicked,
but the horns of the righteous will
be lifted up.[j]

Psalm 76

For the director of music. With stringed instruments. A psalm of Asaph. A song.

IN Judah God is known;
his name is great[k] in Israel.
2His tent is in Salem,[l]
his dwelling place in Zion.[m]
3There he broke the flashing arrows,[n]
the shields and the swords, the
weapons of war.[o] *Selah*
4You are resplendent with light,[p]
more majestic than mountains rich
with game.

74:20 THE CHURCH, Covenant People—In times of trouble people often wonder if God will be faithful. The psalmist prayed for God to remember His covenant. Other Scripture passages demonstrate the faith of believers that God will lead His people through troubled times. Our first step in troubled times is to pray to God, describe our troubles, and seek His help.

75:1–10 EVIL AND SUFFERING, Human Origin—Human pride brings suffering and wickedness to the earth. The basis for such pride is short-lived. God will judge the wicked.

75:1–10 PRAYER, Thanksgiving—See note on 18:1–50. This is an unusual prayer, a dialogue between heaven and earth. The psalmist began with plural thanksgiving and ended in singular praise. Thanksgiving acknowledges God as the source of all good. God responded with His declaration that He is the Judge and will deal with the arrogant who do not acknowledge Him (vv 2–5). The psalmist agreed (vv 6–8) and proceeded with praise. God had the final word. Thanksgiving can be a congregational act. It can represent dialogue with God. It leads to renewed assurance for the future. The individual should praise God as a result of the congregational thanks.

75:2,7 GOD, Judge—As Judge, God has the sovereign authority to rule this world. He judges fairly, bringing the thanks of His people. See notes on Ge 3:8–24; Ro 2:2.

76:1 REVELATION, Events—God's presence is revealed when He acts to save His people. Deliverance from enemy armies revealed God is powerful, present among His people, active in the land He chose for them, and able to redeem. God's love and purpose were manifested in the saving of His children from destruction. V 1 did not limit revelation geographically but confessed what God had done among His people.

76:1–10 HISTORY, Deliverance—God's acts in history are a major source of revelation for His people. They show that no one and nothing else should be worshiped.

76:1–12 PRAYER, Sovereignty of God—One of the paradoxes of prayer is stated here. God rules earth from heaven (v 8) and yet expressed His presence peculiarly in Jerusalem (v 2). His universal presence finds peculiar local expression. Before His unique power, people and nature are paralyzed. Prayer focuses on and claims the presence of God for the present situation. See note on 48:1–14.

5Valiant men[q] lie plundered,
they sleep their last sleep;[r]
not one of the warriors
can lift his hands.
6At your rebuke,[s] O God of Jacob,
both horse and chariot[t] lie still.
7You alone are to be feared.[u]
Who can stand[v] before you when
you are angry?[w]
8From heaven you pronounced
judgment,
and the land feared[x] and was
quiet—
9when you, O God, rose up to judge,[y]
to save all the afflicted[z] of the land.
Selah
10Surely your wrath against men brings
you praise,[a]
and the survivors of your wrath are
restrained.[f]
11Make vows to the LORD your God and
fulfill them;[b]
let all the neighboring lands
bring gifts[c] to the One to be feared.
12He breaks the spirit of rulers;
he is feared by the kings of the
earth.

Psalm 77

For the director of music. For Jeduthun.
Of Asaph. A psalm.

I cried out to God[d] for help;
I cried out to God to hear me.
2When I was in distress,[e] I sought the
Lord;
at night[f] I stretched out untiring
hands[g]
and my soul refused to be
comforted.[h]
3I remembered[i] you, O God, and I
groaned;[j]
I mused, and my spirit grew faint.[k]
Selah
4You kept my eyes from closing;
I was too troubled to speak.[l]
5I thought about the former days,[m]
the years of long ago;
6I remembered my songs in the night.
My heart mused and my spirit
inquired:
7"Will the Lord reject forever?[n]
Will he never show his favor[o]
again?
8Has his unfailing love[p] vanished
forever?
Has his promise[q] failed for all time?
9Has God forgotten to be merciful?[r]
Has he in anger withheld his
compassion?[s]"
Selah
10Then I thought, "To this I will appeal:
the years of the right hand[t] of the
Most High."
11I will remember the deeds of the
LORD;
yes, I will remember your miracles[u]
of long ago.
12I will meditate[v] on all your works
and consider all your mighty
deeds.[w]
13Your ways, O God, are holy.
What god is so great as our God?[x]
14You are the God who performs
miracles;[y]
you display your power among the
peoples.
15With your mighty arm you redeemed
your people,[z]
the descendants of Jacob and Joseph.
Selah
16The waters[a] saw you, O God,
the waters saw you and writhed;[b]
the very depths were convulsed.
17The clouds poured down water,[c]
the skies resounded with thunder;[d]
your arrows[e] flashed back and forth.
18Your thunder was heard in the
whirlwind,[f]
your lightning[g] lit up the world;

76:5 [q]S Jdg 20:44 [r]S Ps 13:3; S Mt 9:24
76:6 [s]S Ps 50:21 [t]S Ex 15:1
76:7 [u]S 1Ch 16:25 [v]S Ezr 9:15; Rev 6:17 [w]Ps 2:5; Na 1:6
76:8 [x]S 1Ch 16:30; Eze 38:20
76:9 [y]S Ps 9:8; 58:11; 74:22; 82:8; 96:13 [z]S Ps 72:4
76:10 [a]Ex 9:16; Ro 9:17
76:11 [b]S Lev 22:18; S Ps 50:14; Ecc 5:4-5 [c]S 2Ch 32:23
77:1 [d]S 1Ki 8:52
77:2 [e]S Ge 32:7; S 2Sa 22:7; S Ps 118:5 [f]Ps 6:6; 22:2; 88:1 [g]S Ex 9:29; S Job 11:13 [h]S Ge 37:35; Mt 2:18
77:3 [i]Ps 78:35 [j]Ex 2:23; S Ps 6:6; Jer 45:3 [k]S Ps 6:2
77:4 [l]S Ps 39:2
77:5 [m]Dt 32:7; Ps 44:1; 143:5; Ecc 7:10
77:7 [n]S 1Ch 28:9 [o]Ps 85:1; 102:13; 106:4
77:8 [p]S Ps 6:4; 90:14 [q]2Pe 3:9
77:9 [r]Ps 25:6; 40:11; 51:1 [s]Isa 49:15
77:10 [t]S Ex 15:6
77:11 [u]S Ne 9:17
77:12 [v]S Ge 24:63 [w]Ps 143:5
77:13 [x]S Ex 15:11; S Ps 71:19; 86:8
77:14 [y]S Ex 3:20; S 34:10
77:15 [z]S Ex 6:6
77:16 [a]Ex 14:21, 28; Isa 50:2; Hab 3:8 [b]Ps 114:4; Hab 3:10
77:17 [c]S Jdg 5:4 [d]S Ex 9:23; S Ps 29:3 [e]S Dt 32:23
77:18 [f]S Ps 55:8 [g]S 2Sa 22:13

[f]10 Or *Surely the wrath of men brings you praise, / and with the remainder of wrath you arm yourself*

76:7,10–11 GOD, Wrath—See note on 69:24.
76:8–9 GOD, Judge—God as Judge and Savior might seem to be opposites, but these verses relate the ideas closely. Whether as Judge or as Savior, all God does is righteous and seeks to help the afflicted and needy.
76:11 EVANGELISM, Obedience—God has acted in wrath against all powers of evil. His people respond with vows, promising to serve the Lord. Obedience to our Lord demands such a response. One vow God wants us to make is to tell the world of His salvation.
77:1–20 EVIL AND SUFFERING, Endurance—See note on 3:1–8. Is God's love temporary? Can anger be His final word? Suffering and despair may lead us to think so. A long look at God's history with His people will change our minds. He has repeatedly shown us His everlasting love. His anger acts only to discipline us and call us back to Him. In suffering we need to look back and remember what God has done for us.
77:1–20 REVELATION, History—Memories from the past bring revelation to help in present trouble. A sleepless night of prayer led the psalmist back to the Exodus. Reflection on God's history of salvation renewed confidence to face the new crisis. Such reflection reveals anew the nature of God.
77:1–20 PRAYER, Lament—This singularly depressed prayer states the dread questions which occur often to Christians in affliction (vv 7–9). The psalmist, however, based faith not on present circumstances but on the past record of God's might and His redemptive use of that might on behalf of His people (vv 10–20). The hope of the future is not in the disastrous potential of circumstances but in the unchanging record of God's salvation in the past. Prayer can raise any question with God and find hope in past experiences with Him.
77:8 GOD, Faithfulness—In despair the psalmist questioned both the love and the faithfulness of God. He feared God's wrath had taken the upper hand. In vv 11–20 the psalmist gained reassurance by rehearsing God's history with His people. See notes on 69:13,16; 71:5–6,15–22.
77:11–20 HISTORY, Confession—See note on 26:7.

the earth trembled and quaked.[h]
19Your path[i] led through the sea,[j]
your way through the mighty
waters,
though your footprints were not
seen.

20You led your people[k] like a flock[l]
by the hand of Moses and Aaron.[m]

Psalm 78

A *maskil*[g] of Asaph.

O my people, hear my teaching;[n]
listen to the words of my mouth.
2I will open my mouth in parables,[o]
I will utter hidden things, things
from of old—
3what we have heard and known,
what our fathers have told us.[p]
4We will not hide them from their
children;[q]
we will tell the next generation[r]
the praiseworthy deeds[s] of the LORD,
his power, and the wonders[t] he has
done.
5He decreed statutes[u] for Jacob[v]
and established the law in Israel,
which he commanded our forefathers
to teach their children,

77:18 hS Jdg 5:4
77:19 iS Ex 14:22 jS Job 9:8
77:20 kS Ex 13:21 lPs 78:52; Isa 63:11 mS Ex 4:16; S Nu 33:1
78:1 nIsa 51:4; 55:3
78:2 oS Ps 49:4; S Mt 13:35*
78:3 pS Jdg 6:13
78:4 qS Dt 11:19 rS Dt 32:7; S Ps 71:18 sPs 26:7; 71:17 tS Job 5:9
78:5 uPs 19:7; 81:5 vPs 147:19
78:6 wS Ps 22:31
78:7 xS Dt 6:12 yS Dt 5:29
78:8 zS 2Ch 30:7 aS Ex 32:9 bS Ex 23:21; S Dt 21:18; Isa 30:9; 65:2
78:9 cver 57; 1Ch 12:2; Hos 7:16 dS Jdg 20:39
78:10 eS Jos 7:11; S 2Ki 17:15 fS Ex 16:28; S Jer 11:8
78:11 gPs 106:13
78:12 hS Ne 9:17; Ps 106:22 iEx 11:9 jS Nu 13:22
78:13 kS Ex 14:21; Ps 66:6; 136:13

6so the next generation would know
them,
even the children yet to be born,[w]
and they in turn would tell their
children.
7Then they would put their trust in God
and would not forget[x] his deeds
but would keep his commands.[y]
8They would not be like their
forefathers[z]—
a stubborn[a] and rebellious[b]
generation,
whose hearts were not loyal to God,
whose spirits were not faithful to
him.

9The men of Ephraim, though armed
with bows,[c]
turned back on the day of battle;[d]
10they did not keep God's covenant[e]
and refused to live by his law.[f]
11They forgot what he had done,[g]
the wonders he had shown them.
12He did miracles[h] in the sight of their
fathers
in the land of Egypt,[i] in the region
of Zoan.[j]
13He divided the sea[k] and led them
through;

[g]Title: Probably a literary or musical term

78:1–72 GOD, Wrath—This long psalm has numerous expressions of the wrath of God against the sin of the people, as they failed to live in faithful obedience. Such examples of wrath serve to teach the next generation. See note on 30:5.

78:1–22 EVIL AND SUFFERING, Punishment—Especially in times of hurt and trouble we need to look back in history and see how God had just reason to punish His people. History should be the story of God testing His people and finding us faithful. Too often it is the story of our testing God and complaining that He does not act as we demand. Our patient God restrains His anger in mercy but eventually punishes us for habitual, unrepented sins.

78:1–72 SIN, Serious—The next generation must know how serious sin is in disrupting individual and communal life and in alienating us from God. We must use our experiences and our traditions to teach our children the nature of sin. The next generation needs to learn the faithfulness and loyalty to God we did not practice. They need to see the various characteristics of sin: broken covenants, disobeyed law, saving acts forgotten, rebellion against His leadership, making demands which test God, doubting God's power, not trusting God to save in time of need, lying to God with flattery, being unreliable, and worshiping other gods. Sin takes many forms. Each is serious, and the next generation needs warning against all forms of sin.

78:1–6 HOLY SCRIPTURE, Word—The worship leader affirmed the teachings of God learned from previous generations. God's Word included narratives of God's actions and statements of God's expectations. The psalmist incorporated teachings learned in worship into his teaching psalm, which God led His people to incorporate into Holy Scripture.

78:1–72 HISTORY, God's Will—God's actions and His revealed moral will are closely connected. He delivered His people in the Exodus to lead them to the mountain of revelation where they received His commandments. Forgetfulness of His commandments proved disastrous in their history. History can thus be confessed as a history of human sin and divine mercy. Such a history calls the present generation to teach both God's acts and God's will to the next generation.

78:1–72 PRAYER, Instruction—See note on 15:1–5. Public instruction became collected among the prayers in the psalter. The call to people to listen thus became a call to God to keep proper teaching alive among His people.

78:1–6 EDUCATION, Parents—Though scattered and persecuted, the Jews have managed to maintain their ethnic and religious identity from ancient times until the present day. One of the important reasons for this perserverance lies in their continued teaching of the faith from one generation to another. The psalmist reflected the long-range perspective of his people when he stressed the importance of teaching not only the next generation but even the children of those who are not yet born. See note on Dt 6:1–10.

78:1–8 FAMILY, Bible Study—The psalmist prayed that the commandments and actions of the Lord would be studied and communicated to the next generation in the home. Only in this way can children be led to put their trust in the Lord and obey His teachings. No generation becomes Christian at birth. Each individual must learn to love and obey God. Parental love and teaching is the biblical model to lead children to God. No other institution can be more effective than the home.

78:2 JESUS CHRIST, Foretold—In quoting this verse, Matthew described and defended Jesus' favorite method of teaching, teaching by parables (Mt 13:35).

78:5–8 CHRISTIAN ETHICS, Covenant—God's covenant demands grow out of His loving, saving deeds. These deeds show us we can trust Him and His goodness. See note on Ge 18:19.

78:10,37 THE CHURCH, Covenant People—History teaches the reality of God's judgment on a disobedient covenant people. In His faithfulness God seeks to save and lead His people, but He will discipline a people who reject Him (v 67). See notes on 1 Ki 19:10,14; 2 Ch 13:1–20.

78:13–72 MIRACLE, Redemption—Miracles should be unforgettable and form the heart of the tradition we teach our children. Miracles should help keep us from rebelling against God and being unfaithful to Him. Forgetting God's miracles is a beginning point for sin and disobedience. The psalmist sang of God's mighty acts in redeeming His people. He sang with

he made the water stand firm like a
wall.[l]
14He guided them with the cloud by day
and with light from the fire all
night.[m]
15He split the rocks[n] in the desert
and gave them water as abundant as
the seas;
16he brought streams out of a rocky crag
and made water flow down like
rivers.

17But they continued to sin[o] against
him,
rebelling in the desert against the
Most High.
18They willfully put God to the test[p]
by demanding the food they
craved.[q]
19They spoke against God,[r] saying,
"Can God spread a table in the
desert?
20When he struck the rock, water
gushed out,[s]
and streams flowed abundantly.
But can he also give us food?
Can he supply meat[t] for his
people?"
21When the LORD heard them, he was
very angry;
his fire broke out[u] against Jacob,
and his wrath rose against Israel,
22for they did not believe in God
or trust[v] in his deliverance.
23Yet he gave a command to the skies
above
and opened the doors of the
heavens;[w]
24he rained down manna[x] for the people
to eat,
he gave them the grain of heaven.
25Men ate the bread of angels;
he sent them all the food they could
eat.
26He let loose the east wind[y] from the
heavens
and led forth the south wind by his
power.
27He rained meat down on them like
dust,
flying birds[z] like sand on the
seashore.
28He made them come down inside their
camp,
all around their tents.
29They ate till they had more than
enough,[a]
for he had given them what they
craved.

78:13 [l]S Ex 14:22; S 15:8
78:14 [m]Ex 13:21; Ps 105:39
78:15 [n]S Nu 20:11; 1Co 10:4
78:17 [o]ver 32,40; Dt 9:22; Isa 30:1; 63:10; Heb 3:16
78:18 [p]S Ex 17:2; 1Co 10:9 [q]S Ex 15:24; Nu 11:4
78:19 [r]Nu 21:5
78:20 [s]S Nu 20:11; S Isa 35:6 [t]Nu 11:18
78:21 [u]S Nu 11:1
78:22 [v]S Dt 1:32; Heb 3:19
78:23 [w]Ge 7:11; S 2Ki 7:2
78:24 [x]Ex 16:4; Jn 6:31*
78:26 [y]S Nu 11:31
78:27 [z]S Ex 16:13; Nu 11:31
78:29 [a]S Nu 11:20
78:30 [b]S Nu 11:33
78:31 [c]Isa 10:16
78:32 [d]S ver 17 [e]ver 11 [f]ver 22
78:33 [g]Nu 14:29, 35
78:34 [h]S Dt 4:29; Hos 5:15
78:35 [i]S Ge 49:24 [j]S Dt 9:26
78:36 [k]Eze 33:31
78:37 [l]ver 8; Ac 8:21
78:38 [m]S Ex 34:6 [n]Isa 1:25; 27:9; 48:10; Da 11:35 [o]Ps 25:11; 85:2 [p]S Job 9:13; S Isa 30:18
78:39 [q]S Ge 6:3; S Isa 29:5 [r]S Job 7:7; Jas 4:14
78:40 [s]S Ex 23:21 [t]Ps 95:8; 106:14 [u]Eph 4:30
78:41 [v]S Ex 17:2 [w]S 2Ki 19:22; Ps 71:22; 89:18
78:42 [x]S Jdg 3:7; S Ne 9:17 [y]S Ps 27:11
78:43 [z]Ex 10:1 [a]S Ex 3:20
78:44 [b]Ex 7:20-21; Ps 105:29
78:45 [c]Ex 8:24; Ps 105:31 [d]S Ex 8:2,6

30But before they turned from the food
they craved,
even while it was still in their
mouths,[b]
31God's anger rose against them;
he put to death the sturdiest[c]
among them,
cutting down the young men of
Israel.

32In spite of all this, they kept on
sinning;[d]
in spite of his wonders,[e] they did
not believe.[f]
33So he ended their days in futility[g]
and their years in terror.
34Whenever God slew them, they would
seek[h] him;
they eagerly turned to him again.
35They remembered that God was their
Rock,[i]
that God Most High was their
Redeemer.[j]
36But then they would flatter him with
their mouths,[k]
lying to him with their tongues;
37their hearts were not loyal[l] to him,
they were not faithful to his
covenant.
38Yet he was merciful;[m]
he forgave[n] their iniquities[o]
and did not destroy them.
Time after time he restrained his
anger[p]
and did not stir up his full wrath.
39He remembered that they were but
flesh,[q]
a passing breeze[r] that does not
return.

40How often they rebelled[s] against him
in the desert[t]
and grieved him[u] in the wasteland!
41Again and again they put God to the
test;[v]
they vexed the Holy One of Israel.[w]
42They did not remember[x] his power—
the day he redeemed them from the
oppressor,[y]
43the day he displayed his miraculous
signs[z] in Egypt,
his wonders[a] in the region of
Zoan.
44He turned their rivers to blood;[b]
they could not drink from their
streams.
45He sent swarms of flies[c] that devoured
them,
and frogs[d] that devastated them.

---

tears because the redeemed rebelled. We must always keep the miraculous history of redemption bright in our memory.

78:32–42 HUMANITY, Relationship to God—God's punishment comes upon those who have broken their relationship to Him. God is merciful to forgive and redeem. He punishes a forgetful, rebellious people to lead us back to Him.

78:39 HUMANITY, Life—At its very best, life is always temporary. God knows this and patiently restrains His anger to give us further opportunity to live our brief life in relationship to Him.

46He gave their crops to the
grasshopper,[e]
their produce to the locust.[f]
47He destroyed their vines with hail[g]
and their sycamore-figs with sleet.
48He gave over their cattle to the hail,
their livestock[h] to bolts of lightning.
49He unleashed against them his hot
anger,[i]
his wrath, indignation and
hostility—
a band of destroying angels.[j]
50He prepared a path for his anger;
he did not spare them from death
but gave them over to the plague.
51He struck down all the firstborn of
Egypt,[k]
the firstfruits of manhood in the
tents of Ham.[l]
52But he brought his people out like a
flock;[m]
he led them like sheep through the
desert.
53He guided them safely, so they were
unafraid;
but the sea engulfed[n] their
enemies.[o]
54Thus he brought them to the border of
his holy land,
to the hill country his right hand[p]
had taken.
55He drove out nations[q] before them
and allotted their lands to them as
an inheritance;[r]
he settled the tribes of Israel in their
homes.

56But they put God to the test
and rebelled against the Most High;
they did not keep his statutes.
57Like their fathers[s] they were disloyal
and faithless,
as unreliable as a faulty bow.[t]
58They angered him[u] with their high
places;[v]
they aroused his jealousy with their
idols.[w]
59When God heard[x] them, he was very
angry;[y]
he rejected Israel[z] completely.
60He abandoned the tabernacle of
Shiloh,[a]
the tent he had set up among
men.[b]
61He sent ⌊the ark of⌋ his might[c] into
captivity,[d]
his splendor into the hands of the
enemy.
62He gave his people over to the
sword;[e]
he was very angry with his
inheritance.[f]
63Fire consumed[g] their young men,
and their maidens had no wedding
songs;[h]
64their priests were put to the sword,[i]
and their widows could not weep.
65Then the Lord awoke as from sleep,[j]
as a man wakes from the stupor of
wine.
66He beat back his enemies;
he put them to everlasting shame.[k]
67Then he rejected the tents of Joseph,
he did not choose the tribe of
Ephraim;[l]
68but he chose the tribe of Judah,[m]
Mount Zion,[n] which he loved.
69He built his sanctuary[o] like the
heights,
like the earth that he established
forever.
70He chose David[p] his servant
and took him from the sheep pens;
71from tending the sheep[q] he brought
him
to be the shepherd[r] of his people
Jacob,
of Israel his inheritance.
72And David shepherded them with
integrity of heart;[s]
with skillful hands he led them.

Psalm 79

A psalm of Asaph.

O God, the nations have invaded your
inheritance;[t]
they have defiled[u] your holy temple,
they have reduced Jerusalem to
rubble.[v]
2They have given the dead bodies of
your servants
as food to the birds of the air,[w]
the flesh of your saints to the beasts
of the earth.[x]
3They have poured out blood like water
all around Jerusalem,
and there is no one to bury[y] the
dead.[z]
4We are objects of reproach to our
neighbors,
of scorn[a] and derision to those
around us.[b]
5How long,[c] O LORD? Will you be
angry[d] forever?

78:46 [e]Na 3:15 [f]S Ex 10:13
78:47 [g]Ex 9:23; Ps 105:32; 147:17
78:48 [h]Ex 9:25
78:49 [i]Ex 15:7 [j]S Ge 19:13; 1Co 10:10
78:51 [k]S Ex 12:12; Ps 135:8 [l]Ps 105:23; 106:22
78:52 [m]S Job 21:11; S Ps 28:9; 77:20
78:53 [n]S Ex 14:28 [o]Ex 15:7; Ps 106:10
78:54 [p]Ps 44:3
78:55 [q]Ps 44:2 [r]S Dt 1:38; S Jos 13:7; Ac 13:19
78:57 [s]S 2Ch 30:7; Eze 20:27 [t]S ver 9
78:58 [u]S Jdg 2:12 [v]S Lev 26:30 [w]Ex 20:4; S Dt 5:8; 32:21
78:59 [x]Ps 55:19 [y]S Lev 26:28; S Nu 32:14 [z]S Dt 32:19
78:60 [a]S Jos 18:1 [b]Eze 8:6
78:61 [c]Ps 132:8 [d]S 1Sa 4:17
78:62 [e]S Dt 28:25 [f]S 1Sa 10:1
78:63 [g]S Nu 11:1 [h]S 1Ki 4:32; Jer 7:34; 16:9; 25:10
78:64 [i]1Sa 4:17
78:65 [j]Ps 44:23
78:66 [k]1Sa 5:6
78:67 [l]Jer 7:15; Hos 9:13; 12:1
78:68 [m]S Nu 1:7; Ps 108:8 [n]S Ex 15:17; S Ps 68:16
78:69 [o]S Ps 15:1
78:70 [p]S 1Sa 16:1
78:71 [q]S Ge 37:2 [r]S Ps 28:9
78:72 [s]S Ge 17:1
79:1 [t]S Ex 34:9 [u]S Lev 20:3 [v]S 2Ki 25:9; S Ne 4:2; S Isa 6:11
79:2 [w]Rev 19:17-18 [x]S Dt 28:26; Jer 7:33
79:3 [y]Jer 25:33; Rev 11:9 [z]Jer 16:4
79:4 [a]S Ps 39:8; S Eze 5:14 [b]Ps 44:13; 80:6
79:5 [c]S Ps 74:10 [d]Ps 74:1; 85:5

79:1–13 EVIL AND SUFFERING, Endurance—See notes on 3:1–8; 35:1–28; 74:1–23.
79:1–13 PRAYER, Lament—The psalmist stated the case in vv 1–4 and identified brutalized Israel with God—she was God's inheritance, His servants, His saints. Although Israel was guilty and needed forgiveness (vv 8–9), the apostasy was now ended. The basis for the prayer is the mercy of God and the glory of God's name. See notes on 5:10; 7:1–17.
79:3–4 HUMANITY, Burial—Burial was considered important for the dead. The tragedy of destruction was heightened when burial of the dead became impossible. We need the opportunity to pay last respects to the dead.

How long will your jealousy burn
like fire?[e]
6Pour out your wrath[f] on the nations
that do not acknowledge[g] you,
on the kingdoms
that do not call on your name;[h]
7for they have devoured[i] Jacob
and destroyed his homeland.
8Do not hold against us the sins of the
fathers;[j]
may your mercy come quickly to
meet us,
for we are in desperate need.[k]
9Help us,[l] O God our Savior,
for the glory of your name;
deliver us and forgive our sins
for your name's sake.[m]
10Why should the nations say,
"Where is their God?"[n]
Before our eyes, make known among
the nations
that you avenge[o] the outpoured
blood[p] of your servants.
11May the groans of the prisoners come
before you;
by the strength of your arm
preserve those condemned to die.
12Pay back into the laps[q] of our
neighbors seven times[r]
the reproach they have hurled at
you, O Lord.
13Then we your people, the sheep of
your pasture,[s]
will praise you forever;[t]
from generation to generation
we will recount your praise.

Psalm 80

For the director of music. To ⌊the tune of⌋ "The Lilies of the Covenant." Of Asaph. A psalm.

HEAR us, O Shepherd of Israel,
you who lead Joseph like a flock;[u]
you who sit enthroned between the
cherubim,[v] shine forth
2 before Ephraim, Benjamin and
Manasseh.[w]
Awaken[x] your might;
come and save us.[y]
3Restore[z] us,[a] O God;
make your face shine upon us,
that we may be saved.[b]
4O LORD God Almighty,
how long[c] will your anger smolder[d]
against the prayers of your people?
5You have fed them with the bread of
tears;[e]
you have made them drink tears by
the bowlful.[f]
6You have made us a source of
contention to our neighbors,
and our enemies mock us.[g]
7Restore us, O God Almighty;
make your face shine upon us,
that we may be saved.[h]
8You brought a vine[i] out of Egypt;
you drove out[j] the nations and
planted[k] it.
9You cleared the ground for it,
and it took root and filled the land.
10The mountains were covered with its
shade,
the mighty cedars with its branches.
11It sent out its boughs to the Sea,[h]
its shoots as far as the River.[i] [l]
12Why have you broken down its walls[m]
so that all who pass by pick its
grapes?
13Boars from the forest ravage[n] it
and the creatures of the field feed on
it.
14Return to us, O God Almighty!
Look down from heaven and see![o]
Watch over this vine,
15 the root your right hand has planted,
the son[j] you have raised up for
yourself.

79:5 [e]S Dt 29:20; Ps 89:46; Zep 3:8
79:6 [f]S Ps 2:5; 69:24; 110:5; Rev 16:1 [g]Ps 147:20; Jer 10:25 [h]S Ps 14:4
79:7 [i]Isa 9:12; Jer 10:25
79:8 [j]S Ge 9:25; Jer 44:21 [k]Ps 116:6; 142:6
79:9 [l]S 2Ch 14:11 [m]Ps 25:11; 31:3; Jer 14:7
79:10 [n]S Ps 42:3 [o]Ps 94:1; S Rev 6:10 [p]ver 3
79:12 [q]Isa 65:6; Jer 32:18 [r]S Ge 4:15
79:13 [s]S Ps 74:1 [t]Ps 44:8
80:1 [u]Ps 77:20 [v]S Ex 25:22
80:2 [w]Nu 2:18-24 [x]S Ps 35:23 [y]Ps 54:1; 69:1; 71:2; 109:26; 116:4; 119:94
80:3 [z]S Ps 71:20; 85:4; Jer 31:18; La 5:21 [a]S Nu 6:25 [b]ver 7,19
80:4 [c]S Ps 74:10 [d]S Dt 29:20
80:5 [e]S Job 3:24 [f]Isa 30:20
80:6 [g]S Ps 79:4
80:7 [h]ver 3
80:8 [i]Isa 5:1-2; Jer 2:21; Mt 21:33-41 [j]Ex 23:28-30; S Jos 13:6; Ac 7:45 [k]S Ex 15:17
80:11 [l]Ps 72:8
80:12 [m]Ps 89:40; Isa 5:5; 30:13; Jer 39:8
80:13 [n]Jer 5:6
80:14 [o]S Dt 26:15

[h]*11* Probably the Mediterranean [i]*11* That is, the Euphrates [j]*15* Or *branch*

79:5 GOD, Jealous—Jealousy is an emotion felt between lovers. God has such love for His people He zealously acts to maintain their fidelity. His jealous acts are perceived as wrath at times by His people. See notes on Ex 34:14; Dt 6:10–25.
79:8 SIN, Responsibility—Although persons must bear the responsibility for their own sins, some sins have consequences that pass from generation to generation and serve as reminders for repentance. God does not hold us accountable for another generation's sins. He does let us endure the environment produced by their sins and His judgment on their sins.
79:9 GOD, Glory—God's very name, the sacred, personal word Yahweh, shows His glorious presence to His people. See notes on Ex 16:7,10; 40:34–38; Lk 2:9,14; Jn 11:4.
80:1–19 EVIL AND SUFFERING, Prayer—See note on 3:1–8. What do I do when God ignores prayer? The psalmist wrestled with this question after desperate military defeat and long periods of prayer with no apparent answer. The psalmist appealed to God for action three times with the same refrain: vv 3,7,19. Our ultimate source of help in times of trouble is God. When we feel abandoned by God, we should still appeal to Him. He has helped in the past and will do so again. Prayer is not a panic button summoning immediate help. It is a communication line maintaining relationships with our only Source of hope.
80:1–19 HISTORY, Hope—See note on 74:9–23.
80:1–19 PRAYER, Lament—See note on 3:1–8. The two names for God summarize the intent of this prayer. Israel had been victimized, and the psalmist described her pitiable condition to God. God does not need information. Such description is simply assuming God's viewpoint of the situation. As victim, Israel appealed to God as caring Shepherd and as powerful God Almighty. Unanswered prayer was part of Israel's problem. God's anger can express itself in refusing to give prayed-for deliverance.
80:2–3,7,19 GOD, Savior—Here we see one part of the biblical definition of salvation: life in proper relationship with God. See notes on 38:22; 62:1–2,6–8; Lk 1:47; 1 Ti 1:1.
80:4 GOD, Wrath—See notes on 30:5; 69:24.

16Your vine is cut down, it is burned
with fire;[p]
at your rebuke[q] your people perish.
17Let your hand rest on the man at your
right hand,
the son of man[r] you have raised up
for yourself.
18Then we will not turn away from you;
revive[s] us, and we will call on your
name.

19Restore us, O LORD God Almighty;
make your face shine upon us,
that we may be saved.

Psalm 81

For the director of music. According to *gittith*.[k] Of Asaph.

SING for joy to God our strength;
shout aloud to the God of Jacob![t]
2Begin the music, strike the
tambourine,[u]
play the melodious harp[v] and lyre.[w]
3Sound the ram's horn[x] at the New
Moon,[y]
and when the moon is full, on the
day of our Feast;
4this is a decree for Israel,
an ordinance of the God of Jacob.[z]
5He established it as a statute for Joseph
when he went out against Egypt,[a]
where we heard a language we did
not understand.[l] [b]
6He says, "I removed the burden[c] from
their shoulders;[d]
their hands were set free from the
basket.
7In your distress you called[e] and I
rescued you,
I answered[f] you out of a
thundercloud;
I tested you at the waters of
Meribah.[g] *Selah*

8"Hear, O my people,[h] and I will warn
you—
if you would but listen to me,
O Israel!
9You shall have no foreign god[i] among
you;
you shall not bow down to an alien
god.
10I am the LORD your God,
who brought you up out of Egypt.[j]
Open[k] wide your mouth and I will
fill[l] it.

11"But my people would not listen to
me;
Israel would not submit to me.[m]
12So I gave them over[n] to their stubborn
hearts
to follow their own devices.

13"If my people would but listen to me,[o]
if Israel would follow my ways,
14how quickly would I subdue[p] their
enemies
and turn my hand against[q] their
foes!
15Those who hate the LORD would
cringe[r] before him,
and their punishment would last
forever.
16But you would be fed with the finest of
wheat;[s]
with honey from the rock I would
satisfy you."

Psalm 82

A psalm of Asaph.

GOD presides in the great assembly;
he gives judgment[t] among the
"gods":[u]
2"How long will you[m] defend the unjust

80:16 [p]Ps 79:1 [q]S Dt 28:20
80:17 [r]S Job 25:6
80:18 [s]Ps 85:6; Isa 57:15; Hos 6:2
81:1 [t]S Ps 66:1
81:2 [u]S Ex 15:20 [v]Ps 92:3 [w]S Job 21:12
81:3 [x]S Ex 19:13 [y]S Ne 10:33
81:4 [z]ver 1
81:5 [a]S Ex 11:4 [b]Ps 114:1
81:6 [c]S Ex 1:14 [d]Isa 9:4; 52:2
81:7 [e]S Ex 2:23 [f]Ex 19:19 [g]S Ex 17:7; S Dt 33:8
81:8 [h]Ps 50:7; 78:1
81:9 [i]S Ex 20:3
81:10 [j]S Ex 6:6; S 13:3; S 29:46 [k]Eze 2:8 [l]Ps 107:9
81:11 [m]Ex 32:1-6
81:12 [n]Eze 20:25; Ac 7:42; Ro 1:24
81:13 [o]S Dt 5:29
81:14 [p]Ps 47:3 [q]Am 1:8
81:15 [r]S 2Sa 22:45
81:16 [s]S Dt 32:14
82:1 [t]Ps 7:8; 58:11; Isa 3:13; 66:16; Joel 3:12 [u]S Job 21:22

[k]Title: Probably a musical term [l]*5* Or / *and we heard a voice we had not known* [m]*2* The Hebrew is plural.

81:1–14 REVELATION, Commitment—Annual festivals (Ex 23: 14–17) reviewed God's history with His people, revealed His will, and called for commitment. The festivals were based on past historical acts. They were celebrated in response to specific divine command. They resulted in written revelation such as this Psalm.

81:1–16 PRAYER, Corporate—See note on Est 9:30–31. The first five verses are a call to celebrate one of the annual feasts, probably the Feast of Tabernacles (Lev 23:33–36). Vv 6–16 are the voice of the Lord probably spoken by a priest calling Israel to remember and to listen to the voice of the Lord. Israel's book of prayers thus includes a worship program for an annual festival.

81:5 HISTORY, Worship—The great feast days of Israel's worship celebrated God's deeds in history. See notes on 78:1–72; Lev 23:4–43.

81:9–10 GOD, One God—In worship God's people hear anew His expectations of total loyalty. A people who do not listen suffer God's judgment. See note on Ne 1:5.

82:1–8 EVIL AND SUFFERING, Punishment—The heavens are concerned about earthly evil. God presides over the heavenly council. Other nations talked of a heavenly council of gods with various authority and rank. Israel said the one God ruled over His angelic messengers. The apearance of "gods" (Hebrew *'elohim*) in vv 1,6 is unusual for the Bible. Various interpreters have understood the term as a reference to Israel's wicked rulers or judges, foreign kings who claimed to be divine, gods of foreign nations reduced to God's servants, or angels responsible for various nations. Whatever the precise meaning, the theological intent is clear. God reigns supreme over the world. Even those who have claimed to appear in heaven as deities must face His judgment if they are responsible for evil on the earth. They, too, can die. Only God is immortal and will not die. Anyone who exercises power on earth must help the helpless and promote good, not evil. God's kingship over all the earth assures that right will eventually prevail and evil disappear.

82:1–8 PRAYER, Lament—See note on 3:1–8. Strong language characterizes Israel's prayers to God. This psalm traced the cause of injustice to the heavenly throne and presented the call for God to straighten out the heavenly council. Prayer seeks to express honest impressions to God and trusts God to accept our language and minister to our situation.

82:2–4 CHRISTIAN ETHICS, Justice—All beings in

and show partiality[v] to the
wicked?[w] *Selah*
3Defend the cause of the weak and
fatherless;[x]
maintain the rights of the poor[y] and
oppressed.
4Rescue the weak and needy;
deliver them from the hand of the
wicked.

5"They know nothing, they understand
nothing.[z]
They walk about in darkness;[a]
all the foundations[b] of the earth are
shaken.

6"I said, 'You are "gods";[c]
you are all sons of the Most High.'
7But you will die[d] like mere men;
you will fall like every other ruler."

8Rise up,[e] O God, judge[f] the earth,
for all the nations are your
inheritance.[g]

Psalm 83

A song. A psalm of Asaph.

O God, do not keep silent;[h]
be not quiet, O God, be not still.
2See how your enemies are astir,[i]
how your foes rear their heads.[j]
3With cunning they conspire[k] against
your people;
they plot against those you cherish.[l]
4"Come," they say, "let us destroy[m]
them as a nation,[n]
that the name of Israel be
remembered[o] no more."

5With one mind they plot together;[p]
they form an alliance against you—
6the tents of Edom[q] and the
Ishmaelites,
of Moab[r] and the Hagrites,[s]
7Gebal,[n][t] Ammon[u] and Amalek,[v]
Philistia,[w] with the people of Tyre.[x]
8Even Assyria[y] has joined them
to lend strength to the descendants
of Lot.[z] *Selah*

9Do to them as you did to Midian,[a]
as you did to Sisera[b] and Jabin[c] at
the river Kishon,[d]
10who perished at Endor[e]
and became like refuse[f] on the
ground.
11Make their nobles like Oreb and
Zeeb,[g]
all their princes like Zebah and
Zalmunna,[h]
12who said, "Let us take possession[i]
of the pasturelands of God."

13Make them like tumbleweed, O my
God,
like chaff[j] before the wind.
14As fire consumes the forest
or a flame sets the mountains
ablaze,[k]
15so pursue them with your tempest[l]
and terrify them with your storm.[m]
16Cover their faces with shame[n]
so that men will seek your name,
O LORD.

17May they ever be ashamed and
dismayed;[o]
may they perish in disgrace.[p]
18Let them know that you, whose name
is the LORD[q]—
that you alone are the Most High[r]
over all the earth.[s]

Psalm 84

For the director of music. According to *gittith*.[o] Of the Sons of Korah. A psalm.

HOW lovely is your dwelling place,[t]
O LORD Almighty!
2My soul yearns,[u] even faints,
for the courts of the LORD;
my heart and my flesh cry out
for the living God.[v]
3Even the sparrow has found a home,
and the swallow a nest for herself,
where she may have her young—
a place near your altar,[w]
O LORD Almighty,[x] my King[y] and
my God.[z]
4Blessed are those who dwell in your
house;
they are ever praising you. *Selah*
5Blessed are those whose strength[a] is
in you,
who have set their hearts on
pilgrimage.[b]
6As they pass through the Valley of
Baca,
they make it a place of springs;[c]

82:2 [v]Dt 1:17 [w]Ps 58:1-2; Pr 18:5 **82:3** [x]S Dt 24:17 [y]Ps 140:12; Jer 5:28; 22:16 **82:5** [z]S Ps 14:4; S 53:2 [a]Job 30:26; Isa 5:30; 8:21-22; 9:2; 59:9; 60:2; Jer 13:16; 23:12; La 3:2 [b]S Jdg 5:4; S Ps 11:3 **82:6** [c]Jn 10:34* **82:7** [d]Ps 49:12; Eze 31:14 **82:8** [e]Ps 12:5 [f]S Ps 76:9 [g]Ps 2:8 **83:1** [h]Ps 28:1; 35:22; Isa 42:14; 57:11; 62:1; 64:12 **83:2** [i]Ps 2:1; Isa 17:12 [j]Jdg 8:28 **83:3** [k]S Ex 1:10; S Ps 31:13 [l]Ps 17:14 **83:4** [m]S Est 3:6 [n]Jer 33:24 [o]Jer 11:19 **83:5** [p]Ps 2:2 **83:6** [q]Ps 137:7; Isa 34:5; Jer 49:7; Am 1:11 [r]2Ch 20:1 [s]S Ge 25:16 **83:7** [t]S Jos 13:5 [u]Ge 19:38 [v]S Ge 14:7; S Ex 17:14 [w]Ex 15:14 [x]Isa 23:3; Eze 27:3 **83:8** [y]S Ge 10:11 [z]S Dt 2:9 **83:9** [a]S Ge 25:2; Jdg 7:1-23 [b]S Jdg 4:2 [c]S Jos 11:1 [d]S Jdg 4:23-24 **83:10** [e]S 1Sa 28:7 [f]S 2Ki 9:37; Isa 5:25; Jer 8:2; 9:22; 16:4; 25:33; Zep 1:17 **83:11** [g]Jdg 7:25 [h]S Jdg 8:5 **83:12** [i]2Ch 20:11; Eze 35:10 **83:13** [j]S Job 13:25 **83:14** [k]Dt 32:22; Isa 9:18 **83:15** [l]S Ps 50:3 [m]S Job 9:17 **83:16** [n]S Ps 34:5; 109:29; 132:18 **83:17** [o]S 2Ki 19:26 [p]S Ps 35:4 **83:18** [q]S Ps 68:4 [r]Ps 7:8; 18:13 [s]S Job 34:29 **84:1** [t]S Dt 33:27; Ps 27:4; 43:3; 90:1; 132:5 **84:2** [u]S Job 19:27 [v]S Jos 3:10 **84:3** [w]S Ps 43:4 [x]Jer 44:11 [y]Ps 2:6 [z]Ps 5:2 **84:5** [a]Ps 81:1 [b]Jer 31:6 **84:6** [c]S Job 38:26

[n]*7* That is, Byblos [o]Title: Probably a musical term

God's creation are responsible to use their power and position to help the needy and to establish justice.

83:1–18 PRAYER, Persistence—See note on 5:10. The prayer principle of continuity is seen here. The psalmist appealed for God to demonstrate His power and justice as He did in the days of Gideon. God will act as He has acted in the past. It is helpful to keep a record of answered prayers to understand how God works in one's life.

84:1–12 PRAYER, Fellowship with God—This prayer expresses intense yearning for the presence of God. Ps 42 yearns for God's presence in difficult circumstances; Ps 90 deals with dwelling in the awesomeness of God's presence; and Ps 91, dwelling under the protection of His presence. This psalm, possibly by an exiled Levite in time of war, is a song of yearning for God Himself in His dwelling place, the Temple. Vv 5–7 probably refer to the joy of those in pilgrimage to one of the annual feasts. No other joy can be compared with the joy of His presence. Prayer seeks fellowship with God and provides that fellowship even when we are far removed from the house of worship.

the autumn[d] rains also cover it with
pools.[p]
7They go from strength to strength,[e]
till each appears[f] before God in
Zion.[g]

8Hear my prayer,[h] O LORD God
Almighty;
listen to me, O God of Jacob. *Selah*
9Look upon our shield,[q][i] O God;
look with favor on your anointed
one.[j]

10Better is one day in your courts
than a thousand elsewhere;
I would rather be a doorkeeper[k] in the
house of my God
than dwell in the tents of the
wicked.
11For the LORD God is a sun[l] and
shield;[m]
the LORD bestows favor and honor;
no good thing does he withhold[n]
from those whose walk is blameless.

12O LORD Almighty,
blessed[o] is the man who trusts in
you.

Psalm 85

For the director of music. Of the Sons of
Korah. A psalm.

YOU showed favor to your land,
O LORD;
you restored the fortunes[p] of Jacob.
2You forgave[q] the iniquity[r] of your
people
and covered all their sins. *Selah*
3You set aside all your wrath[s]
and turned from your fierce anger.[t]

4Restore[u] us again, O God our Savior,[v]
and put away your displeasure
toward us.
5Will you be angry with us forever?[w]
Will you prolong your anger through
all generations?
6Will you not revive[x] us again,
that your people may rejoice[y] in
you?
7Show us your unfailing love,[z] O LORD,
and grant us your salvation.[a]

8I will listen to what God the LORD will
say;
he promises peace[b] to his people,
his saints—
but let them not return to folly.[c]
9Surely his salvation[d] is near those who
fear him,
that his glory[e] may dwell in our
land.

10Love and faithfulness[f] meet together;
righteousness[g] and peace kiss each
other.
11Faithfulness springs forth from the
earth,
and righteousness[h] looks down from
heaven.
12The LORD will indeed give what is
good,[i]
and our land will yield[j] its harvest.
13Righteousness goes before him
and prepares the way for his steps.

Psalm 86

A prayer of David.

HEAR, O LORD, and answer[k] me,
for I am poor and needy.

84:6 [d]Joel 2:23
84:7 [e]S Job 17:9 [f]S Dt 16:16 [g]1Ki 8:1
84:8 [h]Ps 4:1
84:9 [i]S Ps 59:11 [j]1Sa 16:6; Ps 2:2; 18:50; 132:17
84:10 [k]1Ch 23:5
84:11 [l]Isa 60:19; Jer 43:13; Rev 21:23 [m]S Ge 15:1 [n]Ps 34:10
84:12 [o]Ps 2:12
85:1 [p]S Dt 30:3; Ps 14:7
85:2 [q]S Nu 14:19 [r]S Ex 32:30; S Ps 78:38
85:3 [s]Ps 106:23; Da 9:16 [t]Ex 32:12; Dt 13:17; Ps 78:38; Jnh 3:9
85:4 [u]S Ps 71:20 [v]S Ps 65:5
85:5 [w]S Ps 50:21
85:6 [x]S Ps 80:18 [y]Php 3:1
85:7 [z]S Ps 6:4 [a]Ps 27:1
85:8 [b]S Lev 26:6; S Isa 60:17; S Jn 14:27; 2Th 3:16 [c]Pr 26:11; 27:22
85:9 [d]Ps 27:1; Isa 43:3; 45:8; 46:13; 51:5; 56:1; 62:11 [e]S Ex 29:43; Isa 60:19; Hag 2:9; Zec 2:5
85:10 [f]Ps 89:14; 115:1; Pr 3:3 [g]Ps 72:2-3; Isa 32:17
85:11 [h]Isa 45:8
85:12 [i]Ps 84:11; Jas 1:17 [j]Lev 26:4; S Ps 67:6; Zec 8:12
86:1 [k]Ps 17:6

[p]6 Or *blessings* [q]9 Or *sovereign*

84:11 GOD, Goodness—God in His goodness graciously provides what His people need. See notes on Ge 19:12–19,29; 39:21–23; 45:5–9; Mt 19:17; Lk 1:30.
85:1–7 GOD, Savior—As Savior, God withdraws His wrathful judgment and forgives His people's sins. See notes on 38:22; 62:1–2,6–8; Lk 1:47; 1 Ti 1:1.
85:1–13 EVIL AND SUFFERING, Endurance—Suffering is not something to be endured one time and then forgotten. God's people may endure repeated suffering as God deals with us in a world dominated by sin. Suffering, however, does not endure forever. God's righteousness and salvation do. See note on 3:1–8.
85:1–13 PRAYER, Petition—The psalmist appealed on the basis of God's former favor. See note on Ps 83:1–18. He appealed to the Lord's expression of His nature in covenant and committed himself to hear God's word. He looked to God in time of drought and famine, confident He would faithfully give a rich harvest.
85:4–7 EVANGELISM, Holy Life—The power of a holy, revived life is great in evangelism. Revival comes when God's people seek forgiveness and a new sense of God's love. All believers are to seek that constant spiritual renewing that they may be holy people, powerful in God's hands. Holy lives are vital to evangelism and revival. See Guide to Applying the Word, pp. 1811–1812.
85:7–8 REVELATION, Oracles—God reveals Himself to those who truly wish to know who He is. The wise choose to hear, the foolish to ignore Him. See note on 42:8–11.
85:9 GOD, Glory—God's salvation means His glorious presence is with His people. See notes on Ex 16:7,10; 40:34–38; Lk 2:9,14; Jn 11:4.
85:9 SALVATION, Fear of God—This verse unmistakably ties salvation to the fear of God. God's glory dwells with those who worship Him. Being in His presence is salvation. See note on Ex 20:20.
85:10–13 GOD, Faithfulness—Three characteristics of God are used together almost synonymously. Salvation means God in faithfulness has renewed His covenant love with His people through righteous acts which restore the peace and welfare of His people.
85:10–13 CREATION, Confidence—God's restoration of Israel from Babylonian captivity showed He loved her, but bad times soon fell upon the nation because of sin. The psalmist prayed for a new demonstration of God's concern. He believed God would answer him because he knew the world was structured in righteousness. God created a world that He will never surrender to the forces of evil. Sin may win temporary skirmishes, but the final victory belongs to the Lord who made heaven and earth. Since this is true, we can serve Him confidently, knowing He will vindicate us at the time He feels is proper.
86:1–7 GOD, Personal—God is addressed in a very personal way, expecting an answer. God's faithful servants can count on His personal, loving attention. See notes on Ex

2Guard my life, for I am devoted to you.
You are my God; save your servant
who trusts in you.[l]
3Have mercy[m] on me, O Lord,
for I call[n] to you all day long.
4Bring joy to your servant,
for to you, O Lord,
I lift[o] up my soul.
5You are forgiving and good, O Lord,
abounding in love[p] to all who call to
you.
6Hear my prayer, O LORD;
listen to my cry[q] for mercy.
7In the day of my trouble[r] I will call[s]
to you,
for you will answer[t] me.
8Among the gods[u] there is none like
you,[v] O Lord;
no deeds can compare with yours.
9All the nations you have made
will come[w] and worship[x] before
you, O Lord;
they will bring glory[y] to your name.
10For you are great[z] and do marvelous
deeds;[a]
you alone[b] are God.
11Teach me your way,[c] O LORD,
and I will walk in your truth;[d]
give me an undivided[e] heart,
that I may fear[f] your name.
12I will praise you, O Lord my God, with
all my heart;[g]
I will glorify your name forever.
13For great is your love toward me;
you have delivered me[h] from the
depths of the grave.[r] [i]
14The arrogant are attacking me, O God;
a band of ruthless men seeks my
life—
men without regard for you.[j]
15But you, O Lord, are a compassionate
and gracious[k] God,
slow to anger,[l] abounding[m] in love
and faithfulness.[n]
16Turn to me[o] and have mercy[p] on me;
grant your strength[q] to your servant
and save the son of your
maidservant.[s] [r]
17Give me a sign[s] of your goodness,
that my enemies may see it and be
put to shame,
for you, O LORD, have helped me
and comforted me.

Psalm 87

Of the Sons of Korah. A psalm. A song.

He has set his foundation on the holy
mountain;[t]
2 the LORD loves the gates of Zion[u]
more than all the dwellings of Jacob.
3Glorious things are said of you,
O city of God:[v] *Selah*
4"I will record Rahab[t] [w] and Babylon
among those who acknowledge
me—
Philistia[x] too, and Tyre[y], along with
Cush[u]—
and will say, 'This[v] one was born in
Zion.[z]' "
5Indeed, of Zion it will be said,
"This one and that one were born in
her,

86:2 [l]Ps 25:2; 31:14 **86:3** [m]Ps 4:1; S 9:13; 57:1 [n]Ps 88:9 **86:4** [o]Ps 46:5; 143:8 **86:5** [p]Ex 34:6; Ne 9:17; Ps 103:8; 145:8; Joel 2:13; Jnh 4:2 **86:6** [q]Ps 5:2; 17:1 **86:7** [r]Ps 27:5; S 50:15; 94:13; Hab 3:16 [s]Job 22:27; Ps 4:3; 80:18; 91:15; Isa 30:19; 58:9; 65:24; Zec 13:9 [t]Ps 3:4 **86:8** [u]S Ex 8:10; S Job 21:22 [v]S Ps 18:31 **86:9** [w]S Ps 65:2 [x]Ps 66:4; Isa 19:21; 27:13; 49:7; Zec 8:20-22; 14:16; Rev 15:4 [y]Isa 43:7; 44:23 **86:10** [z]S 2Sa 7:22; S Ps 48:1 [a]S Ex 3:20; S Ps 71:17; 72:18 [b]S Dt 6:4; S Isa 43:10; Mk 12:29; 1Co 8:4 **86:11** [c]S Ex 33:13; S 1Sa 12:23; Ps 25:5 [d]S Ps 26:3 [e]Jer 24:7; 32:39; Eze 11:19; 1Co 7:35 [f]S Dt 6:24 **86:12** [g]S Ps 9:1 **86:13** [h]S Ps 34:4; 49:15; 116:8 [i]S Ps 16:10; S 56:13 **86:14** [j]Ps 54:3 **86:15** [k]S Ps 51:1; 103:8; 111:4; 116:5; 145:8 [l]Nu 14:18 [m]ver 5 [n]S Ex 34:6; S Ne 9:17; Joel 2:13 **86:16** [o]S Ps 6:4 [p]S Ps 9:13 [q]Ps 18:1 [r]Ps 116:16 **86:17** [s]S Ex 3:12; Mt 24:3; S Jn 2:11 **87:1** [t]S Ps 48:1 **87:2** [u]Ps 2:6 **87:3** [v]S Ps 46:4 **87:4** [w]S Job 9:13 [x]S 2Sa 8:1; Ps 83:7 [y]Ps 45:12; Joel 3:4 [z]Isa 19:25

[r]*13* Hebrew *Sheol* [s]*16* Or *save your faithful son* [t]*4* A poetic name for Egypt [u]*4* That is, the upper Nile region [v]*4* Or *"O Rahab and Babylon, / Philistia, Tyre and Cush, / I will record concerning those who acknowledge me: / 'This*

3:12–16; Mt 18:10–14.

86:1–17 EVIL AND SUFFERING, Prayer—See note on 3:1–8. God's characteristics of love, forgiveness, faithfulness, mercy, grace, and compassion offer the greatest comfort to the sufferer. When we endure in prayer, we know He will answer.

86:1–17 PRAYER, Lament—See note on 3:1–8. The psalmist elaborately prepared for his petition. Vv 1–7 make an impassioned plea for God to hear. Vv 8–10 tell God He is the only God who can hear. V 11 is a prayer and a pledge to be God's obedient servant. Vv 12–13 praise the loving, saving God. Vv 14–17 petition for help when enemies are attacking. The petition maintains the spirit of humility and reverent praise established in the first thirteen verses.

86:5,13,15 GOD, Love—In committed covenant love God listens to His people's prayers and delivers them from the threat of death. See notes on Ex 3:7; Dt 32:10–12,36; Mt 10:29–31; Jn 3:16.

86:8–10 HISTORY, Universal—God's unique saving actions were not done just for one people. They serve as reason for all peoples to worship God.

86:8–10 EVANGELISM, Call to Salvation—The day will come when all will bow before the Lord. That is the final judgment. Before that hour, however, God's call to faith in Christ goes out to all nations. He wants all to know of His saving acts and to believe He alone is God. We share in that divine call to salvation because we have tasted God's redemption. God is patient with those who do not know Him. He waits for us to go tell them the gospel story. God's salvation call to the lost comes through the saved.

86:9 GOD, Creator—God is ultimately the Creator of all persons and things on the earth. Each nation owes its existence to Him and is invited to worship Him. See notes on Ge 1:3—2:25; Ro 4:17.

86:9 GOD, Glory—Glory is the weight, the honor, and the prestige which belongs to God alone. In worship people recognize and testify to God's unique glory. See notes on Ex 16:7, 10; 40:34–38; Lk 2:9,14; Jn 11:4.

86:11 EDUCATION, Guidance—The godly person does not depend upon previous learning to keep walking in the way of truth but upon God's continued guidance. The child of God never graduates from the school of divine instruction; every day is "commencement." See 143:10.

86:13 HUMANITY, Life—Life, as God's gift, is the result of His love. The psalmist experienced that love as deliverance from certain death. We experience it in Jesus Christ as total victory over death (1 Co 15:20–28).

86:13 SALVATION, As Deliverance—God saves us from physical death as well as from spiritual death. The grave here is Sheol, the place of departed spirits. Salvation is based on God's love and brings forth human praise.

86:13 LAST THINGS, Intermediate State—See note on Isa 14:9.

and the Most High himself will
establish her."
6The LORD will write in the register[a] of
the peoples:
"This one was born in Zion." *Selah*
7As they make music[b] they will sing,
"All my fountains[c] are in you."

Psalm 88

A song. A psalm of the Sons of Korah. For the director of music. According to *mahalath leannoth.*[w] A *maskil*[x] of Heman the Ezrahite.

O LORD, the God who saves me,[d]
day and night I cry out[e] before
you.
2May my prayer come before you;
turn your ear to my cry.
3For my soul is full of trouble[f]
and my life draws near the grave.[y] [g]
4I am counted among those who go
down to the pit;[h]
I am like a man without strength.[i]
5I am set apart with the dead,
like the slain who lie in the grave,
whom you remember no more,
who are cut off[j] from your care.
6You have put me in the lowest pit,
in the darkest depths.[k]
7Your wrath[l] lies heavily upon me;
you have overwhelmed me with all
your waves.[m] *Selah*
8You have taken from me my closest
friends[n]
and have made me repulsive to
them.
I am confined[o] and cannot escape;[p]
9 my eyes[q] are dim with grief.

I call[r] to you, O LORD, every day;
I spread out my hands[s] to you.
10Do you show your wonders to the
dead?
Do those who are dead rise up and
praise you?[t] *Selah*
11Is your love declared in the grave,
your faithfulness[u] in Destruction[z] ?
12Are your wonders known in the place
of darkness,
or your righteous deeds in the land
of oblivion?

13But I cry to you for help,[v] O LORD;
in the morning[w] my prayer comes
before you.[x]
14Why, O LORD, do you reject[y] me
and hide your face[z] from me?
15From my youth[a] I have been afflicted[b]
and close to death;
I have suffered your terrors[c] and am
in despair.[d]
16Your wrath[e] has swept over me;
your terrors[f] have destroyed me.
17All day long they surround me like a
flood;[g]
they have completely engulfed me.
18You have taken my companions[h] and
loved ones from me;
the darkness is my closest friend.

Psalm 89

A *maskil*[x] of Ethan the Ezrahite.

I will sing[i] of the LORD's great love
forever;

87:6 [a]Ex 32:32; Ps 69:28; Isa 4:3; Mal 3:16
87:7 [b]Ps 149:3 [c]S Ps 36:9
88:1 [d]S Ps 51:14 [e]Ps 3:4; 22:2; Lk 18:7
88:3 [f]Ps 6:3; 25:17 [g]S Job 33:22
88:4 [h]S Ps 31:12 [i]Ps 18:1
88:5 [j]S Ps 31:22
88:6 [k]Ps 30:1; S 69:15; La 3:55; Jnh 2:3
88:7 [l]Ps 7:11 [m]S Ps 42:7
88:8 [n]S Job 19:13; Ps 31:11 [o]Jer 32:2; 33:1 [p]S Job 3:23
88:9 [q]S Ps 38:10 [r]Ps 5:2 [s]Job 11:13; Ps 143:6
88:10 [t]S Ps 6:5
88:11 [u]S Ps 30:9
88:13 [v]S Ps 30:2 [w]Ps 5:3; S 55:17 [x]Ps 119:147
88:14 [y]S Ps 43:2 [z]Ps 13:1
88:15 [a]Ps 129:1; Jer 22:21; Eze 16:22; Hos 2:15 [b]Ps 9:12 [c]Job 6:4; S 18:11 [d]2Co 4:8
88:16 [e]Ps 7:11 [f]Job 6:4
88:17 [g]Ps 124:4
88:18 [h]ver 8; Ps 38:11
89:1 [i]Ps 59:16

[w]Title: Possibly a tune, "The Suffering of Affliction"
[x]Title: Probably a literary or musical term
[y]3 Hebrew *Sheol* [z]11 Hebrew *Abaddon*

88:1 GOD, Savior—See note on 85:1–7.
88:1–18 EVIL AND SUFFERING, Prayer—Approaching death does not separate us from God, even when it causes friends and relatives to ignore us. We may feel totally rejected and think God has rejected us. We can take these honest feelings to Him and know He hears us. Though the Old Testament writer feared death and the grave would separate us from God, the New Testament reveals the resurrection hope in Christ. Life may be constant suffering and sorrow, but God is as near as our next whisper. See note on 3:1–8.
88:1–18 PRAYER, Lament—See note on 3:1–8. This is unquestionably the most despairing prayer in the Bible. The only hopeful note in it is in the opening address. The psalmist was close to death. The Bible emphatically affirms that God hears such cries. Prayer is not graded on pious language, for prayer is the expression of our depths to the depth of God. See note on Ex 2:23–24.
88:3–5 HUMANITY, Nature of Death—Death is the last trouble which comes into human experience. Its onset is seen as the departure of natural strength, and its end is the final separation from God. Until Jesus offered a greater hope, the onset of death was usually viewed with great pessimism.
88:3–5, 10–11 LAST THINGS, Intermediate State—See note on Isa 14:9.
88:10–12 HUMANITY, Nature of Death—See note on 88:3–5. Until Jesus gave a vivid hope of life beyond death, the dead were often viewed as being unable to relate to God in any way.
88:15–18 GOD, Wrath—In moments of despair God's people see their life as encompassed by God's wrath and pray to Him for relief. See note on 69:24.
88:15 HUMANITY, Childhood and Youth—Youth is the time of great expectations. To have to face death at such a time is an exceptional tragedy. To believe that God has been behind such tragedy is almost unbearable. Still, in such tragic desperation we can call to God for help. No trouble or tragedy is horrible enough to separate us from God.
89:1–49 GOD, Faithfulness—God's faithfulness is an eternal characteristic which leads Him to enter into covenant with His people. His faithfulness makes Him different from all created beings, pointing to His place as the unique God. His faithfulness forms the foundation for our praise. It is also the foundation for the messianic hope through David's line. See notes on Ge 8:1; Nu 26:65; Dt 10:11,22; Jos 1:6; 1 Co 1:9.
89:1–49 GOD, Love—The love of God is a recurring refrain running through this psalm. God remains faithful to His people not only because His faithfulness requires it but because His love binds Him to us. See note on 69:13,16.
89:1–51 ELECTION, Faithfulness—In worship Israel celebrated the eternal promise to David to provide leadership from His house for Israel. They also joined the king in mourning a massive defeat which showed God had rejected the king. Dark days sometimes hide God's faithfulness and raise questions concerning His commitment to His covenant promises. In Jesus, Christians celebrate God's faithfulness precisely in the dark hour of the cross.

with my mouth I will make your
faithfulness known[j] through
all generations.
2I will declare that your love stands firm
forever,
that you established your
faithfulness in heaven itself.[k]

3You said, "I have made a covenant
with my chosen one,
I have sworn to David my servant,
4'I will establish your line forever
and make your throne firm through
all generations.' "[l] *Selah*

5The heavens[m] praise your wonders,
O LORD,
your faithfulness too, in the
assembly[n] of the holy ones.
6For who in the skies above can
compare with the LORD?
Who is like the LORD among the
heavenly beings?[o]
7In the council[p] of the holy ones[q] God
is greatly feared;
he is more awesome than all who
surround him.[r]
8O LORD God Almighty,[s] who is like
you?[t]
You are mighty, O LORD, and your
faithfulness surrounds you.

9You rule over the surging sea;
when its waves mount up, you still
them.[u]
10You crushed Rahab[v] like one of the
slain;
with your strong arm you scattered[w]
your enemies.
11The heavens are yours,[x] and yours
also the earth;[y]
you founded the world and all that is
in it.[z]
12You created the north and the south;
Tabor[a] and Hermon[b] sing for joy[c]
at your name.
13Your arm is endued with power;
your hand is strong, your right hand
exalted.[d]
14Righteousness and justice are the
foundation of your throne;[e]
love and faithfulness go before you.[f]
15Blessed are those who have learned to
acclaim you,
who walk[g] in the light[h] of your
presence, O LORD.
16They rejoice in your name[i] all day
long;
they exult in your righteousness.
17For you are their glory and strength,[j]
and by your favor you exalt our
horn.[a] [k]
18Indeed, our shield[b] [l] belongs to the
LORD,
our king[m] to the Holy One of Israel.

19Once you spoke in a vision,
to your faithful people you said:
"I have bestowed strength on a
warrior;
I have exalted a young man from
among the people.
20I have found David[n] my servant;[o]
with my sacred oil[p] I have
anointed[q] him.
21My hand will sustain him;
surely my arm will strengthen him.[r]
22No enemy will subject him to tribute;[s]
no wicked man will oppress[t] him.
23I will crush his foes before him[u]
and strike down his adversaries.[v]
24My faithful love will be with him,[w]
and through my name his horn[c]
will be exalted.
25I will set his hand over the sea,
his right hand over the rivers.[x]
26He will call out to me, 'You are my
Father,[y]
my God, the Rock[z] my Savior.'[a]
27I will also appoint him my firstborn,[b]

89:1 [j]S Ps 36:5; 40:10
89:2 [k]S Ps 36:5
89:4 [l]2Sa 7:12-16; 1Ki 8:16; Ps 132:11-12; Isa 9:7; Eze 37:24-25; S Mt 1:1; S Lk 1:33
89:5 [m]S Ps 19:1 [n]S Ps 1:5
89:6 [o]S Ge 1:26; S Ex 9:14; S Ps 18:31; 113:5
89:7 [p]Ps 111:1 [q]S Job 5:1 [r]Ps 47:2
89:8 [s]Isa 6:3 [t]S Ps 71:19
89:9 [u]S Ps 65:7
89:10 [v]S Job 9:13 [w]S Ps 59:11; S 68:1; 92:9
89:11 [x]S Dt 10:14; Ps 115:16 [y]1Ch 29:11; S Ps 24:1 [z]S Ge 1:1
89:12 [a]S Jos 19:22 [b]S Dt 3:8; S 4:48 [c]Ps 98:8
89:13 [d]S Jos 4:24
89:14 [e]Ps 97:2 [f]Ps 85:10-11
89:15 [g]Ps 1:1 [h]Ps 44:3
89:16 [i]Ps 30:4; 105:3
89:17 [j]Ps 18:1 [k]ver 24; Ps 75:10; 92:10; 112:9; 148:14
89:18 [l]Ps 18:2 [m]Ps 47:9; Isa 16:5; 33:17,22
89:20 [n]Ac 13:22 [o]Ps 78:70 [p]S Ex 29:7; S 1Ki 1:39 [q]S 1Sa 2:35; S 2Sa 22:51
89:21 [r]ver 13; Ps 18:35
89:22 [s]S Jdg 3:15 [t]2Sa 7:10
89:23 [u]Ps 18:40 [v]2Sa 7:9
89:24 [w]S 2Sa 7:15
89:25 [x]Ps 72:8
89:26 [y]S 2Sa 7:14; S Jer 3:4; Heb 1:5 [z]S Ps 62:2 [a]S 2Sa 22:47
89:27 [b]S Col 1:18

[a]*17 Horn* here symbolizes strong one. [b]*18* Or *sovereign* [c]*24 Horn* here symbolizes strength.

89:1–51 PRAYER, Lament—See note on 3:1–8. The plea for God to remember His love and faithfulness to the Davidic kingship (vv 38–51) follows a long eulogy of God's love and faithfulness to David (vv 1–37). God's love and faithfulness work together and formed the basis for Ethan's appeal. Praise and petition are parts of the same prayer. Lament over God's anger grows out of a life of faith and praise. Only the person who praises and trusts God can be honest in petitioning God seriously.

89:3–4,18–37 JESUS CHRIST, Foretold—God's promise to Abraham to extend his line to bless all the earth was repeated through the promise to David. Ps 89 extols the blessing promised to David. The promise was realized through Jesus Christ who was descended from David. Compare Lk 1:32–33.

89:3,28–37 THE CHURCH, Covenant People—See note on 2 Sa 23:5.

89:9–13 CREATION, Power—Creation shows God's power over all forces which might threaten human existence. Neither the fearful ocean depths nor Rahab, the mysterious monster of chaos, threaten God. Surely human enemies cannot. If this Psalm is to be read in light of 87:4, then the name Rahab is to be extended to include a reference to the ancient enemy Egypt. Then this passage would also call on us to recall the Exodus victory at the Red Sea (Ex 14). God possesses and rules over all creation. No one has power to take it from Him.

89:9–10 EVIL AND SUFFERING, Satan—See notes on Job 26:12–13; Ps 74:1–23; Isa 30:7.

89:14 GOD, Righteous—God's righteousness, justice, love, and faithfulness are linked together in this verse, suggesting the very close relationship of these basic qualities of the nature of God. God's sovereign rule over the world rests on His enduring faithfulness, His righteous character which leads Him to establish justice, and His love which binds Him to His people whom He created.

89:18,35 GOD, Holy—Holiness underlies all else that is said about God. God's awesome holiness is the only safe protection for an earthly ruler. His holy, moral purity guarantees His word can be trusted and His promises counted on. See notes on Ex 3:5–6; 19:10–24; Lev 11:44–45; 2 Co 7:1.

89:26 GOD, Father—The ideas of Father and Savior are related here. The heavenly Father saves His earthly leader and protects Him. See notes on 68:5, 19–20; 85:1–7.

the most exalted[c] of the kings[d] of
the earth.
28I will maintain my love to him forever,
and my covenant with him will
never fail.[e]
29I will establish his line forever,
his throne as long as the heavens
endure.[f]

30"If his sons forsake my law
and do not follow my statutes,
31if they violate my decrees
and fail to keep my commands,
32I will punish their sin with the rod,
their iniquity with flogging;[g]
33but I will not take my love from him,[h]
nor will I ever betray my
faithfulness.
34I will not violate my covenant
or alter what my lips have uttered.[i]
35Once for all, I have sworn by my
holiness—
and I will not lie to David—
36that his line will continue forever
and his throne endure before me
like the sun;[j]
37it will be established forever like the
moon,
the faithful witness in the sky."[k]
Selah

38But you have rejected,[l] you have
spurned,
you have been very angry with your
anointed one.
39You have renounced the covenant with
your servant
and have defiled his crown in the
dust.[m]
40You have broken through all his walls[n]
and reduced his strongholds[o] to
ruins.
41All who pass by have plundered[p] him;
he has become the scorn of his
neighbors.[q]
42You have exalted the right hand of his
foes;
you have made all his enemies
rejoice.[r]
43You have turned back the edge of his
sword
and have not supported him in
battle.[s]
44You have put an end to his splendor
and cast his throne to the ground.
45You have cut short[t] the days of his
youth;
you have covered him with a mantle
of shame.[u] *Selah*

46How long, O LORD? Will you hide
yourself forever?
How long will your wrath burn like
fire?[v]
47Remember how fleeting is my life.[w]
For what futility you have created all
men!
48What man can live and not see death,
or save himself from the power of
the grave[d]?[x] *Selah*
49O Lord, where is your former great
love,
which in your faithfulness you swore
to David?
50Remember, Lord, how your servant
has[e] been mocked,[y]
how I bear in my heart the taunts of
all the nations,
51the taunts with which your enemies
have mocked, O LORD,
with which they have mocked every
step of your anointed one.[z]

52Praise be to the LORD forever!
Amen and Amen.[a]

BOOK IV

Psalms 90–106

Psalm 90

A prayer of Moses the man of God.

LORD, you have been our dwelling
place[b]
throughout all generations.

89:27 [c]S Nu 24:7 [d]Ps 2:6; Rev 1:5; 19:16
89:28 [e]ver 33-34; Isa 55:3
89:29 [f]ver 4,36
89:32 [g]2Sa 7:14
89:33 [h]S 2Sa 7:15
89:34 [i]S Nu 23:19
89:36 [j]ver 4
89:37 [k]Jer 33:20-21
89:38 [l]1Ch 28:9; Ps 44:9; 78:59
89:39 [m]La 5:16
89:40 [n]S Ps 80:12 [o]Isa 22:5; La 2:2
89:41 [p]S Jdg 2:14 [q]S Ps 44:13
89:42 [r]Ps 13:2; 80:6
89:43 [s]Ps 44:10
89:45 [t]S Ps 39:5 [u]Ps 44:15; 109:29
89:46 [v]Ps 79:5
89:47 [w]S Ge 47:9; S Job 7:7; Ps 39:5; 1Pe 1:24
89:48 [x]S Ge 5:24; Ps 22:29
89:50 [y]Ps 69:19
89:51 [z]Ps 74:10
89:52 [a]S Ps 41:13; S 72:19
90:1 [b]S Dt 33:27; Eph 2:22; Rev 21:3

[d]48 Hebrew *Sheol* [e]50 Or *your servants have*

89:30–32 SIN, Responsibility—One generation's sins could not nullify God's promises to His chosen people. The sin would bring painful consequences. Human sin is serious, but it is not strong enough to defeat God's purposes.
89:39 THE CHURCH, Covenant People—God's everlasting covenant with David (2 Sa 23:5) did not release the kings from responsibility. When they relied on military might and political covenants rather than on God, He disciplined them. Eventually He took the kingship away from Israel. He did not forget His covenant. He reestablished it in a new form through Jesus Christ, the eternal King. See note on 74:20.
89:47–48 HUMANITY, Nature of Death—People always face the temporality of life and its ultimate limits. Life as it is always ends in death. Facing death without the confidence of God's presence and love is life's most dreadful experience.
89:48 LAST THINGS, Intermediate State—See note on Isa 14:9.
89:52 HOLY SCRIPTURE, Collection—See note on 41:13.
89:52 PRAYER, Corporate—See note on 41:13.
90:1–17 EVIL AND SUFFERING, Divine Origin—Belief in the existence and rule of only one God is the basis of the theological problem of evil. Belief in more than one god would let us blame evil and suffering on a "bad" god while still loving and serving the good god(s). We must relate suffering and evil to God's sovereignty. The psalmist contrasted God's eternity to the brief span of human life and confessed that God not only created humans from dust but also caused us to return to dust in death. Divine anger at human sin was the motivation behind God's act. See notes on Ge 3:1–13, 14–24. Our limited, troubled days make it imperative we learn to use our time wisely and seek God's compassion and forgiveness.
90:1–17 PRAYER, Sovereignty of God—This prayer contrasts the eternity of God with the temporal nature of man. See note on Ps 84:1–12. Prayer seeks the meaning of the transitory in view of the eternal. The work of even mortal man can be

2Before the mountains were born[c]
or you brought forth the earth and the world,
from everlasting to everlasting[d] you are God.[e]

3You turn men back to dust,
saying, "Return to dust, O sons of men."[f]
4For a thousand years in your sight
are like a day that has just gone by,
or like a watch in the night.[g]
5You sweep men away[h] in the sleep of death;
they are like the new grass of the morning—
6though in the morning it springs up new,
by evening it is dry and withered.[i]

7We are consumed by your anger
and terrified by your indignation.
8You have set our iniquities before you,
our secret sins[j] in the light of your presence.[k]
9All our days pass away under your wrath;
we finish our years with a moan.[l]
10The length of our days is seventy years[m]—
or eighty,[n] if we have the strength;
yet their span[t] is but trouble and sorrow,[o]
for they quickly pass, and we fly away.[p]
11Who knows the power of your anger?
For your wrath[q] is as great as the fear that is due you.[r]
12Teach us to number our days[s] aright,
that we may gain a heart of wisdom.[t]

13Relent, O LORD! How long[u] will it be?
Have compassion on your servants.[v]
14Satisfy[w] us in the morning with your unfailing love,[x]
that we may sing for joy[y] and be glad all our days.[z]
15Make us glad for as many days as you have afflicted us,
for as many years as we have seen trouble.
16May your deeds be shown to your servants,
your splendor to their children.[a]
17May the favor[g] of the Lord our God rest upon us;
establish the work of our hands for us—
yes, establish the work of our hands.[b]

Psalm 91

HE who dwells in the shelter[c] of the Most High
will rest in the shadow[d] of the Almighty.[h]
2I will say[i] of the LORD, "He is my refuge[e] and my fortress,[f]
my God, in whom I trust."

3Surely he will save you from the fowler's snare[g]
and from the deadly pestilence.[h]
4He will cover you with his feathers,
and under his wings you will find refuge;[i]
his faithfulness will be your shield[j] and rampart.
5You will not fear[k] the terror of night,
nor the arrow that flies by day,
6nor the pestilence that stalks in the darkness,
nor the plague that destroys at midday.
7A thousand may fall at your side,

90:2 [c]S Job 15:7 [d]Isa 9:6; 57:15 [e]S Ge 21:33; S Job 10:5; Ps 102:24-27; Pr 8:23-26
90:3 [f]S Ge 2:7; S Job 7:21; 34:15; 1Co 15:47
90:4 [g]S Job 10:5; 2Pe 3:8
90:5 [h]S Ge 19:15
90:6 [i]Isa 40:6-8; Mt 6:30; Jas 1:10
90:8 [j]S Ps 19:12; 2Co 4:2; Eph 5:12 [k]S Heb 4:13
90:9 [l]Ps 78:33
90:10 [m]Isa 23:15, 17; Jer 25:11 [n]2Sa 19:35 [o]S Job 5:7 [p]S Job 20:8; S 34:15
90:11 [q]Ps 7:11 [r]Ps 76:7
90:12 [s]Ps 39:4; 139:16; Pr 16:9; 20:24 [t]Dt 32:29
90:13 [u]Ps 6:3 [v]S Dt 32:36
90:14 [w]Ps 103:5; 107:9; 145:16,19 [x]S Ps 77:8; 143:8 [y]S Ps 5:11 [z]Ps 31:7
90:16 [a]Ps 44:1; Hab 3:2
90:17 [b]Isa 26:12
91:1 [c]S Ex 33:22 [d]Ps 63:7; Isa 49:2; La 4:20
91:2 [e]ver 9; S 2Sa 22:3; Ps 9:9 [f]S 2Sa 22:2
91:3 [g]Ps 124:7; Pr 6:5 [h]1Ki 8:37
91:4 [i]S Ru 2:12; Ps 17:8 [j]S Dt 32:10; Ps 35:2; Isa 27:3; 31:5; Zec 12:8
91:5 [k]S Job 5:21

[t]10 Or *yet the best of them* [g]17 Or *beauty* [h]1 Hebrew *Shaddai* [i]2 Or *He says*

established; only the Eternal knows the meaning of the word "establish" (v 17).
90:5–6 HUMANITY, Life—Death is a natural end to life even as sleep is the natural end of having been awake. See note on 89:47–48. The brevity of human life provides a sharp contrast to God's relationship to time. It also calls us to use our time wisely (v 12).
90:7–11 GOD, Wrath—God's wrath leads His troubled people to cry for His love and compassion. See note on 88:15–18.
90:9–10 HUMANITY, Life—Life has limits. It is limited in duration. Most of us cannot expect to live more than seventy or eighty years. Life's joys also have limits. Life is filled with sorrow. No one escapes grief. Under such limits we need a sense of God's unfailing love and care.
90:12 HUMANITY, Intellectual Nature—As usual, the heart in the Old Testament is understood as the seat of the mind, the intellect, the will. Life should be so lived that people become wise as God intends. Only He can teach us to plan our lives and use our time in such a manner that we reach the full measure of wisdom He plans for us. Such wisdom leads us to accept the sorrows life brings and to be grateful for signs of God's love and care.
90:13–17 GOD, Love—Note the emphasis here on God's love, grace, and compassion, following the preceeding emphasis on His wrath.
91:1–16 GOD, Savior—This entire psalm praises God as Savior. In saving us God responds to our love for Him (v 14). See notes on 38:22; 62:1–2,6–8; Lk 1:47; 1 Ti 1:1.
91:1–16 EVIL AND SUFFERING, God's Present Help—Those who rely on God need not fear evil. Satan quoted vv 11–12 in response to Jesus (Mt 4:6; Lk 4:10–11). Jesus' own experience in Pilate's court, Gethsemane, and on Golgotha shows that God's faithful people suffer physical harm and pain. In all suffering and trouble we can turn to God, experience His presence, and feel the spiritual security He gives. Our problems never outnumber God's resources.
91:1–16 PRAYER, Intercession—God provides protection for troubled people. This prayer functioned as a blessing by a Temple priest for worshipers seeking God's help. See note on Nu 6:22–27. Such intercession provides comfort and hope. The divine response (vv 14–16) solidifies the worshiper's faith. See note on 6:1–10.

ten thousand at your right hand,
but it will not come near you.
8You will only observe with your eyes
and see the punishment of the wicked.[l]

9If you make the Most High your dwelling—
even the LORD, who is my refuge—
10then no harm[m] will befall you,
no disaster will come near your tent.
11For he will command his angels[n] concerning you
to guard you in all your ways;[o]
12they will lift you up in their hands,
so that you will not strike your foot against a stone.[p]
13You will tread upon the lion and the cobra;
you will trample the great lion and the serpent.[q]

14"Because he loves me," says the LORD,
"I will rescue him;
I will protect him, for he acknowledges my name.
15He will call upon me, and I will answer him;
I will be with him in trouble,
I will deliver him and honor him.[r]
16With long life[s] will I satisfy him
and show him my salvation.[t]"

Psalm 92

A psalm. A song. For the Sabbath day.

1It is good to praise the LORD
and make music[u] to your name,[v] O Most High,[w]
2to proclaim your love in the morning[x]
and your faithfulness at night,
3to the music of the ten-stringed lyre[y]
and the melody of the harp.[z]

91:8 [l]Ps 37:34; S 58:10
91:10 [m]Pr 12:21
91:11 [n]S Ge 32:1; Heb 1:14 [o]Ps 34:7
91:12 [p]Mt 4:6*; Lk 4:10-11*
91:13 [q]Da 6:22; Lk 10:19
91:15 [r]S 1Sa 2:30; Jn 12:26
91:16 [s]Dt 6:2; S Ps 21:4 [t]S Ps 50:23
92:1 [u]S Ps 27:6 [v]S Ps 9:2; 147:1 [w]Ps 135:3
92:2 [x]S Ps 55:17
92:3 [y]S Ps 71:22 [z]S 1Sa 10:5; S Ne 12:27; S Ps 33:2; 81:2
92:4 [a]S Ps 5:11; 27:6 [b]S Ps 8:6; 111:7; 143:5
92:5 [c]S Job 36:24; Rev 15:3 [d]Ps 40:5; 139:17; Isa 28:29; 31:2; Ro 11:33
92:6 [e]S Ps 73:22
92:7 [f]S Ps 37:2
92:9 [g]S Ps 45:5 [h]S Ps 68:1; S 89:10
92:10 [i]S Ps 89:17 [j]S Ps 29:6 [k]S Ps 23:5
92:11 [l]S Ps 54:7; 91:8
92:12 [m]S Ps 72:7 [n]S Ps 1:3; 52:8; Jer 17:8; Hos 14:6
92:13 [o]Ps 135:2
92:14 [p]S Ps 1:3; S Jn 15:2
92:15 [q]S Job 34:10
93:1 [r]S 1Ch 16:31; S Ps 97:1 [s]S Job 40:10; S Ps 21:5

4For you make me glad by your deeds, O LORD;
I sing for joy[a] at the works of your hands.[b]
5How great are your works,[c] O LORD,
how profound your thoughts![d]
6The senseless man[e] does not know,
fools do not understand,
7that though the wicked spring up like grass
and all evildoers flourish,
they will be forever destroyed.[f]

8But you, O LORD, are exalted forever.

9For surely your enemies[g], O LORD,
surely your enemies will perish;
all evildoers will be scattered.[h]
10You have exalted my horn[i][j] like that of a wild ox;[j]
fine oils[k] have been poured upon me.
11My eyes have seen the defeat of my adversaries;
my ears have heard the rout of my wicked foes.[l]

12The righteous will flourish[m] like a palm tree,
they will grow like a cedar of Lebanon;[n]
13planted in the house of the LORD,
they will flourish in the courts of our God.[o]
14They will still bear fruit[p] in old age,
they will stay fresh and green,
15proclaiming, "The LORD is upright;
he is my Rock, and there is no wickedness in him.[q]"

Psalm 93

1THE LORD reigns,[r] he is robed in majesty;[s]

[i]10 *Horn* here symbolizes strength.

91:14–15 SALVATION, As Deliverance—Contrast 50:15. God honors those whom He delivers. He delivers those who love Him and know Him personally.
91:16 HUMANITY, Life—As long as life was thought to be limited by death, then God's greatest act of mercy was understood to be the granting of long life under God's protection. In Jesus Christ we have learned that life is His greatest gift and that it goes on beyond the grave. See 1 Co 15:19.
92:1–15 EVIL AND SUFFERING, Punishment—See note on 11:1–7. Suffering must be viewed in long-term perspective. Evil exists but not eternally. God is opposed to evil and will destroy it.
92:1–15 PRAYER, Praise—See note on 33:1–22. Praise is good. It is what God deserves and wants. It is what people need to do. Music enhances praise. Praise describes the nature and actions of God and the consequences of those on human life.
92:2 GOD, Faithfulness—The love and faithfulness of God are virtually synonymous here. God's love is constant, dependable, unchanging.
92:4–7 REVELATION, *Events*—The redemptive actions of God brought the worshiper gladness. He celebrated the faithfulness of God in the constant revelation of His love for His people through deeds of mercy and salvation. God is at work because of His nature of love to make good out of every event. The joy the believer experiences is based upon God's unfailing presence and work in all that happens.
92:4 HISTORY, Individual—The history of God's acts for His people brings joy and hope to individual worshipers.
92:4 SALVATION, Joy—God's deeds make His people glad and enable them to sing with joy. See note on 4:7.
92:15 GOD, Righteous—The righteous God is totally devoid of wickedness. See notes on Lev 1:1; Jos 23:1–16; 2 Sa 10:12; Jn 17:25.
93:1 GOD, Creator—By creating the world, God established His power and authority to rule it. This calls for our praise. See note on 86:9.
93:1–5 PRAYER, Praise—See notes on 33:1–22; 47:1–9. This psalm is unusual in that the praise is for God Himself. The majority of the praise psalms celebrate what He does or has done for people. This rare kind of praise also appears in Ps 96; 97; 100; 150. The universal reign of the Lord is an important basis of praise throughout the psalter. Pss 47 and 117 are a shout of joy over that reign; Ps 72 celebrates the reign of the universal King. Ps 93 begins a series of praise and prayers about the universality of God's reign in stability (Ps 93), justice (Pss 94; 98), supremacy (Ps 96), and exaltation in history (Ps 99).

the LORD is robed in majesty
and is armed with strength.[t]
The world is firmly established;[u]
it cannot be moved.[v]
2Your throne was established[w] long ago;
you are from all eternity.[x]

3The seas[y] have lifted up, O LORD,
the seas have lifted up their voice;[z]
the seas have lifted up their pounding waves.[a]
4Mightier than the thunder[b] of the great waters,
mightier than the breakers[c] of the sea—
the LORD on high is mighty.[d]

5Your statutes stand firm;
holiness[e] adorns your house[f]
for endless days, O LORD.

Psalm 94

O LORD, the God who avenges,[g]
O God who avenges, shine forth.[h]
2Rise up,[i] O Judge[j] of the earth;
pay back[k] to the proud what they deserve.
3How long will the wicked, O LORD,
how long will the wicked be jubilant?[l]

4They pour out arrogant[m] words;
all the evildoers are full of boasting.[n]
5They crush your people,[o] O LORD;
they oppress your inheritance.[p]
6They slay the widow[q] and the alien;
they murder the fatherless.[r]
7They say, "The LORD does not see;[s]
the God of Jacob[t] pays no heed."

8Take heed, you senseless ones[u] among the people;
you fools, when will you become wise?
9Does he who implanted the ear not hear?
Does he who formed the eye not see?[v]
10Does he who disciplines[w] nations not punish?
Does he who teaches[x] man lack knowledge?
11The LORD knows the thoughts[y] of man;
he knows that they are futile.[z]

12Blessed is the man you discipline,[a] O LORD,
the man you teach[b] from your law;
13you grant him relief from days of trouble,[c]
till a pit[d] is dug for the wicked.
14For the LORD will not reject his people;[e]
he will never forsake his inheritance.
15Judgment will again be founded on righteousness,[f]
and all the upright in heart[g] will follow it.

16Who will rise up[h] for me against the wicked?
Who will take a stand for me against evildoers?[i]
17Unless the LORD had given me help,[j]

93:1 [t]S Ps 65:6 [u]Ps 24:2; 78:69; 119:90 [v]1Ch 16:30; Ps 96:10 **93:2** [w]S 2Sa 7:16 [x]S Ge 21:33 **93:3** [y]Ps 96:11; 98:7; Isa 5:30; 17:12-13; Jer 6:23 [z]S Ps 46:3 [a]Job 9:8; Ps 107:25,29; Isa 51:15; Jer 31:35; Hab 3:10 **93:4** [b]Ps 65:7; Jer 6:23 [c]S Ps 18:4; Jnh 1:15 [d]S Ne 9:32; S Job 9:4 **93:5** [e]Ps 29:2; 96:9 [f]Ps 5:7; 23:6 **94:1** [g]S Ge 4:24; Ro 12:19 [h]S Dt 33:2; Ps 80:1 **94:2** [i]S Nu 10:35 [j]S Ge 18:25; Heb 12:23; S Jas 5:9 [k]S Ps 31:23 **94:3** [l]Ps 13:2 **94:4** [m]Jer 43:2 [n]S Ps 52:1 **94:5** [o]Ps 44:2; 74:8; Isa 3:15; Jer 8:21 [p]Ps 28:9 **94:6** [q]S Dt 10:18; S Isa 1:17 [r]Dt 24:19 **94:7** [s]S Job 22:14 [t]S Ge 24:12 **94:8** [u]S Dt 32:6; S Ps 73:22 **94:9** [v]Ex 4:11; Pr 20:12 **94:10** [w]S Ps 39:11 [x]S Ex 35:34; Job 35:11; Isa 28:26 **94:11** [y]Ps 139:2; Pr 15:26; S Mt 9:4 [z]1Co 3:20* **94:12** [a]S Job 5:17; 1Co 11:32; Heb 12:5 [b]S Dt 8:3; S 1Sa 12:23 **94:13** [c]S Ps 86:7 [d]S Ps 7:15; S 55:23 **94:14** [e]S Dt 31:6; Ps 37:28; Ro 11:2 **94:15** [f]Ps 97:2 [g]Ps 7:10; 11:2; S 36:10 **94:16** [h]Nu 10:35; Ps 17:13; Isa 14:22 [i]S Ps 59:2 **94:17** [j]Ps 124:2

Ps 95 speaks of submission; 97, of awe; and 98 of singing in view of God's reign. Ps 100 is a climactic expression of thanksgiving.

93:2 GOD, Eternal—God has no time limits. He always was God and always will be. He never had to defeat another god to gain His eternal throne. No one can ever usurp His power. See notes on Ge 1:1; 21:33; Ro 16:25–27.

93:5 GOD, Holy—See notes on Ex 3:5–6; 19:10–24; Lev 11:44–45; 2 Co 7:1.

94:1–2,22–23 GOD, Justice—God's justice ensures that wickedness will not triumph no matter how bad circumstances appear. See notes on 7:6,8,11; 72:1; Job 40:8; 41:11; 42:7–9.

94:1–23 EVIL AND SUFFERING, Endurance—See notes on 3:1–8; 35:1–28. Atheistic human opinion does not change reality. God is aware of and will take care of human wickedness. The successful person is one who experiences God's discipline and learns from it. The failure is the one who ignores God. God's people know He will never totally reject us.

94:1–23 CHRISTIAN ETHICS, Justice—The portrayal of injustice should be vivid to each of us. The psalmist encourages us with his sense of hope that God's relief will come. He is the supreme Judge and is constantly aware of oppression and injustice. Corrupt leaders and judges cannot claim God's support.

94:1–23 PRAYER, Lament—See notes on 3:1–8; 93:1–5. The psalmist appealed to God as Judge to deal with the arrogant. Because God is the Judge of the universe, we can appeal to Him for justice. Public prayer represents the desires of the individual as part of the congregation. Thus it often fluctuates between singular and plural subject, I and we.

94:10–11 GOD, Wisdom—Human wisdom cannot be compared to God's. He knows all we know and much more. We need to let Him teach us His ways for us. See note on 73:11.

94:10–12 EDUCATION, God—God's instruction is closely related to His punishment and discipline. The happy, secure individual learns from life's difficult experiences and acknowledges that God's law points to discipline for the disobedient. See note on 25:4–9.

94:11 HUMANITY, Intellectual Nature—"Futile" is literally "vanity," "insignificant," "like a breath." The greatest human intellectual achievements are insignificant in comparison to God's wisdom. Only fools take so much pride in their knowledge and intelligence that they ignore God, His purposes, and commands.

94:12 CHRISTIAN ETHICS, Moral Imperatives—The moral law acts as God's entry level teacher to His ethical expectations of individuals and the larger society. See notes on Ge 2:16–17; Lev 18:3–30.

94:14 ELECTION, Faithfulness—God will not reject His elect, but He will discipline them when it is necessary.

94:17 HUMANITY, Life—Only God's power provides life for people. Amid all the threats to our life, we can call on God for help and deliverance. Without Him we slip into the silence of death.

I would soon have dwelt in the
silence of death.[k]
18When I said, "My foot is slipping,[l]"
your love, O LORD, supported me.
19When anxiety[m] was great within me,
your consolation[n] brought joy to my
soul.

20Can a corrupt throne[o] be allied with
you—
one that brings on misery by its
decrees?[p]
21They band together[q] against the
righteous
and condemn the innocent[r] to
death.[s]
22But the LORD has become my fortress,
and my God the rock[t] in whom I
take refuge.[u]
23He will repay[v] them for their sins
and destroy[w] them for their
wickedness;
the LORD our God will destroy them.

Psalm 95

COME,[x] let us sing for joy[y] to the
LORD;
let us shout aloud[z] to the Rock[a] of
our salvation.
2Let us come before him[b] with
thanksgiving[c]
and extol him with music[d] and
song.

3For the LORD is the great God,[e]
the great King[f] above all gods.[g]
4In his hand are the depths of the
earth,[h]
and the mountain peaks belong to
him.
5The sea is his, for he made it,
and his hands formed the dry land.[i]

6Come, let us bow down[j] in worship,[k]
let us kneel[l] before the LORD our
Maker;[m]
7for he is our God
and we are the people of his
pasture,[n]
the flock under his care.

Today, if you hear his voice,
8 do not harden your hearts[o] as you
did at Meribah,[k] [p]
as you did that day at Massah[l] in
the desert,[q]
9where your fathers tested[r] and tried
me,
though they had seen what I did.
10For forty years[s] I was angry with that
generation;
I said, "They are a people whose
hearts go astray,[t]
and they have not known my
ways."[u]
11So I declared on oath[v] in my anger,
"They shall never enter my rest."[w]

Psalm 96

96:1-13pp — 1Ch 16:23-33

SING to the LORD[x] a new song;[y]
sing to the LORD, all the earth.
2Sing to the LORD, praise his name;[z]
proclaim his salvation[a] day after
day.
3Declare his glory[b] among the nations,
his marvelous deeds[c] among all
peoples.

4For great is the LORD and most worthy
of praise;[d]
he is to be feared[e] above all gods.[f]
5For all the gods of the nations are
idols,[g]
but the LORD made the heavens.[h]
6Splendor and majesty[i] are before him;
strength and glory[j] are in his
sanctuary.

94:17 [k]S Ps 31:17 **94:18** [l]S Dt 32:35; S Job 12:5 **94:19** [m]Ecc 11:10 [n]S Job 6:10 **94:20** [o]Jer 22:30; 36:30 [p]S Ps 58:2 **94:21** [q]S Ps 56:6 [r]Ps 106:38; Pr 17:15,26; 28:21; Isa 5:20,23; Mt 27:4 [s]S Ge 18:23 **94:22** [t]S Ps 61:2 [u]S 2Sa 22:3; S Ps 18:2 **94:23** [v]S Ex 32:34; S Ps 54:5 [w]Ps 9:5; 37:38; 145:20 **95:1** [x]Ps 34:11; 80:2 [y]S Ps 5:11 [z]Ps 81:1; Isa 44:23; Zep 3:14 [a]S 2Sa 22:47 **95:2** [b]Ps 100:2; Mic 6:6 [c]S Ps 42:4 [d]Ps 81:2; S Eph 5:19 **95:3** [e]Ps 48:1; 86:10; 145:3; 147:5 [f]S Ps 47:2 [g]Ps 96:4; 97:9 **95:4** [h]S Ps 63:9 **95:5** [i]S Ge 1:9; Ps 146:6 **95:6** [j]S 2Sa 12:16; Php 2:10 [k]S Ps 22:29 [l]2Ch 6:13 [m]Ps 100:3; 149:2; Isa 17:7; 54:5; Da 6:10-11; Hos 8:14 **95:7** [n]S Ps 74:1 **95:8** [o]Mk 10:5; Heb 3:8 [p]S Ex 17:7; S Dt 33:8; Heb 3:15*; 4:7 [q]S Ps 78:40 **95:9** [r]S Nu 14:22; 1Co 10:9 **95:10** [s]S Ex 16:35; S Nu 14:34; Ac 7:36; Heb 3:17 [t]Ps 58:3; 119:67, 176; Pr 12:26; 16:29; Isa 53:6; Jer 31:19; 50:6; Eze 34:6 [u]S Dt 8:6 **95:11** [v]S Nu 14:23 [w]Dt 1:35; Heb 3:7-11*; 4:3* **96:1** [x]Ps 30:4 [y]Ps 33:3; S 40:3; 98:1; 144:9; 149:1; Isa 42:10; S Rev 5:9 **96:2** [z]S Ps 68:4 [a]Ps 27:1; 71:15 **96:3** [b]Ps 8:1 [c]S Ps 71:17; Rev 15:3 **96:4** [d]S Ps 48:1 [e]S Dt 28:58; S 1Ch 16:25; Ps 89:7 [f]S Ps 95:3 **96:5** [g]S Lev 19:4 [h]S Ge 1:1; S 2Ch 2:12 **96:6** [i]S Ps 21:5 [j]Ps 29:1; 89:17

[k]8 *Meribah* means *quarreling.* [l]8 *Massah* means *testing.*

94:23 SIN, Judgment—See note on 68:21.
95:1–11 PRAYER, Praise—See notes on 33:1–22; 93:1–5. We should enter His presence with thanksgiving and submission. The call to worship is a vital prayer in the congregation's worship. It calls for worship and obedience. Its speech to the congregation is at the same time prayer to God.
95:3–7 GOD, Creator—God created and controls everything—heights and depths, land and sea. Thus He rules all, and we respond naturally in humble worship. Note the Creator is also the kind Shepherd. Compare Ps 23.
95:7–11 EVIL AND SUFFERING, Punishment—God rejects a people who claim to be His but refuse to obey Him. The history of human rebellion and divine punishment should call us to worship and loyalty. Compare Heb 3:7–11; 4:3–11.
95:8–11 SIN, Judgment—Past sin should warn the present generation of God's power and will to intervene in history and discipline sinners. See note on Nu 14:23.
95:8–11 ELECTION, Condemnation—Compare Ex 17:7; Nu 20:8–12. Beyond praise in worship is obedience to God. Reverent humility must enable God's elect to be true to the calling of their election. Rebellion brings God's anger and punishment, robbing a generation of the blessings of the elect.
95:10–11 GOD, Wrath—History teaches us the reality of God's wrath. See notes on Ge 6:5–8; 17:14; 19:13,24–26; Jos 7:1,25–26; Mt 3:7–10.
96:1–13 PRAYER, Praise—See note on 93:1–5. Praise raises our prayer life beyond ourselves to encompass the universe and all its inhabitants.
96:3,6–8 GOD, Glory—In worship and witness we spread the news of God's prestige and honor which outranks all others. We let others know His glory by telling the miraculous acts He has performed for us. All people are invited to worship the glorious One. See notes on Ex 16:7,10; 40:34–38; Lk 2:9,14; Jn 11:4.
96:4–6 GOD, Creator—Creation shows the uniqueness of God. Nothing else can rival Him because everything else has been created. No one created God. He is eternal. See notes on 93:1; 95:3–7.

7Ascribe to the LORD,[k] O families of
nations,[l]
ascribe to the LORD glory and
strength.
8Ascribe to the LORD the glory due his
name;
bring an offering[m] and come into his
courts.[n]
9Worship the LORD[o] in the splendor of
his[m] holiness;[p]
tremble[q] before him, all the earth.[r]
10Say among the nations, "The LORD
reigns.[s]"
The world is firmly established,[t] it
cannot be moved;[u]
he will judge[v] the peoples with
equity.[w]
11Let the heavens rejoice,[x] let the earth
be glad;[y]
let the sea resound, and all that is in
it;
12 let the fields be jubilant, and
everything in them.
Then all the trees of the forest[z] will
sing for joy;[a]
13 they will sing before the LORD, for
he comes,
he comes to judge[b] the earth.
He will judge the world in
righteousness[c]
and the peoples in his truth.[d]

Psalm 97

THE LORD reigns,[e] let the earth be
glad;[f]
let the distant shores[g] rejoice.

2Clouds[h] and thick darkness[i] surround
him;
righteousness and justice are the
foundation of his throne.[j]
3Fire[k] goes before[l] him
and consumes[m] his foes on every
side.
4His lightning[n] lights up the world;
the earth[o] sees and trembles.[p]
5The mountains melt[q] like wax[r] before
the LORD,
before the Lord of all the earth.[s]
6The heavens proclaim his
righteousness,[t]
and all the peoples see his glory.[u]

7All who worship images[v] are put to
shame,[w]
those who boast in idols[x] —
worship him,[y] all you gods![z]

8Zion hears and rejoices
and the villages of Judah are glad[a]
because of your judgments,[b]
O LORD.
9For you, O LORD, are the Most High[c]
over all the earth;[d]
you are exalted[e] far above all gods.

10Let those who love the LORD hate
evil,[f]
for he guards[g] the lives of his
faithful ones[h]
and delivers[i] them from the hand of
the wicked.[j]
11Light is shed[k] upon the righteous[l]
and joy on the upright in heart.[m]
12Rejoice in the LORD,[n] you who are
righteous,
and praise his holy name.[o]

Psalm 98

A psalm.

SING to the LORD[p] a new song,[q]
for he has done marvelous things;[r]
his right hand[s] and his holy arm[t]
have worked salvation[u] for him.
2The LORD has made his salvation
known[v]

96:7 [k]Ps 29:1 [l]Ps 22:27 **96:8** [m]Ps 45:12; S 51:19; 72:10 [n]Ps 65:4; 84:10; 92:13; 100:4 **96:9** [o]Ex 23:25; Jnh 1:9 [p]S Ps 93:5 [q]S Ex 15:14; Ps 114:7 [r]Ps 33:8 **96:10** [s]Ps 97:1 [t]Ps 24:2; 78:69; 119:90 [u]S Ps 93:1 [v]Ps 58:11 [w]Ps 67:4; 98:9 **96:11** [x]S Rev 12:12 [y]Ps 97:1; Isa 49:13 **96:12** [z]Isa 44:23; 55:12; Eze 17:24 [a]Ps 65:13 **96:13** [b]Rev 19:11 [c]S Ps 7:11; Ac 17:31 [d]Ps 86:11 **97:1** [e]Ex 15:18; Ps 93:1; 96:10; 99:1; Isa 24:23; 52:7 [f]S Ps 96:11 [g]S Est 10:1 **97:2** [h]S Job 22:14 [i]S Ex 19:9 [j]Ps 89:14 **97:3** [k]Isa 9:19; Da 7:10; Joel 1:19; 2:3 [l]Hab 3:5 [m]S 2Sa 22:9 **97:4** [n]S Job 36:30 [o]S 2Sa 22:8 [p]S Ps 18:7; 104:32; S Rev 6:12 **97:5** [q]S Ps 46:2,6 [r]S Ps 22:14 [s]S Jos 3:11 **97:6** [t]Ps 50:6; 98:2 [u]S Ps 19:1 **97:7** [v]S Lev 26:1 [w]Isa 42:17; Jer 10:14 [x]S Dt 5:8 [y]Heb 1:6 [z]Ex 12:12; Ps 16:4 **97:8** [a]S Ps 9:2 [b]Ps 48:11 **97:9** [c]Ps 7:8 [d]S Job 34:29 [e]S Ps 47:9 **97:10** [f]S Job 28:28; Am 5:15; Ro 12:9 [g]Ps 145:20 [h]Ps 31:23; 37:28; Pr 2:8 [i]S Ps 34:7; Da 3:28; 6:16 [j]Ps 37:40; Jer 15:21; 20:13 **97:11** [k]S Job 22:28 [l]Ps 11:5 [m]Ps 7:10 **97:12** [n]S Job 22:19; Ps 104:34; Isa 41:16; Php 4:4 [o]S Ex 3:15; S Ps 99:3 **98:1** [p]Ps 30:4 [q]S Ps 96:1 [r]Ex 15:1; Ps 96:3; Isa 12:5; Lk 1:51 [s]S Ex 15:6 [t]S Jos 4:24; Job 40:9; Isa 51:9; 52:10; 53:1; 63:5 [u]S Ps 44:3; Isa 59:16 **98:2** [v]Isa 52:10; Lk 3:6

[m]9 Or *LORD with the splendor of*

96:9 WORSHIP, Reverence—God's holiness often produces such awe in us that we tremble in adoration before Him. See note on Lev 9:23–24.

96:10–13 GOD, Judge—Note the close relationship between the idea of the righteousness of God and God acting as judge of all the earth. His judgment will be carried out on the basis of righteousness. His righteous judgment brings joy and praise to His creation.

97:1,5,9 GOD, Sovereignty—See note on 59:5,13.

97:1–12 PRAYER, Praise—See note on 93:1–5. God's rule brings joy and praise to His people but shame and fear to others.

97:2,6 GOD, Righteous—The glorious order of the skies shows God is right in all He does. See notes on 89:14; Lev 1:1; Jos 23:1–16; 2 Sa 10:12; Jn 17:25.

97:10–12 CHRISTIAN ETHICS, Character—The promise of God's protection, blessing, and joy resides with those who "love the Lord." To love Him is more than emotion. It is a commitment to hate evil and thus avoid evil actions.

98:1–3 GOD, Savior—God's saving work is not hidden, a special secret shared only by the initiated. He acts in full view of all people, in human history, to provide salvation. He invites all people to accept His saving acts. See notes on 38:22; 62:1–2,6–8; Lk 1:47; 1 Ti 1:1.

98:1 GOD, Holy—God's awesome holiness does not separate Him from His people. It enables Him to bring salvation. See note on 89:18,35.

98:1–3 HISTORY, Praise—God's saving involvement in Israel's national and individual lives called forth praise from His people and from the nations. They showed God's love was more than an abstract idea used by theologians. God's love gained concrete expression in His historical actions.

98:1–9 PRAYER, Praise—See note on 93:1–5. This is a psalm of universal music welcoming God's just judgment.

98:2–3 GOD, Love—Note the close relationship between God's love and righteousness and salvation. Letting His people see His salvation reveals to all people that He is righteous. He acts to save because He loves and is faithful to His purposes and promises. See notes on 89:1–49; 97:2,6.

and revealed his righteousness[w] to
the nations.[x]
3He has remembered[y] his love
and his faithfulness to the house of
Israel;
all the ends of the earth[z] have seen
the salvation of our God.[a]

4Shout for joy[b] to the LORD, all the
earth,
burst into jubilant song with music;
5make music to the LORD with the
harp,[c]
with the harp and the sound of
singing,[d]
6with trumpets[e] and the blast of the
ram's horn[f] —
shout for joy[g] before the LORD, the
King.[h]

7Let the sea[i] resound, and everything
in it,
the world, and all who live in it.[j]
8Let the rivers clap their hands,[k]
let the mountains[l] sing together for
joy;
9let them sing before the LORD,
for he comes to judge the earth.
He will judge the world in
righteousness
and the peoples with equity.[m]

Psalm 99

THE LORD reigns,[n]
let the nations tremble;[o]
he sits enthroned[p] between the
cherubim,[q]
let the earth shake.
2Great is the LORD[r] in Zion;[s]
he is exalted[t] over all the nations.
3Let them praise[u] your great and
awesome name[v] —
he is holy.[w]

4The King[x] is mighty, he loves
justice[y] —
you have established equity;[z]
in Jacob you have done
what is just and right.[a]
5Exalt[b] the LORD our God
and worship at his footstool;
he is holy.

6Moses[c] and Aaron[d] were among his
priests,
Samuel[e] was among those who
called on his name;
they called on the LORD
and he answered[f] them.
7He spoke to them from the pillar of
cloud;[g]
they kept his statutes and the
decrees he gave them.

8O LORD our God,
you answered them;
you were to Israel[n] a forgiving God,[h]
though you punished[i] their
misdeeds.[o]
9Exalt the LORD our God
and worship at his holy mountain,
for the LORD our God is holy.

Psalm 100

A psalm. For giving thanks.

SHOUT for joy[j] to the LORD, all the
earth.
2 Worship the LORD[k] with gladness;
come before him[l] with joyful songs.
3Know that the LORD is God.[m]
It is he who made us,[n] and we are
his[p];
we are his people,[o] the sheep of his
pasture.[p]

4Enter his gates with thanksgiving[q]
and his courts[r] with praise;
give thanks to him and praise his
name.[s]
5For the LORD is good[t] and his love
endures forever;[u]

98:2 [w]S Ps 97:6 [x]S Ps 67:2
98:3 [y]S 1Ch 16:15 [z]S Ge 49:10; S Ps 48:10 [a]S Ps 50:23
98:4 [b]Ps 20:5; Isa 12:6; 44:23; 52:9; 54:1; 55:12
98:5 [c]Ps 33:2; 92:3; 147:7 [d]Isa 51:3
98:6 [e]S Nu 10:2; S 2Sa 6:15 [f]S Ex 19:13 [g]Ps 20:5; 100:1; Isa 12:6 [h]Ps 2:6; 47:7
98:7 [i]S Ps 93:3 [j]S Ps 24:1
98:8 [k]S 2Ki 11:12 [l]Ps 148:9; Isa 44:23; 55:12
98:9 [m]S Ps 96:10
99:1 [n]S 1Ch 16:31; S Ps 97:1 [o]S Ex 15:14; S 1Ch 16:30 [p]S 2Sa 6:2 [q]S Ex 25:22
99:2 [r]S Ps 48:1 [s]Ps 2:6 [t]Ex 15:1; Ps 46:10; 97:9; 113:4; 148:13
99:3 [u]Ps 30:4; 33:21; 97:12; 103:1; 106:47; 111:9; 145:21; 148:5 [v]Ps 76:1 [w]S Ex 15:11; S Lev 11:44; Rev 4:8
99:4 [x]Ps 2:6 [y]S 1Ki 10:9 [z]Ps 98:9 [a]S Ge 18:19; Rev 15:3
99:5 [b]S Ex 15:2
99:6 [c]S Ex 24:6 [d]S Ex 28:1 [e]1Sa 7:5 [f]Ps 4:3; 91:15
99:7 [g]S Ex 13:21; S 19:9; S Nu 11:25
99:8 [h]S Ex 22:27; S Nu 14:20 [i]S Lev 26:18
100:1 [j]S Ps 98:6
100:2 [k]S Dt 10:12 [l]S Ps 95:2
100:3 [m]S 1Ki 18:21; S Ps 46:10 [n]S Job 10:3 [o]Ps 79:13; Isa 19:25; 63:8, 17-19; 64:9 [p]S 2Sa 24:17; S Ps 74:1
100:4 [q]S Ps 42:4 [r]S Ps 96:8 [s]Ps 116:17
100:5 [t]S 1Ch 16:34 [u]S Ezr 3:11; Ps 106:1

[n]8 Hebrew *them* [o]8 Or / *an avenger of the wrongs done to them* [p]3 Or *and not we ourselves*

98:9 GOD, Judge—When God judges, the world rejoices, for He will judge justly and fairly. See notes on 96:10–13; Ge 3:8–24; Ro 2:2.
99:1–2 GOD, Sovereignty—God's people praise the holy God because He rules all creation. Note the sovereign Lord is also the forgiving God (v 8). See notes on Ge 15:13–16; 18:14; 24:3,7,50; Dt 1:10.
99:1–9 PRAYER, Praise—See note on 93:1–5. God's position as King of the universe and His past history hearing and forgiving His people are reasons to praise Him.
99:3,5,9 GOD, Holy—See notes on Ex 3:5–6; 19:10–24; Lev 11:44–45; 2 Co 7:1.
99:8 SALVATION, Forgiveness—God showed Himself to Israel as a forgiving God, but He was not soft on sin. His past forgiveness calls forth praise and provides assurance that forgiveness remains a possibility.
100:1–5 PRAYER, Praise—See notes on 93:1–5; 95:1–11. The climax to this series of praises of the Lord's universal reign is a shout of joy. We praise Him joyfully as God, Creator, and Shepherd. We give thanks because He is good, loving, and forever faithful.
100:3 GOD, Creator—Because God created us, we belong to Him. We find joy in the relationship because the Creator God is our good, loving Shepherd. See note on 96:4–6.
100:3 THE CHURCH, God's Community—God's people have abundant reasons to praise Him. This verse gives three reasons. (1) The Lord is God. He alone created the universe and is, therefore, Lord of creation. (2) God made us in His image. We are not our own makers. (3) God shepherds His people. He is involved intimately in the lives of His people. God's people are thus a worshiping, praising community.
100:4 WORSHIP, Thanksgiving—Thanksgiving is a vital part of the community's coming together in God's house for worship. See note on 1 Ch 16:4.
100:5 GOD, Faithfulness—God is not fickle. His good, loving faithfulness remains the same forever. We can count on Him.

his faithfulness[v] continues through
all generations.

Psalm 101

Of David. A psalm.

I will sing of your love[w] and justice;
to you, O LORD, I will sing praise.
2I will be careful to lead a blameless
life[x]—
when will you come to me?

I will walk[y] in my house
with blameless heart.
3I will set before my eyes
no vile thing.[z]

The deeds of faithless men I hate;[a]
they will not cling to me.
4Men of perverse heart[b] shall be far
from me;
I will have nothing to do with evil.

5Whoever slanders his neighbor[c] in
secret,
him will I put to silence;
whoever has haughty eyes[d] and a
proud heart,
him will I not endure.

6My eyes will be on the faithful in the
land,
that they may dwell with me;
he whose walk is blameless[e]
will minister to me.

7No one who practices deceit
will dwell in my house;
no one who speaks falsely
will stand in my presence.

8Every morning[f] I will put to silence
all the wicked[g] in the land;
I will cut off every evildoer[h]
from the city of the LORD.[i]

Psalm 102

A prayer of an afflicted man. When he is faint and pours out his lament before the LORD.

HEAR my prayer,[j] O LORD;
let my cry for help[k] come to you.
2Do not hide your face[l] from me
when I am in distress.
Turn your ear[m] to me;
when I call, answer me quickly.

3For my days vanish like smoke;[n]
my bones[o] burn like glowing
embers.
4My heart is blighted and withered like
grass;[p]
I forget to eat my food.[q]
5Because of my loud groaning[r]
I am reduced to skin and bones.
6I am like a desert owl,[s]
like an owl among the ruins.
7I lie awake;[t] I have become
like a bird alone[u] on a roof.
8All day long my enemies[v] taunt me;[w]
those who rail against me use my
name as a curse.[x]
9For I eat ashes[y] as my food
and mingle my drink with tears[z]
10because of your great wrath,[a]
for you have taken me up and
thrown me aside.
11My days are like the evening
shadow;[b]
I wither[c] away like grass.

12But you, O LORD, sit enthroned
forever;[d]
your renown endures[e] through all
generations.[f]
13You will arise[g] and have compassion[h]
on Zion,
for it is time[i] to show favor[j] to
her;
the appointed time[k] has come.

100:5 [v]Ps 108:4; 119:90
101:1 [w]Ps 33:1; 51:14; 89:1; 145:7
101:2 [x]S Ge 17:1; Php 1:10 [y]S 1Ki 3:14
101:3 [z]Jer 16:18; Eze 11:21; Hos 9:10 [a]S Ps 5:5
101:4 [b]Pr 3:32; 6:16-19; 11:20
101:5 [c]S Ex 20:16; S Lev 19:16 [d]S Ps 10:5
101:6 [e]ver 2; Ps 119:1
101:8 [f]Ps 5:3; Jer 21:12 [g]Ps 75:10 [h]S 2Sa 3:39; Ps 118:10-12 [i]S Ps 46:4
102:1 [j]Ps 4:1 [k]S Ex 2:23
102:2 [l]S Ps 22:24 [m]S 2Ki 19:16; Ps 31:2; 88:2
102:3 [n]S Ps 37:20; S Jas 4:14 [o]La 1:13
102:4 [p]S Ps 37:2; 90:5-6 [q]S 1Sa 1:7; S Ezr 10:6; S Job 33:20
102:5 [r]S Ps 6:6
102:6 [s]S Dt 14:15-17; Job 30:29; Isa 34:11; Zep 2:14
102:7 [t]Ps 77:4 [u]Ps 38:11
102:8 [v]S Ps 31:11 [w]S Ps 42:10; Lk 22:63-65; 23:35-37 [x]S Ex 22:28; Isa 65:15; Jer 24:9; 25:18; 42:18; 44:12; Eze 14:8; Zec 8:13
102:9 [y]Isa 44:20 [z]Ps 6:6; 42:3; 80:5
102:10 [a]Ps 7:11; 38:3
102:11 [b]S 1Ch 29:15; S Job 14:2; S Ps 39:6 [c]S Job 8:12; Jas 1:10
102:12 [d]S Ex 15:18 [e]Ps 135:13; Isa 55:13; 63:12 [f]S Ex 3:15
102:13 [g]S Ps 44:26 [h]S Dt 32:36; S 1Ki 3:26; Isa 54:8; 60:10; Zec 10:6 [i]Ps 119:126
[j]S Ps 77:7 [k]S Ex 13:10; Da 8:19; Ac 1:7

101:1 GOD, Justice—God's love and justice are perfectly coordinated, not in conflict with one another. In love God has given His law, His guidelines for life under His rule. As Judge, He establishes and maintains a just order in which the rights of all people—particularly the poor and underprivileged—are protected.

101:1–8 PRAYER, Commitment—Prayer is commitment to the high purposes of God's righteousness. The commitments derive from the divine qualities of love and justice (v 1). The psalm belonged originally in a king's mouth but can be properly used by any person of faith.

102:1–28 EVIL AND SUFFERING, Prayer—One of the traditional penitential psalms (6,32,38,51,102,130,143), this lament stresses the call for healing of the individual and the nation. See notes on 3:1–8; 74:1–23. The sufferer knows God has a time He has chosen to act and asks Him to show His compassion so all nations may know and worship Him. Human suffering must be measured in the light of God's eternal purpose.

102:1–28 PRAYER, Lament—See note on 3:1–8. The despair of vv 1–11 and 23–24 strongly contrasts with the faith and insight of vv 12–22, 25–28. Circumstances change; God does not. The situation of man is temporary; the character of God is eternal. God will hear the needy and bring them to His praise. Lament apparently occurs in the silent absence of God, but He hears and responds to our most desperate pleas. Written testimony and prayer (v 18) lets future generations benefit from our experiences.

102:10 GOD, Wrath—The sufferer may interpret distress as due to God's wrath. Even so, we turn to God for compassion and help. See notes on Ge 6:5–8; 17:14; 19:13,24–26; Jos 7:1,25–26; Mt 3:7–10.

102:12 GOD, Eternal—Distress drives God's people back to Him in trust that His eternal rule ensures ultimate deliverance and security. See notes on Ge 1:1; 21:33; Ro 16:25–27.

102:13–17 GOD, Grace—God may discipline in His wrath, but in His grace He always has time to respond to the prayers of His people. See note on 67:1.

[14]For her stones are dear to your servants;
her very dust moves them to pity.
[15]The nations will fear[l] the name of the LORD,
all the kings[m] of the earth will revere your glory.
[16]For the LORD will rebuild Zion[n]
and appear in his glory.[o]
[17]He will respond to the prayer[p] of the destitute;
he will not despise their plea.

[18]Let this be written[q] for a future generation,
that a people not yet created[r] may praise the LORD:
[19]"The LORD looked down[s] from his sanctuary on high,
from heaven he viewed the earth,
[20]to hear the groans of the prisoners[t]
and release those condemned to death."
[21]So the name of the LORD will be declared[u] in Zion
and his praise[v] in Jerusalem
[22]when the peoples and the kingdoms
assemble to worship[w] the LORD.

[23]In the course of my life[q] he broke my strength;
he cut short my days.[x]
[24]So I said:
"Do not take me away, O my God,
in the midst of my days;
your years go on[y] through all generations.
[25]In the beginning[z] you laid the foundations of the earth,
and the heavens[a] are the work of your hands.[b]
[26]They will perish,[c] but you remain;
they will all wear out like a garment.
Like clothing you will change them
and they will be discarded.
[27]But you remain the same,[d]
and your years will never end.[e]
[28]The children of your servants[f] will live in your presence;
their descendants[g] will be established before you."

Psalm 103

Of David.

PRAISE the LORD,[h] O my soul;[i]
all my inmost being, praise his holy name.[j]
[2]Praise the LORD,[k] O my soul,
and forget not[l] all his benefits—
[3]who forgives all your sins[m]
and heals[n] all your diseases,
[4]who redeems your life[o] from the pit

102:15 [l]1Ki 8:43; Ps 67:7; Isa 2:2 [m]Ps 76:12; 138:4; 148:11 **102:16** [n]S Ps 51:18 [o]Ps 8:1; Isa 60:1-2 **102:17** [p]S 1Ki 8:29; Ps 4:1; 6:9 **102:18** [q]S Ro 4:24 [r]S Ps 22:31 **102:19** [s]Ps 53:2 **102:20** [t]S Ps 68:6; S Lk 4:19 **102:21** [u]Ps 22:22 [v]Ps 9:14 **102:22** [w]S Ps 22:27; Isa 49:22-23; Zec 8:20-23 **102:23** [x]S Ps 39:5 **102:24** [y]S Ge 21:33; Job 36:26; Ps 90:2 **102:25** [z]S Ge 1:1; Heb 1:10-12* [a]S 2Ch 2:12 [b]S Ps 8:3 **102:26** [c]Isa 13:10, 13; 34:4; 51:6; Eze 32:8; Joel 2:10; Mt 24:35; 2Pe 3:7-10; Rev 20:11 **102:27** [d]S Nu 23:19; Heb 13:8; Jas 1:17 [e]Ps 9:7 **102:28** [f]Ps 69:36 [g]Ps 25:13; 89:4 **103:1** [h]Ps 28:6 [i]Ps 104:1 [j]S Ps 30:4 **103:2** [k]Ps 106:1; 117:1 [l]S Dt 6:12; Ps 77:11 **103:3** [m]S Ex 34:7 [n]S Ex 15:26; Col 3:13; 1Pe 2:24; 1Jn 1:9 **103:4** [o]Ps 34:22; 56:13; Isa 43:1

[q]23 Or *By his power*

102:15 EVANGELISM, Salvation—See note on 67:1–2.
102:18 CREATION, Sovereignty—God creates (Hebrew *bara'*) each new generation of people. Deliverance from current troubles should be recorded to encourage the new generation to praise God. "A people" may refer to the nation, underlining God's sovereign power to create history. See note on Ge 1:1.
102:18–20 HOLY SCRIPTURE, Writing—Prayers addressed to God from human distress increase personal faith. They are placed in writing to testify to future generations. Normally psalms were oral songs or prayers used in worship. This psalmist consciously wrote out his prayer. God inspired and used both oral and written composition.
102:24–27 JESUS CHRIST, Foretold—God is eternal, and so is His Messiah. Humans seek the nonperishing and the constantly abiding. The author of Hebrews quoted these verses as evidence of the permanence, stability, and enduring qualities of Jesus Christ, God's Messiah (Heb 1:10–12).
102:25 GOD, Eternal—The Creator is eternal, without beginning or end. All creation is temporary, with beginning and ending. This means I must look to my own death, but I can take comfort that the eternal God will continue to rule and love my descendants. See notes on Ge 1:3—2:25; Ro 4:17.
102:25–28 REVELATION, Author of Creation—Creation reveals God's eternity. Human understanding sees the universe as the stable, ongoing factor of life. Compared to God, the universe has the lifespan of a suit of clothes. God's people can be assured of His presence forever.
103:1 GOD, Holy—Holiness stresses God's purity and uniqueness and is cause for us to praise and worship. See notes on Ex 3:5–6; 19:10–24; Lev 11:44–45; 2 Co 7:1.
103:1–22 EVIL AND SUFFERING, God's Compassion—Deserved punishment does not always come. Because of His love, God did not punish the psalmist for his sins. In His love, the just God is willing to forgive. God is like a father who has compassion or pity on his children (v 13). We can rely on God because of His love and compassion. Our complaints should turn to praise of the eternal God.
103:1–14 REVELATION, Author of Grace—God is the loving, intervening Lord of life. He does not forget His people, and they are not to forget what He does. He forgives, heals, and redeems from death. Such personal experiences affirm the tradition of the Exodus deliverance and lead us to understand God's nature as love and compassion.
103:1–22 PRAYER, Praise—See note on 33:1–22. This is one of the highest and most comprehensive statements of praise in the Bible. The outer stanzas (vv 1–6,20–22) frame statements of personal praise from those who need God in weakness of mortality, and of corporate praise from the mighty who serve Him in strength. The inner stanzas (vv 7–12, 13–17) praise Him for His mercy for sinners and for His immortal greatness in dealing with mortality. The word "all" is important in understanding the intent of this praise pointing to the incomprehensible greatness of His nature and works. Those who know human sin and weakness overcome by divine forgiveness and strength join in praise to God.
103:3,10,12 SALVATION, Forgiveness—God forgives all our sins, but not in accordance with what we as sinners deserve. Forgiving is God's merciful act of forgetting every sin for which we repent and claim His promise of forgiveness. Our sins are separated as far from us as east is from west.
103:3 SALVATION, Healing—The jubilant experience of forgiveness and healing led the psalmist to extravagant praise of God. He testified to his situation of the moment and to his confidence in God's power. He did not establish a general rule binding God to heal every disease of a believer. Nor did he give us a way to judge others' faith by seeing if they are healed. Healing is a part of salvation, but complete healing will come only when Christ returns.
103:4,8,11,17 GOD, Love—Forgiveness of sin and freedom from guilt prove God's love to us. His love has no limits in space or time. See notes on Ex 3:7; Dt 32:10–12,36; Mt

and crowns you with love and
compassion,[p]
5who satisfies[q] your desires with good
things
so that your youth is renewed[r] like
the eagle's.[s]

6The LORD works righteousness[t]
and justice for all the oppressed.[u]

7He made known[v] his ways[w] to Moses,
his deeds[x] to the people of Israel:
8The LORD is compassionate and
gracious,[y]
slow to anger, abounding in love.
9He will not always accuse,
nor will he harbor his anger
forever;[z]
10he does not treat us as our sins
deserve[a]
or repay us according to our
iniquities.
11For as high as the heavens are above
the earth,
so great is his love[b] for those who
fear him;[c]
12as far as the east is from the west,
so far has he removed our
transgressions[d] from us.
13As a father has compassion[e] on his
children,
so the LORD has compassion on
those who fear him;
14for he knows how we are formed,[f]
he remembers that we are dust.[g]
15As for man, his days are like grass,[h]
he flourishes like a flower[i] of the
field;
16the wind blows[j] over it and it is gone,
and its place[k] remembers it no
more.
17But from everlasting to everlasting
the LORD's love is with those who
fear him,
and his righteousness with their
children's children[l]—
18with those who keep his covenant[m]
and remember[n] to obey his
precepts.[o]

19The LORD has established his throne[p]
in heaven,
and his kingdom rules[q] over all.

20Praise the LORD,[r] you his angels,[s]
you mighty ones[t] who do his
bidding,[u]
who obey his word.
21Praise the LORD, all his heavenly
hosts,[v]
you his servants[w] who do his will.
22Praise the LORD, all his works[x]
everywhere in his dominion.

Praise the LORD, O my soul.[y]

Psalm 104

PRAISE the LORD, O my soul.[z]
O LORD my God, you are very great;
you are clothed with splendor and
majesty.[a]

103:4 [p]S Ps 8:5; 23:6 **103:5** [q]S Ps 90:14; S 104:28 [r]Job 33:25; Ps 119:25,93; 2Co 4:16 [s]S Ex 19:4 **103:6** [t]Ps 9:8; 65:5; Isa 9:7 [u]S Ps 74:21; S Lk 4:19 **103:7** [v]Ps 99:7; 147:19 [w]S Ex 33:13 [x]Ps 106:22 **103:8** [y]S Ex 22:27; S Ps 86:15; Mic 7:18-19; Jas 5:11 **103:9** [z]Ps 30:5; 79:5; Isa 57:16; Jer 3:5,12; Mic 7:18 **103:10** [a]S Ezr 9:13; Ro 6:23 **103:11** [b]Ps 13:5; 57:10; 100:5; 106:45; 117:2; La 3:22; Eph 3:18 [c]S 2Ch 6:31 **103:12** [d]S 2Sa 12:13; Ro 4:7; Eph 2:5 **103:13** [e]Mal 3:17; 1Jn 3:1 **103:14** [f]Ps 119:73; 139:13-15; Isa 29:16 [g]S Ge 2:7; S Ps 146:4 **103:15** [h]Ps 37:2; 90:5; 102:11; Isa 40:6 [i]S Job 14:2; Jas 1:10 **103:16** [j]Isa 40:7; Hag 1:9 [k]S Job 7:8 **103:17** [l]S Ge 48:11; S Ezr 9:12 **103:18** [m]S Dt 29:9 [n]Ps 119:52 [o]S Nu 15:40; Jn 14:15 **103:19** [p]Ps 47:8; 80:1; 113:5 [q]Ps 22:28; 66:7; Da 4:17 **103:20** [r]Ps 28:6 [s]S Ne 9:6; Lk 2:13; Heb 1:14 [t]S Ps 29:1 [u]Ps 107:25; 135:7; 148:8 **103:21** [v]S 1Ki 22:19 [w]S Ne 7:73 **103:22** [x]Ps 19:1; 67:3; 145:10; 150:6 [y]ver 1; Ps 104:1 **104:1** [z]S Ps 103:22 [a]S Job 40:10

10:29–31; Jn 3:16.

103:6–7 CHRISTIAN ETHICS, Justice—See note on 146:5–9.

103:7 HISTORY, God—Historical involvement lets people see God at work and thus come to know the nature of God as righteous, just, compassionate, gracious, slow to anger, and loving.

103:8–10 GOD, Wrath—The wrath of God is qualified by His love. See note on 102:10.

103:8,13 GOD, Father—God's grace takes priority over His wrath. The Father may discipline us but never stops loving us. See notes on Ge 19:12–19,29; 39:21–23; 45:5–9; Lk 1:30.

103:13–18 HUMANITY, Life—Human beings are animated dust. Life at its very best is always temporary. As our Creator, God knows our fragile nature, loves us, and provides hope and meaning for our limited time on earth.

103:17 GOD, Righteous—God's righteousness is closely associated with His love. He expresses His love through His righteous, saving acts. See note on 97:2,6.

103:17–18 THE CHURCH, Covenant People—Humans have a limited time on earth. God's covenant love (*chesed*) continues forever with His people. See note on 2 Ch 6:14.

103:19 THE CHURCH, God's Kingdom—The kingdom of God is God's rule over the universe. As Creator and Sustainer of life, God is Master of all. In the Old Testament, the kingdom of God is often equated with the kingdom of Israel. The rebellion of Israel and its kings against God demonstrated that this equation is not always true. God's throne is in the heavens. Israel is too small to be the sole kingdom of the King of the universe. God's kingdom consists of the whole earth. He reigns and will reign over all creation forever (Ps 93). His reign is universal and complete. The Lord is Master of all the earth, controlling all nature. The Lord's reign over His kingdom is not evident to all; yet, God is reigning. One day all people will recognize His rule. Visible evidence of the kingdom of God is reflected in the coming of the Messiah Jesus.

104:1–35 GOD, Sovereignty—This whole psalm praises God's sovereignty. God is in full control of His world and does wondrous things in it. He is not a tyrant but designed creation to meet the needs of people and animals. God's sovereignty is shown by His power (v 4), His wisdom (v 24), His work as Creator (vv 2–9), and His glory (v 31). See note on 99:1–2.

104:1–35 REVELATION, Author of Creation—The entire created order, especially the mysterious forces of nature, are used by God to reveal Himself and His will. God's power is shown by His control of the raging, chaotic waters. His glory shines through the beauty of His creation. His sovereignty appears in His control of natural powers—clouds, wind, lightning—and in the stability of creation. His love comes through in the ecology of creation, providing the needs of plant, animal, and human life. His reliability reveals itself in the ordered processes of creation—day and night, seasons, time for work and play. His wisdom shows through the total order of an immense universe suited to the needs and habits of each inhabitant. His nature as the only God is implied by His control of life and death. The natural human response to a close look at creation is to praise the Creator.

104:1–35 PRAYER, Praise—See note on 33:1–22. Creation points us to the glorious Creator before whom we sing a song of praise. Compare 19; 24. Such praise reminds us of Ge 1 and points us to God's final victory over evil.

2He wraps[b] himself in light[c] as with a
garment;
he stretches[d] out the heavens[e] like
a tent[f]
3 and lays the beams[g] of his upper
chambers on their waters.[h]
He makes the clouds[i] his chariot[j]
and rides on the wings of the
wind.[k]
4He makes winds his messengers,[r] [l]
flames of fire[m] his servants.

5He set the earth[n] on its foundations;[o]
it can never be moved.
6You covered it[p] with the deep[q] as
with a garment;
the waters stood[r] above the
mountains.
7But at your rebuke[s] the waters fled,
at the sound of your thunder[t] they
took to flight;
8they flowed over the mountains,
they went down into the valleys,
to the place you assigned[u] for them.
9You set a boundary[v] they cannot
cross;
never again will they cover the
earth.

10He makes springs[w] pour water into the
ravines;
it flows between the mountains.
11They give water[x] to all the beasts of
the field;
the wild donkeys[y] quench their
thirst.
12The birds of the air[z] nest by the
waters;
they sing among the branches.[a]
13He waters the mountains[b] from his
upper chambers;[c]
the earth is satisfied by the fruit of
his work.[d]
14He makes grass grow[e] for the cattle,
and plants for man to cultivate—
bringing forth food[f] from the earth:
15wine[g] that gladdens the heart of man,
oil[h] to make his face shine,
and bread that sustains[i] his heart.
16The trees of the LORD[j] are well
watered,
the cedars of Lebanon[k] that he
planted.
17There the birds[l] make their nests;
the stork has its home in the pine
trees.
18The high mountains belong to the wild
goats;[m]
the crags are a refuge for the
coneys.[s] [n]

19The moon marks off the seasons,[o]
and the sun[p] knows when to go
down.
20You bring darkness,[q] it becomes
night,[r]
and all the beasts of the forest[s]
prowl.
21The lions roar for their prey[t]
and seek their food from God.[u]
22The sun rises, and they steal away;
they return and lie down in their
dens.[v]
23Then man goes out to his work,[w]
to his labor until evening.[x]

24How many are your works,[y] O LORD!
In wisdom you made[z] them all;
the earth is full of your creatures.[a]
25There is the sea,[b] vast and spacious,
teeming with creatures beyond
number—
living things both large and small.[c]
26There the ships[d] go to and fro,
and the leviathan,[e] which you
formed to frolic[f] there.[g]

27These all look to you
to give them their food[h] at the
proper time.
28When you give it to them,
they gather it up;
when you open your hand,
they are satisfied[i] with good things.
29When you hide your face,[j]
they are terrified;
when you take away their breath,
they die and return to the dust.[k]
30When you send your Spirit,[l]
they are created,
and you renew the face of the earth.

31May the glory of the LORD[m] endure
forever;

104:2 [b]Isa 49:18; Jer 43:12 [c]Ps 18:12; 1Ti 6:16 [d]Job 9:8; Jer 51:15 [e]Job 37:18; Isa 40:22; 42:5; 44:24; Zec 12:1 [f]S Ps 19:4 **104:3** [g]Am 9:6 [h]S Ps 24:2 [i]S Dt 33:26; Isa 19:1; Na 1:3 [j]S 2Ki 2:11 [k]Ps 18:10 **104:4** [l]Ps 148:8; Heb 1:7* [m]Ge 3:24; 2Ki 2:11 **104:5** [n]Ex 31:17; Job 26:7; Ps 24:1-2; 102:25; 121:2 [o]S 1Sa 2:8 **104:6** [p]Ge 7:19 [q]S Ge 1:2 [r]2Pe 3:6 **104:7** [s]S Ps 18:15 [t]S Ex 9:23; Ps 29:3 **104:8** [u]Ps 33:7 **104:9** [v]S Ge 1:9; S Ps 16:6 **104:10** [w]Ps 107:33; Isa 41:18 **104:11** [x]ver 13 [y]S Ge 16:12; Isa 32:14; Jer 14:6 **104:12** [z]ver 17; Mt 8:20 [a]Mt 13:32 **104:13** [b]Ps 135:7; 147:8; Jer 10:13; Zec 10:1 [c]S Lev 26:4 [d]Am 9:6 **104:14** [e]S Job 38:27; Ps 147:8 [f]S Ge 1:30; S Job 28:5 **104:15** [g]S Ge 14:18; S Jdg 9:13 [h]Ps 23:5; 92:10; Lk 7:46 [i]S Dt 8:3; Mt 6:11 **104:16** [j]Ge 1:11 [k]S Ps 72:16 **104:17** [l]ver 12 **104:18** [m]S Dt 14:5 [n]Pr 30:26 **104:19** [o]S Ge 1:14 [p]Ps 19:6 **104:20** [q]Isa 45:7; Am 5:8 [r]Ps 74:16 [s]S Ps 50:10 **104:21** [t]Am 3:4 [u]Ps 145:15; Joel 1:20; S Mt 6:26 **104:22** [v]S Job 37:8 **104:23** [w]S Ge 3:19 [x]Jdg 19:16 **104:24** [y]Ps 40:5 [z]S Ge 1:31 [a]Ps 24:1; 50:10-11 **104:25** [b]Ps 69:34 [c]Eze 47:10 **104:26** [d]Ps 107:23; Eze 27:9; Jnh 1:3 [e]S Job 3:8; 41:1 [f]Job 40:20 [g]S Ge 1:21 **104:27** [h]Job 36:31; Ps 145:15; 147:9 **104:28** [i]Ps 103:5; 145:16; Isa 58:11 **104:29** [j]S Dt 31:17 [k]S Job 7:21 **104:30** [l]S Ge 1:2 **104:31** [m]Ex 40:35; Ps 8:1; S Ro 11:36

[r]4 Or *angels* [s]18 That is, the hyrax or rock badger

104:5–30 CREATION, Nature—This brief Psalm sketches the universe, the heavens, and the earth, with a few beautiful strokes. It praises God's revelation in nature and is a companion to the preceding one which praises His revelation in history. Ge 1 provides the general arrangement. Creation reveals the incomparable majesty of God. The forces of nature are an expression of His almighty power. He has made a delightful place for people to live in and should be praised for His incomparable work. The elements of creation serve God's purposes. None can rage beyond His control. He sustains what He created, satisfying the needs of earth and its creatures. Even threatening waters, darkness, and sea monsters have their proper place in God's wise rule of the universe. Each new birth can be called a new creative act through God's life-giving Spirit.

104:14–15 CHRISTIAN ETHICS, Alcohol—The Hebrews viewed wine with other agricultural products as one of the good gifts of God to humankind. Wine symbolized joyousness and gladness of heart in addition to describing prosperity and success before God. See note on Pr 23:20,29–35.

104:23 HUMANITY, Work—Daily labor is the common and expected lot of all people. It is part of the order God created and cause for us to praise God. Work fills a large part of our limited time on earth and should give meaning to our life and reason to thank the Creator.

may the LORD rejoice in his works[n]—
32he who looks at the earth, and it trembles,[o]
who touches the mountains,[p] and they smoke.[q]

33I will sing[r] to the LORD all my life;
I will sing praise to my God as long as I live.
34May my meditation be pleasing to him,
as I rejoice[s] in the LORD.
35But may sinners vanish[t] from the earth
and the wicked be no more.[u]

Praise the LORD, O my soul.

Praise the LORD.[t] [v]

Psalm 105

105:1–15pp — 1Ch 16:8–22

1GIVE thanks to the LORD,[w] call on his name;[x]
make known among the nations what he has done.
2Sing to him,[y] sing praise[z] to him;
tell of all his wonderful acts.[a]
3Glory in his holy name;[b]
let the hearts of those who seek the LORD rejoice.
4Look to the LORD and his strength;
seek his face[c] always.

5Remember the wonders[d] he has done,
his miracles, and the judgments he pronounced,[e]
6O descendants of Abraham his servant,[f]
O sons of Jacob, his chosen[g] ones.
7He is the LORD our God;
his judgments are in all the earth.

8He remembers his covenant[h] forever,
the word he commanded, for a thousand generations,
9the covenant he made with Abraham,[i]
the oath he swore to Isaac.
10He confirmed it[j] to Jacob as a decree,
to Israel as an everlasting covenant:[k]
11"To you I will give the land of Canaan[l]
as the portion you will inherit."[m]

12When they were but few in number,[n]
few indeed, and strangers in it,[o]
13they wandered from nation to nation,[p]
from one kingdom to another.
14He allowed no one to oppress[q] them;
for their sake he rebuked kings:[r]
15"Do not touch[s] my anointed ones;
do my prophets[t] no harm."

16He called down famine[u] on the land
and destroyed all their supplies of food;
17and he sent a man before them—
Joseph, sold as a slave.[v]
18They bruised his feet with shackles,[w]
his neck was put in irons,
19till what he foretold[x] came to pass,
till the word[y] of the LORD proved him true.
20The king sent and released him,
the ruler of peoples set him free.[z]
21He made him master of his household,
ruler over all he possessed,
22to instruct his princes[a] as he pleased
and teach his elders wisdom.[b]

23Then Israel entered Egypt;[c]
Jacob lived[d] as an alien in the land of Ham.[e]
24The LORD made his people very fruitful;
he made them too numerous[f] for their foes,
25whose hearts he turned[g] to hate his people,
to conspire[h] against his servants.
26He sent Moses[i] his servant,
and Aaron,[j] whom he had chosen.[k]
27They performed[l] his miraculous signs[m] among them,
his wonders[n] in the land of Ham.
28He sent darkness[o] and made the land dark—
for had they not rebelled against[p] his words?

104:31 [n]S Ge 1:4 **104:32** [o]S Ps 97:4 [p]S Ex 19:18 [q]Ps 144:5 **104:33** [r]S Ex 15:1; Ps 108:1 **104:34** [s]S Ps 2:11; 9:2; 32:11 **104:35** [t]Ps 37:38 [u]S Job 7:10 [v]Ps 28:6; 105:45; 106:48 **105:1** [w]S 1Ch 16:34 [x]Ps 80:18; 99:6; 116:13; Joel 2:32; Ac 2:21 **105:2** [y]Ps 30:4; 33:3; 96:1 [z]Ps 7:17; 18:49; 27:6; 59:17; 71:22; 146:2 [a]S Ps 75:1 **105:3** [b]S Ps 89:16 **105:4** [c]S Ps 24:6 **105:5** [d]S Ps 40:5 [e]S Dt 7:18 **105:6** [f]ver 42 [g]S Dt 10:15; Ps 106:5 **105:8** [h]S Ge 9:15; Ps 106:45; 111:5; Eze 16:60; S Lk 1:72 **105:9** [i]Ge 12:7; S 15:18; S 22:16-18; Lk 1:73; Gal 3:15-18 **105:10** [j]Ge 28:13-15 [k]Isa 55:3 **105:11** [l]S Ge 12:7 [m]S Nu 34:2 **105:12** [n]Dt 7:7 [o]Ge 23:4; Heb 11:9 **105:13** [p]Ge 15:13-16; Nu 32:13; 33:3-49 **105:14** [q]Ge 35:5 [r]Ge 12:17-20; S 20:3; S Ps 9:5 **105:15** [s]S Ge 26:11; S 1Sa 12:3 [t]S Ge 20:7 **105:16** [u]S Ge 12:10; S Lev 26:26; Isa 3:1; Eze 4:16 **105:17** [v]S Ge 37:28; Ac 7:9 **105:18** [w]S Ge 40:15 **105:19** [x]S Ge 12:10; 40:20-22 [y]Ge 41:40 **105:20** [z]Ge 41:14 **105:22** [a]Ge 41:43-44 [b]S Ge 41:40 **105:23** [c]Ge 46:6; Ac 7:15; 13:17 [d]Ge 47:28 [e]S Ps 78:51 **105:24** [f]Ex 1:7,9; Ac 7:17 **105:25** [g]S Ex 4:21 [h]Ex 1:6-10; Ac 7:19 **105:26** [i]S Ex 3:10 [j]S Ex 4:16; S Nu 33:1 [k]S Nu 16:5; 17:5-8 **105:27** [l]ver 28-37; Ex 7:8-12:51 [m]S Ex 4:17; S 10:1 [n]S Ex 3:20; Da 4:3 **105:28** [o]S Ge 1:4; S Ex 10:22 [p]S Ex 7:22

[t]*35* Hebrew *Hallelu Yah*; in the Septuagint this line stands at the beginning of Psalm 105.

105:1–45 REVELATION, History—History reveals God's faithfulness to His people. He has promised His people what He would do in history and has kept His promises. History is in God's loving hands. He redeems each event to make it useful for His ultimate purposes. God's people respond to His historical acts with thanksgiving and obedience.

105:1–45 HISTORY, Confession—Worship is memory of what God has done which leads to praise for who He is, thanks for the salvation He brings, and proclamation to others of what relationship to Him means.

105:1–45 PRAYER, Thanksgiving—A recital of God's previous acts is an appropriate subject for prayer if that recital prompts worship and commitment. Memory should cause us to give thanks. We can be thankful because God remembers His covenant. Vv 1–15 are quoted in 1 Ch 16:8–22 as a "psalm of thanks."

105:1–45 EVANGELISM, Gospel—The story of God acting in the history of His people formed the Old Testament gospel which God's people celebrated and recited in worship. They obeyed His commands. So must we. See note on 71:14–18.

105:3,42 GOD, Holy—God's morally pure holiness means His covenant promises are also pure and holy. We can count on them. See notes on Ex 3:5–6; 19:10–24; Lev 11:44–45; 2 Co 7:1.

105:8–11 THE CHURCH, Covenant People—God's regard for His people continues forever. Thus, we thank Him. See note on Ge 17:1–21.

29He turned their waters into blood,[q]
causing their fish to die.[r]
30Their land teemed with frogs,[s]
which went up into the bedrooms of their rulers.
31He spoke,[t] and there came swarms of flies,[u]
and gnats[v] throughout their country.
32He turned their rain into hail,[w]
with lightning throughout their land;
33he struck down their vines[x] and fig trees[y]
and shattered the trees of their country.
34He spoke,[z] and the locusts came,[a]
grasshoppers[b] without number;[c]
35they ate up every green thing in their land,
ate up the produce of their soil.
36Then he struck down all the firstborn[d] in their land,
the firstfruits of all their manhood.
37He brought out Israel, laden with silver and gold,[e]
and from among their tribes no one faltered.
38Egypt was glad when they left,
because dread of Israel[f] had fallen on them.
39He spread out a cloud[g] as a covering,
and a fire to give light at night.[h]
40They asked,[i] and he brought them quail[j]
and satisfied them with the bread of heaven.[k]
41He opened the rock,[l] and water gushed out;
like a river it flowed in the desert.
42For he remembered his holy promise[m]
given to his servant Abraham.
43He brought out his people with rejoicing,[n]
his chosen ones with shouts of joy;
44he gave them the lands of the nations,[o]
and they fell heir to what others had toiled[p] for—
45that they might keep his precepts
and observe his laws.[q]
Praise the LORD.[u] [r]

Psalm 106

106:1,47–48pp — 1Ch 16:34–36

PRAISE the LORD.[v] [s]
Give thanks to the LORD, for he is good;[t]
his love endures forever.[u]
2Who can proclaim the mighty acts[v] of the LORD
or fully declare his praise?
3Blessed are they who maintain justice,[w]
who constantly do what is right.[x]
4Remember me,[y] O LORD, when you show favor[z] to your people,
come to my aid[a] when you save them,
5that I may enjoy the prosperity[b] of your chosen ones,[c]
that I may share in the joy[d] of your nation
and join your inheritance[e] in giving praise.
6We have sinned,[f] even as our fathers[g] did;

105:29 [q]S Ps 78:44 [r]Ex 7:21 **105:30** [s]S Ex 8:2,6 **105:31** [t]Ps 107:25; 148:8 [u]Ex 8:21-24; S Ps 78:45 [v]Ex 8:16-18 **105:32** [w]Ex 9:22-25; S Job 38:22; S Ps 78:47 **105:33** [x]Ps 78:47 [y]Ex 10:5,12 **105:34** [z]Ps 107:25 [a]S Ex 10:4,12-15 [b]S 1Ki 8:37 [c]Joel 1:6 **105:36** [d]S Ex 4:23; S 12:12 **105:37** [e]S Ex 3:21, 22 **105:38** [f]Ex 15:16 **105:39** [g]S Ex 13:21; 1Co 10:1 [h]S Ps 78:14 **105:40** [i]Ps 78:18, 24 [j]S Ex 16:13 [k]S Ex 16:4; Jn 6:31 **105:41** [l]S Nu 20:11; 1Co 10:4 **105:42** [m]Ge 12:1-3; 13:14-17; 15:13-16 **105:43** [n]Ex 15:1-18; Ps 106:12 **105:44** [o]Ex 32:13; Jos 11:16-23; 12:8; 13:6-7; Ps 111:6 [p]Dt 6:10-11; Ps 78:55 **105:45** [q]S Dt 4:40; 6:21-24; Ps 78:5-7 [r]S Ps 104:35 **106:1** [s]S Ps 22:23; S 103:2 [t]S Ps 119:68 [u]S Ezr 3:11; Ps 136:1-26; Jer 33:11 **106:2** [v]S Ps 71:16 **106:3** [w]Ps 112:5; Hos 12:6 [x]Ps 15:2 **106:4** [y]Ps 25:6,7 [z]S Ps 77:7 [a]S Ge 50:24 **106:5** [b]S Dt 30:15; Ps 1:3 [c]S Ps 105:6 [d]Ps 20:5; 27:6; 47:5; 118:15 [e]S Ex 34:9

106:6 [f]S 1Ki 8:47; S Ro 3:9 [g]S 2Ch 30:7

[u]*45* Hebrew *Hallelu Yah* [v]*1* Hebrew *Hallelu Yah*; also in verse 48

105:42 ELECTION, God's Promise—The Exodus proved God remembers promises He makes to His elect. Praise in worship is the proper response to the faithful God who remembers. Obedience to God's election expectations is the corresponding response.

106:1 GOD, Goodness—God's goodness and love are closely tied. See notes on 100:5; Mt 19:17.

106:1,45 GOD, Love—See note on 103:4,8,11,17.

106:1–48 EVIL AND SUFFERING, Repentance—Repentance is the key theme for a people consciously suffering under God's wrath and discipline. Israel in exile confessed their sins, acknowledging that their history was a story of God's grace to a rebellious people. They deserved their punishment, were grateful for the grace God was showing to them in captivity, and prayed for restoration to their land. As God's people Christian disciples must constantly be aware of our history with Him and confess our sins to Him. We have no right to complain of punishment we deserve. We can call only on His grace. See note on 78:1–22.

106:1–47 REVELATION, Events—As God revealed Himself in historical acts, Israel regularly interrupted His plans by their selfish will. Thus history revealed God's anger at a disobedient people, His compassion for a suffering people, and His faithfulness to His covenant promises. A punished people plead for God's salvation, praise Him for His faithfulness, and express confidence in His plans. See note on Ps 105:1–45.

106:1–48 PRAYER, Confession—Ps 105 reviews history from God's perspective. Ps 106 reviews history from the human perspective, listing lessons learned in rebellion. Rebellion may pervert the very answers to prayer (vv 14–15), cause God to give a person over to the consequences of rebellion (v 41), and produce physical weakness in the sinner (v 43). One righteous prayer may interrupt the consequences (vv 30–31). In spite of the consequences, God remains loving and disposed to preserve His people (vv 44–46). That disposition is a basis for sinners to pray. A history of rebellion should not prevent the present generation from praising God. Human rebellion often reveals God's love. That love should lead to confession of sin as a prelude to praise and petition.

106:2 HISTORY, God—Humans can never adequately know all God has done. Nor can we adequately praise Him. History thus reveals human weakness and leads us to confess our sinfulness.

106:3 SALVATION, Blessing—Those who do justice are blessed. Salvation by a righteous God leads us to act as He acts in righteousness.

106:4,8,10,21 GOD, Savior—God acts to save us so we will make His name—His reputation—known to others. Too often we forget our Savior. See note on 98:1–3.

106:6–46 SIN, Forgiveness—History calls God's people

we have done wrong and acted
wickedly.[h]
7When our fathers were in Egypt,
they gave no thought[i] to your
miracles;
they did not remember[j] your many
kindnesses,
and they rebelled by the sea,[k] the
Red Sea.[w]
8Yet he saved them[l] for his name's
sake,[m]
to make his mighty power[n] known.
9He rebuked[o] the Red Sea, and it dried
up;[p]
he led them through[q] the depths as
through a desert.
10He saved them[r] from the hand of the
foe;[s]
from the hand of the enemy he
redeemed them.[t]
11The waters covered[u] their adversaries;
not one of them survived.
12Then they believed his promises
and sang his praise.[v]

13But they soon forgot[w] what he had
done
and did not wait for his counsel.[x]
14In the desert[y] they gave in to their
craving;
in the wasteland[z] they put God to
the test.[a]
15So he gave them[b] what they asked for,
but sent a wasting disease[c] upon
them.
16In the camp they grew envious[d] of
Moses
and of Aaron, who was consecrated
to the LORD.
17The earth opened[e] up and swallowed
Dathan;[f]
it buried the company of Abiram.[g]
18Fire blazed[h] among their followers;
a flame consumed the wicked.

19At Horeb they made a calf[i]
and worshiped an idol cast from
metal.
20They exchanged their Glory[j]
for an image of a bull, which eats
grass.
21They forgot the God[k] who saved
them,
who had done great things[l] in
Egypt,
22miracles in the land of Ham[m]
and awesome deeds[n] by the Red
Sea.
23So he said he would destroy[o] them—
had not Moses, his chosen one,
stood in the breach[p] before him
to keep his wrath from destroying
them.

24Then they despised[q] the pleasant
land;[r]
they did not believe[s] his promise.
25They grumbled[t] in their tents
and did not obey the LORD.
26So he swore[u] to them with uplifted
hand
that he would make them fall in the
desert,[v]
27make their descendants fall among the
nations
and scatter[w] them throughout the
lands.

28They yoked themselves to the Baal of
Peor[x]
and ate sacrifices offered to lifeless
gods;
29they provoked the LORD to anger[y] by
their wicked deeds,[z]
and a plague[a] broke out among
them.
30But Phinehas[b] stood up and
intervened,
and the plague was checked.[c]
31This was credited to him[d] as
righteousness
for endless generations[e] to come.
32By the waters of Meribah[f] they
angered the LORD,
and trouble came to Moses because
of them;
33for they rebelled[g] against the Spirit[h]
of God,
and rash words came from Moses'
lips.[x] [i]

106:6 [h]Ne 1:7 **106:7** [i]S Jdg 3:7 [j]Ps 78:11,42 [k]Ex 14:11-12 **106:8** [l]Ex 14:30; S Ps 80:3; 107:13; Isa 25:9; Joel 2:32 [m]S Ex 9:16; S Ps 23:3 [n]S Ex 14:31 **106:9** [o]Ps 18:15; Isa 50:2 [p]S Ex 14:21; Na 1:4 [q]Ps 78:13; Isa 63:11-14 **106:10** [r]Ex 14:30; Ps 107:13 [s]S Ps 78:53 [t]Ps 78:42; 107:2; Isa 35:9; 62:12 **106:11** [u]S Ex 14:28 **106:12** [v]Ex 15:1-21; S Ps 105:43 **106:13** [w]S Ex 15:24 [x]S Ex 16:28; S Nu 27:21 **106:14** [y]S Ps 78:40 [z]S Ps 68:7 [a]S Ex 17:2; 1Co 10:9 **106:15** [b]S Ex 16:13; Ps 78:29 [c]S Nu 11:33 **106:16** [d]Nu 16:1-3 **106:17** [e]Dt 11:6 [f]S Ex 15:12 [g]S Nu 16:1 **106:18** [h]S Lev 10:2 **106:19** [i]S Ex 32:4; Ac 7:41 **106:20** [j]Jer 2:11; Ro 1:23 **106:21** [k]Ps 78:11 [l]Dt 10:21; Ps 75:1 **106:22** [m]S Ps 78:51 [n]S Ex 3:20; S Dt 4:34 **106:23** [o]S Ex 32:10 [p]Ex 32:11-14; S Nu 11:2; S Dt 9:19 **106:24** [q]Nu 14:30-31 [r]S Dt 8:7; S Jer 3:19 [s]S Nu 14:11; Heb 3:18-19 **106:25** [t]S Ex 15:24; Dt 1:27; 1Co 10:10 **106:26** [u]S Nu 14:23; Heb 4:3 [v]S Dt 2:14; Heb 3:17 **106:27** [w]S Lev 26:33 **106:28** [x]S Nu 23:28 **106:29** [y]Nu 25:3 [z]S Ps 64:2; 141:4 [a]S Nu 16:46; 25:8 **106:30** [b]S Ex 6:25 [c]Nu 25:8 **106:31** [d]S Ge 15:6; S Nu 25:11-13 [e]Ps 49:11 **106:32** [f]S Ex 17:7; Nu 20:2-13 **106:33** [g]S Ex 23:21; Ps 107:11 [h]S Ps 51:11; Isa 63:10 [i]Ex 17:4-7; Nu 20:8-12

[w]*7* Hebrew *Yam Suph*; that is, Sea of Reeds; also in verses 9 and 22 [x]*33* Or *against his spirit, / and rash words came from his lips*

to confession. We cannot confess our ancestors' sins to gain forgiveness or salvation for them. We can confess we have not learned history's lesson and have repeated their sins. We confess our sins, ask God's help to escape the environment produced by our ancestors' sins, and accept the forgiveness and salvation He gives us. See notes on 78:1–72; Nu 14:23.

106:6 SALVATION, Confession—In confession, we take responsibility for our sins. We do not blame previous generations or other people.

106:20 GOD, Glory—How ironic that people would turn to a sculptured animal rather than to the glorious Savior. See notes on Ex 16:7,10; 40:34–38; Lk 2:9,14; Jn 11:4.

106:29,32,40 GOD, Wrath—God is not naturally angry. His anger is His reaction to human sin. See note on 103:8–10.

106:32–33 HOLY SPIRIT, Resisted—God's Spirit has all power because God the Creator has all power. The Spirit does not use His power to force us to obey. We can rebel against God's Spirit. The translation of the text is difficult here. The Hebrew has pronouns without explicit mention of "Lord" or "God." Some Bible students interpret these as references to Moses, not God. The end result is the same, for God's Spirit led Moses. We need to know the Spirit can be resisted, but resistance is sin. We must commit ourselves to Him. We must not resist His work. See 1 Th 5:19; note on Eph 4:30.

34They did not destroy[j] the peoples
as the LORD had commanded[k] them,
35but they mingled[l] with the nations
and adopted their customs.
36They worshiped their idols,[m]
which became a snare[n] to them.
37They sacrificed their sons[o]
and their daughters to demons.[p]
38They shed innocent blood,
the blood of their sons[q] and daughters,
whom they sacrificed to the idols of Canaan,
and the land was desecrated by their blood.
39They defiled themselves[r] by what they did;
by their deeds they prostituted[s] themselves.

40Therefore the LORD was angry[t] with his people
and abhorred his inheritance.[u]
41He handed them over[v] to the nations,
and their foes ruled over them.
42Their enemies oppressed[w] them
and subjected them to their power.
43Many times he delivered them,[x]
but they were bent on rebellion[y]
and they wasted away in their sin.

44But he took note of their distress
when he heard their cry;[z]
45for their sake he remembered his covenant[a]
and out of his great love[b] he relented.[c]
46He caused them to be pitied[d]
by all who held them captive.

47Save us,[e] O LORD our God,
and gather us[f] from the nations,
that we may give thanks[g] to your holy name[h]
and glory in your praise.

48Praise be to the LORD, the God of Israel,
from everlasting to everlasting.
Let all the people say, "Amen!"[i]

Praise the LORD.

BOOK V

Psalms 107–150

Psalm 107

GIVE thanks to the LORD,[j] for he is good;[k]
his love endures forever.
2Let the redeemed[l] of the LORD say this—
those he redeemed from the hand of the foe,
3those he gathered[m] from the lands,
from east and west, from north and south.[y]

4Some wandered in desert[n] wastelands,
finding no way to a city[o] where they could settle.
5They were hungry[p] and thirsty,[q]
and their lives ebbed away.
6Then they cried out[r] to the LORD in their trouble,
and he delivered them from their distress.
7He led them by a straight way[s]
to a city[t] where they could settle.
8Let them give thanks[u] to the LORD for his unfailing love[v]
and his wonderful deeds[w] for men,
9for he satisfies[x] the thirsty
and fills the hungry with good things.[y]

106:34 [j]S Jos 9:15; Jdg 1:27-36 [k]Ex 23:24; S Dt 2:34; 7:16; 20:17 **106:35** [l]Jdg 3:5-6; Ezr 9:1-2 **106:36** [m]S Dt 7:16 [n]S Ex 10:7 **106:37** [o]S Lev 18:21; S Dt 12:31; Eze 16:20-21 [p]S Ex 22:20; S Dt 32:17; 1Co 10:20 **106:38** [q]S Lev 18:21; S Dt 18:10; S 2Ki 3:27 **106:39** [r]S Ge 3:17; Lev 18:24; Eze 20:18 [s]S Nu 15:39 **106:40** [t]S Lev 26:28 [u]S Ex 34:9; S Dt 9:29 **106:41** [v]S Jdg 2:14 **106:42** [w]S Jdg 4:3 **106:43** [x]S Jos 10:14; Jdg 7:1-25; S Ne 9:28; Ps 81:13-14 [y]S Jdg 2:16-19; 6:1-7 **106:44** [z]S Jdg 3:9 **106:45** [a]S Ge 9:15; Ps 105:8; S Lk 1:72 [b]S Ps 17:7; S 103:11 [c]S Ex 32:14 **106:46** [d]S Ex 3:21; S 1Ki 8:50 **106:47** [e]S Ps 28:9 [f]Ps 107:3; 147:2; Isa 11:12; 27:13; 56:8; 66:20; Jer 31:8; Eze 20:34; Mic 4:6 [g]Ps 105:1 [h]Ps 30:4; S 99:3 **106:48** [i]S Ps 41:13; S 72:19 **107:1** [j]S 1Ch 16:8; S 2Ch 5:13 [k]S 2Ch 7:3 **107:2** [l]S Ps 106:10; S Isa 35:9 **107:3** [m]S Ne 1:9 **107:4** [n]S Jos 5:6 [o]ver 36 **107:5** [p]Ex 16:3 [q]S Ex 15:22; S 17:2 **107:6** [r]S Ex 14:10 **107:7** [s]S Ezr 8:21 [t]ver 36 **107:8** [u]Ps 105:1 [v]Ps 6:4 [w]S Ps 75:1 **107:9** [x]Ps 22:26; 63:5; Isa 58:11; Mt 5:6; Lk 1:53 [y]S Ps 23:1; Jer 31:25

[y]3 Hebrew *north and the sea*

106:45 THE CHURCH, Covenant People—The history of God's people may be viewed as a history of sin (Ps 78). Still the psalmist thanked God because He is good and showed mercy to His people after He disciplined them through the Babylonian captivity (2 Ki 25). A covenant people can count on God's faithfulness. Discipline and judgment are not God's final words for His people because of His covenant love for us. See note on 2 Ch 6:14.
106:48 HOLY SCRIPTURE, Collection—See note on 41:13.
106:48 PRAYER, Corporate—See note on 41:13.
107:1 GOD, Goodness—See note on 106:1.
107:1,8,15,21,31,43 GOD, Love—See note on 106:1,45.
107:1–43 EVIL AND SUFFERING, God's Present Help—Help lies ahead for the suffering, lonely, imprisoned, and troubled. God can and does reveal His goodness in all life's circumstances when His people cry for help. Some of life's desperate circumstances result from divine punishment on human sin. God hears the prayers of penitent sufferers and helps in their circumstances. We should learn from others' experiences, join them in praising God for His deliverance, and call on God for help in our troubles. See note on 32:1–11.
107:1–43 REVELATION, Events—God acts in the different experiences of His people to meet their individual needs. Events in individual lives thus reveal God's love. God's people respond to such revelation with praise, thanksgiving, offerings, testimony, worship, and reflection.
107:1–43 PRAYER, Thanksgiving—The thought of the opening verse is repeated five times in thanksgiving for the deliverance of God's unfailing love (vv 8,15,21,31). Each time the thanksgiving is for a type of deliverance: from exile and hunger, imprisonment, rebellion, and storms. The concluding verses (33–43) see all of history and nature under the control of God. Reciting the prayer instructs us and lets God speak His wisdom even as we give thanks to Him. See note on 15:1–5.
107:2 HISTORY, Confession—Each of God's people has a unique history with God. Each is called to confess that history to the congregation so others may learn from individual experiences. See Guide to Personal Testimony, pp. 1786–1788.
107:2 SALVATION, Redemption—Those whom God has redeemed should not hesitate to thank Him for His steadfast love or to tell others about it. Redemption is rescue from enemies to serve God.

10Some sat in darkness[z] and the deepest
gloom,
prisoners suffering[a] in iron chains,[b]
11for they had rebelled[c] against the
words of God
and despised[d] the counsel[e] of the
Most High.
12So he subjected them to bitter labor;
they stumbled, and there was no
one to help.[f]
13Then they cried to the LORD in their
trouble,
and he saved them[g] from their
distress.
14He brought them out of darkness[h] and
the deepest gloom[i]
and broke away their chains.[j]
15Let them give thanks[k] to the LORD for
his unfailing love[l]
and his wonderful deeds[m] for men,
16for he breaks down gates of bronze
and cuts through bars of iron.

17Some became fools[n] through their
rebellious ways[o]
and suffered affliction[p] because of
their iniquities.
18They loathed all food[q]
and drew near the gates of death.[r]
19Then they cried[s] to the LORD in their
trouble,
and he saved them[t] from their
distress.
20He sent forth his word[u] and healed
them;[v]
he rescued[w] them from the grave.[x]
21Let them give thanks[y] to the LORD for
his unfailing love[z]
and his wonderful deeds[a] for men.
22Let them sacrifice thank offerings[b]
and tell of his works[c] with songs of
joy.[d]

23Others went out on the sea[e] in
ships;[f]
they were merchants on the mighty
waters.
24They saw the works of the LORD,[g]
his wonderful deeds in the deep.
25For he spoke[h] and stirred up a
tempest[i]
that lifted high the waves.[j]
26They mounted up to the heavens and
went down to the depths;
in their peril[k] their courage
melted[l] away.
27They reeled[m] and staggered like
drunken men;
they were at their wits' end.

107:10 [z]ver 14; Ps 88:6; 143:3; Isa 9:2; 42:7,16; 49:9; Mic 7:9 [a]Ps 102:20; Isa 61:1 [b]S Job 36:8 **107:11** [c]S Ps 5:10 [d]S Nu 14:11 [e]S 1Ki 22:5; 2Ch 36:16 **107:12** [f]S 2Ki 14:26; Ps 72:12 **107:13** [g]S Ps 106:8 **107:14** [h]S ver 10; Isa 9:2; 42:7; 50:10; 59:9; 60:2; S Lk 1:79 [i]Ps 86:13; Isa 29:18 [j]S Job 36:8; Ps 116:16; Ac 12:7 **107:15** [k]ver 8,21, 31; Ps 105:1 [l]Ps 6:4 [m]S Ps 75:1 **107:17** [n]S Ps 53:1 [o]S Ps 25:7 [p]S Lev 26:16; Isa 65:6-7; Jer 30:14-15; Gal 6:7-8 **107:18** [q]S Job 3:24; S 6:6 [r]S Job 17:16; S 33:22 **107:19** [s]ver 28; Ps 5:2 [t]ver 13; Ps 34:4 **107:20** [u]S Dt 32:2; Ps 147:15; Mt 8:8; Lk 7:7 [v]S Ex 15:26 [w]S Job 33:28 [x]Ps 16:10; 30:3; S 56:13 **107:21** [y]S ver 15 [z]Ps 6:4 [a]Ps 75:1 **107:22** [b]S Lev 7:12 [c]Ps 9:11; 73:28; 118:17 [d]S Job 8:21; S Ps 65:8 **107:23** [e]Isa 42:10 [f]S Ps 104:26 **107:24** [g]Ps 64:9; 111:2; 143:5 **107:25** [h]S Ps 105:31 [i]S Ps 50:3 [j]S Ps 93:3 **107:26** [k]Lk 8:23 [l]S Jos 2:11 **107:27** [m]Isa 19:14; 24:20; 28:7 **107:28** [n]S ver 19 [o]Ps 4:1; Jnh 1:6 **107:29** [p]Lk 8:24 [q]S Ps 93:3 [r]S Ps 65:7; Jnh 1:15 **107:30** [s]ver 7 **107:31** [t]S ver 15 [u]Ps 6:4 [v]Ps 75:1; 106:2 **107:32** [w]Ps 30:1; 34:3; 99:5 [x]S Ps 1:5; 22:22, 25; 26:12; 35:18 **107:33** [y]1Ki 17:1; Ps 74:15; Isa 41:15; 42:15; 50:2 [z]S Ps 104:10 **107:34** [a]S Ge 13:10 **107:35** [b]S 2Ki 3:17; Ps 105:41; 126:4; Isa 43:19; 51:3 [c]S Job 38:26; S Isa 35:7 **107:37**

28Then they cried[n] out to the LORD in
their trouble,
and he brought them out of their
distress.[o]
29He stilled the storm[p] to a whisper;
the waves[q] of the sea were
hushed.[r]
30They were glad when it grew calm,
and he guided them[s] to their
desired haven.
31Let them give thanks[t] to the LORD for
his unfailing love[u]
and his wonderful deeds[v] for men.
32Let them exalt[w] him in the assembly[x]
of the people
and praise him in the council of the
elders.

33He turned rivers into a desert,[y]
flowing springs[z] into thirsty ground,
34and fruitful land into a salt waste,[a]
because of the wickedness of those
who lived there.
35He turned the desert into pools of
water[b]
and the parched ground into flowing
springs;[c]
36there he brought the hungry to live,
and they founded a city where they
could settle.
37They sowed fields and planted
vineyards[d]
that yielded a fruitful harvest;
38he blessed them, and their numbers
greatly increased,[e]
and he did not let their herds
diminish.[f]

39Then their numbers decreased,[g] and
they were humbled[h]
by oppression, calamity and sorrow;
40he who pours contempt on nobles[i]
made them wander in a trackless
waste.[j]
41But he lifted the needy[k] out of their
affliction
and increased their families like
flocks.[l]
42The upright see and rejoice,[m]
but all the wicked shut their
mouths.[n]

43Whoever is wise,[o] let him heed these
things

[d]S 2Ki 19:29; S Isa 37:30 **107:38** [e]S Ge 12:2; S Dt 7:13 [f]S Ge 49:25 **107:39** [g]S 2Ki 10:32; Eze 5:12 [h]S Ps 44:9 **107:40** [i]S Job 12:18 [j]S Dt 32:10 **107:41** [k]S 1Sa 2:8; Ps 113:7-9 [l]S Job 21:11 **107:42** [m]S Job 22:19; Ps 97:10-12 [n]S Job 5:16; Ro 3:19 **107:43** [o]Jer 9:12; Hos 14:9

107:18 HUMANITY, Physical Nature—Life is dependent upon food. When it is rejected, starvation begins. Its end is death. Sin can cause humans to suffer and become foolish to the point of rejecting food. Even in a weakened, starving condition they can call to God and find healing. Such experiences call us to give thanks to our Creator and Savior.

107:20 HUMANITY, Life—God's spoken word created life. It also sustains life; healing weak, sick bodies near death.

107:43 HUMANITY, Intellectual Nature—Human intellect should lead people to remember and ponder the great acts of God. The wisest people ponder God's love and learn from the mistakes of others.

and consider the great love[p] of the
LORD.

Psalm 108

108:1–5pp — Ps 57:7–11
108:6–13pp — Ps 60:5–12

A song. A psalm of David.

MY heart is steadfast,[q] O God;
I will sing[r] and make music with
all my soul.
2Awake, harp and lyre![s]
I will awaken the dawn.
3I will praise you, O LORD, among the
nations;
I will sing of you among the peoples.
4For great is your love,[t] higher than
the heavens;
your faithfulness[u] reaches to the
skies.[v]
5Be exalted, O God, above the
heavens,[w]
and let your glory be over all the
earth.[x]

6Save us and help us with your right
hand,[y]
that those you love may be
delivered.
7God has spoken[z] from his sanctuary:[a]
"In triumph I will parcel out
Shechem[b]
and measure off the Valley of
Succoth.[c]
8Gilead is mine, Manasseh is mine;
Ephraim is my helmet,
Judah[d] my scepter.
9Moab[e] is my washbasin,
upon Edom[f] I toss my sandal;
over Philistia[g] I shout in triumph."
10Who will bring me to the fortified city?
Who will lead me to Edom?
11Is it not you, O God, you who have
rejected us
and no longer go out with our
armies?[h]
12Give us aid against the enemy,
for the help of man is worthless.[i]
13With God we will gain the victory,
and he will trample down[j] our
enemies.

Psalm 109

For the director of music. Of David.
A psalm.

O God, whom I praise,[k]
do not remain silent,[l]
2for wicked and deceitful men[m]
have opened their mouths against
me;
they have spoken against me with
lying tongues.[n]
3With words of hatred[o] they surround
me;
they attack me without cause.[p]
4In return for my friendship they accuse
me,
but I am a man of prayer.[q]

107:43 [p]Ps 103:11
108:1 [q]Ps 112:7; 119:30,112 [r]S Ps 18:49
108:2 [s]S Job 21:12
108:4 [t]Nu 14:18; Ps 106:45 [u]S Ex 34:6 [v]S Ps 36:5
108:5 [w]S Ps 8:1 [x]S Ps 57:5
108:6 [y]S Job 40:14
108:7 [z]Ps 89:35 [a]Ps 68:35; 102:19 [b]S Ge 12:6 [c]S Ge 33:17
108:8 [d]S Ps 78:68
108:9 [e]S Ge 19:37 [f]S 2Sa 8:13-14 [g]S 2Sa 8:1
108:11 [h]S Ps 44:9
108:12 [i]Ps 118:8; 146:3; Isa 10:3; 30:5; 31:3; Jer 2:36; 17:5
108:13 [j]Ps 44:5; Isa 22:5; 63:3,6
109:1 [k]S Ex 15:2; Jer 17:14 [l]S Job 34:29
109:2 [m]S Ps 43:1 [n]S Ps 52:4
109:3 [o]Ps 69:4 [p]Ps 35:7; Jn 15:25
109:4 [q]Ps 69:13; 141:5

108:1–13 PRAYER, Praise—Psalms are personal or congregational prayers in poetic form and most likely originally set to music. As such, they are human words directed in lament, thanks, praise, and confession to God. All have been written and included in the collection of Scripture. The writing process is clearly seen here in the combination of 57:7–11 and 60:5–12 to form this psalm. In writing, the human prayers become more clearly seen as words inspired by God. They function both as expressions of our prayer to God and as God's inspired teaching to us. This psalm allows us to praise God, call for His help, gain confidence in His deliverance, and confess our faith. It also teaches us of God's sovereignty.

108:4 GOD, Faithfulness—See notes on 89:1–49; 92:2; 100:5.

108:5 GOD, Glory—God's purpose is to be present and recognized in all His glory by all people. See notes on Ex 16:7,10; 40:34–38; Lk 2:9,14; Jn 11:4.

108:6–13 SALVATION, Definition—God is Lord over all nations and over all parts of all nations. Because He is Lord over all, He is the Savior of all. Biblical passages like this teach us the inclusiveness of God's saving nature, the utter impossibility of human beings saving themselves, and love as God's motive in saving His people.

108:7 HOLY SCRIPTURE, God's Initiative—Unlike the gods worshiped by surrounding nations, the true Maker of life began the conversation with His children Israel by declaring Himself in their worship, being vitally interested in their welfare, and dwelling with them in every circumstance. The nature and character of God is being revealed to those who seek Him in true worship. Ps 108 combines two other psalms—*57:7–11; 60:5–12—into one.* The combination transforms lamentation and pleas for mercy into praise. This arrangement points to the freedom of the worshiping community to take inspired song texts and use them to meet new situations. God's inspired words are powerful to people in widely different circumstances, bringing forth varying responses. See note on 2 Sa 22:1–51.

109:1–31 EVIL AND SUFFERING, Vindication—See notes on 3:1–8; 35:1–28. Wicked people do return evil for good. Such actions rouse our righteous anger. We must express that anger to God and trust Him to deal with the situation. We should not expect our angry feelings to be carried out by Him. Depending on His will and way causes us to develop calmer and more rational desires. Jesus calls us to love and pray for our enemies (Mt 5:44).

109:1–31 SIN, Death—Sinful people persecuted God's people, who prayed for deliverance. Sin involves false accusations, hatred, unreasonable attacks, betrayal of friendship, absence of kindness, unjust treatment of the poor, and scorn for the righteous. The falsely-accused sufferer asked God to give the sinner what he deserved—death, the just payment for sin. Such death would involve more than the individual; it would cut off the entire family name and memory. Reputation, wealth, and fame earned through sin deserve to be destroyed and forgotten. See note on 68:21.

109:1–31 CHRISTIAN ETHICS, Justice—Though horrible vengeance is called on his enemies, the writer did not take this into his own hands but left it with God in whose sovereignty judgment resides. Vengeful thoughts must not lead to vengeful deeds. See note on 69:22–28.

109:1–31 PRAYER, Lament—See notes on 3:1–8; 5:10. David placed his stance as a "man of prayer" alongside the fact that he had been a friend to those who were now his enemies. He rejoiced in God's blessing although they cursed him. In extraordinary need, we can use strong language to call for God's justice. In so doing we leave action in His hands, aware that perpetual cursing of others is wrong. Lament properly concludes with a vow to praise. See note on 7:1–17.

[5]They repay me evil for good,[r]
and hatred for my friendship.

[6]Appoint[z] an evil man[a] to oppose him;
let an accuser[b][s] stand at his right hand.
[7]When he is tried, let him be found guilty,[t]
and may his prayers condemn[u] him.
[8]May his days be few;[v]
may another take his place[w] of leadership.
[9]May his children be fatherless
and his wife a widow.[x]
[10]May his children be wandering beggars;[y]
may they be driven[c] from their ruined homes.
[11]May a creditor[z] seize all he has;
may strangers plunder[a] the fruits of his labor.[b]
[12]May no one extend kindness to him
or take pity[c] on his fatherless children.
[13]May his descendants be cut off,[d]
their names blotted out[e] from the next generation.
[14]May the iniquity of his fathers[f] be remembered before the LORD;
may the sin of his mother never be blotted out.
[15]May their sins always remain before[g] the LORD,
that he may cut off the memory[h] of them from the earth.

[16]For he never thought of doing a kindness,
but hounded to death the poor
and the needy[i] and the brokenhearted.[j]
[17]He loved to pronounce a curse—
may it[d] come on him;[k]
he found no pleasure in blessing—
may it be[e] far from him.
[18]He wore cursing[l] as his garment;
it entered into his body like water,[m]
into his bones like oil.
[19]May it be like a cloak wrapped[n] about him,
like a belt tied forever around him.
[20]May this be the LORD's payment[o] to my accusers,
to those who speak evil[p] of me.

[21]But you, O Sovereign LORD,
deal well with me for your name's sake;[q]
out of the goodness of your love,[r]
deliver me.[s]
[22]For I am poor and needy,
and my heart is wounded within me.
[23]I fade away like an evening shadow;[t]
I am shaken off like a locust.
[24]My knees give[u] way from fasting;[v]
my body is thin and gaunt.[w]
[25]I am an object of scorn[x] to my accusers;
when they see me, they shake their heads.[y]

[26]Help me,[z] O LORD my God;
save me in accordance with your love.
[27]Let them know[a] that it is your hand,
that you, O LORD, have done it.
[28]They may curse,[b] but you will bless;
when they attack they will be put to shame,
but your servant will rejoice.[c]
[29]My accusers will be clothed with disgrace
and wrapped in shame[d] as in a cloak.
[30]With my mouth I will greatly extol the LORD;
in the great throng[e] I will praise him.
[31]For he stands at the right hand[f] of the needy one,
to save his life from those who condemn him.

Psalm 110

Of David. A psalm.

[1]THE LORD says[g] to my Lord:
"Sit at my right hand[h]
until I make your enemies
a footstool for your feet."[i]
[2]The LORD will extend your mighty scepter[j] from Zion;[k]
you will rule[l] in the midst of your enemies.

109:5 [r]S Ge 44:4 **109:6** [s]1Ch 21:1; Job 1:6; Zec 3:1 **109:7** [t]Ps 1:5 [u]Pr 28:9; Isa 41:24 **109:8** [v]S Job 15:32 [w]Ac 1:20* **109:9** [x]Ex 22:24; Jer 18:21 **109:10** [y]S Ge 4:12 **109:11** [z]Ne 5:3 [a]S Nu 14:3; Isa 1:7; 6:11; 36:1; La 5:2 [b]Job 20:18 **109:12** [c]S Job 5:4 **109:13** [d]Job 18:19; Ps 21:10 [e]S Nu 14:12; Ps 9:5; Pr 10:7 **109:14** [f]Ex 20:5; Nu 14:18; Isa 65:6-7; Jer 32:18 **109:15** [g]Ps 90:8 [h]S Ex 17:14; S Dt 32:26 **109:16** [i]S Job 20:19; S Ps 35:10 [j]S Ps 34:18 **109:17** [k]Pr 28:27; S Mt 7:2 **109:18** [l]Ps 10:7 [m]Nu 5:22 **109:19** [n]ver 29; Ps 73:6; Eze 7:27 **109:20** [o]S Ex 32:34; Ps 54:5; 94:23; Isa 3:11; 2Ti 4:14 [p]Ps 71:10 **109:21** [q]S Ex 9:16; S Ps 23:3 [r]Ps 69:16 [s]S Ps 3:7 **109:23** [t]S Job 14:2 **109:24** [u]Heb 12:12 [v]S Ps 35:13 [w]S Job 16:8 **109:25** [x]S Ps 22:6 [y]S Job 16:4; S Mt 27:39; Mk 15:29 **109:26** [z]Ps 12:1; 119:86 **109:27** [a]S Job 37:7 **109:28** [b]S 2Sa 16:12 [c]Ps 66:4; Isa 35:10; 51:11; 54:1; 65:14 **109:29** [d]S Ps 35:26 **109:30** [e]S Ps 35:18 **109:31** [f]Ps 16:8; 108:6 **110:1** [g]Mt 22:44*; Mk 12:36*; Lk 20:42*; Ac 2:34* [h]S Mk 16:19; Heb 1:13*; 12:2 [i]S Jos 10:24; S 1Ki 5:3; 1Co 15:25 **110:2** [j]S Ge 49:10; Ps 45:6; Isa 14:5; Jer 48:17 [k]S Ps 2:6 [l]Ps 72:8

[z]6 Or ⌊*They say:*⌋ *"Appoint* (with quotation marks at the end of verse 19) [a]6 Or *the Evil One* [b]6 Or *let Satan* [c]10 Septuagint; Hebrew *sought* [d]17 Or *curse, / and it has* [e]17 Or *blessing, / and it is*

109:21,26 GOD, Love—We do not deserve God's saving deliverance. It comes from His love for us. See notes on Ex 3:7; Dt 32:10–12,36; Mt 10:29–31; Jn 3:16.

109:26–27,31 SALVATION, Definition—See note on 108:6–13. God's salvation extends to all of our needs, even to the need to let vengeance belong to Him. Only through God's grace can persons rise above their human selfishness and immaturity. God's salvation is a sign to all people that He controls history.

110:1–7 JESUS CHRIST, Foretold—This royal psalm was used at the crowning of the kings of Judah. Christians apply it to the exaltation of Jesus Christ, God's Messiah. To sit at the right hand is the highest honor, the place of privilege. The New Testament frequently uses this expression to refer to Jesus in relation to God (Mt 22:44; Mk 12:36; Lk 20:42–43; Eph 1:20). Hebrews, in addition to using the idea of exaltation to God's right hand (Heb 1:13), makes the Melchizedek priesthood a cornerstone in the argument for Christ as High Priest (Heb 5:6; 7:17,21).

3Your troops will be willing
on your day of battle.
Arrayed in holy majesty,[m]
from the womb of the dawn
you will receive the dew of your
youth.[f] [n]

4The LORD has sworn
and will not change his mind:[o]
"You are a priest forever,[p]
in the order of Melchizedek.[q]"

5The Lord is at your right hand;[r]
he will crush kings[s] on the day of
his wrath.[t]
6He will judge the nations,[u] heaping up
the dead[v]
and crushing the rulers[w] of the
whole earth.
7He will drink from a brook beside the
way[g];
therefore he will lift up his head.[x]

Psalm 111[h]

PRAISE the LORD.[i]
I will extol the LORD[y] with all my
heart[z]
in the council[a] of the upright and in
the assembly.[b]

2Great are the works[c] of the LORD;
they are pondered by all[d] who
delight in them.
3Glorious and majestic are his deeds,
and his righteousness endures[e]
forever.
4He has caused his wonders to be
remembered;
the LORD is gracious and
compassionate.[f]
5He provides food[g] for those who fear
him;[h]
he remembers his covenant[i]
forever.
6He has shown his people the power of
his works,[j]
giving them the lands of other
nations.[k]
7The works of his hands[l] are faithful
and just;
all his precepts are trustworthy.[m]
8They are steadfast for ever[n] and ever,
done in faithfulness and uprightness.
9He provided redemption[o] for his
people;
he ordained his covenant forever—
holy and awesome[p] is his name.

10The fear of the LORD[q] is the beginning
of wisdom;[r]
all who follow his precepts have
good understanding.[s]
To him belongs eternal praise.[t]

Psalm 112[h]

PRAISE the LORD.[i] [u]
Blessed is the man[v] who fears the
LORD,[w]
who finds great delight[x] in his
commands.

110:3 [m]S Ex 15:11 [n]Mic 5:7 110:4 [o]S Nu 23:19 [p]Zec 6:13; Heb 5:6*; 7:21* [q]S Ge 14:18; Heb 5:10; 7:15-17* 110:5 [r]Ps 16:8 [s]S Dt 7:24; Ps 2:12; 68:21; 76:12; Isa 60:12; Da 2:44 [t]S Ps 2:5; Ro 2:5; Rev 6:17; 11:18 110:6 [u]S Ps 9:19 [v]Isa 5:25; 34:3; 66:24 [w]S Ps 18:38 110:7 [x]Ps 3:3; 27:6 111:1 [y]Ps 34:1; 109:30; 115:18; 145:10 [z]S Ps 9:1 [a]Ps 89:7 [b]S Ps 1:5 111:2 [c]S Job 36:24; Ps 143:5; Rev 15:3 [d]Ps 64:9 111:3 [e]Ps 112:3,9; 119:142 111:4 [f]S Dt 4:31; S Ps 86:15 111:5 [g]S Ge 1:30; S Ps 37:25; Mt 6:26,31-33 [h]Ps 103:11 [i]S 1Ch 16:15; S Ps 105:8 111:6 [j]Ps 64:9; S 66:3,5 [k]S Ps 105:44 111:7 [l]S Ps 92:4 [m]Ps 19:7; 119:128 111:8 [n]Ps 119:89, 152,160; Isa 40:8; S Mt 5:18 111:9 [o]Ps 34:22; S 103:4; 130:7; Lk 1:68 [p]Ps 30:4; 99:3; Lk 1:49 111:10 [q]S Job 23:15; S Ps 19:9 [r]Dt 4:6 [s]S Dt 4:6; Ps 119:98,104,130 [t]Ps 28:6; 89:52 112:1 [u]Ps 33:2; 103:1; 150:1 [v]Ps 1:1-2 [w]S Job 1:8; Ps 103:11; 115:13; 128:1 [x]S Ps 1:2; 119:14,16,47,92

[f]3 Or / *your young men will come to you like the dew* [g]7 Or / *The One who grants succession will set him in authority* [h]This psalm is an acrostic poem, the lines of which begin with the successive letters of the Hebrew alphabet. [i]1 Hebrew *Hallelu Yah*

110:5 GOD, Wrath—No one, not even powerful political rulers, can escape God's wrath. See notes on Ge 6:5–8; 17:14; 19:13,24–26; Jos 7:1,25–26; Mt 3:7–10.

111:1–10 THE CHURCH, Covenant People—The history of God's people gives proof of God's enduring covenant love. His love and mercy are more than theological teachings we have to believe to be part of God's people. They are the life experiences of God's people to which we testify in praise and thanksgiving. See note on Ex 2:24.

111:1–10 PRAYER, Praise—Pss 111 and 112 begin with "Praise the LORD" (Hebrew *halelu yah*). The two psalms mirror one another. Ps 111 extols the virtues of the Lord; Ps 112, the blessedness of a godly person who faithfully reproduces the character of the Lord. Ps 111:10 links the two. The wonders of the Lord will be remembered (111:4); the righteous man will be remembered (112:6). The Lord provides for those who fear Him (111:5); good will come to those who mirror God's compassion (112:5). The works and precepts of the Lord are steadfast forever (111:7–8); the righteousness of the righteous will endure forever (112:9). Both God's compassionate acts and human character formed by God's love are reasons to praise (Hebrew *hillel*) Yahweh, our God.

111:3 GOD, Righteous—God's righteous actions are not a thing of the past. He continues to perform majestic works for His people. See notes on Lev 1:1; Jos 23:1–16; 2 Sa 10:12; Jn 17:25.

111:4 GOD, Grace—See notes on Ge 19:12–19,29; 39:21–23; 45:5–9; Lk 1:30.

111:9 GOD, Holy—God's redeeming acts and covenant promises are so far beyond our comprehension that we see how holy and unique God is through them. See notes on Ex 3:5–6; 19:10–24; Lev 11:44–45; 2 Co 7:1.

111:10 HUMANITY, Intellectual Nature—Here the fear of the Lord appears to be a Hebrew idiom referring to a reverential attitude which leads us to obey God's law and revelation. This relationship to Him and His revealed Word lets people find true wisdom. Such wisdom centers on obedience to God rather than demanding obedience to or acceptance of our opinions and knowledge.

112:1–10 EVIL AND SUFFERING, Deserved—See note on 1:1–6.

112:1 SALVATION, Fear of God—Fear of God brings happiness. Happiness comes from appreciating the guidelines God has set out for life and following them. Obedience is a joy rather than a burden.

112:1–10 CHRISTIAN ETHICS, Justice—See note on 1 Sa 30:1–25. Security and confidence are built on deeds of justice and generosity. Just deeds or righteousness means being right with God in an eternal relationship.

112:1–3 CHRISTIAN ETHICS, Property Rights—Proper relationship with God leads a person to give proper priority to other concerns. Family life and economic relationships will reflect a sense of stewardship and responsibility. Though literal accumulation of wealth may not follow, the quality of one's life will reflect the true wealth of fulfillment and righteousness.

112:1 CHRISTIAN ETHICS, Obedience—See notes on 1:1–11; Dt 10:12–13.

112:1–10 PRAYER, Praise—See note on 111:1–10.

2His children[y] will be mighty in the land;
the generation of the upright will be blessed.
3Wealth and riches[z] are in his house,
and his righteousness endures[a] forever.
4Even in darkness light dawns[b] for the upright,
for the gracious and compassionate and righteous[c] man.[j]
5Good will come to him who is generous and lends freely,[d]
who conducts his affairs with justice.
6Surely he will never be shaken;[e]
a righteous man will be remembered[f] forever.
7He will have no fear of bad news;
his heart is steadfast,[g] trusting in the LORD.[h]
8His heart is secure, he will have no fear;[i]
in the end he will look in triumph on his foes.[j]
9He has scattered abroad his gifts to the poor,[k]
his righteousness endures[l] forever;
his horn[k] will be lifted[m] high in honor.

10The wicked man will see[n] and be vexed,
he will gnash his teeth[o] and waste away;[p]
the longings of the wicked will come to nothing.[q]

Psalm 113

PRAISE the LORD.[1] [r]

Praise, O servants of the LORD,[s]
praise the name of the LORD.
2Let the name of the LORD be praised,[t]
both now and forevermore.[u]
3From the rising of the sun[v] to the place where it sets,
the name of the LORD is to be praised.

4The LORD is exalted[w] over all the nations,
his glory above the heavens.[x]
5Who is like the LORD our God,[y]
the One who sits enthroned[z] on high,[a]
6who stoops down to look[b]
on the heavens and the earth?

7He raises the poor[c] from the dust
and lifts the needy[d] from the ash heap;
8he seats them[e] with princes,
with the princes of their people.
9He settles the barren[f] woman in her home
as a happy mother of children.

Praise the LORD.

Psalm 114

WHEN Israel came out of Egypt,[g]
the house of Jacob from a people of foreign tongue,
2Judah[h] became God's sanctuary,[i]
Israel his dominion.

3The sea looked and fled,[j]
the Jordan turned back;[k]
4the mountains skipped[l] like rams,
the hills like lambs.

5Why was it, O sea, that you fled,[m]
O Jordan, that you turned back,
6you mountains, that you skipped like rams,
you hills, like lambs?

7Tremble, O earth,[n] at the presence of the Lord,
at the presence of the God of Jacob,
8who turned the rock into a pool,
the hard rock into springs of water.[o]

112:2 [y]Ps 25:13; 37:26; 128:2-4 112:3 [z]S Dt 8:18 [a]S Ps 37:6; S 111:3 112:4 [b]S Ps 18:28 [c]Ps 5:12 112:5 [d]S Ps 37:21, 26; Lk 6:35 112:6 [e]S Ps 15:5; S 55:22 [f]Pr 10:7; Ecc 2:16 112:7 [g]Ps 57:7; 108:1 [h]S Ps 28:7; 56:3-4; S Isa 12:2 112:8 [i]Ps 3:6; 27:1; 56:11; Pr 1:33; Isa 12:2 [j]S Ps 54:7 112:9 [k]Lk 19:8; Ac 9:36; 2Co 9:9* [l]S Ps 111:3 [m]S Ps 75:10 112:10 [n]Ps 86:17 [o]S Ps 37:12; S Mt 8:12 [p]S Ps 34:21 [q]S Job 8:13 113:1 [r]S Ps 22:23 [s]Ps 34:22; S 103:21; 134:1 113:2 [t]S Ps 30:4; 48:10; 145:21; 148:13; 149:3; Isa 12:4 [u]Ps 115:18; 131:3; Da 2:20 113:3 [v]Isa 24:15; 45:6; 59:19; Mal 1:11 113:4 [w]S Ps 99:2 [x]S Ps 8:1; S 57:11 113:5 [y]S Ex 8:10; S Ps 35:10 [z]S Ps 103:19 [a]S Job 16:19 113:6 [b]Ps 11:4; 138:6; Isa 57:15 113:7 [c]1Sa 2:8; Ps 35:10; 68:10; 140:12 [d]Ps 107:41 113:8 [e]S 2Sa 9:11 113:9 [f]S 1Sa 2:5 114:1 [g]S Ex 13:3; S 29:46 114:2 [h]Ps 76:1 [i]S Ex 15:17; Ps 78:68-69 114:3 [j]Ex 14:21; Ps 77:16 [k]S Ex 15:8; S Jos 3:16 114:4 [l]S Jdg 5:5 114:5 [m]S Ex 14:21 114:7 [n]S Ex 15:14; S 1Ch 16:30 114:8 [o]S Ex 17:6; S Nu 20:11

j4 Or / *for* ⌊*the LORD*⌋ *is gracious and compassionate and righteous* k9 *Horn* here symbolizes dignity.
l1 Hebrew *Hallelu Yah*; also in verse 9

112:7 SALVATION, Belief—See notes on 4:5; 56:3–4,11. Those who trust in God do not need to be afraid of bad news, knowing God's final word is good news.
112:10 SIN, Judgment—Sin may appear to bring prosperity, but in the long run the wicked do not achieve their dreams.
113:1–9 EVIL AND SUFFERING, God's Present Help—Social conditions cause undeserved, innocent suffering. God especially helps the poor, needy, and barren. Social standing does not reflect standing with God.
113:1–9 PRAYER, Praise—Pss 113—118 form the "Hallel" psalms of high praise and were sung at the Jewish festivals. This opening hymn calls for the universal praise of the Lord in time (v 2) and space (v 3). It is characteristic of the praise of the Lord that He who is highest stoops to the lowest (vv 7–9). Praise comes from a servant to the universal God.
113:1–9 EVANGELISM, Worship—See note on 48:9.
113:4–9 GOD, Sovereignty—The basis for praising God here is His sovereignty, His authority and majesty. Just to see our marvelous universe, He has to bend over because He is so far above us. Still He takes note of our needs. See notes on Ge 15:13–16; 18:14; 24:3,7,50; Dt 1:10.
113:4 GOD, Glory—God's prestige and honor have no limits. They extend beyond earth into the heavens. See note on 108:5.
114:1–8 REVELATION, History—Worship relives God's revelation through the great moments of salvation in history. Reexperiencing history brings the worshipers a renewed sense of God's presence and thus a renewal of worship.
114:1–8 HISTORY, Presence—Remembering God's history with His people leads to an awareness of God's presence.
114:1–8 PRAYER, Corporate—God's people need holy days of celebration to recall God's great acts of salvation. Prayer may praise God by simply reciting what He has done. Such prayer gains added meaning in the context of holiday worship with a congregation. Israel celebrated the Exodus and conquest (Ex 14; Jos 3—4). Christians celebrate Christ's birth at Christmas and Christ's death and resurrection at Easter.

Psalm 115

115:4–11pp — Ps 135:15–20

NOT to us, O LORD, not to us
but to your name be the glory,[p]
because of your love and
faithfulness.[q]
2Why do the nations say,
"Where is their God?"[r]
3Our God is in heaven;[s]
he does whatever pleases him.[t]
4But their idols are silver and gold,[u]
made by the hands of men.[v]
5They have mouths, but cannot speak,[w]
eyes, but they cannot see;
6they have ears, but cannot hear,
noses, but they cannot smell;
7they have hands, but cannot feel,
feet, but they cannot walk;
nor can they utter a sound with
their throats.
8Those who make them will be like
them,
and so will all who trust in them.

9O house of Israel, trust[x] in the
LORD—
he is their help and shield.
10O house of Aaron,[y] trust in the
LORD—
he is their help and shield.
11You who fear him,[z] trust in the
LORD—
he is their help and shield.

12The LORD remembers[a] us and will
bless us:[b]
He will bless the house of Israel,
he will bless the house of Aaron,
13he will bless those who fear[c] the
LORD—
small and great alike.

14May the LORD make you increase,[d]
both you and your children.
15May you be blessed by the LORD,
the Maker of heaven[e] and earth.

16The highest heavens belong to the
LORD,[f]
but the earth he has given[g] to man.
17It is not the dead[h] who praise the
LORD,
those who go down to silence;
18it is we who extol the LORD,[i]
both now and forevermore.[j]

Praise the LORD.[m k]

115:1 [p]Ps 29:2; 66:2; 96:8 [q]S Ex 34:6
115:2 [r]S Ps 42:3
115:3 [s]Ezr 5:11; Ne 1:4; Ps 103:19; 136:26; Mt 6:9 [t]Ps 135:6
115:4 [u]Rev 9:20 [v]S 2Ki 19:18; S 2Ch 32:19; Jer 10:3-5; Ac 19:26
115:5 [w]Jer 10:5
115:9 [x]Ps 37:3; 62:8
115:10 [y]Ex 30:30; Ps 118:3
115:11 [z]Ps 22:23; 103:11; 118:4
115:12 [a]S 1Ch 16:15 [b]S Ge 12:2
115:13 [c]S Ps 112:1
115:14 [d]Dt 1:11
115:15 [e]S Ge 1:1; Ac 14:15; S Rev 10:6
115:16 [f]S Ps 89:11 [g]S Ge 1:28; Ps 8:6-8
115:17 [h]Ps 88:10-12
115:18 [i]S Ps 111:1 [j]S Ps 113:2 [k]Ps 28:6; 33:2; 103:1
116:1 [l]Ps 18:1 [m]S Ps 31:22; S 40:1 [n]S Ps 6:9; S 28:2
116:2 [o]S Ps 5:1
116:3 [p]S 2Sa 22:6; Ps 18:4-5
116:4 [q]Ps 80:18; 118:5 [r]S Ps 80:2
116:5 [s]S Ex 9:27; S 2Ch 12:6; S Ezr 9:15 [t]S Ex 22:27; S Ps 86:15
116:6 [u]S Ps 79:8 [v]Ps 18:3; 22:5; 107:13
116:7 [w]Ps 46:10; 62:1; 131:2; Mt 11:29

Psalm 116

I love the LORD,[l] for he heard my
voice;
he heard my cry[m] for mercy.[n]
2Because he turned his ear[o] to me,
I will call on him as long as I live.

3The cords of death[p] entangled me,
the anguish of the grave[n] came
upon me;
I was overcome by trouble and
sorrow.
4Then I called on the name[q] of the
LORD:
"O LORD, save me![r]"

5The LORD is gracious and righteous;[s]
our God is full of compassion.[t]
6The LORD protects the simplehearted;
when I was in great need,[u] he
saved me.[v]

7Be at rest[w] once more, O my soul,

[m]18 Hebrew *Hallelu Yah* [n]3 Hebrew *Sheol*

115:1 GOD, Glory—Prestige and honor belong to God, not to us, no matter what our position and authority. God has earned His glorious position by showing love and faithfulness to us. See note on 113:4.

115:1–18 HOLY SCRIPTURE, Collection—Many Hebrew and Greek manuscripts connect Pss 114—115 into one psalm, possibly because 114 ends so abruptly. See note on 9:20.

115:1–18 PRAYER, Praise—Hard times may give rise to praise. The psalmist spoke for a weak and threatened people calling for trust in God. This psalm exemplifies common themes of praise—ascription of glory to the Lord's name because of His expression of His covenant in love and faithfulness (v 1) and a particular expression of His blessing in the private relationship with Israel (vv 9–15). Vv 2–8 praise the superiority of Israel's understanding of God as invisible and spiritual over those who make false gods in the visible form of human-like idols. Pss 115—118, or possibly only Ps 118, may have constituted the hymn which Christ and the disciples sang after the Lord's Supper (Mt 26:30). See notes on 113:1–9; Ge 14:18–20; Nu 6:22–27.

115:15 GOD, Creator—See note on 100:3.

115:16 HUMANITY, Human Nature—God is the sovereign Creator to whom alone belongs glory and praise. He rules the highest heavens, so He certainly controls our insignificant planet. With all His power, wisdom, and authority, God has chosen to let humans live on and maintain control over our planet. Our authority is only a gift which may be taken back. We maintain authority only so long as we acknowledge His supreme authority. See Ge 1:26–30; 2:15.

115:17 HUMANITY, Nature of Death—See note on 88:10–12.

116:1–2 GOD, Personal—Only a personal God can hear. God relates to us person to person, hearing what we say to Him. See notes on Ex 3:12–16; Mt 18:10–14.

116:1–19 EVIL AND SUFFERING, God's Present Help—See note on 88:1–18.

116:1–19 HOLY SCRIPTURE, Collection—The Septuagint, the earliest Greek translation, divides this psalm into two psalms (vv 1–9,10–19). See note on 9:20.

116:1–19 PRAYER, Thanksgiving—Thanksgiving is the appropriate prayer for deliverance from death. In thanking the Lord for this deliverance, the psalmist expressed an extraordinary promise: the Lord closely guards and monitors the death of His saints (v 15).

116:3–6 SALVATION, Definition—When in trouble, God's people simply call on Him for salvation. God's salvation includes deliverance from sickness and dangerous illness. See notes on 103:3; 2 Ch 30:20. He is the Savior of our bodies from destruction and will one day give us a new body (1 Co 15:42–44). Because He loves us so tenderly in all of our afflictions, we cannot but love, praise, worship, and serve Him as long as we live.

for the LORD has been good[x] to you.

8For you, O LORD, have delivered my
soul[y] from death,
my eyes from tears,
my feet from stumbling,
9that I may walk before the LORD[z]
in the land of the living.[a]
10I believed;[b] therefore[o] I said,
"I am greatly afflicted."[c]
11And in my dismay I said,
"All men are liars."[d]

12How can I repay the LORD
for all his goodness[e] to me?
13I will lift up the cup of salvation
and call on the name[f] of the LORD.
14I will fulfill my vows[g] to the LORD
in the presence of all his people.

15Precious in the sight[h] of the LORD
is the death of his saints.[i]
16O LORD, truly I am your servant;[j]
I am your servant, the son of your
maidservant[p];[k]
you have freed me from my chains.[l]

17I will sacrifice a thank offering[m] to you
and call on the name of the LORD.
18I will fulfill my vows[n] to the LORD
in the presence of all his people,
19in the courts[o] of the house of the
LORD—
in your midst, O Jerusalem.[p]

Praise the LORD.[q]

Psalm 117

PRAISE the LORD,[q] all you nations;[r]
extol him, all you peoples.
2For great is his love[s] toward us,
and the faithfulness of the LORD[t]
endures forever.

Praise the LORD.[q]

Psalm 118

GIVE thanks to the LORD,[u] for he is
good;[v]
his love endures forever.[w]

2Let Israel say:[x]
"His love endures forever."[y]
3Let the house of Aaron say:[z]
"His love endures forever."
4Let those who fear the LORD[a] say:
"His love endures forever."

5In my anguish[b] I cried to the LORD,
and he answered[c] by setting me
free.
6The LORD is with me;[d] I will not be
afraid.
What can man do to me?[e]
7The LORD is with me; he is my
helper.[f]
I will look in triumph on my
enemies.[g]

8It is better to take refuge in the LORD[h]
than to trust in man.[i]
9It is better to take refuge in the LORD
than to trust in princes.[j]

10All the nations surrounded me,
but in the name of the LORD I cut
them off.[k]
11They surrounded me[l] on every side,[m]
but in the name of the LORD I cut
them off.
12They swarmed around me like bees,[n]
but they died out as quickly as
burning thorns;[o]
in the name of the LORD I cut them
off.[p]

13I was pushed back and about to fall,
but the LORD helped me.[q]
14The LORD is my strength[r] and my
song;
he has become my salvation.[s]

15Shouts of joy[t] and victory
resound in the tents of the
righteous:
"The LORD's right hand[u] has done
mighty things![v]
16 The LORD's right hand is lifted high;
the LORD's right hand has done
mighty things!"

116:7 [x]Ps 13:6; 106:1; 142:7 **116:8** [y]S Ps 86:13 **116:9** [z]S Ge 5:22; Ps 56:13; 89:15 [a]S Job 28:13; Ps 27:13; Isa 38:11; Jer 11:19 **116:10** [b]2Co 4:13* [c]Ps 9:18; 72:2; S 107:17; 119:67, 71,75 **116:11** [d]Jer 9:3-5; Hos 7:13; Mic 6:12; Ro 3:4 **116:12** [e]Ps 103:2; 106:1 **116:13** [f]S Ps 105:1 **116:14** [g]S Nu 30:2; S Ps 66:13 **116:15** [h]Ps 72:14 [i]S Nu 23:10 **116:16** [j]Ps 119:125; 143:12 [k]S Ps 86:16 [l]S Job 12:18 **116:17** [m]S Lev 7:12; S Ezr 1:4 **116:18** [n]ver 14; S Lev 22:18 **116:19** [o]Ps 92:13; 96:8; 100:4; 135:2 [p]Ps 102:21 **117:1** [q]S Ps 22:23; S 103:2 [r]Ro 15:11* **117:2** [s]S Ps 17:7; S 103:11 [t]Ps 119:90; 146:6 **118:1** [u]S 1Ch 16:8 [v]S 2Ch 5:13; S 7:3 [w]S Ezr 3:11 **118:2** [x]Ps 115:9 [y]Ps 106:1; 136:1-26 **118:3** [z]Ex 30:30; Ps 115:10 **118:4** [a]S Ps 115:11 **118:5** [b]Ps 18:6; 31:7; 77:2; 120:1 [c]ver 21; Ps 34:4; 86:7; 116:1; 138:3 **118:6** [d]S Dt 31:6; Heb 13:6* [e]S Ps 56:4 **118:7** [f]S Dt 33:29 [g]S Ps 54:7 **118:8** [h]Ps 2:12; 5:11; 9:9; 37:3; 40:4; Isa 25:4; 57:13 [i]2Ch 32:7-8; S Ps 108:12; S Isa 2:22 **118:9** [j]Ps 146:3 **118:10** [k]S Ps 37:9 **118:11** [l]Ps 88:17 [m]Ps 3:6 **118:12** [n]Dt 1:44 [o]S Ps 58:9 [p]Ps 37:9 **118:13** [q]ver 7; 2Ch 18:31; Ps 86:17 **118:14** [r]S Ex 15:2 [s]S Ps 62:2 **118:15** [t]S Job 8:21; S Ps 106:5 [u]S Ex 15:6; Ps 89:13; 108:6 [v]Lk 1:51

[o]*10* Or *believed even when* [p]*16* Or *servant, your faithful son* [q]*19,2* Hebrew *Hallelu Yah*

116:15 HUMANITY, Worth—The Psalms make much of human insignificance compared to God's eternal majesty. Human value comes because God values us. He watches over every part of our life, even our death. We may call gems and gold precious. God places such value only on the persons He created. Knowledge that God's love has given us worth does not lead to pride and the need to impress others with our worth. A sense of personal worth leads us to commit our worth to God as His servants.

117:1–3 PRAYER, Praise—See notes on 113:1–9; 115:1–18. The psalmist called on all peoples to praise the love and faithfulness characteristic of God's covenant. No people has a monopoly on praise.

118:1–4,29 GOD, Love—Deliverance from trouble reveals God's love to us, assuring us He never forgets or stops loving us. See note on 109:21,26.

118:1,29 GOD, Goodness—See note on 106:1.

118:1–29 EVIL AND SUFFERING, God's Present Help—See note on 21:1–13.

118:1–29 REVELATION, Divine Presence—God reveals His presence in the tough situations of life as well as in the solemn quietness of worship. Such experiences reveal God's personal love for the individual and His power to overcome evil. They lead God's people to give thanks. See note on 107:1–43.

118:1–19 PRAYER, Thanksgiving—See notes on 30:1–12; 113:1–9; 115:1–18. The "Hallel" psalms climax with thanksgiving for the opportunity to worship in God's house. Freedom to worship should always lead us to give thanks. Compare Mt 21:42; Mk 12:10–11; Lk 20:17.

118:8–9 SALVATION, As Refuge—Taking refuge in God is the opposite of trusting in human beings.

[17]I will not die[w] but live,
and will proclaim[x] what the LORD
has done.
[18]The LORD has chastened[y] me severely,
but he has not given me over to
death.[z]

[19]Open for me the gates[a] of
righteousness;
I will enter[b] and give thanks to the
LORD.
[20]This is the gate of the LORD[c]
through which the righteous may
enter.[d]
[21]I will give you thanks, for you
answered me;[e]
you have become my salvation.[f]

[22]The stone[g] the builders rejected
has become the capstone;[h]
[23]the LORD has done this,
and it is marvelous[i] in our eyes.
[24]This is the day the LORD has made;
let us rejoice and be glad[j] in it.

[25]O LORD, save us;[k]
O LORD, grant us success.
[26]Blessed is he who comes[l] in the name
of the LORD.
From the house of the LORD we
bless you.[r] [m]
[27]The LORD is God,[n]
and he has made his light shine[o]
upon us.
With boughs in hand,[p] join in the
festal procession
up[s] to the horns of the altar.[q]

[28]You are my God, and I will give you
thanks;
you are my God,[r] and I will exalt[s]
you.

[29]Give thanks to the LORD, for he is
good;
his love endures forever.

Psalm 119[t]

א Aleph

BLESSED are they whose ways are
blameless,[t]
who walk[u] according to the law of
the LORD.[v]
[2]Blessed[w] are they who keep his
statutes[x]
and seek him[y] with all their heart.[z]
[3]They do nothing wrong;[a]
they walk in his ways.[b]
[4]You have laid down precepts[c]
that are to be fully obeyed.[d]
[5]Oh, that my ways were steadfast
in obeying your decrees![e]
[6]Then I would not be put to shame[f]
when I consider all your
commands.[g]
[7]I will praise you with an upright heart
as I learn your righteous laws.[h]
[8]I will obey your decrees;

118:17 [w]Hab 1:12 [x]S Dt 32:3; Ps 64:9; 71:16; 73:28 **118:18** [y]Jer 31:18; 1Co 11:32; Heb 12:5 [z]Ps 86:13 **118:19** [a]S Ps 24:7 [b]Ps 100:4 **118:20** [c]Ps 122:1-2 [d]Ps 15:1-2; 24:3-4; Rev 22:14 **118:21** [e]S ver 5 [f]Ps 27:1 **118:22** [g]Isa 8:14 [h]Isa 17:10; 19:13; 28:16; Zec 4:7; 10:4; Mt 21:42; Mk 12:10; Lk 20:17*; S Ac 4:11*; 1Pe 2:7 **118:23** [i]Mt 21:42*; Mk 12:11* **118:24** [j]S Ps 70:4 **118:25** [k]S Ps 28:9; 116:4 **118:26** [l]S Mt 11:3; 21:9*; 23:39; Mk 11:9*; Lk 13:35*; 19:38; Jn 12:13* [m]Ps 129:8 **118:27** [n]S 1Ki 18:21 [o]Ps 27:1; Isa 58:10; 60:1,19,20; Mal 4:2; 1Pe 2:9 [p]S Lev 23:40 [q]Ex 27:2 **118:28** [r]S Ge 28:21; S Ps 16:2; 63:1; Isa 25:1 [s]S Ex 15:2 **119:1** [t]S Ge 17:1; S Dt 18:13; Pr 11:20 [u]Ps 128:1 [v]S Ps 1:2 **119:2** [w]Ps 112:1; Isa 56:2 [x]ver 146; Ps 99:7 [y]S 1Ch 16:11; S Ps 40:16 [z]S Dt 10:12 **119:3** [a]S Ps 59:4; 1Jn 3:9; 5:18 [b]Ps 128:1; Jer 6:16; 7:23 **119:4** [c]Ps 103:18 [d]S ver 56; S Dt 6:17 **119:5** [e]S Lev 19:37 **119:6** [f]ver 46,80 [g]ver 117 **119:7** [h]S Dt 4:8

[r]26 The Hebrew is plural. [s]27 Or *Bind the festal sacrifice with ropes / and take it* [t]This psalm is an acrostic poem; the verses of each stanza begin with the same letter of the Hebrew alphabet.

118:17–18 HUMANITY, Life—Death and life are clearly opposites. Only those who live have the opportunity to relate to God. We live only because God chooses for us to live rather than punishing us fully for our sins so that we die.

118:22,23 JESUS CHRIST, Foretold—A "capstone" was either a crucial stone used to secure the foundation or a keystone used as the primary stone in an arch. According to this psalm, a rejected stone became the chief building block in God's building plan. New Testament Christians with their sensitivity toward Jesus' rejection and their certainty of His significance saw this as a reference to Jesus. There are at least six direct references to v 22 in the New Testament (Mt 21:42; Mk 12:10; Lk 20:17; Ac 4:11; Eph 2:20; 1 Pet 2:7).

118:26 JESUS CHRIST, Foretold—The greeting of this verse was given annually, possibly at the Feast of the Tabernacles. The greeting echoes 2 Sa 7:12–16. The cry of joy was called out by the crowd on Palm Sunday (Mt 21:9). This is the greeting which Christians will call out at the ultimate coming of Christ (Mt 23:39). The welcome to the ancient Temple and Holy City reverberates as the glad cry of the new Jerusalem.

119:1–176 HOLY SCRIPTURE, Commitment—Revelation began with God working in an individual life. Such revelation produced an inspired literary document, the written Word of God. The written document became the source of revelation for readers or listeners. The people of God accepted the written revelation as God's inspired, authoritative Word and committed themselves to study and follow its teachings. This psalm reflects a worshiper's enthusiastic commitment to the part of the Scriptures known at that time. The written Word leads us to praise God, live morally pure lives, teach the Word to others, want greater understanding, know God's grace, pray for help in trouble, find hope for life, meditate, be angry at sin, sing, evaluate our lives, appreciate God's love, see the goodness of God, understand our afflictions, recognize the value of God's Word, become an example for others, confess the eternal trustworthiness of God's Word, gain self-confidence, recognize God's righteousness, experience God's peace, confess our sins, and trust God's promises.

119:1–2 SALVATION, Blessing—Those who keep God's law are blessed. God's law here is His statutes, precepts, decrees, commands, and word. This entire psalm is devoted to the love of God's word.

119:1–176 PRAYER, Instruction—See notes on 15:1–5; 34:1–22. Ps 119 is a lengthy meditation on the values and delights of God's Word, or His law. Most of the meditation is expressed in the form of prayer in direct address to God, but the language and total effect of the psalm show its intention to be instruction of believers as well as communication with God. The basic message is that God's continual blessings through all stages and circumstances of life fall on those who study and follow His Word, a Word known in written, permanent form available for study. The psalmist is an example of people Jesus described in Mt 5:6. Sorrow and pain turned him to God and His Word, not away. He prayed for understanding, knowing God is the only source of proper understanding of His Word. Security and freedom come only to one who serves God's Word. It gives power and courage to obey in the face of powerful opposition. Faithful study of God's Word leads one to praise the Word, obey its teachings, and freely petition God for help in time of need and suffering and to ask forgiveness when devotion to the law does not always bring obedience to it. See Guide to Extended Prayer, pp. 1767–1769.

do not utterly forsake me.[i]

ב Beth

9How can a young man keep his way
pure?[j]
By living according to your word.[k]
10I seek you with all my heart;[l]
do not let me stray from your
commands.[m]
11I have hidden your word in my heart[n]
that I might not sin[o] against you.
12Praise be[p] to you, O LORD;
teach me[q] your decrees.[r]
13With my lips I recount
all the laws that come from your
mouth.[s]
14I rejoice in following your statutes[t]
as one rejoices in great riches.
15I meditate on your precepts[u]
and consider your ways.
16I delight[v] in your decrees;
I will not neglect your word.

ג Gimel

17Do good to your servant,[w] and I will
live;
I will obey your word.[x]
18Open my eyes that I may see
wonderful things in your law.
19I am a stranger on earth;[y]
do not hide your commands from
me.
20My soul is consumed[z] with longing
for your laws[a] at all times.
21You rebuke the arrogant,[b] who are
cursed[c]
and who stray[d] from your
commands.
22Remove from me scorn[e] and
contempt,
for I keep your statutes.[f]
23Though rulers sit together and slander
me,
your servant will meditate on your
decrees.
24Your statutes are my delight;
they are my counselors.

ד Daleth

25I am laid low in the dust;[g]
preserve my life[h] according to your
word.[i]

119:8 [i]S Ps 38:21
119:9 [j]S Ps 39:1 [k]ver 65,169
119:10 [l]S Ps 9:1 [m]ver 21,118
119:11 [n]S Dt 6:6; S Job 22:22 [o]ver 133,165; Ps 18:22-23; 19:13; Pr 3:23; Isa 63:13
119:12 [p]Ps 28:6 [q]Ps 143:8,10 [r]S Ex 18:20
119:13 [s]ver 72
119:14 [t]ver 111
119:15 [u]ver 97, 148; Ps 1:2
119:16 [v]S Ps 112:1
119:17 [w]Ps 13:6; 116:7 [x]ver 67; Ps 103:20
119:19 [y]S Ge 23:4; Heb 11:13
119:20 [z]Ps 42:2; 84:2 [a]ver 131; S Ps 63:1; Isa 26:9
119:21 [b]ver 51; Job 30:1; Ps 5:5; Jer 20:7; 50:32; Da 4:37; Mal 3:15 [c]Dt 27:26 [d]S ver 10
119:22 [e]Ps 39:8 [f]ver 2
119:25 [g]Ps 44:25 [h]ver 50,107; Ps 143:11 [i]ver 9
119:26 [j]Ps 25:4; 27:11; 86:11
119:27 [k]Ps 105:2; 145:5
119:28 [l]Ps 6:7; 116:3; Isa 51:11; Jer 45:3 [m]Ps 18:1; Isa 40:29; 41:10 [n]ver 9
119:29 [o]Ps 26:4 [p]S Nu 6:25
119:30 [q]S Jos 24:22 [r]S Ps 26:3 [s]S Ps 108:1
119:31 [t]S Dt 10:20
119:33 [u]ver 12
119:34 [v]ver 27,73, 144,169; S Job 32:8; Pr 2:6; Da 2:21; Jas 1:5 [w]S Dt 6:25 [x]ver 69
119:35 [y]Ps 25:4-5 [z]ver 32 [a]S Ps 1:2
119:36 [b]S Jos 24:23 [c]Eze 33:31
119:37 [d]ver 25; Ps 71:20 [e]ver 9
119:38 [f]S Nu 23:19
119:39 [g]ver 22; Ps 69:9; 89:51; Isa 25:8; 51:7; 54:4
119:40 [h]ver 20 [i]ver 25,149,154
119:41 [j]S Ps 6:4 [k]ver 76,116,154, 170

26I recounted my ways and you
answered me;
teach me your decrees.[j]
27Let me understand the teaching of
your precepts;
then I will meditate on your
wonders.[k]
28My soul is weary with sorrow;[l]
strengthen me[m] according to your
word.[n]
29Keep me from deceitful ways;[o]
be gracious to me[p] through your
law.
30I have chosen[q] the way of truth;[r]
I have set my heart[s] on your laws.
31I hold fast[t] to your statutes, O LORD;
do not let me be put to shame.
32I run in the path of your commands,
for you have set my heart free.

ה He

33Teach me,[u] O LORD, to follow your
decrees;
then I will keep them to the end.
34Give me understanding,[v] and I will
keep your law[w]
and obey it with all my heart.[x]
35Direct me[y] in the path of your
commands,[z]
for there I find delight.[a]
36Turn my heart[b] toward your statutes
and not toward selfish gain.[c]
37Turn my eyes away from worthless
things;
preserve my life[d] according to your
word.[u][e]
38Fulfill your promise[f] to your servant,
so that you may be feared.
39Take away the disgrace[g] I dread,
for your laws are good.
40How I long[h] for your precepts!
Preserve my life[i] in your
righteousness.

ו Waw

41May your unfailing love[j] come to me,
O LORD,
your salvation according to your
promise;[k]

[u]*37* Two manuscripts of the Masoretic Text and Dead Sea Scrolls; most manuscripts of the Masoretic Text *life in your way*

119:9–11 EDUCATION, Guidance—How may persons guard against sin in their lives? The psalmist gave a straightforward answer: live according to God's Word. This answer highlights the need to be a lifelong student of the Scriptures. We cannot live according to His Word without being personally acquainted with it. The Bible provides resources for resolving life's dilemmas, making right decisions, and distinguishing true values from worldly banalities.

119:10 SIN, Responsibility—Sin is not necessary. Memorizing and obeying God's Word leads us to avoid sin. Thus, we bear responsibility when we do not use His Word to fight temptation. See vv 28–29,36–37.

119:40,75,137,142 GOD, Righteous—In trouble we trust God to do what is right and preserve our life from our enemies. See note on 111:3.

119:41,64,76,88,124,149,156,159 GOD, Love—Trusting in God's never failing love, we seek to learn and obey His law, His guidelines for life. See notes on Ex 3:7; Dt 32:10–12,36; Mt 10:29–31; Jn 3:16.

119:41,81,123,155,166,174 SALVATION, Definition—God's salvation is connected with His word. See note on 1 Sa 3:7. Both the first creation (Ge 1) and the new creation (1 Pe 1:23) are by the word of God. We know His spoken word as the inspired, written Word. There we find promises of His unfailing love and promises, reason for hope, judgment on the wicked who oppose us, and commands to guide our life.

42 then I will answer[l] the one who
taunts me,[m]
for I trust in your word.
43 Do not snatch the word of truth from
my mouth,[n]
for I have put my hope[o] in your
laws.
44 I will always obey your law,[p]
for ever and ever.
45 I will walk about in freedom,
for I have sought out your
precepts.[q]
46 I will speak of your statutes before
kings[r]
and will not be put to shame,[s]
47 for I delight[t] in your commands
because I love them.[u]
48 I lift up my hands to[v] your commands,
which I love,
and I meditate[v] on your decrees.

ז Zayin

49 Remember your word[w] to your
servant,
for you have given me hope.[x]
50 My comfort in my suffering is this:
Your promise preserves my life.[y]
51 The arrogant mock me[z] without
restraint,
but I do not turn[a] from your law.
52 I remember[b] your ancient laws,
O LORD,
and I find comfort in them.
53 Indignation grips me[c] because of the
wicked,
who have forsaken your law.[d]
54 Your decrees are the theme of my
song[e]
wherever I lodge.
55 In the night I remember[f] your name,
O LORD,
and I will keep your law.[g]
56 This has been my practice:
I obey your precepts.[h]

ח Heth

57 You are my portion,[i] O LORD;
I have promised to obey your
words.[j]
58 I have sought[k] your face with all my
heart;
be gracious to me[l] according to
your promise.[m]

119:42 [l]Pr 27:11 [m]S Ps 42:10 **119:43** [n]S 1Ki 17:24 [o]ver 74,81,114,147 **119:44** [p]ver 33,34, 55; S Dt 6:25 **119:45** [q]ver 94,155 **119:46** [r]Mt 10:18; Ac 26:1-2 [s]S ver 6 **119:47** [t]ver 77, 143; S Ps 112:1 [u]ver 97,127,159, 163,165 **119:48** [v]S Ge 24:63 **119:49** [w]ver 9 [x]ver 43 **119:50** [y]S ver 25 **119:51** [z]S ver 21; S Job 16:10; S 17:2 [a]S Job 23:11 **119:52** [b]Ps 103:18 **119:53** [c]S Ex 32:19; S 33:4 [d]Ps 89:30 **119:54** [e]ver 172; Ps 101:1; 138:5 **119:55** [f]ver 62,72; Ps 1:2; 42:8; S 63:6; 77:2; Isa 26:9; Ac 16:25 [g]S ver 44 **119:56** [h]ver 4,100, 134,168; S Nu 15:40 **119:57** [i]S Dt 32:9; Jer 51:19; La 3:24 [j]ver 17,67,101 **119:58** [k]S Dt 4:29; S 1Ch 16:11; Ps 34:4 [l]S Ge 43:29; S Ezr 9:8 [m]ver 41 **119:59** [n]Jos 24:14-15; S Ps 39:1 **119:60** [o]ver 115 **119:61** [p]ver 83, 109,153,176 **119:62** [q]S ver 55; Ac 16:25 [r]ver 7 **119:63** [s]Ps 15:4; 101:6-7; 103:11 [t]ver 56; Ps 111:10 **119:64** [u]Ps 33:5 [v]ver 12,108 **119:65** [w]ver 17; Ps 125:4; Isa 50:2; 59:1; Mic 2:7 [x]S ver 9 **119:66** [y]S Ps 51:6 **119:67** [z]S Ps 116:10 [a]S Ps 95:10; S Jer 8:4 [b]S ver 17 **119:68** [c]Ps 100:5; 106:1; 107:1; 135:3 [d]S Ex 18:20 **119:69** [e]Job 13:4; Ps 109:2 **119:70** [f]S Ps 17:10; Isa 29:13; Ac 28:27 **119:71** [g]ver 67,75 **119:72** [h]S Job 28:17; S Ps 19:10 **119:73** [i]S Ge 1:27; S Job 4:17; 10:8; Ps 138:8; 139:13-16 **119:74** [j]S Ps 34:2 [k]ver 9; Ps 130:5

59 I have considered my ways[n]
and have turned my steps to your
statutes.
60 I will hasten and not delay
to obey your commands.[o]
61 Though the wicked bind me with
ropes,
I will not forget[p] your law.
62 At midnight[q] I rise to give you thanks
for your righteous laws.[r]
63 I am a friend to all who fear you,[s]
to all who follow your precepts.[t]
64 The earth is filled with your love,[u]
O LORD;
teach me your decrees.[v]

ט Teth

65 Do good[w] to your servant
according to your word,[x] O LORD.
66 Teach me knowledge[y] and good
judgment,
for I believe in your commands.
67 Before I was afflicted[z] I went astray,[a]
but now I obey your word.[b]
68 You are good,[c] and what you do is
good;
teach me your decrees.[d]
69 Though the arrogant have smeared me
with lies,[e]
I keep your precepts with all my
heart.
70 Their hearts are callous[f] and
unfeeling,
but I delight in your law.
71 It was good for me to be afflicted[g]
so that I might learn your decrees.
72 The law from your mouth is more
precious to me
than thousands of pieces of silver
and gold.[h]

י Yodh

73 Your hands made me[i] and formed me;
give me understanding to learn your
commands.
74 May those who fear you rejoice[j] when
they see me,
for I have put my hope in your
word.[k]

[v]*48* Or *for*

119:53 SIN, Covenant Breach—Wicked people ignore God's covenant guidelines and disobey them. To refuse to learn and follow God's ways is sin.

119:65–72 EVIL AND SUFFERING, Testing—The psalmist recognized that his suffering made him appreciate God's law. Suffering reveals human limitations and the beneficial nature of God's commands.

119:66 HUMANITY, Intellectual Nature—Human wisdom finds its basis in God's revelation. True knowledge and judgment come from study of God's Word and will, not from human philosophy and reasoning. Human philosophy helps us understand life when that philosophy is built on trust in God and His revelation.

119:68 GOD, Goodness—God's very nature is good, so all He does is good. Thus we willingly listen to His teaching. See note on 106:1.

119:70 SIN, Depravity—Sin robs a person of the ability to care for others. Sinful hearts grow fat, shutting out all interest in other people and in God's commandments.

119:73 HUMANITY, Relationship to God—Because we are the creatures and God is the Creator, we can find understanding of and meaning in life only as we listen to the Creator's directions.

75 I know, O LORD, that your laws are
righteous,[l]
and in faithfulness[m] you have
afflicted me.
76 May your unfailing love[n] be my
comfort,
according to your promise[o] to your
servant.
77 Let your compassion[p] come to me that
I may live,
for your law is my delight.[q]
78 May the arrogant[r] be put to shame for
wronging me without cause;[s]
but I will meditate on your
precepts.
79 May those who fear you turn to me,
those who understand your
statutes.[t]
80 May my heart be blameless[u] toward
your decrees,[v]
that I may not be put to shame.[w]

כ Kaph

81 My soul faints[x] with longing for your
salvation,[y]
but I have put my hope[z] in your
word.
82 My eyes fail,[a] looking for your
promise;[b]
I say, "When will you comfort me?"
83 Though I am like a wineskin in the
smoke,
I do not forget[c] your decrees.
84 How long[d] must your servant wait?
When will you punish my
persecutors?[e]
85 The arrogant[f] dig pitfalls[g] for me,
contrary to your law.
86 All your commands are trustworthy;[h]
help me,[i] for men persecute me[j]
without cause.[k]
87 They almost wiped me from the earth,
but I have not forsaken[l] your
precepts.
88 Preserve my life[m] according to your
love,[n]
and I will obey the statutes[o] of your
mouth.

ל Lamedh

89 Your word, O LORD, is eternal;[p]
it stands firm in the heavens.
90 Your faithfulness[q] continues through
all generations;[r]
you established the earth, and it
endures.[s]
91 Your laws endure[t] to this day,
for all things serve you.[u]
92 If your law had not been my delight,[v]
I would have perished in my
affliction.[w]
93 I will never forget[x] your precepts,
for by them you have preserved my
life.[y]
94 Save me,[z] for I am yours;
I have sought out your precepts.[a]
95 The wicked are waiting to destroy
me,[b]
but I will ponder your statutes.[c]
96 To all perfection I see a limit;
but your commands are boundless.[d]

מ Mem

97 Oh, how I love your law![e]
I meditate[f] on it all day long.
98 Your commands make me wiser[g] than
my enemies,
for they are ever with me.
99 I have more insight than all my
teachers,
for I meditate on your statutes.[h]
100 I have more understanding than the
elders,
for I obey your precepts.[i]
101 I have kept my feet[j] from every evil
path
so that I might obey your word.[k]
102 I have not departed from your laws,[l]
for you yourself have taught[m] me.
103 How sweet are your words to my
taste,
sweeter than honey[n] to my
mouth![o]
104 I gain understanding[p] from your
precepts;
therefore I hate every wrong path.[q]

נ Nun

105 Your word is a lamp[r] to my feet
and a light[s] for my path.
106 I have taken an oath[t] and confirmed
it,
that I will follow your righteous
laws.[u]
107 I have suffered much;
preserve my life,[v] O LORD,
according to your word.

119:75 [l]ver 7,138, 172 [m]Heb 12:5-11 **119:76** [n]Ps 6:4 [o]S ver 41 **119:77** [p]Ps 90:13; 103:13 [q]S ver 47 **119:78** [r]ver 51; Jer 50:32 [s]ver 86, 161; Ps 35:19 **119:79** [t]ver 27,125 **119:80** [u]ver 1; S 1Ki 8:61 [v]S Ge 26:5 [w]S ver 6 **119:81** [x]ver 20; Ps 84:2 [y]ver 123 [z]S ver 43 **119:82** [a]S Ps 6:7; 69:3; La 2:11 [b]ver 41,123 **119:83** [c]S ver 61 **119:84** [d]Ps 6:3; Rev 6:10 [e]ver 51; Jer 12:3; 15:15; 20:11 **119:85** [f]ver 51 [g]Ps 35:7; 57:6; Jer 18:20,22 **119:86** [h]ver 138 [i]S Ps 109:26 [j]S Ps 7:1 [k]S ver 78 **119:87** [l]ver 150; Isa 1:4,28; 58:2; 59:13 **119:88** [m]S Ps 41:2 [n]ver 124; Ps 51:1; 109:26 [o]ver 2,100, 129,134,168 **119:89** [p]ver 111, 144; S Ps 111:8; Isa 51:6; S Mt 5:18; 1Pe 1:25 **119:90** [q]S Ps 36:5 [r]S Ps 45:17 [s]S Job 8:19; Ps 148:6 **119:91** [t]Jer 33:25 [u]Ps 104:2-4; Jer 31:35 **119:92** [v]Ps 37:4; S 112:1 [w]ver 50,67 **119:93** [x]ver 83 [y]S Ps 103:5 **119:94** [z]ver 146; Ps 54:1; 116:4; Jer 17:14; 31:18; 42:11 [a]S ver 45 **119:95** [b]S Ps 69:4 [c]ver 99 **119:96** [d]Ps 19:7 **119:97** [e]S ver 47 [f]S ver 15 **119:98** [g]ver 130; S Dt 4:6; Ps 19:7; 2Ti 3:15 **119:99** [h]ver 15 **119:100** [i]S ver 56; S Dt 6:17 **119:101** [j]Pr 1:15 [k]S ver 57 **119:102** [l]S Dt 17:20 [m]S Dt 4:5 **119:103** [n]S Ps 19:10 [o]Pr 24:13-14 **119:104** [p]S Ps 111:10 [q]ver 128 **119:105** [r]Pr 20:27; 2Pe 1:19 [s]ver 130; Pr 6:23 **119:106** [t]S Ne 10:29 [u]ver 7 **119:107** [v]S ver 25

119:75–76,86,90,138,160 GOD, Faithfulness—Even in affliction and persecution we can affirm God's faithfulness to His purposes, His promises, and His precepts. His faithfulness means His Word is faithful and trustworthy. See notes on Ge 8:1; Nu 26:65; Dt 10:11,22; Jos 1:6; 1 Co 1:9.

119:97–104 HUMANITY, Intellectual Nature—Learning has many sources. Powerful humans build up ways to rule and control. Teachers study human traditions and use human reasoning to gain knowledge. Elders rely on long experience in life. Such wisdom used correctly can be good and helpful, but it needs to be secondary. Genuine wisdom comes from God and the study of His Word.

119:99–102 EDUCATION, Obedience—The psalmist taught an important educational principle. Only one who obeys the Word of the Lord can fully understand it. See 119:33–34. Divine truth is not something to be contemplated from a distance. It must be grappled with in the arena of everyday experience. True wisdom depends upon obedience to God's precepts. See note on 86:11.

108Accept, O LORD, the willing praise of
my mouth,[w]
and teach me your laws.[x]
109Though I constantly take my life in
my hands,[y]
I will not forget[z] your law.
110The wicked have set a snare[a] for me,
but I have not strayed[b] from your
precepts.
111Your statutes are my heritage forever;
they are the joy of my heart.[c]
112My heart is set[d] on keeping your
decrees
to the very end.[e]

ס Samekh

113I hate double-minded men,[f]
but I love your law.[g]
114You are my refuge and my shield;[h]
I have put my hope[i] in your word.
115Away from me,[j] you evildoers,
that I may keep the commands of
my God!
116Sustain me[k] according to your
promise,[l] and I will live;
do not let my hopes be dashed.[m]
117Uphold me,[n] and I will be
delivered;[o]
I will always have regard for your
decrees.[p]
118You reject all who stray[q] from your
decrees,
for their deceitfulness is in vain.
119All the wicked of the earth you
discard like dross;[r]
therefore I love your statutes.[s]
120My flesh trembles[t] in fear of you;[u]
I stand in awe[v] of your laws.

ע Ayin

121I have done what is righteous and
just;[w]
do not leave me to my oppressors.
122Ensure your servant's well-being;[x]
let not the arrogant oppress me.[y]
123My eyes fail,[z] looking for your
salvation,[a]
looking for your righteous promise.[b]
124Deal with your servant according to
your love[c]
and teach me your decrees.[d]
125I am your servant;[e] give me
discernment
that I may understand your
statutes.[f]
126It is time for you to act, O LORD;
your law is being broken.[g]
127Because I love your commands[h]
more than gold,[i] more than pure
gold,[j]
128and because I consider all your
precepts right,[k]
I hate every wrong path.[l]

פ Pe

129Your statutes are wonderful;[m]
therefore I obey them.[n]
130The unfolding of your words gives
light;[o]
it gives understanding to the
simple.[p]
131I open my mouth and pant,[q]
longing for your commands.[r]
132Turn to me[s] and have mercy[t] on
me,
as you always do to those who love
your name.[u]
133Direct my footsteps according to your
word;[v]
let no sin rule[w] over me.
134Redeem me from the oppression of
men,[x]
that I may obey your precepts.[y]
135Make your face shine[z] upon your
servant
and teach me your decrees.[a]
136Streams of tears[b] flow from my eyes,
for your law is not obeyed.[c]

צ Tsadhe

137Righteous are you,[d] O LORD,
and your laws are right.[e]
138The statutes you have laid down are
righteous;[f]
they are fully trustworthy.[g]
139My zeal wears me out,[h]
for my enemies ignore your words.
140Your promises[i] have been thoroughly
tested,[j]
and your servant loves them.[k]
141Though I am lowly and despised,[l]
I do not forget your precepts.[m]
142Your righteousness is everlasting
and your law is true.[n]

119:108 [w]Ps 51:15; 63:5; 71:8; 109:30 [x]S ver 64 **119:109** [y]S Jdg 12:3 [z]S ver 61 **119:110** [a]Ps 25:15; S 64:5; Isa 8:14; Am 3:5 [b]ver 10 **119:111** [c]ver 14, 162 **119:112** [d]S Ps 108:1 [e]ver 33 **119:113** [f]S 1Ki 18:21; Jas 1:8; 4:8 [g]ver 47 **119:114** [h]S Ge 15:1; S Ps 18:2 [i]S ver 43 **119:115** [j]S Ps 6:8 **119:116** [k]S Ps 18:35; 41:3; 55:22; Isa 46:4 [l]S ver 41 [m]Ro 5:5 **119:117** [n]Isa 41:10; 46:4 [o]Ps 34:4 [p]ver 6 **119:118** [q]S ver 10 **119:119** [r]Isa 1:22, 25; Eze 22:18,19 [s]ver 47 **119:120** [t]S Job 4:14; S Isa 64:2 [u]S Jos 24:14 [v]Jer 10:7; Hab 3:2 **119:121** [w]S 2Sa 8:15; S Job 27:6 **119:122** [x]S Job 17:3 [y]ver 21, 121,134; Ps 106:42 **119:123** [z]Isa 38:14 [a]ver 81 [b]S ver 82 **119:124** [c]S ver 88; S Ps 25:7 [d]ver 12 **119:125** [e]S Ps 116:16 [f]S ver 79 **119:126** [g]S Nu 15:31 **119:127** [h]S ver 47 [i]Ps 19:10 [j]S Job 3:21 **119:128** [k]S Ps 19:8 [l]ver 104,163; Ps 31:6; Pr 13:5 **119:129** [m]ver 18 [n]ver 22,S 88 **119:130** [o]S ver 105 [p]S Ps 19:7 **119:131** [q]Ps 42:1 [r]S ver 20 **119:132** [s]S Ps 6:4 [t]S 2Sa 24:14; S Ps 9:13 [u]S Ps 5:11 **119:133** [v]ver 9 [w]S ver 11; S Ro 6:16 **119:134** [x]S ver 122 [y]S ver 56,S 88 **119:135** [z]S Nu 6:25; Ps 4:6; 67:1; 80:3 [a]ver 12 **119:136** [b]Ps 6:6; Isa 22:4; Jer 9:1,18; 13:17; 14:17; La 1:16; 3:48 [c]ver 158; Ps 106:25; Isa 42:24; Eze 9:4

119:137 [d]S Ex 9:27; S Ezr 9:15 [e]S Ne 9:13 **119:138** [f]S ver 75; S Ps 19:7 [g]ver 86 **119:139** [h]Ps 69:9; Jn 2:17 **119:140** [i]S Jos 23:14 [j]Ps 12:6 [k]ver 47 **119:141** [l]S Ps 22:6 [m]ver 61,134 **119:142** [n]ver 151,160; Ps 19:7

119:118 SIN, Alienation—Sin makes us think we can deceive God. We forget God controls the universe. Sin only causes Him to judge us.

119:121 CHRISTIAN ETHICS, Justice—In bleak times we may forget the promises of 112:3,6. Such times lead us to make bold claims before God. We do cry out for justice knowing our suffering is not just return for our devotion to God and His way of life. God hears our cries for justice and will act on them in His time.

119:132 GOD, Grace—God faithfully shows His grace to help people who love Him. See note on 102:13–17.

119:133 SIN, Slavery—Sin allures us with false promises of grandeur. Its real intent is to control and rule our lives. A person can have only one type of relationship to sin—slave to master. The alternative is to let God's Word rule our lives.

119:134,154 SALVATION, Redemption—God's redemption is for the sake of His Word, here called "precepts" and "promise." Redemption brings victory in God's court over false accusations and frees us to obey God.

143Trouble and distress have come upon
me,
but your commands are my
delight.[o]
144Your statutes are forever right;
give me understanding[p] that I may
live.

ק Qoph

145I call with all my heart;[q] answer me,
O LORD,
and I will obey your decrees.[r]
146I call out to you; save me[s]
and I will keep your statutes.
147I rise before dawn[t] and cry for help;
I have put my hope in your word.
148My eyes stay open through the
watches of the night,[u]
that I may meditate on your
promises.
149Hear my voice[v] in accordance with
your love;[w]
preserve my life,[x] O LORD,
according to your laws.
150Those who devise wicked schemes[y]
are near,
but they are far from your law.
151Yet you are near,[z] O LORD,
and all your commands are true.[a]
152Long ago I learned from your
statutes[b]
that you established them to last
forever.[c]

ר Resh

153Look upon my suffering[d] and deliver
me,[e]
for I have not forgotten[f] your law.
154Defend my cause[g] and redeem me;[h]
preserve my life[i] according to your
promise.[j]
155Salvation is far from the wicked,
for they do not seek out[k] your
decrees.
156Your compassion is great,[l] O LORD;
preserve my life[m] according to your
laws.[n]
157Many are the foes who persecute
me,[o]
but I have not turned[p] from your
statutes.
158I look on the faithless with loathing,[q]
for they do not obey your word.[r]
159See how I love your precepts;
preserve my life,[s] O LORD,
according to your love.
160All your words are true;
all your righteous laws are eternal.[t]

ש Sin and Shin

161Rulers persecute me[u] without cause,
but my heart trembles[v] at your
word.
162I rejoice[w] in your promise
like one who finds great spoil.[x]
163I hate and abhor[y] falsehood
but I love your law.[z]
164Seven times a day I praise you
for your righteous laws.[a]
165Great peace[b] have they who love
your law,
and nothing can make them
stumble.[c]
166I wait for your salvation,[d] O LORD,
and I follow your commands.
167I obey your statutes,
for I love them[e] greatly.
168I obey your precepts[f] and your
statutes,[g]
for all my ways are known[h]
to you.

ת Taw

169May my cry come[i] before you,
O LORD;
give me understanding[j] according
to your word.[k]
170May my supplication come[l] before
you;
deliver me[m] according to your
promise.[n]
171May my lips overflow with praise,[o]
for you teach me[p] your decrees.
172May my tongue sing[q] of your word,
for all your commands are
righteous.[r]
173May your hand be ready to help[s]
me,
for I have chosen[t] your precepts.
174I long for your salvation,[u] O LORD,
and your law is my delight.[v]
175Let me live[w] that I may praise you,
and may your laws sustain me.
176I have strayed like a lost sheep.[x]
Seek your servant,
for I have not forgotten[y] your
commands.

119:143 [o]ver 24, S 47 **119:144** [p]S ver 34 **119:145** [q]ver 10 [r]ver 22,55 **119:146** [s]S ver 94 **119:147** [t]Ps 5:3; 57:8; 108:2 **119:148** [u]S Ps 63:6 **119:149** [v]S Ps 27:7 [w]ver 124 [x]S ver 40 **119:150** [y]S Ps 37:7 **119:151** [z]S Ps 34:18; Php 4:5 [a]S ver 142 **119:152** [b]ver 7,73 [c]S ver 89; S Ps 111:8; Lk 21:33 **119:153** [d]S Ps 13:3 [e]S Ps 3:7 [f]S Ps 44:17 **119:154** [g]Ps 35:1; Jer 50:34; Mic 7:9 [h]S 1Sa 24:15 [i]ver 25 [j]S ver 41 **119:155** [k]ver 94, 118 **119:156** [l]S Ne 9:27; Jas 5:11 [m]ver 25 [n]ver 149 **119:157** [o]S Ps 7:1 [p]S Ps 44:18 **119:158** [q]ver 104; S Ex 32:19 [r]S ver 136 **119:159** [s]ver 25; S Ps 41:2 **119:160** [t]S ver 89; S Ps 111:8 **119:161** [u]ver 23, 122,157; 1Sa 24:14-15 [v]ver 120 **119:162** [w]S ver 111 [x]1Sa 30:16; Isa 9:3; 53:12 **119:163** [y]S ver 128 [z]ver 47 **119:164** [a]ver 7,160 **119:165** [b]Ps 37:11; Isa 26:3, 12; 27:5; 32:17; 57:19; 66:12 [c]S ver 11; S Ps 37:24; 1Jn 2:10 **119:166** [d]ver 81 **119:167** [e]ver 47 **119:168** [f]S ver 56, S 88 [g]ver 2,22 [h]S Job 10:4; S 23:10; Ps 139:3; Pr 5:21 **119:169** [i]S Job 16:18 [j]S ver 34 [k]S ver 9 **119:170** [l]1Ki 8:30; 2Ch 6:24; Ps 28:2; 140:6; 143:1 [m]Ps 3:7; 22:20; 59:1 [n]S ver 41 **119:171** [o]Ps 51:15; 63:3 [p]Ps 94:12; Isa 2:3; Mic 4:2 **119:172** [q]Ps 51:14 [r]ver 7,S 75 **119:173** [s]Ps 37:24; 73:23; Isa 41:10 [t]S Jos 24:22 **119:174** [u]ver 166 [v]ver 16,24 **119:175** [w]ver 116,159; Isa 55:3 **119:176** [x]ver 10; S Ps 95:10; Jer 50:17; Eze 34:11; S Lk 15:4 [y]S Ps 44:17

119:145 SALVATION, Obedience—The saved will obey God's Word, here called His decrees. Compare v 134.
119:151 REVELATION, Faithfulness—The psalmist affirmed the reliability of God, both in remaining available and in being true to His word. Personal history is publicly celebrated as the proof of God's nearness and trustworthiness. The written documents reveal a steadfast God to a people assembled for worship.
119:170 SALVATION, As Deliverance—God delivers us according to His promise recorded in His Word and in answer to our prayers.
119:176 SIN, Universal Nature—The psalmist devoted the longest of the Psalms to the praise of God's Word. Then he concluded by acknowledging that one as devoted as he was only a sinful lost sheep whom God needed to seek. Knowing God's Word is a strong weapon against temptation (v 10), but we must also obey God's Word. None of us does this perfectly. We all sin.

Psalm 120

A song of ascents.

I call on the LORD[z] in my distress,[a]
and he answers me.
2Save me, O LORD, from lying lips[b]
and from deceitful tongues.[c]

3What will he do to you,
and what more besides, O deceitful tongue?
4He will punish you with a warrior's sharp arrows,[d]
with burning coals of the broom tree.

5Woe to me that I dwell in Meshech,
that I live among the tents of Kedar![e]
6Too long have I lived
among those who hate peace.
7I am a man of peace;
but when I speak, they are for war.

Psalm 121

A song of ascents.

I lift up my eyes to the hills—
where does my help come from?
2My help comes from the LORD,
the Maker of heaven[f] and earth.[g]

3He will not let your foot slip—
he who watches over you will not slumber;
4indeed, he who watches[h] over Israel
will neither slumber nor sleep.

5The LORD watches over[i] you—
the LORD is your shade at your right hand;
6the sun[j] will not harm you by day,
nor the moon by night.

7The LORD will keep you from all harm[k]—
he will watch over your life;
8the LORD will watch over your coming and going
both now and forevermore.[l]

Psalm 122

A song of ascents. Of David.

I rejoiced with those who said to me,
"Let us go to the house of the LORD."
2Our feet are standing
in your gates, O Jerusalem.

3Jerusalem is built like a city
that is closely compacted together.
4That is where the tribes go up,
the tribes of the LORD,
to praise the name of the LORD

120:1 [z]S Ps 18:6 [a]S 2Sa 22:7; S Ps 118:5
120:2 [b]S Ps 31:18 [c]S Ps 52:4
120:4 [d]S Dt 32:23
120:5 [e]S Ge 25:13; Jer 2:10
121:2 [f]S Ge 1:1 [g]S Ps 104:5; Ps
121:4 [h]Ps 127:1
121:5 [i]S Ps 1:6
121:6 [j]Isa 49:10
121:7 [k]S Ps 9:9
121:8 [l]Dt 28:6

120:1 GOD, Personal—Impersonal images and idols do not hear and answer when we need help. The personal God does. See note on 116:1–2.
120:1–7 EVIL AND SUFFERING, Endurance—See note on 3:1–8. Life in a foreign culture among people with different values and life-styles is often viewed as personal punishment and suffering. God is not confined to any culture or geographical area. He can help us in all situations, as the homesick psalmist discovered.
120:1–7 PRAYER, Lament—See note on 3:1–8. Pss 120—134 are the "Songs of Ascents," probably sung by pilgrims as they approached Mt. Zion in the annual feasts. They are concerned with Jerusalem (122; 127:1; 128:5), the house of the Lord (122; 132:3–5; 134:1–2), and Zion (125; 126; 128:5; 129:5; 132:13–16; 133:3; 134:3). The series begins with a lament of a person stationed far from Jerusalem and being falsely condemned. Prayer is the path to God no matter where one lives.
120:2–3 SIN, Estrangement—Sin works through human beings. It controls our speech mechanism, leading us to lie and deceive other people. They cry for vengeance. Sin separates us from our fellow human beings.
120:2 SALVATION, Definition—God's salvation is from lies and deceit. His salvation is for a life-style characterized by truth and honesty. Salvation has to do with our personal moral conduct—the way we use the members of our body. Saved persons should have tamed tongues and truthful lips (Jas 3:3–12).
120:6–7 CHRISTIAN ETHICS, War and Peace—Isolation in a foreign land often brings a feeling of persecution and a desire for revenge. The psalmist met the challenge by leaving revenge to God and experiencing a reaffirmation of dedication to peace. The only hope to end war is for God's people to love peace even in a world clamoring for war. See note on 55:20–21.
121:1–8 EVIL AND SUFFERING, God's Present Help—Our situation in life affects the way we pray to and understand God. This grateful psalmist testified to the ever-alert God who offers constant protection from all harm. Job and the writers of the psalms of lament offered a different perspective. They complained of God's silence and asked how long He would wait to help. They felt lonely and rejected (Ps 88). Theological reflection must take all perspectives into view. God is eternally aware of the situation of each of us. He will accomplish His ultimate purpose of salvation for His people. He does respect human freedom. This means He allows His people to suffer the consequences of our sin and that of the human race. He even uses suffering to test us (Job) and discipline us. Looking to the past, we can see God's direction even through our troubles. We can confess that He protected us from ultimate harm. He does not let evil finally conquer. We can follow Him faithfully through all life's twists and turns.
121:1–8 PRAYER, Confidence—See note on 120:1–7. Prayer expresses confidence in God's protection through daily problems. This prayer was probably used in worship in the Temple. It functions as a blessing on a worried worshiper. See note on Nu 6:22–27.
121:2 GOD, Creator—See notes on Ge 1:3—2:25; Ro 4:17.
121:3–8 GOD, Personal—God is always personally on guard watching over His people. We can rest assured knowing God never rests. Israel's neighbors often depended on rather insignificant personal gods to hear their needs and report them to the "high gods." We know the one and only God is watching and listening to our needs. See notes on 44:23; 116:1–2; Ro 4:17.
122:1–9 PRAYER, God's Presence—See note on 120:1–7. This hymn celebrated Jerusalem both as the site of the annual pilgrimages and as the place on earth where God had chosen to reside. The city's peace was dependent on the people whom God placed there. They had to pray for her peace. To pray for our town and our worship place is one way to pray for God's presence with His worshiping congregation.

according to the statute given to
Israel.
5There the thrones for judgment stand,
the thrones of the house of David.

6Pray for the peace of Jerusalem:
"May those who love[m] you be
secure.
7May there be peace[n] within your walls
and security within your citadels.[o]"
8For the sake of my brothers and
friends,
I will say, "Peace be within you."
9For the sake of the house of the LORD
our God,
I will seek your prosperity.[p]

Psalm 123

A song of ascents.

I lift up my eyes to you,
to you whose throne[q] is in heaven.
2As the eyes of slaves look to the hand
of their master,
as the eyes of a maid look to the
hand of her mistress,
so our eyes look to the LORD[r] our
God,
till he shows us his mercy.

3Have mercy on us, O LORD, have
mercy on us,
for we have endured much
contempt.
4We have endured much ridicule from
the proud,
much contempt from the arrogant.

Psalm 124

A song of ascents. Of David.

IF the LORD had not been on our side—
let Israel say[s]—
2if the LORD had not been on our side
when men attacked us,
3when their anger flared against us,
they would have swallowed us alive;
4the flood[t] would have engulfed us,
the torrent[u] would have swept over
us,
5the raging waters
would have swept us away.

6Praise be to the LORD,
who has not let us be torn by their
teeth.
7We have escaped like a bird
out of the fowler's snare;[v]
the snare has been broken,[w]
and we have escaped.
8Our help is in the name[x] of the LORD,
the Maker of heaven[y] and earth.

Psalm 125

A song of ascents.

THOSE who trust in the LORD are like
Mount Zion,[z]
which cannot be shaken[a] but
endures forever.
2As the mountains surround
Jerusalem,[b]
so the LORD surrounds[c] his people
both now and forevermore.

3The scepter[d] of the wicked will not
remain[e]
over the land allotted to the
righteous,
for then the righteous might use
their hands to do evil.[f]

4Do good, O LORD,[g] to those who are
good,
to those who are upright in heart.[h]
5But those who turn[i] to crooked ways[j]
the LORD will banish[k] with the
evildoers.

Peace be upon Israel.[l]

Psalm 126

A song of ascents.

WHEN the LORD brought back[m] the
captives to[w] Zion,

122:6 [m]S Ps 26:8
122:7 [n]S 1Sa 25:6 [o]S Ps 48:3
122:9 [p]Ps 128:5
123:1 [q]S Ps 68:5; Isa 6:1; 63:15
123:2 [r]S Ps 25:15
124:1 [s]Ps 129:1
124:4 [t]Ps 88:17 [u]S Ps 18:4
124:7 [v]S Ps 91:3 [w]Ps 25:15
124:8 [x]S 1Sa 17:45 [y]Ge 1:1; Ps 115:15; 121:2; 134:3
125:1 [z]Ps 48:12; Isa 33:20 [a]Ps 46:5; 48:2-5
125:2 [b]S 1Ch 21:15 [c]Ps 32:10; Zec 2:4-5
125:3 [d]S Est 4:11 [e]Ps 89:22; Pr 22:8; Isa 13:11; 14:5 [f]1Sa 24:10
125:4 [g]S Ps 119:65 [h]S Ps 36:10
125:5 [i]S Job 23:11 [j]Pr 2:15; Isa 59:8 [k]Ps 92:7 [l]Ps 128:6; Pr 17:6; Gal 6:16
126:1 [m]Ezr 1:1-3; Ps 85:1; Hos 6:11

[w] 1 Or *LORD restored the fortunes of*

123:1–4 EVIL AND SUFFERING, Endurance—See note on 3:1–8.
123:1–4 PRAYER, Commitment—See note on 120:1–7. Prayer is commitment of the servant of God to depend on and serve the Lord. Such commitment is an acknowledgment of dependence on His mercy. The alert servant is both obedient and dependent. The obedient servant can ask for the Master's protection.
123:2–3 GOD, Grace—We are servants who must depend on the Master for everything. He is not an unfeeling taskmaster but a merciful Lord ready to supply our needs. See note on 119:132.
124:1–8 GOD, Grace—No matter how numerous or powerful the enemy, God's people will win because He is graciously present on our side. See note on 123:2–3.
124:1–8 EVIL AND SUFFERING, God's Present Help—Only the Lord can defeat the enemies of His people. See note on 21:1–13.
124:1–8 PRAYER, Praise—See notes on 93:1–5; 120:1–7. Much of the praise in the psalter is for what God has done or does for His people. As such, praise becomes a way of expressing thanks. Praise acknowledges dependence on the Creator.
124:8 GOD, Creator—See notes on Ge 1:3—2:25; Ro 4:17.
125:1–5 EVIL AND SUFFERING, Endurance—See notes on 3:1–8; 121:1–8.
125:1–5 PRAYER, Faith—See note on 120:1–7. The psalmist declared the unshakability of faith and then made his petition. Thus personal prayer becomes public instruction as prayer expresses testimony to encourage others. Petition turns to blessing. See note on Nu 6:22–27.
125:2 SALVATION, As Refuge—God surrounds those who take refuge in Him like the mountains surround Jerusalem. See note on 34:8.
126:1–6 EVIL AND SUFFERING, Endurance—See

we were like men who dreamed.[x]
2Our mouths were filled with
laughter,[n]
our tongues with songs of joy.[o]
Then it was said among the nations,
"The LORD has done great things[p]
for them."
3The LORD has done great things[q] for
us,
and we are filled with joy.[r]

4Restore our fortunes,[y][s] O LORD,
like streams in the Negev.[t]
5Those who sow in tears[u]
will reap[v] with songs of joy.[w]
6He who goes out weeping,[x]
carrying seed to sow,
will return with songs of joy,
carrying sheaves with him.

Psalm 127

A song of ascents. Of Solomon.

UNLESS the LORD builds[y] the house,
its builders labor in vain.
Unless the LORD watches[z] over the
city,
the watchmen stand guard in vain.
2In vain you rise early
and stay up late,
toiling for food[a] to eat—
for he grants sleep[b] to[z] those he
loves.[c]

3Sons are a heritage from the LORD,
children a reward[d] from him.
4Like arrows[e] in the hands of a warrior
are sons born in one's youth.
5Blessed is the man
whose quiver is full of them.[f]
They will not be put to shame
when they contend with their
enemies[g] in the gate.[h]

Psalm 128

A song of ascents.

BLESSED are all who fear the LORD,[i]
who walk in his ways.[j]
2You will eat the fruit of your labor;[k]
blessings and prosperity[l] will be
yours.
3Your wife will be like a fruitful vine[m]
within your house;
your sons[n] will be like olive shoots[o]
around your table.
4Thus is the man blessed[p]
who fears the LORD.[q]

5May the LORD bless you from Zion[r]
all the days of your life;
may you see the prosperity of
Jerusalem,[s]
6 and may you live to see your
children's children.[t]

Peace be upon Israel.[u]

Psalm 129

A song of ascents.

THEY have greatly oppressed[v] me
from my youth[w]—

126:2 [n]S Ge 21:6 [o]S Job 8:21; S Ps 65:8 [p]S Dt 10:21; Ps 71:19; Lk 1:49
126:3 [q]Ps 106:21; Joel 2:21,26 [r]S Ps 9:2; 16:11
126:4 [s]S Dt 30:3 [t]S Ps 107:35; Isa 43:19; 51:3
126:5 [u]Ps 6:6; 80:5; Jer 50:4 [v]Gal 6:9 [w]Ps 16:11; 20:5; 23:6; Isa 35:10; 51:11; 60:15; 61:7; Jer 31:6-7,12
126:6 [x]S Nu 25:6; S Ps 30:5
127:1 [y]Ps 78:69 [z]Ps 121:4
127:2 [a]S Ge 3:17 [b]S Nu 6:26; S Job 11:18 [c]S Dt 33:12; Ecc 2:25
127:3 [d]S Ge 1:28
127:4 [e]Ps 112:2
127:5 [f]Ps 128:2-3 [g]S Ge 24:60 [h]S Ge 23:10
128:1 [i]Ps 103:11; S 112:1 [j]Ps 119:1-3
128:2 [k]S Ps 58:11; 109:11; Isa 3:10 [l]S Ge 39:3; Pr 10:22
128:3 [m]S Ge 49:22 [n]S Job 29:5 [o]Ps 52:8; 144:12
128:4 [p]S Ps 1:1 [q]Ps 112:1
128:5 [r]S Ps 20:2 [s]Ps 122:9
128:6 [t]S Ge 48:11 [u]S Ps 125:5
129:1 [v]S Ex 1:13 [w]S Ps 88:15

[x]*1* Or *men restored to health* [y]*4* Or *Bring back our captives* [z]*2* Or *eat— / for while they sleep he provides for*

notes on 3:1–8; 74:1–23; 106:1–48.

126:1–6 REVELATION, Author of Hope—This preserved song of return from exile is an affirmation that the gathered worshipers might safely believe in the God who already had returned them to the Promised Land. The writer had hope for the future because of what God had already done. The joy of the Hebrews in worship preceded the actual occurrences which they celebrated. The people celebrated in advance, counting on God to be true. Salvation history extended beyond the Exodus and conquest to the Exile and beyond. Revelation shows God at work in past history and in our history.

126:1–3 HISTORY, Deliverance—God's delivering acts are not limited to one period in a people's history. Israel confessed the great acts of God from creation to Exodus to restoration from Exile. Still they looked forward to new acts. History calls God's people to ask for and expect His deliverance.

126:1–6 PRAYER, Petition—See note on 120:1–7. This prayer celebrated restoration from Exile and petitioned God to complete the work of restoration. Petition is not complete until God's work with His people is complete. Momentary joy does not guarantee permanent satisfaction. Constant prayer assures eventual joy with God.

127:1–2 HUMANITY, Work—Accomplishments in life, of whatever dimension, come as the result of God's gift. He provides the skill for accomplishment and allows us to complete projects we start. This does not call us to idleness in the face of His sovereignty but to gratitude as we labor with Him to accomplish His purposes on earth.

127:1–5 PRAYER, Instruction—See notes on 15:1–5; 120:1–7. Prayer expressing confidence in God's direction in all life's activities is also instruction to the congregation about the nature of life with God.

127:3–5 FAMILY, Childbearing—Loyal children are parents' greatest blessing. The psalmist praised God for His gift of children who would defend their falsely accused father from charges made in the city gate where local courts met. Families should be characterized by a feeling of gratitude and blessing for each family member. See note on Ge 4:1–2.

128:1 SALVATION, Blessing—All who have reverential fear for the Lord are blessed. Fear of God leads to obedience to His ways. Compare Pr 28:14.

128:1–6 PRAYER, Instruction—See notes on 15:1–5; 120:1–7. Wisdom teaching used prayer forms to assure Israel of happiness and blessing for faithful people. Such prayers ended in blessing on the nation and on individual worshipers.

128:3–6 FAMILY, Childbearing—Children add richness and joy to life. They do not represent human achievements for the parents but blessings from God. Grandchildren bring joy and hope to aging adults. See note on Ge 4:1–2.

128:5–6 CHRISTIAN ETHICS, War and Peace—Praying for the abundant life of peace and wholeness (Hebrew *shalom*) is part of prayer responsibilities for the people of God (125:5). Peace must be more than the absence of international conflict. It includes prosperity, life, and justice for all people. See Isa 2:1–5; notes on Ps 34:14; Mic 4:1–5.

129:1–8 EVIL AND SUFFERING, Endurance—See notes on 3:1–8; 35:1–28.

129:1–8 PRAYER, Curse—See notes on 5:10; 120:1–7. Past experience shows God delivers His people from wicked enemies, so prayer delivers enemies into God's justice rather

let Israel say[x]—
2they have greatly oppressed me from
my youth,
but they have not gained the
victory[y] over me.
3Plowmen have plowed my back
and made their furrows long.
4But the LORD is righteous;[z]
he has cut me free[a] from the cords
of the wicked.[b]

5May all who hate Zion[c]
be turned back in shame.[d]
6May they be like grass on the roof,[e]
which withers[f] before it can grow;
7with it the reaper cannot fill his
hands,[g]
nor the one who gathers fill his
arms.
8May those who pass by not say,
"The blessing of the LORD be upon
you;
we bless you[h] in the name of the
LORD."

Psalm 130

A song of ascents.

OUT of the depths[i] I cry to you,[j]
O LORD;
2 O Lord, hear my voice.[k]
Let your ears be attentive[l]
to my cry for mercy.[m]

3If you, O LORD, kept a record of sins,
O Lord, who could stand?[n]
4But with you there is forgiveness;[o]
therefore you are feared.[p]

5I wait for the LORD,[q] my soul waits,[r]
and in his word[s] I put my hope.
6My soul waits for the Lord
more than watchmen[t] wait for the
morning,
more than watchmen wait for the
morning.[u]

7O Israel, put your hope[v] in the LORD,
for with the LORD is unfailing love[w]
and with him is full redemption.[x]

129:1 [x]Ps 124:1
129:2 [y]Jer 1:19; 15:20; 20:11; Mt 16:18
129:4 [z]S Ex 9:27 [a]Ps 37:9 [b]Ps 140:5
129:5 [c]Mic 4:11 [d]S Ps 70:2
129:6 [e]Isa 37:27 [f]S 2Ki 19:26; Ps 102:11
129:7 [g]S Dt 28:38; Ps 79:12
129:8 [h]Ps 118:26
130:1 [i]S Job 30:19; Ps 42:7; La 3:55 [j]Ps 22:2; 55:17; 142:5
130:2 [k]S Ps 27:7; 28:2 [l]S 2Ch 6:40 [m]S Ps 28:6; 31:22; 86:6; 140:6
130:3 [n]S 1Sa 6:20; S Ezr 9:15; Ps 143:2; Na 1:6; Rev 6:17
130:4 [o]S Ex 34:7; S 2Sa 24:14; S Jer 31:34 [p]S 1Ki 8:40
130:5 [q]S Ps 27:14; Isa 8:17; 26:8; 30:18; 49:23 [r]S Ps 5:3 [s]S Ps 119:74
130:6 [t]Ps 63:6 [u]S 2Sa 23:4
130:7 [v]S Ps 25:5; S 71:14 [w]S 1Ch 21:13 [x]S Ps 111:9; S Ro 3:24
130:8 [y]Lk 1:68 [z]S Ex 34:7; S Mt 1:21
131:1 [a]Ps 101:5; Isa 2:12; Ro 12:16 [b]S 2Sa 22:28; S Job 41:34 [c]Jer 45:5 [d]S Job 5:9; Ps 139:6
131:2 [e]S Ps 116:7 [f]Mt 18:3; 1Co 13:11; 14:20
131:3 [g]S Ps 25:5; 119:43; 130:7 [h]S Ps 113:2
132:1 [i]1Sa 18:11; S 2Sa 15:14
132:2 [j]S Ge 49:24; Isa 49:26; 60:16
132:3 [k]S 2Sa 7:2, 27
132:5 [l]S 1Ki 8:17; Ac 7:46
132:6 [m]S 1Sa 17:12 [n]S Jos 9:17; S 1Sa 7:2

8He himself will redeem[y] Israel
from all their sins.[z]

Psalm 131

A song of ascents. Of David.

MY heart is not proud,[a] O LORD,
my eyes are not haughty;[b]
I do not concern myself with great
matters[c]
or things too wonderful for me.[d]
2But I have stilled and quieted my
soul;[e]
like a weaned child with its mother,
like a weaned child is my soul[f]
within me.

3O Israel, put your hope[g] in the LORD
both now and forevermore.[h]

Psalm 132

132:8–10pp — 2Ch 6:41–42

A song of ascents.

O LORD, remember David
and all the hardships he endured.[i]

2He swore an oath to the LORD
and made a vow to the Mighty One
of Jacob:[j]
3"I will not enter my house[k]
or go to my bed—
4I will allow no sleep to my eyes,
no slumber to my eyelids,
5till I find a place[l] for the LORD,
a dwelling for the Mighty One of
Jacob."

6We heard it in Ephrathah,[m]
we came upon it in the fields of
Jaar[a]:[b] [n]
7"Let us go to his dwelling place;[o]
let us worship at his footstool[p]—

132:7 [o]S 2Sa 15:25; Ps 5:7; 122:1 [p]S 1Ch 28:2

[a]*6* That is, Kiriath Jearim [b]*6* Or *heard of it in Ephrathah, / we found it in the fields of Jaar.* (And no quotes around verses 7-9)

---

than taking personal vengeance.
129:4 GOD, Righteous—See note on 119:40,75,137,142.
130:1–8 EVIL AND SUFFERING, Endurance—See notes on 3:1–8; 51:1–19. This psalm is one of the traditional penitential psalms (6,32,38,51,102,130,143), stressing repentance and forgiveness for sins. Without God's forgiveness, we would be crushed under the weight of our own sins. We do not suffer all the punishment our sins deserve.
130:1–8 PRAYER, Repentance—See notes on 6:1–10; 120:1–7. This is one of the clearest expressions of God's mercy in the Old Testament. The redemption is "full." For the Christian, redemption in Christ is not merely from sins, but from a natural inclination and dedication to sin. God hears our cry of repentance, grants us mercy, and forgives our sin through Jesus Christ.
130:3–4 SALVATION, Forgiveness—God is ready to forgive our sins rather than to eliminate us because of them. He does not keep a list of our sins at His fingertips.
130:7 GOD, Love—God's people call to Him from the depths because we know Him as the loving Redeemer who will satisfy our hopes. God saves not only from physical distress but also from the spiritual distress caused by sin. See notes on 106:4,8,10,21; 119:41,64,76,88,124,149,156,159.
131:1–3 PRAYER, Humility—See note on 120:1–7. It is rare in biblical prayers to confess humility. Here, humility is an act of the will. Humility is the starting point for prayer and the basis for testimony to others.
132:1–18 PRAYER, Politics—See note on 120:1–7. In festival worship Israel prayed for their king. Such prayer looked back to David's faithfulness in preparing a place for Yahweh to be worshiped and to God's covenant to maintain David's descendants on the throne. Whatever the form of national government, God's people have a responsibility to pray that the government will maintain order in society and that God will work out His will in the affairs of state. Through blessing political processes God blesses His people.

[8]arise, O LORD,[q] and come to your
resting place,
you and the ark of your might.
[9]May your priests be clothed with
righteousness;[r]
may your saints[s] sing for joy."

[10]For the sake of David your servant,
do not reject your anointed one.

[11]The LORD swore an oath to David,[t]
a sure oath that he will not
revoke:
"One of your own descendants[u]
I will place on your throne—
[12]if your sons keep my covenant[v]
and the statutes I teach them,
then their sons will sit
on your throne[w] for ever and
ever."

[13]For the LORD has chosen Zion,[x]
he has desired it for his
dwelling:[y]
[14]"This is my resting place for ever and
ever;[z]
here I will sit enthroned,[a] for I have
desired it—
[15]I will bless her with abundant
provisions;
her poor will I satisfy with food.[b]
[16]I will clothe her priests[c] with
salvation,
and her saints will ever sing for
joy.[d]

[17]"Here I will make a horn[c] grow[e] for
David
and set up a lamp[f] for my anointed
one.[g]
[18]I will clothe his enemies with shame,[h]
but the crown on his head[i] will be
resplendent."

132:8 [q]S Nu 10:35 **132:9** [r]S Job 27:6; Isa 61:3,10; Zec 3:4; Mal 3:3; Eph 6:14 [s]Ps 16:3; 30:4; 149:5 **132:11** [t]S Ps 89:3-4,35 [u]S 1Ch 17:11-14; S Mt 1:1; Lk 3:31 **132:12** [v]2Ch 6:16; S Ps 25:10 [w]Lk 1:32; Ac 2:30 **132:13** [x]S Ex 15:17; Ps 48:1-2; S 68:16 [y]S 1Ki 8:13 **132:14** [z]ver 8; Ps 68:16 [a]S 2Sa 6:2; Ps 80:1 **132:15** [b]Ps 107:9; 147:14 **132:16** [c]S 2Ch 6:41 [d]S Job 8:21; Ps 149:5 **132:17** [e]S 1Sa 2:10; Ps 92:10; Eze 29:21; S Lk 1:69 [f]1Ki 11:36; 2Ki 8:19; 2Ch 21:7; Ps 18:28 [g]S Ps 84:9 **132:18** [h]S Job 8:22 [i]S 2Sa 12:30 **133:1** [j]S Ge 13:8; S Ro 12:10 [k]Jn 17:11 **133:2** [l]S Ex 29:7 **133:3** [m]Job 29:19; Pr 19:12; Isa 18:4; 26:19; 45:8; Hos 14:5; Mic 5:7 [n]S Dt 3:8; S 4:48 [o]S Ex 15:17; S Ps 2:6; 74:2 [p]S Lev 25:21 [q]S Ps 21:4 **134:1** [r]S Ps 113:1; 135:1-2; Rev 19:5 [s]S Nu 16:9; S 1Ch 15:2 [t]S 1Ch 23:30 **134:2** [u]S Ps 28:2; 1Ti 2:8 [v]Ps 15:1 [w]Ps 33:2; 103:1 **134:3** [x]S Ps 124:8 [y]S Lev 25:21; S Ps 20:2 **135:1** [z]Ne 7:73 **135:2** [a]S 1Ch 15:2; Lk 2:37

Psalm 133

A song of ascents. Of David.

HOW good and pleasant it is
when brothers live together[j] in
unity![k]
[2]It is like precious oil poured on the
head,[l]
running down on the beard,
running down on Aaron's beard,
down upon the collar of his robes.
[3]It is as if the dew[m] of Hermon[n]
were falling on Mount Zion.[o]
For there the LORD bestows his
blessing,[p]
even life forevermore.[q]

Psalm 134

A song of ascents.

PRAISE the LORD, all you servants[r] of
the LORD
who minister[s] by night[t] in the
house of the LORD.
[2]Lift up your hands[u] in the sanctuary[v]
and praise the LORD.[w]

[3]May the LORD, the Maker of heaven[x]
and earth,
bless you from Zion.[y]

Psalm 135

135:15–20pp — Ps 115:4–11

PRAISE the LORD.[d]
Praise the name of the LORD;
praise him, you servants[z] of the
LORD,
[2]you who minister in the house[a] of the
LORD,

[c] *17 Horn* here symbolizes strong one, that is, king.
[d] *1* Hebrew *Hallelu Yah;* also in verses 3 and 21

132:11 JESUS CHRIST, Foretold—This verse recalls once more the promise of a perpetual heir for David's throne. It is related to Ps 89 and is reaffirmed in the New Testament (Mt 1:1; Lk 1:32; Ac 2:30; 13:23; Ro 1:3; 2 Ti 2:8). No physical kingdom lasts forever. Jesus as David's heir is the rightful successor and the fulfillment of the promise. His kingdom is eternal.

132:11–12 THE CHURCH, Covenant People—God established an everlasting covenant with David, promising a descendant would sit on David's throne forever. Even everlasting promises have stipulations of obedience. Herein lies a paradox. The covenant is everlasting, but the covenant stipulations must be kept. God made the covenant with His people out of His abundant grace. He promised to keep the covenant. To receive the full blessings of God, we must serve Him. Only then will we enjoy the fullness of the relationship God initiated with His people. See note on 2 Sa 23:5.

132:14 GOD, Eternal—See notes on 55:19; 102:25.

132:16 SALVATION, Sanctification—See note on 9:14. God's salvation is sanctification, or setting persons apart to His service. All of God's people should progress toward moral and spiritual perfection.

133:1 HUMANITY, Family Relationships—Although not always attained in reality, the ideal family relationship is that of oneness of purpose and action. This is true not only for the immediate family but also for the family of God.

133:1–3 PRAYER, God's Presence—See notes on 48:1–14; 120:1–7; Nu 6:22–27. God's presence, symbolized by the worship place at Zion, unifies His people and provides blessing. Congregational prayer can praise God for His presence by exclaiming over its good results.

134:1–3 WORSHIP, Buildings—See note on Ge 28:16–22.

134:1–3 PRAYER, Praise—See notes on 33:1–22; 120:1–7; Nu 6:22–27. Some of the continuous Levitical praise in the Temple was to be offered at night (1 Ch 9:33; 23:30). The ending is probably a priestly blessing. Prayer and worship are appropriate at all times.

134:3 GOD, Creator—See note on 100:3.

135:1–21 PRAYER, Praise—See notes on 33:1–22; 111:1–10. This is a "hallelujah" psalm—one which begins and ends with "Praise the LORD" (113; 117; 146—150). It praises God for who He is in Himself as well as for what He has done for His people. Vv 15–20 are nearly identical with 115:4–11. In praise we not only speak to God, we also encourage one another to praise Him.

in the courts[b] of the house of our God.

3Praise the LORD, for the LORD is good;[c]
sing praise to his name,[d] for that is pleasant.[e]
4For the LORD has chosen Jacob[f] to be his own,
Israel to be his treasured possession.[g]

5I know that the LORD is great,[h]
that our Lord is greater than all gods.[i]
6The LORD does whatever pleases him,[j]
in the heavens and on the earth,[k]
in the seas and all their depths.
7He makes clouds rise from the ends of the earth;
he sends lightning with the rain[l]
and brings out the wind[m] from his storehouses.[n]

8He struck down the firstborn[o] of Egypt,
the firstborn of men and animals.
9He sent his signs[p] and wonders into your midst, O Egypt,
against Pharaoh and all his servants.[q]
10He struck down many[r] nations
and killed mighty kings—
11Sihon[s] king of the Amorites,[t]
Og king of Bashan[u]
and all the kings of Canaan[v]—
12and he gave their land as an inheritance,[w]
an inheritance to his people Israel.

13Your name, O LORD, endures forever,[x]
your renown,[y] O LORD, through all generations.
14For the LORD will vindicate his people[z]
and have compassion on his servants.[a]

15The idols of the nations[b] are silver and gold,
made by the hands of men.[c]
16They have mouths, but cannot speak,[d]
eyes, but they cannot see;
17they have ears, but cannot hear,
nor is there breath[e] in their mouths.
18Those who make them will be like them,
and so will all who trust in them.

19O house of Israel, praise the LORD;[f]
O house of Aaron, praise the LORD;
20O house of Levi, praise the LORD;
you who fear him, praise the LORD.
21Praise be to the LORD from Zion,[g]
to him who dwells in Jerusalem.[h]

Praise the LORD.

Psalm 136

GIVE thanks[i] to the LORD, for he is good.[j]
His love endures forever.[k]
2Give thanks[l] to the God of gods.[m]
His love endures forever.
3Give thanks[n] to the Lord of lords:[o]
His love endures forever.

4to him who alone does great wonders,[p]
His love endures forever.
5who by his understanding[q] made the heavens,[r]
His love endures forever.
6who spread out the earth[s] upon the waters,[t]
His love endures forever.

135:2 [b]S Ps 116:19 **135:3** [c]S 1Ch 16:34; S Ps 119:68 [d]S Ps 68:4 [e]S Ps 92:1; 147:1 **135:4** [f]S Dt 10:15 [g]Ex 19:5; Dt 7:6; Mal 3:17; S Tit 2:14 **135:5** [h]S Ps 48:1; 145:3 [i]S Ex 12:12; S 1Ch 16:25; S Job 21:22 **135:6** [j]Ps 115:3; Da 4:35 [k]Mt 6:10 **135:7** [l]S Job 5:10; Ps 68:9; Isa 30:23; Jer 10:13; 51:16; Joel 2:23; Zec 10:1 [m]Am 4:13 [n]S Dt 28:12 **135:8** [o]S Ex 4:23; S 12:12 **135:9** [p]S Ex 7:9 [q]Ps 136:10-15 **135:10** [r]Nu 21:21-25; Jos 24:8-11; Ps 44:2; 78:55; 136:17-21 **135:11** [s]S Nu 21:21 [t]S Nu 21:26 [u]S Nu 21:33 [v]S Jos 12:7-24; 24:12 **135:12** [w]S Dt 29:8 **135:13** [x]S Ex 3:15 [y]S Ps 102:12 **135:14** [z]S 1Sa 24:15; Heb 10:30* [a]S Dt 32:36 **135:15** [b]Ps 96:5; Rev 9:20 [c]Isa 2:8; 31:7; 37:19; 40:19; Jer 1:16; 10:5 **135:16** [d]S 1Ki 18:26 **135:17** [e]Jer 10:14; Hab 2:19 **135:19** [f]S Ps 22:23 **135:21** [g]Ps 128:5; 134:3 [h]S 1Ki 8:13; S 2Ch 6:2 **136:1** [i]Ps 105:1 [j]Ps 100:5; 106:1; 145:9; Jer 33:11; Na 1:7 [k]ver 2-26; S 2Ch 5:13; S Ezr 3:11; Ps 118:1-4 **136:2** [l]Ps 105:1 [m]S Dt 10:17 **136:3** [n]Ps 105:1 [o]S Dt 10:17; S 1Ti 6:15 **136:4** [p]S Ex 3:20; S Job 9:10 **136:5** [q]Pr 3:19; Jer 51:15 [r]S Ge 1:1 **136:6** [s]S Ge 1:1; Isa 42:5; Jer 10:12; 33:2 [t]S Ge 1:6

135:5–7 CREATION, Freedom—God has established laws in this world, but He is not a slave to them. He is a free, personal Spirit and acts in accordance with His wishes. He created the world apart from Himself and yet controls that which happens in it. No human or supernatural power can prevent Him from accomplishing His purpose. Nothing in heaven or earth is equal to Him. He rules over the powers of weather and fertility as well as all other powers.
135:5–18 HISTORY, Praise—History shows God's uniqueness compared to all others who claim to be God. Seeing God's uniqueness leads us to praise.
135:6 GOD, Sovereignty—See note on 113:4–9.
135:13 GOD, Eternal—See notes on 102:25.
135:14 GOD, Grace—History teaches us that evil forces cannot keep God's people down forever. God's grace comes to the aid of His people. See note on 124:1–8.
136:1–26 GOD, Love—This whole psalm is a commentary on God's never-ending, faithful love. Creation and history testify to God's love. See note on 118:1–4,29.
136:1–26 EVIL AND SUFFERING, God's Present Help—The psalmist recited God's help throughout Hebrew history, stressing God's enduring love as a refrain in every verse. Although we face many challenges in life, we can be assured of God's enduring love.
136:1 REVELATION, Faithfulness—The people, awed by the fidelity and reliability of their God, sang a continuous chant in His honor. The revealed deity is a God who remains by His people and His promises, even if time is required to make them good. The Psalm was designed to assist worshipers in recalling God's saving presence throughout their history.
136:1–26 HISTORY, Praise—See notes on 26:7; 66:5–7; 98:1–3; 135:5–18.
136:1–26 PRAYER, Thanksgiving—See note on 30:1–12. This is a litany, a liturgical form with a repeated phrase of thanking God as Creator and as Deliverer of Israel. Such responsive worship is one way of congregational prayer. God's enduring love is the basis of everything for which we give thanks.
136:4–9 GOD, Creator—The Bible testifies that the mighty Creator loves us. See note on 100:3.
136:4–26 CREATION, Love—Creation is an example of God's eternal love and of His unique miraculous powers. Creation was accomplished through His divine understanding and skill. The sun and moon are not high gods ruling the nations. They are simple creations of God given assignments to provide the needed light and darkness for human activities.

7who made the great lights[u] —
His love endures forever.
8the sun to govern[v] the day,
His love endures forever.
9the moon and stars to govern the night;
His love endures forever.

10to him who struck down the firstborn[w] of Egypt
His love endures forever.
11and brought Israel out[x] from among them
His love endures forever.
12with a mighty hand[y] and outstretched arm;[z]
His love endures forever.

13to him who divided the Red Sea[e] [a] asunder
His love endures forever.
14and brought Israel through[b] the midst of it,
His love endures forever.
15but swept Pharaoh and his army into the Red Sea;[c]
His love endures forever.

16to him who led his people through the desert,[d]
His love endures forever.
17who struck down great kings,[e]
His love endures forever.
18and killed mighty kings[f] —
His love endures forever.
19Sihon king of the Amorites[g]
His love endures forever.
20and Og king of Bashan[h] —
His love endures forever.
21and gave their land[i] as an inheritance,[j]
His love endures forever.
22an inheritance[k] to his servant Israel;[l]
His love endures forever.

23to the One who remembered us[m] in our low estate
His love endures forever.
24and freed us[n] from our enemies,[o]
His love endures forever.
25and who gives food[p] to every creature.
His love endures forever.

136:7 [u]Ge 1:14,16; Ps 74:16; Jas 1:17 **136:8** [v]S Ge 1:16 **136:10** [w]S Ex 4:23; S 12:12 **136:11** [x]S Ex 6:6; 13:3; Ps 105:43 **136:12** [y]S Ex 3:20; S Dt 5:15 [z]S Dt 9:29 **136:13** [a]S Ps 78:13 **136:14** [b]Ex 14:22; Ps 106:9 **136:15** [c]S Ex 14:27 **136:16** [d]S Ex 13:18; Ps 78:52 **136:17** [e]Nu 21:23-25; Jos 24:8-11; Ps 78:55; 135:9-12 **136:18** [f]Dt 29:7; S Jos 12:7-24 **136:19** [g]Nu 21:21-25 **136:20** [h]Nu 21:33-35 **136:21** [i]Jos 12:1 [j]S Dt 1:38; S Jos 14:1 **136:22** [k]S Dt 29:8; Ps 78:55 [l]Isa 20:3; 41:8; 42:19; 43:10; 44:1,21; 45:4; 49:5-7 **136:23** [m]Ps 78:39; 103:14; 115:12 **136:24** [n]S Jos 10:14; S Ne 9:28 [o]S Dt 6:19 **136:25** [p]S Ge 1:30; S Mt 6:26 **136:26** [q]Ps 105:1 [r]S Ps 115:3 [s]S Ezr 3:11 **137:1** [t]Eze 1:1,3; 3:15; 10:15 [u]Ne 1:4 [v]Isa 3:26; La 1:4 **137:2** [w]S Lev 23:40 [x]Job 30:31; Isa 24:8; Eze 26:13; Am 6:5 **137:3** [y]Ps 79:1-4; La 1:5 [z]S Job 30:9; Ps 80:6 [a]Eze 16:57; 22:4; 34:29 **137:4** [b]S Ne 12:46 **137:5** [c]Isa 2:3; 56:7; 65:11; 66:20 **137:6** [d]S Ps 22:15 [e]Ne 2:3 [f]S Dt 4:29; Jer 51:50; Eze 6:9 **137:7** [g]S Ge 25:30; S 2Ch 28:17; S Ps 83:6; La 4:21-22 [h]2Ki 25:1-10; Ob 1:11 [i]Ps 74:8 **137:8** [j]Isa 13:1,19; 47:1-15; Jer 25:12, 26; 50:1; 50:2-51:58 **137:9** [k]S 2Ki 8:12; S Isa 13:16; Lk 19:44 **138:1** [l]Ps 95:3; 96:4 [m]Ps 27:6; 108:1 **138:2** [n]S 1Ki 8:29; S Ps 5:7

26Give thanks[q] to the God of heaven.[r]
His love endures forever.[s]

Psalm 137

By the rivers of Babylon[t] we sat and wept[u]
when we remembered Zion.[v]
2There on the poplars[w]
we hung our harps,[x]
3for there our captors[y] asked us for songs,
our tormentors demanded[z] songs of joy;
they said, "Sing us one of the songs of Zion!"[a]

4How can we sing the songs of the LORD[b]
while in a foreign land?
5If I forget you,[c] O Jerusalem,
may my right hand forget ⌊its skill⌋.
6May my tongue cling to the roof[d] of my mouth
if I do not remember[e] you,
if I do not consider Jerusalem[f]
my highest joy.

7Remember, O LORD, what the Edomites[g] did
on the day Jerusalem fell.[h]
"Tear it down," they cried,
"tear it down to its foundations!"[i]
8O Daughter of Babylon, doomed to destruction,[j]
happy is he who repays you
for what you have done to us—
9he who seizes your infants
and dashes them[k] against the rocks.

Psalm 138

Of David.

I will praise you, O LORD, with all my heart;
before the "gods"[l] I will sing[m] your praise.
2I will bow down toward your holy temple[n]

[e] *13* Hebrew *Yam Suph*; that is, Sea of Reeds; also in verse 15

137:1–9 EVIL AND SUFFERING, Vindication—Covenant disobedience led Israel to punishment in Exile. The Hebrews' anguish in the Exile led to a cry for God's vengeance. See notes on 35:1–28; 109:1–31. This psalm offers an extreme example of honesty before God in the face of suffering and evil. We have the responsibility to take our cries of righteous outrage to God.

137:1–9 PRAYER, Curse—Loyalty to God and country caused intense reaction from Jews in Exile when their Babylonian captors taunted them. Mourning led to anger, which erupted in vows and curses. The actions described fell far below anyone's ethical standards. The feelings in the situation are easily understood by all. Prayer helps direct such strong feelings to the only One who can help us deal with them constructively. See note on 5:10.

138:1–8 PRAYER, Thanksgiving—See note on 33:1–22. Answered prayer leads to prayers of thanks. Answered prayer not only helps the person but even more exalts God. Thanks leads us to invite the universe to join us in praise, to gain confidence of God's help for the future, to catch a new vision of God's purpose for us, and to petition God with renewed energy.

138:2 GOD, Faithfulness—See notes on 89:1–49; 92:2; 100:5; 119:75–76,86,90,138,160.

138:2,8 GOD, Love—See note on 136:1–26.

and will praise your name[o]
for your love and your faithfulness,[p]
for you have exalted above all things
your name and your word.[q]
3 When I called,[r] you answered me;[s]
you made me bold[t] and
stouthearted.[u]

4 May all the kings of the earth[v] praise
you, O LORD,
when they hear the words of your
mouth.
5 May they sing[w] of the ways of the
LORD,
for the glory of the LORD[x] is great.

6 Though the LORD is on high, he looks
upon the lowly,[y]
but the proud[z] he knows from afar.
7 Though I walk[a] in the midst of
trouble,
you preserve my life;[b]
you stretch out your hand[c] against the
anger of my foes,[d]
with your right hand[e] you save
me.[f]
8 The LORD will fulfill ⌊his purpose⌋[g] for
me;
your love, O LORD, endures
forever[h]—
do not abandon[i] the works of your
hands.[j]

Psalm 139

For the director of music. Of David.
A psalm.

O LORD, you have searched me[k]
and you know[l] me.

2 You know when I sit and when I
rise;[m]
you perceive my thoughts[n] from
afar.
3 You discern my going out[o] and my
lying down;
you are familiar with all my ways.[p]
4 Before a word is on my tongue
you know it completely,[q] O LORD.

5 You hem me in[r]—behind and before;
you have laid your hand upon me.
6 Such knowledge is too wonderful for
me,[s]
too lofty[t] for me to attain.

7 Where can I go from your Spirit?
Where can I flee[u] from your
presence?
8 If I go up to the heavens,[v] you are
there;
if I make my bed[w] in the depths,[f]
you are there.
9 If I rise on the wings of the dawn,
if I settle on the far side of the sea,
10 even there your hand will guide me,[x]
your right hand[y] will hold me fast.

11 If I say, "Surely the darkness will hide
me
and the light become night around
me,"
12 even the darkness will not be dark[z] to
you;
the night will shine like the day,
for darkness is as light to you.

13 For you created my inmost being;[a]

138:2 [o]Ps 74:21; 97:12; 140:13 [p]Ps 108:4; 115:1 [q]Ps 119:9
138:3 [r]Ps 18:6; 30:2; 99:6; 116:4 [s]S Ps 118:5 [t]Pr 28:1; S Ac 4:29 [u]Ps 28:7
138:4 [v]Ps 72:11; 102:15
138:5 [w]S Ps 51:14; 71:16; 145:7 [x]Ps 21:5
138:6 [y]S Ps 113:6 [z]S Ps 40:4; S Mt 23:12
138:7 [a]Ps 23:4 [b]S Ps 41:2 [c]S Ex 7:5 [d]Ps 7:6 [e]Ps 20:6; 60:5; 108:6 [f]Ps 17:7,14
138:8 [g]Php 1:6 [h]S Ezr 3:11; Ps 100:5 [i]S Ps 51:11 [j]S Job 10:3,8
139:1 [k]S Ps 17:3; Ro 8:27 [l]Ps 44:21
139:2 [m]2Ki 19:27 [n]Ps 94:11; Pr 24:12; Jer 12:3
139:3 [o]2Ki 19:27 [p]S Job 31:4
139:4 [q]S Heb 4:13
139:5 [r]S 1Sa 25:16; Ps 32:10; 34:7; 125:2
139:6 [s]S Ps 131:1 [t]Ro 11:33
139:7 [u]Jer 23:24; Jnh 1:3
139:8 [v]Dt 30:12-15; Am 9:2-3 [w]Job 17:13
139:10 [x]Ps 23:3 [y]Ps 108:6; Isa 41:10
139:12 [z]Job 34:22; Da 2:22
139:13 [a]Ps 119:73

[f]8 Hebrew *Sheol*

138:4 EVANGELISM, Power—There is power in proclamation. When people hear God's word, even the kings of the earth are moved to praise the Lord. Thus we can count on the power inherent in the gospel when we witness and share the message.
138:5 GOD, Glory—See note on 115:1.
138:7 GOD, Savior—See notes on 38:22; 62:1–2,6–8; 98:1–3; Lk 1:47; 1 Ti 1:1.
139:1–18 GOD, Wisdom—Wisdom is not limited to philosophical concepts or objective facts. The Bible praises God because He takes a personal interest in each individual. He has personal, detailed knowledge of what is going on in my world. Thus I praise Him. See note on 94:10–11.
139:1–24 EVIL AND SUFFERING, Prayer—The innocent suffer, as we learn from Job. They call on God's justice to deal with personal enemies, who are also God's enemies. See notes on 35:1–28; 109:1–31. They count on and rejoice in God's presence. They commit themselves to God's continued testing and leadership. See note on 3:1–8.
139:1–24 HUMANITY, Life—Both our emotional and physical natures result from God's creative activity. The entire process of life from conception onwards occurs through God's creative power and wisdom. In His care and concern He knows everything about us. We can never escape God's attention. How do we respond to a life totally under God's control? We can respond in fear because of our sin. We can resign and quit trying because of God's power. The psalmist showed a different way. We can praise God for His greatness, because He guides us faithfully through life, because He made us so well, because He is interested in each of our days, because we can take our complaints to Him, and because He reveals our sin and leads us away from it.
139:1–24 PRAYER, Lament—Praise of God's all-encompassing knowledge and presence led the psalmist to protest the unjust situation. Wicked people opposed God and thus were the psalmist's enemies. The psalmist could testify to personal innocence undeserving of the troubled situation. Thus God was asked to curse the enemies. See notes on 3:1–8; 5:10; 7:1–17. Prayer identifies us as God's people fighting God's enemies but trusting victory to His actions.
139:7–10 GOD, Immanent—One cannot escape the presence of God in His universe. Every place is accessible to God, even the depths, the home of the dead. See notes on Dt 4:7; Heb 11:27.
139:7 HOLY SPIRIT, Presence of God—The Bible usually describes the Spirit of God as coming to an individual at a specific time to give a specific gift and to carry out a specific task. This does not limit the Spirit to certain times and certain people. The Spirit may be found everywhere. The Spirit of God brings the presence of God to every part of creation, even in Sheol (NIV footnote), the abode of the dead. The Spirit is not a creation of God, but rather is the divine Presence within which human beings always live. You can never escape God's presence. When you need Him, He is already with you. The Spirit is God's presence in His world aware of all that occurs in the world.
139:8 LAST THINGS, Intermediate State—See note on Isa 14:9.
139:13–16 CREATION, Persons—Each person is a creative work of God. The physical processes in a mother's womb

you knit me together[b] in my
mother's womb.[c]
14I praise you[d] because I am fearfully
and wonderfully made;
your works are wonderful,[e]
I know that full well.
15My frame was not hidden from
you
when I was made[f] in the secret
place.
When I was woven together[g] in the
depths of the earth,[h]
16 your eyes saw my unformed
body.
All the days ordained[i] for me
were written in your book
before one of them came to be.

17How precious to[g] me are your
thoughts,[j] O God![k]
How vast is the sum of them!
18Were I to count them,[l]
they would outnumber the grains of
sand.[m]
When I awake,[n]
I am still with you.

19If only you would slay the wicked,[o]
O God!
Away from me,[p] you bloodthirsty
men![q]
20They speak of you with evil intent;
your adversaries[r] misuse your
name.[s]
21Do I not hate those[t] who hate you,
O LORD,
and abhor[u] those who rise up
against you?
22I have nothing but hatred for
them;
I count them my enemies.[v]
23Search me,[w] O God, and know my
heart;[x]
test me and know my anxious
thoughts.
24See if there is any offensive way[y] in
me,
and lead me[z] in the way
everlasting.

139:13 [b]S Job 10:11 [c]Isa 44:2,24; 46:3; 49:5; Jer 1:5
139:14 [d]Ps 119:164; 145:10 [e]S Job 40:19
139:15 [f]Ecc 11:5 [g]S Job 10:11 [h]S Ps 63:9
139:16 [i]S Job 33:29; S Ps 90:12
139:17 [j]S Ps 92:5 [k]S Job 5:9
139:18 [l]Ps 40:5 [m]S Job 29:18 [n]S Ps 3:5
139:19 [o]Ps 5:6; Isa 11:4 [p]S Ps 6:8 [q]S Ps 59:2
139:20 [r]S Ps 65:7 [s]S Dt 5:11
139:21 [t]2Ch 19:2; Ps 31:6; 119:113 [u]S Ps 26:5
139:22 [v]Mt 5:43
139:23 [w]Job 31:6 [x]S 1Sa 16:7; S 1Ch 29:17; S Ps 7:9; Pr 17:3; Jer 11:20; S Rev 2:23
139:24 [y]Jer 25:5; 36:3 [z]Ps 5:8; 23:2; 143:10
140:1 [a]Ps 17:13; S 25:20; 59:2; 71:4; 142:6; 143:9 [b]ver 11; Ps 86:14
140:2 [c]Ps 36:4; 52:2; Pr 6:14; 16:27; Isa 59:4; Hos 7:15 [d]S Ps 68:30
140:3 [e]Ps 57:4 [f]Ps 58:4; Ro 3:13*; Jas 3:8
140:4 [g]Ps 141:9 [h]S Ps 36:11
140:5 [i]S Job 34:30; S Ps 119:110 [j]S Job 18:8 [k]Job 18:9; Ps 31:4; S 38:12
140:6 [l]S Ps 16:2 [m]S Ps 28:2,6
140:7 [n]Ps 68:20
140:8 [o]Ps 10:2-3; S 66:7
140:9 [p]Pr 18:7
140:10 [q]Ps 11:6; 21:9; S Mt 3:10; Lk 12:49; Rev 20:15
140:11 [r]S Ps 34:21
140:12 [s]S Ps 82:3

Psalm 140

For the director of music. A psalm of David.

RESCUE me,[a] O LORD, from evil men;
protect me from men of violence,[b]
2who devise evil plans[c] in their hearts
and stir up war[d] every day.
3They make their tongues as sharp as[e]
a serpent's;
the poison of vipers[f] is on their
lips. *Selah*
4Keep me,[g] O LORD, from the hands of
the wicked;[h]
protect me from men of violence
who plan to trip my feet.
5Proud men have hidden a snare[i] for
me;
they have spread out the cords of
their net[j]
and have set traps[k] for me along my
path. *Selah*

6O LORD, I say to you, "You are my
God."[l]
Hear, O LORD, my cry for mercy.[m]
7O Sovereign LORD,[n] my strong
deliverer,
who shields my head in the day of
battle—
8do not grant the wicked[o] their desires,
O LORD;
do not let their plans succeed,
or they will become proud. *Selah*

9Let the heads of those who surround
me
be covered with the trouble their
lips have caused.[p]
10Let burning coals fall upon them;
may they be thrown into the fire,[q]
into miry pits, never to rise.
11Let slanderers not be established in the
land;
may disaster hunt down men of
violence.[r]

12I know that the LORD secures justice
for the poor[s]

[g]17 Or *concerning*

---

and in the process of birth do not fully explain the formation of a new person. God is involved in each instance, performing a new wonder. The newborn child does not have to face meaningless existence. The Creator has plans and purposes for the people He creates.

139:16 SALVATION, Human Freedom—God saw us when we were embryos. He had formed or created our days from the start; yet He has given us the real freedom to choose between life and death.

139:23–24 CHRISTIAN ETHICS, Character—God is the believer's ultimate judge of character, advocate of character, and resource for activating righteous character. The person seeking growth in Christian graces and character should therefore begin and continue in the ethical light and warmth of God Himself.

140:1–13 EVIL AND SUFFERING, Endurance—See notes on 3:1–8; 109:1–31.

140:1–13 PRAYER, Lament—The psalmist prayed that God would deliver him from the craftiness of evil men. The confidence of faith in vv 12–13 was based on an understanding of God's character. A curse on enemies could be pronounced because God is just and protects the needy. See note on 5:10.

140:6 GOD, Grace—Mercy is an expression of God's grace. In mercy God listens and acts when I need him. See notes on Ge 19:12–19,29; 39:21–23; 45:5–9; Lk 1:30.

140:12–13 CHRISTIAN ETHICS, Justice—God's character and ways on behalf of the down and out are well-known. We can trust His help. Those who are God's people will surely act as He does. People who do not act like God reveal some of their true character. See note on Mt 25:37–46.

and upholds the cause[t] of the
needy.[u]
13Surely the righteous will praise your
name[v]
and the upright will live[w] before
you.[x]

Psalm 141

A psalm of David.

O LORD, I call to you; come quickly[y]
to me.
Hear my voice[z] when I call to you.
2May my prayer be set before you like
incense;[a]
may the lifting up of my hands[b] be
like the evening sacrifice.[c]
3Set a guard over my mouth,[d] O LORD;
keep watch over the door of my
lips.[e]
4Let not my heart[f] be drawn to what is
evil,
to take part in wicked deeds[g]
with men who are evildoers;
let me not eat of their delicacies.[h]

5Let a righteous man[h] strike me—it is
a kindness;
let him rebuke me[i]—it is oil on my
head.[j]
My head will not refuse it.

Yet my prayer is ever against the deeds
of evildoers;
6 their rulers will be thrown down
from the cliffs,[k]
and the wicked will learn that my
words were well spoken.
7They will say, "As one plows[l] and
breaks up the earth,[m]
so our bones have been scattered at
the mouth[n] of the grave.[i]"

8But my eyes are fixed[o] on you,
O Sovereign LORD;
in you I take refuge[p]—do not give
me over to death.
9Keep me[q] from the snares they have
laid[r] for me,
from the traps set[s] by evildoers.
10Let the wicked fall[t] into their own
nets,
while I pass by in safety.[u]

Psalm 142

A *maskil*[j] of David. When he was in the
cave.[v] A prayer.

I cry aloud[w] to the LORD;
I lift up my voice to the LORD for
mercy.[x]
2I pour out my complaint[y] before him;
before him I tell my trouble.[z]

3When my spirit grows faint[a] within
me,
it is you who know my way.
In the path where I walk
men have hidden a snare for me.
4Look to my right and see;
no one is concerned for me.
I have no refuge;[b]
no one cares[c] for my life.

5I cry to you, O LORD;
I say, "You are my refuge,[d]
my portion[e] in the land of the
living."[f]
6Listen to my cry,[g]
for I am in desperate need;[h]
rescue me[i] from those who pursue
me,
for they are too strong[j] for me.
7Set me free from my prison,[k]
that I may praise your name.[l]

Then the righteous will gather about
me
because of your goodness to me.[m]

Psalm 143

A psalm of David.

O LORD, hear my prayer,[n]
listen to my cry for mercy;[o]

h5 Or *Let the Righteous One* i7 Hebrew *Sheol*
jTitle: Probably a literary or musical term

140:12 tS 1Ki 8:45 uS Ps 35:10
140:13 vS Ps 138:2 wS Ps 11:7 xPs 16:11
141:1 yS Ps 22:19 zS Ps 4:1; 5:1-2; 27:7; 143:1
141:2 aS Lk 1:9; Rev 5:8; 8:3 bS Ps 28:2; 63:4; 1Ti 2:8 cS Ex 29:39,41; 30:8
141:3 dS Ps 34:13; Jas 1:26; 3:8 eS Ps 12:2
141:4 fS Jos 24:23 gS Ps 106:29 hPr 23:1-3
141:5 iPr 9:8; 19:25; 25:12; Ecc 7:5 jS Ex 29:7; Ps 23:5
141:6 kS 2Ch 25:12
141:7 lPs 129:3 mNu 16:32-33 nS Nu 16:30
141:8 oPs 123:2 pPs 2:12; 11:1
141:9 qPs 140:4 rS Ps 64:5 sS Ps 38:12
141:10 tPs 7:15; 35:8; 57:6 uPs 124:7
142:1 v142 Title 1Sa 22:1; 24:3; Ps 57 Title wS 1Ki 8:52; Ps 3:4 xPs 30:8
142:2 yPs 64:1 zS Ps 50:15
142:3 aPs 6:2; 77:3; 84:2; 88:4; 143:4,7; Jer 8:18; La 1:22
142:4 bJer 25:35 cJer 30:17
142:5 dS Ps 46:1 eS Dt 32:9; Ps 16:5 fS Job 28:13; Ps 27:13
142:6 gS Ps 17:1 hS Ps 79:8 iS Ps 25:20 jJer 31:11
142:7 kS Ps 66:11 lPs 7:17; 9:2 mS 2Ch 6:41
143:1 nS Ps 141:1 oS Ps 28:2; 130:2

141:1–10 EVIL AND SUFFERING, Prayer—See note on 3:1–8. Suffering tempts us to follow the example of the wicked. We must pray for strength and guidance to resist such temptation. We must ask God to act to restore His righteousness. See note on 109:1–31.
141:1–10 PRAYER, Lament—See notes on 3:1–8; 5:10. Lament and petition are based on identity with God's way of life, making God's enemies our enemies and committing ourselves to obey His teaching. Lifting hands to heaven is a prayer posture symbolizing dependence on God. To be God's people we must be protected from His enemies and their temptations.
141:4 CHRISTIAN ETHICS, Character—Good company builds good character (Ps 1). Participation in evil practices with evil people destroys character. See note on 97:10–12.
142:1–7 EVIL AND SUFFERING, Endurance—Lonely isolation separated from all who care and love us may be the hardest type of suffering to endure. We need to lift our cry to God and experience His caring love. He often acts by establishing for us a righteous community who cares. See note on 3:1–8.
142:1–7 PRAYER, Lament—Some prayers in the Bible are a cry or groaning. See note on Ex 2:23–24. God is especially inclined toward those in desperation. Dramatic deliverance gives opportunity to encourage God's righteous people. Prayer brings hope to those who feel isolated and persecuted.
142:7 CHRISTIAN ETHICS, Justice—Mercy, or compassion, and grace are part of the attitudes inherent in a righteous person.
143:1 GOD, Mercy—Mercy comes as the result of God's faithfulness and His righteousness. He is constant and unchanging. He always does what is right, bringing all people of faith into a right relationship with Himself. Thus He honors a cry for mercy. All these qualities are closely related to the love cited in v 11. See note on 98:2–3.
143:1–12 EVIL AND SUFFERING, Endurance—See note on 3:1–8. We all deserve to suffer, for none of us are

in your faithfulness[p] and
righteousness[q]
come to my relief.
2Do not bring your servant into
judgment,
for no one living is righteous[r]
before you.

3The enemy pursues me,
he crushes me to the ground;
he makes me dwell in darkness[s]
like those long dead.[t]
4So my spirit grows faint within me;
my heart within me is dismayed.[u]

5I remember[v] the days of long ago;
I meditate[w] on all your works
and consider what your hands have
done.
6I spread out my hands[x] to you;
my soul thirsts for you like a
parched land. *Selah*

7Answer me quickly,[y] O LORD;
my spirit fails.[z]
Do not hide your face[a] from me
or I will be like those who go down
to the pit.
8Let the morning bring me word of your
unfailing love,[b]
for I have put my trust in you.
Show me the way[c] I should go,
for to you I lift up my soul.[d]
9Rescue me[e] from my enemies,[f]
O LORD,
for I hide myself in you.
10Teach me[g] to do your will,
for you are my God;[h]
may your good Spirit
lead[i] me on level ground.[j]

11For your name's sake,[k] O LORD,
preserve my life;[l]
in your righteousness,[m] bring me
out of trouble.
12In your unfailing love, silence my
enemies;[n]
destroy all my foes,[o]
for I am your servant.[p]

Psalm 144

Of David.

PRAISE be to the LORD my Rock,[q]
who trains my hands for war,
my fingers for battle.
2He is my loving God and my fortress,[r]
my stronghold[s] and my deliverer,
my shield,[t] in whom I take refuge,
who subdues peoples[k][u] under me.

3O LORD, what is man[v] that you care
for him,
the son of man that you think of
him?
4Man is like a breath;[w]
his days are like a fleeting shadow.[x]

5Part your heavens,[y] O LORD, and come
down;[z]
touch the mountains, so that they
smoke.[a]
6Send forth lightning[b] and scatter[c] ⌞the
enemies⌟;
shoot your arrows[d] and rout them.
7Reach down your hand from on high;[e]
deliver me and rescue me[f]
from the mighty waters,[g]
from the hands of foreigners[h]
8whose mouths are full of lies,[i]
whose right hands[j] are deceitful.[k]

143:1 [p]S Ex 34:6; Ps 89:1-2 [q]Ps 71:2 **143:2** [r]S Ps 14:3; Ro 3:10 **143:3** [s]S Ps 107:10 [t]La 3:6 **143:4** [u]Ps 30:7 **143:5** [v]Ps 77:6 [w]S Ge 24:63 **143:6** [x]S Ex 9:29; S Job 11:13 **143:7** [y]S Ps 69:17 [z]S Ps 142:3 [a]S Ps 22:24; 27:9; 30:7 **143:8** [b]Ps 6:4; 90:14 [c]S Ex 33:13; S Job 34:32; Ps 27:11; 32:8 [d]Ps 25:1-2; S 86:4 **143:9** [e]S Ps 140:1 [f]S Ps 18:17; 31:15 **143:10** [g]S Ps 119:12 [h]Ps 31:14 [i]S Ne 9:20; Ps 25:4-5 [j]Ps 26:12 **143:11** [k]Ps 25:11 [l]S Ps 41:2 [m]Ps 31:1; 71:2 **143:12** [n]Ps 8:2 [o]Ps 54:5 [p]S Ps 116:16 **144:1** [q]S Ge 49:24 **144:2** [r]Ps 59:9; 91:2 [s]Ps 27:1; 37:39; 43:2 [t]S Ge 15:1; S Ps 18:2 [u]S Jdg 4:23; S Ps 18:39 **144:3** [v]Heb 2:6 **144:4** [w]S Job 7:7; 27:3; Isa 2:22 [x]S 1Ch 29:15; S Job 14:2; S Jas 4:14 **144:5** [y]Ps 18:9; Isa 64:1 [z]S Ge 11:5; S Ps 57:3 [a]Ps 104:32 **144:6** [b]Hab 3:11; Zec 9:14 [c]S Ps 59:11; S 68:1 [d]Ps 7:12-13; 18:14 **144:7** [e]S 2Sa 22:17 [f]Ps 3:7; S 57:3 [g]Ps 69:2 [h]S Ps 18:44 **144:8** [i]Ps 12:2; 41:6 [j]Ge 14:22; Dt 32:40 [k]S Ps 36:3

[k]*2* Many manuscripts of the Masoretic Text, Dead Sea Scrolls, Aquila, Jerome and Syriac; most manuscripts of the Masoretic Text *subdues my people*

righteous. We throw ourselves on God's mercy, knowing that unendurable suffering comes with a sense of His absence. Even in suffering, we must commit ourselves to learn and do His will. God's love is our hope in desperate situations.

143:1–12 PRAYER, Lament—See notes on 3:1–8; 6:1–10; 142:1–7. Past experiences with God give hope in desperate circumstances. Prayer seeks God's teaching and direction as well as His action. We can cooperate with God in acting to escape trouble. God's righteousness and love as our Lord give us reasons to pray with confidence.

143:5–7 REVELATION, History—Reflecting on God's revelation of Himself in past deeds, the writer reached out to find God again, fearful but hopeful that God would not ignore him. The psalmist struggled to understand God's delay in answering a fervent and sincere prayer request. Revelation does not occur in every prayer. At times we must struggle long in prayer before God speaks to us.

143:5–6 HISTORY, Individual—See note on 92:4.

143:7 HUMANITY, Nature of Death—Death, in a real sense, is the absence of God from a person's life. True life comes from God's unfailing love working to deliver us.

143:10 GOD, Personal—The psalmist trusted God to teach and lead personally. See note on 121:3–8.

144:1–15 EVIL AND SUFFERING, God's Present Help—Who does God help in war? God's people naturally ask Him for help against foreign enemies. This proved little problem as long as God worked through one nation. To label enemies as foreigners no longer guarantees they are godless or unrelated to God's people. We must at least be certain our cause is right before we invoke God's direction and help in battle. We can ask God to establish His kingdom on earth (Mt 6:10) and make us part of His blessing to coming generations.

144:1–15 PRAYER, Petition—Praying as the king facing enemies, David used picturesque language to describe God as His teacher and strength. The prayer for victory showed David expected the work to be unmistakably divine. As reason for God's help, David listed the consequences for the nation—a future for the next generation, abundant harvest not destroyed or stolen by enemy soldiers, and peace rather than war and exile. God's people are responsible to pray in national emergencies.

144:2 GOD, Savior—We praise the Savior who can deliver us from trouble and who will deliver because He loves us. See notes on 38:22; 62:1–2,6–8; 98:1–3; Lk 1:47; 1 Ti 1:1.

144:2 SALVATION, As Refuge—God is our refuge and salvation because He loves us. See note on 34:8.

144:3–4 HUMANITY, Worth—Mortal, temporary humans would appear to have little worth. God's love provides worth. See notes on 8:3–8; 116:15.

[9]I will sing a new song[l] to you, O God;
on the ten-stringed lyre[m] I will make music to you,
[10]to the One who gives victory to kings,[n]
who delivers his servant David[o]
from the deadly sword.[p]

[11]Deliver me and rescue me[q]
from the hands of foreigners[r]
whose mouths are full of lies,[s]
whose right hands are deceitful.[t]

[12]Then our sons in their youth
will be like well-nurtured plants,[u]
and our daughters will be like pillars[v]
carved to adorn a palace.
[13]Our barns will be filled[w]
with every kind of provision.
Our sheep will increase by thousands,
by tens of thousands in our fields;
[14] our oxen[x] will draw heavy loads.[1]
There will be no breaching of walls,[y]
no going into captivity,
no cry of distress in our streets.[z]

[15]Blessed are the people[a] of whom this is true;
blessed are the people whose God is the LORD.

Psalm 145[m]

A psalm of praise. Of David.

[1]I will exalt you,[b] my God the King;[c]
I will praise your name[d] for ever and ever.
[2]Every day I will praise[e] you
and extol your name[f] for ever and ever.

[3]Great is the LORD[g] and most worthy of praise;[h]
his greatness no one can fathom.[i]
[4]One generation[j] will commend your works to another;
they will tell[k] of your mighty acts.[l]
[5]They will speak of the glorious splendor[m] of your majesty,
and I will meditate on your wonderful works.[n] [n]
[6]They will tell[o] of the power of your awesome works,[p]
and I will proclaim[q] your great deeds.[r]
[7]They will celebrate your abundant goodness[s]
and joyfully sing[t] of your righteousness.[u]

[8]The LORD is gracious and compassionate,[v]
slow to anger and rich in love.[w]

[9]The LORD is good[x] to all;
he has compassion[y] on all he has made.
[10]All you have made will praise you,[z] O LORD;
your saints will extol[a] you.[b]
[11]They will tell of the glory of your kingdom[c]
and speak of your might,[d]
[12]so that all men may know of your mighty acts[e]
and the glorious splendor of your kingdom.[f]

144:9 [l]S Ps 28:7; S 96:1 [m]Ps 33:2-3; S 71:22
144:10 [n]S 2Sa 8:14 [o]Ps 18:50 [p]S Job 5:20
144:11 [q]Ps 3:7; S 25:20 [r]S Ps 18:44 [s]Ps 41:6-7 [t]Ps 12:2; S 36:3; 106:26; Isa 44:20
144:12 [u]Ps 92:12-14; S 128:3 [v]SS 4:4; 7:4
144:13 [w]Pr 3:10
144:14 [x]Pr 14:4 [y]2Ki 25:11 [z]Isa 24:11; Jer 14:2-3
144:15 [a]Dt 28:3
145:1 [b]Ps 30:1; 34:1 [c]Ps 2:6; 5:2 [d]S Ps 54:6
145:2 [e]S Ps 71:6 [f]Ps 34:1; Isa 25:1; 26:8
145:3 [g]S Ps 95:3 [h]S 2Sa 22:4; Ps 96:4 [i]S Job 5:9
145:4 [j]Ps 22:30 [k]S Dt 11:19 [l]S Ps 71:16
145:5 [m]Ps 96:6; 148:13 [n]S Ps 75:1
145:6 [o]Ps 78:4 [p]S Ps 66:3 [q]S Dt 32:3 [r]Ps 75:1; 106:22
145:7 [s]S Ex 18:9; S Ps 27:13 [t]S Ps 5:11; S 101:1 [u]S Ps 138:5
145:8 [v]S Ps 86:15; 103:8 [w]S Ps 86:5
145:9 [x]S 1Ch 16:34; S Ps 136:1; Mt 19:17; Mk 10:18 [y]Ps 103:13-14
145:10 [z]S Ps 8:6; S 103:22; S 139:14 [a]Ps 30:4; 148:14; 149:9 [b]Ps 115:17-18
145:11 [c]ver 12-13; S Ex 15:2; Mt 6:33 [d]Ps 21:13
145:12 [e]S Ps 75:1; 105:1 [f]ver 11; Ps 103:19; Isa 2:10,19,21

[1]*14* Or *our chieftains will be firmly established*
[m]This psalm is an acrostic poem, the verses of which (including verse 13b) begin with the successive letters of the Hebrew alphabet. [n]*5* Dead Sea Scrolls and Syriac (see also Septuagint); Masoretic Text *On the glorious splendor of your majesty / and on your wonderful works I will meditate*

144:12–15 CHRISTIAN ETHICS, Property Rights—The psalmist affirmed that security and love of family, fulfillment and accomplishment in one's work, peace and protection for the community, and economic security reflect God's blessing. Such security depends on our sense that God cares for us (v 3).

145:1–21 HISTORY, Praise—Individual worship involves meditation on God's historical acts. This reveals God's majestic personal characteristics: greatness, majesty, power, goodness, righteousness, grace, compassion, loving, glory, splendor, faithfulness, presence, giving, saving, holy. His character leads us to praise. See note on 136:1–26.

145:1–21 PRAYER, Praise—Although God is called "King" elsewhere in the psalter (5:2; 44:4; 68:24; 84:3), this prayer is unique in its conception of the kingly qualities of God as perfect Ruler. God's kingdom is unlike others in its glory and eternity. All are dependent on Him. He hears those who call on Him in truth. Prayer is the adoring address of the human subject to the divine Ruler. Prayer is possible because the King of the universe is compassionate, patient, gracious, loving, righteous, and good. He is near when we call, ready to supply our needs.

145:3–13 EVANGELISM, Obedience—It is a *command* to make known God's mighty deeds to all, but it is also a great *privilege.*

145:4–7 HOLY SCRIPTURE, Word—Temple worshipers had God's written Word in the form achieved in their day along with teachings from earlier generations not yet in written form. The Temple worship hour was the regular atmosphere for the transmission of God's truth. The constant repetition in the singing and praying was an exercise in remembering God's word and passing it on. Psalms like this one contain and reveal God's will and nature to the worshiper, who is called to reflect on and take seriously the character of God.

145:8–9,17 GOD, Love—God's love is magnified above His wrath. See note on 136:1–26.

145:8 GOD, Wrath—See note on 110:5.

145:10–13 THE CHURCH, God's Kingdom—God's kingdom has no boundaries in time or space. The reign of near eastern gods often came to an end when the earthly king lost power. New rulers brought new gods. New, young gods might retire an old, traditional god to a more remote or lesser position in the ranking of the gods. Military defeat and the passing of time did not affect the kingdom of Yahweh, the God of Israel. He was not limited to one people. He ruled over and could use all nations to accomplish His purposes. He began His rule before creation and will continue when this world passes away under His judgment. He wants all people of all nations to worship Him. They should because He has shown His love in His redeeming acts in history. The greatest of these was the sending of His Son Jesus with whom the kingdom of God is near (Mk 1:15). See note on Ps 103:19.

13Your kingdom is an everlasting kingdom,[g]
and your dominion endures through all generations.

The LORD is faithful[h] to all his promises[i]
and loving toward all he has made.[o]
14The LORD upholds[j] all those who fall
and lifts up all[k] who are bowed down.[l]
15The eyes of all look to you,
and you give them their food[m] at the proper time.
16You open your hand
and satisfy the desires[n] of every living thing.

17The LORD is righteous[o] in all his ways
and loving toward all he has made.[p]
18The LORD is near[q] to all who call on him,[r]
to all who call on him in truth.
19He fulfills the desires[s] of those who fear him;[t]
he hears their cry[u] and saves them.[v]
20The LORD watches over[w] all who love him,[x]
but all the wicked he will destroy.[y]

21My mouth will speak[z] in praise of the LORD.
Let every creature[a] praise his holy name[b]
for ever and ever.

Psalm 146

PRAISE the LORD.[p]

Praise the LORD,[c] O my soul.
2 I will praise the LORD all my life;[d]
I will sing praise[e] to my God as long as I live.[f]

3Do not put your trust in princes,[g]
in mortal men,[h] who cannot save.
4When their spirit departs, they return to the ground;[i]
on that very day their plans come to nothing.[j]

5Blessed is he[k] whose help[l] is the God of Jacob,
whose hope is in the LORD his God,
6the Maker of heaven[m] and earth,
the sea, and everything in them—
the LORD, who remains faithful[n] forever.
7He upholds[o] the cause of the oppressed[p]
and gives food to the hungry.[q]
The LORD sets prisoners free,[r]
8 the LORD gives sight[s] to the blind,[t]
the LORD lifts up those who are bowed down,[u]
the LORD loves the righteous.[v]
9The LORD watches over the alien[w]
and sustains the fatherless[x] and the widow,[y]
but he frustrates the ways of the wicked.

10The LORD reigns[z] forever,
your God, O Zion, for all generations.

Praise the LORD.

Psalm 147

PRAISE the LORD.[q]

How good it is to sing praises to our God,

145:13 [g]S Ex 15:18; 1Ti 1:17; 2Pe 1:11; Rev 11:15 [h]S Dt 7:9; S 1Co 1:9 [i]S Jos 23:14 **145:14** [j]S Ps 37:17 [k]S 1Sa 2:8; Ps 146:8 [l]S Ps 38:6 **145:15** [m]S Ge 1:30; S Job 28:5; S Ps 37:25; S Mt 6:26 **145:16** [n]S Ps 90:14; S 104:28 **145:17** [o]S Ex 9:27; S Ezr 9:15 [p]ver 13 **145:18** [q]S Nu 23:21; S Ps 46:1; Php 4:5 [r]Ps 18:6; 80:18 **145:19** [s]S Ps 20:4 [t]S Job 22:28 [u]S Ps 31:22; S 40:1 [v]S 1Sa 10:19; Ps 7:10; 34:18 **145:20** [w]S Ps 1:6 [x]Ps 31:23; 91:14; 97:10 [y]S Ps 94:23 **145:21** [z]Ps 71:8 [a]Ps 65:2; 150:6 [b]S Ex 3:15; S Ps 30:4; S 99:3 **146:1** [c]Ps 103:1; 104:1 **146:2** [d]Ps 104:33 [e]S Ps 105:2 [f]S Ps 63:4 **146:3** [g]Ps 118:9 [h]Ps 60:11; S 108:12; Isa 2:22 **146:4** [i]S Ge 3:19; S Job 7:21; Ps 103:14; Ecc 12:7 [j]Ps 33:10; 1Co 2:6 **146:5** [k]Ps 33:18; 37:9; 119:43; 144:15; Jer 17:7 [l]Ps 70:5; 71:5; 121:2 **146:6** [m]S 2Ch 2:12; Ps 115:15; Ac 14:15; S Rev 10:6 [n]S Dt 7:9; S Ps 18:25; 108:4; 117:2 **146:7** [o]S Ps 37:17 [p]Ps 103:6 [q]Ps 107:9; 145:15 [r]S Ps 66:11; S 68:6 **146:8** [s]Pr 20:12; Isa 29:18; 32:3; 35:5; 42:7,18-19; 43:8; Mt 11:5 [t]S Ex 4:11 [u]S Ps 38:6 [v]S Dt 7:13; S Job 23:10 **146:9** [w]S Lev 19:34 [x]S Ps 10:18 [y]S Ex 22:22; Jas 1:27 **146:10** [z]S Ge 21:33; S 1Ch 16:31; Ps 93:1; 99:1; Rev 11:15

[o]*13* One manuscript of the Masoretic Text, Dead Sea Scrolls and Syriac (see also Septuagint); most manuscripts of the Masoretic Text do not have the last two lines of verse 13. [p]*1* Hebrew *Hallelu Yah;* also in verse 10 [q]*1* Hebrew *Hallelu Yah;* also in verse 20

145:17 GOD, Righteous—God's righteousness in no way conflicts with His love, also mentioned here. See note on 119:40,75,137,142.

146:1–10 EVIL AND SUFFERING, God's Present Help—See note on 21:1–13. The only true hope of relief for those who are oppressed is the faithful God, Lord of all heaven and earth. He knows and cares for the needy, whom we tend to ignore.

146:1–10 PRAYER, Sovereignty of God—This "hallelujah" psalm praises the sovereign, eternal God rather than temporary, mortal rulers. See notes on 47:1–9; 135:1–21. God's creation and His faithful care of the oppressed and needy show His sovereign power. Praise belongs only to the One who rules forever.

146:5–9 CHRISTIAN ETHICS, Justice—God works for the oppressed, those for whom no one else will speak. The expectation is that people who call themselves after God's name will also execute justice.

146:6 GOD, Creator—God's sovereignty and faithfulness are emphasized in this reference to God as Creator. See notes on 95:3–7; Ge 1:3—2:25; Ro 4:17.

146:7–10 GOD, Sovereignty—God's sovereignty expresses itself in compassionate acts of mercy and grace to the unfortunate. This is the result of the faithfulness cited in v 6.

147:1–20 EVIL AND SUFFERING, God's Present Help—See notes on 21:1–13; 106:1–48. Our God is the God who gathers and rebuilds His people after they have been torn down and scattered.

147:1–20 REVELATION, Events—The God of the Bible makes Himself known to His people through specific actions in individual lives, national history, and nature. Such events reveal God's unlimited power and knowledge. His special attention to His people reveals His love and calls forth our praise and obedience. His people can obey because He has revealed His word and His laws.

147:1–20 PRAYER, Praise—See note on 135:1–21. This "hallelujah" psalm sings of the delight the psalmist felt in praising the Lord and notes that the Lord's delight is in those who seek a relationship with Him. To know God and have His unique revelation is a strong reason to praise Him. He restores, renews, heals, controls, knows, sustains, supplies, provides, and strengthens. The only reasonable response is praise.

how pleasant[a] and fitting to praise
him![b]

2The LORD builds up Jerusalem;[c]
he gathers the exiles[d] of Israel.
3He heals the brokenhearted[e]
and binds up their wounds.[f]

4He determines the number of the
stars[g]
and calls them each by name.
5Great is our Lord[h] and mighty in
power;[i]
his understanding has no limit.[j]
6The LORD sustains the humble[k]
but casts the wicked[l] to the ground.

7Sing to the LORD[m] with thanksgiving;[n]
make music[o] to our God on the
harp.[p]
8He covers the sky with clouds;[q]
he supplies the earth with rain[r]
and makes grass grow[s] on the hills.
9He provides food[t] for the cattle
and for the young ravens[u] when
they call.
10His pleasure is not in the strength[v] of
the horse,[w]
nor his delight in the legs of a man;
11the LORD delights[x] in those who fear
him,[y]
who put their hope[z] in his unfailing
love.[a]

12Extol the LORD, O Jerusalem;[b]
praise your God, O Zion,
13for he strengthens the bars of your
gates[c]
and blesses your people[d] within
you.
14He grants peace[e] to your borders
and satisfies you[f] with the finest of
wheat.[g]

15He sends his command[h] to the earth;
his word runs[i] swiftly.
16He spreads the snow[j] like wool
and scatters the frost[k] like ashes.
17He hurls down his hail[l] like pebbles.
Who can withstand his icy blast?
18He sends his word[m] and melts them;
he stirs up his breezes,[n] and the
waters flow.

19He has revealed his word[o] to Jacob,[p]
his laws and decrees[q] to Israel.
20He has done this for no other nation;[r]
they do not know[s] his laws.

Praise the LORD.[t]

Psalm 148

PRAISE the LORD.[r] [u]

Praise the LORD from the heavens,[v]
praise him in the heights above.
2Praise him, all his angels,[w]
praise him, all his heavenly hosts.[x]
3Praise him, sun[y] and moon,
praise him, all you shining stars.
4Praise him, you highest heavens[z]
and you waters above the skies.[a]
5Let them praise the name[b] of the
LORD,
for he commanded[c] and they were
created.
6He set them in place for ever and ever;
he gave a decree[d] that will never
pass away.

7Praise the LORD[e] from the earth,
you great sea creatures[f] and all
ocean depths,[g]
8lightning and hail,[h] snow and clouds,
stormy winds that do his bidding,[i]
9you mountains and all hills,[j]
fruit trees and all cedars,
10wild animals[k] and all cattle,
small creatures and flying birds,
11kings[l] of the earth and all nations,
you princes and all rulers on earth,
12young men and maidens,
old men and children.

13Let them praise the name of the
LORD,[m]
for his name alone is exalted;
his splendor[n] is above the earth and
the heavens.[o]

147:1 [a]S Ps 135:3 [b]Ps 33:1 **147:2** [c]S Ps 51:18 [d]S Ps 106:47 **147:3** [e]S Ps 34:18 [f]S Nu 12:13; S Job 5:18; Isa 1:6; Eze 34:16 **147:4** [g]S Ge 15:5 **147:5** [h]S Ps 48:1 [i]S Ex 14:31 [j]Ps 145:3; Isa 40:28 **147:6** [k]S 2Ch 33:23; Ps 146:8-9 [l]Ps 37:9-10; 145:20 **147:7** [m]Ps 30:4; 33:3 [n]S Ps 42:4 [o]S Ps 27:6 [p]S Ps 98:5 **147:8** [q]S Job 26:8 [r]S Dt 11:14; S 32:2; S 2Sa 1:21; S Job 5:10 [s]S Job 28:26; S Ps 104:14 **147:9** [t]S Ge 1:30; Ps 104:27-28; S Mt 6:26 [u]S Ge 8:7 **147:10** [v]S 1Sa 16:7 [w]S Job 39:11; Ps 33:16-17 **147:11** [x]S Ps 35:27 [y]Ps 33:18; 103:11 [z]Ps 119:43 [a]Ps 6:4 **147:12** [b]Ps 48:1 **147:13** [c]S Dt 33:25 [d]S Lev 25:21; Ps 128:5; 134:3 **147:14** [e]S Lev 26:6; S 2Sa 7:10; S Isa 48:18 [f]S Ps 132:15 [g]S Dt 32:14 **147:15** [h]Job 37:12; Ps 33:9; 148:5 [i]Isa 55:11 **147:16** [j]Ps 148:8 [k]S Job 37:12; 38:29 **147:17** [l]Ex 9:22-23; S Job 38:22; S Ps 78:47 **147:18** [m]ver 15; Ps 33:9; 107:20 [n]S Ps 50:3 **147:19** [o]S Ex 20:1; Ro 3:2 [p]Ps 78:5 [q]S Dt 33:4; Jos 1:8; 2Ki 22:8; Mal 4:4; Ro 9:4 **147:20** [r]Dt 4:7-8, 32-34 [s]S Ps 79:6 [t]Ps 33:2; 103:1 **148:1** [u]Ps 33:2; 103:1 [v]Ps 19:1; 69:34; 150:1 **148:2** [w]Ps 103:20 [x]S 1Ki 22:19 **148:3** [y]S Ps 19:1 **148:4** [z]S Dt 10:14 [a]S Ge 1:7 **148:5** [b]Ps 145:21 [c]S Ps 147:15 **148:6** [d]Jer 31:35-36; 33:25 **148:7** [e]Ps 33:2 [f]S Ge 1:21; Ps 74:13-14 [g]S Dt 33:13 **148:8** [h]S Ex 9:18; S Jos 10:11 [i]Job 37:11-12; S Ps 103:20; 147:15-18 **148:9** [j]Isa 44:23; 49:13; 55:12 **148:10** [k]Isa 43:20; Hos 2:18 **148:11** [l]S Ps 102:15 **148:13** [m]S Ps 113:2; 138:4 [n]S Ps 145:5 [o]S Ps 8:1

[r]1 Hebrew *Hallelu Yah*; also in verse 14

147:2–3 GOD, Grace—God extends grace to homeless, hurting people.
147:5 GOD, Wisdom—See note on 139:1–18.
147:11 GOD, Love—The all-powerful God delights in us, His people, and extends His faithful love to us. See note on 145:8–9,17.
148:1–14 CREATION, Praise—Praise of God is a central purpose of creation. Every element of existence, even the heavenly bodies so often worshiped by humans, exists because God had a purpose for it and created it. Each can function only in the place and manner the Creator decreed in creation. Chaotic ocean depths and fearful sea monsters should not frighten earth's inhabitants, for they have a place in the chorus of praise to God. Storms and animals do not frighten God. They, too, are His creation under His sovereign control. Foreign nations may exercise military might, but ultimately they must sing God's song.
148:1–14 PRAYER, Praise—See note on 135:1–21. A "hallelujah" psalm calls on all creation to praise the Lord. Only loud voices can give adequate voice to God's praise. Humans alone cannot give sufficient praise to the Creator, who gives political leadership to His people.
148:13 GOD, Transcendent—In His sovereignty over all the earth, God is high and lifted up, above all persons and things. He is qualitatively superior to everything and everyone. He is Lord, and there is none like Him. Still His people are close to Him.

14 He has raised up for his people a
horn,[s] [p]
the praise[q] of all his saints,[r]
of Israel, the people close to his
heart.[s]

Praise the LORD.

Psalm 149

PRAISE the LORD.[t] [t]

Sing to the LORD a new song,[u]
his praise in the assembly[v] of the
saints.

2 Let Israel rejoice[w] in their Maker;[x]
let the people of Zion be glad in
their King.[y]
3 Let them praise his name with
dancing[z]
and make music to him with
tambourine and harp.[a]
4 For the LORD takes delight[b] in his
people;
he crowns the humble with
salvation.[c]
5 Let the saints rejoice[d] in this honor
and sing for joy on their beds.[e]

6 May the praise of God be in their
mouths[f]
and a double-edged[g] sword in their
hands,[h]
7 to inflict vengeance[i] on the nations
and punishment[j] on the peoples,
8 to bind their kings with fetters,[k]
their nobles with shackles of iron,[l]
9 to carry out the sentence written
against them.[m]
This is the glory of all his saints.[n]

Praise the LORD.

Psalm 150

PRAISE the LORD.[u] [o]

Praise God in his sanctuary;[p]
praise him in his mighty heavens.[q]
2 Praise him for his acts of power;[r]
praise him for his surpassing
greatness.[s]
3 Praise him with the sounding of the
trumpet,[t]
praise him with the harp and lyre,[u]
4 praise him with tambourine and
dancing,[v]
praise him with the strings[w] and
flute,[x]
5 praise him with the clash of cymbals,[y]
praise him with resounding cymbals.
6 Let everything[z] that has breath praise
the LORD.

Praise the LORD.

[s] *14 Horn* here symbolizes strong one, that is, king.
[t] *1* Hebrew *Hallelu Yah*; also in verse 9
[u] *1* Hebrew *Hallelu Yah*; also in verse 6

148:14 *p*S 1Sa 2:1 *q*S Ex 15:2; Ps 22:3 *r*S Ps 145:10 *s*S Dt 26:19
149:1 *t*Ps 33:2; 103:1 *u*S Ps 28:7; S 96:1; Rev 5:9 *v*S Ps 1:5
149:2 *w*Isa 13:3; Jer 51:48 *x*S Job 10:3; Ps 95:6; Isa 44:2; 45:11; 54:5 *y*Ps 10:16; 47:6; Isa 32:1; Zec 9:9
149:3 *z*S Ex 15:20 *a*S Ps 57:8
149:4 *b*Ps 35:27; 147:11 *c*Ps 132:16
149:5 *d*S Ps 132:16 *e*Job 35:10; Ps 42:8
149:6 *f*Ps 66:17 *g*Heb 4:12; Rev 1:16 *h*Ne 4:17
149:7 *i*S Nu 31:3; S Dt 32:41 *j*Ps 81:15
149:8 *k*S 2Sa 3:34; S Isa 14:1-2 *l*2Ch 33:11
149:9 *m*Dt 7:1; Eze 28:26 *n*S Ps 145:10
150:1 *o*S Ps 112:1 *p*Ps 68:24-26; 73:17; 102:19 *q*S Ps 148:1
150:2 *r*S Dt 3:24 *s*S Ex 15:7
150:3 *t*S Nu 10:2 *u*S Ps 57:8
150:4 *v*S Ex 15:20 *w*S Ps 45:8 *x*S Ge 4:21
150:5 *y*S 2Sa 6:5
150:6 *z*S Ps 103:22

149:1–9 PRAYER, Praise—Ps 148 calls on nature and all creation to praise God. This "hallelujah" psalm calls on His people for praise. See note on 135:1–21. His purpose becomes the purpose of His praying people. Public worship is a proper time for such praise. A multitude of activities help people praise God properly. Praise gives way to petition for God to punish His enemies, the nation's enemies.

149:2 GOD, Creator—God is Creator not only of His world but also of us, His people.

149:5 SALVATION, Joy—God's people can always rejoice in the Lord. See notes on 4:7; 16:11; Php 3:1.

150:1–6 PRAYER, Praise—See note on 135:1–21. The full sounds of a human orchestra are needed to sound God's praises through the earth. In praise we do not exclude anyone. We invite all people to join in public worship of our Lord. Praise should be high, loud, and joyous.

150:6 HOLY SCRIPTURE, Collection—See note on 41:13.

Proverbs

Theological Setting

Ancient thinkers apparently recognized quite early the orderliness of the world in which they lived. They understood that if they tried to live in harmony with that set order, life would be much more enjoyable and fulfilling. We call these early thinkers "wise men" and their writing "wisdom writings."

The goal of such instruction appears to have been to enable its learners to master their lives and thereby to discover happiness. Since they believed the gods had set up the world to follow a fixed order, all one had to do was to observe nature, learn that order, and then live in accordance with it. However, any conduct that varied from that order would bring quick and severe penalties, if not death.

In Israel "wisdom" thinking probably began among the clans or early tribes. Such early Israelite wisdom consisted of simple observations about life. One generation handed these down to another in a continuing search for the answers to life's perplexing problems. Such observations probably dealt with topics such as integrity, contentment, and sexual and family relationships. Unlike their neighbors' wisdom, for Israel "the fear of the Lord" provided the central theme, tying all wisdom teaching together (1:7; 31:30).

Theological Outline

Proverbs: The Path to Life

I. Proverbs Is Designed to Impart Divine Wisdom Concerning Life. (1:1-6)

II. Wisdom's Contribution to Life Is to Be Praised. (1:7—9:18)
- A. The goal of all wisdom is that people "fear . . . the Lord." (1:7)
- B. Wisdom identifies sin and calls sinners to repentance. (1:8-33)
- C. Wisdom enables the sinner to be set free and experience meaningful life. (2:1-22)
- D. Wisdom produces a sense of divine presence, joy, and peace in the believer. (3:1-26)
- E. Wisdom admonishes believers to share God's love with others. (3:27-35)
- F. Wisdom helps a father instruct his son how to obtain a meaningful life. (4:1-27)
- G. Wisdom calls for purity and honesty in all marriage relationships. (5:1-23)
- H. Wisdom admonishes the believer to work hard and spend wisely. (6:1-19)
- I. Wisdom warns against the peril of adultery. (6:20—7:27)
- J. Through divine wisdom, God offers Himself to mankind. (8:1-36)
- K. Wisdom presents us with two choices, life or death. (9:1-18)

III. One's Response to Wisdom Brings About Earthly Consequences. (10:1—22:16)
- A. The righteous find blessings, but the wicked suffer greatly. (10:1-32)
- B. The deceitful pay a terrible price, but the honest find God's favor. (11:1-31)
- C. The righteous are open to instruction, but the wicked are not. (12:1-28)
- D. The righteous are obedient to God's will; however, the wicked rebel. (13:1-25)
- E. The foolish will be judged, but the righteous will be accepted by God. (14:1-35)
- F. The Lord watches over all mankind and judges each accordingly. (15:1-33)
- G. The Lord is the fountain of life for the faithful. (16:1-33)
- H. The foolish thrive on bribery, but the wise are honest yet merciful. (17:1-28)
- I. The foolish are haughty, but the righteous are humble. (18:1-24)
- J. The poor are to be pitied, but the wealthy are honored by God. (19:1-29)
- K. The wise work hard and treat both friend and foe with love. (20:1-30)
- L. God requires holy lives and not just holy rituals. (21:1-31)
- M. The wise discipline themselves to follow God in everything. (22:1-16)

IV. Wisdom Provides Prudent Counsel for Both the Present and the Future. (22:17—24:34)
- A. Wisdom tells one when to speak and when to be silent. (22:17-21)
- B. The wise ones care for and protect the poor. (22:22-29)

C. Wisdom warns one not to fall into the trap of another's craftiness. (23:1-11)
D. Youth need instruction and correction to become what they should be. (23:12-28)
E. The drunkard destroys his life and that of others. (23:29-35)
F. Wisdom leads to a meaningful life, but wickedness leads to destruction. (24:1-9)
G. The wise ones steadfastly trust God in both the good and bad times. (24:10-22)
H. Wisdom promotes true justice. (24:23-34)

V. Wisdom Constantly Reminds People of Their Past Heritage. (25:1—29:27)
A. The king shares in the responsibility for promoting wisdom. (25:1-14)
B. The righteous exercise self-discipline and love in all of life. (25:15-28)
C. The foolish fail the test of life and face God's judgment. (26:1-28)
D. Life's quest for meaning is brief and frustrating at times. (27:1-22)
E. People should learn to live as responsible stewards. (27:23-27)
F. God expects justice from His followers. (28:1-28)
G. Discipline is an essential part of life. (29:1-27)

VI. The True Source of Meaningful Existence Can Be Found Only in God. (30:1—31:31)
A. Human beings cannot fully discover or understand God's wisdom. (30:1-33)
B. Humans can practice righteousness and show loving-kindness. (31:1-9)
C. The key to meaningful existence is found in one's faith relationship to God. (31:10-31)

Theological Conclusions

The Book of Proverbs clearly defines how God expects His people to find meaningful existence. In doing this, two doctrines are emphasized: the human search for meaning and the nature of God. Though all mankind has searched constantly for meaningful existence, Israel's search is unique in at least two ways. First, though the Wisdom Literature recognizes an orderliness to the world, it never pretends that one can know that order fully (30:5-33) or that knowing it will automatically bring about riches (27:22-27) or a meaningful existence (24:10-34). The revealed wisdom of Proverbs clearly tells God's people how to relate to both God and other people. More explicitly, it teaches honesty (11:1), truthfulness (12:19,22), sobriety (23:29-35), hard work (10:4-5,26), compassion toward one's enemies (25:1-22), humility (16:18-19), proper sexual and marriage relationships (5:3-11; 31:10-31), proper parent-child relationships (4:1-4; 22:6), and trust in God (3:5-6; 16:3). No doubt all of these individually and collectively, if followed, will provide a more meaningful life.

The inspired biblical wisdom centers uniquely on God. Wisdom outside the Bible speaks of gods who provide an orderliness to creation and of the need for people to discover that orderliness. The wisdom of Israel's neighbors does not speak of the god or gods seeking to reveal that order. Nor does it speak of such an orderliness leading to eternal salvation. Certainly from the very beginning to the end of the Book of Proverbs, the "fear of the Lord" (in the sense of a reverence for God that produces a willing obedience) is not only its overarching context but also its constant theme. The first chapter clearly states that the "fear of the Lord is the beginning of knowledge" (1:7). This is followed up by a call to repent of sin and to trust in God as Lord and Savior (1:20—2:8). In different forms, this theme is followed up throughout the book (3:5-7; 8:22-36; 14:27; 21:1-3; 30:5). Finally the book ends by reaffirming that the one who "fears the Lord is to be praised" (31:30). Certainly this book, like the others of the Bible, clearly teaches that meaningful existence can come only from the proper relationship with God. God inspired the Book of Proverbs to make these very practical teachings readily available for His people to follow and thus find meaningful life with Him. Unfortunately, the children of Israel never seemed to understand nor to follow such wise precepts, and thus they had to face God's judgment (Pr 1:27-33; Isa 5:20-30; Jer 22:3-9; 52:1-30).

Contemporary Teaching

Proverbs clearly reminds us that we are all walking down the road of life, a road with two branches. The one chosen by the wise produces joy, happiness, and a meaningful existence as well as an eternal hope. The other chosen by the foolish brings about heartache, sorrow, and ultimate destruction.

Since there is clearly no middle ground, Dame Wisdom (that is the personification of wisdom in Proverbs) pleads with us: (1) to acknowledge God as the Creator and Sustainer of the world; (2) to repent of our sin and to trust in God as Lord and Savior; (3) to so order our lives in accordance with His will that His love will clearly be reflected in our relationships with our families, friends, neighbors, strangers, and even our enemies; (4) to teach these precepts diligently to our children both in word and in deed; and (5) to praise God for the fullness and joy that He provides along life's way.

Chapter 1

Prologue: Purpose and Theme

THE proverbs[a] of Solomon[b] son of David, king of Israel:[c]

2for attaining wisdom and discipline;
for understanding words of insight;
3for acquiring a disciplined and prudent life,
doing what is right and just and fair;
4for giving prudence to the simple,[d]
knowledge and discretion[e] to the young—
5let the wise listen and add to their learning,[f]
and let the discerning get guidance—
6for understanding proverbs and parables,[g]
the sayings and riddles[h] of the wise.[i]

7The fear of the LORD[j] is the beginning of knowledge,
but fools[a] despise wisdom[k] and discipline.[l]

Exhortations to Embrace Wisdom

Warning Against Enticement

8Listen, my son,[m] to your father's[n] instruction
and do not forsake your mother's teaching.[o]
9They will be a garland to grace your head
and a chain to adorn your neck.[p]

10My son, if sinners entice[q] you,
do not give in[r] to them.[s]
11If they say, "Come along with us;
let's lie in wait[t] for someone's blood,
let's waylay some harmless soul;
12let's swallow[u] them alive, like the grave,[b]
and whole, like those who go down to the pit;[v]
13we will get all sorts of valuable things
and fill our houses with plunder;
14throw in your lot with us,
and we will share a common purse[w]"—
15my son, do not go along with them,

1:1 [a]Mt 13:3 [b]1Ki 4:29-34 [c]Pr 10:1; 25:1; Ecc 1:1
1:4 [d]Pr 8:5 [e]Pr 8:12
1:5 [f]Pr 9:9
1:6 [g]S Ps 49:4; Mt 13:10-17 [h]S Nu 12:8; S Jdg 14:12 [i]Pr 22:17; 24:23
1:7 [j]S Ex 20:20; S Job 23:15; Ps 34:4-22; S 112:1; Pr 9:10; 15:33; Isa 33:6; 50:10; 59:19 [k]S Dt 4:6; Jer 8:9 [l]Pr 8:33-36; 9:7-9; 12:1; 13:18; 15:32
1:8 [m]ver 8-9; Pr 2:1; 3:1; 4:1; 5:1; 6:1; 7:1; 19:27; 22:17; 23:26-28 [n]Jer 35:8 [o]S Dt 21:18; Pr 6:20
1:9 [p]Pr 3:21-22; 4:1-9
1:10 [q]S Job 24:15 [r]Dt 13:8 [s]ver 15; Ps 1:1; Pr 16:29
1:11 [t]S Ps 10:8
1:12 [u]S Ps 35:25 [v]ver 16-18; S Job 33:18; S Ps 30:3
1:14 [w]ver 19

[a]*7* The Hebrew words rendered *fool* in Proverbs, and often elsewhere in the Old Testament, denote one who is morally deficient. [b]*12* Hebrew *Sheol*

1:1–33 EVIL AND SUFFERING, Deserved—A father warns his son of the suffering the wicked would experience as punishment for their actions. Much of the Book of Proverbs follows the view that the wise (righteous) will succeed and the wicked (foolish) will suffer. The "fool" is morally corrupt rather than intellectually limited. Like the Book of Deuteronomy, Proverbs stresses that the rewards and punishments will come in this life and are primarily material consequences for actions. Proverbs focuses on the individual's actions rather than the nation's actions and often suggests that the rewards or punishments are the "natural" consequences of the actions rather than the direct action of God. Proverbs' view of rewards and punishments was intended as a generalization about life, not a guarantee that the good would always succeed in human terms. Proverbs offers practical, general guidance for living daily life rather than rules we can use to check if we are wise or if God is just.

1:1–7 HUMANITY, Intellectual Nature—Our intellect's purpose is to build life, not facts. God's revelation is the place to begin intellectual development. We can build a disciplined and well-ordered life on that foundation. To fail to follow this process is the path of folly. This holds true for young and old, unlearned and wise. See note on Ps 111:10.

1:1–5 HOLY SCRIPTURE, Writing—God inspired Solomon to write and/or collect proverbs calling readers to wisdom, discipline, and insight. Read in solemn assemblies or shared from person to person, the gathered sayings of Solomon and other wise Jewish leaders disclosed God's will and purposes to hearers through generations.

1:7,29 SALVATION, Fear of God—Compare with Job 28:28; Ps 111:10. Reverence and awe for the covenant-making and covenant-keeping God is the chief part of knowledge. Knowledge here is more than a recognition of God. It is recognition of Him as the self-revealing One, the Lord of grace and history. Fools live without taking God into account and become morally corrupt. Those who fear God see Him as the most important part of all knowledge. The saved are the wise ones so committed to God as the Source of all wisdom that they could never become fools and act as if God did not exist.

1:7 EDUCATION, Wisdom—God is the starting point for the education that leads to wisdom. True knowledge, in the biblical sense, is something more than a collection of factual information. It includes knowing how to conduct oneself in the practical affairs of everyday life, to make wise choices, to do the right thing in relation to others, and to have insight into the true nature of things. Wisdom of this kind can only grow out of an awareness of God and His purpose in the world. Fools may acquire encyclopedic information, but they cannot attain wisdom because they fail to take God into account.

1:8–9 EDUCATION, Parents—The first and most important classroom in the school of life is the home. Both father and mother are expected to assume responsibility for training and nurturing the minds of children. Though school and church might contribute significantly to the process of education, no outside agency can equal the influence of parents as an educative force. Note that the words of the wisdom writer are addressed to the son rather than to the parents. The learner has a responsibility for attending to parental instruction. See note on 4:1–10.

1:8–9 FAMILY, Symbolic Nature—Wisdom in Proverbs is intellectual, experiential, and religious. Parental guidance was the inspired writer's model for the teacher-student relationship. Parental teachings are basic to family living and to society's larger educational program. Such teachings should lead to commitment to the Lord, the source of all wisdom.

1:10–19 EVIL AND SUFFERING, Punishment—Evil should not attract us. Evil actions often contain their own punishment and destruction within them. Doing evil is self-destructive. Proverbs often emphasizes this "natural consequences" view of wickedness and punishment. Behind the view lies the conviction that God made the world so that actions lead to corresponding consequences. God can use the natural order He created to punish sinners just as He can intervene in a specific historical event to punish His enemies. The natural consequences teaching must not be turned around to conclude that all suffering is the natural result of sin. Job teaches us the innocent also suffer.

1:10–19 CHRISTIAN ETHICS, Moral Limits—Stepping over God's moral limits is suicide. See notes on Ge 31:1–55; Ex 34:11–26,32.

do not set foot[x] on their paths;[y]
16for their feet rush into sin,[z]
they are swift to shed blood.[a]
17How useless to spread a net
in full view of all the birds!
18These men lie in wait[b] for their own
blood;
they waylay only themselves![c]
19Such is the end of all who go after
ill-gotten gain;
it takes away the lives of those who
get it.[d]

Warning Against Rejecting Wisdom

20Wisdom calls aloud[e] in the street,
she raises her voice in the public
squares;
21at the head of the noisy streets[c] she
cries out,
in the gateways of the city she
makes her speech:

22"How long will you simple ones[d] [f]
love your simple ways?
How long will mockers delight in
mockery
and fools hate[g] knowledge?
23If you had responded to my rebuke,
I would have poured out my heart to
you
and made my thoughts known to
you.
24But since you rejected[h] me when I
called[i]
and no one gave heed[j] when I
stretched out my hand,
25since you ignored all my advice
and would not accept my rebuke,
26I in turn will laugh[k] at your disaster;[l]
I will mock[m] when calamity
overtakes you[n] —
27when calamity overtakes you like a
storm,
when disaster[o] sweeps over you like
a whirlwind,
when distress and trouble
overwhelm you.

1:15 xS Ps 119:101 yS Ge 49:6; Pr 4:14
1:16 zS Job 15:31 aPr 6:18; Isa 59:7
1:18 bS Ps 71:10 cS ver 11-12
1:19 dS ver 13-14; Pr 4:14-17; 11:19
1:20 eS Job 28:12; Pr 7:10-13; 9:1-3, 13-15
1:22 fPr 6:32; 7:7; 8:5; 9:4,16 gPs 50:17
1:24 hJer 26:5; 35:17; 36:31 iIsa 65:12; 66:4; Jer 7:13 jS 1Sa 8:19
1:26 kS Ps 2:4 lver 33; S Ps 59:8 mS 2Ki 19:21 nDt 28:63
1:27 oS Ps 18:18; Pr 5:12-14
1:28 pS Dt 1:45; S 1Sa 8:18; S Jer 11:11 qS Job 27:9; Pr 8:17; Eze 8:18; Hos 5:6; Zec 7:13
1:29 rS Job 21:14
1:30 sver 25
1:31 tS 2Ch 36:16; Pr 14:14; Jer 6:19; 14:16; 21:14; 30:15
1:32 uPr 5:22; 15:10; Isa 66:4
1:33 vS Nu 24:21; S Dt 33:28; Pr 3:23 wS ver 21-26; S Ps 112:8
2:1 xS Pr 1:8
2:2 yPr 22:17; 23:12
2:3 zJas 1:5
2:4 aS Job 3:21; Mt 13:44
2:5 bS Dt 4:6
2:6 cS Job 12:13; S Ps 119:34 dS Job 9:4; S 22:22

28"Then they will call to me but I will
not answer;[p]
they will look for me but will not
find me.[q]
29Since they hated knowledge
and did not choose to fear the
LORD,[r]
30since they would not accept my advice
and spurned my rebuke,[s]
31they will eat the fruit of their ways
and be filled with the fruit of their
schemes.[t]
32For the waywardness of the simple will
kill them,
and the complacency of fools will
destroy them;[u]
33but whoever listens to me will live in
safety[v]
and be at ease, without fear of
harm."[w]

Chapter 2

Moral Benefits of Wisdom

MY son,[x] if you accept my words
and store up my commands within
you,
2turning your ear to wisdom
and applying your heart to
understanding,[y]
3and if you call out for insight[z]
and cry aloud for understanding,
4and if you look for it as for silver
and search for it as for hidden
treasure,[a]
5then you will understand the fear of
the LORD
and find the knowledge of God.[b]
6For the LORD gives wisdom,[c]
and from his mouth come
knowledge and
understanding.[d]

[c]21 Hebrew; Septuagint / *on the tops of the walls*
[d]22 The Hebrew word rendered *simple* in Proverbs generally denotes one without moral direction and inclined to evil.

1:20–33 EVIL AND SUFFERING, Deserved—God's wisdom is personified, warning the foolish of the consequences of their actions. See note on vv 10–19. Failure to listen to the wise teachings of God and His Word leads to disaster. We cannot avoid such disaster by choosing to follow God at the last moment before disaster strikes. We must not spurn the opportunity God gives us. Security comes only by following God's wisdom now.
1:20–33 HUMANITY, Intellectual Nature—Wisdom is personified as calling to people, making herself available to all who will respond. God is the ultimate source of wisdom. Those who reject wisdom have no sense of moral direction.
1:20 HOLY SCRIPTURE, Word—Biblical writers used many literary devices to affirm the divine power behind their words. In Proverbs, God's wisdom is pictured as a woman walking the streets of Jerusalem seeking to win people away from the alluring streetwalkers. The personification of Wisdom seen here forms part of the background of Jn 1, describing Jesus as the Word become flesh.
1:28–29 PRAYER, Hindrances—God will not answer those who willfully reject Him.
2:1–22 EVIL AND SUFFERING, Deserved—The world offers alternatives to draw us away from God's wisdom. We face the choice of walking wisdom's way or the world's. If we choose the world's, we deserve the destruction we ultimately will experience. See note on 1:20–33.
2:1–6 HUMANITY, Intellectual Nature—Wisdom is the gift of God. Those who accept His wisdom will find it a firm basis for understanding His revelation as well as all of life's knowledge. See note on 1:20–33.
2:1–22 REVELATION, Inspiration—Wisdom comes from God and has the ability to rescue people from evil choices and poor decisions. God can speak through the awakened mind and imagination of a believer. God not only uses the mind in dreams and visions at night or in an event that communicates His will, but He also gives insight to the average individual in reading and reflecting on His truth (Ps 145:5). See note on 1:20.

7He holds victory in store for the upright,
he is a shield[e] to those whose walk is blameless,[f]
8for he guards the course of the just
and protects the way of his faithful ones.[g]

9Then you will understand[h] what is right and just
and fair—every good path.
10For wisdom will enter your heart,[i]
and knowledge will be pleasant to your soul.
11Discretion will protect you,
and understanding will guard you.[j]

12Wisdom will save[k] you from the ways of wicked men,
from men whose words are perverse,
13who leave the straight paths
to walk in dark ways,[l]
14who delight in doing wrong
and rejoice in the perverseness of evil,[m]
15whose paths are crooked[n]
and who are devious in their ways.[o]

16It will save you also from the adulteress,[p]
from the wayward wife with her seductive words,
17who has left the partner of her youth
and ignored the covenant she made before God.[e] [q]
18For her house leads down to death
and her paths to the spirits of the dead.[r]
19None who go to her return
or attain the paths of life.[s]

20Thus you will walk in the ways of good men
and keep to the paths of the righteous.
21For the upright will live in the land,[t]
and the blameless will remain in it;
22but the wicked[u] will be cut off from the land,[v]
and the unfaithful will be torn from it.[w]

Chapter 3

Further Benefits of Wisdom

3 My son,[x] do not forget my teaching,[y]
but keep my commands in your heart,
2for they will prolong your life many years[z]
and bring you prosperity.[a]

3Let love and faithfulness[b] never leave you;
bind them around your neck,
write them on the tablet of your heart.[c]
4Then you will win favor and a good name
in the sight of God and man.[d]

5Trust in the LORD[e] with all your heart
and lean not on your own understanding;
6in all your ways acknowledge him,
and he will make your paths[f] straight.[f] [g]

7Do not be wise in your own eyes;[h]
fear the LORD[i] and shun evil.[j]
8This will bring health to your body[k]
and nourishment to your bones.[l]

9Honor the LORD with your wealth,
with the firstfruits[m] of all your crops;
10then your barns will be filled[n] to overflowing,
and your vats will brim over with new wine.[o]

2:7 [e]S Ge 15:1; Pr 30:5-6 [f]S Ge 6:9; Ps 84:11 **2:8** [g]1Sa 2:9; S Ps 18:25; S 97:10 **2:9** [h]S Dt 1:16 **2:10** [i]Pr 14:33 **2:11** [j]Pr 4:6 **2:12** [k]ver 16; Pr 3:13-18; 4:5 **2:13** [l]Pr 4:19 **2:14** [m]Pr 10:23; 15:21 **2:15** [n]S Ps 125:5 [o]Pr 21:8 **2:16** [p]Pr 5:1-6; 6:20-29; 7:5-27 **2:17** [q]Mal 2:14 **2:18** [r]Pr 5:5; 7:27; 9:18 **2:19** [s]Pr 3:16-18; 5:8; Ecc 7:26 **2:21** [t]S Ps 37:29 **2:22** [u]S Ps 5:4 [v]S Job 18:17 [w]Dt 28:63; S 29:28; Ps 37:9, 28-29; Pr 10:30 **3:1** [x]S Pr 1:8 [y]S Ps 44:17 **3:2** [z]S Dt 11:21 [a]S Dt 5:16; S 30:15, 16; S 1Ki 3:13,14; Pr 9:6,10-11 **3:3** [b]S Ps 85:10 [c]S Ex 13:9; S Dt 6:6; Pr 6:21; 7:3; S 2Co 3:3 **3:4** [d]S 1Sa 2:26; Lk 2:52 **3:5** [e]S Ps 4:5 **3:6** [f]S Job 33:11; S Isa 30:11 [g]S Ps 5:8; Pr 16:3; Isa 40:3; Jer 42:3 **3:7** [h]Pr 26:5,12; Isa 5:21 [i]Ps 111:10 [j]S Ex 20:20; S Dt 4:6; S Job 1:1 **3:8** [k]S Ps 38:3; Pr 4:22 [l]Job 21:24 **3:9** [m]S Ex 22:29; Dt 26:1-15 **3:10** [n]Ps 144:13 [o]S Job 22:21; Joel 2:24; Mal 3:10-12

[e]17 Or *covenant of her God* [f]6 Or *will direct your paths*

2:9–11 HUMANITY, Intellectual Nature—See note on 2:1–6.

2:18 LAST THINGS, Intermediate State—See note on Isa 14:9.

2:20–22 CHRISTIAN ETHICS, Moral Imperatives—Fellowship in community with other people is basic to life. We must exercise care in choosing the community with whom we identify. Friends help form our character. We do not choose friends to reform them. We want them to continue forming our character, leading us to righteousness. See notes on Lev 26:3–45; Dt 28:25.

3:1–35 EVIL AND SUFFERING, Deserved—See note on 1:10–19. Accepting God's discipline is a part of being God's people. Discipline is one expression of the Father's love for us, His children.

3:1–4 HOLY SCRIPTURE, Obedience—See note on 1:20. The wisdom teacher assumed the role of father to his students and tried to motivate them to learn and put into practice his teachings. Obeying the inspired teaching of Scripture develops character which pleases both God and other people.

3:3–4 CHRISTIAN ETHICS, Character—Love and faithfulness are two key biblical virtues. They are the focal point for the understanding and implementation of other virtues such as peace, mercy, justice, and righteousness. Love (Hebrew *chesed*) is a self-denying readiness to help other people. It represents a reciprocal relationship of service beyond social duties. Faithfulness (Hebrew *'emeth*) indicates trustworthiness, reliability, and loyalty. These characteristics can be found in people who please God.

3:5–6 SALVATION, Belief—God directs the paths of those who wholeheartedly trust in Him.

3:9–10 STEWARDSHIP, Rewards—The experience of God's people through the years is distilled into a pithy proverb by the inspired writer. It shows that God's people can count on His blessings when we honor Him with our offerings. As with all proverbial wisdom, this is not an ironclad rule without exceptions. It is a principle proved through experience and inspired by God. Stewardship is not an attempt to bribe God and ensure our own wealth. It is a committed response to the God who never forgets the needs of His people. See note on Lk 6:38.

11My son,[p] do not despise the LORD's
discipline[q]
and do not resent his rebuke,
12because the LORD disciplines those he
loves,[r]
as a father[g] the son he delights in.[s]

13Blessed is the man who finds wisdom,
the man who gains understanding,
14for she is more profitable than silver
and yields better returns than gold.[t]
15She is more precious than rubies;[u]
nothing you desire can compare
with her.[v]
16Long life is in her right hand;[w]
in her left hand are riches and
honor.[x]
17Her ways are pleasant ways,
and all her paths are peace.[y]
18She is a tree of life[z] to those who
embrace her;
those who lay hold of her will be
blessed.[a]

19By wisdom[b] the LORD laid the earth's
foundations,[c]
by understanding he set the
heavens[d] in place;
20by his knowledge the deeps were
divided,
and the clouds let drop the dew.

21My son,[e] preserve sound judgment
and discernment,
do not let them out of your sight;[f]
22they will be life for you,[g]
an ornament to grace your neck.[h]
23Then you will go on your way in
safety,[i]
and your foot will not stumble;[j]
24when you lie down,[k] you will not be
afraid;[l]
when you lie down, your sleep[m] will
be sweet.
25Have no fear of sudden disaster
or of the ruin that overtakes the
wicked,

3:11 [p]Pr 1:8-9 [q]S Job 5:17
3:12 [r]Pr 13:24; Rev 3:19 [s]S Dt 8:5; S Job 5:17; Heb 12:5-6*
3:14 [t]S Job 28:15; Pr 8:19; 16:16
3:15 [u]S Job 28:18 [v]S Job 28:17-19
3:16 [w]S Ge 15:15 [x]S 1Ki 3:13,14
3:17 [y]Mt 11:28-30
3:18 [z]S Ge 2:9; S Pr 10:11; S Rev 2:7 [a]S Pr 2:12; 4:3-9,8; 8:17-21
3:19 [b]S Ge 1:31; Ps 136:5-9 [c]S Job 28:25-27 [d]Pr 8:27-29
3:21 [e]Pr 1:8-9; 6:20 [f]Pr 4:20-22
3:22 [g]S Dt 30:20; Pr 4:13 [h]S Pr 1:8-9
3:23 [i]S Pr 1:33 [j]S Ps 37:24; S 119:11; Pr 4:12
3:24 [k]S Lev 26:6 [l]Ps 91:5; 112:8 [m]S Job 11:18; Jer 31:26
3:26 [n]S 2Ki 18:5; S Job 4:6 [o]S 1Sa 2:9 [p]S Job 5:19
3:28 [q]Lev 19:13; Dt 24:15; Lk 10:25-37
3:29 [r]Zec 8:17
3:31 [s]S Ps 37:1; Pr 24:1-2
3:32 [t]S Ps 101:4 [u]S Job 29:4
3:33 [v]S Job 5:3 [w]Zec 5:4 [x]Ps 37:22; Pr 14:11
3:34 [y]S 2Ki 19:21 [z]S Ps 40:4 [a]S Ps 18:25-27; S Mt 23:12; Jas 4:6*; 1Pe 5:5*
4:1 [b]S Pr 1:8 [c]Pr 19:20 [d]S Job 8:10

26for the LORD will be your confidence[n]
and will keep your foot[o] from being
snared.[p]

27Do not withhold good from those who
deserve it,
when it is in your power to act.
28Do not say to your neighbor,
"Come back later; I'll give it
tomorrow"—
when you now have it with you.[q]
29Do not plot harm against your
neighbor,
who lives trustfully near you.[r]
30Do not accuse a man for no reason—
when he has done you no harm.

31Do not envy[s] a violent man
or choose any of his ways,
32for the LORD detests a perverse man[t]
but takes the upright into his
confidence.[u]

33The LORD's curse[v] is on the house of
the wicked,[w]
but he blesses the home of the
righteous.[x]
34He mocks[y] proud mockers[z]
but gives grace to the humble.[a]
35The wise inherit honor,
but fools he holds up to shame.

Chapter 4

Wisdom Is Supreme

LISTEN, my sons,[b] to a father's
instruction;[c]
pay attention and gain
understanding.[d]
2I give you sound learning,
so do not forsake my teaching.
3When I was a boy in my father's
house,

[g]*12* Hebrew; Septuagint / *and he punishes*

3:11–12 GOD, Father—God is our Father who wants to teach us the wise path of life. He disciplines us in love when we require it. See notes on Dt 8:1–5; 14:1–29; Mt 5:43–48; 6:1–34.

3:13,33 SALVATION, Blessing—Those who find wisdom and gain understanding are blessed. Compare Ps 1:1–6. Wisdom here means knowledge of the moral law of God as it concerns the practical affairs of life.

3:13–18 CHRISTIAN ETHICS, Property Rights—Wisdom is knowing the way of the Lord. Wisdom comes through experience with God in His world and includes experiencing His discipline (vv 11–12). Worth more than any material value we can place on it, wisdom causes us to have the upward look (toward God) and outward look (toward our neighbor). Without wisdom material goods tempt us to look only toward ourselves. Material goods cannot buy a pleasant life of peace. Wisdom puts peace as our top priority in our life under God.

3:13–18 EDUCATION, Happiness—True wisdom promotes health, well-being, and happiness. Many of the problems that plague human existence spring from poor judgment, foolish choices, and confused values. God-given wisdom helps us avoid these pitfalls and heightens the quality of life. See note on 2 Ki 17:27–28.

3:19–20 GOD, Wisdom—God's wisdom directed His mighty acts of creation, making creation very good. See note on Ps 139:1–18.

3:19–20 CREATION, Purposeful—Creation has purpose and meaning. Divine wisdom guided each step of the universe's origin. Nothing was accidental or opposed to God's wise purposes. The wisdom behind creation proves the wisdom of letting divine wisdom guide each of life's choices.

4:1–27 EVIL AND SUFFERING, Deserved—See note on 1:10–19. Life needs goals. Two major alternatives face us—obedience to God or dedication to evil. Those on evil's path deserve the punishment that comes.

4:1 HOLY SCRIPTURE, Obedience—See note on 3:1–4.

4:1–10 EDUCATION, Discipline—"Instruction" refers to a process of training in which the learner submits to the teaching and guidance of a wiser person. To benefit from such instruction, we must cultivate a teachable spirit and accept the discipline of firm guidance. The ultimate reward of such training will be a long and useful life. See 3:1–2.

still tender, and an only child of my
mother,
[4]he taught me and said,
"Lay hold[e] of my words with all
your heart;
keep my commands and you will
live.[f]
[5]Get wisdom,[g] get understanding;
do not forget my words or swerve
from them.
[6]Do not forsake wisdom, and she will
protect you;[h]
love her, and she will watch over
you.[i]
[7]Wisdom is supreme; therefore get
wisdom.
Though it cost all[j] you have,[h] get
understanding.[k]
[8]Esteem her, and she will exalt you;
embrace her, and she will honor
you.[l]
[9]She will set a garland of grace on your
head
and present you with a crown of
splendor.[m]"

[10]Listen, my son,[n] accept what I say,
and the years of your life will be
many.[o]
[11]I guide[p] you in the way of wisdom
and lead you along straight paths.[q]
[12]When you walk, your steps will not be
hampered;
when you run, you will not
stumble.[r]
[13]Hold on to instruction, do not let it go;
guard it well, for it is your life.[s]
[14]Do not set foot on the path of the
wicked
or walk in the way of evil men.[t]
[15]Avoid it, do not travel on it;
turn from it and go on your way.
[16]For they cannot sleep till they do
evil;[u]
they are robbed of slumber till they
make someone fall.
[17]They eat the bread of wickedness
and drink the wine of violence.[v]

[18]The path of the righteous[w] is like the
first gleam of dawn,[x]
shining ever brighter till the full
light of day.[y]
[19]But the way of the wicked is like deep
darkness;[z]
they do not know what makes them
stumble.[a]

4:4 [e]S 1Ki 9:4 [f]Pr 7:2
4:5 [g]S Pr 2:12; 3:13-18
4:6 [h]2Th 2:10 [i]S Pr 2:11
4:7 [j]Mt 13:44-46 [k]Pr 23:23
4:8 [l]S Pr 3:18
4:9 [m]S Pr 1:8-9
4:10 [n]Ps 34:11-16; Pr 1:8-9 [o]S Dt 11:21
4:11 [p]S 1Sa 12:23 [q]2Sa 22:37; Ps 5:8
4:12 [r]S Job 18:7; Pr 3:23
4:13 [s]S Pr 3:22
4:14 [t]Ps 1:1; S Pr 1:15
4:16 [u]Ps 36:4; Mic 7:3
4:17 [v]Ge 49:5; Ps 73:6; Pr 1:10-19; 14:22; Isa 59:6; Jer 22:3; Hab 1:2; Mal 2:16
4:18 [w]Job 17:9 [x]S Job 22:28 [y]S 2Sa 23:4; Da 12:3; Mt 5:14; Jn 8:12; Php 2:15
4:19 [z]S Pr 2:13 [a]S Dt 32:35; S Job 3:23; Pr 13:9; S Isa 8:15
4:20 [b]Ps 34:11-16; Pr 1:8-9 [c]Pr 5:1
4:21 [d]Pr 3:21
4:22 [e]S Pr 3:8
4:23 [f]S 2Ki 10:31 [g]Pr 10:11; Lk 6:45
4:25 [h]S Job 31:1
4:26 [i]Heb 12:13*
4:27 [j]S Lev 10:11; S Dt 5:32
5:1 [k]S Pr 1:8 [l]Pr 4:20
5:3 [m]S Ps 55:21; Pr 7:5
5:4 [n]Ecc 7:26
5:5 [o]S Ps 9:17; S Pr 2:18; 7:26-27
5:6 [p]Pr 9:13; 30:20
5:7 [q]Pr 1:8-9
5:8 [r]S Pr 2:16-19; 6:20-29; 7:1-27
5:10 [s]Pr 29:3

[20]My son,[b] pay attention to what I say;
listen closely to my words.[c]
[21]Do not let them out of your sight,[d]
keep them within your heart;
[22]for they are life to those who find
them
and health to a man's whole body.[e]
[23]Above all else, guard[f] your heart,
for it is the wellspring of life.[g]
[24]Put away perversity from your mouth;
keep corrupt talk far from your lips.
[25]Let your eyes[h] look straight ahead,
fix your gaze directly before you.
[26]Make level[i] paths for your feet[i]
and take only ways that are firm.
[27]Do not swerve to the right or the
left;[j]
keep your foot from evil.

Chapter 5

Warning Against Adultery

MY son,[k] pay attention to my
wisdom,
listen well to my words[l] of insight,
[2]that you may maintain discretion
and your lips may preserve
knowledge.
[3]For the lips of an adulteress drip
honey,
and her speech is smoother than
oil;[m]
[4]but in the end she is bitter as gall,[n]
sharp as a double-edged sword.
[5]Her feet go down to death;
her steps lead straight to the
grave.[j] [o]
[6]She gives no thought to the way of life;
her paths are crooked, but she
knows it not.[p]

[7]Now then, my sons, listen[q] to me;
do not turn aside from what I say.
[8]Keep to a path far from her,[r]
do not go near the door of her
house,
[9]lest you give your best strength to
others
and your years to one who is cruel,
[10]lest strangers feast on your wealth
and your toil enrich another man's
house.[s]
[11]At the end of your life you will groan,
when your flesh and body are spent.

[h]7 Or *Whatever else you get* [i]26 Or *Consider the* [j]5 Hebrew *Sheol*

4:18 CHRISTIAN ETHICS, Righteousness—Relationship with God promises a clearer sense of the way to go in life as God provides light for that life. The righteous person is one on God's pathway of life.

5:1–23 EVIL AND SUFFERING, Deserved—See note on 1:10–19. The focus here is on the consequences for associating with an immoral woman. Wisdom warns against conceding to a very strong but temporary desire that has long-term, destructive results.

5:1 HOLY SCRIPTURE, Obedience—See note on 3:1–4.

5:3–6 HUMANITY, Death and Sin—Adultery is specifically identified, but all infidelity appears to be implied as being the kind of life which leads to death. Living only to satisfy the pleasures of the flesh is the way of folly. Eventually moral corruption robs us of the ability to distinguish right from wrong.

12You will say, "How I hated discipline!
How my heart spurned correction![t]
13I would not obey my teachers
or listen to my instructors.
14I have come to the brink of utter ruin[u]
in the midst of the whole
assembly."[v]

15Drink water from your own cistern,
running water from your own well.
16Should your springs overflow in the
streets,
your streams of water in the public
squares?
17Let them be yours alone,
never to be shared with strangers.
18May your fountain[w] be blessed,
and may you rejoice in the wife of
your youth.[x]
19A loving doe, a graceful deer[y] —
may her breasts satisfy you always,
may you ever be captivated by her
love.
20Why be captivated, my son, by an
adulteress?
Why embrace the bosom of another
man's wife?

21For a man's ways are in full view[z] of
the LORD,
and he examines[a] all his paths.[b]
22The evil deeds of a wicked man
ensnare him;[c]
the cords of his sin hold him fast.[d]
23He will die for lack of discipline,[e]
led astray by his own great folly.[f]

Chapter 6

Warnings Against Folly

MY son,[g] if you have put up
security[h] for your neighbor,[i]
if you have struck hands in pledge[j]
for another,
2if you have been trapped by what you
said,
ensnared by the words of your
mouth,
3then do this, my son, to free yourself,
since you have fallen into your
neighbor's hands:
Go and humble yourself;
press your plea with your neighbor!
4Allow no sleep to your eyes,
no slumber to your eyelids.[k]
5Free yourself, like a gazelle[l] from the
hand of the hunter,[m]
like a bird from the snare of the
fowler.[n]

6Go to the ant, you sluggard;[o]
consider its ways and be wise!
7It has no commander,
no overseer or ruler,
8yet it stores its provisions in summer[p]
and gathers its food at harvest.[q]

9How long will you lie there, you
sluggard?[r]
When will you get up from your
sleep?
10A little sleep, a little slumber,
a little folding of the hands to
rest[s] —
11and poverty[t] will come on you like a
bandit
and scarcity like an armed man.[k]

12A scoundrel and villain,
who goes about with a corrupt
mouth,
13 who winks with his eye,[u]
signals with his feet

5:12 [t]Pr 12:1
5:14 [u]Pr 1:24-27; 6:33 [v]Pr 31:3
5:18 [w]SS 4:12-15 [x]S Dt 20:7; Pr 2:17; Ecc 9:9; Mal 2:14
5:19 [y]SS 4:5; 8:14
5:21 [z]S Ps 119:168 [a]Jer 29:23 [b]S Job 10:4; S 14:16; Pr 15:3; Jer 32:19; S Heb 4:13
5:22 [c]Ps 9:16 [d]Nu 32:23; S Job 18:9; Ps 7:15-16; S Pr 1:31-32
5:23 [e]S Job 4:21; Pr 10:21 [f]Job 34:21-25; Pr 11:5
6:1 [g]S Pr 1:8 [h]Job 17:3 [i]Pr 17:18 [j]Pr 11:15; 22:26-27
6:4 [k]Ps 132:4
6:5 [l]S 2Sa 2:18 [m]Isa 13:14 [n]S Ps 91:3
6:6 [o]ver 6-11; Pr 20:4
6:8 [p]Pr 30:24-25 [q]Pr 10:4
6:9 [r]Pr 24:30-34; 26:13-16
6:10 [s]Pr 24:33; Ecc 4:5
6:11 [t]ver 10-11; Pr 20:13; 24:30-34
6:13 [u]S Ps 35:19; Pr 16:30

[k]11 Or *like a vagrant / and scarcity like a beggar*

5:15–23 FAMILY, Sexual Fulfillment—Sexual pleasure between husband and wife is a basic motivation for avoiding adultery in addition to the fear of God's judgment (vv 21–23). Symbolic language describes the wife as cistern, well, and fountain. She is the source of great pleasure to the man. Sexual fascination and mutual pleasuring are part of God's purpose for sex in marriage as can be seen in this passage and in the Song of Songs. The latter book describes in vivid detail the loving sexual embrace (SS 2:3–6; 7:7–10) and the attractiveness of male and female bodies to each other (SS 4:1–7; 5:10–16; 6:4–7; 7:1–6). The satisfaction of healthy sexual experience is clearly set forth in Song of Songs 8:10. Such experience is designed for the commitment and trust of marriage. Outside marriage sex ultimately leads to guilt and loss of self-respect.
5:21–23 SIN, Slavery—Sin brings its own punishment in the life of the individual. Sinners eventually discover they are trapped. Sin has captured them so they cannot get loose. They are slaves to sin. Lack of self-discipline has resulted in loss of power not to sin. The final word is spiritual death. No one intends for life to turn out this way. We just get caught in a habit of sin.
5:22–23 HUMANITY, Death and Sin—Death is more than physical. It always has a spiritual dimension. It is the end of a life of sin. Such a life is foolishly built upon the absence of discipline. Without personal discipline exercising moral choices under God, we do not have life.
6:1–35 EVIL AND SUFFERING, Deserved—See note on 1:10–19. Evil destroys human relationships as well as our relationship with God. Certain actions and attitudes are always evil. We can never justify pride, lying, evil schemes against others, dedication to evil projects, false testimony, adultery, or stirring up dissension. Such actions lead naturally to ultimate disaster.
6:1 HOLY SCRIPTURE, Obedience—See note on 3:1–4.
6:1–5 CHRISTIAN ETHICS, Language—Our tongue can get us into trouble (11:15). We may agree without thinking to a contract made by a dishonest person. When we recognize the wrongness of our attitudes and words, we need to act immediately. We must not quit until we are reconciled to the other person and nullify the agreement. In so doing we must admit our wrongness.
6:6–8 HUMANITY, Work—No one should have to force us to work. Planning for the future and hard work in the present are the bases for life. These, however, are also expected to be coupled with cooperative relations with those around us.
6:12–19 SIN, Death—Sin has one reward—destruction, death. To earn the reward you simply use filthy language, give deceitful or cheating gestures, plan how to take advantage of other people, create controversy, be proud, lie, murder, testify falsely, and stir up every possible evil. All represent sin against the community. They break God's guidelines for life, and He will punish the sinner.

and motions with his fingers,[v]
14 who plots evil[w] with deceit in his
heart—
he always stirs up dissension.[x]
15Therefore disaster will overtake him in
an instant;[y]
he will suddenly[z] be
destroyed—without remedy.[a]

16There are six things the LORD hates,[b]
seven that are detestable to him:
17 haughty eyes,[c]
a lying tongue,[d]
hands that shed innocent blood,[e]
18 a heart that devises wicked
schemes,
feet that are quick to rush into
evil,[f]
19 a false witness[g] who pours out
lies[h]
and a man who stirs up dissension
among brothers.[i]

Warning Against Adultery

20My son,[j] keep your father's
commands
and do not forsake your mother's
teaching.[k]
21Bind them upon your heart forever;
fasten them around your neck.[l]
22When you walk, they will guide you;
when you sleep, they will watch
over you;
when you awake, they will speak to
you.
23For these commands are a lamp,
this teaching is a light,[m]
and the corrections of discipline
are the way to life,[n]
24keeping you from the immoral woman,
from the smooth tongue of the
wayward wife.[o]
25Do not lust in your heart after her
beauty
or let her captivate you with her
eyes,
26for the prostitute reduces you to a loaf
of bread,
and the adulteress preys upon your
very life.[p]
27Can a man scoop fire into his lap
without his clothes being burned?

6:13 [v]Isa 58:9
6:14 [w]S Ps 140:2 [x]ver 16-19
6:15 [y]S Ps 55:15 [z]Job 5:3 [a]Pr 14:32; 29:1
6:16 [b]ver 16-19; Pr 3:32; 8:13; 15:8, 9,26; 16:5
6:17 [c]S Job 41:34; S Ps 10:5 [d]Pr 12:22 [e]S Dt 19:10; Pr 1:16; Isa 1:21; 59:7; Jer 2:34; Mic 7:2
6:18 [f]S Job 15:31
6:19 [g]S Dt 19:16 [h]S Ps 12:2 [i]ver 12-15; Pr 15:18; Zec 8:17
6:20 [j]S Pr 3:21 [k]Pr 1:8
6:21 [l]Dt 6:8; S Pr 3:3; 7:1-3
6:23 [m]S Ps 119:105 [n]Pr 10:17
6:24 [o]Ge 39:8; S Ps 55:21; Pr 2:16; 7:5
6:26 [p]Pr 7:22-23
6:29 [q]S Ex 20:14 [r]Pr 2:16-19; S 5:8
6:31 [s]Ex 22:1-14
6:32 [t]S Ex 20:14 [u]Pr 7:7; 9:4,16
6:33 [v]Pr 5:9-14
6:34 [w]S Nu 5:14 [x]S Ge 34:7
6:35 [y]Job 31:9-11; SS 8:7
7:1 [z]S Pr 1:8
7:2 [a]Pr 4:4
7:3 [b]S Pr 3:3
7:5 [c]ver 21; S Job 31:9; S Pr 2:16; 6:24
7:7 [d]S Pr 1:22; S 6:32

28Can a man walk on hot coals
without his feet being scorched?
29So is he who sleeps[q] with another
man's wife;[r]
no one who touches her will go
unpunished.

30Men do not despise a thief if he steals
to satisfy his hunger when he is
starving.
31Yet if he is caught, he must pay
sevenfold,[s]
though it costs him all the wealth of
his house.
32But a man who commits adultery[t]
lacks judgment;[u]
whoever does so destroys himself.
33Blows and disgrace are his lot,
and his shame will never[v] be wiped
away;
34for jealousy[w] arouses a husband's
fury,[x]
and he will show no mercy when he
takes revenge.
35He will not accept any compensation;
he will refuse the bribe, however
great it is.[y]

Chapter 7

Warning Against the Adulteress

MY son,[z] keep my words
and store up my commands within
you.
2Keep my commands and you will
live;[a]
guard my teachings as the apple of
your eye.
3Bind them on your fingers;
write them on the tablet of your
heart.[b]
4Say to wisdom, "You are my sister,"
and call understanding your
kinsman;
5they will keep you from the adulteress,
from the wayward wife with her
seductive words.[c]

6At the window of my house
I looked out through the lattice.
7I saw among the simple,
I noticed among the young men,
a youth who lacked judgment.[d]

6:20–35 FAMILY, Sexual Sin—Parental teaching helps young adults avoid tragic mistakes. Among such tragedies is the disaster of sexual sins with immoral women and wayward wives. Such sin begins with flirtatious looks and ends with disastrous punishment. Shame, disgrace, and revenge chart life's course for the adulterer. Sex brings true joy and pleasure only within marriage. See note on 5:15–23.

7:1–27 EVIL AND SUFFERING, Deserved—See notes on 1:10–19; 5:1–23. Evil may be alluring and offer temporary pleasure. It never produces long-term good for an individual or society. The young are especially susceptible to the temptation of sex outside marriage. They often do not exercise mature judgment to consider the broken life resulting from yielding to sexual allures.

7:1–3 HOLY SCRIPTURE, Writing—The collecting and retaining of God's wisdom gives the reader genuine life. Faithful Israelites were asked to keep symbolic records of God's law on their hands and foreheads as constant reminders of God's purposes and plans. Yet the symbol was to establish God's way of life inside of His people, that is in their hearts, the seat of thinking and directing (Dt 6:8). See note on 3:1–4.

7:1–5 EDUCATION, Moral Purity—Instruction in the Word of God and a serious commitment to live by it provide a safeguard against moral lapses. This truth, a recurrent theme in Old Testament wisdom writings (see Ps 119:9–11; Pr 5:1–14), also appears in the New Testament. See 2 Ti 2:16.

8He was going down the street near her corner,
walking along in the direction of her house
9at twilight,[e] as the day was fading,
as the dark of night set in.

10Then out came a woman to meet him,
dressed like a prostitute and with crafty intent.
11(She is loud[f] and defiant,
her feet never stay at home;
12now in the street, now in the squares,
at every corner she lurks.)[g]
13She took hold of him[h] and kissed him
and with a brazen face she said:[i]
14"I have fellowship offerings[1][j] at home;
today I fulfilled my vows.
15So I came out to meet you;
I looked for you and have found you!
16I have covered my bed
with colored linens from Egypt.
17I have perfumed my bed[k]
with myrrh,[l] aloes and cinnamon.
18Come, let's drink deep of love till morning;
let's enjoy ourselves with love![m]
19My husband is not at home;
he has gone on a long journey.
20He took his purse filled with money
and will not be home till full moon."

21With persuasive words she led him astray;
she seduced him with her smooth talk.[n]
22All at once he followed her
like an ox going to the slaughter,
like a deer[m] stepping into a noose[n] [o]
23 till an arrow pierces[p] his liver,
like a bird darting into a snare,
little knowing it will cost him his life.[q]

24Now then, my sons, listen[r] to me;
pay attention to what I say.
25Do not let your heart turn to her ways
or stray into her paths.[s]
26Many are the victims she has brought down;
her slain are a mighty throng.
27Her house is a highway to the grave,[o]
leading down to the chambers of death.[t]

7:9 [e]Job 24:15
7:11 [f]Pr 9:13
7:12 [g]Pr 8:1-36; 23:26-28
7:13 [h]S Ge 39:12 [i]S Pr 1:20
7:14 [j]S Lev 7:11-18
7:17 [k]S Est 1:6; Isa 57:7; Eze 23:41; Am 6:4 [l]S Ge 37:25
7:18 [m]S Ge 39:7
7:21 [n]S ver 5
7:22 [o]S Job 18:10
7:23 [p]S Job 15:22; S 16:13 [q]S Pr 6:26; Ecc 7:26
7:24 [r]Pr 1:8-9; 8:32
7:25 [s]Pr 5:7-8
7:27 [t]Jdg 16:19; S Pr 2:18; Rev 22:15
8:1 [u]S Job 28:12
8:3 [v]Pr 7:6-13
8:4 [w]Isa 42:2
8:5 [x]S Pr 1:22 [y]Pr 1:4
8:7 [z]Jn 8:14
8:10 [a]S Job 28:17; S Ps 19:10
8:11 [b]ver 19; S Job 28:17-19 [c]Pr 3:13-15
8:12 [d]Pr 1:4
8:13 [e]S Ge 22:12 [f]S Ex 20:20; S Job 28:28 [g]Jer 44:4

Chapter 8

Wisdom's Call

DOES not wisdom call out?[u]
Does not understanding raise her voice?
2On the heights along the way,
where the paths meet, she takes her stand;
3beside the gates leading into the city,
at the entrances, she cries aloud:[v]
4"To you, O men, I call out;[w]
I raise my voice to all mankind.
5You who are simple,[x] gain prudence;[y]
you who are foolish, gain understanding.
6Listen, for I have worthy things to say;
I open my lips to speak what is right.
7My mouth speaks what is true,[z]
for my lips detest wickedness.
8All the words of my mouth are just;
none of them is crooked or perverse.
9To the discerning all of them are right;
they are faultless to those who have knowledge.
10Choose my instruction instead of silver,
knowledge rather than choice gold,[a]
11for wisdom is more precious[b] than rubies,
and nothing you desire can compare with her.[c]

12"I, wisdom, dwell together with prudence;
I possess knowledge and discretion.[d]
13To fear the LORD[e] is to hate evil;[f]
I hate[g] pride and arrogance,
evil behavior and perverse speech.

[1]*14* Traditionally *peace offerings* [m]*22* Syriac (see also Septuagint); Hebrew *fool* [n]*22* The meaning of the Hebrew for this line is uncertain. [o]*27* Hebrew *Sheol*

7:10–27 HUMANITY, Death and Sin—See note on 5:3–6.

8:1—9:16 HUMANITY, Intellectual Nature—Wisdom is personified here, being viewed as God's companion from before creation. It is described in feminine terms. Wisdom is revealed as the basis of all great accomplishments of humanity. Its origin is seen in God and was His companion in creation and is the basis of His revelation. This divine wisdom is offered to all who know and admit their own ignorance. See notes on 1:1–7, 20–33; 2:1–6.

8:1–7,11 EDUCATION, Wisdom—Viewed as a person, wisdom extends an invitation to learning to everyone she meets. She is not confined to academic halls or classrooms. She walks the streets, moves among the people, stands in crowded thoroughfares. Here is a biblical picture of the modern ideal of universal, lifelong learning, in which people can gain treasures of the mind and heart worth far more than material resources. God wants to teach us His ways through every experience of life.

8:10–21 CHRISTIAN ETHICS, Property Rights—Choosing to seek and follow God's wisdom lets us see wealth in proper perspective, so seeking wealth does not become the all-consuming goal of life. See note on 3:13–18.

8:12–31 GOD, Wisdom—God's wisdom stands at the very heart of God's being. Personified wisdom here prepares the way for the deeper New Testament description of Jesus as the Word and Wisdom of God (Jn 1:1–3; 1 Co 1:24,30; Col 2:3). Wisdom is the basis of all God does. See notes on Ex 6:5; Dt 31:21; 1 Sa 2:3; Ps 94:10–11; 139:1–18.

14Counsel and sound judgment are
mine;
I have understanding and power.[h]
15By me kings reign
and rulers[i] make laws that are just;
16by me princes govern,[j]
and all nobles who rule on earth.[p]
17I love those who love me,[k]
and those who seek me find me.[l]
18With me are riches and honor,[m]
enduring wealth and prosperity.[n]
19My fruit is better than fine gold;[o]
what I yield surpasses choice
silver.[p]
20I walk in the way of righteousness,[q]
along the paths of justice,
21bestowing wealth on those who love
me
and making their treasuries full.[r]

22"The LORD brought me forth as the
first of his works,[q] [r]
before his deeds of old;
23I was appointed[s] from eternity,
from the beginning, before the
world began.
24When there were no oceans, I was
given birth,
when there were no springs
abounding with water;[s]
25before the mountains were settled in
place,[t]
before the hills, I was given birth,[u]
26before he made the earth or its fields
or any of the dust of the world.[v]
27I was there when he set the heavens
in place,[w]
when he marked out the horizon[x]
on the face of the deep,
28when he established the clouds
above[y]
and fixed securely the fountains of
the deep,[z]
29when he gave the sea its boundary[a]
so the waters would not overstep his
command,[b]
and when he marked out the
foundations of the earth.[c]
30 Then I was the craftsman at his
side.[d]
I was filled with delight day after day,
rejoicing always in his presence,
31rejoicing in his whole world
and delighting in mankind.[e]

8:14 [h]S Job 9:4; Pr 21:22; Ecc 7:19
8:15 [i]S Ps 2:10
8:16 [j]S 2Ch 1:10; Pr 29:4
8:17 [k]S 1Sa 2:30; Jn 14:21-24 [l]S 1Ch 16:11; S Pr 1:28; 3:13-18; Mt 7:7-11
8:18 [m]S 1Ki 3:13 [n]S Dt 8:18
8:19 [o]S Job 28:17-19 [p]S Pr 3:13-14
8:20 [q]S Ps 5:8
8:21 [r]Pr 15:6; 24:4
8:24 [s]S Ge 7:11
8:25 [t]S Job 38:6 [u]S Job 15:7
8:26 [v]S Ps 90:2
8:27 [w]S Job 26:7 [x]S Job 22:14
8:28 [y]S Job 36:29 [z]S Ge 1:7; S Job 9:8; S 26:10
8:29 [a]S Ge 1:9; S Ps 16:6 [b]S Job 38:8 [c]S 1Sa 2:8; S Job 38:5
8:30 [d]Pr 3:19-20; Rev 3:14
8:31 [e]S Job 28:25-27; 38:4-38; Ps 104:1-30; Pr 30:4; Jn 1:1-4; Col 1:15-20
8:32 [f]S Pr 7:24 [g]Lk 11:28 [h]S 2Sa 22:22; S Ps 18:21
8:34 [i]1Ki 10:8
8:35 [j]Pr 3:13-18 [k]Pr 9:6; Jn 5:39-40 [l]S Job 33:26
8:36 [m]Pr 15:32; Isa 3:9; Jer 40:2 [n]S Job 28:22
9:1 [o]Eph 2:20-22; 1Pe 2:5
9:2 [p]Isa 25:6; 62:8 [q]Lk 14:16-23
9:3 [r]S Pr 1:20; 8:1-3 [s]ver 14
9:4 [t]S Pr 1:22 [u]ver 16; S Pr 6:32
9:5 [v]Jn 7:37-38 [w]S Ps 42:2; 63:1; 143:6; Isa 44:3; 55:1
9:6 [x]S Pr 8:35 [y]S Pr 3:1-2
9:7 [z]Pr 23:9; Mt 7:6
9:8 [a]Pr 15:12 [b]Ps 141:5
9:9 [c]Pr 1:5,7; 12:15; 13:10; 14:6; 15:31; 19:25

32"Now then, my sons, listen[f] to me;
blessed are[g] those who keep my
ways.[h]
33Listen to my instruction and be wise;
do not ignore it.
34Blessed is the man who listens[i] to me,
watching daily at my doors,
waiting at my doorway.
35For whoever finds me[j] finds life[k]
and receives favor from the LORD.[l]
36But whoever fails to find me harms
himself;[m]
all who hate me love death."[n]

Chapter 9

Invitations of Wisdom and of Folly

WISDOM has built[o] her house;
she has hewn out its seven pillars.
2She has prepared her meat and mixed
her wine;[p]
she has also set her table.[q]
3She has sent out her maids, and she
calls[r]
from the highest point of the city.[s]
4"Let all who are simple[t] come in
here!"
she says to those who lack
judgment.[u]
5"Come,[v] eat my food
and drink the wine I have mixed.[w]
6Leave your simple ways and you will
live;[x]
walk in the way of understanding.[y]

7"Whoever corrects a mocker invites
insult;
whoever rebukes a wicked man
incurs abuse.[z]
8Do not rebuke a mocker[a] or he will
hate you;
rebuke a wise man and he will love
you.[b]
9Instruct a wise man and he will be
wiser still;
teach a righteous man and he will
add to his learning.[c]

[p]*16* Many Hebrew manuscripts and Septuagint; most Hebrew manuscripts *and nobles—all righteous rulers*
[q]*22* Or *way;* or *dominion* [r]*22* Or *The LORD possessed me at the beginning of his work;* or *The LORD brought me forth at the beginning of his work*
[s]*23* Or *fashioned*

8:22–31 CREATION, Purposeful—See note on 3:19–20. Wisdom should be the guide and goal for life because wisdom was a possession (NIV footnote) of God in creation, is an eternal aspect of God's being, and underlies all other elements of creation. It gives the world continuity. All elements are interrelated. The world is constituted in such a way that those who cooperate with God's basic laws find the natural world sustains their life. God's natural and moral laws make sense when viewed from the Creator's wisdom. To obey these laws shows good judgment.

9:1–18 EVIL AND SUFFERING, Deserved—God's wisdom, personified as a hostess, is contrasted with a foolish woman. Two forces within and without us beckon. One, wisdom, invites us to dine with her and truly enjoy the benefits of the Lord. The other, folly, tempts us to destroy ourselves on what only appears to be good for us.

9:9 EDUCATION, Wisdom—Long before modern educators learned of a "predisposition toward learning," the biblical writer pointed out that a wise and knowledgeable person is receptive to further instruction. Learning kindles a desire for more learning. See note on 15:14.

10"The fear of the LORD[d] is the
beginning of wisdom,
and knowledge of the Holy One[e] is
understanding.[f]
11For through me your days will be
many,
and years will be added to your
life.[g]
12If you are wise, your wisdom will
reward you;
if you are a mocker, you alone will
suffer."

13The woman Folly is loud;[h]
she is undisciplined and without
knowledge.[i]
14She sits at the door of her house,
on a seat at the highest point of the
city,[j]
15calling out[k] to those who pass by,
who go straight on their way.
16"Let all who are simple come in
here!"
she says to those who lack
judgment.[l]
17"Stolen water is sweet;
food eaten in secret is delicious![m]"
18But little do they know that the dead
are there,
that her guests are in the depths of
the grave.[t] [n]

Chapter 10

Proverbs of Solomon

THE proverbs[o] of Solomon:[p]
A wise son brings joy to his father,[q]
but a foolish son grief to his mother.

2Ill-gotten treasures are of no value,[r]
but righteousness delivers from
death.[s]

3The LORD does not let the righteous go
hungry[t]
but he thwarts the craving of the
wicked.[u]

4Lazy hands make a man poor,[v]
but diligent hands bring wealth.[w]

5He who gathers crops in summer is a
wise son,
but he who sleeps during harvest is
a disgraceful son.[x]

6Blessings crown the head of the
righteous,
but violence overwhelms the mouth
of the wicked.[u] [y]

7The memory of the righteous[z] will be
a blessing,
but the name of the wicked[a] will
rot.[b]

8The wise in heart accept commands,
but a chattering fool comes to ruin.[c]

9The man of integrity[d] walks
securely,[e]
but he who takes crooked paths will
be found out.[f]

10He who winks maliciously[g] causes
grief,
and a chattering fool comes to ruin.

11The mouth of the righteous is a
fountain of life,[h]
but violence overwhelms the mouth
of the wicked.[i]

12Hatred stirs up dissension,
but love covers over all wrongs.[j]

13Wisdom is found on the lips of the
discerning,[k]

9:10 [d]S Pr 1:7 [e]Ps 22:3; Pr 30:3 [f]S Dt 4:6
9:11 [g]S Ge 15:15; S Dt 11:21; S Pr 3:1-2; 10:27
9:13 [h]Pr 7:11 [i]S Pr 5:6
9:14 [j]ver 3; Eze 16:25
9:15 [k]S Pr 1:20
9:16 [l]S Pr 1:22
9:17 [m]Pr 20:17
9:18 [n]S Pr 2:18; 7:26-27
10:1 [o]S 1Ki 4:32 [p]S Pr 1:1 [q]Pr 15:20; 17:21; 19:13; 23:22-25; 27:11; 29:3
10:2 [r]Pr 13:11; 21:6 [s]ver 16; Pr 11:4,19; 12:28
10:3 [t]Mt 6:25-34 [u]Pr 13:25
10:4 [v]Pr 6:6-8; 19:15; 24:30-34 [w]Pr 12:24; 21:5
10:5 [x]Pr 24:30-34
10:6 [y]ver 8,11,14; Pr 12:13; 13:3; Ecc 10:12
10:7 [z]S Ps 112:6 [a]S Job 18:17; S Ps 109:13 [b]S Job 18:17; Ps 9:6
10:8 [c]ver 14; S Job 33:33; Mt 7:24-27
10:9 [d]S Ps 25:21 [e]S Ps 37:24 [f]Pr 28:18
10:10 [g]S Ps 35:19
10:11 [h]ver 27; S Pr 3:18; S 4:23; 11:30; 13:12,14, 19; 14:27; 15:4; 16:22 [i]S ver 6
10:12 [j]Pr 17:9; 1Co 13:4-7; 1Pe 4:8
10:13 [k]ver 31; S Ps 37:30; Pr 15:7

[t]*18* Hebrew *Sheol* [u]*6* Or *but the mouth of the wicked conceals violence*; also in verse 11

9:10 GOD, Holy—We cannot approach God without proper respect for His holiness. See notes on Ex 3:5–6; 19:10–24; Lev 11:44–45; Ps 89:18,35; 2 Co 7:1.
9:18 HUMANITY, Death and Sin—See note on 5:3–6.
9:18 LAST THINGS, Intermediate State—See note on Isa 14:9.
10:1—22:16 EVIL AND SUFFERING, Deserved—This major collection of Solomon's proverbs stresses two ways of life or two value systems, wisdom (righteousness) and folly (sin). The comparisons normally come in parallel verses. The wise will prosper, and the foolish will suffer. The theologian must understand the biblical intent here. Proverbs offers the inspired generalization of the experiences of generations of God's people. Such generalizations prove true in the overwhelming majority of cases. They cannot be considered natural laws which prove true in every instance. They must not be used as criteria for judgment to condemn ourselves or others of ungodly lives because we do not reach a certain standard of prosperity. Proverbs does promise God's rich blessings on people who follow inspired wise advice through life. See note on 1:10–19.
10:2,24–25,29–32 CHRISTIAN ETHICS, Righteousness—Marks of righteousness are those actions which reflect perseverance, courage, compassion, consistency, integrity, peace, joy, and a sense of what is appropriate. The rewards are the respect of your neighbor and the care of God.
10:4 CHRISTIAN ETHICS, Property Rights—Gaining wealth should not become an end in itself. This effort does not provide the godly person reason to be lazy and not work. Wisdom leads to work by which we reap material security. See note on 8:10–21.
10:5 HUMANITY, Work—Wisdom teaches us work is important, but it calls us to use wise judgment in our work. It is most important to work when we can anticipate gaining the greatest results.
10:9 CHRISTIAN ETHICS, Character—One with integrity of purpose and character will live a life of openness before God and others. Those without such integrity must constantly work at keeping up a front wondering when they will be caught in their own trap of lies.
10:12 CHRISTIAN ETHICS, Character—The work of love is to bring smoothness to relationships. Such love does not gloss over difficulties; rather, it provides the energy needed to bring the sometimes difficult results of forgiveness and reconciliation.
10:13 HUMANITY, Intellectual Nature—People are expected to develop their wisdom to their highest potential. Those who fail to do so can expect to suffer the consequences of their own folly.

but a rod is for the back of him who
lacks judgment.[l]

14Wise men store up knowledge,[m]
but the mouth of a fool invites
ruin.[n]

15The wealth of the rich is their fortified
city,[o]
but poverty is the ruin of the poor.[p]

16The wages of the righteous bring them
life,[q]
but the income of the wicked brings
them punishment.[r]

17He who heeds discipline shows the
way to life,[s]
but whoever ignores correction
leads others astray.

18He who conceals his hatred has lying
lips,[t]
and whoever spreads slander is a
fool.

19When words are many, sin is not
absent,
but he who holds his tongue is
wise.[u]

20The tongue of the righteous is choice
silver,
but the heart of the wicked is of
little value.

21The lips of the righteous nourish
many,
but fools die for lack of judgment.[v]

22The blessing of the LORD[w] brings
wealth,[x]
and he adds no trouble to it.[y]

23A fool finds pleasure in evil conduct,[z]
but a man of understanding delights
in wisdom.

24What the wicked dreads[a] will
overtake him;[b]
what the righteous desire will be
granted.[c]

25When the storm has swept by, the
wicked are gone,
but the righteous stand firm[d]
forever.[e]

10:13 [l]S Dt 25:2; Pr 14:3; 26:3
10:14 [m]Pr 11:13; 12:23 [n]S ver 6; S Ps 59:12; S Pr 14:3; 18:6,7; S Mt 12:37
10:15 [o]Pr 18:11 [p]Pr 19:7
10:16 [q]S Dt 30:15 [r]Pr 11:18-19; 15:6; S Ro 6:23
10:17 [s]Pr 6:23; 15:5
10:18 [t]S Ps 31:18
10:19 [u]S Job 1:22; S 6:24; Pr 17:28; S 20:25; 21:23; Jas 1:19; 3:2-12
10:21 [v]Pr 5:22-23; Isa 5:13; Jer 5:4; Hos 4:1,6,14
10:22 [w]S Ps 128:2 [x]S Ge 13:2; S 49:25; S Dt 8:18 [y]S 2Ch 25:9
10:23 [z]S Pr 2:14
10:24 [a]Isa 65:7; 66:4 [b]S Ge 42:36 [c]S Ps 37:4; 145:17-19; Eze 11:8
10:25 [d]S Ps 20:8 [e]Pr 12:3,7; Mt 7:24-27
10:26 [f]Isa 65:5 [g]Pr 13:17; 25:13; 26:6
10:27 [h]S ver 11; Dt 11:9; Pr 9:10-11; 19:23; 22:4 [i]S Job 15:32
10:28 [j]Est 7:10; S Job 8:13; Ps 112:10; Pr 11:7
10:29 [k]Pr 21:15; Hos 14:9
10:30 [l]Ps 37:9, 28-29; S Pr 2:20-22
10:31 [m]S ver 13; S Pr 15:2; 31:26 [n]S Ps 52:4
10:32 [o]Ecc 10:12 [p]S Ps 59:7
11:1 [q]S Lev 19:36; Dt 25:13-16; S Job 6:2; Pr 20:10, 23 [r]Pr 16:11; Eze 45:10
11:2 [s]Pr 16:18 [t]Pr 18:12; 29:23
11:3 [u]ver 5; Pr 13:6
11:4 [v]Eze 27:27 [w]S Job 20:20; S Eze 7:19 [x]S Pr 10:2
11:5 [y]S 1Ki 8:36

26As vinegar to the teeth and smoke[f] to
the eyes,
so is a sluggard to those who send
him.[g]

27The fear of the LORD adds length to
life,[h]
but the years of the wicked are cut
short.[i]

28The prospect of the righteous is joy,
but the hopes of the wicked come to
nothing.[j]

29The way of the LORD is a refuge for the
righteous,
but it is the ruin of those who do
evil.[k]

30The righteous will never be uprooted,
but the wicked will not remain in
the land.[l]

31The mouth of the righteous brings
forth wisdom,[m]
but a perverse tongue[n] will be cut
out.

32The lips of the righteous know what is
fitting,[o]
but the mouth of the wicked only
what is perverse.[p]

Chapter 11

THE LORD abhors dishonest scales,[q]
but accurate weights are his
delight.[r]

2When pride comes, then comes
disgrace,[s]
but with humility comes wisdom.[t]

3The integrity of the upright guides
them,
but the unfaithful are destroyed by
their duplicity.[u]

4Wealth[v] is worthless in the day of
wrath,[w]
but righteousness delivers from
death.[x]

5The righteousness of the blameless
makes a straight way[y] for
them,

10:28 SALVATION, Joy—Those who are in fellowship with God can look forward to joy, but those not in a right relationship with Him can look forward to nothing (Ps 1:6).

11:1 REVELATION, God's Nature—God's laws reveal not only what people should do but also who God is. Laws against unjust business practices (Dt 25:13–16) reveal the righteousness of the God behind the laws. Proverbial sayings can teach law in a memorable way that may have more effect than formal laws.

11:1 CHRISTIAN ETHICS, Property Rights—Dishonesty is the opposite of the character traits God calls for and honors: justice, mercy, loving-kindness, righteousness. If we use dishonesty to supply material needs, we need to ask God for wisdom to put life back in perspective. See note on 10:4.

11:4,16,18,28 CHRISTIAN ETHICS, Property Rights—Wealth is not the final good; it carries potentially devastating power for character. It cannot satisfy the claim for righteousness demanded by God and fulfilled only through a faith relationship with Him. Wealth cannot purchase respect and good relationships in this life. Neither can it provide safety from God's judgment. Even in this life a good salary does not purchase life's truly basic needs.

11:5–11,18,21,23,28,30–31 CHRISTIAN ETHICS, Righteousness—Two groups of people comprise every society—the righteous and the wicked. The righteous are in right standing with God, standing in God's way of life, experiencing God's deliverance and society's admiration. The wicked oppose God and His ways depending rather on human guile,

but the wicked are brought down by
their own wickedness.[z]

6The righteousness of the upright
delivers them,
but the unfaithful are trapped by evil
desires.[a]

7When a wicked man dies, his hope
perishes;[b]
all he expected from his power
comes to nothing.[c]

8The righteous man is rescued from
trouble,
and it comes on the wicked
instead.[d]

9With his mouth the godless destroys
his neighbor,
but through knowledge the
righteous escape.[e]

10When the righteous prosper, the city
rejoices;[f]
when the wicked perish, there are
shouts of joy.[g]

11Through the blessing of the upright a
city is exalted,[h]
but by the mouth of the wicked it is
destroyed.[i]

12A man who lacks judgment derides his
neighbor,[j]
but a man of understanding holds
his tongue.[k]

13A gossip betrays a confidence,[l]
but a trustworthy man keeps a
secret.[m]

14For lack of guidance a nation falls,[n]
but many advisers make victory
sure.[o]

15He who puts up security[p] for another
will surely suffer,
but whoever refuses to strike hands
in pledge is safe.[q]

16A kindhearted woman gains respect,[r]
but ruthless men gain only wealth.

17A kind man benefits himself,
but a cruel man brings trouble on
himself.

18The wicked man earns deceptive
wages,
but he who sows righteousness
reaps a sure reward.[s]

19The truly righteous man attains life,[t]
but he who pursues evil goes to his
death.[u]

20The LORD detests men of perverse
heart[v]
but he delights[w] in those whose
ways are blameless.[x]

21Be sure of this: The wicked will not go
unpunished,
but those who are righteous will go
free.[y]

22Like a gold ring in a pig's snout
is a beautiful woman who shows no
discretion.

23The desire of the righteous ends only
in good,
but the hope of the wicked only in
wrath.

24One man gives freely, yet gains even
more;
another withholds unduly, but
comes to poverty.

25A generous[z] man will prosper;
he who refreshes others will himself
be refreshed.[a]

26People curse the man who hoards
grain,
but blessing crowns him who is
willing to sell.

27He who seeks good finds goodwill,
but evil comes to him who searches
for it.[b]

28Whoever trusts in his riches will fall,[c]
but the righteous will thrive like a
green leaf.[d]

29He who brings trouble on his family
will inherit only wind,
and the fool will be servant to the
wise.[e]

30The fruit of the righteous is a tree of
life,[f]
and he who wins souls is wise.

31If the righteous receive their due[g] on
earth,

11:5 [z]S ver 3; Pr 5:21-23; 13:6; 21:7
11:6 [a]S Est 7:9
11:7 [b]S Job 8:13 [c]S Pr 10:28
11:8 [d]Pr 21:18
11:9 [e]Pr 12:6; Jer 45:5
11:10 [f]S 2Ki 11:20 [g]S Est 8:17
11:11 [h]Pr 14:34 [i]Pr 29:8
11:12 [j]Pr 14:21 [k]S Job 6:24
11:13 [l]Pr 20:19 [m]S Pr 10:14
11:14 [n]Pr 20:18 [o]S 2Sa 15:34; Pr 15:22; 24:6
11:15 [p]S Pr 6:1 [q]Pr 17:18; 22:26-27
11:16 [r]Pr 31:31
11:18 [s]S Ex 1:20; S Job 4:8; Hos 10:12-13
11:19 [t]S Dt 30:15; S Pr 10:2 [u]1Sa 2:6; Ps 89:48; Pr 1:18-19; Ecc 7:2; Jer 43:11
11:20 [v]Pr 3:32 [w]S Nu 14:8 [x]S 1Ch 29:17; S Ps 15:2; 101:1-4; S 119:1; Pr 12:2, 22; 15:9
11:21 [y]Pr 16:5
11:25 [z]1Ch 29:17; Isa 32:8 [a]Pr 22:9; 2Co 9:6-9
11:27 [b]Ps 7:15-16
11:28 [c]Job 31:24-28; S Ps 49:6; S 52:7; 62:10; Jer 9:23; 48:7 [d]Ps 52:8; 92:12-14
11:29 [e]Pr 14:19
11:30 [f]S Ge 2:9; S Pr 10:11
11:31 [g]Jer 25:29; 49:12; 1Pe 4:18

---

desires, and wealth. Life awaits the righteous; judgment awaits the wicked. Such categorization is not a simplistic blindness to the evil in the best of us or to the good in the worst of us. It is a recognition that relationship to God is the basic ethical category. See note on 10:2,24–25,29–32.

11:7 HUMANITY, Nature of Death—Worldly power, prestige, and authority are often the goals of people without God. All people are mortal. We die. We may have achieved part of our goals, but we cannot then enjoy them. Death brings an end to all human, earthly hopes. Only hope built on Christ endures.

11:11–13 CHRISTIAN ETHICS, Language—Loose treatment of the power of words can erode friendships or even lead to the destruction of a nation. Learn the secret of silence.

11:19 HUMANITY, Death and Sin—From a physical perspective death is the normal end of human life. See notes on Ge 15:15; Jos 23:14. Theologically explained, death is the consequence of sinful rebellion. True life comes from doing what God has shown to be right. See notes on Ge 2:17; Lev 10:1–2.

11:24–25 STEWARDSHIP, Rewards—See notes on 3:9–10; Lk 6:38.

how much more the ungodly and
the sinner!

Chapter 12

WHOEVER loves discipline loves
knowledge,
but he who hates correction is
stupid.[h]
2A good man obtains favor from the
LORD,[i]
but the LORD condemns a crafty
man.[j]
3A man cannot be established through
wickedness,
but the righteous cannot be
uprooted.[k]
4A wife of noble character[l] is her
husband's crown,
but a disgraceful wife is like decay in
his bones.[m]
5The plans of the righteous are just,
but the advice of the wicked is
deceitful.
6The words of the wicked lie in wait for
blood,
but the speech of the upright
rescues them.[n]
7Wicked men are overthrown and are
no more,[o]
but the house of the righteous
stands firm.[p]
8A man is praised according to his
wisdom,
but men with warped[q] minds are
despised.
9Better to be a nobody and yet have a
servant
than pretend to be somebody and
have no food.
10A righteous man cares for the needs of
his animal,[r]
but the kindest acts of the wicked
are cruel.
11He who works his land will have
abundant food,
but he who chases fantasies lacks
judgment.[s]
12The wicked desire the plunder of evil
men,
but the root of the righteous
flourishes.
13An evil man is trapped by his sinful
talk,[t]
but a righteous man escapes
trouble.[u]
14From the fruit of his lips a man is filled
with good things[v]
as surely as the work of his hands
rewards him.[w]
15The way of a fool seems right to him,[x]
but a wise man listens to advice.[y]
16A fool[z] shows his annoyance at
once,[a]
but a prudent man overlooks an
insult.[b]
17A truthful witness gives honest
testimony,
but a false witness tells lies.[c]
18Reckless words pierce like a sword,[d]
but the tongue of the wise brings
healing.[e]
19Truthful lips endure forever,
but a lying tongue lasts only a
moment.
20There is deceit in the hearts of those
who plot evil,
but joy for those who promote
peace.[f]
21No harm befalls the righteous,[g]
but the wicked have their fill of
trouble.

12:1 [h]Pr 5:11-14; S 9:7-9; 13:1,18; 15:5,10,12,32
12:2 [i]S Job 33:26; Ps 84:11 [j]2Sa 15:3; S Pr 11:20
12:3 [k]S Pr 10:25
12:4 [l]S Ru 3:11; Pr 31:10-11 [m]Pr 18:22
12:6 [n]S Pr 11:9; 14:3
12:7 [o]S Ps 37:36 [p]S Pr 10:25; 14:11; 15:25
12:8 [q]Isa 19:14; 29:24
12:10 [r]S Nu 22:29
12:11 [s]Pr 28:19
12:13 [t]S Ps 59:12; S Pr 10:6; 18:7 [u]Pr 21:23
12:14 [v]Pr 13:2; 15:23; 18:20 [w]Pr 14:14
12:15 [x]Pr 14:12; 16:2,25 [y]S Pr 9:7-9; 19:20
12:16 [z]S 1Sa 25:25 [a]S Job 5:2 [b]Pr 29:11
12:17 [c]S Ps 12:2; Pr 14:5,25
12:18 [d]S Ps 55:21; Pr 25:18 [e]Pr 15:4
12:20 [f]S Ro 14:19
12:21 [g]S Job 4:7

12:1 FAMILY, Education—Parents must discipline children for the children to have a chance in life. Without discipline and correction we never learn. Many verses in Proverbs stress the value of discipline in child guidance and point out the foolishness of resisting discipline. Some representative passages are: 13:1,24; 19:18; 22:15; 23:13–14; 29:15,17.
12:2,22 REVELATION, God's Nature—Pithy statements which summarize the nature and will of God appear throughout the book. Goodness is a moral attribute, reflecting who we should be because our Maker is so. Deception and falsehood are foreign enough to Him that He must reject them. He deeply enjoys truth in His own people. See note on 11:1.
12:3,5,7,10,21,28 CHRISTIAN ETHICS, Righteousness—See notes on 10:2,24–25,29–32; 11:5–11,18,21, 23,28,30–31. Cruelty characterizes the wicked; kindness characterizes the righteous.
12:4 FAMILY, Role Relationships—Strong contrasts are made in Proverbs between wives who are acceptable in their behavior and those who are not. The good wife is valued as a gift from the Lord (18:22; 19:14), but the bad wife is generally a quarrelsome one (19:13; 21:9,19; 25:24; 27:15–17). The good wife is respected by her husband and brings honor to his name (31:23). Only a relationship of trust and commitment from both parties can lead to the respect and honor needed for family success.
12:11 HUMANITY, Work—Consistent work, not idle dreaming of things past or future, brings necessary provisions for life. Planning is essential, but the majority of time must be dedicated to work which achieves the plans.
12:13–24 CHRISTIAN ETHICS, Language—Words can hurt or heal. Wise use of the power of words leads one to know the importance of timing, both knowing when to speak and when to listen. Language backed by the integrity of the speaker builds confidence and leaves lasting results.
12:15–16 CHRISTIAN ETHICS, Character—Persons of integrity are marked by patience, slowness to anger, and humility. They are teachable.
12:20 CHRISTIAN ETHICS, War and Peace—Contrasting the intent, loyalties, and actions of persons distinguishes peace lovers from peace despisers.

22The LORD detests lying lips,[h]
but he delights[i] in men who are truthful.[j]

23A prudent man keeps his knowledge to himself,[k]
but the heart of fools blurts out folly.[l]

24Diligent hands will rule,
but laziness ends in slave labor.[m]

25An anxious heart weighs a man down,[n]
but a kind word cheers him up.

26A righteous man is cautious in friendship,[v]
but the way of the wicked leads them astray.[o]

27The lazy man does not roast[w] his game,
but the diligent man prizes his possessions.

28In the way of righteousness there is life;[p]
along that path is immortality.

Chapter 13

A wise son heeds his father's instruction,
but a mocker does not listen to rebuke.[q]

2From the fruit of his lips a man enjoys good things,[r]
but the unfaithful have a craving for violence.

3He who guards his lips[s] guards his life,[t]
but he who speaks rashly will come to ruin.[u]

4The sluggard craves and gets nothing,[v]
but the desires of the diligent are fully satisfied.

5The righteous hate what is false,[w]
but the wicked bring shame and disgrace.

6Righteousness guards the man of integrity,
but wickedness overthrows the sinner.[x]

7One man pretends to be rich, yet has nothing;[y]
another pretends to be poor, yet has great wealth.[z]

8A man's riches may ransom his life,
but a poor man hears no threat.[a]

9The light of the righteous shines brightly,
but the lamp of the wicked is snuffed out.[b]

10Pride only breeds quarrels,
but wisdom is found in those who take advice.[c]

11Dishonest money dwindles away,[d]
but he who gathers money little by little makes it grow.

12Hope deferred makes the heart sick,
but a longing fulfilled is a tree of life.[e]

13He who scorns instruction will pay for it,[f]
but he who respects[g] a command is rewarded.[h]

14The teaching of the wise is a fountain of life,[i]

12:22 [h]1Ki 13:18; Pr 6:17 [i]Ps 18:19 [j]S Pr 11:20
12:23 [k]S Pr 10:14 [l]S Ps 38:5; S 59:7; Pr 18:2
12:24 [m]S Pr 10:4
12:25 [n]Pr 15:13
12:26 [o]S Ps 95:10
12:28 [p]S Dt 30:15; S Pr 10:2
13:1 [q]S Pr 12:1; 15:5
13:2 [r]S Pr 12:14
13:3 [s]S Ps 12:2; S 34:13 [t]S Pr 10:6; 21:23 [u]S Job 1:22; Pr 18:7,20-21
13:4 [v]Pr 21:25-26
13:5 [w]S Ps 119:128
13:6 [x]S Pr 11:3,5; Jer 44:5
13:7 [y]Rev 3:17 [z]2Co 6:10
13:8 [a]Pr 15:16
13:9 [b]S Job 18:5; S Pr 4:18-19
13:10 [c]S Jdg 19:30; S Pr 9:9
13:11 [d]S Pr 10:2
13:12 [e]S Pr 10:11
13:13 [f]S Nu 15:31 [g]Ex 9:20 [h]Pr 16:20
13:14 [i]S Pr 10:11

[v]26 Or *man is a guide to his neighbor* [w]27 The meaning of the Hebrew for this word is uncertain.

12:23 HUMANITY, Human Nature—Wisdom is self-evident and does not have to be advertised. People with little wisdom and much foolishness tend to talk more than the wise.
12:24 HUMANITY, Work—Those who work hard have an opportunity to achieve, while people who are lazy are most likely to lose even that which they have, including freedom itself.
12:26 HUMANITY, Relationships—Those who are in a right relationship with God are careful in the human relationships which they establish. Wrong human relationships can lead us away from God.
12:27 HUMANITY, Work—We prize possessions for which we have worked because of the labor invested in them. However, patience must be exercised to achieve greater accomplishments. Long-term goals should not be sacrificed for short-term gain.
12:28 HUMANITY, Death—No Old Testament word exists for immortality. The Hebrew expression is literally "not death." Sin brings death, and righteousness is the way of "not death."
13:2–3 CHRISTIAN ETHICS, Language—See note on 12:13–24.
13:4 HUMANITY, Work—Desire, no matter how intense, will lead nowhere until people are willing to work for what they desire.
13:5–6 CHRISTIAN ETHICS, Righteousness—See note on 10:2,24–25,29–32.
13:8 CHRISTIAN ETHICS, Property Rights—Wealth may pay the ransom when greedy persons threaten us. Righteous people without wealth do not have to endure such threats. What has wealth really purchased?
13:9 HUMANITY, Death and Sin—Light, which the eyes see while people are living, is gone when death comes. Death follows upon sin. See note on 11:19.
13:10 HUMANITY, Relationships—A wise person recognizes areas of personal ignorance and is willing to learn from others in such places. Pride robs us of the riches of others' knowledge, leading only to fights between friends.
13:14 EDUCATION, Law—"Teaching" (Hebrew *torah*) originally denoted religious instruction in general (see "teaching" in 3:1; 4:2) but later referred especially to the Law as it appears in the first five books of the Old Testament. See note on Ex 24:12. *Torah* denotes both the process and the content of instruction based on the Word of God. Therefore, the teaching activity of the wise cannot be separated from the substance of their teachings. Wise teaching provides a source of life and well-being to those who will listen. For this reason *Torah*, instruction in God's life-giving Word, will be an important aspect of the Messianic Age. See note on Isa 2:3.

turning a man from the snares of
death.[j]
15Good understanding wins favor,
but the way of the unfaithful is
hard.[x]
16Every prudent man acts out of
knowledge,
but a fool exposes[k] his folly.[l]
17A wicked messenger falls into
trouble,[m]
but a trustworthy envoy brings
healing.[n]
18He who ignores discipline comes to
poverty and shame,[o]
but whoever heeds correction is
honored.[p]
19A longing fulfilled is sweet to the
soul,[q]
but fools detest turning from evil.
20He who walks with the wise grows
wise,
but a companion of fools suffers
harm.[r]
21Misfortune pursues the sinner,[s]
but prosperity[t] is the reward of the
righteous.[u]
22A good man leaves an inheritance for
his children's children,
but a sinner's wealth is stored up for
the righteous.[v]
23A poor man's field may produce
abundant food,
but injustice sweeps it away.
24He who spares the rod[w] hates his son,
but he who loves him is careful to
discipline[x] him.[y]
25The righteous eat to their hearts'
content,
but the stomach of the wicked goes
hungry.[z]

Chapter 14

THE wise woman builds her house,[a]
but with her own hands the foolish
one tears hers down.
2He whose walk is upright fears the
LORD,
but he whose ways are devious
despises him.
3A fool's talk brings a rod to his back,[b]
but the lips of the wise protect
them.[c]
4Where there are no oxen, the manger
is empty,
but from the strength of an ox[d]
comes an abundant harvest.
5A truthful witness does not deceive,
but a false witness pours out lies.[e]
6The mocker seeks wisdom and finds
none,
but knowledge comes easily to the
discerning.[f]
7Stay away from a foolish man,
for you will not find knowledge on
his lips.
8The wisdom of the prudent is to give
thought to their ways,[g]
but the folly of fools is deception.[h]
9Fools mock at making amends for sin,
but goodwill is found among the
upright.
10Each heart knows its own bitterness,
and no one else can share its joy.
11The house of the wicked will be
destroyed,[i]
but the tent of the upright will
flourish.[j]
12There is a way that seems right to a
man,[k]
but in the end it leads to death.[l]
13Even in laughter[m] the heart may ache,
and joy may end in grief.
14The faithless will be fully repaid for
their ways,[n]
and the good man rewarded for
his.[o]
15A simple man believes anything,

13:14 [j]Pr 14:27
13:16 [k]Ecc 10:3 [l]Est 5:11; S Ps 38:5
13:17 [m]S Pr 10:26 [n]Pr 25:13
13:18 [o]S Pr 1:7; S 12:1 [p]Ps 141:5; Pr 25:12; Ecc 7:5
13:19 [q]S Pr 10:11
13:20 [r]2Ch 10:8
13:21 [s]2Sa 3:39; Jer 40:3; 50:7; Eze 14:13; 18:4 [t]Ps 25:13 [u]Ps 32:10
13:22 [v]S Est 8:2; S Job 27:17; Ecc 2:26
13:24 [w]S 2Sa 7:14 [x]S Pr 3:12 [y]Pr 19:18; 22:15; 23:13-14; 29:15, 17; Eph 6:4; Heb 12:7
13:25 [z]Pr 10:3
14:1 [a]S Ru 3:11; Pr 24:3
14:3 [b]S Pr 10:14; Ecc 10:12 [c]S Pr 10:13; S 12:6
14:4 [d]Ps 144:14
14:5 [e]S Ps 12:2; S Pr 12:17
14:6 [f]S Pr 9:9
14:8 [g]ver 15; Pr 15:28; 21:29 [h]ver 24
14:11 [i]S Job 8:22; Pr 21:12 [j]S Ps 72:7; S Pr 3:33; S 12:7
14:12 [k]S Pr 12:15 [l]Pr 16:25
14:13 [m]Ecc 2:2; 7:3,6
14:14 [n]S Pr 1:31 [o]S 2Ch 15:7; Pr 12:14

[x]15 Or *unfaithful does not endure*

13:20 EDUCATION, Example—We learn a great deal, both good and bad, by imitating the behavior of others. This educational principle, widely recognized by contemporary psychologists, is mentioned repeatedly in Proverbs. See 4:14; 16:29; 23:20; note on 22:24–25.

14:1 HUMANITY, Work—Wisdom put into action leads people to choose constructive ways of living and working. Foolishness self-destructs.

14:4 HUMANITY, Relationship to Nature—The proper use of the natural resources of the world offers the opportunity for prosperity for all.

14:8 HUMANITY, Intellectual Nature—Those seeking to develop their wisdom and knowledge are willing to be open to the examination of themselves and others. This is the way of intellectual stimulation and growth.

14:11,19,32,34 CHRISTIAN ETHICS, Righteousness—Righteousness is more than an individual characteristic. It is a necessity for nations to survive. See note on 10:2, 24–25,29–32.

14:12 HUMANITY, Human Nature—Unaided human nature leads people to make wrong choices leading ultimately to death. The untrained conscience cannot be a trusted guide.

14:15 HUMANITY, Intellectual Nature—God has given people minds with the expectation that we will use them to evaluate everything we hear and see. We must decide for ourselves, not simply accept another's opinion blindly regardless of the position or education of the other person.

but a prudent man gives thought to
his steps.[p]

16A wise man fears the LORD and shuns
evil,[q]
but a fool[r] is hotheaded and
reckless.

17A quick-tempered[s] man does foolish
things,[t]
and a crafty man is hated.[u]

18The simple inherit folly,
but the prudent are crowned with
knowledge.

19Evil men will bow down in the
presence of the good,
and the wicked at the gates of the
righteous.[v]

20The poor are shunned even by their
neighbors,
but the rich have many friends.[w]

21He who despises his neighbor sins,[x]
but blessed is he who is kind to the
needy.[y]

22Do not those who plot evil go astray?[z]
But those who plan what is good
find[y] love and faithfulness.

23All hard work brings a profit,
but mere talk leads only to poverty.

24The wealth of the wise is their crown,
but the folly of fools yields folly.[a]

25A truthful witness saves lives,
but a false witness is deceitful.[b]

26He who fears the LORD has a secure
fortress,[c]
and for his children it will be a
refuge.[d]

27The fear of the LORD is a fountain of
life,[e]
turning a man from the snares of
death.[f]

28A large population is a king's glory,
but without subjects a prince is
ruined.[g]

29A patient man has great
understanding,[h]
but a quick-tempered man displays
folly.[i]

30A heart at peace gives life to the body,
but envy rots the bones.[j]

31He who oppresses the poor shows
contempt for their Maker,[k]
but whoever is kind to the needy
honors God.[l]

32When calamity comes, the wicked are
brought down,[m]
but even in death the righteous have
a refuge.[n]

33Wisdom reposes in the heart of the
discerning[o]
and even among fools she lets
herself be known.[z]

34Righteousness exalts a nation,[p]
but sin is a disgrace to any people.

35A king delights in a wise servant,
but a shameful servant incurs his
wrath.[q]

Chapter 15

A gentle answer[r] turns away wrath,[s]
but a harsh word stirs up anger.

[y]22 Or *show* [z]33 Hebrew; Septuagint and Syriac / *but in the heart of fools she is not known*

14:15 [p]S ver 8
14:16 [q]S Ex 20:20; Pr 22:3 [r]S 1Sa 25:25
14:17 [s]S 2Ki 5:12 [t]ver 29; Pr 15:18; 16:28; 26:21; 28:25; 29:22 [u]S Est 5:9
14:19 [v]Pr 11:29
14:20 [w]Pr 19:4,7
14:21 [x]Pr 11:12 [y]Pr 19:17
14:22 [z]Pr 4:16-17
14:24 [a]ver 8
14:25 [b]S Pr 12:17
14:26 [c]Pr 18:10 [d]Ps 9:9
14:27 [e]S Pr 10:11 [f]Ps 18:5; Pr 13:14
14:28 [g]S 2Sa 19:7
14:29 [h]S 2Ki 5:12; Pr 17:27 [i]S ver 17; Ecc 7:8-9
14:30 [j]Pr 17:22
14:31 [k]Pr 17:5 [l]S Dt 24:14; S Job 20:19; S Mt 10:42
14:32 [m]S Ps 34:21; S Pr 6:15 [n]S Job 13:15
14:33 [o]Pr 2:6-10
14:34 [p]Pr 11:11
14:35 [q]S Est 8:2; Mt 24:45-51; 25:14-30
15:1 [r]1Ki 12:7; 2Ch 10:7 [s]Pr 25:15

14:23 HUMANITY, Work—Work does not necessarily produce financial profit immediately, but usually pays off in the long run. Empty words unaccompanied by work never produce profit of any kind.
14:23 CHRISTIAN ETHICS, Language—Talk, no matter how spiritual its application, must be backed by action. Words without work lead to the spiritual poorhouse. See notes on Jas 1:26; 3:1–12.
14:27 HUMANITY, Spiritual Nature—The life based upon the proper attitude to and revelation from God is like a fresh spring with its life-giving qualities. See note on Ps 111:10.
14:27 REVELATION, Commitment—Revelation through wisdom literature seeks to lead people to give utmost respect to God. Fear is a quality associated in the Old Testament with three characteristics: awe, high regard, and deep respect, all of which inspire the follower to drink deeply from the Source of life. Compare 1:7.
14:29–31 CHRISTIAN ETHICS, Character—Character traits affect our physical health as well as our relationships with God and man. Quick temper, envy, and oppression are foolish traits to cultivate. Patience is the opposite of quick temper. Peaceful hearts do not envy others, and kindness leaves no room for envy.
14:31 GOD, Grace—Our loving response to persons in need pleases and honors God because He has shown Himself to be a God of grace and love, greatly concerned for persons who are needy and in distress.
14:31 CREATION, Good—Poverty and human suffering are not adequate reasons for doubting the goodness of creation or the Creator. Human injustice is one major source of poverty. The Creator constantly shows concern and compassion for the poor. Compare 17:5.
14:32 SALVATION, As Refuge—The righteous have God as their refuge even in death. This advanced view of the afterlife previews the New Testament meaning of salvation as eternal life. Compare 15:24.
14:33 HUMANITY, Intellectual Nature—Even a person who is a fool can have access to the wisdom of God. God does not have secret knowledge He wants to give only a few.
15:1–2 CHRISTIAN ETHICS, Language—Language communicates our emotions and our intellect. In so doing it attracts or repels people. See note on 12:13–24.
15:1,4,23 FAMILY, Communication—Good communication is at the heart of good human relationships. This is especially true of family relationships. These verses celebrate gentleness, encouragement, and appropriateness in verbal communication. Pr 18:2,13,17 point out common communication faults that cause tension in personal relationships. Honesty in speech (24:26) is contrasted with using humor that hurts (26:18–19). Open confrontation is described as better than refusal to care enough to face issues (27:5). The inspired writer recognized nonverbal communication in showing

[2]The tongue of the wise commends
knowledge,[t]
but the mouth of the fool gushes
folly.[u]

[3]The eyes[v] of the LORD are
everywhere,[w]
keeping watch on the wicked and
the good.[x]

[4]The tongue[y] that brings healing is a
tree of life,[z]
but a deceitful tongue crushes the
spirit.[a]

[5]A fool spurns his father's discipline,
but whoever heeds correction shows
prudence.[b]

[6]The house of the righteous contains
great treasure,[c]
but the income of the wicked brings
them trouble.[d]

[7]The lips of the wise spread
knowledge;[e]
not so the hearts of fools.

[8]The LORD detests the sacrifice[f] of the
wicked,[g]
but the prayer of the upright pleases
him.[h]

[9]The LORD detests the way of the
wicked[i]
but he loves those who pursue
righteousness.[j]

[10]Stern discipline awaits him who leaves
the path;
he who hates correction will die.[k]

[11]Death and Destruction[a] lie open
before the LORD[l] —
how much more the hearts of
men![m]

[12]A mocker resents correction;[n]
he will not consult the wise.

[13]A happy heart makes the face
cheerful,[o]
but heartache crushes the spirit.[p]

[14]The discerning heart seeks
knowledge,[q]
but the mouth of a fool feeds on
folly.

[15]All the days of the oppressed are
wretched,
but the cheerful heart has a
continual feast.[r]

[16]Better a little with the fear of the LORD
than great wealth with turmoil.[s]

[17]Better a meal of vegetables where
there is love
than a fattened calf with hatred.[t]

[18]A hot-tempered man stirs up
dissension,[u]
but a patient man calms a quarrel.[v]

[19]The way of the sluggard is blocked
with thorns,[w]
but the path of the upright is a
highway.

[20]A wise son brings joy to his father,[x]
but a foolish man despises his
mother.

[21]Folly delights a man who lacks
judgment,[y]
but a man of understanding keeps a
straight course.

[22]Plans fail for lack of counsel,[z]
but with many advisers[a] they
succeed.[b]

[23]A man finds joy in giving an apt
reply[c] —
and how good is a timely word![d]

[24]The path of life leads upward for the
wise

15:2 [t]ver 7; S Pr 10:31 [u]S Ps 59:7; Ecc 10:12
15:3 [v]S 2Ch 16:9 [w]S Job 10:4; S 31:4; S Heb 4:13 [x]S Job 34:21; Pr 5:21; Jer 16:17
15:4 [y]S Ps 5:9 [z]S Pr 10:11 [a]Pr 12:18
15:5 [b]S Pr 10:17; S 12:1; S 13:1
15:6 [c]S Pr 8:21 [d]S Pr 10:16
15:7 [e]S ver 2; S Pr 10:13
15:8 [f]S Ps 51:17; S Isa 1:13 [g]S Pr 6:16; 21:27 [h]ver 29; Job 35:13; Pr 28:9; S Jn 9:31
15:9 [i]S Pr 6:16 [j]S Dt 7:13; S Pr 11:20
15:10 [k]S Pr 1:31-32; S 12:1
15:11 [l]S Job 26:6 [m]S 1Sa 2:3; S 2Ch 6:30; S Ps 44:21; S Rev 2:23
15:12 [n]S Pr 9:8; S 12:1
15:13 [o]ver 15 [p]S Pr 12:25; 17:22; 18:14
15:14 [q]Pr 18:15
15:15 [r]ver 13
15:16 [s]ver 17; Ps 37:16-17; Pr 13:8; 16:8; 17:1
15:17 [t]S ver 16; Pr 17:1; Ecc 4:6
15:18 [u]S Pr 6:16-19; S 14:17 [v]S Ge 13:8
15:19 [w]Pr 22:5
15:20 [x]S Pr 10:1
15:21 [y]S Pr 2:14
15:22 [z]S Ps 16:7 [a]1Ki 1:12; Pr 24:6 [b]S Pr 11:14
15:23 [c]S Pr 12:14 [d]Pr 25:11

[a]*11* Hebrew *Sheol and Abaddon*

feelings (16:30).
15:3,11 GOD, Wisdom—See note on 8:12–31.
15:8 PRAYER, Hindrances—Sacrifice without righteousness is meaningless. It gains no favor with God. The prayer of the righteous pleases God.
15:9 CHRISTIAN ETHICS, Righteousness—Those who choose righteousness over wickedness can be assured of the presence and protection of God.
15:14 EDUCATION, Wisdom—A hunger for knowledge is the mark of a wise person. Wisdom makes us understand our need for learning. The fool is a "know-it-all," self-satisfied in ignorance. See 12:1.
15:15 HUMANITY, Psychological Nature—Those who keep a sense of festival within their lives find the days more pleasant. People who dwell on their problems never know joy.
15:16–18 STEWARDSHIP, Rewards—God promises to reward His faithful servants (3:9–10), but rewards and wealth must not become our major concern in life. Possessing little and being faithful is greater than wealth without devotion to God. See Ps 37:16–17; notes on Ge 26:12–16; Lk 6:38.
15:22 HUMANITY, Relationships—Those who are willing to work with others find better accomplishments through pooled wisdom.
15:24 LAST THINGS, Believers' Resurrection—See note on Isa 14:9. Following the teaching of Proverbs and fearing God (1:7) was wise and led upward so that the person did not die. The Old Testament contains many sentences like this with tantalizing language about escaping death. How much the original inspired authors understood about life beyond death is not precisely known. Some interpreters think Isa 26:19 and Da 12:2 are the clearest statements of resurrection in the Old Testament. Others argue from Egyptian beliefs, contemporary burial customs, the tree of life (Ge 2:9), and statements like the one in this verse, 2 Sa 12:23; Job 19:25–27, and other passages, particularly in Psalms, that at least some, if not all Israelites, hoped for life beyond the grave at a very early date. Most, if not all, interpreters agree the Old Testament literature is not as clear on the doctrine as is the New. Christ's resurrection gave clear definition to the resurrection hope and invites Christian disciples to read Old Testament passages in light of Christ. Compare Pr 14:14; 23:18.

to keep him from going down to the
grave.[b]

25The LORD tears down the proud man's
house[e]
but he keeps the widow's
boundaries intact.[f]

26The LORD detests the thoughts[g] of the
wicked,[h]
but those of the pure[i] are pleasing
to him.

27A greedy man brings trouble to his
family,
but he who hates bribes will live.[j]

28The heart of the righteous weighs its
answers,[k]
but the mouth of the wicked gushes
evil.[l]

29The LORD is far from the wicked
but he hears the prayer of the
righteous.[m]

30A cheerful look brings joy to the heart,
and good news gives health to the
bones.[n]

31He who listens to a life-giving rebuke
will be at home among the wise.[o]

32He who ignores discipline despises
himself,[p]
but whoever heeds correction gains
understanding.[q]

33The fear of the LORD[r] teaches a man
wisdom,[c]
and humility comes before honor.[s]

Chapter 16

1To man belong the plans of the heart,
but from the LORD comes the reply
of the tongue.[t]

2All a man's ways seem innocent to
him,[u]
but motives are weighed[v] by the
LORD.[w]

3Commit to the LORD whatever you do,
and your plans will succeed.[x]

4The LORD works out everything for his
own ends[y] —
even the wicked for a day of
disaster.[z]

5The LORD detests all the proud of
heart.[a]
Be sure of this: They will not go
unpunished.[b]

6Through love and faithfulness sin is
atoned for;
through the fear of the LORD[c] a man
avoids evil.[d]

7When a man's ways are pleasing to the
LORD,
he makes even his enemies live at
peace[e] with him.[f]

8Better a little with righteousness
than much gain[g] with injustice.[h]

9In his heart a man plans his course,
but the LORD determines his steps.[i]

10The lips of a king speak as an oracle,
and his mouth should not betray
justice.[j]

11Honest scales and balances are from
the LORD;
all the weights in the bag are of his
making.[k]

12Kings detest wrongdoing,
for a throne is established through
righteousness.[l]

15:25 [e]S Pr 12:7 [f]S Dt 19:14; Pr 23:10-11
15:26 [g]S Ps 94:11 [h]S Pr 6:16 [i]S Ps 18:26
15:27 [j]S Ex 23:8; S Ps 15:5; Isa 1:23; 33:15
15:28 [k]S Pr 14:8 [l]S Ps 59:7
15:29 [m]S ver 8; S Job 15:31; Ps 145:18-19; Isa 59:2; S Jn 9:31
15:30 [n]Pr 25:25
15:31 [o]S Pr 9:7-9; S 12:1
15:32 [p]S Pr 1:7; S 12:1 [q]S Pr 9:7-9; S 12:1; Ecc 7:5
15:33 [r]S Pr 1:7 [s]Pr 16:18; 18:12; 22:4; 29:23; Isa 66:2
16:1 [t]ver 9; Pr 19:21
16:2 [u]S Pr 12:15; 30:12 [v]S 1Sa 2:3 [w]S 2Ch 6:30; Pr 20:27; 21:2; Lk 16:15
16:3 [x]S 2Ch 20:20; S Ps 20:4; 37:5-6; S Pr 3:5-6
16:4 [y]Ex 9:16 [z]S 2Ch 34:24; S Ps 18:18; Ro 9:22
16:5 [a]S Ps 40:4; S Pr 6:16 [b]Pr 11:20-21
16:6 [c]S Ge 20:11; S Ex 1:17 [d]S Ex 20:20
16:7 [e]S Ge 39:21 [f]Ps 105:15; Jer 39:12; 40:1; 42:12; Da 1:9
16:8 [g]S Ps 37:16 [h]S Pr 15:16; 17:1; Ecc 4:6
16:9 [i]S ver 1; S Job 33:29; S Ps 90:12
16:10 [j]Pr 17:7
16:11 [k]S Pr 11:1; Eze 45:10
16:12 [l]Pr 20:28; 25:5; 29:14; 31:5

[b]24 Hebrew *Sheol* [c]33 Or *Wisdom teaches the fear of the LORD*

15:25–27 REVELATION, God's Nature—By declaring what God is pleased and displeased with, the writer revealed the nature and will of God. He is a God who rejects pride, supports the weak, despises divided loyalties, and blesses the undivided heart. See note on 11:1.

15:26 HUMANITY, Relationship to God—Not only the deeds but the very thoughts of people determine their relationship with God.

15:27 CHRISTIAN ETHICS, Property Rights—Material greed has destructive implications not only for one's self but also for all other relationships. Prosperity is never more valuable than people. Duty to family reputation and needs far outweighs any responsibility to gain material goods.

15:29 PRAYER, Faithfulness of God—The wicked alienate themselves. "Hears" implies God will answer. He is faithful to His faithful people.

15:31–33 EDUCATION, Discipline—The biblical writer repeatedly emphasized the relationship between learning and the quality of "teachableness." Just as children can learn from parental discipline, so can we learn from constructive criticism all through life, if we have the humility to accept corrective advice. See 15:12.

15:33 HUMANITY, Intellectual Nature—See note on Ps 111:10.

16:1–7 REVELATION, Actions—Following God's revealed purpose is the only effective way to conduct life. We are free to choose as we will, but God takes every event and works His own will into it. No suggestion is made that He causes all events. He is active in each event to produce His own purposes. Thus God's gift of individual freedom is balanced by His fidelity to His own purposes: He will work in every situation to save and redeem in accordance with His will. The author asked: Would it not be much better if the human will were submissive to God's will and purposes from the beginning?

16:6 SALVATION, Atonement—This text teaches atonement for sin through love and faithfulness. Love (Hebrew *chesed*) is the loyal love of a covenant relationship with God. Faithfulness (Hebrew *'emeth*) is belief or trust which is reliable and continuing. The two are frequently coupled in the Old Testament. Here atonement is lifted out of the ceremonial or priestly realm and put into the moral or prophetic sphere of action (Hos 6:6). The poetic parallelism of the verse shows that atonement through love and faithfulness is the same as atonement through fearing the Lord. Right relations with God are restored through spiritual regeneration, not through physical acts. See note on Ex 20:20.

13 Kings take pleasure in honest lips;
they value a man who speaks the truth.[m]

14 A king's wrath is a messenger of death,[n]
but a wise man will appease it.[o]

15 When a king's face brightens, it means life;[p]
his favor is like a rain cloud in spring.[q]

16 How much better to get wisdom than gold,
to choose understanding[r] rather than silver![s]

17 The highway of the upright avoids evil;
he who guards his way guards his life.[t]

18 Pride[u] goes before destruction,
a haughty spirit[v] before a fall.[w]

19 Better to be lowly in spirit and among the oppressed
than to share plunder with the proud.

20 Whoever gives heed to instruction prospers,[x]
and blessed is he who trusts in the LORD.[y]

21 The wise in heart are called discerning,
and pleasant words promote instruction.[d] [z]

22 Understanding is a fountain of life to those who have it,[a]
but folly brings punishment to fools.

23 A wise man's heart guides his mouth,[b]
and his lips promote instruction.[e] [c]

24 Pleasant words are a honeycomb,[d]
sweet to the soul and healing to the bones.[e]

25 There is a way that seems right to a man,[f]
but in the end it leads to death.[g]

26 The laborer's appetite works for him;
his hunger drives him on.

27 A scoundrel[h] plots evil,
and his speech is like a scorching fire.[i]

28 A perverse man stirs up dissension,[j]
and a gossip separates close friends.[k]

29 A violent man entices his neighbor
and leads him down a path that is not good.[l]

30 He who winks[m] with his eye is plotting perversity;
he who purses his lips is bent on evil.

31 Gray hair is a crown of splendor;[n]
it is attained by a righteous life.

32 Better a patient man than a warrior,
a man who controls his temper than one who takes a city.

33 The lot is cast[o] into the lap,
but its every decision[p] is from the LORD.[q]

Chapter 17

BETTER a dry crust with peace and quiet
than a house full of feasting,[f] with strife.[r]

2 A wise servant will rule over a disgraceful son,
and will share the inheritance as one of the brothers.

3 The crucible for silver and the furnace for gold,[s]
but the LORD tests the heart.[t]

4 A wicked man listens to evil lips;
a liar pays attention to a malicious tongue.

5 He who mocks the poor[u] shows contempt for their Maker;[v]
whoever gloats over disaster[w] will not go unpunished.[x]

16:13 [m]Pr 22:11
16:14 [n]S Ge 40:2; S Job 29:24; Pr 20:2 [o]Pr 25:15; 29:8; Ecc 10:4
16:15 [p]S Ge 40:2; S Job 29:24 [q]Pr 19:12; 25:2-7
16:16 [r]Ps 49:20 [s]S Job 28:15; S Pr 3:13-14
16:17 [t]Pr 19:16
16:18 [u]S 1Sa 17:42 [v]Ps 18:27; Isa 13:11; Jer 48:29 [w]S Est 5:12; Pr 11:2; S 15:33; 18:12; 29:23
16:20 [x]Pr 13:13 [y]S Ps 32:10; 40:4; Pr 19:8; 29:25; Jer 17:7
16:21 [z]ver 23
16:22 [a]S Pr 10:11
16:23 [b]Job 15:5 [c]ver 21
16:24 [d]S 1Sa 14:27 [e]Pr 24:13-14
16:25 [f]S Pr 12:15 [g]Est 3:6; Pr 14:12
16:27 [h]S Ps 140:2 [i]Jas 3:6
16:28 [j]S Pr 14:17 [k]Pr 17:9
16:29 [l]S Pr 1:10; 12:26
16:30 [m]S Pr 6:13
16:31 [n]Pr 20:29
16:33 [o]S Lev 16:8; S 1Sa 10:21; Eze 21:21 [p]1Sa 14:41 [q]Jos 7:14; Pr 18:18; 29:26; Jnh 1:7
17:1 [r]S Pr 15:16, 17; S 16:8
17:3 [s]Pr 27:21 [t]S 1Ch 29:17; Ps 26:2; S 139:23; 1Pe 1:7
17:5 [u]S Job 5:16 [v]Pr 14:31 [w]S Job 31:29 [x]Eze 25:3; Ob 1:12

[d]*21* Or *words make a man persuasive* [e]*23* Or *mouth / and makes his lips persuasive* [f]*1* Hebrew *sacrifices*

16:16 HUMANITY, Intellectual Nature—Wisdom is a far more lasting attainment than wealth.
16:18–19 CHRISTIAN ETHICS, Character—Pride and humility contrasted in this proverb provide some insight into the overarching biblical perspective that pride is a negative virtue while humility is to be cultivated.
16:25 HUMANITY, Human Nature—See note on 14:12.
16:26 HUMANITY, Work—If nothing else motivates, physical need should drive people to diligent work.
16:31 CHRISTIAN ETHICS, Righteousness—Age does not bring wisdom automatically. One who has sought the life of righteousness will reflect that righteousness in old age. Respect and praise will crown the life of the righteous elderly.
16:33 GOD, Sovereignty—Here is an ancient expression of the belief that God causes and controls everything that happens. He controls the lots—probably specially marked stones—used in determining God's will.
17:1 CHRISTIAN ETHICS, Character—Financial prosperity and social acceptance do not indicate a person is successful in life or right with God. Contentment and strong personal relationships are more important. Wealth gained by war and strife with family and associates is worthless.
17:4 CHRISTIAN ETHICS, Language—The company we keep feeds our tongue. We will communicate to others what we listen to. Eventually we usually believe and become what we constantly hear.
17:5 GOD, Righteous—God is concerned for persons who suffer in any way.
17:5 CREATION, Good—See note on 14:31.

6Children's children[y] are a crown to
the aged,
and parents are the pride of their
children.

7Arrogant[g] lips are unsuited to a fool—
how much worse lying lips to a
ruler![z]

8A bribe is a charm to the one who
gives it;
wherever he turns, he succeeds.[a]

9He who covers over an offense
promotes love,[b]
but whoever repeats the matter
separates close friends.[c]

10A rebuke impresses a man of
discernment
more than a hundred lashes a fool.

11An evil man is bent only on rebellion;
a merciless official will be sent
against him.

12Better to meet a bear robbed of her
cubs
than a fool in his folly.[d]

13If a man pays back evil[e] for good,[f]
evil will never leave his house.

14Starting a quarrel is like breaching a
dam;
so drop the matter before a dispute
breaks out.[g]

15Acquitting the guilty and condemning
the innocent[h]—
the LORD detests them both.[i]

16Of what use is money in the hand of a
fool,
since he has no desire to get
wisdom?[j]

17A friend loves at all times,
and a brother is born for adversity.[k]

18A man lacking in judgment strikes
hands in pledge
and puts up security for his
neighbor.[l]

19He who loves a quarrel loves sin;
he who builds a high gate invites
destruction.

20A man of perverse heart does not
prosper;
he whose tongue is deceitful falls
into trouble.

21To have a fool for a son brings grief;
there is no joy for the father of a
fool.[m]

22A cheerful heart is good medicine,
but a crushed[n] spirit dries up the
bones.[o]

23A wicked man accepts a bribe[p] in
secret
to pervert the course of justice.[q]

24A discerning man keeps wisdom in
view,
but a fool's eyes[r] wander to the
ends of the earth.

25A foolish son brings grief to his father
and bitterness to the one who bore
him.[s]

26It is not good to punish an innocent
man,[t]
or to flog officials for their integrity.

27A man of knowledge uses words with
restraint,[u]
and a man of understanding is
even-tempered.[v]

28Even a fool is thought wise if he keeps
silent,
and discerning if he holds his
tongue.[w]

Chapter 18

An unfriendly man pursues selfish
ends;
he defies all sound judgment.

2A fool finds no pleasure in
understanding

[g]7 Or *Eloquent*

17:6 [y]S Ps 125:5
17:7 [z]Pr 16:10
17:8 [a]S Ex 23:8; Pr 19:6
17:9 [b]S Pr 10:12 [c]Pr 16:28
17:12 [d]S 1Sa 25:25
17:13 [e]S 1Sa 19:4 [f]S Ge 44:4; S Ps 35:12
17:14 [g]Mt 5:25-26
17:15 [h]S Ps 94:21; S Pr 18:5 [i]Ex 23:6-7; Isa 5:23; La 3:34-36
17:16 [j]Pr 23:23
17:17 [k]S 2Sa 15:21; Pr 27:10
17:18 [l]Pr 6:1-5; S 11:15; 22:26-27
17:21 [m]S Pr 10:1
17:22 [n]S Ps 38:8 [o]S Ex 12:46; Pr 14:30; S 15:13; 18:14
17:23 [p]S Ex 18:21; S 23:8; S 1Sa 8:3 [q]S Job 34:33
17:24 [r]S Job 31:1
17:25 [s]S Pr 10:1
17:26 [t]S Ps 94:21
17:27 [u]S Job 6:24 [v]S Pr 14:29
17:28 [w]S Job 2:13; 13:5; S Pr 10:19

17:9 CHRISTIAN ETHICS, Character—A right understanding of love will issue in forgiveness and forgetfulness about an offensive act.
17:10 EDUCATION, Discipline—Observant parents and teachers know by experience that learners react differently to various forms of criticism and correction. Some children seem unaffected by even the harshest punishment; others wither under the mildest scolding. To a sensitive, intelligent child, a rebuke can sometimes accomplish more than a hundred stripes. The wise and effective teacher stays attuned to such individual differences.
17:15,23,26 CHRISTIAN ETHICS, Justice—The courtroom is of all places expected to uphold integrity. Unfair decisions, bribery, punishment of the innocent, and persecution of just officials have no place in society.
17:17 HUMANITY, Relationships—Genuine friends love one another regardless of the situations which they face. People especially need to sustain both friends and family in times of adversity.
17:17 CHRISTIAN ETHICS, Character—Character is shown by our ability to form friendships. Friends never desert or ignore you. In life's toughest times friends find ways to help.
17:20,27 CHRISTIAN ETHICS, Language—See note on 12:13–24.
17:22 HUMANITY, Psychological Nature—Our outlook on life has a significant effect on our physical well-being.
17:25 HUMANITY, Parenthood—The behavior of children affects their parents. The very nature of parenting is to suffer for the problems of children.
17:28 HUMANITY, Intellectual Nature—Words expose a person's ignorance quicker than silence.
18:1 HUMANITY, Relationships—The Hebrew term for "unfriendly" describes a person who separates from others. Those who do so are depriving both themselves and others of the benefits of working together. Such an approach to life is foolish.

but delights in airing his own
opinions.[x]

3When wickedness comes, so does
contempt,
and with shame comes disgrace.

4The words of a man's mouth are deep
waters,[y]
but the fountain of wisdom is a
bubbling brook.

5It is not good to be partial to the
wicked[z]
or to deprive the innocent of
justice.[a]

6A fool's lips bring him strife,
and his mouth invites a beating.[b]

7A fool's mouth is his undoing,
and his lips are a snare[c] to his
soul.[d]

8The words of a gossip are like choice
morsels;
they go down to a man's inmost
parts.[e]

9One who is slack in his work
is brother to one who destroys.[f]

10The name of the LORD is a strong
tower;[g]
the righteous run to it and are safe.[h]

11The wealth of the rich is their fortified
city;[i]
they imagine it an unscalable wall.

12Before his downfall a man's heart is
proud,
but humility comes before honor.[j]

13He who answers before listening—
that is his folly and his shame.[k]

14A man's spirit sustains him in sickness,
but a crushed spirit who can bear?[l]

15The heart of the discerning acquires
knowledge;[m]
the ears of the wise seek it out.

16A gift[n] opens the way for the giver
and ushers him into the presence of
the great.

17The first to present his case seems
right,
till another comes forward and
questions him.

18Casting the lot settles disputes[o]
and keeps strong opponents apart.

19An offended[p] brother is more
unyielding than a fortified city,
and disputes are like the barred
gates of a citadel.

20From the fruit of his mouth a man's
stomach is filled;
with the harvest from his lips he is
satisfied.[q]

21The tongue has the power of life and
death,[r]
and those who love it will eat its
fruit.[s]

22He who finds a wife finds what is
good[t]
and receives favor from the LORD.[u]

23A poor man pleads for mercy,
but a rich man answers harshly.

24A man of many companions may come
to ruin,
but there is a friend who sticks
closer than a brother.[v]

Chapter 19

BETTER a poor man whose walk is
blameless
than a fool whose lips are
perverse.[w]

2It is not good to have zeal without
knowledge,
nor to be hasty and miss the way.[x]

3A man's own folly[y] ruins his life,
yet his heart rages against the
LORD.[z]

4Wealth brings many friends,

18:2 [x]S Pr 12:23
18:4 [y]S Ps 18:16
18:5 [z]Pr 24:23-25; 28:21 [a]S Ps 82:2; S Pr 17:15
18:6 [b]S Pr 10:14
18:7 [c]Ps 140:9 [d]S Ps 64:8; S Pr 10:14; S 12:13; S 13:3; Ecc 10:12
18:8 [e]Pr 26:22
18:9 [f]Pr 28:24
18:10 [g]S Ps 61:3 [h]S Ps 20:1; Pr 14:26
18:11 [i]Pr 10:15
18:12 [j]S Pr 11:2; 15:33; S 16:18
18:13 [k]Pr 20:25
18:14 [l]S Pr 15:13; S 17:22
18:15 [m]S Pr 15:14
18:16 [n]S Ge 32:13; S 1Sa 10:4; Pr 19:6
18:18 [o]S Pr 16:33
18:19 [p]S 1Sa 17:28
18:20 [q]S Pr 12:14
18:21 [r]S Ps 12:4 [s]Pr 13:2-3; S Mt 12:37
18:22 [t]S Pr 12:4 [u]S Job 33:26; Pr 19:14; 31:10
18:24 [v]S 1Sa 20:42; Jn 15:13-15
19:1 [w]Pr 28:6
19:2 [x]Pr 29:20
19:3 [y]Ps 14:1; Pr 9:13; 24:9; Isa 32:6 [z]Jas 1:13-15

18:2,13,17 FAMILY, Communication—See note on 15:1,4,23. Poor communication destroys family relationships. Communication faults which lead to interpersonal tension include the love of one's own voice rather than love of wisdom, the failure to listen, and the inability to discuss questions frankly and openly.

18:9 HUMANITY, Work—In evaluating the importance of work, those who destroy are seen to be of the same type as those who do not work with diligence. See 14:1.

18:10 SALVATION, As Refuge—The Lord's name stands for His person, since it reflects His character and qualities. Here the name of God is His covenant name by which He made Himself known to Israel (Ex 3:14). Persons may confidently and safely take refuge in the covenant name of God.

18:13 CHRISTIAN ETHICS, Language—We must know the question before we give an answer. Otherwise, we appear foolish. See note on 12:13–24.

18:14 HUMANITY, Psychological Nature—See note on 17:22. Emotional strength gives physical strength.

18:19 HUMANITY, Relationships—Destroyed relationships create barriers between people. God's Word calls us to maintain good relationships with others.

18:20–21 CHRISTIAN ETHICS, Language—The power of the tongue to sway is awesome. One who realizes that and uses the tongue rightly will enjoy a rich, meaningful life. Our use of language should be productive, helping us reach our goals.

18:24 HUMANITY, Relationships—People need the strength of a few solid relationships rather than a large number of superficial ones which offer no support.

19:4,7 CHRISTIAN ETHICS, Property Rights—Compare 14:20. Some friends last only as long as one has money to spend on them. Proper relatedness to God teaches us that the true value of people is not to be measured in how much they have or do not have materially. Poverty is not a value to be set as life's goal, but neither is wealth. See note on 15:27.

but a poor man's friend deserts
him.[a]

5A false witness[b] will not go
unpunished,[c]
and he who pours out lies will not
go free.[d]

6Many curry favor with a ruler,[e]
and everyone is the friend of a man
who gives gifts.[f]

7A poor man is shunned by all his
relatives—
how much more do his friends avoid
him![g]
Though he pursues them with
pleading,
they are nowhere to be found.[h] [h]

8He who gets wisdom loves his own
soul;
he who cherishes understanding
prospers.[i]

9A false witness will not go unpunished,
and he who pours out lies will
perish.[j]

10It is not fitting for a fool[k] to live in
luxury—
how much worse for a slave to rule
over princes![l]

11A man's wisdom gives him patience;[m]
it is to his glory to overlook an
offense.

12A king's rage is like the roar of a lion,[n]
but his favor is like dew[o] on the
grass.[p]

13A foolish son is his father's ruin,[q]
and a quarrelsome wife is like a
constant dripping.[r]

14Houses and wealth are inherited from
parents,[s]
but a prudent wife is from the
LORD.[t]

15Laziness brings on deep sleep,
and the shiftless man goes hungry.[u]

16He who obeys instructions guards his
life,
but he who is contemptuous of his
ways will die.[v]

17He who is kind to the poor lends to
the LORD,[w]
and he will reward him for what he
has done.[x]

18Discipline your son, for in that there is
hope;
do not be a willing party to his
death.[y]

19A hot-tempered man must pay the
penalty;
if you rescue him, you will have to
do it again.

20Listen to advice and accept
instruction,[z]
and in the end you will be wise.[a]

21Many are the plans in a man's heart,
but it is the LORD's purpose that
prevails.[b]

22What a man desires is unfailing love[i];
better to be poor than a liar.

23The fear of the LORD leads to life:
Then one rests content, untouched
by trouble.[c]

24The sluggard buries his hand in the
dish;
he will not even bring it back to his
mouth![d]

25Flog a mocker, and the simple will
learn prudence;
rebuke a discerning man,[e] and he
will gain knowledge.[f]

26He who robs his father and drives out
his mother[g]
is a son who brings shame and
disgrace.

27Stop listening to instruction, my son,[h]
and you will stray from the words of
knowledge.

28A corrupt witness mocks at justice,
and the mouth of the wicked gulps
down evil.[i]

29Penalties are prepared for mockers,
and beatings for the backs of fools.[j]

19:4 [a]ver 7; Pr 14:20
19:5 [b]S Ex 23:1 [c]S Ps 56:7 [d]ver 9; S Dt 19:19; Pr 21:28
19:6 [e]Pr 29:26 [f]S Pr 17:8; S 18:16
19:7 [g]Pr 10:15 [h]S ver 4
19:8 [i]S Pr 16:20
19:9 [j]S ver 5; S Dt 19:19
19:10 [k]Pr 26:1 [l]Pr 30:21-23; Ecc 10:5-7
19:11 [m]S 2Ki 5:12
19:12 [n]Pr 20:2 [o]S Ps 133:3 [p]S Est 1:12; S 7:7; Ps 72:5-6; Pr 16:14-15
19:13 [q]S Pr 10:1 [r]S Est 1:18; Pr 21:9
19:14 [s]2Co 12:14 [t]S Pr 18:22
19:15 [u]S Pr 10:4; 20:13
19:16 [v]S Pr 16:17; S Ro 10:5
19:17 [w]S Dt 24:14 [x]S Dt 24:19; Pr 14:21; 22:9; S Mt 10:42
19:18 [y]S Pr 13:24; 23:13-14
19:20 [z]Pr 4:1 [a]S Pr 12:15
19:21 [b]Ps 33:11; Pr 16:9; 20:24; Isa 8:10; 14:24,27; 31:2; 40:8; 46:10; 48:14; 55:11; Jer 44:29; La 3:37
19:23 [c]S Job 4:7; S Pr 10:27
19:24 [d]Pr 26:15
19:25 [e]S Ps 141:5 [f]S Pr 9:9; 21:11
19:26 [g]Pr 28:24
19:27 [h]S Pr 1:8
19:28 [i]S Job 15:16
19:29 [j]S Dt 25:2

[h]*7* The meaning of the Hebrew for this sentence is uncertain. [i]*22* Or *A man's greed is his shame*

19:8 HUMANITY, Intellectual Nature—The search for wisdom is far more profitable than the search for wealth.
19:13 HUMANITY, Family Relationships—The maintenance of family relationships is the responsibility of each member of the family. Bad family relationships destroy its members. The family should teach us cooperation through shared responsibilities and joint projects.
19:15 HUMANITY, Work—"Shiftless" carries the idea of idleness, the opposite of being involved in work. See note on 12:24.
19:18 EDUCATION, Discipline—Parents can spare their children grief later in life if they will correct and guide them in their younger years. The Hebrew *yasser* means both discipline or rebuke and teach or guide. Parental discipline should always be corrective in nature, never vindictive. Laissez-faire ("let them do as they choose") parenthood can contribute to trouble and unhappiness in the lives of children, and sometimes even to their untimely deaths.
19:20 HUMANITY, Intellectual Nature—An ingredient of wisdom is the recognition of personal intellectual need combined with the ability to accept and utilize education.
19:21 GOD, Sovereignty—See note on 16:33.

Chapter 20

WINE[k] is a mocker[l] and beer a brawler;
whoever is led astray[m] by them is not wise.[n]

2A king's wrath is like the roar of a lion;[o]
he who angers him forfeits his life.[p]

3It is to a man's honor to avoid strife,
but every fool[q] is quick to quarrel.[r]

4A sluggard[s] does not plow in season;
so at harvest time he looks but finds nothing.[t]

5The purposes of a man's heart are deep waters,[u]
but a man of understanding draws them out.

6Many a man claims to have unfailing love,
but a faithful man who can find?[v]

7The righteous man leads a blameless life;[w]
blessed are his children after him.[x]

8When a king sits on his throne to judge,[y]
he winnows out all evil with his eyes.[z]

9Who can say, "I have kept my heart pure;[a]
I am clean and without sin"?[b]

10Differing weights and differing measures—
the LORD detests them both.[c]

11Even a child is known by his actions,
by whether his conduct is pure[d] and right.

12Ears that hear and eyes that see—
the LORD has made them both.[e]

13Do not love sleep or you will grow poor;[f]
stay awake and you will have food to spare.

14"It's no good, it's no good!" says the buyer;
then off he goes and boasts about his purchase.

15Gold there is, and rubies in abundance,
but lips that speak knowledge are a rare jewel.

16Take the garment of one who puts up security for a stranger;
hold it in pledge[g] if he does it for a wayward woman.[h]

17Food gained by fraud tastes sweet to a man,[i]
but he ends up with a mouth full of gravel.[j]

18Make plans by seeking advice;
if you wage war, obtain guidance.[k]

19A gossip betrays a confidence;[l]
so avoid a man who talks too much.

20If a man curses his father or mother,[m]
his lamp will be snuffed out in pitch darkness.[n]

21An inheritance quickly gained at the beginning
will not be blessed at the end.

22Do not say, "I'll pay you back for this wrong!"[o]
Wait for the LORD, and he will deliver you.[p]

23The LORD detests differing weights,
and dishonest scales do not please him.[q]

24A man's steps are directed[r] by the LORD.[s]
How then can anyone understand his own way?[t]

25It is a trap for a man to dedicate something rashly

20:1 [k]S Lev 10:9; Hab 2:5 [l]S 1Sa 25:36 [m]1Ki 20:16 [n]Pr 31:4
20:2 [o]S Pr 19:12 [p]S Est 7:7; S Pr 16:14
20:3 [q]S 1Sa 25:25 [r]S Ge 13:8
20:4 [s]S Pr 6:6 [t]Ecc 10:18
20:5 [u]S Ps 18:16
20:6 [v]Ps 12:1
20:7 [w]S Ps 26:1 [x]Ps 37:25-26; 112:2
20:8 [y]S 1Ki 7:7 [z]ver 26; Pr 25:4-5
20:9 [a]S Job 15:14 [b]1Ki 8:46; Ecc 7:20; 1Jn 1:8
20:10 [c]ver 23; S Pr 11:1
20:11 [d]S Ps 39:1
20:12 [e]S Ps 94:9
20:13 [f]S Pr 6:11; S 19:15
20:16 [g]S Ex 22:26 [h]Pr 27:13
20:17 [i]Pr 9:17 [j]Job 20:14; La 3:16
20:18 [k]Pr 11:14; 24:6
20:19 [l]Pr 11:13
20:20 [m]Pr 30:11 [n]Ex 21:17; S Job 18:5
20:22 [o]Pr 24:29 [p]Isa 37:20; Jer 1:19; 42:11; Ro 12:19
20:23 [q]S ver 10; S Dt 25:13
20:24 [r]S Ps 90:12 [s]S Job 33:29 [t]S Pr 19:21; Jer 10:23

20:1 CHRISTIAN ETHICS, Alcohol—This verse is part of the lengthy chain of thought stretching from Ge 9:21 to Isa 5:11–12 and beyond which expresses consciousness of the dangers inherent in wine. Wise people do not give alcoholic drinks the opportunity to control their minds and take away their wisdom. They do not want to become silly braggarts and stupid brawlers.
20:4 HUMANITY, Work—See note on 13:4.
20:9 SIN, Universal Nature—Rhetorical questions with obvious answers abound in the Bible. We all know no person is sinless. We know this from our own experiences. I cannot claim to be sinless; nor can anyone I know. Our experience is confirmed by God's Word. Sin is the universal thread uniting all mankind.
20:10,23 CHRISTIAN ETHICS, Honesty—The proverb's ability to condense a thought adds to the power of realizing God's displeasure with dishonesty. See note on Lev 19:35–36.
20:12 REVELATION, Word—Human ability to perceive and understand God has much to do with our alertness and openness. To see and hear God is a question of being aware and seeking what God wishes to communicate. God's revelation is available far more often than God's people are available to see and hear Him.
20:13 HUMANITY, Work—See note on v 4.
20:14–15 CHRISTIAN ETHICS, Language—Language can be used to secure goods through proper bargaining procedures. One expects, particularly in Near Eastern bargaining, to downgrade the quality of goods being offered until the sale is final. Then the buyer claims to have gotten the best of the deal. Material wealth is not, however, the highest value of life. Lips devoted to wisdom rank high on the priority scale and low on the availability scale.
20:18 HUMANITY, Relationships—See note on 15:22.
20:22 CHRISTIAN ETHICS, Character—One with godly integrity will leave to God the place of revenge for harshness suffered at the hands of others.
20:24 GOD, Sovereignty—See note on 16:33.
20:25 CHRISTIAN ETHICS, Language—Words express-

and only later to consider his
vows.[u]

26A wise king winnows out the wicked;
he drives the threshing wheel over
them.[v]

27The lamp of the LORD[w] searches the
spirit of a man[j];
it searches out his inmost being.[x]

28Love and faithfulness keep a king safe;
through love[y] his throne is made
secure.[z]

29The glory of young men is their
strength,
gray hair the splendor of the old.[a]

30Blows and wounds cleanse[b] away evil,
and beatings[c] purge the inmost
being.

Chapter 21

THE king's heart is in the hand of the
LORD;
he directs it like a watercourse
wherever he pleases.[d]

2All a man's ways seem right to him,
but the LORD weighs the heart.[e]

3To do what is right and just
is more acceptable to the LORD than
sacrifice.[f]

4Haughty eyes[g] and a proud heart,
the lamp of the wicked, are sin!

5The plans of the diligent lead to
profit[h]
as surely as haste leads to poverty.

6A fortune made by a lying tongue
is a fleeting vapor and a deadly
snare.[k] [i]

7The violence of the wicked will drag
them away,[j]
for they refuse to do what is right.

8The way of the guilty is devious,[k]
but the conduct of the innocent is
upright.

9Better to live on a corner of the roof
than share a house with a
quarrelsome wife.[l]

10The wicked man craves evil;
his neighbor gets no mercy from
him.

11When a mocker is punished, the
simple gain wisdom;
when a wise man is instructed, he
gets knowledge.[m]

12The Righteous One[l] takes note of the
house of the wicked
and brings the wicked to ruin.[n]

13If a man shuts his ears to the cry of the
poor,
he too will cry out[o] and not be
answered.[p]

14A gift given in secret soothes anger,
and a bribe concealed in the cloak
pacifies great wrath.[q]

15When justice is done, it brings joy to
the righteous
but terror to evildoers.[r]

16A man who strays from the path of
understanding
comes to rest in the company of the
dead.[s]

17He who loves pleasure will become
poor;
whoever loves wine and oil will
never be rich.[t]

18The wicked become a ransom[u] for the
righteous,
and the unfaithful for the upright.

19Better to live in a desert
than with a quarrelsome and
ill-tempered wife.[v]

20In the house of the wise are stores of
choice food and oil,
but a foolish man devours all he has.

21He who pursues righteousness and
love
finds life, prosperity[m] [w] and honor.[x]

22A wise man attacks the city of the
mighty[y]
and pulls down the stronghold in
which they trust.

23He who guards his mouth[z] and his
tongue
keeps himself from calamity.[a]

[j]27 Or *The spirit of man is the LORD's lamp*
[k]6 Some Hebrew manuscripts, Septuagint and Vulgate; most Hebrew manuscripts *vapor for those who seek death*
[l]12 Or *The righteous man*
[m]21 Or *righteousness*

20:25 [u]S Pr 10:19; 18:13; Ecc 5:2,4-5; Jer 44:25
20:26 [v]S ver 8
20:27 [w]S Ps 119:105 [x]S Pr 16:2
20:28 [y]Ps 40:11 [z]S Pr 16:12; Isa 16:5
20:29 [a]Pr 16:31
20:30 [b]S Ps 51:2; Pr 22:15 [c]Isa 1:5
21:1 [d]Est 5:1; Jer 39:11-12
21:2 [e]S Pr 16:2
21:3 [f]S 1Sa 15:22; Isa 1:11; Mic 6:6-8
21:4 [g]S Job 41:34
21:5 [h]S Pr 10:4
21:6 [i]S Pr 10:2
21:7 [j]S Pr 11:5
21:8 [k]S Pr 2:15
21:9 [l]ver 19; Pr 19:13; 25:24
21:11 [m]S Pr 19:25
21:12 [n]S Pr 14:11
21:13 [o]S Ex 11:6 [p]S Job 29:12
21:14 [q]S Ge 32:20
21:15 [r]S Pr 10:29
21:16 [s]Eze 18:24
21:17 [t]Pr 23:20-21, 29-35
21:18 [u]Pr 11:8; Isa 43:3
21:19 [v]S ver 9
21:21 [w]Ps 25:13 [x]Mt 5:6
21:22 [y]S Pr 8:14
21:23 [z]S Ps 34:13 [a]S Pr 10:19; 12:13; S 13:3

ing religious commitment often come easily. Fulfillment of promises made may bring sorrow and personal loss (Jdg 11:29–39). We must not trap ourselves with our words.

21:1,30 GOD, Sovereignty—These verses express confidence in the sovereignty of God, His ultimate control over all things.

21:3 CHRISTIAN ETHICS, Worship—Acts of worship play a central role in biblical teaching, but they remain secondary through all parts of Scripture to the call for righteousness and justice. See Isa 1:11–17; note on Mic 6:6–8.

21:11 HUMANITY, Intellectual Nature—God's wisdom leads to self-discipline through the power of His Spirit and the teaching of His Word. External discipline then becomes less needed. See 19:25.

21:16 LAST THINGS, Intermediate State—See note on Isa 14:9.

24 The proud and arrogant[b]
man—"Mocker" is his name;
he behaves with overweening pride.

25 The sluggard's craving will be the
death of him,[c]
because his hands refuse to work.
26 All day long he craves for more,
but the righteous[d] give without
sparing.[e]

27 The sacrifice of the wicked is
detestable[f] —
how much more so when brought
with evil intent![g]
28 A false witness[h] will perish,[i]
and whoever listens to him will be
destroyed forever.[n]

29 A wicked man puts up a bold front,
but an upright man gives thought to
his ways.[j]
30 There is no wisdom,[k] no insight, no
plan
that can succeed against the LORD.[l]

31 The horse is made ready for the day of
battle,
but victory rests with the LORD.[m]

Chapter 22

A good name is more desirable than
great riches;
to be esteemed is better than silver
or gold.[n]

2 Rich and poor have this in common:
The LORD is the Maker of them all.[o]

3 A prudent man sees danger and takes
refuge,[p]
but the simple keep going and suffer
for it.[q]

4 Humility and the fear of the LORD
bring wealth and honor[r] and life.[s]

21:24 [b]Jer 43:2
21:25 [c]Pr 13:4
21:26 [d]S 2Sa 17:27 [e]S Lev 25:35
21:27 [f]S 1Ki 14:24 [g]S Pr 15:8
21:28 [h]Isa 29:21 [i]S Pr 19:5
21:29 [j]S Pr 14:8
21:30 [k]S Job 12:13; S 15:25 [l]S 2Ch 13:12; S Job 5:13; Isa 8:10
21:31 [m]Ps 33:12-19; Isa 31:1
22:1 [n]Ecc 7:1
22:2 [o]S Job 31:15; Pr 29:13; Mt 5:45
22:3 [p]S Pr 14:16 [q]Pr 27:12
22:4 [r]S Pr 15:33 [s]S Pr 10:27; Da 4:36
22:5 [t]Pr 15:19
22:6 [u]S Ge 14:14 [v]Eph 6:4 [w]S Dt 6:7
22:8 [x]S Ex 1:20; S Job 4:8; Gal 6:7-8 [y]Hos 8:7
22:9 [z]S Dt 14:29 [a]S Pr 11:25; S 19:17; 28:27
22:10 [b]Pr 26:20
22:11 [c]Pr 16:13; Mt 5:8
22:13 [d]Pr 26:13
22:14 [e]S Pr 5:3-5; 23:27 [f]Ecc 7:26

5 In the paths of the wicked lie thorns
and snares,[t]
but he who guards his soul stays far
from them.

6 Train[o][u] a child in the way he should
go,[v]
and when he is old he will not turn
from it.[w]

7 The rich rule over the poor,
and the borrower is servant to the
lender.

8 He who sows wickedness reaps
trouble,[x]
and the rod of his fury will be
destroyed.[y]

9 A generous man will himself be
blessed,[z]
for he shares his food with the
poor.[a]

10 Drive out the mocker, and out goes
strife;
quarrels and insults are ended.[b]

11 He who loves a pure heart and whose
speech is gracious
will have the king for his friend.[c]

12 The eyes of the LORD keep watch over
knowledge,
but he frustrates the words of the
unfaithful.

13 The sluggard says, "There is a lion
outside!"[d]
or, "I will be murdered in the
streets!"

14 The mouth of an adulteress is a deep
pit;[e]
he who is under the LORD's wrath
will fall into it.[f]

15 Folly is bound up in the heart of a
child,

[n]28 Or / *but the words of an obedient man will live on*   [o]6 Or *Start*

21:25–26 CHRISTIAN ETHICS, Justice—Righteousness and justice demand that all citizens work hard and make positive contributions to society.

21:27 STEWARDSHIP, Service to God—The worth of one's gift is measured by the spirit and intent of the giver. Wicked, godless persons think they can maintain a proper relationship with God through observing worship rituals and giving enough money to God's work. They are wrong. God measures by intention and attitude rather than by amount. We must serve God, not selfish ambition. See notes on Ps 37:21–26; Ac 4:32—5:11.

21:31 CHRISTIAN ETHICS, War and Peace—See note on Ps 20:7–8.

22:2 CREATION, Justice—Wealth and poverty may appear to show that creation is unfair and unjust. Such differences are extinguished when people stand before their Creator. He made every person and treats all with justice.

22:7,9,26–27 CHRISTIAN ETHICS, Property Rights—Indebtedness is a kind of slavery. Overextension of credit without an appropriate repayment agreement can mean loss of one's possessions, one's reputation, and, if a constant theme of life, loss of one's integrity. To become rich and exercise oppressive rule over the helpless poor is not the goal of life.

22:9 STEWARDSHIP, Care of Needy—The caring person who enjoys helping others receives blessings abundantly. Jesus taught that giving brings the reward of inward blessings. Stewardship involves more than regular gifts to God's work. It also involves a caring attitude that leads to caring actions for people in need. See notes on Ac 4:32—5:11; 1 Jn 3:17.

22:10 CHRISTIAN ETHICS, War and Peace—International war grows out of personal strife. Such strife roots in insecure people who mock the achievements of others and in jealousy fight for undeserved attention. Society begins the road to peace when it helps these people change their ways.

22:11 CHRISTIAN ETHICS, Language—One who loves truth and knows how to communicate truth tactfully will have many supporters.

22:13 HUMANITY, Work—Those who do not wish to work will always find an excuse for not doing so.

but the rod of discipline will drive it
far from him.[g]

16He who oppresses the poor to increase
his wealth
and he who gives gifts to the
rich—both come to poverty.

Sayings of the Wise

17Pay attention[h] and listen to the
sayings of the wise;[i]
apply your heart to what I teach,[j]
18for it is pleasing when you keep them
in your heart
and have all of them ready on your
lips.
19So that your trust may be in the LORD,
I teach you today, even you.
20Have I not written thirty[p] sayings for
you,
sayings of counsel and knowledge,
21teaching you true and reliable words,[k]
so that you can give sound answers
to him who sent you?

22Do not exploit the poor[l] because they
are poor
and do not crush the needy in
court,[m]
23for the LORD will take up their case[n]
and will plunder those who plunder
them.[o]

24Do not make friends with a
hot-tempered man,
do not associate with one easily
angered,
25or you may learn his ways
and get yourself ensnared.[p]

26Do not be a man who strikes hands in
pledge[q]
or puts up security for debts;
27if you lack the means to pay,
your very bed will be snatched from
under you.[r]

28Do not move an ancient boundary
stone[s]
set up by your forefathers.

29Do you see a man skilled[t] in his
work?
He will serve[u] before kings;[v]
he will not serve before obscure
men.

Chapter 23

WHEN you sit to dine with a ruler,
note well what[q] is before you,
2and put a knife to your throat
if you are given to gluttony.
3Do not crave his delicacies,[w]
for that food is deceptive.

4Do not wear yourself out to get rich;
have the wisdom to show restraint.
5Cast but a glance at riches, and they
are gone,[x]
for they will surely sprout wings
and fly off to the sky like an eagle.[y]

6Do not eat the food of a stingy man,
do not crave his delicacies;[z]
7for he is the kind of man
who is always thinking about the
cost.[r]
"Eat and drink," he says to you,
but his heart is not with you.
8You will vomit up the little you have
eaten
and will have wasted your
compliments.

9Do not speak to a fool,
for he will scorn the wisdom of your
words.[a]

10Do not move an ancient boundary
stone[b]
or encroach on the fields of the
fatherless,
11for their Defender[c] is strong;[d]
he will take up their case against
you.[e]

12Apply your heart to instruction[f]
and your ears to words of
knowledge.

13Do not withhold discipline from a
child;
if you punish him with the rod, he
will not die.

22:15 [g]S Pr 13:24; S 20:30
22:17 [h]S Pr 1:8 [i]S Pr 1:6; 30:1; 31:1 [j]S Pr 2:2
22:21 [k]Ecc 12:10
22:22 [l]S Lev 25:17; S Job 5:16 [m]S Ex 23:6
22:23 [n]S Job 29:16; Ps 140:12 [o]Est 8:1; S 9:1; Pr 23:10-11
22:25 [p]1Co 15:33
22:26 [q]Pr 6:1-5
22:27 [r]S Pr 11:15; S 17:18
22:28 [s]S Dt 19:14
22:29 [t]S 1Ki 11:28 [u]S Ge 41:46 [v]S Ge 39:4
23:3 [w]ver 6-8; Ps 141:4
23:5 [x]S Mt 6:19 [y]Pr 27:24
23:6 [z]ver 1-3; Ps 141:4
23:9 [a]S Pr 9:7
23:10 [b]S Dt 19:14
23:11 [c]S Job 19:25 [d]Ps 24:8 [e]Ex 22:22-24; Pr 15:25; 22:22-23
23:12 [f]S Pr 2:2

[p]20 Or *not formerly written;* or *not written excellent*
[q]1 Or *who* [r]7 Or *for as he thinks within himself, / so he is;* or *for as he puts on a feast, / so he is*

22:17 EDUCATION, Discipline—The learner's self-discipline is more important than externally imposed discipline. The presence of good teaching does not guarantee learning, for learning is an active process in which learners seek truth and apply themselves to the task. See 23:12. Indifference, self-sufficiency, or dullness of mind and heart can close our ears to words of wisdom. We do not acquire knowledge by sitting passively and waiting for it. We must search for it as though it were a hidden treasure. See 2:4.

22:24–25 EDUCATION, Example—Beginning in infancy, human beings learn by imitating the behavior of others. The examples others set are not always positive. The biblical writer had this in mind when he warned against association with persons who are habitually angry. Negative emotions are contagious. Unfortunately, children whose parents are temperamental have no choice in the matter. Brought up under the daily influence of angry parents, they learn to be hot-tempered persons themselves. By self-discipline and associating with the right people, we can unlearn bad habits acquired as children. We cannot blame our problems on our parents. We must take responsibility for ourselves and set good examples for our families, friends, and associates.

23:1–8 CHRISTIAN ETHICS, Property Rights—Wealth for its own sake is deceptive in its promise of satisfaction. It leads to loss of personal integrity and values serving the rich and powerful, to fleeting success with riches which do not provide the emotional and spiritual riches we seek, or to deception and dishonesty.

14 Punish him with the rod
and save his soul from death.[s] [g]

15 My son, if your heart is wise,
then my heart will be glad;
16 my inmost being will rejoice
when your lips speak what is right.[h]

17 Do not let your heart envy[i] sinners,
but always be zealous for the fear of
the LORD.
18 There is surely a future hope for you,
and your hope will not be cut off.[j]

19 Listen, my son,[k] and be wise,
and keep your heart on the right
path.
20 Do not join those who drink too much
wine[l]
or gorge themselves on meat,
21 for drunkards and gluttons become
poor,[m]
and drowsiness clothes them in rags.

22 Listen to your father, who gave you
life,
and do not despise your mother
when she is old.[n]
23 Buy the truth and do not sell it;
get wisdom, discipline and
understanding.[o]
24 The father of a righteous man has great
joy;
he who has a wise son delights in
him.[p]
25 May your father and mother be glad;
may she who gave you birth
rejoice![q]

26 My son,[r] give me your heart
and let your eyes keep to my ways,[s]
27 for a prostitute is a deep pit[t]
and a wayward wife is a narrow
well.
28 Like a bandit she lies in wait,[u]
and multiplies the unfaithful among
men.

29 Who has woe? Who has sorrow?
Who has strife? Who has
complaints?
Who has needless bruises? Who has
bloodshot eyes?
30 Those who linger over wine,[v]
who go to sample bowls of mixed
wine.
31 Do not gaze at wine when it is red,
when it sparkles in the cup,
when it goes down smoothly!
32 In the end it bites like a snake

23:14 [g]S Pr 13:24; S 19:18
23:16 [h]ver 24; Pr 27:11; 29:3
23:17 [i]S Ps 37:1; S 73:3
23:18 [j]S Ps 9:18; 37:1-4; Pr 24:14, 19-20
23:19 [k]Dt 4:9; Pr 28:7
23:20 [l]Isa 5:11,22; 56:12; Hab 2:15
23:21 [m]S Pr 21:17
23:22 [n]S Lev 19:32
23:23 [o]Pr 4:7; 17:16
23:24 [p]S ver 15-16
23:25 [q]S Pr 10:1
23:26 [r]Pr 5:1-6 [s]S Ps 18:21
23:27 [t]S Pr 22:14
23:28 [u]Pr 7:11-12
23:30 [v]ver 20-21; Isa 5:11
23:35 [w]Pr 20:1
24:1 [x]Pr 3:31-32; 23:17-18
24:2 [y]S Ps 2:1; Isa 32:6; 55:7-8; 59:7; 65:2; 66:18; Hos 4:1 [z]Ps 10:7
24:3 [a]S Pr 14:1
24:4 [b]S Pr 8:21
24:6 [c]S Pr 11:14; S 20:18; Lk 14:31
24:10 [d]S Job 4:5
24:11 [e]Ps 82:4
24:12 [f]S Ps 139:2 [g]S 1Sa 2:3 [h]S Ps 54:5 [i]Job 34:11; Ps 62:12; S Mt 16:27; Ro 2:6*

and poisons like a viper.
33 Your eyes will see strange sights
and your mind imagine confusing
things.
34 You will be like one sleeping on the
high seas,
lying on top of the rigging.
35 "They hit me," you will say, "but I'm
not hurt!
They beat me, but I don't feel it!
When will I wake up
so I can find another drink?"[w]

Chapter 24

Do not envy[x] wicked men,
do not desire their company;
2 for their hearts plot violence,[y]
and their lips talk about making
trouble.[z]

3 By wisdom a house is built,[a]
and through understanding it is
established;
4 through knowledge its rooms are filled
with rare and beautiful treasures.[b]

5 A wise man has great power,
and a man of knowledge increases
strength;
6 for waging war you need guidance,
and for victory many advisers.[c]

7 Wisdom is too high for a fool;
in the assembly at the gate he has
nothing to say.

8 He who plots evil
will be known as a schemer.
9 The schemes of folly are sin,
and men detest a mocker.

10 If you falter in times of trouble,
how small is your strength![d]

11 Rescue those being led away to death;
hold back those staggering toward
slaughter.[e]
12 If you say, "But we knew nothing
about this,"
does not he who weighs[f][g] the
heart perceive it?
Does not he who guards your life
know it?
Will he not repay[h] each person
according to what he has
done?[i]

13 Eat honey, my son, for it is good;

[s]14 Hebrew *Sheol*

23:13–16 HUMANITY, Parenthood—A necessary responsibility of parents is disciplining children. This training prepares them for life, bringing satisfaction to the parents.
23:20,29–35 CHRISTIAN ETHICS, Alcohol—See note on 20:1. Extremely vivid, this passage may have been written by one who had personally experienced the trauma of drunkenness. Rather than being proud of this, however, the writer wants to warn abusers of strong drink of the consequences they face: quarreling, fights, injuries, ugly physical appearance, confused minds, separation from reality, dangerous loss of feeling, drowsiness, and addiction.
24:3–4 HUMANITY, Intellectual Nature—Wisdom leads to careful planning for the future.

honey from the comb is sweet to
your taste.
14Know also that wisdom is sweet to
your soul;
if you find it, there is a future hope
for you,
and your hope will not be cut off.[j k]
15Do not lie in wait like an outlaw
against a righteous man's
house,
do not raid his dwelling place;
16for though a righteous man falls seven
times, he rises again,
but the wicked are brought down by
calamity.[l]
17Do not gloat[m] when your enemy falls;
when he stumbles, do not let your
heart rejoice,[n]
18or the LORD will see and disapprove
and turn his wrath away from him.[o]
19Do not fret[p] because of evil men
or be envious of the wicked,
20for the evil man has no future hope,
and the lamp of the wicked will be
snuffed out.[q]
21Fear the LORD and the king,[r] my son,
and do not join with the rebellious,
22for those two will send sudden
destruction[s] upon them,
and who knows what calamities they
can bring?

Further Sayings of the Wise

23These also are sayings of the wise:[t]

To show partiality[u] in judging is not
good:[v]
24Whoever says to the guilty, "You are
innocent"[w]—
peoples will curse him and nations
denounce him.
25But it will go well with those who
convict the guilty,
and rich blessing will come upon
them.

24:14 [j]Ps 119:103; Pr 16:24 [k]Pr 23:18
24:16 [l]S Job 5:19; S Ps 34:21
24:17 [m]Ob 1:12 [n]S 2Sa 3:32; Mic 7:8
24:18 [o]S Job 31:29
24:19 [p]Ps 37:1
24:20 [q]S Job 18:5; S Pr 23:17-18
24:21 [r]Ro 13:1-5
24:22 [s]S Ps 73:19
24:23 [t]S Pr 1:6 [u]S Ex 18:16; S Lev 19:15 [v]Ps 72:2; Pr 28:21; 31:8-9; Jer 22:16
24:24 [w]S Pr 17:15
24:28 [x]S Ps 7:4
24:29 [y]Pr 20:22; Mt 5:38-41
24:30 [z]Pr 6:6-11; 26:13-16
24:33 [a]S Pr 6:10
24:34 [b]S Pr 10:4; Ecc 10:18
25:1 [c]S 1Ki 4:32 [d]S Pr 1:1
25:2 [e]Pr 16:10-15

26An honest answer
is like a kiss on the lips.
27Finish your outdoor work
and get your fields ready;
after that, build your house.
28Do not testify against your neighbor
without cause,[x]
or use your lips to deceive.
29Do not say, "I'll do to him as he has
done to me;
I'll pay that man back for what he
did."[y]
30I went past the field of the sluggard,[z]
past the vineyard of the man who
lacks judgment;
31thorns had come up everywhere,
the ground was covered with weeds,
and the stone wall was in ruins.
32I applied my heart to what I observed
and learned a lesson from what I
saw:
33A little sleep, a little slumber,
a little folding of the hands to
rest[a]—
34and poverty will come on you like a
bandit
and scarcity like an armed man.[t b]

Chapter 25

More Proverbs of Solomon

THESE are more proverbs[c] of Solomon,
copied by the men of Hezekiah king
of Judah:[d]

2It is the glory of God to conceal a
matter;
to search out a matter is the glory of
kings.[e]
3As the heavens are high and the earth
is deep,
so the hearts of kings are
unsearchable.
4Remove the dross from the silver,

[t]34 Or *like a vagrant / and scarcity like a beggar*

24:14 HUMANITY, Intellectual Nature—See note on 24:3–4.
24:15–16 CHRISTIAN ETHICS, Righteousness—See note on 10:2,24–25,29–32.
24:17–18 GOD, Wrath—God's wrath is not cause for us to rejoice. That sin would bring His wrath upon us.
24:26 CHRISTIAN ETHICS, Language—Truth and honesty have their own satisfying reward.
24:26 FAMILY, Communication—See note on 15:1,4,23.
24:28–29 CHRISTIAN ETHICS, Language—See note on Ex 20:16. Even if a neighbor has done us wrong, vengeance is to be left with God. See note on Mt 5:38–48.
24:30–34 HUMANITY, Work—Laziness and refusal to work not only rob a person of personal accomplishments and meaning, they destroy through negligence what previous generations have accomplished. To make "rest" a top priority creates poverty.
24:32 HUMANITY, Intellectual Nature—The wise person learns from the experience of others. See note on Ps 90:12.
25:1 HOLY SCRIPTURE, Collection—Hezekiah ruled 200 years after Solomon. The collectors of wise comments, most of which are attributed to Solomon, assembled the inspired material to form a recorded witness of God's revelation over the years. Revelation and inspiration included preserving the material and passing it on from generation to generation in both oral and written form to produce God's Book.
25:2 REVELATION, Divine Presence—God's revelation gives what His people need to know, not all that could be known about God. The unique nature of God is that He is greater than the human mind and imagination. Even kings with all their power and human resources cannot search out the mysterious side of God's nature.
25:4–5 CHRISTIAN ETHICS, Righteousness—Work for good and justice. The results will allow others more possibili-

and out comes material for[u] the
silversmith;
5remove the wicked from the king's
presence,[f]
and his throne will be established[g]
through righteousness.[h]
6Do not exalt yourself in the king's
presence,
and do not claim a place among
great men;
7it is better for him to say to you,
"Come up here,"[i]
than for him to humiliate you before
a nobleman.

What you have seen with your eyes
8 do not bring[v] hastily to court,
for what will you do in the end
if your neighbor puts you to
shame?[j]
9If you argue your case with a neighbor,
do not betray another man's
confidence,
10or he who hears it may shame you
and you will never lose your bad
reputation.

11A word aptly spoken
is like apples of gold in settings of
silver.[k]
12Like an earring of gold or an ornament
of fine gold
is a wise man's rebuke to a listening
ear.[l]
13Like the coolness of snow at harvest
time
is a trustworthy messenger to those
who send him;
he refreshes the spirit of his
masters.[m]
14Like clouds and wind without rain
is a man who boasts of gifts he does
not give.
15Through patience a ruler can be
persuaded,[n]
and a gentle tongue can break a
bone.[o]
16If you find honey, eat just enough—
too much of it, and you will vomit.[p]
17Seldom set foot in your neighbor's
house—
too much of you, and he will hate
you.

25:5 [f]S Pr 20:8 [g]S 2Sa 7:13 [h]S Pr 16:12; 29:14
25:7 [i]Lk 14:7-10
25:8 [j]Mt 5:25-26
25:11 [k]ver 12; Pr 15:23
25:12 [l]S ver 11; Ps 141:5; S Pr 13:18
25:13 [m]S Pr 10:26; 13:17
25:15 [n]Ecc 10:4 [o]Pr 15:1
25:16 [p]ver 27
25:18 [q]S Pr 12:18
25:22 [r]S Ps 18:8 [s]S 2Ch 28:15; Mt 5:44; Ro 12:20*
25:24 [t]S Pr 21:9
25:25 [u]Pr 15:30
25:27 [v]ver 16 [w]Pr 27:2; S Mt 23:12
26:1 [x]S 1Sa 12:17 [y]ver 8; Pr 19:10
26:2 [z]S Dt 23:5
26:3 [a]Ps 32:9 [b]S Pr 10:13

18Like a club or a sword or a sharp arrow
is the man who gives false testimony
against his neighbor.[q]
19Like a bad tooth or a lame foot
is reliance on the unfaithful in times
of trouble.
20Like one who takes away a garment on
a cold day,
or like vinegar poured on soda,
is one who sings songs to a heavy
heart.
21If your enemy is hungry, give him food
to eat;
if he is thirsty, give him water to
drink.
22In doing this, you will heap burning
coals[r] on his head,
and the LORD will reward you.[s]
23As a north wind brings rain,
so a sly tongue brings angry looks.
24Better to live on a corner of the roof
than share a house with a
quarrelsome wife.[t]
25Like cold water to a weary soul
is good news from a distant land.[u]
26Like a muddied spring or a polluted
well
is a righteous man who gives way to
the wicked.
27It is not good to eat too much honey,[v]
nor is it honorable to seek one's
own honor.[w]
28Like a city whose walls are broken
down
is a man who lacks self-control.

Chapter 26

LIKE snow in summer or rain[x] in
harvest,
honor is not fitting for a fool.[y]
2Like a fluttering sparrow or a darting
swallow,
an undeserved curse does not come
to rest.[z]
3A whip for the horse, a halter for the
donkey,[a]
and a rod for the backs of fools![b]

[u]4 Or *comes a vessel from* [v]7,8 Or *nobleman / on whom you had set your eyes. / 8Do not go*

ties for doing the works of justice. Wicked advisers can destroy a ruler.
25:11 CHRISTIAN ETHICS, Language—See note on 12:13–24.
25:13–14 CHRISTIAN ETHICS, Language—A message appropriately delivered can lift our spirits. One who boasts actually declares his emptiness of spirit. Unfulfilled words wear us out; good news refreshes us.
25:16–17 HUMANITY, Life—Self-discipline leads to moderation in all of life.
25:18 CHRISTIAN ETHICS, Language—To falsely convict a person of crime is to fight a war against our neighbor. See note on 24:28–29.
26:2 CHRISTIAN ETHICS, Language—Language does not give us unlimited power. To place another person under an undeserved curse has no effect on the other person. It does reveal the foolishness of the speaker.

4 Do not answer a fool according to his folly,
or you will be like him yourself.[c]

5 Answer a fool according to his folly,
or he will be wise in his own eyes.[d]

6 Like cutting off one's feet or drinking violence
is the sending of a message by the hand of a fool.[e]

7 Like a lame man's legs that hang limp
is a proverb in the mouth of a fool.[f]

8 Like tying a stone in a sling
is the giving of honor to a fool.[g]

9 Like a thornbush in a drunkard's hand
is a proverb in the mouth of a fool.[h]

10 Like an archer who wounds at random
is he who hires a fool or any passer-by.

11 As a dog returns to its vomit,[i]
so a fool repeats his folly.[j]

12 Do you see a man wise in his own eyes?[k]
There is more hope for a fool than for him.[l]

13 The sluggard says,[m] "There is a lion in the road,
a fierce lion roaming the streets!"[n]

14 As a door turns on its hinges,
so a sluggard turns on his bed.[o]

15 The sluggard buries his hand in the dish;
he is too lazy to bring it back to his mouth.[p]

16 The sluggard is wiser in his own eyes
than seven men who answer discreetly.

17 Like one who seizes a dog by the ears
is a passer-by who meddles in a quarrel not his own.

18 Like a madman shooting
firebrands or deadly arrows
19 is a man who deceives his neighbor
and says, "I was only joking!"

20 Without wood a fire goes out;
without gossip a quarrel dies down.[q]

21 As charcoal to embers and as wood to fire,
so is a quarrelsome man for kindling strife.[r]

22 The words of a gossip are like choice morsels;
they go down to a man's inmost parts.[s]

23 Like a coating of glaze[w] over earthenware
are fervent lips with an evil heart.

24 A malicious man disguises himself with his lips,[t]
but in his heart he harbors deceit.[u]

25 Though his speech is charming,[v] do not believe him,
for seven abominations fill his heart.[w]

26 His malice may be concealed by deception,
but his wickedness will be exposed in the assembly.

27 If a man digs a pit,[x] he will fall into it;[y]
if a man rolls a stone, it will roll back on him.[z]

28 A lying tongue hates those it hurts,
and a flattering mouth[a] works ruin.

Chapter 27

1 Do not boast[b] about tomorrow,
for you do not know what a day may bring forth.[c]

2 Let another praise you, and not your own mouth;
someone else, and not your own lips.[d]

3 Stone is heavy and sand[e] a burden,
but provocation by a fool is heavier than both.

26:4 [c]ver 5; Isa 36:21
26:5 [d]ver 4; S Pr 3:7
26:6 [e]S Pr 10:26
26:7 [f]ver 9
26:8 [g]S ver 1
26:9 [h]ver 7
26:11 [i]2Pe 2:22* [j]S Ps 85:8
26:12 [k]S Pr 3:7 [l]Pr 29:20
26:13 [m]Pr 6:6-11; 24:30-34 [n]Pr 22:13
26:14 [o]S Pr 6:9
26:15 [p]Pr 19:24
26:20 [q]Pr 22:10
26:21 [r]S Pr 14:17
26:22 [s]Pr 18:8
26:24 [t]S Ps 31:18 [u]Ps 41:6
26:25 [v]Ps 28:3 [w]Jer 9:4-8
26:27 [x]S Ps 7:15 [y]S Est 6:13 [z]S Est 2:23; S 7:9; Ps 35:8; 141:10; Pr 28:10; 29:6; Isa 50:11
26:28 [a]S Ps 12:3; Pr 29:5
27:1 [b]S 1Ki 20:11 [c]Mt 6:34; Jas 4:13-16
27:2 [d]S Pr 25:27
27:3 [e]S Job 6:3

[w]*23* With a different word division of the Hebrew; Masoretic Text *of silver dross*

26:4–5 CHRISTIAN ETHICS, Language—The careful listener recognizes a foolish speaker. It is a losing battle to attempt to engage such people on their level. The mature person in God attempts to raise the level of conversation and to guide the fool away from foolish conceit.
26:12 HUMANITY, Intellectual Nature—Genuine wisdom recognizes its own limitations and is ready to learn more. Self-centered pride robs us of the chance to improve.
26:13–16 HUMANITY, Work—See 21:25–26; 22:13; 24:30–34.
26:18–19 CHRISTIAN ETHICS, Language—Making jokes at another's expense shows foolishness. Playing on another's emotions and intentions is dishonest and malicious. We need to find better ways to gain attention.
26:18–19 FAMILY, Communication—See note on 15:1, 4,23.
26:20 CHRISTIAN ETHICS, Language—How do we treat gossip? We are not to give it credence by ever responding to it. Such an approach will soon see the end of the gossip and cause us to avoid fights with other persons.
26:24–28 CHRISTIAN ETHICS, Language—Language can deceive for a while. We need to refuse to trust charmers whose hearts oppose their lips. Charming lies can ruin the speaker and other people. Eventually the charmer is found out. We need to resist all temptations to speak anything but the truth. See note on 26:18–19.
27:1 HISTORY, Individual—Individual hope does not come in length of days or accomplishment of all plans. God controls each individual's destiny. We will never fulfill all our plans. Our only source of pride and security is in God.

[4]Anger is cruel and fury overwhelming,
but who can stand before jealousy?[f]

[5]Better is open rebuke
than hidden love.

[6]Wounds from a friend can be trusted,
but an enemy multiplies kisses.[g]

[7]He who is full loathes honey,
but to the hungry even what is bitter tastes sweet.

[8]Like a bird that strays from its nest[h]
is a man who strays from his home.

[9]Perfume[i] and incense bring joy to the heart,
and the pleasantness of one's friend springs from his earnest counsel.

[10]Do not forsake your friend and the friend of your father,
and do not go to your brother's house when disaster[j] strikes you—
better a neighbor nearby than a brother far away.

[11]Be wise, my son, and bring joy to my heart;[k]
then I can answer anyone who treats me with contempt.[l]

[12]The prudent see danger and take refuge,
but the simple keep going and suffer for it.[m]

[13]Take the garment of one who puts up security for a stranger;
hold it in pledge if he does it for a wayward woman.[n]

[14]If a man loudly blesses his neighbor early in the morning,
it will be taken as a curse.

[15]A quarrelsome wife is like
a constant dripping[o] on a rainy day;
[16]restraining her is like restraining the wind
or grasping oil with the hand.

[17]As iron sharpens iron,
so one man sharpens another.

[18]He who tends a fig tree will eat its fruit,[p]
and he who looks after his master will be honored.[q]

[19]As water reflects a face,
so a man's heart reflects the man.

[20]Death and Destruction[x] are never satisfied,[r]
and neither are the eyes of man.[s]

[21]The crucible for silver and the furnace for gold,[t]
but man is tested by the praise he receives.

[22]Though you grind a fool in a mortar,
grinding him like grain with a pestle,
you will not remove his folly from him.

[23]Be sure you know the condition of your flocks,[u]
give careful attention to your herds;
[24]for riches do not endure forever,[v]
and a crown is not secure for all generations.
[25]When the hay is removed and new growth appears
and the grass from the hills is gathered in,
[26]the lambs will provide you with clothing,
and the goats with the price of a field.
[27]You will have plenty of goats' milk
to feed you and your family
and to nourish your servant girls.

Chapter 28

THE wicked man flees[w] though no one pursues,[x]
but the righteous are as bold as a lion.[y]

[2]When a country is rebellious, it has many rulers,
but a man of understanding and knowledge maintains order.

[3]A ruler[y] who oppresses the poor

27:4 [f]S Nu 5:14
27:6 [g]Ps 141:5; Pr 28:23
27:8 [h]Isa 16:2
27:9 [i]S Est 2:12; S Ps 45:8
27:10 [j]S Pr 17:17
27:11 [k]S Pr 10:1; S 23:15-16 [l]S Ge 24:60
27:12 [m]Pr 22:3
27:13 [n]Pr 20:16
27:15 [o]S Est 1:18
27:18 [p]1Co 9:7 [q]Lk 19:12-27
27:20 [r]Pr 30:15-16; Hab 2:5 [s]Ecc 1:8; 6:7
27:21 [t]S Pr 17:3
27:23 [u]Pr 12:10
27:24 [v]Pr 23:5
28:1 [w]S 2Ki 7:7 [x]S Lev 26:17 [y]S Ps 138:3

[x]20 Hebrew *Sheol and Abaddon* [y]3 Or *A poor man*

27:5 FAMILY, Communication—See note on 15:1,4,23.
27:9–10 HUMANITY, Relationships—Everyone needs friends who are supportive and honest.
27:10 FAMILY, Friendships—The strange-sounding advice of this verse is actually being practiced by older adults today. Friends are often called upon for assistance when family members live at a distance. Because of the value of friends to family relationships, nurturing friendships is important to marital and family happiness. Friendship is honored in 17:17; 18:24. Being friends with one's mate is celebrated by the lover in SS 5:16.
27:17 HUMANITY, Intellectual Nature—Genuine friends in honest discussion whet the skill and wisdom of each other. We can never be so wise we do not need to learn in dialogue with others of opposing viewpoints.
27:20 HUMANITY, Life—No life is without its catastrophes, the last one of which is death, the end of life itself. Human greed is as easily satisfied as the graveyard.
27:20 CHRISTIAN ETHICS, Property Rights—A wise person learns the limits of material needs and lives within those rather than constantly responding to the drive of personal wants, which are never satisfied.
28:1,10,12,28 CHRISTIAN ETHICS, Righteousness—Wickedness generates fear; righteousness brings joy. See note on 10:2,24–25,29–32.

is like a driving rain that leaves no
crops.

4 Those who forsake the law praise the
wicked,
but those who keep the law resist
them.

5 Evil men do not understand justice,
but those who seek the LORD
understand it fully.

6 Better a poor man whose walk is
blameless
than a rich man whose ways are
perverse.[z]

7 He who keeps the law is a discerning
son,
but a companion of gluttons
disgraces his father.[a]

8 He who increases his wealth by
exorbitant interest[b]
amasses it for another,[c] who will be
kind to the poor.[d]

9 If anyone turns a deaf ear to the law,
even his prayers are detestable.[e]

10 He who leads the upright along an evil
path
will fall into his own trap,[f]
but the blameless will receive a good
inheritance.

11 A rich man may be wise in his own
eyes,
but a poor man who has
discernment sees through him.

12 When the righteous triumph, there is
great elation;[g]
but when the wicked rise to power,
men go into hiding.[h]

13 He who conceals his sins[i] does not
prosper,
but whoever confesses[j] and
renounces them finds mercy.[k]

14 Blessed is the man who always fears
the LORD,
but he who hardens his heart falls
into trouble.

15 Like a roaring lion or a charging bear
is a wicked man ruling over a
helpless people.

16 A tyrannical ruler lacks judgment,

28:6 [z]Pr 19:1
28:7 [a]Pr 23:19-21
28:8 [b]S Ex 18:21; Eze 18:8 [c]S Job 27:17 [d]S Job 3:15; Ps 112:9; Lk 14:12-14
28:9 [e]S Ps 109:7; S Pr 15:8; S Isa 1:13
28:10 [f]S Ps 57:6; S Pr 26:27
28:12 [g]S 2Ki 11:20 [h]ver 28; Job 24:4; Pr 29:2
28:13 [i]S 2Sa 12:13; S Job 31:33 [j]S Lev 5:5 [k]Ps 32:1-5; Da 4:27; 1Jn 1:9
28:17 [l]1Sa 30:17; 1Ki 20:20; Jer 41:15; 44:14
28:18 [m]Jer 39:18 [n]S Est 6:13; Pr 10:9
28:19 [o]Pr 12:11
28:20 [p]ver 22
28:21 [q]S Lev 19:15 [r]S Ps 94:21; S Pr 18:5 [s]Eze 13:19
28:22 [t]ver 20
28:23 [u]S Pr 27:5-6
28:24 [v]Pr 19:26 [w]S Pr 18:9
28:25 [x]S Pr 14:17 [y]Pr 29:25
28:26 [z]S Ps 4:5; Pr 3:5 [a]1Co 3:18
28:27 [b]S Dt 24:19; S Pr 22:9 [c]S Ps 109:17
28:28 [d]S ver 12; S Job 20:19
29:1 [e]S Ex 32:9; S Dt 9:27

but he who hates ill-gotten gain will
enjoy a long life.

17 A man tormented by the guilt of
murder
will be a fugitive[l] till death;
let no one support him.

18 He whose walk is blameless is kept
safe,[m]
but he whose ways are perverse will
suddenly fall.[n]

19 He who works his land will have
abundant food,
but the one who chases fantasies
will have his fill of poverty.[o]

20 A faithful man will be richly blessed,
but one eager to get rich will not go
unpunished.[p]

21 To show partiality[q] is not good[r] —
yet a man will do wrong for a piece
of bread.[s]

22 A stingy man is eager to get rich
and is unaware that poverty awaits
him.[t]

23 He who rebukes a man will in the end
gain more favor
than he who has a flattering
tongue.[u]

24 He who robs his father or mother[v]
and says, "It's not wrong"—
he is partner to him who destroys.[w]

25 A greedy man stirs up dissension,[x]
but he who trusts in the LORD[y] will
prosper.

26 He who trusts in himself is a fool,[z]
but he who walks in wisdom is kept
safe.[a]

27 He who gives to the poor will lack
nothing,[b]
but he who closes his eyes to them
receives many curses.[c]

28 When the wicked rise to power,
people go into hiding;[d]
but when the wicked perish, the
righteous thrive.

Chapter 29

A man who remains stiff-necked[e] after
many rebukes

28:6,22,25,27 CHRISTIAN ETHICS, Property Rights—The stingy rich show by their actions where their hearts are. They care little for those without material things. They reveal little true wisdom. Poverty of spirit awaits them even though they may amass a fortune. Only generous, giving persons are truly rich.

28:13 SALVATION, Confession—Confessing our sins is uncovering and renouncing them. It is the path to God's mercy.

28:19 HUMANITY, Work—See 26:13–16.

28:20–22 STEWARDSHIP, Attitudes—God's people do not set their sights on material prosperity. God's people seek to be faithful to Him, to be fair and just with other people, and to help others. These attitudes lead to God's blessings. Selfish commitment to wealth leads to eventual ruin. See note on Mt 6:19–33.

28:23 CHRISTIAN ETHICS, Language—We need to be cordial and tactful in confronting others, but we need to face differences honestly. In the long run confrontation gains more respect than saying simply what the other wants to hear.

will suddenly be destroyed[f] —
without remedy.[g]

2When the righteous thrive, the people rejoice;[h]
when the wicked rule,[i] the people groan.[j]

3A man who loves wisdom brings joy to his father,[k]
but a companion of prostitutes squanders his wealth.[l]

4By justice a king gives a country stability,[m]
but one who is greedy for bribes tears it down.

5Whoever flatters his neighbor
is spreading a net for his feet.[n]

6An evil man is snared by his own sin,[o]
but a righteous one can sing and be glad.

7The righteous care about justice for the poor,[p]
but the wicked have no such concern.

8Mockers stir up a city,
but wise men turn away anger.[q]

9If a wise man goes to court with a fool,
the fool rages and scoffs, and there is no peace.

10Bloodthirsty men hate a man of integrity
and seek to kill the upright.[r]

11A fool gives full vent to his anger,[s]
but a wise man keeps himself under control.[t]

12If a ruler[u] listens to lies,
all his officials become wicked.[v]

13The poor man and the oppressor have this in common:
The LORD gives sight to the eyes of both.[w]

14If a king judges the poor with fairness,
his throne will always be secure.[x]

15The rod of correction imparts wisdom,
but a child left to himself disgraces his mother.[y]

16When the wicked thrive, so does sin,
but the righteous will see their downfall.[z]

17Discipline your son, and he will give you peace;
he will bring delight to your soul.[a]

18Where there is no revelation, the people cast off restraint;
but blessed is he who keeps the law.[b]

19A servant cannot be corrected by mere words;
though he understands, he will not respond.

20Do you see a man who speaks in haste?
There is more hope for a fool than for him.[c]

21If a man pampers his servant from youth,
he will bring grief[z] in the end.

22An angry man stirs up dissension,
and a hot-tempered one commits many sins.[d]

23A man's pride brings him low,[e]
but a man of lowly spirit gains honor.[f]

24The accomplice of a thief is his own enemy;
he is put under oath and dare not testify.[g]

25Fear[h] of man will prove to be a snare,
but whoever trusts in the LORD[i] is kept safe.[j]

26Many seek an audience with a ruler,[k]
but it is from the LORD that man gets justice.[l]

29:1 [f]Jer 19:15; 36:31; Hab 2:7 [g]S 2Ch 36:16; Pr 6:15
29:2 [h]S 2Ki 11:20 [i]Pr 30:22; Ecc 10:6 [j]S Pr 28:12
29:3 [k]S Pr 10:1; S 23:15-16 [l]Pr 5:8-10; Lk 15:11-32
29:4 [m]ver 14; S Pr 8:15-16
29:5 [n]S Job 32:21; S Pr 26:28
29:6 [o]S Job 5:13; S Pr 26:27; Ecc 9:12
29:7 [p]Pr 31:8-9
29:8 [q]Pr 11:11; S 16:14
29:10 [r]ver 27; 1Jn 3:12
29:11 [s]S Job 15:13 [t]Pr 12:16
29:12 [u]2Ki 21:9 [v]S Job 34:30
29:13 [w]S Pr 22:2; Mt 5:45
29:14 [x]S ver 4; Ps 72:1-5; S Pr 16:12
29:15 [y]ver 17; S Pr 13:24
29:16 [z]S Ps 91:8; S 92:11
29:17 [a]S ver 15
29:18 [b]Ps 1:1-2; 19:11; 119:1-2
29:20 [c]Pr 19:2; 26:12
29:22 [d]S Pr 14:17
29:23 [e]S Est 5:12 [f]S Pr 11:2; S 15:33; S 16:18
29:24 [g]S Lev 5:1
29:25 [h]S 1Sa 15:24 [i]Pr 28:25 [j]S Pr 16:20
29:26 [k]Pr 19:6 [l]S Pr 16:33

[z]*21* The meaning of the Hebrew for this word is uncertain.

29:1 EDUCATION, Self-preservation—We can fail to learn through indifference and apathy. See note on 22:17. Stubbornness can also stand as a barrier to learning, often with disastrous results. Refusal to learn and change is a sin against God.
29:2,6,7,27 CHRISTIAN ETHICS, Righteousness—The wicked and righteous do not mix. They totally oppose each other. Joy and concern for the underpriviledged characterize righteous behavior. See note on 10:2,24–25,29–32.
29:3 EDUCATION, Moral Purity—In modern society a man who has technical knowledge may be regarded as highly educated, without any regard to moral standards and practice. In the Scriptures, wisdom has a definite moral component. A person who has true wisdom does not associate with prostitutes or show other signs of moral illiteracy.
29:6 SIN, Slavery—See note on 5:21–23.
29:10 CHRISTIAN ETHICS, Murder—Wicked people cannot stand the presence of righteous people. The righteous become murder victims because their presence witnesses to the guilt of the wicked.
29:18 HOLY SCRIPTURE, Visions—The absence of God's revelation leads to the loss of controls and disciplined living. The word for revelation (Hebrew *chazon*) normally refers to prophetic visions. People who maintain the laws of life revealed by God are blessed, for they have found the genuine meaning of life. Within this wisdom writing is affirmation of prophetic vision and the law, thus a combination of the three major sections of the Hebrew Bible—Law, Prophets, Writings. All three types of inspired literature seek to bring people to know and do God's will so they will have meaning in life.
29:20 CHRISTIAN ETHICS, Language—Cautious use of language is necessary to succeed in any area of life. Constant speaking without thinking or listening leads nowhere. See note on 12:13–24.

27The righteous detest the dishonest;
the wicked detest the upright.[m]

Chapter 30

Sayings of Agur

THE sayings[n] of Agur son of Jakeh—an oracle[a]:
This man declared to Ithiel,
to Ithiel and to Ucal:[b]

2"I am the most ignorant of men;
I do not have a man's understanding.
3I have not learned wisdom,
nor have I knowledge of the Holy One.[o]
4Who has gone up[p] to heaven and come down?
Who has gathered up the wind in the hollow[q] of his hands?
Who has wrapped up the waters[r] in his cloak?[s]
Who has established all the ends of the earth?
What is his name,[t] and the name of his son?
Tell me if you know!

5"Every word of God is flawless;[u]
he is a shield[v] to those who take refuge in him.
6Do not add[w] to his words,
or he will rebuke you and prove you a liar.

7"Two things I ask of you, O LORD;
do not refuse me before I die:
8Keep falsehood and lies far from me;
give me neither poverty nor riches,
but give me only my daily bread.[x]
9Otherwise, I may have too much and disown[y] you
and say, 'Who is the LORD?'[z]
Or I may become poor and steal,
and so dishonor the name of my God.[a]

10"Do not slander a servant to his master,
or he will curse you, and you will pay for it.

11"There are those who curse their fathers
and do not bless their mothers;[b]
12those who are pure in their own eyes[c]
and yet are not cleansed of their filth;[d]
13those whose eyes are ever so haughty,[e]
whose glances are so disdainful;
14those whose teeth[f] are swords
and whose jaws are set with knives[g]
to devour[h] the poor[i] from the earth,
the needy from among mankind.[j]

15"The leech has two daughters.
'Give! Give!' they cry.

"There are three things that are never satisfied,[k]
four that never say, 'Enough!':
16the grave,[c][l] the barren womb,
land, which is never satisfied with water,
and fire, which never says, 'Enough!'

17"The eye that mocks[m] a father,
that scorns obedience to a mother,
will be pecked out by the ravens of the valley,
will be eaten by the vultures.[n]

18"There are three things that are too amazing for me,
four that I do not understand:
19the way of an eagle in the sky,
the way of a snake on a rock,

29:27 [m]S ver 10
30:1 [n]S Pr 22:17
30:3 [o]S Pr 9:10
30:4 [p]Dt 30:12; Ps 24:1-2; S Pr 8:22-31; Jn 3:13; Eph 4:7-10 [q]Isa 40:12 [r]Job 26:8 [s]S Ge 1:2 [t]Rev 19:12
30:5 [u]S Ps 12:6; S 18:30 [v]S Ge 15:1
30:6 [w]S Dt 4:2
30:8 [x]Mt 6:11
30:9 [y]Jos 24:27; Isa 1:4; 59:13 [z]Dt 6:12; 8:10-14; Hos 13:6 [a]S Dt 8:12
30:11 [b]S Pr 20:20
30:12 [c]S Pr 16:2 [d]Jer 2:23,35
30:13 [e]S 2Sa 22:28; S Job 41:34
30:14 [f]S Job 4:11; S Ps 3:7 [g]Ps 57:4 [h]S Job 24:9 [i]Am 8:4; Mic 2:2 [j]S Job 19:22
30:15 [k]Pr 27:20
30:16 [l]Isa 5:14; 14:9,11; Hab 2:5
30:17 [m]Dt 21:18-21 [n]S Job 15:23

[a]*1* Or *Jakeh of Massa* [b]*1* Masoretic Text; with a different word division of the Hebrew *declared, "I am weary, O God; / I am weary, O God, and faint.* [c]*16* Hebrew *Sheol*

30:1–4 HOLY SCRIPTURE, Inspired—More than one inspired person contributed to the formulation of Proverbs. Agur is unknown otherwise and illustrates the wide variety of people God used in inspiring Scripture. Agur points to the weakness even of the persons God inspired. They remained deeply aware of human ignorance in the face of God's mystery. See notes on 25:1; 31:1.
30:2–4 GOD, Wisdom—God's creative acts establish His control over the world and show His surpassing wisdom. See note on 8:12–31.
30:4 JESUS CHRIST, Foretold—This Old Testament riddle became a New Testament affirmation. The answer Christians give to each of these questions is Jesus Christ. He has gone up to and come down from heaven. See notes on Ps 68:18; Eph 4:7–12. The angel of the annunciation identified Him as the Son of God (Lk 1:35). Jesus was declared to be the Son of God at His baptism (Mt 3:17). He acknowledged His sonship before the high priest (Mk 14:62). Paul affirmed the special sonship of Jesus (Ro 1:4). Peter's confession (Mt 16:16) identified Jesus as "Christ, the Son of the living God." This obscure proverb gave early Christians and us as well an opportunity to identify and confess our knowledge of the name.
30:5–6 HOLY SCRIPTURE, Canonization—The declared wisdom of God, oral and written, is pure. God is a Lord of no deception, and what He reveals has no flaw. It can be counted on to sustain the believer. The reader is admonished not to add or subtract from what God has made known and called His people to follow. See note on Dt 4:2.
30:8 CHRISTIAN ETHICS, Property Rights—Honesty and satisfaction are basic values leading to the good life. Daily bread, not assured luxurious retirement, is what we should ask of God. Compare Mt 6:11.
30:10–33 EVIL AND SUFFERING, Deserved—Evil is not always apparent to the evildoer. We are too prone to supply our own definitions of evil. They always fit the other person. God and His inspired Word define evil. Setting oneself as superior to another person or doing anything which harms another person is evil. Pride and greed are cornerstones of evil behavior.

the way of a ship on the high seas,
and the way of a man with a
maiden.
20"This is the way of an adulteress:
She eats and wipes her mouth
and says, 'I've done nothing
wrong.'[o]
21"Under three things the earth
trembles,
under four it cannot bear up:
22a servant who becomes king,[p]
a fool who is full of food,
23an unloved woman who is married,
and a maidservant who displaces her
mistress.
24"Four things on earth are small,
yet they are extremely wise:
25Ants are creatures of little strength,
yet they store up their food in the
summer;[q]
26coneys[d][r] are creatures of little power,
yet they make their home in the
crags;
27locusts[s] have no king,
yet they advance together in ranks;
28a lizard can be caught with the hand,
yet it is found in kings' palaces.
29"There are three things that are stately
in their stride,
four that move with stately bearing:
30a lion, mighty among beasts,
who retreats before nothing;
31a strutting rooster, a he-goat,
and a king with his army around
him.[e]
32"If you have played the fool and
exalted yourself,
or if you have planned evil,
clap your hand over your mouth![t]
33For as churning the milk produces
butter,
and as twisting the nose produces
blood,
so stirring up anger produces strife."

Chapter 31

Sayings of King Lemuel

THE sayings[u] of King Lemuel—an oracle[f] his mother taught him:
2"O my son, O son of my womb,
O son of my vows,[g][v]
3do not spend your strength on women,
your vigor on those who ruin
kings.[w]
4"It is not for kings, O Lemuel—
not for kings to drink wine,[x]
not for rulers to crave beer,
5lest they drink[y] and forget what the
law decrees,[z]
and deprive all the oppressed of
their rights.
6Give beer to those who are perishing,
wine[a] to those who are in anguish;
7let them drink[b] and forget their
poverty
and remember their misery no
more.
8"Speak[c] up for those who cannot
speak for themselves,
for the rights of all who are
destitute.
9Speak up and judge fairly;
defend the rights of the poor and
needy."[d]

Epilogue: The Wife of Noble Character

10[h]A wife of noble character[e] who can
find?[f]

30:20 [o]Pr 5:6
30:22 [p]S Pr 19:10; S 29:2
30:25 [q]Pr 6:6-8
30:26 [r]S Ps 104:18
30:27 [s]S Ex 10:4
30:32 [t]S Job 29:9
31:1 [u]S Pr 22:17
31:2 [v]S Jdg 11:30
31:3 [w]S Dt 17:17; S 1Ki 11:3; Pr 5:1-14
31:4 [x]S Pr 20:1; Ecc 10:16-17; Isa 5:22
31:5 [y]S 1Ki 16:9 [z]S Pr 16:12
31:6 [a]S Ge 14:18
31:7 [b]S Est 1:10
31:8 [c]S 1Sa 19:4
31:9 [d]S Pr 24:23; 29:7
31:10 [e]S Ru 3:11; S Pr 18:22 [f]Pr 8:35

[d]*26* That is, the hyrax or rock badger [e]*31* Or *king secure against revolt* [f]*1* Or *of Lemuel king of Massa, which* [g]*2* Or */ the answer to my prayers* [h]*10* Verses 10-31 are an acrostic, each verse beginning with a successive letter of the Hebrew alphabet.

30:24–28 HUMANITY, Life—Lack of individual power is no hindrance to great accomplishments if there is cooperative effort and wise planning.

31:1–9 EVIL AND SUFFERING, Human Origin—Rulers have power to cause great evil for others, especially the underprivileged in society. Thus, rulers must exercise discipline in their private lives so they can exercise fairness in their public lives. Sexual sins and drunkenness can ruin a leader's ability to govern people fairly. Much suffering and injustice originates through the evil practices of political and judicial leaders.

31:1 HOLY SCRIPTURE, Inspired—See note on 30:1–4. Lemuel is not named among the kings of Israel or Judah. Thus, this portion of inspired Scripture was written by a foreigner. The ultimate human source was a woman, the king's mother. Inspiration here includes a mother's oral teaching, a king's writing, and Israelite collection of foreign writing into the Book of Proverbs. Note the influence of other inspired women in Ex 15:21; Jdg 5.

31:1 DISCIPLESHIP, Women—God uses women to teach His people. A godly mother received an oracle, a communication from God, and taught it to her son. Eventually the God-inspired word was written down and became a part of Holy Scripture.

31:4–7 CHRISTIAN ETHICS, Alcohol—Civil leaders cannot afford to have their judgment and actions impaired from misuse of alcohol. They should refrain from those things which would work against justice being done.

31:10–31 HUMANITY, Work—The accomplishments of a wise and industrious woman are magnificent to behold and a source of strength and encouragement to all who know her. A wise woman's potential reaches out to many fields of endeavor.

31:10–31 FAMILY, Role Relationships—See note on 12:4. Women may play many roles in a successful family relationship. This appears to be a composite picture of the ideal wife and mother. One woman could hardly perform all the functions mentioned within one day. The woman is equally active in home and business duties. She is trusted by her husband and seeks to help him at all times. She works hard, makes difficult decisions, earns and invests money well, is compassionate and helpful to the needy, is prepared for the future, and has wisdom to teach other people. She has earned a high reputation in her family, in the business world, and in

She is worth far more than rubies.
11 Her husband[g] has full confidence in
her
and lacks nothing of value.[h]
12 She brings him good, not harm,
all the days of her life.
13 She selects wool and flax
and works with eager hands.[i]
14 She is like the merchant ships,
bringing her food from afar.
15 She gets up while it is still dark;
she provides food for her family
and portions for her servant girls.
16 She considers a field and buys it;
out of her earnings she plants a
vineyard.
17 She sets about her work vigorously;
her arms are strong for her tasks.
18 She sees that her trading is profitable,
and her lamp does not go out at
night.
19 In her hand she holds the distaff
and grasps the spindle with her
fingers.
20 She opens her arms to the poor
and extends her hands to the
needy.[j]
21 When it snows, she has no fear for her
household;
for all of them are clothed in
scarlet.
22 She makes coverings for her bed;
she is clothed in fine linen and
purple.
23 Her husband is respected at the city
gate,
where he takes his seat among the
elders[k] of the land.
24 She makes linen garments and sells
them,
and supplies the merchants with
sashes.
25 She is clothed with strength and
dignity;
she can laugh at the days to come.
26 She speaks with wisdom,
and faithful instruction is on her
tongue.[l]
27 She watches over the affairs of her
household
and does not eat the bread of
idleness.
28 Her children arise and call her blessed;
her husband also, and he praises
her:
29 "Many women do noble things,
but you surpass them all."
30 Charm is deceptive, and beauty is
fleeting;
but a woman who fears the LORD is
to be praised.
31 Give her the reward she has earned,
and let her works bring her praise[m]
at the city gate.

31:11 [g]S Ge 2:18 [h]S Pr 12:4
31:13 [i]1Ti 2:9-10
31:20 [j]Dt 15:11
31:23 [k]S Ex 3:16
31:26 [l]S Pr 10:31
31:31 [m]Pr 11:16

the community. All of this is possible because her life is centered on God. The Bible thus challenges women to use their talents in as many areas as possible to bring honor to God, their family, and themselves. It does not seek to bring a guilt trip on the woman who cannot succeed in all these areas. Few can succeed, but all should have the opportunity to try.

31:26 EDUCATION, Parents—More than any other book of the Old Testament, Proverbs stresses the importance of mothers as teachers in the home. See note on 1:8–9. With all her other laudable traits, the ideal woman pictured in this passage is also an excellent teacher.

Ecclesiastes

Theological Setting

The Book of Ecclesiastes addressed people trying desperately to find meaning and identity and retain the security of their homeland. It shows us the value of the present world without hope of eternal life and resurrection. The basic conclusion of a person facing death after the brief allotted span of years: all of life equals zero, so the only prudent path is to fear God and be careful.

We are often disillusioned by how much time we have left. Many of the people who first heard or read Ecclesiastes were wasting their lives foolishly. The Teacher confessed he had wasted much of his long life. He was too old to correct his ways, but it was not too late for the young people (12:1).

Some among the hearers must have believed the wise and righteous would always prosper and be happy. Like Job, the Teacher appeared to say, "not so." He made it clear that wisdom, wealth, materialism, education, and religion all claimed in one way or another to be able to make life worth living. The Teacher tried each in turn. None worked. He tried to encourage his audience to opt for simplicity in food, entertainment, and work. He tried to encourage them to look for joy in the companionship of their mates, a cheerful disposition, and a reverence of God.

Chapter 12 makes clear the writer was an old man who had come to the end but still had a passion for life. He tended to be skeptical and cynical. He shared his life's experiences to temper the unrealistic optimism of the younger generation. He did not fear to question God. He refused to accept traditional, simplistic answers to life's tough questions. He loved the beauty of the sun and was intrigued with the mystery of the wind. He knew about farming, gardens, and orchards. He was acquainted with fine music and enjoyed good food. He was familiar with war, construction, and fine houses.

The Teacher loved life and justice. He became more skeptical in old age as he observed the injustices of life. He experienced hopelessness as he found himself unable to correct the injustices of life. Even in his skepticism he was a realist, not a pessimist. He remained a believer, not an agnostic.

The aged Teacher wanted his congregation to avoid the pitfalls of life. He wanted his readers to change their lives before it was too late. He wanted them to understand how life can best be lived.

Theological Outline

Ecclesiastes: Is Life Worth Living?

Introductory Statement: Outlining Ecclesiastes is similar to outlining Psalms or Proverbs—almost impossible. The writer *often repeats* himself. For this reason a sequential outline is presented followed by a thematic outline. In discussing a major subject in the thematic outline the author will often come back to minor subjects he has already discussed, so a verse is often listed more than once.

Sequential Outline

I. Introduction: Life Is Meaningless Because Nothing New Ever Occurs. (1:1-11)
II. Wisdom Is Meaningless. (1:12-18)
III. Pleasure and Possessions Are Meaningless. (2:1-11)
IV. Wisdom Is Not Any Better Than Folly. (2:12-17)
V. Labor Is Meaningless. (2:18-26)
VI. God Plans the World But Hides the Plan. (3:1-11)
VII. The Rational Conclusion: Seek to Enjoy Life. (3:12-22)
VIII. Illustrations: Life Is Without Meaning. (4:1-16)
XI. The Wise Conclusion: Fear God. (5:1-7)
X. Wealth Is No Advantage. (5:8—6:12)
XI. Proverbs Illustrate the Way of Wisdom. (7:1-14)
XII. Righteousness Is Meaningless. (7:15-25)
XIII. The Teacher Warns About the Wiles and Devices of Women. (7:26-29)

XIV. Obey the King. (8:1-9)
XV. Righteousness Goes Unrewarded. (8:10-17)
XVI. All Share the Same Ultimate Fate. (9:1-12)
XVII. Wisdom Does Not Provide the Ultimate Answer. (9:13—10:20)
XVIII. The Teacher Calls to Action in the Face of Meaninglessness. (11:1-8)
XIX. The Advantage Lies with Youth. (11:9—12:7)
XX. Conclusion: Eveything Is Meaningless. (12:8)
XXI. Parting Advice: Hear the Experienced Teacher and Obey God. (12:9-14)

Thematic Outline

I. The Futility of Life
  A. The futility of vocational fulfillment
    1. Life's labors do not bring fulfillment. (1:2-4; 2:10-11,18-23; 4:4-6; 8:15)
    2. Life's professions do not bring fulfillment. (1:12-14; 2:9*a*; 4:13-16)
  B. The futility of worldliness
    1. Pleasure does not bring fulfillment. (2:1,9-11; 6:9-12; 9:7-10)
    2. Laughter does not bring fulfillment. (2:2)
    3. Wine does not bring fulfillment. (2:3)
    4. Entertainment does not bring fulfillment. (2:8*b*)
    5. Food does not bring fulfillment. (6:7)
    6. Sex does not bring fulfillment. (7:25-29)
  C. The futility of materialism
    1. Things you can build do not bring fulfillment. (2:4-6)
    2. Having others serve you does not bring fulfillment. (2:7)
    3. Wealth does not bring fulfillment. (2:8,26; 5:10-20; 6:1-6)
  D. The futility of human ability
    1. Humans cannot understand eternity. (3:9-11)
    2. Humans cannot alter the fact of death. (3:19-22; 8:8)
    3. Humans cannot alter their destiny. (9:1-6,10-12; 11:1-6)
    4. Humans cannot bring about justice. (3:16; 4:1-3; 5:8; 8:14; 10:5-6)
    5. Humans cannot affect life's events. (7:13-24; 8:16-17)
  E. The futility of government (5:8-9; 8:2-7)
    1. The futility of government when run by the wicked (8:10-17)
    2. The futility of government when run by fools or commoners (10:16-17)
  F. The futility of foolishness
    1. The futility of foolish worship (5:1-7)
    2. The futility of foolish neglect (10:18)
    3. The futility of foolish speech (10:20)
  G. The futility of study (12:12)
  H. The futility of youthfulness (11:7-10; 12:1-8)
  I. Summary: All is meaningless. (1:16-18; 3:1-22; 7:13-24; 8:16-17; 9:1-6,11-16; 11:6-8)

II. The Hope of Life
  A. Pleasures can add meaning to life. (10:19)
  B. Wisdom can add meaning to life. (2:14; 7:1-12,19; 9:17-18; 10:1-15)
  C. Friendship can add meaning to life. (4:7-12)
  D. The Teacher's advice can add meaning to life. (12:9-11)
  E. An understanding of timeliness can add meaning to life. (3:1-8)
  F. Relationship to God can add meaning to life.
    1. Relationship to God can add meaning to life's pleasures. (2:24-25; 3:12)
    2. Relationship to God can add meaning to life's labor. (2:24; 3:13)
    3. Relationship to God can add meaning to life's wisdom. (2:26)
    4. Relationship to God can add meaning to life's joy. (2:26)
    5. Relationship to God can add meaning to life's worship. (3:14; 7:18)
    6. Relationship to God can add meaning to life's injustice. (3:17-18)
  G. Summary: Obedience to God can add meaning to life. (12:13-14)

Theological Conclusions

The primary contribution of this work may be a negative one. It forces the world's claims to the good life to face the spotlight of truth. Work, pleasure, drink, sex, wealth, human abilities, government, knowledge, youthful pleasures—all entice us to follow them into paradise, hope, and fulfillment. None can deliver on their promises. None is an adequate master for life.

Ecclesiastes depicts life as futile so that we will not follow his footsteps, not make the same mistakes, not fail in the same ways he did. It has been said, "the light is never brighter than when it shines in total darkness." The Teacher creates a darkness that makes "the Light of the world" appear even brighter when the Messiah finally comes. He prepared the world for Jesus by showing how hopeless life is without Him. Ecclesiastes is not totally dark. A few glimpses of light flicker in the book. If we grant that the contenders to the throne of life are not adequate masters, then we can find some simple pleasures to brighten life. Pleasure, wisdom, friendship, good advice, timely action, and proper relationship to God can be helpful companions on life's road. They help, however, only when fear of God and obedience to His way of life dominate life. As much as any other biblical book, Ecclesiastes shows the sovereignty of God over His created world. No human can fully understand God and His ways. Only God knows fully the secrets of the created order.

Contemporary Teaching

To paraphrase the apostle Paul, the Teacher could "see but a poor reflection as in a mirror" (1 Co 13:12). He looked at life from the other side of the incarnation event. If the Book of Ecclesiastes describes for you the hopelessness of life before Jesus, you have comprehended a major message of the author.

The Book of Ecclesiastes is amazingly applicable to the contemporary scene.

A. Similarity of Philosophies

The author of Ecclesiastes reflected a world with an impersonal view of God. The majority of our world knows nothing about a personal relationship with Him. The author saw the hopelessness of human existence. Many modern philosophers reflect such fatalism. His mood is also mirrored by people wearied by international terrorism, worldwide political unrest, and faltering economies. Nowhere is the author's fatalism more evident than among those today who keep reminding us of the realistic possibility of nuclear annihilation.

B. What Makes Life Worth Living?

Ancient man thought he could find pleasure in materialism, wealth, vocational success, fame, fortune, and the pleasures of the world (good food, good wine, slaves, and women). Today's mass media spreads the same misconceptions. The advertising industry tells the same lies. The end is the same—futility.

C. Avoid the Extremes.

In 7:16-17 the author reminded his hearers to avoid extremes. We would do well to avoid extremism in our day as well. We find repeated invitations to have us "go out on their limb." We must see the good and the bad in such invitations. We would do well to take the middle way most of the time.

D. The Mystery of Evil

Life is not always fair. It was not then. It is not now. The wicked are not always punished, and the righteous are not always rewarded. Government authorities are not always just, wise, or righteous. We do not always understand the ramifications of life.

E. The Difficulty of Aging

The Teacher had acquired a skeptical bent in his old age. Skepticism is not all bad. We need to be skeptical of the world's claims to make life meaningful when such claims can never be realized. Aging does not necessarily make you skeptical; but if you are inclined in that direction, aging may intensify an unhealthy skepticism. The losses one experiences in the aging process can cause skepticism. As we age, we lose our energy, our jobs, our mates, our friends, and often our health. We lose the opportunity to "begin again." We often lose contact with the church. In an era when people are living longer and the problems of aging are becoming more prominent, the church must program for and minister to the aging.

F. Hope

The Teacher did not give up on life completely. He could not answer the larger questions of overcoming death and escaping futility. He could find hope in the simple pleasures and duties of life—pleasure, wisdom, friendship, listening to advice, acting at the right times, and relating each of life's activities to God.

Thus, Ecclesiastes does not offer the final light for a worthwhile life. It does point the way to hope in the simple activities of life while warning us of paths which seem so sure to bring worth to life but lead to futility. In the final analysis, Ecclesiastes leads us to praise Jesus Christ all the more for bringing the final Light that gives supreme worth to life.

Chapter 1

Everything Is Meaningless

THE words of the Teacher,[a][a] son of David, king in Jerusalem:[b]

2"Meaningless! Meaningless!"
says the Teacher.
"Utterly meaningless!
Everything is meaningless."[c]

3What does man gain from all his labor
at which he toils under the sun?[d]
4Generations come and generations go,
but the earth remains forever.[e]
5The sun rises and the sun sets,
and hurries back to where it rises.[f]
6The wind blows to the south
and turns to the north;
round and round it goes,
ever returning on its course.
7All streams flow into the sea,
yet the sea is never full.
To the place the streams come from,
there they return again.[g]
8All things are wearisome,
more than one can say.
The eye never has enough of seeing,[h]
nor the ear its fill of hearing.
9What has been will be again,
what has been done will be done
again;[i]
there is nothing new under the sun.
10Is there anything of which one can say,
"Look! This is something new"?
It was here already, long ago;
it was here before our time.
11There is no remembrance of men of
old,[j]
and even those who are yet to come
will not be remembered
by those who follow.[k]

Wisdom Is Meaningless

12I, the Teacher,[l] was king over Israel
in Jerusalem.[m] 13I devoted myself to
study and to explore by wisdom all that is
done under heaven.[n] What a heavy burden God has laid on men![o] 14I have seen
all the things that are done under the
sun; all of them are meaningless, a chasing after the wind.[p]

15What is twisted cannot be
straightened;[q]
what is lacking cannot be counted.

16I thought to myself, "Look, I have
grown and increased in wisdom more
than anyone who has ruled over Jerusalem before me;[r] I have experienced
much of wisdom and knowledge."
17Then I applied myself to the understanding of wisdom,[s] and also of madness and folly,[t] but I learned that this,
too, is a chasing after the wind.

18For with much wisdom comes much
sorrow;[u]
the more knowledge, the more
grief.[v]

Chapter 2

Pleasures Are Meaningless

I thought in my heart, "Come now, I
will test you with pleasure[w] to find out
what is good." But that also proved to be
meaningless. 2"Laughter,"[x] I said, "is
foolish. And what does pleasure accomplish?" 3I tried cheering myself with
wine,[y] and embracing folly[z]—my mind
still guiding me with wisdom. I wanted to
see what was worthwhile for men to do
under heaven during the few days of their
lives.

4I undertook great projects: I built
houses for myself[a] and planted vineyards.[b] 5I made gardens and parks and
planted all kinds of fruit trees in them. 6I
made reservoirs to water groves of flour-

1:1 [a]ver 12; Ecc 7:27; 12:10 [b]S Pr 1:1
1:2 [c]Ps 39:5-6; 62:9; Ecc 12:8; Ro 8:20-21
1:3 [d]Ecc 2:11,22; 3:9; 5:15-16
1:4 [e]S Job 8:19
1:5 [f]Ps 19:5-6
1:7 [g]Job 36:28
1:8 [h]Pr 27:20
1:9 [i]Ecc 2:12; 3:15
1:11 [j]Ge 40:23; Ecc 9:15 [k]Ps 88:12; Ecc 2:16; 8:10; 9:5
1:12 [l]S ver 1 [m]Ecc 2:9
1:13 [n]S Job 28:3 [o]S Ge 3:17; Ecc 3:10
1:14 [p]Ecc 2:11,17; 4:4; 6:9
1:15 [q]Ecc 7:13
1:16 [r]S 1Ki 3:12
1:17 [s]Ecc 7:23; 8:16 [t]Ecc 2:3,12; 7:25
1:18 [u]Jer 45:3 [v]Ecc 2:23; 12:12
2:1 [w]ver 24; Ecc 7:4; 8:15
2:2 [x]S Pr 14:13
2:3 [y]ver 24-25; S Jdg 9:13; Ru 3:3; Ecc 3:12-13; 5:18; 8:15 [z]S Ecc 1:17
2:4 [a]2Ch 2:1; 8:1-6 [b]SS 8:11

[a]1 Or *leader of the assembly*; also in verses 2 and 12

1:1–11 EVIL AND SUFFERING, Deserved—The Teacher was convinced that life was often futile and empty of meaning. Generations come and go, only to be forgotten, having made no progress. The Book of Ecclesiastes frequently criticizes the traditional view that the good will succeed and the wicked will suffer. According to this writer's experiences and observations, that formula will not always work. Sometimes the bad will succeed and the good will suffer. This teaching warns us not to make an ironclad rule out of proverbial wisdom. See notes on 12:13–14; Pr 1:1–33, 10–19. Some suffering is a testing of our faith. See notes on Job 1:6–12; 4:7–8. Our suffering might also fit into God's redemptive purpose. See note on Isa 52:13—53:12.

1:11 HUMANITY, Death—Death brings a quick end to fame. For most people, no matter how great they appear to be, little will be remembered of them after death. Almost no human accomplishment is long remembered. The resurrection hope revealed clearly in Christ provides a new dimension to fame. The resurrection will reveal how influential our Christian witness has been.

1:12–18 HUMANITY, Intellectual Nature—Human wisdom ultimately reveals human frailties and the emptiness of most of that for which people strive. Knowledge may simply reveal more problems to be solved and more awareness of human pain that we cannot relieve.

1:12–14 REVELATION, Events—The writer reflected from his position as a student of life and history and declared that events have no meaning. The teacher saw no value in the daily routine and habits of his life. Such an opinion is inevitable if faith requires God's immediate intervention and rescue from suffering. Any life-style focused on self-entertainment also finds this conclusion about life quite accurate. A person finds meaning only by looking above the heavens and trusting God's inspired promises. Without God's inspired interpretation, the events of human history reveal neither hope nor meaning.

2:1–16 HUMANITY, Death—No accomplishment of people can finally avoid the last enemy—death. Pleasure is fleeting; death, permanent. See note on 1 Co 15:19.

2:4–11 CHRISTIAN ETHICS, Property Rights—The wealthy can testify with the wise writer of this book that wealth is not ultimately fulfilling. Yet, we retain the compelling desire to get more.

ishing trees. 7I bought male and female
slaves and had other slaves[c] who were
born in my house. I also owned more
herds and flocks than anyone in Jerusalem before me. 8I amassed silver and
gold[d] for myself, and the treasure of
kings and provinces.[e] I acquired men
and women singers,[f] and a harem[b] as
well—the delights of the heart of man. 9I
became greater by far than anyone in Jerusalem[g] before me.[h] In all this my wisdom stayed with me.

10I denied myself nothing my eyes
desired;
I refused my heart no pleasure.
My heart took delight in all my work,
and this was the reward for all my
labor.
11Yet when I surveyed all that my hands
had done
and what I had toiled to achieve,
everything was meaningless, a chasing
after the wind;[i]
nothing was gained under the sun.[j]

Wisdom and Folly Are Meaningless

12Then I turned my thoughts to consider
wisdom,
and also madness and folly.[k]
What more can the king's successor do
than what has already been done?[l]
13I saw that wisdom[m] is better than
folly,[n]
just as light is better than darkness.
14The wise man has eyes in his head,
while the fool walks in the darkness;
but I came to realize
that the same fate overtakes them
both.[o]
15Then I thought in my heart,
"The fate of the fool will overtake me
also.
What then do I gain by being
wise?"[p]
I said in my heart,
"This too is meaningless."
16For the wise man, like the fool, will
not be long remembered;[q]
in days to come both will be
forgotten.[r]
Like the fool, the wise man too must
die![s]

Toil Is Meaningless

17So I hated life, because the work that
is done under the sun was grievous to
me. All of it is meaningless, a chasing after the wind.[t] 18I hated all the things I
had toiled for under the sun, because I
must leave them to the one who comes
after me.[u] 19And who knows whether he
will be a wise man or a fool?[v] Yet he will
have control over all the work into which
I have poured my effort and skill under
the sun. This too is meaningless. 20So my
heart began to despair over all my toilsome labor under the sun. 21For a man
may do his work with wisdom, knowledge and skill, and then he must leave all
he owns to someone who has not worked
for it. This too is meaningless and a great
misfortune. 22What does a man get for all
the toil and anxious striving with which
he labors under the sun?[w] 23All his days
his work is pain and grief;[x] even at night
his mind does not rest.[y] This too is
meaningless.
24A man can do nothing better than to
eat and drink[z] and find satisfaction in his
work.[a] This too, I see, is from the hand
of God,[b] 25for without him, who can eat
or find enjoyment?[c] 26To the man who
pleases him, God gives wisdom,[d] knowledge and happiness, but to the sinner he
gives the task of gathering and storing up
wealth[e] to hand it over to the one who
pleases God.[f] This too is meaningless, a
chasing after the wind.

Chapter 3

A Time for Everything

THERE is a time[g] for everything,
and a season for every activity under
heaven:

2:7 [c]2Ch 8:7-8
2:8 [d]S 1Ki 9:28 [e]S Jdg 3:15 [f]S 2Sa 19:35
2:9 [g]Ecc 1:12 [h]1Ch 29:25
2:11 [i]S Ecc 1:14 [j]S Ecc 1:3
2:12 [k]S Ecc 1:17 [l]S Ecc 1:9
2:13 [m]Ecc 7:19; 9:18 [n]Ecc 7:11-12
2:14 [o]Ps 49:10; Ecc 3:19; 6:6; 7:2; 9:3,11-12
2:15 [p]ver 19; Ecc 6:8
2:16 [q]S Ps 112:6 [r]S Ecc 1:11 [s]Ps 49:10
2:17 [t]S Ecc 1:14
2:18 [u]Ps 39:6; 49:10
2:19 [v]S ver 15
2:22 [w]S Ecc 1:3
2:23 [x]S Ecc 1:18 [y]S Ge 3:17; S Job 7:2
2:24 [z]ver 3; 1Co 15:32 [a]S ver 1; Ecc 3:22 [b]S Job 2:10; Ecc 3:12-13; 5:17-19; 7:14; 9:7-10; 11:7-10
2:25 [c]S Ps 127:2
2:26 [d]S Job 9:4 [e]S Job 27:17 [f]S Pr 13:22
3:1 [g]ver 11,17; Ecc 8:6

[b]8 The meaning of the Hebrew for this phrase is uncertain.

2:17–26 EVIL AND SUFFERING, Endurance—Work occupies much of our time and often seems meaningless and boring. We save our earnings for the next generation who promptly waste them. How can we endure such a life? Is anxiety and stress our only reward? The Teacher encourages us to find work that satisfies us and to learn to enjoy life's simple pleasures. The secret is a life pleasing to God rather than trying to satisfy the world's demands.

2:18–19 HUMANITY, Attitudes to Death—The unrelieved prospect of death snuffing out life and its achievements leads to a sense of utter futility. We may accumulate much in our brief lifetime, but death snatches possessions from us and presents them to one whose attitudes, actions, and achievements we cannot control.

2:24–26 REVELATION, Fellowship—The simple pleasures of life can reveal God's work. Human greed discounts such pleasures, finding meaning only in the accumulation of goods over which we have no ultimate control. Such a self-centered view of life loses God's purposes of fellowship, service, love, and value in human community.

2:26 HUMANITY, Intellectual Nature—God-given wisdom alone brings joy.

3:1–8 CREATION, Purposeful—God has so constructed His world that different events come and go on schedule. Opportunities arise, and we find joy or sorrow as we realize the importance of acting on them during their lifetime. God did not make a haphazard world void of meaning. He made one that offers chances at various intervals of our days. The world God created has a well-balanced structure. Nothing is accidental in God's world. He holds everything in His wise and omnipotent hand.

3:1–9 EVIL AND SUFFERING, Endurance—Giving a

2 a time to be born and a time to die,
a time to plant and a time to
uproot,[h]
3 a time to kill[i] and a time to heal,
a time to tear down and a time to
build,
4 a time to weep and a time to laugh,
a time to mourn and a time to
dance,
5 a time to scatter stones and a time
to gather them,
a time to embrace and a time to
refrain,
6 a time to search and a time to give
up,
a time to keep and a time to throw
away,
7 a time to tear and a time to mend,
a time to be silent[j] and a time to
speak,
8 a time to love and a time to hate,
a time for war and a time for peace.

9What does the worker gain from his
toil?[k] 10I have seen the burden God has
laid on men.[l] 11He has made everything
beautiful in its time.[m] He has also set
eternity in the hearts of men; yet they
cannot fathom[n] what God has done from
beginning to end.[o] 12I know that there is
nothing better for men than to be happy
and do good while they live. 13That everyone may eat and drink,[p] and find satisfaction[q] in all his toil—this is the gift of
God.[r] 14I know that everything God does
will endure forever; nothing can be added to it and nothing taken from it. God
does it so that men will revere him.[s]

15Whatever is has already been,[t]
and what will be has been before;[u]
and God will call the past to
account.[c]

16And I saw something else under the
sun:

In the place of judgment—wickedness
was there,
in the place of justice—wickedness
was there.

17I thought in my heart,

"God will bring to judgment[v]
both the righteous and the wicked,
for there will be a time for every
activity,
a time for every deed."[w]

18I also thought, "As for men, God tests

3:2 [h]Isa 28:24
3:3 [i]S Dt 5:17
3:7 [j]S Est 4:14
3:9 [k]S Ecc 1:3
3:10 [l]S Ecc 1:13
3:11 [m]S ver 1 [n]S Job 11:7 [o]S Job 28:23; Ro 11:33
3:13 [p]Ecc 2:3 [q]Ps 34:12 [r]S Dt 12:7,18; S Ecc 2:24
3:14 [s]S Job 23:15; Ecc 5:7; 7:18; 8:12-13
3:15 [t]Ecc 6:10 [u]S Ecc 1:9
3:17 [v]S Job 19:29; Ecc 11:9; 12:14 [w]ver 1

[c]15 Or *God calls back the past*

realistic view of ordinary life, the writer mentioned the good and the bad that characterize life. It would be unrealistic and naive to expect a life without some pain, sorrow, or trouble.

3:1–8 HUMANITY, Life—Although each life is unique, every life has its common experiences which are a part of our humanity.

3:1–8 HISTORY, Time—God made time to be filled with activities. Humans do not exercise ultimate control over time. We must seek to use time as God has made it to be used. If we demand the right to ultimate control over time and to certainty as to the results of our labor in time, we are doomed to hopelessness. If we can trust God with our time and let Him control its use, then the activities of life can gain joy and meaning.

3:8 CHRISTIAN ETHICS, War and Peace—In the enumeration of "a time for everything," the wise man included the contrasting concepts of love/hate and war/peace. Rather than providing a prooftext for outright hate of neighbor and legitimizing of war, the writer of this text raises the question, "What are we to hate, and what are we to go to war about?" A proper response is that we are to hate injustice and the lack of mercy and that we are to be ready to battle the forces and power of the evil one.

3:9–14 CREATION, Purposeful—The Book of Ecclesiastes represents a human struggle to find meaning in life. Did the Creator place a hopeless burden or a hope-filled challenge before us? Even a limited human view sees that God has created an ordered, beautiful universe, but unaided human reason does not discover the true meaning of life. Rather, we want to see eternal results of our lives but cannot. We see only unending labor. Hope comes only as we let God's gift of life satisfy us by reverencing and fearing Him. God controls the events of His created order. Finding purpose in that order is not a natural human discovery. It is a discovery of faith in the Creator who sees and acts beyond our limited time.

3:11–14 GOD, Sovereignty—God is in full control of His world. This unsettles the person who wants to know and control everything. Only God does that. We need to learn to live contently and let God control His world.

3:11–17 REVELATION, Divine Presence—Without a sense of God's intimate presence, a person sees life as an impossible burden. Visions of eternity are destroyed by the brief span of human life. Life with God sees simple pleasures as His gift. Total meaning comes in faith God will establish His justice to help His people.

3:13 HUMANITY, Human Nature—The ability to find pleasure in one's accomplishments is not natural but God's gift. The natural human is never pleased but always greedy for more.

3:14 CREATION, Sovereignty—The Teacher varied between frustration and faith. The Teacher refused to give up his monotheism or his confidence that an all-wise Intelligence was in charge of the world. Yet he had great difficulty deciding where he and other people whom God created fitted into the scheme of things. Underlying all his philosophical pursuits, however, was one firm conviction. God is in charge, and what He does is right. Because of this, nothing He has had a part in will perish. No one can improve on His work. His purpose is always present whether we realize it or not. Sometimes we must wait for greater maturity to realize the goal toward which God was working in a situation where we, at first, could not see His presence. Often we must wait until we join Him in eternity.

3:16–22 EVIL AND SUFFERING, Deserved—Justice does not always prevail in life, although God will eventually judge the wicked. The writer even questioned whether people have a different end than animals. His conclusion is not despair but satisfaction with his work in this life. Belief in life after death is clearer in Da 12:2. See note there. The New Testament clearly affirms belief in the resurrection of the dead (1 Co 15).

3:16–17 CHRISTIAN ETHICS, Justice—The sovereignty of God in spite of the apparent victory of evil is the underlying note of Ecclesiastes. The author observed life closely and knew the evidence of injustice abounded. Ultimately, however, God's control would be manifested for him and will be manifested for us. The present must be measured in terms of God's future. See note on 8:11–14.

3:18–21 HUMANITY, Life—The physical nature of people is like that of animals. See note on Ge 2:7. Both end in

them so that they may see that they are
like the animals.[x] 19Man's fate[y] is like
that of the animals; the same fate awaits
them both: As one dies, so dies the other.
All have the same breath[d]; man has no
advantage over the animal. Everything is
meaningless. 20All go to the same place;
all come from dust, and to dust all return.[z] 21Who knows if the spirit of man
rises upward[a] and if the spirit of the animal[e] goes down into the earth?"
22So I saw that there is nothing better
for a man than to enjoy his work,[b] because that is his lot.[c] For who can bring
him to see what will happen after him?

Chapter 4

Oppression, Toil, Friendlessness

AGAIN I looked and saw all the oppression[d] that was taking place under
the sun:

I saw the tears of the oppressed—
  and they have no comforter;
power was on the side of their
    oppressors—
  and they have no comforter.[e]
2And I declared that the dead,[f]
  who had already died,
are happier than the living,
  who are still alive.[g]
3But better than both
  is he who has not yet been,[h]
who has not seen the evil
  that is done under the sun.[i]

4And I saw that all labor and all
achievement spring from man's envy of
his neighbor. This too is meaningless, a
chasing after the wind.[j]

5The fool folds his hands[k]
  and ruins himself.
6Better one handful with tranquillity
  than two handfuls with toil[l]
  and chasing after the wind.

7Again I saw something meaningless
under the sun:

8There was a man all alone;

3:18 [x]S Ps 73:22
3:19 [y]S Ecc 2:14
3:20 [z]S Ge 2:7; S Job 34:15
3:21 [a]Ecc 12:7
3:22 [b]S Ecc 2:24 [c]S Job 31:2
4:1 [d]S Ps 12:5 [e]La 1:16
4:2 [f]Jer 20:17-18; 22:10 [g]S Job 3:17; S 10:18
4:3 [h]S Job 3:16 [i]S Job 3:22
4:4 [j]S Ecc 1:14
4:5 [k]S Pr 6:10
4:6 [l]Pr 15:16-17; S 16:8
4:8 [m]Pr 27:20

  he had neither son nor brother.
There was no end to his toil,
  yet his eyes were not content[m] with
    his wealth.
"For whom am I toiling," he asked,
  "and why am I depriving myself of
    enjoyment?"
This too is meaningless—
  a miserable business!

9Two are better than one,
  because they have a good return for
    their work:
10If one falls down,
  his friend can help him up.
But pity the man who falls
  and has no one to help him up!
11Also, if two lie down together, they
    will keep warm.
  But how can one keep warm alone?
12Though one may be overpowered,
  two can defend themselves.
A cord of three strands is not quickly
    broken.

Advancement Is Meaningless

13Better a poor but wise youth than an
old but foolish king who no longer knows
how to take warning. 14The youth may
have come from prison to the kingship, or
he may have been born in poverty within
his kingdom. 15I saw that all who lived
and walked under the sun followed the
youth, the king's successor. 16There was
no end to all the people who were before
them. But those who came later were not
pleased with the successor. This too is
meaningless, a chasing after the wind.

Chapter 5

Stand in Awe of God

GUARD your steps when you go to the
house of God. Go near to listen rather than to offer the sacrifice of fools, who
do not know that they do wrong.

2Do not be quick with your mouth,

[d]*19* Or *spirit* [e]*21* Or *Who knows the spirit of man, which rises upward, or the spirit of the animal, which*

death. Ultimately humans have advantage over animals only if resurrection is a reality. Otherwise, both simply fade into oblivion. Jesus revealed the full reality of God's resurrection victory (1 Co 15:20–28).

3:22 HUMANITY, Work—Work is not a burden but should be enjoyed if a person is to find satisfaction in life.

4:4–8 CHRISTIAN ETHICS, Property Rights—Envy's appetite will never be satisfied. It provides proper motive for no undertaking. See note on 2:4–11.

4:4–6 STEWARDSHIP, Life-style—Living modestly is better than "chasing after the wind" of wealth. Labor should be done to meet God's goals for our lives not to meet the standard set by our neighbor. Christ said that life does not consist of things, no matter how abundant. Real living is in giving and serving, not in getting and indulging. Inner peace and tranquility, not personal wealth and prestige, mark true success. See Mk 10:40–45; note on Lk 12:16–31.

4:9–12 HUMANITY, Relationships—We are usually better off when we have a vital relationship with someone else. This supplies the pooling of strength, resources, and wisdom. Being alone can be nonproductive, dangerous, and uncomfortable.

5:1–7 WORSHIP, Buildings—See note on Ge 28:16–22. Being in God's house is not automatically worship. The attitude of the person, not the location, determines true worship. Worship is to be done with serious purpose and honest intentions.

5:2 GOD, Sovereignty—God's authority, majesty, and transcendence should make us cautious as we communicate with Him. He is exalted over us.

5:2 PRAYER, Humility—Consider carefully how you speak to God. It is wise to approach God in humility.

do not be hasty in your heart
to utter anything before God.[n]
God is in heaven
and you are on earth,
so let your words be few.[o]
3As a dream[p] comes when there are
many cares,
so the speech of a fool when there
are many words.[q]

4When you make a vow to God, do not
delay in fulfilling it.[r] He has no pleasure
in fools; fulfill your vow.[s] 5It is better not
to vow than to make a vow and not fulfill
it.[t] 6Do not let your mouth lead you into
sin. And do not protest to the ⌊temple⌋
messenger, "My vow was a mistake."
Why should God be angry at what you say
and destroy the work of your hands?
7Much dreaming and many words are
meaningless. Therefore stand in awe of
God.[u]

Riches Are Meaningless

8If you see the poor oppressed[v] in a
district, and justice and rights denied, do
not be surprised at such things; for one
official is eyed by a higher one, and over
them both are others higher still. 9The
increase from the land is taken by all; the
king himself profits from the fields.

10Whoever loves money never has
money enough;
whoever loves wealth is never
satisfied with his income.
This too is meaningless.

11As goods increase,
so do those who consume them.
And what benefit are they to the
owner
except to feast his eyes on them?

12The sleep of a laborer is sweet,
whether he eats little or much,
but the abundance of a rich man
permits him no sleep.[w]

13I have seen a grievous evil under the
sun:[x]

wealth hoarded to the harm of its
owner,
14 or wealth lost through some
misfortune,
so that when he has a son
there is nothing left for him.
15Naked a man comes from his mother's
womb,
and as he comes, so he departs.[y]
He takes nothing from his labor[z]
that he can carry in his hand.[a]

16This too is a grievous evil:

As a man comes, so he departs,
and what does he gain,
since he toils for the wind?[b]
17All his days he eats in darkness,
with great frustration, affliction and
anger.

18Then I realized that it is good and
proper for a man to eat and drink,[c] and
to find satisfaction in his toilsome labor[d]
under the sun during the few days of life
God has given him—for this is his lot.
19Moreover, when God gives any man
wealth and possessions,[e] and enables
him to enjoy them,[f] to accept his lot[g]
and be happy in his work—this is a gift of
God.[h] 20He seldom reflects on the days of
his life, because God keeps him occupied
with gladness of heart.[i]

Chapter 6

I have seen another evil under the sun,
and it weighs heavily on men: 2God
gives a man wealth, possessions and hon-
or, so that he lacks nothing his heart desires, but God does not enable him to enjoy them,[j] and a stranger enjoys them
instead. This is meaningless, a grievous
evil.[k]
3A man may have a hundred children
and live many years; yet no matter how

5:2 [n]S Jdg 11:35 [o]S Job 6:24; S Pr 20:25
5:3 [p]S Job 20:8 [q]Ecc 10:14
5:4 [r]S Dt 23:21; S Jdg 11:35; Ps 119:60 [s]S Nu 30:2; Ps 66:13-14
5:5 [t]Nu 30:2-4; Jnh 2:9
5:7 [u]Ecc 3:14
5:8 [v]S Ps 12:5
5:12 [w]Job 20:20
5:13 [x]Ecc 6:1-2
5:15 [y]S Job 1:21 [z]Ps 49:17; 1Ti 6:7 [a]Ecc 1:3
5:16 [b]S Ecc 1:3
5:18 [c]S Ecc 2:3 [d]Ecc 2:10,24
5:19 [e]S 1Ch 29:12 [f]Ecc 6:2 [g]S Job 31:2 [h]S Ecc 2:24
5:20 [i]S Dt 12:7,18
6:2 [j]Ecc 5:19 [k]Ecc 5:13

5:4–7 GOD, Wrath—Improper worship can bring down God's wrath.
5:4–6 SIN, Responsibility—Inaction may be more sinful than wrong action. To make a promise to God and not carry through represents lack of gratitude or trust in God. We must not make promises to God lightly. He does not take His words or ours lightly. He expects us to do what we promise, no turning back.
5:10–17 EVIL AND SUFFERING, Deserved—See notes on 1:1–11; 2:17–26. To make your livelihood and life-style into gods is to invite death's mockery of your labor. Satisfaction in life, not accumulation of goods, should be among our goals.
5:15 HUMANITY, Attitudes to Death—Wealth dies with us. We need to recognize that nothing gained in this life can be carried beyond the grave.
5:18–20 GOD, Grace—We need to accept everything and every opportunity we have as God's gift.
5:18–20 HUMANITY, Life—Life by itself offers few activities which provide real pleasure. Eating, drinking, and daily work should provide basic satisfaction. Any extras we receive are a bonus from God. Enjoying the simple pleasures leaves no time to worry about life's unsolvable problems. See note on 3:13.
5:18–20 CHRISTIAN ETHICS, Property Rights—This testimony is of one who has recognized the true source of his wealth, the satisfaction of a job well done, and the proper use of the good gifts of God.
6:1–2 EVIL AND SUFFERING, Divine Origin—God has established an order that often frustrates humans. We do not control our ultimate fate. We cannot be sure of keeping forever what we accumulate. We face death and the changing fortunes of life. We would like to change God's order. We might even think His established order evil. The Bible calls us to change our thinking. Accumulation of goods must not occupy all our time. We must control our schedules so we have time to enjoy the life God has graciously given us.
6:3–6 HUMANITY, Burial—The person who finds no pleasure in this life or who is not buried with proper honor and respect would have been as well off to die at birth according to Old Testament thought. This underscores the importance

long he lives, if he cannot enjoy his prosperity and does not receive proper burial,
I say that a stillborn[l] child is better off
than he.[m] 4It comes without meaning, it
departs in darkness, and in darkness its
name is shrouded. 5Though it never saw
the sun or knew anything, it has more
rest than does that man— 6even if he
lives a thousand years twice over but fails
to enjoy his prosperity. Do not all go to
the same place?[n]

7All man's efforts are for his mouth,
 yet his appetite is never satisfied.[o]
8What advantage has a wise man
 over a fool?[p]
What does a poor man gain
 by knowing how to conduct himself
 before others?
9Better what the eye sees
 than the roving of the appetite.
This too is meaningless,
 a chasing after the wind.[q]

10Whatever exists has already been
 named,[r]
 and what man is has been known;
no man can contend
 with one who is stronger than he.
11The more the words,
 the less the meaning,
 and how does that profit anyone?

12For who knows what is good for a
man in life, during the few and meaningless days[s] he passes through like a shadow?[t] Who can tell him what will happen
under the sun after he is gone?

Chapter 7

Wisdom

A good name is better than fine
 perfume,[u]
 and the day of death better than the
 day of birth.[v]
2It is better to go to a house of
 mourning
 than to go to a house of feasting,

6:3 [l]S Job 3:16 [m]S Job 3:3
6:6 [n]Ecc 2:14
6:7 [o]S Pr 27:20
6:8 [p]S Ecc 2:15
6:9 [q]S Ecc 1:14
6:10 [r]Ecc 3:15
6:12 [s]S Job 10:20; S 20:8 [t]S 1Ch 29:15; S Job 14:2; S Ps 39:6
7:1 [u]Pr 22:1; SS 1:3 [v]S Job 10:18
7:2 [w]S Pr 11:19 [x]S Ecc 2:14
7:3 [y]S Pr 14:13
7:4 [z]S Ecc 2:1; Jer 16:8
7:5 [a]S Pr 13:18; 15:31-32
7:6 [b]S Ps 58:9 [c]S Pr 14:13
7:7 [d]S Ex 18:21; S 23:8
7:8 [e]Pr 14:29
7:9 [f]S Mt 5:22 [g]S Pr 14:29
7:10 [h]S Ps 77:5
7:11 [i]Ecc 2:13 [j]Ecc 11:7
7:13 [k]Ecc 2:24 [l]Ecc 1:15
7:14 [m]S Job 1:21; S Ecc 2:24

for death[w] is the destiny[x] of every
 man;
 the living should take this to heart.
3Sorrow is better than laughter,[y]
 because a sad face is good for the
 heart.
4The heart of the wise is in the house
 of mourning,
 but the heart of fools is in the house
 of pleasure.[z]
5It is better to heed a wise man's
 rebuke[a]
 than to listen to the song of fools.
6Like the crackling of thorns[b] under
 the pot,
 so is the laughter[c] of fools.
 This too is meaningless.
7Extortion turns a wise man into a fool,
 and a bribe[d] corrupts the heart.
8The end of a matter is better than its
 beginning,
 and patience[e] is better than pride.
9Do not be quickly provoked[f] in your
 spirit,
 for anger resides in the lap of fools.[g]
10Do not say, "Why were the old days[h]
 better than these?"
 For it is not wise to ask such
 questions.
11Wisdom, like an inheritance, is a good
 thing[i]
 and benefits those who see the
 sun.[j]
12Wisdom is a shelter
 as money is a shelter,
but the advantage of knowledge is this:
 that wisdom preserves the life of its
 possessor.
13Consider what God has done:[k]

Who can straighten
 what he has made crooked?[l]
14When times are good, be happy;
 but when times are bad, consider:
God has made the one
 as well as the other.[m]

placed upon burial and magnifies the good news proclaimed in Christ's resurrection.

6:11 CHRISTIAN ETHICS, Language—Language proves a paradox. Quantity of words does not produce quantity of information and meaning. People who say the least often contribute the most to a conversation.

7:1–2 HUMANITY, Attitudes to Death—Without hope of life after death, people can live only to build a personal reputation. Reflection on life's sad experiences and brief duration lead to maturity, whereas constant partying brings no improvement. The New Testament resurrection message brings deeper meaning to life and death.

7:11–12 HUMANITY, Intellectual Nature—Genuine wisdom is both life-giving and a refuge in times of trouble.

7:13–14 GOD, Sovereignty—God's full control of everything means we must expect both good and bad times. We cannot predict when one or the other will come. We must trust God.

7:13–14 CREATION, Evil—The human perspective sees crooked places and bad times in life. One Creator God must bear final responsibility for these. Human life is not a predictable path which an individual controls. It is a path to be walked in faith, knowing that God controls its destiny. Bad times are part of a life in which God has allowed human freedom and in which moral laws operate.

7:14 EVIL AND SUFFERING, Divine Origin—Ultimately the good and bad experiences of life come from God. We need to learn to enjoy the good times in happiness but not expect all days to be good. We must enjoy today and be prepared to accept and deal with what comes tomorrow.

7:14 REVELATION, Author of Hope—Mortals cannot see all of life at once. We must face all of life, the good and the bad. The bad does not prove a lack of revelation. It opens the door to faith for humans with our mortal limits. Faith knows God as the Author and Revealer of hope. Without faith meaninglessness is the ultimate description of life.

Therefore, a man cannot discover
anything about his future.

15 In this meaningless life[n] of mine I
have seen both of these:

a righteous man perishing in his
righteousness,
and a wicked man living long in his
wickedness.[o]
16 Do not be overrighteous,
neither be overwise—
why destroy yourself?
17 Do not be overwicked,
and do not be a fool—
why die before your time?[p]
18 It is good to grasp the one
and not let go of the other.
The man who fears God[q] will avoid
all ⌊extremes⌋.[f]
19 Wisdom[r] makes one wise man more
powerful[s]
than ten rulers in a city.
20 There is not a righteous man[t] on
earth
who does what is right and never
sins.[u]
21 Do not pay attention to every word
people say,
or you[v] may hear your servant
cursing you—
22 for you know in your heart
that many times you yourself have
cursed others.

23 All this I tested by wisdom and I said,

"I am determined to be wise"[w]—
but this was beyond me.
24 Whatever wisdom may be,
it is far off and most profound—
who can discover it?[x]
25 So I turned my mind to understand,
to investigate and to search out
wisdom and the scheme of
things[y]
and to understand the stupidity of
wickedness
and the madness of folly.[z]

26 I find more bitter than death
the woman who is a snare,[a]
whose heart is a trap
and whose hands are chains.

7:15 [n]S Job 7:7 [o]S Job 21:7; Ecc 8:12-14; Jer 12:1
7:17 [p]Job 15:32
7:18 [q]S Ecc 3:14
7:19 [r]S Ecc 2:13 [s]S Pr 8:14
7:20 [t]S Ps 14:3 [u]S 2Ch 6:36; S Job 4:17; S Pr 20:9; Ro 3:12
7:21 [v]Pr 30:10
7:23 [w]S Ecc 1:17
7:24 [x]S Job 28:12
7:25 [y]S Job 28:3 [z]S Ecc 1:17
7:26 [a]S Ex 10:7; S Jdg 14:15 [b]S Pr 2:16-19; 5:3-5; S 7:23; 22:14
7:27 [c]S Ecc 1:1
7:28 [d]1Ki 11:3
8:3 [e]Ecc 10:4
8:4 [f]Est 1:19
8:6 [g]Ecc 3:1

The man who pleases God will escape
her,
but the sinner she will ensnare.[b]

27 "Look," says the Teacher,[g][c] "this is
what I have discovered:

"Adding one thing to another to
discover the scheme of
things—
28 while I was still searching
but not finding—
I found one ⌊upright⌋ man among a
thousand,
but not one ⌊upright⌋ woman[d]
among them all.
29 This only have I found:
God made mankind upright,
but men have gone in search of
many schemes."

Chapter 8

WHO is like the wise man?
Who knows the explanation of
things?
Wisdom brightens a man's face
and changes its hard appearance.

Obey the King

2 Obey the king's command, I say, because you took an oath before God. 3 Do
not be in a hurry to leave the king's presence.[e] Do not stand up for a bad cause,
for he will do whatever he pleases. 4 Since
a king's word is supreme, who can say to
him, "What are you doing?[f]"

5 Whoever obeys his command will
come to no harm,
and the wise heart will know the
proper time and procedure.
6 For there is a proper time and
procedure for every matter,[g]
though a man's misery weighs
heavily upon him.

7 Since no man knows the future,
who can tell him what is to come?
8 No man has power over the wind to
contain it[h];
so no one has power over the day of
his death.

[f] 18 Or *will follow them both* [g] 27 Or *leader of the assembly* [h] 8 Or *over his spirit to retain it*

7:15–18 EVIL AND SUFFERING, Deserved—Sometimes the wicked succeed and the righteous do not. See notes on 1:1–11; 2:17–26. This is no reason to despair. It is not a call to forget righteousness and be totally wicked. It is not a demand to become a moral legalist, proud of my righteousness and critical of everyone else's life. It tells us to seek God's will and follow His wise path through life.

7:15–16 CHRISTIAN ETHICS, Justice—The cynic's reaction to wickedness is not uncommon. His question is, "How long shall evil prevail?" A helpful response is, "What is your time line of perspective?" We must remember God's timetable is longer, but His sovereignty is absolute. See note on 3:16–17.

7:20 SIN, Universal Nature—Long experience in many areas of life led to this proverbial teaching. No matter how wise or powerful a person becomes in the world's eyes, that person cannot truthfully claim to be righteous or sinless. See note on Pr 20:9.

7:23–25 HUMANITY, Intellectual Nature—The first step to attain wisdom is to recognize the utter folly of doing wrong.

8:1 HUMANITY, Intellectual Nature—See note on 7:11–12.

As no one is discharged in time of war,
so wickedness will not release those
who practice it.

9 All this I saw, as I applied my mind to
everything done under the sun. There is a
time when a man lords it over others to
his own[i] hurt. 10 Then too, I saw the
wicked buried[h]—those who used to
come and go from the holy place and receive praise[j] in the city where they did
this. This too is meaningless.
11 When the sentence for a crime is not
quickly carried out, the hearts of the people are filled with schemes to do wrong.
12 Although a wicked man commits a hundred crimes and still lives a long time, I
know that it will go better[i] with God-
fearing men,[j] who are reverent before
God.[k] 13 Yet because the wicked do not
fear God,[l] it will not go well with them,
and their days[m] will not lengthen like a
shadow.
14 There is something else meaningless
that occurs on earth: righteous men who
get what the wicked deserve, and wicked
men who get what the righteous deserve.[n] This too, I say, is meaningless.[o]
15 So I commend the enjoyment of life[p],
because nothing is better for a man under
the sun than to eat and drink[q] and be
glad.[r] Then joy will accompany him in
his work all the days of the life God has
given him under the sun.
16 When I applied my mind to know
wisdom[s] and to observe man's labor on
earth[t]—his eyes not seeing sleep day or
night— 17 then I saw all that God has
done.[u] No one can comprehend what
goes on under the sun. Despite all his efforts to search it out, man cannot discover its meaning. Even if a wise man claims
he knows, he cannot really comprehend it.[v]

Chapter 9

A Common Destiny for All

So I reflected on all this and concluded
that the righteous and the wise and
what they do are in God's hands, but no
man knows whether love or hate awaits
him.[w] 2 All share a common destiny—the
righteous and the wicked, the good and
the bad,[k] the clean and the unclean,
those who offer sacrifices and those who
do not.

As it is with the good man,
so with the sinner;
as it is with those who take oaths,
so with those who are afraid to take
them.[x]

3 This is the evil in everything that happens under the sun: The same destiny
overtakes all.[y] The hearts of men, moreover, are full of evil and there is madness
in their hearts while they live,[z] and after-

8:10 [h]S Ecc 1:11
8:12 [i]S Dt 12:28 [j]S Ex 1:20 [k]Ecc 3:14
8:13 [l]Ecc 3:14 [m]Dt 4:40; Job 5:26; Ps 34:12; Isa 65:20
8:14 [n]S Job 21:7 [o]S Ecc 7:15
8:15 [p]S Ps 42:8 [q]S Ex 32:6; S Ecc 2:3 [r]S Ecc 2:1
8:16 [s]S Ecc 1:17 [t]Ecc 1:13
8:17 [u]S Job 28:3 [v]S Job 28:23; Ro 11:33
9:1 [w]Ecc 10:14
9:2 [x]Job 9:22; Ecc 2:14
9:3 [y]S Job 9:22; S Ecc 2:14 [z]Jer 11:8; 13:10; 16:12; 17:9

[i]*9* Or *to their* [j]*10* Some Hebrew manuscripts and Septuagint (Aquila); most Hebrew manuscripts *and are forgotten* [k]*2* Septuagint (Aquila), Vulgate and Syriac; Hebrew does not have *and the bad.*

8:9–15 EVIL AND SUFFERING, Deserved—Despite the apparent success of the wicked, God still will reward the reverent. Praise for human accomplishments quickly passes. Punishment for crime should be swift but often is not. Righteous people may suffer what the wicked deserve. Life does not follow the logical pattern we might like. The author of Ecclesiastes openly faced the injustice of life by writing his book. His short-term solution was to enjoy life's daily pleasures. The long-term is in God's hands.

8:11–13 HUMANITY, Life—Concrete evidence may seem to prove wickedness is not punished and reverence not rewarded. Yet confidence in God's justice leads to the opposite conclusion.

8:11–14 CHRISTIAN ETHICS, Justice—A society which does not punish crime invites more. The short-term outlook recognizes inconsistencies and injustice in the rewards people receive on earth. The long-term perspective looks to God's justice and judgment. See note on 7:15–16.

8:16–17 GOD, Wisdom—God's sovereign wisdom surpasses all human knowledge and intellect. Trying to know everything is meaningless.

8:16–17 EVIL AND SUFFERING, Humility—The human mind cannot totally comprehend the meaning of life. We cannot judge things or events as good or evil because we cannot see their total results. We cannot claim life has meaning, nor can we declare it meaningless. Only God can answer such ultimate questions. Still, we, like the Teacher, use the intellectual capacities God has given us to struggle with and seek answers to life's complex questions. We trust Him to let us see the answers we need. The Teacher concluded that enjoying life was the best solution.

8:16–17 HUMANITY, Intellectual Nature—For all the greatness of human achievements, ultimate wisdom is still beyond human attainment. Only the eternal God knows everything.

9:1–18 EVIL AND SUFFERING, Rejoicing—Ignorance of the future colors our perspective on life. The Teacher could not see beyond the grave as Da 12:2 and the New Testament do. Without resurrection hope, life may seem meaningless and unfair. Life, and its relationships and activities, is certainly better than death. Living amid life's uncertainties, we still need to learn to rejoice in the good things of life available to us. Concentration on life's simple joys is much more satisfactory than emphasizing its sorrows and injustice. Such a wise approach is much better than using might and violence to try to establish our desires.

9:1–6 HUMANITY, Death—Regardless of human achievements, death comes to everyone. Death is final and disillusioning without hope of resurrection. Christ provides this hope.

9:1–10 REVELATION, Author of Hope—Revelation points to hope through Jesus Christ. Without such faith death blocks the door to all meaning. In Christ we know love awaits us at the end. If eternal life is not available, then God-talk brings no meaning, and life's simple pleasures are the only source of hope.

9:1–6 LAST THINGS, Judgment—The future for mankind, both the good and the sinner, is in God's hands. Left to discover it for themselves, persons might conclude death ends it all for everyone. This text, as much of Ecclesiastes, does not reflect the fuller revelation of the New Testament. The pessimistic view of life and death reveals what human eyes see which do not see beyond death's veil. Out of the fact that future destiny is in God's hands grows the God-given expectation of divine judgment. What mortals cannot know about the future, God by revelation can and does make known.

ward they join the dead.[a] 4Anyone who
is among the living has hope[l]—even a
live dog is better off than a dead lion!

5For the living know that they will die,
but the dead know nothing;[b]
they have no further reward,
and even the memory of them[c] is
forgotten.[d]
6Their love, their hate
and their jealousy have long since
vanished;
never again will they have a part
in anything that happens under the
sun.[e]

7Go, eat your food with gladness, and
drink your wine[f] with a joyful heart,[g]
for it is now that God favors what you do.
8Always be clothed in white,[h] and always
anoint your head with oil. 9Enjoy life with
your wife,[i] whom you love, all the days
of this meaningless life that God has giv-
en you under the sun— all your meaningless days. For this is your lot[j] in life and
in your toilsome labor under the sun.
10Whatever[k] your hand finds to do, do it
with all your might,[l] for in the grave,[m][m]
where you are going, there is neither
working nor planning nor knowledge nor
wisdom.[n]

11I have seen something else under the
sun:

The race is not to the swift
or the battle to the strong,[o]
nor does food come to the wise[p]
or wealth to the brilliant
or favor to the learned;
but time and chance[q] happen to them
all.[r]

12Moreover, no man knows when his
hour will come:

As fish are caught in a cruel net,
or birds are taken in a snare,
so men are trapped by evil times[s]
that fall unexpectedly upon them.[t]

Wisdom Better Than Folly

13I also saw under the sun this example
of wisdom[u] that greatly impressed me:
14There was once a small city with only a
few people in it. And a powerful king
came against it, surrounded it and built
huge siegeworks against it. 15Now there
lived in that city a man poor but wise,
and he saved the city by his wisdom. But
nobody remembered that poor man.[v]
16So I said, "Wisdom is better than
strength." But the poor man's wisdom is
despised, and his words are no longer
heeded.[w]

17The quiet words of the wise are more
to be heeded
than the shouts of a ruler of fools.
18Wisdom[x] is better than weapons of
war,
but one sinner destroys much good.

Chapter 10

As dead flies give perfume a bad smell,
so a little folly[y] outweighs wisdom
and honor.
2The heart of the wise inclines to the
right,
but the heart of the fool to the left.
3Even as he walks along the road,
the fool lacks sense
and shows everyone[z] how stupid he
is.
4If a ruler's anger rises against you,
do not leave your post;[a]
calmness can lay great errors to
rest.[b]

5There is an evil I have seen under the
sun,
the sort of error that arises from a
ruler:
6Fools are put in many high positions,[c]
while the rich occupy the low ones.
7I have seen slaves on horseback,
while princes go on foot like
slaves.[d]

8Whoever digs a pit may fall into it;[e]
whoever breaks through a wall may
be bitten by a snake.[f]
9Whoever quarries stones may be
injured by them;
whoever splits logs may be
endangered by them.[g]

10If the ax is dull
and its edge unsharpened,
more strength is needed
but skill will bring success.

11If a snake bites before it is charmed,
there is no profit for the charmer.[h]

12Words from a wise man's mouth are
gracious,[i]
but a fool is consumed by his own
lips.[j]
13At the beginning his words are folly;
at the end they are wicked
madness—
14 and the fool multiplies words.[k]

9:3 [a]S Job 21:26
9:5 [b]S Job 14:21 [c]S Ps 9:6 [d]S Ecc 1:11
9:6 [e]S Job 21:21
9:7 [f]S Nu 6:20 [g]S Ecc 2:24
9:8 [h]S Rev 3:4
9:9 [i]S Pr 5:18 [j]S Job 31:2
9:10 [k]S 1Sa 10:7 [l]Ecc 11:6 [m]Nu 16:33; S Ps 6:5; Isa 38:18 [n]S Ecc 2:24
9:11 [o]Am 2:14-15 [p]Job 32:13; Isa 47:10; Jer 9:23 [q]Ecc 2:14 [r]S Dt 8:18
9:12 [s]S Pr 29:6 [t]S Ps 73:22; S Ecc 2:14
9:13 [u]S 2Sa 20:22
9:15 [v]S Ge 40:14; S Ecc 1:11
9:16 [w]Est 6:3
9:18 [x]S Ecc 2:13
10:1 [y]Pr 13:16; 18:2
10:3 [z]Pr 13:16
10:4 [a]Ecc 8:3 [b]S Pr 16:14
10:6 [c]S Pr 29:2
10:7 [d]Pr 19:10
10:8 [e]S Ps 57:6 [f]S Est 2:23; Ps 9:16; Am 5:19
10:9 [g]S Pr 26:27
10:11 [h]S Ps 58:5; S Isa 3:3
10:12 [i]Pr 10:32 [j]S Pr 10:6; S 14:3; S 15:2; S 18:7
10:14 [k]Ecc 5:3

[l]4 Or *What then is to be chosen? With all who live, there is hope* [m]10 Hebrew *Sheol*

9:10 LAST THINGS, Intermediate State—See note on Isa 14:9.

9:15–18 HUMANITY, Intellectual Nature—While wisdom is of great value, not everyone recognizes or accepts it as such. Too often we listen to the loudest voice backed by the most powerful weapons.

No one knows what is coming—
who can tell him what will happen
after him?[l]
15A fool's work wearies him;
he does not know the way to town.
16Woe to you, O land whose king was a
servant[n] [m]
and whose princes feast in the
morning.
17Blessed are you, O land whose king is
of noble birth
and whose princes eat at a proper
time—
for strength and not for
drunkenness.[n]
18If a man is lazy, the rafters sag;
if his hands are idle, the house
leaks.[o]
19A feast is made for laughter,
and wine[p] makes life merry,
but money is the answer for
everything.
20Do not revile the king[q] even in your
thoughts,
or curse the rich in your bedroom,
because a bird of the air may carry
your words,
and a bird on the wing may report
what you say.

Chapter 11

Bread Upon the Waters

CAST[r] your bread upon the waters,
for after many days you will find it
again.[s]
2Give portions to seven, yes to eight,
for you do not know what disaster
may come upon the land.
3If clouds are full of water,
they pour rain upon the earth.
Whether a tree falls to the south or to
the north,
in the place where it falls, there will
it lie.

10:14 [l]Ecc 9:1
10:16 [m]Isa 3:4-5, 12
10:17 [n]S Dt 14:26; S 1Sa 25:36; S Pr 31:4
10:18 [o]Pr 20:4; S 24:30-34
10:19 [p]S Ge 14:18; S Jdg 9:13
10:20 [q]S Ex 22:28
11:1 [r]ver 6; Isa 32:20; Hos 10:12 [s]S Dt 24:19
11:5 [t]Jn 3:8-10 [u]Ps 139:14-16
11:6 [v]S Ecc 9:10
11:7 [w]Ecc 7:11
11:8 [x]Ecc 12:1
11:9 [y]S Job 19:29; S Ecc 2:24; S 3:17
11:10 [z]Ps 94:19 [a]S Ecc 2:24

4Whoever watches the wind will not
plant;
whoever looks at the clouds will not
reap.
5As you do not know the path of the
wind,[t]
or how the body is formed[o] in a
mother's womb,[u]
so you cannot understand the work of
God,
the Maker of all things.
6Sow your seed in the morning,
and at evening let not your hands be
idle,[v]
for you do not know which will
succeed,
whether this or that,
or whether both will do equally
well.

Remember Your Creator While Young

7Light is sweet,
and it pleases the eyes to see the
sun.[w]
8However many years a man may live,
let him enjoy them all.
But let him remember[x] the days of
darkness,
for they will be many.
Everything to come is meaningless.
9Be happy, young man, while you are
young,
and let your heart give you joy in
the days of your youth.
Follow the ways of your heart
and whatever your eyes see,
but know that for all these things
God will bring you to judgment.[y]
10So then, banish anxiety[z] from your
heart
and cast off the troubles of your
body,
for youth and vigor are
meaningless.[a]

[n]16 Or *king is a child* [o]5 Or *know how life* (or *the spirit*) / *enters the body being formed*

10:20 CHRISTIAN ETHICS, Language—Insincere and malicious ideas get communicated to those whom we would want to be the very last to hear. Our words should reveal thoughts that are pure and truthful.
11:1–8 EVIL AND SUFFERING, Humility—Life involves some uncertainties and risks. No one understands God's work in the world completely. Hard work does not guarantee success. How do we respond to such a world? The beginning point is to do our assigned work with hope for some success and to share with others in humility, knowing some day we may need help. Whatever we do should be enjoyable.
11:3–5 GOD, Sovereignty—See note on 8:16–17.
11:6 HUMANITY, Work—The worker needs to be industrious at all tasks, recognizing that not all may succeed. Failure must not stifle the will to work.
11:9—12:8 EVIL AND SUFFERING, Rejoicing—Rejoice while you can in life. Each of us eventually reaches the point of physical and mental decline. We should not let fear, anxiety, and frustration dominate life. Neither should we interpret joy as moral restraint forgetting God's judgment. We should take every opportunity God gives us to enjoy life without expecting complete success and understanding. Life must be lived in faith in God, not in expectation of being able to control our destiny.
11:9–10 HUMANITY, Childhood and Youth—Youth is the time of development and experimentation. The young should find satisfaction in their youth but must recognize they are still responsible to God for all youthful acts. While not to be belittled, undue value should not be placed upon youth as such. A generation which strives for youthfulness has missed the point of life itself, for youth is only an introductory stage of life.
11:9 LAST THINGS, Judgment—One does not sin with impunity. A life of self-indulgence and self-chosen ways ultimately answers to God in judgment. See note on 12:14.

Chapter 12

REMEMBER[b] your Creator
in the days of your youth,
before the days of trouble[c] come
and the years approach when you will say,
"I find no pleasure in them"—
2before the sun and the light
and the moon and the stars grow dark,
and the clouds return after the rain;
3when the keepers of the house tremble,
and the strong men stoop,
when the grinders cease because they are few,
and those looking through the windows grow dim;
4when the doors to the street are closed
and the sound of grinding fades;
when men rise up at the sound of birds,
but all their songs grow faint;[d]
5when men are afraid of heights
and of dangers in the streets;
when the almond tree blossoms
and the grasshopper drags himself along
and desire no longer is stirred.
Then man goes to his eternal home[e]
and mourners[f] go about the streets.

6Remember him—before the silver cord is severed,
or the golden bowl is broken;
before the pitcher is shattered at the spring,
or the wheel broken at the well,
7and the dust returns[g] to the ground it came from,
and the spirit returns to God[h] who gave it.[i]
8"Meaningless! Meaningless!" says the Teacher.[p] [j]
"Everything is meaningless![k]"

The Conclusion of the Matter

9Not only was the Teacher wise, but
also he imparted knowledge to the people. He pondered and searched out and
set in order many proverbs.[l] 10The
Teacher[m] searched to find just the right
words, and what he wrote was upright
and true.[n]

11The words of the wise are like goads,
their collected sayings like firmly embedded nails[o]—given by one Shepherd. 12Be
warned, my son, of anything in addition
to them.

Of making many books there is no end,
and much study wearies the body.[p]

13Now all has been heard;

12:1 [b]Ecc 11:8 [c]S 2Sa 19:35
12:4 [d]Jer 25:10
12:5 [e]S Job 10:21 [f]Jer 9:17; Am 5:16
12:7 [g]S Ge 2:7; S Ps 146:4 [h]Ecc 3:21 [i]S Job 20:8
12:8 [j]Ecc 1:1 [k]S Ecc 1:2
12:9 [l]1Ki 4:32
12:10 [m]S Ecc 1:1 [n]Pr 22:20-21
12:11 [o]S Ezr 9:8; S Job 6:25
12:12 [p]S Ecc 1:18
12:13 [q]S Ex 20:20; S 1Sa 12:24; S Job 23:15; S Ps 19:9 [r]S Dt 4:2 [s]S Dt 4:6; S Job 37:24

[p]8 Or *the leader of the assembly*; also in verses 9 and 10

12:1 CREATION, Purposeful—After searching for the thing most meaningful in life, the Teacher reached "full circle" and came back to a profound fact about himself. He did not arrive in the universe accidentally. All of us are part of a purpose because we begin with a divine Creator. Recognition of this fact paved the way for his conclusion of the matter. Since we have a limited time to fit into the plan of God for our lives, we should begin early. Physical functions become impaired almost before we are aware the process is starting to take place. For those who indulge in things outside God's purpose, the spirit becomes cynical. Despite human ignorance, fears, and limits, the best path is to live life from beginning to end according to God's will.

12:1–7 HUMANITY, Age—The onset of age takes away the opportunities of youth, while it leads onward to death. Separation of the body's "dust" and the life-giving spirit breathed in by God does not signify hope. Rather, it describes graphically the finality of death with the loss of the vital life-giving divine breath. Biblical hope centers on resurrection of our body, not on separation of body and spirit. All life should be lived conscious of our responsibility to our Creator.

12:7 LAST THINGS, Intermediate State—At death the spirit leaves the body. It returns to God. The original meaning here may well have been a reflection on Ge 2:7. God created the human body from dust and breathed into it the breath or life-giving spirit (Hebrew *ruach*). Ecclesiastes apparently meant that dust went to dust and breath back to God. His words left open room for further interpretation. From the whole of Scripture those interpreters who believe in a disembodied intermediate state for the righteous see it as a time of being with God waiting for resurrection. The limited vision of the writer is reflected in v 8, whereas the New Testament believer exclaims eternity's blessings. See note on 2 Co 5:1–10.

12:8 HUMANITY, Life—The Teacher began with an understanding of life as "meaningless" (1:2). His exploration of human experience led him to maintain his opinion. No life experiences gave the human being sufficient control of events and of the future to find true meaning and hope. He thought old age and death sealed the matter. In a world where human control led to such meaningless, the Teacher turned outside human efforts. Obedient worship for the Creator is the only hope for meaning (12:13).

12:9–14 HOLY SCRIPTURE, Writing—The author of Ecclesiastes was originally a wise Teacher who collected proverbial wisdom from past generations and taught it orally to young people. He wrote down his teaching in a book. Reference to the Teacher in the third person in v 9 may indicate one of his students or disciples was inspired to describe and summarize the Teacher's work. See note on Pr 30:1–4. The purpose of Ecclesiastes was to prod people into thought and action so they would reverence and serve God, the one Author of all inspired Scripture. No words outside Scripture should ever be placed on the same level or considered acceptable alternatives to Scripture.

12:13–14 EVIL AND SUFFERING, Worship—The conclusion to Ecclesiastes is unexpected. Having echoed the refrain of "meaningless," the book concludes with a call to worship. Is this more than a pious footnote seeking to make the radical conclusions of the book acceptable? Calls to joy echo through the book (2:24; 3:12–13,22; 5:18–20; 8:15; 9:7–9). These are tied to descriptions of God's work for people. The Book of Ecclesiastes underlines strongly the dark side of existence lived according to human understanding and worldly desires. Life lived without considering God is evil and

here is the conclusion of the matter:
Fear God[q] and keep his
commandments,[r]
for this is the whole ⌊duty⌋ of man.[s]
14For God will bring every deed into
judgment,[t]
including every hidden thing,[u]
whether it is good or evil.

12:14 [t]S Job 19:29; S Ecc 3:17 [u]S Job 34:21; S Ps 19:12; Jer 16:17; 23:24

without meaning. Purpose comes only as we seize the opportunities for joy God gives and follow the path of worship and obedience He has set out. Life lived under God's judgment is not negative. Only He is qualified to judge and to point us to the pathway of meaning.

12:13 SALVATION, Obedience—Life may appear meaningless, but God has a way of meaning. Worship and obedience will eventually lead to the light of God's hope. See note on Pr 1:7,29.

12:14 LAST THINGS, Judgment—God's judgment is thorough. He considers every deed, even the secret things. His judgment is fair. He considers both the good things done and the evil. New Testament distinctions in judgment for the wicked and the good show that the evil are punished and the good are rewarded. See notes on 2 Co 5:10; Rev 20:11–15.

Song of Songs

Theological Setting

Love—how does the believer express love to another human being? That is the issue in the Song of Songs.

The issue was real for God's people when these love songs were written and sung for them. Relationships between the sexes were not simply a private matter for Israel. The worship services of their neighbors involved sexual relationships between the worshiper and a member of the staff of the high places where worship was held. We refer to such practices as cultic prostitution and the staff members of the high places as cultic prostitutes.

The Baal religion of Canaan taught that this use of sexual relationships in the worship of Baal guaranteed rain, good crops, and fertility for human parents. Those who refused to participate in such worship faced outrage from their neighbors when drought or plagues brought a poor crop year.

The Bible resolutely declares that all of life stands under God's control. The one God who created everything rules over the agricultural and fertility realms just as He rules over the political and historical realms.

The Song of Songs declares the independence of God's people from religion which imprisons love and sexual relationships within the realm of Baal worship or any other false ruler. The sexual acts of the Baal worship constitute neither a ritual of worship nor a sign of love. Instead, the Song of Songs gives new definition to love. Love and sexual union are a God-given privilege for a man and a woman to share. God's people in the privacy of their existence together, not in the worship place, may participate properly and happily in this dimension of life.

Later traditions of Judaism and Christianity have used allegorical and typological methods of interpretation to extend the meaning of the Song of Songs to God's love with His people and Christ's love for the church. See Guide to Interpreting the Bible, pp. 1769–1772.

Theological Outline

Song of Songs: Celebrating Human Love

I. Longing Is a Part of Love. (1:1-8)
II. Love Will Not Be Silent. (1:9—2:7)
III. Spring and Love Go Together. (2:8-17)
IV. Love Is Exclusive. (3:1-5)
V. Love Is Enhanced by Friendship. (3:6-11)
VI. Love Sees Only the Beautiful. (4:1-7)
VII. Love Involves Giving and Receiving. (4:8—5:1)
VIII. Love Means Risking the Possibility of Pain. (5:2—6:3)
IX. Words Fail for Expressing Love. (6:4—7:9)
X. Love Must Be Given Freely. (7:10-13)
XI. True Love Is Priceless. (8:1-14)

Theological Conclusions

The theology of the Song of Songs must be discovered by the implications, presuppositions, and suggestions of the book rather than by its direct teachings. God is never mentioned in the book. No clear historical situation can be reconstructed which prompted the writing. There is little structure or movement to be found in this book. The beauty of expression and the theme of love will surely prompt some degree of appreciation of what is there, but can more be gained from this part of the Bible?

Looking beyond as well as directly at the text itself, the following doctrinal truths are evident:

1. God made man and woman to complement each other in every way.
2. God made man and woman physically attractive to each other.

3. God meant for human sexuality to be expressed in an exclusive relationship.

In a real sense the Song of Songs picks up where the account of the creation of man and woman in Genesis 1—2 leaves off. There both man and woman were made in God's image. This means they were to have a responsible and meaningful relationship with their Creator. They were made to have an enriching relationship with each other. This included sexual suitability, for they were to multiply upon the earth. The Song of Songs reflects such doctrine but does not expressly state it.

The delightful fact that God made man and woman physically attractive to each other is clearly evident throughout the Song of Songs. The groom used all the resources of human language to express the beauty of his beloved. In explicit and frank words he described her bodily features (4:1-7; 7:1-9). To him she was perfect (4:7), although she seemed to think of herself as less than attractive (1:6-7). She was probably a peasant maiden, but to him she was a queen (7:1). She, too, spoke freely and honestly of his physical attractiveness (5:10-16; 7:10-13). Each thrilled with the anticipation of physical union (7:6-13). The longing and pain of separation was contrasted with the surge of joy in reunion (3:1-5). The desire of lovers to flee from others to their own little love nest can surely be understood by everyone who has experienced love's mysterious power (2:8-15).

It should be carefully noted that this intense human love in the Song of Songs was an exclusive love. It was a love so completely shared with each other that nothing was left for others. The groom spoke of his bride as his own (1:15), and she described him in the same way (1:16). When asked what was so special about her beloved, the maiden was quick to let others know that he was unique (5:9-16).

If such an exclusive relationship is threatened from without, the feeling of jealousy will inevitably come (8:6). This emotion is normal and healthy if kept under control. Such an overwhelming desire of one man for one woman in an exclusive union is consistent with the biblical ideal of marriage and the home. How powerful and how priceless is such a love (8:6-7).

Contemporary Teaching

The practice within our modern culture of degrading human sexuality for gain offers a very real temptation to the reader of the Song of Songs. Should one apologize for, gloss over, explain away, or seek to hide the explicit language describing the eagerness of these lovers to consummate their love? The temptation to do this must be resisted. Such bold words about sexual matters are kept within the context of an exclusive love relationship. The satisfying of a natural or biological urge is not the point. These love songs are private and personal. The maiden is willing to give herself only to her beloved. He reserves himself only for his bride. The Song of Songs is not the only word, not the last word, on human sexuality in the Bible. It is, however, a refreshing reminder of the beauty and wonder of love shared by a man and a woman. The church needs to teach its people this wonder and beauty in the proper relationship.

Chapter 1

SOLOMON'S Song of Songs.[a]

Beloved[a]

2Let him kiss me with the kisses of his
mouth—
for your love[b] is more delightful
than wine.[c]
3Pleasing is the fragrance of your
perfumes;[d]
your name[e] is like perfume poured
out.
No wonder the maidens[f] love you!
4Take me away with you—let us hurry!
Let the king bring me into his
chambers.[g]

Friends

We rejoice and delight[h] in you[b];
we will praise your love[i] more than
wine.

Beloved

How right they are to adore you!

5Dark am I, yet lovely,[j]
O daughters of Jerusalem,[k]
dark like the tents of Kedar,[l]
like the tent curtains of Solomon.[c]
6Do not stare at me because I am dark,
because I am darkened by the sun.
My mother's sons were angry with me
and made me take care of the
vineyards;[m]
my own vineyard I have neglected.
7Tell me, you whom I love, where you
graze your flock
and where you rest your sheep[n] at
midday.
Why should I be like a veiled[o] woman
beside the flocks of your friends?

Friends

8If you do not know, most beautiful of
women,[p]
follow the tracks of the sheep
and graze your young goats
by the tents of the shepherds.

Lover

9I liken you, my darling, to a mare
harnessed to one of the chariots[q] of
Pharaoh.
10Your cheeks[r] are beautiful with
earrings,
your neck with strings of jewels.[s]
11We will make you earrings of gold,
studded with silver.

Beloved

12While the king was at his table,
my perfume spread its fragrance.[t]
13My lover is to me a sachet of myrrh[u]
resting between my breasts.
14My lover[v] is to me a cluster of henna[w]
blossoms
from the vineyards of En Gedi.[x]

Lover

15How beautiful[y] you are, my darling!
Oh, how beautiful!
Your eyes are doves.[z]

Beloved

16How handsome you are, my lover![a]
Oh, how charming!
And our bed is verdant.

Lover

17The beams of our house are cedars;[b]
our rafters are firs.

Chapter 2

Beloved[d]

I am a rose[e][c] of Sharon,[d]
a lily[e] of the valleys.

Lover

2Like a lily among thorns
is my darling among the maidens.

Beloved

3Like an apple tree among the trees of
the forest
is my lover[f] among the young men.
I delight[g] to sit in his shade,
and his fruit is sweet to my taste.[h]
4He has taken me to the banquet hall,[i]
and his banner[j] over me is love.
5Strengthen me with raisins,
refresh me with apples,[k]
for I am faint with love.[l]
6His left arm is under my head,
and his right arm embraces me.[m]
7Daughters of Jerusalem, I charge you[n]
by the gazelles and by the does of
the field:
Do not arouse or awaken love
until it so desires.[o]
8Listen! My lover!

1:1 [a]S 1Ki 4:32; Ps 45 Title
1:2 [b]ver 4; SS 4:10; 8:6 [c]S Ge 14:18; S Jdg 9:13
1:3 [d]S Est 2:12; S Ps 45:8 [e]S Ecc 7:1 [f]Ps 45:14
1:4 [g]Ps 45:15 [h]SS 2:3 [i]S ver 2
1:5 [j]SS 2:14; 4:3 [k]SS 5:16 [l]S Ge 25:13
1:6 [m]SS 2:15; 7:12; 8:12
1:7 [n]Isa 13:20 [o]S Ge 24:65
1:8 [p]SS 5:9; 6:1
1:9 [q]2Ch 1:17
1:10 [r]SS 5:13 [s]Isa 61:10
1:12 [t]SS 4:11-14
1:13 [u]S Ge 37:25
1:14 [v]ver 16; SS 2:3,17; 5:8 [w]SS 4:13 [x]S 1Sa 23:29; S 2Ch 20:2
1:15 [y]SS 4:7; 7:6 [z]Ps 74:19; SS 2:14; 4:1; 5:2,12; 6:9; Jer 48:28
1:16 [a]S ver 14
1:17 [b]1Ki 6:9
2:1 [c]Isa 35:1 [d]S 1Ch 27:29 [e]SS 5:13; Hos 14:5
2:3 [f]S SS 1:14 [g]SS 1:4 [h]SS 4:16
2:4 [i]Est 1:11 [j]S Nu 1:52
2:5 [k]SS 7:8 [l]SS 5:8
2:6 [m]SS 8:3
2:7 [n]SS 5:8 [o]SS 3:5; 8:4

[a]Primarily on the basis of the gender of the Hebrew pronouns used, male and female speakers are indicated in the margins by the captions *Lover* and *Beloved* respectively. The words of others are marked *Friends.* In some instances the divisions and their captions are debatable. [b]*4* The Hebrew is masculine singular. [c]*5* Or *Salma* [d]*1* Or *Lover* [e]*1* Possibly a member of the crocus family

2:3–6 FAMILY, Sexual Fulfillment—Poetic descriptions portray the fruitful results of a loving, committed sexual embrace. The Bible does not condemn sex. It condemns the false claims made for sex and the cheapening of sex outside the marriage commitment. See 7:7–10; note on Pr 5:15–23.

those watchmen of the walls!
8O daughters of Jerusalem, I charge
you[t] —
if you find my lover,[u]
what will you tell him?
Tell him I am faint with love.[v]

Friends

9How is your beloved better than
others,
most beautiful of women?[w]
How is your beloved better than
others,
that you charge us so?

Beloved

10My lover is radiant and ruddy,
outstanding among ten thousand.[x]
11His head is purest gold;
his hair is wavy
and black as a raven.
12His eyes are like doves[y]
by the water streams,
washed in milk,[z]
mounted like jewels.
13His cheeks[a] are like beds of spice[b]
yielding perfume.
His lips are like lilies[c]
dripping with myrrh.[d]
14His arms are rods of gold
set with chrysolite.
His body is like polished ivory
decorated with sapphires.[k] [e]
15His legs are pillars of marble
set on bases of pure gold.
His appearance is like Lebanon,[f]
choice as its cedars.
16His mouth[g] is sweetness itself;
he is altogether lovely.
This is my lover,[h] this my friend,
O daughters of Jerusalem.[i]

Chapter 6

Friends

WHERE has your lover[j] gone,
most beautiful of women?[k]
Which way did your lover turn,
that we may look for him with you?

Beloved

2My lover has gone[l] down to his
garden,[m]
to the beds of spices,[n]
to browse in the gardens
and to gather lilies.
3I am my lover's and my lover is
mine;[o]
he browses among the lilies.[p]

5:8 [t]SS 2:7 [u]S SS 1:14 [v]SS 2:5
5:9 [w]S SS 1:8
5:10 [x]Ps 45:2
5:12 [y]S SS 1:15 [z]Ge 49:12
5:13 [a]SS 1:10 [b]SS 6:2 [c]S SS 2:1 [d]ver 5
5:14 [e]S Job 28:6
5:15 [f]1Ki 4:33; SS 7:4
5:16 [g]SS 4:3 [h]SS 7:9 [i]SS 1:5
6:1 [j]SS 5:6 [k]S SS 1:8
6:2 [l]SS 5:6 [m]S SS 4:12 [n]SS 5:13
6:3 [o]SS 7:10 [p]S SS 2:16
6:4 [q]S Jos 12:24; S 1Ki 15:33 [r]Ps 48:2; 50:2 [s]S Nu 1:52
6:5 [t]S SS 4:1
6:6 [u]SS 4:2
6:7 [v]S Ge 24:65 [w]SS 4:3
6:8 [x]Ps 45:9 [y]S Ge 22:24; S Est 2:14
6:9 [z]S SS 1:15 [a]SS 5:2 [b]S SS 3:4
6:11 [c]SS 7:12
6:13 [d]S Ex 15:20

Lover

4You are beautiful, my darling, as
Tirzah,[q]
lovely as Jerusalem,[r]
majestic as troops with banners.[s]
5Turn your eyes from me;
they overwhelm me.
Your hair is like a flock of goats
descending from Gilead.[t]
6Your teeth are like a flock of sheep
coming up from the washing.
Each has its twin,
not one of them is alone.[u]
7Your temples behind your veil[v]
are like the halves of a
pomegranate.[w]
8Sixty queens[x] there may be,
and eighty concubines,[y]
and virgins beyond number;
9but my dove,[z] my perfect one,[a] is
unique,
the only daughter of her mother,
the favorite of the one who bore
her.[b]
The maidens saw her and called her
blessed;
the queens and concubines praised
her.

Friends

10Who is this that appears like the dawn,
fair as the moon, bright as the sun,
majestic as the stars in procession?

Lover

11I went down to the grove of nut trees
to look at the new growth in the
valley,
to see if the vines had budded
or the pomegranates were in
bloom.[c]
12Before I realized it,
my desire set me among the royal
chariots of my people.[1]

Friends

13Come back, come back, O
Shulammite;
come back, come back, that we may
gaze on you!

Lover

Why would you gaze on the
Shulammite
as on the dance[d] of Mahanaim?

[k]14 Or *lapis lazuli* [1]12 Or *among the chariots of Amminadab*; or *among the chariots of the people of the prince*

5:10–16 FAMILY, Sexual Fulfillment—See Pr 4:1–7; note on Pr 5:15–23.

Chapter 7

HOW beautiful your sandaled feet,
O prince's[e] daughter!
Your graceful legs are like jewels,
the work of a craftsman's hands.
2Your navel is a rounded goblet
that never lacks blended wine.
Your waist is a mound of wheat
encircled by lilies.
3Your breasts[f] are like two fawns,
twins of a gazelle.
4Your neck is like an ivory tower.[g]
Your eyes are the pools of Heshbon[h]
by the gate of Bath Rabbim.
Your nose is like the tower of
Lebanon[i]
looking toward Damascus.
5Your head crowns you like Mount
Carmel.[j]
Your hair is like royal tapestry;
the king is held captive by its
tresses.
6How beautiful[k] you are and how
pleasing,
O love, with your delights![l]
7Your stature is like that of the palm,
and your breasts[m] like clusters of
fruit.
8I said, "I will climb the palm tree;
I will take hold of its fruit."
May your breasts be like the clusters of
the vine,
the fragrance of your breath like
apples,[n]
9 and your mouth like the best wine.

Beloved

May the wine go straight to my lover,[o]
flowing gently over lips and teeth.[m]
10I belong to my lover,
and his desire[p] is for me.[q]
11Come, my lover, let us go to the
countryside,
let us spend the night in the
villages.[n]
12Let us go early to the vineyards[r]
to see if the vines have budded,[s]
if their blossoms[t] have opened,
and if the pomegranates[u] are in
bloom[v] —
there I will give you my love.
13The mandrakes[w] send out their
fragrance,
and at our door is every delicacy,
both new and old,
that I have stored up for you, my
lover.[x]

Chapter 8

IF only you were to me like a brother,
who was nursed at my mother's
breasts!
Then, if I found you outside,
I would kiss you,
and no one would despise me.
2I would lead you
and bring you to my mother's
house[y] —
she who has taught me.
I would give you spiced wine to drink,
the nectar of my pomegranates.
3His left arm is under my head
and his right arm embraces me.[z]
4Daughters of Jerusalem, I charge you:
Do not arouse or awaken love
until it so desires.[a]

Friends

5Who is this coming up from the
desert[b]
leaning on her lover?

Beloved

Under the apple tree I roused you;
there your mother conceived[c] you,
there she who was in labor gave you
birth.
6Place me like a seal over your heart,
like a seal on your arm;
for love[d] is as strong as death,
its jealousy[o][e] unyielding as the
grave.[p]
It burns like blazing fire,
like a mighty flame.[q]
7Many waters cannot quench love;
rivers cannot wash it away.
If one were to give
all the wealth of his house for love,
it[r] would be utterly scorned.[f]

Friends

8We have a young sister,
and her breasts are not yet grown.
What shall we do for our sister
for the day she is spoken for?
9If she is a wall,

7:1 [e]Ps 45:13
7:3 [f]SS 4:5
7:4 [g]S Ps 144:12 [h]Nu 21:26 [i]S SS 5:15
7:5 [j]Isa 35:2
7:6 [k]S SS 1:15 [l]SS 4:10
7:7 [m]SS 4:5
7:8 [n]SS 2:5
7:9 [o]S S 5:16
7:10 [p]Ps 45:11 [q]SS 2:16; 6:3
7:12 [r]S SS 1:6 [s]SS 2:15 [t]SS 2:13 [u]S SS 4:13 [v]SS 6:11
7:13 [w]S Ge 30:14 [x]SS 4:16
8:2 [y]SS 3:4
8:3 [z]SS 2:6
8:4 [a]SS 2:7; S 3:5
8:5 [b]SS 3:6 [c]S SS 3:4
8:6 [d]S SS 1:2 [e]S Nu 5:14
8:7 [f]S Pr 6:35

[m]9 Septuagint, Aquila, Vulgate and Syriac; Hebrew *lips of sleepers* [n]11 Or *henna bushes* [o]6 Or *ardor* [p]6 Hebrew *Sheol* [q]6 Or / *like the very flame of the LORD* [r]7 Or *he*

7:1–9 FAMILY, Sexual Fulfillment—Physical attraction is God's gift. As with all gifts, it can be misused. Rightly used by marriage partners, it brings ecstatic joy. See Pr 4:1–7; note on Pr 5:15–23.

8:6–7 FAMILY, Authentic Love—This passage is an excellent summary of the whole book in its celebration of human love between the sexes. The Hebrew term (*'ahabah*) defined as "love" involves the whole person in an intensity of feelings for the other which expresses itself both in desire for that person and in self-giving to that person. The Hebrew word encompasses sexual love, friendship love, and self-giving love. The marriage relationship involves all three types of love. Such love outlives death and produces a protective jealousy which allows no competition. Marital love is commitment and trust forever. It cannot be destroyed, nor can it be purchased. God gives such love to two people committed to Him and to one another.

we will build towers of silver on
her.
If she is a door,
we will enclose her with panels of
cedar.

Beloved

10 I am a wall,
and my breasts are like towers.
Thus I have become in his eyes
like one bringing contentment.
11 Solomon had a vineyard[g] in Baal
Hamon;
he let out his vineyard to tenants.
Each was to bring for its fruit
a thousand shekels[s][h] of silver.
12 But my own vineyard[i] is mine to give;
the thousand shekels are for you,
O Solomon,
and two hundred[t] are for those
who tend its fruit.

Lover

13 You who dwell in the gardens
with friends in attendance,
let me hear your voice!

Beloved

14 Come away, my lover,
and be like a gazelle[j]
or like a young stag[k]
on the spice-laden mountains.[l]

8:11 [g] Ecc 2:4 [h] Isa 7:23
8:12 [i] S SS 1:6
8:14 [j] S Pr 5:19 [k] S SS 2:9 [l] S SS 2:8, 17

[s] *11* That is, about 25 pounds (about 11.5 kilograms); also in verse 12 [t] *12* That is, about 5 pounds (about 2.3 kilograms)

8:10 FAMILY, One Flesh—Dedicated love between marriage partners should bring fulfillment and contentment. The thought or sight of the beloved should flood the lover with happiness and joy. The end result of shared love is contentment.

Isaiah

Theological Setting

The Book of Isaiah presents an exciting challenge to the reader both by its size and its content. The book's riches open only to those diligent and persistent. Little is known of the origin of the book. The content falls easily into two distinct divisions: 1-39 historically set in the eighth century BC, and 40-66 historically set in the sixth century BC. Such a striking and unusual phenomenon within one book has caused serious students of the Bible to reach differing conclusions as to exactly what happened. Did God reveal to Isaiah truth for his own day (eighth century) and truth relevant two hundred years in the future (sixth century)? Were there perhaps two prophets involved in bringing this truth to us, Isaiah and a nameless one who lived and ministered two hundred years later? Each one who takes up the Book of Isaiah should remember: (1) that such a difference in time does exist between the two parts; (2) that scholars will forever be divided on how to explain this difference; and (3) that the question is not a question of what God could or could not do. Either position fits comfortably within the belief that God is all powerful. More important than the explanation accepted is the realization that these two parts of the book are not contradictory but complementary. Together they reveal the total message of the inspired book.

Isaiah, son of Amoz, lived in a troubled time when everything that was supposedly nailed down seemed to be coming loose. Three hundred years before the prophet ministered, David had drawn the struggling tribes together, subdued the neighboring groups, and carved out a secure Israelite state. David's was the golden age. Following David's time, destructive forces began to chip away at this rather idealistic situation causing the golden age to lose its luster. Solomon followed his father on the throne but created great discontent with his luxurious living and oppressive ways. The division of this kingdom followed close on the death of Solomon. Military struggle, false worship, weak leadership, internal confusion, and external threat characterized the life of these two kingdoms down to the eighth century.

In the first half of the eighth century both of these kingdoms reached a strength, prosperity, and security they had not known before. They were free from the danger of being destroyed by other powers and were being ruled over by capable kings, Jeroboam II (793-753 BC) in the north and Uzziah (792-740) in the south. The last half of the eighth century was quite a different story. Assyria began a policy of expansion and conquest which would bring the destruction of the Northern Kingdom, Israel, and leave the Southern Kingdom, Judah, in the position of paying tribute to this great power.

The prophet Isaiah was a citizen of the Southern Kingdom, Judah, and ministered during a forty year period which witnessed the subjection of Judah to Assyria in the days of King Ahaz (735-715 BC; 2 Ki 16) and the attempt of King Hezekiah (715-686 BC) to free his people from Assyrian control (2 Ki 18—20).

Surely God's elect people must have pondered the meaning of such tumultuous events. Is our nation in this crisis because our God is weaker than the gods of Assyria? Is military strength the determining force in the history of nations? Could it be that bad times had to come for us to see some things that we could never see in the good times? Did our love and confidence in good King Uzziah cause us to forget God, our true King? Is the external plight of our nation in any way related to the moral and ethical living of those within the nation? What does the future hold? Wherein is hope and security? Who speaks for God in such a time?

In the very year that good King Uzziah died, God called Isaiah to help the people answer such questions as these (Isa 6:1-8). After seeking and finding cleansing for his own sins, he responded to God's call for a spokesman with his well-known words, "Here am I. Send me!" (6:8). His task was not to be an easy one, but he must faithfully help his people understand what God was saying to them for the present and the future through the events of history.

History and doctrine are closely intertwined in the Book of Isaiah. To appreciate the teachings, one must keep in mind the history. Isaiah lived in the eighth century when his people, the nation of Judah, were under Assyrian control. The doctrinal points of chapters 1—39 are linked with this historical setting.

Assyria continued her control of Judah until the last half of the seventh century when she crumbled and fell. After a brief period of independence Judah came under Babylonian control, and in 587 BC was destroyed by this world power. A few thousand citizens of Judah were carried into exile and settled in the vicinity of the ancient city of Babylon. There they stayed for about fifty years. Around 538 BC, Cyrus the Persian took control of the Babylonian empire and, thereby, gained control of the Jews in exile. His policy toward captive peoples was more lenient than that of the Assyrians and Babylonians. Cyrus' offer to the Jews to return to their homeland was accepted by some according to the history in the Book of Ezra. The last part (40—66) of the Book of Isaiah relates closely to the rise of Cyrus (45:1) and how God planned to use him to bring deliverance to His people.

Theological Outline

Isaiah: The Holy God in Judgment and Redemption

I. God Knows His Peoples' Sins But Calls Them Back to Himself. (1:1—12:6)
 A. Though your sins are many, forgiveness is possible. (1:1—5:30)
 B. People need God, but God also needs people to call His people. (6:1-13)
 C. National leaders may refuse God's help. (7:1—8:15)
 D. Waiting for God to act is part of serving Him. (8:16-22)
 E. With God the future is bright. (9:1-7)
 F. Fallen nations teach lessons. (9:8—10:4)
 G. Pride destroys individuals and nations. (10:5-19)
 H. God can do His work with a righteous few. (10:20-23)
 I. Faith in God conquers fear of all else. (10:24-34)
 J. An ideal age is a human dream, but a divine accomplishment. (11:1-16)
 K. Anytime is the right time for thanksgiving. (12:1-6)

II. God's Sovereignty Extends to All Nations Whether Acknowledged or Not. (13:1—23:18)
 A. God's judgment is real. (13:1—21:17)
 B. God's judgment is impartial. (22:1—23:18)

III. God's Triumph Over Evil Means Deliverance for His People. (24:1—27:13)
 A. God's judgment time is a time of mourning and singing. (24:1-23)
 B. God's judgment time is a time of thanksgiving. (25:1-12)
 C. God's judgment time is a time of victory. (26:1—27:13)

IV. God's People Must Be Different. (28:1—39:8)
 A. Tragedy strikes when leaders fail. (28:1—29:4)
 B. The power of God overshadows the power of nations. (30:1—35:10)
 C. A triumphant faith is a faith that will not let go. (36:1—39:8)

V. God's Word for His Confused People. (40:1—55:13)
 A. God comes to His people when judgment has passed. (40:1-31)
 B. God holds His people by the hand. (41:1-29)
 C. Send the light of truth to those in darkness. (42:1-25)
 D. God alone is Savior of His people. (43:1-28)
 E. Homemade gods can never save. (44:1-28)
 F. God may use an unbeliever. (45:1-25)
 G. False gods make life's load heavier. (46:1-13)
 H. Ruin follows wickedness as night follows day. (47:1-15)
 I. Let the redeemed of the Lord proclaim it. (48:1—52:15)
 J. Healing comes to many through the suffering of One. (53:1-12)
 K. God keeps His promises. (54:1-17)
 L. God's finest invitation: Return to Me. (55:1-13)

VI. God's Word to His Imperfect People (56:1—66:24)
 A. Salvation is for all people. (56:1-12)
 B. Idolatry is an ever present temptation. (57:1-21)
 C. Worship and right living are inseparable. (58:1-14)
 D. Repentance brings reconciliation with God. (59:1-21)
 E. Light from God brings life. (60:1—62:12)
 F. Prayer brings God's help. (63:1—65:25)
 G. Judgment and deliverance are rights of God alone. (66:1-24)

Theological Conclusions

The major doctrinal points in the Book of Isaiah are the following:

1. God is One.
2. God is sovereign over creation and history.
3. God is holy.
4. God is Judge.
5. God is Redeemer.

While the Book of Isaiah refers to the gods of other nations (46:1), these are named to ridicule them and declare them nonexistent. In Isaiah's lifetime the people who knew the true God were tempted to become involved with other gods (2:8). This temptation must have intensified for those carried into exile. Surely they wondered if their captor's gods were stronger than their own in the light of their nation's destruction. Thus, for these, the message that there is only one God was a welcome answer to a burning issue. The idol worshiper is pictured as one destined to disappointment because these gods have no power to save (42:17). They cannot even help themselves but must be placed on a beast of burden and carried from one place to another (46:1-2). The one true God, however, lifts and carries His people (46:3). The idol worshipers are mocked and scorned for believing they can make a god from a chunk of wood (44:9-20). The people of the true God must not be so foolish. Has not God Himself eliminated all rivals by identifying Himself as the first and the last and declaring "apart from me there is no God" (44:6)?

Should not those who know this true and only God tell others about Him? The message of the Book of Isaiah is a resounding "yes." This missionary vocation for God's people is especially stressed in the second half of the book. When God brings His people out of exile, Israel must take up the work of a servant of God to be "light for the Gentiles" (42:6).

Closely related to the doctrine of one God is the thought of God's sovereignty over creation and history. The teaching of God as the Creator of this world is clear but not prominent in the Bible. One of the clearest and most dramatic presentations of this doctrine is in the Book of Isaiah (40:12-31). This passage, however, sets the stage for emphasizing God's sovereign control of history.

With a mind and heart attuned to the working of God, Isaiah sought to convince the kings of his day that God was the controlling force in the lives of nations. King Ahaz refused to believe this fact when Isaiah told him that God would deliver him from his enemies. The powers of Israel and Syria were pressuring Judah under Ahaz to enter an alliance with them against threatening Assyria (2 Ki 16:1-9). Isaiah assured Ahaz that God would remove these two troublesome powers but would use Assyria as an instrument for judging the people of Judah (Isa 7:1-25). Soon after these words were spoken, Assyria destroyed Syria and Israel and made Judah pay tribute.

Later, during the reign of Hezekiah, Isaiah again proclaimed that God was exercising His power over nations. On this occasion Hezekiah had revolted against Assyrian control bringing an Assyrian army which overran the land of Judah and laid siege to Jerusalem (30:1-17; 2 Ki 18:1—19:37). Isaiah's promise to King Hezekiah that the Assyrian army would not enter Jerusalem must have appeared as an idle dream at the time. The intervention of God in human history was never more dramatically portrayed than in the subsequent events. The destruction of the Assyrian army and the retreat of the Assyrian ruler back to his homeland should have convinced the people of Judah that their God was in control of human affairs.

Much later, when the citizens of Judah were in exile, God manifested His power over history by choosing and using a pagan ruler, Cyrus the Persian, as an instrument to deliver His people. God even allowed Cyrus to build an empire by military victories over others (41:2-4). Cyrus was not aware he was being used, but God had directed his every step (45:1). The purposes of God within history would be realized. Thus, Cyrus conquered Babylon, found God's elect people in exile, and issued a decree allowing them to return to their homeland (Ezr 1:1-4).

The one God who created this world and runs history is in His nature holy. Isaiah's favorite title for the God he served was, "the Holy One of Israel" (Isa 5:19,24; 10:20; 30:15; 31:1; 40:25; 41:14,20). The primary meaning of the word "Holy" is set apart or separated. Thus, God's holiness means, first of all, that God is not a human being. He cannot be put into human categories. More specifically Isaiah meant to stress the complete purity and the unlimited power of God. In his call, the prophet saw God in a vision and heard those words that would help mold the prophet's conception of God: "Holy, holy, holy" (6:1-3). Thrice holy suggests complete holiness or purity. As a fitting response to God's holiness, the prophet confessed his lack of holiness and his need for cleansing. Only after he was forgiven was this one ready to be God's spokesman (6:5-7).

Holiness also suggests God is not human because God's power is unlimited. The thought was applied by Isaiah with particular reference to the question of Judah's security as a nation. While the kings sought to find security in military might or alliances with other nations, Isaiah pleaded with them to lean on their God with His unlimited power (7:1-16). The Egyptians, from whom Judah often sought help, were human and not divine (31:3). Their power was partial. Quiet and confident faith in the Holy One would mean the nation had a future.

God is Judge of all people. This follows from God's uniqueness and holiness. All nations are accountable to Him (13:1—23:18). Even greater attention is given to the sinfulness of God's people and God's judgment upon them. God's people are accused of being in rebellion against God (1:2), a people sick with the disease of sin (1:5-6). Failure to live in righteousness in moral and ethical matters makes worship a false thing which God rejects (1:10-17). God lavished His attention on His people, yet they were like a vineyard which does not produce good fruit and must be destroyed (5:1-7). God's people were ripe for judgment, but God is reluctant. He would have us do the reasonable thing—repent and experience cleansing and forgiveness (1:18-19). Even when His judgment does fall upon us, it is not meant simply as punishment. It is to purify us and make us usable (1:25).

Such thinking brought Isaiah to one of his key concepts: the remnant idea. After judgment God would save a remnant of the people and would continue His work with this purified and forgiven group (10:20-23; 11:11). Isaiah even gave his two sons names suggesting the swiftness of coming judgment (8:1) and a remnant being saved (7:3). In time this announced judgment would fall on Judah, and the nation would be destroyed. But God did save a remnant. From those taken into exile He, through Cyrus the Persian, rescued a portion of His people and brought them back to their homeland.

God as Redeemer permeates the Book of Isaiah but is particularly evident in the last part of the book. Already it has been shown that the sovereign and holy God uses His power to deliver His people from other nations which would destroy them. There is, however, much more to the story of God as Redeemer in this book. He is the God of all people and extends His redemption to all people. He calls upon His servant, understood at this point to be His elect people, to take that message of redemption to others. The acceptance of the true God by other nations was part of the picture of the ideal age to come as envisioned by Isaiah. This new age was described as a time when a king from the line of David would reign (11:1). He would delight in God (11:3). His eternal kingdom would be one where righteousness and peace prevail (9:7; 11:3-9; 2:4). This glorious time of the Messiah would also mean that others would come to know God and experience His salvation (2:1-3; 11:9).

In the last half of the Book of Isaiah the figure who would be God's instrument for bringing redemption to others was known only as God's servant. While it was reasonable to identify this servant with the people of God coming out of exile with a missionary task as has already been done, a higher application suggested One who would be God's servant in a very special way. He would establish justice in the earth (42:1-4). This act would mean the Servant would suffer at the hands of those He would serve (53:3). Finally, He would be brought to death (53:8). He would die willingly (53:7), although He had done only good (53:9). Yet death was not the end. This Servant of God would experience victory beyond suffering and death—the victory of knowing that His suffering had brought God's redemption to others (53:10-13).

Who is this Servant? A careful reading of the Gospels leads one to realize that Jesus understood His mission in the world in terms of the two great figures in Isaiah—the Messiah King and the Suffering Servant. In combining these roles, Jesus fulfilled God's plan of redemption (Mk 8:31; 10:45).

Contemporary Teaching

So much that was relevant to an understanding of Isaiah the prophet has long since vanished from the scene of history. But the God who guided and inspired this prophet is our God today, and we who follow His Son are His elect people. The Book of Isaiah calls us to live by these ageless truths.

1. God is both separated from us by His holiness yet ever with us in love and power.
2. God calls us individually and as His people to find our security for the future in Him and not in our own human schemes.
3. God is first no matter where we choose to put Him in our lives.
4. God's kingdom of righteousness is the only eternal kingdom.
5. As God's people we are called to be missionaries.
6. Jesus, God's Messiah, looked for by Isaiah, walks with us through life's experiences.
7. The temptation is always with us to make our own gods and bow down to them.
8. God still controls nations and is working out His purposes in history.

These and other great thoughts from the Book of Isaiah will, if pondered and applied, lead us to that abundant life which our God meant for us to experience.

Chapter 1

THE vision[a] concerning Judah and Jerusalem[b] that Isaiah son of Amoz saw[c] during the reigns of Uzziah,[d] Jotham,[e] Ahaz[f] and Hezekiah,[g] kings of Judah.

A Rebellious Nation

2Hear, O heavens! Listen, O earth![h]
For the LORD has spoken:[i]
"I reared children[j] and brought them up,
but they have rebelled[k] against me.
3The ox knows[l] his master,
the donkey his owner's manger,[m]
but Israel does not know,[n]
my people do not understand.[o]"

4Ah, sinful nation,
a people loaded with guilt,[p]
a brood of evildoers,[q]
children given to corruption![r]
They have forsaken[s] the LORD;
they have spurned the Holy One[t] of Israel
and turned their backs[u] on him.

5Why should you be beaten[v] anymore?
Why do you persist[w] in rebellion?[x]
Your whole head is injured,
your whole heart[y] afflicted.[z]
6From the sole of your foot to the top of your head[a]
there is no soundness[b]—
only wounds and welts[c]
and open sores,
not cleansed or bandaged[d]
or soothed with oil.[e]

7Your country is desolate,[f]
your cities burned with fire;[g]
your fields are being stripped by foreigners[h]
right before you,
laid waste as when overthrown by strangers.[i]
8The Daughter of Zion[j] is left[k]
like a shelter in a vineyard,
like a hut[l] in a field of melons,
like a city under siege.
9Unless the LORD Almighty
had left us some survivors,[m]
we would have become like Sodom,
we would have been like Gomorrah.[n]

10Hear the word of the LORD,[o]
you rulers of Sodom;[p]
listen to the law[q] of our God,
you people of Gomorrah![r]
11"The multitude of your sacrifices—
what are they to me?" says the LORD.
"I have more than enough of burnt offerings,
of rams and the fat of fattened animals;[s]
I have no pleasure[t]
in the blood of bulls[u] and lambs and goats.[v]

1:1 [a]1Sa 3:1; Isa 22:1,5; Ob 1:1; Na 1:1 [b]Isa 40:9; 44:26 [c]Isa 2:1; 13:1 [d]S 2Ki 14:21; S 2Ch 26:22 [e]S 1Ch 3:12 [f]S 2Ki 16:1 [g]S 1Ch 3:13 **1:2** [h]S Dt 4:26 [i]Jdg 11:10; Jer 42:5; Mic 1:2 [j]Isa 23:4; 63:16 [k]ver 4,23; Isa 24:5, 20; 30:1,9; 46:8; 48:8; 57:4; 65:2; 66:24; Eze 24:3; Hag 1:12; Mal 1:6; 3:5 **1:3** [l]Job 12:9 [m]S Ge 42:27 [n]Jer 4:22; 5:4; 9:3, 6; Hos 2:8; 4:1 [o]S Dt 32:28; Isa 42:25; 48:8; Hos 4:6; 7:9 **1:4** [p]Isa 5:18 [q]S ver 2; Isa 9:17; 14:20; 31:2; Jer 23:14 [r]Ps 14:3 [s]S Dt 32:15; S Ps 119:87 [t]S 2Ki 19:22; Isa 5:19,24; 31:1; 37:23; 41:14; 43:14; 45:11; 47:4; Eze 39:7 [u]S Pr 30:9; Isa 59:13 **1:5** [v]Pr 20:30 [w]Jer 2:30; 5:3; 8:5 [x]S ver 2; Isa 31:6; Jer 44:16-17; Heb 3:16 [y]La 2:11; 5:17 [z]Isa 30:26; 33:6,24; 58:8; Jer 30:17 **1:6** [a]S Dt 28:35 [b]Ps 38:3 [c]Isa 53:5 [d]S Ps 147:3; Isa 30:26; Jer 8:22; 14:19; 30:17; La 2:13; Eze 34:4 [e]2Sa 14:2; Ps 23:5; 45:7; 104:15; Isa 61:3; Lk 10:34 **1:7** [f]S Lev 26:34 [g]S Lev 26:31; S Dt 29:23 [h]Lev 26:16; Jdg 6:3-6; Isa 62:8; Jer 5:17 [i]S 2Ki 18:13; S Ps 109:11 **1:8** [j]S Ps 9:14; S Isa 10:32 [k]Isa 30:17; 49:21 [l]S Job 27:18 **1:9** [m]S Ge 45:7; S 2Ki 21:14; Isa 4:2; 6:13; 27:12; 28:5; 37:4,31-32; 45:25; 56:8; Jer 23:3; Joel 2:32 [n]S Ge 19:24; Ro 9:29* **1:10** [o]Isa 28:14 [p]S Ge 13:13; S 18:20; Eze 16:49; Ro 9:29; Rev 11:8 [q]Isa 5:24; 8:20; 30:9 [r]Isa 13:19 **1:11** [s]Ps 50:8; Am 6:4 [t]S Job 22:3 [u]Isa 66:3; Jer 6:20 [v]1Sa 15:22; S Ps 40:6; Mal 1:10; Heb 10:4

1:2–4 SIN, Rebellion—God called His children to court. They rebelled and turned from the Father's love. Sin is unreasonable rejection of love. Sin causes us to look at the world from a perverted point of view so we no longer understand the basic realities of life. Such sin involves several elements. The basic one is rebellion (Hebrew *pasha'*), a conscious breach of relationship, disavowing a loyalty, refusing to accept authority. God's children decide they have matured and need no longer live under the Father's authority. We rebels forget our Father provides the basic necessities of life. Rebellion gains nothing but a larger ego. It costs us our entire life support system. Rebelling, God's people become a sinful (Hebrew *chote'*) nation. This is the Old Testament's dominant word for sin. See note on Ne 1:6–7. Sinners are weighted down by guilt (Hebrew *'awon*), a bending or twisting of life so it is bad rather than good as God created it (Ge 1:31). Thus, the crooked deed leads to a crooked life which must be bent back into shape by the Master's discipline. Evildoers (Hebrew *mere'im*) cause others to suffer and hurt. They are thus corrupt people (Hebrew *mashchitim*) who destroy and corrupt others. This is a military term and relates to destruction of the possibility for human welfare. All such sin shows alienation from God, not because God has left His people but because they have forsaken Him. See note on 2 Ch 24:17–26.

1:2–3 HOLY SCRIPTURE, Word—God inspired His prophets to use many literary forms to communicate His message. The Book of Isaiah begins with a trial. Creation was called to testify against the chosen children who had rejected God's revealed plan. God's revealed Word is more easily understood when the reader recognizes the literary form God inspired the writer to use.

1:3 SALVATION, Knowledge of God—Knowledge of God is a proper human response to His salvation. One of God's charges against His people was that although He had been a Father to them, they did not know Him. Their elaborate worship rites had not led them to a personal experience with God (v 11). We begin to see something here of the cross in the heart of God. The text foreshadows the full disclosure of the loving fatherhood of God in Jesus Christ, who has shown us the Father (Jn 14:6–11). Compare Jer 4:22.

1:4 GOD, Holy—Isaiah in his call experience met the holy, pure God (ch 6). He adopted the term holy One of Israel as his favorite expression for God. The holiness of God stands in the sharpest possible contrast to human sinfulness.

1:7–9 THE CHURCH, Remnant—Isaiah proclaimed the destruction of the land by a foreign invader, possibly the invasions by the Assyrians in 735 or 701 BC. The word for remnant or survivor here refers only to something left over, not to the holy remnant. See note on 2 Ch 34:9. Isaiah emphasized the completeness of the destruction rather than God's action in preserving a righteous remnant. The very survival of God's people rests on His grace.

1:10–17 WORSHIP, False—See note on Ex 22:20.

1:10–17 PRAYER, Sincerity—Israel had become satisfied with outward observance without inner character. God hates sham and will not hear prayer as mere form, if the character of the one praying betrays God's purposes. See note on Lev 1:9.

1:12–16 SIN, Transgression—To pray is to sin—when the person praying is hypocritical. To do evil and destroy other people does not qualify you to go to worship and offer prayers

12When you come to appear before me,
who has asked this of you,[w]
this trampling of my courts?
13Stop bringing meaningless offerings![x]
Your incense[y] is detestable[z] to me.
New Moons,[a] Sabbaths and
convocations[b] —
I cannot bear your evil assemblies.
14Your New Moon[c] festivals and your
appointed feasts[d]
my soul hates.[e]
They have become a burden to me;[f]
I am weary[g] of bearing them.
15When you spread out your hands[h] in
prayer,
I will hide[i] my eyes from you;
even if you offer many prayers,
I will not listen.[j]
Your hands[k] are full of blood;[l]
16 wash[m] and make yourselves clean.
Take your evil deeds
out of my sight![n]
Stop doing wrong,[o]
17 learn to do right![p]
Seek justice,[q]
encourage the oppressed.[a] [r]
Defend the cause of the fatherless,[s]
plead the case of the widow.[t]

18"Come now, let us reason together,"[u]
says the LORD.
"Though your sins are like scarlet,
they shall be as white as snow;[v]
though they are red as crimson,
they shall be like wool.[w]
19If you are willing and obedient,[x]
you will eat the best from the land;[y]
20but if you resist and rebel,[z]
you will be devoured by the
sword."[a]
For the mouth of the LORD
has spoken.[b]

21See how the faithful city
has become a harlot![c]
She once was full of justice;
righteousness[d] used to dwell in
her—
but now murderers![e]
22Your silver has become dross,[f]
your choice wine is diluted with
water.
23Your rulers are rebels,[g]
companions of thieves;[h]
they all love bribes[i]
and chase after gifts.
They do not defend the cause of the
fatherless;
the widow's case does not come
before them.[j]
24Therefore the Lord, the LORD
Almighty,
the Mighty One[k] of Israel, declares:
"Ah, I will get relief from my foes
and avenge[l] myself on my
enemies.[m]
25I will turn my hand against you;[n]
I will thoroughly purge[o] away your
dross[p]
and remove all your impurities.[q]
26I will restore your judges as in days of
old,[r]
your counselors as at the beginning.
Afterward you will be called[s]

1:12 [w]Ex 23:17; Dt 31:11 **1:13** [x]Pr 15:8; Isa 66:3; Hag 2:14 [y]Jer 7:9; 18:15; 44:8 [z]S 1Ki 14:24; Ps 115:8; Pr 28:9; Isa 41:24; Mal 2:11 [a]S Nu 10:10 [b]1Ch 23:31 **1:14** [c]S Ne 10:33 [d]Ex 12:16; Lev 23:1-44; Nu 28:11-29:39; Dt 16:1-17; Isa 5:12; 29:1; Hos 2:11 [e]S Ps 11:5 [f]S Job 7:12 [g]Ps 69:3; Isa 7:13; 43:22,24; Jer 44:22; Mal 2:17; 3:14 **1:15** [h]S Ex 9:29 [i]S Dt 31:17; Isa 57:17; 59:2 [j]S Dt 1:45; S 1Sa 8:18; S Job 15:31; S Jn 9:31 [k]S Job 9:30 [l]Isa 4:4; 59:3; Jer 2:34; Eze 7:23; Hos 4:2; Joel 3:21 **1:16** [m]S Ru 3:3; Mt 27:24; Jas 4:8 [n]Nu 19:11,16; Isa 52:11 [o]Isa 55:7; Jer 25:5 **1:17** [p]S Ps 34:14 [q]S Ps 72:1; Isa 11:4; 33:5; 56:1; 61:8; Am 5:14-15; Mic 6:8; Zep 2:3 [r]S Dt 14:29 [s]ver 23; Job 22:9; Ps 82:3; 94:6; Isa 10:2 [t]S Ex 22:22; Eze 18:31; 22:7; Lk 18:3; Jas 1:27 **1:18** [u]S 1Sa 2:25; Isa 41:1; 43:9,26 [v]S Ps 51:7; Rev 7:14 [w]Isa 55:7 **1:19** [x]S Job 36:11; S Isa 50:10 [y]Dt 30:15-16; Ezr 9:12; Ps 34:10; Isa 30:23; 55:2; 58:14; 62:9; 65:13, 21-22 **1:20** [z]S 1Sa 12:15

[a]S Job 15:22; Isa 3:25; 27:1; 65:12; 66:16; Jer 17:27 [b]Nu 23:19; Isa 21:17; 34:16; 40:5; 58:14; Jer 49:13; Mic 4:4; Zec 1:6; Rev 1:16 **1:21** [c]Isa 57:3-9; Jer 2:20; 3:2,9; 13:27; Eze 23:3; Hos 2:1-13 [d]Isa 5:7; 46:13; 59:14; Am 6:12 [e]S Pr 6:17 **1:22** [f]S Ps 119:119 **1:23** [g]S ver 2 [h]S Dt 19:14; Mic 2:1-2; 6:12 [i]S Ex 23:8; Am 5:12 [j]Isa 10:2; Jer 5:28; Eze 22:6-7; Mic 3:9; Hab 1:4 **1:24** [k]S Ge 49:24 [l]Isa 34:2,8; 35:4; 47:3; 59:17; 61:2; 63:4; Jer 51:6; Eze 5:13 [m]S Dt 32:43; S Isa 10:3 **1:25** [n]Dt 28:63 [o]S Ps 78:38 [p]S Ps 119:119 [q]2Ch 29:15; Isa 48:10; Jer 6:29; 9:7; Eze 22:22; Mal 3:3 **1:26** [r]Jer 33:7,11; Mic 4:8 [s]S Ge 32:28

[a] *17* Or / *rebuke the oppressor*

---

of praise and gratitude. Sin puts a barrier between people and God, making proper worship impossible until the sin barrier is removed through repentance and forgiveness. People must stop being wicked, causing others to suffer, if they want to be counted among God's people. See notes on 1:2–4; 1 Ki 14:22–24.

1:18–20 SALVATION, Atonement—This text is often wrenched out of its context and interpreted as an unconditional promise of forgiveness, but God's forgiveness of sin is conditioned on our repentance for sin (1 Jn 1:9). God will not be mocked by a faith which ignores His moral demands. God offers atonement but does not force it on a people unwilling to serve Him.

1:20 SIN, Judgment—Because Judah's sins were many and persistent, God had no choice but to deliver her to her adversaries. This threat was repeated many times in the prophecies of Isaiah and Jeremiah and in the funeral dirges of Lamentations. God prefers compassionate fellowship with His people and appeals to judgment only as a last resort to bring them back to His will.

1:21–27 CHRISTIAN ETHICS, Righteousness—Justice and righteousness ultimately belong to God. In Him we find the power to restore these characteristics where they once were found in a society. He seeks to establish a people in right relationship with Him and seeks to ensure fair treatment for all people. Murder, trickery, deceit, theft, bribery, and unjust courts mark a nation as God's enemy.

1:24 GOD, Power—Isaiah piled up ancient names for God connected with the glory days of the patriarchs in Genesis to emphasize the sovereign power of God to be turned against His people. God's power comforts an obedient people but threatens judgment on a sinful people.

1:24–26 HISTORY, National—The basic prophetic message dealt with the national history of God's rebellious people. The prophets described the sin which deserved judgment, announced the judgment God would bring, and then pointed beyond judgment to hope for renewal and righteousness. In so doing the prophets revealed how seriously God takes human history and demonstrated the concrete foundation of the biblical definition of salvation. Salvation always has an historical beginning point and effects a change in historical existence. Salvation leads to fuller life and meaning in the world, not escape from the world.

1:25 SALVATION, As Cleansing—God's salvation is His cleansing, or purging us. When He saves us, He purges away our dross and impurities. Salvation involves discipline at times to lead us to obedience.

1:26 SALVATION, Renewal—See note on Ps 53:6. Israel's hope for the future included God's restoration to her former glory. God's restored people will reflect His righteousness and faithfulness.

the City of Righteousness,[t]
the Faithful City.[u]"

27Zion will be redeemed with justice,
her penitent[v] ones with righteousness.[w]
28But rebels and sinners[x] will both be broken,
and those who forsake[y] the LORD will perish.[z]

29"You will be ashamed[a] because of the sacred oaks[b]
in which you have delighted;
you will be disgraced because of the gardens[c]
that you have chosen.
30You will be like an oak with fading leaves,[d]
like a garden without water.
31The mighty man will become tinder
and his work a spark;
both will burn together,
with no one to quench the fire.[e]"

Chapter 2

The Mountain of the LORD

2:1–4pp — Mic 4:1–3

THIS is what Isaiah son of Amoz saw concerning Judah and Jerusalem:[f]

2In the last days[g]
the mountain[h] of the LORD's temple will be established
as chief among the mountains;[i]
it will be raised[j] above the hills,
and all nations will stream to it.[k]

3Many peoples[l] will come and say,
"Come, let us go[m] up to the mountain[n] of the LORD,
to the house of the God of Jacob.
He will teach us his ways,
so that we may walk in his paths."
The law[o] will go out from Zion,
the word of the LORD from Jerusalem.[p]
4He will judge[q] between the nations
and will settle disputes[r] for many peoples.
They will beat their swords into plowshares
and their spears into pruning hooks.[s]
Nation will not take up sword against nation,[t]
nor will they train for war anymore.

5Come, O house of Jacob,[u]
let us walk in the light[v] of the LORD.

The Day of the LORD

6You have abandoned[w] your people,
the house of Jacob.[x]
They are full of superstitions from the East;
they practice divination[y] like the Philistines[z]
and clasp hands[a] with pagans.[b]
7Their land is full of silver and gold;[c]
there is no end to their treasures.[d]

1:26 [t]Isa 32:16; 33:5; 46:13; 48:18; 61:11; 62:1; Jer 31:23; Zec 8:3 [u]Isa 4:3; 48:2; 52:1; 60:14; 62:2; 64:10; Da 9:24 **1:27** [v]Isa 30:15; 31:6; 59:20; Eze 18:30 [w]Isa 35:10; 41:14; 43:1; 52:3; 62:12; 63:4; Hos 2:19 **1:28** [x]Isa 33:14; 43:27; 48:8; 50:1; 59:2; Jer 4:18 [y]S Dt 32:15 [z]Ps 9:5; Isa 24:20; 66:24; Jer 16:4; 42:22; 44:12; 2Th 1:8-9 **1:29** [a]Ps 97:7; Isa 42:17; 44:9,11; 45:16; Jer 10:14 [b]Isa 57:5; Eze 6:13; Hos 4:13 [c]Isa 65:3; 66:17 **1:30** [d]S Ps 1:3 **1:31** [e]Isa 4:4; 5:24; 9:18-19; 10:17; 24:6; 26:11; 30:27,33; 33:14; 34:10; 66:15-16, 24; Jer 5:14; 7:20; 21:12; Ob 1:18; Mal 3:2; 4:1; S Mt 25:41 **2:1** [f]Isa 1:1 **2:2** [g]Ac 2:17; Heb 1:2 [h]Isa 11:9; 24:23; 25:6,10; 27:13; 56:7; 57:13; 65:25; 66:20; Jer 31:23; Da 11:45; Joel 3:17; Mic 4:7 [i]Isa 65:9 [j]Zec 14:10 [k]S Ps 102:15; Jer 16:19 **2:3** [l]Isa 45:23; 49:1; 60:3-6,14; 66:18; Jer 3:17; Joel 3:2; Zep 3:8; Zec 14:2 [m]Isa 45:14; 49:12, 23; 55:5 [n]S Dt 33:19; S Ps 137:5 [o]S Isa 1:10; 33:22; 51:4,7 [p]Lk 24:47; S Jn 4:22 **2:4** [q]Ps 7:6; S 9:19; 96:13; 98:9; Isa 1:27; 3:13; 9:7; 42:4; 51:4; Joel 3:14 [r]S Ge 49:10 [s]Joel 3:10 [t]Ps 46:9; Isa 9:5; 11:6-9; 32:18; 57:19; 65:25; Jer 30:10; Da 11:45; Hos 2:18; Mic 4:3; Zec 9:10 **2:5** [u]Isa 58:1 [v]Isa 60:1,19-20; 1Jn 1:5,7 **2:6** [w]S Dt 31:17 [x]Jer 12:7 [y]S Dt 18:10; S Isa 44:25 [z]S 2Ki 1:2; S 2Ch 26:6 [a]Pr 6:1 [b]S 2Ki 16:7; Mic 5:12 **2:7** [c]S Dt 17:17 [d]S Ps 17:14

1:27 SALVATION, Redemption—God's redemption is tied to His justice and righteousness and to the repentance of His people. He sets us free when we turn from our sins. Redemption transforms the social order because it changes individuals.

1:28–29 SIN, Rebellion—God's redemption is for people willing to follow His moral teachings, not for proud worshipers who hurt other people and serve other gods. Sinners face ruin, not redemption. See note on 1:2–4.

2:1–4 HOLY SCRIPTURE, Collection—See note on Mic 4:1–2.

2:1–5 SALVATION, Preparation—Compare Mic 4:1–5; Zec 2:11. The prophet foresaw a day of universal peace among nations. Christians view this as a prophecy which can be completely fulfilled only through Jesus Christ the Lord. God was preparing the world for the salvation of humankind through the teaching of His inspired prophets.

2:1–4 LAST THINGS, Last Days—The prophetic vision is of a future time when Jerusalem and its Temple would be central, the place to which the peoples of the earth come to learn the ways of God. When the word of the Lord gets into the fabric of the nations, the implements of war are turned into the instruments of peace. Some look for a literal fulfillment in a future millennial period with Jerusalem made the political and religious center of the world; some believe Zion refers to a literal kingdom but leave its location open; others see a poetic expectation of the messianic age when the Prince of peace makes harmony possible between persons and nations. See note on Rev 20:1–6.

2:3 SALVATION, Obedience—Obeying God means walking in His paths. It includes religious belief and the moral behavior accompanying that belief. All Christians belong to "the Way" (Ac 9:2).

2:3 EDUCATION, God—Divine teaching will be a major characteristic of the Messianic Age. See Jer 31:33; Mic 4:2. As the Lord Himself instructs the people in His perfect Law (*Torah*—see note on Pr 13:14), justice, righteousness, harmony, and universal peace will prevail. See note on Job 36:22.

2:3 EVANGELISM, Teaching—God's teaching in God's worship place should attract people of all nations to Him. God has entrusted His people with His Word to teach the peoples. Such teaching should lead people to faith.

2:4 CHRISTIAN ETHICS, War and Peace—See note on Mic 4:1–5.

2:6–9 SIN, Depravity—"Do not forgive" may be the most shocking, horrible prayer in the Bible. A people seeking religious rites and beliefs from everyone except God cannot expect God's blessing. Rather the riches they enjoy briefly will be their only reward. Such depravity of character can lead only to destruction and judgment. Even a prophet cannot find hope for forgiveness for such sinners. See note on 1 Ki 14:22–24.

2:6 ELECTION, Condemnation—Because of the superstitions, divination, love of idols, greed for gold, and worship of human invention and technology, God abandoned His elect. People cannot expect the blessings of the elect when they refuse to live the life of the elect.

Their land is full of horses;[e]
there is no end to their chariots.[f]
8Their land is full of idols;[g]
they bow down[h] to the work of
their hands,[i]
to what their fingers[j] have made.
9So man will be brought low[k]
and mankind humbled[l] —
do not forgive them.[b] [m]

10Go into the rocks,
hide[n] in the ground
from dread of the LORD
and the splendor of his majesty![o]
11The eyes of the arrogant[p] man will be
humbled[q]
and the pride[r] of men brought
low;[s]
the LORD alone will be exalted[t] in that
day.[u]

12The LORD Almighty has a day[v] in store
for all the proud[w] and lofty,[x]
for all that is exalted[y]
(and they will be humbled),[z]
13for all the cedars of Lebanon,[a] tall and
lofty,[b]
and all the oaks of Bashan,[c]
14for all the towering mountains
and all the high hills,[d]
15for every lofty tower[e]
and every fortified wall,[f]
16for every trading ship[c] [g]
and every stately vessel.
17The arrogance of man will be brought
low[h]
and the pride of men humbled;[i]
the LORD alone will be exalted in that
day,[j]
18 and the idols[k] will totally
disappear.[l]

19Men will flee to caves[m] in the rocks
and to holes in the ground[n]
from dread[o] of the LORD
and the splendor of his majesty,[p]
when he rises to shake the earth.[q]
20In that day[r] men will throw away
to the rodents and bats[s]
their idols of silver and idols of gold,[t]
which they made to worship.[u]
21They will flee to caverns in the rocks[v]
and to the overhanging crags
from dread of the LORD
and the splendor of his majesty,[w]
when he rises[x] to shake the earth.[y]
22Stop trusting in man,[z]
who has but a breath[a] in his
nostrils.
Of what account is he?[b]

Chapter 3

Judgment on Jerusalem and Judah

SEE now, the Lord,
the LORD Almighty,
is about to take from Jerusalem and
Judah
both supply and support:[c]
all supplies of food[d] and all supplies of
water,[e]
2 the hero and warrior,[f]
the judge and prophet,
the soothsayer[g] and elder,[h]
3the captain of fifty[i] and man of rank,[j]
the counselor, skilled craftsman[k]
and clever enchanter.[l]

4I will make boys their officials;
mere children will govern them.[m]
5People will oppress each other—
man against man, neighbor against
neighbor.[n]
The young will rise up against the old,
the base against the honorable.

6A man will seize one of his brothers
at his father's home, and say,
"You have a cloak, you be our leader;
take charge of this heap of ruins!"
7But in that day[o] he will cry out,
"I have no remedy.[p]
I have no food[q] or clothing in my
house;
do not make me the leader of the
people."[r]

8Jerusalem staggers,

2:7 [e]S Dt 17:16 [f]S Ge 41:43; Isa 31:1; Mic 5:10 **2:8** [g]Isa 10:9-11; Rev 9:20 [h]Isa 44:17 [i]S 2Ch 32:19; S Ps 135:15; Mic 5:13 [j]Isa 17:8 **2:9** [k]Ps 62:9 [l]ver 11,17; Isa 5:15; 13:11 [m]S Ne 4:5 **2:10** [n]ver 19; Na 3:11 [o]S Ps 145:12; 2Th 1:9; Rev 6:15-16 **2:11** [p]S Ne 9:29; Hab 2:5 [q]S ver 9 [r]Isa 5:15; 10:12; 37:23; Eze 31:10 [s]S Job 40:11 [t]S Ps 46:10 [u]ver 17, 20; Isa 3:7,18; 4:1, 2; 5:30; 7:18; 17:4, 7; 24:21; 25:9; 26:1; 27:1 **2:12** [v]Isa 13:6,9; 22:5,8,12; 34:8; 61:2; Jer 30:7; La 1:12; Eze 7:7; 30:3; Joel 1:15; 2:11; Am 5:18; Zep 1:14 [w]S Ps 59:12 [x]S 2Sa 22:28 [y]Ps 76:12; Isa 24:4, 21; 60:11; Mal 4:1 [z]S Job 40:11 **2:13** [a]S Jdg 9:15; Isa 10:34; 29:17; Eze 27:5 [b]Isa 10:33 [c]S Ps 22:12; Zec 11:2 **2:14** [d]Isa 30:25; 40:4 **2:15** [e]Isa 30:25; 32:14; 33:18 [f]Isa 25:2,12; Zep 1:16 **2:16** [g]fn S Ge 10:4; S 1Ki 9:26 **2:17** [h]S 2Sa 22:28; S Job 40:11 [i]S ver 9 [j]S ver 11 **2:18** [k]S 1Sa 5:2; Eze 36:25 [l]S Dt 9:21; Isa 21:9; Jer 10:11; Mic 5:13 **2:19** [m]S Jdg 6:2; Isa 7:19 [n]S Jdg 6:2; S Job 30:6; Lk 23:30; Rev 6:15 [o]S Dt 2:25 [p]S Ps 145:12 [q]ver 21; S Job 9:6; S Isa 14:16; Heb 12:26 **2:20** [r]S ver 11 [s]Lev 11:19 [t]S Job 22:24; Eze 36:25; Rev 9:20 [u]Eze 7:19-20; 14:6 **2:21** [v]S Ex 33:22 [w]S Ps 145:12 [x]Isa 33:10 [y]S ver 19 **2:22** [z]Ps 118:6,8; 146:3; Isa 51:12; Jer 17:5 [a]S Ge 2:7; S Ps 144:4 [b]S Job 12:19; Ps 8:4; 18:42; 144:3; Isa 17:13; 29:5; 40:15; S Jas 4:14 **3:1** [c]S Ps 18:18 [d]S Lev 26:26; Am 4:6 [e]Isa 5:13; 65:13; Eze 4:16 **3:2** [f]Eze 17:13 [g]Dt 18:10 [h]Isa 9:14-15 **3:3** [i]S 2Ki 1:9 [j]S Job 22:8 [k]2Ki 24:14 [l]S Ecc 10:11; Jer 8:17 **3:4** [m]ver 12; Ecc 10:16 *fn* **3:5** [n]Ps 28:3; Isa 9:19; Jer 9:8; Mic 7:2,6 **3:7** [o]S Isa 2:11 [p]Jer 30:12; Eze 34:4; Hos 5:13 [q]Joel 1:16 [r]Isa 24:2

[b]9 Or *not raise them up* [c]16 Hebrew *every ship of Tarshish*

2:8,18,20 GOD, One God—God expected Israel to bow down in worship and praise. Instead they bowed to idols. God vowed to show He is the only God by bringing the people low. God will be exalted. He may achieve that by humbling us if we do not recognize Him as the only God.

2:9 SALVATION, Forgiveness—See note on Jos 24:19.

2:11–18 CHRISTIAN ETHICS, Character—Arrogance has no place in the believer's character. All that we are comes by God's grace. Thus, those who preen and posture before others will suffer God's judgment because of their lack of humility.

2:22 HUMANITY, Physical Nature—The physical, human nature of people is of little significance in contrast to the divine nature of God. Humans are only one breath away from death, and God is the giver of breath (Ge 2:7). Human nature at its best is no basis for ultimate trust by anyone.

3:8–17 EVIL AND SUFFERING, Deserved—The wicked bring evil upon themselves as Judah learned. Some suffering is innocent, however, brought on by the sin of others. For example, the rich oppress the poor. When we suffer, we should try to determine if it is deserved as a punishment for sin. If it is undeserved, it may be a test of our faith or part of God's redemptive purpose. It may result from evil political systems which must be endured if they cannot be changed. See notes on 52:13—53:12; Job 4:7–8.

3:8–9 SIN, Depravity—Moral depravity is apparent when

Judah is falling;[s]
their words[t] and deeds[u] are against
the LORD,
defying[v] his glorious presence.
9The look on their faces testifies[w]
against them;
they parade their sin like Sodom;[x]
they do not hide it.
Woe to them!
They have brought disaster[y] upon
themselves.

10Tell the righteous it will be well[z] with
them,
for they will enjoy the fruit of their
deeds.[a]
11Woe to the wicked![b] Disaster[c] is
upon them!
They will be paid back[d] for what their
hands have done.[e]

12Youths[f] oppress my people,
women rule over them.
O my people, your guides lead you
astray;[g]
they turn you from the path.

13The LORD takes his place in court;[h]
he rises to judge[i] the people.
14The LORD enters into judgment[j]
against the elders and leaders of his
people:
"It is you who have ruined my
vineyard;
the plunder[k] from the poor[l] is in
your houses.
15What do you mean by crushing my
people[m]
and grinding[n] the faces of the
poor?"[o]
declares the Lord,
the LORD Almighty.[p]

16The LORD says,
"The women of Zion[q] are haughty,
walking along with outstretched
necks,[r]
flirting with their eyes,
tripping along with mincing steps,
with ornaments jingling on their
ankles.
17Therefore the Lord will bring sores on
the heads of the women of
Zion;
the LORD will make their scalps
bald.[s]"

18In that day[t] the Lord will snatch
away their finery: the bangles and headbands and crescent necklaces,[u] 19the earrings and bracelets[v] and veils,[w] 20the
headdresses[x] and ankle chains and
sashes, the perfume bottles and charms,
21the signet rings and nose rings,[y] 22the
fine robes and the capes and cloaks,[z] the
purses 23and mirrors, and the linen garments[a] and tiaras[b] and shawls.

24Instead of fragrance[c] there will be a
stench;[d]
instead of a sash,[e] a rope;
instead of well-dressed hair,
baldness;[f]
instead of fine clothing, sackcloth;[g]
instead of beauty,[h] branding.[i]
25Your men will fall by the sword,[j]
your warriors in battle.[k]
26The gates[l] of Zion will lament and
mourn;[m]
destitute,[n] she will sit on the
ground.[o]

Chapter 4

IN that day[p] seven women
will take hold of one man[q]
and say, "We will eat our own food[r]
and provide our own clothes;
only let us be called by your name.
Take away our disgrace!"[s]

The Branch of the LORD

2In that day[t] the Branch of the LORD[u]

3:8 [s]Isa 1:7 [t]Isa 9:15,17; 28:15; 30:9; 59:3,13 [u]2Ch 33:6 [v]S Job 1:11; Ps 73:9,11; Isa 65:7 **3:9** [w]Nu 32:23; Isa 59:12; Jer 14:7; Hos 5:5 [x]S Ge 13:13 [y]S 2Ch 34:24; S Pr 8:36; Ro 6:23 **3:10** [z]S Dt 5:33; S 12:28; 28:1-14; Ps 37:17; Jer 22:15 [a]S Ge 15:1; S Ps 128:2 **3:11** [b]S Job 9:13; Isa 57:20 [c]Dt 28:15-68 [d]S 2Ch 6:23 [e]Jer 21:14; La 5:16; Eze 24:14 **3:12** [f]S ver 4 [g]Isa 9:16; 19:14; 28:7; 29:9; Jer 23:13; 25:16; Mic 3:5 **3:13** [h]S Job 10:2 [i]S Ps 82:1; S Isa 2:4 **3:14** [j]S 1Sa 12:7; S Job 22:4 [k]S Job 24:9; Jas 2:6 [l]Isa 11:4; 25:4 **3:15** [m]S Ps 94:5 [n]S Job 24:14 [o]Isa 10:6; 11:4; 26:6; 29:19; 32:6; 51:23 [p]Isa 5:7 **3:16** [q]S SS 3:11 [r]S Job 15:25 **3:17** [s]ver 24; Eze 27:31; Am 8:10 **3:18** [t]S Isa 2:11 [u]Ge 41:42; S Jdg 8:21 **3:19** [v]S Ge 24:47 [w]Eze 16:11-12 **3:20** [x]Ex 39:28; Eze 24:17,23; 44:18 **3:21** [y]S Ge 24:22 **3:22** [z]Ru 3:15 **3:23** [a]Eze 16:10; 23:26 [b]S Ex 29:6; SS 3:11; Isa 61:3; 62:3 **3:24** [c]S Est 2:12 [d]Isa 4:4 [e]Pr 31:24 [f]S ver 17; S Lev 13:40; S Job 1:20 [g]S Ge 37:34; Job 16:15; Isa 20:2; Jer 4:8; La 2:10; Eze 27:30-31; Jnh 3:5-8 [h]1Pe 3:3 [i]S 2Sa 10:4; Isa 20:4 **3:25** [j]S Isa 1:20 [k]Jer 15:8 **3:26** [l]Isa 14:31; 24:12; 45:2 [m]S Ps 137:1; Isa 24:4,7; 29:2; 33:9; Jer 4:28; 14:2 [n]S Lev 26:31 [o]S Job 2:13; La 4:5 **4:1** [p]S Isa 2:11 [q]Isa 13:12; 32:9 [r]2Th 3:12 [s]S Ge 30:23 **4:2** [t]S Isa 2:11 [u]Isa 11:1-5; 52:13; 53:2; Jer 23:5-6; 33:15-16; Eze 17:22; Zec 3:8; 6:12

---

those who claim to be God's people parade their perversion proudly. Blatant sin assures disaster. Bragging of sin when God's glory is available invites the end. See note on 1 Ki 14:22–24.

3:10–11 CHRISTIAN ETHICS, Righteousness—God has created a world order in which people and nations eventually receive what they have given others. See note on Pr 10:2,24–25,29–32.

3:14–15 SIN, Unrighteousness—The divine judge announced the verdict on the leaders of His people. They had not established justice for the poor and needy. They enriched their account by mistreating the poor. Failure to help the poor and actions that cause poverty are sins calling forth God's judgment on us. See note on 1:20.

3:14–15 DISCIPLESHIP, Poor—The people of God have been guilty of injustice and cruelty many times in their treatment of the poor. God confronts leaders of His people with their guilt and pronounces His judgment against them. The people of God today are not free from such guilt. We need to hear God's judgment on our behavior. The pulpits of today should allow no one to feel comfortable in their mistreatment of the poor. Christian disciples need to be challenged to provide loving care that is appropriate for followers of Christ. See note on Lev 25:35–37,39–43.

4:2–6 THE CHURCH, Remnant—For Israel, the doctrine of the remnant helped to solve the theological dilemma concerning God's judgment of Israel. How could God punish and destroy a nation which He had promised to keep forever? The answer lies in the doctrine of the remnant. God punished the wicked but preserved a holy and righteous remnant who would serve Him and faithfully proclaim His name. God promised Israel He would cleanse the remnant of His people. God's promises remain true. God intends to do good toward His people. He provides continued protection and care. The passage looks forward to the coming of the Messiah, the Lord's Branch and the only One who has been perfectly righteous as God wants His remnant to be.

will be beautiful[v] and glorious, and the
fruit[w] of the land will be the pride and
glory[x] of the survivors[y] in Israel. 3Those
who are left in Zion,[z] who remain[a] in
Jerusalem, will be called holy,[b] all who
are recorded[c] among the living in Jerusalem. 4The Lord will wash away the filth[d]
of the women of Zion;[e] he will cleanse[f]
the bloodstains[g] from Jerusalem by a
spirit[d] of judgment[h] and a spirit[d] of
fire.[i] 5Then the LORD will create[j] over
all of Mount Zion[k] and over those who
assemble there a cloud of smoke by day
and a glow of flaming fire by night;[l] over
all the glory[m] will be a canopy.[n] 6It will
be a shelter[o] and shade from the heat of
the day, and a refuge[p] and hiding place
from the storm[q] and rain.

Chapter 5

The Song of the Vineyard

I will sing for the one I love
a song about his vineyard:[r]
My loved one had a vineyard
on a fertile hillside.
2He dug it up and cleared it of stones
and planted it with the choicest
vines.[s]
He built a watchtower[t] in it
and cut out a winepress[u] as well.
Then he looked for a crop of good
grapes,
but it yielded only bad fruit.[v]

3"Now you dwellers in Jerusalem and
men of Judah,
judge between me and my
vineyard.[w]
4What more could have been done for
my vineyard
than I have done for it?[x]
When I looked for good grapes,
why did it yield only bad?[y]
5Now I will tell you
what I am going to do to my
vineyard:
I will take away its hedge,
and it will be destroyed;[z]
I will break down its wall,[a]
and it will be trampled.[b]
6I will make it a wasteland,[c]
neither pruned nor cultivated,
and briers and thorns[d] will grow
there.
I will command the clouds
not to rain[e] on it."

7The vineyard[f] of the LORD Almighty
is the house of Israel,
and the men of Judah
are the garden of his delight.
And he looked for justice,[g] but saw
bloodshed;
for righteousness,[h] but heard cries
of distress.[i]

Woes and Judgments

8Woe[j] to you who add house to house
and join field to field[k]
till no space is left
and you live alone in the land.

9The LORD Almighty[l] has declared in
my hearing:[m]

4:2 [v]Isa 33:17; 53:2 [w]S Ps 72:16; Eze 36:8 [x]Isa 60:15; Eze 34:29 [y]S Isa 1:9 **4:3** [z]S Isa 1:26 [a]Isa 1:9; Ro 11:5 [b]S Ex 19:6; Isa 26:2; 45:25; 52:1; 60:21; Joel 3:17; Ob 1:17; Zep 3:13 [c]S Ps 56:8; S 87:6; S Lk 10:20 **4:4** [d]Isa 3:24 [e]S SS 3:11 [f]S Ps 51:2 [g]S Isa 1:15 [h]Isa 28:6 [i]S Isa 1:31; S 30:30; S Zec 13:9; Mt 3:11; Lk 3:17 **4:5** [j]Isa 41:20; 65:18 [k]Rev 14:1 [l]S Ex 13:21 [m]Isa 35:2; 58:8; 60:1 [n]S Ps 18:11; Rev 7:15 **4:6** [o]Lev 23:34-43; Ps 27:5; Isa 8:14; 25:4; Eze 11:16 [p]Isa 14:32; 25:4; 30:2; 57:13 [q]S Ps 55:8 **5:1** [r]Ps 80:8-9; Isa 27:2; Jn 15:1 **5:2** [s]S Ex 15:17; Isa 16:8 [t]1Sa 2:9; Isa 27:3; 31:5; 49:8; Mt 21:33 [u]S Job 24:11 [v]Mt 21:19; Mk 11:13; Lk 13:6 **5:3** [w]Mt 21:40 **5:4** [x]S 2Ch 36:15; Jer 2:5-7; Mic 6:3-4; Mt 23:37 [y]Jer 2:21; 24:2; 29:17 **5:5** [z]2Ch 36:21; Isa 6:12; 27:10 [a]S Ps 80:12; S Isa 22:5 [b]Isa 10:6; 26:6; 28:3,18; 41:25; 63:3; Jer 12:10; 34:22; La 1:15; Hos 2:12; Mic 7:10; Mal 4:3; S Lk 21:24 **5:6** [c]S Ge 6:13; S Lev 26:32; Isa 6:13; 49:17,19; 51:3; Joel 1:10 [d]ver 10,17; S 2Sa 23:6; Isa 7:23,24; 32:13; 34:13; 55:13; Eze 28:24; Hos 2:12; Heb 6:8 [e]S Dt 28:24; S 2Sa 1:21; Am 4:7 **5:7** [f]Ps 80:8; Isa 17:10; 18:5; 37:30 [g]Isa 10:2; 29:21; 32:7; 59:15; 61:8; Eze 9:9; 22:29 [h]S Isa 1:21 [i]S Ps 12:5 **5:8** [j]ver 11,18,20; Isa 6:5; 10:1; 24:16; Jer 22:13 [k]Job 20:19; Mic 2:2; Hab 2:9-12 **5:9** [l]Jer 44:11 [m]Isa 22:14

[d]4 Or *the Spirit*

4:3 ELECTION, Remnant—God's judgment against His elect had a purpose: creation of a holy remnant who could live securely in His holy presence.

4:5 CREATION, Hope—Creation is not finished. God will create (Hebrew *bara'*) new symbols of His presence in the ideal Jerusalem (2:1–4). Unlike actual Jerusalem (2:5—4:1), the new Jerusalem will be pure. God's presence will insure constant watchcare. Creation is a hope as well as past event.

4:5–6 REVELATION, Divine Presence—The symbols of God's presence in the wilderness are reused here to affirm God's intention of standing by His children. He plans in His day of victory to reveal Himself as He did to the Exodus generation (Ex 33:18–23).

5:1–7 CREATION, Freedom—Divine and human freedom are essential elements of creation. They form the basis for properly understanding divine sovereignty and human responsibility. God created a people as well as a world. He is free to act in accordance with His wishes. He provides all that His people need and reveals His guidelines for life—justice and righteousness. We are free to refuse our allegiance to our Creator and ignore His plans for our lives. He is free to deal with us as we make it necessary by our conduct. Our freedom keeps us from being robots and allows us to choose to relate to God in loving faith. His freedom to interact with His creation prevents Him from becoming an "absentee God," far removed from His creation and powerless to control it.

5:1–7 ELECTION, Love—After giving the house of Israel every advantage, God sang of His disappointment at Israel's bad fruit. Woe and destruction await those who disappoint God with evil and bad fruit. Rejected love turns to wrath when righteousness becomes riotousness and loyalty turns to lament.

5:1–4 GOD, Love—God shows His love for us by providing everything we need to produce fruit as His people. When we do not return His love, He shows His love in judgment and discipline, seeking to save a remnant.

5:5–7 GOD, Wrath—The wrath of God results from His love being rejected. We accept His love by living in righteousness and justice.

5:7–8 CHRISTIAN ETHICS, Justice—Small peasant holdings were passing into the hands of aristocrats. The call of the prophets was for restoration of the poor to their place of economic, social, and political independence. The basis for this call is in the nature of God's justice that calls for relief from injustice. He expects righteousness instead of riots and legality instead of lamentation.

5:8–10 CHRISTIAN ETHICS, Property Rights—God's displeasure and judgment will be revealed against those who have accrued property at the expense of others. They have become ostentatiously rich through the injustice imposed on those who have little. Wealth quickly vanishes. The need for proper relationship with God is eternal.

"Surely the great houses will become
desolate,[n]
the fine mansions left without
occupants.
10A ten-acre[e] vineyard will produce only
a bath[f] of wine,
a homer[g] of seed only an ephah[h] of
grain."[o]

11Woe[p] to those who rise early in the
morning
to run after their drinks,
who stay up late at night
till they are inflamed with wine.[q]
12They have harps and lyres at their
banquets,
tambourines[r] and flutes[s] and wine,
but they have no regard[t] for the deeds
of the LORD,
no respect for the work of his
hands.[u]
13Therefore my people will go into
exile[v]
for lack of understanding;[w]
their men of rank[x] will die of hunger
and their masses will be parched
with thirst.[y]
14Therefore the grave[i] [z] enlarges its
appetite
and opens its mouth[a] without limit;
into it will descend their nobles and
masses
with all their brawlers and
revelers.[b]
15So man will be brought low[c]
and mankind humbled,[d]
the eyes of the arrogant[e] humbled.
16But the LORD Almighty will be
exalted[f] by his justice,[g]
and the holy God will show himself
holy[h] by his righteousness.
17Then sheep will graze as in their own
pasture;[i]
lambs will feed[j] among the ruins of
the rich.

18Woe[j] to those who draw sin along
with cords[k] of deceit,
and wickedness[l] as with cart ropes,
19to those who say, "Let God hurry,
let him hasten[m] his work
so we may see it.
Let it approach,
let the plan of the Holy One[n] of
Israel come,
so we may know it."[o]

20Woe[p] to those who call evil good[q]
and good evil,[r]
who put darkness for light
and light for darkness,[s]
who put bitter for sweet
and sweet for bitter.[t]

21Woe to those who are wise in their
own eyes[u]
and clever in their own sight.

22Woe to those who are heroes at
drinking wine[v]
and champions at mixing drinks,[w]
23who acquit the guilty for a bribe,[x]
but deny justice[y] to the innocent.[z]
24Therefore, as tongues of fire[a] lick up
straw[b]
and as dry grass sinks down in the
flames,
so their roots will decay[c]
and their flowers blow away like
dust;[d]
for they have rejected the law of the
LORD Almighty
and spurned the word[e] of the Holy
One[f] of Israel.
25Therefore the LORD's anger[g] burns
against his people;
his hand is raised and he strikes
them down.
The mountains shake,[h]

5:9 [n]Isa 6:11-12; Mt 23:38 **5:10** [o]S ver 6; Lev 26:26; S Dt 28:38; Zec 8:10 **5:11** [p]S ver 8 [q]S 1Sa 25:36; S Pr 23:29-30 **5:12** [r]Ps 68:25; Isa 24:8 [s]S Job 21:12 [t]S 1Sa 12:24 [u]Ps 28:5; Eze 26:13 **5:13** [v]Isa 49:21 [w]S Pr 10:21; S Isa 1:3; Hos 4:6 [x]S Job 22:8 [y]S Isa 3:1 **5:14** [z]S Pr 30:16 [a]S Nu 16:30 [b]Isa 22:2,13; 23:7; 24:8 **5:15** [c]Isa 10:33 [d]S Isa 2:9 [e]S Isa 2:11 **5:16** [f]Ps 97:9; Isa 33:10 [g]Isa 28:17; 30:18; 33:5; 61:8 [h]S Lev 10:3; Isa 29:23; Eze 36:23 **5:17** [i]Isa 7:25; 17:2; 32:14; Zep 2:6,14 **5:18** [j]S ver 8 [k]Hos 11:4 [l]Isa 59:4-8; Jer 23:14 **5:19** [m]Isa 60:22 [n]S Isa 1:4; 29:23; 30:11,12 [o]Jer 17:15; Eze 12:22; 2Pe 3:4 **5:20** [p]S ver 8 [q]S Ge 18:25; S 1Ki 22:8 [r]S Ps 94:21 [s]S Job 24:13; Mt 6:22-23; Lk 11:34-35 [t]Am 5:7 **5:21** [u]S Pr 3:7; Isa 47:10; Ro 12:16; 1Co 3:18-20 **5:22** [v]S 1Sa 25:36; S Pr 23:20; S Isa 22:13 [w]S Pr 31:4; Isa 65:11; Jer 7:18 **5:23** [x]S Ex 23:8; S Eze 22:12 [y]ver 7; S Isa 1:17; 10:2; 29:21; 59:4,13-15 [z]S Ps 94:21; Am 5:12; Jas 5:6 **5:24** [a]S Isa 1:31 [b]Isa 47:14; Na 1:10 [c]S 2Ki 19:30; S Job 18:16 [d]S Job 24:24; Isa 40:8 [e]Ps 107:11; Isa 8:6; 30:9,12 [f]Job 6:10; Isa 1:4; 10:20; 12:6 **5:25** [g]S 2Ki 22:13; S Job 40:11; Isa 10:17; 26:11; 31:9; 66:15; S Jer 6:12 [h]S Ex 19:18

[e] *10* Hebrew *ten-yoke,* that is, the land plowed by 10 yoke of oxen in one day [f] *10* That is, probably about 6 gallons (about 22 liters) [g] *10* That is, probably about 6 bushels (about 220 liters) [h] *10* That is, probably about 3/5 bushel (about 22 liters) [i] *14* Hebrew *Sheol* [j] *17* Septuagint; Hebrew */ strangers will eat*

5:11–12 SIN, Unbelief—Material well-being can be the greatest snare to keep us from trust in God. Financial security encourages the feeling that we do not need God. Drunken parties are not the way to help God's people or honor God. Such sinful celebration does not even notice God's absence or recognize what He has done. To ignore God is the basic sin. It is unbelief in practice no matter what oral statements the sinner makes.

5:11–12,22 CHRISTIAN ETHICS, Alcohol—These verses pronounce judgment on those who have sought ultimate value for their lives in strong drink. Alcohol makes us forget what God has done for us and so distorts our moral perceptions we do not realize we stand under divine judgment.

5:16 GOD, Justice—In judgment against His own unjust people, the holy, pure God shows His justice because His actions are fair and just.

5:16,19,24 GOD, Holy—God reveals His holiness to us through His righteous acts, which provide salvation for His righteous people but bring judgment on a selfish, oppressive people. See note on 1:4.

5:18–24 SIN, Blindness—Prosperity changes our values, but not God's. The crooked life of sin (*'awon*; see 1:4) is so heavy people have to become like oxen yoked to carts to pull it. Such dedication to sin blinds us to God's actions. Only sin gives rash courage to taunt God and demand action from Him. Sin began with the desire to know good and evil (Ge 3:5–6). Sin totally confuses the two so they become indistinguishable. Sin calls such confusion, "wisdom." Sin must excel, for it knows no humility. Sadly, such sinful persons too often exercise government power and use their positions and wealth to turn justice upside down. All such sin begins when people refuse to trust God's Word, obey His will, and be holy like the holy One.

5:25 GOD, Wrath—God's wrath expresses itself against injustice, even when the guilty ones are God's people. Wrath continues its work until injustice is destroyed.

and the dead bodies[i] are like
refuse[j] in the streets.[k]

Yet for all this, his anger is not turned
away,[l]
his hand is still upraised.[m]
26He lifts up a banner[n] for the distant
nations,
he whistles[o] for those at the ends of
the earth.[p]
Here they come,
swiftly and speedily!
27Not one of them grows tired[q] or
stumbles,
not one slumbers or sleeps;
not a belt[r] is loosened at the
waist,[s]
not a sandal thong is broken.[t]
28Their arrows are sharp,[u]
all their bows[v] are strung;
their horses' hoofs[w] seem like flint,
their chariot wheels like a
whirlwind.[x]
29Their roar is like that of the lion,[y]
they roar like young lions;
they growl as they seize[z] their prey
and carry it off with no one to
rescue.[a]
30In that day[b] they will roar over it
like the roaring of the sea.[c]
And if one looks at the land,
he will see darkness[d] and
distress;[e]
even the light will be darkened[f] by
the clouds.

5:25 [i]S Ps 110:6 [j]S 2Ki 9:37 [k]S 2Sa 22:43 [l]Jer 4:8; Da 9:16 [m]Isa 9:12,17,21; 10:4 **5:26** [n]S Ps 20:5 [o]Isa 7:18; Zec 10:8 [p]Dt 28:49; Isa 13:5; 18:3 **5:27** [q]Isa 14:31; 40:29-31 [r]Isa 22:21; Eze 23:15 [s]S Job 12:18 [t]Joel 2:7-8 **5:28** [u]S Job 39:23; Ps 45:5 [v]S Ps 7:12 [w]Eze 26:11 [x]S 2Ki 2:1; S Job 1:19 **5:29** [y]S 2Ki 17:25; Jer 51:38; Zep 3:3; Zec 11:3 [z]Isa 10:6; 49:24-25 [a]Isa 42:22; Mic 5:8 **5:30** [b]S Isa 2:11 [c]S Ps 93:3; Jer 50:42; Lk 21:25 [d]S 1Sa 2:9; S Job 21:30; Ps 18:28; 44:19; S 82:5 [e]S Jdg 6:2; Isa 22:5; 33:2; Jer 4:23-28 [f]Isa 13:10; 50:3; Joel 2:10 **6:1** [g]S 2Ch 26:22, 23 [h]S 2Ki 15:7 [i]S Ex 24:10; S Nu 12:8; Jn 12:41 [j]S 1Ki 22:19; S Ps 9:4; S 123:1; S Rev 4:2 [k]Isa 52:13; 53:12 [l]Rev 1:13 **6:2** [m]Eze 1:5; 10:15; Rev 4:8 [n]Eze 1:11 **6:3** [o]S Ex 15:11 [p]Ps 89:8 [q]Isa 11:9; 54:5; Mal 1:11

Chapter 6

Isaiah's Commission

IN the year that King Uzziah[g] died,[h] I
saw the Lord[i] seated on a throne,[j]
high and exalted,[k] and the train of his
robe[l] filled the temple. 2Above him were
seraphs,[m] each with six wings: With two
wings they covered their faces, with
two they covered their feet,[n] and with two
they were flying. 3And they were calling
to one another:

"Holy, holy[o], holy is the LORD
Almighty;[p]
the whole earth[q] is full of his
glory."[r]

4At the sound of their voices the doorposts and thresholds shook and the temple was filled with smoke.[s]
5"Woe[t] to me!" I cried. "I am ruined![u] For I am a man of unclean lips,[v w]
and I live among a people of unclean
lips,[x] and my eyes have seen[y] the
King,[z] the LORD Almighty."[a]
6Then one of the seraphs flew to me
with a live coal[b] in his hand, which he

[r]S Ex 16:7; Nu 14:21; Ps 72:19; Rev 4:8 **6:4** [s]S Ex 19:18; S 40:34; Eze 43:5; 44:4; Rev 15:8 **6:5** [t]S Isa 5:8 [u]S Nu 17:12; S Dt 5:26 [v]Lk 5:8 [w]Ex 6:12 [x]Isa 59:3; Jer 9:3-8 [y]S Ex 24:10 [z]Ps 45:3; Isa 24:23; 32:1; 33:17; Jer 51:57 [a]S Job 42:5 **6:6** [b]S Lev 10:1; Eze 10:2

6:1–8 WORSHIP, Reverence—Worship includes two components: the attitudes the worshiper brings and the pattern or ritual of worship. Within the pattern of Temple worship with its beauty and symbolism, Isaiah received a vision of God's holiness and his own sinfulness. He answered God's call to go out in service. The attitudes of humility, reverence, and repentance blessed by God's presence resulted in unforgettable worship. Worship begins with an attitude of reverence and awe and concludes with a commitment to service. See notes on Lev 9:23–24; 1 Sa 15:22–23; Rev 7:11–17.

6:1–13 PROCLAMATION, Call—See note on Jer 1:4–9.

6:1–8 MISSIONS, Call—All Christians are called from sin's darkness and dominion to salvation and service. This passage, along with others (Ex 3:4–10; Jer 1:5; Am 7:14–15), makes it equally clear that God calls some to special ministry and mission. Paul and Barnabas are prime New Testament examples of this missionary call (Ac 13:2). In time of national and personal crisis, Isaiah saw God as the holy Lord of the universe in a way he had never seen Him before. The result in Isaiah is what Christians feel on drawing close to God, that we are sinners and unworthy (v 5). The prophet saw that we are sinners as individuals and as congregations. When we confess our sin, God takes the initiative in cleansing us (Ro 5:8; 1 Jn 1:7,9). Cleansed and forgiven, we can hear God's missionary call. God presents the need, and the Christian with a willing heart responds, "Here am I. Send me." God still speaks and calls. We can make no better response than this. See Knowing and Experiencing the Will of God, pp. 1794–1796.

6:2 REVELATION, Angels—The seraphs are literally "burning ones." They are angelic members of God's heavenly court. They cover their faces in the presence of God's holiness. They carry out God's directions (v 6) but do not become the messengers to God's people here. Seraphs are not mentioned elsewhere in the Old Testament as angels. Rather the word refers to burning serpents in 14:29; 30:6; Nu 21:6,8; Dt 8:15.

6:3 GOD, Glory—In the glorious Temple Isaiah saw only God's glory and became convinced that prestige and honor should be ascribed only to Israel's holy God.

6:3 GOD, Holy—Humans and angels are different from God. He is morally pure and by nature distinct. Only He is holy. So we fall to worship and confess our sin. See note on 1:4.

6:5 HUMANITY, Death and Sin—In the Old Testament that which is unclean is sinful. When the holy God confronts us, personal sinfulness suddenly weighs heavily on our minds. We become deeply aware we deserve death because of our sin. Such a divine confrontation offers opportunity to discover forgiveness of sin and calling to mission in life.

6:5 SIN, Guilt—Guilt is necessary to be part of God's people. Guilt is the recognition of personal sin and its devastating consequences. Guilt occurs when a sinner consciously stands before the holy God and sees the contrast between "sinful me" and pure God. God hears the woebegone cry of the sinner and offers cleansing and salvation. The sinner who accepts God's offer loses his guilt.

6:5–8 REVELATION, Divine Presence—The prophet encountered God in the Temple worship experience, reacting as he should. He was aware of his sin, of the difference between the holy Creator and the unholy creature, and of the consequences of seeing God face to face (Ex 24:10; 33:20; Dt 5:26). Worship makes us aware of God and of our own imperfections. Worship helps us hear God and understand Him as One who meets us, offers grace, and then calls us to volunteer to reveal God's message to others.

6:7 SALVATION, Atonement—Isaiah had a vision of God in which an angelic being, called a seraph, atoned for his sin with a live coal from the altar of Solomon's Temple. God is free to atone for our sins in any way He wishes. Atonement cleanses and makes us ready for God's service.

had taken with tongs from the altar.
7With it he touched my mouth and said,
"See, this has touched your lips;[c] your
guilt is taken away and your sin atoned
for.[d]"
8Then I heard the voice[e] of the Lord
saying, "Whom shall I send?[f] And who
will go for us?[g]"
And I said, "Here am I.[h] Send
me!"
9He said, "Go[i] and tell this people:

" 'Be ever hearing, but never
understanding;
be ever seeing, but never
perceiving.'[j]
10Make the heart of this people
calloused;[k]
make their ears dull
and close their eyes.[k] [l]
Otherwise they might see with their
eyes,
hear with their ears,[m]
understand with their hearts,
and turn and be healed."[n]

11Then I said, "For how long,
O Lord?"[o]
And he answered:

"Until the cities lie ruined[p]
and without inhabitant,
until the houses are left deserted[q]
and the fields ruined and ravaged,[r]
12until the LORD has sent everyone far
away[s]
and the land is utterly forsaken.[t]
13And though a tenth remains[u] in the
land,
it will again be laid waste.[v]
But as the terebinth and oak
leave stumps[w] when they are cut
down,
so the holy[x] seed will be the stump
in the land."[y]

Chapter 7

The Sign of Immanuel

WHEN Ahaz[z] son of Jotham, the son
of Uzziah, was king of Judah, King
Rezin[a] of Aram[b] and Pekah[c] son of
Remaliah[d] king of Israel marched up to
fight against Jerusalem, but they could
not overpower it.
2Now the house of David[e] was told,
"Aram has allied itself with[1] Ephraim[f]";
so the hearts of Ahaz and his people were
shaken,[g] as the trees of the forest are
shaken by the wind.
3Then the LORD said to Isaiah, "Go out,
you and your son Shear-Jashub,[m] [h] to
meet Ahaz at the end of the aqueduct of
the Upper Pool, on the road to the Washerman's Field.[i] 4Say to him, 'Be careful,
keep calm[j] and don't be afraid.[k] Do not
lose heart[l] because of these two smoldering stubs[m] of firewood—because of
the fierce anger[n] of Rezin and Aram and
of the son of Remaliah.[o] 5Aram, Ephraim
and Remaliah's[p] son have plotted[q] your
ruin, saying, 6"Let us invade Judah; let us
tear it apart and divide it among ourselves, and make the son of Tabeel king
over it." 7Yet this is what the Sovereign
LORD says:[r]

" 'It will not take place,
it will not happen,[s]
8for the head of Aram is Damascus,[t]
and the head of Damascus is only
Rezin.[u]

6:7 [c]Jer 1:9; Da 10:16 [d]S Lev 26:41; Isa 45:25; Da 12:3; 1Jn 1:7 **6:8** [e]S Job 40:9; Ac 9:4 [f]Jer 26:12,15 [g]S Ge 1:26 [h]S Ge 22:1; S Ex 3:4 **6:9** [i]Eze 3:11; Am 7:15; Mt 28:19 [j]Jer 5:21; S Mt 13:15*; Lk 8:10* **6:10** [k]S Ex 4:21; Dt 32:15; Ps 119:70 [l]Isa 29:9; 42:18-20; 43:8; 44:18 [m]S Dt 29:4; Eze 12:2; Mk 8:18 [n]S Dt 32:39; Mt 13:13-15; Mk 4:12*; Jn 12:40* **6:11** [o]Ps 79:5 [p]S Lev 26:31; S Jer 4:13 [q]S Lev 26:43; Isa 24:10 [r]Ps 79:1; S 109:11; Jer 35:17 **6:12** [s]S Dt 28:64 [t]S Isa 5:5,9; 60:15; 62:4; Jer 4:29; 30:17 **6:13** [u]S Isa 1:9; 10:22 [v]S Isa 5:6 [w]S Job 14:8 [x]S Lev 27:30; S Dt 14:2 [y]S Job 14:7 **7:1** [z]S 1Ch 3:13 [a]S ver 8; S 2Ki 15:37 [b]2Ch 28:5 [c]S 2Ki 15:25 [d]ver 5, 9; Isa 8:6 **7:2** [e]ver 13; S 2Sa 7:11; Isa 16:5; 22:22; Jer 21:12; Am 9:11 [f]Isa 9:9; Hos 5:3 [g]Isa 6:4; Da 5:6 **7:3** [h]Isa 10:21-22 [i]2Ki 18:17; Isa 36:2 **7:4** [j]Isa 30:15; La 3:26 [k]S Ge 15:1; S Dt 3:2; Isa 8:12; 12:2; 35:4; 37:6; Mt 24:6 [l]S Dt 20:3; S Isa 21:4 [m]Am 4:11; Zec 3:2 [n]Isa 10:24; 51:13; 54:14 [o]S 2Ki 15:27 **7:5** [p]S ver 1 [q]ver 2 **7:7** [r]Isa 24:3; 25:8; 28:16 [s]Ps 2:1; Isa 8:10; 14:24; 28:18; 40:8; 46:10; Ac 4:25 **7:8** [t]S Ge 14:15 [u]ver 1; Isa 9:11

[k]9,10 Hebrew; Septuagint *'You will be ever hearing, but never understanding; / you will be ever seeing, but never perceiving.' / 10This people's heart has become calloused; / they hardly hear with their ears, / and they have closed their eyes* [1]2 Or *has set up camp in* [m]3 *Shear-Jashub* means *a remnant will return.*

6:8 EVANGELISM, Obedience—This great passage motivates us to go and evangelize. Although the call came distinctly to the prophet Isaiah, the same call in principle comes to all. God still cries out, "Who will go for us?" Our response of obedience must always be, "Here I am. Send me!" Millions have heard that call, and millions have responded. As a result, multitudes have come to salvation in Christ. What motivated Isaiah to respond so readily? He "saw the Lord"(v 1). May we see the Lord, be cleansed as was the prophet, then hear God's call and obediently respond. Millions still wait to hear the gospel from our lips and lives.

6:9–10 JESUS CHRIST, Foretold—Jesus saw the reality of this hard saying. His parables were not comprehended by those who lacked faith (Mt 13:14–15). His mighty works were intentionally rejected by those who should have known better and had hardened their hearts in unbelief (Jn 12:39–40). What was true for the Master was true for the servant. Paul also faced hardened unbelief (Ac 28:25–27). Christians can never let opposition to the message or hardened unbelief be a reason for failing to share the message about Jesus Christ.

6:11–13 ELECTION, Remnant—See note on 4:3.

6:13 THE CHURCH, Remnant—In Isaiah's call experience, every major theme of his ministry is found in some form. The promise of the remnant is involved closely with the promise of the Messiah. See note on 4:2–6. Whatever remnant remains will be cleansed by fire (6:6–7). Only then can the remnant be called holy. Thus, the holy remnant is extremely small, the survivors of a tenth of the population. The remnant always reminds us of the punishment and destruction God's people must endure before the remnant is revealed and rescued. See note on 1:7–9.

7:3 ELECTION, Remnant—See note on 2 Ki 19:29–34. Election looks to a returning remnant when the elect fail to trust God. Isaiah vividly conveyed the message by naming his son, "A Remnant Will Return."

7:3 THE CHURCH, Remnant—Isaiah named his son Shear-jashub, meaning "a remnant will return." Isaiah made the son a walking sermon. Every Israelite who heard his name confronted the proclamation of God's judgment and of God's gracious rescue of a remnant after judgment. Early in his ministry Isaiah emphasized the certainty of judgment—*only* a remnant will return. Later, Isaiah spoke of the surety of God's promises by preaching that a remnant surely would return. The doctrine of the remnant emphasizes the steadfast love of the Lord toward His chosen people. See notes on 4:2–6; 6:13; 2 Ch 34:9.

Within sixty-five years
 Ephraim will be too shattered[v] to be
 a people.
9The head of Ephraim is Samaria,[w]
 and the head of Samaria is only
 Remaliah's son.
If you do not stand[x] firm in your
 faith,[y]
 you will not stand at all.' "[z]

10Again the LORD spoke to Ahaz,
11"Ask the LORD your God for a sign,[a]
whether in the deepest depths or in the
highest heights.[b]"
12But Ahaz said, "I will not ask; I will
not put the LORD to the test.[c]"
13Then Isaiah said, "Hear now, you
house of David![d] Is it not enough[e] to try
the patience of men? Will you try the patience[f] of my God[g] also? 14Therefore the
Lord himself will give you[n] a sign:[h] The
virgin[i] will be with child and will give
birth to a son,[j] and[o] will call him Immanuel.[p][k] 15He will eat curds[l] and honey[m] when he knows enough to reject the
wrong and choose the right. 16But before
the boy knows[n] enough to reject the
wrong and choose the right,[o] the land of
the two kings you dread will be laid
waste.[p] 17The LORD will bring on you and
on your people and on the house of your
father a time unlike any since Ephraim
broke away[q] from Judah—he will bring
the king of Assyria.[r]"
18In that day[s] the LORD will whistle[t]
for flies from the distant streams of Egypt
and for bees from the land of Assyria.[u]
19They will all come and settle in the
steep ravines and in the crevices[v] in the
rocks, on all the thornbushes[w] and at all
the water holes. 20In that day[x] the Lord
will use[y] a razor hired from beyond the
River[q][z]—the king of Assyria[a]—to
shave your head and the hair of your legs,
and to take off your beards[b] also.[c] 21In
that day,[d] a man will keep alive a young
cow and two goats.[e] 22And because of
the abundance of the milk they give, he
will have curds to eat. All who remain in
the land will eat curds[f] and honey.[g] 23In
that day,[h] in every place where there
were a thousand vines worth a thousand
silver shekels,[r][i] there will be only briers
and thorns.[j] 24Men will go there with
bow and arrow, for the land will be covered with briers[k] and thorns. 25As for all
the hills[l] once cultivated by the hoe, you
will no longer go there for fear of the briers and thorns;[m] they will become places
where cattle are turned loose and where
sheep run.[n]

7:8 [v]2Ki 17:24; Isa 8:4; 17:1-3 7:9 [w]S 2Ki 15:29; Isa 9:9; 28:1,3 [x]S Ps 20:8; Isa 8:10; 40:8 [y]2Ch 20:20 [z]Isa 8:6-8; 30:12-14 7:11 [a]S Ex 7:9; S Dt 13:2 [b]Ps 139:8 7:12 [c]Dt 4:34 7:13 [d]S ver 2 [e]S Ge 30:15 [f]S Isa 1:14 [g]Ps 63:1; 118:28; Isa 25:1; 49:4; 61:10 7:14 [h]S Ex 3:12; S Lk 2:12 [i]S Ge 24:43 [j]S Ge 3:15; Lk 1:31 [k]S Ge 21:22; Isa 8:8,10; Mt 1:23* 7:15 [l]S Ge 18:8 [m]ver 22 7:16 [n]Isa 8:4 [o]Dt 1:39 [p]S Dt 13:16; Isa 17:3; Jer 7:15; Hos 5:9,13; Am 1:3-5 7:17 [q]1Ki 12:16 [r]S ver 20; S 2Ch 28:20 7:18 [s]ver 20,21; S Isa 2:11 [t]S Isa 5:26 [u]Isa 13:5 7:19 [v]S Isa 2:19 [w]ver 25; Isa 17:9; 34:13; 55:13 7:20 [x]S ver 18 [y]Isa 10:15; 29:16 [z]Isa 11:15; Jer 2:18 [a]ver 17; 2Ki 18:16; Isa 8:7; 10:5 [b]S 2Sa 10:4 [c]S Dt 28:49 7:21 [d]ver 23; Isa 2:17 [e]Jer 39:10 7:22 [f]S Ge 18:8 [g]ver 15; Isa 14:30 7:23 [h]ver 21 [i]S S 8:11 [j]S Isa 5:6; Hos 2:12 7:24 [k]S Isa 5:6 7:25 [l]Hag 1:11 [m]S ver 19 [n]S Isa 5:17 8:1 [o]S Dt 27:8; Job 19:23; Isa 30:8; Jer 51:60 [p]ver 3; Hab 2:2; Jer 20:3; Hos 1:4 8:2 [q]S 2Ki 16:10 [r]ver 16; S Jos 24:22; S Ru 4:9; Jer 32:10, 12,25,44 8:3 [s]S Ex 15:20

Chapter 8

Assyria, the LORD's Instrument

THE LORD said to me, "Take a large
scroll[o] and write on it with an ordinary pen: Maher-Shalal-Hash-Baz.[s][p]
2And I will call in Uriah[q] the priest and
Zechariah son of Jeberekiah as reliable
witnesses[r] for me."
3Then I went to the prophetess,[s] and
she conceived and gave birth to a son.[t]
And the LORD said to me, "Name him
Maher-Shalal-Hash-Baz.[u] 4Before the boy
knows[v] how to say 'My father' or 'My
mother,' the wealth of Damascus[w] and
the plunder of Samaria will be carried off
by the king of Assyria.[x]"
5The LORD spoke to me again:

6"Because this people has rejected[y]
 the gently flowing waters of
 Shiloah[z]
and rejoices over Rezin
 and the son of Remaliah,[a]

[t]S Ge 3:15 [u]S ver 1 8:4 [v]Isa 7:16 [w]S Ge 14:15 [x]S Isa 7:8 8:6 [y]S Isa 5:24 [z]S Ne 3:15; Jn 9:7 [a]S Isa 7:1

[n]*14* The Hebrew is plural. [o]*14* Masoretic Text; Dead Sea Scrolls *and he* or *and they* [p]*14 Immanuel* means *God with us.* [q]*20* That is, the Euphrates [r]*23* That is, about 25 pounds (about 11.5 kilograms) [s]*1 Maher-Shalal-Hash-Baz* means *quick to the plunder, swift to the spoil*; also in verse 3.

7:10–14 PRAYER, Answer—At times God graciously gave a sign to confirm His word or His work (Ex 3:12; 4:1–8; Jdg 6:17–22). See notes on Jdg 6:36–40; 2 Ki 19:20–36. Ahaz's refusal to ask was an affront to God's gracious offer. Prayer is not a sinful lack of faith. Prayer is trusting communication which God welcomes.

7:14 JESUS CHRIST, Foretold—"Virgin" (Hebrew *'almah*) may mean a young woman of marriageable age or a virgin. There is no doubt about which way Matthew saw this term and its prophecy. He applied them (1:23) to the virgin birth of Jesus by using a specific term (Greek *parthenos*) for virgin. People always see promise in the birth of a child. All the world is blessed in the birth of the child Jesus, who is Immanuel, "God with us." Compare Lk 1:27,34.

7:14 REVELATION, Actions—God constantly uses signs to reveal His intentions. Here He employed the most complete sign of communication ever: the birth of a son, whose very name revealed God's intention for His children: Immanuel, God with us.

7:17 HISTORY, Universal—God's sovereign control of history is evident in His announcement of the next events of world history and His mysterious power to use unbelieving world rulers to accomplish His purposes.

7:18–25 THE CHURCH, Remnant—The context clearly declares judgment on Judah because King Ahaz would not trust God. The remnant would be in dire circumstances with only curds and honey to eat. "All who remain" (Hebrew *nothar*) is not the word normally associated with a righteous remnant. See note on 1:7–9.

8:1–4 REVELATION, Actions—Revelation came to the prophet as a direct command. God made the prophet's senses alert to divine communication through dreams, personal visions, or the conscious mind. Isaiah was told to perform a symbolic act. He used the tools of an ordinary secretary to write a public announcement. The child's name and birth symbolized the immediate defeat of Syria and Israel, who had joined to attack Judah. The prophet did not have to preach a sermon to the people. His sign and child announced the message.

7therefore the Lord is about to bring
against them
the mighty floodwaters[b] of the
River[t] —
the king of Assyria[c] with all his
pomp.[d]
It will overflow all its channels,
run over all its banks[e]
8and sweep on into Judah, swirling over
it,[f]
passing through it and reaching up
to the neck.
Its outspread wings[g] will cover the
breadth of your land,
O Immanuel[u]!"[h]

9Raise the war cry,[v][i] you nations, and
be shattered![j]
Listen, all you distant lands.
Prepare[k] for battle, and be shattered!
Prepare for battle, and be shattered!
10Devise your strategy, but it will be
thwarted;[l]
propose your plan, but it will not
stand,[m]
for God is with us.[w][n]

Fear God

11The LORD spoke to me with his
strong hand upon me,[o] warning me not
to follow[p] the way of this people. He
said:

12"Do not call conspiracy[q]
everything that these people call
conspiracy[x];
do not fear what they fear,[r]
and do not dread it.[s]
13The LORD Almighty is the one you are
to regard as holy,[t]
he is the one you are to fear,[u]
he is the one you are to dread,[v]
14and he will be a sanctuary;[w]
but for both houses of Israel he will
be
a stone[x] that causes men to stumble[y]
and a rock that makes them fall.[z]
And for the people of Jerusalem he will
be
a trap and a snare.[a]
15Many of them will stumble;[b]
they will fall and be broken,
they will be snared and captured."

16Bind up the testimony[c]
and seal[d] up the law among my
disciples.
17I will wait[e] for the LORD,
who is hiding[f] his face from the
house of Jacob.
I will put my trust in him.[g]

18Here am I, and the children the LORD
has given me.[h] We are signs[i] and symbols[j] in Israel from the LORD Almighty,
who dwells on Mount Zion.[k]
19When men tell you to consult[l] mediums and spiritists,[m] who whisper and
mutter,[n] should not a people inquire[o] of
their God? Why consult the dead on behalf of the living? 20To the law[p] and to
the testimony![q] If they do not speak according to this word, they have no light[r]
of dawn. 21Distressed and hungry,[s] they
will roam through the land;[t] when they
are famished, they will become enraged

8:7 [b]Isa 17:12-13; 28:2,17; 30:28; 43:2; Da 11:40; Na 1:8 [c]S 2Ch 28:20; S Isa 7:20 [d]Isa 10:16 [e]S Jos 3:15 **8:8** [f]Isa 28:15 [g]Isa 18:6; 46:11; Jer 4:13; 48:40 [h]S Isa 7:14 **8:9** [i]S Jos 6:5; Isa 17:12-13 [j]S Job 34:24 [k]Jer 6:4; 46:3; 51:12,27-28; Eze 38:7; Joel 3:9; Zec 14:2-3 **8:10** [l]S Job 5:12 [m]S Pr 19:21; S 21:30; S Isa 7:7 [n]S Isa 7:14; Mt 1:23; Ro 8:31 **8:11** [o]Eze 1:3; 3:14 [p]Eze 2:8 **8:12** [q]Isa 7:2; 20:5; 30:1; 36:6 [r]S Isa 7:4; Mt 10:28 [s]1Pe 3:14* **8:13** [t]S Nu 20:12 [u]S Ex 20:20 [v]Isa 29:23 **8:14** [w]S Isa 4:6 [x]S Ps 118:22 [y]Jer 6:21; Eze 3:20; 14:3,7; Lk 20:18 [z]S Lk 2:34; Ro 9:33*; 1Pe 2:8* [a]S Ps 119:110; Isa 24:17-18 **8:15** [b]Pr 4:19; Isa 28:13; 59:10; Ro 9:32 **8:16** [c]S Ru 4:7 [d]Isa 29:11-12; Jer 32:14; Da 8:26; 12:4 **8:17** [e]S Ps 27:14 [f]S Dt 31:17 [g]S Ps 22:5; Heb 2:13* **8:18** [h]S Ge 33:5; Heb 2:13* [i]S Ex 3:12; Eze 4:3; 12:6; 24:24; Lk 2:34 [j]S Dt 28:46; S Eze 12:11 [k]Ps 9:11

8:19 [l]S 1Sa 28:8 [m]S Lev 19:31 [n]Isa 29:4 [o]S Nu 27:21 **8:20** [p]S Isa 1:10; Lk 16:29 [q]S Ru 4:7 [r]ver 22; Isa 9:2; 59:9; 60:2; Mic 3:6 **8:21** [s]S Job 18:12 [t]Job 30:3

[t]*7* That is, the Euphrates [u]*8* *Immanuel* means *God with us.* [v]*9* Or *Do your worst* [w]*10* Hebrew *Immanuel* [x]*12* Or *Do not call for a treaty / every time these people call for a treaty*

8:9–10 CHRISTIAN ETHICS, War and Peace—God's purpose and presence represents the decisive factor in history's wars. See note on Ps 20:7–8.

8:10 HISTORY, Presence—God's presence thwarts human political strategy and determines history.

8:13 GOD, Holy—Humans are easily terrified and just as easily tempted to worship heroes. Isaiah learned God is the only hero to be worshiped and the only reason for God's people to express fear, the fear of reverence in His awesome, holy presence. See note on 6:3.

8:13–14 SALVATION, Fear of God—War brings fear, terror, and plotting. Salvation from the enemy is the chief concern. Isaiah called for faith (7:9) and reverential worship of God. God can be a rock of holy refuge.

8:14–15 JESUS CHRIST, Foretold—The gospel is a "stumbling block" (Greek *skandalon*) (1 Co 1:23), and the "stone that causes men to stumble" is Jesus Christ (Ro 9:33). The very stone which some have rejected is a primary support of God's house and the rock over which some fall (1 Pe 2:8). The awesome claim about Jesus, that He is God's Son, is the threshold to belief and the bridge over the chasm of despair. In the original setting of this passage, even God poses the stumbling block over which the prideful pretensions of religious people fall.

8:16 HOLY SCRIPTURE, Collection—Most people rejected the prophet and his inspired message. A few disciples believed and collected the teachings for a time when people would receive them as authoritative Scripture. God used such disciples in His work of revelation and inspiration. Note the prophet's preaching is called "law" (Hebrew *torah*), the term used for the Mosaic law.

8:16 DISCIPLESHIP, Nature—Disciples are God's taught and trained ones. Isaiah committed His prophecies to dedicated disciples to preserve the judgments and promises until they were fulfilled. God counts today on His disciples to preserve His Word, the record of His revelation throughout history. See note on Lk 14:26–33.

8:18 JESUS CHRIST, Foretold—Heb 2:13 rounds out this promise by declaring that Jesus is the one who brings together the family of God. It is encouraging to reflect that Jesus stands with us and for us. He is the elder brother who interprets the Father to us all.

8:18–20 REVELATION, Actions—The prophet understood his mission as a medium of revelation among his people. His reputation had been established. Without further words, he and his children symbolized God's judging presence. Specifically, Isaiah's children had been named to reveal the fate of Israel: Shear-Jashub (7:3, "a remnant will return"), and Maher-Shalal-Hash-Baz (8:3, "quick to the plunder, swift to the spoil"). The people were eager to consult inadequate and dead sources about the future, while ignoring the living God. They had living among them the signs of their own fate and faithlessness. See note on 1 Sa 28:6–25.

and, looking upward, will curse[u] their
king and their God. 22Then they will look
toward the earth and see only distress
and darkness and fearful gloom,[v] and
they will be thrust into utter darkness.[w]

Chapter 9

To Us a Child Is Born

NEVERTHELESS, there will be no
more gloom[x] for those who were in
distress. In the past he humbled the land
of Zebulun and the land of Naphtali,[y] but
in the future he will honor Galilee of the
Gentiles, by the way of the sea, along the
Jordan—

2The people walking in darkness[z]
have seen a great light;[a]
on those living in the land of the
shadow of death[y] [b]
a light has dawned.[c]
3You have enlarged the nation[d]
and increased their joy;[e]
they rejoice before you
as people rejoice at the harvest,
as men rejoice
when dividing the plunder.[f]
4For as in the day of Midian's defeat,[g]
you have shattered[h]
the yoke[i] that burdens them,
the bar across their shoulders,[j]
the rod of their oppressor.[k]
5Every warrior's boot used in battle
and every garment rolled in blood
will be destined for burning,[l]
will be fuel for the fire.
6For to us a child is born,[m]
to us a son is given,[n]
and the government[o] will be on his
shoulders.[p]
And he will be called
Wonderful Counselor,[z] [q] Mighty
God,[r]
Everlasting[s] Father,[t] Prince of
Peace.[u]
7Of the increase of his government[v]
and peace[w]
there will be no end.[x]
He will reign[y] on David's throne
and over his kingdom,
establishing and upholding it
with justice[z] and righteousness[a]
from that time on and forever.[b]
The zeal[c] of the LORD Almighty
will accomplish this.

The LORD's Anger Against Israel

8The Lord has sent a message[d] against
Jacob;
it will fall on Israel.
9All the people will know it—
Ephraim[e] and the inhabitants of
Samaria[f] —
who say with pride
and arrogance[g] of heart,
10"The bricks have fallen down,
but we will rebuild with dressed
stone;[h]
the fig[i] trees have been felled,

8:21 [u]S Ex 22:28; Rev 16:11 8:22 [v]S Job 15:24 [w]S ver 20; S Job 3:13; S Isa 5:30; S Joel 2:2; Mt 25:30; Rev 16:10 9:1 [x]S Job 15:24 [y]S 2Ki 15:29 9:2 [z]S Ps 82:5; S 107:10,14; S Isa 8:20 [a]S Ps 36:9; Isa 42:6; 49:6; 60:19; Mal 4:2; Eph 5:8 [b]S Lk 1:79 [c]Isa 58:8; Mt 4:15-16* 9:3 [d]S Job 12:23 [e]S Ps 4:7; S Isa 25:9 [f]S Ex 15:9; S Jos 22:8; S Ps 119:162 9:4 [g]S Jdg 7:25 [h]S Job 34:24; Isa 37:36-38 [i]Isa 14:25; 58:6,9; Jer 2:20; 30:8; Eze 30:18; Na 1:13; Mt 11:30 [j]S Ps 81:6; S Isa 10:27 [k]Isa 14:4; 16:4; 29:5,20; 49:26; 51:13; 54:14; 60:18 9:5 [l]S Isa 2:4 9:6 [m]S Ge 3:15; Isa 53:2; Lk 2:11 [n]Jn 3:16 [o]S Mt 28:18 [p]Isa 22:22 [q]S Job 15:8; Isa 28:29 [r]S Dt 7:21; Ps 24:8; Isa 10:21; 11:2; 42:13 [s]S Ps 90:2 [t]S Ex 4:22; Isa 64:8; Jn 14:9-10 [u]Isa 26:3,12; 53:5; 66:12; Jer 33:6; Mic 5:5; S Lk 2:14 9:7 [v]S Isa 2:4 [w]S Ps 85:8; 119:165; Isa 11:9; 26:3,12; 32:17; 48:18 [x]Da 2:44; 4:3; S Lk 1:33; Jn 12:34 [y]Isa 1:26; 32:1; 60:17; 1Co 15:25 [z]Isa 11:4; 16:5; 32:1,16; 33:5; 42:1; Jer 23:5; 33:14 [a]S Ps 72:2 [b]S 2Sa 7:13 [c]2Ki 19:31; Isa 26:11; 37:32; 42:13; 59:17; 63:15 9:8 [d]S Dt 32:2 9:9 [e]S Isa 7:2 [f]S Isa 7:9 [g]Isa 46:12; 48:4; Eze 2:4; Zec 7:11 9:10 [h]S Ge 11:3 [i]Am 7:14; Lk 19:4

[y]2 Or *land of darkness* [z]6 Or *Wonderful, Counselor*

9:1–9 JESUS CHRIST, Foretold—Handel did well to make this passage the lyrics for one of his loveliest choruses in *The Messiah.* This poem, originally written to celebrate the birth of a royal heir, sends a message beyond its own time. New Testament writers did not fail to pick up that message. Matthew used vv 1–2 to make the transition from John the Baptist, the last of the old, to Jesus, the first of the new (4:15–16). See note on Lk 1:32–33. Modern Christians adopt this message as a central theme to their mission. His name is and shall be called Wonderful Counselor, Mighty God, Everlasting Father (of the Son), Prince of Peace. This is not Handel's music. This chorus of God's own sphere echoes in Rev 4.

9:1–11 SALVATION, Preparation—Christains like to read or sing these words at Christmas time. Originally the passage may have been used for the anointing or anniversary celebration of a living king in the Davidic line. In view of Christ, this great passage becomes a messianic prophecy fulfilled in the person and mission of the Lord Jesus Christ (Mt 4:12–17).

9:3 SALVATION, Joy—Christ is the One who brings us joy and increases our joy. Salvation fills us with greater joy than any festival or victory.

9:6–7 LAST THINGS, Kingdom Established—The representative kingdom of the house of David, the earthly kingdom during the Old Testament period, gave birth in time to the hope for a messianic kingdom. That hope looked for a future king who would bring about the reign of God and the redemption of His people. This passage describes the hoped-for messianic ruler to reign on the throne of David. His kingdom would be established on the basis of justice and righteousness. It would be a lasting kingdom, taking the Lord Almighty Himself to accomplish it. The New Testament recognized Jesus as the fulfillment of this hope, the Inaugurator of God's ideal reign, who will return to consummate it.

9:7 GOD, Jealous—The same Hebrew word refers to zeal and jealousy, the seriousness with which God takes Himself and His purposes. In jealousy against all rivals and with the zeal of total commitment, God works to fulfill His promises. These characteristics of God assure us the Messianic promises with their fulfillment begun in Christ will find ultimate fulfillment in God's day. See note on Ps 79:5.

9:7 CHRISTIAN ETHICS, Righteousness—Justice and righteousness represent major facets in the messianic reign. These ideals still can be glimpsed in our own experience as we realize the effects of the Kingdom in us and about us. God's goal is a people ruled by righteousness and justice. This is the only way to peace.

9:7 THE CHURCH, God's Kingdom—While God's rule is universal and everlasting, the kingdom of God waited for its ultimate fulfillment in the coming messianic King. The prophet recognized the king would reign on the throne of David. He emphasized the kingdom's everlasting and righteous nature. Justice and righteousness toward all people characterizes God's kingdom. When God's people practice justice and righteousness, they help to make the kingdom of God a reality on earth. Ultimately, however, only God's zealous determination to accomplish His purposes can establish His kingdom perfectly on earth. See notes on Ps 103:19; 145:10–13.

but we will replace them with
cedars.[j] "
11But the LORD has strengthened
Rezin's[k] foes against them
and has spurred their enemies on.
12Arameans[l] from the east and
Philistines[m] from the west
have devoured[n] Israel with open
mouth.

Yet for all this, his anger[o] is not
turned away,
his hand is still upraised.[p]

13But the people have not returned[q] to
him who struck[r] them,
nor have they sought[s] the LORD
Almighty.
14So the LORD will cut off from Israel
both head and tail,
both palm branch and reed[t] in a
single day;[u]
15the elders[v] and prominent men[w] are
the head,
the prophets[x] who teach lies[y] are
the tail.
16Those who guide[z] this people mislead
them,
and those who are guided are led
astray.[a]
17Therefore the Lord will take no
pleasure in the young men,[b]
nor will he pity[c] the fatherless and
widows,
for everyone is ungodly[d] and wicked,[e]
every mouth speaks vileness.[f]

Yet for all this, his anger is not turned
away,
his hand is still upraised.[g]

18Surely wickedness burns like a fire;[h]
it consumes briers and thorns,[i]
it sets the forest thickets ablaze,[j]
so that it rolls upward in a column
of smoke.
19By the wrath[k] of the LORD Almighty
the land will be scorched[l]
and the people will be fuel for the
fire;[m]
no one will spare his brother.[n]
20On the right they will devour,
but still be hungry;[o]
on the left they will eat,[p]
but not be satisfied.
Each will feed on the flesh of his own
offspring[a]:
21 Manasseh will feed on Ephraim, and
Ephraim on Manasseh;[q]
together they will turn against
Judah.[r]

Yet for all this, his anger is not turned
away,
his hand is still upraised.[s]

Chapter 10

WOE[t] to those who make unjust
laws,
to those who issue oppressive
decrees,[u]
2to deprive[v] the poor of their rights
and withhold justice from the
oppressed of my people,[w]
making widows their prey
and robbing the fatherless.[x]
3What will you do on the day of
reckoning,[y]
when disaster[z] comes from afar?
To whom will you run for help?[a]
Where will you leave your riches?
4Nothing will remain but to cringe
among the captives[b]
or fall among the slain.[c]

Yet for all this, his anger is not turned
away,[d]
his hand is still upraised.

God's Judgment on Assyria

5"Woe[e] to the Assyrian,[f] the rod[g] of
my anger,
in whose hand is the club[h] of my
wrath![i]
6I send him against a godless[j] nation,
I dispatch[k] him against a people
who anger me,[l]
to seize loot and snatch plunder,[m]
and to trample[n] them down like
mud in the streets.
7But this is not what he intends,[o]
this is not what he has in mind;
his purpose is to destroy,
to put an end to many nations.

9:10 [j]1Ki 7:2-3 **9:11** [k]S Isa 7:8 **9:12** [l]2Ki 16:6 [m]S 2Ch 28:18 [n]S Ps 79:7 [o]S Job 40:11 [p]S Isa 5:25 **9:13** [q]S 2Ch 28:22; Am 4:9; Zep 3:7; Hag 2:17 [r]Jer 5:3; Eze 7:9 [s]Isa 2:3; 17:7; 31:1; 55:6; Jer 50:4; Da 9:13; Hos 3:5; 7:7,10; Am 4:6,10; Zep 1:6 **9:14** [t]ver 14-15; Isa 19:15 [u]Rev 18:8 **9:15** [v]Isa 3:2-3 [w]S Isa 5:13 [x]Isa 28:7; Eze 13:2 [y]S Job 13:4; S Isa 3:8; 44:20; Eze 13:22; Mt 24:24 **9:16** [z]Mt 15:14; 23:16,24 [a]S Isa 3:12 **9:17** [b]Jer 9:21; 11:22; 18:21; 48:15; 49:26; Am 4:10; 8:13 [c]S Job 5:4; Isa 27:11; Jer 13:14 [d]Isa 10:6; 32:6; Mic 7:2 [e]S Isa 1:4 [f]S Isa 3:8; Mt 12:34; Ro 3:13-14 [g]S Isa 5:25 **9:18** [h]S Dt 29:23; S Isa 1:31 [i]S Isa 5:6 [j]S Ps 83:14 **9:19** [k]S Job 40:11; Isa 13:9,13 [l]Jer 17:27 [m]S Ps 97:3; S Isa 1:31 [n]S Isa 3:5 **9:20** [o]S Lev 26:26; S Job 18:12 [p]Isa 49:26; Zec 11:9 **9:21** [q]S Jdg 7:22; S 12:4 [r]S 2Ch 28:6 [s]S Isa 5:25 **10:1** [t]S Isa 5:8 [u]S Ps 58:2 **10:2** [v]Isa 3:14 [w]S Isa 5:23 [x]S Dt 10:18; S Job 6:27; S Isa 1:17 **10:3** [y]S Job 31:14 [z]ver 25; Ps 59:5; Isa 1:24; 13:6; 14:23; 24:6; 26:14; 47:11; Jer 5:9; 9:9; 50:15; Lk 19:44 [a]S Ps 108:12; Isa 20:6; 30:7; 31:3 **10:4** [b]Isa 24:22; Zec 9:11 [c]Isa 22:2; 34:3; 66:16; Jer 39:6; Na 3:3 [d]S Isa 5:25; 12:1; 63:10; 64:5; Jer 4:8; 30:24; La 1:12 **10:5** [e]S 2Ki 19:21; S Isa 28:1 [f]ver 12, 18; S Isa 7:20; 14:25; 31:8; 37:7; Zep 2:13 [g]Isa 14:5; 54:16 [h]ver 15,24; Isa 30:31; 41:15; 45:1; Jer 50:23; 51:20 [i]Isa 9:4; 13:3,5,13; 26:20; 30:30; 34:2; 63:6; 66:14; Eze 30:24-25 **10:6** [j]S Isa 9:17 [k]Hab 1:12 [l]S 2Ch 28:9; Isa 9:19 [m]S Jdg 6:4; S Isa 5:29; 8:1 [n]S 2Sa 22:43; S Ps 7:5; S Isa 5:5; 37:26-27 **10:7** [o]S Ge 50:20; Ac 4:23-28

[a]*20* Or *arm*

9:12–21 GOD, Wrath—Wrath seeks repentance and may well afflict God's proud, rebellious people until they turn back to God. False, irresponsible leaders must bear the brunt of God's wrath.

10:1–3 DISCIPLESHIP, Oppressed—God pronounced judgment on those who used legal processes to oppress the widows, the fatherless, and the poor. A day of reckoning is ahead for those guilty of such treatment. See note on Isa 3:14–15.

10:4–6,25 GOD, Wrath—God may use godless, pagan people to enforce His wrath against His people. Because God uses a people does not mean He is pleased with them and will continue to bless them. The people God uses may not even realize God is using them. See note on 9:12–21.

10:5–19 HISTORY, Universal—See note on 7:17. God's universal control of history is revealed in His power to punish the conquering nations as well as use them to discipline His people. Power may appear to be in the hands of proud rulers, but they exercise it only as God permits.

8‘Are not my commanders[p] all kings?’
he says.
9 ‘Has not Calno[q] fared like
Carchemish?[r]
Is not Hamath[s] like Arpad,[t]
and Samaria[u] like Damascus?[v]
10As my hand seized the kingdoms of the
idols,[w]
kingdoms whose images excelled
those of Jerusalem and
Samaria—
11shall I not deal with Jerusalem and her
images
as I dealt with Samaria and her
idols?[x]’ ”

12When the Lord has finished all his
work[y] against Mount Zion[z] and Jerusalem, he will say, “I will punish the king
of Assyria[a] for the willful pride[b] of his
heart and the haughty look[c] in his eyes.
13For he says:

“ ‘By the strength of my hand[d] I have
done this,[e]
and by my wisdom, because I have
understanding.
I removed the boundaries of nations,
I plundered their treasures;[f]
like a mighty one I subdued[b] their
kings.[g]
14As one reaches into a nest,[h]
so my hand reached for the wealth[i]
of the nations;
as men gather abandoned eggs,
so I gathered all the countries;[j]
not one flapped a wing,
or opened its mouth to chirp.[k]’ ”

15Does the ax raise itself above him who
swings it,
or the saw boast against him who
uses it?[l]
As if a rod were to wield him who lifts
it up,
or a club[m] brandish him who is not
wood!
16Therefore, the Lord, the LORD
Almighty,
will send a wasting disease[n] upon
his sturdy warriors;[o]
under his pomp[p] a fire[q] will be
kindled
like a blazing flame.
17The Light of Israel will become a fire,[r]
their Holy One[s] a flame;
in a single day it will burn and
consume
his thorns[t] and his briers.[u]
18The splendor of his forests[v] and fertile
fields
it will completely destroy,[w]
as when a sick man wastes away.
19And the remaining trees of his forests[x]
will be so few[y]
that a child could write them down.

The Remnant of Israel

20In that day[z] the remnant of Israel,
the survivors[a] of the house of Jacob,
will no longer rely[b] on him
who struck them down[c]
but will truly rely[d] on the LORD,
the Holy One of Israel.[e]
21A remnant[f] will return,[c][g] a remnant
of Jacob
will return to the Mighty God.[h]
22Though your people, O Israel, be like
the sand[i] by the sea,
only a remnant will return.[j]
Destruction has been decreed,[k]
overwhelming and righteous.
23The Lord, the LORD Almighty, will
carry out
the destruction decreed[l] upon the
whole land.[m]

24Therefore, this is what the Lord, the
LORD Almighty, says:

“O my people who live in Zion,[n]
do not be afraid[o] of the Assyrians,

10:8 [p]2Ki 18:24 **10:9** [q]S Ge 10:10 [r]S 2Ch 35:20 [s]Nu 34:8; 2Ch 8:4; Isa 11:11 [t]2Ki 18:34 [u]2Ki 17:6 [v]S Ge 14:15; 2Ki 16:9; Jer 49:24 **10:10** [w]2Ki 19:18 **10:11** [x]S 2Ki 19:13; S Isa 2:8; 36:18-20; 37:10-13 **10:12** [y]Isa 28:21-22; 65:7; 66:4; Jer 5:29 [z]2Ki 19:31 [a]S ver 5; S 2Ki 19:7; Isa 30:31-33; 37:36-38; Jer 50:18 [b]S Isa 2:11; S Eze 28:17 [c]Ps 18:27 **10:13** [d]S Dt 8:17 [e]S Dt 32:26-27; Isa 47:7; Da 4:30 [f]Eze 28:4 [g]Isa 14:13-14 **10:14** [h]Jer 49:16; Ob 1:4; Hab 2:6-11 [i]S Job 31:25 [j]Isa 14:6 [k]2Ki 19:22-24; Isa 37:24-25 **10:15** [l]S Isa 7:20; 45:9; Ro 9:20-21 [m]S ver 5 **10:16** [n]ver 18; S Nu 11:33; Isa 17:4 [o]Ps 78:31 [p]S Isa 8:7 [q]Jer 21:14 **10:17** [r]S Job 41:21; S Isa 1:31; 31:9; Zec 2:5 [s]Isa 37:23 [t]S Nu 11:1-3; S 2Sa 23:6 [u]S Isa 9:18 **10:18** [v]S 2Ki 19:23 [w]S ver 5 **10:19** [x]ver 33-34; Isa 32:19 [y]Isa 17:6; 21:17; 27:13; Jer 44:28 **10:20** [z]ver 27; Isa 11:10,11; 12:1,4; 19:18,19; 24:21; 28:5; 52:6; Zec 9:16 [a]S Isa 1:9; Eze 7:16 [b]S 2Ki 16:7 [c]2Ch 28:20 [d]2Ch 14:11; Isa 17:7; 48:2; 50:10; Jer 21:2; Hos 3:5; 6:1; Mic 3:11; 7:7 [e]S Isa 5:24 **10:21** [f]S Ge 45:7; Isa 6:13; Zep 3:13 [g]Isa 7:3 [h]S Isa 9:6 **10:22** [i]S Ge 12:2; Isa 48:19; Jer 33:22 [j]Ezr 1:4; Isa 11:11; 46:3 [k]ver 23; Isa 28:22; Jer 40:2; Da 9:27 **10:23** [l]S ver 22 [m]Isa 6:12; 28:22; Ro 9:27-28* **10:24** [n]Ps 87:5-6 [o]S Isa 7:4

[b]*13* Or */ I subdued the mighty,* [c]*21* Hebrew *shear-jashub;* also in verse 22

10:10–11 GOD, One God—God forbade images for Israel’s worship (Ex 20:4), reminding us God is invisible spirit. Still Israel made images, but inferior ones as far as outward appearance. God had to use drastic punishment to teach Israel He is the only God and can destroy any pretenders.

10:17–20 GOD, Holy—The holiness of God speaks of His absolute purity and His utter opposition to sin of whatever kind. When exposed to sin, God’s holiness reacts in burning rage. Faithful believers—the remnant—can trust God’s holiness to protect them. See notes at 1:4; 6:3.

10:20–23 ELECTION, Remnant—See note on 4:3. God’s election goal is to create a remnant who will trust Him fully rather than trusting political systems and political leaders. Thus God chose the faithful remnant as the elect people. Remnant theology is the way election takes seriously the moral demands and judgment of God.

10:20–23 THE CHURCH, Remnant—Judgment often produces cleansing and purification. God desires for His people to lean on Him for comfort and protection rather than depend on weapons of war and military alliances. All Israel refused to do this. God reduced them to a small remnant who would be faithful to Him. “A remnant will return” (vv 21–22) is the name of Isaiah’s son (7:3). The name serves two purposes in emphasizing the certainty of the remnant hope (v 21) and the surety of destruction of the present order (v 22). Return (Hebrew *shub*) is the primary word for repentance in the Old Testament. God expects the remnant He delivers to return to the land and to return to Him in repentance and faith. Only people who turn to God in faith and obedience can be called God’s children.

10:20 SALVATION, Belief—Trust is reliance on God, leaning on Him, putting our weight on Him. Israel was taken into captivity because she relied on one other than God (31:1). Restored Israel would rely only on God.

10:24–27 HISTORY, National—Past historical deliverance gives God’s people hope as they face a new enemy. God

who beat[p] you with a rod[q]
and lift up a club against you, as
Egypt did.
25Very soon[r] my anger against you will
end
and my wrath[s] will be directed to
their destruction.[t]"
26The LORD Almighty will lash[u] them
with a whip,
as when he struck down Midian[v] at
the rock of Oreb;
and he will raise his staff[w] over the
waters,[x]
as he did in Egypt.
27In that day[y] their burden[z] will be
lifted from your shoulders,
their yoke[a] from your neck;[b]
the yoke[c] will be broken
because you have grown so fat.[d]
28They enter Aiath;
they pass through Migron;[d]
they store supplies[e] at Micmash.[f]
29They go over the pass, and say,
"We will camp overnight at
Geba."[g]
Ramah[h] trembles;
Gibeah[i] of Saul flees.[j]
30Cry out, O Daughter of Gallim![k]
Listen, O Laishah!
Poor Anathoth![l]
31Madmenah is in flight;
the people of Gebim take cover.
32This day they will halt at Nob;[m]
they will shake their fist[n]
at the mount of the Daughter of Zion,[o]
at the hill of Jerusalem.
33See, the Lord, the LORD Almighty,
will lop off[p] the boughs with great
power.

10:24 [p]S Ex 5:14 [q]S ver 5 **10:25** [r]Isa 17:14; 29:17; Hag 2:6 [s]ver 5; Ps 30:5; Isa 13:5; 24:21; 26:20; 30:30; 34:2; 66:14; Da 8:19; 11:36 [t]S ver 3; Mic 5:6 **10:26** [u]Isa 37:36-38 [v]S Isa 9:4 [w]Isa 30:32 [x]S Ex 14:16 **10:27** [y]S ver 20 [z]S Ps 66:11 [a]S Lev 26:13; S Isa 9:4 [b]Isa 14:25; 47:6; 52:2 [c]Jer 30:8 **10:28** [d]S 1Sa 14:2 [e]S Jos 1:11 [f]1Sa 13:2 **10:29** [g]S Jos 18:24; S Ne 11:31 [h]S Jos 18:25 [i]S Jdg 19:14 [j]Isa 15:5 **10:30** [k]1Sa 25:44 [l]S Ne 11:32 **10:32** [m]S 1Sa 21:1 [n]S Job 15:25 [o]S Ps 9:14; Isa 16:1; Jer 6:23 **10:33** [p]Isa 18:5; 27:11; Eze 17:4 [q]S Ex 12:12 [r]Isa 2:13; Am 2:9 [s]Isa 5:15 **10:34** [t]Na 1:12; Zec 11:2 [u]S 2Ki 19:23 [v]S Ge 49:24; Ps 93:4; Isa 33:21 **11:1** [w]S 2Ki 19:26; S Job 14:7 [x]S Job 14:8 [y]ver 10; Isa 9:7; S Mt 1:1; S Rev 5:5 [z]S Isa 4:2 [a]S 2Ki 19:30; S Isa 27:6 **11:2** [b]S Jdg 3:10; Isa 32:15; 42:1; 44:3; 48:16; 59:21; 61:1; Eze 37:14; 39:29; Joel 2:28; Mt 3:16; Jn 1:32-33; 16:13 [c]S Ex 28:3;

The lofty trees will be felled,[q]
the tall[r] ones will be brought low.[s]
34He will cut down[t] the forest thickets
with an ax;
Lebanon[u] will fall before the Mighty
One.[v]

Chapter 11

The Branch From Jesse

A shoot[w] will come up from the
stump[x] of Jesse;[y]
from his roots a Branch[z] will bear
fruit.[a]
2The Spirit[b] of the LORD will rest on
him—
the Spirit of wisdom[c] and of
understanding,
the Spirit of counsel and of power,[d]
the Spirit of knowledge and of the
fear of the LORD—
3and he will delight in the fear[e] of the
LORD.

He will not judge by what he sees with
his eyes,[f]
or decide by what he hears with his
ears;[g]
4but with righteousness[h] he will judge
the needy,[i]
with justice[j] he will give decisions
for the poor[k] of the earth.
He will strike[l] the earth with the rod
of his mouth;[m]

S Eph 1:17; S Col 2:3 [d]S Isa 9:6; 2Ti 1:7 **11:3** [e]Isa 33:6 [f]Jn 7:24 [g]Jn 2:25 **11:4** [h]S Ps 72:2 [i]S Ps 72:4; S Isa 14:30 [j]S Isa 9:7; Rev 19:11 [k]S Job 5:16; S Isa 3:14 [l]Isa 27:7; 30:31; Zec 14:12; Mal 4:6 [m]S Job 40:18; Ps 2:9; Rev 19:15

[d]27 Hebrew; Septuagint *broken / from your shoulders*

promised salvation and deliverance to His people beyond judgment in history. See note on 1:24–26.

11:1–10 JESUS CHRIST, Foretold—These messianic prophecies applied first and in a provisional way to the hopes for the prophet's own day. The instrument of their absolute realization, Jesus Christ, was born over seven hundred years later. The ultimate actuality and fulfillment comes at the last day. The Spirit was especially present at Jesus' baptism (Mt 3:16). Paul related Jesus to the Root of Jesse (Ro 15:12). The final parts of the Book of Revelation present a word picture of "The Peaceable Kingdom" celebrating the time when the "kingdom of the world has become the kingdom of our Lord and of his Christ" (Rev 11:15).

11:1–2 HOLY SPIRIT, Hope—Israel's faith was historical; people trusted God because they had experienced His mighty acts in history. Out of historical faith, Israel developed its hope. Because God had acted in the past, they anticipated He would act again in the future, according to His promises. One part of their hope centered on the coming Messiah. The people looked forward to a time when God would send a Man who would deliver the nation from political and other forms of slavery. The Spirit of the Lord would help the promised Deliverer to do His work. The Messiah would be a unique bearer of the Spirit, who would give Him power and knowledge to do the works of justice and judgment. This was fulfilled in Jesus, who received the Spirit in a special way at His baptism and who was guided throughout His ministry by the Spirit. See notes on Lk 3:21–22; 4:14.

11:1–16 THE CHURCH, Remnant—The Messiah was and is the true Remnant of God's people. He came from the felled tree of the house of David. He was the true Israelite, fulfilling all God's covenant commands. He was the righteous One. Hope for God's people rests in following this true remnant. Only those who follow Christ belong to God's chosen remnant. His remnant is not restricted to Israel but comes from all nations. The nations are represented in two ways. God promised to bring scattered Israel back from exile among the nations, and He called on people of other nations to serve Him. Final fulfillment of this prophecy will come only when Jesus comes again. See notes on 6:13; 2 Ch 34:9.

11:2–3 SALVATION, Fear of God—This passage may have originally referred to an expected king of Israel in the Davidic dynasty or in a different branch of David's ancestry. Christians see these verses fulfilled in the person and work of the Lord Jesus Christ (Ac 13:22–23). Ideally, all Spirit-annointed leaders who serve God's people should possess the three leadership qualities enumerated here. Among those qualities, the fear of God is the most prominent. See note on Pr 1:7,29.

11:3–5 CHRISTIAN ETHICS, Justice—The ministry of the Messiah will be marked by His agressive justice and righteousness on behalf of the needy. What human rulers and systems have not achieved, God's Messiah will. See note on 9:7.

with the breath[n] of his lips he will
slay the wicked.[o]
5 Righteousness will be his belt[p]
and faithfulness[q] the sash around
his waist.[r]

6 The wolf will live with the lamb,[s]
the leopard will lie down with the
goat,
the calf and the lion and the yearling[e]
together;
and a little child will lead them.
7 The cow will feed with the bear,
their young will lie down together,
and the lion will eat straw like the
ox.[t]
8 The infant[u] will play near the hole of
the cobra,
and the young child put his hand
into the viper's[v] nest.
9 They will neither harm nor destroy[w]
on all my holy mountain,[x]
for the earth[y] will be full of the
knowledge[z] of the LORD
as the waters cover the sea.

10 In that day[a] the Root of Jesse[b] will
stand as a banner[c] for the peoples; the
nations[d] will rally to him,[e] and his place
of rest[f] will be glorious.[g] 11 In that day[h]
the Lord will reach out his hand a second
time to reclaim the remnant[i] that is left
of his people from Assyria,[j] from Lower
Egypt, from Upper Egypt,[f][k] from
Cush,[g][l] from Elam,[m] from Babylonia,[h]
from Hamath[n] and from the islands[o] of
the sea.[p]

12 He will raise a banner[q] for the nations
and gather[r] the exiles of Israel;[s]
he will assemble the scattered people[t]
of Judah
from the four quarters of the earth.[u]
13 Ephraim's jealousy will vanish,
and Judah's enemies[i] will be cut
off;
Ephraim will not be jealous of Judah,
nor Judah hostile toward Ephraim.[v]
14 They will swoop down on the slopes of
Philistia[w] to the west;
together they will plunder the
people to the east.[x]
They will lay hands on Edom[y] and
Moab,[z]
and the Ammonites[a] will be subject
to them.[b]
15 The LORD will dry up[c]
the gulf of the Egyptian sea;
with a scorching wind[d] he will sweep
his hand[e]
over the Euphrates River.[j][f]
He will break it up into seven streams
so that men can cross over in
sandals.[g]
16 There will be a highway[h] for the
remnant[i] of his people
that is left from Assyria,[j]
as there was for Israel
when they came up from Egypt.[k]

Chapter 12

Songs of Praise

IN that day[l] you will say:
"I will praise[m] you, O LORD.

11:4 [n]S Job 4:9; Ps 18:8; Isa 30:28, 33; 40:24; 59:19; Eze 21:31; 2Th 2:8 [o]S Ps 139:19 **11:5** [p]Ex 12:11; 1Ki 18:46 [q]Isa 25:1 [r]Eph 6:14 **11:6** [s]Isa 65:25 **11:7** [t]S Job 40:15 **11:8** [u]Isa 65:20 [v]Isa 14:29; 30:6; 59:5 **11:9** [w]S Nu 25:12; S Isa 2:4; S 9:7 [x]S Ps 48:1; S Isa 2:2 [y]1Sa 17:46; Ps 98:2-3; Isa 45:22; 48:20; 52:10 [z]Ex 7:5; Isa 19:21; 45:6,14; 49:26; Jer 24:7; 31:34; Hab 2:14 **11:10** [a]S Isa 10:20 [b]S ver 1 [c]S Ps 20:5; Isa 18:3; Jer 4:6; Jn 12:32 [d]Isa 2:4; 14:1; 49:23; 56:3, 6; 60:5,10; Lk 2:32; Ac 11:18 [e]Ro 15:12* [f]S Ps 116:7; Isa 14:3; 28:12; 32:17-18; 40:2; Jer 6:16; 30:10; 46:27 [g]Hag 2:9; Zec 2:5 **11:11** [h]S Isa 10:20 [i]S Dt 30:4; S Isa 1:9 [j]Isa 19:24; Hos 11:11; Mic 7:12; Zec 10:10 [k]Jer 44:1,15; Eze 29:14; 30:14 [l]S Ge 10:6; Ac 8:27 [m]S Ge 10:22 [n]S Isa 10:9 [o]Isa 24:15; 41:1,5; 42:4,10,12; 49:1; 51:5; 59:18; 60:9; 66:19 [p]Isa 49:12; Jer 16:15; 46:27; Eze 38:8; Zec 8:7 **11:12** [q]S Ps 20:5 [r]Isa 14:2; 43:5; 49:22; 54:7; Jer 16:15; 31:10; 32:37 [s]S Ne 1:9; S Ps 106:47; Isa 14:1; 41:14; 49:5 [t]Eze 28:25; Zep 3:10 [u]S Ps 48:10; 67:7; Isa 41:5; Rev 7:1

11:13 [v]S 2Ch 28:6; Jer 3:18; Eze 37:16-17,22; Hos 1:11 **11:14** [w]S 2Ch 26:6; S 28:18 [x]S Jdg 6:3 [y]S Nu 24:18; S Ps 137:7; Isa 34:5-6; 63:1; Jer 49:22; Eze 25:12; Da 11:41; Joel 3:19; Ob 1:1; Mal 1:4 [z]Isa 15:1; 16:14; 25:10; Jer 48:40; Zep 2:8-11 [a]Jdg 11:14-18 [b]Isa 25:3; 60:12 **11:15** [c]S Ex 14:22; S Dt 11:10; Isa 37:25; 42:15; Jer 50:38; 51:36 [d]S Ge 41:6 [e]Isa 19:16; 30:32 [f]S Isa 7:20 [g]S Ex 14:29 **11:16** [h]Isa 19:23; 35:8; 40:3; 49:11; 51:10; 57:14; 62:10; Jer 50:5 [i]S Ge 45:7 [j]S ver 11 [k]Ex 14:26-31 **12:1** [l]S Isa 10:20 [m]Ps 9:1; Isa 25:1

[e] *6* Hebrew; Septuagint *lion will feed* [f] *11* Hebrew *from Pathros* [g] *11* That is, the upper Nile region [h] *11* Hebrew *Shinar* [i] *13* Or *hostility* [j] *15* Hebrew *the River*

11:6–9 CREATION, Hope—God uses His creative powers to make life more bearable for His people. Through Christ, those with sinful natures can be transformed and live together peacefully. Our hope for a nonviolent world is in spreading the message of God's love and forgiveness to sinful people everywhere. Those who share a kindred faith can find a basis for harmonious relations. The total peace described in this passage will be fully realized only when God's kingdom is finally and completely established.

11:9 SALVATION, Knowledge of God—The knowledge of God will one day flood the earth. Every person will know and serve God. That is a part of what salvation is about.

11:9 LAST THINGS, Last Days—The prophetic vision of the day of the Lord saw the earth covered with the knowledge of God. Whether through missionary outreach and/or millennial reign, the manner in which it would be accomplished was not clearly set forth by the prophet. As with many prophetic passages about the ideal last days, some interpreters relate the description literally to a future millennial reign of Christ on earth. See note on Rev 20:1–6. For others symbolic language is used to refer in a general way to the messianic hope in Israel. Christ in either case is the necessary figure for the realization of the promises and warnings of the last days.

11:10–16 HISTORY, Deliverance—The history of salvation, centered in the Exodus, provided linguistic images to use in stirring up hope among God's suffering people. God maintains continuity between past deliverance and future deliverance. The inspired prophet used descriptions of the original Exodus to paint a verbal picture of God's new act of historical deliverance.

11:13 SALVATION, Reconciliation—Israel's future hope involved reconciliation between the two nations of Ephraim (Northern Kingdom) and Judah (Southern Kingdom). Jealousy and hostility would have no place in their relationship. They were to become friends. Likewise, when persons are reconciled to God they become friends; they bury their hostility and jealousy. The reconciliation foreseen here was ultimately fulfilled through Christ. God is the initiator of this reconciled relationship. Reconciliation with Him leads to reconciliation with enemies.

12:1–3 GOD, Savior—God's anger does not last forever (Ps 30:5). He turns to His faithful remnant in salvation. An immediate response to salvation is praise and trust.

12:1–6 WORSHIP, Praise—See note on Ex 15:1–21. Praise will be the agenda on God's day of salvation.

12:1–6 PRAYER, Thanksgiving—The preceding three chapters spoke of deliverance with strong messianic implications. Isaiah provided a psalm of thanks for the people to sing

Although you were angry with me,
your anger has turned away[n]
and you have comforted[o] me.
2Surely God is my salvation;[p]
I will trust[q] and not be afraid.
The LORD, the LORD,[r] is my strength[s]
and my song;
he has become my salvation.[t]"
3With joy you will draw water[u]
from the wells[v] of salvation.

4In that day[w] you will say:

"Give thanks to the LORD, call on his
name;[x]
make known among the nations[y]
what he has done,
and proclaim that his name is
exalted.[z]
5Sing[a] to the LORD, for he has done
glorious things;[b]
let this be known to all the world.
6Shout aloud and sing for joy,[c] people
of Zion,
for great[d] is the Holy One of Israel[e]
among you.[f]"

Chapter 13

A Prophecy Against Babylon

AN oracle[g] concerning Babylon[h] that
Isaiah son of Amoz[i] saw:[j]

2Raise a banner[k] on a bare hilltop,
shout to them;
beckon to them
to enter the gates[l] of the nobles.
3I have commanded my holy ones;
I have summoned my warriors[m] to
carry out my wrath[n]—
those who rejoice[o] in my triumph.
4Listen, a noise on the mountains,
like that of a great multitude![p]
Listen, an uproar[q] among the
kingdoms,
like nations massing together!
The LORD Almighty[r] is mustering[s]
an army for war.
5They come from faraway lands,
from the ends of the heavens[t]—
the LORD and the weapons[u] of his
wrath[v]—
to destroy[w] the whole country.

6Wail,[x] for the day[y] of the LORD is
near;
it will come like destruction[z] from
the Almighty.[k][a]
7Because of this, all hands will go
limp,[b]
every man's heart will melt.[c]
8Terror[d] will seize them,
pain and anguish will grip[e] them;
they will writhe like a woman in
labor.[f]
They will look aghast at each other,
their faces aflame.[g]
9See, the day[h] of the LORD is coming
—a cruel[i] day, with wrath[j] and
fierce anger[k]—
to make the land desolate
and destroy the sinners within it.
10The stars of heaven and their
constellations
will not show their light.[l]
The rising sun[m] will be darkened[n]
and the moon will not give its
light.[o]
11I will punish[p] the world for its evil,
the wicked[q] for their sins.
I will put an end to the arrogance of
the haughty[r]

12:1 [n]S Job 13:16 [o]S Ps 71:21 **12:2** [p]Isa 17:10; 25:9; 33:6; 45:17; 51:5,6; 54:8; 59:16; 61:10; 62:11 [q]S Job 13:15; S Ps 26:1; S 112:7; Isa 26:3; Da 6:23 [r]Isa 26:4; 38:11 [s]S Ps 18:1 [t]S Ex 15:2 **12:3** [u]S 2Ki 3:17; Ps 36:9; Jer 2:13; 17:13; Jn 4:10,14 [v]Ex 15:25 **12:4** [w]S Isa 10:20 [x]Ex 3:15; Ps 80:18; 105:1; Isa 24:15; 25:1; 26:8,13; Hos 12:5 [y]Isa 54:5; 60:3; Jer 10:7; Zep 2:11; Mal 1:11 [z]S Ps 113:2 **12:5** [a]S Ex 15:1 [b]S Ps 98:1 **12:6** [c]S Ge 21:6; S Ps 98:4; Isa 24:14; 48:20; 52:8; Jer 20:13; 31:7; Zec 2:10 [d]Ps 48:1 [e]S Ps 78:41; 99:2; Isa 1:24; 10:20; 17:7; 29:19; 37:23; 43:3,14; 45:11; 49:26; 55:5; Eze 39:7 [f]S Ps 46:5; Zep 3:14-17 **13:1** [g]Isa 14:28; 15:1; 21:1; Na 1:1; Hab 1:1; Zec 9:1; 12:1; Mal 1:1 [h]ver 19; S Ge 10:10; Isa 14:4; 21:9; 46:1-2; 48:14; Jer 24:1; 25:12; Rev 14:8 [i]Isa 20:2; 37:2 [j]S Isa 1:1 **13:2** [k]S Ps 20:5; Jer 50:2; 51:27 [l]Isa 24:12; 45:2; Jer 51:58 **13:3** [m]ver 17; Isa 21:2; Jer 51:11; Da 5:28,31; Joel 3:11 [n]S Job 40:11; S Isa 10:5 [o]S Ps 149:2 **13:4** [p]Joel 3:14 [q]S Ps 46:6 [r]Isa 47:4; 51:15 [s]Isa 42:13; Jer 50:41 **13:5** [t]S Isa 5:26 [u]Isa 45:1; 54:16; Jer 50:25 [v]S Isa 10:25 [w]S Jos 6:17; Isa 24:1; 30:25; 34:2 **13:6** [x]Isa 14:31; 15:2; 16:7; 23:1; Eze 30:2; Jas 5:1 [y]S Isa 2:12 [z]S Isa 10:3; S 14:15 [a]S Ge 17:1 **13:7** [b]S 2Ki 19:26; S Job 4:3; S Jer 47:3 [c]S Jos 2:11; Eze 21:7 **13:8** [d]S Ps 31:13; S 48:5; S Isa 21:4 [e]Ex 15:14 [f]S Ge 3:16; S Jn 16:21 [g]Joel 2:6; Na 2:10 **13:9** [h]S Isa 2:12; Jer 51:2 [i]Jer 6:23 [j]S Isa 9:19 [k]Isa 26:21; 66:16; Jer 25:31; Joel 3:2 **13:10** [l]S Job 9:7 [m]Isa 24:23; Zec 14:7 [n]S Ex 10:22; S Isa 5:30; Rev 8:12 [o]Eze 32:7; Am 5:20; 8:9; S Mt 24:29*; Mk 13:24* **13:11** [p]Isa 3:11; 11:4; 26:21; 65:6-7; 66:16 [q]S Ps 125:3 [r]S Ps 10:5; S Pr 16:18; Da 5:23

[k]*6* Hebrew *Shaddai*

when God fulfills His promises. Praise is the language of the day of the Lord. See note on Ps 30:1–12.

12:3 SALVATION, Joy—See note on Ps 51:8,12. Compare Nu 21:17–18. Hebrew maidens sang as they drew water from their life-giving wells. These words fit well the messianic picture of ch 11. They find their deepest fulfillment in Jesus Christ, the Water of life (Jn 4:10). The living water in God's well of salvation can never be exhausted.

12:4–6 EVANGELISM, Obedience—Obedience to the call of God to evangelize springs from thanksgiving for the Lord's goodness. When we realize all the glorious things He has done, we want to make it known in all the earth. See note on 6:8.

13:1—23:18 HISTORY, Universal—See note on 10:5–19. God renewed hope for Israel by promising judgment on each of her enemies. Temporary defeat must never lead to the conclusion that God has no future for His people. God will never lose control of universal history. He will always direct history to accomplish His ultimate purpose.

13:1 HOLY SCRIPTURE, Oracle—"Oracle" (Hebrew *massa'*) refers to a divine revelation involving judgment. It often appears in prophecies against foreign nations as here. Usually oral, it is revealed to a faithful man of God in dream, meditation, or visionary trance. Isaiah saw this oracle. Compare in 15:1; 17:1; 19:1; 21:1,11,13; 22:1. God's revelation came to Judah. It concerned foreign nations, showing God's power and concern were not limited to Judah. The message was for Judah, assuring God's people of ultimate victory. The message was preserved in writing for future generations to show God keeps His promises and to warn against actions and attitudes like those of the nations.

13:3–13 GOD, Wrath—Proud nations like Babylon face God's fierce wrath after they have accomplished His disciplinary purposes for His people. God's wrath always has a purpose.

13:9–11 SIN, Judgment—Sinners do not always receive justice in this life. Some apparently prosper without enduring discipline or punishment. God promises He will have His day. He will conquer evil and adequately punish sinners. Pride and arrogance will disappear on God's judgment day.

and will humble[s] the pride of the
ruthless.[t]
12I will make man[u] scarcer than pure
gold,
more rare than the gold of Ophir.[v]
13Therefore I will make the heavens
tremble;[w]
and the earth will shake[x] from its
place
at the wrath[y] of the LORD Almighty,
in the day of his burning anger.[z]

14Like a hunted[a] gazelle,
like sheep without a shepherd,[b]
each will return to his own people,
each will flee[c] to his native
land.[d]
15Whoever is captured will be thrust
through;
all who are caught will fall[e] by the
sword.[f]
16Their infants[g] will be dashed to pieces
before their eyes;
their houses will be looted and their
wives ravished.[h]

17See, I will stir up[i] against them the
Medes,[j]
who do not care for silver
and have no delight in gold.[k]
18Their bows[l] will strike down the
young men;[m]
they will have no mercy[n] on infants
nor will they look with compassion
on children.[o]
19Babylon,[p] the jewel of kingdoms,[q]
the glory[r] of the Babylonians'[1]
pride,
will be overthrown[s] by God
like Sodom and Gomorrah.[t]
20She will never be inhabited[u]
or lived in through all generations;
no Arab[v] will pitch his tent there,
no shepherd will rest his flocks
there.
21But desert creatures[w] will lie there,
jackals[x] will fill her houses;
there the owls[y] will dwell,
and there the wild goats[z] will leap
about.
22Hyenas[a] will howl in her
strongholds,[b]
jackals[c] in her luxurious palaces.
Her time is at hand,[d]
and her days will not be prolonged.[e]

Chapter 14

THE LORD will have compassion[f] on
Jacob;
once again he will choose[g] Israel
and will settle them in their own
land.[h]
Aliens[i] will join them
and unite with the house of Jacob.
2Nations will take them
and bring[j] them to their own place.
And the house of Israel will possess
the nations[k]
as menservants and maidservants in
the LORD's land.
They will make captives[l] of their
captors
and rule over their oppressors.[m]
3On the day the LORD gives you relief[n]
from suffering and turmoil[o] and cruel
bondage,[p] 4you will take up this taunt[q]
against the king of Babylon:[r]

How the oppressor[s] has come to an
end!
How his fury[m] has ended!
5The LORD has broken the rod[t] of the
wicked,[u]
the scepter[v] of the rulers,
6which in anger struck down peoples[w]
with unceasing blows,
and in fury subdued[x] nations
with relentless aggression.[y]

13:11 [s]S Isa 2:9; 23:9; Eze 28:2; Da 4:37 [t]Isa 25:3,5; 29:5,20; 49:25,26 **13:12** [u]S Isa 4:1 [v]S Ge 10:29 **13:13** [w]S Ps 102:26; Isa 34:4; 51:6 [x]S Job 9:6; S Isa 14:16; Mt 24:7; Mk 13:8 [y]S Isa 9:19 [z]S Job 9:5 **13:14** [a]Pr 6:5 [b]S 1Ki 22:17; S Mt 9:36; S Jn 10:11 [c]S Ge 11:9; Isa 17:13; 21:15; 22:3; 33:3; Jer 4:9 [d]Jer 46:16; 50:16; 51:9; Na 3:7 **13:15** [e]Jer 51:4 [f]Isa 14:19; Jer 50:25 **13:16** [g]ver 18; S Nu 16:27; S 2Ki 8:12 [h]S Ge 34:29; S Hos 13:16 **13:17** [i]Jer 50:9,41; 51:1 [j]S ver 3 [k]2Ki 18:14-16; Pr 6:34-35 **13:18** [l]S Ps 7:12; Isa 41:2; Jer 50:9, 14,29 [m]S Dt 32:25; Jer 49:26; 50:30; 51:4 [n]Isa 47:6; Jer 6:23; 50:42 [o]S ver 16; Isa 14:22; 47:9 **13:19** [p]S ver 1 [q]Isa 47:5; Da 2:37-38 [r]Da 4:30 [s]S Ps 137:8; S Rev 14:8 [t]S Ge 19:25; Isa 1:9-10; Ro 9:29 **13:20** [u]Isa 14:23; 34:10-15; Jer 51:29, 37-43,62 [v]2Ch 17:11 **13:21** [w]S Ps 74:14; Rev 18:2 [x]Jer 14:6 [y]S Lev 11:16-18; S Dt 14:15-17 [z]Lev 17:7; 2Ch 11:15 **13:22** [a]Isa 34:14 [b]Isa 25:2; 32:14 [c]Isa 34:13; 35:7; 43:20; Jer 9:11; 49:33; 51:37; Mal 1:3 [d]Dt 32:35; Jer 48:16; 51:33 [e]Jer 50:39 **14:1** [f]Ps 102:13; Isa 49:10,13; 54:7-8,10; Jer 33:26; Zec 10:6 [g]Ge 18:19; 2Ch 6:6; Isa 41:8; 42:1; 44:1; 45:4; 49:7; 65:9,22; Zec 1:17; 2:12; 3:2 [h]Jer 3:18; 16:15; 23:8 [i]S Ex 12:43; S Isa 11:10; Eze 47:22; Zec 8:22-23; Eph 2:12-19 **14:2** [j]S Isa 11:12; 60:9 [k]S Ps 49:14; Isa 26:15; 43:14; 49:7,23; 54:3 [l]Ps 149:8; Isa 45:14; 49:25; 60:12; Jer 40:1 [m]Isa 60:14; 61:5; Jer 30:16; 49:2; Eze 39:10; Zep 3:19; Zec 2:9 **14:3** [n]S Isa 11:10 [o]S Job 3:17 [p]S Ex 1:14 **14:4** [q]Mic 2:4; Hab 2:6 [r]S Isa 13:1 [s]S Isa 9:4 **14:5** [t]S Isa 10:15 [u]S Ps 125:3 [v]S Ps 110:2 **14:6** [w]Isa 10:14 [x]S Ps 47:3 [y]S 2Ki 15:29; Isa 47:6; Hab 1:17

[1]*19* Or *Chaldeans'* [m]*4* Dead Sea Scrolls, Septuagint and Syriac; the meaning of the word in the Masoretic Text is uncertain.

14:1–2 GOD, Sovereignty—No one controls God's decisions. Only He knows when and where it is best to act. He chooses to discipline His people in His wrath. He elected to use His authority and power to choose Israel again, after their captivity. He remained free to accomplish His purpose first revealed to Abraham by blessing foreign nations through His people (Ge 12:1–3). He can bring in aliens, Gentiles, to become part of His chosen people.

14:1 GOD, Grace—The grace of God stands in sharp contrast to the wrath pictured in the preceding chapter. God disciplined His people. They still did not deserve His saving acts to restore them. Only God's grace leads Him to deliver His people from trouble.

14:1,32 ELECTION, Remnant—God shows His covenant compassion by giving relief for suffering brought on by past sins. God faithfully renewed His election promises to Israel. He took the remnant left after the Exile to be His people. They were commissioned to accomplish His purposes. This included witnessing for God to the nations. Remnant theology is based on God's parental compassion (Hebrew *richam*). Renewed election included renewed land and a renewed worship place. See note on Dt 14:2.

14:3–23 EVIL AND SUFFERING, Satan—The exiles who returned from Babylonia would taunt the Babylonian king. The king had exalted himself but now was brought low. His aspirations to be like God brought about his defeat. See note on Eze 28:1–10. The king is described as a "morning star." Some understand this passage to refer to the fall of Satan. Part of this rests on the Vulgate or Latin translation "Lucifer." The context points to the fall of an arrogant Babylonian king, not to Satan. See notes on Job 1:6–12; Mt 4:1–11; 2 Pe 2:4; Jude 6.

7All the lands are at rest and at peace;[z]
they break into singing.[a]
8Even the pine trees[b] and the cedars of
Lebanon
exult over you and say,
"Now that you have been laid low,
no woodsman comes to cut us
down."[c]

9The grave[n][d] below is all astir
to meet you at your coming;
it rouses the spirits of the departed[e] to
greet you—
all those who were leaders[f] in the
world;
it makes them rise from their
thrones—
all those who were kings over the
nations.[g]
10They will all respond,
they will say to you,
"You also have become weak, as we
are;
you have become like us."[h]
11All your pomp has been brought down
to the grave,[i]
along with the noise of your harps;[j]
maggots are spread out beneath you
and worms[k] cover you.[l]

12How you have fallen[m] from heaven,
O morning star,[n] son of the dawn!
You have been cast down to the earth,
you who once laid low the nations![o]
13You said in your heart,
"I will ascend[p] to heaven;
I will raise my throne[q]
above the stars of God;
I will sit enthroned on the mount of
assembly,[r]
on the utmost heights[s] of the sacred
mountain.[o]
14I will ascend above the tops of the
clouds;[t]
I will make myself like the Most
High."[u]
15But you are brought down[v] to the
grave,[w]
to the depths[x] of the pit.[y]

16Those who see you stare at you,
they ponder your fate:[z]
"Is this the man who shook[a] the earth
and made kingdoms tremble,
17the man who made the world a
desert,[b]
who overthrew[c] its cities
and would not let his captives go
home?"[d]

18All the kings of the nations lie in state,
each in his own tomb.[e]
19But you are cast out[f] of your tomb
like a rejected branch;
you are covered with the slain,[g]
with those pierced by the sword,[h]
those who descend to the stones of
the pit.[i]
Like a corpse trampled underfoot,
20 you will not join them in burial,[j]
for you have destroyed your land
and killed your people.

14:7 zS Nu 6:26; Jer 50:34; Zec 1:11 aPs 98:1; 126:1-3; Isa 12:6 **14:8** bS 1Ch 16:33; S Ps 65:13; Eze 31:16 cS 2Ki 19:23; Isa 37:24 **14:9** dS Pr 30:16; Eze 32:21 eS Job 26:5 fZec 10:3 gS Job 3:14 **14:10** hEze 26:20; 32:21 **14:11** iS Nu 16:30; S Pr 30:16 jIsa 5:12; Eze 26:13; Am 6:5 kS Job 7:5; 24:20; Isa 51:8; 66:24 lS Job 21:26 **14:12** mLk 10:18 n2Pe 1:19; Rev 2:28; 8:10; 9:1 oEze 26:17 **14:13** pDa 5:23; 8:10; Ob 1:4; Mt 11:23 qEze 28:2; 2Th 2:4 rPs 82:1 sIsa 37:24 **14:14** tS Job 20:6 uS Ge 3:5; S Nu 24:16; Isa 10:13; 47:8; Jer 50:29; 51:53; Da 11:36; 2Th 2:4 **14:15** vIsa 13:6; 45:7; 47:11; Jer 51:8,43 wS Job 21:13 xMt 11:23; Lk 10:15 yS Ps 55:23; Eze 31:16; 32:23 **14:16** zJer 50:23; Rev 18:9 aS Isa 2:19; 13:13; Joel 3:16; Hag 2:6, 21 **14:17** bIsa 15:6; Joel 2:3 cPs 52:7 dEx 7:14; S 2Ki 15:29; Jer 50:33; Rev 18:18

14:18 eJob 21:32 **14:19** fIsa 22:16-18; Jer 8:1; 36:30 gIsa 34:3 hS Isa 13:15 iJer 41:7-9 **14:20** jS 1Ki 21:19

n*9* Hebrew *Sheol*; also in verses 11 and 15 o*13* Or *the north*; Hebrew *Zaphon*

14:9–21 HUMANITY, Death—The prophet promised relief for Israel from Babylonian exile. This meant the mighty Babylonian king would die and enter *Sheol,* the common abode of the dead. No matter how great any person becomes, the ultimate destiny is always death. Further, all people share this fate as the consequence of sin, for all have sinned. For one whose sins had been excessive, the final punishment (in the Old Testament) was to be denied normal burial. The New Testament offers no hope for wicked leaders, rather it intensifies the picture of their punishment under God's wrath.

14:9 LAST THINGS, Intermediate State—The prophet mocked the king of Babylon by picturing his death (vv 4–23). The inspired writer depicted the welcome in the "grave" (Hebrew *She'ol*) where the "spirits of the departed" (Hebrew *repha'im*) live. This chapter is one of the most important in the Old Testament for understanding the state of the dead. The chapter may be considered poetic personification and thus not a literal description of the dead. If taken literally, it describes conscious beings aware of and classed according to their state in the previous life. They can talk (Eze 32:21) but see themselves as weak or exhausted, living among the worms. *Sheol* is a place below the earth (Ps 63:9; 86:13, Pr 15:24). It is synonymous with the state of death apart from hope and meaningfulness (Job 17:13–16; Ecc 9:10). Both good and bad go to *Sheol* (Ge 37:35; Nu 16:30). It is a dark place from which people do not return (Job 10:20–22) and where they cannot praise God (Isa 38:18; Ps 6:5; 88:11). People approaching death fear that God does not remember or put His caring hand on *Sheol's* inhabitants (Ps 88:3–5). The living can claim to have entered *Sheol* in desperate situations (Isa 57:9; 2 Sa 22:6; Ps 30:3; 86:13; 88:4). All people must submit to *Sheol's* power (Ps 89:48). There bodies will decay (Ps 49:14). One does not escape God's presence in *Sheol* (Ps 139:8; Am 9:2). People do not return from *Sheol* (Job 7:9). The wicked appear to enter *Sheol* in prosperity and peace (Job 21:13). *Sheol* has no work, planning, knowledge, or wisdom (Ecc 9:10). "The spirits of the departed" (Hebrew *repha'im*) appear in seven other Old Testament passages in reference to dead people. They suffer (Job 26:5), cannot rise up to praise God (Ps 88:10), represent the destination of adulterers (Pr 2:18; 9:18) and fools (Pr 21:16). God has punished them (Isa 26:14), but hope remains for the earth to give new life to the *repha'im* (Isa 26:19). The most literal meaning of the two important words is "grave" and "dead ones." Isa 14:9–11 seems to imply some form of consciousness for the dead. If so, a simple explanation of *Sheol* as the home of dead bodies and heaven as the resting place of spirits is not satisfactory and must be interpreted in light of the New Testament. The Hebrew concept of humanity resisted the idea of a spirit existence apart from the body; a human was perceived as a unity rather than as a being in two parts, body and soul or spirit. The "spirits" of the dead are therefore by many interpreters identified with "shades," a kind of pale replica of the persons themselves (body and spirit). The concept that life requires the body eventually helped people understand God's revelation that some kind of bodily resurrection is an essential part of ongoing existence. The idea of life beyond death in a resurrection body, however, is clearly taught in the further revelation of the New Testament. See notes on Pr 15:24; 2 Co 5:1–10.

The offspring[k] of the wicked[l]
will never be mentioned[m] again.
21Prepare a place to slaughter his sons[n]
for the sins of their forefathers;[o]
they are not to rise to inherit the land
and cover the earth with their cities.

22"I will rise up[p] against them,"
declares the LORD Almighty.
"I will cut off from Babylon her name[q]
and survivors,
her offspring and descendants,[r]"
declares the LORD.
23"I will turn her into a place for owls[s]
and into swampland;
I will sweep her with the broom of
destruction,[t]"
declares the LORD Almighty.[u]

A Prophecy Against Assyria

24The LORD Almighty has sworn,[v]
"Surely, as I have planned,[w] so it will
be,
and as I have purposed, so it will
stand.[x]
25I will crush the Assyrian[y] in my land;
on my mountains I will trample him
down.
His yoke[z] will be taken from my
people,
and his burden removed from their
shoulders.[a]"
26This is the plan[b] determined for the
whole world;
this is the hand[c] stretched out over
all nations.
27For the LORD Almighty has purposed,[d]
and who can thwart him?
His hand[e] is stretched out, and who
can turn it back?[f]

A Prophecy Against the Philistines

28This oracle[g] came in the year[h] King
Ahaz[i] died:
29Do not rejoice, all you Philistines,[j]
that the rod that struck you is
broken;
from the root of that snake will spring
up a viper,[k]
its fruit will be a darting, venomous
serpent.[l]
30The poorest of the poor will find
pasture,
and the needy[m] will lie down in
safety.[n]
But your root I will destroy by
famine;[o]
it will slay[p] your survivors.[q]
31Wail,[r] O gate![s] Howl, O city!
Melt away, all you Philistines![t]
A cloud of smoke comes from the
north,[u]
and there is not a straggler in its
ranks.[v]
32What answer shall be given
to the envoys[w] of that nation?
"The LORD has established Zion,[x]
and in her his afflicted people will
find refuge.[y]"

Chapter 15

A Prophecy Against Moab

16:6–12pp — Jer 48:29–36

AN oracle[z] concerning Moab:[a]
Ar[b] in Moab is ruined,[c]
destroyed in a night!
Kir[d] in Moab is ruined,
destroyed in a night!
2Dibon[e] goes up to its temple,
to its high places[f] to weep;
Moab wails[g] over Nebo[h] and
Medeba.
Every head is shaved[i]
and every beard cut off.[j]
3In the streets they wear sackcloth;[k]
on the roofs[l] and in the public
squares[m]
they all wail,[n]
prostrate with weeping.[o]
4Heshbon[p] and Elealeh[q] cry out,
their voices are heard all the way to
Jahaz.[r]
Therefore the armed men of Moab cry
out,
and their hearts are faint.

5My heart cries out[s] over Moab;[t]
her fugitives[u] flee as far as Zoar,[v]
as far as Eglath Shelishiyah.
They go up the way to Luhith,
weeping as they go;
on the road to Horonaim[w]
they lament their destruction.[x]
6The waters of Nimrim are dried up[y]
and the grass is withered;[z]
the vegetation is gone[a]
and nothing green is left.[b]
7So the wealth they have acquired[c] and
stored up
they carry away over the Ravine of
the Poplars.
8Their outcry echoes along the border
of Moab;
their wailing reaches as far as
Eglaim,

14:20 [k]S Job 18:19 [l]S Isa 1:4 [m]S Dt 32:26 **14:21** [n]S Nu 16:27 [o]S Ge 9:25; S Lev 26:39 **14:22** [p]S Ps 94:16 [q]S Job 18:17; Ps 109:13; Na 1:14 [r]2Sa 18:18; 1Ki 14:10; Job 18:19; S Ps 9:6; S Isa 13:18 **14:23** [s]S Lev 11:16-18; Isa 34:11-15; Zep 2:14 [t]S Isa 10:3; Jer 25:12 [u]Jer 50:3; 51:62 **14:24** [v]Isa 45:23; 49:18; 54:9; 62:8 [w]Isa 19:12,17; 23:8-9; 25:1; Da 4:35 [x]S Job 9:3; S Isa 7:7; 46:10-11; Eze 12:25; Ac 4:28 **14:25** [y]S Isa 10:5, 12; 37:36-38 [z]S Isa 9:4 [a]S Isa 10:27 **14:26** [b]Isa 23:9 [c]Ex 15:12; S Job 30:21 **14:27** [d]Jer 49:20 [e]S Ex 14:21 [f]S 2Ch 20:6; Isa 43:13; Da 4:35 **14:28** [g]S Isa 13:1 [h]S 2Ki 15:7 [i]S 2Ki 16:1 **14:29** [j]S Jos 13:3; S 2Ki 1:2; S 2Ch 26:6 [k]S Isa 11:8 [l]S Dt 8:15 **14:30** [m]Isa 3:15; 25:4 [n]S Isa 7:21-22 [o]Isa 8:21; 9:20; 51:19 [p]Jer 25:16; Zec 9:5-6 [q]Eze 25:15-17; Zep 2:5 **14:31** [r]S Isa 13:6 [s]S Isa 3:26 [t]S Ge 10:14 [u]Isa 41:25; Jer 1:14; 4:6; 6:1, 22; 10:22; 13:20; 25:9; 46:20,24; 47:2; 50:41; Eze 32:30 [v]S Isa 5:27 **14:32** [w]Isa 37:9 [x]S Ps 51:18; 87:2, 5; Isa 2:2; 26:1; 28:16; 31:5; 33:5, 20; 44:28; 51:21; 54:11 [y]S Isa 4:6; Jas 2:5 **15:1** [z]S Isa 13:1 [a]Nu 22:3-6; S Dt 23:6; S Isa 11:14 [b]S Nu 21:15 [c]S Nu 17:12; Isa 25:12; 26:5; Jer 48:24,41; 51:58 [d]S 2Ki 3:25 **15:2** [e]S Nu 21:30 [f]1Ki 11:7; Isa 16:12; Jer 48:35 [g]S Isa 13:6; 65:14 [h]S Nu 32:38 [i]S Lev 13:40; S Job 1:20 [j]S 2Sa 10:4 **15:3** [k]S Isa 3:24 [l]S Jos 2:8 [m]Jer 48:38 [n]Isa 14:31; Jer 47:2 [o]ver 5; Isa 16:9; 22:4; La 2:11; Eze 7:18; Mic 1:8 **15:4** [p]S Nu 21:25; S Jos 13:26 [q]S Nu 32:3 [r]S Nu 21:23 **15:5** [s]S ver 3 [t]Isa 16:11; Jer 48:31 [u]S Nu 21:29 [v]S Ge 13:10 [w]Jer 48:3,34 [x]Jer 4:20; 48:5 **15:6** [y]Isa 19:5-7; Jer 48:34 [z]Ps 37:2; Isa 16:8; 24:4,7, 11; 33:9; 34:4; 37:27; 40:7; 51:6,12; Hos 4:3; Joel 1:12 [a]S Isa 14:17 [b]Jer 14:5 **15:7** [c]Isa 30:6; Jer 48:36

14:26–27 GOD, Sovereignty—God is at work in His world carrying out His purposes. No opposition can defeat God's plans. No people or nation is automatically excluded from His plan.

their lamentation as far as Beer[d]
Elim.
9Dimon's[p] waters are full of blood,
but I will bring still more upon
Dimon[p] —
a lion[e] upon the fugitives of Moab[f]
and upon those who remain in the
land.

Chapter 16

SEND lambs[g] as tribute[h]
to the ruler of the land,
from Sela,[i] across the desert,
to the mount of the Daughter of
Zion.[j]
2Like fluttering birds
pushed from the nest,[k]
so are the women of Moab[l]
at the fords[m] of the Arnon.[n]

3"Give us counsel,
render a decision.
Make your shadow like night—
at high noon.
Hide the fugitives,[o]
do not betray the refugees.
4Let the Moabite fugitives stay with
you;
be their shelter[p] from the
destroyer."

The oppressor[q] will come to an end,
and destruction will cease;[r]
the aggressor will vanish from the
land.
5In love a throne[s] will be established;[t]
in faithfulness a man will sit on it—
one from the house[q] of David[u] —
one who in judging seeks justice[v]
and speeds the cause of
righteousness.

6We have heard of Moab's[w] pride[x] —
her overweening pride and conceit,
her pride and her insolence—
but her boasts are empty.
7Therefore the Moabites wail,[y]
they wail together for Moab.
Lament and grieve
for the men[r z] of Kir Hareseth.[a]
8The fields of Heshbon[b] wither,[c]
the vines of Sibmah[d] also.
The rulers of the nations
have trampled down the choicest
vines,[e]
which once reached Jazer[f]
and spread toward the desert.
Their shoots spread out[g]
and went as far as the sea.[h]
9So I weep,[i] as Jazer weeps,
for the vines of Sibmah.
O Heshbon, O Elealeh,[j]
I drench you with tears![k]
The shouts of joy[l] over your ripened
fruit
and over your harvests[m] have been
stilled.
10Joy and gladness are taken away from
the orchards;[n]
no one sings or shouts[o] in the
vineyards;
no one treads[p] out wine at the
presses,[q]
for I have put an end to the
shouting.
11My heart laments for Moab[r] like a
harp,[s]
my inmost being[t] for Kir Hareseth.
12When Moab appears at her high
place,[u]
she only wears herself out;
when she goes to her shrine[v] to pray,
it is to no avail.[w]

13This is the word the LORD has already
spoken concerning Moab. 14But now the
LORD says: "Within three years,[x] as a
servant bound by contract[y] would count
them,[z] Moab's splendor and all her many
people will be despised,[a] and her survivors will be very few and feeble."[b]

Chapter 17

An Oracle Against Damascus

AN oracle[c] concerning Damascus:[d]
"See, Damascus will no longer be a
city
but will become a heap of ruins.[e]
2The cities of Aroer[f] will be deserted
and left to flocks,[g] which will lie
down,[h]
with no one to make them afraid.[i]
3The fortified[j] city will disappear from
Ephraim,
and royal power from Damascus;

[p]9 Masoretic Text; Dead Sea Scrolls, some Septuagint manuscripts and Vulgate *Dibon* [q]5 Hebrew *tent* [r]7 Or "*raisin cakes,*" a wordplay

15:8 [d]S Nu 21:16
15:9 [e]S 2Ki 17:25 [f]Eze 25:8-11
16:1 [g]S 2Ki 3:4 [h]S 2Ch 32:23 [i]S Jdg 1:36; Ob 3 *fn* [j]S Isa 10:32
16:2 [k]Pr 27:8 [l]Nu 21:29 [m]Jdg 12:5 [n]Nu 21:13-14; Jer 48:20
16:3 [o]S 1Ki 18:4
16:4 [p]Isa 58:7 [q]S Isa 9:4 [r]Isa 2:2-4
16:5 [s]S 1Sa 13:14; Da 7:14; Mic 4:7 [t]S Pr 20:28 [u]S Isa 7:2; Lk 1:32 [v]S Isa 9:7
16:6 [w]Jer 25:21; Eze 25:8; Am 2:1; Zep 2:8 [x]S Lev 26:19; S Job 20:6; Jer 49:16; Ob 1:3; Zep 2:10
16:7 [y]S Isa 13:6; Jer 48:20; 49:3 [z]S 1Ch 16:3 [a]S 2Ki 3:25
16:8 [b]S Nu 21:25 [c]S Isa 15:6 [d]S Nu 32:3 [e]S Isa 5:2 [f]S Nu 21:32 [g]S Job 8:16 [h]Ps 80:11
16:9 [i]S Isa 15:3; Eze 27:31 [j]S Nu 32:3 [k]S Job 7:3 [l]S Ezr 3:13 [m]Jer 40:12
16:10 [n]Isa 24:7-8 [o]Jer 25:30 [p]S Jdg 9:27 [q]S Job 24:11; S Isa 5:2
16:11 [r]S Isa 15:5 [s]S Job 30:31 [t]Isa 63:15; Hos 11:8; Php 2:1
16:12 [u]1Ki 11:7 [v]S Isa 15:2 [w]S 1Ki 18:29; Ps 115:4-7; Isa 44:17-18; 1Co 8:4
16:14 [x]Isa 20:3; 37:30 [y]S Lev 25:50 [z]S Lev 19:13 [a]Isa 25:10; Jer 48:42 [b]Isa 21:17
17:1 [c]Isa 13:1 [d]S Ge 14:15; Ac 9:2 [e]S Dt 13:16; S Isa 25:2
17:2 [f]S 2Ki 10:33 [g]S Isa 5:17; 7:21; Eze 25:5 [h]Isa 27:10 [i]S Lev 26:6; Jer 7:33; Mic 4:4
17:3 [j]Isa 25:2,12; Hos 10:14

16:4–5 JESUS CHRIST, Foretold—The just and righteous rule over God's kingdom is secured completely and expressly by Jesus, David's heir and God's Son. See note on 9:1–9.
16:5 GOD, Love—Dark days of oppression may make God's people think His purposes are dead. All available evidence may point in that direction. God's love guarantees God's announced plans will be established. God did send Jesus to inherit David's throne. He will send Jesus again to establish justice and righteousness.
16:5 SALVATION, Preparation—New kings often take the throne amid plots and rebellion. Isaiah looked to the day God in love would establish an absolute trustworthy King for His people. Only Jesus fulfilled the role of King of justice. Isaiah's words prepared the way for Him. One day He will establish justice for His people. Salvation points to a social order with justice and righteousness.
17:3–6 ELECTION, Remnant—The glory of Jacob faded, wasted, and became as gleanings in the field when God elected to punish Jacob's sons and daughters even though they were blessed with the election promises of Jacob. Heritage does not

the remnant of Aram will be
like the glory[k] of the Israelites,"[l]
declares the LORD Almighty.

4"In that day[m] the glory[n] of Jacob will fade;
the fat of his body will waste[o] away.
5It will be as when a reaper gathers the standing grain
and harvests[p] the grain with his arm—
as when a man gleans heads of grain[q]
in the Valley of Rephaim.[r]
6Yet some gleanings will remain,[s]
as when an olive tree is beaten,[t]
leaving two or three olives on the topmost branches,
four or five on the fruitful boughs,"
declares the LORD,
the God of Israel.

7In that day[u] men will look[v] to their Maker[w]
and turn their eyes to the Holy One[x] of Israel.
8They will not look to the altars,[y]
the work of their hands,[z]
and they will have no regard for the Asherah poles[s] [a]
and the incense altars their fingers[b] have made.

9In that day their strong cities, which
they left because of the Israelites, will be
like places abandoned to thickets and undergrowth.[c] And all will be desolation.

10You have forgotten[d] God your Savior;[e]
you have not remembered the Rock,[f] your fortress.[g]
Therefore, though you set out the finest plants
and plant imported vines,[h]
11though on the day you set them out,
you make them grow,
and on the morning[i] when you plant them, you bring them to bud,
yet the harvest[j] will be as nothing[k]
in the day of disease and incurable[l] pain.[m]

12Oh, the raging[n] of many nations—
they rage like the raging sea![o]
Oh, the uproar[p] of the peoples—
they roar like the roaring of great waters![q]
13Although the peoples roar[r] like the roar of surging waters,
when he rebukes[s] them they flee[t] far away,
driven before the wind like chaff[u] on the hills,
like tumbleweed before a gale.[v]
14In the evening, sudden[w] terror![x]
Before the morning, they are gone![y]
This is the portion of those who loot us,
the lot of those who plunder us.

Chapter 18

A Prophecy Against Cush

WOE[z] to the land of whirring wings[t]
along the rivers of Cush,[u] [a]
2which sends envoys[b] by sea
in papyrus[c] boats over the water.

Go, swift messengers,
to a people tall and smooth-skinned,[d]
to a people feared far and wide,
an aggressive[e] nation of strange speech,
whose land is divided by rivers.[f]

3All you people of the world,[g]
you who live on the earth,
when a banner[h] is raised on the mountains,
you will see it,
and when a trumpet[i] sounds,
you will hear it.
4This is what the LORD says to me:
"I will remain quiet[j] and will look on from my dwelling place,[k]
like shimmering heat in the sunshine,[l]

17:3 [k]ver 4; Isa 21:16; Hos 9:11 [l]Isa 7:8,16; 8:4 **17:4** [m]S Isa 2:11 [n]S ver 3 [o]S Isa 10:16 **17:5** [p]ver 11; Isa 33:4; Jer 51:33; Joel 3:13; Mt 13:30 [q]Job 24:24 [r]S Jos 17:15; S 1Ch 11:15 **17:6** [s]S Dt 4:27; S Isa 10:19; S 24:13 [t]ver 11; Isa 27:12 **17:7** [u]S Isa 2:11 [v]S Isa 9:13; S 10:20 [w]S Ps 95:6 [x]S Isa 12:6 **17:8** [y]S Lev 26:30 [z]S 2Ch 32:19; Isa 2:18,20; 30:22; 46:6; Rev 9:20 [a]S Jdg 3:7; S 2Ki 17:10 [b]Isa 2:8 **17:9** [c]S Isa 7:19 **17:10** [d]S Dt 6:12; 8:11; Ps 50:22; 106:21; Isa 51:13; 57:11; Jer 2:32; 3:21; 13:25; 18:15; Eze 22:12; 23:35; Hos 8:14; 13:6 [e]S Isa 12:2; S Lk 1:47 [f]S Ge 49:24 [g]S Ps 18:2 [h]S Isa 5:7 **17:11** [i]Ps 90:6 [j]S ver 5 [k]S Lev 26:20; Hos 8:7; Joel 1:11; Hag 1:6 [l]Jer 10:19; 30:12 [m]S Dt 28:39; S Job 4:8 **17:12** [n]ver 13; Isa 41:11 [o]S Ps 18:4; Lk 21:25 [p]S Ps 46:6; Isa 8:9 [q]Isa 8:7 **17:13** [r]S Ps 46:3 [s]S Dt 28:20; S Ps 9:5 [t]S Ps 68:1; S Isa 13:14 [u]S Job 13:25; S Isa 2:22; 41:2, 15-16; Da 2:35 [v]Job 21:18; S Ps 65:7 **17:14** [w]Isa 29:5; 30:13; 47:11; 48:3 [x]Isa 33:18; 54:14 [y]S 2Ki 19:35 **18:1** [z]Isa 5:8 [a]S Ge 10:6; S Ps 68:31; S Eze 29:10 **18:2** [b]Ob 1:1 [c]Ex 2:3; Job 9:26 [d]S Ge 41:14 [e]S Ge 10:8-9; S 2Ch 12:3 [f]ver 7 **18:3** [g]S Ps 33:8 [h]S Ps 60:4; Isa 5:26; 11:10; 13:2; 31:9; Jer 4:21 [i]S Jos 6:20; S Jdg 3:27 **18:4** [j]Isa 62:1; 64:12 [k]Isa 26:21; Hos 5:15; Mic 1:3 [l]S Jdg 5:31; S Ps 18:12; Hab 3:4

[s]*8* That is, symbols of the goddess Asherah [t]*1* Or *of locusts* [u]*1* That is, the upper Nile region

guarantee election. Commitment to human creations rather than the Creator leads to chaos and condemnation. Election theology takes judgment seriously. Israel's remnant was exceedingly small.

17:4–6 THE CHURCH, Remnant—Remnant theology begins with judgment for a proud, prosperous people of God. A complacent people in any age does well to read the warning of the remnant. See note on 7:3; 2 Ch 34:9.

17:7 GOD, Creator—God's judgment seeks to turn His people back to the Creator and away from the worship of products of our own hands which beautify our places of worship.

17:10 GOD, Savior—God delivers people in their need, but disciplines them when they forget Him and His saving acts. See note on 12:1–3.

17:10 SIN, Unbelief—Forgetfulness is a sin when God's people fail to remember what He has done for us. If we do not focus on His saving acts, we will focus on our selfish desires and seek magical solutions to our problems. See note on 1 Ki 12:26–33.

18:4 REVELATION, Word—God reveals Himself in silence also, often choosing not to interrupt evil until it has finished its course. Though able to stop human actions which ignore His will, God is committed enough to the gift of personal free will that He will not force individuals or nations to follow Him. Egypt sought to force Judah into an alliance against Assyria. God announced Egypt's fall in the near future. God's present silence did not mean permanent silence. He was waiting for the opportune moment to defeat Egypt.

like a cloud of dew[m] in the heat of
harvest."
5For, before the harvest, when the
blossom is gone
and the flower becomes a ripening
grape,
he will cut off[n] the shoots with
pruning knives,
and cut down and take away the
spreading branches.[o]
6They will all be left to the mountain
birds of prey[p]
and to the wild animals;[q]
the birds will feed on them all
summer,
the wild animals all winter.

7At that time gifts[r] will be brought to
the LORD Almighty

from a people tall and
smooth-skinned,[s]
from a people feared[t] far and wide,
an aggressive nation of strange speech,
whose land is divided by rivers[u]—

the gifts will be brought to Mount Zion,
the place of the Name of the LORD Almighty.[v]

Chapter 19

A Prophecy About Egypt

AN oracle[w] concerning Egypt:[x] [y]
See, the LORD rides on a swift
cloud[z]
and is coming to Egypt.
The idols of Egypt tremble before him,
and the hearts of the Egyptians
melt[a] within them.

2"I will stir up Egyptian against
Egyptian—
brother will fight against brother,[b]
neighbor against neighbor,
city against city,
kingdom against kingdom.[c]
3The Egyptians will lose heart,[d]
and I will bring their plans[e] to
nothing;[f]
they will consult the idols and the
spirits of the dead,
the mediums and the spiritists.[g]
4I will hand the Egyptians over
to the power of a cruel master,
and a fierce king[h] will rule over
them,"
declares the Lord, the LORD
Almighty.

5The waters of the river will dry up,[i]
and the riverbed will be parched and
dry.[j]
6The canals will stink;[k]
the streams of Egypt will dwindle
and dry up.[l]
The reeds[m] and rushes will wither,[n]
7 also the plants[o] along the Nile,
at the mouth of the river.
Every sown field[p] along the Nile
will become parched, will blow
away and be no more.[q]
8The fishermen[r] will groan and lament,
all who cast hooks[s] into the Nile;
those who throw nets on the water
will pine away.
9Those who work with combed flax[t]
will despair,
the weavers of fine linen[u] will lose
hope.
10The workers in cloth will be dejected,
and all the wage earners will be sick
at heart.

11The officials of Zoan[v] are nothing but
fools;
the wise counselors[w] of Pharaoh
give senseless advice.[x]
How can you say to Pharaoh,
"I am one of the wise men,[y]
a disciple of the ancient kings"?

12Where are your wise men[z] now?
Let them show you and make
known
what the LORD Almighty
has planned[a] against Egypt.
13The officials of Zoan[b] have become
fools,
the leaders of Memphis[v][c] are
deceived;
the cornerstones[d] of her peoples
have led Egypt astray.
14The LORD has poured into them
a spirit of dizziness;[e]
they make Egypt stagger in all that she
does,
as a drunkard staggers[f] around in
his vomit.
15There is nothing Egypt can do—
head or tail, palm branch or reed.[g]

16In that day[h] the Egyptians will be
like women.[i] They will shudder with
fear[j] at the uplifted hand[k] that the LORD
Almighty raises against them. 17And the
land of Judah will bring terror to the
Egyptians; everyone to whom Judah is
mentioned will be terrified,[l] because of
what the LORD Almighty is planning[m]
against them.

18:4 [m]2Sa 1:21; S Ps 133:3; Isa 26:19; Hos 14:5
18:5 [n]S Isa 10:33 [o]Isa 17:10-11; Eze 17:6
18:6 [p]S Isa 8:8 [q]Isa 37:36; 56:9; Jer 7:33; Eze 32:4; 39:17
18:7 [r]S 2Ch 9:24; S Isa 60:7 [s]S Ge 41:14 [t]Hab 1:7 [u]ver 2 [v]Ps 68:31
19:1 [w]Isa 13:1 [x]Isa 20:3; Joel 3:19 [y]S Ex 12:12; S Jer 44:3 [z]S Dt 10:14; S 2Sa 22:10; S Rev 1:7 [a]S Jos 2:11
19:2 [b]S Jdg 7:22; S 12:4; Mt 10:21,36 [c]S 2Ch 15:6; 20:23; Mt 24:7; Mk 13:8; Lk 21:10
19:3 [d]Ps 18:45 [e]ver 11; S Job 5:12 [f]1Ch 10:13 [g]S Lev 19:31; Isa 47:13; Da 2:2, 10; 3:8; 5:7
19:4 [h]Isa 20:4; Jer 46:26; Eze 29:19; 32:11
19:5 [i]Isa 44:27; 50:2; Jer 50:38; 51:36 [j]S 2Sa 14:14
19:6 [k]Ex 7:18 [l]Isa 37:25; Eze 30:12 [m]S Ge 41:2; S Job 8:11 [n]Isa 15:6
19:7 [o]Nu 11:5 [p]Dt 29:23; Isa 23:3 [q]Zec 10:11
19:8 [r]Nu 11:5; Eze 47:10 [s]Am 4:2; Hab 1:15
19:9 [t]S Jos 2:6 [u]Pr 7:16; Eze 16:10; 27:7
19:11 [v]S Nu 13:22 [w]S Ge 41:37 [x]S ver 3 [y]S 1Ki 4:30; Ac 7:22
19:12 [z]1Co 1:20 [a]S Isa 14:24; Ro 9:17
19:13 [b]S Nu 13:22 [c]Jer 2:16; 44:1; 46:14,19; Eze 30:13,16; Hos 9:6 [d]S Ps 118:22
19:14 [e]S Pr 12:8; Mt 17:17 [f]S Ps 107:27
19:15 [g]S Isa 9:14
19:16 [h]Isa 2:17; 11:10 [i]Jer 50:37; 51:30; Na 3:13 [j]S Dt 2:25; Heb 10:31 [k]S Isa 11:15
19:17 [l]S Ge 35:5 [m]S Isa 14:24

[v]*13* Hebrew *Noph*

19:1 GOD, Power—As the one and only God, the Lord is able to exercise judgment against all people and nations. A strong and ancient religious tradition does not protect a people or give them confidence when God comes in judgment. See note on 1:24.

18In that day[n] five cities[o] in Egypt will
speak the language of Canaan and swear
allegiance[p] to the LORD Almighty. One of
them will be called the City of Destruction.[w] [q]
19In that day[r] there will be an altar[s] to
the LORD in the heart of Egypt,[t] and a
monument[u] to the LORD at its border.
20It will be a sign and witness[v] to the
LORD Almighty in the land of Egypt.
When they cry out to the LORD because of
their oppressors, he will send them a savior[w] and defender, and he will rescue[x]
them. 21So the LORD will make himself
known to the Egyptians, and in that day
they will acknowledge[y] the LORD. They
will worship[z] with sacrifices and grain
offerings; they will make vows to the
LORD and keep them.[a] 22The LORD will
strike[b] Egypt with a plague;[c] he will
strike them and heal them. They will
turn[d] to the LORD, and he will respond to
their pleas and heal[e] them.
23In that day[f] there will be a highway[g] from Egypt to Assyria.[h] The Assyrians will go to Egypt and the Egyptians to
Assyria. The Egyptians and Assyrians will
worship[i] together. 24In that day[j] Israel
will be the third, along with Egypt and
Assyria,[k] a blessing[l] on the earth. 25The
LORD Almighty will bless[m] them, saying,
"Blessed be Egypt my people,[n] Assyria
my handiwork,[o] and Israel my inheritance.[p]"

Chapter 20

A Prophecy Against Egypt and Cush

IN the year that the supreme commander,[q] sent by Sargon king of Assyria,
came to Ashdod[r] and attacked and captured it— 2at that time the LORD spoke
through Isaiah son of Amoz.[s] He said to
him, "Take off the sackcloth[t] from your
body and the sandals[u] from your feet."
And he did so, going around stripped[v]
and barefoot.[w]
3Then the LORD said, "Just as my servant[x] Isaiah has gone stripped and barefoot for three years,[y] as sign[z] and
portent[a] against Egypt[b] and Cush,[x] [c] 4so
the king[d] of Assyria will lead away
stripped[e] and barefoot the Egyptian captives[f] and Cushite[g] exiles, young and
old, with buttocks bared[h]—to Egypt's
shame.[i] 5Those who trusted[j] in Cush[k]
and boasted in Egypt[l] will be afraid and
put to shame.[m] 6In that day[n] the people
who live on this coast will say, 'See what
has happened[o] to those we relied on,[p]
those we fled to for help[q] and deliverance from the king of Assyria! How then
can we escape?[r]' "

Chapter 21

A Prophecy Against Babylon

AN oracle[s] concerning the Desert[t] by
the Sea:

Like whirlwinds[u] sweeping through
the southland,[v]
an invader comes from the desert,
from a land of terror.

2A dire[w] vision has been shown to me:
The traitor betrays,[x] the looter takes
loot.
Elam,[y] attack! Media,[z] lay siege!
I will bring to an end all the
groaning she caused.

3At this my body is racked with pain,[a]
pangs seize me, like those of a
woman in labor;[b]
I am staggered by what I hear,
I am bewildered[c] by what I see.
4My heart[d] falters,
fear makes me tremble;[e]
the twilight I longed for
has become a horror[f] to me.

5They set the tables,
they spread the rugs,
they eat, they drink![g]
Get up, you officers,
oil the shields![h]

6This is what the Lord says to me:

"Go, post a lookout[i]
and have him report what he sees.
7When he sees chariots[j]

19:18 [n]S Isa 10:20 [o]Jer 44:1 [p]Ps 22:27; S 63:11; Isa 48:1; Jer 4:2; Zep 3:9 [q]Isa 17:1; 24:12; 32:19; *fn* Jer 43:13 **19:19** [r]S Isa 10:20 [s]S Jos 22:10 [t]S Ps 68:31 [u]S Ge 28:18 **19:20** [v]S Ge 21:30 [w]S Dt 28:29; S Jdg 2:18; S Isa 25:9 [x]Isa 49:24-26 **19:21** [y]S Isa 11:9; S 43:10 [z]ver 19; S Ge 27:29; S Ps 86:9; Isa 56:7; 60:7; Mal 1:11 [a]S Nu 30:2; S Dt 23:21 **19:22** [b]Ex 12:23; Heb 12:11 [c]Ex 11:10 [d]Isa 45:14; Eze 33:11; Hos 6:1; 10:12; 12:6; 14:1; Joel 2:13 [e]S Dt 32:39 **19:23** [f]S ver 16,24; Isa 20:6 [g]S Isa 11:16 [h]Mic 7:12 [i]S Ge 27:29; Isa 2:3; 27:13; 66:23 **19:24** [j]S ver 23 [k]S Isa 11:11 [l]S Ge 12:2 **19:25** [m]S Ge 12:3; Eph 2:11-14 [n]Ps 87:4; S 100:3 [o]Isa 29:23; 43:7; 45:11; 60:21; 64:8; Eph 2:10 [p]S Ex 34:9; Jer 30:22; Hos 2:23 **20:1** [q]2Ki 18:17 [r]S Jos 11:22; S 13:3 **20:2** [s]S Isa 13:1 [t]2Ki 1:8; S Isa 3:24; Zec 13:4; Mt 3:4 [u]Eze 24:17,23 [v]S 1Sa 19:24 [w]Eze 4:1-12; Mic 1:8 **20:3** [x]Isa 22:20; 41:8-9; 42:1; 43:10; 49:3,5-7; 50:10; 52:13; 53:11; Jer 7:25; Hag 2:23; Zec 4:14 [y]S Isa 16:14 [z]S Ex 3:12; S Isa 8:18; 37:30; 38:7; Ac 21:11 [a]S Dt 28:46 [b]S Isa 19:1 [c]ver 5; S Ge 10:6; Isa 37:9; 43:3 **20:4** [d]S Isa 19:4 [e]S Job 12:17 [f]Jer 46:19; Na 3:10 [g]Isa 18:1; Zep 2:12 [h]S Isa 3:24 [i]Isa 47:3; Jer 13:22, 26; Na 3:5 **20:5** [j]S Isa 8:12 [k]S ver 3 [l]S 2Ki 18:21; S Isa 30:5 [m]Eze 29:16

20:6 [n]Isa 2:11; S 19:23 [o]S 2Ki 18:21 [p]Jer 46:25 [q]S Isa 10:3 [r]Jer 30:15-17; 31:2; Mt 23:33; 1Th 5:3; Heb 2:3 **21:1** [s]S Isa 13:1 [t]Isa 13:21; Jer 50:12; 51:43 [u]S Job 1:19 [v]Da 11:40; Zec 9:14 **21:2** [w]Ps 60:3 [x]Isa 24:16; 33:1 [y]S Ge 10:22; Isa 22:6 [z]S Isa 13:3; Jer 25:25; 51:28 **21:3** [a]S Job 14:22 [b]S Ge 3:16; Ps 48:6; Isa 26:17; 37:3; Jer 30:6; 48:41; 49:22; Jn 16:21 [c]Da 7:28; 8:27; 10:16 **21:4** [d]Isa 7:4; 35:4 [e]S Isa 13:8; Da 5:9 [f]S Ps 55:5 **21:5** [g]Isa 5:12; 22:2,13; 23:7; 24:8; 32:13; Jer 25:16,27; 51:39,57; Da 5:2 [h]2Sa 1:21; 1Ki 10:16-17; Jer 46:3; 51:11 **21:6** [i]S 2Ki 9:17 **21:7** [j]ver 9

[w] *18* Most manuscripts of the Masoretic Text; some manuscripts of the Masoretic Text, Dead Sea Scrolls and Vulgate *City of the Sun* (that is, Heliopolis)
[x] *3* That is, the upper Nile region; also in verse 5

19:23–25 ELECTION, Other Nations—Worship of God by Assyria and Egypt reminds us that God is the universal God of Abraham. He owns the universe and welcomes worship from all peoples, even those who first enslaved Jacob and those who conquered the Northern Kingdom. All persons who recognize God are His people. Election is a call to mission, not a call to self-righteous exclusion of others.

20:2 REVELATION, Actions—The prophet was clearly chosen to be the mouthpiece of God. He also used his clothing and body as a symbol of God's message to His disobeying children: mourning was over. God would strip Egypt of its power and pride. The faithful interpreter carried out the message for a long time. Three years is both literal and symbolic of a completed period of time. The prophet was willing to undergo personal humiliation to deliver God's message in unforgettable fashion. Symbolic action often says more than words.

with teams of horses,
riders on donkeys
or riders on camels,[k]
let him be alert,
fully alert."
[8]And the lookout[y][l] shouted,

"Day after day, my lord, I stand on the
watchtower;
every night I stay at my post.
[9]Look, here comes a man in a chariot[m]
with a team of horses.
And he gives back the answer:
'Babylon[n] has fallen,[o] has fallen!
All the images of its gods[p]
lie shattered[q] on the ground!' "

[10]O my people, crushed on the threshing
floor,[r]
I tell you what I have heard
from the LORD Almighty,
from the God of Israel.

A Prophecy Against Edom

[11]An oracle concerning Dumah[z]:[s]

Someone calls to me from Seir,[t]
"Watchman, what is left of the
night?
Watchman, what is left of the
night?"
[12]The watchman replies,
"Morning is coming, but also the
night.
If you would ask, then ask;
and come back yet again."

A Prophecy Against Arabia

[13]An oracle[u] concerning Arabia:[v]

You caravans of Dedanites,[w]
who camp in the thickets of Arabia,
14 bring water for the thirsty;
you who live in Tema,[x]
bring food for the fugitives.
[15]They flee[y] from the sword,[z]
from the drawn sword,
from the bent bow
and from the heat of battle.

[16]This is what the Lord says to me:
"Within one year, as a servant bound by
contract[a] would count it, all the pomp[b]
of Kedar[c] will come to an end. [17]The survivors of the bowmen, the warriors of Kedar, will be few.[d]" The LORD, the God of
Israel, has spoken.[e]

21:7 [k]S Jdg 6:5
21:8 [l]Mic 7:7; Hab 2:1
21:9 [m]ver 7 [n]S Isa 13:1; 47:1,5; S Rev 14:8 [o]Isa 47:11; Jer 51:8; Da 5:30 [p]S Lev 26:30; Isa 46:1; Jer 50:2; 51:44 [q]S Isa 2:18
21:10 [r]Isa 27:12; 28:27,28; 41:15; Jer 51:33; Mic 4:13; Hab 3:12; Mt 3:12
21:11 [s]S Ge 25:14; S Isa 34:11 [t]Ge 32:3
21:13 [u]Isa 13:1 [v]S 2Ch 9:14 [w]S Ge 10:7; S 25:3
21:14 [x]S Ge 25:15
21:15 [y]S Isa 13:14 [z]Isa 31:8
21:16 [a]S Lev 25:50 [b]S Isa 17:3 [c]S Ge 25:13
21:17 [d]S Dt 4:27; S Isa 10:19 [e]S Isa 1:20; 16:14
22:1 [f]Isa 13:1 [g]Ps 125:2; Jer 21:13; Joel 3:2, 12,14 [h]S Isa 1:1 [i]S Jos 2:8; Jer 48:38
22:2 [j]Eze 22:5 [k]S Isa 5:14; S 21:5 [l]S Isa 10:4 [m]S 2Ki 25:3
22:3 [n]S Isa 13:14 [o]S 2Ki 25:6
22:4 [p]S Isa 15:3; S La 1:16; Eze 21:6; Lk 19:41 [q]Jer 9:1
22:5 [r]S Isa 2:12 [s]S Job 40:12; S Ps 108:13 [t]S 2Sa 22:43; Isa 13:3; Jer 30:7; La 1:5; Eze 8:17-18; 9:9-10; Joel 2:31; Am 5:18-20; Zep 1:15 [u]S Isa 1:1 [v]Ne 6:15; S Ps 89:40; Isa 5:5; Jer 39:8; Eze 13:14
22:6 [w]S Isa 21:2 [x]Ps 46:9; Jer 49:35; 51:56 [y]S 2Ki 16:9
22:7 [z]Jos 15:8 [a]S 2Ch 32:1-2
22:8 [b]S Isa 2:12 [c]S 2Ch 32:5 [d]S 1Ki 7:2
22:9 [e]S Ne 1:3 [f]S 2Ki 18:17; S 2Ch 32:4
22:10 [g]Jer 33:4 [h]S 2Ch 32:5
22:11 [i]2Ki 25:4; 2Ch 32:5; Jer 39:4

Chapter 22

A Prophecy About Jerusalem

AN oracle[f] concerning the Valley[g] of
Vision:[h]

What troubles you now,
that you have all gone up on the
roofs,[i]
[2]O town full of commotion,
O city of tumult[j] and revelry?[k]
Your slain[l] were not killed by the
sword,[m]
nor did they die in battle.
[3]All your leaders have fled[n] together;
they have been captured[o] without
using the bow.
All you who were caught were taken
prisoner together,
having fled while the enemy was
still far away.
[4]Therefore I said, "Turn away from me;
let me weep[p] bitterly.
Do not try to console me
over the destruction of my
people."[q]

[5]The Lord, the LORD Almighty, has a
day[r]
of tumult and trampling[s] and
terror[t]
in the Valley of Vision,[u]
a day of battering down walls[v]
and of crying out to the mountains.
[6]Elam[w] takes up the quiver,[x]
with her charioteers and horses;
Kir[y] uncovers the shield.
[7]Your choicest valleys[z] are full of
chariots,
and horsemen are posted at the city
gates;[a]
8 the defenses of Judah are stripped
away.
And you looked in that day[b]
to the weapons[c] in the Palace of the
Forest;[d]
[9]you saw that the City of David
had many breaches[e] in its defenses;
you stored up water
in the Lower Pool.[f]
[10]You counted the buildings in Jerusalem
and tore down houses[g] to
strengthen the wall.[h]
[11]You built a reservoir between the two
walls[i]

[y]*8* Dead Sea Scrolls and Syriac; Masoretic Text *A lion*
[z]*11* *Dumah* means *silence* or *stillness,* a wordplay on *Edom.*

22:1–19 REVELATION, Dreams—In desperate times Israel went to the Valley of Hinnom outside Jerusalem, sacrificed their own sons to foreign *gods (2 Ki 23:10; Jer 7:31–32; 19:2–6; 32:35),* and expected visions from foreign gods concerning the nation's fate. Revelation does not come through such desperate means or such powerless sources. God's prophets called for mourning, not victory celebration. The prophet God chose heard His word clearly and relayed it plainly. To seek revelation apart from God would not be forgiven.

22:11–14 SIN, Unbelief—God's people become a foreign nation in God's day of judgment when they rely on human resources rather than divine strength. Momentary victory over

for the water of the Old Pool,[j]
but you did not look to the One who
made it,
or have regard[k] for the One who
planned[l] it long ago.

12 The Lord, the LORD Almighty,
called you on that day[m]
to weep[n] and to wail,
to tear out your hair[o] and put on
sackcloth.[p]
13 But see, there is joy and revelry,[q]
slaughtering of cattle and killing of
sheep,
eating of meat and drinking of
wine![r]
"Let us eat and drink," you say,
"for tomorrow we die!"[s]

14 The LORD Almighty has revealed this
in my hearing:[t] "Till your dying day this
sin will not be atoned[u] for," says the
Lord, the LORD Almighty.

15 This is what the Lord, the LORD Almighty, says:

"Go, say to this steward,
to Shebna,[v] who is in charge[w] of
the palace:[x]
16 What are you doing here and who gave
you permission
to cut out a grave[y] for yourself[z]
here,
hewing your grave on the height
and chiseling your resting place in
the rock?
17 "Beware, the LORD is about to take
firm hold of you
and hurl[a] you away, O you mighty
man.
18 He will roll you up tightly like a ball
and throw[b] you into a large country.
There you will die
and there your splendid chariots[c]
will remain—
you disgrace to your master's house!
19 I will depose you from your office,
and you will be ousted[d] from your
position.[e]

20 "In that day[f] I will summon my servant,[g] Eliakim[h] son of Hilkiah. 21 I will
clothe him with your robe and fasten
your sash[i] around him and hand your
authority[j] over to him. He will be a father to those who live in Jerusalem and to
the house of Judah. 22 I will place on his
shoulder[k] the key[l] to the house of David;[m] what he opens no one can shut,
and what he shuts no one can open.[n] 23 I
will drive him like a peg[o] into a firm
place;[p] he will be a seat[a] of honor[q] for
the house of his father. 24 All the glory of
his family will hang on him: its offspring
and offshoots—all its lesser vessels, from
the bowls to all the jars.

25 "In that day,[r]" declares the LORD Almighty, "the peg[s] driven into the firm
place will give way; it will be sheared off
and will fall, and the load hanging on it
will be cut down." The LORD has spoken.[t]

22:11 [j]S 2Ch 32:4 [k]S 1Sa 12:24 [l]2Ki 19:25
22:12 [m]S Isa 2:12 [n]Joel 1:9; 2:17 [o]S Lev 13:40; Mic 1:16 [p]S Isa 3:24
22:13 [q]S Isa 21:5 [r]S 1Sa 25:36; Ecc 8:15; Isa 5:22; 28:7-8; 56:12; Lk 17:26-29 [s]1Co 15:32*
22:14 [t]Isa 5:9 [u]S 1Sa 2:25; Isa 13:11; 26:21; 30:13-14; Eze 24:13
22:15 [v]S 2Ki 6:30; S 18:18 [w]ver 21 [x]S Ge 41:40
22:16 [y]Mt 27:60 [z]S Ge 50:5; S Nu 32:42
22:17 [a]Jer 10:18; 13:18; 22:26
22:18 [b]S Job 18:11; Isa 14:19; 17:13 [c]S Ge 41:43
22:19 [d]S 1Sa 2:7; S Ps 52:5 [e]Lk 16:3
22:20 [f]ver 25 [g]S Isa 20:3 [h]S 2Ki 18:18; S Isa 36:3
22:21 [i]S Isa 5:27 [j]ver 15
22:22 [k]Isa 9:6 [l]1Ch 9:27; Mt 16:19; Rev 3:7 [m]S Isa 7:2 [n]S Job 12:14
22:23 [o]ver 25; Eze 15:3; Zec 10:4 [p]S Ezr 9:8; S Job 6:25 [q]S 1Sa 2:7-8; S Job 36:7
22:25 [r]ver 20 [s]S ver 23 [t]Isa 46:11; Mic 4:4
23:1 [u]Jos 19:29; 1Ki 5:1; Jer 47:4; Joel 3:4-8; Am 1:9-10 [v]S Isa 13:6 [w]S 1Ki 10:22 [x]S Ge 10:4; Isa 2:16 fn [y]S Ge 1:2; Eze 26:4
23:2 [z]S Job 2:13 [a]Eze 27:5-24 [b]Jdg 1:31
23:3 [c]S Ge 41:5 [d]S Isa 19:7 [e]S Ps 83:7
23:4 [f]S Ge 10:15, 19 [g]Isa 54:1
23:5 [h]Eze 30:9 [i]Eze 26:17-18
23:6 [j]S Ge 10:4

Chapter 23

A Prophecy About Tyre

AN oracle concerning Tyre:[u]
Wail,[v] O ships[w] of Tarshish![x]
For Tyre is destroyed[y]
and left without house or harbor.
From the land of Cyprus[b]
word has come to them.

2 Be silent,[z] you people of the island
and you merchants[a] of Sidon,[b]
whom the seafarers have enriched.
3 On the great waters
came the grain of the Shihor;[c]
the harvest of the Nile[c][d] was the
revenue of Tyre,[e]
and she became the marketplace of
the nations.

4 Be ashamed, O Sidon,[f] and you,
O fortress of the sea,
for the sea has spoken:
"I have neither been in labor nor
given birth;[g]
I have neither reared sons nor
brought up daughters."
5 When word comes to Egypt,
they will be in anguish[h] at the
report from Tyre.[i]

6 Cross over to Tarshish;[j]

[a]23 Or *throne* [b]1 Hebrew *Kittim*
[c]2,3 Masoretic Text; one Dead Sea Scroll *Sidon, / who cross over the sea; / your envoys* 3*are on the great waters. / The grain of the Shihor, / the harvest of the Nile,*

an enemy does not call for wild celebration. Certainly, if death is tomorrow's fate, parties are not on today's schedule. Crisis calls for repentance and faith. Refusing to exercise faith in God is the unforgiveable sin. Nothing atones for unbelief.

22:20–25 THE CHURCH, Servants—God's servants often do not hold public or church office. They serve God where they are and in the ways He leads. To be a servant of God, whether in office or not, requires faithfulness to God. One cannot serve God apart from commitment and obedience to Him. Too often God's faithful servants change when they gain the power and authority of office.

22:21–24 JESUS CHRIST, Foretold—Corrupt officials (Shebna, v 15) would be replaced by incorrupt ones (Eliakim, v 20). The incorrupt would eventually become corrupt and be replaced (v 25). Is there anyone with the keys of authority who is worthy to open and close the doors of justice and eternal life? John had One in mind and commended Him to the church at Philadelphia (Rev 3:7–13). Contemporary churches need confidence in Him who can open and shut what no one else can (Rev 3:7).

wail, you people of the island.
7Is this your city of revelry,[k]
the old, old city,
whose feet have taken her
to settle in far-off lands?
8Who planned this against Tyre,
the bestower of crowns,
whose merchants[l] are princes,
whose traders[m] are renowned in the earth?
9The LORD Almighty planned[n] it,
to bring low[o] the pride of all glory
and to humble[p] all who are
renowned[q] on the earth.
10Till[d] your land as along the Nile,
O Daughter of Tarshish,
for you no longer have a harbor.
11The LORD has stretched out his hand[r]
over the sea
and made its kingdoms tremble.[s]
He has given an order concerning
Phoenicia[e]
that her fortresses be destroyed.[t]
12He said, "No more of your reveling,[u]
O Virgin Daughter[v] of Sidon, now
crushed!

"Up, cross over to Cyprus[f];[w]
even there you will find no rest."
13Look at the land of the Babylonians,[g][x]
this people that is now of no
account!
The Assyrians[y] have made it
a place for desert creatures;[z]
they raised up their siege towers,[a]
they stripped its fortresses bare
and turned it into a ruin.[b]

14Wail, you ships[c] of Tarshish;[d]
your fortress is destroyed![e]

15At that time Tyre[f] will be forgotten
for seventy years,[g] the span of a king's
life. But at the end of these seventy years,
it will happen to Tyre as in the song of
the prostitute:

16"Take up a harp, walk through the
city,
O prostitute[h] forgotten;
play the harp well, sing many a song,
so that you will be remembered."

17At the end of seventy years,[i] the
LORD will deal with Tyre. She will return
to her hire as a prostitute[j] and will ply
her trade with all the kingdoms on the
face of the earth.[k] 18Yet her profit and
her earnings will be set apart for the
LORD;[l] they will not be stored up or
hoarded. Her profits will go to those who
live before the LORD,[m] for abundant food
and fine clothes.[n]

Chapter 24

The LORD's Devastation of the Earth

SEE, the LORD is going to lay waste the
earth[o]
and devastate[p] it;
he will ruin its face
and scatter[q] its inhabitants—
2it will be the same
for priest as for people,[r]
for master as for servant,
for mistress as for maid,
for seller as for buyer,[s]
for borrower as for lender,
for debtor as for creditor.[t]
3The earth will be completely laid
waste[u]
and totally plundered.[v]
The LORD has spoken[w]
this word.

4The earth dries up[x] and withers,[y]
the world languishes and withers,
the exalted[z] of the earth languish.[a]
5The earth is defiled[b] by its people;
they have disobeyed[c] the laws,
violated the statutes
and broken the everlasting
covenant.[d]
6Therefore a curse[e] consumes the
earth;
its people must bear their guilt.
Therefore earth's inhabitants are
burned up,[f]
and very few are left.
7The new wine dries up[g] and the vine
withers;[h]
all the merrymakers groan.[i]
8The gaiety of the tambourines[j] is
stilled,

[d]*10* Dead Sea Scrolls and some Septuagint manuscripts; Masoretic Text *Go through*
[e]*11* Hebrew *Canaan* [f]*12* Hebrew *Kittim*
[g]*13* Or *Chaldeans*

23:7 [k]ver 12; S Isa 5:14; S 21:5; 32:13; Eze 26:13
23:8 [l]Na 3:16 [m]Eze 28:5; Rev 18:23
23:9 [n]S Isa 14:24 [o]S Job 40:11 [p]S Isa 13:11 [q]Isa 5:13; 9:15; Eze 27:3
23:11 [r]S Ex 14:21 [s]S Ps 46:6 [t]ver 14; Isa 25:2; Eze 26:4; Zec 9:3-4
23:12 [u]S ver 7; Rev 18:22 [v]Isa 37:22; 47:1; Jer 14:17; 46:11; La 2:13; Zep 3:14; Zec 2:10 [w]S Ge 10:4
23:13 [x]Isa 43:14; Jer 51:12 [y]Isa 10:5 [z]S Ps 74:14; Isa 18:6 [a]S 2Ki 25:1 [b]Isa 10:7
23:14 [c]S 1Ki 10:22 [d]S Ge 10:4; Isa 2:16 *fn* [e]S ver 11
23:15 [f]Jer 25:22 [g]S Ps 90:10
23:16 [h]Pr 7:10
23:17 [i]S Ps 90:10 [j]Dt 23:17-18; Eze 16:26; Na 3:4; Rev 17:1; 18:3,9 [k]Jer 25:26
23:18 [l]Ex 28:36; S 39:30; Jos 6:17-19; Ps 72:10 [m]Isa 18:7; 60:5-9; 61:6; Mic 4:13 [n]Am 1:9-10; Zec 14:1,14
24:1 [o]ver 20; Isa 2:19-21; 33:9; Jer 25:29 [p]S Jos 6:17; S Isa 13:5 [q]S Ge 11:9
24:2 [r]Hos 4:9 [s]Eze 7:12; 1Co 7:29-31 [t]S Lev 25:35-37; Dt 23:19-20; Isa 3:1-7
24:3 [u]S Ge 6:13 [v]Isa 6:11-12; 10:6 [w]S Isa 7:7
24:4 [x]Jer 12:11; 14:4; Joel 1:10 [y]S Isa 15:6 [z]S Isa 2:12 [a]S Isa 3:26
24:5 [b]S Ge 3:17 [c]S Isa 1:2; 9:17; 10:6; 59:12; Jer 7:28 [d]S Ge 9:11; S Jer 11:10
24:6 [e]S Jos 23:15 [f]S Isa 1:31
24:7 [g]Jer 48:33; Joel 1:5 [h]Isa 7:23; S 15:6; 32:10 [i]S Isa 3:26; 16:8-10
24:8 [j]S Ge 31:27; S Isa 5:12

23:9 GOD, Sovereignty—The mighty fall. Surprise overtakes us until we realize the sovereign God planned it to reveal who truly controls history and deserves praise and fame.
24:1—27:13 HISTORY, Hope—Present conditions may generate despair and hopelessness. God's Word uses apocalyptic language to rouse new hopes based on new actions of God to show His control of history and eternity. Ultimately all history will erupt into universal *praise for the one true Lord* of *history who will have* exercised judgment on all sin.
24:5–6 SIN, Universal Nature—Oracles or sermons against foreign nations fill Isa 13—23. Add them up; they teach one truth. Every known people are sinners. God's everlasting covenant in Ge 9:8–17 promised the earth would never again be destroyed by flood. Universal sin seen by Isaiah and repeated daily means God must act in punishment again. He will have His day of destruction. Guilt cannot escape unpunished. Why? Because God has created all people with a sense of moral justice. No one can claim to have lived life as morally as they know how. The moral laws of the universe condemn each of us. We are sinners without excuse. See note on 1 Ki 14:22–24.

the noise[k] of the revelers[l] has
stopped,
the joyful harp[m] is silent.[n]
9No longer do they drink wine[o] with a
song;
the beer is bitter[p] to its drinkers.
10The ruined city[q] lies desolate;[r]
the entrance to every house is
barred.
11In the streets they cry out[s] for wine;[t]
all joy turns to gloom,[u]
all gaiety is banished from the earth.
12The city is left in ruins,[v]
its gate[w] is battered to pieces.
13So will it be on the earth
and among the nations,
as when an olive tree is beaten,[x]
or as when gleanings are left after
the grape harvest.[y]

14They raise their voices, they shout for
joy;[z]
from the west[a] they acclaim the
LORD's majesty.
15Therefore in the east[b] give glory[c] to
the LORD;
exalt[d] the name[e] of the LORD, the
God of Israel,
in the islands[f] of the sea.
16From the ends of the earth[g] we hear
singing:[h]
"Glory[i] to the Righteous One."[j]

But I said, "I waste away, I waste
away![k]
Woe[l] to me!
The treacherous[m] betray!
With treachery the treacherous
betray![n]"
17Terror[o] and pit and snare[p] await you,
O people of the earth.[q]
18Whoever flees[r] at the sound of terror
will fall into a pit;[s]
whoever climbs out of the pit
will be caught in a snare.[t]

The floodgates of the heavens[u] are
opened,
the foundations of the earth shake.[v]
19The earth is broken up,[w]
the earth is split asunder,[x]
the earth is thoroughly shaken.
20The earth reels like a drunkard,[y]
it sways like a hut[z] in the wind;
so heavy upon it is the guilt of its
rebellion[a]
that it falls[b]—never to rise again.[c]

21In that day[d] the LORD will punish[e]
the powers[f] in the heavens above
and the kings[g] on the earth below.
22They will be herded together
like prisoners[h] bound in a
dungeon;[i]
they will be shut up in prison
and be punished[h] after many days.[j]
23The moon will be abashed, the sun[k]
ashamed;
for the LORD Almighty will reign[l]
on Mount Zion[m] and in Jerusalem,
and before its elders, gloriously.[n]

Chapter 25

Praise to the LORD

O LORD, you are my God;[o]
I will exalt you and praise your
name,[p]
for in perfect faithfulness[q]
you have done marvelous things,[r]
things planned[s] long ago.
2You have made the city a heap of
rubble,[t]
the fortified[u] town a ruin,[v]
the foreigners' stronghold[w] a city no
more;
it will never be rebuilt.[x]
3Therefore strong peoples will honor
you;[y]
cities of ruthless[z] nations will
revere you.
4You have been a refuge[a] for the
poor,[b]
a refuge for the needy[c] in his
distress,
a shelter from the storm[d]

24:8 [k]Jer 7:34; 16:9; 25:10; 33:11; Hos 2:11 [l]S Isa 5:14; S 21:5 [m]S Ps 137:2; Rev 18:22 [n]La 5:14; Eze 26:13 **24:9** [o]Isa 5:11,22 [p]Isa 5:20 **24:10** [q]Isa 25:2; 26:5 [r]S Ge 1:2; S Isa 6:11 **24:11** [s]S Ps 144:14 [t]La 2:12 [u]S Isa 15:6; 16:10; 32:13; Jer 14:3 **24:12** [v]S Isa 19:18 [w]S Isa 3:26; S 13:2 **24:13** [x]S Dt 30:4; S Isa 17:6 [y]Ob 1:5; Mic 7:1 **24:14** [z]S Isa 12:6 [a]Isa 43:5; 49:12 **24:15** [b]S Ps 113:3 [c]Isa 42:12; 66:19; 2Th 1:12 [d]S Ex 15:2; Isa 25:3; 59:19; Mal 1:11 [e]S Isa 12:4 [f]S Isa 11:11 **24:16** [g]S Ps 48:10 [h]S Ps 65:8 [i]Isa 28:5; 60:1,19 [j]S Ezr 9:15 [k]S Lev 26:39 [l]1Sa 4:8; S Isa 5:8; Jer 10:19; 45:3 [m]S Ps 25:3 [n]Isa 21:2; 33:1; Jer 3:6,20; 5:11; 9:2; Hos 5:7; 9:1 **24:17** [o]Dt 32:23-25 [p]Isa 8:14; Jer 48:43 [q]Lk 21:35 **24:18** [r]S Job 20:24 [s]Isa 42:22 [t]S Job 18:9; S Isa 8:14; La 3:47; Eze 12:13 [u]S Ge 7:11 [v]S Jdg 5:4; S Job 9:6; S Ps 11:3; S Eze 38:19 **24:19** [w]S Ps 46:2 [x]S Dt 11:6 **24:20** [y]S Job 12:25 [z]S Job 27:18 [a]S Isa 1:2,28; 43:27; 58:1 [b]S Ps 46:2 [c]S Job 12:14 **24:21** [d]S Isa 2:11; S 10:20; Rev 16:14 [e]Isa 10:12; 13:11; Jer 25:29 [f]1Co 6:3; Eph 6:11-12 [g]S Isa 2:12 **24:22** [h]S Isa 10:4 [i]Isa 42:7,22; Lk 8:31; Rev 20:7-10 [j]Eze 38:8 **24:23** [k]S Isa 13:10 [l]S Ps 97:1; Rev 22:5 [m]S Isa 2:2; Heb 12:22 [n]Isa 28:5; 41:16; 45:25; 60:19; Eze 48:35; Zec 2:5; Rev 21:23 **25:1** [o]S Isa 7:13 [p]S Ps 145:2; S Isa 12:1,4 [q]Isa 11:5 [r]Ps 40:5; 98:1; Joel 2:21,26 [s]Nu 23:19; S Isa 14:24; 37:26; 46:11; Eph 1:11 **25:2** [t]Isa 17:1; 26:5; 37:26 [u]S Isa 17:3 [v]S Dt 13:16 [w]S Isa 13:22 [x]S Job 12:14 **25:3** [y]S Ex 6:2; S Ps 22:23; S Isa 11:14 [z]S Isa 13:11 **25:4** [a]S 2Sa 22:3; S Ps 118:8; S Isa 4:6; 17:10; 27:5; 33:16; Joel 3:16 [b]S Isa 3:14 [c]S Isa 14:30; 29:19 [d]S Ps 55:8

h22 Or *released*

24:14–16 EVANGELISM, Glory to God—When people realize the goodness and majesty of the Lord, they "shout" in praise. This incites others to give glory to God. Finally, the ends *of the earth hear songs* of praise. When nations truly know the Lord, they praise Him, and *He is glorified*. Thus we are to tell them of His majesty and glory—that is evangelism.

24:15 GOD, Glory—God's final judgment and victory serves to bring worldwide recognition of and praise for God's glory, His overwhelming revelation of His presence.

24:16 GOD, Righteous—Righteousness is such a basic part of God's being that He can be called the Righteous One. He acts fairly in judgment, even the final judgment, bringing praise from people around the world.

25:1,9 GOD, Personal—Only one God proves His deity through marvelous saving acts. Remarkably, He is personal, a God who thinks, plans, works, and relates to us. See note on Ps 121:3–8.

25:1–12 PRAYER, Thanksgiving—See note on 12:1–6. Ch 24 spoke of the devastating judgments of God on the earth which would deliver Zion to the reign of God. Ch 25 is a psalm of thanks for that deliverance, with eschatological statements of great encouragement for those who lay claim on God. Praise will be the program at the heavenly banquet. Prayer is based on a deeply personal relationship with "my God."

25:3 EVANGELISM, Salvation—When the gospel is proclaimed, even strong and ruthless people are brought to surrender and to believe, thus fearing the Lord. The glorious salvation of God completely transforms lives.

and a shade from the heat.
For the breath of the ruthless[e]
is like a storm driving against a wall
5 and like the heat of the desert.
You silence[f] the uproar of
foreigners;[g]
as heat is reduced by the shadow of
a cloud,
so the song of the ruthless[h] is
stilled.

6On this mountain[i] the LORD Almighty
will prepare
a feast[j] of rich food for all peoples,
a banquet of aged wine—
the best of meats and the finest of
wines.[k]
7On this mountain he will destroy
the shroud[l] that enfolds all
peoples,[m]
the sheet that covers all nations;
8 he will swallow up death[n] forever.
The Sovereign LORD will wipe away
the tears[o]
from all faces;
he will remove the disgrace[p] of his
people
from all the earth.
The LORD has spoken.[q]

9In that day[r] they will say,

"Surely this is our God;[s]
we trusted[t] in him, and he saved[u]
us.
This is the LORD, we trusted in him;
let us rejoice[v] and be glad in his
salvation."[w]

10The hand of the LORD will rest on this
mountain;[x]
but Moab[y] will be trampled under
him
as straw is trampled down in the
manure.
11They will spread out their hands in it,
as a swimmer spreads out his hands
to swim.
God will bring down[z] their pride[a]
despite the cleverness[i] of their
hands.
12He will bring down your high fortified
walls[b]
and lay them low;[c]
he will bring them down to the
ground,
to the very dust.

Chapter 26

A Song of Praise

IN that day[d] this song will be sung[e] in
the land of Judah:

We have a strong city;[f]
God makes salvation
its walls[g] and ramparts.[h]
2Open the gates[i]
that the righteous[j] nation may
enter,
the nation that keeps faith.
3You will keep in perfect peace[k]
him whose mind is steadfast,
because he trusts[l] in you.
4Trust[m] in the LORD forever,[n]
for the LORD, the LORD, is the Rock[o]
eternal.
5He humbles those who dwell on high,
he lays the lofty city low;
he levels it to the ground[p]

25:4 [e]Isa 29:5; 49:25 **25:5** [f]Jer 51:55 [g]S Ps 18:44 [h]S Isa 13:11 **25:6** [i]S Isa 2:2 [j]S Ge 29:22; 1Ki 1:25; Isa 1:19; 55:1-2; 66:11; Joel 3:18; Mt 8:11; 22:4; Rev 19:9 [k]S Ps 36:8; S Pr 9:2 **25:7** [l]2Co 3:15-16; Eph 4:18 [m]S Job 4:9 **25:8** [n]Isa 26:19; Hos 13:14; 1Co 15:54-55* [o]Isa 15:3; 30:19; 35:10; 51:11; 65:19; Jer 31:16; Rev 7:17; 21:4 [p]S Ge 30:23; S Ps 119:39; Mt 5:11; 1Pe 4:14; Rev 7:14 [q]S Isa 7:7 **25:9** [r]S Isa 2:11; S 10:20 [s]Isa 40:9 [t]S Ps 22:5; S Isa 12:2 [u]Ps 145:19; Isa 19:20; 33:22; 35:4; 43:3,11; 45:15,21; 49:25-26, 26; 60:16; 63:8; Jer 14:8 [v]S Dt 32:43; S Ps 9:2; Isa 9:3; 35:2,10; 41:16; 51:3; 61:7,10; 66:14 [w]S Ps 13:5; S Isa 12:2 **25:10** [x]S Isa 2:2 [y]S Ge 19:37; S Nu 21:29; S Dt 23:6; S Isa 11:14; Am 2:1-3 **25:11** [z]Isa 5:25; 14:26; 16:14 [a]S Lev 26:19; S Job 40:12 **25:12** [b]S Isa 2:15 [c]S Job 40:11; S Isa 15:1; S Jer 51:44 **26:1** [d]S Isa 10:20 [e]Isa 30:29 [f]S Isa 14:32 [g]Isa 32:18; 60:18; Zec 2:5; 9:8 [h]S Ps 48:13 **26:2** [i]S Ps 24:7 [j]Ps 24:3-4; 85:13; S Isa 1:26; S 4:3; 9:7; 50:8; 53:11; 54:14; 58:8; 62:2 **26:3** [k]S Job 22:21; S Isa 9:6,7; Php 4:7 [l]S 1Ch 5:20; S Ps 22:5; S 28:7; S Isa 12:2 **26:4** [m]S Isa 12:2; 50:10 [n]S Ps 62:8 [o]S Ge 49:24 **26:5** [p]S Isa 25:12; Eze 26:11

[i] *11* The meaning of the Hebrew for this word is uncertain.

25:6 CHRISTIAN ETHICS, Alcohol—Coupled with other passages such as Ps 104:14–15, this verse notes the availability of wine at the day of the Lord. See notes on 5:11–12,22; Jn 2:1–11.

25:7–8 HUMANITY, Death—Victory over death is not a fanciful wish projected into reality by the human mind. Nor is it an achievement of human scientists curing all diseases. Victory over death comes only through the active intervention of God. We see His actions fully in the ministry and resurrection of Jesus and in the proclamation of the gospel. See Jn 14:18; 1 Co 15:54. God's victory removes the disgrace, grief, and finality of death.

25:8 JESUS CHRIST, Foretold—This promise at God's feast given on God's mountain was that death will be overcome. Paul exulted that this promise was realized through God's Christ, who has overcome death (1 Co 15). John acknowledged a time when, through Jesus Christ, God will wipe away all human tears (Rev 21:4). Christians need to celebrate these gifts expressed so well in the language of promise and fulfillment and anchored in Jesus Christ.

25:9 GOD, Savior—God's destructive judgment on evil leads His people to recognize He is our *Savior and to trust Him.* Our natural *reaction is to acknowledge* Him as Lord and rejoice *in His salvation.* See note on Ps 98:1–3.

26:1–11 CHRISTIAN ETHICS, Righteousness—Righteousness is the theme of Israel's hope. Israel looks forward to a final victory song by the righteous nation that keeps faith with God. The oppressed and poor celebrate the downfall of the proud. In the present we yearn for the final day as we humbly obey God. We know one day all nations will experience God's just judgment (Hebrew *mishpat*) and righteous, saving actions (Hebrew *tsedeq*) bringing peace for His people and punishment for the wicked. See note on Hos 2:19–20.

26:1–21 PRAYER, Praise—Ch 26 is a psalm of praise for peace and deliverance. Redeemed Israel was given a song of the glories of the redeemed. The words are addressed to God, so it is a prayer. This prayer is a statement, not a petition. Prayer is agreeing with God and proclaiming the work of God. The hymn teaches the initiative of God; therefore His people honor Him alone. A special reason for praise is the hope of resurrection.

26:3 SALVATION, Belief—Perfect peace is one of God's gifts to those who trust in Him. Confidence in God rules out fear and anxiety over lesser things.

26:3 CHRISTIAN ETHICS, War and Peace—The prophet looked to peace in the last days. The mark of peace is ultimately individual rather than national. Peace is based on steadfast trust in God. Such trust produces internal, personal peace, the only basis for peace on a larger scale. See note on Pr 22:10.

set on the head of a fertile valley[j] —
to that city, the pride of those laid
low by wine![k]
2See, the Lord has one who is
powerful[l] and strong.
Like a hailstorm[m] and a destructive
wind,[n]
like a driving rain and a flooding[o]
downpour,
he will throw it forcefully to the
ground.
3That wreath, the pride of Ephraim's[p]
drunkards,
will be trampled[q] underfoot.
4That fading flower, his glorious beauty,
set on the head of a fertile valley,[r]
will be like a fig[s] ripe before
harvest—
as soon as someone sees it and takes
it in his hand,
he swallows it.

5In that day[t] the LORD Almighty
will be a glorious[u] crown,[v]
a beautiful wreath
for the remnant[w] of his people.
6He will be a spirit of justice[x]
to him who sits in judgment,[y]
a source of strength
to those who turn back the battle[z]
at the gate.

7And these also stagger[a] from wine[b]
and reel[c] from beer:
Priests[d] and prophets[e] stagger from
beer
and are befuddled with wine;
they reel from beer,
they stagger when seeing visions,[f]
they stumble when rendering
decisions.
8All the tables are covered with vomit[g]
and there is not a spot without filth.

9"Who is it he is trying to teach?[h]
To whom is he explaining his
message?[i]
To children weaned[j] from their
milk,[k]
to those just taken from the breast?
10For it is:
Do and do, do and do,
rule on rule, rule on rule[o];
a little here, a little there.[l]"
11Very well then, with foreign lips and
strange tongues[m]
God will speak to this people,[n]
12to whom he said,
"This is the resting place, let the
weary rest";[o]
and, "This is the place of repose"—
but they would not listen.
13So then, the word of the LORD to them
will become:
Do and do, do and do,
rule on rule, rule on rule;
a little here, a little there[p] —
so that they will go and fall backward,
be injured[q] and snared and
captured.[r]

14Therefore hear the word of the LORD,[s]
you scoffers[t]
who rule this people in Jerusalem.
15You boast, "We have entered into a
covenant with death,[u]
with the grave[p] we have made an
agreement.
When an overwhelming scourge
sweeps by,[v]
it cannot touch us,
for we have made a lie[w] our refuge
and falsehood[q] our hiding place.[x]"

28:1 [j]ver 4 [k]S Lev 10:9; Isa 5:11; Hos 7:5; Am 6:6 **28:2** [l]Isa 40:10 [m]S Jos 10:11 [n]Isa 29:6 [o]S Isa 8:7; S Da 9:26 **28:3** [p]S ver 1 [q]S Job 40:12; S Isa 5:5 **28:4** [r]ver 1 [s]S SS 2:13; Hos 9:10; Na 3:12 **28:5** [t]S Isa 10:20; S 27:1; 29:18; 30:23 [u]S Isa 24:16, 23 [v]Isa 62:3; Jer 13:18; Eze 16:12; 21:26; Zec 9:16 [w]S Isa 1:9 **28:6** [x]S 2Sa 14:20; Isa 11:2-4; 32:1,16; 33:5 [y]Isa 4:4; Jn 5:30 [z]Jdg 9:44-45; S 2Ch 32:8 **28:7** [a]S Isa 3:12 [b]S Lev 10:9; S Isa 22:13; S Eph 5:18 [c]S Ps 107:27 [d]Isa 24:2 [e]S Isa 9:15 [f]S Isa 1:1; 29:11 **28:8** [g]Jer 48:26 **28:9** [h]ver 26; Ps 32:8; Isa 2:3; 30:20; 48:17; 50:4; 54:13; Jer 31:34; 32:33 [i]Isa 52:7; 53:1 [j]Ps 131:2 [k]Heb 5:12-13; 1Pe 2:2 **28:10** [l]ver 13 **28:11** [m]S Ge 11:7; Isa 33:19; Jer 5:15 [n]Eze 3:5; 1Co 14:21* **28:12** [o]S Ex 14:14; S Jos 1:13; S Job 11:18; S Isa 11:10; Mt 11:28-29 **28:13** [p]ver 10 [q]Mt 21:44 [r]S Isa 8:15 **28:14** [s]Isa 1:10 [t]2Ch 36:16 **28:15** [u]S Job 5:23; Isa 8:19 [v]ver 2,18; Isa 8:7-8; 10:26; 29:6; 30:28; Da 11:22 [w]S Isa 9:15 [x]S Jdg 9:35; Isa 29:15; Jer 23:24

[o] *10* Hebrew / *sav lasav sav lasav* / *kav lakav kav lakav* (possibly meaningless sounds; perhaps a mimicking of the prophet's words); also in verse 13 [p] *15* Hebrew *Sheol*; also in verse 18 [q] *15* Or *false gods*

God's "strange work" (v 21). See note on 26:20–21.

28:5–6 THE CHURCH, Remnant—Membership in God's faithful remnant will ultimately bring glory and prestige. For His remnant, God would care for every need and insure justice and safety. This is certainly a better guarantee and hope than that provided by drunken political leaders (v 1).

28:9–10 EDUCATION, Repetition—The drunken priests were mocking Isaiah as they asked sarcastically, "Are you here to teach us, as though we were small children?" In the process, they shed light on ancient Hebrew elementary education. Apparently, drill and repetition were important methods in the teaching of small children. So it is today. Modern instructional technology has never replaced guided practice as a major teaching strategy. Computer-assisted instruction often provides an electronic medium for learning "rule on rule." We need to learn to use the best technology to apply old and true methods of education.

28:14–21 REVELATION, Word—God speaks even to those who ridicule Him. He revealed His plans to the leadership of Jerusalem, calling them away from false oaths in the names of false gods with foreign nations. His will and plan is like an immovable foundation stone secured by God. He planned to test their faith and faithfulness through a strange work of defeating His chosen people.

28:15 HUMANITY, Death—In the prophets, the term "lie" is often used as a synonym for idolatry which is false faith. False religion can lead people to believe they have a commitment which will overcome death. Religious rites can seek to appease gods who supposedly rule the underworld. Only the true God controls death and has power to give victory over death. Even He does not promise escape from death.

28:15–18 THE CHURCH, Covenant People—A covenant establishes a relationship. Just as God established a relationship with His people for good purposes, a covenant can be made for evil purposes. God promises to judge evil so that ultimately it will not stand. Israel's covenant with death probably referred to political treaties with foreign kings which obligated Israel to worship the foreigners' gods. Such worship may have involved rituals of dying and rising gods or rituals seeking to appease a "god of the underworld." God bluntly said such agreements led to war, defeat, and death of the nation. God's people must be true to their covenant agreements with God and make such agreements with no one else.

16So this is what the Sovereign LORD says:

"See, I lay a stone in Zion,[y]
a tested stone,[z]
a precious cornerstone for a sure foundation;[a]
the one who trusts will never be dismayed.[b]
17I will make justice[c] the measuring line
and righteousness the plumb line;[d]
hail[e] will sweep away your refuge, the lie,
and water will overflow[f] your hiding place.
18Your covenant with death will be annulled;
your agreement with the grave will not stand.[g]
When the overwhelming scourge sweeps by,[h]
you will be beaten down[i] by it.
19As often as it comes it will carry you away;[j]
morning after morning,[k] by day and by night,
it will sweep through."

The understanding of this message
will bring sheer terror.[l]
20The bed is too short to stretch out on,
the blanket too narrow to wrap around you.[m]
21The LORD will rise up as he did at Mount Perazim,[n]
he will rouse himself as in the Valley of Gibeon[o]—
to do his work,[p] his strange work,
and perform his task, his alien task.
22Now stop your mocking,[q]
or your chains will become heavier;
the Lord, the LORD Almighty, has told me
of the destruction decreed[r] against the whole land.[s]

23Listen[t] and hear my voice;
pay attention and hear what I say.
24When a farmer plows for planting,[u]
does he plow continually?
Does he keep on breaking up and harrowing the soil?
25When he has leveled the surface,
does he not sow caraway and scatter cummin?[v]
Does he not plant wheat in its place,[r]
barley[w] in its plot,[r]
and spelt[x] in its field?
26His God instructs him
and teaches[y] him the right way.
27Caraway is not threshed[z] with a sledge,[a]
nor is a cartwheel rolled over cummin;
caraway is beaten out with a rod,[b]
and cummin with a stick.
28Grain must be ground to make bread;
so one does not go on threshing it forever.
Though he drives the wheels of his threshing cart[c] over it,
his horses do not grind it.
29All this also comes from the LORD Almighty,
wonderful in counsel[d] and magnificent in wisdom.[e]

Chapter 29

Woe to David's City

WOE[f] to you, Ariel, Ariel,[g]
the city[h] where David settled!
Add year to year
and let your cycle of festivals[i] go on.
2Yet I will besiege Ariel;[j]
she will mourn and lament,[k]
she will be to me like an altar hearth.[s] [l]
3I will encamp against you all around;
I will encircle[m] you with towers
and set up my siege works[n] against you.
4Brought low, you will speak from the ground;
your speech will mumble[o] out of the dust.[p]
Your voice will come ghostlike[q] from the earth;
out of the dust your speech will whisper.[r]
5But your many enemies will become like fine dust,[s]

28:16 [y]S Isa 14:32 [z]Ps 118:22; Isa 8:14-15; Da 2:34-35,45; Zec 12:3; S Ac 4:11 [a]Jer 51:26; 1Co 3:11; 2Ti 2:19 [b]Isa 29:22; 45:17; 50:7; 54:4; Ro 9:33*; 10:11*; 1Pe 2:6*
28:17 [c]S Ps 11:7; S Isa 5:16 [d]S 2Ki 21:13 [e]S Jos 10:11 [f]S Isa 8:7
28:18 [g]S Isa 7:7 [h]S ver 15 [i]S Isa 5:5; 63:18; Da 8:13
28:19 [j]2Ki 24:2 [k]S Ps 5:3 [l]S Job 18:11
28:20 [m]Isa 59:6
28:21 [n]S Ge 38:29; S 1Ch 14:11 [o]S Jos 9:3 [p]Isa 10:12; 65:7; Lk 19:41-44
28:22 [q]S 2Ch 36:16; Jer 29:18; La 2:15; Zep 2:15 [r]S Isa 10:22 [s]S Isa 10:23
28:23 [t]Isa 32:9
28:24 [u]Ecc 3:2
28:25 [v]Mt 23:23 [w]S Ex 9:31 [x]Ex 9:32; Eze 4:9
28:26 [y]S Ps 94:10
28:27 [z]S Isa 21:10 [a]S Job 41:30 [b]Isa 10:5
28:28 [c]S Isa 21:10
28:29 [d]S Isa 9:6 [e]S Ps 92:5; Ro 11:33
29:1 [f]Isa 22:12-13; S 28:1 [g]ver 2,7 [h]S 2Sa 5:7 [i]S Isa 1:14
29:2 [j]S ver 1 [k]S Isa 3:26; La 2:5 [l]Eze 43:15
29:3 [m]Lk 19:43-44 [n]S 2Ki 25:1
29:4 [o]Isa 8:19 [p]Isa 47:1; 52:2 [q]S Lev 19:31 [r]Isa 26:16
29:5 [s]S Dt 9:21; Ps 78:39; 103:15; S Isa 2:22; 37:27; 40:6; 51:12

[r]*25* The meaning of the Hebrew for this word is uncertain. [s]*2* The Hebrew for *altar hearth* sounds like the Hebrew for *Ariel.*

28:16 JESUS CHRIST, Foretold—Real cornerstones are meant to carry the weight of a building. Christians see Jesus Christ as God's cornerstone for the house of God (Ro 9:33; 1 Pe 2:6). See note on Isa 8:14–15.

28:18 HUMANITY, Death—"Annulled" is the normal word for burial. In a graphic play on words, the false commitment the people depended on to avoid death would one day be buried. Political actions do not provide an escape from death. Treaty partners may turn against us and become agents of death. Humans cannot avoid death. See note on 28:15.

28:29 GOD, Wisdom—God's knowledge or wisdom is infinite, far surpassing anyone else's. We should learn from His warnings.

29:5–8 CREATION, Freedom—God chose Jerusalem as a special city. He planned to make it the center of His redemptive program. When it disappointed Him, however, He was free to bring judgment against the people to purify them for future service. We must never try to force God "into a corner" and demand that He act in a certain way. He operates from a moral base which comes from His holiness. He is free to make any choices necessary and perform any acts He feels proper to vindicate His holiness and implement His goals.

the ruthless[t] hordes like blown
chaff.[u]
Suddenly,[v] in an instant,
6 the LORD Almighty will come[w]
with thunder[x] and earthquake[y] and
great noise,
with windstorm and tempest[z] and
flames of a devouring fire.[a]
7Then the hordes of all the nations[b]
that fight against Ariel,[c]
that attack her and her fortress and
besiege her,
will be as it is with a dream,[d]
with a vision in the night—
8as when a hungry man dreams that he
is eating,
but he awakens,[e] and his hunger
remains;
as when a thirsty man dreams that he
is drinking,
but he awakens faint, with his thirst
unquenched.[f]
So will it be with the hordes of all the
nations
that fight against Mount Zion.[g]

9Be stunned and amazed,[h]
blind yourselves and be sightless;[i]
be drunk,[j] but not from wine,[k]
stagger,[l] but not from beer.
10The LORD has brought over you a deep
sleep:[m]
He has sealed your eyes[n] (the
prophets);[o]
he has covered your heads (the
seers).[p]

11For you this whole vision[q] is nothing
but words sealed[r] in a scroll. And if you
give the scroll to someone who can read,
and say to him, "Read this, please," he
will answer, "I can't; it is sealed." 12Or if
you give the scroll to someone who cannot read, and say, "Read this, please," he
will answer, "I don't know how to read."

13The Lord says:

"These people[s] come near to me with
their mouth
and honor me with their lips,[t]
but their hearts are far from me.[u]
Their worship of me
is made up only of rules taught by
men.[t] [v]
14Therefore once more I will astound
these people
with wonder upon wonder;[w]
the wisdom of the wise[x] will perish,
the intelligence of the intelligent
will vanish.[y]"
15Woe to those who go to great depths
to hide[z] their plans from the LORD,
who do their work in darkness and
think,
"Who sees us?[a] Who will know?"[b]
16You turn things upside down,
as if the potter were thought to be
like the clay![c]
Shall what is formed say to him who
formed[d] it,
"He did not make me"?
Can the pot say of the potter,[e]
"He knows nothing"?[f]

17In a very short time,[g] will not
Lebanon[h] be turned into a
fertile field[i]
and the fertile field seem like a
forest?[j]
18In that day[k] the deaf[l] will hear the
words of the scroll,
and out of gloom and darkness[m]
the eyes of the blind will see.[n]
19Once more the humble[o] will rejoice in
the LORD;

29:5 [t]S Isa 13:11 [u]S Isa 17:13 [v]S Ps 55:15; S Isa 17:14; 1Th 5:3 **29:6** [w]S Isa 26:21; Zec 14:1-5 [x]S Ex 19:16 [y]Mt 24:7; Mk 13:8; Lk 21:11; S Rev 6:12; 11:19 [z]S Ps 50:3; S 55:8; S Isa 28:15 [a]S Lev 10:2; Ps 83:13-15 **29:7** [b]Mic 4:11-12; Zec 12:9 [c]S ver 1 [d]S Job 20:8 **29:8** [e]S Ps 73:20 [f]ver 5,7; Isa 41:11, 15; Jer 30:16; Zec 12:3 [g]Isa 17:12-14; 54:17 **29:9** [h]ver 14; Jer 4:9; Hab 1:5 [i]S Isa 6:10 [j]Isa 51:17; 63:6; Jer 13:13; 25:27 [k]S Lev 10:9; Isa 28:1; 51:21-22 [l]S Ps 60:3; S Isa 3:12 **29:10** [m]S Jdg 4:21; Jnh 1:5 [n]Ps 69:23; S Isa 6:9-10; 44:18; Ro 11:8*; 2Th 2:9-11 [o]Mic 3:6 [p]S 1Sa 9:9 **29:11** [q]S Isa 28:7 [r]S Isa 8:16; Da 8:26; 12:9; Mt 13:11; Rev 5:1-2 **29:13** [s]Jer 14:11; Hag 1:2; 2:14 [t]S Ps 50:16 [u]S Ps 119:70; Isa 58:2; Jer 12:2; Eze 33:31 [v]Mt 15:8-9*; Mk 7:6-7*; Col 2:22 **29:14** [w]S Job 10:16 [x]S Job 5:13; Jer 8:9; 49:7 [y]Isa 6:9-10; 1Co 1:19* **29:15** [z]S Ge 3:8; S Isa 28:15 [a]S Job 8:3; Ps 10:11-13; 94:7; Isa 47:10; 57:12; Eze 8:12; 9:9 [b]S 2Ki 21:16; S Job 22:13 **29:16** [c]S Job 10:9; S Isa 10:15 [d]S Ge 2:7 [e]Isa 45:9; 64:8; Jer 18:6; Ro 9:20-21* [f]S Job 9:12 **29:17** [g]S Isa 10:25 [h]S Isa 2:13 [i]Ps 84:6; 107:33 [j]Isa 32:15 **29:18** [k]S Isa 28:5 [l]Mk 7:37 [m]S Ps 107:14 [n]S Ps 146:8; S Isa 32:3; Mt 11:5; Lk 7:22 **29:19** [o]Ps 25:9; 37:11; Isa 61:1; Mt 5:5; 11:29

[t]*13* Hebrew; Septuagint *They worship me in vain; / their teachings are but rules taught by men*

29:13–21 GOD, Wisdom—People cannot hide from God or deceive Him. Human wisdom is no match for His. God will accomplish His purposes both of discipline and salvation through His authority, power, and wisdom.

29:13–14 HUMANITY, Intellectual Nature—Hypocritical worship calls down God's harshest judgment. God promised new miracles for Israel, not the miracles of salvation as in the Exodus from Egypt but miracles of judgment. He would pull a disappearing act. Israel's wisdom would vanish. Human wisdom lasts only as long as God allows.

29:13 EDUCATION, Obedience—A fundamental weakness in much religious instruction is that it becomes a matter of mere words that make little difference to anyone. The purpose of biblical teaching is to transform lives (see note on Ro 12:2) not to pay lip service to verbal propositions. God wants obedience which comes from dedicated hearts, not just words falling from articulate lips.

29:14–16 CREATION, Sovereignty—Though Jerusalem was excited with festivities, Isaiah saw her shallow superficiality. God would do extraordinary things to punish the people. God had acted at other times to show His miraculous power over His creation. He would not allow the present inhabitants of Jerusalem to exalt themselves and pretend to have greater knowledge than their Creator. The more sophisticated our present generation becomes, the more we are tempted to imagine ourselves superior to our all-knowing Lord. Such an attitude, in any generation, is a dead-end street. We are creatures dependent on the Creator.

29:14 MIRACLE, Power—False worship can lead God to bring forth miracles of judgment. God does not accept lip-service religion or people-pleasing rites. God promises miraculous judgment robbing such sinners of their own judgment capacities. Here miracles are a part of God's wonderful work that uses historical events and historical persons to accomplish His purpose.

29:18 JESUS CHRIST, Foretold—Blindness and deafness were special burdens in biblical times. Remedies were unknown. Messiah could do this great work of God and did. In this way, John the Baptist recognized Him (Mt 11:4–6). Jesus came to heal blindness both of the eyes and of the heart (Jn 9:39).

the needy[p] will rejoice in the Holy
One[q] of Israel.
20The ruthless[r] will vanish,[s]
the mockers[t] will disappear,
and all who have an eye for evil[u]
will be cut down—
21those who with a word make a man
out to be guilty,
who ensnare the defender in court[v]
and with false testimony[w] deprive
the innocent of justice.[x]

22Therefore this is what the LORD, who
redeemed[y] Abraham,[z] says to the house
of Jacob:

"No longer will Jacob be ashamed;[a]
no longer will their faces grow
pale.[b]
23When they see among them their
children,[c]
the work of my hands,[d]
they will keep my name holy;[e]
they will acknowledge the holiness
of the Holy One[f] of Jacob,
and will stand in awe of the God of
Israel.
24Those who are wayward[g] in spirit will
gain understanding;[h]
those who complain will accept
instruction."[i]

Chapter 30

Woe to the Obstinate Nation

"WOE[j] to the obstinate
children,"[k]
declares the LORD,
"to those who carry out plans that are
not mine,
forming an alliance,[l] but not by my
Spirit,
heaping sin upon sin;

29:19 [p]S Ps 72:4; S Isa 3:15; S 14:30; Mt 11:5; Lk 7:22; Jas 1:9; 2:5 [q]ver 23; Isa 1:4; S 5:19; S 12:6; 30:11 **29:20** [r]S Isa 9:4; S 13:11 [s]Isa 34:12 [t]S 2Ch 36:16; Isa 28:22 [u]S Job 15:35; Ps 7:14; Isa 32:7; 33:11; 59:4; Eze 11:2; Mic 2:1; Na 1:11 **29:21** [v]Am 5:10,15 [w]Pr 21:28 [x]S Isa 2:7; Hab 1:4 **29:22** [y]S Ex 6:6 [z]Ge 17:16; Isa 41:8; 51:2; 63:16 [a]Ps 22:5; 25:3; S Isa 28:16; 49:23; 61:7; Joel 2:26; Zep 3:11 [b]Jer 30:6,10; Joel 2:6,21; Na 2:10 **29:23** [c]Isa 49:20-26; 53:10; 54:1-3 [d]S Ps 8:6; S Isa 19:25 [e]Mt 6:9 [f]S ver 19; S Isa 5:19 **29:24** [g]Ps 95:10; S Pr 12:8; Isa 28:7; Heb 5:2 [h]Isa 1:3; 32:4; 41:20; 60:16 [i]Isa 30:21; 42:16 **30:1** [j]S Isa 28:1 [k]S Dt 21:18; S Isa 1:2 [l]S 2Ki 17:4; S Isa 8:12 **30:2** [m]2Ki 25:26; Isa 31:1; 36:6; Jer 2:18,36; 42:14; Eze 17:15; 29:16 [n]S Ge 25:22; S Nu 27:21 [o]Isa 36:9 [p]S Isa 4:6 **30:3** [q]Jdg 9:8-15 [r]ver 5; S Ps 44:13; Isa 20:4-5; 36:6 **30:4** [s]S Nu 13:22 **30:5** [t]ver 7; Isa 20:5; 31:1; 36:6 [u]S 2Ki 18:21 [v]S Ps 108:12; Jer 37:3-5 [w]S ver 3; S 2Ki 18:21; Eze 17:15 **30:6** [x]Isa 13:1

2who go down to Egypt[m]
without consulting[n] me;
who look for help to Pharaoh's
protection,[o]
to Egypt's shade for refuge.[p]
3But Pharaoh's protection will be to
your shame,
Egypt's shade[q] will bring you
disgrace.[r]
4Though they have officials in Zoan[s]
and their envoys have arrived in
Hanes,
5everyone will be put to shame
because of a people[t] useless[u] to
them,
who bring neither help[v] nor
advantage,
but only shame and disgrace."[w]

6An oracle[x] concerning the animals of
the Negev:[y]

Through a land of hardship and
distress,[z]
of lions[a] and lionesses,
of adders and darting snakes,[b]
the envoys carry their riches on
donkeys'[c] backs,
their treasures[d] on the humps of
camels,
to that unprofitable nation,
7 to Egypt, whose help is utterly
useless.[e]
Therefore I call her
Rahab[f] the Do-Nothing.

8Go now, write it on a tablet[g] for them,
inscribe it on a scroll,[h]
that for the days to come

[y]S Jdg 1:9 [z]S Ex 1:13; 5:10,21; Isa 5:30; 8:22; Jer 11:4 [a]S Isa 5:29; 35:9 [b]S Dt 8:15 [c]S Ge 42:26; S 1Sa 25:18 [d]S Isa 15:7 **30:7** [e]S 2Ki 18:21; S Jer 2:36 [f]S Job 9:13 **30:8** [g]S Dt 27:8 [h]S Ex 17:14; S Isa 8:1; Jer 25:13; 30:2; 36:28; Hab 2:2

29:22 REVELATION, Author of Hope—Even in the midst of gloomy descriptions of judgment, God revealed Himself as the consistent Author of hope for Israel. His people would not be grieved permanently, regardless of their inappropriate behavior. God's chastisements are always intermediate steps toward His recurring redemption.
29:22 SALVATION, Redemption—God has a long history of redemption. We can count on His promises to redeem us.
30:1–7 GOD, Sovereignty—God is in complete control of His world and will ultimately accomplish His purposes. It is futile for people to trust in their own plans, strength, and alliances rather than in God.
30:1–3 SIN, Unbelief—Sin invades international politics. Judah discovered an international ally—Egypt—to deliver her from Assyrian threats. She trusted political skills rather than God. Any action not led by God's Spirit is sin. Any action not based on trust in God is sin. Sin leads to disgrace. See note on 1 Ki 14:22–24.
30:1–5 HISTORY, Judgment—See note on 2 Ch 16:7–9.
30:6–11 REVELATION, Messengers—Seers of many factions claimed to predict the future. Such self-appointed prophets often speak what people want to hear. Isaiah disclosed them as the false voices they were and confronted the people as seekers of comfort and easy judgments. The true Revealer of God's word will not quit speaking the truth in love. Harsh as the vision may be, God wants His children to face it. The prophetic messenger delivered His message to his own generation orally in person. His inspired message spoke to more than one generation. Thus God instructed Him to write the message so future generations would know God's people had been forewarned of judgment and that God's judgment is always deserved. God's people may not want His revelation. Still He gives it to them, seeking to call them back to Him.
30:7 EVIL AND SUFFERING, God's Present Help—Rahab was a sea monster controlled by God. Rahab became a symbol for Egypt. See notes on Job 26:12–13; Ps 74:1–23. We should rely on God for help in the face of trouble. Even Rahab, or any chaotic force, is powerless when confronted by God.
30:8–14 SIN, Rebellion—Refusal to listen to God's word is sin. The heavenly Father wants to teach us, His children, the best way to live. Trying to deceive God into believing we listen when we do not is sin. Determining our standards of right and refusing to let God correct them is sin. Shooing God off our path so we can go our own selfish ways without being bothered by Him is sin. Oppressing the poor to line our pockets is sin. Added together these sins are rebellion against our Father. The sin of rebellion provides no wall of defense against God's sure intervention and punishment. See note on 2 Ki 24:1–4.

it may be an everlasting witness.[i]
9These are rebellious[j] people,
deceitful[k] children,
children unwilling to listen to the
LORD's instruction.[l]
10They say to the seers,[m]
"See no more visions[n]!"
and to the prophets,
"Give us no more visions of what is
right!
Tell us pleasant things,[o]
prophesy illusions.[p]
11Leave this way,[q]
get off this path,
and stop confronting[r] us
with the Holy One[s] of Israel!"

12Therefore, this is what the Holy
One[t] of Israel says:

"Because you have rejected this
message,[u]
relied on oppression[v]
and depended on deceit,
13this sin will become for you
like a high wall,[w] cracked and
bulging,
that collapses[x] suddenly,[y] in an
instant.
14It will break in pieces like pottery,[z]
shattered so mercilessly
that among its pieces not a fragment
will be found
for taking coals from a hearth
or scooping water out of a cistern."

15This is what the Sovereign[a] LORD,
the Holy One[b] of Israel, says:

"In repentance and rest[c] is your
salvation,
in quietness and trust[d] is your
strength,
but you would have none of it.[e]
16You said, 'No, we will flee[f] on
horses.'[g]
Therefore you will flee!
You said, 'We will ride off on swift
horses.'
Therefore your pursuers will be
swift!
17A thousand will flee
at the threat of one;
at the threat of five[h]
you will all flee[i] away,
till you are left[j]
like a flagstaff on a mountaintop,
like a banner[k] on a hill."

18Yet the LORD longs[l] to be gracious to
you;
he rises to show you compassion.[m]
For the LORD is a God of justice.[n]
Blessed are all who wait for him![o]

19O people of Zion, who live in Jerusalem, you will weep no more.[p] How gracious he will be when you cry for help![q]
As soon as he hears, he will answer[r] you.
20Although the Lord gives you the bread[s]
of adversity and the water of affliction,
your teachers[t] will be hidden[u] no more;
with your own eyes you will see them.
21Whether you turn to the right or to the
left, your ears will hear a voice[v] behind
you, saying, "This is the way;[w] walk in
it." 22Then you will defile your idols[x]
overlaid with silver and your images covered with gold;[y] you will throw them
away like a menstrual[z] cloth and say to
them, "Away with you![a]"

23He will also send you rain[b] for the
seed you sow in the ground, and the food
that comes from the land will be rich[c]
and plentiful.[d] In that day[e] your cattle
will graze in broad meadows.[f] 24The
oxen[g] and donkeys that work the soil
will eat fodder[h] and mash, spread out
with fork[i] and shovel. 25In the day of
great slaughter,[j] when the towers[k] fall,
streams of water will flow[l] on every high
mountain and every lofty hill. 26The
moon will shine like the sun,[m] and the
sunlight will be seven times brighter, like
the light of seven full days, when the
LORD binds up the bruises of his people
and heals[n] the wounds he inflicted.

30:8 [i]Jos 24:26-27 **30:9** [j]S Ps 78:8; S Isa 1:2; S Eze 2:6 [k]Isa 28:15; 59:3-4 [l]S Isa 1:10 **30:10** [m]S 1Sa 9:9 [n]Jer 11:21; 32:3; Am 7:13 [o]S 1Ki 22:8; S Jer 4:10 [p]Jer 23:26; 25:9; 26:9; 36:29; Eze 13:7; Ro 16:18; 2Ti 4:3-4 **30:11** [q]ver 21; Pr 3:6; Isa 35:8-9; 48:17 [r]S Job 21:14 [s]S Isa 29:19 **30:12** [t]ver 15; S Isa 5:19; 31:1 [u]S Isa 5:24 [v]S Ps 10:7; S 12:5; S Isa 5:7 **30:13** [w]S Ne 2:17; Ps 62:3; S 80:12 [x]S 1Ki 20:30 [y]S Isa 17:14 **30:14** [z]S Ps 2:9 **30:15** [a]Jer 7:20; Eze 3:11 [b]S ver 12 [c]S Ex 14:14; S Jos 1:13 [d]S 2Ch 20:12; Isa 32:17 [e]Isa 8:6; 42:24; 57:17 **30:16** [f]Jer 46:6 [g]S Dt 17:16; 1Ki 10:28-29; S Ps 20:7; Isa 31:1, 3; 36:8 **30:17** [h]S Lev 26:8 [i]Lev 26:36; Dt 28:25; S 2Ki 7:7 [j]S Isa 1:8 [k]S Ps 20:5 **30:18** [l]S Ge 43:31; Isa 42:14; 2Pe 3:9, 15 [m]Ps 78:38; Isa 48:9; Jnh 3:10 [n]S Ps 11:7; S Isa 5:16 [o]S Ps 27:14; Isa 25:9; 33:2; 40:31; 64:4; La 3:25; Da 12:12 **30:19** [p]S Isa 25:8; 60:20; 61:3 [q]S Job 24:12 [r]Job 22:27; Ps 50:15; S 86:7; Isa 41:17; 58:9; 65:24; Zec 13:9; Mt 7:7-11 **30:20** [s]1Ki 22:27 [t]S Isa 28:9 [u]Ps 74:9; Am 8:11 **30:21** [v]S Isa 29:24 [w]S ver 11; S Job 33:11 **30:22** [x]S Ex 32:4; S Isa 17:8 [y]S Job 22:24; Isa 31:7 [z]Lev 15:19-23 [a]Eze 7:19-20 **30:23** [b]S Dt 28:12; Isa 65:21-22 [c]Isa 25:6; 55:2; Jer 31:14 [d]S Job 36:31; Isa 62:8 [e]S Isa 28:5 [f]S Ps 65:13 **30:24** [g]Isa 32:14,20 [h]S Job 6:5 [i]Mt 3:12; Lk 3:17 **30:25** [j]S Isa 13:5; 34:6; 65:12; Jer 25:32; 50:27 [k]S Isa 2:15 [l]S Ex 17:6; Isa 32:2; 41:18; Joel 3:18; Zec 14:8 **30:26** [m]Isa 24:23; 60:19-20; Zec 14:7; Rev 21:23; 22:5 [n]S Dt 32:39; S 2Ch 7:14; Ps 107:20; S Isa 1:5; Jer 3:22; 17:14; Hos 14:4

30:11–12,15 GOD, Holy—Part of the preaching task is to lead people to confront the morally pure and awesomely holy God. This exposes our sin. Too often the reaction is to shut up the preacher. See note on 10:17–20.
30:15 SALVATION, Repentance—Salvation belongs to those who return to God and surrender to Him. God is the Lord of history. His people should trust Him and act accordingly. He does not force them. When they choose to have none of His way, He gives them freedom to be away from Him.
30:18–19 GOD, Justice—Justice is not God's angry side. It is His righteousness working for His people. He wants to be able in fairness to show love and compassion.
30:19–26 CREATION, Hope—Hope rests in the Creator's new actions, not in human achievements. God can renew the fertility of the land. The Lord who created the moon and the sun can make them shine even brighter for us when we trust Him to deliver us from our sorrows. When He gives us resources to cope with our problems, we find a new world emerges. We may be bruised by our sin, but God promises healing. The hopes of this passage will be fully realized when Christ returns.
30:19–21 PRAYER, Answer—This chapter had chided Israel for relying on sources other than God. The Lord longs to answer prayer, but the relationship with Him must be two-way. God demanded that Israel depend on Him. Then He would make His guidance explicit.
30:22 GOD, Jealous—The only God is a jealous God who will not tolerate idols or other forms of false gods. See note on 26:11.

27See, the Name[o] of the LORD comes
from afar,
with burning anger[p] and dense
clouds of smoke;
his lips are full of wrath,[q]
and his tongue is a consuming fire.[r]
28His breath[s] is like a rushing torrent,[t]
rising up to the neck.[u]
He shakes the nations in the sieve[v] of
destruction;
he places in the jaws of the peoples
a bit[w] that leads them astray.
29And you will sing
as on the night you celebrate a holy
festival;[x]
your hearts will rejoice[y]
as when people go up with flutes[z]
to the mountain[a] of the LORD,
to the Rock[b] of Israel.
30The LORD will cause men to hear his
majestic voice[c]
and will make them see his arm[d]
coming down
with raging anger[e] and consuming
fire,[f]
with cloudburst, thunderstorm[g] and
hail.[h]
31The voice of the LORD will shatter
Assyria;[i]
with his scepter he will strike[j]
them down.
32Every stroke the LORD lays on them
with his punishing rod[k]
will be to the music of tambourines[l]
and harps,
as he fights them in battle with the
blows of his arm.[m]
33Topheth[n] has long been prepared;
it has been made ready for the king.
Its fire pit has been made deep and
wide,
with an abundance of fire and wood;
the breath[o] of the LORD,
like a stream of burning sulfur,[p]
sets it ablaze.[q]

Chapter 31

Woe to Those Who Rely on Egypt

WOE[r] to those who go down to
Egypt[s] for help,
who rely on horses,[t]
who trust in the multitude of their
chariots[u]
and in the great strength of their
horsemen,
but do not look to the Holy One[v] of
Israel,
or seek help from the LORD.[w]
2Yet he too is wise[x] and can bring
disaster;[y]
he does not take back his words.[z]
He will rise up against the house of the
wicked,[a]
against those who help evildoers.
3But the Egyptians[b] are men and not
God;[c]
their horses[d] are flesh and not
spirit.
When the LORD stretches out his
hand,[e]
he who helps will stumble,
he who is helped[f] will fall;
both will perish together.[g]

4This is what the LORD says to me:

"As a lion[h] growls,
a great lion over his prey—
and though a whole band of
shepherds[i]
is called together against him,
he is not frightened by their shouts
or disturbed by their clamor[j]—
so the LORD Almighty will come
down[k]
to do battle on Mount Zion and on
its heights.
5Like birds hovering[l] overhead,
the LORD Almighty will shield[m]
Jerusalem;
he will shield it and deliver[n] it,
he will 'pass over'[o] it and will
rescue it."

6Return[p] to him you have so greatly
revolted[q] against, O Israelites. 7For in
that day[r] every one of you will reject the
idols of silver and gold[s] your sinful hands
have made.[t]

8"Assyria[u] will fall by a sword that is
not of man;

30:27 [o]1Ki 18:24; Ps 20:1; Isa 59:19; 64:2 [p]Isa 26:20; 66:14; Eze 22:31 [q]Isa 10:5; 13:5 [r]S ver 30; S Job 41:21 **30:28** [s]S Isa 11:4 [t]S Ps 50:3; S Isa 28:15 [u]S Isa 8:8 [v]Am 9:9 [w]2Ki 19:28 **30:29** [x]Isa 25:6 [y]Isa 12:1 [z]S 1Sa 10:5 [a]S Ps 42:4; Mt 26:30 [b]S Ge 49:24 **30:30** [c]S Ps 68:33 [d]Isa 9:12; 40:10; 51:9; 52:10; 53:1; 59:16; 62:8; 63:12 [e]S ver 27; S Isa 10:25 [f]S Isa 4:4; 47:14 [g]Ex 20:18; Ps 29:3 [h]S Ex 9:18 **30:31** [i]S Isa 10:5, 12 [j]S Isa 11:4 **30:32** [k]Isa 10:26 [l]S Ex 15:20 [m]S Isa 11:15; Eze 32:10 **30:33** [n]S 2Ki 23:10 [o]S Ex 15:10; S 2Sa 22:16 [p]S Ge 19:24; S Rev 9:17 [q]S Isa 1:31 **31:1** [r]S Isa 28:1 [s]S Dt 17:16; S Isa 30:2,5; S Jer 37:5 [t]S Isa 30:16 [u]S Isa 2:7 [v]Job 6:10; S Isa 1:4; S 30:12 [w]S Dt 20:1; S Pr 21:31; S Isa 9:13; Jer 46:9; Eze 29:16 **31:2** [x]S Ps 92:5; Ro 16:27 [y]Isa 45:7; 47:11; Am 3:6 [z]Nu 23:19; S Pr 19:21 [a]S Isa 1:4; 29:15; 32:6 **31:3** [b]Isa 20:5; 36:9 [c]S Ps 9:20; Eze 28:9; 2Th 2:4 [d]S Isa 30:16 [e]Ne 1:10; S Job 30:21; Isa 9:17,21; Jer 51:25; Eze 20:34 [f]Isa 10:3; 30:5-7 [g]S Isa 20:6; Jer 17:5 **31:4** [h]Nu 24:9; S 1Sa 17:34; Hos 11:10; Am 3:8 [i]Jer 3:15; 23:4; Eze 34:23; Na 3:18 [j]Ps 74:23 [k]Isa 42:13 **31:5** [l]S Ge 1:2; S Mt 23:37 [m]S Ps 91:4; S Isa 5:2; S Zec 9:15 [n]S Ps 34:7; Isa 37:35; 38:6 [o]S Ex 12:23 **31:6** [p]S Job 22:23; S Isa 1:27 [q]S Isa 1:5 **31:7** [r]Isa 29:18 [s]S Isa 30:22 [t]S Ps 135:15 **31:8** [u]S Isa 10:12

30:27–33 GOD, Wrath—God's wrath against His enemies gives joy to His people.
31:1 GOD, Holy—God's people trust in the awesome holy God and no one else to deliver us. Only He has divine will and power to save. See note on 30:11–12,15.
31:1–3 HISTORY, Judgment—See note on 30:1–5.
31:1–9 CHRISTIAN ETHICS, War and Peace—International treaties of submission do not promise peace and hope. Negotiations should seek justice for all sides not dominance by one, as Egypt desired. Only God can bring victory and peace. Repentance and turning to God is the first step to peace. See notes on 2 Ch 16:1–10; Ps 20:7–8.
31:2 GOD, Wisdom—In His perfect wisdom, God knows fully all that is happening in His world and what to do about it.
31:3 HUMANITY, Physical Nature—Material success and political victory puff our pride till we forget our limitations. The Egyptians tried to proclaim their Pharaoh as a god on earth. Egyptian soldiers appeared bigger than life to Israel. Only One is Spirit. All humans are flesh depending on God's breath to give them spirit and life. All will die.
31:5–7 SALVATION, As Deliverance—See 36:15,18; 37:20; 38:5–6. God rescues His people from their own folly. Human history is the scene of His action. At times He chooses to protect a faithless people, using the joy of salvation as a call to repent and turn from other gods.

a sword, not of mortals, will
devour[v] them.
They will flee before the sword
and their young men will be put to
forced labor.[w]
9Their stronghold[x] will fall because of
terror;
at sight of the battle standard[y] their
commanders will panic,[z]"
declares the LORD,
whose fire[a] is in Zion,
whose furnace[b] is in Jerusalem.

Chapter 32

The Kingdom of Righteousness

SEE, a king[c] will reign in
righteousness
and rulers will rule with justice.[d]
2Each man will be like a shelter[e] from
the wind
and a refuge from the storm,[f]
like streams of water[g] in the desert[h]
and the shadow of a great rock in a
thirsty land.
3Then the eyes of those who see will no
longer be closed,[i]
and the ears[j] of those who hear will
listen.
4The mind of the rash will know and
understand,[k]
and the stammering tongue[l] will be
fluent and clear.
5No longer will the fool[m] be called
noble
nor the scoundrel be highly
respected.
6For the fool speaks folly,[n]
his mind is busy with evil:[o]
He practices ungodliness[p]
and spreads error[q] concerning the
LORD;
the hungry he leaves empty[r]
and from the thirsty he withholds
water.
7The scoundrel's methods are wicked,[s]
he makes up evil schemes[t]
to destroy the poor with lies,
even when the plea of the needy[u] is
just.[v]
8But the noble man makes noble plans,
and by noble deeds[w] he stands.[x]

The Women of Jerusalem

9You women[y] who are so complacent,
rise up and listen[z] to me;
you daughters who feel secure,[a]
hear what I have to say!
10In little more than a year[b]
you who feel secure will tremble;
the grape harvest will fail,[c]
and the harvest of fruit will not
come.
11Tremble,[d] you complacent women;
shudder, you daughters who feel
secure![e]
Strip off your clothes,[f]
put sackcloth[g] around your waists.
12Beat your breasts[h] for the pleasant
fields,
for the fruitful vines[i]
13and for the land of my people,
a land overgrown with thorns and
briers[j] —
yes, mourn[k] for all houses of
merriment
and for this city of revelry.[l]
14The fortress[m] will be abandoned,
the noisy city deserted;[n]
citadel and watchtower[o] will become
a wasteland forever,
the delight of donkeys,[p] a pasture
for flocks,[q]
15till the Spirit[r] is poured upon us from
on high,

31:8 [v]S Ex 12:12; Isa 10:12; 14:25; S 27:1; 33:1; 37:7; Jer 25:12; Hab 2:8 [w]S Ge 49:15; S Dt 20:11 **31:9** [x]Dt 32:31,37 [y]S Isa 18:3; S Jer 4:6 [z]Jer 51:9; Na 3:7 [a]S Isa 10:17 [b]Ps 21:9; Mal 4:1 **32:1** [c]S Ps 149:2; S Isa 6:5; 55:4; Eze 37:24 [d]Ps 72:1-4; S Isa 9:7; S 28:6 **32:2** [e]S 1Ki 18:4 [f]S Ps 55:8 [g]S Ps 23:2; S Isa 30:25; 49:10; Jer 31:9 [h]S Ps 107:35; Isa 44:3 **32:3** [i]S Isa 29:18; 35:5; 42:7,16 [j]S Dt 29:4 **32:4** [k]Isa 6:10; S 29:24 [l]Isa 35:6 **32:5** [m]S 1Sa 25:25 **32:6** [n]S Pr 19:3 [o]S Pr 24:2; S Isa 26:10 [p]S Isa 9:17 [q]Isa 3:12; 9:16 [r]S Isa 3:15 **32:7** [s]Jer 5:26-28; Da 12:10 [t]S Isa 29:20; Mic 7:3 [u]S Ps 72:4; Isa 29:19; 61:1 [v]S Isa 29:21 **32:8** [w]1Ch 29:9; S Pr 11:25 [x]Isa 14:24 **32:9** [y]S Isa 4:1 [z]Isa 28:23 [a]ver 11; Isa 47:8; Da 4:4; Am 6:1; Zep 2:15 **32:10** [b]Isa 37:30 [c]Isa 5:5-6; S 24:7 **32:11** [d]Isa 33:14 [e]S ver 9 [f]Isa 47:2; Mic 1:8; Na 3:5 [g]S Isa 3:24 **32:12** [h]Na 2:7 [i]Isa 16:9 **32:13** [j]S Isa 5:6; Hos 10:8 [k]S Isa 24:11 [l]S Isa 23:7 **32:14** [m]S Isa 13:22 [n]S Isa 6:11; S 27:10 [o]S Isa 2:15; 34:13 [p]S Ps 104:11 [q]S Isa 5:17 **32:15** [r]S Isa 11:2; S Eze 37:9

32:1–8 SALVATION, As Refuge—Isaiah saw hope of Israel in an ideal king to rule over them. These rulers would be a refuge for the people of God. No human ruler fulfilled the vision of a wise, good, God-fearing king. The doctrine of salvation teaches that while leaders and people should seek to be the kind of refuge here described, ultimately only Jesus Christ can perfectly fulfill this hope. He alone brings true nobility to our world. Compare 3:1–12; 6:10; 29:9–10,21; 30:9–11; 31:2.
32:1 CHRISTIAN ETHICS, Righteousness—See notes on 9:7; 11:3–5.
32:1–8 THE CHURCH, God's Kingdom—God is the only true King. All others rule with His permission. The King became flesh in the Messiah—Jesus. His rule will eventually be established, bringing justice and righteousness, opening people's ears and eyes to heed God's Word. Only under the messianic King will society recognize people correctly and follow wise leaders rather than fools. Then all people will be treated as God desires.
32:9–15 PRAYER, Lament—At times lamentation is the only proper prayer. Economic recession and military crisis are not the major reasons for lamentation. Spiritual poverty in the nation should call us to cry out humbly to God. See note on Ps 3:1–8.
32:14–18 HOLY SPIRIT, Hope—Peace and justice are realistic hopes. The Spirit will bring them. Through Isaiah, God warned Jerusalem of the coming of judgment and destruction. He also gave hope for a future in which the people would again be free and live in peace. The metaphor describing the promised age of peace is agricultural; the new age will replace the old as a forest replaces a desert. God will give this new life, pouring out His Spirit upon the people. This promise and others like it were partially fulfilled on the day of Pentecost. See Ac 2. God's people continue to wait for the day when God's Spirit will lead to peace and justice. The qualities which the Spirit will produce in the people include justice, righteousness, peace, quietness, and security. These fruits of the Spirit are all given to Christians. See Gal 5:22. Only when the Spirit's fruits become ripe in our lives can we expect the hope to be fulfilled. See Isa 42:1–2.
32:14–20 CHRISTIAN ETHICS, War and Peace—Righteousness and peace have an intimate relationship. The presence of righteousness more than implies peace. Peace is the work of God's Spirit establishing justice among people and leading people to act rightly toward one another. Peace will bring security, confidence, freedom from danger, and adequate resources. See note on Ps 34:14.

and the desert becomes a fertile field,[s]
and the fertile field seems like a forest.[t]
16Justice[u] will dwell in the desert[v]
and righteousness[w] live in the fertile field.
17The fruit of righteousness[x] will be peace;[y]
the effect of righteousness will be quietness and confidence[z] forever.
18My people will live in peaceful[a] dwelling places,
in secure homes,[b]
in undisturbed places of rest.[c]
19Though hail[d] flattens the forest[e]
and the city is leveled[f] completely,
20how blessed you will be,
sowing[g] your seed by every stream,[h]
and letting your cattle and donkeys range free.[i]

Chapter 33

Distress and Help

WOE[j] to you, O destroyer,
you who have not been destroyed!
Woe to you, O traitor,
you who have not been betrayed!
When you stop destroying,
you will be destroyed;[k]
when you stop betraying,
you will be betrayed.[l]

2O LORD, be gracious[m] to us;
we long for you.
Be our strength[n] every morning,
our salvation[o] in time of distress.[p]
3At the thunder of your voice,[q] the peoples flee;[r]
when you rise up,[s] the nations scatter.
4Your plunder,[t] O nations, is harvested[u] as by young locusts;[v]
like a swarm of locusts men pounce on it.
5The LORD is exalted,[w] for he dwells on high;[x]
he will fill Zion with justice[y] and righteousness.[z]
6He will be the sure foundation for your times,
a rich store of salvation[a] and wisdom and knowledge;
the fear[b] of the LORD is the key to this treasure.[u] [c]

7Look, their brave men[d] cry aloud in the streets;
the envoys[e] of peace weep bitterly.
8The highways are deserted,
no travelers[f] are on the roads.[g]
The treaty is broken,[h]
its witnesses[v] are despised,
no one is respected.
9The land mourns[w] [i] and wastes away,
Lebanon[j] is ashamed and withers;[k]
Sharon[l] is like the Arabah,
and Bashan[m] and Carmel[n] drop their leaves.

10"Now will I arise,[o]" says the LORD.
"Now will I be exalted;[p]
now will I be lifted up.
11You conceive[q] chaff,
you give birth[r] to straw;
your breath is a fire[s] that consumes you.
12The peoples will be burned as if to lime;[t]
like cut thornbushes[u] they will be set ablaze.[v]"

13You who are far away,[w] hear[x] what I have done;
you who are near, acknowledge my power!
14The sinners[y] in Zion are terrified;
trembling[z] grips the godless:
"Who of us can dwell with the consuming fire?[a]
Who of us can dwell with everlasting burning?"
15He who walks righteously[b]
and speaks what is right,[c]
who rejects gain from extortion[d]

32:15 sPs 107:35; Isa 35:1-2 tIsa 29:17 **32:16** uS Isa 9:7; S 28:6 vIsa 35:1,6; 42:11 wS Ps 48:1; S Isa 1:26 **32:17** xS Ps 85:10 yS Ps 119:165; S Isa 9:7; Ro 14:17; Heb 12:11; Jas 3:18 zS Isa 30:15 **32:18** aS Isa 2:4 bS Isa 26:1; 33:20; 37:33; 65:21; 66:14; Am 9:14 cS Jos 1:13; S Job 11:18; Hos 2:18-23 **32:19** dIsa 28:17 eS Isa 10:19; Zec 11:2 fS Job 40:11; S Isa 19:18; 24:10; 27:10 **32:20** gS Ecc 11:1 hS Dt 28:12 iJob 39:8; S Isa 30:24 **33:1** jS 2Ki 19:21; S Isa 28:1 kS Isa 31:8; S Mt 7:2 lS Isa 21:2; Jer 30:16; Eze 39:10 **33:2** mS Ge 43:29; S Ezr 9:8 nIsa 40:10; 51:9; 59:16; 63:5 oS Ps 13:5; S Isa 12:2 pS Isa 5:30 **33:3** qS Ps 46:6; S 68:33 rS Ps 68:1; S Isa 13:14 sver 10; Nu 10:35; Ps 12:5; Isa 59:16-18 **33:4** tS Nu 14:3; S 2Ki 7:16 uS Isa 17:5; Joel 3:13 vJoel 1:4 **33:5** wS Isa 5:16 xS Job 16:19 yS Isa 9:7; S 28:6 zS Isa 1:26 **33:6** aS Isa 12:2; 26:1; 51:6; 60:18 bS Pr 1:7; Isa 11:2-3; Mt 6:33 cS Ge 39:3; S Job 22:25 **33:7** dIsa 10:34 eS 2Ki 18:37 **33:8** fIsa 60:15; Zec 7:14 gS Jdg 5:6; Isa 30:21; 35:8 hS 2Ki 18:14 **33:9** iS Isa 3:26 jS 2Ki 19:23; Isa 2:13; 35:2; 37:24; Jer 22:6 kS Isa 15:6 lS 1Ch 27:29 mMic 7:14 n1Ki 18:19; Isa 35:2; Na 1:4 **33:10** oS ver 3; Isa 2:21 pS Isa 5:16 **33:11** qPs 7:14; Isa 59:4; Jas 1:15 rS Isa 26:18 sIsa 1:31 **33:12** tAm 2:1 uS Isa 5:6 vS Isa 10:17; S 27:11 **33:13** wPs 48:10; 49:1 xIsa 34:1; 48:16; 49:1 **33:14** yS Isa 1:28 zS Isa 32:11 aS Isa 1:31; S 30:30; S Zec 13:9; Heb 12:29 **33:15** bIsa 58:8 cPs 15:2; 24:4 dEze 22:13; 33:31

u6 Or *is a treasure from him* v8 Dead Sea Scrolls; Masoretic Text / *the cities* w9 Or *dries up*

33:2 SALVATION, Grace—God's graciousness is our strength and salvation. There is power in God's grace. See note on Ps 26:11.
33:5,10,21–22 GOD, Sovereignty—God rules the world and is at work to lead the nations to recognize His sovereign authority. Sinners tremble before Him (v 14), but His faithful people trust Him for salvation.
33:5–6 SALVATION, Fear of God—Isaiah saw the fear of the Lord as the key to God's rich store of salvation. Rulers of empires set the world in confusion, robbing the treasuries of conquered peoples. The supreme Ruler treats all people right and fair as He establishes a foundation for international security. The only treasures He desires are a wise people who worship Him in reverence. See note on Ex 20:20.
33:14–16 CHRISTIAN ETHICS, Character—Compare 15:1–5; Ps 24:3–6. The righteous person who wants to participate in God's final salvation will not cheat the poor, try to bribe the court systems to avoid justice, hurt innocent people, or be involved in evil plots or activities. Righteous people avoid all appearances of evil.

and keeps his hand from accepting
bribes,[e]
who stops his ears against plots of
murder
and shuts his eyes[f] against
contemplating evil—
16this is the man who will dwell on the
heights,[g]
whose refuge[h] will be the mountain
fortress.[i]
His bread will be supplied,
and water will not fail[j] him.
17Your eyes will see the king[k] in his
beauty[l]
and view a land that stretches
afar.[m]
18In your thoughts you will ponder the
former terror:[n]
"Where is that chief officer?
Where is the one who took the
revenue?
Where is the officer in charge of the
towers?[o]"
19You will see those arrogant people[p] no
more,
those people of an obscure speech,
with their strange,
incomprehensible tongue.[q]
20Look upon Zion,[r] the city of our
festivals;
your eyes will see Jerusalem,
a peaceful abode,[s] a tent[t] that will
not be moved;[u]
its stakes will never be pulled up,
nor any of its ropes broken.
21There the LORD will be our Mighty[v]
One.
It will be like a place of broad rivers
and streams.[w]
No galley with oars will ride them,
no mighty ship[x] will sail them.
22For the LORD is our judge,[y]
the LORD is our lawgiver,[z]
the LORD is our king;[a]
it is he who will save[b] us.
23Your rigging hangs loose:
The mast is not held secure,
the sail is not spread.
Then an abundance of spoils will be
divided
and even the lame[c] will carry off
plunder.[d]
24No one living in Zion will say, "I am
ill";[e]
and the sins of those who dwell
there will be forgiven.[f]

33:15 [e]S Pr 15:27 [f]Ps 119:37 **33:16** [g]S Dt 32:13 [h]S Ps 46:1; S Isa 25:4 [i]Ps 18:1-2; Isa 26:1 [j]Isa 48:21; 49:10; 65:13 **33:17** [k]S Isa 6:5 [l]S Isa 4:2 [m]S Isa 26:15 **33:18** [n]S Isa 17:14 [o]S Isa 2:15 **33:19** [p]S Ps 5:5 [q]S Ge 11:7; S Isa 28:11 **33:20** [r]S Ps 125:1 [s]S Isa 32:18 [t]S Ge 26:22 [u]ver 6; Ps 46:5 **33:21** [v]S Isa 10:34 [w]S Ex 17:6; S Ps 1:3; Isa 32:2; 41:18; 48:18; 49:10; 66:12; Na 3:8 [x]Isa 23:1 **33:22** [y]Isa 11:4 [z]S Isa 2:3; Jas 4:12 [a]S Ps 89:18 [b]S Isa 25:9 **33:23** [c]S 2Ki 7:8 [d]S 2Ki 7:16 **33:24** [e]S Isa 30:26 [f]S Nu 23:21; S 2Ch 6:21; Isa 43:1; 48:20; Jer 31:34; 33:8; 1Jn 1:7-9 **34:1** [g]S Isa 33:13 [h]Isa 41:1; 43:9 [i]S Dt 4:26; Ps 49:1 [j]Ps 24:1 **34:2** [k]S Isa 10:25 [l]S Isa 13:5; S Zec 5:3 [m]S Isa 30:25 **34:3** [n]S Isa 5:25; S 10:4 [o]S Ps 110:6; Eze 39:11 [p]Joel 2:20; Am 4:10 [q]ver 7; S 2Sa 1:22; Isa 63:6; Eze 5:17; 14:19; 32:6; 35:6; 38:22 **34:4** [r]S Job 9:7; S Isa 13:13; 2Pe 3:10 [s]Isa 38:12; Heb 1:12 [t]S Mt 24:29*; Mk 13:24-25* [u]S Job 8:12; S Isa 15:6; Mt 21:19 **34:5** [v]Dt 32:41-42; Jer 47:6; Eze 21:5; Zec 13:7 [w]S 2Sa 8:13-14; S 2Ch 28:17; Am 1:11-12 [x]S Dt 13:15; S Jos 6:17; Isa 24:6; Am 3:14-15; 6:11 **34:6** [y]S Dt 32:41; S Isa 27:1 [z]S Lev 3:9 [a]S Ge 36:33 [b]S Isa 30:25; S Jer 25:34; Rev 19:17 **34:7** [c]S Nu 23:22 [d]S Ps 68:30 [e]S 2Sa 1:22 **34:8** [f]S Isa 2:12 [g]S Isa 1:24; 35:4; 47:3; 63:4 [h]Isa 59:18; Eze 25:12-17; Joel 3:4; Am 1:6-8,9-10 **34:9** [i]S Ge 19:24

Chapter 34

Judgment Against the Nations

COME near, you nations, and listen;[g]
pay attention, you peoples![h]
Let the earth[i] hear, and all that is in
it,
the world, and all that comes out of
it![j]
2The LORD is angry with all nations;
his wrath[k] is upon all their armies.
He will totally destroy[x][l] them,
he will give them over to
slaughter.[m]
3Their slain[n] will be thrown out,
their dead bodies[o] will send up a
stench;[p]
the mountains will be soaked with
their blood.[q]
4All the stars of the heavens will be
dissolved[r]
and the sky rolled up[s] like a scroll;
all the starry host will fall[t]
like withered[u] leaves from the vine,
like shriveled figs from the fig tree.
5My sword[v] has drunk its fill in the
heavens;
see, it descends in judgment on
Edom,[w]
the people I have totally destroyed.[x]
6The sword[y] of the LORD is bathed in
blood,
it is covered with fat—
the blood of lambs and goats,
fat from the kidneys of rams.
For the LORD has a sacrifice[z] in
Bozrah[a]
and a great slaughter[b] in Edom.
7And the wild oxen[c] will fall with
them,
the bull calves and the great bulls.[d]
Their land will be drenched with
blood,[e]
and the dust will be soaked with fat.
8For the LORD has a day[f] of
vengeance,[g]
a year of retribution,[h] to uphold
Zion's cause.
9Edom's streams will be turned into
pitch,
her dust into burning sulfur;[i]

[x]2 The Hebrew term refers to the irrevocable giving over of things or persons to the LORD, often by totally destroying them; also in verse 5.

33:20–24 CHRISTIAN ETHICS, War and Peace—God's vision for His people looks to peace under God's rule and protection. Material prosperity, help for the sick and handicapped, and forgiveness of sins are all included in peace.

34:1–17 HISTORY, Universal—See note on 13:1—23:18. National power lasts only as long as God permits.

34:2,5–15 GOD, Wrath—God exercises His wrath to defend His people. See note on 30:27–33.

34:4 CREATION, Hope—The hope of the world for God's people is that He will vindicate His righteousness by destroying those who oppose Him. As He can make the sun and moon shine brighter for the righteous, He can do the opposite for those who seek to destroy His people. See note on 30:19–26.

her land will become blazing pitch!
10It will not be quenched[j] night and day;
its smoke will rise forever.[k]
From generation to generation[l] it will lie desolate;[m]
no one will ever pass through it again.
11The desert owl[y n] and screech owl[y] will possess it;
the great owl[y] and the raven[o] will nest there.
God will stretch out over Edom[p]
the measuring line of chaos[q]
and the plumb line[r] of desolation.
12Her nobles will have nothing there to be called a kingdom,
all her princes[s] will vanish[t] away.
13Thorns[u] will overrun her citadels,
nettles and brambles her strongholds.[v]
She will become a haunt for jackals,[w]
a home for owls.[x]
14Desert creatures[y] will meet with hyenas,[z]
and wild goats will bleat to each other;
there the night creatures[a] will also repose
and find for themselves places of rest.
15The owl will nest there and lay eggs,
she will hatch them, and care for her young under the shadow of her wings;[b]
there also the falcons[c] will gather,
each with its mate.

16Look in the scroll[d] of the LORD and read:

None of these will be missing,[e]
not one will lack her mate.
For it is his mouth[f] that has given the order,[g]
and his Spirit will gather them together.
17He allots their portions;[h]
his hand distributes them by measure.
They will possess it forever
and dwell there from generation to generation.[i]

Chapter 35

Joy of the Redeemed

THE desert[j] and the parched land will be glad;
the wilderness will rejoice and blossom.[k]
Like the crocus,[l] 2it will burst into bloom;
it will rejoice greatly and shout for joy.[m]
The glory of Lebanon[n] will be given to it,
the splendor of Carmel[o] and Sharon;[p]
they will see the glory[q] of the LORD,
the splendor of our God.[r]

3Strengthen the feeble hands,
steady the knees[s] that give way;
4say[t] to those with fearful hearts,[u]
"Be strong, do not fear;[v]
your God will come,[w]
he will come with vengeance;[x]
with divine retribution
he will come to save[y] you."

5Then will the eyes of the blind be opened[z]
and the ears of the deaf[a] unstopped.
6Then will the lame[b] leap like a deer,[c]
and the mute tongue[d] shout for joy.[e]
Water will gush forth in the wilderness
and streams[f] in the desert.
7The burning sand will become a pool,
the thirsty ground[g] bubbling springs.[h]
In the haunts where jackals[i] once lay,
grass and reeds[j] and papyrus will grow.
8And a highway[k] will be there;

34:10 [j]S Isa 1:31 [k]Rev 14:10-11; 19:3 [l]ver 17 [m]Isa 13:20; 24:1; Jer 49:18; Eze 29:12; 35:3; Mal 1:3 **34:11** [n]S Lev 11:16-18; S Dt 14:15-17; Rev 18:2 [o]S Ge 8:7 [p]Isa 21:11; Eze 35:15; Joel 3:19; Ob 1:1; Mal 1:4 [q]S Ge 1:2 [r]S 2Ki 21:13; Am 7:8 **34:12** [s]Job 12:21; Ps 107:40; Isa 40:23; Jer 21:7; 27:20; 39:6; Eze 24:5 [t]Isa 29:20; 41:11-12 **34:13** [u]S Isa 5:6; S 7:19 [v]S Isa 13:22 [w]Ps 44:19; S Isa 13:22; Jer 9:11; 10:22 [x]S Lev 11:16-18 **34:14** [y]S Ps 74:14 [z]Isa 13:22 [a]Rev 18:2 **34:15** [b]S Ps 17:8 [c]Dt 14:13 **34:16** [d]Isa 30:8 [e]Isa 40:26; 48:13 [f]Isa 1:20; 58:14 [g]S Isa 1:20 **34:17** [h]Isa 17:14; Jer 13:25 [i]ver 10 **35:1** [j]Isa 27:10; 32:15,16; 41:18-19 [k]Isa 27:6; 51:3 [l]SS 2:1 **35:2** [m]S Ge 21:6; Ps 105:43; Isa 12:6; S 25:9; 44:23; 51:11; 52:9; 55:12 [n]S Ezr 3:7; S Isa 33:9 [o]SS 7:5 [p]S 1Ch 27:29; Isa 65:10 [q]S Ex 16:7; S Isa 4:5; S 59:19 [r]S Isa 25:9 **35:3** [s]S Job 4:4; Heb 12:12 **35:4** [t]2Ch 32:6; Isa 40:2; Zec 1:13 [u]S Dt 20:3; S Isa 21:4 [v]S Jos 1:9; S Isa 7:4; Da 10:19 [w]Isa 40:9, 10-11; 51:5; 62:11; Rev 22:12 [x]S Isa 1:24; S 34:8 [y]S Isa 25:9 **35:5** [z]S Ps 146:8; Jn 9:6-7; Ac 26:18 [a]Isa 29:18; 42:18; 50:4 **35:6** [b]Mt 15:30; Lk 7:22; Jn 5:8-9; Ac 3:8 [c]S 2Sa 22:34 [d]Isa 32:4; Mt 9:32-33; 12:22; Mk 7:35; Lk 11:14 [e]Ps 20:5 [f]S Ex 17:6; Jn 7:38 **35:7** [g]S Ps 68:6; Isa 41:17; 44:3; 55:1 [h]Ps 107:35; Isa 49:10; 58:11 [i]S Isa 13:22 [j]S Job 8:11; S 40:21 **35:8** [k]S Isa 11:16; S 33:8; S Jer 31:21; Mt 7:13-14

[y]*11* The precise identification of these birds is uncertain.

34:16 HOLY SCRIPTURE, Authoritative—History proves Scripture right (Dt 18:22; 1 Sa 3:19–20; 1 Ki 22:28; Jer 28:9). The inspired prophet invited future readers to understand the destruction of the nations in light of the Lord's scroll or book. Prophecy did not come from human dreams, wishes, or ambitions. It came from God's mouth, collected by His Spirit. We can count on the promises and warnings of Scripture to come true in history, for God has issued them.

35:1–10 CREATION, Hope—Our own lives, like God's glorious creation, sometimes become barren and nonproductive. As wild animals frequent the beautiful areas God made, ferocious obstacles can present difficulties to our happiness and security. *The God of creation* can intervene with His marvelous grace, bringing fresh meaning to fruitless and discouraged lives. He does it, however, as we are willing to be instruments of His redemptive purpose for the world. See note on 30:19–26.

35:2 GOD, Glory—God's salvation restores all parts of creation, but the crown of salvation is seeing the personal glory of God. See notes on 6:3; 26:10,15.

35:4–10 JESUS CHRIST, Foretold—God's Messiah would bring in God's kingdom. The news of the kingdom is especially good news for the poor, the disenfranchised, the sick. God intends good for His creation, and He intends to secure it through Jesus Christ (Mt 9:27–31; Lk 4:16–19; Jn 5:1–8). Christians are to be ambassadors for the kingdom of God (2 Co 5:20). It is, therefore, our task to be involved in Jesus' concern for healing, for the poor, and for those society ignores.

35:8 GOD, Holy—To save His people, God promised to prepare a holy highway on which only His holy, pure people

it will be called the Way of
Holiness.[l]
The unclean[m] will not journey on it;
it will be for those who walk in that
Way;
wicked fools will not go about on
it.[z]
9No lion[n] will be there,
nor will any ferocious beast[o] get up
on it;
they will not be found there.
But only the redeemed[p] will walk
there,
10 and the ransomed[q] of the LORD will
return.
They will enter Zion with singing;[r]
everlasting joy[s] will crown their
heads.
Gladness[t] and joy will overtake them,
and sorrow and sighing will flee
away.[u]

Chapter 36

Sennacherib Threatens Jerusalem

36:1–22pp — 2Ki 18:13,17–37; 2Ch 32:9–19

IN the fourteenth year of King Hezekiah's[v] reign, Sennacherib[w] king of Assyria attacked all the fortified cities of Judah and captured them.[x] 2Then the king
of Assyria sent his field commander with
a large army from Lachish[y] to King Hezekiah at Jerusalem. When the commander
stopped at the aqueduct of the Upper
Pool, on the road to the Washerman's
Field,[z] 3Eliakim[a] son of Hilkiah the palace administrator,[b] Shebna[c] the secretary,[d] and Joah[e] son of Asaph the recorder[f] went out to him.

4The field commander said to them,
"Tell Hezekiah,

" 'This is what the great king, the
king of Assyria, says: On what are
you basing this confidence of yours?
5You say you have strategy and military strength—but you speak only
empty words. On whom are you depending, that you rebel[g] against me?
6Look now, you are depending[h] on
Egypt,[ij] that splintered reed[k] of a
staff, which pierces a man's hand and
wounds him if he leans on it! Such is
Pharaoh king of Egypt to all who depend on him. 7And if you say to me,
"We are depending[l] on the LORD
our God"—isn't he the one whose
high places and altars Hezekiah removed,[m] saying to Judah and Jerusalem, "You must worship before this
altar"?[n]

8" 'Come now, make a bargain
with my master, the king of Assyria: I
will give you two thousand horses[o]
—if you can put riders on them!
9How then can you repulse one officer of the least of my master's officials, even though you are depending
on Egypt[p] for chariots[q] and horsemen?[r] 10Furthermore, have I come
to attack and destroy this land without the LORD? The LORD himself
told[s] me to march against this country and destroy it.' "

11Then Eliakim, Shebna and Joah[t] said
to the field commander, "Please speak to
your servants in Aramaic,[u] since we understand it. Don't speak to us in Hebrew
in the hearing of the people on the wall."

12But the commander replied, "Was it
only to your master and you that my master sent me to say these things, and not to
the men sitting on the wall—who, like
you, will have to eat their own filth and
drink their own urine?[v] "

13Then the commander stood and
called out in Hebrew,[w] "Hear the words
of the great king, the king of Assyria![x]
14This is what the king says: Do not let
Hezekiah deceive[y] you. He cannot deliver you! 15Do not let Hezekiah persuade
you to trust in the LORD when he says,
'The LORD will surely deliver[z] us; this
city will not be given into the hand of the
king of Assyria.'[a]

16"Do not listen to Hezekiah. This is
what the king of Assyria says: Make
peace with me and come out to me. Then
every one of you will eat from his own
vine and fig tree[b] and drink water from
his own cistern,[c] 17until I come and take

[z]8 Or / *the simple will not stray from it*

35:8 [l]Isa 4:3; 1Pe 1:15 [m]Isa 52:1
35:9 [n]S Isa 30:6 [o]Isa 11:6; 13:22; 34:14 [p]S Ex 6:6; Lev 25:47-55; Isa 51:11; 62:12; 63:4
35:10 [q]S Job 19:25; S Isa 1:27 [r]Isa 30:29 [s]S Ps 4:7; S 126:5; S Isa 25:9 [t]S Ps 51:8; S Isa 51:3 [u]S Isa 30:19; Rev 7:17; 21:4
36:1 [v]S 2Ki 18:9 [w]S 2Ch 32:1 [x]S Ps 109:11
36:2 [y]S Jos 10:3 [z]S Isa 7:3
36:3 [a]Isa 22:20-21; 37:2 [b]S Ge 41:40 [c]S 2Ki 18:18 [d]S 2Sa 8:17 [e]ver 11 [f]S 2Sa 8:16
36:5 [g]S 2Ki 18:7
36:6 [h]S 2Ki 17:4; S Isa 8:12 [i]Eze 17:17 [j]S Isa 30:2,5 [k]Isa 42:3; 58:5; Eze 29:6-7
36:7 [l]Ps 22:8; Mt 27:43 [m]S 2Ki 18:4 [n]Dt 12:2-5; S 2Ch 31:1
36:8 [o]S Ps 20:7; S Isa 30:16
36:9 [p]S Isa 31:3 [q]Isa 37:24 [r]S Ps 20:7; Isa 30:2-5
36:10 [s]S 1Ki 13:18; Isa 10:5-7
36:11 [t]ver 3 [u]S Ezr 4:7
36:12 [v]2Ki 6:25; Eze 4:12
36:13 [w]S 2Ch 32:18 [x]Isa 37:4
36:14 [y]S 2Ch 32:15
36:15 [z]S Ps 3:2,7 [a]Isa 37:10
36:16 [b]S 1Ki 4:25 [c]Pr 5:15

can walk as He leads. See note on 31:1.

35:8 SALVATION, As Cleansing—Holiness and cleansing from sins cannot be separated. The Way of Holiness is so called because it leads to Zion, the holy place. Those who want to travel on God's highway of holiness will have to be clean from sin. See note on 1:25.

35:9–10 SALVATION, Redemption—God freely ransoms His people. The prophet looked to the return of Israel from Exile when a cleansed and disciplined people would joyfully march across the wilderness back to Jerusalem. God's people continue to look to the final day of God's cleansing when sorrows and sighs disappear from human history.

35:10 SALVATION, Joy—Israel's joy over her restoration from Exile was but a foretaste of the joy experienced by those whom God delivers from the bondage of sin. Compare 51:11.

36:1—37:38 GOD, One God—The Assyrian commander ridiculed Israel's hopes in her God. He used history to show no other gods had been able to resist him. Hezekiah's prayers led God to use the occasion to show truly He is the only God and can control any human power.

36:1—39:8 HOLY SCRIPTURE, Writing—These chapters basically repeat 2 Ki 8:12—20:19. Compare 2 Ch 32:1–31. An Assyrian account of the events has also been preserved. In collecting Isaiah's work, his faithful, inspired disciples took over this historical account and interpreted it to show historical proof of Isaiah's prophetic power and, thus, to encourage readers who looked to the fulfillment of his prophecies. See notes on Isa 8:16; 2 Sa 22:1–51; Jer 51:64.

you to a land like your own[d]—a land of
grain and new wine,[e] a land of bread and
vineyards.
18"Do not let Hezekiah mislead you
when he says, 'The LORD will deliver us.'
Has the god of any nation ever delivered
his land from the hand of the king of Assyria? 19Where are the gods of Hamath
and Arpad?[f] Where are the gods of Sepharvaim?[g] Have they rescued Samaria[h]
from my hand? 20Who of all the gods[i] of
these countries has been able to save his
land from me? How then can the LORD
deliver Jerusalem from my hand?"[j]
21But the people remained silent and
said nothing in reply, because the king
had commanded, "Do not answer
him."[k]
22Then Eliakim[l] son of Hilkiah the palace administrator, Shebna the secretary,
and Joah son of Asaph the recorder[m]
went to Hezekiah, with their clothes
torn,[n] and told him what the field commander had said.

Chapter 37

Jerusalem's Deliverance Foretold

37:1–13pp — 2Ki 19:1–13

WHEN King Hezekiah heard this, he
tore his clothes[o] and put on sackcloth[p] and went into the temple[q] of the
LORD. 2He sent Eliakim[r] the palace administrator, Shebna[s] the secretary, and
the leading priests, all wearing sackcloth,
to the prophet Isaiah son of Amoz.[t]
3They told him, "This is what Hezekiah
says: This day is a day of distress[u] and
rebuke and disgrace, as when children
come to the point of birth[v] and there is
no strength to deliver them. 4It may be
that the LORD your God will hear the
words of the field commander, whom his
master, the king of Assyria, has sent to
ridicule[w] the living God,[x] and that he
will rebuke him for the words the LORD
your God has heard.[y] Therefore pray[z]
for the remnant[a] that still survives."
5When King Hezekiah's officials came
to Isaiah, 6Isaiah said to them, "Tell your
master, 'This is what the LORD says: Do
not be afraid[b] of what you have heard—
those words with which the underlings of
the king of Assyria have blasphemed[c]
me. 7Listen! I am going to put a spirit[d] in
him so that when he hears a certain report,[e] he will return to his own country,
and there I will have him cut down[f] with
the sword.' "
8When the field commander heard that
the king of Assyria had left Lachish,[g] he
withdrew and found the king fighting
against Libnah.[h]
9Now Sennacherib[i] received a report[j] that Tirhakah, the Cushite[a][k] king
⌊of Egypt⌋, was marching out to fight
against him. When he heard it, he sent
messengers to Hezekiah with this word:
10"Say to Hezekiah king of Judah: Do not
let the god you depend on deceive[l] you
when he says, 'Jerusalem will not be
handed over to the king of Assyria.'[m]
11Surely you have heard what the kings of
Assyria have done to all the countries, destroying them completely. And will you
be delivered?[n] 12Did the gods of the nations that were destroyed by my forefathers[o] deliver them—the gods of Gozan,
Haran,[p] Rezeph and the people of Eden[q]
who were in Tel Assar? 13Where is the
king of Hamath, the king of Arpad,[r] the
king of the city of Sepharvaim,[s] or of
Hena or Ivvah?"[t]

Hezekiah's Prayer

37:14–20pp — 2Ki 19:14–19

14Hezekiah received the letter[u] from
the messengers and read it. Then he
went up to the temple[v] of the LORD and
spread it out before the LORD. 15And Hezekiah prayed[w] to the LORD: 16"O LORD
Almighty, God of Israel, enthroned[x] between the cherubim,[y] you alone are
God[z] over all the kingdoms[a] of the
earth. You have made heaven and earth.[b]
17Give ear, O LORD, and hear;[c] open
your eyes, O LORD, and see;[d] listen to all
the words Sennacherib[e] has sent to insult[f] the living God.[g]
18"It is true, O LORD, that the Assyrian
kings have laid waste all these peoples
and their lands.[h] 19They have thrown
their gods into the fire[i] and destroyed
them,[j] for they were not gods[k] but only
wood and stone, fashioned by human

36:17 [d]S 2Ki 15:29 [e]S Ge 27:28; S Dt 28:51
36:19 [f]S 2Ki 18:34 [g]S 2Ki 17:24 [h]S 2Ki 15:29
36:20 [i]S 1Ki 20:23 [j]Ex 5:2; 2Ch 25:15; Isa 10:8-11; 37:10-13,18-20; 40:18; Da 3:15
36:21 [k]Pr 9:7-8; S 26:4
36:22 [l]S 2Ki 18:18 [m]S 2Sa 8:16 [n]S Ge 37:29; S 2Ch 34:19
37:1 [o]S Ge 37:29; S 2Ch 34:19 [p]S Ge 37:34 [q]S ver 14; S 1Ki 8:33; Mt 21:13
37:2 [r]S 2Ki 18:18; S Isa 36:3 [s]S 2Ki 18:18 [t]ver 21; Isa 1:1; S 13:1; 38:1
37:3 [u]S Jdg 6:2; S Isa 5:30 [v]Isa 26:18; 66:9; Hos 13:13
37:4 [w]ver 23-24; S 2Ch 32:17 [x]S Jos 3:10 [y]Isa 36:13,18-20 [z]S 1Sa 7:8 [a]S Isa 1:9; Am 7:2
37:6 [b]S Jos 1:9; S Isa 7:4 [c]S Nu 15:30
37:7 [d]1Ch 5:26 [e]ver 9 [f]S Isa 31:8
37:8 [g]S Jos 10:3 [h]S Nu 33:20
37:9 [i]S 2Ch 32:1 [j]ver 7 [k]S Isa 20:3
37:10 [l]2Ch 32:11, 15 [m]Isa 36:15
37:11 [n]Isa 36:18-20
37:12 [o]2Ki 18:11 [p]Ge 11:31; 12:1-4; Ac 7:2 [q]Eze 27:23; Am 1:5
37:13 [r]Isa 10:9 [s]S 2Ki 17:24 [t]S Isa 36:20
37:14 [u]2Ch 32:17 [v]ver 1,38; S 1Ki 8:33
37:15 [w]S 2Ch 32:20
37:16 [x]S Ps 2:4 [y]S Ge 3:24 [z]Dt 10:17; S Ps 46:10; 86:10; 136:2-3 [a]Da 4:34 [b]S Ge 1:1; S Isa 11:12; 41:9; 43:6; Ac 4:24
37:17 [c]S 1Ki 8:29; S 2Ch 6:40 [d]Jer 25:29; Da 9:18 [e]S 2Ch 32:1 [f]S 2Ch 32:17 [g]S Jos 3:10
37:18 [h]S 2Ki 15:29; Na 2:11-12
37:19 [i]S Jos 7:15 [j]Isa 26:14; 36:20 [k]2Ch 13:9; Isa 40:17; 41:24,29; Jer 2:11; 5:7; 16:20; Gal 4:8

[a]9 That is, from the upper Nile region

37:4,19 GOD, Living—God is a living God in contrast to the inanimate, man-made gods of the nations. He responds to the needs and prayers of His people.

37:4 THE CHURCH, Remnant—King Hezekiah realized God had reduced His people to a remnant as Isaiah had prophesied (7:18–25). He knew the only hope for a powerless remnant was prayer. God can do for a remnant what the most powerful human rulers cannot. *See note on 2 Ch 34:9.*

37:14–20 PRAYER, Sovereignty of God—Hezekiah's prayers are remarkable. See notes on 2 Ki 19:14–19; 20:3. He based his prayer on the identification of Israel with God and His purposes. Belief in God as the only One able to answer prayer is a requirement for prayer.

37:16 GOD, Creator—The one true God is the Creator of heaven and earth but still hears His people's prayers.

37:16,22–29 GOD, Sovereignty—Mocking and ridiculing the sovereign God does not pay. Human success comes only as it fits God's plans. God ultimately punishes those who let success blind them to God's power and sovereignty.

hands.[l] 20Now, O LORD our God, deliver[m] us from his hand, so that all kingdoms on earth[n] may know that you
alone, O LORD, are God.[b] [o]"

Sennacherib's Fall

37:21–38pp — 2Ki 19:20–37; 2Ch 32:20–21

21Then Isaiah son of Amoz[p] sent a
message to Hezekiah: "This is what the
LORD, the God of Israel, says: Because
you have prayed to me concerning Sennacherib king of Assyria, 22this is the
word the LORD has spoken against him:

"The Virgin Daughter[q] of Zion[r]
despises and mocks you.
The Daughter of Jerusalem
tosses her head[s] as you flee.
23Who is it you have insulted and
blasphemed?[t]
Against whom have you raised your
voice[u]
and lifted your eyes in pride?[v]
Against the Holy One[w] of Israel!
24By your messengers
you have heaped insults on the Lord.
And you have said,
'With my many chariots[x]
I have ascended the heights of the
mountains,
the utmost heights[y] of Lebanon.[z]
I have cut down its tallest cedars,
the choicest of its pines.[a]
I have reached its remotest heights,
the finest of its forests.
25I have dug wells in foreign lands[c]
and drunk the water there.
With the soles of my feet
I have dried up[b] all the streams of
Egypt.[c]'

26"Have you not heard?
Long ago I ordained[d] it.
In days of old I planned[e] it;
now I have brought it to pass,
that you have turned fortified cities
into piles of stone.[f]
27Their people, drained of power,
are dismayed and put to shame.
They are like plants in the field,
like tender green shoots,
like grass[g] sprouting on the roof,[h]
scorched[d] before it grows up.

28"But I know where you stay
and when you come and go[i]
and how you rage[j] against me.
29Because you rage against me
and because your insolence[k] has
reached my ears,
I will put my hook[l] in your nose[m]
and my bit in your mouth,
and I will make you return
by the way you came.[n]

30"This will be the sign[o] for you, O
Hezekiah:

"This year[p] you will eat what grows
by itself,
and the second year what springs
from that.
But in the third year[q] sow and reap,
plant vineyards[r] and eat their
fruit.[s]
31Once more a remnant of the house of
Judah
will take root[t] below and bear
fruit[u] above.
32For out of Jerusalem will come a
remnant,[v]
and out of Mount Zion a band of
survivors.[w]
The zeal[x] of the LORD Almighty
will accomplish this.

33"Therefore this is what the LORD says
concerning the king of Assyria:

"He will not enter this city[y]
or shoot an arrow here.
He will not come before it with shield
or build a siege ramp[z] against it.
34By the way that he came he will
return;[a]
he will not enter this city,"
declares the LORD.
35"I will defend[b] this city and save it,
for my sake[c] and for the sake of
David[d] my servant!"

36Then the angel[e] of the LORD went
out and put to death[f] a hundred and
eighty-five thousand men in the Assyrian[g] camp. When the people got up the
next morning—there were all the dead

37:19 [l]S 2Ch 32:19; S Ps 135:15; Isa 40:18-20; 44:9-11
37:20 [m]S Ps 3:2,7; S Pr 20:22 [n]S Jos 4:24 [o]S 1Sa 17:46; S Ps 46:10
37:21 [p]S ver 2
37:22 [q]S Isa 23:12 [r]S Isa 10:32 [s]S Job 16:4
37:23 [t]ver 4; S Nu 15:30; Isa 52:5; Eze 36:20, 23; Da 7:25 [u]S Job 15:25 [v]S Isa 2:11 [w]S Isa 1:4; S 12:6
37:24 [x]Isa 36:9 [y]Isa 14:13 [z]S 1Ki 7:2; S Isa 14:8; S 33:9 [a]1Ki 5:8-10; Isa 41:19; 55:13; 60:13; Hos 14:8
37:25 [b]S Isa 19:6; 44:27 [c]S Dt 11:10; S Isa 10:14; Da 4:30
37:26 [d]Ac 2:23; 4:27-28; 1Pe 2:8 [e]Isa 10:6; S 25:1 [f]S Dt 13:16; S Isa 25:2
37:27 [g]S Isa 15:6 [h]Ps 129:6
37:28 [i]Ps 139:1-3 [j]Ps 2:1
37:29 [k]Isa 10:12 [l]S 2Ch 33:11 [m]S Job 40:24 [n]ver 34
37:30 [o]S Isa 20:3 [p]Isa 32:10 [q]S Isa 16:14 [r]S Lev 25:4 [s]Ps 107:37; Isa 30:23; 65:21; Jer 31:5
37:31 [t]Isa 11:10 [u]S Isa 27:6
37:32 [v]S Isa 11:11 [w]S Isa 1:9 [x]S Isa 9:7
37:33 [y]S Isa 32:18 [z]S 2Sa 20:15
37:34 [a]ver 29
37:35 [b]S Isa 31:5 [c]Isa 43:25; 48:9, 11; Eze 36:21-22 [d]S 1Ch 17:19
37:36 [e]S Ex 12:23 [f]S Ex 12:12 [g]S Isa 10:12

[b]*20* Dead Sea Scrolls (see also 2 Kings 19:19); Masoretic Text *alone are the LORD* [c]*25* Dead Sea Scrolls (see also 2 Kings 19:24); Masoretic Text does not have *in foreign lands.* [d]*27* Some manuscripts of the Masoretic Text, Dead Sea Scrolls and some Septuagint manuscripts (see also 2 Kings 19:26); most manuscripts of the Masoretic Text *roof / and terraced fields*

37:21–29 PRAYER, Answer—See note on 2 Ki 19:20–36. God answers out of His long-established purposes for His people.
37:30–32 PRAYER, Answer—See note on 7:10–14. God confirmed His word with a sign pointing to future fulfillment of prophecy. Compare Dt 18:21–22.
37:31–32 THE CHURCH, Remnant—A remnant does not have to remain small. God makes His faithful remnant fruitful and rebuilds His people. See note on 27:12–13.
37:32 GOD, Jealous—See note on 30:22.
37:35 ELECTION, Protection—God promised Jerusalem protection against Sennacherib and Assyria. For the sake of God's election promises to David and His own reputation, God preserved Jerusalem. God keeps His promises to protect His elect. No human power can defeat God's eternal purposes.
37:35 THE CHURCH, Servants—David, above all others, is called the servant of God. See note on Eze 34:1–24. David, though a sinner, sought to obey God. He gave himself to God in humbleness and repentance. He became the symbol of what it means to be God's servant.

bodies! 37So Sennacherib[h] king of Assyria
broke camp and withdrew. He returned
to Nineveh[i] and stayed there.
38One day, while he was worshiping in
the temple[j] of his god Nisroch, his sons
Adrammelech and Sharezer cut him
down with the sword, and they escaped
to the land of Ararat.[k] And Esarhaddon[l]
his son succeeded him as king.[m]

Chapter 38

Hezekiah's Illness

38:1–8pp — 2Ki 20:1–11; 2Ch 32:24–26

In those days Hezekiah became ill and
was at the point of death. The prophet
Isaiah son of Amoz[n] went to him and
said, "This is what the LORD says: Put
your house in order,[o] because you are
going to die; you will not recover."[p]
2Hezekiah turned his face to the wall
and prayed to the LORD, 3"Remember, O
LORD, how I have walked[q] before you
faithfully and with wholehearted devotion[r] and have done what is good in your
eyes.[s]" And Hezekiah wept[t] bitterly.
4Then the word[u] of the LORD came to
Isaiah: 5"Go and tell Hezekiah, 'This is
what the LORD, the God of your father
David,[v] says: I have heard your prayer
and seen your tears;[w] I will add fifteen
years[x] to your life. 6And I will deliver you
and this city from the hand of the king of
Assyria. I will defend[y] this city.
7" 'This is the LORD's sign[z] to you that
the LORD will do what he has promised:
8I will make the shadow cast by the sun
go back the ten steps it has gone down on
the stairway of Ahaz.' " So the sunlight
went back the ten steps it had gone
down.[a]

9A writing of Hezekiah king of Judah
after his illness and recovery:

10I said, "In the prime of my life[b]
must I go through the gates of
death[e c]
and be robbed of the rest of my
years?[d]"
11I said, "I will not again see the LORD,
the LORD,[e] in the land of the
living;[f]
no longer will I look on mankind,
or be with those who now dwell in
this world.[f]
12Like a shepherd's tent[g] my house
has been pulled down[h] and taken
from me.
Like a weaver I have rolled[i] up my
life,
and he has cut me off from the
loom;[j]
day and night[k] you made an end of
me.
13I waited patiently[l] till dawn,
but like a lion he broke[m] all my
bones;[n]
day and night[o] you made an end of
me.
14I cried like a swift or thrush,
I moaned like a mourning dove.[p]
My eyes grew weak[q] as I looked to the
heavens.
I am troubled; O Lord, come to my
aid!"[r]

15But what can I say?[s]
He has spoken to me, and he
himself has done this.[t]
I will walk humbly[u] all my years
because of this anguish of my soul.[v]
16Lord, by such things men live;
and my spirit finds life in them too.
You restored me to health
and let me live.[w]
17Surely it was for my benefit[x]
that I suffered such anguish.[y]
In your love you kept me
from the pit[z] of destruction;
you have put all my sins[a]
behind your back.[b]
18For the grave[e c] cannot praise you,

[e] *10,18* Hebrew *Sheol* [f] *11* A few Hebrew manuscripts; most Hebrew manuscripts *in the place of cessation*

37:37 [h]S 2Ch 32:1 [i]S Ge 10:11; S Na 1:1 **37:38** [j]S ver 14 [k]Ge 8:4; Jer 51:27 [l]S 2Ki 17:24 [m]S Isa 9:4; 10:26; S 14:25 **38:1** [n]S Isa 37:2 [o]2Sa 17:23 [p]2Ki 8:10 **38:3** [q]Ps 26:3 [r]S 1Ki 8:61; S 1Ch 29:19 [s]S Dt 6:18; S 10:20 [t]Ps 6:8 **38:4** [u]1Sa 13:13; Isa 39:5 **38:5** [v]2Ki 18:3 [w]Ps 6:6 [x]S 2Ki 18:2 **38:6** [y]S Isa 31:5 **38:7** [z]S Ge 24:14; S 2Ch 32:31; Isa 7:11,14; S 20:3 **38:8** [a]Jos 10:13 **38:10** [b]Ps 102:24 [c]S Job 17:16; Ps 107:18; 2Co 1:9 [d]S Job 17:11 **38:11** [e]S Isa 12:2 [f]S Job 28:13; S Ps 116:9 **38:12** [g]Isa 33:20; 2Co 5:1,4; 2Pe 1:13-14 [h]S Job 4:21 [i]S Isa 34:4; Heb 1:12 [j]S Nu 11:15; S Job 7:6; S Ps 31:22 [k]ver 13; Ps 32:4; 73:14 **38:13** [l]S Ps 37:7 [m]S Job 9:17; Ps 51:8 [n]S Job 10:16; Jer 34:17; La 3:4; Da 6:24 [o]S ver 12 **38:14** [p]S Ge 8:8; S Isa 59:11 [q]S Ps 6:7 [r]S Ge 50:24; S Job 17:3 **38:15** [s]2Sa 7:20 [t]S Ps 39:9 [u]1Ki 21:27 [v]S Job 7:11 **38:16** [w]Ps 119:25; Heb 12:9 **38:17** [x]Ro 8:28; Heb 12:11 [y]S Job 7:11; Ps 119:71,75 [z]S Job 17:16; S Ps 30:3 [a]Ps 103:3; Jer 31:34 [b]S Ps 103:12; Isa 43:25; Mic 7:19 **38:18** [c]S Nu 16:30; S Ecc 9:10

38:1–22 EVIL AND SUFFERING, God's Present Help—See note on 2 Ki 20:1–11.
38:1–6 HUMANITY, Life—Illness was perceived to be the onset of death and, thus, as much related to sin as was death. God, however, as the Author of life can grant additional life by the postponement of death. It should be noted that miraculous intervention is not His normal way of dealing with people. In His sovereign will He chooses when to intervene and for whom.
38:2–7 PRAYER, Lament—See note on 2 Ki 20:3. Lament may be expressed in acts such as weeping as much as in words. The protest of innocence is one way of crying for help. See note on Ps 7:1–17.
38:9–19 HUMANITY, Death—A vivid portrayal of the onset of death is made all the more meaningful by praise for life. People need to recognize that all life is a gift from God and should not be taken for granted. Illness may be a punishment for sin as here but is not necessarily so. See Job 1:1—2:10. Whatever the case, we need to learn from illness the great meaning of life and seek to find how God is working in our illness.
38:9–20 PRAYER, Thanksgiving—See notes on Ps 7:1–17; 30:1–12. Hezekiah composed a psalm of gratitude for the answer to his prayer. Thanksgiving relives troubled times to recall the wonder of God's intervention. It leads to a vow of humble devotion.
38:17 GOD, Love—Escape from serious illness and death makes us appreciate more deeply the saving love of God.
38:17,20 GOD, Savior—Deliverance from sickness and death is a part of God's salvation. It causes us to express heartfelt thanks to Him in public worship (v 20).
38:17 SALVATION, Forgiveness—When God forgives our sins, He puts them behind His back. This is a human way of saying God does not see our sins any more. Forgiveness of sin and recovery from mortal illness are often two sides of the same experience of God's saving power.

death cannot sing your praise;[d]
those who go down to the pit[e]
cannot hope for your faithfulness.
19The living, the living—they praise[f] you,
as I am doing today;
fathers tell their children[g]
about your faithfulness.

20The LORD will save me,
and we will sing[h] with stringed instruments[i]
all the days of our lives[j]
in the temple[k] of the LORD.

21Isaiah had said, "Prepare a poultice
of figs and apply it to the boil, and he will
recover."
22Hezekiah had asked, "What will be
the sign[l] that I will go up to the temple
of the LORD?"

Chapter 39

Envoys From Babylon

39:1–8pp — 2Ki 20:12–19

AT that time Merodach-Baladan son of
Baladan king of Babylon[m] sent Hezekiah letters and a gift, because he had
heard of his illness and recovery. 2Hezeki-
ah received the envoys[n] gladly and
showed them what was in his storehouses—the silver, the gold,[o] the spices,
the fine oil, his entire armory and everything found among his treasures.[p] There
was nothing in his palace or in all his
kingdom that Hezekiah did not show
them.
3Then Isaiah the prophet went to King
Hezekiah and asked, "What did those
men say, and where did they come
from?"
"From a distant land,[q]" Hezekiah replied. "They came to me from Babylon."

38:18 [d]Ps 6:5; 88:10-11; 115:17 [e]S Ps 30:9
38:19 [f]Ps 118:17; 119:175 [g]S Dt 11:19
38:20 [h]Ps 68:25 [i]S Ps 33:2; S 45:8 [j]Ps 23:6; S 63:4; 116:2 [k]Ps 116:17-19
38:22 [l]S 2Ch 32:31
39:1 [m]S 2Ch 32:31
39:2 [n]2Ch 32:31 [o]S 2Ki 18:15 [p]2Ch 32:27-29
39:3 [q]S Dt 28:49
39:5 [r]S Isa 38:4
39:6 [s]S Jdg 6:4; S 2Ki 24:13
39:7 [t]S 2Ki 24:15; Da 1:1-7
39:8 [u]S Jdg 10:15; Job 1:21; Ps 39:9 [v]S 2Ch 32:26
40:1 [w]Isa 12:1; 49:13; 51:3,12; 52:9; 57:18; 61:2; 66:13; Jer 31:13; Zep 3:14-17; Zec 1:17; 2Co 1:3
40:2 [x]S Ge 34:3; S Isa 35:4 [y]S Job 7:1 [z]Isa 41:11-13; 49:25 [a]S Lev 26:41 [b]Isa 51:19; 61:7; Jer 16:18; 17:18; Zec 9:12; Rev 18:6
40:3 [c]S Isa 11:16; 43:19; Mal 3:1 [d]S Pr 3:5-6 [e]Mt 3:3*; Mk 1:3*; Jn 1:23*
40:4 [f]Isa 49:11

4The prophet asked, "What did they
see in your palace?"
"They saw everything in my palace,"
Hezekiah said. "There is nothing among
my treasures that I did not show them."
5Then Isaiah said to Hezekiah, "Hear
the word[r] of the LORD Almighty: 6The
time will surely come when everything in
your palace, and all that your fathers have
stored up until this day, will be carried off
to Babylon.[s] Nothing will be left, says
the LORD. 7And some of your descendants, your own flesh and blood who will
be born to you, will be taken away, and
they will become eunuchs in the palace
of the king of Babylon.[t]"
8"The word of the LORD you have spoken is good,[u]" Hezekiah replied. For he
thought, "There will be peace and security in my lifetime.[v]"

Chapter 40

Comfort for God's People

COMFORT, comfort[w] my people,
says your God.
2Speak tenderly[x] to Jerusalem,
and proclaim to her
that her hard service[y] has been completed,[z]
that her sin has been paid for,[a]
that she has received from the LORD's hand
double[b] for all her sins.

3A voice of one calling:
"In the desert prepare
the way[c] for the LORD[g];
make straight[d] in the wilderness
a highway for our God.[h] [e]
4Every valley shall be raised up,[f]

[g]3 Or *A voice of one calling in the desert: / "Prepare the way for the LORD* [h]3 Hebrew; Septuagint *make straight the paths of our God*

38:18 LAST THINGS, Intermediate State—See note on 14:9.
38:19 FAMILY, Bible Study—See notes on Dt 6:4–9; Ps 78:1–8.
38:20 WORSHIP, Music—Hezekiah promised to praise God in Temple worship accompanied by music for the rest of his life. Such vows are a common part of worship celebrating or looking forward to God's deliverance. See notes on 1 Ch 6:31–32; Ps 61:8.
39:5–6 HOLY SCRIPTURE, Inspired—The prophet dared to speak to the king about the future of his palace and kingdom. He represented God to Hezekiah just as an ambassador represents one king to another. The revealed words were God-breathed to the prophet.
40:1 SALVATION, Grace—God's comfort to His people is an expression of His grace and mercy. The twice repeated imperative strikes the note of urgency. God was answering the lamentations of His people (La 1:2,9,16–17,21; 2:13). Compare Lk 2:25–35.
40:1–8 PROCLAMATION, Call—See notes on Jer 1:4–9; 19:14–15.
40:2 SALVATION, Redemption—The sufferings of God's people are tied to the purpose and sovereignty of God. He never forgets His people. They were Babylon's prisoner and His prisoner in Exile. They had paid what they owed plus damages (Ex 22:1,7,9). God was ready to set them free even if Babylon was not. No matter how the present appears, God's people can be sure He is working to liberate His people.
40:3–11 JESUS CHRIST, Foretold—Isa 40 begins a new rhythm played for a time of desolation. Comfort becomes the dominant theme; poetry is the idiom. The Messiah's forerunner was predicted. His task would be to make straight the path for the coming King. Early Christians recognized this crying voice as that of John the Baptist (Mt 3:3). John himself perceived this as his task (Jn 1:23). John's Gospel highlights the magnificent metaphor of caring by portraying Jesus as the Good Shepherd (Isa 40:11; Jn 10:14). Christians as recipients of such care must also learn to care in their tasks of making ready the climactic royal appearance. Patient preparation through concern and care is our ministry of comfort as we wait for Jesus to return.
40:3 SALVATION, Preparation—Originally this was a message of hope to the Jewish exiles in Babylon. Christians see it as a messianic prophecy pointing to God's preparation for Christ. The New Testament identifies John the Baptist as the messenger (Mt 3:3; Mk 1:3; Lk 3:4).

every mountain and hill[g] made low;
the rough ground shall become level,[h]
the rugged places a plain.
5And the glory[i] of the LORD will be revealed,
and all mankind together will see it.[j]
For the mouth of the LORD has spoken."[k]

6A voice says, "Cry out."
And I said, "What shall I cry?"

"All men are like grass,[l]
and all their glory is like the flowers of the field.
7The grass withers[m] and the flowers fall,
because the breath[n] of the LORD blows[o] on them.
Surely the people are grass.
8The grass withers and the flowers[p] fall,
but the word[q] of our God stands[r] forever.[s]"

9You who bring good tidings[t] to Zion,
go up on a high mountain.
You who bring good tidings to Jerusalem,[i] [u]
lift up your voice with a shout,
lift it up, do not be afraid;
say to the towns of Judah,
"Here is your God!"[v]
10See, the Sovereign LORD comes[w] with power,[x]
and his arm[y] rules[z] for him.
See, his reward[a] is with him,
and his recompense accompanies him.
11He tends his flock like a shepherd:[b]
He gathers the lambs in his arms[c]
and carries them close to his heart;[d]
he gently leads[e] those that have young.[f]

12Who has measured the waters[g] in the hollow of his hand,[h]
or with the breadth of his hand marked off the heavens?[i]
Who has held the dust of the earth in a basket,
or weighed the mountains on the scales
and the hills in a balance?[j]
13Who has understood the mind[j] [k] of the LORD,
or instructed him as his counselor?[l]
14Whom did the LORD consult to enlighten him,
and who taught him the right way?
Who was it that taught him knowledge[m]
or showed him the path of understanding?[n]

15Surely the nations are like a drop in a bucket;
they are regarded as dust on the scales;[o]
he weighs the islands as though they were fine dust.[p]
16Lebanon[q] is not sufficient for altar fires,
nor its animals[r] enough for burnt offerings.
17Before him all the nations[s] are as nothing;[t]
they are regarded by him as worthless
and less than nothing.[u]

18To whom, then, will you compare God?[v]

40:4 [g]S Isa 2:14 [h]S Ps 26:12; S Isa 26:7; 45:2,13; Jer 31:9 **40:5** [i]S Ex 16:7; S Nu 14:21; S Isa 59:19 [j]Isa 52:10; 62:2; Lk 2:30; 3:4-6* [k]S Isa 1:20; 58:14 **40:6** [l]S Ge 6:3; S Isa 29:5 **40:7** [m]S Job 8:12; S Isa 15:6 [n]S Ex 15:10; S Job 41:21 [o]S Ps 103:16; S Eze 22:21 **40:8** [p]S Isa 5:24; Jas 1:10 [q]Isa 55:11; 59:21 [r]S Pr 19:21; S Isa 7:7,9; S Jer 39:16 [s]S Ps 119:89; S Mt 5:18; 1Pe 1:24-25* **40:9** [t]Isa 41:27; 44:28; 52:7-10; 61:1; Na 1:15; S Ac 13:32; Ro 10:15; 1Co 15:1-4 [u]S Isa 1:1 [v]Isa 25:9 **40:10** [w]Isa 35:4; 59:20; Mt 21:5; Rev 22:7 [x]Isa 28:2 [y]S Ps 44:3; S Isa 30:30; S 33:2 [z]Isa 9:6-7 [a]S Isa 35:4; Rev 22:12 **40:11** [b]S Ge 48:15; S Ps 28:9; S Mic 5:4; S Jn 10:11 [c]S Nu 11:12 [d]S Dt 26:19 [e]Isa 49:10 [f]S Ge 33:13; S Dt 30:4 **40:12** [g]S Job 12:15; S 38:10 [h]Pr 30:4 [i]S Job 38:5; Heb 1:10-12 [j]S Job 38:18; Pr 16:11 **40:13** [k]Isa 11:2; 42:1 [l]S Job 15:8; Ro 11:34*; 1Co 2:16* **40:14** [m]Job 21:22; Col 2:3 [n]S Job 12:13; S 34:13; Isa 55:9 **40:15** [o]S Ps 62:9 [p]S Dt 9:21; Isa 2:22 **40:16** [q]Isa 33:9; 37:24 [r]Ps 50:9-11; Mic 6:7; Heb 10:5-9 **40:17** [s]Isa 30:28 [t]S Job 12:19; Isa 29:7 [u]S Isa 37:19; Da 4:35 **40:18** [v]S Ex 8:10; S 1Sa 2:2

[i]9 Or *O Zion, bringer of good tidings, / go up on a high mountain. / O Jerusalem, bringer of good tidings*
[j]13 Or *Spirit*; or *spirit*

40:4 CREATION, Hope—As God's miraculous power can level the mountains and exalt the valleys of His created world, so He can bring hope to discouraged lives. His promises keep us from being drowned in discouragement and frustration. Periods of fresh starts come to us after great crises. They cause us to realize we need to reevaluate our priorities and face the future optimistically with the One who created and sustains us.

40:6–7 HUMANITY, Human Nature—We are not permanent fixtures on this earth. Our life is so fragile we serve as a good contrast to the faithful, everlasting Word of God.

40:8 HOLY SCRIPTURE, Authoritative—Human words come and go, making their impact for a moment and then dying in the mists of history. God's Word never dies. It has eternal authority. The comfort He offers His people is sure. We can count on Scripture when all else seems to fail.

40:10,26,28–31 GOD, Power—God's unceasing power reaches out to help those people who respond to Him. In His grace God uses His power to lead and deliver His people just as He used it to create the perfection of the heavens.

40:11 GOD, Love—The powerful Creator reaches down in love to care for us tenderly as a shepherd with his sheep. See notes on Jn 3:16; 1 Jn 4:7–16.

40:12–31 CREATION, Sovereignty—No one can rival the incomparable Creator who controls everything related to that which He made. Neither gods made with human hands nor rulers temporarily in power can compete with Him. All who oppose Him stand ineffectual and even worthless before His power. No one can understand Him, for He created the world by Himself with no aid or advice from anyone. He is completely knowledgeable concerning every element of His world. We who live in His presence can find fresh motivation and endurance as we recognize His complete lordship and plan our lives according to His will for us.

40:15–17,21–24 GOD, Transcendent—God is greater than the whole power structure of the nations. See notes on Ge 15:13–16; 18:14; 24:3,7,50; Dt 1:10.

40:15–17 HISTORY, Universal—Political power does not measure up on God's scales. No human ruler can compare with His power.

40:18–20,25 GOD, One God—An exiled people were tempted to give credit to the gods of their captors. Such gods are only products of human hands and have no claim to authority over human history and destiny. No one compares to the true God.

40:18–24 HISTORY, God—God's judgment on political powers points to His unique position in the world.

What image[w] will you compare him
to?
19As for an idol,[x] a craftsman casts it,
and a goldsmith[y] overlays it with
gold[z]
and fashions silver chains for it.
20A man too poor to present such an
offering
selects wood[a] that will not rot.
He looks for a skilled craftsman
to set up an idol[b] that will not
topple.[c]

21Do you not know?
Have you not heard?[d]
Has it not been told[e] you from the
beginning?[f]
Have you not understood[g] since the
earth was founded?[h]
22He sits enthroned[i] above the circle of
the earth,
and its people are like
grasshoppers.[j]
He stretches out the heavens[k] like a
canopy,[l]
and spreads them out like a tent[m] to
live in.[n]
23He brings princes[o] to naught
and reduces the rulers of this world
to nothing.[p]
24No sooner are they planted,
no sooner are they sown,
no sooner do they take root[q] in the
ground,
than he blows[r] on them and they
wither,[s]
and a whirlwind sweeps them away
like chaff.[t]

25"To whom will you compare me?[u]
Or who is my equal?" says the Holy
One.[v]
26Lift your eyes and look to the
heavens:[w]
Who created[x] all these?
He who brings out the starry host[y]
one by one,
and calls them each by name.
Because of his great power and mighty
strength,[z]
not one of them is missing.[a]

27Why do you say, O Jacob,
and complain, O Israel,
"My way is hidden from the LORD;
my cause is disregarded by my
God"?[b]
28Do you not know?
Have you not heard?[c]
The LORD is the everlasting[d] God,
the Creator[e] of the ends of the
earth.[f]
He will not grow tired or weary,[g]
and his understanding no one can
fathom.[h]
29He gives strength[i] to the weary[j]
and increases the power of the
weak.
30Even youths grow tired and weary,
and young men[k] stumble and fall;[l]
31but those who hope[m] in the LORD
will renew their strength.[n]
They will soar on wings like eagles;[o]
they will run and not grow weary,
they will walk and not be faint.[p]

Chapter 41

The Helper of Israel

"BE silent[q] before me, you islands![r]
Let the nations renew their
strength![s]
Let them come forward[t] and speak;
let us meet together[u] at the place of
judgment.

2"Who has stirred[v] up one from the
east,[w]
calling him in righteousness[x] to his
service[k]?[y]
He hands nations over to him
and subdues kings before him.
He turns them to dust[z] with his
sword,
to windblown chaff[a] with his bow.[b]
3He pursues them and moves on
unscathed,[c]
by a path his feet have not traveled
before.
4Who has done this and carried it
through,
calling[d] forth the generations from
the beginning?[e]

40:18 [w]S Dt 4:15; Ac 17:29 **40:19** [x]S Ex 20:4; Ps 115:4; S Isa 37:19; 42:17; Jer 2:8,28; 10:8; 16:19; Hab 2:18; Zec 10:2 [y]Isa 41:7; 46:6; Jer 10:3 [z]Isa 2:20; 31:7 **40:20** [a]Isa 44:19 [b]S 1Sa 12:21 [c]S 1Sa 5:3 **40:21** [d]ver 28; 2Ki 19:25; Isa 41:22; 42:9; 44:8; 48:3,5 [e]Ps 19:1; 50:6; Ac 14:17 [f]S Ge 1:1 [g]Ro 1:19 [h]Isa 48:13; 51:13 **40:22** [i]S 2Ch 6:18; S Ps 2:4 [j]S Nu 13:33 [k]S Ge 1:1; S Isa 48:13 [l]S Ge 1:8; S Job 22:14 [m]S Job 36:29 [n]S Job 26:7 **40:23** [o]S Job 12:18; S Isa 34:12 [p]S Job 12:19; Am 2:3 **40:24** [q]S Job 5:3 [r]S 2Sa 22:16; S Isa 11:4; 41:16 [s]S Job 8:12; S 18:16 [t]S Job 24:24; S Isa 41:2 **40:25** [u]S 1Sa 2:2; S 1Ch 16:25 [v]Isa 1:4; 37:23 **40:26** [w]Isa 51:6 [x]ver 28; Ps 89:11-13; Isa 42:5; 66:2 [y]S 2Ki 17:16; S Ne 9:6; S Job 38:32 [z]S Job 9:4; S Isa 45:24; Eph 1:19 [a]S Isa 34:16 **40:27** [b]S Job 6:29; S 27:2; Lk 18:7-8 **40:28** [c]S ver 21 [d]S Dt 33:27; S Ps 90:2 [e]S ver 26 [f]S Isa 37:16 [g]Isa 44:12 [h]S Ps 147:5; Ro 11:33 **40:29** [i]S Ge 18:14; S Ps 68:35; S 119:28 [j]Isa 50:4; 57:19; Jer 31:25 **40:30** [k]Isa 9:17; Jer 6:11; 9:21 [l]S Ps 20:8; Isa 5:27 **40:31** [m]S Ps 37:9; 40:1; S Isa 30:18; Lk 18:1 [n]S 1Sa 2:4; S 2Ki 6:33; S 2Co 4:16 [o]S Ex 19:4 [p]2Co 4:1; Heb 12:1-3 **41:1** [q]Ps 37:7; Hab 2:20; Zep 1:7; Zec 2:13 [r]S Isa 11:11 [s]S 1Sa 2:4 [t]Isa 48:16; 57:3 [u]S Isa 1:18; 34:1; 50:8 **41:2** [v]S Ezr 1:2 [w]ver 25; Isa 13:4,17; 44:28; 45:1,13; 48:14; Jer 50:3; 51:11 [x]Isa 45:8, 13 [y]Isa 44:28; Jer 25:9 [z]S 2Sa 22:43 [a]Ps 1:4; Isa 40:24 [b]S Isa 13:18 **41:3** [c]Da 8:4 **41:4** [d]ver 9; Isa 43:7 [e]ver 26; S Ge 1:1; Isa 46:10

[k]2 Or / *whom victory meets at every step*

40:29–31 DISCIPLESHIP, Enabling Power—Disciples find God's strength in their times of weakness. Those who trust in God with expectancy find power to accomplish His purposes. Paul had that kind of faith. He boasted of his own weakness in order to experience Christ's power. See 2 Co 12:7–10. Acknowledged weakness is the first step in receiving God's enabling power. Those who feel strong in themselves do not reach out with expectancy for God's power. In our sense of weakness and need God has opportunity to strengthen us. When we receive God's strength, we soar like eagles and run like champions on God's mission. We then give God the glory for all He accomplishes through us.

40:31 SALVATION, Renewal—Compare Ex 19:4. When God renews His people, they soar like eagles. God gives the saved renewed strength, keeps them from growing weary, and prevents their fainting. Endurance is a part of salvation.

41:2–4 HISTORY, Universal—Cyrus of Persia appeared to be dominating the world. He was only answering God's call. Credit belongs to God not to temporary figures of history.

41:2 ELECTION, Other Nations—See note on 2 Ch 36:22–23.

I, the LORD—with the first of them
and with the last[f]—I am he.[g]"

5The islands[h] have seen it and fear;
the ends of the earth[i] tremble.
They approach and come forward;
6 each helps the other
and says to his brother, "Be strong![j]"
7The craftsman[k] encourages the goldsmith,[l]
and he who smooths with the hammer
spurs on him who strikes the anvil.
He says of the welding, "It is good."
He nails down the idol so it will not topple.[m]

8"But you, O Israel, my servant,[n]
Jacob, whom I have chosen,[o]
you descendants of Abraham[p] my friend,[q]
9I took you from the ends of the earth,[r]
from its farthest corners I called[s] you.
I said, 'You are my servant';[t]
I have chosen[u] you and have not rejected you.
10So do not fear,[v] for I am with you;[w]
do not be dismayed, for I am your God.
I will strengthen[x] you and help[y] you;
I will uphold you[z] with my righteous right hand.[a]

11"All who rage[b] against you
will surely be ashamed and disgraced;[c]
those who oppose[d] you
will be as nothing and perish.[e]
12Though you search for your enemies,
you will not find them.[f]
Those who wage war against you
will be as nothing[g] at all.
13For I am the LORD, your God,
who takes hold of your right hand[h]
and says to you, Do not fear;
I will help[i] you.
14Do not be afraid,[j] O worm[k] Jacob,
O little Israel,
for I myself will help[l] you," declares the LORD,
your Redeemer,[m] the Holy One[n] of Israel.
15"See, I will make you into a threshing sledge,[o]
new and sharp, with many teeth.
You will thresh the mountains[p] and crush them,
and reduce the hills to chaff.[q]
16You will winnow[r] them, the wind will pick them up,
and a gale[s] will blow them away.[t]
But you will rejoice[u] in the LORD
and glory[v] in the Holy One[w] of Israel.

17"The poor and needy search for water,[x]

41:4 [f]Isa 44:6; 48:12; Rev 1:8,17 [g]S Dt 32:39 **41:5** [h]S Isa 11:11; Eze 26:17-18 [i]S Dt 30:4; S Isa 11:12 **41:6** [j]S Jos 1:6 **41:7** [k]Isa 44:13; Jer 10:3-5 [l]S Isa 40:19 [m]S 1Sa 5:3; Isa 46:7 **41:8** [n]S Ps 136:22; S Isa 27:11 [o]S Isa 14:1 [p]S Isa 29:22; 51:2; 63:16 [q]2Ch 20:7; Jas 2:23 **41:9** [r]Isa 11:12; S 37:16 [s]S ver 4 [t]S Isa 20:3 [u]S Dt 7:6 **41:10** [v]S Ge 15:1 [w]S Dt 3:22; Jos 1:9; Isa 43:2,5; Jer 30:10; 46:27-28; Ro 8:31 [x]S Ps 68:35; S 119:28 [y]ver 13-14; Isa 44:2; 49:8; 50:7,9 [z]S Ps 18:35; S 119:117 [a]S Ex 3:20; S Job 40:14 **41:11** [b]S Isa 17:12 [c]Isa 29:22; 45:24; 54:17 [d]S Ex 23:22 [e]S Isa 29:8; S Jer 2:3 **41:12** [f]Ps 37:35-36; S Isa 34:12 [g]S Job 7:8; Isa 17:14; 29:20 **41:13** [h]Ps 73:23; Isa 42:6; 45:1; 51:18 [i]ver 10 **41:14** [j]S Ge 15:1 [k]S Job 4:19; S Ps 22:6 [l]S ver 10 [m]S Ex 15:13; S Job 19:25; S Isa 1:27 [n]ver 16, 20; S Isa 1:4

41:15 [o]S Job 41:30; S Isa 10:5; S 21:10 [p]S Ex 19:18; S Ps 107:33; Jer 9:10; Eze 33:28 [q]S ver 2 **41:16** [r]Jer 15:7; 51:2 [s]Isa 40:24 [t]Da 2:35 [u]S Isa 25:9 [v]Isa 45:25; 60:19 [w]S ver 14; S Mk 1:24 **41:17** [x]Isa 43:20

41:7,22–29 GOD, One God—Foreign idols are not gods because they cannot predict history and then cause their predictions to come true. The true God can. See note on 40:18–20,25.

41:8–16 HISTORY, National—Israel's hope rested on God's plans not on political power and strategy. Israel needed to worry about fulfilling their mission as God's servant to the nations rather than about seeking ways to gain international power and influence.

41:8–20 ELECTION, God's Servants—God gave renewed hope to His people in Exile by calling them to be His servants. The destruction of city, Temple, and throne did not mean ultimate rejection of the elect. Election is not disproved by historical crises. The faithful God continues to work to create a faithful servant people to do His will among the nations.

41:8–9 THE CHURCH, Servants—God chose His people Israel for a special purpose. See note on Ex 19:4–8. The Lord called Israel to serve Him and to proclaim His name among the nations. God promised to care for His people in the difficult time of the Exile. Punishment and discipline do not mean God has rejected us. They offer new opportunity for Him to call us to be His servants. We can answer the call because He promises to give us the strength and help we need to accomplish His mission.

41:10–13 GOD, Personal—God the transcendent Creator is intimately related to His people by His personal presence helping us through troubled times. See notes on Ex 3:12–16; Mt 18:10–14.

41:10 GOD, *Righteous*—*Note the close relationship* between the righteousness of God and His grace in helping His people. God's righteousness is sometimes expressed as opposition to evil, sometimes as help for the helpless.

41:10 REVELATION, Divine Presence—The prophets promised salvation as well as judgment. The oracle of salvation included the comforting call "do not fear." Salvation was based on God's promised presence with His people. God's presence would give exiled Israel strength to return to their land and reestablish themselves. There they would serve God.

41:10–12,14 SALVATION, Definition—See note on 1 Sa 14:6. Salvation is redemption by God the Redeemer. God is with His people in exile and suffering. He knows our fears, speaks words of comfort, and promises to help. Salvation is no bed of roses. Being saved involves struggle, suffering, and growth. The good news is that we can count on God to help us with our fears and heartaches, to deliver us from our failures, and to strengthen us in our weaknesses. We call this process sanctification.

41:14,16,20 GOD, Holy—The God whose purity and awesome character separate Him from us and our sinful world chooses to be our personal Redeemer. See note on 35:8.

41:14 SALVATION, Redemption—"Worm" here is an expression of endearment. No matter how small and insignificant we as God's people may seem or think ourselves to be, God is our Redeemer. See note on Ex 13:13–15.

41:17–20 CREATION, Redemption—The return from Exile was part of God's creation of redemption for His people. The prophet saw God's mighty work for Israel as a part of His redemptive plan for the world. In bringing back Israel from Babylon, He made a fresh start in preparing them to be His servants. His creative work included providing for every need of His people as they journeyed through the desert back to Jerusalem. His new creative acts like His first ones sought to reveal Himself to the people He created.

but there is none;
their tongues are parched with
thirst.[y]
But I the LORD will answer[z] them;
I, the God of Israel, will not
forsake[a] them.
18I will make rivers flow[b] on barren
heights,
and springs within the valleys.
I will turn the desert[c] into pools of
water,[d]
and the parched ground into
springs.[e]
19I will put in the desert[f]
the cedar and the acacia,[g] the
myrtle and the olive.
I will set pines[h] in the wasteland,
the fir and the cypress[i] together,[j]
20so that people may see and know,[k]
may consider and understand,[l]
that the hand[m] of the LORD has done
this,
that the Holy One[n] of Israel has
created[o] it.

21"Present your case,[p]" says the LORD.
"Set forth your arguments," says
Jacob's King.[q]
22"Bring in ⌊your idols⌋ to tell us
what is going to happen.[r]
Tell us what the former things[s] were,
so that we may consider them
and know their final outcome.
Or declare to us the things to come,[t]
23 tell us what the future holds,
so we may know[u] that you are gods.
Do something, whether good or bad,[v]
so that we will be dismayed[w] and
filled with fear.
24But you are less than nothing[x]
and your works are utterly
worthless;[y]
he who chooses you is detestable.[z]

25"I have stirred[a] up one from the
north,[b] and he comes—
one from the rising sun who calls on
my name.
He treads[c] on rulers as if they were
mortar,
as if he were a potter treading the
clay.
26Who told of this from the beginning,[d]
so we could know,
or beforehand, so we could say, 'He
was right'?
No one told of this,
no one foretold[e] it,
no one heard any words[f] from you.
27I was the first to tell[g] Zion, 'Look,
here they are!'
I gave to Jerusalem a messenger of
good tidings.[h]
28I look but there is no one[i]—
no one among them to give
counsel,[j]
no one to give answer[k] when I ask
them.
29See, they are all false!
Their deeds amount to nothing;[l]
their images[m] are but wind[n] and
confusion.

Chapter 42

The Servant of the LORD

"HERE is my servant,[o] whom I
uphold,

41:17 [y]S Isa 35:7 [z]S Isa 30:19 [a]S Dt 31:6; S Ps 27:9 **41:18** [b]S Isa 30:25 [c]Isa 43:19 [d]S 2Ki 3:17 [e]S Job 38:26; S Isa 35:7 **41:19** [f]S Isa 35:1; 51:3 [g]Ex 25:5,10, 13 [h]S Isa 37:24 [i]Isa 44:14 [j]Isa 60:13 **41:20** [k]S Ex 6:7 [l]S Isa 29:24 [m]Ezr 7:6; 8:31; Isa 50:2; 51:9; 59:1; 66:14; Jer 32:17 [n]S ver 14; Isa 43:3,14 [o]S Isa 4:5 **41:21** [p]S ver 1 [q]Isa 43:15; 44:6 **41:22** [r]ver 26; Isa 43:9; 44:7; 45:21; 48:14 [s]Isa 43:18,26; 46:9; 48:3 [t]Isa 42:9; 43:19; 46:10; 48:6; 65:17; Jn 13:19 **41:23** [u]Isa 45:3 [v]Jer 10:5 [w]S 2Ki 19:26 **41:24** [x]S Isa 37:19; 1Co 8:4 [y]S 1Sa 12:21; Jer 8:19; 10:5,8,15 [z]S Ps 109:7; S Isa 1:13; S 48:8 **41:25** [a]S Ezr 1:2 [b]S ver 2; Jer 50:9, 41; 51:48 [c]S 2Sa 22:43; S Isa 5:5; Na 3:14 **41:26** [d]S ver 4 [e]S ver 22; Isa 52:6 [f]S 1Ki 18:26; Hab 2:18-19 **41:27** [g]Isa 48:3,16 [h]S Isa 40:9 **41:28** [i]Ps 22:11; Isa 50:2; 59:16; 63:5; 64:7; Eze 22:30 [j]Isa 40:13-14 [k]S 1Ki 18:26; Isa 65:12; 66:4; Jer 25:4 **41:29** [l]S 1Sa 12:21 [m]S Isa 37:19 [n]Jer 5:13 **42:1** [o]S Isa 20:3; S Mt 20:28

41:21–29 HISTORY, God—God's power to predict the fortunes of history through His prophets marked Him as different from all other gods. He called on other gods to provide historical evidence of their divine power or quit claiming to be gods. Their silence proved they had no personal existence. Control of history involves prediction of history.

42:1–16 JESUS CHRIST, Servant—Servanthood is a messianic motif. These four poems of the Servant (42:1–4; 49:1–9; 50:4–11; 52:13—53:12) came from a crisis in Israel's history. The prophet looked for help from one who was obedient to God, who served the nation, and who ministered to all peoples by submission, suffering, and Spirit-filled ministry. These poems became anthems in the New Testment and gave shape to the very description and ministry of God's Messiah. In the New Testament Jesus Christ is the suffering Messiah who, by the conscious fulfillment of these songs, added a new and definitive interpretation of messiahship through suffering. Explicit and implicit references to Jesus as the Suffering Servant based on this passage include: Mt 3:17; 12:18–21; 17:5; Mk 1:11; 10:45; 14:24; Lk 3:22; 9:35; 22:37; Ac 3:13,26; 4:27,30; Php 2:7; 1 Pe 2:4. Suffering on behalf of others is the godliest act and the best way Christians can imitate Christ. Although our sufferings do not bring atonement for sins, our suffering may help to make the gospel believable as we identify with a hurting world. See note on Ac 3:13.

42:1–2 HOLY SPIRIT, Hope—Hope rests in God's action, not ours. He promised His Spirit-filled Servant to establish justice, a righteous cooperation in peace among all nations. He sent Jesus as the righteous, Suffering Servant. See Mt 3:17; notes on 12:15–21; Lk 4:14. We still await the day when all nations will recognize that Jesus is Lord. In that day the Spirit's power will provide justice for the world. See notes on Isa 11:1–2; 32:14–18.

42:1–4 REVELATION, Spirit—The purposes of God were to be most daringly fulfilled in the use of a servant in whom the presence and will of God resided. God revealed the particular way in which He would provide justice and complete His will on earth: the tender gift of a servant-leader. The servant would be an instrument of revelation because God's Spirit would direct His life. Israel refused to accept the servant role for the nation and never recognized that Messiah had to be a servant. Israel was blinded by their royal, political ambitions and did not learn to see their promised King as a suffering servant. Jesus centered His ministry and messianic understanding on the servant role, which thus became the center of biblical revelation.

42:1–9 ELECTION, God's Servants—The election of God is always to responsible service as a light to the Gentiles, eyes for the blind, and the release of captives in prison. God's election is not one of privilege but of being chosen as the servant of the Lord. See note on 41:8–20.

42:1–4 DISCIPLESHIP, Involvement—God's intention to establish justice in our world is clear. Mt 12:18–21 shows this passage refers to the Messiah. It follows that those who are indwelt by the Holy Spirit and following Christ should be about Christ's business of establishing justice. Like Jesus, we should

my chosen one[p] in whom I
delight;[q]
I will put my Spirit[r] on him
and he will bring justice[s] to the
nations.[t]
2He will not shout or cry out,[u]
or raise his voice in the streets.
3A bruised reed[v] he will not break,[w]
and a smoldering wick he will not
snuff out.[x]
In faithfulness he will bring forth
justice;[y]
4 he will not falter or be
discouraged
till he establishes justice[z] on earth.
In his law[a] the islands[b] will put
their hope."[c]

5This is what God the LORD says—
he who created the heavens[d] and
stretched them out,
who spread out the earth[e] and all
that comes out of it,[f]
who gives breath[g] to its people,
and life to those who walk on it:
6"I, the LORD, have called[h] you in
righteousness;[i]
I will take hold of your hand.[j]
I will keep[k] you and will make you
to be a covenant[l] for the people
and a light[m] for the Gentiles,[n]
7to open eyes that are blind,[o]
to free[p] captives from prison[q]
and to release from the dungeon
those who sit in darkness.[r]

42:1 [p]S Isa 14:1; Lk 9:35; 23:35; 1Pe 2:4,6 [q]Mt 3:17 [r]S Isa 11:2; S 44:3; Mt 3:16-17; S Jn 3:34 [s]S Isa 9:7 [t]S Ge 49:10 **42:2** [u]Pr 8:1-4 **42:3** [v]S Isa 36:6 [w]S Job 30:24 [x]S Job 13:25 [y]Ps 72:2; 96:13 **42:4** [z]S Isa 2:4 [a]ver 21; Ex 34:29; Isa 51:4 [b]S Isa 11:11 [c]S Ge 49:10; Mt 12:18-21* **42:5** [d]S Ge 1:6; Ps 102:25; Isa 48:13 [e]S Ge 1:1 [f]Ps 24:2; Ac 17:24 [g]S Ge 2:7; Ac 17:25 **42:6** [h]Ex 31:2; S Jdg 4:10; Isa 41:9-10; 43:1 [i]Isa 45:24; Jer 23:6; Da 9:7 [j]Isa 41:13; 45:1 [k]Isa 26:3; 27:3 [l]Isa 49:8; 54:10; 59:21; 61:8; Jer 31:31; 32:40; Mal 3:1; S Lk 22:20 [m]S Isa 9:2 [n]S Isa 26:18; S Lk 2:32 **42:7** [o]S Ps 146:8; S Isa 32:3; Mt 11:5 [p]Isa 49:9; 51:14; 52:2; Zec 2:7 [q]S Ps 66:11; S Isa 24:22; 48:20; Zec 9:11; S Lk 4:19; 2Ti 2:26; Heb 2:14-15 [r]S Ps 107:10,14; Ac 26:18 **42:8** [s]Ps 81:10; Isa 43:3,11,15; 46:9; 49:23 [t]S Ex 3:15; S 6:3 [u]Isa 48:11

8"I am the LORD;[s] that is my name![t]
I will not give my glory to another[u]
or my praise to idols.[v]
9See, the former things[w] have taken
place,
and new things I declare;
before they spring into being
I announce[x] them to you."

Song of Praise to the LORD

10Sing[y] to the LORD a new song,[z]
his praise[a] from the ends of the
earth,[b]
you who go down to the sea, and all
that is in it,[c]
you islands,[d] and all who live in
them.
11Let the desert[e] and its towns raise
their voices;
let the settlements where Kedar[f]
lives rejoice.
Let the people of Sela[g] sing for joy;
let them shout from the
mountaintops.[h]
12Let them give glory[i] to the LORD
and proclaim his praise[j] in the
islands.[k]
13The LORD will march out like a
mighty[l] man,

[v]S Ex 8:10; S 20:4 **42:9** [w]S Isa 41:22 [x]S Isa 40:21; Eze 2:4 **42:10** [y]S Ex 15:1 [z]S Ps 96:1 [a]1Ki 10:9; Isa 60:6 [b]S Dt 30:4; S Ps 48:10; 65:5; Isa 49:6 [c]S 1Ch 16:32; Ps 96:11 [d]S Isa 11:11 **42:11** [e]S Isa 32:16 [f]S Ge 25:13; Isa 60:7 [g]S Jdg 1:36 [h]Isa 52:7; Na 1:15 **42:12** [i]S 1Ch 16:24; S Isa 24:15 [j]S Ps 26:7; S 66:2; 1Pe 2:9 [k]S Isa 11:11 **42:13** [l]S Isa 9:6

not stop or become discouraged until it is established. See note on Mic 6:6–8.

42:1–4 CHRISTIAN ETHICS, Justice—God's chosen servant has one mission—to establish international justice. Jesus took up this messianic mission (Mt 12:18–21). He expects His disciples to dedicate themselves to the same ministry.

42:1–4 THE CHURCH, Servants—God defined the work of His servant. God's servant must bring justice and order to the world for all nations. The servant did not use normal means—public proclamation, political or military action—to accomplish his purposes. Rather, he quietly but faithfully worked without harming anyone or anything. The Spirit of God provides the power and motivation for the servant. The servant's task challenges all God's people in all generations. Only One has fulfilled it—Jesus of Nazareth. He continues to send the Spirit to lead His church to be God's servants.

42:5 GOD, Creator—God the Creator cares for His people, giving them the breath of life and sending His Servant to establish justice and hope for the needy. In so doing He establishes His sovereignty over all nations and gods.

42:5 CREATION, Personal Creator—God is the One who created the world. Both morality and redemption are rooted in monotheism. Only when people recognize the oneness of God are they able to comprehend His insistence on one standard of conduct and one universal kingdom of righteousness. He refuses to recognize anyone else as having a part in bringing His world into existence. Our very breath depends on Him. As personal Creator, He has the right to call us to righteous service for Him and for His world.

42:5 HUMANITY, Relationship to God—Everyone is related to God through His creative act. He has given life and breath to all *people. He, thus, has the right to call* us to His *mission.*

42:6–7 THE CHURCH, Covenant People—Isa 42:1–4; 49:1–9; 50:4–11; 52:13—53:12 have been called Servant Songs or poems. These songs describe the Lord's chosen Servant. The Servant serves the Lord in humility and faith, living righteously and helping the oppressed. The identity of the servant has been interpreted in various ways, including the nation Israel, the ideal Israel, various individuals, and the Messiah. When the Ethiopian eunuch asked Philip to explain Isa 53, Philip gave the inspired interpretation of the early church by telling about Jesus (Ac 8:30–35). The Servant's mission is described here. The Lord gave the Servant as a covenant to the people to be a light to the nations, bringing hope to those imprisoned by sin. God's people are to take up Jesus' servant role and extend His hope to all nations. To be covenant people of God is to be missionary people.

42:6–7 EVANGELISM, Involves—God called His Spirit-filled servant to bring righteousness to His world and fulfill His covenant to bless the nations (Ge 12:1–3). Jesus took the role of God's Servant and invites us also to be God's servants to bring God's light to all peoples. God calls, leads, and keeps us. We respond by involving ourselves in the world's needs and leading people to God.

42:8,17 GOD, One God—Idol worship does not pay. See notes on 40:18–20,25; 41:7,22–29.

42:10–12 EVANGELISM, Universality—All the nations of the earth are to praise the Lord for His grace. Salvation puts a "new song" in the heart of everyone who will embrace the gospel. From the top of the mountain, to the desert, to the coastland, to the end of the earth, all are to sing to the Lord because of His great salvation. The gospel is universal; it is for all.

42:13 *CHRISTIAN ETHICS, War and Peace*—God is about the business of triumphing ultimately over the powers of evil. When nations represent and practice evil, God turns from them. His purpose is to restore rest and peace to His people.

like a warrior[m] he will stir up his
zeal;[n]
with a shout[o] he will raise the battle
cry
and will triumph over his enemies.[p]

14"For a long time I have kept silent,[q]
I have been quiet and held myself
back.[r]
But now, like a woman in childbirth,
I cry out, I gasp and pant.[s]
15I will lay waste[t] the mountains[u] and
hills
and dry up all their vegetation;
I will turn rivers into islands
and dry up[v] the pools.
16I will lead[w] the blind[x] by ways they
have not known,
along unfamiliar paths I will guide
them;
I will turn the darkness into light[y]
before them
and make the rough places
smooth.[z]
These are the things I will do;
I will not forsake[a] them.
17But those who trust in idols,
who say to images, 'You are our
gods,'[b]
will be turned back in utter shame.[c]

Israel Blind and Deaf

18"Hear, you deaf;[d]
look, you blind, and see!
19Who is blind[e] but my servant,[f]
and deaf like the messenger[g] I
send?
Who is blind like the one committed[h]
to me,
blind like the servant of the LORD?
20You have seen many things, but have
paid no attention;
your ears are open, but you hear
nothing."[i]
21It pleased the LORD
for the sake[j] of his righteousness
to make his law[k] great and glorious.
22But this is a people plundered[l] and
looted,
all of them trapped in pits[m]
or hidden away in prisons.[n]
They have become plunder,
with no one to rescue them;[o]
they have been made loot,
with no one to say, "Send them
back."

23Which of you will listen to this
or pay close attention[p] in time to
come?
24Who handed Jacob over to become
loot,
and Israel to the plunderers?[q]
Was it not the LORD,[r]
against whom we have sinned?
For they would not follow[s] his ways;
they did not obey his law.[t]
25So he poured out on them his burning
anger,[u]
the violence of war.
It enveloped them in flames,[v] yet they
did not understand;[w]
it consumed them, but they did not
take it to heart.[x]

Chapter 43

Israel's Only Savior

BUT now, this is what the LORD
says—
he who created[y] you, O Jacob,
he who formed[z] you, O Israel:[a]

42:13 [m]S Ex 14:14 [n]S Isa 26:11 [o]S Jos 6:5; Jer 25:30; Hos 11:10; Joel 3:16; Am 1:2; 3:4,8 [p]Isa 66:14 **42:14** [q]S Est 4:14; S Ps 50:21 [r]S Ge 43:31; Lk 18:7; 2Pe 3:9 [s]Jer 4:31 **42:15** [t]Eze 38:20 [u]S Ps 107:33 [v]S Isa 11:15; 50:2; Na 1:4-6 **42:16** [w]S Isa 29:24; 40:11; 57:18; 58:11; Jer 31:8-9; Lk 1:78-79 [x]S Isa 32:3 [y]S Ps 18:28; Isa 58:8,10; S Ac 26:18 [z]S Isa 26:7; Lk 3:5 [a]S Dt 4:31; Heb 13:5 **42:17** [b]S Ex 32:4 [c]S Ps 97:7; S Isa 1:29 **42:18** [d]S Isa 35:5 **42:19** [e]Isa 43:8; Eze 12:2 [f]Isa 41:8-9 [g]Isa 44:26; Hag 1:13 [h]Isa 26:3 **42:20** [i]Isa 6:9-10; 43:8; Jer 5:21; 6:10 **42:21** [j]Isa 43:25 [k]S ver 4; 2Co 3:7 **42:22** [l]S Jdg 6:4; S 2Ki 24:13 [m]S Isa 24:18 [n]S Ps 66:11; S Isa 24:22 [o]S Isa 5:29 **42:23** [p]Dt 32:29; Ps 81:13; Isa 47:7; 48:18; 57:11 **42:24** [q]S 2Ki 17:6; Isa 43:28; 47:6 [r]Isa 10:5-6 [s]S Isa 30:15 [t]S Jos 1:7; S Ps 119:136; Isa 5:24; Jer 44:10 **42:25** [u]S 2Ki 22:13; S Job 40:11; S Isa 51:17; S Eze 7:19 [v]2Ki 25:9; Isa 66:15; Jer 4:4; 21:12; La 2:3; Na 1:6 [w]S Isa 1:3 [x]Isa 29:13; 47:7; 57:1,11; Hos 7:9 **43:1** [y]S Isa 27:11 [z]S ver 7; S Ge 2:7 [a]Ge 32:28; Isa 44:21

See note on 2 Sa 7:1,11.
42:18–20 SIN, Blindness—The people would not answer the call to repent. They would not be the servant of Yahweh as He called them to be. Ignoring God long enough leads to spiritual blindness and deafness. Then the Word of God makes no impact. Exile from God is the ultimate destiny for the spiritually blind.
42:18–22 THE CHURCH, Servants—Israel, called to provide light and sight to the nations (41:8–9; 42:1,6–7), was blind to its mission. Most of the people of the nation lacked insight into the purpose of God. The real danger for believers is that the church may neglect its mission to go into all the world with the good news of Jesus Christ. To miss the work of being servants is to miss the meaning of being the church.
42:24 GOD, Sovereignty—Foreign powers and gods may claim power over God's people. In reality God gave them the power because His people sinned.
42:24 SIN, Against God—"How do you explain the miserable destiny of our history?" Israel asked. "Your sin provides the answer," the prophet answered. Breaking a law here, not doing God's will there is sin. It is not an unimportant moral mistake. It is unbelief in God, distrust in His goodness, and doubt of His will or power to punish. The result of sin is divine anger. See note on 1:20.
43:1–21 GOD, Creator—God's work as Creator involved creating a special people for Himself through the Exodus from Egypt (see Ex 3—15). His creative and redemptive work is done to lead people to recognize and praise His glory. Despite stories told among the Babylonians and other peoples, only the God of Israel ever created anything. As sole Creator, God is our only hope for redemption and the only claimant to rule the world eternally.
43:1–7 GOD, Father—God the sovereign Creator acts for the special people He created with the love of a father. God's love is the only reason God's people can ever experience salvation. See notes on Dt 8:1–5; 14:1–29; Mt 5:43–48.
43:1–7 CREATION, Confidence—Forming an obedient people was and is an essential part of God's creation. Since He had created the nation and redeemed them from Babylon, He would continue to protect them. Israel could face the future in their own land once more with confidence, knowing that they could cope with new situations, including enemies that threatened their existence. The confident people of God give glory and praise to their Creator.
43:1–7 HISTORY, National—God promised a new Exodus for His people. See note on 11:10–16. This showed His love for His people and His presence with them.
43:1–13 ELECTION, Love—God initiated a new Exodus for the Exiles in Babylon, showing His continued love for His elect remnant. In love God creates, redeems, protects, and

"Fear not, for I have redeemed[b] you;
I have summoned you by name;[c]
you are mine.[d]
2When you pass through the waters,[e]
I will be with you;[f]
and when you pass through the rivers,
they will not sweep over you.
When you walk through the fire,[g]
you will not be burned;
the flames will not set you ablaze.[h]
3For I am the LORD, your God,[i]
the Holy One[j] of Israel, your Savior;[k]
I give Egypt[l] for your ransom,
Cush[l][m] and Seba[n] in your stead.[o]
4Since you are precious and honored[p] in my sight,
and because I love[q] you,
I will give men in exchange for you,
and people in exchange for your life.
5Do not be afraid,[r] for I am with you;[s]
I will bring your children[t] from the east
and gather[u] you from the west.[v]
6I will say to the north, 'Give them up!'
and to the south,[w] 'Do not hold them back.'
Bring my sons from afar
and my daughters[x] from the ends of the earth[y]—
7everyone who is called by my name,[z]
whom I created[a] for my glory,[b]
whom I formed and made.[c]"

8Lead out those who have eyes but are blind,[d]
who have ears but are deaf.[e]
9All the nations gather together[f]
and the peoples assemble.
Which of them foretold[g] this
and proclaimed to us the former things?
Let them bring in their witnesses to prove they were right,
so that others may hear and say, "It is true."
10"You are my witnesses,[h]" declares the LORD,
"and my servant[i] whom I have chosen,
so that you may know[j] and believe me
and understand that I am he.
Before me no god[k] was formed,
nor will there be one after me.[l]
11I, even I, am the LORD,[m]
and apart from me there is no savior.[n]
12I have revealed and saved and proclaimed—
I, and not some foreign god[o] among you.
You are my witnesses,[p]" declares the LORD, "that I am God.
13 Yes, and from ancient days[q] I am he.[r]
No one can deliver out of my hand.
When I act, who can reverse it?"[s]

God's Mercy and Israel's Unfaithfulness

14This is what the LORD says—
your Redeemer,[t] the Holy One[u] of Israel:
"For your sake I will send to Babylon
and bring down as fugitives[v] all the Babylonians,[m][w]
in the ships in which they took pride.

43:1 [b]S Ex 6:6; S Job 19:25 [c]S Isa 42:6; 45:3-4; 49:1 [d]S Dt 7:6; Mal 3:17 **43:2** [e]S Isa 8:7 [f]S Ge 26:3; S Ex 14:22 [g]Isa 29:6; 30:27 [h]Ps 66:12; Da 3:25-27 **43:3** [i]S Ex 20:2 [j]S Isa 41:20 [k]S Ex 14:30; S Jdg 2:18; S Ps 3:8; S Isa 25:9 [l]S Ps 68:31; Isa 19:1; Eze 29:20 [m]S Isa 20:3 [n]S Ge 10:7 [o]S Pr 21:18 **43:4** [p]Ex 19:5; Isa 49:5 [q]Isa 63:9; Rev 3:9 **43:5** [r]S Ge 15:1; Isa 44:2 [s]S Ge 21:22; S Ex 14:22; Jer 30:10-11 [t]Isa 41:8; 54:3; 61:9; 66:22 [u]S Isa 11:12; S 49:18 [v]S Isa 24:14; Zec 8:7; S Mt 8:11 **43:6** [w]Ps 107:3 [x]Isa 60:4; Eze 16:61; 2Co 6:18 [y]S Dt 30:4; S Isa 11:12; Jer 23:8; Eze 36:24 **43:7** [z]Isa 48:1; 56:5; 62:2; 63:19; 65:1; Jer 15:16; Jas 2:7 [a]S Isa 27:11 [b]S Ps 86:9 [c]ver 1, 21; Ps 100:3; Eph 2:10; S Isa 19:25 **43:8** [d]S Isa 6:9-10 [e]S Isa 42:20; Eze 12:2 **43:9** [f]S Isa 41:1; 45:20; 48:14 [g]S Isa 41:26 **43:10** [h]ver 12; S Jos 24:22 [i]S Isa 20:3; 41:8-9 [j]S Ex 6:7 [k]ver 11; S Ps 86:10; Isa 19:21; 44:6,8; 45:5-6,14 [l]S Dt 4:35; S 32:39; Jer 14:22 **43:11** [m]S Ex 6:2; S Isa 42:8 [n]S ver 10; S Ps 3:8; S 18:31; S Isa 25:9; 64:4 **43:12** [o]S Dt 32:12 [p]S ver 10 **43:13** [q]Ps 90:2 [r]S Dt 32:39; Isa 46:4; 48:12 [s]S Nu 23:8; S Job 9:12 **43:14** [t]S Ex 15:13; S Job 19:25 [u]S Isa 1:4; S 41:20 [v]Isa 13:14-15 [w]S Isa 23:13

[l]*3* That is, the upper Nile region [m]*14* Or *Chaldeans*

forgives His elect people. Response to such love should come in witnessing to others as God's chosen servant. See note on 42:1–9.

43:2 EVIL AND SUFFERING, God's Present Help—God would preserve Israel through fiery experiences such as the Exile. Similarly, He guides us through the trials of this life to find rest with Him. The poetic quality of this passage must be appreciated. God is not guaranteeing here that a believer is immune to the pain caused by fire. Compare Ps 66:12.

43:3,14,15 GOD, Holy—See note on 41:14,16,20.

43:10–15 GOD, One God—God's creation and His historical acts of salvation show He alone is God.

43:10 SALVATION, Belief—God chose Israel to believe in Him and to bear witness that others might believe in Him as the one true God. That call and mission is extended to Christians also (Ac 1:8).

43:10 THE CHURCH, Servants—"Witnesses" and "servants" are parallel in usage. Servants and witnesses tell others that the Lord alone is God. They learn this great truth and other truths from God. Servants of God proclaim to all the world that only the Lord can forgive sin and restore lives. God's servant people must witness to *what God has done for us* so the *world's multitudes* may be delivered from serving gods that are not God. See notes on 41:8–9; 42:1–4; 42:18–22.

43:10–13 EVANGELISM, Personal—Witnesses declare what God has done. Effective witnesses need to be knowledgeable of the mighty acts of God in history—and in the contemporary moment also. This requires study and sensitivity to all God has revealed in His Word, in history, and in one's daily life. Witnesses take up the role of God's servant. See note on 42:6–7. Witnesses believe in, obey, and worship God. They share what they have experienced with all who do not know God. They want everyone in the world to let the true God be their Savior and to commit their lives to Him. Witnessing is the believer's essential task.

43:14–21 CREATION, Progressive—God's creative work never ends. He constantly works to create a people. See note on vv 1–7. As holy King, He is morally perfect and absolute ruler. He will not let His people totally perish. He will destroy enemies and renew His disciplined people. The Creator God is not a figure of the past who has become senile and forgetful. He is the Creator bringing new redemption to His people. Because God is holy, He cannot overlook iniquity. Because He is a God of redemption, He forgives and restores His people. He is constantly creating new things for His people so we can serve Him and bring His purposes to pass in the world.

15I am the LORD,[x] your Holy One,
Israel's Creator,[y] your King.[z]"

16This is what the LORD says—
he who made a way through the sea,
a path through the mighty waters,[a]
17who drew out[b] the chariots and
horses,[c]
the army and reinforcements
together,[d]
and they lay[e] there, never to rise
again,
extinguished, snuffed out like a
wick:[f]
18"Forget the former things;[g]
do not dwell on the past.
19See, I am doing a new thing![h]
Now it springs up; do you not
perceive it?
I am making a way in the desert[i]
and streams in the wasteland.[j]
20The wild animals[k] honor me,
the jackals[l] and the owls,
because I provide water[m] in the desert
and streams in the wasteland,
to give drink to my people, my chosen,
21 the people I formed[n] for myself[o]
that they may proclaim my praise.[p]

22"Yet you have not called upon me,
O Jacob,
you have not wearied[q] yourselves
for me, O Israel.[r]
23You have not brought me sheep for
burnt offerings,[s]
nor honored[t] me with your
sacrifices.[u]
I have not burdened[v] you with grain
offerings
nor wearied you with demands[w] for
incense.[x]
24You have not bought any fragrant
calamus[y] for me,
or lavished on me the fat[z] of your
sacrifices.
But you have burdened me with your
sins
and wearied[a] me with your
offenses.[b]

25"I, even I, am he who blots out
your transgressions,[c] for my own
sake,[d]
and remembers your sins[e] no
more.[f]
26Review the past for me,
let us argue the matter together;[g]
state the case[h] for your innocence.
27Your first father[i] sinned;
your spokesmen[j] rebelled[k] against
me.
28So I will disgrace the dignitaries of
your temple,
and I will consign Jacob to
destruction[n] [l]
and Israel to scorn.[m]

Chapter 44

Israel the Chosen

"BUT now listen, O Jacob, my
servant,[n]
Israel, whom I have chosen.[o]
2This is what the LORD says—
he who made[p] you, who formed
you in the womb,[q]
and who will help[r] you:
Do not be afraid,[s] O Jacob, my
servant,[t]
Jeshurun,[u] whom I have chosen.
3For I will pour water[v] on the thirsty
land,
and streams on the dry ground;[w]
I will pour out my Spirit[x] on your
offspring,
and my blessing[y] on your
descendants.[z]
4They will spring up like grass[a] in a
meadow,
like poplar trees[b] by flowing
streams.[c]
5One will say, 'I belong[d] to the LORD';

43:15 [x]S Isa 42:8 [y]S Isa 27:11; 45:11 [z]S Isa 41:21 **43:16** [a]S Ex 14:29; S 15:8; S Isa 11:15 **43:17** [b]Ps 118:12; Isa 1:31 [c]S Ex 14:22 [d]S Ex 14:9 [e]Ps 76:5-6 [f]S Job 13:25; Jer 51:21; Eze 38:4 **43:18** [g]S Isa 41:22 **43:19** [h]S Isa 41:22; Jer 16:14-15; 23:7-8; 2Co 5:17; Rev 21:5 [i]S Isa 40:3 [j]S Ps 126:4; S Isa 33:21; S 35:7 **43:20** [k]S Ps 148:10 [l]S Isa 13:22 [m]S Nu 20:8 **43:21** [n]S ver 7; S Ge 2:7 [o]Mal 3:17 [p]S Ps 66:2; 102:18; 1Pe 2:9 **43:22** [q]S Jos 22:5; S Isa 1:14 [r]Isa 30:11 **43:23** [s]S Ex 29:41 [t]Zec 7:5-6; Mal 1:6-8 [u]Am 5:25 [v]Mic 6:3; Mal 1:12-13 [w]Jer 7:22 [x]Ex 30:35; S Lev 2:1 **43:24** [y]S Ex 30:23 [z]Lev 3:9 [a]S Isa 1:14; S 7:13; S Jer 8:21 [b]Jer 44:22; Mal 2:17 **43:25** [c]S 2Sa 12:13; S 2Ch 6:21; Mk 2:7; Lk 5:21; Ac 3:19 [d]S Isa 37:35; S Eze 20:44 [e]Isa 64:9; Mic 7:18 [f]S Job 7:21; S Isa 38:17 **43:26** [g]S Isa 1:18 [h]S Isa 41:1; 49:25; 50:8 **43:27** [i]S Ge 12:18 [j]Isa 9:15; 28:7; Jer 5:31 [k]S Isa 24:20; S 48:8 **43:28** [l]S Nu 5:27; S Dt 13:15; S Isa 42:24; S Zec 5:3 [m]S Ps 39:8; Jer 24:9; Eze 5:15 **44:1** [n]ver 21 [o]S Ge 16:11; S Isa 14:1 **44:2** [p]ver 21; S Ps 149:2 [q]S Ge 2:7; S Ps 139:13; S Isa 27:11 [r]S Isa 41:10 [s]S Isa 43:5 [t]Jer 30:10; 46:27 [u]S Nu 23:21; S Dt 32:15 **44:3** [v]Joel 3:18; Jn 4:10 [w]S Pr 9:5; S Isa 32:2; S 35:7 [x]S Isa 11:2; Eze 36:27; S Mk 1:8; S Ac 2:17 [y]Mal 3:10 [z]Isa 61:9; 65:23 **44:4** [a]S Job 5:25; S Ps 72:16 [b]S Lev 23:40 [c]S Job 40:22 **44:5** [d]Ps 116:16; Isa 19:21; Jer 50:5

[n]*28* The Hebrew term refers to the irrevocable giving over of things or persons to the LORD, often by totally destroying them.

43:22–24 SIN, Transgression—God does not promise to bear unrepentant sin and neglect. He will not do slave labor for us, bearing our burdens and wearying Himself with our problems when we do nothing for Him. He is Master. We are servants. He provides all He has promised when we do our part for Him. To expect God to forgive our sins when we do not serve Him is sin.

43:25 GOD, Grace—Israel suffered exile because they sinned. They did nothing to deserve deliverance from exile. God in His grace to accomplish His purposes and plans chooses to forgive sins and save His people.

44:1–4 HOLY SPIRIT, Hope—Renewal will come to God's people. Israel tried to make God the servant rather than the Master (43:24), letting Him carry their burdens. The result was the Exile of 586 BC. Judgment was not God's final word. He wanted to restore proper relationships with His servant, Israel. He wanted to renew the people as water renews parched earth. Renewal for humans comes through God's Spirit. God's Spirit makes us proud of our identity as God's people.

44:1–8 ELECTION, Israel—Israel's God is King and Redeemer. He promised never to forget He had chosen Israel for service. Israel experienced the deep meaning of election in their experiences in Egyptian slavery and Babylonian captivity.

44:1 THE CHURCH, Servants—See note on 43:10.

44:2,21,24 GOD, Creator—See note on 43:1–21.

44:5 SALVATION, Confession—This is a missionary text. Our salvation is never mature until we begin to see others confess the Lord and become part of His community. These outsiders confessed that they belonged to the covenant Lord and to the community of Israel.

another will call himself by the
name of Jacob;
still another will write on his hand,[e]
'The LORD's,'[f]
and will take the name Israel.

The LORD, Not Idols

6"This is what the LORD says—
Israel's King[g] and Redeemer,[h] the
LORD Almighty:
I am the first and I am the last;[i]
apart from me there is no God.[j]
7Who then is like me?[k] Let him
proclaim it.
Let him declare and lay out before
me
what has happened since I established
my ancient people,
and what is yet to come—
yes, let him foretell[l] what will
come.
8Do not tremble, do not be afraid.
Did I not proclaim[m] this and foretell
it long ago?
You are my witnesses. Is there any
God[n] besides me?
No, there is no other Rock;[o] I know
not one."

9All who make idols[p] are nothing,
and the things they treasure are
worthless.[q]
Those who would speak up for them
are blind;[r]
they are ignorant, to their own
shame.[s]
10Who shapes a god and casts an idol,[t]
which can profit him nothing?[u]
11He and his kind will be put to
shame;[v]
craftsmen are nothing but men.
Let them all come together and take
their stand;
they will be brought down to terror
and infamy.[w]

12The blacksmith[x] takes a tool
and works with it in the coals;
he shapes an idol with hammers,
he forges it with the might of his
arm.[y]
He gets hungry and loses his strength;
he drinks no water and grows
faint.[z]
13The carpenter[a] measures with a line
and makes an outline with a marker;
he roughs it out with chisels
and marks it with compasses.
He shapes it in the form of man,[b]
of man in all his glory,
that it may dwell in a shrine.[c]
14He cut down cedars,
or perhaps took a cypress or oak.
He let it grow among the trees of the
forest,
or planted a pine,[d] and the rain
made it grow.
15It is man's fuel[e] for burning;
some of it he takes and warms
himself,
he kindles a fire and bakes bread.
But he also fashions a god and
worships[f] it;
he makes an idol and bows[g] down
to it.
16Half of the wood he burns in the fire;
over it he prepares his meal,
he roasts his meat and eats his fill.
He also warms himself and says,
"Ah! I am warm; I see the fire.[h]"
17From the rest he makes a god, his idol;
he bows down to it and worships.[i]
He prays[j] to it and says,
"Save[k] me; you are my god."
18They know nothing, they understand[l]
nothing;
their eyes[m] are plastered over so
they cannot see,
and their minds closed so they
cannot understand.
19No one stops to think,
no one has the knowledge or
understanding[n] to say,
"Half of it I used for fuel;[o]
I even baked bread over its coals,
I roasted meat and I ate.
Shall I make a detestable[p] thing from
what is left?
Shall I bow down to a block of
wood?"[q]
20He feeds on ashes,[r] a deluded[s] heart
misleads him;
he cannot save himself, or say,
"Is not this thing in my right hand a
lie?[t] [u]"

21"Remember[v] these things, O Jacob,
for you are my servant, O Israel.[w]
I have made you, you are my servant;[x]
O Israel, I will not forget you.[y]
22I have swept away[z] your offenses like
a cloud,

44:5 [e]Ex 13:9 [f]Isa 60:3; 66:23; Zec 8:20-22; 13:9; 14:16
44:6 [g]S Isa 41:21 [h]S Job 19:25; Isa 43:1 [i]S Isa 41:4; Rev 1:8,17 [j]S Dt 6:4; S 1Ch 17:20; S Ps 18:31; S Isa 43:10
44:7 [k]S Dt 32:39 [l]S Isa 41:22,26
44:8 [m]S Isa 40:21; S 42:9 [n]S Isa 43:10 [o]S Ge 49:24
44:9 [p]S Ex 20:4; S Lev 19:4; Isa 40:19 [q]S Isa 41:24 [r]S Isa 26:11 [s]S Isa 1:29; 65:13; 66:5; Jer 22:22
44:10 [t]S Isa 40:19 [u]Isa 41:29; Jer 10:5; Ac 19:26
44:11 [v]S ver 9; S Isa 1:29 [w]S 2Ki 19:18; S Isa 37:19
44:12 [x]S Isa 40:19; 41:6-7; 54:16 [y]Ac 17:29 [z]Isa 40:28
44:13 [a]S Isa 41:7 [b]Ps 115:4-7 [c]S Jdg 17:4-5
44:14 [d]S Isa 41:19
44:15 [e]ver 19 [f]S Ex 20:5; Rev 9:20 [g]S 2Ch 25:14
44:16 [h]Isa 47:14
44:17 [i]S Ex 20:5; Isa 2:8; Jer 1:16 [j]S 1Ki 18:26 [k]S Jdg 10:14; Isa 45:20; 46:7; 47:15
44:18 [l]Isa 1:3; S 16:12; Jer 4:22; 10:8,14,14-15 [m]S Isa 6:9-10; S 29:10
44:19 [n]ver 18-19; Isa 5:13; 27:11; 45:20 [o]ver 15 [p]S Dt 27:15 [q]Isa 40:20
44:20 [r]Ps 102:9 [s]S Job 15:31; Ro 1:21-23,28; 2Th 2:11; 2Ti 3:13 [t]S Dt 4:28; Hos 10:5; 13:2 [u]Isa 59:3,4,13; Jer 9:3; 10:14; 51:17; Ro 1:25
44:21 [v]Isa 46:8; Zec 10:9 [w]S Isa 43:1 [x]S Ps 136:22; S Isa 27:11 [y]Ps 27:10; Isa 49:15; Jer 31:20
44:22 [z]S 2Sa 12:13; S 2Ch 6:21; Ac 3:19

44:6–28 GOD, One God—The eternal existence of God—without beginning or ending—supports His claim to be the only God. Worship of idols goes against all logic. See notes on 40:18–20,25; 41:7,22–29.

44:8 EVANGELISM, Personal—The witness has one essential message: *God is. There is no other god. He is the only ultimate Reality. He, therefore, is the Rock upon which to build* one's life. He is the Foundation for all that is meaningful. Witnesses are to share that truth with all who will hear.

44:21 THE CHURCH, Servants—A servant must be loyal to his master. God is loyal to His servants. He will neither forget nor forsake us. He forgives our sins, calls us to repent and turn back to Him, and redeems us. Certainly we need to remember and testify to what He has done for us. See notes on 41:8–9; 43:10; Ps 27:9.

44:22 SALVATION, Forgiveness—Forgiveness of sin is so certain a reality that it is here represented as prior to repentance. The experience of salvation is that God has been seeking

your sins like the morning mist.
Return[a] to me,
for I have redeemed[b] you."

23 Sing for joy,[c] O heavens, for the LORD
has done this;
shout aloud, O earth[d] beneath.
Burst into song, you mountains,[e]
you forests and all your trees,[f]
for the LORD has redeemed[g] Jacob,
he displays his glory[h] in Israel.

Jerusalem to Be Inhabited

24 "This is what the LORD says—
your Redeemer,[i] who formed[j] you
in the womb:[k]

I am the LORD,
who has made all things,
who alone stretched out the heavens,[l]
who spread out the earth[m] by myself,
25 who foils[n] the signs of false prophets
and makes fools of diviners,[o]
who overthrows the learning of the
wise[p]
and turns it into nonsense,[q]
26 who carries out the words[r] of his
servants
and fulfills[s] the predictions of his
messengers,

who says of Jerusalem,[t] 'It shall be
inhabited,'
of the towns of Judah, 'They shall be
built,'
and of their ruins,[u] 'I will restore
them,'[v]
27 who says to the watery deep, 'Be dry,
and I will dry up[w] your streams,'
28 who says of Cyrus,[x] 'He is my
shepherd
and will accomplish all that I please;
he will say of Jerusalem,[y] "Let it be
rebuilt,"
and of the temple,[z] "Let its
foundations[a] be laid." '

Chapter 45

"THIS is what the LORD says to his
anointed,[b]
to Cyrus,[c] whose right hand I take
hold[d] of
to subdue nations[e] before him
and to strip kings of their armor,
to open doors before him
so that gates will not be shut:
2 I will go before you[f]
and will level[g] the mountains°;
I will break down gates[h] of bronze
and cut through bars of iron.[i]
3 I will give you the treasures[j] of
darkness,
riches stored in secret places,[k]
so that you may know[l] that I am the
LORD,
the God of Israel, who summons you
by name.[m]
4 For the sake of Jacob my servant,[n]
of Israel my chosen,
I summon you by name
and bestow on you a title of honor,
though you do not acknowledge[o]
me.
5 I am the LORD, and there is no other;[p]
apart from me there is no God.[q]
I will strengthen you,[r]
though you have not acknowledged
me,
6 so that from the rising of the sun

44:22 [a]S Job 22:23; Isa 45:22; 55:7; Jer 36:3; Mal 3:7 [b]S Isa 33:24; S Mt 20:28; 1Co 6:20 **44:23** [c]S Ps 98:4; S Isa 12:6 [d]S 1Ch 16:31; Ps 148:7 [e]S Ps 98:8 [f]S Ps 65:13 [g]S Ex 6:6; Isa 51:11; 62:12 [h]S Ex 16:7; S Lev 10:3; S Isa 4:2; 43:7; 46:13; 49:3; 52:1; 55:5; 60:9,21; 61:3; Jer 30:19 **44:24** [i]S Job 19:25; Isa 43:14 [j]S Isa 27:11 [k]S Ps 139:13 [l]S Ge 2:1; S Isa 42:5 [m]S Ge 1:1 **44:25** [n]Ps 33:10 [o]Lev 19:26; 1Sa 6:2; Isa 2:6; 8:19; 47:13; Jer 27:9; Da 2:2,10; 4:7; Mic 3:7; Zec 10:2 [p]S Job 5:13; 1Co 1:27 [q]2Sa 15:31; 1Co 1:19-20 **44:26** [r]Isa 59:21; Zec 1:6 [s]Isa 46:10; 55:11; Jer 23:20; 39:16; La 2:17; Da 9:12; S Mt 5:18 [t]S Isa 1:1 [u]S Ps 74:3; S Isa 51:3 [v]S Ezr 9:9; S Ps 51:18; Isa 49:8-21; S 61:4 **44:27** [w]S Isa 11:15; S 19:5; Rev 16:12 **44:28** [x]S 2Ch 36:22; S Isa 41:2 [y]S Isa 14:32 [z]Ezr 1:2-4 [a]S Isa 28:16; 58:12 **45:1** [b]S Ps 45:7 [c]S 2Ch 36:22; S Isa 41:2 [d]Ps 73:23; Isa 41:13; 42:6 [e]Isa 48:14; Jer 50:35; 51:20, 24; Mic 4:13 **45:2** [f]Ex 23:20 [g]S Isa 40:4 [h]S Isa 13:2 [i]Ps 107:16; 147:13; Jer 51:30; La 2:9; Na 3:13 **45:3** [j]S 2Ki 24:13; Jer 50:37; 51:13 [k]Jer 41:8 [l]Isa 41:23 [m]S Ex 33:12; S Isa 43:1 **45:4** [n]S Isa 14:1; 41:8-9 [o]Ac 17:23 **45:5** [p]S Isa 44:8 [q]S Dt 32:12; S Ps 18:31; S Isa 43:10 [r]S Ps 18:39; Eze 30:24-25

°*2* Dead Sea Scrolls and Septuagint; the meaning of the word in the Masoretic Text is uncertain.

---

after us long before we ever sought Him. Our sins hang over us like a cloud or a morning mist, but God, like the rising sun, quickly and quietly sweeps them away. God has already accomplished the work of redemption. He calls all people to appropriate that redemption for their own lives. See Guide to Accepting Christ (pp. 1745–1747).

44:23 WORSHIP, Praise—See note on Ex 15:1–21.

44:24–28 REVELATION, Messengers—God not only sends His message, He confuses the false messages, and is faithful to carry out His messenger's revelation about His will. Israel often doubted God's word and believed false prophets because the fulfillment of the true prophecy was delayed. God has His own timing. We do not know when He will fulfill His prophetic revelations. We can be sure He will fulfill them.

45:1–3,11–13 GOD, Sovereignty—God controls His world so completely He could even work through Cyrus, a foreign king, to accomplish His purposes. All His work in our world is done to introduce Himself and His sovereign rule to all peoples.

45:1–7 HISTORY, Universal—See note on 41:2–4. In His mysterious way God uses unbelieving rulers without their knowledge to bring about His purposes for His people.

45:4,12 ELECTION, Other Nations—Even a Gentile king could be chosen of God to bring blessings to those who enjoy God's election. See note on 2 Ch 36:22–23.

45:4 THE CHURCH, Servants—Cyrus, king of Persia, served God although he did not know God. God used Cyrus to bring the people of Israel out of the Exile in Babylon. God works on behalf of those who serve Him. He does not forget His people. See note on 44:21.

45:5,14–24 GOD, One God—As the only God, Yahweh, the God of Israel, can use people who do not recognize His sovereign lordship to accomplish His purposes. As the only God, He is responsible for all that occurs in His world, both good and bad from human perspective. He works in everything to accomplish His purposes. As the only God, He is the only hope for salvation for all people.

45:5–13 CREATION, Sovereignty—God's calling of Cyrus, a nonbeliever, to deliver His people was an act of both grace and sovereignty. It demonstrated God's claim to be the one, universal God. All things, whether seen from our perspective as good or bad, were created by God to serve His purpose. He alone determines if acts are justified. People do not have the right to quarrel with the One who brought them into existence. Since God created the world and all that is in it, He has the wisdom to choose His servants and accomplish His purposes. He is working to create righteousness, a just world order.

to the place of its setting[s]
men may know[t] there is none besides
me.[u]
I am the LORD, and there is no
other.
7I form the light and create darkness,[v]
I bring prosperity and create
disaster;[w]
I, the LORD, do all these things.

8"You heavens above, rain[x] down
righteousness;[y]
let the clouds shower it down.
Let the earth open wide,
let salvation[z] spring up,
let righteousness grow with it;
I, the LORD, have created it.

9"Woe to him who quarrels[a] with his
Maker,[b]
to him who is but a potsherd[c]
among the potsherds on the
ground.
Does the clay say to the potter,[d]
'What are you making?'[e]
Does your work say,
'He has no hands'?[f]
10Woe to him who says to his father,
'What have you begotten?'
or to his mother,
'What have you brought to birth?'

11"This is what the LORD says—
the Holy One[g] of Israel, and its
Maker:[h]
Concerning things to come,
do you question me about my
children,
or give me orders about the work of
my hands?[i]
12It is I who made the earth[j]
and created mankind upon it.
My own hands stretched out the
heavens;[k]
I marshaled their starry hosts.[l]
13I will raise up Cyrus[p] [m] in my
righteousness:
I will make all his ways straight.[n]
He will rebuild my city[o]
and set my exiles free,
but not for a price or reward,[p]
says the LORD Almighty."

14This is what the LORD says:

"The products[q] of Egypt and the
merchandise of Cush,[q]
and those tall Sabeans[r]—
they will come over to you[s]
and will be yours;
they will trudge behind you,[t]
coming over to you in chains.[u]
They will bow down before you
and plead[v] with you, saying,
'Surely God is with you,[w] and there is
no other;
there is no other god.[x]' "

15Truly you are a God who hides[y]
himself,
O God and Savior[z] of Israel.

45:6 [s]S Ps 113:3; Isa 43:5 [t]S Isa 11:9 [u]ver 5,18; Isa 14:13-14; 47:8, 10; Zep 2:15 **45:7** [v]S Ge 1:4; S Ex 10:22 [w]S Isa 14:15; S 31:2; La 3:38 **45:8** [x]Ps 72:6; S 133:3; Joel 3:18 [y]ver 24; Ps 85:11; S Isa 41:2; 46:13; 48:18; 60:21; 61:10,11; 62:1; Hos 10:12; Joel 2:23; Am 5:24; Mal 4:2 [z]S Ps 85:9; Isa 12:3 **45:9** [a]S Job 12:13; S 15:25; S 27:2; 1Co 10:22 [b]S Job 33:13 [c]Ps 22:15 [d]S Isa 29:16; Ro 9:20-21* [e]S Job 9:12; Da 4:35 [f]S Isa 10:15 **45:11** [g]S Isa 1:4 [h]S Ps 149:2; S Isa 51:13 [i]S Ps 8:6; S Isa 19:25 **45:12** [j]S Ge 1:1 [k]S Ge 2:1; S Isa 48:13 [l]S Ne 9:6; S Job 38:32 **45:13** [m]S 2Ch 36:22; S Isa 41:2 [n]S 1Ki 8:36; S Ps 26:12; S Isa 40:4 [o]S Ezr 1:2 [p]Isa 52:3 **45:14** [q]2Sa 8:2; Isa 18:7; 60:5 [r]S Isa 2:3; 60:11; 62:2; Zec 8:20-22 [s]S Isa 2:3 [t]S Ge 27:29 [u]S 2Sa 3:34; S Isa 14:1-2 [v]Jer 16:19; Zec 8:20-23 [w]1Co 14:25 [x]S Ps 18:31; S Isa 11:9; S 43:10 **45:15** [y]S Dt 31:17; Ps 44:24; S Isa 1:15 [z]S Isa 25:9

[p] *13* Hebrew *him* [q] *14* That is, the upper Nile region

45:6 EVANGELISM, Universality—See note on 42:10–12.

45:7–9,11–12,18 GOD, Creator—God creates the world and the events of human history. Here we stand in the mystery of divine sovereignty and human freedom. Free human choices lead to historical consequences such as Cyrus of Persia dominating the world. Even when enemy kings such as Cyrus appear to be in control, God is the One working to establish justice and righteousness. If we question the way God is creating history, we reveal how inadequate we are compared to our Creator. All this gives further evidence He is the only God.

45:7 EVIL AND SUFFERING, Divine Origin—Isaiah stressed God's sovereignty in the universe. God remains in control of all He created. This does not mean that God is directly responsible for every specific experience of suffering. Isaiah stressed that the God of Israel was the only true God (44:6–8; 45:5,18,20–21; 46:8–9). Israel's situation was, however indirect, due to the true God, not to pagan gods or idols. God directly causes some suffering, especially when it is punishment for sin or is a means of testing faith. Nothing happens outside of God's ultimate sovereign will. He allows some innocent suffering to occur. For example, the misuse of human freedom, given by God, is the direct cause of much suffering. See note on Ge 1:1–3.

45:8 SALVATION, Definition—Salvation and righteousness are inseparable. Compare 46:13. Salvation is God's desired status for people. Righteousness is the proper social order of the world. The *heavens and earth participate* in God's *salvation. Israel's* restoration from the Exile was the beginning of the consummation of all history.

45:8 CHRISTIAN ETHICS, Righteousness—God creates and calls forth righteousness. Without God's work in human history, hope for a just society is vain. God's work to achieve righteousness surprises us. He could even work through a foreign king such as Cyrus of Persia. See notes on Hos 2:19–20; Am 5:7–24.

45:9–13 HUMANITY, Relationship to God—The word "Maker" is frequently used of a potter who works with clay. People are the clay worked by the divine Potter who become the products of His creative and shaping acts. As such, we have no right to complain that He is not just. We must trust God even when He does something so beyond our logic, such as raising up a pagan ruler to carry out His plans for us. The Psalms show God gives us freedom to express our complaints; but when it comes to God's sovereign plan to save His people, we must trust Him. See note on 42:5.

45:10–11 GOD, Father—Both father and mother images are used to illustrate God's sovereignty. See 49:15. This is appropriate in a culture often dominated by a female fertility deity and for a people devoted to the worship of only one God. See note on 43:1–7.

45:11–13 REVELATION, Persons—God surprises His people by choosing unexpected people to reveal and carry out His will. He used Cyrus, a foreign conqueror, to be His anointed agent (v 1) to restore His people to the Promised Land. The Creator can use anyone from anywhere He chooses to bring about His historical purposes.

45:15,21 GOD, Savior—Humans do not always understand God's actions. At times He appears to hide. We can see no actions, as when Israel was in exile. Still we trustingly proclaim, He is our Savior.

16All the makers of idols will be put to
shame and disgraced;[a]
they will go off into disgrace
together.
17But Israel will be saved[b] by the LORD
with an everlasting salvation;[c]
you will never be put to shame or
disgraced,[d]
to ages everlasting.

18For this is what the LORD says—
he who created the heavens,
he is God;
he who fashioned and made the
earth,[e]
he founded it;
he did not create it to be empty,[f]
but formed it to be inhabited[g]—
he says:
"I am the LORD,
and there is no other.[h]
19I have not spoken in secret,[i]
from somewhere in a land of
darkness;[j]
I have not said to Jacob's
descendants,[k]
'Seek[l] me in vain.'
I, the LORD, speak the truth;
I declare what is right.[m]

20"Gather together[n] and come;
assemble, you fugitives from the
nations.
Ignorant[o] are those who carry[p] about
idols of wood,
who pray to gods that cannot save.[q]
21Declare what is to be, present it—
let them take counsel together.
Who foretold[r] this long ago,
who declared it from the distant
past?[s]
Was it not I, the LORD?
And there is no God apart from
me,[t]
a righteous God[u] and a Savior;[v]
there is none but me.

22"Turn[w] to me and be saved,[x]
all you ends of the earth;[y]
for I am God, and there is no
other.[z]
23By myself I have sworn,[a]
my mouth has uttered in all
integrity[b]
a word that will not be revoked:[c]
Before me every knee will bow;[d]
by me every tongue will swear.[e]
24They will say of me, 'In the LORD alone
are righteousness[f] and strength.'[g]"
All who have raged against him
will come to him and be put to
shame.[h]
25But in the LORD all the descendants[i]
of Israel
will be found righteous[j] and will
exult.[k]

Chapter 46

Gods of Babylon

BEL[l] bows down, Nebo stoops low;
their idols[m] are borne by beasts of
burden.[r]
The images that are carried[n] about are
burdensome,
a burden for the weary.
2They stoop and bow down together;
unable to rescue the burden,
they themselves go off into
captivity.[o]

3"Listen[p] to me, O house of Jacob,
all you who remain[q] of the house of
Israel,

45:16 [a]S Ps 35:4; S Isa 1:29 **45:17** [b]Jer 23:6; 33:16; Ro 11:26 [c]S Isa 12:2 [d]S Ge 30:23; S Isa 29:22; S 41:11 **45:18** [e]S Ge 1:1 [f]S Ge 1:2 [g]S Ge 1:26 [h]ver 5; Dt 4:35 **45:19** [i]Isa 48:16; 65:4 [j]Jer 2:31 [k]ver 25; Isa 41:8; 65:9; Jer 31:36 [l]S Dt 4:29; S 2Ch 15:2 [m]S Dt 30:11 **45:20** [n]S Isa 43:9 [o]S Isa 44:19 [p]Ps 115:7; Isa 46:1; Jer 10:5 [q]Dt 32:37; S Isa 44:17; Jer 1:16; 2:28 **45:21** [r]S Isa 41:22 [s]Isa 46:10 [t]ver 5; S Ps 46:10; Isa 46:9; Mk 12:32 [u]Ps 11:7 [v]S Ps 3:8; S Isa 25:9 **45:22** [w]S Isa 44:22; Zec 12:10 [x]Nu 21:8-9; S 2Ch 20:12 [y]S Ge 49:10; S Isa 11:9,12; 49:6, 12 [z]Hos 13:4 **45:23** [a]S Ge 22:16; S Isa 14:24 [b]S Dt 30:11; Heb 6:13 [c]Isa 55:11 [d]S ver 14 [e]S Ps 63:11; S Isa 19:18; Ro 14:11*; Php 2:10-11 **45:24** [f]S ver 8; Jer 33:16 [g]S Dt 33:29; S Ps 18:39; S Isa 40:26; 63:1 [h]S Isa 41:11 **45:25** [i]S ver 19 [j]S Isa 4:3; S 49:4 [k]S Isa 24:23; S 41:16 **46:1** [l]S Isa 21:9; Jer 50:2; 51:44 [m]S 1Sa 5:2 [n]ver 7; S Isa 45:20 **46:2** [o]S Jdg 18:17-18; S 2Sa 5:21; Jer 51:47 **46:3** [p]ver 12; Isa 48:12; 51:1 [q]S Isa 1:9

[r]*1* Or *are but beasts and cattle*

45:18 CREATION, Purposeful—Though God waited until the sixth day to create persons, humans were not an afterthought. Rather, they were the crown of creation. God prepared the world for people before placing them in it. From the beginning, He had people in mind. The choice of Israel to be His servants to produce the Redeemer was but the implementation of a plan conceived before the foundation of the world. The starry elements and the good, green earth are insignificant compared to people (Ps 8:3–8).
45:18–22 HISTORY, God—See note on 41:21–29.
45:21,24 GOD, Righteous—The only God could be an immoral tyrant making unreasonable demands. Instead He is the righteous God who acts to see all people ultimately gain fair treatment.
45:22–24 EVANGELISM, Call to Salvation—God's call to salvation excludes no one. It rings out to the ends of the earth. God is always calling people to redemption—to look to Him and live. Those who do, engage in the task of taking the message to others that God might call them to salvation. They can deliver the message with assurance, for God has sworn to let every person in the world see His victory. The task of a witness is to bring people to bow in worship, before judgment leads them to bow down in defeat and submission. Evangelism leads people to see the ultimate importance of obeying the call to salvation and thus to experience God's grace in the present rather than His wrath in the future.
45:25 SALVATION, Justification—Israel's hope for the future was that God would justify all her descendants. Apart from God's righteousness there is not hope for anyone's future.
46:1–13 GOD, One God—God's people do not need to carry our gods in parade. He will carry us through our problems. See note on 45:5,14–24.
46:3–4 ELECTION, Remnant—God has no equal, nor can He be compared. None is like the God of election who carries, sustains, and rescues His people. He called the remnant of Israel to remember their history with Him and renew their commitment to Him. Election is a call to acknowledge the only God and to serve Him.
46:3–4 THE CHURCH, Remnant—When faced with discouraging situations, God's people have the assurance that He will carry them through difficult times of life. Being part of the remnant might bring discouragement which causes persons to feel small and insignificant. It could also raise fears that the judgment which left only a remnant will continue and destroy even the remnant. The God who created a people for Himself does not give up on His plans. He has shown Himself faithful to His remnant in the past and will continue to do so. Being part of the remnant is reason for faith. See note on 2 Ch 34:9.

you whom I have upheld since you
were conceived,[r]
and have carried[s] since your birth.[t]
4Even to your old age and gray hairs[u]
I am he,[v] I am he who will sustain
you.
I have made you and I will carry you;
I will sustain[w] you and I will rescue
you.

5"To whom will you compare me or
count me equal?
To whom will you liken me that we
may be compared?[x]
6Some pour out gold from their bags
and weigh out silver on the scales;
they hire a goldsmith[y] to make it into
a god,
and they bow down and worship
it.[z]
7They lift it to their shoulders and
carry[a] it;
they set it up in its place, and there
it stands.
From that spot it cannot move.[b]
Though one cries out to it, it does not
answer;[c]
it cannot save[d] him from his
troubles.

8"Remember[e] this, fix it in mind,
take it to heart, you rebels.[f]
9Remember the former things,[g] those
of long ago;[h]
I am God, and there is no other;
I am God, and there is none like
me.[i]
10I make known the end from the
beginning,[j]
from ancient times,[k] what is still to
come.[l]
I say: My purpose will stand,[m]
and I will do all that I please.
11From the east I summon[n] a bird of
prey;[o]
from a far-off land, a man to fulfill
my purpose.
What I have said, that will I bring
about;
what I have planned,[p] that will I
do.[q]
12Listen[r] to me, you stubborn-hearted,[s]
you who are far from
righteousness.[t]
13I am bringing my righteousness[u] near,
it is not far away;
and my salvation[v] will not be
delayed.

46:3 [r]S Ps 139:13; Isa 44:2 [s]S Dt 1:31; S Ps 28:9 [t]S Ps 22:10 **46:4** [u]Ps 71:18 [v]S Dt 32:39; S Isa 43:13 [w]S Ps 18:35; S 119:117 **46:5** [x]S Ex 15:11; Job 41:10; Isa 40:18,25; Jer 49:19 **46:6** [y]S Isa 40:19 [z]S Ex 20:5; Isa 44:17; Hos 13:2 **46:7** [a]S ver 1 [b]S 1Sa 5:3; S Isa 41:7 [c]S 1Ki 18:26 [d]S Isa 44:17; S 47:13 **46:8** [e]S Isa 44:21 [f]S Isa 1:2 **46:9** [g]S Isa 41:22 [h]S Dt 32:7 [i]S Ex 8:10; S Isa 45:5,21; Mk 12:32 **46:10** [j]S Isa 41:4 [k]S Isa 45:21 [l]S Isa 41:22 [m]S Pr 19:21; S Isa 7:7,9; S 44:26; Ac 5:39; Eph 1:11 **46:11** [n]S Jdg 4:10; S Ezr 1:2 [o]S Isa 8:8 [p]S Isa 25:1 [q]S Ge 41:25; Jer 44:28 **46:12** [r]S ver 3 [s]S Ex 32:9; S Isa 9:9 [t]Ps 119:150; Isa 48:1; Jer 2:5 **46:13** [u]S Isa 1:26; S 45:8; Ro 3:21 [v]S Ps 85:9 [w]S Ps 74:2; Joel 2:32 [x]S Isa 44:23 **47:1** [y]S Job 2:13; S Isa 29:4 [z]S Isa 21:9; S 23:12 [a]Ps 137:8; Jer 50:42; 51:33; Zec 2:7 [b]Dt 28:56 **47:2** [c]Ex 11:5; Mt 24:41 [d]S Jdg 16:21 [e]S Ge 24:65 [f]S Isa 32:11 **47:3** [g]S Ge 2:25; Eze 16:37; Na 3:5 [h]S Isa 20:4 [i]S Isa 1:24; S 34:8 [j]Isa 13:18-19 **47:4** [k]S Job 19:25 [l]S Isa 13:4 [m]Isa 48:2; Jer 50:34; Am 4:13 [n]S Isa 1:4; 48:17 **47:5** [o]S Job 2:13 [p]Isa 9:2; 13:10 [q]S Isa 21:9 [r]ver 7; La 1:1; Rev 18:7 [s]S Isa 13:19; Rev 17:18 **47:6** [t]S 2Ch 28:9 [u]S Dt 13:15; S Isa 42:24; Jer 2:7; 50:11 [v]Isa 10:13 [w]S Isa 14:6 **47:7** [x]S Isa 10:13; Da 4:30 [y]S ver 5;

I will grant salvation to Zion,[w]
my splendor[x] to Israel.

Chapter 47

The Fall of Babylon

"GO down, sit in the dust,[y]
Virgin Daughter[z] of Babylon;
sit on the ground without a throne,
Daughter of the Babylonians.[s][a]
No more will you be called
tender or delicate.[b]
2Take millstones[c] and grind[d] flour;
take off your veil.[e]
Lift up your skirts,[f] bare your legs,
and wade through the streams.
3Your nakedness[g] will be exposed
and your shame[h] uncovered.
I will take vengeance;[i]
I will spare no one.[j]"

4Our Redeemer[k]—the LORD Almighty[l]
is his name[m]—
is the Holy One[n] of Israel.

5"Sit in silence,[o] go into darkness,[p]
Daughter of the Babylonians;[q]
no more will you be called
queen[r] of kingdoms.[s]
6I was angry[t] with my people
and desecrated my inheritance;[u]
I gave them into your hand,[v]
and you showed them no mercy.[w]
Even on the aged
you laid a very heavy yoke.
7You said, 'I will continue forever[x]—
the eternal queen!'[y]
But you did not consider these things
or reflect[z] on what might happen.[a]

8"Now then, listen, you wanton
creature,
lounging in your security[b]
and saying to yourself,
'I am, and there is none besides
me.[c]
I will never be a widow[d]
or suffer the loss of children.'
9Both of these will overtake you
in a moment,[e] on a single day:
loss of children[f] and widowhood.[g]
They will come upon you in full
measure,

Rev 18:7 [z]S Isa 42:23,25 [a]S Dt 32:29 **47:8** [b]S Isa 32:9 [c]S Isa 45:6 [d]Isa 49:21; 54:4; La 1:1; Rev 18:7 **47:9** [e]S Ps 55:15; 73:19; 1Th 5:3; Rev 18:8-10 [f]S Isa 13:18 [g]Isa 4:1; Jer 15:8; 18:21

[s]*1* Or *Chaldeans*; also in verse 5

46:8–13 HISTORY, Hope—Present historical conditions do not reveal the ultimate reality of history. Historical memories of what God has done must live on to kindle hopes of what He is going to do. God *can and will do what He pleases to bring about His purposes.*

46:13 GOD, Righteous—God is not only righteous in His own nature, but He is seeking to establish righteousness in all His people on the earth.

47:1–15 GOD, Wrath—God uses nations to judge His people, but the wickedness of the nations cannot escape God's wrath. Note the supreme irony of Babylon's claim in vv 8,10. See note on 34:2,5–15.

47:1–15 HISTORY, Universal—No one can save a nation from God's judgment. See note on 10:5–19.

in spite of your many sorceries[h]
and all your potent spells.[i]
10You have trusted[j] in your wickedness
and have said, 'No one sees me.'[k]
Your wisdom[l] and knowledge
mislead[m] you
when you say to yourself,
'I am, and there is none besides
me.'
11Disaster[n] will come upon you,
and you will not know how to
conjure it away.
A calamity will fall upon you
that you cannot ward off with a
ransom;
a catastrophe you cannot foresee
will suddenly[o] come upon you.

12"Keep on, then, with your magic spells
and with your many sorceries,[p]
which you have labored at since
childhood.
Perhaps you will succeed,
perhaps you will cause terror.
13All the counsel you have received has
only worn you out![q]
Let your astrologers[r] come forward,
those stargazers who make predictions
month by month,
let them save[s] you from what is
coming upon you.
14Surely they are like stubble;[t]
the fire[u] will burn them up.
They cannot even save themselves
from the power of the flame.[v]
Here are no coals to warm anyone;
here is no fire to sit by.
15That is all they can do for you—
these you have labored with
and trafficked[w] with since
childhood.
Each of them goes on in his error;
there is not one that can save[x] you.

47:9 [h]ver 12; Na 3:4; Mal 3:5 [i]Dt 18:10-11; Rev 9:21; 18:23
47:10 [j]S Job 15:31; Ps 52:7; 62:10 [k]S 2Ki 21:16; S Isa 29:15 [l]S Isa 5:21 [m]Isa 44:20
47:11 [n]S Isa 10:3; S 14:15; S 21:9; S 31:2; Lk 17:27 [o]S Ps 55:15; S Isa 17:14; 1Th 5:3
47:12 [p]S ver 9; S Ex 7:11
47:13 [q]Isa 57:10; Jer 51:58; Hab 2:13 [r]S Isa 19:3; S 44:25 [s]ver 15; S Isa 5:29; 43:13; 46:7
47:14 [t]S Isa 5:24 [u]S Isa 30:30 [v]Isa 10:17; Jer 51:30,32,58
47:15 [w]Rev 18:11 [x]S ver 13; S Isa 44:17
48:1 [y]S Ge 17:5 [z]S Ge 29:35 [a]S Isa 19:18 [b]S 1Sa 20:42; S Isa 43:7 [c]Ex 23:13; 2Sa 14:11; Ps 50:16; Isa 58:2; Jer 7:9-10; 44:26 [d]Isa 59:14; Jer 4:2; 5:2; Da 8:12; Zec 8:3
48:2 [e]S Ne 11:1; S Isa 1:26; S Mt 4:5 [f]S Isa 10:20; Ro 2:17 [g]S Isa 47:4
48:3 [h]S Isa 41:22 [i]S Isa 40:21; 45:21 [j]S Isa 17:14; 30:13
48:4 [k]S Isa 9:9 [l]S Ex 32:9; S Dt 9:27; Ac 7:51 [m]Eze 3:9
48:5 [n]S Isa 40:21; S 42:9 [o]Jer 44:15-18
48:6 [p]S Isa 41:22; S Ro 16:25
48:7 [q]Isa 65:18 [r]Isa 45:21

Chapter 48

Stubborn Israel

"LISTEN to this, O house of Jacob,
you who are called by the name
of Israel[y]
and come from the line of Judah,[z]
you who take oaths[a] in the name of
the LORD[b]
and invoke[c] the God of Israel—
but not in truth[d] or righteousness—
2you who call yourselves citizens of the
holy city[e]
and rely[f] on the God of Israel—
the LORD Almighty is his name:[g]
3I foretold the former things[h] long ago,
my mouth announced[i] them and I
made them known;
then suddenly[j] I acted, and they
came to pass.
4For I knew how stubborn[k] you were;
the sinews of your neck[l] were iron,
your forehead[m] was bronze.
5Therefore I told you these things long
ago;
before they happened I announced[n]
them to you
so that you could not say,
'My idols did them;[o]
my wooden image and metal god
ordained them.'
6You have heard these things; look at
them all.
Will you not admit them?

"From now on I will tell you of new
things,[p]
of hidden things unknown to you.
7They are created[q] now, and not long
ago;[r]

47:10 HUMANITY, Intellectual Nature—An international ruler like the King of Babylon is tempted to place too much trust in human might and knowledge. Human wisdom unaided by divine guidance and revelation cannot be trusted as a safe guide to life. We cannot claim to have God's unequaled wisdom or power. Nothing we do goes unnoticed by Him.
47:11 EVIL AND SUFFERING, Punishment—God punished Babylon for their sins. They could not escape God's wrath even with their expertise in divination, astrology, and magic. God had used them to punish His chosen people, but that did not exempt them from deserved punishment for their pride and injustice. No source of evil stands outside God's power to punish. See note on 3:8–17.
48:1–9 SIN, Rebellion—Sin is unfaithfulness to a relationship, or treachery (Hebrew *bagad*), Israel was born as a people in Egypt, but rebelled against God from that point on. They played the game of religion with God, wanting all the privileges of being His people, but they lied under oath and refused to act as He directed. They attributed His acts to other gods. In His love for His people God promised the exiles He would give them one more chance. This did not mean God takes His expectations of His people lightly. The Exile showed He carries out His threats. This text does show God is merciful even to the sinner who is unfaithful to the relationship with God.
48:1–22 ELECTION, God's Purpose—Judgment is not God's goal or delight. God's mercy was slow to execute wrath against stubborn Israel. He granted time to the rebellious, elect people. He wanted them to be true to His covenant. Finally judgment came to test and refine the elect. In all this the purpose was to protect God's reputation and to prevent idols from receiving the glory due Him. Ultimately election can be explained only as God's determination to relate personally in freedom to His created people. Obedience and following His direction is best for His people, resulting in the promised election blessings. He may redeem the rebellious, but He leaves those who persist in wickedness without peace.
48:5,14 GOD, One God—See note on 45:5,14–24.
48:6–7 CREATION, Progressive—In every generation, God has a fresh word for His people. He had predicted Israel's Babylonian Exile, and He gave the nation a new word as they prepared to return home. The history of His people is part of God's ongoing creation (Hebrew *bara'*). See note on Ge 1:1. This continuous creation gives every succeeding generation assurance that He has a message for them in their day. Prophetic preaching is not merely telling what will happen but what must happen because God is holy. It deals with contemporary issues related to the problems people are facing as the prophet speaks. It interprets God's ongoing activity as Creator of history and redemption.

you have not heard of them before
today.
So you cannot say,
'Yes, I knew[s] of them.'
8You have neither heard nor
understood;[t]
from of old your ear[u] has not been
open.
Well do I know how treacherous[v] you
are;
you were called a rebel[w] from birth.
9For my own name's sake[x] I delay my
wrath;[y]
for the sake of my praise I hold it
back from you,
so as not to cut you off.[z]
10See, I have refined[a] you, though not
as silver;
I have tested[b] you in the furnace[c]
of affliction.
11For my own sake,[d] for my own sake, I
do this.
How can I let myself be defamed?[e]
I will not yield my glory to
another.[f]

Israel Freed

12"Listen[g] to me, O Jacob,
Israel, whom I have called:[h]
I am he;[i]
I am the first and I am the last.[j]
13My own hand laid the foundations of
the earth,[k]
and my right hand spread out the
heavens;[l]
when I summon them,
they all stand up together.[m]

14"Come together,[n] all of you, and
listen:
Which of ⌊the idols⌋ has foretold[o]
these things?
The LORD's chosen ally[p]
will carry out his purpose[q] against
Babylon;[r]
his arm will be against the
Babylonians.[t]
15I, even I, have spoken;
yes, I have called[s] him.
I will bring him,
and he will succeed[t] in his mission.

16"Come near[u] me and listen[v] to this:

"From the first announcement I have
not spoken in secret;[w]
at the time it happens, I am there."

And now the Sovereign LORD[x] has
sent[y] me,
with his Spirit.[z]

17This is what the LORD says—
your Redeemer,[a] the Holy One[b] of
Israel:
"I am the LORD your God,
who teaches[c] you what is best for
you,
who directs[d] you in the way[e] you
should go.
18If only you had paid attention[f] to my
commands,
your peace[g] would have been like a
river,[h]
your righteousness[i] like the waves
of the sea.
19Your descendants[j] would have been
like the sand,[k]
your children like its numberless
grains;[l]
their name would never be cut off[m]
nor destroyed from before me."

20Leave Babylon,
flee[n] from the Babylonians!
Announce this with shouts of joy[o]
and proclaim it.
Send it out to the ends of the earth;[p]

48:7 [s]S Ex 6:7
48:8 [t]S Isa 1:3 [u]S Dt 29:4 [v]Isa 41:24; Mal 2:11,14 [w]Dt 9:7,24; Ps 58:3; S Isa 1:2; 43:27; 58:1
48:9 [x]S 1Sa 12:22; S Isa 37:35 [y]S Job 9:13; S Isa 30:18 [z]S Ne 9:31
48:10 [a]S Isa 1:25; Zec 13:9; Mal 3:3; 1Pe 1:7 [b]S Ex 15:25 [c]S Ex 1:13; S 1Ki 8:51
48:11 [d]S 1Sa 12:22; S Isa 37:35 [e]S Lev 18:21; Dt 32:27; Jer 14:7, 21; Eze 20:9,14,22, 44 [f]Isa 42:8
48:12 [g]S Isa 46:3 [h]Isa 41:8; 42:6; 43:1 [i]S Isa 43:13 [j]S Isa 41:4; S Rev 1:17
48:13 [k]Heb 1:10-12 [l]S Ge 2:1; Ex 20:11; Job 9:8; Isa 40:22; S 42:5; 45:18; 51:16; 65:17 [m]S Isa 34:16
48:14 [n]S Isa 43:9 [o]S Isa 41:22 [p]S Isa 41:2 [q]Isa 46:10-11 [r]S Isa 21:9; S 45:1; Jer 50:45
48:15 [s]S Jdg 4:10; Isa 45:1 [t]Isa 44:28-45:4
48:16 [u]S Isa 41:1 [v]S Isa 33:13 [w]S Isa 45:19 [x]Isa 50:5,7,9 [y]Zec 2:9,11 [z]S Isa 11:2
48:17 [a]S Job 19:25; Isa 49:7; 54:8 [b]S Isa 47:4 [c]S Isa 28:9; S Jer 7:13 [d]Isa 49:10; 57:18; 58:11 [e]S Isa 30:11
48:18 [f]S Isa 42:23 [g]Ps 147:14; S Isa 9:7; 54:13; 66:12 [h]S Isa 33:21 [i]S Isa 1:26; S 45:8
48:19 [j]Isa 43:5; 44:3; 61:9 [k]S Ge 12:2 [l]S Job 5:25
[m]Isa 56:5; 65:23; 66:22; Jer 35:19 **48:20** [n]Isa 52:11; Jer 48:6; 50:8; 51:6,45; Zec 2:6-7; Rev 18:4 [o]S Isa 12:6; 49:13; 51:11 [p]S Ge 49:10; S Dt 30:4; S Jer 25:22

[t]*14* Or *Chaldeans*; also in verse 20

48:8–10 EVIL AND SUFFERING, Testing—Israel was tested in the Exile just as silver is refined in fire. Even in Exile Israel did not learn her lesson. Israel continued to rebel against God, worshiping the gods of her captors. Punishment was due people who failed to learn from God's test, but God chose to act in saving grace for His people, so all nations could see His power. Punishment for sin is not an automatic device triggered instantly. Punishment is always God's personal choice used to accomplish His purposes with His people and His world. See note on Ps 66:1–20.

48:9 SALVATION, Grace—Were it not for God's grace, His wrath would consume us. We deserve wrath, but He gives us grace.

48:12–13 GOD, Creator—See note on 45:7–9,11–12,18.

48:17 GOD, Savior—In the midst of many passages depicting His wrath, God wants us to know He is primarily a God who wants to save, to bless. *Part of His salvation is to teach us what is best for us.*

48:17–19 REVELATION, Commitment—God is committed to reveal Himself and His ways to His people. Though they refused to obey His revelation to Moses and the prophets, He willingly started over again bringing them out of the Exile. God wants His people to believe His revealed teachings lead to the best life possible in the Creator's world. To leave Him is to lose the way. To follow Him is to find true peace and just living.

48:17–19 CHRISTIAN ETHICS, War and Peace—Obedience to God's ethical imperatives is integrally tied to the results of peace. Peace and blessing have continued to be God's goal since He called Abraham (Ge 12:1–7). See note on 32:14–20.

48:18–19 CHRISTIAN ETHICS, Righteousness—Obedience to God is rewarded individually and socially in the fruit of justice and righteousness. We do not have the just society we desire because we do not obey. Thus, God has to work in strange ways such as using Cyrus of Persia. See note on 45:8. God is working to create a people who will fulfill the promise to and mission of Abraham (Ge 12:1–3).

48:20 THE CHURCH, Servants—God does not forsake His people. See note on 44:21. As God redeemed His servant Jacob from Babylon, He will care for His servants today who minister in His name.

say, "The LORD has redeemed[q] his
servant Jacob."
21They did not thirst[r] when he led them
through the deserts;
he made water flow[s] for them from
the rock;
he split the rock
and water gushed out.[t]

22"There is no peace,"[u] says the LORD,
"for the wicked."[v]

Chapter 49

The Servant of the LORD

LISTEN[w] to me, you islands;[x]
hear this, you distant nations:
Before I was born[y] the LORD called[z]
me;
from my birth he has made mention
of my name.[a]
2He made my mouth[b] like a sharpened
sword,[c]
in the shadow of his hand[d] he hid
me;
he made me into a polished arrow[e]
and concealed me in his quiver.
3He said to me, "You are my servant,[f]
Israel, in whom I will display my
splendor.[g]"
4But I said, "I have labored to no
purpose;
I have spent my strength in vain[h]
and for nothing.
Yet what is due me is in the LORD's
hand,[i]
and my reward[j] is with my God."[k]

5And now the LORD says—
he who formed me in the womb[l] to
be his servant
to bring Jacob back to him
and gather Israel[m] to himself,
for I am honored[n] in the eyes of the
LORD

48:20 [q]S Ex 6:6; S Isa 33:24; 52:9; 63:9; Mic 4:10 **48:21** [r]S Isa 33:16 [s]S Isa 30:25 [t]S Nu 20:11; S Isa 35:6 **48:22** [u]S Job 3:26 [v]S Isa 3:11; 57:21 **49:1** [w]S Isa 33:13 [x]S Isa 11:11 [y]Isa 44:24; 46:3; Mt 1:20 [z]Isa 7:14; 9:6; 44:2; Jer 1:5; Gal 1:15 [a]S Ex 33:12; S Isa 43:1 **49:2** [b]S Job 40:18 [c]S Ps 64:3; Eph 6:17; S Rev 1:16 [d]S Ex 33:22; S Ps 91:1 [e]S Dt 32:23; Zec 9:13 **49:3** [f]S Isa 20:3; Zec 3:8 [g]S Lev 10:3; S Isa 44:23 **49:4** [h]S Lev 26:20; Isa 55:2; 65:23 [i]Isa 45:25; 50:8; 53:10; 54:17 [j]S Isa 35:4 [k]S Job 27:2 **49:5** [l]S Ps 139:13; Gal 1:15 [m]S Dt 30:4; S Isa 11:12 [n]S Isa 43:4 [o]S Ps 18:1 **49:6** [p]S ver 3 [q]Isa 1:9 [r]S Isa 9:2; Jn 1:9 [s]S Isa 26:18; 55:5; Zec 8:22; S Lk 2:32 [t]S Dt 30:4; S Ps 48:10; S Mt 28:19; Jn 11:52; Ac 13:47* **49:7** [u]S Isa 48:17 [v]S Ps 22:6; 69:7-9 [w]S Ezr 1:2; Isa 52:15 [x]S Ge 27:29; S Ps 22:29; S 86:9 [y]S Dt 7:9; S 1Co 1:9 [z]S Isa 14:1 **49:8** [a]Ps 69:13; Isa 60:10; 61:2 [b]S Isa 41:10; 2Co 6:2* [c]S Isa 5:2; 26:3 [d]S Isa 42:6 [e]Lev 25:10; S Ps 37:9; Isa 44:26; 58:12; 61:4; Eze 36:10,33; Am 9:11,14 [f]S Nu 34:13; S Isa 60:21 **49:9** [g]Isa 42:7; 61:1; S Lk 4:19 [h]S Ps 107:10 [i]Isa 41:18

and my God has been my
strength[o]—
6he says:
"It is too small a thing for you to be
my servant[p]
to restore the tribes of Jacob
and bring back those of Israel I have
kept.[q]
I will also make you a light[r] for the
Gentiles,[s]
that you may bring my salvation to
the ends of the earth."[t]

7This is what the LORD says—
the Redeemer and Holy One of
Israel[u]—
to him who was despised[v] and
abhorred by the nation,
to the servant of rulers:
"Kings[w] will see you and rise up,
princes will see and bow down,[x]
because of the LORD, who is faithful,[y]
the Holy One of Israel, who has
chosen[z] you."

Restoration of Israel

8This is what the LORD says:

"In the time of my favor[a] I will
answer you,
and in the day of salvation I will
help you;[b]
I will keep[c] you and will make you
to be a covenant for the people,[d]
to restore the land[e]
and to reassign its desolate
inheritances,[f]
9to say to the captives,[g] 'Come out,'
and to those in darkness,[h] 'Be free!'

"They will feed beside the roads
and find pasture on every barren
hill.[i]

48:22 CHRISTIAN ETHICS, War and Peace—Peace, God's goal for His creation, cannot come when evil rules a person or a nation. See note on Jer 6:14.

49:1–6 JESUS CHRIST, Foretold—This is the second servant poem. See note on 42:1–16. The missionary task of the Messiah and His people is the point of emphasis. Paul identified his own mission to the Gentiles by quoting v 6 (Ac 13:47). Jesus said His disciples are the light of the world (Mt 5:14). The aged Simeon pointed to the source of all this light when he identified the Christ child (Lk 2:32).

49:1–7 JESUS CHRIST, Servant—See note on Ac 3:13.

***49:1–7* ELECTION, Israel**—See notes on 42:1–9; 44:1–8. Election began *before* Israel did. The elect have no evidence that they deserve election. The elect are the remnant in Israel with a mission to rebellious Israel and to the nations. Through the elect servants God radiates His splendor to the world.

49:1–7 THE CHURCH, Servants—See note on 42:1–4. God's chosen people are God's servants. As such, we have a dual task. We are called by God to turn the rebels and sinners in our own midst, or among our own members, back to God. We are also sent as missionaries to the nations. Israel in Exile wanted to complain about its plight. God called them to use the opportunity to testify to the nations and to bring salvation to all people.

49:1–6 EVANGELISM, Universality—Evangelism is an Old Testament teaching as well as one from the New Testament. From her birth as a people, Israel was called to be God's servant through whom God would display His splendor to the nations. Israel's experience in Babylonian Exile appeared futile and without purpose. Instead, it opened opportunities to expand their witness to the nations. Thus God's message of salvation could reach the ends of the world. See notes on 42:10–12; 45:22–24.

49:7,26 GOD, Savior—See note on 48:17.

49:8 SALVATION, Renewal—The Hebrew uses perfect tenses here to indicate the certainty of God's salvation. God would in the time of His favor save His people from Exile and return them to their homeland. In Christ, God has provided a sure salvation, incorporating all who trust Him into His covenant by which we become witnesses "for the people."

49:8 THE CHURCH, Covenant People—See note on 42:6–7.

10 They will neither hunger nor thirst,[j]
nor will the desert heat or the sun
beat upon them.[k]
He who has compassion[l] on them will
guide[m] them
and lead them beside springs[n] of
water.
11 I will turn all my mountains into roads,
and my highways[o] will be raised
up.[p]
12 See, they will come from afar[q]—
some from the north, some from the
west,[r]
some from the region of Aswan.[u]"

13 Shout for joy,[s] O heavens;
rejoice, O earth;[t]
burst into song, O mountains![u]
For the LORD comforts[v] his people
and will have compassion[w] on his
afflicted ones.[x]

14 But Zion[y] said, "The LORD has
forsaken[z] me,
the Lord has forgotten me."

15 "Can a mother forget the baby at her
breast
and have no compassion on the
child[a] she has borne?
Though she may forget,
I will not forget you![b]
16 See, I have engraved[c] you on the
palms of my hands;
your walls[d] are ever before me.
17 Your sons hasten back,
and those who laid you waste[e]
depart from you.
18 Lift up your eyes and look around;
all your sons gather[f] and come to
you.
As surely as I live,[g]" declares the
LORD,
"you will wear[h] them all as
ornaments;
you will put them on, like a bride.

19 "Though you were ruined and made
desolate[i]
and your land laid waste,[j]
now you will be too small for your
people,[k]
and those who devoured[l] you will
be far away.
20 The children born during your
bereavement
will yet say in your hearing,
'This place is too small for us;
give us more space to live in.'[m]
21 Then you will say in your heart,
'Who bore me these?[n]
I was bereaved[o] and barren;
I was exiled and rejected.[p]
Who brought these[q] up?
I was left[r] all alone,[s]
but these—where have they come
from?' "

22 This is what the Sovereign LORD[t]
says:

"See, I will beckon to the Gentiles,
I will lift up my banner[u] to the
peoples;
they will bring[v] your sons in their
arms
and carry your daughters on their
shoulders.[w]
23 Kings[x] will be your foster fathers,
and their queens your nursing
mothers.[y]
They will bow down[z] before you with
their faces to the ground;
they will lick the dust[a] at your feet.
Then you will know that I am the
LORD;[b]
those who hope[c] in me will not be
disappointed.[d]"

24 Can plunder be taken from warriors,[e]
or captives rescued from the
fierce[v]?

25 But this is what the LORD says:

"Yes, captives[f] will be taken from
warriors,[g]
and plunder retrieved from the
fierce;[h]
I will contend with those who contend
with you,[i] [j]
and your children I will save.[k]
26 I will make your oppressors[l] eat[m]
their own flesh;

49:10 [j]S Isa 33:16 [k]Ps 121:6; Rev 7:16 [l]S Isa 14:1 [m]S Ps 48:14; S Isa 42:16; S 48:17 [n]S Isa 33:21; S 35:7 **49:11** [o]S Isa 11:16 [p]Isa 40:4; Jer 31:9 **49:12** [q]S Isa 2:3; S 11:11; 43:5-6 [r]Isa 59:19; S Mt 8:11 **49:13** [s]S Isa 48:20 [t]S Ps 96:11 [u]S Ps 65:12-13; 98:4; Isa 44:23 [v]S Ps 71:21; S Isa 40:1; S 2Co 1:4 [w]S Isa 14:1 [x]S Ps 9:12 **49:14** [y]Isa 40:9 [z]S Ps 9:10; S 71:11; S Isa 27:8 **49:15** [a]S 1Ki 3:26; Isa 66:13 [b]S Isa 44:21 **49:16** [c]S Ge 38:18; S Ex 28:9 [d]Ps 48:12-13; Isa 62:6 **49:17** [e]S Isa 5:6; 10:6; 37:18 **49:18** [f]S Isa 11:12; 14:1; 43:5; 51:3; 54:7 [g]S Nu 14:21; Isa 45:23; 54:9; 62:8; Ro 14:11* [h]Isa 52:1; 61:10; Jer 2:32 **49:19** [i]S Lev 26:33; Isa 54:1,3; 60:18; 62:4 [j]S Isa 5:6 [k]Eze 36:10-11; Zec 10:10 [l]S Isa 1:20 **49:20** [m]Isa 54:1-3; Zec 2:4; 10:10 **49:21** [n]Isa 29:23; 66:7-8 [o]S Isa 47:8; 54:1 [p]Isa 5:13; 54:6 [q]Isa 60:8 [r]S Isa 1:8 [s]S Ps 142:4; Isa 51:18; Jer 10:20 **49:22** [t]S Ge 15:2 [u]S Isa 11:10 [v]S Isa 11:12; S 14:2 [w]Lk 15:5 **49:23** [x]Isa 60:3, 10-11 [y]S Nu 11:12; S Isa 60:16 [z]S Ge 27:29; Rev 3:9 [a]S Ge 3:14; Ps 72:9 [b]S Ex 6:2; S Ps 22:23; S Isa 42:8 [c]S Ps 37:9; S 130:5 [d]S Ps 22:5; S Isa 29:22; S 41:11 **49:24** [e]Mt 12:29; Mk 3:27; Lk 11:21 **49:25** [f]S Isa 14:2 [g]Jer 50:33-34; Mk 3:27 [h]S Isa 13:11; S 25:4 [i]Isa 25:5; S 43:26; 51:22; Jer 50:34 [j]S 1Sa 24:15 [k]Isa 25:9; 33:22; 35:4 **49:26** [l]S Isa 9:4; S 13:11 [m]S Isa 9:20

[u] *12* Dead Sea Scrolls; Masoretic Text *Sinim*
[v] *24* Dead Sea Scrolls, Vulgate and Syriac (see also Septuagint and verse 25); Masoretic Text *righteous*

49:10,13–18 GOD, Grace—God's people may suffer, but we are never forgotten. Strong words have described the wrath of God. Now His grace is set forth in strong language.

49:14–23 HISTORY, Hope—See notes on 46:8–13; 1 Ki 20:13. God does not forget His people. He plans new actions to introduce Himself as God.

49:22–26 GOD, Sovereignty—The sovereign God knows the plight of His people and plans unexpected ways to use even foreign rulers to save His people. His actions will eventually lead all people to recognize His lordship.

***49:22–26* SALVATION, As Deliverance**—Israel's story and the story of world redemption are inseparably intertwined. God delivered Israel again and again that He might in the end deliver all peoples. He wants to introduce His name to all nations and let all humans experience Him as Savior and Redeemer. God saves His children from seemingly impossible situations to reveal Himself to the nations.

49:26 EVANGELISM, Judgment—Even the judgment of God upon the sins of people aids the evangelistic task. As God judges the *rebellious people* who oppress His people, all the *world* comes to know God as the "Redeemer" and the "Mighty One" who saves His own. This, in turn, motivates people to become one of God's own. God's purpose in all He does is to evangelize the world.

they will be drunk on their own
blood,[n] as with wine.
Then all mankind will know[o]
that I, the LORD, am your Savior,[p]
your Redeemer,[q] the Mighty One of
Jacob.[r]"

Chapter 50

Israel's Sin and the Servant's Obedience

THIS is what the LORD says:
"Where is your mother's certificate
of divorce[s]
with which I sent her away?
Or to which of my creditors
did I sell[t] you?
Because of your sins[u] you were sold;[v]
because of your transgressions your
mother was sent away.
2When I came, why was there no one?
When I called, why was there no
one to answer?[w]
Was my arm too short[x] to ransom
you?
Do I lack the strength[y] to rescue
you?
By a mere rebuke[z] I dry up the sea,[a]
I turn rivers into a desert;[b]
their fish rot for lack of water
and die of thirst.
3I clothe the sky with darkness[c]
and make sackcloth[d] its covering."

4The Sovereign LORD[e] has given me an
instructed tongue,[f]
to know the word that sustains the
weary.[g]
He wakens me morning by morning,[h]
wakens my ear to listen like one
being taught.[i]
5The Sovereign LORD[j] has opened my
ears,[k]
and I have not been rebellious;[l]
I have not drawn back.
6I offered my back to those who beat[m]
me,
my cheeks to those who pulled out
my beard;[n]
I did not hide my face
from mocking and spitting.[o]

49:26 [n]Nu 23:24; Jer 25:27; Na 1:10; 3:11; Rev 16:6 [o]Ex 6:7; S Isa 11:9; Eze 39:7 [p]S Isa 25:9 [q]S Job 19:25; S Isa 48:17 [r]S Ge 49:24; S Ps 132:2
50:1 [s]S Dt 24:1; Hos 2:2; Mt 19:7; Mk 10:4 [t]S Ne 5:5; S Mt 18:25 [u]S Isa 1:28 [v]S Dt 32:30; S Jdg 3:8
50:2 [w]S 1Sa 8:19; S Isa 41:28 [x]Nu 11:23; Isa 59:1 [y]S Ge 18:14; S Ps 68:35; Jer 14:9 [z]S Ps 18:15 [a]S Ex 14:22 [b]S Ps 107:33
50:3 [c]S Ex 10:22; S Isa 5:30 [d]Rev 6:12
50:4 [e]ver 5; Isa 61:1 [f]S Ex 4:12 [g]S Isa 40:29; Mt 11:28 [h]Ps 5:3; 88:13; 119:147; 143:8 [i]S Isa 28:9
50:5 [j]S Isa 48:16 [k]Isa 35:5 [l]Eze 2:8; 24:3; S Mt 26:39; Jn 8:29; 14:31; 15:10; Ac 26:19; Heb 5:8
50:6 [m]Isa 53:5; Mt 27:30; Mk 14:65; 15:19; Lk 22:63; Jn 19:1 [n]S 2Sa 10:4 [o]S Nu 12:14; La 3:30; Mt 26:67; Mk 10:34
50:7 [p]S Isa 48:16 [q]S Isa 41:10; 42:1 [r]Jer 1:18; 15:20; Eze 3:8-9 [s]S Isa 28:16; S 29:22
50:8 [t]S Isa 26:2; S 49:4 [u]S Ps 34:18 [v]S Job 13:19; S Isa 43:26; Ro 8:32-34 [w]S Isa 41:1
50:9 [x]S Isa 48:16 [y]S Isa 41:10 [z]Ro 8:1,34 [a]S Job 13:28; S Isa 51:8
50:10 [b]S Pr 1:7 [c]Isa 1:19; Hag 1:12 [d]S Isa 49:3 [e]S Ps 107:14; Ac 26:18 [f]S Isa 10:20; S 26:4
50:11 [g]Pr 26:18 [h]Isa 1:31; Jas 3:6 [i]S Dt 21:22-23; S Pr 26:27 [j]S Job 15:20; Isa 65:13-15

7Because the Sovereign LORD[p] helps[q]
me,
I will not be disgraced.
Therefore have I set my face like
flint,[r]
and I know I will not be put to
shame.[s]
8He who vindicates[t] me is near.[u]
Who then will bring charges against
me?[v]
Let us face each other![w]
Who is my accuser?
Let him confront me!
9It is the Sovereign LORD[x] who helps[y]
me.
Who is he that will condemn[z] me?
They will all wear out like a garment;
the moths[a] will eat them up.

10Who among you fears[b] the LORD
and obeys[c] the word of his
servant?[d]
Let him who walks in the dark,
who has no light,[e]
trust[f] in the name of the LORD
and rely on his God.
11But now, all you who light fires
and provide yourselves with flaming
torches,[g]
go, walk in the light of your fires[h]
and of the torches you have set
ablaze.
This is what you shall receive from my
hand:[i]
You will lie down in torment.[j]

Chapter 51

Everlasting Salvation for Zion

"LISTEN[k] to me, you who pursue
righteousness[l]
and who seek[m] the LORD:
Look to the rock[n] from which you
were cut
and to the quarry from which you
were hewn;
2look to Abraham,[o] your father,
and to Sarah, who gave you birth.

51:1 [k]S Isa 46:3 [l]ver 7; S Dt 7:13; 16:20; Ps 94:15; Isa 63:8; Ro 9:30-31 [m]Isa 55:6; 65:10 [n]Isa 17:10
51:2 [o]S Ge 17:6; S Isa 29:22; Ro 4:16; Heb 11:11

50:1 SIN, Unbelief—The sinner cannot take God to court and prove Him guilty. He did not divorce His people (Dt 24:1–4) or sell them into slavery (Ex 21:7–11). Israel had separated themselves from God to worship idols and made themselves slaves through treaties with other nations. Still Yahweh, the God of Israel, held legal claim to them and in love would exercise His claim. The fault was Judah's. God's people did not believe He would act. To quit waiting expectantly for God's saving intervention in your life is sin.
50:4–11 JESUS CHRIST, Servant—See note on Ac 3:13.
50:4–11 THE CHURCH, Servants—God's servant can face adversity and persecution with confidence. Such confidence comes from listening to and learning from God. God helps His servant in distress and shows the servant has reason for confidence. Jesus lived out this servant role perfectly. He stands as a worthy model for all who seek to serve God. See notes on 41:8–9; 42:1–4, 18–22; 49:1–7.
50:6 JESUS CHRIST, Foretold—This verse is in the middle of the third servant poem which spells out in detail how God's Servant would suffer. The suffering Messiah was to endure scourging, spitting, and the pulling of His beard. This ancient description of contempt is spelled out in all four Gospels (Mt 26:67; Mk 14:65; Lk 22:63–65; Jn 19:1).
51:1–3 CHRISTIAN ETHICS, Righteousness—To be God's people is to worship Him and to pursue right actions which give stability to society. If God could achieve so much through one family, surely He can fulfill all His promises of a just society to His people.
51:2–3 ELECTION, God's Promise—Fulfillment of past election promises is reason to believe renewed promises.

When I called him he was but one,
and I blessed him and made him
many.[p]
3The LORD will surely comfort[q] Zion[r]
and will look with compassion on all
her ruins;[s]
he will make her deserts like Eden,[t]
her wastelands[u] like the garden of
the LORD.
Joy and gladness[v] will be found in her,
thanksgiving[w] and the sound of
singing.

4"Listen to me, my people;[x]
hear me,[y] my nation:
The law[z] will go out from me;
my justice[a] will become a light to
the nations.[b]
5My righteousness draws near speedily,
my salvation[c] is on the way,[d]
and my arm[e] will bring justice to
the nations.
The islands[f] will look to me
and wait in hope[g] for my arm.
6Lift up your eyes to the heavens,
look at the earth beneath;
the heavens will vanish like smoke,[h]
the earth will wear out like a
garment[i]
and its inhabitants die like flies.
But my salvation[j] will last forever,[k]
my righteousness will never fail.[l]

7"Hear me, you who know what is
right,[m]
you people who have my law in your
hearts:[n]
Do not fear the reproach of men
or be terrified by their insults.[o]
8For the moth will eat them up like a
garment;[p]
the worm[q] will devour them like
wool.
But my righteousness will last
forever,[r]
my salvation through all
generations."

9Awake, awake![s] Clothe yourself with
strength,[t]
O arm[u] of the LORD;
awake, as in days gone by,
as in generations of old.[v]
Was it not you who cut Rahab[w] to
pieces,
who pierced that monster[x] through?
10Was it not you who dried up the
sea,[y]
the waters of the great deep,[z]
who made a road in the depths of the
sea[a]
so that the redeemed[b] might cross
over?
11The ransomed[c] of the LORD will
return.
They will enter Zion with singing;[d]
everlasting joy will crown their
heads.
Gladness and joy[e] will overtake
them,
and sorrow and sighing will flee
away.[f]

12"I, even I, am he who comforts[g] you.
Who are you that you fear[h] mortal
men,[i]
the sons of men, who are but
grass,[j]

51:2 [p]S Ge 12:2 **51:3** [q]S Isa 40:1 [r]S Ps 51:18; S Isa 61:4 [s]Isa 44:26; 52:9; 61:4 [t]S Ge 2:8 [u]S Isa 5:6; S 41:19 [v]S Isa 25:9; 35:10; 65:18; 66:10; Jer 16:9 [w]Jer 17:26; 30:19; 33:11 **51:4** [x]Ex 6:7; Ps 50:7; Isa 3:15; 63:8; 64:9 [y]S Ps 78:1 [z]S Dt 18:18 [a]S Isa 2:4 [b]S Isa 26:18; S 49:6 **51:5** [c]S Ps 85:9; S Isa 12:2 [d]S Isa 35:4 [e]Ps 98:1; Isa 40:10; 50:2; 52:10; 59:16; 63:1,5 [f]S Isa 11:11 [g]S Ge 49:10; S Ps 37:9 **51:6** [h]S Ps 37:20; S 102:26; Mt 24:35; Lk 21:33; 2Pe 3:10 [i]Ps 102:25-26; Heb 1:10-12 [j]S Isa 12:2 [k]ver 8; S Ps 119:89 [l]Ps 89:33; Isa 54:10 **51:7** [m]S ver 1 [n]S Dt 6:6; Ps 119:11 [o]S Ps 119:39; Isa 50:7; 54:4; Mt 5:11; Lk 6:22; Ac 5:41 **51:8** [p]S Job 13:28; Jas 5:2 [q]S Isa 14:11 [r]S ver 6 **51:9** [s]S Jdg 5:12 [t]S Ge 18:14; S Ps 65:6; Isa 40:31; 52:1 [u]S Ps 98:1; S Isa 30:30; S 33:2 [v]Ex 6:6; Dt 4:34; S 32:7 [w]S Job 9:13 [x]S Ps 68:30; S 74:13 **51:10** [y]S Ex 14:22; Zec 10:11; Rev 16:12 [z]Ex 15:5, 8 [a]S Job 36:30 [b]S Ex 15:13 **51:11** [c]S Isa 35:9; S 44:23 [d]S Ps 109:28; Isa 65:14; Jer 30:19; Zep 3:14 [e]S Isa 48:20; Jer 33:11 [f]S Isa 30:19; Jer 31:13; S Rev 7:17 **51:12** [g]S Isa 40:1; S 2Co 1:4 [h]S 2Ki 1:15 [i]S Isa 2:22 [j]S Isa 15:6; 40:6-7; 1Pe 1:24

51:3,12 GOD, Grace—See note on 49:10,13–18.

51:3 CREATION, Freedom—God's freedom often extends to those who are in the depths of despair. He can and often chooses to extend His grace to those who are suffering, even though they may be reaping the result of their own sinful ways. He creates new opportunities and delivers them in new ways. In His freedom, God acts in ways that seem strange to us. He does so to call His erring creation back to Himself.

51:3,11 SALVATION, Joy—See note on 35:10. Salvation history moves from Eden to Eden. These verses foreshadow the new heaven and new earth of Rev 21:1. God's compassionate acts of salvation create joy in His people.

51:4,15–16 GOD, Sovereignty—The one true God is sovereign over all the earth. He will establish a just order which will attract the nations to Him.

51:4–8 CHRISTIAN ETHICS, Justice—God's design for His world is eternal justice and righteousness for all people and nations. He will act in righteousness to establish His salvation.

51:4–8 LAST THINGS, Salvation's Completion—God knew the Israelites in Exile would complain of their impoverished situation. God promised salvation. Salvation will not be complete until it is established forever. God is at work to establish new heavens and a new earth wherein dwells righteousness forever. Then people will no longer suffer ridicule or complain to God. See note on Rev 21:1–5.

51:5–6,22 GOD, Savior—God had repeatedly saved Israel from her enemies. God's eternal plan provided for an eternal salvation. See note on 48:17.

51:5,7–8 GOD, Righteous—God's righteousness is not only a characteristic of His own nature. It is also a quality that He is spreading through the earth. The relationship between God and His people is a relationship of righteousness. Note the close connection between righteousness and salvation. See notes on Ps 92:15; 98:2–3.

51:6 CREATION, Hope—The earth which God created is not His ultimate handiwork. This material dwelling place, as we know it, will some day be destroyed. It is already now in the process of dying. Even the heavens shall dissolve some day and be created anew. The only eternal things are those of the spirit, values related to God's unalterable principles. Our hope for the future is rooted in God's righteousness and the justice that proceeds from it. He creates that hope as we are properly related to Him.

51:7 CHRISTIAN ETHICS, Character—Building our lives around the moral expectations of God will produce a shield of encouragement against the insults of those alienated from God.

51:12 HUMANITY, Human Nature—Whom can we trust? A God who showed His power in Egypt centuries ago? Or the King of Babylon who has captured and enslaved us? So the exiles questioned God. He gave a simple alternative—trust the Creator or trust a dying man. Mortal humans are quickly seen to be an insufficient source of strength when God's strength is available.

13that you forget[k] the LORD your
Maker,[l]
who stretched out the heavens[m]
and laid the foundations of the
earth,
that you live in constant terror[n] every
day
because of the wrath of the
oppressor,
who is bent on destruction?
For where is the wrath of the
oppressor?[o]
14 The cowering prisoners will soon be
set free;[p]
they will not die in their dungeon,
nor will they lack bread.[q]
15For I am the LORD your God,
who churns up the sea[r] so that its
waves roar[s] —
the LORD Almighty[t] is his name.
16I have put my words in your mouth[u]
and covered you with the shadow of
my hand[v] —
I who set the heavens in place,
who laid the foundations of the
earth,[w]
and who say to Zion, 'You are my
people.[x]' "

The Cup of the LORD's Wrath

17Awake, awake![y]
Rise up, O Jerusalem,
you who have drunk from the hand of
the LORD
the cup[z] of his wrath,[a]
you who have drained to its dregs[b]
the goblet that makes men stagger.[c]
18Of all the sons[d] she bore
there was none to guide her;[e]
of all the sons she reared
there was none to take her by the
hand.[f]
19These double calamities[g] have come
upon you—
who can comfort you?[h] —
ruin and destruction,[i] famine[j] and
sword[k] —
who can[w] console you?
20Your sons have fainted;
they lie at the head of every street,[l]
like antelope caught in a net.[m]
They are filled with the wrath[n] of the
LORD
and the rebuke[o] of your God.
21*Therefore hear* this, you afflicted[p] one,
made drunk,[q] but not with wine.
22This is what your Sovereign LORD says,
your God, who defends[r] his people:
"See, I have taken out of your hand
the cup[s] that made you stagger;
from that cup, the goblet of my wrath,
you will never drink again.
23I will put it into the hands of your
tormentors,[t]
who said to you,
'Fall prostrate[u] that we may walk[v]
over you.'
And you made your back like the
ground,
like a street to be walked over."[w]

Chapter 52

AWAKE, awake,[x] O Zion,
clothe yourself with strength.[y]
Put on your garments of splendor,[z]
O Jerusalem, the holy city.[a]
The uncircumcised[b] and defiled[c]
will not enter you again.[d]
2Shake off your dust;[e]
rise up,[f] sit enthroned,
O Jerusalem.
Free yourself from the chains on your
neck,[g]
O captive Daughter of Zion.[h]
3For this is what the LORD says:

"You were sold for nothing,[i]
and without money[j] you will be
redeemed.[k]"

4For this is what the Sovereign LORD
says:

"At first my people went down to
Egypt[l] to live;
lately, Assyria[m] has oppressed them.

5"And now what do I have here?" declares the LORD.

"For my people have been taken away
for nothing,
and those who rule them mock,[x]"
declares the LORD.
"And all day long
my name is constantly
blasphemed.[n]
6Therefore my people will know[o] my
name;[p]
therefore in that day[q] they will
know
that it is I who foretold[r] it.
Yes, it is I."

7How beautiful on the mountains[s]

51:13 [k]S Job 8:13; S Isa 17:10 [l]S Job 4:17; Isa 17:7; 45:11; 54:5 [m]S Ge 1:1; S Isa 48:13 [n]S Isa 7:4 [o]S Isa 9:4 **51:14** [p]S Isa 42:7 [q]Isa 49:10 **51:15** [r]S Ex 14:21 [s]S Ps 93:3 [t]S Isa 13:4 **51:16** [u]S Ex 4:12, 15 [v]S Ex 33:22 [w]S Isa 48:13 [x]Jer 7:23; 11:4; 24:7; Eze 14:11; Zec 8:8 **51:17** [y]S Jdg 5:12; Isa 52:1 [z]S ver 22; S Ps 16:5; S Mt 20:22 [a]ver 20; Job 21:20; Isa 42:25; 66:15; Rev 14:10; 16:19 [b]S Ps 75:8 [c]S ver 23; S Ps 60:3 **51:18** [d]Ps 88:18 [e]S Job 31:18; S Isa 49:21 [f]S Isa 41:13 **51:19** [g]S Isa 40:2; 47:9 [h]Isa 49:13; 54:11; Jer 15:5; Na 3:7 [i]Isa 60:18; 62:4; Jer 48:3; La 3:47 [j]S Isa 14:30 [k]Jer 14:12; 24:10 **51:20** [l]Isa 5:25; Jer 14:16; La 2:19 [m]S Job 18:10 [n]S ver 17; S Job 40:11; Jer 44:6 [o]S Dt 28:20 **51:21** [p]S Isa 14:32 [q]ver 17; S Isa 29:9 **51:22** [r]S Isa 49:25 [s]S ver 17; Jer 25:15; 51:7; Hab 2:16; S Mt 20:22 **51:23** [t]Isa 14:4; 49:26; Jer 25:15-17, 26,28; 49:12 [u]ver 17; Zec 12:2 [v]S Jos 10:24 [w]Ps 66:12; Mic 7:10 **52:1** [x]S Isa 51:17 [y]S 1Sa 2:4; S Isa 51:9 [z]Ex 28:2, 40; Est 6:8; Ps 110:3; Isa 49:18; 61:10; Zec 3:4 [a]S Ne 11:1; S Isa 1:26; Mt 4:5; S Rev 21:2 [b]S Ge 34:14 [c]S Isa 35:8 [d]Joel 3:17; Na 1:15; Zec 9:8; Rev 21:27 **52:2** [e]S Isa 29:4 [f]Isa 60:1 [g]S Ps 81:6; S Isa 10:27 [h]Ps 9:14 **52:3** [i]S Ps 44:12 [j]Isa 45:13 [k]S Isa 1:27; 1Pe 1:18 **52:4** [l]S Ge 46:6 [m]Isa 10:24 **52:5** [n]S Isa 37:23; Ro 2:24* **52:6** [o]S Isa 49:23 [p]S Ex 6:3 [q]S Isa 10:20 [r]S Isa 41:26 **52:7** [s]S Isa 42:11

[w]*19* Dead Sea Scrolls, Septuagint, Vulgate and Syriac; Masoretic Text */ how can I* [x]*5* Dead Sea Scrolls and Vulgate; Masoretic Text *wail*

51:17–23 GOD, Wrath—God acts in wrath to discipline His people. See note on 47:1–15.
51:17–23 EVIL AND SUFFERING, Punishment—The suffering of the Exile was God's punishment for Israel's sin. Here God was ready to punish their oppressors. See note on 3:8–17. Today God allows us to suffer the consequences of our actions. He still works in human history to bring about justice and the end of oppression.

are the feet of those who bring good
news,[t]
who proclaim peace,[u]
who bring good tidings,
who proclaim salvation,
who say to Zion,
"Your God reigns!"[v]
8Listen! Your watchmen[w] lift up their
voices;[x]
together they shout for joy.[y]
When the LORD returns[z] to Zion,[a]
they will see it with their own eyes.
9Burst into songs of joy[b] together,
you ruins[c] of Jerusalem,
for the LORD has comforted[d] his
people,
he has redeemed Jerusalem.[e]
10The LORD will lay bare his holy arm[f]
in the sight of all the nations,[g]
and all the ends of the earth[h] will see
the salvation[i] of our God.

11Depart,[j] depart, go out from there!
Touch no unclean thing![k]
Come out from it and be pure,[l]
you who carry the vessels[m] of the
LORD.
12But you will not leave in haste[n]
or go in flight;
for the LORD will go before you,[o]
the God of Israel will be your rear
guard.[p]

The Suffering and Glory of the Servant

13See, my servant[q] will act wisely[y];
he will be raised and lifted up and
highly exalted.[r]
14Just as there were many who were
appalled[s] at him[z]—
his appearance was so disfigured[t]
beyond that of any man
and his form marred beyond human
likeness[u]—
15so will he sprinkle[v] many nations,[a]
and kings[w] will shut their mouths[x]
because of him.
For what they were not told, they will
see,
and what they have not heard, they
will understand.[y]

Chapter 53

WHO has believed our message[z]
and to whom has the arm[a] of the
LORD been revealed?[b]
2He grew up before him like a tender
shoot,[c]
and like a root[d] out of dry ground.
He had no beauty or majesty to attract
us to him,
nothing in his appearance[e] that we
should desire him.
3He was despised and rejected by men,
a man of sorrows,[f] and familiar
with suffering.[g]
Like one from whom men hide[h] their
faces

52:7 [t]S 2Sa 18:26; S Isa 40:9; Ro 10:15* [u]Na 1:15; Lk 2:14; Eph 6:15 [v]S 1Ch 16:31; S Ps 97:1; 1Co 15:24-25 **52:8** [w]S 1Sa 14:16; Isa 56:10; 62:6; Jer 6:17; 31:6; Eze 3:17; 33:7 [x]Isa 40:9 [y]S Isa 12:6 [z]S Nu 10:36 [a]Isa 59:20; Zec 8:3 **52:9** [b]S Ps 98:4; S Isa 35:2 [c]S Ps 74:3; S Isa 51:3 [d]S Isa 40:1; Lk 2:25 [e]S Ezr 9:9; S Isa 48:20 **52:10** [f]S 2Ch 32:8; S Ps 44:3; S Isa 30:30 [g]Isa 66:18 [h]S Jos 4:24; S Isa 11:9 [i]S Ps 67:2; Lk 2:30; 3:6 **52:11** [j]S Isa 48:20 [k]S Isa 1:16; 2Co 6:17* [l]S Nu 8:6; 2Ti 2:19 [m]S 2Ch 36:10 **52:12** [n]S Ex 12:11 [o]Mic 2:13; Jn 10:4 [p]S Ex 14:19 **52:13** [q]S Jos 1:8; S Isa 4:2; S 20:3 [r]S Isa 6:1; 57:15; Ac 3:13; S Php 2:9 **52:14** [s]S Lev 26:32; S Job 18:20 [t]S 2Sa 10:4 [u]S Job 2:12; S 16:16 **52:15** [v]S Lev 14:7; S 16:14-15 [w]S Isa 49:7 [x]S Jdg 18:19; Ps 107:42 [y]Ro 15:21*; Eph 3:4-5 **53:1** [z]S Isa 28:9; Ro 10:16* [a]S Ps 98:1; S Isa 30:30 [b]Jn 12:38* **53:2** [c]S 2Ki 19:26; S Job 14:7; S Isa 4:2 [d]S Isa 11:10 [e]Isa 52:14 **53:3** [f]Ps 69:29 [g]ver 4,10; S Ex 1:10; S Mt 16:21; Lk 18:31-33; Heb 5:8 [h]S Dt 31:17; Isa 1:15

[y]13 Or *will prosper* [z]14 Hebrew *you*
[a]15 Hebrew; Septuagint *so will many nations marvel at him*

52:10 EVANGELISM, Salvation—As God reveals His mighty acts and people come to realize who He is and what He does, they cry out to God for salvation. Evangelism, therefore, is to share the mighty acts of God in redemption that all the ends of the earth will see and turn to Him. For the prophet's audience, God's great act was the return from Exile. For Christians, it is Christ's ministry, death, and resurrection, bringing us salvation.

52:13—53:12 JESUS CHRIST, Servant—See note on Ac 3:13. Israel's destiny was to suffer on behalf of the faithless among her own people. Christ's destiny was to suffer on behalf of all the world. In this fourth servant poem, God vindicated Israel. The suffering of God's Messiah vindicates sinful humanity. The New Testament found the ministry of Jesus forecast in this song stanza by stanza. The general tone of the trial and suffering of Jesus foretold in this song is found in Mt 26:63–64. Jesus' patient example in suffering sets a pattern for us. We may hope our suffering will be caught up in His purpose and plan.

52:13—53:12 EVIL AND SUFFERING, Redemptive—Isaiah described an anonymous "servant" who would save God's people through his suffering. The servant suffers vicariously for the guilty. Isaiah's description of the Suffering Servant anticipated the ministry and death of Jesus (Lk 22:37; Ac 8:32–35). The notion of innocent, vicarious suffering is the deepest truth in the Old Testament about suffering. The traditional view was that suffering was normally a punishment for sin. See note on Job 1:6–12; Pr 1:10–19. Job's friends represent the attempt to explain all suffering as a direct result of sin. See note on Job 4:7–8. However, Job was the exception: a good man experiencing undeserved suffering. In Job's case, his suffering was a testing of his faith in God. Ecclesiastes also criticizes the assumption that all suffering is the result of sin. See note on Ecc 1:1–11. Sometimes we suffer because we deserve it. Sometimes we suffer because others sin and mistreat us, or we suffer as part of God's redemptive purpose. Isaiah's servant represents the deepest truth of an innocent person suffering for the sins of the guilty. Christians can suffer redemptively when their innocent suffering witnesses to the vicarious suffering of Jesus. See note on 1 Pe 2:18–25.

52:13—53:12 THE CHURCH, Servants—The servant appears to be an individual out of the nation Israel. The servant is described as lowly, despised and rejected, suffering for others, accepting of his punishment without murmur, and triumphant. The servant's ministry cannot be evaluated according to physical characteristics. This servant appeared to be the least likely to be chosen of God for special service. No one would have picked such a servant for significant ministry. Rather than being accepted by other people, the servant was despised and rejected by men. Being a servant means suffering on behalf of others. Servants do not assert their rights or seek by secular power to control others for selfish ends. God's Suffering Servant took on Himself the sins of others. By His suffering, humiliation, and death, He provided forgiveness and new life. Though beaten and killed, the Servant was triumphant. He triumphed because God chose to deliver and to exalt Him. This servant is unique because he bore the sins of other people and continues to make intercession for them. Jesus perfectly fulfilled the portrait of the servant of God. He serves as the model for Christians who seek to serve their Lord. See note on 50:4–11.

he was despised,[i] and we esteemed
him not.

4Surely he took up our infirmities
and carried our sorrows,[j]
yet we considered him stricken by
God,[k]
smitten by him, and afflicted.[l]
5But he was pierced[m] for our
transgressions,[n]
he was crushed[o] for our iniquities;
the punishment[p] that brought us
peace[q] was upon him,
and by his wounds[r] we are
healed.[s]
6We all, like sheep, have gone astray,[t]
each of us has turned to his own
way;[u]
and the LORD has laid on him
the iniquity[v] of us all.

7He was oppressed[w] and afflicted,
yet he did not open his mouth;[x]
he was led like a lamb[y] to the
slaughter,[z]
and as a sheep before her shearers is
silent,
so he did not open his mouth.
8By oppression[b] and judgment[a] he was
taken away.
And who can speak of his
descendants?
For he was cut off from the land of the
living;[b]
for the transgression[c] of my people
he was stricken.[c]
9He was assigned a grave with the
wicked,[d]
and with the rich[e] in his death,
though he had done no violence,[f]
nor was any deceit in his mouth.[g]

10Yet it was the LORD's will[h] to crush[i]
him and cause him to suffer,[j]
and though the LORD makes[d] his life
a guilt offering,[k]
he will see his offspring[l] and prolong
his days,
and the will of the LORD will
prosper[m] in his hand.
11After the suffering[n] of his soul,
he will see the light[o] ⌊of life⌋[e] and
be satisfied[f];
by his knowledge[g] my righteous
servant[p] will justify[q] many,
and he will bear their iniquities.[r]
12Therefore I will give him a portion
among the great,[h][s]
and he will divide the spoils[t] with
the strong,[i]
because he poured out his life unto
death,[u]
and was numbered with the
transgressors.[v]
For he bore[w] the sin of many,[x]
and made intercession[y] for the
transgressors.

Chapter 54

The Future Glory of Zion

"SING, O barren woman,[z]
you who never bore a child;
burst into song, shout for joy,[a]
you who were never in labor;[b]
because more are the children[c] of the
desolate[d] woman
than of her who has a husband,[e]"
says the LORD.
2"Enlarge the place of your tent,[f]
stretch your tent curtains wide,
do not hold back;
lengthen your cords,
strengthen your stakes.[g]
3For you will spread out to the right and
to the left;
your descendants[h] will dispossess
nations[i]

53:3 [i]S 1Sa 2:30; S Ps 22:6; Mt 27:29; Jn 1:10-11 **53:4** [j]Mt 8:17* [k]S Dt 5:24; S Job 4:5; Jer 23:5-6; 25:34; Eze 34:23-24; Mic 5:2-4; Zec 13:7; Jn 19:7 [l]S ver 3; S Ge 12:17; S Ru 1:21 **53:5** [m]S Ps 22:16 [n]S Ex 28:38; S Ps 39:8; S Jn 3:17; Ro 4:25; 1Co 15:3; Heb 9:28 [o]Ps 34:18 [p]S Isa 50:6 [q]S Isa 9:6; Ro 5:1 [r]Isa 1:6; Mt 27:26; Jn 19:1 [s]S Dt 32:39; S 2Ch 7:14; 1Pe 2:24-25 **53:6** [t]S Ps 95:10; 1Pe 2:24-25 [u]S 1Sa 8:3; Isa 56:11; 57:17; Mic 3:5 [v]ver 12; S Ex 28:38; Ro 4:25 **53:7** [w]Isa 49:26 [x]S Mk 14:61; 1Pe 2:23 [y]Mt 27:31; S Jn 1:29 [z]S Ps 44:22 **53:8** [a]Mk 14:49 [b]Ps 88:5; Da 9:26; Ac 8:32-33* [c]ver 12; S Ps 39:8 **53:9** [d]Mt 27:38; Mk 15:27; Lk 23:32; Jn 19:18 [e]Mt 27:57-60; Mk 15:43-46; Lk 23:50-53; Jn 19:38-41 [f]Isa 42:1-3 [g]S Job 16:17; 1Pe 2:22*; 1Jn 3:5; Rev 14:5 **53:10** [h]Isa 46:10; 55:11; Ac 2:23 [i]ver 5 [j]S ver 3; S Ge 12:17 [k]S Lev 5:15; Jn 3:17 [l]S Ps 22:30 [m]S Jos 1:8; S Isa 49:4 **53:11** [n]Jn 10:14-18 [o]S Job 33:30 [p]S Isa 20:3; Ac 7:52 [q]S Isa 6:7; Jn 1:29; Ac 10:43; S Ro 4:25 [r]S Ex 28:38 **53:12** [s]S Isa 6:1; S Php 2:9 [t]S Ex 15:9; S Ps 119:162; Lk 11:22 [u]Mt 26:28,38,39,42 [v]Mt 27:38; Mk 15:27*; Lk 22:37*; 23:32 [w]S ver 6; 1Pe 2:24 [x]Heb 9:28 [y]Isa 59:16; S Ro 8:34 **54:1** [z]S Ge 30:1 [a]S Ge 21:6; S Ps 98:4 [b]Isa 66:7 [c]Isa 49:20 [d]S Isa 49:19 [e]S 1Sa 2:5; Gal 4:27* **54:2** [f]S Ge 26:22; Isa 26:15; 49:19-20 [g]Ex 35:18; 39:40 **54:3** [h]S Ge 13:14; S Isa 48:19 [i]S Job 12:23; S Isa 14:2; 60:4-11

[b]*8* Or *From arrest* [c]*8* Or *away. / Yet who of his generation considered / that he was cut off from the land of the living / for the transgression of my people, / to whom the blow was due?* [d]*10* Hebrew *though you make* [e]*11* Dead Sea Scrolls (see also Septuagint); Masoretic Text does not have *the light ⌊of life⌋.* [f]*11* Or (with Masoretic Text) *11He will see the result of the suffering of his soul / and be satisfied* [g]*11* Or *by knowledge of him* [h]*12* Or *many* [i]*12* Or *numerous*

53:4–12 SALVATION, Atonement—Isaiah pointed to a loving Suffering Servant whom God would provide as an atonement for sin. The personal pronouns of vv 4–6 indicate that the Servant is neither Israel, the remnant, nor the prophet. The New Testament identifies Him as Jesus Christ (1 Pe 2:21–25).

53:6 SIN, Universal Nature—Unexpected love shocks us into confessing our sin. In face of the Suffering Servant our only response is to say we belong to a dumb race which has all followed the leader into sin and destruction. We have followed our own path instead of following our Shepherd. That is the essence of sin.

53:11 SALVATION, Justification—God promised His Suffering Servant would justify many. See note on 53:4–12.

53:12 PRAYER, Intercession—The Old Testament mentions the intercession of the Messiah. See notes on Ro 8:34; Heb 7:25.

54:1–5 EVANGELISM, Involves—Christians are to branch out with a vision of a needy world and become involved in ministry so that all may hear of Jesus Christ and His saving grace. We are not to "hold back" from anyone who needs the gospel. It will mean lengthening our views from the narrow and provincial. It also demands strengthening our often limited involvement. This we must do if we are to evangelize the whole world. Our humble, barren condition is no excuse. God promises strength and blessing to His faithful witnesses. As God restored and repopulated Jerusalem after the Exile, He seeks to restore His church to accomplish His evangelistic mission.

and settle in their desolate[j] cities.

4"Do not be afraid;[k] you will not suffer
shame.[l]
Do not fear disgrace;[m] you will not
be humiliated.
You will forget the shame of your
youth[n]
and remember no more the
reproach[o] of your
widowhood.[p]
5For your Maker[q] is your husband[r]—
the LORD Almighty is his name—
the Holy One[s] of Israel is your
Redeemer;[t]
he is called the God of all the
earth.[u]
6The LORD will call you back[v]
as if you were a wife deserted[w] and
distressed in spirit—
a wife who married young,[x]
only to be rejected," says your God.
7"For a brief moment[y] I abandoned[z]
you,
but with deep compassion[a] I will
bring you back.[b]
8In a surge of anger[c]
I hid[d] my face from you for a
moment,
but with everlasting kindness[e]
I will have compassion[f] on you,"
says the LORD your Redeemer.[g]

9"To me this is like the days of Noah,
when I swore that the waters of
Noah would never again cover
the earth.[h]
So now I have sworn[i] not to be
angry[j] with you,
never to rebuke[k] you again.
10Though the mountains be shaken[l] [m]
and the hills be removed,
yet my unfailing love[n] for you will not
be shaken[o]
nor my covenant[p] of peace[q] be
removed,"
says the LORD, who has
compassion[r] on you.

11"O afflicted[s] city, lashed by storms[t]
and not comforted,[u]
I will build you with stones of
turquoise,[j] [v]
your foundations[w] with
sapphires.[k] [x]
12I will make your battlements of rubies,
your gates[y] of sparkling jewels,
and all your walls of precious stones.
13All your sons will be taught by the
LORD,[z]
and great will be your children's
peace.[a]
14In righteousness[b] you will be
established:[c]
Tyranny[d] will be far from you;
you will have nothing to fear.[e]
Terror[f] will be far removed;
it will not come near you.
15If anyone does attack you, it will not
be my doing;
whoever attacks you will surrender[g]
to you.
16"See, it is I who created the
blacksmith[h]
who fans the coals into flame
and forges a weapon[i] fit for its
work.
And it is I who have created the
destroyer[j] to work havoc;
17 no weapon forged against you will
prevail,[k]

54:3 [j]S Isa 49:19 **54:4** [k]Jer 30:10; Joel 2:21 [l]S Isa 28:16; S 29:22 [m]S Ge 30:23; S Ps 119:39; S Isa 41:11 [n]S Ps 25:7; S Jer 2:2; S 22:21 [o]S Isa 51:7 [p]S Isa 47:8 **54:5** [q]S Ps 95:6; S 149:2; S Isa 51:13 [r]S SS 3:11; Jer 3:14; 31:32; Hos 2:7,16 [s]S Isa 1:4; 49:7; 55:5; 60:9 [t]S Isa 48:17 [u]S Isa 6:3; S 12:4 **54:6** [v]Isa 49:14-21 [w]ver 6-7; Isa 1:4; 50:1-2; 60:15; 62:4,12; Jer 44:2; Hos 1:10 [x]S Ex 20:14; Mal 2:15 **54:7** [y]S Job 14:13; Isa 26:20 [z]S Ps 71:11; S Isa 27:8 [a]S Ps 51:1 [b]S Isa 49:18 **54:8** [c]Isa 9:12; 26:20; 60:10 [d]S Isa 1:15 [e]ver 10; S Ps 25:6; 92:2; Isa 55:3; 63:7 [f]S Ps 102:13; S Isa 14:1; Hos 2:19 [g]S Isa 48:17 **54:9** [h]S Ge 8:21 [i]S Isa 14:24; S 49:18 [j]Ps 13:1; 103:9; Isa 12:1; 57:16; Jer 3:5,12; Eze 39:29; Mic 7:18 [k]S Dt 28:20 **54:10** [l]Rev 6:14 [m]S Ps 46:2 [n]S Ps 6:4 [o]S Isa 51:6; Heb 12:27 [p]S Ge 9:16; Ex 34:10; Ps 89:34; S Isa 42:6 [q]S Nu 25:12 [r]ver 8; S Isa 14:1; 55:7 **54:11** [s]S Isa 14:32 [t]Isa 28:2; 29:6 [u]S Isa 51:19 [v]1Ch 29:2; Rev 21:18 [w]S Isa 28:16; Rev 21:19-20 [x]S Ex 24:10; S Job 28:6 **54:12** [y]Rev 21:21 **54:13** [z]S Isa 28:9; Mic 4:2; Jn 6:45*; Heb 8:11 [a]S Lev 26:6; S Isa 48:18 **54:14** [b]S Isa 26:2 [c]Jer 30:20 [d]S 2Sa 7:10; S Isa 9:4 [e]Zep 3:15; Zec 9:8 [f]S Isa 17:14 **54:15** [g]S Isa 41:11-16 **54:16** [h]S Isa 44:12 [i]S Isa 10:5 [j]S Isa 13:5 **54:17** [k]S Isa 29:8

[j]11 The meaning of the Hebrew for this word is uncertain. [k]11 Or *lapis lazuli*

54:5,16 GOD, Creator—With a play on the Hebrew word *ba'al,* the prophet explained that the all-powerful Creator God was also a loving husband, unlike Baal, the Canaanite god who claimed to control fertility but was not the creator. Baal also played the husband in the fertility rituals but was certainly not a dedicated, loving husband to his worshipers. Our God has the power to create and the compassion to love.

54:7–10 GOD, Love—God's love is eternal while His wrath was displayed for a moment. See note on 51:17–23.

54:9–10 THE CHURCH, Covenant People—Peace and a relationship of mutual love are God's intentions for His people. As in the days of Noah, God once again promised His steadfast love to the people after their punishment in Exile. Peace involves fullness or completeness. Peace is more than the absence of conflict. When we have peace, we experience the fullness of life, with the joys of health, family, prosperity, and right relationships with God and other individuals. God's covenant of peace signifies His never-ending desire to do good for His chosen people. See notes on Ge 9:8–17; 2 Ch 6:14.

54:11–17 CREATION, Evil—*Sometimes God finds it necessary to chastise His* people. He chooses the instrument and even gives the strength to perform the task. Assyria and Babylon humbled Israel and Judah; but when they completed their God-assigned task, they passed into oblivion. When such people are at the height of their power, they become puffed up with their importance. They do not realize God is the Creator and that His creative goal is a new, majestic city in which people will heed His teaching, the righteous world order will be established, terror will vanish, and weapons of war will become ineffective.

54:11–17 CHRISTIAN ETHICS, War and Peace—Peace is God's vision and promise for His people. Peace is initiated by God's actions and by His people learning and doing His will. Peace includes righteousness, freedom from tyrants, absence of fear and terror, and protection from attackers and false accusations.

54:14 CHRISTIAN ETHICS, Righteousness—When God achieves His goal of a righteous people, tyrants will no longer rule, so terror and terrorism will vanish. See note on 51:1–3.

54:17 THE CHURCH, Servants—God's servants inherit security and hope because God is the Creator (v 5) and Covenant-maker (vv 9–10). Every person who commits life to God becomes His servant with a call to witness (49:1–7). As servants, we may be punished; but we will never lose our security, for He promises His help against all our enemies.

and you will refute[l] every tongue
that accuses you.
This is the heritage of the servants[m] of
the LORD,
and this is their vindication[n] from
me,"
declares the LORD.

Chapter 55

Invitation to the Thirsty

"COME, all you who are thirsty,[o]
come to the waters;[p]
and you who have no money,
come, buy[q] and eat!
Come, buy wine and milk[r]
without money and without cost.[s]
2Why spend money on what is not
bread,
and your labor on what does not
satisfy?[t]
Listen, listen to me, and eat what is
good,[u]
and your soul will delight in the
richest[v] of fare.
3Give ear and come to me;
hear[w] me, that your soul may live.[x]
I will make an everlasting covenant[y]
with you,
my faithful love[z] promised to
David.[a]
4See, I have made him a witness[b] to
the peoples,
a leader and commander[c] of the
peoples.
5Surely you will summon nations[d] you
know not,
and nations that do not know you
will hasten to you,[e]
because of the LORD your God,
the Holy One[f] of Israel,
for he has endowed you with
splendor."[g]

6Seek[h] the LORD while he may be
found;[i]
call[j] on him while he is near.
7Let the wicked forsake[k] his way
and the evil man his thoughts.[l]
Let him turn[m] to the LORD, and he will
have mercy[n] on him,
and to our God, for he will freely
pardon.[o]
8"For my thoughts[p] are not your
thoughts,
neither are your ways my ways,"[q]
declares the LORD.
9"As the heavens are higher than the
earth,[r]
so are my ways higher than your
ways
and my thoughts than your
thoughts.[s]
10As the rain[t] and the snow
come down from heaven,
and do not return to it
without watering the earth
and making it bud and flourish,[u]
so that it yields seed[v] for the sower
and bread for the eater,[w]
11so is my word[x] that goes out from my
mouth:
It will not return to me empty,[y]
but will accomplish what I desire
and achieve the purpose[z] for which
I sent it.
12You will go out in joy[a]
and be led forth in peace;[b]
the mountains and hills
will burst into song[c] before you,
and all the trees[d] of the field
will clap their hands.[e]

54:17 [l]S Isa 41:11 [m]Isa 56:6-8; 63:17; 65:8,9,13-15; 66:14 [n]S Ps 17:2; Zec 1:20-21 **55:1** [o]S Pr 9:5; S Isa 35:7; Mt 5:6; Lk 6:21; Jn 4:14; 7:37 [p]Jer 2:13; Eze 47:1,12; Zec 14:8 [q]La 5:4; Mt 13:44; Rev 3:18 [r]S SS 5:1; 1Pe 2:2 [s]Hos 14:4; Mt 10:8; Rev 21:6; 22:17 **55:2** [t]Ps 22:26; Ecc 6:2; Isa 49:4; Jer 12:13; Hos 4:10; 8:7; Mic 6:14; Hag 1:6 [u]S Isa 1:19 [v]S Isa 30:23 **55:3** [w]S Ps 78:1 [x]S Lev 18:5; S Jn 6:27; Ro 10:5 [y]S Ge 9:16; S Isa 54:10; S Heb 13:20 [z]S Isa 54:8 [a]Ac 13:34* **55:4** [b]Rev 1:5 [c]S 1Sa 13:14; S 2Ch 7:18; S Isa 32:1 **55:5** [d]S Isa 49:6 [e]S Isa 2:3 [f]S Isa 12:6; S 54:5 [g]S Isa 44:23 **55:6** [h]S Dt 4:29; S 2Ch 15:2; S Isa 9:13 [i]Ps 32:6; Isa 49:8; Ac 17:27; 2Co 6:1-2 [j]S Ps 50:15; Isa 65:24; Jer 29:12; 33:3 **55:7** [k]S 2Ch 7:14; S 30:9; Eze 18:27-28 [l]Isa 32:7; 59:7 [m]S Isa 44:22; S Jer 26:3; S Eze 18:32 [n]S Isa 54:10 [o]S 2Ch 6:21; Isa 1:18; 40:2 **55:8** [p]Php 2:5; 4:8 [q]Isa 53:6; Mic 4:12 **55:9** [r]S Job 11:8; Ps 103:11 [s]S Nu 23:19; S Isa 40:13-14 **55:10** [t]Isa 30:23 [u]S Lev 25:19; S Job 14:9; S Ps 67:6 [v]S Ge 47:23 [w]2Co 9:10 **55:11** [x]S Dt 32:2; Jn 1:1 [y]Isa 40:8; 45:23; S Mt 5:18; Heb 4:12 [z]S Pr 19:21; S Isa 44:26; Eze 12:25 **55:12** [a]S Ps 98:4; S Isa 35:2 [b]Isa 54:10,13 [c]S Ps 65:12-13; S 96:12-13 [d]S 1Ch 16:33 [e]Ps 98:8

55:1–13 EVANGELISM, Call to Salvation—This most significant chapter for evangelism presents ten vital truths: (1) God calls all to receive His free grace (v 1); (2) only God's salvation truly satisfies (v 2); (3) all can have new life as nations and people come into the new covenant (vv 3–5); (4) God warns everyone to seek Him while He can be found (v 6); (5) the human response must be one of true repentance (v 7a); (6) pardon and forgiveness are wonderfully possible (v 7b); (7) God is above all, but He can still be experienced (vv 8–9); (8) God's Word is powerful and will do its saving work (vv 10–11); (9) great joy erupts everywhere when people come to salvation (v 12); and (10) fruit that glorifies God is the everlasting result of effective evangelism (v 13). In the light of these realities, how wise it is to evangelize and call people to God's great salvation.

55:3 GOD, Love—God renewed His promise of Messiah, a promise issuing from His covenant love for His people. See note on 54:7–10.

55:3 THE CHURCH, Covenant People—God pursues His people, desiring to do good for them. When people come in commitment and faith, God promises to be their God. God wants to make an everlasting covenant with each individual (55:1). The everlasting covenant indicates God's desire that all people belong to Him forever. Every person can have the same assurance David had of God's faithful love. Receiving the assurance, we also receive the commission to witness to all nations (v 4).

55:6–13 GOD, Transcendent—God's total difference in power, authority, and sphere of influence forms the basis of His invitation to salvation. Because He is so much greater than we are, we can trust Him though we do not understand everything which happens.

55:6–7 SALVATION, Repentance—God offers a free pardon to those who repent. Repentance is an inward reversal of life, a radical change of thought and conduct. The gospel of repentance does not contradict the gospel of grace. Compare Mk 1:15. See note on 2 Ch 30:6.

55:7 SALVATION, Grace—The Lord shows mercy to those who forsake wickedness and evil. Wicked conduct and evil thoughts obstruct God's grace.

55:12 SALVATION, Joy—The prophet conceived of the exiles' return as a new exodus. Nature itself would join the triumphant chorus of God's pilgrims. The wonders of the new exodus surpass those of the old. This text previews the incomparable joy of the Lord's salvation of His people through Jesus Christ His Son.

13Instead of the thornbush will grow the pine tree,
and instead of briers[f] the myrtle[g] will grow.
This will be for the LORD's renown,[h]
for an everlasting sign,
which will not be destroyed."

Chapter 56

Salvation for Others

THIS is what the LORD says:
"Maintain justice[i]
and do what is right,[j]
for my salvation[k] is close at hand
and my righteousness[l] will soon be revealed.
2Blessed[m] is the man who does this,
the man who holds it fast,
who keeps the Sabbath[n] without desecrating it,
and keeps his hand from doing any evil."

3Let no foreigner[o] who has bound himself to the LORD say,
"The LORD will surely exclude me from his people."[p]
And let not any eunuch[q] complain,
"I am only a dry tree."

4For this is what the LORD says:

"To the eunuchs[r] who keep my Sabbaths,
who choose what pleases me
and hold fast to my covenant[s] —
5to them I will give within my temple and its walls[t]
a memorial[u] and a name
better than sons and daughters;
I will give them an everlasting name[v]
that will not be cut off.[w]
6And foreigners[x] who bind themselves to the LORD
to serve[y] him,
to love the name[z] of the LORD,
and to worship him,
all who keep the Sabbath[a] without desecrating it
and who hold fast to my covenant—
7these I will bring to my holy mountain[b]
and give them joy in my house of prayer.
Their burnt offerings and sacrifices[c]
will be accepted on my altar;
for my house will be called
a house of prayer for all nations.[d]"[e]
8The Sovereign LORD declares—
he who gathers the exiles of Israel:
"I will gather[f] still others to them
besides those already gathered."

God's Accusation Against the Wicked

9Come, all you beasts of the field,[g]
come and devour, all you beasts of the forest!
10Israel's watchmen[h] are blind,
they all lack knowledge;[i]
they are all mute dogs,
they cannot bark;
they lie around and dream,
they love to sleep.[j]
11They are dogs with mighty appetites;
they never have enough.
They are shepherds[k] who lack understanding;[l]
they all turn to their own way,[m]
each seeks his own gain.[n]
12"Come," each one cries, "let me get wine![o]
Let us drink our fill of beer!
And tomorrow will be like today,
or even far better."[p]

55:13 [f]S Nu 33:55; S Isa 5:6 [g]Isa 41:19 [h]S Ps 102:12; Isa 63:12; Jer 32:20; 33:9
56:1 [i]S Ps 11:7; S Isa 1:17; S Jer 22:3 [j]S Isa 26:8 [k]S Ps 85:9 [l]Jer 23:6; Da 9:24
56:2 [m]S Ps 119:2 [n]S Ex 20:8,10
56:3 [o]S Ex 12:43; S 1Ki 8:41; S Isa 11:10; Zec 8:20-23 [p]Dt 23:3 [q]S Lev 21:20; Jer 38:7 *fn*; Ac 8:27
56:4 [r]Jer 38:7 *fn* [s]S Ex 31:13
56:5 [t]Isa 26:1; 60:18 [u]S Nu 32:42; 1Sa 15:12 [v]S Isa 43:7 [w]S Isa 48:19; 55:13
56:6 [x]S Ex 12:43; S 1Ki 8:41 [y]S 1Ch 22:2; Isa 60:7,10; 61:5 [z]Mal 1:11 [a]ver 2,4
56:7 [b]S Isa 2:2; Eze 20:40 [c]S Isa 19:21; Ro 12:1; Php 4:18; Heb 13:15 [d]Mt 21:13*; Lk 19:46* [e]Mk 11:17*
56:8 [f]S Dt 30:4; S Isa 1:9; S 11:12; 60:3-11; Eze 34:12; Jn 10:16
56:9 [g]Isa 18:6; Jer 12:9; Eze 34:5, 8; 39:17-20
56:10 [h]S Isa 52:8; 62:6; Jer 6:17; 31:6; Eze 3:17; 33:7 [i]Jer 2:8; 10:21; 14:13-14 [j]Na 3:18
56:11 [k]Jer 23:1; Eze 34:2 [l]Isa 1:3 [m]S Isa 53:6; Hos 4:7-8 [n]Isa 57:17; Jer 6:13; 8:10; 22:17; Eze 13:19; Mic 3:11
56:12 [o]S Lev 10:9; S Pr 23:20; S Isa 22:13 [p]Ps 10:6; Lk 12:18-19

56:1–8 SALVATION, Definition—God's salvation includes foreigners and eunuchs as well as His exiled people. He goes beyond the Law (Dt 23:1–3) in His saving grace. His grace extends to physically mutilated persons (Ac 8:26–40) and to Gentiles (Isa 51:4–5; 52:10). Jesus quoted from v 7 when He cleansed the Temple (Mk 11:17). None is excluded from salvation because of race, nationality, color, economic condition, or the like. Salvation is available to any person ready to trust and serve God.

56:1 CHRISTIAN ETHICS, Righteousness—Impatient people must let God fulfill His promises His way. Return from Exile and rebuilding the Temple had not brought the renewed glory Israel expected. God called on them for renewed dedication to worship and social justice. Then He would reveal full salvation and righteous acts which would fulfill His promises and their hopes. Participation in God's salvation is not passive. We must be actively involved in God's work of righteousness.

56:3–8 GOD, Love—God's *love and His salvation* are *intended for all persons*, Gentiles and Jews alike. No physical disability disqualifies a person from God's salvation. God is the one true God, with love and compassion for all humans. Compare 23:1–8. See notes on Ex 3:7; Dt 32:10–12,36; Mt 10:29–31; Jn 3:16.

56:3–8 EVANGELISM, Universality—Nothing separates us from accepting God's salvation. Foreign origin or physical handicap may raise questions with people, but they serve as God's opportunity to reveal His grace. God accepts and promises blessing to all people who accept Him. The door to God is open to everyone. God's witnesses must announce this to all.

56:4–8 THE CHURCH, Covenant People—Physical traits do not disqualify us from being part of God's people. In sharp contrast to much of official Judaism in biblical times, God includes people with handicaps and deficiencies in His covenant. God desires that all people come to Him. God accepts those whom others cast out. He receives eunuchs and foreigners. God's only requirement is to keep the covenant He has made. Covenant stipulations include the worship of God on His day. See note on Ex 19:4–8.

56:7 PRAYER, Universality of—The prophet promised salvation will be available to all, and all will come to the Temple to pray. Therefore Jesus called it a "house of prayer for all nations" (Mk 11:17). See note on Mt 21:13. God wants all people to pray to Him. He sets no preconditions.

Chapter 57

THE righteous perish,[q]
and no one ponders it in his heart;[r]
devout men are taken away,
and no one understands
that the righteous are taken away
to be spared from evil.[s]
2Those who walk uprightly[t]
enter into peace;
they find rest[u] as they lie in death.

3"But you—come here, you sons of a
sorceress,[v]
you offspring of adulterers[w] and
prostitutes![x]
4Whom are you mocking?
At whom do you sneer
and stick out your tongue?
Are you not a brood of rebels,[y]
the offspring of liars?
5You burn with lust among the oaks[z]
and under every spreading tree;[a]
you sacrifice your children[b] in the
ravines
and under the overhanging crags.
6⌊The idols⌋[c] among the smooth stones
of the ravines are your
portion;
they, they are your lot.
Yes, to them you have poured out
drink offerings[d]
and offered grain offerings.
In the light of these things, should I
relent?[e]
7You have made your bed on a high and
lofty hill;[f]
there you went up to offer your
sacrifices.[g]
8Behind your doors and your doorposts
you have put your pagan symbols.
Forsaking me, you uncovered your
bed,
you climbed into it and opened it
wide;
you made a pact with those whose
beds you love,[h]
and you looked on their
nakedness.[i]
9You went to Molech[l][j] with olive oil
and increased your perfumes.[k]
You sent your ambassadors[m][l] far
away;
you descended to the grave[n][m] itself!
10You were wearied[n] by all your ways,
but you would not say, 'It is
hopeless.'[o]
You found renewal of your strength,[p]
and so you did not faint.

11"Whom have you so dreaded and
feared[q]
that you have been false to me,
and have neither remembered[r] me
nor pondered[s] this in your hearts?
Is it not because I have long been
silent[t]
that you do not fear me?
12I will expose your righteousness and
your works,[u]
and they will not benefit you.
13When you cry out[v] for help,
let your collection ⌊of idols⌋ save[w]
you!
The wind will carry all of them off,
a mere breath will blow[x] them
away.
But the man who makes me his
refuge[y]
will inherit the land[z]
and possess my holy mountain."[a]

Comfort for the Contrite

14And it will be said:

"Build up, build up, prepare the
road![b]
Remove the obstacles out of the way
of my people."[c]
15For this is what the high and lofty[d]
One says—
he who lives forever,[e] whose name
is holy:

57:1 [q]S Ps 12:1; Eze 21:3 [r]S Isa 42:25 [s]S 2Ki 22:20 **57:2** [t]Isa 26:7 [u]Da 12:13 **57:3** [v]S Ex 22:18; Mal 3:5 [w]ver 7-8; Mt 16:4; Jas 4:4 [x]Isa 1:21; Jer 2:20 **57:4** [y]S Isa 1:2 **57:5** [z]S Isa 1:29 [a]S Dt 12:2; 2Ki 16:4 [b]S Lev 18:21; S Dt 18:10; Ps 106:37-38; Eze 16:20 **57:6** [c]S 2Ki 17:10; Jer 3:9; Hab 2:19 [d]Jer 7:18; 19:13; 44:18 [e]Jer 5:9,29; 9:9 **57:7** [f]Jer 3:6; Eze 6:3; 16:16; 20:29 [g]Isa 65:7; Jer 13:27; Eze 6:13; 20:27-28 **57:8** [h]Eze 16:26; 23:7 [i]Eze 16:15,36; 23:18 **57:9** [j]S Lev 18:21; S 1Ki 11:5 [k]S SS 4:10 [l]Eze 23:16,40 [m]S Isa 8:19 **57:10** [n]S Isa 47:13 [o]Jer 2:25; 18:12; Mal 3:14 [p]S 1Sa 2:4 **57:11** [q]S 2Ki 1:15; Pr 29:25; Isa 7:2 [r]S Isa 17:10; Jer 2:32; 3:21; 13:25; 18:15; Eze 22:12 [s]S Isa 42:23 [t]S Est 4:14; S Ps 50:21; S 83:1 **57:12** [u]Isa 29:15; 58:1; 59:6,12; 65:7; 66:18; Eze 16:2; Mic 3:2-4,8 **57:13** [v]Jer 22:20; 30:15 [w]S Jdg 10:14 [x]Isa 40:7,24 [y]S Ps 118:8 [z]S Ps 37:9 [a]Isa 2:2-3; 56:7; 65:9-11 **57:14** [b]S Isa 11:16 [c]Isa 62:10; Jer 18:15 **57:15** [d]S Isa 52:13 [e]S Dt 33:27; S Ps 90:2

[l]9 Or *to the king* [m]9 Or *idols* [n]9 Hebrew *Sheol*

57:1–13 GOD, One God—Temporary misfortune and the seeming silence of God are no reason to forsake Him for sin and idolatry. Idols can never save. God's eternally valid and inspired promise guarantees salvation to His faithful people. Only He is God.

57:1–2 CREATION, Evil—The prophet's caustic attack upon the Israelites' folly for worshiping idols forms the background for this chapter. God wanted the people returning from captivity in Babylon to be thoroughly purged of all evil practices. Instead, He found immoral conduct comparable to the days of Jeremiah and Ezekiel. God created a wonderful world, but wicked people have contaminated it by participating in immorality. God takes good people away from this evil world for one important reason. They can then be safe from the impure things that constantly threaten to contaminate them. Godly people find ultimate security only when they leave their present habitation to be with their Creator.

57:1–2 HUMANITY, Death and Sin—A new dimension is added to the understanding of death. It can be a deliverance from catastrophe and suffering, rather than merely a punishment for sin. God can use death to spare His righteous people worse horrors. Sadly, many people go through so many unnecessary, even wicked, religious ceremonies they do not notice the righteous person's death.

57:9 LAST THINGS, Intermediate State—See note on 14:9.

57:14–21 CREATION, Hope—New opportunity does not mean paradise achieved. Returning from Exile, Israel returned to her greedy ways. God determined a new course of action. Life remained His goal for the creature into whose nostrils He breathed life (Ge 2:7). He would heal His people, creating them anew, removing greed, and creating (Hebrew *bara'*) praise on mourning lips. See note on Ge 1:1. The wicked would, however, still exist and would continue to seek peace and wholeness fruitlessly.

57:14–19 HUMANITY, Human Nature—The weak creature faces death when the Creator becomes angry. God's desire is to heal His sinful people.

57:15 GOD, Grace—While God is great in power and authority, exalted far above humans, He is also a God of grace,

"I live in a high[f] and holy place,
but also with him who is contrite[g]
and lowly in spirit,[h]
to revive the spirit of the lowly
and to revive the heart of the
contrite.[i]
16 I will not accuse[j] forever,
nor will I always be angry,[k]
for then the spirit of man would grow
faint before me—
the breath[l] of man that I have
created.
17 I was enraged by his sinful greed;[m]
I punished him, and hid[n] my face in
anger,
yet he kept on in his willful ways.[o]
18 I have seen his ways, but I will heal[p]
him;
I will guide[q] him and restore
comfort[r] to him,
19 creating praise on the lips[s] of the
mourners in Israel.
Peace, peace,[t] to those far and
near,"[u]
says the LORD. "And I will heal
them."
20 But the wicked[v] are like the tossing
sea,[w]
which cannot rest,
whose waves cast up mire[x] and
mud.
21 "There is no peace,"[y] says my God,
"for the wicked."[z]

Chapter 58

True Fasting

"SHOUT it aloud,[a] do not hold back.
Raise your voice like a trumpet.[b]
Declare to my people their rebellion[c]
and to the house of Jacob their
sins.[d]
2 For day after day they seek[e] me out;
they seem eager to know my ways,
as if they were a nation that does what
is right
and has not forsaken[f] the
commands of its God.

57:15 [f]S Job 16:19 [g]Ps 147:3 [h]Ps 34:18; 51:17; Isa 66:2; Mic 6:8; Mt 5:3 [i]S 2Ki 22:19; S Job 5:18; S Mt 23:12 **57:16** [j]S Ps 50:21; Isa 3:13-14 [k]S Ps 103:9; S Isa 54:9 [l]S Ge 2:7; Zec 12:1 **57:17** [m]S Isa 56:11; Jer 8:10 [n]S Isa 1:15 [o]Isa 1:4; S 30:15; S 53:6; 66:3 **57:18** [p]S Dt 32:39; S 2Ch 7:14; S Isa 30:26 [q]S Ps 48:14; S Isa 42:16; S 48:17 [r]Isa 49:13; 61:1-3 **57:19** [s]Isa 6:7; 51:16; 59:21; Heb 13:15 [t]S Isa 2:4; 26:3,12; 32:17; S Lk 2:14 [u]Ac 2:39 **57:20** [v]Job 18:5-21 [w]S Ge 49:4; Eph 4:14; Jude 1:13 [x]Ps 69:14 **57:21** [y]S Isa 26:3; 59:8; Eze 13:16 [z]S Isa 48:22 **58:1** [a]Isa 40:6 [b]S Ex 20:18 [c]S Isa 24:20; S 48:8 [d]S Isa 57:12; Eze 3:17 **58:2** [e]S Isa 48:1; Tit 1:16; Jas 4:8 [f]S Dt 32:15; S Ps 119:87 [g]Isa 29:13 **58:3** [h]S Lev 16:29 [i]S Ex 10:3; S 2Ch 6:37; Jer 44:10 [j]Mal 3:14 [k]Isa 22:13; Zec 7:5-6 **58:4** [l]1Ki 21:9-13; Isa 59:6; Jer 6:7; Eze 7:11; Mal 2:16 [m]S 1Sa 8:18; Isa 59:2; La 3:44; Eze 8:18; Mic 3:4 **58:5** [n]Zec 7:5 [o]1Ki 21:27; Mt 6:16 [p]S Isa 36:6 [q]S Job 2:8 **58:6** [r]Joel 2:12-14 [s]Ne 5:10-11 [t]S Dt 14:29; Isa 61:1; Jer 34:9; Am 4:1; S Lk 4:19 [u]S Isa 9:4 **58:7** [v]S Job 22:7; Eze 18:16; Lk 3:11 [w]Isa 16:4; Heb 13:2 [x]Job 31:19-20; S Mt 25:36 [y]S Ge 29:14; Lk 10:31-32 **58:8** [z]S Job 11:17; S Isa 9:2 [a]S Isa 1:5; S 30:26

They ask me for just decisions
and seem eager for God to come
near[g] them.
3 'Why have we fasted,'[h] they say,
'and you have not seen it?
Why have we humbled[i] ourselves,
and you have not noticed?'[j]

"Yet on the day of your fasting, you do
as you please[k]
and exploit all your workers.
4 Your fasting ends in quarreling and
strife,[l]
and in striking each other with
wicked fists.
You cannot fast as you do today
and expect your voice to be heard[m]
on high.
5 Is this the kind of fast[n] I have
chosen,
only a day for a man to humble[o]
himself?
Is it only for bowing one's head like a
reed[p]
and for lying on sackcloth and
ashes?[q]
Is that what you call a fast,
a day acceptable to the LORD?

6 "Is not this the kind of fasting[r] I have
chosen:
to loose the chains of injustice[s]
and untie the cords of the yoke,
to set the oppressed[t] free
and break every yoke?[u]
7 Is it not to share your food with the
hungry[v]
and to provide the poor wanderer
with shelter[w]—
when you see the naked, to clothe[x]
him,
and not to turn away from your own
flesh and blood?[y]
8 Then your light will break forth like
the dawn,[z]
and your healing[a] will quickly
appear;

---

a God of love, who draws people to Himself.
57:15 CHRISTIAN ETHICS, Character—Contriteness or sadness over one's spiritual state is a mark of one who seeks God's face. Such contriteness will be honored by God's comforting presence.
57:16–18 GOD, Wrath—Notice that while God's wrath is real, it is also temporary and is superseded by His love. He truly understands our weakness and impatience.
58:1–14 EVIL AND SUFFERING, Humility—Sufferers should come humbly before God seeking to know and do His will. Israel ritualized humility. They established fasting ceremonies and rites to express sorrow to God. They were sorry for their condition, not for their deeds. *That is not humility. God questioned their motives, for their* actions were unjust and oppressive. God seeks humility expressed by concerned action in behalf of the poor, hungry, and needy. Only such acts show true humility. Even in our suffering we must be more concerned for the needs of others than for our own.
58:1–9 SIN, Unrighteousness—Religion mixed with unrighteousness and injustice is sin. Going through the motions of worship and repentance does not gain favor with God when we exploit the poor and gain social standing by mistreating other people. A contentious spirit does not fit a religious heart. If we expect God to answer our prayers, we must help the helpless and establish justice for all people. True worship comes only from righteous living.
58:6–7 DISCIPLESHIP, Poor—God desires that His people be set free from the chains of injustice and that they share their blessings with those who are less fortunate. Disciples *choose* service to others rather than ritual observances to express devotion to God. See note on Lev 19:1–2,9–19.
58:8 GOD, Glory—A people in need must help others in need before they can expect the glorious presence of God to come protect them.

then your righteousness[o][b] will go
before you,
and the glory of the LORD will be
your rear guard.[c]
9Then you will call,[d] and the LORD will
answer;[e]
you will cry for help, and he will
say: Here am I.

"If you do away with the yoke of
oppression,
with the pointing finger[f] and
malicious talk,[g]
10and if you spend yourselves in behalf
of the hungry
and satisfy the needs of the
oppressed,[h]
then your light[i] will rise in the
darkness,
and your night will become like the
noonday.[j]
11The LORD will guide[k] you always;
he will satisfy your needs[l] in a
sun-scorched land[m]
and will strengthen[n] your frame.
You will be like a well-watered
garden,[o]
like a spring[p] whose waters never
fail.
12Your people will rebuild the ancient
ruins[q]
and will raise up the age-old
foundations;[r]
you will be called Repairer of Broken
Walls,[s]
Restorer of Streets with Dwellings.

13"If you keep your feet from breaking
the Sabbath[t]
and from doing as you please on my
holy day,
if you call the Sabbath a delight[u]
and the LORD's holy day honorable,
and if you honor it by not going your
own way
and not doing as you please or
speaking idle words,[v]
14then you will find your joy[w] in the
LORD,
and I will cause you to ride on the
heights[x] of the land
and to feast on the inheritance[y] of
your father Jacob."
The mouth of the LORD
has spoken.[z]

Chapter 59

Sin, Confession and Redemption

SURELY the arm[a] of the LORD is not
too short[b] to save,
nor his ear too dull to hear.[c]
2But your iniquities have separated[d]
you from your God;
your sins have hidden his face from
you,
so that he will not hear.[e]
3For your hands are stained with
blood,[f]
your fingers with guilt.[g]
Your lips have spoken lies,[h]
and your tongue mutters wicked
things.
4No one calls for justice;[i]
no one pleads his case with
integrity.
They rely[j] on empty arguments and
speak lies;[k]
they conceive trouble and give birth
to evil.[l]
5They hatch the eggs of vipers[m]
and spin a spider's web.[n]
Whoever eats their eggs will die,
and when one is broken, an adder is
hatched.
6Their cobwebs are useless for clothing;
they cannot cover themselves with
what they make.[o]
Their deeds are evil deeds,
and acts of violence[p] are in their
hands.
7Their feet rush into sin;
they are swift to shed innocent
blood.[q]
Their thoughts are evil thoughts;[r]
ruin and destruction mark their
ways.[s]
8The way of peace they do not know;[t]
there is no justice in their paths.

58:8 [b]S Isa 26:2 [c]S Ex 14:19
58:9 [d]S Ps 50:15 [e]S Job 8:6; S Isa 30:19; Da 9:20; S Zec 10:6 [f]S Pr 6:13 [g]Ps 12:2; Isa 59:13
58:10 [h]Dt 15:7-8 [i]S Isa 42:16 [j]S Job 11:17
58:11 [k]S Ps 48:14; S Isa 42:16; S 48:17 [l]S Ps 104:28; S 107:9 [m]S Ps 68:6 [n]S Ps 72:16 [o]S SS 4:15 [p]S Isa 35:7; Jn 4:14
58:12 [q]S Isa 49:8 [r]S Isa 44:28 [s]Ne 2:17
58:13 [t]S Ex 20:8 [u]Ps 37:4; 42:4; 84:2,10 [v]Isa 59:3
58:14 [w]S Job 22:26 [x]S Dt 32:13 [y]Ps 105:10-11 [z]S Isa 1:20
59:1 [a]S Isa 41:20 [b]S Isa 50:2 [c]Isa 30:19; 58:9; 65:24
59:2 [d]Jer 5:25; Eze 39:23 [e]S Ps 18:41; S Isa 58:4; S Jer 11:11; S Jn 9:31
59:3 [f]S 2Ki 21:16; S Isa 1:15; S Eze 22:9 [g]Ps 7:3 [h]S Isa 3:8
59:4 [i]S Isa 5:23 [j]S Job 15:31 [k]S Isa 44:20 [l]S Job 4:8; S Isa 29:20; Jas 1:15
59:5 [m]S Isa 11:8; Mt 3:7 [n]S Job 8:14
59:6 [o]Isa 28:20 [p]S Ps 55:9; S Pr 4:17; S Isa 58:4
59:7 [q]S 2Ki 21:16; S Pr 6:17; S Mic 3:10 [r]S Pr 24:2; S Isa 26:10; Mk 7:21-22 [s]Ro 3:15-17*
59:8 [t]Ro 3:15-17*

[o]8 Or *your righteous One*

58:9 PRAYER, Answer—God is eager to answer prayer, but He does not guarantee an answer to people who consistently oppose His will and then go through empty prayer rituals. True prayer makes us willing to help others.
59:1–20 GOD, Power—Human sin, not God's lack of power or will, separate us from His salvation. God promises salvation to those who repent.
59:1–20 REVELATION, History—Israel feared revelation had ended and God's saving power was lost. The prophet showed sin separated them from new saving revelations in history. The promised redemption applied to all who would repent.
59:1–2 PRAYER, Hindrances—Sin separates us from God and blocks His answers to prayer. The honest prayer of repentance removes the hindrances to answered prayer.
59:2–15 SIN, Depravity—God cannot look upon sin in His people; sin alienates us from God. Judah neglected its relationship with the Lord and reaped the results—exile. A people who are expert in sinning become unconscious of their sin. We can act in depravity and think we are God's people because we have lost the sense of right and wrong. When we lose all sense of peace and justice, we cannot expect God to hear us. Confession of sin to God and hope in Him for renewal are the only answers for a depraved people (vv 9–15).
59:6–8 CHRISTIAN ETHICS, War and Peace—The one who is separated from God does not know God's peace in any of its dimensions. Thus, life is marked by the lack of justice. Such a life leads ultimately away from God. Sin, lack of respect for other people, violent actions all lead away from peace toward war.

They have turned them into crooked
roads;[u]
no one who walks in them will
know peace.[v]

9So justice is far from us,
and righteousness does not reach us.
We look for light, but all is darkness;[w]
for brightness, but we walk in deep
shadows.
10Like the blind[x] we grope along the
wall,
feeling our way like men without
eyes.
At midday we stumble[y] as if it were
twilight;
among the strong, we are like the
dead.[z]
11We all growl like bears;
we moan mournfully like doves.[a]
We look for justice, but find none;
for deliverance, but it is far away.

12For our offenses[b] are many in your
sight,
and our sins testify[c] against us.
Our offenses are ever with us,
and we acknowledge our
iniquities:[d]
13rebellion[e] and treachery against the
LORD,
turning our backs[f] on our God,
fomenting oppression[g] and revolt,
uttering lies[h] our hearts have
conceived.
14So justice[i] is driven back,
and righteousness[j] stands at a
distance;
truth[k] has stumbled in the streets,
honesty cannot enter.
15Truth[l] is nowhere to be found,
and whoever shuns evil becomes a
prey.

The LORD looked and was displeased
that there was no justice.[m]
16He saw that there was no one,[n]
he was appalled that there was no
one to intervene;[o]
so his own arm worked salvation[p] for
him,
and his own righteousness[q]
sustained him.
17He put on righteousness as his
breastplate,[r]
and the helmet[s] of salvation on his
head;
he put on the garments[t] of
vengeance[u]
and wrapped himself in zeal[v] as in a
cloak.
18According to what they have done,
so will he repay[w]
wrath to his enemies
and retribution to his foes;
he will repay the islands[x] their due.
19From the west,[y] men will fear the
name of the LORD,
and from the rising of the sun,[z]
they will revere his glory.[a]
For he will come like a pent-up flood
that the breath[b] of the LORD drives
along.[p]

20"The Redeemer[c] will come to Zion,[d]
to those in Jacob who repent of their
sins,"[e]
declares the LORD.

21"As for me, this is my covenant[f]
with them," says the LORD. "My Spirit,[g]
who is on you, and my words that I have
put in your mouth[h] will not depart from
your mouth,[i] or from the mouths of your
children, or from the mouths of their descendants from this time on and forever,"
says the LORD.

Chapter 60

The Glory of Zion

"ARISE,[j] shine, for your light[k] has
come,

59:8 [u]S Jdg 5:6 [v]S Isa 57:21; Lk 1:79 **59:9** [w]S Job 19:8; S Ps 107:14; S Isa 5:30; S 8:20; S Lk 1:79 **59:10** [x]Dt 28:29; S Isa 6:9-10; 56:10; La 4:14; Zep 1:17 [y]S Job 3:23; S Isa 8:15; Jn 11:9-10 [z]La 3:6 **59:11** [a]S Ge 8:8; Ps 74:19; Isa 38:14; Jer 48:28; Eze 7:16; Na 2:7 **59:12** [b]S Ezr 9:6; S Isa 57:12 [c]S Ge 4:7; S Isa 3:9; S Jer 2:19 [d]Ps 51:3 **59:13** [e]Isa 46:8; 48:8 [f]S Nu 11:20; S Pr 30:9; Mt 10:33; Tit 1:16 [g]S Ps 12:5; S Isa 5:7 [h]S Isa 3:8; S 44:20; Mk 7:21-22 **59:14** [i]S Isa 29:21 [j]S Isa 1:21 [k]S Isa 48:1; S Jer 33:16 **59:15** [l]Jer 7:28; 9:5; Da 8:12 [m]S Isa 5:7 **59:16** [n]S Isa 41:28 [o]S Isa 53:12 [p]S Isa 51:5 [q]Isa 45:8,13; 46:13 **59:17** [r]Eph 6:14; 1Th 5:8 [s]Eph 6:17; 1Th 5:8 [t]S Job 27:6; Isa 63:3 [u]S Isa 1:24 [v]S Isa 9:7; Eze 5:13 **59:18** [w]S Lev 26:28; S Nu 10:35; S Isa 34:8; S Mt 16:27 [x]Isa 11:11; 41:5 **59:19** [y]S Isa 49:12; S Mt 8:11 [z]S Ps 113:3 [a]Ps 97:6; S Isa 24:15; 35:2; 40:5; 52:10; 66:18 [b]S Isa 11:4 **59:20** [c]S Job 19:25; Isa 60:16; 63:16 [d]S Isa 52:8; S Joel 3:21 [e]S Job 22:23; S Isa 1:27; S Jer 35:15; Ac 2:38-39; Ro 11:26-27* **59:21** [f]S Ge 9:16; S Dt 29:14; S Isa 42:6 [g]S Isa 11:2; S 44:3 [h]S Ex 4:15 [i]S Jos 1:8

60:1 [j]Isa 52:2 [k]S Ps 36:9; S 118:27; S Isa 9:2; Jn 8:12; Eph 5:14

[p]*19* Or *When the enemy comes in like a flood, / the Spirit of the LORD will put him to flight*

59:12–15 PRAYER, Confession—The prophet led the people in confessing their sins. Confession involves admitting guilt, listing specific sins, acknowledging that sin is against God, and seeking forgiveness. God responded to Israel's confession with determination to act. See note on Ps 32:1–11.

59:17–18 GOD, Wrath—God exercises wrath against His enemies to bring salvation to His repentant people. See note on 57:16–18.

59:20–21 THE CHURCH, Covenant People—God's covenant people are redeemed sinners who have turned away from sin. God's covenant with us includes the gift of the Spirit which inspired the prophets. The Spirit will continue to convict us of sin, lead us to repentance, and comfort us with hope. This promise gained fullness at Pentecost (Ac 2).

59:21 *HOLY SPIRIT, Hope*—God's Spirit seeks to make everyone a prophet. Our hope lies in being part of God's covenant people. To do this we must be faithful to His covenant and that requires knowing and living His Word. God's Spirit makes this possible. See note on Nu 11:25–29. Two things distinguish this promise from the other experiences of Israel in the Old Testament. First, the Spirit would be given to all the people, not just to outstanding leaders. Second, the Spirit will remain with the people forever. The particular gift of the Spirit to the people is prophecy; the people will know and speak the message from God. These promises were fulfilled at Pentecost, when the Spirit equipped the church to preach the gospel of Christ (Ac 2).

59:21 REVELATION, Spirit—God's people need constant revelation. God promised the Spirit would supply this. The Spirit or breath of God would breath His words into the mouths of His people, not just selected prophets. Every generation of God's people has access to His revealing Spirit and has no excuse for not obeying.

60:1–2 GOD, Glory—To a people burdened by darkness and trouble, God promised the redeeming light of His glorious presence.

and the glory[l] of the LORD rises
upon you.
2See, darkness[m] covers the earth
and thick darkness[n] is over the
peoples,
but the LORD rises upon you
and his glory appears over you.
3Nations[o] will come to your light,[p]
and kings[q] to the brightness of your
dawn.

4"Lift up your eyes and look about you:
All assemble[r] and come to you;
your sons come from afar,[s]
and your daughters[t] are carried on
the arm.[u]
5Then you will look and be radiant,[v]
your heart will throb and swell with
joy;[w]
the wealth[x] on the seas will be
brought to you,
to you the riches of the nations will
come.
6Herds of camels[y] will cover your land,
young camels of Midian[z] and
Ephah.[a]
And all from Sheba[b] will come,
bearing gold and incense[c]
and proclaiming the praise[d] of the
LORD.
7All Kedar's[e] flocks will be gathered to
you,
the rams of Nebaioth will serve you;
they will be accepted as offerings[f] on
my altar,[g]
and I will adorn my glorious
temple.[h]

8"Who are these[i] that fly along like
clouds,[j]
like doves to their nests?
9Surely the islands[k] look to me;
in the lead are the ships of
Tarshish,[q] [l]
bringing[m] your sons from afar,
with their silver and gold,[n]
to the honor[o] of the LORD your God,
the Holy One[p] of Israel,
for he has endowed you with
splendor.[q]

10"Foreigners[r] will rebuild your walls,
and their kings[s] will serve you.
Though in anger I struck you,
in favor[t] I will show you
compassion.[u]
11Your gates[v] will always stand open,
they will never be shut, day or
night,
so that men may bring you the wealth
of the nations[w]—
their kings[x] led in triumphal
procession.
12For the nation or kingdom that will not
serve[y] you will perish;
it will be utterly ruined.[z]

13"The glory of Lebanon[a] will come to
you,
the pine, the fir and the cypress
together,[b]
to adorn the place of my sanctuary;[c]
and I will glorify the place of my
feet.[d]
14The sons of your oppressors[e] will
come bowing before you;
all who despise you will bow down[f]
at your feet
and will call you the City[g] of the
LORD,
Zion[h] of the Holy One[i] of Israel.

15"Although you have been forsaken[j]
and hated,
with no one traveling[k] through,
I will make you the everlasting pride[l]
and the joy[m] of all generations.
16You will drink the milk of nations
and be nursed[n] at royal breasts.
Then you will know[o] that I, the LORD,
am your Savior,[p]
your Redeemer,[q] the Mighty One of
Jacob.[r]
17Instead of bronze I will bring you
gold,[s]
and silver in place of iron.
Instead of wood I will bring you
bronze,
and iron in place of stones.
I will make peace[t] your governor
and righteousness your ruler.[u]
18No longer will violence[v] be heard in
your land,

60:1 [l]S Ex 16:7; S Isa 4:5; Rev 21:11 60:2 [m]S 1Sa 2:9; S Ps 82:5; S 107:14; S Isa 8:20 [n]Jer 13:16; Col 1:13 60:3 [o]S Isa 44:5; S 45:14; Mt 2:1-11; Rev 21:24 [p]S Isa 9:2; 42:6 [q]S Isa 49:23 60:4 [r]S Isa 11:12 [s]S Isa 2:3; Jer 30:10 [t]S Isa 43:6 [u]Isa 49:20-22 60:5 [v]S Ex 34:29 [w]Isa 35:2; 65:13; 66:14; Zec 10:7 [x]S Dt 33:19; S Jdg 3:15; Rev 21:26 60:6 [y]S Jdg 6:5 [z]S Ge 25:2 [a]Ge 25:4 [b]S Ge 10:7,28 [c]Isa 43:23; Jer 6:20; Mt 2:11 [d]S 1Ki 5:7; S Isa 42:10 60:7 [e]S Ge 25:13 [f]Isa 18:7; Eze 20:40; 43:27; Zep 3:10 [g]S Isa 19:21 [h]ver 13; Hag 2:3,7, 9 60:8 [i]Isa 49:21 [j]Isa 19:1 60:9 [k]S Isa 11:11 [l]S Ge 10:4; Isa 2:16 *fn* [m]S Isa 14:2; S 43:6 [n]S 1Ki 10:22 [o]S Ps 22:23 [p]ver 14; Isa 1:4; S 54:5 [q]S Isa 44:23; 55:5; Jer 30:19 60:10 [r]S Ex 1:11; S Isa 14:1-2; S 56:6 [s]S Ezr 1:2; Rev 21:24 [t]S Isa 49:8 [u]S Ps 102:13 60:11 [v]ver 18; S Ps 24:7; Isa 62:10; Mic 2:13; Rev 21:25 [w]S ver 5; Isa 61:6; Rev 21:26 [x]Ps 149:8; S Isa 2:12 60:12 [y]S Isa 11:14; S 14:2 [z]S Ge 27:29; S Ps 110:5; Da 2:34 60:13 [a]S Ezr 3:7 [b]Isa 41:19 [c]S ver 7 [d]S 1Ch 28:2 60:14 [e]S Isa 14:2 [f]S Ge 27:29; S Isa 2:3; Rev 3:9 [g]S Ge 32:28; S Isa 1:26 [h]Heb 12:22 [i]S ver 9 60:15 [j]Isa 1:7-9; S 6:12; S 54:6 [k]S Isa 33:8 [l]S Isa 4:2 [m]S Ps 126:5; Isa 65:18

60:16 [n]S Ex 6:2; Isa 49:23; 66:11,12 [o]S Ex 6:7 [p]S Ex 14:30; S Isa 25:9 [q]S Job 19:25; S Isa 59:20 [r]S Ge 49:24; S Ps 132:2 60:17 [s]1Ki 10:21 [t]S Ps 85:8; Isa 66:12; Hag 2:9 [u]S Isa 9:7 60:18 [v]S Lev 26:6; S 2Sa 7:10; S Isa 9:4

[q]9 Or *the trading ships*

60:1–3 JESUS CHRIST, Foretold—This messianic promise given to Zion (the people of God) was recounted by Simeon at Jesus' presentation in the Temple (Lk 2:28–32). The birth of any child is an occasion for joy, but the birth of God's Holy Child was the beginning of the fulfillment of all our expectations.

60:1–14 EVANGELISM, Universality—Evangelistic opportunities often rise from the darkest circumstances. God promised the returned exiles they would see His glory at work among the nations. God would take the initiative to lead the nations to serve Him. God's people need to recognize God's initiative, reflect His shining glory, and accept those God leads to them. Joy is the result. Evangelism takes advantage of opportunities to reach internationals and rejoices in the results.

60:9,14 GOD, Holy—See note on 41:14,16,20.

60:10 GOD, Love—See note on 57:16–18.

60:15–16 GOD, Love—An exiled people heard God's promise to save them in royal fashion. Why? Because He loves His people.

60:17 CHRISTIAN ETHICS, Righteousness—See notes on 26:1–11; 56:1.

nor ruin or destruction[w] within your borders,
but you will call your walls Salvation[x]
and your gates Praise.[y]
19The sun will no more be your light by day,
nor will the brightness of the moon shine on you,
for the LORD will be your everlasting light,[z]
and your God will be your glory.[a]
20Your sun[b] will never set again,
and your moon will wane no more;
the LORD will be your everlasting light,
and your days of sorrow[c] will end.
21Then will all your people be righteous[d]
and they will possess[e] the land forever.
They are the shoot I have planted,[f]
the work of my hands,[g]
for the display of my splendor.[h]
22The least of you will become a thousand,
the smallest a mighty nation.[i]
I am the LORD;
in its time I will do this swiftly."[j]

60:18 [w]S Isa 49:19; S 51:19 [x]S Isa 33:6 [y]Isa 61:11; 62:7; Jer 33:9; Zep 3:20 60:19 [z]S Ps 36:9; S 118:27; Rev 22:5 [a]S Ps 85:9; S Isa 24:16,23; Rev 21:23 60:20 [b]Isa 30:26 [c]S Isa 30:19; S 35:10; S Rev 7:17 60:21 [d]S Isa 4:3; S 26:2; Rev 21:27 [e]Ps 37:11,22; Isa 49:8; 57:13; 61:7; 65:9; Zec 8:12 [f]S Ex 15:17; Ps 44:2; 80:8-11; Jer 32:41; Am 9:15; Mt 15:13 [g]S Job 10:3; S Ps 8:6; S Isa 19:25; Eph 2:10 [h]S Lev 10:3; S Isa 44:23 60:22 [i]S Ge 12:2; S Dt 1:10 [j]Isa 5:19 61:1 [k]S Isa 11:2; 2Co 3:17 [l]S Isa 50:4 [m]S Ps 45:7; S Da 9:24-26; S Ac 4:26 [n]S 2Sa 18:26; S Isa 40:9 [o]S Job 5:16; S Mt 11:5; Lk 7:22 [p]S 2Ki 22:19; S Job 5:18 [q]S Lev 25:10 [r]S Ps 68:6; S Isa 49:9 61:2 [s]S Isa 49:8; S Lk 4:18-19* [t]S Isa 1:24 [u]S Isa 40:1; Mt 5:4 [v]S Job 5:11; Lk 6:21 61:3 [w]S Isa 3:23 [x]S Job 2:8 [y]S Ru 3:3; S Isa 1:6; Heb 1:9 [z]Jer 31:13; Mt 5:4 [a]Ps 1:3; 92:12-13; Mt 15:13; 1Co 3:9 [b]S Isa 44:23 61:4 [c]S Isa 44:26; 51:3; 65:21; Eze 36:33; Am 9:14; Zec 1:16-17

Chapter 61

The Year of the LORD's Favor

THE Spirit[k] of the Sovereign LORD[l] is on me,
because the LORD has anointed[m] me
to preach good news[n] to the poor.[o]
He has sent me to bind up[p] the brokenhearted,
to proclaim freedom[q] for the captives[r]
and release from darkness for the prisoners,[r]
2to proclaim the year of the LORD's favor[s]
and the day of vengeance[t] of our God,
to comfort[u] all who mourn,[v]
3 and provide for those who grieve in Zion—
to bestow on them a crown[w] of beauty instead of ashes,[x]
the oil[y] of gladness
instead of mourning,[z]
and a garment of praise
instead of a spirit of despair.
They will be called oaks of righteousness,
a planting[a] of the LORD
for the display of his splendor.[b]
4They will rebuild the ancient ruins[c]
and restore the places long devastated;
they will renew the ruined cities
that have been devastated for generations.

[r]*1* Hebrew; Septuagint *the blind*

60:21 GOD, Sovereignty—God's eternal plan is to create a wholly righteous people who will reflect His splendor and glory to the world. Because He is the sovereign ruler of the world, we can be sure He will carry out His plan.

61:1–3 JESUS CHRIST, Foretold—This passage was originally intended to give comfort to the exiles. Jesus used it as His manifesto delivered in the synagogue at Nazareth at the beginning of His ministry (Lk 4:16–19). He lived the fulfillment out in the years of His earthly ministry. He intends His followers to continue living it out in our own time. Compare Jas 1:27.

61:1–3 HOLY SPIRIT, Hope—The Spirit makes ministry for God possible. Jesus used this passage as a text for the first sermon He preached. He claimed to fulfill Isaiah's promise in His ministry (Lk 4:16–22). So Jesus understood that the Spirit of God gave Him prophetic power to preach God's message and to provide salvation for oppressed people. Jesus calls us to minister as He did. The Spirit will empower our ministry as it did His.

61:1–11 CHRISTIAN ETHICS, Righteousness—Righteous actions marked the ministry to which God called His prophet. Jesus saw this as His calling, too (Lk 4:16–21). We will do well to take up the same calling to help the needy, be priests to the nations (Ex 19:6), and establish the justice God loves. Then the blessings promised Abraham will be realized. The world will see God's new order of righteousness. See note on 56:1.

61:1–2 WORSHIP, Proclamation—See note on Jer 26:2–7.

61:1–3 PROCLAMATION, Anointing—When we faithfully proclaim the gospel, God *anoints that proclamation.* He *fills it* with power (Mic 3:8; Lk 4:17–19; 1 Th 1:4–5). What God commands us to do, He enables us to do. God does not call the equipped. He equips the called. We experience great joy when we sense the anointing of God upon our lives. When we rest wholly on Him and are in obedience to His Word, He fills us with His presence and power. Compare Ac 4:31–33; 1 Co 2:1–5; 2 Ti 4:17. Some proclamation is without this anointing. Even this kind of proclamation is not without effect (Php 1:14–18) because the Word of God is alive, powerful, and as sharp as a two-edged sword (Heb 4:12). How tragic it is, however, for God to have to work through sin and rebellion in the life of the proclaimer. The anointed proclamation of the prophet was directed to groups of people often ignored by society's power brokers. Proclamation has content bringing hope to people in need.

61:1–3 MISSIONS, Nature—This passage may have applied first to the prophet and/or to the remnant nation Israel. Jesus applied it to Himself and said it found fulfillment in Him (Lk 4:16–20). When we couple this fulfillment with Christ sending out His disciples in the same manner (Jn 20:21), the prophetic call becomes an important description of the nature of missions for all times: (1) missions is a divine activity of the Sovereign God; (2) the Spirit of God calls persons to the task; (3) the Spirit of God anoints or selects; (4) the nature of missions includes preaching the good news to the poor; (5) missions goes beyond proclamation and extends to deeds of love; and (6) the gospel brings freedom from fear, sin, vice, superstition, and oppressive conditions. Missions is God's work through His anointed people to meet the spiritual and physical needs of people. The "year of the LORD's favor" seems to refer to the Year of Jubilee, which came every fifty years. It included freedom for slaves, the forgiveness of debts, and the restoration of lost properties (Lev 25:3–13). The Christian understanding of this message includes the proclamation of freedom, forgiveness, and new life in Christ Jesus. Christian messengers must be committed to helping persons become all they can become in Christ.

5Aliens[d] will shepherd your flocks;
foreigners will work your fields and vineyards.
6And you will be called priests[e] of the LORD,
you will be named ministers of our God.
You will feed on the wealth[f] of nations,
and in their riches you will boast.

7Instead of their shame[g]
my people will receive a double[h] portion,
and instead of disgrace
they will rejoice in their inheritance;
and so they will inherit[i] a double portion in their land,
and everlasting joy[j] will be theirs.

8"For I, the LORD, love justice;[k]
I hate robbery and iniquity.
In my faithfulness I will reward them
and make an everlasting covenant[l] with them.
9Their descendants[m] will be known among the nations
and their offspring among the peoples.
All who see them will acknowledge
that they are a people the LORD has blessed."[n]

10I delight greatly in the LORD;
my soul rejoices[o] in my God.
For he has clothed me with garments of salvation
and arrayed me in a robe of righteousness,[p]
as a bridegroom adorns his head[q] like a priest,
and as a bride[r] adorns herself with her jewels.
11For as the soil makes the sprout come up
and a garden[s] causes seeds to grow,
so the Sovereign LORD will make righteousness[t] and praise
spring up before all nations.

61:5 [d]S Isa 14:1-2; S 56:6
61:6 [e]S Ex 19:6; 1Pe 2:5 [f]Dt 33:19; S Isa 60:11
61:7 [g]S Isa 29:22; S 41:11 [h]S Dt 21:17; S Isa 40:2 [i]S Isa 60:21 [j]S Ps 126:5; S Isa 25:9
61:8 [k]S Ps 11:7; S Isa 1:17; S 5:16 [l]S Ge 9:16; S Isa 42:6; S Heb 13:20
61:9 [m]S Isa 43:5; S 48:19 [n]S Ge 12:2; S Dt 28:3-12
61:10 [o]S Ps 2:11; S Isa 7:13; S 25:9; Hab 3:18; S Lk 1:47 [p]S Job 27:6; S Ps 132:9; S Isa 52:1; Rev 19:8 [q]S Ex 39:28 [r]S Isa 49:18; Rev 21:2
61:11 [s]S Ge 47:23; Isa 58:11 [t]S Isa 45:8
62:1 [u]S Est 4:14; S Ps 50:21; S 83:1 [v]S Isa 1:26; S 45:8 [w]S Job 11:17 [x]S Ps 67:2
62:2 [y]S Ps 67:2; S Isa 40:5; S 45:14; 52:10 [z]S Ge 32:28; S Isa 1:26; Rev 2:17; 3:12
62:3 [a]S Isa 28:5; 1Th 2:19
62:4 [b]S Lev 26:43; S Isa 6:12; S 54:6 [c]S Isa 49:19; S 51:19 [d]2Ki 21:1 [e]Isa 65:19; Jer 32:41; Zep 3:17; Mal 3:12 [f]Isa 54:5; Jer 3:14; Hos 2:19
62:5 [g]S SS 3:11 [h]S Dt 28:63; Isa 65:19; Jer 31:12; Zep 3:17
62:6 [i]S Isa 52:8; Heb 13:17 [j]Ps 132:4
62:7 [k]Mt 15:21-28; Lk 18:1-8 [l]S Dt 26:19; S Isa 60:18
62:8 [m]S Ge 22:16; S Isa 14:24; S 49:18 [n]Dt 28:30-33; S Isa 1:7

Chapter 62

Zion's New Name

FOR Zion's sake I will not keep silent,[u]
for Jerusalem's sake I will not remain quiet,
till her righteousness[v] shines out like the dawn,[w]
her salvation[x] like a blazing torch.
2The nations[y] will see your righteousness,
and all kings your glory;
you will be called by a new name[z]
that the mouth of the LORD will bestow.
3You will be a crown[a] of splendor in the LORD's hand,
a royal diadem in the hand of your God.
4No longer will they call you Deserted,[b]
or name your land Desolate.[c]
But you will be called Hephzibah,[s] [d]
and your land Beulah[t];
for the LORD will take delight[e] in you,
and your land will be married.[f]
5As a young man marries a maiden,
so will your sons[u] marry you;
as a bridegroom[g] rejoices over his bride,
so will your God rejoice[h] over you.

6I have posted watchmen[i] on your walls, O Jerusalem;
they will never be silent day or night.
You who call on the LORD,
give yourselves no rest,[j]
7and give him no rest[k] till he establishes Jerusalem
and makes her the praise[l] of the earth.

8The LORD has sworn[m] by his right hand
and by his mighty arm:
"Never again will I give your grain[n]

[s]4 *Hephzibah* means *my delight is in her.*
[t]4 *Beulah* means *married.* [u]5 Or *Builder*

61:6 EVANGELISM, Involves—Persons who declare the gospel are seen as priests (Ex 19:6) and ministers. They stand before God in prayer for people and minister the gospel. That depth of involvement wins others to Christ. God calls us to serve people's needs (vv 1–3) and to evangelize the nations. Service, prayer, and proclamation are all parts of the evangelistic task.

61:8 THE CHURCH, Covenant People—Learning what God is like helps us know what He wants His people to be and do. God loves justice. He wants righteousness extended to every sphere of life. He hates attitudes and actions which harm people. He swiftly judges robbery and oppression. God's promise to His people is to establish justice among us as the distinguishing mark of His people.

61:9 SALVATION, Blessing—Compare 65:23. God promised to bless Israel with an everlasting covenant, which would bring everlasting joy (v 7) to her and her offspring, and be a part of her missionary equipment. Believers in Christ are inheritors of these promised blessings of salvation (2 Co 1:20–21). See note on Ge 1:22,28.

62:1–2 CHRISTIAN ETHICS, Righteousness—We may give up on our dream of a righteous people. God will not be silent forever. He will act in righteousness to save His people and display their righteousness to the nations. See note on 56:1.

62:6–7 PRAYER, Command of God—"Call on the LORD" is a term for prayer. See note on Ge 4:26. God's intention was that Jerusalem exhibit His character and love for the world. The watchmen should pray ceaselessly for that end. Prayer is not a spasmodic activity but a constant involvement in seeking God's will and committing oneself to do His will.

as food for your enemies,
and never again will foreigners drink
the new wine
for which you have toiled;
9but those who harvest it will eat[o] it
and praise the LORD,[p]
and those who gather the grapes will
drink it
in the courts of my sanctuary."[q]

10Pass through, pass through the gates![r]
Prepare the way for the people.
Build up, build up the highway![s] [t]
Remove the stones.
Raise a banner[u] for the nations.

11The LORD has made proclamation
to the ends of the earth:[v]
"Say to the Daughter of Zion,[w]
'See, your Savior comes![x]
See, his reward is with him,
and his recompense accompanies
him.' "[y]
12They will be called[z] the Holy People,[a]
the Redeemed[b] of the LORD;
and you will be called Sought After,
the City No Longer Deserted.[c]

Chapter 63

God's Day of Vengeance and Redemption

WHO is this coming from Edom,[d]
from Bozrah,[e] with his garments
stained crimson?[f]
Who is this, robed in splendor,
striding forward in the greatness of
his strength?[g]

"It is I, speaking in righteousness,
mighty to save."[h]

2Why are your garments red,
like those of one treading the
winepress?[i]

3"I have trodden the winepress[j] alone;
from the nations no one was with
me.
I trampled[k] them in my anger
and trod them down in my wrath;[l]
their blood spattered my garments,[m]
and I stained all my clothing.
4For the day of vengeance[n] was in my
heart,
and the year of my redemption has
come.
5I looked, but there was no one[o] to
help,
I was appalled that no one gave
support;
so my own arm[p] worked salvation for
me,
and my own wrath sustained me.[q]
6I trampled[r] the nations in my anger;
in my wrath I made them drunk[s]
and poured their blood[t] on the
ground."

Praise and Prayer

7I will tell of the kindnesses[u] of the
LORD,
the deeds for which he is to be
praised,
according to all the LORD has done
for us—
yes, the many good things[v] he has
done
for the house of Israel,
according to his compassion[w] and
many kindnesses.
8He said, "Surely they are my people,[x]
sons who will not be false to me";
and so he became their Savior.[y]
9In all their distress he too was
distressed,
and the angel[z] of his presence[a]
saved them.
In his love and mercy he redeemed[b]
them;
he lifted them up and carried[c] them
all the days of old.[d]
10Yet they rebelled[e]

62:9 [o]S Isa 1:19; Am 9:14 [p]S Dt 12:7; Joel 2:26 [q]Lev 23:39
62:10 [r]S Ps 24:7; S Isa 60:11 [s]Isa 57:14 [t]S Isa 11:16 [u]S Isa 11:10
62:11 [v]S Dt 30:4 [w]S Ps 9:14; Zec 9:9; Mt 21:5 [x]S Isa 35:4; Rev 22:12 [y]S Isa 40:10
62:12 [z]S Ge 32:28 [a]S Ex 19:6; 1Pe 2:9 [b]S Ps 106:10; S Isa 35:9; S 44:23 [c]S Ps 27:9; Isa 42:16; S 54:6
63:1 [d]S 2Ch 28:17; S Isa 11:14 [e]S Ge 36:33; Am 1:12 [f]Rev 19:13 [g]S Job 9:4; S Isa 45:24 [h]ver 5; Isa 46:13; S 51:5; Jer 42:11; Zep 3:17
63:2 [i]S Ge 49:11
63:3 [j]S Jdg 6:11; S Rev 14:20 [k]S Job 40:12; S Ps 108:13; S Isa 5:5 [l]S Isa 22:5 [m]Rev 19:13
63:4 [n]S Isa 1:24; S Jer 50:15
63:5 [o]S 2Ki 14:26; S Isa 41:28 [p]S Ps 44:3; S 98:1; S Isa 33:2 [q]Isa 59:16
63:6 [r]S Job 40:12; S Ps 108:13 [s]S Isa 29:9; La 4:21 [t]S Isa 34:3
63:7 [u]S Isa 54:8 [v]S Ex 18:9 [w]S Ps 51:1; Eph 2:4
63:8 [x]S Ps 100:3; S Isa 51:4 [y]S Ex 14:30; S Isa 25:9
63:9 [z]S Ex 14:19 [a]S Ex 33:14 [b]Dt 7:7-8; S Ezr 9:9; S Isa 48:20 [c]S Dt 1:31; S Ps 28:9 [d]S Dt 32:7; S Job 37:23
63:10 [e]S Ps 78:17; Eze 20:8; Ac 7:39-42

62:12 GOD, Holy—Holiness is the unique nature of God that separates Him from all else. His people can be called holy only because of their relationship to Him in redemption. See note on 41:14,16,20.
63:1–16 GOD, Savior—In His kindness or covenant love (v 7) for His people, God acts in wrath against their enemies to save them. We can look back at God's history with us and be assured of His saving love for us. Still, when we sin, we must look again for God's discipline and cry anew for His deliverance.
63:1 GOD, Righteous—God does what is right and fair. Thus He acts against His enemies to save His mistreated people.
63:1–6 JESUS CHRIST, Foretold—This image of God as the warrior King who saves His people and defends them from evil was transferred to the triumphant Jesus *(Rev 19:11–16)*. *Vengeance and the* violence necessary to overcome ultimate evil is best left with God, His power, and His justice.
63:3 GOD, Wrath—See note on 57:16–18.
63:7 WORSHIP, Proclamation—See note on Jer 26:2–7.
63:7—64:12 PRAYER, Lament—The prophet provided the people appropriate language to express their frustration to God. The prayer praises the Lord for His kindness to Israel, laments the nation's fall, petitions the Lord for restoration, confesses sin, and asks for forgiveness. An unusual aspect of this prayer is the emphasis on God's Spirit. The whole prayer is based on teaching received about God's past acts of salvation for His people. Prayer grows out of historical knowledge. What we learn about God encourages us to pray to Him even when frustration dominates our lives.
63:8,16 GOD, Father—Because He has chosen to be a Father to His people, God saves us. We can call on Him to deliver us from trouble and danger. See note on 45:10–11.
63:10–14 HOLY SPIRIT, Resisted—Resisting God's Spirit pains God, who grieves over His wayward children. Rebellious Christians need to look at Christ's cross to remember God's acts and renew their commitment. Then the Holy Spirit we once resisted will live in our hearts bringing rest, redemption, and peace. See Ps 51:11; note on Eph 4:30.
63:10 SIN, Against God—The same power that saves, if

and grieved his Holy Spirit.[f]
So he turned and became their
enemy[g]
and he himself fought[h] against
them.
11Then his people recalled[v] the days of
old,
the days of Moses and his people—
where is he who brought them
through the sea,[i]
with the shepherd of his flock?[j]
Where is he who set
his Holy Spirit[k] among them,
12who sent his glorious arm[l] of power
to be at Moses' right hand,
who divided the waters[m] before them,
to gain for himself everlasting
renown,[n]
13who led[o] them through the depths?[p]
Like a horse in open country,
they did not stumble;[q]
14like cattle that go down to the plain,
they were given rest[r] by the Spirit
of the LORD.
This is how you guided your people
to make for yourself a glorious
name.
15Look down from heaven[s] and see
from your lofty throne,[t] holy and
glorious.
Where are your zeal[u] and your might?
Your tenderness and compassion[v]
are withheld[w] from us.
16But you are our Father,[x]
though Abraham does not know us
or Israel acknowledge[y] us;
you, O LORD, are our Father,
our Redeemer[z] from of old is your
name.
17Why, O LORD, do you make us
wander[a] from your ways
and harden our hearts[b] so we do
not revere[c] you?
Return[d] for the sake of your servants,
the tribes that are your
inheritance.[e]
18For a little while[f] your people
possessed your holy place,
but now our enemies have
trampled[g] down your
sanctuary.[h]

63:10 [f]S Ps 51:11; Ac 7:51; Eph 4:30 [g]Ps 106:40; S Isa 10:4 [h]S Jos 10:14 **63:11** [i]S Ex 14:22, 30 [j]S Ps 77:20 [k]S Nu 11:17 **63:12** [l]S Ge 49:24; S Ex 3:20 [m]Ex 14:21-22; Isa 11:15 [n]S Ps 102:12; S Isa 55:13; S Jer 13:11 **63:13** [o]S Dt 32:12 [p]S Ex 14:22 [q]S Ps 119:11; Jer 31:9 **63:14** [r]S Ex 33:14; S Dt 12:9 **63:15** [s]S Dt 26:15; La 3:50 [t]S 1Ki 22:19; S Ps 123:1 [u]S Isa 9:7; S 26:11 [v]S 1Ki 3:26; S Ps 25:6 [w]S Ge 43:31; Isa 64:12 **63:16** [x]S Ex 4:22; S Jer 3:4; Jn 8:41 [y]S Job 14:21 [z]Isa 41:14; 44:6; S 59:20 **63:17** [a]S Ge 20:13; La 3:9 [b]S Ex 4:21 [c]Isa 29:13 [d]S Nu 10:36 [e]S Ex 34:9 **63:18** [f]Dt 4:26; 11:17 [g]S Isa 28:18; Da 8:13; S Lk 21:24 [h]S Lev 26:31; S 2Ki 25:9 **63:19** [i]S Isa 43:7; S Jer 14:9 **64:1** [j]Ps 18:9; 144:5 [k]ver 3; Mic 1:3 [l]S Ex 19:18 **64:2** [m]S Isa 30:27 [n]Ps 99:1; 119:120; Jer 5:22; 33:9 **64:3** [o]S Ps 65:5 [p]S Ps 18:7 **64:4** [q]S Isa 43:10-11 [r]S Isa 30:18; 1Co 2:9* **64:5** [s]S Isa 26:8 [t]S Isa 10:4 **64:6** [u]S Lev 5:2; S 12:2 [v]Isa 46:12; 48:1 [w]S Ps 1:3; 90:5-6 [x]Ps 1:4; Jer 4:12 **64:7** [y]S Isa 41:28; 59:4; 63:5; Jer 8:6; Eze 22:30 [z]S Ps 14:4 [a]Dt 31:18; Isa 1:15; 54:8 [b]S Isa 9:18; Eze 22:18-22 **64:8** [c]S Ex 4:22; S Jer 3:4 [d]S Isa 29:16; Ro 9:20-21

19We are yours from of old;
but you have not ruled over them,
they have not been called by your
name.[w] [i]

Chapter 64

OH, that you would rend the
heavens[j] and come down,[k]
that the mountains[l] would tremble
before you!
2As when fire sets twigs ablaze
and causes water to boil,
come down to make your name[m]
known to your enemies
and cause the nations to quake[n]
before you!
3For when you did awesome[o] things
that we did not expect,
you came down, and the mountains
trembled[p] before you.
4Since ancient times no one has heard,
no ear has perceived,
no eye has seen any God besides you,[q]
who acts on behalf of those who
wait for him.[r]
5You come to the help of those who
gladly do right,[s]
who remember your ways.
But when we continued to sin against
them,
you were angry.[t]
How then can we be saved?
6All of us have become like one who is
unclean,[u]
and all our righteous[v] acts are like
filthy rags;
we all shrivel up like a leaf,[w]
and like the wind our sins sweep us
away.[x]
7No one[y] calls on your name[z]
or strives to lay hold of you;
for you have hidden[a] your face from
us
and made us waste away[b] because
of our sins.
8Yet, O LORD, you are our Father.[c]
We are the clay, you are the
potter;[d]

[v]*11* Or *But may he recall* [w]*19* Or *We are like those you have never ruled, / like those never called by your name*

resisted, becomes the power that torments and punishes. Human sin is not a mark God checks off on His record book until we reach a limit that must be punished. Sin is a personal hurt to God. The Holy Spirit attempts to guide our lives to godly actions. When we rebel to follow our desires instead of His, we bring distress and grief to God. See notes on Ac 7:51–53; Eph 4:29–32.

64:1–12 EVANGELISM, Lostness—People experience their own sinfulness and the absence of God. God's anger stands over the lost person. Good deeds are worthless when the person is not rightly related to God. The only hope for a lost person is to confess sins and call on God for salvation.

64:4 GOD, One God—Yahweh, the God of Israel, is the only One who has demonstrated His deity by acting for His people.

64:4–7 SIN, Discipline—Sin destroys us spiritually and physically because God intervenes in our lives to discipline sinners. Habitual sin brings God's judging anger from which salvation appears impossible. Such sin makes us feel filthy, unworthy of speaking to God. We see our basic sin as failing to call on God in moments of distress because we feel He will not hear us. Still we have hope. We can express our feelings to God as the prophet did in this strong prayer of lament and confession.

64:5,9 GOD, Wrath—Sinners suffering under God's wrath may pray for relief. See note on Ps 27:9.

we are all the work of your hand.[e]
9Do not be angry[f] beyond measure,
O LORD;
do not remember our sins[g] forever.
Oh, look upon us, we pray,
for we are all your people.[h]
10Your sacred cities[i] have become a
desert;
even Zion is a desert, Jerusalem a
desolation.[j]
11Our holy and glorious temple,[k] where
our fathers praised you,
has been burned with fire,
and all that we treasured[l] lies in
ruins.
12After all this, O LORD, will you hold
yourself back?[m]
Will you keep silent[n] and punish us
beyond measure?

Chapter 65

Judgment and Salvation

"I revealed myself to those who did
not ask for me;
I was found by those who did not
seek me.[o]
To a nation[p] that did not call on my
name,[q]
I said, 'Here am I, here am I.'
2All day long I have held out my hands
to an obstinate people,[r]
who walk in ways not good,
pursuing their own imaginations[s]—
3a people who continually provoke me
to my very face,[t]
offering sacrifices in gardens[u]
and burning incense[v] on altars of
brick;
4who sit among the graves[w]
and spend their nights keeping
secret vigil;
who eat the flesh of pigs,[x]
and whose pots hold broth of
unclean meat;
5who say, 'Keep away; don't come near
me,
for I am too sacred[y] for you!'
Such people are smoke[z] in my
nostrils,
a fire that keeps burning all day.
6"See, it stands written before me:
I will not keep silent[a] but will pay
back[b] in full;
I will pay it back into their laps[c]—
7both your sins[d] and the sins of your
fathers,"[e]
says the LORD.
"Because they burned sacrifices on the
mountains
and defied me on the hills,[f]
I will measure into their laps
the full payment[g] for their former
deeds."
8This is what the LORD says:

"As when juice is still found in a
cluster of grapes[h]
and men say, 'Don't destroy it,
there is yet some good in it,'
so will I do in behalf of my servants;[i]
I will not destroy them all.
9I will bring forth descendants[j] from
Jacob,
and from Judah those who will
possess[k] my mountains;
my chosen[l] people will inherit them,
and there will my servants live.[m]
10Sharon[n] will become a pasture for
flocks,[o]
and the Valley of Achor[p] a resting
place for herds,
for my people who seek[q] me.
11"But as for you who forsake[r] the LORD
and forget my holy mountain,[s]
who spread a table for Fortune
and fill bowls of mixed wine[t] for
Destiny,
12I will destine you for the sword,[u]
and you will all bend down for the
slaughter;[v]
for I called but you did not answer,[w]

64:8 [e]S Job 10:3; S Isa 19:25 **64:9** [f]Isa 54:8; 57:17; 60:10; La 5:22 [g]S Isa 43:25 [h]S Ps 100:3; S Isa 51:4 **64:10** [i]Ps 78:54; S Isa 1:26 [j]S Dt 29:23 **64:11** [k]S Lev 26:31; S 2Ki 25:9; Ps 74:3-7; La 2:7 [l]ver 10-11; La 1:7, 10 **64:12** [m]S Ge 43:31; Ps 74:10-11 [n]S Est 4:14; S Ps 50:21; S 83:1 **65:1** [o]Hos 1:10; Ro 9:24-26; 10:20* [p]Ro 9:30; Eph 2:12 [q]S Ps 14:4; S Isa 43:7 **65:2** [r]S Ps 78:8; S Isa 1:2,23; Ro 10:21* [s]Ps 81:11-12; S Pr 24:2; Isa 66:18 **65:3** [t]S Job 1:11 [u]S Isa 1:29 [v]S Lev 2:2; Jer 41:5; 44:17; Eze 23:41 **65:4** [w]S Lev 19:31; S Isa 8:19 [x]S Lev 11:7 **65:5** [y]S Ps 40:4; Mt 9:11; Lk 7:39; 18:9-12 [z]Pr 10:26 **65:6** [a]S Ps 50:3 [b]S 2Ch 6:23; Isa 59:18; Jer 16:18 [c]S Ps 79:12; Eze 9:10; Lk 6:38 **65:7** [d]S Isa 22:14 [e]Ex 20:5; Jer 32:18 [f]S Isa 57:7 [g]S Pr 10:24; S Isa 10:12 **65:8** [h]Isa 5:2 [i]S Isa 54:17 **65:9** [j]S Isa 45:19 [k]S Nu 34:13; S Isa 60:21; Jer 50:19; Am 9:11-15 [l]S Isa 14:1 [m]Isa 32:18 **65:10** [n]S 1Ch 27:29; S Isa 35:2; Ac 9:35 [o]Jer 31:12; 33:12; Eze 34:13-14 [p]S Jos 7:26 [q]S Isa 51:1 **65:11** [r]Dt 28:20; 29:24-25; S 32:15; Isa 1:28; Jer 2:13; 19:4 [s]S Dt 33:19; S Ps 137:5 [t]S Isa 5:22 **65:12** [u]S Isa 1:20; S 27:1 [v]S Isa 30:25 [w]S Pr 1:24-25; S Isa 41:28; 66:4; Jer 7:27

64:8 GOD, Father—As Father, God is also praised as sovereign Creator. The heavenly Father listens to the cries of His sinful children.
64:8–12 CREATION, Personal Creator—The Creator is not far removed from His creation. We can still cry out to Him and claim the personal relationship of Father-child because He is our Creator. The Creator is also the One who listens and forgives.
64:8–9 THE CHURCH, God's Community—The people of God are His sons, totally dependent on our Father and Creator. As such, we can pray for forgiveness and ask God to take away His anger. He hears our prayers even when they are bold laments expressing our dissatisfaction and impatience.
65:1–7 SIN, Rebellion—God works to save sinners. We stay too busy showing others how good and religious we are to pay attention to His efforts to save us. Repeated sin produces an "obstinate people" (Hebrew *sarar*), a people with an attitude of stubborn rebellion against God like a sullen son stubbornly refusing to obey parents. We know to do right, but our attitude is wrong, so we go on strike against God, refusing to do anything that pleases Him. Obstinate, stubborn sin produces a life following the wrong paths of self-centered objectives. Such sin brings divine discipline and robs the sinner of potential for good.
65:1–22 ELECTION, Remnant—God distinguished clearly between His chosen servants who were still good and those who forsook Him. Each faced a different future. Election applies only to the faithful. Unbelieving people have no reason to claim to be part of God's elect. Election is God taking the initiative to create a people out of obstinate rebels.
65:8–10 THE CHURCH, Remnant—The remnant consists of righteous people who love God and do His will. All who claim to be God's people are not God's people. God takes those who are willing to commit their lives to Him and makes them His chosen people. They do good and seek to know Him and His will. See notes on 4:2–6; 2 Ch 34:9.

I spoke but you did not listen.[x]
You did evil in my sight
and chose what displeases me."[y]

13Therefore this is what the Sovereign LORD says:

"My servants will eat,[z]
but you will go hungry;[a]
my servants will drink,[b]
but you will go thirsty;[c]
my servants will rejoice,[d]
but you will be put to shame.[e]
14My servants will sing[f]
out of the joy of their hearts,
but you will cry out[g]
from anguish of heart
and wail in brokenness of spirit.
15You will leave your name
to my chosen ones as a curse;[h]
the Sovereign LORD will put you to death,
but to his servants he will give
another name.[i]
16Whoever invokes a blessing[j] in the land
will do so by the God of truth;[k]
he who takes an oath in the land
will swear[l] by the God of truth.
For the past troubles[m] will be forgotten
and hidden from my eyes.

New Heavens and a New Earth

17"Behold, I will create
new heavens and a new earth.[n]
The former things will not be remembered,[o]
nor will they come to mind.
18But be glad and rejoice[p] forever
in what I will create,
for I will create Jerusalem[q] to be a delight
and its people a joy.
19I will rejoice[r] over Jerusalem
and take delight[s] in my people;
the sound of weeping and of crying[t]
will be heard in it no more.

20"Never again will there be in it
an infant[u] who lives but a few days,
or an old man who does not live out
his years;[v]
he who dies at a hundred
will be thought a mere youth;
he who fails to reach[x] a hundred
will be considered accursed.
21They will build houses[w] and dwell in them;
they will plant vineyards and eat
their fruit.[x]
22No longer will they build houses and
others live in them,[y]
or plant and others eat.
For as the days of a tree,[z]
so will be the days[a] of my people;
my chosen[b] ones will long enjoy
the works of their hands.
23They will not toil in vain[c]
or bear children doomed to
misfortune;[d]
for they will be a people blessed[e] by
the LORD,
they and their descendants[f] with
them.
24Before they call[g] I will answer;[h]
while they are still speaking[i] I will
hear.
25The wolf and the lamb[j] will feed
together,
and the lion will eat straw like the
ox,[k]

65:12 [x]2Ch 36:15-16; Jer 7:13; 13:11; 25:3; 26:5 [y]Ps 149:7; Isa 1:24; 66:4; Mic 5:15 **65:13** [z]S Isa 1:19 [a]S Job 18:12; Lk 6:25 [b]S Isa 33:16 [c]S Isa 3:1; 41:17 [d]S Isa 60:5; 61:7 [e]S Isa 44:9 **65:14** [f]S Ps 109:28; Zep 3:14-20; Jas 5:13 [g]S Isa 15:2; Mt 8:12; Lk 13:28 **65:15** [h]S Nu 5:27; S Ps 102:8 [i]S Ge 32:28; Rev 2:17 **65:16** [j]S Dt 29:19 [k]Ps 31:5; Rev 3:14 [l]S Ps 63:11; S Isa 19:18 [m]S Job 11:16 **65:17** [n]S Isa 41:22; 66:22; 2Co 5:17; S 2Pe 3:13 [o]Isa 43:18; Jer 3:16; S Rev 7:17 **65:18** [p]S Dt 32:43; Ps 98:1-9; S Isa 25:9 [q]Rev 21:2 **65:19** [r]S Isa 35:10; S 62:5 [s]S Dt 30:9 [t]S Isa 25:8; Rev 7:17 **65:20** [u]Isa 11:8 [v]Ge 5:1-32; S 15:15; S Ecc 8:13; Zec 8:4 **65:21** [w]S Isa 32:18; S 61:4 [x]S 2Ki 19:29; S Isa 37:30; Eze 28:26; Am 9:14 **65:22** [y]S Dt 28:30 [z]Ps 1:3; 92:12-14 [a]Ps 21:4; 91:16 [b]S Isa 14:1 **65:23** [c]S Isa 49:4; 1Co 15:58 [d]Dt 28:32,41; Jer 16:3-4 [e]S Ge 12:2; S Dt 28:3-12 [f]S Isa 44:3; Ac 2:39 **65:24** [g]S Isa 55:6; Mt 6:8 [h]S Job 8:6; S Isa 30:19; S Zec 10:6 [i]Da 9:20-23; 10:12 **65:25** [j]Isa 11:6 [k]S Job 40:15

[x]*20* Or / *the sinner who reaches*

65:13–16 THE CHURCH, Servants—See note on 54:17. A strong contrast exists between the righteous and the unrighteous. God promises to bless those who serve Him with the basic necessities of life and with the joy of service to Him.

65:17 GOD, Creator—God, who created the first heavens and earth, has the power and wisdom and authority to create new heavens and earth. He has promised to do so. This illustrates His sovereignty.

65:17–25 JESUS CHRIST, Foretold—This last great picture of the messianic kingdom in Isaiah became a prototype for the messianic kingdom described in Rev 21:1–7. In their trinitarian theology, Christians associate God's kingdom with Christ's accomplishments, and the glory of the Father is also attributed to the Son. Isaiah's visions of peace which foreshadowed Jesus' final kingdom are goals and models of what Christians want to demonstrate in history.

65:17–25 CREATION, Hope—A new creation so glorious it eliminates past memories is the ultimate hope of God's people. God's new creation will eliminate mourning and untimely death. Fear and fighting among God's creatures will vanish. God's new heaven and new earth for restored Israel were a foregleam of the heavenly home to which we look forward with hope and expectation. The One who created the first will also provide the second. Those who, on earth, follow the Lord in faith shall fellowship with one another throughout eternity. Transformed natures will serve as the basis for spiritual communion. Those who oppose the Lord during their lifetime will not only cease from hindering Him and His people but will also suffer the humiliation and misery of defeat and hopelessness.

65:17–25 LAST THINGS, History's Goal—The hope of new heavens and a new earth is the ultimate hope of the people of God (66:22) and the final goal toward which redemptive history is moving. Even natural enemies in the animal world will eat together instead of eating one another. God expects His people to pray for this day to come. See note on Rev 21:1.

65:18 SALVATION, Joy—God's people are to be glad and rejoice forever in His new creation (Ro 8:19–23; Rev 21:1–5).

65:20–23 FAMILY, Accepting Covenant—Family renewal was one element of God's promise to Judah when the people would return to Him in renewed covenant devotion. The text describes family values in Hebrew thought: absence of infant mortality, long life, secure homes, rewarding work, and many descendants. Basic to all of this is the continued presence of God, who hears and answers prayers of His people. God's plan centers on family relationships on this earth. Eventually, in the eternal family of God, the small family unit will not be needed (Mt 22:30).

65:24 PRAYER, Faithfulness of God—Prayer will be an integral part of God's new creation. The faithful God will respond instantly to His people's call.

but dust will be the serpent's[l] food.
They will neither harm nor destroy
on all my holy mountain,"[m]
says the LORD.

Chapter 66

Judgment and Hope

THIS is what the LORD says:

"Heaven is my throne,[n]
and the earth is my footstool.[o]
Where is the house[p] you will build for me?
Where will my resting place be?
2Has not my hand made all these things,[q]
and so they came into being?"
declares the LORD.

"This is the one I esteem:
he who is humble and contrite in spirit,[r]
and trembles at my word.[s]
3But whoever sacrifices a bull[t]
is like one who kills a man,
and whoever offers a lamb,
like one who breaks a dog's neck;
whoever makes a grain offering
is like one who presents pig's[u] blood,
and whoever burns memorial incense,[v]
like one who worships an idol.
They have chosen their own ways,[w]
and their souls delight in their abominations;[x]
4so I also will choose harsh treatment for them
and will bring upon them what they dread.[y]
For when I called, no one answered,[z]
when I spoke, no one listened.
They did evil[a] in my sight
and chose what displeases me."[b]

5Hear the word of the LORD,
you who tremble at his word:[c]
"Your brothers who hate[d] you,
and exclude you because of my name, have said,
'Let the LORD be glorified,
that we may see your joy!'
Yet they will be put to shame.[e]

65:25 [l]Ge 3:14; Mic 7:17 [m]S Job 5:23; S Isa 2:4
66:1 [n]S 2Ch 6:18; S Ps 2:4; S 9:7; Mt 23:22 [o]S 1Ki 8:27; Mt 5:34-35 [p]S 2Sa 7:7; Jn 4:20-21; Ac 7:48; 17:24
66:2 [q]S Isa 40:26; Ac 7:50*; 17:24 [r]S Isa 57:15; Mt 5:3-4; Lk 18:13-14 [s]S Ezr 9:4
66:3 [t]S Isa 1:11 [u]S Lev 11:7 [v]S Lev 2:2 [w]S Isa 57:17 [x]ver 17; S Dt 27:15; Eze 8:9-13
66:4 [y]S Pr 10:24; S Isa 10:12 [z]S 1Sa 8:19; S Isa 41:28 [a]2Ki 21:2,4,6; Isa 59:12 [b]S Isa 65:12
66:5 [c]S Ezr 9:4 [d]Ps 38:20; Isa 60:15; Jn 15:21 [e]S Isa 44:9; Lk 13:17
66:6 [f]S 1Sa 2:10; S Ps 68:33 [g]S Lev 26:28; Isa 65:6; Joel 3:7
66:7 [h]S Isa 54:1 [i]Rev 12:5
66:8 [j]Isa 64:4; Jer 18:13 [k]S Isa 49:20 [l]S Isa 49:21
66:9 [m]S Isa 37:3
66:10 [n]S Dt 32:43; S Isa 25:9; Ro 15:10 [o]S Ps 26:8 [p]Isa 57:19; 61:2
66:11 [q]S Nu 11:12; S Isa 60:16 [r]Ge 49:25 [s]S Nu 25:1; S Isa 25:6
66:12 [t]S Ps 119:165; S Isa 9:6 [u]S Isa 33:21 [v]Ps 72:3; Isa 60:5; 61:6 [w]S Nu 11:12; Isa 60:4
66:13 [x]S Isa 49:15; 1Th 2:7 [y]S Isa 40:1; S 2Co 1:4
66:14 [z]S Isa 25:9; S 60:5; S Joel 2:23 [a]S Ps 72:16 [b]S Ezr 5:5; S Isa 41:20 [c]S Isa 54:17

6Hear that uproar from the city,
hear that noise from the temple!
It is the sound[f] of the LORD
repaying[g] his enemies all they deserve.

7"Before she goes into labor,[h]
she gives birth;
before the pains come upon her,
she delivers a son.[i]
8Who has ever heard of such a thing?
Who has ever seen[j] such things?
Can a country be born in a day[k]
or a nation be brought forth in a moment?
Yet no sooner is Zion in labor
than she gives birth to her children.[l]
9Do I bring to the moment of birth[m]
and not give delivery?" says the LORD.
"Do I close up the womb
when I bring to delivery?" says your God.
10"Rejoice[n] with Jerusalem and be glad for her,
all you who love[o] her;
rejoice greatly with her,
all you who mourn[p] over her.
11For you will nurse[q] and be satisfied
at her comforting breasts;[r]
you will drink deeply
and delight in her overflowing abundance."[s]

12For this is what the LORD says:

"I will extend peace[t] to her like a river,[u]
and the wealth[v] of nations like a flooding stream;
you will nurse and be carried[w] on her arm
and dandled on her knees.
13As a mother comforts her child,[x]
so will I comfort[y] you;
and you will be comforted over Jerusalem."

14When you see this, your heart will rejoice[z]
and you will flourish[a] like grass;
the hand[b] of the LORD will be made known to his servants,[c]

66:1–2 GOD, Sovereignty—God's people may be disappointed at the inadequacy of the worship place we build for God. We can be assured all such places are inadequate, for no human creation can house the sovereign Creator. See note on 65:17.

66:1–4 SIN, Discipline—The opposite of sin is not religion but humble obedience. Religious rites combining what God asks and what people practice in other religions is not acceptable. To delight in false worship ceremonies rather than answer God's call to obedient service is sin. When we choose to displease God, He chooses the proper discipline for us. See note on 63:10.

66:1–4 ELECTION, Condemnation—The doctrine of election often centers on God's choices. Human choice is also involved. People must individually and as a community choose how to respond to God. Israel chose to emphasize sacrifices and ceremonies. They followed rituals God commanded and imitated those of their neighbors' religions. They thus chose to displease God. He, in turn, chose to punish them. The constant wordplay on the technical Hebrew term (*bachar*) for choose or elect shows the interplay between divine freedom and human free will in the teaching on election. The biblical teaching on election gives no room for salvation by ceremony.

66:5–6,14–16,24 GOD, Wrath—See note on 59:17–18.

but his fury[d] will be shown to his
foes.
15See, the LORD is coming with fire,[e]
and his chariots[f] are like a
whirlwind;[g]
he will bring down his anger with fury,
and his rebuke[h] with flames of fire.
16For with fire[i] and with his sword[j]
the LORD will execute judgment[k]
upon all men,
and many will be those slain[l] by
the LORD.

17"Those who consecrate and purify
themselves to go into the gardens,[m] following the one in the midst of[y] those
who eat the flesh of pigs[n] and rats[o] and
other abominable things—they will meet
their end[p] together," declares the LORD.

18"And I, because of their actions and
their imaginations,[q] am about to come[z]
and gather all nations[r] and tongues, and
they will come and see my glory.[s]

19"I will set a sign[t] among them, and I
will send some of those who survive[u] to
the nations—to Tarshish,[v] to the Libyans[a] and Lydians[w] (famous as archers),
to Tubal[x] and Greece,[y] and to the distant islands[z] that have not heard of my
fame or seen my glory.[a] They will proclaim my glory among the nations. 20And
they will bring[b] all your brothers, from
all the nations, to my holy mountain[c] in
Jerusalem as an offering to the LORD—on
horses, in chariots and wagons, and on
mules and camels,"[d] says the LORD.
"They will bring them, as the Israelites
bring their grain offerings, to the temple
of the LORD in ceremonially clean vessels.[e] 21And I will select some of them
also to be priests[f] and Levites," says the
LORD.

22"As the new heavens and the new
earth[g] that I make will endure before
me," declares the LORD, "so will your
name and descendants endure.[h] 23From
one New Moon to another and from one
Sabbath[i] to another, all mankind will
come and bow down[j] before me," says
the LORD. 24"And they will go out and
look upon the dead bodies[k] of those who
rebelled[l] against me; their worm[m] will
not die, nor will their fire be quenched,[n]
and they will be loathsome to all mankind."

66:14 [d]S Isa 10:5; S 30:27 **66:15** [e]S Isa 1:31; S 42:25 [f]S 2Ki 2:11; S Ps 68:17 [g]S 2Ki 2:1 [h]S Dt 28:20; S Ps 9:5; S 39:11 **66:16** [i]Isa 30:30; Am 7:4; Mal 4:1 [j]S Isa 1:20; S 27:1; S Eze 14:21 [k]S Isa 13:9,11; S Jer 2:35; S Eze 36:5 [l]S Isa 10:4 **66:17** [m]S Isa 1:29 [n]S Lev 11:7 [o]Lev 11:29 [p]Ps 37:20; Isa 1:28 **66:18** [q]S Pr 24:2; S Isa 65:2 [r]S Isa 2:3; S Zec 12:3 [s]S Ex 16:7; S Isa 59:19 **66:19** [t]Isa 11:10; 49:22; Mt 24:30 [u]S 2Ki 19:31 [v]S Isa 2:16 [w]Jer 46:9; Eze 27:10 [x]S Ge 10:2 [y]Jer 31:10; Da 11:18 [z]Isa 11:11 [a]S 1Ch 16:24; S Isa 24:15 **66:20** [b]S Isa 11:12; S Jer 25:22; Eze 34:13 [c]S Dt 33:19; S Isa 2:2; Jer 31:23 [d]S Ezr 2:66 [e]Isa 52:11 **66:21** [f]S Ex 19:6; 1Pe 2:5,9 **66:22** [g]S Isa 65:17; Heb 12:26-27; S 2Pe 3:13 [h]S Isa 48:19; Jn 10:27-29; 1Pe 1:4-5 **66:23** [i]Eze 46:1-3 [j]S Ps 22:29; S Isa 19:21; S 44:5; Rev 15:4 **66:24** [k]S Ps 110:6 [l]S Isa 1:2 [m]S Isa 14:11 [n]S Isa 1:31; S Mt 25:41; Mk 9:48*

[y] *17* Or *gardens behind one of your temples, and* [z] *18* The meaning of the Hebrew for this clause is uncertain. [a] *19* Some Septuagint manuscripts *Put* (Libyans); Hebrew *Pul*

66:17–24 HISTORY, Eternal—Human history on this earth is not eternal. God has announced its end. Hope rests on God's new creation not on human achievement in bringing perfection to this world. God acts in history, but He will finally act beyond history. God's new creation beyond history will have continuity with the historical existence we know on earth. It will involve hope for His faithful people who will worship Him obediently but eternal judgment on those who rebelled against God.

66:17–24 EVANGELISM, Universality—God calls believers, those who know God, to carry the message far and wide. The prophet pictured evangelists going to the exotic, unknown lands at the farthest reaches of the known world. Their work would extend the worship of the true God beyond all racial limits. God's promise of universal results for His evangelists did not include perfect acceptance. Many reject the gospel and must suffer the eternal results.

66:18–19 GOD, Glory—See note on 35:2; 58:8; 60:1–2.

66:18–21 GOD, One God—God wishes to be known as the one true God for all persons, in all places. He is not just the God of the Hebrews but of all the earth. This was implied in the covenant established with Abraham (Ge 12:1–3), and restated in the covenant with Israel at Sinai (Ex 19:1–6). God's redemptive work results in the obliteration of all the racial and national barriers between persons (Gal 3:28).

66:18–21 ELECTION, Other Nations—Election is not limited to one race or one locality. God's election has always sought to create a people to carry His glory to the nations. He even seeks to create religious leadership among foreigners.

66:19–23 MISSIONS, Sending—God's eternal purpose has been to send His people to bless the nations (Ge 12:1–3) and to introduce the nations to Him. He finally used judgment to disperse His people away from their homeland to be signs among the nations of His power and glory. Missionaries who, voluntarily leave their homeland to share God's message among the nations continue to fulfill God's intention that "all mankind will come and bow down before me."

Jeremiah

Theological Setting

Jeremiah began his prophetic ministry in the thirteenth year of the reign of Josiah, king of Judah (1:2), probably 626 BC. He continued until sometime after he was forcibly carried off to Egypt, probably about 584 BC. Jeremiah's ministry began a few years before Josiah's reform (2 Ki 23); it ended shortly after the destruction of Judah, Jerusalem, and the Temple of Solomon. Jeremiah, thus, witnessed both the last flowering of Judean independence and Judah's swift demise after the death of her last good king, Josiah. See introduction to Zephaniah.

Judah, after the death of her last great king, Josiah, in 609 BC, faced three religious options, which were also tied up with the political realities of the time:

1. They could continue on the course of unswerving and exclusive faithfulness to the God of Israel on which Josiah's reform had set them.

2. They could continue to worship their own God, at the same time reincorporating the worship of other gods alongside the Temple ritual, as had been the practice before Josiah's reform.

3. They could abandon the worship of their own God altogether, and give themselves over completely to the worship of the gods of Canaan, Egypt, and Mesopotamia.

Judah, from her kings and other leaders down to the poorest of the land, chose the second option, which they undoubtedly regarded as the wisest and the safest, the sensible middle ground. We know that in Judah people worshiped the sun, the moon, the constellations (principally the various signs of the Zodiac), and "all the host of heaven," meaning primarily the planets.

Besides this astrological worship, the Judeans were involved in the worship of the more specifically Canaanite deities—Baal, the Canaanite fertility god, both in his universal and localized manifestations; Ashtoreth, his earth-goddess consort; Molech, the god of the Ammonites, who demanded the sacrifice by fire of sons and daughters; and Chemosh, the god of the Moabites.

Why did the Judeans of Jeremiah's day bring the worship of virtually all the gods of their neighbors into the very precincts of the Temple of Israel's God and mix up their worship with His own? A part of the reason was political power; Judah did not have it, and two of her neighbors did. Usually in the ancient Near East, a vassal king was expected to acknowledge the gods of his overlord. Yet the rule of an outside power is not the whole answer. We see from the records of earlier Judean kings that some of them had decided to be faithful to the God of Israel in the face of their overlord's demands, and God had honored them for it. Judah's last kings knew this. The great majority of Judah's people returned to those gods after Josiah's death ended his reform. For people and leaders alike, the reform had been only skin-deep, something to be tolerated because the king directed it. Any Judean who knew much about the world knew that his own country could not match those great centers of civilization in any significant area of achievement. If the Judeans' devotion to the God of Israel was not firm, total, and unshakable, they were likely to conclude the God of their fathers was no match for the gods of their neighbors. In a polytheistic world, the easy and obvious solution, the "right" solution, was to incorporate the worship of their neighbors' gods alongside and into the worship of Judah's God. The sophistication and the learning of Judah's neighbors were even more effective than their political domination in enticing Judah to compromise her devotion to God.

Within religious compromise in Judah, only a few persons remained completely faithful to God alone. Jeremiah was one of the few. His faithfulness by itself might not have brought him trouble, but Jeremiah was commissioned by God to deliver a very unpopular message. His first unwelcome point was that Judah's unfaithfulness was sin and would be punished. His second point was labeled treasonous in an increasingly independence-minded nation. God intended to use the Babylonians under Nebuchadnezzar to punish Judah, and her only chance of survival as a nation lay in submission to the great empire, God's rod of judgment. Revolt and intrigue with Egypt in the attempt to throw off the Babylonian yoke could bring only disaster.

Needless to say, Jeremiah's message earned him the animosity of most Judeans. Furthermore, God had told him ahead of time that his message would be rejected and he himself would be persecuted. Nevertheless, the continual rejection, both of the message which he knew was from God, and of himself as God's prophet, was at times such a burden to Jeremiah that he quit proclaiming God's message for a time (Jer 20:9), and even cursed the day of his birth (20:14). Jeremiah—the man and his message—stands as a beacon of faithfulness in the midst of a nation which did not consider its ways to be evil and did not think that God would really punish. Jeremiah's only immediate result was to leave his people without excuse for their unfaithfulness through the example of his own faithfulness.

Theological Outline

Jeremiah: Crying for Surrender

I. God Calls His Spokesman. (1:1-19)

II. God's Spokesman Warns His People. (2:1—6:30)
- A. God brings a lawsuit against His unfaithful people. (2:1-37)
- B. God pleads with His faithless people to return. (3:1—4:4)
- C. God threatens judgment through invasion. (4:5—6:30)

III. Prophetic Theology Opposes Traditional Theology. (7:1—11:17)
- A. A place of worship cannot save. (7:1-15)
- B. A prophet cannot fulfill his traditional role for a people who forsake God. (7:16-20)
- C. Obedience, not ritual, is the most important tradition. (7:21-28)
- D. False worship will have its terrible reward. (7:29—8:13)
- E. Lamentation, not praise, is the appropriate worship in face of desolation and deceitfulness. (8:14—9:22)
- F. Worship of images is folly in light of God's creative power. (9:23—10:16)
- G. God threatens judgment through exile. (10:17-25)
- H. A covenant brings disaster on God's people. (11:1-17)

IV. Struggle with God Defines the Prophetic Role. (11:18—20:18)
- A. Prophesying can be life-threatening. (11:18—12:6)
- B. God laments His errant people. (12:7-17)
- C. God's purpose is to punish pride and promote humility. (13:1-27)
- D. God can reject and prohibit prayers for forgiveness. (14:1—15:9)
- E. God's spokesman makes personal sacrifices because of God's calling. (15:10—16:21)
- F. Trust in humans rather than God leads to destruction. (17:1-11)
- G. God's spokesman must keep listening to God and preaching. (17:12-27)
- H. God's spokesman centers his message on God's freedom, not on human expectations. (18:1-23)
- I. God's message leads to persecution of His spokesman. (19:1—20:6)
- J. God's spokesman struggles with God over the hostility of the people. (20:7-18)

V. God's Spokesman Confronts Unfaithful Leaders. (21:1—29:32)
- A. God's spokesman calls for sorrow and judgment based on the king's injustice. (21:1—22:30)
- B. God's spokesman bases hope on future righteous leaders. (23:1-8)
- C. God's spokesman must condemn those who preach lies. (23:9-40)
- D. God's word of hope is based in faithful, suffering people, not in institutions. (24:1—25:38)
- E. Prophetic hope lies in repentance, not in the Temple. (26:1-6)
- F. A prophetic precedent protects the endangered prophet. (26:7-24)
- G. God can condemn faithless leaders to serve enemies to fulfill His purpose. (27:1-22)
- H. God's true prophet overcomes false prophecy through God's divine Word. (28:1-17)
- I. Hope rests in dependence on God, not on popular prophecies or political power. (29:1-32)

VI. God Promises Restoration. (30:1—33:26)
- A. Restoration is based on God's promises in His preserved Word. (30:1-24)
- B. Restoration is based on God's faithfulness. (31:1-14)
- C. Restoration is based on God's mercy. (31:15-26)
- D. Restoration is based on God's promises to establish a new covenant with His people. (31:27-40)
- E. God's spokesman demonstrates his trust by a purchase of land. (32:1-44)
- F. Restoration is based on God's promises to restore the nation and David's dynasty. (33:1-26)

VII. God Protects His Spokesman. (34:1—40:6)
- A. God promises punishment upon the privileged for their treachery to their slaves. (34:1-22)
- B. God commends the Rechabites for their faithfulness. (35:1-19)
- C. God protects His servants and His Word from a wicked ruler. (36:1-32)

D. God protects His servant from a weak and foolish ruler. (37:1—38:28)
E. Prophetic preaching proves true. (39:1-10)
F. Even foreign leaders acknowledge prophetic authority. (39:11-14)
G. God protects His servant during a national crisis. (39:15—40:6)

VIII. God's Spokesman Warns Those Who Continue in Unfaithfulness. (40:7—45:5)
A. Political intrigue offers no basis for hope. (40:7—41:18)
B. Disobeying God's Word brings disaster, not hope, for the remnant. (42:1—43:13)
C. Disobeying God's law of loyal worship brings disaster, not hope, for the remnant. (44:1-14)
D. The people answer God's spokesman with continued defiance. (44:15-19)
E. Jeremiah promises punishment for the people. (44:20-30)
F. God promises His faithful servant his life despite desperate changes. (45:1-5)

IX. God's Spokesman Warns the Nations. (46:1—51:64)
A. God promises judgment upon Judah's pagan neighbors. (46:1—49:39)
B. God promises perpetual desolation for the destroyer of His people. (50:1—51:64)

X. Unfaithfulness Causes Destruction for God's People. (52:1-34)

Theological Conclusions

Five principal doctrinal teachings emerge from Jeremiah's prophetic ministry:

1. The sovereignty of God
2. The faithfulness of God
3. The necessity of faithfulness in God's people
4. The grace of God
5. God's promise of a new covenant.

God is sovereign over individuals, as demonstrated in His calling, sending, and protecting His prophet Jeremiah. God is sovereign over His covenant community, as demonstrated in His calling Judah back to faithfulness and His judgment of them when they refused to change their ways. God is sovereign over all the nations of the earth, as demonstrated in His using Babylon to chastise His people, and in the oracles of judgment on all Judah's neighbors, including Babylon, even though none of them acknowledged Him.

God is faithful to His people, both to assist them in living the life to which He has called them and to protect them when danger threatens. He is also faithful to His Word, performing what He has promised when His people are faithful to Him, and executing the judgment He has proclaimed when His people become unfaithful and refuse to repent.

God's people must be faithful to Him. Especially is this true of leaders who are responsible for influencing and directing the course which the people take. Ultimately, faithfulness is the responsibility of each individual member of the covenant community, because each member, by remaining within the community, has made a personal commitment to the covenant.

God is gracious to His people. God's first calling and the initial establishment of a relationship with His people is of grace. God is gracious to warn His people when they begin to stray from faithfulness to Him and the covenant. Even God's judgment is of grace, for to let His people go on unimpeded in their rebellion would be ultimately to allow them to destroy themselves completely. God's judgment rescues them from themselves. God is gracious in the promise of restoration after judgment. The present judgment is not the end of God's dealing with His people. He will restore them to Himself in righteousness.

In Jeremiah, of course, the restoration was foreseen in the promise of the new covenant. Jeremiah's vision of the new covenant was his most distinctive contribution. God would not allow His people to repeat forever the cycle of rebellion and failure. He would initiate a new covenant and engrave it upon the heart, so that the old problem of chronic disobedience would be solved. It was in the events of Calvary and Pentecost that Jeremiah's vision of the new covenant was fulfilled.

Contemporary Teaching

God's message through Jeremiah came to Judah in her most desperate hour. Yet many in Judah did not recognize the seriousness of their position. If we will take seriously God's instructions through Jeremiah, the church and individual believers will avoid the spiritual blindness and bankruptcy which doomed Judah.

Jeremiah teaches us to: 1) Take our new covenant relationship with God seriously; 2) Believe God; 3) Trust God; 4) Take our relationships with fellow believers seriously; 5) Take our agreements (covenants) seriously; 6) Be alert to recognize and apply God's correction; and 7) Live in joyful expectation of God's final restoration of His people and His creation.

Chapter 1

THE words of Jeremiah son of Hilkiah,
one of the priests at Anathoth[a] in
the territory of Benjamin. 2 The word of
the LORD came[b] to him in the thirteenth
year of the reign of Josiah[c] son of Amon
king of Judah, 3 and through the reign of
Jehoiakim[d] son of Josiah king of Judah,
down to the fifth month of the eleventh
year of Zedekiah[e] son of Josiah king of
Judah, when the people of Jerusalem
went into exile.[f]

The Call of Jeremiah

4 The word of the LORD came to me,
saying,

5 "Before I formed you in the womb[g] I
knew[a][h] you,
before you were born[i] I set you
apart;[j]
I appointed you as a prophet to the
nations.[k]"

6 "Ah, Sovereign LORD," I said, "I do
not know how to speak;[l] I am only a
child."[m]
7 But the LORD said to me, "Do not say,
'I am only a child.' You must go to everyone I send you to and say whatever I command you. 8 Do not be afraid[n] of them,
for I am with you[o] and will rescue[p]
you," declares the LORD.[q]
9 Then the LORD reached out his hand
and touched[r] my mouth and said to me,
"Now, I have put my words in your
mouth.[s] 10 See, today I appoint you over
nations[t] and kingdoms to uproot[u] and
tear down, to destroy and overthrow, to
build and to plant."[v]
11 The word of the LORD came to me:
"What do you see, Jeremiah?"[w]
"I see the branch of an almond tree," I
replied.
12 The LORD said to me, "You have seen
correctly, for I am watching[b][x] to see that
my word is fulfilled."
13 The word of the LORD came to me
again: "What do you see?"[y]
"I see a boiling pot, tilting away from
the north," I answered.
14 The LORD said to me, "From the
north[z] disaster will be poured out on all
who live in the land. 15 I am about to summon all the peoples of the northern kingdoms," declares the LORD.

"Their kings will come and set up
their thrones
in the entrance of the gates of
Jerusalem;
they will come against all her
surrounding walls

1:1 [a]S Jos 21:18
1:2 [b]Eze 1:3; Hos 1:1; Joel 1:1 [c]S 2Ki 22:1
1:3 [d]S 2Ki 23:34 [e]S 2Ki 24:17 [f]Ezr 5:12; Jer 52:15
1:5 [g]S Ps 139:13 [h]Ps 139:16 [i]S Isa 49:1 [j]Jn 10:36 [k]ver 10; Jer 25:15-26
1:6 [l]S Ex 3:11; S 6:12 [m]1Ki 3:7
1:8 [n]S Ge 15:1; S Jos 8:1 [o]S Ge 26:3; S Jos 1:5; Jer 15:20 [p]ver 19; Jer 15:21; 26:24; 36:26; 42:11 [q]Jer 20:11
1:9 [r]S Isa 6:7 [s]S Ex 4:12
1:10 [t]Jer 25:17; 46:1 [u]Jer 12:17 [v]Jer 18:7-10; 24:6; 31:4,28
1:11 [w]Jer 24:3; Am 7:8
1:12 [x]S Job 29:2; Jer 44:27
1:13 [y]Jer 24:3; Zec 4:2; 5:2
1:14 [z]S Isa 14:31

[a] *5* Or *chose* [b] *12* The Hebrew for *watching* sounds like the Hebrew for *almond tree.*

1:4–9 REVELATION, Messengers—God frequently chooses messengers who see themselves as inadequate for the task. God reveals Himself to them and empowers them to do His will. Jeremiah, like predecessors Moses and Elijah, tried to resist God's call but found himself pressed to obey and encouraged by the promise of God's steady presence. God can be depended on to support those of whom He makes requests. Compare Ex 3:11; Jdg 6:15; 1 Ki 19:3; Isa 6:5. God's calls to individuals differ, since God does not set up qualification lists. He called Moses in middle age but Jeremiah as a youngster. A purified Isaiah volunteered for service. Jeremiah was chosen prior to birth. The prophetic task involved Jeremiah in being God's messenger to royal courts to announce God's plans in international politics. The prophet announced both salvation and judgment.

1:4–9 PROCLAMATION, Call—In Old Testament times God selected certain individuals to proclaim His message. This call to proclaim was vital to effective proclamation. God set Jeremiah apart even before he was born! On the other hand, God called Jonah in his adult years to proclaim a certain message in a certain place (Jnh 1:2; 3:2–4). In New Testament times God called people to preach His revealed truth in the manner of the Lord Jesus Himself (Mt 4:17–22; Mk 3:13–14; Lk 9:1–2). This call established these men as servant leaders of the Christian movement (Ro 15:15–22; 1 Co 1:17–18; 2 Co 1:17–24; Eph 3:8–9; Col 1:25; 2 Ti 1:11). In addition, in the New Testament as the early church was scattered in persecution, each believer became a preacher of the good news (Ac 8:4–5; Ro 10:14–15). See note on Ro 10:14–15.

1:5,10 GOD, Sovereignty—God chose to exercise His sovereign authority over His world in a special way in Jeremiah's life. Before God placed Jeremiah in his mother's womb, God planned to use him as the instrument to announce God's world-changing word to the nations. God is free to act in individual lives and among nations as He chooses.

1:5 HUMANITY, Birth—Conception and birth are a natural process and acts of God, the Creator of life. As Creator, God has a purpose for each of His creatures.

1:5 ELECTION, Leadership—Jeremiah sensed God's purposeful direction of his life from the beginning. God has a purpose for individual lives as well as for the community of His people. He creates individuals for definite purposes in His election plan. Individuals have the freedom to argue and complain about God's purpose, as did Jeremiah. Inner peace comes only as individuals find, accept, and follow God's purpose.

1:5–10 EVANGELISM, Obedience—The prophetic call to declare God's message has several significant evangelistic principles: (1) God calls in His sovereign purpose (v 5a); (2) the appointment comes from God, not human agency (v 5b); (3) human limitations are not important (v 6); (4) human obedience is expected (v 7); (5) God is with those He calls for the task (v 8); (6) God enables His witness to speak His word (v 9); and (7) the message will provoke a crisis of decision (v 10). In the light of all these marvelous truths, we ought to evangelize faithfully, for to this He has called us all (Mt 28:19–20).

1:6–7 HUMANITY, Childhood and Youth—The Hebrew word indicates immaturity, more likely referring to a young person than a child. Immaturity makes people feel inadequate to the tasks of adulthood. Immaturity, however, must never be misconstrued as inability. God enables people of every age to do what He calls them to do.

1:11–16 REVELATION, Visions—God used different means to reveal His will and word to prophets. Some prophetic visions included dialog with God about a common, everyday object (24:3; Am 7:8; 8:2; Zec 4:2; 5:2). Through the visions God taught Jeremiah His word would happen in history. He summoned the people to hear a new interpretation of their history. Saving acts would become judging, destroying acts. Thus God prepared Judah for Babylon's destruction of Jerusalem in 586 BC.

1:14–19 HISTORY, Judgment—The prophetic task involved opposing God's disobedient people and announcing historical judgment on them. God's Word does not proclaim false hope to an unfaithful people.

and against all the towns of Judah.[a]
16I will pronounce my judgments[b] on
my people
because of their wickedness[c] in
forsaking me,[d]
in burning incense to other gods[e]
and in worshiping[f] what their
hands have made.[g]

17"Get yourself ready! Stand up and
say[h] to them whatever I command you.
Do not be terrified[i] by them, or I will
terrify you before them. 18Today I have
made you[j] a fortified city, an iron pillar
and a bronze wall to stand against the
whole land—against the kings of Judah,
its officials, its priests and the people of
the land. 19They will fight against you but
will not overcome[k] you, for I am with
you[l] and will rescue[m] you," declares the
LORD.

Chapter 2

Israel Forsakes God

THE word[n] of the LORD came to me:
2"Go and proclaim in the hearing of
Jerusalem:

" 'I remember the devotion of your
youth,[o]
how as a bride you loved me
and followed me through the desert,[p]

1:15 [a]Jer 4:16; 9:11; 10:22
1:16 [b]Jer 4:12 [c]S Ge 6:5; Jer 44:5 [d]Jer 2:13; 17:13 [e]S Ex 20:3; Jer 7:9; 19:4; 44:3 [f]S Nu 25:3 [g]Ps 115:4-8; S 135:15
1:17 [h]ver 7; Jer 7:27; 26:2,15; 42:4 [i]S Dt 31:6; S 2Ki 1:15
1:18 [j]S Isa 50:7
1:19 [k]S Ps 129:2 [l]S Ge 26:3; Isa 43:2; Jer 20:11 [m]S ver 8; S Pr 20:22; Ac 26:17
2:1 [n]Isa 38:4; Eze 1:3; Mic 1:1
2:2 [o]Ps 71:17; Isa 54:4; Jer 3:4; Eze 16:8-14,60; Hos 2:15; 11:1; Rev 2:4 [p]S Ex 13:21; S Dt 1:19
2:3 [q]S Dt 7:6 [r]S Ex 19:6; S Dt 7:6 [s]Lev 23:9-14; Jas 1:18; Rev 14:4 [t]Isa 41:11; Jer 10:25; 30:16 [u]Jer 50:7
2:5 [v]S Dt 32:21; S 1Sa 12:21; Ps 31:6 [w]2Ki 17:15
2:6 [x]S Ex 6:6; Hos 13:4 [y]S Dt 1:19 [z]S Dt 32:10
[a]Jer 51:43
2:7 [b]S Nu 13:27; Dt 8:7-9; 11:10-12

through a land not sown.
3Israel was holy[q] to the LORD,[r]
the firstfruits[s] of his harvest;
all who devoured[t] her were held
guilty,[u]
and disaster overtook them,' "
declares the LORD.

4Hear the word of the LORD, O house of
Jacob,
all you clans of the house of Israel.

5This is what the LORD says:

"What fault did your fathers find in
me,
that they strayed so far from me?
They followed worthless idols[v]
and became worthless[w] themselves.
6They did not ask, 'Where is the LORD,
who brought us up out of Egypt[x]
and led us through the barren
wilderness,
through a land of deserts[y] and
rifts,[z]
a land of drought and darkness,[c]
a land where no one travels[a] and no
one lives?'
7I brought you into a fertile land
to eat its fruit and rich produce.[b]
But you came and defiled my land

[c]6 Or *and the shadow of death*

1:16 GOD, One God—Sharing worship that belonged only to the one true God with handmade idols led Israel into captivity.

1:16 SIN, Transgression—Judgment comes on God's people when they forsake Him for social or political convenience. Past history does not protect us against present sin. See note on 2 Ch 24:17–26.

1:17–19 REVELATION, Messengers—Prophets became enemies of God's people, announcing their judgment and destruction. God armed His messengers to protect them from the people. God's presence was sufficient protection against the angry people.

2:1—3:5 SIN, Against God—Freedom led Judah to slavery. God saved her in the Exodus and established her on her land. Still she vaunted her freedom and wooed other nations into defense treaties. The treaties included provisions for recognition and worship of national gods. Judah exercised her freedom still further. She saw how the Canaanite farmers "ensured" fertility for crops through exciting ceremonies involving ritual prostitution. Judah joined in to share the fun and reap the harvests. God had other words for Judah's exercise of freedom. They "strayed" (2:5) or distanced themselves from God. To place any god, any material possession, or any activity in first place in life is to separate ourselves from God. Such obvious sin comes when religious and political leaders set up personal achievement priorities ahead of humble service of God (2:8). Any time we devote our time and energies totally to one project, we are in danger of doing the unthinkable, of changing the true God for an idol (2:11). We must glory only in the glorious One. When we do not, we are "backsliding" or turning around from God (Hebrew root *shub,* the same root for repentance). Any time we do not fear God in reverence, respect, and awe, we can expect bitter consequences. No human efforts can wash away our sin of rebellion, wrong exercise of freedom, false worship, and backsliding. Turning to God in humble repentance can bring His forgiveness.

2:1—3:5 HISTORY, Judgment—History can serve as evidence against God's people. Ignoring or denying history's evidence is no excuse. God's judgment eventually comes to a sinful people. See note on Ps 106:2.

2:1–37 ELECTION, Free Will—Israel's relationship to God was like that of an unfaithful wife. God had remorse over Israel's rejected love. Sin breaks God's heart, but He gives His elect the freedom to reject Him. He retains freedom to discipline His chosen. People cannot exercise freedom to roam religiously and change gods at will while still claiming innocence before God.

2:1–3 THE CHURCH, Covenant People—Jeremiah used two analogies—those of the bride and the firstfruits—to teach that Israel was the covenant people of God. Early in Israel's history, the people loved God as a bride loves her husband and followed Him obediently in the wilderness. In later years, the people rebelled against God, looking to other "lovers." The firstfruits (Ex 23:19) belonged to God alone. Any other use of the firstfruits brought judgment upon the owner. As the firstfruits of God's harvest, Israel was holy to the Lord. The people were set apart for God's service. God desires that His covenant people serve Him in a manner like the people of Israel in the earlier period. God's covenant people are holy to the Lord. We must yield ourselves to God's work.

2:1–3 FAMILY, Symbolic Nature—Marriage can symbolize the covenant relationship between Israel and God. Consequently, the prophet also used adultery and divorce as symbols of the broken relationship caused when Israel turned to other gods resulting in God's judgment on them (2:20,24; 3:1, 8–10).

2:2 PROCLAMATION, Fearless—See note on 19:14–15.

2:3 GOD, Holy—The holy God chose to establish a people holy, set apart for Himself. The holy God then protected them from enemies, but still Israel strayed.

2:5–13,26–28 GOD, One God—The unthinkable sin is to switch gods, losing confidence in God, who proved His claim to be the only God so often in history. The new gods certainly never demonstrate power to save. See note on 1:16.

and made my inheritance
detestable.[c]
8The priests did not ask,
'Where is the LORD?'
Those who deal with the law did not
know me;[d]
the leaders[e] rebelled against me.
The prophets prophesied by Baal,[f]
following worthless idols.[g]

9"Therefore I bring charges[h] against
you again,"
declares the LORD.
"And I will bring charges against
your children's children.
10Cross over to the coasts of Kittim[d] [i]
and look,
send to Kedar[e] [j] and observe
closely;
see if there has ever been anything
like this:
11Has a nation ever changed its gods?
(Yet they are not gods[k] at all.)
But my people have exchanged their[f]
Glory[l]
for worthless idols.
12Be appalled at this, O heavens,
and shudder with great horror,"
declares the LORD.
13"My people have committed two sins:
They have forsaken[m] me,
the spring of living water,[n]
and have dug their own cisterns,
broken cisterns that cannot hold
water.
14Is Israel a servant, a slave[o] by birth?
Why then has he become plunder?
15Lions[p] have roared;
they have growled at him.
They have laid waste[q] his land;
his towns are burned[r] and
deserted.[s]
16Also, the men of Memphis[g] [t] and
Tahpanhes[u]
have shaved the crown of your
head.[h]
17Have you not brought this on
yourselves[v]
by forsaking[w] the LORD your God
when he led you in the way?
18Now why go to Egypt[x]
to drink water from the Shihor[i] ?[y]
And why go to Assyria[z]
to drink water from the River[j] ?[a]
19Your wickedness will punish you;
your backsliding[b] will rebuke[c] you.
Consider then and realize
how evil and bitter[d] it is for you
when you forsake[e] the LORD your God
and have no awe[f] of me,"
declares the Lord,
the LORD Almighty.

2:7 [c]Ps 106:34-39; Jer 3:9; 7:30; 16:18; Eze 11:21; 36:17
2:8 [d]S 1Sa 2:12; Jer 4:22 [e]Jer 3:15; 23:1; 25:34; 50:6 [f]S 1Ki 18:22 [g]ver 25; S Isa 40:19; S 56:10; Jer 5:19; 9:14; 16:19; 22:9
2:9 [h]Jer 25:31; Hos 4:1; Mic 6:2
2:10 [i]S Ge 10:4 [j]S Ge 25:13
2:11 [k]S Isa 37:19; Jer 16:20; Gal 4:8 [l]S 1Sa 4:21; Ro 1:23
2:13 [m]S Dt 31:16; S Isa 65:11 [n]S Isa 12:3; Jn 4:14
2:14 [o]Ex 4:22; Jer 31:9
2:15 [p]Jer 4:7; 50:17 [q]S Isa 1:7 [r]S 2Ki 25:9 [s]S Lev 26:43
2:16 [t]S Isa 19:13 [u]Jer 43:7-9
2:17 [v]Jer 4:18 [w]S Isa 1:28; Jer 17:13; 19:4
2:18 [x]S Isa 30:2 [y]S Jos 13:3 [z]S 2Ki 16:7; Hos 5:13; 7:11; 8:9 [a]S Isa 7:20
2:19 [b]Jer 3:11,22; 7:24; 11:10; 14:7; Hos 14:4 [c]Isa 3:9; 59:12; Hos 5:5 [d]S Job 20:14; Am 8:10 [e]Jer 19:4 [f]S Ps 36:1
2:20 [g]S Lev 26:13 [h]Ps 2:3; Jer 5:5 [i]S Job 21:14 [j]Isa 57:7; Jer 3:23; 17:2 [k]S Dt 12:2 [l]S Isa 1:21; Eze 16:15
2:21 [m]S Ex 15:17 [n]S Ps 80:8 [o]S Isa 5:4
2:22 [p]S Ps 51:2; La 1:8,17 [q]S Job 9:30 [r]Jer 17:1
2:23 [s]S Pr 30:12 [t]ver 25; Jer 9:14; 23:27 [u]S 2Ki 23:10; Jer 7:31; 19:2; 31:40 [v]ver 33; Jer 31:22
2:24 [w]S Ge 16:12; Jer 14:6 [x]S Job 39:6
2:25 [y]S Isa 57:10 [z]Dt 32:16; Jer 3:13; 14:10 [a]S ver 8,S 23
2:26 [b]Jer 48:27; La 1:7; Eze 16:54; 36:4 [c]Eze 22:26 [d]Jer 32:32; 44:17, 21
2:27 [e]Jer 10:8 [f]Jer 3:9 [g]S 1Ki 14:9; S 2Ch 29:6; Ps 14:3; Eze 8:16 [h]Jer 18:17; 32:33; Eze 7:22 [i]Jdg 10:10; Isa 26:16 [j]Isa 37:20; Hos 5:15
2:28 [k]S Isa 45:20 [l]S Dt 32:37; S Isa 40:19 [m]S 2Ki 17:29

20"Long ago you broke off your yoke[g]
and tore off your bonds;[h]
you said, 'I will not serve you!'[i]
Indeed, on every high hill[j]
and under every spreading tree[k]
you lay down as a prostitute.[l]
21I had planted[m] you like a choice vine[n]
of sound and reliable stock.
How then did you turn against me
into a corrupt,[o] wild vine?
22Although you wash[p] yourself with
soda[q]
and use an abundance of soap,
the stain of your guilt is still before
me,"
declares the Sovereign LORD.[r]
23"How can you say, 'I am not defiled;[s]
I have not run after the Baals'?[t]
See how you behaved in the valley;[u]
consider what you have done.
You are a swift she-camel
running[v] here and there,
24a wild donkey[w] accustomed to the
desert,[x]
sniffing the wind in her craving—
in her heat who can restrain her?
Any males that pursue her need not
tire themselves;
at mating time they will find her.
25Do not run until your feet are bare
and your throat is dry.
But you said, 'It's no use![y]
I love foreign gods,[z]
and I must go after them.'[a]

26"As a thief is disgraced[b] when he is
caught,
so the house of Israel is disgraced—
they, their kings and their officials,
their priests[c] and their prophets.[d]
27They say to wood,[e] 'You are my
father,'
and to stone,[f] 'You gave me birth.'
They have turned their backs[g] to me
and not their faces;[h]
yet when they are in trouble,[i] they
say,
'Come and save[j] us!'
28Where then are the gods[k] you made
for yourselves?
Let them come if they can save you
when you are in trouble![l]
For you have as many gods
as you have towns,[m] O Judah.

29"Why do you bring charges against
me?

[d]*10* That is, Cyprus and western coastlands
[e]*10* The home of Bedouin tribes in the Syro-Arabian desert
[f]*11* Masoretic Text; an ancient Hebrew scribal tradition *my*
[g]*16* Hebrew *Noph*
[h]*16* Or *have cracked your skull*
[i]*18* That is, a branch of the Nile
[j]*18* That is, the Euphrates

2:11 GOD, Glory—See notes on Ex 16:7,10; 40:34–38; Lk 2:9,14; Jn 11:4.

You have all[n] rebelled against me,"
declares the LORD.
30 "In vain I punished your people;
they did not respond to correction.[o]
Your sword has devoured your
prophets[p]
like a ravening lion.

31 "You of this generation, consider the word of the LORD:

"Have I been a desert to Israel
or a land of great darkness?[q]
Why do my people say, 'We are free to
roam;
we will come to you no more'?[r]
32 Does a maiden forget her jewelry,
a bride her wedding ornaments?
Yet my people have forgotten[s] me,
days without number.
33 How skilled you are at pursuing[t] love!
Even the worst of women can learn
from your ways.
34 On your clothes men find
the lifeblood[u] of the innocent poor,
though you did not catch them
breaking in.[v]
Yet in spite of all this
35 you say, 'I am innocent;[w]
he is not angry with me.'
But I will pass judgment[x] on you
because you say, 'I have not
sinned.'[y]
36 Why do you go about so much,
changing[z] your ways?
You will be disappointed by Egypt[a]
as you were by Assyria.
37 You will also leave that place
with your hands on your head,[b]
for the LORD has rejected those you
trust;
you will not be helped[c] by them.

Chapter 3

"IF a man divorces[d] his wife
and she leaves him and marries
another man,
should he return to her again?
Would not the land be completely
defiled?[e]
But you have lived as a prostitute with
many lovers[f] —
would you now return to me?"[g]
declares the LORD.
2 "Look up to the barren heights[h] and
see.
Is there any place where you have
not been ravished?
By the roadside[i] you sat waiting for
lovers,
sat like a nomad[k] in the desert.
You have defiled the land[j]
with your prostitution[k] and
wickedness.
3 Therefore the showers have been
withheld,[l]
and no spring rains[m] have fallen.
Yet you have the brazen[n] look of a
prostitute;
you refuse to blush with shame.[o]
4 Have you not just called to me:
'My Father,[p] my friend from my
youth,[q]
5 will you always be angry?[r]
Will your wrath continue forever?'
This is how you talk,
but you do all the evil you can."

Unfaithful Israel

6 During the reign of King Josiah,[s] the
LORD said to me, "Have you seen what
faithless[t] Israel has done? She has gone
up on every high hill and under every
spreading tree[u] and has committed adultery[v] there. 7 I thought that after she had
done all this she would return to me but
she did not, and her unfaithful sister[w] Judah saw it.[x] 8 I gave faithless Israel[y] her
certificate of divorce[z] and sent her away
because of all her adulteries. Yet I saw
that her unfaithful sister Judah had no
fear;[a] she also went out and committed
adultery. 9 Because Israel's immorality
mattered so little to her, she defiled the
land[b] and committed adultery[c] with
stone[d] and wood.[e] 10 In spite of all this,
her unfaithful sister Judah did not return[f] to me with all her heart, but only
in pretense,[g]" declares the LORD.[h]
11 The LORD said to me, "Faithless Israel is more righteous[i] than unfaithful[j] Ju-

2:29 [n]Jer 5:1; 6:13; Da 9:11; Mic 3:11; 7:2 **2:30** [o]S Lev 26:23 [p]S Ne 9:26; S Jer 11:21; Ac 7:52; 1Th 2:15 **2:31** [q]Isa 45:19 [r]S Job 21:14 **2:32** [s]S Dt 32:18; S Isa 57:11 **2:33** [t]S ver 23 **2:34** [u]S 2Ki 21:16; S Pr 6:17 [v]S Ex 22:2 **2:35** [w]S Pr 30:12 [x]Isa 66:16; Jer 25:31; 39:7; 45:5; Eze 17:20; 20:35; Joel 3:2 [y]S 2Sa 12:13; 1Jn 1:8,10 **2:36** [z]Jer 31:22 [a]S Ps 108:12; S Isa 30:2,3,7; Jer 37:7 **2:37** [b]2Sa 13:19 [c]Jer 37:7 **3:1** [d]Dt 24:1-4 [e]S Ge 3:17 [f]S 2Ki 16:7; S Isa 1:21; Jer 2:20,25; 4:30; La 1:2; Eze 16:26,29; Hos 2:5,12; 3:1 [g]Hos 2:7 **3:2** [h]ver 21 [i]Ge 38:14; Eze 16:25 [j]ver 9 [k]S Nu 15:39; S Isa 1:21 **3:3** [l]Lev 26:19; Jer 5:25; Am 4:7 [m]S Dt 11:14; Jer 14:4; Joel 1:10 [n]Eze 3:7; 16:30 [o]Jer 6:15; 8:12; Zep 2:1; 3:5 **3:4** [p]ver 19; S Dt 32:6; S Ps 89:26; Isa 63:16; 64:8; Jer 31:9 [q]S Jer 2:2 **3:5** [r]S Ps 103:9; S Isa 54:9 **3:6** [s]S 1Ch 3:14 [t]ver 12,22; S Isa 24:16; Jer 31:22; 49:4 [u]S Dt 12:2; Jer 17:2; Eze 20:28; Hos 4:13 [v]S Lev 17:7; Jer 2:20 **3:7** [w]Eze 16:46; 23:2,11 [x]Am 4:8 **3:8** [y]Jer 11:10 [z]S Dt 4:27; S 24:1 [a]Eze 16:47; 23:11 **3:9** [b]ver 2 [c]S Lev 17:7; S Isa 1:21 [d]S Isa 57:6 [e]Jer 2:27 **3:10** [f]Isa 31:6; Am 4:9; Hag 2:17 [g]Jer 12:2; Eze 33:31 [h]S 2Ki 17:19 **3:11** [i]Eze 16:52; 23:11 [j]ver 7

[k]2 Or *an Arab*

3:4,19 GOD, Father—Pious prayer language claiming God as Father is worthless without matching deeds.
3:5,12 GOD, Wrath—See notes on Ge 6:5–8; 17:14; 19:13,24–26; Jos 7:1,25–26; Ps 30:5; Isa 30:18–19; Mt 3:7–10.
3:6–10 SIN, Against God—"Faithless" (v 6) comes from the same Hebrew root as "backsliding."
3:6–10 ELECTION, Forgiveness—God requires sincere and genuine repentance. Judah's return to God was only in pretense. Election depends on God forgiving sinful people, but forgiveness comes only to those willing to change guilty ways and follow God.
3:6–18 SALVATION, Repentance—Israel here refers to the Northern Kingdom which had been destroyed in 721 BC. Judah is the Southern Kingdom. Faithless is sometimes translated backsliding (v 22), which contains a play on the two senses of the Hebrew root—implying both to turn the back on God and to turn back to Him. Repentance is turning back to God and turning away from idolatry (4:1). God promises mercy to those who repent.
3:11–18 THE CHURCH, Remnant—Repentance is a spiritual necessity. God promises to do good to His people who turn to Him in faith. God's people are the repentant remnant who accept His discipline, confess sins, trust His mercy, and follow His leadership.

dah.[k] 12 Go, proclaim this message toward the north:[l]

" 'Return,[m] faithless[n] Israel,' declares
the LORD,
'I will frown on you no longer,
for I am merciful,'[o] declares the LORD,
'I will not be angry[p] forever.
13 Only acknowledge[q] your guilt—
you have rebelled against the LORD
your God,
you have scattered your favors to
foreign gods[r]
under every spreading tree,[s]
and have not obeyed[t] me,' "
declares the LORD.

14 "Return,[u] faithless people," declares
the LORD, "for I am your husband.[v] I will
choose you—one from a town and two
from a clan—and bring you to Zion.
15 Then I will give you shepherds[w] after
my own heart,[x] who will lead you with
knowledge and understanding. 16 In those
days, when your numbers have increased
greatly in the land," declares the LORD,
"men will no longer say, 'The ark[y] of the
covenant of the LORD.' It will never enter
their minds or be remembered;[z] it will
not be missed, nor will another one be
made. 17 At that time they will call Jerusalem The Throne[a] of the LORD, and all
nations[b] will gather in Jerusalem to hon-
or[c] the name of the LORD. No longer will
they follow the stubbornness of their evil
hearts.[d] 18 In those days the house of Judah will join the house of Israel,[e] and
together[f] they will come from a northern[g] land to the land[h] I gave your forefathers as an inheritance.
19 "I myself said,

" 'How gladly would I treat you like
sons
and give you a desirable land,[i]
the most beautiful inheritance[j] of
any nation.'
I thought you would call me 'Father'[k]
and not turn away from following
me.

3:11 [k]S Jer 2:19
3:12 [l]2Ki 17:3-6 [m]ver 14; S Dt 4:30; Jer 31:21,22; Eze 14:6; 33:11; Hos 14:1 [n]S ver 6 [o]S 1Ki 3:26; S Ps 6:2 [p]S Ps 103:9; S Isa 54:9
3:13 [q]Dt 30:1-3; Jer 14:20; 1Jn 1:9 [r]S Jer 2:25 [s]S Dt 12:2 [t]ver 25; Jer 22:21
3:14 [u]S ver 12; S Job 22:23; Jer 4:1 [v]S Isa 54:5
3:15 [w]S Isa 31:4 [x]Ac 13:22
3:16 [y]S Nu 3:31; S 1Ch 15:25 [z]S Isa 65:17
3:17 [a]S Ps 47:8; Jer 17:12; 33:16; Eze 1:26; 43:7; 48:35 [b]S Isa 2:3; Mic 4:1 [c]S Ps 22:23; Jer 13:11; 33:9 [d]Ps 81:12; Jer 7:24; 9:14; 11:8; 13:10; 16:12; 18:12
3:18 [e]Jer 30:3; Eze 37:19 [f]S Isa 11:13; Jer 50:4 [g]Jer 16:15; 31:8 [h]Dt 31:7; S Isa 14:1; Eze 11:17; 37:22; Am 9:15
3:19 [i]S Dt 8:7 [j]Ps 106:24; Eze 20:6 [k]S ver 4; S Ex 4:22; S 2Sa 7:14
3:20 [l]S Isa 24:16
3:21 [m]ver 2 [n]Jer 31:18 [o]S Isa 57:11
3:22 [p]S ver 12; S Job 22:23 [q]S Isa 30:26; 57:18; Jer 33:6; Hos 6:1 [r]S Jer 2:19
3:23 [s]S Jer 2:20 [t]Ps 3:8; Jer 17:14
3:24 [u]Jer 11:13; Hos 9:10
3:25 [v]S Ezr 9:6; Jer 31:19; Da 9:7 [w]S Jdg 10:10; S 1Ki 8:47 [x]Jer 14:20 [y]S Ps 25:7; S Jer 22:21 [z]S ver 13; Eze 2:3
4:1 [a]S Dt 4:30; S 2Ki 17:13; S Hos 12:6 [b]S 2Ki 21:4; Jer 16:18; 35:15; Eze 8:5

20 But like a woman unfaithful to her
husband,
so you have been unfaithful[l] to me,
O house of Israel,"
declares the LORD.

21 A cry is heard on the barren heights,[m]
the weeping[n] and pleading of the
people of Israel,
because they have perverted their
ways
and have forgotten[o] the LORD their
God.

22 "Return,[p] faithless people;
I will cure[q] you of backsliding."[r]

"Yes, we will come to you,
for you are the LORD our God.
23 Surely the ⌞idolatrous⌟ commotion on
the hills[s]
and mountains is a deception;
surely in the LORD our God
is the salvation[t] of Israel.
24 From our youth shameful[u] gods have
consumed
the fruits of our fathers' labor—
their flocks and herds,
their sons and daughters.
25 Let us lie down in our shame,[v]
and let our disgrace cover us.
We have sinned[w] against the LORD our
God,
both we and our fathers;[x]
from our youth[y] till this day
we have not obeyed[z] the LORD our
God."

Chapter 4

"If you will return,[a] O Israel,
return to me,"
declares the LORD.
"If you put your detestable idols[b] out
of my sight
and no longer go astray,
2 and if in a truthful, just and righteous
way

3:12,14 GOD, Grace—God in grace chooses to deliver faithless people if they repent. See notes on Ge 19:12–19,29; 39:21–23; 45:5–9; Lk 1:30.

3:13,22–25 SALVATION, Confession—Confession is the acknowledgment of our guilt. It is returning from our backsliding. It is commitment to the Lord as the only God and rejection of all deceptive "gods." It is turning to obey God. Compare Isa 59:12–15; 64:5–12. See note on Ps 106:6.

3:14–17 ELECTION, Remnant—God chose to start over with a small remnant He would lead out of captivity. The promises of the old covenant would be superseded by the promises of the new covenant. Gentiles would come to Zion in a fellowship where evil would not exist. Election purposes hold true even when election people are faithless and have to be rejected for a remnant.

3:17 GOD, Sovereignty—The sovereign God will one day reveal Himself as King over all nations.

3:20–22 SIN, Rebellion—Unfaithful (Hebrew *bagad*) means literally treachery or betrayal. See note on Isa 48:1–9. On backsliding, see Jer 2:1—3:5. Going to God in repentance cures this sin against Him.

3:23 SALVATION, Initiative—Our salvation is not in idols and the worship of false gods, but in a covenant relationship with the living God.

4:1–2 EVANGELISM, Call to Salvation—God's call to the lost is always to return. They are to turn to Him—not to the church, or to religious exercises, or to themselves in new resolves. They turn to God Himself. All those secondary things will follow as they answer the call to turn to God. It is in Him they are blessed (Ge 12:3).

4:2 SALVATION, Blessing—See note on Isa 61:9. The refusal of God's people truly to return to Him can block His blessings on them and others. Returning to Him they again assume the mission of blessing the nations (Ge 12:1–3).

you swear,[c] 'As surely as the LORD
lives,'[d]
then the nations will be blessed[e] by
him
and in him they will glory.[f] "

3This is what the LORD says to the men
of Judah and to Jerusalem:

"Break up your unplowed ground[g]
and do not sow among thorns.[h]
4Circumcise yourselves to the LORD,
circumcise your hearts,[i]
you men of Judah and people of
Jerusalem,
or my wrath[j] will break out and burn
like fire[k]
because of the evil[l] you have
done—
burn with no one to quench[m] it.

Disaster From the North

5"Announce in Judah and proclaim[n] in
Jerusalem and say:
'Sound the trumpet[o] throughout the
land!'
Cry aloud and say:
'Gather together!
Let us flee to the fortified cities!'[p]
6Raise the signal[q] to go to Zion!
Flee for safety without delay!
For I am bringing disaster[r] from the
north,[s]
even terrible destruction."

7A lion[t] has come out of his lair;[u]
a destroyer[v] of nations has set out.
He has left his place
to lay waste[w] your land.
Your towns will lie in ruins[x]
without inhabitant.
8So put on sackcloth,[y]
lament[z] and wail,
for the fierce anger[a] of the LORD
has not turned away from us.

9"In that day," declares the LORD,
"the king and the officials will lose
heart,[b]
the priests will be horrified,
and the prophets will be appalled."[c]

10Then I said, "Ah, Sovereign LORD,
how completely you have deceived[d] this
people and Jerusalem by saying, 'You will
have peace,'[e] when the sword is at our
throats."

11At that time this people and Jerusalem will be told, "A scorching wind[f]
from the barren heights in the desert
blows toward my people, but not to winnow or cleanse; 12a wind[g] too strong for
that comes from me.[1] Now I pronounce
my judgments[h] against them."

13Look! He advances like the clouds,[i]
his chariots[j] come like a
whirlwind,[k]
his horses[l] are swifter than eagles.[m]
Woe to us! We are ruined![n]
14O Jerusalem, wash[o] the evil from your
heart and be saved.[p]
How long[q] will you harbor wicked
thoughts?
15A voice is announcing from Dan,[r]
proclaiming disaster from the hills of
Ephraim.[s]
16"Tell this to the nations,
proclaim it to Jerusalem:
'A besieging army is coming from a
distant land,[t]
raising a war cry[u] against the cities
of Judah.[v]
17They surround[w] her like men guarding
a field,
because she has rebelled[x] against
me,' "
declares the LORD.
18"Your own conduct and actions[y]
have brought this upon you.[z]
This is your punishment.
How bitter[a] it is!
How it pierces to the heart!"

19Oh, my anguish, my anguish![b]
I writhe in pain.[c]
Oh, the agony of my heart!
My heart pounds[d] within me,
I cannot keep silent.[e]
For I have heard the sound of the
trumpet;[f]
I have heard the battle cry.[g]
20Disaster follows disaster;[h]
the whole land lies in ruins.[i]

4:2 [c]Dt 10:20; S Isa 19:18; 65:16 [d]S Nu 14:21; Jer 5:2; 12:16; 44:26; Hos 4:15 [e]S Ge 12:2; Gal 3:8 [f]Jer 9:24 **4:3** [g]Hos 10:12 [h]Mk 4:18 **4:4** [i]S Lev 26:41 [j]Zep 1:18; 2:2 [k]S Job 41:21 [l]S Ex 32:22 [m]Isa 1:31; Am 5:6 **4:5** [n]Jer 5:20; 11:2, 6 [o]S ver 21; S Nu 10:2,7; S Job 39:24 [p]S Jos 10:20 **4:6** [q]ver 21; Ps 74:4; S Isa 11:10; 31:9; Jer 50:2 [r]Jer 11:11; 18:11 [s]S Isa 14:31; Jer 50:3 **4:7** [t]S 2Ki 24:1; S Jer 2:15 [u]Jer 25:38; Hos 5:14; 13:7; Na 2:12 [v]Jer 6:26; 15:8; 22:7; 48:8; 51:1,53; Eze 21:31; 25:7 [w]S Isa 1:7; Eze 12:20 [x]ver 29; S Lev 26:31; S Isa 6:11 **4:8** [y]1Ki 21:27; S Isa 3:24; Jer 6:26; Eze 7:18; Joel 1:8 [z]Jer 7:29; 9:20; Am 5:1 [a]S Isa 10:4; S Jer 30:24 **4:9** [b]S 1Sa 17:32 [c]S Isa 29:9 **4:10** [d]S Ex 5:23; 2Th 2:11 [e]Isa 30:10; Jer 6:14; 8:11; 14:13; 23:17; Eze 13:10; Mic 3:5; 1Th 5:3 **4:11** [f]S Ge 41:6; S Lev 26:33; S Job 1:19 **4:12** [g]S Isa 64:6 [h]Jer 1:16 **4:13** [i]S 2Sa 22:10; Isa 19:1 [j]Isa 66:15; Eze 26:10; Na 2:4 [k]S 2Ki 2:1 [l]Hab 3:8 [m]S Dt 28:49; Hab 1:8 [n]ver 20,27; Isa 6:11; 24:3; Jer 7:34; 9:11,19; 12:11; 25:11; 44:6; Mic 2:4 **4:14** [o]S Ru 3:3; S Ps 51:2; Jas 4:8 [p]Isa 45:22 [q]S Ps 6:3 **4:15** [r]S Ge 30:6 [s]Jer 31:6 **4:16** [t]S Dt 28:49 [u]ver 19; Eze 21:22 [v]S Jer 1:15 **4:17** [w]S 2Ki 25:1,4 [x]S 1Sa 12:15; Jer 5:23 **4:18** [y]Ps 107:17; S Isa 1:28; Jer 5:25 [z]Jer 2:17 [a]Jer 2:19 **4:19** [b]Isa 22:4; Jer 6:24; 9:10; La 1:20 [c]S Job 6:10; S 14:22; Jer 10:19 [d]S Job 37:1; Jer 23:9 [e]S Job 4:2; Jer 20:9 [f]S ver 21; S Nu 10:2; S Job 39:24 [g]S ver 16; Nu 10:9; Jer 49:2; Zep 1:16 **4:20** [h]S Dt 31:17 [i]S ver 13

[1]12 Or *comes at my command*

4:3–6 REVELATION, Word—God's word was given directly to the prophet to be announced to the people. The prophet was so closely identified as God's messenger he could refer to God in third person (v 4) and in first person (v 6). The prophet's revelation of God's intention sounds harsh, but such words from God introduced His redemptive purifying. The God who chastised and allowed Judah to hurt is the God who used their *self-induced* pain as a means to call them back to their commitment to Him. God sought to restore Judah by stunning her back to her senses.

4:4,8,26 GOD, Wrath—The basic purpose of God is to express His love and grace. Sometimes His wrath must be expressed instead. He gives His people warning of wrath to come.

4:13–31 HISTORY, Judgment—See note on 1:14–19.

4:17–18 SIN, Punishment—God's intervention in our lives to punish sin is deserved, yet shockingly unexpected. We can blame no one but ourselves. We know God is as true to His word of threat as He is to His word of promise. We can suffer no more bitter experience than to know we are being punished by our God. Such may cause physical suffering, but the most bitter part is what it does to the heart.

In an instant my tents[j] are destroyed,
my shelter in a moment.
21How long must I see the battle
standard[k]
and hear the sound of the trumpet?[l]
22"My people are fools;[m]
they do not know me.[n]
They are senseless children;
they have no understanding.[o]
They are skilled in doing evil;[p]
they know not how to do good."[q]
23I looked at the earth,
and it was formless and empty;[r]
and at the heavens,
and their light[s] was gone.
24I looked at the mountains,
and they were quaking;[t]
all the hills were swaying.
25I looked, and there were no people;
every bird in the sky had flown
away.[u]
26I looked, and the fruitful land was a
desert;[v]
all its towns lay in ruins[w]
before the LORD, before his fierce
anger.[x]

27This is what the LORD says:

"The whole land will be ruined,[y]
though I will not destroy[z] it
completely.
28Therefore the earth will mourn[a]
and the heavens above grow dark,[b]
because I have spoken and will not
relent,[c]
I have decided and will not turn
back.[d]"
29At the sound of horsemen and
archers[e]
every town takes to flight.[f]
Some go into the thickets;
some climb up among the rocks.[g]
All the towns are deserted;[h]
no one lives in them.
30What are you doing,[i] O devastated
one?
Why dress yourself in scarlet
and put on jewels[j] of gold?
Why shade your eyes with paint?[k]
You adorn yourself in vain.
Your lovers[l] despise you;
they seek your life.[m]
31I hear a cry as of a woman in labor,[n]
a groan as of one bearing her first
child—
the cry of the Daughter of Zion[o]
gasping for breath,[p]
stretching out her hands[q] and
saying,
"Alas! I am fainting;
my life is given over to
murderers."[r]

Chapter 5

Not One Is Upright

"GO up and down[s] the streets of
Jerusalem,
look around and consider,[t]
search through her squares.
If you can find but one person[u]
who deals honestly[v] and seeks the
truth,
I will forgive[w] this city.
2Although they say, 'As surely as the
LORD lives,'[x]
still they are swearing falsely.[y]"
3O LORD, do not your eyes[z] look for
truth?
You struck[a] them, but they felt no
pain;
you crushed them, but they refused
correction.[b]
They made their faces harder than
stone[c]
and refused to repent.[d]
4I thought, "These are only the poor;
they are foolish,[e]
for they do not know[f] the way of the
LORD,
the requirements of their God.
5So I will go to the leaders[g]
and speak to them;
surely they know the way of the LORD,
the requirements of their God."
But with one accord they too had
broken off the yoke
and torn off the bonds.[h]
6Therefore a lion from the forest[i] will
attack them,
a wolf from the desert will ravage[j]
them,
a leopard[k] will lie in wait near their
towns
to tear to pieces any who venture
out,

4:20 [j]S Nu 24:5; Jer 10:20; La 2:4
4:21 [k]S ver 6; S Nu 2:2; S Isa 18:3 [l]ver 5,19; S Jos 6:20; Jer 6:1; Hos 5:8; Am 3:6; Zep 1:16
4:22 [m]Jer 5:21; 10:8 [n]S Isa 1:3; 27:11; Jer 2:8; 8:7; Hos 5:4; 6:6 [o]S Ps 14:4; S 53:2 [p]Jer 13:23; S 1Co 14:20 [q]S Ps 36:3
4:23 [r]S Ge 1:2 [s]ver 28; S Job 9:7; 30:26; S Isa 5:30; 59:9; La 3:2
4:24 [t]S Ex 19:18; S Job 9:6
4:25 [u]Jer 7:20; 9:10; 12:4; Hos 4:3; Zep 1:3
4:26 [v]S Ge 13:10; Jer 12:4; 23:10 [w]S Isa 6:11 [x]Jer 12:13; 25:38
4:27 [y]S ver 13 [z]S Lev 26:44; Jer 5:10,18; 12:12; 30:11; 46:28; Eze 20:17; Am 9:8
4:28 [a]Jer 12:4,11; 14:2; Hos 4:3 [b]S ver 23 [c]S Nu 23:19 [d]ver 8; Jer 23:20; 30:24
4:29 [e]S ver 13; Jer 6:23; 8:16 [f]2Ki 25:4 [g]S Ex 33:22; S 1Sa 26:20 [h]S ver 7; S Isa 6:12
4:30 [i]Isa 10:3-4 [j]Eze 16:11; 23:40 [k]S 2Ki 9:30 [l]Job 19:14; La 1:2; Eze 23:9,22 [m]S Ps 35:4
4:31 [n]S Ge 3:16; Jer 6:24; 13:21; 22:23; 30:6; Mic 4:10 [o]S Ps 9:14 [p]Isa 42:14 [q]Isa 1:15; La 1:17 [r]S Dt 32:25; La 2:21
5:1 [s]2Ch 16:9; Eze 22:30 [t]Ps 45:10 [u]Ge 18:32; S Jer 2:29 [v]ver 31; Jer 14:14; Eze 13:6 [w]S Ge 18:24
5:2 [x]S Jer 4:2 [y]S Lev 19:12
5:3 [z]2Ch 16:9 [a]S Isa 9:13 [b]S Lev 26:23 [c]Jer 7:26; 19:15; Eze 3:8-9; 36:26; Zec 7:12 [d]S 2Ch 28:22; S Isa 1:5; Eze 2:4-5; Am 4:6; Zec 7:11
5:4 [e]S ver 21; S Jer 4:22 [f]S Pr 10:21; S Isa 1:3
5:5 [g]Mic 3:1,9 [h]S Jer 2:20
5:6 [i]S Ps 17:12 [j]S Lev 26:22 [k]Hos 13:7

5:1–6 EVIL AND SUFFERING, Testing—God sent suffering to provoke repentance, but Judah did not accept His instruction. Suffering may be redemptive. God patiently deals with us, calling us to repentance. Enduring suffering has no merit in itself. We do not gain favor with God because we suffer. God expects us to learn from His correction and change our way of living. See note on Isa 48:8–10.

5:1 CHRISTIAN ETHICS, Justice—This verse reminds of Abraham's and God's exchange about righteous people in Sodom. The despairing part of Jeremiah's experience, too, is that no upright person could be found. Judgment is certain for such a society. "Deals honestly" is literally "doing justice" (Hebrew *mishpat*). God demands that His people protect the rights of all members of society. See note on Hos 2:19–20.

5:3 SALVATION, Repentance—God did His best to get Israel to turn from her wicked ways, but she stubbornly refused. We are free to refuse to repent, but like Israel we are also responsible for our choice. Compare 18:5–12.

for their rebellion is great
and their backslidings many.[l]

7"Why should I forgive you?
Your children have forsaken me
and sworn[m] by gods that are not gods.[n]
I supplied all their needs,
yet they committed adultery[o]
and thronged to the houses of prostitutes.[p]
8They are well-fed, lusty stallions,
each neighing for another man's wife.[q]
9Should I not punish them for this?"[r]
declares the LORD.
"Should I not avenge[s] myself
on such a nation as this?

10"Go through her vineyards and ravage them,
but do not destroy them completely.[t]
Strip off her branches,
for these people do not belong to the LORD.
11The house of Israel and the house of Judah
have been utterly unfaithful[u] to me,"
declares the LORD.

12They have lied[v] about the LORD;
they said, "He will do nothing!
No harm will come to us;[w]
we will never see sword or famine.[x]
13The prophets[y] are but wind[z]
and the word is not in them;
so let what they say be done to them."

14Therefore this is what the LORD God Almighty says:

"Because the people have spoken these words,
I will make my words in your mouth[a] a fire[b]
and these people the wood it consumes.[c]
15O house of Israel," declares the LORD,
"I am bringing a distant nation[d] against you—
an ancient and enduring nation,
a people whose language[e] you do not know,
whose speech you do not understand.
16Their quivers[f] are like an open grave;
all of them are mighty warriors.
17They will devour[g h] your harvests and food,
devour[i j] your sons and daughters;
they will devour[k] your flocks and herds,
devour your vines and fig trees.[l]
With the sword[m] they will destroy
the fortified cities[n] in which you trust.[o]

18"Yet even in those days," declares
the LORD, "I will not destroy[p] you completely. 19And when the people ask,[q]
'Why has the LORD our God done all this
to us?' you will tell them, 'As you have
forsaken me and served foreign gods[r] in
your own land, so now you will serve foreigners[s] in a land not your own.'

20"Announce this to the house of Jacob
and proclaim[t] it in Judah:
21Hear this, you foolish and senseless people,[u]
who have eyes[v] but do not see,
who have ears but do not hear:[w]
22Should you not fear[x] me?" declares the LORD.
"Should you not tremble[y] in my presence?
I made the sand a boundary for the sea,[z]
an everlasting barrier it cannot cross.
The waves may roll, but they cannot prevail;

5:6 [l]Jer 14:7; 30:14
5:7 [m]S Jos 23:7 [n]Dt 32:21; Jer 2:11; 16:20; Gal 4:8 [o]S Nu 25:1 [p]Jer 13:27
5:8 [q]Jer 29:23; Eze 22:11; 33:26
5:9 [r]ver 29; Jer 9:9 [s]S Isa 57:6
5:10 [t]S Jer 4:27; Am 9:8
5:11 [u]S 1Ki 19:10; S Ps 73:27; S Isa 24:16
5:12 [v]Isa 28:15 [w]Jer 23:17 [x]Jer 14:13; 27:8
5:13 [y]Jer 14:15 [z]S 2Ch 36:16; S Job 6:26
5:14 [a]Hos 6:5 [b]S Ps 39:3; Jer 23:29 [c]S Isa 1:31
5:15 [d]S Dt 28:49; S 2Ki 24:2 [e]S Ge 11:7; S Isa 28:11
5:16 [f]S Job 39:23
5:17 [g]S Isa 1:7; Jer 8:16; 30:16 [h]Lev 26:16 [i]Jer 50:7,17 [j]Dt 28:32 [k]Dt 28:31 [l]S Nu 16:14; Jer 8:13; Hos 2:12 [m]S Lev 26:25 [n]S Jos 10:20 [o]Dt 28:33
5:18 [p]S Jer 4:27
5:19 [q]S Dt 4:28; S 1Ki 9:9 [r]S Jer 2:8; 15:14; 16:13; 17:4 [s]Dt 28:48
5:20 [t]S Jer 4:5
5:21 [u]ver 4; S Dt 32:6; S Jer 4:22; Hab 2:18 [v]Isa 6:10; Eze 12:2 [w]S Dt 29:4; S Isa 42:20; S Mt 13:15; Mk 8:18
5:22 [x]S Dt 28:58 [y]S Job 4:14; S Isa 64:2 [z]S Ge 1:9

5:7–13 GOD, One God—Worshiping anyone or anything except the one true God removes any reason for God to forgive us. Such conduct leads people to believe foolishly that God either cannot or will not act to punish. See note on 1:5,10.
5:7–13 SIN, Rebellion—Forgiveness is not an option for an unfaithful people (see 3:20–22) who deny God's power or will to act. To lie about God and deny His will to save is the highest human presumption and the unforgiveable sin.
5:10–13 ELECTION, Remnant—Israel and Judah and the prophets were unfaithful to God. The people, priests, and prophets were breakers of God's covenant. God severely punished them but not completely. He retained an elect remnant for His purposes.
5:12–17 REVELATION, Word—Even when people reject God, their life and its consequences bear witness to God's will and purposes. Judah's rejection forced God to use them as fuel for His revelation. They themselves fanned the flame of His will. People take great risk when they reject the prophetic word. God's word is never a lie. His word becomes a fire burning up those who reject it. The prophetic judgment speech paved the way for God's judging actions.
5:15–17 HISTORY, Judgment—See note on 1:14–19.
5:19 SIN, Punishment—God does not have to justify His actions to us. He is just. We must justify our actions because we sin against Him. He often sends punishment to fit the sin.
5:21–31 SIN, Blindness—Devoting ourselves religiously to fill our pockets leads to spiritual blindness so that we do not do what is obviously right. We have no right to expect "nature's" blessings when we go against God's teachings and treat other people unjustly or even cruelly just to improve our cash flow. On "stubborn," see note on Isa 65:1–7. To turn away from society's needy is to turn away from God. To turn leaders away from godly actions to follow popular opinion is also to turn from God. When religious leaders play to the galleries instead of following God, God's people must fear the end. See note on Isa 5:18–24.
5:22–25 GOD, Creator—The sovereign God and Creator certainly has the capability to chastise His faithless people.

they may roar,[a] but they cannot
cross it.
23But these people have stubborn and
rebellious[b] hearts;
they have turned aside[c] and gone
away.
24They do not say to themselves,
'Let us fear[d] the LORD our God,
who gives autumn and spring rains[e] in
season,
who assures us of the regular weeks
of harvest.'[f]
25Your wrongdoings have kept these
away;
your sins have deprived you of
good.[g]

26"Among my people are wicked[h] men
who lie in wait[i] like men who
snare birds
and like those who set traps[j] to
catch men.
27Like cages full of birds,
their houses are full of deceit;[k]
they have become rich[l] and powerful
28 and have grown fat[m] and sleek.
Their evil deeds have no limit;
they do not plead the case of the
fatherless[n] to win it,
they do not defend the rights of the
poor.[o]
29Should I not punish them for this?"
declares the LORD.
"Should I not avenge[p] myself
on such a nation as this?

30"A horrible[q] and shocking thing
has happened in the land:
31The prophets prophesy lies,[r]
the priests[s] rule by their own
authority,
and my people love it this way.
But what will you do in the end?[t]

Chapter 6

Jerusalem Under Siege

"FLEE for safety, people of Benjamin!
Flee from Jerusalem!
Sound the trumpet[u] in Tekoa![v]
Raise the signal over Beth
Hakkerem![w]
For disaster looms out of the north,[x]
even terrible destruction.
2I will destroy the Daughter of Zion,[y]
so beautiful and delicate.[z]
3Shepherds[a] with their flocks will
come against her;
they will pitch their tents around[b]
her,
each tending his own portion."

4"Prepare for battle against her!
Arise, let us attack at noon![c]
But, alas, the daylight is fading,
and the shadows of evening grow
long.
5So arise, let us attack at night
and destroy her fortresses!"

6This is what the LORD Almighty says:

"Cut down the trees[d]
and build siege ramps[e] against
Jerusalem.
This city must be punished;
it is filled with oppression.[f]
7As a well pours out its water,
so she pours out her wickedness.
Violence[g] and destruction[h] resound in
her;
her sickness and wounds are ever
before me.
8Take warning, O Jerusalem,
or I will turn away[i] from you
and make your land desolate
so no one can live in it."

9This is what the LORD Almighty says:

"Let them glean the remnant[j] of
Israel
as thoroughly as a vine;
pass your hand over the branches
again,
like one gathering grapes."

10To whom can I speak and give
warning?
Who will listen[k] to me?
Their ears are closed[m][l]
so they cannot hear.[m]
The word[n] of the LORD is offensive to
them;
they find no pleasure in it.
11But I am full of the wrath[o] of the
LORD,
and I cannot hold it in.[p]

5:22 [a]S Ps 46:3
5:23 [b]S Dt 21:18 [c]Ps 14:3
5:24 [d]Dt 6:24 [e]S Lev 26:4; S 2Sa 1:21; Jas 5:7 [f]S Ge 8:22; Ac 14:17
5:25 [g]Ps 84:11
5:26 [h]S Mt 7:15 [i]S Ps 10:8 [j]Ecc 9:12; Jer 9:8; Hos 5:1; Mic 7:2
5:27 [k]Jer 8:5; 9:6 [l]Jer 12:1
5:28 [m]S Dt 32:15 [n]Zec 7:10 [o]Ex 22:21-24; S Ps 82:3; S Isa 1:23; Jer 7:6; Eze 16:49; Am 5:12
5:29 [p]S Isa 57:6
5:30 [q]ver 30-31; Jer 18:13; 23:14; Hos 6:10
5:31 [r]S ver 1; Mic 2:11 [s]La 4:13 [t]Hos 9:5
6:1 [u]S Nu 10:7; S Jer 4:21 [v]2Ch 11:6; Am 1:1 [w]Ne 3:14 [x]S Jer 4:6
6:2 [y]S Ps 9:14 [z]La 4:5
6:3 [a]Jer 12:10 [b]S 2Ki 25:4; Lk 19:43
6:4 [c]Jer 15:8; 22:7
6:6 [d]Dt 20:19-20 [e]S 2Sa 20:15; Jer 32:24; 52:4; Eze 26:8 [f]S Dt 28:33; Jer 25:38; Zep 3:1
6:7 [g]S Ps 55:9; S Isa 58:4 [h]Jer 20:8
6:8 [i]Eze 23:18
6:9 [j]S Ge 45:7
6:10 [k]Jer 7:13,24; 35:15 [l]Jer 4:4; Ac 7:51 [m]S Isa 42:20 [n]Jer 15:10,15; 20:8
6:11 [o]Jer 7:20; 15:17 [p]Job 32:20; Jer 20:9

[m] *10* Hebrew *uncircumcised*

5:26–29 CHRISTIAN ETHICS, Property Rights—The rich are often guilty of economic injustice. Rather than defend the widows, orphans, or poor as God expects (Ex 22:21; Dt 10:18; 27:19), they became rich off them. They will suffer the judgment of God.
6:1–30 HISTORY, Judgment—History becomes the story of God's rejection of His people when they refuse to accept warning and when they trust religious ritual rather than spiritual obedience. See note on 1:14–19.
6:9 THE CHURCH, Remnant—See Isa 6:13; 7:3. A rebellious remnant is not safe. God judges His people when they are not committed to Him. He calls His remnant to be faithful.
6:10–11 GOD, Wrath—God's preacher must proclaim faithfully God's announcement of wrath even when the people refuse to listen.
6:10–11 REVELATION, Word—Despite God's regular communication of Himself, revelation can be thwarted by the refusal of listeners to hear. Jeremiah expressed frustration that people refused to be alert to Him. God reveals far more than His people ever hear. God's messenger feels constrained to speak even when people refuse to listen.

"Pour it out on the children in the street
and on the young men[q] gathered together;
both husband and wife will be caught in it,
and the old, those weighed down with years.[r]
12Their houses will be turned over to others,[s]
together with their fields and their wives,[t]
when I stretch out my hand[u]
against those who live in the land,"
declares the LORD.
13"From the least to the greatest,
all[v] are greedy for gain;[w]
prophets and priests alike,
all practice deceit.[x]
14They dress the wound of my people
as though it were not serious.
'Peace, peace,' they say,
when there is no peace.[y]
15Are they ashamed of their loathsome conduct?
No, they have no shame at all;
they do not even know how to blush.[z]
So they will fall among the fallen;
they will be brought down when I punish[a] them,"
says the LORD.

16This is what the LORD says:

"Stand at the crossroads and look;
ask for the ancient paths,[b]
ask where the good way[c] is, and walk in it,
and you will find rest[d] for your souls.
But you said, 'We will not walk in it.'
17I appointed watchmen[e] over you and said,
'Listen to the sound of the trumpet!'[f]
But you said, 'We will not listen.'[g]
18Therefore hear, O nations;
observe, O witnesses,
what will happen to them.
19Hear, O earth:[h]
I am bringing disaster[i] on this people,
the fruit of their schemes,[j]
because they have not listened to my words[k]
and have rejected my law.[l]
20What do I care about incense from Sheba[m]
or sweet calamus[n] from a distant land?
Your burnt offerings are not acceptable;[o]
your sacrifices[p] do not please me."[q]

21Therefore this is what the LORD says:

"I will put obstacles before this people.
Fathers and sons alike will stumble[r] over them;
neighbors and friends will perish."

22This is what the LORD says:

"Look, an army is coming
from the land of the north;[s]
a great nation is being stirred up
from the ends of the earth.[t]
23They are armed with bow and spear;
they are cruel and show no mercy.[u]
They sound like the roaring sea[v]
as they ride on their horses;[w]
they come like men in battle formation
to attack you, O Daughter of Zion.[x]"
24We have heard reports about them,
and our hands hang limp.[y]
Anguish[z] has gripped us,
pain like that of a woman in labor.[a]
25Do not go out to the fields
or walk on the roads,
for the enemy has a sword,
and there is terror on every side.[b]
26O my people, put on sackcloth[c]
and roll in ashes;[d]
mourn with bitter wailing[e]
as for an only son,[f]
for suddenly the destroyer[g]
will come upon us.

27"I have made you a tester[h] of metals
and my people the ore,
that you may observe
and test their ways.
28They are all hardened rebels,[i]
going about to slander.[j]
They are bronze and iron;[k]
they all act corruptly.

6:11 [q]S 2Ch 36:17; S Isa 40:30 [r]La 2:21
6:12 [s]S Dt 28:30; Mic 2:4 [t]1Ki 11:4; Jer 8:10; 29:23; 38:22; 43:6; 44:9, 15 [u]Isa 5:25; Jer 21:5; 32:21; Eze 6:14; 35:3; Zep 1:4
6:13 [v]S Jer 2:29 [w]S Isa 56:11 [x]La 4:13
6:14 [y]S Isa 30:10; S Jer 4:10
6:15 [z]Jer 3:3; 8:10-12; Mic 3:7; Zec 13:4 [a]2Ch 25:16; Jer 27:15
6:16 [b]Jer 18:15 [c]S 1Ki 8:36; S Ps 119:3 [d]S Jos 1:13; S Isa 11:10; Mt 11:29
6:17 [e]S Isa 52:8 [f]S Ex 20:18 [g]Jer 11:7-8; Eze 33:4; Zec 1:4
6:19 [h]S Dt 4:26; Jer 22:29; Mic 1:2 [i]S Jos 23:15; Jer 11:11; 19:3 [j]Pr 1:31 [k]Jer 29:19 [l]Jer 8:9; Eze 20:13; Am 2:4
6:20 [m]S Ge 10:7 [n]S Ex 30:23 [o]Am 5:22; Mal 1:9 [p]Ps 50:8-10; Jer 7:21; Mic 6:7-8 [q]S Isa 1:11; Jer 14:12; Hos 8:13; 9:4
6:21 [r]S Lev 26:37; S Isa 8:14
6:22 [s]S Jer 4:6 [t]S Dt 28:49
6:23 [u]S Isa 13:18 [v]S Ps 18:4; S 93:3 [w]S Jer 4:29 [x]S Isa 10:32
6:24 [y]Isa 13:7 [z]S Jer 4:19 [a]S Jer 4:31; 50:41-43
6:25 [b]S Job 15:21; S Ps 31:13; Jer 49:29
6:26 [c]S Jer 4:8 [d]S Job 2:8; Jer 25:34; Eze 27:30; Jnh 3:6 [e]Jer 9:1; 18:22; 20:16; 25:36 [f]S Ge 21:16 [g]S Ex 12:23; S Jer 4:7
6:27 [h]Jer 9:7; Zec 13:9
6:28 [i]Jer 5:23 [j]S Lev 19:16 [k]Eze 22:18

6:12–15 SIN, Blindness—Sin should lead to shame, guilt, repentance. When sin no longer produces shame, a people is spiritually blind. Only spiritual deafness can lead a minister of the Word to promise peace to a materialistic, deceitful people. See notes on 5:21–31; Isa 5:18–24.

6:12–15 HOLY SCRIPTURE, Writing—See note on 30:1–11.

6:14 CHRISTIAN ETHICS, War and Peace—Peace is more than empty words and false promises. Even preachers get caught in the worldly desire for money and popularity, promising prosperity to people facing judgment. Peace can come only when God's people live peaceably with one another instead of imitating the world. See note on Ps 34:14.

6:18–20 SIN, Punishment—Religious bribery does not buy off God and prevent His punishment.

6:22–24 HOLY SCRIPTURE, Writing—See note on 30:1–11.

6:27–30 ELECTION, Condemnation—Like silver ore unsuccessfully subjected to the refining process, the people were impure and rejected by God. Physical membership in the elect group did not bring spiritual blessing. The people had to choose to follow God.

29The bellows blow fiercely
to burn away the lead with fire,
but the refining[l] goes on in vain;
the wicked are not purged out.
30They are called rejected silver,[m]
because the LORD has rejected
them."[n]

Chapter 7

False Religion Worthless

THIS is the word that came to Jeremiah
from the LORD: 2"Stand[o] at the gate
of the LORD's house and there proclaim
this message:
" 'Hear the word of the LORD, all you
people of Judah who come through these
gates to worship the LORD. 3This is what
the LORD Almighty, the God of Israel,
says: Reform your ways[p] and your actions, and I will let you live[q] in this
place. 4Do not trust[r] in deceptive[s]
words and say, "This is the temple of the
LORD, the temple of the LORD, the temple
of the LORD!" 5If you really change[t] your
ways and your actions and deal with each
other justly,[u] 6if you do not oppress[v] the
alien, the fatherless or the widow and do
not shed innocent blood[w] in this place,
and if you do not follow other gods[x] to
your own harm, 7then I will let you live
in this place, in the land[y] I gave your
forefathers[z] for ever and ever. 8But look,
you are trusting[a] in deceptive[b] words
that are worthless.
9" 'Will you steal[c] and murder,[d] commit adultery[e] and perjury,[n][f] burn incense to Baal[g][h] and follow other gods[i]
you have not known, 10and then come
and stand[j] before me in this house,[k]
which bears my Name, and say, "We are
safe"—safe to do all these detestable
things?[l] 11Has this house,[m] which bears
my Name, become a den of robbers[n] to
you? But I have been watching![o] declares
the LORD.
12" 'Go now to the place in Shiloh[p]
where I first made a dwelling[q] for my
Name,[r] and see what I did[s] to it because
of the wickedness of my people Israel.
13While you were doing all these things,
declares the LORD, I spoke[t] to you again
and again,[u] but you did not listen;[v] I
called[w] you, but you did not answer.[x]
14Therefore, what I did to Shiloh[y] I will
now do to the house that bears my
Name,[z] the temple[a] you trust in, the
place I gave to you and your fathers. 15I
will thrust you from my presence,[b] just
as I did all your brothers, the people of
Ephraim.'[c]
16"So do not pray for this people nor
offer any plea[d] or petition for them; do
not plead with me, for I will not listen[e]
to you. 17Do you not see what they are
doing in the towns of Judah and in the
streets of Jerusalem? 18The children gather wood, the fathers light the fire, and the
women knead the dough and make cakes
of bread for the Queen of Heaven.[f] They
pour out drink offerings[g] to other gods to
provoke[h] me to anger. 19But am I the one
they are provoking?[i] declares the LORD.
Are they not rather harming themselves,
to their own shame?[j]
20" 'Therefore this is what the Sovereign[k] LORD says: My anger[l] and my
wrath will be poured[m] out on this place,
on man and beast, on the trees of the
field and on the fruit of the ground, and it
will burn and not be quenched.[n]
21" 'This is what the LORD Almighty,
the God of Israel, says: Go ahead, add
your burnt offerings to your other sacrifices[o] and eat[p] the meat yourselves!
22For when I brought your forefathers out
of Egypt and spoke to them, I did not just
give them commands[q] about burnt offerings and sacrifices,[r] 23but I gave them
this command:[s] Obey[t] me, and I will be

6:29 [l]Mal 3:3 **6:30** [m]Pr 17:3; Eze 22:18 [n]Ps 53:5; 119:119; Jer 7:29; La 5:22; Hos 9:17 **7:2** [o]Jer 17:19 **7:3** [p]Jer 18:11; 26:13; 35:15 [q]ver 7 **7:4** [r]S Job 15:31 [s]ver 8; Jer 28:15; Mic 3:11 **7:5** [t]ver 3; Jer 18:11; 26:13; 35:15 [u]S Ex 22:22; S Lev 25:17; S Isa 1:17 **7:6** [v]S Jer 5:28; Eze 22:7 [w]S 2Ki 21:16; Jer 2:34; 19:4; 22:3 [x]S Ex 20:3; S Dt 8:19 **7:7** [y]S Dt 4:40 [z]S Jos 1:6 **7:8** [a]S Job 15:31 [b]S ver 4 **7:9** [c]Ex 20:15 [d]Ex 20:13 [e]Ex 20:14; S Nu 25:1 [f]Ex 20:16; S Lev 19:12; Zec 8:17; Mal 3:5 [g]S Isa 1:13 [h]Jer 11:13,17; 32:29 [i]S Ex 20:3; Hos 2:13 **7:10** [j]S Isa 48:1 [k]ver 30; 2Ki 21:4-5; Jer 23:11; 32:34; Eze 23:38-39 [l]Eze 33:25 **7:11** [m]Isa 56:7 [n]Mt 21:13*; Mk 11:17*; Lk 19:46 [o]Ge 31:50; Jdg 11:10; Jer 29:23; 42:5 **7:12** [p]S Jos 18:1; S 1Sa 2:32 [q]S Ex 40:2; S Jos 18:10 [r]Da 9:18 [s]S 1Sa 4:10-11,22; Ps 78:60-64 **7:13** [t]Ps 71:17; Isa 48:17; Jer 32:33 [u]S 2Ch 36:15 [v]S ver 26; S Isa 65:12 [w]S Pr 1:24 [x]Jer 35:17 **7:14** [y]S Jdg 18:31; S 1Sa 2:32 [z]S 1Ki 9:7 [a]ver 4; Eze 24:21 **7:15** [b]S Ge 4:14; S Ex 33:15; S 2Ki 17:20; Jer 23:39 [c]S Ps 78:67 **7:16** [d]S Ex 32:10; Dt 9:14; Jer 15:1 [e]S Nu 23:19 **7:18** [f]Jer 44:17-19 [g]S Isa 57:6 [h]S Dt 31:17; S 1Ki 14:9 **7:19** [i]Dt 32:21, Jer 44:3 [j]S Job 7:20; Jer 9:19; 20:11; 22:22 **7:20** [k]S Isa 30:15 [l]S Job 40:11; Jer 42:18; La 2:3-5 [m]Jer 6:11-12; La 4:11 [n]S Isa 1:31; Jer 11:16; 13:14; 15:6,14; 17:4,27; Eze 20:47-48 **7:21** [o]S Jer 6:20; Am 5:21-22 [p]S 1Sa 2:12-17; Hos 8:13 **7:22** [q]Isa 43:23 [r]S 1Sa 15:22 **7:23** [s]1Jn 3:23 [t]S Ex 19:5

[n]9 Or *and swear by false gods*

7:5–7 CHRISTIAN ETHICS, Justice—Obedient actions to help the needy and thus reestablish justice form the basis of confidence for God's people. Religious tradition and holy places are insecure roots for confidence for an unjust society. See note on Zec 7:8–10.

7:9 CHRISTIAN ETHICS, Character—One cannot compartmentalize worship into one phase of life while carrying on a life-style of overt hypocrisy and detestable actions. All of life is under God's judgment. All of life should be offered to God.

7:16–19 SIN, Alienation—A preacher could not pray for God's people when they worshiped other gods blatantly. Such sin is presumptuous. Sin eventually boomerangs on us. We may think sinful action will bring security, popularity, political freedom. In the end sin harms the sinner.

7:16 PRAYER, Sovereignty of God—Times come when people cannot pray (1 Jn 5:16). The initiative in prayer is with God. He allows people to communicate with Him in His grace. God declared Israel beyond the reach even of prayer. God does not change His mind (1 Sa 15:29). His present purposes must be worked out (v 20). God will not hear prayer for a faithless people who have brought forth His wrath and judgment. Later God responded to Jeremiah's prayer in time of drought with another command not to pray (14:11).

7:18 GOD, One God—God's minister cannot intercede for a people who worship other gods. See note on 1:16.

7:20,29 GOD, Wrath—God's wrath represents His rejection of a people no matter how faithful they are to religious ritual.

7:22–29 HISTORY, God's Will—See note on Ps 78:1–72. God's people need to understand all of God's history, not just the parts they may like. Israel chose to remember the call for glorious ritual but conveniently forgot the call to moral obedience. Judgment resulted.

7:23 THE CHURCH, Covenant People—These words

your God and you will be my people.[u]
Walk in all the ways[v] I command you,
that it may go well[w] with you. 24But they
did not listen[x] or pay attention;[y] instead, they followed the stubborn inclinations of their evil hearts.[z] They went
backward[a] and not forward. 25From the
time your forefathers left Egypt until
now, day after day, again and again[b] I
sent you my servants[c] the prophets.[d]
26But they did not listen to me or pay
attention.[e] They were stiff-necked[f] and
did more evil than their forefathers.'[g]

27"When you tell[h] them all this, they
will not listen[i] to you; when you call to
them, they will not answer.[j] 28Therefore
say to them, 'This is the nation that has
not obeyed the LORD its God or responded to correction.[k] Truth[l] has perished;
it has vanished from their lips. 29Cut off[m]
your hair and throw it away; take up a
lament[n] on the barren heights, for the
LORD has rejected and abandoned[o] this
generation that is under his wrath.

The Valley of Slaughter

30" 'The people of Judah have done
evil[p] in my eyes, declares the LORD. They
have set up their detestable idols[q] in the
house that bears my Name and have defiled[r] it. 31They have built the high
places of Topheth[s] in the Valley of Ben
Hinnom[t] to burn their sons and daughters[u] in the fire—something I did not
command, nor did it enter my mind.[v]
32So beware, the days are coming, declares the LORD, when people will no longer call it Topheth or the Valley of Ben
Hinnom, but the Valley of Slaughter,[w] for
they will bury[x] the dead in Topheth until
there is no more room. 33Then the carcasses[y] of this people will become food[z]
for the birds of the air and the beasts of
the earth, and there will be no one to
frighten them away.[a] 34I will bring an
end to the sounds[b] of joy and gladness
and to the voices of bride and bridegroom[c] in the towns of Judah and the
streets of Jerusalem,[d] for the land will
become desolate.[e]

7:23 [u]S Lev 26:12; S Isa 51:16 [v]S 1Ki 8:36; S Ps 119:3 [w]S Dt 5:33 **7:24** [x]S Jer 6:10 [y]Jer 11:8; 17:23; 34:14 [z]S Jer 3:17 [a]S Jer 2:19; Eze 37:23 **7:25** [b]S 2Ch 36:15 [c]S Isa 20:3 [d]S Nu 11:29; Jer 25:4; 35:15 **7:26** [e]ver 13,24; S 2Ch 36:16; Ps 81:11; Jer 13:11; 22:21; 25:3; 35:15; Eze 20:8,21 [f]S Ex 32:9; Ac 7:51 [g]Jer 16:12; Mal 3:7; Lk 11:47 **7:27** [h]Eze 2:7 [i]ver 13; Eze 3:7; Zec 7:13 [j]S Isa 65:12 **7:28** [k]S Lev 26:23; Zep 3:7 [l]S Ps 15:2; S Isa 59:15 **7:29** [m]S Lev 21:5; S Job 1:20 [n]S Jer 4:8; S Eze 19:1 [o]S Jer 6:30; 12:7; Hos 11:8; Mic 5:3 **7:30** [p]S ver 10; S Lev 18:21 [q]S Jer 2:7; S 4:1; Eze 7:20-22 [r]S Lev 20:3; Jer 32:34 **7:31** [s]S 2Ki 23:10 [t]S Jos 15:8; 2Ch 33:6 [u]S Lev 18:21; Eze 16:20 [v]Jer 19:5; 32:35; Eze 20:31; Mic 6:7 **7:32** [w]Jer 19:6 [x]Jer 19:11 **7:33** [y]S Ge 15:11 [z]S Dt 28:26; Eze 29:5 [a]Jer 6:11; 14:16 **7:34** [b]S Isa 24:8 [c]Rev 18:23 [d]Isa 24:7-12; Jer 33:10 [e]S Lev 26:34; Zec 7:14; Mt 23:38 **8:1** [f]S Ps 53:5 [g]S Isa 14:19 **8:2** [h]S 2Ki 23:5; Jer 19:13; Zep 1:5; Ac 7:42 [i]S Job 31:27 [j]Jer 14:16; Eze 29:5; 37:1 [k]S 2Ki 9:37; Jer 31:40; 36:30 **8:3** [l]Dt 29:28 [m]S Job 3:22; Rev 9:6 **8:4** [n]Pr 24:16; Mic 7:8

Chapter 8

" 'AT that time, declares the LORD,
the bones of the kings and officials of Judah, the bones of the priests and
prophets, and the bones[f] of the people of
Jerusalem will be removed[g] from their
graves. 2They will be exposed to the sun
and the moon and all the stars of the
heavens, which they have loved and
served[h] and which they have followed
and consulted and worshiped.[i] They will
not be gathered up or buried,[j] but will
be like refuse lying on the ground.[k]
3Wherever I banish them,[l] all the survivors of this evil nation will prefer death to
life,[m] declares the LORD Almighty.'

Sin and Punishment

4"Say to them, 'This is what the LORD
says:

" 'When men fall down, do they not
get up?[n]
When a man turns away,[o] does he
not return?
5Why then have these people turned
away?
Why does Jerusalem always turn
away?
They cling to deceit;[p]
they refuse to return.[q]
6I have listened[r] attentively,
but they do not say what is right.
No one repents[s] of his wickedness,
saying, "What have I done?"
Each pursues his own course[t]
like a horse charging into battle.
7Even the stork in the sky
knows her appointed seasons,
and the dove, the swift and the thrush
observe the time of their migration.
But my people do not know[u]
the requirements of the LORD.
8" 'How can you say, "We are wise,
for we have the law[v] of the LORD,"
when actually the lying pen of the
scribes

[o]Ps 119:67; Jer 31:19 **8:5** [p]S Jer 5:27 [q]Zec 7:11 **8:6** [r]Mal 3:16 [s]Rev 9:20 [t]Ps 14:1-3 **8:7** [u]S Dt 32:28; S Jer 4:22 **8:8** [v]Ro 2:17

form the ideal of the covenant relationship (Dt 26:16–19). God's desire for His people involves relationship rather than ritual. God's ideal is that He should be the God of all people with all serving Him. Being God's people means obeying Him.

7:26–31 SIN, Punishment—Ignore God's Word, and God will ignore you. God intervenes in history to correct His people and lead us back to Him. Ignoring His correction leads to His rejection of us. Obedience is the only path away from God's disciplinary actions.

7:28 EVIL AND SUFFERING, Testing—See note on 5:1–6.

7:28 CHRISTIAN ETHICS, Language—A whole society will find itself in a state of moral erosion when true and honest communication has been lost.

7:32—8:2 HUMANITY, Burial—Burial rites distinguish people from animals. Both are made of flesh. Humans can give honor and gratitude to one another. Burial rites express such honor. When burial is denied, humans are reduced to the lot of animals, mere carcasses to be forgotten and devoured. At times burial is impossible. Honor can be given the dead through other ceremonies.

8:3 HUMANITY, Death—When death becomes preferable to life, life has indeed become tragic. God's wrath can bring such tragedy.

8:7 CHRISTIAN ETHICS, Moral Imperatives—The moral guidelines of God to a large extent are obvious, expecially to those who desire them. Those who let their relationship to God deteriorate do not easily recognize these guidelines. We are responsible before God to learn what He expects of us.

8:8–9 HUMANITY, Intellectual Nature—Humans have

has handled it falsely?
9The wise[w] will be put to shame;
they will be dismayed[x] and trapped.[y]
Since they have rejected the word[z] of the LORD,
what kind of wisdom[a] do they have?
10Therefore I will give their wives to other men
and their fields to new owners.[b]
From the least to the greatest,
all are greedy for gain;[c]
prophets[d] and priests alike,
all practice deceit.[e]
11They dress the wound of my people
as though it were not serious.
"Peace, peace," they say,
when there is no peace.[f]
12Are they ashamed of their loathsome conduct?
No, they have no shame[g] at all;
they do not even know how to blush.
So they will fall among the fallen;
they will be brought down when they are punished,[h]
says the LORD.[i]

13" 'I will take away their harvest,
declares the LORD.
There will be no grapes on the vine.[j]
There will be no figs[k] on the tree,
and their leaves will wither.[l]
What I have given them
will be taken[m] from them.[o] ' "

14"Why are we sitting here?
Gather together!
Let us flee to the fortified cities[n]
and perish there!
For the LORD our God has doomed us to perish
and given us poisoned water[o] to drink,
because we have sinned[p] against him.
15We hoped for peace[q]
but no good has come,
for a time of healing
but there was only terror.[r]
16The snorting of the enemy's horses[s]
is heard from Dan;[t]
at the neighing of their stallions
the whole land trembles.[u]
They have come to devour[v]
the land and everything in it,
the city and all who live there."
17"See, I will send venomous snakes[w] among you,
vipers that cannot be charmed,[x]
and they will bite you,"
declares the LORD.

18O my Comforter[p] in sorrow,
my heart is faint[y] within me.
19Listen to the cry of my people
from a land far away:[z]
"Is the LORD not in Zion?
Is her King[a] no longer there?"
"Why have they provoked[b] me to anger with their images,
with their worthless[c] foreign idols?"[d]

20"The harvest is past,
the summer has ended,
and we are not saved."
21Since my people are crushed,[e] I am crushed;
I mourn,[f] and horror grips me.
22Is there no balm in Gilead?[g]
Is there no physician[h] there?
Why then is there no healing[i]
for the wound of my people?

Chapter 9

1OH, that my head were a spring of water
and my eyes a fountain of tears![j]
I would weep[k] day and night
for the slain of my people.[l]
2Oh, that I had in the desert[m]

8:9 [w]S Isa 29:14 [x]S 2Ki 19:26 [y]S Job 5:13 [z]S Jer 6:19 [a]Pr 1:7; 1Co 1:20
8:10 [b]S Jer 6:12 [c]S Isa 56:11 [d]Jer 14:14; La 2:14 [e]Jer 23:11,15
8:11 [f]ver 15; S Jer 4:10; Eze 7:25
8:12 [g]S Jer 3:3 [h]Ps 52:5-7; Isa 3:9 [i]S Jer 6:15
8:13 [j]Hos 2:12; Joel 1:7 [k]Lk 13:6 [l]Mt 21:19 [m]S Jer 5:17
8:14 [n]S Jos 10:20; Jer 35:11 [o]S Dt 29:18; Jer 9:15; 23:15 [p]Jer 14:7,20; Da 9:5
8:15 [q]S ver 11 [r]S Job 19:8; Jer 14:19
8:16 [s]S Jer 4:29 [t]S Ge 30:6 [u]Jer 51:29 [v]S Jer 5:17
8:17 [w]Nu 21:6; S Dt 32:24 [x]S Ps 58:5; S Isa 3:3
8:18 [y]La 5:17
8:19 [z]Dt 28:64; Jer 9:16 [a]Mic 4:9 [b]Jer 44:3 [c]S Isa 41:24 [d]S Dt 32:21
8:21 [e]S Ps 94:5 [f]Ps 78:40; Isa 43:24; Jer 4:19; 10:19; 14:17; 30:14; La 2:13; Eze 6:9
8:22 [g]S Ge 37:25 [h]Job 13:4 [i]S Isa 1:6; Jer 30:12
9:1 [j]S Ps 119:136 [k]Jer 13:17; 14:17; La 2:11,18; 3:48 [l]Isa 22:4
9:2 [m]Ps 55:7

[o] *13* The meaning of the Hebrew for this sentence is uncertain. [p] *18* The meaning of the Hebrew for this word is uncertain.

---

many sources of knowledge. Human wisdom which rejects God's revelation is foolish and false. What is worse is human wisdom which claims to be based on divine revelation but actually comes from false human interpretation of God's Word.
8:10–12 HOLY SCRIPTURE, Writing—See note on 30:1–11.
8:11 CHRISTIAN ETHICS, War and Peace—See note on 6:14.
8:12–14 SIN, Blindness—See note on 6:12–15.
8:13–17 ELECTION, Condemnation—God pronounced doom upon the people. He would send serpents and consume them for their wickedness. However, the people had become used to their wickedness and would settle for man-made shelters which would allow them to perish with pride. Sin makes persons satisfied with their self-destructive behavior. God is free to take away what He gives if people respond unfaithfully.
8:14–17 GOD, Wrath—Graphic terms seek to awaken senseless people not heeding God. God can work through the natural processes of harvest or the historical processes of war to effect His wrath.
8:20–22 EVANGELISM, Judgment—This tragic word, although it had an immediate meaning to Israel, is relevant to all times and places. It is sad to think of all that has been done to share the saving grace of God in faithful evangelism and then to realize the day of opportunity is about over, and still people refuse the gospel. Little wonder the prophet was crushed. He realized God's judgment is sure in such a situation. Healing does not come for a people who do not return to God. See note on 4:1–2.
8:22 SALVATION, Healing—See Ge 37:25; notes on 2 Ch 30:20; Ps 103:3. Balm was resin from trees and was used medicinally. It was plentiful in Gilead, so much so that they exported it. God is able to heal but does not do so when His people forsake Him and do not trust Him.

a lodging place for travelers,
so that I might leave my people
and go away from them;
for they are all adulterers,[n]
a crowd of unfaithful[o] people.

3"They make ready their tongue
like a bow, to shoot lies;[p]
it is not by truth
that they triumph[q] in the land.
They go from one sin to another;
they do not acknowledge[q] me,"
declares the LORD.
4"Beware of your friends;[r]
do not trust your brothers.[s]
For every brother is a deceiver,[r] [t]
and every friend a slanderer.[u]
5Friend deceives friend,[v]
and no one speaks the truth.[w]
They have taught their tongues to lie;[x]
they weary themselves with sinning.
6You[s] live in the midst of deception;[y]
in their deceit they refuse to
acknowledge me,"
declares the LORD.

7Therefore this is what the LORD Almighty says:

"See, I will refine[z] and test[a] them,
for what else can I do
because of the sin of my people?
8Their tongue[b] is a deadly arrow;
it speaks with deceit.
With his mouth each speaks cordially
to his neighbor,[c]
but in his heart he sets a trap[d] for
him.[e]
9Should I not punish them for this?"
declares the LORD.
"Should I not avenge[f] myself
on such a nation as this?"

10I will weep and wail for the mountains
and take up a lament concerning the
desert pastures.[g]
They are desolate and untraveled,
and the lowing of cattle is not heard.
The birds of the air[h] have fled
and the animals are gone.

9:2 [n]S Nu 25:1; Jer 23:10; Hos 4:2; 7:4 [o]S 1Ki 19:10; S Isa 24:16
9:3 [p]ver 8; S Ex 20:16; Ps 64:3; S Isa 44:20; Jer 18:18; Mic 6:12 [q]S Isa 1:3
9:4 [r]S 2Sa 15:12 [s]Mic 7:5-6 [t]S Ge 27:35 [u]S Ex 20:16; S Lev 19:16
9:5 [v]S Lev 6:2 [w]S Ps 15:2; S Isa 59:15 [x]S Ps 52:3
9:6 [y]S Jer 5:27
9:7 [z]S Job 28:1; S Isa 1:25 [a]S Jer 6:27
9:8 [b]S ver 3; S Ps 35:20 [c]S Isa 3:5 [d]S Jer 5:26 [e]ver 4
9:9 [f]S Dt 32:43; S Isa 10:3
9:10 [g]Jer 23:10; Joel 1:19 [h]S Jer 4:25; 12:4; Hos 4:3; Joel 1:18
9:11 [i]Jer 26:18 [j]S Job 30:29; S Isa 34:13 [k]S Jer 1:15 [l]S Lev 26:31; Isa 25:2; S Jer 4:13; 26:9; 33:10; 50:3, 13; 51:62; La 1:4
9:12 [m]S Ps 107:43
9:13 [n]S 2Ch 7:19; S Ps 89:30-32
9:14 [o]S Jer 2:8,23; Am 2:4 [p]S Jer 3:17; S 7:24
9:15 [q]La 3:15 [r]S Jer 8:14
9:16 [s]S Lev 26:33 [t]S Dt 4:32; S Jer 8:19 [u]Jer 14:12; 24:10; Eze 5:2 [v]Jer 44:27; Eze 5:12
9:17 [w]S Ecc 12:5
9:18 [x]S Ps 119:136; La 3:48
9:19 [y]S Jer 4:13

11"I will make Jerusalem a heap[i] of
ruins,
a haunt of jackals;[j]
and I will lay waste the towns of
Judah[k]
so no one can live there."[l]

12What man is wise[m] enough to understand this? Who has been instructed by
the LORD and can explain it? Why has the
land been ruined and laid waste like a
desert that no one can cross?
13The LORD said, "It is because they
have forsaken my law, which I set before
them; they have not obeyed me or followed my law.[n] 14Instead, they have followed[o] the stubbornness of their
hearts;[p] they have followed the Baals, as
their fathers taught them." 15Therefore,
this is what the LORD Almighty, the God
of Israel, says: "See, I will make this people eat bitter food[q] and drink poisoned
water.[r] 16I will scatter them among nations[s] that neither they nor their fathers
have known,[t] and I will pursue them
with the sword[u] until I have destroyed
them."[v]

17This is what the LORD Almighty says:

"Consider now! Call for the wailing
women[w] to come;
send for the most skillful of them.
18Let them come quickly
and wail over us
till our eyes overflow with tears
and water streams from our
eyelids.[x]
19The sound of wailing is heard from
Zion:
'How ruined[y] we are!
How great is our shame!
We must leave our land
because our houses are in ruins.' "

q3 Or *lies; / they are not valiant for truth* r4 Or *a deceiving Jacob* s6 That is, Jeremiah (the Hebrew is singular)

9:3–6 SIN, Blindness—To know God is to obey Him. To make sin your life-style is to prove you do not know God. No matter what your lips say, such a life-style robs a society of its necessary cornerstone—trust.
9:3–8 CHRISTIAN ETHICS, Language—Can one win by deceit? Of course, but it will finally be brought to judgment because lying reflects broken relationships with God and other people. Society is the loser when lying, deceit, mistrust, slander, and enmity rule its tongues.
9:4–6 HUMANITY, Relationships—Jeremiah wept over a great tragedy. Friends had become deceivers, no longer worthy of trust. Such betrayal of relationships is founded upon a false or empty relationship with God.
9:13–16 ELECTION, Condemnation—The elect people forsook God's law and stubbornly served idols. God sent judgment upon His elect. Election is not protection for a people of defection.
9:13–16 FAMILY, God's Judgment—Judgment comes upon families when fathers lead the family into idolatry. The Old Testament prophets described in graphic terms God's judgment upon the nation, including families, when the people followed false gods instead of remaining faithful to their covenant with Him (16:1–13; 18:21). Families today that worship the gods of this age may likewise reap the results of unhappiness and meaninglessness in their personal and family lives. Family devotion is the heart of a nation's religious identity.
9:14 SIN, Rebellion—See note on Isa 65:1–7.
9:14 EDUCATION, False Teachers—Parental instruction is not always for the better. Fathers can corrupt the faith of children and undermine their ability to believe in the living God. The seed of false religious belief, planted in the minds of children, can keep on growing through successive generations.

[20]Now, O women, hear the word of the
LORD;
open your ears to the words of his
mouth.[z]
Teach your daughters how to wail;
teach one another a lament.[a]
[21]Death has climbed in through our
windows[b]
and has entered our fortresses;
it has cut off the children from the
streets
and the young men[c] from the public
squares.

[22]Say, "This is what the LORD
declares:

" 'The dead bodies of men will lie
like refuse[d] on the open field,
like cut grain behind the reaper,
with no one to gather them.' "

[23]This is what the LORD says:

"Let not the wise man boast of his
wisdom[e]
or the strong man boast of his
strength[f]
or the rich man boast of his
riches,[g]
[24]but let him who boasts boast[h] about
this:
that he understands and knows[i]
me,
that I am the LORD,[j] who exercises
kindness,[k]
justice and righteousness[l] on
earth,
for in these I delight,"
declares the LORD.

[25]"The days are coming," declares the
LORD, "when I will punish all who are
circumcised only in the flesh[m]— [26]Egypt,
Judah, Edom, Ammon, Moab and all who
live in the desert in distant places.[t][n] For
all these nations are really uncircumcised,[o] and even the whole house of Israel is uncircumcised in heart.[p]"

9:20 [z]Jer 23:16 [a]Isa 32:9-13
9:21 [b]Joel 2:9 [c]S 2Ch 36:17; S Isa 40:30; S Jer 16:6
9:22 [d]S 2Ki 9:37
9:23 [e]S Job 4:12; S Ecc 9:11 [f]S 1Ki 20:11 [g]Ps 62:10; S Pr 11:28; Jer 48:7; 49:4; Eze 28:4-5
9:24 [h]S Ps 34:2; 1Co 1:31*; Gal 6:14 [i]S Ps 36:10 [j]2Co 10:17* [k]Ps 51:1 [l]Ps 36:6
9:25 [m]S Lev 26:41; Ro 2:25
9:26 [n]Jer 25:23; 49:32 [o]S 1Sa 14:6; Eze 31:18 [p]Ac 7:51
10:2 [q]S Ex 23:24; S Lev 20:23 [r]S Ge 1:14
10:3 [s]S Isa 40:19 [t]Dt 9:21; S 1Ki 8:36; Jer 44:8; Eze 7:20
10:4 [u]Ps 135:15; Hos 13:2; Hab 2:19 [v]S 1Sa 5:3; Isa 41:7
10:5 [w]S 1Ki 18:26; 1Co 12:2 [x]S Isa 45:20 [y]Isa 41:23 [z]S Isa 41:24; 44:9-20; 46:7; Ac 19:26
10:6 [a]S Ex 8:10 [b]S 2Sa 7:22; S Ps 48:1
10:7 [c]Jer 5:22 [d]Ps 22:28; S Isa 12:4; Rev 15:4
10:8 [e]S Isa 44:18 [f]S Isa 40:19; S Jer 4:22 [g]S Dt 32:21
10:9 [h]S Ge 10:4 [i]Ps 115:4; S Isa 40:19

Chapter 10

God and Idols

10:12–16pp — Jer 51:15–19

HEAR what the LORD says to you, O
house of Israel. [2]This is what the
LORD says:

"Do not learn the ways of the nations[q]
or be terrified by signs[r] in the sky,
though the nations are terrified by
them.
[3]For the customs of the peoples are
worthless;
they cut a tree out of the forest,
and a craftsman[s] shapes it with his
chisel.[t]
[4]They adorn it with silver[u] and gold;
they fasten it with hammer and nails
so it will not totter.[v]
[5]Like a scarecrow in a melon patch,
their idols cannot speak;[w]
they must be carried
because they cannot walk.[x]
Do not fear them;
they can do no harm[y]
nor can they do any good."[z]
[6]No one is like you,[a] O LORD;
you are great,[b]
and your name is mighty in power.
[7]Who should not revere[c] you,
O King of the nations?[d]
This is your due.
Among all the wise men of the nations
and in all their kingdoms,
there is no one like you.
[8]They are all senseless[e] and foolish;[f]
they are taught by worthless wooden
idols.[g]
[9]Hammered silver is brought from
Tarshish[h]
and gold from Uphaz.
What the craftsman and goldsmith
have made[i]
is then dressed in blue and purple—
all made by skilled workers.
[10]But the LORD is the true God;

[t]26 Or *desert and who clip the hair by their foreheads*

9:21 HUMANITY, Nature of Death—Death is expected to come at the end of a long life. However, when death comes to children and youth, it is especially tragic. Tragedy increases when war causes premature deaths. Tragedy escalates further when God has to resort to war to punish His unfaithful people.
9:23–24 HUMANITY, Relationship to God—Human nature leads us to be proud of our attainments. We need to recognize that our greatest attainment is being rightly related to God.
9:24 GOD, Nature—This verse presents a concise description of God's character. He seeks to know the people He creates in personal relationship, a relationship based on God's covenant love, justice, and righteousness. God works to establish a world order of justice based on fair dealings with all. He expects us to return His love by acting as He acts.
10:1–16 GOD, One God—Idols are inert, unable to do either good or evil. The wise Creator God controls history and terrifies evil nations with His power and wrath. No other god fits in the same category. They will all perish, but He is the living God forever. See note on 1:16.
10:6 GOD, Power—God's unique power is one part of His uniqueness as the only true God. All people should worship Him because of His all-surpassing power.
10:7–8 HUMANITY, Intellectual Nature—Babylon proudly pointed to an ancient wisdom tradition. The Babylonians were guilty of the height of human folly. They turned to idols they made and away from the King of the universe. No wise person rejects God.
10:9–10 GOD, Living—Worshipers must create and dress dead, inanimate idols, but God lives, able to know and commune with His people, able to bless and to judge them. No other is the true God.
10:10,24–25 GOD, Wrath—All people—enemy nations and pious worshipers—fear God's wrath. Note that the verse

he is the living God,[j] the eternal
King.[k]
When he is angry,[l] the earth
trembles;[m]
the nations cannot endure his
wrath.[n]

11"Tell them this: 'These gods, who
did not make the heavens and the earth,
will perish[o] from the earth and from under the heavens.' "[u]

12But God made[p] the earth[q] by his
power;
he founded the world by his
wisdom[r]
and stretched out the heavens[s] by
his understanding.
13When he thunders,[t] the waters in the
heavens roar;
he makes clouds rise from the ends
of the earth.
He sends lightning[u] with the rain[v]
and brings out the wind from his
storehouses.[w]

14Everyone is senseless and without
knowledge;
every goldsmith is shamed[x] by his
idols.
His images are a fraud;[y]
they have no breath in them.
15They are worthless,[z] the objects of
mockery;
when their judgment comes, they
will perish.
16He who is the Portion[a] of Jacob is not
like these,
for he is the Maker of all things,[b]
including Israel, the tribe of his
inheritance[c] —
the LORD Almighty is his name.[d]

Coming Destruction

17Gather up your belongings[e] to leave
the land,
you who live under siege.
18For this is what the LORD says:
"At this time I will hurl[f] out
those who live in this land;
I will bring distress[g] on them
so that they may be captured."

19Woe to me because of my injury!
My wound[h] is incurable!
Yet I said to myself,
"This is my sickness, and I must
endure[i] it."
20My tent[j] is destroyed;
all its ropes are snapped.
My sons are gone from me and are no
more;[k]
no one is left now to pitch my tent
or to set up my shelter.
21The shepherds[l] are senseless[m]
and do not inquire of the LORD;[n]
so they do not prosper[o]
and all their flock is scattered.[p]
22Listen! The report is coming—
a great commotion from the land of
the north![q]
It will make the towns of Judah
desolate,[r]
a haunt of jackals.[s]

Jeremiah's Prayer

23I know, O LORD, that a man's life is
not his own;
it is not for man to direct his steps.[t]
24Correct me, LORD, but only with
justice—
not in your anger,[u]
lest you reduce me to nothing.[v] [w]
25Pour out your wrath on the nations[x]
that do not acknowledge you,
on the peoples who do not call on
your name.[y]
For they have devoured[z] Jacob;
they have devoured him completely
and destroyed his homeland.[a]

Chapter 11

The Covenant Is Broken

THIS is the word that came to Jeremiah
from the LORD: 2"Listen to the terms

10:10 [j]S Jos 3:10; S Mt 16:16 [k]S Ge 21:33; Da 6:26 [l]S Ps 18:7 [m]S Jdg 5:4; S Job 9:6; Ps 29:8 [n]Ps 76:7; Jer 21:12; Na 1:6
10:11 [o]S Isa 2:18
10:12 [p]S 1Sa 2:8 [q]S ver 16 [r]S Ge 1:31 [s]S Ge 1:1,8
10:13 [t]S Job 36:29 [u]S Job 36:30 [v]S Ps 104:13; S 135:7 [w]S Dt 28:12
10:14 [x]S Ps 97:7; S Isa 1:29 [y]S Isa 44:20
10:15 [z]S Isa 41:24; S Jer 14:22
10:16 [a]S Dt 32:9; S Ps 119:57 [b]ver 12; Jer 32:17; 33:2 [c]S Ex 34:9; Ps 74:2 [d]Jer 31:35; 32:18
10:17 [e]Eze 12:3-12
10:18 [f]S 1Sa 25:29; S Isa 22:17 [g]S Dt 28:52
10:19 [h]Job 34:6; Jer 14:17; 15:18; 30:12,15; La 2:13; Mic 1:9; Na 3:19 [i]Mic 7:9
10:20 [j]S Jer 4:20 [k]Jer 31:15; La 1:5
10:21 [l]Jer 22:22; 23:1; 25:34; 50:6 [m]ver 8 [n]S Isa 56:10 [o]Jer 22:30 [p]Jer 23:2; Eze 34:6
10:22 [q]Jer 6:22; 27:6; 49:28,30 [r]Eze 12:19 [s]S Isa 34:13
10:23 [t]S Job 33:29; S Pr 3:5-6; 20:24
10:24 [u]Ps 6:1; 38:1; S Jer 7:20; 18:23 [v]Jer 46:28 [w]Jer 30:11
10:25 [x]S Ps 69:24; Zep 2:2; 3:8 [y]S Ps 14:4 [z]S Ps 79:7; S Jer 2:3 [a]Ps 79:6-7

[u]*11* The text of this verse is in Aramaic.

---

does not set up a contradiction between God's wrath and justice. God's people must accept God's discipline as deserved correction. God's people join the nations in fearing a full display of God's anger which would destroy the nation. Sadly, God had to act in such anger for His people to learn total loyalty to Him.

10:12–16 GOD, Creator—The created order is not an accident. It reflects the wisdom and understanding of the Master Designer. God's wise and powerful creation shows His superiority over the false gods and emphasizes His sovereignty, His power and authority to accomplish His purposes and to judge His people when necessary. God's creative work is not limited to the beginning of the world. He continues to create a people for Himself.

10:12–16 HOLY SCRIPTURE, Writing—See note on 30:1–11.

10:23–25 PRAYER, Petition—Discouraged, Jeremiah prayed for guidance. V 25 is repeated in Ps 79:6–7. There the appeal is clearly for justice. Jeremiah sought justice for the nations and correction in his own life. Troubled times call for prayer seeking God's changes for our lives.

11:1–14 HISTORY, Judgment—Prayer becomes useless for a people who forget they made a covenant to obey God and who ignore the lessons of judgment from history. Faithfulness to the one God is the first lesson of history. Judgment is the only other option.

11:1–8 THE CHURCH, Covenant People—God's covenant leaves people two choices—blessings or cursings (Dt 27:12—28:68). To accept God's covenant is to commit oneself to obey God. This does not represent a way of earning salvation through good works. It represents the reality of spiritual life. God acted in love and grace to make the covenant relationship possible (Ge 17; Ex 19—24; Jer 11:4–5). Accepting the covenant is not earning salvation. It is committing oneself to God and His way of life, a way that leads to blessing. Sin is a rebellion against the relationship, the choice of another

of this covenant[b] and tell them to the
people of Judah and to those who live in
Jerusalem. 3 Tell them that this is what
the LORD, the God of Israel, says:
'Cursed[c] is the man who does not obey
the terms of this covenant— 4 the terms I
commanded your forefathers when I
brought them out of Egypt,[d] out of the
iron-smelting furnace.[e] I said, 'Obey[f]
me and do everything I command you,
and you will be my people,[g] and I will be
your God. 5 Then I will fulfill the oath I
swore[h] to your forefathers, to give them
a land flowing with milk and honey'[i] —
the land you possess today."
I answered, "Amen,[j] LORD."
6 The LORD said to me, "Proclaim[k] all
these words in the towns of Judah and in
the streets of Jerusalem: 'Listen to the
terms of this covenant and follow[l] them.
7 From the time I brought your forefathers
up from Egypt until today, I warned them
again and again,[m] saying, "Obey me."
8 But they did not listen or pay attention;[n]
instead, they followed the stubbornness
of their evil hearts.[o] So I brought on
them all the curses[p] of the covenant I
had commanded them to follow but that
they did not keep.[q]' "
9 Then the LORD said to me, "There is a
conspiracy[r] among the people of Judah
and those who live in Jerusalem. 10 They
have returned to the sins of their forefathers,[s] who refused to listen to my
words.[t] They have followed other gods[u]
to serve them.[v] Both the house of Israel
and the house of Judah have broken the
covenant[w] I made with their forefathers.
11 Therefore this is what the LORD says: 'I
will bring on them a disaster[x] they cannot escape.[y] Although they cry[z] out to
me, I will not listen[a] to them. 12 The
towns of Judah and the people of Jerusalem will go and cry out to the gods to
whom they burn incense,[b] but they will
not help them at all when disaster[c]

11:2 [b]S Dt 5:2
11:3 [c]Dt 11:26-28; 27:26; 28:15-68; Gal 3:10
11:4 [d]ver 7 [e]S 1Ki 8:51 [f]S Ex 24:8; Jer 7:23 [g]Jer 7:23; 31:33; Eze 11:20
11:5 [h]S Ex 6:8; 13:5; Dt 7:12; Ps 105:8-11 [i]S Ex 3:8 [j]S Dt 27:26
11:6 [k]S Jer 4:5 [l]S Ex 15:26; S Dt 15:5; Jas 1:22
11:7 [m]S 2Ch 36:15
11:8 [n]S Jer 7:26 [o]S Ecc 9:3; S Jer 3:17 [p]Lev 26:14-43; Dt 28:15-68; S Jos 23:15 [q]S 2Ch 7:19; Ps 78:10; Jer 26:4; 32:23; 44:10
11:9 [r]Eze 22:25
11:10 [s]Dt 9:7; S 2Ch 30:7 [t]Zec 7:11 [u]S Jdg 2:12-13; S 10:13 [v]Jer 16:11; Eze 20:8 [w]Isa 24:5; Jer 34:18; Hos 6:7; 8:1
11:11 [x]S 2Ki 22:16; S Jer 4:6 [y]S Job 11:20; La 2:22 [z]S Job 27:9; Jer 14:12; Eze 8:18; Mal 2:13 [a]ver 14; S Ps 66:18; Pr 1:28; S Isa 1:15; 59:2; Eze 8:8; Zec 7:13
11:12 [b]S Dt 32:38; S Jer 44:17 [c]S Dt 32:37; S Jdg 10:14
11:13 [d]S Ex 20:3; Jer 19:4 [e]S 2Ki 17:29 [f]S Jer 7:9; 44:21 [g]S Jer 3:24
11:14 [h]S Ex 32:10 [i]S ver 11
11:15 [j]Hag 2:12 [k]S Jer 7:9-10
11:16 [l]S Ps 1:3; Hos 14:6 [m]S Jer 7:20; 21:14 [n]S Isa 27:11; Ro 11:17-24
11:17 [o]S Ex 15:17; Isa 5:2; Jer 12:2; 45:4 [p]ver 11 [q]Jer 7:18 [r]S Jer 7:9
11:19 [s]S Ps 44:22

strikes. 13 You have as many gods[d] as you
have towns,[e] O Judah; and the altars you
have set up to burn incense[f] to that
shameful[g] god Baal are as many as the
streets of Jerusalem.'
14 "Do not pray[h] for this people nor offer any plea or petition for them, because
I will not listen[i] when they call to me in
the time of their distress.

15 "What is my beloved doing in my
temple
as she works out her evil schemes
with many?
Can consecrated meat[j] avert ⌊your
punishment⌋?[k]
When you engage in your wickedness,
then you rejoice.[v] "

16 The LORD called you a thriving olive
tree[l]
with fruit beautiful in form.
But with the roar of a mighty storm
he will set it on fire,[m]
and its branches will be broken.[n]

17 The LORD Almighty, who planted[o] you,
has decreed disaster[p] for you, because
the house of Israel and the house of Judah
have done evil and provoked[q] me to anger by burning incense to Baal.[r]

Plot Against Jeremiah

18 Because the LORD revealed their plot
to me, I knew it, for at that time he
showed me what they were doing. 19 I had
been like a gentle lamb led to the slaughter;[s] I did not realize that they had plotted[t] against me, saying,

"Let us destroy the tree and its fruit;
let us cut him off from the land of
the living,[u]

[t]ver 21; S Ps 44:16; 54:3; 71:10; Jer 18:18; 20:10
[u]S Job 28:13; S Ps 116:9; Isa 53:8

[v] *15* Or *Could consecrated meat avert your punishment? / Then you would rejoice*

---

way of life, a way leading to curse. The passage indicates the abiding nature of the covenant. God has not forgotten His people or His covenant with them. God expects His people to obey the commands of the covenant and to live in fellowship with Him.

11:8–13 SIN, Covenant Breach—The life of God's people depends on the covenant relationship He initiated at Mt. Sinai (Ex 19—24). To disobey God's teachings is to display lack of faith in Him which is to bring disaster on yourself. Religion is not measured by the number of gods but by faithfulness to the one God.

11:14 PRAYER, Sovereignty of God—See note on 7:16.

11:17 ELECTION, Condemnation—Time and again God told the nation about His covenant with them. Stubbornly both Israel and Judah provoked God's anger with their wicked living. They were without excuse (Ro 1:20). Persons have no excuse for being the object of God's judgment.

11:18—12:6 EVIL AND SUFFERING, Vindication—Jeremiah complained to God about his personal suffering. These "confessions" (11:18—12:6; 15:10–21; 17:14–18; 18:18–23; 20:7–12,14–18) are very candid, personal statements similar to the psalms of lament. See note on Ps 3:1–8. Jeremiah's confessions include a sometimes vindictive plea for God to punish his enemies (11:20; 12:3). See note on Ps 35:1–28. Jeremiah was perplexed by the prosperity of the wicked (12:1). He had questions about God's justice. God responded that Jeremiah's present suffering was a preparation for later struggles. Today we can still complain to God about our disappointments and frustrations. Jeremiah's pleas give us a model for honest prayer. We must not expect our prayers to provide immediate relief from suffering. Suffering may simply strengthen us for even more difficult times ahead. We must trust God to provide needed strength to face suffering and to use our suffering to accomplish His purposes.

11:18–23 PRAYER, Curse—Jeremiah courageously took his case against his enemies to God in five monumental confessions. In life's hopeless situations prayer is the only avenue of hope. Here God agreed to Jeremiah's request. This was not always the case. See note on Ps 5:10.

that his name be remembered[v] no
more."
20But, O LORD Almighty, you who judge
righteously[w]
and test the heart[x] and mind,[y]
let me see your vengeance[z] upon
them,
for to you I have committed my
cause.

21"Therefore this is what the LORD says
about the men of Anathoth[a] who are
seeking your life[b] and saying, 'Do not
prophesy[c] in the name of the LORD or
you will die[d] by our hands'— 22therefore
this is what the LORD Almighty says: 'I
will punish them. Their young men[e] will
die by the sword, their sons and daughters by famine. 23Not even a remnant[f]
will be left to them, because I will bring
disaster on the men of Anathoth in the
year of their punishment.[g]' "

Chapter 12

Jeremiah's Complaint

YOU are always righteous,[h] O LORD,
when I bring a case[i] before you.
Yet I would speak with you about your
justice:[j]
Why does the way of the wicked
prosper?[k]
Why do all the faithless live at ease?
2You have planted[l] them, and they
have taken root;
they grow and bear fruit.[m]
You are always on their lips
but far from their hearts.[n]
3Yet you know me, O LORD;
you see me and test[o] my thoughts
about you.
Drag them off like sheep[p] to be
butchered!
Set them apart for the day of
slaughter![q]
4How long will the land lie parched[w][r]
and the grass in every field be
withered?[s]
Because those who live in it are
wicked,
the animals and birds have
perished.[t]
Moreover, the people are saying,
"He will not see what happens to
us."

God's Answer

5"If you have raced with men on foot
and they have worn you out,
how can you compete with horses?
If you stumble in safe country,[x]
how will you manage in the
thickets[u] by[y] the Jordan?
6Your brothers, your own family—
even they have betrayed you;
they have raised a loud cry against
you.[v]
Do not trust them,
though they speak well of you.[w]

7"I will forsake[x] my house,
abandon[y] my inheritance;
I will give the one I love[z]
into the hands of her enemies.[a]
8My inheritance has become to me
like a lion[b] in the forest.
She roars at me;
therefore I hate her.[c]
9Has not my inheritance become to me
like a speckled bird of prey
that other birds of prey surround
and attack?
Go and gather all the wild beasts;
bring them to devour.[d]
10Many shepherds[e] will ruin my
vineyard
and trample down my field;
they will turn my pleasant field
into a desolate wasteland.[f]
11It will be made a wasteland,[g]
parched and desolate before me;[h]

11:19 [v]Ps 83:4
11:20 [w]Ps 7:11 [x]S 1Sa 2:3; S 1Ch 29:17 [y]S Ps 26:2 [z]S Ps 58:10; La 3:60
11:21 [a]S Jos 21:18 [b]S ver 19; Jer 12:6; 21:7; 34:20 [c]S Isa 30:10 [d]Jer 2:30; 18:23; 26:8,11; 38:4
11:22 [e]S Isa 9:17; Jer 18:21
11:23 [f]Jer 6:9 [g]Jer 23:12
12:1 [h]S Ezr 9:15; Job 8:3; Da 9:14 [i]S Job 5:8 [j]Eze 18:25 [k]S Job 21:7,13; Ps 37:7; Jer 5:27-28
12:2 [l]S Jer 11:17 [m]S Job 5:3 [n]S Isa 29:13; S Jer 3:10; S Eze 22:27; Mt 15:8; Mk 7:6; Tit 1:16
12:3 [o]Ps 7:9; 11:5; 139:1-4 [p]S Ps 44:11 [q]Jer 16:18; 17:18; 20:11
12:4 [r]S Jer 4:28 [s]S ver 11; S Jer 4:26; Joel 1:10-12; Am 1:2 [t]Dt 28:15-18; S Jer 4:25; S 9:10
12:5 [u]Jer 49:19; 50:44
12:6 [v]S Pr 26:24-25; Jer 9:4 [w]Ps 12:2
12:7 [x]S 2Ki 21:14 [y]S Jer 7:29 [z]Isa 5:1 [a]Jer 17:4
12:8 [b]S Ps 17:12 [c]Ps 5:5; Hos 9:15; Am 6:8
12:9 [d]S Dt 28:26; Isa 56:9; Jer 15:3; Eze 23:25; 39:17-20
12:10 [e]Jer 23:1; 25:34; Eze 34:2-10 [f]Isa 5:1-7; Jer 9:10; 25:11
12:11 [g]S Isa 5:6; S 24:4 [h]ver 4; Jer 9:12; 14:4; 23:10

[w]4 Or *land mourn* [x]5 Or *If you put your trust in a land of safety* [y]5 Or *the flooding of*

11:20 GOD, Righteous—God is righteous in all that He does. When other people treat us unjustly, we can turn to God for righteous intervention. What is right in the case is His decision, not ours.

11:21 HUMANITY, Community Relationships—People expect to be able to trust neighbors. When that trust is betrayed, we are overwhelmed. See note on 9:4–6. Such betrayal invites divine action. God refused to leave even a remnant of such people.

12:1–17 GOD, Righteous—God's people confess that He always does what is right. Still we have times when we cannot see or understand the rightness of present events. At such times we can join Jeremiah in taking our complaints to God. See note on 11:20.

12:1–6 PRAYER, Answer—Jeremiah used the language of the courtroom to seek God's intervention against his enemies. God told him to keep trying and to separate himself from his own family who opposed him. At times God's answers are demanding rather than granting our desires. See note on 11:18–23.

12:5 HUMANITY, Potentiality—People fail to recognize their God-given potential by giving up too quickly, rather than struggling on to achieve their very best. At times the call to perseverance is hard to follow, but we must continue in God's mission regardless of the cost.

12:6 HUMANITY, Family Relationships—Family ties are supposed to bind people together. When hatred breaks such ties, the tragedy is extreme. See note on 11:21.

12:7,14–17 GOD, Love—God's loving nature does not mean He is blind or indifferent to the character and actions of the persons He loves. His love means He will chastise those whom He loves when that is needed. Even those who are not God's people receive compassionate treatment as God seeks to lead them to worship Him.

12:7–13 ELECTION, Freedom—The individual or nation who disobeys God is destroyed (Ro 3:23). A claim to election does not save a people without commitment. God retains freedom to respond to a rebellious people.

the whole land will be laid waste
because there is no one who cares.
12Over all the barren heights in the desert
destroyers will swarm,
for the sword[i] of the LORD[j] will devour[k]
from one end of the land to the other;[l]
no one will be safe.[m]
13They will sow wheat but reap thorns;
they will wear themselves out but gain nothing.[n]
So bear the shame of your harvest
because of the LORD's fierce anger."[o]

14This is what the LORD says: "As for
all my wicked neighbors who seize the
inheritance[p] I gave my people Israel, I
will uproot[q] them from their lands and I
will uproot[r] the house of Judah from
among them. 15But after I uproot them, I
will again have compassion[s] and will
bring[t] each of them back to his own inheritance and his own country. 16And if
they learn[u] well the ways of my people
and swear by my name, saying, 'As surely
as the LORD lives'[v]—even as they once
taught my people to swear by Baal[w]—
then they will be established among my
people.[x] 17But if any nation does not listen, I will completely uproot and destroy[y] it," declares the LORD.

Chapter 13

A Linen Belt

THIS is what the LORD said to me: "Go and buy a linen belt and put it around your waist, but do not let it touch
water." 2So I bought a belt, as the LORD
directed, and put it around my waist.
3Then the word of the LORD came to
me a second time:[z] 4"Take the belt you
bought and are wearing around your
waist, and go now to Perath[z][a] and hide
it there in a crevice in the rocks." 5So I
went and hid it at Perath, as the LORD
told me.[b]
6Many days later the LORD said to me,
"Go now to Perath and get the belt I told

12:12 [i]Eze 21:3-4 [j]S Dt 32:41; Isa 31:8; Jer 46:10; 47:6; Eze 14:17; 21:28; 33:2 [k]S Dt 32:42 [l]Jer 3:2 [m]Jer 7:10
12:13 [n]S Lev 26:20; S Dt 28:38 [o]S Ex 15:7; S Jer 4:26
12:14 [p]S Dt 29:28; S 2Ch 7:20 [q]S Ps 9:6; Zec 2:7-9 [r]S Dt 28:63
12:15 [s]S Ps 6:2 [t]S Dt 30:3; Am 9:14-15
12:16 [u]Jer 18:8 [v]S Jer 4:2 [w]S Jos 23:7 [x]S Isa 26:18; 49:6; Jer 3:17
12:17 [y]S Ge 27:29
13:3 [z]Jer 33:1
13:4 [a]S Ge 2:14
13:5 [b]Ex 40:16
13:9 [c]S Lev 26:19; S Mt 23:12; S Lk 1:51
13:10 [d]Jer 22:21 [e]S Ecc 9:3; S Jer 3:17 [f]S Dt 8:19; Jer 9:14 [g]S Jdg 10:13 [h]Eze 15:3
13:11 [i]Isa 63:12; Jer 32:20 [j]Ex 19:5-6; Isa 43:21; S Jer 3:17 [k]S Isa 65:12; S Jer 7:26
13:13 [l]Ps 60:3; 75:8; S Isa 29:9; Jer 25:18; 51:57
13:14 [m]Eze 7:4; 8:18; 9:5,10; 24:14; Zec 11:6 [n]S Isa 9:17; Jer 16:5 [o]Dt 29:20; Isa 9:19-21; S Jer 7:20; 49:32, 36; La 2:21; Eze 5:10
13:15 [p]S Ex 23:21; Ps 95:7-8
13:16 [q]S Jos 7:19 [r]S Lev 26:37; S Job 3:23; Isa 51:17; Jer 23:12 [s]S 1Sa 2:9; S Job 3:5; S Ps 82:5
13:17 [t]Mal 2:2

you to hide there." 7So I went to Perath
and dug up the belt and took it from the
place where I had hidden it, but now it
was ruined and completely useless.
8Then the word of the LORD came to
me: 9"This is what the LORD says: 'In the
same way I will ruin the pride of Judah
and the great pride[c] of Jerusalem.
10These wicked people, who refuse to listen[d] to my words, who follow the stubbornness of their hearts[e] and go after
other gods[f] to serve and worship them,[g]
will be like this belt—completely useless![h] 11For as a belt is bound around a
man's waist, so I bound the whole house
of Israel and the whole house of Judah to
me,' declares the LORD, 'to be my people
for my renown[i] and praise and honor.[j]
But they have not listened.'[k]

Wineskins

12"Say to them: 'This is what the LORD,
the God of Israel, says: Every wineskin
should be filled with wine.' And if they
say to you, 'Don't we know that every
wineskin should be filled with wine?'
13then tell them, 'This is what the LORD
says: I am going to fill with drunkenness[l]
all who live in this land, including the
kings who sit on David's throne, the
priests, the prophets and all those living
in Jerusalem. 14I will smash them one
against the other, fathers and sons alike,
declares the LORD. I will allow no pity[m] or
mercy or compassion[n] to keep me from
destroying[o] them.' "

Threat of Captivity

15Hear and pay attention,
do not be arrogant,
for the LORD has spoken.[p]
16Give glory[q] to the LORD your God
before he brings the darkness,
before your feet stumble[r]
on the darkening hills.
You hope for light,
but he will turn it to thick darkness
and change it to deep gloom.[s]
17But if you do not listen,[t]
I will weep in secret

[z]4 Or possibly *the Euphrates*; also in verses 5-7

12:14–17 EVANGELISM, Judgment—Here is a fearsome passage to those who refuse to submit to God's will and drink of His salvation. God loves and abounds in mercy; but God also judges the wicked. Evangelism means to warn them lest they see God "completely uproot and destroy." If they open their ears and listen, then they shall be "established." The evangelist shares these realities of salvation and judgment.
13:9–10 SIN, Judgment—See notes on Isa 1:20; 64:4–7.
13:11–27 ELECTION, Freedom—As the girdle cleaves close to the human body, so God wanted Judah and Israel to cling close to Him. He called them to spread His reputation among the nations. Their sinful pride influenced them to reject God and brought them to destruction. Such is the penalty for rejecting an intimate relationship with God. God chooses a people and its leaders. He is free to choose to punish them when they proudly become addicted to sin.
13:11 THE CHURCH, Covenant People—The waistcloth symbolizes God's intimate relationship with His people. God wants fellowship with His people. He wants His people to serve Him and spread His wonderful name throughout the earth. One who belongs to God listens to Him and gives Him praise.
13:14,17 GOD, Love—God's merciful love reveals itself in His righteous anger against a rebellious people. See note on 12:7,14–17.
13:16 GOD, Glory—See notes on Ex 16:7,10; 40:34–38; Ps 96:3,6–8; Lk 2:9,14; Jn 11:4.

because of your pride;
my eyes will weep bitterly,
overflowing with tears,[u]
because the LORD's flock[v] will be
taken captive.[w]

18Say to the king[x] and to the queen
mother,[y]
"Come down from your thrones,
for your glorious crowns[z]
will fall from your heads."
19The cities in the Negev will be shut
up,
and there will be no one to open
them.
All Judah[a] will be carried into exile,
carried completely away.

20Lift up your eyes and see
those who are coming from the
north.[b]
Where is the flock[c] that was entrusted
to you,
the sheep of which you boasted?
21What will you say when ⌊the LORD⌋ sets
over you
those you cultivated as your special
allies?[d]
Will not pain grip you
like that of a woman in labor?[e]
22And if you ask yourself,
"Why has this happened to
me?"[f]—
it is because of your many sins[g]
that your skirts have been torn off[h]
and your body mistreated.[i]
23Can the Ethiopian[a] change his skin
or the leopard its spots?
Neither can you do good
who are accustomed to doing evil.[j]

24"I will scatter you like chaff[k]
driven by the desert wind.[l]
25This is your lot,
the portion[m] I have decreed for
you,"
declares the LORD,
"because you have forgotten[n] me
and trusted in false gods.[o]
26I will pull up your skirts over your face
that your shame may be seen[p]—
27your adulteries and lustful neighings,
your shameless prostitution![q]
I have seen your detestable acts
on the hills and in the fields.[r]

13:17 [u]S Jer 9:1 [v]Ps 80:1; Jer 23:1 [w]Jer 14:18; 29:1
13:18 [x]Jer 21:11; 22:1 [y]S 1Ki 2:19; S 2Ki 24:8; S Isa 22:17 [z]S 2Sa 12:30; La 5:16; Eze 16:12; 21:26
13:19 [a]Jer 20:4; 52:30; La 1:3
13:20 [b]Jer 6:22; Hab 1:6 [c]Jer 23:2
13:21 [d]S Ps 41:9; Jer 4:30; 20:10; 38:22; Ob 1:7 [e]S Jer 4:31
13:22 [f]S 1Ki 9:9 [g]Jer 9:2-6; 16:10-12 [h]S Isa 20:4 [i]La 1:8; Eze 16:37; 23:26; Na 3:5-6
13:23 [j]S 2Ch 6:36
13:24 [k]S Ps 1:4 [l]S Lev 26:33; S Job 1:19; S 27:21
13:25 [m]S Job 20:29; Mt 24:51 [n]S Isa 17:10 [o]S Dt 31:20; S Ps 4:2; 106:19-21
13:26 [p]La 1:8; Eze 16:37; Na 3:5
13:27 [q]Eze 23:29 [r]S Isa 57:7; Eze 6:13 [s]Hos 8:5
14:1 [t]S Dt 28:22; S Isa 5:6
14:2 [u]S Isa 3:26
14:3 [v]S Dt 28:48; S 2Ki 18:31; Job 6:19-20 [w]S Est 6:12
14:4 [x]S Jer 3:3; S 12:11; Am 4:8; Zec 14:17
14:5 [y]Isa 15:6
14:6 [z]S Job 39:5-6; S Ps 104:11; S Jer 2:24 [a]S Ge 47:4
14:7 [b]S Isa 3:9; Hos 5:5 [c]S 1Sa 12:22; S Ps 79:9 [d]S Jer 2:19; 5:6 [e]S Jer 8:14
14:8 [f]S Ps 9:18; Jer 17:13; 50:7 [g]Ps 18:46; S Isa 25:9 [h]Ps 46:1
14:9 [i]S Isa 50:2 [j]S Ge 17:7; Jer 8:19 [k]Isa 63:19; Jer 15:16 [l]S Ps 27:9

Woe to you, O Jerusalem!
How long will you be unclean?"[s]

Chapter 14

Drought, Famine, Sword

THIS is the word of the LORD to Jeremiah concerning the drought:[t]

2"Judah mourns,[u]
her cities languish;
they wail for the land,
and a cry goes up from Jerusalem.
3The nobles send their servants for
water;
they go to the cisterns
but find no water.[v]
They return with their jars unfilled;
dismayed and despairing,
they cover their heads.[w]
4The ground is cracked
because there is no rain in the
land;[x]
the farmers are dismayed
and cover their heads.
5Even the doe in the field
deserts her newborn fawn
because there is no grass.[y]
6Wild donkeys stand on the barren
heights[z]
and pant like jackals;
their eyesight fails
for lack of pasture."[a]

7Although our sins testify[b] against us,
O LORD, do something for the sake
of your name.[c]
For our backsliding[d] is great;
we have sinned[e] against you.
8O Hope[f] of Israel,
its Savior[g] in times of distress,[h]
why are you like a stranger in the land,
like a traveler who stays only a
night?
9Why are you like a man taken by
surprise,
like a warrior powerless to save?[i]
You are among[j] us, O LORD,
and we bear your name;[k]
do not forsake[l] us!

10This is what the LORD says about this
people:

[a]23 Hebrew *Cushite* (probably a person from the upper Nile region)

13:22–25 SIN, Depravity—Sin is not a harmless companion we can drop at will. Sin is an addiction which so changes our spiritual chemistry we lose the ability to do good. Sin masters us so we can no longer refuse to sin. Putting something in God's place is the first step to depravity. See note on Ps 10:1–18. Such depravity leads us to destruction.

14:3–4 GOD, Sovereignty—Even famine and drought testify to God's sovereignty—His power and authority to work in the world as He pleases to accomplish His purposes in blessing or judging His people. No other god controls fertility and harvest. The Lord rules over all areas of our life.

14:7–11 PRAYER, Petition—Jeremiah based his prayer on the honor of God's name with which Israel was identified by other people. God refused to answer because of their sin. We cannot rely solely on past history and tradition as we approach God. A rebellious people cannot expect God's intervention in times of disaster. See note on 7:16.

14:8–9 GOD, Savior—Past experiences show God is our Savior. Dark times may blind us to His presence, making Him appear to be a stranger among us. Still we can pray in repentance and trust Him to deliver us. He is never powerless to save.

"They greatly love to wander;
they do not restrain their feet.[m]
So the LORD does not accept[n] them;
he will now remember[o] their
wickedness
and punish them for their sins."[p]

11Then the LORD said to me, "Do not
pray[q] for the well-being of this people.
12Although they fast, I will not listen to
their cry;[r] though they offer burnt offerings[s] and grain offerings,[t] I will not accept[u] them. Instead, I will destroy them
with the sword,[v] famine[w] and plague."[x]

13But I said, "Ah, Sovereign LORD, the
prophets[y] keep telling them, 'You will
not see the sword or suffer famine.[z] Indeed, I will give you lasting peace[a] in
this place.' "

14Then the LORD said to me, "The
prophets are prophesying lies[b] in my
name. I have not sent[c] them or appointed them or spoken to them. They are
prophesying to you false visions,[d] divinations,[e] idolatries[b] and the delusions of
their own minds. 15Therefore, this is
what the LORD says about the prophets
who are prophesying in my name: I did
not send them, yet they are saying, 'No
sword or famine will touch this land.'
Those same prophets will perish[f] by
sword and famine.[g] 16And the people
they are prophesying to will be thrown
out into the streets of Jerusalem because
of the famine and sword. There will be no
one to bury[h] them or their wives, their
sons or their daughters.[i] I will pour out
on them the calamity they deserve.[j]

17"Speak this word to them:

" 'Let my eyes overflow with tears[k]
night and day without ceasing;
for my virgin[l] daughter—my
people—
has suffered a grievous wound,
a crushing blow.[m]
18If I go into the country,
I see those slain by the sword;
if I go into the city,
I see the ravages of famine.[n]
Both prophet and priest
have gone to a land they know
not.[o] ' "

19Have you rejected Judah completely?[p]
Do you despise Zion?
Why have you afflicted us
so that we cannot be healed?[q]
We hoped for peace
but no good has come,
for a time of healing
but there is only terror.[r]
20O LORD, we acknowledge[s] our
wickedness
and the guilt of our fathers;[t]
we have indeed sinned[u] against
you.
21For the sake of your name[v] do not
despise us;
do not dishonor your glorious
throne.[w]
Remember your covenant[x] with us
and do not break it.
22Do any of the worthless idols[y] of the
nations bring rain?[z]
Do the skies themselves send down
showers?
No, it is you, O LORD our God.
Therefore our hope is in you,
for you are the one who does all
this.[a]

Chapter 15

THEN the LORD said to me: "Even if
Moses[b] and Samuel[c] were to stand
before me, my heart would not go out to
this people.[d] Send them away from my
presence![e] Let them go! 2And if they ask
you, 'Where shall we go?' tell them, 'This
is what the LORD says:

14:10 [m]Ps 119:101; Jer 2:25 [n]Jer 6:20; Am 5:22 [o]Hos 7:2; 9:9; Am 8:7 [p]Jer 44:21-23; Hos 8:13; Am 3:2 **14:11** [q]S Ex 32:10; S 1Sa 2:25 **14:12** [r]S Dt 1:45; S 1Sa 8:18; S Jer 11:11 [s]Lev 1:1-17; Jer 7:21 [t]S Lev 2:1-16 [u]Am 5:22 [v]S Isa 51:19; S Jer 9:16 [w]Jer 15:2; 16:4 [x]Jer 21:6; 27:8,13; 32:24; 34:17; Eze 14:21 **14:13** [y]Dt 18:22; Jer 27:14; 37:19 [z]S Jer 5:12 [a]S Isa 30:10; S Jer 4:10 **14:14** [b]S Jer 5:1; 23:25; 27:14; Eze 13:2 [c]Jer 23:21, 32; 29:31; Eze 13:6 [d]Jer 23:16; La 2:9 [e]Eze 12:24 **14:15** [f]Jer 20:6; Eze 14:9 [g]Jer 5:12-13; 16:4; La 1:19 **14:16** [h]Ps 79:3 [i]S Jer 7:33 [j]S Pr 1:31; S Jer 17:10 **14:17** [k]S Ps 119:136 [l]S 2Ki 19:21; S Isa 23:12 [m]S Jer 8:21 **14:18** [n]Eze 7:15 [o]S 2Ch 36:10; S Jer 13:17 **14:19** [p]Jer 7:29 [q]S Isa 1:6; Jer 30:12-13 [r]S Job 19:8; S Jer 8:15 **14:20** [s]S Jer 3:13 [t]S Lev 26:40; S 1Ki 8:47; S Ezr 9:6 [u]S Jdg 10:10; Da 9:7-8 **14:21** [v]ver 7; S Jos 7:9 [w]Isa 62:7; Jer 3:17 [x]S Ex 2:24 **14:22** [y]S Isa 41:24; S 44:10; Jer 10:15; 16:19; Hab 2:18 [z]S 1Ki 8:36; S Ps 135:7 [a]S Isa 43:10 **15:1** [b]S Ex 32:11; Nu 14:13-20 [c]S 1Sa 1:20; S 7:8 [d]S 1Sa 2:25; S Jer 7:16 [e]S 2Ki 17:20; Jer 16:13

[b]*14* Or *visions, worthless divinations*

14:10 SIN, Depravity—Sin becomes a love affair. We dance to sin's tune. God cannot accept a habitual sinner. Punishment must come. See note on Isa 1:20.

14:14–16 REVELATION, Messengers—Not all prophets speak the revealed word of God. Some appoint themselves to be false spokesmen for God. They invent their own illusions. They have been neither called nor empowered and thus have no divine revelation. Then and now, the task of the listener is to discern God's revelation among many voices claiming to be His (15:19). See note on Dt 18:21–22.

14:19—15:9 PRAYER, Intercession—Jeremiah called on the honor of God's name and appealed to His covenant faithfulness. He confessed the sin of the nation and testified to God as the only true God and source of hope. He said the right things in the right attitude and still got no for an answer. God's mightiest prayer warriors could not have changed God's mind in that situation. See note on 14:7–11.

14:20–21 THE CHURCH, Covenant People—Confession and repentance are necessary for a healthy relationship. Prayer is vital in maintaining a relationship with God. God will never forget His covenant, but He does want His people to pray.

14:22 CREATION, Nature—God's creative power is not limited to one sphere of life with other gods having control of other areas of existence. God controls the weather and agricultural fertility as well as politics, history, and human relationships. Only He is God. He is the only source of hope in every area of life.

15:1 SIN, Judgment—Sin eventually stretches its luck too far. No one, no matter how powerful in prayer, can intercede when God serves the eviction notice. Absence from God is death.

15:1–2 ELECTION, Condemnation—No amount of intercession would save Israel and Judah. Not even the pleadings of Moses and Samuel could save them. Such bad news of total rejection brought Jeremiah to the point of despondency. A people cannot rest in a theology of election when their sins destine them for death.

" 'Those destined for death, to death;
those for the sword, to the sword;[f]
those for starvation, to starvation;[g]
those for captivity, to captivity.'[h]

3"I will send four kinds of destroyers[i]
against them," declares the LORD, "the
sword[j] to kill and the dogs[k] to drag
away and the birds[l] of the air and the
beasts of the earth to devour and destroy.[m] 4I will make them abhorrent[n] to
all the kingdoms of the earth[o] because of
what Manasseh[p] son of Hezekiah king of
Judah did in Jerusalem.

5"Who will have pity[q] on you,
O Jerusalem?
Who will mourn for you?
Who will stop to ask how you are?
6You have rejected[r] me," declares the
LORD.
"You keep on backsliding.
So I will lay hands[s] on you and
destroy you;
I can no longer show compassion.[t]
7I will winnow[u] them with a
winnowing fork
at the city gates of the land.
I will bring bereavement[v] and
destruction on my people,[w]
for they have not changed their
ways.[x]
8I will make their widows[y] more
numerous
than the sand of the sea.
At midday I will bring a destroyer[z]
against the mothers of their young
men;
suddenly I will bring down on them
anguish and terror.[a]
9The mother of seven will grow
faint[b]
and breathe her last.[c]
Her sun will set while it is still day;
she will be disgraced[d] and
humiliated.
I will put the survivors to the sword[e]
before their enemies,"[f]
declares the LORD.

10Alas, my mother, that you gave me
birth,[g]
a man with whom the whole land
strives and contends![h]
I have neither lent[i] nor borrowed,
yet everyone curses[j] me.
11The LORD said,

"Surely I will deliver you[k] for a good
purpose;
surely I will make your enemies
plead[l] with you
in times of disaster and times of
distress.

12"Can a man break iron—
iron from the north[m]—or bronze?
13Your wealth[n] and your treasures
I will give as plunder,[o] without
charge,[p]
because of all your sins
throughout your country.[q]
14I will enslave you to your enemies
in[c] a land you do not know,[r]
for my anger will kindle a fire[s]
that will burn against you."

15You understand, O LORD;
remember me and care for me.
Avenge me on my persecutors.[t]
You are long-suffering[u]—do not take
me away;
think of how I suffer reproach for
your sake.[v]
16When your words came, I ate[w] them;

15:2 [f]Jer 42:22; 43:11; 44:13 [g]S Dt 28:26; S Jer 14:12; La 4:9 [h]Eze 12:11; Rev 13:10
15:3 [i]S Nu 33:4 [j]S Lev 26:25 [k]S 1Ki 21:19; S 2Ki 9:36 [l]S Dt 28:26 [m]S Lev 26:22; Eze 14:21; 33:27
15:4 [n]Jer 24:9; 29:18; 34:17 [o]S Dt 28:25; S Job 17:6 [p]S 2Ki 21:2; 23:26-27
15:5 [q]Isa 27:11; 51:19; S Jer 13:14; 16:13; 21:7; Na 3:7
15:6 [r]S Dt 32:15; Jer 6:19 [s]Isa 31:3; Zep 1:4 [t]S Jer 7:20; Am 7:8
15:7 [u]S Isa 41:16 [v]Isa 3:26 [w]Jer 18:21 [x]S 2Ch 28:22
15:8 [y]S Isa 47:9 [z]S Jer 4:7; S 6:4 [a]S Job 18:11
15:9 [b]1Sa 2:5 [c]S Job 8:13 [d]Jer 7:19 [e]Jer 21:7; 25:31 [f]2Ki 25:7; Jer 19:7
15:10 [g]S Job 3:1; S 10:18-19 [h]Jer 1:19 [i]S Lev 25:36; Ne 5:1-12 [j]S Jer 6:10
15:11 [k]ver 21; Jer 40:4 [l]Jer 21:1-2; 37:3; 42:1-3
15:12 [m]S Dt 28:48; Jer 28:14; La 1:14; Hos 10:11
15:13 [n]S 2Ki 25:15 [o]S 2Ki 24:13; Eze 38:12-13 [p]S Ps 44:12 [q]Jer 17:3
15:14 [r]S Dt 28:36; S Jer 5:19 [s]S Ps 21:9
15:15 [t]Jdg 16:28; S Ps 119:84 [u]S Ex 34:6 [v]Ps 44:22; 69:7-9; S Jer 6:10
15:16 [w]Eze 2:8; 3:3; Rev 10:10

[c]*14* Some Hebrew manuscripts, Septuagint and Syriac (see also Jer. 17:4); most Hebrew manuscripts *I will cause your enemies to bring you / into*

15:6 SIN, Against God—Backsliding is the rejection of God (Hebrew *natash*), that is the conscious decision to ignore God and leave Him alone, to isolate ourselves from Him. Rejection breeds rejection. God withdraws His warm compassion from His people and destroys them.

15:10–21 EVIL AND SUFFERING, Repentance—Suffering may make even Christians question why we were born. Suffering can cause life to lose its sense of meaning. Our obedience to God seems vain and stupid. We may even ask God if He has tricked us. God's answer may be more shocking than our questions. He demanded that Jeremiah repent. Suffering, no matter how severe, must not cause us to adopt the world's attitudes and lose our trust in God. God's promise to save His people remains true even as we walk through the darkest night. Suffering may be God's road for us. See note on 11:18—12:6.

15:10–21 PRAYER, Lament—Jeremiah used the funeral language of mourning to express his despair to God. He yearned never to have been born if the only alternative was the life he had to live. In dialog with God he gained assurance of deliverance and assured God of his innocent faithfulness. God called him to repent so he could receive further commissions to work. Any area of life may provide the language of prayer. Answers may surprise us with new divine expectations. Faith in God's redemption leads us to continue praying. See note on 11:18–23.

15:16 HOLY SCRIPTURE, Purpose—God's Word seeks to bring joy to human life, but that joy is not always readily apparent. Jeremiah remembered his joy at learning God's word and being called to be a prophet of the word (1:9). That joy did not prove eternal. God's word and the prophetic office isolated Jeremiah from the normal privileges of life (16:2) and from his family and friends (15:10). His loneliness seemed to indicate God had deceived him (15:18), but still Jeremiah called to the God who had called him. The past joys of God's word were sufficient to turn him to God even in the midst of uncertainty, despair, and isolation. Reading and responding to God's Word gives us resources to call on in time of darkness and need.

15:16–18 REVELATION, Messengers—The true prophet takes in God's revelation so that it becomes part of his very being. God's word becomes his deepest feeling and his driving direction. God's word brought both joy and bitterness to Jeremiah. He argued with God in his confessions. Thus we see that revelation occurred in dialog between God and His chosen messenger, God at times having to call the prophet to repent (15:19). Revelation involved use of the prophet's total person-

they were my joy and my heart's
delight,[x]
for I bear your name,[y]
O LORD God Almighty.
17I never sat[z] in the company of
revelers,
never made merry with them;
I sat alone because your hand[a] was on
me
and you had filled me with
indignation.
18Why is my pain unending
and my wound grievous and
incurable?[b]
Will you be to me like a deceptive
brook,
like a spring that fails?[c]

19Therefore this is what the LORD says:

"If you repent, I will restore you
that you may serve[d] me;
if you utter worthy, not worthless,
words,
you will be my spokesman.[e]
Let this people turn to you,
but you must not turn to them.
20I will make you a wall[f] to this people,
a fortified wall of bronze;
they will fight against you
but will not overcome[g] you,
for I am with you
to rescue and save you,"[h]
declares the LORD.
21"I will save[i] you from the hands of
the wicked[j]
and redeem[k] you from the grasp of
the cruel."[l]

Chapter 16

Day of Disaster

THEN the word of the LORD came to
me: 2"You must not marry[m] and
have sons or daughters in this place."
3For this is what the LORD says about the
sons and daughters born in this land and
about the women who are their mothers
and the men who are their fathers:[n]

15:16 [x]S Job 15:11; Ps 119:72,103 [y]S Isa 43:7; S Jer 14:9
15:17 [z]Ru 3:3; Ps 1:1; 26:4-5; Jer 16:8 [a]S 2Ki 3:15
15:18 [b]S Job 6:4; S Jer 10:19; 30:12; Mic 1:9 [c]S Job 6:15; S Ps 9:10
15:19 [d]Zec 3:7 [e]S Ex 4:16
15:20 [f]S Isa 50:7 [g]S Ps 129:2 [h]S Jer 1:8; 20:11; 42:11; Eze 3:8
15:21 [i]S Jer 1:8 [j]S Ps 97:10 [k]Jer 50:34 [l]S Ge 48:16
16:2 [m]Mt 19:12; 1Co 7:26-27
16:3 [n]Jer 6:21
16:4 [o]ver 6; Jer 25:33 [p]S Jer 9:22 [q]S Jer 14:15 [r]S Dt 28:26; Ps 79:1-3; S Jer 14:12; 19:7
16:5 [s]S Jer 15:5
16:6 [t]Jer 9:21; Eze 9:5-6 [u]S ver 4 [v]S Lev 19:28 [w]S Lev 21:5; S Job 1:20
16:7 [x]S 2Sa 3:35 [y]Jer 22:10; Eze 24:17; Hos 9:4 [z]La 1:9,16
16:8 [a]S Ex 32:6; S Ecc 7:2-4; S Jer 15:17
16:9 [b]S Isa 24:8; S 51:3; Eze 26:13; Am 6:4-7 [c]S Ps 78:63 [d]Isa 22:12-14; Rev 18:23
16:10 [e]S Dt 29:24; Jer 5:19
16:11 [f]S Job 31:27 [g]Dt 29:25-26; S 1Ki 9:9; Ps 106:35-43
16:12 [h]S Ex 32:8; S Jer 7:26; Eze 20:30; Am 2:4 [i]S Ecc 9:3; S Jer 3:17
16:13 [j]S 2Ch 7:20 [k]S Dt 28:36; S Jer 5:19 [l]S Dt 4:28; S 1Ki 9:9 [m]S Jer 15:5
16:14 [n]Jer 29:10; 30:3; 31:27,38

4"They will die of deadly diseases. They
will not be mourned or buried[o] but will
be like refuse lying on the ground.[p] They
will perish by sword and famine,[q] and
their dead bodies will become food for
the birds of the air and the beasts of the
earth."[r]
5For this is what the LORD says: "Do
not enter a house where there is a funeral
meal; do not go to mourn or show sympathy, because I have withdrawn my blessing, my love and my pity[s] from this people," declares the LORD.
6"Both high and
low will die in this land.[t] They will not
be buried or mourned,[u] and no one will
cut[v] himself or shave[w] his head for
them.
7No one will offer food[x] to comfort
those who mourn[y] for the dead—not
even for a father or a mother—nor will
anyone give them a drink to console[z]
them.
8"And do not enter a house where
there is feasting and sit down to eat and
drink.[a]
9For this is what the LORD Almighty, the God of Israel, says: Before
your eyes and in your days I will bring an
end to the sounds[b] of joy and gladness
and to the voices of bride[c] and bridegroom in this place.[d]
10"When you tell these people all this
and they ask you, 'Why has the LORD decreed such a great disaster against us?
What wrong have we done? What sin
have we committed against the LORD our
God?'[e]
11then say to them, 'It is because
your fathers forsook me,' declares the
LORD, 'and followed other gods and
served and worshiped[f] them. They forsook me and did not keep my law.[g]
12But
you have behaved more wickedly than
your fathers.[h] See how each of you is following the stubbornness of his evil
heart[i] instead of obeying me.
13So I will
throw you out of this land[j] into a land
neither you nor your fathers have
known,[k] and there you will serve other
gods[l] day and night, for I will show you
no favor.'[m]
14"However, the days are coming,"[n]

ality—emotions, intellect, will, communication skills. Revelation spoke to the personal needs of the prophet as well as to the purpose of God for the nation. Revelation protected the prophet from disaster but not from isolation, imprisonment, anger, doubt, mockery, and mental anguish.

15:17 SALVATION, Obedience—Compare Job 6:10. Jeremiah separated himself in order to obey God. Obedience to God can bring loneliness to God's servants. Jeremiah was alone for and before the people. He was alone for and before God. Salvation is not protection from isolation and loneliness.

16:1–18 EVIL AND SUFFERING, Punishment—God may demand unusual behavior in crisis situations. He may even deprive us of the normal relationships and respect we assume to be our rights. Jeremiah had to tell his people marriage, mourning, funerals, and ministry to the grieving would no longer be possible. People naturally asked why. God's patience with a sinful people was exhausted. Even the prophet had to forego marriage and family. The people failed to learn from their history of God's discipline. Thus they had to suffer more. With such punishment also came the word of hope and restoration for the future. Present suffering may seem extraordinary, but we must listen for God's word in it and learn faithfulness to Him through it. See note on 5:1–6.

16:5,13 GOD, Grace—See note on 12:7,14–17.

16:10–11 SIN, Transgression—Sin can be learned but is never excusable. Each generation in Judah learned to ignore God's threats and repeat or exceed their ancestors' sins. Finally, God acted to judge one generation through defeat and exile. That generation could not understand why they suffered. They wanted to protest their innocence, God saw the evidence otherwise. They excelled in sin. For "stubborn," see note on Isa 65:1–7. God desires obedience, not excuses.

16:10–18 HISTORY, Hope—See note on Isa 1:24–26.

16:14–15 HOLY SCRIPTURE, Writing—See note on

declares the LORD, "when men will no
longer say, 'As surely as the LORD lives,
who brought the Israelites up out of
Egypt,'[o] 15but they will say, 'As surely as
the LORD lives, who brought the Israelites
up out of the land of the north[p] and out
of all the countries where he had banished them.'[q] For I will restore[r] them to
the land I gave their forefathers.[s]

16"But now I will send for many fishermen," declares the LORD, "and they will
catch them.[t] After that I will send for
many hunters, and they will hunt[u] them
down on every mountain and hill and
from the crevices of the rocks.[v] 17My
eyes are on all their ways; they are not
hidden[w] from me, nor is their sin concealed from my eyes.[x] 18I will repay[y]
them double[z] for their wickedness and
their sin, because they have defiled my
land[a] with the lifeless forms of their vile
images[b] and have filled my inheritance
with their detestable idols.[c]"[d]

19O LORD, my strength and my fortress,
my refuge[e] in time of distress,
to you the nations will come[f]
from the ends of the earth and say,
"Our fathers possessed nothing but
false gods,[g]
worthless idols[h] that did them no
good.[i]
20Do men make their own gods?
Yes, but they are not gods!"[j]

21"Therefore I will teach them—
this time I will teach them
my power and might.
Then they will know
that my name[k] is the LORD.

Chapter 17

"JUDAH'S sin is engraved with an
iron tool,[l]
inscribed with a flint point,
on the tablets of their hearts[m]
and on the horns[n] of their altars.
2Even their children remember
their altars and Asherah poles[d] [o]
beside the spreading trees
and on the high hills.[p]
3My mountain in the land
and your[e] wealth and all your
treasures
I will give away as plunder,[q]
together with your high places,[r]
because of sin throughout your
country.[s]
4Through your own fault you will lose
the inheritance[t] I gave you.
I will enslave you to your enemies[u]
in a land[v] you do not know,
for you have kindled my anger,
and it will burn[w] forever."

5This is what the LORD says:

"Cursed is the one who trusts in
man,[x]
who depends on flesh for his
strength
and whose heart turns away from
the LORD.[y]
6He will be like a bush in the
wastelands;
he will not see prosperity when it
comes.
He will dwell in the parched places[z]
of the desert,
in a salt[a] land where no one lives.

7"But blessed[b] is the man who trusts[c]
in the LORD,
whose confidence is in him.
8He will be like a tree planted by the
water
that sends out its roots by the
stream.[d]
It does not fear when heat comes;
its leaves are always green.
It has no worries in a year of drought[e]
and never fails to bear fruit."[f]

9The heart[g] is deceitful above all things

16:14 [o]S Dt 15:15 **16:15** [p]S Jer 3:18 [q]S Isa 11:11; Jer 23:8 [r]Ps 53:6; S Isa 11:12; Jer 30:3; 32:44; Eze 38:14; Joel 3:1 [s]S Dt 30:3; S Isa 14:1 **16:16** [t]Am 4:2; Hab 1:14-15 [u]Am 9:3; Mic 7:2 [v]S 1Sa 26:20 **16:17** [w]S Ge 3:8; S Ecc 12:14; S Mk 4:22; 1Co 4:5; S Heb 4:13 [x]S Ps 51:9; Pr 15:3; Zep 1:12 **16:18** [y]S Isa 65:6 [z]S Isa 40:2; S Jer 12:3; Rev 18:6 [a]Nu 35:34; Jer 2:7 [b]S Ps 101:3 [c]S 1Ki 14:24 [d]S Jer 2:7; S 4:1; Eze 5:11; 8:10 **16:19** [e]S 2Sa 22:3; S Ps 46:1 [f]S Isa 2:2; Jer 3:17 [g]S Ps 4:2 [h]S Dt 32:21; S 1Sa 12:21 [i]S Isa 40:19; S Jer 14:22 **16:20** [j]Ps 115:4-7; S Jer 2:11; Ro 1:23 **16:21** [k]S Ex 3:15 **17:1** [l]Job 19:24 [m]S Dt 6:6; S 2Co 3:3 [n]S Ex 27:2 **17:2** [o]S 2Ch 24:18 [p]S Jer 2:20 **17:3** [q]S 2Ki 24:13 [r]Jer 26:18; Mic 3:12 [s]Jer 15:13 **17:4** [t]La 5:2 [u]Dt 28:48; S Jer 12:7 [v]Jer 16:13; 22:28 [w]S Jer 7:20 **17:5** [x]S Ps 108:12; S Isa 2:22 [y]2Co 1:9 **17:6** [z]Job 30:3 [a]Dt 29:23; S Job 39:6; Ps 107:34; Jer 48:9 **17:7** [b]S Ps 146:5 [c]S Ps 26:1; 34:8; 40:4; Pr 16:20; Jer 39:18 **17:8** [d]S Job 14:9 [e]Jer 14:1-6 [f]Ps 1:3; 92:12-14; Eze 19:10; 47:12 **17:9** [g]S Ecc 9:3; Mt 13:15; Mk 7:21-22

[d]2 That is, symbols of the goddess Asherah [e]2,3 Or *hills / 3and the mountains of the land. / Your*

30:1–11.

16:16–18 SIN, Punishment—Judah's guile could not fool God or hide from Him. He would require double payment—punishment and restitution from Judah (Ex 22:1,7,9). Sin brings punishment. History and experience teach us this. Yet we add to our sin by trying to hide it. See note on Isa 64:4–7.

16:17 GOD, Wisdom—Nothing is hidden from God. He knows our sins and will not ignore them.

16:19–21 GOD, Power—The power of God testifies that He is the one true God. God seeks to teach this to all nations.

16:19 SALVATION, As Refuge—God is the refuge for all the nations of the earth. His salvation requires the destruction of all idols. His salvation is available to all who will acknowledge Him.

16:19–21 EVANGELISM, Teaching—Evangelistic opportunities may come unexpectedly. People dissatisfied with their way of life come seeking the truth. The evangelist should be a teacher for God to teach God's power and might and introduce God by name to those who seek Him.

17:1–4 SIN, Transgression—See note on 16:10–11.

17:4,13 GOD, Wrath—People bring upon themselves the wrath of God with their sins.

17:5–7 HUMANITY, Relationships—Human relationships are important. Times come, however, when we must choose between human relationships and a relationship with God. Too often we trust human solutions to our crises rather than trusting God.

17:7 SALVATION, Belief—Trusting the Lord is putting one's confidence in Him. Compare Ps 1:1–6.

17:9–10 EVIL AND SUFFERING, Human Origin—Evil actions spring from the human heart, the center of reason and decision according to Hebrew understanding. The dominating creature of God's very good creation (Ge 1) became the deceitful, self-centered creature whose sin problem rages totally out of control. The nature of human wickedness is beyond all human understanding and cure, but God knows us better than we know ourselves and has an answer for our sin problem and our wickedness. See note on Mk 7:14–23.

and beyond cure.
Who can understand it?

10"I the LORD search the heart[h]
and examine the mind,[i]
to reward[j] a man according to his
conduct,
according to what his deeds
deserve."[k]

11Like a partridge that hatches eggs it
did not lay
is the man who gains riches by
unjust means.
When his life is half gone, they will
desert him,
and in the end he will prove to be a
fool.[l]

12A glorious throne,[m] exalted from the
beginning,
is the place of our sanctuary.
13O LORD, the hope[n] of Israel,
all who forsake[o] you will be put to
shame.
Those who turn away from you will be
written in the dust[p]
because they have forsaken the
LORD,
the spring of living water.[q]

14Heal me, O LORD, and I will be
healed;[r]
save[s] me and I will be saved,
for you are the one I praise.[t]
15They keep saying to me,
"Where is the word of the LORD?
Let it now be fulfilled!"[u]
16I have not run away from being your
shepherd;
you know I have not desired the day
of despair.
What passes my lips[v] is open before
you.
17Do not be a terror[w] to me;
you are my refuge[x] in the day of
disaster.[y]
18Let my persecutors be put to shame,
but keep me from shame;
let them be terrified,
but keep me from terror.
Bring on them the day of disaster;
destroy them with double
destruction.[z]

Keeping the Sabbath Holy

19This is what the LORD said to me:
"Go and stand at the gate of the people,
through which the kings of Judah go in
and out; stand also at all the other gates
of Jerusalem.[a] 20Say to them, 'Hear the
word of the LORD, O kings of Judah and
all people of Judah and everyone living in
Jerusalem[b] who come through these
gates.[c] 21This is what the LORD says: Be
careful not to carry a load on the Sabbath[d] day or bring it through the gates of
Jerusalem. 22Do not bring a load out of
your houses or do any work on the Sabbath, but keep the Sabbath day holy, as I
commanded your forefathers.[e] 23Yet they
did not listen or pay attention;[f] they
were stiff-necked[g] and would not listen
or respond to discipline.[h] 24But if you are
careful to obey me, declares the LORD,
and bring no load through the gates of
this city on the Sabbath, but keep the Sabbath day holy[i] by not doing any work on
it, 25then kings who sit on David's
throne[j] will come through the gates of
this city with their officials. They and
their officials will come riding in chariots
and on horses, accompanied by the men
of Judah and those living in Jerusalem,
and this city will be inhabited forever.[k]
26People will come from the towns of Judah and the villages around Jerusalem,
from the territory of Benjamin and the
western foothills, from the hill country
and the Negev,[l] bringing burnt offerings
and sacrifices, grain offerings, incense
and thank offerings to the house of the

17:10 [h]S Jos 22:22; S 2Ch 6:30; S Rev 2:23 [i]Ps 17:3; 139:23; Jer 11:20; 20:12; Eze 11:5; 38:10 [j]S Lev 26:28; Ps 62:12; Jer 32:19; S Mt 16:27 [k]Jer 12:13; 14:16; 21:14; 32:19
17:11 [l]Lk 12:20
17:12 [m]S Jer 3:17
17:13 [n]Ps 71:5; Jer 14:8 [o]S Jer 2:17 [p]S Ps 69:28; 87:6; Eze 13:9; Da 12:1 [q]S Isa 12:3; Jn 4:10
17:14 [r]S Isa 30:26; Jer 15:18 [s]S Ps 119:94 [t]S Ex 15:2; S Ps 109:1
17:15 [u]S Isa 5:19; 2Pe 3:4
17:16 [v]Ps 139:4
17:17 [w]Ps 88:15-16 [x]S Ps 46:1; Jer 16:19; Na 1:7 [y]S Ps 18:18
17:18 [z]Ps 35:1-8; S Isa 40:2; S Jer 12:3
17:19 [a]Jer 7:2; 26:2
17:20 [b]Jer 19:3 [c]Jer 22:2
17:21 [d]Nu 15:32-36; S Dt 5:14; Ne 13:15-21; Jn 5:10
17:22 [e]S Ge 2:3; S Ex 20:8; Isa 56:2-6
17:23 [f]Jer 7:26 [g]Jer 19:15 [h]S 2Ch 28:22; S Jer 7:28; Zec 7:11
17:24 [i]ver 22
17:25 [j]S 2Sa 7:13; Isa 9:7; Jer 22:2,4; Lk 1:32 [k]Jer 30:10; 33:16; Eze 28:26
17:26 [l]Jer 32:44; 33:13; Zec 7:7

17:9 SIN, Universal Nature—Jeremiah struggled with God and learned the nature of his heart and the human heart in general. Without God's love and Spirit, the human being is so self-centered that deception and dishonesty rule the day. We try to fool others, ourselves, and God. We know we cannot succeed. Still we try. We must confess our own personal sinful nature, a confession shared by every human being.

17:11 CHRISTIAN ETHICS, Property Rights—The utter folly of depending on material wealth for soul sustenance is graphically portrayed here. See note on Pr 23:1–8.

17:14–18 EVIL AND SUFFERING, Prayer—God and His word caused Jeremiah to suffer. The prophet carried out the task God assigned him without apparent success. What he predicted did not come true immediately. Jeremiah confessed his confusion. Was God a cause of panic or a place to hide from trouble? We may find faithfulness to God isolates us from other people without providing immediate rewards. We may share Jeremiah's confusion. We need to follow Jeremiah's pattern, taking our troubles to God, confessing our troubled state, and seeking His direction. See notes on 11:18—12:6; Ps 109:1–31.

17:14 SALVATION, Healing—See note on 8:22. God's salvation includes His healing. He, and He alone, can heal us from the sickness of sin and a broken heart. Healing from sickness and forgiveness of sin are often closely tied in the Bible (2 Ch 7:14; 36:16; Ps 41:4; 103:3; 147:3; Isa 53:5; 57:18).

17:15 REVELATION, Events—People wait anxiously to see God's word fulfilled in specific human events. For the Hebrew, deliverance was a very concrete human experience, not an abstract thought. "Word" (Hebrew *dabar*) means word, matter, thing. God's words were not abstract propositions but concrete promises which took on reality at God's bidding. The unfulfilled word made the people doubt Jeremiah's calling as a prophet. Jeremiah complained to God and then had to preach and wait. See note on 15:16–18.

17:19–27 ELECTION, Condemnation—Jeremiah loved his people. Preaching God's judgment to them was painful. Yet he pleaded with them to obey God's rules and to observe the sabbath. He warned them of the severe penalty of disobedience. God's unquenchable fire would consume Jerusalem. The wrath of God is the holy expression of God toward wickedness, even toward those who enjoy the status of His election.

LORD. 27But if you do not obey[m] me to
keep the Sabbath[n] day holy by not carrying any load as you come through the
gates of Jerusalem on the Sabbath day,
then I will kindle an unquenchable fire[o]
in the gates of Jerusalem that will consume her fortresses.' "[p]

Chapter 18

At the Potter's House

THIS is the word that came to Jeremiah
from the LORD: 2"Go down to the
potter's house, and there I will give you
my message." 3So I went down to the
potter's house, and I saw him working at
the wheel. 4But the pot he was shaping
from the clay was marred in his hands; so
the potter formed it into another pot,
shaping it as seemed best to him.

5Then the word of the LORD came to
me: 6"O house of Israel, can I not do with
you as this potter does?" declares the
LORD. "Like clay[q] in the hand of the potter, so are you in my hand,[r] O house of
Israel. 7If at any time I announce that a
nation or kingdom is to be uprooted,[s]
torn down and destroyed, 8and if that nation I warned repents of its evil, then I
will relent[t] and not inflict on it the disaster[u] I had planned. 9And if at another
time I announce that a nation or kingdom
is to be built[v] up and planted, 10and if it
does evil[w] in my sight and does not obey
me, then I will reconsider[x] the good I
had intended to do for it.[y]

11"Now therefore say to the people of
Judah and those living in Jerusalem, 'This
is what the LORD says: Look! I am preparing a disaster[z] for you and devising a
plan[a] against you. So turn[b] from your
evil ways,[c] each one of you, and reform
your ways and your actions.'[d] 12But they
will reply, 'It's no use.[e] We will continue
with our own plans; each of us will follow
the stubbornness of his evil heart.[f] ' "

17:27 [m]S 1Ki 9:6; Jer 22:5 [n]S Ne 10:31 [o]S Jer 7:20 [p]S 2Ki 25:9; Hos 8:14; Am 2:5 **18:6** [q]S Isa 29:16; 45:9; Ro 9:20-21 [r]S Ge 2:7 **18:7** [s]Jer 1:10 **18:8** [t]S Ex 32:14; Ps 25:11; Jer 26:13; 36:3; Jnh 3:8-10 [u]Jer 31:28; 42:10; Da 9:14; Hos 11:8-9; Joel 2:13; Jnh 4:2 **18:9** [v]Jer 1:10; 31:28 **18:10** [w]Eze 33:18 [x]1Sa 2:29-30; 13:13 [y]S Jer 1:10 **18:11** [z]S 2Ki 22:16; S Jer 4:6 [a]ver 18 [b]S Dt 4:30; S 2Ki 17:13; Isa 1:16-19 [c]S Jer 7:3 [d]S Job 16:17 **18:12** [e]S Isa 57:10 [f]S Jer 3:17 **18:13** [g]S Isa 66:8 [h]S Jer 5:30 [i]S 2Ki 19:21 **18:15** [j]S Isa 17:10 [k]S Isa 1:13; Jer 44:15,19 [l]Jer 10:15; 51:18; Hos 11:2 [m]Eze 44:12; Mal 2:8 [n]Jer 6:16 [o]S Isa 57:14; 62:10 **18:16** [p]S Dt 28:37; Jer 25:9; Eze 33:28-29 [q]Jer 19:8; 42:18 [r]S Lev 26:32 [s]S 2Ki 19:21; S Job 16:4; Ps 22:7; La 1:12 **18:17** [t]S Job 7:10; Jer 13:24 [u]S 2Ch 29:6; S Jer 2:27 **18:18** [v]ver 11; Jer 11:19 [w]Jer 2:8; Hag 2:11; Mal 2:7 [x]S Job 5:13; Eze 7:26 [y]Jer 5:13 [z]Ps 52:2; 64:2-8; S Jer 9:3 **18:19** [a]Ps 71:13 **18:20** [b]S Ge 44:4 [c]Ps 35:7; 57:6; S 119:85 [d]Jer 15:1 [e]S Ge 20:7; S Dt 9:19; Ps 106:23; Jer 14:7-9

13Therefore this is what the LORD says:
"Inquire among the nations:
Who has ever heard anything like
this?[g]
A most horrible[h] thing has been done
by Virgin[i] Israel.
14Does the snow of Lebanon
ever vanish from its rocky slopes?
Do its cool waters from distant sources
ever cease to flow?[f]
15Yet my people have forgotten[j] me;
they burn incense[k] to worthless
idols,[l]
which made them stumble[m] in their
ways
and in the ancient paths.[n]
They made them walk in bypaths
and on roads not built up.[o]
16Their land will be laid waste,[p]
an object of lasting scorn;[q]
all who pass by will be appalled[r]
and will shake their heads.[s]
17Like a wind[t] from the east,
I will scatter them before their
enemies;
I will show them my back and not my
face[u]
in the day of their disaster."

18They said, "Come, let's make plans[v]
against Jeremiah; for the teaching of the
law by the priest[w] will not be lost, nor
will counsel from the wise,[x] nor the
word from the prophets.[y] So come, let's
attack him with our tongues[z] and pay no
attention to anything he says."

19Listen to me, O LORD;
hear what my accusers[a] are saying!
20Should good be repaid with evil?[b]
Yet they have dug a pit[c] for me.
Remember that I stood[d] before you
and spoke in their behalf[e]
to turn your wrath away from them.

[f]*14* The meaning of the Hebrew for this sentence is uncertain.

18:1–17 EVIL AND SUFFERING, Repentance—The visit to the potter's house taught Jeremiah that God would not destroy the house of Judah if they repented of their sins. God is willing to withhold punishment if we are repentant and cooperative. This is not an automatic, mechanical reaction. To punish or not to punish is God's free, personal decision in light of His purpose. However, our stubborn rebellion will finally result in punishment and suffering. See note on 19:1–15.

18:5–12 CREATION, Freedom—No people or nation can claim God as their unconditional ally. Only those who serve Him with implicit obedience can expect to enjoy the favor of His blessing and approval. This conditional element expresses the Creator's freedom.

18:6–17 GOD, Sovereignty—God has the power and the authority as the sovereign Lord to accomplish His own purposes in human history as He sees fit. He is Creator and owns all. We are like clay in His hand; yet we can trust Him to act fairly with us, warning us and seeking to redeem us prior to judgment.

18:6 HUMANITY, Relationship to God—We do not rule our own destinies. God does. Our Maker can shape us like clay. No laws of human reason bind God. He has bound Himself to do what is right for us. As we respond to Him, He is free to respond to us.

18:15 SIN, Rebellion—See note on Isa 1:2–4.

18:18–23 EVIL AND SUFFERING, Vindication—Evil for good is what we often receive when we seek to obey God. Jeremiah interceded with God for his people. They responded with evil plots and words. Jeremiah wanted vindication. Instead of acting himself, thus increasing the evil, Jeremiah expressed his desires to God. When we have such horrible desires, we should tell God and no one else. We know He will act in love and justice, where we would act in anger and pride. See notes on 11:18—12:6; Ps 109:1–31.

18:18–23 PRAYER, Curse—When life is not fair, prayer is in order. Jeremiah based his prayer on the fact he had prayed for his accusers. He turned former intercession into curse. See notes on 11:18–23; Ps 5:10.

21So give their children over to famine;[f]
hand them over to the power of the
sword.[g]
Let their wives be made childless and
widows;[h] ... put to death,
let their men ... slain by the
their young ... battle.
sword ... from their houses
22Let a cry[i] ... when you ... bring invaders
... them
for they ... dug a pit[k] to capture me
and ... hidden snares[l] for my
... O LORD,
... plots to kill[m] me.
23But ... forgive[n] their crimes
... blot out their sins from your
sight.
... them be overthrown before you;
deal with them in the time of your
anger.

Chapter 19

THIS is what the LORD says: "Go and
buy a ... from a potter.[p] Take
along some ... elders[q] of the people
and of the ... 2and go out to the Valley of Ben ... m,[r] near the entrance of
the Pots ... ate. There proclaim the
words I ... 3and say, 'Hear the word
of the ... kings[s] of Judah and people of ... h. This is what the LORD
Almighty, the God of Israel, says: Listen! I
am ... bring a disaster[t] on this
place ... make the ears of everyone
who ... it tingle.[u] 4For they have
for ... and made this a place of
... they have burned sacrifices ... gods that neither they nor
... nor the kings of Judah ever
... they have filled this place with
the ... the innocent.[y] 5They have
... places of Baal to burn their
... fire as offerings to Baal—
... did not command or men-
... it enter my mind.[a] 6So be-
... days are coming, declares the
... people will no longer call
... Topheth[b] or the Valley of Ben

18:21 [f]Jer 11:22; 14:16 [g]S Ps 63:10 [h]S 1Sa 15:33; Ps 109:9; S Isa 47:9; La 5:3 [i]S Isa 9:17
18:22 [j]S Jer 6:26 [k]S Ps 119:85 [l]Ps 35:15; 140:5; Jer 5:26; 20:10
18:23 [m]S Jer 11:21; 37:15 [n]S Ne 4:5 [o]Ps 59:5; S Jer 10:24
19:1 [p]Jer 18:2 [q]S Nu 11:17; 1Ki 8:1
19:2 [r]S Jos 15:8
19:3 [s]Jer 17:20 [t]S Jer 6:19 [u]S 1Sa 3:11
19:4 [v]S Dt 31:16; Dt 28:20; S Isa 65:11 [w]S Ex 20:3; S Jer 1:16 [x]S Lev 18:21 [y]S 2Ki 21:16
19:5 [z]S Lev 18:21; S 2Ki 3:27; Ps 106:37-38 [a]S Jer 7:31; Eze 16:36
19:6 [b]S 2Ki 23:10 [c]S Jos 15:8 [d]Jer 7:32
19:7 [e]Ps 33:10-11 [f]S ver 9; S Lev 26:17; S Dt 28:25 [g]S Jer 16:4; 34:20 [h]S Dt 28:26
19:8 [i]S Dt 28:37; S Jer 18:16; 25:9 [j]S Lev 26:32; La 2:15-16 [k]S Dt 29:22
19:9 [l]S Lev 26:29; Dt 28:49-57; La 4:10 [m]S ver 7; Jer 21:7; 34:20
19:10 [n]ver 1; S Ps 2:9; Jer 13:14
19:11 [o]Ps 2:9; Isa 30:14 [p]Jer 7:32
19:13 [q]Jer 32:29; 52:13; Eze 16:41 [r]Ps 74:7 [s]S 2Ki 23:12 [t]Dt 4:19; S 2Ki 17:16; S Job 38:32; Jer 8:2; Ac 7:42 [u]S Isa 57:6; Eze 20:28
19:14 [v]2Ch 20:5; S Jer 7:2; 26:2
19:15 [w]ver 3; Jer 11:11 [x]S Ne 9:16; Ac 7:51 [y]Jer 22:21
20:1 [z]S 1Ch 24:14 [a]2Ki 25:18; Lk 22:52

Hinnom,[c] but the Valley of Slaughter.[d]
7" 'In this place I will ruin[g] the plans[e]
of Judah and Jerusalem. I will make them
fall by the sword before their enemies,[f]
at the hands of those who seek their
lives, and I will give their carcasses[g] as
food[h] to the birds of the air and the
beasts of the earth. 8I will devastate this
city and make it an object of scorn;[i] all
who pass by will be appalled[j] and will
scoff because of all its wounds.[k] 9I will
make them eat[l] the flesh of their sons
and daughters, and they will eat one another's flesh during the stress of the siege
imposed on them by the enemies[m] who
seek their lives.'
10"Then break the jar[n] while those
who go with you are watching, 11and say
to them, 'This is what the LORD Almighty
says: I will smash[o] this nation and this
city just as this potter's jar is smashed and
cannot be repaired. They will bury[p] the
dead in Topheth until there is no more
room. 12This is what I will do to this place
and to those who live here, declares the
LORD. I will make this city like Topheth.
13The houses[q] in Jerusalem and those of
the kings of Judah will be defiled[r] like
this place, Topheth—all the houses
where they burned incense on the roofs[s]
to all the starry hosts[t] and poured out
drink offerings[u] to other gods.' "
14Jeremiah then returned from Topheth, where the LORD had sent him to
prophesy, and stood in the court[v] of the
LORD's temple and said to all the people,
15"This is what the LORD Almighty, the
God of Israel, says: 'Listen! I am going to
bring on this city and the villages around
it every disaster[w] I pronounced against
them, because they were stiff-necked[x]
and would not listen[y] to my words.' "

Chapter 20

Jeremiah and Pashhur

WHEN the priest Pashhur son of Immer,[z] the chief officer[a] in the

[g]7 The Hebrew for *ruin* sounds like the Hebrew for *jar* (see verses 1 and 10).

... **VIL AND SUFFERING, Punishment**—The ... Judah is compared to a broken clay jar that ... ded (vv 10–11). See note on 18:1–17. As long ... as soft, the potter could work with it. Once it was ... beyond repair. God patiently works with us as long ... epentant and pliable. Persistent sin, however, hard- ... d results in punishment.

... **SIN, Discipline**—See notes on 1 Ki 14:22–24; ...–7.

...**6 GOD, One God**—New gods do not arise with a ... generation. One God has ruled through all eternity. We ... no other god. See note on 1:16.

...**7–9 GOD, Sovereignty**—See note on 14:3–4.

...**:14–15 PROCLAMATION, Fearless**—Proclamation ... as been accomplished primarily through individual human beings, though at times God used angels to announce His word (Ge 16:9–11; 31:11; Nu 22:16–35; Jdg 6:20; 13:3–21; 1 Ki 13:18; 2 Ki 1:3; Zec 1:9—6:5; Mt 1:20–24; 28:2–5; Lk 1:13, 26–38; 2:9–13; Ac 7:38; 8:26; 10:3–7; 12:7–23; Rev 5:2). In the Old Testament prophets were the major proclaimers of God's word (Dt 18:9–22; 30:12–13; Isa 40:2; Jer 2:2; Hos 5:9; Joel 3:9; Am 3:7–10; Jnh 3:2; Mic 1:2; 3:5; Na 1:15; Zec 1:14,17). Prophets carried God's messages from the divine council (Isa 6) to kings, congregations, and individuals. The prophets did not control the content of the proclamation. They spoke the word God gave them in a way the audience would hear and remember. At times they surprised people with words of doom and rebuke. Other times they spoke words of comfort and salvation. At all times they fearlessly announced the given message.

temple of the LORD, heard Jeremiah
prophesying these things, 2he had Jeremiah the prophet beaten[b] and put in the
stocks[c] at the Upper Gate of Benjamin[d]
at the LORD's temple. 3The next day,
when Pashhur released him from the
stocks, Jeremiah said to him, "The LORD's
name[e] for you is not Pashhur, but
Magor-Missabib.[h][f] 4For this is what the
LORD says: 'I will make you a terror to
yourself and to all your friends; with your
own eyes[g] you will see them fall by the
sword of their enemies. I will hand[h] all
Judah over to the king of Babylon, who
will carry[i] them away to Babylon or put
them to the sword. 5I will hand over to
their enemies all the wealth[j] of this city
—all its products, all its valuables and all
the treasures of the kings of Judah. They
will take it away[k] as plunder and carry it
off to Babylon. 6And you, Pashhur, and all
who live in your house will go into exile
to Babylon. There you will die and be buried, you and all your friends to whom you
have prophesied[l] lies.' "

Jeremiah's Complaint

7O LORD, you deceived[i][m] me, and I was deceived[i];
you overpowered[n] me and prevailed.
I am ridiculed[o] all day long;
everyone mocks[p] me.
8Whenever I speak, I cry out
proclaiming violence and destruction.[q]
So the word of the LORD has brought me
insult and reproach[r] all day long.
9But if I say, "I will not mention him
or speak any more in his name,"[s]
his word is in my heart like a fire,[t]
a fire shut up in my bones.
I am weary of holding it in;[u]
indeed, I cannot.
10I hear many whispering,
"Terror[v] on every side!
Report[w] him! Let's report him!"

20:2 [b]Dt 25:2-3; S Jer 1:19; 15:15; 37:15; 2Co 11:24 [c]S Job 13:27; Jer 29:26; Ac 16:24; Heb 11:36 [d]S Job 29:7; Jer 37:13; 38:7; Zec 14:10 **20:3** [e]Hos 1:4 [f]S ver 10; S Ps 31:13 **20:4** [g]Jer 29:21 [h]Jer 21:10; 25:9 [i]Jer 13:19; 39:9; 52:27 **20:5** [j]S 2Ki 25:15; Jer 17:3 [k]S 2Ki 20:17 **20:6** [l]S Jer 14:15; La 2:14 **20:7** [m]S Ex 5:23; 22:16 [n]Isa 8:11; Am 3:8; 1Co 9:16 [o]Job 12:4 [p]S Job 17:2; S Ps 119:21 **20:8** [q]Jer 6:7; 28:8 [r]S 2Ch 36:16; S Jer 6:10 **20:9** [s]Jer 44:16 [t]S Ps 39:3; S Jer 4:19 [u]S Job 4:2; S Jer 6:11; Am 3:8; Ac 4:20 **20:10** [v]Jer 6:25 [w]Ne 6:6-13; Isa 29:21 [x]S Job 19:14; S Jer 13:21 [y]S Ps 57:4; S Jer 18:22; Lk 11:53-54 [z]S 1Ki 19:2 [a]S 1Sa 18:25; S Jer 11:19 **20:11** [b]Jer 1:8; Ro 8:31 [c]Jer 15:15; 17:18 [d]S Ps 129:2 [e]S Jer 7:19; 23:40 **20:12** [f]S Ps 7:9; S Jer 17:10 [g]Dt 32:35; S Ro 12:19 [h]Ps 62:8; Jer 11:20 **20:13** [i]S Isa 12:6 [j]Ps 34:6; 35:10 [k]S Ps 97:10 **20:14** [l]S Job 3:8, 16; Jer 15:10 **20:16** [m]S Ge 19:25 [n]S Jer 6:26 **20:17** [o]S Job 3:16; S 10:18-19 **20:18** [p]S Job 3:10-11; S Ecc 4:2 [q]S Ge 3:17; S Job 5:7 [r]S 1Ki 19:4; Ps 90:9; 102:3

All my friends[x]
are waiting for me to slip,[y]
saying,
"Perhaps he will be deceived;
then we will pi
and take our revenge[z] over him
on him."[a]
11But the LORD[b] is with me like a
mighty warrior;
so my persecutors[c] will stumble and
not prevail.[d]
They will fail and be thoroughly
disgraced;[e]
their dishonor will never be
forgotten.
12O LORD Almighty, you who examine
the righteous
and probe the heart and mind,[f]
let me see your vengeance[g] upon
them,
for to you I have committed[h] my
cause.

13Sing[i] to the LORD!
Give praise to the Lo
He rescues[j] the life of t
from the hands of the needy
[k]

14Cursed be the day I was b
May the day my mother
be blessed! not
15Cursed be the man who bro
father the news,
who made him very glad,
"A child is born to you—a
16May that man be like the tow
the LORD overthrew withou
May he hear wailing[n] in the m
a battle cry at noon.
17For he did not kill me in the wo
with my mother as my grave,
her womb enlarged forever.
18Why did I ever come out of the
womb[p]
to see trouble[q] and sorrow
and to end my days in shame?[r]

[h]3 *Magor-Missabib* means *terror on every side.*
[i]7 Or *persuaded*

20:7–12 EVIL AND SUFFERING, Vindication—See note on 11:18—12:6. Obeying God may bring suffering under human persecution and ridicule. God's call to obedience is not silenced. We must maintain confidence in His eventual victory in and through us. We must leave the timing and action to Him.

20:7–18 PRAYER, Lament—Jeremiah expressed faith and entrusted vengeance to the Lord. His human weakness is seen in the conclusion of the prayer. His frustrated anger is seen in its beginning. Prayer does not always express proper theology. Jeremiah in more reflective moments would not have called God a deceiver or contemplated the advantages of death or stillbirth. Prayer expresses honest feelings and trusts God to deal with them as He knows best. See note on 11:18–23.

20:13 DISCIPLESHIP, Poor—God not only cares for the poor and the needy; He rescues them from the cruelty of the wicked. God most often provides such rescue through the faithful service of His people. See note on Isa 3:14–15.

20:14–18 EVIL AND SUFFERING, Endurance—S note on 11:18—12:6. Expressing anger may be the only w to deal with the suffering and evil we experience. God accep such expressions as part of our communication with Him Jeremiah protested life itself and placed a curse on everything involved in his entrance into the world. Jeremiah did more than protest. He endured the dark days by faithfully fulfilling the task God gave him. Endurance is more than expressing anger. We must remain involved with God and with life.

20:14–18 HUMANITY, Death—Depression makes people wish they had never been born or had already died. At such times, life appears almost to become a form of death. Even God's greatest servants may exhibit radical signs of depression. In love, God listens to our darkest feelings then sends us back to His mission. Creative purpose is the path away from depression.

23You who live in 'Lebanon,[m][f]'
who are nestled in cedar buildings,
how you will groan when pangs come
upon you,
pain[g] like that of a woman in labor!

24"As surely as I live," declares the
LORD, "even if you, Jehoiachin[n][h] son of
Jehoiakim king of Judah, were a signet
ring[i] on my right hand, I would still pull
you off. 25I will hand you over[j] to those
who seek your life, those you fear—to
Nebuchadnezzar king of Babylon and to
the Babylonians.[o] 26I will hurl[k] you and
the mother[l] who gave you birth into another country, where neither of you was
born, and there you both will die. 27You
will never come back to the land you long
to return[m] to."

28Is this man Jehoiachin[n] a despised,
broken pot,[o]
an object no one wants?
Why will he and his children be
hurled[p] out,
cast into a land[q] they do not know?
29O land,[r] land, land,
hear the word of the LORD!
30This is what the LORD says:
"Record this man as if childless,[s]
a man who will not prosper[t] in his
lifetime,
for none of his offspring[u] will prosper,
none will sit on the throne[v] of
David
or rule anymore in Judah."

Chapter 23

The Righteous Branch

"WOE to the shepherds[w] who are
destroying and scattering[x] the
sheep of my pasture!"[y] declares the
LORD. 2Therefore this is what the LORD,
the God of Israel, says to the shepherds[z]
who tend my people: "Because you have
scattered my flock[a] and driven them
away and have not bestowed care on
them, I will bestow punishment on you
for the evil[b] you have done," declares
the LORD. 3"I myself will gather the remnant[c] of my flock out of all the countries
where I have driven them and will bring
them back to their pasture,[d] where they
will be fruitful and increase in number. 4I
will place shepherds[e] over them who
will tend them, and they will no longer
be afraid[f] or terrified, nor will any be
missing,[g]" declares the LORD.

5"The days are coming," declares the
LORD,
"when I will raise up to David[p] a
righteous Branch,[h]
a King[i] who will reign[j] wisely
and do what is just and right[k] in the
land.
6In his days Judah will be saved
and Israel will live in safety.[l]
This is the name[m] by which he will be
called:
The LORD Our Righteousness.[n]

7"So then, the days are coming,"[o] declares the LORD, "when people will no
longer say, 'As surely as the LORD lives,
who brought the Israelites up out of
Egypt,'[p] 8but they will say, 'As surely as
the LORD lives, who brought the descendants of Israel up out of the land of the
north and out of all the countries where
he had banished them.' Then they will
live in their own land."[q]

Lying Prophets

9Concerning the prophets:

22:23 [f]S 1Ki 7:2; Eze 17:3 [g]S Jer 4:31
22:24 [h]S 2Ki 24:6, 8 [i]S Ge 38:18
22:25 [j]S 2Ki 24:16; S 2Ch 36:10
22:26 [k]S 1Sa 25:29; S 2Ki 24:8; 2Ch 36:10; S Isa 22:17; Eze 19:9-14 [l]S 1Ki 2:19
22:27 [m]S ver 10
22:28 [n]S 2Ki 24:6 [o]Ps 31:12; S Jer 19:10; 25:34; 48:38 [p]Jer 15:1 [q]S Jer 17:4
22:29 [r]S Jer 6:19
22:30 [s]1Ch 3:18; Jer 38:23; 52:10; Mt 1:12 [t]Jer 10:21 [u]S Job 18:19 [v]S Ps 94:20
23:1 [w]Jer 10:21; 12:10; 25:36; Eze 34:1-10; Zec 10:2; Zec 11:15-17 [x]S Isa 56:11 [y]Ps 100:3; S Jer 13:17; Eze 34:31
23:2 [z]Jn 10:8 [a]S Jer 10:21; 13:20 [b]Jer 21:12; Eze 34:8-10
23:3 [c]Isa 11:10-12; Jer 32:37; Eze 34:11-16 [d]S 1Ki 8:48
23:4 [e]S Ge 48:15; S Isa 31:4; Jer 31:10 [f]Jer 30:10; 46:27-28 [g]S Jn 6:39
23:5 [h]S 2Ki 19:26; S Isa 4:2; Eze 17:22 [i]S Mt 2:2 [j]Isa 9:7; S Mt 1:1 [k]S Ge 18:19
23:6 [l]S Lev 25:18; S Dt 32:8; Hos 2:18 [m]Ex 23:21; Jer 33:16; Mt 1:21-23 [n]S Ezr 9:15; S Isa 42:6; Ro 3:21-22; S 1Co 1:30
23:7 [o]Jer 30:3 [p]S Dt 15:15
23:8 [q]S Isa 14:1; S 43:5-6; Jer 30:10; Eze 20:42; 34:13; Am 9:14-15

[m]23 That is, the palace in Jerusalem (see 1 Kings 7:2)
[n]24 Hebrew *Coniah,* a variant of *Jehoiachin;* also in verse 28
[o]25 Or *Chaldeans*
[p]5 Or *up from David's line*

23:1–4 THE CHURCH, Remnant—God judges leaders who do not care for His remnant people. He protects and blesses His faithful remnant and provides them the needed leadership. As God's righteous, faithful remnant, we have no reason to fear.
23:5–6 JESUS CHRIST, Foretold—Jeremiah, who lived at the end of Judah's last days, spoke eloquently of God's new day. The early Christians saw this day dawn in the birth of Jesus, the seed of David, the righteous Branch, the just King (Lk 1:32). Compare Isa 4:2; 11:1; Zec 3:8.
23:5–6 HOLY SCRIPTURE, Writing—See note on 30:1–11.
23:6 GOD, Righteous—Not only is God righteous in Himself, but He seeks to produce righteousness in those who are relating to Him. Righteousness for people is living in right relationship with God.
23:7–8 HOLY SCRIPTURE, Writing—See note on 30:1–11.
23:7–8 HISTORY, Deliverance—Deliverance is not simply tradition handed down from past ages. Deliverance is a possibility for a faithful generation needing God's help. Because He is involved in history rather than being isolated in the heavens, God can meet new historical needs of His people with even greater acts than previous generations experienced. He promised such an act to the Exiles.
23:9–15 SIN, Transgression—Preaching God's Word can be sinful. When the preaching office becomes only a power tool to manipulate other people and to gain fame and fortune, the preacher has become a repulsive sinner. Sinful preachers break God's heart and the people's will to do right. Preachers should not preach the truth and live a lie. See notes on 1 Ki 12:26–33; 14:22–24.
23:9–40 HOLY SCRIPTURE, Inspired—Prophetic inspiration with its awesome experience of the Spirit and its world-changing content deeply affected the prophet (v 9). Others claimed the prophetic office but were not overcome by God's "holy words." They joined with priests in wicked actions, even promoting foreign gods. They practiced physical and spiritual adultery in the name of religion. They raised false hopes based on their communication skills rather than on God's words. To be a prophet a person had to receive a word in God's heavenly council (1 Ki 22:19–22; Job 1:6–12; 2:1–7; Isa 6:1–13). There one saw His word in a vision or heard a direct commission (Jer 23:18). True prophets turn from the

My heart[r] is broken within me;
all my bones tremble.[s]
I am like a drunken man,
like a man overcome by wine,
because of the LORD
and his holy words.[t]
10The land is full of adulterers;[u]
because of the curse[q][v] the land lies
parched[r]
and the pastures[w] in the desert are
withered.[x]
The ⌊prophets⌋ follow an evil course
and use their power unjustly.

11"Both prophet and priest are godless;[y]
even in my temple[z] I find their
wickedness,"
declares the LORD.
12"Therefore their path will become
slippery;[a]
they will be banished to darkness
and there they will fall.
I will bring disaster on them
in the year they are punished,[b]"
declares the LORD.

13"Among the prophets of Samaria
I saw this repulsive thing:
They prophesied by Baal[c]
and led my people Israel astray.[d]
14And among the prophets of Jerusalem
I have seen something horrible:[e]
They commit adultery and live a
lie.[f]
They strengthen the hands of
evildoers,[g]
so that no one turns from his
wickedness.[h]
They are all like Sodom[i] to me;
the people of Jerusalem are like
Gomorrah."[j]

15Therefore, this is what the LORD Almighty says concerning the prophets:

"I will make them eat bitter food
and drink poisoned water,[k]
because from the prophets of
Jerusalem
ungodliness[l] has spread throughout
the land."

16This is what the LORD Almighty says:

"Do not listen[m] to what the prophets
are prophesying to you;
they fill you with false hopes.
They speak visions[n] from their own
minds,
not from the mouth[o] of the LORD.
17They keep saying[p] to those who
despise me,
'The LORD says: You will have
peace.'[q]
And to all who follow the
stubbornness[r] of their hearts
they say, 'No harm[s] will come to
you.'
18But which of them has stood in the
council[t] of the LORD
to see or to hear his word?
Who has listened and heard his
word?
19See, the storm[u] of the LORD
will burst out in wrath,
a whirlwind[v] swirling down
on the heads of the wicked.
20The anger[w] of the LORD will not turn
back[x]
until he fully accomplishes
the purposes of his heart.
In days to come
you will understand it clearly.
21I did not send[y] these prophets,
yet they have run with their
message;
I did not speak to them,
yet they have prophesied.
22But if they had stood in my council,[z]
they would have proclaimed[a] my
words to my people
and would have turned[b] them from
their evil ways
and from their evil deeds.[c]

23"Am I only a God nearby,[d]"
declares the LORD,
"and not a God far away?
24Can anyone hide[e] in secret places
so that I cannot see him?"
declares the LORD.
"Do not I fill heaven and earth?"[f]
declares the LORD.

25"I have heard what the prophets say
who prophesy lies[g] in my name. They
say, 'I had a dream![h] I had a dream!'
26How long will this continue in the
hearts of these lying prophets, who
prophesy the delusions[i] of their own
minds?[j] 27They think the dreams they
tell one another will make my people forget[k]
my name, just as their fathers forgot[l]
my name through Baal worship.[m]
28Let the prophet who has a dream[n] tell
his dream, but let the one who has my

23:9 [r]S Jer 4:19 [s]S Job 4:14 [t]Jer 20:8-9
23:10 [u]S Jer 9:2 [v]Dt 28:23-24 [w]Ps 107:34; S Jer 9:10 [x]S Jer 4:26; S 12:11
23:11 [y]Jer 6:13; S 8:10; Zep 3:4 [z]S 2Ki 21:4; S Jer 7:10
23:12 [a]S Dt 32:35; S Job 3:23; Jer 13:16 [b]Jer 11:23
23:13 [c]S 1Ki 18:22 [d]ver 32; S Isa 3:12; Eze 13:10
23:14 [e]S Jer 5:30; Hos 6:10 [f]Jer 29:23 [g]ver 22 [h]S Isa 5:18 [i]S Ge 18:20; Mt 11:24 [j]Jer 20:16; Am 4:11
23:15 [k]S Jer 8:14; 9:15 [l]S Jer 8:10
23:16 [m]Jer 27:9-10,14; S Mt 7:15 [n]S Jer 14:14; Eze 13:3 [o]Jer 9:20
23:17 [p]ver 31 [q]S 1Ki 22:8; S Jer 4:10 [r]S Jer 13:10 [s]Jer 5:12; Am 9:10; Mic 3:11
23:18 [t]S 1Ki 22:19; S Ro 11:34
23:19 [u]Isa 30:30; Jer 25:32; 30:23 [v]Zec 7:14
23:20 [w]S 2Ki 23:26 [x]S Jer 4:28
23:21 [y]S Jer 14:14; 27:15
23:22 [z]S 1Ki 22:19 [a]S Dt 33:10 [b]S 2Ki 17:13; Jer 25:5; Zec 1:4 [c]ver 14; Am 3:7
23:23 [d]Ps 139:1-10
23:24 [e]S Ge 3:8; S Job 11:20; 22:12-14; S Ecc 12:14; S Isa 28:15; 1Co 4:5 [f]S 1Ki 8:27
23:25 [g]ver 16; Jer 14:14; 27:10 [h]ver 28,32; S Dt 13:1; Jer 27:9; 29:8
23:26 [i]S Isa 30:10; 1Ti 4:1-2 [j]Jer 14:14; Eze 13:2
23:27 [k]Dt 13:1-3; Jer 29:8 [l]S Jdg 3:7; S 8:33-34 [m]S Jer 2:23
23:28 [n]S ver 25

[q]10 Or *because of these things* [r]10 Or *land mourns*

experience with God to proclaim His full message to the people, knowing God will bring it to pass. Claiming a proper means of inspiration—a dream or oracle—did not mean a person was inspired by God (v 26). Such false prophets even stole words from other prophets to gain prestige and power. False prophets face true punishment.

23:19–20 GOD, Wrath—God's wrath is not irrational or irresponsible. It accomplishes His purposes. As humans, we often understand His wrath only as we look back on it through the perspective of history.

23:19–20 HOLY SCRIPTURE, Writing—See note on 30:1–11.

word[o] speak it faithfully. For what has
straw to do with grain?" declares the
LORD. 29"Is not my word like fire,"[p] declares the LORD, "and like a hammer[q]
that breaks a rock in pieces?
30"Therefore," declares the LORD, "I
am against[r] the prophets[s] who steal
from one another words supposedly from
me. 31Yes," declares the LORD, "I am
against the prophets who wag their own
tongues and yet declare, 'The LORD declares.'[t] 32Indeed, I am against those
who prophesy false dreams,[u]" declares
the LORD. "They tell them and lead my
people astray[v] with their reckless lies,[w]
yet I did not send[x] or appoint them. They
do not benefit[y] these people in the
least," declares the LORD.

False Oracles and False Prophets

33"When these people, or a prophet or
a priest, ask you, 'What is the oracle[s][z] of
the LORD?' say to them, 'What oracle?[t] I
will forsake[a] you, declares the LORD.' 34If
a prophet or a priest or anyone else
claims, 'This is the oracle[b] of the LORD,' I
will punish[c] that man and his household.
35This is what each of you keeps on saying to his friend or relative: 'What is the
LORD's answer?'[d] or 'What has the LORD
spoken?' 36But you must not mention 'the
oracle of the LORD' again, because every
man's own word becomes his oracle and
so you distort[e] the words of the living
God,[f] the LORD Almighty, our God.
37This is what you keep saying to a prophet: 'What is the LORD's answer to you?' or
'What has the LORD spoken?' 38Although
you claim, 'This is the oracle of the
LORD,' this is what the LORD says: You
used the words, 'This is the oracle of the
LORD,' even though I told you that you
must not claim, 'This is the oracle of the
LORD.' 39Therefore, I will surely forget
you and cast[g] you out of my presence
along with the city I gave to you and your
fathers. 40I will bring upon you everlasting disgrace[h]—everlasting shame that
will not be forgotten."

Chapter 24

Two Baskets of Figs

AFTER Jehoiachin[u][i] son of Jehoiakim
king of Judah and the officials, the
craftsmen and the artisans of Judah were
carried into exile from Jerusalem to Babylon by Nebuchadnezzar king of Babylon,
the LORD showed me two baskets of figs[j]
placed in front of the temple of the LORD.
2One basket had very good figs, like those
that ripen early;[k] the other basket had
very poor[l] figs, so bad they could not be
eaten.
3Then the LORD asked me, "What do
you see,[m] Jeremiah?"
"Figs," I answered. "The good ones
are very good, but the poor ones are so
bad they cannot be eaten."
4Then the word of the LORD came to
me: 5"This is what the LORD, the God of
Israel, says: 'Like these good figs, I regard
as good the exiles from Judah, whom I
sent[n] away from this place to the land of
the Babylonians.[v] 6My eyes will watch
over them for their good, and I will bring
them back[o] to this land. I will build[p]
them up and not tear them down; I will
plant[q] them and not uproot them. 7I will
give them a heart to know[r] me, that I am
the LORD. They will be my people,[s] and I
will be their God, for they will return[t] to
me with all their heart.[u]
8" 'But like the poor[v] figs, which are
so bad they cannot be eaten,' says the
LORD, 'so will I deal with Zedekiah[w] king
of Judah, his officials[x] and the survivors[y]
from Jerusalem, whether they remain in
this land or live in Egypt.[z] 9I will make
them abhorrent[a] and an offense to all the
kingdoms of the earth, a reproach and a
byword,[b] an object of ridicule and cursing,[c] wherever I banish[d] them. 10I will
send the sword,[e] famine[f] and plague[g]

23:28 [o]S 1Sa 3:17
23:29 [p]S Ps 39:3; Jer 5:14; S 1Co 3:13 [q]Heb 4:12
23:30 [r]S Ps 34:16 [s]ver 2; Dt 18:20; Jer 14:15; S 21:13
23:31 [t]ver 17
23:32 [u]S ver 25 [v]S ver 13; S Jer 50:6 [w]S Job 13:4; Eze 13:3; 22:28 [x]S Jer 14:14 [y]Jer 7:8; La 2:14
23:33 [z]Mal 1:1 [a]S 2Ki 21:14
23:34 [b]La 2:14 [c]Zec 13:3
23:35 [d]Jer 33:3; 42:4
23:36 [e]Gal 1:7-8; 2Pe 3:16 [f]S Jos 3:10
23:39 [g]S Jer 7:15
23:40 [h]S Jer 20:11; Eze 5:14-15
24:1 [i]S 2Ki 24:16; S 2Ch 36:9 [j]Ex 23:19; Dt 26:2; Am 8:1-2
24:2 [k]S SS 2:13 [l]S Isa 5:4
24:3 [m]Jer 1:11; Am 8:2
24:5 [n]Jer 29:4,20
24:6 [o]S Dt 30:3; Jer 27:22; 29:10; 30:3; Eze 11:17 [p]Jer 33:7; 42:10 [q]S Dt 30:9; S Jer 1:10; Am 9:14-15
24:7 [r]S Isa 11:9 [s]S Lev 26:12; S Isa 51:16; S Zec 2:11; Heb 8:10 [t]Jer 32:40 [u]S 2Ch 6:37; Eze 11:19
24:8 [v]Jer 29:17 [w]Jer 32:4-5; 38:18, 23; 39:5; 44:30 [x]Jer 39:6 [y]Jer 39:9 [z]Jer 44:1,26; 46:14
24:9 [a]S Jer 15:4; 25:18 [b]S Dt 28:25; S 1Ki 9:7 [c]S 2Ki 22:19; S Jer 29:18 [d]S Dt 28:37; Da 9:7
24:10 [e]S Isa 51:19; S Jer 9:16; Rev 6:8 [f]Jer 15:2 [g]Jer 27:8

[s]33 Or *burden* (see Septuagint and Vulgate)
[t]33 Hebrew; Septuagint and Vulgate *'You are the burden.* (The Hebrew for *oracle* and *burden* is the same.)
[u]1 Hebrew *Jeconiah,* a variant of *Jehoiachin*
[v]5 Or *Chaldeans*

23:33–40 ELECTION, Leadership—The plight of God's elect was not erased but made more acute because false prophets who had not been elected to speak for God were speaking lies that the people believed to be true. The popularity of false prophets makes difficult the unpopular message of God's elected prophets. Self-appointment does not make a prophet. God elects spiritual leaders and gives them His true word.

24:4–10 ELECTION, Remnant—Sword, famine, plague, death, and loss of the land given to their fathers and mothers by the election of God became the punishment and destruction of Israel and Judah. Sin must be punished. Destruction is the end of the disobedient. Still God saved a remnant in Exile to be His faithful people fulfilling His election purposes.

24:7 SALVATION, Repentance—God is proud to call those His people who return to Him with all their heart. Here it is those who have suffered exile who repent with their whole hearts. Repentance is not a human accomplishment to be rewarded. God offers forgiveness to those who repent and experience God in personal relationship. They are the good figs in Jeremiah's vision (v 5).

24:7 THE CHURCH, Covenant People—After the judgment of the Exile in Babylon, God promised to restore His purified people and give them a heart to know and serve Him. This verse reveals a remarkable new step in God's dealings with His people. God chooses His people by His own initiative. He gives them what they need in order to know Him. "Know" indicates intimate, experiential knowledge. The heart is the seat of the will and the motive center of the personality. When people know God, the ideal of the covenant relationship will be a reality. Then the people will be God's people, and He will be their God. This kind of relationship becomes possible when people repent. The word "return" defines true repentance: it is turning or returning to God. Life in sin under judgment need not be permanent. God calls people to turn to Him for renewal.

against them until they are destroyed
from the land I gave to them and their
fathers.[h] ' "

Chapter 25

Seventy Years of Captivity

THE word came to Jeremiah concerning all the people of Judah in the
fourth year of Jehoiakim[i] son of Josiah
king of Judah, which was the first year of
Nebuchadnezzar[j] king of Babylon. 2So
Jeremiah the prophet said to all the people of Judah[k] and to all those living in
Jerusalem: 3For twenty-three years—
from the thirteenth year of Josiah[l] son of
Amon king of Judah until this very day—
the word of the LORD has come to me and
I have spoken to you again and again,[m]
but you have not listened.[n]
4And though the LORD has sent all his
servants the prophets[o] to you again and
again, you have not listened or paid any
attention.[p] 5They said, "Turn[q] now,
each of you, from your evil ways and your
evil practices, and you can stay in the
land[r] the LORD gave to you and your fathers for ever and ever. 6Do not follow
other gods[s] to serve and worship them;
do not provoke me to anger with what
your hands have made. Then I will not
harm you."
7"But you did not listen to me," declares the LORD, "and you have provoked[t] me with what your hands have
made,[u] and you have brought harm[v] to
yourselves."
8Therefore the LORD Almighty says
this: "Because you have not listened to
my words, 9I will summon[w] all the peoples of the north[x] and my servant[y] Nebuchadnezzar[z] king of Babylon," declares
the LORD, "and I will bring them against
this land and its inhabitants and against
all the surrounding nations. I will completely destroy[w] [a] them and make them
an object of horror and scorn,[b] and an
everlasting ruin.[c] 10I will banish from
them the sounds[d] of joy and gladness,
the voices of bride and bridegroom,[e] the
sound of millstones[f] and the light of the
lamp.[g] 11This whole country will become
a desolate wasteland,[h] and these nations
will serve[i] the king of Babylon seventy
years.[j]

12"But when the seventy years[k] are
fulfilled, I will punish the king of Babylon[l] and his nation, the land of the Babylonians,[x] for their guilt," declares the
LORD, "and will make it desolate[m] forever. 13I will bring upon that land all the
things I have spoken against it, all that
are written[n] in this book and prophesied
by Jeremiah against all the nations.
14They themselves will be enslaved[o] by
many nations[p] and great kings; I will repay[q] them according to their deeds and
the work of their hands."

The Cup of God's Wrath

15This is what the LORD, the God of
Israel, said to me: "Take from my hand
this cup[r] filled with the wine of my
wrath and make all the nations to whom I
send[s] you drink it. 16When they drink[t]
it, they will stagger[u] and go mad[v] because of the sword[w] I will send among
them."
17So I took the cup from the LORD's
hand and made all the nations to whom
he sent[x] me drink it: 18Jerusalem[y] and
the towns of Judah, its kings and officials,
to make them a ruin[z] and an object of
horror and scorn[a] and cursing,[b] as they
are today;[c] 19Pharaoh king[d] of Egypt,[e]
his attendants, his officials and all his
people, 20and all the foreign people there;
all the kings of Uz;[f] all the kings of the
Philistines[g] (those of Ashkelon,[h] Gaza,[i]
Ekron, and the people left at Ashdod);
21Edom,[j] Moab[k] and Ammon;[l] 22all the
kings of Tyre[m] and Sidon;[n] the kings of
the coastlands[o] across the sea; 23De-
dan,[p] Tema,[q] Buz[r] and all who are in
distant places[y];[s] 24all the kings of Arabia[t] and all the kings of the foreign people[u] who live in the desert; 25all the
kings of Zimri,[v] Elam[w] and Media;[x]
26and all the kings of the north,[y] near
and far, one after the other—all the kingdoms[z] on the face of the earth. And after

24:10 [h]S Dt 28:21
25:1 [i]S 2Ki 24:2 [j]S 2Ki 24:1
25:2 [k]Jer 18:11
25:3 [l]S 1Ch 3:14 [m]Jer 11:7; 26:5 [n]S Isa 65:12; S Jer 7:26
25:4 [o]Jer 6:17; S 7:25; 29:19 [p]S Jer 7:26; 34:14; 44:5
25:5 [q]S Jdg 6:8; S 2Ch 7:14; S 30:9; S Jer 23:22 [r]S Ge 12:7; S Dt 4:40
25:6 [s]S Ex 20:3; S Dt 8:19
25:7 [t]Jer 30:14; 32:35; 44:5 [u]Dt 32:21 [v]2Ki 17:20; 21:15
25:9 [w]Isa 13:3-5 [x]S Isa 14:31 [y]S Isa 41:2; Jer 27:6 [z]S 2Ch 36:6 [a]S Nu 21:2 [b]S 2Ch 29:8 [c]S Jer 19:8; S 20:4; Eze 12:20
25:10 [d]S Isa 24:8; Eze 26:13 [e]Jer 7:34; 33:11 [f]Ecc 12:3-4 [g]S Job 18:5; La 5:15; Rev 18:22-23
25:11 [h]S Lev 26:31,32; Jer 4:26-27; 12:11-12 [i]Jer 28:14 [j]S 2Ch 36:21
25:12 [k]Jer 27:7; 29:10 [l]S Ge 10:10; S Ps 137:8 [m]S Isa 13:19-22; 14:22-23
25:13 [n]S Isa 30:8
25:14 [o]Isa 14:6; Jer 27:7 [p]Jer 50:9; 51:27-28 [q]S Dt 32:41; S Job 21:19; S Jer 51:6
25:15 [r]S Isa 51:17; Jer 49:12; La 4:21; Eze 23:31; Rev 14:10 [s]Jer 1:5
25:16 [t]ver 26 [u]S Ps 60:3 [v]Jer 51:7 [w]ver 27-29
25:17 [x]Jer 1:10; 27:3
25:18 [y]S Jer 13:13 [z]S Job 12:19 [a]S 2Ch 29:8 [b]S Jer 24:9 [c]S Ge 19:13; Jer 44:22
25:19 [d]S 2Ki 18:21 [e]Isa 19:1; 20:3; Jer 44:30; Eze 29:2
25:20 [f]S Ge 10:23 [g]S Jos 13:3; S 2Ch 26:6; S 28:18; Zep 2:4-7 [h]Jer 47:5; Am 1:7-8 [i]S Ge 10:19
25:21 [j]S Ge 25:30 [k]S Ge 19:37; S Dt 23:6 [l]S Ge 19:38; Jer 27:3; 49:1
25:22 [m]S Jos 19:29 [n]S Ge 10:15 [o]Isa 11:11; 48:20; 66:20; Jer 31:10; Eze 27:15; 39:6; Da 11:18
25:23 [p]S Ge 25:3 [q]S Ge 25:15 [r]S Ge 2 2:21 [s]Jer 9:26; 49:32
25:24 [t]S 2Ch 9:14 [u]ver 20
25:25 [v]Ge 25:2 [w]S Ge 10:22 [x]S Isa 21:2
25:26 [y]ver 9; Jer 50:3,9; 51:11,48 [z]Isa 23:17

[w]9 The Hebrew term refers to the irrevocable giving over of things or persons to the LORD, often by totally destroying them. [x]12 Or *Chaldeans* [y]23 Or *who clip the hair by their foreheads*

25:1–38 GOD, Wrath—God's wrath comes upon us after we have rejected His warnings and His calls to repent. God's acts of wrath discipline His people and punish His enemies. They fulfill the promises God has made.

25:3–4 REVELATION, Messengers—Jeremiah described the many years and the many ways in which God's revelation had been interpreted to a rejecting people. The prophet was a persistent witness against Judah, standing in their midst to remind them of how many times God's revealed will had come to them and how they had set it aside. See note on 6:10–11.

25:8–14 HISTORY, National—See notes on 1:14–19; Isa 1:24–26; 10:5–19.

25:13 HOLY SCRIPTURE, Writing—The prophet's words were written and could be checked by later generations.

25:15–38 GOD, Sovereignty—God's sovereignty leads to drastic actions to maintain His rule over the nations.

all of them, the king of Sheshach[z] [a] will
drink it too.

[27]"Then tell them, 'This is what the
LORD Almighty, the God of Israel, says:
Drink, get drunk[b] and vomit, and fall to
rise no more because of the sword[c] I will
send among you.' [28]But if they refuse to
take the cup from your hand and drink[d],
tell them, 'This is what the LORD Almighty says: You must drink it! [29]See, I
am beginning to bring disaster[e] on the
city that bears my Name,[f] and will you
indeed go unpunished?[g] You will not go
unpunished, for I am calling down a
sword[h] upon all[i] who live on the
earth,[j] declares the LORD Almighty.'

[30]"Now prophesy all these words
against them and say to them:

" 'The LORD will roar[k] from on high;
he will thunder[l] from his holy
dwelling[m]
and roar mightily against his land.
He will shout like those who tread[n]
the grapes,
shout against all who live on the
earth.
[31]The tumult[o] will resound to the ends
of the earth,
for the LORD will bring charges[p]
against the nations;
he will bring judgment[q] on all[r]
mankind
and put the wicked to the
sword,[s] ' "
declares the LORD.

[32]This is what the LORD Almighty says:

"Look! Disaster[t] is spreading
from nation to nation;[u]
a mighty storm[v] is rising
from the ends of the earth."[w]

[33]At that time those slain[x] by the LORD
will be everywhere—from one end of the
earth to the other. They will not be
mourned or gathered[y] up or buried,[z] but
will be like refuse lying on the ground.

[34]Weep and wail, you shepherds;[a]
roll[b] in the dust, you leaders of the
flock.
For your time to be slaughtered[c] has
come;
you will fall and be shattered like
fine pottery.[d]
[35]The shepherds will have nowhere to
flee,
the leaders of the flock no place to
escape.[e]
[36]Hear the cry[f] of the shepherds,[g]
the wailing of the leaders of the
flock,
for the LORD is destroying their
pasture.
[37]The peaceful meadows will be laid
waste
because of the fierce anger of the
LORD.
[38]Like a lion[h] he will leave his lair,
and their land will become
desolate[i]
because of the sword[a] of the
oppressor[j]
and because of the LORD's fierce
anger.[k]

Chapter 26

Jeremiah Threatened With Death

EARLY in the reign of Jehoiakim[l] son
of Josiah king of Judah, this word
came from the LORD: [2]"This is what the
LORD says: Stand in the courtyard[m] of the
LORD's house and speak to all the people
of the towns of Judah who come to worship in the house of the LORD.[n] Tell[o]
them everything I command you; do not
omit[p] a word. [3]Perhaps they will listen
and each will turn[q] from his evil way.
Then I will relent[r] and not bring on
them the disaster I was planning because
of the evil they have done. [4]Say to them,
'This is what the LORD says: If you do not
listen[s] to me and follow my law,[t] which
I have set before you, [5]and if you do not
listen to the words of my servants the
prophets, whom I have sent to you
again and again (though you have not

[z] *26 Sheshach* is a cryptogram for Babylon.
[a] *38* Some Hebrew manuscripts and Septuagint (see also Jer. 46:16 and 50:16); most Hebrew manuscripts *anger*

25:26 [a]Jer 51:41
25:27 [b]ver 16,28; S Isa 29:9; S 49:26; Jer 51:57; Eze 23:32-34; Na 3:18; Hab 2:16 [c]S Jer 12:12; Eze 14:17; 21:4
25:28 [d]S Isa 51:23
25:29 [e]S 2Sa 5:7; Isa 10:12; Jer 13:12-14; 39:1 [f]S Dt 28:10; S Isa 37:17 [g]S Pr 11:31 [h]ver 27 [i]ver 30-31; Isa 34:2 [j]S Isa 24:1
25:30 [k]Isa 16:10; S 42:13 [l]S Ps 46:6 [m]S Ps 68:5 [n]Isa 63:3; Joel 3:13; Rev 14:19-20
25:31 [o]Jer 23:19 [p]S Jer 2:9 [q]S 1Sa 12:7; S Jer 2:35; S Eze 36:5 [r]S ver 29 [s]S Jer 15:9
25:32 [t]S Isa 30:25 [u]Isa 34:2 [v]S Jer 23:19 [w]S Dt 28:49
25:33 [x]Isa 66:16; Eze 39:17-20 [y]S Jer 8:2 [z]S Ps 79:3
25:34 [a]S Jer 2:8; Zec 10:3 [b]S Jer 6:26 [c]S Ps 44:22; S Isa 34:6; Jer 50:27; 51:40; Zec 11:4,7 [d]S Jer 22:28
25:35 [e]S Job 11:20
25:36 [f]S Jer 6:26 [g]S Jer 23:1; Zec 11:3
25:38 [h]S Job 10:16; S Jer 4:7 [i]Jer 44:22 [j]Jer 46:16; 50:16 [k]S Ex 15:7; S Jer 4:26
26:1 [l]2Ki 23:36
26:2 [m]Jer 19:14 [n]S Jer 17:19 [o]S ver 12; S Jer 1:17; Mt 28:20; Ac 20:27 [p]Dt 4:2
26:3 [q]Dt 30:2; 2Ch 33:12-13; Isa 55:7; Jer 35:15; 36:7 [r]S Jer 18:8
26:4 [s]Lev 26:14; Jer 25:3 [t]Ex 20:1-23:33; S 1Ki 9:6; S Jer 11:8

26:1–19 REVELATION, Messengers—God does not quit on His people even when they consistently quit Him. God's word offered a choice: forgiveness and restoration if they repented or destruction if they did not. The prophetic messenger at times preached in the Temple. There he met other prophets, probably professionals on the Temple staff. Compare 1 Ki 22:6–8. They joined priests in seeking to condemn Jeremiah to death. Jeremiah faithfully preached every word God commanded and depended on God for protection. An earlier prophecy from Micah (3:12) was regarded as authoritative Scripture by the officials and thus saved Jeremiah's life. Micah's example showed that the choice in prophecy is real. Repentance brought God's turning from the word of judgment He had announced.

26:2–7 WORSHIP, Proclamation—God instructed the prophet to preach to the people in the house of God when they came to worship. Proclamation of God's Word is a part of genuine worship. This aspect of worship is most clearly seen in the time of the prophets (44:20–29; Isa 61:1–2; 63:7; Eze 33:31). It continued as a pattern in worship in the New Testament church (Lk 4:15–21; Ac 20:20–21). One of the prominent features seen in these passages is the reading of the Word of God, a vital aspect of proclamation. See note on Ne 8:1–6.

26:3,19–24 GOD, Sovereignty—God's sovereignty does not set each decision in concrete. He retains the freedom to react to the personal decisions we make in our relationship to Him. See note on 14:3–4.

listened[u]), 6then I will make this house
like Shiloh[v] and this city an object of cursing[w] among all the nations of the
earth.' "

7The priests, the prophets and all the
people heard Jeremiah speak these words
in the house of the LORD. 8But as soon as
Jeremiah finished telling all the people
everything the LORD had commanded[x]
him to say, the priests, the prophets and
all the people seized[y] him and said, "You
must die![z] 9Why do you prophesy in the
LORD's name that this house will be like
Shiloh and this city will be desolate and
deserted?"[a] And all the people crowded[b] around Jeremiah in the house of the
LORD.

10When the officials[c] of Judah heard
about these things, they went up from
the royal palace to the house of the LORD
and took their places at the entrance of
the New Gate[d] of the LORD's house.
11Then the priests and the prophets said
to the officials and all the people, "This
man should be sentenced to death[e] because he has prophesied against this city.
You have heard it with your own ears!"[f]

12Then Jeremiah said to all the officials[g] and all the people: "The LORD sent
me to prophesy[h] against this house and
this city all the things you have heard.[i]
13Now reform[j] your ways and your actions and obey[k] the LORD your God.
Then the LORD will relent[l] and not bring
the disaster he has pronounced against
you. 14As for me, I am in your hands;[m] do
with me whatever you think is good and
right. 15Be assured, however, that if you
put me to death, you will bring the guilt
of innocent blood[n] on yourselves and on
this city and on those who live in it, for in
truth the LORD has sent me to you to
speak all these words[o] in your hearing."

16Then the officials[p] and all the people
said to the priests and the prophets,
"This man should not be sentenced to
death![q] He has spoken to us in the name
of the LORD our God."

17Some of the elders of the land
stepped forward and said to the entire assembly of people, 18"Micah[r] of Moresheth prophesied in the days of Hezekiah
king of Judah. He told all the people of
Judah, 'This is what the LORD Almighty
says:

" 'Zion[s] will be plowed like a field,
Jerusalem will become a heap of
rubble,[t]
the temple hill[u] a mound
overgrown with thickets.'[b] [v]

19"Did Hezekiah king of Judah or anyone
else in Judah put him to death? Did not
Hezekiah[w] fear the LORD and seek[x] his
favor? And did not the LORD relent,[y] so
that he did not bring the disaster[z] he
pronounced against them? We are about
to bring a terrible disaster[a] on ourselves!"

20(Now Uriah son of Shemaiah from
Kiriath Jearim[b] was another man who
prophesied in the name of the LORD; he
prophesied the same things against this
city and this land as Jeremiah did.
21When King Jehoiakim[c] and all his officers and officials[d] heard his words, the
king sought to put him to death.[e] But
Uriah heard of it and fled[f] in fear to
Egypt. 22King Jehoiakim, however, sent
Elnathan[g] son of Acbor to Egypt, along
with some other men. 23They brought
Uriah out of Egypt and took him to King
Jehoiakim, who had him struck down
with a sword[h] and his body thrown into
the burial place of the common people.)[i]

24Furthermore, Ahikam[j] son of Shaphan supported Jeremiah, and so he was
not handed over to the people to be put
to death.

Chapter 27

Judah to Serve Nebuchadnezzar

EARLY in the reign of Zedekiah[c] [k] son
of Josiah king of Judah, this word
came to Jeremiah from the LORD: 2This is
what the LORD said to me: "Make a
yoke[l] out of straps and crossbars and put
it on your neck. 3Then send[m] word to the
kings of Edom, Moab, Ammon,[n] Tyre
and Sidon[o] through the envoys who have
come to Jerusalem to Zedekiah king of Judah. 4Give them a message for their masters and say, 'This is what the LORD Almighty, the God of Israel, says: "Tell this
to your masters: 5With my great power
and outstretched arm[p] I made[q] the earth
and its people and the animals[r] that are
on it, and I give[s] it to anyone I please.
6Now I will hand all your countries over

26:5 [u]S Pr 1:24; S Isa 65:12; Jer 25:4; 44:5
26:6 [v]S Jos 18:1; S Jdg 18:31 [w]S Dt 28:25; S 2Ki 22:19
26:8 [x]Jer 43:1 [y]Ac 6:12; 21:27 [z]Lev 24:15-16; S Ne 9:26; S Jer 11:21
26:9 [a]S Lev 26:32; S Jer 9:11 [b]Ac 21:32
26:10 [c]ver 16; Jer 34:19; Eze 22:27 [d]S Ge 23:10
26:11 [e]Dt 18:20; S Jer 11:21; 18:23; Mt 26:66; Ac 6:11 [f]S Ps 44:1
26:12 [g]Jer 1:18 [h]S Isa 6:8; Am 7:15; Ac 4:18-20; 5:29 [i]S ver 2,15
26:13 [j]S Jer 7:5; Joel 2:12-14 [k]Jer 11:4 [l]S Jer 18:8
26:14 [m]Jos 9:25; Jer 38:5
26:15 [n]S Dt 19:10 [o]S ver 12; S Jer 1:17
26:16 [p]S ver 10; S Ac 23:9 [q]Ac 23:29
26:18 [r]Mic 1:1 [s]Isa 2:3 [t]S 2Ki 25:9; S Ne 4:2; Jer 9:11 [u]Mic 4:1; Zec 8:3 [v]S Jer 17:3
26:19 [w]S 1Ch 3:13; 2Ch 32:24-26; Isa 37:14-20 [x]S 1Sa 13:12 [y]S Ex 32:14; S Jer 18:8 [z]Jer 44:7 [a]Hab 2:10
26:20 [b]S Jos 9:17
26:21 [c]S 1Ki 19:2 [d]ver 10 [e]Jer 2:30; Mt 23:37 [f]S Ge 31:21; Mt 10:23
26:22 [g]Jer 36:12, 25
26:23 [h]Heb 11:37 [i]2Ki 23:6
26:24 [j]S 2Ki 22:12
27:1 [k]S 2Ch 36:11
27:2 [l]S Lev 26:13; S 1Ki 22:11
27:3 [m]S Jer 25:17 [n]S Jer 25:21 [o]S Ge 10:15; S Jer 25:22
27:5 [p]S Dt 9:29 [q]S Ge 1:1 [r]S Ge 1:25 [s]Ps 115:16; Da 4:17

[b]*18* Micah 3:12 [c]*1* A few Hebrew manuscripts and Syriac (see also Jer. 27:3, 12 and 28:1); most Hebrew manuscripts *Jehoiakim* (Most Septuagint manuscripts do not have this verse.)

26:19 SALVATION, Fear of God—Hezekiah is an example of one who feared God (2 Ki 18:3–6). Those who fear God seek His favor and listen to His prophets. Devotion to God can avert the disaster of His announced judgment.

26:20–23 REVELATION, Messengers—God protected His faithful messengers. He did not protect Uriah. This may be because Uriah used human means for safety—escape—rather than trusting God, but inspired Scripture does not explicitly say this. God exercised His freedom to achieve His purpose.

27:5–22 GOD, Creator—As Creator, God maintains His right to distribute territory among nations as He chooses. No nation, not even His people, can make lasting territorial claims which restrict God's sovereignty, power, or freedom. See note on 14:3–4.

to my servant[t] Nebuchadnezzar[u] king of Babylon; I will make even the wild animals subject to him.[v] 7All nations will serve[w] him and his son and his grandson until the time[x] for his land comes; then many nations and great kings will subjugate[y] him.

8" ' "If, however, any nation or kingdom will not serve Nebuchadnezzar king of Babylon or bow its neck under his yoke, I will punish[z] that nation with the sword,[a] famine[b] and plague,[c] declares the LORD, until I destroy it by his hand. 9So do not listen to your prophets,[d] your diviners,[e] your interpreters of dreams,[f] your mediums[g] or your sorcerers[h] who tell you, 'You will not serve[i] the king of Babylon.' 10They prophesy lies[j] to you that will only serve to remove[k] you far from your lands; I will banish you and you will perish. 11But if any nation will bow its neck under the yoke[l] of the king of Babylon and serve him, I will let that nation remain in its own land to till it and to live[m] there, declares the LORD." ' "

12I gave the same message to Zedekiah king of Judah. I said, "Bow your neck under the yoke[n] of the king of Babylon; serve him and his people, and you will live.[o] 13Why will you and your people die[p] by the sword, famine and plague[q] with which the LORD has threatened any nation that will not serve the king of Babylon? 14Do not listen[r] to the words of the prophets[s] who say to you, 'You will not serve the king of Babylon,' for they are prophesying lies[t] to you. 15'I have not sent[u] them,' declares the LORD. 'They are prophesying lies in my name.[v] Therefore, I will banish you and you will perish,[w] both you and the prophets who prophesy to you.' "

16Then I said to the priests and all these people, "This is what the LORD says: Do not listen to the prophets who say, 'Very soon now the articles[x] from the LORD's house will be brought back from Babylon.' They are prophesying lies to you. 17Do not listen[y] to them. Serve the king of Babylon, and you will live.[z] Why should this city become a ruin? 18If they are prophets and have the word of the LORD, let them plead[a] with the LORD Almighty that the furnishings remaining in the house of the LORD and in the palace of the king of Judah and in Jerusalem not be taken to Babylon. 19For this is what the LORD Almighty says about the pillars, the Sea,[b] the movable stands and the other furnishings[c] that are left in this city, 20which Nebuchadnezzar king of Babylon did not take away when he carried[d] Jehoiachin[d][e] son of Jehoiakim king of Judah into exile from Jerusalem to Babylon, along with all the nobles of Judah and Jerusalem— 21yes, this is what the LORD Almighty, the God of Israel, says about the things that are left in the house of the LORD and in the palace of the king of Judah and in Jerusalem: 22'They will be taken[f] to Babylon and there they will remain until the day[g] I come for them,' declares the LORD. 'Then I will bring[h] them back and restore them to this place.' "

Chapter 28

The False Prophet Hananiah

IN the fifth month of that same year, the fourth year, early in the reign of Zedekiah[i] king of Judah, the prophet Hananiah son of Azzur, who was from Gibeon,[j] said to me in the house of the LORD in the presence of the priests and all the people: 2"This is what the LORD Almighty, the God of Israel, says: 'I will break the yoke[k] of the king of Babylon. 3Within two years I will bring back to this place all the articles[l] of the LORD's house that Nebuchadnezzar king of Babylon removed from here and took to Babylon. 4I will also bring back to this place Jehoiachin[d][m] son of Jehoiakim king of Judah and all the other exiles from Judah who went to Babylon,' declares the LORD, 'for I will break the yoke of the king of Babylon.' "[n]

5Then the prophet Jeremiah replied to the prophet Hananiah before the priests and all the people who were standing in the house of the LORD. 6He said, "Amen! May the LORD do so! May the LORD fulfill the words you have prophesied by bringing the articles of the LORD's house and all the exiles back to this place from Babylon.[o] 7Nevertheless, listen to what I have to say in your hearing and in the hearing of all the people: 8From early times the prophets who preceded you and me have prophesied war, disaster and plague[p] against many countries and great kingdoms. 9But the prophet who prophesies peace will be recognized as

27:6 [t]S Jer 25:9 [u]S Jer 21:7 [v]Jer 28:14; Da 2:37-38
27:7 [w]S 2Ch 36:20; Da 5:18 [x]S Jer 25:12 [y]S Jer 25:14; 51:47; Da 5:28
27:8 [z]Jer 9:16 [a]Jer 21:9 [b]S Jer 5:12 [c]S Jer 14:12
27:9 [d]Eze 13:1-23 [e]S Ge 30:27; S Isa 44:25 [f]S Dt 13:1; S Jer 23:25 [g]S Dt 18:11 [h]S Ex 7:11 [i]Jer 6:14
27:10 [j]S Jer 23:25; S Mk 13:5 [k]S 2Ki 23:27
27:11 [l]S Jer 21:9 [m]Dt 6:2
27:12 [n]Jer 17:4 [o]S Jer 21:9
27:13 [p]Eze 18:31 [q]S Jer 14:12
27:14 [r]S Jer 23:16 [s]S Jer 14:13 [t]S Jer 14:14; S Mt 7:15
27:15 [u]S Jer 23:21 [v]Jer 29:9; 44:16 [w]S Jer 6:15; Mt 15:12-14
27:16 [x]1Ki 7:48-50; S 2Ki 24:13
27:17 [y]Jer 23:16 [z]Jer 42:11
27:18 [a]S Nu 21:7; S 1Sa 7:8
27:19 [b]1Ki 7:23-26 [c]S 1Ki 7:51; Jer 52:17-23
27:20 [d]S Dt 28:36; S 2Ch 36:10 [e]Jer 22:24; Mt 1:11
27:22 [f]S 2Ki 20:17; 25:13 [g]S 2Ch 36:21; S Jer 24:6 [h]S Ezr 7:19
28:1 [i]S 2Ch 36:11 [j]S Jos 9:3
28:2 [k]Jer 27:12
28:3 [l]S 2Ki 24:13
28:4 [m]S 2Ki 25:30; Jer 22:24-27 [n]Hos 7:3
28:6 [o]Zec 6:10
28:8 [p]Lev 26:14-17; Isa 5:5-7; Na 1:14

[d]*20,4* Hebrew *Jeconiah,* a variant of *Jehoiachin*

27:20–22 HOLY SCRIPTURE, Collection—Collecting Jeremiah's preaching into written form was part of God's revelatory process. See note on 30:1–11. The process produced two slightly different forms of written text as seen in the Hebrew text and in the earliest translation—the Greek Septuagint. The Greek translation of Jeremiah is about one-eighth shorter than the Hebrew text. It does not include passages such as 27:20–22; 33:14–26; 39:3–14; 48:45–47. The marvel of inspiration is that God could provide a faithful scribe like Baruch and other faithful followers who preserved Jeremiah's preaching even as the nation was destroyed and the prophet forcibly taken to Egypt.

one truly sent by the LORD only if his prediction comes true.[q]"
10Then the prophet Hananiah took the
yoke[r] off the neck of the prophet Jeremiah and broke it, 11and he said[s] before all
the people, "This is what the LORD says:
'In the same way will I break the yoke of
Nebuchadnezzar king of Babylon off the
neck of all the nations within two
years.'" At this, the prophet Jeremiah
went on his way.
12Shortly after the prophet Hananiah
had broken the yoke off the neck of the
prophet Jeremiah, the word of the LORD
came to Jeremiah: 13"Go and tell Hananiah, 'This is what the LORD says: You have
broken a wooden yoke, but in its place
you will get a yoke of iron. 14This is what
the LORD Almighty, the God of Israel,
says: I will put an iron yoke[t] on the
necks of all these nations to make them
serve[u] Nebuchadnezzar[v] king of Babylon, and they will serve him. I will even
give him control over the wild animals.[w]'"
15Then the prophet Jeremiah said to
Hananiah the prophet, "Listen, Hananiah! The LORD has not sent[x] you, yet you
have persuaded this nation to trust in
lies.[y] 16Therefore, this is what the LORD
says: 'I am about to remove you from the
face of the earth.[z] This very year you are
going to die,[a] because you have preached
rebellion[b] against the LORD.'"
17In the seventh month of that same
year, Hananiah the prophet died.[c]

Chapter 29

A Letter to the Exiles

THIS is the text of the letter[d] that the
prophet Jeremiah sent from Jerusalem to the surviving elders among the exiles and to the priests, the prophets and
all the other people Nebuchadnezzar had
carried into exile from Jerusalem to Babylon.[e] 2(This was after King Jehoiachin[e][f] and the queen mother,[g] the
court officials and the leaders of Judah
and Jerusalem, the craftsmen and the artisans had gone into exile from Jerusalem.)
3He entrusted the letter to Elasah son of
Shaphan and to Gemariah son of Hilkiah,
whom Zedekiah king of Judah sent to
King Nebuchadnezzar in Babylon. It said:

4This is what the LORD Almighty,
the God of Israel, says to all those I
carried[h] into exile from Jerusalem to
Babylon: 5"Build[i] houses and settle
down; plant gardens and eat what
they produce. 6Marry and have sons
and daughters; find wives for your
sons and give your daughters in marriage, so that they too may have sons
and daughters. Increase in number
there; do not decrease.[j] 7Also,
seek[k] the peace and prosperity of the
city to which I have carried you into
exile. Pray[l] to the LORD for it, because if it prospers, you too will prosper." 8Yes, this is what the LORD Almighty, the God of Israel, says: "Do
not let the prophets[m] and diviners
among you deceive[n] you. Do not listen to the dreams[o] you encourage
them to have.[p] 9They are prophesying lies[q] to you in my name. I have
not sent[r] them," declares the LORD.
10This is what the LORD says:
"When seventy years[s] are completed for Babylon, I will come to you[t]
and fulfill my gracious promise[u] to
bring you back[v] to this place. 11For I
know the plans[w] I have for you," declares the LORD, "plans to prosper[x]
you and not to harm you, plans to
give you hope and a future.[y] 12Then
you will call[z] upon me and come and

28:9 qS Dt 18:22; Eze 33:33
28:10 rS Lev 26:13; S 1Ki 22:11
28:11 sJer 14:14; 27:10
28:14 tS Dt 28:48; S Jer 15:12 uJer 25:11 vJer 39:1; Da 1:1; 5:18 wS Jer 27:6
28:15 xJer 29:31 yS Jer 7:4; 20:6; 29:21; La 2:14; Eze 13:6
28:16 zS Ge 7:4 aDt 18:20; Zec 13:3 bDt 13:5; Jer 29:32
28:17 cS 2Ki 1:17
29:1 dver 28 eS 2Ch 36:10; S Jer 13:17
29:2 fS 2Ki 24:12 gS 2Ki 24:8
29:4 hS Jer 24:5
29:5 iver 28
29:6 jJer 30:19
29:7 kS Est 3:8 l1Ti 2:1-2
29:8 m1Jn 4:1 nJer 37:9 oS Dt 13:1; S Jer 23:25 pS Jer 23:27
29:9 qS Jer 27:15; La 2:14; Eze 13:6 rJer 23:21
29:10 sS 2Ch 36:21; S Da 9:2 tS Ru 1:6 u1Ki 8:56; Jer 32:42; 33:14 vS Jer 16:14; S 24:6
29:11 wPs 40:5 xIsa 55:12 yS Job 8:7; Zec 8:15
29:12 zHos 2:23; Zep 3:12; Zec 13:9

e2 Hebrew *Jeconiah,* a variant of *Jehoiachin*

28:16–17 HUMANITY, Death and Sin—Human sinfulness causes spiritual death. At times physical death is the immediate result of sin.
28:16 SIN, Punishment—False preaching brings ominous divine action. See note on 23:9–15.
29:1–32 REVELATION, Oracles—Even in exile the Hebrews continued to look to false prophets and to diviners who sought God's word from natural forces or animal parts. See note on 1 Sa 28:6–25. Change of scenery and economic conditions did nothing to change their sinful attempts to create revelation rather than depending on God for it. Prophets receiving divine revelation appeared to some observers to be mad (v 26). Compare 1 Sa 21:15; 2 Ki 9:11.
29:4–23 GOD, Sovereignty—God rules foreign lands as well as the land of His chosen people. Geography does not restrict God. Neither do prophets who preach without receiving words from God. We can trust God in His sovereign rule because we know ultimately His plans give us hope and a future. See note on 14:3–4.
29:7 PRAYER, Command of God—Prayer is at God's initiative. He will not reverse consequences but will weave the future to the good of those who obey Him. In Babylon, the captives should pray for its peace and prosperity. What God wants us to pray for sometimes surprises us. We need to let God change our will rather than trying to reverse His.
29:10 REVELATION, History—Revelation for Israel centered on God's actions in their history in response to the people's faith or lack of it. Such revelation was often general, pointing to a future moment of judgment or day of salvation. It could be quite specific as Jeremiah's pointing seventy years ahead. Seventy years could be a normal human life (Ps 90:10; Isa 23:15). In Jer 25:11–12 the seventy years may refer to the period from 605, the date in 25:1, to 538 when Israel first returned from Exile, or from 587, the destruction of the Temple, to 515, the Temple rededication. Later literature used the expression in different ways. Compare 2 Ch 36:20–23; (586 BC); Ezr 1:1 (538 BC); Zec 1:12 (519 BC); Da 9:2 (538 BC); 9:24–27.
29:10–11 SALVATION, Grace—God graciously promised to bring the scattered Jewish exiles in Babylon back to their homeland after seventy years (25:11–12). His plans for His people are always pregnant with grace.

pray[a] to me, and I will listen[b] to
you. 13You will seek[c] me and find
me when you seek me with all your
heart.[d] 14I will be found by you," declares the LORD, "and will bring you
back[e] from captivity.[f] I will gather
you from all the nations and places
where I have banished you," declares the LORD, "and will bring you
back to the place from which I carried you into exile."[f]

15You may say, "The LORD has
raised up prophets for us in Babylon," 16but this is what the LORD
says about the king who sits on David's throne and all the people who
remain in this city, your countrymen
who did not go with you into exile—
17yes, this is what the LORD Almighty
says: "I will send the sword, famine
and plague[g] against them and I will
make them like poor figs[h] that are so
bad they cannot be eaten. 18I will
pursue them with the sword, famine
and plague and will make them abhorrent[i] to all the kingdoms of the
earth and an object of cursing[j] and
horror,[k] of scorn[l] and reproach,
among all the nations where I drive
them. 19For they have not listened to
my words,"[m] declares the LORD,
"words that I sent to them again and
again[n] by my servants the prophets.[o] And you exiles have not listened either," declares the LORD.

20Therefore, hear the word of the
LORD, all you exiles whom I have
sent[p] away from Jerusalem to Babylon. 21This is what the LORD Almighty, the God of Israel, says about
Ahab son of Kolaiah and Zedekiah
son of Maaseiah, who are prophesying lies[q] to you in my name: "I will
hand them over to Nebuchadnezzar
king of Babylon, and he will put them
to death before your very eyes. 22Be-
cause of them, all the exiles from Judah who are in Babylon will use this
curse: 'The LORD treat you like Zedekiah and Ahab, whom the king of
Babylon burned[r] in the fire.' 23For
they have done outrageous things in
Israel; they have committed adultery[s] with their neighbors' wives
and in my name have spoken lies,
which I did not tell them to do. I
know[t] it and am a witness[u] to it,"
declares the LORD.

Message to Shemaiah

24Tell Shemaiah the Nehelamite,
25"This is what the LORD Almighty, the
God of Israel, says: You sent letters in
your own name to all the people in Jerusalem, to Zephaniah[v] son of Maaseiah
the priest, and to all the other priests.
You said to Zephaniah, 26'The LORD has
appointed you priest in place of Jehoiada
to be in charge of the house of the LORD;
you should put any madman[w] who acts
like a prophet into the stocks[x] and neck-
irons. 27So why have you not reprimanded Jeremiah from Anathoth, who
poses as a prophet among you? 28He has
sent this message[y] to us in Babylon: It
will be a long time.[z] Therefore build[a]
houses and settle down; plant gardens
and eat what they produce.' "

29Zephaniah[b] the priest, however,
read the letter to Jeremiah the prophet.
30Then the word of the LORD came to Jeremiah: 31"Send this message to all the
exiles: 'This is what the LORD says about
Shemaiah[c] the Nehelamite: Because Shemaiah has prophesied to you, even
though I did not send[d] him, and has led
you to believe a lie, 32this is what the
LORD says: I will surely punish Shemaiah
the Nehelamite and his descendants.[e]
He will have no one left among this people, nor will he see the good[f] things I
will do for my people, declares the LORD,
because he has preached rebellion[g]
against me.' "

Chapter 30

Restoration of Israel

THIS is the word that came to Jeremiah
from the LORD: 2"This is what the
LORD, the God of Israel, says: 'Write[h] in a
book all the words I have spoken to you.
3The days[i] are coming,' declares the
LORD, 'when I will bring[j] my people Israel and Judah back from captivity[g] and re-

29:12 [a]S 1Ki 8:30 [b]Ps 145:19; S Isa 55:6
29:13 [c]Mt 7:7 [d]S Dt 4:29; S 2Ch 6:37
29:14 [e]S Dt 30:3; Jer 30:3; Eze 39:25; Am 9:14; Zep 3:20 [f]Jer 23:3-4; 30:10; 46:27; Eze 37:21
29:17 [g]Jer 27:8 [h]S Isa 5:4
29:18 [i]S Jer 15:4 [j]S Nu 5:27; S Jer 18:16; S 22:10; 44:12 [k]S Dt 28:25 [l]S Dt 28:37; S Isa 28:22; S Mic 2:6
29:19 [m]Jer 6:19 [n]Jer 7:25 [o]S Jer 25:4
29:20 [p]S Jer 24:5
29:21 [q]ver 9; Jer 14:14
29:22 [r]Da 3:6
29:23 [s]S Jer 23:14 [t]S Heb 4:13 [u]S Ge 31:48; S Jer 7:11
29:25 [v]S 2Ki 25:18
29:26 [w]S 1Sa 10:11; Hos 9:7; S Jn 10:20 [x]Jer 20:2
29:28 [y]ver 1 [z]ver 10 [a]ver 5
29:29 [b]Jer 21:1
29:31 [c]ver 24 [d]S Jer 14:14
29:32 [e]S 1Sa 2:30-33 [f]ver 10 [g]S Jer 28:16
30:2 [h]S Isa 30:8; S Jer 36:2
30:3 [i]S Jer 16:14; S 24:6 [j]S Jer 29:14

[f]14 Or *will restore your fortunes* [g]3 Or *will restore the fortunes of my people Israel and Judah*

29:12–14 PRAYER, Sovereignty of God—The purpose of the captivity was to produce repentance. When that was accomplished, their prayer life could return to normal. See note on 7:16.

30:1–11 HOLY SCRIPTURE, Writing—God revealed His message to the prophet as a spoken word. Later He explicitly commanded the prophet to write the words so generations returning from Exile could learn from them. Writing the words of Jeremiah resulted in recording the same oracle twice in a few cases. Compare 6:12–15 and 8:10–12; 6:22–24 and 50:41–43; 10:12–16 and 51:15–19; 16:14–15 and 23:7–8; 23:5–6 and 33:15–16; 23:19–20 and 30:23–24; 30:10–11 and 46:27–28. God's process of revelation leading from sermon to book included such repetition. See note on 2 Sa 22:1–51. Such repetition shows the importance of the passages in God's plan and their power to speak in different contexts.

30:3,18 SALVATION, Renewal—God's restoration brings a new unity to His people and results from His compassion.

store[k] them to the land I gave their forefathers to possess,' says the LORD."

4These are the words the LORD spoke concerning Israel and Judah: 5"This is what the LORD says:

" 'Cries of fear[l] are heard—
terror, not peace.
6Ask and see:
Can a man bear children?
Then why do I see every strong man
with his hands on his stomach like a woman in labor,[m]
every face turned deathly pale?[n]
7How awful that day[o] will be!
None will be like it.
It will be a time of trouble[p] for Jacob,
but he will be saved[q] out of it.

8" 'In that day,' declares the LORD Almighty,
'I will break the yoke[r] off their necks
and will tear off their bonds;[s]
no longer will foreigners enslave them.[t]
9Instead, they will serve the LORD their God
and David[u] their king,[v]
whom I will raise up for them.

10" 'So do not fear,[w] O Jacob my servant;[x]
do not be dismayed, O Israel,'
declares the LORD.
'I will surely save[y] you out of a distant place,
your descendants from the land of their exile.
Jacob will again have peace and security,[z]
and no one will make him afraid.[a]
11I am with you[b] and will save you,'
declares the LORD.
'Though I completely destroy all the nations
among which I scatter you,
I will not completely destroy[c] you.
I will discipline[d] you but only with justice;
I will not let you go entirely unpunished.'[e]

12"This is what the LORD says:

" 'Your wound[f] is incurable,
your injury beyond healing.[g]
13There is no one to plead your cause,[h]
no remedy for your sore,
no healing[i] for you.
14All your allies[j] have forgotten you;
they care nothing for you.
I have struck you as an enemy[k] would
and punished you as would the cruel,[l]
because your guilt is so great
and your sins[m] so many.
15Why do you cry out over your wound,
your pain that has no cure?[n]
Because of your great guilt and many sins
I have done these things to you.[o]

16" 'But all who devour[p] you will be devoured;
all your enemies will go into exile.[q]
Those who plunder[r] you will be plundered;
all who make spoil of you I will despoil.
17But I will restore you to health
and heal[s] your wounds,'
declares the LORD,
'because you are called an outcast,[t]
Zion for whom no one cares.'[u]

18"This is what the LORD says:

" 'I will restore the fortunes[v] of Jacob's tents[w]
and have compassion[x] on his dwellings;
the city will be rebuilt[y] on her ruins,
and the palace will stand in its proper place.
19From them will come songs[z] of thanksgiving[a]
and the sound of rejoicing.[b]
I will add to their numbers,[c]
and they will not be decreased;
I will bring them honor,[d]
and they will not be disdained.
20Their children[e] will be as in days of old,
and their community will be established[f] before me;

30:3 [k]S Jer 16:15
30:5 [l]Jer 6:25
30:6 [m]S Jer 4:31 [n]S Isa 29:22
30:7 [o]S Isa 2:12 [p]S Isa 22:5; Zep 1:15 [q]ver 10; Jer 23:3
30:8 [r]S Isa 9:4 [s]Ps 107:14 [t]Jer 25:14; 27:7; Eze 34:27
30:9 [u]S Mt 1:1 [v]ver 21; S 1Sa 13:14; Jer 33:15; Eze 34:23-24; 37:24; Hos 1:11; 3:5
30:10 [w]S Isa 41:10 [x]S Isa 44:2 [y]S ver 7; S Jer 29:14 [z]Isa 35:9; S Jer 17:25 [a]S Isa 29:22; S 54:4; S Jer 23:4; Eze 34:25-28
30:11 [b]S Jos 1:5 [c]S Lev 26:44; S Jer 5:18; 46:28 [d]S Jer 10:24 [e]Hos 11:9; Am 9:8
30:12 [f]S Job 6:4; S Jer 10:19 [g]S Jer 8:22
30:13 [h]S Jdg 6:31 [i]S Jer 8:22; 14:19; 46:11; Na 3:19
30:14 [j]S Jer 22:20; La 1:2 [k]S Job 13:24 [l]S Job 30:21 [m]S Jer 25:7
30:15 [n]S Jer 10:19 [o]S Pr 1:31; La 1:5
30:16 [p]S Isa 29:8; S 33:1; S Jer 2:3 [q]S Isa 14:2; Joel 3:4-8 [r]Jer 49:2; 50:10
30:17 [s]S Isa 1:5; Hos 6:1 [t]S Isa 6:12; Jer 33:24 [u]Ps 142:4
30:18 [v]ver 3; S Dt 30:3; Jer 31:23; 32:44 [w]S Nu 24:5 [x]Ps 102:13; Jer 33:26; Eze 39:25 [y]Jer 31:4, 24,38; 33:7; Eze 36:10,33; Am 9:14
30:19 [z]S Ps 9:2; Isa 35:10; S 51:11 [a]S Isa 51:3 [b]Ps 126:1-2; Jer 31:4 [c]S Ge 15:5; 22:17; Jer 33:22; Eze 37:26; Zec 2:4 [d]S Isa 44:23; S 60:9
30:20 [e]Isa 54:13; Jer 31:17; Zec 8:5 [f]Isa 54:14

30:9 JESUS CHRIST, Foretold—Jeremiah lived after David, yet he promised a new David, a new King. Christians see Jesus as this new King (Jn 18:37). Just as spirituals celebrate "King Jesus," so our lives should reflect loyalty and submission to Him.

30:10–17 SIN, Punishment—Sin is an incurable sickness leading to death. God brings just judgment on sin, not letting it go unpunished. He also becomes the Great Physician, healing our incurable wounds. God's compassion means no sinner is beyond hope, but we must be willing to learn from discipline. See note on Isa 64:4–7.

30:11 GOD, Justice—All God does is just. He is present among His people to save us, but will punish us if necessary. Such punishment is deserved and just. We can be sure His punishment will not totally obliterate His people.

30:11 THE CHURCH, Remnant—God removes reason to fear from His remnant. We know His discipline is just and will eventually destroy God's enemies. His purpose is not to destroy but to save a people for Himself. Judgment is a part of God's love. He intends to bring a purified and redeemed people to Himself.

30:18 GOD, Love—God's love will ultimately be expressed when His wrath has accomplished its purpose.

30:18–22 THE CHURCH, Remnant—Thanksgiving and joy mark God's remnant. We celebrate God's mercy and compassion for us while devoting ourselves to be close to Him. The remnant is comprised of those people who have renewed covenant commitments to God. See note on Isa 4:2–6.

I will punish[g] all who oppress them.
21Their leader[h] will be one of their own;
their ruler will arise from among them.[i]
I will bring him near[j] and he will come close to me,
for who is he who will devote himself
to be close to me?'
declares the LORD.
22" 'So you will be my people,[k]
and I will be your God.[l] ' "

23See, the storm[m] of the LORD
will burst out in wrath,
a driving wind swirling down
on the heads of the wicked.
24The fierce anger[n] of the LORD will not turn back[o]
until he fully accomplishes
the purposes of his heart.
In days to come
you will understand[p] this.

Chapter 31

"AT that time," declares the LORD, "I
will be the God[q] of all the clans
of Israel, and they will be my people."
2This is what the LORD says:

"The people who survive the sword
will find favor[r] in the desert;
I will come to give rest[s] to Israel."

3The LORD appeared to us in the past,[h]
saying:

"I have loved[t] you with an everlasting love;
I have drawn[u] you with loving-kindness.
4I will build you up again
and you will be rebuilt,[v] O Virgin[w] Israel.
Again you will take up your tambourines[x]
and go out to dance[y] with the joyful.[z]
5Again you will plant[a] vineyards
on the hills of Samaria;[b]
the farmers will plant them
and enjoy their fruit.[c]
6There will be a day when watchmen[d] cry out
on the hills of Ephraim,
'Come, let us go up to Zion,
to the LORD our God.' "[e]

7This is what the LORD says:

"Sing[f] with joy for Jacob;
shout for the foremost[g] of the nations.
Make your praises heard, and say,
'O LORD, save[h] your people,
the remnant[i] of Israel.'
8See, I will bring them from the land of the north[j]
and gather[k] them from the ends of the earth.
Among them will be the blind[l] and the lame,[m]
expectant mothers and women in labor;
a great throng will return.
9They will come with weeping;[n]
they will pray as I bring them back.
I will lead[o] them beside streams of water[p]
on a level[q] path where they will not stumble,
because I am Israel's father,[r]
and Ephraim is my firstborn son.

10"Hear the word of the LORD,
O nations;
proclaim it in distant coastlands:[s]

30:20 [g]S Ex 23:22
30:21 [h]S ver 9; Jer 23:5-6 [i]Dt 17:15 [j]Nu 16:5
30:22 [k]S Isa 19:25; Hos 2:23 [l]S Lev 26:12
30:23 [m]S Jer 23:19
30:24 [n]Jer 4:8; La 1:12 [o]S Jer 4:28 [p]Jer 23:19-20
31:1 [q]S Lev 26:12
31:2 [r]Nu 14:20 [s]S Ex 33:14; S Dt 12:9
31:3 [t]S Dt 4:37 [u]Hos 11:4; Jn 6:44
31:4 [v]S Jer 1:10; S 30:18 [w]S 2Ki 19:21 [x]S Ge 31:27 [y]S Ex 15:20 [z]S Jer 30:19
31:5 [a]S Dt 20:6 [b]Jer 33:13; 50:19; Ob 1:19 [c]S Isa 37:30; Am 9:14
31:6 [d]S Isa 52:8; S 56:10 [e]ver 12; S Dt 33:19; Jer 50:4-5; Mic 4:2
31:7 [f]S Isa 12:6 [g]Dt 28:13; Isa 61:9 [h]Ps 14:7; 28:9 [i]S Isa 37:31
31:8 [j]S Jer 3:18 [k]S Ge 33:13; S Dt 30:4; S Ps 106:47; Eze 34:12-14 [l]Isa 42:16 [m]Eze 34:16; Mic 4:6
31:9 [n]S Ezr 3:12; Ps 126:5 [o]Isa 63:13 [p]S Nu 20:8; S Ps 1:3; S Isa 32:2 [q]S Isa 40:4; S 49:11 [r]S Ex 4:22; S Jer 3:4
31:10 [s]Isa 49:1; S 66:19; S Jer 25:22

[h]3 Or *LORD has appeared to us from afar*

30:22 GOD, Personal—God's intention in all His actions, both disciplining and saving, is to establish a personal relationship of commitment and love with His people. God wants to create His kind of people in this world.
30:22 THE CHURCH, Covenant People—The covenant relationship is summarized in this brief formula. God initiated the relationship in the Exodus (Ex 6:7). He worked constantly to maintain or reestablish the relationship. In the relationship with Israel and with us God promises to be the personal, caring God from whom we learn what is expected from our lives. When we accept God's promise to be our God, we commit to Him our absolute loyalty. God continues to look to the day when the relationship He desires will be perfectly realized. Compare Ex 6:7; Lev 26:12; Dt 14:1–2; 26:16–19; Jer 7:23; 11:4; 24:7; 30:22; 31:1; 31:33; 32:38; Eze 11:20; 14:11; 36:28; 37:23; 37:27; Zec 8:8; 13:9.
30:23–24 GOD, Wrath—God acts in wrath to achieve His purposes which come from a heart of love.
30:23–24 HOLY SCRIPTURE, Writing—See note on 30:1–11.
30:24 GOD, Sovereignty—See note on 18:6–17.
31:1–14 THE CHURCH, Remnant—See notes on 2 Ch 34:9; Isa 4:2–6. God's people should praise Him continually because He loves them and restores them unto Himself. The remnant exists because of God's love, not because of human qualifications or accomplishments.
31:1 THE CHURCH, Covenant People—God does not place limits on who can be part of His people. He sought to create a people Israel as His own. Rebellion brought division and then exile. Still He promised to reunite them as His people. He did not want any group excluded. He continues to work to incorporate all groups and classes of people into His church. See note on 30:22.
31:7 PRAYER, Command of God—After the stern prohibitions of 7:16; 11:14; 14:11, God called for this prayer. Israel was to rejoice loudly with the expectation of the salvation of a remnant. The prayer of praise sometimes needs to be raised for what we expect God to do in the future.
31:9,20 GOD, Father—By creation, God is Father of all peoples, but He has a special deep, fatherly interest in His people. They are His "first born" whom He created in the Exodus and whom He promised to deliver even from the punishment He imposed.
31:9 PRAYER, Thanksgiving—Participation in God's saving acts is done with tears of joy and prayers of gratitude.

'He who scattered[t] Israel will gather[u]
them
and will watch over his flock like a
shepherd.'[v]
11 For the LORD will ransom Jacob
and redeem[w] them from the hand of
those stronger[x] than they.
12 They will come and shout for joy[y] on
the heights[z] of Zion;
they will rejoice in the bounty[a] of
the LORD—
the grain, the new wine and the oil,[b]
the young of the flocks[c] and herds.
They will be like a well-watered
garden,[d]
and they will sorrow[e] no more.
13 Then maidens will dance and be glad,
young men and old as well.
I will turn their mourning[f] into
gladness;
I will give them comfort[g] and joy[h]
instead of sorrow.
14 I will satisfy[i] the priests[j] with
abundance,
and my people will be filled with my
bounty,[k]"
declares the LORD.

15 This is what the LORD says:

"A voice is heard in Ramah,[l]
mourning and great weeping,
Rachel weeping for her children
and refusing to be comforted,[m]
because her children are no
more."[n]

16 This is what the LORD says:

"Restrain your voice from weeping
and your eyes from tears,[o]
for your work will be rewarded,[p]"
declares the LORD.
"They will return[q] from the land of
the enemy.
17 So there is hope[r] for your future,"
declares the LORD.
"Your children[s] will return to their
own land.
18 "I have surely heard Ephraim's
moaning:
'You disciplined[t] me like an unruly
calf,[u]
and I have been disciplined.
Restore[v] me, and I will return,
because you are the LORD my God.
19 After I strayed,[w]
I repented;
after I came to understand,
I beat[x] my breast.
I was ashamed[y] and humiliated
because I bore the disgrace of my
youth.'[z]
20 Is not Ephraim my dear son,
the child[a] in whom I delight?
Though I often speak against him,
I still remember[b] him.
Therefore my heart yearns for him;
I have great compassion[c] for him,"
declares the LORD.

21 "Set up road signs;
put up guideposts.[d]
Take note of the highway,[e]
the road that you take.
Return,[f] O Virgin[g] Israel,
return to your towns.
22 How long will you wander,[h]
O unfaithful[i] daughter?
The LORD will create a new thing[j] on
earth—
a woman will surround[i][k] a man."

23 This is what the LORD Almighty, the
God of Israel, says: "When I bring them
back from captivity,[j][l] the people in the
land of Judah and in its towns will once
again use these words: 'The LORD bless[m]
you, O righteous dwelling,[n] O sacred
mountain.'[o] 24 People will live[p] together
in Judah and all its towns—farmers and
those who move about with their flocks.[q]
25 I will refresh the weary[r] and satisfy the
faint."[s]
26 At this I awoke[t] and looked around.
My sleep had been pleasant to me.
27 "The days are coming,"[u] declares
the LORD, "when I will plant[v] the house
of Israel and the house of Judah with the
offspring of men and of animals. 28 Just as
I watched[w] over them to uproot[x] and
tear down, and to overthrow, destroy and
bring disaster,[y] so I will watch over them
to build and to plant,"[z] declares the
LORD. 29 "In those days people will no longer say,

31:10 [t]S Lev 26:33 [u]S Dt 30:4; S Isa 11:12; Jer 50:19 [v]Isa 40:11; Eze 34:12 **31:11** [w]S Ex 6:6; Zec 9:16 [x]Ps 142:6 **31:12** [y]S Ps 126:5 [z]Eze 17:23; 20:40; 40:2; Mic 4:1 [a]S Ps 36:8; Joel 3:18 [b]S Nu 18:12; Hos 2:21-22; Joel 2:19 [c]ver 24; S Isa 65:10 [d]S SS 4:15 [e]S Isa 30:19; S 62:5; Jn 16:22; S Rev 7:17 **31:13** [f]S Isa 61:3 [g]S Isa 40:1 [h]Ps 30:11; S Isa 51:11 **31:14** [i]ver 25 [j]Lev 7:35-36 [k]S Ps 36:8; S Isa 30:23 **31:15** [l]S Jos 18:25 [m]S Ge 37:35 [n]S Jer 10:20; Mt 2:17-18* **31:16** [o]S Ps 30:5; S Isa 25:8; 30:19 [p]S Ru 2:12; S 2Ch 15:7 [q]Jer 30:3; Eze 11:17 **31:17** [r]S Job 8:7; La 3:29 [s]S Jer 30:20 **31:18** [t]S Job 5:17 [u]Jer 50:11; Hos 4:16; 10:11 [v]S Ps 80:3 **31:19** [w]S Ps 95:10; S Jer 8:4; Eze 36:31 [x]Eze 21:12; Lk 18:13 [y]Ezr 9:6 [z]S Ps 25:7; S Jer 22:21 **31:20** [a]La 3:33 [b]S Isa 44:21 [c]S 1Ki 3:26; S Ps 6:2; Isa 55:7; Mic 7:18 **31:21** [d]Eze 21:19 [e]Isa 35:8; Jer 50:5 [f]Isa 52:11; S Jer 3:12 [g]ver 4 **31:22** [h]S Jer 2:23 [i]S Jer 3:6 [j]Isa 43:19 [k]S Dt 32:10 **31:23** [l]S Jer 30:18 [m]S Ge 28:3; S Nu 6:24 [n]S Isa 1:26 [o]S Ps 48:1; S Isa 2:2 **31:24** [p]S Jer 30:18; Zec 8:4-8 [q]S ver 12 **31:25** [r]S Isa 40:29 [s]Jn 4:14 **31:26** [t]Zec 4:1 **31:27** [u]S Jer 16:14 [v]Hos 2:23 **31:28** [w]S Job 29:2 [x]S Dt 29:28 [y]S Jer 18:8 [z]S Dt 28:63; S 30:9; S Jer 1:10; Eze 36:10-11; Am 9:14

[i]22 Or *will go about ⌊seeking⌋;* or *will protect*
[j]23 Or *I restore their fortunes*

31:15 JESUS CHRIST, Foretold—In the midst of Israel's desolation, God promised hope (v 16). After the birth of Jesus, Herod's slaughter of the innocents recapitulated the agony of the crisis of Israel (Mt 2:18).
31:20 SALVATION, Remembrance—God's salvation is remembrance. Israel is like a beloved child to God. He can never forget them. It is His remembrance of them, and their remembrance of Him, which brings restoration. Memory, both God's and ours, plays a large role in salvation.
31:27–30 ELECTION, Free Will—Election does not bind a person to the fate of the family. Parents cannot be blamed for an individual's punishment. God calls for individual, personal accountability for life before Him.
31:29–30 EVIL AND SUFFERING, Deserved—See note on Eze 18:1–32. Suffering cannot be blamed on our ancestors. Their sin and evil have left us in an environment which is far from perfect and may encourage the growth of evil and suffering. We have received from them a nature prone to sin. We, however, freely choose to sin and add to the suffering and wickedness in the world. We are not innocent.
31:29–30 HUMANITY, Death and Sin—Whom can I blame for my problems? Israel wanted to blame earlier

'The fathers[a] have eaten sour grapes,
and the children's teeth are set on edge.'[b]

30Instead, everyone will die for his own
sin;[c] whoever eats sour grapes—his own
teeth will be set on edge.

31"The time is coming," declares the LORD,
"when I will make a new covenant[d]
with the house of Israel
and with the house of Judah.
32It will not be like the covenant[e]
I made with their forefathers[f]
when I took them by the hand
to lead them out of Egypt,[g]
because they broke my covenant,
though I was a husband[h] to[k] them,[l] "
declares the LORD.
33"This is the covenant I will make with
the house of Israel
after that time," declares the LORD.
"I will put my law in their minds[i]
and write it on their hearts.[j]
I will be their God,
and they will be my people.[k]
34No longer will a man teach[l] his neighbor,
or a man his brother, saying, 'Know the LORD,'
because they will all know[m] me,
from the least of them to the greatest,"
declares the LORD.
"For I will forgive[n] their wickedness
and will remember their sins[o] no more."

35This is what the LORD says,

he who appoints[p] the sun
to shine by day,
who decrees the moon and stars
to shine by night,[q]
who stirs up the sea[r]
so that its waves roar[s]—
the LORD Almighty is his name:[t]
36"Only if these decrees[u] vanish from my sight,"
declares the LORD,
"will the descendants[v] of Israel ever cease
to be a nation before me."

37This is what the LORD says:

"Only if the heavens above can be measured[w]
and the foundations of the earth below be searched out

31:29 [a]S Ge 9:25; Dt 24:16; La 5:7 [b]Eze 18:2
31:30 [c]S 2Ki 14:6; S Isa 3:11; Gal 6:7
31:31 [d]S Dt 29:14; S Isa 42:6; S 54:10; S Lk 22:20; Heb 8:8-12*; 10:16-17
31:32 [e]S Ex 24:8 [f]Dt 5:3 [g]Jer 11:4 [h]S Isa 54:5
31:33 [i]S Ex 4:15 [j]S Dt 6:6; S 2Co 3:3 [k]S Jer 11:4; Heb 10:16
31:34 [l]1Jn 2:27 [m]S Isa 11:9; S Jn 6:45 [n]Ps 85:2; 130:4; Jer 33:8; 50:20 [o]S Job 7:21; S Isa 38:17; Mic 7:19; Heb 10:17*
31:35 [p]Ps 136:7-9 [q]S Ge 1:16 [r]S Ex 14:21 [s]S Ps 93:3 [t]S Jer 10:16
31:36 [u]S Job 38:33; Jer 33:20-26 [v]Ps 89:36-37
31:37 [w]S Job 38:5; Jer 33:22

[k]32 Hebrew; Septuagint and Syriac */ and I turned away from* [l]32 Or *was their master*

generations. Some may want to go all the way back to Adam and Eve, the first sinners. Certainly an individual's sin affects the entire community, and we learn sin from the early generation's example. We cannot, however, blame our punishment for sin on anyone else. I have sinned. I deserve to die. See Ge 2:17; Jos 7:1–26.

31:31–34 JESUS CHRIST, Foretold—The new covenant promised by Jeremiah was fulfilled by the death of Jesus (Mt 26:28; 1 Co 11:25). It was promised at the last supper and instituted at the cross. The author of Hebrews rejoiced in the new covenant (10:15–17). We Christians continue to celebrate God's new covenant in Jesus Christ each time we share the Lord's Supper. In so doing, we remember Him and renew our vows to Him.

31:31–34 THE CHURCH, Covenant People—God has worked since creation to create a people for whom He can truly be related as their God. See note on 30:22. He worked through the masses of humanity, narrowed His work to the individual patriarchs, and then created the nation Israel, which soon divided. With the nation He created the old covenant, centering on community worship and community dedication to the covenant obligations. Each individual was responsible to God and could be excluded from the community for being unfaithful to God's covenant, but the emphasis on the community continued. Israel made the new covenant necessary because of their refusal to abide by the obligations they accepted under the old covenant. Making prophetic promises, God prepared the way for the new covenant relationship with His people based on the renewal of their inner will and desires (Isa 61:8; Eze 11:19–21; 16:60–63; 37:24–28; Heb 8:8–12; 10:16–17). Jesus formally instituted the new covenant during the Last Supper (Lk 22:20). The new covenant reemphasized God's desire to form a people who would let Him be Master of their lives. It also included obligations which covenant members accept. The new covenant has at least four radically new elements: (1) The instructions or law which make up the covenant obligations are no longer external documents taught by human teachers; they are internal desires of the transformed heart. (2) The new covenant is not restricted to one nation or worship community; all people are invited to know God in a personal, experiential way. (3) The new covenant is offered to individuals who can know God's personal forgiveness rather than emphasizing the nation as a worshiping community. (4) Forgiveness by God rather than covenant renewal by people stands at the center of the new covenant. God forgets our sins. This was made possible by Jesus, God's Son, through His life, death, and resurrection. He fulfilled the obligations of the old covenant and opened the door of forgiveness to the new. This brought two divisions to God's inspired Word—the Old and New Testaments.

31:33 GOD, Personal—God is a personal God entering into intimate relationships with His people. Because His people would not maintain that relationship through the Sinai covenant, He promised to initiate a new covenant which would change their hearts. This He did through the saving work of Jesus. See notes on Ex 3:12–16; Mt 18:10–14.

31:33–37 ELECTION, Faithfulness—The new covenant with the new Israel is as secure as the created order of the heavens. God used a remnant of Israel after the Exile to establish permanently His purpose of election, the creation of a truly obedient people. God punishes but does not abandon His elect.

31:33 CHRISTIAN ETHICS, Moral Imperatives—The picture of the new covenant for Jeremiah parallels the working of the Holy Spirit as described by Jesus in Jn 14:26. Moral imperatives do not form an arbitrary checklist for God to use to punish. Nor are they a minimum standard we use to see if we are still making passing grades with God. Moral imperatives are seeds God plants in our hearts to let us grow and realize the potential He created in us.

31:34 SALVATION, Knowledge of God—Universal knowledge of God was promised in God's new covenant with His people. Such knowledge is possible only where forgiveness abounds. Compare Heb 8:7–13.

31:35–37 GOD, Creator—The Creator promises to exercise sovereign protection over His people until the very order He created quits functioning. Only He can stop it.

will I reject[x] all the descendants of
Israel
because of all they have done,"
declares the LORD.
[38]"The days are coming," declares the
LORD, "when this city will be rebuilt[y] for
me from the Tower of Hananel[z] to the
Corner Gate.[a] [39]The measuring line[b]
will stretch from there straight to the hill
of Gareb and then turn to Goah. [40]The
whole valley[c] where dead bodies[d] and
ashes are thrown, and all the terraces out
to the Kidron Valley[e] on the east as far as
the corner of the Horse Gate,[f] will be
holy[g] to the LORD. The city will never
again be uprooted or demolished."

Chapter 32

Jeremiah Buys a Field

THIS is the word that came to Jeremiah
from the LORD in the tenth[h] year of
Zedekiah king of Judah, which was the
eighteenth[i] year of Nebuchadnezzar.
[2]The army of the king of Babylon was
then besieging[j] Jerusalem, and Jeremiah
the prophet was confined[k] in the courtyard of the guard[l] in the royal palace of
Judah.
[3]Now Zedekiah king of Judah had imprisoned him there, saying, "Why do you
prophesy[m] as you do? You say, 'This is
what the LORD says: I am about to hand
this city over to the king of Babylon, and
he will capture[n] it. [4]Zedekiah[o] king of
Judah will not escape[p] out of the hands
of the Babylonians[m][q] but will certainly
be handed over to the king of Babylon,
and will speak with him face to face and
see him with his own eyes. [5]He will
take[r] Zedekiah to Babylon, where he will
remain until I deal with him,[s] declares
the LORD. If you fight against the Babylonians, you will not succeed.' "[t]

31:37 [x]Jer 33:24-26; Ro 11:1-5
31:38 [y]S Jer 30:18 [z]S Ne 3:1 [a]S 2Ki 14:13; S 2Ch 25:23
31:39 [b]S 1Ki 7:23
31:40 [c]S Jer 2:23; 7:31-32 [d]S Jer 8:2 [e]S 2Sa 15:23; Jn 18:1 [f]S 2Ki 11:16 [g]S Isa 4:3; Joel 3:17; Zec 14:21
32:1 [h]2Ki 25:1 [i]Jer 25:1
32:2 [j]S 2Ki 25:1 [k]S Ps 88:8 [l]S Ne 3:25
32:3 [m]Jer 26:8-9 [n]ver 28; Jer 21:4; 34:2-3
32:4 [o]Jer 34:21; 44:30 [p]S Jer 21:7; 38:18,23; 39:5-7; 52:9 [q]ver 24
32:5 [r]Jer 39:7; Eze 12:13 [s]S 2Ki 25:7 [t]Jer 21:4; La 1:14
32:7 [u]S Jos 21:18 [v]Lev 25:24-25; S Ru 4:3-4; Mt 27:10*
32:8 [w]ver 25
32:9 [x]Jer 37:12 [y]S Ge 23:16
32:10 [z]Ge 23:20 [a]S Ru 4:9; S Isa 8:2
32:12 [b]ver 16; Jer 36:4; 43:3,6; 45:1 [c]Jer 51:59
32:14 [d]S Isa 8:16
32:15 [e]ver 43-44; Isa 44:26; Jer 30:18; Eze 28:26; Am 9:14-15
32:16 [f]S ver 12
32:17 [g]Jer 1:6 [h]S Ge 1:1; S Jer 10:16

[6]Jeremiah said, "The word of the LORD
came to me: [7]Hanamel son of Shallum
your uncle is going to come to you and
say, 'Buy my field at Anathoth,[u] because
as nearest relative it is your right and
duty[v] to buy it.'
[8]"Then, just as the LORD had said, my
cousin Hanamel came to me in the courtyard of the guard and said, 'Buy my field[w]
at Anathoth in the territory of Benjamin.
Since it is your right to redeem it and
possess it, buy it for yourself.'
"I knew that this was the word of the
LORD; [9]so I bought the field[x] at Anathoth
from my cousin Hanamel and weighed
out for him seventeen shekels[n] of silver.[y] [10]I signed and sealed the deed,[z]
had it witnessed,[a] and weighed out the
silver on the scales. [11]I took the deed of
purchase—the sealed copy containing
the terms and conditions, as well as the
unsealed copy— [12]and I gave this deed to
Baruch[b] son of Neriah,[c] the son of Mahseiah, in the presence of my cousin Hanamel and of the witnesses who had signed
the deed and of all the Jews sitting in the
courtyard of the guard.
[13]"In their presence I gave Baruch
these instructions: [14]'This is what the
LORD Almighty, the God of Israel, says:
Take these documents, both the sealed[d]
and unsealed copies of the deed of purchase, and put them in a clay jar so they
will last a long time. [15]For this is what the
LORD Almighty, the God of Israel, says:
Houses, fields and vineyards will again be
bought in this land.'[e]
[16]"After I had given the deed of purchase to Baruch[f] son of Neriah, I prayed
to the LORD:

[17]"Ah, Sovereign LORD,[g] you have
made the heavens and the earth[h] by

[m]4 Or *Chaldeans*; also in verses 5, 24, 25, 28, 29 and 43 [n]9 That is, about 7 ounces (about 200 grams)

32:1–5,16–44 GOD, Sovereignty—God, the ruler of the universe, has power and freedom to hand the king of His people over to the enemy. He can also fulfill His promise to restore His people. God has power and authority to do whatever He desires. Both creation and history prove this.

32:6–15 REVELATION, Actions—The prophet followed instructions which became symbolic of God's hope and plans for Judah. A purchased field represented God's vote of confidence in their future after destruction and His revealed purposes for His people. The land would again be the home of the children of God. Prophets frequently acted out their messages symbolically rather than simply preaching them. Compare 13:1–11; 16:1–4,5–7,8–9; 19:1–11; 27:2–7,10–12; 28:10–11; 1 Sa 15:27–28; 1 Ki 11:30–32; 2 Ki 13:15–19; Isa 7:3; 8:1–4; 20:1–6; Hos 1:1–9; 3:1–5.

32:15,37,42–44 SALVATION, Renewal—Compare 31:4, 16–17,23–25. When God renews His people, they experience new prosperity and peace. His restoration gives us a new start.

32:16–25 HISTORY, Judgment—History reveals the complex nature of God's relationship with His people. God can do whatever He chooses in history. He shows mercy but also punishes. He works both with nations and individuals. History points to His saving acts, but the present often reveals His judgment. His saving acts gain fame for Him among all nations, yet He is willing to turn from saving acts to disciplining acts. The continuity in the complexity comes in God's working out His purpose to create a holy, obedient people for Himself.

32:16–27 PRAYER, Faith—Prayer expresses faith in God even when we do not understand current events. Jeremiah's purchase of land in view of the imminent fall to Babylon would be foolish without an understanding of the power of the Lord to do the seemingly impossible in restoring the land to Israel (30:3). He began his prayer with an important declaration that nothing is too hard for the Lord. The prayer praised the great power of the Lord and confessed the nation's disobedience. God validated Jeremiah's understanding.

32:17–23 MIRACLE, Faith—Miracles teach us the nature of God, His power and love. They give reason to pray to Him in our need. Past marvelous works were a part of the nation's faith and served as examples for the prophet's prayer requests. Miraculous examples pointed to God's creation, redemption, and judgment. A balanced faith may call on God in time of need. See note on 21:2.

your great power and outstretched
arm.[i] Nothing is too hard[j] for you.
18You show love[k] to thousands but
bring the punishment for the fathers'
sins into the laps[l] of their children[m]
after them. O great and powerful
God,[n] whose name is the LORD Almighty,[o] 19great are your purposes
and mighty are your deeds.[p] Your
eyes are open to all the ways of
men;[q] you reward everyone according to his conduct and as his deeds
deserve.[r] 20You performed miraculous signs and wonders[s] in Egypt[t]
and have continued them to this day,
both in Israel and among all mankind, and have gained the renown[u]
that is still yours. 21You brought your
people Israel out of Egypt with signs
and wonders, by a mighty hand[v] and
an outstretched arm[w] and with great
terror.[x] 22You gave them this land
you had sworn to give their forefathers, a land flowing with milk and
honey.[y] 23They came in and took
possession[z] of it, but they did not
obey you or follow your law;[a] they
did not do what you commanded
them to do. So you brought all this
disaster[b] upon them.

24"See how the siege ramps[c] are
built up to take the city. Because of
the sword, famine and plague,[d] the
city will be handed over to the Babylonians who are attacking it. What
you said[e] has happened,[f] as you
now see. 25And though the city will
be handed over to the Babylonians,
you, O Sovereign LORD, say to me,
'Buy the field[g] with silver and have
the transaction witnessed.[h]' "

26Then the word of the LORD came to
Jeremiah: 27"I am the LORD, the God of
all mankind.[i] Is anything too hard for
me?[j] 28Therefore, this is what the LORD
says: I am about to hand this city over to
the Babylonians and to Nebuchadnezzar[k]
king of Babylon, who will capture it.[l]
29The Babylonians who are attacking this
city will come in and set it on fire; they
will burn it down,[m] along with the
houses[n] where the people provoked me
to anger by burning incense on the roofs
to Baal and by pouring out drink offerings[o] to other gods.[p]

30"The people of Israel and Judah have
done nothing but evil in my sight from
their youth;[q] indeed, the people of Israel
have done nothing but provoke[r] me with
what their hands have made,[s] declares
the LORD. 31From the day it was built until now, this city[t] has so aroused my anger and wrath that I must remove[u] it
from my sight. 32The people of Israel and
Judah have provoked[v] me by all the evil[w]
they have done—they, their kings and officials,[x] their priests and prophets, the
men of Judah and the people of Jerusalem. 33They turned their backs[y] to me
and not their faces; though I taught[z]
them again and again, they would not listen or respond to discipline.[a] 34They set
up their abominable idols[b] in the house
that bears my Name[c] and defiled[d] it.
35They built high places for Baal in the
Valley of Ben Hinnom[e] to sacrifice their
sons and daughters° to Molech,[f] though
I never commanded, nor did it enter my
mind,[g] that they should do such a detestable[h] thing and so make Judah sin.[i]

36"You are saying about this city, 'By
the sword, famine and plague[j] it will be

32:17 iS Dt 9:29; 2Ki 19:15; Ps 102:25 jS 2Ki 3:18; Jer 51:15; S Mt 19:26 **32:18** kS Dt 5:10 lS Ps 79:12 mS Ex 20:5; S Ps 109:14 nJer 10:6 oS Jer 10:16 **32:19** pS Job 12:13; Da 2:20 qS Job 14:16; S Pr 5:21; Jer 16:17 rS Job 34:11; S Mt 16:27 **32:20** sS Ex 3:20; S Job 9:10 tEx 9:16 uS Isa 55:13; S Jer 13:11 **32:21** vS Ex 6:6; Da 9:15 wS Dt 5:15; S Jer 6:12 xS Dt 26:8 **32:22** yS Ex 3:8; Eze 20:6 **32:23** zS Ps 44:2; 78:54-55 aS Ex 16:28; S Jos 1:7; S 1Ki 9:6; S Jer 11:8 bS Dt 28:64; 31:29; Da 9:14 **32:24** cS 2Sa 20:15; S Jer 6:6 dS Jer 14:12 eDt 4:25-26; Jos 23:15-16 fS Dt 28:2 **32:25** gS ver 8 hS Isa 8:2 **32:27** iS Nu 16:22 jS Ge 18:14; S 2Ki 3:18 **32:28** kS 2Ch 36:17 lS ver 3; S Jer 21:10 **32:29** mS 2Ch 36:19 nS Jer 19:13 oJer 44:18 pS Jer 7:9 **32:30** qS Ps 25:7; S Jer 22:21 rJer 8:19 sJer 25:7 **32:31** t1Ki 11:7-8; 2Ki 21:4-5; Mt 23:37 uS 2Ki 23:27 **32:32** vS 1Ki 14:9 wDa 9:8 xS Jer 2:26; S 44:9

32:33 yS 1Ki 14:9; S Ps 14:3; Jer 2:27; Eze 8:16; Zec 7:11 zS Dt 4:5; S Isa 28:9; S Jer 7:13 aS Jer 7:28 **32:34** bS 2Ki 21:4; Eze 8:3-16 cJer 7:10; 34:15 dS Jer 7:30 **32:35** eJer 19:2 fS Lev 18:21 gS Jer 19:5 hS 1Ki 14:24 iS Jer 25:7 **32:36** jver 24

°35 Or *to make their sons and daughters pass through the fire*

32:18 HUMANITY, Family Relationships—We face death, the ultimate punishment for sin, strictly because of our own sins. Still, the sins of parents do affect their children. We have to live in the environment our parents create. See note on 31:29–30.

32:19 SALVATION, Grace—God's purposes for humankind are not stingy and narrow. They are governed by His righteousness and grace.

32:29,37 GOD, Wrath—See notes on 21:4–7,12; 30:18.

32:29–35 SIN, Discipline—Sin is creative, devising evil which never entered God's mind. The ways we find to divert worship from the Creator to the created seem limitless. Such creative sin stretches God's patience to the breaking point. When we do not accept and learn from His discipline, He finally intervenes in a horribly creative way to destroy.

32:33 EDUCATION, God—Even when God Himself was their Teacher, the children of Judah failed to learn. God's teaching included punishment and discipline for His people. Even divine discipline failed. What more forceful way to illustrate the necessity of the learner's willing participation in the teaching-learning transaction? When we resist learning, no one can teach us.

32:36–44 ELECTION, Faithfulness—God assured Jeremiah of days when His punishment of His elect would cease. Peaceful days would follow calamity. The end of judgment would become the guarantee of future restoration. A new and everlasting covenant would be established. God's elect would return to Jerusalem. The deed of Jeremiah's property purchase that was placed in an earthen vessel and given to Baruch would be redeemed by Jeremiah's heirs. Nothing is impossible for the God of election who redeems His elect. He is faithful to do good for His elect and to establish His purpose of creating a faithful people. The elect are those devoted to God in singleness of heart and action.

32:36–41 THE CHURCH, Covenant People—God wants His people to obey and serve Him. By giving singleness of heart and way, God gives His people the desire to do righteousness. Fearing God does not imply cringing in terror but living in awe and reverence before the Lord. Wrath, punishment, and anger are not God's final words to His people. God's promises are everlasting. He desires that we live in relationship with Him forever, letting Him be God and never turning away from Him. See note on 31:31–34.

handed over to the king of Babylon'; but
this is what the LORD, the God of Israel,
says: 37 I will surely gather[k] them from all
the lands where I banish them in my furious anger[l] and great wrath; I will bring
them back to this place and let them live
in safety.[m] 38 They will be my people,[n]
and I will be their God. 39 I will give them
singleness[o] of heart and action, so that
they will always fear[p] me for their own
good and the good of their children after
them. 40 I will make an everlasting covenant[q] with them: I will never stop doing good to them, and I will inspire[r]
them to fear me, so that they will never
turn away from me.[s] 41 I will rejoice[t] in
doing them good[u] and will assuredly
plant[v] them in this land with all my heart
and soul.[w]

42 "This is what the LORD says: As I
have brought all this great calamity[x] on
this people, so I will give them all the
prosperity I have promised[y] them.
43 Once more fields will be bought[z] in
this land of which you say, 'It is a desolate[a] waste, without men or animals, for
it has been handed over to the Babylonians.' 44 Fields will be bought for silver,
and deeds[b] will be signed, sealed and
witnessed[c] in the territory of Benjamin,
in the villages around Jerusalem, in the
towns of Judah and in the towns of the
hill country, of the western foothills and
of the Negev,[d] because I will restore[e]
their fortunes,[p] declares the LORD."

Chapter 33

Promise of Restoration

WHILE Jeremiah was still confined[f]
in the courtyard[g] of the guard, the
word of the LORD came to him a second
time:[h] 2 "This is what the LORD says, he
who made the earth,[i] the LORD who
formed it and established it—the LORD is
his name:[j] 3 'Call[k] to me and I will answer you and tell you great and unsearchable[l] things you do not know.' 4 For this
is what the LORD, the God of Israel, says

32:37 [k]S Isa 11:12 [l]Jer 21:5 [m]S Lev 25:18; Eze 34:28; 39:26 **32:38** [n]Jer 24:7; 2Co 6:16* **32:39** [o]S 2Ch 30:12; S Ps 86:11; Jn 17:21; Ac 4:32 [p]S Dt 6:24; S 10:16 **32:40** [q]S Ge 9:16; S Isa 42:6 [r]S Dt 4:10 [s]S Jer 24:7 **32:41** [t]S Dt 28:63; S Isa 62:4 [u]S Dt 28:3-12 [v]Jer 24:6; 31:28 [w]Mic 7:18 **32:42** [x]La 3:38 [y]S Jer 29:10 **32:43** [z]ver 15 [a]Jer 33:12 **32:44** [b]ver 10 [c]S Ru 4:9; S Isa 8:2 [d]S Jer 17:26 [e]S Ezr 9:9; Ps 14:7 **33:1** [f]S Ps 88:8 [g]Jer 37:21; 38:28 [h]Jer 13:3 **33:2** [i]S Ps 136:6; S Jer 10:16 [j]S Ex 3:15 **33:3** [k]S Isa 55:6 [l]S Job 28:11 **33:4** [m]S 2Ki 25:1; Eze 4:2 [n]Jer 32:24; Eze 26:8; Hab 1:10 **33:5** [o]Jer 21:4-7 [p]S Dt 31:17; S Isa 8:17 **33:6** [q]S Dt 32:39; S Isa 30:26 [r]S Isa 9:6 **33:7** [s]Jer 32:44 [t]Jer 30:3; Eze 39:25; Am 9:14 [u]S Jer 24:6 [v]S Isa 1:26 **33:8** [w]S Lev 16:30; Heb 9:13-14 [x]S 2Sa 24:14; S Jer 31:34 **33:9** [y]S Isa 55:13 [z]S Isa 60:18 [a]S Jer 3:17 [b]S Isa 64:2 **33:10** [c]Jer 32:43 [d]S Lev 26:32; S Jer 9:11 **33:11** [e]S Ps 51:8; S Isa 24:8; S 51:3 [f]S Lev 7:12 [g]S 2Ch 7:3; Ps 25:8; S 136:1; Na 1:7 [h]S 1Ch 16:34; 2Ch 5:13; Ps 100:4-5 [i]Ps 14:7 [j]S Isa 1:26 **33:12** [k]Jer 32:43 [l]ver 10

about the houses in this city and the royal
palaces of Judah that have been torn
down to be used against the siege[m]
ramps[n] and the sword 5 in the fight with
the Babylonians[q]: 'They will be filled
with the dead bodies of the men I will
slay in my anger and wrath.[o] I will hide
my face[p] from this city because of all its
wickedness.

6 " 'Nevertheless, I will bring health
and healing to it; I will heal[q] my people
and will let them enjoy abundant peace[r]
and security. 7 I will bring Judah[s] and Israel back from captivity[r][t] and will rebuild[u] them as they were before.[v] 8 I will
cleanse[w] them from all the sin they have
committed against me and will forgive[x]
all their sins of rebellion against me.
9 Then this city will bring me renown,[y]
joy, praise[z] and honor[a] before all nations on earth that hear of all the good
things I do for it; and they will be in awe
and will tremble[b] at the abundant prosperity and peace I provide for it.'

10 "This is what the LORD says: 'You say
about this place, "It is a desolate waste,
without men or animals."[c] Yet in the
towns of Judah and the streets of Jerusalem that are deserted,[d] inhabited by neither men nor animals, there will be heard
once more 11 the sounds of joy and gladness,[e] the voices of bride and bridegroom, and the voices of those who bring
thank offerings[f] to the house of the
LORD, saying,

"Give thanks to the LORD Almighty,
for the LORD is good;[g]
his love endures forever."[h]

For I will restore the fortunes[i] of the
land as they were before,[j] says the
LORD.

12 "This is what the LORD Almighty
says: 'In this place, desolate[k] and without men or animals[l]—in all its towns

[p]44 Or *will bring them back from captivity* [q]5 Or *Chaldeans* [r]7 Or *will restore the fortunes of Judah and Israel*

32:39 CHRISTIAN ETHICS, Character—Integrity of character can be marked by one's sense of purpose in life. Is this purpose of a single strand, that is, seeking the will of God? Or, does it reflect a fragmentation, going off in many directions? Singleness of heart and action after God's purposes reveal one in whom God is working His grace.
32:42 HISTORY, National—See note on Isa 1:24–26.
33:1–9 CHRISTIAN ETHICS, War and Peace—God's intention is to bring peace to His people. At times He must act in wrath and judgment to discipline and purify His people before He can act to bring peace. Peace involves a secure homeland, a cleansed, forgiven people dedicated to God's glory instead of their own, and a life of prosperity and meaning. Peace attracts attention from all nations. See note on Ps 34:14.
33:2 GOD, Creator—The Creator God wants to reveal His great plans to His people, but first we must call on Him in prayer.
33:3 HUMANITY, Relationship to God—The relationship between God and people becomes real through prayer.
33:3 PRAYER, Faithfulness of God—See notes on Ge 4:26; Eph 3:20–21. God constantly reassures of His willingness to provide answers beyond human understanding. We need only ask.
33:6–9 EVANGELISM, God's Provision—All that God provides in salvation is glorious beyond description. The "good things" and "abundant prosperity" of redemption cause multitudes to turn to Christ and share in those wonders. Evangelism means telling people of God's wonderful provision of salvation.
33:8 SALVATION, As Cleansing—God cleanses His people from guilt and rebellion. Forgiveness accompanies His cleansing. The doctrine of salvation teaches that God does not give up on His people when they go astray.
33:11,26 GOD, Goodness—See note on Ps 100:5.

before the men of the Recabite family and
said to them, "Drink some wine."
6But they replied, "We do not drink
wine, because our forefather Jonadab[m]
son of Recab gave us this command: 'Neither you nor your descendants must ever
drink wine.[n] 7Also you must never build
houses, sow seed or plant vineyards; you
must never have any of these things, but
must always live in tents.[o] Then you will
live a long time in the land[p] where you
are nomads.' 8We have obeyed everything our forefather[q] Jonadab son of Recab commanded us. Neither we nor our
wives nor our sons and daughters have
ever drunk wine 9or built houses to live
in or had vineyards, fields or crops.[r]
10We have lived in tents and have fully
obeyed everything our forefather Jonadab
commanded us. 11But when Nebuchadnezzar king of Babylon invaded[s] this
land, we said, 'Come, we must go to Jerusalem[t] to escape the Babylonian[w] and
Aramean armies.' So we have remained
in Jerusalem."
12Then the word of the LORD came to
Jeremiah, saying: 13"This is what the
LORD Almighty, the God of Israel, says:
Go and tell[u] the men of Judah and the
people of Jerusalem, 'Will you not learn a
lesson[v] and obey my words?' declares
the LORD. 14'Jonadab son of Recab ordered his sons not to drink wine and this
command has been kept. To this day they
do not drink wine, because they obey
their forefather's command.[w] But I have
spoken to you again and again,[x] yet you
have not obeyed[y] me. 15Again and again
I sent all my servants the prophets[z] to
you. They said, "Each of you must turn[a]
from your wicked ways and reform[b] your
actions; do not follow other gods[c] to
serve them. Then you will live in the
land[d] I have given to you and your fathers." But you have not paid attention or
listened[e] to me. 16The descendants of
Jonadab son of Recab have carried out the
command their forefather[f] gave them,
but these people have not obeyed me.'
17"Therefore, this is what the LORD
God Almighty, the God of Israel, says:
'Listen! I am going to bring on Judah and
on everyone living in Jerusalem every disaster[g] I pronounced against them. I
spoke to them, but they did not listen;[h] I
called to them, but they did not answer.'"[i]
18Then Jeremiah said to the family of
the Recabites, "This is what the LORD Almighty, the God of Israel, says: 'You have
obeyed the command of your forefather[j]
Jonadab and have followed all his instructions and have done everything he ordered.' 19Therefore, this is what the LORD
Almighty, the God of Israel, says: 'Jonadab son of Recab will never fail[k] to have
a man to serve[l] me.'"

Chapter 36

Jehoiakim Burns Jeremiah's Scroll

IN the fourth year of Jehoiakim[m] son of
Josiah king of Judah, this word came to
Jeremiah from the LORD: 2"Take a scroll[n]
and write on it all the words[o] I have spoken to you concerning Israel, Judah and
all the other nations from the time I began speaking to you in the reign of Josiah[p] till now. 3Perhaps[q] when the people
of Judah hear[r] about every disaster I plan
to inflict on them, each of them will
turn[s] from his wicked way; then I will
forgive[t] their wickedness and their sin."
4So Jeremiah called Baruch[u] son of Neriah,[v] and while Jeremiah dictated[w] all
the words the LORD had spoken to him,
Baruch wrote them on the scroll.[x] 5Then
Jeremiah told Baruch, "I am restricted; I
cannot go to the LORD's temple. 6So you
go to the house of the LORD on a day of
fasting[y] and read to the people from the
scroll the words of the LORD that you
wrote as I dictated.[z] Read them to all the
people of Judah[a] who come in from their
towns. 7Perhaps they will bring their petition[b] before the LORD, and each will
turn[c] from his wicked ways, for the anger[d] and wrath pronounced against this
people by the LORD are great."
8Baruch son of Neriah did everything
Jeremiah the prophet told him to do; at
the LORD's temple he read the words of
the LORD from the scroll. 9In the ninth

[w]11 Or *Chaldean*

35:6 [m]S 2Ki 10:15 [n]S Lev 10:9; Nu 6:2-4; S Lk 1:15
35:7 [o]Heb 11:9 [p]S Ex 20:12; Eph 6:2-3
35:8 [q]Pr 1:8; Col 3:20
35:9 [r]1Ti 6:6
35:11 [s]2Ki 24:1 [t]S Jos 10:20; Jer 8:14
35:13 [u]Jer 11:6 [v]Jer 6:10; 32:33
35:14 [w]ver 6-10,16 [x]S Jer 7:13 [y]Isa 30:9
35:15 [z]S Jer 7:25 [a]S 2Ki 17:13; S Jer 26:3 [b]S Isa 1:16-17; S 59:20; Jer 4:1; 18:11; Eze 14:6; 18:30 [c]S Ex 20:3 [d]S Dt 4:40; Jer 25:5 [e]S Jer 6:10; S 7:26; 44:4-5
35:16 [f]S Lev 20:9; Mal 1:6
35:17 [g]S Jos 23:15; S 1Ki 13:34; Jer 21:4-7 [h]S Pr 1:24; Ro 10:21 [i]Jer 7:13
35:18 [j]S Ge 31:35
35:19 [k]S Isa 48:19; Jer 33:17 [l]Jer 15:19
36:1 [m]S 2Ch 36:5
36:2 [n]S ver 4; S Ex 17:14; S Ps 40:7; Jer 30:2; Hab 2:2 [o]Eze 2:7 [p]Jer 1:2; 25:3
36:3 [q]ver 7; Eze 12:3; Am 5:15 [r]Isa 6:9; Mk 4:12 [s]S 2Ki 17:13; S Isa 44:22; S Jer 26:3; Ac 3:19 [t]S Jer 18:8
36:4 [u]S Jer 32:12 [v]Jer 51:59 [w]ver 18 [x]ver 2; Eze 2:9; Da 7:1; Zec 5:1
36:6 [y]ver 9 [z]S Ex 4:16 [a]2Ch 20:4
36:7 [b]Jer 37:20; 42:2 [c]S Jer 26:3 [d]S Dt 31:17

35:14–15 SIN, Transgression—Obedience is possible. People do not have to sin. The Recabites had been obedient to their forefathers' command to abstain from wine. How much easier should it be for God's children to keep His commands, especially when He sent prophets to help. Sin is refusing to do the possible. See 2 Ki 10:15–16.

35:15 REVELATION, Messengers—See note on 6:10–11. Compare 7:13.

35:17 SALVATION, Human Freedom—Israel's captivity was caused by her own choice. If we do not listen to God and answer His call, disaster will befall us.

36:1–32 HOLY SCRIPTURE, Inspiration—Jeremiah was basically a preacher. God chose to use his words far beyond Jeremiah's generation. He instructed the prophet with his faithful scribe Baruch to collect and write down his sermons. When the king tried to destroy the words God had inspired, God enabled Jeremiah to have the words copied again. This served as the basis for the eventual Book of Jeremiah, formed when "many similar words were added to them." God produced His written Word through the inspired prophet's preaching, collecting, transcribing, rewriting, and gradual addition of other preaching.

36:7 GOD, Wrath—God does not want to act in wrath. He wants His sinful people to repent. Knowledge of the devastating greatness of His wrath should lead us to repentance.

month[e] of the fifth year of Jehoiakim son of Josiah king of Judah, a time of fasting[f] before the LORD was proclaimed for all the people in Jerusalem and those who had come from the towns of Judah. 10From the room of Gemariah[g] son of Shaphan[h] the secretary,[i] which was in the upper courtyard at the entrance of the New Gate[j] of the temple, Baruch read to all the people at the LORD's temple the words of Jeremiah from the scroll.

11When Micaiah son of Gemariah, the son of Shaphan, heard all the words of the LORD from the scroll, 12he went down to the secretary's[k] room in the royal palace, where all the officials were sitting: Elishama the secretary, Delaiah son of Shemaiah, Elnathan[l] son of Acbor, Gemariah son of Shaphan, Zedekiah son of Hananiah, and all the other officials.[m] 13After Micaiah told them everything he had heard Baruch read to the people from the scroll, 14all the officials sent Jehudi[n] son of Nethaniah, the son of Shelemiah, the son of Cushi, to say to Baruch, "Bring the scroll[o] from which you have read to the people and come." So Baruch son of Neriah went to them with the scroll in his hand. 15They said to him, "Sit down, please, and read it to us."

So Baruch read it to them. 16When they heard all these words, they looked at each other in fear[p] and said to Baruch, "We must report all these words to the king." 17Then they asked Baruch, "Tell us, how did you come to write[q] all this? Did Jeremiah dictate it?"

18"Yes," Baruch replied, "he dictated[r] all these words to me, and I wrote them in ink on the scroll."

19Then the officials[s] said to Baruch, "You and Jeremiah, go and hide.[t] Don't let anyone know where you are."

20After they put the scroll in the room of Elishama the secretary, they went to the king in the courtyard and reported everything to him. 21The king sent Jehudi[u] to get the scroll, and Jehudi brought it from the room of Elishama the secretary and read it to the king[v] and all the officials standing beside him. 22It was the ninth month and the king was sitting in the winter apartment,[w] with a fire burning in the firepot in front of him. 23Whenever Jehudi had read three or four columns of the scroll,[x] the king cut them off with a scribe's knife and threw them into the firepot, until the entire scroll was burned in the fire.[y] 24The king and all his attendants who heard all these words showed no fear,[z] nor did they tear their clothes.[a] 25Even though Elnathan, Delaiah[b] and Gemariah[c] urged the king not to burn the scroll, he would not listen to them. 26Instead, the king commanded Jerahmeel, a son of the king, Seraiah son of Azriel and Shelemiah son of Abdeel to arrest[d] Baruch the scribe and Jeremiah the prophet. But the LORD had hidden[e] them.

27After the king burned the scroll containing the words that Baruch had written at Jeremiah's dictation,[f] the word of the LORD came to Jeremiah: 28"Take another scroll[g] and write on it all the words that were on the first scroll, which Jehoiakim king of Judah burned up. 29Also tell Jehoiakim king of Judah, 'This is what the LORD says: You burned that scroll and said, "Why did you write on it that the king of Babylon would certainly come and destroy this land and cut off both men and animals[h] from it?"[i] 30Therefore, this is what the LORD says about Jehoiakim[j] king of Judah: He will have no one to sit on the throne of David; his body will be thrown out[k] and exposed[l] to the heat by day and the frost by night.[m] 31I will punish him and his children[n] and his attendants for their wickedness; I will bring on them and those living in Jerusalem and the people of Judah every disaster[o] I pronounced against them, because they have not listened.[p]' "

32So Jeremiah took another scroll and gave it to the scribe Baruch son of Neriah, and as Jeremiah dictated,[q] Baruch wrote[r] on it all the words of the scroll that Jehoiakim king of Judah had burned[s] in the fire. And many similar words were added to them.

Chapter 37

Jeremiah in Prison

ZEDEKIAH[t] son of Josiah was made king[u] of Judah by Nebuchadnezzar king of Babylon; he reigned in place of Jehoiachin[x][v] son of Jehoiakim. 2Neither he nor his attendants nor the people of the land paid any attention[w] to the words the LORD had spoken through Jeremiah the prophet.

3King Zedekiah, however, sent[x] Jehucal[y] son of Shelemiah with the priest Zephaniah[z] son of Maaseiah to Jeremiah

x *1* Hebrew *Coniah,* a variant of *Jehoiachin*

36:9 [e]ver 22 [f]S 2Ch 20:3
36:10 [g]ver 12,25; Jer 29:3 [h]Jer 26:24 [i]Jer 52:25 [j]S Ge 23:10
36:12 [k]S 2Sa 8:17 [l]S Jer 26:22 [m]Jer 38:4
36:14 [n]ver 21 [o]ver 4
36:16 [p]S Ps 36:1
36:17 [q]Jer 30:2
36:18 [r]ver 4
36:19 [s]Jer 26:16 [t]S 1Ki 17:3
36:21 [u]ver 14 [v]2Ki 22:10
36:22 [w]Am 3:15
36:23 [x]ver 2 [y]1Ki 22:8
36:24 [z]S Ps 36:1 [a]S Ge 37:29; S Nu 14:6
36:25 [b]ver 12 [c]S ver 10
36:26 [d]Mt 23:34 [e]S 1Ki 17:3; Ps 11:1; S Jer 1:8; 15:21
36:27 [f]ver 4
36:28 [g]ver 2
36:29 [h]Jer 33:12 [i]S Isa 30:10
36:30 [j]Jer 52:2 [k]S Isa 14:19 [l]S 2Ki 24:6 [m]S Jer 8:2
36:31 [n]Ex 20:5 [o]S Pr 29:1 [p]S Pr 1:24
36:32 [q]ver 4 [r]Ex 34:1; Jer 30:2 [s]ver 23
37:1 [t]S 2Ki 24:17 [u]1Sa 11:1; Eze 17:13 [v]S 2Ki 24:8,12; Jer 22:24
37:2 [w]S 2Ki 24:19
37:3 [x]ver 17; Jer 38:14 [y]Jer 38:1 [z]S 2Ki 25:18; Jer 29:25; 52:24

36:30 THE CHURCH, Covenant People—Human beings can place themselves outside God's promises by rebellion. Although Jehoiakim would not have a son to sit on the throne of David, the promise concerning David's everlasting dynasty continued and was fulfilled in Jesus Christ. See note on 2 Sa 23:5. God takes seriously and acts on His warnings of judgment.

36:31 SIN, Judgment—See note on 2 Ki 24:1–4.

the prophet with this message: "Please
pray[a] to the LORD our God for us."
4Now Jeremiah was free to come and
go among the people, for he had not yet
been put in prison.[b] 5Pharaoh's army had
marched out of Egypt,[c] and when the
Babylonians[y] who were besieging Jerusalem heard the report about them, they
withdrew[d] from Jerusalem.[e]
6Then the word of the LORD came to
Jeremiah the prophet: 7"This is what the
LORD, the God of Israel, says: Tell the
king of Judah, who sent you to inquire[f]
of me, 'Pharaoh's army, which has
marched[g] out to support you, will go
back to its own land, to Egypt.[h] 8Then
the Babylonians will return and attack
this city; they will capture[i] it and burn[j]
it down.'
9"This is what the LORD says: Do not
deceive[k] yourselves, thinking, 'The Babylonians will surely leave us.' They will
not! 10Even if you were to defeat the entire Babylonian[z] army that is attacking
you and only wounded men were left in
their tents, they would come out and
burn[l] this city down."
11After the Babylonian army had withdrawn[m] from Jerusalem because of Pharaoh's army, 12Jeremiah started to leave
the city to go to the territory of Benjamin
to get his share of the property[n] among
the people there. 13But when he reached
the Benjamin Gate,[o] the captain of the
guard, whose name was Irijah son of Shelemiah, the son of Hananiah, arrested him
and said, "You are deserting to the Babylonians!"[p]
14"That's not true!" Jeremiah said. "I
am not deserting to the Babylonians." But
Irijah would not listen to him; instead, he
arrested[q] Jeremiah and brought him to
the officials. 15They were angry with Jeremiah and had him beaten[r] and imprisoned[s] in the house[t] of Jonathan the secretary, which they had made into a prison.
16Jeremiah was put into a vaulted cell
in a dungeon, where he remained a long
time. 17Then King Zedekiah sent[u] for
him and had him brought to the palace,
where he asked[v] him privately,[w] "Is
there any word from the LORD?"
"Yes," Jeremiah replied, "you will be
handed over[x] to the king of Babylon."
18Then Jeremiah said to King Zedekiah,
"What crime[y] have I committed against
you or your officials or this people, that
you have put me in prison? 19Where are
your prophets[z] who prophesied to you,
'The king of Babylon will not attack you
or this land'? 20But now, my lord the
king, please listen. Let me bring my petition before you: Do not send me back to
the house of Jonathan the secretary, or I
will die there."[a]
21King Zedekiah then gave orders for
Jeremiah to be placed in the courtyard of
the guard and given bread from the street
of the bakers each day until all the
bread[b] in the city was gone.[c] So Jeremiah remained in the courtyard of the
guard.[d]

Chapter 38

Jeremiah Thrown Into a Cistern

SHEPHATIAH son of Mattan, Gedaliah
son of Pashhur[e], Jehucal[a][f] son of
Shelemiah, and Pashhur son of Malkijah
heard what Jeremiah was telling all the
people when he said, 2"This is what the
LORD says: 'Whoever stays in this city will
die by the sword, famine or plague,[g] but
whoever goes over to the Babylonians[b]
will live. He will escape with his life; he
will live.'[h] 3And this is what the LORD
says: 'This city will certainly be handed
over to the army of the king of Babylon,
who will capture it.' "[i]
4Then the officials[j] said to the king,
"This man should be put to death.[k] He is
discouraging[l] the soldiers who are left in
this city, as well as all the people, by the
things he is saying to them. This man is
not seeking the good of these people but
their ruin."
5"He is in your hands,"[m] King Zedekiah answered. "The king can do nothing[n]
to oppose you."
6So they took Jeremiah and put him
into the cistern of Malkijah, the king's
son, which was in the courtyard of the
guard.[o] They lowered Jeremiah by
ropes[p] into the cistern; it had no water
in it,[q] only mud, and Jeremiah sank
down into the mud.[r]
7But Ebed-Melech,[s] a Cushite,[c] an official[d][t] in the royal palace, heard that
they had put Jeremiah into the cistern.
While the king was sitting in the Benjamin Gate,[u] 8Ebed-Melech went out of
the palace and said to him, 9"My lord the
king, these men have acted wickedly in
all they have done to Jeremiah the prophet. They have thrown him into a cistern,[v] where he will starve to death
when there is no longer any bread[w] in
the city."

[y] *5* Or *Chaldeans*; also in verses 8, 9, 13 and 14
[z] *10* Or *Chaldean*; also in verse 11 [a] *1* Hebrew *Jucal*, a variant of *Jehucal* [b] *2* Or *Chaldeans*; also in verses 18, 19 and 23 [c] *7* Probably from the upper Nile region [d] *7* Or *a eunuch*

37:3 [a]S Ex 8:28; S Nu 21:7; 1Sa 12:19; 1Ki 13:6; 2Ki 19:4; Jer 42:2
37:4 [b]ver 15; Jer 32:2
37:5 [c]S Ge 15:18; Isa 31:1; Eze 17:15 [d]Jer 34:21 [e]S Isa 30:5; Jer 34:11
37:7 [f]S Ge 25:22; S 2Ki 22:18 [g]ver 5 [h]S 2Ki 18:21; S Jer 2:36; La 1:7; 4:17
37:8 [i]Jer 38:3 [j]Jer 21:10; 38:18; 39:8
37:9 [k]Jer 29:8; S Mk 13:5
37:10 [l]Jer 21:10
37:11 [m]ver 5
37:12 [n]S Jer 32:9
37:13 [o]S Jer 20:2 [p]Jer 21:9
37:14 [q]Isa 58:6; Jer 40:4
37:15 [r]S Jer 20:2; Heb 11:36 [s]S 1Ki 22:27 [t]ver 20; Jer 38:26
37:17 [u]S ver 3 [v]S Ge 25:22; Jer 15:11 [w]Jer 38:16 [x]S Jer 21:7
37:18 [y]S 1Sa 26:18; Jn 10:32; Ac 25:8
37:19 [z]S Jer 14:13; Eze 13:2
37:20 [a]S ver 15
37:21 [b]S Lev 26:26; Isa 33:16; Jer 38:9; La 1:11 [c]S 2Ki 25:3 [d]Jer 32:2; 38:6,13, 28; 39:13-14
38:1 [e]S 1Ch 9:12 [f]Jer 37:3
38:2 [g]Jer 34:17 [h]ver 17; S Jer 21:9; 39:18; 45:5
38:3 [i]S Jer 21:4,10
38:4 [j]S Jer 36:12 [k]S Jer 11:21 [l]S 1Sa 17:32
38:5 [m]S Jer 26:14 [n]1Sa 15:24
38:6 [o]S Jer 37:21 [p]S Jos 2:15 [q]S Ge 37:24 [r]S Job 30:19; La 3:53
38:7 [s]Jer 39:16 [t]fn Isa 56:3-5; Ac 8:27 [u]S Job 29:7
38:9 [v]S Ge 37:20 [w]S Jer 37:21

37:4–10 HISTORY, Faith—See note on 2 Ch 16:7–9.

10Then the king commanded Ebed-Melech the Cushite, "Take thirty men from
here with you and lift Jeremiah the
prophet out of the cistern before he
dies."
11So Ebed-Melech took the men with
him and went to a room under the treasury in the palace. He took some old rags
and worn-out clothes from there and let
them down with ropes[x] to Jeremiah in
the cistern. 12Ebed-Melech the Cushite
said to Jeremiah, "Put these old rags and
worn-out clothes under your arms to pad
the ropes." Jeremiah did so, 13and they
pulled him up with the ropes and lifted
him out of the cistern. And Jeremiah remained in the courtyard of the guard.[y]

Zedekiah Questions Jeremiah Again

14Then King Zedekiah sent[z] for Jeremiah the prophet and had him brought to
the third entrance to the temple of the
LORD. "I am going to ask you something,"
the king said to Jeremiah. "Do not hide[a]
anything from me."
15Jeremiah said to Zedekiah, "If I give
you an answer, will you not kill me? Even
if I did give you counsel, you would not
listen to me."
16But King Zedekiah swore this oath secretly[b] to Jeremiah: "As surely as the
LORD lives, who has given us breath,[c] I
will neither kill you nor hand you over to
those who are seeking your life."[d]
17Then Jeremiah said to Zedekiah,
"This is what the LORD God Almighty,
the God of Israel, says: 'If you surrender[e]
to the officers of the king of Babylon, your
life will be spared and this city will not be
burned down; you and your family will
live.[f] 18But if you will not surrender to
the officers of the king of Babylon, this
city will be handed over[g] to the Babylonians and they will burn[h] it down; you
yourself will not escape[i] from their
hands.'"
19King Zedekiah said to Jeremiah, "I
am afraid[j] of the Jews who have gone
over[k] to the Babylonians, for the Babylonians may hand me over to them and
they will mistreat me."
20"They will not hand you over," Jeremiah replied. "Obey[l] the LORD by doing
what I tell you. Then it will go well[m] with
you, and your life[n] will be spared. 21But if
you refuse to surrender, this is what the
LORD has revealed to me: 22All the wom-
en[o] left in the palace of the king of Judah
will be brought out to the officials of the
king of Babylon. Those women will say to
you:

"'They misled you and overcame
you—
those trusted friends[p] of yours.
Your feet are sunk in the mud;[q]
your friends have deserted you.'

23"All your wives and children[r] will
be brought out to the Babylonians. You
yourself will not escape[s] from their
hands but will be captured[t] by the king
of Babylon; and this city will[e] be burned
down."[u]
24Then Zedekiah said to Jeremiah, "Do
not let anyone know[v] about this conversation, or you may die. 25If the officials
hear that I talked with you, and they
come to you and say, 'Tell us what you
said to the king and what the king said to
you; do not hide it from us or we will kill
you,' 26then tell[w] them, 'I was pleading
with the king not to send me back to Jonathan's house[x] to die there.'"
27All the officials did come to Jeremiah
and question him, and he told them everything the king had ordered him to say.
So they said no more to him, for no one
had heard his conversation with the king.
28And Jeremiah remained in the courtyard of the guard[y] until the day Jerusalem was captured.

Chapter 39

The Fall of Jerusalem

39:1–10pp — 2Ki 25:1–12; Jer 52:4–16

THIS is how Jerusalem[z] was taken: 1In
the ninth year of Zedekiah[a] king of
Judah, in the tenth month, Nebuchadnezzar[b] king of Babylon marched against Jerusalem with his whole army and laid
siege[c] to it. 2And on the ninth day of the
fourth[d] month of Zedekiah's eleventh
year, the city wall[e] was broken
through.[f] 3Then all the officials[g] of the
king of Babylon came and took seats in
the Middle Gate: Nergal-Sharezer of Sam-
gar, Nebo-Sarsekim[f] a chief officer, Nergal-Sharezer a high official and all the other officials of the king of Babylon. 4When
Zedekiah king of Judah and all the soldiers saw them, they fled; they left the
city at night by way of the king's garden,
through the gate between the two
walls,[h] and headed toward the Arabah.[g] [i]
5But the Babylonian[h] army pursued
them and overtook Zedekiah[j] in the
plains of Jericho. They captured[k] him
and took him to Nebuchadnezzar king of

38:11 [x]S Jos 2:15
38:13 [y]S Jer 37:21
38:14 [z]S Jer 37:3 [a]S 1Sa 3:17
38:16 [b]Jer 37:17 [c]Isa 42:5; 57:16 [d]ver 4
38:17 [e]Jer 27:8 [f]S Jer 21:9
38:18 [g]ver 3 [h]S Jer 37:8 [i]S Jer 24:8; S 32:4
38:19 [j]Isa 51:12; Jn 12:42 [k]Jer 39:9; 52:15
38:20 [l]Jer 11:4 [m]S Dt 5:33; Jer 40:9 [n]Isa 55:3
38:22 [o]S Jer 6:12 [p]S Job 19:14; S Jer 13:21 [q]S Job 30:19; Ps 69:14
38:23 [r]S 2Ki 25:6 [s]S Jer 32:4; Eze 17:15 [t]S Jer 24:8 [u]Jer 21:10; 37:8
38:24 [v]Jer 37:17
38:26 [w]1Sa 16:2 [x]S Jer 37:15
38:28 [y]S Jer 37:21
39:1 [z]S Jer 25:29 [a]S 2Ch 36:11 [b]S 2Ki 24:1; S Jer 28:14 [c]S 2Ki 25:1; Jer 52:4; Eze 4:3; 24:2
39:2 [d]Zec 8:19 [e]S 2Ki 14:13 [f]Eze 33:21
39:3 [g]ver 13; Jer 21:4
39:4 [h]S Isa 22:11 [i]Eze 12:12
39:5 [j]S Jer 24:8; S 32:4 [k]S Jer 21:7

[e]23 Or *and you will cause this city to* [f]3 Or *Nergal-Sharezer, Samgar-Nebo, Sarsekim* [g]4 Or *the Jordan Valley* [h]5 Or *Chaldean*

39:3–14 HOLY SCRIPTURE, Collection—See note on 27:20–22.

Babylon at Riblah[l] in the land of Hamath, where he pronounced sentence on
him. 6There at Riblah the king of Babylon
slaughtered the sons of Zedekiah before
his eyes and also killed all the nobles[m] of
Judah. 7Then he put out Zedekiah's eyes[n]
and bound him with bronze shackles to
take him to Babylon.[o]

8The Babylonians[1] set fire[p] to the royal palace and the houses of the people
and broke down the walls[q] of Jerusalem.
9Nebuzaradan commander of the imperial
guard carried into exile to Babylon the
people who remained in the city, along
with those who had gone over to him,[r]
and the rest of the people.[s] 10But Nebuzaradan the commander of the guard left
behind in the land of Judah some of the
poor people, who owned nothing; and at
that time he gave them vineyards and
fields.

11Now Nebuchadnezzar king of Babylon had given these orders about Jeremiah through Nebuzaradan commander of
the imperial guard: 12"Take him and look
after him; don't harm[t] him but do for
him whatever he asks." 13So Nebuzaradan the commander of the guard, Nebu-
shazban a chief officer, Nergal-Sharezer a
high official and all the other officers[u] of
the king of Babylon 14sent and had Jeremiah taken out of the courtyard of the
guard.[v] They turned him over to Gedaliah[w] son of Ahikam,[x] the son of Shaphan,[y] to take him back to his home. So
he remained among his own people.[z]

15While Jeremiah had been confined in
the courtyard of the guard, the word of
the LORD came to him: 16"Go and tell
Ebed-Melech[a] the Cushite, 'This is what
the LORD Almighty, the God of Israel,
says: I am about to fulfill my words[b]
against this city through disaster,[c] not
prosperity. At that time they will be fulfilled before your eyes. 17But I will rescue[d] you on that day, declares the LORD;
you will not be handed over to those you
fear. 18I will save[e] you; you will not fall
by the sword[f] but will escape with your
life,[g] because you trust[h] in me, declares
the LORD.' "

Chapter 40

Jeremiah Freed

THE word came to Jeremiah from the
LORD after Nebuzaradan commander
of the imperial guard had released him at
Ramah.[i] He had found Jeremiah bound
in chains among all the captives[j] from
Jerusalem and Judah who were being carried into exile to Babylon. 2When the
commander[k] of the guard found Jeremiah, he said to him, "The LORD your God
decreed[l] this disaster[m] for this place.[n]
3And now the LORD has brought it about;
he has done just as he said he would. All
this happened because you people
sinned[o] against the LORD and did not
obey[p] him. 4But today I am freeing[q] you
from the chains[r] on your wrists. Come
with me to Babylon, if you like, and I will
look after you; but if you do not want to,
then don't come. Look, the whole country lies before you; go wherever you
please."[s] 5However, before Jeremiah
turned to go,[j] Nebuzaradan added, "Go
back to Gedaliah[t] son of Ahikam,[u] the
son of Shaphan, whom the king of Babylon has appointed[v] over the towns[w] of
Judah, and live with him among the people, or go anywhere else you please."[x]

Then the commander gave him provisions and a present[y] and let him go. 6So
Jeremiah went to Gedaliah son of Ahikam
at Mizpah[z] and stayed with him among
the people who were left behind in the
land.

Gedaliah Assassinated

40:7–9; 41:1–3pp — 2Ki 25:22–26

7When all the army officers and their
men who were still in the open country
heard that the king of Babylon had appointed Gedaliah son of Ahikam as governor[a] over the land and had put him in
charge of the men, women and children
who were the poorest[b] in the land and
who had not been carried into exile to
Babylon, 8they came to Gedaliah at Mizpah[c]—Ishmael[d] son of Nethaniah, Johanan[e] and Jonathan the sons of Kareah,
Seraiah son of Tanhumeth, the sons of
Ephai the Netophathite,[f] and Jaazaniah[k]
the son of the Maacathite,[g] and their
men. 9Gedaliah son of Ahikam, the son of
Shaphan, took an oath to reassure them
and their men. "Do not be afraid to
serve[h] the Babylonians,[l][i]" he said.
"Settle down in the land and serve the
king of Babylon, and it will go well with
you.[j] 10I myself will stay at Mizpah[k] to
represent you before the Babylonians
who come to us, but you are to harvest

39:5 [l]S Nu 34:11
39:6 [m]S Isa 34:12
39:7 [n]S Nu 16:14; Eze 12:13
[o]S Jer 2:35
39:8 [p]S Jer 34:22
[q]S Ne 1:3; S Ps 80:12; S Isa 22:5; La 2:8
39:9 [r]Jer 21:9
[s]Jer 40:1; La 1:5
39:12 [t]S Pr 16:7; Jer 15:20-21; 1Pe 3:13
39:13 [u]S ver 3
39:14 [v]S Ne 3:25; Jer 37:21
[w]S 2Ki 25:22
[x]S 2Ki 22:12
[y]S 2Ki 22:3
[z]Jer 40:5
39:16 [a]Jer 38:7
[b]Ps 33:11; Isa 14:27; 40:8; Jer 44:28; La 2:17; S Mt 1:22
[c]S Jos 23:15; Jer 21:10
39:17 [d]Ps 34:22; 41:1-2
39:18 [e]S 1Sa 17:47; Ac 16:31
[f]S Job 5:20
[g]S Jer 21:9; S 38:2
[h]S Jer 17:7; Ro 10:11
40:1 [i]S Jos 18:25; 1Sa 8:4; Mt 2:18
[j]S Dt 21:10; S 2Ki 24:1; S 2Ch 36:10; Na 3:10
40:2 [k]Ro 13:4
[l]S Isa 10:22
[m]S 2Ch 34:24; S Ps 18:18; S Pr 8:36; Gal 6:7-8
[n]S Jos 23:15
40:3 [o]S Pr 13:21; Ro 6:23; Jas 1:15
[p]S Lev 26:33; Dt 28:45-52; 29:24-28; 31:17-18; S 1Ki 9:9; Jer 22:8-9; Da 9:14; Ac 7:39; Ro 2:5-9
40:4 [q]Ps 105:18-20; S Jer 37:14 [r]La 3:7
[s]S Ge 13:9
40:5 [t]S 2Ki 25:22
[u]2Ki 22:12-14
[v]Ne 5:14; Jer 41:2
[w]Jer 44:2; Zec 1:12
[x]Jer 39:14
[y]S Ge 32:20; S 1Sa 9:7
40:6 [z]ver 10; Jdg 20:1; 1Sa 7:5-17
40:7 [a]S Ge 41:41; S Ne 5:14
[b]S 2Ki 24:14; S Ac 24:17; Jas 2:5
40:8 [c]ver 13
[d]ver 14; Jer 41:1,2
[e]ver 15; Jer 41:11
[f]S 2Sa 23:28
[g]S Dt 3:14
40:9 [h]Jer 5:19; 27:11; Ro 13:1-2; Eph 6:5-8
[i]Eze 23:23
[j]S Jer 38:20; La 1:1
40:10 [k]S ver 6

[1]8 Or *Chaldeans* [j]5 Or *Jeremiah answered* [k]8 Hebrew *Jezaniah,* a variant of *Jaazaniah* [l]9 Or *Chaldeans;* also in verse 10

39:16–17 GOD, Faithfulness—What God says, He will do. He is faithful, dependable, unchanging. Whether He promises salvation or destruction, He will carry out His promises. We can trust Him to be just as He does. See note on 26:3, 19–24. God's faithful servants need not fear.

40:1–6 GOD, Faithfulness—God is faithful to carry out His promises (39:15–18) and to take care of His servants who have been faithful to Him.

40:3 SIN, Discipline—See note on 2 Ki 25:1–21.

the wine,[l] summer fruit and oil, and put
them in your storage jars,[m] and live in
the towns you have taken over."[n]
11When all the Jews in Moab,[o] Ammon, Edom[p] and all the other countries[q]
heard that the king of Babylon had left a
remnant in Judah and had appointed Gedaliah son of Ahikam, the son of Shaphan,
as governor over them, 12they all came
back to the land of Judah, to Gedaliah at
Mizpah, from all the countries where
they had been scattered.[r] And they harvested an abundance of wine and summer fruit.
13Johanan[s] son of Kareah and all the
army officers still in the open country
came to Gedaliah at Mizpah[t] 14and said
to him, "Don't you know that Baalis king
of the Ammonites[u] has sent Ishmael[v]
son of Nethaniah to take your life?" But
Gedaliah son of Ahikam did not believe
them.
15Then Johanan[w] son of Kareah said
privately to Gedaliah in Mizpah, "Let me
go and kill[x] Ishmael son of Nethaniah,
and no one will know it. Why should he
take your life and cause all the Jews who
are gathered around you to be scattered[y]
and the remnant[z] of Judah to perish?"
16But Gedaliah son of Ahikam said to
Johanan[a] son of Kareah, "Don't do such
a thing! What you are saying about Ishmael is not true."

Chapter 41

IN the seventh month Ishmael[b] son of
Nethaniah, the son of Elishama, who
was of royal blood and had been one of
the king's officers, came with ten men to
Gedaliah son of Ahikam at Mizpah. While
they were eating together there, 2Ishma-
el[c] son of Nethaniah and the ten men
who were with him got up and struck
down Gedaliah son of Ahikam, the son of
Shaphan, with the sword,[d] killing the
one whom the king of Babylon had appointed[e] as governor over the land.[f]
3Ishmael also killed all the Jews who
were with Gedaliah at Mizpah, as well as
the Babylonian[m] soldiers who were
there.
4The day after Gedaliah's assassination,
before anyone knew about it, 5eighty men
who had shaved off their beards,[g] torn
their clothes[h] and cut[i] themselves came
from Shechem,[j] Shiloh[k] and Samaria,[l]
bringing grain offerings and incense[m]
with them to the house of the LORD.[n]
6Ishmael son of Nethaniah went out from
Mizpah to meet them, weeping[o] as he
went. When he met them, he said,
"Come to Gedaliah son of Ahikam."[p]
7When they went into the city, Ishmael
son of Nethaniah and the men who were
with him slaughtered them and threw
them into a cistern.[q] 8But ten of them
said to Ishmael, "Don't kill us! We have
wheat and barley, oil and honey, hidden
in a field."[r] So he let them alone and did
not kill them with the others. 9Now the
cistern where he threw all the bodies of
the men he had killed along with Gedaliah was the one King Asa[s] had made as
part of his defense[t] against Baasha[u] king
of Israel. Ishmael son of Nethaniah filled
it with the dead.
10Ishmael made captives of all the rest
of the people[v] who were in Mizpah—the
king's daughters[w] along with all the others who were left there, over whom Nebuzaradan commander of the imperial
guard had appointed Gedaliah son of Ahikam. Ishmael son of Nethaniah took them
captive and set out to cross over to the
Ammonites.[x]
11When Johanan[y] son of Kareah and
all the army officers who were with him
heard about all the crimes Ishmael son of
Nethaniah had committed, 12they took all
their men and went to fight[z] Ishmael son
of Nethaniah. They caught up with him
near the great pool[a] in Gibeon. 13When
all the people[b] Ishmael had with him
saw Johanan son of Kareah and the army
officers who were with him, they were
glad. 14All the people Ishmael had taken
captive at Mizpah[c] turned and went over
to Johanan son of Kareah. 15But Ishmael
son of Nethaniah and eight of his men
escaped[d] from Johanan and fled to the
Ammonites.

Flight to Egypt

16Then Johanan son of Kareah and all
the army officers[e] who were with him
led away all the survivors[f] from Mizpah
whom he had recovered from Ishmael
son of Nethaniah after he had assassinated Gedaliah son of Ahikam: the soldiers,
women, children and court officials he
had brought from Gibeon. 17And they
went on, stopping at Geruth Kimham[g]
near Bethlehem[h] on their way to Egypt[i]
18to escape the Babylonians.[n] They were
afraid[j] of them because Ishmael son of
Nethaniah had killed Gedaliah[k] son of

m3 Or *Chaldean* n18 Or *Chaldeans*

40:10 [l]S Ge 27:28; S Ex 23:16 [m]Ex 7:19; 2Co 4:7 [n]Dt 1:39
40:11 [o]S Nu 21:11; 25:1 [p]S Ge 25:30 [q]Jer 12:14
40:12 [r]Jer 43:5
40:13 [s]Jer 42:1 [t]ver 8
40:14 [u]S Ge 19:38; 2Sa 10:1-19; Jer 25:21; 41:10; 49:1 [v]S ver 8
40:15 [w]S ver 8 [x]S Dt 5:17; Mt 5:21-22 [y]S Ge 11:4; S Lev 26:33; Mt 26:31; Jn 11:52; Jas 1:1 [z]S 2Ki 21:14; S Isa 1:9; Ro 11:5
40:16 [a]Jer 43:2
41:1 [b]S Jer 40:8
41:2 [c]Ps 41:9; 109:5 [d]S Jos 11:10; Jer 40:15; Heb 11:37 [e]S Jer 40:5 [f]2Sa 3:27; 20:9-10; S Jer 40:8
41:5 [g]S Lev 19:27; Jer 47:5; 48:37 [h]S Ge 37:29; S Lev 10:6; S Mk 14:63 [i]S Lev 19:28 [j]Ge 12:6; 33:18; Jdg 9:1-57; 1Ki 12:1 [k]S Jos 18:1 [l]1Ki 16:24 [m]S Nu 16:40; S Lk 1:9 [n]1Ki 3:2; 6:38; 2Ki 25:9
41:6 [o]2Sa 3:16 [p]Ps 5:9; Hos 7:11; Rev 20:10
41:7 [q]S Ge 37:24; 2Ki 10:14
41:8 [r]Isa 45:3
41:9 [s]S 1Ki 15:22; S 2Ch 16:6 [t]S Jdg 6:2 [u]S 2Ch 16:1
41:10 [v]Jer 40:7,12 [w]Jer 38:23 [x]S Jer 40:14
41:11 [y]S Jer 40:8
41:12 [z]S Ex 14:14; Jn 18:36 [a]S Jos 9:3; Jn 9:7
41:13 [b]ver 10
41:14 [c]Jer 40:6
41:15 [d]Job 21:30; S Pr 28:17
41:16 [e]Jer 42:1; 43:2 [f]Isa 1:9; Jer 43:4; Eze 7:16; 14:22; Zep 2:9
41:17 [g]2Sa 19:37 [h]Ge 35:19; Mic 5:2 [i]Jer 42:14
41:18 [j]S Nu 14:9; Isa 51:12; Jer 42:16; Lk 12:4-5 [k]S 2Ki 25:22

40:11–12 THE CHURCH, Remnant—God's remnant attracts others to it. Many Jews had fled to neighboring lands fearing the Babylonian army. When they saw a remnant functioning in Judah after the destruction of Jerusalem, they returned to join the remnant. God's people are always a remnant from the entire world which God loves and wants to save. See note on 2 Ch 34:9.

Ahikam, whom the king of Babylon had
appointed as governor over the land.

Chapter 42

THEN all the army officers, including
Johanan[l] son of Kareah and Jezaniah[o] son of Hoshaiah,[m] and all the people
from the least to the greatest[n] approached 2Jeremiah the prophet and said
to him, "Please hear our petition and
pray[o] to the LORD your God for this entire remnant.[p] For as you now see,
though we were once many, now only a
few[q] are left. 3Pray that the LORD your
God will tell us where we should go and
what we should do."[r]

4"I have heard you," replied Jeremiah
the prophet. "I will certainly pray[s] to the
LORD your God as you have requested; I
will tell[t] you everything the LORD says
and will keep nothing back from you."[u]

5Then they said to Jeremiah, "May the
LORD be a true[v] and faithful[w] witness[x]
against us if we do not act in accordance
with everything the LORD your God sends
you to tell us. 6Whether it is favorable or
unfavorable, we will obey the LORD our
God, to whom we are sending you, so
that it will go well[y] with us, for we will
obey[z] the LORD our God."

7Ten days later the word of the LORD
came to Jeremiah. 8So he called together
Johanan son of Kareah and all the army
officers[a] who were with him and all the
people from the least to the greatest.[b]
9He said to them, "This is what the LORD,
the God of Israel, to whom you sent me
to present your petition,[c] says:[d] 10'If you
stay in this land,[e] I will build[f] you up
and not tear you down; I will plant[g] you
and not uproot you,[h] for I am grieved
over the disaster I have inflicted on you.[i]
11Do not be afraid of the king of Babylon,[j] whom you now fear.[k] Do not be
afraid of him, declares the LORD, for I am
with you and will save[l] you and deliver
you from his hands.[m] 12I will show you
compassion[n] so that he will have compassion on you and restore you to your
land.'[o]

13"However, if you say, 'We will not
stay in this land,' and so disobey[p] the
LORD your God, 14and if you say, 'No, we
will go and live in Egypt,[q] where we will
not see war or hear the trumpet[r] or be
hungry for bread,'[s] 15then hear the word
of the LORD,[t] O remnant of Judah. This is
what the LORD Almighty, the God of Israel, says: 'If you are determined to go to
Egypt and you do go to settle there,
16then the sword[u] you fear[v] will overtake you there, and the famine[w] you
dread will follow you into Egypt, and
there you will die.[x] 17Indeed, all who are
determined to go to Egypt to settle there
will die by the sword, famine and
plague;[y] not one of them will survive or
escape the disaster I will bring on them.'
18This is what the LORD Almighty, the
God of Israel, says: 'As my anger and
wrath[z] have been poured out on those
who lived in Jerusalem,[a] so will my
wrath be poured out on you when you go
to Egypt. You will be an object of cursing[b] and horror,[c] of condemnation and
reproach;[d] you will never see this place
again.'[e]

19"O remnant[f] of Judah, the LORD has
told you, 'Do not go to Egypt.'[g] Be sure of
this: I warn you today 20that you made a
fatal mistake[p] when you sent me to the
LORD your God and said, 'Pray to the
LORD our God for us; tell us everything he
says and we will do it.'[h] 21I have told you
today, but you still have not obeyed the
LORD your God in all he sent me to tell
you.[i] 22So now, be sure of this: You will
die by the sword, famine[j] and plague[k]
in the place where you want to go to settle."[l]

Chapter 43

WHEN Jeremiah finished telling the
people all the words of the LORD
their God—everything the LORD had sent
him to tell them[m]— 2Azariah son of

42:1 [l]S Jer 40:13 [m]S Jer 41:16 [n]Jer 6:13; 44:12 **42:2** [o]S Ge 20:7; S Jer 36:7; Ac 8:24; Jas 5:16 [p]S Isa 1:9 [q]S Lev 26:22; La 1:1 **42:3** [r]ver 20; Ps 86:11; S Pr 3:6; S Jer 15:11 **42:4** [s]Ex 8:29; 1Sa 12:23 [t]S Jer 1:17 [u]S Nu 22:18; S 1Sa 3:17 **42:5** [v]1Ki 22:16; Ps 119:160; Ro 3:4 [w]S Dt 7:9; Jn 8:26; S 1Co 1:9 [x]S Ge 31:48; S Dt 4:26; S Isa 1:2; S Ro 1:9; Rev 1:5 **42:6** [y]Dt 5:29; 6:3; Jer 7:23; 22:15 [z]S ver 19; S Ex 24:7; S Jos 24:24 **42:8** [a]ver 1 [b]Jer 41:16; S Mk 9:35; Lk 7:28; Heb 8:11 **42:9** [c]ver 2 [d]2Ki 22:15 **42:10** [e]Jer 43:4 [f]S Jer 24:6 [g]S Dt 30:9 [h]S Dt 29:28; Ecc 3:2; Jer 45:4; Eze 36:36; Da 11:4 [i]S 2Ch 34:24; Isa 30:26; S Jer 18:8 **42:11** [j]Jer 27:11 [k]S Nu 14:9; S 1Sa 15:24; Ps 23:4; Mt 10:28; 2Ti 1:7 [l]Ps 18:27; 69:35; S 119:94; S Isa 63:1; Heb 7:25 [m]S Ps 3:7; S Pr 20:22; S Jer 1:8; Ro 8:31 **42:12** [n]S Ex 3:21; S 2Sa 24:14; 2Co 1:3 [o]S Ge 31:3; S Ne 1:9; Ps 106:44-46 **42:13** [p]S Dt 11:28 **42:14** [q]Nu 11:4-5; S Dt 17:16; S Isa 30:2 [r]S Jos 6:20; S Mt 24:31 [s]S Dt 8:3; 1Sa 2:5; Pr 10:3; Isa 65:13; Mt 4:2-4 **42:15** [t]Jer 44:24 **42:16** [u]S Lev 26:33; Eze 11:8; 14:17 [v]S Jer 41:18 [w]S Ge 41:55 [x]S Ge 2:17; 2Ch 25:4; S Job 21:20; Eze 3:19; 18:4 **42:17** [y]ver 22; S Jer 21:7; 44:13 **42:18** [z]Dt 29:18-20; S 2Ch 12:7 [a]S 2Ch 36:19; Jer 39:1-9 [b]S Nu 5:27; S Jer 25:18 [c]S Dt 28:25, 37 [d]S Ps 44:13 [e]S Jer 22:10 **42:19** [f]Jer 40:15 [g]S ver 6; Dt 17:16; Isa 30:7; Jer 43:2; 44:16 **42:20** [h]ver 2; Eze 14:7-8 **42:21** [i]S Ex 24:7; Jer 40:3; Eze 2:7; 12:2; Zec 7:11-12 **42:22** [j]S Isa 1:28 [k]S ver 17; Jer 24:10; Eze 6:11 [l]S Jer 15:2; Hos 9:6 **43:1** [m]Jer 26:8; 42:9-22

[o]*1* Hebrew; Septuagint (see also 43:2) *Azariah*
[p]*20* Or *you erred in your hearts*

42:1–3 THE CHURCH, Remnant—The prophetic warning of judgment that left only a small remnant came true (Isa 7:3, 18–25). Their only hope was prayer. Sadly, when God answered their prayers, they refused to believe (Jer 43:2). Being part of the remnant does not guarantee a person is God's faithful servant. God's remnant must have more than pious actions. They must trust and follow God's words. See note on 2 Ch 34:9.

42:2—43:4 PRAYER, Answer—The officers realized how dependent they were on God and asked Jeremiah to pray for their guidance. They refused to accept God's answer. Prayer is of no avail if we do not trust God's answer.

42:7–11 REVELATION, Word—The word of God did not come automatically to the prophets. They had to wait until God spoke. Jeremiah waited ten days. The word did come in response to prophetic prayer but in God's timing. As so often, this word from God placed conditional demands on the hearers. They had to stay in the land rather than flee to Egypt. They had to show their faith in God's promised presence as greater than the Babylonian army. Compare 44:1–30.

42:11–12 GOD, Savior—God is primarily a saving God, a God of love. His love means we need not fear earthly powers and enemies.

42:18 GOD, Wrath—We cannot escape God's announced wrath by leaving the country. His wrath is directed towards sinful persons, not geographic features. See note on 4:4,8,26.

Hoshaiah[n] and Johanan[o] son of Kareah
and all the arrogant[p] men said to Jeremiah,
"You are lying![q] The LORD our God has
not sent you to say, 'You must not go to
Egypt to settle there.'[r] 3But Baruch[s] son
of Neriah is inciting you against us to
hand us over to the Babylonians,[q] so they
may kill us or carry us into exile to Babylon."[t]

4So Johanan son of Kareah and all the
army officers and all the people[u] disobeyed the LORD's command[v] to stay in
the land of Judah.[w] 5Instead, Johanan son
of Kareah and all the army officers led
away all the remnant of Judah who had
come back to live in the land of Judah
from all the nations where they had been
scattered.[x] 6They also led away all the
men, women[y] and children and the
king's daughters whom Nebuzaradan
commander of the imperial guard had left
with Gedaliah son of Ahikam, the son of
Shaphan, and Jeremiah the prophet and
Baruch[z] son of Neriah. 7So they entered
Egypt[a] in disobedience to the LORD and
went as far as Tahpanhes.[b]

8In Tahpanhes[c] the word of the LORD
came to Jeremiah: 9"While the Jews are
watching, take some large stones[d] with
you and bury them in clay in the brick[e]
pavement at the entrance to Pharaoh's
palace[f] in Tahpanhes. 10Then say to
them, 'This is what the LORD Almighty,
the God of Israel, says: I will send for my
servant[g] Nebuchadnezzar[h] king of Babylon, and I will set his throne[i] over these
stones I have buried here; he will spread
his royal canopy[j] above them. 11He will
come and attack Egypt,[k] bringing death[l]
to those destined[m] for death, captivity to
those destined for captivity,[n] and the
sword to those destined for the sword.[o]
12He[r] will set fire[p] to the temples[q] of
the gods[r] of Egypt; he will burn their
temples and take their gods captive.[s] As
a shepherd wraps[t] his garment around
him, so will he wrap Egypt around himself and depart from there unscathed.
13There in the temple of the sun[s][u] in
Egypt he will demolish the sacred pillars[v]
and will burn down the temples of the
gods of Egypt.'"

Chapter 44

Disaster Because of Idolatry

THIS word came to Jeremiah concerning all the Jews living in Lower
Egypt[w]—in Migdol,[x] Tahpanhes[y] and
Memphis[t][z]—and in Upper Egypt[u]:[a]
2"This is what the LORD Almighty, the
God of Israel, says: You saw the great disaster[b] I brought on Jerusalem and on all
the towns of Judah.[c] Today they lie deserted and in ruins[d] 3because of the
evil[e] they have done. They provoked me
to anger[f] by burning incense[g] and by
worshiping other gods[h] that neither they
nor you nor your fathers[i] ever knew.
4Again and again[j] I sent my servants the
prophets,[k] who said, 'Do not do this detestable[l] thing that I hate!' 5But they did
not listen or pay attention;[m][n] they did
not turn from their wickedness[o] or stop
burning incense[p] to other gods.[q] 6There-
fore, my fierce anger was poured out;[r] it
raged against the towns of Judah and the
streets of Jerusalem and made them the
desolate ruins[s] they are today.

7"Now this is what the LORD God Almighty, the God of Israel, says: Why

43:2 [n]S Jer 41:16 [o]Jer 40:16 [p]S Ne 9:29; 1Co 4:18-21 [q]S Ge 19:14; S Dt 13:3; Ro 9:1; 2Co 11:31; 1Ti 2:7 [r]S Ex 24:7; 2Ki 25:24; Jer 18:19; S 42:19; Eze 37:14 **43:3** [s]S Jer 32:12 [t]Jer 38:4; 41:18; 52:30 **43:4** [u]S Jer 41:16 [v]2Ch 25:16; Jer 42:5-6 [w]Jer 42:10 **43:5** [x]Jer 40:12 **43:6** [y]S Jer 6:12 [z]S Jer 32:12 **43:7** [a]S 2Ki 25:26 [b]Jer 2:16; 44:1; 46:14; Eze 30:18 **43:8** [c]Ps 139:7; Jer 2:16 **43:9** [d]Ge 31:45-53; Jos 4:1-7; 1Ki 18:31-32 [e]S Ge 11:3 [f]S Ge 47:14 **43:10** [g]Isa 44:28; 45:1; Jer 25:9; 27:6 [h]Jer 46:13 [i]Jer 49:38 [j]S Ps 18:11 **43:11** [k]Jer 46:13-26; Eze 29:19-20 [l]S Pr 11:19; Ro 6:23 [m]S Ps 49:14; Heb 9:27 [n]S Dt 28:64; Rev 13:10 [o]S Jer 15:2; Eze 32:11; Zec 11:9 **43:12** [p]S Jos 7:15 [q]S 1Ki 16:32 [r]ver 13; S Ex 12:12; S Isa 2:18; Jer 46:25; Eze 30:13; Zec 13:2 [s]Da 11:8 [t]S Ps 104:2; 109:18-19 **43:13** [u]S Ge 1:16; Isa 19:18 *fn*; S Dt 4:19 [v]Jer 52:17; Eze 26:11 **44:1** [w]S Dt 32:42; S Jer 24:8 [x]S Ex 14:2 [y]S Jer 43:7,8 [z]S Isa 19:13 [a]S Isa 11:11 **44:2** [b]S 2Ch 34:24 [c]S Jer 40:5 [d]S Lev 26:31; S Dt 29:23; S Isa 6:11 **44:3** [e]S Ex 32:22 [f]S Nu 11:33 [g]S Nu 16:40 [h]ver 8; S Nu 25:3; Dt 13:6-11; 29:26; Isa 19:1 [i]S Jdg 2:19 **44:4** [j]S Jer 7:13 [k]S Nu 11:29 [l]S Dt 18:9; S 1Ki 14:24; 1Pe 4:3 **44:5** [m]Da 9:6 [n]S Jer 25:4 [o]S Ge 6:5; Ro 1:18; 2Ti 2:19 [p]ver 21; Jer 1:16; Eze 8:11; 16:18; 23:41 [q]Jer 11:8-10; S 25:7 **44:6** [r]Eze 8:18; 20:34 [s]S Lev 26:31,34; S Dt 29:23; La 1:13; Zec 7:14

[q]3 Or *Chaldeans* [r]12 Or *I* [s]13 Or *in Heliopolis* [t]1 Hebrew *Noph* [u]1 Hebrew *in Pathros*

43:10 THE CHURCH, Servants—God can use even the most unlikely people to serve Him. Nebuchadnezzar, the king of Babylon, sought to destroy Jerusalem and Judah. The Lord used Nebuchadnezzar's greed for plunder and power to punish rebellious Judah. He even promised Nebuchadnezzar power in Egypt to punish the rebellious Jews there. In this sense, Nebuchadnezzar could be called the servant of the Lord (25:9). Like the nation of Assyria (Isa 10:5–19) and Cyrus (Isa 45:4), the Lord used Nebuchadnezzar to serve Him, even though Nebuchadnezzar did not know the Lord.

43:11 ELECTION, Predestination—The translation might be interpreted as teaching eternal predestination for certain people or groups. The Hebrew text does not have a verb "destined." English syntax requires a verb for meaningful communication. The meaning is that God had pronounced prophetic judgment on Egyptians and they would suffer what He pronounced.

44:1–30 EVIL AND SUFFERING, Punishment—Punishment is not an empty threat as the Jews learned in 587 BC. Nor can we escape responsibility by fleeing to another environment and worshiping other gods. The one God controls all the world and tries every method to lead us to serve Him and know true life. His punishing work may not be immediately evident. Prosperity may come to the wicked for a time. In the end God's word of threat becomes reality. Prosperity is neither the goal of life nor a criteria by which to choose an object of worship.

44:1–30 REVELATION, Faithfulness—God is faithful to fulfill His revealed word whether it brings salvation or judgment. Salvation does not automatically follow judgment. A people who refuse to learn the lessons of judgment face further punishment. The Hebrews who fled to Egypt after Jerusalem was destroyed had to learn this lesson the hard way. They learned God's word has no geographical limits, being effective throughout His creation. The sign of God's power was the fulfillment of His word in Egypt's history. See note on Dt 18:21–22.

44:3,6,8 GOD, Wrath—Provoking God to wrath brings no profit, only the opportunity to face His anger. See note on 4:4,8,26.

44:3,8,15–29 GOD, One God—Change of address does not authorize change of gods. No interpretation of historical evidence can justify worshiping a god other than the one true God. See note on 1:16.

44:7–30 THE CHURCH, Remnant—Escaping disaster

bring such great disaster[t] on yourselves
by cutting off from Judah the men and
women,[u] the children and infants, and so
leave yourselves without a remnant?[v]
8Why provoke me to anger with what
your hands have made,[w] burning incense[x] to other gods in Egypt,[y] where
you have come to live?[z] You will destroy
yourselves and make yourselves an object
of cursing and reproach[a] among all the
nations on earth. 9Have you forgotten the
wickedness committed by your fathers[b]
and by the kings[c] and queens[d] of Judah
and the wickedness committed by you
and your wives[e] in the land of Judah and
the streets of Jerusalem?[f] 10To this day
they have not humbled[g] themselves or
shown reverence,[h] nor have they followed my law[i] and the decrees[j] I set
before you and your fathers.[k]

11"Therefore, this is what the LORD Almighty,[l] the God of Israel, says: I am determined to bring disaster[m] on you and to
destroy all Judah. 12I will take away the
remnant[n] of Judah who were determined
to go to Egypt to settle there. They will all
perish in Egypt; they will fall by the
sword or die from famine. From the least
to the greatest,[o] they will die by sword or
famine.[p] They will become an object of
cursing and horror, of condemnation and
reproach.[q] 13I will punish[r] those who
live in Egypt with the sword,[s] famine
and plague,[t] as I punished Jerusalem.
14None of the remnant of Judah who have
gone to live in Egypt will escape or survive to return to the land of Judah, to
which they long to return and live; none
will return except a few fugitives."[u]

15Then all the men who knew that
their wives[v] were burning incense[w] to
other gods, along with all the women[x]
who were present—a large assembly—
and all the people living in Lower and
Upper Egypt,[v][y] said to Jeremiah, 16"We
will not listen[z] to the message you have
spoken to us in the name of the LORD![a]
17We will certainly do everything we said
we would:[b] We will burn incense[c] to
the Queen of Heaven[d] and will pour out
drink offerings to her just as we and our
fathers, our kings and our officials[e] did in
the towns of Judah and in the streets of
Jerusalem.[f] At that time we had plenty of
food[g] and were well off and suffered no
harm.[h] 18But ever since we stopped
burning incense to the Queen of Heaven
and pouring out drink offerings[i] to her,
we have had nothing and have been perishing by sword and famine.[j] [k]"

19The women added, "When we
burned incense[l] to the Queen of Heav-
en[m] and poured out drink offerings to
her, did not our husbands[n] know that we
were making cakes[o] like her image[p] and
pouring out drink offerings to her?"

20Then Jeremiah said to all the people,
both men and women, who were answering him, 21"Did not the LORD remember[q]
and think about the incense[r] burned in
the towns of Judah and the streets of Jerusalem[s] by you and your fathers,[t] your
kings and your officials and the people of
the land?[u] 22When the LORD could no
longer endure[v] your wicked actions and
the detestable things you did, your land
became an object of cursing[w] and a desolate waste[x] without inhabitants, as it is
today.[y] 23Because you have burned incense and have sinned against the LORD
and have not obeyed him or followed[z]
his law or his decrees[a] or his stipulations, this disaster[b] has come upon you,
as you now see."[c]

24Then Jeremiah said to all the people,
including the women,[d] "Hear the word
of the LORD, all you people of Judah in
Egypt.[e] 25This is what the LORD Almighty, the God of Israel, says: You and
your wives[f] have shown by your actions
what you promised when you said, 'We
will certainly carry out the vows we made
to burn incense and pour out drink offerings to the Queen of Heaven.'[g]

"Go ahead then, do what you promised! Keep your vows![h] 26But hear the
word of the LORD, all Jews living in
Egypt:[i] 'I swear[j] by my great name,'
says the LORD, 'that no one from Judah
living anywhere in Egypt will ever again
invoke my name or swear, "As surely as
the Sovereign[k] LORD lives."[l] 27For I am
watching[m] over them for harm,[n] not for

44:7 [t]Jer 26:19 [u]Jer 51:22 [v]S 2Ki 21:14 **44:8** [w]S Isa 40:18-20; S Jer 10:3; Ro 1:23 [x]ver 17-25; Jer 41:5 [y]S ver 3; S Ex 12:12 [z]S 1Co 10:22 [a]S Ps 44:13 **44:9** [b]S Jdg 2:19 [c]S 2Ki 23:11 [d]1Ki 21:25 [e]S Pr 31:10; S Jer 6:12 [f]ver 17, 21; Jer 11:12; 32:32 **44:10** [g]S Dt 8:3; S Mt 23:12; Php 2:8 [h]S Dt 6:13; S Ps 5:7 [i]S Jos 1:7; S Jer 11:8; Mt 5:17-20; Gal 3:19; 1Jn 3:4 [j]S Lev 18:4 [k]1Ki 9:6-9; 2Ki 17:17 **44:11** [l]Rev 4:8 [m]S 2Ch 34:24; Am 9:4 **44:12** [n]ver 7; Jer 40:15 [o]S Jer 42:1 [p]S Isa 1:28 [q]S Dt 28:25; S Jer 29:18 **44:13** [r]S Ex 32:34; Lev 26:14-17 [s]S Jer 15:2 [t]S Jer 42:17 **44:14** [u]Jer 22:24-27; 49:5; La 4:15; Eze 6:8; S Ro 9:27 **44:15** [v]S Pr 31:10; S Jer 6:12 [w]S Jer 18:15 [x]S Ge 3:6; 1Ti 2:14 [y]S Isa 11:11 **44:16** [z]S 1Sa 8:19; Job 15:25-26; Jer 11:8-10 [a]S Jer 42:19 **44:17** [b]ver 28; Dt 23:23; Zec 1:6 [c]S Isa 65:3 [d]ver 25; Jer 11:12 [e]Ne 9:34 [f]S ver 9; S Jer 2:26 [g]S Ex 16:3; Nu 11:4-6 [h]S Job 21:15; Isa 3:9; Hos 2:5-13; 9:1 **44:18** [i]Lev 23:18 [j]Mal 3:13-15 [k]Jer 42:16 **44:19** [l]S Jer 18:15 [m]Jer 7:18 [n]S Ge 3:6; Eph 5:22 [o]Lev 7:12 [p]S Lev 26:1; Ac 17:29 **44:21** [q]Isa 64:9; S Jer 14:10; Hos 8:13 [r]S Jer 11:13 [s]ver 9 [t]S Ps 79:8 [u]S Jer 2:26 **44:22** [v]S Isa 1:14 [w]S Jer 25:18 [x]S Lev 26:31,32 [y]S Ge 19:13; Ps 107:33-34; Eze 33:28-29 **44:23** [z]S 1Ki 9:6 [a]S Lev 18:4 [b]Jer 40:2 [c]S Lev 26:33; S 1Ki 9:9; Jer 7:13-15; Eze 39:23; Da 9:11-12 **44:24** [d]S Ge 3:6 [e]Jer 43:7 **44:25** [f]S Pr 31:10 [g]S ver 17; S Dt 32:38 [h]S Pr 20:25; Eze 20:39; Jas 1:13-15 **44:26** [i]S Jer 24:8 [j]S Ge 22:16; S Isa 48:1; Ac 19:13; Heb 6:13-17 [k]S Ge 15:2 [l]Dt 32:40; Ps 50:16; S Jer 4:2 **44:27** [m]S Jer 1:12 [n]S Jer 21:10

[v]*15* Hebrew *in Egypt and Pathros*

does not guarantee membership in God's remnant. The people who escaped to Egypt (41:16—43:7) continued to rebel against God, signifying that they had no part in the people of God. God warned them they would destroy the remnant through their disobedience. God's people continue to call upon Him in awe and reverence, obeying His word. They remember the rebellion which caused them to be a remnant in the first place.

44:19 HUMANITY, Marriage—The Hebrew expression indicates the men knew and participated in their wives' sin. In marriage, the partners share values and participate in joint activities. When values are wrong and activities sinful, the individuals and the marriage suffer.

44:20–29 WORSHIP, Proclamation—See note on 26:2-7.

44:25–28 FAMILY, God's Judgment—See note on 9:13-16.

good; the Jews in Egypt will perish[o] by
sword and famine[p] until they are all destroyed.[q] 28Those who escape the
sword[r] and return to the land of Judah
from Egypt will be very few.[s] Then the
whole remnant[t] of Judah who came to
live in Egypt will know whose word will
stand[u]—mine or theirs.[v]
29" 'This will be the sign[w] to you that I
will punish[x] you in this place,' declares
the LORD, 'so that you will know that my
threats of harm against you will surely
stand.'[y] 30This is what the LORD says: 'I
am going to hand Pharaoh[z] Hophra king
of Egypt over to his enemies who seek his
life, just as I handed Zedekiah[a] king of
Judah over to Nebuchadnezzar king of
Babylon, the enemy who was seeking his
life.' "[b]

Chapter 45

A Message to Baruch

THIS is what Jeremiah the prophet told
Baruch[c] son of Neriah[d] in the
fourth year of Jehoiakim[e] son of Josiah
king of Judah, after Baruch had written
on a scroll[f] the words Jeremiah was then
dictating: 2"This is what the LORD, the
God of Israel, says to you, Baruch: 3You
said, 'Woe[g] to me! The LORD has added
sorrow[h] to my pain;[i] I am worn out
with groaning[j] and find no rest.' "[k]
4The LORD said, "Say this to him:
'This is what the LORD says: I will overthrow what I have built and uproot[l]
what I have planted,[m] throughout the
land.[n] 5Should you then seek great[o]
things for yourself? Seek them not.[p] For I
will bring disaster[q] on all people,[r] declares the LORD, but wherever you go I
will let you escape[s] with your life.' "[t]

Chapter 46

A Message About Egypt

THIS is the word of the LORD that came
to Jeremiah the prophet concerning
the nations:[u]

44:27 [o]S Lev 26:38; S Job 15:22; 2Pe 3:9 [p]S Ge 41:55 [q]S Jer 9:16; Da 9:14; Am 9:8 **44:28** [r]Jer 45:5; Eze 6:8 [s]ver 13-14; S Isa 10:19 [t]S 2Ki 21:14 [u]S Isa 7:9; S Jer 39:16; 42:15-18 [v]S ver 17, 25-26 **44:29** [w]S Ge 24:14; S Ex 3:12; S Nu 16:38; S Mt 12:38; 24:3 [x]S Ex 32:34 [y]S Pr 19:21 **44:30** [z]S Jer 25:19; 46:26; Eze 30:21; 32:32 [a]2Ki 25:1-7; S Jer 24:8 [b]Jer 43:9-13 **45:1** [c]S Jer 32:12 [d]Jer 51:59 [e]S 2Ch 36:5 [f]S Ex 17:14; S Ps 40:7 **45:3** [g]S Isa 24:16; 1Co 9:16 [h]S Ps 119:28; Mk 14:34; Ro 9:2 [i]S Job 6:10 [j]S Job 23:2; Ps 69:3 [k]S Jos 1:13; Mt 11:28; Heb 4:3 **45:4** [l]S Jer 42:10 [m]S Jer 11:17 [n]S Dt 28:63; S 30:9; Isa 5:5-7; Jer 18:7-10 **45:5** [o]Ps 131:1 [p]Mt 6:25-27,33 [q]Jer 11:11; 40:2 [r]S Jer 2:35 [s]S Ps 68:20; S Jer 44:28 [t]S Jer 21:9 **46:1** [u]S Jer 1:10 **46:2** [v]S Ex 1:8 [w]S 2Ki 23:29 [x]S 2Ch 35:20 [y]S Ge 2:14 [z]Jer 1:3; 25:1; 35:1; 36:1; 45:1; Da 1:1 **46:3** [a]S Isa 21:5 **46:4** [b]Eze 21:9-11 [c]1Sa 17:5,38; 2Ch 26:14; Ne 4:16 **46:5** [d]ver 21; Jer 48:44 [e]S Ps 31:13; S 48:5 **46:6** [f]Isa 30:16 [g]Ge 2:14; 15:18 [h]ver 12,16; S Ps 20:8 **46:7** [i]Jer 47:2 **46:8** [j]Eze 29:3,9; 30:12; Am 8:8 [k]Da 11:10 **46:9** [l]Jer 47:3; Eze 26:10; Na 3:2 [m]S Ge 10:6 [n]S Isa 66:19 **46:10** [o]Eze 32:10; Joel 1:15; Ob 1:15

2Concerning Egypt:[v]

This is the message against the army of
Pharaoh Neco[w] king of Egypt, which was
defeated at Carchemish[x] on the Euphrates[y] River by Nebuchadnezzar king of
Babylon in the fourth year of Jehoiakim[z]
son of Josiah king of Judah:

3"Prepare your shields,[a] both large and
small,
and march out for battle!
4Harness the horses,
mount the steeds!
Take your positions
with helmets on!
Polish[b] your spears,
put on your armor![c]
5What do I see?
They are terrified,
they are retreating,
their warriors are defeated.
They flee[d] in haste
without looking back,
and there is terror[e] on every side,"
declares the LORD.
6"The swift cannot flee[f]
nor the strong escape.
In the north by the River Euphrates[g]
they stumble and fall.[h]
7"Who is this that rises like the Nile,
like rivers of surging waters?[i]
8Egypt rises like the Nile,[j]
like rivers of surging waters.
She says, 'I will rise and cover the
earth;
I will destroy cities and their
people.'[k]
9Charge, O horses!
Drive furiously, O charioteers![l]
March on, O warriors—
men of Cush[w][m] and Put who carry
shields,
men of Lydia[n] who draw the bow.
10But that day[o] belongs to the Lord, the
LORD Almighty—

[w]9 That is, the upper Nile region

45:1 REVELATION, Word—God's word can be intensely personal. This inspired chapter concerned the problem of one faithful individual—Baruch, Jeremiah's scribe.

45:1–5 ELECTION, Remnant—Baruch, Jeremiah's faithful scribe, was forced by the king into seclusion with Jeremiah. Sorrow and pain made life uncomfortable for Baruch. He could take comfort in knowing that in the middle of great turmoil, he would escape with his life. God rewards faithful servants for enduring pain on behalf of the people of God. Thus He established His faithful remnant even as He overthrew the unfaithful remnant He had built up.

46:1—51:64 GOD, Sovereignty—God can tell what is coming to a people and then proceed to bring it to pass. God can work in His world to carry out His purposes, His judgments, and His blessings.

46:1 HOLY SCRIPTURE, Collection—See notes on 27:20–22; 30:1–11. The inspired Book of Jeremiah was collected in two different orders. The community in Egypt which preserved Hebrew Scripture and translated it into Greek produced the Septuagint. Jer 46:1—51:64 appears immediately after 25:13 in the Greek translation in the following order: 49:34–39; 46:2–28; 50:1—51:64; 47:1–7; 49:7–22, 1–6,28–33,23–27; 48:1–44. God used both collections of His inspired Word to bless His people for centuries. The early Christian church used the Septuagint effectively in its ministry. The ongoing church is directed by translations based on the inspired Hebrew text.

46:1—51:64 HISTORY, Universal—See note on Isa 13:1—23:18. Destruction was not God's final word even for Israel's enemies. He looked to a day to restore them and give them new opportunity to hear His Word and worship Him (46:26; 48:47; 49:6,39).

a day of vengeance[p], for vengeance
on his foes.
The sword will devour[q] till it is
satisfied,
till it has quenched its thirst with
blood.[r]
For the Lord, the LORD Almighty, will
offer sacrifice[s]
in the land of the north by the River
Euphrates.[t]

11"Go up to Gilead and get balm,[u]
O Virgin[v] Daughter of Egypt.
But you multiply remedies in vain;
there is no healing[w] for you.
12The nations will hear of your shame;
your cries will fill the earth.
One warrior will stumble over
another;
both will fall[x] down together."

13This is the message the LORD spoke
to Jeremiah the prophet about the coming
of Nebuchadnezzar king of Babylon[y] to
attack Egypt:[z]

14"Announce this in Egypt, and proclaim
it in Migdol;
proclaim it also in Memphis[x][a] and
Tahpanhes:[b]
'Take your positions and get ready,
for the sword devours[c] those
around you.'
15Why will your warriors be laid low?
They cannot stand, for the LORD will
push them down.[d]
16They will stumble[e] repeatedly;
they will fall[f] over each other.
They will say, 'Get up, let us go back
to our own people[g] and our native
lands,
away from the sword of the
oppressor.'[h]
17There they will exclaim,
'Pharaoh king of Egypt is only a loud
noise;[i]
he has missed his opportunity.[j]'
18"As surely as I live," declares the
King,[k]
whose name is the LORD Almighty,
"one will come who is like Tabor[l]
among the mountains,
like Carmel[m] by the sea.
19Pack your belongings for exile,[n]
you who live in Egypt,
for Memphis[o] will be laid waste[p]
and lie in ruins without inhabitant.

20"Egypt is a beautiful heifer,
but a gadfly is coming
against her from the north.[q]
21The mercenaries[r] in her ranks

46:10 [p]S Nu 31:3; S Dt 32:41; 2Ki 23:29-30 [q]S Dt 32:42; S 2Sa 2:26; Zep 2:12 [r]S Dt 32:42 [s]S Lev 3:9; Zep 1:7 [t]Ge 2:14; 15:18
46:11 [u]S Ge 37:25 [v]S 2Ki 19:21 [w]S Jer 30:13; S Mic 1:9
46:12 [x]S ver 6; Isa 19:4; Na 3:8-10
46:13 [y]ver 26; Eze 32:11 [z]Isa 19:1; Jer 27:7
46:14 [a]S Isa 19:13 [b]S Jer 43:8 [c]S Dt 32:42; S 2Sa 2:26; S Jer 24:8
46:15 [d]S Jos 23:5; Isa 66:15-16
46:16 [e]S Lev 26:37 [f]S ver 6 [g]S Isa 13:14 [h]S Jer 25:38
46:17 [i]1Ki 20:10-11 [j]Isa 19:11-16
46:18 [k]Jer 48:15 [l]S Jos 19:22 [m]1Ki 18:42
46:19 [n]S Isa 20:4 [o]S Isa 19:13 [p]Eze 29:10,12; 35:7
46:20 [q]ver 24; S Isa 14:31; Jer 47:2
46:21 [r]S 2Ki 7:6 [s]Lk 15:27 [t]S ver 5; S Job 20:24 [u]Ps 18:18; 37:13; Jer 18:17 [v]S Job 18:20
46:22 [w]Ps 74:5
46:23 [x]S Dt 28:42; S Jdg 7:12
46:24 [y]S 2Ki 24:7
46:25 [z]Eze 30:14; Na 3:8 [a]2Ki 24:7; Eze 30:22 [b]S Jer 43:12 [c]Isa 20:6
46:26 [d]S Jer 44:30 [e]S ver 13; S Isa 19:4 [f]Eze 29:11-16
46:27 [g]Isa 43:5; Jer 51:46 [h]Isa 41:8; 44:1; Mal 1:2 [i]S Isa 44:2 [j]S Isa 11:11; S Jer 29:14; 50:19
46:28 [k]S Ex 14:22; S Nu 14:9; Isa 8:9-10 [l]S Jer 4:27

are like fattened calves.[s]
They too will turn and flee[t] together,
they will not stand their ground,
for the day[u] of disaster is coming upon
them,
the time[v] for them to be punished.
22Egypt will hiss like a fleeing serpent
as the enemy advances in force;
they will come against her with axes,
like men who cut down trees.[w]
23They will chop down her forest,"
declares the LORD,
"dense though it be.
They are more numerous than
locusts,[x]
they cannot be counted.
24The Daughter of Egypt will be put to
shame,
handed over to the people of the
north.[y]"

25The LORD Almighty, the God of Israel, says: "I am about to bring punishment
on Amon god of Thebes,[y][z] on Pharaoh,[a]
on Egypt and her gods[b] and her kings,
and on those who rely[c] on Pharaoh. 26I
will hand them over[d] to those who seek
their lives, to Nebuchadnezzar king[e] of
Babylon and his officers. Later, however,
Egypt will be inhabited[f] as in times
past," declares the LORD.

27"Do not fear,[g] O Jacob[h] my servant;[i]
do not be dismayed, O Israel.
I will surely save you out of a distant
place,
your descendants from the land of
their exile.[j]
Jacob will again have peace and
security,
and no one will make him afraid.
28Do not fear, O Jacob my servant,
for I am with you,"[k] declares the
LORD.
"Though I completely destroy[l] all the
nations
among which I scatter you,
I will not completely destroy you.
I will discipline you but only with
justice;
I will not let you go entirely
unpunished."

Chapter 47

A Message About the Philistines

THIS is the word of the LORD that came
to Jeremiah the prophet concerning

[x]*14* Hebrew *Noph;* also in verse 19 [y]*25* Hebrew *No*

46:27–28 HOLY SCRIPTURE, Writing—See note on 30:1–11.
46:28 THE CHURCH, Servants—God's servants remain in His care. Through times of testing and judgment, God continues His caring rule over His people. The servants of God never escape His loving presence. See note on 30:11.

the Philistines[m] before Pharaoh attacked
Gaza:[n]

2This is what the LORD says:

"See how the waters are rising in the
north;[o]
they will become an overflowing
torrent.
They will overflow the land and
everything in it,
the towns and those who live in
them.
The people will cry out;
all who dwell in the land will wail[p]
3at the sound of the hoofs of galloping
steeds,
at the noise of enemy chariots[q]
and the rumble of their wheels.
Fathers will not turn to help their
children;
their hands will hang limp.[r]
4For the day has come
to destroy all the Philistines
and to cut off all survivors
who could help Tyre[s] and Sidon.[t]
The LORD is about to destroy the
Philistines,[u]
the remnant from the coasts of
Caphtor.[z] [v]
5Gaza will shave[w] her head in
mourning;
Ashkelon[x] will be silenced.
O remnant on the plain,
how long will you cut[y] yourselves?

6" 'Ah, sword[z] of the LORD,' ⌞you cry,⌟
'how long till you rest?
Return to your scabbard;
cease and be still.'[a]
7But how can it rest
when the LORD has commanded it,
when he has ordered it
to attack Ashkelon and the coast?"[b]

Chapter 48

A Message About Moab

48:29–36pp — Isa 16:6–12

CONCERNING Moab:[c]
This is what the LORD Almighty, the
God of Israel, says:

"Woe to Nebo,[d] for it will be ruined.
Kiriathaim[e] will be disgraced and
captured;
the stronghold[a] will be disgraced
and shattered.
2Moab will be praised[f] no more;
in Heshbon[b] [g] men will plot her
downfall:
'Come, let us put an end to that
nation.'[h]
You too, O Madmen,[c] will be
silenced;
the sword will pursue you.
3Listen to the cries from Horonaim,[i]
cries of great havoc and destruction.
4Moab will be broken;
her little ones will cry out.[d]
5They go up the way to Luhith,[j]
weeping bitterly as they go;
on the road down to Horonaim[k]
anguished cries over the destruction
are heard.
6Flee![l] Run for your lives;
become like a bush[e] in the desert.[m]
7Since you trust in your deeds and
riches,[n]
you too will be taken captive,
and Chemosh[o] will go into exile,[p]
together with his priests and
officials.[q]
8The destroyer[r] will come against
every town,
and not a town will escape.
The valley will be ruined
and the plateau[s] destroyed,
because the LORD has spoken.
9Put salt[t] on Moab,
for she will be laid waste[f];[u]
her towns will become desolate,
with no one to live in them.

10"A curse on him who is lax in doing
the LORD's work!
A curse on him who keeps his
sword[v] from bloodshed![w]

11"Moab has been at rest[x] from youth,
like wine left on its dregs,[y]
not poured from one jar to another—
she has not gone into exile.
So she tastes as she did,
and her aroma is unchanged.
12But days are coming,"
declares the LORD,
"when I will send men who pour from
jars,
and they will pour her out;
they will empty her jars
and smash her jugs.
13Then Moab will be ashamed[z] of
Chemosh,[a]
as the house of Israel was ashamed
when they trusted in Bethel.[b]

14"How can you say, 'We are warriors,[c]
men valiant in battle'?
15Moab will be destroyed and her towns
invaded;
her finest young men[d] will go down
in the slaughter,[e]"
declares the King,[f] whose name is
the LORD Almighty.[g]

[z]4 That is, Crete [a]1 Or / Misgab [b]2 The Hebrew for *Heshbon* sounds like the Hebrew for *plot.* [c]2 The name of the Moabite town Madmen sounds like the Hebrew for *be silenced.* [d]4 Hebrew; Septuagint / *proclaim it to Zoar* [e]6 Or *like Aroer* [f]9 Or *Give wings to Moab, / for she will fly away*

47:1 [m]S Ge 10:14; S Jdg 3:31 [n]S Ge 10:19; Zec 9:5-7
47:2 [o]S Isa 14:31 [p]S Isa 15:3
47:3 [q]S Jer 46:9; S Eze 23:24 [r]Isa 13:7; Jer 50:43; Eze 7:17; 21:7
47:4 [s]S Isa 23:1; Am 1:9-10; Zec 9:2-4 [t]S Ge 10:15; S Jer 25:22 [u]S Ge 10:14; Joel 3:4 [v]S Dt 2:23
47:5 [w]S Jer 41:5 [x]S Jer 25:20 [y]S Lev 19:28
47:6 [z]S Isa 34:5; Jer 12:12; 48:10; 50:35 [a]Eze 21:30
47:7 [b]Eze 25:15-17
48:1 [c]S Ge 19:37; S Dt 23:6 [d]S Nu 32:38 [e]S Nu 32:37; S Jos 13:19
48:2 [f]Isa 16:14 [g]S Nu 21:25; S Jos 13:26 [h]ver 42
48:3 [i]S Isa 15:5
48:5 [j]Isa 15:5 [k]ver 3
48:6 [l]S Ge 19:17 [m]Jer 17:6
48:7 [n]S Ps 49:6; S Pr 11:28 [o]S Nu 21:29 [p]Isa 46:1-2; Jer 49:3 [q]Am 2:3
48:8 [r]S Ex 12:23; S Jer 4:7 [s]S Jos 13:9
48:9 [t]Jdg 9:45 [u]Jer 51:29
48:10 [v]S Jer 47:6 [w]S 1Sa 15:11; 1Ki 20:42; 2Ki 13:15-19
48:11 [x]Zec 1:15 [y]Zep 1:12
48:13 [z]Hos 10:6 [a]ver 7 [b]S Jos 7:2
48:14 [c]Ps 33:16
48:15 [d]S Isa 9:17 [e]Jer 51:40 [f]S Jer 46:18 [g]Jer 51:57

become a ruin and an object of horror,[h] of reproach[i] and of cursing; and all its towns will be in ruins forever."[j]

14I have heard a message from the LORD:
An envoy was sent to the nations to say,
"Assemble yourselves to attack it!
Rise up for battle!"

15"Now I will make you small among the nations,
despised among men.
16The terror you inspire
and the pride[k] of your heart have deceived you,
you who live in the clefts of the rocks,[l]
who occupy the heights of the hill.
Though you build your nest[m] as high as the eagle's,
from there I will bring you down,"
declares the LORD.
17"Edom will become an object of horror;[n]
all who pass by will be appalled and will scoff
because of all its wounds.[o]
18As Sodom[p] and Gomorrah[q] were overthrown,
along with their neighboring towns,"
says the LORD,
"so no one will live there;
no man will dwell[r] in it.

19"Like a lion[s] coming up from Jordan's thickets[t]
to a rich pastureland,
I will chase Edom from its land in an instant.
Who is the chosen one I will appoint for this?
Who is like[u] me and who can challenge me?[v]
And what shepherd[w] can stand against me?"
20Therefore, hear what the LORD has planned against Edom,[x]
what he has purposed[y] against those who live in Teman:[z]
The young of the flock[a] will be dragged away;
he will completely destroy[b] their pasture because of them.[c]
21At the sound of their fall the earth will tremble;[d]
their cry[e] will resound to the Red Sea.[i]
22Look! An eagle will soar and swoop[f] down,
spreading its wings over Bozrah.[g]
In that day the hearts of Edom's warriors[h]
will be like the heart of a woman in labor.[i]

A Message About Damascus

23Concerning Damascus:[j]

"Hamath[k] and Arpad[l] are dismayed,
for they have heard bad news.
They are disheartened,
troubled like[k] the restless sea.[m]
24Damascus has become feeble,
she has turned to flee
and panic has gripped her;
anguish and pain have seized her,
pain like that of a woman in labor.[n]
25Why has the city of renown not been abandoned,
the town in which I delight?
26Surely, her young men[o] will fall in the streets;
all her soldiers will be silenced[p] in that day,"
declares the LORD Almighty.
27"I will set fire[q] to the walls of Damascus;[r]
it will consume[s] the fortresses of Ben-Hadad.[t]"

A Message About Kedar and Hazor

28Concerning Kedar[u] and the kingdoms of Hazor,[v] which Nebuchadnezzar[w] king of Babylon attacked:

This is what the LORD says:
"Arise, and attack Kedar
and destroy the people of the East.[x]
29Their tents and their flocks[y] will be taken;
their shelters will be carried off
with all their goods and camels.
Men will shout to them,
'Terror[z] on every side!'

30"Flee quickly away!
Stay in deep caves,[a] you who live in Hazor,[b]"
declares the LORD.
"Nebuchadnezzar[c] king of Babylon
has plotted against you;
he has devised a plan against you.
31"Arise and attack a nation at ease,
which lives in confidence,"
declares the LORD,
"a nation that has neither gates nor bars;[d]
its people live alone.
32Their camels[e] will become plunder,
and their large herds[f] will be booty.
I will scatter to the winds[g] those who are in distant places[l][h]

49:13 [h]ver 17 [i]Jer 42:18 [j]S Jer 19:8; Eze 35:9
49:16 [k]Eze 35:13; Ob 1:12 [l]S Job 39:28 [m]S Job 39:27
49:17 [n]ver 13 [o]S Dt 29:22; Eze 35:7
49:18 [p]Jer 23:14 [q]S Ge 19:24 [r]ver 33; S Isa 34:10
49:19 [s]S 1Sa 17:34 [t]S Jer 12:5 [u]S Ex 8:10; S 2Ch 20:6; S Isa 46:5 [v]S Job 9:19; Jer 50:44 [w]1Sa 17:35
49:20 [x]Isa 34:5 [y]Isa 14:27 [z]ver 7; S Ge 36:11 [a]Jer 50:45 [b]ver 10; Ob 1:10; Mal 1:3-4 [c]Jer 50:45
49:21 [d]Ps 114:7; Eze 26:15; 27:28; 31:16 [e]Jer 50:46; 51:29; Eze 26:18
49:22 [f]S Dt 28:49; Hos 8:1; Hab 1:8 [g]S Ge 36:33 [h]Jer 50:36; Na 3:13 [i]Isa 13:8
49:23 [j]S Ge 14:15; 2Ki 14:28; 2Ch 16:2; Ac 9:2 [k]1Ki 8:65; Isa 10:9; Eze 47:16; Am 6:2; Zec 9:2 [l]S 2Ki 18:34; S 19:13 [m]S Ge 49:4
49:24 [n]Jer 13:21
49:26 [o]S Isa 9:17; S 13:18 [p]Isa 17:12-14
49:27 [q]Jer 21:14; 43:12; 50:32; Eze 30:8; 39:6; Am 1:4 [r]S Ge 14:15 [s]Isa 17:1 [t]S 1Ki 15:18
49:28 [u]S Ge 25:13 [v]S Jos 11:1 [w]S Jer 10:22 [x]S Jdg 6:3
49:29 [y]ver 32 [z]S Jer 6:25
49:30 [a]S Jdg 6:2 [b]Jos 11:1 [c]S Jer 10:22
49:31 [d]Eze 38:11
49:32 [e]S Jdg 6:5 [f]ver 29 [g]ver 36; Jer 13:24 [h]S Jer 9:26

[i]21 Hebrew *Yam Suph*; that is, Sea of Reeds
[k]23 Hebrew *on* or *by*
[l]32 Or *who clip the hair by their foreheads*

and will bring disaster on them from
every side,"
declares the LORD.
33"Hazor[i] will become a haunt of
jackals,[j]
a desolate[k] place forever.
No one will live there;
no man will dwell[l] in it."

A Message About Elam

34This is the word of the LORD that
came to Jeremiah the prophet concerning
Elam,[m] early in the reign of Zedekiah[n]
king of Judah:
35This is what the LORD Almighty says:

"See, I will break the bow[o] of Elam,
the mainstay of their might.
36I will bring against Elam the four
winds[p]
from the four quarters of the
heavens;[q]
I will scatter them to the four winds,
and there will not be a nation
where Elam's exiles do not go.
37I will shatter Elam before their foes,
before those who seek their lives;
I will bring disaster upon them,
even my fierce anger,"[r]
declares the LORD.
"I will pursue them with the sword[s]
until I have made an end of them.
38I will set my throne in Elam
and destroy her king and officials,"
declares the LORD.
39"Yet I will restore[t] the fortunes of
Elam
in days to come,"
declares the LORD.

Chapter 50

A Message About Babylon

51:15–19pp — Jer 10:12–16

THIS is the word the LORD spoke
through Jeremiah the prophet concerning Babylon[u] and the land of the
Babylonians[m]:

2"Announce and proclaim[v] among the
nations,
lift up a banner[w] and proclaim it;
keep nothing back, but say,
'Babylon will be captured;[x]
Bel[y] will be put to shame,[z]
Marduk[a] filled with terror.
Her images will be put to shame
and her idols[b] filled with terror.'
3A nation from the north[c] will attack
her
and lay waste her land.
No one will live[d] in it;
both men and animals[e] will flee
away.

4"In those days, at that time,"
declares the LORD,
"the people of Israel and the people of
Judah together[f]
will go in tears[g] to seek[h] the LORD
their God.
5They will ask the way[i] to Zion
and turn their faces toward it.
They will come[j] and bind themselves
to the LORD
in an everlasting covenant[k]
that will not be forgotten.

6"My people have been lost sheep;[l]
their shepherds[m] have led them
astray[n]
and caused them to roam on the
mountains.
They wandered over mountain and
hill[o]
and forgot their own resting place.[p]
7Whoever found them devoured[q]
them;
their enemies said, 'We are not
guilty,[r]
for they sinned against the LORD, their
true pasture,
the LORD, the hope[s] of their
fathers.'

8"Flee[t] out of Babylon;[u]
leave the land of the Babylonians,
and be like the goats that lead the
flock.
9For I will stir[v] up and bring against
Babylon
an alliance of great nations[w] from
the land of the north.[x]
They will take up their positions
against her,
and from the north she will be
captured.[y]
Their arrows[z] will be like skilled
warriors

[m] *1* Or *Chaldeans;* also in verses 8, 25, 35 and 45

49:33 [i]S Jos 11:1 [j]S Isa 13:22 [k]Jer 48:9 [l]S ver 18; Jer 51:37
49:34 [m]S Ge 10:22 [n]2Ki 24:18
49:35 [o]S Ps 37:15; S Isa 22:6
49:36 [p]S ver 32 [q]Da 11:4
49:37 [r]Jer 30:24 [s]Jer 9:16; Eze 32:24
49:39 [t]S Jer 48:47
50:1 [u]S Ge 10:10; S Ps 137:8
50:2 [v]S Dt 30:4; Jer 4:16 [w]S Ps 20:5; S Isa 13:2 [x]ver 9; Jer 51:31 [y]S Isa 21:9; S 46:1 [z]Ps 97:7; Jer 51:52 [a]ver 38; Isa 46:6; Jer 51:47 [b]S Lev 26:30
50:3 [c]S ver 26; S Isa 41:25; S Jer 25:26 [d]S ver 13; S Isa 14:22-23; S Jer 9:11 [e]Zep 1:3
50:4 [f]S Jer 3:18; Eze 37:22 [g]S Ezr 3:12 [h]S Isa 9:13; Eze 37:17; Hos 3:5
50:5 [i]S Isa 11:16; S Jer 31:21 [j]S 1Sa 29:1; Jer 33:7 [k]S Dt 29:14; Isa 55:3; Jer 32:40; Heb 8:6-10
50:6 [l]S Ps 119:176; Mt 9:36; 10:6 [m]S Jer 2:8; S 10:21 [n]S Ps 95:10; Jer 23:32; Eze 13:10 [o]Jer 3:6; Eze 34:6 [p]ver 19
50:7 [q]S Jer 5:17; 10:25; Eze 35:12 [r]Jer 2:3 [s]S Jer 14:8
50:8 [t]S Isa 48:20 [u]ver 28
50:9 [v]S Isa 13:17 [w]S Jer 25:14 [x]S Isa 41:25; S Jer 25:26 [y]S ver 2 [z]S Isa 13:18

49:39 EVANGELISM, God's Provision—See note on 48:47.

50:2,38,44 GOD, One God—One of the primary goals of God, as seen in Jeremiah, is to convince His people that there is only one God. All other gods are false, helpless objects, and empty ideas. Even the high gods worshiped by the most powerful political rulers in the world have no real existence. They offer no challenge to God's sovereign rule over the world. See note on 1:16.

50:4–5 THE CHURCH, Covenant People—People must pledge themselves to God in covenant relationship. Repentance is the proper attitude and action with which to come before the Lord. Even Exile in Babylon could not derail God's plans. The eternal covenant is His way of working with His people. See note on 31:31–34.

50:6–7 SIN, Alienation—Sin brings separation from God, home, and hope. Sinners are lost sheep wandering the hills without a shepherd. Often the shepherd or political leader has raised false hopes and led the flock astray. God's final note is a call to come home to Him, our true Pasture and Hope. Sin's separation does not have to be final. The lost sheep can return to the Good Shepherd.

who do not return empty-handed.
10So Babylonia[n] will be plundered;[a]
all who plunder her will have their fill,"
declares the LORD.

11"Because you rejoice and are glad,
you who pillage my inheritance,[b]
because you frolic like a heifer[c]
threshing grain
and neigh like stallions,
12your mother will be greatly ashamed;
she who gave you birth will be disgraced.[d]
She will be the least of the nations—
a wilderness, a dry land, a desert.[e]
13Because of the LORD's anger she will not be inhabited
but will be completely desolate.[f]
All who pass Babylon will be horrified[g] and scoff[h]
because of all her wounds.[i]

14"Take up your positions around Babylon,
all you who draw the bow.[j]
Shoot at her! Spare no arrows,[k]
for she has sinned against the LORD.
15Shout[l] against her on every side!
She surrenders, her towers fall,
her walls[m] are torn down.
Since this is the vengeance[n] of the LORD,
take vengeance on her;
do to her[o] as she has done to others.[p]
16Cut off from Babylon the sower,
and the reaper with his sickle at harvest.
Because of the sword[q] of the oppressor
let everyone return to his own people,[r]
let everyone flee to his own land.[s]

17"Israel is a scattered flock[t]
that lions[u] have chased away.
The first to devour[v] him
was the king[w] of Assyria;
the last to crush his bones[x]
was Nebuchadnezzar[y] king[z] of Babylon."

18Therefore this is what the LORD Almighty, the God of Israel, says:

"I will punish the king of Babylon and his land
as I punished the king[a] of Assyria.[b]
19But I will bring[c] Israel back to his own pasture
and he will graze on Carmel and Bashan;
his appetite will be satisfied[d]
on the hills[e] of Ephraim and Gilead.[f]
20In those days, at that time,"
declares the LORD,
"search will be made for Israel's guilt,
but there will be none,[g]
and for the sins[h] of Judah,
but none will be found,
for I will forgive[i] the remnant[j] I spare.

21"Attack the land of Merathaim
and those who live in Pekod.[k]
Pursue, kill and completely destroy[o] them,"
declares the LORD.
"Do everything I have commanded you.
22The noise[l] of battle is in the land,
the noise of great destruction!
23How broken and shattered
is the hammer[m] of the whole earth![n]
How desolate[o] is Babylon
among the nations!
24I set a trap[p] for you, O Babylon,
and you were caught before you knew it;
you were found and captured[q]
because you opposed[r] the LORD.
25The LORD has opened his arsenal
and brought out the weapons[s] of his wrath,
for the Sovereign LORD Almighty has work to do
in the land of the Babylonians.[t]
26Come against her from afar.[u]
Break open her granaries;
pile her up like heaps of grain.[v]
Completely destroy[w] her
and leave her no remnant.
27Kill all her young bulls;[x]
let them go down to the slaughter![y]
Woe to them! For their day[z] has come,
the time[a] for them to be punished.
28Listen to the fugitives[b] and refugees from Babylon
declaring in Zion[c]
how the LORD our God has taken vengeance,[d]
vengeance for his temple.[e]

29"Summon archers against Babylon,
all those who draw the bow.[f]
Encamp all around her;

50:10 [a]Isa 47:11; S Jer 30:16
50:11 [b]S Isa 47:6 [c]S Jer 31:18
50:12 [d]Jer 51:47 [e]ver 13; S Isa 21:1; Jer 25:12; 51:26
50:13 [f]ver 3,S 12; S Jer 9:11; 48:9; 51:62 [g]Jer 51:41 [h]S Jer 18:16; 51:37; Eze 27:36; Hab 2:6 [i]S Dt 29:22
50:14 [j]ver 29,42 [k]S Isa 13:18
50:15 [l]Jer 51:14 [m]S 2Ki 25:4; S Jer 51:44,58 [n]ver 28; S Isa 10:3; 63:4; Jer 51:6 [o]ver 29; Ps 137:8; Rev 18:6 [p]Jer 51:24; Hab 2:7-8
50:16 [q]S Jer 25:38 [r]S Isa 13:14 [s]Jer 51:9
50:17 [t]S Lev 26:33; S Ps 119:176 [u]S 2Ki 24:1; S Jer 2:15 [v]S Jer 5:17 [w]S Dt 4:27; S 2Ki 15:29 [x]S Nu 24:8; La 3:4 [y]Jer 51:34 [z]S 2Ki 24:17; S 25:7
50:18 [a]S Isa 10:12 [b]Eze 31:3; Zep 2:13
50:19 [c]S Jer 31:10; Eze 34:13 [d]Jer 31:14 [e]S Jer 31:5 [f]Mic 7:14; Zec 10:10
50:20 [g]S Ps 17:3 [h]Ps 103:12; S Isa 38:17; Eze 33:16; Mic 7:18,19; Zec 3:4,9 [i]S Isa 33:24 [j]S Ge 45:7; Isa 1:9; 10:20-22; S Ro 9:27
50:21 [k]Eze 23:23
50:22 [l]Jer 4:19-21; 51:54
50:23 [m]S Isa 10:5 [n]Jer 51:25 [o]S Isa 14:16
50:24 [p]Jer 51:12 [q]Jer 51:31 [r]Job 9:4
50:25 [s]S Isa 13:5 [t]Jer 51:25,55
50:26 [u]ver 3,41; Jer 51:11 [v]S Ru 3:7 [w]S Isa 14:22-23
50:27 [x]S Ps 68:30; Jer 48:15 [y]S Isa 30:25; S Jer 25:34 [z]S Job 18:20 [a]Jer 51:6
50:28 [b]ver 8 [c]Isa 48:20; Jer 51:10 [d]S ver 15 [e]2Ki 24:13; Jer 51:11; 52:13
50:29 [f]S ver 14

[n]*10* Or *Chaldea* [o]*21* The Hebrew term refers to the irrevocable giving over of things or persons to the LORD, often by totally destroying them; also in verse 26.

50:19 SALVATION, Renewal—When God renews His people, He relates to them like the Good Shepherd (Ps 23:1–6).

50:20 THE CHURCH, Remnant—God fully and freely forgives those who turn to Him in faith. He plans to produce a remnant in perfect relation to Him.

let no one escape.[g]
Repay[h] her for her deeds;[i]
do to her as she has done.
For she has defied[j] the LORD,
the Holy One[k] of Israel.
30Therefore, her young men[l] will fall in
the streets;
all her soldiers will be silenced in
that day,"
declares the LORD.
31"See, I am against[m] you, O arrogant
one,"
declares the Lord, the LORD
Almighty,
"for your day[n] has come,
the time for you to be punished.
32The arrogant[o] one will stumble and
fall[p]
and no one will help her up;[q]
I will kindle a fire[r] in her towns
that will consume all who are
around her."

33This is what the LORD Almighty says:

"The people of Israel are oppressed,[s]
and the people of Judah as well.
All their captors hold them fast,
refusing to let them go.[t]
34Yet their Redeemer[u] is strong;
the LORD Almighty[v] is his name.
He will vigorously defend their cause[w]
so that he may bring rest[x] to their
land,
but unrest to those who live in
Babylon.
35"A sword[y] against the Babylonians!"[z]
declares the LORD—
"against those who live in Babylon
and against her officials and wise[a]
men!
36A sword against her false prophets!
They will become fools.
A sword against her warriors![b]
They will be filled with terror.[c]
37A sword against her horses and
chariots[d]
and all the foreigners in her
ranks!
They will become women.[e]
A sword against her treasures![f]
They will be plundered.
38A drought on[p] her waters![g]
They will dry[h] up.
For it is a land of idols,[i]
idols that will go mad with
terror.

50:29 [g]S Isa 13:18; Jer 51:3 [h]S Dt 32:41; S Job 21:19; S Jer 51:6; Rev 18:6 [i]Eze 35:11; Ob 1:15 [j]S Isa 14:13-14; 47:10; Da 5:23 [k]Ps 78:41; Isa 41:20; Jer 51:5
50:30 [l]S Isa 13:18
50:31 [m]S Jer 21:13 [n]S Job 18:20; Rev 18:7-8
50:32 [o]S Ps 119:21 [p]S Ps 20:8 [q]Am 5:2 [r]S Jer 49:27
50:33 [s]Isa 58:6 [t]S Isa 14:17
50:34 [u]S Ex 6:6; S Job 19:25 [v]Jer 31:35; 51:19 [w]S Ps 119:154; S Isa 49:25; Jer 15:21; 51:36; La 3:58 [x]S Isa 14:7
50:35 [y]S Jer 47:6 [z]S Isa 45:1 [a]Da 5:7
50:36 [b]S Jer 49:22 [c]Jer 51:30,32
50:37 [d]S 2Ki 19:23; Jer 51:21 [e]S Isa 19:16 [f]S Isa 45:3
50:38 [g]Ps 137:1; Jer 51:13 [h]S Isa 11:15; Jer 51:36 [i]S ver 2
50:39 [j]S Ps 74:14 [k]Isa 13:19-22; 34:13-15; Jer 51:37; Rev 18:2
50:40 [l]S Ge 19:24; S Mt 10:15 [m]Jer 51:62
50:41 [n]S ver 26; S Isa 41:25 [o]S Isa 13:17 [p]S Isa 13:4; Jer 51:22-28
50:42 [q]S ver 14 [r]S Job 30:21 [s]S Isa 13:18 [t]S Isa 5:30 [u]S Isa 47:1
50:43 [v]S Jer 47:3 [w]Jer 6:22-24
50:44 [x]S Jer 12:5 [y]S Nu 16:5 [z]S Job 41:10; Isa 46:9; S Jer 49:19
50:45 [a]Ps 33:11; Jer 51:11 [b]S Isa 48:14
50:46 [c]S Jdg 5:4; S Jer 49:21

39"So desert creatures[j] and hyenas will
live there,
and there the owl will dwell.
It will never again be inhabited
or lived in from generation to
generation.[k]
40As God overthrew Sodom and
Gomorrah[l]
along with their neighboring
towns,"
declares the LORD,
"so no one will live there;
no man will dwell in it.[m]
41"Look! An army is coming from the
north;[n]
a great nation and many kings
are being stirred[o] up from the ends
of the earth.[p]
42They are armed with bows[q] and
spears;
they are cruel[r] and without
mercy.[s]
They sound like the roaring sea[t]
as they ride on their horses;
they come like men in battle formation
to attack you, O Daughter of
Babylon.[u]
43The king of Babylon has heard reports
about them,
and his hands hang limp.[v]
Anguish has gripped him,
pain like that of a woman in labor.[w]
44Like a lion coming up from Jordan's
thickets[x]
to a rich pastureland,
I will chase Babylon from its land in an
instant.
Who is the chosen[y] one I will
appoint for this?
Who is like me and who can challenge
me?[z]
And what shepherd can stand
against me?"
45Therefore, hear what the LORD has
planned against Babylon,
what he has purposed[a] against the
land of the Babylonians:[b]
The young of the flock will be dragged
away;
he will completely destroy their
pasture because of them.
46At the sound of Babylon's capture the
earth will tremble;[c]

[p]38 Or *A sword against*

50:34 GOD, Savior—At a particular moment in history, the enemies of God's people may oppress God's people. This is not evidence of God's weakness. When He chooses, He acts to redeem His people and punish the enemies. The gods of the nations are helpless and worthless, but God is the Savior of His people. He can be depended upon.
50:41–43 HOLY SCRIPTURE, Writing—See note on 30:1–11.

50:44 ELECTION, Freedom—Oppressed Judah and Israel were released from captivity by God's humbling of Babylon. The God of election had purposed and planned revenge against Babylon. God controls history to establish His election purposes. He can appoint whom He chooses over any people He chooses. Nebuchadnezzar, the Babylonian king, could be His servant (43:10), but Babylon could also face His destruction.

its cry[d] will resound among the
nations.

Chapter 51

THIS is what the LORD says:
"See, I will stir[e] up the spirit of a
destroyer
against Babylon[f] and the people of
Leb Kamai.[q]
2I will send foreigners[g] to Babylon
to winnow[h] her and to devastate
her land;
they will oppose her on every side
in the day[i] of her disaster.
3Let not the archer string his bow,[j]
nor let him put on his armor.[k]
Do not spare her young men;
completely destroy[r] her army.
4They will fall[l] down slain in
Babylon,[s]
fatally wounded in her streets.[m]
5For Israel and Judah have not been
forsaken[n]
by their God, the LORD Almighty,
though their land[t] is full of guilt[o]
before the Holy One of Israel.

6"Flee[p] from Babylon!
Run for your lives!
Do not be destroyed because of her
sins.[q]
It is time[r] for the LORD's vengeance;[s]
he will pay[t] her what she deserves.
7Babylon was a gold cup[u] in the LORD's
hand;
she made the whole earth drunk.
The nations drank her wine;
therefore they have now gone mad.
8Babylon will suddenly fall[v] and be
broken.
Wail over her!
Get balm[w] for her pain;
perhaps she can be healed.

9" 'We would have healed Babylon,
but she cannot be healed;
let us leave[x] her and each go to his
own land,
for her judgment[y] reaches to the
skies,
it rises as high as the clouds.'

10" 'The LORD has vindicated[z] us;
come, let us tell in Zion
what the LORD our God has done.'[a]

11"Sharpen the arrows,[b]
take up the shields![c]
The LORD has stirred up the kings[d] of
the Medes,[e]
because his purpose[f] is to destroy
Babylon.
The LORD will take vengeance,[g]
vengeance for his temple.[h]
12Lift up a banner[i] against the walls of
Babylon!
Reinforce the guard,
station the watchmen,[j]
prepare an ambush![k]
The LORD will carry out his purpose,[l]
his decree against the people of
Babylon.
13You who live by many waters[m]
and are rich in treasures,[n]
your end has come,
the time for you to be cut off.[o]
14The LORD Almighty has sworn by
himself:[p]
I will surely fill you with men, as
with a swarm of locusts,[q]
and they will shout[r] in triumph
over you.

15"He made the earth by his power;
he founded the world by his
wisdom[s]
and stretched[t] out the heavens by
his understanding.[u]
16When he thunders,[v] the waters in the
heavens roar;
he makes clouds rise from the ends
of the earth.
He sends lightning with the rain[w]
and brings out the wind from his
storehouses.[x]

17"Every man is senseless and without
knowledge;

q*1 Leb Kamai* is a cryptogram for Chaldea, that is, Babylonia. r*3* The Hebrew term refers to the irrevocable giving over of things or persons to the LORD, often by totally destroying them. s*4* Or *Chaldea* t*5* Or */ and the land ⌊of the Babylonians⌋*

50:46 dS Job 24:12; Rev 18:9-10
51:1 eS Isa 13:17 fJer 25:12
51:2 gIsa 13:5 hS Isa 41:16; Mt 3:12 iS Isa 13:9
51:3 jS Jer 50:29 kJer 46:4
51:4 lIsa 13:15 mS Isa 13:18
51:5 nS Lev 26:44; Isa 54:6-8 oHos 4:1
51:6 pS Isa 48:20 qNu 16:26; Rev 18:4 rJer 50:27 sS Isa 1:24; S Jer 50:15 tver 24, 56; Dt 32:35; S Job 21:19; Jer 25:14; 50:29; La 3:64
51:7 uS Isa 51:22; Jer 25:15-16; 49:12; Rev 14:8-10
51:8 vS Isa 14:15; S 21:9; S Rev 14:8 wJer 8:22; 46:11
51:9 xS Isa 13:14; S 31:9; Jer 50:16 yRev 18:4-5
51:10 zMic 7:9 aPs 64:9; S Jer 50:28
51:11 bJer 50:9 cS Isa 21:5 dS Isa 41:2 ever 28; S Isa 13:3; S 41:25 fS Jer 50:45 gS Lev 26:25 hS Jer 50:28
51:12 iver 27; S Ps 20:5 j2Sa 18:24; Eze 33:2 kJer 50:24 lS Ps 33:11
51:13 mS Jer 50:38 nS Isa 45:3; Eze 22:27; Hab 2:9 oJer 50:3
51:14 pS Ge 22:16; Am 6:8 qver 27; Am 7:1; Na 3:15 rJer 50:15
51:15 sPs 104:24 tS Ge 1:1; S Ps 104:2 uS Ps 136:5
51:16 vPs 18:11-13 wS Job 28:26 xS Dt 28:12; S Ps 135:7; Jnh 1:4

51:1–16 CREATION, Freedom—God chooses His goals and also how to implement them. Because Israel sinned, He sent them into captivity, using Babylon as His chastening agent. When, however, He decided He was ready to return the nation to her homeland, He raised up Persia against Babylon. From the beginning, God's resources guided the world's creation. He retains for Himself the freedom to act toward His people according to His sovereign will and their moral choices.
51:10,36 SALVATION, Vindication—God's salvation is referred to as His vindication. This represents courtroom language. God defends the rights of His people and punishes all who abuse those rights. Thus, humans do not need to seek revenge. We are to be witnesses testifying to what God has done. The Lord promised to defend Israel's cause and to avenge her against Babylonia. He vindicates all who trust in Him (Dt 32:35; Ro 12:19).
51:10 EVANGELISM, Personal—God's people share their personal testimonies to encourage others to worship God and participate in His salvation. The returning exiles were to share their deliverance and freedom from Babylon. We share our deliverance and freedom in Christ.
51:15–19 GOD, One God—No idol can do what the true God has done.
51:15 GOD, Wisdom—The superiority of God is shown in His infinite wisdom, a wisdom evidenced by the created order.
51:15–19 HOLY SCRIPTURE, Writing—See note on 30:1–11.
51:17 HUMANITY, Human Nature—The Hebrew word for "senseless" describes one becoming like an animal. Those who make their own gods have given up their human nature

every goldsmith is shamed by his idols.
His images are a fraud;[y]
they have no breath in them.
18They are worthless,[z] the objects of mockery;
when their judgment comes, they will perish.
19He who is the Portion[a] of Jacob is not like these,
for he is the Maker of all things,
including the tribe of his inheritance[b] —
the LORD Almighty is his name.

20"You are my war club,[c]
my weapon for battle—
with you I shatter[d] nations,[e]
with you I destroy kingdoms,
21with you I shatter horse and rider,[f]
with you I shatter chariot[g] and driver,
22with you I shatter man and woman,
with you I shatter old man and youth,
with you I shatter young man and maiden,[h]
23with you I shatter shepherd and flock,
with you I shatter farmer and oxen,
with you I shatter governors and officials.[i]

24"Before your eyes I will repay[j] Babylon[k] and all who live in Babylonia[u] for
all the wrong they have done in Zion,"
declares the LORD.

25"I am against[l] you, O destroying mountain,
you who destroy the whole earth,"[m]
declares the LORD.
"I will stretch out my hand[n] against you,
roll you off the cliffs,
and make you a burned-out mountain.[o]
26No rock will be taken from you for a cornerstone,
nor any stone for a foundation,
for you will be desolate[p] forever,"
declares the LORD.

27"Lift up a banner[q] in the land!
Blow the trumpet among the nations!
Prepare the nations for battle against her;
summon against her these kingdoms:[r]
Ararat,[s] Minni and Ashkenaz.[t]
Appoint a commander against her;
send up horses like a swarm of locusts.[u]
28Prepare the nations for battle against her—
the kings of the Medes,[v]
their governors and all their officials,
and all the countries they rule.[w]
29The land trembles[x] and writhes,
for the LORD's purposes[y] against Babylon stand—
to lay waste[z] the land of Babylon
so that no one will live there.[a]
30Babylon's warriors[b] have stopped fighting;
they remain in their strongholds.
Their strength is exhausted;
they have become like women.[c]
Her dwellings are set on fire;[d]
the bars[e] of her gates are broken.
31One courier[f] follows another
and messenger follows messenger
to announce to the king of Babylon
that his entire city is captured,[g]
32the river crossings seized,
the marshes set on fire,[h]
and the soldiers terrified.[i] "

33This is what the LORD Almighty, the
God of Israel, says:

"The Daughter of Babylon[j] is like a threshing floor[k]
at the time it is trampled;
the time to harvest[l] her will soon come.[m]"

34"Nebuchadnezzar[n] king of Babylon
has devoured[o] us,[p]
he has thrown us into confusion,
he has made us an empty jar.
Like a serpent he has swallowed us
and filled his stomach with our delicacies,
and then has spewed[q] us out.
35May the violence[r] done to our flesh[v]
be upon Babylon,"
say the inhabitants of Zion.
"May our blood be on those who live in Babylonia,"
says Jerusalem.[s]

36Therefore, this is what the LORD says:

"See, I will defend your cause[t]
and avenge[u] you;
I will dry up[v] her sea
and make her springs dry.
37Babylon will be a heap of ruins,
a haunt[w] of jackals,
an object of horror and scorn,[x]
a place where no one lives.[y]
38Her people all roar like young lions,[z]
they growl like lion cubs.

[u]24 Or *Chaldea;* also in verse 35 [v]35 Or *done to us and to our children*

51:17 [y]S Isa 44:20; Hab 2:18-19
51:18 [z]S Jer 18:15
51:19 [a]S Ps 119:57 [b]S Ex 34:9
51:20 [c]S Isa 10:5; Zec 9:13 [d]S Job 34:24; Mic 4:13 [e]S Isa 45:1
51:21 [f]S Ex 15:1 [g]S Isa 43:17; S Jer 50:37
51:22 [h]S 2Ch 36:17; Isa 13:17-18
51:23 [i]ver 57
51:24 [j]S ver 6,35; S Dt 32:41; S Jer 50:15; La 3:64 [k]S Isa 45:1
51:25 [l]S Jer 21:13 [m]Jer 50:23 [n]S Ex 3:20 [o]Zec 4:7
51:26 [p]ver 29; S Isa 13:19-22; S Jer 50:12
51:27 [q]S Ps 20:5; S Isa 13:2 [r]S Jer 25:14 [s]S Ge 8:4 [t]Ge 10:3 [u]S ver 14
51:28 [v]S ver 11 [w]ver 48
51:29 [x]S Jdg 5:4; S Jer 49:21 [y]S Ps 33:11 [z]Jer 48:9 [a]ver 43; S Isa 13:20
51:30 [b]S Jer 50:36 [c]S Isa 19:16 [d]S Isa 47:14 [e]S Isa 45:2
51:31 [f]2Sa 18:19-31 [g]S Jer 50:2; Da 5:30
51:32 [h]S Isa 47:14 [i]S Jer 50:36
51:33 [j]S Isa 47:1 [k]S Isa 21:10 [l]S Isa 17:5 [m]S Isa 13:22
51:34 [n]S Jer 50:17 [o]Na 2:12 [p]Hos 8:8 [q]ver 44; S Lev 18:25
51:35 [r]Joel 3:19; Hab 2:17 [s]S ver 24; Ps 137:8
51:36 [t]Ps 140:12; Jer 50:34; La 3:58 [u]ver 6; Jer 20:12; S Ro 12:19 [v]S Isa 11:15; S 19:5; Hos 13:15
51:37 [w]S Isa 13:22; Rev 18:2 [x]Na 3:6; Mal 2:9 [y]S Jer 50:13,39
51:38 [z]S Isa 5:29

for that of animals.
51:20–26 HISTORY, Universal—See note on Isa 10:5–19. God shattered the greatness of Babylon.

39But while they are aroused,
I will set out a feast for them
and make them drunk,[a]
so that they shout with laughter—
then sleep forever[b] and not awake,"
declares the LORD.[c]
40"I will bring them down
like lambs to the slaughter,
like rams and goats.[d]

41"How Sheshach[w][e] will be captured,[f]
the boast of the whole earth seized!
What a horror[g] Babylon will be
among the nations!
42The sea will rise over Babylon;
its roaring waves[h] will cover her.
43Her towns will be desolate,
a dry and desert[i] land,
a land where no one lives,
through which no man travels.[j]
44I will punish Bel[k] in Babylon
and make him spew out[l] what he
has swallowed.
The nations will no longer stream to
him.
And the wall[m] of Babylon will fall.

45"Come out[n] of her, my people!
Run[o] for your lives!
Run from the fierce anger[p] of the
LORD.
46Do not lose heart[q] or be afraid[r]
when rumors[s] are heard in the
land;
one rumor comes this year, another
the next,
rumors of violence in the land
and of ruler against ruler.
47For the time will surely come
when I will punish the idols[t] of
Babylon;
her whole land will be disgraced[u]
and her slain will all lie fallen within
her.[v]
48Then heaven and earth and all that is
in them
will shout[w] for joy over Babylon,
for out of the north[x]
destroyers[y] will attack her,"
declares the LORD.

49"Babylon must fall because of Israel's
slain,
just as the slain in all the earth
have fallen because of Babylon.[z]
50You who have escaped the sword,
leave[a] and do not linger!
Remember[b] the LORD in a distant
land,[c]

51:39 [a]S Isa 21:5 [b]S Ps 13:3 [c]ver 57; S Jer 50:24
51:40 [d]Eze 39:18
51:41 [e]S Jer 25:26 [f]Isa 13:19 [g]Jer 50:13
51:42 [h]S Ps 18:4; Isa 8:7
51:43 [i]S Isa 21:1 [j]S ver 29,62; S Isa 13:20; Jer 2:6
51:44 [k]S Isa 21:9; S 46:1 [l]S ver 34 [m]ver 58; S 2Ki 25:4; Isa 25:12; Jer 50:15
51:45 [n]ver 50 [o]S Isa 48:20 [p]Ps 76:10; 79:6
51:46 [q]Ps 18:45 [r]S Jer 46:27 [s]S 2Ki 19:7
51:47 [t]S Isa 46:1-2; S Jer 50:2 [u]Jer 50:12 [v]S Jer 27:7
51:48 [w]S Job 3:7; S Ps 149:2; Rev 18:20 [x]ver 11; S Isa 41:25; S Jer 25:26 [y]ver 53, 56
51:49 [z]Ps 137:8; S Jer 50:29
51:50 [a]ver 45 [b]S Ps 137:6 [c]Jer 23:23
51:51 [d]Ps 44:13-16; 79:4 [e]La 1:10
51:52 [f]ver 47 [g]S Job 24:12
51:53 [h]S Ge 11:4; S Isa 14:13-14 [i]S ver 48; S Job 15:21
51:54 [j]S Job 24:12 [k]S Jer 50:22
51:55 [l]Isa 25:5 [m]S Ps 18:4
51:56 [n]S ver 48; S Job 15:21 [o]Ps 46:9 [p]S ver 6; S Ge 4:24; S Dt 32:41; Ps 94:1-2; Hab 2:8
51:57 [q]S ver 23 [r]S Job 5:13 [s]S Isa 21:5 [t]S ver 39; Ps 76:5; S Jer 25:27 [u]S Isa 6:5
51:58 [v]S ver 44; S 2Ki 25:4; S Isa 15:1 [w]S Isa 13:2 [x]ver 64 [y]S Isa 47:13 [z]S Isa 47:14
51:59 [a]Jer 36:4 [b]Jer 52:1 [c]Jer 28:1
51:60 [d]S Ex 17:14; Jer 30:2; 36:2

and think on Jerusalem."

51"We are disgraced,[d]
for we have been insulted
and shame covers our faces,
because foreigners have entered
the holy places of the LORD's
house."[e]

52"But days are coming," declares the
LORD,
"when I will punish her idols,[f]
and throughout her land
the wounded will groan.[g]
53Even if Babylon reaches the sky[h]
and fortifies her lofty stronghold,
I will send destroyers[i] against her,"
declares the LORD.

54"The sound of a cry[j] comes from
Babylon,
the sound of great destruction[k]
from the land of the Babylonians.[x]
55The LORD will destroy Babylon;
he will silence[l] her noisy din.
Waves[m] ⌞of enemies⌟ will rage like
great waters;
the roar of their voices will resound.
56A destroyer[n] will come against
Babylon;
her warriors will be captured,
and their bows will be broken.[o]
For the LORD is a God of retribution;
he will repay[p] in full.
57I will make her officials[q] and wise[r]
men drunk,[s]
her governors, officers and warriors
as well;
they will sleep[t] forever and not
awake,"
declares the King,[u] whose name is
the LORD Almighty.

58This is what the LORD Almighty says:
"Babylon's thick wall[v] will be leveled
and her high gates[w] set on fire;
the peoples[x] exhaust[y] themselves for
nothing,
the nations' labor is only fuel for the
flames."[z]

59This is the message Jeremiah gave to
the staff officer Seraiah son of Neriah,[a]
the son of Mahseiah, when he went to
Babylon with Zedekiah[b] king of Judah in
the fourth[c] year of his reign. 60Jeremiah
had written on a scroll[d] about all the

[w]41 *Sheshach* is a cryptogram for Babylon. [x]54 Or *Chaldeans*

51:45,56 GOD, Wrath—God commissioned Babylon to capture and punish His people Judah. This was not evidence of Babylon's goodness. Rather God announced judgment on the wickedness of Babylon and called His own people to flee the disaster.

51:60 HOLY SCRIPTURE, Collection—Jeremiah recorded all the various revelations of God concerning the fate of his people and preserved them in a scroll. He sent the scroll to Babylon where the concluding chapters pronouncing doom on Babylon would bring hope to God's exiled people. The scroll became not only an historical document for Judah but also inspired Scripture, revealing God's nature and will.

disasters that would come upon Babylon
—all that had been recorded concerning
Babylon. 61He said to Seraiah, "When you
get to Babylon, see that you read all these
words aloud. 62Then say, 'O LORD, you
have said you will destroy this place, so
that neither man nor animal will live in
it; it will be desolate[e] forever.' 63When
you finish reading this scroll, tie a stone
to it and throw it into the Euphrates.[f]
64Then say, 'So will Babylon sink to rise
no more[g] because of the disaster I will
bring upon her. And her people[h] will
fall.' "[i]

The words of Jeremiah end[j] here.

Chapter 52

The Fall of Jerusalem

52:1–3pp — 2Ki 24:18–20; 2Ch 36:11–16
52:4–16pp — Jer 39:1–10
52:4–21pp — 2Ki 25:1–21; 2Ch 36:17–20

ZEDEKIAH[k] was twenty-one years old
when he became king, and he
reigned in Jerusalem eleven years. His
mother's name was Hamutal daughter of
Jeremiah; she was from Libnah.[l] 2He did
evil in the eyes of the LORD, just as Jehoiakim[m] had done. 3It was because of the
LORD's anger that all this happened to Jerusalem and Judah,[n] and in the end he
thrust them from his presence.[o]

Now Zedekiah rebelled[p] against the
king of Babylon.

4So in the ninth year of Zedekiah's
reign, on the tenth[q] day of the tenth
month, Nebuchadnezzar king of Babylon
marched against Jerusalem[r] with his
whole army. They camped outside the
city and built siege works[s] all around it.[t]
5The city was kept under siege until the
eleventh year of King Zedekiah.

6By the ninth day of the fourth month
the famine in the city had become so severe that there was no food for the people
to eat.[u] 7Then the city wall was broken
through, and the whole army fled.[v] They
left the city at night through the gate between the two walls near the king's garden, though the Babylonians[y] were surrounding the city. They fled toward the
Arabah,[z] 8but the Babylonian[a] army pursued King Zedekiah and overtook him in
the plains of Jericho. All his soldiers were
separated from him and scattered, 9and
he was captured.[w]

He was taken to the king of Babylon at
Riblah[x] in the land of Hamath,[y] where
he pronounced sentence on him. 10There
at Riblah the king of Babylon slaughtered
the sons[z] of Zedekiah before his eyes; he
also killed all the officials of Judah.
11Then he put out Zedekiah's eyes, bound
him with bronze shackles and took him
to Babylon, where he put him in prison
till the day of his death.[a]

12On the tenth day of the fifth[b] month,
in the nineteenth year of Nebuchadnezzar king of Babylon, Nebuzaradan[c] commander of the imperial guard, who
served the king of Babylon, came to Jerusalem. 13He set fire[d] to the temple[e] of
the LORD, the royal palace and all the
houses[f] of Jerusalem. Every important
building he burned down. 14The whole
Babylonian army under the commander
of the imperial guard broke down all the
walls[g] around Jerusalem. 15Nebuzaradan
the commander of the guard carried into
exile[h] some of the poorest people and
those who remained in the city, along
with the rest of the craftsmen[b] and those
who had gone over[i] to the king of Babylon. 16But Nebuzaradan left behind[j] the
rest of the poorest people of the land to
work the vineyards and fields.

17The Babylonians broke up the bronze
pillars,[k] the movable stands[l] and the
bronze Sea[m] that were at the temple of
the LORD and they carried all the bronze
to Babylon.[n] 18They also took away the
pots, shovels, wick trimmers, sprinkling
bowls,[o] dishes and all the bronze articles
used in the temple service.[p] 19The commander of the imperial guard took away
the basins, censers,[q] sprinkling bowls,
pots, lampstands,[r] dishes[s] and bowls
used for drink offerings[t]—all that were
made of pure gold or silver.[u]

[y] 7 Or *Chaldeans*; also in verse 17 [z] 7 Or *the Jordan Valley* [a] 8 Or *Chaldean*; also in verse 14 [b] 15 Or *populace*

51:62 [e]S Isa 13:20; S Jer 9:11; S 50:13, 39
51:63 [f]S Ge 2:14
51:64 [g]Eze 26:21; 28:19 [h]S ver 58 [i]Rev 18:21 [j]S Job 31:40
52:1 [k]S 2Ki 24:17 [l]S Nu 33:20; Jos 10:29; 2Ki 8:22
52:2 [m]S Jer 36:30
52:3 [n]Isa 3:1 [o]S Ge 4:14; S Ex 33:15 [p]Eze 17:12-16
52:4 [q]Zec 8:19 [r]Jer 34:1 [s]S Jer 6:6 [t]Eze 24:1-2
52:6 [u]S Lev 26:26; S Isa 3:1; La 1:11
52:7 [v]La 4:19
52:9 [w]S Jer 21:7; S 32:4 [x]S Nu 34:11 [y]S Nu 13:21
52:10 [z]S Jer 22:30
52:11 [a]Jer 34:4; Eze 12:13; 17:16
52:12 [b]Zec 7:5; 8:19 [c]ver 26
52:13 [d]S 2Ch 36:19; S Ps 74:8; La 2:6 [e]S Dt 29:24; Ps 79:1; Mic 3:12 [f]S Dt 13:16; S Jer 19:13
52:14 [g]S Ne 1:3; La 2:8
52:15 [h]S 2Ki 24:1; S Jer 1:3 [i]S Jer 38:19
52:16 [j]Jer 40:6
52:17 [k]S 1Ki 7:15 [l]1Ki 7:27-37 [m]S 1Ki 7:23 [n]Jer 27:19-22
52:18 [o]S Nu 4:14 [p]S Ex 27:3; 1Ki 7:45
52:19 [q]S Lev 10:1; S 1Ki 7:50 [r]S Nu 3:31 [s]Ex 25:29 [t]S Nu 4:7 [u]S Ezr 1:7; Da 5:2

51:64 HOLY SCRIPTURE, Collection—Baruch or another follower of Jeremiah added a final note to the inspired book noting prophetic preaching ended at this point. Apparently this inspired editor or another one also added ch 52 to show how Jeremiah's prophecies were fulfilled. Ch 52 basically repeats 2 Ki 24:18—25:21. Within Scripture we see the use of inspired Scripture to give authority and power to another part of God's Word. Such use of written Scripture is an important part of God's work in revelation and inspiration. See note on Isa 36:1—39:8.

52:1–34 GOD, Sovereignty—The unthinkable happened. God's holy city suffered destruction. Why? The sovereign God can bring judgment upon His people when necessary. He has the power and authority to work in His world as He sees fit. No one can indefinitely escape His judgment.

52:2–3 SIN, Discipline—See notes on 1 Ki 14:22–24; 2 Ki 25:1–21.

52:3 REVELATION, Divine Presence—The prophet expressed God's anger with Judah and interpreted the events which followed as a consequence of God's reaction to infidelity. God's anger is associated with His deep care for His children and His painful disappointment over their choosing destructive ways (3:2–5). God's anger removed Judah from Jerusalem and the Temple, the symbol of His presence. Isaiah 40—55 shows how deeply involved God was with the exiled people in Babylon, as does Ezekiel. Going into Exile, the Israelites felt God's absence but soon discovered He faithfully cared for them wherever they were.

20 The bronze from the two pillars, the
Sea and the twelve bronze bulls[v] under
it, and the movable stands, which King
Solomon had made for the temple of the
LORD, was more than could be weighed.[w]
21 Each of the pillars was eighteen cubits
high and twelve cubits in circumference[c]; each was four fingers thick, and
hollow.[x] 22 The bronze capital[y] on top of
the one pillar was five cubits[d] high and
was decorated with a network and pomegranates[z] of bronze all around. The other
pillar, with its pomegranates, was similar.
23 There were ninety-six pomegranates on
the sides; the total number of pomegranates[a] above the surrounding network
was a hundred.[b]
24 The commander of the guard took as
prisoners Seraiah[c] the chief priest, Zephaniah[d] the priest next in rank and the
three doorkeepers.[e] 25 Of those still in
the city, he took the officer in charge of
the fighting men, and seven royal advisers. He also took the secretary[f] who was
chief officer in charge of conscripting the
people of the land and sixty of his men
who were found in the city. 26 Nebuzaradan[g] the commander took them
all and brought them to the king of
Babylon at Riblah. 27 There at Riblah,[h]
in the land of Hamath, the king had them
executed.

So Judah went into captivity, away[i]
from her land. 28 This is the number of the
people Nebuchadnezzar carried into exile:[j]

in the seventh year, 3,023 Jews;
29 in Nebuchadnezzar's eighteenth
year,
832 people from Jerusalem;
30 in his twenty-third year,
745 Jews taken into exile[k] by
Nebuzaradan the commander of
the imperial guard.
There were 4,600 people in all.[l]

Jehoiachin Released

52:31–34pp — 2Ki 25:27–30

31 In the thirty-seventh year of the exile
of Jehoiachin[m] king of Judah, in the year
Evil-Merodach[e] became king of Babylon,
he released Jehoiachin king of Judah and
freed him from prison on the twenty-fifth
day of the twelfth month. 32 He spoke
kindly to him and gave him a seat of hon-
or higher than those of the other kings
who were with him in Babylon. 33 So Jehoiachin put aside his prison clothes and
for the rest of his life ate regularly at the
king's table.[n] 34 Day by day the king of
Babylon gave Jehoiachin a regular allowance[o] as long as he lived, till the day of
his death.

52:20 [v]1Ki 7:25 [w]S 1Ki 7:47
52:21 [x]S 1Ki 7:15
52:22 [y]S 1Ki 7:16 [z]S Ex 28:33
52:23 [a]1Ki 7:20 [b]S ver 17; S Jer 27:19
52:24 [c]S 2Ki 25:18 [d]S 2Ki 25:18; S Jer 37:3 [e]S 2Ki 12:9
52:25 [f]Jer 36:10
52:26 [g]S ver 12
52:27 [h]S Nu 34:11 [i]S Jer 20:4
52:28 [j]S Dt 28:36; S 2Ch 36:20; S Ne 1:2
52:30 [k]S Jer 43:3 [l]S Jer 13:19
52:31 [m]S 2Ch 36:9
52:33 [n]S 2Sa 9:7
52:34 [o]2Sa 9:10

[c] *21* That is, about 27 feet (about 8.1 meters) high and 18 feet (about 5.4 meters) in circumference
[d] *22* That is, about 7 1/2 feet (about 2.3 meters)
[e] *31* Also called *Amel-Marduk*

52:31–34 HISTORY, Hope—Jeremiah's inspired book does not end with a ringing proclamation of victory and hope. Instead it concludes with a modest historical report of kindness to an old, exiled king in his last days. From the small historical glimmer, God's people were expected to read a note of hope signalling the beginning point of fulfillment for Jeremiah's prophecies. The king was dead. The promise of hope of God's Word lives on forever.

Lamentations

Theological Setting

Can God be defeated? Israel had reason to wonder!

The year was 586 BC. Jerusalem had fallen. The nation had been destroyed. The Temple had been demolished, its sacred vessels taken as spoils of war. The priests had been killed or taken captive to Babylon. Jeremiah had warned of impending disaster, and now it had come.

How would the inhabitants of the land respond to this loss? Where was God when all this happened? Had God permitted barbaric Babylonians to devastate His elect people with impunity? Or had the Lord Himself been defeated? The Book of Lamentations poses such questions.

Lamentations, as its name suggests, is a series of five independent laments, each of whose subject is the fall of Judah and Jerusalem. Chapters 1 through 4 are alphabetic acrostics, a poetic device in which successive verses or groups of verses begin with successive letters of the Hebrew alphabet. All five chapters center on one question: How can one respond to the loss of all security?

Those who had experienced the horrors of defeat, disruption of the economy, and the ensuing famine and pestilence must have felt at times that God had abandoned them. In such dire circumstances the people had several theological options:

1. They could decide their God had been defeated and was impotent. Thus they might abandon their God and turn to the worship of the victorious Babylonian deity.

2. They might decide God did not really exist and become basically atheistic.

3. They might abandon their religious zeal for a fanatical political program, becoming those zealots who would try to overthrow foreign conquerors by violence. Ishmael, the son of Nethaniah (Jer 40—41), was such a revolutionary.

4. Or they might try to understand how God could have brought the Exile and could be working through it.

This latter response is the position of Lamentations. In spite of the despair over defeat, personal suffering, and loss, still the community must have hope. Even if God seemed to have abandoned them, they must be hopeful. For, the poet tells them, hope is all they have left.

Theological Outline

Lamentations: Hope Is All We Have.

I. The Appalling Price of Sin (1:1-22)
  - A. Description of punishment for sins (1:1-17)
  - B. Admission of sin (1:18-20)
  - C. Cry for vengeance (1:21-22)

II. God Is the One Who Punishes Sin (2:1-22)
  - A. God has done as He said. (2:1-17)
  - B. Call the people to repent. (2:18-19)
  - C. Call on the Lord to relent. (2:20-22)

III. A Personal Cry to God (3:1-66)
  - A. I am suffering. (3:1-18)
  - B. I cry to God in hope. (3:19-21)
  - C. God will hear and help. (3:22-33)
  - D. God knows our unacceptable actions. (3:34-36)
  - E. God punishes unforgiven sin. (3:37-54)
  - F. God will hear, respond, and requite the enemy. (3:55-66)

IV. A Graphic Portrayal of Suffering Caused by Sin (4:1-22)

V. A Plea to God (5:1-22)
  A. Remember us, O God. (5:1-18)
  B. Restore us, O God. (5:19-22)

Theological Conclusions

The Book of Lamentations honestly and forthrightly expresses both individual and community despair over the plight of Jerusalem and Judah. From bittersweet reminiscences of the greatness the nation had known (1:1-6) to the vengeful word that those who rejoice over Zion's fall will have to answer for their own sins (4:21-22), the book laments what had been but is no more.

Several theological themes stand out in this brief book: (1) God is a just God; (2) sinful people will be punished for sins; (3) God is not partial; even His own elect people will be held accountable for their sins; and (4) if a people will repent and trust in God, they may have hope for the future.

The book describes in horrifying detail the ravages of war, famine, and pestilence (4:1-10). But just as plainly, the book states that the punishment was richly deserved. Jerusalem had grievously sinned (1:8); Jerusalem rebelled against God's Word (1:18); Jerusalem committed spiritual adultery by worshiping false gods (1:19). The prophets had failed to expose the people's sins and had given false prophecies (2:14).

God had been just in His punishment of His people. He is no capricious God (1:18). A just God must deal with a sinful and rebellious people, and that is exactly what God had done (3:37-39). God had long before spoken through Moses of the covenant requirements. If the people would keep the covenant, then God would bless them. But if they disobeyed the covenant, then He would put them under a curse. Now the people of Judah had sinned; therefore, God had brought about the punishment (2:17). Election did not protect Israel from punishment for their sins. Indeed, more was expected of Israel because of their unique covenant relationship.

Yet despite the sin and punishment, the Book of Lamentations still offers hope. In the midst of the book, surrounded by laments, the author cries out to God in hope (3:19-21) and then sings a psalm of assurance that God will hear and respond (3:22-33). Hope is based on past experience when the people called out to God and He responded (3:55-57). Thus they can justifiably hope that once again He will respond to those who call to Him (3:64-66; 5:20-21). But a change is necessary. The people must examine their ways, repent, confess their sins, and return to God (3:40-42). Then perhaps God will be gracious and forgiving. Such hope is all they have.

Contemporary Teaching

Lamentations reminds us of the appalling consequences of sin. God does not treat our sin lightly. Furthermore, we are responsible for our sins; we cannot "pass the buck." Nevertheless, there is also good news. None of us is beyond help. If we repent and confess, our gracious God will forgive. We still have the opportunity to respond to God through Jesus Christ. Therein lies our only hope.

Chapter 1[a]

HOW deserted[a] lies the city,
once so full of people![b]
How like a widow[c] is she,
who once was great[d] among the nations!
She who was queen among the provinces
has now become a slave.[e]

2Bitterly she weeps[f] at night,
tears are upon her cheeks.
Among all her lovers[g]
there is none to comfort her.
All her friends have betrayed[h] her;
they have become her enemies.[i]

3After affliction and harsh labor,
Judah has gone into exile.[j]
She dwells among the nations;
she finds no resting place.[k]
All who pursue her have overtaken her[l]
in the midst of her distress.

4The roads to Zion mourn,[m]
for no one comes to her appointed feasts.
All her gateways are desolate,[n]
her priests groan,
her maidens grieve,
and she is in bitter anguish.[o]

5Her foes have become her masters;
her enemies are at ease.
The LORD has brought her grief[p]
because of her many sins.[q]
Her children have gone into exile,[r]
captive before the foe.[s]

6All the splendor has departed
from the Daughter of Zion.[t]
Her princes are like deer
that find no pasture;
in weakness they have fled[u]
before the pursuer.

7In the days of her affliction and wandering
Jerusalem remembers all the treasures
that were hers in days of old.
When her people fell into enemy hands,
there was no one to help her.[v]
Her enemies looked at her
and laughed[w] at her destruction.

8Jerusalem has sinned[x] greatly
and so has become unclean.[y]
All who honored her despise her,
for they have seen her nakedness;[z]
she herself groans[a]
and turns away.

9Her filthiness clung to her skirts;
she did not consider her future.[b]
Her fall[c] was astounding;
there was none to comfort[d] her.
"Look, O LORD, on my affliction,[e]
for the enemy has triumphed."

10The enemy laid hands
on all her treasures;[f]
she saw pagan nations
enter her sanctuary[g] —
those you had forbidden[h]
to enter your assembly.

11All her people groan[i]
as they search for bread;[j]
they barter their treasures for food
to keep themselves alive.
"Look, O LORD, and consider,
for I am despised."

12"Is it nothing to you, all you who pass by?[k]
Look around and see.
Is any suffering like my suffering[l]
that was inflicted on me,
that the LORD brought on me
in the day of his fierce anger?[m]

13"From on high he sent fire,
sent it down into my bones.[n]
He spread a net[o] for my feet

[a]This chapter is an acrostic poem, the verses of which begin with the successive letters of the Hebrew alphabet.

1:1 [a]S Lev 26:43 [b]S Jer 42:2 [c]S Isa 47:8 [d]S 1Ki 4:21 [e]Isa 3:26; S Jer 40:9; Eze 5:5
1:2 [f]Ps 6:6 [g]S Jer 3:1 [h]S Jer 4:30; Mic 7:5 [i]ver 16; S Jer 30:14
1:3 [j]S Jer 13:19 [k]Dt 28:65 [l]S Ex 15:9
1:4 [m]S Ps 137:1 [n]S Isa 27:10; S Jer 9:11 [o]ver 21; Joel 1:8-13
1:5 [p]S Isa 22:5; S Jer 30:15 [q]S Ps 5:10 [r]S Jer 10:20; S 39:9; 52:28-30 [s]S Ps 137:3; La 2:17
1:6 [t]S Ps 9:14; Jer 13:18 [u]S Lev 26:36
1:7 [v]S 2Ki 14:26; S Jer 37:7; La 4:17 [w]S Jer 2:26
1:8 [x]ver 20; Isa 59:2-13 [y]S Jer 2:22 [z]S Jer 13:22,26 [a]ver 21,22; S Ps 6:6; S 38:8
1:9 [b]Dt 32:28-29; Eze 24:13 [c]Jer 13:18 [d]S Ecc 4:1; S Jer 16:7 [e]Ps 25:18
1:10 [f]S Isa 64:11 [g]Ps 74:7-8; 79:1; Jer 51:51 [h]Dt 23:3
1:11 [i]S Ps 6:6; S 38:8 [j]S Jer 37:21; S 52:6
1:12 [k]S Jer 18:16 [l]ver 18 [m]S Isa 10:4; 13:13; S Jer 30:24
1:13 [n]S Job 30:30; Ps 102:3 [o]S Job 18:8

1:1—5:22 PRAYER, Lament—The book represents a collection of prayers mourning over the destroyed Jerusalem and searching for God's direction. As collected prayers they provided vivid memory of the results of rebellion and prayers suitable for public and private use to commemorate past disasters and to pray concerning present predicaments. See notes on Ps 3:1–8; 34:1–22. Loneliness, isolation, weakness, affliction, defeat, confession, shame, agony, suffering, rejection, weeping, betrayal, emotional torment, distress, divine anger, hunger, scoffing, injustice, bitterness, grief, vengeance, poverty, punishment, and destruction are the central words of lament. They have a proper place in prayer for people in desperate situations.

1:1 HUMANITY, Marriage—Loss of a marriage partner may be the world's loneliest and saddest feeling. Humans cannot provide sufficient comfort.

1:5 EVIL AND SUFFERING, Punishment—To forsake God is to become a servant to a cruel, oppressive master. People of Jerusalem could sing only sad laments because they had not taken God's word and covenant seriously.

1:5 SIN, Discipline—See notes on 2 Ki 25:1–21; Isa 64:4–7.

1:8 SIN, Transgression—See notes on 1 Ki 14:22–24; 2 Ki 25:1–21; Ne 1:6–7.

1:10–16 SIN, Punishment—Sin's punishment may include suffering and destitution. "Friends" gained in sinful pursuits become mockers in sin's punishment. See notes on 2 Ki 25:1–21; Isa 1:20; 64:4–7.

1:12 GOD, Wrath—The misery of life in the destroyed Jerusalem evoked desperate pleas from God's people, who thought they lived in the worst of all possible worlds. They confessed that God's anger had caused their plight. Still they turned to Him in prayer to find a way out. Exercise of God's wrath does not cut us off from God. God's primary desire is to show His love, but sometimes it is necessary for Him to show His wrath.

let your tears[t] flow like a river
day and night;[u]
give yourself no relief,
your eyes no rest.[v]

19Arise, cry out in the night,
as the watches of the night begin;
pour out your heart[w] like water
in the presence of the Lord.[x]
Lift up your hands[y] to him
for the lives of your children,
who faint[z] from hunger
at the head of every street.

20"Look, O LORD, and consider:
Whom have you ever treated like
this?
Should women eat their offspring,[a]
the children they have cared for?[b]
Should priest and prophet be killed[c]
in the sanctuary of the Lord?[d]

21"Young and old lie together
in the dust of the streets;
my young men and maidens
have fallen by the sword.[e]
You have slain them in the day of your
anger;
you have slaughtered them without
pity.[f]

22"As you summon to a feast day,
so you summoned against me
terrors[g] on every side.
In the day of the LORD's anger
no one escaped[h] or survived;
those I cared for and reared,[i]
my enemy has destroyed."

Chapter 3[h]

I am the man who has seen affliction[j]
by the rod of his wrath.[k]
2He has driven me away and made me
walk
in darkness[l] rather than light;
3indeed, he has turned his hand against
me[m]
again and again, all day long.

4He has made my skin and my flesh
grow old[n]
and has broken my bones.[o]
5He has besieged me and surrounded
me
with bitterness[p] and hardship.[q]
6He has made me dwell in darkness
like those long dead.[r]

7He has walled me in so I cannot
escape;[s]
he has weighed me down with
chains.[t]
8Even when I call out or cry for help,[u]
he shuts out my prayer.[v]
9He has barred[w] my way with blocks of
stone;
he has made my paths crooked.[x]

10Like a bear lying in wait,
like a lion[y] in hiding,[z]
11he dragged me from the path and
mangled[a] me
and left me without help.
12He drew his bow[b]
and made me the target[c] for his
arrows.[d]

13He pierced[e] my heart
with arrows from his quiver.[f]
14I became the laughingstock[g] of all my
people;[h]
they mock me in song[i] all day long.
15He has filled me with bitter herbs
and sated me with gall.[j]

16He has broken my teeth with gravel;[k]
he has trampled me in the dust.[l]
17I have been deprived of peace;
I have forgotten what prosperity is.
18So I say, "My splendor is gone
and all that I had hoped from the
LORD."[m]

19I remember my affliction and my
wandering,
the bitterness[n] and the gall.[o]
20I well remember them,
and my soul is downcast[p] within
me.[q]
21Yet this I call to mind
and therefore I have hope:

[h]This chapter is an acrostic poem; the verses of each stanza begin with the successive letters of the Hebrew alphabet, and the verses within each stanza begin with the same letter.

2:18 [t]S La 1:16 [u]S Jer 9:1 [v]La 3:49
2:19 [w]1Sa 1:15 [x]S ver 11; Isa 26:9 [y]S Ps 28:2 [z]S Isa 51:20
2:20 [a]S Dt 28:53; Jer 19:9; Eze 5:10 [b]La 4:10 [c]Ps 78:64; S Jer 14:15; 23:11-12 [d]S La 1:19
2:21 [e]S Dt 32:25; S 2Ch 36:17; Ps 78:62-63; Jer 6:11 [f]S Jer 13:14; La 3:43; Zec 11:6
2:22 [g]S Ps 31:13; S Jer 20:10 [h]S Jer 11:11 [i]Job 27:14; Hos 9:13
3:1 [j]Jer 15:17-18 [k]S Job 19:21; Ps 88:7
3:2 [l]S Job 19:8; S Ps 82:5; S Jer 4:23
3:3 [m]Ps 38:2; Isa 5:25
3:4 [n]S Job 30:30; La 4:8 [o]Ps 51:8; S Isa 38:13; S Jer 50:17
3:5 [p]ver 19 [q]Jer 23:15
3:6 [r]Ps 88:5-6; 143:3; Isa 59:10
3:7 [s]S Job 3:23 [t]Jer 40:4
3:8 [u]Ps 5:2 [v]ver 44; S Dt 1:45; S Job 30:20; Ps 22:2
3:9 [w]S Job 19:8 [x]S Job 9:24; S Isa 63:17; Hos 2:6
3:10 [y]S Job 10:16 [z]Hos 13:8; Am 5:18-19
3:11 [a]Hos 6:1
3:12 [b]S La 2:4 [c]Job 7:20 [d]S Job 16:12; Ps 7:12-13; 38:2
3:13 [e]S Job 16:13 [f]Job 6:4
3:14 [g]S Ge 38:23; Ps 22:6-7; Jer 20:7 [h]S Job 17:2 [i]S Job 30:9
3:15 [j]ver 19; Jer 9:15
3:16 [k]S Pr 20:17 [l]S Ps 7:5
3:18 [m]S ver 54; S Job 17:15
3:19 [n]ver 5 [o]S ver 15
3:20 [p]S Ps 42:5 [q]Ps 42:11; 43:5

2:19 PRAYER, Command of God—Jerusalem's destruction called for sleep-denying prayer.
2:22 THE CHURCH, Remnant—In the midst of crisis the faithful may feel isolated and complain that God has let even the remnant be destroyed. God does let His people face extreme disaster, but He listens to our desperate prayers. He preserves a few faithful to carry on His name. See note on Isa 1:7–9.
3:1,43 GOD, Wrath—God pities and has compassion on His people. That is a basic part of His nature. His people can sin and call forth His wrath. Then His pity vanishes—for a time.
3:1–66 EVIL AND SUFFERING, Repentance—Suffering must ultimately be brought into relationship to our understanding of God. Sufferers in Jerusalem during the Exile recognized God caused their suffering as punishment for their sins. A great part of their suffering was their isolation from God, who did not even accept their prayers. The sufferer maintained hope because of God's character. Love and compassion comprise God's basic being (1 Jn 4:8). He is faithful to His people and purposes. Therefore, we can patiently endure suffering confident of God's help in the time He chooses. God's basic desire is never to bring suffering to people (v 33). Punishment for sin is no reason to complain to God (v 39). Repentance and confession of sin are the way back to God (v 42). This brings confidence in God's salvation and vindication. See note on Ps 109:1–31.
3:8 PRAYER, Hindrances—Judah had sinned almost beyond hope. See note on Isa 59:1–2.

22 Because of the LORD's great love[r] we
are not consumed,[s]
for his compassions never fail.[t]
23 They are new every morning;
great is your faithfulness.[u]
24 I say to myself, "The LORD is my
portion;[v]
therefore I will wait for him."

25 The LORD is good to those whose hope
is in him,
to the one who seeks him;[w]
26 it is good to wait quietly[x]
for the salvation of the LORD.[y]
27 It is good for a man to bear the yoke
while he is young.

28 Let him sit alone in silence,[z]
for the LORD has laid it on him.
29 Let him bury his face in the dust[a] —
there may yet be hope.[b]
30 Let him offer his cheek to one who
would strike him,[c]
and let him be filled with disgrace.[d]

31 For men are not cast off
by the Lord forever.[e]
32 Though he brings grief, he will show
compassion,
so great is his unfailing love.[f]
33 For he does not willingly bring
affliction
or grief to the children of men.[g]

34 To crush underfoot
all prisoners in the land,
35 to deny a man his rights
before the Most High,[h]
36 to deprive a man of justice—
would not the Lord see such
things?[i]

37 Who can speak and have it happen
if the Lord has not decreed it?[j]
38 Is it not from the mouth of the Most
High
that both calamities and good things
come?[k]
39 Why should any living man complain
when punished for his sins?[l]

40 Let us examine our ways and test
them,[m]
and let us return to the LORD.[n]
41 Let us lift up our hearts and our hands
to God in heaven,[o] and say:
42 "We have sinned and rebelled[p]
and you have not forgiven.[q]

43 "You have covered yourself with anger
and pursued[r] us;
you have slain without pity.[s]
44 You have covered yourself with a
cloud[t]
so that no prayer[u] can get
through.[v]
45 You have made us scum[w] and refuse
among the nations.

46 "All our enemies have opened their
mouths
wide[x] against us.[y]
47 We have suffered terror and pitfalls,[z]
ruin and destruction."[a]
48 Streams of tears[b] flow from my eyes[c]
because my people are destroyed.[d]

49 My eyes will flow unceasingly,
without relief,[e]
50 until the LORD looks down
from heaven and sees.[f]
51 What I see brings grief to my soul
because of all the women of my city.

3:22 [r]S Ps 103:11 [s]S Job 34:15; S Hos 11:9 [t]Ps 78:38; 130:7 **3:23** [u]S Ex 34:6; Zep 3:5 **3:24** [v]S Ps 119:57 **3:25** [w]S Ps 33:18; Isa 25:9; S 30:18 **3:26** [x]S Isa 7:4 [y]Ps 37:7; 40:1 **3:28** [z]Jer 15:17; La 2:10 **3:29** [a]S Job 2:8 [b]S Jer 31:17 **3:30** [c]S Job 16:10; S Isa 50:6 [d]Mic 5:1 **3:31** [e]Ps 94:14; Isa 54:7 **3:32** [f]Ps 78:38; 106:43-45; Hos 11:8; Na 1:12 **3:33** [g]S Job 37:23; S Jer 31:20; Eze 18:23; 33:11 **3:35** [h]Ge 14:18,19,20,22 **3:36** [i]Ps 140:12; S Pr 17:15; S Jer 22:3; Hab 1:13 **3:37** [j]Ps 33:9-11; S Pr 19:21; S 21:30 **3:38** [k]S Job 2:10; S Isa 45:7; Jer 32:42 **3:39** [l]S Jer 30:15; Mic 7:9 **3:40** [m]2Co 13:5 [n]Ps 119:59; 139:23-24 **3:41** [o]S Ps 25:1; S 28:2 **3:42** [p]Jer 14:20; Da 9:5 [q]S 2Ki 24:4; Jer 5:7-9 **3:43** [r]ver 66; Ps 35:6 [s]S La 2:2, 17,21 **3:44** [t]Ps 97:2; La 2:1 [u]S ver 8; Zec 7:13 [v]S Isa 58:4 **3:45** [w]1Co 4:13 **3:46** [x]Ps 22:13 [y]La 2:16 **3:47** [z]Jer 48:43 [a]S Isa 24:17-18; S 51:19 **3:48** [b]S Ps 119:136 [c]S Jer 9:1,18; La 1:16 [d]La 2:11 **3:49** [e]Jer 14:17; S La 2:18 **3:50** [f]S Ps 14:2; 80:14; S Isa 63:15

3:22–33 GOD, Love—Deepest trouble cannot hide the memory of nor kill the hope for God's love, His abiding characteristic.

3:22 GOD, Faithfulness—God's compassion, His love deeper than any parent's, springs forth fresh to us each day, ready to receive His penitent people. Wrath may mark yesterday, but today can be the day of love when we relate rightly to Him. God is always faithful to His people and to His own basic character.

3:22–23 REVELATION, Events—God reveals Himself in daily experiences as well as in His mighty saving acts in history. Each day we can recognize His compassionate acts in our personal and community lives.

3:25 GOD, Goodness—While bemoaning our fate under God's wrath, we must confess God is good to those who seek Him. He is good to let those He is punishing seek Him. God's goodness includes His righteousness, faithfulness, and love. See note on Mt 19:17.

3:31–33 ELECTION, Love—Judgment bringing grief and pain to people is not God's election purpose. He does not abandon His election purposes. Love dominates His work with the people He created and delivered. Compare Jn 3:16. In trouble God's people can cry to Him and find mercy.

3:32–36 CHRISTIAN ETHICS, Justice—The sovereignty of God brings hope to the oppressed. Those who act unjustly face certain judgment. God is aware of all who suffer in innocence and will in His time and way make the situation right.

3:37–39 GOD, Sovereignty—We have no reason for complaint when God punishes us for our sins. We can be sure He is carrying out His sovereign plan which is best for us in the long run.

3:39–42 SIN, Punishment—We have no recourse and should make no complaint when we receive just punishment for sins committed. Punishment should discipline us to return to God in repentance. Such confession to God comes before He has forgiven our sins. For rebellion, see notes on 1:18–22; Isa 1:2–4.

3:40 SALVATION, Repentance—In suffering and trouble we may think God has dealt cruelly with us. We are called to examine our ways, recognize where we have failed God, and repent.

3:40–42 PRAYER, Confession—God's purpose had been to bring Judah to repentance. Although the writer despaired, he knew that the Lord's compassions were faithfully fresh every morning (vv 22–23).

3:44–50 REVELATION, Fellowship—People who cut themselves off from God believe He also has permanently cut Himself off from them. The nature of God, however, is to remain open for redemption and reconciliation. People who continue to pray eventually experience God's fellowship.

3:44 PRAYER, Hindrances—See note on v 8.

52 Those who were my enemies without cause
hunted me like a bird.[g]
53 They tried to end my life in a pit[h]
and threw stones at me;
54 the waters closed over my head,[i]
and I thought I was about to be cut off.[j]

55 I called on your name, O LORD,
from the depths[k] of the pit.[l]
56 You heard my plea:[m] "Do not close your ears
to my cry for relief."
57 You came near[n] when I called you,
and you said, "Do not fear."[o]

58 O Lord, you took up my case;[p]
you redeemed my life.[q]
59 You have seen, O LORD, the wrong done to me.[r]
Uphold my cause![s]
60 You have seen the depth of their vengeance,
all their plots against me.[t]

61 O LORD, you have heard their insults,[u]
all their plots against me—
62 what my enemies whisper and mutter
against me all day long.[v]
63 Look at them! Sitting or standing,
they mock me in their songs.[w]

64 Pay them back what they deserve, O LORD,
for what their hands have done.[x]
65 Put a veil over their hearts,[y]
and may your curse be on them!
66 Pursue[z] them in anger and destroy them
from under the heavens of the LORD.

Chapter 4[i]

HOW the gold has lost its luster,
the fine gold become dull!
The sacred gems are scattered
at the head of every street.[a]

2 How the precious sons of Zion,[b]
once worth their weight in gold,
are now considered as pots of clay,
the work of a potter's hands!

3:52 [g]Ps 35:7
3:53 [h]Jer 37:16; S 38:6
3:54 [i]Ps 69:2; Jnh 2:3-5 [j]ver 18; Ps 88:5; Eze 37:11
3:55 [k]S Ps 88:6 [l]Ps 130:1; Jnh 2:2
3:56 [m]S Ps 55:1; 116:1-2
3:57 [n]S Ps 46:1 [o]Isa 41:10
3:58 [p]S Jer 51:36 [q]Ps 34:22; S Jer 50:34
3:59 [r]Jer 18:19-20 [s]Ps 35:23; 43:1
3:60 [t]S Jer 11:20; 18:18
3:61 [u]Ps 89:50; Zep 2:8
3:62 [v]Eze 36:3
3:63 [w]S Job 30:9
3:64 [x]S Ps 28:4; S Jer 51:6
3:65 [y]Ex 14:8; Dt 2:30; Isa 6:10
3:66 [z]S ver 43
4:1 [a]Eze 7:19
4:2 [b]Isa 51:18
4:3 [c]S Job 39:16
4:4 [d]S Dt 28:48; S 2Ki 18:31 [e]S Ps 22:15 [f]La 2:11,12
4:5 [g]Jer 6:2 [h]S Isa 3:26; Am 6:3-7
4:6 [i]S Ge 19:25
4:8 [j]S Job 30:28 [k]Ps 102:3-5; S La 3:4
4:9 [l]S 2Ki 25:3 [m]S Jer 15:2; S 16:4; La 5:10
4:10 [n]S Lev 26:29; Dt 28:53-57; Jer 19:9; La 2:20; Eze 5:10
4:11 [o]S Job 20:23 [p]S 2Ch 34:21 [q]Na 1:6; Zep 2:2; 3:8 [r]Jer 17:27 [s]S Dt 32:22; S Jer 7:20; Eze 22:31

3 Even jackals offer their breasts
to nurse their young,
but my people have become heartless
like ostriches in the desert.[c]
4 Because of thirst[d] the infant's tongue
sticks to the roof of its mouth;[e]
the children beg for bread,
but no one gives it to them.[f]

5 Those who once ate delicacies
are destitute in the streets.
Those nurtured in purple[g]
now lie on ash heaps.[h]

6 The punishment of my people
is greater than that of Sodom,[i]
which was overthrown in a moment
without a hand turned to help her.

7 Their princes were brighter than snow
and whiter than milk,
their bodies more ruddy than rubies,
their appearance like sapphires.[j]
8 But now they are blacker[j] than soot;
they are not recognized in the streets.
Their skin has shriveled on their bones;[k]
it has become as dry as a stick.

9 Those killed by the sword are better off
than those who die of famine;[l]
racked with hunger, they waste away
for lack of food from the field.[m]

10 With their own hands compassionate women
have cooked their own children,[n]
who became their food
when my people were destroyed.

11 The LORD has given full vent to his wrath;[o]
he has poured out[p] his fierce anger.[q]
He kindled a fire[r] in Zion
that consumed her foundations.[s]

12 The kings of the earth did not believe,

[i] This chapter is an acrostic poem, the verses of which begin with the successive letters of the Hebrew alphabet. [j] 7 Or *lapis lazuli*

3:55–66 PRAYER, Curse—An agonizing series of prayers ended with a cry that anticipated God's action. The petitioner had faith to give enemies over to God's action because he knew God had heard his prayer. God's answer brings assurance of redemption.

3:61–66 SALVATION, Vindication—The prophet sought vindication from God against his enemies. Compare 1:20–22. God hears our frustrated, angry cry for vengeance but does not want us to take vengeance in our own hands. As we share our dark feelings with God, we need to forgive our enemies. See note on Jer 51:10,36; Mt 18:21–35.

4:1–22 GOD, Wrath—After long bitter complaint and vivid description of suffering, God's faithful can affirm that salvation will come. See notes on 1:12; Ps 30:5; Isa 30:18–19.

4:1–2 CHRISTIAN ETHICS, Property Rights—Sometimes only tragedy and crisis can teach the true value of material things. It took a time of judgment for the people of Israel to recognize the folly of trusting in gold and gems for their sense of security. The prophetic warnings against their oppressive economic practices came true. See notes on Isa 5:8–10; Jer 22:11–17; Am 6:4–7.

4:12–13 SALVATION, Belief—Contrary to popular opinion, Jerusalem was not permanently secure from enemy destruction (Jer 27:14). Israel's unbelief brought about Jerusalem's destruction. Our belief in God should not be taken for granted. Faith is no license to sin. Participation in worship services is no guarantee of protection and salvation.

nor did any of the world's people,
that enemies and foes could enter
the gates of Jerusalem.[t]

13But it happened because of the sins of
her prophets
and the iniquities of her priests,[u]
who shed within her
the blood[v] of the righteous.

14Now they grope through the streets
like men who are blind.[w]
They are so defiled with blood[x]
that no one dares to touch their
garments.

15"Go away! You are unclean!" men cry
to them.
"Away! Away! Don't touch us!"
When they flee and wander[y] about,
people among the nations say,
"They can stay here no longer."[z]

16The LORD himself has scattered them;
he no longer watches over them.[a]
The priests are shown no honor,
the elders[b] no favor.[c]

17Moreover, our eyes failed,
looking in vain[d] for help;[e]
from our towers we watched
for a nation[f] that could not save us.

18Men stalked us at every step,
so we could not walk in our streets.
Our end was near, our days were
numbered,
for our end had come.[g]

19Our pursuers were swifter
than eagles[h] in the sky;
they chased us[i] over the mountains
and lay in wait for us in the desert.[j]

20The LORD's anointed,[k] our very life
breath,
was caught in their traps.[l]
We thought that under his shadow[m]
we would live among the nations.

21Rejoice and be glad, O Daughter of
Edom,
you who live in the land of Uz.[n]
But to you also the cup[o] will be
passed;
you will be drunk and stripped
naked.[p]

22O Daughter of Zion, your punishment
will end;[q]
he will not prolong your exile.

4:12 [t]S 1Ki 9:9; S Jer 21:13
4:13 [u]Jer 5:31; 6:13; Eze 22:28; Mic 3:11 [v]S 2Ki 21:16
4:14 [w]S Isa 59:10 [x]Jer 19:4
4:15 [y]S Jer 44:14 [z]Lev 13:46; Mic 2:10
4:16 [a]Isa 9:14-16 [b]La 5:12 [c]S La 2:6
4:17 [d]S Ge 15:18; S Isa 20:5; Eze 29:16 [e]S La 1:7 [f]Jer 37:7
4:18 [g]Eze 7:2-12; Am 8:2
4:19 [h]S Dt 28:49 [i]S Lev 26:36; Isa 5:26-28 [j]Jer 52:7
4:20 [k]S 1Sa 26:9; 2Sa 19:21 [l]Jer 39:5; Eze 12:12-13; 19:4, 8 [m]S Ps 91:1
4:21 [n]S Ge 10:23 [o]S Ps 16:5; S Jer 25:15 [p]Isa 34:6-10; S 63:6; Eze 35:15; Am 1:11-12; Ob 1:16; Hab 2:16
4:22 [q]Isa 40:2; Jer 33:8 [r]S Ps 137:7; Eze 25:12-14; Mal 1:4
5:1 [s]Ps 44:13-16; 89:50
5:2 [t]Ps 79:1 [u]S Ps 109:11 [v]Zep 1:13 [w]Jer 17:4
5:3 [x]S Ex 22:24; Jer 15:8; S 18:21
5:4 [y]S Isa 55:1; Eze 4:16-17 [z]Isa 3:1
5:5 [a]S Ne 9:37; Isa 47:6 [b]S Jos 1:13
5:6 [c]Jer 2:36; Hos 5:13; 7:11; 9:3
5:7 [d]S Jer 31:29 [e]Jer 14:20; 16:12
5:8 [f]Ne 5:15 [g]Zec 11:6
5:10 [h]S Job 30:30; S La 4:8-9
5:11 [i]S Ge 34:29; Zec 14:2
5:12 [j]S Lev 19:32 [k]S La 2:6; 4:16
5:14 [l]S Isa 24:8; Jer 7:34
5:15 [m]S Jer 25:10; Am 8:10
5:16 [n]Ps 89:39; S Jer 13:18 [o]S Job 19:9 [p]S Isa 3:11; Jer 14:20
5:17 [q]S Isa 1:5 [r]S Jer 8:18 [s]Ps 6:7 [t]S Job 16:8
5:18 [u]Ps 74:2-3 [v]S Isa 27:10; Mic 3:12
5:19 [w]S 1Ch 16:31

But, O Daughter of Edom, he will
punish your sin
and expose your wickedness.[r]

Chapter 5

REMEMBER, O LORD, what has
happened to us;
look, and see our disgrace.[s]
2Our inheritance[t] has been turned
over to aliens,[u]
our homes[v] to foreigners.[w]
3We have become orphans and
fatherless,
our mothers like widows.[x]
4We must buy the water we drink;[y]
our wood can be had only at a
price.[z]
5Those who pursue us are at our heels;
we are weary[a] and find no rest.[b]
6We submitted to Egypt and Assyria[c]
to get enough bread.
7Our fathers[d] sinned and are no more,
and we bear their punishment.[e]
8Slaves[f] rule over us,
and there is none to free us from
their hands.[g]
9We get our bread at the risk of our
lives
because of the sword in the desert.
10Our skin is hot as an oven,
feverish from hunger.[h]
11Women have been ravished[i] in Zion,
and virgins in the towns of Judah.
12Princes have been hung up by their
hands;
elders[j] are shown no respect.[k]
13Young men toil at the millstones;
boys stagger under loads of wood.
14The elders are gone from the city gate;
the young men have stopped their
music.[l]
15Joy is gone from our hearts;
our dancing has turned to
mourning.[m]
16The crown[n] has fallen from our
head.[o]
Woe to us, for we have sinned![p]
17Because of this our hearts[q] are faint,[r]
because of these things our eyes[s]
grow dim[t]
18for Mount Zion,[u] which lies
desolate,[v]
with jackals prowling over it.
19You, O LORD, reign forever;[w]

5:7 EVIL AND SUFFERING, Deserved—Some of the exiles felt they were suffering the penalty for their parents' sin. See note on Eze 18:1–32. Our generation leaves a legacy for the next. They may have to suffer because of our sin and failure to plan for the future.

5:7 HUMANITY, Family Relationships—See note on Jer 32:18.

5:15 SALVATION, Joy—When Jerusalem fell to Nebuchadnezzar in 587 BC, Israel lost her joy. This text is part of a prayer for the return of that joy. Catastrophe does strike God's people. Sometimes we backslide and lose our joy. Whatever may befall us as the people of God, we can always repent and ask the Lord to restore the joy of our salvation. See note on Ps 4:7.

5:19 GOD, Eternal—Amidst woeful complaint and pleas for mercy, the inspired writer affirmed that God has and will

Theological Outline

Ezekiel: The Sovereignty of God's Glory in the Lives of His People

I. Introduction: Yahweh's Glory Watches Over the Captives in Babylon. (1:1-28)

II. The Glory Brings Divine Judgment on Israel. (2:1—24:27)
   A. By calling Ezekiel to be a prophet (2:1—3:27)
   B. By predicting the fall of Jerusalem (4:1—5:17)
   C. By condemning Jerusalem's idolatry and sins (6:1—7:27)
   D. By describing and explaining why the Glory departed from the city (8:1—11:25)
   E. By showing the futility of the nation's leadership (12:1—15:8)
      1. The Davidic ruler would be taken into captivity. (12:1-28)
      2. The false prophets and prophetesses would be swept away by a storm. (13:1-23)
      3. The idolatrous community leaders had created such a state of alienation from Yahweh that prayer for deliverance would be ineffectual. (14:1-23)
      4. Like a useless vine the city would be burned up. (15:1-8)
   F. As a means of providing reconciliation (16:1—18:32)
      1. In spite of Israel's ingratitude and unfaithfulness, Israel will be restored. (16:1-63)
      2. In spite of the king's failure, a universal kingdom will flourish. (17:1-24)
      3. On the basis of individual responsibility, the relationship between God and Israel will be maintained. (18:1-32)
   G. Resulting in the nation's destruction (19:1—23:49)
      1. In spite of the hopeless situations of their rulers (19:1-14)
      2. Because of Israel's constant state of apostasy (20:1-49)
      3. By means of a sword (21:1-32)
      4. Because Israel refused to live by God's covenant demands (22:1-31)
      5. Because of the two sisters' (Oholah and Oholibah) incessant immoralities (23:1-49)
   H. As seen in two events of unparalleled sadness (24:1-27)
      1. In the siege and destruction of Jerusalem (24:1-14)
      2. In the death of Ezekiel's wife (24:15-27)

III. The Glory Brings Divine Judgment to the Nations. (25:1—32:32)
   A. Against Ammon because of her joy over Israel's distress (25:1-7)
   B. Against Moab because of her failure to recognize Israel's revelatory status (25:8-11)
   C. Against Edom because of her lust for vengeance (25:12-14)
   D. Against Philistia because of her perpetual hostility (25:15-17)
   E. Against Tyre because of her greed for self-gain at Israel's expense (26:1—28:19)
   F. Against Sidon because of her constant threat to Israel's welfare (28:20-26)
   G. Against Egypt because of her pride and deceit (29:1—32:32)

IV. The Glory Brings Restoration to Israel. (33:1—48:35)
   A. Through Ezekiel's faithful role as a watchman (33:1-33)
   B. By means of the messianic leader, "my servant David" (34:1-31)
   C. For the entire land (35:1—36:38)
      1. By the total destruction of Edom (35:1-15)
      2. In the deliverance of Israel (36:1-21)
      3. In the implementation of the new covenant (36:22-38)
   D. To revive the hopeless state of the people who felt they had perished (37:1-28)
   E. By defeating the ungodly forces of the nations under Gog of Magog (38:1—39:29)
   F. Resulting in the pure worship of the restored people (40:1—48:35)
      1. With the throne of Yahweh's glory replacing the ark (40:1—43:12)
      2. With the presence of Yahweh's glory providing far-reaching blessings (44:1—47:12)
      3. With a firm inheritance in the land (47:13—48:35)

Theological Conclusions

From 593 BC (1:2) to at least 571 BC (29:17), Ezekiel ministered to his generation who were both exceedingly sinful and thoroughly hopeless. By means of his prophetic ministry, he attempted to bring them to immediate repentance and to confidence in the distant future. He taught that:

1. God works through human messengers. Ninety-three times Ezekiel is called "Son of man." See 3:1. Yahweh used the title to address the human messenger. Such a usage, occurring so infrequently elsewhere in the Old Testament, identified the prophet with his people. God chose to work through a common man who could identify with his people in their grief, pain, and despair.

2. Even in defeat and despair, God's people need to affirm God's sovereign lordship. The term "I am Yahweh" ("I am the LORD," 7:27) appears at least forty-nine times in the book. Such a phrase indicated God's sovereignty. Nothing could prohibit the accomplishment of His will. God's sovereignty is universal. His presence was not limited to Israel. He was also present in Babylon. He ruled over nations, using them as tools in His hands to accomplish His will. Ultimately, He called all peoples under His judgment. His own people were not exempt when they rebelled. Nevertheless, His wrath gave way to love and redemption for those who would accept and serve Him (36:22-32).

3. God's Word never fails. No person or nation can prevent the fulfillment of God's true Word. God's Word may seem bitter at times. As Ezekiel received the word, he found it to be sweet and effective (3:3). As he studied the scrolls of earlier prophets, God's Word met his desperate needs. Thus, he proclaimed it faithfully, for it possessed the power to deliver Israel once again as God had delivered the nation from Egypt.

4. God is present and can be worshiped anywhere. Geography has no bearing on God. In Ezekiel's era the people had so associated the worship of God with Temple sacrifices, rituals, and services they thought moving from the Jerusalem Temple made worship an impossibility. In Babylon, Yahweh had no Temple. Did that mean they could no longer worship Him effectively? Ezekiel would reply, "By no means!" He himself fell before the God of Israel in reverence and submission out on the Babylonian plain (1:28). Thus, God had become "a little sanctuary" for them in a foreign land (11:16,19-20). Worship did not depend upon impressive buildings but upon submissive hearts. Worship was in essence spiritual in nature. Anything less bordered on idolatry. With that concept, the Babylonian captives began the practice that produced synagogue worship: prayer, hymns, and Scripture.

5. People are personally responsible for their actions. Ezekiel's generation was swift to blame their circumstances on someone else (18:2). Ezekiel forcefully declared the doctrine of individual responsibility (chs 3,18). Each person is responsible for his or her own response to God.

6. God's people must obey God if they expect to receive God's blessings. In Ezekiel's day the people tended to emphasize only the blessings of being a covenant people. They ignored the demands of faith and obedience and the stipulations of God's covenant commandments. The prophet repeatedly noted the fallacy of such religious presumption. He called the people back to the obligations of covenant relationship.

7. God's kingdom will come. With the collapse of the nation and the demise of the people's aspirations, Ezekiel sought to focus the people's attention on the future. He described a kingdom established by God with a coming messianic ruler, "my servant David" (34:23), that would be without end. In Him their hopes and God's promises would ultimately be fulfilled. Thus, the future belonged to people of faith who would faithfully serve Him.

8. God's promised new covenant is superior to the old Mosaic one. While Jeremiah preached in Jerusalem about a new covenant being implemented in the place of the Mosaic Covenant (Jer 31:27-34), Ezekiel assured the people of the exile that God would one day make a new covenant with His people (Eze 11:19-20). That covenant would be associated with the coming Messiah. In it they would know peace (34:25) and an inward inclination to serve God (36:27).

9. God provides for the worship needs of His people. In looking to the distant future, Ezekiel saw a time that Israel's worship would center around a new Temple (chs 40-48). The new Temple would be vastly different from the Temple Ezekiel had known from his youth. Even though its size and design would be different, the most radical difference was the absence of Israel's most sacred symbol, the ark of the covenant. Instead, the very glory of Yahweh would inhabit the house, and His followers would serve Him.

Contemporary Teaching

The Book of Ezekiel calls us to join in a fresh and living encounter with the God of Abraham, Moses, and the prophets. We must be overcomers, or we will be overcome. Ezekiel challenges us:

(1) To experience a life-changing vision of God's power, knowledge, eternal presence, and holiness.

(2) To let God direct us from the expected paths of service to the existing avenues of ministry.

(3) To realize the sweetness and effectiveness of God's Word to challenge and direct our lives.

(4) To comprehend the depth of, and commitment to, evil that lodges in each human heart.

(5) To identify with the humanity of the very ones whose life-styles we must understand and condemn.

(6) To recognize that God holds His servants responsible for warning wicked men of their peril.

(7) To understand that momentary tragedies are not God's ultimate purpose for our lives.

(8) To experience a living relationship with Jesus Christ, who said that the new covenant is to be found in His blood (Lk 22:20).

(9) To depend upon God daily, being confident that His kingdom will suffice both now and forever.

Chapter 1

The Living Creatures and the Glory of the LORD

IN the[a] thirtieth year, in the fourth
month on the fifth day, while I was
among the exiles[a] by the Kebar River,[b]
the heavens were opened[c] and I saw visions[d] of God.
2On the fifth of the month—it was the
fifth year of the exile of King Jehoiachin[e]— 3the word of the LORD came to
Ezekiel[f] the priest, the son of Buzi,[b] by
the Kebar River in the land of the Babylonians.[c] There the hand of the LORD was
upon him.[g]
4I looked, and I saw a windstorm[h]
coming out of the north[i]—an immense
cloud with flashing lightning and surrounded by brilliant light. The center of
the fire looked like glowing metal,[j] 5and
in the fire was what looked like four living creatures.[k] In appearance their form
was that of a man,[l] 6but each of them
had four faces[m] and four wings. 7Their
legs were straight; their feet were like
those of a calf and gleamed like burnished
bronze.[n] 8Under their wings on their
four sides they had the hands of a man.[o]
All four of them had faces and wings,
9and their wings touched one another.
Each one went straight ahead; they did
not turn as they moved.[p]
10Their faces looked like this: Each of
the four had the face of a man, and on the
right side each had the face of a lion, and
on the left the face of an ox; each also had
the face of an eagle.[q] 11Such were their
faces. Their wings[r] were spread out upward; each had two wings, one touching
the wing of another creature on either
side, and two wings covering its body.
12Each one went straight ahead. Wherever the spirit would go, they would go,
without turning as they went.[s] 13The appearance of the living creatures was like
burning coals[t] of fire or like torches. Fire
moved back and forth among the creatures; it was bright, and lightning[u]
flashed out of it. 14The creatures sped
back and forth like flashes of lightning.[v]
15As I looked at the living creatures,[w] I
saw a wheel[x] on the ground beside each
creature with its four faces. 16This was
the appearance and structure of the
wheels: They sparkled like chrysolite,[y]
and all four looked alike. Each appeared
to be made like a wheel intersecting a
wheel. 17As they moved, they would go
in any one of the four directions the creatures faced; the wheels did not turn[z]
about[d] as the creatures went. 18Their
rims were high and awesome, and all four
rims were full of eyes[a] all around.
19When the living creatures moved,
the wheels beside them moved; and
when the living creatures rose from the
ground, the wheels also rose. 20Wherever
the spirit would go, they would go,[b] and
the wheels would rise along with them,
because the spirit of the living creatures
was in the wheels. 21When the creatures
moved, they also moved; when the creatures stood still, they also stood still; and
when the creatures rose from the ground,
the wheels rose along with them, because
the spirit of the living creatures was in
the wheels.[c]
22Spread out above the heads of the living creatures was what looked like an expanse,[d] sparkling like ice, and awesome.
23Under the expanse their wings were
stretched out one toward the other, and
each had two wings covering its body.
24When the creatures moved, I heard the
sound of their wings, like the roar of
rushing[e] waters, like the voice[f] of the
Almighty,[e] like the tumult of an army.[g]
When they stood still, they lowered their
wings.
25Then there came a voice from above
the expanse over their heads as they
stood with lowered wings. 26Above the
expanse over their heads was what
looked like a throne[h] of sapphire,[f][i] and
high above on the throne was a figure
like that of a man.[j] 27I saw that from
what appeared to be his waist up he
looked like glowing metal, as if full of fire,
and that from there down he looked like
fire; and brilliant light surrounded him.[k]
28Like the appearance of a rainbow[l] in

1:1 [a]S Dt 21:10; Eze 11:24-25 [b]S Ps 137:1 [c]S Mt 3:16 [d]S Ex 24:10
1:2 [e]S 2Ki 24:15
1:3 [f]Eze 24:24 [g]S 2Ki 3:15; Isa 8:11; Eze 3:14, 22; 8:1; 33:22; 37:1; 40:1
1:4 [h]S Job 38:1 [i]Jer 1:14 [j]Eze 8:2
1:5 [k]S Isa 6:2; Rev 4:6 [l]ver 26; Da 7:13
1:6 [m]Eze 10:14
1:7 [n]Eze 40:3; Da 10:6; S Rev 1:15
1:8 [o]Eze 10:8
1:9 [p]Eze 10:22
1:10 [q]Eze 10:14; Rev 4:7
1:11 [r]Isa 6:2
1:12 [s]Eze 10:16-19
1:13 [t]S 2Sa 22:9 [u]Rev 4:5
1:14 [v]S Ps 29:7
1:15 [w]Eze 3:13 [x]Eze 10:2; Da 7:9
1:16 [y]S Ex 28:20
1:17 [z]ver 9
1:18 [a]Rev 4:6
1:20 [b]ver 12
1:21 [c]Eze 10:9-12
1:22 [d]Eze 10:1
1:24 [e]S Ps 46:3; Eze 3:13 [f]Eze 10:5; 43:2; Da 10:6; Rev 1:15; 14:2; 19:6 [g]S 2Ki 7:6
1:26 [h]S 1Ki 22:19; Isa 6:1; S Jer 3:17 [i]S Ex 24:10 [j]S ver 5; S Eze 2:1; S Rev 1:13
1:27 [k]Eze 8:2
1:28 [l]S Ge 9:13; Rev 10:1

[a] *1* Or ⌞*my*⌟ [b] *3* Or *Ezekiel son of Buzi the priest* [c] *3* Or *Chaldeans* [d] *17* Or *aside* [e] *24* Hebrew *Shaddai* [f] *26* Or *lapis lazuli*

1:1–28 REVELATION, Visions—God introduced the priest Ezekiel to his prophetic office through an intricate vision combining natural elements of a thunderstorm and supernatural elements of four creatures. The colorful vision incorporates representatives of all classes of creatures who live on land. The vision as a whole shows God's sovereign control of the entire world, but the vision's separate elements and interpretation serve only as a preface to the central symbol, the vision of God's glory. Ezekiel could speak God's inspired message because he had been permitted to catch a vision of God's glory. Ezekiel's vision revealed to the exiles that God was present with them even in a foreign land. The wheels represented the mobility of God's word, able to reach His people anywhere even without the Jerusalem Temple. See note on Isa 6:5–8. Visions differ from dreams in that the person is awake and sees something in the natural world which gives the setting for the revelatory vision. See note on Jer 1:11–16. Compare Eze 8:4; 10:1–22; 11:22–23; 43:3.

1:25–28 GOD, Sovereignty—Ezekiel's vision from God provided vivid imagery to attempt to describe the sovereign God who is above all persons and all things. Newly arrived in foreign captivity, Ezekiel and his friends needed strong reassurance God was still in control and was present with them so far away from His land.

the clouds on a rainy day, so was the radiance around him.[m]

This was the appearance of the likeness of the glory[n] of the LORD. When I saw it, I fell facedown,[o] and I heard the voice of one speaking.

Chapter 2

Ezekiel's Call

HE said to me, "Son of man,[p] stand[q] up on your feet and I will speak to you.[r]" 2As he spoke, the Spirit came into me and raised me[s] to my feet, and I heard him speaking to me.

3He said: "Son of man, I am sending you to the Israelites, to a rebellious nation that has rebelled against me; they and their fathers have been in revolt against me to this very day.[t] 4The people to whom I am sending you are obstinate and stubborn.[u] Say to them, 'This is what the Sovereign LORD says.'[v] 5And whether they listen or fail to listen[w]—for they are a rebellious house[x]—they will know that a prophet has been among them.[y] 6And you, son of man, do not be afraid[z] of them or their words. Do not be afraid, though briers and thorns[a] are all around you and you live among scorpions. Do not be afraid of what they say or terrified by them, though they are a rebellious house.[b] 7You must speak[c] my words to them, whether they listen or fail to listen, for they are rebellious.[d] 8But you, son of man, listen to what I say to you. Do not rebel[e,f] like that rebellious house;[g] open your mouth and eat[h] what I give you."

9Then I looked, and I saw a hand[i] stretched out to me. In it was a scroll,[j] 10which he unrolled before me. On both sides of it were written words of lament and mourning and woe.[k]

Chapter 3

AND he said to me, "Son of man, eat what is before you, eat this scroll; then go and speak to the house of Israel." 2So I opened my mouth, and he gave me the scroll to eat.

3Then he said to me, "Son of man, eat this scroll I am giving you and fill your stomach with it." So I ate[l] it, and it tasted as sweet as honey[m] in my mouth.

4He then said to me: "Son of man, go now to the house of Israel and speak my words to them.[n] 5You are not being sent to a people of obscure speech and difficult language,[o] but to the house of Israel— 6not to many peoples of obscure speech and difficult language, whose words you cannot understand. Surely if I had sent you to them, they would have listened to you.[p] 7But the house of Israel is not willing to listen[q] to you because they are not willing to listen to me, for the whole house of Israel is hardened and obstinate.[r] 8But I will make you as unyielding and hardened as they are.[s] 9I will make your forehead[t] like the hardest stone, harder than flint.[u] Do not be afraid of

1:28 mS Rev 4:2 nS Ex 16:7; S 24:16; Lk 2:9 oS Ge 17:3; S Nu 14:5 **2:1** pS Job 25:6; Ps 8:4; S Eze 1:26; Da 7:13; 8:15 qDa 10:11; Ac 14:10; 26:16 rAc 9:6 **2:2** sEze 3:24; Da 8:18 **2:3** tS Jer 3:25; Eze 5:6; 20:8-24; 24:3 **2:4** uS Ex 32:9; S Isa 9:9; Eze 3:7 vAm 7:15 **2:5** wEze 3:11 xEze 3:27 yS Jer 5:3; Eze 33:33; Jn 15:22 **2:6** zS Dt 31:6; S 2Ki 1:15 aS Nu 33:55; Isa 9:18; Mic 7:4 bS Isa 1:2; 30:9; Eze 24:3; 44:6 **2:7** cJer 7:27 dJer 1:7; S 42:21; Eze 3:10-11 **2:8** eNu 20:10-13 fIsa 8:11 gS Isa 50:5 hPs 81:10; S Jer 15:16; Rev 10:9 **2:9** iEze 8:3 jS Ps 40:7; S Jer 36:4; Rev 5:1-5; 10:8-10 **2:10** kIsa 3:11; Rev 8:13 **3:3** lS Jer 15:16 mS Ps 19:10; Rev 10:9-10 **3:4** nEze 11:4,25 **3:5** oS Isa 28:11; Jnh 1:2 **3:6** pJnh 3:5-10; Mt 11:21-23; Ac 13:46-48 **3:7** qS Jer 7:27 rIsa 48:4; Jer 3:3; S Eze 2:4; Jn 15:20-23 **3:8** sJer 1:18; S 15:20 **3:9** tS Isa 48:4 uS Jer 5:3

1:28 GOD, Glory—Inspired biblical writers were careful not to try to describe the invisible God. They described only what seemed to be a likeness of His brilliant glory, which was so bright no one could see beyond it to God Himself. The glory of the Lord does signify His presence with His discouraged people. See notes on Ex 16:7,10; 40:34–38; Lk 2:9,14; Jn 11:4.

2:1–2 HOLY SPIRIT, Leaders—The Spirit frequently lifted Ezekiel up (2:2; 3:12,14,24; 8:3; 11:1,24; 43:5) and transported him to other locations (3:14; 8:3; 11:1,24). Similar work of the Spirit appears in 1 Ki 18:12; 2 Ki 2:16; Ac 8:39; Rev 17:3; 21:10. The unusual action of the Spirit did not matter as much as the prophetic message that followed. The action of the Spirit drew attention to the prophet so that the message would be heard.

2:1–10 REVELATION, Faithfulness—God's prophet represented God's faithfulness to His people even when they rejected Him. The prophet's task was to be faithful in proclamation and not worry about being rejected.

2:3–4 SIN, Rebellion—Judah's sin of rebellion had become so entrenched that her fate was sealed: exile in Babylon. God sent the prophet Ezekiel to proclaim the message of judgment upon Judah. Even when God's people become hopeless rebels, He does not leave them without a prophetic word of warning and hope. For rebellion, see note on Isa 1:2–4. The parallel expression, "revolt" (Hebrew *marad*), comes from Near Eastern laws and covenant treaties. It refers to mutiny against a legally-established vassal relationship. Sin is agreeing to be God's servant and then actively backing out of and refusing to abide by the agreement. Only an obstinate and stubborn people (literally stiff of face and firm of heart) would dare mutiny against God.

2:7 SIN, Rebellion—See notes on 2:3–4; La 1:18–22.

3:1–3 REVELATION, Actions—Ezekiel's commission to proclaim God's word took concrete form. Symbolic actions normally displayed God's message concretely to the nation. This one was for the prophet's personal benefit. For the dedicated proclaimer of the word, God's message can be sweet. Compare, however, Jeremiah's confessions. See note on Jer 15:16–18.

3:5–11 EVANGELISM, Results—God seeks faithful witnesses to share His Word. He knows our audience may be stubborn and refuse to respond. We are to be just as stubborn in our commitment to witness. God does not demand large numbers of converts as our result. He calls for faithful devotion to the task He has given.

3:7 SIN, Rebellion—A preacher of God's Word must always remember whose Word is proclaimed and understand any rejection accordingly. A sinful people become "hardened and obstinate" (literally firm of forehead and stiff of heart). They choose not to listen to God's Word. That choice is sinful.

3:8–17 REVELATION, Messengers—Delivering God's word is a difficult task. The messenger must face hard opposition without fear. The messenger of judgment must personify God's anger against the sinful people. God's Spirit leads the messenger and gives strength for the task. One aspect of the messenger's task is that of watchman, hearing God's warning and applying it to the life of the people, seeking to turn them back to God's ways.

them or terrified by them, though they
are a rebellious house.[v]"
10And he said to me, "Son of man, listen carefully and take to heart[w] all the
words I speak to you. 11Go[x] now to your
countrymen in exile and speak to them.
Say to them, 'This is what the Sovereign
LORD says,'[y] whether they listen or fail to
listen.[z]"
12Then the Spirit lifted me up,[a] and I
heard behind me a loud rumbling sound
—May the glory of the LORD be praised in
his dwelling place!— 13the sound of the
wings of the living creatures[b] brushing
against each other and the sound of the
wheels beside them, a loud rumbling
sound.[c] 14The Spirit[d] then lifted me up[e]
and took me away, and I went in bitterness and in the anger of my spirit, with
the strong hand of the LORD[f] upon me.
15I came to the exiles who lived at Tel
Abib near the Kebar River.[g] And there,
where they were living, I sat among them
for seven days[h]—overwhelmed.

Warning to Israel

16At the end of seven days the word of
the LORD came to me:[i] 17"Son of man, I
have made you a watchman[j] for the
house of Israel; so hear the word I speak
and give them warning from me.[k]
18When I say to a wicked man, 'You will
surely die,'[l] and you do not warn him or
speak out to dissuade him from his evil
ways in order to save his life, that wicked
man will die for[g] his sin, and I will hold
you accountable for his blood.[m] 19But if
you do warn the wicked man and he does
not turn[n] from his wickedness[o] or from
his evil ways, he will die[p] for his sin; but
you will have saved yourself.[q]
20"Again, when a righteous man
turns[r] from his righteousness and does
evil, and I put a stumbling block[s] before
him, he will die. Since you did not warn
him, he will die for his sin. The righteous
things he did will not be remembered,
and I will hold you accountable for his
blood.[t] 21But if you do warn the righteous man not to sin and he does not sin,
he will surely live because he took warning, and you will have saved yourself.[u]"
22The hand of the LORD[v] was upon me
there, and he said to me, "Get up and
go[w] out to the plain,[x] and there I will
speak to you." 23So I got up and went out
to the plain. And the glory of the LORD
was standing there, like the glory I had
seen by the Kebar River,[y] and I fell facedown.[z]
24Then the Spirit came into me and
raised me[a] to my feet. He spoke to me
and said: "Go, shut yourself inside your
house.[b] 25And you, son of man, they will
tie with ropes; you will be bound so that
you cannot go out among the people.[c] 26I
will make your tongue stick to the roof[d]
of your mouth so that you will be silent
and unable to rebuke them, though they
are a rebellious house.[e] 27But when I
speak to you, I will open your mouth and
you shall say to them, 'This is what the
Sovereign LORD says.'[f] Whoever will listen let him listen, and whoever will refuse let him refuse; for they are a rebellious house.[g]

Chapter 4

Siege of Jerusalem Symbolized

"NOW, son of man, take a clay tablet, put it in front of you and
draw the city of Jerusalem on it. 2Then
lay siege to it: Erect siege works against
it, build a ramp[h] up to it, set up camps
against it and put battering rams around

3:9 [v]Isa 50:7; Eze 2:6; 44:6; Mic 3:8
3:10 [w]S Job 22:22
3:11 [x]S Isa 6:9 [y]ver 27 [z]Eze 2:4-5, 7; 11:24-25
3:12 [a]ver 14; Eze 8:3; 43:5
3:13 [b]Eze 1:15 [c]Eze 1:24; 10:5, 16-17
3:14 [d]S 1Ki 18:12 [e]S ver 12 [f]ver 22; S Isa 8:11; Eze 37:1
3:15 [g]S Ps 137:1 [h]S Ge 50:10
3:16 [i]Jer 42:7
3:17 [j]S Isa 52:8 [k]S Isa 58:1; Jer 1:17; Eze 11:4; Hab 2:1
3:18 [l]S Ge 2:17; Jn 8:21,24 [m]ver 20
3:19 [n]S Ps 7:12 [o]S Ge 6:5 [p]S Jer 42:16 [q]S 2Ki 17:13; Eze 14:14,20; Ac 18:6; 20:26; 1Ti 4:14-16
3:20 [r]S Jer 34:16 [s]S Lev 26:37; S Isa 8:14; S Eze 7:19 [t]ver 18; Ps 125:5; Eze 18:24; 33:12, 18
3:21 [u]Ac 20:31
3:22 [v]S ver 14; S Eze 1:3 [w]Ac 9:6 [x]Eze 8:4
3:23 [y]Eze 1:1 [z]S Ge 17:3
3:24 [a]S Eze 2:2 [b]Jer 15:17
3:25 [c]Eze 4:8
3:26 [d]S Ps 22:15 [e]Eze 2:5; 24:27; 33:22; Hos 4:4
3:27 [f]ver 11 [g]Eze 2:5; 12:3; 24:27; 29:21; 33:22; Rev 22:11
4:2 [h]S Jer 6:6; Eze 17:17; Da 11:15

[g]*18* Or *in*; also in verses 19 and 20

3:12,23 GOD, Glory—See note on 1:28.
3:12 WORSHIP, Praise—See note on Ex 15:1–21.
3:15 HUMANITY, Psychological Nature—People who fully share the suffering of others can be overcome emotionally. The compassionate sharing of grief is a part of the prophetic calling. Silent presence is a powerful expression of sharing.
3:16–21 HUMANITY, Responsibility—A part of an individual's responsibility to God is to share His Word with those who have not heard. Ignoring the responsibility makes a person liable to God for that failure.
3:16–21 SIN, Rebellion—To refuse to warn sinners of the consequence of sin is sin, bringing God's judgment as strongly as the original sin. Wickedness brings death. See note on Ps 10:1–18.
3:16–21 ELECTION, Responsibility—Ezekiel was given responsibility as a prophet to be a watchman to warn both the wicked and the righteous. He was to prophesy not only to the nation but also to individuals. As a prophet, he was accountable for the souls he was called to warn. Election to a task for God brings responsibility and accountability before God. Election is not a free ride on God's grace. It is a responsible service in God's mission.
3:19–21 SALVATION, Definition—The apostle Paul took this passage seriously (Ac 18:6; 20:26). Compare Jas 5:19–20. God's people are to watch over themselves and others and warn persons of the dire consequences of their sins. We cannot save ourselves, nor can we save others through warnings or any other good work. God will use our warnings to turn us and others from wickedness and sin (Eph 2:8–10). Persons are free to accept or reject salvation. Failure to let other people know the "wages of sin" (Ro 6:23) is sin.
3:20 CHRISTIAN ETHICS, Character—This verse illustrates the individual/corporate tension in moral responsibility for God's people. The individual carries an ethical obligation toward righteousness. The community has an obligation as well to aid the individual toward righteousness. The community must bear some of the blame and guilt when one of its individuals exhibits ethical failure.
4:1—5:17 REVELATION, Actions—In Exile, Ezekiel needed dramatic ways to catch people's attention. God gave him symbolic actions which preached God's message of Jerusalem's siege and destruction, the Exile as a time of atonement, and the Exile as punishment. The extreme action of ritual defilement was too much for the priest-prophet Ezekiel, so he complained to God. This shows the freedom to respond that God gave His inspired messengers. See note on Jer 32:6–15.

it.[i] 3Then take an iron pan,[j] place it as
an iron wall between you and the city and
turn your face toward[k] it. It will be under
siege, and you shall besiege it. This will
be a sign[l] to the house of Israel.[m]
4"Then lie on your left side and put the
sin of the house of Israel upon yourself.[h]
You are to bear their sin for the number
of days you lie on your side. 5I have assigned you the same number of days as
the years of their sin. So for 390 days you
will bear the sin of the house of Israel.
6"After you have finished this, lie
down again, this time on your right side,
and bear the sin[n] of the house of Judah. I
have assigned you 40 days, a day for each
year.[o] 7Turn your face[p] toward the siege
of Jerusalem and with bared arm prophesy against her. 8I will tie you up with
ropes so that you cannot turn from one
side to the other until you have finished
the days of your siege.[q]
9"Take wheat and barley, beans and
lentils, millet and spelt;[r] put them in a
storage jar and use them to make bread
for yourself. You are to eat it during the
390 days you lie on your side. 10Weigh
out twenty shekels[i][s] of food to eat each
day and eat it at set times. 11Also measure
out a sixth of a hin[j] of water and drink it
at set times.[t] 12Eat the food as you would
a barley cake; bake it in the sight of the
people, using human excrement[u] for
fuel." 13The LORD said, "In this way the
people of Israel will eat defiled food
among the nations where I will drive
them."[v]
14Then I said, "Not so, Sovereign
LORD![w] I have never defiled myself. From
my youth until now I have never eaten
anything found dead[x] or torn by wild animals. No unclean meat has ever entered
my mouth.[y]"
15"Very well," he said, "I will let you
bake your bread over cow manure instead
of human excrement."
16He then said to me: "Son of man, I
will cut off[z] the supply of food in Jerusalem. The people will eat rationed food in
anxiety and drink rationed water in despair,[a] 17for food and water will be
scarce.[b] They will be appalled at the
sight of each other and will waste away
because of[k] their sin.[c]

Chapter 5

"NOW, son of man, take a sharp
sword and use it as a barber's razor[d] to shave[e] your head and your
beard.[f] Then take a set of scales and divide up the hair. 2When the days of your
siege come to an end, burn a third[g] of
the hair with fire[h] inside the city. Take a
third and strike it with the sword all
around the city. And scatter a third to the
wind.[i] For I will pursue them with
drawn sword.[j] 3But take a few strands of
hair and tuck them away in the folds of
your garment.[k] 4Again, take a few of
these and throw them into the fire[l] and
burn them up. A fire will spread from
there to the whole house of Israel.
5"This is what the Sovereign LORD
says: This is Jerusalem, which I have set
in the center of the nations, with countries all around her.[m] 6Yet in her wickedness she has rebelled against my laws and
decrees more than the nations and countries around her. She has rejected my
laws and has not followed my decrees.[n]
7"Therefore this is what the Sovereign
LORD says: You have been more unruly
than the nations around you and have not
followed my decrees or kept my laws.
You have not even[l] conformed to the
standards of the nations around you.[o]
8"Therefore this is what the Sovereign
LORD says: I myself am against you, Jerusalem, and I will inflict punishment on
you in the sight of the nations.[p] 9Because
of all your detestable idols, I will do to
you what I have never done before and
will never do again.[q] 10Therefore in your
midst fathers will eat their children, and
children will eat their fathers.[r] I will in-

4:2 [i]S Jer 33:4; Eze 21:22
4:3 [j]S Lev 2:5 [k]ver 7; Eze 20:46; 21:2 [l]S Isa 8:18; S 20:3; Jer 13:1-7; 18:1-4; 19:1-2; Eze 5:1-4; 12:3-6 [m]S Jer 39:1
4:6 [n]S Ex 28:38 [o]Nu 14:34; Da 9:24-26; 12:11-12
4:7 [p]S ver 3; Eze 6:2; S 13:17
4:8 [q]Eze 3:25
4:9 [r]S Isa 28:25
4:10 [s]S Ex 30:13
4:11 [t]ver 16
4:12 [u]S Isa 36:12
4:13 [v]Hos 9:3; Am 7:17
4:14 [w]Jer 1:6; Eze 9:8; 20:49 [x]S Lev 11:39 [y]S Ex 22:31; Dt 14:3; 32:37-38; Da 1:8; Hos 9:3-4
4:16 [z]S Ps 105:16 [a]ver 10-11; S Lev 26:26; Isa 3:1; Eze 12:19
4:17 [b]La 5:4; Eze 5:16; 12:18-19; Am 4:8 [c]S Lev 26:39; Eze 24:23; 33:10
5:1 [d]S Nu 6:5 [e]Eze 44:20 [f]S Lev 21:5; S 2Sa 10:4
5:2 [g]Zec 13:8 [h]Jer 21:10; Eze 15:7 [i]ver 10; Jer 13:24 [j]ver 12; S Lev 26:33; S Jer 9:16; S 39:1-2
5:3 [k]2Ki 25:12; S Ps 74:11; Jer 39:10
5:4 [l]Eze 10:7; 15:7
5:5 [m]S Dt 4:6; S La 1:1; Eze 16:14
5:6 [n]S 2Ki 17:15; Ne 9:17; Jer 11:10; S Eze 2:3; 16:47-51; Zec 7:11
5:7 [o]S 2Ki 21:9; S 2Ch 33:9; Jer 2:10-11; Eze 16:47
5:8 [p]S Jer 21:5,13; 24:9; Eze 11:9; 15:7; Zec 14:2
5:9 [q]Da 9:12; S Mt 24:21
5:10 [r]S Lev 26:29; S La 2:20

[h]4 Or *your side* [i]10 That is, about 8 ounces (about 0.2 kilogram) [j]11 That is, about 2/3 quart (about 0.6 liter) [k]17 Or *away in* [l]7 Most Hebrew manuscripts; some Hebrew manuscripts and Syriac *You have*

4:4–8 SIN, Serious—Sin cannot be confessed and forgiven until we understand its gravity. Ezekiel had to bear Israel's sins symbolically to understand the immense importance of His task of calling them to repentance. Sin is not an idea or theory to be debated. It is an enemy to be fought.
5:5–17 ELECTION, Condemnation—The idolatry of Jerusalem placed her against God. God would therefore punish her. God has a standard to which He expects His people to conform. The elect's actions should distinguish them from the nations. When they do not, they face discipline.
5:6–7 SIN, Transgression—Sin is conscious action against a known standard. For the Old Testament covenant, God gave His people specific laws recorded in the five books of Moses. For other people God gave the moral conscience with its understanding of basic universal moral laws of right and justice. See note on Ro 1:18–25. For the New Testament God gave Christ's interpretation of the law in light of the commands to love God, self, and neighbor (Lk 10:25–28). Whatever God has revealed to us as His will, we sin when we rebel against that will. For obstinate rebellion, see note on La 1:18–22; for wickedness, see note on Ps 10:1–8. To reject God's will as revealed through His Word is to reject Him.
5:8–17 GOD, Wrath—God's wrath is His inevitable expression against persistent sin. When God's love does not win a response of faith and obedience, God's wrath is the inevitable result. Wrath is the withdrawal of His pity. The total destruction of His chosen land was a unique, never to be repeated expression of His wrath (v 9). See note on La 3:1,43.
5:8–17 SIN, Discipline—See note on 2 Ki 25:1–21.

flict punishment on you and will scatter all your survivors to the winds.[s] 11 Therefore as surely as I live,[t] declares the Sovereign[u] LORD, because you have defiled my sanctuary[v] with all your vile images[w] and detestable practices,[x] I myself will withdraw my favor; I will not look on you with pity or spare you.[y] 12 A third of your people will die of the plague or perish by famine inside you; a third will fall by the sword outside your walls; and a third I will scatter to the winds[z] and pursue with drawn sword.[a]

13 "Then my anger will cease and my wrath[b] against them will subside, and I will be avenged.[c] And when I have spent my wrath upon them, they will know that I the LORD have spoken in my zeal.[d]

14 "I will make you a ruin and a reproach among the nations around you, in the sight of all who pass by.[e] 15 You will be a reproach[f] and a taunt, a warning[g] and an object of horror to the nations around you when I inflict punishment on you in anger and in wrath and with stinging rebuke.[h] I the LORD have spoken.[i] 16 When I shoot at you with my deadly and destructive arrows of famine, I will shoot to destroy you. I will bring more and more famine upon you and cut off your supply of food.[j] 17 I will send famine and wild beasts[k] against you, and they will leave you childless. Plague and bloodshed[l] will sweep through you, and I will bring the sword against you. I the LORD have spoken.[m]"

Chapter 6

A Prophecy Against the Mountains of Israel

THE word of the LORD came to me: 2 "Son of man, set your face[n] against the mountains[o] of Israel; prophesy against them[p] 3 and say: 'O mountains of Israel, hear the word of the Sovereign LORD. This is what the Sovereign LORD says to the mountains and hills, to the ravines and valleys:[q] I am about to bring a sword against you, and I will destroy your high places.[r] 4 Your altars will be demolished and your incense altars[s] will be smashed; and I will slay your people in front of your idols.[t] 5 I will lay the dead bodies of the Israelites in front of their idols, and I will scatter your bones[u] around your altars.[v] 6 Wherever you live,[w] the towns will be laid waste and the high places[x] demolished, so that your altars will be laid waste and devastated, your idols[y] smashed and ruined, your incense altars[z] broken down, and what you have made wiped out.[a] 7 Your people will fall slain[b] among you, and you will know that I am the LORD.[c]

8 " 'But I will spare some, for some of you will escape[d] the sword when you are scattered among the lands and nations.[e] 9 Then in the nations where they have been carried captive, those who escape will remember[f] me—how I have been grieved[g] by their adulterous hearts, which have turned away from me, and by their eyes, which have lusted after their idols.[h] They will loathe themselves for the evil[i] they have done and for all their detestable practices.[j] 10 And they will know that I am the LORD;[k] I did not threaten in vain to bring this calamity on them.[l]

11 " 'This is what the Sovereign LORD says: Strike your hands together and stamp your feet and cry out "Alas!" because of all the wicked and detestable practices of the house of Israel, for they will fall by the sword, famine and plague.[m] 12 He that is far away will die of the plague, and he that is near will fall by the sword, and he that survives and is spared will die of famine. So will I spend my wrath[n] upon them.[o] 13 And they will know that I am the LORD, when their people lie slain among their idols[p] around their altars, on every high hill and on all the mountaintops, under every spreading tree and every leafy oak[q]—places where they offered fragrant incense to all their idols.[r] 14 And I will stretch out my hand[s] against them and make the land a desolate waste from the desert to Diblah[m]—wherever they live. Then they will know that I am the LORD.[t] ' "

5:10 [s]S Lev 26:33; S Ps 44:11; S Jer 13:14; Eze 12:14 **5:11** [t]S Nu 14:21 [u]S Ge 15:2 [v]S Lev 15:31 [w]Eze 7:20; 11:18 [x]2Ch 36:14; Eze 8:6 [y]S Job 27:22; S Jer 16:18; S La 2:17; Eze 7:4, 9; 8:18; 9:5 **5:12** [z]ver 10; Jer 13:24 [a]S ver 2, 17; S Ps 107:39; S Jer 15:2; S 21:9; Eze 6:11-12; 7:15; 12:14; Am 9:4; Zec 13:8; Rev 6:8 **5:13** [b]S 2Ch 12:7; S Job 20:23; Eze 21:17; 24:13 [c]S Isa 1:24 [d]S Isa 59:17; Eze 16:42; 38:19; Hos 10:10; Zec 6:8 **5:14** [e]S Lev 26:32; Ne 2:17; Ps 74:3-10; 79:1-4; Isa 64:11; Eze 6:6; 22:4; Da 9:16; Mic 3:12 **5:15** [f]S Isa 43:28 [g]S Dt 28:46 [h]S Dt 28:20; S 1Ki 9:7; S Jer 22:8-9; 24:9; Eze 14:8 [i]S Jer 23:40 **5:16** [j]S Lev 26:26; S Dt 32:24 **5:17** [k]Eze 14:15 [l]Eze 38:22 [m]S ver 12; S Lev 26:25; Eze 14:21; 28:23 **6:2** [n]S Eze 4:7 [o]Eze 18:6; Mic 6:1 [p]ver 13 **6:3** [q]Eze 36:4 [r]S Lev 26:30 **6:4** [s]S 2Ch 14:5 [t]Eze 9:6; 14:3; 20:16 **6:5** [u]S Nu 19:16; S Ps 53:5; Jer 8:1-2 [v]ver 13; S Lev 26:30 **6:6** [w]S Ex 12:20 [x]Hos 10:8 [y]Eze 30:13; Mic 1:7; Zec 13:2 [z]S Lev 26:30 [a]S 1Sa 5:4; Isa 6:11; S Eze 5:14 **6:7** [b]Eze 9:7 [c]ver 10,13,14; Eze 11:10-12 **6:8** [d]S Ps 68:20; S Jer 44:28 [e]S Ge 11:4; S Ps 44:11; Isa 6:13; S Jer 44:14; Eze 7:16; 12:16; 14:22 **6:9** [f]S Ps 137:6; Zec 10:9 [g]S Isa 7:13; S Jer 8:21 [h]S Ex 22:20; Eze 20:7,24; Mic 5:13 [i]S Ex 32:22 [j]S Job 42:6; Eze 20:43; 23:14-16; 36:31 **6:10** [k]S ver 7 [l]S Dt 28:52; Jer 40:2 **6:11** [m]S Jer 42:22; Eze 21:14,17; 22:13; 25:6 **6:12** [n]S Job 20:23 [o]S Eze 5:12; 7:15 **6:13** [p]S Lev 26:30 [q]S Isa 1:29 [r]S 1Ki 14:23; S Jer 2:20; Eze 18:6; 20:28; Hos 4:13 **6:14** [s]S Ex 7:5; S Job 30:21; S Jer 6:12; 51:25; Eze 20:34 [t]Eze 12:19; 14:13

[m] *14* Most Hebrew manuscripts; a few Hebrew manuscripts *Riblah*

6:1–2 REVELATION, Word—God's judging word strikes at the places of sin as well as the people of sin. God promised destruction for worship places dedicated to false gods.

6:1–14 HISTORY, Judgment—See notes on 1 Ki 20:13; Jer 1:14–19.

6:3–7 GOD, One God—The failure to recognize that God is the one and only God brought the renewed captivity of the people of God. God was teaching them to recognize Him only as God.

6:8–10 THE CHURCH, Remnant—God's judgment of His people has a purpose. He intends to present to Himself a purified remnant. The remnant, recognizing God's grace, repent and call upon the Lord. They know God carries out His threats against a rebellious people.

6:9 SALVATION, Remembrance—See note on Jer 31:20. God's character and His saving actions make us hate our sins and turn to Him.

6:11 REVELATION, Actions—See note on Jer 32:6–15.

Chapter 7

The End Has Come

THE word of the LORD came to me:
2“Son of man, this is what the Sovereign LORD says to the land of Israel: The
end![u] The end has come upon the four
corners[v] of the land. 3The end is now
upon you and I will unleash my anger
against you. I will judge you according to
your conduct[w] and repay you for all your
detestable practices.[x] 4I will not look on
you with pity[y] or spare you; I will surely
repay you for your conduct and the detestable practices among you. Then you
will know that I am the LORD.[z]
5“This is what the Sovereign LORD
says: Disaster![a] An unheard-of[n] disaster
is coming. 6The end[b] has come! The end
has come! It has roused itself against you.
It has come! 7Doom has come upon you
—you who dwell in the land. The time
has come, the day[c] is near;[d] there is
panic, not joy, upon the mountains. 8I am
about to pour out my wrath[e] on you and
spend my anger against you; I will judge
you according to your conduct and repay
you for all your detestable practices.[f] 9I
will not look on you with pity or spare
you;[g] I will repay you in accordance with
your conduct and the detestable practices
among you.[h] Then you will know that it
is I the LORD who strikes the blow.[i]
10“The day is here! It has come! Doom
has burst forth, the rod[j] has budded, arrogance has blossomed! 11Violence[k] has
grown into[o] a rod to punish wickedness;
none of the people will be left, none of
that crowd—no wealth, nothing of value.[l] 12The time has come, the day has
arrived. Let not the buyer[m] rejoice nor
the seller grieve, for wrath is upon the
whole crowd.[n] 13The seller will not recover the land he has sold as long as both
of them live, for the vision concerning
the whole crowd will not be reversed. Because of their sins, not one of them will
preserve his life.[o] 14Though they blow
the trumpet[p] and get everything ready,
no one will go into battle, for my wrath[q]
is upon the whole crowd.
15“Outside is the sword, inside are
plague and famine; those in the country
will die by the sword, and those in the
city will be devoured by famine and
plague.[r] 16All who survive[s] and escape
will be in the mountains, moaning like
doves[t] of the valleys, each because of his
sins.[u] 17Every hand will go limp,[v] and
every knee will become as weak as water.[w] 18They will put on sackcloth[x] and
be clothed with terror.[y] Their faces will
be covered with shame and their heads
will be shaved.[z] 19They will throw their
silver into the streets,[a] and their gold
will be an unclean thing. Their silver and
gold will not be able to save them in the
day of the LORD's wrath.[b] They will not
satisfy[c] their hunger or fill their stomachs with it, for it has made them stumble[d] into sin.[e] 20They were proud of
their beautiful jewelry and used it to
make[f] their detestable idols and vile images.[g] Therefore I will turn these into an
unclean thing for them.[h] 21I will hand it
all over as plunder[i] to foreigners and as
loot to the wicked of the earth, and they
will defile it.[j] 22I will turn my face[k]
away from them, and they will desecrate
my treasured place; robbers will enter it
and desecrate it.[l]
23“Prepare chains, because the land is
full of bloodshed[m] and the city is full of
violence.[n] 24I will bring the most wicked
of the nations to take possession of their
houses; I will put an end to the pride of
the mighty, and their sanctuaries[o] will
be desecrated.[p] 25When terror comes,
they will seek peace, but there will be
none.[q] 26Calamity upon calamity[r] will
come, and rumor upon rumor. They will
try to get a vision from the prophet;[s] the
teaching of the law by the priest will be
lost, as will the counsel of the elders.[t]
27The king will mourn, the prince will be
clothed with despair,[u] and the hands of
the people of the land will tremble. I will
deal with them according to their conduct,[v] and by their own standards I will
judge them. Then they will know that I
am the LORD.[w]”

Chapter 8

Idolatry in the Temple

IN the sixth year, in the sixth month on
the fifth day, while I was sitting in my
house and the elders[x] of Judah were sit-

7:2 [u]Am 8:2,10 [v]Rev 7:1; 20:8 **7:3** [w]Eze 18:30 [x]S Ge 6:13 **7:4** [y]S Jer 13:14; S Eze 5:11 [z]S Eze 5:11; 23:49 **7:5** [a]S 2Ki 21:12 **7:6** [b]Eze 39:8 **7:7** [c]S Job 18:20; S Isa 2:12; Am 5:18-20 [d]Eze 12:23; 30:3; Zep 1:14; Mal 3:2 **7:8** [e]Isa 42:25; Eze 9:8; 14:19; 22:22; Hos 5:10; Na 1:6 [f]Eze 20:8, 21; 36:19 **7:9** [g]S Jer 21:7; S Eze 5:11 [h]Eze 22:31 [i]Dt 32:35; S Ps 39:10; S Isa 9:13 **7:10** [j]Ps 89:32; Isa 10:5 **7:11** [k]S Ps 55:9; S Isa 58:4 [l]Jer 16:6; Zep 1:18 **7:12** [m]S Isa 24:2 [n]ver 7; Isa 5:13-14; Eze 30:3 **7:13** [o]Lev 25:24-28 **7:14** [p]S Job 39:24 [q]Jer 25:38 **7:15** [r]S Dt 32:25; Jer 14:18; S La 1:20; S Eze 5:12; 33:27 **7:16** [s]S Isa 10:20; S Jer 41:16; 42:17 [t]S Ge 8:8; S Isa 59:11 [u]S Ezr 9:15; Jer 9:19; S Eze 6:8 **7:17** [v]S 2Ki 19:26; S Jer 47:3; Eze 21:7; 22:14 [w]Da 5:6 **7:18** [x]S Jer 4:8; 48:37; 49:3 [y]S Ps 55:5 [z]S Isa 15:2-3; Eze 27:31; Am 8:10 **7:19** [a]S La 4:1 [b]Isa 42:25; Eze 13:5; 30:3; Joel 1:15; 2:1; Zep 1:7,18; 2:2 [c]Isa 55:2 [d]Eze 3:20; 14:3; Hos 4:5 [e]S Pr 11:4 **7:20** [f]S Jer 10:3 [g]S Eze 5:11 [h]S Isa 2:20; 30:22; Eze 16:17 **7:21** [i]S Nu 14:3 [j]S 2Ki 24:13 **7:22** [k]S Jer 2:27; Eze 39:23-24 [l]Ps 74:7-8; Jer 19:13; S La 2:7 **7:23** [m]S 2Ki 21:16; S Isa 1:15; S Eze 22:9 [n]S Ge 6:11; Eze 11:6 **7:24** [o]La 2:7; Eze 24:21 [p]2Ch 7:20; Eze 28:7 **7:25** [q]Jer 6:14; S 8:11; Eze 13:10, 16 **7:26** [r]S Dt 29:21; S 31:17 [s]S 1Sa 3:1 [t]Isa 47:11; S Jer 18:18; Eze 20:1-3; Am 8:11; Mic 3:6 **7:27** [u]S Ps 109:19; Eze 26:16 [v]S Isa 3:11; Eze 18:20 [w]S ver 4 **8:1** [x]S 2Ki 6:32; Eze 14:1

[n]*5* Most Hebrew manuscripts; some Hebrew manuscripts and Syriac *Disaster after* [o]*11* Or *The violent one has become*

7:1–27 SIN, Rebellion—Whoever dismisses the Lord's will from future plans will soon run out of time. God intervenes in judgment to reintroduce Himself to His own people (v 27). See note on 2 Ki 25:1–21.

7:1–27 HISTORY, Judgment—See notes on 1 Ki 20:13; Jer 1:14–19.

7:8,12–14,19 GOD, Wrath—Sin inevitably brings God's wrath. See note on 5:8–17.

7:16–19 SIN, Responsibility—Material refuge cannot protect a people from the guilt of their sins. Material wealth cannot buy protection from the punishment our sins bring. We must accept responsibility for our sins.

8:1–18 SIN, Against God—The worship place can become the sinful place. God's people insisted on being like their

ting before[y] me, the hand of the Sovereign LORD came upon me there.[z] 2I
looked, and I saw a figure like that of a
man.[p] From what appeared to be his
waist down he was like fire, and from
there up his appearance was as bright as
glowing metal.[a] 3He stretched out what
looked like a hand[b] and took me by the
hair of my head. The Spirit lifted me up[c]
between earth and heaven and in visions[d] of God he took me to Jerusalem, to
the entrance to the north gate of the inner court,[e] where the idol that provokes
to jealousy[f] stood. 4And there before me
was the glory[g] of the God of Israel, as in
the vision I had seen in the plain.[h]

5Then he said to me, "Son of man, look
toward the north." So I looked, and in
the entrance north of the gate of the altar
I saw this idol[i] of jealousy.

6And he said to me, "Son of man, do
you see what they are doing—the utterly
detestable[j] things the house of Israel is
doing here, things that will drive me far
from my sanctuary?[k] But you will see
things that are even more detestable."

7Then he brought me to the entrance
to the court. I looked, and I saw a hole in
the wall. 8He said to me, "Son of man,
now dig into the wall." So I dug into the
wall and saw a doorway there.

9And he said to me, "Go in and see the
wicked and detestable things they are doing here." 10So I went in and looked, and
I saw portrayed all over the walls[l] all
kinds of crawling things and detestable[m]
animals and all the idols of the house of
Israel.[n] 11In front of them stood seventy
elders[o] of the house of Israel, and Jaazaniah son of Shaphan was standing among
them. Each had a censer[p] in his hand,
and a fragrant cloud of incense[q] was rising.[r]

12He said to me, "Son of man, have you
seen what the elders of the house of Israel are doing in the darkness,[s] each at the
shrine of his own idol? They say, 'The
LORD does not see[t] us; the LORD has forsaken the land.'" 13Again, he said, "You
will see them doing things that are even
more detestable."

14Then he brought me to the entrance
to the north gate of the house of the
LORD, and I saw women sitting there,
mourning for Tammuz.[u] 15He said to me,
"Do you see this, son of man? You will
see things that are even more detestable
than this."

16He then brought me into the inner
court[v] of the house of the LORD, and
there at the entrance to the temple, between the portico and the altar,[w] were
about twenty-five men. With their backs
toward the temple of the LORD and their
faces toward the east, they were bowing
down to the sun[x] in the east.[y]

17He said to me, "Have you seen this,
son of man? Is it a trivial matter for the
house of Judah to do the detestable
things[z] they are doing here? Must they
also fill the land with violence[a] and continually provoke me to anger?[b] Look at
them putting the branch to their nose!
18Therefore I will deal with them in anger;[c] I will not look on them with pity[d]
or spare them. Although they shout in my
ears, I will not listen[e] to them."

Chapter 9

Idolaters Killed

THEN I heard him call out in a loud
voice, "Bring the guards of the city
here, each with a weapon in his hand."
2And I saw six men coming from the direction of the upper gate, which faces
north, each with a deadly weapon in his

8:1 [y]Eze 33:31 [z]Eze 1:1-3; 24:1; 40:1
8:2 [a]Eze 1:4,26-27
8:3 [b]S Eze 2:9 [c]S Eze 3:12; 11:1 [d]S Ex 24:10 [e]ver 16 [f]ver 5; Ex 20:5; Dt 32:16
8:4 [g]S Ex 24:16 [h]Eze 3:22
8:5 [i]Ps 78:58; S Jer 4:1; 32:34
8:6 [j]Ps 78:60; S Eze 5:11 [k]Hos 5:6
8:10 [l]S Jdg 17:4-5; Eze 23:14 [m]Jer 44:4 [n]Ex 20:4; Dt 4:15-18; S Jer 16:18; Eze 11:12
8:11 [o]S Ex 3:16 [p]S Lev 10:1; Nu 16:17 [q]Nu 16:35; S Jer 44:5 [r]Eze 11:1-2
8:12 [s]S Job 22:13 [t]S 2Ki 21:16; Ps 10:11; S Isa 29:15; Eze 9:9; Zep 1:12
8:14 [u]Eze 11:12
8:16 [v]ver 3 [w]Joel 2:17 [x]S Ge 1:16 [y]Dt 4:19; S 17:3; S Job 31:28; S Jer 2:27; Eze 9:6; 11:1,12; 40:6; 43:1
8:17 [z]Eze 16:2 [a]S Ge 6:11 [b]S Nu 11:33; S 1Ki 14:9; Eze 16:26
8:18 [c]S Jer 44:6 [d]S Jer 13:14; S Eze 5:11; 9:10; 24:14 [e]S 1Sa 8:18; S Isa 58:4; S Jer 11:11

[p]2 Or *saw a fiery figure*

neighbors and making a visible image of God. God's jealous zeal reacted in wrath against such sin. God makes Himself known in His glory to His people. Making an idol is a failure to trust God to reveal Himself to His people. Such lack of trust is sin. Worshiping the idol or any part of the natural world is open rebellion against God.

8:1–18 REVELATION, Visions—Ezekiel felt God's hand on him producing a powerful sense of divine presence and setting the prophet in an emotional state to experience God's vision (1:3; 3:14,22; 33:22; 37:1; 40:1). Compare 1 Ki 18:46 (where the Hebrew reads literally "hand of the LORD"); Isa 8:11; Jer 15:17. Ezekiel's vision involved changing geographical locations to see the sin of the people. Ezekiel learned God would ignore a people who ignored Him.

8:3 HOLY SPIRIT, Revelation—The Spirit inspired the prophets. Often we cannot tell how a prophet received his oracle from God. In this instance, however, the Spirit brought Ezekiel to Jerusalem in a vision, one of God's methods of inspiration. See Nu 12:6; Isa 6:1–4; Jer 14:14; note on Joel 2:28–32.

8:4 GOD, Glory—God's glory was present with His people in the Temple. How shocking to see an immense idol there! See note on 1:28.

8:12 GOD, Wisdom—God knows what is happening in His world and in the hearts of His people. Nothing is hidden from Him. See notes on Dt 31:21; 1 Sa 2:3; Pr 8:12–31.

8:17–18 GOD, Wrath—False worship among God's people drives Him to extreme means to show His disciplinary wrath. He puts aside pity and turns deaf to prayer while He acts in wrath. See note on 5:8–17.

8:18 PRAYER, Hindrances—After the detestable idolatry described in this chapter, God said even fervent shouting would not cause Him to listen. Shouting could not get His attention; idolatry had done that. Sin separates our prayers from God. See note on Isa 59:1–2.

9:1–11 REVELATION, Divine Presence—God's presence (as in the deliverance in Egypt) is active to identify and redeem those who are repentant. God is always seeking ways to save and reconcile not hurt or destroy. He marked off His faithful people before leaving Jerusalem to destruction. In Ezekiel's vision God symbolically left the Temple, refusing to live among an unholy people. Ezekiel faithfully carried out the prophet's role, interceding for His people. God was present to see the destruction of His faithless people.

hand. With them was a man clothed in
linen[f] who had a writing kit at his side.
They came in and stood beside the
bronze altar.
3Now the glory[g] of the God of Israel
went up from above the cherubim,[h]
where it had been, and moved to the
threshold of the temple. Then the LORD
called to the man clothed in linen who
had the writing kit at his side 4and said to
him, "Go throughout the city of Jerusalem[i] and put a mark[j] on the foreheads
of those who grieve and lament[k] over all
the detestable things that are done in
it.[l]"
5As I listened, he said to the others,
"Follow him through the city and kill,
without showing pity[m] or compassion.[n]
6Slaughter[o] old men, young men and
maidens, women and children,[p] but do
not touch anyone who has the mark.[q]
Begin at my sanctuary." So they began
with the elders[r] who were in front of the
temple.[s]
7Then he said to them, "Defile the
temple and fill the courts with the slain.[t]
Go!" So they went out and began killing
throughout the city. 8While they were
killing and I was left alone, I fell facedown,[u] crying out, "Ah, Sovereign
LORD![v] Are you going to destroy the entire remnant of Israel in this outpouring
of your wrath[w] on Jerusalem?[x]"
9He answered me, "The sin of the
house of Israel and Judah is exceedingly
great; the land is full of bloodshed and
the city is full of injustice.[y] They say,
'The LORD has forsaken the land; the
LORD does not see.'[z] 10So I will not look
on them with pity[a] or spare them, but I
will bring down on their own heads what
they have done.[b]"
11Then the man in linen with the writing kit at his side brought back word,
saying, "I have done as you commanded."

Chapter 10

The Glory Departs From the Temple

I looked, and I saw the likeness of a
throne[c] of sapphire[q][d] above the expanse[e] that was over the heads of the
cherubim.[f] 2The LORD said to the man
clothed in linen,[g] "Go in among the
wheels[h] beneath the cherubim. Fill[i]
your hands with burning coals[j] from
among the cherubim and scatter them
over the city." And as I watched, he went
in.
3Now the cherubim were standing on
the south side of the temple when the
man went in, and a cloud filled the inner
court. 4Then the glory of the LORD[k] rose
from above the cherubim and moved to
the threshold of the temple. The cloud
filled the temple, and the court was full of
the radiance of the glory of the LORD.
5The sound of the wings of the cherubim
could be heard as far away as the outer
court, like the voice[l] of God Almighty[r]
when he speaks.[m]
6When the LORD commanded the man
in linen, "Take fire from among the
wheels,[n] from among the cherubim,"
the man went in and stood beside a
wheel. 7Then one of the cherubim
reached out his hand to the fire[o] that was
among them. He took up some of it and
put it into the hands of the man in linen,
who took it and went out. 8(Under the

9:2 [f]S Lev 16:4; Eze 10:2; Da 10:5; 12:6; Rev 15:6
9:3 [g]S 1Sa 4:21; Eze 10:4 [h]Eze 11:22
9:4 [i]Jer 25:29 [j]S Ge 4:15; Ex 12:7; 2Co 1:22; S Rev 7:3 [k]Ps 119:136; Jer 7:29; 13:17; Eze 21:6; Am 6:6 [l]Ps 119:53
9:5 [m]S Jer 13:14; S Eze 5:11 [n]S Ex 32:27; Isa 13:18
9:6 [o]Jer 7:32 [p]S Jer 16:6 [q]S Ge 4:15; S Ex 12:7 [r]Eze 8:11-13,16 [s]S 2Ch 36:17; Jer 25:29; S Eze 6:4; 1Pe 4:17
9:7 [t]Eze 6:7
9:8 [u]S Jos 7:6 [v]S Eze 4:14 [w]S Eze 7:8 [x]Eze 11:13; Am 7:1-6
9:9 [y]S Ps 58:2; Jer 12:1; Eze 22:29; Hab 1:4 [z]S Job 22:13; S Eze 8:12; 14:23
9:10 [a]S Jer 13:14; S Eze 8:18 [b]S Isa 22:5; S 65:6; Eze 11:21; 23:49
10:1 [c]S Rev 4:2 [d]S Ex 24:10 [e]Eze 1:22 [f]S Ge 3:24
10:2 [g]S Eze 9:2 [h]S Eze 1:15 [i]Rev 8:5 [j]S 2Sa 22:9
10:4 [k]S Ex 24:16; Eze 9:3; 44:4
10:5 [l]S Job 40:9 [m]S Eze 3:13
10:6 [n]Da 7:9
10:7 [o]S Eze 5:4

[q]*1* Or *lapis lazuli* [r]*5* Hebrew *El-Shaddai*

9:3–11 GOD, Wrath—Even in executing wrath, God protects those who are faithful to Him. See comments at 5:8–17.
9:3–11 ELECTION, Remnant—God marked out a faithful remnant for Himself even as He destroyed the wicked among elect Israel. Participating in worship ceremonies in the Temple did not distinguish the elect remnant. Sadness over sin did.
9:3–11 CHRISTIAN ETHICS, Moral Limits—The vision communicates in an extreme form in order for the audience to understand the perverseness which they had reached and their guilt before God. God's holiness demanded purity from His people. Unless they turned from their ways of bloodshed, the symbolic judgment would become real. God enforces the moral limits He sets for His people.
9:8–10 THE CHURCH, Remnant—Destruction does not please God's spokespersons even though they have predicted it. Ezekiel pleaded with God to spare His remnant, but God refused to spare a guilty people. God expects obedience from His remnant. See note on 6:8–10.
9:9–10 EVIL AND SUFFERING, Punishment—God's punishment is often delayed in His grace. He does not delay forever. At the time best suiting His purposes, He exercises unrelenting judgment on a sinful people.
9:9–10 SIN, Responsibility—We destroy society through injustice and greed. Then we complain that God has ignored us and cannot see our troubles or help us. God will not take responsibility for our sins. We must. See notes on 8:3–18; 18:1–32.
9:9–10 CHRISTIAN ETHICS, Justice—An unjust people who think they can fool God face His inevitable judgment. See note on La 3:32–36.
10:1 GOD, Sovereignty—See note on 1:25–28.
10:1–22 REVELATION, Angels—Cherubim appear in Ezekiel's vision because they are represented in the Temple as standing figures where God was present in the Most Holy Place over the ark (Ex 25:18–22; 1 Ki 6:23–35; 8:6–7). God was pictured by Israel as riding on cherubim (1 Sa 4:4; 2 Sa 6:2; 22:11; Ps 18:11). God placed cherubim as guards of the garden (Ge 3:24). Cherubim thus represent God's presence and guard unauthorized entry into that presence.
10:3–5 REVELATION, Divine Presence—God was seen and heard in the Temple sanctuary. Elements of the Exodus revelations are evident (cloud, wind, brightness). Each symbolic occurrence confirmed that God was present to the prophet. The vision also showed God was leaving His Temple and thus condemning His people to destruction.
10:4,18–19 GOD, Glory—Ezekiel used glory to express God's active presence on behalf of His people. See note on 1:28.

wings of the cherubim could be seen
what looked like the hands of a man.)[p]
9I looked, and I saw beside the cherubim four wheels, one beside each of the
cherubim; the wheels sparkled like chrysolite.[q] 10As for their appearance, the four
of them looked alike; each was like a
wheel intersecting a wheel. 11As they
moved, they would go in any one of the
four directions the cherubim faced; the
wheels did not turn about[s] as the cherubim went. The cherubim went in whatever direction the head faced, without turning as they went. 12Their entire bodies,
including their backs, their hands and
their wings, were completely full of
eyes,[r] as were their four wheels.[s] 13I
heard the wheels being called "the whirl-
ing wheels." 14Each of the cherubim[t]
had four faces:[u] One face was that of a
cherub, the second the face of a man, the
third the face of a lion,[v] and the fourth
the face of an eagle.[w]
15Then the cherubim rose upward.
These were the living creatures[x] I had
seen by the Kebar River.[y] 16When the
cherubim moved, the wheels beside
them moved; and when the cherubim
spread their wings to rise from the
ground, the wheels did not leave their
side. 17When the cherubim stood still,
they also stood still; and when the cherubim rose, they rose with them, because
the spirit of the living creatures was in
them.[z]
18Then the glory[a] of the LORD departed
from over the threshold of the temple and
stopped above the cherubim.[b] 19While I
watched, the cherubim spread their
wings and rose from the ground, and as
they went, the wheels went with them.[c]
They stopped at the entrance to the
east gate of the LORD's house, and the
glory[d] of the God of Israel was above
them.
20These were the living creatures I had
seen beneath the God of Israel by the Kebar River,[e] and I realized that they were
cherubim. 21Each had four faces[f] and
four wings,[g] and under their wings was
what looked like the hands of a man.
22Their faces had the same appearance as
those I had seen by the Kebar River.[h]
Each one went straight ahead.

10:8 [p]Eze 1:8
10:9 [q]S Ex 28:20; Rev 21:20
10:12 [r]Rev 4:6-8 [s]Eze 1:15-21
10:14 [t]1Ki 7:36 [u]Eze 1:6 [v]1Ki 7:29 [w]Eze 1:10; 41:19; Rev 4:7
10:15 [x]S Isa 6:2 [y]S Ps 137:1
10:17 [z]S Eze 3:13
10:18 [a]S 1Sa 4:21 [b]S Ps 18:10
10:19 [c]Eze 11:1,22 [d]Eze 43:4
10:20 [e]Eze 1:1
10:21 [f]Eze 41:18 [g]Eze 1:6
10:22 [h]Eze 1:1
11:1 [i]ver 13 [j]Jer 5:5 [k]S Eze 8:16; S 10:19; 43:4-5
11:2 [l]S Isa 29:20; Na 1:11 [m]Eze 8:11
11:3 [n]Jer 1:13; Eze 24:3 [o]ver 7,11; Eze 12:22,27; Mic 3:3
11:4 [p]S Eze 3:4,17
11:5 [q]S Ps 26:2; S Jer 17:10
11:6 [r]S Eze 7:23; 22:6
11:7 [s]Jer 1:13 [t]ver 3; Eze 24:3-13; Mic 3:2-3
11:8 [u]S Lev 26:25; S Jer 42:16 [v]S Pr 10:24; Isa 66:4
11:9 [w]Ps 106:41 [x]Dt 28:36; S Eze 5:8
11:10 [y]2Ki 14:25
11:11 [z]ver 3; Eze 24:6
11:12 [a]S Eze 6:7 [b]S Lev 18:4; Eze 18:9 [c]Eze 8:10
11:13 [d]ver 1 [e]S Eze 9:8; Am 7:2

Chapter 11

Judgment on Israel's Leaders

THEN the Spirit lifted me up and
brought me to the gate of the house
of the LORD that faces east. There at the
entrance to the gate were twenty-five
men, and I saw among them Jaazaniah
son of Azzur and Pelatiah[i] son of Benaiah, leaders[j] of the people.[k] 2The LORD
said to me, "Son of man, these are the
men who are plotting evil[l] and giving
wicked advice in this city.[m] 3They say,
'Will it not soon be time to build
houses?[t] This city is a cooking pot,[n] and
we are the meat.'[o] 4Therefore prophesy[p]
against them; prophesy, son of man."
5Then the Spirit of the LORD came
upon me, and he told me to say: "This is
what the LORD says: That is what you are
saying, O house of Israel, but I know
what is going through your mind.[q] 6You
have killed many people in this city and
filled its streets with the dead.[r]
7"Therefore this is what the Sovereign
LORD says: The bodies you have thrown
there are the meat and this city is the
pot,[s] but I will drive you out of it.[t] 8You
fear the sword,[u] and the sword is what I
will bring against you, declares the Sovereign LORD.[v] 9I will drive you out of the
city and hand you over[w] to foreigners and
inflict punishment on you.[x] 10You will
fall by the sword, and I will execute judgment on you at the borders of Israel.[y]
Then you will know that I am the LORD.
11This city will not be a pot[z] for you, nor
will you be the meat in it; I will execute
judgment on you at the borders of Israel.
12And you will know that I am the
LORD,[a] for you have not followed my decrees[b] or kept my laws but have conformed to the standards of the nations
around you.[c]"
13Now as I was prophesying, Pelatiah[d]
son of Benaiah died. Then I fell facedown
and cried out in a loud voice, "Ah, Sovereign LORD! Will you completely destroy
the remnant of Israel?[e]"
14The word of the LORD came to me:
15"Son of man, your brothers—your

[s]*11* Or *aside* [t]*3* Or *This is not the time to build houses.*

11:1–12 SIN, Punishment—The leaders in Jerusalem after the destruction of 597 BC (2 Ki 24:8–17) decided they were God's choice, preserved meat, and those exiled to Babylon were the bones. They proudly led Jerusalem back to its wicked, idolatrous ways. God taught them He is not limited to one time or way of punishment. He would punish their transgression. They learned the hard way (2 Ki 25). See notes on 5:6–7; 1 Ki 14:22–24; 2 Ki 25:1–21.
11:1–21 HISTORY, National—See note on Isa 1:24–26.
11:7–12 REVELATION, History—God detailed the events a disobedient Jerusalem faced, showing the price people pay for ignoring God's purposes. When people ignore God's revealed will, He uses history to reveal His anger.
11:13 THE CHURCH, Remnant—See 6:8–10; 9:8–10.
11:15 ELECTION, Remnant—The law of judgment is followed by the gospel of hope. God does not practice total destruction. He saves the remnant and gives them undivided commitment to Him. God does everything possible to create a people who will freely let Him be their God. Those serving other gods do not qualify for the elect remnant.

brothers who are your blood relatives[u]
and the whole house of Israel—are those
of whom the people of Jerusalem have
said, ‘They are[v] far away from the LORD;
this land was given to us as our possession.’[f]

Promised Return of Israel

16“Therefore say: ‘This is what the
Sovereign LORD says: Although I sent
them far away among the nations and
scattered them among the countries, yet
for a little while I have been a sanctuary[g]
for them in the countries where they
have gone.’

17“Therefore say: ‘This is what the
Sovereign LORD says: I will gather you
from the nations and bring you back from
the countries where you have been scattered, and I will give you back the land of
Israel again.’[h]

18“They will return to it and remove all
its vile images[i] and detestable idols.[j] 19I
will give them an undivided heart[k] and
put a new spirit in them; I will remove
from them their heart of stone[l] and give
them a heart of flesh.[m] 20Then they will
follow my decrees and be careful to keep
my laws.[n] They will be my people,[o] and
I will be their God.[p] 21But as for those
whose hearts are devoted to their vile images and detestable idols,[q] I will bring
down on their own heads what they have
done, declares the Sovereign LORD.[r]”

22Then the cherubim, with the wheels
beside them, spread their wings, and the
glory[s] of the God of Israel was above
them.[t] 23The glory[u] of the LORD went up
from within the city and stopped above
the mountain[v] east of it. 24The Spirit[w]
lifted me up and brought me to the exiles
in Babylonia[w] in the vision[x] given by the
Spirit of God.

Then the vision I had seen went up
from me, 25and I told the exiles everything the LORD had shown me.[y]

Chapter 12

The Exile Symbolized

THE word of the LORD came to me:
2“Son of man, you are living among a
rebellious people.[z] They have eyes to see
but do not see and ears to hear but do not
hear, for they are a rebellious people.[a]

3“Therefore, son of man, pack your belongings for exile and in the daytime, as
they watch, set out and go from where
you are to another place. Perhaps[b] they
will understand,[c] though they are a rebellious house.[d] 4During the daytime,
while they watch, bring out your belongings packed for exile. Then in the evening, while they are watching, go out like
those who go into exile.[e] 5While they
watch, dig through the wall[f] and take
your belongings out through it. 6Put them
on your shoulder as they are watching
and carry them out at dusk. Cover your
face so that you cannot see the land, for I
have made you a sign[g] to the house of
Israel.”

7So I did as I was commanded.[h] During the day I brought out my things
packed for exile. Then in the evening I
dug through the wall with my hands. I
took my belongings out at dusk, carrying
them on my shoulders while they
watched.

8In the morning the word of the LORD

11:15 [f]Eze 33:24
11:16 [g]Ps 31:20; 90:1; 91:9; S Isa 4:6
11:17 [h]S Ne 1:9; S Jer 3:18; 24:5-6; S 31:16; Eze 20:41; 28:25; 34:13; 36:28
11:18 [i]S Eze 5:11 [j]Eze 37:23
11:19 [k]S 2Ch 30:12; S Ps 86:11 [l]Zec 7:12; Ro 2:5 [m]Eze 18:31; S 2Co 3:3
11:20 [n]S Ps 1:2 [o]S Jer 11:4; 32:38 [p]S Ex 6:7; Eze 14:11; 34:30; 36:26-28; Hos 1:9; Zec 8:8; Heb 8:10
11:21 [q]Jer 16:18 [r]Jer 16:11; S Eze 9:10; 16:43
11:22 [s]S Ex 24:16 [t]Eze 9:3; S 10:19
11:23 [u]Eze 1:28; S 10:4 [v]Zec 14:4
11:24 [w]Eze 37:1; 43:5 [x]2Co 12:2-4
11:25 [y]S Eze 3:4, 11
12:2 [z]Ps 78:40; S Jer 42:21 [a]S Isa 6:10; S Mt 13:15; Mk 4:12; 8:18
12:3 [b]S Jer 36:3 [c]Jer 26:3 [d]ver 11; S Eze 3:27; 2Ti 2:25-26
12:4 [e]ver 12; 2Ki 25:4; S Jer 39:4
12:5 [f]Jer 52:7; Am 4:3
12:6 [g]ver 12; S Isa 8:18; S 20:3
12:7 [h]Eze 24:18; 37:10

[u]15 Or *are in exile with you* (see Septuagint and Syriac) [v]15 Or *those to whom the people of Jerusalem have said, ‘Stay* [w]24 Or *Chaldea*

11:16 SALVATION, As Refuge—See note on Isa 8:13–14. God always provides a refuge, or sanctuary, for His people. That sanctuary of refuge is the Lord Himself (Ps 90:1; 91:9; Isa 4:6).

11:17–21 SALVATION, Renewal—God’s promised restoration of Israel included giving her a new spirit and a new heart. Here we can see a decisive turn in the doctrine of salvation as it developed in salvation history. God’s new covenant was to be written on hearts of flesh rather than upon tables of stone like the Ten Commandments. God has done everything possible to be our God and let us be His obedient people.

11:17–20 THE CHURCH, Covenant People—God graciously provides the motivation for obedience. He changes the lives of those who respond to Him in repentance and faith. In the day of restoration from the Exile in Babylon, God promised to give His people a new heart and spirit. A single or undivided heart probably indicates a heart focused on God. See note on Jer 31:31–34. A new spirit probably refers to the human spirit. The spirit is the dominant disposition of the individual, reflected in attitudes and actions. A new spirit indicates that God will replace the old disposition which opposed Him with a spirit which follows in His way. With a new spirit and a dedicated heart, God’s people may faithfully follow Him.

11:18–21 HUMANITY, Human Nature—See note on Ps 90:12. Heart here refers to a common “mind” or commitment on the part of God’s people. False religion destoys our relationship with God, so our mental capacities no longer function properly. The merciful power of God can restore our ability and our will to commit ourselves to Him.

11:18–21 SALVATION, Obedience—The new spirit and new heart bring with them a new obedience. Ezekiel’s good news was that God would so renew His people that they would obey Him from the heart.

11:21 GOD, One God—See note on 6:3–7.

12:1–6 REVELATION, Actions—God used Ezekiel’s actions as a clear parable to His children of what was about to happen. The revealed future may hopefully call them to follow their Lord. God’s revelation of Israel’s captivity was designed to stun them into returning to Him. See note on Jer 32:6–15.

12:1–28 HISTORY, Judgment—See notes on 1 Ki 20:13; Jer 1:14–19. Israel heard so much preaching of judgment they became skeptical. They refused to believe judgment would come in their generation. Ezekiel called for a turn away from skepticism. God would bring judgment immediately. Israel learned God’s Word is true. God judges a disobedient people. Ignoring God’s Word does not allow one to escape the historical reality of the judgment He announces.

12:2 SIN, Rebellion—See note on La 1:18–22.

came to me: 9"Son of man, did not that
rebellious house of Israel ask you, 'What
are you doing?'[i]
10"Say to them, 'This is what the Sovereign LORD says: This oracle concerns
the prince in Jerusalem and the whole
house of Israel who are there.' 11Say to
them, 'I am a sign[j] to you.'
"As I have done, so it will be done to
them. They will go into exile as captives.[k]
12"The prince among them will put his
things on his shoulder at dusk[l] and
leave, and a hole will be dug in the wall
for him to go through. He will cover his
face so that he cannot see the land.[m] 13I
will spread my net[n] for him, and he will
be caught in my snare;[o] I will bring him
to Babylonia, the land of the Chaldeans,[p]
but he will not see[q] it, and there he will
die.[r] 14I will scatter to the winds all
those around him—his staff and all his
troops—and I will pursue them with
drawn sword.[s]
15"They will know that I am the LORD,
when I disperse them among the nations[t] and scatter them through the
countries. 16But I will spare a few of them
from the sword, famine and plague, so
that in the nations where they go they
may acknowledge all their detestable
practices. Then they will know that I am
the LORD."[u]
17The word of the LORD came to me:
18"Son of man, tremble as you eat your
food,[v] and shudder in fear as you drink
your water. 19Say to the people of the
land: 'This is what the Sovereign LORD
says about those living in Jerusalem and
in the land of Israel: They will eat their
food in anxiety and drink their water in
despair, for their land will be stripped of
everything[w] in it because of the violence
of all who live there.[x] 20The inhabited
towns will be laid waste and the land will
be desolate. Then you will know that I am
the LORD.[y]' "
21The word of the LORD came to me:
22"Son of man, what is this proverb[z] you
have in the land of Israel: 'The days go by
and every vision comes to nothing'?[a]
23Say to them, 'This is what the Sovereign
LORD says: I am going to put an end to
this proverb, and they will no longer
quote it in Israel.' Say to them, 'The days
are near[b] when every vision will be fulfilled.[c] 24For there will be no more false
visions or flattering divinations[d] among
the people of Israel. 25But I the LORD will
speak what I will, and it shall be fulfilled
without delay.[e] For in your days, you rebellious house, I will fulfill[f] whatever I
say, declares the Sovereign LORD.[g]' "
26The word of the LORD came to me:
27"Son of man, the house of Israel is saying, 'The vision he sees is for many years
from now, and he prophesies about the
distant future.'[h]
28"Therefore say to them, 'This is what
the Sovereign LORD says: None of my
words will be delayed any longer; whatever I say will be fulfilled, declares the
Sovereign LORD.' "

Chapter 13

False Prophets Condemned

THE word of the LORD came to me:
2"Son of man, prophesy against the
prophets[i] of Israel who are now prophesying. Say to those who prophesy out of
their own imagination:[j] 'Hear the word
of the LORD![k] 3This is what the Sovereign
LORD says: Woe to the foolish[x] prophets[l] who follow their own spirit and
have seen nothing![m] 4Your prophets, O
Israel, are like jackals among ruins. 5You
have not gone up to the breaks in the wall
to repair[n] it for the house of Israel so that
it will stand firm in the battle on the day
of the LORD.[o] 6Their visions are false[p]
and their divinations a lie. They say,
"The LORD declares," when the LORD has
not sent[q] them; yet they expect their
words to be fulfilled.[r] 7Have you not
seen false visions[s] and uttered lying divinations when you say, "The LORD declares," though I have not spoken?
8" 'Therefore this is what the Sover-

12:9 [i]Eze 17:12; 20:49; 24:19
12:11 [j]Isa 8:18; Zec 3:8 [k]S 2Ki 25:7; S Jer 15:2; 52:15
12:12 [l]S Jer 39:4 [m]Jer 52:7
12:13 [n]Eze 17:20; 19:8; 32:3; Hos 7:12 [o]S Isa 24:17-18 [p]Eze 1:3 [q]S Jer 39:7 [r]S Jer 24:8; S 52:11; S La 4:20; Eze 17:16
12:14 [s]S 2Ki 25:5; S Jer 21:7; S Eze 5:10,12; 17:21
12:15 [t]S Lev 26:33
12:16 [u]S Jer 22:8-9; Eze 6:8-10; 14:22; 36:20
12:18 [v]La 5:9
12:19 [w]Jer 10:22; S Eze 6:6-14; Mic 7:13; Zec 7:14 [x]S Eze 4:16; 23:33
12:20 [y]Isa 7:23-24; S Jer 4:7; S 25:9
12:22 [z]S Ps 49:4 [a]S Isa 5:19; Eze 11:3; Am 6:3; 2Pe 3:4
12:23 [b]S Eze 7:7 [c]S Ps 37:13; Eze 18:3; Joel 2:1; Zep 1:14
12:24 [d]Jer 14:14; Eze 13:23; Mic 3:6; Zec 13:2-4
12:25 [e]Hab 2:3 [f]S Nu 11:23; Eze 13:6 [g]Nu 14:28-34; S Isa 14:24; S 55:11; Jer 16:9; Hab 1:5
12:27 [h]S Eze 11:3; Da 10:14; Mt 24:48-50; 2Pe 3:4
13:2 [i]S Isa 9:15 [j]Jer 28:15 [k]ver 17; S Jer 23:16; S 37:19; Eze 22:28
13:3 [l]S La 2:14; Hos 9:7 [m]S Jer 23:25-32
13:5 [n]Isa 58:12; Eze 22:30 [o]S Eze 7:19; 30:3
13:6 [p]S Jer 5:1; 23:16 [q]S Jer 14:14 [r]S Jer 28:15; S 29:9; Eze 12:24-25; 22:28
13:7 [s]S Isa 30:10

[x]3 Or *wicked*

12:16 THE CHURCH, Remnant—Part of the responsibility of the remnant is to proclaim the goodness of God among the nations. They have to repent before they can witness. See note on 6:8–10. The true remnant knows God.

12:17–20 REVELATION, Actions—Ezekiel acted out events which symbolized Israel's bleak future. See note on vv 1–6.

12:19 SIN, Violence—Acts which harm our neighbors, diminish the neighbor's rights or environment, or threaten our society can be classified as violence (Hebrew *chamas*). When violence becomes the accepted life-style of a community, the community must get ready for God's intervention. God accepts no excuses for violent behavior. It is sin.

12:25–28 GOD, Faithfulness—We may become impatient for God to fulfill His promises. We can be sure what God says, He will do. He is dependable, unchangeable. See note on La 3:22.

13:1–23 REVELATION, Messengers—God deals with those who predict wrongly because they do not represent His will and purpose. They will not be heard, and their words will be lost to history. Only the spiritually blind follow such prophets. Magical charms and secret powers to divine the future do not work, for they do not come from God. Only God's revelation is preserved for future generations and recorded as Scripture.

13:1–23 HISTORY, Judgment—Preaching to win popularity or money cannot reverse the reality of God's judgment. Neither can magic or folk religion. God judges those who try to shield God's people from His Word of wrath and judgment. See notes on 1 Ki 20:13; Jer 1:14–19.

eign LORD says: Because of your false
words and lying visions, I am against
you,[t] declares the Sovereign LORD. 9My
hand will be against the prophets who
see false visions and utter lying[u] divinations. They will not belong to the council
of my people or be listed in the records[v]
of the house of Israel, nor will they enter
the land of Israel. Then you will know
that I am the Sovereign LORD.[w]

10" 'Because they lead my people
astray,[x] saying, "Peace,"[y] when there is
no peace, and because, when a flimsy
wall is built, they cover it with whitewash,[z] 11therefore tell those who cover
it with whitewash that it is going to fall.
Rain will come in torrents, and I will send
hailstones[a] hurtling down,[b] and violent
winds will burst forth.[c] 12When the wall
collapses, will people not ask you,
"Where is the whitewash you covered it
with?"

13" 'Therefore this is what the Sovereign LORD says: In my wrath I will unleash a violent wind, and in my anger
hailstones[d] and torrents of rain[e] will fall
with destructive fury.[f] 14I will tear down
the wall[g] you have covered with whitewash and will level it to the ground so
that its foundation[h] will be laid bare.
When it[y] falls,[i] you will be destroyed in
it; and you will know that I am the LORD.
15So I will spend my wrath against the
wall and against those who covered it
with whitewash. I will say to you, "The
wall is gone and so are those who whitewashed it, 16those prophets of Israel who
prophesied to Jerusalem and saw visions
of peace for her when there was no
peace, declares the Sovereign LORD.[j] " '

17"Now, son of man, set your face[k]
against the daughters[l] of your people
who prophesy out of their own imagination. Prophesy against them[m] 18and say,
'This is what the Sovereign LORD says:
Woe to the women who sew magic
charms on all their wrists and make veils
of various lengths for their heads in order
to ensnare people. Will you ensnare the
lives of my people but preserve your
own? 19You have profaned[n] me among
my people for a few handfuls of barley
and scraps of bread.[o] By lying to my people, who listen to lies, you have killed
those who should not have died and have
spared those who should not live.[p]

20" 'Therefore this is what the Sovereign LORD says: I am against your magic
charms with which you ensnare people
like birds and I will tear them from your
arms; I will set free the people that you
ensnare like birds.[q] 21I will tear off your
veils and save my people from your
hands, and they will no longer fall prey to
your power. Then you will know that I
am the LORD.[r] 22Because you disheartened the righteous with your lies,[s] when
I had brought them no grief, and because
you encouraged the wicked not to turn
from their evil ways and so save their
lives,[t] 23therefore you will no longer see
false visions[u] or practice divination.[v] I
will save[w] my people from your hands.
And then you will know that I am the
LORD.[x] ' "

Chapter 14

Idolaters Condemned

SOME of the elders of Israel came to me
and sat down in front of me.[y] 2Then
the word of the LORD came to me: 3"Son
of man, these men have set up idols in
their hearts[z] and put wicked stumbling
blocks[a] before their faces. Should I let
them inquire of me at all?[b] 4Therefore
speak to them and tell them, 'This is what
the Sovereign LORD says: When any Israelite sets up idols in his heart and puts a
wicked stumbling block before his face
and then goes to a prophet, I the LORD
will answer him myself in keeping with
his great idolatry. 5I will do this to recapture the hearts of the people of Israel,
who have all deserted[c] me for their
idols.'[d]

6"Therefore say to the house of Israel,

[y] 14 Or *the city*

13:8 [t]S Jer 21:13
13:9 [u]S Dt 13:3 [v]S Ex 32:32; S Jer 17:13 [w]S Ex 6:2; Jer 20:3-6; Eze 20:38
13:10 [x]S Jer 23:13; S 50:6 [y]S Jer 4:10 [z]S Eze 7:25; 22:28
13:11 [a]S Jos 10:11 [b]S Job 38:23 [c]Ps 11:6; Eze 38:22
13:13 [d]S Jos 10:11; Rev 11:19; 16:21 [e]Job 14:19 [f]S Ex 9:25; S Job 38:23; Isa 30:30
13:14 [g]S Isa 22:5 [h]Mic 1:6 [i]Jer 6:15
13:16 [j]S Isa 57:21; Jer 6:14; S Eze 7:25
13:17 [k]S Eze 4:7; 25:2; 28:21 [l]S Ex 15:20; Rev 2:20 [m]S ver 2
13:19 [n]Jer 44:26; Eze 20:39; 22:26; 36:20; 39:7 [o]S Isa 56:11 [p]Pr 28:21; Mic 3:11
13:20 [q]Ps 124:7
13:21 [r]Ps 91:3
13:22 [s]S Isa 9:15 [t]Jer 23:14; Eze 18:21; 33:14-16
13:23 [u]Ne 6:12 [v]S Eze 12:24 [w]S Ps 72:14 [x]Mic 3:6
14:1 [y]S Eze 8:1; 20:1
14:3 [z]S Eze 6:4 [a]S ver 7; S Eze 7:19 [b]Isa 1:15; Eze 20:31
14:5 [c]S Dt 32:15; Eze 16:45; Hos 5:7; Zec 11:8 [d]Jer 2:11

13:8–16 CHRISTIAN ETHICS, War and Peace—The judgment of God awaits those who falsely proclaim peace. See note on Jer 6:14.
13:13–16 GOD, Wrath—God's wrath is intended to introduce Himself to His people. See note on 5:8–17.
13:17–23 CHRISTIAN ETHICS, Justice—False religious leadership can support and promote injustice. Religious leaders must not be motivated by greed or ego needs. Those who are face God's wrath.
14:1–11 GOD, One God—God deals with idolatry with a call to repent and with judgment against those who do not. God works toward the day when He will truly have a people dedicated wholly to the one God. See note on 6:3–7.
14:1–5 ELECTION, Condemnation—God's judgment is redemptive. His purpose is to recapture the hearts of the elect who desert Him for idols. God acts in every way possible among His people to lead them to know Him and be His devoted people.
14:6–9 GOD, Faithfulness—These difficult verses illustrate the faithfulness and the wrath of God. God's character is unchanging, and He will not be manipulated by shallow, sinful, conniving people. He not only will not be manipulated or used by them, He will oppose them in His wrath. Vv 3–4, 7 refer to people who were determined in their idolatry. V 9 suggests that a responsible prophet would have nothing to do with them in their attempt to give a righteous veneer to their idolatry. If a prophet did pay attention to them, God would deal very seriously with the prophet as well as those who were engaged in idolatry. The statement that the Lord has "enticed that prophet" represents absolute monotheistic thought which ascribes everything directly or indirectly to God.

'This is what the Sovereign LORD says:
Repent![e] Turn from your idols and renounce all your detestable practices![f]
7" 'When any Israelite or any alien[g]
living in Israel separates himself from me
and sets up idols in his heart and puts a
wicked stumbling block[h] before his face
and then goes to a prophet to inquire[i] of
me, I the LORD will answer him myself. 8I
will set my face against[j] that man and
make him an example[k] and a byword.[l] I
will cut him off from my people. Then
you will know that I am the LORD.[m]
9" 'And if the prophet[n] is enticed[o] to
utter a prophecy, I the LORD have enticed
that prophet, and I will stretch out my
hand against him and destroy him from
among my people Israel.[p] 10They will
bear their guilt—the prophet will be as
guilty as the one who consults him.
11Then the people of Israel will no longer
stray[q] from me, nor will they defile
themselves anymore with all their sins.
They will be my people,[r] and I will be
their God, declares the Sovereign
LORD.[s] ' "

Judgment Inescapable

12The word of the LORD came to me:
13"Son of man, if a country sins[t] against
me by being unfaithful and I stretch out
my hand against it to cut off its food supply[u] and send famine upon it and kill its
men and their animals,[v] 14even if these
three men—Noah,[w] Daniel[z x] and Job[y]
—were in it, they could save only themselves by their righteousness,[z] declares
the Sovereign LORD.
15"Or if I send wild beasts[a] through
that country and they leave it childless
and it becomes desolate so that no one
can pass through it because of the
beasts,[b] 16as surely as I live, declares the
Sovereign LORD, even if these three men

14:6 [e]Ne 1:9; S Jer 3:12; S 35:15 [f]S Isa 2:20; S 30:22
14:7 [g]Ex 12:48; 20:10 [h]ver 3; S Isa 8:14; Hos 4:5; 5:5 [i]S Ge 25:22
14:8 [j]Eze 15:7 [k]S Nu 16:38 [l]S Ps 102:8; S Eze 5:15 [m]S Jer 42:20
14:9 [n]S Jer 14:15 [o]Isa 63:17; Jer 4:10 [p]1Ki 22:23; S 2Ch 18:22; Zec 13:3
14:11 [q]Eze 48:11 [r]S Isa 51:16 [s]S Eze 11:19-20; 37:23
14:13 [t]S Pr 13:21 [u]S Lev 26:26 [v]S Eze 5:16; 6:14; 15:8
14:14 [w]Ge 6:8 [x]ver 20; Eze 28:3; Da 1:6; 6:13 [y]S Job 1:1 [z]S Ge 6:9; S Job 42:9; Jer 15:1; S Eze 3:19; 18:20
14:15 [a]Eze 5:17 [b]S Lev 26:22
14:16 [c]S Ge 19:29; Eze 18:20
14:17 [d]S Lev 26:25; S Jer 25:27; S 42:16 [e]Eze 25:13; Zep 1:3
14:19 [f]S Eze 7:8 [g]S Isa 34:3 [h]Jer 14:12; Eze 38:22
14:20 [i]S ver 14
14:21 [j]S Nu 33:4 [k]Isa 31:8; 34:6; 66:16; Eze 21:3,19 [l]S 2Sa 24:13 [m]S Jer 14:12; 27:8 [n]S Jer 15:3; S Eze 5:17; 33:27; Am 4:6-10; Rev 6:8
14:22 [o]S Jer 41:16 [p]S Eze 12:16 [q]Eze 20:43 [r]Eze 31:16; 32:31
14:23 [s]S Jer 22:8-9; Eze 8:6-18; S 9:9

were in it, they could not save their own
sons or daughters. They alone would be
saved, but the land would be desolate.[c]
17"Or if I bring a sword[d] against that
country and say, 'Let the sword pass
throughout the land,' and I kill its men
and their animals,[e] 18as surely as I live,
declares the Sovereign LORD, even if
these three men were in it, they could
not save their own sons or daughters.
They alone would be saved.
19"Or if I send a plague into that land
and pour out my wrath[f] upon it through
bloodshed,[g] killing its men and their animals,[h] 20as surely as I live, declares the
Sovereign LORD, even if Noah, Daniel and
Job were in it, they could save neither
son nor daughter. They would save only
themselves by their righteousness.[i]
21"For this is what the Sovereign LORD
says: How much worse will it be when I
send against Jerusalem my four dreadful
judgments[j]—sword[k] and famine[l] and
wild beasts and plague[m]—to kill its men
and their animals![n] 22Yet there will be
some survivors[o]—sons and daughters
who will be brought out of it.[p] They will
come to you, and when you see their conduct[q] and their actions, you will be consoled[r] regarding the disaster I have
brought upon Jerusalem—every disaster I
have brought upon it. 23You will be consoled when you see their conduct and
their actions, for you will know that I
have done nothing in it without cause,
declares the Sovereign LORD.[s] "

Chapter 15

Jerusalem, A Useless Vine

THE word of the LORD came to me:
2"Son of man, how is the wood of a

[z] 14 Or *Danel*; the Hebrew spelling may suggest a person other than the prophet Daniel; also in verse 20.

14:7–10 SIN, Responsibility—Prophecy can be an instrument of God's punishment. God's Word is intended for His faithful people who will follow it. People who try to use God's Word or God's minister for their own sinful purposes will find that Word turned against them. The minister of the Word who is foolish enough to cooperate with the wicked shares their guilt. God Himself will use that prophet as an agent of punishment—bringing punishment on both wicked sinner and foolish prophet. Such sin produces crooked guilt (Isa 1:2–4). Death is the ultimate result. See note on 18:1–32.

14:7–8 REVELATION, Faithfulness—People separate themselves from God. In the heart people decide to follow other gods. God threatens to make such persons examples to others of what happens to people who abandon God's plans and will for their lives. People cannot expect to receive God's revelation in time of need when they have dedicated their lives to other gods.

14:11 THE CHURCH, Covenant People—The Lord desires that His people obey Him. He wants us to be faithful and obedient. See note on Jer 30:22.

14:12–23 HISTORY, Judgment—Judgment is not blind anger lashing out without reason. God's judgment, just as His deliverance, works to accomplish God's eternal purpose of forming a permanent relationship with a faithful people. He uses all elements of creation to judge His people—human armies, natural disaster, wild animals, and sickness.

14:12–20 PRAYER, Intercession—Lot's righteousness and Abraham's prayers (Ge 18:23–33) could not save Sodom. The most proverbial righteousness cannot save a country once God moves against it. God does not change His mind (1 Sa 15:29). A people's ongoing sin eventually makes intercessory prayer fruitless. See note on 8:18.

14:16,18,20 GOD, Living—God has no one greater in whose name He can swear an oath to tell the truth, so He swears by His own life. In contrast to dead idols, the one true God is the living God.

14:22–23 THE CHURCH, Remnant—The remnant testifies to God's justice. The people who were exiled to Babylon in 597 BC could not understand why God was letting Babylon destroy Jerusalem in 587 BC. When they saw the evil conduct of the new exiles, they would understand why God had to punish His people. We need to look forward and find God's directions into the future rather than look to the past and question God's actions. See note on 6:8–10.

vine[t] better than that of a branch on any
of the trees in the forest? 3 Is wood ever
taken from it to make anything useful?[u]
Do they make pegs[v] from it to hang
things on? 4 And after it is thrown on the
fire as fuel and the fire burns both ends
and chars the middle, is it then useful for
anything?[w] 5 If it was not useful for anything when it was whole, how much less
can it be made into something useful
when the fire has burned it and it is
charred?

6 "Therefore this is what the Sovereign
LORD says: As I have given the wood of
the vine among the trees of the forest as
fuel for the fire, so will I treat the people
living in Jerusalem. 7 I will set my face
against[x] them. Although they have come
out of the fire[y][z], the fire will yet consume them. And when I set my face
against them, you will know that I am the
LORD.[a] 8 I will make the land desolate[b]
because they have been unfaithful,[c] declares the Sovereign LORD."

Chapter 16

An Allegory of Unfaithful Jerusalem

THE word of the LORD came to me:
2 "Son of man, confront[d] Jerusalem
with her detestable practices[e] 3 and say,
'This is what the Sovereign LORD says to
Jerusalem: Your ancestry[f] and birth
were in the land of the Canaanites; your
father[g] was an Amorite[h] and your mother a Hittite.[i] 4 On the day you were
born[j] your cord was not cut, nor were
you washed with water to make you
clean, nor were you rubbed with salt or
wrapped in cloths. 5 No one looked on you
with pity or had compassion enough to do
any of these things for you. Rather, you
were thrown out into the open field, for
on the day you were born you were despised.

6 " 'Then I passed by and saw you kicking about in your blood, and as you lay
there in your blood I said to you,
"Live!"[a][k] 7 I made you grow[l] like a
plant of the field. You grew up and developed and became the most beautiful of
jewels.[b] Your breasts were formed and
your hair grew, you who were naked and
bare.[m]

8 " 'Later I passed by, and when I
looked at you and saw that you were old
enough for love, I spread the corner of my
garment[n] over you and covered your nakedness. I gave you my solemn oath and
entered into a covenant[o] with you, declares the Sovereign LORD, and you became mine.[p]

9 " 'I bathed[c] you with water and
washed[q] the blood from you and put
ointments on you. 10 I clothed you with an
embroidered[r] dress and put leather sandals on you. I dressed you in fine linen[s]
and covered you with costly garments.[t]
11 I adorned you with jewelry:[u] I put
bracelets[v] on your arms and a necklace[w]
around your neck, 12 and I put a ring on
your nose,[x] earrings[y] on your ears and a
beautiful crown[z] on your head.[a] 13 So
you were adorned with gold and silver;
your clothes[b] were of fine linen and cost-

15:2 [t]Ps 80:8-16; Isa 5:1-7; 27:2-6; Jer 2:21; Hos 10:1; S Jn 15:2
15:3 [u]Jer 13:10 [v]S Isa 22:23
15:4 [w]Eze 17:3-10; 19:14; Jn 15:6
15:7 [x]S Lev 26:17; Ps 34:16; Eze 14:8 [y]S Eze 5:2 [z]S Eze 5:4 [a]Isa 24:18; Am 9:1-4
15:8 [b]S Eze 14:13 [c]Eze 17:20; 18:24
16:2 [d]S Isa 57:12; Eze 23:36 [e]Eze 8:17; 20:4; 22:2
16:3 [f]Ge 11:25-29; Eze 21:30 [g]S Ge 12:18 [h]S Ge 15:16 [i]ver 45; S Ge 10:15; S Dt 7:1; Jos 24:14-15
16:4 [j]Hos 2:3
16:6 [k]ver 22; S Ex 19:4; Eze 18:23,32
16:7 [l]S Dt 1:10 [m]S Ex 1:7
16:8 [n]Ru 3:9 [o]ver 59; S Jer 11:10; Mal 2:14 [p]Jer 2:2; Hos 2:7,19-20
16:9 [q]S Ru 3:3
16:10 [r]S Ex 26:36; S Isa 19:9 [s]Eze 27:16 [t]ver 18; S Isa 3:23
16:11 [u]S Jer 4:30; Eze 23:40 [v]Isa 3:19; Eze 23:42 [w]S Ge 41:42; S Ps 73:6
16:12 [x]Isa 3:21 [y]S Ge 35:4 [z]S Isa 28:5; S Jer 13:18 [a]Pr 1:9; S Isa 3:19
16:13 [b]Est 5:1

[a]6 A few Hebrew manuscripts, Septuagint and Syriac; most Hebrew manuscripts *"Live!" And as you lay there in your blood I said to you, "Live!"* [b]7 Or *became mature* [c]9 Or *I had bathed*

15:6–8 SIN, Lack of Faith—See notes on 11:1–12; 1 Ch 10:13.

15:6–8 HISTORY, Judgment—God's judgment comes when His people are unfaithful to Him. Judgment reveals the divine nature and power of God to a people who have forgotten the lessons of God's deliverance.

16:1–63 GOD, Love—Ezekiel often pictures God as a God of wrath, but God is primarily a God of love. God is like a parent who found an abandoned newborn baby and raised it as His own to become a beautiful person. Even repeated rejection does not kill God's love. See notes on Ex 3:7; Dt 32:10–12,36; Mt 10:29–31; Jn 3:16.

16:1–63 REVELATION, History—Historical review shows God's covenant love for helpless Israel and her sinful search for other lovers. History thus reveals both God's love and His people's sin. See note on Ps 105:1–45; 106:1–47.

16:1–63 HISTORY, Confession—The prophet confessed Israel's history in his own unique way to bring judgment and eventual hope. See note on Isa 1:24–26. He reminded the people that Jerusalem's history was a mixed one, since Jerusalem's origins were deeply rooted in unbelief and idolatry. Only God's covenant love had saved Jerusalem from destruction. Jerusalem forgot God's grace and trusted in her own attributes. See note on 2 Ch 16:7–9. This led to immorality and false worship (1 Ki 11). God finally judged Jerusalem because they would not be true to Him. They behaved worse than history's worst examples—Samaria and Sodom. Judgment was a preface to God's new beginning with a new, everlasting covenant. Then His people would be willing to learn history's lesson and renew their vows with God in faithfulness.

16:1–14 ELECTION, God's Initiative—Jerusalem was the soul of Judah, a source of pride and power. God gave Judah a history lesson. He had taken Jerusalem as an abandoned baby and raised her to be a young woman ready for marriage. He transformed her into a queen and lavished on her the richest of gifts, garments, and jewels. After she became His beautiful and attractive wife, she became faithless, living as a prostitute. She even sacrificed her children (2 Ki 16:3). Instead of receiving gifts from her lovers, she gave to them. Judah and Jerusalem had no reason for pride. They deserved nothing they had. Only God's grace in election endowed them with wealth and fame. The biblical teaching of election is a confession of God's initiative behind every good thing we have and are.

16:1–8 THE CHURCH, Covenant People—God's people can never claim a right to be His people. Ancestry, religious ritual, and social class are not qualifications to be God's people. One thing qualifies us to be His—the gracious love He shows in initiating the relationship with us. See note on Dt 7:6–8.

16:8–9 FAMILY, Symbolic Nature—Marital intimacy offers appropriate language to symbolize God's relationship to His people. Ezekiel used the sexual union to symbolize God's establishment of covenant with Judah. In the remainder of the chapter he symbolized the infidelity of Judah by using marital and family terms. In spite of her infidelity, the covenant love of God would never be totally lost (16:59–63).

ly fabric and embroidered cloth. Your
food was fine flour, honey and olive oil.[c]
You became very beautiful and rose to be
a queen.[d] 14And your fame[e] spread
among the nations on account of your
beauty,[f] because the splendor I had giv-
en you made your beauty perfect, declares the Sovereign LORD.[g]

15" 'But you trusted in your beauty and
used your fame to become a prostitute.
You lavished your favors on anyone who
passed by[h] and your beauty became
his.[d] [i] 16You took some of your garments
to make gaudy high places,[j] where you
carried on your prostitution.[k] Such
things should not happen, nor should
they ever occur. 17You also took the fine
jewelry I gave you, the jewelry made of
my gold and silver, and you made for
yourself male idols and engaged in prostitution with them.[l] 18And you took your
embroidered clothes to put on them, and
you offered my oil and incense[m] before
them. 19Also the food I provided for you
—the fine flour, olive oil and honey I
gave you to eat—you offered as fragrant
incense before them. That is what happened, declares the Sovereign LORD.[n]

20" 'And you took your sons and daughters[o] whom you bore to me[p] and sacrificed them as food to the idols. Was your
prostitution not enough?[q] 21You slaughtered my children and sacrificed them[e]
to the idols.[r] 22In all your detestable
practices and your prostitution you did
not remember the days of your youth,[s]
when you were naked and bare,[t] kicking
about in your blood.[u]

23" 'Woe![v] Woe to you, declares the
Sovereign LORD. In addition to all your
other wickedness, 24you built a mound
for yourself and made a lofty shrine[w] in
every public square.[x] 25At the head of
every street[y] you built your lofty shrines
and degraded your beauty, offering your
body with increasing promiscuity to anyone who passed by.[z] 26You engaged in
prostitution[a] with the Egyptians,[b] your
lustful neighbors, and provoked[c] me to
anger with your increasing promiscuity.[d]
27So I stretched out my hand[e] against
you and reduced your territory; I gave
you over[f] to the greed of your enemies,
the daughters of the Philistines,[g] who
were shocked by your lewd conduct.
28You engaged in prostitution with the
Assyrians[h] too, because you were insatiable; and even after that, you still were not
satisfied.[i] 29Then you increased your
promiscuity to include Babylonia,[f] [j] a
land of merchants, but even with this you
were not satisfied.[k]

30" 'How weak-willed you are, declares
the Sovereign LORD, when you do all
these things, acting like a brazen prostitute![l] 31When you built your mounds at
the head of every street and made your
lofty shrines[m] in every public square, you
were unlike a prostitute, because you
scorned payment.

32" 'You adulterous wife! You prefer
strangers to your own husband! 33Every
prostitute receives a fee,[n] but you give
gifts[o] to all your lovers, bribing them to
come to you from everywhere for your
illicit favors.[p] 34So in your prostitution
you are the opposite of others; no one
runs after you for your favors. You are the
very opposite, for you give payment and
none is given to you.

35" 'Therefore, you prostitute, hear the
word of the LORD! 36This is what the Sovereign LORD says: Because you poured
out your wealth[g] and exposed your nakedness in your promiscuity with your
lovers, and because of all your detestable
idols, and because you gave them your
children's blood,[q] 37therefore I am going
to gather all your lovers, with whom you
found pleasure, those you loved as well as
those you hated. I will gather them
against you from all around and will
strip[r] you in front of them, and they will
see all your nakedness.[s] 38I will sentence
you to the punishment of women who
commit adultery and who shed blood;[t] I
will bring upon you the blood vengeance
of my wrath and jealous anger.[u] 39Then I
will hand you over[v] to your lovers, and
they will tear down your mounds and destroy your lofty shrines. They will strip
you of your clothes and take your fine
jewelry and leave you naked and bare.[w]
40They will bring a mob against you, who

16:13 [c]1Sa 10:1 [d]Dt 32:13-14; S 1Ki 4:21; S Est 2:9,17
16:14 [e]1Ki 10:24 [f]S Est 1:11; S Ps 48:2; S La 2:15 [g]S Eze 5:5
16:15 [h]ver 25 [i]S Isa 57:8; S Jer 2:20; Eze 23:3; 27:3
16:16 [j]S Isa 57:7 [k]S 2Ki 23:7
16:17 [l]S Eze 7:20; Hos 2:13
16:18 [m]S Jer 44:5
16:19 [n]Hos 2:8
16:20 [o]S Jer 7:31 [p]Ex 13:2 [q]Ps 106:37-38; S Isa 57:5; Eze 23:37
16:21 [r]S 2Ki 17:17; S Jer 19:5
16:22 [s]S Ps 25:7; S 88:15; Jer 2:2; Hos 2:15; 11:1 [t]Hos 2:3 [u]ver 6
16:23 [v]Eze 24:6
16:24 [w]ver 31; Isa 57:7 [x]Ps 78:58; S Jer 2:20; 3:2; S 44:21; Eze 20:28
16:25 [y]S Jer 3:2 [z]ver 15; S Pr 9:14
16:26 [a]S Isa 23:17 [b]S Jer 3:1 [c]S 1Ki 14:9; S Eze 8:17 [d]S Isa 57:8; Jer 11:15; Eze 20:8; 23:19-21
16:27 [e]Eze 20:33; 25:13 [f]S Jer 34:20 [g]S 2Ch 28:18
16:28 [h]S 2Ki 16:7 [i]Isa 57:8
16:29 [j]S Jer 3:1; Eze 23:14-17 [k]Na 3:4
16:30 [l]S Jer 3:3
16:31 [m]S ver 24
16:33 [n]S Ge 30:15 [o]Isa 30:6; 57:9 [p]Hos 8:9-10
16:36 [q]S Jer 19:5; Eze 23:10
16:37 [r]Hos 2:3 [s]S Isa 47:3; S Jer 13:22; Eze 23:22; Hos 2:10; 8:10; Rev 17:16
16:38 [t]S Ge 38:24 [u]S Lev 20:10; Ps 79:3,5; Eze 23:25; Zep 1:17
16:39 [v]S 2Ki 18:11 [w]Eze 21:31; Hos 2:3

[d]*15* Most Hebrew manuscripts; one Hebrew manuscript (see some Septuagint manuscripts) *by. Such a thing should not happen* [e]*21* Or *and made them pass through* ⌞*the fire*⌟ [f]*29* Or *Chaldea* [g]*36* Or *lust*

16:15–34 SIN, Against God—Ingratitude is sin. God provided all Israel needed and provides all we need for life with Him. We sin against Him when we take His gifts and prostitute them to serve purposes other than His. Our beauty, fame, fortune, and skills are His gifts to us. We can use them in gratitude to worship Him. When we use them selfishly to attract other people whose favors we desire, we sin. When we use them to buy protection from other powers, we sin. When we use them to pay homage to anyone or thing besides God, we sin. When such sin leads us to violent treatment of others, we multiply our sin. We think our brazen actions against God show our strength and independence. God says they show how weak our mental, moral, and spiritual capacities are.

16:23,35–42 GOD, Wrath—God's wrath is effective but not eternal. See note on 5:8–17.

16:38 GOD, Jealous—Jealousy is a term between lovers. God has no "female god" as His companion. Rather He turns all His love to His children, His chosen people. When we fail Him, His love expresses itself in jealous anger, disciplining His beloved children. See notes on Ex 34:14; Isa 9:7; 26:11.

will stone[x] you and hack you to pieces
with their swords. 41They will burn
down[y] your houses and inflict punishment on you in the sight of many wom-
en.[z] I will put a stop[a] to your prostitution, and you will no longer pay your lovers. 42Then my wrath against you will
subside and my jealous anger will turn
away from you; I will be calm and no longer angry.[b]
43" 'Because you did not remember[c]
the days of your youth but enraged me
with all these things, I will surely bring
down[d] on your head what you have
done, declares the Sovereign LORD. Did
you not add lewdness to all your other
detestable practices?[e]
44" 'Everyone who quotes proverbs[f]
will quote this proverb about you: "Like
mother, like daughter." 45You are a true
daughter of your mother, who despised[g]
her husband[h] and her children; and you
are a true sister of your sisters, who despised their husbands and their children.
Your mother was a Hittite and your father
an Amorite.[i] 46Your older sister[j] was Samaria, who lived to the north of you with
her daughters; and your younger sister,
who lived to the south of you with her
daughters, was Sodom.[k] 47You not only
walked in their ways and copied their detestable practices, but in all your ways
you soon became more depraved than
they.[l] 48As surely as I live, declares the
Sovereign[m] LORD, your sister Sodom[n]
and her daughters never did what you
and your daughters have done.[o]
49" 'Now this was the sin of your sister
Sodom:[p] She and her daughters were arrogant,[q] overfed and unconcerned;[r]
they did not help the poor and needy.[s]
50They were haughty[t] and did detestable
things before me. Therefore I did away
with them as you have seen.[u] 51Samaria
did not commit half the sins you did. You
have done more detestable things than
they, and have made your sisters seem
righteous by all these things you have
done.[v] 52Bear your disgrace, for you have
furnished some justification for your sisters. Because your sins were more vile
than theirs, they appear more righteous[w]
than you. So then, be ashamed and bear[x]
your disgrace, for you have made your sisters appear righteous.
53" 'However, I will restore[y] the fortunes of Sodom and her daughters and of
Samaria and her daughters, and your fortunes along with them,[z] 54so that you
may bear your disgrace[a] and be ashamed
of all you have done in giving them comfort. 55And your sisters, Sodom with her
daughters and Samaria with her daughters, will return to what they were before; and you and your daughters will return to what you were before.[b] 56You
would not even mention your sister Sodom in the day of your pride, 57before your
wickedness was uncovered. Even so, you
are now scorned[c] by the daughters of
Edom[h][d] and all her neighbors and the
daughters of the Philistines—all those
around you who despise you. 58You will
bear the consequences of your lewdness
and your detestable practices, declares
the LORD.[e]
59" 'This is what the Sovereign LORD
says: I will deal with you as you deserve,
because you have despised my oath by
breaking the covenant.[f] 60Yet I will remember the covenant[g] I made with you
in the days of your youth,[h] and I will
establish an everlasting covenant[i] with
you. 61Then you will remember your
ways and be ashamed[j] when you receive
your sisters, both those who are older
than you and those who are younger. I
will give them to you as daughters,[k] but
not on the basis of my covenant with you.
62So I will establish my covenant[l] with
you, and you will know that I am the
LORD.[m] 63Then, when I make atone-

16:40 [x]Jn 8:5,7
16:41 [y]S Dt 13:16; S Jer 19:13 [z]Eze 23:10 [a]Eze 22:15; 23:27, 48
16:42 [b]2Sa 24:25; Isa 40:1-2; 54:9; S Eze 5:13; 39:29
16:43 [c]S Ex 15:24; Ps 78:42 [d]Eze 22:31 [e]Eze 11:21
16:44 [f]S Ps 49:4
16:45 [g]S Eze 14:5 [h]Jer 44:19 [i]ver 3; Eze 23:2
16:46 [j]S Jer 3:7 [k]Ge 13:10-13; S 18:20; Jer 3:8-11; Eze 23:4; Rev 11:8
16:47 [l]S Eze 5:7
16:48 [m]S Ge 15:2 [n]S Ge 19:25 [o]Mt 10:15; 11:23-24
16:49 [p]S Isa 1:10 [q]Ps 138:6; Eze 28:2 [r]Isa 22:13 [s]S Ge 13:13; 19:9; S Jer 5:28; Eze 18:7,12,16; Am 6:4-6; Lk 12:16-20; 16:19; Jas 5:5
16:50 [t]Ps 18:27 [u]Ge 18:20-21; S 19:5
16:51 [v]Jer 3:8-11; Eze 5:6-7; 23:11
16:52 [w]S Jer 3:11 [x]Eze 23:35
16:53 [y]S Dt 30:3; Isa 19:24-25; S Jer 48:47 [z]Eze 39:25
16:54 [a]S Jer 2:26
16:55 [b]Eze 36:11; Mal 3:4
16:57 [c]S Ps 137:3 [d]2Ki 16:6
16:58 [e]Eze 23:49
16:59 [f]S ver 8; Eze 17:19
16:60 [g]S Ge 6:18; S 9:15 [h]S Ps 25:7; S Jer 2:2 [i]S Ge 9:16; Eze 37:26
16:61 [j]ver 63; Eze 20:43; 43:10; 44:13 [k]S Isa 43:6
16:62 [l]S Dt 29:14 [m]S Jer 24:7; Eze 20:37,43-44; 34:25; 37:26; Hos 2:19-20

[h]*57* Many Hebrew manuscripts and Syriac; most Hebrew manuscripts, Septuagint and Vulgate *Aram*

16:43 SALVATION, Remembrance—See note on Jer 31:20. God judges His people who fail to remember His goodness and who backslide on His love. See Rev 2:4.

16:44–52 SIN, Depravity—Sin is not inherited. I am not guilty because mother was guilty. I do inherit a nature prone to sin from Adam (Ro 5:17). I am sinful like my parents because all influences on my life give me the tendency to sin and I choose to let their influence outweigh God's on my life. I increase my guilt by condemning my neighbors for their sins when mine are worse than theirs. For "depraved" (Hebrew *hishchit*), see note on Isa 1:2–4. Ezekiel described Jerusalem as more corrupt than Israel's favorite example of wicked people: Sodom (Ge 13:13; 18–19) and Samaria, the capital of the Northern Kingdom exiled and inhabited by a mixed race with a mixed religion (2 Ki 17:24–41; Ezr; Ne). Such corruption came because the people of Jerusalem chose to act more corruptly than the other nations ever imagined (v 48). Their "depravity" represented one generation's choices, not their inheritance from their ancestors.

16:59–63 THE CHURCH, Covenant People—God overcomes even the rebellion of His people. The everlasting covenant is based on God's action, not on our actions. God forgives and restores. He judges to reform and purify. We can make no claims of injustice against God. We can only praise Him for the love and faithfulness which surpasses any hope human imagination could ever devise. We are His only because He wants us to be and makes it possible. See note on Jer 31:31–34.

16:60–63 ELECTION, Faithfulness—Embarrassment and shame were all Judah had earned. They deserved punishment and destruction. God gave new life in a new covenant. Why? Because He is the faithful God committed to the election of His people and ever willing to start over with a new, humbled remnant. Election teaches God's faithfulness in creating a people to be His people and to serve Him as their God.

16:63 SALVATION, Atonement—God promised to establish an everlasting covenant with Israel in which He would make atonement for their sins. Sodom and Samaria are includ-

ment[n] for you for all you have done, you
will remember and be ashamed[o] and
never again open your mouth[p] because
of your humiliation, declares the Sovereign LORD.[q]' "

Chapter 17

Two Eagles and a Vine

THE word of the LORD came to me:
2"Son of man, set forth an allegory
and tell the house of Israel a parable.[r]
3Say to them, 'This is what the Sovereign
LORD says: A great eagle[s] with powerful
wings, long feathers and full plumage of
varied colors came to Lebanon.[t] Taking
hold of the top of a cedar, 4he broke off[u]
its topmost shoot and carried it away to a
land of merchants, where he planted it in
a city of traders.

5" 'He took some of the seed of your
land and put it in fertile soil. He planted it
like a willow by abundant water,[v] 6and it
sprouted and became a low, spreading
vine. Its branches[w] turned toward him,
but its roots remained under it. So it became a vine and produced branches and
put out leafy boughs.[x]

7" 'But there was another great eagle
with powerful wings and full plumage.
The vine now sent out its roots toward
him from the plot where it was planted
and stretched out its branches to him for
water.[y] 8It had been planted in good soil
by abundant water so that it would produce branches,[z] bear fruit and become a
splendid vine.'

9"Say to them, 'This is what the Sovereign LORD says: Will it thrive? Will it not
be uprooted and stripped of its fruit so
that it withers? All its new growth will
wither. It will not take a strong arm or
many people to pull it up by the roots.[a]
10Even if it[b] is transplanted, will it
thrive? Will it not wither completely
when the east wind strikes it—wither
away in the plot where it grew?[c]' "

11Then the word of the LORD came to
me: 12"Say to this rebellious house, 'Do
you not know what these things mean?[d]'
Say to them: 'The king of Babylon went to
Jerusalem and carried off her king and
her nobles,[e] bringing them back with
him to Babylon.[f] 13Then he took a member of the royal family and made a treaty[g]
with him, putting him under oath.[h] He
also carried away the leading men[i] of the
land, 14so that the kingdom would be
brought low,[j] unable to rise again, surviving only by keeping his treaty. 15But
the king rebelled[k] against him by sending his envoys to Egypt[l] to get horses
and a large army.[m] Will he succeed? Will
he who does such things escape? Will he
break the treaty and yet escape?[n]

16" 'As surely as I live, declares the
Sovereign LORD, he shall die[o] in Babylon,
in the land of the king who put him on
the throne, whose oath he despised and
whose treaty he broke.[p] 17Pharaoh[q]
with his mighty army and great horde
will be of no help to him in war, when
ramps[r] are built and siege works erected
to destroy many lives.[s] 18He despised the
oath by breaking the covenant. Because
he had given his hand in pledge[t] and yet
did all these things, he shall not escape.

19" 'Therefore this is what the Sovereign LORD says: As surely as I live, I will
bring down on his head my oath that he
despised and my covenant that he
broke.[u] 20I will spread my net[v] for him,
and he will be caught in my snare. I will
bring him to Babylon and execute judgment[w] upon him there because he was
unfaithful[x] to me. 21All his fleeing troops
will fall by the sword,[y] and the survivors[z] will be scattered to the winds.[a]
Then you will know that I the LORD have
spoken.[b]

22" 'This is what the Sovereign LORD
says: I myself will take a shoot[c] from the
very top of a cedar and plant it; I will
break off a tender sprig from its topmost
shoots and plant it on a high and lofty
mountain.[d] 23On the mountain heights[e]
of Israel I will plant it; it will produce
branches and bear fruit[f] and become a
splendid cedar. Birds of every kind will
nest in it; they will find shelter in the

16:63 [n]Ps 65:3; 78:38; 79:9 [o]Eze 36:31-32 [p]Ro 3:19 [q]Ps 39:9; Da 9:7-8
17:2 [r]S Jdg 14:12; S Eze 20:49
17:3 [s]S Dt 28:49; Jer 49:22; Da 7:4; Hos 8:1 [t]S Jer 22:23
17:4 [u]S Isa 10:33
17:5 [v]Dt 8:7-9; Ps 1:3; Isa 44:4; Eze 31:5
17:6 [w]S Isa 18:5 [x]S Job 5:3
17:7 [y]Eze 31:4
17:8 [z]Job 18:19; Mal 4:1
17:9 [a]Jer 42:10; Am 2:9
17:10 [b]S Job 1:19; Hos 12:1; 13:15 [c]S Eze 15:4
17:12 [d]S Eze 12:9 [e]S 2Ki 24:15 [f]S Dt 21:10; S 2Ch 36:10; Eze 24:19
17:13 [g]S Ex 23:32; S Jer 37:1 [h]2Ch 36:13 [i]Isa 3:2
17:14 [j]Eze 29:14
17:15 [k]Jer 52:3 [l]S Isa 30:2; S Jer 37:5 [m]S Dt 17:16 [n]S Ps 56:7; S Isa 30:5; Jer 34:3; 38:18; Eze 29:16
17:16 [o]S Jer 52:11; Eze 12:13 [p]S 2Ki 24:17
17:17 [q]Jer 37:7 [r]S Eze 4:2 [s]S Isa 36:6; Jer 37:5; Eze 29:6-7
17:18 [t]S 2Ki 10:15; 1Ch 29:24
17:19 [u]Jer 7:9; S Eze 16:59; 21:23; Hos 10:4
17:20 [v]S Eze 12:13; 32:3 [w]S Jer 2:35 [x]S Eze 15:8
17:21 [y]S Eze 12:14 [z]2Ki 25:11 [a]S Lev 26:33; S 2Ki 25:5; Zec 2:6 [b]S Jer 27:8
17:22 [c]S 2Ki 19:30; S Isa 4:2 [d]ver 23; Isa 2:2; S Jer 23:5; Eze 20:40; 36:1,36; 37:22; 40:2; 43:12
17:23 [e]S ver 22; S Jer 31:12 [f]S Isa 27:6

ed in this new covenant. If there is hope for Sodom, there is hope for all. God was progressively setting the stage for a once-for-all atonement for the sins of the world in the death of His Son.

17:1–6,9 HOLY SCRIPTURE, Word—God's Word comes in many literary forms. God spoke through Ezekiel in allegory here, revealing God's initial purpose for Israel, His care in beginning her growth, and Israel's dismal future for not having strong roots in God. Ezekiel, more than any other Old Testament prophet, interpreted God's revelations to His people through creative literary forms.

17:1–24 HISTORY, National—Judgment was needed to make God's people quit trusting in other nations. See note on 2 Ch 16:7–9. Judgment would prepare for a new historical deliverance through a messianic Savior. See note on Isa 1:24–26.

17:19 THE CHURCH, Covenant People—See note on 2 Ki 18:11–12.

17:22–24 JESUS CHRIST, Foretold—Ezekiel saw the Babylonian kingdom spreading its branches over the known world, choking out all growth. He saw King Zedekiah plotting with Egypt against Babylon to no avail. He saw something mysterious and great—hope coming out of the exiled Jewish community in Babylon. God would restore His people and establish His kingdom. Present historical conditions made deliverance appear impossible, but God could still accomplish His purposes. Similarly, Jesus' ministry and death did not appear to be the foundation of a universal kingdom to human eyes, but He knew how God's kingdom grows (Mt 13:31–32). Compare Jer 33:15–17; Eze 31:6; Da 4:12.

shade of its branches.[g] 24All the trees of
the field[h] will know that I the LORD bring
down[i] the tall tree and make the low
tree grow tall. I dry up the green tree and
make the dry tree flourish.[j]
"'I the LORD have spoken, and I will
do it.[k]'"

Chapter 18

The Soul Who Sins Will Die

THE word of the LORD came to me:
2"What do you people mean by quoting this proverb about the land of Israel:

"'The fathers eat sour grapes,
and the children's teeth are set on
edge'?[l]

3"As surely as I live, declares the Sovereign LORD, you will no longer quote
this proverb[m] in Israel. 4For every living
soul belongs to me, the father as well as
the son—both alike belong to me. The
soul who sins[n] is the one who will die.[o]

5"Suppose there is a righteous man
who does what is just and right.
6He does not eat at the mountain[p]
shrines
or look to the idols[q] of the house of
Israel.
He does not defile his neighbor's wife
or lie with a woman during her
period.[r]
7He does not oppress[s] anyone,
but returns what he took in pledge[t]
for a loan.
He does not commit robbery[u]
but gives his food to the hungry[v]
and provides clothing for the
naked.[w]
8He does not lend at usury
or take excessive interest.[i] [x]
He withholds his hand from doing
wrong
and judges fairly[y] between man and
man.
9He follows my decrees[z]
and faithfully keeps my laws.
That man is righteous;[a]
he will surely live,[b]
declares the Sovereign LORD.

10"Suppose he has a violent son, who
sheds blood[c] or does any of these other
things[j] 11(though the father has done
none of them):

"He eats at the mountain shrines.[d]
He defiles his neighbor's wife.
12He oppresses the poor[e] and needy.
He commits robbery.
He does not return what he took in
pledge.[f]
He looks to the idols.
He does detestable things.[g]
13He lends at usury and takes excessive
interest.[h]

Will such a man live? He will not! Because he has done all these detestable
things, he will surely be put to death and
his blood will be on his own head.[i]
14"But suppose this son has a son who
sees all the sins his father commits, and
though he sees them, he does not do such
things:[j]

17:23 [g]Ps 92:12; S Isa 2:2; Eze 31:6; Da 4:12; Hos 14:5-7; S Mt 13:32 **17:24** [h]S Ps 96:12; Isa 2:13 [i]S Ps 52:5 [j]S Nu 17:8; Da 5:21 [k]S 1Sa 2:7-8; Eze 19:12; 21:26; 22:14; 37:13; Am 9:11 **18:2** [l]S Job 21:19; Isa 3:15; Jer 31:29 **18:3** [m]S Ps 49:4 **18:4** [n]S 2Ki 14:6; S Pr 13:21 [o]ver 20; S Ge 18:23; S Ex 17:14; S Job 21:20; Isa 42:5; Eze 33:8; S Ro 6:23 **18:6** [p]S Eze 6:2 [q]Dt 4:19; S Eze 6:13; 20:24; Am 5:26 [r]S Lev 12:2; S 15:24 **18:7** [s]Ex 22:21; Mal 3:5; Jas 5:4 [t]S Ex 22:26 [u]S Ex 20:15 [v]S Job 22:7 [w]Dt 15:11; S Eze 16:49; S Mt 25:36; Lk 3:11 **18:8** [x]S Ex 18:21; 22:25; S Lev 25:35-37; Dt 23:19-20 [y]S Jer 22:3; Zec 8:16 **18:9** [z]S Lev 19:37 [a]Hab 2:4 [b]S Lev 18:5; S Eze 11:12; 20:11; Am 5:4 **18:10** [c]Ex 21:12; Eze 22:6 **18:11** [d]Eze 22:9 **18:12** [e]S Ex 22:22; S Job 24:9; Am 4:1 [f]S Ex 22:27 [g]2Ki 21:11; Isa 59:6-7; S Jer 22:17; S Eze 16:49; Hab 2:6 **18:13** [h]Ex 22:25 [i]S Lev 20:9; Eze 33:4-5; Hos 12:14 **18:14** [j]2Ch 34:21; S Pr 23:24

[i]*8* Or *take interest*; similarly in verses 13 and 17
[j]*10* Or *things to a brother*

18:1–32 EVIL AND SUFFERING, Deserved—Complaining and blaming come easily. In Exile, Israel blamed their suffering on their parents' sins (Jer 31:29–30; La 5:7). Ezekiel removed Israel's right to blame and complain. Most often we suffer for our sins, not someone else's. Someone else may set the pattern, but people are responsible when they adopt the pattern for themselves and sin. Participation in group sin brings the threat of participation in group suffering. Ezekiel set up God's way of dealing with people. He did not attempt to set out a full doctrine of evil and suffering. Job and Jesus show us the innocent do suffer from sinful plots and plans of others. See notes on Job 4:7–8; Isa 52:13—53:12.

18:1–32 HUMANITY, Death and Sin—See note on Jer 31:29–30. God is just in giving the sinner a new chance to live for Him. Thus, in grace God delays sin's punishment to call us to repent.

18:1–32 SIN, Responsibility—The Old Testament emphasizes corporate responsibility for sin (see Jos 7:1–26) but places a stronger emphasis on individual responsibility. The exiles in Babylon tried to shift the responsibility for their suffering in the Exile to the sins of previous generations. Ezekiel lifted his prophetic cry against such reasoning to declare that we must each accept responsibility for our personal sins. This principle is maintained throughout Scripture. All persons are sinners without exception. Our inherited tendencies, our environment, our history, and our friends and relatives all lead us to sin. We have to bear suffering and unpleasant circumstances provoked by the sins of former generations. We may have reason to complain, but we do not have reason to blame. The Lamentations show how to take complaints to God. Ezekiel shows how to bear our responsibility. We do not focus on our fathers' faults. We focus on God's call to us for religious loyalty, sexual faithfulness and purity, just treatment of other people including the poor and underprivileged, charity for the needy, respect for other people's property, fair judgment in decisions affecting other people, and obedience to God's will. When we live within this focus, we know we are rightly related to God. When we do not, we know we must seek forgiveness through our repentance and God's grace. We cannot draw benefits from our ancestors, nor can we pass on righteousness to our children. Each is personally responsible. Accepting such responsibility is not a onetime act but a daily relationship with God. Refusing responsibility means death.

18:1–32 CHRISTIAN ETHICS, Character—Compare Ps 15; 24; Job 31; Zec 7:8–10. God judges individuals for their own wickedness or righteousness. This was not a totally new emphasis in the predominantly corporate framework seen in the Old Testament. Rather, it is a reemphasis needed in Ezekiel's generation and our own. Basic to character development is the commitment to take responsibility for and to repent of sins. The godly person worships only God, respects marriage vows, helps the poor instead of causing their poverty, does not rob, engages in fair economic practices, mediates between people fairly, and makes God's teaching the guide of life.

15"He does not eat at the mountain
shrines[k]
or look to the idols[l] of the house of
Israel.
He does not defile his neighbor's wife.
16He does not oppress anyone
or require a pledge for a loan.
He does not commit robbery
but gives his food to the hungry[m]
and provides clothing for the
naked.[n]
17He withholds his hand from sin[k]
and takes no usury or excessive
interest.
He keeps my laws[o] and follows my
decrees.

He will not die for his father's sin; he will
surely live. 18But his father will die for his
own sin, because he practiced extortion,
robbed his brother and did what was
wrong among his people.

19"Yet you ask, 'Why does the son not
share the guilt of his father?' Since the
son has done what is just and right and
has been careful to keep all my decrees,
he will surely live.[p] 20The soul who sins
is the one who will die.[q] The son will not
share the guilt of the father, nor will the
father share the guilt of the son. The
righteousness of the righteous man will
be credited to him, and the wickedness of
the wicked will be charged against him.[r]

21"But if[s] a wicked man turns away
from all the sins he has committed and
keeps all my decrees[t] and does what is
just and right, he will surely live; he will
not die.[u] 22None of the offenses he has
committed will be remembered against
him. Because of the righteous things he
has done, he will live.[v] 23Do I take any
pleasure in the death of the wicked? declares the Sovereign LORD. Rather, am I
not pleased[w] when they turn from their
ways and live?[x]

24"But if a righteous man turns[y] from
his righteousness and commits sin and
does the same detestable things the wicked man does, will he live? None of the

18:15 [k]Eze 22:9 [l]S Ps 24:4
18:16 [m]Isa 58:7 [n]S Ex 22:27; Ps 41:1; Isa 58:10; S Eze 16:49
18:17 [o]S Ps 1:2
18:19 [p]Ex 20:5; Dt 5:9; Jer 15:4; Zec 1:3-6
18:20 [q]S Nu 15:31 [r]Dt 24:16; S 1Ki 8:32; 2Ki 14:6; Isa 3:11; S Eze 7:27; S 14:14; S Mt 16:27; Jn 9:2
18:21 [s]Jer 18:8 [t]S Ge 26:5 [u]S Eze 13:22; 36:27
18:22 [v]Ps 18:20-24; S Isa 43:25; Da 4:27; Mic 7:19
18:23 [w]Ps 147:11 [x]S Job 37:23; S La 3:33; S Eze 16:6; Mic 7:18; S 1Ti 2:4
18:24 [y]S Jer 34:16 [z]S Eze 15:8 [a]S 1Sa 15:11; 2Ch 24:17-20; S Job 35:8; Pr 21:16; S Eze 3:20; 20:27; 2Pe 2:20-22
18:25 [b]Jer 2:29 [c]S Ge 18:25; Jer 12:1; Eze 33:17; Zep 3:5; Mal 2:17; 3:13-15
18:27 [d]S Isa 1:18; S Eze 13:22
18:28 [e]S Isa 55:7
18:30 [f]S Isa 1:27; S Jer 35:15; Mt 3:2 [g]Eze 7:3; 24:14; 33:20; Hos 12:6; 1Pe 1:17
18:31 [h]S Jdg 6:8 [i]Ps 51:10 [j]Jer 27:13 [k]S Isa 1:16-17; S Eze 11:19; 36:26
18:32 [l]S Job 22:23; Isa 55:7; Mal 3:7 [m]S 2Ch 7:14; S Job 37:23; S Eze 16:6; 33:11
19:1 [n]ver 14; Jer 7:29; 9:10,20; Eze 26:17; 27:2,32; 28:12; 32:2,16; Am 5:1 [o]S 2Ki 24:6
19:2 [p]S Nu 23:24 [q]S Ge 49:9

righteous things he has done will be remembered. Because of the unfaithfulness[z] he is guilty of and because of the
sins he has committed, he will die.[a]

25"Yet you say, 'The way of the Lord is
not just.'[b] Hear, O house of Israel: Is my
way unjust?[c] Is it not your ways that are
unjust? 26If a righteous man turns from
his righteousness and commits sin, he
will die for it; because of the sin he has
committed he will die. 27But if a wicked
man turns away from the wickedness he
has committed and does what is just and
right, he will save his life.[d] 28Because he
considers all the offenses he has committed and turns away from them, he will
surely live; he will not die.[e] 29Yet the
house of Israel says, 'The way of the Lord
is not just.' Are my ways unjust, O house
of Israel? Is it not your ways that are unjust?

30"Therefore, O house of Israel, I will
judge you, each one according to his
ways, declares the Sovereign LORD. Repent![f] Turn away from all your offenses;
then sin will not be your downfall.[g]
31Rid[h] yourselves of all the offenses you
have committed, and get a new heart[i]
and a new spirit. Why[j] will you die, O
house of Israel?[k] 32For I take no pleasure
in the death of anyone, declares the Sovereign LORD. Repent[l] and live![m]

Chapter 19

A Lament for Israel's Princes

"TAKE up a lament[n] concerning the
princes[o] of Israel 2and say:

" 'What a lioness[p] was your mother
among the lions!
She lay down among the young lions
and reared her cubs.[q]
3She brought up one of her cubs,
and he became a strong lion.
He learned to tear the prey
and he devoured men.

[k]*17* Septuagint (see also verse 8); Hebrew *from the poor*

18:21–32 SALVATION, Repentance—Life and death are the two ways set before all persons. God wants us to live and not die in our sins. Repentance is the path to life. The way to get a new heart and a new spirit is to turn away from our sins and turn to God. The doctrine of salvation teaches that we can be freed from our own past through repentance in the present. We do not have to die in our sins. We can repent of them. We can change our attitude to God, sin, self, others, and the world. See note on Lk 13:1–5.

18:23 HUMANITY, Relationship to God—The Hebrew word for repentance means "turn." Each individual has the opportunity and the responsibility of turning his or her life to God and re-establishing the relationship broken by sin.

18:25–32 GOD, Justice—God has sovereign authority over all persons. His ways are just. He will judge us all according to standards of justice. As long as we are alive, God gives us a chance to repent and not face condemnation.

18:25 CREATION, Evil—Faced with Ezekiel's outline of moral responsibility, the people in captivity claimed the Lord was unjust. The prophet, however, insisted that those who committed the evil must accept the blame. God made a beautiful world and established it in righteousness. Sin entered because people made deliberate choices to do wrong things. Every generation must face moral responsibility for its actions. God's moral law is both sensible and fair.

18:30–32 HUMANITY, Life—God is the Author of all life, both physical and spiritual. He does not want to pay the wages of sin to anyone. True life comes from Him when we turn from sin to serve Him.

19:1–14 HISTORY, Confession—The confession form which Israel used in worship to remember, teach, and praise God for their history of salvation proved meaningful in the midst of judgment. History could become the content of lament as God's people cried to God for help after judgment.

4The nations heard about him,
and he was trapped in their pit.
They led him with hooks[r]
to the land of Egypt.[s]

5" 'When she saw her hope unfulfilled,
her expectation gone,
she took another of her cubs[t]
and made him a strong lion.[u]
6He prowled among the lions,
for he was now a strong lion.
He learned to tear the prey
and he devoured men.[v]
7He broke down[1] their strongholds
and devastated[w] their towns.
The land and all who were in it
were terrified by his roaring.
8Then the nations[x] came against him,
those from regions round about.
They spread their net[y] for him,
and he was trapped in their pit.[z]
9With hooks[a] they pulled him into a cage
and brought him to the king of Babylon.[b]
They put him in prison,
so his roar[c] was heard no longer
on the mountains of Israel.[d]

10" 'Your mother was like a vine in your vineyard[m][e]
planted by the water;[f]
it was fruitful and full of branches
because of abundant water.[g]
11Its branches were strong,
fit for a ruler's scepter.
It towered high
above the thick foliage,
conspicuous for its height
and for its many branches.[h]
12But it was uprooted[i] in fury
and thrown to the ground.
The east wind[j] made it shrivel,
it was stripped of its fruit;
its strong branches withered
and fire consumed them.[k]
13Now it is planted in the desert,[l]
in a dry and thirsty land.[m]
14Fire spread from one of its main[n] branches
and consumed[n] its fruit.
No strong branch is left on it
fit for a ruler's scepter.'[o]

This is a lament[p] and is to be used as a lament."

Chapter 20

Rebellious Israel

IN the seventh year, in the fifth month
on the tenth day, some of the elders of
Israel came to inquire[q] of the LORD, and
they sat down in front of me.[r]
2Then the word of the LORD came to
me: 3"Son of man, speak to the elders[s] of
Israel and say to them, 'This is what the
Sovereign LORD says: Have you come to
inquire[t] of me? As surely as I live, I will
not let you inquire of me, declares the
Sovereign LORD.[u]'
4"Will you judge them? Will you judge
them, son of man? Then confront them
with the detestable practices of their fathers[v] 5and say to them: 'This is what
the Sovereign LORD says: On the day I
chose[w] Israel, I swore with uplifted
hand[x] to the descendants of the house of
Jacob and revealed myself to them in
Egypt. With uplifted hand I said to them,
"I am the LORD your God.[y]" 6On that

19:4 [r]S Job 41:2 [s]2Ki 23:33-34; 2Ch 36:4; S La 4:20
19:5 [t]S Ge 49:9 [u]2Ki 23:34
19:6 [v]2Ki 24:9; 2Ch 36:9
19:7 [w]Eze 29:10; 30:12
19:8 [x]2Ki 24:2 [y]S Eze 12:13 [z]2Ki 24:11; S La 4:20
19:9 [a]S 2Ki 19:28 [b]S 2Ki 25:7; S 2Ch 36:6 [c]Zec 11:3 [d]S 2Ki 24:15
19:10 [e]S Ge 49:22 [f]S Jer 17:8 [g]Ps 80:8-11
19:11 [h]Eze 31:3; Da 4:11
19:12 [i]S Dt 29:28 [j]S Ge 41:6 [k]S Isa 27:11; S Eze 17:24; 28:17; Hos 13:15
19:13 [l]Eze 20:35; Hos 2:14 [m]Hos 2:3
19:14 [n]Eze 20:47 [o]S Eze 15:4 [p]S ver 1
20:1 [q]S Ge 25:22 [r]Eze 1:1-2; S 8:1; 21:1
20:3 [s]S Eze 7:26 [t]S Ge 25:22; Eze 14:3 [u]S 1Sa 28:6; Isa 1:15; Am 8:12; Mic 3:7
20:4 [v]S Eze 16:2; 22:2; Mt 23:32
20:5 [w]S Dt 7:6 [x]S Ge 14:22; S Nu 14:30 [y]S Lev 11:44

[1]7 Targum (see Septuagint); Hebrew *He knew* [m]*10* Two Hebrew manuscripts; most Hebrew manuscripts *your blood* [n]*14* Or *from under its*

20:1–44 GOD, One God—Throughout her history, from Egypt on, Israel imitated her neighbors and worshiped other gods. Despite the Israelite's history of idolatry, God still sought to bring them to worship Himself and forsake all other gods. He exercised both love and wrath to accomplish this. He continues to seek to create a completely loyal people. See note on 6:3–7.
20:1–44 CREATION, Evil—Ezekiel insisted to his audience that God does not arbitrarily bring judgment upon people. When they sin, He acts. To ignore sin would violate God's insistence for justice. He demands that His created beings practice justice toward one another and acknowledge Him in worship as the only God. He creates evil only in the sense that He allows the consequences of sin to occur. Moral choices in God's universe always have consequences. Our choices determine the type of future we shall experience. God will ultimately redeem His people and vindicate His reputation.
20:1–38 SIN, Rebellion—See notes on Jer 16:10–11; La 1:18–22.
20:1–44 REVELATION, History—God planned to repeat history with a new Exodus. He wanted His people to learn from history and renew their covenant with Him. See note on 16:1–63. God's anger at a nation is an indication that they have lived below their potential and His hope. His anger becomes the springboard for His next restoring actions.
20:1–44 HISTORY, National—See note on Isa 1:24–26. From Israel's perspective history was the narrative of rebellion, of seeking to be like the nations rather than to serve God. Thus their history became a history under God's judgment. From God's perspective history was His work to establish His holy reputation among all the nations of the world by working through Israel. Thus history became a narrative of anger, pity, discipline, and renewed deliverance. History pointed to a time of purging when rebels and idolaters would be weeded out of the exiled community so a new faithful community could be established. Then God's holy purpose would be established. His people would be related to Him in faithful, intimate trust. History would cause them shame and teach them obedience.
20:5 ELECTION, Israel—By a special act of love, God chose Israel (Ex 3:6—15:21). The covenant carried obligations on Israel's part (Lev 18:24). The people deserved to perish, but for God's name sake He spared them. The election of Israel cannot be explained with human logic. God's love and commitment to the human race He created is the only explanation. Election is God's plan to make His name known among all people so He can create a true people devoted to and blessed by Him.
20:5 THE CHURCH, Covenant People—God's people become God's own through His grace. He chose to call out and develop a holy people dedicated to Him. He promised to be God for His people. He keeps His promises and expects us to do the same. See note on Dt 7:6–8.

day I swore[z] to them that I would bring
them out of Egypt into a land I had
searched out for them, a land flowing
with milk and honey,[a] the most beautiful
of all lands.[b] 7And I said to them, "Each
of you, get rid of the vile images[c] you
have set your eyes on, and do not defile
yourselves with the idols[d] of Egypt. I am
the LORD your God.[e] "
8" 'But they rebelled against me and
would not listen to me;[f] they did not get
rid of the vile images they had set their
eyes on, nor did they forsake the idols of
Egypt.[g] So I said I would pour out my
wrath on them and spend my anger
against them in Egypt.[h] 9But for the sake
of my name I did what would keep it from
being profaned[i] in the eyes of the nations they lived among and in whose
sight I had revealed myself to the Israelites by bringing them out of Egypt.[j]
10Therefore I led them out of Egypt and
brought them into the desert.[k] 11I gave
them my decrees and made known to
them my laws, for the man who obeys
them will live by them.[l] 12Also I gave
them my Sabbaths[m] as a sign[n] between
us,[o] so they would know that I the LORD
made them holy.[p]
13" 'Yet the people of Israel rebelled[q]
against me in the desert. They did not
follow my decrees but rejected my laws[r]
—although the man who obeys them will
live by them—and they utterly desecrated my Sabbaths.[s] So I said I would pour
out my wrath[t] on them and destroy[u]
them in the desert.[v] 14But for the sake of
my name I did what would keep it from
being profaned[w] in the eyes of the nations in whose sight I had brought them
out.[x] 15Also with uplifted hand I swore[y]
to them in the desert that I would not
bring them into the land I had given
them—a land flowing with milk and honey, most beautiful of all lands[z]— 16be-
cause they rejected my laws[a] and did not
follow my decrees and desecrated my
Sabbaths. For their hearts[b] were devoted
to their idols.[c] 17Yet I looked on them
with pity and did not destroy[d] them or
put an end to them in the desert. 18I said
to their children in the desert, "Do not
follow the statutes of your fathers[e] or
keep their laws or defile yourselves[f]
with their idols. 19I am the LORD your
God;[g] follow my decrees and be careful
to keep my laws.[h] 20Keep my Sabbaths[i]
holy, that they may be a sign[j] between
us. Then you will know that I am the
LORD your God.[k] "
21" 'But the children rebelled against
me: They did not follow my decrees, they
were not careful to keep my laws[l] —although the man who obeys them will live
by them—and they desecrated my Sabbaths. So I said I would pour out my
wrath on them and spend my anger[m]
against them in the desert.[n] 22But I withheld[o] my hand, and for the sake of my
name[p] I did what would keep it from being profaned in the eyes of the nations in
whose sight I had brought them out.
23Also with uplifted hand I swore to them
in the desert that I would disperse them
among the nations and scatter[q] them
through the countries, 24because they
had not obeyed my laws but had rejected
my decrees[r] and desecrated my Sabbaths,[s] and their eyes ⌊lusted⌋ after[t] their
fathers' idols.[u] 25I also gave them over[v]
to statutes that were not good and laws
they could not live by;[w] 26I let them become defiled through their gifts—the sacrifice[x] of every firstborn[o]—that I might
fill them with horror so they would know
that I am the LORD.[y] '
27"Therefore, son of man, speak to the
people of Israel and say to them, 'This is
what the Sovereign LORD says: In this
also your fathers[z] blasphemed[a] me by
forsaking me:[b] 28When I brought them
into the land[c] I had sworn to give them
and they saw any high hill or any leafy
tree, there they offered their sacrifices,
made offerings that provoked me to anger, presented their fragrant incense and
poured out their drink offerings.[d] 29Then
I said to them: What is this high place[e]
you go to?' " (It is called Bamah[p] to this
day.)

Judgment and Restoration

30"Therefore say to the house of Israel:
'This is what the Sovereign LORD says:
Will you defile yourselves[f] the way your
fathers did and lust after their vile images?[g] 31When you offer your gifts—the
sacrifice of your sons[h] in[q] the fire—you

20:6 [z]S Ex 6:8 [a]S Ex 3:8 [b]S Dt 8:7; Da 8:9; 11:41; Mal 3:12 **20:7** [c]Ex 20:4 [d]S Eze 6:9 [e]S Ex 20:2; Lev 18:3; Dt 29:18 **20:8** [f]S Jer 7:26 [g]S Jer 11:10; S Eze 7:8; S 16:26 [h]S Ex 32:7; Dt 9:7; S Isa 63:10 **20:9** [i]S Isa 48:11 [j]Eze 36:22; 39:7 **20:10** [k]S Ex 13:18; 19:1 **20:11** [l]Ex 20:1-23; Lev 18:5; Dt 4:7-8; S Eze 18:9; S Ro 10:5 **20:12** [m]S Ex 20:10 [n]S Ex 31:13 [o]Jer 17:22 [p]S Lev 20:8 **20:13** [q]Ps 78:40 [r]S Jer 6:19; 11:8 [s]ver 24 [t]S Dt 9:8 [u]S Ex 32:10 [v]Lev 26:15,43; S Nu 14:29; Ps 95:8-10; Isa 56:6 **20:14** [w]S Isa 48:11 [x]Eze 36:23 **20:15** [y]S Dt 1:34 [z]Nu 14:22-23; Ps 95:11; 106:26; Heb 3:11 **20:16** [a]Jer 11:8; Am 2:4 [b]S Nu 15:39 [c]ver 24; S Eze 6:4; Am 5:26 **20:17** [d]S Jer 4:27 **20:18** [e]S 2Ch 30:7; Zec 1:4 [f]S Ps 106:39 **20:19** [g]S Ex 20:2 [h]Dt 5:32-33; 6:1-2; S 8:1; 11:1; S 12:1 **20:20** [i]S Ex 20:10 [j]S Ex 31:13 [k]Jer 17:22 **20:21** [l]S Jer 7:26 [m]Nu 25:3 [n]S Eze 7:8 **20:22** [o]Ps 78:38 [p]S Isa 48:11 **20:23** [q]S Lev 26:33; S Ps 9:11 **20:24** [r]Am 2:4 [s]ver 13 [t]S Eze 6:9 [u]S ver 16; S Eze 2:3; S 18:6 **20:25** [v]S Ps 81:12; Ro 1:28 [w]Isa 66:4; 2Th 2:11 **20:26** [x]S Lev 18:21 [y]Lev 20:2-5; 2Ki 17:17 **20:27** [z]S Ps 78:57 [a]S Nu 15:30; Ro 2:24 [b]S Eze 18:24 **20:28** [c]Ne 9:23; Ps 78:55,58 [d]S Jer 2:7; S 3:6; S 19:13; S Eze 6:13 **20:29** [e]Eze 16:16; 43:7

20:30 [f]ver 43 [g]S Jdg 2:16-19; S Jer 16:12 **20:31** [h]S Eze 16:20

[o]26 Or *—making every firstborn pass through ⌊the fire⌋*
[p]29 Bamah means *high place.*
[q]31 Or *—making your sons pass through*

20:11–26 CHRISTIAN ETHICS, Moral Imperatives—The power of sin to blind us to God's moral guidance is tragically awesome. Eventually even God will not intervene to stop our rebellion.

20:12,14,40,41 GOD, Holy—God created Israel to be a holy people completely devoted to Him and to moral purity. Israel could be called holy only as she related to the holy God. With her sin Israel violated the holiness of God, forgetting the supreme characteristic of God. For this reason God would not hear them when they called upon Him (vv 3,31,33) and poured out His wrath upon them (vv 8,13,21,28,33,34).

20:17 GOD, Grace—God had good reason to destroy Israel before He even gave them the land. Instead, He pitied them and endured centuries of idolatry. Truly His love and grace are great, much greater than His wrath.

continue to defile yourselves with all your
idols to this day. Am I to let you inquire
of me, O house of Israel? As surely as I
live, declares the Sovereign LORD, I will
not let you inquire of me.[i]
32" 'You say, "We want to be like the
nations, like the peoples of the world,
who serve wood and stone." But what
you have in mind will never happen. 33As
surely as I live, declares the Sovereign
LORD, I will rule over you with a mighty
hand and an outstretched arm[j] and with
outpoured wrath.[k] 34I will bring you
from the nations[l] and gather[m] you from
the countries where you have been scattered—with a mighty hand[n] and an outstretched arm and with outpoured
wrath.[o] 35I will bring you into the
desert[p] of the nations and there, face to
face, I will execute judgment[q] upon you.
36As I judged your fathers in the desert of
the land of Egypt, so I will judge you, declares the Sovereign LORD.[r] 37I will take
note of you as you pass under my rod,[s]
and I will bring you into the bond of the
covenant.[t] 38I will purge[u] you of those
who revolt and rebel against me. Although I will bring them out of the land
where they are living, yet they will not
enter the land of Israel. Then you will
know that I am the LORD.[v]
39" 'As for you, O house of Israel, this
is what the Sovereign LORD says: Go and
serve your idols,[w] every one of you! But
afterward you will surely listen to me and
no longer profane my holy name[x] with
your gifts and idols.[y] 40For on my holy
mountain, the high mountain of Israel,[z]
declares the Sovereign LORD, there in the
land the entire house of Israel will serve
me, and there I will accept them. There I
will require your offerings[a] and your
choice gifts,[r] along with all your holy sacrifices.[b] 41I will accept you as fragrant incense[c] when I bring you out from the
nations and gather[d] you from the countries where you have been scattered, and
I will show myself holy[e] among you in
the sight of the nations.[f] 42Then you will
know that I am the LORD,[g] when I bring
you into the land of Israel,[h] the land I
had sworn with uplifted hand to give to
your fathers.[i] 43There you will remember your conduct[j] and all the actions by
which you have defiled yourselves, and
you will loathe yourselves[k] for all the evil
you have done.[l] 44You will know that I
am the LORD, when I deal with you for
my name's sake[m] and not according to
your evil ways and your corrupt practices,
O house of Israel, declares the Sovereign
LORD.[n]' "

Prophecy Against the South

45The word of the LORD came to me:
46"Son of man, set your face toward[o] the
south; preach against the south and
prophesy against[p] the forest of the southland.[q] 47Say to the southern forest:[r]
'Hear the word of the LORD. This is what
the Sovereign LORD says: I am about to
set fire to you, and it will consume[s] all
your trees, both green and dry. The blazing flame will not be quenched, and every face from south to north[t] will be
scorched by it.[u] 48Everyone will see that
I the LORD have kindled it; it will not be
quenched.[v]' "
49Then I said, "Ah, Sovereign LORD![w]
They are saying of me, 'Isn't he just telling parables?[x]' "

Chapter 21

Babylon, God's Sword of Judgment

THE word of the LORD came to me:[y]
2"Son of man, set your face against[z]
Jerusalem and preach against the sanctuary.[a] Prophesy against[b] the land of Israel
3and say to her: 'This is what the LORD
says: I am against you.[c] I will draw my
sword[d] from its scabbard and cut off from
you both the righteous and the wicked.[e]
4Because I am going to cut off the righteous and the wicked, my sword[f] will be
unsheathed against everyone from south
to north.[g] 5Then all people will know

20:31 [i]Ps 106:37-39; S Jer 7:31; S Eze 14:3; Am 8:12; Zec 7:13 **20:33** [j]S Eze 16:27 [k]Jer 21:5; Eze 25:16 **20:34** [l]2Co 6:17* [m]S Dt 30:4; S Ps 106:47 [n]S Isa 31:3 [o]Isa 27:12-13; S Jer 44:6; S La 2:4; S Eze 6:14 **20:35** [p]S Eze 19:13 [q]S 1Sa 12:7; S Job 22:4; S Jer 2:35 **20:36** [r]Nu 11:1-35; 14:28-30; 1Co 10:5-10 **20:37** [s]S Lev 27:32 [t]S Eze 16:62 **20:38** [u]Eze 34:17-22; Am 9:9-10 [v]Ps 95:11; Jer 44:14; S Eze 13:9; 23:49; Hos 2:14; Zec 13:8-9; Mal 3:3; 4:1-3; Heb 4:3 **20:39** [w]S Jer 44:25 [x]S Ex 20:7; S Eze 13:19 [y]Eze 43:7; Am 4:4 **20:40** [z]S Eze 17:22; 34:14 [a]S Isa 60:7 [b]S Isa 56:7; Mal 3:4 **20:41** [c]S 2Co 2:14 [d]S Dt 30:4 [e]Eze 28:25; 36:23 [f]S Isa 5:16; S Eze 11:17; 2Co 6:17 **20:42** [g]Eze 38:23 [h]S Jer 23:8; Eze 34:13; 36:24 [i]Jer 30:3; Eze 34:27; 37:21 **20:43** [j]Eze 14:22 [k]S Lev 26:41 [l]S Eze 6:9; S 16:61; Hos 5:15 **20:44** [m]Ps 109:21; Isa 43:25; Eze 36:22 [n]S Eze 16:62; 36:32 **20:46** [o]S Eze 4:3; S 13:17 [p]Eze 21:2; Am 7:16 [q]Isa 30:6; Jer 13:19 **20:47** [r]S 2Ki 19:23 [s]Eze 19:14 [t]Eze 21:4 [u]Isa 9:18-19; S 13:8 **20:48** [v]S Jer 7:20; Eze 21:5,32; 23:25 **20:49** [w]S Eze 4:14 [x]S Jdg 14:12; S Ps 78:2; S Eze 12:9; Mt 13:13; S Jn 16:25 **21:1** [y]S Eze 20:1 **21:2** [z]S Eze 13:17 [a]Eze 9:6 [b]Jer 26:11-12; S Eze 20:46 **21:3** [c]S Jer 21:13 [d]S Isa 27:1; S Eze 14:21 [e]ver 9-11; S Job 9:22; S Isa 57:1; Jer 47:6-7 **21:4** [f]S Lev 26:25; S Jer 25:27 [g]Eze 20:47

[r]40 Or *and the gifts of your firstfruits*

20:32–38 THE CHURCH, Remnant—God has a purpose for His remnant. They are to become His covenant people, knowing and serving Him. If they refuse to do so, He will continue to punish the remnant people until the survivors are faithful. God will not continually let people who claim to serve Him shame His name. See note on Mic 2:12.

20:33 GOD, Sovereignty—God delivered Israel from Egypt with a mighty hand and outstretched arm. He finally decided to treat Israel as He had treated Egypt. Thus He showed His sovereign rule over all people. See note on 1:25–28. He judged the people He had delivered.

20:35–38 GOD, Judge—God's judgment on His people is not a rare occurrence. Its long history reaches back to the wilderness. His judgment is not a total destruction, but a purging of the rebels. See note on 18:25–32.

20:39–44 ELECTION, God's Purpose—God elected Israel to have a people who would worship only Him and would know Him in intimate relationship as the only God. He worked in love and wrath to lead them freely to conform to His will.

20:40 SALVATION, Acceptance—God gives us salvation by accepting us as we serve Him. Acceptance is an appropriate human response to God's salvation. Salvation requires our acceptance of God's acceptance.

20:44 SALVATION, Grace—See note on Isa 48:9.

21:1–27 HISTORY, Judgment—See note on Jer 1:14–19.

21:3–5 GOD, Judge—God judges His people to let all people see His power and know Him. See note on 18:25–32.

that I the LORD have drawn my sword[h]
from its scabbard; it will not return[i]
again.’[j]
6“Therefore groan, son of man! Groan
before them with broken heart and bitter
grief.[k] 7And when they ask you, ‘Why
are you groaning?’[l] you shall say, ‘Because of the news that is coming. Every
heart will melt[m] and every hand go
limp;[n] every spirit will become faint[o]
and every knee become as weak as water.’[p] It is coming! It will surely take
place, declares the Sovereign LORD.”
8The word of the LORD came to me:
9“Son of man, prophesy and say, ‘This is
what the Lord says:

“ ‘A sword, a sword,
sharpened and polished—
10sharpened for the slaughter,[q]
polished to flash like lightning!

“ ‘Shall we rejoice in the scepter of my
son ⌞Judah⌟? The sword despises every
such stick.[r]

11“ ‘The sword is appointed to be
polished,[s]
to be grasped with the hand;
it is sharpened and polished,
made ready for the hand of the
slayer.
12Cry out and wail, son of man,
for it is against my people;
it is against all the princes of Israel.
They are thrown to the sword
along with my people.
Therefore beat your breast.[t]

13“ ‘Testing will surely come. And
what if the scepter ⌞of Judah⌟, which the
sword despises, does not continue? declares the Sovereign LORD.’

14“So then, son of man, prophesy
and strike your hands[u] together.
Let the sword strike twice,
even three times.
It is a sword for slaughter—
a sword for great slaughter,
closing in on them from every
side.[v]
15So that hearts may melt[w]
and the fallen be many,
I have stationed the sword for
slaughter[s]
at all their gates.
Oh! It is made to flash like lightning,
it is grasped for slaughter.[x]
16O sword, slash to the right,
then to the left,
wherever your blade is turned.
17I too will strike my hands[y] together,

21:5 [h]S Isa 34:5 [i]ver 30 [j]S Eze 20:47-48; Na 1:9
21:6 [k]ver 12; S Isa 22:4; Jer 30:6; S Eze 9:4
21:7 [l]S Job 23:2 [m]S Jos 7:5 [n]S Jer 47:3; Eze 22:14 [o]S Ps 6:2 [p]S Lev 26:36; S Job 11:16
21:10 [q]Ps 110:5-6; Isa 34:5-6 [r]Dt 32:41
21:11 [s]Jer 46:4
21:12 [t]Jer 31:19
21:14 [u]ver 17; S Nu 24:10 [v]S Eze 6:11; 30:24
21:15 [w]S 2Sa 17:10 [x]Ps 22:14
21:17 [y]ver 14; Eze 22:13 [z]S Eze 5:13 [a]S Eze 6:11; S 16:42
21:19 [b]S Eze 14:21; 32:11 [c]Jer 31:21
21:20 [d]S Dt 3:11
21:21 [e]S Pr 16:33 [f]Zec 10:2 [g]Nu 22:7; S 23:23
21:22 [h]S Jer 4:16 [i]Jer 32:24 [j]S 2Ki 25:1; S Eze 4:2; 26:9
21:23 [k]S Nu 5:15 [l]S Eze 17:19
21:25 [m]Eze 22:4 [n]Eze 35:5
21:26 [o]S Isa 28:5; S Jer 13:18 [p]S Ps 75:7; Isa 40:4; S Eze 17:24; S Mt 23:12
21:27 [q]Ge 49:10 [r]Ps 2:6; Jer 23:5-6; Eze 37:24; Hag 2:21-22
21:28 [s]S Ge 19:38; Zep 2:8 [t]S Jer 12:12
21:29 [u]Jer 27:9 [v]ver 25; Eze 22:28; 35:5
21:30 [w]ver 5; Jer 47:6

and my wrath[z] will subside.
I the LORD have spoken.[a]”

18The word of the LORD came to me:
19“Son of man, mark out two roads for
the sword[b] of the king of Babylon to take,
both starting from the same country.
Make a signpost[c] where the road
branches off to the city. 20Mark out one
road for the sword to come against Rabbah of the Ammonites[d] and another
against Judah and fortified Jerusalem.
21For the king of Babylon will stop at the
fork in the road, at the junction of the
two roads, to seek an omen: He will cast
lots[e] with arrows, he will consult his
idols,[f] he will examine the liver.[g] 22Into
his right hand will come the lot for Jerusalem, where he is to set up battering
rams, to give the command to slaughter,
to sound the battle cry,[h] to set battering
rams against the gates, to build a ramp[i]
and to erect siege works.[j] 23It will seem
like a false omen to those who have
sworn allegiance to him, but he will remind[k] them of their guilt[l] and take
them captive.
24“Therefore this is what the Sovereign
LORD says: ‘Because you people have
brought to mind your guilt by your open
rebellion, revealing your sins in all that
you do—because you have done this, you
will be taken captive.
25“ ‘O profane and wicked prince of Israel, whose day has come,[m] whose time
of punishment has reached its climax,[n]
26this is what the Sovereign LORD says:
Take off the turban, remove the crown.[o]
It will not be as it was: The lowly will be
exalted and the exalted will be brought
low.[p] 27A ruin! A ruin! I will make it a
ruin! It will not be restored until he
comes to whom it rightfully belongs;[q] to
him I will give it.’[r]
28“And you, son of man, prophesy and
say, ‘This is what the Sovereign LORD says
about the Ammonites[s] and their insults:

“ ‘A sword,[t] a sword,
drawn for the slaughter,
polished to consume
and to flash like lightning!
29Despite false visions concerning you
and lying divinations[u] about you,
it will be laid on the necks
of the wicked who are to be slain,
whose day has come,
whose time of punishment has
reached its climax.[v]
30Return the sword to its scabbard.[w]

[s]15 Septuagint; the meaning of the Hebrew for this word is uncertain.

21:14–17,28–32 GOD, Wrath—See note on 5:8–17.

21:23–25 SIN, Rebellion—See notes on Ne 1:6–7; Isa 1:2–4. Rebellion leads to destruction.

21:30 CREATION, Sovereignty—God created (Hebrew

In the place where you were
created,
in the land of your ancestry,[x]
I will judge you.
31 I will pour out my wrath upon you
and breathe[y] out my fiery anger[z]
against you;
I will hand you over to brutal men,
men skilled in destruction.[a]
32 You will be fuel for the fire,[b]
your blood will be shed in your land,
you will be remembered[c] no more;
for I the LORD have spoken.' "

Chapter 22

Jerusalem's Sins

THE word of the LORD came to me:
2 "Son of man, will you judge her?
Will you judge this city of bloodshed?[d]
Then confront her with all her detestable
practices[e] 3 and say: 'This is what the
Sovereign LORD says: O city that brings
on herself doom by shedding blood[f] in
her midst and defiles herself by making
idols, 4 you have become guilty because of
the blood you have shed[g] and have become defiled by the idols you have made.
You have brought your days to a close,
and the end of your years has come.[h]
Therefore I will make you an object of
scorn[i] to the nations and a laughingstock
to all the countries.[j] 5 Those who are
near and those who are far away will
mock you, O infamous city, full of turmoil.[k]
6 " 'See how each of the princes of Israel who are in you uses his power to shed
blood.[l] 7 In you they have treated father
and mother with contempt;[m] in you they
have oppressed the alien[n] and mistreated
the fatherless and the widow.[o] 8 You have
despised my holy things and desecrated
my Sabbaths.[p] 9 In you are slanderous
men[q] bent on shedding blood;[r] in you
are those who eat at the mountain
shrines[s] and commit lewd acts.[t] 10 In
you are those who dishonor their fathers'
bed;[u] in you are those who violate wom-
en during their period,[v] when they are
ceremonially unclean.[w] 11 In you one man
commits a detestable offense with his
neighbor's wife,[x] another shamefully defiles his daughter-in-law,[y] and another violates his sister,[z] his own father's daughter.[a] 12 In you men accept bribes[b] to
shed blood; you take usury[c] and excessive interest[t] and make unjust gain from
your neighbors[d] by extortion. And you
have forgotten[e] me, declares the Sovereign LORD.[f]
13 " 'I will surely strike my hands[g] together at the unjust gain[h] you have made
and at the blood[i] you have shed in your
midst.[j] 14 Will your courage endure[k] or
your hands[l] be strong in the day I deal
with you? I the LORD have spoken,[m] and I
will do it.[n] 15 I will disperse you among
the nations and scatter[o] you through the
countries; and I will put an end to[p] your
uncleanness.[q] 16 When you have been defiled[u] in the eyes of the nations, you will
know that I am the LORD.' "
17 Then the word of the LORD came to
me: 18 "Son of man, the house of Israel
has become dross[r] to me; all of them are
the copper, tin, iron and lead left inside a
furnace.[s] They are but the dross of silver.[t] 19 Therefore this is what the Sovereign LORD says: 'Because you have all become dross,[u] I will gather you into Jerusalem. 20 As men gather silver, copper,
iron, lead and tin into a furnace to melt it
with a fiery blast, so will I gather you in
my anger and my wrath and put you inside the city and melt you.[v] 21 I will gather you and I will blow[w] on you with my
fiery wrath, and you will be melted inside
her.[x] 22 As silver is melted[y] in a furnace,
so you will be melted inside her, and you

21:30 [x]S Eze 16:3
21:31 [y]Ps 18:15; S Isa 11:4 [z]Ps 79:6; Eze 22:20-21 [a]S Jer 4:7; 51:20-23; S Eze 16:39
21:32 [b]S Eze 20:47-48; Mal 4:1 [c]Eze 25:10
22:2 [d]Eze 24:6,9; Hos 4:2; Na 3:1; Hab 2:12 [e]S Eze 16:2; 23:36
22:3 [f]ver 6,13,27; Eze 23:37,45; 24:6
22:4 [g]S 2Ki 21:16 [h]Eze 21:25 [i]S Ps 137:3 [j]Ps 44:13-14; S Eze 5:14
22:5 [k]S Isa 22:2
22:6 [l]S Eze 11:6; 18:10; 33:25
22:7 [m]S Dt 5:16; Mic 7:6 [n]S Ex 23:9 [o]S Ex 22:21-22
22:8 [p]S Ex 20:8; Eze 23:38-39
22:9 [q]S Lev 19:16 [r]Isa 59:3; S Eze 11:6; Hos 4:2; 6:9 [s]Eze 18:11 [t]Eze 23:29; Hos 4:10,14
22:10 [u]Lev 18:7 [v]S Lev 12:2 [w]S Lev 18:8,19
22:11 [x]S Jer 5:8 [y]S Ge 11:31; Lev 18:15 [z]S Lev 18:9; S 2Sa 13:14 [a]Eze 18:6
22:12 [b]S Ex 18:21; Dt 27:25; Ps 26:10; Isa 5:23; Am 5:12; Mic 7:3 [c]S Eze 18:8 [d]Lev 19:13 [e]Ps 106:21; S Isa 17:10; S 57:11 [f]S Eze 11:6
22:13 [g]S Nu 24:10; S Eze 21:17 [h]S ver 27; S Isa 33:15 [i]S ver 3 [j]S Eze 6:11
22:14 [k]Ps 76:7; Joel 2:11; Na 1:6; Mal 3:2 [l]S Eze 7:17 [m]Eze 24:14 [n]S Eze 17:24
22:15 [o]S Lev 26:33; Dt 4:27; Zec 7:14 [p]S Eze 16:41 [q]Eze 24:11
22:18 [r]S Ps 119:119 [s]Isa 48:10 [t]Jer 6:28-30
22:19 [u]S Ps 119:119 **22:20** [v]Hos 8:10; Mal 3:2 **22:21** [w]Isa 40:7; Hag 1:9 [x]Ps 68:2; Eze 21:31 **22:22** [y]S Isa 1:25

[t] 12 Or *usury and interest* [u] 16 Or *When I have allotted you your inheritance*

bara') the Ammonites in their land. See note on Ge 1:1. His creative power extends to all people, and, therefore, His moral law includes all nations. His judgment knows no distinction nor favoritism. No one will escape the wrath of His punitive hand. He is not limited by geographical distance nor manipulated by heathen nations and their gods.

22:1–31 CHRISTIAN ETHICS, Justice—God establishes leaders of His people to create and maintain a just social order. When they become the problem, they face destruction. God looks for people who will stand in the gap between Him and His people to intercede for them and build up the wall of justice. See note on 13:17–23.

22:2–16 SIN, Lawlessness—Continual sinning leads to loss of moral judgment. All laws are broken. Nothing is respected. Murder, idolatry, loss of respect and care for parents, injustice against the needy, destruction of others' reputations, sexual sin, bribery, loss of respect for God's day and His place of worship, illegal business practices—lawless sinfulness pervades and perverts life. One action stands behind such sin: we forget God, losing respect for His holiness. God does not forget. He punishes such lawlessness drastically. See note on 8:3–18.

22:6–11 FAMILY, Sexual Sin—Sexual sins show the destruction of a people. Only people who forget God can commit such sins. See note on Lev 18:6–20.

22:12,27–29 CHRISTIAN ETHICS, Property Rights—The horrible enumeration of economic injustices and abridgment of human rights which Ezekiel made could be applied to our own day. The signs of forgetting God's ways are seen in overcharging, extortion, oppression of the poor, and the denial of justice to those who have no advocate. Religious leaders face judgment when they ensure the support of their institution by ignoring or even supporting economic injustice.

22:15–16 HISTORY, Judgment—See notes on 1 Ki 20:13; Jer 1:14–19.

22:20–31 GOD, Wrath—See note on 5:8–17.

will know that I the LORD have poured out my wrath[z] upon you.' "[a]

23 Again the word of the LORD came to me: 24 "Son of man, say to the land, 'You are a land that has had no rain or showers[v] in the day of wrath.'[b] 25 There is a conspiracy[c] of her princes[w] within her like a roaring lion[d] tearing its prey; they devour people,[e] take treasures and precious things and make many widows[f] within her. 26 Her priests do violence to my law[g] and profane my holy things; they do not distinguish between the holy and the common;[h] they teach that there is no difference between the unclean and the clean;[i] and they shut their eyes to the keeping of my Sabbaths, so that I am profaned[j] among them.[k] 27 Her officials[l] within her are like wolves[m] tearing their prey; they shed blood and kill people[n] to make unjust gain.[o] 28 Her prophets whitewash[p] these deeds for them by false visions and lying divinations.[q] They say, 'This is what the Sovereign LORD says'—when the LORD has not spoken.[r] 29 The people of the land practice extortion and commit robbery;[s] they oppress the poor and needy and mistreat the alien,[t] denying them justice.[u]

30 "I looked for a man among them who would build up the wall[v] and stand before me in the gap on behalf of the land so I would not have to destroy it, but I found none.[w] 31 So I will pour out my wrath on them and consume them with my fiery anger,[x] bringing down[y] on their own heads all they have done, declares the Sovereign LORD.[z]"

Chapter 23

Two Adulterous Sisters

THE word of the LORD came to me: 2 "Son of man, there were two women, daughters of the same mother.[a] 3 They became prostitutes in Egypt,[b] engaging in prostitution[c] from their youth.[d] In that land their breasts were fondled and their virgin bosoms caressed.[e] 4 The older was named Oholah, and her sister was Oholibah. They were mine and gave birth to sons and daughters. Oholah is Samaria, and Oholibah is Jerusalem.[f]

5 "Oholah engaged in prostitution while she was still mine; and she lusted after her lovers, the Assyrians[g]—warriors[h] 6 clothed in blue, governors and commanders, all of them handsome young men, and mounted horsemen. 7 She gave herself as a prostitute to all the elite of the Assyrians and defiled herself with all the idols of everyone she lusted after.[i] 8 She did not give up the prostitution she began in Egypt,[j] when during her youth men slept with her, caressed her virgin bosom and poured out their lust upon her.[k]

9 "Therefore I handed her over[l] to her lovers,[m] the Assyrians, for whom she lusted.[n] 10 They stripped[o] her naked, took away her sons and daughters and killed her with the sword. She became a byword among women,[p] and punishment was inflicted[q] on her.[r]

11 "Her sister Oholibah saw this,[s] yet in her lust and prostitution she was more depraved than her sister.[t] 12 She too lusted after the Assyrians—governors and commanders, warriors in full dress, mounted horsemen, all handsome young men.[u] 13 I saw that she too defiled herself; both of them went the same way.[v]

14 "But she carried her prostitution still further. She saw men portrayed on a wall,[w] figures of Chaldeans[x] portrayed in red,[x] 15 with belts[y] around their waists and flowing turbans on their heads; all of them looked like Babylonian chariot officers, natives of Chaldea.[y] 16 As soon as she saw them, she lusted after them and sent messengers[z] to them in Chaldea.[a]

22:22 [z]S Eze 7:8 [a]S Isa 64:7 **22:24** [b]Eze 24:13 **22:25** [c]Jer 11:9 [d]S Ps 22:13 [e]Hos 6:9 [f]Jer 15:8; 18:21 **22:26** [g]Hos 9:7-8; Zep 3:4; Mal 2:7-8 [h]Eze 42:20; 44:23 [i]S Lev 20:25 [j]S Lev 18:21; S Eze 13:19 [k]ver 8; S 1Sa 2:12-17; Jer 2:8,26; Hag 2:11-14 **22:27** [l]S Jer 26:10; Zep 3:3 [m]Mt 7:15 [n]S ver 3; S Eze 11:6; 33:25; 34:2-3; Mic 3:2,10 [o]ver 13; S Ge 37:24; S Isa 1:23; S Jer 12:2; S 51:13; Eze 33:31 **22:28** [p]S Eze 13:10 [q]S La 2:14; S 4:13; S Eze 21:29 [r]S Eze 13:2,6-7 **22:29** [s]S Ps 62:10 [t]S Ex 22:21 [u]S Isa 5:7 **22:30** [v]S Eze 13:5 [w]Ps 106:23; S Isa 64:7; Jer 5:1 **22:31** [x]Ex 32:10; S Isa 30:27; S La 4:11 [y]Eze 16:43 [z]Eze 7:8-9; Ro 2:8 **23:2** [a]S Jer 3:7; S Eze 16:45 **23:3** [b]Jos 24:14 [c]S Lev 17:7; S Isa 1:21 [d]S Ps 25:7 [e]S Eze 16:15 **23:4** [f]S Eze 16:46 **23:5** [g]S 2Ki 16:7; Hos 5:13 [h]Hos 8:9 **23:7** [i]Isa 57:8; Hos 5:3; 6:10 **23:8** [j]Ex 32:4 [k]S Eze 16:15 **23:9** [l]S 2Ki 18:11 [m]S Jer 4:30 [n]Hos 11:5 **23:10** [o]Hos 2:10 [p]Eze 16:41 [q]Jer 42:10 [r]Eze 16:36 **23:11** [s]S Jer 3:7 [t]Jer 3:8-11; S Eze 16:51 **23:12** [u]2Ki 16:7-15; S 2Ch 28:16; S Eze 16:15,28 **23:13** [v]S 2Ki 17:19; Hos 12:2 **23:14** [w]S Eze 8:10 [x]Jer 22:14; Na 2:3 **23:15** [y]S Isa 5:27 **23:16** [z]S Isa 57:9 [a]S Eze 6:9

[v]*24* Septuagint; Hebrew *has not been cleansed or rained on* [w]*25* Septuagint; Hebrew *prophets* [x]*14* Or *Babylonians* [y]*15* Or *Babylonia*; also in verse 16

22:23–29 SIN, Unrighteousness—Leaders stamp a society with their moral values. Materialistic leaders produce self-centered people. This principle works in politics, business, and religion. When religious leaders echo the materialistic, selfish values of society's leaders, a nation has no hope of a spiritual foundation. God targets such a people for destruction.

22:26–31 GOD, Holy—Ministers are consecrated to handle the holy worship and word of God. When they fail, the people have little hope. See notes on 20:12,14,40,41.

22:28 REVELATION, Messengers—See note on 13:1–23. Revelation does not come automatically when humans call. God must send it.

22:30 PRAYER, Command of God—This could refer either to lack of prophets and teachers warning the land or to lack of intercessors. One task of a prophet was intercessory prayer. God wants people strong in prayer to intercede for His sinful people. See note on Isa 59:1–2.

23:1–49 REVELATION, Word—Using the analogy of prostitution as lack of fidelity to God, the prophet declared the story of two nations—Judah and Israel. Both nations left God for other gods and thus defaced their own identity. They had to face the consequences of their actions. International alliances cannot replace faithfulness to God's covenant.

23:1–49 HISTORY, Judgment—See notes on 16:1–63; 20:1–44; 1 Ki 20:13; Jer 1:14–19. God described Israel's history as that of two prostitutes making alliances with the most available suitors. God sent their illicit lovers to punish them. A history of calling oneself God's people does not make a community God's people assured of His blessings. Rather a people's historical actions of faith or faithlessness show their true identity and bring God's actions on them.

17Then the Babylonians[b] came to her, to
the bed of love, and in their lust they defiled her. After she had been defiled by
them, she turned away from them in disgust.[c] 18When she carried on her prostitution openly and exposed her nakedness,[d] I turned away[e] from her in disgust, just as I had turned away from her
sister.[f] 19Yet she became more and more
promiscuous as she recalled the days of
her youth, when she was a prostitute in
Egypt. 20There she lusted after her lovers,
whose genitals were like those of donkeys and whose emission was like that of
horses. 21So you longed for the lewdness
of your youth, when in Egypt your bosom
was caressed and your young breasts
fondled.[z] [g]

22"Therefore, Oholibah, this is what
the Sovereign LORD says: I will stir up
your lovers[h] against you, those you
turned away from in disgust, and I will
bring them against you from every
side[i]— 23the Babylonians[j] and all the
Chaldeans,[k] the men of Pekod[l] and
Shoa and Koa, and all the Assyrians with
them, handsome young men, all of them
governors and commanders, chariot officers and men of high rank, all mounted
on horses.[m] 24They will come against you
with weapons,[a] chariots and wagons[n]
and with a throng of people; they will
take up positions against you on every
side with large and small shields and with
helmets. I will turn you over to them for
punishment,[o] and they will punish you
according to their standards. 25I will direct my jealous anger[p] against you, and
they will deal with you in fury. They will
cut off your noses and your ears, and
those of you who are left will fall by the
sword. They will take away your sons and
daughters,[q] and those of you who are left
will be consumed by fire.[r] 26They will
also strip[s] you of your clothes and take
your fine jewelry.[t] 27So I will put a stop[u]
to the lewdness and prostitution you began in Egypt. You will not look on these
things with longing or remember Egypt
anymore.

28"For this is what the Sovereign LORD
says: I am about to hand you over[v] to
those you hate, to those you turned away
from in disgust. 29They will deal with you
in hatred and take away everything you
have worked for. They will leave you naked[w] and bare, and the shame of your
prostitution will be exposed.[x] Your lewdness[y] and promiscuity[z] 30have brought
this upon you, because you lusted after
the nations and defiled yourself with
their idols.[a] 31You have gone the way of
your sister; so I will put her cup[b] into
your hand.[c]

32"This is what the Sovereign LORD
says:

"You will drink your sister's cup,
 a cup large and deep;
it will bring scorn and derision,[d]
 for it holds so much.[e]
33You will be filled with drunkenness
 and sorrow,
 the cup of ruin and desolation,
 the cup of your sister Samaria.[f]
34You will drink it[g] and drain it dry;
 you will dash it to pieces
 and tear your breasts.

I have spoken, declares the Sovereign
LORD.[h]

35"Therefore this is what the Sovereign
LORD says: Since you have forgotten[i] me
and thrust me behind your back,[j] you
must bear[k] the consequences of your
lewdness and prostitution."

36The LORD said to me: "Son of man,
will you judge Oholah and Oholibah?
Then confront[l] them with their detestable practices,[m] 37for they have committed adultery and blood is on their hands.
They committed adultery with their idols;
they even sacrificed their children, whom
they bore to me,[b] as food for them.[n]
38They have also done this to me: At that
same time they defiled my sanctuary[o]
and desecrated my Sabbaths.[p] 39On the
very day they sacrificed their children to
their idols, they entered my sanctuary
and desecrated[q] it. That is what they did
in my house.[r]

40"They even sent messengers for men
who came from far away,[s] and when
they arrived you bathed yourself for
them, painted your eyes[t] and put on
your jewelry.[u] 41You sat on an elegant
couch,[v] with a table[w] spread before it on
which you had placed the incense[x] and
oil that belonged to me.[y]

42"The noise of a carefree[z] crowd was
around her; Sabeans[c] [a] were brought
from the desert along with men from the

23:17 [b]Jer 40:9 [c]S Eze 16:29
23:18 [d]S Isa 57:8 [e]Ps 78:59; 106:40; Jer 6:8 [f]Jer 12:8; Am 5:21
23:21 [g]S Eze 16:26
23:22 [h]S Jer 4:30 [i]S Eze 16:37
23:23 [j]2Ki 20:14-18; S Jer 40:9 [k]S Ge 11:28 [l]Jer 50:21 [m]S 2Ki 24:2
23:24 [n]Jer 47:3; Eze 26:7,10; Na 2:4 [o]Jer 39:5-6
23:25 [p]S Dt 29:20 [q]ver 47; Eze 24:21 [r]S Jer 12:9; S Eze 16:38; S 20:47-48
23:26 [s]S Jer 13:22 [t]S Isa 3:18-23; S Eze 16:39
23:27 [u]S Eze 16:41
23:28 [v]S Jer 34:20
23:29 [w]Mic 1:11 [x]S Jer 13:27 [y]S Eze 22:9 [z]Dt 28:48; S Eze 16:36
23:30 [a]Ps 106:37-38; Zep 3:1
23:31 [b]S Jer 25:15 [c]2Ki 21:13
23:32 [d]Ps 44:13; Hos 7:16 [e]Ps 60:3; Isa 51:17; Jer 25:15
23:33 [f]Jer 25:15-16; S Eze 12:19
23:34 [g]S Ps 16:5 [h]S Jer 25:27
23:35 [i]S Dt 32:18; S Isa 17:10 [j]S 1Ki 14:9; S 2Ch 29:6 [k]Eze 16:52
23:36 [l]S Eze 16:2 [m]Isa 58:1; S Eze 22:2; Mic 3:8
23:37 [n]S Eze 16:36
23:38 [o]S Lev 15:31 [p]S Ne 10:31
23:39 [q]S 2Ki 21:4 [r]S Jer 7:10; Eze 22:8
23:40 [s]S Isa 57:9 [t]2Ki 9:30 [u]S Jer 4:30; Eze 16:13-19; Hos 2:13
23:41 [v]S Est 1:6; S Pr 7:17 [w]Isa 65:11; Eze 41:22; 44:16; Mal 1:7,12 [x]Isa 57:9; S 65:3; S Jer 44:5 [y]S Nu 18:12
23:42 [z]S Ps 73:5 [a]S 2Ch 9:1

[z]*21* Syriac (see also verse 3); Hebrew *caressed because of your young breasts* [a]*24* The meaning of the Hebrew for this word is uncertain. [b]*37* Or *even made the children they bore to me pass through* ⌞*the fire*⌟ [c]*42* Or *drunkards*

23:25 GOD, Jealous—See note on 16:38. Jealous love produces zealous judgment.
23:35–41 SIN, Responsibility—Sin may bring fame, fortune, and fun for awhile. Crowds may gather around the sinner. When political advantage is at stake, the lure of sin becomes all the greater. When religious apostasy results, sin becomes all the graver. God soon enters the picture to destroy sin and its "profit." The sinner must bear personal responsibility to God for sin, weighing its short-term gain against ultimate destruction.

rabble, and they put bracelets[b] on the
arms of the woman and her sister and
beautiful crowns on their heads.[c] 43 Then
I said about the one worn out by adultery,
'Now let them use her as a prostitute,[d]
for that is all she is.' 44 And they slept
with her. As men sleep with a prostitute,
so they slept with those lewd women,
Oholah and Oholibah. 45 But righteous
men will sentence them to the punishment of women who commit adultery
and shed blood,[e] because they are adulterous and blood is on their hands.[f]

46 "This is what the Sovereign LORD
says: Bring a mob[g] against them and give
them over to terror and plunder.[h] 47 The
mob will stone them and cut them down
with their swords; they will kill their
sons and daughters[i] and burn[j] down
their houses.[k]

48 "So I will put an end[l] to lewdness in
the land, that all women may take warning and not imitate you.[m] 49 You will suffer the penalty for your lewdness and
bear the consequences of your sins of
idolatry.[n] Then you will know that I am
the Sovereign LORD.[o]"

Chapter 24

The Cooking Pot

IN the ninth year, in the tenth month on
the tenth day, the word of the LORD
came to me:[p] 2 "Son of man, record[q] this
date, this very date, because the king of
Babylon has laid siege to Jerusalem this
very day.[r] 3 Tell this rebellious house[s] a
parable[t] and say to them: 'This is what
the Sovereign LORD says:

" 'Put on the cooking pot;[u] put it on
and pour water into it.
4 Put into it the pieces of meat,
all the choice pieces—the leg and
the shoulder.
Fill it with the best of these bones;[v]
5 take the pick of the flock.[w]
Pile wood beneath it for the bones;
bring it to a boil
and cook the bones in it.[x]

6 " 'For this is what the Sovereign LORD
says:

" 'Woe[y] to the city of bloodshed,[z]
to the pot now encrusted,
whose deposit will not go away!
Empty it piece by piece
without casting lots[a] for them.[b]

23:42 [b]S Ge 24:30 [c]S Eze 16:11-12
23:43 [d]ver 3
23:45 [e]S Eze 22:3 [f]S Lev 20:10; S Eze 16:38; Hos 2:2; 6:5
23:46 [g]Eze 16:40 [h]S Dt 28:25; S Jer 25:9
23:47 [i]S ver 25 [j]2Ch 36:19; S Jer 34:22 [k]S 2Ch 36:17
23:48 [l]Eze 16:41 [m]2Pe 2:6
23:49 [n]Eze 24:13 [o]S Eze 7:4; S 9:10; 16:58; S 20:38
24:1 [p]S Eze 8:1; 26:1; 29:17
24:2 [q]Isa 30:8; Hab 2:2 [r]2Ki 25:1; S Jer 39:1
24:3 [s]S Isa 1:2; S Eze 2:3,6 [t]S Eze 20:49 [u]S Eze 11:3
24:4 [v]S Eze 11:7
24:5 [w]S Isa 34:12; Jer 52:10 [x]Jer 52:24-27; Mic 3:2-3
24:6 [y]S Eze 16:23 [z]S Eze 22:2 [a]S Job 6:27; Joel 3:3; Ob 1:11; Na 3:10 [b]S Eze 11:11
24:7 [c]S Lev 17:13
24:11 [d]Jer 21:10
24:13 [e]S Isa 22:14 [f]Jer 6:28-30; La 1:9; S Eze 16:42; 22:24; 23:36-49; Hos 7:1; Zec 6:8
24:14 [g]Eze 22:14 [h]S Nu 11:23 [i]S Eze 8:18 [j]S Job 27:22 [k]Eze 36:19; Zec 8:14 [l]S Isa 3:11; S Eze 18:30
24:16 [m]S Ps 39:10 [n]ver 21; Ps 84:1; S La 2:4 [o]Jer 13:17; 16:5; S 22:10
24:17 [p]Ps 39:9 [q]S Ex 28:39; S Isa 3:20 [r]S Isa 20:2 [s]S Lev 13:45 [t]ver 22; S Jer 16:7
24:18 [u]S Eze 12:7
24:19 [v]Eze 12:9; 37:18

7 " 'For the blood she shed is in her
midst:
She poured it on the bare rock;
she did not pour it on the ground,
where the dust would cover it.[c]
8 To stir up wrath and take revenge
I put her blood on the bare rock,
so that it would not be covered.

9 " 'Therefore this is what the Sovereign
LORD says:

" 'Woe to the city of bloodshed!
I, too, will pile the wood high.
10 So heap on the wood
and kindle the fire.
Cook the meat well,
mixing in the spices;
and let the bones be charred.
11 Then set the empty pot on the coals
till it becomes hot and its copper
glows
so its impurities may be melted
and its deposit burned away.[d]
12 It has frustrated all efforts;
its heavy deposit has not been
removed,
not even by fire.

13 " 'Now your impurity is lewdness.
Because I tried to cleanse you but you
would not be cleansed[e] from your impurity, you will not be clean again until my
wrath against you has subsided.[f]

14 " 'I the LORD have spoken.[g] The
time has come for me to act.[h] I will not
hold back; I will not have pity,[i] nor will I
relent.[j] You will be judged according to
your conduct and your actions,[k] declares
the Sovereign LORD.[l]' "

Ezekiel's Wife Dies

15 The word of the LORD came to me:
16 "Son of man, with one blow[m] I am
about to take away from you the delight
of your eyes.[n] Yet do not lament or weep
or shed any tears.[o] 17 Groan quietly;[p] do
not mourn for the dead. Keep your turban[q] fastened and your sandals[r] on your
feet; do not cover the lower part of your
face[s] or eat the customary food ⌞of
mourners⌟.[t]"

18 So I spoke to the people in the morning, and in the evening my wife died. The
next morning I did as I had been commanded.[u]

19 Then the people asked me, "Won't
you tell us what these things have to do
with us?[v]"

20 So I said to them, "The word of the

24:13 GOD, Wrath—God's wrath seeks to reform God's people, but even active wrath is not eternal. In love God restores His people. See note on 5:8–17.

24:15–24 REVELATION, Actions—Ezekiel had to endure the death of his beloved wife without the usual funeral rites and mourning. His actions were a sign to Judah of their actions at the nation's imminent destruction. See note on 12:1–6.

LORD came to me: 21Say to the house of
Israel, 'This is what the Sovereign LORD
says: I am about to desecrate my sanctuary[w]—the stronghold in which you take
pride,[x] the delight of your eyes,[y] the object of your affection. The sons and
daughters[z] you left behind will fall by the
sword.[a] 22And you will do as I have
done. You will not cover the lower part of
your face[b] or eat the customary food ⌞of
mourners⌟.[c] 23You will keep your turbans[d] on your heads and your sandals[e]
on your feet. You will not mourn[f] or
weep but will waste away[g] because of[d]
your sins and groan among yourselves.[h]
24Ezekiel[i] will be a sign[j] to you; you
will do just as he has done. When this
happens, you will know that I am the Sovereign LORD.'

25"And you, son of man, on the day I
take away their stronghold, their joy and
glory, the delight of their eyes,[k] their
heart's desire,[l] and their sons and
daughters[m] as well— 26on that day a fugitive will come to tell you[n] the news. 27At
that time your mouth will be opened; you
will speak with him and will no longer be
silent.[o] So you will be a sign to them, and
they will know that I am the LORD.[p]"

Chapter 25

A Prophecy Against Ammon

THE word of the LORD came to me:
2"Son of man, set your face against[q]
the Ammonites[r] and prophesy against
them.[s] 3Say to them, 'Hear the word of
the Sovereign LORD. This is what the Sovereign LORD says: Because you said
"Aha![t]" over my sanctuary when it was
desecrated[u] and over the land of Israel
when it was laid waste and over the people of Judah when they went into exile,[v]
4therefore I am going to give you to the
people of the East[w] as a possession. They
will set up their camps[x] and pitch their
tents among you; they will eat your fruit
and drink your milk.[y] 5I will turn Rabbah[z] into a pasture for camels and Ammon into a resting place for sheep.[a] Then
you will know that I am the LORD. 6For
this is what the Sovereign LORD says: Because you have clapped your hands[b] and
stamped your feet, rejoicing with all the
malice of your heart against the land of
Israel,[c] 7therefore I will stretch out my
hand[d] against you and give you as plunder[e] to the nations. I will cut you off
from the nations and exterminate you
from the countries. I will destroy[f] you,
and you will know that I am the
LORD.[g]' "

A Prophecy Against Moab

8"This is what the Sovereign LORD
says: 'Because Moab[h] and Seir[i] said,
"Look, the house of Judah has become
like all the other nations," 9therefore I
will expose the flank of Moab, beginning
at its frontier towns—Beth Jeshimoth[j],
Baal Meon[k] and Kiriathaim[l]—the glory
of that land. 10I will give Moab along with
the Ammonites to the people of the East
as a possession, so that the Ammonites
will not be remembered[m] among the nations; 11and I will inflict punishment on
Moab. Then they will know that I am the
LORD.' "[n]

A Prophecy Against Edom

12"This is what the Sovereign LORD
says: 'Because Edom[o] took revenge on
the house of Judah and became very
guilty by doing so, 13therefore this is what
the Sovereign LORD says: I will stretch
out my hand[p] against Edom and kill its
men and their animals.[q] I will lay it
waste, and from Teman[r] to Dedan[s] they
will fall by the sword.[t] 14I will take vengeance on Edom by the hand of my people Israel, and they will deal with Edom
in accordance with my anger[u] and my
wrath; they will know my vengeance, declares the Sovereign LORD.' "[v]

A Prophecy Against Philistia

15"This is what the Sovereign LORD
says: 'Because the Philistines[w] acted in
vengeance and took revenge with malice[x] in their hearts, and with ancient
hostility sought to destroy Judah, 16there-
fore this is what the Sovereign LORD says:
I am about to stretch out my hand against
the Philistines,[y] and I will cut off the
Kerethites[z] and destroy those remaining
along the coast.[a] 17I will carry out great
vengeance[b] on them and punish[c] them
in my wrath. Then they will know that I
am the LORD,[d] when I take vengeance on
them.[e][f]' "

24:21 [w]S Lev 26:31; S Eze 7:24 [x]S Lev 26:19 [y]S ver 16; Ps 27:4 [z]S Eze 23:25 [a]Jer 7:14,15; Hos 9:12,16; Mal 2:12 **24:22** [b]S Lev 13:45 [c]Jer 16:7 **24:23** [d]S Ex 28:39; S Isa 3:20 [e]S Isa 20:2 [f]Ex 33:4 [g]S Lev 26:16 [h]Ps 78:64 **24:24** [i]Eze 1:3 [j]S Isa 20:3; Eze 12:11 **24:25** [k]S La 2:4 [l]S Ps 20:4 [m]Dt 28:32; Jer 11:22 **24:26** [n]S 1Sa 4:12; Job 1:15-19 **24:27** [o]Da 10:15 [p]S Eze 3:26; 33:22 **25:2** [q]S Eze 13:17; 29:2 [r]S Eze 21:28 [s]Jer 49:1-6 **25:3** [t]S Ps 35:21; Eze 26:2; 36:2 [u]Zep 2:8 [v]S Pr 17:5 **25:4** [w]S Ge 25:6; S Jdg 6:3 [x]S Nu 31:10 [y]Dt 28:33,51; S Jdg 6:33 **25:5** [z]S Dt 3:11 [a]S S Isa 17:2 **25:6** [b]S Nu 24:10 [c]S Eze 6:11; Ob 1:12; Zep 2:8 **25:7** [d]Zep 1:4 [e]S Nu 14:3 [f]Eze 21:31 [g]ver 13-14,17; Am 1:14-15 **25:8** [h]S Ge 19:37; S Dt 23:6; S Isa 16:6 [i]S Ge 14:6 **25:9** [j]S Nu 33:49 [k]S Nu 32:3; S Jos 13:17 [l]S Nu 32:37; S Jos 13:19 **25:10** [m]Eze 21:32 **25:11** [n]Isa 15:9; 16:1-14; Jer 48:1; Am 2:1-3 **25:12** [o]S 2Sa 8:13-14; S 2Ch 28:17; S Isa 11:14 **25:13** [p]S Ex 7:5; S Eze 16:27 [q]Eze 29:8 [r]S Ge 36:11,15,34 [s]Jer 25:23 [t]S Jer 49:10; S Eze 14:17 **25:14** [u]Eze 35:11 [v]S Ps 137:7; Eze 32:29; 35:2-3; 36:5; Am 1:11; Ob 1:1,10-16; Mal 1:4 **25:15** [w]S Jos 13:3; S 2Ch 28:18 [x]S Ps 73:8 **25:16** [y]S 2Ch 26:6; Am 1:8 [z]S 1Sa 30:14 [a]S Eze 20:33 **25:17** [b]S Nu 31:3 [c]Jer 44:13 [d]S Ex 6:2; S 8:22 [e]S Isa 11:14 [f]S Isa 14:30; Jer 47:7; Joel 3:4

[d]23 Or *away in*

25:1—32:32 HISTORY, Universal—See note on Isa 13:1—23:18. God's judgment against the nations demonstrated His position as the only God. Gaining vengeance against the nations introduced Yahweh, the God of Israel, as Yahweh, the God of the universe (Eze 25:5,7,11,14,17; 26:6,14; 28:22, 23,24,26; 29:6,9,16,21; 30:8,19,25,26; 32:15). See note on 1 Ki 20:13.

25:14,17 GOD, Wrath—God uses human instruments to execute His wrath. See note on 5:8–17.

Chapter 26

A Prophecy Against Tyre

IN the eleventh year, on the first day of
the month, the word of the LORD came
to me:[g] 2“Son of man, because Tyre[h]
has said of Jerusalem, ‘Aha![i] The gate to
the nations is broken, and its doors have
swung open to me; now that she lies in
ruins I will prosper,’ 3therefore this is
what the Sovereign LORD says: I am
against you, O Tyre, and I will bring
many nations against you, like the sea[j]
casting up its waves. 4They will destroy[k]
the walls of Tyre[l] and pull down her
towers; I will scrape away her rubble and
make her a bare rock. 5Out in the sea[m]
she will become a place to spread fishnets,[n] for I have spoken, declares the
Sovereign LORD. She will become plunder[o] for the nations,[p] 6and her settlements on the mainland will be ravaged by
the sword. Then they will know that I am
the LORD.

7“For this is what the Sovereign LORD
says: From the north I am going to bring
against Tyre Nebuchadnezzar[e][q] king of
Babylon, king of kings,[r] with horses and
chariots,[s] with horsemen and a great
army. 8He will ravage your settlements on
the mainland with the sword; he will set
up siege works[t] against you, build a
ramp[u] up to your walls and raise his
shields against you. 9He will direct the
blows of his battering rams against your
walls and demolish your towers with his
weapons.[v] 10His horses will be so many
that they will cover you with dust. Your
walls will tremble at the noise of the war
horses, wagons and chariots[w] when he
enters your gates as men enter a city
whose walls have been broken through.
11The hoofs[x] of his horses will trample all
your streets; he will kill your people with
the sword, and your strong pillars[y] will
fall to the ground.[z] 12They will plunder
your wealth and loot your merchandise;
they will break down your walls and demolish your fine houses and throw your
stones, timber and rubble into the sea.[a]
13I will put an end[b] to your noisy songs,[c]
and the music of your harps[d] will be
heard no more.[e] 14I will make you a bare
rock, and you will become a place to
spread fishnets. You will never be rebuilt,[f] for I the LORD have spoken, declares the Sovereign LORD.

15“This is what the Sovereign LORD
says to Tyre: Will not the coastlands[g]
tremble[h] at the sound of your fall, when
the wounded groan[i] and the slaughter
takes place in you? 16Then all the princes
of the coast will step down from their
thrones and lay aside their robes and take
off their embroidered[j] garments.
Clothed[k] with terror, they will sit on the
ground,[l] trembling[m] every moment, appalled[n] at you. 17Then they will take up a
lament[o] concerning you and say to you:

“ ‘How you are destroyed, O city of
renown,
peopled by men of the sea!
You were a power on the seas,
you and your citizens;
you put your terror
on all who lived there.[p]
18Now the coastlands tremble[q]
on the day of your fall;
the islands in the sea
are terrified at your collapse.’[r]

19“This is what the Sovereign LORD
says: When I make you a desolate city,
like cities no longer inhabited, and when
I bring the ocean depths[s] over you and
its vast waters cover you,[t] 20then I will
bring you down with those who go down
to the pit,[u] to the people of long ago. I
will make you dwell in the earth below,
as in ancient ruins, with those who go
down to the pit, and you will not return
or take your place[f] in the land of the
living.[v] 21I will bring you to a horrible
end and you will be no more.[w] You will
be sought, but you will never again be
found, declares the Sovereign LORD.”[x]

Chapter 27

A Lament for Tyre

THE word of the LORD came to me:
2“Son of man, take up a lament[y]
concerning Tyre. 3Say to Tyre,[z] situated
at the gateway to the sea,[a] merchant of
peoples on many coasts, ‘This is what the
Sovereign LORD says:

“ ‘You say, O Tyre,
“I am perfect in beauty.[b]”
4Your domain was on the high seas;
your builders brought your beauty to
perfection.[c]
5They made all your timbers
of pine trees from Senir[g];[d]
they took a cedar from Lebanon[e]
to make a mast for you.
6Of oaks[f] from Bashan

26:1 [g]S Eze 24:1; 29:1; 30:20
26:2 [h]S Jos 19:29; 2Sa 5:11 [i]S Eze 25:3
26:3 [j]ver 19; Isa 5:30; Jer 50:42; 51:42
26:4 [k]S Isa 23:1,11 [l]Am 1:10
26:5 [m]Eze 27:32 [n]Eze 47:10 [o]S Nu 14:3; Eze 29:19 [p]Zec 9:2-4
26:7 [q]Jer 27:6; 39:1 [r]S Ezr 7:12 [s]S Eze 23:24; Na 2:3-4
26:8 [t]S Jer 6:6 [u]S Jer 33:4
26:9 [v]S Eze 21:22
26:10 [w]S Jer 4:13; S 46:9; S Eze 23:24
26:11 [x]Isa 5:28 [y]S Jer 43:13 [z]S Isa 26:5
26:12 [a]Isa 23:8; S Jer 4:7; Eze 27:3-27; 28:8; Hab 1:8
26:13 [b]S Jer 7:34 [c]S Isa 23:7 [d]S Ps 137:2; S Isa 14:11 [e]S Job 30:31; S Jer 16:9; S 25:10; Rev 18:22
26:14 [f]S Job 12:14; Mal 1:4
26:15 [g]Isa 41:5; Eze 27:35 [h]S Jer 49:21 [i]S Job 24:12
26:16 [j]S Ex 26:36 [k]S Job 8:22 [l]S Job 2:8,13 [m]Hos 11:10 [n]S Lev 26:32; Eze 32:10
26:17 [o]S Eze 19:1 [p]Isa 14:12
26:18 [q]S Ps 46:6; S Jer 49:21 [r]Isa 23:5; S 41:5; Eze 27:35
26:19 [s]S Ge 7:11 [t]S ver 3; Isa 8:7-8
26:20 [u]Nu 16:30; Ps 28:1; 88:6; Eze 31:14; 32:18; Am 9:2; Jnh 2:2,6 [v]S Job 28:13; S Isa 14:9-10; Eze 32:24,30
26:21 [w]S Jer 51:64; Da 11:19 [x]Jer 20:4; Eze 27:36; 28:19; Rev 18:21
27:2 [y]S Eze 19:1
27:3 [z]S Ps 83:7 [a]ver 33; Hos 9:13 [b]S Isa 23:9; S Eze 16:15
27:4 [c]Eze 28:12
27:5 [d]S Dt 3:9 [e]S Isa 2:13
27:6 [f]Nu 21:33; S Ps 29:9; Jer 22:20; Zec 11:2

[e]*7* Hebrew *Nebuchadrezzar,* of which *Nebuchadnezzar* is a variant; here and often in Ezekiel and Jeremiah [f]*20* Septuagint; Hebrew *return, and I will give glory* [g]*5* That is, Hermon

26:19–21 HUMANITY, Nature of Death—Through most of the Old Testament, death was viewed as the end of life, with no escape from its clutches. It was the final event from which there was neither escape nor return. Jesus' resurrection offered hope beyond this. See notes on 37:1–14; Isa 25:7–8; 1 Co 15:38–57.

they made your oars;
of cypress wood[h] from the coasts of
Cyprus[i g]
they made your deck, inlaid with
ivory.
7Fine embroidered linen[h] from Egypt
was your sail
and served as your banner;
your awnings were of blue and
purple[i]
from the coasts of Elishah.[j]
8Men of Sidon and Arvad[k] were your
oarsmen;
your skilled men, O Tyre, were
aboard as your seamen.[l]
9Veteran craftsmen of Gebal[j m] were on
board
as shipwrights to caulk your seams.
All the ships of the sea[n] and their
sailors
came alongside to trade for your
wares.
10" 'Men of Persia,[o] Lydia[p] and Put[q]
served as soldiers in your army.
They hung their shields[r] and helmets
on your walls,
bringing you splendor.
11Men of Arvad and Helech
manned your walls on every side;
men of Gammad
were in your towers.
They hung their shields around your
walls;
they brought your beauty to
perfection.[s]

12" 'Tarshish[t] did business with you
because of your great wealth of goods;[u]
they exchanged silver, iron, tin and lead
for your merchandise.
13" 'Greece,[v] Tubal and Meshech[w]
traded with you; they exchanged slaves[x]
and articles of bronze for your wares.
14" 'Men of Beth Togarmah[y] exchanged work horses, war horses and
mules for your merchandise.
15" 'The men of Rhodes[k z] traded with
you, and many coastlands[a] were your
customers; they paid you with ivory[b]
tusks and ebony.
16" 'Aram[l c] did business with you because of your many products; they exchanged turquoise,[d] purple fabric, embroidered work, fine linen,[e] coral[f] and
rubies for your merchandise.
17" 'Judah and Israel traded with you;
they exchanged wheat[g] from Minnith[h]
and confections,[m] honey, oil and balm[i]
for your wares.[j]
18" 'Damascus,[k] because of your many
products and great wealth of goods,[l] did
business with you in wine from Helbon
and wool from Zahar.
19" 'Danites and Greeks[m] from Uzal[n]

27:6 [g]S Ge 10:4; Isa 23:12
27:7 [h]S Ex 26:36; S Isa 19:9 [i]Ex 25:4; Jer 10:9 [j]Ge 10:4
27:8 [k]Ge 10:18 [l]1Ki 9:27
27:9 [m]S Jos 13:5 [n]S Ps 104:26
27:10 [o]2Ch 36:20; Ezr 1:1; Eze 38:5; Da 8:20 [p]S Isa 66:19 [q]S Ge 10:6; Eze 30:5; Na 3:9 [r]SS 4:4
27:11 [s]ver 27
27:12 [t]S Ge 10:4 [u]ver 18,33
27:13 [v]Joel 3:6 [w]Ge 10:2; Isa 66:19; Eze 32:26; 38:2; 39:1 [x]Rev 18:13
27:14 [y]S Ge 10:3
27:15 [z]S Ge 10:7 [a]S Jer 25:22 [b]1Ki 10:22; Rev 18:12
27:16 [c]Jdg 10:6; Isa 7:1-8 [d]Ex 28:18; 39:11; Eze 28:13 [e]S Eze 16:10 [f]Job 28:18
27:17 [g]S 1Ki 5:9 [h]Jdg 11:33 [i]S Ge 43:11 [j]Ac 12:20
27:18 [k]S Ge 14:15; Eze 47:16-18 [l]S ver 12
27:19 [m]S Ge 10:2 [n]Ge 10:27 [o]S Ex 30:24
27:20 [p]S Ge 10:7
27:21 [q]S 2Ch 9:14 [r]S Ge 25:13; Isa 21:17
27:22 [s]S Ge 10:7, 28 [t]S Ge 43:11 [u]Rev 18:12
27:23 [v]S Ge 11:26 [w]S Isa 37:12 [x]S Ge 10:22; S Nu 24:24
27:25 [y]S Ge 10:4; Isa 2:16 *fn* [z]Rev 18:3
27:26 [a]S Ge 41:6; Jer 18:17
27:27 [b]Pr 11:4 [c]Eze 28:8
27:28 [d]S Jer 49:21
27:30 [e]S Jos 7:6; S 2Sa 1:2 [f]S Jer 6:26 [g]Rev 18:18-19
27:31 [h]S Lev 13:40; S Job 1:20; S Isa 3:17; S Jer 48:37 [i]S Isa 16:9; Rev 18:15 [j]S Est 4:1; Job 3:20; Isa 22:12; Jer 6:26; S La 2:10; S Eze 7:18
27:32 [k]S Eze 19:1 [l]Isa 23:1-6; Eze 26:5

bought your merchandise; they exchanged wrought iron, cassia[o] and calamus for your wares.
20" 'Dedan[p] traded in saddle blankets
with you.
21" 'Arabia[q] and all the princes of Kedar[r] were your customers; they did business with you in lambs, rams and goats.
22" 'The merchants of Sheba[s] and Raamah traded with you; for your merchandise they exchanged the finest of all kinds
of spices[t] and precious stones, and
gold.[u]
23" 'Haran,[v] Canneh and Eden[w] and
merchants of Sheba, Asshur[x] and Kilmad
traded with you. 24In your marketplace
they traded with you beautiful garments,
blue fabric, embroidered work and multi-
colored rugs with cords twisted and tightly knotted.

25" 'The ships of Tarshish[y] serve
as carriers for your wares.
You are filled with heavy cargo
in the heart of the sea.[z]
26Your oarsmen take you
out to the high seas.
But the east wind[a] will break you to
pieces
in the heart of the sea.
27Your wealth,[b] merchandise and wares,
your mariners, seamen and
shipwrights,
your merchants and all your soldiers,
and everyone else on board
will sink into the heart of the sea[c]
on the day of your shipwreck.
28The shorelands will quake[d]
when your seamen cry out.
29All who handle the oars
will abandon their ships;
the mariners and all the seamen
will stand on the shore.
30They will raise their voice
and cry bitterly over you;
they will sprinkle dust[e] on their heads
and roll[f] in ashes.[g]
31They will shave their heads[h] because
of you
and will put on sackcloth.
They will weep[i] over you with
anguish of soul
and with bitter mourning.[j]
32As they wail and mourn over you,
they will take up a lament[k]
concerning you:
"Who was ever silenced like Tyre,
surrounded by the sea?[l]"

[h]*6* Targum; the Masoretic Text has a different division of the consonants. [i]*6* Hebrew *Kittim* [j]*9* That is, Byblos [k]*15* Septuagint; Hebrew *Dedan* [l]*16* Most Hebrew manuscripts; some Hebrew manuscripts and Syriac *Edom* [m]*17* The meaning of the Hebrew for this word is uncertain.

33When your merchandise went out on
the seas,[m]
you satisfied many nations;
with your great wealth[n] and your
wares
you enriched the kings of the earth.
34Now you are shattered by the sea
in the depths of the waters;
your wares and all your company
have gone down with you.[o]
35All who live in the coastlands[p]
are appalled[q] at you;
their kings shudder with horror
and their faces are distorted with
fear.[r]
36The merchants among the nations hiss
at you;[s]
you have come to a horrible end
and will be no more.[t] ' "

Chapter 28

A Prophecy Against the King of Tyre

THE word of the LORD came to me:
2"Son of man[u], say to the ruler of
Tyre, 'This is what the Sovereign LORD
says:

" 'In the pride of your heart
you say, "I am a god;
I sit on the throne[v] of a god
in the heart of the seas."[w]
But you are a man and not a god,
though you think you are as wise as
a god.[x]
3Are you wiser than Daniel[n]?[y]
Is no secret hidden from you?
4By your wisdom and understanding
you have gained wealth for yourself
and amassed gold and silver
in your treasuries.[z]
5By your great skill in trading[a]
you have increased your wealth,[b]
and because of your wealth
your heart has grown proud.[c]

6" 'Therefore this is what the Sovereign LORD says:

" 'Because you think you are wise,
as wise as a god,

27:33 [m]S ver 3 [n]S ver 12; Eze 28:4-5
27:34 [o]Zec 9:4
27:35 [p]S Eze 26:15 [q]S Lev 26:32; S Job 18:20 [r]S Eze 26:17-18; 32:10
27:36 [s]Jer 19:8; S 49:17; S 50:13; Zep 2:15 [t]S Ps 37:10,36; S Eze 26:21
28:2 [u]S Isa 13:11 [v]S Isa 14:13 [w]Zep 2:15 [x]S Ge 3:5; S Ps 9:20; 82:6-7; S Eze 16:49; 2Th 2:4
28:3 [y]S Eze 14:14; Da 1:20; 2:20-23, 28; 5:11-12
28:4 [z]Isa 10:13; Zec 9:3
28:5 [a]S Isa 23:8 [b]S Jer 9:23; S Eze 27:33 [c]S Job 31:25; Ps 52:7; 62:10; Hos 12:8; 13:6
28:7 [d]Eze 30:11; 31:12; 32:12; Hab 1:6 [e]Jer 9:23 [f]S Eze 7:24
28:8 [g]S Ps 55:23; Eze 32:30 [h]Rev 18:7 [i]S Eze 26:12; 27:27
28:9 [j]S Isa 31:3 [k]S Eze 16:49
28:10 [l]S 1Sa 14:6; S Jer 9:26; Eze 32:19,24
28:12 [m]S Eze 19:1 [n]Eze 27:2-4
28:13 [o]S Ge 2:8 [p]Eze 31:8-9 [q]Rev 17:4 [r]S Eze 27:16 [s]Isa 14:11; Rev 21:20
28:14 [t]Ex 30:26; 40:9 [u]Ex 25:17-20

7I am going to bring foreigners against
you,
the most ruthless of nations;[d]
they will draw their swords against
your beauty and wisdom[e]
and pierce your shining splendor.[f]
8They will bring you down to the pit,[g]
and you will die a violent death[h]
in the heart of the seas.[i]
9Will you then say, "I am a god,"
in the presence of those who kill
you?
You will be but a man, not a god,[j]
in the hands of those who slay you.[k]
10You will die the death of the
uncircumcised[l]
at the hands of foreigners.

I have spoken, declares the Sovereign
LORD.' "

11The word of the LORD came to me:
12"Son of man, take up a lament[m] concerning the king of Tyre and say to him:
'This is what the Sovereign LORD says:

" 'You were the model of perfection,
full of wisdom and perfect in
beauty.[n]
13You were in Eden,[o]
the garden of God;[p]
every precious stone[q] adorned you:
ruby, topaz and emerald,
chrysolite, onyx and jasper,
sapphire,[o] turquoise[r] and beryl.[p]
Your settings and mountings[q] were
made of gold;
on the day you were created they
were prepared.[s]
14You were anointed[t] as a guardian
cherub,[u]
for so I ordained you.
You were on the holy mount of God;
you walked among the fiery stones.
15You were blameless in your ways
from the day you were created

[n]3 Or *Danel*; the Hebrew spelling may suggest a person other than the prophet Daniel. [o]13 Or *lapis lazuli* [p]13 The precise identification of some of these precious stones is uncertain. [q]13 The meaning of the Hebrew for this phrase is uncertain.

28:1–10 GOD, One God—No human, no matter how powerful, can be compared to God. See note on 6:3–7.

28:1–10 EVIL AND SUFFERING, Punishment—The ruler of Tyre was punished for claiming to be a god. Similar claims were made by the king of Babylon. See note on Isa 14:3–23. The most powerful of humans has no reason for such pride. Pride brings punishment from God. Geographic isolation, economic power, and political alliances may seem to offer security. No sinner is secure when God decides to punish.

28:1–10 HUMANITY, Intellectual Nature—Human wisdom may enable persons to amass great fortunes. The danger is wisdom will enable persons to amass great pride, believing themselves to be beyond God's touch. God's judgment will show the weakness of such wisdom.

28:8–9 HUMANITY, Death—Humans die. God does not. Death demonstrates we are human rather than divine.

28:12–15 CREATION, Sin—The foreign prophecies represented a unique type of message from God's spokesmen. One of their favorite formats was to personify the object of their condemnation. Ezekiel compared the innocence of life in creation's garden to the king of Tyre's early days. God created him, all his wealth, and a wealth of opportunity. Sin, however, destroyed him in the same way that it made desolation of the entire world. God created a good earth, but His creature's deliberate choice to sin transformed creation into a fragmented dwelling place for coming generations. Continued wicked choices have forced us to face this same struggle as we try to live righteously in a hostile setting. Sin will do the same today that it did for Tyre's once mighty king, dragging us to the ground in sorrow and humiliation. Some Bible students see in this passage a comparison between the king of Tyre and Satan.

till wickedness was found in you.
16Through your widespread trade
you were filled with violence,[v]
and you sinned.
So I drove you in disgrace from the
mount of God,
and I expelled you, O guardian
cherub,[w]
from among the fiery stones.
17Your heart became proud[x]
on account of your beauty,
and you corrupted your wisdom
because of your splendor.
So I threw you to the earth;
I made a spectacle of you before
kings.[y]
18By your many sins and dishonest trade
you have desecrated your
sanctuaries.
So I made a fire[z] come out from you,
and it consumed you,
and I reduced you to ashes[a] on the
ground
in the sight of all who were
watching.[b]
19All the nations who knew you
are appalled[c] at you;
you have come to a horrible end
and will be no more.[d]' "

A Prophecy Against Sidon

20The word of the LORD came to me:
21"Son of man, set your face against[e] Sidon;[f] prophesy against her 22and say:
'This is what the Sovereign LORD says:

" 'I am against you, O Sidon,
and I will gain glory[g] within you.
They will know that I am the LORD,
when I inflict punishment[h] on her
and show myself holy[i] within her.
23I will send a plague upon her
and make blood flow in her streets.
The slain will fall within her,
with the sword against her on every
side.
Then they will know that I am the
LORD.[j]

24" 'No longer will the people of Israel
have malicious neighbors who are painful
briers and sharp thorns.[k] Then they will
know that I am the Sovereign LORD.
25" 'This is what the Sovereign LORD
says: When I gather[l] the people of Israel
from the nations where they have been
scattered,[m] I will show myself holy[n]
among them in the sight of the nations.
Then they will live in their own land,
which I gave to my servant Jacob.[o]
26They will live there in safety[p] and will
build houses and plant[q] vineyards; they
will live in safety when I inflict punishment[r] on all their neighbors who maligned them. Then they will know that I
am the LORD their God.[s]' "

Chapter 29

A Prophecy Against Egypt

IN the tenth year, in the tenth month on
the twelfth day, the word of the LORD
came to me:[t] 2"Son of man, set your face
against[u] Pharaoh king of Egypt[v] and
prophesy against him and against all
Egypt.[w] 3Speak to him and say: 'This is
what the Sovereign LORD says:

" 'I am against you, Pharaoh[x] king of
Egypt,
you great monster[y] lying among
your streams.
You say, "The Nile[z] is mine;
I made it for myself."
4But I will put hooks[a] in your jaws
and make the fish of your streams
stick to your scales.
I will pull you out from among your
streams,
with all the fish sticking to your
scales.[b]
5I will leave you in the desert,
you and all the fish of your streams.
You will fall on the open field
and not be gathered[c] or picked up.
I will give you as food
to the beasts of the earth and the
birds of the air.[d]

6Then all who live in Egypt will know
that I am the LORD.

" 'You have been a staff of reed[e] for
the house of Israel. 7When they grasped
you with their hands, you splintered[f]
and you tore open their shoulders; when
they leaned on you, you broke and their
backs were wrenched.[r] [g]
8" 'Therefore this is what the Sovereign LORD says: I will bring a sword
against you and kill your men and their
animals.[h] 9Egypt will become a desolate
wasteland. Then they will know that I am
the LORD.
" 'Because you said, "The Nile[i] is
mine; I made it,[j]" 10therefore I am
against you[k] and against your streams,
and I will make the land of Egypt[l] a ruin

[r] 7 Syriac (see also Septuagint and Vulgate); Hebrew *and you caused their backs to stand*

28:16 [v]S Ge 6:11; Hab 2:17 [w]S Ge 3:24
28:17 [x]Isa 10:12; Eze 16:49; 31:10 [y]S Eze 19:12
28:18 [z]Ob 1:18 [a]Mal 4:3 [b]Zec 9:2-4
28:19 [c]S Lev 26:32 [d]S Jer 51:64; S Eze 26:21
28:21 [e]S Eze 13:17 [f]S Ge 10:15; S Jer 25:22
28:22 [g]Eze 39:13 [h]Eze 30:19 [i]S Lev 10:3
28:23 [j]S Eze 5:17; 38:22
28:24 [k]S Isa 5:6; S Eze 2:6
28:25 [l]Ps 106:47; Jer 32:37 [m]S Isa 11:12 [n]S Eze 20:41 [o]Jer 12:15; 23:8; S Eze 11:17; 34:27; 37:25
28:26 [p]S Lev 25:18; S 1Ki 4:25; S Jer 17:25 [q]S Dt 20:6 [r]S Ps 149:9 [s]S Isa 65:21; S Jer 32:15; Eze 38:8; 39:26-27; Hos 2:15; 11:11; Am 9:14-15
29:1 [t]ver 17; S Eze 26:1
29:2 [u]S Eze 25:2 [v]S Jer 25:19 [w]Isa 19:1-17; Jer 46:2; Eze 30:1-26; 31:1-18; 32:1-32
29:3 [x]Jer 44:30 [y]S Ps 68:30; S 74:13; Eze 32:2 [z]S Jer 46:8
29:4 [a]S 2Ki 19:28; S Job 41:2 [b]Eze 38:4
29:5 [c]S Jer 8:2 [d]S Jer 7:33; 34:20; Eze 31:13; 32:4-6; 39:4
29:6 [e]S 2Ki 18:21
29:7 [f]2Ki 18:21; Isa 36:6 [g]Jer 17:5; Eze 17:15-17
29:8 [h]Eze 25:13; 32:11-13
29:9 [i]S Jer 46:8 [j]Eze 30:7-8,13-19
29:10 [k]S Jer 21:13 [l]S Ex 3:22

28:22 GOD, Glory—By defeating glorious, proud kingdoms, God shows all glory, honor, and prestige belong to Himself alone. See note on 1:28.

28:24–26 ELECTION, Remnant—Israel's existence after the Exile was due to God's holy love and power. He proved faithful to His elect people and restored their fortune. God created the remnant to have a people who would recognize Him as their God. God wants His people to live in trusting security not in fear of punishment.

and a desolate waste[m] from Migdol[n] to
Aswan,[o] as far as the border of Cush.[s] [p]
11No foot of man or animal will pass
through it; no one will live there for forty
years.[q] 12I will make the land of Egypt
desolate[r] among devastated lands, and
her cities will lie desolate forty years
among ruined cities. And I will disperse
the Egyptians among the nations and scatter them through the countries.[s]

13" 'Yet this is what the Sovereign
LORD says: At the end of forty years I will
gather the Egyptians from the nations
where they were scattered. 14I will bring
them back from captivity and return them
to Upper Egypt,[t] [t] the land of their ancestry. There they will be a lowly[u] kingdom.[v] 15It will be the lowliest of kingdoms and will never again exalt itself
above the other nations.[w] I will make it
so weak that it will never again rule over
the nations. 16Egypt will no longer be a
source of confidence[x] for the people of
Israel but will be a reminder[y] of their sin
in turning to her for help.[z] Then they
will know that I am the Sovereign
LORD.[a] ' "

17In the twenty-seventh year, in the
first month on the first day, the word of
the LORD came to me:[b] 18"Son of man,
Nebuchadnezzar[c] king of Babylon drove
his army in a hard campaign against Tyre;
every head was rubbed bare[d] and every
shoulder made raw.[e] Yet he and his army
got no reward from the campaign he led
against Tyre. 19Therefore this is what the
Sovereign LORD says: I am going to give
Egypt to Nebuchadnezzar king[f] of Babylon, and he will carry off its wealth. He
will loot and plunder[g] the land as pay for
his army.[h] 20I have given him Egypt[i] as
a reward for his efforts because he and
his army did it for me, declares the Sovereign LORD.[j]

21"On that day I will make a horn[u] [k]
grow for the house of Israel, and I will
open your mouth[l] among them. Then
they will know that I am the LORD.[m]"

Chapter 30

A Lament for Egypt

THE word of the LORD came to me:
2"Son of man, prophesy and say:
'This is what the Sovereign LORD says:

" 'Wail[n] and say,
"Alas for that day!"
3For the day is near,[o]
the day of the LORD[p] is near—
a day of clouds,

29:10 [m]S Jer 46:19 [n]S Ex 14:2 [o]Eze 30:6 [p]Isa 18:1; Eze 30:4
29:11 [q]Eze 32:13
29:12 [r]S Isa 34:10 [s]S Jer 46:19; Eze 30:7,23,26
29:14 [t]S Isa 11:11; Eze 30:14 [u]Eze 17:14 [v]S Isa 19:22; Jer 46:26
29:15 [w]Zec 10:11
29:16 [x]2Ch 32:10 [y]S Nu 5:15 [z]S La 4:17 [a]Isa 20:5; S 30:2; Hos 8:13
29:17 [b]S ver 1; S Eze 24:1; 30:20; 40:1
29:18 [c]Jer 27:6; 39:1 [d]S Lev 13:40; S Job 1:20; S Jer 48:37 [e]Ge 49:15
29:19 [f]S Isa 19:4 [g]S Eze 26:5 [h]Jer 43:10-13; Eze 30:4,10,24-25; 32:11
29:20 [i]S Isa 43:3 [j]Isa 10:6-7; 45:1; S Jer 25:9
29:21 [k]S Ps 132:17; S Lk 1:69 [l]Eze 33:22 [m]S Eze 3:27
30:2 [n]S Isa 13:6; Jas 5:1
30:3 [o]S Eze 7:7; Joel 1:15; 2:1,11; Ob 1:15 [p]ver 18; S Eze 7:12,19; 32:7; 34:12
30:4 [q]Jer 25:19; Da 11:43 [r]S Ge 10:6; S Eze 29:10 [s]S Eze 29:19
30:5 [t]S Eze 27:10 [u]S 2Ch 9:14 [v]Jer 25:20 [w]Na 3:9
30:6 [x]Eze 29:10
30:7 [y]S Eze 29:12
30:8 [z]S Jer 49:27; Eze 39:6; Am 1:4,7,10; Na 1:6 [a]S Eze 29:9
30:9 [b]S Ge 10:6 [c]Isa 23:5 [d]Eze 32:9-10; Zep 2:12
30:10 [e]Jer 39:1 [f]S Eze 29:19
30:11 [g]S Eze 28:7 [h]ver 24-25
30:12 [i]S Isa 19:6 [j]S Jer 46:8; Eze 29:9 [k]S Eze 19:7
30:13 [l]S Jer 43:12; S Eze 6:6

a time of doom for the nations.
4A sword will come against Egypt,[q]
and anguish will come upon
Cush.[v] [r]
When the slain fall in Egypt,
her wealth will be carried away
and her foundations torn down.[s]

5Cush and Put,[t] Lydia and all Arabia,[u]
Libya[w] and the people[v] of the covenant
land will fall by the sword along with
Egypt.[w]

6" 'This is what the LORD says:

" 'The allies of Egypt will fall
and her proud strength will fail.
From Migdol to Aswan[x]
they will fall by the sword within
her,
declares the Sovereign LORD.
7" 'They will be desolate
among desolate lands,
and their cities will lie
among ruined cities.[y]
8Then they will know that I am the
LORD,
when I set fire[z] to Egypt
and all her helpers are crushed.[a]

9" 'On that day messengers will go out
from me in ships to frighten Cush[b] out of
her complacency. Anguish[c] will take
hold of them on the day of Egypt's doom,
for it is sure to come.[d]

10" 'This is what the Sovereign LORD
says:

" 'I will put an end to the hordes of
Egypt
by the hand of Nebuchadnezzar[e]
king of Babylon.[f]
11He and his army—the most ruthless of
nations[g]—
will be brought in to destroy the
land.
They will draw their swords against
Egypt
and fill the land with the slain.[h]
12I will dry up[i] the streams of the Nile[j]
and sell the land to evil men;
by the hand of foreigners
I will lay waste[k] the land and
everything in it.

I the LORD have spoken.

13" 'This is what the Sovereign LORD
says:

" 'I will destroy the idols[l]

[s]*10* That is, the upper Nile region [t]*14* Hebrew *to Pathros* [u]*21 Horn* here symbolizes strength.
[v]*4* That is, the upper Nile region; also in verses 5 and 9 [w]*5* Hebrew *Cub*

30:13 GOD, One God—God displays His power and authority over the nations by destroying their worthless idols. See note on 6:3–7. Governments reign only as long as God allows.

and put an end to the images in
Memphis.[x] [m]
No longer will there be a prince in
Egypt,[n]
and I will spread fear throughout the
land.
14I will lay[o] waste Upper Egypt,[y]
set fire to Zoan[p]
and inflict punishment on
Thebes.[z] [q]
15I will pour out my wrath on
Pelusium,[a]
the stronghold of Egypt,
and cut off the hordes of Thebes.
16I will set fire[r] to Egypt;
Pelusium will writhe in agony.
Thebes will be taken by storm;
Memphis[s] will be in constant
distress.
17The young men of Heliopolis[b] [t] and
Bubastis[c]
will fall by the sword,
and the cities themselves will go
into captivity.
18Dark will be the day at Tahpanhes[u]
when I break the yoke of Egypt;[v]
there her proud strength will come
to an end.
She will be covered with clouds,
and her villages will go into
captivity.[w]
19So I will inflict punishment[x] on Egypt,
and they will know that I am the
LORD.' "

20In the eleventh year, in the first
month on the seventh day, the word of
the LORD came to me:[y] 21"Son of man, I
have broken the arm[z] of Pharaoh[a] king
of Egypt. It has not been bound up for
healing[b] or put in a splint so as to become strong enough to hold a sword.
22Therefore this is what the Sovereign
LORD says: I am against Pharaoh king of
Egypt.[c] I will break both his arms, the
good arm as well as the broken one, and
make the sword fall from his hand.[d] 23I
will disperse the Egyptians among the nations and scatter them through the countries.[e] 24I will strengthen[f] the arms of
the king of Babylon and put my sword[g]
in his hand, but I will break the arms of
Pharaoh, and he will groan[h] before him
like a mortally wounded man. 25I will
strengthen the arms of the king of Babylon, but the arms of Pharaoh will fall
limp. Then they will know that I am the
LORD, when I put my sword[i] into the
hand of the king of Babylon and he bran-
dishes it against Egypt.[j] 26I will disperse
the Egyptians among the nations and
scatter them through the countries.
Then they will know that I am the
LORD.[k]"

30:13 [m]S Isa 19:13 [n]Zec 10:11
30:14 [o]S Eze 29:14 [p]S Nu 13:22 [q]S Jer 46:25
30:16 [r]S Jos 7:15 [s]S Isa 19:13
30:17 [t]Ge 41:45
30:18 [u]S Jer 43:7 [v]S Lev 26:13; S Isa 9:4 [w]S ver 3
30:19 [x]Eze 28:22
30:20 [y]S Eze 26:1; S 29:17; 31:1; 32:1
30:21 [z]S Jer 48:25 [a]S Jer 44:30 [b]Jer 30:13; 46:11
30:22 [c]S Ge 15:18; S Jer 46:25 [d]Ps 37:17; Zec 11:17
30:23 [e]S Eze 29:12
30:24 [f]Zec 10:6, 12; 12:5 [g]S Eze 21:14; Zep 2:12 [h]Jer 51:52
30:25 [i]1Ch 21:12 [j]S Isa 10:5; 45:1,5; S Eze 29:19
30:26 [k]S Eze 29:12
31:1 [l]Jer 52:5 [m]S Eze 30:20; 32:17
31:3 [n]S Jer 50:18 [o]S 2Ki 19:23; Hab 2:17; Zec 11:1 [p]Isa 10:34; S Eze 19:11
31:4 [q]Eze 17:7 [r]Da 4:10
31:5 [s]ver 10 [t]S Nu 24:6; S Eze 17:5
31:6 [u]S Ge 31:7-9 [v]S Eze 17:23; S Mt 13:32
31:7 [w]S Job 14:9
31:8 [x]Ps 80:10 [y]S Ge 30:37 [z]Ge 2:8-9
31:9 [a]S Ge 2:8 [b]S Ge 13:10; Eze 28:13
31:10 [c]S Isa 2:11; S 14:13-14; S Eze 28:17
31:11 [d]Da 5:20
31:12 [e]S Eze 28:7

Chapter 31

A Cedar in Lebanon

IN the eleventh year,[l] in the third
month on the first day, the word of the
LORD came to me:[m] 2"Son of man, say to
Pharaoh king of Egypt and to his hordes:
" 'Who can be compared with you in
majesty?
3Consider Assyria,[n] once a cedar in
Lebanon,[o]
with beautiful branches
overshadowing the forest;
it towered on high,
its top above the thick foliage.[p]
4The waters[q] nourished it,
deep springs made it grow tall;
their streams flowed
all around its base
and sent their channels
to all the trees of the field.[r]
5So it towered higher[s]
than all the trees of the field;
its boughs increased
and its branches grew long,
spreading because of abundant
waters.[t]
6All the birds of the air
nested in its boughs,
all the beasts of the field
gave birth[u] under its branches;
all the great nations
lived in its shade.[v]
7It was majestic in beauty,
with its spreading boughs,
for its roots went down
to abundant waters.[w]
8The cedars[x] in the garden of God
could not rival it,
nor could the pine trees
equal its boughs,
nor could the plane trees[y]
compare with its branches—
no tree in the garden of God
could match its beauty.[z]
9I made it beautiful
with abundant branches,
the envy of all the trees of Eden[a]
in the garden of God.[b]

10" 'Therefore this is what the Sovereign LORD says: Because it towered on
high, lifting its top above the thick foliage, and because it was proud[c] of its
height, 11I handed it over to the ruler of
the nations, for him to deal with according to its wickedness. I cast it aside,[d]
12and the most ruthless of foreign nations[e] cut it down and left it. Its boughs
fell on the mountains and in all the val-

[x] *13* Hebrew *Noph;* also in verse 16 [y] *14* Hebrew *waste Pathros* [z] *14* Hebrew *No;* also in verses 15 and 16 [a] *15* Hebrew *Sin;* also in verse 16 [b] *17* Hebrew *Awen* (or *On*) [c] *17* Hebrew *Pi Beseth*

leys;[f] its branches lay broken in all the
ravines of the land. All the nations of the
earth came out from under its shade and
left it.[g] 13All the birds of the air settled
on the fallen tree, and all the beasts of the
field were among its branches.[h] 14There-
fore no other trees by the waters are ever
to tower proudly on high, lifting their
tops above the thick foliage. No other
trees so well-watered are ever to reach
such a height; they are all destined[i] for
death,[j] for the earth below, among mortal men, with those who go down to the
pit.[k]
15" 'This is what the Sovereign LORD
says: On the day it was brought down to
the grave[d] I covered the deep springs
with mourning for it; I held back its
streams, and its abundant waters were restrained. Because of it I clothed Lebanon
with gloom, and all the trees of the field
withered away.[l] 16I made the nations
tremble[m] at the sound of its fall when I
brought it down to the grave with those
who go down to the pit. Then all the
trees[n] of Eden,[o] the choicest and best of
Lebanon, all the trees that were well-watered, were consoled[p] in the earth below.[q] 17Those who lived in its shade, its
allies among the nations, had also gone
down to the grave with it, joining those
killed by the sword.[r]
18" 'Which of the trees of Eden can be
compared with you in splendor and majesty? Yet you, too, will be brought down
with the trees of Eden to the earth below;
you will lie among the uncircumcised,[s]
with those killed by the sword.
" 'This is Pharaoh and all his hordes,
declares the Sovereign LORD.' "

Chapter 32

A Lament for Pharaoh

IN the twelfth year, in the twelfth
month on the first day, the word of the
LORD came to me:[t] 2"Son of man, take
up a lament[u] concerning Pharaoh king of
Egypt and say to him:

" 'You are like a lion[v] among the
nations;
you are like a monster[w] in the seas[x]
thrashing about in your streams,
churning the water with your feet
and muddying the streams.[y]

3" 'This is what the Sovereign LORD
says:

" 'With a great throng of people
I will cast my net over you,
and they will haul you up in my
net.[z]
4I will throw you on the land

31:12 [f]Eze 32:5; 35:8 [g]Eze 32:11-12; Da 4:14
31:13 [h]S Isa 18:6; S Eze 29:5; 32:4
31:14 [i]S Ps 49:14 [j]S Ps 82:7 [k]S Nu 14:11; Ps 63:9; S Eze 26:20; 32:24
31:15 [l]S 2Sa 1:21
31:16 [m]S Jer 49:21 [n]S Isa 14:8 [o]S Ge 2:8 [p]S Eze 14:22 [q]S Isa 14:15; Eze 32:18
31:17 [r]Ps 9:17
31:18 [s]S Jer 9:26
32:1 [t]S Eze 31:1; 33:21
32:2 [u]2Sa 1:17; 3:33; 2Ch 35:25; S Eze 19:1 [v]S 2Ki 24:1; Na 2:11-13 [w]S Job 3:8; S Ps 74:13 [x]S Ge 1:21 [y]ver 13; Job 41:31; S Eze 29:3; 34:18
32:3 [z]S Eze 12:13; Hab 1:15
32:4 [a]S Isa 18:6; Eze 31:12-13; 39:4-5,17
32:5 [b]S Eze 31:12
32:6 [c]S Isa 34:3 [d]S Eze 29:5
32:7 [e]S Isa 13:10; 34:4; S Eze 30:3; Joel 2:2,31; 3:15; S Mt 24:29; Rev 8:12
32:8 [f]S Ps 102:26 [g]S Job 9:7; S Jer 4:23; Joel 2:10
32:10 [h]S Isa 30:32 [i]S Jer 46:10 [j]S Eze 26:16; S 27:35; 30:9; Rev 18:9-10
32:11 [k]S Eze 21:19 [l]S Isa 19:4; S Jer 46:13 [m]S Eze 29:19
32:12 [n]S Eze 28:7 [o]Eze 31:11-12
32:13 [p]S ver 2; S Eze 29:8,11

and hurl you on the open field.
I will let all the birds of the air settle
on you
and all the beasts of the earth gorge
themselves on you.[a]
5I will spread your flesh on the
mountains
and fill the valleys[b] with your
remains.
6I will drench the land with your
flowing blood[c]
all the way to the mountains,
and the ravines will be filled with
your flesh.[d]
7When I snuff you out, I will cover the
heavens
and darken their stars;
I will cover the sun with a cloud,
and the moon will not give its
light.[e]
8All the shining lights in the heavens
I will darken[f] over you;
I will bring darkness over your
land,[g]
declares the Sovereign LORD.
9I will trouble the hearts of many
peoples
when I bring about your destruction
among the nations,
among[e] lands you have not known.
10I will cause many peoples to be
appalled at you,
and their kings will shudder with
horror because of you
when I brandish my sword[h] before
them.
On the day[i] of your downfall
each of them will tremble
every moment for his life.[j]

11" 'For this is what the Sovereign
LORD says:

" 'The sword[k] of the king of Babylon[l]
will come against you.[m]
12I will cause your hordes to fall
by the swords of mighty men—
the most ruthless of all nations.[n]
They will shatter the pride of Egypt,
and all her hordes will be
overthrown.[o]
13I will destroy all her cattle
from beside abundant waters
no longer to be stirred by the foot of
man
or muddied by the hoofs of cattle.[p]
14Then I will let her waters settle
and make her streams flow like oil,
declares the Sovereign LORD.
15When I make Egypt desolate
and strip the land of everything in it,
when I strike down all who live there,

[d] *15* Hebrew *Sheol;* also in verses 16 and 17
[e] *9* Hebrew; Septuagint *bring you into captivity among the nations, / to*

then they will know that I am the
LORD.[q]'

[16]"This is the lament[r] they will chant
for her. The daughters of the nations will
chant it; for Egypt and all her hordes they
will chant it, declares the Sovereign
LORD."

[17]In the twelfth year, on the fifteenth
day of the month, the word of the LORD
came to me:[s] [18]"Son of man, wail for the
hordes of Egypt and consign[t] to the earth
below both her and the daughters of
mighty nations, with those who go down
to the pit.[u] [19]Say to them, 'Are you more
favored than others? Go down and be laid
among the uncircumcised.'[v] [20]They will
fall among those killed by the sword. The
sword is drawn; let her be dragged[w] off
with all her hordes.[x] [21]From within the
grave[f][y] the mighty leaders will say of
Egypt and her allies, 'They have come
down and they lie with the uncircumcised,[z] with those killed by the sword.'
[22]"Assyria is there with her whole
army; she is surrounded by the graves of
all her slain, all who have fallen by the
sword. [23]Their graves are in the depths of
the pit[a] and her army lies around her
grave.[b] All who had spread terror in the
land of the living are slain, fallen by the
sword.
[24]"Elam[c] is there, with all her hordes
around her grave. All of them are slain,
fallen by the sword.[d] All who had spread
terror in the land of the living[e] went
down uncircumcised to the earth below.
They bear their shame with those who go
down to the pit.[f] [25]A bed is made for her
among the slain, with all her hordes
around her grave. All of them are uncircumcised,[g] killed by the sword. Because
their terror had spread in the land of the
living, they bear their shame with those
who go down to the pit; they are laid
among the slain.
[26]"Meshech and Tubal[h] are there,
with all their hordes around their graves.
All of them are uncircumcised, killed by
the sword because they spread their terror in the land of the living. [27]Do they not
lie with the other uncircumcised[i] warriors who have fallen, who went down to
the grave with their weapons of war,
whose swords were placed under their
heads? The punishment for their sins
rested on their bones, though the terror
of these warriors had stalked through the
land of the living.
[28]"You too, O Pharaoh, will be broken
and will lie among the uncircumcised,
with those killed by the sword.
[29]"Edom[j] is there, her kings and all
her princes; despite their power, they are
laid with those killed by the sword. They
lie with the uncircumcised, with those
who go down to the pit.[k]
[30]"All the princes of the north[l] and all
the Sidonians[m] are there; they went
down with the slain in disgrace despite
the terror caused by their power. They lie
uncircumcised[n] with those killed by the
sword and bear their shame with those
who go down to the pit.[o]
[31]"Pharaoh—he and all his army—will
see them and he will be consoled[p] for all
his hordes that were killed by the sword,
declares the Sovereign LORD. [32]Although I
had him spread terror in the land of the
living, Pharaoh[q] and all his hordes will
be laid among the uncircumcised, with
those killed by the sword, declares the
Sovereign LORD."[r]

Chapter 33

Ezekiel a Watchman

THE word of the LORD came to me:
[2]"Son of man, speak to your countrymen and say to them: 'When I bring the
sword[s] against a land, and the people of
the land choose one of their men and
make him their watchman,[t] [3]and he sees
the sword coming against the land and
blows the trumpet[u] to warn the people,
[4]then if anyone hears the trumpet but
does not take warning[v] and the sword

32:15 [q]Ex 7:5; S 14:4,18; Ps 107:33-34
32:16 [r]S Ge 50:10; S Eze 19:1
32:17 [s]S ver 1
32:18 [t]Jer 1:10 [u]Eze 26:20; S 31:14,16; Mic 1:8
32:19 [v]ver 29-30; S Eze 28:10
32:20 [w]Ps 28:3 [x]Eze 31:17-18
32:21 [y]S Isa 14:9 [z]Eze 28:10
32:23 [a]S Isa 14:15 [b]Na 1:14
32:24 [c]S Ge 10:22 [d]S Jer 49:37 [e]S Job 28:13 [f]S Eze 26:20
32:25 [g]Eze 28:10
32:26 [h]S Eze 27:13
32:27 [i]Eze 28:10
32:29 [j]S Ps 137:7; Isa 34:5-15; Jer 49:7; Eze 35:15; Ob 1:1 [k]Eze 25:12-14
32:30 [l]S Isa 14:31; Jer 25:26; Eze 38:6; 39:2 [m]S Ge 10:15; S Jer 25:22 [n]Eze 28:10 [o]S Eze 26:20; S 28:8
32:31 [p]S Eze 14:22
32:32 [q]S Jer 44:30 [r]S Job 3:14
33:2 [s]S Lev 26:25; S Jer 12:12 [t]S 1Sa 14:16; Isa 21:6-9; S Jer 51:12
33:3 [u]S Ex 20:18; S Nu 10:7; Hos 5:8; 8:1
33:4 [v]2Ch 25:16

[f]*21* Hebrew *Sheol*; also in verse 27

32:17–32 HUMANITY, Nature of Death—Human rulers and armies may spread terror over the world. Their great power cannot save them from suffering the same destiny they handed out to others. The world's most terrifying leaders also die.

32:21,27 LAST THINGS, Intermediate State—See note on Isa 14:9.

33:1–20 EVIL AND SUFFERING, Deserved—The complex chain of responsibility for sin and suffering is clarified here. People are responsible for their own sin. See note on 18:1–32. Sin does not bring irreversible responsibility. God forgives those who repent. Those who do not repent find themselves being destroyed by guilt, evil's natural results, and God's punishment. To repent, a person must have a clear understanding of personal guilt and responsibility. God calls His people to stand watch and warn sinners. God's commission makes us responsible for our sins and gives us responsibility for those we are to warn (Gal 6:1–5).

33:1–20 HUMANITY, Responsibility—Sin against God leads to death. God introduced Ezekiel to a new angle of the relationship. Those entrusted with God's message of grace are responsible for sharing it. Not to share God's message is sin. To rest on one's righteous laurels and quit being righteous is sin. To accuse God continually of injustice is sin. Each person is responsible for personal sin. God invites each of us to turn back to Him in repentance. We are responsible if we do not. See note on 3:16–21.

33:1–20 SIN, Responsibility—Punishment, destruction, and death are not God's will for the sinner. God seeks repentance and life, but He lets the sinner choose freely between sin/death and obedience/life. See notes on 3:16–21; 18:1–32.

comes and takes his life, his blood will be
on his own head.[w] [5]Since he heard the
sound of the trumpet but did not take
warning, his blood will be on his own
head.[x] If he had taken warning, he
would have saved himself.[y] [6]But if the
watchman sees the sword coming and
does not blow the trumpet to warn the
people and the sword comes and takes
the life of one of them, that man will be
taken away because of his sin, but I will
hold the watchman accountable for his
blood.'[z]

[7]"Son of man, I have made you a
watchman[a] for the house of Israel; so
hear the word I speak and give them
warning from me.[b] [8]When I say to the
wicked, 'O wicked man, you will surely
die,[c]' and you do not speak out to dissuade him from his ways, that wicked
man will die for[g] his sin, and I will hold
you accountable for his blood.[d] [9]But if
you do warn the wicked man to turn from
his ways and he does not do so,[e] he will
die for his sin, but you will have saved
yourself.[f]

[10]"Son of man, say to the house of Israel, 'This is what you are saying: "Our offenses and sins weigh us down, and we
are wasting away[g] because of[h] them.
How then can we live?[h]" ' [11]Say to them,
'As surely as I live, declares the Sovereign
LORD, I take no pleasure in the death of
the wicked, but rather that they turn
from their ways and live.[i] Turn![j] Turn
from your evil ways! Why will you die, O
house of Israel?'[k]

[12]"Therefore, son of man, say to your
countrymen,[l] 'The righteousness of the
righteous man will not save him when he
disobeys, and the wickedness of the wicked man will not cause him to fall when he
turns from it. The righteous man, if he
sins, will not be allowed to live because
of his former righteousness.'[m] [13]If I tell
the righteous man that he will surely live,
but then he trusts in his righteousness
and does evil, none of the righteous
things he has done will be remembered;
he will die for the evil he has done.[n]
[14]And if I say to the wicked man, 'You
will surely die,' but he then turns away

33:4 [w]S Lev 20:9; S Jer 6:17; Zec 1:4; Ac 18:6
33:5 [x]S Lev 20:9 [y]S Ex 9:21
33:6 [z]Isa 56:10-11; S Eze 3:18
33:7 [a]S Isa 52:8 [b]Jer 1:17; 26:2
33:8 [c]ver 14 [d]S Isa 3:11; S Eze 18:4
33:9 [e]S Ps 7:12 [f]Eze 3:17-19
33:10 [g]S Lev 26:16 [h]S Lev 26:39; S Eze 4:17
33:11 [i]S La 3:33 [j]S 2Ch 30:9; S Isa 19:22; S Jer 3:12 [k]Jer 44:7-8; S Eze 18:23; Hos 11:8; Joel 2:12; S 1Ti 2:4
33:12 [l]ver 2 [m]2Ch 7:14; S Eze 3:20; S 18:21
33:13 [n]Heb 10:38; 2Pe 2:20-21
33:14 [o]S Jer 22:3
33:15 [p]S Ex 22:26 [q]Ex 22:1-4; S Lev 6:2-5 [r]Isa 55:7; Jer 18:7-8; S Lk 19:8
33:16 [s]S Jer 50:20 [t]S Isa 43:25
33:18 [u]Jer 18:10 [v]S Eze 3:20
33:19 [w]S ver 14-15
33:20 [x]S Job 34:11
33:21 [y]Eze 24:26 [z]S 2Ki 25:4,10; Jer 39:1-2; 52:4-7; S Eze 32:1
33:22 [a]S Eze 1:3 [b]Eze 29:21; Lk 1:64 [c]Eze 3:26-27; S 24:27
33:24 [d]Eze 36:4 [e]S Dt 1:10 [f]Isa 51:2; Jer 40:7; Eze 11:15; Lk 3:8; Ac 7:5
33:25 [g]Jer 7:21 [h]S Ge 9:4 [i]Jer 7:9-10; S Eze 22:6,27
33:26 [j]Jer 41:7 [k]Eze 22:11

from his sin and does what is just[o] and
right— [15]if he gives back what he took in
pledge[p] for a loan, returns what he has
stolen,[q] follows the decrees that give life,
and does no evil, he will surely live; he
will not die.[r] [16]None of the sins[s] he has
committed will be remembered against
him. He has done what is just and right;
he will surely live.[t]

[17]"Yet your countrymen say, 'The way
of the Lord is not just.' But it is their way
that is not just. [18]If a righteous man turns
from his righteousness and does evil,[u] he
will die for it.[v] [19]And if a wicked man
turns away from his wickedness and does
what is just and right, he will live by doing so.[w] [20]Yet, O house of Israel, you say,
'The way of the Lord is not just.' But I
will judge each of you according to his
own ways."[x]

Jerusalem's Fall Explained

[21]In the twelfth year of our exile, in the
tenth month on the fifth day, a man who
had escaped[y] from Jerusalem came to me
and said, "The city has fallen![z]" [22]Now
the evening before the man arrived, the
hand of the LORD was upon me,[a] and he
opened my mouth[b] before the man came
to me in the morning. So my mouth was
opened and I was no longer silent.[c]

[23]Then the word of the LORD came to
me: [24]"Son of man, the people living in
those ruins[d] in the land of Israel are saying, 'Abraham was only one man, yet he
possessed the land. But we are many;[e]
surely the land has been given to us as
our possession.'[f] [25]Therefore say to
them, 'This is what the Sovereign LORD
says: Since you eat[g] meat with the
blood[h] still in it and look to your idols
and shed blood, should you then possess
the land?[i] [26]You rely on your sword, you
do detestable things,[j] and each of you
defiles his neighbor's wife.[k] Should you
then possess the land?'

[27]"Say this to them: 'This is what the
Sovereign LORD says: As surely as I live,
those who are left in the ruins will fall by
the sword, those out in the country I will

[g]*8* Or *in;* also in verse 9 [h]*10* Or *away in*

33:11 GOD, Grace—This passage suggests the priority of God's grace over His wrath. Wrath comes only when the purposes of grace and love are rejected. His first desire is our repentance.

33:13 SALVATION, Belief—See notes on 11:18–21; Hab 2:4. Trusting in our own righteousness to save us is like trusting in filthy rags. The prophet here emphasizes God's justice rather than His mercy. V 14 balances what is said. Salvation changes the heart and leads to obedient trust in God. Compare Eze 18:24.

33:17–20 GOD, Justice—God's grace is not cause to condemn Him as unjust. See note on 18:25–32.

33:21–25 REVELATION, Messengers—Those who speak for God reveal God's purposes at His command and remain silent until God's chosen time to reveal and explain. God silenced His spokesman until the fall of Jerusalem. Then He opened a new era in the prophet's career. Compare 3:22–27; 24:25–27.

33:23–33 HISTORY, Judgment—See note on Isa 1:24–26. History does not guarantee God's blessings. A people who do not live according to God's will so clearly revealed in history cannot expect to receive the blessings enjoyed by the patriarchs. Judgment is the only expectation for disobedient people. Judgment justifies the thankless work of God's messenger.

33:25–29 SIN, Intervention—See note on 11:1–12.

give to the wild animals to be devoured,
and those in strongholds and caves will
die of a plague.[l] 28I will make the land a
desolate waste, and her proud strength
will come to an end, and the mountains[m]
of Israel will become desolate so that no
one will cross them.[n] 29Then they will
know that I am the LORD, when I have
made the land a desolate[o] waste because
of all the detestable things they have
done.'[p]
30"As for you, son of man, your countrymen are talking together about you by
the walls and at the doors of the houses,
saying to each other, 'Come and hear the
message that has come from the LORD.'
31My people come to you, as they usually
do, and sit before[q] you to listen to your
words, but they do not put them into
practice. With their mouths they express
devotion, but their hearts are greedy[r] for
unjust gain.[s] 32Indeed, to them you are
nothing more than one who sings love
songs[t] with a beautiful voice and plays
an instrument well, for they hear your
words but do not put them into practice.[u]
33"When all this comes true—and it
surely will—then they will know that a
prophet has been among them.[v]"

Chapter 34

Shepherds and Sheep

THE word of the LORD came to me:
2"Son of man, prophesy against the
shepherds of Israel; prophesy and say to
them: 'This is what the Sovereign LORD
says: Woe to the shepherds of Israel who
only take care of themselves! Should not
shepherds take care of the flock?[w] 3You
eat the curds, clothe yourselves with the
wool and slaughter the choice animals,
but you do not take care of the flock.[x]
4You have not strengthened the weak or
healed[y] the sick or bound up[z] the injured. You have not brought back the
strays or searched for the lost. You have
ruled them harshly and brutally.[a] 5So
they were scattered because there was no
shepherd,[b] and when they were scattered they became food for all the wild
animals.[c] 6My sheep wandered over all
the mountains and on every high hill.[d]
They were scattered[e] over the whole
earth, and no one searched or looked for
them.[f]
7" 'Therefore, you shepherds, hear the
word of the LORD: 8As surely as I live,
declares the Sovereign LORD, because my
flock lacks a shepherd and so has been
plundered[g] and has become food for all
the wild animals,[h] and because my shepherds did not search for my flock but
cared for themselves rather than for my
flock,[i] 9therefore, O shepherds, hear the
word of the LORD: 10This is what the Sovereign LORD says: I am against[j] the shepherds and will hold them accountable for
my flock. I will remove them from tending the flock so that the shepherds can no
longer feed themselves. I will rescue[k] my
flock from their mouths, and it will no
longer be food for them.[l]
11" 'For this is what the Sovereign
LORD says: I myself will search for my
sheep[m] and look after them. 12As a shepherd[n] looks after his scattered flock
when he is with them, so will I look after
my sheep. I will rescue them from all the
places where they were scattered on a
day of clouds and darkness.[o] 13I will
bring them out from the nations and gather[p] them from the countries, and I will
bring them into their own land.[q r s t] I
will pasture them on the mountains of
Israel, in the ravines and in all the settlements in the land.[u v w] 14I will tend them
in a good pasture, and the mountain
heights of Israel[x] will be their grazing
land. There they will lie down in good
grazing land, and there they will feed in a
rich pasture[y] on the mountains of Israel.[z] 15I myself will tend my sheep and
have them lie down,[a] declares the Sovereign LORD.[b] 16I will search for the lost
and bring back the strays. I will bind up[c]
the injured and strengthen the weak,[d]
but the sleek and the strong I will destroy.[e] I will shepherd the flock with justice.[f]
17" 'As for you, my flock, this is what

33:27 [l]1Sa 13:6; Isa 2:19; S Jer 42:22; S Eze 7:15; S 14:21; 39:4
33:28 [m]S Isa 41:15 [n]S Ge 6:7; Jer 9:10
33:29 [o]S Lev 26:34 [p]S Jer 18:16; S 44:22; Eze 36:4; Mic 7:13
33:31 [q]S Eze 8:1 [r]Ps 119:36 [s]Ps 78:36-37; S Isa 29:13; S 33:15; S Jer 3:10; S 6:17; S Eze 22:27; Mt 13:22; 1Jn 3:18
33:32 [t]S 1Ki 4:32 [u]Mk 6:20
33:33 [v]S 1Sa 3:20; S Jer 28:9; S Eze 2:5
34:2 [w]Ps 78:70-72; Isa 40:11; Jer 3:15; S 23:1; Mic 3:11; Jn 10:11; 21:15-17; Jude 1:12
34:3 [x]Isa 56:11; S Eze 22:27; Am 6:4; Zec 11:5
34:4 [y]S Isa 3:7 [z]S Isa 1:6 [a]ver 16; S Lev 25:43; Mic 3:3; Zec 11:15-17
34:5 [b]S Nu 27:17 [c]ver 28; S Isa 56:9; Ac 20:29
34:6 [d]S Jer 50:6 [e]S Lev 26:33; S Ps 95:10; S Jer 10:21 [f]2Ch 18:16; Ps 142:4; Hos 7:13; S Mt 9:36; 18:12-13; Lk 15:5; 1Pe 2:25
34:8 [g]S Jdg 2:14 [h]S Isa 56:9 [i]Jude 1:12
34:10 [j]S Jer 21:13 [k]S Ps 72:14 [l]1Sa 2:29-30; S Jer 23:2; Zec 10:3
34:11 [m]S Ps 119:176
34:12 [n]Isa 40:11; S Jer 31:10; Zec 10:3; Lk 19:10 [o]S Eze 32:7
34:13 [p]S Ge 48:21; S Dt 30:4 [q]Mic 4:6 [r]S Eze 11:17 [s]S Jer 23:8 [t]S Isa 66:20 [u]S Eze 28:25; 36:24 [v]S Jer 50:19 [w]Jer 23:3
34:14 [x]S Eze 20:40 [y]Ps 23:2; S 37:3 [z]S Isa 65:10; Eze 36:29-30; 37:22; Am 9:14; Mic 7:14
34:15 [a]Zep 3:13 [b]Ps 23:1-2; S Jer 33:12; Mic 5:4
34:16 [c]S Ps 147:3 [d]Mic 4:6; Zep 3:19 [e]Lk 19:10 [f]Isa 10:16; S Jer 31:8; Lk 5:32

33:31 CHRISTIAN ETHICS, Property Rights—True religion is more than mere ritual. Attitudes changed and actions which match are the signs of God working in one's inner being.
34:1–30 GOD, Savior—Human rulers are appointed to care for the needs of their people. Too often they only feed on their oppressed people. God never takes advantage of His people. He is the Good Shepherd who works to meet our every need. He is our Savior. This whole chapter suggests the loving heart of God who wants above all else to be Savior to His people. See note on Jer 50:34.
34:1–24 THE CHURCH, God's Community—God describes His people in tender terms as His sheep. He cares for His sheep, condemning shepherds (leaders) who lead the sheep astray. The Lord loves His people and provides leaders who will protect them. He condemns and punishes selfish leaders who have profited at the expense of other people. God knows the weaknesses of His people and protects us. He promised to send a new David to lead His people. Jesus did come as the Good Shepherd (Jn 10:11).
34:17–20 HUMANITY, Relationships—Responsibility does not end with the effect of my acts on my own life. My acts can have significant impact upon others. I am responsible for the harm my acts cause other people. Leaders bear responsibility for the harm they inflict on their followers. Oppression and injustice are two sins the prophets condemn the most.
34:17–31 SALVATION, Blessing—Ezekiel judged Isra-

the Sovereign LORD says: I will judge between one sheep and another, and between rams and goats.[g] 18Is it not
enough[h] for you to feed on the good pasture? Must you also trample the rest of
your pasture with your feet?[i] Is it not
enough for you to drink clear water?
Must you also muddy the rest with your
feet? 19Must my flock feed on what you
have trampled and drink what you have
muddied with your feet?
20" 'Therefore this is what the Sovereign LORD says to them: See, I myself will
judge between the fat sheep and the lean
sheep.[j] 21Because you shove with flank
and shoulder, butting all the weak sheep
with your horns[k] until you have driven
them away, 22I will save my flock, and
they will no longer be plundered. I will
judge between one sheep and another.[l]
23I will place over them one shepherd,
my servant David, and he will tend[m]
them; he will tend them and be their
shepherd.[n] 24I the LORD will be their
God,[o] and my servant David[p] will be
prince among them.[q] I the LORD have
spoken.[r]
25" 'I will make a covenant[s] of peace[t]
with them and rid the land of wild
beasts[u] so that they may live in the
desert and sleep in the forests in safety.[v]
26I will bless[w] them and the places surrounding my hill.[1] I will send down
showers in season;[x] there will be showers of blessing.[y] 27The trees of the field
will yield their fruit[z] and the ground will
yield its crops;[a] the people will be secure[b] in their land. They will know that I
am the LORD, when I break the bars of
their yoke[c] and rescue them from the
hands of those who enslaved them.[d]
28They will no longer be plundered by the
nations, nor will wild animals devour
them. They will live in safety,[e] and no
one will make them afraid.[f] 29I will provide for them a land renowned[g] for its
crops, and they will no longer be victims
of famine[h] in the land or bear the scorn[i]
of the nations.[j] 30Then they will know
that I, the LORD their God, am with them
and that they, the house of Israel, are my
people, declares the Sovereign LORD.[k]
31You my sheep,[l] the sheep of my pasture,[m] are people, and I am your God,
declares the Sovereign LORD.' "

Chapter 35

A Prophecy Against Edom

THE word of the LORD came to me:
2"Son of man, set your face against
Mount Seir;[n] prophesy against it 3and
say: 'This is what the Sovereign LORD
says: I am against you, Mount Seir, and I
will stretch out my hand[o] against you
and make you a desolate waste.[p] 4I will
turn your towns into ruins[q] and you will
be desolate. Then you will know that I am
the LORD.[r]

34:17 [g]Mt 25:32-33 **34:18** [h]S Ge 30:15 [i]S Eze 32:2 **34:20** [j]Mt 25:32 **34:21** [k]S Dt 33:17 **34:22** [l]Ps 72:12-14; Jer 23:2-3; Eze 20:37-38 **34:23** [m]Isa 40:11 [n]S Isa 31:4; Mic 5:4 **34:24** [o]Eze 36:28 [p]Ps 89:49 [q]S Isa 53:4; Zec 13:7 [r]Jer 23:4-5; S 30:9; S 33:14; Jn 10:16; Rev 7:17 **34:25** [s]S Eze 16:62 [t]S Nu 25:12 [u]Lev 26:6 [v]S Lev 25:18; Isa 11:6-9; Hos 2:18 **34:26** [w]S Ge 12:2 [x]Ps 68:9; Joel 2:23 [y]Dt 11:13-15; S 28:12; Isa 44:3 **34:27** [z]S Ps 72:16 [a]S Job 14:9; S Ps 67:6 [b]S Nu 24:21 [c]S Lev 26:13 [d]S Jer 30:8; S Eze 20:42; S 28:25 **34:28** [e]S Jer 32:37 [f]S Jer 30:10; S Eze 28:26; 39:26; Hos 11:11; Am 9:15; Zep 3:13; Zec 14:11 **34:29** [g]S Isa 4:2 [h]Eze 36:29 [i]S Ps 137:3; Eze 36:6; Joel 2:19 [j]Eze 36:15 **34:30** [k]S Eze 14:11; 37:27 **34:31** [l]S Ps 28:9 [m]S Jer 23:1 **35:2** [n]S Ge 14:6 **35:3** [o]S Jer 6:12 [p]S Isa 34:10; Eze 25:12-14

35:4 [q]Jer 44:2 [r]ver 9; S Jer 49:10

[1]26 Or *I will make them and the places surrounding my hill a blessing*

el's rulers, often called shepherds in near eastern culture. God promised to become the Shepherd and send a new King from David's line to tend His people. This blessing would also transform nature so nothing would threaten His people. This messianic prophecy was fulfilled only through Jesus Christ. Compare 37:26; Isa 54:10.

34:23–24 JESUS CHRIST, Foretold—Ezekiel did not invent shepherd imagery (Ps 23; Isa 40:10–11; Jer 23:1–6). Compare Zec 13:7; Mt 18:12–14. Ezekiel did see his people scattered to the winds and looked to God to shepherd them home. Jesus is the tender Shepherd who cares for His people's wounds. See note on Jer 30:9. Compare Jn 10:1–18.

34:24,30–31 GOD, Personal—God is as closely related to us as a shepherd is to the sheep. See note on Jer 30:22.

34:25–31 CREATION, Freedom—Ezekiel's first 24 chapters, delivered between 592 and 586 BC, told the people that the captivity would be a long one. He warned those in Babylon they would not be returning shortly to Jerusalem and declared forcefully to those in Jerusalem that they would be exiled to Babylon soon. After the final fall of Jerusalem in 587 BC, Ezekiel became a comforter. He delivered oracles against Israel's enemies (chs 25—32). See also prophecies of hope (chs 33—48). The message concerning Israel's shepherds condemned the unfaithful leaders but closed with a promise that God would gather the sheep and give them a new leader. God had decreed their punishment, but He remained free to revoke His sentence. He caused the land to suffer when the people sinned, but He was free to restore it to beauty and productivity. God promised them protection so they could fulfill His redemptive purpose in the world He created. Because God has perfect freedom, He can adopt any method He chooses to implement His plan for the world's salvation. Though Israel was often far from what He wished for them to be, God used them to produce the Messiah, our Good Shepherd. That was one reason He brought Israel back from Babylonian Exile.

34:25–31 REVELATION, Author of Creation—God promised a lasting peace for His children. The land and the people would one day live in harmony. Creation's renewed safety would reveal God at work and present among them as their protecting and leading Shepherd.

34:25–31 ELECTION, God's Purpose—Bad leadership could not prevent God from achieving His election purposes. He judged and disciplined false kings, prophets, and priests to establish Himself as the Good Shepherd and prepare the way for the new David with a covenant of peace. God wants a secure people enjoying His blessings because they serve Him faithfully. The basis of security is God's presence. Over seventy times Ezekiel used the recognition formula "You will know that I am Yahweh" to show God's election purpose of introducing Himself to and seeking personal relationship with His people.

34:25–31 THE CHURCH, Covenant People—God's promises include a covenant of peace which insures God's blessings for His people. Instead of an unproductive land filled with uncertainty concerning daily bread, God gives the blessings of the good land to His people. When God fulfills all these promises, the people will know He is God. See note on 36:28.

35:1–15 GOD, Sovereignty—God works against guilty nations to reveal His divine power to all people. No power can prevent God from accomplishing His purposes. See note on 1:25–28.

35:1–15 HISTORY, Universal—See note on 25:1—32:32.

5“ ‘Because you harbored an ancient
hostility and delivered the Israelites over
to the sword[s] at the time of their calamity,[t] the time their punishment reached
its climax,[u] 6therefore as surely as I live,
declares the Sovereign LORD, I will give
you over to bloodshed[v] and it will pursue
you.[w] Since you did not hate bloodshed,
bloodshed will pursue you. 7I will make
Mount Seir a desolate waste[x] and cut off
from it all who come and go.[y] 8I will fill
your mountains with the slain; those
killed by the sword will fall on your hills
and in your valleys and in all your ravines.[z] 9I will make you desolate forever;[a] your towns will not be inhabited.
Then you will know that I am the LORD.[b]
10“ ‘Because you have said, “These
two nations and countries will be ours
and we will take possession[c] of them,”
even though I the LORD was there,
11therefore as surely as I live, declares the
Sovereign LORD, I will treat you in accordance with the anger[d] and jealousy you
showed in your hatred of them and I will
make myself known among them when I
judge you.[e] 12Then you will know that I
the LORD have heard all the contemptible
things you have said against the mountains of Israel. You said, “They have been
laid waste and have been given over to us
to devour.[f]” 13You boasted[g] against me
and spoke against me without restraint,
and I heard it.[h] 14This is what the Sovereign LORD says: While the whole earth
rejoices, I will make you desolate.[i] 15Be-
cause you rejoiced[j] when the inheritance of the house of Israel became desolate, that is how I will treat you. You will
be desolate, O Mount Seir,[k] you and all
of Edom.[l] Then they will know that I am
the LORD.’ ”

Chapter 36

A Prophecy to the Mountains of Israel

“SON of man, prophesy to the mountains of Israel[m] and say, ‘O mountains of Israel, hear the word of the LORD.
2This is what the Sovereign LORD says:[n]
The enemy said of you, “Aha![o] The ancient heights[p] have become our possession.[q]” ’ 3Therefore prophesy and say,
‘This is what the Sovereign LORD says:
Because they ravaged[r] and hounded you
from every side so that you became the
possession of the rest of the nations and
the object of people’s malicious talk and
slander,[s] 4therefore, O mountains of Israel, hear the word of the Sovereign LORD:
This is what the Sovereign LORD says to
the mountains and hills, to the ravines
and valleys,[t] to the desolate ruins[u] and
the deserted[v] towns that have been plundered and ridiculed[w] by the rest of the
nations around you[x]— 5this is what the
Sovereign LORD says: In my burning[y]
zeal I have spoken against the rest of the
nations, and against all Edom, for with
glee and with malice in their hearts they
made my land their own possession so
that they might plunder its pastureland.’[z] 6Therefore prophesy concerning
the land of Israel and say to the mountains and hills, to the ravines and valleys:
‘This is what the Sovereign LORD says: I
speak in my jealous wrath because you
have suffered the scorn of the nations.[a]
7Therefore this is what the Sovereign
LORD says: I swear with uplifted hand[b]
that the nations around you will also suffer scorn.[c]
8“ ‘But you, O mountains of Israel, will
produce branches and fruit[d] for my people Israel, for they will soon come home.
9I am concerned for you and will look on
you with favor; you will be plowed and
sown,[e] 10and I will multiply the number
of people upon you, even the whole
house of Israel. The towns will be inhabited and the ruins[f] rebuilt.[g] 11I will increase the number of men and animals
upon you, and they will be fruitful[h] and
become numerous. I will settle people[i]
on you as in the past[j] and will make you
prosper more than before.[k] Then you
will know that I am the LORD. 12I will
cause people, my people Israel, to walk
upon you. They will possess you, and
you will be their inheritance;[l] you will
never again deprive them of their
children.
13“ ‘This is what the Sovereign LORD
says: Because people say to you, “You devour men[m] and deprive your nation of its
children,” 14therefore you will no longer
devour men or make your nation childless, declares the Sovereign LORD. 15No

35:5 [s]S Ps 63:10 [t]Ob 1:13 [u]Ps 137:7; S Eze 21:29
35:6 [v]S Isa 34:3 [w]Isa 63:2-6
35:7 [x]S Jer 46:19 [y]S Jer 49:17
35:8 [z]S Eze 31:12
35:9 [a]Ob 1:10 [b]S Isa 34:5-6; S Jer 49:13
35:10 [c]S Ps 83:12; Eze 36:2,5
35:11 [d]Eze 25:14 [e]S Ps 9:16; Ob 1:15; S Mt 7:2
35:12 [f]S Jer 50:7
35:13 [g]S Jer 49:16 [h]Da 11:36
35:14 [i]Jer 51:48
35:15 [j]Eze 36:5; Ob 1:12 [k]ver 3 [l]S Isa 34:5-6,11; Jer 50:11-13; S La 4:21; S Eze 32:29
36:1 [m]S Eze 17:22
36:2 [n]Eze 6:2-3 [o]S Eze 25:3 [p]S Dt 32:13 [q]S Eze 35:10
36:3 [r]Ob 1:13 [s]Ps 44:13-14; S La 2:16; 3:62
36:4 [t]Eze 6:3 [u]Eze 33:24 [v]S Lev 26:43 [w]S Jer 2:26 [x]Dt 11:11; S Ps 79:4; S Eze 33:28-29
36:5 [y]S Dt 29:20 [z]Isa 66:16; Jer 25:31; 50:11; Eze 25:12-14; S 35:10,15; 38:22; Joel 3:2,14
36:6 [a]Ps 123:3-4; Eze 34:29
36:7 [b]S Nu 14:30 [c]S Jer 25:9
36:8 [d]S Isa 4:2; S 27:6; Eze 47:12
36:9 [e]ver 34-36; Jer 31:27
36:10 [f]S Isa 49:8 [g]Isa 49:17-23; S Jer 30:18
36:11 [h]S Ge 1:22 [i]S Isa 49:19 [j]Mic 7:14 [k]Lev 26:9; Job 42:13; S Jer 31:28; S Eze 16:55; Zec 10:8
36:12 [l]Eze 47:14, 22
36:13 [m]S Nu 13:32

36:1–38 GOD, Wrath—God’s wrath protects His people from their enemies, protects His holy name from ridicule, and leads His people to repentance and renewal. See note on 5:8–17.

36:1–38 HISTORY, National—Israel’s judgment was deserved. Her deliverance was not. God delivered His people from Exile to restore the reputation of His holy name among the nations, to express His jealous wrath against the nations, to make a new covenant relationship which His people would keep, and to cause Israel and the nations to know Him as the only God in control of history. See notes on 1 Ki 20:13; Isa 1:24–26.

36:5–6 GOD, Jealous—Zeal and jealousy are translations of the same Hebrew word. See note on 16:38.

36:8–12 GOD, Grace—God turns from His wrath to renew His people in His grace. See note on 20:17.

36:8–12 REVELATION, Author of Hope—The God of redemption and hope declared Israel’s future to be good, beginning with the land and its yield, and the people and their development. The fulfillment of His promises would introduce Him anew to His people. See note on 34:25–31.

longer will I make you hear the taunts of
the nations, and no longer will you suffer
the scorn of the peoples or cause your
nation to fall, declares the Sovereign
LORD.[n] ' "
16Again the word of the LORD came to
me: 17"Son of man, when the people of
Israel were living in their own land, they
defiled it by their conduct and their actions. Their conduct was like a woman's
monthly uncleanness[o] in my sight.[p] 18So
I poured out[q] my wrath on them because
they had shed blood in the land and because they had defiled it with their idols.
19I dispersed them among the nations,
and they were scattered[r] through the
countries; I judged them according to
their conduct and their actions.[s] 20And
wherever they went among the nations
they profaned[t] my holy name, for it was
said of them, 'These are the LORD's people, and yet they had to leave his land.'[u]
21I had concern for my holy name, which
the house of Israel profaned among the
nations where they had gone.[v]
22"Therefore say to the house of Israel,
'This is what the Sovereign LORD says: It
is not for your sake, O house of Israel,
that I am going to do these things, but for
the sake of my holy name,[w] which you
have profaned[x] among the nations where
you have gone.[y] 23I will show the holiness of my great name,[z] which has been
profaned[a] among the nations, the name
you have profaned among them. Then the
nations will know that I am the LORD,[b]
declares the Sovereign LORD, when I
show myself holy[c] through you before
their eyes.[d]
24" 'For I will take you out of the nations; I will gather you from all the coun-

36:15 [n]Ps 89:50-51; Isa 54:4; S Eze 34:29 **36:17** [o]S Lev 5:2; S 12:2 [p]Ps 106:37-38; S Jer 2:7 **36:18** [q]S 2Ch 34:21 **36:19** [r]Dt 28:64 [s]Lev 18:24-28; S Eze 7:8; S 24:14; 39:24 **36:20** [t]S Lev 18:21; S Eze 13:19; Ro 2:24 [u]Isa 52:5; S Jer 33:24; S Eze 12:16 **36:21** [v]Ps 74:18; Isa 48:9 **36:22** [w]S Isa 37:35; S Eze 20:44 [x]Ro 2:24* [y]Dt 9:5-6; Ps 106:8; S Eze 20:9 **36:23** [z]S Nu 6:27 [a]S Isa 37:23 [b]S Ps 46:10 [c]S Eze 20:41 [d]Ps 126:2; S Isa 5:16; Eze 20:14; 38:23; 39:7,27-28 **36:24** [e]S Isa 43:5-6; S Eze 34:13; 37:21 **36:25** [f]S Lev 14:7; S 16:14-15; Heb 9:13 [g]S Ps 51:2,7 [h]S Ezr 6:21 [i]Isa 2:18; Joel 3:21; Zec 3:4; 13:2; S Ac 22:16 **36:26** [j]Jer 24:7 [k]S Jer 5:3 [l]S Ps 51:10; S Eze 18:31; S 2Co 3:3 **36:27** [m]S Isa 44:3; Joel 2:29; Jn 3:5 [n]S Eze 18:21 [o]Jer 50:20; 1Th 4:8 **36:28** [p]Jer 30:22; 31:33 [q]S Eze 11:17; S 14:11; 34:24; 37:14,27; Zec 8:8 **36:29** [r]Eze 34:29 **36:30** [s]Lev 26:4-5; S Eze 34:13-14; Hos 2:21-22 **36:31** [t]Isa 6:5; S Jer 31:19; S Eze 6:9 **36:32** [u]Eze 16:63 [v]Dt 9:5 **36:33** [w]S Lev 16:30 [x]S Lev 26:31 [y]S Isa 49:8 **36:35** [z]S Ge 2:8

tries and bring you back into your own
land.[e] 25I will sprinkle[f] clean water on
you, and you will be clean; I will
cleanse[g] you from all your impurities[h]
and from all your idols.[i] 26I will give you
a new heart[j] and put a new spirit in you;
I will remove from you your heart of
stone[k] and give you a heart of flesh.[l]
27And I will put my Spirit[m] in you and
move you to follow my decrees[n] and be
careful to keep my laws.[o] 28You will live
in the land I gave your forefathers; you
will be my people,[p] and I will be your
God.[q] 29I will save you from all your uncleanness. I will call for the grain and
make it plentiful and will not bring famine[r] upon you. 30I will increase the fruit
of the trees and the crops of the field, so
that you will no longer suffer disgrace
among the nations because of famine.[s]
31Then you will remember your evil ways
and wicked deeds, and you will loathe
yourselves for your sins and detestable
practices.[t] 32I want you to know that I
am not doing this for your sake, declares
the Sovereign LORD. Be ashamed[u] and
disgraced for your conduct, O house of
Israel![v]
33" 'This is what the Sovereign LORD
says: On the day I cleanse[w] you from all
your sins, I will resettle your towns, and
the ruins[x] will be rebuilt.[y] 34The desolate land will be cultivated instead of lying desolate in the sight of all who pass
through it. 35They will say, "This land
that was laid waste has become like the
garden of Eden;[z] the cities that were lying in ruins, desolate and destroyed, are

---

36:20–23 GOD, Holy—God's people are His only representatives that many people see. When we sin, we profane His name before the peoples. God acts to defend His holy name. He wants all people to know the awesome holiness which separates Him from all other gods. See note on 20:12,14,40,41.

36:22–28 REVELATION, History—The release from Babylonian captivity would be God's revelation of Himself to the nations to carry out His purposes and honor His name. God redeemed not because of Israel's behavior or repentance but because of His character. His historical revelation occurred to continue His purposes in the original Exodus—to create a loyal people for Himself (11:20; Ex 6:7).

36:24 GOD, Savior—God is our Savior, intimately related to His people. See note on Jer 50:34.

36:24–30 HOLY SPIRIT, Indwells—Only God's Spirit in our lives can lead us to obey. After the destruction of Jerusalem, the prophets Jeremiah (31:31–34) and Ezekiel gave messages of hope. They prophesied that in a coming age God would restore His people. This action included physical restoration of the city and spiritual renewal. The people would experience a new covenant or relationship with God (Jer 31:31), a new heart, and a new spirit (Eze 36:26). God would put His Spirit in His people. The Spirit would help the people obey the law (v 27). Jesus fulfilled these promises. He gave His life to establish a new covenant (1 Co 11:25) and poured out the Spirit of God on His followers at Pentecost (Ac 2). The Spirit produces love, joy, peace, and other qualities in Christians today as then (Gal 5:22), changing us from spiritually lifeless people to living, fruitful people of God.

36:24–28 SALVATION, Definition—God's salvation is His cleansing from sin. The new covenant which He has made with us through the death of Christ makes possible cleansing from all impurities. He gives us a new heart or will and puts His Spirit in us to lead us to obey and serve Him. See note on 11:17–21.

36:25,33 SALVATION, As Cleansing—God is determined to cleanse His people from their sins. He provided a new covenant in which His people will be cleansed from all impurities, idols, and sins. This cleansing is fully accomplished only in Christ (1 Jn 1:7). See note on Jer 33:8.

36:26 HUMANITY, Human Nature—See note on 11:18–21.

36:26 THE CHURCH, Covenant People—God gives that which is necessary to change our lives and to enable us to follow Him. See notes on 11:17–20; Jer 31:31–34.

36:28 THE CHURCH, Covenant People—Through the ages God's ideal remains the same. He wants to be our God, receiving worship, praise, and right living from His people. He wants us to be His people, receiving blessings from Him, our gracious Lord. Some interpreters look for a literal fulfillment in which Jews will be restored to the land and converted to Christ. See note on Jer 30:22.

now fortified and inhabited.[a]" 36Then the nations around you that remain will know that I the LORD have rebuilt what was destroyed and have replanted what was desolate. I the LORD have spoken, and I will do it.'[b]

37"This is what the Sovereign LORD says: Once again I will yield to the plea[c] of the house of Israel and do this for them: I will make their people as numerous as sheep,[d] 38as numerous as the flocks for offerings[e] at Jerusalem during her appointed feasts. So will the ruined cities be filled with flocks of people. Then they will know that I am the LORD.[f]"

Chapter 37

The Valley of Dry Bones

THE hand of the LORD was upon me,[g] and he brought me out by the Spirit[h] of the LORD and set me in the middle of a valley;[i] it was full of bones.[j] 2He led me back and forth among them, and I saw a great many bones on the floor of the valley, bones that were very dry. 3He asked me, "Son of man, can these bones live?"

I said, "O Sovereign LORD, you alone know.[k]"

4Then he said to me, "Prophesy to these bones and say to them, 'Dry bones, hear the word of the LORD![l] 5This is what the Sovereign LORD says to these bones: I will make breath[j] enter you, and you will come to life.[m] 6I will attach tendons to you and make flesh come upon you and cover you with skin; I will put breath in you, and you will come to life. Then you will know that I am the LORD.[n]' "

7So I prophesied as I was commanded. And as I was prophesying, there was a noise, a rattling sound, and the bones came together, bone to bone. 8I looked, and tendons and flesh appeared on them and skin covered them, but there was no breath in them.

9Then he said to me, "Prophesy to the breath;[o] prophesy, son of man, and say to it, 'This is what the Sovereign LORD says: Come from the four winds,[p] O breath, and breathe into these slain, that they may live.' " 10So I prophesied as he commanded[q] me, and breath entered them; they came to life and stood up on their feet—a vast army.[r]

11Then he said to me: "Son of man, these bones are the whole house of Israel. They say, 'Our bones are dried up and our hope is gone; we are cut off.'[s] 12Therefore prophesy and say to them: 'This is what the Sovereign LORD says: O my people, I am going to open your graves and bring you up from them; I will bring you back to the land of Israel.[t] 13Then you, my people, will know that I am the LORD,[u] when I open your graves and bring you up from them.[v] 14I will put my Spirit[w] in you and you will live, and I will settle[x] you in your own land. Then you will know that I the LORD have spoken, and I have done it, declares the LORD.[y]' "

One Nation Under One King

15The word of the LORD came to me: 16"Son of man, take a stick of wood and write on it, 'Belonging to Judah and the Israelites[z] associated with him.[a]' Then take another stick of wood, and write on it, 'Ephraim's stick, belonging to Joseph and all the house of Israel associated with him.' 17Join them together into one stick so that they will become one in your hand.[b]

18"When your countrymen ask you, 'Won't you tell us what you mean by this?'[c] 19say to them, 'This is what the Sovereign LORD says: I am going to take the stick of Joseph—which is in Ephraim's hand—and of the Israelite tribes associated with him, and join it to Judah's stick, making them a single stick of wood, and they will become one in my hand.'[d]

36:35 [a]Am 9:14
36:36 [b]S Jer 42:10; S Eze 17:22; 37:14; 39:27-28
36:37 [c]Zec 10:6; 13:9 [d]Ps 102:17; Jer 29:12-14
36:38 [e]1Ki 8:63; 2Ch 35:7-9 [f]S Ex 6:2
37:1 [g]S Eze 1:3 [h]S Eze 11:24; Lk 4:1; Ac 8:39 [i]Jer 7:32 [j]S Jer 8:2; Eze 40:1
37:3 [k]Dt 32:39; S 1Sa 2:6; Isa 26:19; 1Co 15:35
37:4 [l]Jer 22:29
37:5 [m]S Ge 2:7; Ps 104:29-30; Rev 11:11
37:6 [n]S Ex 6:2; Eze 38:23
37:9 [o]ver 14; Ps 104:30; Isa 32:15; Eze 39:29; Zec 12:10 [p]Jer 49:36; Da 7:2; 8:8; 11:4; Zec 2:6; 6:5; Rev 7:1
37:10 [q]S Eze 12:7 [r]Rev 11:11
37:11 [s]S Job 17:15; S La 3:54
37:12 [t]ver 21; Dt 32:39; 1Sa 2:6; Isa 26:19; Jer 29:14; Hos 13:14; Am 9:14-15; Zep 3:20; Zec 8:8
37:13 [u]S Ex 6:2 [v]S Eze 17:24; Hos 13:14
37:14 [w]S ver 9; S Isa 11:2; Joel 2:28-29 [x]S Jer 43:2 [y]Eze 36:27-28,36; Rev 11:11
37:16 [z]S 1Ki 12:20; 2Ch 10:17-19 [a]Nu 17:2-3; 2Ch 15:9
37:17 [b]ver 24; Isa 11:13; S Jer 50:4; Hos 1:11
37:18 [c]S Eze 24:19
37:19 [d]Zec 10:6

[j]5 The Hebrew for this word can also mean *wind* or *spirit* (see verses 6-14).

37:1–14 GOD, Power—God has sovereign power over a dead nation (v 11). No realm—even death—is beyond His control. He can save His people no matter what human judgment would say the possibilities are. All God's actions seek to introduce Himself to all people as Lord.

37:1–14 HUMANITY, Life—The Hebrew nation was in exile—dead. God used the graphic symbol of dry bones to show how dead they were. Dry bones can live. God promised Ezekiel He would make the dead nation live again (v 14). Jesus has shown us dead believers will rise again to eternal life.

37:11–14 SALVATION, Renewal—Israel's coming restoration was to be like scattered dry bones being brought back together and given new life or like a resurrection from the grave. God would put His Spirit upon His people. See note on 11:17–21. They would have a new body as well as a new heart and mind. In fact, they would be a new creation of God's making. This promise foreshadows the new birth (Jn 3) and the new creation of which Paul and John spoke. God takes people dead and hopeless because of their sin and recreates them to be His people. This is salvation.

37:12–14 HOLY SPIRIT, Hope—The valley of dry bones represented dead Israel in the Babylonian captivity. Ezekiel assured the people that God would restore Israel to life. Life would come through God's Spirit. The language of the Spirit suggests life. The Hebrew word *ruach* may mean spirit, wind, or breath. Breath is the essential sign of life. So God calls the winds to put breath into the bones (vv 9–10), and they live again. Only God can put spiritual life, or breath, into spiritually dead people. See notes on Jn 3:5–6; Ro 8:1–17.

37:15–28 ELECTION, God's Purpose—God seeks to create a unified people under unified leadership living in moral unity under His moral guidelines in His presence. Achievement of the purpose is a witness to all nations.

20Hold before their eyes the sticks you
have written on 21and say to them, 'This
is what the Sovereign LORD says: I will
take the Israelites out of the nations
where they have gone. I will gather them
from all around and bring them back into
their own land.[e] 22I will make them one
nation in the land, on the mountains of
Israel.[f] There will be one king over all of
them and they will never again be two
nations or be divided into two kingdoms.[g] 23They will no longer defile[h]
themselves with their idols and vile images or with any of their offenses, for I
will save them from all their sinful backsliding,[k][i] and I will cleanse them. They
will be my people, and I will be their
God.[j]
24" 'My servant David[k] will be king[l]
over them, and they will all have one
shepherd.[m] They will follow my laws and
be careful to keep my decrees.[n] 25They
will live in the land I gave to my servant
Jacob, the land where your fathers
lived.[o] They and their children and their
children's children will live there forever,[p] and David my servant will be their
prince forever.[q] 26I will make a covenant
of peace[r] with them; it will be an everlasting covenant.[s] I will establish them
and increase their numbers,[t] and I will
put my sanctuary among them[u] forever.[v]
27My dwelling place[w] will be with them;
I will be their God, and they will be my
people.[x] 28Then the nations will know
that I the LORD make Israel holy,[y] when
my sanctuary is among them forever.[z][a] ' "

37:21 [e]S ver 12; S Isa 43:5-6; S Eze 20:42; 39:27; Mic 4:6 **37:22** [f]S Eze 17:22; S 34:13-14 [g]Isa 11:13; Jer 33:24; S 50:4; Hos 1:11 **37:23** [h]Eze 43:7 [i]S Jer 7:24 [j]Eze 11:18; S 36:28; Na 2:2 **37:24** [k]Isa 55:4; Hos 3:5 [l]S 1Sa 13:14; S Isa 32:1 [m]Zec 13:7 [n]Ps 78:70-71; S Jer 30:21; S Eze 21:27 **37:25** [o]S Eze 28:25 [p]S Ezr 9:12; Am 9:15 [q]S Ps 89:3-4; Isa 11:1; S Eze 34:23-24 **37:26** [r]S Nu 25:12 [s]S Ge 9:16; S Dt 29:14; S Heb 13:20 [t]S Jer 30:19 [u]Lev 26:11 [v]S Eze 16:62 **37:27** [w]S Lev 26:11 [x]S Eze 34:30; S 36:28; S 2Co 6:16* **37:28** [y]S Ex 31:13 [z]Hos 1:10-11 [a]Eze 43:9; Zep 3:15 **38:2** [b]ver 14; Eze 39:11 [c]S Ge 10:2 [d]S Eze 27:13 **38:3** [e]Eze 39:1 **38:4** [f]S 2Ki 19:28 [g]S Isa 43:17; Eze 29:4; 39:2; Da 11:40 **38:5** [h]S Ge 10:6 [i]S Ge 10:6; S Eze 27:10 **38:6** [j]S Ge 10:2 [k]S Ge 10:3

Chapter 38

A Prophecy Against Gog

THE word of the LORD came to me:
2"Son of man, set your face against
Gog,[b] of the land of Magog,[c] the chief
prince of[l] Meshech and Tubal;[d] prophesy against him 3and say: 'This is what the
Sovereign LORD says: I am against you, O
Gog, chief prince of[m] Meshech and Tubal.[e] 4I will turn you around, put hooks[f]
in your jaws and bring you out with your
whole army—your horses, your horsemen fully armed, and a great horde with
large and small shields, all of them bran-
dishing their swords.[g] 5Persia, Cush[n][h]
and Put[i] will be with them, all with
shields and helmets, 6also Gomer[j] with
all its troops, and Beth Togarmah[k] from
the far north[l] with all its troops—the
many nations with you.
7" 'Get ready; be prepared,[m] you and
all the hordes gathered about you, and
take command of them. 8After many
days[n] you will be called to arms. In future years you will invade a land that has
recovered from war, whose people were
gathered from many nations[o] to the
mountains of Israel, which had long been
desolate. They had been brought out from
the nations, and now all of them live in

[l]S Eze 32:30 **38:7** [m]S Isa 8:9 **38:8** [n]Isa 24:22 [o]S Isa 11:11

[k] *23* Many Hebrew manuscripts (see also Septuagint); most Hebrew manuscripts *all their dwelling places where they sinned* [l] *2* Or *the prince of Rosh,* [m] *3* Or *Gog, prince of Rosh,* [n] *5* That is, the upper Nile region

---

37:23 SALVATION, As Cleansing—See note on 36:25, 33. God's cleansing is from idolatry. Saving and cleansing are synonymous in this text.

37:23 THE CHURCH, Covenant People—See note on 36:28.

37:24–28 THE CHURCH, Covenant People—God's people have a future because God plans and controls the future. The Jews in Babylonian exile did not appear to have much hope. God promised a new king, unity, obedience, and life in their land. This would center in a new worship place showing God was with them. All the promises to Abraham (Ge 12:1–7) would again be fulfilled. They would be holy and totally dedicated to God. Their holiness would be a testimony to all other peoples, fulfilling the mission first given Abraham (Ge 12:1–3). God continues to create a future for an obedient people. See notes on 16:59–63; 34:1–24, 25–31; 36:28.

37:28 EVANGELISM, Holy Life—God seeks to live with and in His people. His presence leads His people to a holy, pure life (Lev 19:1–37). Worship of God leads to holy living which leads others to acknowledge and worship God. A holy life makes evangelistic efforts effective.

38:1—39:29 GOD, Holy—God knows human plans and has plans of His own to counter any attacks upon His chosen people. He will use the opportunity presented by enemy greed and aggression to display His awesome holiness which uniquely sets Him apart from all people and gods. He wants all nations to recognize Him as the only God. See note on 20:12, 14,40,41.

38:1—39:29 HISTORY, Eternal—See note on 25:1—32:32. God's people in historical circumstances live under fear of enemies. Even the restored exiles looked to fearful invaders. Ezekiel looked to the day of the final invasion. God would show His control of history by dictating when the invasion would come. He would show Himself powerful enough to defeat this final invader. He would make it possible to burn all weapons of war. No matter how powerful the enemy, God's faithful people have no reason to fear. God can and will defeat all His people's enemies. In so doing He will introduce Himself in all His holiness to the world. Everyone will recognize His incomparable glory. Finally Israel will quit blaming God for their problems and learn from history that unfaithfulness leads to destruction.

38:1—39:29 LAST THINGS, Great Tribulation—The idea of an intense uprising of evil is described in a prophecy concerning Gog and Magog. Ezekiel pointed Israel to a new day in her land before showing how God's power would be revealed to the nations and Israel's fear of international coalitions would be relieved. God would lead an otherwise unknown leader named Gog of an unknown place, Magog, to attack Judah. Then God would use His power and resources to destroy the attackers. This would fulfill earlier prophecies and let both the nations and Israel know of God's holiness. A connection is made between this prophecy and end time events in Rev 20:7–10 by a symbolic use of the ancient invaders from the north. The ultimate expression of organized evil is found in the concept of a future tribulation period and the New Testament idea of antichrist, which many scholars believe will be personified in the last days. See note on 1 Jn 2:18.

safety.[p] 9You and all your troops and the
many nations with you will go up, advancing like a storm;[q] you will be like a
cloud[r] covering the land.[s]
10" 'This is what the Sovereign LORD
says: On that day thoughts will come into
your mind[t] and you will devise an evil
scheme.[u] 11You will say, "I will invade a
land of unwalled villages; I will attack a
peaceful and unsuspecting people[v] —all
of them living without walls and without
gates and bars.[w] 12I will plunder and loot
and turn my hand against the resettled
ruins and the people gathered from the
nations, rich in livestock and goods, living at the center of the land." 13Sheba[x]
and Dedan[y] and the merchants of Tarshish[z] and all her villages[o] will say to
you, "Have you come to plunder? Have
you gathered your hordes to loot, to carry
off silver and gold, to take away livestock
and goods and to seize much plunder?[a]" '
14"Therefore, son of man, prophesy
and say to Gog: 'This is what the Sovereign LORD says: In that day, when my
people Israel are living in safety,[b] will
you not take notice of it? 15You will come
from your place in the far north,[c] you
and many nations with you, all of them
riding on horses, a great horde, a mighty
army.[d] 16You will advance against my
people Israel like a cloud[e] that covers the
land.[f] In days to come, O Gog, I will
bring you against my land, so that the nations may know me when I show myself
holy[g] through you before their eyes.[h]
17" 'This is what the Sovereign LORD
says: Are you not the one I spoke of in
former days by my servants the prophets
of Israel? At that time they prophesied for
years that I would bring you against
them. 18This is what will happen in that
day: When Gog attacks the land of Israel,
my hot anger will be aroused, declares
the Sovereign LORD. 19In my zeal and fiery wrath I declare that at that time there
shall be a great earthquake[i] in the land
of Israel.[j] 20The fish of the sea, the birds
of the air, the beasts of the field, every
creature that moves along the ground,
and all the people on the face of the earth
will tremble[k] at my presence. The mountains will be overturned,[l] the cliffs will
crumble[m] and every wall will fall to the
ground.[n] 21I will summon a sword[o]
against Gog on all my mountains, declares the Sovereign LORD. Every man's
sword will be against his brother.[p] 22I
will execute judgment[q] upon him with
plague and bloodshed;[r] I will pour down
torrents of rain, hailstones[s] and burning
sulfur[t] on him and on his troops and on
the many nations with him.[u] 23And so I
will show my greatness and my holiness,
and I will make myself known in the sight
of many nations. Then they will know
that I am the LORD.[v] '

Chapter 39

"SON of man, prophesy against Gog[w]
and say: 'This is what the Sovereign LORD says: I am against you, O Gog,
chief prince of[p] Meshech[x] and Tubal.[y]
2I will turn you around and drag you
along. I will bring you from the far
north[z] and send you against the mountains of Israel.[a] 3Then I will strike your
bow[b] from your left hand and make your
arrows[c] drop from your right hand. 4On
the mountains of Israel you will fall, you
and all your troops and the nations with
you. I will give you as food to all kinds of
carrion birds[d] and to the wild animals.[e]
5You will fall in the open field, for I have
spoken, declares the Sovereign LORD.[f] 6I
will send fire[g] on Magog[h] and on those
who live in safety in the coastlands,[i] and
they will know[j] that I am the LORD.
7" 'I will make known my holy name
among my people Israel. I will no longer
let my holy name be profaned,[k] and the
nations will know[l] that I the LORD am
the Holy One in Israel.[m] 8It is coming! It
will surely take place, declares the Sovereign LORD. This is the day[n] I have spoken
of.
9" 'Then those who live in the towns of
Israel will go out and use the weapons for
fuel and burn them up—the small and
large shields, the bows and arrows,[o] the
war clubs and spears. For seven years
they will use them for fuel.[p] 10They will
not need to gather wood from the fields
or cut it from the forests, because they
will use the weapons for fuel. And they
will plunder[q] those who plundered them
and loot those who looted them, declares
the Sovereign LORD.[r]

[o] 13 Or *her strong lions* [p] 1 Or *Gog, prince of Rosh,*

38:8 [p]ver 14; Jer 23:6; S Eze 28:26; Joel 3:1
38:9 [q]Isa 25:4; 28:2 [r]ver 16; Jer 4:13; Joel 2:2 [s]Rev 20:8
38:10 [t]S Jer 17:10 [u]Ps 36:4; Mic 2:1
38:11 [v]S Ge 34:25 [w]Jer 49:31; Zec 2:4
38:13 [x]S Ge 10:7 [y]S Ge 25:3 [z]S Ge 10:4 [a]Isa 10:6; 33:23; S Jer 15:13
38:14 [b]S ver 8; S Lev 25:18; S Jer 16:15; Zec 2:5
38:15 [c]Eze 32:30 [d]Eze 39:2; Rev 20:8
38:16 [e]S ver 9 [f]Joel 3:11 [g]S Lev 10:3 [h]Isa 29:23; Eze 39:21
38:19 [i]Isa 24:18; Joel 2:10; 3:16; S Rev 6:12 [j]Ps 18:7; S Eze 5:13; Hag 2:6, 21
38:20 [k]S Ex 15:14 [l]Isa 42:15 [m]Job 14:18 [n]S Ps 76:8; Hos 4:3; Na 1:5
38:21 [o]Isa 66:16; Jer 25:29 [p]S 1Sa 14:20; S 2Ch 20:23; Hag 2:22
38:22 [q]Isa 66:16; Jer 25:31; S Eze 36:5 [r]S Eze 14:19; S 28:23 [s]S Ex 9:18; Ps 18:12; Rev 16:21 [t]S Ge 19:24; S Rev 9:17 [u]S Eze 13:11
38:23 [v]Eze 20:42; S 36:23; S 37:6
39:1 [w]Rev 20:8 [x]S Ge 10:2 [y]S Eze 27:13; S 38:2,3
39:2 [z]S Eze 32:30 [a]S Eze 38:4,15
39:3 [b]Hos 1:5; Am 2:15 [c]Ps 76:3
39:4 [d]S Ge 40:19 [e]ver 17-20; S Jer 25:33; S Eze 29:5; S 33:27
39:5 [f]S Eze 32:4
39:6 [g]S Eze 30:8; Rev 20:9 [h]S Ge 10:2 [i]S Jer 25:22 [j]S Ex 6:7
39:7 [k]S Ex 20:7; S Eze 13:19 [l]S Isa 49:26 [m]S Isa 12:6; S 54:5; S Eze 20:9; S 36:16, 23
39:8 [n]Eze 7:6
39:9 [o]Ps 76:3 [p]S Ps 46:9
39:10 [q]S Ex 3:22 [r]S Isa 14:2; S 33:1; Hab 2:8

38:16 EVANGELISM, Mass—God often uses strange methods to bring the mass of the people to an awareness of His glory. Here He even used Gog, a godless source, to declare His greatness. But our Lord uses all means. Therefore, if He will use Gog, how much more will He use us, as we attempt the evangelization of the masses.

38:18–19 GOD, Wrath—God zealousy guards His chosen people. See note on 5:8–17.

38:22 GOD, Judge—See note on 18:25–32.

38:23 EVANGELISM, Power—God is the power source in making known to all people that He is the holy Lord. He reveals Himself and His glorious holiness. He will not allow anyone to fail to see that He is holy, great, and majestic. Although He uses agents in that divine work, He is the ultimate source of the power to convince people of their need of Him.

39:7 EVANGELISM, Power—See note on 38:23.

11“ ‘On that day I will give Gog a burial
place in Israel, in the valley of those who
travel east toward[q] the Sea.[r] It will
block the way of travelers, because Gog
and all his hordes will be buried[s] there.
So it will be called the Valley of Hamon
Gog.[s] [t]
12“ ‘For seven months the house of Israel will be burying them in order to
cleanse the land.[u] 13All the people of the
land will bury them, and the day I am
glorified[v] will be a memorable day for
them, declares the Sovereign LORD.
14“ ‘Men will be regularly employed to
cleanse the land. Some will go throughout the land and, in addition to them, others will bury those that remain on the
ground. At the end of the seven months
they will begin their search. 15As they go
through the land and one of them sees a
human bone, he will set up a marker beside it until the gravediggers have buried
it in the Valley of Hamon Gog. 16(Also a
town called Hamonah[t] will be there.)
And so they will cleanse the land.’
17“Son of man, this is what the Sovereign LORD says: Call out to every kind of
bird[w] and all the wild animals: ‘Assemble
and come together from all around to the
sacrifice I am preparing for you, the great
sacrifice on the mountains of Israel.
There you will eat flesh and drink
blood.[x] 18You will eat the flesh of mighty
men and drink the blood of the princes of
the earth as if they were rams and lambs,
goats and bulls—all of them fattened animals from Bashan.[y] 19At the sacrifice[z] I
am preparing for you, you will eat fat till
you are glutted and drink blood till you
are drunk. 20At my table you will eat your
fill of horses and riders, mighty men and
soldiers of every kind,’ declares the Sovereign LORD.[a]
21“I will display my glory among the
nations, and all the nations will see the
punishment I inflict and the hand I lay
upon them.[b] 22From that day forward the
house of Israel will know that I am the
LORD their God. 23And the nations will
know that the people of Israel went into
exile for their sin, because they were unfaithful to me. So I hid my face from them
and handed them over to their enemies,
and they all fell by the sword.[c] 24I dealt
with them according to their uncleanness
and their offenses, and I hid my face from
them.[d]
25“Therefore this is what the Sovereign
LORD says: I will now bring Jacob back
from captivity[u] [e] and will have compassion[f] on all the people of Israel, and I
will be zealous for my holy name.[g]
26They will forget their shame and all the
unfaithfulness they showed toward me
when they lived in safety[h] in their land
with no one to make them afraid.[i]
27When I have brought them back from
the nations and have gathered them from
the countries of their enemies, I will
show myself holy through them in the
sight of many nations.[j] 28Then they will
know that I am the LORD their God, for
though I sent them into exile among the
nations, I will gather them[k] to their own
land, not leaving any behind.[l] 29I will no
longer hide my face[m] from them, for I
will pour out my Spirit[n] on the house of
Israel, declares the Sovereign LORD.[o]”

Chapter 40

The New Temple Area

IN the twenty-fifth year of our exile, at
the beginning of the year, on the tenth
of the month, in the fourteenth year after
the fall of the city[p]—on that very day the
hand of the LORD was upon me[q] and he
took me there. 2In visions[r] of God he
took me to the land of Israel and set me
on a very high mountain,[s] on whose

[q]*11* Or *of* [r]*11* That is, the Dead Sea
[s]*11* *Hamon Gog* means *hordes of Gog.*
[t]*16* *Hamonah* means *horde.* [u]*25* Or *now restore the fortunes of Jacob*

39:11 [s]S Isa 34:3 [t]S Eze 38:2
39:12 [u]Dt 21:23
39:13 [v]Eze 28:22
39:17 [w]S Job 15:23 [x]S Eze 32:4
39:18 [y]S Ps 22:12; Jer 51:40
39:19 [z]S Lev 3:9
39:20 [a]S Isa 56:9; S Jer 12:9; Rev 19:17-18
39:21 [b]Ex 9:16; Isa 37:20; S Eze 38:16
39:23 [c]Isa 1:15; 59:2; S Jer 22:8-9; S 44:23
39:24 [d]2Ki 17:23; Jer 2:17,19; 4:18; S Eze 7:22; Da 9:7
39:25 [e]S Jer 33:7 [f]S Jer 30:18 [g]Isa 27:12-13; S Eze 16:53
39:26 [h]S 1Ki 4:25; S Jer 32:37; S Eze 38:8 [i]Isa 17:2; Eze 34:28; Mic 4:4
39:27 [j]S Eze 37:21
39:28 [k]Ps 147:2 [l]S Eze 36:23,36
39:29 [m]S Dt 31:17 [n]S Isa 11:2; S Eze 37:9; S Ac 2:17 [o]S Eze 16:42
40:1 [p]S 2Ki 25:7; Jer 39:1-10; 52:4-11 [q]S Eze 1:3; S 29:17
40:2 [r]S Ex 24:10; Da 7:1,7 [s]S Jer 31:12; S Eze 17:22; Rev 21:10

39:13,21 GOD, Glory—God's victory over His enemies will make His glorious presence and prestige known before all peoples. That is His plan. See note on 1:28.

39:23–24 SIN, Unbelief—God's punishment has purpose. God can use it to reveal Himself to His people and the world. Punishment comes when we sin through a crooked, guilty life (Isa 2:1–4), are unfaithful to God (see note on 1 Ch 10:13), become unclean (Hebrew *tame'*), and offend or rebel against God (Isa 1:2–4). Unclean is a term referring to a person's acceptability for worship in God's house. The unclean cannot enter the holy presence of God (Lev 11—16). Sin makes a person unclean, impure, unfit for worshiping God. God determines what is unclean. Human laws do not make such decisions. See note on 2 Ki 25:1–21.

39:25 GOD, Grace—Israel did not deserve to be delivered from captivity. Only God's love and jealous zeal lead Him to be gracious to His people.

39:27 EVANGELISM, Power—God acts in power to deliver His people from trouble so He can cause unbelieving peoples to realize His greatness and holiness. Part of the evangelistic task is to be available to God so He can show His power through us.

39:29 HOLY SPIRIT, Hope—See 36:27; 37:14.

40:1—48:35 HISTORY, Presence—God's goal for history is to be able to dwell with His holy people. Once God's glory had to leave the Temple because of the people's unfaithfulness (chs 8—11). The goal is the return of God's glory to a restored Temple and a holy people. Such a return is both God's promise to His people and God's command for a new life-style for His people.

40:2–5 REVELATION, Visions—God transported His messenger through space in a vision which allowed Him to see and hear what God was revealing. The prophet was to tell Israel what he understood. He thus became a mediator of God's revelation to the people. Prophets, like other messengers of God in the Old Testament, received and passed on manifestations of God in dreams, visions, and insights derived from religious meditation and reflection. See note on 1:1–28.

south side were some buildings that
looked like a city. 3He took me there, and
I saw a man whose appearance was like
bronze;[t] he was standing in the gateway
with a linen cord and a measuring rod[u]
in his hand. 4The man said to me, "Son of
man, look with your eyes and hear with
your ears and pay attention to everything
I am going to show you,[v] for that is why
you have been brought here. Tell[w] the
house of Israel everything you see.[x]"

The East Gate to the Outer Court

5I saw a wall completely surrounding
the temple area. The length of the measuring rod in the man's hand was six long
cubits, each of which was a cubit[v] and a
handbreadth.[w] He measured[y] the wall; it
was one measuring rod thick and one rod
high.
6Then he went to the gate facing east.[z]
He climbed its steps and measured the
threshold of the gate; it was one rod
deep.[x] 7The alcoves[a] for the guards
were one rod long and one rod wide, and
the projecting walls between the alcoves
were five cubits thick. And the threshold
of the gate next to the portico facing the
temple was one rod deep.
8Then he measured the portico of the
gateway; 9it[y] was eight cubits deep and
its jambs were two cubits thick. The portico of the gateway faced the temple.
10Inside the east gate were three alcoves on each side; the three had the
same measurements, and the faces of the
projecting walls on each side had the
same measurements. 11Then he measured the width of the entrance to the
gateway; it was ten cubits and its length
was thirteen cubits. 12In front of each alcove was a wall one cubit high, and the
alcoves were six cubits square. 13Then he
measured the gateway from the top of the
rear wall of one alcove to the top of the
opposite one; the distance was twenty-
five cubits from one parapet opening to
the opposite one. 14He measured along
the faces of the projecting walls all
around the inside of the gateway—sixty
cubits. The measurement was up to the
portico[z] facing the courtyard.[a][b] 15The
distance from the entrance of the gateway
to the far end of its portico was fifty cubits. 16The alcoves and the projecting
walls inside the gateway were surmount-
ed by narrow parapet openings all
around, as was the portico; the openings
all around faced inward. The faces of the
projecting walls were decorated with
palm trees.[c]

The Outer Court

17Then he brought me into the outer

40:3 [t]S Eze 1:7; Rev 1:15 [u]Eze 47:3; Zec 2:1-2; Rev 11:1; 21:15
40:4 [v]S Dt 6:6 [w]Jer 26:2 [x]Eze 44:5
40:5 [y]Eze 42:20
40:6 [z]S Eze 8:16
40:7 [a]ver 36
40:14 [b]S Ex 27:9
40:16 [c]ver 21-22; 2Ch 3:5; Eze 41:26
40:17 [d]Rev 11:2 [e]Eze 41:6 [f]Eze 42:1
40:19 [g]Eze 46:1 [h]ver 23,27
40:21 [i]ver 7 [j]ver 30
40:22 [k]ver 49 [l]S ver 16,26
40:23 [m]S ver 19
40:24 [n]ver 32,35
40:25 [o]ver 33
40:26 [p]S ver 22
40:27 [q]ver 32 [r]S ver 19
40:28 [s]ver 35
40:29 [t]ver 7

court.[d] There I saw some rooms and a
pavement that had been constructed all
around the court; there were thirty
rooms[e] along the pavement.[f] 18It abut-
ted the sides of the gateways and was as
wide as they were long; this was the lower pavement. 19Then he measured the
distance from the inside of the lower
gateway to the outside of the inner
court;[g] it was a hundred cubits[h] on the
east side as well as on the north.

The North Gate

20Then he measured the length and
width of the gate facing north, leading
into the outer court. 21Its alcoves[i]—
three on each side—its projecting walls
and its portico[j] had the same measurements as those of the first gateway. It was
fifty cubits long and twenty-five cubits
wide. 22Its openings, its portico[k] and its
palm tree decorations had the same measurements as those of the gate facing east.
Seven steps led up to it, with its portico
opposite them.[l] 23There was a gate to
the inner court facing the north gate, just
as there was on the east. He measured
from one gate to the opposite one; it was
a hundred cubits.[m]

The South Gate

24Then he led me to the south side and
I saw a gate facing south. He measured its
jambs and its portico, and they had the
same measurements[n] as the others.
25The gateway and its portico had narrow
openings all around, like the openings of
the others. It was fifty cubits long and
twenty-five cubits wide.[o] 26Seven steps
led up to it, with its portico opposite
them; it had palm tree decorations on the
faces of the projecting walls on each
side.[p] 27The inner court[q] also had a gate
facing south, and he measured from this
gate to the outer gate on the south side; it
was a hundred cubits.[r]

Gates to the Inner Court

28Then he brought me into the inner
court through the south gate, and he measured the south gate; it had the same
measurements[s] as the others. 29Its alcoves,[t] its projecting walls and its portico had the same measurements as the
others. The gateway and its portico had

[v]*5* The common cubit was about 1 1/2 feet (about 0.5 meter). [w]*5* That is, about 3 inches (about 8 centimeters) [x]*6* Septuagint; Hebrew *deep, the first threshold, one rod deep* [y]*8,9* Many Hebrew manuscripts, Septuagint, Vulgate and Syriac; most Hebrew manuscripts *gateway facing the temple; it was one rod deep. 9Then he measured the portico of the gateway; it* [z]*14* Septuagint; Hebrew *projecting wall* [a]*14* The meaning of the Hebrew for this verse is uncertain.

openings all around. It was fifty cubits long and twenty-five cubits wide.[u] 30(The porticoes[v] of the gateways around the inner court were twenty-five cubits wide and five cubits deep.) 31Its portico[w] faced the outer court; palm trees decorated its jambs, and eight steps led up to it.[x]

32Then he brought me to the inner court on the east side, and he measured the gateway; it had the same measurements[y] as the others. 33Its alcoves,[z] its projecting walls and its portico had the same measurements as the others. The gateway and its portico had openings all around. It was fifty cubits long and twenty-five cubits wide. 34Its portico[a] faced the outer court; palm trees decorated the jambs on either side, and eight steps led up to it.

35Then he brought me to the north gate[b] and measured it. It had the same measurements[c] as the others, 36as did its alcoves,[d] its projecting walls and its portico, and it had openings all around. It was fifty cubits long and twenty-five cubits wide. 37Its portico[b][e] faced the outer court; palm trees decorated the jambs on either side, and eight steps led up to it.[f]

The Rooms for Preparing Sacrifices

38A room with a doorway was by the portico in each of the inner gateways, where the burnt offerings[g] were washed. 39In the portico of the gateway were two tables on each side, on which the burnt offerings,[h] sin offerings[i] and guilt offerings[j] were slaughtered.[k] 40By the outside wall of the portico of the gateway, near the steps at the entrance to the north gateway were two tables, and on the other side of the steps were two tables. 41So there were four tables on one side of the gateway and four on the other—eight tables in all—on which the sacrifices were slaughtered. 42There were also four tables of dressed stone[l] for the burnt offerings, each a cubit and a half long, a cubit and a half wide and a cubit high. On them were placed the utensils for slaughtering the burnt offerings and the other sacrifices.[m] 43And double-pronged hooks, each a handbreadth long, were attached to the wall all around. The tables were for the flesh of the offerings.

Rooms for the Priests

44Outside the inner gate, within the inner court, were two rooms, one[c] at the side of the north gate and facing south, and another at the side of the south[d] gate and facing north. 45He said to me, "The room facing south is for the priests who have charge of the temple,[n] 46and the room facing north[o] is for the priests who have charge of the altar.[p] These are the sons of Zadok,[q] who are the only Levites who may draw near to the LORD to minister before him.[r]"

47Then he measured the court: It was square—a hundred cubits long and a hundred cubits wide. And the altar was in front of the temple.[s]

The Temple

48He brought me to the portico of the temple[t] and measured the jambs of the portico; they were five cubits wide on either side. The width of the entrance was fourteen cubits and its projecting walls were[e] three cubits wide on either side. 49The portico[u] was twenty cubits wide, and twelve[f] cubits from front to back. It was reached by a flight of stairs,[g] and there were pillars[v] on each side of the jambs.

Chapter 41

THEN the man brought me to the outer sanctuary[w] and measured the jambs; the width of the jambs was six cubits[h] on each side.[i] 2The entrance was ten cubits wide, and the projecting walls on each side of it were five cubits wide. He also measured the outer sanctuary; it was forty cubits long and twenty cubits wide.[x]

3Then he went into the inner sanctuary and measured the jambs of the entrance; each was two cubits wide. The entrance was six cubits wide, and the projecting walls on each side of it were seven cubits wide. 4And he measured the length of the inner sanctuary; it was twenty cubits, and its width was twenty cubits across the end of the outer sanctuary.[y] He said to me, "This is the Most Holy Place.[z]"

5Then he measured the wall of the temple; it was six cubits thick, and each side room around the temple was four cubits wide. 6The side rooms were on three levels, one above another, thirty[a] on each level. There were ledges all around the wall of the temple to serve as supports for the side rooms, so that the supports were not inserted into the wall of the temple.[b] 7The side rooms all around the temple were wider at each successive level. The structure surrounding the temple was built in ascending stages, so that the rooms widened as one went upward. A stairway[c] went up from the lowest

40:29 uver 25
40:30 vver 21
40:31 wver 22 xver 34,37
40:32 yS ver 24
40:33 zver 7
40:34 aver 22
40:35 bEze 44:4; 47:2 cS ver 24
40:36 dver 7
40:37 ever 22 fver 34
40:38 gS 2Ch 4:6; Eze 42:13
40:39 hEze 46:2 iLev 4:3,28 jS Lev 7:1 kver 42
40:42 lEx 20:25 mver 39
40:45 n1Ch 9:23
40:46 oEze 42:13 pNu 18:5 qS 2Sa 8:17; S Ezr 7:2 rNu 16:5; Eze 43:19; 44:15; 45:4; 48:11
40:47 sEze 41:13-14
40:48 t1Ki 6:2
40:49 uver 22; 1Ki 6:3 vS 1Ki 7:15
41:1 wver 23
41:2 x2Ch 3:3
41:4 y1Ki 6:20 zS Ex 26:33; Heb 9:3-8
41:6 aEze 40:17 bS 1Ki 6:5
41:7 c1Ki 6:8

b37 Septuagint (see also verses 31 and 34); Hebrew *jambs* c44 Septuagint; Hebrew *were rooms for singers, which were* d44 Septuagint; Hebrew *east*
e48 Septuagint; Hebrew *entrance was*
f49 Septuagint; Hebrew *eleven* g49 Hebrew; Septuagint *Ten steps led up to it* h1 The common cubit was about 1 1/2 feet (about 0.5 meter).
i1 One Hebrew manuscript and Septuagint; most Hebrew manuscripts *side, the width of the tent*

floor to the top floor through the middle floor.

[8]I saw that the temple had a raised base all around it, forming the foundation of the side rooms. It was the length of the rod, six long cubits. [9]The outer wall of the side rooms was five cubits thick. The open area between the side rooms of the temple [10]and the ⌞priests'⌟ rooms was twenty cubits wide all around the temple. [11]There were entrances to the side rooms from the open area, one on the north and another on the south; and the base adjoining the open area was five cubits wide all around.

[12]The building facing the temple courtyard on the west side was seventy cubits wide. The wall of the building was five cubits thick all around, and its length was ninety cubits.

[13]Then he measured the temple; it was a hundred cubits long, and the temple courtyard and the building with its walls were also a hundred cubits long. [14]The width of the temple courtyard on the east, including the front of the temple, was a hundred cubits.[d]

[15]Then he measured the length of the building facing the courtyard at the rear of the temple, including its galleries[e] on each side; it was a hundred cubits.

The outer sanctuary, the inner sanctuary and the portico facing the court, [16]as well as the thresholds and the narrow windows[f] and galleries around the three of them—everything beyond and including the threshold was covered with wood. The floor, the wall up to the windows, and the windows were covered.[g] [17]In the space above the outside of the entrance to the inner sanctuary and on the walls at regular intervals all around the inner and outer sanctuary [18]were carved[h] cherubim[i] and palm trees.[j] Palm trees alternated with cherubim. Each cherub had two faces:[k] [19]the face of a man toward the palm tree on one side and the face of a lion toward the palm tree on the other. They were carved all around the whole temple.[l] [20]From the floor to the area above the entrance, cherubim and palm trees were carved on the wall of the outer sanctuary.

[21]The outer sanctuary[m] had a rectangular doorframe, and the one at the front of the Most Holy Place was similar. [22]There was a wooden altar[n] three cubits high and two cubits square[j]; its corners, its base[k] and its sides were of wood. The man said to me, "This is the table[o] that is before the LORD." [23]Both the outer sanctuary[p] and the Most Holy Place had double doors.[q] [24]Each door had two leaves—two hinged leaves[r] for each door. [25]And on the doors of the outer sanctuary were carved cherubim and palm trees like those carved on the walls, and there was a wooden overhang on the front of the portico. [26]On the sidewalls of the portico were narrow windows with palm trees carved on each side. The side rooms of the temple also had overhangs.[s]

41:14 [d]Eze 40:47
41:15 [e]Eze 42:3
41:16 [f]1Ki 6:4 [g]ver 25-26; 1Ki 6:15; Eze 42:3
41:18 [h]S 1Ki 6:18 [i]Ex 37:7; S 2Ch 3:7 [j]S 1Ki 6:29; 7:36 [k]Eze 10:21
41:19 [l]S Eze 10:14
41:21 [m]ver 1
41:22 [n]S Ex 30:1 [o]S Ex 25:23; S Eze 23:41
41:23 [p]ver 1 [q]1Ki 6:32
41:24 [r]1Ki 6:34
41:26 [s]ver 15-16; Eze 40:16
42:1 [t]ver 13 [u]S Ex 27:9; Eze 41:12-14 [v]Eze 40:17
42:3 [w]Eze 41:15 [x]Eze 41:16
42:4 [y]Eze 46:19
42:9 [z]Eze 44:5; 46:19
42:10 [a]Eze 41:12-14 [b]ver 1
42:13 [c]Eze 40:46 [d]ver 1 [e]Eze 41:12-14

Chapter 42

Rooms for the Priests

THEN the man led me northward into the outer court and brought me to the rooms[t] opposite the temple courtyard[u] and opposite the outer wall on the north side.[v] [2]The building whose door faced north was a hundred cubits[l] long and fifty cubits wide. [3]Both in the section twenty cubits from the inner court and in the section opposite the pavement of the outer court, gallery[w] faced gallery at the three levels.[x] [4]In front of the rooms was an inner passageway ten cubits wide and a hundred cubits[m] long. Their doors were on the north.[y] [5]Now the upper rooms were narrower, for the galleries took more space from them than from the rooms on the lower and middle floors of the building. [6]The rooms on the third floor had no pillars, as the courts had; so they were smaller in floor space than those on the lower and middle floors. [7]There was an outer wall parallel to the rooms and the outer court; it extended in front of the rooms for fifty cubits. [8]While the row of rooms on the side next to the outer court was fifty cubits long, the row on the side nearest the sanctuary was a hundred cubits long. [9]The lower rooms had an entrance[z] on the east side as one enters them from the outer court.

[10]On the south side[n] along the length of the wall of the outer court, adjoining the temple courtyard[a] and opposite the outer wall, were rooms[b] [11]with a passageway in front of them. These were like the rooms on the north; they had the same length and width, with similar exits and dimensions. Similar to the doorways on the north [12]were the doorways of the rooms on the south. There was a doorway at the beginning of the passageway that was parallel to the corresponding wall extending eastward, by which one enters the rooms.

[13]Then he said to me, "The north[c] and south rooms[d] facing the temple courtyard[e] are the priests' rooms, where the

[j]*22* Septuagint; Hebrew *long* [k]*22* Septuagint; Hebrew *length* [l]*2* The common cubit was about 1 1/2 feet (about 0.5 meter). [m]*4* Septuagint and Syriac; Hebrew *and one cubit* [n]*10* Septuagint; Hebrew *Eastward*

priests who approach the LORD will eat the most holy offerings. There they will put the most holy offerings—the grain offerings,[f] the sin offerings[g] and the guilt offerings[h]—for the place is holy.[i] 14Once the priests enter the holy precincts, they are not to go into the outer court until they leave behind the garments[j] in which they minister, for these are holy. They are to put on other clothes before they go near the places that are for the people.[k]"

15When he had finished measuring what was inside the temple area, he led me out by the east gate[l] and measured the area all around: 16He measured the east side with the measuring rod; it was five hundred cubits.[o] 17He measured the north side; it was five hundred cubits[p] by the measuring rod. 18He measured the south side; it was five hundred cubits by the measuring rod. 19Then he turned to the west side and measured; it was five hundred cubits by the measuring rod. 20So he measured[m] the area[n] on all four sides. It had a wall around it,[o] five hundred cubits long and five hundred cubits wide,[p] to separate the holy from the common.[q]

Chapter 43

The Glory Returns to the Temple

THEN the man brought me to the gate facing east,[r] 2and I saw the glory of the God of Israel coming from the east. His voice was like the roar of rushing waters,[s] and the land was radiant with his glory.[t] 3The vision I saw was like the vision I had seen when he[q] came to destroy the city and like the visions I had seen by the Kebar River, and I fell facedown. 4The glory[u] of the LORD entered the temple through the gate facing east.[v] 5Then the Spirit[w] lifted me up[x] and brought me into the inner court, and the glory[y] of the LORD filled the temple.[z]

6While the man was standing beside me, I heard someone speaking to me from inside the temple. 7He said: "Son of man, this is the place of my throne[a] and the place for the soles of my feet. This is where I will live among the Israelites forever. The house of Israel will never again defile[b] my holy name—neither they nor their kings—by their prostitution[r] and the lifeless idols[s] of their kings at their high places.[c] 8When they placed their threshold next to my threshold and their doorposts beside my doorposts, with only a wall between me and them, they defiled my holy name by their detestable practices. So I destroyed them in my anger. 9Now let them put away from me their prostitution and the lifeless idols of their kings, and I will live among them forever.[d]

10"Son of man, describe the temple to the people of Israel, that they may be ashamed[e] of their sins. Let them consider the plan, 11and if they are ashamed of all they have done, make known to them the design of the temple—its arrangement, its exits and entrances—its whole design and all its regulations[t] and laws. Write these down before them so that they may be faithful to its design and follow all its regulations.[f]

12"This is the law of the temple: All the surrounding area[g] on top of the mountain will be most holy.[h] Such is the law of the temple.

The Altar

13"These are the measurements of the altar[i] in long cubits, that cubit being a cubit[u] and a handbreadth[v]: Its gutter is a

42:13 [f]Jer 41:5 [g]S Lev 10:17 [h]Lev 14:13 [i]S Ex 29:31; S Lev 6:29; 7:6; 10:12-13; Nu 18:9-10
42:14 [j]Lev 16:23; Eze 44:19 [k]Ex 29:9; S Lev 8:7-9
42:15 [l]Eze 43:1
42:20 [m]Eze 40:5 [n]Eze 43:12 [o]Zec 2:5 [p]Eze 45:2; Rev 21:16 [q]S Eze 22:26
43:1 [r]S 1Ch 9:18; S Eze 8:16; 42:15; 44:1
43:2 [s]S Ps 18:4; S Rev 1:15 [t]Isa 6:3; Rev 18:1; 21:11
43:4 [u]Eze 1:28 [v]Eze 10:19; 44:2
43:5 [w]S Eze 11:24 [x]S Eze 3:12 [y]S Ex 16:7 [z]S Isa 6:4
43:7 [a]S Jer 3:17 [b]S Eze 37:23 [c]S Lev 26:30; S Eze 20:29,39
43:9 [d]Eze 37:26-28
43:10 [e]S Eze 16:61
43:11 [f]Eze 44:5
43:12 [g]Eze 42:20 [h]S Eze 17:22
43:13 [i]S Ex 20:24; 2Ch 4:1

[o] *16* See Septuagint of verse 17; Hebrew *rods*; also in verses 18 and 19. [p] *17* Septuagint; Hebrew *rods* [q] *3* Some Hebrew manuscripts and Vulgate; most Hebrew manuscripts *I* [r] *7* Or *their spiritual adultery*; also in verse 9 [s] *7* Or *the corpses*; also in verse 9 [t] *11* Some Hebrew manuscripts and Septuagint; most Hebrew manuscripts *regulations and its whole design* [u] *13* The common cubit was about 1 1/2 feet (about 0.5 meter). [v] *13* That is, about 3 inches (about 8 centimeters)

42:13,14,20 GOD, Holy—God sets apart people and places to serve His people as they worship. Because these are in God's presence, they are holy and must be kept pure. Entering God's presence is an awesome, purifying experience.

43:2,4–5 GOD, Glory—The destruction of God's worship place did not separate His people from His presence. God came in His glorious presence. See note on 1:28.

43:6–7 REVELATION, Divine Presence—God reaffirmed an age-old promise realized by the released Israelites on their exit from Egypt. He would live among them, provide the strength for them to remain faithful, and let them become the nation God purposed them to be. A new Temple would represent God's presence among a renewed people.

43:7 GOD, Personal—The invisible God provides a place where His people can experience His personal presence among them in an extraordinary way. This is extremely important because He does not allow any image to represent His presence and because we know He is too great to be contained by any house of worship. Still He wants us to know He is personally present with us.

43:7,12 GOD, Holy—God had plans for a new Temple where His holy presence could be symbolized among His people. See note on 42:13,14,20.

43:7,9 ELECTION, Worship—Ezekiel spoke of the day when unholy practices would be put away from the holy city and the Temple. God will live among His people forever. The glory will return to the Temple. The new age will have come to pass. Holy lives united in holy worship is God's election goal. Compare Rev 21:1–22.

43:11 HOLY SCRIPTURE, Writing—The prophet was asked to record God's plans for the Temple and worship in hope that a repentant and committed Israel might return to faithful pursuit of God's will. Rebuilding the Temple became a major part of Israel's mission after the Exile. See Haggai; Zechariah.

cubit deep and a cubit wide, with a rim of
one span[w] around the edge. And this is
the height of the altar: 14From the gutter
on the ground up to the lower ledge it is
two cubits high and a cubit wide, and
from the smaller ledge up to the larger
ledge it is four cubits high and a cubit
wide. 15The altar hearth[j] is four cubits
high, and four horns[k] project upward
from the hearth. 16The altar hearth is
square, twelve cubits long and twelve cubits wide.[l] 17The upper ledge[m] also is
square, fourteen cubits long and fourteen
cubits wide, with a rim of half a cubit and
a gutter of a cubit all around. The steps[n]
of the altar face east.[o]"
18Then he said to me, "Son of man,
this is what the Sovereign LORD says:
These will be the regulations for sacrificing burnt offerings[p] and sprinkling
blood[q] upon the altar when it is built:
19You are to give a young bull[r] as a sin
offering to the priests, who are Levites, of
the family of Zadok,[s] who come near[t] to
minister before me, declares the Sovereign LORD. 20You are to take some of its
blood and put it on the four horns of the
altar[u] and on the four corners of the upper ledge[v] and all around the rim, and so
purify the altar[w] and make atonement for
it. 21You are to take the bull for the sin
offering and burn it in the designated part
of the temple area outside the sanctuary.[x]
22"On the second day you are to offer a
male goat without defect for a sin offering, and the altar is to be purified as it
was purified with the bull. 23When you
have finished purifying it, you are to offer
a young bull and a ram from the flock,
both without defect.[y] 24You are to offer
them before the LORD, and the priests are
to sprinkle salt[z] on them and sacrifice
them as a burnt offering to the LORD.
25"For seven days[a] you are to provide
a male goat daily for a sin offering; you
are also to provide a young bull and a ram
from the flock, both without defect.[b]
26For seven days they are to make atonement for the altar and cleanse it; thus
they will dedicate it. 27At the end of these
days, from the eighth day[c] on, the priests
are to present your burnt offerings[d] and
fellowship offerings[x][e] on the altar. Then
I will accept you, declares the Sovereign
LORD."

Chapter 44

The Prince, the Levites, the Priests

THEN the man brought me back to the
outer gate of the sanctuary, the one
facing east,[f] and it was shut. 2The LORD
said to me, "This gate is to remain shut.
It must not be opened; no one may enter
through it.[g] It is to remain shut because
the LORD, the God of Israel, has entered
through it. 3The prince himself is the only
one who may sit inside the gateway to eat
in the presence[h] of the LORD. He is to
enter by way of the portico of the gateway
and go out the same way.[i]"
4Then the man brought me by way of
the north gate[j] to the front of the temple. I looked and saw the glory of the
LORD filling the temple[k] of the LORD, and
I fell facedown.[l]
5The LORD said to me, "Son of man,
look carefully, listen closely and give attention to everything I tell you concerning all the regulations regarding the temple of the LORD. Give attention to the entrance[m] of the temple and all the exits of
the sanctuary.[n] 6Say to the rebellious
house[o] of Israel, 'This is what the Sovereign LORD says: Enough of your detestable practices, O house of Israel! 7In addition to all your other detestable practices,
you brought foreigners uncircumcised in
heart[p] and flesh into my sanctuary, desecrating my temple while you offered me
food, fat and blood, and you broke my
covenant.[q] 8Instead of carrying out your
duty in regard to my holy things, you put
others in charge of my sanctuary.[r] 9This
is what the Sovereign LORD says: No foreigner uncircumcised in heart and flesh is
to enter my sanctuary, not even the foreigners who live among the Israelites.[s]
10" 'The Levites who went far from me
when Israel went astray[t] and who wandered from me after their idols must bear
the consequences of their sin.[u] 11They
may serve in my sanctuary, having charge

43:15 [j]Isa 29:2 [k]S Ex 27:2
43:16 [l]Rev 21:16
43:17 [m]ver 20; Eze 45:19 [n]Ex 20:26 [o]S Ex 27:1
43:18 [p]Ex 40:29 [q]Lev 1:5,11; Heb 9:21-22
43:19 [r]S Lev 4:3 [s]S 2Sa 8:17; S Ezr 7:2 [t]Nu 16:40; S Eze 40:46
43:20 [u]S Lev 4:7 [v]S ver 17 [w]Lev 16:19
43:21 [x]Ex 29:14; Heb 13:11
43:23 [y]Ex 29:1; S Lev 22:20
43:24 [z]S Lev 2:13; Mk 9:49-50
43:25 [a]S Lev 8:33 [b]S Ex 29:37
43:27 [c]Lev 9:1 [d]S Isa 60:7 [e]S Ex 32:6; S Lev 17:5
44:1 [f]S Eze 43:1
44:2 [g]Eze 43:4-5
44:3 [h]S Ex 24:9-11 [i]Eze 46:2,8
44:4 [j]S Eze 40:35 [k]S Isa 6:4; S Eze 10:4; Rev 15:8 [l]Da 8:17
44:5 [m]S Eze 42:9 [n]Eze 40:4; 43:10-11
44:6 [o]S Eze 3:9
44:7 [p]S Lev 26:41 [q]Ge 17:14; Ex 12:48; Lev 22:25
44:8 [r]Lev 22:2; Nu 18:7
44:9 [s]Joel 3:17; Zec 14:21
44:10 [t]Ps 95:10 [u]Nu 18:23

[w]*13* That is, about 9 inches (about 22 centimeters)
[x]*27* Traditionally *peace offerings*

44:4 GOD, Glory—See notes on 1:28; 43:2,4–5.
44:6–9 SIN, Rebellion—Worship is a holy moment not to be taken lightly. Failure to take worship seriously is rebellion against God. See note on La 1:18–22. Worship sins are detestable practices or abominations (Hebrew *to'ebah*). The very essence of these practices is opposed to and incompatible with belief in and worship of the God of Israel. The worshiping community cannot function when such practices are present. The practices endanger the life of the worshiping community. Israel learned by sad experience that foreign people brought abominable practices into Israelite worship. See note on 1 Ki 11:1–13. Such practices represent a breach of God's covenant. We as God's people must take seriously our worship responsibilities. When we do not, we sin against God's holiness.
44:7 THE CHURCH, Covenant People—See note on Lev 26:15–17.
44:8–9,23 GOD, Holy—God knows the history of His people. Even priests had led His people into sin. As He started over, He issued stringent restrictions on who were permitted to be His ministers. This did not result from bias against or hatred for foreigners. They were welcome to worship, but worship leaders must have proved themselves in the test of time. See note on 42:13,14,20.

of the gates of the temple and serving in
it; they may slaughter the burnt offerings[v] and sacrifices for the people and
stand before the people and serve them.[w]
12But because they served them in the
presence of their idols and made the
house of Israel fall[x] into sin, therefore I
have sworn with uplifted hand[y] that they
must bear the consequences of their sin,
declares the Sovereign LORD.[z] 13They are
not to come near to serve me as priests or
come near any of my holy things or my
most holy offerings; they must bear the
shame[a] of their detestable practices.[b]
14Yet I will put them in charge of the duties of the temple and all the work that is
to be done in it.[c]
15" 'But the priests, who are Levites
and descendants of Zadok[d] and who
faithfully carried out the duties of my
sanctuary when the Israelites went astray
from me, are to come near to minister
before me; they are to stand before me to
offer sacrifices of fat[e] and blood, declares
the Sovereign LORD.[f] 16They alone are to
enter my sanctuary; they alone are to
come near my table[g] to minister before
me and perform my service.[h]
17" 'When they enter the gates of the
inner court, they are to wear linen
clothes;[i] they must not wear any woolen
garment while ministering at the gates of
the inner court or inside the temple.
18They are to wear linen turbans[j] on
their heads and linen undergarments[k]
around their waists. They must not wear
anything that makes them perspire.[l]
19When they go out into the outer court
where the people are, they are to take off
the clothes they have been ministering in
and are to leave them in the sacred
rooms, and put on other clothes, so that
they do not consecrate[m] the people by
means of their garments.[n]
20" 'They must not shave[o] their heads
or let their hair grow long, but they are to
keep the hair of their heads trimmed.[p]
21No priest is to drink wine when he enters the inner court.[q] 22They must not
marry widows or divorced women; they
may marry only virgins of Israelite descent or widows of priests.[r] 23They are to
teach my people the difference between
the holy and the common[s] and show
them how to distinguish between the unclean and the clean.[t]
24" 'In any dispute, the priests are to
serve as judges[u] and decide it according
to my ordinances. They are to keep my
laws and my decrees for all my appointed
feasts,[v] and they are to keep my Sabbaths
holy.[w]
25" 'A priest must not defile himself by
going near a dead person; however, if the
dead person was his father or mother,
son or daughter, brother or unmarried
sister, then he may defile himself.[x] 26Af-
ter he is cleansed, he must wait seven
days.[y] 27On the day he goes into the inner court of the sanctuary[z] to minister in
the sanctuary, he is to offer a sin offering[a] for himself, declares the Sovereign
LORD.
28" 'I am to be the only inheritance[b]
the priests have. You are to give them no
possession in Israel; I will be their possession. 29They will eat[c] the grain offerings,
the sin offerings and the guilt offerings;
and everything in Israel devoted[y] to the
LORD[d] will belong to them.[e] 30The best
of all the firstfruits[f] and of all your special gifts will belong to the priests. You
are to give them the first portion of your
ground meal[g] so that a blessing[h] may
rest on your household.[i] 31The priests
must not eat anything, bird or animal,
found dead[j] or torn by wild animals.[k]

Chapter 45

Division of the Land

" 'WHEN you allot the land as an
inheritance,[l] you are to
present to the LORD a portion of the land
as a sacred district, 25,000 cubits long
and 20,000[z] cubits wide; the entire area
will be holy.[m] 2Of this, a section 500 cubits square[n] is to be for the sanctuary,
with 50 cubits around it for open land.
3In the sacred district, measure off a section 25,000 cubits[a] long and 10,000 cubits[b] wide. In it will be the sanctuary,
the Most Holy Place. 4It will be the sacred
portion of the land for the priests,[o] who
minister in the sanctuary and who draw
near to minister before the LORD. It will
be a place for their houses as well as a
holy place for the sanctuary.[p] 5An area
25,000 cubits long and 10,000 cubits
wide will belong to the Levites, who

[y]*29* The Hebrew term refers to the irrevocable giving over of things or persons to the LORD. [z]*1* Septuagint (see also verses 3 and 5 and 48:9); Hebrew *10,000*
[a]*3* That is, about 7 miles (about 12 kilometers)
[b]*3* That is, about 3 miles (about 5 kilometers)

44:11 [v]2Ch 29:34 [w]Nu 3:5-37; S 16:9; S 1Ch 26:12-19
44:12 [x]S Jer 18:15 [y]Ps 106:26 [z]2Ki 16:10-16; Jer 14:10
44:13 [a]S Eze 16:61 [b]Nu 18:3; Hos 5:1
44:14 [c]1Sa 2:36; 2Ki 23:9; S 1Ch 23:28-32
44:15 [d]S 2Sa 8:17; S Ezr 7:2 [e]S Ex 29:13 [f]S Jer 33:18; S Eze 40:46; Zec 3:7
44:16 [g]S Eze 41:22 [h]Lev 3:16-17; 17:5-6; Nu 18:5; S 1Sa 2:35; Zec 3:7
44:17 [i]Rev 19:8
44:18 [j]S Ex 28:39; S Isa 3:20 [k]S Ex 28:42 [l]S Lev 16:4
44:19 [m]S Lev 6:27 [n]Ex 39:27-29; Lev 6:10-11; S Eze 42:14
44:20 [o]Eze 5:1 [p]S Lev 21:5; Nu 6:5
44:21 [q]S Lev 10:9
44:22 [r]Lev 21:7
44:23 [s]S Eze 22:26 [t]S Ge 7:2; Lev 13:50; 15:31; Jer 15:19; Hag 2:11-13
44:24 [u]Dt 17:8-9; 19:17; 21:5; S 1Ch 23:4 [v]S Lev 23:2 [w]2Ch 19:8
44:25 [x]Lev 21:1-4
44:26 [y]Nu 19:14
44:27 [z]S Nu 3:28 [a]S Lev 4:28; Nu 6:11
44:28 [b]S Nu 18:20; Dt 18:1-2; S Jos 13:33
44:29 [c]Lev 6:16 [d]S Lev 27:21 [e]Nu 18:9,14; S Jos 13:14
44:30 [f]Nu 18:12-13; S 2Ch 31:5 [g]S Nu 15:18-21 [h]S Lev 25:21 [i]S 2Ch 31:10; Ne 10:35-37
44:31 [j]S Lev 11:39 [k]S Ex 22:31; S Lev 11:40
45:1 [l]S Nu 34:13 [m]Eze 48:8-9,29
45:2 [n]Eze 42:20
45:4 [o]S Eze 40:46 [p]Eze 48:10-11

44:23 EDUCATION, Priests—See Dt 33:10; note on Lev 10:11.

44:29–30 STEWARDSHIP, Giving in Worship—Giving is a part of worship. The gifts help support the leaders of worship. This was true for Israel's life as a nation, for Ezekiel's vision of a restored nation, and for Christ's church. See note on Mt 5:23–24.

45:1,3,4 GOD, Holy—In grace God restored His people. Central to His restoration plans was a holy place of worship marking His presence among His people. See note on 42:13, 14,20.

serve in the temple, as their possession
for towns to live in.[c] [q]
6" 'You are to give the city as its property an area 5,000 cubits wide and 25,
000 cubits long, adjoining the sacred portion; it will belong to the whole house of
Israel.[r]
7" 'The prince will have the land bordering each side of the area formed by
the sacred district and the property of the
city. It will extend westward from the
west side and eastward from the east
side, running lengthwise from the western to the eastern border parallel to one
of the tribal portions.[s] 8This land will be
his possession in Israel. And my princes
will no longer oppress my people but will
allow the house of Israel to possess the
land according to their tribes.[t]
9" 'This is what the Sovereign LORD
says: You have gone far enough, O
princes of Israel! Give up your violence
and oppression[u] and do what is just and
right.[v] Stop dispossessing my people, declares the Sovereign LORD. 10You are to
use accurate scales,[w] an accurate
ephah[d][x] and an accurate bath.[e] 11The
ephah[y] and the bath are to be the same
size, the bath containing a tenth of a homer[f] and the ephah a tenth of a homer;
the homer is to be the standard measure
for both. 12The shekel[g] is to consist of
twenty gerahs.[z] Twenty shekels plus
twenty-five shekels plus fifteen shekels
equal one mina.[h]

Offerings and Holy Days

13" 'This is the special gift you are to
offer: a sixth of an ephah from each homer of wheat and a sixth of an ephah
from each homer of barley. 14The prescribed portion of oil, measured by the
bath, is a tenth of a bath from each cor
(which consists of ten baths or one homer, for ten baths are equivalent to a homer). 15Also one sheep is to be taken
from every flock of two hundred from the
well-watered pastures of Israel. These
will be used for the grain offerings, burnt
offerings[a] and fellowship offerings[i] to
make atonement[b] for the people, declares the Sovereign LORD. 16All the people of the land will participate in this special gift for the use of the prince in Israel.
17It will be the duty of the prince to provide the burnt offerings, grain offerings
and drink offerings at the festivals, the
New Moons[c] and the Sabbaths[d]—at all
the appointed feasts of the house of Israel. He will provide the sin offerings, grain
offerings, burnt offerings and fellowship
offerings to make atonement for the
house of Israel.[e]
18" 'This is what the Sovereign LORD
says: In the first month[f] on the first day
you are to take a young bull without defect[g] and purify the sanctuary.[h] 19The
priest is to take some of the blood of the
sin offering and put it on the doorposts of
the temple, on the four corners of the
upper ledge[i] of the altar[j] and on the
gateposts of the inner court. 20You are to
do the same on the seventh day of the
month for anyone who sins unintentionally[k] or through ignorance; so you are to
make atonement for the temple.
21" 'In the first month on the fourteenth day you are to observe the Passover,[l] a feast lasting seven days, during
which you shall eat bread made without
yeast. 22On that day the prince is to provide a bull as a sin offering for himself
and for all the people of the land.[m] 23Ev-
ery day during the seven days of the Feast
he is to provide seven bulls and seven
rams[n] without defect as a burnt offering
to the LORD, and a male goat for a sin
offering.[o] 24He is to provide as a grain
offering[p] an ephah for each bull and an
ephah for each ram, along with a hin[j] of
oil for each ephah.[q]
25" 'During the seven days of the
Feast,[r] which begins in the seventh
month on the fifteenth day, he is to make
the same provision for sin offerings, burnt
offerings, grain offerings and oil.[s]

Chapter 46

"'THIS is what the Sovereign LORD
says: The gate of the inner
court[t] facing east[u] is to be shut on the
six working days, but on the Sabbath day
and on the day of the New Moon[v] it is to
be opened. 2The prince is to enter from
the outside through the portico[w] of the
gateway and stand by the gatepost. The
priests are to sacrifice his burnt offering[x]
and his fellowship offerings.[k] He is to
worship at the threshold of the gateway
and then go out, but the gate will not be
shut until evening.[y] 3On the Sabbaths[z]

45:5 [q]Eze 48:13
45:6 [r]Eze 48:15-18
45:7 [s]Eze 48:21
45:8 [t]S Nu 26:53; Eze 46:18
45:9 [u]Ps 12:5 [v]S Jer 22:3; Zec 7:9-10; 8:16
45:10 [w]Dt 25:15; S Pr 11:1; Am 8:4-6; Mic 6:10-11 [x]S Lev 19:36
45:11 [y]Isa 5:10
45:12 [z]Ex 30:13; Lev 27:25; Nu 3:47
45:15 [a]S Lev 1:4 [b]Lev 6:30
45:17 [c]S Nu 10:10 [d]S Lev 23:38; Isa 66:23 [e]S 1Ki 8:62; S 2Ch 31:3; Eze 46:4-12
45:18 [f]Ex 12:2 [g]S Lev 22:20; Heb 9:14 [h]S Lev 16:16,33
45:19 [i]S Eze 43:17 [j]Lev 16:18-19
45:20 [k]Lev 4:27
45:21 [l]S Ex 12:11
45:22 [m]Lev 4:14
45:23 [n]S Nu 22:40; S Job 42:8 [o]Nu 28:16-25
45:24 [p]Nu 28:12-13 [q]Eze 46:5-7
45:25 [r]Dt 16:13 [s]Lev 23:34-43; Nu 29:12-38
46:1 [t]S Eze 40:19 [u]S 1Ch 9:18 [v]ver 6; Isa 66:23
46:2 [w]ver 8 [x]Eze 40:39 [y]ver 12; S Eze 44:3
46:3 [z]S Isa 66:23

[c]5 Septuagint; Hebrew *temple; they will have as their possession 20 rooms* [d]10 An ephah was a dry measure. [e]10 A bath was a liquid measure. [f]11 A homer was a dry measure. [g]12 A shekel weighed about 2/5 ounce (about 11.5 grams). [h]12 That is, 60 shekels; the common mina was 50 shekels. [i]15 Traditionally *peace offerings*; also in verse 17 [j]24 That is, probably about 4 quarts (about 4 liters) [k]2 Traditionally *peace offerings*; also in verse 12

45:9–12 CHRISTIAN ETHICS, Justice—See note on Lev 19:35–36; Ps 72:1–14.
45:13–18 STEWARDSHIP, Sacrifice Giving—Stewardship is a part of renewal. Ezekiel described life for a nation restored from exile and captivity. They would give sacrifices to seek atonement and to express worship. See note on Lev 1:2.

and New Moons the people of the land
are to worship in the presence of the
LORD at the entrance to that gateway.[a]
4The burnt offering the prince brings to
the LORD on the Sabbath day is to be six
male lambs and a ram, all without defect.
5The grain offering given with the ram is
to be an ephah,[l] and the grain offering
with the lambs is to be as much as he
pleases, along with a hin[m] of oil for each
ephah.[b] 6On the day of the New Moon[c]
he is to offer a young bull, six lambs and a
ram, all without defect.[d] 7He is to provide as a grain offering one ephah with
the bull, one ephah with the ram, and
with the lambs as much as he wants to
give, along with a hin of oil with each
ephah.[e] 8When the prince enters, he is
to go in through the portico[f] of the gateway, and he is to come out the same
way.[g]
9" 'When the people of the land come
before the LORD at the appointed feasts,[h]
whoever enters by the north gate to worship is to go out the south gate; and whoever enters by the south gate is to go out
the north gate. No one is to return
through the gate by which he entered,
but each is to go out the opposite gate.
10The prince is to be among them, going
in when they go in and going out when
they go out.[i]
11" 'At the festivals and the appointed
feasts, the grain offering is to be an ephah
with a bull, an ephah with a ram, and
with the lambs as much as one pleases,
along with a hin of oil for each ephah.[j]
12When the prince provides[k] a freewill
offering[l] to the LORD—whether a burnt
offering or fellowship offerings—the gate
facing east is to be opened for him. He
shall offer his burnt offering or his fellowship offerings as he does on the Sabbath
day. Then he shall go out, and after he
has gone out, the gate will be shut.[m]
13" 'Every day you are to provide a
year-old lamb without defect for a burnt
offering to the LORD; morning by morning[n] you shall provide it.[o] 14You are also
to provide with it morning by morning a
grain offering, consisting of a sixth of an
ephah with a third of a hin of oil[p] to
moisten the flour. The presenting of this
grain offering to the LORD is a lasting ordinance.[q] 15So the lamb and the grain offering and the oil shall be provided morning by morning for a regular[r] burnt offering.[s]
16" 'This is what the Sovereign LORD
says: If the prince makes a gift from his
inheritance to one of his sons, it will also
belong to his descendants; it is to be their
property by inheritance.[t] 17If, however,
he makes a gift from his inheritance to
one of his servants, the servant may keep
it until the year of freedom;[u] then it will
revert to the prince. His inheritance belongs to his sons only; it is theirs. 18The
prince must not take[v] any of the inheritance[w] of the people, driving them off
their property. He is to give his sons their
inheritance out of his own property, so
that none of my people will be separated
from his property.' "
19Then the man brought me through
the entrance[x] at the side of the gate to
the sacred rooms facing north,[y] which
belonged to the priests, and showed me a
place at the western end. 20He said to me,
"This is the place where the priests will
cook the guilt offering and the sin offering
and bake the grain offering, to avoid
bringing them into the outer court and
consecrating[z] the people."[a]
21He then brought me to the outer
court and led me around to its four corners, and I saw in each corner another
court. 22In the four corners of the outer
court were enclosed[n] courts, forty cubits
long and thirty cubits wide; each of the
courts in the four corners was the same
size. 23Around the inside of each of the
four courts was a ledge of stone, with
places for fire built all around under the
ledge. 24He said to me, "These are the
kitchens where those who minister at the
temple will cook the sacrifices of the people."

Chapter 47

The River From the Temple

THE man brought me back to the entrance of the temple, and I saw water[b] coming out from under the threshold of the temple toward the east (for the
temple faced east). The water was coming
down from under the south side of the
temple, south of the altar.[c] 2He then
brought me out through the north gate[d]
and led me around the outside to the outer gate facing east, and the water was
flowing from the south side.
3As the man went eastward with a
measuring line[e] in his hand, he measured off a thousand cubits[o] and then led
me through water that was ankle-deep.
4He measured off another thousand cubits and led me through water that was
knee-deep. He measured off another
thousand and led me through water that
was up to the waist. 5He measured off
another thousand, but now it was a

46:3 [a]Lk 1:10
46:5 [b]ver 11
46:6 [c]ver 1; S Nu 10:10 [d]S Lev 22:20
46:7 [e]Eze 45:24
46:8 [f]ver 2 [g]Eze 44:3
46:9 [h]S Ex 23:14; S 34:20
46:10 [i]2Sa 6:14-15; Ps 42:4
46:11 [j]ver 5
46:12 [k]S Eze 45:17 [l]S Lev 7:16 [m]ver 2
46:13 [n]S Ps 5:3 [o]Ex 29:38; S Nu 28:3
46:14 [p]Nu 15:6 [q]Da 8:11
46:15 [r]S Ex 29:42 [s]S Ex 29:38; Nu 28:5-6
46:16 [t]2Ch 21:3
46:17 [u]S Lev 25:10
46:18 [v]1Sa 8:14 [w]S Lev 25:23; Eze 45:8; Mic 2:1-2
46:19 [x]S Eze 42:9 [y]Eze 42:4
46:20 [z]S Lev 6:27 [a]ver 24; Zec 14:20
47:1 [b]S Isa 55:1 [c]Ps 46:4; Joel 3:18; Rev 22:1
47:2 [d]S Eze 40:35
47:3 [e]S Eze 40:3

[l]*5* That is, probably about 3/5 bushel (about 22 liters)
[m]*5* That is, probably about 4 quarts (about 4 liters)
[n]*22* The meaning of the Hebrew for this word is uncertain.
[o]*3* That is, about 1,500 feet (about 450 meters)

river[f] that I could not cross, because the
water had risen and was deep enough to
swim in—a river that no one could
cross.[g] 6He asked me, "Son of man, do
you see this?"

Then he led me back to the bank of the
river. 7When I arrived there, I saw a great
number of trees on each side of the river.[h] 8He said to me, "This water flows
toward the eastern region and goes down
into the Arabah,[p][i] where it enters the
Sea.[q] When it empties into the Sea,[q] the
water there becomes fresh.[j] 9Swarms of
living creatures will live wherever the
river flows. There will be large numbers
of fish, because this water flows there
and makes the salt water fresh; so where
the river flows everything will live.[k]
10Fishermen[l] will stand along the shore;
from En Gedi[m] to En Eglaim there will be
places for spreading nets.[n] The fish will
be of many kinds[o]—like the fish of the
Great Sea.[r][p] 11But the swamps and
marshes will not become fresh; they will
be left for salt.[q] 12Fruit trees of all kinds
will grow on both banks of the river.[r]
Their leaves will not wither, nor will
their fruit[s] fail. Every month they will
bear, because the water from the sanctuary[t] flows to them. Their fruit will serve
for food and their leaves for healing.[u]"

The Boundaries of the Land

13This is what the Sovereign LORD says:
"These are the boundaries[v] by which
you are to divide the land for an inheritance among the twelve tribes of Israel,
with two portions for Joseph.[w] 14You are
to divide it equally among them. Because
I swore with uplifted hand to give it to
your forefathers, this land will become
your inheritance.[x]

15"This is to be the boundary of the
land:[y]

"On the north side it will run from the
Great Sea[z] by the Hethlon road[a]
past Lebo[s] Hamath to Zedad, 16Be-
rothah[t][b] and Sibraim (which lies
on the border between Damascus
and Hamath),[c] as far as Hazer Hat-
ticon, which is on the border of Hauran. 17The boundary will extend
from the sea to Hazar Enan,[u] along
the northern border of Damascus,
with the border of Hamath to the
north. This will be the north
boundary.[d]
18"On the east side the boundary will run
between Hauran and Damascus,
along the Jordan between Gilead
and the land of Israel, to the eastern
sea and as far as Tamar.[v] This will
be the east boundary.[e]
19"On the south side it will run from Tamar as far as the waters of Meribah
Kadesh,[f] then along the Wadi ⌊of
Egypt⌋[g] to the Great Sea.[h] This will
be the south boundary.
20"On the west side, the Great Sea will
be the boundary to a point opposite
Lebo[w] Hamath.[i] This will be the
west boundary.[j]

21"You are to distribute this land
among yourselves according to the tribes
of Israel. 22You are to allot it as an inheritance[k] for yourselves and for the aliens[l]
who have settled among you and who
have children. You are to consider them
as native-born Israelites; along with you
they are to be allotted an inheritance
among the tribes of Israel.[m] 23In whatever tribe the alien settles, there you are to
give him his inheritance," declares the
Sovereign LORD.[n]

Chapter 48

The Division of the Land

"THESE are the tribes, listed by
name: At the northern frontier,
Dan[o] will have one portion; it will follow
the Hethlon road[p] to Lebo[x] Hamath;[q]
Hazar Enan and the northern border of
Damascus next to Hamath will be part of
its border from the east side to the west
side.
2"Asher[r] will have one portion; it will
border the territory of Dan from east to
west.
3"Naphtali[s] will have one portion; it
will border the territory of Asher from
east to west.
4"Manasseh[t] will have one portion; it

47:5 [f]S Ge 2:10 [g]Isa 11:9; Hab 2:14
47:7 [h]ver 12; Rev 22:2
47:8 [i]S Dt 1:1; S 3:17 [j]Isa 41:18
47:9 [k]Isa 12:3; 55:1; Jn 4:14; 7:37-38
47:10 [l]S Isa 19:8; Mt 4:19 [m]S Jos 15:62 [n]Eze 26:5 [o]S Ps 104:25; Mt 13:47 [p]S Nu 34:6
47:11 [q]S Dt 29:23
47:12 [r]ver 7; Rev 22:2 [s]S Ps 1:3 [t]S Isa 55:1 [u]S Ge 2:9; S Jer 17:8; Eze 36:8
47:13 [v]Nu 34:2-12 [w]S Ge 48:16; S 49:26
47:14 [x]S Ge 12:7; S Dt 1:8; S Eze 36:12
47:15 [y]Nu 34:2 [z]ver 19; S Nu 34:6 [a]Eze 48:1
47:16 [b]2Sa 8:8 [c]Nu 13:21; S Jer 49:23; Eze 48:1
47:17 [d]Eze 48:1
47:18 [e]S Eze 27:18
47:19 [f]Dt 32:51 [g]S Ge 15:18; Isa 27:12 [h]S ver 15; Eze 48:28
47:20 [i]S Nu 13:21; Eze 48:1 [j]Nu 34:6
47:22 [k]S Eze 36:12 [l]S Dt 24:19; S Isa 14:1; Mal 3:5 [m]S Lev 24:22; Nu 15:29; 26:55-56; Isa 56:6-7; Ro 10:12; Eph 2:12-16; 3:6; Col 3:11
47:23 [n]S Dt 10:19
48:1 [o]S Ge 30:6 [p]Eze 47:15-17 [q]S Eze 47:20
48:2 [r]Jos 19:24-31
48:3 [s]Jos 19:32-39
48:4 [t]Jos 17:1-11

[p]8 Or *the Jordan Valley* [q]8 That is, the Dead Sea [r]10 That is, the Mediterranean; also in verses 15, 19 and 20 [s]15 Or *past the entrance to* [t]15,16 See Septuagint and Ezekiel 48:1; Hebrew *road to go into Zedad, 16Hamath, Berothah* [u]17 Hebrew *Enon,* a variant of *Enan* [v]18 Septuagint and Syriac; Hebrew *Israel. You will measure to the eastern sea* [w]20 Or *opposite the entrance to* [x]1 Or *to the entrance to*

47:7-23 SALVATION, Renewal—Ezekiel's vision of restored Israel has a life-giving river flowing from underneath the Temple altar. His vision has some elements in common with John's in Rev 21:1—22:5. The boundaries of restored Israel are reduced from the frontiers of David and Solomon. Aliens are given full citizens' rights in renewed Israel. The power of God can accomplish the impossible in salvation. The Lord can give new life to the dead. He can redeem the waste places of nations and individuals. Nothing is beyond the reach of God's grace in Christ Jesus.

47:22 EVANGELISM, Mass—God surprised the exiles with His restoration plan which included full citizenship rights for foreign believers. No one is to be exempted from the household of faith. All who believe become part of God's family. Our evangelistic ministry must extend to all.

will border the territory of Naphtali from
east to west.
5"Ephraim[u] will have one portion; it
will border the territory of Manasseh[v]
from east to west.[w]
6"Reuben[x] will have one portion; it
will border the territory of Ephraim from
east to west.
7"Judah[y] will have one portion; it will
border the territory of Reuben from east
to west.
8"Bordering the territory of Judah from
east to west will be the portion you are to
present as a special gift. It will be 25,000
cubits[y] wide, and its length from east to
west will equal one of the tribal portions;
the sanctuary will be in the center of it.[z]
9"The special portion you are to offer
to the LORD will be 25,000 cubits long
and 10,000 cubits[z] wide.[a] 10This will be
the sacred portion for the priests. It will
be 25,000 cubits long on the north side,
10,000 cubits wide on the west side,
10,000 cubits wide on the east side and
25,000 cubits long on the south side. In
the center of it will be the sanctuary of the
LORD.[b] 11This will be for the consecrated
priests, the Zadokites,[c] who were faithful
in serving me[d] and did not go astray as
the Levites did when the Israelites went
astray.[e] 12It will be a special gift to them
from the sacred portion of the land, a
most holy portion, bordering the territory
of the Levites.
13"Alongside the territory of the
priests, the Levites will have an allotment
25,000 cubits long and 10,000 cubits
wide. Its total length will be 25,000 cubits and its width 10,000 cubits.[f] 14They
must not sell or exchange any of it. This
is the best of the land and must not pass
into other hands, because it is holy to the
LORD.[g]
15"The remaining area, 5,000 cubits
wide and 25,000 cubits long, will be for
the common use of the city, for houses
and for pastureland. The city will be in
the center of it 16and will have these measurements: the north side 4,500 cubits,
the south side 4,500 cubits, the east side
4,500 cubits, and the west side 4,500 cubits.[h] 17The pastureland for the city will
be 250 cubits on the north, 250 cubits on
the south, 250 cubits on the east, and
250 cubits on the west. 18What remains
of the area, bordering on the sacred portion and running the length of it, will be
10,000 cubits on the east side and
10,000 cubits on the west side. Its produce will supply food for the workers of
the city.[i] 19The workers from the city who
farm it will come from all the tribes of
Israel. 20The entire portion will be a
square, 25,000 cubits on each side. As a
special gift you will set aside the sacred
portion, along with the property of the
city.
21"What remains on both sides of the
area formed by the sacred portion and the
city property will belong to the prince. It
will extend eastward from the 25,000 cubits of the sacred portion to the eastern
border, and westward from the 25,000
cubits to the western border. Both these
areas running the length of the tribal portions will belong to the prince, and the
sacred portion with the temple sanctuary
will be in the center of them.[j] 22So the
property of the Levites and the property
of the city will lie in the center of the area
that belongs to the prince. The area belonging to the prince will lie between the
border of Judah and the border of Benjamin.
23"As for the rest of the tribes: Benjamin[k] will have one portion; it will extend from the east side to the west side.
24"Simeon[l] will have one portion; it
will border the territory of Benjamin from
east to west.
25"Issachar[m] will have one portion; it
will border the territory of Simeon from
east to west.
26"Zebulun[n] will have one portion; it
will border the territory of Issachar from
east to west.
27"Gad[o] will have one portion; it will
border the territory of Zebulun from east
to west.
28"The southern boundary of Gad will
run south from Tamar[p] to the waters of
Meribah Kadesh, then along the Wadi ⌊of
Egypt⌋ to the Great Sea.[a] [q]
29"This is the land you are to allot as an
inheritance to the tribes of Israel, and
these will be their portions," declares the
Sovereign LORD.[r]

The Gates of the City

30"These will be the exits of the city:
Beginning on the north side, which is
4,500 cubits long, 31the gates of the city
will be named after the tribes of Israel.
The three gates on the north side will be
the gate of Reuben, the gate of Judah and
the gate of Levi.
32"On the east side, which is 4,500 cubits long, will be three gates: the gate of
Joseph, the gate of Benjamin and the gate
of Dan.
33"On the south side, which measures

48:5 [u]Jos 16:5-9 [v]Jos 17:7-10 [w]Jos 17:17
48:6 [x]Jos 13:15-21
48:7 [y]Jos 15:1-63
48:8 [z]ver 21
48:9 [a]S Eze 45:1
48:10 [b]ver 21; S Eze 45:3-4
48:11 [c]S 2Sa 8:17 [d]S Lev 8:35 [e]Eze 14:11; S 44:15
48:13 [f]Eze 45:5
48:14 [g]S Lev 25:34; 27:10,28
48:16 [h]Rev 21:16
48:18 [i]Eze 45:6
48:21 [j]ver 8,10; Eze 45:7
48:23 [k]Jos 18:11-28
48:24 [l]S Ge 29:33; Jos 19:1-9
48:25 [m]Jos 19:17-23
48:26 [n]Jos 19:10-16
48:27 [o]Jos 13:24-28
48:28 [p]S Ge 14:7 [q]S Nu 34:6; Eze 47:19
48:29 [r]S Eze 45:1

[y]*8* That is, about 7 miles (about 12 kilometers)
[z]*9* That is, about 3 miles (about 5 kilometers)
[a]*28* That is, the Mediterranean

48:12,18 GOD, Holy—See notes on 42:13,14,20; 45:1,3,4.

4,500 cubits, will be three gates: the gate
of Simeon, the gate of Issachar and the
gate of Zebulun.
34"On the west side, which is 4,500
cubits long, will be three gates: the gate
of Gad, the gate of Asher and the gate of
Naphtali.[s]
35"The distance all around will be
18,000 cubits.

"And the name of the city from that
time on will be:

THE LORD IS THERE.[t]"

48:34 [s]S 2Ch 4:4; Rev 21:12-13
48:35 [t]S Isa 12:6; S 24:23; S Jer 3:17; 14:9; Joel 3:21; Rev 3:12; S 21:3

48:35 ELECTION, Presence—Election is God's way of creating a people to dwell eternally in His presence. Ezekiel pointed forward to a day when all nations would recognize God as the sovereign Lord of history, Israel would be a holy people restored to a land newly distributed to the twelve tribes of Israel, and God in His glory and holiness would dwell among a cleansed and holy people. The holy people would dedicate themselves to worship of the God who lived among them in the worship place dedicated to His service.

Daniel

Theological Setting

In every generation some people feel radically threatened. They seek encouragement and hope. They want to know if God still exists and if God is concerned about their plight. The Book of Daniel provides support and understanding for persons living under constant fear.

The author of Daniel adopted a radically different form of communication from that of other Old Testament writers. He took thought forms, imagery, and literary forms from the worlds of wisdom and prophecy to challenge the prevailing fear and hopelessness of his day. He began Israel's use of apocalyptic writing as a way of communicating God's message to His people. Isaiah 24-27, Zechariah, and portions of Ezekiel use related language but not to the extent Daniel does. Revelation is the New Testament example of apocalyptic.

Apocalyptic expression involves the use of elaborate visions and images to describe God's revelation of the last days of history when the world order is rescued from indescribable threats and evil. Apocalyptic writing tells its readers the ethical requirements of the faithful remnant during the terrible threat and often divides the final stages of history into periods which are each described by rich and mysterious symbolism. Only those who know the symbols can fully understand the message of such writing.

The Book of Daniel used six stories about four Israelite captives in Babylon after 597 BC to demonstrate the necessity of proper behavior during the perilous days. Daniel then offered a series of symbol-laden visions to help readers understand their own place in history and the hope God wants to give them for the last days.

Students have honest differences in their interpretations of the figures and images used in Daniel. All agree that the Babylonian, Persian (with the Medes), and Greek empires are involved, along with the later subdivisions of the Greek Empire including the Ptolemy rulers in Egypt and the Seleucid rulers in Syria. A major figure is the Seleucid ruler Antiochus Epiphanes, who violated the holy Temple in Jerusalem in 165 BC. Some scholars see the Roman Empire or a revival of the Roman Empire as the final kingdom.

Whatever the exact progression of historical references, the book presented important options to its readers. The rush of time and history brought an ever-deepening threat to God's people. Successive rulers brought them closer to despair. How could an enslaved people hold on to their faith? What incentive did they have to look to the future? Had their God been defeated? Should they follow the life-styles of their enemies to avoid persecution? Would they dare to die to be true to the teachings God gave them? Dared they live their faith, exposing themselves to all kinds of dangers?

Theological Outline

Daniel: God is Alive! Don't Capitulate to Evil.

I. Historical Change Brings Temptations to God's People. (1:1-7)

II. Historical Experiences Teach Fidelity and Perseverance. (1:8—6:28)
- A. God's wisdom wins in the secular world. (1:8-21)
- B. God's wisdom wins in the realm of dreams and revelation. (2:1-49)
- C. God's people are faithful even unto death. (3:1—4:3)
- D. God's wisdom wins in the realm of personal behavior. (4:4-37)
- E. God's judgment defeats human conspiracies. (5:1-30)
- F. God's wisdom wins despite human conspiracies. (5:31—6:28)

III. Fidelity and Perseverance for God Will Win in the Future. (7:1—12:13)
- A. The Son of man and God's kingdom will defeat the most terrible human powers. (7:1-28)
- B. God allows deceitful persecutors temporary powers but promises their ultimate defeat. (8:1-27)
- C. In desperate times God's people need to confess their sins and seek forgiveness. (9:1-19)
- D. God controls all history, punishing His sinful people but defeating violent conquerors. (9:20-27)
- E. God gives insight, strength, and courage to His faithful interpreter. (10:1—11:1)
- F. God's wise servants will teach the truth even under persecution. (11:2-35)

G. The fiercest enemy will meet his end. (11:36-45)
H. God will bring victory and resurrection for His people. (12:1-13)

Theological Conclusions

Amid its visions, symbols, and images the Book of Daniel makes strong theological statements about the nature of God, the nature of the Christian life, the nature of history, prayer, and the last things.

God, the God of the Hebrews, is a demanding God. He expects His people to remain faithful to Him and His way of life for them even in the darkest moments of history and under the most horrible threats. God is a dependable God. He will keep His promises to His people.

Perseverance is necessary. The central message of Daniel is the call for His people to keep on being faithful when human circumstances appear to hide all hope. Life with God does not guarantee good times always. God's people must persevere through the dark days. In a world filled with "voices" clamoring for allegiance, God's people are called to follow Him at all costs. The example of Daniel and his friends stands as a role model for each person who wants to be listed among God's people. Faith involves risk. Just as Daniel and his friends had to act in faith against immensely powerful opposition, so God's people must risk even their lives to remain faithful.

History involves God's judgment of His sinful people. God's people cannot complain of injustice when their own sins have brought judgment upon them. God mysteriously uses the forces of history, even arrogant rulers, to discipline and judge His people. The meaning of history is not crystal clear on the surface. Events may appear to contradict traditional theological interpretations and beliefs. God provides inspired speakers to interpret His historical acts for His people. Only with such inspired interpreters can God's people understand God's ways with His world. History leads to God's victory. Present defeat must not hide God's march to victory for His people. Amid the shadows of persecution and sacrilege, God works to accomplish His ultimate purpose. History does not naturally lead to such victory through natural forces. God's activity alone brings final victory.

Prayer keeps God's people faithful. Only through constant communication with God can His people persevere and follow the life He sets out for them. Prayer is the highway to proper ethics for God's people. Prayer brings hope in the midst of travail and threat. When enemies surround God's people, prayer is the link that gives vision and hope. Through prayer God's people confess their sins and seek God's new directions for life. The leaders of God's people must confess the people's sins and intercede for them.

God has ultimate purpose for His people and His world. God knows the powers which oppose Him and knows they will be defeated. Evil rulers may hold sway momentarily, but God holds the ultimate key to victory. No human power or kingdom is superior to Yahweh and His kingdom. The kingdom of God is composed of those who believe and are faithful to the end. The persevering saints will see God's victory and experience the joy of His kingdom come. The faithful will inherit eternal life. This book provides the Old Testament's clearest teaching on resurrection. God will reward His faithful servants with eternal life, raising the dead from the grave.

Contemporary Teaching

1. This book is a contagious word of encouragement through personal examples. Daniel is a consistent role model. His actions were grounded in history. He was a real person who confronted real issues and led many persons in the life of faith. Danger never dampened his daily dedication to God. The laws or threats of a dictator could not deter Daniel from exalting God.

2. Evil may prosper for a time. That time may extend beyond an individual's lifetime. Our calling is not to have constant victory but to have constant faith. Evil will be punished, *eventually.*

3. God's message will be unchanging even though the medium may vary. The Book of Daniel reflects the time when the power of prophetic utterances was not paramount. Other types of proclamation were needed. Apocalyptic expressions began to be understood as an avenue of God's voice.

4. God calls persons continually. That call may involve threats of tyrants, unrighteous laws, inordinate pressures, and personal suffering. In all situations God calls people to lead and instruct His people.

5. Our actions must be prompted by glorification of God and not by gratification of selfish desires. God created the whole world. All nations are under God's requirements. The faithful must exalt the living God constantly in the whole world under all circumstances.

6. God is alive and at work. Hard times and suffering may dim our vision. God does not call us to explain our circumstances. He calls us to trust Him and His Word of promise.

7. Resurrection hope is the answer for a world falling apart. Just reward and punishment does not always come in this life. The righteous may die for their faithfulness. God will reward them through personal resurrection.

Chapter 1

Daniel's Training in Babylon

IN the third year of the reign of Jehoiakim[a] king of Judah, Nebuchadnezzar[b] king of Babylon[c] came to Jerusalem and besieged it.[d] 2And the Lord delivered Jehoiakim king of Judah into his hand, along with some of the articles from the temple of God. These he carried[e] off to the temple of his god in Babylonia[a] and put in the treasure house of his god.[f]

3Then the king ordered Ashpenaz, chief of his court officials, to bring in some of the Israelites from the royal family and the nobility[g]— 4young men without any physical defect, handsome,[h] showing aptitude for every kind of learning,[i] well informed, quick to understand, and qualified to serve in the king's palace. He was to teach them the language[j] and literature of the Babylonians.[b] 5The king assigned them a daily amount of food and wine[k] from the king's table.[l] They were to be trained for three years,[m] and after that they were to enter the king's service.[n]

6Among these were some from Judah: Daniel,[o] Hananiah, Mishael and Azariah.[p] 7The chief official gave them new names: to Daniel, the name Belteshazzar;[q] to Hananiah, Shadrach; to Mishael, Meshach; and to Azariah, Abednego.[r]

8But Daniel resolved not to defile[s] himself with the royal food and wine, and he asked the chief official for permission not to defile himself this way. 9Now God had caused the official to show favor[t] and sympathy[u] to Daniel, 10but the official told Daniel, "I am afraid of my lord the king, who has assigned your[c] food and drink.[v] Why should he see you looking worse than the other young men your age? The king would then have my head because of you."

11Daniel then said to the guard whom the chief official had appointed over Daniel, Hananiah, Mishael and Azariah, 12"Please test[w] your servants for ten days: Give us nothing but vegetables to eat and water to drink. 13Then compare our appearance with that of the young men who eat the royal food, and treat your servants in accordance with what you see."[x] 14So he agreed to this and tested[y] them for ten days.

15At the end of the ten days they looked healthier and better nourished than any of the young men who ate the royal food.[z] 16So the guard took away their choice food and the wine they were to drink and gave them vegetables instead.[a]

17To these four young men God gave knowledge and understanding[b] of all kinds of literature and learning.[c] And Daniel could understand visions and dreams of all kinds.[d]

18At the end of the time[e] set by the king to bring them in, the chief official presented them to Nebuchadnezzar. 19The king talked with them, and he found none equal to Daniel, Hananiah, Mishael and Azariah; so they entered the king's service.[f] 20In every matter of wisdom and understanding about which the king questioned them, he found them ten times better than all the magicians[g] and enchanters in his whole kingdom.[h]

21And Daniel remained there until the first year of King Cyrus.[i]

Chapter 2

Nebuchadnezzar's Dream

IN the second year of his reign, Nebuchadnezzar had dreams;[j] his mind was troubled[k] and he could not sleep.[l] 2So the king summoned the magicians,[m] enchanters, sorcerers[n] and astrologers[d][o] to tell him what he had dreamed.[p] When they came in and stood before the king, 3he said to them, "I have had a dream that troubles[q] me and I want to know what it means.[e]"

4Then the astrologers answered the

[a]2 Hebrew *Shinar* [b]4 Or *Chaldeans* [c]10 The Hebrew for *your* and *you* in this verse is plural.
[d]2 Or *Chaldeans*; also in verses 4, 5 and 10
[e]3 Or *was*

1:1 [a]S Jer 46:2 [b]S 2Ki 24:1; S Jer 28:14 [c]Jer 50:1 [d]2Ki 24:1; S 2Ch 36:6; Jer 35:11
1:2 [e]S 2Ki 24:13 [f]S 2Ch 36:7; Jer 27:19-20; Zec 5:5-11
1:3 [g]S 2Ki 20:18; S 24:15; Isa 39:7
1:4 [h]S Ge 39:6 [i]ver 17 [j]S Ezr 4:7
1:5 [k]ver 8,10 [l]S Est 2:9 [m]ver 18 [n]ver 19; S Est 2:5-6
1:6 [o]S Eze 14:14 [p]Da 2:17,25
1:7 [q]Da 2:26; 4:8; 5:12; 10:1 [r]S Isa 39:7; Da 2:49; 3:12
1:8 [s]S Eze 4:13-14
1:9 [t]S Ge 39:21; S Pr 16:7 [u]S 1Ki 8:50
1:10 [v]ver 5
1:12 [w]Rev 2:10
1:13 [x]ver 16
1:14 [y]Rev 2:10
1:15 [z]Ex 23:25
1:16 [a]ver 12-13
1:17 [b]S Job 12:13 [c]Da 2:23; Col 1:9; Jas 1:5 [d]Da 2:19, 30; 5:11; 7:1; 8:1
1:18 [e]ver 5
1:19 [f]S Ge 41:46
1:20 [g]S Ge 41:8 [h]S 1Ki 4:30; Est 2:15; S Eze 28:3; Da 2:13,28; 4:18; 6:3
1:21 [i]S 2Ch 36:22; Da 6:28; 10:1
2:1 [j]ver 3; S Ge 20:3; S Job 33:15,18; Da 4:5 [k]Ge 41:8 [l]S Est 6:1
2:2 [m]S Ge 41:8 [n]Ex 7:11; Jer 27:9 [o]S ver 10; S Isa 19:3; S 44:25 [p]Da 4:6
2:3 [q]Da 4:5

1:4 HUMANITY, Physical Nature—Physical or intellectual qualities do not determine a person's character. Such qualities do make good first impressions and can point to leadership potential. They do not guarantee leadership capability. Many persons with "physical defects" and without outstanding mental "aptitude" have been outstanding leaders.

1:8–16 CHRISTIAN ETHICS, Health—Good eating habits lead to good health. Young Daniel bravely chose to follow God's guidance and seek permission for a special, God-approved diet rather than seeking to please the Babylonian rulers.

1:9 GOD, Sovereignty—God works through foreign officials without their knowledge to accomplish His purposes for His faithful people. See note on Eze 1:25–28.

1:12–16 HUMANITY, Physical Nature—The food people eat has a significant effect upon their ultimate physical and intellectual well-being. Avoidance of excesses and of rich foods helps maintain the best physical health. The elimination of alcohol allows the full utilization of the mental processes.

1:17 HUMANITY, Relationship to God—Any person's skills and abilities come as the gift of God. This is true whether or not it is so acknowledged. Visions and dreams are often viewed as means of revelation. The ability to understand such revelations is also a gift of God.

1:19–20 HUMANITY, Work—God prepares His people for the tasks which He calls them to do. A person's work should allow the full use of all God-given skills and abilities. People should devote these skills to the fulfillment of the tasks God sets before them.

2:4 HOLY SCRIPTURE, Writing—At the mention of Aramaic, the written language of Daniel changes from Hebrew to

king in Aramaic,[f][r] "O king, live forever![s] Tell your servants the dream, and we will interpret it."

5The king replied to the astrologers, "This is what I have firmly decided:[t] If you do not tell me what my dream was and interpret it, I will have you cut into pieces[u] and your houses turned into piles of rubble.[v] 6But if you tell me the dream and explain it, you will receive from me gifts and rewards and great honor.[w] So tell me the dream and interpret it for me."

7Once more they replied, "Let the king tell his servants the dream, and we will interpret it."

8Then the king answered, "I am certain that you are trying to gain time, because you realize that this is what I have firmly decided: 9If you do not tell me the dream, there is just one penalty[x] for you. You have conspired to tell me misleading and wicked things, hoping the situation will change. So then, tell me the dream, and I will know that you can interpret it for me."[y]

10The astrologers[z] answered the king, "There is not a man on earth who can do what the king asks! No king, however great and mighty, has ever asked such a thing of any magician or enchanter or astrologer.[a] 11What the king asks is too difficult. No one can reveal it to the king except the gods,[b] and they do not live among men."

12This made the king so angry and furious[c] that he ordered the execution[d] of all the wise men of Babylon. 13So the decree was issued to put the wise men to death, and men were sent to look for Daniel and his friends to put them to death.[e]

14When Arioch, the commander of the king's guard, had gone out to put to death the wise men of Babylon, Daniel spoke to him with wisdom and tact. 15He asked the king's officer, "Why did the king issue such a harsh decree?" Arioch then explained the matter to Daniel. 16At this, Daniel went in to the king and asked for time, so that he might interpret the dream for him.

17Then Daniel returned to his house and explained the matter to his friends Hananiah, Mishael and Azariah.[f] 18He urged them to plead for mercy[g] from the God of heaven[h] concerning this mystery,[i] so that he and his friends might not be executed with the rest of the wise men of Babylon. 19During the night the mystery[j] was revealed to Daniel in a vision.[k] Then Daniel praised the God of heaven[l] 20and said:

"Praise be to the name of God for ever
and ever;[m]
wisdom and power[n] are his.
21He changes times and seasons;[o]
he sets up kings[p] and deposes[q] them.
He gives wisdom[r] to the wise
and knowledge to the discerning.[s]
22He reveals deep and hidden things;[t]
he knows what lies in darkness,[u]
and light[v] dwells with him.
23I thank and praise you, O God of my fathers:[w]
You have given me wisdom[x] and power,
you have made known to me what we asked of you,
you have made known to us the dream of the king.[y]"

Daniel Interprets the Dream

24Then Daniel went to Arioch,[z] whom the king had appointed to execute the wise men of Babylon, and said to him, "Do not execute the wise men of Babylon. Take me to the king, and I will interpret his dream for him."

25Arioch took Daniel to the king at once and said, "I have found a man among the exiles[a] from Judah[b] who can tell the king what his dream means."

2:4 [r]S Ezr 4:7 [s]S Ne 2:3
2:5 [t]Ge 41:32 [u]ver 12 [v]Ezr 6:11; Da 3:29
2:6 [w]ver 48; Da 5:7,16
2:9 [x]Est 4:11 [y]Isa 41:22-24
2:10 [z]ver 2; Da 3:8; 4:7 [a]ver 27; Da 5:8
2:11 [b]S Ge 41:38
2:12 [c]Da 3:13,19 [d]ver 5
2:13 [e]S Da 1:20; 5:19
2:17 [f]S Da 1:6
2:18 [g]S Isa 37:4 [h]Ezr 1:2; Ne 1:4; Jnh 1:9; Rev 11:13 [i]ver 23; Jer 33:3
2:19 [j]ver 28 [k]S Job 33:15; S Da 1:17 [l]S Jos 22:33
2:20 [m]S Ps 113:2; 145:1-2 [n]S Job 9:4; S Jer 32:19
2:21 [o]Da 7:25 [p]Da 4:17 [q]S Job 12:19; Ps 75:6-7; Ro 13:1 [r]S Ps 119:34; Jas 1:5 [s]S 2Sa 14:17
2:22 [t]S Ge 40:8; S Job 12:22; Da 5:11; 1Co 2:10 [u]Job 12:22; Ps 139:11-12; Jer 23:24; S Heb 4:13 [v]Isa 45:7; Jas 1:17
2:23 [w]S Ge 31:5; S Ex 3:15 [x]S Da 1:17 [y]S Eze 28:3
2:24 [z]ver 14
2:25 [a]S Dt 21:10 [b]S Da 1:6; 5:13; 6:13

[f]4 The text from here through chapter 7 is in Aramaic.

Aramaic, the language of international commerce and diplomacy. At 8:1 the language returns to Hebrew. Many theories seek to explain the change. God showed in this way that revelation is not limited to one language. He also showed He could use educated, linguistically skilled persons to record His revelation.

2:11,47 GOD, One God—God's ability to reveal the mysteries of the future to His servant shows He is the only God. Belief in one true God is not simply a dogmatic statement of faith. It is a valid interpretation of the experiences of history. See note on Jer 1:16.

2:14 HUMANITY, Relationships—A wise gentleness in talking with others opens the doors of communication in personal and business relationships. Use of wisdom and tact may save innocent lives.

2:18–44 GOD, Sovereignty—God's gift of wisdom shows His sovereign control over all human affairs. Through Jesus He has begun to set up His kingdom which will never be destroyed. See note on 1:9.

2:18–19 PRAYER, Intercession—Daniel asked his friends to pray for God to reveal the interpretation of the dream. The answer was immediate. God responds to intercessory prayer. Agreement of a group to pray on a subject adds strength to prayer.

2:20–23 PRAYER, Praise—Daniel praised God's total power and knowledge and omniscience, His revelation of divine knowledge, and His sovereign control of human history. He expressed thanks for answered prayer.

2:25–28 REVELATION, Dreams—Magicians and diviners cannot interpret dreams correctly. Only the true God can give the revelation necessary to interpret dreams. Dreams were perceived by ancients to be an approach divine beings used to reveal themselves to humans. The king's dream revealed God's coming actions in history. God used a foreign king's dream as the basis of inspired Scripture.

26 The king asked Daniel (also called Belteshazzar),[c] "Are you able to tell me what I saw in my dream and interpret it?"

27 Daniel replied, "No wise man, enchanter, magician or diviner can explain to the king the mystery he has asked about,[d] 28 but there is a God in heaven who reveals mysteries.[e] He has shown King Nebuchadnezzar what will happen in days to come.[f] Your dream and the visions that passed through your mind[g] as you lay on your bed[h] are these:[i]

29 "As you were lying there, O king, your mind turned to things to come, and the revealer of mysteries showed you what is going to happen.[j] 30 As for me, this mystery has been revealed[k] to me, not because I have greater wisdom than other living men, but so that you, O king, may know the interpretation and that you may understand what went through your mind.

31 "You looked, O king, and there before you stood a large statue—an enormous, dazzling statue,[l] awesome[m] in appearance. 32 The head of the statue was made of pure gold, its chest and arms of silver, its belly and thighs of bronze, 33 its legs of iron, its feet partly of iron and partly of baked clay. 34 While you were watching, a rock was cut out, but not by human hands.[n] It struck the statue on its feet of iron and clay and smashed[o] them.[p] 35 Then the iron, the clay, the bronze, the silver and the gold were broken to pieces at the same time and became like chaff on a threshing floor in the summer. The wind swept them away[q] without leaving a trace. But the rock that struck the statue became a huge mountain[r] and filled the whole earth.[s]

36 "This was the dream, and now we will interpret it to the king.[t] 37 You, O king, are the king of kings.[u] The God of heaven has given you dominion[v] and power and might and glory; 38 in your hands he has placed mankind and the beasts of the field and the birds of the air. Wherever they live, he has made you ruler over them all.[w] You are that head of gold.

39 "After you, another kingdom will rise, inferior to yours. Next, a third kingdom, one of bronze, will rule over the whole earth.[x] 40 Finally, there will be a fourth kingdom, strong as iron—for iron breaks and smashes everything—and as iron breaks things to pieces, so it will crush and break all the others.[y] 41 Just as you saw that the feet and toes were partly of baked clay and partly of iron, so this will be a divided kingdom; yet it will have some of the strength of iron in it, even as you saw iron mixed with clay. 42 As the toes were partly iron and partly clay, so this kingdom will be partly strong and partly brittle. 43 And just as you saw the iron mixed with baked clay, so the people will be a mixture and will not remain united, any more than iron mixes with clay.

44 "In the time of those kings, the God of heaven will set up a kingdom that will never be destroyed, nor will it be left to another people. It will crush[z] all those kingdoms[a] and bring them to an end, but it will itself endure forever.[b] 45 This is the meaning of the vision of the rock[c] cut out of a mountain, but not by human hands[d]—a rock that broke the iron, the bronze, the clay, the silver and the gold to pieces.

"The great God has shown the king what will take place in the future.[e] The dream is true[f] and the interpretation is trustworthy."

2:26 [c] S Da 1:7
2:27 [d] S ver 10; S Ge 41:8
2:28 [e] S Ge 40:8; Jer 10:7; Am 4:13 [f] S Ge 49:1; Da 10:14; Mt 24:6; Rev 1:1; 22:6 [g] Da 4:5 [h] S Ps 4:4 [i] S Eze 28:3; S Da 1:20
2:29 [j] S Ge 41:25
2:30 [k] Isa 45:3; S Da 1:17; Am 4:13
2:31 [l] Hab 1:7 [m] Isa 25:3-5
2:34 [n] S Job 12:19; Zec 4:6 [o] S Job 34:24 [p] ver 44-45; Ps 2:9; S Isa 60:12; Da 8:25
2:35 [q] Ps 1:4; 37:10; S Isa 17:13; 41:15-16 [r] Isa 2:3; Mic 4:1 [s] Zec 12:3
2:36 [t] S Ge 40:12
2:37 [u] S Ezr 7:12 [v] S Jer 27:7; Da 4:26
2:38 [w] S Jer 27:6; Da 4:21-22; 5:18
2:39 [x] Da 7:5
2:40 [y] Da 7:7,23
2:44 [z] S Ge 27:29; Ps 2:9; S 110:5; Mt 21:43-44; 1Co 15:24 [a] S 1Sa 9:20; Hag 2:22 [b] Ps 145:13; S Isa 9:7; Da 4:34; 6:26; 7:14,27; Ob 1:21; Mic 4:7, 13; S Lk 1:33; Rev 11:15
2:45 [c] S Isa 28:16 [d] Da 8:25 [e] S Ge 41:25 [f] Rev 22:6

2:27–28 HUMANITY, Intellectual Nature—Solving difficult problems involves honestly admitting our limitations and seeking God's help.

2:30 HUMANITY, Relationship to God—God gives us gifts not so much for our own benefit but to help others. We are responsible to God to use our gifts to share His revelation and glorify Him.

2:30 REVELATION, Messengers—Daniel humbly admitted he possessed no special power to interpret God's purposes. God wished to be known and chose to reveal Himself to the king. Messengers of God are rarely unique in ability. God often chooses unlikely and unskilled intermediaries. Compare Ex 3:4; Jer 1:6.

2:36–45 HISTORY, Eternal—God knows all history and is ultimately responsible for placing all earthly rulers in power. He holds rulers responsible for their influence on history. He is leading history to the establishment of His kingdom. No earthly ruler will take over after God's kingdom, for it will be set up for eternity.

2:44–45 JESUS CHRIST, Foretold—Christians see Daniel's prediction of an everlasting kingdom as referring to the kingdom of God begun in the ministry of Jesus (Lk 1:32–33). The only abiding things are what God initiates and secures. It is an important part of our faith to pray, "your kingdom come" (Mt 6:10).

2:44 LAST THINGS, Coming Kingdom—This reference to a kingdom of the God of heaven that will never be destroyed but endure forever prophesies the New Testament kingdom of God and its ultimate coming in fullness. In times of oppression or difficulty the idea of God's rule of Israel took on futuristic dimensions. The reality of oppressive kingdoms over which evil men ruled was made more bearable with the hope of a coming kingdom in which God would rule. The ultimate hope lay in a coming kingdom that would be everlasting and triumphant, bringing an end to all earthly kingdoms. The realization of this everlasting kingdom would involve a direct intervention of God to set it up (Da 4:3,34; 6:26; 7:14,18,27). The triumph of God's kingdom over the kingdoms of the world is assured. The rule of God which Christ made possible in the lives of individual believers will one day be manifest in a realm over which Christ reigns in righteousness. God's covenant with Old Testament Israel was to be King over the nation, but Israel violated the covenant. Jesus brought the new covenant and announced the kingdom to be near (Mt 4:17). At His second coming in glory the kingdom will be fully established, never to be destroyed.

46 Then King Nebuchadnezzar fell prostrate[g] before Daniel and paid him honor
and ordered that an offering[h] and incense be presented to him. 47 The king
said to Daniel, "Surely your God is the
God of gods[i] and the Lord of kings[j] and
a revealer of mysteries,[k] for you were
able to reveal this mystery.[l]"
48 Then the king placed Daniel in a
high[m] position and lavished many gifts on
him. He made him ruler over the entire
province of Babylon and placed him in
charge of all its wise men.[n] 49 Moreover,
at Daniel's request the king appointed
Shadrach, Meshach and Abednego administrators over the province of Babylon,[o] while Daniel himself remained at
the royal court.[p]

Chapter 3

The Image of Gold and the Fiery Furnace

KING Nebuchadnezzar made an image[q] of gold, ninety feet high and
nine feet[g] wide, and set it up on the
plain of Dura in the province of Babylon.
2 He then summoned the satraps,[r] prefects, governors, advisers, treasurers,
judges, magistrates and all the other provincial officials[s] to come to the dedication of the image he had set up. 3 So the
satraps, prefects, governors, advisers,
treasurers, judges, magistrates and all the
other provincial officials assembled for
the dedication of the image that King
Nebuchadnezzar had set up, and they
stood before it.
4 Then the herald loudly proclaimed,
"This is what you are commanded to do,
O peoples, nations and men of every language:[t] 5 As soon as you hear the sound
of the horn, flute, zither, lyre, harp,[u]
pipes and all kinds of music, you must fall
down and worship the image[v] of gold
that King Nebuchadnezzar has set up.[w]
6 Whoever does not fall down and worship
will immediately be thrown into a blazing
furnace."[x]
7 Therefore, as soon as they heard the
sound of the horn, flute, zither, lyre, harp
and all kinds of music, all the peoples,
nations and men of every language fell
down and worshiped the image of gold
that King Nebuchadnezzar had set up.[y]
8 At this time some astrologers[h][z] came
forward and denounced the Jews. 9 They
said to King Nebuchadnezzar, "O king,
live forever![a] 10 You have issued a decree,[b] O king, that everyone who hears
the sound of the horn, flute, zither, lyre,
harp, pipes and all kinds of music must
fall down and worship the image of
gold,[c] 11 and that whoever does not fall
down and worship will be thrown into a
blazing furnace. 12 But there are some
Jews whom you have set over the affairs
of the province of Babylon—Shadrach,
Meshach and Abednego[d]—who pay no
attention[e] to you, O king. They neither
serve your gods nor worship the image of
gold you have set up."[f]
13 Furious[g] with rage, Nebuchadnezzar
summoned Shadrach, Meshach and
Abednego. So these men were brought
before the king, 14 and Nebuchadnezzar
said to them, "Is it true, Shadrach, Meshach and Abednego, that you do not
serve my gods[h] or worship the image[i] of
gold I have set up? 15 Now when you hear
the sound of the horn, flute, zither, lyre,
harp, pipes and all kinds of music, if you
are ready to fall down and worship the
image I made, very good. But if you do
not worship it, you will be thrown immediately into a blazing furnace. Then what
god[j] will be able to rescue[k] you from my
hand?"
16 Shadrach, Meshach and Abednego[l]
replied to the king, "O Nebuchadnezzar,
we do not need to defend ourselves before you in this matter. 17 If we are
thrown into the blazing furnace, the God
we serve is able to save[m] us from it, and
he will rescue[n] us from your hand, O
king. 18 But even if he does not, we want

2:46 [g]Da 8:17; Ac 10:25 [h]Ac 14:13
2:47 [i]S Dt 10:17; Da 11:36 [j]Da 4:25; 1Ti 6:15 [k]S ver 22, 28 [l]Da 4:9; 1Co 14:25
2:48 [m]S 2Ki 25:28 [n]S ver 6; S Est 8:2; S Da 1:20; 4:9; 5:11; 8:27
2:49 [o]S Da 1:7; 3:30 [p]Da 6:2
3:1 [q]ver 14; S Isa 46:6; Jer 16:20; Hab 2:19
3:2 [r]S Est 1:1 [s]ver 27; Da 6:7
3:4 [t]Da 4:1; 6:25; Rev 10:11
3:5 [u]S Ge 4:21 [v]Rev 13:12 [w]ver 10,15
3:6 [x]ver 11,15,21; Jer 29:22; Da 5:19; 6:7; Mt 13:42,50; Rev 13:15
3:7 [y]S ver 5
3:8 [z]S Isa 19:3; S Da 2:10
3:9 [a]S Ne 2:3; Da 5:10; 6:6
3:10 [b]Da 6:12 [c]ver 4-6
3:12 [d]S Da 2:49 [e]Da 6:13 [f]S Est 3:3
3:13 [g]S Da 2:12
3:14 [h]Isa 46:1; Jer 50:2 [i]S ver 1
3:15 [j]S Isa 36:18-20 [k]S 2Ch 32:15
3:16 [l]S Da 1:7
3:17 [m]S Ge 48:16; S Ps 18:48; 27:1-2 [n]S Job 5:19; Jer 1:8; Da 6:20

[g]*1* Aramaic *sixty cubits high and six cubits wide* (about 27 meters high and 2.7 meters wide) [h]*8* Or *Chaldeans*

3:1–30 GOD, Power—God can save His people from circumstances humans consider impossible. Other gods cannot defend their interests against Him. See note on 1:9.

3:1–30 MIRACLE, Exception—Miracles distinguish God from all false gods served by other people. The miracle here shows that miracle may be an exception to the normal rules of existence. Normally fire kills and destroys people. God's presence saved the three Jews in an exceptional way because God chose this time to reveal His saving power to the Babylonians. Even the pagan king had to acknowledge the unique saving power of Israel's God.

3:16–18,28–30 GOD, Savior—When God's people prove faithful to Him, He saves them in ways no other powers and authorities can. Human faithfulness may mean risking death to stay true to God. See note on Jer 50:34.

3:16–18 EVIL AND SUFFERING, Endurance—Shadrach, Meshach, and Abednego believed God was able to deliver them from the fiery furnace. If God chose not to deliver them, they would still remain faithful to Him. God did deliver them (vv 24–27), but their faith was not based on expectation of a miracle. Similarly, our faith in God is based on His basic character, not the absence or presence of suffering. God is able to relieve our suffering, but sometimes we will not experience miraculous divine intervention. God may choose to sustain us in the midst of our difficulty rather than removing the problem. See note on 2 Co 12:1–10.

3:17–18,28 SALVATION, As Deliverance—The God who rescued Shadrach, Meshach, and Abednego from Nebuchadnezzar's fiery furnace can deliver us from anything.

3:18,28 SALVATION, Belief—Shadrach, Meshach, and Abednego are examples of the kind of faith God wants persons to have in Him. Faith has such trust in God's love and power

you to know, O king, that we will not
serve your gods or worship the image of
gold you have set up.[o]"
19 Then Nebuchadnezzar was furious
with Shadrach, Meshach and Abednego,
and his attitude toward them changed.
He ordered the furnace heated seven[p]
times hotter than usual 20 and commanded some of the strongest soldiers in his
army to tie up Shadrach, Meshach and
Abednego[q] and throw them into the
blazing furnace. 21 So these men, wearing
their robes, trousers, turbans and other
clothes, were bound and thrown into the
blazing furnace. 22 The king's command
was so urgent and the furnace so hot that
the flames of the fire killed the soldiers
who took up Shadrach, Meshach and
Abednego,[r] 23 and these three men, firmly tied, fell into the blazing furnace.
24 Then King Nebuchadnezzar leaped to
his feet in amazement and asked his advisers, "Weren't there three men that we
tied up and threw into the fire?"
They replied, "Certainly, O king."
25 He said, "Look! I see four men walking around in the fire, unbound and unharmed, and the fourth looks like a son of
the gods."
26 Nebuchadnezzar then approached
the opening of the blazing furnace and
shouted, "Shadrach, Meshach and Abednego, servants of the Most High God,[s]
come out! Come here!"
So Shadrach, Meshach and Abednego
came out of the fire, 27 and the satraps,
prefects, governors and royal advisers[t]
crowded around them.[u] They saw that
the fire[v] had not harmed their bodies,
nor was a hair of their heads singed; their
robes were not scorched, and there was
no smell of fire on them.
28 Then Nebuchadnezzar said, "Praise
be to the God of Shadrach, Meshach and
Abednego, who has sent his angel[w] and
rescued[x] his servants! They trusted[y] in
him and defied the king's command and
were willing to give up their lives rather
than serve or worship any god except
their own God.[z] 29 Therefore I decree[a]
that the people of any nation or language

3:18 [o]ver 28; S Ex 1:17; S Jos 24:15
3:19 [p]Lev 26:18-28
3:20 [q]S Da 1:7
3:22 [r]S Da 1:7
3:26 [s]Da 4:2,34
3:27 [t]ver 2; Da 6:7 [u]Ps 91:3-11; S Isa 43:2; Heb 11:32-34 [v]Da 6:23
3:28 [w]S Ps 34:7; Da 6:22; Ac 5:19 [x]S Ps 97:10; Ac 12:11 [y]S Dt 31:20; S Job 13:15; S Ps 26:1; 84:12 [z]S ver 18
3:29 [a]Da 6:26 [b]S Ezr 6:11 [c]Da 6:27
3:30 [d]S Da 2:49
4:1 [e]S Da 3:4 [f]Da 6:25
4:2 [g]Ps 74:9 [h]S Da 3:26
4:3 [i]S Ps 105:27; Da 6:27 [j]Da 2:44
4:4 [k]Ps 30:6; S Isa 32:9
4:5 [l]S Da 2:1 [m]Ps 4:4 [n]Da 2:28 [o]ver 19; S Ge 41:8; S Job 3:26; Da 2:3; 5:6
4:6 [p]Da 2:2
4:7 [q]S Ge 41:8 [r]S Isa 44:25; S Da 2:2 [s]S Da 2:10
4:8 [t]S Da 1:7 [u]S Ge 41:38
4:9 [v]Da 2:48

who say anything against the God of Shadrach, Meshach and Abednego be cut
into pieces and their houses be turned
into piles of rubble,[b] for no other god can
save[c] in this way."
30 Then the king promoted Shadrach,
Meshach and Abednego in the province
of Babylon.[d]

Chapter 4

Nebuchadnezzar's Dream of a Tree

KING Nebuchadnezzar,
To the peoples, nations and men
of every language,[e] who live in all
the world:

May you prosper greatly![f]

2 It is my pleasure to tell you about
the miraculous signs[g] and wonders
that the Most High God[h] has performed for me.

3 How great are his signs,
how mighty his wonders![i]
His kingdom is an eternal
kingdom;
his dominion endures[j] from
generation to generation.

4 I, Nebuchadnezzar, was at home
in my palace, contented[k] and prosperous. 5 I had a dream[l] that made
me afraid. As I was lying in my bed,[m]
the images and visions that passed
through my mind[n] terrified me.[o]
6 So I commanded that all the wise
men of Babylon be brought before
me to interpret[p] the dream for me.
7 When the magicians,[q] enchanters,
astrologers[1] and diviners[r] came, I
told them the dream, but they could
not interpret it for me.[s] 8 Finally,
Daniel came into my presence and I
told him the dream. (He is called Belteshazzar,[t] after the name of my
god, and the spirit of the holy gods[u]
is in him.)
9 I said, "Belteshazzar, chief[v] of
the magicians, I know that the spirit

[1]7 Or *Chaldeans*

that believers hold to God no matter what happens, no matter who seeks to change their minds, or what threats they face.

4:1–37 GOD, Sovereignty—God spoke through Daniel to tell what was to come, and then brought it to pass. The dream's message shows God's power over the ruler of the world's mightiest empire (vv 32,34–35). See note on Eze 1:25–28.

4:2–28 REVELATION, Events—The Babylonian king became a proclaimer of God's mighty acts. God's historical actions sought to reach the entire world, calling even a foreign king to repent. God's Spirit enabled Daniel to interpret the dream. See note on 2:25–28.

4:3 LAST THINGS, Kingdom Established—Hope for the universal, everlasting reign of God was part of prophetic hope in Israel. Out of it God led His people to expect a future kingdom that endures, ruled over by an everlasting King (Da 4:34; 6:26; 7:14,27). The meaning of history is to be found in the future establishment of this kingdom. Jesus inaugurated God's kingdom and will establish it at His return. See note on Rev 11:15.

4:4–23 GOD, Holy—Other religions speak of the awesome otherness of the gods. Nebuchadnezzar spoke more than he knew. He thought revelation came from holy gods like he worshiped. Revelation actually came through the Spirit of the one and only holy God. See note on Eze 20:12,14,40,41.

4:9 HOLY SPIRIT, Revelation—The Spirit enabled Daniel, like Joseph before him (Ge 41:38), to interpret dreams. See Da 5:11,14. The Aramaic language of the original text makes a subtle wordplay. The word "gods" may be understood either

of the holy gods[w] is in you, and no
mystery is too difficult for you. Here
is my dream; interpret it for me.
10These are the visions I saw while
lying in my bed:[x] I looked, and there
before me stood a tree in the middle
of the land. Its height was enormous.[y] 11The tree grew large and
strong and its top touched the sky; it
was visible to the ends of the earth.[z]
12Its leaves were beautiful, its fruit
abundant, and on it was food for all.
Under it the beasts of the field found
shelter, and the birds of the air lived
in its branches;[a] from it every creature was fed.
13"In the visions I saw while lying
in my bed,[b] I looked, and there before me was a messenger,[j] a holy
one,[c] coming down from heaven.
14He called in a loud voice: 'Cut
down the tree[d] and trim off its
branches; strip off its leaves and scatter its fruit. Let the animals flee from
under it and the birds from its
branches.[e] 15But let the stump and
its roots, bound with iron and
bronze, remain in the ground, in the
grass of the field.
" 'Let him be drenched with the
dew of heaven, and let him live with
the animals among the plants of the
earth. 16Let his mind be changed
from that of a man and let him be
given the mind of an animal, till sev-
en times[k] pass by for him.[f]
17" 'The decision is announced by
messengers, the holy ones declare
the verdict, so that the living may
know that the Most High[g] is sovereign[h] over the kingdoms of men and
gives them to anyone he wishes and
sets over them the lowliest[i] of men.'
18"This is the dream that I, King
Nebuchadnezzar, had. Now, Belteshazzar, tell me what it means, for
none of the wise men in my kingdom
can interpret it for me.[j] But you
can,[k] because the spirit of the holy
gods[l] is in you."[m]

Daniel Interprets the Dream

19Then Daniel (also called Belteshazzar) was greatly perplexed for a
time, and his thoughts terrified[n]
him. So the king said, "Belteshazzar,
do not let the dream or its meaning
alarm you."[o]
Belteshazzar answered, "My lord,
if only the dream applied to your enemies and its meaning to your adversaries! 20The tree you saw, which
grew large and strong, with its top
touching the sky, visible to the whole
earth, 21with beautiful leaves and
abundant fruit, providing food for all,
giving shelter to the beasts of the
field, and having nesting places in its
branches for the birds of the air[p] —
22you, O king, are that tree![q] You
have become great and strong; your
greatness has grown until it reaches
the sky, and your dominion extends
to distant parts of the earth.[r]
23"You, O king, saw a messenger,
a holy one,[s] coming down from
heaven and saying, 'Cut down the
tree and destroy it, but leave the
stump, bound with iron and bronze,
in the grass of the field, while its
roots remain in the ground. Let him
be drenched with the dew of heaven;
let him live like the wild animals, until seven times pass by for him.'[t] [u]
24"This is the interpretation, O
king, and this is the decree[v] the
Most High has issued against my lord
the king: 25You will be driven away
from people and will live with the
wild animals; you will eat grass like
cattle and be drenched[w] with the
dew of heaven. Seven times will pass
by for you until you acknowledge that
the Most High[x] is sovereign over the
kingdoms of men and gives them to
anyone he wishes.[y] 26The command
to leave the stump of the tree with its
roots[z] means that your kingdom will
be restored to you when you acknowledge that Heaven rules.[a]
27Therefore, O king, be pleased to accept my advice: Renounce your sins
by doing what is right, and your

j13 Or *watchman*; also in verses 17 and 23 k16 Or *years*; also in verses 23, 25 and 32

4:9 wDa 5:11-12
4:10 xS ver 5; Ps 4:4 yEze 31:3-4
4:11 zS Eze 19:11; 31:5
4:12 aS Eze 17:23; S Mt 13:32
4:13 bver 10; Da 7:1 cS ver 23; S Dt 33:2
4:14 dS Job 24:20 eS Eze 31:12; S Mt 3:10
4:16 fver 23,32
4:17 gver 2,25; Ps 83:18 hS Ps 103:19; Jer 27:5-7; Da 2:21; 5:18-21; Ro 13:1 iDa 11:21; Mt 23:12
4:18 jS Ge 41:8; Da 5:8,15 kS Ge 41:15 lS Ge 41:38 mver 7-9; S Da 1:20
4:19 nS ver 5; S Ge 41:8; Da 7:15, 28; 8:27; 10:16-17 oS Ge 40:12
4:21 pS Eze 31:6
4:22 qS 2Sa 12:7 rJer 27:7; Da 5:18-19
4:23 sver 13; Da 8:13 tDa 5:21 uS Eze 31:3-4
4:24 vJob 40:12; Ps 107:40; Jer 40:2
4:25 wS Job 24:8 xS ver 17 yJer 27:5; S Da 2:47; 5:21
4:26 zver 15 aS Da 2:37

as singular or plural. Nebuchadnezzar intended it as plural. The inspired writer meant readers of the Bible to hear the singular. The one God, through His one Spirit, reveals Himself in dreams to His chosen interpreter to instruct His people and give hope for the future.

4:17 ELECTION, Sovereignty—The God of election is the sovereign Lord of history. He has the first and final say about the kingdoms of this world. He elevates the lowliest of persons, and He pulls down the mighty from their thrones (Lk 1:46–55,67–79). God is in charge of this world.

4:19–33 EVIL AND SUFFERING, Punishment—Loss of mental capacities may reduce humans to a mere animal existence. No person is too powerful or wealthy to be immune to mental illness. Such illness has many causes. Nebuchadnezzar lost his mental functions as a direct result of God's punishment on his pride. His example shows us God's punishment may take this form, but the one example must not be used as a rule to condemn as sinners all who endure mental illness.

4:25 HISTORY, Universal—Every earthly kingdom is subject to God. God is not Ruler only of Israel's history. He directs all history to His goals. He can punish any ruler, no matter how much earthly power the ruler exercises.

4:27 SALVATION, Repentance—Daniel called upon Nebuchadnezzar to renounce his sins and do right. "Renounce"

wickedness by being kind to the oppressed.[b] It may be that then your
prosperity[c] will continue.[d]"

The Dream Is Fulfilled

28All this happened[e] to King Nebuchadnezzar. 29Twelve months later,
as the king was walking on the roof
of the royal palace of Babylon, 30he
said, "Is not this the great Babylon I
have built as the royal residence, by
my mighty power and for the glory[f]
of my majesty?"[g]

31The words were still on his lips
when a voice came from heaven,
"This is what is decreed for you,
King Nebuchadnezzar: Your royal authority has been taken from you.[h]
32You will be driven away from people and will live with the wild animals; you will eat grass like cattle.
Seven times will pass by for you until
you acknowledge that the Most High
is sovereign over the kingdoms of
men and gives them to anyone he
wishes."[i]

33Immediately what had been said
about Nebuchadnezzar was fulfilled.
He was driven away from people and
ate grass like cattle. His body was
drenched[j] with the dew of heaven
until his hair grew like the feathers of
an eagle and his nails like the claws
of a bird.[k]

34At the end of that time, I, Nebuchadnezzar, raised my eyes toward
heaven, and my sanity[l] was restored. Then I praised the Most High;
I honored and glorified him who lives
forever.[m]

His dominion is an eternal dominion;
his kingdom[n] endures from
generation to generation.[o]
35All the peoples of the earth
are regarded as nothing.[p]
He does as he pleases[q]
with the powers of heaven
and the peoples of the earth.
No one can hold back[r] his hand[s]
or say to him: "What have you
done?"[t]

36At the same time that my sanity
was restored, my honor and splendor
were returned to me for the glory of
my kingdom.[u] My advisers and nobles sought me out, and I was restored to my throne and became
even greater than before. 37Now I,
Nebuchadnezzar, praise and exalt[v]
and glorify[w] the King of heaven, because everything he does is right and
all his ways are just.[x] And those who
walk in pride[y] he is able to humble.[z]

Chapter 5

The Writing on the Wall

KING Belshazzar[a] gave a great banquet[b] for a thousand of his nobles[c]
and drank wine with them. 2While Belshazzar was drinking[d] his wine, he gave
orders to bring in the gold and silver goblets[e] that Nebuchadnezzar his father[1]
had taken from the temple in Jerusalem,
so that the king and his nobles, his wives
and his concubines[f] might drink from
them.[g] 3So they brought in the gold goblets that had been taken from the temple
of God in Jerusalem, and the king and his
nobles, his wives and his concubines
drank from them. 4As they drank the
wine, they praised the gods[h] of gold and
silver, of bronze, iron, wood and stone.[i]

5Suddenly the fingers of a human hand
appeared and wrote on the plaster of the
wall, near the lampstand in the royal palace. The king watched the hand as it
wrote. 6His face turned pale[j] and he was
so frightened[k] that his knees knocked[l]
together and his legs gave way.[m]

7The king called out for the enchanters,[n] astrologers[m][o] and diviners[p] to be
brought and said to these wise[q] men of
Babylon, "Whoever reads this writing
and tells me what it means will be
clothed in purple and have a gold chain
placed around his neck,[r] and he will be
made the third[s] highest ruler in the kingdom."[t]

8Then all the king's wise men[u] came
in, but they could not read the writing or
tell the king what it meant.[v] 9So King

[1]2 Or *ancestor*; or *predecessor*; also in verses 11, 13 and 18 [m]7 Or *Chaldeans*; also in verse 11

4:27 [b]Isa 55:6-7 [c]Jer 29:7 [d]S Dt 24:13; 1Ki 21:29; S Ps 41:3; S Pr 28:13; S Eze 18:22
4:28 [e]Nu 23:19
4:30 [f]Isa 13:19 [g]S Isa 10:13; S 37:24-25; Da 5:20; Hab 1:11; 2:4
4:31 [h]S 2Sa 22:28; Da 5:20
4:32 [i]S Job 9:12
4:33 [j]S Job 24:8 [k]Da 5:20-21
4:34 [l]S Job 12:20 [m]Da 12:7 [n]Isa 37:16 [o]Ps 145:13; S Da 2:44; 5:21; 6:26; Lk 1:33
4:35 [p]S Isa 40:17 [q]Dt 21:8; Ps 115:3; S 135:6; Jnh 1:14 [r]S Isa 14:27 [s]S Dt 32:39 [t]S Job 9:4; S Isa 14:24; S 45:9; Da 5:21; Ro 9:20
4:36 [u]S Pr 22:4; Da 5:18
4:37 [v]S Ex 15:2 [w]S Ps 34:3 [x]Dt 32:4; Ps 33:4-5 [y]Ps 18:27; S 119:21 [z]S Job 31:4; 40:11-12; S Isa 13:11; Da 5:20,23; Mt 23:12
5:1 [a]ver 30; Da 7:1; 8:1 [b]S 1Ki 3:15 [c]Jer 50:35
5:2 [d]S Isa 21:5 [e]S 2Ki 24:13; S 2Ch 36:10; S Jer 52:19 [f]S Est 2:14 [g]S Est 1:7; Da 1:2
5:4 [h]Jdg 16:24 [i]S Est 1:10; Ps 135:15-18; Hab 2:19; Rev 9:20
5:6 [j]S Job 4:15 [k]S Da 4:5 [l]S Isa 7:2 [m]S Ps 22:14; Eze 7:17
5:7 [n]S Ge 41:8 [o]S Isa 19:3 [p]Isa 44:25 [q]Jer 50:35; Da 4:6-7 [r]S Ge 41:42 [s]Est 10:3 [t]Da 2:5-6, 48
5:8 [u]S Ex 8:18 [v]S Da 2:10,27; S 4:18

means "to break off," like breaking a yoke off one's neck. Repentance is breaking off our sins and proving it by doing them no more.

4:27 CHRISTIAN ETHICS, Justice—God's invitation to justice is unrestricted. He expects rulers of all peoples to establish justice by helping the oppressed. See note on Ps 72:1–14.

4:34 LAST THINGS, Kingdom Established—See note on 4:3.

4:37 GOD, Justice—Even a humbled, disciplined foreign emperor must look back at his humiliation and say the one true God of Daniel was responsible and was justified and fair in what He did. See note on Eze 18:25–32.

5:2–5 REVELATION, Signs—God interrupted Belshazzar's blasphemous party with a written message. God uses His own mysterious ways to communicate His will. God's Spirit gave Daniel wisdom to read and interpret the writing. Such revelation came to overcome human pride and reveal God's sovereignty.

5:7–9 HUMANITY, Intellectual Nature—God can confound the wisest human. For all of humanity's intellectual accomplishments, the areas of ignorance still abound.

Belshazzar became even more terrified[w]
and his face grew more pale. His nobles
were baffled.

10The queen,[n] hearing the voices of
the king and his nobles, came into the
banquet hall. "O king, live forever!"[x]
she said. "Don't be alarmed! Don't look
so pale! 11There is a man in your kingdom
who has the spirit of the holy gods[y] in
him. In the time of your father he was
found to have insight and intelligence and
wisdom[z] like that of the gods.[a] King
Nebuchadnezzar your father—your father the king, I say—appointed him chief
of the magicians, enchanters, astrologers
and diviners.[b] 12This man Daniel, whom
the king called Belteshazzar,[c] was found
to have a keen mind and knowledge and
understanding, and also the ability to interpret dreams, explain riddles[d] and
solve difficult problems.[e] Call for Daniel,
and he will tell you what the writing
means.[f]"

13So Daniel was brought before the
king, and the king said to him, "Are you
Daniel, one of the exiles my father the
king brought from Judah?[g] 14I have heard
that the spirit of the gods[h] is in you and
that you have insight, intelligence and
outstanding wisdom.[i] 15The wise men
and enchanters were brought before me
to read this writing and tell me what it
means, but they could not explain it.[j]
16Now I have heard that you are able to
give interpretations and to solve difficult
problems.[k] If you can read this writing
and tell me what it means, you will be
clothed in purple and have a gold chain
placed around your neck,[l] and you will
be made the third highest ruler in the
kingdom."

17Then Daniel answered the king,
"You may keep your gifts for yourself and
give your rewards to someone else.[n]
Nevertheless, I will read the writing for
the king and tell him what it means.

18"O king, the Most High God gave
your father Nebuchadnezzar[o] sovereignty and greatness and glory and splendor.[p]
19Because of the high position he gave
him, all the peoples and nations and men
of every language dreaded and feared
him. Those the king wanted to put to
death, he put to death;[q] those he wanted
to spare, he spared; those he wanted to
promote, he promoted; and those he
wanted to humble, he humbled.[r] 20But
when his heart became arrogant and
hardened with pride,[s] he was deposed
from his royal throne[t] and stripped[u] of
his glory.[v] 21He was driven away from
people and given the mind of an animal;
he lived with the wild donkeys and ate
grass like cattle; and his body was
drenched with the dew of heaven, until
he acknowledged that the Most High God
is sovereign[w] over the kingdoms of men
and sets over them anyone he wishes.[x]

22"But you his son,[o] O Belshazzar,
have not humbled[y] yourself, though you
knew all this. 23Instead, you have set
yourself up against[z] the Lord of heaven.
You had the goblets from his temple
brought to you, and you and your nobles,
your wives[a] and your concubines drank
wine from them. You praised the gods of
silver and gold, of bronze, iron, wood and
stone, which cannot see or hear or understand.[b] But you did not honor the God
who holds in his hand your life[c] and all
your ways.[d] 24Therefore he sent the
hand that wrote the inscription.

25"This is the inscription that was written:

MENE, MENE, TEKEL, PARSIN[p]

26"This is what these words mean:

Mene[q]: God has numbered the
days[e] of your reign and
brought it to an end.[f]
27*Tekel*[r]: You have been weighed
on the scales[g] and found
wanting.[h]
28*Peres*[s]: Your kingdom is divided
and given to the Medes[i]
and Persians."[j]

29Then at Belshazzar's command, Daniel was clothed in purple, a gold chain
was placed around his neck,[k] and he was
proclaimed the third highest ruler in the
kingdom.[l]

30That very night Belshazzar,[m] king[n]
of the Babylonians,[t] was slain,[o] 31and
Darius[p] the Mede[q] took over the kingdom, at the age of sixty-two.

5:9 [w]S Ps 48:5; S Isa 21:4
5:10 [x]S Ne 2:3; S Da 3:9
5:11 [y]S Ge 41:38 [z]ver 14; S Da 1:17 [a]S Da 2:22 [b]Da 2:47-48
5:12 [c]S Da 1:7 [d]S Nu 12:8 [e]ver 14-16; Da 6:3 [f]S Eze 28:3
5:13 [g]S Est 2:5-6; Da 6:13
5:14 [h]S Ge 41:38 [i]S Da 2:22
5:15 [j]S Da 4:18
5:16 [k]S Ge 41:15 [l]S Ge 41:42
5:17 [m]S Est 5:3; S Da 2:6 [n]S 2Ki 5:16
5:18 [o]S Jer 28:14 [p]S Jer 27:7; S Da 2:37-38; S 4:36
5:19 [q]Da 2:12-13; S 3:6 [r]S Da 4:22
5:20 [s]Da 4:30 [t]Jer 43:10 [u]Jer 13:18; S Da 4:31 [v]S Job 40:12; Isa 14:13-15; Eze 31:10-11; Da 8:8
5:21 [w]S Eze 17:24 [x]Da 4:16-17,35
5:22 [y]S Ex 10:3
5:23 [z]S Isa 14:13; S Jer 50:29 [a]Jer 44:9 [b]Ps 115:4-8; Hab 2:19; Rev 9:20 [c]Job 12:10; Ac 17:28 [d]S Job 31:4; S Isa 13:11; Jer 10:23; S 48:26
5:26 [e]Jer 27:7 [f]Isa 13:6
5:27 [g]S Job 6:2 [h]Ps 62:9
5:28 [i]Isa 13:17 [j]S Jer 27:7; 50:41-43; Da 6:28
5:29 [k]S Ge 41:42 [l]S Da 2:6
5:30 [m]S ver 1 [n]Jer 50:35 [o]S Isa 21:9; S Jer 51:31
5:31 [p]Jer 50:41; Da 6:1; 9:1; 11:1 [q]S Isa 13:3

[n]*10* Or *queen mother* [o]*22* Or *descendant*; or *successor* [p]*25* Aramaic *UPARSIN* (that is, *AND PARSIN*) [q]*26* *Mene* can mean *numbered* or *mina* (a unit of money). [r]*27* *Tekel* can mean *weighed* or *shekel*. [s]*28* *Peres* (the singular of *Parsin*) can mean *divided* or *Persia* or *a half mina* or *a half shekel*. [t]*30* Or *Chaldeans*

5:12 HUMANITY, Intellectual Nature—Wise leaders admit the limits of their abilities and seek persons with the needed God-given skills to solve problems.

5:14 HUMANITY, Relationships—A good reputation opens doors of service for God and others which might otherwise be closed.

5:17–30 EVIL AND SUFFERING, Punishment—See notes on 4:19–33; Eze 28:1–10.

5:25–28 REVELATION, Signs—The translation of the four written words is a revelation of God's purposes in the immediate history of Belshazzar and nations which surrounded him. God used Daniel to reveal God's will to the king. The message involved word plays on weights and monetary units. God used the mysterious word game to first confuse, then give meaning to the king. See NIV note.

5:25–31 HISTORY, Universal—See note on 4:25.

Chapter 6

Daniel in the Den of Lions

IT pleased Darius[r] to appoint 120 satraps[s] to rule throughout the kingdom, 2with three administrators over them, one of whom was Daniel.[t] The satraps were made accountable[u] to them so that the king might not suffer loss. 3Now Daniel so distinguished himself among the administrators and the satraps by his exceptional qualities that the king planned to set him over the whole kingdom.[v] 4At this, the administrators and the satraps tried to find grounds for charges[w] against Daniel in his conduct of government affairs, but they were unable to do so. They could find no corruption in him, because he was trustworthy and neither corrupt nor negligent. 5Finally these men said, "We will never find any basis for charges against this man Daniel unless it has something to do with the law of his God."[x]

6So the administrators and the satraps went as a group to the king and said: "O King Darius, live forever![y] 7The royal administrators, prefects, satraps, advisers and governors[z] have all agreed that the king should issue an edict and enforce the decree that anyone who prays to any god or man during the next thirty days, except to you, O king, shall be thrown into the lions' den.[a] 8Now, O king, issue the decree and put it in writing so that it cannot be altered—in accordance with the laws of the Medes and Persians, which cannot be repealed."[b] 9So King Darius put the decree in writing.

10Now when Daniel learned that the decree had been published, he went home to his upstairs room where the windows opened toward[c] Jerusalem. Three times a day he got down on his knees[d] and prayed, giving thanks to his God, just as he had done before.[e] 11Then these men went as a group and found Daniel praying and asking God for help.[f] 12So they went to the king and spoke to him about his royal decree: "Did you not publish a decree that during the next thirty days anyone who prays to any god or man except to you, O king, would be thrown into the lions' den?"

The king answered, "The decree stands—in accordance with the laws of the Medes and Persians, which cannot be repealed."[g]

13Then they said to the king, "Daniel, who is one of the exiles from Judah,[h] pays no attention[i] to you, O king, or to the decree you put in writing. He still prays three times a day." 14When the king heard this, he was greatly distressed;[j] he was determined to rescue Daniel and made every effort until sundown to save him.

15Then the men went as a group to the king and said to him, "Remember, O king, that according to the law of the Medes and Persians no decree or edict that the king issues can be changed."[k]

16So the king gave the order, and they brought Daniel and threw him into the lions' den.[l] The king said to Daniel, "May your God, whom you serve continually, rescue[m] you!"

17A stone was brought and placed over the mouth of the den, and the king sealed[n] it with his own signet ring and with the rings of his nobles, so that Daniel's situation might not be changed. 18Then the king returned to his palace and spent the night without eating[o] and without any entertainment being brought to him. And he could not sleep.[p]

19At the first light of dawn, the king got up and hurried to the lions' den. 20When he came near the den, he called to Daniel in an anguished voice, "Daniel, servant of the living God, has your God, whom you serve continually, been able to rescue you from the lions?"[q]

21Daniel answered, "O king, live forever![r] 22My God sent his angel,[s] and he shut the mouths of the lions.[t] They have not hurt me, because I was found

6:1 [r]S Da 5:31 [s]S Est 1:1
6:2 [t]Da 2:48-49 [u]Ezr 4:22
6:3 [v]S Ge 41:41; S Est 10:3; S Da 1:20; 5:12-14
6:4 [w]Jer 20:10
6:5 [x]Ac 24:13-16
6:6 [y]S Ne 2:3
6:7 [z]S Da 3:2 [a]Ps 59:3; 64:2-6; S Da 3:6
6:8 [b]S Est 1:19
6:10 [c]S 1Ki 8:29 [d]Ps 95:6 [e]Mt 6:6; Ac 5:29
6:11 [f]1Ki 8:48-50; Ps 55:17; 1Th 5:17-18
6:12 [g]S Est 1:19; Da 3:8-12
6:13 [h]S Eze 14:14; Da 2:25 [i]S Est 3:8
6:14 [j]Mk 6:26
6:15 [k]S Est 8:8
6:16 [l]S ver 7 [m]S Job 5:19; Ps 37:39-40; S 97:10
6:17 [n]Mt 27:66
6:18 [o]S 2Sa 12:17; Da 10:3 [p]S Est 6:1
6:20 [q]S Da 3:17
6:21 [r]S Ne 2:3; Da 3:9
6:22 [s]S Ge 32:1; S Da 3:28 [t]ver 27; Ps 91:11-13; Heb 11:33

6:1–2 HUMANITY, Work—Work becomes more effective when it is efficiently and cooperatively organized with a specific purpose in view.

6:4–5 CHRISTIAN ETHICS, Character—Daniel's trustworthy character gained him the reputation of being obedient to his God no matter what. Ethical behavior is rooted in strong personal devotion.

6:10–11 PRAYER, Persistence—Daniel knew of Darius' decree. He knelt, a token of humility. He maintained his regular prayer habits. Compare 2 Ch 6:36–39. God vindicated Daniel's courage. Prayer should not be an emergency measure. It should represent habitual communication and fellowship with God. Thanks and petition are parts of regular prayer.

6:16–28 SALVATION, As Deliverance—No human authority can prevent God from rescuing His people when He chooses. God delivered Daniel from the Persian authorities, the most powerful empire of the day. What God did for Daniel, He can do for all. The Lord is a God of power, able to save His people.

6:19–24 EVIL AND SUFFERING, God's Present Help—Daniel refused to stop praying to God, and God rescued him from the lions' den. The evil of other people may bring danger and suffering to us. No matter what the danger, God is able to protect His people. We must trust Him whether He chooses to exercise His power or not. Even the natural order with its storms and wild animals cannot harm us when God chooses to protect us. See note on 3:16–18.

6:20,26–27 GOD, Living—Saving Daniel from the lions showed God was alive and active. Only He is the living God who knows and can act and save. He is not like the gods of the nations, inanimate idols of wood or stone. See note on Eze 14:16,18,20.

innocent in his sight.[u] Nor have I ever
done any wrong before you, O king."
23The king was overjoyed and gave orders to lift Daniel out of the den. And
when Daniel was lifted from the den, no
wound[v] was found on him, because he
had trusted[w] in his God.
24At the king's command, the men
who had falsely accused Daniel were
brought in and thrown into the lions'
den,[x] along with their wives and children.[y] And before they reached the floor
of the den, the lions overpowered them
and crushed all their bones.[z]
25Then King Darius wrote to all the
peoples, nations and men of every language[a] throughout the land:

"May you prosper greatly![b]

26"I issue a decree that in every
part of my kingdom people must fear
and reverence[c] the God of Daniel.[d]

"For he is the living God[e]
and he endures forever;[f]
his kingdom will not be destroyed,
his dominion will never end.[g]
27He rescues and he saves;[h]
he performs signs and wonders[i]
in the heavens and on the earth.
He has rescued Daniel
from the power of the lions."[j]

28So Daniel prospered during the reign
of Darius and the reign of Cyrus[u][k] the
Persian.[l]

Chapter 7

Daniel's Dream of Four Beasts

IN the first year of Belshazzar[m] king of
Babylon, Daniel had a dream, and visions[n] passed through his mind[o] as he
was lying on his bed.[p] He wrote[q] down
the substance of his dream.

2Daniel said: "In my vision at night I
looked, and there before me were the
four winds of heaven[r] churning up the
great sea. 3Four great beasts,[s] each different from the others, came up out of the
sea.
4"The first was like a lion,[t] and it had
the wings of an eagle.[u] I watched until its
wings were torn off and it was lifted from
the ground so that it stood on two feet
like a man, and the heart of a man was
given to it.
5"And there before me was a second
beast, which looked like a bear. It was
raised up on one of its sides, and it had
three ribs in its mouth between its teeth.
It was told, 'Get up and eat your fill of
flesh!'[v]
6"After that, I looked, and there before
me was another beast, one that looked
like a leopard.[w] And on its back it had
four wings like those of a bird. This beast
had four heads, and it was given authority
to rule.
7"After that, in my vision[x] at night I
looked, and there before me was a fourth
beast—terrifying and frightening and
very powerful. It had large iron[y] teeth; it
crushed and devoured its victims and
trampled[z] underfoot whatever was left.[a]
It was different from all the former
beasts, and it had ten horns.[b]
8"While I was thinking about the
horns, there before me was another horn,
a little[c] one, which came up among
them; and three of the first horns were
uprooted before it. This horn had eyes
like the eyes of a man[d] and a mouth that
spoke boastfully.[e]
9"As I looked,

"thrones were set in place,

[u]28 Or *Darius, that is, the reign of Cyrus*

6:22 [u]Ac 12:11; 2Ti 4:17
6:23 [v]Da 3:27 [w]S 1Ch 5:20; S Isa 12:2
6:24 [x]Dt 19:18-19; Est 7:9-10; Ps 54:5 [y]Dt 24:16; 2Ki 14:6 [z]S Isa 38:13
6:25 [a]S Da 3:4 [b]Da 4:1
6:26 [c]S Ps 5:7 [d]S Est 8:17; Ps 99:1-3; Da 3:29 [e]S Jos 2:11; S 3:10 [f]S Jer 10:10; Da 12:7; Rev 1:18 [g]S Da 2:44
6:27 [h]Da 3:29 [i]S Da 4:3 [j]S ver 22
6:28 [k]S 2Ch 36:22; S Da 1:21 [l]S Da 5:28
7:1 [m]S Da 5:1 [n]S Eze 40:2 [o]S Da 1:17 [p]Ps 4:4; S Da 4:13 [q]S Jer 36:4
7:2 [r]S Eze 37:9; Da 8:8; 11:4; Rev 7:1
7:3 [s]Rev 13:1
7:4 [t]S 2Ki 24:1; Ps 7:2; Jer 4:7; Rev 13:2 [u]S Eze 17:3
7:5 [v]Da 2:39
7:6 [w]Rev 13:2
7:7 [x]S Eze 40:2 [y]S Da 2:40 [z]Da 8:10 [a]Da 8:7 [b]S Rev 12:3
7:8 [c]Da 8:9 [d]Rev 9:7 [e]S Ps 12:3; Rev 13:5-6

6:26 GOD, Eternal—Political circumstances made nations change gods. Israel's political captivity made no difference to God's power. He is the only eternal One. Everyone else is created. See note on La 5:19.
6:26 SALVATION, Fear of God—Daniel so feared and reverenced God that King Darius issued a decree for his whole kingdom to do likewise. Our fear of God should inspire others to fear Him. Fear of God cannot, however, be legislated by government decree. Reverence and worship depend on personal experience with and loyalty to God.
6:26 LAST THINGS, Kingdom Established—See note on 4:3.
6:26 EVANGELISM, Mass—The message of God's greatness went to the masses through the decree of King Darius, an unlikely source. Regardless of the source of the message, the whole of humanity needs to hear "he is the living God." That is good news. Those who know it are to tell it, especially those who are God's own people.
6:27 GOD, Savior—See note on Jer 50:34.
6:27 REVELATION, Events—The endangered servant was kept safe. Daniel's safety revealed God's power and superiority over all Babylonian gods. God's presence was felt as a controlling influence on the lions and as a source of peace for Daniel. One miraculous event gained fame and respect for God through the Persian empire.
7:1–28 GOD, Sovereignty—God is the eternal Ruler who holds power over all earthly kingdoms in all generations. No one can destroy His kingdom. See note on 4:1–37.
7:1 HOLY SCRIPTURE, Visions—Daniel both interpreted and received dreams of revelation as God revealed His will to Darius. Daniel's dream was also a vision. God spoke in symbols which explained events about to occur in the histories of several nations near Babylon. God's servant heard the dream, interpreted it, and wrote it down for future use. Eventually other narratives and visions of Daniel and his friends were collected, written, and became part of Scripture. Daniel's visions represent a literary form called apocalyptic literature in which symbols are used to hide meaning from enemies of God's people but reveal it to God's informed people. The apocalyptic imagery had strong revelatory power for Daniel's day. Later generations of Bible students have debated strongly over the correct ways to interpret apocalyptic writings. See Introduction to Revelation.
7:9–10,22,26 GOD, Judge—God is the eternal Judge who holds records of each kingdom and individual. No one will be treated unfairly when He pronounces the ultimate decision.

and the Ancient of Days[f] took his
seat.[g]
His clothing was as white as snow;[h]
the hair of his head was white like
wool.[i]
His throne was flaming with fire,
and its wheels[j] were all ablaze.
10A river of fire[k] was flowing,
coming out from before him.[l]
Thousands upon thousands attended
him;
ten thousand times ten thousand
stood before him.
The court was seated,
and the books[m] were opened.

11"Then I continued to watch because
of the boastful words the horn was speaking.[n] I kept looking until the beast was
slain and its body destroyed and thrown
into the blazing fire.[o] 12(The other beasts
had been stripped of their authority, but
were allowed to live for a period of time.)
13"In my vision at night I looked, and
there before me was one like a son of
man,[p] coming[q] with the clouds of heav-
en.[r] He approached the Ancient of Days
and was led into his presence. 14He was
given authority,[s] glory and sovereign
power; all peoples, nations and men of
every language worshiped him.[t] His dominion is an everlasting dominion that
will not pass away, and his kingdom[u] is
one that will never be destroyed.[v]

The Interpretation of the Dream

15"I, Daniel, was troubled in spirit, and
the visions that passed through my mind
disturbed me.[w] 16I approached one of
those standing there and asked him the
true meaning of all this.
"So he told me and gave me the interpretation[x] of these things: 17'The four
great beasts are four kingdoms that will
rise from the earth. 18But the saints[y] of
the Most High will receive the kingdom[z]
and will possess it forever—yes, for ever
and ever.'[a]
19"Then I wanted to know the true
meaning of the fourth beast, which was
different from all the others and most terrifying, with its iron teeth and bronze
claws—the beast that crushed and devoured its victims and trampled underfoot whatever was left. 20I also wanted to
know about the ten horns[b] on its head
and about the other horn that came up,
before which three of them fell—the
horn that looked more imposing than the
others and that had eyes and a mouth that
spoke boastfully.[c] 21As I watched, this
horn was waging war against the saints
and defeating them,[d] 22until the Ancient
of Days came and pronounced judgment
in favor of the saints of the Most High,
and the time came when they possessed
the kingdom.[e]
23"He gave me this explanation: 'The
fourth beast is a fourth kingdom that will
appear on earth. It will be different from
all the other kingdoms and will devour
the whole earth, trampling it down and
crushing it.[f] 24The ten horns[g] are ten
kings who will come from this kingdom.
After them another king will arise, different from the earlier ones; he will subdue
three kings. 25He will speak against the
Most High[h] and oppress his saints[i] and
try to change the set times[j] and the laws.
The saints will be handed over to him for
a time, times and half a time.[v] [k]
26" 'But the court will sit, and his power will be taken away and completely destroyed[l] forever. 27Then the sovereignty,
power and greatness of the kingdoms[m]
under the whole heaven will be handed
over to the saints,[n] the people of the
Most High.[o] His kingdom will be an
everlasting[p] kingdom, and all rulers will
worship[q] and obey him.'
28"This is the end of the matter. I,

7:9 [f]ver 22 [g]S 1Ki 22:19; 2Ch 18:18; Mt 19:28; Rev 4:2; 20:4 [h]S Mt 28:3 [i]Rev 1:14 [j]S Eze 1:15; 10:6
7:10 [k]Ps 50:3; 97:3; Isa 30:27 [l]S Dt 33:2; Ps 68:17; Jude 1:14; Rev 5:11 [m]S Ex 32:32; S Ps 56:8; Rev 20:11-15
7:11 [n]Rev 13:5-6 [o]Rev 19:20
7:13 [p]S Eze 1:5; S 2:1; Mt 8:20*; Rev 1:13*; 14:14* [q]Isa 13:6; Zep 1:14; Mal 3:2; 4:1 [r]S Dt 33:26; S Rev 1:7
7:14 [s]S Mt 28:18 [t]Ps 72:11; 102:22 [u]S Isa 16:5 [v]S Da 2:44; Heb 12:28; Rev 11:15
7:15 [w]S Job 4:15; S Da 4:19
7:16 [x]Da 8:16; 9:22; Zec 1:9
7:18 [y]S Ps 16:3 [z]S Ps 49:14 [a]Isa 60:12-14; Lk 12:32; Heb 12:28; Rev 2:26; 20:4
7:20 [b]Rev 17:12 [c]Rev 13:5-6
7:21 [d]Rev 13:7
7:22 [e]Mk 8:35
7:23 [f]S Da 2:40
7:24 [g]Rev 17:12
7:25 [h]S Isa 37:23; Da 11:36 [i]Rev 16:6 [j]Da 2:21; Mk 1:15; Lk 21:8; Ac 1:6-7 [k]Da 8:24; 12:7; S Rev 11:2
7:26 [l]Rev 19:20
7:27 [m]S Isa 14:2 [n]1Co 6:2 [o]Ge 14:18 [p]S 2Sa 7:13; Ps 145:13; S Da 2:44; S 4:34; S Lk 1:33; Rev 11:15; 22:5 [q]S Ps 22:27; 72:11; 86:9

[v]25 Or *for a year, two years and half a year*

His judgment is favorable to His saints. See notes on Ge 3:8–24; Ro 2:2.

7:9,14,22,27 GOD, Eternal—God is the Ancient of Days, as old as the universe and more. He has always existed. There was never a time when He was not. See notes on Ge 1:1; 21:33; Ro 16:25–27.

7:13–14 JESUS CHRIST, Foretold—After the kingdoms of history have waned and ebbed, God's eternal kingdom will come fully. The finality of God's kingdom is heralded by the coming of "one like a son of man, coming with the clouds of heaven." Daniel's vision, expressed in apocalyptic language, was taken up in the New Testament; and a son of man became Jesus, *the* Son of man. The kingdom of earth will pass away when the returning Messiah ushers in God's eternal order (Mt 24:30; 26:64; Rev 1:7). The images of God's coming kingdom are designed to give us assurance, keep us watchful, and help us be diligent and faithful in our service.

7:14,18,27 LAST THINGS, Kingdom Established—God's saints will inherit His kingdom and possess it for eternity. How this inheritance will be fulfilled has been variously interpreted. See note on 4:3.

7:15–27 HISTORY, Universal—See note on 2:36–45. Earthly kings through blasphemy and oppression may terrify God's faithful people. They may persecute and kill God's saints. Their power is only temporary. Only God's kingdom will last forever. All earthly rulers will obey Him. The saints will find blessing and exercise power under God's rule.

7:18–27 THE CHURCH, God's Kingdom—The saints of the Most High God are the people of God. "Saints" refers to the people of God in every age who yield to God's reign over their lives. Saint means one set apart for God's service. The word does not indicate sinlessness. It is used for citizens of God's kingdom in general. The saints of God will endure the persecution of this world and reign with Him forever.

7:26–28 ELECTION, God's Purpose—Election points to the final kingdom of God when His saints will exercise control forever, and the entire world will worship and obey Him. Election thus concerns saints dedicated wholly to Him, the entire world, all eternity, spiritual worship, and moral living.

Daniel, was deeply troubled[r] by my thoughts,[s] and my face turned pale,[t] but I kept the matter to myself."

Chapter 8

Daniel's Vision of a Ram and a Goat

IN the third year of King Belshazzar's[u] reign, I, Daniel, had a vision,[v] after the one that had already appeared to me. 2In my vision I saw myself in the citadel of Susa[w] in the province of Elam;[x] in the vision I was beside the Ulai Canal. 3I looked up,[y] and there before me was a ram[z] with two horns, standing beside the canal, and the horns were long. One of the horns was longer than the other but grew up later. 4I watched the ram as he charged toward the west and the north and the south. No animal could stand against him, and none could rescue from his power.[a] He did as he pleased[b] and became great.

5As I was thinking about this, suddenly a goat with a prominent horn between his eyes came from the west, crossing the whole earth without touching the ground. 6He came toward the two-horned ram I had seen standing beside the canal and charged at him in great rage. 7I saw him attack the ram furiously, striking the ram and shattering his two horns. The ram was powerless to stand against him; the goat knocked him to the ground and trampled on him,[c] and none could rescue the ram from his power.[d] 8The goat became very great, but at the height of his power his large horn was broken off,[e] and in its place four prominent horns grew up toward the four winds of heaven.[f]

9Out of one of them came another horn, which started small[g] but grew in power to the south and to the east and toward the Beautiful Land.[h] 10It grew until it reached[i] the host of the heavens, and it threw some of the starry host down to the earth[j] and trampled[k] on them. 11It set itself up to be as great as the Prince[l] of the host;[m] it took away the daily sacrifice[n] from him, and the place of his sanctuary was brought low.[o] 12Because of rebellion, the host ⌊of the saints⌋[w] and the daily sacrifice were given over to it. It prospered in everything it did, and truth was thrown to the ground.[p]

13Then I heard a holy one[q] speaking, and another holy one said to him, "How long will it take for the vision to be fulfilled[r]—the vision concerning the daily sacrifice, the rebellion that causes desolation, and the surrender of the sanctuary and of the host that will be trampled[s] underfoot?"

14He said to me, "It will take 2,300 evenings and mornings; then the sanctuary will be reconsecrated."[t]

The Interpretation of the Vision

15While I, Daniel, was watching the vision[u] and trying to understand it, there before me stood one who looked like a man.[v] 16And I heard a man's voice from the Ulai[w] calling, "Gabriel,[x] tell this man the meaning of the vision."[y]

17As he came near the place where I was standing, I was terrified and fell prostrate.[z] "Son of man," he said to me, "understand that the vision concerns the time of the end."[a]

18While he was speaking to me, I was in a deep sleep, with my face to the ground.[b] Then he touched me and raised me to my feet.[c]

19He said: "I am going to tell you what will happen later in the time of wrath,[d] because the vision concerns the appointed time[e] of the end.[x][f] 20The two-horned ram that you saw represents the kings of Media and Persia.[g] 21The shaggy goat is the king of Greece,[h] and the large horn between his eyes is the first king.[i] 22The four horns that replaced the one that was broken off represent four kingdoms that will emerge from his nation but will not have the same power.

23"In the latter part of their reign, when rebels have become completely wicked, a stern-faced king, a master of intrigue, will arise. 24He will become very strong, but not by his own power. He will cause astounding devastation and will succeed in whatever he does. He will destroy the mighty men and the holy people.[j] 25He will cause deceit[k] to prosper, and he will consider himself superior. When they feel secure, he will destroy many and take his stand against the Prince of princes.[l] Yet he will be destroyed, but not by human power.[m]

[w] 12 Or *rebellion, the armies* [x] 19 Or *because the end will be at the appointed time*

7:28 [r]S Isa 21:3; S Da 4:19 [s]S Ps 13:2 [t]S Job 4:15
8:1 [u]S Da 5:1 [v]S Da 1:17
8:2 [w]S Ezr 4:9; S Est 2:8 [x]S Ge 10:22
8:3 [y]Da 10:5 [z]Rev 13:11
8:4 [a]Isa 41:3 [b]Da 11:3,16
8:7 [c]S Da 7:7 [d]Da 11:11,16
8:8 [e]2Ch 26:16-21; S Da 5:20 [f]S Da 7:2; Rev 7:1
8:9 [g]Da 7:8 [h]S Eze 20:6; Da 11:16
8:10 [i]S Isa 14:13 [j]Rev 8:10; 12:4 [k]S Da 7:7
8:11 [l]ver 25 [m]Da 11:36-37 [n]Eze 46:13-14 [o]Da 11:31; 12:11
8:12 [p]S Isa 48:1
8:13 [q]S Dt 33:2; S Da 4:23 [r]Da 12:6 [s]S Isa 28:18; S Lk 21:24; Rev 11:2
8:14 [t]Da 12:11-12
8:15 [u]ver 1 [v]S Eze 2:1; Da 10:16-18
8:16 [w]ver 2 [x]Da 9:21; S Lk 1:19 [y]S Da 7:16
8:17 [z]Eze 1:28; 44:4; S Da 2:46; Rev 1:17 [a]ver 19; Hab 2:3
8:18 [b]Da 10:9 [c]S Eze 2:2; Da 10:16-18; Zec 4:1
8:19 [d]S Isa 10:25 [e]S Ps 102:13 [f]Hab 2:3
8:20 [g]S Eze 27:10
8:21 [h]Da 10:20 [i]Da 11:3
8:24 [j]S Da 7:25; 11:36
8:25 [k]Da 11:23 [l]Da 11:36 [m]S Da 2:34; 11:21

8:11,24–25 GOD, Sovereignty—Human monarchs may establish famous empires through treachery, intrigue, and evil; but their success will be temporary. No one can oppose God and escape punishment. Only God rules forever. See note on Eze 1:25–28.

8:17–19,26 LAST THINGS, Last Days—Prophecy often had both an immediate (near history) and a distant fulfillment, thus applying to the situation the prophet faced and also to a future time. This multiple fulfillment theory is one way of explaining how historical events can anticipate eschatological ones. See note on Joel 2:28–32. The time of "the end" will be a "time of wrath." It was so in the immediate history of the time (vv 20–22); it will be so in the ultimate level of fulfillment, called in v 26 "the distant future." Compare Rev 15:1; 16:1–21.

26“The vision of the evenings and
mornings that has been given you is
true,[n] but seal[o] up the vision, for it concerns the distant future.”[p]
27I, Daniel, was exhausted and lay ill[q]
for several days. Then I got up and went
about the king’s business.[r] I was appalled[s] by the vision; it was beyond understanding.

Chapter 9

Daniel’s Prayer

IN the first year of Darius[t] son of
Xerxes[y][u] (a Mede by descent), who
was made ruler over the Babylonian[z] kingdom— 2in the first year of his reign, I,
Daniel, understood from the Scriptures,
according to the word of the LORD given
to Jeremiah the prophet, that the desolation of Jerusalem would last seventy[v]
years. 3So I turned to the Lord God and
pleaded with him in prayer and petition,
in fasting,[w] and in sackcloth and ashes.[x]
4I prayed to the LORD my God and confessed:[y]

“O Lord, the great and awesome
God,[z] who keeps his covenant of
love[a] with all who love him and
obey his commands, 5we have
sinned[b] and done wrong.[c] We have
been wicked and have rebelled; we
have turned away[d] from your commands and laws.[e] 6We have not listened[f] to your servants the prophets,[g] who spoke in your name to our
kings, our princes and our fathers,[h]
and to all the people of the land.
7“Lord, you are righteous,[i] but
this day we are covered with
shame[j]—the men of Judah and people of Jerusalem and all Israel, both
near and far, in all the countries
where you have scattered[k] us because of our unfaithfulness[l] to you.[m]
8O LORD, we and our kings, our
princes and our fathers are covered
with shame because we have sinned
against you.[n] 9The Lord our God is
merciful and forgiving,[o] even though
we have rebelled against him;[p] 10we
have not obeyed the LORD our God or
kept the laws he gave us through his
servants the prophets.[q] 11All Israel
has transgressed[r] your laws[s] and
turned away, refusing to obey you.
“Therefore the curses[t] and sworn
judgments[u] written in the Law of
Moses, the servant of God, have been
poured out on us, because we have
sinned[v] against you. 12You have

8:26 [n]Da 10:1 [o]S Isa 8:16; S 29:11; Rev 10:4; 22:10 [p]Da 10:14 **8:27** [q]Da 10:8 [r]S Da 2:48 [s]S Isa 21:3; S Da 4:19 **9:1** [t]S Da 5:31 [u]S Ezr 4:6 **9:2** [v]S 2Ch 36:21; Jer 29:10; Zec 1:12; 7:5 **9:3** [w]S 2Ch 20:3 [x]S 2Sa 13:19; S Ne 1:4; Jer 29:12; Da 10:12; Jnh 3:6 **9:4** [y]S 1Ki 8:30 [z]S Dt 7:21 [a]Dt 7:9; S 1Ki 8:23 **9:5** [b]S Jer 8:14 [c]Ps 106:6 [d]Isa 53:6 [e]ver 11; La 1:20; S 3:42 **9:6** [f]S 2Ki 18:12 [g]S 2Ch 36:16; S Jer 44:5; Jas 5:10; Rev 10:7 [h]S 2Ch 29:6 **9:7** [i]S Ezr 9:15; S Isa 42:6 [j]Ezr 9:7; Ps 44:15 [k]Dt 4:27; Am 9:9 [l]S Dt 7:3 [m]S Jer 3:25; S 24:9; S Eze 39:23-24 **9:8** [n]S Ne 9:33; S Jer 14:20; S Eze 16:63 **9:9** [o]S Ex 34:7; S 2Sa 24:14; Jer 42:12 [p]S Ne 9:17; Jer 14:7 **9:10** [q]2Ki 17:13-15; S 18:12; Rev 10:7 **9:11** [r]S Jer 2:29 [s]2Ki 22:16 [t]S Dt 11:26; S 13:15; S 28:15 [u]2Ki 17:23 [v]Isa 1:4-6; Jer 8:5-10

[y]1 Hebrew *Ahasuerus* [z]1 Or *Chaldean*

8:26 HISTORY, Future—God knows the future. At times He chooses to reveal future history to His chosen spokesperson. Such revelation seeks to encourage God’s people, particularly as they face dark times. Such knowledge of the future is usually in general outlines rather than specific details. God’s knowledge does not predetermine history. Humans remain free to make decisions which affect history.

9:3–19 PRAYER, Confession—Daniel began with worship and continued with confession of national sin. Sin stands in sharp contrast to the righteousness of God. In confession Daniel recognized God’s justice in punishing His people. Confession led to petition for forgiveness and restoration, a petition based on God’s mercy and not on justice. The answer was immediate. God responds to humble confession and works out His purposes for His people.

9:4 GOD, Love—Note the emphasis here on the love of God in the midst of a book about the power and sovereignty of God. See note on Eze 16:1–63.

9:4–19 SIN, Rebellion—Rebellion has a cure: confession. Confession admits that sin has been committed and that God’s punishment is justified. People must confess when we sin or miss God’s mark for our life (see note on Ne 1:6–7), do wrong by living a crooked life (see note on Isa 1:2–4), act wickedly (see note on Ps 10:1–18), turn away (Hebrew *sur*) from God’s commands (see note on Eze 5:6–7), refuse to listen to God’s Word (see note on Eze 3:7), cover ourselves with shame (Hebrew *bosheth*) by acting in ways that bring disgrace to ourselves and our community, are unfaithful to God (see note on 1 Ch 10:13), rebel against God (see note on Eze 2:3–4), or refuse to obey His will. These are all sins. They represent transgression or passing over (Hebrew *'abar*) God’s law. To pass back over to God’s grace, we must follow Daniel’s example and confess our sins.

9:4,10–11 SALVATION, Obedience—The covenant between God and Israel required obedience of God’s commands. Those commands were contained in the teachings of Israel’s prophets and in the Law of Moses. Saved persons exist in a new covenant relationship with God. Obedience to the will of God is expected in the new covenant as in the old.

9:4 SALVATION, Love of God—God is awesome and loving. His people are to fear Him and love Him. His faithful covenant love evokes the obedient love of His people. Love of God is a proper response to salvation.

9:4–18 CHRISTIAN ETHICS, Obedience—Biblical ethics centers in the righteousness of God. Humans acknowledge our imperfect response to God’s known will and confess that God is perfect. God becomes the ethical standard rather than a list of rules and regulations. The Bible’s laws and prophetic teaching reflect God’s holy righteousness and provide guidelines for us to follow in seeking to be holy and righteous as He is.

9:4 THE CHURCH, Covenant People—See note on 2 Ch 6:14.

9:7,14,16 GOD, Righteous—Even as we suffer from His judgment, we must confess what God does is right. The sinner can pray to such a God for forgiveness and ask for new historical acts establishing righteousness for the repentant sufferer.

9:9–16 REVELATION, Messengers—The prayer is a confession of rebellion by God’s people and an affirmation of God’s patient mercy and revelation in the law and through the prophets. God used many forms of literature—Law, prophecy, wisdom, apocalyptic—to reveal His will. Daniel clearly shows that Law and prophecy were acknowledged as authoritative Scripture in his day.

9:11 THE CHURCH, Servants—Like David (Isa 37:35), Moses could be identified as the servant of God. Both men, and many other unnamed people, served God in humility and faith. God’s servants are not confined to the famous or powerful. All people who love and trust God become His servants. The main requirement for service to God is willingness to serve Him. Those who refuse to serve Him face His judgment.

fulfilled[w] the words spoken against us
and against our rulers by bringing
upon us great disaster.[x] Under the
whole heaven nothing has ever been
done like[y] what has been done to
Jerusalem.[z] 13Just as it is written in
the Law of Moses, all this disaster has
come upon us, yet we have not
sought the favor of the LORD[a] our
God by turning from our sins and giving attention to your truth.[b] 14The
LORD did not hesitate to bring the disaster[c] upon us, for the LORD our
God is righteous in everything he
does;[d] yet we have not obeyed
him.[e]

15"Now, O Lord our God, who
brought your people out of Egypt
with a mighty hand[f] and who made
for yourself a name[g] that endures to
this day, we have sinned, we have
done wrong. 16O Lord, in keeping
with all your righteous acts,[h] turn
away[i] your anger and your wrath[j]
from Jerusalem,[k] your city, your holy
hill.[l] Our sins and the iniquities of
our fathers have made Jerusalem and
your people an object of scorn[m] to all
those around us.

17"Now, our God, hear the prayers
and petitions of your servant. For
your sake, O Lord, look with favor[n]
on your desolate sanctuary. 18Give
ear,[o] O God, and hear;[p] open your
eyes and see[q] the desolation of the
city that bears your Name.[r] We do
not make requests of you because we
are righteous, but because of your
great mercy.[s] 19O Lord, listen! O
Lord, forgive![t] O Lord, hear and act!
For your sake,[u] O my God, do not
delay, because your city and your
people bear your Name."

The Seventy "Sevens"

20While I was speaking and praying,
confessing[v] my sin and the sin of my people Israel and making my request to the
LORD my God for his holy hill[w]— 21while
I was still in prayer, Gabriel,[x] the man I
had seen in the earlier vision, came to me
in swift flight about the time of the evening sacrifice.[y] 22He instructed me and
said to me, "Daniel, I have now come to
give you insight and understanding.[z]
23As soon as you began to pray,[a] an answer was given, which I have come to tell
you, for you are highly esteemed.[b]
Therefore, consider the message and understand the vision:[c]

24"Seventy 'sevens'[a] are decreed for

9:12 [w]S Isa 44:26; Zec 1:6 [x]S Jer 44:23 [y]Jer 30:7 [z]Jer 44:2-6; Eze 5:9; Da 12:1; Joel 2:2; Zec 7:12 **9:13** [a]S Dt 4:29; S Isa 31:1 [b]S Isa 9:13; Jer 2:30 **9:14** [c]S Jer 18:8; S 44:27 [d]S Ge 18:25; S 2Ch 12:6; S Jer 12:1 [e]S Ne 9:33; S Jer 32:23; S 40:3 **9:15** [f]S Ex 3:20; S Jer 32:21 [g]S Ne 9:10 **9:16** [h]S Jdg 5:11; Ps 31:1 [i]S Isa 5:25 [j]S Ps 85:3 [k]Jer 32:32 [l]S Ex 15:17; S Ps 48:1 [m]S Ps 39:8; S Eze 5:14 **9:17** [n]Nu 6:24-26; Ps 80:19 **9:18** [o]S Ps 5:1 [p]Ps 116:1 [q]Ps 80:14 [r]S Dt 28:10; S Isa 37:17; Jer 7:10-12; 25:29 [s]Lk 18:13 **9:19** [t]Ps 44:23 [u]S 1Sa 12:22 **9:20** [v]S Ezr 10:1 [w]S ver 3; Ps 145:18; S Isa 58:9 **9:21** [x]S Da 8:16; S Lk 1:19 [y]S Ex 29:39 **9:22** [z]S Da 7:16; 10:14; Am 3:7 **9:23** [a]S Isa 65:24 [b]Da 10:19; Lk 1:28 [c]Da 10:11-12; Mt 24:15

[a]*24* Or *'weeks'*; also in verses 25 and 26

9:13 SALVATION, Repentance—Repentance is closely related to seeking God's favor and paying attention to the truth. The good news of salvation is that we have God's favor and that His Word is truth. Yet both are fully appropriated only through repentance.

9:14 SIN, Discipline—Confessing sin we recognize the justice of His disciplinary intervention in our lives. See note on Isa 64:4–7.

9:16 GOD, Wrath—Wrath is not God's constant disposition. He turns from it in answer to repentant prayers. See note on La 3:1,43.

9:16,20,24 GOD, Holy—God's holy presence separates off a part of the earth as holy. See note on Eze 20:12,14,40,41.

9:17–19 THE CHURCH, Servants—In crisis God's servants depend on His mercy. We ask for forgiveness as we look for deliverance. See note on Ps 27:9.

9:19 SALVATION, Forgiveness—God forgives sin for His name's sake as well as for our sake. Believers who use God's personal name indicate they belong to God and represent His name to the world. He seeks to cleanse and forgive so His name will be seen as pure and holy by the world.

9:22 HUMANITY, Intellectual Nature—A person's intellectual abilities are a gift from God. Their development may also come as an additional divine gift, as God reveals His purposes to people.

9:24–27 JESUS CHRIST, Foretold—History moves according to a divine plan. Calamity and catastrophe are a part of the fabric of human history as it moves inexorably toward the final climax of Messiah's fully accomplished kingdom. Compare Mt 24:15–31.

9:24 SALVATION, Sanctification—Daniel's vision for the future of his people included their sanctification. It takes time to be holy. Sanctification is the process of putting an end to sin. Both people and places may be sanctified, or set apart to God's service. The text makes three negative and three positive assertions about the removal of evil. Sanctification has both negative and positive aspects. It is a turning away from sin and a turning to God.

9:24 CHRISTIAN ETHICS, Righteousness—The apocalyptic vision and the history to which it points have an ethical goal. God seeks to inform, assure, and motivate His people by revealing His eternal purpose of establishing eternal righteousness. Apocalyptic is a call to be a faithful citizen of God's eternal kingdom of righteousness.

9:24–27 LAST THINGS, Great Tribulation—This difficult passage has received many interpretations. The "seventy" may be related to Jer 25:11–14; 29:10–14. It is a major focal point in spite of its difficulties for some people's doctrine of last things. Three major interpretations include: (1) The Historical—The period in view is from Jeremiah about 587 BC to Antiochus Epiphanes about 164 BC. The anointed one is either Cyrus (Isa 45:1), Zerubbabel (Hag 2:21–23), or Joshua the high priest (Hag 1:1). The first seven weeks ended with the return of the Exiles in 538 BC. The intervening period ended in 171 BC with the murder of Onias, the high priest. Compare Da 11:22. The last week was from 171–164 BC, when Antiochus desecrated the Temple by sacrificing a pig. (2) The Messianic—The period in view is from 538 BC to AD 70 or until the death of Christ. The anointed one is Jesus. The numbers are symbolical, not mathematical. The first seven weeks were from 538 BC to Ezra and Nehemiah. The sixty-two weeks were from Ezra to Christ. The last week was the Lord's life climaxing in the tearing of the veil of the Temple. V 26 refers to the destruction of the Temple by Titus, the Roman emperor, in AD 70. (3) The Dispensational Premillennial—The starting point is the command to Cyrus to restore the Temple in 539 BC (Ezr 1:1–2) or from the decree of Artaxerxes to restore Jerusalem in 444 BC (Ezr 7:13–26). Sixty-nine weeks were completed at the time of Christ's death. The seventieth week is seen as a future tribulation period of seven years or a week of years. The present church age is a gap or parenthesis between the sixty-ninth and seventieth weeks which God had not revealed through His inspired prophets. In this view the future seven-year tribulation period will be divided at its midpoint. The focal

will take many of them, but a commander
will put an end to his insolence and will
turn his insolence back upon him.[b] 19After
this, he will turn back toward the fortresses of his own country but will stumble and fall,[c] to be seen no more.[d]

20"His successor will send out a tax collector to maintain the royal splendor.[e] In
a few years, however, he will be destroyed, yet not in anger or in battle.

21"He will be succeeded by a contemptible[f] person who has not been given the honor of royalty.[g] He will invade
the kingdom when its people feel secure,
and he will seize it through intrigue.
22Then an overwhelming army will be
swept away[h] before him; both it and a
prince of the covenant will be destroyed.[i] 23After coming to an agreement
with him, he will act deceitfully,[j] and
with only a few people he will rise to
power. 24When the richest provinces feel
secure, he will invade them and will
achieve what neither his fathers nor his
forefathers did. He will distribute plunder, loot and wealth among his followers.[k] He will plot the overthrow of fortresses—but only for a time.

25"With a large army he will stir up his
strength and courage against the king of
the South. The king of the South will
wage war with a large and very powerful
army, but he will not be able to stand
because of the plots devised against him.
26Those who eat from the king's provisions will try to destroy him; his army
will be swept away, and many will fall in
battle. 27The two kings, with their hearts
bent on evil,[l] will sit at the same table
and lie[m] to each other, but to no avail,
because an end will still come at the appointed time.[n] 28The king of the North
will return to his own country with great
wealth, but his heart will be set against
the holy covenant. He will take action
against it and then return to his own
country.

29"At the appointed time he will invade the South again, but this time the
outcome will be different from what it
was before. 30Ships of the western coastlands[o] will oppose him, and he will lose
heart.[p] Then he will turn back and vent
his fury[q] against the holy covenant. He
will return and show favor to those who
forsake the holy covenant.

31"His armed forces will rise up to desecrate the temple fortress and will abolish
the daily sacrifice.[r] Then they will set up
the abomination that causes desolation.[s]
32With flattery he will corrupt those who
have violated the covenant, but the people who know their God will firmly resist[t] him.

33"Those who are wise will instruct[u]
many, though for a time they will fall by
the sword or be burned or captured or
plundered.[v] 34When they fall, they will
receive a little help, and many who are
not sincere[w] will join them. 35Some of
the wise will stumble, so that they may
be refined,[x] purified and made spotless
until the time of the end, for it will still
come at the appointed time.

The King Who Exalts Himself

36"The king will do as he pleases. He
will exalt and magnify himself[y] above every god and will say unheard-of things[z]
against the God of gods.[a] He will be successful until the time of wrath[b] is completed, for what has been determined
must take place.[c] 37He will show no regard for the gods of his fathers or for the
one desired by women, nor will he regard
any god, but will exalt himself above
them all. 38Instead of them, he will honor
a god of fortresses; a god unknown to his
fathers he will honor with gold and silver,
with precious stones and costly gifts. 39He
will attack the mightiest fortresses with
the help of a foreign god and will greatly
honor those who acknowledge him. He
will make them rulers over many people
and will distribute the land at a price.[p]

40"At the time of the end the king of
the South[d] will engage him in battle, and

[o]30 Hebrew *of Kittim* [p]39 Or *land for a reward*

11:18 [b]Hos 12:14
11:19 [c]S Ps 27:2; S 46:2 [d]S Ps 37:36; S Eze 26:21
11:20 [e]Isa 60:17
11:21 [f]Da 4:17 [g]S Da 8:25
11:22 [h]S Isa 28:15 [i]Da 8:10-11
11:23 [j]Da 8:25
11:24 [k]Ne 9:25
11:27 [l]Ps 64:6 [m]Ps 12:2; Jer 9:5 [n]Hab 2:3
11:30 [o]S Ge 10:4 [p]S 1Sa 17:32 [q]S Job 15:13
11:31 [r]Hos 3:4 [s]S Jer 19:4; Da 8:11-13; S 9:27; Mt 24:15*; Mk 13:14*
11:32 [t]Mic 5:7-9
11:33 [u]Da 12:3; Mal 2:7 [v]Mt 24:9; Jn 16:2; Heb 11:32-38
11:34 [w]Mt 7:15; Ro 16:18
11:35 [x]S Job 28:1; S Ps 78:38; S Isa 48:10; Da 12:10; Zec 13:9; Jn 15:2
11:36 [y]Jude 1:16 [z]Rev 13:5-6 [a]S Dt 10:17; S Isa 14:13-14; S Da 7:25; 8:11-12, 25; 2Th 2:4 [b]S Isa 10:25; 26:20 [c]Eze 35:13; S Da 8:24
11:40 [d]S Isa 21:1

11:28–35 THE CHURCH, Covenant People—God used foreign rulers and armies such as those of Assyria, Babylon, and Persia to discipline His people. That does not mean every enemy ruler was God's instrument against a disobedient people. God condemned enemy rulers such as the Syrian Antiochus Epiphanes IV, who acted against God's will and looted the Jerusalem Temple of its sacred objects in 169 BC. This was an action against the holy God's commitment to His people and against His eternal plan to create a people for Himself. Such action prompted God's response to protect His people (v 45). God's people must live with evil people (Jn 3:19), but we do not have to be evil. We can be part of God's holy covenant. He will purify us even though we stumble briefly. God's people may endure wicked political leadership, but in the end time God will triumph for His people.

11:32–35 CHRISTIAN ETHICS, Covenant—Apocalyptic teachings call for God's people to be faithful to His covenant, resist those who oppose it, and accept tribulation as an instrument of moral purification. See note on 9:24.

11:32 THE CHURCH, Covenant People—Disobedience is possible. God's people must guard themselves from rebelling against God and His purpose in the world. See note on Dt 17:2.

11:35 SALVATION, Sanctification—Daniel saw the death and martyrdom of so many pious leaders (v 33) as bringing about the refining, purifying, and making spotless of God's people for the end times. That is a good way to describe the process of sanctification. Sanctification refines, purifies, and cleanses us. The holy examples of others challenge us to stronger commitment to God's way of life.

11:36–45 HISTORY, Universal—See note on 7:15–27. The strongest opponents of God will come to an end.

the king of the North will storm[e] out
against him with chariots and cavalry and
a great fleet of ships. He will invade many
countries and sweep through them like a
flood.[f] 41 He will also invade the Beautiful
Land.[g] Many countries will fall, but
Edom,[h] Moab[i] and the leaders of Ammon
will be delivered from his hand.
42 He will extend his power over many
countries; Egypt will not escape. 43 He
will gain control of the treasures of gold
and silver and all the riches of Egypt,[j]
with the Libyans[k] and Nubians in submission.
44 But reports from the east and
the north will alarm him, and he will set
out in a great rage to destroy and annihilate
many. 45 He will pitch his royal tents
between the seas at[q] the beautiful holy
mountain.[l] Yet he will come to his end,
and no one will help him.

Chapter 12

The End Times

12 "At that time Michael,[m] the great
prince who protects your people,
will arise. There will be a time of distress[n]
such as has not happened from the
beginning of nations until then. But at
that time your people—everyone whose
name is found written in the book[o]—
will be delivered.[p] 2 Multitudes who
sleep in the dust of the earth will
awake:[q] some to everlasting life, others
to shame and everlasting contempt.[r]
3 Those who are wise[r] [s] will shine[t] like
the brightness of the heavens, and those
who lead many to righteousness,[u] like
the stars for ever and ever.[v] 4 But you,
Daniel, close up and seal[w] the words of
the scroll until the time of the end.[x]
Many will go here and there[y] to increase
knowledge."

5 Then I, Daniel, looked, and there before
me stood two others, one on this
bank of the river and one on the opposite
bank.[z] 6 One of them said to the man
clothed in linen,[a] who was above the waters
of the river, "How long will it be
before these astonishing things are fulfilled?"[b]

7 The man clothed in linen, who was
above the waters of the river, lifted his
right hand[c] and his left hand toward
heaven, and I heard him swear by him
who lives forever,[d] saying, "It will be for
a time, times and half a time.[s] [e] When
the power of the holy people[f] has been
finally broken, all these things will be
completed.[g]"

8 I heard, but I did not understand. So I
asked, "My lord, what will the outcome
of all this be?"

9 He replied, "Go your way, Daniel, because
the words are closed up and

[q] 45 Or *the sea and* [r] 3 Or *who impart wisdom*
[s] 7 Or *a year, two years and half a year*

11:40 [e] Isa 5:28 [f] S Isa 8:7; S Eze 38:4
11:41 [g] S Eze 20:6; Mal 3:12 [h] S Isa 11:14 [i] S Jer 48:47
11:43 [j] S Eze 30:4 [k] 2Ch 12:3; Na 3:9
11:45 [l] S Isa 2:2,4; Da 8:9
12:1 [m] S Da 10:13; Jude 1:9 [n] S Da 9:12; S Mt 24:21; Mk 13:19; Rev 16:18 [o] S Ex 32:32; S Ps 56:8; S Jer 17:13; S Lk 10:20 [p] Jer 30:7
12:2 [q] Jn 11:24 [r] S Isa 26:19; Mt 25:46
12:3 [s] S Da 11:33 [t] Mt 13:43; Jn 5:35; Php 2:15 [u] S Isa 6:7 [v] S Pr 4:18; 1Co 15:42
12:4 [w] S Isa 8:16 [x] ver 9,13; Rev 22:10 [y] Jer 5:1
12:5 [z] Da 10:4
12:6 [a] S Eze 9:2 [b] Da 8:13
12:7 [c] S Ge 14:22 [d] S Da 6:26; Rev 10:5-6 [e] S Da 7:25; S Rev 11:2 [f] S Da 8:24 [g] Lk 21:24; Rev 10:7

12:1 REVELATION, Angels—See note on 10:18—11:1.

12:1 LAST THINGS, Great Tribulation—A time of unparalleled trouble is predicted. See Mk 13:18–19. Fulfillment of such an announcement can be found within history, such as the atrocities inflicted by Antiochus in the second century BC or by the Roman army in AD 70. The more distant reference is like that of Jesus in Mk 13 or Mt 24, where end time tribulation announcements merged with the more immediate one about Jerusalem's destruction. God's people are not protected from distress but are delivered in the midst of it. God's true people will be those whose names are in the book of life. See Rev 20:15. The ultimate fulfillment will be in the coming of the messianic kingdom and its triumph.

12:1–13 THE CHURCH, Covenant People—God promises to protect His people no matter what power the enemy might possess. God's people can depend on Him in every situation of life. God's people will not be free from distress, suffering, and persecution. They will have the spiritual and emotional freedom that God's promises of final protection and eternal hope give. Resurrection hope is the ultimate promise for God's people.

12:2 EVIL AND SUFFERING, God's Future Help—The righteous will be rewarded, and the wicked will be punished. Although the Old Testament generally stressed rewards and punishments in the present life, this passage is one of the clearest in the Old Testament concerning future judgment. The elimination of suffering for the righteous in the life after death is a strong theme in the New Testament. See note on Rev 21:1–8. Suffering will be the eternal lot of the wicked.

12:2 HUMANITY, Death—To sleep in the dust is an idiom for death. Throughout most of the Old Testament, death was viewed as the end of life, although a few hints of life beyond death were given. See notes on Isa 25:7–8; Eze 37:1–14. This passage clearly reveals that both the wicked and the good have a continued existence after death. In that existence the ultimate justice of God will be fully evident.

12:2 LAST THINGS, Unbelievers' Resurrection—This, along with Isa 26:19, are perhaps the clearest expressions of personal resurrection in the Old Testament. While the resurrection of believers is a prominent part of biblical hope, references to unbelievers being resurrected are much more limited. Here the matter is strongly asserted. Some shall awake to everlasting contempt, just as some to everlasting life. The full experiencing of eternal destiny calls for personal resurrection from the "dust of the earth." See notes on Jn 5:25–29; Rev 20:11–15.

12:3 HUMANITY, Relationships—The ultimate in human wisdom is demonstrated by those who lead others into paths of goodness.

12:3,10 CHRISTIAN ETHICS, Righteousness—See note on 11:32–35.

12:3 EVANGELISM, Rewards—Witnessing is wise. When we lead someone to faith in Christ, eternal rewards are promised. We shall shine as the stars forever. All of that is for the glory of God. It is wise to share one's faith with others—eternity will record the effort.

12:4–9 HOLY SCRIPTURE, Redemption—God commanded the preservation and setting aside of the sacred recordings the prophet had received because they were to be for another time. The "time of the end" refers to several incidents described in this book from 9:27 on. Apocalyptic revelation brought comfort to the present generation but also pointed forward to the time of extreme crisis. See Rev 22:10.

12:7 GOD, Holy—At times God's purposes involve momentary defeat for His holy people. People are holy only by virtue of being in a right relationship to God, who alone is holy. See note on Eze 20:12,14,40,41.

sealed[h] until the time of the end.[i]
[10]Many will be purified, made spotless
and refined,[j] but the wicked will continue to be wicked.[k] None of the wicked
will understand, but those who are wise
will understand.[l]
[11]"From the time that the daily sacrifice[m] is abolished and the abomination
that causes desolation[n] is set up, there
will be 1,290 days.[o] [12]Blessed is the one
who waits[p] for and reaches the end of
the 1,335 days.[q]
[13]"As for you, go your way till the
end.[r] You will rest,[s] and then at the end
of the days you will rise to receive your
allotted inheritance.[t] [u]"

12:9 [h]S Isa 29:11 [i]S ver 4
12:10 [j]S Isa 1:25; S Da 11:35 [k]S Isa 32:7; Rev 22:11 [l]Hos 14:9
12:11 [m]S Ex 29:38 [n]S Da 8:11; S 9:27; Mt 24:15*; Mk 13:14* [o]Rev 11:2
12:12 [p]S Isa 30:18 [q]S Eze 4:5-6; Da 8:14
12:13 [r]S ver 4 [s]Isa 57:2 [t]Ps 16:5; Rev 14:13 [u]Mt 10:22; Jas 1:12

12:10 HUMANITY, Intellectual Nature—The ability to discern or perceive God's work comes from the wisdom which He alone imparts.

12:13 HISTORY, Eternal—All history—good days and dark days—point forward to the end. God's people can live and die in confidence. They will receive eternal rewards. God will not let history lead to nothing. The end will reveal the full meaning of history.

Hosea

Theological Setting

Why does God continue to put up with an unfaithful people? Unfaithfulness was Israel's besetting sin. The people of the land had fallen for the tempting promises of the Baal cult. Their attraction to the fertility rites associated with Baal worship began even before they occupied the land of Canaan (9:10; Nu 25:1-18). The high places dedicated to local Baals continued to lure Israel throughout their history. That fact was especially true in the days of Hosea (Hos 1:2*b*; 2:5-10,13; 4:11-14; 5:3-4; 9:1-3; 11:2).

The appeal of Baal worship to the base lusts of sexual immorality and greed for gain may explain Israel's eager involvement in it. Then again, the lure of Baal worship may have been its promise of reward in the form of fertile flocks, fields, and families. Perhaps the Israelites observed the farming methods of the original inhabitants of the land of Canaan, especially their rituals of seeking productivity for their herds and crops through magic. Influenced by their "successful" neighbors, Israelites flocked to the Baal shrines and engaged in the immoral fertility rites. They left believing Baal would give them needed rain, bountiful harvests, productive herds, and many children. See Introduction to Song of Songs.

In so doing they turned away from their covenant God. They committed spiritual adultery, pursuing pagan deities as "lovers" in the place of God. How would a faithful God react to such an unfaithful people? What could a faithless people expect from a loving God? Could God's covenant election be detoured or destroyed by the people's sin? These were Hosea's questions.

Hosea's ministry as prophet to Israel, the breakaway Northern Kingdom, came toward the close of an era of peace and prosperity for both Israel and Judah (ca. 750 BC). Both nations had trouble handling the good times in faithfulness. Hosea witnessed the rapid deterioration of Israel's society, religion, and politics. He had the dubious honor of preaching God's Word to a nation sick unto death. Amos had announced the end of Israel (Am 5:2; 7:7-9; 8:1-3), and Hosea watched the fulfillment of his words.

Apparently, Hosea was a native of Israel. At least that relationship seems to be indicated by his personal identification with the plight of the people and by his intimate knowledge of their moral, religious, and political activities. God did more than tell Hosea to preach. The Lord commanded Hosea to take "an adulterous wife and children of unfaithfulness" (Hos 1:2*a*). By this action, the prophet symbolized in his family life the nation's life. The land was "guilty of the vilest adultery in departing from the LORD" (1:2*b*). Later God commanded the prophet to "Go, show your love to your wife again" (3:1*a*), though she had turned to other lovers. The prophet's faithful obedience boldly symbolized the fact that "the LORD loves the Israelites, though they turn to other gods" (3:1*b*). Hosea's relationship to his family was a miniature of God's relationship to Israel.

Hosea's domestic problems and his prophetic ministry became tools in God's hands aimed at turning Israel away from Baalism and back to God. The prophet magnified the love of God as the initiating force in his relationship to Israel (11:1). He threatened God's judgment upon faithless people, priests, and prophets (4:1-9). He promised a new beginning if only they would turn back (repent) to God. He said God would "heal their waywardness," "love them freely," and "be like the dew" to them (14:4-5*a*). Hosea hoped to negate the false teachings of the Baal cult and to lead Israel to trust God alone for their life and prosperity. Thus, the nation might avert the disaster and doom Hosea had announced.

Theological Outline

Hosea: God's Faithful Love for Unfaithful People

I. God Loves His Unfaithful People. (1:1—3:5)
   A. God's forgiveness has its limits. (1:1-9)
   B. God promises a future reversal of His judgment upon His people. (1:10—2:1)
      1. The promise is based on God's earlier word to Abraham. (1:10*a*)
      2. The promise will result in a united people. (2:1)
      3. The promise is a prediction of restored relationships. (2:1*b*)

C. God works with His people to bring about reconciliation. (2:2-15)
   1. God's legal actions call for His people's reform. (2:2-5)
   2. God places obstacles in the path of His people to turn them back to God. (2:6-8)
   3. God removes the bounty of His people to remind them that God is the Giver. (2:9-13)
   4. God lures His people into the wilderness to open a door of hope. (2:14-15)

D. God initiates a new covenant with His people. (2:16-23)
   1. God will remove the pagan elements of their worship. (2:16-17)
   2. God will restore His people to a right relationship with the animal kingdom. (2:18*a*)
   3. God will abolish war and grant peace and security to His people. (2:18*b*)
   4. God will establish a new and permanent relationship with His people based on His character. (2:19-20)
   5. God will bless His restored covenant people. (2:21-23)

E. God's love is the basis of future hope for His people. (3:1-5)
   1. God's love is strong enough to overcome the unfaithfulness of His people. (3:1)
   2. God's love is deep enough to redeem His people. (3:2)
   3. God's love is courageous enough to discipline His people. (3:3-4)
   4. God's love will ultimately win the return of His people. (3:5)

II. Unfaithfulness Is the Basis of God's Controversy with His People. (4:1—9:9)

A. Unfaithful people break covenant commitments. (4:1-3)

B. Unfaithful ministers bring judgment on the people and on themselves. (4:4-12*a*)

C. An alien spirit dominates unfaithful people. (4:12*b*-19)

D. God chastises His unfaithful people. (5:1-15)
   1. God disciplines unfaithful leaders. (5:1-2)
   2. God disciplines because He knows His people fully. (5:3)
   3. Pride prevents repentance and promotes stumbling. (5:4-5)
   4. Extravagant giving is no substitute for lapses in living. (5:6-7)
   5. God is the agent of punishment for His people. (5:8-14)
   6. God seeks the return of His people through discipline. (5:15)

E. Surface repentance does not satisfy the sovereign God. (6:1-3)

F. Sharp judgment comes upon fleeting loyalty. (6:4-5)

G. Loyal love and personal knowledge of God meet His requirements. (6:6)

H. Covenant-breaking hinders restoration of God's people. (6:7—7:2)

I. Making leaders by power politics shuts God out of the process. (7:3-7)

J. Compromise leads to loss of strength and alienation from God. (7:8-10)

K. Diplomatic duplicity interferes with God's redemptive activity. (7:11-13)

L. Religious perversion ends in apostasy and bondage. (7:14-16)

M. God's unfaithful people reap more than they sow. (8:1—9:9)
   1. The unfaithful disregard divine law. (8:1-2)
   2. The unfaithful reject God's goodness. (8:3)
   3. The unfaithful practice idolatry. (8:4-6)
   4. The unfaithful will reap foreign domination. (8:7-10)
   5. The unfaithful will reap religious and moral corruption. (8:11-13*a*)
   6. The unfaithful will reap national destruction. (8:13*b*-14)
   7. The unfaithful will reap exile in a foreign land. (9:1-4)
   8. The unfaithful will reap punishment for their sins. (9:5-9)

III. God's Loyal Love Is the Only Basis for a Lasting Relationship with His People. (9:10—14:9)

A. Without God's love His people perish. (9:10-17)

B. Without reverence for God, His people have no future. (10:1-8)
   1. Ornate altars cannot hide deceitful hearts. (10:1-2)
   2. Bad leaders produce bad times. (10:3-8)

C. Without righteousness God's people cannot experience God's unfailing love. (10:9-15)

D. God's love for His people will not allow Him to give them up. (11:1-11)

E. Covenant-making with alien powers is infidelity to God. (11:12—12:1)

F. Judgment according to deeds is a universal principle. (12:2-6)

G. Deception is repaid by destruction. (12:7-14)

H. Rebellion against God leads to death. (13:1-16)

I. Repentance results in restoration and life for God's people. (14:1-9)

Theological Conclusions

The love of God is the doctrinal foundation for the Book of Hosea. The book contains strong warnings to God's rebellious, unfaithful people. At the same time, it contains promises of forgiveness, hope, and blessing for those who repent. God's love is the basis for both the warnings to the unfaithful and for the promises to the repentant. From that base the author presents five conclusions:

1. God's love prompts Him to enter into a covenant relationship with His people.
2. God's love for His people is consistent in spite of their unfaithfulness.
3. God's love leads Him to discipline and to judge His unfaithful people.
4. God's love for His people causes Him to expect them to love Him consistently.
5. Genuine repentance on the part of God's people results in divine forgiveness, love, and blessing.

God initiated a relationship with Israel based on love (11:1-4). He chose them to be His people (13:4). Not only was Israel young and inexperienced as a nation, but they were also slaves in Egypt when God chose them to be His people and gave them His covenant (Ex 20—24). God's care was constant and tender, like that of a father for his son. God's steady hand was upon the nation as it began to grow and develop. His love sustained them through hard and trying times as they struggled to establish themselves in the land God gave them (Hos 13:5-6).

God's love remained consistent in the face of Israel's repeated lapses in her love for God. The nation fell into the trap of Baal worship even before they entered the Promised Land (9:10). Again and again the fertility rites associated with the worship of pagan deities lured Israel away from God. Hosea's children bore names that made them walking sermons, expressing Israel's deteriorating relationship to God (1:4-9). God's love for faithless Israel was the model for Hosea to go and love his unfaithful wife (3:1-3).

God's love is tender, but it is not weak. In love God disciplined His wayward wife Israel (2:1-13). Election and covenant did not protect an unfaithful people from discipline and judgment. Through judgment upon the nation He deprived them of a king, of sacrifice, and of the normal means of seeking God (3:4). Punishment was not aimed at the nation's destruction, but at their future repentance and restoration to God.

What God wanted from His people was not more and more offerings, not more elaborate rituals of worship, but more consistency in their love. His controversy with the nation was over the absence of expected faithfulness, loyal love, and the knowledge of God. The whole nation failed to live by the covenant principles God had established. Priests and prophets failed to fulfill their calling, and the people plunged deeper and deeper into their sin. Social injustice, immorality, and political anarchy all revealed Israel's lack of loyal love. Their loyal love was like a morning cloud and like the dew that goes early away. God wanted their love to be as faithful as His.

Under the heavy hand of God's judgment the nation would fall. Still God's great love for His people offered forgiveness, love, and blessing if the nation would repent. God promised a repentant people that He would heal their backsliding, love them freely, and be like the dew to them. A faithful God would love anew a faithful people who responded to His loving discipline.

Contemporary Teaching

The word of the Lord that came to Hosea in the prosperous eighth century BC is relevant to the "successful" church in the twentieth century AD. God's people are lured by local gods and material greed to turn away from the true and living God. Social injustice, immorality, and political intrigue mar modern life and need to be addressed. Repentant sinners need to know that God's forgiveness, love, and blessing are available to them. The church should learn the following lessons from Hosea:

1. God's judgment comes upon His people when they turn away from Him to seek pagan gods and to devote themselves to material prosperity.
2. God disciplines His people to turn them away from false gods and false goals and return to Himself.
3. God opens a door of hope out of the valley of trouble.
4. God loves His people even when they turn to other gods.
5. God has ways of calling His unfaithful people to account for their infidelity.
6. God's ministers are not immune to judgment when they lead God's people astray and engage in the same sins as the people.
7. Immorality and drunkenness take away the ability to think straight and to make good moral decisions.
8. Large offerings and elaborate rituals are not acceptable substitutes for loyal love.
9. The Holy God is restrained from expressing His wrath by His overpowering compassion.
10. When God's people repent, they can expect God to forgive them, love them, and bless them.

Chapter 1

THE word of the LORD that came[a] to
Hosea son of Beeri during the reigns
of Uzziah,[b] Jotham,[c] Ahaz[d] and Hezekiah,[e] kings of Judah,[f] and during the
reign of Jeroboam[g] son of Jehoash[a] king
of Israel:[h]

Hosea's Wife and Children

2When the LORD began to speak
through Hosea, the LORD said to him,
"Go, take to yourself an adulterous[i] wife
and children of unfaithfulness, because
the land is guilty of the vilest adultery[j] in
departing from the LORD." 3So he married
Gomer[k] daughter of Diblaim, and she
conceived and bore him a son.
4Then the LORD said to Hosea, "Call
him Jezreel,[l] because I will soon punish
the house of Jehu for the massacre at Jezreel, and I will put an end to the kingdom
of Israel. 5In that day I will break Israel's
bow in the Valley of Jezreel.[m]"
6Gomer[n] conceived again and gave
birth to a daughter. Then the LORD said to
Hosea, "Call her Lo-Ruhamah,[b][o] for I
will no longer show love to the house of
Israel,[p] that I should at all forgive them.
7Yet I will show love to the house of Judah; and I will save them—not by bow,[q]
sword or battle, or by horses and horsemen, but by the LORD their God.[r]"
8After she had weaned Lo-Ruhamah,[s]
Gomer had another son. 9Then the LORD
said, "Call him Lo-Ammi,[c] for you are
not my people, and I am not your God.[t]
10"Yet the Israelites will be like the
sand on the seashore, which cannot be
measured or counted.[u] In the place
where it was said to them, 'You are not
my people,' they will be called 'sons of
the living God.'[v][w] 11The people of Judah
and the people of Israel will be reunited,[x] and they will appoint one leader[y]
and will come up out of the land,[z] for
great will be the day of Jezreel.[a]

Chapter 2

"SAY of your brothers, 'My people,'
and of your sisters, 'My loved
one.'[b]

1:1 [a]S Jer 1:2 [b]S 2Ki 14:21 [c]S 1Ch 3:12 [d]S 1Ch 3:13 [e]S 1Ch 3:13 [f]Isa 1:1; Mic 1:1 [g]S 2Ki 13:13 [h]Am 1:1
1:2 [i]S Jer 3:1; Hos 2:2,5; 3:1 [j]Dt 31:16; Jer 3:14; Eze 23:3-21; Hos 5:3
1:3 [k]ver 6
1:4 [l]ver 11; S 1Sa 29:1; 1Ki 18:45; 2Ki 10:1-14; Hos 2:22
1:5 [m]S Jos 15:56; S 1Sa 29:1; 2Ki 15:29
1:6 [n]ver 3 [o]ver 8; Hos 2:23 [p]Hos 2:4
1:7 [q]S Ps 44:6 [r]Zec 4:6
1:8 [s]S ver 6
1:9 [t]ver 10; S Eze 11:19-20; 1Pe 2:10
1:10 [u]S Ge 22:17; S Jer 33:22 [v]S ver 9; Hos 2:23; Ro 9:26* [w]S Jos 3:10
1:11 [x]S Isa 11:12, 13 [y]Jer 23:5-8; 30:9 [z]S Eze 37:15-28 [a]S ver 4
2:1 [b]ver 23; 1Pe 2:10

[a] *1* Hebrew *Joash,* a variant of *Jehoash*
[b] *6* *Lo-Ruhamah* means *not loved.* [c] *9* *Lo-Ammi* means *not my people.*

1:1–2 REVELATION, Word—Hosea received God's revelation during the reign of four kings. He communicated the word with words and with his family life. God's word in this sense is the intention God wanted to reveal to His people and their leaders.

1:1–8 FAMILY, Symbolic Nature—Hosea's marriage became a prophetic sign symbolizing Judah's rejection of God in favor of Baal. Marriage language was appropriate because Baal worship included sexual fertility rites. Hosea denounced the actions of the people and declared that only God could enter into a true marriage alliance with Israel. The symbolic names given to his children and the purchasing again of Gomer are designed to show both the separation of the people from Yahweh, their God, and His intention to bring them back into an intimate relationship with Himself.

1:2 SIN, Against God—Sex filled a central spot in Canaanite worship of Baal. The worship place employed prostitutes, so men could participate in sinful rites supposed to ensure good harvests. This made adultery a powerful word to describe Israel's rejection of God for Baal or their mixture of Baal and Yahweh worship. To worship another god is as shameful and disgusting as breaking the trust of the marriage relationship through adultery. See note on 1 Ki 12:26–33.

1:2—3:5 REVELATION, Actions—The prophet became totally identified with God and His word. His marriage relationship and his children's names were living sermons. Every time a member of Hosea's family appeared on the street, God's judgment of Israel was proclaimed. See note on Jer 32:6–15.

1:6—2:1 GOD, Wrath—God threatened to withhold His love. This involved refusing to forgive them. This defines God's wrath: an absence of divine love and forgiveness. Love, not wrath, is God's final word. See notes on Ps 30:5; Isa 30:18–19.

1:7 SALVATION, Definition—God saves His people through suffering love, not by weapons of traditional or modern warfare. Compare 13:10; 14:3.

1:8–9 THE CHURCH, Covenant People—Hosea, as a message to unfaithful Israel, gave his children symbolic names. Lo-Ruhamah, meaning "not pitied," was the name of the second child. Israel would not find pity. Hosea named the third child Lo-Ammi, meaning "not my people." Instead of being God's people, the people had broken the covenant relationship by their evil deeds. God's covenant love keeps the covenant, but human sin breaks the covenant. God desires to continue the relationship with His people, but each believer is responsible to maintain the relationship by serving and obeying God. God, of course, has never forsaken His people. He remains faithful even when unfaithful people break the covenant. Hosea spoke of a new day when God would bring His people back to Himself. See note on 2:14–23.

1:10 SALVATION, Blessing—Compare Ge 22:17–18. Israel's name would be changed from Lo-Ammi (Not my People) to Ammi (My People) when God restored her from her whoredom with other gods. Peter applied this promised blessing to the church (1 Pe 2:10). Compare Hos 2:23. Only a committed people can hope to receive God's promised blessing.

1:10–11 THE CHURCH, God's Community—Israel became the sons of God because God chose them for His own and established His covenant with them. See note on Dt 7:6–8. Because of rebellion, Israel could no longer be called the people of God. God chose to restore them unto Himself and to call them the sons of God. God chooses by His grace to restore His people despite our sin. The loving Father does everything possible to woo His people back to loyalty to Himself and His covenant. He wants to call all of us "My people." He remains faithful to us even when we are unfaithful. See note on Ge 6:18.

2:1–23 GOD, Love—God uses allure and punishment to renew His vows with His beloved people. When they love other gods more, He is forced to drastic action. Still the goal is renewal of the love relationship. His love calls for faithful response. See note on Eze 16:1–63.

2:1–23 EVIL AND SUFFERING, Redemptive—God punished Israel to bring her back to Him. Sometimes our suffering is part of God's dealing with us redemptively, aiming for our repentance and reconciliation. Our sin and unfaithfulness does not destroy His love for us.

2:1–20 ELECTION, God's Initiative—God spoke as an aggrieved husband. Israel was the adulterous wife. The few Israelites true to God's covenant were urged to argue with their guilty mother, Israel. God makes the advances toward restoration and reconciliation. God always takes the lead. We love Him because He first loved us. Human worship does not initiate the relationship described by election. God's love does.

Israel Punished and Restored

2"Rebuke your mother,[c] rebuke her,
for she is not my wife,
and I am not her husband.
Let her remove the adulterous[d] look
from her face
and the unfaithfulness from between
her breasts.
3Otherwise I will strip[e] her naked
and make her as bare as on the day
she was born;[f]
I will make her like a desert,[g]
turn her into a parched land,
and slay her with thirst.
4I will not show my love to her
children,[h]
because they are the children of
adultery.[i]
5Their mother has been unfaithful
and has conceived them in
disgrace.
She said, 'I will go after my lovers,[j]
who give me my food and my water,
my wool and my linen, my oil and
my drink.'[k]
6Therefore I will block her path with
thornbushes;
I will wall her in so that she cannot
find her way.[l]
7She will chase after her lovers but not
catch them;
she will look for them but not find
them.[m]
Then she will say,
'I will go back to my husband[n] as at
first,[o]
for then I was better off[p] than now.'
8She has not acknowledged[q] that I was
the one
who gave her the grain, the new
wine and oil,[r]
who lavished on her the silver and
gold[s]—
which they used for Baal.[t]

9"Therefore I will take away my grain[u]
when it ripens,
and my new wine[v] when it is
ready.
I will take back my wool and my
linen,
intended to cover her nakedness.
10So now I will expose[w] her lewdness
before the eyes of her lovers;[x]
no one will take her out of my
hands.[y]
11I will stop[z] all her celebrations:[a]
her yearly festivals, her New Moons,
her Sabbath days—all her appointed
feasts.[b]
12I will ruin her vines[c] and her fig
trees,[d]
which she said were her pay from
her lovers;[e]
I will make them a thicket,[f]
and wild animals will devour
them.[g]
13I will punish her for the days
she burned incense[h] to the Baals;[i]
she decked herself with rings and
jewelry,[j]
and went after her lovers,[k]
but me she forgot,[l]"
declares the LORD.[m]

2:2 [c]ver 5; S Isa 50:1; S Hos 1:2; 4:5 [d]S Isa 1:21; S Eze 23:45
2:3 [e]S Eze 16:37 [f]Eze 16:4,22 [g]Isa 32:13-14
2:4 [h]S Eze 8:18; Hos 1:6 [i]Hos 5:7
2:5 [j]S Jer 3:6; S Hos 1:2 [k]Jer 44:17-18
2:6 [l]S Job 3:23; S 19:8; S La 3:9
2:7 [m]Hos 5:13 [n]S Isa 54:5 [o]Jer 2:2; S 3:1 [p]S Eze 16:8
2:8 [q]S Isa 1:3 [r]S Nu 18:12 [s]S Dt 8:18 [t]ver 13; Eze 16:15-19; Hos 8:4
2:9 [u]Hos 8:7 [v]Hos 9:2
2:10 [w]Eze 23:10 [x]Jer 13:26 [y]S Eze 16:37
2:11 [z]Jer 7:34 [a]S Isa 24:8 [b]S Isa 1:14; Jer 16:9; Hos 3:4; 9:5; Am 5:21; 8:10
2:12 [c]S Isa 7:23; S Jer 8:13 [d]S Jer 5:17 [e]S Jer 3:1 [f]S Isa 5:6 [g]Hos 5:7; 13:8
2:13 [h]Isa 65:7 [i]ver 8; S Jer 7:9; Hos 11:2 [j]S Eze 16:17; S 23:40 [k]Hos 4:13 [l]Hos 4:6; 8:14; 13:6 [m]S Jer 44:17; Hos 13:1

That love often involves condemnation and discipline to achieve its purposes.

2:1 THE CHURCH, Covenant People—God wants to reverse the horrible consequences caused when His people rebel. "Not loved" becomes "My loved one," and "Not my people" becomes "My people." God's final word to His people is acceptance and love. This is not a reason to rebel but a call to love and be faithful to the loving, faithful God.

2:2–23 GOD, One God—Both Judah and Israel had a history of prostituting themselves with the fertility gods of Canaan. They failed to recognize God as the one true God, who gave them good harvests and prosperity. The true God continues working to lure His people back in faithful love and righteousness. He wants His people to confess Him as our only God and Source of blessing.

2:7–8 SIN, Against God—See note on Eze 16:15–34.

2:9–13 CREATION, Freedom—Brokenhearted because of his wife's unfaithfulness, Hosea saw a parallel between his experience with her and God's with Israel. Though God had blessed the nation and promised her a glorious future, she had refused to follow Him in faithful obedience. He has the freedom to confiscate gifts if the receiver fails to show proper gratitude. If a group of people become unusable, God can do one of two things. He can throw them away completely as His instrument of blessing, or He can discipline them until they have been purified sufficiently. That which applied to Israel as His Servant applies to us as *individuals. God calls us to His service and expects us to respond* to His loving call in faithful service.

2:13 SIN, Punishment—We forget. God does not. Enamored with other exciting priorities, we push God aside to a more convenient time. When the time is right for Him, He punishes our forgetfulness. See note on 1:2.

2:14–23 THE CHURCH, Covenant People—God offers hope for broken and rebellious people by establishing a new relationship which is possible through God's grace. He takes the initiative to turn His people to a better way of life. He willingly waits to bring contrary people to a proper relationship with Himself. Hosea saw a future time when God would restore His people to proper relationship with Him. Four new elements are contained in these verses: (1) God establishes a new love. God takes the initiative in helping unfaithful people turn to Him. The Hebrew term *Baal* means husband, master, or lord. Because of its use in the worship of pagan gods, God promised to give the people a new term to reflect the new faith which He promised to give. (2) God gives a new environment of peace. See note on Ge 9:8–17. (3) God establishes His new relationship on right living. Righteousness means to meet the demands of a relationship. A person is righteous before God when the person meets the demands of the relationship with God. Justice means that righteousness is carried over into the legal sphere. Steadfast love, mercy, faithfulness, and knowledge are all associated with the responsibilities of a relationship with God. God promised to give these qualities to His people and does so through Christ. See notes on 2 Ch 6:14; Ps 25:10; Jer 31:31–34. (4) Nature will rejoice in the renewed and right *relationship*. When people return to God and God restores His people, then God's ideal for His people will be realized—they will indeed be His people. We look for that day.

because they have deserted[u] the LORD
to give themselves [11]to
prostitution,[v]
to old wine[w] and new,
which take away the
understanding[x] [12]of my
people.
They consult a wooden idol[y]
and are answered by a stick of
wood.[z]
A spirit of prostitution[a] leads them
astray;[b]
they are unfaithful[c] to their God.
13They sacrifice on the mountaintops
and burn offerings on the hills,
under oak,[d] poplar and terebinth,
where the shade is pleasant.[e]
Therefore your daughters turn to
prostitution[f]
and your daughters-in-law to
adultery.[g]
14"I will not punish your daughters
when they turn to prostitution,
nor your daughters-in-law
when they commit adultery,
because the men themselves consort
with harlots[h]
and sacrifice with shrine
prostitutes[i] —
a people without understanding[j]
will come to ruin![k]
15"Though you commit adultery,
O Israel,
let not Judah become guilty.

"Do not go to Gilgal;[l]
do not go up to Beth Aven.[s] [m]
And do not swear, 'As surely as the
LORD lives!'[n]
16The Israelites are stubborn,[o]
like a stubborn heifer.[p]
How then can the LORD pasture them
like lambs[q] in a meadow?
17Ephraim is joined to idols;
leave him alone!
18Even when their drinks are gone,
they continue their prostitution;
their rulers dearly love shameful
ways.
19A whirlwind[r] will sweep them
away,
and their sacrifices will bring them
shame.[s]

4:10 [u]Hos 7:14; 9:17
4:11 [v]ver 14; Hos 5:4 [w]S Lev 10:9; S 1Sa 25:36 [x]S Pr 20:1
4:12 [y]Jer 2:27 [z]Hab 2:19 [a]S Nu 15:39 [b]S Isa 44:20 [c]S Ps 73:27
4:13 [d]S Isa 1:29 [e]S Jer 3:6; Hos 10:8; 11:2 [f]Jer 2:20; Am 7:17 [g]Hos 2:13
4:14 [h]S ver 11 [i]S Ge 38:21; Hos 9:10 [j]S Pr 10:21 [k]ver 19
4:15 [l]Hos 9:15; 12:11; Am 4:4; 5:5 [m]S Jos 7:2; S Hos 5:8 [n]S Jer 4:2
4:16 [o]S Ex 32:9 [p]S Jer 31:18 [q]Isa 5:17; 7:25
4:19 [r]Hos 12:1; 13:15 [s]ver 13-14; Isa 1:29
5:1 [t]S Job 10:2 [u]Hos 6:9; 9:8 [v]S Jer 5:26
5:2 [w]S Hos 4:2 [x]Hos 9:15
5:3 [y]Am 5:12 [z]S Eze 23:7; S Hos 1:2; 6:10
5:4 [a]Hos 7:10 [b]S Hos 4:11 [c]S Jer 4:22; S Hos 4:6
5:5 [d]S Isa 3:9; S Jer 2:19; Hos 7:10 [e]S Eze 14:7 [f]Hos 14:1
5:6 [g]Mic 6:6-7 [h]S Pr 1:28; Isa 1:15; Eze 8:6; Mal 1:10
5:7 [i]S Isa 24:16; Hos 6:7 [j]Hos 2:4 [k]Isa 1:14 [l]S Hos 2:11-12
5:8 [m]S Nu 10:2; S Jer 4:21; S Eze 33:3 [n]Jdg 19:12; Hos 9:9; 10:9 [o]S Isa 10:29 [p]S Jos 7:2; Hos 4:15; 10:5
5:9 [q]S Isa 7:16 [r]Isa 37:3; Hos 9:11-17 [s]Isa 46:10; Zec 1:6
5:10 [t]S Dt 19:14 [u]S Eze 7:8

Chapter 5

Judgment Against Israel

"HEAR this, you priests!
Pay attention, you Israelites!
Listen, O royal house!
This judgment[t] is against you:
You have been a snare[u] at Mizpah,
a net[v] spread out on Tabor.
2The rebels are deep in slaughter.[w]
I will discipline all of them.[x]
3I know all about Ephraim;
Israel is not hidden[y] from me.
Ephraim, you have now turned to
prostitution;
Israel is corrupt.[z]

4"Their deeds do not permit them
to return[a] to their God.
A spirit of prostitution[b] is in their
heart;
they do not acknowledge[c] the LORD.
5Israel's arrogance testifies[d] against
them;
the Israelites, even Ephraim,
stumble[e] in their sin;
Judah also stumbles with them.[f]
6When they go with their flocks and
herds
to seek the LORD,[g]
they will not find him;
he has withdrawn[h] himself from
them.
7They are unfaithful[i] to the LORD;
they give birth to illegitimate[j]
children.
Now their New Moon festivals[k]
will devour[l] them and their fields.

8"Sound the trumpet[m] in Gibeah,[n]
the horn in Ramah.[o]
Raise the battle cry in Beth Aven[s];[p]
lead on, O Benjamin.
9Ephraim will be laid waste[q]
on the day of reckoning.[r]
Among the tribes of Israel
I proclaim what is certain.[s]
10Judah's leaders are like those
who move boundary stones.[t]
I will pour out my wrath[u] on them
like a flood of water.

[s]*15,8* *Beth Aven* means *house of wickedness* (a name for Bethel, which means *house of God*).

5:1–15 GOD, Wrath—People can become so corrupt they cannot repent and return to God. Sometimes the wrath of God is necessary to awaken people and bring them to the point where the love of God can be expressed.

5:1–15 SIN, Alienation—Repentance becomes impossible for a people totally devoted to sin. Evil deeds raise a barrier between a sinner and God. They raise wicked pride in people's hearts, barring saving humility and repentance. Adulterous Israel (1:2) had become totally corrupt or unclean (see note on Eze 39:23–24), unfit for God's presence. Instead of letting God's Spirit lead them, they followed the "spirit of prostitution." They did not even know God (4:1–2). They stumbled along a crooked path of sin (Isa 1:2–4). Such a path certainly cannot lead the way to God, who cannot accept unfaithful, treacherous people (see note on Isa 48:1–9). Political allies cannot cure sin sickness. They cannot fight God's discipline. Only confession of sin and guilt or shame (see note on 2 Ch 28:9–13) can bridge the sin gap which separates us from God.

5:3 GOD, Wisdom—We may try to hide sins from God. We will always fail. Nothing escapes His attention. God knows fully what is happening in His world and in the hearts of His people. See note on Eze 8:12.

5:9 PROCLAMATION, Authoritative—See note on Jer 19:14–15.

11Ephraim is oppressed,
trampled in judgment,
intent on pursuing idols.[t] [v]
12I am like a moth[w] to Ephraim,
like rot[x] to the people of Judah.

13"When Ephraim[y] saw his sickness,
and Judah his sores,
then Ephraim turned to Assyria,[z]
and sent to the great king for help.[a]
But he is not able to cure[b] you,
not able to heal your sores.[c]
14For I will be like a lion[d] to Ephraim,
like a great lion to Judah.
I will tear them to pieces[e] and go away;
I will carry them off, with no one to rescue them.[f]
15Then I will go back to my place[g]
until they admit their guilt.[h]
And they will seek my face;[i]
in their misery[j] they will earnestly seek me.[k]"

Chapter 6

Israel Unrepentant

"COME, let us return[l] to the LORD.
He has torn us to pieces[m]
but he will heal us;[n]
he has injured us
but he will bind up our wounds.[o]
2After two days he will revive us;[p]
on the third day[q] he will restore[r] us,
that we may live in his presence.
3Let us acknowledge the LORD;
let us press on to acknowledge him.
As surely as the sun rises,
he will appear;
he will come to us like the winter rains,[s]
like the spring rains that water the earth.[t]"

4"What can I do with you, Ephraim?[u]
What can I do with you, Judah?
Your love is like the morning mist,
like the early dew that disappears.[v]
5Therefore I cut you in pieces with my prophets,
I killed you with the words of my mouth;[w]
my judgments flashed like lightning upon you.[x]
6For I desire mercy, not sacrifice,[y]
and acknowledgment[z] of God rather than burnt offerings.[a]
7Like Adam,[u] they have broken the covenant[b]—
they were unfaithful[c] to me there.
8Gilead is a city of wicked men,[d]
stained with footprints of blood.
9As marauders lie in ambush for a man,[e]
so do bands of priests;
they murder[f] on the road to Shechem,
committing shameful crimes.[g]
10I have seen a horrible[h] thing
in the house of Israel.
There Ephraim is given to prostitution
and Israel is defiled.[i]

11"Also for you, Judah,
a harvest[j] is appointed.

Chapter 7

"WHENEVER I would restore the fortunes[k] of my people,

5:11 [v]Hos 9:16; Mic 6:16 **5:12** [w]S Job 13:28; S Isa 51:8 [x]S Job 18:16 **5:13** [y]S Isa 7:16 [z]S Eze 23:5; Hos 7:11; 8:9; 12:1 [a]S La 5:6; Hos 7:8; 10:6 [b]S Isa 3:7; Hos 14:3 [c]Hos 2:7 **5:14** [d]S Job 10:16; S Jer 4:7; Am 3:4 [e]Hos 6:1 [f]S Dt 32:39; Mic 5:8 **5:15** [g]S Isa 18:4 [h]S Lev 26:40 [i]S Nu 21:7; S Ps 24:6; S Hos 3:5 [j]Ps 50:15; S Jer 2:27 [k]Isa 64:9; S Eze 20:43 **6:1** [l]S Isa 10:20; S 19:22 [m]S Job 16:9; La 3:11; Hos 5:14 [n]S Nu 12:13; S Jer 3:22 [o]S Dt 32:39; S Job 5:18; S Jer 30:17; Hos 14:4 **6:2** [p]Ps 30:5; S 80:18 [q]S Mt 16:21 [r]S Ps 71:20 **6:3** [s]S Job 4:3; Joel 2:23 [t]Ps 72:6; Hos 11:10; 12:6 **6:4** [u]Hos 11:8 [v]Hos 7:1; 13:3 **6:5** [w]Jer 1:9-10; 5:14; 23:29 [x]Heb 4:12 **6:6** [y]S 1Sa 15:22; S Isa 1:11; Mt 9:13*; 12:7*; Mk 12:33 [z]S Jer 4:22; S Hos 2:20 [a]S Ps 40:6; Mic 6:8 **6:7** [b]S Ge 9:11; S Jer 11:10; Hos 8:1 [c]S Hos 5:7 **6:8** [d]Hos 12:11 **6:9** [e]Ps 10:8 [f]S Hos 4:2 [g]Jer 5:30-31; 7:9-10; S Eze 22:9; S Hos 5:1; 7:1 **6:10** [h]S Jer 5:30 [i]S Jer 23:14; S Eze 23:7; S Hos 5:3 **6:11** [j]Jer 51:33; Joel 3:13 **7:1** [k]S Ps 126:1; Zep 2:7

[t]*11* The meaning of the Hebrew for this word is uncertain. [u]*7* Or *As at Adam;* or *Like men*

5:13 SALVATION, Healing—Ephraim turned to a false physician. See note on La 2:13. Only God can heal the sores of sin.

6:1–2 REVELATION, Author of Grace—The call to restore the relationship to God acknowledges the discipline of God and His healing intentions. Rescue on the third day to the Hebrew was a complete number of days and in the New Testament became the waiting period for the resurrection. Revelation leads to knowledge of God's forgiving grace and sure salvation.

6:1–3 SALVATION, Healing—Israel's judgment was from God and so would be her healing. God "has torn" that He may heal. His punishment is always disciplinary and remedial. The prophet provided His people language to use to express their repentance ("return"), their faith, and their hope. To "acknowledge God" (literally to know God) means to follow the guidelines He has given for life. See note on 4:1.

6:2 SALVATION, Renewal—God is ready to restore His people whenever they return to Him, provided they sincerely repent (7:1). The prophet used the language of resurrection to describe the people's hope.

6:3 GOD, Faithfulness—When we repent and turn to God, He is always there to receive us. The problem is our fickleness (v 4), not His faithfulness. See note on 3:1.

6:4–5 SIN, Punishment—Inconsistent, sporadic love is a sin. Yahweh, our God, will not be one among many lovers waiting His turn for our affections. Carrying out regular religious rituals is no substitute for daily devotion and service to the one love of our lives. We cannot breach God's covenant and expect to go free. God punishes unfaithfulness or treachery (see note on Isa 48:1–9). Hands stained by human blood cannot spread out in prayer to Him.

6:5 REVELATION, Messengers—Prophets spoke words of God's mouth judging and destroying the people. The spoken word of God was a promise sure to be fulfilled.

6:6 SALVATION, Obedience—God wants the loving obedience of His people more than He wants their animal sacrifices. Compare 1 Sa 15:22. See note on Hos 4:1.

6:6 WORSHIP, Obedience—Worship comes from an obedient heart filled with God's attitudes, such as mercy. See note on 1 Sa 15:22–23.

6:6 PRAYER, Humility—Offerings given in pride and with demands on God are not acceptable. Acknowledging God's sovereign rule over us is the prelude to prayer and the requirement for genuine relationship with God. See notes on Lev 1:9; Mt 9:13.

7:1–16 SIN, Blindness—Solving the sin problem takes more than God's desire. He heals us from the sin disease only when we turn fully to Him and away from sin. The problem is that sin blinds us. We do not realize we are sick. We forget our

1 whenever I would heal Israel,
the sins of Ephraim are exposed
and the crimes of Samaria
revealed.[l]
They practice deceit,[m]
thieves break into houses,[n]
bandits rob in the streets;[o]
2but they do not realize
that I remember[p] all their evil
deeds.[q]
Their sins engulf them;[r]
they are always before me.

3"They delight the king with their
wickedness,
the princes with their lies.[s]
4They are all adulterers,[t]
burning like an oven
whose fire the baker need not stir
from the kneading of the dough till
it rises.
5On the day of the festival of our king
the princes become inflamed with
wine,[u]
and he joins hands with the
mockers.[v]
6Their hearts are like an oven;[w]
they approach him with intrigue.
Their passion smolders all night;
in the morning it blazes like a
flaming fire.
7All of them are hot as an oven;
they devour their rulers.
All their kings fall,[x]
and none of them calls[y] on me.

8"Ephraim mixes[z] with the nations;
Ephraim is a flat cake not turned
over.
9Foreigners sap his strength,[a]
but he does not realize it.
His hair is sprinkled with gray,
but he does not notice.
10Israel's arrogance testifies against
him,[b]
but despite all this
he does not return[c] to the LORD his
God
or search[d] for him.

11"Ephraim is like a dove,[e]
easily deceived and senseless—
now calling to Egypt,[f]
now turning to Assyria.[g]
12When they go, I will throw my net[h]
over them;
I will pull them down like birds of
the air.
When I hear them flocking together,
I will catch them.
13Woe[i] to them,
because they have strayed[j] from
me!
Destruction to them,
because they have rebelled against
me!
I long to redeem them
but they speak lies[k] against me.[l]
14They do not cry out to me from their
hearts[m]
but wail upon their beds.
They gather together[v] for grain and
new wine[n]
but turn away from me.[o]
15I trained[p] them and strengthened
them,
but they plot evil[q] against me.
16They do not turn to the Most High;[r]
they are like a faulty bow.[s]
Their leaders will fall by the sword
because of their insolent[t] words.
For this they will be ridiculed[u]
in the land of Egypt.[v]

Chapter 8

Israel to Reap the Whirlwind

"PUT the trumpet[w] to your lips!
An eagle[x] is over the house of
the LORD
because the people have broken my
covenant[y]
and rebelled against my law.[z]
2Israel cries out to me,
'O our God, we acknowledge you!'
3But Israel has rejected what is good;
an enemy will pursue him.[a]
4They set up kings without my consent;
they choose princes without my
approval.[b]
With their silver and gold
they make idols[c] for themselves
to their own destruction.

7:1 [l]S Eze 24:13; S Hos 6:4 [m]ver 13 [n]S Ex 22:2; Hos 4:2 [o]S Hos 6:9; 12:1
7:2 [p]S Jer 14:10; S 44:21; S Hos 8:13 [q]S Job 35:15; Hos 9:15 [r]Jer 2:19; 4:18
7:3 [s]Jer 28:1-4; S Hos 4:2; 10:13; Mic 7:3
7:4 [t]S Jer 9:2
7:5 [u]S Isa 28:1,7 [v]S Ps 1:1
7:6 [w]Ps 21:9
7:7 [x]Hos 13:10 [y]ver 16; S Ps 14:4; S Isa 9:13; Zep 1:6
7:8 [z]ver 11; Ps 106:35; S Hos 5:13
7:9 [a]Isa 1:7; Hos 8:7
7:10 [b]Hos 5:5 [c]Hos 5:4 [d]ver 14; S Isa 9:13
7:11 [e]S Ge 8:8 [f]ver 16; Hos 9:6 [g]S ver 8; S Jer 2:18; S La 5:6; Hos 9:3; 12:1
7:12 [h]S Eze 12:13; S 32:3
7:13 [i]Hos 9:12 [j]Jer 14:10; S Eze 34:4-6; Hos 9:17 [k]S Ps 116:11 [l]ver 1; Jer 51:9; Mt 23:37
7:14 [m]Jer 3:10 [n]Am 2:8 [o]S ver 10; S Hos 4:10; 9:1; 13:16
7:15 [p]Hos 11:3 [q]Ps 2:1; S 140:2; Na 1:9,11
7:16 [r]S ver 7 [s]S Ps 78:9,57 [t]Mal 3:14 [u]S Eze 23:32 [v]S ver 11; Hos 9:3; 11:5
8:1 [w]S Nu 10:2; S Eze 33:3 [x]S Dt 28:49; Jer 4:13 [y]S Jer 11:10 [z]S Hos 4:6; S 6:7
8:3 [a]S Mt 7:23; Tit 1:16
8:4 [b]Hos 13:10 [c]S Hos 2:8; 13:1-2

[v]14 Most Hebrew manuscripts; some Hebrew manuscripts and Septuagint *They slash themselves*

sins and forget that God does not forget. He looks at us and sees only a gulf of sins surrounding us. Blind Israel continued her adultery (1:2) and political intrigue, blind to God's absence from all her activities. Thus, the people did not call on God, search for Him, or return in repentance to Him. Sin had blinded them to their need for God. God wanted to redeem. They rebelled (see note on Isa 1:2–4). To rebel against the Redeemer is the end of the line; all hope is gone.

7:1 SALVATION, Healing—God's healing exposes our sins and those of others. Israel and Ephraim are the same people. Salvation is not a one-way street. Even God will not heal us unless we repent.

7:13 GOD, Savior—God does not force us to be saved. God is Savior, but sometimes people set in their sinfulness and stubbornness refuse His salvation. See note on Jer 50:34.

8:1–10 SIN, Covenant Breach—Being in covenant relation with God means letting Him be King and direct our decisions. Excluding Him from our decision-making processes is rebellion, a breach of the conditions of His covenant law. See note on Jer 11:8–13.

8:1 THE CHURCH, Covenant People—See note on 2 Ki 17:35–39.

8:4–6 GOD, One God—When we set materialistic man-made things in place of God, His anger burns. Nothing can replace Him in our lives. See note on 2:2–23.

5Throw out your calf-idol, O Samaria![d]
My anger burns against them.
How long will they be incapable of
purity?[e]
6 They are from Israel!
This calf—a craftsman has made it;
it is not God.[f]
It will be broken in pieces,
that calf[g] of Samaria.[h]

7"They sow the wind
and reap the whirlwind.[i]
The stalk has no head;
it will produce no flour.[j]
Were it to yield grain,
foreigners would swallow it up.[k]
8Israel is swallowed up;[l]
now she is among the nations
like a worthless[m] thing.
9For they have gone up to Assyria[n]
like a wild donkey[o] wandering
alone.
Ephraim has sold herself to lovers.[p]
10Although they have sold themselves
among the nations,
I will now gather them together.[q]
They will begin to waste away[r]
under the oppression of the mighty
king.
11"Though Ephraim built many altars for
sin offerings,
these have become altars for
sinning.[s]
12I wrote for them the many things of
my law,
but they regarded them as
something alien.[t]
13They offer sacrifices given to me
and they eat[u] the meat,
but the LORD is not pleased with
them.[v]
Now he will remember[w] their
wickedness
and punish their sins:[x]
They will return to Egypt.[y]
14Israel has forgotten[z] his Maker[a]
and built palaces;
Judah has fortified many towns.
But I will send fire upon their cities
that will consume their
fortresses."[b]

Chapter 9

Punishment for Israel

Do not rejoice, O Israel;
do not be jubilant[c] like the other
nations.
For you have been unfaithful[d] to your
God;
you love the wages of a prostitute[e]
at every threshing floor.
2Threshing floors and winepresses will
not feed the people;
the new wine[f] will fail them.
3They will not remain[g] in the LORD's
land;
Ephraim will return to Egypt[h]
and eat unclean[w] food in Assyria.[i]
4They will not pour out wine offerings[j]
to the LORD,
nor will their sacrifices please[k] him.
Such sacrifices will be to them like the
bread of mourners;[l]
all who eat them will be unclean.[m]
This food will be for themselves;
it will not come into the temple of
the LORD.[n]
5What will you do[o] on the day of your
appointed feasts,[p]
on the festival days of the LORD?
6Even if they escape from destruction,
Egypt will gather them,[q]
and Memphis[r] will bury them.[s]
Their treasures of silver[t] will be taken
over by briers,
and thorns[u] will overrun their tents.
7The days of punishment[v] are coming,
the days of reckoning[w] are at hand.
Let Israel know this.
Because your sins[x] are so many
and your hostility so great,
the prophet is considered a fool,[y]
the inspired man a maniac.[z]
8The prophet, along with my God,
is the watchman over Ephraim,[x]
yet snares[a] await him on all his paths,
and hostility in the house of his
God.[b]

[w] *3* That is, ceremonially unclean [x] *8* Or *The prophet is the watchman over Ephraim, / the people of my God*

8:5 [d]ver 6; Hos 10:5 [e]Jer 13:27 **8:6** [f]S Jer 16:20; Hos 14:3 [g]S Ex 32:4 [h]S ver 5 **8:7** [i]S Job 4:8; Pr 22:8; Isa 66:15; Hos 10:12-13; Na 1:3; Gal 6:8 [j]S Dt 28:38; S Isa 17:11; Hos 9:16 [k]Hos 2:9; S 7:9 **8:8** [l]Jer 51:34 [m]Jer 22:28 **8:9** [n]S Jer 2:18 [o]S Ge 16:12 [p]S Jer 22:20; Eze 23:5; S Hos 5:13 **8:10** [q]S Eze 16:37; S 22:20 [r]Jer 42:2 **8:11** [s]Hos 10:1; 12:11 **8:12** [t]S ver 1 **8:13** [u]S Jer 7:21 [v]S Jer 6:20; Hos 9:4 [w]Hos 7:2; 9:9; Am 8:7 [x]S Hos 4:9 [y]Hos 9:3,6 **8:14** [z]S Dt 32:18; S Isa 17:10; S Hos 2:13 [a]S Ps 95:6 [b]Jer 5:17; S 17:27; Am 2:5 **9:1** [c]Isa 22:12-13 [d]S Ps 73:27; S Isa 24:16; S Hos 7:14; 10:5 [e]S Ge 30:15 **9:2** [f]Isa 24:7; Hos 2:9; Joel 1:10 **9:3** [g]Lev 25:23 [h]S Hos 7:16; S 8:13 [i]Eze 4:13; S Hos 7:11; 10:5; Am 7:17 **9:4** [j]Joel 1:9,13; 2:14 [k]S Hos 8:13 [l]S Jer 16:7 [m]S Dt 26:14; Hag 2:13-14 [n]S Eze 4:13-14 **9:5** [o]Isa 10:3; Jer 5:31 [p]S Hos 2:11 **9:6** [q]S Hos 7:11; S 8:13 [r]S Isa 19:13 [s]S Jer 42:22 [t]Zep 1:11 [u]Isa 5:6; Hos 10:8 **9:7** [v]Isa 34:8; Jer 10:15; Mic 7:4; Lk 21:22 [w]S Job 31:14 [x]Jer 16:18 [y]S 1Sa 10:11; Isa 44:25; S La 2:14; Eze 14:9-10 [z]S Jer 29:26; Hos 14:1 **9:8** [a]S Hos 5:1 [b]S Eze 22:26

8:7 EVIL AND SUFFERING, Punishment—The prophet took up a proverb to echo the wise men's teaching that actions have consequences. Wicked deeds result in suffering and sorrow. See note on Pr 1:10–19.

8:11–14 SIN, Transgression—Altars were made for sin offerings to deal with Israel's sin problem. They became places for sin because Israel refused to worship how and whom God's laws directed. Their wickedness or crookedness (see note on Isa 1:2–4) and their sins in missing God's target for their lives (see note on Ne 1:6–7) called forth God's threat to reverse their entire national history. Ignoring God's directions for life leads us backward to oppression, not forward to hope. See note on Eze 5:6–7.

8:12 HOLY SCRIPTURE, Writing—Hosea knew a written law which his people should have regarded as authoritative Scripture but which they disregarded. To ignore these directions from God is to ignore God's will for His people. See 4:2.

9:1 SIN, Against God—See note on 1:2.

9:7–9 SIN, Discipline—The unpopular preacher is often God's servant. God's word of discipline often does not sit well with the audience. A sinful people does not relish hearing God's Word. Preaching it does not win popularity contests. Judgment preaching is in order when sin or crookedness (see note on Isa 1:2–4), hostility or grudge-bearing animosity (Hebrew *satam*), corruption or destructiveness (see note on Isa 1:2–4), and sins missing God's target (see note on Ne 1:6–7) dominate the life of God's people.

9They have sunk deep into corruption,[c]
as in the days of Gibeah.[d]
God will remember[e] their wickedness
and punish them for their sins.[f]

10"When I found Israel,
it was like finding grapes in the
desert;
when I saw your fathers,
it was like seeing the early fruit[g] on
the fig[h] tree.
But when they came to Baal Peor,[i]
they consecrated themselves to that
shameful idol[j]
and became as vile as the thing they
loved.
11Ephraim's glory[k] will fly away like a
bird[l] —
no birth, no pregnancy, no
conception.[m]
12Even if they rear children,
I will bereave[n] them of every one.
Woe[o] to them
when I turn away from them![p]
13I have seen Ephraim,[q] like Tyre,
planted in a pleasant place.[r]
But Ephraim will bring out
their children to the slayer."[s]

14Give them, O LORD—
what will you give them?
Give them wombs that miscarry
and breasts that are dry.[t]

15"Because of all their wickedness in
Gilgal,[u]
I hated them there.
Because of their sinful deeds,[v]
I will drive them out of my house.
I will no longer love them;[w]
all their leaders are rebellious.[x]
16Ephraim[y] is blighted,
their root is withered,
they yield no fruit.[z]
Even if they bear children,

9:9 [c]Zep 3:7 [d]Jdg 19:16-30; S Hos 5:8 [e]S Hos 8:13 [f]S Hos 4:9
9:10 [g]S SS 2:13 [h]S Isa 28:4 [i]Nu 25:1-5; Ps 106:28-29 [j]Jer 11:13; S Hos 4:14
9:11 [k]S Isa 17:3 [l]S Hos 4:7; 10:5 [m]ver 14
9:12 [n]ver 16; S Eze 24:21 [o]Hos 7:13 [p]S Dt 31:17
9:13 [q]S Ps 78:67 [r]S Eze 27:3 [s]S Job 15:22; S La 2:22
9:14 [t]ver 11; Lk 23:29
9:15 [u]S Hos 4:15 [v]S Hos 7:2 [w]S Jer 12:8 [x]S Isa 1:23; S Hos 4:9; 5:2
9:16 [y]S Hos 5:11 [z]S Job 15:32; S Hos 8:7 [a]S ver 12
9:17 [b]S Jer 6:30 [c]S Hos 4:10 [d]S Dt 28:65; S Hos 7:13
10:1 [e]S Eze 15:2 [f]S 1Ki 14:23 [g]Hos 13:15 [h]Hos 3:4; S 4:7; S 8:11; 12:11
10:2 [i]1Ki 18:21 [j]Hos 13:16 [k]ver 8 [l]Mic 5:13
10:4 [m]S Hos 4:2 [n]S Eze 17:19; Am 5:7 [o]Am 6:12
10:5 [p]S Ex 32:4; S Isa 44:17-20 [q]ver 8; S Hos 5:8 [r]S 2Ki 23:5; Zep 1:4 [s]S Jdg 18:17-18; S Hos 8:5; S 9:1,3, 11
10:6 [t]S 2Ki 16:7; Hos 11:5 [u]S Jdg 3:15 [v]S Hos 5:13 [w]Isa 30:3; S Hos 4:7

I will slay[a] their cherished
offspring."
17My God will reject[b] them
because they have not obeyed[c] him;
they will be wanderers among the
nations.[d]

Chapter 10

ISRAEL was a spreading vine;[e]
he brought forth fruit for himself.
As his fruit increased,
he built more altars;[f]
as his land prospered,[g]
he adorned his sacred stones.[h]
2Their heart is deceitful,[i]
and now they must bear their
guilt.[j]
The LORD will demolish their altars[k]
and destroy their sacred stones.[l]

3Then they will say, "We have no king
because we did not revere the LORD.
But even if we had a king,
what could he do for us?"
4They make many promises,
take false oaths[m]
and make agreements;[n]
therefore lawsuits spring up
like poisonous weeds[o] in a plowed
field.
5The people who live in Samaria fear
for the calf-idol[p] of Beth Aven.[y] [q]
Its people will mourn over it,
and so will its idolatrous priests,[r]
those who had rejoiced over its
splendor,
because it is taken from them into
exile.[s]
6It will be carried to Assyria[t]
as tribute[u] for the great king.[v]
Ephraim will be disgraced;[w]

[y]5 *Beth Aven* means *house of wickedness* (a name for Bethel, which means *house of God*).

9:10–17 GOD, Wrath—Idolatry utterly corrupts human values and brings on God's angry reaction. He rejects His people. See note on 5:1–15.

9:10–17 HISTORY, Judgment—See note on Jer 1:14–19. Israel's history should have been a love affair with God. Instead it was a shameful affair with the gods. Even their worship was sinful. Rejection was the only logical step for God.

9:10–13 ELECTION, Israel—At first Israel was as delectable as luscious grapes and good figs, but at Baal-peor she left God to worship Baal (Nu 25:1–3; Dt 4:3). Moral decay set in. Ephraim, like the city of Tyre, would be given up to destruction. Nations and individuals can lose their status of moral beauty and spiritual health. Election does not place a people in a moral and spiritual vacuum. The elect continue to face moral and spiritual decisions of utmost importance.

9:15 SIN, Rebellion—God hates pretense. Worship in God's house by uncaring sinners sparks God's wrath. He withdraws His love, totally rejecting a people who say the right words in worship but do all the wrong things in daily life. False worship starts with leaders who must maintain their image in God's house but stubbornly rebel against His expectations outside it. See note on Isa 65:1–7.

9:15–17 ELECTION, Condemnation—Hosea lamented the wickedness of the nation he loved. He pitied the nation while hating its sinfulness. He believed it would be better if the nation were barren, rather than fertile. Their wickedness began in Gilgal, where Israel crowned its human king (1 Sa 11:14–15). The wicked worship continued in Gilgal (Hos 4:15). Because of their sins, Israel would suffer punishment by the God who elected them. The people who prided in being God's elect became His rejects. Election is a call to faithfulness.

10:1–2 SIN, Judgment—See note on 8:11–14.

10:1–15 HISTORY, Moral—See note on 9:10–17. Prosperity can deceive. God can change history's fortunes suddenly to discipline His people as Israel discovered. Wicked seeds will never produce lasting success. Only righteousness does that, for God has installed a moral foundation to history.

10:5–8 GOD, One God—Idols are only worth something to conquering kings who want to show off their power over enemy gods or desire to strip off valuable gold for their treasures. The only power of idols is to bring down the wrath of God. See note on 2:2–23.

10:5–15 SIN, Against God—See note on Eze 8:3–18.

Israel will be ashamed[x] of its
wooden idols.[z]
7Samaria and its king will float away[y]
like a twig on the surface of the
waters.
8The high places[z] of wickedness[a] [a]
will be destroyed—
it is the sin of Israel.
Thorns[b] and thistles will grow up
and cover their altars.[c]
Then they will say to the mountains,
"Cover us!"[d]
and to the hills, "Fall on us!"[e]

9"Since the days of Gibeah,[f] you have
sinned,[g] O Israel,
and there you have remained.[b]
Did not war overtake
the evildoers in Gibeah?
10When I please, I will punish[h] them;
nations will be gathered against
them
to put them in bonds for their
double sin.
11Ephraim is a trained heifer
that loves to thresh;
so I will put a yoke[i]
on her fair neck.
I will drive Ephraim,
Judah must plow,
and Jacob must break up the ground.
12Sow[j] for yourselves righteousness,[k]
reap the fruit of unfailing love,
and break up your unplowed ground;[l]
for it is time to seek[m] the LORD,
until he comes
and showers righteousness[n] on you.
13But you have planted wickedness,
you have reaped evil,[o]
you have eaten the fruit of
deception.[p]
Because you have depended on your
own strength
and on your many warriors,[q]
14the roar of battle will rise against your
people,
so that all your fortresses will be
devastated[r]—
as Shalman[s] devastated Beth Arbel on
the day of battle,
when mothers were dashed to the
ground with their children.[t]
15Thus will it happen to you, O Bethel,
because your wickedness is great.
When that day dawns,
the king of Israel will be completely
destroyed.[u]

Chapter 11

God's Love for Israel

"WHEN Israel was a child,[v] I
loved[w] him,
and out of Egypt I called my son.[x]
2But the more I[c] called Israel,
the further they went from me.[d] [y]
They sacrificed to the Baals[z]
and they burned incense to
images.[a]
3It was I who taught Ephraim to walk,
taking them by the arms;[b]
but they did not realize
it was I who healed[c] them.
4I led them with cords of human
kindness,
with ties of love;[d]
I lifted the yoke[e] from their neck

10:6 [x]Jer 48:13
10:7 [y]ver 15; Hos 13:11
10:8 [z]S Eze 6:6 [a]S ver 5; 1Ki 12:28-30; S Hos 4:13 [b]S Hos 9:6 [c]ver 2; S Isa 32:13 [d]S Job 30:6; Am 3:14-15 [e]Am 7:9; Lk 23:30*; Rev 6:16
10:9 [f]S Hos 5:8 [g]S Jos 7:11
10:10 [h]S Eze 5:13; S Hos 4:9
10:11 [i]S Jer 15:12; S 31:18
10:12 [j]S Ecc 11:1 [k]S Pr 11:18; Jas 3:18 [l]Jer 4:3 [m]S Isa 19:22; Hos 12:6 [n]S Isa 45:8
10:13 [o]S Job 4:8; S Hos 7:3; 11:12; Gal 6:7-8 [p]S Pr 11:18; S Hos 8:7 [q]Ps 33:16
10:14 [r]S Isa 17:3; Mic 5:11 [s]S 2Ki 17:3 [t]S Isa 13:16; Hos 13:16
10:15 [u]S ver 7
11:1 [v]S Jer 2:2; S Eze 16:22 [w]S Dt 4:37 [x]S Ex 4:22; Hos 12:9,13; 13:4; Mt 2:15*
11:2 [y]ver 7 [z]S Hos 2:13 [a]S 2Ki 17:15; Isa 65:7; S Jer 18:15; S Hos 4:13; 13:1
11:3 [b]S Dt 1:31; S 32:11; Hos 7:15 [c]S Ex 15:26; Jer 30:17
11:4 [d]Jer 31:2-3 [e]S Lev 26:13

[z]6 Or *its counsel* [a]8 Hebrew *aven,* a reference to Beth Aven (a derogatory name for Bethel) [b]9 Or *there a stand was taken* [c]2 Some Septuagint manuscripts; Hebrew *they* [d]2 Septuagint; Hebrew *them*

10:12–13 CHRISTIAN ETHICS, Righteousness—Righteousness and justice sowed in the name of God will bear its fruit in due time. God's people cannot wait passively for His salvation. They must act in ways to give stability and hope to society. In His time God will act righteously to save us. See note on 2:19–20.

10:15 ELECTION, Condemnation—Israel faced destruction because of her superficiality. She scratched the surface of her soil, refusing to go deep to the depths of her heart by breaking up the fallow ground. Destruction was the result of her sinful life-style.

11:1–11 GOD, Father—God is Father of His people because He took them in their weakness and raised them to be a mature nation. This resulted from God's love. See note on Jer 31:9,20.

11:1–4,8 GOD, Love—As long as they have existed, God's people have known His love. They grew up in His love. His love cured their ills. His love sought to steer them on the right track. Still they rebelled. The only option left seemed clear. God must harshly discipline His people in His anger. But God does not give up easily. He loves His people too much. His holy otherness distinguishes even His love from anything we have experienced. He exercises patient, divine, self-giving love with even His rebellious people.

11:1 JESUS CHRIST, Foretold—Hosea's reference to Israel's deliverance from Egypt is given new meaning by the flight and return from Egypt of the holy family (Mt 2:13–15). The long journey to the cross began on the long journey into Egypt. Our salvation comes through one who made a long journey into an alien land.

11:1–7 SIN, Blindness—Sin blinds in two ways. We do not see what God has done for us. We stubbornly refuse to repent because we cannot see our own sin.

11:1–11 EVIL AND SUFFERING, God's Compassion—Evil behavior deserves God's punishment, but God's basic relationship to His people is love. His heart fills with compassion when time for punishment comes. Sometimes His great love leads to even greater patience and protection for His people. Still, the time of punishment cannot be put off forever, as the Northern Kingdom found out in 721 BC.

11:1–11 HISTORY, National—See note on Isa 1:24–26. God's love and Israel's stupid commitment to the practices of their neighbors marked Israel's history. Justice called for an unrepentant people to face justice. Love could not give up on the beloved, so the final word is hope beyond judgment.

11:1–11 ELECTION, Love—When Israel was young, God loved her. She grew old with ingratitude and infidelity. God would have preserved Israel in the vigor of youth, but Israel rejected the election love of God. God's unconditional love melted with compassion. In His faithfulness He could not totally give up His people.

11:3 EDUCATION, God—As the Teacher of His people, God is gentle and loving, like a father helping a toddler take his first steps. See Mic 4:2.

and bent down to feed[f] them.[g]
5"Will they not return to Egypt[h]
and will not Assyria[i] rule over them
because they refuse to repent?[j]
6Swords[k] will flash in their cities,
will destroy the bars[l] of their gates
and put an end to their plans.
7My people are determined to turn[m]
from me.[n]
Even if they call to the Most High,
he will by no means exalt them.

8"How can I give you up,[o] Ephraim?[p]
How can I hand you over, Israel?
How can I treat you like Admah?
How can I make you like Zeboiim?[q]
My heart is changed within me;
all my compassion[r] is aroused.[s]
9I will not carry out my fierce anger,[t]
nor will I turn and devastate[u]
Ephraim.
For I am God, and not man[v]—
the Holy One[w] among you.
I will not come in wrath.[e]
10They will follow the LORD;
he will roar[x] like a lion.[y]
When he roars,
his children will come trembling[z]
from the west.[a]
11They will come trembling
like birds from Egypt,
like doves[b] from Assyria.[c]
I will settle them in their homes,"[d]
declares the LORD.

Israel's Sin

12Ephraim has surrounded me with
lies,[e]
the house of Israel with deceit.
And Judah is unruly against God,
even against the faithful[f] Holy
One.[g]

Chapter 12

1EPHRAIM[h] feeds on the wind;[i]
he pursues the east wind all day
and multiplies lies and violence.[j]
He makes a treaty with Assyria[k]
and sends olive oil to Egypt.[l]
2The LORD has a charge[m] to bring
against Judah;[n]
he will punish[o] Jacob[f] according to
his ways
and repay him according to his
deeds.[p]
3In the womb he grasped his brother's
heel;[q]
as a man he struggled[r] with God.
4He struggled with the angel and
overcame him;
he wept and begged for his favor.
He found him at Bethel[s]
and talked with him there—
5the LORD God Almighty,
the LORD is his name[t] of renown!
6But you must return[u] to your God;
maintain love and justice,[v]
and wait for your God always.[w]

7The merchant uses dishonest scales;[x]
he loves to defraud.
8Ephraim boasts,[y]
"I am very rich; I have become
wealthy.[z]
With all my wealth they will not find
in me
any iniquity or sin."

9"I am the LORD your God,
⌞who brought you⌟ out of[g] Egypt;[a]
I will make you live in tents[b] again,
as in the days of your appointed
feasts.
10I spoke to the prophets,
gave them many visions
and told parables[c] through them."[d]

11Is Gilead wicked?[e]
Its people are worthless!
Do they sacrifice bulls in Gilgal?[f]
Their altars will be like piles of
stones
on a plowed field.[g]
12Jacob fled to the country of Aram[h];[h]
Israel served to get a wife,
and to pay for her he tended
sheep.[i]
13The LORD used a prophet to bring
Israel up from Egypt,[j]
by a prophet he cared for him.[k]
14But Ephraim has bitterly provoked him
to anger;
his Lord will leave upon him the
guilt of his bloodshed[l]

[e]9 Or *come against any city* [f]2 *Jacob* means *he grasps the heel* (figuratively, *he deceives*). [g]9 Or *God / ever since you were in* [h]12 That is, Northwest Mesopotamia

11:4 [f]Ex 16:32; Ps 78:25 [g]Jer 31:20 **11:5** [h]S Hos 7:16 [i]S Hos 10:6 [j]S Ex 13:17 **11:6** [k]Hos 13:16 [l]S La 2:9 **11:7** [m]S Isa 26:10 [n]ver 2; Jer 3:6-7; 8:5 **11:8** [o]S Jer 7:29 [p]Hos 6:4 [q]S Ge 14:8; S La 3:32 [r]S 1Ki 3:26; S Ps 25:6 [s]S Eze 33:11; Am 7:3 **11:9** [t]Dt 13:17; S Jer 18:8; S 30:11 [u]La 3:22; Mal 3:6 [v]S Nu 23:19 [w]S 2Ki 19:22; S Isa 31:1 **11:10** [x]S Isa 42:13 [y]S Isa 31:4 [z]S Ps 18:45 [a]S Hos 3:5; S 6:1-3 **11:11** [b]S Ge 8:8 [c]S Isa 11:11 [d]S Eze 28:26; S 34:25-28 **11:12** [e]S Hos 4:2 [f]S Dt 7:9 [g]S Hos 10:13 **12:1** [h]S Ps 78:67 [i]S Ge 41:6; S Eze 17:10 [j]S Hos 4:19; S 7:1 [k]Hos 5:13; S 7:11 [l]S 2Ki 17:4 **12:2** [m]S Job 10:2; Mic 6:2 [n]Am 2:4 [o]S Ex 32:34 [p]S Hos 4:9; S 9:15 **12:3** [q]Ge 25:26 [r]Ge 32:24-29 **12:4** [s]S Ge 12:8; S 35:15 **12:5** [t]S Ex 3:15 **12:6** [u]S Isa 19:22; Jer 4:1; Joel 2:12 [v]S Ps 106:3; S Jer 22:3 [w]S Eze 18:30; Hos 6:1-3; 10:12; Mic 7:7 **12:7** [x]S Lev 19:36; Am 8:5 **12:8** [y]S Eze 28:5 [z]Ps 62:10; Rev 3:17 **12:9** [a]Lev 23:43; S Hos 2:15; S 11:1 [b]S Ne 8:17 **12:10** [c]S Jdg 14:12; S Eze 20:49 [d]2Ki 17:13; Jer 7:25 **12:11** [e]S Hos 6:8 [f]S Hos 4:15 [g]S Hos 8:11 **12:12** [h]Ge 28:5 [i]S Ge 29:18 **12:13** [j]S Hos 11:1 [k]Ex 13:3; 14:19-22; Isa 63:11-14 **12:14** [l]S Eze 18:13

11:10 THE CHURCH, God's Community—See note on 1:10–11.
12:1–14 HISTORY, Faith—See note on 2 Ch 16:7–9. Political strategy and sly conniving do not lead to historical success. Love for and faith in God do. Israel had to return to isolation with God in Exile and wilderness to learn the lesson.
12:3–4 PRAYER, Sincerity—See note on Ge 32:24.
12:6 CHRISTIAN ETHICS, Justice—See note on 2:19–20.
12:10–14 REVELATION, History—God described Israel's history and His loving persistence in saving her. Moses was a prophet called to guide God's children to safety from Egypt and to reveal God's deep care for His children. God manifested His care also through guiding visions and parables which prophets delivered. In act and word God's history with His people is a call to salvation. God's people too often make it a history of God's disciplining anger. Compare 6:4–11.
12:14 GOD, Wrath—See note on 5:1–15.
12:14 SIN, Judgment—God eventually squares accounts. People can spill innocent blood and heap scorn, contempt, and reproach on other people and God only so long. God promises to pay us our due for our sin when we remain in it without

and will repay him for his
contempt.[m]

Chapter 13

The LORD's Anger Against Israel

WHEN Ephraim spoke, men
trembled;[n]
he was exalted[o] in Israel.
But he became guilty of Baal
worship[p] and died.
2Now they sin more and more;
they make[q] idols for themselves
from their silver,[r]
cleverly fashioned images,
all of them the work of craftsmen.[s]
It is said of these people,
"They offer human sacrifice
and kiss[i][t] the calf-idols.[u]"
3Therefore they will be like the
morning mist,
like the early dew that disappears,[v]
like chaff[w] swirling from a threshing
floor,[x]
like smoke[y] escaping through a
window.

4"But I am the LORD your God,
⌞who brought you⌟ out of[j] Egypt.[z]
You shall acknowledge[a] no God but
me,[b]
no Savior[c] except me.
5I cared for you in the desert,[d]
in the land of burning heat.
6When I fed them, they were satisfied;
when they were satisfied, they
became proud;[e]
then they forgot[f] me.[g]
7So I will come upon them like a lion,[h]
like a leopard I will lurk by the path.
8Like a bear robbed of her cubs,[i]
I will attack them and rip them
open.
Like a lion[j] I will devour them;
a wild animal will tear them apart.[k]

9"You are destroyed, O Israel,
because you are against me,[l]
against your helper.[m]
10Where is your king,[n] that he may save
you?
Where are your rulers in all your
towns,
of whom you said,
'Give me a king and princes'?[o]
11So in my anger I gave you a king,[p]
and in my wrath I took him away.[q]
12The guilt of Ephraim is stored up,
his sins are kept on record.[r]
13Pains as of a woman in childbirth[s]
come to him,
but he is a child without wisdom;
when the time[t] arrives,
he does not come to the opening of
the womb.[u]

14"I will ransom them from the power of
the grave[k];[v]
I will redeem them from death.[w]
Where, O death, are your plagues?
Where, O grave,[k] is your
destruction?[x]

"I will have no compassion,
15 even though he thrives[y] among his
brothers.
An east wind[z] from the LORD will
come,
blowing in from the desert;
his spring will fail
and his well dry up.[a]
His storehouse will be plundered[b]
of all its treasures.
16The people of Samaria[c] must bear
their guilt,[d]
because they have rebelled[e] against
their God.
They will fall by the sword;[f]
their little ones will be dashed[g] to
the ground,
their pregnant women[h] ripped
open."

12:14 [m]Da 11:18 **13:1** [n]Jdg 12:1 [o]S Jdg 8:1 [p]S Hos 11:2 **13:2** [q]Jer 44:8 [r]S Isa 46:6; S Jer 10:4 [s]Hos 14:3 [t]1Ki 19:18 [u]S Isa 44:17-20; S Hos 8:4 **13:3** [v]S Hos 6:4 [w]S Job 13:25; Ps 1:4; S Isa 17:13 [x]Da 2:35 [y]Ps 68:2 **13:4** [z]S Jer 2:6; S Hos 12:9 [a]S Hos 2:20 [b]S Ex 20:3 [c]S Dt 28:29; Ps 18:46; Isa 43:11; 45:21-22 **13:5** [d]S Dt 1:19 **13:6** [e]S Eze 28:5 [f]S Dt 32:18; S Isa 17:10 [g]Dt 32:12-15; S Pr 30:7-9; S Jer 5:7; S Hos 2:13; S 4:7 **13:7** [h]S Job 10:16; S Jer 4:7 **13:8** [i]2Sa 17:8 [j]S 1Sa 17:34; Ps 17:12 [k]Ps 50:22; S La 3:10; S Hos 2:12 **13:9** [l]Jer 2:17-19 [m]S Dt 33:29 **13:10** [n]2Ki 17:4; Hos 7:7 [o]1Sa 8:6; Hos 8:4 **13:11** [p]S Nu 11:20 [q]S Jos 24:20; S 1Sa 13:14; S 1Ki 14:10; Hos 3:4; S 10:7 **13:12** [r]S Dt 32:34 **13:13** [s]Isa 13:8; Mic 4:9-10 [t]2Ki 19:3 [u]Isa 66:9 **13:14** [v]S Ps 16:10; 49:15; S Eze 37:12-13 [w]S Isa 25:8 [x]1Co 15:55* **13:15** [y]S Hos 10:1 [z]S Job 1:19; S Eze 19:12; S Hos 4:19 [a]S Jer 51:36 [b]Jer 20:5 **13:16** [c]2Ki 17:5 [d]Hos 10:2 [e]S Hos 7:14 [f]Hos 11:6 [g]S 2Ki 8:12; S Hos 10:14 [h]2Ki 15:16; Isa 13:16; Am 1:13

[i]2 Or *"Men who sacrifice / kiss* [j]4 Or *God / ever since you were in* [k]14 Hebrew *Sheol*

asking forgiveness.
13:1–3 SIN, Transgression—See notes on 1:2; Eze 8:3–18.
13:4–13 HISTORY, God—God made His case in Israel's history. He was the only God and Savior. No one else cared or provided for their needs. Israel forgot and searched for a better helper. They found God's anger.
13:14 HUMANITY, Death—God used resurrection language to reveal to Hosea hope for a dead nation. Christians join Paul in seeing that God brought an ultimate victory over the grave through Jesus. See 1 Co 15:35–56, especially v 55.
13:14 SALVATION, Redemption—Hosea appears to be saying that Ephraim (another name for Israel) cannot now be saved. The nation is spiritually dead; therefore, let death and the grave have them. However, as the New Testament teaches us, with God all things are possible, even the resurrection from the dead. God can redeem His people when our case appears to be hopeless. Compare 6:2; 1 Co 15:55.
13:14 LAST THINGS, Unbelievers' Death—"Grave" (Hebrew *She'ol*) is the realm of the dead. See note on Isa 14:9. The idea of destruction, despair, and desolation is often associated with *Sheol.* There God's purpose is lost but not His presence (Ps 139:8). The ultimate despair would be to be where God is but be unable to know Him. In this text God promised to rescue the dead nation Israel from *Sheol,* rather than individuals. Even death cannot destroy its victims if God chooses otherwise. The Old Testament concept of *Sheol* found its way into the New Testament in the idea of Hades, where it appears as the intermediate abode of the wicked dead and where torment could be experienced. See note on Lk 16:19–26. Some interpreters believe that because the nation was made up of individuals, the promise about resurrection here can be applied to believing individuals. Compare 1 Co 15:55.
13:16 SIN, Responsibility—Our sins may bring judgment that affects innocent people. We must bear responsibility and recognize the seriousness of our sin. To rebel against God (La 1:8–22) asks for trouble for our whole community. See note on Eze 18:1–32.

Chapter 14

Repentance to Bring Blessing

RETURN,[i] O Israel, to the LORD your God.
Your sins[j] have been your downfall![k]
2Take words with you
and return to the LORD.
Say to him:
"Forgive[l] all our sins
and receive us graciously,[m]
that we may offer the fruit of our lips.[1] [n]
3Assyria cannot save us;[o]
we will not mount war-horses.[p]
We will never again say 'Our gods'[q]
to what our own hands have made,[r]
for in you the fatherless[s] find compassion."
4"I will heal[t] their waywardness[u]
and love them freely,[v]
for my anger has turned away[w] from them.
5I will be like the dew[x] to Israel;
he will blossom like a lily.[y]
Like a cedar of Lebanon[z]
he will send down his roots;[a]
6his young shoots will grow.
His splendor will be like an olive tree,[b]
his fragrance like a cedar of Lebanon.[c]
7Men will dwell again in his shade.[d]
He will flourish like the grain.
He will blossom[e] like a vine,
and his fame will be like the wine[f]
from Lebanon.[g]
8O Ephraim, what more have I[m] to do with idols?[h]
I will answer him and care for him.
I am like a green pine[i] tree;
your fruitfulness comes from me."
9Who is wise?[j] He will realize these things.
Who is discerning? He will understand them.[k]
The ways of the LORD are right;[l]
the righteous walk[m] in them,
but the rebellious stumble in them.

14:1 [i]S Isa 19:22; S Jer 3:12 [j]S Hos 4:8 [k]S Hos 5:5; S 9:7 **14:2** [l]S Ex 34:9 [m]Ps 51:16-17; Mic 7:18-19 [n]Heb 13:15 **14:3** [o]S Hos 5:13 [p]Ps 33:17; S Isa 31:1; Mic 5:10 [q]Hos 8:6 [r]ver 28; Hos 13:2 [s]Ps 10:14; 68:5; Jer 49:11 **14:4** [t]S Isa 30:26; S Hos 6:1 [u]S Jer 2:19 [v]S Isa 55:1; Jer 31:20; Zep 3:17 [w]S Job 13:16 **14:5** [x]S Ge 27:28; S Isa 18:4 [y]S SS 2:1 [z]Isa 35:2 [a]Job 29:19 **14:6** [b]Ps 52:8; S Jer 11:16 [c]S Ps 92:12; S SS 4:11 **14:7** [d]Ps 91:1-4 [e]S Ge 40:10 [f]S Hos 2:22 [g]S Eze 17:23 **14:8** [h]S ver 3 [i]S Isa 37:24 **14:9** [j]S Ps 107:43 [k]S Pr 10:29; S Isa 1:28; Da 12:10 [l]Ps 111:7-8; Zep 3:5; Ac 13:10 [m]Isa 26:7

[1]2 Or *offer our lips as sacrifices of bulls* [m]8 Or *What more has Ephraim*

14:1–8 GOD, Love—God gladly turns away from His anger for a people who ask forgiveness because love is His basic characteristic. See notes on 3:1; 7:13; 11:1–11.

14:1–4 SALVATION, Healing—Waywardness (backsliding) is a spiritual disease which requires healing. See note on Jer 3:6–18. Neither political and military power nor human products offer hope. When God's people genuinely repent of their sins and confess them to Him, He heals their spiritual disease. Only God's freely-given love can provide the healing we need. Salvation is a continuing healing process.

14:1–2 SALVATION, Repentance—Israel's suffering and ruin was caused by her sins—not by political misfortunes. She had willfully turned her back on God and worshiped Baal. Her only hope was to repent of her sins by turning to God and forsaking idolatry. Instead of taking animal sacrifices to God, she was to take penitent words of confession. Heartfelt confession and prayer accompany repentance.

14:2 SALVATION, Grace—God's grace forgives our sins in answer to the prayer of repentance. Those who turn to Him in penitent confession will in no wise be cast out. The prophet provided words to use in confession. The people needed to use them in heartfelt sorrow for sin to experience God's grace.

14:9 HUMANITY, Intellectual Nature—God's wisdom helps people perceive that His way is the best way for us to live. Wisdom leads us to read God's inspired Book and live by it.

14:9 CHRISTIAN ETHICS, Righteousness—God's righteous ones can be recognized by their pattern of life. Human righteousness reflects God's character. The prophet's message is thus summarized as a call to righteous living.

Joel

Theological Setting

The land of Judah was devastated. Locusts, like a huge army, had destroyed much of the vegetation. A severe drought made the situation worse. Although there had been locust plagues before, no one could remember one as bad as this (1:2). Humans and beasts alike were suffering greatly.

In the midst of this tragedy, God called one of the citizens of Judah, a man named Joel, to provide a proper interpretation of the terrible events and to recommend a course of action for the people to follow. We know very little about this man. Even the date of his ministry is uncertain. Perhaps it was in the ninth century BC, or perhaps it was as late as 400 BC. No one can be sure. We know his name means "the Lord is God," and we know he suffered along with the people.

Joel understood that the problem was primarily a theological matter. He knew the solution would have to be theological in nature. He interpreted the calamity as a judgment God sent because of the sin and unfaithfulness of His people. The day of the LORD, a day of judgment, was near at hand.

Joel still held out hope, but only if the people repented and sought God with prayer and fasting. He earnestly encouraged all the citizens of Judah (1:14; 2:12-17) to return in genuine faith to God and to seek His grace and mercy.

Joel provided a rarity among biblical prophets. Israel most often ignored or rejected prophetic counsel. Apparently they heeded the words of Joel. The people repented, and God forgave them. He removed the plague of locusts and sent rain upon the parched land. The fields brought forth a good harvest (2:18-27). Once again joy reigned in Judah.

But God had more to say to His people. In the last half of the book (2:28—3:21), Joel turned his attention to the more distant future. He described a time in which God would pour out His Spirit on all flesh. Signs in heaven and on earth would accompany God's action. Another day of the LORD, a day of decision for all persons and all nations, would be ushered in. Those who would welcome the gracious presence of God in their lives would be forever blessed. Those who rejected Him would be judged severely and separated from the people of God.

Theological Outline

I. The Day of the LORD Calls for God's People to Respond. (1:1—2:17)
   A. Witness to future generations. (1:1-4)
   B. Mourn and grieve over the destruction. (1:5-20)
   C. Sound the alarm because the day of the LORD is dreadful. (2:1-11)
   D. Repent inwardly because your gracious, patient God may have pity. (2:12-14)
   E. Assemble the congregation for mourning and repentance. (2:15-17)

II. God Will Respond to His People's Mourning and Repentance. (2:18-27)
   A. God will have pity. (2:18)
   B. God will provide food needs and remove shame from His people. (2:19)
   C. God will defeat the enemy. (2:20)
   D. God will replace fear and shame with joy and praise. (2:21-26)
   E. God will cause His people to know and worship Him, and Him alone. (2:27)

III. God Is Preparing a Great Day of Salvation. (2:28—3:21)
   A. God will pour out His Spirit to bring salvation to the remnant. (2:28-32)
   B. God will judge all nations. (3:1-17)
   C. God will bless His people. (3:18-21)

Theological Conclusions

The day of the LORD is the center of Joel's theology. He used traditional language to interpret a natural catastrophe. God never ignores sin. Judgment is certain to come sooner or later. The Lord often uses natural means to accomplish this, as He did in the time of Joel. Joel, like many other writers of Scripture, taught that the entire universe suffers when people disobey God and live a life of unfaithfulness. See Ge 3:17-18; Ro 8:22-23. No sins are insignificant—all have cosmic implications.

God, however, is a gracious and merciful God. He is eager for sinners to turn from their evil ways. He is always ready to forgive those who come to Him in genuine repentance. Restoration of a correct relationship between God and His people brings healing and joy to the land as well as to people (Isa 55:12-13).

Restoration is not automatic. It involves repentance from the heart (Joel 2:12-13), not simple participation in public rites and ceremonies. God calls His people to observe such rites as public testimony to a sincere change of life's direction. Only such change signals true repentance.

Those who live in accord with God's purpose, in obedience and faithfulness, will be forever blessed. Those who spurn Him will ultimately be cut off completely. Each person decides his or her own eternal destiny. The locust plague was not simply a freak happening of nature; it was an act of God. It was God's way of judging a sinful nation. Such a day of the LORD was not God's final act, however. That would come "afterwards," when God poured out His Spirit so all people would know His will, just as God's prophets knew His will by receiving His Spirit (Nu 11:29). Thus, Joel pointed forward to Pentecost (Ac 2:16-21) and beyond to the final day of the LORD.

Contemporary Teaching

Few of life's tragedies are the direct judgment of God. The unfair and dangerous idea that every calamity is due to personal sin in the life of the sufferer still haunts and hurts people. (Remember Jn 9:1-3.) On the other hand, when serious difficulties come to an individual or a nation, it is wise to take time for self-examination. Perhaps individual or corporate sin needs to be confessed and removed. If so, no other solution will be adequate.

Members of the body of Christ are the benefactors of God's outpoured Spirit. Peter interpreted the promise of God as given by Joel to have been fulfilled at Pentecost (Ac 2:17-21). Through Christ and the Holy Spirit, Christians have been given a fuller knowledge of God than was even possible to Joel. The Spirit now dwells within us to guide and instruct. He helps us understand what God is doing in our present world.

As Christians, we need to remember that God's richest blessings have been freely given to us, not because we deserve them but because we decided to accept the grace and forgiveness offered through Christ. Without Him we are helpless, but nothing can separate us from Him (Ro 8:31-39).

Even Christians sin, and our sins are serious. They dilute our joy, harm others, and have an adverse effect on the world in which we live. The Book of Joel continues to remind us of the ongoing need for confession and for lives of faithfulness. We are also reminded of the need to encourage non-Christians to decide to turn to the Lord for forgiveness and abundant life.

Chapter 1

THE word of the LORD that came[a] to Joel[b] son of Pethuel.

An Invasion of Locusts

2Hear this,[c] you elders;[d]
listen, all who live in the land.[e]
Has anything like this ever happened in your days
or in the days of your forefathers?[f]
3Tell it to your children,[g]
and let your children tell it to their children,
and their children to the next generation.[h]
4What the locust[i] swarm has left
the great locusts have eaten;
what the great locusts have left
the young locusts have eaten;
what the young locusts have left[j]
other locusts[a] have eaten.[k]

5Wake up, you drunkards, and weep!
Wail, all you drinkers of wine;[l]
wail because of the new wine,
for it has been snatched[m] from your lips.
6A nation has invaded my land,
powerful and without number;[n]
it has the teeth[o] of a lion,
the fangs of a lioness.
7It has laid waste[p] my vines
and ruined my fig trees.[q]
It has stripped off their bark
and thrown it away,
leaving their branches white.

8Mourn like a virgin[b] in sackcloth[r]
grieving for the husband[c] of her youth.
9Grain offerings and drink offerings[s]
are cut off from the house of the LORD.
The priests are in mourning,[t]
those who minister before the LORD.
10The fields are ruined,
the ground is dried up[d];[u]
the grain is destroyed,
the new wine[v] is dried up,
the oil fails.[w]
11Despair, you farmers,[x]
wail, you vine growers;
grieve for the wheat and the barley,[y]
because the harvest of the field is destroyed.[z]
12The vine is dried up
and the fig tree is withered;[a]
the pomegranate,[b] the palm and the apple tree—
all the trees of the field—are dried up.[c]
Surely the joy of mankind
is withered away.

A Call to Repentance

13Put on sackcloth,[d] O priests, and mourn;
wail, you who minister[e] before the altar.
Come, spend the night in sackcloth,
you who minister before my God;
for the grain offerings and drink offerings[f]
are withheld from the house of your God.
14Declare a holy fast;[g]
call a sacred assembly.
Summon the elders
and all who live in the land[h]
to the house of the LORD your God,
and cry out[i] to the LORD.[j]

15Alas for that[k] day!
For the day of the LORD[l] is near;
it will come like destruction from the Almighty.[e][m]

16Has not the food been cut off[n]
before our very eyes—
joy and gladness[o]
from the house of our God?[p]
17The seeds are shriveled
beneath the clods.[f][q]
The storehouses are in ruins,
the granaries have been broken down,
for the grain has dried up.
18How the cattle moan!

1:1 [a]S Jer 1:2 [b]Ac 2:16
1:2 [c]Hos 5:1 [d]Joel 2:16 [e]S Hos 4:1 [f]Joel 2:2
1:3 [g]S Ex 10:2 [h]S Ps 71:18
1:4 [i]S Ex 10:14 [j]S Ex 10:5 [k]S Ex 10:15; S Dt 28:39; Am 7:1; Na 3:15
1:5 [l]Joel 3:3 [m]S Isa 24:7
1:6 [n]Ps 105:34; Joel 2:2,11,25 [o]Rev 9:8
1:7 [p]Isa 5:6 [q]Am 4:9
1:8 [r]ver 13; Isa 22:12; Am 8:10
1:9 [s]S Hos 9:4 [t]S Isa 22:12
1:10 [u]S Isa 5:6; S 24:4; S Jer 3:3 [v]S Hos 9:2 [w]S Nu 18:12
1:11 [x]S Job 6:20; Am 5:16 [y]S Ex 9:31 [z]S Isa 17:11
1:12 [a]S Isa 15:6 [b]S Ex 28:33 [c]S Isa 16:8; Hag 2:19
1:13 [d]S Ge 37:34; S Jer 4:8 [e]Joel 2:17 [f]ver 9; S Hos 9:4; Joel 2:14
1:14 [g]S 2Ch 20:3 [h]S Hos 4:1 [i]Jnh 3:8 [j]2Ch 20:4
1:15 [k]S Isa 2:12; Jer 30:7; S 46:10; S Eze 30:3; Mal 4:5 [l]Joel 2:1,11,31; 3:14; Am 5:18; Zep 1:14; Zec 14:1 [m]S Ge 17:1
1:16 [n]Isa 3:7 [o]S Ps 51:8 [p]Dt 12:7
1:17 [q]S Isa 17:10-11

[a]4 The precise meaning of the four Hebrew words used here for locusts is uncertain. [b]8 Or *young woman* [c]8 Or *betrothed* [d]10 Or *ground mourns* [e]15 Hebrew *Shaddai* [f]17 The meaning of the Hebrew for this word is uncertain.

1:1–20 REVELATION, Author of Creation—The sustenance of the land was cut off as the sustenance of God was withdrawn from the people: fellowship and food dried up. The very created order revealed God's judgment over Judah. God used locusts to destroy the crops and point the people to His day of judgment, mourning, and repentance.

1:8 HUMANITY, Attitudes to Death—Death is normal and is to be expected at the end of a long life. We grieve because of our loss. Grief may overwhelm us when death comes early and unexpectedly to a young person. However expressed, grief is normal and needs to be worked through. Communities as well as individuals experience grief.

1:12 SALVATION, Joy—Compare Isa 55:12. The Hebrews did not make neat distinctions between the physical and the spiritual. God often brings spiritual joy through physical blessings. Sin does wither away joy, but repentance and salvation restore it.

1:13–14 WORSHIP, Humility—Often the humility required for true worship is evidenced by weeping, fasting, and repentance. Joel called upon the priests to proclaim a national ceremony of lamentation. Times of distress are times for humble community worship, crying to God for help. See note on Jdg 20:26.

1:14 PRAYER, Sincerity—Fasting was a sign of mourning for the devastation of the locusts. In crisis God's people need to join in public and private lamentation earnestly seeking God's direction for a way out.

The herds mill about
because they have no pasture;[r]
even the flocks of sheep are
suffering.[s]

19To you, O LORD, I call,[t]
for fire[u] has devoured the open
pastures[v]
and flames have burned up all the
trees of the field.
20Even the wild animals pant for you;[w]
the streams of water have dried up[x]
and fire has devoured the open
pastures.[y]

Chapter 2

An Army of Locusts

BLOW the trumpet[z] in Zion;[a]
sound the alarm on my holy hill.[b]
Let all who live in the land tremble,
for the day of the LORD[c] is coming.
It is close at hand[d] —
2 a day of darkness[e] and gloom,[f] [g]
a day of clouds[h] and blackness.[i]
Like dawn spreading across the
mountains
a large and mighty army[j] comes,
such as never was of old[k]
nor ever will be in ages to come.
3Before them fire[l] devours,
behind them a flame blazes.
Before them the land is like the garden
of Eden,[m]
behind them, a desert waste[n] —
nothing escapes them.
4They have the appearance of horses;[o]
they gallop along like cavalry.
5With a noise like that of chariots[p]
they leap over the mountaintops,
like a crackling fire[q] consuming
stubble,
like a mighty army drawn up for
battle.

6At the sight of them, nations are in
anguish;[r]
every face turns pale.[s]
7They charge like warriors;[t]
they scale walls like soldiers.
They all march in line,[u]
not swerving[v] from their course.
8They do not jostle each other;
each marches straight ahead.
They plunge through defenses
without breaking ranks.
9They rush upon the city;
they run along the wall.
They climb into the houses;[w]
like thieves they enter through the
windows.[x]

10Before them the earth shakes,[y]
the sky trembles,[z]
the sun and moon are darkened,[a]
and the stars no longer shine.[b]
11The LORD[c] thunders[d]
at the head of his army;[e]
his forces are beyond number,
and mighty are those who obey his
command.
The day of the LORD is great;[f]
it is dreadful.
Who can endure it?[g]

Rend Your Heart

12"Even now," declares the LORD,
"return[h] to me with all your
heart,[i]
with fasting and weeping and
mourning."
13Rend your heart[j]
and not your garments.[k]
Return[l] to the LORD your God,
for he is gracious and
compassionate,[m]
slow to anger and abounding in love,[n]
and he relents from sending
calamity.[o]
14Who knows? He may turn[p] and have
pity[q]
and leave behind a blessing[r] —
grain offerings and drink offerings[s]
for the LORD your God.

15Blow the trumpet[t] in Zion,[u]
declare a holy fast,[v]

1:18 [r]S Ge 47:4 [s]S Jer 9:10 **1:19** [t]Ps 50:15 [u]S Ps 97:3; Am 7:4 [v]S Jer 9:10 **1:20** [w]S Ps 42:1; S 104:21 [x]1Ki 17:7 [y]Joel 2:22 **2:1** [z]S Nu 10:2,7 [a]ver 15 [b]S Ex 15:17 [c]S Joel 1:15; Zep 1:14-16 [d]S Eze 12:23; S 30:3; Ob 1:15 **2:2** [e]ver 10,31; S Job 9:7; S Isa 8:22; S 13:10; Am 5:18 [f]S Da 9:12; S Mt 24:21 [g]S Eze 34:12 [h]S Eze 38:9 [i]Zep 1:15; Rev 9:2 [j]S Joel 1:6 [k]Joel 1:2 **2:3** [l]S Ps 97:3; S Isa 1:31 [m]S Ge 2:8 [n]Ex 10:12-15; Ps 105:34-35; S Isa 14:17 **2:4** [o]Rev 9:7 **2:5** [p]Rev 9:9 [q]Isa 5:24; 30:30 **2:6** [r]S Isa 13:8 [s]S Isa 29:22 **2:7** [t]S Job 16:14 [u]Pr 30:27 [v]Isa 5:27 **2:9** [w]Ex 10:6 [x]Jer 9:21 **2:10** [y]Ps 18:7; Na 1:5 [z]S Eze 38:19 [a]S ver 2; S Isa 5:30; S Mt 24:29; Mk 13:24; Rev 9:2 [b]S Job 9:7; S Ps 102:26; Isa 13:10; S Eze 32:8 **2:11** [c]S Isa 2:12; S Eze 30:3; S Joel 1:15; Ob 1:15 [d]S Ps 29:3 [e]S ver 2, 25 [f]Zep 1:14 [g]S Eze 22:14; Zep 2:11; Rev 6:17 **2:12** [h]S Dt 4:30; S Eze 33:11; S Hos 12:6 [i]S 1Sa 7:3 **2:13** [j]Ps 51:17; Isa 57:15 [k]S Ge 37:29; S Nu 14:6; Job 1:20 [l]S Isa 19:22 [m]S Dt 4:31 [n]Ex 34:6; S Ps 86:5, 15 [o]S Jer 18:8; Jnh 4:2 **2:14** [p]Jer 26:3; Jnh 3:9 [q]Am 5:15; Jnh 1:6 [r]Jer 31:14; Hag 2:19; Zec 8:13; Mal 3:10 [s]S Joel 1:13

2:15 [t]S Nu 10:2 [u]ver 1 [v]S 2Ch 20:3; Jer 36:9

1:19 PRAYER, Sincerity—Joel obeyed his own injunction (v 14) to cry to the Lord. Prayer is a private practice as well as a doctrine to teach others.

2:10–14 EVIL AND SUFFERING, Repentance—Repentance is the order of the day as God's people anticipate the day of the Lord. God's people too easily look forward to a day of salvation. The day of the Lord can surprise us, revealing we are God's enemies facing His judgment. We must repent from the heart and change our way of life. This is God's desire. He wants His final day to bring salvation for us. We can endure that day only if we are rightly related to Him through repentance and forgiveness. See note on Jer 18:1–17.

2:12–14 SALVATION, Repentance—Fasting, weeping, and mourning were usual expressions of repentance in Israel. See note on Ezr 9:3–7. Tearing of garments was a sign of grief. What God wants in repentance is a torn heart (Ps 51:17). The heart in Hebrew psychology was the seat of the will even more than of the affections. The surprise to many in this passage is its emphasis on double repentance (Zec 1:3; Mal 3:7). Not only should persons repent, but God repents when we repent. He turns from His announced intention, responds to us as persons, and changes His plan of action from judgment to mercy. Compare Ex 32:14; Dt 13:17; Jos 7:26; 2 Ch 30:6; Jer 12:15; Jnh 3:9. When we turn to Him, He turns to us. The good news of salvation is that we have a High Priest who is touched with our infirmities (Heb 4:15).

2:13–14 GOD, Wrath—God warned His people that the day of the Lord will bring judgment instead of the salvation they expected. Judgment is not necessary. Repentance remains an option, the preferred option. Grace and love, not wrath and judgment, reflect God's basic character. Note that day of the Lord here points to God's intervention in national history, not the final judgment. See notes on Hos 1:6—2:1.

call a sacred assembly.[w]
16Gather the people,
consecrate[x] the assembly;
bring together the elders,[y]
gather the children,
those nursing at the breast.
Let the bridegroom[z] leave his room
and the bride her chamber.
17Let the priests, who minister[a] before
the LORD,
weep[b] between the temple porch
and the altar.[c]
Let them say, "Spare your people,
O LORD.
Do not make your inheritance an
object of scorn,[d]
a byword[e] among the nations.
Why should they say among the
peoples,
'Where is their God?[f]' "

The LORD's Answer

18Then the LORD will be jealous[g] for his
land
and take pity[h] on his people.

19The LORD will reply[g] to them:

"I am sending you grain, new wine[i]
and oil,[j]
enough to satisfy you fully;[k]
never again will I make you
an object of scorn[l] to the nations.

20"I will drive the northern army[m] far
from you,
pushing it into a parched and barren
land,
with its front columns going into the
eastern[n] sea[h]
and those in the rear into the
western sea.[i]
And its stench[o] will go up;
its smell will rise."

2:15 [w]S Ex 32:5; Nu 10:3
2:16 [x]S Ex 19:10, 22 [y]Joel 1:2 [z]Ps 19:5
2:17 [a]Joel 1:13 [b]S Isa 22:12 [c]Eze 8:16; Mt 23:35 [d]Dt 9:26-29; Ps 44:13 [e]S 1Ki 9:7; S Job 17:6 [f]S Ps 42:3
2:18 [g]S Isa 26:11; Zec 1:14; 8:2 [h]S Ps 72:13
2:19 [i]Ps 4:7 [j]S Jer 31:12 [k]S Lev 26:5 [l]S Eze 34:29
2:20 [m]Jer 1:14-15 [n]Zec 14:8 [o]S Isa 34:3
2:21 [p]S Isa 29:22; S 54:4; Zep 3:16-17 [q]S Ps 9:2 [r]S Ps 126:3; S Isa 25:1
2:22 [s]S Ps 65:12 [t]S 1Ki 4:25 [u]S Nu 16:14 [v]Joel 1:18-20; Zec 8:12
2:23 [w]Ps 33:21; 97:12; 149:2; Isa 12:6; 41:16; 66:14; Hab 3:18; Zec 10:7 [x]S Isa 45:8 [y]S Job 36:28; S Eze 34:26 [z]Ps 84:6 [a]S Lev 26:4; S Ps 135:7; Jas 5:7
2:24 [b]Lev 26:10; Mal 3:10 [c]S Pr 3:10; Joel 3:18; Am 9:13
2:25 [d]S Ex 10:14; Am 4:9 [e]S Dt 28:39 [f]S Joel 1:6
2:26 [g]S Lev 26:5 [h]S Lev 23:40; S Isa 62:9 [i]S Ps 126:3; S Isa 25:1 [j]S Isa 29:22

Surely he has done great things.[j]
21 Be not afraid,[p] O land;
be glad and rejoice.[q]
Surely the LORD has done great
things.[r]
22 Be not afraid, O wild animals,
for the open pastures are becoming
green.[s]
The trees are bearing their fruit;
the fig tree[t] and the vine[u] yield
their riches.[v]
23Be glad, O people of Zion,
rejoice[w] in the LORD your God,
for he has given you
the autumn rains in
righteousness.[k] [x]
He sends you abundant showers,[y]
both autumn[z] and spring rains,[a] as
before.
24The threshing floors will be filled with
grain;
the vats will overflow[b] with new
wine[c] and oil.

25"I will repay you for the years the
locusts[d] have eaten[e] —
the great locust and the young
locust,
the other locusts and the locust
swarm[l] —
my great army[f] that I sent among you.
26You will have plenty to eat, until you
are full,[g]
and you will praise[h] the name of
the LORD your God,
who has worked wonders[i] for you;
never again will my people be
shamed.[j]

[g]*18,19* Or *LORD was jealous . . . / and took pity . . . / 19The LORD replied* [h]*20* That is, the Dead Sea [i]*20* That is, the Mediterranean [j]*20* Or *rise. / Surely it has done great things."* [k]*23* Or / *the teacher for righteousness:* [l]*25* The precise meaning of the four Hebrew words used here for locusts is uncertain.

2:17 REVELATION, Divine Presence—God's judgment on His people and their land indicated His absence to some. God is present in the work of discipline as well as in the work of salvation.

2:17 DISCIPLESHIP, Spiritual Leaders—Priests were God's servants, mediating between the people and God. They interceded with God for the people's needs. Under the new covenant all Christian disciples are priests. See notes on Ex 19:5–8; 1 Pe 2:5,9–10.

2:17 PRAYER, Intercession—The priests were mediators before God for the people. Moses had prayed that God would spare Israel because she was His inheritance (Dt 9:19–20). Preachers should intercede for their people as well as preach to them.

2:18 GOD, Jealous—Jealousy does not always reflect God's wrath when His people reject His love. Community worship expressing repentance and seeking mercy arouses God's zealous jealousy for His people. In love and pity God defends and protects His repentant people. He is jealous to protect His reputation among the nations. See note on Eze 16:38.

2:18–31 MIRACLE, Redemption—God works wonders in history, in nature, and in the heavens. His miracles provide political, personal, and eternal redemption for His people. Joel looked back to the Exodus miracles (v 26) to promise agricultural miracles for individuals (vv 19, 22–26) and military deliverance miracles (v 20). Joel looked ahead to God's day of deliverance to promise spiritual miracles for individuals (vv 28–29) and heavenly miracles indicating God's victory in the last days (vv 30–32). God poured out His Spirit at Pentecost. See Ac 2:19–20. He works all types of miracles to redeem His people and let us know His unique nature.

2:18–27 ELECTION, God's Purpose—God saved Israel from the destruction of the locusts. Grain, new wine, and oil would be given to replace the material necessities destroyed by the locusts. As a result of God's blessings, Israel would know that the Lord is the one and only God who provides, protects, and saves His elect. They, in turn, would praise Him. Election seeks to create a mutual relationship of blessing and praise between God and His elect.

2:21–24 REVELATION, Author of Creation—Even the day of judgment can be the day of gladness. Hope with God can still arrive as late as a fall rain. Creation can show God's salvation as well as His judgment. Israel did not have to look to Baal or other fertility gods to care for creation. The God of Israel created the world, cares for it, and reveals Himself in it. See note on 1:1–20.

27Then you will know[k] that I am in
Israel,
that I am the LORD[l] your God,
and that there is no other;
never again will my people be
shamed.[m]

The Day of the LORD

28"And afterward,
I will pour out my Spirit[n] on all
people.[o]
Your sons and daughters will
prophesy,[p]
your old men will dream
dreams,[q]
your young men will see
visions.
29Even on my servants,[r] both men and
women,
I will pour out my Spirit in those
days.[s]
30I will show wonders in the
heavens[t]
and on the earth,[u]
blood and fire and billows of
smoke.
31The sun will be turned to darkness[v]
and the moon to blood
before the coming of the great and
dreadful day of the LORD.[w]
32And everyone who calls
on the name of the LORD[x] will be
saved;[y]
for on Mount Zion[z] and in
Jerusalem
there will be deliverance,[a]
as the LORD has said,
among the survivors[b]
whom the LORD calls.[c]

2:27 [k]S Ex 6:7 [l]S Ex 6:2; S Isa 44:8; Joel 3:17 [m]Isa 45:17; 54:4; Zep 3:11 **2:28** [n]S Isa 11:2; S 44:3 [o]S Nu 11:17; S Mk 1:8; Gal 3:14 [p]S 1Sa 19:20 [q]Jer 23:25 **2:29** [r]1Co 12:13; Gal 3:28 [s]S Eze 36:27 **2:30** [t]Lk 21:11 [u]Mk 13:24-25 **2:31** [v]S ver 2; S Isa 22:5; S Jer 4:23; S Mt 24:29 [w]S Joel 1:15; Ob 1:15; Mal 3:2; 4:1,5 **2:32** [x]S Ge 4:26; S Ps 105:1 [y]S Ps 106:8; Ac 2:17-21*; Ro 10:13* [z]S Isa 46:13 [a]Ob 1:17 [b]S Isa 1:9; 11:11; Mic 4:7; 7:18; S Ro 9:27 [c]Ac 2:39 **3:1** [d]S Dt 30:3; S Jer 16:15; S Eze 38:8; Zep 3:20 [e]Jer 40:5 **3:2** [f]Zep 3:8 [g]ver 12; S Isa 22:1 [h]S Isa 13:9; S Jer 2:35; S Eze 36:5 [i]S Ge 11:4; S Lev 26:33 **3:3** [j]S Job 6:27; S Eze 24:6 [k]Joel 1:5; Am 2:6 **3:4** [l]S Ge 10:15; S Mt 11:21 [m]S Ps 87:4; Isa 14:29-31; Jer 47:1-7 [n]S Lev 26:28; S Isa 34:8; S Eze 25:15-17; Zec 9:5-7 **3:5** [o]S 1Ki 15:18; S 2Ch 21:16-17 **3:6** [p]Eze 27:13; Zec 9:13 **3:7** [q]S Isa 43:5-6; Jer 23:8 [r]S Isa 66:6

Chapter 3

The Nations Judged

"IN those days and at that time,
when I restore the fortunes[d] of
Judah[e] and Jerusalem,
2I will gather[f] all nations
and bring them down to the Valley
of Jehoshaphat.[m] [g]
There I will enter into judgment[h]
against them
concerning my inheritance, my
people Israel,
for they scattered[i] my people among
the nations
and divided up my land.
3They cast lots[j] for my people
and traded boys for prostitutes;
they sold girls for wine[k]
that they might drink.

4"Now what have you against me, O
Tyre and Sidon[l] and all you regions of
Philistia?[m] Are you repaying me for something I have done? If you are paying me
back, I will swiftly and speedily return on
your own heads what you have done.[n]
5For you took my silver and my gold and
carried off my finest treasures to your
temples.[o] 6You sold the people of Judah
and Jerusalem to the Greeks,[p] that you
might send them far from their homeland.
7"See, I am going to rouse them out of
the places to which you sold them,[q] and I
will return[r] on your own heads what you

[m] 2 *Jehoshaphat* means *the LORD judges*; also in verse 12.

2:27 GOD, One God—God's restoring of His people and their land showed them again He was their God present to help them. See note on Hos 2:2–23.
2:28–32 HOLY SPIRIT, Hope—Locusts brought dark days for God's people (1:4). The prophet called for repentance (2:12–13). In response God promised hope produced by the Spirit. All people without age, sexual, or social barriers would become prophets, knowing God's will. They would have all God's media of revelation at their disposal—prophetic ecstasies, dreams, and visions. At Pentecost (Ac 2) God gave His prophetic Spirit to the church to proclaim His gospel. The proclamation of the gospel by all Christians brings hope to the world. See note on Nu 11:25–29.
2:28–29 REVELATION, Spirit—The Spirit is the power behind prophecy. It is God's desire for all to be instruments of His revelation to the world.
2:28–32 SALVATION, Preparation—Joel foretold a time when God would pour out His Spirit upon all people. The world would be shaken, and everyone who called on the name of the Lord would be saved. Both Peter and Paul taught this prophecy was fulfilled in the coming of Christ and the outpouring of the Spirit at Pentecost (Ac 2:16–21; Ro 10:13).
2:28–32 LAST THINGS, Day of the Lord—The hope for an historical day of the Lord gradually took the shape of future, eschatological hope. Often the two were intertwined as in this passage. This prophecy found direct fulfillment at Pentecost (Ac 2:16–21), yet ultimate fulfillment awaits the end time, as expressed in the apocalyptic language of the passage. Some aspects of the prophecy are fulfilled as people accept salvation provided through the work of Christ and the administration of the Spirit. In regard to end times, the prophecy refers to God's final intervention to complete His redemptive work. In this aspect the day of the Lord includes both judgment upon unrighteousness and reward for righteousness. See note on Am 5:18–20.
2:29 THE CHURCH, Servants—All God's servants participate in the blessings of God. God's Spirit comes to all who trust in Him. Both men and women anticipate God's promises and receive the Spirit's power. Pentecost introduced the Spirit in all His power to the church (Ac 2).
2:32 THE CHURCH, Remnant—God's remnant are those who call on Him in faith for salvation. Joel looked to deliverance during a time of judgment on Jerusalem. God's truth also applies to spiritual salvation. People can take hope because God remains in charge of His world and plans salvation for His faithful remnant.
3:1–8 GOD, Sovereignty—Having punished His people, God has power and authority to turn and punish their punishers. No nation is beyond His rule and control.
3:1–21 HISTORY, Universal—See notes on Isa 1:24–26; 13:1—23:18. Nations which punish and misuse God's people face punishment in return. God will have history's last word. All nations will recognize God as history's Judge and will recognize His holy presence with His people.
3:2,12 GOD, Judge—See note on Da 7:9–10,22,26.

have done. 8I will sell your sons[s] and
daughters to the people of Judah,[t] and
they will sell them to the Sabeans,[u] a nation far away." The LORD has spoken.[v]

9Proclaim this among the nations:
Prepare for war![w]
Rouse the warriors![x]
Let all the fighting men draw near
and attack.
10Beat your plowshares into swords
and your pruning hooks[y] into
spears.[z]
Let the weakling[a] say,
"I am strong!"[b]
11Come quickly, all you nations from
every side,
and assemble[c] there.

Bring down your warriors,[d] O LORD!

12"Let the nations be roused;
let them advance into the Valley of
Jehoshaphat,[e]
for there I will sit
to judge[f] all the nations on every
side.
13Swing the sickle,[g]
for the harvest[h] is ripe.
Come, trample the grapes,[i]
for the winepress[j] is full
and the vats overflow—
so great is their wickedness!"

14Multitudes,[k] multitudes
in the valley[l] of decision!
For the day of the LORD[m] is near
in the valley of decision.[n]
15The sun and moon will be darkened,
and the stars no longer shine.[o]
16The LORD will roar[p] from Zion
and thunder from Jerusalem;[q]
the earth and the sky will tremble.[r]
But the LORD will be a refuge[s] for his
people,
a stronghold[t] for the people of
Israel.

Blessings for God's People

17"Then you will know[u] that I, the LORD
your God,[v]
dwell in Zion,[w] my holy hill.[x]
Jerusalem will be holy;[y]
never again will foreigners invade
her.[z]

18"In that day the mountains will drip
new wine,[a]
and the hills will flow with milk;[b]
all the ravines of Judah will run with
water.[c]
A fountain will flow out of the LORD's
house[d]
and will water the valley of
acacias.[n] [e]
19But Egypt[f] will be desolate,
Edom[g] a desert waste,
because of violence[h] done to the
people of Judah,
in whose land they shed innocent
blood.
20Judah will be inhabited forever[i]
and Jerusalem through all
generations.
21Their bloodguilt,[j] which I have not
pardoned,
I will pardon.[k]"

The LORD dwells in Zion![l]

3:8 [s]Isa 60:14 [t]Isa 14:2 [u]S Ge 10:7; S 2Ch 9:1 [v]S Isa 23:1; S Jer 30:16 **3:9** [w]S Isa 8:9 [x]Jer 46:4 **3:10** [y]Isa 2:4 [z]S Nu 25:7 [a]Zec 12:8 [b]S Jos 1:6 **3:11** [c]Eze 38:15-16; Zep 3:8 [d]S Isa 13:3 **3:12** [e]S ver 2 [f]S Ps 82:1; S Isa 2:4 **3:13** [g]Mk 4:29 [h]S Isa 17:5; S Hos 6:11; Mt 13:39; Rev 14:15-19 [i]S Jer 25:30 [j]S Jdg 6:11; S Rev 14:20 **3:14** [k]Isa 13:4 [l]S Isa 22:1 [m]Isa 34:2-8; S Joel 1:15; S Zep 1:7 [n]S Isa 2:4; S Eze 36:5 **3:15** [o]S Job 9:7; S Eze 32:7 **3:16** [p]S Isa 42:13 [q]Am 1:2 [r]S Jdg 5:4; S Isa 14:16; S Eze 38:19 [s]S Ps 46:1; S Isa 25:4; Zec 12:8 [t]S 2Sa 22:3; Jer 16:19; Zec 9:12 **3:17** [u]S Ex 6:7 [v]S Joel 2:27 [w]S Ps 74:2; S Isa 4:3 [x]Ps 2:6; S Isa 2:2; S Eze 17:22 [y]S Jer 31:40 [z]S Isa 52:1; S Eze 44:9; Zec 9:8 **3:18** [a]S Joel 2:24 [b]Ex 3:8; S SS 5:1 [c]S Isa 30:25; 35:6; S 44:3 [d]Rev 22:1-2 [e]S Nu 25:1; S Isa 25:6; S Jer 31:12; S Eze 47:1; Am 9:13 **3:19** [f]S Isa 19:1 [g]S Isa 11:14; S 34:11 [h]S Jer 51:35; Ob 1:10 **3:20** [i]S Ezr 9:12; Am 9:15 **3:21** [j]S Isa 1:15 [k]S Eze 36:25 [l]S Ps 74:2; Isa 59:20; S Eze 48:35; Zec 8:3

n *18* Or *Valley of Shittim*

3:9 PROCLAMATION, Authoritative—See note on Jer 19:14–15.
3:14–21 LAST THINGS, Day of the Lord—This passage illustrates how prophecy merged into eschatology. Nations like Israel, Egypt, and Edom are involved, but the day of the Lord will be no ordinary day. Supernatural events are prophesied to accompany that day. It will be a time of God's intervention and the end of the present order. God will provide protection for His people but destruction for their enemies. Forgiveness will be given God's people. See note on Am 5:18–20.
3:16 SALVATION, As Refuge—The Lord is a refuge to His people, even when He roars like a hungry lion against His enemies (Jer 25:30; Am 1:2).
3:17–18 REVELATION, Author of Creation—The created order will reveal the day of God's salvation. When God redeems the people and the land, all creation will return to His original purposes.
3:17–21 ELECTION, God's Purpose—See note on 2:18–27. Blessings from the God of election would give security to Israel. No fear of foreign invaders destroying the Land of Promise would invade the hearts and minds of Israel. Judah would be forgiven for their sins. The Lord would dwell among His chosen, who would live in prosperity. Intimate relationship with God, security, prosperity, forgiveness, and God's presence among His people are election's goals.

Amos

Theological Setting

Amos saw himself called to be the spokesman of God, not a professional religious leader. He sought to call his people to a relationship with God that would result in the proper relationship with their fellow human beings and that would in turn result in proper worship. He called them to a righteousness that reflected a right relation with God. He warned his people that a failure to respond ultimately would bring the judgment and wrath of God.

The ministry of Amos was set near the end of the first half of the eighth century BC (about 765 BC) in the Northern Kingdom of Israel, during the reign of Jeroboam II. Amos was the first of the great eighth-century prophets, followed by Hosea, Micah, and Isaiah. God called Amos from the Southern Kingdom of Judah to confront the sins of the people of the Northern Kingdom.

The times in which Amos ministered were times of great prosperity in the Northern Kingdom. The economic wealth of the nation was unprecedented. Israel controlled more territory than at any other time in its history except during the reigns of David and Solomon. In addition, religious observance was at an all-time high, with shrines and sanctuaries thronged with people. To all appearances, everything in the Northern Kingdom was going well. The popular theology of that day, even as in ours, indicated that external prosperity was clearly an indication of the blessings of God. But was such a belief correct?

To a large extent the Northern Kingdom became prosperous because the wealthy political leaders oppressed the poor, especially the poor farmers. The courts had been corrupted by bribery. Many of the poor had been forced to give up their land received as part of the tribal inheritances (see Jos 13—19). Frequently they even had to sell themselves into slavery. The leaders apparently believed this was merely an indication the poor were unrighteous and the rich were righteous.

The religion of the day was primarily an assimilation of the worship of the God of Israel with that of the Baals of Canaan. Canaanite religion centered in a fertility cult that appealed to the sexual urges of the people. Gradually it led Israel astray from the God of their fathers. They assumed their prosperity resulted from their faithfulness in ritual and worship. Unfortunately, they missed the fact that worship, to have any value, must affect the way people live.

Thus Amos faced a crowd that needed to rearrange the theological system and practice of the day. Could they change their way of living amid such prosperity?

Theological Outline

Amos: God's Call to Practical Righteousness

- I. The Sermons: God Confronts His People's Sin. (1:1—6:14)
  - A. God's Word is revealed in human words. (1:1-2)
  - B. God identifies and condemns all human sin. (1:3—2:16)
    1. Acts against common human decency are sinful. (1:3—2:3)
    2. The rejection of God's law by substituting one's own wisdom is sin. (2:4-5)
    3. Rejecting God's love is sin. (2:6-16)
  - C. God condemns empty religion. (3:1-15)
    1. The privilege of being loved by God brings responsibility. (3:1-2)
    2. God reveals His purposes to His people. (3:3-8)
    3. God uses historical agents in His judgment. (3:9-12)
    4. Centers of empty religion and ill-gotten prosperity will all fall. (3:13-15)
  - D. God's love confronts His disobedient people in judgment. (4:1-13)
    1. Insatiable desire leads to sin. (4:1-3)
    2. Empty and meaningless worship is sin. (4:4-5)
    3. Temporal judgment is intended to lead God's people to repentance. (4:6-11)
    4. God's rebellious people face an ultimate confrontation with Him. (4:12-13)

- E. God calls His people to practice justice and righteousness. (5:1-27)
  1. God sees the end of His sinful people. (5:1-3)
  2. God's rebellious people are invited to seek Him. (5:4-9,14-15)
  3. God's inescapable judgment is on His people. (5:10-13,16-20)
  4. Practical righteousness is God's ultimate demand of His people. (5:21-27)
- F. False security in national strength leads to ultimate downfall. (6:1-14)

II. The Visions: Seeing God Properly Reveals Both His Judgment and His Mercy. (7:1—9:15)

- A. God extends mercy in response to serious intercession. (7:1-6)
- B. Ultimate confrontation with God can never be escaped. (7:7-9)
- C. A proper view of God brings everything else into perspective. (7:10-17)
  1. A false view of the nature of God's message leads to wrong decisions. (7:10-13)
  2. A person transformed by a vision of God sees people and things as they really are. (7:14-17)
- D. The final consequences of sin offers judgment without hope. (8:1—9:4)
  1. An overripe, rotten religion is worthless. (8:1-3)
  2. The empty observance of meaningless ritual leaves our morality unaffected. (8:4-6)
  3. God's final judgment is a horrible sight. (8:7—9:4)
- E. God's mercy can be seen beyond His judgment. (9:5-15)
  1. God is Sovereign over all the universe. (9:5-6)
  2. God's mercy still offers hope beyond temporal judgment. (9:7-10)
  3. God's ultimate purpose of good for His people will be fulfilled. (9:11-15)

Theological Conclusions

Amos set before the people of Israel several themes that they (and we) desperately need to hear. He began with the popular beliefs of the day, attacked them with vehemence, and then pointed out the true concepts on which the covenant relation with God was to be based.

1. Merely observing proper forms of worship is not sufficient for a right relation with God. Any religion that does not result in the right treatment of the poor and helpless is worthless. Greed had led the leaders of Israel to oppress the helpless. These oppressed people had been rendered even more helpless by corrupt courts and politicians who sought for and received bribes. Even the women, in their insatiable lust for luxury, had lost their compassion and added to the burdens of the helpless poor. To such people Amos issued a call for practical righteousness as a foundation for proper worship.

2. Being a part of God's people does not guarantee exemption from judgment. The people of Israel had ignored the basic idea that privilege carries responsibility. They had assumed, rightly, that the day of the Lord would bring judgment on God's enemies. They also had assumed wrongly that it would bring deliverance for God's people. Their own actions of social oppression had made them into enemies of God. Instead of deliverance, judgment had become an inescapable certainty. Rebellion will be judged.

3. Not all judgment seeks to penalize and hurt. In fact, Amos described most temporal judgments as being redemptive in purpose, designed to bring people into a right relation with God (4:6-11).

4. God calls whom He wills to be an agent of His revelation. God's prophet becomes a prophet in response to the divine call, not through training or as the result of vocational choice. On the other hand, it is also clear that the prophet proclaimed the divine Word in his own human words. God spoke through a particular person to a specific people at a particular time. This revelation lays the foundation for the idea that He can and still does do the same.

Contemporary Teaching

God is involved in and concerned with life as it is and as He intends it to be. Basic to this confrontation are several specific ideas: (1) Greed for the things of this world can distort our thinking and our living, leading us to oppress or be indifferent to our fellows and to be alienated from God. (2) Beliefs that are popular with people and that the majority of God's people hold are not necessarily true. Each must be measured against God's Word, not against popular preaching. (3) Beliefs in the standard theological propositions, accompanied by the proper observance of religious ritual, are of no value if they are not also accompanied by practical righteousness in our dealings with others. (4) God sometimes uses historical tragedy and natural calamity to call people to an honest confrontation with sin, seeking to lead us to repent, turning from sin to God. (5) God is sovereign Ruler of the universe and ultimately will accomplish His purposes, with or without the obedient service of His people. (6) God expects us to be ready to obey Him, even to the point of facing hostile situations as servants of His love.

Chapter 1

THE words of Amos, one of the shepherds of Tekoa[a]—what he saw concerning Israel two years before the earthquake,[b] when Uzziah[c] was king of Judah and Jeroboam[d] son of Jehoash[a] was king of Israel.[e]

2He said:

"The LORD roars[f] from Zion
and thunders[g] from Jerusalem;[h]
the pastures of the shepherds dry up,[b]
and the top of Carmel[i] withers."[j]

Judgment on Israel's Neighbors

3This is what the LORD says:

"For three sins of Damascus,[k]
even for four, I will not turn back ⌊my wrath⌋.[l]
Because she threshed Gilead
with sledges having iron teeth,
4I will send fire[m] upon the house of Hazael[n]
that will consume the fortresses[o] of Ben-Hadad.[p]
5I will break down the gate[q] of Damascus;
I will destroy the king who is in[c] the Valley of Aven[d]
and the one who holds the scepter in Beth Eden.[r]
The people of Aram will go into exile to Kir,[s]"
says the LORD.[t]

6This is what the LORD says:

"For three sins of Gaza,[u]
even for four, I will not turn back ⌊my wrath⌋.[v]
Because she took captive whole communities
and sold them to Edom,[w]
7I will send fire upon the walls of Gaza
that will consume her fortresses.
8I will destroy the king[e] of Ashdod[x]
and the one who holds the scepter in Ashkelon.
I will turn my hand[y] against Ekron,
till the last of the Philistines[z] is dead,"[a]
says the Sovereign LORD.[b]

9This is what the LORD says:

"For three sins of Tyre,[c]
even for four, I will not turn back ⌊my wrath⌋.[d]
Because she sold whole communities of captives to Edom,
disregarding a treaty of brotherhood,[e]
10I will send fire upon the walls of Tyre
that will consume her fortresses."[f]

11This is what the LORD says:

"For three sins of Edom,[g]
even for four, I will not turn back ⌊my wrath⌋.
Because he pursued his brother with a sword,[h]
stifling all compassion,[f]
because his anger raged continually
and his fury flamed unchecked,[i]
12I will send fire upon Teman[j]
that will consume the fortresses of Bozrah."[k]

13This is what the LORD says:

"For three sins of Ammon,[l]
even for four, I will not turn back ⌊my wrath⌋.
Because he ripped open the pregnant women[m] of Gilead
in order to extend his borders,

1:1 [a]S 2Sa 14:2 [b]Zec 14:5 [c]S 2Ki 14:21; S 2Ch 26:23 [d]S 2Ki 14:23 [e]S Hos 1:1
1:2 [f]S Isa 42:13 [g]S Ps 29:3 [h]Joel 3:16 [i]Am 9:3 [j]S Jer 12:4
1:3 [k]Isa 7:8; 8:4; 17:1-3 [l]ver 6,9,11, 13; Am 2:6
1:4 [m]S Jer 49:27; S Eze 30:8 [n]S 1Ki 19:17; 2Ki 8:7-15 [o]Jer 17:27 [p]1Ki 20:1; 2Ki 6:24; Jer 49:23-27
1:5 [q]Jer 51:30 [r]S Isa 37:12 [s]S 2Ki 16:9; S Isa 22:6; Zec 9:1 [t]S Isa 7:16; Jer 49:27
1:6 [u]S Ge 10:19; 1Sa 6:17; Zep 2:4 [v]S ver 3 [w]S Ge 14:6; Ob 1:11
1:8 [x]S 2Ch 26:6 [y]Ps 81:14 [z]S Eze 25:16 [a]S Isa 34:8 [b]Isa 14:28-32; Zep 2:4-7
1:9 [c]1Ki 5:1; 9:11-14; Jer 25:22; Joel 3:4; S Mt 11:21 [d]ver 3 [e]S 1Ki 5:12
1:10 [f]Isa 23:1-18; S 34:8; S Jer 47:4; Eze 26:2-4; Zec 9:1-4
1:11 [g]Nu 20:14-21; S 2Ch 28:17; S Ps 83:6 [h]S Ps 63:10 [i]S Eze 25:12-14; Zec 1:15
1:12 [j]S Ge 36:11, 15 [k]S Isa 34:5; 63:1-6; Jer 25:21; Eze 25:12-14; 35:1-15; Ob 1:1; Mal 1:2-5
1:13 [l]S Ge 19:38; S Eze 21:28 [m]S Ge 34:29; S 2Ki 8:12; S Hos 13:16

[a] *1* Hebrew *Joash,* a variant of *Jehoash* [b] *2* Or *shepherds mourn* [c] *5* Or *the inhabitants of* [d] *5 Aven* means *wickedness.* [e] *8* Or *inhabitants* [f] *11* Or *sword / and destroyed his allies*

1:1—2:16 SIN, Universal Nature—Sin is not limited to the chosen people of God. Every person knows the difference between right and wrong, justice and injustice. The prophet condemned the nations for cruelty in war, breach of political treaties, and disrespect for a foreign leader. He condemned Judah for refusing to obey God's law (see note on Eze 5:6–7) and worshiping idols (see note on Eze 8:3–18). Israel faced God's wrath for social injustice and sexual sins in the name of worship (see note on Hos 1:2). God expects moral behavior from all people. No exceptions are allowed.

1:1,3 REVELATION, Messengers—The shepherd prophet revealed that God uses whom He will to manifest Himself and His will. Amos was not a professional prophet employed by Temple or king (7:12–14). He spoke the message he received from God regardless of its impact on institutions. He gained a hearing by speaking first of Israel's enemies and then adding Judah and Israel to the list of God's enemies (1:3—2:16).

1:2—2:16 EVIL AND SUFFERING, Punishment—God's law extends beyond His chosen people to all humanity, making everyone accountable to Him. Judgment comes on all who break the moral standards obvious to all people.

1:3–15 GOD, Wrath—God's wrath is His judgment upon sin. No sinful nation or people can escape His wrath. See note on La 3:1,43.

1:3—2:16 GOD, Sovereignty—God knows the actions of every nation. He can intervene in any nation's history. He rules the world. See note on Eze 1:25–28.

1:3 HOLY SCRIPTURE, Oracle—See note on Isa 13:1.

1:3—2:16 HISTORY, Moral—All inhabitants of history stand under the basic moral laws God has built into history. Immoral, unjust treatment of other people(s) leads to judgment. As often with the prophets, Amos pronounced judgment on foreign nations building hope for salvation for God's nation. Then Israel and Judah found themselves in the list of nations foreign to God and facing His judgment. See note on Isa 13:1—23:18.

1:3—2:16 CHRISTIAN ETHICS, Justice—Amos' strategy was to get Israel's attention by pronouncing God's judgment on Israel's neighbors. God's judgment is not partial. His call for righteousness is imposed on Israel, too. Justice is an ethical norm recognized by and expected of all nations.

1:9 HUMANITY, Community Relationships—Covenants establish a firm commitment in a relationship between two parties. The betrayal of such a relationship is utterly despicable. Such betrayal is sin even for peoples who do not know or serve the true God.

[14]I will set fire to the walls of Rabbah[n]
that will consume[o] her fortresses
amid war cries[p] on the day of battle,
amid violent winds[q] on a stormy
day.
[15]Her king[g] will go into exile,
he and his officials together,[r]"
says the LORD.[s]

Chapter 2

THIS is what the LORD says:
"For three sins of Moab,[t]
even for four, I will not turn back
⌞my wrath⌟.
Because he burned, as if to lime,[u]
the bones of Edom's king,
[2]I will send fire upon Moab
that will consume the fortresses of
Kerioth.[h] [v]
Moab will go down in great tumult
amid war cries[w] and the blast of the
trumpet.[x]
[3]I will destroy her ruler[y]
and kill all her officials with him,"[z]
says the LORD.[a]

[4]This is what the LORD says:

"For three sins of Judah,[b]
even for four, I will not turn back
⌞my wrath⌟.
Because they have rejected the law[c] of
the LORD
and have not kept his decrees,[d]
because they have been led astray[e] by
false gods,[i] [f]
the gods[j] their ancestors followed,[g]
[5]I will send fire[h] upon Judah
that will consume the fortresses[i] of
Jerusalem.[j]"

Judgment on Israel

[6]This is what the LORD says:

"For three sins of Israel,
even for four, I will not turn back
⌞my wrath⌟.[k]
They sell the righteous for silver,
and the needy for a pair of sandals.[l]
[7]They trample on the heads of the poor
as upon the dust of the ground
and deny justice to the oppressed.
Father and son use the same girl
and so profane my holy name.[m]
[8]They lie down beside every altar
on garments taken in pledge.[n]
In the house of their god
they drink wine[o] taken as fines.[p]

[9]"I destroyed the Amorite[q] before
them,
though he was tall[r] as the cedars
and strong as the oaks.[s]
I destroyed his fruit above
and his roots[t] below.

[10]"I brought you up out of Egypt,[u]
and I led[v] you forty years in the
desert[w]
to give you the land of the
Amorites.[x]

[11]I also raised up prophets[y] from among
your sons
and Nazirites[z] from among your
young men.
Is this not true, people of Israel?"
declares the LORD.

[12]"But you made the Nazirites drink
wine
and commanded the prophets not to
prophesy.[a]

[13]"Now then, I will crush you
as a cart crushes when loaded with
grain.[b]
[14]The swift will not escape,[c]
the strong[d] will not muster their
strength,
and the warrior will not save his
life.[e]
[15]The archer[f] will not stand his ground,
the fleet-footed soldier will not get
away,
and the horseman[g] will not save his
life.[h]
[16]Even the bravest warriors[i]
will flee naked on that day,"
declares the LORD.

1:14 [n]S Dt 3:11 [o]Isa 30:30 [p]S Job 39:25 [q]Jer 23:19
1:15 [r]S Jer 25:21 [s]1Ch 20:1; S Jer 49:1; Eze 21:28-32; 25:2-7
2:1 [t]S Isa 16:6 [u]Isa 33:12
2:2 [v]Jer 48:24 [w]S Job 39:25 [x]S Jos 6:20
2:3 [y]S Ps 2:10 [z]S Isa 40:23 [a]Isa 15:1-9; 16:1-14; S 25:10; Jer 48:1; S Eze 25:8-11; Zep 2:8-9
2:4 [b]2Ki 17:19; Hos 12:2 [c]S Jer 6:19 [d]S Eze 20:24 [e]Isa 9:16 [f]S Ex 34:15; S Dt 31:20; S Ps 4:2 [g]S 2Ki 22:13; S Jer 9:14; S 16:12
2:5 [h]S 2Ki 25:9; S 2Ch 36:19 [i]Am 3:11 [j]S Jer 17:27; S Hos 8:14
2:6 [k]S Am 1:3 [l]S Joel 3:3; Am 8:6
2:7 [m]S Lev 18:21; Am 5:11-12; 8:4
2:8 [n]S Ex 22:26; Dt 24:12-13 [o]Hos 7:14; Am 4:1; 6:6 [p]Hab 2:6
2:9 [q]Nu 21:23-26; Jos 10:12 [r]S Isa 10:33 [s]S Ps 29:9 [t]S 2Ki 19:30; S Job 18:16; S Eze 17:9
2:10 [u]S Ex 6:6; 20:2; Am 3:1 [v]S Dt 8:2 [w]S Dt 2:7 [x]S Ex 3:8; S Nu 21:25; S Jos 13:4; Am 9:7
2:11 [y]Dt 18:18; Jer 7:25 [z]S Jdg 13:5
2:12 [a]Isa 30:10; Jer 11:21; Am 7:12-13; Mic 2:6
2:13 [b]Am 7:16-17
2:14 [c]S Job 11:20 [d]S 1Ki 20:11 [e]Ps 33:16; Isa 30:16-17
2:15 [f]S Eze 39:3 [g]S Ex 15:21; Zec 10:5 [h]Ecc 9:11
2:16 [i]Jer 48:41

[g]*15* Or / *Molech*; Hebrew *malcam* [h]*2* Or *of her cities* [i]*4* Or *by lies* [j]*4* Or *lies*

2:4 GOD, One God—See note on Hos 2:2–23.
2:6–7 DISCIPLESHIP, Spiritual Leaders—The Hebrew prophets claimed to have a word from God for the people. They sounded the note of repentance and social righteousness over and over. God's leaders teach His Word and lead in helping the needy. See note on 3:7.
2:7 GOD, Holy—God expects His people to be morally pure, holy as He is. When we are not, we reflect on His reputation for holiness. This He cannot allow. See notes on Lev 11:44–45; Eze 20:12,14,40,41.
2:9–12 *REVELATION, History*—*The history of prophecy was part of God's salvation history* for His people. It was also part of Israel's history of sin against God.
2:9–12 ELECTION, Condemnation—Israel, having forgotten to be true to their calling as God's chosen, had become prisoners of greed and immorality. Judgment came to Israel because of her unethical and immoral ways. Israel would have to pay for her sins along with Gentile nations like Gaza, Tyre, Edom, Moab, and Ammon. Being the elect of God did not excuse Israel from living lives of justice and righteousness. As He had taken initiative in creating the elect nation, He would take the initiative in disciplining them. God demands repentance and righteousness from His elect.
2:14–16 HUMANITY, Physical Nature—Outstanding physical skills and qualities are generally admired. Yet the most outstanding physical ability is as nothing when compared with the power of God. No human skills can overcome God's punishing wrath.

Chapter 3

Witnesses Summoned Against Israel

HEAR this word the LORD has spoken against you,[j] O people of Israel—against the whole family I brought up out of Egypt:[k]

2"You only have I chosen[l]
of all the families of the earth;
therefore I will punish[m] you
for all your sins.[n]"

3Do two walk together
unless they have agreed to do so?
4Does a lion roar[o] in the thicket
when he has no prey?[p]
Does he growl in his den
when he has caught nothing?
5Does a bird fall into a trap on the ground
where no snare[q] has been set?
Does a trap spring up from the earth
when there is nothing to catch?
6When a trumpet[r] sounds in a city,
do not the people tremble?
When disaster[s] comes to a city,
has not the LORD caused it?[t]

7Surely the Sovereign LORD does nothing
without revealing his plan[u]
to his servants the prophets.[v]

8The lion[w] has roared[x]—
who will not fear?
The Sovereign LORD has spoken—
who can but prophesy?[y]

9Proclaim to the fortresses of Ashdod[z]
and to the fortresses of Egypt:
"Assemble yourselves on the mountains of Samaria;[a]
see the great unrest within her
and the oppression among her people."

10"They do not know how to do right,[b]"
declares the LORD,
"who hoard plunder[c] and loot in
their fortresses."[d]

11Therefore this is what the Sovereign LORD says:

"An enemy will overrun the land;
he will pull down your strongholds
and plunder your fortresses.[e]"

12This is what the LORD says:

"As a shepherd saves from the lion's[f] mouth
only two leg bones or a piece of an ear,
so will the Israelites be saved,
those who sit in Samaria
on the edge of their beds
and in Damascus on their couches.[k] [g]"

13"Hear this and testify[h] against the house of Jacob," declares the Lord, the LORD God Almighty.

14"On the day I punish[i] Israel for her sins,
I will destroy the altars of Bethel;[j]
the horns[k] of the altar will be cut off
and fall to the ground.
15I will tear down the winter house[l]
along with the summer house;[m]
the houses adorned with ivory[n] will be destroyed
and the mansions[o] will be demolished,[p]"
declares the LORD.[q]

3:1 [j]Zep 2:5 [k]S Am 2:10
3:2 [l]S Ex 19:6; Dt 7:6; Lk 12:47 [m]ver 14 [n]S Jer 14:10; Mic 2:3; 1Pe 4:17
3:4 [o]S Isa 42:13 [p]Ps 104:21; S Hos 5:14
3:5 [q]S Ps 119:110
3:6 [r]S Nu 10:2; S Job 39:24; S Jer 4:21 [s]S Isa 31:2 [t]Isa 14:24-27
3:7 [u]Ge 18:17; S 1Sa 3:7; S Da 9:22; Jn 15:15; Rev 10:7 [v]S Jer 23:22
3:8 [w]S Isa 31:4 [x]S Isa 42:13 [y]S Jer 20:9; Jnh 1:1-3; 3:1-3; Ac 4:20
3:9 [z]S Jos 13:3; S 2Ch 26:6 [a]Am 4:1; 6:1
3:10 [b]Am 5:7; 6:12 [c]Hab 2:8 [d]S Ps 36:3; Mic 6:10; Zep 1:9
3:11 [e]Am 2:5; 6:14
3:12 [f]S 1Sa 17:34 [g]S Est 1:6; Am 6:4
3:13 [h]Eze 2:7
3:14 [i]S ver 2; S Lev 26:18 [j]S Ge 12:8; Am 5:5-6 [k]S Ex 27:2
3:15 [l]Jer 36:22 [m]Jdg 3:20 [n]S 1Ki 22:39 [o]Am 5:11; 6:11 [p]S Isa 34:5 [q]Hos 10:5-8,14-15

[k]*12* The meaning of the Hebrew for this line is uncertain.

3:1–14 SIN, Discipline—God's chosen people will be chosen for judgment if they stubbornly oppose God. When God's people become so depraved they forget how to act rightly, they are ripe for God's discipline. False worship and greed rob people of moral sensitivity and make judgment necessary. See note on Hos 8:11–14.

3:2–6 GOD, Sovereignty—God has the sovereign right to choose a people for Himself. He has the sovereign freedom to punish us when we disobey. Historical acts are not accidents. God controls them in His sovereignty. See note on Eze 1:25–28.

3:2 ELECTION, Condemnation—Election makes God's people unique in responsibility. Only Israel had been chosen of all the families of the earth. Yet Israel would not walk in unity or agreement with God. Her disobedience grew out of disrespect for the election requirements of living holy with the holy God of the universe. Her material prosperity had led her to believe she did not need to walk in justice with the God who elected her. Election security comes in spiritual obedience, not in material possessions.

3:7–8 REVELATION, Messengers—God is committed to declare His plans to His people through His messengers. He acts only as His purposes are made clear (Ge 18:17). God rules all and wants His children to know and understand what He does in His world. Prophesying is not a task people choose but one God compels them to fulfill.

3:7 DISCIPLESHIP, Spiritual Leaders—"Prophet" (Hebrew *nabi'*) means literally "one called out." The Hebrew prophets believed God had revealed His secrets to them and called them to announce His message. They could not resist speaking to others what God had revealed. All the prophets considered themselves to be spiritual leaders commissioned by God to warn the people concerning the perils of wickedness and to give guidance on moral issues. The prophets were the moral leaders of Israel. They also announced and interpreted God's actions in history. Under God they were the creative force in the development of Israel's spiritual greatness. Prophets always have been on the cutting edge in advancing the work of God in the world. All have been filled with enthusiasm as they have sought to advance God's will. God uses the prophetic voices of His leaders today, to warn and inspire His people. A prophetic dimension should characterize the ministries of all who preach the good news of the gospel. God still needs His leaders to be on the moral cutting edge.

3:7–10 PROCLAMATION, Authoritative—See note on Jer 19:14–15.

3:12 THE CHURCH, Remnant—God judges a rebellious people—even those He calls His own. Here the emphasis lies on the completeness of the judgment rather than on the restoration of a surviving righteous remnant. See note on Isa 1:7–9.

Chapter 4

Israel Has Not Returned to God

HEAR this word, you cows of Bashan[r]
on Mount Samaria,[s]
you women who oppress the poor[t]
and crush the needy[u]
and say to your husbands,[v] "Bring
us some drinks![w]"
2The Sovereign LORD has sworn by his
holiness:
"The time[x] will surely come
when you will be taken away[y] with
hooks,[z]
the last of you with fishhooks.
3You will each go straight out
through breaks in the wall,[a]
and you will be cast out toward
Harmon,[1] "
declares the LORD.
4"Go to Bethel[b] and sin;
go to Gilgal[c] and sin yet more.
Bring your sacrifices every morning,[d]
your tithes[e] every three years.[m][f]
5Burn leavened bread[g] as a thank
offering
and brag about your freewill
offerings[h] —
boast about them, you Israelites,
for this is what you love to do,"
declares the Sovereign LORD.
6"I gave you empty stomachs[n] in every
city
and lack of bread in every town,
yet you have not returned to me,"
declares the LORD.[i]

7"I also withheld[j] rain from you
when the harvest was still three
months away.
I sent rain on one town,
but withheld it from another.[k]
One field had rain;
another had none and dried up.
8People staggered from town to town
for water[l]
but did not get enough[m] to drink,
yet you have not returned[n] to me,"
declares the LORD.[o]

9"Many times I struck your gardens and
vineyards,
I struck them with blight and
mildew.[p]
Locusts[q] devoured your fig and olive
trees,[r]
yet you have not returned[s] to me,"
declares the LORD.

10"I sent plagues[t] among you
as I did to Egypt.[u]
I killed your young men[v] with the
sword,
along with your captured horses.
I filled your nostrils with the stench[w]
of your camps,
yet you have not returned to me,"[x]
declares the LORD.[y]

11"I overthrew some of you
as I[o] overthrew Sodom and
Gomorrah.[z]
You were like a burning stick[a]
snatched from the fire,
yet you have not returned to me,"
declares the LORD.[b]

12"Therefore this is what I will do to
you, Israel,

4:1 [r]S Ps 22:12 [s]S Am 3:9 [t]S Isa 58:6; S Eze 18:12 [u]S Dt 24:14 [v]Jer 44:19 [w]S Am 2:8; 5:11; 8:6
4:2 [x]Jer 31:31 [y]Am 6:8 [z]S 2Ki 19:28; S 2Ch 33:11; S Isa 19:8
4:3 [a]S Eze 12:5
4:4 [b]S Jos 7:2 [c]S Hos 4:15 [d]S Nu 28:3 [e]Dt 14:28 [f]S Eze 20:39; Am 5:21-22
4:5 [g]S Lev 7:13 [h]S Lev 22:18-21
4:6 [i]S Isa 3:1; S 9:13; S Jer 5:3; Hag 2:17
4:7 [j]S Jer 3:3; Zec 14:17 [k]Ex 9:4,26; Dt 11:17; S 2Ch 7:13; S Isa 5:6
4:8 [l]S Eze 4:16-17 [m]Hag 1:6 [n]S Jer 3:7 [o]S Job 36:31; S Jer 14:4
4:9 [p]S Dt 28:22 [q]S Ex 10:13; S Joel 2:25 [r]Joel 1:7 [s]S Isa 9:13; S Jer 3:10
4:10 [t]S Ex 9:3 [u]Ex 11:5 [v]S Isa 9:17 [w]S Isa 34:3 [x]S Dt 28:21 [y]S Isa 9:13
4:11 [z]S Ge 19:24; S Jer 23:14 [a]S Isa 7:4; Jude 1:23 [b]S Job 36:13

[1]*3* Masoretic Text; with a different word division of the Hebrew (see Septuagint) *out, O mountain of oppression* [m]*4* Or *tithes on the third day* [n]*6* Hebrew *you cleanness of teeth* [o]*11* Hebrew *God*

4:1–13 GOD, Wrath—History under God's wrath should teach God's people to repent. Often we fail to learn the lesson. Then we face the fearsome call to meet the Creator in His wrath. God may express His wrath by refusing to accept our worship, taking away daily necessities, withholding the rain, striking our crops, sending sickness, and destroying our cities.

4:1–2 DISCIPLESHIP, Oppressed—God is displeased with the oppression of the poor and needy. The elite women were guilty of such mistreatment. God showed the end result of such an irresponsible and foolish life-style. They needed to repent and turn to God, but they would not do so. God expects both men and women to center life on helping others rather than fulfilling selfish desires. See note on Isa 10:1–3.

4:1 CHRISTIAN ETHICS, Alcohol—When alcohol, rather than service to the needy, is the uniting factor of family life, the nation is in trouble.

4:2 GOD, Holy—God has no one higher than Himself by whom to swear an oath, emphasizing the certainty that His word will become historical reality. Thus He swears by His own holy nature. See note on Eze 20:12,14,40,41.

4:4–6 STEWARDSHIP, Tithe—A person cannot earn nor buy the good pleasure of God. Regular observance of the ceremonial acts of giving required by Levitical law did not please God when the giver was rebellious and sinful. God delights in the gift of the righteous who give out of reverence and love. See notes on Nu 18:21–32; Ps 51:16–17.

4:6–12 EVIL AND SUFFERING, Testing—God's punishment of Israel came in stages and was intended to induce a repentance which did not come. He used the natural order to punish Israel. At times, God must resort to increasingly severe measures to rivet His people's attention to their sin and His will. Meeting God can be the ultimate punishment for people who are not rightly related to Him.

4:6–12 HISTORY, Judgment—God uses all forces of nature and political history to call His people to repentance. Failure to repent means summons to meet God in judgment.

4:6–11 SALVATION, Repentance—The Lord brought these stern calamities on Israel to summon them to repentance. They were actually expressions of His concern for His people. Amos wanted Israel to know that God was not just another Baal who could be placated with ritual singsong and perfunctory sacrifices. He was Lord over nature, history, and the forces that make death and destruction. Compare Hag 2:17. The doctrine of salvation teaches us to turn to God in extreme situations of life. The hard and bad things that happen to us are intended to prepare us to meet the living God. Without repentance that meeting will bring eternal catastrophe. In repentance we find eternal life.

4:12–13 REVELATION, Author of Creation—The God who creates has purposes which He shares with His people (3:7). He is present in all He makes and is still in control of creation. His plans are revealed to His people, who must face

and because I will do this to you,
prepare to meet your God,
O Israel."

13He who forms the mountains,[c]
creates the wind,[d]
and reveals his thoughts[e] to man,
he who turns dawn to darkness,
and treads the high places of the earth[f] —
the LORD God Almighty is his name.[g]

Chapter 5

A Lament and Call to Repentance

HEAR this word, O house of Israel, this
lament[h] I take up concerning you:

2"Fallen is Virgin[i] Israel,
never to rise again,
deserted in her own land,
with no one to lift her up.[j]"

3This is what the Sovereign LORD says:

"The city that marches out a thousand strong for Israel
will have only a hundred left;
the town that marches out a hundred strong
will have only ten left.[k]"

4This is what the LORD says to the
house of Israel:

"Seek[l] me and live;[m]
5 do not seek Bethel,
do not go to Gilgal,[n]
do not journey to Beersheba.[o]
For Gilgal will surely go into exile,
and Bethel will be reduced to nothing.[p] [p]"

6Seek[q] the LORD and live,[r]
or he will sweep through the house of Joseph like a fire;[s]
it will devour,
and Bethel[t] will have no one to quench it.[u]

7You who turn justice into bitterness[v]
and cast righteousness[w] to the ground[x]

8(he who made the Pleiades and Orion,[y]
who turns blackness into dawn[z]
and darkens day into night,[a]
who calls for the waters of the sea
and pours them out over the face of the land—
the LORD is his name[b] —
9he flashes destruction on the stronghold
and brings the fortified city to ruin),[c]

10you hate the one who reproves in court[d]
and despise him who tells the truth.[e]

11You trample on the poor[f]
and force him to give you grain.
Therefore, though you have built stone mansions,[g]
you will not live in them;[h]
though you have planted lush vineyards,

4:13 [c]Ps 65:6 [d]Ps 135:7 [e]S Da 2:28 [f]Mic 1:3 [g]S Isa 47:4; Am 5:8, 27; 9:6
5:1 [h]S Jer 4:8; S Eze 19:1
5:2 [i]S 2Ki 19:21; Jer 14:17 [j]Jer 50:32; Am 8:14
5:3 [k]Isa 6:13; Am 6:9
5:4 [l]S Dt 4:29 [m]Dt 32:46-47; Isa 55:3; Jer 29:13; S Eze 18:9
5:5 [n]1Sa 11:14; S Hos 4:15 [o]Ge 21:31; Am 8:14 [p]S 1Sa 7:16; S 8:2
5:6 [q]Ps 22:26; 105:4; S Isa 31:1; 55:6; Zep 2:3 [r]ver 14; S Lev 18:5 [s]Dt 4:24 [t]S Am 3:14 [u]S Jer 4:4
5:7 [v]Isa 5:20; Am 6:12 [w]S Am 3:10 [x]S Hos 10:4
5:8 [y]S Ge 1:16; S Job 38:31 [z]S Job 38:12; Isa 42:16 [a]S Ps 104:20; Am 8:9 [b]Ps 104:6-9; Jer 16:21; S Am 4:13
5:9 [c]Mic 5:11
5:10 [d]S Isa 29:21 [e]1Ki 22:8; Gal 4:16
5:11 [f]Am 8:6 [g]S Am 3:15 [h]S Dt 28:30; Mic 1:6

[p]5 Or *grief*; or *wickedness*; Hebrew *aven*, a reference to Beth Aven (a derogatory name for Bethel)

who God is and what God wants (4:2; Jer 5:22). Amos apparently used excerpts from hymns praising the Creator to contrast the people's weak sinfulness with God's creative might (Am 5:8; 9:5).

4:12 EVANGELISM, Judgment—Repent or perish summarizes the Bible's inspired message. Israel refused to repent. Thus they had to prepare to meet God in judgment. The evangelistic efforts of God's people seek to prepare others to meet God as Savior and to warn them of judgment if they refuse. All shall meet Him as Judge or Savior.

4:13 GOD, Creator—As Creator, God has power and control to carry out His threats against His people. Ominous hymnic language shows God can turn dawn to darkness and tread down sacred places humans build. See note on Ps 95:3–7.

4:13 CREATION, Personal Creator—Judgment demands that God be personal. A moral law works, and those who violate it suffer. Some people, however, live out their days on earth and never reap what they have sown. Amos made it clear that the One who will judge people at the end of time is more than a divine law. He is the Creator who made the world and controls the elements in it. Though He is a God who redeems, He also has a stern side, demanding holiness and justice. Failure to respond in obedience to the personal Creator, who established righteousness as the standard of conduct for people, means a terrible judgment. No escape is possible because the One who created the world will have the final word with His creation. Compare 5:8–9; 9:5–6.

5:3 THE CHURCH, Remnant—See note on 3:12.

5:4–6 GOD, Savior—Salvation comes when we personally seek to meet the living God, not when we regularly and routinely carry out meaningless acts of worship. God, the Savior, issues a personal call to life in Him.

5:4–6,14 PRAYER, Humility—Going to public worship is not necessarily prayer. Public worship can turn into self-serving ceremony without God's presence. Humble service of God and the oppressed He protects is a necessary partner to true prayer. Prayer is seeking God's presence. Prayer results in true, meaningful life. Compare Mt 7:7–8.

5:7–24 CHRISTIAN ETHICS, Justice—Injustice invites graphic description and grave judgment. A society which builds its gross national product on the graves of oppressed citizens cannot expect to enjoy its luxurious standard of living for long. Justice must move from the worship house to the economic and judicial centers of society. Without justice in the streets prayer in the pulpit is meaningless. Justice and righteousness cannot be temporary measures for political expediency. They must be constant streams watering all policy statements and actions in a society. See note on Hos 2:19–20.

5:8–9 GOD, Creator—God created the constellations and still controls all nature as He exercises His punishing wrath. See note on 4:13.

5:8–9 CREATION, Personal Creator—See note on 4:13. Creation shows God has personal power to execute the judgment the prophet announced.

5:8 REVELATION, Author of Creation—The Creator God originated all things. Creation itself bears His character and mark and displays His power. Creation obeys the One in whose identity it was formed and shaped. See note on 4:12–13.

you will not drink their wine.[i]
12For I know how many are your offenses
and how great your sins.[j]

You oppress the righteous and take bribes[k]
and you deprive the poor[l] of justice in the courts.[m]
13Therefore the prudent man keeps quiet[n] in such times,
for the times are evil.[o]

14Seek good, not evil,
that you may live.[p]
Then the LORD God Almighty will be with you,
just as you say he is.
15Hate evil,[q] love good;[r]
maintain justice in the courts.[s]
Perhaps[t] the LORD God Almighty will have mercy[u]
on the remnant[v] of Joseph.

16Therefore this is what the Lord, the LORD God Almighty, says:

"There will be wailing[w] in all the streets[x]
and cries of anguish in every public square.
The farmers[y] will be summoned to weep
and the mourners to wail.
17There will be wailing[z] in all the vineyards,
for I will pass through[a] your midst,"
says the LORD.[b]

The Day of the LORD

18Woe to you who long
for the day of the LORD![c]
Why do you long for the day of the LORD?[d]
That day will be darkness,[e] not light.[f]
19It will be as though a man fled from a lion
only to meet a bear,[g]
as though he entered his house
and rested his hand on the wall
only to have a snake bite him.[h]
20Will not the day of the LORD be darkness,[i] not light—
pitch-dark, without a ray of brightness?[j]

21"I hate,[k] I despise your religious feasts;[l]
I cannot stand your assemblies.[m]
22Even though you bring me burnt offerings[n] and grain offerings,
I will not accept them.[o] [p]

5:11 [i]S Jdg 9:27; S Am 4:1; 9:14; Mic 6:15; Zep 1:13 **5:12** [j]Hos 5:3 [k]S Job 36:18; S Isa 1:23; S Eze 22:12 [l]S Jer 5:28 [m]S Job 5:4; S Isa 5:23; S Am 2:6-7 **5:13** [n]S Est 4:14 [o]Mic 2:3 **5:14** [p]S ver 6 **5:15** [q]S Ps 52:3; S 97:10; Ro 12:9 [r]S Ge 18:25 [s]S Isa 1:17; S 29:21; Zec 8:16 [t]S Jer 36:3 [u]S Joel 2:14 [v]Mic 5:7,8; 7:18 **5:16** [w]Jer 9:17; Am 8:3; Zep 1:10 [x]Jer 7:34 [y]S Joel 1:11 **5:17** [z]S Ex 11:6 [a]Ex 12:12 [b]Isa 16:10; S Jer 48:33 **5:18** [c]S Isa 2:12; S Joel 1:15 [d]S Jer 30:5 [e]S 1Sa 2:9; S Joel 2:2 [f]S Job 20:28; Isa 5:19,30; Jer 30:7 **5:19** [g]S La 3:10 [h]S Dt 32:24; Job 20:24; S Ecc 10:8; Isa 24:17-18; Jer 15:2-3; 48:44 **5:20** [i]S 1Sa 2:9 [j]S Isa 13:10; S Eze 7:7; Ob 1:15; Zep 1:15 **5:21** [k]Jer 44:4 [l]S Lev 26:31; S Hos 2:11 [m]S Eze 23:18 **5:22** [n]Lev 26:31 [o]S Jer 7:21 [p]S Ps 40:6

5:12 GOD, Wisdom—You cannot sin in secret. God knows what is going on in His world and in the hearts of His people. See note on Eze 8:12.
5:14 GOD, Personal—God wants to be personally present with us. He is not present just because we make loud claims He is. We must be faithful, obedient servants for Him to be present, blessing us.
5:14–15 DISCIPLESHIP, Involvement—God always will be with His people when we are seeking justice—when we are seeking good rather than evil. He holds us responsible for providing justice for all. Faithful disciples will go beyond mere actions; we will desire justice. Justice will become a controlling motive in our lives. Neighbor love will express itself in justice for all others. It will never place selfish interests above the interests of others. See notes on Mt 22:37–40; Lk 6:27–35.
5:14–15 CHRISTIAN ETHICS, Moral Imperatives—Throughout the Bible, this decision-making principle appears: look for the good, shun evil (Col 3). See note on Ps 34:14.
5:15 GOD, Grace—When judgment is sure and wrath certain to afflict His people, God still issues the call to repent. God's condemned people still have hope because of His mercy. See note on Eze 20:17.
5:15 THE CHURCH, Remnant—God is gracious toward those who call upon His name. "Have mercy" (Hebrew *chanan*) means to bow down to help. Except for the grace of God, no one could stand before Him. Our obedience does not win His favor and guarantee deliverance. As the remnant, we must constantly look to His grace. See note on 2 Ch 34:9.
5:17 REVELATION, Divine Presence—The sounds of grief describe a people separated from God, as a loved one is separated by death from another. To reject God's life-style of justice and mercy is to reject God's identify and nature, and thus to die to one's *true self. God passes through* as the *messenger of death,* or life, as in Egypt, to bring life where His people follow, and to bring isolation and death where people fail to follow His will and way.
5:18–20 LAST THINGS, Day of the Lord—Israel expected the day of the Lord to be a future time when God would vindicate both Himself and His covenant people against their common opposition, the ungodly. This passage enlarged the expectation and called for Israel to understand that they, not only Gentiles, would be the targets of God's judgment because of their unfaithfulness. The day of the Lord will involve judgment upon all ungodliness, whether among the covenant people or the ungodly opposition. Those with greater opportunities for knowing and doing God's will have more to fear from divine judgment at that day, if that greater privilege has not resulted in greater righteousness of life. Amos' immediate prophecy was to the fall of Israel at the hands of Assyria; many scholars do not believe the text calls for future application beyond that time. However, Amos' reference to the day of the Lord shows how the term came to be expressed as apocalyptic language and eventually eschatological expectations. See note on Joel 2:28–32. The later prophets envisioned the day of the Lord as the time when God would manifest His righteous kingship (Zec 14:9), fill the earth with His knowledge, gather a remnant (Isa 11:1), and vindicate His saints. See note on Isa 11:9.
5:21–24 DISCIPLESHIP, Involvement—The people of God should not neglect assembling for religious activity, but such activity does not please God unless the people are involved in righteous living that produces and maintains justice in all human affairs and relationships. See note on Mic 6:6–8.
5:21–24 STEWARDSHIP, Giving in Worship—God's people must live according to His standards before we can expect God to accept our gifts as proper expressions of worship. He expects righteousness to precede rites of worship. See notes on 4:4–6; Mt 5:23–24.
5:21–27 WORSHIP, False—See note on Ex 22:20.
5:21–24 PRAYER, Worship—See notes on vv 4–6,14; Lev 1:9; Hos 6:6; Mt 9:13.

Though you bring choice fellowship
offerings,[q]
I will have no regard for them.[q r]
23Away with the noise of your songs!
I will not listen to the music of your
harps.[s]
24But let justice[t] roll on like a river,
righteousness[u] like a never-failing
stream![v]

25"Did you bring me sacrifices[w] and
offerings
forty years[x] in the desert, O house
of Israel?
26You have lifted up the shrine of your
king,
the pedestal of your idols,[y]
the star of your god[r] —
which you made for yourselves.
27Therefore I will send you into exile[z]
beyond Damascus,"
says the LORD, whose name is God
Almighty.[a]

Chapter 6

Woe to the Complacent

WOE to you[b] who are complacent[c]
in Zion,
and to you who feel secure[d] on
Mount Samaria,[e]
you notable men of the foremost
nation,
to whom the people of Israel
come![f]
2Go to Calneh[g] and look at it;
go from there to great Hamath,[h]
and then go down to Gath[i] in
Philistia.
Are they better off than[j] your two
kingdoms?
Is their land larger than yours?
3You put off the evil day
and bring near a reign of terror.[k]
4You lie on beds inlaid with ivory
and lounge on your couches.[l]
You dine on choice lambs
and fattened calves.[m]

5:22 [q]Jer 14:12; S Am 4:4; Mic 6:6-7 [r]Isa 1:11-16; S 66:3
5:23 [s]Am 6:5
5:24 [t]S Jer 22:3 [u]S Isa 45:8 [v]Mic 6:8
5:25 [w]S Isa 43:23 [x]S Ex 16:35
5:26 [y]S Eze 18:6; S 20:16
5:27 [z]Am 6:7; 7:11,17; Mic 1:16 [a]Dt 32:17-19; Jer 38:17; S Am 4:13; Ac 7:42-43*
6:1 [b]Lk 6:24 [c]Zep 1:12 [d]S Job 24:23 [e]S Am 3:9 [f]Isa 32:9-11
6:2 [g]S Ge 10:10 [h]S 2Ki 17:24; S Jer 49:23 [i]S Jos 11:22; 2Ch 26:6 [j]Na 3:8
6:3 [k]S Isa 56:12; S Eze 12:22; Am 9:10
6:4 [l]S Est 1:6; S Pr 7:17 [m]S Isa 1:11; S Eze 34:2-3; S Am 3:12
6:5 [n]S Ps 137:2; S Isa 14:11; Am 5:23 [o]S 1Ch 15:16
6:6 [p]S Isa 28:1; S Am 2:8 [q]S Eze 9:4 [r]S Eze 16:49
6:7 [s]S Am 5:27 [t]S Jer 16:9; S La 4:5
6:8 [u]S Ge 22:16; Heb 6:13 [v]S Lev 26:30 [w]S Ps 47:4 [x]S Jer 12:8 [y]Am 4:2 [z]S Lev 26:19; Dt 32:19
6:9 [a]S Am 5:3
6:10 [b]S 1Sa 31:12 [c]Am 8:3
6:11 [d]S Isa 34:5 [e]S Am 3:15 [f]Isa 55:11
6:12 [g]Hos 10:4 [h]S Am 3:10 [i]S Isa 1:21; S Am 5:7

5You strum away on your harps[n] like
David
and improvise on musical
instruments.[o]
6You drink wine[p] by the bowlful
and use the finest lotions,
but you do not grieve[q] over the ruin
of Joseph.[r]
7Therefore you will be among the first
to go into exile;[s]
your feasting and lounging will
end.[t]

The LORD Abhors the Pride of Israel

8The Sovereign LORD has sworn by
himself[u]—the LORD God Almighty declares:

"I abhor[v] the pride of Jacob[w]
and detest his fortresses;[x]
I will deliver up[y] the city
and everything in it.[z]"

9If ten[a] men are left in one house, they
too will die. 10And if a relative who is to
burn the bodies[b] comes to carry them
out of the house and asks anyone still hiding there, "Is anyone with you?" and he
says, "No," then he will say, "Hush![c]
We must not mention the name of the
LORD."

11For the LORD has given the command,
and he will smash[d] the great
house[e] into pieces
and the small house into bits.[f]

12Do horses run on the rocky crags?
Does one plow there with oxen?
But you have turned justice into
poison[g]
and the fruit of righteousness[h] into
bitterness[i] —
13you who rejoice in the conquest of Lo
Debar[s]

[q]22 Traditionally *peace offerings* [r]26 Or *lifted up Sakkuth your king / and Kaiwan your idols, / your star-gods;* Septuagint *lifted up the shrine of Molech / and the star of your god Rephan, / their idols* [s]13 *Lo Debar* means *nothing.*

6:1–8 SIN, Unrighteousness—Religion brings confidence and security based on God's grace. False religion brings complacency and false security based on human pride and forgetfulness. Our complacent, secure feelings do not protect us from God's judgment. The history of powerful empires should teach us that fact. Wealth and parties do not mark God's favor. They may mark the passing profit of sin which God plans to snatch away.

6:1 ELECTION, Eternal Security—Complacency in Zion brought woe upon the elected of God. A ceremonial and ritualistic religion that had no place for personal integrity, social justice, and spiritual sensitivity to the living God brought God's judgment and resulted in Israel traveling into exile beyond Damascus. Israel learned eternal security does not come from political influence or economic power.

6:4–7 CHRISTIAN ETHICS, Property Rights—Too often our ease and comfort veil us from seeing the economic injustice in our world. Our actions show we think if all is well with us, all must be well with everyone else. Our complacency is no excuse for not grieving over injustice to others. Riches cannot protect from God's judgment.

6:6 CHRISTIAN ETHICS, Alcohol—A value system that finds no higher level than being an expert on wines and lotions misses the intention of God for us to work on behalf of justice. See note on Isa 5:11–12,22.

6:12 CHRISTIAN ETHICS, Justice—Using two illustrations of impossibility, Amos drilled his point home. The Hebrews were so far away from reflecting God's character that they had perverted justice and righteousness. Qualities which should flavor society poisoned it. Only a godless society could accomplish such impossible perversion. See note on Hos 2:19–20.

6:13–14 HISTORY, Judgment—Human conquest is no basis for pride and self-confidence. God stands behind and above all conquest. Trust in self brings God's conquest of the arrogant.

and say, "Did we not take Karnaim[t]
by our own strength?[j] "

14For the LORD God Almighty declares,
"I will stir up a nation[k] against you,
O house of Israel,
that will oppress you all the way
from Lebo[u] Hamath[l] to the valley
of the Arabah.[m]"

Chapter 7

Locusts, Fire and a Plumb Line

THIS is what the Sovereign LORD
showed me:[n] He was preparing
swarms of locusts[o] after the king's share
had been harvested and just as the second crop was coming up. 2When they had
stripped the land clean,[p] I cried out,
"Sovereign LORD, forgive! How can Jacob
survive?[q] He is so small![r]"
3So the LORD relented.[s]
"This will not happen," the LORD
said.[t]
4This is what the Sovereign LORD
showed me: The Sovereign LORD was
calling for judgment by fire;[u] it dried up
the great deep and devoured[v] the land.
5Then I cried out, "Sovereign LORD, I beg
you, stop! How can Jacob survive? He is
so small![w]"
6So the LORD relented.[x]
"This will not happen either," the Sovereign LORD said.[y]

7This is what he showed me: The Lord
was standing by a wall that had been built
true to plumb, with a plumb line in his
hand. 8And the LORD asked me, "What do
you see,[z] Amos?[a]"
"A plumb line,[b]" I replied.
Then the Lord said, "Look, I am setting
a plumb line among my people Israel; I
will spare them no longer.[c]

6:13 [j]S Job 8:15; Isa 28:14-15
6:14 [k]Jer 5:15 [l]S Nu 13:21 [m]S Am 3:11
7:1 [n]ver 7; Am 8:1 [o]Ps 78:46; S Jer 51:14; S Joel 1:4
7:2 [p]S Ex 10:15 [q]S Isa 37:4 [r]S Eze 11:13; S Am 4:9
7:3 [s]S Ex 32:14; Dt 32:36; S Jer 18:8; 26:19 [t]S Hos 11:8
7:4 [u]S Isa 66:16; S Joel 1:19 [v]Dt 32:22
7:5 [w]S ver 1-2; Joel 2:17
7:6 [x]S Ex 32:14; S Jer 18:8; Jnh 3:10 [y]Jer 42:10; S Eze 9:8
7:8 [z]Jer 1:11,13 [a]Am 8:2 [b]S 2Ki 21:13 [c]S Jer 15:6; Eze 7:2-9
7:9 [d]S Lev 26:30 [e]S Lev 26:31 [f]S 1Ki 13:34; 2Ki 15:9; Isa 63:18; S Hos 10:8
7:10 [g]S Jos 7:2 [h]S 2Ki 14:23 [i]Jer 38:4 [j]2Ki 14:24; Jer 26:8-11
7:11 [k]S Am 5:27 [l]Jer 36:16
7:12 [m]S 1Sa 9:9 [n]Mt 8:34
7:13 [o]S Jos 7:2; S 1Ki 12:29 [p]Jer 36:5 [q]S Jer 20:2; S Am 2:12; Ac 4:18
7:14 [r]S 1Sa 10:5; 2Ki 2:5; 4:38; Zec 13:5 [s]S 1Ki 10:27; S Isa 9:10
7:15 [t]S Ge 37:2; S 2Sa 7:8 [u]S Isa 6:9 [v]S Jer 26:12 [w]Jer 7:1-2; S Eze 2:3-4
7:16 [x]Jer 22:2 [y]S Eze 20:46; Mic 2:6
7:17 [z]S Hos 4:13

9"The high places[d] of Isaac will be
destroyed
and the sanctuaries[e] of Israel will be
ruined;
with my sword I will rise against the
house of Jeroboam.[f]"

Amos and Amaziah

10Then Amaziah the priest of Bethel[g]
sent a message to Jeroboam[h] king of Israel: "Amos is raising a conspiracy[i] against
you in the very heart of Israel. The land
cannot bear all his words.[j] 11For this is
what Amos is saying:

" 'Jeroboam will die by the sword,
and Israel will surely go into exile,[k]
away from their native land.' "[l]

12Then Amaziah said to Amos, "Get
out, you seer![m] Go back to the land of
Judah. Earn your bread there and do your
prophesying there.[n] 13Don't prophesy
anymore at Bethel,[o] because this is the
king's sanctuary and the temple[p] of the
kingdom.[q]"
14Amos answered Amaziah, "I was neither a prophet[r] nor a prophet's son, but I
was a shepherd, and I also took care of
sycamore-fig trees.[s] 15But the LORD took
me from tending the flock[t] and said to
me, 'Go,[u] prophesy[v] to my people Israel.'[w] 16Now then, hear[x] the word of the
LORD. You say,

" 'Do not prophesy against[y] Israel,
and stop preaching against the house
of Isaac.'

17"Therefore this is what the LORD
says:

" 'Your wife will become a prostitute[z]
in the city,

[t]*13 Karnaim* means *horns*; *horn* here symbolizes strength. [u]*14* Or *from the entrance to*

6:14 GOD, Sovereignty—Israel's illogical sin brought God's condemnation. He showed He has the sovereign power to use any nation, no matter how strong or wicked, to carry out His purposes. See notes on 1:3—2:16.

7:1–9 GOD, Grace—God repents. He reacts to the cries of His people and does not carry out to completion the judgment He planned and announced. God is not so bound by His word of judgment that He cannot respond to the cry for forgiveness. See note on Eze 20:17.

7:1—9:15 EVIL AND SUFFERING, Punishment—God's punishment may be delayed through the intercession of His people. Amos' pleas for the people led God to turn back from His plan to punish (7:3,6). When the people's sin continued, God announced judgment from which He would no longer spare His people (8:2). God will not always overlook His people's injustice. His judgment does not, however, nullify His promise or defeat His saving purpose. Salvation after suffering and through suffering is His word for the faithful remnant. See note on Hos 11:1–11.

7:1–9 PRAYER, Intercession—Twice Amos interceded, once for the stopping of the locust plague (v 2) and once for the stopping of the fiery destruction (v 5). The third time God showed him the irregularities in the "wall" by means of a plumb line, and he did not intercede. See note on Ex 32:32.

7:12–17 REVELATION, Messengers—Amaziah wanted Amos out of his territory because the prophet represented a truth he did not wish to hear. The king thought of the sanctuary as his, not God's. A messenger is often sent away for bearing the truth from God to those who most need to hear it. Amos contradicted Amaziah's definition of a prophet. The priest saw prophets as professionals on the king's or Temple's staff serving the purposes of the institution. Amos saw himself as a lay person answering God's roaring call (3:8).

7:12–17 PROCLAMATION, Call—See note on Jer 1:4–9. Jeremiah and Isaiah had close ties to the priests and the Temple when God called them. Amos denied any such ties. He was a rural man of the soil. God can call any person from any vocation to proclaim His Word.

7:15 GOD, Sovereignty—God exercises His sovereign will in the lives of individuals as well as of nations. He uses a person without apparent qualifications to accomplish His purposes. In doing so the sovereign Lord relates in a very personal, intimate way to the person involved.

and your sons and daughters will fall
by the sword.
Your land will be measured and
divided up,
and you yourself will die in a
pagan[v] country.
And Israel will certainly go into exile,[a]
away from their native land.[b] ' "

Chapter 8

A Basket of Ripe Fruit

THIS is what the Sovereign LORD
showed me:[c] a basket of ripe fruit.
2"What do you see,[d] Amos?[e]" he asked.
"A basket[f] of ripe fruit," I answered.
Then the LORD said to me, "The time is
ripe for my people Israel; I will spare
them no longer.[g]
3"In that day," declares the Sovereign
LORD, "the songs in the temple will turn
to wailing.[w][h] Many, many bodies—flung
everywhere! Silence![i] "

4Hear this, you who trample the needy
and do away with the poor[j] of the
land,[k]

5saying,

"When will the New Moon[l] be over
that we may sell grain,
and the Sabbath be ended
that we may market[m] wheat?"[n] —
skimping the measure,
boosting the price
and cheating[o] with dishonest
scales,[p]
6buying the poor[q] with silver
and the needy for a pair of sandals,
selling even the sweepings with the
wheat.[r]

7The LORD has sworn by the Pride of
Jacob:[s] "I will never forget[t] anything
they have done.[u]

8"Will not the land tremble[v] for this,
and all who live in it mourn?
The whole land will rise like the Nile;
it will be stirred up and then sink
like the river of Egypt.[w]

7:17 [a]S Am 5:27 [b]S 2Ki 17:6; S Eze 4:13; S Hos 9:3; Am 2:12-13
8:1 [c]S Am 7:1
8:2 [d]Jer 1:13; 24:3 [e]Am 7:8 [f]S Ge 40:16 [g]S La 4:18; Eze 7:2-9
8:3 [h]S Am 5:16 [i]Am 6:10
8:4 [j]S Pr 30:14 [k]S Job 20:19; S Ps 14:4; S Am 2:7
8:5 [l]S Nu 10:10 [m]Isa 58:13 [n]S Ne 10:31 [o]S Ge 31:7 [p]Dt 25:15; 2Ki 4:23; Ne 13:15-16; Eze 45:10-12; S Hos 12:7; Mic 6:10-11; Zec 5:6
8:6 [q]Am 5:11 [r]S Am 2:6; S 4:1
8:7 [s]S Ps 47:4 [t]S Hos 8:13 [u]S Job 35:15
8:8 [v]S Job 9:6; Jer 51:29 [w]Ps 18:7; S Jer 46:8; Am 9:5
8:9 [x]S Job 5:14; Isa 59:9-10; Jer 13:16; 15:9; S Eze 32:7; S Am 5:8; Mic 3:6; Mt 27:45; Mk 15:33; Lk 23:44-45
8:10 [y]S Lev 26:31 [z]S La 5:15; S Hos 2:11 [a]S Joel 1:8 [b]S Lev 13:40; S Isa 3:17 [c]S Ge 21:16 [d]S Jer 2:19; S Eze 7:18
8:11 [e]Jer 30:3; 31:27 [f]S Isa 30:20 [g]S 1Sa 3:1; S 28:6; S 2Ch 15:3
8:12 [h]S Eze 20:3, 31
8:13 [i]S Isa 9:17 [j]Isa 41:17; Hos 2:3
8:14 [k]Mic 1:5 [l]S 1Ki 12:29 [m]S Am 5:5 [n]S Ps 46:2 [o]S Am 5:2

9"In that day," declares the Sovereign
LORD,

"I will make the sun go down at noon
and darken the earth in broad
daylight.[x]
10I will turn your religious feasts[y] into
mourning
and all your singing into weeping.[z]
I will make all of you wear sackcloth[a]
and shave[b] your heads.
I will make that time like mourning for
an only son[c]
and the end of it like a bitter day.[d]

11"The days are coming,"[e] declares the
Sovereign LORD,
"when I will send a famine through
the land—
not a famine of food or a thirst for
water,
but a famine[f] of hearing the words
of the LORD.[g]
12Men will stagger from sea to sea
and wander from north to east,
searching for the word of the LORD,
but they will not find it.[h]

13"In that day

"the lovely young women and strong
young men[i]
will faint because of thirst.[j]
14They who swear by the shame[x] of
Samaria,[k]
or say, 'As surely as your god lives,
O Dan,'[l]
or, 'As surely as the god[y] of
Beersheba[m] lives'—
they will fall,[n]
never to rise again.[o] "

Chapter 9

Israel to Be Destroyed

I saw the Lord standing by the altar, and
he said:

"Strike the tops of the pillars

[v] *17* Hebrew *an unclean* [w] *3* Or *"the temple singers will wail* [x] *14* Or *by Ashima*; or *by the idol* [y] *14* Or *power*

8:4–6 SIN, Moral Insensitivity—Sin can become such a way of life that we have no consciousness of wrongdoing. This is the result of continued, blatant sin. An impaired conscience is always anxious to engage in injustices against its acquaintances. To do nothing about injustice is sin just as to cause injustice to the poor by misusing our wealth is sin.
8:4–6 CHRISTIAN ETHICS, Property Rights—A sad time had come when the sabbath held no respect by the people. They could hardly wait to get back to their economic exploitation. Impatient participation in public worship does not protect a person from God's judgment on greed, cheating, slavery, and injustice. See note on La 4:1–2.
8:4–6 CHRISTIAN ETHICS, Justice—Serving God must be top priority for a society seeking justice. We must help people become self-supporting not support ourselves by buying their labor cheaply. Without honest market and labor practices, we cannot please God or build a stable society. See note on Isa 5:7–8.
8:9 CREATION, Nature—Natural laws and natural elements are not sovereign. God controls them for His purposes. He can overturn the created order and bring the day of judgment on His people.
8:10 HUMANITY, Attitudes to Death—An only son represented survival and hope for Old Testament people. They hoped they would live on in the memory and through the work of their children, in particular their sons. When a person's only son died, it marked not only death but the end of the family line. At such times grief was intense.
8:11–14 GOD, Wrath—The most horrible expression of God's wrath comes when He withholds His word from His people. Improper worship leads to this. See note on 1:3–15.
9:1–6 GOD, Sovereignty—In God's house Israel found

so that the thresholds shake.
Bring them down on the heads[p] of all the people;
those who are left I will kill with the sword.
Not one will get away,
none will escape.[q]
2Though they dig down to the depths of the grave,[z r]
from there my hand will take them.
Though they climb up to the heavens,[s]
from there I will bring them down.[t]
3Though they hide themselves on the top of Carmel,[u]
there I will hunt them down and seize them.[v]
Though they hide from me at the bottom of the sea,[w]
there I will command the serpent[x] to bite them.[y z]
4Though they are driven into exile by their enemies,
there I will command the sword[a] to slay them.
I will fix my eyes upon them
for evil[b] and not for good.[c]"[d]

5The Lord, the LORD Almighty,
he who touches the earth and it melts,[e]
and all who live in it mourn—
the whole land rises like the Nile,
then sinks like the river of Egypt[f] —
6he who builds his lofty palace[a g] in the heavens
and sets its foundation[b] on the earth,
who calls for the waters of the sea
and pours them out over the face of the land—
the LORD is his name.[h]

7"Are not you Israelites
the same to me as the Cushites[c] ?"[i]
declares the LORD.
"Did I not bring Israel up from Egypt,
the Philistines[j] from Caphtor[d k]

9:1 [p]Ps 68:21 [q]Jer 11:11
9:2 [r]S Job 7:9; S Eze 26:20 [s]Jer 51:53 [t]Ob 1:4
9:3 [u]Am 1:2 [v]Ps 139:8-10 [w]Ps 68:22 [x]Isa 27:1 [y]Jer 16:16-17 [z]S Ge 49:17; S Job 11:20
9:4 [a]S Lev 26:33; S Eze 5:12 [b]S Jer 21:10 [c]Jer 39:16; S Eze 15:7 [d]S Jer 44:11
9:5 [e]S Ps 46:2 [f]S Am 8:8
9:6 [g]Jer 43:9 [h]Ps 104:1-3,5-6,13; S Am 5:8
9:7 [i]S 2Ch 12:3; Isa 20:4; 43:3 [j]S Ge 10:14 [k]S Dt 2:23 [l]S 2Ki 16:9; S Isa 22:6; S Am 2:10
9:8 [m]S Jer 4:27 [n]S Jer 44:27
9:9 [o]Lk 22:31 [p]Isa 30:28 [q]S Jer 31:36; S Da 9:7
9:10 [r]Jer 49:37 [s]Jer 5:12; S 23:17; S Eze 20:38; S Am 6:3
9:11 [t]S Isa 7:2 [u]S Ge 26:22 [v]Ps 53:6; S Isa 49:8 [w]Ps 80:12; S Eze 17:24; Mic 7:8,11; Zec 12:7; 14:10
9:12 [x]S Nu 24:18 [y]Isa 43:7; Jer 25:29 [z]Ac 15:16-17*
9:13 [a]Jer 31:38; 33:14 [b]S Ru 2:3 [c]Lev 26:5 [d]S Jdg 9:27

and the Arameans from Kir?[l]

8"Surely the eyes of the Sovereign LORD
are on the sinful kingdom.
I will destroy[m] it
from the face of the earth—
yet I will not totally destroy
the house of Jacob,"
declares the LORD.[n]
9"For I will give the command,
and I will shake the house of Israel
among all the nations
as grain[o] is shaken in a sieve,[p]
and not a pebble will reach the ground.[q]
10All the sinners among my people
will die by the sword,[r]
all those who say,
'Disaster will not overtake or meet us.'[s]

Israel's Restoration

11"In that day I will restore
David's[t] fallen tent.[u]
I will repair its broken places,
restore its ruins,[v]
and build it as it used to be,[w]
12so that they may possess the remnant of Edom[x]
and all the nations that bear my name,[e y]"
declares the LORD, who will do these things.[z]

13"The days are coming," [a] declares the LORD,

"when the reaper[b] will be overtaken by the plowman[c]
and the planter by the one treading[d] grapes.

[z]2 Hebrew *to Sheol* [a]6 The meaning of the Hebrew for this phrase is uncertain. [b]6 The meaning of the Hebrew for this word is uncertain. [c]7 That is, people from the upper Nile region [d]7 That is, Crete [e]12 Hebrew; Septuagint *so that the remnant of men / and all the nations that bear my name may seek* ⌊*the Lord*⌋

wrath instead of worship. They turned to flee. They learned you cannot flee from God. His sovereign presence rules everywhere. His presence can signify judgment and wrath, not love and salvation. See note on Eze 1:25–28.

9:1–4 REVELATION, Visions—God appeared in the Temple to reveal His ongoing presence with Israel and to begin again the conversation of reconciliation. Compare Isa 6:1. Even Amos, the prophet farthest removed from professional prophecy (Am 7:14), received a vision in the Temple, but the vision marked the Temple's end.

9:2 LAST THINGS, Intermediate State—See note on Isa 14:9.

9:5–6 GOD, Creator—See note on 5:8–9.

9:5–6 CREATION, Personal Creator—See note on 4:13.

9:5 REVELATION, Author of Creation—See note on 4:12–13.

9:7 HISTORY, Deliverance—Historical confessions of faith are not religious warranties or reasons to have superiority feelings. As great as God's Exodus deliverance from Egypt was, it did not mean Israel had an eternal monopoly on God's love. God directs the fates of all peoples and seeks to accomplish His purposes through every nation.

9:7–15 ELECTION, Freedom—People of the God of election cannot take comfort in their status as privileged persons. They cannot expect to be excused for sinful and permissive life-styles. God's decree was that all the sinners among His people would die by the sword. The remnant that remained true to God's election requirements would be planted in their own land, never to be replanted or uprooted so that all nations would bear the name of God. Election means not special privilege but special responsibility. God is free to treat all sinners the same no matter their nation, race, or religious tradition.

9:11–15 GOD, Savior—The harsh words of the Book of Amos end with God's promise of salvation. God's purpose always is to save His people. History is the story of His attempts to provide salvation for a rebellious people.

New wine[e] will drip from the
mountains
and flow from all the hills.[f]
14I will bring[g] back my exiled[f][h] people
Israel;
they will rebuild the ruined cities[i]
and live in them.
They will plant vineyards[j] and drink
their wine;
they will make gardens and eat their
fruit.[k]
15I will plant[l] Israel in their own land,[m]
never again to be uprooted[n]
from the land I have given them,"[o]
says the LORD your God.[p]

9:13 [e]S Joel 2:24 [f]S Joel 3:18
9:14 [g]S Jer 29:14 [h]S Jer 33:7 [i]S Isa 32:18; S 49:8; S 61:4 [j]S 2Ki 19:29 [k]S Isa 62:9; S Jer 30:18; S 31:28; Eze 28:25-26; S 34:13-14; S Am 5:11
9:15 [l]S Ex 15:17; S Isa 60:21 [m]S Jer 23:8 [n]S Joel 3:20 [o]S Isa 65:9; S Jer 3:18; Ob 1:17 [p]S Jer 18:9; S 24:6; S 32:15; S Eze 28:26; S 34:25-28; S 37:12,25

[f]*14* Or *will restore the fortunes of my*

9:14 CHRISTIAN ETHICS, Alcohol—See note on Isa 25:6.

Obadiah

Theological Setting

Does God have a future for a defeated people? This question focuses the primary concern of the people of God as they first heard the "revelation of Obadiah." The most likely setting is 587 BC, when the Babylonian armies destroyed Jerusalem and brought chaos to the lives of her citizens. Other Bible students see different disasters—such as that of about 845 BC under Jehoram (2 Ki 8:20-22).

The conquered people were marched into exile in a foreign land. Adding to their sorrows was the fact their own "kin" had betrayed them. The people of Edom, descended from Israel's brother Esau (Ge 36:1), had gloated over the fall of Jerusalem and helped the Babylonians capture the citizens of Judah. They even participated in the destruction of the city (Ps 137:7; La 4:21-22; Eze 25:12-14; 35:5-7). The apocryphal book of I Esdras says, "You also vowed to build the temple, which the Edomites burned when Judea was laid waste by the Chaldeans" (4:45).

In the face of such defeat, the hopeless, helpless remnant of Judah had several options:

1. They could fall into a deepening state of despair. They were in exile. Where was God? Was there any hope for the future?
2. They could even forget God and begin to worship Babylonian deities. Had not their gods won the victory?
3. They could fall into the trap of clinging to hatred against the unbrotherly Edomites. That is, the exiled people of God might simply seek revenge because of their defeat.
4. They could wait upon God to restore His people and judge their enemies.

Into this setting came Obadiah. His name means "servant or worshiper of the Lord." The prophet knew the pain of the people and the disaster they had experienced. Yet, he prophesied a future when God would restore the remnant of Judah to the fullness of life and bring judgment upon the Edomites because of their cruelty toward Judah.

Does God have a future for a defeated people? Obadiah's answer is yes! He rejected despair and the frustration of harboring hatred in favor of the revelation of God's justice and hope.

Theological Outline

Obadiah: A Vision of Hope for a Defeated People

I. God Knows and Will Judge the Sins of His People's Enemies. (1—14)
- A. Pride deceives people into thinking they can escape God's judgment. (1—4)
- B. Deceitful people will be deceived by their "friends." (5—7)
- C. Human wisdom cannot avoid divine judgment. (8—9)
- D. Conspiracy against "brothers" will not go unpunished. (10—14)

II. The Day of the Lord Offers Judgment for the Nations but Deliverance for God's People. (15—21)
- A. Sinful peoples will receive just recompense. (15—16)
- B. God will deliver His people in holiness. (17—18)
- C. God's remnant will be restored. (19—20)
- D. The Kingdom belongs to God alone. (21)

Theological Conclusions

The Book of Obadiah records how God's servant brought identity and hope to a defeated and broken people. The book concentrates on two affirmations:

1. The justice of God
2. The grace of God

The prophetic word proclaimed the justice of God in a renewed way. Edom and other nations who wronged the people of God would receive just retribution for their evil. In fact, Edom already faced invasion (v. 7). Archeologists have uncovered ruined and desolate Edomite cities from this era.

In addition, God spoke a word of grace: the remnant of Judah had suffered but would have a future in the coming day of the Lord. God is sovereign and would bring in the kingdom. The justice and grace of God would prevail. Obadiah's word offered hope for the people of Yahweh (God).

Obadiah's doctrinal conclusions relate to themes found in other prophecies. In fact, Obadiah 1-9 is quite similar to Jeremiah 49:7-22; perhaps Obadiah applied an older prophetic word to his own setting. The prophets affirmed that God judged the sin of Judah and Jerusalem and the sin of other nations. However, God's last word was not a word of judgment but a word of grace, of hope for the future—a hope fulfilled in the incarnation in the New Testament.

Contemporary Teaching

The proclamation of Obadiah applies to the people of God wherever they find themselves defeated. Even in the throes of overwhelming military defeat and abject despair which followed, the prophet affirmed the justice of God and hope for the future.

The Book of Obadiah is sometimes perceived as a ventilation of despair or bitterness. That perception errs. The book works out of a theological base which emphasizes the justice of God and God's involvement in life. It also assumes a setting of oppression. When the community of faith is oppressed, says Obadiah, they may, nonetheless, have hope beyond the current crisis (vv. 19-20). Such a word encourages communities of faith suffering under totalitarian regimes. The text also affirms the reality of justice for oppressors. They reap their own destruction. Obadiah declares good news: God meets people at the point of their greatest need. The prophet speaks of justice and hope in the face of oppression.

Obadiah calls us (1) to believe in the Word of God; (2) to live in light of God's faithfulness; (3) to renew our vision of God's justice; (4) to aid in the liberation of oppressed people.

THE vision[a] of Obadiah.

1–4pp — Jer 49:14–16
5–6pp — Jer 49:9–10

This is what the Sovereign LORD says about Edom[b] —

We have heard a message from the
LORD:
An envoy[c] was sent to the nations
to say,
"Rise, and let us go against her for
battle"[d] —

2"See, I will make you small[e] among
the nations;
you will be utterly despised.
3The pride[f] of your heart has deceived
you,
you who live in the clefts of the
rocks[a] [g]
and make your home on the heights,
you who say to yourself,
'Who can bring me down to the
ground?'[h]
4Though you soar like the eagle
and make your nest[i] among the
stars,
from there I will bring you down,"[j]
declares the LORD.[k]
5"If thieves came to you,
if robbers in the night—
Oh, what a disaster awaits you—
would they not steal only as much as
they wanted?
If grape pickers came to you,
would they not leave a few grapes?[l]
6But how Esau will be ransacked,
his hidden treasures pillaged!
7All your allies[m] will force you to the
border;
your friends will deceive and
overpower you;
those who eat your bread[n] will set a
trap for you,[b]
but you will not detect it.

8"In that day," declares the LORD,
"will I not destroy[o] the wise men of
Edom,
men of understanding in the
mountains of Esau?
9Your warriors, O Teman,[p] will be
terrified,
and everyone in Esau's mountains
will be cut down in the slaughter.
10Because of the violence[q] against your
brother Jacob,[r]
you will be covered with shame;
you will be destroyed forever.[s]
11On the day you stood aloof
while strangers carried off his
wealth
and foreigners entered his gates
and cast lots[t] for Jerusalem,
you were like one of them.[u]
12You should not look down[v] on your
brother
in the day of his misfortune,[w]
nor rejoice[x] over the people of Judah
in the day of their destruction,[y]
nor boast[z] so much
in the day of their trouble.[a]
13You should not march through the
gates of my people
in the day of their disaster,
nor look down on them in their
calamity[b]
in the day of their disaster,
nor seize their wealth
in the day of their disaster.
14You should not wait at the crossroads
to cut down their fugitives,[c]
nor hand over their survivors
in the day of their trouble.

15"The day of the LORD is near[d]
for all nations.
As you have done, it will be done to
you;
your deeds[e] will return upon your
own head.
16Just as you drank[f] on my holy hill,[g]
so all the nations will drink[h]
continually;
they will drink and drink
and be as if they had never been.[i]
17But on Mount Zion will be
deliverance;[j]
it will be holy,[k]
and the house of Jacob
will possess its inheritance.[l]
18The house of Jacob will be a fire
and the house of Joseph a flame;

1:1 [a]S Isa 1:1 [b]S Ge 25:14; S Isa 11:14; S 34:11; 63:1-6; Jer 49:7-22; S Eze 25:12-14; S 32:29; S Am 1:11-12 [c]Isa 18:2 [d]Jer 6:4-5
1:2 [e]Nu 24:18
1:3 [f]S Isa 16:6 [g]fn Isa 16:1 [h]S 2Ch 25:11-12
1:4 [i]S Isa 10:14 [j]S Isa 14:13 [k]S Job 20:6
1:5 [l]S Dt 4:27; 24:21; S Isa 24:13
1:7 [m]Jer 30:14 [n]S Ps 41:9
1:8 [o]Job 5:12; Isa 29:14
1:9 [p]S Ge 36:11,34
1:10 [q]S Joel 3:19 [r]Ps 137:7; Am 1:11-12 [s]S Ps 137:7; S Eze 25:12-14; 35:9
1:11 [t]S Job 6:27; S Eze 24:6 [u]S Am 1:6
1:12 [v]Pr 24:17 [w]S Job 31:29 [x]S Eze 35:15 [y]S Pr 17:5 [z]Ps 137:7 [a]S Eze 25:6; Mic 4:11; 7:8
1:13 [b]S Eze 35:5
1:14 [c]S 1Ki 18:4
1:15 [d]S Jer 46:10; S Eze 30:3; S Joel 2:31; S Am 5:18 [e]S Jer 50:29; Hab 2:8
1:16 [f]Isa 51:17 [g]S Ex 15:17 [h]Jer 25:15; 49:12; S La 4:21-22 [i]S La 4:21; S Eze 25:12-14
1:17 [j]S Ps 69:35; S Isa 14:1-2; Joel 2:32; S Am 9:11-15 [k]S Ps 74:2; S Isa 4:3 [l]Zec 8:12

[a]3 Or *of Sela* [b]7 The meaning of the Hebrew for this clause is uncertain.

1 REVELATION, Messengers—An unknown prophet responded to God by becoming a messenger of doom to Edom. He declared God's deep disappointment in a nation which abandoned her brothers and sisters in their hour of suffering. God cared even about the descendants of Esau, their apathy, and their refusal to assist Judah. The entire sermon against Edom is called a vision.

3 CHRISTIAN ETHICS, Character—Pride in human ingenuity and security is blind to the matter of God's all-seeing eye. Such pride is antithetical to the person of God.

8–14 GOD, Justice—God brings judgment on people and nations because they deserve it. God can list the crimes calling for punishment.

8 HUMANITY, Intellectual Nature—In the ancient Near East, Edom was considered to be a major center of human wisdom and intellectual achievement. Human wisdom, however, is ultimately worthless when it is not dedicated to God's purposes.

10–12 HUMANITY, Family Relationships—Edom and Israel were descended from the two brothers, Esau and Jacob. To deny or betray such a relationship was a violation of family commitments and a denial of family responsibilities. Edom applauded Jerusalem's fall. God would certainly avenge their actions.

the house of Esau will be stubble,
and they will set it on fire[m] and
consume[n] it.
There will be no survivors[o]
from the house of Esau."
The LORD has spoken.

19 People from the Negev will occupy
the mountains of Esau,
and people from the foothills will
possess
the land of the Philistines.[p]
They will occupy the fields of Ephraim
and Samaria,[q]
and Benjamin[r] will possess Gilead.

20 This company of Israelite exiles who
are in Canaan
will possess ⌞the land⌟ as far as
Zarephath;[s]
the exiles from Jerusalem who are in
Sepharad
will possess the towns of the
Negev.[t]
21 Deliverers[u] will go up on[c] Mount
Zion
to govern the mountains of Esau.
And the kingdom will be the
LORD'S.[v]

1:18 [m]S Isa 1:31 [n]Zec 12:6 [o]S Jer 49:10
1:19 [p]Isa 11:14 [q]S Jer 31:5 [r]S Nu 1:36
1:20 [s]1Ki 17:9-10; Lk 4:26 [t]S Jer 33:13
1:21 [u]S Dt 28:29; S Jdg 3:9 [v]S Ps 22:28; 47:9; 66:4; S Da 2:44; Zec 14:9,16; Mal 1:14; Rev 11:15

[c] *21* Or *from*

21 GOD, Sovereignty—Present conditions may be chaotic with no one seeming to be in control. God's inspired Word promises us God's kingdom will eventually be revealed for all the world to see.

21 HISTORY, Kingdom—History points to a goal: God's kingdom. Establishing that kingdom involves historical judgment on God's enemies. God has plans for history. No nation can prevent Him from fulfilling His plans and establishing His kingdom. Even in the darkness of defeat, God's people can live in hope, expecting the kingdom to come.

Jonah

Theological Setting

Does God's love have limits? Jonah found enemies he could not love and did not expect God to love. The Book of Jonah teaches us a lesson about the nature of God and His love.

Jonah lived shortly before or during the early years of Jeroboam II's reign (805-764 BC) in Israel (2 Ki 14:24). Some scholars contend this book is an autobiographical work written shortly after Jonah returned from Nineveh or by someone of that day to whom he told the events. Increasingly, however, more are suggesting it was written centuries later about the great prophet who had become a national hero. After 538 BC, when the Jews returned from Babylonian captivity, their religion took on an intensely exclusive coloring. They felt God had no use for any other nation. In this theological climate, they needed to hear the story of one of their greatest prophets who once had had a similar attitude.

The book is more than the story of a disobedient prophet. It focuses on the nature of Israel's God. The writer, probably a person held in high esteem, wrote to show the people their opinions and life-styles were not consistent with God's love for all people. God's redemptive program included everyone. The Messiah, whom He would send, was to be for inhabitants of all nations. Only when Israel understood this theological truth could she become His instrument.

Of all Israel's enemies, Assyria had been the cruelest. See introduction to Nahum. If the writer could lead the Jews to understand God loved such a nation, they could see He loved all enemies and all nations.

Jonah's readers faced two major choices. They could remain belligerent in their hatred and self-pity, or they could join God's mission and seek the conversion of all people, even their enemies.

Theological Outline

Jonah: God's Limitless Love.

I. People with Bad Reputations Can Be Pious and Know God. (1:1-16)
II. God Hears the Distress Calls of His People. (1:17—2:10)
III. God in His Compassion Turns Away from Judgment When Any People Repent. (3:1-10)
IV. God's People Should Mirror God's Compassion for All People. (4:1-11)

A more extensive outline shows the doctrinal emphases.

I. Doctrine of God
  A. Omnipotent (all powerful)
    1. Elements subservient to His command (1:4,15)
    2. Creatures controlled by His word (1:17; 2:10)
    3. Vegetation directed by His wish (4:6-7)
  B. Omnipresent (present everywhere)
    1. On the storm-troubled sea (1:4-15)
    2. In the ocean and the belly of the great fish (2:2-9)
    3. At Nineveh when Jonah preached (3:10)
    4. When Jonah pouted (4:4-11)
  C. Holy
    1. Confronts evil (1:2)
    2. Rebukes pride (4:4-11)
    3. Threatens judgment (3:4*b*)
  D. Resourceful
    1. Uses events to declare His will (1:7)
    2. Uses people to accomplish His purpose (1:8-15)
    3. Uses adversity to prepare His servants (1:17—2:8)
  E. Merciful
    1. To sailors when they prayed (1:13-15)

2. To Jonah when he disobeyed (2:1-9)
3. To Ninevites when they repented (3:5-10)
4. To those who cannot understand (4:10-11)

II. Doctrine of Humanity
A. Responsible to God for moral actions (1:2)
B. Rebellious because of pride (1:3; 4:1-8)
C. Fearful before that which is not understood (1:5-15)
D. Willing to change loyalties for self-preservation (1:14)
E. Capable of giving thanks for deliverance (1:16; 2:9)

III. Doctrine of Sin
A. Offensive to God (1:2)
B. Leads to confusion, violence, and misery (1:4-5; 2:3,4*a*,5-8)
C. Affects others (1:5)
D. Will be punished (1:4,17)
E. Can be forgiven through repentance (2:2,4,7; 3:5-10)

IV. Doctrine of Salvation
A. Originates with God (2:9)
B. Intended for everyone (4:10-11)
C. Available because of divine mercy (3:10)
D. Effected through repentance (3:5-9)

Theological Conclusions

This book reaffirms the traditional doctrines of Israel. In addition, it underscores the basic thesis of prophecy. God is not bound by His previous decrees but, like humans, possesses a free will. He responds appropriately to the moral choices of people.

The book's major contribution, however, went far beyond where most Israelites were. Jonah showed us that God's love is not confined to one nation. Even though He had chosen a people for a special mission, He would never allow Himself to be possessed exclusively by any one group.

No other Old Testament book is so clearly missionary. Some have this teaching implicit in parts of their messages, but this book trumpets the imperative from beginning to end. God's plan for the ages, taught so clearly in Ephesians, finds its Old Testament counterpart in this account of a popular prophet who learned the hard way that God's love must never be limited to any one nation. The Book of Acts, filled with missionary activity, finds its roots in the prophet Jonah who was a foreign missionary long before Paul answered the Macedonian call. The author struck the high-water mark of practical Old Testament theology. Nothing else in Jewish Scriptures sets forth more clearly the character of God, His love for all mankind, and His willingness to forgive the most sinful of people.

Contemporary Teaching

Never, since Jonah's day, has the message of this book been as needed as now. Prejudice and hatred abound. Many Christians contend Jesus Christ is not the only answer to our sin. They insist His gospel is not the final word for the world's salvation. According to them, our missionary programs are not only unnecessary but, in some cases, may be counterproductive for harmony across the nations. Jonah reminds us we must call all people to repentance. Missionary programs form the essence of the Christian gospel.

The Book of Jonah shouts for its message to be heeded. Christianity cannot, as ancient Judaism sought to do, identify religious faith exclusively with national interests. God's kingdom in Christ transcends all geographical and ethnic boundaries. When the storms of life are raging, we cannot afford to be asleep, imagining things are well. Several lessons should be learned from the book.

(1) Sin offends God's holiness and must be dealt with drastically.
(2) When God calls, we have no option but to obey.
(3) God's redeeming grace is for all people, no matter who they are or where they are.
(4) God will accomplish His purpose—with us if He can or without us if He must.
(5) Even after the fiercest message of prophetic condemnation, repentance can avert the threatened judgment.

Chapter 1

Jonah Flees From the LORD

THE word of the LORD came to Jonah[a]
son of Amittai:[b] 2"Go to the great
city of Nineveh[c] and preach against it,
because its wickedness has come up before me."
3But Jonah ran[d] away from the LORD
and headed for Tarshish[e]. He went down
to Joppa,[f] where he found a ship bound
for that port. After paying the fare, he
went aboard and sailed for Tarshish to
flee from the LORD.[g]
4Then the LORD sent a great wind on
the sea, and such a violent storm arose
that the ship threatened to break up.[h]
5All the sailors were afraid and each cried
out to his own god. And they threw the
cargo into the sea to lighten the ship.[i]
But Jonah had gone below deck, where
he lay down and fell into a deep sleep.

1:1 [a]Mt 12:39-41; 16:4; Lk 11:29-32 [b]2Ki 14:25
1:2 [c]S Ge 10:11; S Na 1:1
1:3 [d]Ps 139:7 [e]S Ge 10:4 [f]S Jos 19:46; Ac 9:36,43 [g]Ex 4:13; S Jer 20:9; S Am 3:8
1:4 [h]Ps 107:23-26
1:5 [i]Ac 27:18-19
1:6 [j]Jnh 3:8 [k]S Ps 107:28
1:7 [l]Nu 32:23; Jos 7:10-18; S 1Sa 14:42 [m]S Pr 16:33
1:9 [n]S Ps 96:9 [o]S Da 2:18; Ac 17:24 [p]S Ne 9:6 [q]S Ge 1:9

6The captain went to him and said, "How
can you sleep? Get up and call[j] on your
god! Maybe he will take notice of us, and
we will not perish."[k]
7Then the sailors said to each other,
"Come, let us cast lots to find out who is
responsible for this calamity."[l] They cast
lots and the lot fell on Jonah.[m]
8So they asked him, "Tell us, who is
responsible for making all this trouble for
us? What do you do? Where do you come
from? What is your country? From what
people are you?"
9He answered, "I am a Hebrew and I
worship the LORD,[n] the God of heaven,[o]
who made the sea[p] and the land.[q]"
10This terrified them and they asked,
"What have you done?" (They knew he
was running away from the LORD, because he had already told them so.)
11The sea was getting rougher and
rougher. So they asked him, "What

1:1—4:11 HISTORY, Universal—God recorded a history of an individual prophet to teach a lesson about universal history. People with power remain sinners facing God's judgment. God wants even our enemies to repent and find relationship with Him apart from judgment. Jonah wanted to destroy the hated national enemy. God wanted to save for His purposes the international power, seeing them in their innocence and need (4:11).

1:1—4:11 ELECTION, Mission—God welcomes the worship of pagan sailors and hated enemies. Election is a call to mission, not an excuse to withdraw. Jonah learned the hard way that God had elected him and his people to be a witness to the nations, so the nations could join God's elect in worship.

1:1—4:11 EVANGELISM, Obedience—Jonah's message concerns disobedience, surrender, and triumph. It is a picture of many of us: (1) God calls to unusual tasks, even preaching in the enemy's capital (1:2). That means going across many cultural barriers and being misunderstood by many. (2) God's call can be rejected (1:3). God calls, but we are not forced to respond. (3) God will chastise us if we are disobedient (1:17). To refuse God's call is tragic, inviting His discipline. (4) We can repent, and God will forgive (2:2). We can find restoration to obedience. (5) God will give a second chance (3:1–2). Even when we sin, God will give us a second chance if we repent. (6) Success will attend our obedience (3:5). How wonderful to know that obedience to the call to evangelize the "Ninevites" of our day will bring glorious fruits of salvation to the wayward people of our world.

1:1—2:10 MIRACLE, Redemption—Jonah's miracle arouses our interest in the size and nature of the fish. The greater miracle is Nineveh's repentance and redemption and God's desire through the inspired narrative to redeem us from hateful prejudice. God's redeeming miracle is more important than the scientific classification of the fish. God who created the cosmos and its biology can prepare a fish for His redemptive purpose. In miracles God can use the natural order of creation, or He can choose to do something unique and exceptional within the natural order. Our calling is not to debate the how of God's miracles but to claim and proclaim the redemption provided by the miracle-working God.

1:1–2 REVELATION, Messengers—Jonah was a reluctant prophet, who ran from the responsibility of revealing God's message. God uses unskilled, unrefined, and even involuntary messengers as interpreters of His will. Jonah thought God's message should benefit only God's chosen people. God seeks to share His call to repentance with all people.

1:1–3 MISSIONS, Call—God called Jonah to a missionary venture—to preach to Nineveh, the capital of Assyria and Israel's prime enemy. God called Jonah to go to a different people with a strange culture and a foreign language. God was grieved over the wickedness of Nineveh. He gave Jonah a message of judgment, announcing His plans to destroy Nineveh. Jonah rebelled. He fled in precisely the opposite direction. God allowed him to retreat from the missionary call. When we seek to run away from the presence and the call of God, we can usually find others ready to help us escape. Jonah's purpose was to flee from the mission to which God called him. In so doing he sought to hide from God's presence. Such a step is always utter futility (Ps 139:7–12). The cost of fleeing in rebellion to God's call and command always carries a price tag with it as Jonah quickly discovered.

1:2 PROCLAMATION, Call—See note on Jer 1:4–9.

1:3 SIN, Rebellion—Jonah sinned by rebelling against the known will of God. When a person knows and refuses to do what God requires, this is a grevious sin. Human rights do not exempt us from God's direct command. To refuse to witness to other people for any reason is sin.

1:4–17 EVIL AND SUFFERING, Natural Origin—Nature brings human suffering. Innocent people suffer. Many times we have no explanation. Evil in nature is one of the great mysteries ultimately beyond human explanation. Jonah teaches us God retains control of the natural order. He used the storm to punish Jonah and the fish to rescue him. God will not allow the storm to destroy all civilized life (Ge 9:11). Humans are not responsible for the damage and death God's punishing storms send. The crisis of storm can lead people to a right relationship with God. We must trust God to control nature and to bring out of its storms His own purposes (Ro 8:28).

1:4–11 HUMANITY, Community Relationships—Tragedy promotes community togetherness. Only the worst of people fail to cooperate. How unbelievable a prophet would not pray. The deeds of one person clearly affected the lives of those around him.

1:4–7 REVELATION, Author of Creation—The sailors saw in the storm the anger of one of the gods. Revelation of divine anger through creation was a belief Israel shared with her neighbors. The sailors attempted to find out who was responsible by casting lots. See note on Jdg 1:1–2. When people seek God's will, there are many ways to discern His response.

1:6,14–16 GOD, One God—In the ancient world people believed in many gods. The pious sea captain did the best he knew. He roused people to call on the gods. He learned quickly from Jonah's reluctant testimony and offered prayer and sacrifice to the one true God. See note on Jer 1:16.

1:9 GOD, Creator—The one true God is the God who is Creator. Sailors quickly learn to respect the Creator of the sea and land.

should we do to you to make the sea calm
down for us?"
12"Pick me up and throw me into the
sea," he replied, "and it will become
calm. I know that it is my fault that this
great storm has come upon you."[r]
13Instead, the men did their best to
row back to land. But they could not, for
the sea grew even wilder than before.[s]
14Then they cried to the LORD, "O LORD,
please do not let us die for taking this
man's life. Do not hold us accountable for
killing an innocent man,[t] for you, O
LORD, have done as you pleased."[u]
15Then they took Jonah and threw him
overboard, and the raging sea grew
calm.[v] 16At this the men greatly feared[w]
the LORD, and they offered a sacrifice to
the LORD and made vows[x] to him.
17But the LORD provided[y] a great fish
to swallow Jonah,[z] and Jonah was inside
the fish three days and three nights.

Chapter 2

Jonah's Prayer

FROM inside the fish Jonah prayed to
the LORD his God. 2He said:

"In my distress I called[a] to the LORD,[b]
and he answered me.
From the depths of the grave[a][c] I
called for help,
and you listened to my cry.
3You hurled me into the deep,[d]
into the very heart of the seas,
and the currents swirled about me;
all your waves[e] and breakers
swept over me.[f]
4I said, 'I have been banished
from your sight;[g]
yet I will look again
toward your holy temple.'[h]
5The engulfing waters threatened me,[b]
the deep surrounded me;
seaweed was wrapped around my
head.[i]
6To the roots of the mountains[j] I sank
down;
the earth beneath barred me in
forever.
But you brought my life up from the
pit,[k]
O LORD my God.

7"When my life was ebbing away,
I remembered[l] you, LORD,
and my prayer[m] rose to you,
to your holy temple.[n]

8"Those who cling to worthless idols[o]
forfeit the grace that could be theirs.
9But I, with a song of thanksgiving,[p]
will sacrifice[q] to you.
What I have vowed[r] I will make good.
Salvation[s] comes from the LORD."

10And the LORD commanded the fish,
and it vomited Jonah onto dry land.

Chapter 3

Jonah Goes to Nineveh

THEN the word of the LORD came to
Jonah[t] a second time: 2"Go to the

1:12 [r]2Sa 24:17; 1Ch 21:17
1:13 [s]S Pr 21:30
1:14 [t]Dt 21:8 [u]S Da 4:35
1:15 [v]S Ps 107:29; Lk 8:24
1:16 [w]Mk 4:41 [x]S Nu 30:2; Ps 66:13-14
1:17 [y]Jnh 4:6,7 [z]Mt 12:40; 16:4; Lk 11:30
2:2 [a]La 3:55 [b]Ps 18:6; 120:1 [c]Ps 86:13
2:3 [d]S Ps 88:6 [e]S 2Sa 22:5 [f]S Ps 42:7
2:4 [g]Ps 31:22; Jer 7:15 [h]S 1Ki 8:48
2:5 [i]Ps 69:1-2
2:6 [j]Job 28:9 [k]S Job 17:16; S 33:18; S Ps 30:3
2:7 [l]Ps 77:11-12 [m]2Ch 30:27 [n]S Ps 11:4; 18:6
2:8 [o]S Dt 32:21; S 1Sa 12:21
2:9 [p]S Ps 42:4 [q]Ps 50:14,23; Heb 13:15 [r]S Nu 30:2; Ps 116:14; S Ecc 5:4-5 [s]S Ex 15:2; S Ps 3:8
3:1 [t]Jnh 1:1

[a]2 Hebrew *Sheol* [b]5 Or *waters were at my throat*

1:9 CREATION, Power—The Creator can still reveal His power through the elements He created (vv 4–5,15). Power in creation shows He is more than a local or tribal god. Worldly-wise sailors recognized His power and turned from their gods (v 5) to the Creator God (v 16). The feared chaotic waters had no power against the Creator during creation (Ge 1:2, 6–7,9–10,20–22). They had no power over Jonah in face of the Creator's redemptive answer to his prayer (Jnh 2:1–10).

1:12–13 HUMANITY, Community Relationships—Pagan sailors taught more about communal relationships than God's prophet. Even the toughest people shrink from placing total guilt on and demanding the ultimate penalty from another person.

1:14–16 PRAYER, Universality of—The sailors had called to their own gods (v 5). They understood Jonah's reference to the universal God (v 9). When Jonah revealed the reason for the storm, they called on Jonah's God. Pagans are welcome at God's altar when they learn to acknowledge Him. Prophets' prayers lack meaning when not backed by obedience.

1:17 GOD, Sovereignty—God controls even the feared creatures of the deep to accomplish His purposes.

1:17 JESUS CHRIST, Foretold—The experience of Jonah became a sign to Israel both of the call to repent and of the necessity for the Messiah to die and be raised (Mt 12:39–41; 16:4; Lk 11:29–32). God did not send the Messiah with overwhelming evidence so everyone would follow Him automatically. He sent His Son to give true fulfillment of Scripture so that people truly seeking God's will in faith would repent and follow Him even to death.

2:1–9 PRAYER, Petition—Jonah, like many other humans, prayed when he was driven to it. His prayer, however, indicated his understanding of the principle of obedience in relation to prayer. Sin does not have to separate us from God forever. We do not have to wait for pleasant circumstances to seek forgiveness and call to God for help. Jonah's prayer is structured like a thanksgiving prayer. See note on Ps 30:1–12.

2:2,6 LAST THINGS, Hell—Temporal destruction faced Jonah in the fish's belly. In this context, the "grave" (Hebrew *She'ol*) was the sea or the fish's belly where he faced certain death. See notes on Isa 14:9; Hos 13:14. The idea of the grave is parallel to that of the "pit," generally a deep place. Figuratively, it stands for death, as does grave and *Sheol*. From this it leads to the New Testament revelation about the abyss or pit. See note on Lk 8:31.

2:6 GOD, Personal—In deepest distress the rebellious missionary prophet can still commune with "my God." No circumstances can separate us from the personal God who seeks personal relationship with us. Prayer is the deepest expression of that personal relationship.

2:8–9 GOD, One God—Just as the sailors in chapter 1, Jonah discovered worship of other gods has no value. Only one God answers prayer. He is our only Savior. See note on Jer 50:34.

3:1—4:11 EVIL AND SUFFERING, Repentance—The people of Nineveh repented, and God did not destroy the city. God does not wish the destruction of any people, even those who turn from Him. All people are acceptable to Him upon His terms. We are not to follow Jonah wanting to exclude national enemies from God's grace and salvation. God's mercy often runs counter to our passion for human justice. Suffering should

great city of Nineveh and proclaim to it
the message I give you."

3 Jonah obeyed the word of the LORD
and went to Nineveh. Now Nineveh was
a very important city—a visit required
three days. 4 On the first day, Jonah started into the city. He proclaimed:[u] "Forty
more days and Nineveh will be overturned." 5 The Ninevites believed God.
They declared a fast, and all of them, from
the greatest to the least, put on sackcloth.[v]

6 When the news reached the king of
Nineveh, he rose from his throne, took
off his royal robes, covered himself with
sackcloth and sat down in the dust.[w]
7 Then he issued a proclamation in Nineveh:

"By the decree of the king and his nobles:

Do not let any man or beast, herd
or flock, taste anything; do not let
them eat or drink.[x] 8 But let man and
beast be covered with sackcloth. Let
everyone call[y] urgently on God. Let
them give up[z] their evil ways[a] and
their violence.[b] 9 Who knows?[c] God
may yet relent[d] and with compassion turn[e] from his fierce anger[f] so
that we will not perish."

10 When God saw what they did and
how they turned from their evil ways, he
had compassion[g] and did not bring upon
them the destruction[h] he had threatened.[i]

Chapter 4

Jonah's Anger at the LORD's Compassion

BUT Jonah was greatly displeased and
became angry.[j] 2 He prayed to the
LORD, "O LORD, is this not what I said
when I was still at home? That is why I
was so quick to flee to Tarshish. I knew[k]
that you are a gracious[l] and compassionate God, slow to anger and abounding in
love,[m] a God who relents[n] from sending
calamity.[o] 3 Now, O LORD, take away my
life,[p] for it is better for me to die[q] than
to live."[r]

4 But the LORD replied, "Have you any
right to be angry?"[s]

5 Jonah went out and sat down at a
place east of the city. There he made himself a shelter, sat in its shade and waited
to see what would happen to the city.
6 Then the LORD God provided[t] a vine
and made it grow up over Jonah to give
shade for his head to ease his discomfort,
and Jonah was very happy about the vine.
7 But at dawn the next day God provided a
worm, which chewed the vine so that it
withered.[u] 8 When the sun rose, God provided a scorching east wind, and the sun
blazed on Jonah's head so that he grew
faint. He wanted to die,[v] and said, "It
would be better for me to die than to
live."

9 But God said to Jonah, "Do you have a
right to be angry about the vine?"[w]

"I do," he said. "I am angry enough to
die."

10 But the LORD said, "You have been
concerned about this vine, though you
did not tend it or make it grow. It sprang

3:4 [u]S Jer 18:7-10
3:5 [v]Da 9:3; Mt 11:21; 12:41; Lk 11:32
3:6 [w]Est 4:1-3; S Job 2:8,13; S Eze 27:30-31
3:7 [x]S 2Ch 20:3; S Ezr 10:6
3:8 [y]Ps 130:1; Jnh 1:6 [z]Jer 25:5 [a]Jer 7:3 [b]S Job 16:17
3:9 [c]2Sa 12:22 [d]S Jer 18:8 [e]S Joel 2:14 [f]S Ps 85:3
3:10 [g]S Am 7:6 [h]S Jer 18:8 [i]S Ex 32:14
4:1 [j]ver 4; Mt 20:11; Lk 15:28
4:2 [k]Jer 20:7-8 [l]S Dt 4:31; Ps 103:8 [m]S Ex 22:27; Ps 86:5,15 [n]S Nu 14:18 [o]S Joel 2:13
4:3 [p]S Nu 11:15 [q]S Job 7:15 [r]Jer 8:3
4:4 [s]Ge 4:6; Mt 20:11-15
4:6 [t]S Jnh 1:17
4:7 [u]Joel 1:12
4:8 [v]S 1Ki 19:4
4:9 [w]ver 4

---

never be an occasion of delight for us. We should let God use us to call all people to repentance.

3:1 REVELATION, Messengers—God revealed Himself again to the rebellious prophet and communicated a message for the disobedient people of Nineveh. God is both patient with the people who disobey and the prophet who disobeys. God works to see His message is finally delivered.

3:2–4 PROCLAMATION, Call—See notes on Jer 1:4–9; 19:14–15.

3:3–5 SALVATION, Obedience—When Jonah finally obeyed the Lord, the city of Nineveh repented. Our obedience can result in the salvation of others.

3:5 SALVATION, Belief—The penitent Ninevites are an example of what it means to believe in God. The fasting and sackcloth indicate profound repentance. Through faith, Ninevites, as well as Israelites and all others, can have fellowship with God.

3:8 GOD, Righteous—The people of Nineveh recognized that God is a righteous God who does not turn away the confession of sin and plea for forgiveness no matter how severe the announced judgment. See note on Da 9:7,14,16.

3:8 SALVATION, Repentance—Those who repent experience a moral transformation as they focus life totally on God and His mercy.

3:9 GOD, Love—In His love God listens to the prayer of repentance from all people, even those who have had no previous experience with Him and His worshipers. See note on Hos 11:1–11

3:9 GOD, Wrath—Wrath is never God's last word to a repentant people. The preacher's announcement does not force God to appear in judgment. See note on Am 4:1–13.

4:1–11 PRAYER, Curse—Jonah's anger because God spared an enemy of Israel indicated a basic flaw in his understanding of God. God was long-suffering with Jonah's initial disobedience, with this anger, and with the Ninevites. A prayer condemning God's mercy and seeking death can be uttered to God. God's answer is an attempt to teach more about His nature. Angry words to God can bring us closer to Him if we are willing to listen and learn.

4:2 GOD, Love—God's patient love often overrules His anger. We do not always love this. God's love made Jonah angry. He did not want God to have the freedom to repent of His anger. See note on Am 7:1–9.

4:6 GOD, Grace—In His grace God expressed concrete concern for a single individual's needs, even when the person was complaining bitterly about God's actions. See note on Eze 20:17.

4:6–10 REVELATION, Author of Creation—God used a special vine to reveal His nature and being to Jonah and to confront Jonah with his vengeful attitude.

4:8 HUMANITY, Attitudes to Death—Embarrassment, disappointment, and discomfort can all make people feel sorry for themselves. When life appears unbearable, they may long for death as a welcome relief. Jonah became uncomfortable because he thought God loved too much, forgave too easily, and punished too slowly. Jonah wanted forgiveness and grace for himself but not for his enemies. No reason justifies anger that leads to the desire to die.

up overnight and died overnight. [11]But Nineveh[x] has more than a hundred and twenty thousand people who cannot tell their right hand from their left, and many cattle as well. Should I not be concerned[y] about that great city?"

4:11 [x]Jnh 1:2; 3:2 [y]Jnh 3:10

4:11 GOD, Grace—God's grace goes beyond legal duty to express personal concern and emotion. God had every right to destroy Assyria for their renowned wickedness. Instead God looked at innocent multitudes who needed His love and cried in repentance for His grace. The human mind seeking to justify self and gain revenge cannot understand and accept God's grace. Jonah was ready to die because God was gracious. We cannot establish a monopoly on God's grace. He will be gracious to whom He chooses.

4:11 MISSIONS, Source—The biblical teachings on missions rests on one foundation: the unique, all-encompassing love of God. Humans see other people and feel envy, hatred, pride, and need for revenge. God looks at people and see helpless need and hopeless evil. The call to missions is a call to share God's perspective on the world, recognizing the spiritual needs of those with the greatest material wealth and the strongest political power. We answer God's call to go when we share His love of spiritually-bankrupt people.

Micah

Theological Setting

What is the outlook for a people who disregard God's expectations? Micah had to show God's people the unexpected truth.

When Micah began his ministry about 735 BC, both Israel and Judah were enjoying times of unaccustomed peace and prosperity. The westward advance of the Assyrians had compelled the Syrians to withdraw from Israel's eastern border. Freed from the threat of war, both the Northern and Southern Kingdom were at liberty to develop their economic, social, and political life.

But this situation also had its ominous sides. The rich began to emulate the life-styles of pagan nations. When the peasant farmers found difficulty in producing the required luxury goods, the rich landowners took over their holdings and influenced court decisions by bribing the judges. The unemployed farm workers then drifted to the cities seeking shelter. For the first time in Hebrew history serious overcrowding threatened large settled areas, along with the squalor and disease that accompanied poverty.

The religious condition of the nation as a whole was even more serious. The Israelites had been liberated from Egypt under Moses and provided with a home in Canaan so they might live as "a kingdom of priests and a holy nation" (Ex 19:6). At Mount Sinai they covenanted with God to serve Him alone as the one true God and promised to obey all His laws. Once they occupied Canaan, however, they discovered the inhabitants practiced one of the most depraved forms of religion the world has ever known.

The Canaanites worshiped Baal ("lord," "master") and his consort, Anath, at four principal festivals each year. Their celebrations included orgiastic and degrading rites that included ceremonial prostitution, drunkenness, incest, homosexuality, and violent assaults. The Canaanite priests sanctioned these activities as legitimate acts of worship. The acts often occurred in the groves of trees that surrounded their hilltop shrines. See Introduction to Song of Songs.

Under Jeroboam I (930-909 BC) the holy places at Bethel and Dan were introduced to Egyptian calf-worship, thus enabling the ten tribes to participate in pagan worship, despite the fact that such activity was expressly forbidden by the Sinai covenant. When Ahab ruled Israel (874-853 BC), his pagan wife, Jezebel, a Canaanite high priestess, made the idolatrous religion of Canaan the norm for the Israelites. Most of the people welcomed priestly sanction for indulging in the lewd Canaanite rites, although a few were troubled by the repudiation of God's covenant laws. Periodically God sent prophetic messengers to warn the Israelites of the consequences attached to breaking the oath of obedience to the covenant (Dt 28:15-68), but the people chose to ignore the fact that covenantal privileges entailed the responsibility of their living holy lives under God's commandments.

While Canaanite religion was particularly strong in the north, its influence also was felt in the south among the Judeans. Baal and the true Lord were being worshiped side by side in Jerusalem. The poor were being exploited mercilessly by the upper classes. Justice was perverted through bribery. Instead of treating the peasants as equal members of a holy community under God, the rich reduced them to the level of slaves. Amos and Isaiah had already denounced these gross iniquities. It fell to Micah to expose again the injustices committed by the covenant people.

Little is known about Micah except that he prophesied in the reigns of Jotham (750-735 BC), Ahaz (735-715 BC), and Hezekiah (715-686 BC). Concerning his occupation, Scripture is silent. Since he lived at Moresheth Gath, some twenty-five miles southwest of Jerusalem in a rich agricultural area, we may suppose he farmed. A firm supporter of the Sinai covenant, Micah prophesied that the Israelites would be punished severely if they continued to reject its provisions. He looked among the Judeans for repentance and faith, but saw little to reassure him. Priests and prophets alike had misled the people, so that Micah could only pronounce Judah as incurably ill. Still he begged for justice to prevail among his countrymen before it was too late.

Theological Outline

Micah: Covenant or Chaos?

I. God's Word Witnesses Against All People. (1:1-2)
II. God Judges His People for Their Sins. (1:3—3:12)
  A. God judges religious infidelity. (1:3-16)
  B. God judges economic injustice. (2:1-5)
  C. God judges false preaching. (2:6-11)
  D. God's judgment looks to the remnant's restoration. (2:12-13)
  E. God judges unjust leaders. (3:1-4)
  F. God judges those who preach peace and prosperity for sinners. (3:5-7)
  G. God judges through His Spirit-filled messenger. (3:8)
  H. God judges corrupt, greedy officials. (3:9-12)
III. God Promises a Day of International Peace and Worship. (4:1—5:15)
  A. God plans for His people to teach His way to the nations. (4:1-5)
  B. God plans to redeem and rule His weakened remnant. (4:6-11)
  C. God plans to show the world His universal rule. (4:12-13)
  D. God plans to raise up a Shepherd from Bethlehem to bring peace and victory to His beleagured flock. (5:1-9)
  E. God plans to destroy weapons and idolatry from His people. (5:10-15)
IV. God Has a Case Against His People. (6:1—7:6)
  A. God has done His part, redeeming His people. (6:1-5)
  B. God's expectations are clear: justice, mercy, piety. (6:6-8)
  C. God's people have not met His expectations. (6:9-12)
  D. God's punishment is sure for a corrupt people. (6:13—7:6)
V. God in Righteousness, Love, and Faithfulness Will Forgive and Renew His People. (7:7-20)
  A. God's people can trust Him for salvation. (7:7)
  B. God's repentant people can expect better days ahead. (7:8-14)
  C. God's enemies face shameful judgment. (7:15-17)
  D. The incomparable God of patience, mercy, compassion, and faithfulness will forgive and renew His people. (7:18-20)

Theological Conclusions

For Micah, fidelity to God's covenant was fundamental. Idolatry and apostasy were grave evils that had to be resisted if the nation were to survive. The covenant people had to reflect God's own nature in terms of justice, fidelity, mercy, and holiness. Though the community had sinned, a loving God would pardon iniquity on the basis of sincere repentance and would renew the fellowship between Himself and His people. Micah's teachings are in full accord with those of his contemporaries Amos, Hosea, and Isaiah, but his specific doctrinal contribution relates to the promises of the Messiah.

As a teacher of righteousness, Micah saw idolatry, corruption, and injustice had deep roots in the spiritual condition of the nation. He sought to teach them God's requirements, warn them of God's judgment, and assure them of God's promises for the faithful remnant.

God's requirements of His people:

1. God demands that they act with justice towards all because that is characteristic of His dealings with them.

2. Mercy must be a recognizable part of their mental and spiritual attitude. The Hebrew word *chesed* ("mercy," "lovingkindness") is difficult to render adequately in one word, but describes the all-encompassing, altruistic love of God from which every form of divine activity proceeds.

3. Instead of behaving arrogantly and flaunting an improper independence, they must repent of their rebellion against the covenant and do God's will consciously and continuously in humble obedience.

God's judgment of His people:

1. The religious leaders of God's people bear responsibility to help God's people remember what God has done to redeem them and to teach what God expects of them. Leaders who reject their responsibility face God's covenant curses (Dt 28:15-68).

2. Political leaders have no right to exploit the people, treating them as slaves instead of brothers and sisters. God protects and saves the victims of exploitation and injustice and gathers together under His leadership those who are faithful to His commands. Their unjust leaders face destruction.

3. Dedication to social and spiritual evils means any hope of salvation must be preceded by a period

of punishment for sins. Only after the covenant curses for disobedience and infidelity can God's people look for a just God to show His mercy to the penitent sinners.

God's promises for His people:

1. Judgment for disobedience. When God's people are unwilling to repent of their disobedience, God has no alternative to drastic punishment. This fate is unthinkable to persons who imagine that, because of the covenant relationship, God will protect and deliver them no matter how disobedient, idolatrous, and perverted they become.

2. The coming Messiah. In His Word, God tinges even the most severe forebodings of disaster with hope for the future. Salvation and hope are God's major themes. Salvation is achieved by the Messiah, who will institute a time of peace and prosperity when God's people will live in obedience to God's will (4:1-5; 5:4). Micah is the most explicit of all Old Testament prophets in predicting the birthplace of the Messiah some 700 years before the actual event (5:2; compare Mt 2:5-6). Whatever the future might hold for Judah, those who were loyal to the covenant had this marvelous assurance that God was sending His own Deliverer.

3. The coming salvation. The very promise of the Messiah was a guarantee that a loving God would sustain His people through their trials and judgment. Ultimately, He would bring them to true repentance. This done, He would shower His blessings on them. The faithful remnant will be governed by a messianic King who will purge His people from sin and institute peace and justice in the land. Then God's people will become a model for all other people to imitate and would witness to the true nature of the covenant God.

Contemporary Teaching

The world of Micah is curiously like the modern world. The moral perversions of ancient Canaan are being flaunted brazenly, and even given the status of "rights" in some quarters. The faith of the new covenant is all but submerged under secularism, humanism, and the influence of pagan oriental religions.

In an age of unprecedented communication, Christians are still largely ignorant of the contents of Scripture, and especially of the demands of Christ in the new covenant. Because the principles of godly living have not been made explicit, many believers have become conformed to the world and have begun to ignore and even deny the conditions of their salvation. What is even worse is a rampant spirit of antinomianism opposing all religious and ethical regulations. This encourages believers to think that, because they have been "saved," they are above the law. They are tempted to see enactments such as the Ten Commandments and the Sermon on the Mount are for other inferior people to follow. Thus Christians are committing adultery through multiple marriages in sublime indifference to the teachings of the law and the gospel, while maintaining arrogantly that their religious experience places them above such precepts. The chuch must learn the following lessons from this prophetic book: (1) Life under biblical covenants is distinctive. It comprises a relationship in which the believer accepts the overlordship of God and agrees to submit to it in obedience and faith. (2) On this basis a loving God guarantees provision for human needs and His blessing on the believer's life. (3) That life must be lived in submission to the known, revealed will of God, and must be holy, as God is holy (Lev 11:44; 1 Pe 1:16). (4) The privileges of covenantal life are matched by obligations. The believer must witness to God's holiness, mercy, and justice in society, ministering to the oppressed and exploited, and protesting against social injustice. (5) The believer must maintain a distinctive faith that rests on the inspiration and authority of God's Word. The Christian must proclaim the centrality of Jesus as our Messiah, Savior, and Lord and look for His second coming in glory to establish God's kingdom.

Chapter 1

THE word of the LORD that came to Micah of Moresheth[a] during the reigns of Jotham,[b] Ahaz[c] and Hezekiah,[d] kings of Judah[e]—the vision[f] he saw concerning Samaria and Jerusalem.

2Hear,[g] O peoples, all of you,[h]
listen, O earth[i] and all who are in it,
that the Sovereign LORD may witness[j] against you,
the Lord from his holy temple.[k]

Judgment Against Samaria and Jerusalem

3Look! The LORD is coming from his dwelling[l] place;
he comes down[m] and treads the high places of the earth.[n]
4The mountains melt[o] beneath him[p]
and the valleys split apart,[q]
like wax before the fire,
like water rushing down a slope.
5All this is because of Jacob's transgression,
because of the sins of the house of Israel.
What is Jacob's transgression?
Is it not Samaria?[r]
What is Judah's high place?
Is it not Jerusalem?

6"Therefore I will make Samaria a heap of rubble,
a place for planting vineyards.[s]
I will pour her stones[t] into the valley
and lay bare her foundations.[u]
7All her idols[v] will be broken to pieces;[w]
all her temple gifts will be burned with fire;
I will destroy all her images.[x]
Since she gathered her gifts from the wages of prostitutes,[y]
as the wages of prostitutes they will again be used."

Weeping and Mourning

8Because of this I will weep[z] and wail;
I will go about barefoot[a] and naked.
I will howl like a jackal
and moan like an owl.
9For her wound[b] is incurable;[c]
it has come to Judah.[d]
It[a] has reached the very gate[e] of my people,
even to Jerusalem itself.
10Tell it not in Gath[b];
weep not at all.[c]
In Beth Ophrah[d]
roll in the dust.
11Pass on in nakedness[f] and shame,
you who live in Shaphir.[e]
Those who live in Zaanan[f]
will not come out.
Beth Ezel is in mourning;
its protection is taken from you.
12Those who live in Maroth[g] writhe in pain,
waiting for relief,[g]
because disaster[h] has come from the LORD,
even to the gate of Jerusalem.
13You who live in Lachish,[h] [i]
harness the team to the chariot.
You were the beginning of sin
to the Daughter of Zion,[j]
for the transgressions of Israel
were found in you.
14Therefore you will give parting gifts[k]
to Moresheth[l] Gath.
The town of Aczib[i] [m] will prove deceptive[n]
to the kings of Israel.
15I will bring a conqueror against you
who live in Mareshah.[j] [o]
He who is the glory of Israel
will come to Adullam.[p]
16Shave[q] your heads in mourning
for the children in whom you delight;
make yourselves as bald as the vulture,
for they will go from you into exile.[r]

1:1 [a]ver 14; Jer 26:18 [b]S 1Ch 3:12 [c]S 1Ch 3:13 [d]S 1Ch 3:13 [e]Hos 1:1 [f]Isa 1:1
1:2 [g]S Dt 32:1 [h]Ps 50:7 [i]S Jer 6:19 [j]S Ge 31:50; S Dt 4:26; S Isa 1:2 [k]S Ps 11:4
1:3 [l]S Isa 18:4 [m]S Isa 64:1 [n]S Am 4:13
1:4 [o]S Ps 46:2,6 [p]S Job 9:5 [q]S Nu 16:31; Na 1:5
1:5 [r]Am 8:14
1:6 [s]S Dt 20:6 [t]S Am 5:11 [u]Eze 13:14
1:7 [v]S Eze 6:6 [w]S Ex 32:20 [x]S Dt 9:21 [y]Dt 23:17-18
1:8 [z]S Isa 15:3 [a]S Isa 20:2
1:9 [b]Jer 46:11 [c]S Jer 10:19 [d]S 2Ki 18:13 [e]Isa 3:26
1:11 [f]Eze 23:29
1:12 [g]Jer 14:19 [h]Jer 40:2
1:13 [i]S Jos 10:3 [j]S Ps 9:14
1:14 [k]2Ki 16:8 [l]S ver 1 [m]S Jos 15:44 [n]Jer 15:18
1:15 [o]Jos 15:44 [p]S Jos 12:15
1:16 [q]S Lev 13:40; S Job 1:20 [r]S Dt 4:27; S Am 5:27

[a]9 Or *He* [b]10 *Gath* sounds like the Hebrew for *tell.* [c]10 Hebrew; Septuagint may suggest *not in Acco.* The Hebrew for *in Acco* sounds like the Hebrew for *weep.* [d]10 *Beth Ophrah* means *house of dust.* [e]11 *Shaphir* means *pleasant.* [f]11 *Zaanan* sounds like the Hebrew for *come out.* [g]12 *Maroth* sounds like the Hebrew for *bitter.* [h]13 *Lachish* sounds like the Hebrew for *team.* [i]14 *Aczib* means *deception.* [j]15 *Mareshah* sounds like the Hebrew for *conqueror.*

1:1–3 REVELATION, Messengers—The prophet represented God during reigns of three kings. The brief book thus probably contains only a fraction of the prophet's preaching. Choosing the part of a prophet's sermons to be preserved in Scripture was a part of revelation and inspiration. Compare the very brief ministry and preserved material from Obadiah. God came to judge His people from His earthly and heavenly Temple. His coming was revealed by reactions in the created order. Compare Dt 33; Ps 68; Hab 3. Micah's message was revealed in a vision. See note on Ob 1. Each confrontation by a messenger was designed by God not to solicit terror from His people but to create fear (respect for a God of standards) and action toward repentance and reconciliation with God.

1:2 PROCLAMATION, Authoritative—See note on Jer 19:14–15. The prophet's word was God's witness against a rebellious world.

1:3–16 GOD, Wrath—The wrath of God is His reaction to sin and unfaithfulness in His people. God can use enemy conquerors without their knowledge to execute His wrath. See note on Am 4:1–13.

1:5 SIN, Against God—In the capital city God's house may become the king's house. To turn worship into a political activity is sin.

1:7 GOD, One God—See note on Hos 2:2–23.

Chapter 2

Man's Plans and God's

WOE to those who plan iniquity,
to those who plot evil[s] on their beds![t]
At morning's light they carry it out
because it is in their power to do it.
2 They covet fields[u] and seize them,[v]
and houses, and take them.
They defraud[w] a man of his home,
a fellowman of his inheritance.[x]
3 Therefore, the LORD says:

"I am planning disaster[y] against this people,
from which you cannot save yourselves.
You will no longer walk proudly,[z]
for it will be a time of calamity.
4 In that day men will ridicule you;
they will taunt you with this mournful song:
'We are utterly ruined;[a]
my people's possession is divided up.[b]
He takes it from me!
He assigns our fields to traitors.' "
5 Therefore you will have no one in the assembly of the LORD
to divide the land[c] by lot.[d]

False Prophets

6 "Do not prophesy," their prophets say.
"Do not prophesy about these things;
disgrace[e] will not overtake us.[f] "
7 Should it be said, O house of Jacob:

2:1 [s]S Isa 29:20 [t]Ps 36:4
2:2 [u]Isa 5:8 [v]S Pr 30:14 [w]S Jer 22:17 [x]S 1Sa 8:14; S Isa 1:23; S Eze 46:18
2:3 [y]Jer 18:11; S Am 3:1-2 [z]Isa 2:12
2:4 [a]S Lev 26:31; S Jer 4:13 [b]S Jer 6:12
2:5 [c]Dt 32:13; Jos 18:4 [d]S Nu 34:13
2:6 [e]Ps 44:13; Jer 18:16; 19:8; 25:18; 29:18; Mic 6:16 [f]S Am 2:12
2:7 [g]S Ps 119:65 [h]Ps 15:2; 84:11
2:9 [i]Jer 10:20
2:10 [j]S Dt 12:9 [k]Lev 18:25-29; Ps 106:38-39; S La 4:15
2:11 [l]S 2Ch 36:16; Jer 5:31 [m]S Lev 10:9 [n]Isa 30:10
2:12 [o]Mic 4:7; 5:7; 7:18 [p]S Ne 1:9
2:13 [q]S Isa 52:12 [r]S Isa 60:11

"Is the Spirit of the LORD angry?
Does he do such things?"
"Do not my words do good[g]
to him whose ways are upright?[h]
8 Lately my people have risen up
like an enemy.
You strip off the rich robe
from those who pass by without a care,
like men returning from battle.
9 You drive the women of my people
from their pleasant homes.[i]
You take away my blessing
from their children forever.
10 Get up, go away!
For this is not your resting place,[j]
because it is defiled,[k]
it is ruined, beyond all remedy.
11 If a liar and deceiver[l] comes and says,
'I will prophesy for you plenty of wine and beer,'[m]
he would be just the prophet for this people![n]

Deliverance Promised

12 "I will surely gather all of you,
O Jacob;
I will surely bring together the remnant[o] of Israel.
I will bring them together like sheep in a pen,
like a flock in its pasture;
the place will throng with people.[p]
13 One who breaks open the way will go up before[q] them;
they will break through the gate[r] and go out.
Their king will pass through before them,
the LORD at their head."

2:1–5 GOD, Wrath—Injustice and oppression bring God's wrath against His people. See note on 1:3–16.

2:1–5 EVIL AND SUFFERING, Punishment—The rich often seem to escape suffering. No matter how evil their deeds, as they pile up wealth they seem to escape all judgment and punishment. They cannot, however, buy their way out of God's judgment. Often powerful leaders think they are necessary to carry on God's work. Israel's leaders ignored God's just plan of dividing the land among the tribes (Jos 13:1—19:5). Instead, they plotted evil ways to secure as much land as possible for themselves. No person is indispensable to God's work. He will punish the wicked.

2:1–2,8–9 SIN, Moral Insensitivity—When sin so dominates a person that every hour is filled with evil scheming against helpless people, moral values have disappeared. The person has no more moral character. This condition does not excuse a person. It prevents repentance and invites God's judgment. See note on Am 8:4–6.

2:1–7 CHRISTIAN ETHICS, Justice—Dreams become reality. A society which concentrates its dreams on personal economic matters instead of on the good of the community faces a future of nightmares. The family farm is a vital heritage which society abandons at its own risk. God pronounces the funeral woe on such societies.

2:6–7 REVELATION, Word—God's word is designed to help His people, but too often we prefer the word of the false prophet. God is angry because He cares for His believers and for His people, whose actions He hopes can be superior to the behavior they have settled for. God sends His prophets so people may live the abundant, right quality of life.

2:8–9 HUMANITY, Community Relationships—Communities exist because people trust one another to help and not hurt each other. If people take advantage of one another, they have denied their responsibilities, destroyed the community, and become enemies.

2:12–13 GOD, Savior—Amid pronouncements of wrath, God promised to gather His people as the Good Shepherd and lead His faithful remnant to salvation. Salvation is God's desire for us. He plans for it even as He expresses His wrath.

2:12–13 REVELATION, Actions—The One who creates is always leading the way to redemption and deliverance. God promised to gather up those who were left, guide them with the care of a shepherd, and lead them into freedom and new hope.

2:12 THE CHURCH, Remnant—God's blessings continually flow toward His people. In the most difficult circumstances, God cares for His people and delivers them from bondage. He refuses to let human sin thwart His purpose of gathering a covenant people.

Chapter 3

Leaders and Prophets Rebuked

THEN I said,
"Listen, you leaders[s] of Jacob,
you rulers of the house of Israel.
Should you not know justice,
2 you who hate good and love evil;
who tear the skin from my people
and the flesh from their bones;[t]
3who eat my people's flesh,[u]
strip off their skin
and break their bones in pieces;[v]
who chop[w] them up like meat for the pan,
like flesh for the pot?[x]"
4Then they will cry out to the LORD,
but he will not answer them.[y]
At that time he will hide his face[z]
from them
because of the evil they have done.[a]

5This is what the LORD says:

"As for the prophets
who lead my people astray,[b]
if one feeds them,
they proclaim 'peace';[c]
if he does not,
they prepare to wage war against him.
6Therefore night will come over you,
without visions,
and darkness, without divination.[d]
The sun will set for the prophets,[e]
and the day will go dark for them.[f]
7The seers will be ashamed[g]
and the diviners disgraced.[h]
They will all cover[i] their faces[j]
because there is no answer from God.[k]"
8But as for me, I am filled with power,
with the Spirit of the LORD,
and with justice and might,
to declare to Jacob his transgression,
to Israel his sin.[l]
9Hear this, you leaders of the house of Jacob,
you rulers of the house of Israel,
who despise justice
and distort all that is right;[m]
10who build[n] Zion with bloodshed,[o]
and Jerusalem with wickedness.[p]
11Her leaders judge for a bribe,[q]
her priests teach for a price,[r]
and her prophets tell fortunes for money.[s]
Yet they lean[t] upon the LORD and say,
"Is not the LORD among us?
No disaster will come upon us."[u]
12Therefore because of you,
Zion will be plowed like a field,

3:1 [s]S Jer 5:5
3:2 [t]Ps 53:4; S Eze 22:27
3:3 [u]S Ps 14:4 [v]S Eze 34:4; Zep 3:3 [w]S Job 24:14 [x]S Eze 11:7; S 24:4-5
3:4 [y]S Dt 1:45; S 1Sa 8:18; S Isa 58:4; S Jer 11:11 [z]S Dt 31:17 [a]S Job 15:31; S Eze 8:18
3:5 [b]S Isa 3:12; S 9:16; S 53:6 [c]S Jer 4:10
3:6 [d]Isa 8:19-22; S Eze 12:24 [e]Isa 29:10 [f]S Eze 7:26; S Am 8:11
3:7 [g]S Jer 6:15; Mic 7:16 [h]S Isa 44:25 [i]S Est 6:12 [j]S Lev 13:45 [k]S Eze 20:3
3:8 [l]S Isa 57:12; 61:2
3:9 [m]Ps 58:1-2; S Isa 1:23
3:10 [n]S Jer 22:13 [o]Isa 59:7; Mic 7:2; Na 3:1; Hab 2:12 [p]Jer 22:17; S Eze 22:27
3:11 [q]S Ex 23:8; S Lev 19:15; Mal 2:9 [r]S Eze 13:19 [s]Isa 1:23; S 56:11; Jer 6:13; S La 4:13; S Hos 4:8,18 [t]S Isa 10:20 [u]Jer 7:4; S Eze 34:2

3:1–3 HUMANITY, Community Relationships—Denial of relationship or responsibility between members of a community turns people into little more than emotional, intellectual, or spiritual cannibals.

3:1–4 SIN, Unrighteousness—A community is seldom righteous when its leaders are unrighteous. The political heads of the Northern Kingdom were trained in Israel's legal tradition. They knew a just God demanded justice from His people, especially for the unprotected poor and needy (Dt 24:10–22). In Eden, the first humans sought to control their own destiny by knowing good and evil (Ge 3:5). Amos had to call Israel to seek good and not evil (Am 5:14). Micah found Israel openly hated the good. Why? They could not get wealthy enough doing good, they thought. They did not want to share the wealth with the poor. They mistreated the poor every way possible to pad their own pockets. Such would not last. God would hide His face and bring the covenant curses on them. An unrighteous people cannot talk to God or expect to receive His blessings.

3:1–12 CHRISTIAN ETHICS, Justice—Leaders from all areas of life can let greed destroy their value systems. Devotion to evil and disregard for the value of persons mark the end of justice and hope for a nation. God supplied justice and power to His faithful, courageous speaker to call society to renewal. Religious words alone do not bring God's protection for a selfish society. See notes on Ps 72:1–14; Zec 7:8–10.

3:4 GOD, Presence—Sin shuts us off from God's presence. Withdrawing His presence is one way God shows His wrath.

3:4 PRAYER, Sovereignty of God—Sins can carry a nation beyond the reach of prayer. See note on Jer 7:16.

3:5–7 REVELATION, Messengers—Those who purposefully misdirect God's people will be cut off and disgraced in their behavior. God is silent to those who speak for their own gain and not His will. See note on 2:6–7.

3:5–6 PROCLAMATION, Fearless—Prophets had to preach against the false preaching of other popular prophets. See note on Jer 19:14–15.

3:8 HOLY SPIRIT, Revelation—The Spirit makes preaching possible. Micah emphasized more forcefully than most writing prophets that the Spirit gave him the prophetic gift. The gift of prophecy included both the content of the message (justice) and the power and courage to deliver the message effectively. Prophecy, therefore, included both medium and message. The Spirit continues to lead people to recognize and confess sin. Sadly, false preachers, not led by the Spirit, continue to please people rather than listen to God (vv 5–7).

3:8–11 SIN, Unrighteousness—The prophet had a job in facing the people's sin. He had to teach a morally inept people they were sinners facing God's judgment. The people did not listen. They had prophets they could pay to preach what they wanted to hear. Deaf ears and bribes could not avoid God's judgment. When people in charge of creating justice despise it, a nation has no future. Prayer and worship do not secure the future for a greedy, unrighteous people. A people cannot say with confidence, "No disaster will come upon us." God is sovereign and determines the future. We do not.

3:8 HOLY SCRIPTURE, Inspired—The honest spokesman felt God's inbreathing presence and spoke for Him. God's Spirit led the prophet to demand justice in the people's lives, to confront the people with their sin, and to demonstrate God's power to eliminate His people's wrong.

3:8 PROCLAMATION, Anointing—See note on Isa 61:1–3.

3:11–12 EVIL AND SUFFERING, Punishment—Some sinners assume they will escape destruction by religious acts and pious language. Religious professionals are especially apt to excuse their misdeeds. Apparently they think religious leadership justifies certain actions which would be improper for anyone else. God promises punishment for all wickedness, even that done in the name of religion.

3:11 EDUCATION, Priests—In every generation, some teachers of religion have been guilty of commercializing their services, thus becoming pawns of the rich rather than servants of the Word of God.

Jerusalem will become a heap of
rubble,[v]
the temple[w] hill a mound
overgrown with thickets.[x]

Chapter 4

The Mountain of the LORD

4:1–3pp — Isa 2:1–4

IN the last days
the mountain[y] of the LORD's temple
will be established
as chief among the mountains;
it will be raised above the hills,[z]
and peoples will stream to it.[a]

2Many nations will come and say,

"Come, let us go up to the mountain
of the LORD,[b]
to the house of the God of Jacob.[c]
He will teach us[d] his ways,[e]
so that we may walk in his paths."
The law[f] will go out from Zion,
the word of the LORD from
Jerusalem.
3He will judge between many peoples
and will settle disputes for strong
nations far and wide.[g]
They will beat their swords into
plowshares
and their spears into pruning
hooks.[h]
Nation will not take up sword against
nation,
nor will they train for war[i]
anymore.[j]
4Every man will sit under his own vine
and under his own fig tree,[k]
and no one will make them afraid,[l]
for the LORD Almighty has spoken.[m]
5All the nations may walk
in the name of their gods;[n]
we will walk in the name of the LORD
our God for ever and ever.[o]

The LORD*'s Plan*

6"In that day," declares the LORD,

"I will gather the lame;[p]
I will assemble the exiles[q]
and those I have brought to grief.[r]
7I will make the lame a remnant,[s]
those driven away a strong nation.[t]
The LORD will rule over them in
Mount Zion[u]
from that day and forever.[v]
8As for you, O watchtower of the flock,
O stronghold[k] of the Daughter of
Zion,
the former dominion will be restored[w]
to you;
kingship will come to the Daughter
of Jerusalem.[x]"

9Why do you now cry aloud—
have you no king?[y]
Has your counselor perished,
that pain seizes you like that of a
woman in labor?[z]
10Writhe in agony, O Daughter of Zion,
like a woman in labor,
for now you must leave the city
to camp in the open field.
You will go to Babylon;[a]
there you will be rescued.
There the LORD will redeem[b] you

3:12 [v]S 2Ki 25:9; S Isa 6:11 [w]S Jer 52:13 [x]S Lev 26:31; S Jer 17:3; S 22:6; S La 5:18; S Eze 5:14
4:1 [y]S Ps 48:1; Zec 8:3 [z]S Eze 17:22 [a]S Ps 22:27; 86:9; S Jer 3:17; S 31:12; S Da 2:35
4:2 [b]S Jer 31:6; S Eze 20:40 [c]Zec 2:11; 14:16 [d]S Ps 119:171 [e]Ps 25:8-9; S Isa 54:13 [f]S Dt 18:18
4:3 [g]S Isa 11:4 [h]Joel 3:10; Zec 9:10 [i]S Ps 46:9 [j]Zec 8:20-22
4:4 [k]S 1Ki 4:25 [l]S Lev 26:6; S Eze 39:26 [m]S Isa 1:20
4:5 [n]2Ki 17:29; Ac 14:16 [o]Jos 24:14-15; Isa 26:8; Zec 10:12
4:6 [p]S Jer 31:8 [q]S Ps 106:47 [r]S Eze 34:13,16; S 37:21; Zep 3:19
4:7 [s]S Joel 2:32; S Mic 2:12 [t]S Ge 12:2 [u]S Isa 2:2 [v]S Da 2:44; S 7:14; S Lk 1:33; Rev 11:15
4:8 [w]S Isa 1:26 [x]Zec 9:9
4:9 [y]Jer 8:19 [z]S Ge 3:16; Jer 30:6; 48:41
4:10 [a]S Dt 21:10; 2Ki 20:18; Isa 43:14 [b]S Isa 48:20

[k]8 Or *hill*

4:1–8 JESUS CHRIST, Foretold—Micah joined Isaiah (2:1–4) in picturing God's kingdom of peace, contentment, and trust. The Messiah is the only One who can establish such a kingdom. See Isa 7; 9; 40; 49; 60; 65; Mic 5; Zec 10.

4:1–2 HOLY SCRIPTURE, Collection—Micah revealed the ultimate end God has for all His people: everyone will gather under the leadership of the only true God. The people will want to know God's will and way. They will seek to live it with one another. Both law and prophetic word will be available to reveal God to all people. The oracle here also appears in Isa 2:1–4. The two prophets must have been associated with one another and preached the same inspired message. Each added a different ending to reflect a specific emphasis. See note on 2 Sa 22:1–51.

4:1–5 ELECTION, Other Nations—Micah went about barefooted and naked, mourning and wailing like an owl and jackal because of the incurable wounds and sin sickness of Judah. He was hurt over the exploitation and immorality of the priests and prophets. He had a noble vision when nations would not take up the sword against each other. The law of God would go out from Zion. All nations would come to the mountain of the Lord to learn about Him. Israel's election purpose of pointing the nations to God would be realized.

4:1–5 CHRISTIAN ETHICS, War and Peace—Micah joined Isaiah (2:1–4) to provide a provocative picture of God's promised kingdom. Peace, not conflict, will be the rule of that time. Peace will attract the nations of the world to worship the one true God. God's teaching will be the basis of peace and of settling international disputes. Weapons of war will become unnecessary, for war will vanish from the earth. Security at home and faithfulness to God will be the order of the day. God calls His people to share and work toward His vision of peace.

4:2 EDUCATION, God—Education is a part of the prophetic vision of a glorious Messianic Age. God Himself will teach His ways to the people who come streaming to acknowledge His sovereignty. The purpose of this divine instruction will go beyond intellectual understanding; those who learn from the Lord will "walk in his paths." See note on Isa 2:3.

4:2 EVANGELISM, Teaching—The gospel, although in many respects simple, is still most profound and needs to be carefully taught. Faithful teaching explains all the various elements and implications of the message of salvation. We need to pray God will "teach us his ways" that we may "walk in his paths." Teaching evangelism is as important as preaching evangelism. See note on Isa 2:3.

4:5,13 GOD, One God—When God establishes His messianic kingdom, His people will ignore all practices of their neighbors to worship and serve the only true God. See note on Hos 2:2–23.

4:6–7 THE CHURCH, Remnant—See note on 2:12; Isa 4:2–6.

4:7–8 GOD, Sovereignty—As sovereign Lord, God works to establish His kingdom so He can rule His people according to His purposes. See note on Eze 1:25–28.

4:10 SALVATION, As Deliverance—The suffering of God's people has a redemptive intent. His deliverance takes place in real places and in historical events.

out of the hand of your enemies.

[11]But now many nations
are gathered against you.
They say, "Let her be defiled,
let our eyes gloat[c] over Zion!"
[12]But they do not know
the thoughts of the LORD;
they do not understand his plan,[d]
he who gathers them like sheaves to
the threshing floor.
[13]"Rise and thresh,[e] O Daughter of
Zion,
for I will give you horns of iron;
I will give you hoofs of bronze
and you will break to pieces many
nations."[f]
You will devote their ill-gotten gains to
the LORD,[g]
their wealth to the Lord of all the
earth.

Chapter 5

A Promised Ruler From Bethlehem

MARSHAL your troops, O city of
troops,[1]
for a siege is laid against us.
They will strike Israel's ruler
on the cheek[h] with a rod.
[2]"But you, Bethlehem[i] Ephrathah,[j]
though you are small among the
clans[m] of Judah,
out of you will come for me
one who will be ruler[k] over Israel,
whose origins[n] are from of old,[l]
from ancient times.[o]"[m]
[3]Therefore Israel will be abandoned[n]
until the time when she who is in
labor gives birth
and the rest of his brothers return
to join the Israelites.
[4]He will stand and shepherd his flock[o]
in the strength of the LORD,
in the majesty of the name of the
LORD his God.
And they will live securely, for then
his greatness[p]

4:11 [c]S La 2:16; S Ob 1:12; Mic 7:8
4:12 [d]S Ge 50:20; S Isa 55:8; Ro 11:33-34
4:13 [e]S Isa 21:10 [f]S Isa 45:1; S Da 2:44 [g]S Isa 23:18
5:1 [h]La 3:30
5:2 [i]S Jn 7:42 [j]S Ge 35:16; S 48:7 [k]S Nu 24:19; S 1Sa 13:14; S 2Sa 6:21; S 2Ch 7:18 [l]Ps 102:25 [m]Mt 2:6*
5:3 [n]S Jer 7:29
5:4 [o]Isa 40:11; 49:9; S Eze 34:11-15,23; Mic 7:14 [p]Isa 52:13; Lk 1:32
5:5 [q]S Isa 9:6; S Lk 2:14; Col 1:19-20 [r]Isa 8:7 [s]Isa 10:24-27
5:6 [t]Ge 10:8 [u]Zep 2:13 [v]Na 2:11-13
5:7 [w]S Am 5:15; S Mic 2:12 [x]S Ps 133:3 [y]Isa 44:4
5:8 [z]S Ge 49:9 [a]Mic 4:13; Zec 10:5 [b]S Ps 50:22; S Isa 5:29; S Hos 5:14
5:9 [c]S Ps 10:12
5:10 [d]Ex 15:4,19; S Hos 14:3; Hag 2:22; Zec 9:10
5:11 [e]S Dt 29:23; Isa 6:11 [f]S La 2:2; S Hos 10:14; Am 5:9
5:12 [g]Dt 18:10-12; Isa 2:6; 8:19
5:13 [h]Na 1:14 [i]Hos 10:2

will reach to the ends of the earth.
5 And he will be their peace.[q]

Deliverance and Destruction

When the Assyrian invades[r] our land
and marches through our fortresses,
we will raise against him seven
shepherds,
even eight leaders of men.[s]
[6]They will rule[p] the land of Assyria
with the sword,
the land of Nimrod[t] with drawn
sword.[q] [u]
He will deliver us from the Assyrian
when he invades our land
and marches into our borders.[v]
[7]The remnant[w] of Jacob will be
in the midst of many peoples
like dew[x] from the LORD,
like showers on the grass,[y]
which do not wait for man
or linger for mankind.
[8]The remnant of Jacob will be among
the nations,
in the midst of many peoples,
like a lion among the beasts of the
forest,[z]
like a young lion among flocks of
sheep,
which mauls and mangles[a] as it goes,
and no one can rescue.[b]
[9]Your hand will be lifted up[c] in
triumph over your enemies,
and all your foes will be destroyed.

[10]"In that day," declares the LORD,

"I will destroy your horses from among
you
and demolish your chariots.[d]
[11]I will destroy the cities[e] of your land
and tear down all your strongholds.[f]
[12]I will destroy your witchcraft
and you will no longer cast spells.[g]
[13]I will destroy your carved images[h]
and your sacred stones from among
you;[i]

[1]1 Or *Strengthen your walls, O walled city* [m]2 Or *rulers* [n]2 Hebrew *goings out* [o]2 Or *from days of eternity* [p]6 Or *crush* [q]6 Or *Nimrod in its gates*

4:11–12 HUMANITY, Intellectual Nature—Humans make great plans and expect to accomplish them. We forget human intellect is always limited. We will never be wise enough to understand totally the will and purposes of God. Through His revelation we can determine His will for our individual lives and the contribution we can make to the accomplishment of His universal purpose.

5:1–5 JESUS CHRIST, Foretold—The prophet led Israel to expect David's line would be restored in Bethlehem, the city of David's birth. What was unexpected was the humble circumstances of the birth. Royalty birthed in a stable, placed in a manger, born to poverty-stricken parents? Highly unlikely! Yet it happened (Mt 1; Lk 2). Shepherds praised; Mary marveled; the Magi wondered; God provided. We need to learn that God comes in unexpected places, ways, and events.

5:2–5 CHRISTIAN ETHICS, War and Peace—The Messiah is God's key to peace. He will come to establish the Kingdom. Not only will He speak the words of peace, but He will incarnate the way of peace. He is the Good Shepherd who will provide security for His people.

5:7–8 THE CHURCH, Remnant—God's remnant is not forsaken even when they must live far from home. He plans to use His remnant to accomplish His purposes throughout His world. Victory is His final word for His people. See note on Isa 4:2–6.

5:12–15 GOD, One God—God's people refused to learn that God has no rivals. Thus they repeatedly suffered God's wrath. God works in His wrath to destroy all idols and foolish religious practices so His people will recognize Him as the only God.

you will no longer bow down
to the work of your hands.[j]
14I will uproot from among you your
Asherah poles[r] [k]
and demolish your cities.
15I will take vengeance[l] in anger and
wrath
upon the nations that have not
obeyed me."

Chapter 6

The LORD's Case Against Israel

LISTEN to what the LORD says:
"Stand up, plead your case before
the mountains;[m]
let the hills hear what you have to
say.
2Hear,[n] O mountains, the LORD's
accusation;[o]
listen, you everlasting foundations of
the earth.
For the LORD has a case[p] against his
people;
he is lodging a charge[q] against
Israel.
3"My people, what have I done to you?
How have I burdened[r] you?[s]
Answer me.
4I brought you up out of Egypt[t]
and redeemed you from the land of
slavery.[u]
I sent Moses[v] to lead you,
also Aaron[w] and Miriam.[x]
5My people, remember
what Balak[y] king of Moab counseled
and what Balaam son of Beor
answered.
Remember [your journey] from
Shittim[z] to Gilgal,[a]
that you may know the righteous
acts[b] of the LORD."
6With what shall I come before[c] the
LORD
and bow down before the exalted
God?
Shall I come before him with burnt
offerings,
with calves a year old?[d]
7Will the LORD be pleased with
thousands of rams,[e]
with ten thousand rivers of oil?[f]
Shall I offer my firstborn[g] for my
transgression,
the fruit of my body for the sin of
my soul?[h]
8He has showed you, O man, what is
good.
And what does the LORD require of
you?
To act justly[i] and to love mercy
and to walk humbly[j] with your
God.[k]

Israel's Guilt and Punishment

9Listen! The LORD is calling to the
city—
and to fear your name is wisdom—
"Heed the rod[l] and the One who
appointed it.[s]
10Am I still to forget, O wicked house,
your ill-gotten treasures
and the short ephah,[t] which is
accursed?[m]

[r] *14* That is, symbols of the goddess Asherah [s] *9* The meaning of the Hebrew for this line is uncertain. [t] *10* An ephah was a dry measure.

5:13 [j]S Isa 2:18; S Eze 6:9; Zec 13:2
5:14 [k]S Ex 34:13; S Jdg 3:7; S 2Ki 17:10
5:15 [l]S Isa 65:12
6:1 [m]S Ps 50:1; S Eze 6:2
6:2 [n]Dt 32:1 [o]S Hos 12:2 [p]S Isa 3:13 [q]Ps 50:7; S Jer 2:9
6:3 [r]Jer 2:5 [s]Jer 2:5
6:4 [t]S Ex 3:10; S 6:6 [u]Dt 7:8 [v]S Ex 4:16 [w]S Nu 33:1; Ps 77:20 [x]S Ex 15:20
6:5 [y]S Nu 22:2 [z]S Nu 25:1 [a]S Dt 11:30; Jos 5:9-10 [b]Jdg 5:11; 1Sa 12:7
6:6 [c]S Ps 95:2 [d]Ps 40:6-8; 51:16-17
6:7 [e]S Isa 1:11; S 40:16 [f]Ps 50:8-10 [g]S Lev 18:21; S 2Ki 3:27 [h]Hos 5:6; S Am 5:22
6:8 [i]S Isa 1:17; S Jer 22:3 [j]S 2Ki 22:19; S Isa 57:15 [k]S Ge 5:22; Dt 10:12-13; 1Sa 15:22; Hos 6:6; Zec 7:9-10; Mt 9:13; 23:23; Mk 12:33; Lk 11:42
6:9 [l]S Ge 17:1; Isa 11:4
6:10 [m]Eze 45:9-10; S Am 3:10; 8:4-6

6:1–16 GOD, Judge—As the just Judge, God brings charges against His people. He demonstrates that in His righteous acts of salvation He has done all He could for them. He shows His just expectations of His people, points out their sins, and pronounces judgment upon them. Every generation must approach the bench to face the holy Judge.

6:3–5 HISTORY, Confession—Israel's worship was supposed to center on confession of God's historical acts. Too often it centered on complaint about God's lack of action. God called Israel to remember what He had done and know He would continue to be their Redeemer. Correctly seen, history justifies God. It does not condemn God. It calls to praise and confession not complaint and self-pity.

6:6–8 DISCIPLESHIP, Involvement—People do many things to try to please God. Micah raised the question of priority for all who desire God's acceptance. God gave a clear answer. Pleasing Him requires a person to be rightly related to others. Nothing we bring to Him will be acceptable apart from a life characterized by properly motivated justice in relation to others. Our actions must result in justice for all people, not special privilege for a few. Our hearts must love mercy rather than demand justice for self. Every act must come from a relationship to God, making Him Lord and us His humble servants. God requires this of every person. The people of God are to be loving and merciful in all of their relationships. In this way others will recognize the people of God. See notes on Jn 13:34–35; 1 Jn 3:17–18.

6:6–8 CHRISTIAN ETHICS, Justice—Society must be built on God's requirements rather than on human ambitions. See notes on Hos 2:19–20; Am 5:7–24.

6:6–8 STEWARDSHIP, Giving in Worship—Even those gifts that comply with the letter of the law may not please God, for their value cannot be separated from the life of the giver. Giving or offering sacrifices never substitutes for being a godly person who shows mercy to others and a personal commitment to God. See notes on Am 5:21–24; Mt 5:23–24; 23:23–24.

6:6–8 WORSHIP, Service—Outward service is an act of worship. See note on Dt 11:13.

6:7–8 SALVATION, Atonement—Compare Isa 1:10–17. Micah saw that it took more to please God than farm, barn, orchard, or human sacrifices. More than externals, God wants persons to have fellowship with Him and with one another. We see here the futility of ritualistic worship which thinks divine favor can be obtained by offering sacrifices to God. Spiritual change and moral transformation mark the atonement of God's people.

6:9–13 SIN, Judgment—Sin is not limited to church matters. God pays attention to our business practices. Cheating our customers is sin. Forgetting truth and honesty to get rich never pays in the long run. God intervenes to judge business sin. Missing God's mark in our business life brings ultimate destruction.

[11]Shall I acquit a man with dishonest
scales,[n]
with a bag of false weights?[o]
[12]Her rich men are violent;[p]
her people are liars[q]
and their tongues speak deceitfully.[r]
[13]Therefore, I have begun to destroy[s]
you,
to ruin you because of your sins.
[14]You will eat but not be satisfied;[t]
your stomach will still be empty.[u]
You will store up but save nothing,[u]
because what you save I will give to
the sword.
[15]You will plant but not harvest;[v]
you will press olives but not use the
oil on yourselves,
you will crush grapes but not drink
the wine.[w]
[16]You have observed the statutes of
Omri[x]
and all the practices of Ahab's[y]
house,
and you have followed their
traditions.[z]
Therefore I will give you over to ruin[a]
and your people to derision;
you will bear the scorn[b] of the
nations.[v]"

Chapter 7

Israel's Misery

WHAT misery is mine!
I am like one who gathers summer
fruit
at the gleaning of the vineyard;
there is no cluster of grapes to eat,
none of the early figs[c] that I crave.
[2]The godly have been swept from the
land;[d]
not one[e] upright man remains.
All men lie in wait[f] to shed blood;[g]
each hunts his brother[h] with a
net.[i]
[3]Both hands are skilled in doing evil;[j]
the ruler demands gifts,
the judge accepts bribes,[k]

6:11 [n]S Lev 19:36 [o]S Dt 25:13
6:12 [p]S Isa 1:23 [q]S Ps 116:11; Isa 3:8 [r]S Ps 35:20; S Jer 9:3
6:13 [s]Isa 1:7; 6:11
6:14 [t]S Isa 9:20; S Hos 4:10 [u]Isa 30:6
6:15 [v]S Dt 28:38; Jer 12:13 [w]Job 24:11; S Am 5:11; Zep 1:13
6:16 [x]S 1Ki 16:25 [y]1Ki 16:29-33 [z]Jer 7:24 [a]S Jer 25:9 [b]S Dt 28:37; S Jer 51:51; S Mic 2:6
7:1 [c]S SS 2:13
7:2 [d]S Ps 12:1 [e]S Jer 2:29; 8:6 [f]Ps 10:8 [g]S Pr 6:17; S Mic 3:10 [h]S Isa 3:5 [i]S Jer 5:26
7:3 [j]S Pr 4:16 [k]S Ex 23:8; S Eze 22:12
7:4 [l]S Nu 33:55; S Eze 2:6 [m]S 2Sa 23:6 [n]S Job 31:14; Isa 22:5; S Hos 9:7
7:5 [o]Jer 9:4
7:6 [p]S Eze 22:7 [q]Mt 10:35-36*; S Mk 13:12
7:7 [r]S Isa 21:8 [s]Ps 130:5; Isa 25:9 [t]S Ps 4:3
7:8 [u]S Ps 22:17; S Pr 24:17; S Mic 4:11 [v]Ps 20:8; 37:24; S Am 9:11 [w]S 2Sa 22:29; Isa 9:2
7:9 [x]La 3:39-40 [y]S Ps 119:154 [z]S Ps 107:10 [a]Isa 46:13
7:10 [b]S Ps 35:26 [c]S Ps 42:3 [d]S Isa 51:23 [e]S 2Sa 22:43; S Job 40:12; S Isa 5:5; Zec 10:5

the powerful dictate what they
desire—
they all conspire together.
[4]The best of them is like a brier,[l]
the most upright worse than a
thorn[m] hedge.
The day of your watchmen has come,
the day God visits you.
Now is the time of their confusion.[n]
[5]Do not trust a neighbor;
put no confidence in a friend.[o]
Even with her who lies in your
embrace
be careful of your words.
[6]For a son dishonors his father,
a daughter rises up against her
mother,[p]
a daughter-in-law against her
mother-in-law—
a man's enemies are the members of
his own household.[q]
[7]But as for me, I watch[r] in hope[s] for
the LORD,
I wait for God my Savior;
my God will hear[t] me.

Israel Will Rise

[8]Do not gloat over me,[u] my enemy!
Though I have fallen, I will rise.[v]
Though I sit in darkness,
the LORD will be my light.[w]
[9]Because I have sinned against him,
I will bear the LORD's wrath,[x]
until he pleads my case[y]
and establishes my right.
He will bring me out into the light;[z]
I will see his righteousness.[a]
[10]Then my enemy will see it
and will be covered with shame,[b]
she who said to me,
"Where is the LORD your God?"[c]
My eyes will see her downfall;[d]
even now she will be trampled[e]
underfoot
like mire in the streets.

[u]*14* The meaning of the Hebrew for this word is uncertain. [v]*16* Septuagint; Hebrew *scorn due my people*

7:1–7 CHRISTIAN ETHICS, Character—Micah related the hopelessness of the human condition around him. Despair, frustration, and futility typified the reactions of some, but Hosea hoped in God's sovereign justice. Such hope is a shaper of character and conduct. This hope in God can inspire such hope in others. See note on Eze 9:3–11.
7:5–6 HUMANITY, Relationships—People ought to be able to trust one another. The closer the relationship between people, the greater should be the degree of trust. Human sinfulness leads even those closest in relationship to betray trust. Such betrayal leaves us able only to trust in God. He never betrays us.
7:5–6 FAMILY, Conflict—Micah described family conflict during the troubled times of God's judgment on Israel's sinfulness. Family members could not trust each other. Self-preservation became more important than family commitment. Micah highlighted the consequences of sin to celebrate the renewal to come when the people would return to their faith in God. Sin, distrust, and self-centeredness lie at the center of family conflict. Families cannot function without deep communication and trust.
7:7 GOD, Savior—Amidst total moral collapse, God's faithful have only one hope. The one true God is the Savior, who hears our cries for help. See note on Jer 50:34.
7:7 PRAYER, Mercy of God—A stricken nation returns to her only hope, God Himself. In times of moral confusion and rebellion, the faithful can still turn to God in hope.
7:9 SALVATION, Confession—Repentance and confession of sin do not guarantee immediate escape from trouble. God removes His disciplining judgment when He chooses. We can depend on Him to establish justice ultimately.

[11]The day for building your walls[f] will
come,
the day for extending your
boundaries.
[12]In that day people will come to you
from Assyria[g] and the cities of
Egypt,
even from Egypt to the Euphrates
and from sea to sea
and from mountain to mountain.[h]
[13]The earth will become desolate
because of its inhabitants,
as the result of their deeds.[i]

Prayer and Praise

[14]Shepherd[j] your people with your
staff,[k]
the flock of your inheritance,
which lives by itself in a forest,
in fertile pasturelands.[w] [l]
Let them feed in Bashan[m] and Gilead[n]
as in days long ago.[o]

[15]"As in the days when you came out of
Egypt,
I will show them my wonders.[p]"

[16]Nations will see and be ashamed,[q]
deprived of all their power.
They will lay their hands on their
mouths[r]
and their ears will become deaf.
[17]They will lick dust[s] like a snake,
like creatures that crawl on the
ground.
They will come trembling[t] out of their
dens;
they will turn in fear[u] to the LORD
our God
and will be afraid of you.
[18]Who is a God[v] like you,
who pardons sin[w] and forgives[x] the
transgression
of the remnant[y] of his
inheritance?[z]
You do not stay angry[a] forever
but delight to show mercy.[b]
[19]You will again have compassion on us;
you will tread our sins underfoot
and hurl all our iniquities[c] into the
depths of the sea.[d]
[20]You will be true to Jacob,
and show mercy to Abraham,[e]
as you pledged on oath to our fathers[f]
in days long ago.[g]

7:11 [f]Isa 54:11; S Am 9:11
7:12 [g]S Isa 11:11 [h]Isa 19:23-25; 60:4
7:13 [i]Isa 3:10-11; S Eze 12:19; S 33:28-29
7:14 [j]S Ps 28:9; S Mic 5:4 [k]Ps 23:4 [l]Ps 95:7 [m]S Isa 33:9 [n]S SS 4:1; S Jer 50:19 [o]Eze 36:11
7:15 [p]S Ex 3:20; Ps 78:12
7:16 [q]Isa 26:11 [r]S Jdg 18:19
7:17 [s]S Ge 3:14 [t]2Sa 22:46 [u]Isa 25:3; 59:19
7:18 [v]S Ex 8:10; S 1Sa 2:2 [w]S Isa 43:25; S Jer 50:20; Zec 3:4 [x]S 2Ch 6:21; Ps 103:8-13 [y]S Joel 2:32; S Am 5:15; S Mic 2:12 [z]S Ex 34:9 [a]S Ps 103:9; S Isa 54:9 [b]S 2Ch 30:9; S Jer 31:20; 32:41; S Eze 18:23
7:19 [c]S Isa 43:25 [d]S Jer 31:34
7:20 [e]Gal 3:16 [f]Dt 7:8; Lk 1:72 [g]Ps 108:4

[w] *14* Or *in the middle of Carmel*

7:14–20 GOD, One God—The distinguishing characteristic of God is His love which leads Him to pardon sinners. Love replaces wrath. Salvation follows punishment. The loving God does miracles for His flock.
7:14–20 PRAYER, Mercy of God—Micah called on God to shepherd Israel as His inheritance. God promised to do so. The closing three verses are a doxology, giving glory and praise to God for answered prayer.
7:15 MIRACLE, Faith—Past miracles give foundation for present faith and future hope. Events surrounding the Exodus continued to be remembered for hundreds of years as God's wonderful works. Weak and persecuted by enemies, Israel waited for the new Exodus when God would restore His people. Such faith persisted because the miracle-working God is a forgiving, merciful God.
7:15 HISTORY, Deliverance—God used history as an illustration of His future delivering acts. History teaches what God can do and gives reason to believe that the God whose mission and loving nature do not change will act in the future as He has in the past.
7:18–19 SALVATION, Forgiveness—Micah's name meant "Who Is Like the Lord?" None is like the Lord in forgiving sin. He treads our sins under His feet and casts them into the depths of the ocean. These words were originally spoken of the faithful remnant of Israel just before their return from Exile, but should be seen now in the fullness of God's revelation as applying to all of God's people. Forgiveness includes the turning of God's anger.
7:18 THE CHURCH, Remnant—Our greatness does not compare with the greatness of God. He continually forgives us when we forget Him and passes over our rebellion. God forgives because He loves the remnant He restored. He is slow to anger and abounding in steadfast love (Ex 34:6–7).

Nahum

Theological Setting

The people of ancient Israel had suffered for many years under the harsh oppression of the Assyrians, who in 722 BC had conquered the Northern Kingdom of Israel. Judah's vassalage to Assyria began under King Ahaz (735-715 BC). By the time of Nahum, the Southern Kingdom was but a small state in a region dominated by the brutal Assyrians. Tiglath-Pileser III had come to the Assyrian throne in 745 BC to begin a renewal of Assyrian power in the ancient Near East. He and his armies conquered much territory and promoted Assyrian culture and religion throughout the region. Assyrian dominance continued for more than a century under Shalmaneser V (726-722 BC), Sargon II (721-705 BC), Sennacherib (704-681 BC), and Esarhaddon (680-669 BC). Ashurbanipal (668-627 BC) was their last great ruler. Nineveh, their capital city and chief fortress, was an impressive achievement in the ancient world.

The Assyrians were known not only for their power but also for their cruelty. Their archives reflect pride in the complete devastation of enemies. Assyrian kings boasted of dragging women and children away from their dead husbands and fathers and taking the captives to Nineveh as part of the spoils of war. The Assyrians also bragged of flaying skin from rebels to display to their enemies.

Nahum, too, described the cruelty of Assyria. (3:1). He also complained that Assyria practiced harlotry in state craft, betraying weaker nations (3:4). The evil of the Assyrian Empire, in fact, touched the whole region (3:19). Judah felt betrayed and frustrated under the heavy hand of Assyria. Was there any hope in the face of such oppression?

In the midst of this apparent hopelessness, the people of Judah had several options:

1. They could sink into an ever deepening state of despair. They had been oppressed for over a century. Was there no hope for the future? Where was God?

2. They could decide that God had been conquered by the Assyrians and could no longer help them. Their response would be to join in the worship of the Assyrian gods.

3. They could decide that compromise with the Assyrians was the best path. The result would be to make Yahweh one of the many gods the peoples of the Assyrian Empire worshiped.

4. They could fall into the frustrating habit of harboring hatred against the oppressive Assyrians, which would drain their energies away from the task of building a responsible future.

5. They could be true to God and look to God for their hope.

The book does not specify the date, but it does give us some clues. Nahum prophesied the fall of Nineveh. This happened in 612 BC. In chapter three of his book, the prophet used the fall of Thebes as an analogy for what will happen to Nineveh. This analogy assumed that the fall of Thebes in 663 BC had already taken place. A time between 663 and 612 is thus required. The most probable date was around 625 BC. At that time, Nahum saw the Assyrian Empire beginning to weaken and Judah beginning to assert some independence under King Josiah. The prophet declared that God would remove the affliction from Judah and create a future for the people. God would also bring judgment upon Assyria for the cruelty they had perpetrated against Judah.

Nahum knew the pain and oppression of Judah. The faithful among the people were frustrated with Assyrian dominance. Other Judahites, however, desiring to emulate Assyrian ways, would not like this word from Nahum. Nonetheless, the prophet spoke and did so in eloquent poetry. Nahum spoke of hope. He described God as judging oppressors and freeing the oppressed. He saw that God's deliverance was at hand, and of this reality he was an evangel.

Theological Outline

Nahum: A Vision of Hope for an Oppressed People

I. The Sovereign God Makes Himself Known. (1:1-11)
   A. The jealous, patient Lord takes vengeance on His adversaries. (1:1-3)
   B. The earth quakes at the arrival of God. (1:4-5)

C. Who can endure the heat of God's anger? (1:6)
D. The good Lord is a refuge for His troubled, trusting people. (1:7)
E. God protects those who seek Him but will destroy the enemy. (1:8-9)
F. The enemy must drink the cup of God's wrath. (1:10-11)

II. In the Enemy's Fall, God Offers Hope for His Oppressed People. (1:12-15)
A. God can defeat the enemies no matter how strong and numerous they are. (1:12-13)
B. God judges the enemy because of its false gods. (1:14)
C. God calls His delivered people to grateful worship. (1:15)

III. God Will Bring Judgment Upon His Wicked Enemy. (2:1—3:19)
A. The enemy will fall, but God's people will be restored. (2:1-2)
B. Armies and wealth cannot prevent God's judgment. (2:3-12)
C. When God declares war, the enemy is helpless. (2:13)
D. God humiliates wicked peoples. (3:1-19)

Theological Conclusions

The Book of Nahum brings encouragement and hope to an oppressed people. The book emphasizes four themes:

1. The sovereignty of God
2. The justice of God
3. The grace of God
4. Hope for God's People

For over a century, the Assyrians oppressed Judah. Then Nahum came, reminding the oppressed people that God was sovereign, that He created the world and still ruled over it. The Assyrian gods and military forces were defenseless in the face of God's penetrating presence. This sovereignty would be demonstrated in the destruction of the proud city of Nineveh. Nahum vividly portrayed this coming destruction.

God was also a God of justice. Yahweh brought judgment upon Assyria because of their cruel oppression of many peoples. Such destruction of the wicked was a sign of God's grace toward Judah, as well as a sign of His justice. Judah's actions did not earn victory over her enemies. God, in love, chose to give victory. God did indeed have a future for the people of Judah. This hope found some expression in expansion and renewal under King Josiah (640-609 BC). Nahum's prophecy was fruitful. His call to return to faithfulness (1:12-15) provided support for Josiah's attempts to reform the people and to rid them of Assyrian influence.

We need to view the message of Nahum in light of other Old Testament passages. His word was similar to other prophecies about oppressive foreign nations like Edom, Babylon, Philistia, and Syria. They all suffered the consequences of their inhumanity; such was the just activity of God. Note, however, that the primary addressee in such prophecies was the oppressed people of God. A sovereign, gracious God offered the hope of deliverance. In short, such prophecies functioned for the community as a powerful word of encouragement and hope based on God's power, justice, and grace, themes found throughout the biblical revelation. The messenger who brings such tidings of peace (1:15) is called blessed.

Contemporary Teaching

Nahum speaks to all communities of faith which face oppression. Judah had experienced the ruthless tyranny of Assyria for many years, so Nahum focused on tyranny. In the face of such oppression, the prophet reaffirmed the sovereignty, justice, and grace of God.

Unfortunately, the Book of Nahum has sometimes been described as a tract of nationalism or even of hatred born of despair. On the contrary, the book presents a universal message. Assyria oppressed many; that oppression was met by the justice of God. Dire consequences await oppressors then and now. That is, God delivers His afflicted people—God offers hope in the midst of affliction.

Nahum calls us (1) to recognize the presence of evil in the world; (2) to believe that God is opposed to all evil; (3) to examine our attitudes toward oppression and to understand that oppression sows its own destruction; (4) to live in hope; (5) to renew our vision of God's sovereign power in a world ruled by political expediency; (6) to resist the temptation to live only by societal norms rather than by the Word of God; (7) to act on the belief that God is indeed involved in life and history.

Nahum proclaims a significant message to a world often dominated by chaos and confusion. God is powerful. He creates a future for the oppressed and for the community of faith. The reality of God's justice brings hope and sustenance for living.

'Nineveh[w] is in ruins[x]—who will
mourn for her?'[y]
Where can I find anyone to
comfort[z] you?"

8Are you better than[a] Thebes,[e] [b]
situated on the Nile,[c]
with water around her?
The river was her defense,
the waters her wall.
9Cush[f] [d] and Egypt were her boundless
strength;
Put[e] and Libya[f] were among her
allies.
10Yet she was taken captive[g]
and went into exile.
Her infants were dashed[h] to pieces
at the head of every street.
Lots[i] were cast for her nobles,
and all her great men were put in
chains.[j]
11You too will become drunk;[k]
you will go into hiding[l]
and seek refuge from the enemy.
12All your fortresses are like fig trees
with their first ripe fruit;[m]
when they are shaken,
the figs[n] fall into the mouth of the
eater.
13Look at your troops—
they are all women![o]
The gates[p] of your land
are wide open to your enemies;
fire has consumed their bars.[q]

14Draw water for the siege,[r]
strengthen your defenses![s]
Work the clay,
tread the mortar,
repair the brickwork!
15There the fire[t] will devour you;
the sword[u] will cut you down
and, like grasshoppers, consume
you.
Multiply like grasshoppers,
multiply like locusts![v]
16You have increased the number of
your merchants
till they are more than the stars of
the sky,
but like locusts[w] they strip the land
and then fly away.
17Your guards are like locusts,[x]
your officials like swarms of locusts
that settle in the walls on a cold
day—
but when the sun appears they fly
away,
and no one knows where.

18O king of Assyria, your shepherds[g]
slumber;[y]
your nobles lie down to rest.[z]
Your people are scattered[a] on the
mountains
with no one to gather them.
19Nothing can heal your wound;[b]
your injury is fatal.
Everyone who hears the news about
you
claps his hands[c] at your fall,
for who has not felt
your endless cruelty?[d]

3:7 [w]S Na 1:1 [x]S Job 3:14 [y]S Jer 15:5 [z]S Isa 51:19
3:8 [a]Am 6:2 [b]S Jer 46:25 [c]Isa 19:6-9
3:9 [d]S Ge 10:6; S 2Ch 12:3 [e]S Eze 27:10 [f]Eze 30:5
3:10 [g]S Isa 20:4 [h]S 2Ki 8:12; S Isa 13:16; Hos 13:16 [i]S Job 6:27; S Eze 24:6 [j]S Jer 40:1
3:11 [k]S Isa 49:26 [l]S Isa 2:10
3:12 [m]S SS 2:13 [n]S Isa 28:4
3:13 [o]S Isa 19:16 [p]S Na 2:6 [q]S Isa 45:2
3:14 [r]S 2Ch 32:4 [s]Na 2:1
3:15 [t]S Isa 27:1 [u]S 2Sa 2:26 [v]S Jer 51:14; S Joel 1:4
3:16 [w]S Ex 10:13
3:17 [x]Jer 51:27
3:18 [y]Ps 76:5-6; S Jer 25:27 [z]Isa 56:10 [a]S 1Ki 22:17
3:19 [b]S Jer 30:13; S Mic 1:9 [c]S Job 27:23; S La 2:15; Zep 2:15 [d]Isa 37:18

[e]8 Hebrew *No Amon* [f]9 That is, the upper Nile region [g]18 Or *rulers*

3:19 HUMANITY, Attitudes to Death—Cruel people endure cruel funerals. Humans tend to rejoice rather than mourn when extremely wicked people die. Christians can never rejoice when a person must face eternal judgment separated from God. All people need to reflect on how their death will be received.

Habakkuk

Theological Setting

Why would a good God who controls the world also allow the righteous to suffer and the wicked to prosper? God knew His people had failed Him, but why did God use the Chaldeans as an instrument of chastisement? Habakkuk argued with God that a wicked Judah was more righteous than a wicked Chaldea.

Habakkuk may have been a contemporary of Jeremiah during the time of Judah's decline. The reference to the Chaldeans (the Babylonians) as a people whom God was raising points, in all probability, to the last quarter of the seventh century BC. During that time, Babylonia reasserted her independence and replaced Assyria as the dominant power in Western Asia. See introduction to Zephaniah.

The book begins in dialog form. The prophet uttered a complaint (1:1-4), and God answered, promising only an even worse situation (1:5-11). Again the prophet complained (1:12—2:1). God responded in a vision assuring salvation (2:2-20). The psalm in chapter 3 consists of a description of God's coming in judgment (vv 2-6) and an assertion of utter faith in God's goodness in spite of adversity (vv 17-19).

Habakkuk and his people posed honest questions as they struggled to understand and trust God. The book is designed to answer the questions:

(1) How could God use such a wicked instrument as the Chaldeans to execute His purpose?
(2) Could the divine purpose be justified in such events?
(3) Why do the wicked seem to triumph while the righteous suffer?

Theological Outline

Habakkuk: A Pilgrimage from Doubt to Faith

I. A Prophet Perplexed: Why Does God Permit Injustice? (1:1-17)
   A. Prophet's first protest: A cry for deliverance from violence and iniquity. (1:1-4)
   B. God's first reply: The worst is yet to be. (1:5-11)
   C. Prophet's second protest: How can a holy God use such a cruel instrument as this evil people? (1:12-17)

II. A Prophet Perceiving: The Righteous Shall Live by Faithfulness. (2:1-20)
   A. God's second reply (2:1-5)
      1. Revelation comes to one prepared to wait. (2:1)
      2. Revelation must be easy to understand. (2:2)
      3. Revelation will prove true in God's time. (2:3)
      4. Persistent faith—not pride, parties, nor plunder—is the distinguishing mark of the righteous. (2:4-5)
   B. God taunts His materialistic enemy. (2:6-20)
      1. First taunt song: Woe because of pride and ambition (2:6-8)
      2. Second taunt song: Woe because of arrogance and greed (2:9-11)
      3. Third taunt song: Woe because of cruelty (2:12-14)
      4. Fourth taunt song: Woe because of drunkenness (2:15-17)
      5. Fifth taunt song: Woe because of idolatry (2:18-19)
      6. Conclusion: A call for universal worship of the holy God (2:20)

III. A Prophet Praying and Praising: A Psalm of Confidence Is the Proper Response to Revelation. (3:1-19)
   A. Prayer asks God to repeat His acts of deliverance. (3:1-2)
   B. Prayer gains confidence by recounting the holy God's redeeming acts. (3:3-15)
   C. Prayer responds in awesome fear and confident joy to God's history with His people. (3:16-18)
   D. Prayer claims God's strength for present crisis. (3:19)

Theological Conclusions

(1) God's government is moral. The prophet was practical rather than philosophical in dealing with his defense of God's goodness and omnipotence in view of the existence of evil. He learned that God is moral in relation with the universe. In the outcome God will turn the worst to a good end. This does not completely solve the problem of suffering and evil, but it provides a part of the right response to a harsh reality. God's just government of His world may not be immediately apparent to us. In the long run it will become apparent. Meanwhile, God calls His people to fidelity through good or evil times until God's day shall finally come.

(2) Tyranny is suicide. Evil carries in it the seeds of its own destruction. Greed and pride will eventually lead to a realization "that the people's labor is only fuel for the fire" (2:13). In the affairs of nations, a law of retribution is assumed (2:8). The taunt songs in chapter 2 give a total picture of self-destruction.

(3) "The righteous will live by his faith [faithfulness, NIV footnote]" (2:4*b*). Faithfulness is steadfastness and trustworthiness. The "righteous" are not morally perfect but persistently faithful, even amid present perils and perplexity. The "righteous" will "live" prosperously, successfully, and permanently. The meaning of "live" carries the germs of belief in future life, thus being both qualitative and quantitative. This declaration of faith is quoted by Paul who adds to the meaning (Ro 1:17; Gal 3:11) of this important truth.

Contemporary Teaching

The Book of Habakkuk is relevant today since injustice and violence so often plague Christians. The facts of life do not always agree with traditional teachings about God. Our question, like the prophet's, is why God seems to be inactive when difficulties occur. This question should be directed to God, and not against Him. Out of our doubts, we may forge a new belief in the character of the Infinite and discover the grace of God which is sufficient.

For Habakkuk, the righteous shall live by faithfulness or moral steadfastness. We can live in the assurance God will come to our aid to achieve His goals. Righteousness will triumph, even though wickedness often seems to go unchecked. We are encouraged to trust God and wait. Take a long look. God will do right in the government of the whole world.

The concluding verses of the book express true faith of one in fellowship with God. This magnificent passage echoes the thought of 2:4. In spite of all losses, a true believer rests in the Lord and waits patiently for Him, strengthened to walk on higher ground.

Chapter 1

THE oracle[a] that Habakkuk the prophet received.

Habakkuk's Complaint

2How long,[b] O LORD, must I call for
help,
but you do not listen?[c]
Or cry out to you, "Violence!"
but you do not save?[d]
3Why do you make me look at injustice?
Why do you tolerate[e] wrong?[f]
Destruction and violence[g] are before
me;
there is strife,[h] and conflict
abounds.
4Therefore the law[i] is paralyzed,
and justice never prevails.
The wicked hem in the righteous,
so that justice[j] is perverted.[k]

The LORD's Answer

5"Look at the nations and watch—
and be utterly amazed.[l]
For I am going to do something in your
days
that you would not believe,
even if you were told.[m]
6I am raising up the Babylonians,[a] [n]
that ruthless and impetuous people,
who sweep across the whole earth[o]
to seize dwelling places not their
own.[p]
7They are a feared and dreaded
people;[q]
they are a law to themselves
and promote their own honor.
8Their horses are swifter[r] than
leopards,
fiercer than wolves[s] at dusk.
Their cavalry gallops headlong;
their horsemen come from afar.
They fly like a vulture swooping to
devour;
9 they all come bent on violence.
Their hordes[b] advance like a desert
wind
and gather prisoners[t] like sand.
10They deride kings
and scoff at rulers.[u]
They laugh at all fortified cities;
they build earthen ramps[v] and
capture them.
11Then they sweep past like the wind[w]
and go on—
guilty men, whose own strength is
their god."[x]

Habakkuk's Second Complaint

12O LORD, are you not from
everlasting?[y]
My God, my Holy One,[z] we will not
die.[a]
O LORD, you have appointed[b] them to
execute judgment;
O Rock,[c] you have ordained them
to punish.
13Your eyes are too pure[d] to look on
evil;
you cannot tolerate wrong.[e]
Why then do you tolerate[f] the
treacherous?[g]
Why are you silent while the wicked

[a]6 Or *Chaldeans* [b]9 The meaning of the Hebrew for this word is uncertain.

1:1 [a]S Na 1:1
1:2 [b]S Ps 6:3 [c]Ps 13:1-2; 22:1-2 [d]Jer 14:9; Zec 1:12
1:3 [e]ver 13 [f]S Job 9:23 [g]Jer 20:8 [h]S Ps 55:9
1:4 [i]Ps 119:126 [j]S Isa 29:21 [k]S Job 19:7; S Isa 1:23; 5:20; S Eze 9:9
1:5 [l]S Isa 29:9 [m]Ac 13:41*
1:6 [n]S Dt 28:49; S 2Ki 24:2 [o]Rev 20:9 [p]S Jer 13:20; S 21:7
1:7 [q]Isa 18:7; Jer 39:5-9
1:8 [r]S Jer 4:13 [s]S Ge 49:27
1:9 [t]Hab 2:5
1:10 [u]S 2Ch 36:6 [v]S Jer 33:4
1:11 [w]Jer 4:11-12 [x]S Da 4:30
1:12 [y]S Ge 21:33 [z]Isa 31:1; 37:23 [a]Ps 118:17 [b]Isa 10:6 [c]S Ge 49:24; S Ex 33:22
1:13 [d]Ps 18:26 [e]S La 3:34-36 [f]ver 3 [g]S Ps 25:3

1:1 HOLY SCRIPTURE, Oracle—Habakkuk's preaching is called an oracle which he received (literally, he saw). The contents of the book show a dialogue of questions and answers between the prophet and God. The prophetic vision includes convictions received in prayerful meditation with God. See notes on Isa 13:1; Na 1:1.

1:2–11 GOD, Justice—We want to see God move immediately into action when we suffer injustice. God answers our prayers and establishes justice but only on His timetable. He may even use violent people as His instruments to establish justice. See note on Eze 18:25–32.

1:2–4 EVIL AND SUFFERING, Prayer—Habakkuk was perplexed at the apparent injustice of his day. We often do not understand why there is so much injustice in the world. We wonder if God really cares about us. Like Habakkuk, we should feel free to approach God with our questions about injustice. See notes on 2:4; Jer 11:18—12:6.

1:2–4 PROCLAMATION, Call—See note on Jer 1:4–9. Habakkuk saw the need for God's word in the seemingly unjust situation of his day. He thus sought a word from God and received it. Humans can take the initiative in seeking God's word to proclaim.

1:5–11 EVIL AND SUFFERING, Providence—God still controls history. He used the Babylonians to punish Judah. From our limited perspective, we may not understand God's purposes in history. We tend to judge events in relation to self-interest or national concerns instead of God's providential guidance of history. Our suffering and the world's evil can be explained only in light of God's perspectives and purposes, including His purpose of relating to free humans who choose to sin.

1:5–7 REVELATION, History—God intended to use the irreverent and self-serving Babylonians to accomplish His justice. The prophet was bewildered but recorded the revelation. God can use unrighteous people to correct human abuses. Habakkuk withheld judgment, waiting for God to explain and complete His work. Faithful followers interpret even when they do not fully understand what God is doing. God is active amid the confusion of human history.

1:5–11 HISTORY, Universal—See note on Isa 7:17.

1:12–13 GOD, Holy—God's holiness marks the infinite qualitative difference between God and humans. A major area of difference is moral purity. Because God is holy, we can pray to Him when immoral people oppress us.

1:12 GOD, Eternal—See note on Da 7:9,14,22,27.

1:12–17 EVIL AND SUFFERING, Human Origin—Our theology forces us to ask questions about the kind of world we live in. Habakkuk knew God was pure and could not tolerate the presence of evil. He also knew of the treacherous and inhumane treatment his people were suffering from Babylon. Could God allow such unjust sinners to punish His people? The prophet knew his people deserved punishment, but he questioned whether a holy God would punish them through such an unjust agent. We live in a world in which God allows human evil to win at times to accomplish His ultimate purposes. Living under the momentary triumph of evil, we raise serious questions and wait for God to answer. We may have to endure His silence before we receive His answer.

swallow up those more righteous
than themselves?[h]
14You have made men like fish in the
sea,
like sea creatures that have no ruler.
15The wicked[i] foe pulls all of them up
with hooks,[j]
he catches them in his net,[k]
he gathers them up in his dragnet;
and so he rejoices and is glad.
16Therefore he sacrifices to his net
and burns incense[l] to his dragnet,
for by his net he lives in luxury
and enjoys the choicest food.
17Is he to keep on emptying his net,
destroying nations without mercy?[m]

Chapter 2

I will stand at my watch[n]
and station myself on the ramparts;[o]
I will look to see what he will say[p] to
me,
and what answer I am to give to this
complaint.[c] [q]

The LORD's Answer

2Then the LORD replied:

"Write[r] down the revelation
and make it plain on tablets
so that a herald[d] may run with it.
3For the revelation awaits an appointed
time;[s]
it speaks of the end[t]
and will not prove false.
Though it linger, wait[u] for it;
it[e] will certainly come and will not
delay.[v]

4"See, he is puffed up;
his desires are not upright—
but the righteous[w] will live by his
faith[f] [x] —
5indeed, wine[y] betrays him;
he is arrogant[z] and never at rest.
Because he is as greedy as the grave[g]
and like death is never satisfied,[a]
he gathers to himself all the nations
and takes captive[b] all the peoples.

6"Will not all of them taunt[c] him with
ridicule and scorn, saying,

" 'Woe to him who piles up stolen
goods
and makes himself wealthy by
extortion![d]
How long must this go on?'
7Will not your debtors[h] suddenly arise?
Will they not wake up and make you
tremble?
Then you will become their victim.[e]
8Because you have plundered many
nations,
the peoples who are left will plunder
you.[f]
For you have shed man's blood;[g]
you have destroyed lands and cities
and everyone in them.[h]

9"Woe to him who builds[i] his realm by
unjust gain[j]
to set his nest[k] on high,
to escape the clutches of ruin!
10You have plotted the ruin[l] of many
peoples,
shaming[m] your own house and
forfeiting your life.
11The stones[n] of the wall will cry out,
and the beams of the woodwork will
echo it.

12"Woe to him who builds a city with
bloodshed[o]

1:13 [h]S Job 21:7
1:15 [i]Jer 5:26 [j]S Isa 19:8 [k]S Job 18:8; Jer 16:16
1:16 [l]Jer 44:8
1:17 [m]S Isa 14:6; 19:8
2:1 [n]S Isa 21:8 [o]S Ps 48:13 [p]Ps 85:8 [q]S Ps 5:3; S Eze 3:17
2:2 [r]S Isa 30:8; S Jer 36:2; S Eze 24:2; S Ro 4:24; Rev 1:19
2:3 [s]Da 11:27 [t]Da 8:17 [u]S Ps 27:14 [v]S Eze 12:25
2:4 [w]S Eze 18:9 [x]Ro 1:17*; Gal 3:11*; Heb 10:37-38*
2:5 [y]S Pr 20:1 [z]S Isa 2:11 [a]S Pr 27:20; S 30:15-16 [b]Hab 1:9
2:6 [c]S Isa 14:4 [d]Am 2:8
2:7 [e]S Pr 29:1
2:8 [f]Isa 33:1; Jer 50:17-18; S Ob 1:15; Zec 2:8-9 [g]ver 17 [h]S Eze 39:10
2:9 [i]S Jer 22:13 [j]S Jer 51:13 [k]S Job 39:27; S Isa 10:14
2:10 [l]Jer 26:19 [m]ver 16; S Na 3:6
2:11 [n]S Jos 24:27; Zec 5:4; Lk 19:40
2:12 [o]S Eze 22:2; S Mic 3:10

[c]*1* Or *and what to answer when I am rebuked* [d]*2* Or *so that whoever reads it* [e]*3* Or *Though he linger, wait for him; / he* [f]*4* Or *faithfulness* [g]*5* Hebrew *Sheol* [h]*7* Or *creditors*

2:1–3 HOLY SCRIPTURE, Writing—The prophet declared his willingness to wait on the revelation of God, even when he did not like what he heard and saw. God's own Spirit then breathed truth into the prophet, who was to write plainly what he perceived. The message was to be made public and available at the time God chose. God's Word is genuine and can be relied upon. The prophet showed revelation can be asked for by God's messenger representing God's people.
2:4 EVIL AND SUFFERING, Humility—God did not give Habakkuk a philosophical answer to the problem of suffering. Humans must live by faith in God, who is ultimately just and in control of history. Even when some events seem to contradict this belief, we are to trust in God. See note on 3:16–19.
2:4–17 SIN, Lawlessness—Habakkuk attacked Babylon's sins. These sins were not violations of covenant law, since Babylon was not part of God's covenant. These were sins against moral conscience, against the universal sense of right and wrong which distinguishes the human race. These universal sins include self-centered pride, drunkenness, greed, theft, extortion, violent war crimes, murder, unjust economic practices, cruel expansionist policies (v 12), and inhumane treatment of prisoners (v 15). God promised the same treatment for a lawless people who ignored all human rights and decency.
2:4 SALVATION, Belief—This text is the Mount Everest in the biblical understanding of salvation. Faith in God and faithfulness (NIV footnote) to God are the path to life. Unbelief and unfaithfulness are the path to death. Faithfulness (Hebrew *'emunah*) includes moral steadfastness—integrity. It is characteristic of God (Dt 32:4) and represents the faithful carrying out of an assignment (1 Ch 9:22). The righteous will live in the day of judgment. They will be vindicated by God Himself. The proud wicked, like the King of Babylon, do not swallow up the righteous forever. God delivers His people and judges their persecutors. God has chosen to honor commitment and faithfulness to Him as the only requirement for His salvation.
2:4 CHRISTIAN ETHICS, Justice—Living by faith is always a prerequisite in the Bible to experiencing the righteous life. Right actions do not come by human effort to meet written or traditional standards. Right actions come as God's people trust Him and let Him lead life. See note on Php 3:9.
2:5 HUMANITY, Death—Death is personified as always reaching for its next victim. All who live will die. Greedy people seeking personal glory will suffer God's judgment.
2:12–17 GOD, Sovereignty—The prophet could not understand why the sovereign Ruler of the universe did not act to establish His righteous order. Sometimes our theology does not square with current reality. We have to join the prophet on the watch tower praying and waiting for God to act.

and establishes a town by crime!
13Has not the LORD Almighty determined
that the people's labor is only fuel for the fire,[p]
that the nations exhaust themselves for nothing?[q]
14For the earth will be filled with the knowledge of the glory[r] of the LORD,
as the waters cover the sea.[s]

15"Woe to him who gives drink[t] to his neighbors,
pouring it from the wineskin till they are drunk,
so that he can gaze on their naked bodies.
16You will be filled with shame[u] instead of glory.[v]
Now it is your turn! Drink[w] and be exposed[i]![x]
The cup[y] from the LORD's right hand is coming around to you,
and disgrace will cover your glory.
17The violence[z] you have done to Lebanon will overwhelm you,
and your destruction of animals will terrify you.[a]
For you have shed man's blood;[b]
you have destroyed lands and cities and everyone in them.

18"Of what value[c] is an idol,[d] since a man has carved it?
Or an image[e] that teaches lies?
For he who makes it trusts in his own creation;
he makes idols that cannot speak.[f]
19Woe to him who says to wood, 'Come to life!'
Or to lifeless stone, 'Wake up!'[g]
Can it give guidance?
It is covered with gold and silver;[h]
there is no breath in it.[i]
20But the LORD is in his holy temple;[j]
let all the earth be silent[k] before him."

Chapter 3

Habakkuk's Prayer

A prayer of Habakkuk the prophet. On *shigionoth.*[j] [l]

2LORD, I have heard[m] of your fame;

2:13 [p]Isa 50:11 [q]S Isa 47:13
2:14 [r]S Ex 16:7; S Nu 14:21 [s]S Isa 11:9
2:15 [t]S Pr 23:20
2:16 [u]S ver 10 [v]S Eze 23:32-34; Hos 4:7 [w]S Lev 10:9 [x]S La 4:21 [y]S Ps 16:5; S Isa 51:22
2:17 [z]S Jer 51:35 [a]S Jer 50:15 [b]ver 8
2:18 [c]S 1Sa 12:21 [d]S Jdg 10:14; S Isa 40:19; S Jer 5:21; S 14:22 [e]S Lev 26:1 [f]Ps 115:4-5; Jer 10:14; 1Co 12:2
2:19 [g]1Ki 18:27 [h]S Jer 10:4 [i]S Da 5:4,23; S Hos 4:12
2:20 [j]S Ps 11:4 [k]S Isa 41:1
3:1 [l]Ps 7 Title
3:2 [m]S Job 26:14; Ps 44:1

[i]*16* Masoretic Text; Dead Sea Scrolls, Aquila, Vulgate and Syriac (see also Septuagint) *and stagger*
[j]*1* Probably a literary or musical term

2:12,17 CHRISTIAN ETHICS, Moral Limits—Violence and bloodshed may bring short-term results to those who impose such methods. God will ultimately reject and punish such methods. See note on Eze 9:3–11.
2:14 GOD, Glory—God works to let his weight—the literal meaning of the Hebrew *kabod,* glory—be felt among all nations so they may acknowledge His sovereign authority and power.
2:14 EVANGELISM, Results—Habakkuk saw the day when the message of the gospel would be known worldwide. God's evangelistic purposes will be realized. This speaks of a great day of culmination, but in the meantime we labor to fulfill the "Great Commission" (Mt 28:19–20), so all may hear of Jesus Christ and His power to save.
2:15 CHRISTIAN ETHICS, Alcohol—One has a personal responsibility to refrain from the dangers of alcohol or any other addictive substance. The judgment of God is also against one who uses the results of the excesses of alcohol to take advantage of a neighbor. Habakkuk condemned both Babylon's international violence and their individual immoral acts.
2:16 GOD, Justice—God in His justice treats oppressive nations as they have treated others. See note on Am 4:1–13.
2:18–20 GOD, One God—Only the one God can create life. Humans certainly cannot create divine life and insert it into the images they carve. The Lord is the only uncreated God. See note on Jer 1:16.
2:18–20 SIN, Transgression—Sin centers life on something less than the unique creator God. See note on Eze 8:3–18.
2:19–20 REVELATION, Divine Presence—God is the only source of revelation. Taunting those who believe in and worship dead objects, God spoke through the prophet to remind His people of God's holy presence. The Temple symbolized His constant availability. Often the true believer's best posture in seeking God is patient silence.
2:20 GOD, Holy—God makes His awesome presence known to His people in the place of worship. The basic response to His holiness is reverent silence. See note on 1:12–13.
3:1–19 HOLY SCRIPTURE, Writing—The final chapter of Habakkuk is the written text of a Temple psalm complete with notations for the choir (vv 1,19). Apparently God inspired the prophet to take up or write a hymn and use it as his response to the revelatory experience in which questions and complaints (1:2; 2:1) turned to reverent praise. Attached in writing to the prophetic book, the hymn praising God became a source of revelation from God to us. It shows that God regularly intervenes in history to redeem His people in crisis.
3:1–19 PRAYER, Faith—For two chapters Habakkuk had questioned God about the Babylonian threat. Now he asked God to demonstrate His power as He did in the Exodus (Ex 14). The key to Habakkuk's remarkable praise is the attitude of waiting. Regardless of circumstance, Habakkuk would praise the Lord. Praise is insisting on the greater, spiritual truth rather than relying on visible evidence. Reviewing God's history with His people increases faith, brings spiritual insight, and encourages waiting for God's new actions.
3:1,19 PRAYER, Corporate—Hab 3 has literary notes for the Temple choir such as appear in the Psalms. Either the psalm was recited by Habakkuk from memory as a result of participation in Temple worship; or the psalm was recognized by collectors of Scripture as a familiar Temple psalm, and the appropriate instructions were attached. Either method enabled the choir to conclude the public reading of Habakkuk with an appropriate anthem. Habakkuk's prayer thus became the congregation's prayer.
3:2–17 GOD, Wrath—Wrath is God's very real reaction against persistent sin. At times He displays His wrath in nature. Experiencing wrath, God's people begged for mercy. God acted in wrath against enemies to save His people. The faithful people trusted God to exercise His wrath and rejoiced in praise even before the signs of God's saving actions became apparent. See note on Am 4:1–13.
3:2 GOD, Grace—Mercy is the deep parental love of God's grace. Only God's mercy can save a people under His wrath.
3:2–19 HISTORY, Confession—In private prayer God's people confess God's historical acts as the basis for hope in His renewed intervention in our history. Even when present conditions testify to God's absence, past history gives faith to expect God's action and rejoice in His presence.

I stand in awe[n] of your deeds,
O LORD.[o]
Renew[p] them in our day,
in our time make them known;
in wrath remember mercy.[q]

3God came from Teman,[r]
the Holy One[s] from Mount Paran.[t]
Selah[k]
His glory covered the heavens[u]
and his praise filled the earth.[v]
4His splendor was like the sunrise;[w]
rays flashed from his hand,
where his power[x] was hidden.
5Plague[y] went before him;
pestilence followed his steps.
6He stood, and shook the earth;
he looked, and made the nations
tremble.
The ancient mountains crumbled[z]
and the age-old hills[a] collapsed.[b]
His ways are eternal.[c]
7I saw the tents of Cushan in distress,
the dwellings of Midian[d] in
anguish.[e]
8Were you angry with the rivers,[f]
O LORD?
Was your wrath against the streams?
Did you rage against the sea[g]
when you rode with your horses
and your victorious chariots?[h]
9You uncovered your bow,
you called for many arrows.[i] *Selah*
You split the earth with rivers;
10 the mountains saw you and
writhed.[j]
Torrents of water swept by;
the deep roared[k]
and lifted its waves[l] on high.

11Sun and moon stood still[m] in the
heavens
at the glint of your flying arrows,[n]
at the lightning[o] of your flashing
spear.
12In wrath you strode through the earth
and in anger you threshed[p] the
nations.
13You came out[q] to deliver[r] your
people,
to save your anointed[s] one.
You crushed[t] the leader of the land of
wickedness,
you stripped him from head to foot.
Selah
14With his own spear you pierced his
head
when his warriors stormed out to
scatter us,[u]
gloating as though about to devour
the wretched[v] who were in hiding.
15You trampled the sea[w] with your
horses,
churning the great waters.[x]

16I heard and my heart pounded,
my lips quivered at the sound;
decay crept into my bones,
and my legs trembled.[y]
Yet I will wait patiently[z] for the day of
calamity
to come on the nation invading us.
17Though the fig tree does not bud
and there are no grapes on the
vines,
though the olive crop fails
and the fields produce no food,[a]
though there are no sheep in the pen
and no cattle in the stalls,[b]
18yet I will rejoice in the LORD,[c]
I will be joyful in God my Savior.[d]

19The Sovereign LORD is my strength;[e]
he makes my feet like the feet of a
deer,
he enables me to go on the
heights.[f]

For the director of music. On my
stringed instruments.

3:2 [n]S Ps 119:120 [o]S Ps 90:16 [p]Ps 85:6 [q]Isa 54:8
3:3 [r]S Ge 36:11,15 [s]Isa 31:1 [t]S Nu 10:12 [u]S Ps 8:1 [v]Ps 48:10
3:4 [w]S Isa 18:4 [x]S Job 9:6
3:5 [y]S Lev 26:25
3:6 [z]S Ps 46:2 [a]Ge 49:26 [b]S Ex 19:18; Ps 18:7; 114:1-6 [c]S Ge 21:33
3:7 [d]S Ge 25:2; S Nu 25:15; Jdg 7:24-25 [e]Ex 15:14
3:8 [f]S Ex 7:20 [g]S Ps 77:16 [h]S 2Ki 2:11; S Ps 68:17
3:9 [i]S Dt 32:23; Ps 7:12-13
3:10 [j]S Ps 77:16 [k]Ps 98:7 [l]S Ps 93:3
3:11 [m]Jos 10:13 [n]Ps 18:14 [o]S Ps 144:6; Zec 9:14
3:12 [p]S Isa 41:15
3:13 [q]S Ex 13:21 [r]S Ps 20:6; S 28:8 [s]S 2Sa 23:1 [t]Ps 68:21; 110:6
3:14 [u]Jdg 7:22 [v]Ps 64:2-5
3:15 [w]S Job 9:8 [x]Ex 15:8
3:16 [y]S Job 4:14 [z]S Ps 37:7
3:17 [a]Joel 1:10-12, 18 [b]Jer 5:17
3:18 [c]Ps 97:12; S Isa 61:10; Php 4:4 [d]S Ex 15:2; S Lk 1:47
3:19 [e]S Dt 33:29; Ps 46:1-5 [f]S Dt 32:13; Ps 18:33

[k]*3* A word of uncertain meaning; possibly a musical term; also in verses 9 and 13

3:16–19 EVIL AND SUFFERING, Humility—Habakkuk was willing to wait for God to punish the wicked. Even though he endured disappointment and hardship, Habakkuk vowed to praise God. Habakkuk's dialog with God enabled him to realize God's presence despite the misfortunes of history. We may not gain a complete understanding of our suffering, but it can empower us still to trust in God (2:20). He may allow us to suffer for a time. He may even use suffering to punish us. He remains the only Savior able to deliver us from trouble.

3:17–18 HUMANITY, Relationship to God—Relationship to God can bring hopeful joy even in the midst of crisis and catastrophe.

3:18 SALVATION, Joy—The prophet affirmed his confidence in the God of his salvation. Although nature failed to yield her fruit, he would rejoice in the Lord. This is the correct attitude of all God's people. Nothing should prevent us from faithfully rejoicing in the Lord. Compare Php 4:4.

Zephaniah

Theological Setting

How much wickedness will God tolerate before He brings judgment? In Zephaniah's day, people had reason to ask this question. After the death of King Hezekiah, his son Manasseh (697-642 BC) quickly abandoned the godly ways of his father. He rebuilt the idolatrous high places his father had destroyed, killed many innocent people, and sacrificed his own son to one of the gods. His son Amon followed Manasseh's policies during his brief reign (642-640 BC).

Amon was succeeded by his eight-year-old son Josiah (640-609 BC). After finding the Book of the Law in the Temple in 622 BC, Josiah instituted thoroughgoing religious reforms. Josiah was personally faithful to God, but his people did not really return to God in their hearts.

Judah had been under Assyrian control since 701 BC, when King Sennacherib devastated the land in a military campaign. Judah was allowed to have her own kings as long as they cooperated with Assyria. With the death of Ashurbanipal, the last of Assyria's great kings (668-627 BC), the once-powerful empire quickly disintegrated under a succession of weak kings and fell to a coalition of nations headed by Babylonia in 612 BC.

God had been patient with His rebellious people. He had sent many prophets over a long period of time to warn them of coming judgment. Now the day of reckoning—"the day of the LORD"—was drawing near (1:18). God raised up the prophet Zephaniah to warn the people in some of the severest language found in the Scriptures that judgment was fast approaching. No nation would escape that judgment, including Judah (1:4).

The prophetic ministry of Zephaniah occurred during the reign of Josiah (1:1). It probably began around 625 BC, as the idolatrous practices which he condemned and which Josiah abolished after 622 BC were still openly taking place (1:4-6).

Little is known about the prophet Zephaniah. His name means "the LORD hides" (i.e., protects). He may have been a member of the royal family, as his genealogy is traced to Hezekiah (1:1), considered by many to be King Hezekiah. His contemporaries included Nahum, Habakkuk, and Jeremiah.

No prophet portrays the religious and moral situation in Judah more clearly than Zephaniah. He understood that Judah would have to learn by bitter experience that though God is patient, His patience has an end. Neither their foreign gods nor their political alliances could save them. Only "the meek and humble, who trust in the name of the LORD" (3:12) would experience the joy of God's deliverance.

Theological Outline

Zephaniah: Messenger of God's Judgment and Hope

I. Identification of the Messenger of God's Word (1:1)

II. God's Warning of Worldwide Judgment (1:2—3:8)

A. God's day of judgment is coming. (1:2—2:3)

1. His judgment will include all mankind. (1:2-3)
2. His judgment will include His own sinful people who forsake Him. (1:4-6)
3. The day of the Lord calls for awesome silence in the face of God's judgment. (1:7-11)
4. God's skeptics will see Him in action on His day. (1:12-13)
5. God's wrath will be poured out against sin on that day. (1:14-17)
6. Wealth is good for nothing on His day. (1:18)
7. God calls His humble people to seek Him before it is too late. (2:1-3)

B. God's judgment will subject His enemies and bless the remnant of His people. (2:4-15)

C. God's righteous justice will be impartial. (3:1-8)

III. God Promises to Form a New People. (3:9-20)

A. The nations will call on God. (3:9-10)

B. A purified remnant will worship Him in humility and with joy. (3:11-13)

C. God will reign as King to remove His people's fears. (3:14-17)
D. His oppressed people will be exalted. (3:18-20)

Theological Conclusions

Zephaniah's messages of judgment and encouragement contain three major doctrines:
1. God is sovereign over all nations.
2. The wicked will be punished and the righteous will be vindicated on the day of judgment.
3. God blesses those who repent and trust in Him.

Zephaniah had the courage to speak bluntly because he knew he was proclaiming the word of the Lord. His book begins with "The word of the LORD" (1:1) and ends with "says the LORD" (3:20). He knew the many gods the people worshiped, or even the might of the Assyrian army, could not save them. God is gracious and compassionate; but when all His warnings are ignored, judgment can be expected.

Zephaniah understood that God's sovereignty includes all nations. God can judge the peoples of all nations because He is their Creator and sovereign Lord.

God's day of judgment is frequently mentioned in the Scriptures. The prophets called it the "day of the LORD." They referred to various events such as the fall of Jerusalem as manifestations of God's day, each of which pointed toward the ultimate day of the Lord. This ultimate day is to be at a time determined solely by God when He will personally intervene to bring this age to an end and judge the nations. It will be a day of punishment for those who have afflicted God's people (2:10) and a day of vindication for the faithful remnant who have trusted God (3:12).

Although the principal emphasis of the prophets is judgment on that day, it will also be a time of joy and blessing for the faithful. The same God who announces judgment also announces hope. The messages are not contradictory. The cross also proclaims both judgment and hope—judgment for those who reject God's Son who died on the cross and hope for those who accept Him.

Contemporary Teaching

Two major emphases highlight Zephaniah's message: judgment of the wicked and hope for the faithful. With a few adjustments in names and situations, this prophet of seventh-century BC could stand in our pulpits today and deliver the same message.

Zephaniah reminds us that: (1) God is offended by the moral and religious sins of His people. (2) God's people will not escape punishment when they sin willfully. (3) Punishment may be painful, but its purpose may be redemptive rather than punitive. (4) The inevitability of the punishment of wickedness gives comfort in a time when it seems that evil is unbridled and victorious. (5) A person has the freedom to disobey God but not the freedom to escape the consequences of that disobedience. (6) Those who are faithful to God may be relatively few, but He does not forget them. They will rejoice in His salvation and in His blessings.

Chapter 1

THE word of the LORD that came to Zephaniah son of Cushi, the son of Gedaliah, the son of Amariah, the son of Hezekiah, during the reign of Josiah[a] son of Amon[b] king of Judah:

Warning of Coming Destruction

2"I will sweep away everything
from the face of the earth,"[c]
declares the LORD.
3"I will sweep away both men and animals;[d]
I will sweep away the birds of the air[e]
and the fish of the sea.
The wicked will have only heaps of rubble[a]
when I cut off man from the face of the earth,"[f]
declares the LORD.[g]

Against Judah

4"I will stretch out my hand[h] against Judah
and against all who live in Jerusalem.
I will cut off from this place every remnant of Baal,[i]
the names of the pagan and the idolatrous priests[j] —
5those who bow down on the roofs
to worship the starry host,[k]
those who bow down and swear by the LORD
and who also swear by Molech,[b] [l]
6those who turn back from following[m] the LORD
and neither seek[n] the LORD nor inquire[o] of him.
7Be silent[p] before the Sovereign LORD,
for the day of the LORD[q] is near.
The LORD has prepared a sacrifice;[r]
he has consecrated those he has invited.
8On the day of the LORD's sacrifice
I will punish[s] the princes
and the king's sons[t]
and all those clad
in foreign clothes.
9On that day I will punish
all who avoid stepping on the threshold,[c] [u]
who fill the temple of their gods
with violence and deceit.[v]
10"On that day,[w]" declares the LORD,
"a cry will go up from the Fish Gate,[x]
wailing[y] from the New Quarter,
and a loud crash from the hills.
11Wail,[z] you who live in the market district[d];
all your merchants will be wiped out,
all who trade with[e] silver will be ruined.[a]
12At that time I will search Jerusalem with lamps
and punish those who are complacent,[b]
who are like wine left on its dregs,[c]
who think, 'The LORD will do nothing,[d]
either good or bad.'[e]
13Their wealth will be plundered,[f]
their houses demolished.
They will build houses
but not live in them;
they will plant vineyards
but not drink the wine.[g]

1:1 [a]2Ki 22:1; 2Ch 34:1-35:25 [b]S 1Ch 3:14
1:2 [c]S Ge 6:7
1:3 [d]Jer 50:3 [e]S Jer 4:25 [f]ver 18; S Hos 4:3 [g]S Eze 14:17
1:4 [h]S Jer 6:12 [i]Mic 5:13; Zep 2:11 [j]S Jer 15:6; S Hos 10:5
1:5 [k]S Jer 8:2 [l]S Lev 18:21; Jer 5:7
1:6 [m]Isa 1:4; Jer 2:13 [n]S Isa 9:13 [o]S Hos 7:7
1:7 [p]S Isa 41:1 [q]ver 14; Isa 13:6; S Eze 7:19; S Joel 3:14; S Am 5:18-20 [r]S Lev 3:9; S Jer 46:10
1:8 [s]Isa 24:21 [t]Jer 39:6
1:9 [u]1Sa 5:5 [v]S Am 3:10
1:10 [w]Isa 22:5 [x]S 2Ch 33:14 [y]S Am 5:16
1:11 [z]Jas 5:1 [a]Hos 9:6
1:12 [b]Am 6:1 [c]Jer 48:11 [d]S 2Ki 21:16; S Eze 8:12 [e]S Job 22:13
1:13 [f]S 2Ki 24:13; Jer 15:13 [g]Dt 28:30,39; La 5:2; S Am 5:11

[a]*3* The meaning of the Hebrew for this line is uncertain. [b]*5* Hebrew *Malcam,* that is, Milcom [c]*9* See 1 Samuel 5:5. [d]*11* Or *the Mortar* [e]*11* Or *in*

1:1,12 REVELATION, Messengers—God revealed Himself to a descendent of a king and declared His displeasure with Jerusalem's behavior. The people thought that God cared little whether they acted rightly or not. God initiated the conversation because He cares for His people's actions and beliefs. Comparison with Amos shows the variety of people God could use as His prophets. See note on Am 1:1,3; Ob 1.

1:1 HISTORY, Narrative—Prophetic books basically record series of prophetic sermons. The introductions of the books give, however, an historical framework to the prophet's ministry. Prophetic preaching is closely tied to historical events and cultural contexts. It gains meaning by relating to historical human existence rather than idealistic spiritual dreams. God's judgment and hope grow out of historical conditions and historical needs. Prophecy retains its power as we find it so natural to relate to the historical conditions of a previous generation and find God's call to them speaks to our historical condition also.

1:2–18 GOD, Wrath—The day of the Lord does not necessarily promise salvation. It means destruction for those who are not true to God. See notes on Am 4:1–13; Hab 3:2–17.

1:4–6 GOD, One God—One god at a time will not do. God destroys people who fail to realize only one true God exists. Nothing else deserves any type of worship or reverence. Neither elements of nature God made nor images people made may be worshiped. None share God's sovereign authority. See note on Jer 1:16.

1:4–13 SIN, Discipline—See note on 2 Ki 25:1–21.

1:4–9 WORSHIP, False—Only the one, true God deserves worship. No matter how elaborate or impressive they may be, ceremonies honoring anyone or anything else are false. They bring judgment on the worshipers. God announced through Zephaniah a sacrifice service in which He would sacrifice the worshipers of false gods. Immoral and unjust lives also lead to false worship.

1:6–7 REVELATION, Oracles—God's people were open-minded, ready to find revelation anywhere and to worship all available gods to obtain it. Only God is living and true. He will not share His worship with anyone or anything else (Ex 20:1–6). Silent reverence is the best attitude as one looks to the day of final revelation.

1:12 HISTORY, God—Atheism apparently was not an option for biblical people. They tended to believe in too many gods rather than not to believe in God at all. Unbelief expressed itself as lack of trust in God's ability or willingness to act for His people. God's judging acts demonstrating His will and power to act came on such people.

The Great Day of the LORD

14"The great day of the LORD[h] is
near[i] —
near and coming quickly.
Listen! The cry on the day of the LORD
will be bitter,
the shouting of the warrior there.
15That day will be a day of wrath,
a day of distress and anguish,
a day of trouble and ruin,
a day of darkness[j] and gloom,
a day of clouds and blackness,[k]
16a day of trumpet and battle cry[l]
against the fortified cities
and against the corner towers.[m]
17I will bring distress[n] on the people
and they will walk like blind[o] men,
because they have sinned against
the LORD.
Their blood will be poured out[p] like
dust
and their entrails like filth.[q]
18Neither their silver nor their gold
will be able to save them
on the day of the LORD's wrath.[r]
In the fire of his jealousy[s]
the whole world will be consumed,[t]
for he will make a sudden end
of all who live in the earth.[u]"

Chapter 2

GATHER together,[v] gather together,
O shameful[w] nation,
2before the appointed time arrives
and that day sweeps on like chaff,[x]
before the fierce anger[y] of the LORD
comes upon you,
before the day of the LORD's wrath[z]
comes upon you.
3Seek[a] the LORD, all you humble of the
land,
you who do what he commands.
Seek righteousness,[b] seek humility;[c]
perhaps you will be sheltered[d]
on the day of the LORD's anger.

Against Philistia

4Gaza[e] will be abandoned
and Ashkelon[f] left in ruins.
At midday Ashdod will be emptied
and Ekron uprooted.
5Woe to you who live by the sea,
O Kerethite[g] people;
the word of the LORD is against you,[h]
O Canaan, land of the Philistines.

"I will destroy you,
and none will be left."[i]

6The land by the sea, where the
Kerethites[f] dwell,
will be a place for shepherds and
sheep pens.[j]
7It will belong to the remnant[k] of the
house of Judah;
there they will find pasture.
In the evening they will lie down
in the houses of Ashkelon.
The LORD their God will care for them;
he will restore their fortunes.[g] [l]

Against Moab and Ammon

8"I have heard the insults[m] of Moab[n]
and the taunts of the Ammonites,[o]
who insulted[p] my people
and made threats against their
land.[q]
9Therefore, as surely as I live,"
declares the LORD Almighty, the God
of Israel,
"surely Moab[r] will become like
Sodom,[s]
the Ammonites[t] like Gomorrah—
a place of weeds and salt pits,
a wasteland forever.

1:14 [h]S ver 7; S Joel 1:15 [i]S Eze 7:7; S Da 7:13
1:15 [j]S 1Sa 2:9 [k]S Isa 22:5; Joel 2:2; Mk 13:24-25
1:16 [l]S Jer 4:19 [m]S Dt 28:52; S Isa 2:15; S Joel 2:1
1:17 [n]S Dt 28:52 [o]S Isa 59:10 [p]Ps 79:3 [q]S Ps 83:10
1:18 [r]S Job 20:20; S 40:11; S Jer 4:4; S Eze 7:19 [s]S Dt 29:20 [t]S ver 2-3; Zep 3:8 [u]S Ge 6:7; S Eze 7:11
2:1 [v]2Ch 20:4; Joel 1:14 [w]S Jer 3:3; 6:15
2:2 [x]Isa 17:13; Hos 13:3 [y]S Jer 10:25; S La 4:11 [z]S Jer 4:4; S Eze 7:19
2:3 [a]S Am 5:6 [b]S Isa 1:17 [c]Ps 45:4 [d]Ps 57:1
2:4 [e]S Ge 10:19; S Am 1:6,7-8; Zec 9:5-7 [f]Jer 47:5
2:5 [g]S 1Sa 30:14 [h]S Lev 26:31; Am 3:1 [i]S Isa 14:30
2:6 [j]S Isa 5:17
2:7 [k]S Ge 45:7 [l]S Dt 30:3; Ps 126:4; Jer 32:44; S Hos 6:11; S Joel 3:1; Am 1:6-8
2:8 [m]S Jer 48:27 [n]S Ge 19:37; S Isa 16:6 [o]S Eze 21:28 [p]Eze 25:3 [q]S La 3:61
2:9 [r]S Dt 23:6; Isa 15:1-16:14; Jer 48:1-47; Eze 25:8-11 [s]Dt 29:23; Isa 13:19; Jer 49:18 [t]Jer 49:1-6; Eze 25:1-7

[f]6 The meaning of the Hebrew for this word is uncertain. [g]7 Or *will bring back their captives*

1:14—2:3 LAST THINGS, Day of the Lord—When God acts decisively in history in judgment upon the sin of individuals and nations, it is the day of the Lord, a day of divine intervention. A past event such as the destruction of Jerusalem could be described as the day of the Lord in His anger (Isa 22:1–13; La 1:12; 2:1,22). More often the reference is to a coming day against Israel's and God's enemies (Isa 34:8; Jer 46:10; Eze 13:5; 30:3; Ob 15). The inspired prophets could speak of the day as God's time of vengeance against sinful Israel (Isa 22:5; Joel 1:15; 2:1,11; Am 5:18–20; Zep 1:7–8,14–18; Zec 14:1). The prophets could also speak of the day of the Lord as the day of universal judgment (Isa 2:12; 13:6; Joel 2:31; 3:14). The idea of judgment is prominent in the prophetic warnings about such a day. The darkness and gloom associated with destruction and overthrow characterize the language about that day. It is a time of God's wrath upon human sin. The glimmer of hope for those who would seek righteousness breaks forth brightly in the other side of the day of the Lord, that which brings deliverance and newness in history (Am 9:11–15) and in the consummation (2 Pe 3:10–13).

1:17 SIN, Universal Nature—See notes on Am 1:1—2:16; Hab 2:4–17.

1:18 GOD, Jealous—See note on Na 1:2.

2:3 SALVATION, Obedience—The prophet presented the possibility that those who obey God's commands may be sheltered from His anger. Obedient believers are saved from the wrath of God. We may suffer from human attacks, but we can take refuge in God's salvation.

2:3 CHRISTIAN ETHICS, Justice—To seek God is more than public or private prayer. It involves humble devotion to God's purpose for society—justice. To "do what He commands" is literally to "do His justice" (Hebrew *mishpat*). Only doers of justice can expect God's protection. See note on Mic 6:6–8.

2:4–15 GOD, Sovereignty—God allows nations to have control of political power for a time. The time always comes when He displays His power to let all nations know they function only with His permission. See note on Eze 1:25–28.

2:6–11 THE CHURCH, Remnant—God promises rich and abundant blessings to those called by His name. Judah may have envied the Philistines and Moabites, but God promised fortunes would be reversed. God's remnant knows He will overcome all opposition in the end. See note on 2 Ch 34:9.

The remnant of my people will
plunder[u] them;
the survivors[v] of my nation will
inherit their land.[w]"

10This is what they will get in return for
their pride,[x]
for insulting[y] and mocking the
people of the LORD Almighty.[z]
11The LORD will be awesome[a] to them
when he destroys all the gods[b] of
the land.[c]
The nations on every shore will
worship him,[d]
every one in its own land.

Against Cush

12"You too, O Cushites,[h] [e]
will be slain by my sword.[f]"

Against Assyria

13He will stretch out his hand against
the north
and destroy Assyria,[g]
leaving Nineveh[h] utterly desolate
and dry as the desert.[i]
14Flocks and herds[j] will lie down there,
creatures of every kind.
The desert owl[k] and the screech
owl[l] [m]
will roost on her columns.
Their calls will echo through the
windows,
rubble will be in the doorways,
the beams of cedar will be exposed.
15This is the carefree[n] city
that lived in safety.[o]
She said to herself,
"I am, and there is none besides
me."[p]
What a ruin she has become,
a lair for wild beasts![q]

2:9 [u]S Isa 11:14 [v]S 2Ki 19:31 [w]S Am 2:1-3
2:10 [x]S Job 40:12; S Isa 16:6 [y]S Jer 48:27 [z]S Ps 9:6
2:11 [a]S Joel 2:11 [b]S Zep 1:4 [c]S 1Ch 19:1; Eze 25:6-7 [d]Ps 86:9; S Isa 12:4; Zep 3:9
2:12 [e]S Ge 10:6; S Isa 20:4 [f]S Jer 46:10
2:13 [g]S Isa 10:5 [h]S Ge 10:11; S Na 1:1 [i]S Mic 5:6; Zec 10:11
2:14 [j]S Isa 5:17 [k]S Isa 14:23 [l]Rev 18:2 [m]S Ps 102:6
2:15 [n]S Isa 32:9 [o]Isa 47:8 [p]Eze 28:2 [q]Jer 49:33 [r]S Isa 28:22; S Na 3:19 [s]S Eze 27:36
3:1 [t]S Jer 6:6 [u]S Dt 21:18 [v]S Eze 23:30
3:2 [w]S Jer 22:21 [x]S Lev 26:23; S Jer 7:28 [y]S Dt 1:32 [z]S Ps 73:28
3:3 [a]S Ps 22:13 [b]S Ge 49:27 [c]S Mic 3:3
3:4 [d]S Ps 25:3; S Isa 48:8; Jer 3:20; 9:4; Mal 2:10 [e]S Jer 23:11; S Eze 22:26
3:5 [f]S Ezr 9:15 [g]Dt 32:4 [h]S Ps 5:3 [i]S La 3:23 [j]S Jer 3:3; S Eze 18:25
3:6 [k]S Lev 26:31
3:7 [l]S Jer 7:28

All who pass by her scoff[r]
and shake their fists.[s]

Chapter 3

The Future of Jerusalem

WOE to the city of oppressors,[t]
rebellious[u] and defiled![v]
2She obeys[w] no one,
she accepts no correction.[x]
She does not trust[y] in the LORD,
she does not draw near[z] to her
God.
3Her officials are roaring lions,[a]
her rulers are evening wolves,[b]
who leave nothing for the
morning.[c]
4Her prophets are arrogant;
they are treacherous[d] men.
Her priests profane the sanctuary
and do violence to the law.[e]
5The LORD within her is righteous;[f]
he does no wrong.[g]
Morning by morning[h] he dispenses his
justice,
and every new day he does not
fail,[i]
yet the unrighteous know no
shame.[j]

6"I have cut off nations;
their strongholds are demolished.
I have left their streets deserted,
with no one passing through.
Their cities are destroyed;[k]
no one will be left—no one at all.
7I said to the city,
'Surely you will fear me
and accept correction!'[l]
Then her dwelling would not be cut
off,

[h]*12* That is, people from the upper Nile region

2:10 SIN, Against God—Attacking God's people is sin against God. Judah's eastern neighbors ridiculed the misfortunes of God's people. They made themselves great at Judah's expense. Why do people heap scorn and reproach on others? It is to bolster their own pride. Such pride is the foundation on which a life of sin is built. Pride makes us focus on self instead of God. Verbal attacks against God's people to boost personal pride are met by God's angry reaction.

2:11 EVANGELISM, Judgment—God's judgment brings about evangelization. As God judges the sins of people, some learn to worship before the Lord. In sincere worship, which implies a true turning to God in repentance, they can find forgiveness and life through faith.

2:15 ELECTION, Sovereignty—God is the sovereign ruler of human history. Gentile nations, therefore, had to be accountable to Him. Complacent and carefree Assyria had to be evaluated and punished by the standards of the electing God, who has His own purposes for each of the nations.

3:1–4 SIN, Depravity—God's elect nation became a depraved people. Morality and values disappeared. Depravity becomes apparent in obstinate rebellion (see note on La 1:18–22); oppressive maltreatment of others; defiled, polluted life-styles (Hebrew *nigalah*) which excluded persons from worship; refusal to listen to, learn from, or obey others; distrust of and refusal to worship God; selfish, vicious leaders; and spiritual leaders who live in arrogant extravagance and treachery (see note on Isa 48:1–9) robbing God's house of its holiness and violating His law. People who show no resemblance to the righteous perfection of God's holiness have begun the road to depravity.

3:5 GOD, Righteous—God's people too often stand in stark contrast to Him. They are unrighteous oppressors. He is perfectly righteous, doing only what is just. When He dispenses absolute justice, such people tremble.

3:5 GOD, Faithfulness—The same God meets us each day. He is faithful to His own character. We can count on Him to do right always.

3:6–13 THE CHURCH, Remnant—The holy remnant of God is characterized by humility, truthfulness, and service to God. God will remove those who are boastful, arrogant, and rebellious.

3:7 SALVATION, Fear of God—Fearing God and accepting His correction are closely linked. God does everything possible to get us to fear Him, that is hold Him in holy reverence; yet, some of us, like Judah, are eager to do evil deeds. We leave God no alternative but to punish us for our sins. See note on Pr 1:7,29.

nor all my punishments come upon
her.
But they were still eager
to act corruptly[m] in all they did.
8Therefore wait[n] for me," declares the
LORD,
"for the day I will stand up to
testify.[i]
I have decided to assemble[o] the
nations,[p]
to gather the kingdoms
and to pour out my wrath[q] on them—
all my fierce anger.[r]
The whole world will be consumed[s]
by the fire of my jealous anger.

9"Then will I purify the lips of the
peoples,
that all of them may call[t] on the
name of the LORD[u]
and serve[v] him shoulder to
shoulder.
10From beyond the rivers of Cush[j] [w]
my worshipers, my scattered people,
will bring me offerings.[x]
11On that day you will not be put to
shame[y]
for all the wrongs you have done to
me,[z]
because I will remove from this city
those who rejoice in their pride.[a]
Never again will you be haughty
on my holy hill.[b]
12But I will leave within you
the meek[c] and humble,
who trust[d] in the name of the LORD.
13The remnant[e] of Israel will do no
wrong;[f]
they will speak no lies,[g]
nor will deceit be found in their
mouths.[h]
They will eat and lie down[i]
and no one will make them
afraid.[j] "

14Sing, O Daughter of Zion;[k]
shout aloud,[l] O Israel!
Be glad and rejoice[m] with all your
heart,
O Daughter of Jerusalem!
15The LORD has taken away your
punishment,
he has turned back your enemy.
The LORD, the King of Israel, is with
you;[n]
never again will you fear[o] any
harm.[p]
16On that day they will say to Jerusalem,
"Do not fear, O Zion;
do not let your hands hang limp.[q]
17The LORD your God is with you,
he is mighty to save.[r]
He will take great delight[s] in you,
he will quiet you with his love,[t]
he will rejoice over you with
singing."[u]
18"The sorrows for the appointed feasts
I will remove from you;
they are a burden and a reproach to
you.[k]
19At that time I will deal
with all who oppressed[v] you;
I will rescue the lame
and gather those who have been
scattered.[w]
I will give them praise[x] and honor
in every land where they were put
to shame.
20At that time I will gather you;
at that time I will bring[y] you home.
I will give you honor[z] and praise[a]
among all the peoples of the earth
when I restore your fortunes[l] [b]
before your very eyes,"
says the LORD.

[i]8 Septuagint and Syriac; Hebrew *will rise up to plunder* [j]10 That is, the upper Nile region [k]18 Or *"I will gather you who mourn for the appointed feasts; / your reproach is a burden to you* [l]20 Or *I bring back your captives*

3:7 [m]S Hos 9:9
3:8 [n]S Ps 27:14 [o]S Joel 3:11 [p]S Isa 2:3 [q]Ps 79:6; Rev 16:1 [r]S Jer 10:25; S La 4:11 [s]S Zep 1:18
3:9 [t]S Zep 2:11 [u]S Ge 4:26 [v]S Isa 19:18
3:10 [w]S Ge 10:6; S Ps 68:31 [x]S 2Ch 32:23; S Isa 60:7
3:11 [y]S Isa 29:22; S Joel 2:26-27 [z]S Ge 50:15 [a]S Ps 59:12 [b]S Ex 15:17; S Lev 26:19
3:12 [c]Isa 14:32 [d]S Jer 29:12; Na 1:7
3:13 [e]S Isa 10:21 [f]Ps 119:3; S Isa 4:3 [g]S Jer 33:16; Rev 14:5 [h]S Job 16:17 [i]Eze 34:15; Zep 2:7 [j]S Lev 26:6; S Eze 34:25-28
3:14 [k]S Ps 9:14; Zec 2:10 [l]S Ps 95:1; Isa 12:6; Zec 2:10 [m]S Ps 9:2; S Isa 51:11
3:15 [n]Eze 37:26-28 [o]S Isa 54:14 [p]Zec 9:9
3:16 [q]S 2Ki 19:26; S Job 4:3; Isa 35:3-4; Heb 12:12
3:17 [r]S Isa 63:1; S Joel 2:21 [s]S Dt 28:63; S Isa 62:4 [t]S Hos 14:4 [u]S Isa 40:1
3:19 [v]S Isa 14:2 [w]S Eze 34:16; S Mic 4:6 [x]Isa 60:18
3:20 [y]S Jer 29:14; S Eze 37:12 [z]Isa 56:5; 66:22 [a]S Dt 26:19; S Isa 60:18 [b]S Joel 3:1

3:8 GOD, Jealous—See note on Na 1:2.
3:9–17 ELECTION, Remnant—God's election purpose aimed at an humble remnant from among all people trusting in God. God promises to be present with the elect remnant.
3:9–10 EVANGELISM, Universality—God plans for all people to join together to worship Him. Different languages can be overcome through God's powers. Evangelism should lead to a purified people calling on God's name in worship.
3:11 GOD, Holy—God established the Temple as a place for holy, morally pure people to worship Him. See Ps 15. Proud, greedy people must be removed. They cannot live in God's holy presence. Worship is for people who are right with God to praise Him, not for sinful people to take pride in the glory of their worship. See note on Hab 1:12–13.
3:12 SALVATION, Belief—Those who trust in the Lord are meek and humble (Mt 5:5). God alone can provide security for His people.
3:14–17 REVELATION, Divine Presence—God promised to redeem His faithful remnant and invited them to celebrate. God thus revealed two crucial aspects of His nature: He is a joyful and a saving God. We can count on Him to be with His faithful people.
3:15 GOD, Sovereignty—The King of the universe stands with His people to protect us againts all harm. Sovereignty should cause sinful people to fear God's wrath, but it comforts His faithful ones. See note on Eze 1:25–28.
3:17 GOD, Savior—God's people can rejoice. He destroys the wicked, but in so doing saves the righteous. See notes on Jer 50:34; Hos 11:1–11.
3:19–20 THE CHURCH, Remnant—See note on 2:6–11.

Haggai

Theological Setting

Will the people of God reconsider their priorities, take courage, and act on the basis of God's promises? God sought to warn the people to heed His words. Not only did God warn them, but He also offered promises through His servant Haggai to motivate them to follow Him.

Because the people of God reversed their priorities and failed to put God in first place in their lives, Judah was sent into Babylonian exile (586-538 BC). In response to Daniel's prayer (Da 9:1-19) and in fulfillment of God's promises (Jer 25:11-12; Isa 44:26—45:4), God directed Cyrus the Persian king to allow the Jews in exile to go back to Jerusalem (Ezr 1:1-4) shortly after 538 BC. A group of Jews (about 50,000) returned to their land with great joy, put God first in their lives, worshiped Him, and began to rebuild the Temple of Jerusalem without the aid of the local people who lived in Palestine (Ezr 3:1—4:5). Their courageous faith was met with opposition from the local people as well as the Persian government for approximately 15 years (Ezr 4). This opposition, several poor harvests in a row, and the broken walls of Jerusalem caused the people of God to center their priorities on their own personal needs rather than on the work of God.

In light of these circumstances the Jews could choose between several possible alternatives:

1. They could give up their old theological priorities and compromise and intermarry with the local inhabitants of Palestine who worshiped other gods. This practice would ease the local tension, might result in some financial assistance, and could possibly bring cooperation from the Persians.
2. They could give up on the idea of rebuilding the Temple destroyed by the Babylonians or decide to wait until more people returned from exile, a new Persian king came to rule, and the people's financial situation looked more positive.
3. They could continue to concentrate on improving their own lot in Jerusalem, maintain a general commitment to their religious ideals but not really stick their neck out in any kind of radical way, and try to be tolerant and peaceable with those who opposed them.
4. They could renew their commitment to God and finish His Temple.

In this situation Haggai (and Zechariah) carried on a short but very effective ministry in 520 BC. (Note the dates attached to each message.) Haggai sought to challenge the people of God concerning their priorities (Hag 1:5,7). He called them to reverence and glorify God by building the Temple in spite of local and official opposition (1:8,12), not to be discouraged because this new Temple would not be quite as richly decorated as Solomon's Temple (2:3-9), to turn from the uncleanness of their ways (2:14), and to trust in God's sovereign power (2:6-7,17-19,21-22) and the promise of His presence and His provisions (1:13; 2:4-5,7-8). The people believed God's promises, demonstrated their reverence for God, and began to rebuild (1:12,14). God dramatically fulfilled His promise of providing for every need, for soon the Persians gave official support for rebuilding the Temple, commanded the local inhabitants not to interfere with the Jews, and even paid the full cost of finishing the Temple building (Ezr 6:1-15).

The Book of Haggai is a reminder of the problems the people of God faced at this time, how the people courageously trusted in God, and how God provided for their needs. Through the ministry and encouragement of Haggai, the people of God set new priorities, acted boldly on the basis of God's promises, and received His grace and blessing.

Theological Outline

Haggai: Encouragement to Reconsider Priorities

I. God's People Must Reconsider Materialistic Priorities in Light of God's Call. (1:1-15)
   A. Materialistic pride and greed must not cause procrastination in fulfilling God's priority tasks. (1:1-4)
   B. God withholds blessing and fertility from a selfish people who do not glorify Him. (1:5-11)

C. Faithful leadership and God's presence can motivate God's people to carry out His priorities. (1:12-15)

II. God's People Must Reconsider Priorities in Light of God's Promises and Power. (2:1-9)

A. Comparisons with past achievements may discourage God's people from doing God's work. (2:1-3)

B. Trust in God's promises and power to provide every need encourages His people to continue His work. (2:4-9)

III. God's People Must Reconsider the Priority of a Pure Life. (2:10-19)

A. Impure people produce only more impurity. (2:10-14)

B. God does not bless an impure people who do not repent. (2:15-17)

C. God will bless His attentive people in the future. (2:18-19)

IV. God's People Must Reconsider God's Power to Overcome Opposition. (2:20-23)

A. God will overcome all opposition. (2:20-22)

B. God will empower His chosen servant. (2:23)

Theological Conclusions

The words of Haggai gave hope and confidence to a group of people who faced economic, social, and political opposition by emphasizing three doctrines:

1. God is in control of all the nations of the earth and can remove political opposition to His work.
2. The people of God need to reject a defeatist attitude and act on the basis of God's promises.
3. God will bless those who strive for purity and those who give priority to His desires.

The Israelities who returned to Jerusalem lost all hope of ever rebuilding the Temple of Jerusalem because of the political opposition from the local inhabitants of Palestine and the Persian government. The Book of Haggai (and Ezra's historical account of this period) shows that God can overturn previous political decisions and use these powers to bring about His glory. He can overthrow kings and great military powers and raise up His own chosen servants. Hope and assurance were strengthened because God's hand was on the leaders of Israel and because He promised that His presence or Spirit would be with His people.

The people of God did not always see the sovereign hand of God at work, for troubles were all around them. They tried to rebuild the Temple, but encountered crop failures, discouragements about the size and glory of this new Temple, and political opposition. Opposition easily led to a defeatist attitude and a rejection of God's priorities. When the crops failed, many felt putting bread on their own table was most important. The rebuilding of the Temple could wait. If the size and glory of the new Temple could not compare with Solomon's Temple, which they remembered as ideal, why not forget the project until it could be done right. Since there was official political opposition, they could only conclude that this was not the time to build the new Temple. The prophet Haggai showed that God was not pleased with this defeatist attitude when opposition arose. God continues to be displeased when opposition today hampers our desire to carry out His work.

The Book of Haggai contains exhortations concerning changes that God desires to see in the lives of His people. They need to reconsider their priorities, to overcome their defeatist attitudes, and to do God's work. If they would put God first, rather than the comfort of their own homes, God could bless them. If they would just build the "Temple" and not put such a priority on its looks, God could bless them. If they remove impurities and live holy and godly lives, God could bless them. In light of God's sovereign power and His promises, He desires that His people step out in faith, act courageously, and bring glory to His name.

Contemporary Teaching

The Book of Haggai draws attention to common problems most people face even today. Although setting and culture are different, it is not difficult to identify with Haggai's situation. Haggai asks us: (1) to examine our priorities to see if we are more interested in our own pleasures than doing the work of God; (2) to reject a defeatist attitude when we run into opposition or discouraging circumstances; (3) to confess our failures and seek to live pure lives before God; (4) to act courageously for God because we have the assurance that He is with us always and is in full control of our circumstances; and (5) to rest secure in God's hands knowing that He will abundantly bless us as we faithfully serve Him.

Chapter 1

A Call to Build the House of the LORD

IN the second year of King Darius,[a] on
the first day of the sixth month, the
word of the LORD came through the
prophet Haggai[b] to Zerubbabel[c] son of
Shealtiel, governor[d] of Judah, and to
Joshua[a][e] son of Jehozadak,[f] the high
priest:[g]
2This is what the LORD Almighty[h] says:
"These people[i] say, 'The time has not
yet come for the LORD's house to be
built.[j]' "
3Then the word of the LORD came
through the prophet Haggai:[k] 4"Is it a
time for you yourselves to be living in
your paneled houses,[l] while this house
remains a ruin?[m]"
5Now this is what the LORD Almighty
says: "Give careful thought[n] to your
ways. 6You have planted much, but have
harvested little.[o] You eat, but never have
enough.[p] You drink, but never have your
fill.[q] You put on clothes, but are not
warm. You earn wages,[r] only to put
them in a purse with holes in it."
7This is what the LORD Almighty says:
"Give careful thought[s] to your ways. 8Go
up into the mountains and bring down
timber[t] and build the house, so that I
may take pleasure[u] in it and be honored,[v]" says the LORD. 9"You expected
much, but see, it turned out to be little.[w]
What you brought home, I blew[x] away.
Why?" declares the LORD Almighty. "Because of my house, which remains a
ruin,[y] while each of you is busy with his
own house. 10Therefore, because of you
the heavens have withheld[z] their dew[a]
and the earth its crops.[b] 11I called for a
drought[c] on the fields and the mountains,[d] on the grain, the new wine,[e] the
oil[f] and whatever the ground produces,
on men and cattle, and on the labor of
your hands.[g]"

12Then Zerubbabel[h] son of Shealtiel,
Joshua son of Jehozadak, the high priest,
and the whole remnant[i] of the people
obeyed[j] the voice of the LORD their God
and the message of the prophet Haggai,
because the LORD their God had sent
him. And the people feared[k] the LORD.
13Then Haggai,[l] the LORD's messenger,[m] gave this message of the LORD to
the people: "I am with[n] you," declares
the LORD. 14So the LORD stirred up[o] the
spirit of Zerubbabel[p] son of Shealtiel,
governor of Judah, and the spirit of Joshua

1:1 [a]S Ezr 4:24 [b]S Ezr 5:1 [c]S 1Ch 3:19; Mt 1:12-13 [d]Ezr 5:3; S Ne 5:14 [e]S Ezr 2:2 [f]S 1Ch 6:15; S Ezr 3:2 [g]Zec 3:8
1:2 [h]Isa 13:4 [i]S Isa 29:13 [j]Ezr 1:2
1:3 [k]S Ezr 5:1
1:4 [l]S 2Sa 7:2 [m]ver 9; Jer 33:12
1:5 [n]ver 7; La 3:40; Hag 2:15,18
1:6 [o]S Lev 26:20; S Isa 5:10 [p]S Isa 9:20; S 55:2 [q]Am 4:8 [r]Hag 2:16; Zec 8:10
1:7 [s]S ver 5
1:8 [t]S 1Ch 14:1 [u]S Job 22:3; Ps 132:13-14 [v]S Ex 29:43; Jer 13:11
1:9 [w]S Dt 28:38; S Isa 5:10 [x]S Ps 103:16; S Eze 22:21 [y]S ver 4; S Ne 13:11
1:10 [z]S Dt 28:24 [a]S Ge 27:28; 1Ki 17:1 [b]Lev 26:19; Dt 28:23
1:11 [c]S Dt 11:26; S 28:22; S Ru 1:1; S 1Ki 17:1; S Isa 5:6 [d]Isa 7:25 [e]S Dt 28:51; Ps 4:7 [f]S Nu 18:12 [g]Hag 2:17
1:12 [h]ver 1 [i]ver 14; Isa 1:9; Hag 2:2 [j]S Job 36:11; S Isa 50:10; Mt 28:20 [k]S Dt 31:12; S Isa 1:2
1:13 [l]ver 1 [m]S Nu 27:21; S 2Ch 36:15 [n]S Ge 26:3; S Nu 14:9; S Mt 28:20; Ro 8:31
1:14 [o]S Ezr 1:5 [p]S Ezr 5:2

[a] *1* A variant of *Jeshua*; here and elsewhere in Haggai

1:1–2 REVELATION, Messengers—God chose Haggai to reveal His displeasure with the exiles' selfish concern for their own material needs. The prophet apparently received his message in meditation and reflection, though no detail is provided. The message was directed to the nation's leaders but came through the prophet as God's chosen instrument of revelation.

1:1–14 SALVATION, Obedience—God's people obeyed the Word of the Lord through Haggai to rebuild the house of the Lord in Jerusalem. The prophet's message was that they were being denied certain blessings because they had put their own houses and welfare before the Lord's house. God's people should obey His commands and place His concerns above their own.

1:2–11 EVIL AND SUFFERING, Punishment—Undisciplined desire for material possessions may bring God's punishment. The returned exiles suffered economically because they neglected rebuilding the Temple in Jerusalem while they rebuilt their own homes. Haggai promised prosperity would return after their priorities returned. Sometimes we suffer because we neglect to do what is really important. When we have the wrong priorities, we neglect what God wants done, and we suffer for it.

1:2–15 WORSHIP, Buildings—Worship is first priority for God's people. Returning from Exile, Israel tended to personal needs before they provided for worship needs. Haggai, Zerubbabel, Joshua, and Zechariah finally led them to rebuild the Temple. God wants His people to have a place to worship. The worship building should reflect the economic position of the people. God is not honored by second-best buildings.

1:3–9 REVELATION, Events—The people neglected the house of God while tending to their own material situations. God revealed His anger by making their lives unsatisfying in every regard. They never reached satisfaction, God declared, because they focused on their own needs. Haggai delivered the inspired word by repeating the people's faithless question and then giving God's answers.

1:4–11 CHRISTIAN ETHICS, Property Rights—Some interpretations do damage to this text by applying it as a prooftext for building huge church buildings. Haggai's point is that the condition of the Temple revealed the attitude of the people toward true faith in God and covenant with Him. They had misplaced their priorities by using their wealth for their own benefit. Self-serving wealth brings God's judgment. Material resources are given to be used for God's purposes.

1:5–11 GOD, Sovereignty—God set up the natural cycles to produce the weather patterns our world needs. He remains in control of all His creation and can use it to accomplish His purposes. He seeks to show His people that placing financial success as priority number one will not work.

1:9 SIN, Against God—Making God's priorities wait is sin against God. Haggai's people were going to build God's Temple when they finished their own houses and got themselves reestablished. Eighteen years after Cyrus let them return from exile, they still had not built God's Temple. They had many excuses. God did not accept them. He did not bless the people.

1:12 SALVATION, Fear of God—The returned exiles of Israel feared the Lord as a proper response to Haggai's message. Obedience and fear are linked together in the doctrine of salvation.

1:12–15 THE CHURCH, Remnant—God's faithful remnant listens to His word and follows His leadership. The remnant in Jerusalem obeyed Haggai's message and rebuilt the Temple. God always has a purpose for His remnant. We need to listen to Him, learn His purpose, and go to work.

1:13 GOD, Presence—God promises His presence to a people who obey and reverence Him. His presence assures our needs will be met. It does not assure financial success.

1:13–15 REVELATION, Divine Presence—God's presence leads people to work for Him. The people respond to God's confrontation. The Lord made His presence felt with the governor, and from him to the entire nation of people. God's Spirit (2:5) made a spiritual impact and changed the priority of the whole community.

son of Jehozadak,[q] the high priest, and
the spirit of the whole remnant[r] of the
people. They came and began to work on
the house of the LORD Almighty, their
God, 15on the twenty-fourth day of the
sixth month[s] in the second year of King
Darius.[t]

Chapter 2

The Promised Glory of the New House

ON the twenty-first day of the seventh
month,[u] the word of the LORD came
through the prophet Haggai:[v] 2"Speak to
Zerubbabel[w] son of Shealtiel, governor of
Judah, to Joshua son of Jehozadak,[x] the
high priest, and to the remnant[y] of the
people. Ask them, 3'Who of you is left
who saw this house[z] in its former glory?
How does it look to you now? Does it not
seem to you like nothing?[a] 4But now be
strong, O Zerubbabel,' declares the LORD.
'Be strong,[b] O Joshua son of Jehozadak,[c]
the high priest. Be strong, all you people
of the land,' declares the LORD, 'and
work. For I am with[d] you,' declares the
LORD Almighty. 5'This is what I covenanted[e] with you when you came out of
Egypt.[f] And my Spirit[g] remains among
you. Do not fear.'[h]

6"This is what the LORD Almighty says:
'In a little while[i] I will once more shake
the heavens and the earth,[j] the sea and
the dry land. 7I will shake all nations, and
the desired[k] of all nations will come, and
I will fill this house[l] with glory,[m]' says
the LORD Almighty. 8'The silver is mine
and the gold[n] is mine,' declares the LORD
Almighty. 9'The glory[o] of this present
house[p] will be greater than the glory of
the former house,' says the LORD Almighty. 'And in this place I will grant
peace,[q]' declares the LORD Almighty."

Blessings for a Defiled People

10On the twenty-fourth day of the
ninth month,[r] in the second year of Darius, the word of the LORD came to the
prophet Haggai: 11"This is what the LORD
Almighty says: 'Ask the priests[s] what the

1:14 [q]S 1Ch 6:15 [r]S ver 12 **1:15** [s]ver 1; Hag 2:10,20 [t]S Ezr 4:24 **2:1** [u]ver 10,20; S Lev 23:34; Jn 7:37 [v]S Ezr 5:1 **2:2** [w]Hag 1:1 [x]S 1Ch 6:15 [y]S Hag 1:12 **2:3** [z]S Ezr 3:12; S Isa 60:7 [a]Zec 4:10 **2:4** [b]S 1Ch 28:20; Zec 8:9; S Eph 6:10 [c]S 1Ch 6:15 [d]S Ex 33:14; S Nu 14:9; S 2Sa 5:10; Ac 7:9 **2:5** [e]S Ge 6:18 [f]S Ex 29:46 [g]S Ne 9:20 [h]S Ge 15:1; 1Ch 28:20; S Ezr 5:2; Zec 8:13 **2:6** [i]S Isa 10:25 [j]S Ex 19:18; S Job 9:6; S Isa 14:16; S Eze 38:19; Heb 12:26* **2:7** [k]S 1Sa 9:20 [l]S Isa 60:7 [m]S Ex 16:7; S 29:43; Lk 2:32 **2:8** [n]S 1Ch 29:2 **2:9** [o]S Ps 85:9; S Isa 11:10 [p]S Ezr 3:12; S Isa 60:7 [q]S Lev 26:6; S Isa 60:17 **2:10** [r]S ver 1; S Hag 1:15 **2:11** [s]S Lev 10:10-11; Dt 17:8-11; 33:8; S Jer 18:18

2:1–9 GOD, Presence—Huge disappointment troubled Haggai's audience. Their building efforts could not match Solomon's. Haggai reassured them. God's presence was with them. Their building needed nothing more for success. God's covenant (Ex 19—20) remained in effect. Our criteria of magnificence do not measure success. God's continued presence and covenant faithfulness determine the success of His people.

2:1–5 THE CHURCH, Remnant—God does not use worldly success standards to measure His remnant's accomplishments. He expects faithfulness at the task. Haggai saw the people's disappointment that the rebuilt Temple appeared inferior to the original. He assured the people of God's presence and covenant blessings. That was all they needed. See note on 1:12–15.

2:3–9 WORSHIP, Buildings—See note on 1:2–15. God's people cannot always match the splendor of theirs, their neighbors', or their ancestors' dreams as they build God's house of worship. God encourages us to do our best and depend on Him to supply the true glory.

2:4–5 HOLY SPIRIT, Mission—Despair quickly engulfs a people when success does not crown their work. Haggai encouraged the people to resume their work in rebuilding the Temple. They compared their work to Solomon's Temple and lost their enthusiasm. Haggai challenged them to look at their God, not their work. The Redeemer of the Exodus (Ex 14) was still with them. His indwelling Spirit continued to guide as He had guided through the wilderness. As God's people, we need to finish our mission for God no matter what discourages us. We can depend on the Spirit to help us when even our leaders lose confidence. See Nu 27:18–20; note on Dt 34:9.

2:4–5 REVELATION, Divine Presence—See note on 1:13–15.

2:4–5 HISTORY, Presence—God's people can be sure of God's presence because He has made historical commitments to be with His people. Israel received the commitment in the Exodus and on Mt. Sinai. Christians received the commitment in the cross and resurrection experience, in the Great Commission of the resurrected Christ (Mt 28:18–20), and in the Lord's Supper.

2:4–5 DISCIPLESHIP, Enabling Power—God promised His enabling power to Zerubbabel and to all the people for the work they were to do. He assured them His Spirit would be with them. Then He sent them to work on the Temple. We can claim those same precious promises. See Mt 28:18–20. We need also to find the task God wants to enable us to do. God's power is given not for personal satisfaction and pride but for the accomplishment of His mission.

2:4–5 THE CHURCH, Covenant People—A rebuilding people may fear God does not accept them because they cannot match the glorious achievements of the past. They can rest assured that God's presence—His Spirit—is with them. God calls people to work productively for Him rather than to match someone else's achievements. See note on Ex 19:4–8.

2:5 ELECTION, Faithfulness—Haggai was able to fire up the people with enthusiasm and courage to complete the Temple. He based this motivation on the promises in God's covenant. God's election assured them of God's approval and presence as they sought to rebuild the Land of Promise. Election points to God's faithfulness to encourage and assure the faithful remnant.

2:7,9 GOD, Glory—Glory may refer to material elegance, personal reputation, or Spiritual presence. All are included here. Only God has and can create true glory. He has the power to bring material and spiritual glory to His house of worship. He can use forces of nature and of history to accomplish His purposes. We may proudly total up our material possessions, but none belong to us. God is sovereign Lord over all His creation's wealth. True wealth comes only when God grants peace.

2:7 REVELATION, Events—God takes the initiative to confirm His promised presence to His people. He would be available again in His sanctuary. See note on 1 Ki 8:1–21. His actions in bringing the remaining exiles along with material wealth from the nations would reveal His glory. Compare Isa 2:2–4; 60:1–22.

2:7–8 CHRISTIAN ETHICS, Property Rights—See note on 1:4–11. The strange paradox is that one would put faith in the created matter (gold and silver) rather than the Creator of this matter.

2:11–12 REVELATION, Oracles—Priests had authority to seek God's will in disputed questions either through interpreting the authoritative Law or using Urim and Thummim. God used a priestly answer or oracle as the springboard for His revelation to His prophet. See note on Nu 27:18–21.

2:11–13 EDUCATION, Priests—The prophet asked the priests to clarify the written Law. God's people will always need teachers who can translate the written Word of God into understanding for contemporary hearers. See Eze 44:23.

law says: 12 If a person carries consecrated
meat[t] in the fold of his garment, and that
fold touches some bread or stew, some
wine, oil or other food, does it become
consecrated?[u]' "

The priests answered, "No."

13 Then Haggai said, "If a person defiled
by contact with a dead body touches one
of these things, does it become defiled?"

"Yes," the priests replied, "it becomes
defiled.[v]"

14 Then Haggai said, " 'So it is with this
people[w] and this nation in my sight,' declares the LORD. 'Whatever they do and
whatever they offer[x] there is defiled.

15 " 'Now give careful thought[y] to this
from this day on[b]—consider how things
were before one stone was laid[z] on another in the LORD's temple.[a] 16 When
anyone came to a heap[b] of twenty measures, there were only ten. When anyone
went to a wine vat[c] to draw fifty measures, there were only twenty.[d] 17 I
struck all the work of your hands[e] with
blight,[f] mildew and hail,[g] yet you did
not turn[h] to me,' declares the LORD.[i]
18 'From this day on, from this twenty-
fourth day of the ninth month, give careful thought[j] to the day when the foundation[k] of the LORD's temple was laid. Give
careful thought: 19 Is there yet any seed
left in the barn? Until now, the vine and
the fig tree, the pomegranate[l] and the
olive tree have not borne fruit.[m]

" 'From this day on I will bless[n]
you.' "

Zerubbabel the LORD's Signet Ring

20 The word of the LORD came to Haggai[o] a second time on the twenty-fourth
day of the month:[p] 21 "Tell Zerubbabel[q]
governor of Judah that I will shake[r] the
heavens and the earth. 22 I will overturn[s]
royal thrones and shatter the power of
the foreign kingdoms.[t] I will overthrow
chariots[u] and their drivers; horses and
their riders[v] will fall, each by the sword
of his brother.[w]

23 " 'On that day,[x]' declares the LORD
Almighty, 'I will take you, my servant[y]
Zerubbabel[z] son of Shealtiel,' declares
the LORD, 'and I will make you like my
signet ring,[a] for I have chosen you,' declares the LORD Almighty."

2:12 [t]Jer 11:15 [u]S Ge 7:2; S Lev 6:27; Mt 23:19
2:13 [v]Lev 22:4-6; Nu 19:13
2:14 [w]S Isa 29:13 [x]S Ps 51:17; S Isa 1:13
2:15 [y]S Hag 1:5 [z]S Ezr 3:10 [a]Ezr 4:24
2:16 [b]S Ru 3:7 [c]S Job 24:11; S Isa 5:2 [d]S Dt 28:38; S Isa 5:10; S Hag 1:6
2:17 [e]Hag 1:11 [f]S Dt 28:22 [g]S Ex 9:18; Ps 78:48 [h]S Isa 9:13; S Jer 3:10 [i]S Am 4:6
2:18 [j]S Hag 1:5 [k]S Ezr 3:11
2:19 [l]S Ex 28:33 [m]S Joel 1:12 [n]S Ge 12:2; S Lev 25:21; Ps 128:1-6; S Joel 2:14
2:20 [o]S Ezr 5:1 [p]S ver 1; S Hag 1:15
2:21 [q]S Ezr 5:2 [r]S Isa 14:16; Eze 38:19-20
2:22 [s]S Ge 19:25; S Job 2:13 [t]S Da 2:44 [u]S Mic 5:10 [v]S Ex 15:21 [w]S Jdg 7:22; S Eze 38:21
2:23 [x]Isa 2:11; 10:20; Zec 4:10 [y]S Isa 20:3; S Da 9:24-26 [z]Mt 1:12 [a]S Ge 38:18; S Ex 28:9; 2Co 1:22

[b]*15* Or *to the days past*

2:20–23 HISTORY, Hope—Language describing God's past historical actions gives assurance of future deliverance. God does not lose the power to control all nations, and He repeatedly affirms His intentions to deliver His people in time of need.

2:23 REVELATION, Persons—God declared His blessing upon Zerubbabel, bestowing upon him power to lead, initiating His work of renewal and care through the king. The king bore God's signature power to reveal God's will in the world. In affirming the descendant of David, God renewed His commitment to His messianic promises through David's line.

2:23 ELECTION, Leadership—God promised leadership to the remnant community. The leader would have authority, being God's signet ring to sign approval on activities among His people. God consistently elects and empowers leaders for His elect people.

2:23 THE CHURCH, Servants—Zerubbabel served as governor of the returned exiles in Jerusalem. All accounts of Zerubbabel picture him as a righteous man who sought to please God. God uses faithful servant leaders to bless and guide His people. Such leaders do not assume leadership positions on their own. God chooses and calls His leaders. See note on Da 9:11.

Zechariah

Theological Setting

In the early days after the exile (539 BC to 520 BC), the people of Judah faced the following set of questions:

1. Why had God punished His people by sending their leaders into exile in 597 and 587?
2. Why had the people not prospered after they returned from Babylon?
3. What did God have in mind for His people in the future?
4. What did they need to do to reap future blessings?

The exiles had returned to Judah under the lenient policy of Cyrus the Great, Emperor of Persia. They returned to a land with few Jewish leaders, little money, no Temple, and no priesthood (or perhaps one viewed as illegitimate by the returnees). The peasants living in Judah had been left behind to cultivate the lands of their former masters in the aftermath of the fall of Jerusalem (587 BC). The peasants and the returning exiles thus claimed the same property, and perhaps competed with each other over religious leadership as well. In addition, the land experienced a famine. Finally, when the Persian Emperor Cambysees (529-521 BC) died and Darius I had to defeat Gautama to claim the throne, the people also confronted political instability. See introduction to Haggai.

Faced with such conditions, God's people had these options:

1. They could follow the lead of many little countries in the Persian Empire and rebel. The option might have looked inviting because the Persians levied taxes against them and seemed too far away and too engrossed in a civil war to collect. The result would have been certain punishment when the Empire restabilized.

2. The people might have given up. In view of the famine and economic hard times, and in view of the fact that most exiles had not returned from Babylon, they might have thought God was unable or unwilling to care for His people. This option might have involved turning to Persian gods or mere secularism. The end result would have been oblivion, the fate suffered by most conquered peoples.

3. The people might have proceeded as they had been, putting self first (building their own houses) and God second (the work on the Temple had stopped dead). The result of this option probably would have been to break into factions, a possibility threatening the tiny community: Judah versus Jerusalem, peasant versus city dweller, priests vesus people, nationalists versus those sympathizing with the Persians.

4. The remaining option was to trust God and follow His plans as revealed through Haggai and Zechariah.

Along with Haggai, Zechariah flourished between 520 BC and 518 BC, urging the people of Judah and Jerusalem to do the following:

1. rebuild the Temple under the leadership of Zerubbabel;
2. reestablish a purified priesthood under Joshua;
3. cast off foreign influences on their religious life; and
4. live proper moral lives.

Zechariah's ministry seems to have been highly successful: the Temple was rebuilt by 515 BC; the priesthood established control and order over the worship and sacrifice in Jerusalem; people were challenged to moral purity. Zechariah's expectation was for God's people to experience the bounteous blessings of God. Probably many did, but the subsequent ministry of a prophet like Malachi and the careers of Ezra and Nehemiah show that the people did not respond whole-heartedly to the call to throw off foreign influence and live morally. Their failure was the failure of God's people in each generation, however, and not an indication of the failure of Zechariah.

Theological Outline

Zechariah: Prosperity through Purification

I. God's Ways Are Just. (1:1-6)

A. God's anger with His sinful people is justified. (1:1-2)
B. God will return to His people if they return to Him. (1:3)
C. History shows the justice of God and the sinfulness of His people. (1:4-6)

II. God Promises Prosperity to His People. (1:7—2:13)
A. Vision One: God's election mercy for His people replaces His anger. (1:7-17)
B. Vision Two: God punishes those who oppress His people. (1:18-21)
C. Vision Three: God's glorious presence will restore, protect, and expand His people. (2:1-13)

III. God Calls His People to Purification. (3:1—6:15)
A. Vision Four: God wants to forgive and purify His people and their leaders. (3:1-10)
B. Vision Five: God exercises His sovereign rule through His Spirit and His messianic leaders. (4:1-14)
C. Vision Six: God condemns stealing and lying. (5:1-4)
D. Vision Seven: God removes the wickedness of His people. (5:5-11)
E. Vision Eight: The universal God defeats the enemies of His people. (6:1-8)
F. God commissions leaders for His obedient people. (6:9-15)

IV. God Seeks Righteousness, Not Ritual. (7:1-14)
A. God has always rejected selfish, insincere worship rituals. (7:1-7)
B. God seeks justice, mercy, and compassion. (7:8-10)
C. God is angry when His people reject His inspired teaching. (7:11-12)
D. God punishes His disobedient people. (7:13-14)

V. God in His Jealousy Restores His Faithful Remnant. (8:1-23)
A. God's jealousy leads to hope for His people. (8:1-5)
B. The faithful God wants to renew His covenant with His people. (8:6-8)
C. God is not bound by the past. (8:9-13)
D. God has punished Judah and now will bless her. (8:14-15)
E. God commands truthfulness, justice, and peace. (8:16-19)
F. God seeks all people to worship Him. (8:20-23)

VI. God Controls the Future for His People. (9:1—11:17)
A. God promises restoration. (9:1-17)
1. God will defeat and convert the enemies of His people. (9:1-8)
2. God promised a messianic King to bring peace for His people. (9:9-10)
3. God will lead His covenant people to victory. (9:11-17)
B. God punishes wicked leaders. (10:1—11:3)
1. God's presence leads His people when leaders deceive them. (10:1-5)
2. God in His compassion redeems His people to obey Him. (10:6-11)
3. Wicked leaders lose their power. The wicked rulers lament their losses. (11:1-3)
C. God is not bound by past covenants from punishing His foolish people and their wicked leaders. (11:4-17)

VII. God Purges and Delivers His People. (12:1—14:21)
A. The universal God exercises His control over all His world. (12:1—13:6)
1. God can defeat any enemy of His people. (12:1-6)
2. God does not play favorites among His people. (12:7-9)
3. God calls His people to prayer and mourning. (12:10-14)
4. God will cleanse His people of immorality, idolatry, and false prophecy in His day. (13:1-6)
B. God will make a new covenant with the remnant of His people after striking His shepherd. (13:7-9)
C. God will rule over the whole earth on the day of the Lord. (14:1-21)
1. God will rescue His defeated people. (14:1-5)
2. God will restore paradise-like conditions. (14:6-8)
3. God will rule the earth from Mt. Zion. (14:9)
4. God will elevate Jerusalem, making it secure. (14:10-11)
5. God will send plagues on non-repentant nations. (14:12-15)
6. The converted nations will go to Jerusalem to worship. (14:16-19)
7. God will purify and sanctify all of Jerusalem. (14:20-21)

Theological Conclusions

Zechariah brought new hope and a new plan of action to the early post-exilic community by teaching his people a number of lessons about God and His relationship to them:

1. Prophets bring God's revelation.
2. God expects morality, not sin.
3. Salvation is offered to all.
4. God is sovereign.

No lesson was more important than the one with which the book opens: God has revealed Himself through His messengers the prophets. Particularly in 1:1-6 and 7:8-14, Zechariah emphasized that God had used His prophets to teach, warn, and correct His people. Unfortunately, they refused to listen. Their sin brought God's punishment. The book also bears evidence (13:2-6) that even prophecy could be corrupted. History shows that in this period prophecy fell into disfavor among the Jews, leading to the period between the Testaments when no lasting prophetic voice spoke to God's people. In the early church a new group of prophets rose in the name of Christ (Ac 19:6; 21:9-10).

Zechariah taught his people that God requires proper moral living. He punishes sin, even the sin of His own people and their leaders. Further, sin has corporate or social consequence. The wickedness of the leaders involved their abuse of their subordinates, but more than that it led the people to sin themselves. On the other hand, moral regeneration could lead to a state of blessing for the people, or at least the repentant ones among the people.

The book of Zechariah also teaches that salvation may be obtained by all. The last chapter depicts peoples from all over the world coming to worship God, who desires that all people follow Him. This is not the doctrine of universalism, i.e., that all people would be saved because it is God's nature to save. Rather, the book teaches that God desires that all people worship Him and accepts those who do, regardless of their national origin. Indeed, in view of the corporate nature of human actions, salvation itself may even take on national or political expressions, as in the freeing of Judah and Jerusalem from their political enemies.

Finally, Zechariah preached that God is sovereign over this world, any appearance to the contrary notwithstanding. His visions of the future indicate that God sees all that will happen. The depictions of God's intervention in the world teach that ultimately He will bring human events to the end He chooses. He does not eliminate the individual's freedom to follow God or rebel, but holds people responsible for the choices they make. In the last chapter, even the forces of nature respond to God's control.

Contemporary Teaching

The book of Zechariah insists that the message of God revealed through His spokesman remains as valid for later generations as it was for the generations who heard the prophets. Such insights prompted old Israel to collect and preserve the books of the Bible. Those books exert their unique power in the life of the individual, however, only when they are read and obeyed. They address us in our sinfulness and call us to God.

God expects sincere worship and moral living of us today, the same as He did of the contemporaries of Zechariah. Sincere worship and good deeds are made possible by the forgiveness and love of God which permeates us.

Zechariah's insistence that proper living and worship would bring God's blessing remains as relevant today as it was to the prophet's community. We must be careful, though, not to commit the error of Job's friends and conclude that financial well-being is evidence of God's blessing and economic or other kinds of hardship prove one's immorality. God will bless the believer spiritually, whether materially or not.

Finally, Zechariah's example of breaking through national prejudice reminds us to reach out into all areas of our society. We must extend God's invitation to salvation to people of all national origins, languages, races, and cultures.

Chapter 1

A Call to Return to the LORD

IN the eighth month of the second year
of Darius,[a] the word of the LORD came
to the prophet Zechariah[b] son of Berekiah,[c] the son of Iddo:[d]
2"The LORD was very angry[e] with your
forefathers. 3Therefore tell the people:
This is what the LORD Almighty says: 'Return[f] to me,' declares the LORD Almighty, 'and I will return to you,'[g] says
the LORD Almighty. 4Do not be like your
forefathers,[h] to whom the earlier prophets[i] proclaimed: This is what the LORD
Almighty says: 'Turn from your evil
ways[j] and your evil practices.' But they
would not listen or pay attention to me,[k]
declares the LORD.[l] 5Where are your
forefathers now? And the prophets, do
they live forever? 6But did not my words[m]
and my decrees, which I commanded my
servants the prophets, overtake your forefathers?[n]
"Then they repented and said, 'The
LORD Almighty has done to us what our
ways and practices deserve,[o] just as he
determined to do.' "[p]

The Man Among the Myrtle Trees

7On the twenty-fourth day of the eleventh month, the month of Shebat, in the
second year of Darius, the word of the
LORD came to the prophet Zechariah son
of Berekiah, the son of Iddo.[q]
8During the night I had a vision—and
there before me was a man riding a red[r]
horse! He was standing among the myrtle
trees in a ravine. Behind him were red,
brown and white horses.[s]
9I asked, "What are these, my lord?"
The angel[t] who was talking with me
answered, "I will show you what they
are."[u]
10Then the man standing among the
myrtle trees explained, "They are the
ones the LORD has sent to go throughout
the earth."[v]
11And they reported to the angel of the
LORD,[w] who was standing among the
myrtle trees, "We have gone throughout
the earth and found the whole world at
rest and in peace."[x]
12Then the angel of the LORD said,
"LORD Almighty, how long[y] will you
withhold mercy[z] from Jerusalem and
from the towns of Judah,[a] which you
have been angry with these seventy[b]
years?" 13So the LORD spoke[c] kind and
comforting words[d] to the angel who
talked with me.[e]
14Then the angel who was speaking to
me said, "Proclaim this word: This is
what the LORD Almighty says: 'I am very
jealous[f] for Jerusalem and Zion, 15but I
am very angry with the nations that feel
secure.[g] I was only a little angry,[h] but
they added to the calamity.'[i]
16"Therefore, this is what the LORD
says: 'I will return[j] to Jerusalem with
mercy, and there my house will be rebuilt. And the measuring line[k] will be
stretched out over Jerusalem,' declares
the LORD Almighty.[l]
17"Proclaim further: This is what the
LORD Almighty says: 'My towns will again
overflow with prosperity, and the LORD
will again comfort[m] Zion and choose[n] Jerusalem.' "[o]

Four Horns and Four Craftsmen

18Then I looked up—and there before
me were four horns! 19I asked the angel
who was speaking to me, "What are
these?"

1:1 [a]S Ezr 4:24; S 6:15 [b]S Ezr 5:1 [c]Mt 23:35; Lk 11:51 [d]ver 7; S Ne 12:4
1:2 [e]S 2Ch 36:16
1:3 [f]S Job 22:23 [g]Mal 3:7; Jas 4:8
1:4 [h]S 2Ch 36:15 [i]Zec 7:7 [j]S 2Ki 17:13; S 2Ch 7:14; Ps 106:6; S Jer 23:22 [k]S 2Ch 24:19; Ps 78:8; S Jer 6:17; 17:23 [l]S Eze 20:18; S 33:4
1:6 [m]S Isa 44:26 [n]S Dt 28:2; S Da 9:12; S Hos 5:9 [o]Jer 12:14-17; La 2:17 [p]Jer 23:20; 39:16; S 44:17
1:7 [q]S ver 1
1:8 [r]Rev 6:4 [s]Zec 6:2-7
1:9 [t]Zec 4:1,4-5; 5:5 [u]S Da 7:16
1:10 [v]Zec 6:5-8
1:11 [w]Ge 16:7 [x]S Isa 14:7
1:12 [y]S Ps 6:3 [z]Ps 40:11 [a]S Jer 40:5 [b]S 2Ch 36:21; S Da 9:2
1:13 [c]S Isa 35:4 [d]S Job 15:11 [e]Zec 4:1
1:14 [f]S Isa 26:11; S Joel 2:18
1:15 [g]Jer 48:11 [h]S 2Ch 28:9 [i]S Ps 69:26; 123:3-4; S Am 1:11
1:16 [j]Zec 8:3 [k]S Job 38:5; Zec 2:1-2 [l]S Ezr 1:1
1:17 [m]S Isa 40:1 [n]S Isa 14:1 [o]S Ezr 9:9; S Ps 51:18; Isa 54:8-10; S 61:4

1:2–17 GOD, Wrath—God's history of anger at His people's sins should be enough to bring us to repentance. His election love for His people turns Him from anger to punish the nations for their cruel treatment of His people.

1:2–6 HISTORY, Judgment—Prophecy had a history. The work and words of earlier prophets gave a basis for later prophets like Zechariah to call God's people to repent. Reciting a history of God's anger provided a foundation for warning of coming judgment.

1:5 HUMANITY, Death—Death comes to everyone regardless of wisdom, power, or accomplishments. Not even the most righteous can avoid it.

1:6 GOD, Justice—Having suffered under God's wrath, His people come to repent of their sins and acknowledge that God is just in exercising His wrath. We deserve the punishment His wrath deals out to us. We must remember, however, that our suffering does not all originate from God's wrath at our sin. See notes on Job 31:35–37; 40:8; 42:2–6.

1:7 REVELATION, Visions—God's call to Zechariah could be dated. Revelation was not a gradual awareness for him but a memorable experience. The word came through a series of visions. Visions are one form God uses to reveal His plans to people. See note on Da 10:1–19. An angel interpreted the vision (v 14), and an angel in human form appeared in the vision, reporting to God about world conditions and interceding with Him for Israel. See note on Da 10:18—11:1.

1:14 GOD, Jealous—When another power exercises authority and control over His beloved people, God's jealous love stirs Him to action to reclaim the affection of His people. See notes on Eze 16:38; Na 1:2.

1:14,17 PROCLAMATION, Divine Source—See note on Jer 19:14–15. God used angels to convey His message to the prophets at times. The prophets then spoke the word to the people. This relay system still produced proclamation with its source in God. All true proclamation must be founded on God's Word.

1:15–17 ELECTION, Love—This jealousy is not a hostile jealousy of God. It is one of special interest and close allegiance which the people owe to God and which God gives to His people. God relates to His elect with tenderness and protection. He follows discipline with renewed signs and promises of His election love. Prosperity may be one sign He gives.

1:16 GOD, Grace—God's wrath results in His withholding mercy from His people. God's jealous, zealous love for His people leads Him to restore them in His mercy. See note on Eze 20:17.

1:18–21 HISTORY, Universal—See note on Isa 10:5–19.

He answered me, "These are the
horns[p] that scattered Judah, Israel and
Jerusalem."
20Then the LORD showed me four
craftsmen. 21I asked, "What are these
coming to do?"
He answered, "These are the horns
that scattered Judah so that no one could
raise his head, but the craftsmen have
come to terrify them and throw down
these horns of the nations who lifted up
their horns[q] against the land of Judah to
scatter its people."[r]

Chapter 2

A Man With a Measuring Line

THEN I looked up—and there before
me was a man with a measuring line
in his hand! 2I asked, "Where are you
going?"
He answered me, "To measure Jerusalem, to find out how wide and how long
it is."[s]
3Then the angel who was speaking to
me left, and another angel came to meet
him 4and said to him: "Run, tell that
young man, 'Jerusalem will be a city without walls[t] because of the great number[u]
of men and livestock in it.[v] 5And I myself
will be a wall[w] of fire[x] around it,' declares the LORD, 'and I will be its glory[y]
within.'[z] [a]
6"Come! Come! Flee from the land of
the north," declares the LORD, "for I have
scattered[b] you to the four winds of heav-
en,"[c] declares the LORD.[d]
7"Come, O Zion! Escape,[e] you who
live in the Daughter of Babylon!"[f] 8For
this is what the LORD Almighty says: "After he has honored me and has sent me
against the nations that have plundered
you—for whoever touches you touches
the apple of his eye[g]— 9I will surely
raise my hand against them so that their
slaves will plunder them.[a] [h] Then you
will know that the LORD Almighty has
sent me.[i]
10"Shout[j] and be glad, O Daughter of
Zion.[k] For I am coming,[l] and I will live
among you,"[m] declares the LORD.[n]
11"Many nations will be joined with the
LORD in that day and will become my people.[o] I will live among you and you will
know that the LORD Almighty has sent me
to you.[p] 12The LORD will inherit[q] Judah[r]
as his portion in the holy land and will
again choose[s] Jerusalem. 13Be still[t] before the LORD, all mankind, because he
has roused himself from his holy dwelling."[u]

Chapter 3

Clean Garments for the High Priest

THEN he showed me Joshua[b] [v] the
high priest standing before the angel
of the LORD, and Satan[c] [w] standing at his
right side to accuse him. 2The LORD said
to Satan, "The LORD rebuke you,[x] Satan!
The LORD, who has chosen[y] Jerusalem,

1:19 [p]Am 6:13 **1:21** [q]S 1Ki 22:11; Ps 75:4 [r]S Ps 75:10; S Isa 54:16-17; Zec 12:9 **2:2** [s]S Eze 40:3; S Zec 1:16; Rev 21:15 **2:4** [t]S Eze 38:11 [u]S Isa 49:20; S Jer 30:19; S 33:22 [v]Zec 14:11 **2:5** [w]S Isa 26:1; Eze 42:20 [x]S Isa 10:17 [y]S Ps 85:9; S Isa 11:10; S 24:23; Rev 21:23 [z]S Ps 125:2 [a]S Ps 46:5; S Eze 38:14 **2:6** [b]S Ps 44:11 [c]S Eze 17:21; S 37:9 [d]Mt 24:31; Mk 13:27 **2:7** [e]S Isa 42:7 [f]S Isa 48:20; Jer 3:18 **2:8** [g]S Dt 32:10 **2:9** [h]S Isa 14:2; S Jer 12:14; S Hab 2:8 [i]S Isa 48:16; Zec 4:9; 6:15 **2:10** [j]S Zep 3:14 [k]S Isa 23:12; S Zep 3:14 [l]Zec 9:9 [m]S Ex 25:8; Lev 26:12; S Nu 23:21; Zec 8:3 [n]S Rev 21:3 **2:11** [o]S Jer 24:7; S Mic 4:2; Zec 8:8, 20-22 [p]Zec 4:9; 6:15 **2:12** [q]S Ex 34:9; Ps 33:12; Jer 10:16 [r]Jer 40:5 [s]S Dt 12:5; S Isa 14:1 **2:13** [t]S Ex 14:14; S Isa 41:1 [u]S Dt 26:15 **3:1** [v]S Ezr 2:2; Zec 6:11 [w]S 2Sa 24:1; S 2Ch 18:21; S Ps 109:6; S Mt 4:10 **3:2** [x]Jude 1:9

[a] *8,9* Or *says after . . . eye:* [9]*"I . . . plunder them."*
[b] *1* A variant of *Jeshua;* here and elsewhere in Zechariah [c] *1* *Satan* means *accuser.*

2:3–5 REVELATION, Angels—Divine messengers from God appear throughout the Old Testament and are either human beings sent on special mission, or mysterious beings of a superhuman nature who represent God. The latter take on a human form so they might be recognizable. The angel announced the revelation of God's glory, the weightiness of His manifestation to Jerusalem. God's presence is also protection for Jerusalem. See note on 1:7.

2:3–10 ELECTION, Protection—In ancient times a major city without walls was unheard of. Cities were walled for security and protection. God's election blessings on the remnant returning from Exile would include a population explosion expanding far beyond the previous limits of Jerusalem and divine protection from enemies. The greatest election blessing would be God's glorious presence among His people.

2:5 GOD, Glory—As humans we spend much time worrying about security and ornamentation that will bring us glory and prestige. God constantly seeks to teach us He is unimpressed with our glorious building projects. His presence can supply our security and glory if we trust Him to do so. See note on Hag 2:7,9.

2:10–13 GOD, Personal—God is not an isolated Creator controlling the universe from His master control tower in the heavens. He is a very personal God who wants all people to be His people and who wants to be present personally with His people. In Jesus He demonstrated how intensely He wants to show His personal interest in and identification with us. See notes on Jer 30:22; Am 5:14.

2:10–11 REVELATION, Divine Presence—The prophetic vision announced the Lord's coming to live with His people. The presence and manifestation of God are assurances that the children of God will live in security. Christ fulfilled this expectation. He became God living with us (Jn 1:10–14).

2:11 EVANGELISM, Universality—All nations are to hear and heed the gospel story, regardless of who or where they are. See note on Isa 49:1–6.

2:12–13 GOD, Holy—"Holy land" appears only here in the Bible. The expression in Ps 78:54 is literally "holy territory." The land is holy, separate, and distinct from all other land, because the holy God chose to live there. He lived there, however, so all nations could be His people and know He lives among them.

2:12 ELECTION, Other Nations—The message of hope came to the elect of God while they were still a small remnant in Jerusalem fresh from the Exile of seventy years. They faced a threefold challenge. They needed to rebuild the Temple, the moral and spiritual life of the people, and a consecrated civic and moral leadership. The prophecy that the Lord would inherit Judah as His portion and would again choose Jerusalem was what the small community needed to hear. The knowledge of the election of God gives the courage and confidence needed to accomplish God's mission in the world. As the blessing to Abraham, so the prophecy of Zechariah saw the nations involved in God's plan of election.

3:1–2 EVIL AND SUFFERING, Satan—Satan means "accuser" in Hebrew. Israel understood one of his roles to be bringing accusations against people in the heavenly council. See notes on 2 Sa 24:1; 1 Ch 21:1; Job 1:6–12; Mt 4:1–11.

rebuke you! Is not this man a burning
stick[z] snatched from the fire?"[a]
3Now Joshua was dressed in filthy
clothes as he stood before the angel.
4The angel said to those who were standing before him, "Take off his filthy
clothes."
Then he said to Joshua, "See, I have
taken away your sin,[b] and I will put rich
garments[c] on you."
5Then I said, "Put a clean turban[d] on
his head." So they put a clean turban on
his head and clothed him, while the angel
of the LORD stood by.
6The angel of the LORD gave this charge
to Joshua: 7"This is what the LORD Almighty says: 'If you will walk in my ways
and keep my requirements,[e] then you
will govern my house[f] and have charge[g]
of my courts, and I will give you a place
among these standing here.[h]
8" 'Listen, O high priest[i] Joshua and
your associates seated before you, who
are men symbolic[j] of things to come: I
am going to bring my servant, the
Branch.[k] 9See, the stone I have set in
front of Joshua![l] There are seven eyes[d] [m]
on that one stone,[n] and I will engrave an
inscription on it,' says the LORD Almighty, 'and I will remove the sin[o] of
this land in a single day.
10" 'In that day each of you will invite
his neighbor to sit[p] under his vine and
fig tree,[q]' declares the LORD Almighty."

Chapter 4

The Gold Lampstand and the Two Olive Trees

THEN the angel who talked with me
returned and wakened[r] me, as a
man is wakened from his sleep.[s] 2He
asked me, "What do you see?"[t]
I answered, "I see a solid gold lampstand[u] with a bowl at the top and seven
lights[v] on it, with seven channels to the
lights. 3Also there are two olive trees[w] by
it, one on the right of the bowl and the
other on its left."
4I asked the angel who talked with me,
"What are these, my lord?"
5He answered, "Do you not know what
these are?"
"No, my lord," I replied.[x]
6So he said to me, "This is the word of
the LORD to Zerubbabel:[y] 'Not[z] by might
nor by power,[a] but by my Spirit,'[b] says
the LORD Almighty.
7"What[e] are you, O mighty mountain?
Before Zerubbabel you will become level
ground.[c] Then he will bring out the capstone[d] to shouts[e] of 'God bless it! God
bless it!' "
8Then the word of the LORD came to
me: 9"The hands of Zerubbabel have laid
the foundation[f] of this temple; his hands
will also complete it.[g] Then you will
know that the LORD Almighty has sent
me[h] to you.
10"Who despises the day[i] of small
things?[j] Men will rejoice when they see
the plumb line in the hand of Zerubbabel.[k]
"(These seven are the eyes[l] of the
LORD, which range throughout the
earth.)"
11Then I asked the angel, "What are
these two olive trees[m] on the right and
the left of the lampstand?"
12Again I asked him, "What are these
two olive branches beside the two gold
pipes that pour out golden oil?"
13He replied, "Do you not know what
these are?"
"No, my lord," I said.
14So he said, "These are the two who
are anointed[n] to[f] serve the Lord of all
the earth."

[d] 9 Or *facets* [e] 7 Or *Who* [f] 14 Or *two who bring oil and*

3:2 [z]S Isa 7:4 [a]Jude 1:23
3:4 [b]S 2Sa 12:13; S Eze 36:25; S Mic 7:18 [c]S Ge 41:42; S Ps 132:9; S Isa 52:1; Rev 19:8
3:5 [d]S Ex 29:6
3:7 [e]S Lev 8:35 [f]Dt 17:8-11; S Eze 44:15-16 [g]2Ch 23:6 [h]Jer 15:19; Zec 6:15
3:8 [i]Hag 1:1 [j]S Dt 28:46; S Eze 12:11 [k]S Isa 4:2; S 49:3; S Eze 17:22
3:9 [l]S Ezr 2:2 [m]S 2Ch 16:9 [n]Isa 28:16 [o]S 2Sa 12:13; S Jer 50:20
3:10 [p]S Job 11:18 [q]S Nu 16:14; S 1Ki 4:25; Mic 4:4
4:1 [r]S Da 8:18 [s]Jer 31:26
4:2 [t]S Jer 1:13 [u]S Ex 25:31; Rev 1:12 [v]Rev 4:5
4:3 [w]ver 11; S Ps 1:3; S Rev 11:4
4:5 [x]S Zec 1:9
4:6 [y]S 1Ch 3:19; S Ezr 5:2 [z]S 1Sa 13:22; S 1Ki 19:12 [a]S 1Sa 2:9 [b]S Ne 9:20; Isa 11:2-4; S Da 2:34; Hos 1:7
4:7 [c]S Ps 26:12; Jer 51:25 [d]S Ps 118:22 [e]S 1Ch 15:28
4:9 [f]S Ezr 3:11 [g]Ezr 3:8; S 6:15; Zec 6:12 [h]S Zec 2:9
4:10 [i]S Hag 2:23 [j]Hag 2:3 [k]S Ezr 5:1; S Ne 12:1; S Job 38:5 [l]S 2Ch 16:9; Rev 5:6
4:11 [m]S ver 3; S Rev 11:4
4:14 [n]Ex 29:7; 40:15; S Ps 45:7; S Isa 20:3; S Da 9:24-26

3:7 WORSHIP, Priesthood—Worship leaders play an essential role for God's people. God expects them to be strong ethical examples for His people. Moral living gives authority to lead worship.
3:8 THE CHURCH, Servants—The Branch symbolized a coming righteous king who would reign on the throne of David (Jer 23:5; 33:15; Isa 4:2–6). Like the Suffering Servant (Isa 42:6–7; 49:1–7; 50:4–11; 52:13—53:12), the Branch provides a model of the true servant of God. Both the Suffering Servant and the righteous Branch were fulfilled in the person of Christ. In all generations God's people need servant leaders.
3:10 HUMANITY, Community Relationships—God has an ideal plan for His community. God's ideal is that people will fulfill their relationships to those surrounding them through hospitality and generosity. One day God will establish His kingdom. Until then we are expected to live in expectancy knowing His kingdom will come.
3:10 ELECTION, God's Purpose—In the day of the Lord, peace will prevail. Neighbors will visit under the trees of self-owned orchards (8:4–8; 1 Ki 4:25; Mic 4:4).
4:1 REVELATION, Angels—See note on 2:3–5.
4:6 HOLY SPIRIT, Mission—The Spirit accomplished what appeared to be an impossible mission. The small Jewish community did not think they had resources to complete the rebuilding of the Temple. The prophetic vision encouraged Zerubbabel, the political leader. He did not need to worry about financial resources, political conditions, or lack of workers. God's Spirit would supply his needs. The Spirit is the power source for all people on mission for God. A review of Old Testament teachings shows the Spirit's power: (1) power of life (notes on Job 33:1–4; Eze 37:12–14); (2) of creation (Ge 1:2); (3) to lead individuals (see notes on Jdg 13:24–25; 1 Sa 10:5–13); (4) to give human skills (see notes on Ex 31:1–11; 2 Sa 23:1–4); (5) to reveal His will through the maze of international politics (see notes on Ge 41:38–39; Eze 2:1–2); (6) to redeem (see note on Isa 63:10–14); (7) to give supernatural gifts (see note on Jdg 15:14); (8) to reveal God's word of judgment and hope (Mic 1:8; see note on Isa 32:14–18). Most of all the Spirit has power because He is the ever-present God. See note on Ps 139:7.

Chapter 5

The Flying Scroll

I looked again—and there before me
was a flying scroll![o]
2He asked me, "What do you see?"[p]
I answered, "I see a flying scroll, thirty
feet long and fifteen feet wide.[g] "
3And he said to me, "This is the curse[q]
that is going out over the whole land; for
according to what it says on one side, every thief[r] will be banished, and according to what it says on the other, everyone
who swears falsely[s] will be banished.
4The LORD Almighty declares, 'I will send
it out, and it will enter the house of the
thief and the house of him who swears
falsely[t] by my name. It will remain in his
house and destroy it, both its timbers and
its stones.[u]' "

The Woman in a Basket

5Then the angel who was speaking to
me came forward and said to me, "Look
up and see what this is that is appearing."
6I asked, "What is it?"
He replied, "It is a measuring basket.[h][v]" And he added, "This is the iniquity[i] of the people throughout the land."
7Then the cover of lead was raised, and
there in the basket sat a woman! 8He
said, "This is wickedness," and he
pushed her back into the basket and
pushed the lead cover down over its
mouth.[w]
9Then I looked up—and there before
me were two women, with the wind in
their wings! They had wings like those of
a stork,[x] and they lifted up the basket
between heaven and earth.
10"Where are they taking the basket?"
I asked the angel who was speaking to
me.
11He replied, "To the country of Babylonia[j][y] to build a house[z] for it. When
it is ready, the basket will be set there in
its place."[a]

Chapter 6

Four Chariots

I looked up again—and there before me
were four chariots[b] coming out from
between two mountains—mountains of
bronze! 2The first chariot had red horses,
the second black,[c] 3the third white,[d]
and the fourth dappled—all of them powerful. 4I asked the angel who was speaking to me, "What are these, my lord?"
5The angel answered me, "These are
the four spirits[k][e] of heaven, going out
from standing in the presence of the Lord
of the whole world.[f] 6The one with the
black horses is going toward the north
country, the one with the white horses
toward the west,[l] and the one with the
dappled horses toward the south."
7When the powerful horses went out,
they were straining to go throughout the
earth.[g] And he said, "Go throughout the
earth!" So they went throughout the
earth.
8Then he called to me, "Look, those
going toward the north country have giv-
en my Spirit[m] rest[h] in the land of the
north."[i]

A Crown for Joshua

9The word of the LORD came to me:
10"Take ⌞silver and gold⌟ from the exiles
Heldai, Tobijah and Jedaiah, who have arrived from Babylon.[j] Go the same day to
the house of Josiah son of Zephaniah.
11Take the silver and gold and make a
crown,[k] and set it on the head of the
high priest, Joshua[l] son of Jehozadak.[m]
12Tell him this is what the LORD Almighty
says: 'Here is the man whose name is the
Branch,[n] and he will branch out from his
place and build the temple of the LORD.[o]
13It is he who will build the temple of the
LORD, and he will be clothed with majesty
and will sit and rule on his throne. And
he will be a priest[p] on his throne. And
there will be harmony between the two.'
14The crown will be given to Heldai,[n] Tobijah, Jedaiah and Hen[o] son of Zephaniah
as a memorial[q] in the temple of the
LORD. 15Those who are far away will
come and help to build the temple of the
LORD,[r] and you will know that the LORD
Almighty has sent me to you.[s] This will
happen if you diligently obey[t] the LORD
your God."

Chapter 7

Justice and Mercy, Not Fasting

IN the fourth year of King Darius, the
word of the LORD came to Zechariah[u]

5:1 [o]S Ps 40:7; S Jer 36:4; Rev 5:1
5:2 [p]S Jer 1:13
5:3 [q]Isa 24:6; 34:2; 43:28; Mal 3:9; 4:6 [r]Ex 20:15; Mal 3:8 [s]Ex 20:7; Isa 48:1
5:4 [t]Zec 8:17 [u]Lev 14:34-45; S Pr 3:33; S Hab 2:9-11; Mal 3:5
5:6 [v]Mic 6:10
5:8 [w]Mic 6:11
5:9 [x]Lev 11:19
5:11 [y]S Ge 10:10 [z]Jer 29:5,28 [a]S Da 1:2
6:1 [b]ver 5; S 2Ki 2:11
6:2 [c]Rev 6:5
6:3 [d]Rev 6:2
6:5 [e]S Eze 37:9; Mt 24:31; Rev 7:1 [f]S Jos 3:11
6:7 [g]Isa 43:6; Zec 1:8
6:8 [h]S Eze 5:13; S 24:13 [i]S Zec 1:10
6:10 [j]Ezr 7:14-16; Jer 28:6
6:11 [k]Ps 21:3 [l]S Ezr 2:2; S Zec 3:1 [m]S 1Ch 6:15; S Ezr 3:2
6:12 [n]S Isa 4:2; S Eze 17:22 [o]Ezr 3:8-10; Zec 4:6-9
6:13 [p]S Ps 110:4
6:14 [q]S Ex 28:12
6:15 [r]Isa 60:10 [s]Zec 2:9-11 [t]Isa 58:12; Jer 7:23; S Zec 3:7
7:1 [u]S Ezr 5:1

[g]2 Hebrew *twenty cubits long and ten cubits wide* (about 9 meters long and 4.5 meters wide) [h]6 Hebrew *an ephah*; also in verses 7-11 [i]6 Or *appearance* [j]11 Hebrew *Shinar* [k]5 Or *winds* [l]6 Or *horses after them* [m]8 Or *spirit* [n]14 Syriac; Hebrew *Helem* [o]14 Or *and the gracious one, the*

5:5–11 SALVATION, Forgiveness—Zechariah's strange vision was of the Babylonian captivity in which God took away Israel's sins. The prophetic vision suggests the idea of a scapegoat. See note on Lev 4:13–35; 16:6–34.

6:1–8 REVELATION, Angels—Four spirits or winds (Hebrew *ruach* means both) represent God in the world. They represent His control over the nations. They let His Spirit control the north where Babylon and Persia had dominated Judah. These spirits function as angels do in other texts. See note on Da 10:18—11:1.

7:1–14 GOD, Wrath—God's wrath is the ultimate explanation for Jerusalem's destruction and the Exile. The people's

on the fourth day of the ninth month, the
month of Kislev.[v] 2The people of Bethel
had sent Sharezer and Regem-Melech, together with their men, to entreat[w] the
LORD[x] 3by asking the priests of the house
of the LORD Almighty and the prophets,
"Should I mourn[y] and fast in the fifth[z]
month, as I have done for so many
years?"

4Then the word of the LORD Almighty
came to me: 5"Ask all the people of the
land and the priests, 'When you fasted[a]
and mourned in the fifth and seventh[b]
months for the past seventy years,[c] was
it really for me that you fasted? 6And
when you were eating and drinking, were
you not just feasting for yourselves?[d]
7Are these not the words the LORD proclaimed through the earlier prophets[e]
when Jerusalem and its surrounding
towns were at rest[f] and prosperous, and
the Negev and the western foothills[g]
were settled?' "[h]

8And the word of the LORD came again
to Zechariah: 9"This is what the LORD Almighty says: 'Administer true justice;[i]
show mercy and compassion to one another.[j] 10Do not oppress the widow[k] or
the fatherless, the alien[l] or the poor.[m] In
your hearts do not think evil of each other.'[n]

11"But they refused to pay attention;
stubbornly[o] they turned their backs[p]
and stopped up their ears.[q] 12They made
their hearts as hard as flint[r] and would
not listen to the law or to the words that
the LORD Almighty had sent by his Spirit
through the earlier prophets.[s] So the
LORD Almighty was very angry.[t]

13" 'When I called, they did not listen;[u] so when they called, I would not
listen,'[v] says the LORD Almighty.[w] 14'I
scattered[x] them with a whirlwind[y]
among all the nations, where they were
strangers. The land was left so desolate
behind them that no one could come or
go.[z] This is how they made the pleasant
land desolate.[a] ' "

Chapter 8

The LORD Promises to Bless Jerusalem

AGAIN the word of the LORD Almighty
came to me. 2This is what the LORD
Almighty says: "I am very jealous[b] for
Zion; I am burning with jealousy for
her."

3This is what the LORD says: "I will
return[c] to Zion[d] and dwell in Jerusa-
lem.[e] Then Jerusalem will be called the
City of Truth,[f] and the mountain[g] of the
LORD Almighty will be called the Holy
Mountain.[h]"

4This is what the LORD Almighty says:
"Once again men and women of ripe old
age will sit in the streets of Jerusalem,[i]
each with cane in hand because of his
age. 5The city streets will be filled with
boys and girls playing there.[j] "

7:1 [v]Ne 1:1 **7:2** [w]Jer 26:19; Zec 8:21 [x]Hag 2:10-14 **7:3** [y]Zec 12:12-14 [z]2Ki 25:9; Jer 52:12-14 **7:5** [a]Isa 58:5 [b]2Ki 25:25 [c]S Da 9:2 **7:6** [d]S Isa 43:23 **7:7** [e]Isa 1:11-20; Zec 1:4 [f]Jer 22:21 [g]S Jer 17:26 [h]Jer 44:4-5 **7:9** [i]S Jer 22:3; 42:5; Zec 8:16 [j]S Dt 22:1 **7:10** [k]Jer 49:11 [l]S Ex 22:21 [m]S Lev 25:17; Isa 1:23 [n]S Ex 22:22; S Job 35:8; S Isa 1:17; S Eze 45:9; S Mic 6:8 **7:11** [o]S Isa 9:9 [p]S Jer 32:33 [q]S Jer 5:3; 8:5; 11:10; S 17:23; S Eze 5:6 **7:12** [r]S Jer 5:3; 17:1; S Eze 11:19 [s]S Ne 9:29 [t]S Jer 42:21; S Da 9:12 **7:13** [u]S Jer 7:27 [v]Isa 1:15; S Jer 11:11; 14:12; S Mic 3:4 [w]S Pr 1:28; S La 3:44; S Eze 20:31 **7:14** [x]S Lev 26:33; Dt 4:27; 28:64-67; S Ps 44:11 [y]Jer 23:19 [z]S Isa 33:8 [a]S Jer 7:34; S 44:6; S Eze 12:19 **8:2** [b]S Joel 2:18 **8:3** [c]Zec 1:16 [d]S Isa 52:8; S Joel 3:21 [e]S Zec 2:10 [f]S Ps 15:2; S Isa 1:26; S 48:1; S Jer 33:16 [g]S Jer 26:18 [h]S Isa 1:26; S Mic 4:1 **8:4** [i]S Isa 65:20 **8:5** [j]S Jer 30:20; 31:13

---

sins of oppression and lack of compassion brought on God's wrath. God's wrath meant He quit listening to the prayers of a hypocritical people and let them suffer what they deserved.

7:4–10 WORSHIP, False—Traditional ceremonies do not constitute worship if they come from false motives. Worship rituals focus on God, not on selfish human desires. Worship is properly offered by people who help the needy and provide justice in the nation.

7:8–10 CHRISTIAN ETHICS, Justice—What is the definition of biblical justice? Zechariah provides an excellent response. It is mercy, compassion, and bringing of balance into things gone wrong for widows, orphans, foreigners, or the poor. These Old Testament categories translate into our own time as those who are the vulnerable people of society, those who have no one to speak for them. Justice begins as an attitude of love in the heart. This expresses itself in actions defending those whom society easily defrauds. See note on Hos 2:19–20.

7:9–10 SALVATION, Obedience—Obedience to God requires justice, mercy, and compassion toward others. The way we treat others shows how obedient we are to God.

7:11–12 SIN, Rebellion—God's people feed on God's Word. The prophetic word consistently taught Israel to establish justice for the needy with mercy and compassion. Israel knew what was right but refused to listen. They paid for their rebellion. A people have reached God's limit when they adamantly refuse to listen to His Word. See note on Eze 2:3–4.

7:11–13 HOLY SCRIPTURE, Writing—God's Law and prophets had become authoritative for Zechariah's generation. We cannot know the content of these materials, but we can see that the principle of written, authoritative teachings had been formulated. The Spirit is the ultimate Source of such Scriptures. Obedience is the expected response to them.

7:12 HOLY SPIRIT, Revelation—The Spirit of God gave various gifts to people in the Old Testament. The most frequently mentioned gift was the gift of prophecy. See notes on Nu 11:25–29; Eze 8:3; Da 4:9. The Spirit is so closely associated with prophecy that Peter could write that prophecy came through men who were moved by the Spirit (2 Pe 1:21). The following prophets were explicitly said to have been given this gift by the Spirit: Eldad and Medad (see note on Nu 11:25–29), Balaam (see note on Nu 24:2), Saul (see note on 1 Sa 10:5–13), David (see note on 2 Sa 23:1–4), Elijah (see note on 1 Ki 18:12), Elisha (see note on 2 Ki 2:1–18), Amasai (see note on 1 Ch 12:18), Azariah (see note on 2 Ch 15:1–2), Zechariah (see note on 2 Ch 24:20), Ezekiel (see note on Eze 2:1–2), and Micah (see note on Mic 3:8). Revelation came in various ways to the prophets. They used various means to communicate their messages. The shocking truth is Zechariah's summary of the reactions to the prophets: God's people would not listen to His word and obey it. Revelation does not help if it is not obeyed.

7:13 PRAYER, Hindrances—The people had practiced false religion. Praying to God includes listening to and obeying Him. See note on Mic 3:4.

8:1–12 THE CHURCH, Remnant—God's saving actions amaze even His faithful remnant. What appears miraculous in our eyes is ordinary for God. He works to create a faithful covenant people to whom He can be faithful and righteous. He plans to bless an obedient, working remnant. See note on Hag 1:12–15.

8:2 GOD, Jealous—See note on 1:14.

8:3 GOD, Holy—See note on 2:12–13.

6This is what the LORD Almighty says:
"It may seem marvelous to the remnant
of this people at that time,[k] but will it
seem marvelous to me?[l]" declares the
LORD Almighty.
7This is what the LORD Almighty says:
"I will save my people from the countries
of the east and the west.[m] 8I will bring
them back[n] to live[o] in Jerusalem; they
will be my people,[p] and I will be faithful
and righteous to them as their God.[q]"
9This is what the LORD Almighty says:
"You who now hear these words spoken
by the prophets[r] who were there when
the foundation[s] was laid for the house of
the LORD Almighty, let your hands be
strong[t] so that the temple may be built.
10Before that time there were no wages[u]
for man or beast. No one could go about
his business safely[v] because of his enemy, for I had turned every man against
his neighbor. 11But now I will not deal
with the remnant of this people as I did in
the past,"[w] declares the LORD Almighty.
12"The seed will grow well, the vine
will yield its fruit,[x] the ground will produce its crops,[y] and the heavens will
drop their dew.[z] I will give all these
things as an inheritance[a] to the remnant
of this people.[b] 13As you have been an
object of cursing[c] among the nations, O
Judah and Israel, so will I save[d] you, and
you will be a blessing.[e] Do not be
afraid,[f] but let your hands be strong.[g]"
14This is what the LORD Almighty says:
"Just as I had determined to bring disaster[h] upon you and showed no pity when
your fathers angered me," says the LORD
Almighty, 15"so now I have determined
to do good[i] again to Jerusalem and Judah.[j] Do not be afraid. 16These are the
things you are to do: Speak the truth[k] to
each other, and render true and sound
judgment[l] in your courts;[m] 17do not plot
evil[n] against your neighbor, and do not
love to swear falsely.[o] I hate all this,"
declares the LORD.
18Again the word of the LORD Almighty
came to me. 19This is what the LORD Almighty says: "The fasts of the fourth,[p]
fifth,[q] seventh[r] and tenth[s] months will
become joyful[t] and glad occasions and
happy festivals for Judah. Therefore love
truth[u] and peace."
20This is what the LORD Almighty says:
"Many peoples and the inhabitants of
many cities will yet come, 21and the inhabitants of one city will go to another
and say, 'Let us go at once to entreat[v] the
LORD and seek[w] the LORD Almighty. I myself am going.' 22And many peoples and
powerful nations will come to Jerusalem
to seek the LORD Almighty and to entreat
him."[x]
23This is what the LORD Almighty says:
"In those days ten men from all languages
and nations will take firm hold of one Jew
by the hem of his robe and say, 'Let us go
with you, because we have heard that
God is with you.'"[y]

Chapter 9

Judgment on Israel's Enemies

An Oracle[z]

THE word of the LORD is against the
land of Hadrach
and will rest upon Damascus[a] —
for the eyes of men and all the tribes
of Israel

8:6 [k]Ps 118:23; 126:1-3 [l]Jer 32:17, 27 **8:7** [m]Ps 107:3; S Isa 11:11; S 43:5 **8:8** [n]S Eze 37:12; Zec 10:10 [o]S Jer 31:24 [p]S Isa 51:16; S Eze 11:19-20; S 36:28; S Zec 2:11; Heb 8:10 [q]Jer 11:4; Zec 10:6 **8:9** [r]S Ezr 5:1 [s]S Ezr 3:11 [t]S Hag 2:4 **8:10** [u]S Isa 5:10; S Hag 1:6 [v]S 2Ch 15:5 **8:11** [w]Isa 12:1 **8:12** [x]S Ps 85:12; S Joel 2:22 [y]S Ps 67:6 [z]S Ge 27:28 [a]S Ps 65:13; S Isa 60:21; Ob 1:17 [b]S Hos 2:21 **8:13** [c]S Nu 5:27; S Dt 13:15; S Ps 102:8; Jer 42:18 [d]S Ps 48:8 [e]S Ge 12:2; S Joel 2:14 [f]S Hag 2:5 [g]ver 9 **8:14** [h]S Eze 24:14 **8:15** [i]ver 13; S Jer 29:11; Mic 7:18-20 [j]Jer 31:28; 32:42 **8:16** [k]S Ps 15:2; S Jer 33:16; S Eph 4:25 [l]S Eze 18:8 [m]S Eze 45:9; S Am 5:15; S Zec 7:9 **8:17** [n]Pr 3:29 [o]S Pr 6:16-19; S Jer 7:9; Zec 5:4 **8:19** [p]S 2Ki 25:7; Jer 39:2 [q]S Jer 52:12 [r]2Ki 25:25 [s]Jer 52:4 [t]Ps 30:11 [u]ver 16 **8:21** [v]S Zec 7:2 [w]Jer 26:19 **8:22** [x]S Ps 86:9; 117:1; Isa 2:2-3; S 44:5; S 45:14; 49:6; S Zec 2:11 **8:23** [y]S Ps 102:22; S Isa 14:1; S 45:14; S 56:3; 1Co 14:25 **9:** [z]S Isa 13:1; Jer 23:33 **9:1** [a]Isa 17:1; S Am 1:5

8:7–8 GOD, Savior—God's saving activity includes salvation from earthly distress. Its purpose is to create a faithful, obedient people. See note on Jer 50:34.

8:8 GOD, Faithfulness—God's promise to be faithful and righteous does not imply that He planned to change to become what He had not been. Rather, He here used covenant language (Ex 6:7) to renew His relationship with His people and reminded them of His eternal purpose to create a people with whom He could live in a relationship of faithfulness and righteousness. God looks to the day when what always should have been will actually be the case.

8:13 EVANGELISM, God's Provision—God has plans to bless His people even when they appear to be cursed. God's provision of salvation is not limited to one particular people. He plans to use His people to reach all the nations. Even in troubled times, we are called to be strong in the evangelistic work.

8:14–17 GOD, Wrath—God's wrath seeks to create an obedient people. See note on 7:1–14.

8:14–17 SIN, Discipline—Sin angers God. He intervenes to punish. That is not His final Word. He seeks to lead His people to do good by doing good to them. A chastened people hear the same requirements from God. He does not change His purpose after disciplining His people. He still expects honesty, justice, and compassion. He still hates sin.

8:14–15 HISTORY, God—History reveals God's freedom to act in response to His people and in accord with His purposes. Neither judgment nor deliverance totally characterizes God's relation to His people and their history. Once God judged a faithless nation without pity. Then He chose to achieve His purposes by doing good to His people.

8:15 GOD, Grace—Wrath is God's temporary work so He can perform His permanent work of grace. Just as creation was a good work of God, so He wants His work in history to create a people that is good.

8:16 CHRISTIAN ETHICS, Justice—Justice is not confined to prophetic judgment sermons. Announcements of hope and renewal echo the call for truth, sound judgment, concern for neighbors, and honest testimony. Every society, whatever its economic and political situation, must strive to encourage these qualities in its citizens. God's people should form the vanguard in the efforts for justice. See notes on Ps 72:1–14; Mic 6:6–8.

8:18–19 SALVATION, Joy—God's salvation can turn fasting into occasions for rejoicing.

8:20–23 EVANGELISM, Mass—When the message of salvation is heralded, nations come to hear and seek the Lord. What a responsibility and joy that is. This is the glory of evangelism—and the duty of the church.

are on the LORD—[p]
2and upon Hamath[b] too, which borders
on it,
and upon Tyre[c] and Sidon,[d] though
they are very skillful.
3Tyre has built herself a stronghold;
she has heaped up silver like dust,
and gold like the dirt of the streets.[e]
4But the Lord will take away her
possessions
and destroy[f] her power on the sea,
and she will be consumed by fire.[g]
5Ashkelon[h] will see it and fear;
Gaza will writhe in agony,
and Ekron too, for her hope will
wither.
Gaza will lose her king
and Ashkelon will be deserted.
6Foreigners will occupy Ashdod,
and I will cut off[i] the pride of the
Philistines.
7I will take the blood from their
mouths,
the forbidden food from between
their teeth.
Those who are left will belong to our
God[j]
and become leaders in Judah,
and Ekron will be like the
Jebusites.[k]
8But I will defend[l] my house
against marauding forces.[m]
Never again will an oppressor overrun
my people,
for now I am keeping watch.[n]

The Coming of Zion's King

9Rejoice greatly, O Daughter of Zion![o]
Shout,[p] Daughter of Jerusalem!
See, your king[q] comes to you,[q]
righteous and having salvation,[r]
gentle and riding on a donkey,[s]
on a colt, the foal of a donkey.[t]
10I will take away the chariots from
Ephraim
and the war-horses from Jerusalem,
and the battle bow will be broken.[u]
He will proclaim peace[v] to the
nations.
His rule will extend from sea to sea
and from the River[r] to the ends of
the earth.[s] [w]
11As for you, because of the blood of my
covenant[x] with you,
I will free your prisoners[y] from the
waterless pit.[z]
12Return to your fortress,[a] O prisoners
of hope;
even now I announce that I will
restore twice[b] as much to you.
13I will bend Judah as I bend my bow[c]
and fill it with Ephraim.[d]
I will rouse your sons, O Zion,
against your sons, O Greece,[e]
and make you like a warrior's
sword.[f]

The LORD Will Appear

14Then the LORD will appear over
them;[g]
his arrow will flash like lightning.[h]
The Sovereign LORD will sound the
trumpet;[i]
he will march in the storms[j] of the
south,
15 and the LORD Almighty will shield[k]
them.
They will destroy
and overcome with slingstones.[l]
They will drink and roar as with
wine;[m]
they will be full like a bowl[n]
used for sprinkling[t] the corners[o] of
the altar.
16The LORD their God will save them on
that day[p]
as the flock of his people.
They will sparkle in his land
like jewels in a crown.[q]

9:2 [b]S Jer 49:23 [c]Eze 28:1-19 [d]S Ge 10:15
9:3 [e]Job 27:16; S Eze 28:4
9:4 [f]S Isa 23:11 [g]S Isa 23:1; Jer 25:22; Eze 26:3-5; 27:32-36; 28:18
9:5 [h]Jer 47:5
9:6 [i]S Isa 14:30
9:7 [j]S Job 25:2 [k]S Jer 47:1; S Joel 3:4; S Zep 2:4
9:8 [l]S Isa 26:1 [m]Zec 14:21 [n]S Isa 52:1; S 54:14; S Joel 3:17
9:9 [o]S Isa 62:11 [p]S 1Ki 1:39 [q]S Ps 24:7; S 149:2; Mic 4:8 [r]Isa 9:6-7; 43:3-11; Jer 23:5-6; Zep 3:14-15; Zec 2:10 [s]S Ge 49:11; S 1Ki 1:33 [t]Mt 21:5*; Jn 12:15*
9:10 [u]Hos 1:7; 2:18; Mic 4:3; 5:10; Zec 10:4 [v]S Isa 2:4 [w]Ps 72:8
9:11 [x]S Ex 24:8; S Mt 26:28; S Lk 22:20 [y]S Isa 10:4; S 42:7 [z]Jer 38:6
9:12 [a]S Joel 3:16 [b]S Dt 21:17; S Isa 40:2
9:13 [c]S 2Sa 22:35 [d]S Isa 49:2 [e]S Joel 3:6 [f]S Jer 51:20
9:14 [g]Isa 31:5 [h]Ps 18:14; S Hab 3:11 [i]S Lev 25:9; S Mt 24:31 [j]Isa 21:1; 66:15
9:15 [k]Isa 31:5; 37:35; Zec 12:8 [l]Zec 14:3 [m]Zec 10:7 [n]Zec 14:20 [o]S Ex 27:2
9:16 [p]S Isa 10:20 [q]S Jer 31:11

[p]1 Or *Damascus. / For the eye of the LORD is on all mankind, / as well as on the tribes of Israel,* [q]9 Or *King* [r]10 That is, the Euphrates [s]10 Or *the end of the land* [t]15 Or *bowl, / like*

9:7 THE CHURCH, Remnant—God not only removes the oppressor but also includes the remnant of the oppressor among the people of Israel. This remarkable teaching shows the character of the church, a fellowship of the redeemed which forgives the oppressor and reaches out to the world with the good news of God.
9:8 ELECTION, Protection—God promised judgment on all Israel's enemies. From Damascus the march of judgment would proceed to the wealthy coastal cities of Tyre and Sidon, then down the shore of the Mediterranean Sea. Ashkelon, Gaza, Ekron, and all of the surrounding nations would become a remnant for God, absorbed by God's elect. The possession of these territories had always been a desire of Israel, but it had never been realized. God protects His elect and remembers His promises to them.
9:9–10 JESUS CHRIST, Foretold—This ancient hymn celebrating the triumph of a warrior riding on a symbolic animal of peace is the prefiguring of Jesus' "triumphal entry" into Jerusalem (Mt 21:1–11; Mk 11:1–10; Lk 19:28–44; Jn 12:12–16). Contemporary Christians need to learn triumphant actions through humility.
9:9 SALVATION, Joy—Israel's hope for the future was expressed in looking for an ideal king who would enable her to rejoice greatly. Christians see that ideal king as Jesus, the Messiah. This prophecy was fulfilled in the triumphal entry of Jesus riding an ass into Jerusalem (Mt 21:1–11).
9:9–13 THE CHURCH, Covenant People—God responds to the needs of His people based on His covenant love. Israel made and renewed its covenant with God through sacrificial ceremonies (Ex 24). Jesus established the new covenant through His blood (Lk 22:20), fulfilling messianic prophecies such as this one.
9:11–16 THE CHURCH, Remnant—Because of God's covenant love, He restores His people unto Himself and continually protects them.
9:16 HISTORY, Deliverance—Deliverance is God's aim for His people. His judgment looks forward to the day when He will again deliver.

17 How attractive and beautiful they will be!
Grain will make the young men thrive,
and new wine the young women.

Chapter 10

The LORD Will Care for Judah

Ask the LORD for rain in the springtime;
it is the LORD who makes the storm clouds.
He gives showers of rain[r] to men,
and plants of the field[s] to everyone.
2 The idols[t] speak deceit,
diviners[u] see visions that lie;
they tell dreams[v] that are false,
they give comfort in vain.[w]
Therefore the people wander like sheep
oppressed for lack of a shepherd.[x]

3 "My anger burns against the shepherds,
and I will punish the leaders;[y]
for the LORD Almighty will care
for his flock, the house of Judah,
and make them like a proud horse in battle.[z]
4 From Judah will come the cornerstone,[a]
from him the tent peg,[b]
from him the battle bow,[c]
from him every ruler.
5 Together they[u] will be like mighty men
trampling the muddy streets in battle.[d]
Because the LORD is with them,
they will fight and overthrow the horsemen.[e]

6 "I will strengthen[f] the house of Judah
and save the house of Joseph.
I will restore them
because I have compassion[g] on them.[h]
They will be as though
I had not rejected them,
for I am the LORD their God
and I will answer[i] them.
7 The Ephraimites will become like mighty men,
and their hearts will be glad as with wine.[j]
Their children will see it and be joyful;
their hearts will rejoice[k] in the LORD.
8 I will signal[l] for them
and gather them in.
Surely I will redeem them;
they will be as numerous[m] as before.
9 Though I scatter them among the peoples,
yet in distant lands they will remember me.[n]
They and their children will survive,
and they will return.
10 I will bring them back from Egypt
and gather them from Assyria.[o]
I will bring them to Gilead[p] and Lebanon,
and there will not be room[q] enough for them.
11 They will pass through the sea of trouble;
the surging sea will be subdued
and all the depths of the Nile will dry up.[r]
Assyria's pride[s] will be brought down
and Egypt's scepter[t] will pass away.[u]
12 I will strengthen[v] them in the LORD
and in his name they will walk,[w]"
declares the LORD.

Chapter 11

Open your doors, O Lebanon,[x]
so that fire[y] may devour your cedars!

10:1 [r]S Lev 26:4; S 1Ki 8:36; S Ps 104:13; S 135:7 [s]S Job 14:9
10:2 [t]Eze 21:21 [u]S Isa 44:25 [v]Jer 23:16 [w]S Isa 40:19 [x]S Nu 27:17; S Jer 23:1; S Hos 3:4; S Mt 9:36
10:3 [y]Isa 14:9; S Jer 25:34 [z]S Eze 34:8-10
10:4 [a]S Ps 118:22; S Ac 4:11 [b]S Isa 22:23 [c]S Zec 9:10
10:5 [d]S 2Sa 22:43; S Mic 7:10 [e]S Am 2:15; S Mic 5:8; Hag 2:22; Zec 12:4
10:6 [f]S Eze 30:24 [g]S Ps 102:13; S Isa 14:1 [h]S Eze 36:37; 37:19; S Zec 8:7-8 [i]Ps 34:17; Isa 58:9; 65:24; Zec 13:9
10:7 [j]Zec 9:15 [k]S 1Sa 2:1; S Isa 60:5; S Joel 2:23
10:8 [l]Isa 5:26 [m]S Jer 33:22; S Eze 36:11
10:9 [n]S Isa 44:21; S Eze 6:9
10:10 [o]S Isa 11:11; S Zec 8:8 [p]S Jer 50:19 [q]S Isa 49:19
10:11 [r]Isa 19:5-7; S 51:10 [s]Zep 2:13 [t]Eze 30:13 [u]Eze 29:15
10:12 [v]S Eze 30:24 [w]S Mic 4:5
11:1 [x]S Eze 31:3 [y]S 2Ch 36:19; Zec 12:6

[u]4,5 Or *ruler, all of them together. / 5 They*

10:1 GOD, Creator—In a world totally dependent on the year's agricultural produce, people invented many rituals and devised many gods to insure the natural forces cooperated to produce abundant crops. Israel had to learn that only the one Creator God can control the forces of nature and promise harvests. Anyone else who makes such promises is a liar. God not only originated all things, He continues to work in His creation.

10:3,6 GOD, Love—God may at times have to move in wrath, but His ultimate purpose is to show His love. Rejection is not His final word to His world. His love leaves a remnant with whom He can begin again, renewing the covenant and listening to and answering their prayers.

10:6–12 HISTORY, Deliverance—See notes on 9:16; Isa 11:10–16. Divine compassion is the basis God's people have to hope for historical deliverance.

10:6 PRAYER, Faithfulness of God—God would not listen to their prayer in 7:13, but in the restoration He promised to answer. See note on Jer 7:16.

10:7 SALVATION, Joy—Salvation brings a joy that is strong, deep, and long-lasting.

10:9,12 REVELATION, History—The prophet declared the end of Israel's dispersion among the nations. God's care and presence would reunite and strengthen them. As in the Exodus, God will reveal His salvation in historical events.

10:9 SALVATION, Remembrance—Compare Eze 6:9. See note on Jer 31:20. Even far from home and from the center of religious activities, memories and traditions taught by family lead us to remember and worship God.

11:1–17 THE CHURCH, Covenant People—This passage appears to be prophetic symbolism which proclaims God's word of judgment against two groups of people: (1) the worthless shepherds or leaders who destroy the sheep (see note on Eze 34:1–24) and (2) the nation Israel for its rebellion against God. Because Israel broke the covenant with God, God removed His hand of protection from the people, allowing His covenant with the people to be broken. This did not mean God gave up His plan to create a covenant people for Himself. It did

2Wail, O pine tree, for the cedar has
fallen;
the stately trees are ruined!
Wail, oaks[z] of Bashan;
the dense forest[a] has been cut
down![b]
3Listen to the wail of the shepherds;
their rich pastures are destroyed!
Listen to the roar of the lions;[c]
the lush thicket of the Jordan is
ruined![d]

Two Shepherds

4This is what the LORD my God says:
"Pasture the flock marked for slaughter.[e]
5Their buyers slaughter them and go unpunished. Those who sell them say,
'Praise the LORD, I am rich!' Their own
shepherds do not spare them.[f] 6For I will
no longer have pity on the people of the
land," declares the LORD. "I will hand everyone over to his neighbor[g] and his
king. They will oppress the land, and I
will not rescue them from their hands."[h]
7So I pastured the flock marked for
slaughter,[i] particularly the oppressed of
the flock. Then I took two staffs and
called one Favor and the other Union,
and I pastured the flock. 8In one month I
got rid of the three shepherds.
The flock detested[j] me, and I grew
weary of them 9and said, "I will not be
your shepherd. Let the dying die, and the
perishing perish.[k] Let those who are left
eat[l] one another's flesh."
10Then I took my staff called Favor[m]
and broke it, revoking[n] the covenant I
had made with all the nations. 11It was
revoked on that day, and so the afflicted
of the flock who were watching me knew
it was the word of the LORD.
12I told them, "If you think it best, give
me my pay; but if not, keep it." So they
paid me thirty pieces of silver.[o]
13And the LORD said to me, "Throw it
to the potter"—the handsome price at
which they priced me! So I took the thirty
pieces of silver[p] and threw them into the
house of the LORD to the potter.[q]
14Then I broke my second staff called
Union, breaking the brotherhood between Judah and Israel.

11:2 [z]S Isa 2:13 [a]Isa 32:19 [b]S Isa 10:34
11:3 [c]S Isa 5:29 [d]Jer 2:15; 50:44; Eze 19:9
11:4 [e]S Jer 25:34
11:5 [f]Jer 50:7; S Eze 34:2-3
11:6 [g]Zec 14:13 [h]Isa 9:19-21; S Jer 13:14; S La 2:21; 5:8; S Mic 5:8; 7:2-6
11:7 [i]S Jer 25:34
11:8 [j]S Eze 14:5
11:9 [k]S Jer 43:11 [l]S Isa 9:20
11:10 [m]ver 7 [n]S Ps 89:39; Jer 14:21
11:12 [o]S Ge 23:16; Mt 26:15
11:13 [p]S Ex 21:32 [q]Mt 27:9-10*; Ac 1:18-19
11:17 [r]Jer 23:1 [s]S Eze 30:21-22 [t]S Jer 23:1
12: [u]S Isa 13:1
12:1 [v]S Ge 1:8; S Ps 104:2; S Jer 51:15 [w]Ps 102:25; Heb 1:10 [x]S Isa 57:16
12:2 [y]S Ps 75:8 [z]S Ps 60:3; S Isa 51:23 [a]Zec 14:14
12:3 [b]Isa 66:18; Zec 14:2 [c]S Isa 28:16; Da 2:34-35 [d]S Isa 29:8
12:4 [e]Ps 76:6; S Zec 10:5
12:5 [f]S Eze 30:24
12:6 [g]Isa 10:17-18; S Zec 11:1 [h]Ob 1:18 [i]Zec 14:10
12:7 [j]Jer 30:18; S Am 9:11

15Then the LORD said to me, "Take
again the equipment of a foolish shepherd. 16For I am going to raise up a shepherd over the land who will not care for
the lost, or seek the young, or heal the
injured, or feed the healthy, but will eat
the meat of the choice sheep, tearing off
their hoofs.

17"Woe to the worthless shepherd,[r]
who deserts the flock!
May the sword strike his arm[s] and his
right eye!
May his arm be completely
withered,
his right eye totally blinded!"[t]

Chapter 12

Jerusalem's Enemies to Be Destroyed

An Oracle[u]

THIS is the word of the LORD concerning Israel. The LORD, who stretches
out the heavens,[v] who lays the foundation of the earth,[w] and who forms the
spirit of man[x] within him, declares: 2"I
am going to make Jerusalem a cup[y] that
sends all the surrounding peoples reel-
ing.[z] Judah[a] will be besieged as well as
Jerusalem. 3On that day, when all the nations[b] of the earth are gathered against
her, I will make Jerusalem an immovable
rock[c] for all the nations. All who try to
move it will injure[d] themselves. 4On that
day I will strike every horse with panic
and its rider with madness," declares the
LORD. "I will keep a watchful eye over
the house of Judah, but I will blind all the
horses of the nations.[e] 5Then the leaders
of Judah will say in their hearts, 'The people of Jerusalem are strong,[f] because the
LORD Almighty is their God.'
6"On that day I will make the leaders
of Judah like a firepot[g] in a woodpile, like
a flaming torch among sheaves. They will
consume[h] right and left all the surrounding peoples, but Jerusalem will remain intact[i] in her place.
7"The LORD will save the dwellings of
Judah first, so that the honor of the house
of David and of Jerusalem's inhabitants
may not be greater than that of Judah.[j]

---

mean He disciplined a people who claimed His promises but refused to be His people.

11:12–13 JESUS CHRIST, Foretold—These prophecies were fulfilled by Judas' tragic betrayal and death (Mt 26:14–15; 27:9). Judas' betrayal of Jesus was traumatic and decisive. There are less dramatic but still very real ways by which His friends betray Him.

12:1–9 GOD, Creator—God the Creator caused earth, heavens, and human life to appear. Certainly He has the sovereign power to take His people in their political weakness, protect them from their enemies, and give them victory. Since He has such power, God's people should trust Him rather than the political agreements they are prone to depend on.

12:1 HUMANITY, Spiritual Nature—The Hebrew word *ruach* means breath, wind, and spirit—that which is vitally present but invisible. It represents the breath of life in humans and animals (Ge 6:17; 7:15–22). The loss of God's *ruach* brings death (Ps 104:29). The *ruach* is the God-given power of humans to recognize, to will, to understand, and to make decisions. We owe all our abilities in these areas not to a process of becoming a better human animal but to God's creative will for us.

12:1–14 REVELATION, History—God's plans point to His final revelation when He establishes His kingdom under His Messiah's rule. This will be the ultimate revelation of God through historical acts.

8 On that day the LORD will shield[k] those
who live in Jerusalem, so that the fee-
blest[l] among them will be like David,
and the house of David will be like God,[m]
like the Angel of the LORD going before[n]
them. 9 On that day I will set out to destroy all the nations[o] that attack Jerusalem.[p]

Mourning for the One They Pierced

10 "And I will pour out on the house of
David and the inhabitants of Jerusalem a
spirit[v][q] of grace and supplication.[r] They
will look on[w] me, the one they have
pierced,[s] and they will mourn for him as
one mourns for an only child,[t] and
grieve bitterly for him as one grieves for a
firstborn son.[u] 11 On that day the weeping[v] in Jerusalem will be great, like the
weeping of Hadad Rimmon in the plain of
Megiddo.[w] 12 The land will mourn,[x] each
clan by itself, with their wives by themselves: the clan of the house of David and
their wives, the clan of the house of Nathan and their wives, 13 the clan of the
house of Levi and their wives, the clan of
Shimei and their wives, 14 and all the rest
of the clans and their wives.[y]

Chapter 13

Cleansing From Sin

"ON that day a fountain[z] will be
opened to the house of David
and the inhabitants of Jerusalem, to
cleanse[a] them from sin and impurity.
2 "On that day, I will banish the names
of the idols[b] from the land, and they will
be remembered no more,"[c] declares the
LORD Almighty. "I will remove both the
prophets[d] and the spirit of impurity from
the land. 3 And if anyone still prophesies,
his father and mother, to whom he was
born, will say to him, 'You must die, because you have told lies[e] in the LORD's
name.' When he prophesies, his own parents will stab him.[f]
4 "On that day every prophet will be
ashamed[g] of his prophetic vision. He will
not put on a prophet's garment[h] of hair[i]
in order to deceive.[j] 5 He will say, 'I am
not a prophet. I am a farmer; the land has
been my livelihood since my youth.[x]'[k]
6 If someone asks him, 'What are these
wounds on your body[y]?' he will answer,
'The wounds I was given at the house of
my friends.'

The Shepherd Struck, the Sheep Scattered

7 "Awake, O sword,[l] against my
shepherd,[m]
against the man who is close to
me!"
declares the LORD Almighty.
"Strike the shepherd,
and the sheep will be scattered,[n]
and I will turn my hand against the
little ones.
8 In the whole land," declares the LORD,
"two-thirds will be struck down and
perish;
yet one-third will be left in it.[o]
9 This third I will bring into the fire;[p]
I will refine them like silver[q]
and test them like gold.[r]
They will call[s] on my name[t]
and I will answer[u] them;
I will say, 'They are my people,'[v]
and they will say, 'The LORD is our
God.[w]' "

Chapter 14

The LORD Comes and Reigns

A day of the LORD[x] is coming when
your plunder[y] will be divided
among you.
2 I will gather all the nations[z] to Jerusalem to fight against it;[a] the city will be
captured, the houses ransacked, and the

12:8 [k]S Ps 91:4; S Joel 3:16; S Zec 9:15 [l]Joel 3:10 [m]Ps 82:6 [n]Mic 7:8 **12:9** [o]S Isa 29:7 [p]S Zec 1:21; 14:2-3 **12:10** [q]S Eze 37:9 [r]Isa 44:3; S Eze 39:29; Joel 2:28-29 [s]S Ps 22:16; Jn 19:34,37* [t]Jdg 11:34 [u]S Ge 21:16; Jer 31:19 **12:11** [v]Jer 50:4 [w]2Ki 23:29 **12:12** [x]Mt 24:30; Rev 1:7 **12:14** [y]Zec 7:3 **13:1** [z]Jer 17:13 [a]S Lev 16:30; S Ps 51:2; Heb 9:14 **13:2** [b]S Jer 43:12; S Eze 6:6; S 36:25; S Hos 2:17 [c]S Mic 5:13 [d]1Ki 22:22; Jer 23:14-15 **13:3** [e]S Jer 28:16 [f]Dt 13:6-11; 18:20; S Ne 6:14; Jer 23:34; S Eze 14:9 **13:4** [g]S Jer 6:15 [h]Mt 3:4 [i]S 1Ki 18:7; S Isa 20:2 [j]S Eze 12:24 **13:5** [k]S Am 7:14 **13:7** [l]S Isa 34:5; Jer 47:6 [m]Isa 40:11; S 53:4; Eze 37:24 [n]S 2Sa 17:2; Mt 26:31*; Mk 14:27* **13:8** [o]S Eze 5:2-4, 12; Zec 14:2 **13:9** [p]S Isa 4:4; 33:14; Mal 3:2 [q]S Ps 12:6; S Da 11:35; 1Pe 1:6-7 [r]S Job 6:29; S Jer 6:27 [s]S Ps 50:15 [t]Ps 105:1 [u]S Ps 86:7; S Isa 30:19; S Zec 10:6 [v]S Lev 26:12; S Jer 30:22 [w]S Isa 44:5; S Jer 29:12; S Eze 20:38 **14:1** [x]Isa 13:6; S Joel 1:15; Mal 4:1 [y]S Isa 23:18 **14:2** [z]S Isa 2:3; S Zec 12:3 [a]S Eze 5:8

[v]10 Or *the Spirit* [w]10 Or *to* [x]5 Or *farmer; a man sold me in my youth* [y]6 Or *wounds between your hands*

12:8 REVELATION, Angels—See note on Da 10:18—11:1.
12:10 JESUS CHRIST, Foretold—Jn 19:37 gives the New Testament setting for the piercing of Jesus. Rev 1:7 gives the final, cosmic expression of looking on the pierced one. We do not often contemplate the wounds of Christ, yet we would do well to reflect on His suffering.
13:6–7 JESUS CHRIST, Foretold—When the shepherd is struck down, the sheep scatter. The New Testament fulfillment of this event came when Jesus died (Mt 26:31; Jn 16:32). Today sheep may also stray from the Shepherd and be disobedient to His leading.
13:8–9 THE CHURCH, Remnant—Judgment is meant to cleanse and purify. See notes on Ge 6:18; 9:8–17. When judgment is complete, God restores a remnant of His people who have been refined in the fires of judgment. These people call on the name of the Lord as God intended. See note on Eze 36:28.
13:9 GOD, One God—The great struggle throughout the Old Testament was establishing a people who truly believed in and relied on one God. This verse looks to the day of the Messiah when a remnant will truly recognize Yahweh, Israel's God, as the only One worthy of worship and service.
13:9 THE CHURCH, Covenant People—God's people face trials and testing. They respond by calling on God for help. God answers the faithful people with the covenant formula. See note on Jer 30:22. He assures His tested and refined people that He still claims them as His own. They respond by committing themselves to Him as their God. See note on Eze 36:28.
13:9 PRAYER, Faithfulness of God—It is the refined who demonstrate a genuine relationship with God. In that state, they will call on Him and own Him as their God. That call is assured an answer. Unanswered prayer may indicate we are unfaithful and need discipline and refining. God is always faithful.

women raped.[b] Half of the city will go
into exile, but the rest of the people will
not be taken from the city.[c]

3Then the LORD will go out and fight[d]
against those nations, as he fights in the
day of battle.[e] 4On that day his feet will
stand on the Mount of Olives,[f] east of
Jerusalem, and the Mount of Olives will
be split[g] in two from east to west, forming a great valley, with half of the mountain moving north and half moving south.
5You will flee by my mountain valley, for
it will extend to Azel. You will flee as you
fled from the earthquake[z] [h] in the days of
Uzziah king of Judah. Then the LORD my
God will come,[i] and all the holy ones
with him.[j]

6On that day there will be no light,[k] no
cold or frost. 7It will be a unique[l] day,
without daytime or nighttime[m]—a day
known to the LORD. When evening
comes, there will be light.[n]

8On that day living water[o] will flow[p]
out from Jerusalem, half to the eastern[q]
sea[a] and half to the western sea,[b] in
summer and in winter.[r]

9The LORD will be king[s] over the
whole earth.[t] On that day there will be
one LORD, and his name the only name.[u]

10The whole land, from Geba[v] to Rimmon,[w] south of Jerusalem, will become
like the Arabah. But Jerusalem will be
raised up[x] and remain in its place,[y] from
the Benjamin Gate[z] to the site of the
First Gate, to the Corner Gate,[a] and from
the Tower of Hananel[b] to the royal winepresses. 11It will be inhabited;[c] never
again will it be destroyed. Jerusalem will
be secure.[d]

12This is the plague with which the
LORD will strike[e] all the nations that
fought against Jerusalem: Their flesh will
rot while they are still standing on their
feet, their eyes will rot in their sockets,
and their tongues will rot in their
mouths.[f] 13On that day men will be
stricken by the LORD with great panic.[g]
Each man will seize the hand of another,
and they will attack each other.[h] 14Ju-
dah[i] too will fight at Jerusalem. The
wealth of all the surrounding nations will
be collected[j]—great quantities of gold
and silver and clothing. 15A similar
plague[k] will strike the horses and mules,
the camels and donkeys, and all the animals in those camps.

16Then the survivors[l] from all the nations that have attacked Jerusalem will go
up year after year to worship[m] the King,[n]
the LORD Almighty, and to celebrate the
Feast of Tabernacles.[o] 17If any of the peoples of the earth do not go up to Jerusalem to worship[p] the King, the LORD Almighty, they will have no rain.[q] 18If the
Egyptian people do not go up and take
part, they will have no rain. The LORD[c]
will bring on them the plague[r] he inflicts
on the nations that do not go up to celebrate the Feast of Tabernacles.[s] 19This
will be the punishment of Egypt and the
punishment of all the nations that do not
go up to celebrate the Feast of Tabernacles.[t]

20On that day HOLY TO THE LORD[u] will
be inscribed on the bells of the horses,
and the cooking pots[v] in the LORD's
house will be like the sacred bowls[w] in
front of the altar. 21Every pot in Jerusalem
and Judah will be holy[x] to the LORD Almighty, and all who come to sacrifice will
take some of the pots and cook in them.
And on that day[y] there will no longer be
a Canaanite[d] [z] in the house[a] of the LORD
Almighty.[b]

14:2 [b]S Ge 34:29; S La 5:11 [c]Isa 13:6; S Zec 13:8 **14:3** [d]Zec 9:14-15 [e]S Isa 8:9; S Zec 12:9 **14:4** [f]Eze 11:23 [g]S Nu 16:31 **14:5** [h]Am 1:1 [i]Isa 29:6; 66:15-16 [j]S Dt 33:2; Mt 16:27; 25:31; Jude 14 **14:6** [k]S Isa 13:10; S Jer 4:23 **14:7** [l]Jer 30:7 [m]Rev 21:23-25; 22:5 [n]S Isa 13:10; S 30:26 **14:8** [o]Eze 47:1-12; Jn 7:38; Rev 22:1-2 [p]S Isa 30:25 [q]Joel 2:20 [r]S Ge 8:22 **14:9** [s]S Ps 22:28; S Ob 1:21 [t]S Dt 6:4; Ps 47:7; Isa 45:24; Rev 11:15 [u]Hab 2:14; Eph 4:5-6 **14:10** [v]1Ki 15:22 [w]S Jos 15:32 [x]Isa 2:2; Jer 30:18; S Am 9:11 [y]Zec 12:6 [z]S Jer 20:2 [a]S 2Ki 14:13 [b]S Ne 3:1 **14:11** [c]Zec 2:4 [d]S Ps 48:8; S Eze 34:25-28 **14:12** [e]S Isa 11:4 [f]ver 18; S Lev 26:16; S Dt 28:22; Job 18:13 **14:13** [g]S Ge 35:5 [h]S Jdg 7:22; S Zec 11:6 **14:14** [i]Zec 12:2 [j]S Isa 23:18 **14:15** [k]ver 12 **14:16** [l]S 2Ki 19:31 [m]S Ps 22:29; S 86:9; S Isa 19:21 [n]S Ob 1:21 [o]S Ex 23:16; Isa 60:6-9; S Mic 4:2 **14:17** [p]S 2Ch 32:23 [q]S Jer 14:4; S Am 4:7 **14:18** [r]S Ge 27:29 [s]S ver 12 **14:19** [t]S Ezr 3:4 **14:20** [u]S Ex 39:30 [v]S Eze 46:20 [w]Zec 9:15 **14:21** [x]S Jer 31:40; Ro 14:6-7; 1Co 10:31 [y]Ne 8:10 [z]Zec 9:8 [a]S Ne 11:1 [b]S Eze 44:9

[z]5 Or *5My mountain valley will be blocked and will extend to Azel. It will be blocked as it was blocked because of the earthquake* [a]8 That is, the Dead Sea [b]8 That is, the Mediterranean [c]18 Or *part, then the LORD* [d]21 Or *merchant*

14:6–9 REVELATION, History—See note on 12:1–14. God revealed the changes which would take place when His revelation is complete in Jerusalem. God will one day have charge over all the people of the earth. No other gods will compete with Him. The nature and character of God will then prevail as the only way of life. Interpreters differ as to whether God's reign will be literally on the earth or figuratively in heaven.

14:9–11 ELECTION, Sovereignty—God shall be King over all the earth. He will be recognized universally as the only true God (Isa 11:9; Ac 2:8–11). Miraculous climatic changes shall transform Jerusalem into a paradise. Jerusalem shall become a sanctuary of all nations. God's election purposes will be fulfilled only when all nations recognize Him as God.

14:16–21 EVANGELISM, Judgment—God wants all people to worship Him. Past history does not exclude people from worship. People who refuse to worship face God's judgment. The principle is applicable to people in all situations. Unless people truly worship God through faith in Jesus Christ, judgment will come. We must come to Jesus Christ, trust Him, and worship Him; or we will incur God's judgment. Worship must result in holy living to be pleasing to God.

14:20–21 GOD, Holy—God created His people in the Exodus to be a kingdom of priests leading the nations to worship the one true God. Israel failed to be what God intended her to be. That did not change God's purpose. He continues to work towards the day when His people will be a holy people, separated from worldly priorities and dedicated to bringing the nations to Him. This would mean every utensil would be handled by a priest and thus would be dedicated to the work of the holy God.

Malachi

Theological Setting

The people who made the trip back to Jerusalem from exile in Babylon (586-538 BC) initially desired to restore the nation (Ezr 1—2) and rebuild the Temple (Ezr 3—6; Hag 1). Before very many years, they once again began to dishonor God's name and to forsake the laws of God. Therefore, God sent Ezra (458 BC) to bring the people back into a covenant relationship with Him (Ezr 9—10). A few years later (445 BC), Nehemiah came to help rebuild the walls of Jerusalem (Ne 1—6), and Ezra again challenged the people to revive their fear of God and separate themselves from foreign influences (Ne 9—10).

Somewhere around the time of Nehemiah, or shortly afterward, some of God's people divorced their Hebrew wives and intermarried with foreigners. The priests failed to teach the people to reverence God. Many did not honor God with proper sacrifices or tithes. Some questioned God's love, and others began to wonder if it really paid to fear God and serve Him.

In light of these circumstances the Jews could choose between several possible alternatives:

1. They could continue to disrespect God with improper sacrifices, to refuse to tithe, to divorce their wives and intermarry with unbelievers, and to blame God for not loving and blessing them.
2. They could turn from their evil ways and become strict observers of the law of Moses, hoping God would be impressed by their zealous good works.
3. They could form an alternative community to prepare the way for the messenger of the Lord to come to His Temple, to judge the wicked, and to bring in the kingdom of God.
4. They could confess their sins and revitalize their stewardship of life before God.

In this situation Malachi ministered the word of the Lord using a unique question and answer style of interaction with his listeners. He sought to challenge the people concerning their lack of honor or respect for God when they worshiped at the Temple (1:6-14), to rebuke the priests for not fearing God and instructing the people in God's ways (2:1-9), to plead with the people to confess their sins and return to God so that God could bless them (3:7-12), and to assure the righteous and the wicked that God is a God of justice who will one day come and judge the wicked and spare those who fear Him (2:17—3:5; 3:13—4:3).

The Book of Malachi is a reminder of how God's people allowed the worldly thinking of their day instead of their reverence for God to determine their behavior. It does matter if the people of God do not truly fear God and magnify His name. God despises those who do not honor Him with the best sacrifice, who refuse to tithe, who divorce and marry unbelievers, who question His love and justice, and who wonder if it is worth it to fear God and serve Him. God has a book of rememberance; He knows those who honor His name and will make them His own and pour out His love on them.

Theological Outline

Malachi: A Challenge to Fear God and Magnify His Name

I. Honor God: Do Not Doubt His Love. (1:1-5)
   A. People may question God's love. (1:1-2)
   B. God has and continues to demonstrate His love for His people. (1:3-4)
   C. God will be magnified for His love. (1:5)

II. Honor God: Do Not Profane His Worship. (1:6—2:9)
   A. God expects and deserves honor from His people. (1:6-14)
   B. God judges unfaithful ministers. (2:1-9)
      1. God curses ministers who do not honor Him. (2:1-3)
      2. God blesses ministers who reverence Him, who instruct His people rightly, who walk with God, and who turn people from sin. (2:4-7)
      3. God humiliates ministers who do not teach His ways. (2:8-9)

III. Honor God: Do Not Be Unfaithful in Marriage Covenants. (2:10-16)
   A. Unfaithfulness results from marriages to unbelievers. (2:10-12)
   B. Proper worship rites cannot replace unfaithfulness brought through divorce. (2:13-16)
IV. Honor God: Do Not Doubt His Justice. (2:17—3:5)
   A. Questioning the justice of God wears out His patience. (2:17)
   B. The "messenger of the covenant" will come to establish justice. (3:1-4)
   C. God will judge those who do not fear Him. (3:5)
V. Honor God: Do Not Withhold the Tithe, and He Will Bless You. (3:6-12)
   A. The changeless God wants His people to change. (3:6-7)
   B. Failure to tithe makes us guilty of robbing God. (3:8-10*a*)
   C. God will bless those who tithe. (3:10*b*-12)
VI. Honoring God Is Worth It: Do Not Think God Will Treat Everyone the Same. (3:13—4:3)
   A. Questioning the value of serving God offends Him. (3:13-15)
   B. God will remember and spare those who reverence and serve Him. (3:16-18)
   C. God will destroy the evildoers in His day. (4:1)
   D. The "sun of righteousness" will bring healing and justice for God's people. (4:2-3)
VII. Honor God: Obey Him and Wait Expectantly. (4:4-6)

Theological Conclusions

The Book of Malachi challenges the people of God to take a fresh look at the way they are thinking about God and at the underlying motives behind their religious activity by emphasizing four doctrines:

1. God is a great King who loves His people and deserves their respect and honor.
2. The people of God demonstrate true reverence for God in worship and in marriage relationships.
3. Spiritual leaders have a responsibility to instruct the people of God in God's ways.
4. God will one day send the "messenger of the covenant" (3:1) to judge those who do not honor Him and bless those who magnify His name.

The Israelites showed more respect for their governor than for God. They did not treat God as the sovereign King who rules the earth or honor Him with appropriate acts of worship. The Book of Malachi reminds the people that one day individuals from all the nations will magnify His name (1:11,14). Surely the people that God has loved and chosen to be His own people should honor Him and not ignore or question His grace and love.

One of Malachi's chief concerns was to demonstrate that the people of God had not honored God in worship or in their marriages. When they came to the Temple to worship and praise God's name, they brought unworthy gifts and were bored with the ceremonies of praise. Such hypocrisy does not fool God. People would be better off not coming to worship at all. Their marriages were also shameful. They intermarried with unbelievers who did not fear God and, thus, tempted them away from God. They were unfaithful to their believing spouses and divorced them (2:10-16). Such acts run contrary to the will of God and suggest a disrespect for God and His ways.

Malachi believed he could explain why the people failed to reverence God. Because their spiritual leaders—the priests—did not fear God or teach the people God's Word, the people did not honor God. The priests should have corrected the people of God when they brought unworthy sacrifices. They should have encouraged a deep love for God, and given God's instructions on tithing; but they did not know God either.

Some believed serving God and living according to His words was a waste of time. Look around; the wicked seem to prosper, and the righteous are not that well off. In response to this kind of thinking, Malachi reminded the people that God is just. He will send his "messenger of the covenant" to purify the nation with judgment. He keeps records and knows who honors God and who does not. In the end, God will distinguish between the wicked and the righteous and pour out His great blessing on His own people.

Contemporary Teaching

The Book of Malachi touches on issues which are significant to our own situation in the church today. Malachi asks us: (1) to take a careful look at our concept of God and evaluate if we truly reverence Him as King in our lives; (2) to honor God with the best that we have to give in worship and in giving our tithes; (3) to confess where we have failed to magnify His name and return to Him in humility; (4) to be faithful to God and our spouses in our marriage relationships; and (5) to be assured that God sees when we honor and serve Him and will richly bless us.

Chapter 1

AN oracle:[a] The word[b] of the LORD to
Israel through Malachi.[a]

Jacob Loved, Esau Hated

2"I have loved[c] you," says the LORD.
"But you ask,[d] 'How have you loved
us?'
"Was not Esau Jacob's brother?" the
LORD says. "Yet I have loved Jacob,[e] 3but
Esau I have hated,[f] and I have turned his
mountains into a wasteland[g] and left his
inheritance to the desert jackals.[h]"
4Edom[i] may say, "Though we have
been crushed, we will rebuild[j] the ruins."
But this is what the LORD Almighty
says: "They may build, but I will demolish.[k] They will be called the Wicked
Land, a people always under the wrath of
the LORD.[l] 5You will see it with your
own eyes and say, 'Great[m] is the LORD—
even beyond the borders of Israel!'[n]

Blemished Sacrifices

6"A son honors his father,[o] and a servant his master.[p] If I am a father, where
is the honor due me? If I am a master,
where is the respect[q] due me?" says the
LORD Almighty.[r] "It is you, O priests,
who show contempt for my name.
"But you ask,[s] 'How have we shown
contempt for your name?'

1:1 [a]S Na 1:1 [b]Ac 7:38; Ro 3:1-2; 1Pe 4:11 **1:2** [c]S Dt 4:37 [d]ver 6,7; Mal 2:14, 17; 3:7,13 [e]S Jer 46:27; Ro 9:13* **1:3** [f]Lk 14:26 [g]S Isa 34:10 [h]S Isa 13:22 **1:4** [i]S Isa 11:14; S 34:11 [j]Isa 9:10 [k]S Isa 34:5 [l]S La 4:22; S Eze 25:12-14; S 26:14 **1:5** [m]Ps 35:27; 48:1; Mic 5:4 [n]Isa 45:22; 52:10; S Am 1:11-12 **1:6** [o]S Lev 20:9; Mt 15:4; 23:9 [p]Lk 6:46 [q]S Dt 31:12; S Isa 1:2 [r]Job 5:17 [s]S ver 2 **1:7** [t]ver 12; Lev 21:6 [u]S ver 2 [v]S Eze 23:41 **1:8** [w]S Lev 1:3; S Dt 15:21 [x]S Ge 32:20 [y]S Isa 43:23 **1:9** [z]Lev 23:33-44; Ps 51:17; Mic 6:6-8; Ro 12:1; Heb 13:16 [a]S Jer 6:20 **1:10** [b]2Ch 28:24 [c]S Hos 5:6 [d]Lev 22:20 [e]ver 13; Isa 1:11-14; Jer 14:12; Mal 2:12 **1:11** [f]S Isa 24:15; 56:6 [g]S Isa 6:3; S 12:4 [h]S Ps 113:3; S Mt 8:11 [i]Isa 60:6-7; Rev 5:8; 8:3 [j]S Isa 19:21; Heb 13:15 **1:12** [k]S Eze 41:22 [l]S ver 7 **1:13** [m]Isa 43:22-24

7"You place defiled food[t] on my altar.
"But you ask,[u] 'How have we defiled
you?'
"By saying that the LORD's table[v] is
contemptible. 8When you bring blind animals for sacrifice, is that not wrong?
When you sacrifice crippled or diseased
animals,[w] is that not wrong? Try offering
them to your governor! Would he be
pleased[x] with you? Would he accept
you?" says the LORD Almighty.[y]
9"Now implore God to be gracious to
us. With such offerings[z] from your
hands, will he accept[a] you?"—says the
LORD Almighty.
10"Oh, that one of you would shut the
temple doors,[b] so that you would not
light useless fires on my altar! I am not
pleased[c] with you," says the LORD Almighty, "and I will accept[d] no offering[e]
from your hands. 11My name will be
great[f] among the nations,[g] from the rising to the setting of the sun.[h] In every
place incense[i] and pure offerings[j] will
be brought to my name, because my
name will be great among the nations,"
says the LORD Almighty.
12"But you profane it by saying of the
Lord's table,[k] 'It is defiled,' and of its
food,[l] 'It is contemptible.' 13And you say,
'What a burden!'[m] and you sniff at it con-

[a]*1 Malachi* means *my messenger.*

1:2–3 ELECTION, Freedom—Mystery surrounds the election of God. One is chosen, and the other is not chosen. God's graciousness, mercy, and compassion are far above and beyond human understanding. Through election He works freely to achieve His just and loving purposes. Those purposes are not limited to one people but extend to all nations. Compare Ro 11:32–36.
1:2–5 THE CHURCH, Covenant People—The ultimate definition of God's people is the people God in His sovereignty chooses to love. The example of Jacob and Esau, the brothers whose descendants became Israel and Edom, illustrates this.
1:4–5 GOD, Sovereignty—The nations saw Yahweh, the God of Israel, as a local god with authority inside the territory of Israel over His own people. God exercised His sovereign power to show He was in charge of all nations, across all geographical and political borders.
1:6 GOD, Father—God as Father calls forth an image of love, concern, and helpfulness in our minds. It must also call us to respect, honor, and serve Him.
1:6—2:9 SIN, Blindness—Ministers can lead religious worship and be spiritually blind. Going through the proper ritual does not make worship acceptable to God. Having the proper attitude to God does. Ministers can look upon their ministry simply as a profession by which they earn a living. They can fulfill a job description while holding God and His house in contempt. A wrong attitude toward ministry leads to self-centered spiritual blindness. Ministry is to bring honor to God, not food and fame to the minister. God would rather shut the doors of His house than have a spiritually blind minister lead His people. A minister is to lead people to obey God and turn from sin. A spiritually blind minister leads them into sin.
1:6–14 STEWARDSHIP, Giving in Worship—Giving reflects our character and the genuineness of our devotion to God. If we truly revere God, we will never offer cast-off or leftover gifts, such as a sick animal or property gained by unethical means. God deserves only the best we have. Anything less shows serving and pleasing Him is not our top priority. See note on Mt 5:23–24. God's ordained ministers are responsible to lead God's people to give their best to God. The failure of ministerial leadership brings failure of the people. Compare 3:3–4.
1:6–14 WORSHIP, Priesthood—Worship leaders focus on pleasing God and honoring Him before the worshipers. Malachi saw priests serving their own financial and ego needs. They offered sacrifices which did not meet minimum standards. God demands the best we have in offering to Him. See note on Ex 22:20.
1:9 PRAYER, Hindrances—The Lord rebuked the priests for offering blemished sacrifices which He would not accept. Going through the motions of worship is not a basis for prayer. Rather false worship blocks prayer. See note on Zec 7:13.
1:11 GOD, One God—God condemns His people, even His ministers, when they do not obediently contribute to the fulfillment of His purpose to let all nations know He is the only God. What Malachi thought was happening or would soon happen outside Jerusalem is not clear from this text. In the biblical view as a whole, we know God does not demand specific rituals limited to one specific place. He wants all people everywhere to worship Him. He wants universal recognition as the only God. See note on Zec 13:9.
1:11 EVANGELISM, Universality—All nations need the Lord. God's entire history with His people has one goal: to bring all nations to worship Him.
1:12–14 GOD, Sovereignty—God is King of the universe and wants to be treated accordingly. He will not accept gifts given to Him with impure motives or unwilling hearts. Gifts do not buy off God or fulfill our obligation to Him. They express our gratitude to Him and our deep desire to share with Him because He is the great Ruler who deserves our worship.

temptuously,[n]" says the LORD Almighty.
"When you bring injured, crippled or
diseased animals and offer them as sacrifices,[o] should I accept them from your
hands?"[p] says the LORD. 14"Cursed is the
cheat who has an acceptable male in his
flock and vows to give it, but then sacrifices a blemished animal[q] to the Lord.
For I am a great king,[r]" says the LORD
Almighty,[s] "and my name is to be
feared[t] among the nations.[u]

Chapter 2

Admonition for the Priests

"AND now this admonition is for you,
O priests.[v] 2If you do not listen,[w]
and if you do not set your heart to honor[x]
my name," says the LORD Almighty, "I
will send a curse[y] upon you, and I will
curse your blessings.[z] Yes, I have already
cursed them, because you have not set
your heart to honor me.

3"Because of you I will rebuke[b] your
descendants[c]; I will spread on your faces
the offal[a] from your festival sacrifices,
and you will be carried off with it.[b] 4And
you will know that I have sent you this
admonition so that my covenant with
Levi[c] may continue," says the LORD Almighty. 5"My covenant was with him, a
covenant[d] of life and peace,[e] and I gave
them to him; this called for reverence[f]
and he revered me and stood in awe of
my name. 6True instruction[g] was in his
mouth and nothing false was found on his
lips. He walked[h] with me in peace[i] and
uprightness,[j] and turned many from
sin.[k]

7"For the lips of a priest[l] ought to preserve knowledge, and from his mouth
men should seek instruction[m]—because
he is the messenger[n] of the LORD Almighty. 8But you have turned from the
way[o] and by your teaching have caused
many to stumble;[p] you have violated the
covenant[q] with Levi,"[r] says the LORD
Almighty. 9"So I have caused you to be
despised[s] and humiliated[t] before all the
people, because you have not followed
my ways but have shown partiality[u] in
matters of the law."[v]

Judah Unfaithful

10Have we not all one Father[d]?[w] Did
not one God create us?[x] Why do we pro-

1:13 [n]S Nu 14:11 [o]S ver 10 [p]S Dt 15:21 **1:14** [q]Ex 12:5; S Lev 22:18-21 [r]Ps 95:3; S Ob 1:21; 1Ti 6:15 [s]Jer 46:18 [t]S Dt 28:58 [u]Ps 72:8-11 **2:1** [v]ver 7 **2:2** [w]Jer 13:17 [x]Mt 15:7-9; Jn 5:23; 1Ti 6:16; Rev 5:12-13 [y]S Dt 11:26; S 28:20 [z]Nu 6:23-27 **2:3** [a]S Ex 29:14; S Lev 4:11; S Job 9:31 [b]1Ki 14:10 **2:4** [c]S Nu 3:12 **2:5** [d]Dt 33:9; Ps 25:10; 103:18; S Mt 26:28; S Lk 22:20; Heb 7:22 [e]S Nu 25:12 [f]S Dt 14:23; S 28:58; Ps 119:161; Heb 12:28 **2:6** [g]S Dt 33:10 [h]S Ge 5:22 [i]Lk 2:14; S Jn 14:27; Gal 5:22 [j]S Ps 25:21 [k]S Ro 11:14; Jas 5:19-20 **2:7** [l]S Jer 18:18 [m]S Lev 10:11; S 2Ch 17:7 [n]S Nu 27:21; S 2Ch 36:15; Mt 11:10; Mk 1:2 **2:8** [o]S Ex 32:8; Jer 2:8 [p]S Jer 18:15 [q]Jer 33:21; S Eze 22:26 [r]S Hos 4:6 **2:9** [s]S 1Sa 2:30; S Ps 22:6; S Jer 51:37 [t]S Ps 35:4; Jer 3:25; Ac 8:32-33 [u]S Ex 18:16; S Lev 19:15; Ac 10:34; Ro 2:11 [v]S 1Sa 2:17 **2:10** [w]S Ex 4:22; Mt 5:16; 6:4,18; Lk 11:2; 1Co 8:6 [x]S Job 4:17; Isa 43:1

[b]3 Or *cut off* (see Septuagint) [c]3 Or *will blight your grain* [d]10 Or *father*

1:14 EVANGELISM, Obedience—What is offered to the Lord in worship must be pure. All are to give the very best in worship of God. This includes motives, not just outward acts. True obedience is from the heart. Evangelization—all service—must be like that. Only the pure life can confirm our words of witness to lead the peoples to faith.

2:1–9 GOD, Wrath—God's ministers bear special responsibility to teach His people. When they neglect or misuse this responsibility, they face God's disciplining wrath. Professional ministry is not a reason for pride but an opportunity for service.

2:1–9 WORSHIP, Priesthood—Worship leaders have specific functions: (1) to listen to God; (2) to honor God; (3) to reverence and worship God; (4) to follow the highest moral standards; (5) to turn other people away from their sinful lives; (6) to instruct God's people; and (7) to be God's messengers.

2:4–6 REVELATION, Faithfulness—God's intention even in chastising was to renew the solemn oath and purpose He had with Israel. Levi, the representative name for the priestly tribe which acted as mediator before God, provided the true teaching and honest interpretation of God's will for His people. Revealed teaching seeks to turn people from sin to God. The agent of God's revelation is expected to live a life of wholeness and moral uprightness.

2:4–8 THE CHURCH, Covenant People—Those who lead others must display characteristics worthy of leadership. Malachi discussed the covenant God made with Levi, a covenant not otherwise explicitly described in the Old Testament. Compare Dt 33:8–11. See note on Nu 25:10–13. Levi was the ancestor of the line of priests. The prophet reminded the priests that their ancestor served God faithfully and discharged his duties in a remarkable way, but many of them were causing people to stumble through false teaching. Malachi presented one of the most exalted views of the Old Testament priesthood. Every minister should exhibit these characteristics: (1) Ministers should fear God, standing in awe before Him. (2) Ministers must instruct others concerning God's way by word and by deed. (3) The minister is the messenger of the Lord of hosts. God had to admonish and discipline unfaithful priests, but His plan was to ensure His covenant with the priests continued. God blesses those who serve Him by giving them meaningful relationships, both with God and with their fellow servants. The blessings of the Lord continue forever.

2:5 SALVATION, Fear of God—God's covenant with Levi promised life and peace, but required reverence and awe of His name. Because all of God's people are now priests, we owe reverence and awe to Him.

2:6–8 EDUCATION, Priests—Every teacher of the Word of God has something in common with the priests of Israel, who bore primary responsibility for teaching the people. As messengers of the Lord, God-called teachers are responsible for the accuracy and soundness of their instruction. When they carry out their teaching duties faithfully, they will have an impact on the behavior of individuals and on the moral standards of the community.

2:7–8 REVELATION, Messengers—The line of priests designated by God to interpret God's law and will were distorting the message and deceiving God's people. The people did not receive the truth of God. Revelation was being thwarted by those trusted to reveal God's truth. No one office has monopoly on God's truth. He used prophets and priests to reveal His will.

2:9 SIN, Transgression—The priests obeyed the law as they chose to and with whom they chose. They were partial in interpreting the law to the various social classes (Lev 19:15). When they were not fair with all people in applying God's law, they transgressed His law. God is not partial to one group over another (Dt 10:17). We must not be either.

2:10 GOD, Father—God's people find common identity as the children of God. He created us as members of the human race and as His special people. This obliges us to serve Him and Him only, doing nothing that would place some other person, power, or thing in His place. Not even human love and marriage should cause us to devote ourselves to someone other than God. See notes on 1:6; Dt 32:6.

2:10 CREATION, Covenant—Creation is the basis for the emotional, physical, and spiritual ties that bind the human family together. The prophet reminded Israel of their common

fane the covenant[y] of our fathers by
breaking faith[z] with one another?
11Judah has broken faith. A detestable[a]
thing has been committed in Israel and in
Jerusalem: Judah has desecrated the sanctuary the LORD loves,[b] by marrying[c] the
daughter of a foreign god.[d] 12As for the
man who does this, whoever he may be,
may the LORD cut him off[e] from the tents
of Jacob[e][f]—even though he brings offerings[g] to the LORD Almighty.
13Another thing you do: You flood the
LORD's altar with tears.[h] You weep and
wail[i] because he no longer pays attention[j] to your offerings or accepts them
with pleasure from your hands.[k] 14You
ask,[l] "Why?" It is because the LORD is
acting as the witness[m] between you and
the wife of your youth,[n] because you
have broken faith with her, though she is
your partner, the wife of your marriage
covenant.[o]
15Has not ⌊the LORD⌋ made them one?[p]
In flesh and spirit they are his. And why
one? Because he was seeking godly offspring.[f][q] So guard yourself[r] in your
spirit, and do not break faith[s] with the
wife of your youth.
16"I hate divorce,[t]" says the LORD God
of Israel, "and I hate a man's covering
himself[g] with violence[u] as well as with
his garment," says the LORD Almighty.
So guard yourself in your spirit,[v] and
do not break faith.

The Day of Judgment

17You have wearied[w] the LORD with
your words.
"How have we wearied him?" you
ask.[x]
By saying, "All who do evil are good in
the eyes of the LORD, and he is pleased[y]
with them" or "Where is the God of justice?[z]"

Chapter 3

"SEE, I will send my messenger,[a]
who will prepare the way before

2:10 [y]Ex 19:5; S 2Ki 17:15; Jer 31:32 [z]S Zep 3:3-4 **2:11** [a]S Isa 1:13; S 48:8 [b]S Dt 4:37 [c]S Ne 13:23 [d]S Ex 34:16; Jer 3:7-9 **2:12** [e]S 1Sa 2:30-33; S Eze 24:21 [f]S Nu 24:5; 2Sa 20:1 [g]S Mal 1:10 **2:13** [h]S Jer 11:11 [i]Ps 39:12 [j]Ps 66:18; Jer 14:12 [k]Isa 58:2 **2:14** [l]S Mal 1:2 [m]S Ge 21:30; S Jos 24:22 [n]S Pr 5:18 [o]S Eze 16:8; Heb 13:4 **2:15** [p]S Ge 2:24; Mt 19:4-6 [q]S Dt 14:2; 1Co 7:14 [r]S Dt 4:15 [s]S Isa 54:6; 1Co 7:10; Heb 13:4 **2:16** [t]S Dt 24:1; Mt 5:31-32; 19:4-9; Mk 10:4-5 [u]S Ge 6:11; 34:25; S Pr 4:17; S Isa 58:4 [v]Ps 51:10 **2:17** [w]S Isa 1:14 [x]S Mal 1:2 [y]Ps 5:4 [z]S Ge 18:25; S Job 8:3; S Eze 18:25 **3:1** [a]S Nu 27:21; S 2Ch 36:15

[e]12 Or *12May the LORD cut off from the tents of Jacob anyone who gives testimony in behalf of the man who does this* [f]15 Or *15But the one ⌊who is our father⌋ did not do this, not as long as life remained in him. And what was he seeking? An offspring from God* [g]16 Or *his wife*

bond with one another. God created them all physically. More important, however, He had united them within the framework of a covenant relationship. The prophet emphasized two things which should result from God's bringing them together through His creative power. They should love one another, and they should be careful to keep their family life tied closely to their religious heritage.

2:10 HUMANITY, Relationships—Creation means we are related to all people. God's election means we belong to a special community, the children of God. Our actions establish the reputation of God's people among the "world's" people. Even the reputation and honor of deceased spiritual ancestors depends on our faithfulness to God's way of life. Actions defaming the community deserve punishment.

2:10–11 SIN, Covenant Breach—God gave Israel a covenant based on trust in and love for both God and fellow members of the covenant. Israel broke faith by dealing treacherously. See note on Isa 48:1–9. This treachery consisted in marrying women with idols for gods and infesting Israel with false worship. See note on 1 Ki 11:1–13.

2:10 THE CHURCH, Covenant People—God's people are tied to Him in two ways—creation and covenant. The covenant ties God's people to God and to one another. Lack of loyalty to a follower of the Lord shows we do not maintain our obligations to God. See note on 1 Jn 3:10.

2:10–12 FAMILY, Intermarriage—See notes on Dt 7:3–4; Ne 10:28–30; 13:23–27.

2:11–12 GOD, One God—Israel lived among peoples who had no problem participating in worship services for several different gods. Marriage meant simply adding another worship service—that of the spouse's god—to the schedule. The one true God does not accept that. He is sufficient to handle all functions attributed to any god. We must devote all worship and reverence to Him.

2:11–14 PRAYER, Hindrances—Two offenses prevented God from accepting the offerings of the people—marriage to a pagan and divorce. A right spirit, not an emotional outpouring, would make the offerings acceptable. Family relationships greatly affect our prayer life.

2:12–13 STEWARDSHIP, Lifestyle—Giving or ceremonial worship does not remove the necessity for right living, including respect within families. See note on Lk 12:16–31.

2:13–16 GOD, Holy—The holiness of God means unforgiven sin separates us from Him. Israel thought nothing of divorcing wives who had long been faithful for younger, more attractive foreigners. Then they entered worship and expected God to hear their prayers and accept their gifts. God refused. We must find forgiveness of sin before we can worship the holy God.

2:13–14 WORSHIP, Obedience—Broken relationships hurt true worship. Malachi's generation thought worship rituals qualified them as God's people even when they openly disobeyed God's will for their marriages. God showed them a different way.

2:13–16 FAMILY, Divorce—Marriage is not a trade-in business. This passage is the strongest statement in the Old Testament against divorce among the covenant people. Dt 24:1–4 describes a divorce process for the Hebrew people. Ezra commanded divorce from heathen wives (Ezr 10:10–44). Malachi condemned the practice of divorcing older wives married within the covenant community to marry younger women or women of the mixed tribes who had remained in Israel during the Babylonian captivity. The prophet anticipated the teaching of Jesus that all divorce is contrary to God's original intention for marriage (Mt 19:4–9).

2:17—3:5 GOD, Righteous—God is righteous and does not approve anything unrighteous. We cannot change the moral laws and expect God to forgive and accept us. We must never think God has given up on establishing justice in His world. We may not see the evidence of God's work to rectify injustice, but we can be sure He is just and will bring just retribution in His time and way.

2:17—3:5 EVIL AND SUFFERING, Punishment—Do the wicked escape punishment for their sins? The people of Judah thought so. God told Malachi He would judge the sinners. Like Judah, we may ignore God, and He may not punish us immediately. Eventually we suffer the consequences of our sins. Evil acts are never good in God's eyes. In His time God reveals His justice. We must trust God's promise to act and must let times of trial refine and purify our lives.

2:17 CHRISTIAN ETHICS, Justice—See notes on Mic 2:1–7; La 3:32–36.

3:1 JESUS CHRIST, Foretold—The Messiah would be preceded by one who announced Him. The New Testament

me.[b] Then suddenly the Lord[c] you are
seeking will come to his temple; the messenger of the covenant,[d] whom you desire,[e] will come," says the LORD Almighty.
2But who can endure[f] the day of his
coming?[g] Who can stand[h] when he appears? For he will be like a refiner's fire[i]
or a launderer's soap.[j] 3He will sit as a
refiner and purifier of silver;[k] he will purify[l] the Levites and refine them like
gold and silver.[m] Then the LORD will have
men who will bring offerings in righteousness,[n] 4and the offerings[o] of Judah
and Jerusalem will be acceptable to the
LORD, as in days gone by, as in former
years.[p]
5"So I will come near to you for judgment. I will be quick to testify against sorcerers,[q] adulterers[r] and perjurers,[s]
against those who defraud laborers of
their wages,[t] who oppress the widows[u]
and the fatherless, and deprive aliens[v] of
justice, but do not fear[w] me," says the
LORD Almighty.

Robbing God

6"I the LORD do not change.[x] So you,
O descendants of Jacob, are not destroyed.[y] 7Ever since the time of your
forefathers you have turned away[z] from
my decrees and have not kept them. Return[a] to me, and I will return to you,"[b]
says the LORD Almighty.
"But you ask,[c] 'How are we to return?'
8"Will a man rob[d] God? Yet you rob
me.
"But you ask, 'How do we rob you?'
"In tithes[e] and offerings. 9You are under a curse[f]—the whole nation of you
—because you are robbing me. 10Bring
the whole tithe[g] into the storehouse,[h]
that there may be food in my house. Test
me in this," says the LORD Almighty,
"and see if I will not throw open the
floodgates[i] of heaven and pour out[j] so
much blessing[k] that you will not have
room enough for it.[l] 11I will prevent
pests from devouring[m] your crops, and
the vines in your fields will not cast their
fruit,[n]" says the LORD Almighty. 12"Then
all the nations will call you blessed,[o] for
yours will be a delightful land,"[p] says the
LORD Almighty.[q]
13"You have said harsh things[r] against
me," says the LORD.
"Yet you ask,[s] 'What have we said
against you?'
14"You have said, 'It is futile[t] to
serve[u] God. What did we gain by carrying out his requirements[v] and going
about like mourners[w] before the LORD Almighty? 15But now we call the arrogant[x]
blessed. Certainly the evildoers[y] prosper,[z] and even those who challenge God
escape.' "
16Then those who feared the LORD
talked with each other, and the LORD lis-

3:1 [b]S Isa 40:3; S Mt 3:3; 11:10*; Mk 1:2*; Lk 7:27* [c]Mic 5:2 [d]S Isa 42:6 [e]S 1Sa 9:20 **3:2** [f]S Eze 22:14; Rev 6:17 [g]S Eze 7:7; S Da 7:13; S Joel 2:31; S Mt 16:27; Jas 5:8; 2Pe 3:4; S Rev 1:7 [h]S 1Sa 6:20 [i]S Isa 1:31; S 30:30; S Zec 13:9; Mt 3:10-12 [j]S Job 9:30 **3:3** [k]S Da 12:10; S 1Co 3:13 [l]S 1Ch 23:28; S Isa 1:25 [m]S Job 28:1; S Ps 12:6; 1Pe 1:7; Rev 3:18 [n]S Ps 132:9 **3:4** [o]2Ch 7:12; Ps 51:19; Mal 1:11 [p]S 2Ch 7:3; S Eze 20:40 **3:5** [q]S Ex 7:11; S Isa 47:9 [r]Ex 20:14; Jas 2:11; 2Pe 2:12-14 [s]Lev 19:11-12; S Jer 7:9 [t]S Lev 19:13; Jas 5:4 [u]S Ex 22:22 [v]S Ex 22:21; S Dt 24:19; S Eze 22:7 [w]S Dt 31:12; S Isa 1:2 **3:6** [x]S Nu 23:19; S Heb 7:21; Jas 1:17 [y]S Job 34:15; S Hos 11:9 **3:7** [z]S Ex 32:8; S Jer 7:26; Ac 7:51 [a]S Isa 44:22; S Eze 18:32 [b]S Zec 1:3; Jas 4:8 [c]S Mal 1:2 **3:8** [d]S Zec 5:3 [e]S Lev 27:30; Nu 18:21; S Ne 13:10-12; Lk 18:12 **3:9** [f]S Dt 11:26; 28:15-68; S Zec 5:3 **3:10** [g]S Ex 22:29 [h]S Ne 13:12 [i]S 2Ki 7:2 [j]Isa 44:3 [k]S Lev 25:21; S Joel 2:14; 2Co 9:8-11 [l]S Joel 2:24 **3:11** [m]S Ex 10:15; S Dt 28:39 [n]S Ex 23:26 **3:12** [o]S Dt 28:3-12; Isa 61:9 [p]S Isa 62:4; S Eze 20:6 [q]S 2Ch 31:10 **3:13** [r]Mal 2:17 [s]S Mal 1:2 **3:14** [t]Ps 73:13; S Isa 57:10 [u]Ps 100:2; Jn 12:26; Ro 12:11 [v]S Jos 22:5; S Isa 1:14 [w]Isa 58:3 **3:15** [x]S Ps 119:21 [y]Ps 14:1; 36:1-2; Jer 7:10 [z]S Job 21:7

identifies John the Baptist as the forerunner of Jesus (Mt 11:10–18; Jn 1:6–9). Lost people continue to need someone to announce the Messiah's coming and thus to prepare the way for the Lord's salvation.

3:1–2 REVELATION, Messengers—God planned and prepared His people to receive His most important revelation. Malachi announced the one who would prepare the way for God's coming to His people. This one is clearly identified with John the Baptist in the New Testament (Mk 1:2).

3:1 THE CHURCH, Covenant People—God does not abandon His people to their own evil choices. He chooses to help people, in this case by sending His messenger to prepare the way before the Lord. John the Baptist fulfilled this role, preparing the way for Jesus (Mk 1:2).

3:3–4 STEWARDSHIP, Lifestyle—God is working to teach His people how to worship Him. He wants to refine and purify us so righteous living will accompany our offerings. Only as we present ourselves acceptable to God can our offerings be acceptable. See notes on Mic 6:6–8; Lk 12:16–31.

3:3–4 WORSHIP, Priesthood—God looked to the day priests would be morally pure and follow the directions He had given for worship. Impure motives and actions make our offerings unacceptable.

3:5 SIN, Judgment—God's presence can be dangerous. People think they can hide their sins and never be convicted. God comes to witness against sinners: those who practice magic or perform sexual sins, who are liars, oppressors of the poor, and perpetrators of injustice. We do not want to face God as a witness against us in His court.

3:6 GOD, Faithfulness—God does not change; He is constant to fulfill His threats and promises. People cannot excuse themselves by blaming God for unfulfilled expectations or for bad times. Such times may reflect God's wrath on a sinful people. God will do what He says. We must ask if we have fulfilled our promises to Him faithfully.

3:6–12 STEWARDSHIP, Tithe—God deplores the sin of turning away from His decrees. Levitical law required the people of Israel to give ten percent of their agricultural products plus various sacrifices and services to God. See note on Nu 18:21–32. Failure to give the tithe and required offerings was robbing God. This Old Testament heritage of required tithes and offerings enriches the Christian understanding of giving. The Old Testament heritage provides a background for the greater revelation of life and service that results from faith in Christ. Giving takes on a greater meaning in the lives of those who follow Jesus Christ and heed His teachings.

3:10 GOD, Grace—God's desire is to bless His people, meeting all their needs. He expects His people to fulfill our obligations to Him.

3:13–18 EVIL AND SUFFERING, Punishment—Some of Judah argued the wicked escaped punishment, and, therefore, it was of no advantage to serve God. God knows who is righteous and rewards them. See note on 2:17—3:5.

3:16–17 HOLY SCRIPTURE, Writing—Those who respect and follow God's way of life were recorded permanently, not only in God's understanding but also in the historical witness of Israel's books of faith. History bears witness to the dramatic difference between those who followed God's lifestyle and those who chose their own. Compare Ex 32:32–33; Ps 69:28; 87:6; Da 12:1.

tened and heard.[a] A scroll[b] of remembrance was written in his presence concerning those who feared[c] the LORD and
honored his name.
17"They will be mine,[d]" says the LORD
Almighty, "in the day when I make up
my treasured possession.[h][e] I will spare[f]
them, just as in compassion a man spares
his son[g] who serves him. 18And you will
again see the distinction between the
righteous[h] and the wicked, between
those who serve God and those who do
not.[i]

Chapter 4

The Day of the LORD

"SURELY the day is coming;[j] it will
burn like a furnace.[k] All the arrogant[l] and every evildoer will be stubble,[m] and that day that is coming will set
them on fire,[n]" says the LORD Almighty.
"Not a root or a branch[o] will be left to
them. 2But for you who revere my
name,[p] the sun of righteousness[q] will
rise with healing[r] in its wings. And you
will go out and leap[s] like calves released
from the stall. 3Then you will trample[t]
down the wicked; they will be ashes[u] under the soles of your feet on the day when
I do these things," says the LORD Almighty.
4"Remember the law[v] of my servant
Moses, the decrees and laws I gave him at
Horeb[w] for all Israel.[x]
5"See, I will send you the prophet Elijah[y] before that great and dreadful day of
the LORD comes.[z] 6He will turn the
hearts of the fathers to their children,[a]
and the hearts of the children to their
fathers; or else I will come and strike[b]
the land with a curse."[c]

3:16 [a]S Ps 34:15 [b]S Ex 32:32; S Ps 56:8; S 87:6; S Lk 10:20 [c]S Dt 28:58; S 31:12; Ps 33:18; S Pr 1:7; Rev 11:18 **3:17** [d]Isa 43:21 [e]S Ex 8:22; S Dt 7:6; S Ro 8:14; S Tit 2:14 [f]Ne 13:22; Ps 103:13; Isa 26:20; Lk 15:1-32 [g]Ro 8:32 **3:18** [h]S Ge 18:25 [i]Dt 32:4; Mt 25:32-33,41 **4:1** [j]S Da 7:13; S Joel 2:31; Mt 11:14; Ac 2:20 [k]S Isa 31:9 [l]S Isa 2:12 [m]S Isa 5:24; S Na 1:10 [n]S Isa 1:31 [o]S 2Ki 10:11; S Eze 17:8; S Mt 3:10 **4:2** [p]S Dt 28:58; Ps 61:5; 111:9; Rev 14:1 [q]S Ps 118:27; S Isa 9:2; S 45:8; Lk 1:78; Eph 5:14 [r]S 2Ch 7:14; S Isa 30:26; S Mt 4:23; Rev 22:2 [s]S Isa 35:6 **4:3** [t]S Job 40:12; Ps 18:40-42 [u]Eze 28:18 **4:4** [v]S Dt 28:61; S Ps 147:19; Mt 5:17; 7:12; Ro 2:13; 4:15; Gal 3:24 [w]S Ex 3:1 [x]S Ex 20:1 **4:5** [y]S 1Ki 17:1; S Mt 11:14; 16:14 [z]S Joel 2:31 **4:6** [a]Lk 1:17 [b]S Isa 11:4; Rev 19:15 [c]S Dt 11:26; S 13:15; S Jos 6:17; S 23:15; S Zec 5:3

[h]17 Or *Almighty, "my treasured possession, in the day when I act*

4:1–3 GOD, Sovereignty—God has elected to bring complete justice to pass only on the day of the Lord, when He will judge all wickedness and destroy it. For the faithful, that will be a day of blessing. In it God will ultimately show He rules the world.

4:1–6 JESUS CHRIST, Foretold—The Old Testament closes with this chapter of expectation. Christians play on the English word sun of righteousness, which equals son of righteousness, which equals Jesus Christ, the Light of the world (Lk 1:78; Jn 8:12). Christians are those who know that the true Light is now shining and that the darkness cannot put it out (1 Jn 2:8).

4:1–3 LAST THINGS, Day of the Lord—See note on Zep 1:14—2:3. The prophetic hope of a future day of the Lord involved both the expectation of a divine overthrow of evildoers and a vindication and rewarding of the righteous. Sometimes one, then the other, of these is emphasized. Here, both are given. The fire of judgment will fall on the arrogant and the evildoer for their destruction. Those who reverence God's name, however, will find that day to be a time of healing, victory, and rejoicing. The main point is that both aspects of that day will be accomplished by the Lord Almighty Himself.

4:4 HOLY SCRIPTURE, Canonization—The prophetic books end with a reminder to the faithful to continue doing the Law, preserved as revelation in writing from its manifestation and deliverance at Horeb (Sinai) by God's messenger Moses. Law had become authoritative Scripture, the criteria for judging the faithfulness of God's people.

THE NEW TESTAMENT

Matthew

Theological Setting

For some years after Jesus' death, resurrection, and ascension, Jewish Christians could worship in the Temple at Jerusalem as well as in Jewish synagogues. This situation changed about the time of the war between the Romans and Jews (AD 66-70).

By the time the Gospel of Matthew was written, a split between Judaism and Christianity had taken place. Synagogue and church were in conflict. Gentile converts had begun to play an increasingly important part in the church, and the church now saw itself as God's true people, the new Israel.

Mark's Gospel had already been written by this time. Helpful though it was, the Gospel of Mark did not include many of Jesus' teachings. Matthew sought to remedy the situation. He likely wrote sometime after AD 80 to a Palestinian or Syrian church.

Matthew wrote for people who had at least these religious options:

1. They could accept or reject Jesus as the promised Jewish Messiah. Most Jews did reject Him as Messiah, though some became believers.

2. They could live strictly according to the Jewish law, as the Pharisees taught. They could, in other words, be legalists, even if they had already become Christians.

3. They could decide that because they were Christians the law was no longer necessary for them. They would, therefore, live as they pleased, without any moral rules.

No doubt the church members in Matthew's time represented a diversity of backgrounds and opinions. In writing his Gospel under the Spirit's inspiration, Matthew hoped to unify that diversity into a central loyalty to Jesus Christ and obedience to His teachings. His book would be an authority to which Christians could turn for answers to such questions as: What was to be the Christians' relationship to the Jewish law? Exactly what were they to believe about Jesus? How were they to conduct their lives, both within and outside the church fellowship?

Theological Outline

Matthew: The King and His Kingdom

I. Jesus' Birth Fulfilled Prophecy. (1:1—2:23)
  A. Jesus was born of the line of David. (1:1-17)
  B. God directed the circumstances of Jesus' birth. (1:18-25)
  C. Even Gentile foreigners worshiped the newborn Jewish king. (2:1-12)
  D. God provided for His Son's survival. (2:13-23)

II. The Obedient Jesus Invites People to Kingdom Service. (3:1—4:25)
  A. Jesus carried out God's will by being baptized by John the Baptist. (3:1-15)
  B. God approved His Son. (3:16-17)
  C. Jesus obeyed God's Word and defeated Satan. (4:1-11)
  D. Jesus called people to God's kingdom through repentance. (4:12-22)
  E. Jesus demonstrated the power of the kingdom. (4:23-25)

III. Jesus Taught God's Way to Live. (5:1—7:29)
  A. Real happiness comes from a right relationship to God. (5:1-12)
  B. Christians must be like salt and light. (5:13-16)
  C. Love, not legalism, is the rule of the kingdom. (5:17-48)
  D. The desire to be seen by others is the wrong motive for good works. (6:1-4)
  E. Prayer is private seeking of forgiveness, not public search for praise. (6:5-15)
  F. Fasting is of value only if the motive behind it is right. (6:16-18)
  G. Only spiritual wealth really lasts. (6:19-21)
  H. Each person must choose whether to give God first place. (6:22-34)
  I. To judge others is wrong; to show discernment is necessary. (7:1-6)

J. The kingdom requires persistence in prayer and faith in God's goodness. (7:7-11)
K. The Golden Rule summarizes the law and the prophets. (7:12)
L. Only the narrow path of submission to God's will leads to life in His kingdom. (7:13-23)
M. Jesus and His teachings form the only lasting foundation for life. (7:24-29)

IV. Jesus' Power and Call Reveal His Authority. (8:1—10:42)
A. Jesus' healing power is available to all persons of faith. (8:1-17)
B. Discipleship is first priority. (8:18-22)
C. Jesus has authority over nature, demons, and sin. (8:23—9:8)
D. Jesus calls sinners to share His authority. (9:9-13)
E. Jesus' gospel requires new forms of piety. (9:14-17)
F. Jesus' authority responds to faith, conquers demons, and does not come from Satan. (9:18-34)
G. The compassionate Lord prays for compassionate helpers. (9:35-38)
H. Jesus entrusts His disciples with His authority in word and deed. (10:1-20)
I. To exercise His authority, disciples must face the dangers Jesus faced. (10:21-25)
J. Jesus' authority removes cause for fear. (10:26-31)
K. Disciples confess Jesus in all situations. (10:32-39)
L. Those who welcome Christian messengers will receive rewards. (10:40-42)

V. Jesus' Work Led to Controversy. (11:1—12:50)
A. Jesus fulfilled messianic prophecy. (11:1-6)
B. John marked the end of the prophetic era. (11:7-15)
C. Blind religion seeks controversy rather than truth. (11:16-19)
D. Repentance is the proper response to Jesus. (11:20-24)
E. Discipleship requires faith in God's Son, not great human wisdom or works. (11:25-30)
F. Mercy, not legalism, is the key to interpreting God's Word. (12:1-14)
G. Jesus fulfilled Isaiah's servant prophecies. (12:15-21)
H. Faith sees Jesus as Messiah, but blindness calls Him satanic. (12:22-37)
I. Resurrection faith is the criterion for eternal judgment. (12:38-45)
J. Obedient believers form God's family. (12:46-50)

VI. Jesus Taught About the Kingdom. (13:1-52)
A. Response to the kingdom depends on the "soil." (13:1-23)
B. God delays separating the true from the false. (13:24-30)
C. God's kingdom, small at first, will finally transform the world. (13:31-33)
D. Jesus' use of parables fulfills Scripture. (13:34-35)
E. The Son of Man controls final judgment and will send those who reject Him to eternal punishment. (13:36-43)
F. The kingdom is worth any sacrifice. (13:44-46)
G. The kingdom involves both traditional and new understandings of Scripture. (13:47-52)

VII. Jesus Confronts Conflict and Critical Events. (13:53—17:27)
A. Jesus faced rejection and sorrow. (13:53—14:12)
B. Jesus placed compassion for others over personal needs. (14:13-21)
C. Jesus' power over nature and disease shows He is God's Son. (14:22-36)
D. Thoughts and motives, not ritual acts, determine spiritual purity. (15:1-20)
E. Faith overcomes all obstacles that would separate us from Jesus. (15:21-28)
F. Jesus' compassionate ministry leads people to praise God. (15:29-39)
G. Unbelieving authorities demand a sign but cannot interpret ones they have. (16:1-12)
H. Confession of Jesus as Messiah and Son of God is the church's foundation. (16:13-20)
I. Willingness to suffer with Jesus is as important as proper confessions of faith. (16:21-28)
J. God revealed Jesus as His Son, whom people should obey. (17:1-13)
K. Faith in God overcomes obstacles. (17:14-21)
L. Jesus expected His coming death and resurrection. (17:22-23)
M. Concern for others may mean forfeiting one's own rights. (17:24-27)

VIII. Jesus Gives Insight into Life in His Kingdom. (18:1—20:34)
A. Entrance into the kingdom requires a childlike trust in God. (18:1-5)
B. Christians must be careful not to lead others into sin. (18:6-7)
C. Radical self-discipline prevents sin. (18:8-9)
D. God takes the initiative in finding the lost. (18:10-14)
E. Reconciliation must be the Christian's aim. (18:15-17)
F. Jesus promises power and authority to His church. (18:18-20)

G. God requires that we forgive if He is to forgive us. (18:21-35)
H. Lifelong marriage is God's plan for most people, but some can accept single devotion to Him. (19:1-12)
I. Children have an important place in God's kingdom. (19:13-15)
J. One must give up any obstacle to discipleship, knowing reward will come. (19:16-30)
K. God's rewards may be different from human expectations. (20:1-16)
L. Jesus taught the necessity of His coming death and resurrection. (20:17-19)
M. The truly great person serves others as Jesus did. (20:20-28)
N. Those who are healed by His mercy become His followers. (20:29-34)

IX. Religious Authorities Reject Jesus as Messiah. (21:1—23:36)
A. Jesus fulfilled messianic prophecy by entering Jerusalem and cleansing the Temple. (21:1-17)
B. God punishes fruitlessness but rewards faith. (21:18-22)
C. Answerless authorities question Jesus' authority. (21:23-27)
D. Authorities must answer the call to repentance to be part of God's kingdom. (21:28-46)
E. God invites even sinners and outcasts to new life in His kingdom. (22:1-14)
F. Taxes belong to the state; we belong to God. (22:15-22)
G. Authorities do not understand Scripture and so do not believe in resurrection. (22:23-33)
H. Authorities must learn love for God and love for neighbor are the greatest commandments. (22:34-40)
I. Authorities must learn the nature of God's Messiah. (22:41-46)
J. Jesus the Authority calls for religious leaders' lives to agree with their teachings. (23:1-36)

X. Jesus Has the Authoritative Word About the Future. (23:37—25:46)
A. Jerusalem faces destruction for rejecting Jesus. (23:37-39)
B. The world will hear the gospel before the end of the age. (24:1-14)
C. Jesus' disciples must flee Jerusalem when a sign appears. (24:15-28)
D. Spectacles in nature will mark Jesus' assured return. (24:29-35)
E. People must prepare for Jesus' return or face judgment. (24:36—25:30)
F. Jesus will judge us by our service to those in need. (25:31-46)

XI. Jesus Prepared for Death, Obeying God and Fulfilling Scripture. (26:1-56)
A. Authorities plotted Jesus' death, as He had foretold. (26:1-5)
B. Jesus' anointing symbolized His messiahship and coming death. (26:6-13)
C. A disciple cooperated in crucifying Jesus. (26:14-16)
D. Jesus transformed Passover to His memorial supper, establishing His covenant. (26:17-30)
E. Jesus prepared His disciples for their time of falling and restoration. (26:31-35)
F. Jesus dedicated Himself to the Father's will. (26:36-46)
G. Jesus' arrest represented fulfillment of God's plan, not evidence of His weakness or God's forsaking Jesus. (26:47-56)

XII. Jesus Conquered Death. (26:57—28:20)
A. The innocent Jesus was convicted on His testimony to His messiahship and to His role as Judge in the last days. (26:57-68)
B. Peter's denial showed Jesus' prophetic powers. (26:69-75)
C. Judas' guilt drove him to suicide and fulfilled Scripture. (27:1-10)
D. Government authority found no guilt in Jesus, but religious authorities accepted full responsibility for His death. (27:11-26)
E. Roman mocking pointed to the truth of Jesus' divine kingship. (27:27-44)
F. Spectacular events pointed to the saving significance of Jesus' death as God's Son. (27:45-56)
G. Jesus' dead body was entombed and could not be stolen. (27:57-66)
H. Jesus was raised from the dead. (28:1-10)
I. Religious leaders bribed people to disprove the resurrection. (28:11-15)
J. The authoritative Jesus gives His disciples a worldwide evangelistic mission. (28:16-20)

Theological Conclusions

The Book of Matthew puts emphasis on four doctrines to give certainty to a questioning church:

1. Jesus is the Messiah prophesied by Scripture.
2. Jesus' teachings are the new law for the church.
3. The kingdom of heaven is both present and future reality.
4. The church is the new community of faith.

Matthew emphasized the fact that Jesus was the Jews' expected Messiah. The term "Messiah" means

"Anointed One." It had come to signify the ideal king, David's descendant, who would free the Jews from Roman rule and establish an earthly kingdom. Jesus did not accept this understanding of messiahship. He was the messianic King, but He chose to take on the role of Isaiah's Suffering Servant (Isa 52:13—53:12). By His death He provides freedom from sin, not from foreign rule. His kingdom is a spiritual one. Matthew used almost seventy quotations from sixteen Old Testament books to prove that Jesus had brought the true fulfillment of Jewish messianic hopes.

Matthew also portrayed Jesus as a Lawgiver, One greater even than Moses. He made this role of Jesus especially clear in his presentation of Jesus' Sermon on the Mount (chs 5-7). Jesus fulfilled the Old Testament law rather than doing away with the old law. Jesus' law goes beyond the letter of the Old Testament law to require an inner purity and love like that of God Himself. Jewish Christians wondering whether to retain their loyalty to the law would be reassured by the knowledge that Jesus' teachings had filled the law with God's intended meaning.

The law Jesus gave is the law for life in His kingdom. In fact, "the kingdom of heaven" may be considered the theme of Matthew's Gospel, since he mentioned it more than thirty times. "Kingdom of heaven" has the same meaning as "kingdom of God." The term means "God's kingly rule." It refers not to a place but to those over whom God rules. Jesus' teaching in Matthew shows that in Him God's rule, or kingdom, has already arrived. Those who become His disciples enter the kingdom now and are given eternal life. Yet, in another sense, the kingdom's fulfillment is future and will be realized only when Christ returns at the end of the age. Many of Jesus' parables in Matthew's Gospel tell about aspects of life in the kingdom. Matthew's readers could rejoice to see themselves living as present and future citizens of God's kingdom.

Only Matthew of the four Gospel writers included teachings about the church. He dealt with the basis of this new community of faith (16:17-19) and provided other teachings relating to the church (18:15-20). He stressed Jesus' call of His church to preach His gospel to all the world (28:16-20). Throughout Matthew's record, however, it is not the church, but the church's Lord who is central. The church members who first read Matthew's Gospel would have found themselves challenged to live in obedience to Him.

Contemporary Teaching

The Gospel of Matthew focuses our attention on Jesus, making our response to Him the main issue. Matthew wrote for a church whose members had differing opinions about important issues. So too, today's church members often disagree. Matthew would have us look beyond the issues that divide and center instead on Jesus and His teachings.

His Gospel would instruct us: (1) to see Jesus as the One who fulfills Old Testament hopes and God's eternal purpose; (2) to accept the salvation Jesus' death has made possible; (3) to follow Jesus' teachings, recognizing that they fulfill the deepest meaning of the law; (4) to live so as to be ready when He returns at the end of the age; and (5) to take the responsibility for sharing the gospel with all the world.

Chapter 1

The Genealogy of Jesus

1:1–17pp — Lk 3:23–38
1:3–6pp — Ru 4:18–22
1:7–11pp — 1Ch 3:10–17

A record of the genealogy of Jesus Christ the son of David,[a] the son of Abraham:[b]

2Abraham was the father of Isaac,[c]
Isaac the father of Jacob,[d]
Jacob the father of Judah and his brothers,[e]
3Judah the father of Perez and Zerah, whose mother was Tamar,[f]
Perez the father of Hezron,
Hezron the father of Ram,
4Ram the father of Amminadab,
Amminadab the father of Nahshon,
Nahshon the father of Salmon,
5Salmon the father of Boaz, whose mother was Rahab,[g]
Boaz the father of Obed, whose mother was Ruth,
Obed the father of Jesse,
6and Jesse the father of King David.[h]

David was the father of Solomon, whose mother had been Uriah's wife,[i]
7Solomon the father of Rehoboam,
Rehoboam the father of Abijah,
Abijah the father of Asa,
8Asa the father of Jehoshaphat,
Jehoshaphat the father of Jehoram,
Jehoram the father of Uzziah,
9Uzziah the father of Jotham,
Jotham the father of Ahaz,
Ahaz the father of Hezekiah,
10Hezekiah the father of Manasseh,[j]
Manasseh the father of Amon,
Amon the father of Josiah,
11and Josiah the father of Jeconiah[a] and his brothers at the time of the exile to Babylon.[k]

12After the exile to Babylon:
Jeconiah was the father of Shealtiel,[l]
Shealtiel the father of Zerubbabel,[m]
13Zerubbabel the father of Abiud,
Abiud the father of Eliakim,
Eliakim the father of Azor,
14Azor the father of Zadok,
Zadok the father of Akim,
Akim the father of Eliud,
15Eliud the father of Eleazar,
Eleazar the father of Matthan,
Matthan the father of Jacob,
16and Jacob the father of Joseph, the husband of Mary,[n] of whom was born Jesus, who is called Christ.[o]

17Thus there were fourteen generations in all from Abraham to David, fourteen from David to the exile to Babylon, and fourteen from the exile to the Christ.[b]

1:1 [a]2Sa 7:12-16; Isa 9:6,7; 11:1; Jer 23:5,6; S Mt 9:27; Lk 1:32, 69; Rev 22:16 [b]Ge 22:18; S Gal 3:16
1:2 [c]Ge 21:3,12 [d]Ge 25:26 [e]Ge 29:35; 49:10
1:3 [f]Ge 38:27-30
1:5 [g]S Heb 11:31
1:6 [h]1Sa 16:1; 17:12 [i]2Sa 12:24
1:10 [j]2Ki 20:21
1:11 [k]2Ki 24:14-16; Jer 27:20; 40:1; Da 1:1,2
1:12 [l]1Ch 3:17 [m]1Ch 3:19; Ezr 3:2
1:16 [n]Lk 1:27 [o]Mt 27:17

[a] *11* That is, Jehoiachin; also in verse 12 [b] *17* Or *Messiah.* "The Christ" (Greek) and "the Messiah" (Hebrew) both mean "the Anointed One."

1:1 JESUS CHRIST, Son of David—The first messianic title applied to Jesus in the New Testament is Son of David. See note on Gal 1:1. This title for Jesus provides a major link between the Old Testament and the New. Both Matthew's and Luke's genealogies are at pains to establish that Jesus is descended from David (Mt 1:69; Lk 3:31). This enabled early believers to claim the Old Testament promise that there would always be an heir to David's throne (2 Sa 7; Ps 132:11–12). Compare Ro 1:3. The crowds and individuals in need often used this title for Jesus (Mt 9:27; 15:22; 20:31; Lk 18:38). Jesus did not use the title for Himself, possibly because it was so open to political interpretation. Jesus had to show He fulfilled Old Testament expectations. He did so by fulfilling the role of the Suffering Servant and letting all other titles be understood in that light. Thus He fulfilled the role of the true kings of Israel, that of servant (2 Sa 7:19) and shepherd (2 Sa 7:7). See note on 1 Ch 17:23–27.

1:1–17 HISTORY, Salvation—The genealogy and virgin birth of Jesus show God's way of salvation. Many people in Jesus' day looked for a heavenly figure to appear and provide earthly salvation. As He always had, God provided salvation within Israel's history. The Son of God became a Son of Abraham to provide salvation for all people in a way all people could see and with which all people could identify.

1:18–25 JESUS CHRIST, Savior—Jesus' saving mission was revealed before His birth. His name, like Joshua, its Hebrew equivalent, meant "Yahweh (the LORD) saves." The name could be understood as predicting political deliverance, but the Gospels show it had a more far-reaching meaning. Jesus provides salvation for all humanity from sin not just for Israel from Rome. Jesus was Immanuel, which in Hebrew means "God with us."

1:18 JESUS CHRIST, Virgin Birth—Jesus was the personal name of our Savior. Christ was a title meaning the anointed one, a translation into Greek of the Hebrew word Messiah. Christ came to be used as part of Jesus' name. See note on Gal 1:1. The story of Jesus' birth emphasizes His unique nature as human child and Son of God. The genealogy or list of human ancestors shows the human side of Jesus and connects Him through Joseph to David and Abraham, with whom God had special covenants to achieve His redemptive purpose (Ge 12:3; 2 Sa 7:12). The virgin birth emphasizes Jesus' divine nature since Mary was with child "through the Holy Spirit." Jesus' complete identity with humanity is revealed by an unusual feature of the genealogies—inclusion of four women with less than perfect reputations: Tamar (v 3), Rahab (v 5), Ruth (v 5), and Bathsheba (v 6).

1:18–20 HOLY SPIRIT, Jesus—Jesus' miraculous conception by the Spirit illustrated that He was the unique bearer of the Spirit. This means that the Spirit was involved in the life of Jesus from the very beginning. He was uniquely human and divine. Conception by the Spirit shows this uniqueness.

1:18–25 MIRACLE, Instruments—That God used women and men to accomplish His purpose of redemption is

The Birth of Jesus Christ

[18]This is how the birth of Jesus Christ
came about: His mother Mary was
pledged to be married to Joseph, but before they came together, she was found to
be with child through the Holy Spirit.[p]
[19]Because Joseph her husband was a
righteous man and did not want to expose her to public disgrace, he had in
mind to divorce[q] her quietly.

[20]But after he had considered this, an
angel[r] of the Lord appeared to him in a
dream[s] and said, "Joseph son of David,
do not be afraid to take Mary home as
your wife, because what is conceived in
her is from the Holy Spirit. [21]She will give
birth to a son, and you are to give him the
name Jesus,[c t] because he will save his
people from their sins."[u]

[22]All this took place to fulfill[v] what the
Lord had said through the prophet:
[23]"The virgin will be with child and will
give birth to a son, and they will call him
Immanuel"[d w]—which means, "God
with us."

[24]When Joseph woke up, he did what
the angel[x] of the Lord had commanded
him and took Mary home as his wife.
[25]But he had no union with her until she
gave birth to a son. And he gave him the
name Jesus.[y]

1:18 [p]Lk 1:35
1:19 [q]Dt 24:1
1:20 [r]S Ac 5:19 [s]S Mt 27:19
1:21 [t]S Lk 1:31 [u]Ps 130:8; S Lk 2:11; S Jn 3:17; Ac 5:31; S Ro 11:14; Tit 2:14
1:22 [v]Mt 2:15,17, 23; 4:14; 8:17; 12:17; 21:4; 26:54, 56; 27:9; Lk 4:21; 21:22; 24:44; Jn 13:18; 19:24,28, 36
1:23 [w]Isa 7:14; 8:8,10
1:24 [x]S Ac 5:19
1:25 [y]ver 21; S Lk 1:31
2:1 [z]Lk 2:4-7 [a]Lk 1:5
2:2 [b]Jer 23:5; Mt 27:11; Mk 15:2; Lk 23:38; Jn 1:49; 18:33-37 [c]Nu 24:17
2:5 [d]Jn 7:42
2:6 [e]Mic 5:2; 2Sa 5:2

Chapter 2

The Visit of the Magi

AFTER Jesus was born in Bethlehem in
Judea,[z] during the time of King Herod,[a] Magi[e] from the east came to Jerusalem [2]and asked, "Where is the one who
has been born king of the Jews?[b] We saw
his star[c] in the east[f] and have come to
worship him."

[3]When King Herod heard this he was
disturbed, and all Jerusalem with him.
[4]When he had called together all the people's chief priests and teachers of the law,
he asked them where the Christ[g] was to
be born. [5]"In Bethlehem[d] in Judea,"
they replied, "for this is what the prophet
has written:

[6]" 'But you, Bethlehem, in the land of
Judah,
are by no means least among the
rulers of Judah;
for out of you will come a ruler
who will be the shepherd of my
people Israel.'[h] "[e]

[7]Then Herod called the Magi secretly
and found out from them the exact time
the star had appeared. [8]He sent them to

[c]*21 Jesus* is the Greek form of *Joshua,* which means *the LORD saves.* [d]*23* Isaiah 7:14 [e]*1* Traditionally *Wise Men* [f]*2* Or *star when it rose* [g]*4* Or *Messiah* [h]*6* Micah 5:2

nowhere clearer than in the story of the virgin birth. Three times in this section (vv 18,20,25) Mary is described as having had no "union" with Joseph. She was "with child through the Holy Spirit." Additional details may be read in Lk 1:26–2:20. We cannot explain the virgin birth. It is another instance of miracle being exception to the natural order of things. In faith we accept the simple truth of the Holy Spirit's action and praise God for keeping His promises and sending our Savior. Against the backdrop of Jesus' ministry and the miracle of the resurrection, it is not so difficult to believe in the virgin birth. The virgin birth does not mean Mary remained a virgin after Jesus' birth. Verse 25 speaks against this: other children were born later to Joseph and Mary (13:55–56). The virgin birth was God's chosen way to become incarnate: the invisible, spiritual God became human.

1:18–19 FAMILY, Divorce—Betrothal vows were as binding as marriage even though the couple did not live together until the wedding. See Dt 22:24, where the betrothed virgin is called a "wife." Thus, in accordance with Jewish legislation which provided for divorce rather than stoning of the woman, Joseph planned to divorce Mary because of her *apparent* sexual unfaithfulness. His concern for her is apparent even though he thought her guilty of sexual sinfulness. He gladly changed his mind when God revealed the miraculous truth about Mary to him. Suspicions too often lead to family problems. Prayer and frank discussion will often reveal the truth that restores trust.

1:20–21 REVELATION, Angels—Messengers from God appeared to Joseph in a dream. The troubled Joseph heard the revelation concerning the unborn Child and its source in the Holy Spirit of God, relieving his fears.

1:23 REVELATION, Jesus Christ—The revelation of God took place in human flesh. The Divine presence was experienced in its most unique manifestation, in the conception of a Child to Mary.

2:1–12 JESUS CHRIST, King—Foreign students of the nighttime skies acknowledged Jesus' birth as a momentous event in world history. These astrologers recognized the royal claims of Jesus and His right to be worshiped. Their coming revealed the corrupt nature of Herod and his government. It showed Jesus as the fulfillment of Micah's prophecy (Mic 5:2). It also confirmed God's power over human rulers and His ability and commitment to protect Jesus. Herod the Great ruled from 37 to 4 BC, so Jesus was born about 6 BC.

2:2,9 MIRACLE, Nature—God uses the natural order He created in exceptional ways to achieve His redemptive purposes. Eastern scholars had studied the stars long and carefully, charting their courses and historical events to see how they affected human life. These students of the skies discovered and followed one special star. They traveled with it to Jerusalem to understand its great significance and to find the new King whose birth it announced. They also depended on other humans for their information: they asked where the child was to be born. They sensed God's guidance to Bethlehem and followed the star there. Various explanations of the unique star have been offered: among the better known is that the planets Saturn and Jupiter joined at about this time. Matthew described one star—a special star. God used His heavenly creation to introduce His eternal Son to earth. Thus began God's greatest miracle—providing our salvation through Jesus.

2:2 PRAYER, Universality of—These Magi were Gentiles. Whatever their office, they perceived that God was manifesting Himself uniquely within the Jewish tradition. Jesus' coming made clear God's open door policy to all peoples.

2:5–6 REVELATION, Word—The birth of Jesus fulfilled a long-time expectation in Israel for a promised liberator to lead God's people in keeping with God's tender care. God had breathed this promise into the prophecy of Micah (5:2) and with it inspired hope in exiled Israel for centuries.

Bethlehem and said, "Go and make a
careful search for the child. As soon as
you find him, report to me, so that I too
may go and worship him."
9After they had heard the king, they
went on their way, and the star they had
seen in the east[i] went ahead of them
until it stopped over the place where the
child was. 10When they saw the star, they
were overjoyed. 11On coming to the
house, they saw the child with his mother Mary, and they bowed down and worshiped him.[f] Then they opened their
treasures and presented him with gifts[g]
of gold and of incense and of myrrh.
12And having been warned[h] in a dream[i]
not to go back to Herod, they returned to
their country by another route.

The Escape to Egypt

13When they had gone, an angel[j] of
the Lord appeared to Joseph in a dream.[k]
"Get up," he said, "take the child and his
mother and escape to Egypt. Stay there
until I tell you, for Herod is going to
search for the child to kill him."[l]
14So he got up, took the child and his
mother during the night and left for
Egypt, 15where he stayed until the death
of Herod. And so was fulfilled[m] what the
Lord had said through the prophet: "Out
of Egypt I called my son."[j] [n]
16When Herod realized that he had
been outwitted by the Magi, he was furious, and he gave orders to kill all the boys
in Bethlehem and its vicinity who were
two years old and under, in accordance
with the time he had learned from the
Magi. 17Then what was said through the
prophet Jeremiah was fulfilled:[o]

18"A voice is heard in Ramah,
weeping and great mourning,
Rachel[p] weeping for her children
and refusing to be comforted,
because they are no more."[k] [q]

The Return to Nazareth

19After Herod died, an angel[r] of the
Lord appeared in a dream[s] to Joseph in
Egypt 20and said, "Get up, take the child
and his mother and go to the land of Israel, for those who were trying to take the
child's life are dead."[t]
21So he got up, took the child and his
mother and went to the land of Israel.
22But when he heard that Archelaus was
reigning in Judea in place of his father
Herod, he was afraid to go there. Having
been warned in a dream,[u] he withdrew
to the district of Galilee,[v] 23and he went
and lived in a town called Nazareth.[w] So
was fulfilled[x] what was said through the
prophets: "He will be called a Nazarene."[y]

Chapter 3

John the Baptist Prepares the Way

3:1–12pp — Mk 1:3–8; Lk 3:2–17

IN those days John the Baptist[z] came,
preaching in the Desert of Judea 2and

i9 Or *seen when it rose* j15 Hosea 11:1
k18 Jer. 31:15

2:11 [f]Isa 60:3 [g]Ps 72:10
2:12 [h]Heb 11:7 [i]ver 13,19,22; S Mt 27:19
2:13 [j]S Ac 5:19 [k]ver 12,19,22; S Mt 27:19 [l]Rev 12:4
2:15 [m]ver 17,23; S Mt 1:22 [n]Hos 11:1; Ex 4:22, 23
2:17 [o]ver 15,23; S Mt 1:22
2:18 [p]Ge 35:19 [q]Jer 31:15
2:19 [r]S Ac 5:19 [s]ver 12,13,22; S Mt 27:19
2:20 [t]Ex 4:19
2:22 [u]ver 12,13,19; S Mt 27:19 [v]Lk 2:39
2:23 [w]Mk 1:9; 6:1; S 1:24; Lk 1:26; 2:39,51; 4:16,23; Jn 1:45,46 [x]ver 15, 17; S Mt 1:22 [y]S Mk 1:24
3:1 [z]ver 13,14; Mt 9:14; 11:2-14; 14:1-12; Lk 1:13, 57-66; 3:2-19; Ac 19:3,4

2:9,12 REVELATION, Author of Creation—A star became a sign to follow for several eastern star experts. God used their expertise and His creation to lead the foreigners to greet Jesus. He warned them in a dream to take another road home, avoiding the capital.

2:11 STEWARDSHIP, Giving in Worship—The Magi's gifts expressed their respect for and joyous worship of the Christ child. Biblical faith calls for worshipers to come before the Lord with gifts that have real value for the worshiper. See notes on 5:23–24; Mal 1:6–14.

2:11 PRAYER, Worship—See note on 2:2. Worship produced voluntary gifts.

2:13–23 JESUS CHRIST, Birth—The shape of current politics would be much different if Ishmael (father of Islam), Isaac (father of the Jews), or Jesus (founder of Christianity) had been killed in infancy. In His providence God preserved all three. In Jesus, hope for salvation is extended to descendants of the other two. Jesus was taken by Mary and Joseph to Egypt (Hos 11:1). Archaelaus, more wicked than his father, Herod the Great, ruled Judea from 4 BC to AD 6. God saw to it that Jesus returned to Nazareth, a safer place. V 23 is possibly a reference to Isa 11:1 with a play on the word *Nezer*, "branch," and therefore, "Nazareth," the place where Jesus grew up. From childhood He knew what it was to be an alien, yet He never knew alienation from God. The suffering of the innocents and the sorrow of their mothers is foreshadowed in Jer 31:15. Matthew's account of Jesus' birth and infancy reminds us of (1) Jesus' place as human among us as seen in the genealogies, (2) Jesus' distinct relation to God, as seen in the virgin birth (virginal conception), and (3) God's preservation of His people and His purpose, even through the birth of a child.

2:13 HUMANITY, Relationships—Refugees afraid to return home represent one of our world's great tragedies. Broken human relationships and oppression force families to become refugees. Failing to acknowledge the interrelatedness of God's human creatures is the ultimate cause. The oppressed on earth can take some comfort knowing their Savior began life as a refugee.

2:13 REVELATION, Angels—God communicated again (1:20–21) to Joseph through an angel in his troubled sleep, warning him of the danger the promised Child was in. God used dreams of angels to guide Joseph as he protected the Baby from jealous, fearful politicians (3:19).

2:16–18 EVIL AND SUFFERING, Human Origin—Traditionally known as the "Slaughter of the Innocents," this story depicts innocent suffering caused by human beings. Not all human suffering is deserved. Human jealousy and ambition lead to evil acts causing innocent people to suffer. God can use even horrible human atrocities to fulfill His Word, bring about His purposes, and lead to His salvation.

2:18 HOLY SCRIPTURE, Inspired—The inspired words of a prophet (Jer 31:15) centuries earlier brought to light the deeper meaning of a horrible human crime. God's Word records the sad event and its prediction years before. The prediction did not force Herod into the act or relieve him of responsibility. The prophecy applied first to the heartache of the Exile before pointing forward to Herod's act to help God's people understand the importance of Jesus as seen by Herod.

2:19–23 REVELATION, Dreams—See note on 2:13.

3:1,8,11 SALVATION, Repentance—John the Baptist's message of repentance was the same as that of God's earlier prophets (Jer 35:15). John announced the nearness of God's

saying, "Repent, for the kingdom of heav-
en[a] is near." 3This is he who was spoken
of through the prophet Isaiah:

"A voice of one calling in the desert,
'Prepare the way for the Lord,
make straight paths for him.' "[l] [b]

4John's[c] clothes were made of camel's
hair, and he had a leather belt around his
waist.[d] His food was locusts[e] and wild
honey. 5People went out to him from Jerusalem and all Judea and the whole region of the Jordan. 6Confessing their sins,
they were baptized[f] by him in the Jordan
River.

7But when he saw many of the Pharisees and Sadducees coming to where he
was baptizing, he said to them: "You
brood of vipers![g] Who warned you to flee
from the coming wrath?[h] 8Produce fruit
in keeping with repentance.[i] 9And do
not think you can say to yourselves, 'We
have Abraham as our father.'[j] I tell you
that out of these stones God can raise up
children for Abraham. 10The ax is already
at the root of the trees, and every tree
that does not produce good fruit will be
cut down and thrown into the fire.[k]

11"I baptize you with[m] water for repentance.[l] But after me will come one who
is more powerful than I, whose sandals I
am not fit to carry. He will baptize you
with the Holy Spirit[m] and with fire.[n]
12His winnowing fork is in his hand, and
he will clear his threshing floor, gathering
his wheat into the barn and burning up
the chaff with unquenchable fire."[o]

The Baptism of Jesus

3:13–17pp — Mk 1:9–11; Lk 3:21,22; Jn 1:31–34

13Then Jesus came from Galilee to the
Jordan to be baptized by John.[p] 14But

3:2 [a]Da 7:14; Mt 4:17; 6:10; 7:21; S 25:34; Lk 11:20; 17:20,21; 19:11; 21:31; Jn 3:3,5; Ac 1:3,6
3:3 [b]Isa 40:3; Mal 3:1; Lk 1:76; Jn 1:23
3:4 [c]S Mt 3:1 [d]2Ki 1:8 [e]Lev 11:22
3:6 [f]ver 11; S Mk 1:4
3:7 [g]Mt 12:34; 23:33 [h]S Ro 1:18
3:8 [i]Ac 26:20
3:9 [j]S Lk 3:8
3:10 [k]Mt 7:19; Lk 3:9; 13:6-9; Jn 15:2,6
3:11 [l]ver 6; S Mk 1:4 [m]S Mk 1:8 [n]Isa 4:4; Ac 2:3,4
3:12 [o]Mt 13:30; S 25:41
3:13 [p]S Mt 3:1; S Mk 1:4

[l]*3* Isaiah 40:3 [m]*11* Or *in*

---

kingdom, called for ethical fruit in keeping with repentance, and baptized in water as a sign of repentance. Compare Mk 1:4; Lk 3:3,8.

3:2–5 REVELATION, Messengers—A prophet laid the foundation for the beginning of Jesus' work. An ancient prophet had prepared the way for John (Isa 40:3). God did everything possible to make His people alert to His revelation.

3:2 DISCIPLESHIP, Kingdom of God—John the Baptist announced that something new was about to begin: the reign of God through the ministry of Christ. Those who want to relate to God and experience the immediacy of the reign of God in and through Christ need a radical change in their lives. John the Baptist made that clear. His call for repentance still needs to be heard today. No one is ready to come under the sovereign rule of God until there is a change of attitude and action with regard to sin and service. There must be a willingness to give up everything to experience the reality of the kingdom of God through the immediacy of Christ's ruling authority. See note on 4:17.

3:2 THE CHURCH, God's Kingdom—Matthew preferred the phrase "kingdom of heaven" because of his Jewish audience. At the time of the Exile (after 587 BC), Jews refrained from speaking the name of God, fearing blasphemy or taking the name of the Lord in vain. John called for repentance in preparation for the coming of God's kingdom. To repent means to change the mind, to turn from sin and toward God. Jesus' coming into the world both inaugurated God's kingdom and brought it to fulfillment. In His life we see what life in the kingdom is like and how God's anointed King rules. The kingdom of God is God's rule in the human heart. When we allow the Lord to be master of our lives, we enter the kingdom of God and look forward in faith to its final establishment.

3:4–17 ORDINANCES, Baptism by John—The most direct background and source of Christian baptism is clearly the baptism of John the Baptist. He baptized faithful Jews as a sign of repentance and preparation for the coming Messiah. All of the elements in John's baptism are taken into the later interpretation of Christian baptism: (1) call to repentance; (2) confession of sins; (3) bearing fruits as evidence of changed lives; (4) warning of coming judgment; and (5) the coming One (Messiah) baptizing with the Holy Spirit. If John's baptism was connected with repentance, why was the sinless Jesus baptized? Jesus' explanation, "to fulfill all righteousness," meant that He approved of John's ministry and message, identified Himself with sinners as their Sin-bearer, and was anointed by the Holy Spirit for His messianic mission. Both the voice from heaven and the coming of the Holy Spirit upon Jesus influenced the understanding of later Christian baptism, as we can see throughout the Book of Acts. The coming of the Spirit was associated with baptism, as was the confession of Jesus as the Christ, the Son of God. See Ac 1:4–5; 2:38,41; 8:12–13,36–39.

3:6 SALVATION, Confession—Confession of sins preceded John's baptism. Compare Mk 1:5.

3:7–10 GOD, Wrath—All who do works of evil, all who sin, should fear the wrath of God that is coming to them. Indeed, it is nearer than they realize. No self-justifying excuses about having the proper form of religion—being descendants of Abraham—will enable them to escape the wrath of the sovereign God who holds us all accountable to Himself. Only responsibility born out of faith can enable us to escape the wrath of God. God's wrath should not be understood as a fit of anger, as though God has some pent-up emotion that must be released. Neither is it merely vindictiveness poured out on those who deserve to be punished. God's nature is basically righteous love—He would rather love and save than destroy the sinner. Love rejected becomes, in a sense, the wrath of God. Each person, before our sovereign and righteous Lord, has only two alternatives: either accept the grace of God in forgiveness or suffer the wrath of God in destruction. We are responsible for our sins and cannot blame God when we suffer the wrath of God.

3:9–10 ELECTION, Israel—See note on Lk 3:8–9.

3:11 JESUS CHRIST, Judgment—Jesus' coming represented judgment as well as salvation. His followers receive the Holy Spirit's power. Those who refuse to follow Him face judgment and destruction. Compare Isa 4:4; Jer 15:7.

3:11 HOLY SPIRIT, Promised—This is the first mention in the Bible of baptism of the Holy Spirit. Jesus would give the Spirit to people in a way John could not. This prophecy was fulfilled at the coming of the Spirit at Pentecost (Ac 2). Luke referred to this experience as a filling (Ac 2:4), a pouring out (Ac 2:33), and a receiving of the Spirit (Ac 2:38). The Spirit would take people who repented and give them power to obey, to follow God's leadership. See Ps 51:10–12; Isa 32:14–18; 44:1–4; Eze 36:24–30; Joel 2:28–32.

3:11–12 LAST THINGS, Judgment—The baptism of fire could be related to the Spirit's coming at Pentecost. However, many believe it refers to future judgment. If so, this statement about Christ's work is given without regard for the interval between His first and second comings. Then the baptism to be performed by Christ is twofold: a Spirit-baptism and a judgment-baptism. The first of these relates to His first coming and His present work through the Spirit in believers. The second refers to future judgment upon the wicked (Mal 4:1). Jesus' coming was good news. Part of the good news is His assurance of the final destruction of evil.

3:13–17 JESUS CHRIST, Servant—John was reluctant to

John tried to deter him, saying, "I need to
be baptized by you, and do you come to
me?"
15 Jesus replied, "Let it be so now; it is
proper for us to do this to fulfill all righteousness." Then John consented.
16 As soon as Jesus was baptized, he
went up out of the water. At that moment
heaven was opened,[q] and he saw the
Spirit of God[r] descending like a dove and
lighting on him. 17 And a voice from heav-
en[s] said, "This is my Son,[t] whom I love;
with him I am well pleased."[u]

Chapter 4

The Temptation of Jesus

4:1-11pp — Mk 1:12,13; Lk 4:1-13

THEN Jesus was led by the Spirit into
the desert to be tempted[v] by the
devil.[w] 2 After fasting forty days and forty
nights,[x] he was hungry. 3 The tempter[y]
came to him and said, "If you are the Son
of God,[z] tell these stones to become
bread."
4 Jesus answered, "It is written: 'Man
does not live on bread alone, but on every
word that comes from the mouth of
God.'[n]"[a]
5 Then the devil took him to the holy
city[b] and had him stand on the highest
point of the temple. 6 "If you are the Son
of God,"[c] he said, "throw yourself down.
For it is written:

" 'He will command his angels
concerning you,
and they will lift you up in their
hands,
so that you will not strike your foot
against a stone.'[o] "[d]

3:16 [q]Eze 1:1; Jn 1:51; Ac 7:56; 10:11; Rev 4:1; 19:11 [r]Isa 11:2; 42:1
3:17 [s]Dt 4:12; Mt 17:5; Jn 12:28 [t]Ps 2:7; Ac 13:33; Heb 1:1-5; 5:5; 2Pe 1:17,18 [u]Isa 42:1; Mt 12:18; 17:5; Mk 1:11; 9:7; Lk 3:22; 9:35; 2Pe 1:17
4:1 [v]Heb 4:15 [w]Ge 3:1-7
4:2 [x]Ex 34:28; 1Ki 19:8
4:3 [y]1Th 3:5 [z]S Mt 3:17; 14:33; 16:16; 27:54; Mk 3:11; Lk 1:35; 22:70; Jn 1:34,49; 5:25; 11:27; 20:31; Ac 9:20; Ro 1:4; 1Jn 5:10-13,20; Rev 2:18
4:4 [a]Dt 8:3; Jn 4:34
4:5 [b]Ne 11:1; Da 9:24; Mt 27:53 **4:6** [c]S ver 3 [d]Ps 91:11,12

[n]*4* Deut. 8:3 [o]*6* Psalm 91:11,12

baptize Jesus because He did not need baptism for repentance. Jesus, who knew God's purpose in His life, insisted. The heavenly voice confirmed Jesus' decision, His sonship, and the kind of Messiah He was to be. The heavenly voice brought together two Old Testament messianic ideas: the exalted beloved Son (Ps 2:7) and the Suffering Servant (Isa 42:1). From the beginning of His ministry, Jesus knew He was to be God's suffering Messiah.

3:15 CHRISTIAN ETHICS, Righteousness—By undergoing the act of baptism, Jesus demonstrated His commitment toward the work of God's kingdom. Such public professions solidify our resolve toward Christian action and represent one of the righteous acts God's people do. Jesus was the righteous Messiah (Jer 33:15–16).

3:16–17 GOD, Trinity—This may well be the first passage in the Bible that points us definitely to a trinitarian understanding of God. No doctrinal teaching is more difficult for the human mind to understand than the doctrine of the Trinity, that is, that one God is known to us in three Persons. It is easy to become unitarian on the one hand, emphasizing the deity and unity of God the Father while playing down the separate divine character of the Holy Spirit and the Son. It is difficult for us not to so emphasize the separate deity of the three Persons—Father, Son, Holy Spirit—that we separate them into three distinct deities. This is called tritheism, belief in three Gods. The trinitarian understanding of God is more of a conclusion that we draw after careful biblical study than a direct statement of Scripture itself. No passage of Scripture discusses or explains the oneness and the threeness of God. Our doctrine of the Trinity is our attempt to do justice to the clear teaching of Scripture: on the one hand, there is only one God; on the other hand, Scripture recognizes three Persons as divine—God the Father, God the Son, and God the Holy Spirit. This is sometimes called a polarity, two pivot points of thought that must be held in relationship to each other. Just as a battery must have both positive and negative poles to function as a battery, so our idea of God must include both the oneness and the threeness to be a complete idea of God. The present passage gives us only a glimpse of the three Persons who make up the Trinity: the voice of God the Father from heaven, a visible manifestation of the Holy Spirit coming down upon Jesus, and Jesus Christ, the Son of God. This glimpse of the three Persons who make up the Trinity must be seen against the clear background of the Old Testament teaching of only one God. Perhaps that is the unique and most important teaching of the entire Old Testament. The present passage shows the apparent distinction of the three Persons of the Trinity. No attempt is made to explain how they are both three and yet one. Love is the key to their relationship, just as love is so fundamental to our very understanding of God. The voice of God from heaven speaks of the love that He has for His Son who is now on earth, while the Spirit of God comes down as the expression or bond of that love.

3:16–17 HOLY SPIRIT, Jesus—God confirmed John's testimony to Jesus through the Spirit. See notes on Nu 11:25–29; 1 Sa 10:5–13. This is the only reference comparing the Spirit to a dove. Through it, God affirmed that Jesus was the promised Messiah. See notes on Isa 11:1–2; 42:1–2; 61:1–3. The baptismal affirmation shows the Spirit guided and empowered Jesus' work throughout His ministry.

3:16–17 REVELATION, Jesus Christ—The dedication of Jesus Christ with the symbol of baptism confirmed John's ministry as God's spokesman and manifested the uniqueness of Jesus' revelation.

4:1–11 JESUS CHRIST, Temptation—The temptations show the humanity of Jesus and His faithfulness to the messianic mission God gave Him. As Israel suffered forty years of temptation and disobedience in the wilderness, so Jesus resisted Satan through forty days of temptation and obedience in the wilderness. The primary point of temptation was the meaning of Jesus' messiahship and lordship. Satan sought to keep Jesus from being a suffering Messiah who would die in love and obedience for God's people. Satan suggested He be (1) a bread Messiah, gaining followers by miraculously meeting physical needs, (2) a spectacular Messiah, gaining followers through displaying miraculous powers, or (3) a compromising Messiah, joining forces with the evil one to accomplish heavenly purposes. Jesus refused each time to follow Satan's ways to accomplish God's will. Knowledge and use of Scripture under the Holy Spirit's power helped Jesus defeat Satan. Thus Jesus knew temptations as difficult to resist as those any human ever faces. He experienced the depth of human moral agony. His obedience and successful resistance to temptation were the first steps to the cross. He chose to do the Father's will the Father's way.

4:1 HOLY SPIRIT, Jesus—The Spirit gives power to resist temptation. Jesus in His humanity relied on the Spirit's direction to face Satan's temptations. The Spirit led Jesus into the temptation situation because Jesus had to be tempted in every way we are. Resisting temptation under the Spirit's leadership showed Jesus was the divine Son of God.

4:1–11 EVIL AND SUFFERING, Satan—In the New Testament Satan, or the devil, was understood to be a tempter who actively opposed God and His people. The New Testament presents a fuller description of Satan than did the Old Testament. This fuller understanding of Satan does not mean God must divide His sovereign power and control of history with an equally powerful demonic god. Satan holds consider-

7Jesus answered him, "It is also written: 'Do not put the Lord your God to the
test.'[p] "[e]

8Again, the devil took him to a very
high mountain and showed him all the
kingdoms of the world and their splendor. 9"All this I will give you," he said,
"if you will bow down and worship me."

10Jesus said to him, "Away from me,
Satan![f] For it is written: 'Worship the
Lord your God, and serve him only.'[q] "[g]

11Then the devil left him,[h] and angels
came and attended him.[i]

Jesus Begins to Preach

12When Jesus heard that John had been
put in prison,[j] he returned to Galilee.[k]
13Leaving Nazareth, he went and lived in
Capernaum,[l] which was by the lake in
the area of Zebulun and Naphtali— 14to
fulfill[m] what was said through the prophet Isaiah:

15"Land of Zebulun and land of Naphtali,
the way to the sea, along the Jordan,
Galilee of the Gentiles—
16the people living in darkness
have seen a great light;
on those living in the land of the
shadow of death
a light has dawned."[r] [n]

17From that time on Jesus began to
preach, "Repent, for the kingdom of
heaven[o] is near."

The Calling of the First Disciples

4:18–22pp — Mk 1:16–20; Lk 5:2–11; Jn 1:35–42

18As Jesus was walking beside the Sea
of Galilee,[p] he saw two brothers, Simon
called Peter[q] and his brother Andrew.
They were casting a net into the lake, for
they were fishermen. 19"Come, follow
me,"[r] Jesus said, "and I will make you
fishers of men." 20At once they left their
nets and followed him.[s]

21Going on from there, he saw two other brothers, James son of Zebedee and his
brother John.[t] They were in a boat with
their father Zebedee, preparing their
nets. Jesus called them, 22and immediately they left the boat and their father and
followed him.[u]

4:7 [e]Dt 6:16
4:10 [f]1Ch 21:1; Job 1:6-9; Mt 16:23; Mk 4:15; Lk 10:18; 13:16; 22:3,31; Ro 16:20; 2Co 2:11; 11:14; 2Th 2:9; Rev 12:9 [g]Dt 6:13
4:11 [h]Jas 4:7 [i]Mt 26:53; Lk 22:43; Heb 1:14
4:12 [j]Mt 14:3 [k]Mk 1:14
4:13 [l]Mk 1:21; 9:33; Lk 4:23,31; Jn 2:12; 4:46,47
4:14 [m]S Mt 1:22
4:16 [n]Isa 9:1,2; Lk 2:32; Jn 1:4,5,9
4:17 [o]S Mt 3:2
4:18 [p]Mt 15:29; Mk 7:31; Jn 6:1 [q]Mt 16:17,18
4:19 [r]ver 20,22; Mt 8:22; Mk 10:21, 28,52; Lk 5:28; Jn 1:43; 21:19,22
4:20 [s]S ver 19
4:21 [t]Mt 17:1; 20:20; 26:37; Mk 3:17; 13:3; Lk 8:51; Jn 21:2
4:22 [u]S ver 19

[p]*7* Deut. 6:16 [q]*10* Deut. 6:13 [r]*16* Isaiah 9:1,2

---

able power in human history. He can even be called the "prince of this world" (Jn 12:31). He cannot force or tempt God to act against God's will or unjustly. As tempter, Satan provides humans an alternative to serving God. This is part of human freedom. Jesus exercised His freedom to serve God and God's purposes. He showed that Satan can be defeated. He also showed that accomplishing God's purposes through Satan's methods is wrong. Providing food for the hungry, displaying God's power and will to care for His own, and establishing Christ's kingdom are all part of God's ultimate purpose. Each must be done under God's leadership, not Satan's. See notes on Job 1:6–12; Gal 1:4.

4:4–10 HOLY SCRIPTURE, Obedience—Jesus met each of the temptations with Scripture, indicating that revelation consists not simply of knowing information about God's truth. Revelation shows us how to apply God's truth to our lives and thus how to do God's will. Satan could quote Scripture but did so to seek to lead Jesus astray. Scripture is to lead us to obey God and not to justify our desires and actions.

4:8–9 CHRISTIAN ETHICS, Property Rights—The father of lies will use the same approach on us as he did with Jesus. The creation is God's not the devil's. Part of our worship of God should include our gratitude for the creation and God's continual care of it. Gaining the world and all its wealth is not a goal for Christians.

4:8–9 STEWARDSHIP, Purpose of Possessions—Material possessions can be used for good or evil. Satan tempted Jesus to become the Messiah of a temporal or material kingdom instead of a spiritual one. The devil seeks to deceive Christ's followers. A Christian who follows Satan's methods sins against God. See note on Dt 8:7–9,10–14,18.

4:10 WORSHIP, Service—Committed and obedient service is a prominent aspect of true worship. To worship (Greek *proskuneō*) means to fall down with face to the ground in humble adoration. The outward act expresses an inward attitude of reverence and humility. See note on 2 Ch 7:3. To worship is to serve (Greek *latreuō*). This Greek term originally referred to wages paid laborers. It came to mean service without wages, then service in the worship place. It may be translated "serve" (2 Ti 1:3) or "worship" (Ac 24:14; Php 3:3). Genuine worship involves committed service (Rev 22:3). See note on Dt 11:13. Committed service grows from a committed heart (Jn 4:23–24).

4:10 PRAYER, Worship—Jesus, quoting Dt 6:13, emphasized the Judaic tradition that God alone is worthy of worship. Prayer should be directed to no one else.

4:17 JESUS CHRIST, Kingdom of God—Jesus represented the climax of God's plans to establish His kingdom. In Jesus the sovereign power of the kingdom was present in flesh among humanity. The only proper response was repentance. Jesus showed us the nature of God's kingdom. He will one day fully establish the kingdom.

4:17 SALVATION, Repentance—Jesus came preaching the same message as John the Baptist. See note on 3:1,8,11. Compare Mk 1:15; Lk 5:32. Turning from sin and exchanging confidence in human systems of rules to trust and reliance on God is the entrance requirement for God's kingdom.

4:17 DISCIPLESHIP, Kingdom of God—God's kingdom is the central focus of the teaching of Jesus. The kingdom of God means, primarily, the sovereign and righteous rule of God over the lives of those who have accepted His rule and are striving to live in accordance with His will. The kingdom of God is both a present reality and a future culminating hope. Life in the kingdom, whether present or future, is God-centered and God-controlled. See notes on 3:2; 6:10, 33.

4:17 THE CHURCH, God's Kingdom—See note on 3:2. John the Baptist and Jesus both called for persons to repent in preparation for the kingdom of heaven. Repentance is necessary for those entering the kingdom of God. We must turn from this world's standards of success and power to God's call for humble faith. We must turn from our sin to His salvation.

4:17 PROCLAMATION, Gospel—See note on Mk 1:14–15.

4:18–22 HUMANITY, Work—In response to Jesus' call to discipleship, people may leave one kind of work for another. See Mk 1:16–20; Lk 5:8–11.

4:19 REVELATION, Commitment—The revelation of God in Jesus Christ called people to follow Him, to become useful employees in the task of bringing followers to commitment to God through Christ. Revelation is a call to action as well as a call to know.

4:19 EVANGELISM, Call to Evangelize—Christ's call to follow Him in discipleship is a call to evangelize other people. The call has only one proper response—immediate obedience. Discipleship always involves the call to witness.

Jesus Heals the Sick

[23]Jesus went throughout Galilee,[v]
teaching in their synagogues,[w] preaching
the good news[x] of the kingdom,[y] and
healing every disease and sickness among
the people.[z] [24]News about him spread all
over Syria,[a] and people brought to him
all who were ill with various diseases,
those suffering severe pain, the demon-
possessed,[b] those having seizures,[c] and
the paralyzed,[d] and he healed them.
[25]Large crowds from Galilee, the Decapolis,[s] Jerusalem, Judea and the region
across the Jordan followed him.[e]

Chapter 5

The Beatitudes

5:3–12pp — Lk 6:20–23

NOW when he saw the crowds, he
went up on a mountainside and sat
down. His disciples came to him, [2]and he
began to teach them, saying:

[3]"Blessed are the poor in spirit,
for theirs is the kingdom of
heaven.[f]
[4]Blessed are those who mourn,
for they will be comforted.[g]
[5]Blessed are the meek,
for they will inherit the earth.[h]
[6]Blessed are those who hunger and
thirst for righteousness,
for they will be filled.[i]
[7]Blessed are the merciful,
for they will be shown mercy.[j]
[8]Blessed are the pure in heart,[k]
for they will see God.[l]
[9]Blessed are the peacemakers,[m]
for they will be called sons of God.[n]

4:23 [v]Mk 1:39; Lk 4:15,44 [w]Mt 9:35; 13:54; Mk 1:21; Lk 4:15; Jn 6:59; 18:20 [x]Mk 1:14 [y]S Mt 3:2; Ac 20:25; 28:23,31 [z]Mt 8:16; 14:14; 15:30; Mk 3:10; Lk 7:22; Ac 10:38 **4:24** [a]S Lk 2:2 [b]Mt 8:16,28; 9:32; 12:22; 15:22; Mk 1:32; 5:15,16, 18 [c]Mt 17:15 [d]Mt 8:6; 9:2; Mk 2:3 **4:25** [e]Mk 3:7,8; Lk 6:17 **5:3** [f]ver 10,19; S Mt 25:34 **5:4** [g]Isa 61:2,3; Rev 7:17 **5:5** [h]Ps 37:11; Ro 4:13 **5:6** [i]Isa 55:1,2 **5:7** [j]S Jas 2:13 **5:8** [k]Ps 24:3,4; 73:1 [l]Ps 17:15; 42:2; Heb 12:14; Rev 22:4 **5:9** [m]Jas 3:18; S Ro 14:19 [n]ver 44,45; S Ro 8:14

[s]*25* That is, the Ten Cities

4:23–25 MIRACLE, Christ—God used human instruments to perform and interpret His miracles. The greatest of His agents was the Man Jesus Christ, God's divine Son. Jesus was known as both Teacher and Healer. His healing miracles attracted suffering humanity, and He compassionately ministered to their needs. These opportunities to teach resulted in large crowds following Him. Miracles allowed Jesus to minister, to attract followers, and to teach.

4:23–24 SALVATION, Healing—Jesus taught, preached, and healed. His salvation was perfectly balanced, providing for the whole person with spiritual, emotional, and physical needs.

4:23 EDUCATION, Jesus—Three major activities marked the Galilean ministry of Jesus—teaching, preaching, and healing. Everywhere He went, He was known as "Teacher." Teaching was His most characteristic function, whether in the synogogue, on a hillside, or in the marketplace. Most of His healings were used as occasions for teaching. Those who teach in the church today are following a pattern established by the Master Himself.

4:23 PROCLAMATION, Gospel—Jesus is the primary example for the Christian preacher. Jesus went where the people were, met their needs, and proclaimed good news to them. The good news did not center on human actions or solutions. The content of proclamation is God's kingdom. God's actions to establish His rule in human hearts is the true good news.

4:23–25 EVANGELISM, Social Action—Jesus healed many of their sicknesses, which opened the door for preaching the gospel. Jesus used all means to help people in their various needs and point them to their greatest need—salvation. There is no conflict between meeting social or physical needs and providing spiritual necessities. Jesus' love for people led Him to minister to all their concerns. The result was that "news about him spread all over," and "large crowds . . . followed him." Jesus' attitude sets the agenda for today's church to join ministry to needs and proclamation of the gospel into one effective program of evangelism. See Guide to Service in Christ's Name, pp. 1823–1826.

5:1—7:27 CHRISTIAN ETHICS, Character—The Sermon on the Mount summarizes Jesus' ethical teachings. It characterizes citizens of His Kingdom. They meet expectations of behavior which go beyond a legalistic application of the moral law. The ethical standards Jesus portrays are active in nature. Their application are both God- and person-oriented. Jesus did not intend the sermon to be dismissed as too demanding and unrealistic. He expects disciples to set these as standards for daily life.

5:1–12 JESUS CHRIST, Teaching—The first Gospel has the most teachings of Jesus. Matthew has five sections of Jesus' teachings: the Sermon on the Mount (5—7), the teaching accompanying the sending of the twelve (10), parables about the kingdom (13), parables about life in the kingdom (18), teaching on judgment (24—25). It is almost as though Matthew, the writer of the most Jewish Gospel, was saying Jesus was the new Moses giving God's final commands in the five new books of God's gospel. Jesus' preaching and teaching both fulfilled and superseded the Old Testament. The theme of Jesus' teaching was the kingdom of God. He described the God of the kingdom, told what the kingdom is like, gave requirements for entering the kingdom, outlined guidelines for living in the kingdom, and told of the future consummation of the kingdom. Jesus' teaching revealed God's purposes for His people in light of Messiah's coming. His teachings are the moral standard by which Christians measure themselves. The Beatitudes refer to both present and future blessings of the kingdom. The kingdom began with Jesus' coming (4:17). The mourning which brings blessedness includes grief at the loss of loved ones and repentance because of sin. God gives comfort to those grieved by the wickedness of this world. "Meek" means "easy or mild." We should be strong enough to be in control of all of the circumstances of our lives under the guidance of God. The quest to be right, what God wants us to be, can be like a powerful hunger or thirst. People who long so intensely after what is right will have their hunger satisfied and their thirst quenched. Compare Lk 6:21. Mercy is a characteristic of God. Those who exercise this quality in human relationships will receive it from God. Compare 6:12.

5:1–12 SALVATION, Blessing—Jesus described the blessings of citizens of the kingdom of God in nine Beatitudes. To be in His kingdom is to be truly happy. Humble service and devotion to God rather than human accomplishments bring happiness. Compare Lk 6:20–22. See note on Ps 1:1.

5:1 THE CHURCH, God's Kingdom—The Ten Commandments were given at Sinai. These commandments give guidelines for faith. With the Sermon on the Mount, Jesus gave a new and extended ethic for the people of the new covenant. All those who make up the kingdom live in a new age governed by the commands of Christ Himself. While the Law of Moses retains its full effect, it is extended by a greater ethic given by One greater than Moses.

5:2 EDUCATION, Jesus—What is widely known as the Sermon on the Mount is actually depicted as a teaching situation. Jesus and His disciples withdrew from the crowds, and Jesus assumed the familiar sitting posture of a teacher. Then He began teaching His followers. His teaching began with blessings or the way to happiness, not with commands.

5:3 HOLY SCRIPTURE, Collection—The heart and will of

10 Blessed are those who are persecuted
because of righteousness,[o]
for theirs is the kingdom of
heaven.[p]

11 "Blessed are you when people insult
you,[q] persecute you and falsely say all
kinds of evil against you because of me.[r]
12 Rejoice and be glad,[s] because great is
your reward in heaven, for in the same
way they persecuted the prophets who
were before you.[t]

Salt and Light

13 "You are the salt of the earth. But if
the salt loses its saltiness, how can it be
made salty again? It is no longer good for
anything, except to be thrown out and
trampled by men.[u]
14 "You are the light of the world.[v] A
city on a hill cannot be hidden. 15 Neither
do people light a lamp and put it under a
bowl. Instead they put it on its stand, and
it gives light to everyone in the house.[w]
16 In the same way, let your light shine
before men,[x] that they may see your
good deeds[y] and praise[z] your Father in
heaven.

The Fulfillment of the Law

17 "Do not think that I have come to
abolish the Law or the Prophets; I have
not come to abolish them but to fulfill
them.[a] 18 I tell you the truth, until heaven
and earth disappear, not the smallest letter, not the least stroke of a pen, will by
any means disappear from the Law until
everything is accomplished.[b] 19 Anyone
who breaks one of the least of these commandments[c] and teaches others to do
the same will be called least in the kingdom of heaven, but whoever practices
and teaches these commands will be
called great in the kingdom of heaven.

5:10 [o]S 1Pe 3:14 [p]ver 3,19; S Mt 25:34
5:11 [q]Isa 51:7 [r]S Jn 15:21
5:12 [s]Ps 9:2; Ac 5:41; S 2Co 6:10; 12:10; Col 1:24; Jas 1:2; 1Pe 1:6; 4:13,16 [t]2Ch 36:16; Mt 23:31,37; Ac 7:52; 1Th 2:15; Heb 11:32-38
5:13 [u]Mk 9:50; Lk 14:34,35
5:14 [v]Jn 8:12
5:15 [w]Mk 4:21; Lk 8:16; 11:33
5:16 [x]1Co 10:31; Php 1:11 [y]S Tit 2:14 [z]S Mt 9:8
5:17 [a]Jn 10:34,35; Ro 3:31
5:18 [b]Ps 119:89; Isa 40:8; 55:11; Mt 24:35; Mk 13:31; Lk 16:17; 21:33
5:19 [c]Jas 2:10

God was being taught as never before. Inspired witnesses preserved for us the teachings of the Son of God. These inspired words were collected by the disciples, taught to the early church, and gathered up to become an ongoing record of God's revelation about who He is, what He commands, and what He promises. God led Matthew to preserve Christ's Sermon on the Mount to teach us the essence of the Christian life.

5:3 THE CHURCH, God's Kingdom—See note on Lk 6:20.

5:6,10,20 CHRISTIAN ETHICS, Justice—A mark of the Spirit within us is a hunger to live out the will of God. Without God's energizing, sustaining, and closeness our fulfillment in life grows weak. By feeding on His presence and guidance, our lives grow and mature. Seeking the will of God causes us to be at cross purposes with our cultural values. Our call is not to be religious experts but humble servants of God's justice. We will be made fun of, and some will even be martyred for Christ's sake. Yet, any righteousness we proclaim and live out is not our own, but that which God's grace works in us through the redemptive acts of Christ.

5:8 JESUS CHRIST, Teaching—Purity is the result of a cleansing. To sinful persons, and that is all of us, being pure at the very core of our being is an awesome task. Small wonder Paul spoke so often of our needing God's mercy and of our rightness being in Christ. Even a radical doctrine of justification must not keep Christians from striving after purity of heart. The term peacemaker occurs in Scripture only in this passage. The verb appears in Col 1:20. The reward of this Beatitude is among the greatest imaginable—to be called a child of God. The Beatitudes work for all who seek the strength of God in accomplishing them. They are specific requirements for Christians. Peacemaking is not just an individual act. It is a corporate responsibility of the Christian community in relationships with individuals, communities, races, and social classes. The people of the Prince of peace should be peaceable people. Modern Christians in free societies know little about active persecution for their faith. The spilled blood and violent oppression of martyrs and those who suffer actual and severe punishment and oppression condemn those who claim this Beatitude for insufficient cause. A faith ready to suffer for Christ marks the citizens of God's kingdom.

5:9 CHRISTIAN ETHICS, War and Peace—Happy, satisfied, fulfilled will be the one who works for and does the things that make for peace. Notice the active and not passive direction of the statement. These people will be known as the children of God, for they will understand and implement in their lives and society the vision of peace articulated in the Old Testament. This vision was an encompassing one recognizing the joy and fulfillment found in right relatedness to God, His creation, and one's neighbor. The way of the peacemaker is not a weak-kneed approach to life, but it is a way of courage. It transcends the world's attitudes and methodologies of bringing change. It makes God's moral teachings the center of community life and seeks to replace weapons of war with tools which will provide basic needs for all the world's population. See notes on Ps 34:14; Mic 4:1–5.

5:9 THE CHURCH, God's Community—As God's sons, Christians are born anew into the new creation. Sonship implies community. In the Old Testament, disciples of the great prophets were called sons of the prophets (1 Ki 20:35). As sons of one Father, Christians are bound to other members of the community as brothers. All are bound to the head of the community, the Father. No greater privilege exists than to be called sons of God. The sons of God follow the Father in bringing peace on earth.

5:10–12 EVIL AND SUFFERING, Endurance—Loyalty to Jesus often brings persecution from evil powers who oppose God. Disciples must show their loyalty to Jesus by enduring the world's wrath. Rather than escaping suffering, we should expect to suffer because we are Christians (Lk 6:22–23).

5:11–12 LAST THINGS, Heaven—Heaven will be a place of rewards for faithful service on earth. The prospect of such is good cause for rejoicing and gladness in the present time. Rewards are to be bestowed on the basis of deeds, while access to heaven is only through faith on the basis of grace (2 Co 5:10). Rewards are to be determined according to faithfulness in light of ability and opportunity (Mt 25:14–30).

5:11–12 EVANGELISM, Persecution—Christ's followers have a difficult message to declare: we must tell people they are in sin, lost, estranged from God, and desperately need salvation in Jesus Christ. That message may cause a severe negative reaction. Christians faithful to their evangelistic responsibility will suffer different forms of persecution. Some will be called upon to forfeit their lives. For others the persecution is no more than ridicule or being excluded. Under any persecution believers are to rejoice. Like their Lord and the prophets before them, great is their reward in heaven.

5:12 SALVATION, Joy—Jesus taught His disciples to rejoice and be glad when they were persecuted for following Him. Their reward will be great in the afterlife.

5:14–16 DISCIPLESHIP, Influence—A Christian's life will have influence, whether good or bad. Jesus commanded His disciples to be like a city on a hill that cannot be hidden. The influential light of our lives should shine forth like the light of a lamp on a stand. We must not try to hide from the world but let our influence count for Christ in such a way that God will get the glory for the good deeds in our lives. We are to live so that everyone will feel our influence. We are vessels for the

20For I tell you that unless your righteousness surpasses that of the Pharisees and
the teachers of the law, you will certainly
not enter the kingdom of heaven.[d]

Murder

5:25,26pp — Lk 12:58,59

21"You have heard that it was said to
the people long ago, 'Do not murder,[t] [e]
and anyone who murders will be subject
to judgment.' 22But I tell you that anyone
who is angry[f] with his brother[u] will be
subject to judgment.[g] Again, anyone who
says to his brother, 'Raca,[v]' is answer-
able to the Sanhedrin.[h] But anyone who
says, 'You fool!' will be in danger of the
fire of hell.[i]
23"Therefore, if you are offering your
gift at the altar and there remember that
your brother has something against you,
24leave your gift there in front of the altar.
First go and be reconciled to your brother; then come and offer your gift.
25"Settle matters quickly with your adversary who is taking you to court. Do it
while you are still with him on the way,
or he may hand you over to the judge,
and the judge may hand you over to the
officer, and you may be thrown into prison. 26I tell you the truth, you will not get
out until you have paid the last penny.[w]

Adultery

27"You have heard that it was said, 'Do
not commit adultery.'[x] [j] 28But I tell you
that anyone who looks at a woman lustfully has already committed adultery with
her in his heart.[k] 29If your right eye
causes you to sin,[l] gouge it out and
throw it away. It is better for you to lose
one part of your body than for your whole
body to be thrown into hell. 30And if your
right hand causes you to sin,[m] cut it off
and throw it away. It is better for you to
lose one part of your body than for your
whole body to go into hell.

Divorce

31"It has been said, 'Anyone who divorces his wife must give her a certificate
of divorce.'[y] [n] 32But I tell you that anyone who divorces his wife, except for
marital unfaithfulness, causes her to become an adulteress, and anyone who
marries the divorced woman commits
adultery.[o]

5:20 [d]Isa 26:2; Mt 18:3; Jn 3:5
5:21 [e]Ex 20:13; 21:12; Dt 5:17
5:22 [f]Ecc 7:9; 1Co 13:5; Eph 4:26; Jas 1:19, 20 [g]1Jn 3:15 [h]Mt 26:59; Jn 11:47; Ac 5:21, 27,34,41; 6:12 [i]Mt 18:9; Mk 9:43, 48; Lk 16:24; Jas 3:6
5:27 [j]Ex 20:14; Dt 5:18
5:28 [k]Pr 6:25; 2Pe 2:14
5:29 [l]ver 30; Mt 18:6,8,9; Mk 9:42-47; Lk 17:2; Ro 14:21; 1Co 8:13; S 2Co 6:3; 11:29
5:30 [m]S ver 29
5:31 [n]Dt 24:1-4
5:32 [o]S Lk 16:18

[t]21 Exodus 20:13 [u]22 Some manuscripts *brother without cause* [v]22 An Aramaic term of contempt [w]26 Greek *kodrantes* [x]27 Exodus 20:14 [y]31 Deut. 24:1

indwelling Spirit of God. Our lives reflect the light of God that burns on the inside.

5:17–48 JESUS CHRIST, Fulfilled—Jesus fulfilled all God had done for, given to, and promised Israel. His teachings did not replace the Old Testament. They represented the completion of and accomplishment of the Old Testament. He lived out what He taught and thus was the only person to be what the Old Testament taught all people should be. Jesus' teachings completed the Old Testament at the level of motivation and intentions. Jesus called people to join God's kingdom and be like God. We trust in Jesus' likeness to God as our Savior even while we work toward godly character in Christ.

5:17–47 HOLY SCRIPTURE, Authoritative—Jesus accepted and used the Old Testament as authoritative Scripture which needed completion through His messianic ministry. Jesus warned against a false, legalistic use and interpretation of Scripture which seeks to determine God's minimum requirements or uses observance of Scripture to gain earthly prestige and power. For Jesus, Scripture included the three-part Hebrew canon: Law—Genesis through Deuteronomy; Prophets—Joshua, Judges, Samuel, Kings, Isaiah, Jeremiah, Ezekiel, twelve minor prophets; Writings—the other Old Testament books. Jesus showed He had the Pharisees' respect for all of Scripture and a higher commitment to the God who inspired Scripture. Scripture laws were not merely intended to regulate a list of specific actions. They motivated an attitude of reverence of life, reconciliation with other people, commitment to marriage and family, hatred of sin, honesty, servanthood, and sacrificial love.

5:21–22 HUMANITY, Relationships—Anger destroys human relationships. At the very least, it destroys compassion. At the worst, it can threaten life itself.

5:21–22 CHRISTIAN ETHICS, Murder—The physical act of taking a life is a grievous thing. Rather than limiting the fulfillment of the moral law to outward conformity, Jesus located the root of murder at the attitude level. Such a perspective should lead the contemporary Christian to give special attention to those attitudes which may cause actions hurtful to others, whether physically, emotionally, or socially. Such discipline of character takes seriously the sanctity and quality of life.

5:22 LAST THINGS, Hell—A progression in describing possible punishment ended with the danger of hell. Literally, Jesus warned of the "Gehenna of fire." The reference was apparently to the Valley of Hinnom (Hebrew *ge'-hinnom*; Neh 11:30) outside Jerusalem where rubbish was burned. Sadly, the valley was remembered as the place where Manasseh (2 Ki 21:6) and others had sacrificed children to Baal or Molech in the valley (2 Ki 23:10; 2 Ch 28:3; 33:6; Jer 2:23; 19:1–13; 32:35). The continual burning of Gehenna afforded a vivid image for the place of eternal torment. Compare Isa 33:10–15. Drastic action is advised to avoid suffering in Gehenna (Mt 5:29–30; 18:9; Mk 9:43–47). Both body and soul are destroyed there (Mt 10:28). It is home to religious hypocrites (23:15,33). God has the power to throw people into Gehenna (Lk 12:5). Hell finds expression through human speech (Jas 3:6). See note on Jnh 2:2,6.

5:23–24 STEWARDSHIP, Giving in Worship—Giving is such a sacred and worshipful act that it should not be thwarted by a person's wrong relationship to another. God so values showing mercy and achieving reconciliation that it justifies temporarily postponing the act of giving. This makes the gift and the worship more meaningful to the individual and more pleasing to God.

5:27–30 FAMILY, Sexual Sin—Actual adultery is a physical act; but the sin begins as a thought, desire, or plan in one's heart or mind. See note on Pr 6:20–35. "Lustfully" (Greek *epithumeō*) describes an intensive and continuing desire to possess another person sexually that becomes obsessive in its control on one's mind. To emphasize the seriousness of allowing one's life to be captured by sensuality, Jesus used the symbolic language of mutilating the body to overcome lust. His vivid description of purging the body of eyes or hand indicates how vital it is to overcome lust in one's heart. Only a change of heart can banish this sin from one's life.

5:31–32 HUMANITY, Marriage—God intends marriage commitments to be kept for life. Anything less falls short of the divine purpose.

5:31–32 FAMILY, Divorce—See note on 19:3–9.

Oaths

33"Again, you have heard that it was
said to the people long ago, 'Do not break
your oath,[p] but keep the oaths you have
made to the Lord.'[q] 34But I tell you, Do
not swear at all:[r] either by heaven, for it
is God's throne;[s] 35or by the earth, for it
is his footstool; or by Jerusalem, for it is
the city of the Great King.[t] 36And do not
swear by your head, for you cannot make
even one hair white or black. 37Simply let
your 'Yes' be 'Yes,' and your 'No,' 'No';[u]
anything beyond this comes from the evil
one.[v]

An Eye for an Eye

38"You have heard that it was said,
'Eye for eye, and tooth for tooth.'[z] [w]
39But I tell you, Do not resist an evil person. If someone strikes you on the right
cheek, turn to him the other also.[x] 40And
if someone wants to sue you and take
your tunic, let him have your cloak as
well. 41If someone forces you to go one
mile, go with him two miles. 42Give to
the one who asks you, and do not turn
away from the one who wants to borrow
from you.[y]

Love for Enemies

43"You have heard that it was said,
'Love your neighbor[a] [z] and hate your enemy.'[a] 44But I tell you: Love your enemies[b] and pray for those who persecute
you,[b] 45that you may be sons[c] of your
Father in heaven. He causes his sun to
rise on the evil and the good, and sends
rain on the righteous and the unrighteous.[d] 46If you love those who love you,
what reward will you get?[e] Are not even
the tax collectors doing that? 47And if you

5:33 [p]Lev 19:12 [q]Nu 30:2; Dt 23:21; Mt 23:16-22 **5:34** [r]Jas 5:12 [s]Isa 66:1; Mt 23:22 **5:35** [t]Ps 48:2 **5:37** [u]Jas 5:12 [v]Mt 6:13; 13:19, 38; Jn 17:15; Eph 6:16; 2Th 3:3; 1Jn 2:13,14; 3:12; 5:18,19 **5:38** [w]Ex 21:24; Lev 24:20; Dt 19:21 **5:39** [x]Lk 6:29; Ro 12:17,19; 1Pe 3:9 **5:42** [y]Dt 15:8; Lk 6:30 **5:43** [z]Lev 19:18; Mt 19:19; 22:39; Mk 12:31; Lk 10:27; Ro 13:9; Gal 5:14; Jas 2:8 [a]Dt 23:6; Ps 139:21,22 **5:44** [b]Lk 6:27,28; 23:34; Jn 15:20; Ac 7:60; Ro 8:35; 12:14; 1Co 4:12; 1Pe 2:23 Lk 6:35; S Ro 8:14 [d]Job 25:3 **5:46** [e]Lk 6:32

[z]*38* Exodus 21:24; Lev. 24:20; Deut. 19:21
[a]*43* Lev. 19:18 [b]*44* Some late manuscripts *enemies, bless those who curse you, do good to those who hate you*

5:33–36 CHRISTIAN ETHICS, Language—We should exhibit such integrity of character that we do not have to make any kind of vow indicating our truthfulness. People should be able to take every word we speak at face value.

5:37 EVIL AND SUFFERING, Satan—The temptation to take unnecessary oaths was from "the evil one" or Satan. Christians can be trusted to tell the truth. We should not have to add long sentences promising to do so. Only people controlled by Satan and, thus, not trusted by the world have to try to convince people of their honesty. Such a statement as this is not trying to teach about human conduct in human courts.

5:38–48 EVIL AND SUFFERING, Endurance—Disciples should respond to evil attacks from enemies with a non-retaliation and a non-vindictive attitude (Lk 6:29–36). God provides the sun and the rain for all people. Disciples should not usurp God's role by attacking evil without God's guidance. The Christian response to evil acts against us must rise above legalism which protects against excess punishment. We must love our attackers and desire the best for them. Divine love rather than self-interest must control our actions. God's character, not human models, is the standard by which to judge our actions. See note on Ro 12:14–21.

5:38–48 CHRISTIAN ETHICS, Character—Jesus' teaching about retaliation surprised His audience as much as an enemy's sudden attack would have. They knew how to deal with enemies. He called for love of an enemy which transcends any action an enemy might perform. We are not to regard persons as enemies but to love them as people God created and as potential followers of Christ.

5:42 STEWARDSHIP, Care of Needy—The Christian cannot ignore human need or refuse to help the needy. Whether we have sufficient resources or not, we help because we love Christ. We measure our giving by Christ, who gave everything, rather than by laws or percentages. Thus, Christian stewards cannot turn away from people seeking help. See notes on Pr 22:9; 1 Jn 3:17.

5:43–48 GOD, Father—Jesus made the fatherhood of God His primary emphasis concerning God. Speaking of God as Father is a figure of speech, a human analogy to help us understand the nature of God. God does not beget children or other gods through sexual procreation on a divine level, as in some of the pagan ideas of god or in the Greek mythologies. God is like a Father in His intense personal interest in us and in the unique relationship that He sustains to Jesus Christ, the incarnate Son of God. God as Father is a rich picture of God, carrying with it a strong emphasis upon God's love for us and His gracious provision for our every need. It is meant to express both the intensity of His loving concern for us and the reason for it. The figure of God as Father is used in three different senses in the New Testament. The three different usages should be seen as separate, distinct emphases with different meaning. First, God is Father of Jesus Christ by incarnation. The relation of God to Jesus is a unique, unshared Father-Son relationship. Only Jesus can call God Father in this sense. Believers may call God Father, but this does not make them divine, nor does it make them brothers to Jesus. Jesus is the *only* begotten Son of God. Second, God is called Father of believers by adoption (Jn 1:12; Ro 8:23; Gal 4:5). He might also be said to be Father of believers by regeneration. Third, God is Father of all persons through His creation of them. This explains His love and concern for all people. This does not at all imply that all persons are therefore saved. In this sense some persons are lost children of God, and some are saved children of God. This passage shows His blessings are not limited to a select group. Jesus elsewhere explained God's deep, driving concern for the lost on the basis of a Father's concern for his lost children. God's interest in saving the lost comes from the fact He is Father to them by creation and therefore has keen, deep interest in saving them.

5:43–48 HUMANITY, Relationships—The Greek word *teleios*, "perfect," refers to maturity and completeness rather than to a gradually achieved moral perfection. Jesus expects us to relate to one another in *agape* love as God relates to us. This is unselfish, enduring devotion. God calls us to relate to all people, even enemies, in this mature way. Only then will people see God's love in us.

5:43–45 THE CHURCH, God's Community—A son is marked by obeying his father and by following in his father's steps. For Christians, sonship means sacrificial love evidenced by loving one's enemies and by praying for one's persecutors. See note on 5:9.

5:44–45 PRAYER, Intercession—Intercession for enemies is an important prayer for Christians. See notes on 6:14–15; Ps 5:10.

5:45 CREATION, Evil—God created a good world, but evil entered because of the first man's and woman's deliberate choices. God does not, however, withhold the normal blessings of life from those who oppose His will. He allows them to function in His world in order that He might lead them to see His love and experience His forgiveness. Since God treats evil people with kindness, we should also. They are a part of the world He created, and we should seek, by every means possible, to lead them to His love and way of life.

greet only your brothers, what are you
doing more than others? Do not even pagans do that? 48Be perfect, therefore, as
your heavenly Father is perfect.[f]

Chapter 6

Giving to the Needy

"BE careful not to do your 'acts of
righteousness' before men, to be
seen by them.[g] If you do, you will have
no reward from your Father in heaven.
2"So when you give to the needy, do
not announce it with trumpets, as the
hypocrites do in the synagogues and on
the streets, to be honored by men. I tell
you the truth, they have received their
reward in full. 3But when you give to the
needy, do not let your left hand know
what your right hand is doing, 4so that
your giving may be in secret. Then your
Father, who sees what is done in secret,
will reward you.[h]

Prayer

6:9–13pp — Lk 11:2–4

5"And when you pray, do not be like
the hypocrites, for they love to pray
standing[i] in the synagogues and on the
street corners to be seen by men. I tell
you the truth, they have received their
reward in full. 6But when you pray, go
into your room, close the door and pray
to your Father,[j] who is unseen. Then
your Father, who sees what is done in
secret, will reward you. 7And when you
pray, do not keep on babbling[k] like
pagans, for they think they will be
heard because of their many words.[l]
8Do not be like them, for your Father
knows what you need[m] before you ask
him.
9"This, then, is how you should pray:

" 'Our Father[n] in heaven,
hallowed be your name,
10your kingdom[o] come,
your will be done[p]
on earth as it is in heaven.
11Give us today our daily bread.[q]
12Forgive us our debts,
as we also have forgiven our
debtors.[r]
13And lead us not into temptation,[s]

5:48 [f]Lev 19:2; 1Pe 1:16
6:1 [g]Mt 5:16; 23:5
6:4 [h]ver 6,18; Col 3:23,24
6:5 [i]Mk 11:25; Lk 18:10-14
6:6 [j]2Ki 4:33
6:7 [k]Ecc 5:2 [l]1Ki 18:26-29
6:8 [m]ver 32
6:9 [n]Jer 3:19; Mal 2:10; 1Pe 1:17
6:10 [o]S Mt 3:2 [p]S Mt 26:39
6:11 [q]Pr 30:8
6:12 [r]Mt 18:21-35
6:13 [s]Jas 1:13

6:1–34 GOD, Father—This chapter makes frequent references to God as Father. God is not the caricature of a doting grandfather. His loving compassion for His children is genuine, but not blind indulgence. The Father's love can be a tough love, a love that withholds blessings that we want and do not deserve. God will not be manipulated, for He is a good Father, with our best interests at heart. Some try to draw a contrast between the New Testament emphasis on God as Father and the Old Testament emphasis on God as Lord as though one is the image of love and the other is the image of stern justice. Such a contrast does justice to neither expression for God. The sovereign justice of God may be a little more prominent in the Old Testament, and the loving warmth more prominent in the New Testament. There is certainly no conflict or contradiction. God as Father not only sees what is said or thought in public. He also sees what is said, done, or thought in secret—and responds accordingly. He blesses or punishes, as may be appropriate. God invites the believer into a relationship of intimacy (6:9–13). We express that intimacy in prayer as we address God as Father. Standing as a sinner before our Creator and Judge, we would never dare be so bold except that we are invited to this intimacy. God encourages us to address a wide range of petitions to our Father: praise, forgiveness of our sins, daily needs, the coming of God's eternal will for time and eternity, relationships with one another, and our relationship with God Himself. We can rest in the assurance that God as our Heavenly Father will faithfully provide for all our basic needs in life if we are properly related to serving Him in our lives (6:25–34).

6:1–34 JESUS CHRIST, Teaching—Chapter six is a small book on Christian spirituality. Our full worship to God should include: ministry to the needy (vv 1–4), prayer (vv 5–14), private forms of spirituality (vv 19–24), and leaving things with God (vv 25–34).

6:1–4 DISCIPLESHIP, Rewarded—We receive no reward for good done for wrong reasons. Motivation determines the reward for acts of righteousness. God does not reward an act done for selfish reasons. The audience before whom we perform the act provides our only reward. God will ultimately reward those who meet the needs of others without thought of personal gain. See note on 25:34–46. Discipleship is serving Christ by serving others.

6:2–4 STEWARDSHIP, Attitudes—Giving is a personal act of worship, not a public demonstration for personal acclaim. Jesus condemned the hypocrites' motives, not their gifts. They made sure everyone knew they were giving to help the poor. They expected God to be pleased. Jesus said public praise from people was the only reward they would receive. God rewards with His loving acceptance those who give to the poor so only God will know and so the needy will be helped as God desires. Jesus did not say we should not gain inspiration from the dedicated stewardship of others. See note on 2 Co 8:1—9:15.

6:5–8 PRAYER, Hindrances—Most of Jesus' teaching on prayer was given in the plural. This is an exception; the command to avoid hypocrisy is in the singular. Jesus' own example was to pray alone. See notes on Lk 18:9–14; Jn 6:15. Prayer is to be thoughtful, not babbling. See note on Ecc 5:2. This does not prohibit long prayers; Jesus prayed all night (Lk 6:12).

6:9–13 PRAYER, Command of God—The Model Prayer both commands and teaches Christians how to pray. The prayer contains six petitions, divided equally. The first three (vv 9–10) concern God's holiness and purposes; the second group (vv 11–13) contain three personal requests. Both types are valid requests, but God's honor and kingdom must take precedence.

6:10 DISCIPLESHIP, Kingdom of God—Praying for God's will to be done is praying for God's kingdom to come among us, for His kingdom comes when His will is done. The kingdom of God is for those who *do* the will of God. See 7:21; note on 6:33.

6:12,14–15 SALVATION, Forgiveness—Forgiveness comes to the forgiving spirit. Christ taught His disciples to ask the Father to forgive their debts as they forgave their debtors. Compare Mk 11:25; Lk 11:4. Those who have become children of God through the new birth have special obligations to members of God's family and to other human beings. Believers are to forgive others as God in Christ has forgiven us (Eph 4:32; Col 3:13). Refusal to forgive makes a person unable to receive God's forgiveness.

6:13 EVIL AND SUFFERING, Satan—Disciples should pray that God will aid us in our struggle with "the evil one," or Satan. Satan is the source of temptation. We seek God's guidance in our lives, not Satan's. We depend on God to lead us away from Satan and his methods. See note on 4:1–11.

but deliver us from the evil one.[c] ' [t]

14 For if you forgive men when they sin
against you, your heavenly Father will
also forgive you.[u] 15 But if you do not forgive men their sins, your Father will not
forgive your sins.[v]

Fasting

16 "When you fast,[w] do not look somber[x] as the hypocrites do, for they disfig-
ure their faces to show men they are fasting. I tell you the truth, they have received their reward in full. 17 But when
you fast, put oil on your head and wash
your face, 18 so that it will not be obvious
to men that you are fasting, but only to
your Father, who is unseen; and your Father, who sees what is done in secret,
will reward you.[y]

Treasures in Heaven

6:22,23pp — Lk 11:34–36

19 "Do not store up for yourselves treasures on earth,[z] where moth and rust destroy,[a] and where thieves break in and
steal. 20 But store up for yourselves treasures in heaven,[b] where moth and rust
do not destroy, and where thieves do not
break in and steal.[c] 21 For where your
treasure is, there your heart will be
also.[d]

22 "The eye is the lamp of the body. If
your eyes are good, your whole body will
be full of light. 23 But if your eyes are bad,
your whole body will be full of darkness.
If then the light within you is darkness,
how great is that darkness!

24 "No one can serve two masters. Either he will hate the one and love the
other, or he will be devoted to the one
and despise the other. You cannot serve
both God and Money.[e]

6:13 [t]S Mt 5:37
6:14 [u]Mt 18:21-35; Mk 11:25,26; Eph 4:32; Col 3:13
6:15 [v]Mt 18:35
6:16 [w]Lev 16:29, 31; 23:27-32; Nu 29:7 [x]Isa 58:5; Zec 7:5; 8:19
6:18 [y]ver 4,6
6:19 [z]Pr 23:4; Lk 12:16-21; Heb 13:5 [a]S Jas 5:2, 3
6:20 [b]Mt 19:21; Lk 12:33; 16:9; 18:22; 1Ti 6:19 [c]Lk 12:33
6:21 [d]Lk 12:34
6:24 [e]Lk 16:13
6:25 [f]ver 27,28,31, 34; Lk 10:41; 12:11,22
6:26 [g]Job 38:41; Ps 104:21; 136:25; 145:15; 147:9 [h]Mt 10:29-31
6:27 [i]Ps 39:5
6:29 [j]1Ki 10:4-7
6:30 [k]Mt 8:26; 14:31; 16:8; Lk 12:28
6:32 [l]ver 8
6:33 [m]S Mt 3:2 [n]Ps 37:4; Mt 19:29
7:1 [o]Lk 6:37; Ro 14:4,10,13; 1Co 4:5; 5:12; Jas 4:11,12

Do Not Worry

6:25–33pp — Lk 12:22–31

25 "Therefore I tell you, do not worry[f]
about your life, what you will eat or
drink; or about your body, what you will
wear. Is not life more important than
food, and the body more important than
clothes? 26 Look at the birds of the air;
they do not sow or reap or store away in
barns, and yet your heavenly Father feeds
them.[g] Are you not much more valuable
than they?[h] 27 Who of you by worrying
can add a single hour to his life[d] ?[i]

28 "And why do you worry about
clothes? See how the lilies of the field
grow. They do not labor or spin. 29 Yet I
tell you that not even Solomon in all his
splendor[j] was dressed like one of these.
30 If that is how God clothes the grass of
the field, which is here today and tomorrow is thrown into the fire, will he not
much more clothe you, O you of little
faith?[k] 31 So do not worry, saying, 'What
shall we eat?' or 'What shall we drink?' or
'What shall we wear?' 32 For the pagans
run after all these things, and your heavenly Father knows that you need them.[l]
33 But seek first his kingdom[m] and his
righteousness, and all these things will be
given to you as well.[n] 34 Therefore do not
worry about tomorrow, for tomorrow will
worry about itself. Each day has enough
trouble of its own.

Chapter 7

Judging Others

7:3–5pp — Lk 6:41,42

"DO not judge, or you too will be
judged.[o] 2 For in the same way

[c] *13* Or *from evil*; some late manuscripts *one, / for yours is the kingdom and the power and the glory forever. Amen.* [d] *27* Or *single cubit to his height*

6:14–15 SIN, Estrangement—Sin ruins human fellowship. Fellowship on the human level is restored through forgiveness. Refusal to forgive and be reconciled to other humans is sin which bars us from God's forgiveness.

6:14–15 PRAYER, Forgiveness—Prayer is agreement with God and must be in agreement with His character. To refuse to forgive is to violate God's claim that vengeance is His alone (Ro 12:19).

6:19–34 CHRISTIAN ETHICS, Property Rights—Material needs are a reality of life all people face. Jesus took our needs seriously and devoted much time to talking about them. Material things are not bad in themselves. They become bad when we place more importance on them than on our relationship with God.

6:19–33 STEWARDSHIP, Attitudes—Money must not dominate life. We give greatest thought and priority to what we really love. Jesus did not condemn money in itself. He condemned obtaining or using money instead of serving God. Anxiety over possessions is also condemned, because it allows one to be troubled over the unknown tomorrow. God's sustaining care allows Christ's followers to serve Him without anxiety. Incomplete loyalty to God, love of money, and anxiety over material things are attitudes which corrupt God's intended role for material possessions. These sins are caused by greed, which robs the steward of the joy and contentment of using material things to serve God (Isa 5:8; Mic 2:1–2). Seeking security in possessions causes much of our frustration. Only God provides true security. Secure in Him, we can meet family needs and serve others.

6:25–34 CHRISTIAN ETHICS, Character—Anxiety over life is a perennial problem. Jesus' remedy for anxiety is to make the kingdom of God and His righteousness the center of our priorities. Trust in the trustworthy, loving Heavenly Father should replace worry, anxiety, and fear in our lives.

6:33 DISCIPLESHIP, Kingdom of God—A Christian's first priority is to seek, find, and follow the will of God. That is the way God's kingdom advances. The kingdom of God is a dynamic reality, not a static idea. It is God breaking into history to redeem and rule all who will accept responsibility for living under His rule. He is willing to give the kingdom to all who are willing to make a covenant with Him through faith in Christ Jesus as Savior and Lord. See Lk 12:32.

7:1–27 JESUS CHRIST, Teaching—Chapter seven goes beneath the surface of our relationship to both God and to other people. Jesus called for care in judging others because we too have faults (vv 1–6). He invited us to ask God for what we

you judge others, you will be judged, and
with the measure you use, it will be measured to you.[p]
3"Why do you look at the speck of sawdust in your brother's eye and pay no attention to the plank in your own eye?
4How can you say to your brother, 'Let
me take the speck out of your eye,' when
all the time there is a plank in your own
eye? 5You hypocrite, first take the plank
out of your own eye, and then you will
see clearly to remove the speck from your
brother's eye.
6"Do not give dogs what is sacred; do
not throw your pearls to pigs. If you do,
they may trample them under their feet,
and then turn and tear you to pieces.

Ask, Seek, Knock

7:7–11pp — Lk 11:9–13

7"Ask and it will be given to you;[q]
seek and you will find; knock and the
door will be opened to you. 8For everyone
who asks receives; he who seeks finds;[r]
and to him who knocks, the door will be
opened.
9"Which of you, if his son asks for
bread, will give him a stone? 10Or if he
asks for a fish, will give him a snake? 11If
you, then, though you are evil, know how
to give good gifts to your children, how
much more will your Father in heaven
give good gifts[s] to those who ask him!
12So in everything, do to others what you
would have them do to you,[t] for this
sums up the Law and the Prophets.[u]

The Narrow and Wide Gates

13"Enter through the narrow gate.[v]
For wide is the gate and broad is the road
that leads to destruction, and many enter
through it. 14But small is the gate and narrow the road that leads to life, and only a
few find it.

A Tree and Its Fruit

15"Watch out for false prophets.[w] They
come to you in sheep's clothing, but inwardly they are ferocious wolves.[x] 16By
their fruit you will recognize them.[y] Do
people pick grapes from thornbushes, or
figs from thistles?[z] 17Likewise every good
tree bears good fruit, but a bad tree bears
bad fruit. 18A good tree cannot bear bad
fruit, and a bad tree cannot bear good
fruit.[a] 19Every tree that does not bear
good fruit is cut down and thrown into
the fire.[b] 20Thus, by their fruit you will
recognize them.
21"Not everyone who says to me,
'Lord, Lord,'[c] will enter the kingdom of
heaven,[d] but only he who does the will
of my Father who is in heaven.[e] 22Many
will say to me on that day,[f] 'Lord, Lord,
did we not prophesy in your name, and in
your name drive out demons and perform
many miracles?'[g] 23Then I will tell them
plainly, 'I never knew you. Away from
me, you evildoers!'[h]

7:2 [p]Eze 35:11; Mk 4:24; Lk 6:38; Ro 2:1
7:7 [q]1Ki 3:5; Mt 18:19; 21:22; Jn 14:13,14; 15:7,16; 16:23,24; Jas 1:5-8; 4:2,3; 5:16; 1Jn 3:22; 5:14,15
7:8 [r]Pr 8:17; Jer 29:12,13
7:11 [s]Jas 1:17
7:12 [t]Lk 6:31 [u]Ro 13:8-10; Gal 5:14
7:13 [v]Lk 13:24; Jn 10:7,9
7:15 [w]Jer 23:16; Mt 24:24; Lk 6:26; 2Pe 2:1; 1Jn 4:1; Rev 16:13 [x]Eze 22:27; Ac 20:29
7:16 [y]Mt 12:33; Lk 6:44 [z]Jas 3:12
7:18 [a]Lk 6:43
7:19 [b]S Mt 3:10
7:21 [c]Hos 8:2; Mt 25:11; S Jn 13:13; 1Co 12:3 [d]S Mt 3:2 [e]Mt 12:50; Ro 2:13; Jas 1:22; 1Jn 3:18
7:22 [f]S Mt 10:15 [g]Lk 10:20; Ac 19:13; 1Co 13:1-3
7:23 [h]Ps 6:8; Mt 25:12,41; Lk 13:25-27

---

need (vv 7–12). The true way to God is narrow. Anyone can walk the broad path to destruction (vv 13–14). You can distinguish good and bad prophets and good and bad disciples as you do good and bad trees—by their fruits (vv 15–23). Discipleship is like building; the foundation is all important (7:24–27).

7:1–5,12 CHRISTIAN ETHICS, Character—Jesus addressed a problem of major proportions in relationships, that of noticing others' personality flaws to the exclusion of our own weaknesses. The approach of true humility recognizes and begins work on our own faults first. We will do this when we step in the other person's shoes and judge things from that perspective. This order builds from the essence of the Law and Prophets sometimes referred to as the Golden Rule. See note on 22:34–40.

7:7–11 PRAYER, Faith—Asking suggests dependence; seeking suggests yearning; knocking suggests persistence. Jesus wanted to encourage faith. These verses should not be applied out of the context of the Sermon on the Mount; they are intended for those asking within the "narrow gate" (vv 13–14) of Jesus' followers. Prayer is to accomplish God's purposes.

7:11 GOD, Father—God as Father is not like the gods of the pagans, whose goodness, at best, was questionable and intermittent. Our Heavenly Father always seeks the best for His children. See note on 6:1–34.

7:12 JESUS CHRIST, Fulfilled—The Golden Rule completes and succinctly summarizes Old Testament teaching by placing emphasis on relationships rather than rules. Jewish rabbis and others taught this in negative form . . . Do not do what you do not want done. Jesus called for positive relationships, not negative fear. See note on 5:17–48.

7:13–14 EVANGELISM, Call to Salvation—The call of the Holy Spirit to all is to enter. The doors to the kingdom of God are always open. Our Lord warns that the large masses of people will go down the broad way to destruction. Most people will reject God's way to life. The Lord urges us to enter the narrow gate. Few find it, but it leads to life. One should strive to find the narrow way through Jesus Christ. Those who seek the Lord will find the way.

7:15 CHURCH LEADERS, False Prophet—False prophets plague the church because they can easily deceive with false claims and mighty works (7:22; 24:24; Rev 19:20). To recognize false prophets, the ordinary Christian must examine the way they live and their message. Do their behavior and character conform to Christ and His teaching? Do they proclaim only what people want to hear that makes life easy and pleasurable while ignoring the demanding and difficult requirements of discipleship?

7:22 MIRACLE, Instruments—Miraculous powers do not give proof of authentic faith. Many in the first century claimed miraculous powers. Like the magicians at Pharaoh's court (Ex 7:11), they sometimes succeeded. The claim here is centered around "in your name." False disciples gain public acclaim for themselves. The source of their success is not easily explained. Their lack of faith is clearly evident. They do not act in accordance with God's will. Love for self, not for others, dominates their lives. Jesus claims as His own only humble, obedient servants. See note on Ac 19:13–16.

7:22–23 LAST THINGS, Day of the Lord—The Old Testament phrase, the day of the Lord, is shortened to "that day." See notes on Joel 2:28–32; Am 5:18–20; Zep 1:14—2:3. It refers to the future day of judgment for those whose lives bear evil fruit. It is the day when the faithful and genuine enter the future kingdom. "That day" will be one of separation based on true character as revealed in outward conduct. It will be a day of surprise for those who performed public actions and even demonstrated unusual power but never committed their lives in submission to Christ.

The Wise and Foolish Builders

7:24–27pp — Lk 6:47–49

24"Therefore everyone who hears
these words of mine and puts them into
practice[i] is like a wise man who built his
house on the rock. 25The rain came
down, the streams rose, and the winds
blew and beat against that house; yet it
did not fall, because it had its foundation
on the rock. 26But everyone who hears
these words of mine and does not put
them into practice is like a foolish man
who built his house on sand. 27The rain
came down, the streams rose, and the
winds blew and beat against that house,
and it fell with a great crash."

28When Jesus had finished saying these
things,[j] the crowds were amazed at his
teaching,[k] 29because he taught as one
who had authority, and not as their teachers of the law.

Chapter 8

The Man With Leprosy

8:2–4pp — Mk 1:40–44; Lk 5:12–14

WHEN he came down from the mountainside, large crowds followed
him. 2A man with leprosy[e] [l] came and
knelt before him[m] and said, "Lord, if you
are willing, you can make me clean."

3Jesus reached out his hand and
touched the man. "I am willing," he said.
"Be clean!" Immediately he was cured[f]
of his leprosy. 4Then Jesus said to him,
"See that you don't tell anyone.[n] But go,
show yourself to the priest[o] and offer the
gift Moses commanded,[p] as a testimony
to them."

The Faith of the Centurion

8:5–13pp — Lk 7:1–10

5When Jesus had entered Capernaum,
a centurion came to him, asking for help.
6"Lord," he said, "my servant lies at
home paralyzed[q] and in terrible suffering."

7Jesus said to him, "I will go and heal
him."

8The centurion replied, "Lord, I do not
deserve to have you come under my roof.
But just say the word, and my servant will
be healed.[r] 9For I myself am a man under
authority, with soldiers under me. I tell
this one, 'Go,' and he goes; and that one,
'Come,' and he comes. I say to my servant, 'Do this,' and he does it."

10When Jesus heard this, he was astonished and said to those following him, "I
tell you the truth, I have not found anyone in Israel with such great faith.[s] 11I
say to you that many will come from the
east and the west,[t] and will take their
places at the feast with Abraham, Isaac
and Jacob in the kingdom of heaven.[u]
12But the subjects of the kingdom[v] will
be thrown outside, into the darkness,
where there will be weeping and gnashing of teeth."[w]

13Then Jesus said to the centurion,
"Go! It will be done just as you believed
it would."[x] And his servant was healed
at that very hour.

Jesus Heals Many

8:14–16pp — Mk 1:29–34; Lk 4:38–41

14When Jesus came into Peter's house,
he saw Peter's mother-in-law lying in bed
with a fever. 15He touched her hand and
the fever left her, and she got up and began to wait on him.

16When evening came, many who
were demon-possessed were brought to
him, and he drove out the spirits with a
word and healed all the sick.[y] 17This was
to fulfill[z] what was spoken through the
prophet Isaiah:

> "He took up our infirmities
> and carried our diseases."[g] [a]

7:24 [i]ver 21; Jas 1:22-25
7:28 [j]Mt 11:1; 13:53; 19:1; 26:1 [k]Mt 13:54; 22:33; Mk 1:22; 6:2; 11:18; Lk 4:32; Jn 7:46
8:2 [l]Lev 13:45; Mt 10:8; 11:5; 26:6; Lk 5:12; 17:12 [m]Mt 9:18; 15:25; 18:26; 20:20
8:4 [n]Mt 9:30; 12:16; Mk 5:43; 7:36; S 8:30; Lk 4:41 [o]Lk 17:14 [p]Lev 14:2-32
8:6 [q]S Mt 4:24
8:8 [r]Ps 107:20
8:10 [s]Mt 15:28
8:11 [t]Ps 107:3; Isa 49:12; 59:19; Mal 1:11 [u]Lk 13:29
8:12 [v]Mt 13:38 [w]Mt 13:42,50; 22:13; 24:51; 25:30; Lk 13:28
8:13 [x]S Mt 9:22
8:16 [y]S Mt 4:23,24
8:17 [z]S Mt 1:22 [a]Isa 53:4

[e] *2* The Greek word was used for various diseases affecting the skin—not necessarily leprosy. [f] *3* Greek *made clean* [g] *17* Isaiah 53:4

7:28 JESUS CHRIST, Authority—Jesus showed He was different from all human teachers in the authority people experienced as He taught. Only God has such authority.

7:28–29 EDUCATION, Jesus—The people were amazed at the teaching of Jesus because His interpretations were original. Only ordained rabbis were permitted to offer unique interpretation of the Law. The function of the scribes, the ordinary teachers of the Law, was to repeat what had been established by rabbinic authority. Jesus did not fit into this mold. See Lk 4:31–32.

8:3 MIRACLE, Christ—See note on Lk 5:12–26.

8:5 JESUS CHRIST, Miracles—See note on Lk 7:1–10.

8:5–13 MIRACLE, Faith—Miracles honor and teach about faith. No group, class, or race of people can claim a monopoly on faith. The Roman officer commanded 100 soldiers but submitted himself to Christ's command. Jesus responded to his faith by healing his paralyzed servant. This teaches that Christ's healings were not confined to Israel. Belonging to the chosen race is not the criterion for belonging to God's kingdom. Submissive faith is. God can still work miracles for persons of all races and nations who submit to Him in faith.

8:5–13,26 SALVATION, Belief—This Roman centurion is an example of the kind of faith Christ wants all persons to have in Him. He believed Christ's word without demanding His physical presence. Compare Jn 20:29. The centurion was a Gentile who came to believe in Jesus and was praised for it. Jesus extends the opportunity to believe and participate in salvation to all people.

8:10–13 PRAYER, Faith—The faith of the centurion gained more for him than the inheritance of the Jews did for them. Personal faith, not family tradition, is the basis of prayer. See note on Lk 7:4–10.

8:13 REVELATION, Commitment—Jesus gave miraculous revelation to people of faith. God seeks belief in a person's heart to bring change and redemption.

8:14–17 MIRACLE, Christ—See note on Lk 4:38–41.

The Cost of Following Jesus

8:19–22pp — Lk 9:57–60

18When Jesus saw the crowd around
him, he gave orders to cross to the other
side of the lake.[b] 19Then a teacher of the
law came to him and said, "Teacher, I
will follow you wherever you go."
20Jesus replied, "Foxes have holes and
birds of the air have nests, but the Son of
Man[c] has no place to lay his head."
21Another disciple said to him, "Lord,
first let me go and bury my father."
22But Jesus told him, "Follow me,[d] and
let the dead bury their own dead."

Jesus Calms the Storm

8:23–27pp — Mk 4:36–41; Lk 8:22–25
8:23–27Ref — Mt 14:22–33

23Then he got into the boat and his disciples followed him. 24Without warning,
a furious storm came up on the lake, so
that the waves swept over the boat. But
Jesus was sleeping. 25The disciples went
and woke him, saying, "Lord, save us!
We're going to drown!"
26He replied, "You of little faith,[e] why
are you so afraid?" Then he got up and
rebuked the winds and the waves, and it
was completely calm.[f]
27The men were amazed and asked,
"What kind of man is this? Even the
winds and the waves obey him!"

The Healing of Two Demon-possessed Men

8:28–34pp — Mk 5:1–17; Lk 8:26–37

28When he arrived at the other side in
the region of the Gadarenes,[h] two demon-possessed[g] men coming from the
tombs met him. They were so violent that
no one could pass that way. 29"What do
you want with us,[h] Son of God?" they
shouted. "Have you come here to torture
us before the appointed time?"[i]
30Some distance from them a large
herd of pigs was feeding. 31The demons
begged Jesus, "If you drive us out, send
us into the herd of pigs."
32He said to them, "Go!" So they came
out and went into the pigs, and the whole
herd rushed down the steep bank into
the lake and died in the water. 33Those
tending the pigs ran off, went into the
town and reported all this, including
what had happened to the demon-possessed men. 34Then the whole town went
out to meet Jesus. And when they saw
him, they pleaded with him to leave their
region.[j]

8:18 [b]Mk 4:35
8:20 [c]Da 7:13; Mt 12:8,32,40; 16:13,27,28; 17:9; 19:28; Mk 2:10; 8:31
8:22 [d]S Mt 4:19
8:26 [e]S Mt 6:30 [f]Ps 65:7; 89:9; 107:29
8:28 [g]S Mt 4:24
8:29 [h]Jdg 11:12; 2Sa 16:10; 1Ki 17:18; Mk 1:24; Lk 4:34; Jn 2:4 [i]2Pe 2:4
8:34 [j]Lk 5:8; Ac 16:39
9:1 [k]Mt 4:13
9:2 [l]S Mt 4:24 [m]S ver 22 [n]Jn 16:33 [o]Lk 7:48
9:3 [p]Mt 26:65; Jn 10:33
9:4 [q]Ps 94:11; Mt 12:25; Lk 6:8; 9:47; 11:17; Jn 2:25
9:6 [r]S Mt 8:20

Chapter 9

Jesus Heals a Paralytic

9:2–8pp — Mk 2:3–12; Lk 5:18–26

JESUS stepped into a boat, crossed over
and came to his own town.[k] 2Some
men brought to him a paralytic,[l] lying on
a mat. When Jesus saw their faith,[m] he
said to the paralytic, "Take heart,[n] son;
your sins are forgiven."[o]
3At this, some of the teachers of the
law said to themselves, "This fellow is
blaspheming!"[p]
4Knowing their thoughts,[q] Jesus said,
"Why do you entertain evil thoughts in
your hearts? 5Which is easier: to say,
'Your sins are forgiven,' or to say, 'Get up
and walk'? 6But so that you may know
that the Son of Man[r] has authority on
earth to forgive sins. . . ." Then he said to
the paralytic, "Get up, take your mat and
go home." 7And the man got up and went
home. 8When the crowd saw this, they

[h]28 Some manuscripts *Gergesenes;* others *Gerasenes*

8:18–22 SALVATION, Obedience—Those who would follow Jesus have to forsake all and obey Him.

8:20 JESUS CHRIST, Son of Man—Son of man is a title Jesus used for Himself. No one else in the Gospels used it to speak of Him. Here the title refers to Jesus' identification with the poor of humanity, an amazing identification for one expected to come on the clouds of heaven to exercise world authority (Da 7:14). To follow the Son of man is not an immediate way to glory. It is a homeless adventure of faith. See note on Mk 10:45.

8:21–22 HUMANITY, Burial—Burial is the final way we can show love, honor, and devotion to the deceased. It plays a significant role for the living. Jesus calls us to a more significant role—being His disciples. That takes priority over all else, even the final rites of love. Service to the living is of more importance than ministry to the dead. See Lk 9:59–60.

8:23–27 MIRACLE, Nature—See note on Lk 8:22–25.

8:26 PRAYER, Hindrances—Little faith produces fear instead of prayer.

8:28–34 MIRACLE, Christ—Miracles show Christ's power over the demonic world and His priority on people. The exorcism of demons was an accepted healing technique (Lk 11:19). People were not sure which powers stood behind the exorcisms of demons. The demons recognized Jesus as "Son of God" and knew His power pointed to the kingdom of God. The religious leaders so strongly opposed Jesus that they charged Him with using Satan's power (Mt 9:34). Jesus showed such claims were nonsense. Only by God's power could He fight the demonic (Lk 11:20). Healing the man endangered the economic life of the pig-farming community. They did not share Christ's compassion for human life. Neither did they share His power over demons. Christ's miracles in casting out demons showed He had the power of God in a unique way.

9:1–8 MIRACLE, Christ—See note on Mk 2:1–12.

9:1–8 EVIL AND SUFFERING, Human Origin—See note on Lk 5:17–26.

9:1–8 SALVATION, Forgiveness—Jesus forgave the paralytic of his sins. He has authority to forgive sins and to heal because He is God. Compare Mk 2:1–12; Lk 5:17–26.

9:1–8,22,28–30 SALVATION, Belief—Faith was a common element in these three healing miracles. Great things are possible for those who believe in Christ—even the forgiveness of sins. Compare Mk 10:52.

9:4 REVELATION, Jesus Christ—The power to forgive sins demonstrated through miraculous healing showed Jesus was God in person, for only God can forgive sins.

9:8 SALVATION, Fear of God—Christ's miracles caused reverent fear and praise because the crowd recognized the

were filled with awe; and they praised
God,[s] who had given such authority to
men.

The Calling of Matthew

9:9–13pp — Mk 2:14–17; Lk 5:27–32

9As Jesus went on from there, he saw a
man named Matthew sitting at the tax
collector's booth. "Follow me,"[t] he told
him, and Matthew got up and followed
him.
10While Jesus was having dinner at
Matthew's house, many tax collectors
and "sinners" came and ate with him
and his disciples. 11When the Pharisees
saw this, they asked his disciples, "Why
does your teacher eat with tax collectors
and 'sinners'?"[u]
12On hearing this, Jesus said, "It is not
the healthy who need a doctor, but the
sick. 13But go and learn what this means:
'I desire mercy, not sacrifice.'[i][v] For I
have not come to call the righteous, but
sinners."[w]

Jesus Questioned About Fasting

9:14–17pp — Mk 2:18–22; Lk 5:33–39

14Then John's[x] disciples came and
asked him, "How is it that we and the
Pharisees fast,[y] but your disciples do not
fast?"
15Jesus answered, "How can the guests
of the bridegroom mourn while he is
with them?[z] The time will come when
the bridegroom will be taken from them;
then they will fast.[a]
16"No one sews a patch of unshrunk
cloth on an old garment, for the patch

9:8 [s]Mt 5:16; 15:31; Lk 7:16; 13:13; 17:15; 23:47; Jn 15:8; Ac 4:21; 11:18; 21:20
9:9 [t]S Mt 4:19
9:11 [u]Mt 11:19; Lk 5:30; 15:2; 19:7; Gal 2:15
9:13 [v]Hos 6:6; Mic 6:6-8; Mt 12:7 [w]Lk 19:10; 1Ti 1:15
9:14 [x]S Mt 3:1 [y]Mt 11:18,19; Lk 18:12
9:15 [z]Jn 3:29 [a]Ac 13:2,3; 14:23
9:18 [b]S Mt 8:2 [c]S Mk 5:23
9:20 [d]Mt 14:36; Mk 3:10; 6:56; Lk 6:19
9:22 [e]ver 2; Jn 16:33 [f]ver 29; Mt 8:13; Mk 10:52; Lk 7:50; 17:19; 18:42 [g]Mt 15:28
9:23 [h]2Ch 35:25; Jer 9:17,18
9:24 [i]Ac 20:10 [j]Da 12:2; Ps 76:5; Jn 11:11-14; Ac 7:60; 13:36; 1Co 11:30; 15:6, 18,20; 1Th 4:13-16
9:25 [k]S Lk 7:14
9:26 [l]ver 31; Mt 4:24; 14:1; Mk 1:28,45; Lk 4:14,37; 5:15; 7:17

will pull away from the garment, making
the tear worse. 17Neither do men pour
new wine into old wineskins. If they do,
the skins will burst, the wine will run out
and the wineskins will be ruined. No,
they pour new wine into new wineskins,
and both are preserved."

A Dead Girl and a Sick Woman

9:18–26pp — Mk 5:22–43; Lk 8:41–56

18While he was saying this, a ruler
came and knelt before him[b] and said,
"My daughter has just died. But come
and put your hand on her,[c] and she will
live." 19Jesus got up and went with him,
and so did his disciples.
20Just then a woman who had been
subject to bleeding for twelve years came
up behind him and touched the edge of
his cloak.[d] 21She said to herself, "If I only
touch his cloak, I will be healed."
22Jesus turned and saw her. "Take
heart,[e] daughter," he said, "your faith
has healed you."[f] And the woman was
healed from that moment.[g]
23When Jesus entered the ruler's house
and saw the flute players and the noisy
crowd,[h] 24he said, "Go away. The girl is
not dead[i] but asleep."[j] But they
laughed at him. 25After the crowd had
been put outside, he went in and took the
girl by the hand, and she got up.[k] 26News
of this spread through all that region.[l]

Jesus Heals the Blind and Mute

27As Jesus went on from there, two

[i]*13* Hosea 6:6

---

superhuman power of God at work in Jesus. Such fear is the first step toward faith. Acknowledgment that God's power is at work in Jesus must be followed by faith commitment to Jesus for salvation. Compare 8:27; 14:26; Mk 4:41; 5:33; Lk 7:16; 8:37; Ac 2:43; 19:17.

9:8 WORSHIP, Reverence—Recognition of God's authority and power leads people to praise and express reverent awe before Him. Belief in Christ is the only basis for proper worship. See note on Lev 9:23–24.

9:9 HUMANITY, Work—See note on 4:18–22.

9:12–13 EVANGELISM, Call to Salvation—Here is the essence of Christ's call to salvation. In great mercy He calls needy sinners to refuse to rely on their own righteousness and to humbly learn from Him. Those who respond positively to Christ's call through repentance and faith find salvation.

9:13 SIN, Alienation—Jesus' ministry focused on sin. This fact shocked the religious establishment of His day. They focused on the society of the righteous, excluding and condemning all others. Jesus recognized all are sinners alienated from God. He offered mercy rather than ritual as the way back to God. Alienation does not have to be our permanent state. We can receive God's mercy and be reconciled.

9:13 CHRISTIAN ETHICS, Righteousness—Righteousness is not a self-satisfied attitude of a religious elite. Self-proclaimed righteous people may be so set in their opposition to God's ways that Christ's message cannot reach them.

9:13 PRAYER, Sincerity—It is not the presentation of the ritual, but the heart the ritual represents, that God wants. See note on Lev 1:9.

9:14–15 PRAYER, Lament—Fasting was normally for the purpose of mourning. Jesus' presence was an occasion for joy. Different types of prayer are appropriate at different times.

9:18–26 MIRACLE, Faith—See note on Mk 5:21–43.

9:18 PRAYER, Humility—See note on Mk 5:23.

9:20–22 PRAYER, Faith—Faith may appear outwardly timid, but be inwardly powerful. The woman was convinced. She expressed prayer through action rather than words. Her faith brought healing.

9:26 EVANGELISM, Mass—Our Lord's ministry of mercy and miracle spread the news of His power far and wide. The masses came to Him, and He did not reject them. Jesus was as concerned for the masses (9:36) as He was for each individual (Lk 7:13). He wanted to see all saved and knew each must come individually to faith.

9:27–34 JESUS CHRIST, Miracles—Miracles pointed to Jesus as God's Messiah who fulfilled Scripture and exercised amazing powers no other humans possessed. The greatest miracle of Jesus was His being a human with flesh and bones and human desires and needs, yet being divine with God's power. His miracles of healing demonstrated God's power over all that harms creation. They showed His redemption of the whole person. Compare 12:22–24; 20:29–34; Mk 10:46–52; Lk 18:35–43. Even the Pharisees who opposed Jesus so strongly recognized His power was superhuman, but they did not have faith to recognize God at work.

9:27–31 MIRACLE, Faith—Miracles demonstrate human faith and divine mercy. In response to the blind men's confession of faith, Jesus healed them. Thus, He answered their plea for mercy. He did not, however, accept their designation as Son of David in the way they meant it, for He did not want people

blind men followed him, calling out,
"Have mercy on us, Son of David!" [m]
28When he had gone indoors, the blind
men came to him, and he asked them,
"Do you believe that I am able to do
this?"
"Yes, Lord," they replied. [n]
29Then he touched their eyes and said,
"According to your faith will it be done to
you"; [o] 30and their sight was restored.
Jesus warned them sternly, "See that no
one knows about this." [p] 31But they went
out and spread the news about him all
over that region. [q]
32While they were going out, a man
who was demon-possessed [r] and could
not talk [s] was brought to Jesus. 33And
when the demon was driven out, the man
who had been mute spoke. The crowd
was amazed and said, "Nothing like this
has ever been seen in Israel." [t]
34But the Pharisees said, "It is by the
prince of demons that he drives out demons." [u]

The Workers Are Few

35Jesus went through all the towns and
villages, teaching in their synagogues,
preaching the good news of the kingdom
and healing every disease and sickness. [v]
36When he saw the crowds, he had compassion on them, [w] because they were harassed and helpless, like sheep without a
shepherd. [x] 37Then he said to his disciples, "The harvest [y] is plentiful but the
workers are few. [z] 38Ask the Lord of the
harvest, therefore, to send out workers
into his harvest field."

Chapter 10

Jesus Sends Out the Twelve

10:2–4pp — Mk 3:16–19; Lk 6:14–16; Ac 1:13
10:9–15pp — Mk 6:8–11; Lk 9:3–5; 10:4–12
10:19–22pp — Mk 13:11–13; Lk 21:12–17
10:26–33pp — Lk 12:2–9
10:34,35pp — Lk 12:51–53

HE called his twelve disciples to him
and gave them authority to drive out
evil [j] spirits [a] and to heal every disease
and sickness. [b]
2These are the names of the twelve
apostles: first, Simon (who is called Peter)
and his brother Andrew; James son of
Zebedee, and his brother John; 3Philip
and Bartholomew; Thomas and Matthew
the tax collector; James son of Alphaeus,
and Thaddaeus; 4Simon the Zealot and Judas Iscariot, who betrayed him. [c]

9:27 [m]S Mt 1:1; 12:23; 15:22; 20:30,31; 21:9,15; 22:42; Mk 10:47
9:28 [n]Ac 14:9
9:29 [o]S ver 22
9:30 [p]S Mt 8:4
9:31 [q]S ver 26; Mk 7:36
9:32 [r]S Mt 4:24 [s]Mt 12:22-24
9:33 [t]Mk 2:12
9:34 [u]Mt 12:24
9:35 [v]S Mt 4:23
9:36 [w]Mt 14:14; 15:32; Mk 8:2 [x]Nu 27:17; 1Ki 22:17; Eze 34:5,6; Zec 10:2
9:37 [y]Jn 4:35 [z]Lk 10:2
10:1 [a]Mk 3:13-15; 6:7; Lk 4:36; 9:1 [b]S Mt 4:23
10:4 [c]Mt 26:14-16, 25,47; 27:3; Mk 14:10; Jn 6:71; 12:4; 13:2,26,27; Ac 1:16

[j]1 Greek *unclean*

looking to Him as a new political David. The healed men could not help telling their own experience. Healing in answer to prayer continues to strengthen faith and motivate witness.

9:31 EVANGELISM, Mass—Salvation from Christ fires an unquenchable desire in our hearts to spread the gospel to all people.

9:32–34 MIRACLE, Revelation—Miracles do not necessarily prove God's presence or power. The crowds could look back to the Exodus and find nothing comparable to Jesus. The Pharisees only saw evil at work. Miracles reveal God only to people willing to believe. Without the mute, faithful friends, the miracle could not have happened.

9:35 EDUCATION, Jesus—See note on 4:23.

9:35–38 MISSIONS, Sending—Jesus' balanced ministry included preaching, teaching, healing, and expressing the compassionate love for the multitudes that motivated Him. He wants His disciples to share His love for the needy multitudes. To have a missionary vision we must be close to Jesus, hear His words, and see our world as Jesus sees it. We may see the multitudes in many ways. Some of these make us ready to condemn the multitudes. Jesus, however, always sees people as a harvest, ready to be gathered. A harvest has several characteristics: (1) it is *valuable*; (2) it must be *gathered*, or it will be lost; and (3) it is *urgent*. Time moves quickly (Jn 9:4), and then the opportunity is gone. Jesus calls for harvesters who care for the multitudes. Prayer moves our own heart to the harvest and moves others to reach out in evangelism and missions. As Christians become concerned about multiplied millions who have never heard the good news of Jesus Christ, prayer is our first recourse. Prayer moves God and brings promise of response. Prayer also opens our vision and the vision of others. Prayer can open our eyes to see our spiritual resources (2 Ki 6:17–18) and to see the person of Christ (Lk 24:30). In this case, our prayer asks God to send harvesters into the field (Mt 24:14).

9:36 DISCIPLESHIP, Oppressed—Jesus looked with compassion upon the crowd of people following Him. They were spiritually destitute and worn out, like a neglected flock of sheep without a shepherd. A compassion for the oppressed seeks action to alleviate their need. Jesus sought to awaken compassion in His disciples and cause them to meet the needs of the spiritually neglected. Workers to reach out to spiritually neglected people were few then, and they still are too few today. See note on Lk 9:12–17. Jesus calls us to compassion, not to condemnation, for the oppressed.

9:37–38 EVANGELISM, Prayer—Christ commanded His disciples to pray that God will call and send out workers to declare the gospel and reap the harvest. Two great needs are for the lost to recognize their desperate condition and for Christians to follow Christ's call to evangelize them. This requires prayer: prayer for the lost and for Christians to share the good news. Prayer is a major key to effective evangelism.

10:1–42 JESUS CHRIST, Mission—Jesus completed His Father's mission by training the disciples and sending them on mission. The mission was divisive and brought rejection and persecution. Participation in Christ's mission means participating in the kingdom of God. The presence of the kingdom involved getting rid of disease and demons. The God who sees all will reveal all even as He cares for all. Disciples of the kingdom openly acknowledge Jesus as Lord even amid controversy and threats, knowing God will reward His faithful servants.

10:1 DISCIPLESHIP, Training—Jesus prepared the twelve for the ministry to which He had called them. He wants His followers to be trained and equipped for ministry. See note on Lk 9:2; Guide to Discovering Your Spiritual Gifts, pp. 1796–1799.

10:1 CHURCH LEADERS, The Twelve—Jesus was sent to renew the people of Israel. Jesus chose twelve men from the wider group of disciples to represent the twelve tribes of Israel. God began His people Israel with twelve sons of Jacob and twelve tribes. He began His church with twelve apostles as witnesses to the saving activity of Jesus. The twelve were chosen to present Jesus to Israel through their preaching and healing. They proclaimed that in Jesus the Messianic Age had dawned upon Israel and the world. See 19:28; Lk 22:28–30.

10:5–42 EVIL AND SUFFERING, Endurance—Disciples can expect opposition. See note on 5:10–12.

5These twelve Jesus sent out with the
following instructions: "Do not go among
the Gentiles or enter any town of the Samaritans.[d] 6Go rather to the lost sheep of
Israel.[e] 7As you go, preach this message:
'The kingdom of heaven[f] is near.' 8Heal
the sick, raise the dead, cleanse those
who have leprosy,[k] drive out demons.
Freely you have received, freely give. 9Do
not take along any gold or silver or copper
in your belts;[g] 10take no bag for the journey, or extra tunic, or sandals or a staff;
for the worker is worth his keep.[h]

11"Whatever town or village you enter,
search for some worthy person there and
stay at his house until you leave. 12As you
enter the home, give it your greeting.[i]
13If the home is deserving, let your peace
rest on it; if it is not, let your peace return
to you. 14If anyone will not welcome you
or listen to your words, shake the dust off
your feet[j] when you leave that home or
town. 15I tell you the truth, it will be
more bearable for Sodom and Gomorrah[k] on the day of judgment[l] than for
that town.[m] 16I am sending you out like
sheep among wolves.[n] Therefore be
as shrewd as snakes and as innocent as
doves.[o]

17"Be on your guard against men; they
will hand you over to the local councils[p]
and flog you in their synagogues.[q] 18On
my account you will be brought before
governors and kings[r] as witnesses to
them and to the Gentiles. 19But when
they arrest you, do not worry about what
to say or how to say it.[s] At that time you
will be given what to say, 20for it will not
be you speaking, but the Spirit of your
Father[t] speaking through you.

21"Brother will betray brother to death,
and a father his child; children will rebel
against their parents[u] and have them put
to death.[v] 22All men will hate you because of me,[w] but he who stands firm to
the end will be saved.[x] 23When you are
persecuted in one place, flee to another. I
tell you the truth, you will not finish go-

10:5 [d]1Ki 16:24; 2Ki 17:24; Lk 9:52; 10:33; 17:16; Jn 4:4-26,39,40; 8:48; Ac 8:5,25
10:6 [e]Jer 50:6; Mt 15:24
10:7 [f]S Mt 3:2
10:9 [g]Lk 22:35
10:10 [h]S 1Ti 5:18
10:12 [i]1Sa 25:6
10:14 [j]Ne 5:13; Mk 6:11; Lk 9:5; 10:11; Ac 13:51; 18:6
10:15 [k]Ge 18:20; 19:24; 2Pe 2:6; Jude 7 [l]Mt 12:36; Ac 17:31; 2Pe 2:9; 3:7; 1Jn 4:17; Jude 6 [m]Mt 11:22, 24
10:16 [n]Lk 10:3; Ac 20:29 [o]S 1Co 14:20
10:17 [p]S Mt 5:22 [q]Mt 23:34; Mk 13:9; Ac 5:40; 22:19; 26:11
10:18 [r]Ac 25:24-26
10:19 [s]Ex 4:12
10:20 [t]Lk 12:11, 12; Ac 4:8
10:21 [u]ver 35,36; Mic 7:6 [v]Mk 13:12
10:22 [w]S Jn 15:21 [x]Mt 24:13; Mk 13:13; Lk 21:19; Rev 2:10

[k]*8* The Greek word was used for various diseases affecting the skin—not necessarily leprosy.

10:5–10 EVANGELISM, Call to Evangelize—Jesus sent the twelve apostles to evangelize with specific, definite instructions. They were to go where He sent them, go to the lost, proclaim the good news of the kingdom, meet people's needs, give of themselves freely, and rely on God's provision. Although the instructions had an immediate and specific application to Jesus' ministry to the Jews, the principles are relevant to God's people in all times. These principles apply in every attempt to reach others with the gospel.

10:5–15 MISSIONS, Examples—The sending of the twelve apostles on mission is closely related to Jesus' sending of the larger group on a similar mission in Lk 10:1–20. Why limit the outreach to Jews in this mission? Obviously, God had prepared the Jews for the message. They had received the promises of the Messiah (Isa 7:14; 42:1–7; 53:1–7; Mic 5:2). Jesus cared for all peoples and commanded that they be reached, but He sent the twelve first to the people He had prepared. Likewise, we must seek God's direction as we plan to enter new fields of mission work. See Guide to Missions Ministries, pp. 1837–1840. Jesus told the twelve the specific nature of their mission. The apostles were to go and proclaim the good news of the kingdom. The word "preach" means "to herald." The sent ones are to herald the good news that sinners can find forgiveness and eternal life in Christ Jesus (Jn 3:16; 10:10). The call to participate in God's kingdom stands at the heart of missionary work. Proclamation is to be accompanied by acts of compassion. Jesus as our example of mission carried out a balanced ministry of word and deed (9:35–36). Jesus seems to have had three teaching purposes in these unique instructions: to teach the apostles to depend on God, to provide their needs, and to let them know that gospel ministry is a calling worthy of support. Missionaries should receive the hospitality of the community and identify with the people among whom they minister and bless. If the message of Christ is received, it carries its own blessing; rejection carries its own judgment. (Note the similarity to instructions in Lk 10.) The destruction of the godless Sodom and Gomorrah stands as a frightening example for those who would reject Christ's claims (Ge 19:1–29, especially v 29).

10:6–8 REVELATION, Persons—Jesus sent His disciples to continue His ministry and thus be agents of God's revelation. Preaching God's kingdom brings revelation of God's good news to people. Jesus described several actions which were ways to proclaim the kingdom.

10:7 THE CHURCH, God's Kingdom—See notes on 3:2; 4:17.

10:7 PROCLAMATION, Central Theme—See note on Lk 10:9.

10:8 DISCIPLESHIP, Sick—Jesus sent the twelve out to minister to the needs of "the lost sheep of Israel." With that limited commission, He gave them power to heal the sick and raise the dead. This was special power for a special need at a particular time. Such power is not promised to all disciples as they go out to serve the Lord, but Christian compassion will cause disciples to minister to the sick and afflicted and to claim every blessing for the sick that God has promised. We must use all means possible to minister to the sick. See notes on 9:36; Lk 9:1–6.

10:11–20 EVANGELISM, In the Marketplace—Christians are to go where the lost live to evangelize them. Every village and town needs Christian witness. Some will receive the message and ministry; some will not. Those who respond positively will experience peace; those who reject the truth incur judgment on themselves. Christian witnesses must expect opposition. Wise action and pure living are necessary to gain a hearing from the lost. Persecution will provide opportunities to witness, even to high government officials. Worry is not necessary in such situations. Faithful witnesses can rely on the Holy Spirit.

10:19–20 HOLY SPIRIT, Protects—Jesus' teaching centered on the kingdom of God. As the unique bearer of the Spirit, Jesus naturally spoke to His disciples concerning the Spirit's work in their lives. He connected the Spirit's work with their witness. One day the Spirit would give them a gift of proclamation. This would lead to conflict with religious and political leaders. When they were put on trial because they were Jesus' followers, the Spirit would provide them with words by which to defend themselves. This is a particular form of the gift of prophecy. It could be called prophetic self-defense. Jn 16:7–11 expands its meaning. Ac 4:5–17 shows the Spirit's protective power at work. See Eph 1:13.

10:21,34–39 FAMILY, Priorities—See note on Lk 12:49–53.

10:22 ELECTION, Eternal Security—Persecution is the lot of the elect. Just as Jesus suffered persecution, so would those who took His teachings seriously. Patient endurance of persecution and suffering to complete the missionary task marks the elect and shows they have eternal salvation.

ing through the cities of Israel before the
Son of Man comes.[y]
24 "A student is not above his teacher,
nor a servant above his master.[z] 25 It is
enough for the student to be like his
teacher, and the servant like his master.
If the head of the house has been called
Beelzebub,[l][a] how much more the members of his household!
26 "So do not be afraid of them. There is
nothing concealed that will not be disclosed, or hidden that will not be made
known.[b] 27 What I tell you in the dark,
speak in the daylight; what is whispered
in your ear, proclaim from the roofs. 28 Do
not be afraid of those who kill the body
but cannot kill the soul. Rather, be afraid
of the One[c] who can destroy both soul
and body in hell. 29 Are not two sparrows
sold for a penny[m]? Yet not one of them
will fall to the ground apart from the will
of your Father. 30 And even the very hairs
of your head are all numbered.[d] 31 So
don't be afraid; you are worth more than
many sparrows.[e]
32 "Whoever acknowledges me before
men,[f] I will also acknowledge him before my Father in heaven. 33 But whoever
disowns me before men, I will disown
him before my Father in heaven.[g]
34 "Do not suppose that I have come to
bring peace to the earth. I did not come
to bring peace, but a sword. 35 For I have
come to turn

" 'a man against his father,
a daughter against her mother,
a daughter-in-law against her
mother-in-law[h] —
36 a man's enemies will be the
members of his own
household.'[n][i]

37 "Anyone who loves his father or
mother more than me is not worthy of
me; anyone who loves his son or daughter more than me is not worthy of me;[j]
38 and anyone who does not take his cross
and follow me is not worthy of me.[k]
39 Whoever finds his life will lose it, and
whoever loses his life for my sake will
find it.[l]
40 "He who receives you receives me,[m]
and he who receives me receives the one
who sent me.[n] 41 Anyone who receives a
prophet because he is a prophet will receive a prophet's reward, and anyone
who receives a righteous man because he
is a righteous man will receive a righteous man's reward. 42 And if anyone gives
even a cup of cold water to one of these
little ones because he is my disciple, I tell
you the truth, he will certainly not lose
his reward."[o]

Chapter 11

Jesus and John the Baptist

11:2–19pp — Lk 7:18–35

AFTER Jesus had finished instructing his
twelve disciples,[p] he went on from
there to teach and preach in the towns of
Galilee.[o]
2 When John[q] heard in prison[r] what
Christ was doing, he sent his disciples 3 to

10:23 [y]S Lk 17:30
10:24 [z]S Jn 13:16
10:25 [a]S Mk 3:22
10:26 [b]Mk 4:22; Lk 8:17
10:28 [c]Isa 8:12,13; Heb 10:31
10:30 [d]1Sa 14:45; 2Sa 14:11; 1Ki 1:52; Lk 21:18; Ac 27:34
10:31 [e]Mt 6:26; 12:12
10:32 [f]Ro 10:9
10:33 [g]Mk 8:38; 2Ti 2:12
10:35 [h]ver 21
10:36 [i]Mic 7:6
10:37 [j]Lk 14:26
10:38 [k]Mt 16:24; Lk 14:27
10:39 [l]S Jn 12:25
10:40 [m]Ex 16:8; Mt 18:5; Gal 4:14 [n]Lk 9:48; 10:16; Jn 12:44; 13:20
10:42 [o]Pr 14:31; 19:17; Mt 25:40; Mk 9:41; Ac 10:4; Heb 6:10
11:1 [p]S Mt 7:28
11:2 [q]S Mt 3:1 [r]Mt 14:3

[l]25 Greek *Beezeboul* or *Beelzeboul* [m]29 Greek *an assarion* [n]36 Micah 7:6 [o]1 Greek *in their towns*

10:26–31 HUMANITY, Worth—See note on Lk 12:6–7.
10:26–28 PROCLAMATION, Fearless—Proclamation is backed by God. The human proclaimer should have no fear in proclaiming His word publicly. God gives His messengers freedom to disclose God's good news of the kingdom to all persons everywhere.
10:29–31 GOD, Love—Jesus laid great stress on the loving, faithful nature of God as Father. In His infinite wisdom God knows our every need. His knowledge of our needs is tantamount to His doing something about our needs. He extends His care to the most common and insignificant appearing birds. How much more can we count on His care. See notes on Jn 3:16; 1 Jn 4:7–21.
10:32–42 JESUS CHRIST, Judgment—Jesus was aware of an intimate relationship with His Heavenly Father. He was also aware of His own power and importance. Final judgment will depend on Jesus' word to the Father concerning each person. Total allegiance to Him and total commitment to His way of life are the criteria for judgment.
10:32–33 SALVATION, Confession—See note on Jer 3:13,22–25. Those who acknowledge Christ before others will be acknowledged by Him to the Father. Jesus expects disciples to make their faith public knowledge.
10:32–33 EVANGELISM, Results—Witnessing reveals our relationship to Christ. Christ left no place for secret disciples. Faith confesses Christ publicly and gains eternal rewards. Without the genuine faith that causes people to witness, we cannot expect God's gracious rewards.
10:34–39 CHRISTIAN ETHICS, War and Peace—Jesus' message will not be received by everyone, for the gospel runs at cross purposes with the values and vision of the world. Thus, in some cases it will cause conflict. Its call reverses worldly priorities so that God takes first place even before family relationships. Family members who do not accept Christ's invitation to the cross will fight against those who do. Jesus did not intend to cause conflict, but the natural reaction of the unbeliever is to oppose all who live out Christ's message.
10:40–42 SALVATION, Acceptance—Those who receive God's sent ones also receive the Son and the Father who sends them. We manifest our acceptance of God's Son by our acceptance of His children.
10:41 CHRISTIAN ETHICS, Righteousness—Righteousness involves honoring and ministering to God's righteous people. See notes on 13:43; 23:28,35; 25:37–46.
11:2–19 JESUS CHRIST, John—John prepared the way (3:1–15) but did not fully understand the way. He expected deliverance but instead was delivered up to Herod. He looked for the coming One, but Jesus' coming had not brought what he or Israel expected. Compare Ps 118:26; Isa 59:20. Jesus pointed to His works for the helpless as signs to identify Him as the expected Messiah. Compare Isa 35:5–6; 61:1–2. This was the advance of God's kingdom. Military advance would not be. Violence is not the way to the kingdom. Forceful faith willing to wait for final victory is the mark of kingdom people. Without faith people find reason to condemn God's servants whatever they do. Following legalistic rules is not the kingdom way. Imitating Christ in helping the needy is.

ask him, "Are you the one who was to
come,[s] or should we expect someone
else?"

[4]**Jesus replied,** "Go back and report to
John what you hear and see: [5]The blind
receive sight, the lame walk, those who
have leprosy[p] are cured, the deaf hear,
the dead are raised, and the good news is
preached to the poor.[t] [6]Blessed is the
man who does not fall away on account of
me."[u]

[7]**As John's[v] disciples were leaving,**
Jesus began to speak to the crowd about
John: "What did you go out into the
desert[w] to see? A reed swayed by the
wind? [8]If not, what did you go out to see?
A man dressed in fine clothes? No, those
who wear fine clothes are in kings' palaces. [9]Then what did you go out to see? A
prophet?[x] Yes, I tell you, and more than
a prophet. [10]This is the one about whom
it is written:

"'I will send my messenger ahead of
you,[y]
who will prepare your way before
you.'[q] [z]

[11]I tell you the truth: Among those born
of women there has not risen anyone
greater than John the Baptist; yet he who
is least in the kingdom of heaven is greater than he. [12]From the days of John the
Baptist until now, the kingdom of heaven
has been forcefully advancing, and forceful men lay hold of it. [13]For all the Prophets and the Law prophesied until John.[a]
[14]And if you are willing to accept it, he is
the Elijah who was to come.[b] [15]He who
has ears, let him hear.[c]

[16]"To what can I compare this generation? They are like children sitting in the
marketplaces and calling out to others:

[17]"'We played the flute for you,
and you did not dance;
we sang a dirge,
and you did not mourn.'

[18]For John came neither eating[d] nor
drinking,[e] and they say, 'He has a demon.' [19]The Son of Man came eating and
drinking, and they say, 'Here is a glutton
and a drunkard, a friend of tax collectors
and "sinners."'[f] But wisdom is proved
right by her actions."

Woe on Unrepentant Cities

11:21–23pp — Lk 10:13–15

[20]**Then Jesus began to denounce the**
cities in which most of his miracles had
been performed, because they did not re-
pent. [21]"Woe to you, Korazin! Woe to
you, Bethsaida![g] If the miracles that were
performed in you had been performed in
Tyre and Sidon,[h] they would have repented long ago in sackcloth and ashes.[i]
[22]But I tell you, it will be more bearable
for Tyre and Sidon on the day of judgment than for you.[j] [23]And you, Capernaum,[k] will you be lifted up to the skies?
No, you will go down to the depths.[r] [l] If
the miracles that were performed in you
had been performed in Sodom, it would
have remained to this day. [24]But I tell you
that it will be more bearable for Sodom
on the day of judgment than for you."[m]

Rest for the Weary

11:25–27pp — Lk 10:21,22

[25]**At that time Jesus said,** "I praise you,
Father,[n] Lord of heaven and earth, because you have hidden these things from

11:3 [s]Ps 118:26; Jn 11:27; Heb 10:37
11:5 [t]Isa 35:4-6; 61:1; Mt 15:31; Lk 4:18,19
11:6 [u]Mt 13:21; 26:31
11:7 [v]S Mt 3:1 [w]Mt 3:1
11:9 [x]Mt 14:5; 21:26; Lk 1:76; 7:26
11:10 [y]Jn 3:28 [z]Mal 3:1; Mk 1:2; Lk 7:27
11:13 [a]Lk 16:16
11:14 [b]Mal 4:5; Mt 17:10-13; Mk 9:11-13; Lk 1:17; Jn 1:21
11:15 [c]Mt 13:9,43; Mk 4:23; Lk 14:35; S Rev 2:7
11:18 [d]Mt 3:4 [e]S Lk 1:15
11:19 [f]S Mt 9:11
11:21 [g]Mk 6:45; 8:22; Lk 9:10; Jn 1:44; 12:21 [h]Joel 3:4; Am 1:9; Mt 15:21; Mk 3:8; Lk 6:17; Ac 12:20 [i]Jnh 3:5-9
11:22 [j]ver 24; Mt 10:15
11:23 [k]S Mt 4:13 [l]Isa 14:13-15
11:24 [m]S Mt 10:15
11:25 [n]Mt 16:17; Lk 22:42; 23:34; Jn 11:41; 12:27,28

[p]*5* The Greek word was used for various diseases affecting the skin—not necessarily leprosy.
[q]*10* Mal. 3:1
[r]*23* Greek *Hades*

11:6 ELECTION, Faith—See note on Lk 7:23.

11:18–19 REVELATION, Jesus Christ—Describing the rejection of John who appeared in a conservative and isolated situation, Jesus confronted the religious community with rejecting Him for participating with and consorting with God's children in their everyday existence. Either way, God's messengers were rejected by people who claimed to be believers. People do not set up rules as to how God can reveal Himself. God chooses His means of revelation. The final proof of whether these messengers convey the truth is to be found by how they live and "flesh out" God's message of love.

11:18–19 CHRISTIAN ETHICS, Alcohol—The difference in the practice of John the Baptist, a Nazirite (Nu 6:1–21), and Jesus were manipulated by Jesus' enemies. The point of the cynical attacks on Jesus and John was not the drinking or nondrinking of wine. There is no basis for believing the charge of Jesus being a glutton and a drunkard. Though John was an ascetic, logic would not allow that he had a demon. Thus, both charges were pointless except for providing means of slander by the Pharisees.

11:20–24 MIRACLE, Vocabulary—See note on Lk 10:13.

11:25–27 GOD, Father—Jesus enjoyed a unique relationship of intimacy with God as His Father, one that is not possible for anyone else. Jesus linked the idea of God as Father and God as Sovereign in one passage. God the Father rules everything—heaven and earth. For Jesus, the two characteristics of God's nature certainly did not stand in conflict. He pictured the loving Heavenly Father acting in His sovereign ways, bringing about His loving will.

11:25–27 REVELATION, Jesus Christ—The prayer is a revelation of how God manifests Himself by making it difficult for those who see themselves as wise to understand but making it clear and simple for those who are open to and subject to learning from Him. Jesus was a walking parable of this truth. He came to reveal God as a simple Carpenter, born in humble surroundings. His simple background made it difficult for the established leaders to understand or accept. He was God's only Son, our clearest revelation of the Father. Father and Son reveal each other. To know Christ is to see and know the Father, who reveals Him. In the same way, Christ the Son has the key to knowing God the Father and is the manifestation which reveals all about God any human needs to know.

11:25–26 PRAYER, Jesus' Example—See note on Lk 10:21–22.

the wise and learned, and revealed them
to little children.[o] 26Yes, Father, for this
was your good pleasure.
27"All things have been committed to
me[p] by my Father.[q] No one knows the
Son except the Father, and no one knows
the Father except the Son and those to
whom the Son chooses to reveal him.[r]
28"Come to me,[s] all you who are weary and burdened, and I will give you
rest.[t] 29Take my yoke upon you and
learn from me,[u] for I am gentle and humble in heart, and you will find rest for
your souls.[v] 30For my yoke is easy and
my burden is light."[w]

Chapter 12

Lord of the Sabbath

12:1–8pp — Mk 2:23–28; Lk 6:1–5
12:9–14pp — Mk 3:1–6; Lk 6:6–11

**AT that time Jesus went through the
grainfields on the Sabbath. His disciples were hungry and began to pick some
heads of grain[x] and eat them. 2When the
Pharisees saw this, they said to him,
"Look! Your disciples are doing what is
unlawful on the Sabbath."[y]**
3He answered, "Haven't you read what
David did when he and his companions
were hungry?[z] 4He entered the house of
God, and he and his companions ate the
consecrated bread—which was not lawful for them to do, but only for the
priests.[a] 5Or haven't you read in the Law
that on the Sabbath the priests in the
temple desecrate the day[b] and yet are innocent? 6I tell you that one[s] greater than
the temple is here.[c] 7If you had known
what these words mean, 'I desire mercy,
not sacrifice,'[t][d] you would not have condemned the innocent. 8For the Son of
Man[e] is Lord of the Sabbath."
**9Going on from that place, he went
into their synagogue, 10and a man with a
shriveled hand was there. Looking for a
reason to accuse Jesus,[f] they asked him,
"Is it lawful to heal on the Sabbath?"[g]
11He said to them, "If any of you has a
sheep and it falls into a pit on the Sabbath, will you not take hold of it and lift it
out?[h] 12How much more valuable is a
man than a sheep![i] Therefore it is lawful
to do good on the Sabbath."
13Then he said to the man, "Stretch
out your hand." So he stretched it out
and it was completely restored, just as
sound as the other. 14But the Pharisees
went out and plotted how they might kill
Jesus.[j]**

God's Chosen Servant

**15Aware of this, Jesus withdrew from
that place. Many followed him, and he
healed all their sick,[k] 16warning them
not to tell who he was.[l] 17This was to
fulfill[m] what was spoken through the
prophet Isaiah:**

**18"Here is my servant whom I have
chosen,
the one I love, in whom I delight;[n]**

11:25 oS Mt 13:11; 1Co 1:26-29
11:27 pS Mt 28:18 qS Jn 3:35 rJn 10:15; 17:25,26
11:28 sJn 7:37 tEx 33:14
11:29 uJn 13:15; Php 2:5; 1Pe 2:21; 1Jn 2:6 vPs 116:7; Jer 6:16
11:30 w1Jn 5:3
12:1 xDt 23:25
12:2 yver 10; Ex 20:10; 23:12; Dt 5:14; Lk 13:14; 14:3; Jn 5:10; 7:23; 9:16
12:3 z1Sa 21:6
12:4 aLev 24:5,9
12:5 bNu 28:9,10; Jn 7:22,23
12:6 cver 41,42
12:7 dHos 6:6; Mic 6:6-8; Mt 9:13
12:8 eS Mt 8:20
12:10 fMk 3:2; 12:13; Lk 11:54; 14:1; 20:20 gS ver 2
12:11 hLk 14:5
12:12 iMt 6:26; 10:31
12:14 jGe 37:18; Ps 71:10; Mt 26:4; 27:1; Mk 3:6; Lk 6:11; Jn 5:18; 7:1,19; 11:53
12:15 kS Mt 4:23
12:16 lS Mt 8:4
12:17 mS Mt 1:22
12:18 nS Mt 3:17

[s]6 Or *something*; also in verses 41 and 42
[t]7 Hosea 6:6

11:27 ELECTION, In Christ—The Son of God has been given unique authority by the Father of heaven and earth to choose the elect. He offers rest to those who respond to His invitation to become disciplined students of His. The New Testament shows that election is in Christ and nowhere else.
11:28–30 EVIL AND SUFFERING, God's Present Help—Jesus promised rest for the weary and troubled. Rest is not the absence of labor, hardship, or suffering. Rest is the absence of guilt, worry, anxiety, and lack of meaning. Jesus promises meaning, hope, assurance, peace, and joy even in the troubles we must endure in life. Following Jesus does not bring the burden and guilt of trying to follow numberless legalistic rules. It brings the confidence of living in His love.
11:28–30 SALVATION, As Rest—God's salvation is rest. This is in some respects comparable to the Old Testament understanding of salvation as refuge. See note on Ps 34:8. Jesus invites the weary and burdened to come to Him and find rest for their souls. The yoke He puts on persons is much easier than that of the legalistic religion taught by the scribes and Pharisees (Mk 7:2–5,8; Ac 15:10). His burdens are lighter than the burdens others may put on us. Especially can He give us rest from the heavy burden of sin.
12:1–14 CHRISTIAN ETHICS, Moral Imperatives—Human need has precedence over ritual law. Mercy, not legalism, is the heart of God's moral imperatives. See notes on Lk 11:37–52; 13:14–17.
12:9–14 MIRACLE, Redemption—Miracles show the priority of people over religion. Jesus was more concerned with healing the handicapped person than with the legalistic observance of the Sabbath. His challenge to the man's faith was clear—your hand has been useless? Use it!
12:13–21 JESUS CHRIST, Secret—Jesus displayed divine power in His healings but asked people to keep His power a secret because they did not fully understand His nature. He sought to involve people in kingdom service. They sought to follow Him to victory over Rome and rule in Jerusalem. See note on 9:27–34. He was the Suffering Servant of Isaiah 42; 53.
12:15–21 HOLY SPIRIT, Hope—As God's Spirit-led Servant, Jesus fulfilled the prophets' messages of hope. Isaiah had written of a servant of the Lord who would provide a new salvation for God's people. This servant would be empowered by the Spirit of the Lord to carry out His mission of preaching, healing, and delivering. Jesus was that Servant as revealed in His healing work (v 15). Empowered by the Spirit, Jesus extended the hope of Israel to all nations. See note on 3:16–17.
12:15–21 MIRACLE, Christ—Miracles symbolize Jesus' identity as the Spirit-filled Servant of God. It was unusual for a miracle-worker not to advertise his work. Jesus fulfilled the prophecy of Isaiah (42:1–4). He sought to help people with divine love, not to proclaim His own power with selfish greed. He worked to establish justice, not to justify a religious establishment.
12:17–21 HOLY SCRIPTURE, Authoritative—Jesus faced crowds with different expectations of Messiah. He chose the servant role as described in Isa 42:1–4. Thus He refused to fight the Pharisees openly and gain institutional power. He did not allow people to proclaim Him openly as Messiah. Rather than interpret Scripture to His own advantage, Jesus fulfilled its meaning. See note on Mt 5:17–47.

I will put my Spirit on him,[o]
and he will proclaim justice to the
nations.
19 He will not quarrel or cry out;
no one will hear his voice in the
streets.
20 A bruised reed he will not break,
and a smoldering wick he will not
snuff out,
till he leads justice to victory.
21 In his name the nations will put
their hope."[u] [p]

Jesus and Beelzebub

12:25–29pp — Mk 3:23–27; Lk 11:17–22

22 Then they brought him a demon-possessed man who was blind and mute, and
Jesus healed him, so that he could both
talk and see.[q] 23 All the people were astonished and said, "Could this be the Son
of David?"[r]
24 But when the Pharisees heard this,
they said, "It is only by Beelzebub,[v] [s] the
prince of demons, that this fellow drives
out demons."[t]
25 Jesus knew their thoughts[u] and said
to them, "Every kingdom divided against
itself will be ruined, and every city or
household divided against itself will not
stand. 26 If Satan[v] drives out Satan, he is
divided against himself. How then can his
kingdom stand? 27 And if I drive out demons by Beelzebub,[w] by whom do your
people[x] drive them out? So then, they
will be your judges. 28 But if I drive out
demons by the Spirit of God, then the
kingdom of God[y] has come upon you.
29 "Or again, how can anyone enter a
strong man's house and carry off his possessions unless he first ties up the strong
man? Then he can rob his house.
30 "He who is not with me is against
me, and he who does not gather with me
scatters.[z] 31 And so I tell you, every sin
and blasphemy will be forgiven men, but
the blasphemy against the Spirit will not
be forgiven.[a] 32 Anyone who speaks a
word against the Son of Man will be forgiven, but anyone who speaks against the
Holy Spirit will not be forgiven, either in
this age[b] or in the age to come.[c]
33 "Make a tree good and its fruit will
be good, or make a tree bad and its fruit
will be bad, for a tree is recognized by its
fruit.[d] 34 You brood of vipers,[e] how can
you who are evil say anything good? For
out of the overflow of the heart the
mouth speaks.[f] 35 The good man brings

12:18 [o]S Jn 3:34
12:21 [p]Isa 42:1-4
12:22 [q]S Mt 4:24
12:23 [r]S Mt 9:27
12:24 [s]S Mk 3:22 [t]Mt 9:34
12:25 [u]S Mt 9:4
12:26 [v]S Mt 4:10
12:27 [w]ver 24 [x]Ac 19:13
12:28 [y]S Mt 3:2
12:30 [z]Mk 9:40; Lk 11:23
12:31 [a]Mk 3:28, 29; Lk 12:10
12:32 [b]Tit 2:12 [c]Mk 10:30; Lk 20:34,35; Eph 1:21; Heb 6:5
12:33 [d]Mt 7:16, 17; Lk 6:43,44
12:34 [e]Mt 3:7; 23:33 [f]Mt 15:18; Lk 6:45

[u]*21* Isaiah 42:1-4 [v]*24* Greek *Beezeboul* or *Beelzeboul*; also in verse 27

12:21 EVANGELISM, Universality—God sent Christ to provide hope for all nations. His salvation is available to all who will accept it.

12:22–24 MIRACLE, Revelation—The description is brief, but the condition was serious: demon-possessed, blind, and mute. To the astonishment of the people Jesus healed him. Some in simple faith responded. Some Pharisees rejected. See note on 9:32–34.

12:22–29 EVIL AND SUFFERING, Satan—See note on Mk 3:22–30.

12:23–28 JESUS CHRIST, Son of David—See note on 1:1. The crowds hoped Jesus would be the promised deliverer but were confused because of Jesus' lack of political involvement. The Pharisees tried to sidetrack popular enthusiasm by identifying Jesus with Satan. Jesus identified Himself as the agent of God's Spirit revealing God's kingdom rather than a human kingdom.

12:28 HOLY SPIRIT, Jesus—Jesus showed His divine nature by casting out demons to heal people. Jesus performed His exorcisms by the power of the Spirit. Religious leaders could not accept this as God's work because Jesus did not follow their religious traditions. They sided with Satan in opposing Jesus. Jesus showed that the Spirit gave Him power against Satan, thus fulfilling Old Testament prophecy. The new age, the kingdom, was dawning. A further phase of the dawning of the new age began when the Spirit was given to Jesus' followers at Pentecost (Ac 2). The Spirit continues to lead our struggle against demonic forces. Too often religious leaders continue to fight against the Spirit rather than against the demons. The Spirit seeks to work through leaders to demonstrate the power of God's kingdom.

12:28 THE CHURCH, God's Kingdom—The kingdom of God is the opposite of the kingdom of Satan. Jesus cast out demons by the Spirit of God which indicates that the kingdom of God came upon the world through Him. Only the eyes of faith could and can recognize God's kingdom. See note on 13:10–17.

12:30 THE CHURCH, People of God—Christians serve Christ. Disobeying Christ shows the person does not belong to the people of God. Every person belongs to Christ or opposes Him.

12:31–32 SIN, Against God—See note on Mk 3:28–29.

12:31–32 SALVATION, Forgiveness—Compare Mk 3:28–30; Lk 12:10. Blasphemy against the Holy Spirit is the one sin which will not be forgiven. Those who commit this sin are so warped and twisted in their values that they attribute to the devil the work of God and to God the work of the devil. Anxiety about having committed this sin is a sure sign that one has not committed it. The words warn against presumption and do not limit God's grace. If you are convicted by the Holy Spirit to ask for forgiveness, you may be sure God will forgive.

12:32 LAST THINGS, Age to Come—This age anticipates an age to come. The idea of two ages is rooted in the prophetic message of the Old Testament but finds clear expression in the New Testament. The present age is characterized by the presence of evil and the activity of Satan (2 Co 4:4; Gal 1:4). Christ's victory was achieved in this age but will be fully revealed in the age to come through the church (Eph 2:7). Believers live in this age but already participate in the age to come through Christ (Gal 1:4; Heb 6:5). Persecuted believers can look to rewards in both ages (Mk 10:30). Relationships and life-styles differ in the two ages (Lk 20:34–35). Christian conduct should not be patterned after that of this age (Ro 12:2). The two ages see wisdom in different lights (1 Co 1:20; 2:6,8; 3:18). Christ's power and authority are greater than anyone else's in either age (Eph 1:21). Persons must be committed to the values of one age or the other. You cannot be committed to both (1 Ti 6:17; 2 Ti 4:10; Tit 2:12).

12:33–37 SIN, Depravity—Sin is not simply a wrong act or wrong thought. It is a depraved way of life, a habitual reaction to circumstances, a common process of making decisions. Persons who develop this way of life become evil, incapable of saying anything good. Words and conversation reflect the spiritual condition of the speaker. A sin-dominated person will utter evil; the good person devoted to and saved by God will utter good. On judgment day our words spoken in our lifetime will truly reflect who we are.

good things out of the good stored up in
him, and the evil man brings evil things
out of the evil stored up in him. 36But I
tell you that men will have to give account on the day of judgment for every
careless word they have spoken. 37For by
your words you will be acquitted, and by
your words you will be condemned."[g]

The Sign of Jonah

12:39–42pp — Lk 11:29–32
12:43–45pp — Lk 11:24–26

**38Then some of the Pharisees and
teachers of the law said to him, "Teacher,
we want to see a miraculous sign[h] from
you."[i]**
**39He answered, "A wicked and adulter-
ous generation asks for a miraculous sign!
But none will be given it except the sign
of the prophet Jonah.[j] 40For as Jonah was
three days and three nights in the belly of
a huge fish,[k] so the Son of Man[l] will be
three days and three nights in the heart
of the earth.[m] 41The men of Nineveh[n]
will stand up at the judgment with this
generation and condemn it; for they repented at the preaching of Jonah,[o] and
now one[w] greater than Jonah is here.
42The Queen of the South will rise at the
judgment with this generation and condemn it; for she came[p] from the ends of
the earth to listen to Solomon's wisdom,
and now one greater than Solomon is
here.**
**43"When an evil[x] spirit comes out of a
man, it goes through arid places seeking
rest and does not find it. 44Then it says, 'I
will return to the house I left.' When it
arrives, it finds the house unoccupied,
swept clean and put in order. 45Then it
goes and takes with it seven other spirits
more wicked than itself, and they go in
and live there. And the final condition of
that man is worse than the first.[q] That is
how it will be with this wicked generation."**

Jesus' Mother and Brothers

12:46–50pp — Mk 3:31–35; Lk 8:19–21

**46While Jesus was still talking to the
crowd, his mother[r] and brothers[s] stood
outside, wanting to speak to him. 47Some-
one told him, "Your mother and brothers
are standing outside, wanting to speak to
you."[y]**
**48He replied to him, "Who is my moth-
er, and who are my brothers?" 49Pointing
to his disciples, he said, "Here are my
mother and my brothers. 50For whoever
does the will of my Father in heaven[t] is
my brother and sister and mother."**

Chapter 13

The Parable of the Sower

13:1–15pp — Mk 4:1–12; Lk 8:4–10
13:16,17pp — Lk 10:23,24
13:18–23pp — Mk 4:13–20; Lk 8:11–15

**THAT same day Jesus went out of the
house[u] and sat by the lake. 2Such
large crowds gathered around him that he**

12:37 [g]Job 15:6; Pr 10:14; 18:21; Jas 3:2
12:38 [h]S Jn 2:11; S 4:48 [i]Mt 16:1; Mk 8:11,12; Lk 11:16; Jn 2:18; 6:30; 1Co 1:22
12:39 [j]Mt 16:4; Lk 11:29
12:40 [k]Jnh 1:17 [l]S Mt 8:20 [m]S Mt 16:21
12:41 [n]Jnh 1:2 [o]Jnh 3:5
12:42 [p]1Ki 10:1; 2Ch 9:1
12:45 [q]2Pe 2:20
12:46 [r]Mt 1:18; 2:11,13,14,20; Lk 1:43; 2:33,34, 48,51; Jn 2:1,5; 19:25,26 [s]Mt 13:55; Jn 2:12; 7:3,5; Ac 1:14; 1Co 9:5; Gal 1:19
12:50 [t]Mt 6:10; Jn 15:14
13:1 [u]ver 36; Mt 9:28

[w]41 Or *something*; also in verse 42 [x]43 Greek *unclean* [y]47 Some manuscripts do not have verse 47.

12:38–42 JESUS CHRIST, Miracles—Miracles were not automatic windows into the nature of Christ. He would not perform miracles on demand. See note on 4:1–11. He pointed only to Jonah, His call to repent, and His approaching death and resurrection. See note on Jnh 1:17. Jesus self-consciously fulfilled His mission leading to the cross.

12:38–42 MIRACLE, Vocabulary—The request for a "sign" (Greek *semeion*) introduces a new concept. The religious leaders could neither understand nor accept the idea that compassion motivated a miracle-worker. They revealed their own lack of faith by asking that a sign be performed. They wanted indisputable evidence Jesus was Messiah. As if they had not witnessed enough "signs"! Jesus pointed them to His death and resurrection to prove His identity. Jesus did not perform miracles to advertise His ministry. He condemned the religious leaders, contrasting them with the citizens of Nineveh and the Queen of the South who had responded in faith to manifest actions of God. Miracles are not signs that convince all people. They offer encouragement to people in need and people in faith. They do not solve all earthly problems. They point to eternal hope beyond death. They call on us to repent rather than to volunteer for power positions.

12:39–41 HOLY SCRIPTURE, Authoritative—Jesus fulfilled Scripture as proof He was Messiah. His Jewish opponents demanded more convincing proof—miracles. Jesus pointed to the sign of Jonah. Here Jesus did not specifically mention resurrection, but certainly Christians are expected to understand the sign of Jonah as pointing to Christ's resurrection. This sign should lead people to repentance, as did Jonah's reluctant preaching. However, the Pharisees did not regard Jesus' resurrection as a sign that was powerful enough.

12:39 PRAYER, Will of God—Jesus condemned the contemptuous dare of the Jewish leaders to establish His credentials by their conditions. Prayer seeks to further God's work, not make selfish demands on God.

12:46–49 JESUS CHRIST, Son of God—Jesus followed His own teaching, being willing to forsake earthly family for His Heavenly Father's mission (10:37–38). He created a new family of persons obedient to God.

12:46–50 THE CHURCH, People of God—People of God obey Him. Serving Christ and belonging to the fellowship of faith transcend all physical relationships. Christ creates a new family through obedience to the Father. See note on 12:30.

12:48–50 HUMANITY, Relationships—See note on Mk 3:33–35.

12:48–49 REVELATION, Fellowship—See note on Mk 3:34.

13:1–43 ELECTION, Righteousness—The elect produce bountiful fruit in face of Satan's opposition and the influence of wicked and unfaithful people in the world and in the church. Proper understanding is not a human achievement to be rewarded. God took the initiative both to establish His kingdom and to give the ability to understand it. The teaching on election affirms God's initiative in salvation along with human responsibility to hear and bear fruit in repentance and righteousness. Election does not relieve people of responsibility. Only those open to hear can receive God's gift and become part of the mysterious amazing growth of the kingdom. Persons who accept Jesus as God's chosen Servant are members of God's elect and bear good fruit.

13:1–23 EVANGELISM, Gospel—The Word of God, the

got into a boat[v] and sat in it, while all the
people stood on the shore. 3Then he told
them many things in parables, saying: "A
farmer went out to sow his seed. 4As he
was scattering the seed, some fell along
the path, and the birds came and ate it
up. 5Some fell on rocky places, where it
did not have much soil. It sprang up
quickly, because the soil was shallow.
6But when the sun came up, the plants
were scorched, and they withered because they had no root. 7Other seed fell
among thorns, which grew up and
choked the plants. 8Still other seed
fell on good soil, where it produced a
crop—a hundred,[w] sixty or thirty times
what was sown. 9He who has ears, let him
hear."[x]
10The disciples came to him and asked,
"Why do you speak to the people in parables?"
11He replied, "The knowledge of the
secrets of the kingdom of heaven[y] has
been given to you,[z] but not to them.
12Whoever has will be given more, and
he will have an abundance. Whoever
does not have, even what he has will be
taken from him.[a] 13This is why I speak to
them in parables:

"Though seeing, they do not see;
though hearing, they do not hear or
understand.[b]
14In them is fulfilled[c] the prophecy of Isaiah:

" 'You will be ever hearing but never
understanding;
you will be ever seeing but never
perceiving.
15For this people's heart has become
calloused;
they hardly hear with their ears,
and they have closed their eyes.
Otherwise they might see with their
eyes,
hear with their ears,
understand with their hearts
and turn, and I would heal them.'[z] [d]

16But blessed are your eyes because they
see, and your ears because they hear.[e]
17For I tell you the truth, many prophets
and righteous men longed to see what
you see[f] but did not see it, and to hear
what you hear but did not hear it.
18"Listen then to what the parable of
the sower means: 19When anyone hears

13:2 [v]Lk 5:3
13:8 [w]Ge 26:12
13:9 [x]S Mt 11:15
13:11 [y]S Mt 3:2 [z]Mt 11:25; 16:17; 19:11; Jn 6:65; 1Co 2:10,14; Col 1:27; 1Jn 2:20, 27
13:12 [a]S Mt 25:29
13:13 [b]Dt 29:4; Jer 5:21; Eze 12:2
13:14 [c]ver 35; S Mt 1:22
13:15 [d]Isa 6:9,10; Jn 12:40; Ac 28:26, 27; Ro 11:8
13:16 [e]Mt 16:17
13:17 [f]Jn 8:56; Heb 11:13; 1Pe 1:10-12

[z] *15* Isaiah 6:9,10

---

good "seed" is powerful (Heb 4:12), but it must be planted in good soil to germinate and produce a crop. Hearing the parable we must ask: what sort of "soil" am I: rocky, shallow, weedy, or fertile? That determines how we will receive the Word of God. God's Word will always have a mixed reception. Even God's people do not always receive it gladly. The lost frequently reject it. God intends His Word to bear fruit—in the saved to bear the fruit of the Spirit and in the lost to bear fruit unto salvation. Many things seek to rob the seed of its opportunity to bear fruit in us and in those to whom we witness. Jesus calls us to receive and obey His Word so we will bear fruit for Him.

13:8–9 REVELATION, Commitment—The truth of God, like a seed, encounters various reactions. The ground or attitude that is receptive and ready produces a response that multiplies God's love and plan in that life. Parables were a favorite ancient way of telling a truth. They were usually designed to communicate one main truth. The four reactions which the seed encountered on different grounds are the ways in which people respond to the revelation of God: unreceptive, unfaithful, unfruitful, and unexpectedly productive.

13:10–17,34–35 JESUS CHRIST, Secret—Jesus did not entrust His teachings to all people but only to believers. His teaching could have evoked dreams of military victory and political dominance. In wrong hands such teaching could have led to charges of treason or to the appearance of a volunteer army ready to follow Him in rebellion against Rome and eager to crown Him King of Israel. Jesus fulfilled His messianic mission by training disciples to help the needy and call people to repent, not by training an army for revolution. Compare Ps 78:2; Isa 6:9–10.

13:10–17 THE CHURCH, God's Kingdom—Those who have ears to hear and eyes to see are blessed to witness the kingdom of God. Others, without the enlightenment of the Holy Spirit, fail to see the new work God did in Jesus Christ and continues to do in the world. Faith is necessary to recognize the kingdom. Its presence is not self-evident to all people because our world trains us to define kingdom in terms of wealth, power, and fame rather than as servant leadership, ministering to human needs, and bringing glory to God.

13:13–15 HOLY SCRIPTURE, Authoritative—Scripture pointed to the rejection Jesus received. Isa 6:9–10 was God's call to Isaiah to an unproductive ministry because hard-hearted people would blind themselves to his truth. Jesus identified with the prophet and taught in parables so believers would understand while the others would continue in their spiritual blindness. Jesus did not cause resistance to repentance. He accepted the situation of the audience, a situation already predicted by Scripture, and taught in the best way to reveal God's kingdom to those who would listen, believe, and follow.

13:18–23 MISSIONS, Results—Drawing upon well-attested conditions that are observable in Jordan and Israel even today, Jesus used a parable to teach a master lesson on four responses to evangelism and missions. The seed is the same in each planting situation—the message of God's kingdom. The hearers, represented by the varied types of soil, are different. (1) *The hard-hearted.* By the side of wheat fields and running through them are paths, packed to asphalt-hardness by centuries of feet walking across them. Hearers, like the soil, have heard and rejected the message so often they have become gospel-hardened. They cannot understand its beauty or its life-giving hope. (2) *The emotional responders.* In the Holy Land, fields sometimes lie in the midst of rocky soil. A seed can fall into a little dirt in the cleft of the rock and spring up, but growing roots cannot penetrate the rock. The hot sun comes out, and the plant withers. So many people make spur-of-the-moment emotional decisions which quickly fade because they have made no personal commitment. The first bit of spiritual trouble sends them running looking for the next emotional pick-up. (3) *Those unwilling to pay the price.* Briars and thistles often grow up in the wheat fields and can crowd out the small wheat. Many people are attracted to Jesus but are unwilling to pay the cost of following Him (6:33; Lk 9:23). (4) *The faithful disciples.* God has always prepared a fourth type of hearer, those with willing hearts who respond to the good news. They have three characteristics: (a) they hear the word willingly; (b) they understand it and respond to it in true commitment and faith; and (c) with the power of God within, they are changed (2 Co 5:17) and produce fruit, that is, they enlist other followers of Jesus. This promise of response encourages the witness, the pastor, and the missionary.

13:19 EVIL AND SUFFERING, Satan—Even Satan understands that the fate of the kingdom of God resides in the

the message about the kingdom[g] and
does not understand it, the evil one[h]
comes and snatches away what was sown
in his heart. This is the seed sown along
the path. 20The one who received the
seed that fell on rocky places is the man
who hears the word and at once receives
it with joy. 21But since he has no root, he
lasts only a short time. When trouble or
persecution comes because of the word,
he quickly falls away.[i] 22The one who
received the seed that fell among the
thorns is the man who hears the word,
but the worries of this life and the deceitfulness of wealth[j] choke it, making it unfruitful. 23But the one who received the
seed that fell on good soil is the man who
hears the word and understands it. He
produces a crop, yielding a hundred, sixty
or thirty times what was sown."[k]

The Parable of the Weeds

24Jesus told them another parable:
"The kingdom of heaven is like[l] a man
who sowed good seed in his field. 25But
while everyone was sleeping, his enemy
came and sowed weeds among the
wheat, and went away. 26When the
wheat sprouted and formed heads, then
the weeds also appeared.
27"The owner's servants came to him
and said, 'Sir, didn't you sow good seed in
your field? Where then did the weeds
come from?'
28" 'An enemy did this,' he replied.
"The servants asked him, 'Do you
want us to go and pull them up?'
29" 'No,' he answered, 'because while
you are pulling the weeds, you may root
up the wheat with them. 30Let both grow
together until the harvest. At that time I
will tell the harvesters: First collect the
weeds and tie them in bundles to be
burned; then gather the wheat and bring
it into my barn.' "[m]

The Parables of the Mustard Seed and the Yeast

13:31,32pp — Mk 4:30–32
13:31–33pp — Lk 13:18–21

31He told them another parable: "The
kingdom of heaven is like[n] a mustard
seed,[o] which a man took and planted in
his field. 32Though it is the smallest of all
your seeds, yet when it grows, it is the
largest of garden plants and becomes a
tree, so that the birds of the air come and
perch in its branches."[p]
33He told them still another parable:
"The kingdom of heaven is like[q] yeast
that a woman took and mixed into a large
amount[a] of flour[r] until it worked all
through the dough."[s]
34Jesus spoke all these things to the
crowd in parables; he did not say anything to them without using a parable.[t]
35So was fulfilled[u] what was spoken
through the prophet:

"I will open my mouth in parables,
I will utter things hidden since the
creation of the world."[b] [v]

The Parable of the Weeds Explained

36Then he left the crowd and went into
the house. His disciples came to him and
said, "Explain to us the parable[w] of the
weeds in the field."
37He answered, "The one who sowed

13:19 [g]Mt 4:23 [h]S Mt 5:37
13:21 [i]Mt 11:6; 26:31
13:22 [j]Mt 19:23; 1Ti 6:9,10,17
13:23 [k]ver 8
13:24 [l]ver 31,33, 45,47; Mt 18:23; 20:1; 22:2; 25:1; Mk 4:26,30
13:30 [m]Mt 3:12
13:31 [n]S ver 24 [o]Mt 17:20; Lk 17:6
13:32 [p]Ps 104:12; Eze 17:23; 31:6; Da 4:12
13:33 [q]S ver 24 [r]Ge 18:6 [s]Gal 5:9
13:34 [t]S Jn 16:25
13:35 [u]ver 14; S Mt 1:22 [v]Ps 78:2; Ro 16:25,26; 1Co 2:7; Eph 3:9; Col 1:26
13:36 [w]Mt 15:15

[a]*33* Greek *three satas* (probably about 1/2 bushel or 22 liters) [b]*35* Psalm 78:2

---

understanding of the Word in the human heart. Satan seeks to make us ignore or not listen to God's Word. He wants to divert us from God's message of salvation.

13:19 THE CHURCH, God's Kingdom—The message of the kingdom leads to life and hope. The evil one seeks to steal life and destroy it. Humans face the choice of accepting Christ as King or following Satan's leadership.

13:22 CHRISTIAN ETHICS, Property Rights—Wealth can rob us of eternal hope with God. The person devoted to riches cannot respond to Jesus' call to the cross.

13:24–30 THE CHURCH, God's Kingdom—Jesus spoke in parables to describe the nature of the kingdom of God. The kingdom of God is not a man planting seed, but the kingdom may be compared to such ordinary human events. This parable emphasizes the present and future aspects of the kingdom. The seed now growing in preparation for the harvest illustrates the present aspect of the kingdom. The harvest pictures the future aspect of God's kingdom. At that time the true character of all people will be revealed and judged. Meanwhile, God's church represents God's kingdom present on earth, not as a separate isolated group, but as God's people living in the midst of evil people influenced by Satan.

13:29–30 REVELATION, Actions—God is aware that some reject and some accept His revelation. He wishes to give every opportunity for acceptance but cannot ignore the difference between following Him (useful wheat) and not following (weeds). Those who follow His revelation are productive and useful, while those who do not will eventually be set aside as wasted products.

13:31–32 THE CHURCH, God's Kingdom—In spite of small beginnings, the kingdom grows to enormous significance. Worldly success standards do not apply to the kingdom. It grows as God chooses. See note on vv 24–30.

13:33–35 HOLY SCRIPTURE, Authoritative—Jesus' practice of teaching in parables fulfilled prophecy. He quoted Ps 78:2, the introduction to a wisdom psalm teaching lessons from God's history with His people. Matthew saw the deeper prophetic meaning of Scripture in the light of Jesus, showing that Jesus gives new perspective for the interpretation of all revelation. The birth of God's revelation to His people is often as a small beginning (seed, yeast) and is often heard as a small truth (parable), but these facts are part of God's design to reveal His purposes which have been hidden from the beginning.

13:33 THE CHURCH, God's Kingdom—The kingdom of God may appear invisible. That does not mean God is not working. God works quietly and continuously to bring His kingdom on earth. Gradually the people of the kingdom influence every part of society. In the end God will establish His kingdom and eliminate all others. See notes on vv 24–30,31–32.

13:36–43 THE CHURCH, God's Kingdom—See note on vv 24–30.

13:37–43 JESUS CHRIST, Son of Man—See note on 8:20. The Son of man was the wandering Preacher sowing

the good seed is the Son of Man.[x] 38The
field is the world, and the good seed
stands for the sons of the kingdom. The
weeds are the sons of the evil one,[y]
39and the enemy who sows them is the
devil. The harvest[z] is the end of the
age,[a] and the harvesters are angels.[b]
40"As the weeds are pulled up and
burned in the fire, so it will be at the end
of the age. 41The Son of Man[c] will send
out his angels,[d] and they will weed out of
his kingdom everything that causes sin
and all who do evil. 42They will throw
them into the fiery furnace, where there
will be weeping and gnashing of teeth.[e]
43Then the righteous will shine like the
sun[f] in the kingdom of their Father. He
who has ears, let him hear.[g]

The Parables of the Hidden Treasure and the Pearl

44"The kingdom of heaven is like[h]
treasure hidden in a field. When a man
found it, he hid it again, and then in his
joy went and sold all he had and bought
that field.[i]
45"Again, the kingdom of heaven is
like[j] a merchant looking for fine pearls.
46When he found one of great value, he
went away and sold everything he had
and bought it.

The Parable of the Net

47"Once again, the kingdom of heaven
is like[k] a net that was let down into the
lake and caught all kinds[l] of fish. 48When
it was full, the fishermen pulled it up on
the shore. Then they sat down and collected the good fish in baskets, but threw
the bad away. 49This is how it will be at
the end of the age. The angels will come
and separate the wicked from the righteous[m] 50and throw them into the fiery
furnace, where there will be weeping and
gnashing of teeth.[n]
51"Have you understood all these
things?" Jesus asked.
"Yes," they replied.
52He said to them, "Therefore every
teacher of the law who has been instructed about the kingdom of heaven is like
the owner of a house who brings out of
his storeroom new treasures as well as
old."

A Prophet Without Honor

13:54–58pp — Mk 6:1–6

53When Jesus had finished these parables,[o] he moved on from there. 54Com-
ing to his hometown, he began teaching
the people in their synagogue,[p] and they
were amazed.[q] "Where did this man get
this wisdom and these miraculous powers?" they asked. 55"Isn't this the carpenter's son?[r] Isn't his mother's[s] name
Mary, and aren't his brothers[t] James, Joseph, Simon and Judas? 56Aren't all his
sisters with us? Where then did this man
get all these things?" 57And they took offense[u] at him.
But Jesus said to them, "Only in his
hometown and in his own house is a
prophet without honor."[v]
58And he did not do many miracles
there because of their lack of faith.

13:37 [x]S Mt 8:20
13:38 [y]Jn 8:44,45; 1Jn 3:10
13:39 [z]Joel 3:13 [a]Mt 24:3; 28:20 [b]Rev 14:15
13:41 [c]S Mt 8:20 [d]Mt 24:31
13:42 [e]S Mt 8:12
13:43 [f]Da 12:3 [g]S Mt 11:15
13:44 [h]S ver 24 [i]Isa 55:1; Mt 19:21; Php 3:7,8
13:45 [j]S ver 24
13:47 [k]S ver 24 [l]Mt 22:10
13:49 [m]Mt 25:32
13:50 [n]S Mt 8:12
13:53 [o]S Mt 7:28
13:54 [p]S Mt 4:23 [q]S Mt 7:28
13:55 [r]Lk 3:23; Jn 6:42 [s]S Mt 12:46 [t]S Mt 12:46
13:57 [u]Jn 6:61 [v]Lk 4:24; Jn 4:44

God's seed, preparing for the final harvest, and thus fulfilling God's mission. The Proclaimer also became the final divine Judge sending out heaven's angels to weed His harvest and destroy those who do not accept the gospel.

13:38–42 EVIL AND SUFFERING, Satan—Satan caused the "weeds" in God's world. Weeds are "sons" or followers of Satan. At the end of this world, those who do evil will be punished. Satan has power to deceive and delay. He does not have power to win the final victory. Both God and Satan seek to win followers in this world. God allows Satan's work to flourish for a while to prevent the destruction of His own followers.

13:41–42 SIN, Alienation—Judgment for sin may be delayed, but it cannot be escaped. In the final analysis, sinners will be separated from God and experience His judgment. Sin will be weeded out of existence.

13:43 CHRISTIAN ETHICS, Righteousness—Present circumstances may indicate righteousness is foolish and unrewarding. Ultimately, the righteous will receive their just rewards.

13:44–46 REVELATION, Commitment—God's revelation in Jesus brought God's kingdom to earth (4:17) forcing commitment for or against it. Commitment to the kingdom means willingness to sacrifice all possessions to be part of God's controlling reign on earth.

13:44 SALVATION, Joy—Nothing is as valuable as God's kingdom. It is like treasure hidden in a field, worth selling everything we have to purchase it. The joy of selling all for the kingdom of God is incomparable. No greater joy can come to persons than to become citizens of God's government. That is part of what it means to be saved.

13:44–46 THE CHURCH, God's Kingdom—The kingdom of God is the ultimate value in life. Nothing compares with the joy, fulfillment, and significance of serving Christ. We must be ready to surrender everything which has worth to us so we may be part of God's kingdom. See note on vv 24–30.

13:47–50 THE CHURCH, God's Kingdom—See note on vv 24–30.

13:52 THE CHURCH, God's Kingdom—As the head of the family cares for his family with new and old goods, the Christian teacher (and every believer) must draw on the old truths of Israel's faith and the new message of Jesus. Both Testaments contain the truths of God. Neither should be neglected. Both point to the kingdom of God present in Jesus Christ.

13:52 EDUCATION, Disciples—Jesus' disciples are teachers instructed in the lore of the Kingdom. As such, they combine the riches of their knowledge of Old Testament Scripture with the new interpretations taught by the Master. Christian teachers are constantly challenged to find new ways to communicate ageless truths, as each successive generation faces unique challenges.

13:53–58 JESUS CHRIST, Wisdom of God—See note on Mk 6:1–6.

13:54 EDUCATION, Jesus—See note on 7:28–29.

13:58 MIRACLE, Faith—See note on Mk 6:5–6.

13:58 SALVATION, Belief—Unbelief limits us and God. Compare 17:17–21.

Chapter 14

John the Baptist Beheaded

14:1–12pp — Mk 6:14–29

AT that time Herod[w] the tetrarch heard
the reports about Jesus,[x] 2and he
said to his attendants, "This is John the
Baptist;[y] he has risen from the dead!
That is why miraculous powers are at
work in him."
3Now Herod had arrested John and
bound him and put him in prison[z] because of Herodias, his brother Philip's
wife,[a] 4for John had been saying to him:
"It is not lawful for you to have her."[b]
5Herod wanted to kill John, but he was
afraid of the people, because they considered him a prophet.[c]
6On Herod's birthday the daughter of
Herodias danced for them and pleased
Herod so much 7that he promised with an
oath to give her whatever she asked.
8Prompted by her mother, she said,
"Give me here on a platter the head of
John the Baptist." 9The king was distressed, but because of his oaths and his
dinner guests, he ordered that her request be granted 10and had John beheaded[d] in the prison. 11His head was
brought in on a platter and given to the
girl, who carried it to her mother.
12John's disciples came and took his body
and buried it.[e] Then they went and told
Jesus.

Jesus Feeds the Five Thousand

14:13–21pp — Mk 6:32–44; Lk 9:10–17; Jn 6:1–13
14:13–21Ref — Mt 15:32–38

13When Jesus heard what had happened, he withdrew by boat privately to a
solitary place. Hearing of this, the crowds
followed him on foot from the towns.
14When Jesus landed and saw a large
crowd, he had compassion on them[f] and
healed their sick.[g]
15As evening approached, the disciples
came to him and said, "This is a remote
place, and it's already getting late. Send
the crowds away, so they can go to the
villages and buy themselves some food."
16Jesus replied, "They do not need to
go away. You give them something to
eat."
17"We have here only five loaves[h] of
bread and two fish," they answered.
18"Bring them here to me," he said.
19And he directed the people to sit down
on the grass. Taking the five loaves and
the two fish and looking up to heaven, he
gave thanks and broke the loaves.[i] Then
he gave them to the disciples, and the
disciples gave them to the people. 20They
all ate and were satisfied, and the disciples picked up twelve basketfuls of broken pieces that were left over. 21The
number of those who ate was about five
thousand men, besides women and children.

Jesus Walks on the Water

14:22–33pp — Mk 6:45–51; Jn 6:15–21
14:34–36pp — Mk 6:53–56

22Immediately Jesus made the disciples
get into the boat and go on ahead of him
to the other side, while he dismissed the
crowd. 23After he had dismissed them, he
went up on a mountainside by himself to
pray.[j] When evening came, he was there
alone, 24but the boat was already a considerable distance[c] from land, buffeted
by the waves because the wind was
against it.
25During the fourth watch of the night

14:1 [w]Mk 8:15; Lk 3:1,19; 13:31; 23:7,8; Ac 4:27; 12:1 [x]Lk 9:7-9
14:2 [y]S Mt 3:1
14:3 [z]Mt 4:12; 11:2 [a]Lk 3:19,20
14:4 [b]Lev 18:16; 20:21
14:5 [c]S Mt 11:9
14:10 [d]Mt 17:12
14:12 [e]Ac 8:2
14:14 [f]S Mt 9:36 [g]S Mt 4:23
14:17 [h]Mt 16:9
14:19 [i]1Sa 9:13; Mt 26:26; Mk 8:6; Lk 9:16; 24:30; Ac 2:42; 20:7,11; 27:35; 1Co 10:16; 1Ti 4:4
14:23 [j]S Lk 3:21

[c]24 Greek *many stadia*

14:1–6 JESUS CHRIST, Authority—See note on 13:10–17,34–35.

14:1 JESUS CHRIST, John—The ministries of Jesus and John were closely related, but they were not identical. Jesus was not John returned to earth. He was the unique Son of God fulfilling God's purpose and mission as prepared for in the Old Testament.

14:2 MIRACLE, Revelation—Herod responded not in faith but in superstition. He had ordered the execution of John the Baptist, and his conscience affected his judgment. Instead of acclaiming Jesus' power for working miracles, he described "powers at work in him." Jesus' miraculous powers were obvious to all. Only faith saw God revealed in them. See note on 12:22–24.

14:9–11 HUMANITY, Moral Consciousness—See note on Mk 6:26–28.

14:13–21 MIRACLE, Christ—Miracles testify to Christ's compassion and call His church to similar compassion for the needy. Jesus sought privacy to rest and teach His disciples. The crowds came seeking help. Jesus surrendered the opportunity to meet His needs because He cared for the needy multitudes. He miraculously healed the sick and then supplied food for the hungry, despite the unbelieving protests of His followers. Bible students have tried to give a natural explanation of the feeding miracle. In so doing they go against the plain biblical statement. Christ was able to do what even His own disciples thought impossible. A needy world continues to wait for a church to have faith to meet their needs.

14:13–14,23 PRAYER, Jesus' Example—Jesus withdrew to pray. See note on Jn 6:15. His withdrawal preceded the feeding of the 5,000. He interrupted His prayer retreat to show compassion to people. See Guide to Extended Prayer, pp. 1767–1769.

14:14 JESUS CHRIST, Miracles—Compassion, not selfish ambition, prompted Jesus to use His divine power. Compare note on 4:1–11.

14:19 PRAYER, Thanksgiving—Blessing the food was characteristic of Jesus. Jesus often looked up to heaven when He prayed (Jn 17:1).

14:22–33 MIRACLE, Christ—Faith is the key to miracles. Jesus walked on water to help the disciples in distress. Instead of recognizing help coming, the disciples let the miracle terrify them. Peter tested Jesus by asking permission to walk on water, too. Jesus tested Peter's faith by inviting him to come. Doubt made Peter fail. Jesus' actions led the disciples to reaffirm their faith in Christ as God's Son. God's miracles reaffirm our faith and lead us to commit ourselves more deeply to His work.

14:25–33 JESUS CHRIST, Son of God—Jesus' miracles and His power to help His disciples do what seemed impossible showed His divine nature. Jesus' response, "It is I" recalls the

Jesus went out to them, walking on the lake. 26 When the disciples saw him walking on the lake, they were terrified. "It's a ghost,"[k] they said, and cried out in fear.

27 But Jesus immediately said to them: "Take courage![l] It is I. Don't be afraid."[m]

28 "Lord, if it's you," Peter replied, "tell me to come to you on the water."

29 "Come," he said.

Then Peter got down out of the boat, walked on the water and came toward Jesus. 30 But when he saw the wind, he was afraid and, beginning to sink, cried out, "Lord, save me!"

31 Immediately Jesus reached out his hand and caught him. "You of little faith,"[n] he said, "why did you doubt?"

32 And when they climbed into the boat, the wind died down. 33 Then those who were in the boat worshiped him, saying, "Truly you are the Son of God."[o]

34 When they had crossed over, they landed at Gennesaret. 35 And when the men of that place recognized Jesus, they sent word to all the surrounding country. People brought all their sick to him 36 and begged him to let the sick just touch the edge of his cloak,[p] and all who touched him were healed.

Chapter 15

Clean and Unclean

15:1–20pp — Mk 7:1–23

THEN some Pharisees and teachers of the law came to Jesus from Jerusalem and asked, 2 "Why do your disciples break the tradition of the elders? They don't wash their hands before they eat!"[q]

3 Jesus replied, "And why do you break the command of God for the sake of your tradition? 4 For God said, 'Honor your father and mother'[d][r] and 'Anyone who curses his father or mother must be put to death.'[e][s] 5 But you say that if a man says to his father or mother, 'Whatever help you might otherwise have received from me is a gift devoted to God,' 6 he is not to 'honor his father[f]' with it. Thus you nullify the word of God for the sake of your tradition. 7 You hypocrites! Isaiah was right when he prophesied about you:

8 " 'These people honor me with their lips,
but their hearts are far from me.
9 They worship me in vain;
their teachings are but rules taught by men.'[t][g][u]"

10 Jesus called the crowd to him and said, "Listen and understand. 11 What goes into a man's mouth does not make him 'unclean,'[v] but what comes out of his mouth, that is what makes him 'unclean.'"[w]

12 Then the disciples came to him and asked, "Do you know that the Pharisees were offended when they heard this?"

13 He replied, "Every plant that my heavenly Father has not planted[x] will be pulled up by the roots. 14 Leave them; they are blind guides.[h][y] If a blind man leads a blind man, both will fall into a pit."[z]

15 Peter said, "Explain the parable to us."[a]

[d] *4* Exodus 20:12; Deut. 5:16 [e] *4* Exodus 21:17; Lev. 20:9 [f] *6* Some manuscripts *father or his mother* [g] *9* Isaiah 29:13 [h] *14* Some manuscripts *guides of the blind*

14:26 [k]Lk 24:37
14:27 [l]Mt 9:2; Ac 23:11 [m]Da 10:12; Mt 17:7; 28:10; Lk 1:13,30; 2:10; Ac 18:9; 23:11; Rev 1:17
14:31 [n]S Mt 6:30
14:33 [o]Ps 2:7; S Mt 4:3
14:36 [p]S Mt 9:20
15:2 [q]Lk 11:38
15:4 [r]Ex 20:12; Dt 5:16; Eph 6:2 [s]Ex 21:17; Lev 20:9
15:9 [t]Col 2:20-22 [u]Isa 29:13; Mal 2:2
15:11 [v]S Ac 10:14, 15 [w]ver 18
15:13 [x]Isa 60:21; 61:3
15:14 [y]Mt 23:16, 24; Ro 2:19 [z]Lk 6:39
15:15 [a]Mt 13:36

Greek reader to Ex 3:14 and the explanation of God's personal name as "I Am." Similarly Peter's call, "Lord," recalls the Jewish use of Lord (Greek *kurios*) instead of pronouncing the holy name of God. Fear and worship are responses appropriate only to the presence of God. Jesus as Son of God represented the divine presence on earth doing what only God can do.

14:30 SALVATION, Definition—Jesus Christ stands for God in all things concerning our salvation. Peter called Him Lord, and so did the apostolic church. Jesus, our Savior, saves us from fear and from all our foes. Fear of natural elements, such as the wind, is different from reverential fear of God. See note on 9:8.

15:1–20 CHRISTIAN ETHICS, Moral Imperatives—The ethical practices of Jesus' listeners had eroded to the point that though they read and talked about the letter of the Law they missed its spirit. Declaring certain goods and services as dedicated to God, these people failed to honor their parents—a ruse to get ahead for themselves. Actions are open windows to the soul. These peoples' attitudes (those dynamics which shape our actions) were apparent. They nurtured evil thoughts until immoral actions emerged. Conversion must work at the attitude level of our personalities. Wanting the right is more important than fulfilling tradition's legalistic requirements and interpretations See note on 12:1–14.

15:3–6 FAMILY, Role Relationships—Family responsibilities are not to be set aside to fulfill religious obligations. The law required faithful Jews to care for their parents in their old age, but oral tradition provided a way for selfish children to avoid this responsibility. By declaring all their property to be "corban," given to God, they could tell their parents they had no money available to help them (Mk 7:1–13). Jesus placed His trust firmly on the biblical revelation and rejected the oral tradition which pious Jews believed was as binding as the law.

15:7–9 HOLY SCRIPTURE, Authoritative—The Old Testament prophet (Isa 29:13) described a major problem of the people who regularly chose to use the right words but rarely worshiped God by following His will. Christ confronted a people who followed laws but missed the attitude inside the laws. Scripture seeks to change the heart and create a new person, not encourage the self-centered person to find new reasons for selfish actions. Jesus fought against human interpretations and traditions that defeated the obvious intention of Scripture.

15:10–20 EVIL AND SUFFERING, Human Origin—See note on Mk 7:14–23.

15:13 GOD, Sovereignty—Jesus was confident that God, our Heavenly Father, is in control of this world and in the end shall accomplish His purposes. God is not only Father to us, but He is also sovereign Lord who is working in the world in times and places and ways that are not always evident to us. When time is over, we will see that the Father's sovereignty has been clearly demonstrated, His purposes fully achieved.

16"Are you still so dull?"[b] Jesus asked
them. 17"Don't you see that whatever enters the mouth goes into the stomach and
then out of the body? 18But the things
that come out of the mouth come from
the heart,[c] and these make a man 'unclean.' 19For out of the heart come evil
thoughts, murder, adultery, sexual immorality, theft, false testimony, slander.[d]
20These are what make a man 'unclean';[e] but eating with unwashed hands
does not make him 'unclean.'"

The Faith of the Canaanite Woman

15:21–28pp — Mk 7:24–30

21Leaving that place, Jesus withdrew to
the region of Tyre and Sidon.[f] 22A Canaanite woman from that vicinity came to
him, crying out, "Lord, Son of David,[g]
have mercy on me! My daughter is suffering terribly from demon-possession."[h]
23Jesus did not answer a word. So his
disciples came to him and urged him,
"Send her away, for she keeps crying out
after us."
24He answered, "I was sent only to the
lost sheep of Israel."[i]
25The woman came and knelt before
him.[j] "Lord, help me!" she said.
26He replied, "It is not right to take the
children's bread and toss it to their
dogs."
27"Yes, Lord," she said, "but even the
dogs eat the crumbs that fall from their
masters' table."
28Then Jesus answered, "Woman, you
have great faith![k] Your request is granted." And her daughter was healed from
that very hour.

Jesus Feeds the Four Thousand

15:29–31pp — Mk 7:31–37
15:32–39pp — Mk 8:1–10
15:32–39Ref — Mt 14:13–21

29Jesus left there and went along the
Sea of Galilee. Then he went up on a
mountainside and sat down. 30Great
crowds came to him, bringing the lame,
the blind, the crippled, the mute and
many others, and laid them at his feet;
and he healed them.[l] 31The people were
amazed when they saw the mute speaking, the crippled made well, the lame
walking and the blind seeing. And they
praised the God of Israel.[m]
32Jesus called his disciples to him and
said, "I have compassion for these people;[n] they have already been with me
three days and have nothing to eat. I do
not want to send them away hungry, or
they may collapse on the way."
33His disciples answered, "Where
could we get enough bread in this remote
place to feed such a crowd?"
34"How many loaves do you have?"
Jesus asked.
"Seven," they replied, "and a few
small fish."
35He told the crowd to sit down on the
ground. 36Then he took the seven loaves
and the fish, and when he had given
thanks, he broke them[o] and gave them to
the disciples, and they in turn to the people. 37They all ate and were satisfied. Afterward the disciples picked up seven
basketfuls of broken pieces that were left
over.[p] 38The number of those who ate
was four thousand, besides women and
children. 39After Jesus had sent the crowd
away, he got into the boat and went to
the vicinity of Magadan.

Chapter 16

The Demand for a Sign

16:1–12pp — Mk 8:11–21

THE Pharisees and Sadducees[q] came to
Jesus and tested him by asking him
to show them a sign from heaven.[r]

15:16 [b]Mt 16:9
15:18 [c]Mt 12:34; Lk 6:45; Jas 3:6
15:19 [d]Gal 5:19-21
15:20 [e]Ro 14:14
15:21 [f]S Mt 11:21
15:22 [g]S Mt 9:27 [h]S Mt 4:24
15:24 [i]Mt 10:6,23; Ro 15:8
15:25 [j]S Mt 8:2
15:28 [k]S Mt 9:22
15:30 [l]S Mt 4:23
15:31 [m]S Mt 9:8
15:32 [n]S Mt 9:36
15:36 [o]S Mt 14:19
15:37 [p]Mt 16:10
16:1 [q]S Ac 4:1 [r]S Mt 12:38

15:17–19 REVELATION, Faithfulness—Fidelity to God's law is not observing the rules which "look" right but observing the rules which change and affect the inside of a person's heart. God is not interested in outside appearances unless they are the true reflection of a corrected and "right" attitude inside.

15:21–28 MIRACLE, Faith—Faith, not race or group membership, makes miracles possible. The woman, though not a Jew, confessed her strong faith. Jesus responded as if He would not heal her daughter. He expressed the primary focus of His personal ministry on the Jews and tested the woman's faith. The woman's faith persisted. Jesus responded to her faith and healed her daughter. Jesus focused on Jews but responded compassionately to Gentiles with faith. Jesus still has power to satisfy our most desperate needs. Our lack of faith is the only thing which robs us of God's power in our lives.

15:21–28 PRAYER, Persistence—Jesus had expressed distress at the disciples' lack of faith. He used the Canaanite woman's persistent faith as an object lesson for the disciples. Prayer is not a onetime test of God but an ongoing communication with Him.

15:22 JESUS CHRIST, Son of David—See note on 1:1. The foreigner correctly identified Jesus as Messiah, but she gained healing for her daughter through persistent faith, not proper identification.

15:29–39 MIRACLE, Christ—Miracles reveal Christ's compassion and lead people to praise God. Jesus' active healing ministry brought needy crowds to Him and resulted in praise for God because such extraordinary power comes only from God. Jesus was moved with compassion on the crowd and fed them with a small amount of food. See note on the similar account in 14:14–33.

15:30–31 DISCIPLESHIP, Handicapped—Jesus did not turn away the handicapped, but blessed them according to their needs. Our compassion as disciples should cause us to minister to the needs of handicapped persons. Churches, wherever possible, should have special programs and make special provision for handicapped people. Our work with the handicapped should bring praise to God. See note on Lk 14:13.

15:36 PRAYER, Thanksgiving—See note on 14:19.

16:1–4 JESUS CHRIST, Temptation—Jesus faced temptation not only from the evil one, but also from His enemies. The politically influential Sadducees tempted Him, as did the popular Pharisees (19:3). Jesus lived in an environment of tempta-

2He replied,[i] "When evening comes,
you say, 'It will be fair weather, for the
sky is red,' 3and in the morning, 'Today it
will be stormy, for the sky is red and
overcast.' You know how to interpret the
appearance of the sky, but you cannot interpret the signs of the times.[s] 4A wicked
and adulterous generation looks for a miraculous sign, but none will be given it
except the sign of Jonah."[t] Jesus then
left them and went away.

The Yeast of the Pharisees and Sadducees

5When they went across the lake, the
disciples forgot to take bread. 6"Be careful," Jesus said to them. "Be on your
guard against the yeast of the Pharisees
and Sadducees."[u]
7They discussed this among themselves
and said, "It is because we didn't bring
any bread."
8Aware of their discussion, Jesus asked,
"You of little faith,[v] why are you talking
among yourselves about having no bread?
9Do you still not understand? Don't you
remember the five loaves for the five
thousand, and how many basketfuls you
gathered?[w] 10Or the seven loaves for the
four thousand, and how many basketfuls
you gathered?[x] 11How is it you don't understand that I was not talking to you
about bread? But be on your guard against
the yeast of the Pharisees and Sadducees." 12Then they understood that he
was not telling them to guard against the
yeast used in bread, but against the teaching of the Pharisees and Sadducees.[y]

Peter's Confession of Christ

16:13–16pp — Mk 8:27–29; Lk 9:18–20

13When Jesus came to the region of
Caesarea Philippi, he asked his disciples,
"Who do people say the Son of Man is?"
14They replied, "Some say John the
Baptist;[z] others say Elijah; and still others, Jeremiah or one of the prophets."[a]
15"But what about you?" he asked.
"Who do you say I am?"
16Simon Peter answered, "You are the
Christ,[j] the Son of the living God."[b]
17Jesus replied, "Blessed are you, Simon son of Jonah, for this was not revealed to you by man,[c] but by my Father
in heaven.[d] 18And I tell you that you are

16:3 [s]Lk 12:54-56
16:4 [t]Mt 12:39
16:6 [u]Lk 12:1
16:8 [v]S Mt 6:30
16:9 [w]Mt 14:17-21
16:10 [x]Mt 15:34-38
16:12 [y]S Ac 4:1
16:14 [z]S Mt 3:1 [a]Mk 6:15; Jn 1:21
16:16 [b]S Mt 4:3; Ps 42:2; Jer 10:10; Ac 14:15; 2Co 6:16; 1Th 1:9; 1Ti 3:15; Heb 10:31; 12:22
16:17 [c]1Co 15:50; Eph 6:12; Heb 2:14 [d]S Mt 13:11

[i]2 Some early manuscripts do not have the rest of verse 2 and all of verse 3. [j]16 Or *Messiah*; also in verse 20

tion and faultfinding (22:15–40; Mk 8:11; 10:2; 12:13–15; Lk 11:16). See note on 12:38–42.

16:1–4 MIRACLE, Vocabulary—Miracles test our faith. We cannot test God with them. See note on 12:38–42. The request was a test question. The reference to weather signs was an appeal to observe spiritual phenomena as skillfully as natural phenomena. God may reveal Himself in such signs, but we cannot force Him to do so. As a preacher of righteousness, Jonah encouraged Nineveh's repentance. Could the religious leaders expect more? Would even resurrection after three days' burial convince them? We must follow God in faith, not on proof. No proof can ever lead to faith. Is there a greater miracle than God's grace provoking us to repent?

16:4 REVELATION, Jesus Christ—The only visible sign any generation needs for repentance and faith is the one God revealed through Jonah, the resurrection hope. The new sign they needed but did not see was the incarnation of truth, Jesus Christ.

16:15–17 REVELATION, Jesus Christ—Peter understood that Jesus, the Son of God, is God's revelation of Himself in flesh for human understanding. Confession of faith in Christ comes not through human logic but through divine revelation.

16:16–17,27 GOD, Trinity—Here is a strategic passage that ties together the person and work of both God the Father and God the Son. Jesus was keenly conscious of His unique relationship to God, His Father. At a strategic turning point in Jesus' teaching ministry, Peter declared that Jesus is the Christ (Messiah) and the Son of the living God. Peter did not yet understand all that that means (vv 22–23). He could not accept the way of suffering Jesus charted out for His ministry, a way that will result in His final appearance in His Father's glory when Jesus Himself will act as Judge of all men. What Jesus did in His ministry of suffering and death and what Jesus did in establishing His church are not something separate and apart from the work of God. These are very much the will of God, the work of God. When Jesus climaxes His work, coming again, it will be in the glory of God His Father, showing that the work of one is virtually the work of the other. These verses suggest that the Persons of the Trinity do not function independently of each other. Even though it is not always apparent, what one does the others are also involved in. We must draw that conclusion if we want to avoid tritheism, the error of separating the three Persons of the Trinity into three separate Gods. Jesus' earthly life developed as a result of the unseen work of God through Him. When Jesus' ministry climaxes at His second coming, we will see His triumph as the full manifestation of God, the glory of God, not just of Jesus Himself. Jesus will then act as Judge, a prerogative of God Himself. There is a distinction between Jesus and God, but there is also an identification between them. That is part of the mystery of the Trinity.

16:16 JESUS CHRIST, Christ—Peter confessed Jesus as "the Anointed One" (Greek *christos*; Hebrew *meshiach*). The title originally applied to the king as anointed by God (1 Sa 10:1; 16:13; Ps 2:2) and was connected to the understanding that the king was God's son (2 Sa 7:14; Ps 2:7). Jesus applauded Peter's insight but did not want the news spread because of the possibility of being misunderstood as a political messiah rather than a Suffering Servant (Mt 16:20–25). Compare 26:63–64; Mk 14:61; Lk 22:67; Gal 3:1).

16:17–19 SALVATION, Confession—Christ builds His church upon the confession that He is the Messiah, the Son of the living God. The confession leads to willingness to die with Jesus rather than hold expectations of earthly power (vv 21–26). Only personal experience with God leads to such confession. The keys of the kingdom are given to those who make that confession. Compare 18:18; Jn 20:23.

16:17 SALVATION, Blessing—Simon Peter was blessed because he made the great confession of v 16. All who confess Jesus as the Messiah, the Son of the living God, are likewise blessed.

16:18–19 THE CHURCH, Intention of Christ—The church exists because of the intention of God to create for Himself a people who would obey Him. Jesus began the church as He ministered among people and called them to repentance. Three general views are held by Christians concerning Christ's intentions for the church. (1) Many Christians believe that the authority of the church resides in Simon Peter. Jesus built the church on Simon Peter, and ultimate authority continues in the successors to the apostle. This interpretation depends on the words "Peter" and "rock" being interpreted as one and the

Peter,[k] [e] and on this rock I will build my
church,[f] and the gates of Hades[l] will
not overcome it.[m] 19I will give you the
keys[g] of the kingdom of heaven; whatever you bind on earth will be[n] bound in
heaven, and whatever you loose on earth
will be[n] loosed in heaven."[h] 20Then he
warned his disciples not to tell anyone[i]
that he was the Christ.

Jesus Predicts His Death

16:21–28pp — Mk 8:31–9:1; Lk 9:22–27

21From that time on Jesus began to explain to his disciples that he must go to
Jerusalem[j] and suffer many things[k] at
the hands of the elders, chief priests and
teachers of the law,[l] and that he must be
killed[m] and on the third day[n] be raised to
life.[o]
22Peter took him aside and began to rebuke him. "Never, Lord!" he said. "This
shall never happen to you!"
23Jesus turned and said to Peter, "Get
behind me, Satan![p] You are a stumbling
block to me; you do not have in mind the
things of God, but the things of men."
24Then Jesus said to his disciples, "If
anyone would come after me, he must
deny himself and take up his cross and
follow me.[q] 25For whoever wants to save
his life[o] will lose it, but whoever loses
his life for me will find it.[r] 26What good
will it be for a man if he gains the whole
world, yet forfeits his soul? Or what can a
man give in exchange for his soul? 27For
the Son of Man[s] is going to come[t] in his
Father's glory with his angels, and then
he will reward each person according to
what he has done.[u] 28I tell you the truth,

16:18 [e]Jn 1:42 [f]S Eph 2:20 **16:19** [g]Isa 22:22; Rev 3:7 [h]Mt 18:18; Jn 20:23 **16:20** [i]S Mk 8:30 **16:21** [j]S Lk 9:51 [k]Ps 22:6; Isa 53:3; Mt 26:67,68; Mk 10:34; Lk 17:25; Jn 18:22, 23; 19:3 [l]Mt 27:1,2 [m]Ac 2:23; 3:13 [n]Hos 6:2; Mt 12:40; Lk 24:21, 46; Jn 2:19; 1Co 15:3,4 [o]Mt 17:22,23; Mk 9:31; Lk 9:22; 18:31-33; 24:6,7 **16:23** [p]S Mt 4:10 **16:24** [q]Mt 10:38; Lk 14:27 **16:25** [r]S Jn 12:25 **16:27** [s]S Mt 8:20 [t]S Lk 17:30; Jn 14:3; Ac 1:11; S 1Co 1:7; S 1Th 2:19; 4:16; S Rev 1:7; 22:7,12, 20 [u]2Ch 6:23; Job 34:11; Ps 62:12; Jer 17:10; Eze 18:20; 1Co 3:12-15; 2Co 5:10; Rev 22:12

[k]*18 Peter* means *rock.* [l]*18* Or *hell* [m]*18* Or *not prove stronger than it* [n]*19* Or *have been* [o]*25* The Greek word means either *life* or *soul*; also in verse 26.

same. The two Greek words are different. Both words mean "rock." "Peter" is the Greek *petros,* which means "pebble." "Rock" (*petra*) refers to a large "foundation stone." Jesus promised to build His church on a foundation stone. The two words are different and appear to call for a different interpretation. (2) Many other Christians believe that the church is built on people with like faith as Simon Peter. When asked the question concerning the true identity of Jesus, Simon answered: "You are the Christ, the Son of the living God." Those who have this kind of faith will make up the church. Simon Peter is a "pebble," who along with many other believers are built on the "foundation stone" of faith. This kind of faith is acquired only by revelation of God. (3) A third view says the "foundation stone" is Jesus, who possibly gestured toward Himself when He said: "On this rock I will build my church." Simon Peter is a small but important "pebble," who along with many others makes up the church which Christ founded. The church is eternal in nature. The greatest forces cannot destroy the church founded by "the Christ, the Son of the living God." "Hades" is a Greek term meaning "the place of the dead." Not even death, the final enemy, can take away those who belong to Christ. The keys of the kingdom of heaven are bestowed upon the church. Again, at least two differing views are held by Christians concerning the authority given by Christ. (1) Those who accept Simon Peter as the foundation of the church usually believe that Jesus gave the keys to the kingdom, i.e. authority, to Simon Peter as well. The authority also extends to His successors. (2) Other Christians understand in accord with the rest of the Bible (1 Pe 2:4–12) that the keys of the kingdom belong to the church in general. Jesus gave the church a stewardship responsibility. "Binding" and "loosing" refer to the work of the church. If forgiveness is preached and extended, forgiveness is possible. If the church shirks its responsibility, forgiveness is less likely, if not impossible, for the vast multitudes of the people of the world. Forgiveness shall be known by other people in direct relation to the proclamation of the way to know forgiveness by the church. As God's visible kingdom, the church uses its authority to represent His purity and holiness on earth. See notes on 3:2; 18:15–20. The church has responsibility to make known God's offer of forgiveness, both in its proclamation to the world and its practice before the world.

16:21–23 JESUS CHRIST, Temptation—Jesus was tempted by a close friend, Simon Peter. The evil one sought to keep Jesus from suffering as God's Messiah. See note on 4:1–11. So did Peter. Jesus recognized the voice of the ancient enemy in the solicitous concern of a friend. To Peter's wish that He should not go to Jerusalem and die, Jesus replied that Peter was speaking the devil's will and that such concerns had to be put behind Him as He set about His determined march to the cross.

16:21–23 JESUS CHRIST, Death—This is the first of Jesus' three predictions of His death (17:22–33; 20:18–19; Mk 8:31–33; 9:31–32; 10:32–34; Lk 9:19–22,44–45; 18:31–34). Despite popular expectations and hopes of new political power, Jesus knew He could fulfill His mission as God's Anointed only by death for their sins (Isa 53).

16:21–27 EVIL AND SUFFERING, Endurance—Peter resisted Jesus' forecast of His suffering and death. Peter's resistance was a temptation from Satan. Peter represents our human tendency to avoid suffering and unwittingly accommodate ourselves to a realm ruled by Satan. Jesus, instead, calls us to His cross and, through it, to His kingdom. To belong to Christ is to follow His way of self-denial. All other roads are laid out by Satan.

16:21–26 SALVATION, Justification—Compare Mk 8:31–38. There is nothing we can give in exchange for our life. We can never save ourselves. Christ, however, came to suffer for us on the cross. He is the One who puts us in right relationship with God through His sacrificial death as the loving Suffering Servant. See note on Isa 53:11.

16:26 HUMANITY, Worth—Nothing in the world is as valuable as a human being. At the very least, the soul is the same totality of life which the Old Testament indicated. The teachings of Jesus appear to heighten its meaning to refer to the very basic spiritual nature of a human being. The soul is that which survives the death of the human body. Yet it also appears to be lacking something until reunited with the resurrection body. See note on Mk 8:36–37.

16:27–28 JESUS CHRIST, Son of Man—See note on 8:20. The Son of man was predicted by Daniel (7:13–14) as coming at the end of time to establish an everlasting kingdom. Jesus pointed away from His appearance on earth in the first century to the second coming when eternal rewards will be given. Compare Ps 62:12. V 28 is difficult to interpret. Perhaps the fall of Jerusalem and its proof that Jerusalem's hopes did not lie in political or military action is the best suggestion.

16:27 LAST THINGS, Return Purposes—Faithful discipleship is motivated by the expectation of Christ's return. Especially so, when the return is seen to have as one purpose the rewarding of a disciple's service (5:12). Conduct or deeds (Greek *praxis*) will be the basis for rewards, not mere professions or verbal claims (7:21). Adding to the majesty of His return will be the accompaniment of the angels. Their presence will not only enhance the glory, but they will serve as God's agents for the final ingathering (24:31). With no distinction made here between the righteous and unrighteous, the indication is that all persons can expect judgment based on their deeds. Only those who have followed Christ in self-denying

some who are standing here will not taste
death before they see the Son of Man
coming in his kingdom."

Chapter 17

The Transfiguration

17:1–8pp — Lk 9:28–36
17:1–13pp — Mk 9:2–13

AFTER six days Jesus took with him Peter, James and John[v] the brother of
James, and led them up a high mountain
by themselves. 2There he was transfigured before them. His face shone like the
sun, and his clothes became as white as
the light. 3Just then there appeared before them Moses and Elijah, talking with
Jesus.
4Peter said to Jesus, "Lord, it is good
for us to be here. If you wish, I will put
up three shelters—one for you, one for
Moses and one for Elijah."
5While he was still speaking, a bright
cloud enveloped them, and a voice from
the cloud said, "This is my Son, whom I
love; with him I am well pleased.[w] Listen
to him!"[x]
6When the disciples heard this, they
fell facedown to the ground, terrified.
7But Jesus came and touched them. "Get
up," he said. "Don't be afraid."[y] 8When
they looked up, they saw no one except
Jesus.
9As they were coming down the mountain, Jesus instructed them, "Don't tell
anyone[z] what you have seen, until the
Son of Man[a] has been raised from the
dead."[b]
10The disciples asked him, "Why then
do the teachers of the law say that Elijah
must come first?"
11Jesus replied, "To be sure, Elijah
comes and will restore all things.[c] 12But I
tell you, Elijah has already come,[d] and
they did not recognize him, but have
done to him everything they wished.[e] In
the same way the Son of Man is going to
suffer[f] at their hands." 13Then the disciples understood that he was talking to
them about John the Baptist.[g]

The Healing of a Boy With a Demon

17:14–19pp — Mk 9:14–28; Lk 9:37–42

14When they came to the crowd, a man
approached Jesus and knelt before him.
15"Lord, have mercy on my son," he said.
"He has seizures[h] and is suffering greatly. He often falls into the fire or into the
water. 16I brought him to your disciples,
but they could not heal him."
17"O unbelieving and perverse generation," Jesus replied, "how long shall I
stay with you? How long shall I put up
with you? Bring the boy here to me."
18Jesus rebuked the demon, and it came
out of the boy, and he was healed from
that moment.
19Then the disciples came to Jesus in
private and asked, "Why couldn't we
drive it out?"
20He replied, "Because you have so little faith. I tell you the truth, if you have
faith[i] as small as a mustard seed,[j] you
can say to this mountain, 'Move from
here to there' and it will move.[k] Nothing
will be impossible for you.[p] "
22When they came together in Galilee,
he said to them, "The Son of Man[l] is
going to be betrayed into the hands of
men. 23They will kill him,[m] and on the
third day[n] he will be raised to life."[o]
And the disciples were filled with grief.

The Temple Tax

24After Jesus and his disciples arrived
in Capernaum, the collectors of the two-
drachma tax[p] came to Peter and asked,
"Doesn't your teacher pay the temple
tax[q] ?"
25"Yes, he does," he replied.
When Peter came into the house, Jesus

17:1 [v]S Mt 4:21
17:5 [w]S Mt 3:17 [x]Ac 3:22,23
17:7 [y]S Mt 14:27
17:9 [z]S Mk 8:30 [a]S Mt 8:20 [b]S Mt 16:21
17:11 [c]Mal 4:6; Lk 1:16,17
17:12 [d]S Mt 11:14 [e]Mt 14:3,10 [f]S Mt 16:21
17:13 [g]S Mt 3:1
17:15 [h]Mt 4:24
17:20 [i]S Mt 21:21 [j]Mt 13:31; Lk 17:6 [k]1Co 13:2
17:22 [l]S Mt 8:20
17:23 [m]Ac 2:23; 3:13 [n]S Mt 16:21 [o]S Mt 16:21
17:24 [p]Ex 30:13

[p]20 Some manuscripts *you.* [21]*But this kind does not go out except by prayer and fasting.* [q]24 Greek *the two drachmas*

faith can expect rewards (16:24).

17:1–13 JESUS CHRIST, Son of God—Jesus is God's Son, worthy of human worship and obedience. God revealed Christ's heavenly glory in the transfiguration and thus confirmed Peter's confession. See note on 16:16. Only the resurrection would reveal the true nature of Christ. Until then public proclamation was dangerous.

17:1–8 WORSHIP, Individual—Worship is the appropriate human response to God's presence. See note on Ex 33:9–11.

17:9–13 JESUS CHRIST, Resurrection—The resurrection was not a surprise. God planned it. Jesus expected it. The resurrection meant Jesus had to die first. Expecting death did not make the experience easier. The agony of Gethsemane was real (26:36–46). The disciples could not understand that. Suffering Messiah was not what they expected.

17:14–20 MIRACLE, Faith—Lack of faith limits God's people. Faith brings Christ's miraculous response. See note on 13:58. This narrative of a onetime incident in the life of Christ teaches us the importance of faith. It does not lay down a rule by which we can judge our own or someone else's faith. Christ does not choose to heal every sickness, even of people of faith. Here demon possession caused epileptic fits. Elsewhere it resulted in insane violence (8:28), blindness and inability to speak (12:23), and departure from normal civilized living habits (Lk 8:27). Whatever powers demons exercised over people, Jesus had the power to expel the demons and restore victims to normal life. He exercised His power in response to human faith.

17:17–20 PRAYER, Hindrances—Lack of faith cripples understanding and spiritual power.

17:22 JESUS CHRIST, Death—See note on 16:21–23; Mk 9:31.

17:24–27 HUMANITY, Relationships—Christians are children of God. At the same time, we live in this world and are related to other peoples. As a part of the world, we are expected to help bear the cost of its government. See 1 Pe 2:13.

was the first to speak. “What do you
think, Simon?” he asked. “From whom
do the kings of the earth collect duty and
taxes[q]—from their own sons or from
others?”
26“From others,” Peter answered.
“Then the sons are exempt,” Jesus said
to him. 27“But so that we may not offend[r] them, go to the lake and throw out
your line. Take the first fish you catch;
open its mouth and you will find a four-
drachma coin. Take it and give it to them
for my tax and yours.”

Chapter 18

The Greatest in the Kingdom of Heaven

18:1–5pp — Mk 9:33–37; Lk 9:46–48

At that time the disciples came to Jesus
and asked, “Who is the greatest in
the kingdom of heaven?”
2He called a little child and had him
stand among them. 3And he said: “I tell
you the truth, unless you change and become like little children,[s] you will never
enter the kingdom of heaven.[t] 4There-
fore, whoever humbles himself like this
child is the greatest in the kingdom of
heaven.[u]
5“And whoever welcomes a little child
like this in my name welcomes me.[v] 6But
if anyone causes one of these little ones
who believe in me to sin,[w] it would be
better for him to have a large millstone
hung around his neck and to be drowned
in the depths of the sea.[x]
7“Woe to the world because of the
things that cause people to sin! Such
things must come, but woe to the man
through whom they come![y] 8If your hand
or your foot causes you to sin[z] cut it off
and throw it away. It is better for you to
enter life maimed or crippled than to
have two hands or two feet and be
thrown into eternal fire. 9And if your eye
causes you to sin,[a] gouge it out and
throw it away. It is better for you to enter
life with one eye than to have two eyes
and be thrown into the fire of hell.[b]

The Parable of the Lost Sheep

18:12–14pp — Lk 15:4–7

10“See that you do not look down on
one of these little ones. For I tell you that
their angels[c] in heaven always see the
face of my Father in heaven.[r]
12“What do you think? If a man owns a
hundred sheep, and one of them wanders
away, will he not leave the ninety-nine
on the hills and go to look for the one that
wandered off? 13And if he finds it, I tell
you the truth, he is happier about that
one sheep than about the ninety-nine
that did not wander off. 14In the same
way your Father in heaven is not willing
that any of these little ones should be
lost.

A Brother Who Sins Against You

15“If your brother sins against you,[s] go

17:25 [q]Mt 22:17-21; Ro 13:7
17:27 [r]Jn 6:61
18:3 [s]Mt 19:14; 1Pe 2:2 [t]S Mt 3:2
18:4 [u]S Mk 9:35
18:5 [v]Mt 10:40
18:6 [w]S Mt 5:29 [x]Mk 9:42; Lk 17:2
18:7 [y]Lk 17:1
18:8 [z]S Mt 5:29
18:9 [a]S Mt 5:29 [b]S Mt 5:22
18:10 [c]Ge 48:16; Ps 34:7; Ac 12:11, 15; Heb 1:14

[r]*10* Some manuscripts *heaven. 11The Son of Man came to save what was lost.* [s]*15* Some manuscripts do not have *against you.*

18:1–5 HUMANITY, Human Nature—Pride is a basic part of human nature. People seek to do things which exalt themselves over others. The only way to be what God intends people to be is to be childlike, casting aside arrogant self-exaltation. At such times persons can honestly see themselves and others as they are. See notes on Mk 9:33–37; Lk 9:46–48.

18:1–10 CHRISTIAN ETHICS, Character—To understand Jesus' instructions about humility, one must observe children. Their sense of innocence, directness, and trust give us keys to comprehending what it means to be humble in the kingdom of God. This humility is acted out before God, but its credibility is visible as we act toward others with a true sense of their worth and of the gifts they bring to the kingdom's work.

18:1–4 THE CHURCH, God's Kingdom—Members of God's kingdom enter the kingdom like children—in humility, faith, and trust. Greatness in the kingdom does not depend on numbers, budgets, or bombs. To be great in the kingdom of God one must humble oneself as a servant of others and of God. Greatness is not an achievement recognized by others but an attitude blessed by God.

18:3 SALVATION, Repentance—Change is a basic meaning of repentance. To repent is to change one's mind and heart about sin and God. Little children are open to God. They naturally and readily believe in Him. See note on 19:13–15.

18:6–9 SIN, Serious—My influence can be my sin. When I lead an impressionable child into wrong behavior and habits, I have darkened two lives. I would be better off buried in the deepest ocean. I must do everything possible to prevent myself from sinning.

18:8–9 LAST THINGS, Hell—“Eternal fire” and the “fire of hell” are mentioned in parallel statements of warning. The punishment (“fire”) of hell is clearly of eternal duration. See note on 5:22. The primary concern of this text is dealing radically with sin in the lives of Jesus' followers. It is enforced by the almost incidental invoking of the danger of eternal punishment in hell. The matter-of-fact employment of the fire of hell as motivation underscores its reality and seriousness. See note on Mk 9:43–48.

18:10–14 GOD, Love—Jesus' own tender, loving interest in the little children, who are so often overlooked by the adult world, is but a reflection of the loving nature of His Heavenly Father. Jesus described the Father as One with great interest for the least and last person on the earth. He used the picture of a shepherd leaving the ninety-nine sheep safely in the fold while going into the wilderness to find the one that is lost. See the similar passage in Lk 15:1–32, where Jesus added the story of the lost coin and the lost boy to the story of the lost sheep to make His case for the Father's unrelenting love for the lost. This is why Jesus Himself associated with the outcasts of His day. He was seeking to find persons who are lost from God and restore them to the Father's love. Jesus came into this world in search of the lost (Lk 19:10). God's tender, fatherly yearning for the lost is the underlying motivating force in God's provision of salvation for the lost.

18:10–14 EVANGELISM, In the Marketplace—Jesus called His followers to leave the security of the worship place and go after that one lost sheep. The ninety-nine in the fold are important, but God seeks the wanderer. We should seek the lost wherever in life's circumstances we may find them. We should search the most difficult places to find and witness to the lost. God loves them all and desires their salvation.

and show him his fault,[d] just between
the two of you. If he listens to you, you
have won your brother over. 16But if he
will not listen, take one or two others
along, so that 'every matter may be established by the testimony of two or three
witnesses.'[t e] 17If he refuses to listen to
them, tell it to the church;[f] and if he
refuses to listen even to the church, treat
him as you would a pagan or a tax collector.[g]
18"I tell you the truth, whatever you
bind on earth will be[u] bound in heaven,
and whatever you loose on earth will be[u]
loosed in heaven.[h]
19"Again, I tell you that if two of you
on earth agree about anything you ask
for, it will be done for you[i] by my Father
in heaven. 20For where two or three
come together in my name, there am I
with them."[j]

The Parable of the Unmerciful Servant

21Then Peter came to Jesus and asked,
"Lord, how many times shall I forgive my
brother when he sins against me?[k] Up to
seven times?"[l]
22Jesus answered, "I tell you, not seven
times, but seventy-seven times.[v m]
23"Therefore, the kingdom of heaven is
like[n] a king who wanted to settle accounts[o] with his servants. 24As he began
the settlement, a man who owed him ten
thousand talents[w] was brought to him.
25Since he was not able to pay,[p] the master ordered that he and his wife and his
children and all that he had be sold[q] to
repay the debt.
26"The servant fell on his knees before
him.[r] 'Be patient with me,' he begged,
'and I will pay back everything.' 27The
servant's master took pity on him, canceled the debt and let him go.
28"But when that servant went out, he
found one of his fellow servants who
owed him a hundred denarii.[x] He
grabbed him and began to choke him.
'Pay back what you owe me!' he demanded.
29"His fellow servant fell to his knees
and begged him, 'Be patient with me, and
I will pay you back.'
30"But he refused. Instead, he went off
and had the man thrown into prison until
he could pay the debt. 31When the other
servants saw what had happened, they
were greatly distressed and went and told
their master everything that had happened.
32"Then the master called the servant
in. 'You wicked servant,' he said, 'I can-

18:15 [d]Lev 19:17; Lk 17:3; Gal 6:1; Jas 5:19,20
18:16 [e]Nu 35:30; Dt 17:6; 19:15; Jn 8:17; 2Co 13:1; 1Ti 5:19; Heb 10:28
18:17 [f]1Co 6:1-6 [g]S Ro 16:17
18:18 [h]Mt 16:19; Jn 20:23
18:19 [i]S Mt 7:7
18:20 [j]S Mt 28:20
18:21 [k]S Mt 6:14 [l]Lk 17:4
18:22 [m]Ge 4:24
18:23 [n]S Mt 13:24 [o]Mt 25:19
18:25 [p]Lk 7:42 [q]Lev 25:39; 2Ki 4:1; Ne 5:5,8
18:26 [r]S Mt 8:2

[t] *16* Deut. 19:15 [u] *18* Or *have been* [v] *22* Or *seventy times seven* [w] *24* That is, millions of dollars [x] *28* That is, a few dollars

18:15–20 SIN, Estrangement—Sin sets one brother against another. We should not let it. We must actively seek to overcome the results of sin and renew our relationships. Refusal to overcome estrangement is sin worthy of exclusion from the church fellowship.

18:15–20 THE CHURCH, Discipline—The church must practice fellowship. Christians must settle disputes to continue fellowship. The church has a three-step plan for solving differences: (1) The two striving parties privately attempt to overcome their differences. (2) Two or three people serve as witnesses and encouragers to solve the problems. (3) The church attempts to settle the disagreement. The time element of the three steps is not mentioned in the Scripture, but the process implies a period of time for the parties to reflect and pray. Persons who do not respond to the three attempts to overcome strife show themselves unconcerned for the fellowship and remove themselves from the church. The church witnesses of Christ's power to forgive. Jesus has given the church the work of bringing people to Him. The church prays, worships, and experiences the presence of Jesus. The church is a powerful body created by Christ Jesus to promote fellowship, forgiveness, witnessing, and worship. See note on 16:18–19.

18:15–17 FAMILY, Conflict Resolution—This passage is not specifically directed toward family conflict, but it does give principles for handling conflict among family members. Having love and courage enough to confront personally the person with whom differences have developed clarifies the actual content of conflict (5:23–24). Since conflict often results from misunderstanding, this is quite important. If there are still strong differences, the help of counselors or other persons who can assist in reconciliation is often helpful.

18:18–20 PRAYER, Corporate—The pronouns throughout this passage are plural. The context (v 17) indicates that this verse is addressed to the church. There is tremendous authority in agreeing prayer. Agreement in Christ's name involves commitment to His purposes. See Guide to Worshiping Together as a Church, pp. 1802–1805.

18:18 CHURCH LEADERS, Authority—The same authority given to Peter to bind and to loose (that is, to define what is permitted and what is forbidden) in 16:18–19 was given also to the church. The congregation as a whole now has the authority originally invested only in the apostles to act on matters of discipline and doctrine. Peter's authority was given him for the unique moment in church history and was passed to the church, not to another individual.

18:21–35 SALVATION, Forgiveness—Jesus taught His disciples to forgive one another an unlimited number of times. That is the meaning of the number in v 22. We are to forgive others as God has forgiven us.

18:21–25 CHRISTIAN ETHICS, Character—One of the greatest barriers to Christian maturity is knowing what to do with forgiveness. Jesus' use of exaggeration makes the point that one forgives and forgives. There is no limit. How long does it take until you have worked through forgiveness? Until you can want the well-being of the other who has trespassed against you. The import of Jesus' teaching here is that our lack of willingness to forgive our neighbor acts as a barrier to accepting God's forgiveness of our own sin.

18:23–35 THE CHURCH, God's Kingdom—Forgiveness characterizes those who enter the kingdom of heaven. An unforgiving spirit demonstrates one not ready to enter the kingdom of God. God does not forgive the unforgiving. See note on 13:24–30.

18:32–35 GOD, Wrath—The idea of God as Father is perfectly compatible with the idea of God as sovereign Lord pouring out wrath on those who deserve it. Jesus here pictured God as Father acting in wrath, seeking stern justice. It is a mistake to interpret the idea of God as Father wholly in terms of kindliness and love. A proper understanding of God as Father must take account of God's righteousness as well as His love. Love which is blind to justice and righteousness would not be a very desirable love ultimately. Conversely, righteousness which is devoid of love would be a mockery of justice. Whether we call Him Father or Lord, God's nature must be

celed all that debt of yours because you
begged me to. 33Shouldn't you have had
mercy on your fellow servant just as I had
on you?' 34In anger his master turned him
over to the jailers to be tortured, until he
should pay back all he owed.
35"This is how my heavenly Father will
treat each of you unless you forgive your
brother from your heart."[s]

Chapter 19

Divorce

19:1–9pp — Mk 10:1–12

**WHEN Jesus had finished saying these
things,[t] he left Galilee and went
into the region of Judea to the other side
of the Jordan. 2Large crowds followed
him, and he healed them[u] there.
3Some Pharisees came to him to test
him. They asked, "Is it lawful for a man
to divorce his wife[v] for any and every
reason?"**
4"Haven't you read," **he replied,** "that
at the beginning the Creator 'made them
male and female,'[y][w] 5and said, 'For this
reason a man will leave his father and
mother and be united to his wife, and the
two will become one flesh'[z]?[x] 6So they
are no longer two, but one. Therefore
what God has joined together, let man
not separate."
7**"Why then," they asked, "did Moses
command that a man give his wife a certificate
of divorce and send her away?"**[y]
8**Jesus replied,** "Moses permitted you
to divorce your wives because your hearts
were hard. But it was not this way from
the beginning. 9I tell you that anyone
who divorces his wife, except for marital
unfaithfulness, and marries another woman
commits adultery."[z]
10**The disciples said to him, "If this is
the situation between a husband and
wife, it is better not to marry."**
11**Jesus replied,** "Not everyone can accept
this word, but only those to whom it
has been given.[a] 12For some are eunuchs
because they were born that way; others
were made that way by men; and others
have renounced marriage[a] because of
the kingdom of heaven. The one who can
accept this should accept it."

The Little Children and Jesus

19:13–15pp — Mk 10:13–16; Lk 18:15–17

13**Then little children were brought to
Jesus for him to place his hands on**

18:35 [s]S Mt 6:14; S Jas 2:13
19:1 [t]S Mt 7:28
19:2 [u]S Mt 4:23
19:3 [v]Mt 5:31
19:4 [w]Ge 1:27; 5:2
19:5 [x]Ge 2:24; 1Co 6:16; Eph 5:31
19:7 [y]Dt 24:1-4; Mt 5:31
19:9 [z]S Lk 16:18
19:11 [a]S Mt 13:11; 1Co 7:7-9,17

[y]4 Gen. 1:27 [z]5 Gen. 2:24 [a]12 Or *have made themselves eunuchs*

---

seen as the perfect blending of love and righteousness, both basic, inseparable aspects of the nature of God.

19:1–6 HUMANITY, Marriage—God intended marriage to be a full physical and emotional union of a man and a woman, superseding prior human ties (Mk 10:1–9). See notes on Ge 2:18; 2:21–25.

19:3–9 FAMILY, Divorce—The husband bears strong responsibility for fulfilling the marriage vows. Jesus surprised His audience with strong talk about marriage and divorce. Jewish teachers debated the meaning of Dt 24:1. A group of rabbis followed Rabbi Hillel in allowing quite superficial and flimsy grounds for divorce. Others agreed with Rabbi Shammai that adultery was the only lawful ground for divorce. The Pharisees hoped to trap Jesus into taking sides in their controversy. Jesus said that the only reason God allowed Moses to make any provision for divorce was a concession to human sin. God's intention is marriage for a lifetime, as seen in Ge 1—2. Biblical students interpret the "except" phrase in Mt 5:32 and 19:9 in different ways. The parallel Bible accounts (Mk 10:5–12; Lk 16:18; note on 1 Co 7:10–11) do not contain the phrase. Some Bible students think the passage discusses a woman with sexual experience prior to marriage, making the marriage invalid by Jewish law. Compare Dt 22:20–21. This would mean Jesus did not approve of divorce for any valid marriage. Other scholars think the text makes adultery a reason for divorce. Jesus affirmed God's intention for permanent marriage. He denied the husband's assumed right to divorce a woman for any reason. He warned husbands not to ruin a wife's reputation *by divorcing her. He* charged husbands with adultery when they divorced an innocent wife and remarried. He placed guilt on a woman whose sexual sins destroyed a marriage. He limited or even prohibited divorce as part of God's will for marriage but did not label divorce as the unforgivable sin. Divorce involves missing the will of God for marriage partners. Both partners should admit their individual fault in not realizing God's purpose for marriage. Both should confess sin in divorce cases. The question of remarriage of divorced persons is then appropriately considered from the perspective of God's forgiveness of repentant sinners. See Jas 2:8–13.

19:10–12 HUMANITY, Celibacy—The Greek expression translated "renounced marriage" literally refers to a man who has castrated himself. Jesus did not refer to a literal self-castration but rather to persons who abstained from sexual relations to devote their full commitment to the kingdom of God. Jesus pointed out that only some can follow this unmarried way of life. This concept was clarified in 1 Co 7:1–9,25–40.

19:10–12 FAMILY, Single—Jesus honored celibacy as a valid life choice just as He honored marriage in the preceding verses. A eunuch is a person physically incapable of sexual union. According to Jewish law such a eunuch could not be validly married. Jesus also affirmed those who remain single by choice to fulfill a vocational commitment to service for God. Jesus' own life illustrates this commitment as does the life of Paul. See note on 1 Co 7:1,7–9. The daughters of Philip were also unmarried by religious commitment (Ac 21:8–9). Since marriage was the normal expectation for all people in the Hebrew faith, the Bible does not deal explicitly with singleness as a life-style. Compare 1 Co 1:7–9. It does offer guidelines to human wholeness that are applicable to singles as well as to married persons.

19:12 THE CHURCH, God's Kingdom—The supreme worth of God's kingdom calls some people to renounce even normal family relationships for it. See note on 13:44–46.

19:13–14 JESUS CHRIST, Mission—Jesus saw His mission as helping the trusting children find acceptance and love rather than as political power struggles.

19:13–15 SALVATION, Definition—God offers salvation to all persons able to respond to Him, to children as well as to adults. The Bible teaches that if children become Christians, they do so just as adults do: by conversion. In early years children cannot consciously confess Christ as Lord and thus be converted (Ro 10:9–10). There comes a time when the child is enabled by God's grace and may become a Christian. The child does so through personal faith, trusting God's grace. The choice is made by the child's individual conscience. No one else can make the decision for the child. This is true because every person sins and becomes alienated from God. God's provision of salvation in Jesus Christ is the only way of salvation

them[b] and pray for them. But the disciples rebuked those who brought them.
14 Jesus said, "Let the little children
come to me, and do not hinder them, for
the kingdom of heaven belongs[c] to such
as these."[d] 15 When he had placed his
hands on them, he went on from there.

The Rich Young Man

19:16–29pp — Mk 10:17–30; Lk 18:18–30

16 Now a man came up to Jesus and
asked, "Teacher, what good thing must I
do to get eternal life[e]?"[f]
17 "Why do you ask me about what is
good?" Jesus replied. "There is only One
who is good. If you want to enter life,
obey the commandments."[g]
18 "Which ones?" the man inquired.
Jesus replied, " 'Do not murder, do not
commit adultery,[h] do not steal, do not
give false testimony, 19 honor your father

19:13 [b]S Mk 5:23
19:14 [c]S Mt 25:34 [d]Mt 18:3; 1Pe 2:2
19:16 [e]S Mt 25:46 [f]Lk 10:25
19:17 [g]Lev 18:5
19:18 [h]Jas 2:11
19:19 [i]Ex 20:12-16; Dt 5:16-20 [j]Lev 19:18; S Mt 5:43
19:21 [k]Mt 5:48 [l]S Ac 2:45 [m]S Mt 6:20
19:23 [n]Mt 13:22; 1Ti 6:9,10

and mother,'[b][i] and 'love your neighbor
as yourself.'[c]"[j]
20 "All these I have kept," the young
man said. "What do I still lack?"
21 Jesus answered, "If you want to be
perfect,[k] go, sell your possessions and
give to the poor,[l] and you will have treasure in heaven.[m] Then come, follow
me."
22 When the young man heard this, he
went away sad, because he had great
wealth.
23 Then Jesus said to his disciples, "I
tell you the truth, it is hard for a rich
man[n] to enter the kingdom of heaven.
24 Again I tell you, it is easier for a camel
to go through the eye of a needle than for
a rich man to enter the kingdom of God."
25 When the disciples heard this, they

[b] *19* Exodus 20:12-16; Deut. 5:16-20
[c] *19* Lev. 19:18

for persons no matter the age. The human will must cooperate with the divine will in bringing about conversion. Salvation is neither automatic nor forced upon any individual. Infants are safe in God's care, and children continue to be safe in God's care until they become capable of responsible decision-making. Sin is not charged against them until they consciously choose to do wrong. Infants and young children who die before they are capable of conversion are a part of God's kingdom. Based on what the Bible tells us about the nature of God, He will not hold young, immature children responsible for making decisions which they are incapable of making. God can be trusted to deal adequately with those who have not yet reached this stage of accountability. Each child develops differently in spiritual awareness as in physical growth. There is no one age of accountability. Children who are accountable before God can experience genuine conversion and be saved.

19:13–15 PRAYER, Blessing—This prayer was a benediction asking God's blessing through the continuing daily needs of life. See note on Ge 14:18–20.

19:14 THE CHURCH, God's Kingdom—The kingdom of God consists of those with the childlike qualities of trust, faith, and humility. See note on 18:1–4.

19:16–26 GOD, Power—God's power is without limit. His capabilities are infinite. This should not be taken in an abstract, speculative sense. In some ages people speculated on such absurd questions as, "Can God make a rock so big He cannot pick it up?" Jesus was not ascribing such speculative absurdities to God. He was saying God has all the power needed to do whatever is necessary, whatever His will requires. God is not lacking in power to accomplish His purposes. Desirable aims that a human cannot accomplish in his finite power, God can easily accomplish in His infinite power. As Jesus illustrated here, a person can no more save himself than a camel can go through the eye of a needle. God has the power to renew and regenerate a sinful heart in salvation.

19:16–30 SALVATION, Human Freedom—The rich young ruler is an example of one who rejected eternal life. Persons are free to accept or reject Christ. Those who accept Him will be abundantly rewarded here and hereafter. Those who think they deserve salvation or who seek to do something good to earn salvation have rejected God's way of salvation by grace through faith (Eph 2:8–9).

19:16–30 SALVATION, Eternal Life—God's salvation is eternal life—the fullness of life which Christ alone gives (Jn 10:10). It is life in Christ here and hereafter, right now and forevermore. We can do nothing in the way of good works to gain eternal life. It is God's free gift to all those who forsake everything and follow Jesus. Not even the very rich can buy eternal life. The wealthy have to be saved in the same way as everybody else.

19:16–30 CHRISTIAN ETHICS, Character—If your priorities are focused on material things, they are off center. Life must center on Christ for it to be truly satisfying and for it to be rewarded by God.

19:17 GOD, Goodness—The goodness of God is such that He is in a category alone. No one else can be compared to God. Only He can truly be called good. God is the very standard of what is good. All else is measured by His goodness (Isa 40:25). Jesus, in His earthly life, was as human as divine (Php 2:5–8; 1 Jn 4:2–3). He chose not to apply this declaration of goodness to Himself, but attributed it to God the Father alone. While Jesus had no sin, He nevertheless recognized the superiority of God the Father over everything earthly and humbled Himself before God. See Mt 3:13–17; 24:36. God is good because only He unites in Himself all that is right, all that is worthwhile. He lives and acts in ways that are the perfect expression of goodness, always faithful to Himself and to His people, unchanging and unswerving in His character. Any person who wants to do good, or be good, must first come into a right relationship with God who alone is good.

19:21–23 HUMANITY, Relationships—See note on Mk 10:21–23.

19:21 DISCIPLESHIP, Poor—The test of devotion to Christ is not the same for all. The rich young man lacked supreme devotion to Christ and was unwilling to renounce his possessions. His test was to let his wealth meet the needs of the poor. He needed to commit his wealth to advancing the purposes of God. It is not easy for a successful rich man to come under the lordship of Christ, but it is possible with God's help. Each of us needs to find God's test for our devotion and use our resources to minister to others' needs. See 19:23–26.

19:21–26 STEWARDSHIP, Attitudes—Devotion to wealth bars us from supreme devotion to God. The rich man wanted to serve two gods—wealth and God. Jesus said he had to choose. God does not share His position with anyone or anything. Wealth may represent God's blessing. All too often it represents our top priority which leads us away from God. Money must be used for God's purposes and the care for the needy, not for achievement of selfish goals and satisfaction of human pride. Only God can give us the proper attitude toward money. See note on 6:19–33.

19:24–26 THE CHURCH, God's Kingdom—In contrast to children, the rich often lack qualities like trust and humility. As believers enter the kingdom with these childlike characteristics, the rich exclude themselves for lack of these qualities. Those who are rich may enter the kingdom, but they must experience the miraculous gift of depending on God and not on

were greatly astonished and asked, "Who
then can be saved?"
26Jesus looked at them and said, "With
man this is impossible, but with God all
things are possible."[o]
27Peter answered him, "We have left
everything to follow you![p] What then
will there be for us?"
28Jesus said to them, "I tell you the
truth, at the renewal of all things, when
the Son of Man sits on his glorious
throne,[q] you who have followed me will
also sit on twelve thrones, judging the
twelve tribes of Israel.[r] 29And everyone
who has left houses or brothers or sisters
or father or mother[d] or children or fields
for my sake will receive a hundred times
as much and will inherit eternal life.[s]
30But many who are first will be last, and
many who are last will be first.[t]

Chapter 20

The Parable of the Workers in the Vineyard

"FOR the kingdom of heaven is like[u]
a landowner who went out early
in the morning to hire men to work in his
vineyard.[v] 2He agreed to pay them a denarius for the day and sent them into his
vineyard.
3"About the third hour he went out
and saw others standing in the marketplace doing nothing. 4He told them, 'You
also go and work in my vineyard, and I
will pay you whatever is right.' 5So they
went.
"He went out again about the sixth
hour and the ninth hour and did the same
thing. 6About the eleventh hour he went
out and found still others standing
around. He asked them, 'Why have you
been standing here all day long doing
nothing?'
7" 'Because no one has hired us,' they
answered.
"He said to them, 'You also go and
work in my vineyard.'
8"When evening came,[w] the owner of
the vineyard said to his foreman, 'Call the
workers and pay them their wages, beginning with the last ones hired and going
on to the first.'
9"The workers who were hired about
the eleventh hour came and each received a denarius. 10So when those came
who were hired first, they expected to
receive more. But each one of them also
received a denarius. 11When they received it, they began to grumble[x] against
the landowner. 12'These men who were
hired last worked only one hour,' they
said, 'and you have made them equal to
us who have borne the burden of the
work and the heat[y] of the day.'
13"But he answered one of them,
'Friend,[z] I am not being unfair to you.
Didn't you agree to work for a denarius?
14Take your pay and go. I want to give the
man who was hired last the same as I
gave you. 15Don't I have the right to do
what I want with my own money? Or are
you envious because I am generous?'[a]
16"So the last will be first, and the first
will be last."[b]

Jesus Again Predicts His Death

20:17–19pp — Mk 10:32–34; Lk 18:31–33

17Now as Jesus was going up to Jerusalem, he took the twelve disciples aside
and said to them, 18"We are going up to
Jerusalem,[c] and the Son of Man[d] will be
betrayed to the chief priests and the

19:26 [o]Ge 18:14; Job 42:2; Jer 32:17; Lk 1:37; 18:27; Ro 4:21
19:27 [p]S Mt 4:19
19:28 [q]Mt 20:21; 25:31 [r]Lk 22:28-30; Rev 3:21; 4:4; 20:4
19:29 [s]Mt 6:33; S 25:46
19:30 [t]Mt 20:16; Mk 10:31; Lk 13:30
20:1 [u]S Mt 13:24 [v]Mt 21:28,33
20:8 [w]Lev 19:13; Dt 24:15
20:11 [x]Jnh 4:1
20:12 [y]Jnh 4:8; Lk 12:55; Jas 1:11
20:13 [z]Mt 22:12; 26:50
20:15 [a]Dt 15:9; Mk 7:22
20:16 [b]S Mt 19:30
20:18 [c]S Lk 9:51 [d]S Mt 8:20

[d]29 Some manuscripts *mother or wife*

---

wealth for meaning and hope in life. See notes on 18:1–4; 19:14.

19:28 JESUS CHRIST, Son of Man—Jesus expected to be King but only in His second coming. See note on 16:27–28.

19:28 LAST THINGS, Creation's Redemption—Personal redemption is a present foretaste in miniature of future cosmic renewal. The time at which Christ sits enthroned is called "the renewal of all things" (Greek *palingenesia*). The broad sweep of the term suggests a new beginning for all creation. Tit 3:5 is the only other New Testament occurrence of the Greek word. The eschatological renewal of all things matches the spiritual renewal that properly follows the rebirth of believers through the Spirit. The meaning of the apostles *sitting* on thrones and judging the twelve tribes has been variously interpreted. See note on Da 9:24–27.

20:1–16 GOD, Grace—Grace is sometimes defined as unmerited favor. God's grace goes beyond our understanding. It is the very nature of God, who is defined as love, to pour out His love upon His people in a way and in a measure that is both undeserved and unexpected. Why did the landowner give so much to those who had not worked for it? He had the resources to do it, on the one hand, and the sovereign right to do it, on the other hand. Most of all, he had a loving nature that sought to reach out to all that he could in bestowing blessings upon them. The grace of God does not defraud anyone of anything. No one earns the grace of God. That any of these had a job was an evidence of grace. Each got at least what he was promised. Most who worked in the vineyard received much more than they expected, much more than they deserved. God's grace is not bestowed on a merit system basis. God's grace is given on the basis of overflowing love out of the free and generous heart of God.

20:1–16 HUMANITY, Work—Jesus assumed people wanted the opportunity to work for wages by which they could support their families. The response to the parable shows people expected their wages to be related to the amount of work they did. Jesus applauded the generosity of an employer who gave more than expected. His main point, however, is that God's grace cannot be earned. It is given freely according to human need.

20:1–16 THE CHURCH, God's Kingdom—The kingdom of God is a gift to be received and used. God graciously blesses His people. No one earns a greater part of the kingdom than another person. God is never in debt to us. Until we humbly admit this and come to God with no demands or expectations, we cannot be part of His kingdom. See note on 13:24–30.

20:17–19 JESUS CHRIST, Death—See note on 16:21–23; Mk 10:32–34.

teachers of the law.[e] They will condemn
him to death 19and will turn him over to
the Gentiles to be mocked and flogged[f]
and crucified.[g] On the third day[h] he will
be raised to life!"[i]

A Mother's Request

20:20–28pp — Mk 10:35–45

20Then the mother of Zebedee's sons[j]
came to Jesus with her sons and, kneeling
down,[k] asked a favor of him.
21"What is it you want?" he asked.
She said, "Grant that one of these two
sons of mine may sit at your right and the
other at your left in your kingdom."[l]
22"You don't know what you are asking," Jesus said to them. "Can you drink
the cup[m] I am going to drink?"
"We can," they answered.
23Jesus said to them, "You will indeed
drink from my cup,[n] but to sit at my right
or left is not for me to grant. These places
belong to those for whom they have been
prepared by my Father."
24When the ten heard about this, they
were indignant[o] with the two brothers.
25Jesus called them together and said,
"You know that the rulers of the Gentiles
lord it over them, and their high officials
exercise authority over them. 26Not so
with you. Instead, whoever wants to become great among you must be your servant,[p] 27and whoever wants to be first

20:18 [e]Mt 27:1,2
20:19 [f]S Mt 16:21 [g]S Ac 2:23 [h]S Mt 16:21 [i]S Mt 16:21
20:20 [j]S Mt 4:21 [k]S Mt 8:2
20:21 [l]Mt 19:28
20:22 [m]Isa 51:17,22; Jer 49:12; Mt 26:39,42; Mk 14:36; Lk 22:42; Jn 18:11
20:23 [n]Ac 12:2; Rev 1:9
20:24 [o]Lk 22:24,25
20:26 [p]S Mk 9:35
20:28 [q]S Mt 8:20 [r]Isa 42:1; Lk 12:37; 22:27; Jn 13:13-16; 2Co 8:9; Php 2:7 [s]Ex 30:12; Isa 44:22; 53:10; Mt 26:28; 1Ti 2:6; Tit 2:14; Heb 9:28; 1Pe 1:18,19
20:30 [t]S Mt 9:27

must be your slave— 28just as the Son of
Man[q] did not come to be served, but to
serve,[r] and to give his life as a ransom[s]
for many."

Two Blind Men Receive Sight

20:29–34pp — Mk 10:46–52; Lk 18:35–43

29As Jesus and his disciples were leaving Jericho, a large crowd followed him.
30Two blind men were sitting by the
roadside, and when they heard that Jesus
was going by, they shouted, "Lord, Son of
David,[t] have mercy on us!"
31The crowd rebuked them and told
them to be quiet, but they shouted all the
louder, "Lord, Son of David, have mercy
on us!"
32Jesus stopped and called them.
"What do you want me to do for you?" he
asked.
33"Lord," they answered, "we want
our sight."
34Jesus had compassion on them and
touched their eyes. Immediately they received their sight and followed him.

Chapter 21

The Triumphal Entry

21:1–9pp — Mk 11:1–10; Lk 19:29–38
21:4–9pp — Jn 12:12–15

AS they approached Jerusalem and came
to Bethphage on the Mount of Ol-

20:20–23 JESUS CHRIST, Kingdom of God—The disciples looked to earthly power and influence. Jesus looked to suffering and death as signs of His kingdom. Jesus showed obedience to the Father even in assigning places of honor in the kingdom.

20:20–28 THE CHURCH, Servants—Service in the kingdom of God is unique. Jesus established no position of authority for one person to "lord it over"others in the kingdom. Greatness in the kingdom is measured differently than in any other group or organization. To be great in the kingdom of God one must assume the role of a servant. The role model for ministry in the church is the one who came as a Suffering Servant (Isa 52:13—53:12). Jesus came to serve rather than to be served. Christian believers must serve others to follow Christ. In Christ, all believers are equal—as servants and slaves of the Lord Jesus. No one in the church should rule over others; all should serve one another in a spirit of humility before Christ.

20:23 GOD, Trinity—God as Father reigns in His world with unqualified sovereignty. His nature as the sovereign Lord appears in both Testaments. He is in complete control, exercising unlimited authority and power. He honors whom He chooses. No one can earn power or prestige in His kingdom. No one else can bestow positions of authority. The sovereign God is at the same time the intimate Father. We can trust Him to make His decisions fairly and lovingly. We will not be cheated. Jesus was saying in this passage that some things are not His to decide, that some things are solely within the authority of God the Father. The three Persons of the Trinity are equal in their deity, but the authority is centered in God the Father.

20:23 ELECTION, Sovereignty—God's elect do not seek status or power. We are servants whose greatness is measured in terms of obedience to God's call. Election requires drinking from the cup of Jesus, that is suffering and dying in service of God. Reward is God's sovereign right, not our deserved choice.

20:25–28 CHURCH LEADERS, Authority—Domination and the exercise of authority is the way of worldly kingdoms but not of Christ's kingdom. Leaders in the church are not to climb ambitiously to places of prominence and privilege. They are to serve with the same spirit as their Lord who gave His life for others. They are to exercise their function, not the power of their office. Authority in the church is not to become an end in itself. Church leaders are church servants.

20:26–28 REVELATION, Jesus Christ—The world prizes rank and position. Jesus in flesh revealed God has different priorities. In God's kingdom the highest calling is servanthood; rank and authority are of little value. Thus Jesus did not seek to rule. He served and died.

20:28 JESUS CHRIST, Redeemer—Jesus knew His mission centered on providing salvation for all who would accept it in faith. To do this He had to die as the ransom price to redeem us from slavery to sin and death. Service and salvation, not power and prestige, were His goals.

20:28 SALVATION, Atonement—Jesus Christ came to give His life to make an atonement for many. His ransom is for all people (1 Ti 2:6). See note on Isa 53:4–12.

20:29–34 JESUS CHRIST, Miracles—Compare Mk 10:46–52; Lk 18:35–43. This healing miracle, as all of Jesus' healing miracles, expressed His compassion for those diseased and impaired. See notes on 9:27–34; 14:14.

20:29–34 MIRACLE, Faith—Miracles heal physically and spiritually. See note on Mk 10:46–52. Blindness was frequent and a miserable condition. These two men were insistent in their pleas for sight. Jesus, moved with compassion, "touched their eyes." They were healed physically and spiritually: they "followed him." The miracle-working ministry of Jesus through the modern church encourages folks to follow Jesus.

20:29–34 PRAYER, Faith—See note on Mk 10:51–52.

21:1–11 JESUS CHRIST, Son of David—As He entered Jerusalem to face the cross, Jesus let the crowds greet Him as a King. Compare 2 Ki 9:13. He showed them His understanding of Messiah—humility. Compare Ps 118:26; Isa 62:11; Zec

ives,[u] Jesus sent two disciples, 2saying to
them, "Go to the village ahead of you,
and at once you will find a donkey tied
there, with her colt by her. Untie them
and bring them to me. 3If anyone says
anything to you, tell him that the Lord
needs them, and he will send them right
away."

4This took place to fulfill[v] what was
spoken through the prophet:

5"Say to the Daughter of Zion,
'See, your king comes to you,
gentle and riding on a donkey,
on a colt, the foal of a donkey.' "[e] [w]

6The disciples went and did as Jesus
had instructed them. 7They brought the
donkey and the colt, placed their cloaks
on them, and Jesus sat on them. 8A very
large crowd spread their cloaks[x] on the
road, while others cut branches from the
trees and spread them on the road. 9The
crowds that went ahead of him and those
that followed shouted,

"Hosanna[f] to the Son of David!"[y]

"Blessed is he who comes in the name
of the Lord!"[g] [z]

"Hosanna[f] in the highest!"[a]

10When Jesus entered Jerusalem, the
whole city was stirred and asked, "Who
is this?"

11The crowds answered, "This is Jesus,
the prophet[b] from Nazareth in Galilee."

Jesus at the Temple

21:12–16pp — Mk 11:15–18; Lk 19:45–47

12Jesus entered the temple area and
drove out all who were buying[c] and selling there. He overturned the tables of the
money changers[d] and the benches of
those selling doves.[e] 13"It is written," he
said to them, " 'My house will be called a
house of prayer,'[h] [f] but you are making it
a 'den of robbers.'[i] "[g]

14The blind and the lame came to him
at the temple, and he healed them.[h]
15But when the chief priests and the
teachers of the law saw the wonderful
things he did and the children shouting
in the temple area, "Hosanna to the Son
of David,"[i] they were indignant.[j]

16"Do you hear what these children
are saying?" they asked him.

"Yes," replied Jesus, "have you never
read,

" 'From the lips of children and infants
you have ordained praise'[j] ?"[k]

17And he left them and went out of the
city to Bethany,[l] where he spent the
night.

The Fig Tree Withers

21:18–22pp — Mk 11:12–14,20–24

18Early in the morning, as he was on
his way back to the city, he was hungry.
19Seeing a fig tree by the road, he went
up to it but found nothing on it except
leaves. Then he said to it, "May you never bear fruit again!" Immediately the tree
withered.[m]

20When the disciples saw this, they

21:1 [u]Mt 24:3; 26:30; Mk 14:26; Lk 19:37; 21:37; 22:39; Jn 8:1; Ac 1:12
21:4 [v]S Mt 1:22
21:5 [w]Zec 9:9; Isa 62:11
21:8 [x]2Ki 9:13
21:9 [y]ver 15; S Mt 9:27 [z]Ps 118:26; Mt 23:39 [a]Lk 2:14
21:11 [b]Dt 18:15; Lk 7:16,39; 24:19; Jn 1:21,25; 6:14; 7:40
21:12 [c]Dt 14:26 [d]Ex 30:13 [e]Lev 1:14
21:13 [f]Isa 56:7 [g]Jer 7:11
21:14 [h]S Mt 4:23
21:15 [i]ver 9; S Mt 9:27 [j]Lk 19:39
21:16 [k]Ps 8:2
21:17 [l]Mt 26:6; Mk 11:1; Lk 24:50; Jn 11:1,18; 12:1
21:19 [m]Isa 34:4; Jer 8:13

[e] *5* Zech. 9:9 [f] *9* A Hebrew expression meaning "Save!" which became an exclamation of praise; also in verse 15 [g] *9* Psalm 118:26 [h] *13* Isaiah 56:7 [i] *13* Jer. 7:11 [j] *16* Psalm 8:2

9:9; 14:4. Jesus consciously transformed Israel's understanding of kingship to emphasize service and peace. See note on Mt 1:1. The triumphal entry began Passion Week, which concluded with the triumphal resurrection from the dead.

21:1–11 REVELATION, Actions—Like the prophets, Jesus acted out His revealed message symbolically. See note on Jer 32:6–15. He began on the traditional mount of judgment (Zec 14:4). He provided opportunity for people to honor Him as King, yet did so with animals that underlined humility rather than power. Jesus did this in light of His understanding of the Scriptural teaching about Messiah, emphasizing service and humility aspects rather than power and authority. Matthew in light of Zec 9:9 emphasized two animals, though Hebrew poetic parallelism may be interpreted to point to only one (Mk 11:2–4; Lk 19:30–33). The crowds also used Scripture to acclaim Jesus. Later events at the cross show how shallow their use of Scripture was.

21:9 PRAYER, Praise—Jesus' miracles repeatedly caused the crowds to praise and glorify God (9:8; 15:31; Lk 7:16; 13:13). The second line of the acclamation came from Ps 118:26, which was used in procession to the Temple at festivals. See notes on Ps 113:1–9; 118:1–19. Such praise was short-lived because it too often looked for physical and political deliverance rather than for the fulfillment of God's purposes.

21:11 JESUS CHRIST, Prophet—Jesus was the fulfillment of Israel's expectations of a prophet like Moses (Dt 18:15,18). Compare Lk 7:16,39; 24:19; Jn 1:21; 6:14; 7:40; Ac 3:22; 7:37.

21:12–16 JESUS CHRIST, Fulfilled—Jesus exercised divine authority over God's house, cleansing it as Malachi prophesied (3:1–4). Jesus transformed the marketplace Temple into a healing Temple for persons Pharisaic law excluded from Temple worship. Jesus accepted messianic worship from children. Compare Ps 8:2; Isa 56:7; Jer 7:11.

21:13 REVELATION, Jesus Christ—God's house was designed to provide free access to God not to oppress and distract people away from God. Instead of concentrating on making money, those who appear at God's house are to seek God's glory. The prophets' words (Isa 56:7; Jer 7:11) are a revelation of God's will, acted out by the Christ. Christ used parts of two Scripture texts to show the total Scriptural application and to reveal Himself as purifier and Lord of the Temple.

21:13 PRAYER, Corporate—See note on Mk 11:17.

21:18–22 MIRACLE, Faith—Faith produces fruitful prayer. The nation's leaders, for all their religious pretense, were fruitless. Jesus' disciples were and are tempted to follow their example. The "cursing" of the fig tree has occasioned more sympathy than the tree deserves. The processes of nature which promise death for a nonproductive tree were hastened . . . the tree immediately withered. Our prayers can also receive immediate answer, if we believe.

21:19–22 PRAYER, Faith—Jesus used similar figures three times. Here, the mountain is thrown into the sea by faith. In 17:20 faith as a mustard seed would move a mountain; in Lk 17:5–6, it would transplant a tree. Elijah commanded the weather (1 Ki 17:1,7; 18:42–45). The object obeys faith.

were amazed. "How did the fig tree wither so quickly?" they asked.
21 Jesus replied, "I tell you the truth, if
you have faith and do not doubt,[n] not
only can you do what was done to the fig
tree, but also you can say to this mountain, 'Go, throw yourself into the sea,'
and it will be done. 22 If you believe, you
will receive whatever you ask for[o] in
prayer."

The Authority of Jesus Questioned

21:23–27pp — Mk 11:27–33; Lk 20:1–8

23 Jesus entered the temple courts, and,
while he was teaching, the chief priests
and the elders of the people came to him.
"By what authority[p] are you doing these
things?" they asked. "And who gave you
this authority?"
24 Jesus replied, "I will also ask you one
question. If you answer me, I will tell you
by what authority I am doing these
things. 25 John's baptism—where did it
come from? Was it from heaven, or from
men?"
They discussed it among themselves
and said, "If we say, 'From heaven,' he
will ask, 'Then why didn't you believe
him?' 26 But if we say, 'From men'—we
are afraid of the people, for they all hold
that John was a prophet."[q]
27 So they answered Jesus, "We don't
know."
Then he said, "Neither will I tell you
by what authority I am doing these
things.

The Parable of the Two Sons

28 "What do you think? There was a
man who had two sons. He went to the
first and said, 'Son, go and work today in
the vineyard.'[r]
29 " 'I will not,' he answered, but later
he changed his mind and went.
30 "Then the father went to the other
son and said the same thing. He answered, 'I will, sir,' but he did not go.

21:21 [n]Mt 17:20; Lk 17:6; 1Co 13:2; Jas 1:6
21:22 [o]S Mt 7:7
21:23 [p]Ac 4:7; 7:27
21:26 [q]S Mt 11:9
21:28 [r]ver 33; Mt 20:1
21:31 [s]Lk 7:29 [t]Lk 7:50
21:32 [u]Mt 3:1-12 [v]Lk 3:12,13; 7:29 [w]Lk 7:36-50 [x]Lk 7:30
21:33 [y]Ps 80:8 [z]Isa 5:1-7 [a]Mt 25:14,15
21:34 [b]Mt 22:3
21:35 [c]2Ch 24:21; Mt 23:34,37; Heb 11:36,37
21:36 [d]Mt 22:4
21:38 [e]Heb 1:2 [f]S Mt 12:14 [g]Ps 2:8
21:41 [h]Mt 8:11,12 [i]S Ac 13:46

31 "Which of the two did what his father wanted?"
"The first," they answered.
Jesus said to them, "I tell you the truth,
the tax collectors[s] and the prostitutes[t]
are entering the kingdom of God ahead of
you. 32 For John came to you to show you
the way of righteousness,[u] and you did
not believe him, but the tax collectors[v]
and the prostitutes[w] did. And even after
you saw this, you did not repent[x] and
believe him.

The Parable of the Tenants

21:33–46pp — Mk 12:1–12; Lk 20:9–19

33 "Listen to another parable: There
was a landowner who planted[y] a vineyard. He put a wall around it, dug a winepress in it and built a watchtower.[z] Then
he rented the vineyard to some farmers
and went away on a journey.[a] 34 When
the harvest time approached, he sent his
servants[b] to the tenants to collect his
fruit.
35 "The tenants seized his servants;
they beat one, killed another, and stoned
a third.[c] 36 Then he sent other servants[d]
to them, more than the first time, and the
tenants treated them the same way.
37 Last of all, he sent his son to them.
'They will respect my son,' he said.
38 "But when the tenants saw the son,
they said to each other, 'This is the heir.[e]
Come, let's kill him[f] and take his inheritance.'[g] 39 So they took him and threw
him out of the vineyard and killed him.
40 "Therefore, when the owner of the
vineyard comes, what will he do to those
tenants?"
41 "He will bring those wretches to a
wretched end,"[h] they replied, "and he
will rent the vineyard to other tenants,[i]
who will give him his share of the crop at
harvest time."
42 Jesus said to them, "Have you never
read in the Scriptures:

21:21–22 SALVATION, Belief—See note on 9:1–8,22,28–30. Faith can move mountains, even the mountains of our unregenerate nature. Answers to prayers are correlated with faith. Compare Mk 11:22–25.
21:23–27 JESUS CHRIST, Authority—Jesus' actions showed He assumed God's authority over the Temple and over nature. He did not verbally claim such authority knowing that would lead to premature arrest.
21:27,36 JESUS CHRIST, Son of Man—See note on 24:25–44.
21:28–32 SALVATION, Obedience—What God wants is actual obedience, not lip service. Compare Lk 6:46.
21:31–32 THE CHURCH, God's Kingdom—The kingdom of God is entered by faith, not by prior rank or social position.
21:33–44 JESUS CHRIST, Teaching—Jesus foretold His own death and God's vengeance on disobedient Israel. People who do not care for God's world and who destroy His prophets and His Son cannot expect His eternal blessings. Jesus applied Scripture to Himself to show His teaching and actions fulfilled the Old Testament's messianic promises. See note on Ps 118:22,23. This parable was so clear in meaning even the religious leaders understood it.
21:42 HOLY SCRIPTURE, Authoritative—Jesus used Ps 118:22 to confirm that God uses unexpected and seemingly unimportant things and people to accomplish His will. The rejected stone and the Christ are explained in the same light. Israel, the accepted nation, was to be rejected in favor of the rejected Gentiles. The psalm quotation originally applied to the Judean king in his fight against national enemies. Jesus applied it to Himself. Compare Mt 22:8–9. See note on 13:33–35.
21:42–44 ELECTION, In Christ—To reject Jesus is to forfeit membership in God's kingdom. Children of Abraham cannot be numbered with God's elect if they renounce Jesus and avoid repentance for sins. As throughout His history with Israel, God chose the faithful remnant for His kingdom. The remnant is in Christ. Remnant teaching in the Bible shows that election is not a determinism which disregards human free will.

" 'The stone the builders rejected
has become the capstone[k] ;
the Lord has done this,
and it is marvelous in our eyes'[l] ?[j]

43"Therefore I tell you that the kingdom of God will be taken away from
you[k] and given to a people who will produce its fruit. 44He who falls on this stone
will be broken to pieces, but he on whom
it falls will be crushed."[m] [l]

45When the chief priests and the Phari-
sees heard Jesus' parables, they knew he
was talking about them. 46They looked for
a way to arrest him, but they were afraid
of the crowd because the people held that
he was a prophet.[m]

Chapter 22

The Parable of the Wedding Banquet

22:2–14Ref — Lk 14:16–24

JESUS spoke to them again in parables,
saying: 2"The kingdom of heaven is
like[n] a king who prepared a wedding
banquet for his son. 3He sent his servants[o] to those who had been invited to
the banquet to tell them to come, but
they refused to come.

4"Then he sent some more servants[p]
and said, 'Tell those who have been invited that I have prepared my dinner: My
oxen and fattened cattle have been butchered, and everything is ready. Come to
the wedding banquet.'

5"But they paid no attention and went
off—one to his field, another to his business. 6The rest seized his servants, mistreated them and killed them. 7The king
was enraged. He sent his army and destroyed those murderers[q] and burned
their city.

8"Then he said to his servants, 'The
wedding banquet is ready, but those I in-

21:42 [j]Ps 118:22, 23; S Ac 4:11
21:43 [k]Mt 8:12
21:44 [l]S Lk 2:34
21:46 [m]S ver 11,26
22:2 [n]S Mt 13:24
22:3 [o]Mt 21:34
22:4 [p]Mt 21:36
22:7 [q]Lk 19:27
22:9 [r]Eze 21:21
22:10 [s]Mt 13:47, 48
22:12 [t]Mt 20:13; 26:50
22:13 [u]S Mt 8:12
22:14 [v]Rev 17:14
22:16 [w]Mk 3:6
22:17 [x]Mt 17:25

vited did not deserve to come. 9Go to the
street corners[r] and invite to the banquet
anyone you find.' 10So the servants went
out into the streets and gathered all the
people they could find, both good and
bad,[s] and the wedding hall was filled
with guests.

11"But when the king came in to see
the guests, he noticed a man there who
was not wearing wedding clothes.
12'Friend,'[t] he asked, 'how did you get in
here without wedding clothes?' The man
was speechless.

13"Then the king told the attendants,
'Tie him hand and foot, and throw him
outside, into the darkness, where there
will be weeping and gnashing of teeth.'[u]

14"For many are invited, but few are
chosen."[v]

Paying Taxes to Caesar

22:15–22pp — Mk 12:13–17; Lk 20:20–26

15Then the Pharisees went out and laid
plans to trap him in his words. 16They
sent their disciples to him along with the
Herodians.[w] **"Teacher," they said, "we**
know you are a man of integrity and that
you teach the way of God in accordance
with the truth. You aren't swayed by
men, because you pay no attention to
who they are. 17Tell us then, what is your
opinion? Is it right to pay taxes[x] **to Cae-**
sar or not?"

18But Jesus, knowing their evil intent,
said, "You hypocrites, why are you trying
to trap me? 19Show me the coin used for
paying the tax." **They brought him a de-**
narius, 20and he asked them, "Whose
portrait is this? And whose inscription?"

[k]*42* Or *cornerstone* [l]*42* Psalm 118:22,23
[m]*44* Some manuscripts do not have verse 44.

22:1–14 JESUS CHRIST, Kingdom of God—Jesus' coming represented God's invitation to Israel to attend the banquet honoring Messiah. They refused to participate. To refuse to honor God's Son is to reject the Father. God in grace invites all people to His kingdom. Compare Lk 14:16–24. We must attend His feast on His terms, not ours.

22:1–14 ELECTION, Free Will—The Jews had the first opportunity to be part of God's kingdom. Having rejected Jesus, they will discover that the believing Gentiles, whom they considered to be last, will join the Jewish faithful remnant as members of God's elect. The inheritance of God is given not as earthly inheritances are, by priority of birth and seniority, but by God's good pleasure. People have freedom to reject God's invitation through indifference, wrong priorities, and hostility. God's invitation continues to go out without preconditions as to membership in social classes or achievement of ethical standards. Election depends on God's grace to all people, not on accident of birth or human works. Acceptance of God's invitation must be in accord with His standard of repentance. Without meeting this standard, one faces expulsion and judgment. In free exercise of will humans respond to God's call to join the elect. Proper response in faith and repentance means a person is among the elect.

22:1–14 THE CHURCH, God's Kingdom—The kingdom of heaven includes those whom others reject. Entrance into God's kingdom depends on His goodness, not on social rank or good deeds. The kingdom's membership is limited. Just being part of the human race or having a vague belief in some kind of God does not qualify you for membership. You must accept God's invitation on His conditions of repentance and faith. See note on 21:31–32.

22:15–22 CHRISTIAN ETHICS, Church and State—The Pharisees intended to trap Jesus in a position which lent loyalty to Caesar and not to God. They wanted to level a charge of blasphemy against Jesus. By getting Him to declare nonallegiance to Caesar, they could get Him charged with a civil crime. Both attempts failed. Jesus' response does not resolve all of our questions regarding the responsibilities we have with church and state, but He does provide some beginning places to inform us. His answer implies we do have responsibilities to the state. These extend only to those 'things' that are Caesar's. A yet higher allegiance pulls upon us, too. We must be faithful to those things of God. See note on Ro 13:1–7.

22:18–21 HUMANITY, Relationships—See note on Lk 20:24–26.

21“Caesar's,” they replied.
Then he said to them, “Give to Caesar
what is Caesar's,[y] and to God what is
God's.”
22When they heard this, they were
amazed. So they left him and went
away.[z]

Marriage at the Resurrection

22:23–33pp — Mk 12:18–27; Lk 20:27–40

23That same day the Sadducees,[a] who
say there is no resurrection,[b] came to
him with a question. 24“Teacher,” they
said, “Moses told us that if a man dies
without having children, his brother
must marry the widow and have children
for him.[c] 25Now there were seven brothers among us. The first one married and
died, and since he had no children, he
left his wife to his brother. 26The same
thing happened to the second and third
brother, right on down to the seventh.
27Finally, the woman died. 28Now then,
at the resurrection, whose wife will she
be of the seven, since all of them were
married to her?”
29Jesus replied, “You are in error because you do not know the Scriptures[d] or
the power of God. 30At the resurrection
people will neither marry nor be given in
marriage;[e] they will be like the angels in
heaven. 31But about the resurrection of
the dead—have you not read what God
said to you, 32‘I am the God of Abraham,
the God of Isaac, and the God of Jacob'[n]?[f] He is not the God of the dead
but of the living.”
33When the crowds heard this, they
were astonished at his teaching.[g]

The Greatest Commandment

22:34–40pp — Mk 12:28–31

34Hearing that Jesus had silenced the
Sadducees,[h] the Pharisees got together.
35One of them, an expert in the law,[i]
tested him with this question: 36“Teacher, which is the greatest commandment
in the Law?”
37Jesus replied: “ ‘Love the Lord your
God with all your heart and with all your
soul and with all your mind.'[o][j] 38This is
the first and greatest commandment.
39And the second is like it: ‘Love your
neighbor as yourself.'[p][k] 40All the Law
and the Prophets hang on these two commandments.”[l]

22:21 [y]Ro 13:7
22:22 [z]Mk 12:12
22:23 [a]S Ac 4:1 [b]Ac 23:8; 1Co 15:12
22:24 [c]Dt 25:5,6
22:29 [d]Jn 20:9
22:30 [e]Mt 24:38
22:32 [f]Ex 3:6; Ac 7:32
22:33 [g]S Mt 7:28
22:34 [h]S Ac 4:1
22:35 [i]Lk 7:30; 10:25; 11:45; 14:3
22:37 [j]Dt 6:5
22:39 [k]Lev 19:18; S Mt 5:43
22:40 [l]Mt 7:12; Lk 10:25-28

[n]*32* Exodus 3:6 [o]*37* Deut. 6:5 [p]*39* Lev. 19:18

22:21 STEWARDSHIP, Taxes—Religious devotion and stewardship to God does not excuse us from responsibilities to civil government. The scribes' intended trap for Jesus backfired. They wanted a reason to keep their money and not support a government they disliked. Jesus said they must give government what was due the government for services rendered. Government loyalty must not exceed or control loyalty to God, but loyalty to God does not eliminate loyalty and responsibility to country.

22:23–33 HUMANITY, Nature of Death—In New Testament times, the Sadducees held to the ancient idea that life ended with death. Jesus assailed the idea that life ended with physical death. See Mk 12:18–27; Lk 20:27–40.

22:23–32 FAMILY, Temporal—Jesus affirmed marital relationships as we know them to be for this life only (Mk 12:18–27; Lk 20:27–38). Individuals experience life after death, but the Bible does not give specific instruction on the nature of personal interaction in heaven by those who have been married on earth.

22:24,36 EDUCATION, Jesus—The fact that Jesus was so often addressed as “Teacher,” even by His opponents, shows that this was His primary role in the eyes of the people around Him.

22:29 HOLY SCRIPTURE, Authoritative—Scriptures are the only source of authority for beliefs and doctrines. The Sadducees prided themselves on being the strict interpreters of Scripture. They were unwilling to believe what they could not find in the books of Moses. Thus they did not believe in resurrection (v 23) and angels and spirits (Ac 23:8). Jesus saw in them an illustration of the fact that false doctrine is built on a false understanding of Scripture. They were more interested in building proper logical connections and constructing theological puzzles to trap Jesus than they were in discovering and obeying the truth. Scripture calls us to careful study of all its words so we may understand more fully God's teachings for us. Proper understanding of Scripture may well correct long-cherished ideas and astonish us (v 33).

22:33 JESUS CHRIST, Authority—See note on 7:28.

22:34–40 CHRISTIAN ETHICS, Character—Personal character grows out of love for God. Loving God leads us to love other people. Such love will result in actions which comply with all God's moral demands. Love is the starting point for Christian ethics.

22:37–40 HUMANITY, Relationships—People are expected to be related both to God and to other persons through a commitment of sacrificial, giving love. Loyalty and faithfulness are to characterize such relationships. See Lev 19:18; Dt 6:5; Mk 12:29–31; 1 Jn 3:16–18.

22:37–39 HOLY SCRIPTURE, Relationship—Jesus provided the best summary possible of all the Old Testament revelation. He focused all Scripture on the priority of a right relationship with God and then with neighbors (Dt 6:5; 10:12; Lev 19:18). See note on Mt 13:33–35.

22:37–39 SALVATION, Obedience—The Law and the Prophets hang on the two commandments to love God supremely and to love neighbor as self. God's people do not have to learn a list of rules or face prophetic judgment. We have to let God plant His love so deep within us that we respond to every situation in love, seeking God's will and the best for the other person(s). Acting in self-giving love is obeying God. As we act in love, we will fulfill the Law's deepest demands (5:17).

22:37–40 DISCIPLESHIP, Neighbor Love—Christian love is the active, vitalizing power necessary in Christian living. Jesus' command to love God is directed primarily to the will rather than the emotions. It means to esteem God, to regard Him above all else, to give Him unchallenged first place, and to give His claims unquestioned priority. This love means, likewise, to esteem all that God esteems, to love what God loves to the extent not only of *doing* but of *being*. Our lives are to radiate Christ's love continuously. Christian relationships must be built on love; Christian fellowship must be maintained in love; and Christian service must be motivated by love. Love, of its own nature, produces the fruits of Christian devotion and service. The love Jesus commands eliminates injustice in human relations. It fulfills the law by abstaining from all that law forbids. See Ro 13:10. Jesus states that the twofold love commandment fulfills “the Law” and “the Prophets,” which when combined indicates the whole Old Testament.

Whose Son Is the Christ?

22:41–46pp — Mk 12:35–37; Lk 20:41–44

41While the Pharisees were gathered
together, Jesus asked them, 42"What do
you think about the Christ[q]? Whose son
is he?"
"The son of David,"[m] they replied.
43He said to them, "How is it then that
David, speaking by the Spirit, calls him
'Lord'? For he says,

44" 'The Lord said to my Lord:
"Sit at my right hand
until I put your enemies
under your feet." '[r] [n]

45If then David calls him 'Lord,' how can
he be his son?" 46No one could say a
word in reply, and from that day on no
one dared to ask him any more questions.[o]

Chapter 23

Seven Woes

23:1–7pp — Mk 12:38,39; Lk 20:45,46
23:37–39pp — Lk 13:34,35

THEN Jesus said to the crowds and to
his disciples: 2"The teachers of the
law[p] and the Pharisees sit in Moses' seat.
3So you must obey them and do everything they tell you. But do not do what
they do, for they do not practice what
they preach. 4They tie up heavy loads and
put them on men's shoulders, but they
themselves are not willing to lift a finger
to move them.[q]
5"Everything they do is done for men
to see:[r] They make their phylacteries[s] [s]
wide and the tassels on their garments[t]
long; 6they love the place of honor at banquets and the most important seats in the
synagogues;[u] 7they love to be greeted in
the marketplaces and to have men call
them 'Rabbi.'[v]
8"But you are not to be called 'Rabbi,'
for you have only one Master and you are
all brothers. 9And do not call anyone on
earth 'father,' for you have one Father,[w]
and he is in heaven. 10Nor are you to be
called 'teacher,' for you have one Teacher, the Christ.[q] 11The greatest among you
will be your servant.[x] 12For whoever exalts himself will be humbled, and whoever humbles himself will be exalted.[y]
13"Woe to you, teachers of the law and
Pharisees, you hypocrites![z] You shut the
kingdom of heaven in men's faces. You
yourselves do not enter, nor will you let
those enter who are trying to.[t] [a]
15"Woe to you, teachers of the law and
Pharisees, you hypocrites! You travel over

22:42 [m]S Mt 9:27
22:44 [n]Ps 110:1; 1Ki 5:3; Ac 2:34,35; 1Co 15:25; Heb 1:13; 10:13
22:46 [o]Mk 12:34; Lk 20:40
23:2 [p]Ezr 7:6,25
23:4 [q]Lk 11:46; Ac 15:10; Gal 6:13
23:5 [r]Mt 6:1,2,5,16 [s]Ex 13:9; Dt 6:8 [t]Nu 15:38; Dt 22:12
23:6 [u]Lk 11:43; 14:7; 20:46
23:7 [v]ver 8; Mt 26:25,49; Mk 9:5; 10:51; Jn 1:38,49; 3:2,26; 20:16
23:9 [w]Mal 1:6; Mt 6:9; 7:11
23:11 [x]S Mk 9:35
23:12 [y]1Sa 2:8; Ps 18:27; Pr 3:34; Isa 57:15; Eze 21:26; Lk 1:52; 14:11
23:13 [z]ver 15,23,25,27,29 [a]Lk 11:52

[q]*42,10* Or *Messiah* [r]*44* Psalm 110:1 [s]*5* That is, boxes containing Scripture verses, worn on forehead and arm [t]*13* Some manuscripts *to.* *[14]Woe to you, teachers of the law and Pharisees, you hypocrites! You devour widows' houses and for a show make lengthy prayers. Therefore you will be punished more severely.*

22:41–46 JESUS CHRIST, Son of David—Son of David applied to Jesus but was inadequate to describe the Messiah's role since Messiah was David's Master, as Ps 110:1 shows. Messiah was Son of God and provided salvation through death and resurrection, not through military victory. See note on Mt 1:1.

22:43 HOLY SPIRIT, Revelation—The Spirit inspired the writing of the Old Testament. Jesus taught that in Ps 110 David spoke by the Spirit. This shows Jesus believed the Hebrew Scriptures had been written under the guidance of the Spirit of the Lord. The same teaching recurs at Mk 12:36; 1 Co 2:10; 2 Ti 3:16; Heb 3:7; 1 Pe 1:11; 2 Pe 1:21.

23:1–11 DISCIPLESHIP, Priesthood—All Christian disciples are brothers, serving one another. No individual disciple or group of disciples is above any other. There is no priestly class because Christ Jesus is the only Mediator between God and us. We are not to seek important titles which distinguish us from or elevate us above others. We are not to set up rules and regulations for others to meet and by which we can judge others. Disciples do nothing to parade their own worth and power in front of others. We must be God-pleasers, not people-pleasers. Humble service, not worldly recognition, identifies the disciple. See Eph 2:18; 3:12; note on 1 Pe 2:5,9–10.

23:3 CHRISTIAN ETHICS, Moral Imperatives—A most unsettling charge lies within Jesus' words for those who dare to teach and to preach. Their verbal witness and their daily lives ought to agree. What they say, they should do. A sad day has come when moral leaders' own morality must be questioned.

23:8–10 JESUS CHRIST, Teaching—The ultimate authority for Christians is Jesus Christ. No one can take His place as Teacher, for only He totally fulfilled God's purposes. His followers are not to compete for positions or titles. They are to serve Him by serving one another.

23:8–10 CHURCH LEADERS, Authority—The church requires structure, but it is not to be like an army with a clearly ranked chain of command. Therefore, the leaders of the church are to renounce all exalted titles of honor that breed pride. The church is a brotherhood of equals under Christ. Status in the kingdom is not to be determined by title. Humility, not power, is the top priority for Christian servant leaders.

23:8 EDUCATION, Jesus—"Rabbi" is a term of respect used to address Jewish teachers of the law. So "Rabbi" is a synonym for "Teacher" in the Gospels. See Jn 1:38. Both titles are applied to Jesus. For all Christians, Jesus is "The Teacher," and no one will ever supersede Him in this role. We are brothers and sisters learning under His tutelage. We owe honor and titles to Him and not to one another. Our teaching task is as His servants and not as persons grasping for worldly honor.

23:9 GOD, Father—God the Father is to occupy a unique place of authority in the hearts of Christians. He is to be given respect, reverence, and love that is not given to any earthly person. God will not share His position of supreme authority with anyone else. No religious leader is to occupy the place of God the Father in our hearts. This verse does not prohibit the recognition of the parent-child relationship, for Jesus magnified human family relationships. He did not say a child must not address a male parent as father. Jesus forbid us to put any human figure in the place of God. We must not compromise the authority of God by projecting some of God's authority on to some human person. Religious leaders are only fellow servants of God (vv 11–12).

23:11 THE CHURCH, Servants—Position, influence, and achievement are not the church's measure of success. Exercising authority over other people does not equal greatness among God's people. God counts greatness by our attitudes towards ourselves and others. They must be viewed as most important and greatest. We must see ourselves as servants of others and, thus, of God. See note on 20:20–28.

23:15 EVANGELISM, Personal—The teachers of the law and the Pharisees were not condemned for seeking converts on

land and sea to win a single convert,[b]
and when he becomes one, you make
him twice as much a son of hell[c] as you
are.
16"Woe to you, blind guides![d] You say,
'If anyone swears by the temple, it means
nothing; but if anyone swears by the gold
of the temple, he is bound by his oath.'[e]
17You blind fools! Which is greater: the
gold, or the temple that makes the gold
sacred?[f] 18You also say, 'If anyone
swears by the altar, it means nothing; but
if anyone swears by the gift on it, he is
bound by his oath.' 19You blind men!
Which is greater: the gift, or the altar that
makes the gift sacred?[g] 20Therefore, he
who swears by the altar swears by it and
by everything on it. 21And he who swears
by the temple swears by it and by the one
who dwells[h] in it. 22And he who swears
by heaven swears by God's throne and by
the one who sits on it.[i]
23"Woe to you, teachers of the law and
Pharisees, you hypocrites! You give a
tenth[j] of your spices—mint, dill and
cummin. But you have neglected the
more important matters of the law—justice, mercy and faithfulness.[k] You should
have practiced the latter, without neglecting the former. 24You blind guides![l] You
strain out a gnat but swallow a camel.
25"Woe to you, teachers of the law and
Pharisees, you hypocrites! You clean the
outside of the cup and dish,[m] but inside
they are full of greed and self-indulgence.[n] 26Blind Pharisee! First clean the
inside of the cup and dish, and then the
outside also will be clean.

23:15 [b]Ac 2:11; 6:5; 13:43 [c]S Mt 5:22
23:16 [d]ver 24; Isa 9:16; Mt 15:14 [e]Mt 5:33-35
23:17 [f]Ex 30:29
23:19 [g]Ex 29:37
23:21 [h]1Ki 8:13; Ps 26:8
23:22 [i]Ps 11:4; Mt 5:34
23:23 [j]Lev 27:30 [k]Mic 6:8; Lk 11:42
23:24 [l]ver 16
23:25 [m]Mk 7:4 [n]Lk 11:39
23:27 [o]Lk 11:44; Ac 23:3
23:29 [p]Lk 11:47, 48
23:31 [q]S Mt 5:12
23:32 [r]1Th 2:16 [s]Eze 20:4
23:33 [t]Mt 3:7; 12:34 [u]S Mt 5:22
23:34 [v]2Ch 36:15, 16; Lk 11:49 [w]S Mt 10:17 [x]Mt 10:23
23:35 [y]Ge 4:8; Heb 11:4 [z]Zec 1:1 [a]2Ch 24:21
23:36 [b]Mt 10:23; 24:34; Lk 11:50,51
23:37 [c]2Ch 24:21; S Mt 5:12

27"Woe to you, teachers of the law and
Pharisees, you hypocrites! You are like
whitewashed tombs,[o] which look beautiful on the outside but on the inside are
full of dead men's bones and everything
unclean. 28In the same way, on the outside you appear to people as righteous but
on the inside you are full of hypocrisy and
wickedness.
29"Woe to you, teachers of the law and
Pharisees, you hypocrites! You build
tombs for the prophets[p] and decorate the
graves of the righteous. 30And you say, 'If
we had lived in the days of our forefathers, we would not have taken part with
them in shedding the blood of the prophets.' 31So you testify against yourselves
that you are the descendants of those
who murdered the prophets.[q] 32Fill up,
then, the measure[r] of the sin of your
forefathers![s]
33"You snakes! You brood of vipers![t]
How will you escape being condemned to
hell?[u] 34Therefore I am sending you
prophets and wise men and teachers.
Some of them you will kill and crucify;[v]
others you will flog in your synagogues[w]
and pursue from town to town.[x] 35And
so upon you will come all the righteous
blood that has been shed on earth, from
the blood of righteous Abel[y] to the blood
of Zechariah son of Berekiah,[z] whom you
murdered between the temple and the altar.[a] 36I tell you the truth, all this will
come upon this generation.[b]
37"O Jerusalem, Jerusalem, you who
kill the prophets and stone those sent to
you,[c] how often I have longed to gather

---

a personal basis. Rather, it was to what they were converting them. They did not lead the people to God's righteousness in Christ, but to a religiosity that had no real spiritual substance. The "converts," being deceived, were worse off than before. We should be anxious to win people personally as did the Scribes and Pharisees, but we must be careful to win them to Christ, not to a shallow set of religious rules.

23:16–22 CHRISTIAN ETHICS, Language—Hypocritical human rules and tradition cannot justify or protect us from lying. Truth is valued. Intricate interpretation of legal rules to avoid the truth is not. See note on 5:33–36.

23:23 CHRISTIAN ETHICS, Justice—Jesus endorsed the prophets' summary of true religion and service of God. Justice not legalism forms the center. Justice must be carried out in mercy for the oppressed. It must be faithfully and constantly acted out. See note on Mic 6:6–8.

23:23–24 STEWARDSHIP, Tithe—In this discussion tithing is given as an example of the Pharisees' hypocrisy. The Old Testament law of the tithe required that they give ten percent of agricultural produce. See note on Nu 18:21–32. They had gone to an exaggerated point on this to prove their righteousness while missing the real meaning of righteousness—mercy and justice. Many believe that here Jesus established the tithe as the plan for Christian giving. He commended the Pharisees' devotion to the law of tithing, but He did not say how this was to apply to His followers. Jesus did say much about giving *during His ministry.*

23:25–26 EDUCATION, False Teachers—Hypocritical teaching is worse than no teaching at all. Teachers who are pious on the outside but corrupt on the inside can delude those who follow them, leaving them worse off spiritually than they were before. See 23:15. Because teaching is an awesome responsibility, false teaching is a terrible sin. See 23:35.

23:28,35 CHRISTIAN ETHICS, Righteousness—Attitudes shape actions. Over a period of time our actions will betray the hypocrisy and evil we harbor. Those whom Jesus addressed prided themselves in outward pious actions, but their attitudes and goals were wicked. Judgment is certain for hypocrites who build their own reputations at any cost. They will have to endure God's vengeance for all the truly righteous people these religious hypocrites persecuted and killed.

23:32 SIN, Depravity—The Jewish leaders were overconscientious about maintaining the traditions of their fathers. In an ironic tone, Jesus said they succeeded well at one point: killing God's messengers. Just as their ancestors ignored, persecuted, and killed prophets, so they were about to bring the tradition to its ultimate fulfillment by rejecting and killing Jesus, the greatest Prophet and more, the anointed Messiah who came to fulfill prophecy and provide God's promised salvation. In their fanatic religious zeal for the tradition, the Pharisees and scribes proved how depraved they were. Jesus tore off their hypocritical masks of self-proclaimed faithfulness to tradition. These religious leaders were not the only or last religious zealots to elevate tradition to God's place and to substitute self-service for God's service.

23:37–39 JESUS CHRIST, Final Coming—Jesus loved and sought to save His own Jewish people. They rejected Him. At the final judgment they will recognize Him whom they rejected.

23:37 REVELATION, Jesus Christ—The heart of God is

your children together, as a hen gathers
her chicks under her wings,[d] but you
were not willing. 38Look, your house is
left to you desolate.[e] 39For I tell you, you
will not see me again until you say,
'Blessed is he who comes in the name of
the Lord.'[u]"[f]

Chapter 24

Signs of the End of the Age

24:1–51pp — Mk 13:1–37; Lk 21:5–36

**JESUS left the temple and was walking
away when his disciples came up to
him to call his attention to its buildings.
2"Do you see all these things?" he asked.**
"I tell you the truth, not one stone here
will be left on another;[g] every one will
be thrown down."

**3As Jesus was sitting on the Mount of
Olives,[h] the disciples came to him privately. "Tell us," they said, "when will
this happen, and what will be the sign of
your coming[i] and of the end of the
age?"[j]**

4Jesus answered: "Watch out that no
one deceives you.[k] 5For many will come
in my name, claiming, 'I am the Christ,[v]'
and will deceive many.[l] 6You will hear of
wars and rumors of wars, but see to it
that you are not alarmed. Such things
must happen, but the end is still to come.
7Nation will rise against nation, and kingdom against kingdom.[m] There will be
famines[n] and earthquakes in various
places. 8All these are the beginning of
birth pains.

9"Then you will be handed over to be
persecuted[o] and put to death,[p] and you
will be hated by all nations because of
me.[q] 10At that time many will turn away
from the faith and will betray and hate
each other, 11and many false prophets[r]
will appear and deceive many people.[s]
12Because of the increase of wickedness,
the love of most will grow cold, 13but he
who stands firm to the end will be
saved.[t] 14And this gospel of the kingdom[u] will be preached in the whole
world[v] as a testimony to all nations, and
then the end will come.

15"So when you see standing in the
holy place[w] 'the abomination that causes
desolation,'[w][x] spoken of through the
prophet Daniel—let the reader understand— 16then let those who are in Judea
flee to the mountains. 17Let no one on the
roof of his house[y] go down to take anything out of the house. 18Let no one in
the field go back to get his cloak. 19How
dreadful it will be in those days for pregnant women and nursing mothers![z]
20Pray that your flight will not take place
in winter or on the Sabbath. 21For then
there will be great distress, unequaled

23:37 [d]Ps 57:1; 61:4; Isa 31:5
23:38 [e]1Ki 9:7,8; Jer 22:5
23:39 [f]Ps 118:26; Mt 21:9
24:2 [g]Lk 19:44
24:3 [h]S Mt 21:1 [i]S Lk 17:30 [j]Mt 13:39; 28:20
24:4 [k]S Mk 13:5
24:5 [l]ver 11,23,24; 1Jn 2:18
24:7 [m]Isa 19:2 [n]Ac 11:28
24:9 [o]Mt 10:17 [p]Jn 16:2 [q]S Jn 15:21
24:11 [r]S Mt 7:15 [s]S Mk 13:5
24:13 [t]S Mt 10:22
24:14 [u]S Mt 4:23 [v]S Ro 10:18; Lk 2:1; 4:5; Ac 11:28; 17:6; Rev 3:10; 16:14
24:15 [w]S Ac 6:13 [x]Da 9:27; 11:31; 12:11
24:17 [y]1Sa 9:25; Mt 10:27; Lk 12:3; Ac 10:9
24:19 [z]Lk 23:29

[u]*39* Psalm 118:26 [v]*5* Or *Messiah*; also in verse 23
[w]*15* Daniel 9:27; 11:31; 12:11

---

clearly known and heard in this loving and painful lamentation over Jerusalem. Jesus' heart ached for people who claimed loyalty to Scripture yet had a history of killing the authors of Scripture. People may reject the love of God, strong as it is. He will not force Himself upon anyone, but He hurts when rejected.

23:39 PRAYER, Blessing—Times will get so bad people will joyfully welcome the returning Messiah with a prayer of benediction.

24:1—25:46 JESUS CHRIST, Final Coming—See note on 5:1–12. This conversation on the final coming combines events which would happen at the destruction of Jerusalem in AD 70 and events which would happen at the end of the age, at Jesus' final coming. Compare Mk 13:1–37; Lk 21:5–36. A special word is used of Jesus' final coming. The Greek *parousia* (24:3,27,37,39) means "presence," but in this special eschatological use it means His final presence or coming.

24:3–14 LAST THINGS, Return Signs—Jesus gave seven signs in this passage that would be precursors of His return. The multiple fulfillment theory of biblical prophecy allows these to have dual meaning. Historically, they were signs of the approaching destruction of the Temple. Eschatologically, they find ultimate fulfillment in association with Christ's return. Both were part of the question Jesus addressed on this occasion. The signs are: the appearance of false messiahs, the occurrence of wars and rumors of wars, multiple famines, frequent earthquakes, apostasy from the faith, abating love, and worldwide proclamation of the gospel. The sign value is not so much in isolated or infrequent occurrences of these precursors but in the converging and intensifying of all of them prior to the coming of the end (Mk 13:3–13).

24:5,23–25 JESUS CHRIST, Christ—Jesus was not the only person looked upon as the Messiah. People had to choose which of several candidates, if any, was actually sent by God. Many people were deceived. False messiahs will continue to plague God's people until Christ's final return.

24:9–14 REVELATION, Events—Persecution and pain occur for Jesus' followers. Many will give up their beliefs under pressure of torture. False revelations from lying messengers will take place. Such events do not disprove the gospel. They confirm God's revelation.

24:10–13 ELECTION, Eternal Security—The church and the elect are not identical. Hard times reveal the elect's true colors. False disciples in the church lead others away into political action or immoral freedom, causing hostility and division in the church. This represents a lack of love and betrayal of Christ and His church. The elect stand firm and will be saved despite the deception and defection of other church members. Endurance in faithful obedience reveals the elect. Christ's return will bring final salvation for the elect.

24:14 PROCLAMATION, Compulsion—See note on 1 Co 9:16–18.

24:14 EVANGELISM, Mass—The gospel will go out to all the world before the end comes. God desires His people to engage in world evangelization. Declaring the gospel to the masses will hasten the day when Jesus comes again.

24:20 PRAYER, Petition—Prayer for protection from final tribulation is in order now. The day is expected when Christians will have to flee persecution and will need open roads without delay.

24:21–22 LAST THINGS, Great Tribulation—In many passages "tribulation" refers to great distress of a general sort, such as may be brought on by national catastrophes or unfortunate circumstances. The amillennial view is that the tribulation refers to the constant and sometimes intense sufferings Christians face because of their faith. Premillennialists believe in such a general application but insist that this reference refers specifically to a particular, intensified period of future distress. Historically, the time of Jerusalem's destruction in AD 70 was an unusual occasion of great distress for its inhabitants. Pro-

from the beginning of the world until
now—and never to be equaled again.[a]
22If those days had not been cut short, no
one would survive, but for the sake of the
elect[b] those days will be shortened. 23At
that time if anyone says to you, 'Look,
here is the Christ!' or, 'There he is!' do
not believe it.[c] 24For false Christs and
false prophets will appear and perform
great signs and miracles[d] to deceive even
the elect—if that were possible. 25See, I
have told you ahead of time.

26"So if anyone tells you, 'There he is,
out in the desert,' do not go out; or, 'Here
he is, in the inner rooms,' do not believe
it. 27For as lightning[e] that comes from
the east is visible even in the west, so
will be the coming[f] of the Son of Man.[g]
28Wherever there is a carcass, there the
vultures will gather.[h]

29"Immediately after the distress of
those days

" 'the sun will be darkened,
and the moon will not give its light;
the stars will fall from the sky,
and the heavenly bodies will be
shaken.'[x] [i]

30"At that time the sign of the Son of
Man will appear in the sky, and all the
nations of the earth will mourn.[j] They
will see the Son of Man coming on the
clouds of the sky,[k] with power and great
glory. 31And he will send his angels[l]
with a loud trumpet call,[m] and they will
gather his elect from the four winds, from
one end of the heavens to the other.

32"Now learn this lesson from the fig
tree: As soon as its twigs get tender and
its leaves come out, you know that summer is near. 33Even so, when you see all
these things, you know that it[y] is near,
right at the door.[n] 34I tell you the truth,
this generation[z] will certainly not pass
away until all these things have happened.[o] 35Heaven and earth will pass
away, but my words will never pass
away.[p]

The Day and Hour Unknown

24:37–39pp — Lk 17:26,27
24:45–51pp — Lk 12:42–46

36"No one knows about that day or
hour, not even the angels in heaven, nor
the Son,[a] but only the Father.[q] 37As it
was in the days of Noah,[r] so it will be at
the coming of the Son of Man. 38For in
the days before the flood, people were
eating and drinking, marrying and giving
in marriage,[s] up to the day Noah entered
the ark; 39and they knew nothing about
what would happen until the flood came
and took them all away. That is how it
will be at the coming of the Son of Man.[t]

24:21 [a]Eze 5:9; Da 12:1; Joel 2:2
24:22 [b]ver 24,31
24:23 [c]Lk 17:23; 21:8
24:24 [d]Ex 7:11,22; 2Th 2:9-11; Rev 13:13; 16:14; 19:20
24:27 [e]Lk 17:24 [f]S Lk 17:30 [g]S Mt 8:20
24:28 [h]Lk 17:37
24:29 [i]Isa 13:10; 34:4; Eze 32:7; Joel 2:10,31; Zep 1:15; Rev 6:12, 13; 8:12
24:30 [j]Rev 1:7 [k]S Rev 1:7
24:31 [l]Mt 13:41 [m]Isa 27:13; Zec 9:14; 1Co 15:52; 1Th 4:16; Rev 8:2; 10:7; 11:15
24:33 [n]Jas 5:9
24:34 [o]Mt 16:28; S 23:36
24:35 [p]S Mt 5:18
24:36 [q]Ac 1:7
24:37 [r]Ge 6:5; 7:6-23
24:38 [s]Mt 22:30
24:39 [t]S Lk 17:30

[x]*29* Isaiah 13:10; 34:4 [y]*33* Or *he* [z]*34* Or *race*
[a]*36* Some manuscripts do not have *nor the Son.*

phetically, a future time of great tribulation, unparalleled in human history, awaits the generation living at the time of Christ's second coming. See note on Da 9:24–27.

24:22–31 ELECTION, Testing—At the time of the appearing of the Son of man, which will occur after days of deep distress, the elect will be gathered from one end of the heavens to the other. Not even the angels in heaven know the precise time. Hence, the elect should be faithful and ready. The elect will endure testing by false religious leaders before the final end of history. God's grace and love for the elect have limited the time of testing.

24:24 MIRACLE, God's Working—Many in the ancient world practised magic and deceived others. Two examples are Simon (Ac 8:9) and Elymas (Ac 13:8). Miracles in themselves do not prove God is at work. We are easily deceived. God's miracles continue His work of creating good in the world and redeeming the world. See Mt 8:22–23.

24:25–44 JESUS CHRIST, Final Coming—Jesus self-consciously exercised God's authority in announcing happenings of the end time. He used His favorite Son of man self-designation to speak of His final coming as a shining appearance (Greek *phaneroō*). Compare Col 3:4; 1 Pe 5:4. He will appear suddenly with divine glory, announced by angelic trumpeters. Jesus showed the limits He assumed as a human being by admitting His ignorance of the exact time. See note on Mt 8:20.

24:27–28,30 LAST THINGS, Return Promises—The coming (Greek *parousia*) of Christ will be unquestionably public, as visible as lightning out of the east visible even unto the west. It will be as impossible to miss as it would be for vultures to fail to see a carcass. All the nations of the earth will see Christ's coming with power and great glory. The hatred of all nations for Jesus' followers (v 9) will turn to the mourning of despair when they see Jesus' glorious return in power.

***24:31* REVELATION, Angels**—At God's appointed time messengers from God will gather all who believe around the world, that they may share in the coming reign of Jesus Christ.

24:35 CREATION, Nature—God created the world and all that is in it. He, however, is more important than the things He has made. The world is so constituted that the spiritual is more important than the physical or material. God has revealed Himself through His Word, both the living Word, Jesus Christ, and His written Word, the Bible. Neither will ever cease to exist. Heaven and earth, as we know them, will someday cease to be.

24:36 GOD, Trinity—Jesus gave to God the Father a unique position of authority and sovereignty, and acknowledged His own submission and obedience to the Father. God the Father has priority even in the trinitarian relationship. While in His earthly life, Jesus plainly subordinated Himself to God, His Father, and experienced at least some of the limitations of human life. One of those limitations is clearly stated here. See notes on 19:17; 20:23. So far as Jesus was concerned some things are only under God the Father's control. The Trinity has an element of mystery. How can the three Persons share a common life as one God, yet one of the three Persons have the priority in sovereign authority? It is a priority of revelation, how the one God is revealed to us in three Persons. It is a priority of function, how the one God in three Persons carries out His work. It is a priority of purpose, the one God in three Persons bringing us under the redemptive power of the Creator-Father who is the one and only true God.

24:36–44 LAST THINGS, Demands Preparedness—The text warns against predictions about the time of Christ's return and cautions believers that not knowing the time of His return demands we stay ever prepared. Like those of Noah's time who were caught unprepared for a flood, so will it be for many at the coming of the Son of man. In their unpreparedness, people will be going about the normal activities of life when the unexpected overtakes them. The good servant is prepared for the Lord at any time. Compare 24:45—25:13.

40Two men will be in the field; one will
be taken and the other left.[u] 41Two wom-
en will be grinding with a hand mill; one
will be taken and the other left.[v]
42"Therefore keep watch, because you
do not know on what day your Lord will
come.[w] 43But understand this: If the
owner of the house had known at what
time of night the thief was coming,[x] he
would have kept watch and would not
have let his house be broken into. 44So
you also must be ready,[y] because the Son
of Man will come at an hour when you do
not expect him.
45"Who then is the faithful and wise
servant,[z] whom the master has put in
charge of the servants in his household to
give them their food at the proper time?
46It will be good for that servant whose
master finds him doing so when he returns.[a] 47I tell you the truth, he will put
him in charge of all his possessions.[b]
48But suppose that servant is wicked and
says to himself, 'My master is staying
away a long time,' 49and he then begins
to beat his fellow servants and to eat and
drink with drunkards.[c] 50The master of
that servant will come on a day when he
does not expect him and at an hour he is
not aware of. 51He will cut him to pieces
and assign him a place with the hypocrites, where there will be weeping and
gnashing of teeth.[d]

Chapter 25

The Parable of the Ten Virgins

"AT that time the kingdom of heaven
will be like[e] ten virgins who took
their lamps[f] and went out to meet the
bridegroom.[g] 2Five of them were foolish
and five were wise.[h] 3The foolish ones
took their lamps but did not take any oil
with them. 4The wise, however, took oil
in jars along with their lamps. 5The bridegroom was a long time in coming, and
they all became drowsy and fell asleep.[i]
6"At midnight the cry rang out: 'Here's
the bridegroom! Come out to meet him!'
7"Then all the virgins woke up and
trimmed their lamps. 8The foolish ones
said to the wise, 'Give us some of your
oil; our lamps are going out.'[j]
9" 'No,' they replied, 'there may not be
enough for both us and you. Instead, go
to those who sell oil and buy some for
yourselves.'
10"But while they were on their way to
buy the oil, the bridegroom arrived. The
virgins who were ready went in with him
to the wedding banquet.[k] And the door
was shut.
11"Later the others also came. 'Sir! Sir!'
they said. 'Open the door for us!'
12"But he replied, 'I tell you the truth, I
don't know you.'[l]
13"Therefore keep watch, because you
do not know the day or the hour.[m]

The Parable of the Talents

25:14–30Ref — Lk 19:12–27

14"Again, it will be like a man going on
a journey,[n] who called his servants and
entrusted his property to them. 15To one
he gave five talents[b] of money, to another two talents, and to another one talent,
each according to his ability.[o] Then he
went on his journey. 16The man who had
received the five talents went at once and

24:40 [u]Lk 17:34
24:41 [v]Lk 17:35
24:42 [w]Mt 25:13; Lk 12:40
24:43 [x]S Lk 12:39
24:44 [y]1Th 5:6
24:45 [z]Mt 25:21, 23
24:46 [a]Rev 16:15
24:47 [b]Mt 25:21, 23
24:49 [c]Lk 21:34
24:51 [d]S Mt 8:12
25:1 [e]S Mt 13:24 [f]Lk 12:35-38; Ac 20:8; Rev 4:5 [g]Rev 19:7; 21:2
25:2 [h]Mt 24:45
25:5 [i]1Th 5:6
25:8 [j]Lk 12:35
25:10 [k]Rev 19:9
25:12 [l]ver 41; S Mt 7:23
25:13 [m]Mt 24:42, 44; Mk 13:35; Lk 12:40
25:14 [n]Mt 21:33; Lk 19:12
25:15 [o]Mt 18:24, 25

[b] *15* A talent was worth more than a thousand dollars.

24:44 REVELATION, Divine Presence—Watchfulness and readiness are critical aspects of preparing for the last days, for no one knows when Christ's reign and coming will take place (25:1–13).
24:51 LAST THINGS, Hell—Those unfaithful to Christ and unprepared for His coming face eternal sorrow and mourning. Hypocrites, in particular, face this fate. See note on 5:22.
25:1–5 HUMANITY, Life—Jesus vividly described a typical group of adolescents. Some were wise and planned ahead. Others were less careful, living only for the moment and not caring about the future. Life should be lived with a constant view to the future insofar as planning and preparation are concerned. Our most careful planning must be to see that we are part of God's kingdom.
25:1–13 SALVATION, Obedience—Salvation leads to obedience over the long run. Obeying the Savior means preparing to serve Him in all circumstances, knowing He may return at any moment.
25:1–13 LAST THINGS, Demands Preparedness—The relation of this parable to last things is variously explained. Seeking meaning in the details, some explain the virgins as professing members of the church awaiting Christ's return. Others see the virgins as representing a faithful Jewish remnant during the tribulation period. Whatever be the application of the details, if any, all see in the parable a lesson about the need to be prepared when Christ returns. Preparedness must be personal. Those unprepared cannot borrow from those who are. Failure to be ready when the Lord comes is to be shut out from His presence and kingdom.
25:1–13 THE CHURCH, God's Kingdom—Christ brought the kingdom of God, making it present in His church. He pointed to the future when He would bring the kingdom in its fullness. Believers must be alert, prepared to greet Christ when He returns. Other people cannot prepare us at the last moment. Christ will admit only the prepared ones to the kingdom. See note on 13:24–30.
25:14–30 HUMANITY, Responsibility—All people have skills, talents, and possessions entrusted to them by God. Our responsibility is to use these in manners that will accomplish God's purposes. No one is responsible for the way others use their gifts. We are responsible for the proper use of our own gifts.
25:14–30 LAST THINGS, Encourages Faithfulness—By use of these parables, Jesus taught the need for faithfulness in service during the time prior to His return. Compare Lk 19:11–27. He expects faithfulness in proportion to ability. He will reward faithfulness and punish unfaithfulness. His return will bring a time of accountability.
25:15–30 STEWARDSHIP, Management—Christ taught accountability and faithfulness to God. Those faithful in managing receive additional trusts. Life and all its possessions are our trust fund from God. We are responsible to manage our time, abilities, and possessions so God and His kingdom will receive the greatest possible return. See note on Ge 39:2–6.

put his money to work and gained five
more. 17So also, the one with the two talents gained two more. 18But the man who
had received the one talent went off, dug
a hole in the ground and hid his master's
money.
19"After a long time the master of
those servants returned and settled accounts with them.[p] 20The man who had
received the five talents brought the other five. 'Master,' he said, 'you entrusted
me with five talents. See, I have gained
five more.'
21"His master replied, 'Well done,
good and faithful servant! You have been
faithful with a few things; I will put you
in charge of many things.[q] Come and
share your master's happiness!'
22"The man with the two talents also
came. 'Master,' he said, 'you entrusted
me with two talents; see, I have gained
two more.'
23"His master replied, 'Well done,
good and faithful servant! You have been
faithful with a few things; I will put you
in charge of many things.[r] Come and
share your master's happiness!'
24"Then the man who had received the
one talent came. 'Master,' he said, 'I
knew that you are a hard man, harvesting
where you have not sown and gathering
where you have not scattered seed. 25So I
was afraid and went out and hid your talent in the ground. See, here is what belongs to you.'
26"His master replied, 'You wicked,
lazy servant! So you knew that I harvest
where I have not sown and gather where
I have not scattered seed? 27Well then,
you should have put my money on deposit with the bankers, so that when I returned I would have received it back with
interest.
28" 'Take the talent from him and give
it to the one who has the ten talents.
29For everyone who has will be given
more, and he will have an abundance.
Whoever does not have, even what he
has will be taken from him.[s] 30And
throw that worthless servant outside, into
the darkness, where there will be weeping and gnashing of teeth.'[t]

The Sheep and the Goats

31"When the Son of Man comes[u] in
his glory, and all the angels with him, he
will sit on his throne[v] in heavenly glory.
32All the nations will be gathered before
him, and he will separate[w] the people
one from another as a shepherd separates
the sheep from the goats.[x] 33He will put
the sheep on his right and the goats on
his left.
34"Then the King will say to those on
his right, 'Come, you who are blessed by

25:19 [p]Mt 18:23
25:21 [q]ver 23; Mt 24:45,47; Lk 16:10
25:23 [r]ver 21
25:29 [s]Mt 13:12; Mk 4:25; Lk 8:18; 19:26
25:30 [t]S Mt 8:12
25:31 [u]S Lk 17:30 [v]Mt 19:28
25:32 [w]Mal 3:18 [x]Eze 34:17,20

25:30 LAST THINGS, Hell—See note on 24:51.

25:31–46 JESUS CHRIST, Judgment—Jesus Christ was the humble Suffering Servant in His earthly ministry. He will return as the all-powerful King executing final judgment. See notes on 8:20; 13:37–43. Even in judgment He will identify with the needy of the world.

25:31–46 EVIL AND SUFFERING, Comfort—Hunger, thirst, loneliness, illness, and imprisonment are evils some of God's people have to endure. Disciples should respond to the problems of the hungry and needy. To ignore such needs will result in eternal punishment.

25:31–46 STEWARDSHIP, Service to God—Serving God's purposes in the world gives value to money and goods. Giving to meet the needs of fellow Christians is one way of serving Christ. We cannot wait until Jesus returns to do something for Him. We must daily seek opportunities to minister to the poor, afflicted, and suffering of our world.

25:31–46 LAST THINGS, Judgment—The specific point of reference for this judgment is interpreted in different ways. Dispensationalists see in it a future judgment of the living nations at the beginning of an earthly millennium. See note on Rev 20:1–6. The purpose of such would be to determine either on a national or individual basis those who enter the millennial kingdom. Other views believe the text portrays a final, general judgment. The purpose of such would be to gather all humanity for the time of separation and assignment of eternal destinies. The basic fact of future judgment is clearly taught, according to both views. The details of the parable may only be to paint a parabolic picture without being intended to be pressed. The point of Jesus is that God's final judgment will result in eternal separation between the righteous and the wicked. Final judgment will be based on what *actual deeds reveal* about the *true inner spiritual* state of persons, not what verbal professions may have claimed. See note on Mt 16:27. Hypocrisy cannot survive the judgment. Final destiny for the unrighteous will be the company of the devil and his angels in everlasting fire, separated from God forever. The same adjective "eternal" (Greek *aiōnion*) describes both the "life" rewarded and the "punishment" given.

25:34 CREATION, Redemption—The physical world with its lavish material wealth was not God's goal in creation. Establishment of His eternal kingdom was His goal. Since we are all His creation, He loves everyone. We will be judged, therefore, by what we have done to help one another, especially those who, being weak, have great need. This passage stands as a great challenge to us and supplements rather than contradicts the doctrine of justification by faith. Those who have been saved by grace and transformed by the Spirit of God will respond affirmatively to such a challenge. Works are the proof of our salvation, not the means of securing it.

25:34 ELECTION, Predestination—The admission of the elect into the blessedness of God's kingdom has been assured from the foundations of the world. God's eternal purpose has been to create a kingdom of holy people devoted to Him. The purpose has always included separation of His people from the unbelieving world. Compare Ex 19:3–6; Eze 34:17; Heb 12:4.

25:34 SALVATION, Blessing—Those who do the Father's will are blessed. Their inheritance is the kingdom of God, prepared for them since the creation of the world.

25:34–46 DISCIPLESHIP, Rewarded—When the Lord returns, the distinction between those who served God and those who did not will be made clear as all stand before the judgment seat for the great separation. The way we served will determine whether or not we are Christ's disciples. Those who serve with proper motives serve the Lord by serving people in need. See note on 6:1–4. They will be rewarded with the inheritance of the kingdom God has prepared since the beginning of time. Those who are not Christ's disciples will receive eternal punishment as their lot. See note on 2 Pe 1:10–11.

my Father; take your inheritance, the
kingdom[y] prepared for you since the creation of the world.[z] 35For I was hungry
and you gave me something to eat, I was
thirsty and you gave me something to
drink, I was a stranger and you invited
me in,[a] 36I needed clothes and you
clothed me,[b] I was sick and you looked
after me,[c] I was in prison and you came
to visit me.'[d]

37"Then the righteous will answer
him, 'Lord, when did we see you hungry
and feed you, or thirsty and give you
something to drink? 38When did we see
you a stranger and invite you in, or needing clothes and clothe you? 39When did
we see you sick or in prison and go to
visit you?'

40"The King will reply, 'I tell you the
truth, whatever you did for one of the
least of these brothers of mine, you did
for me.'[e]

41"Then he will say to those on his left,
'Depart from me,[f] you who are cursed,
into the eternal fire[g] prepared for the
devil and his angels.[h] 42For I was hungry
and you gave me nothing to eat,
I was thirsty and you gave me nothing
to drink, 43I was a stranger and you
did not invite me in, I needed clothes
and you did not clothe me, I was sick
and in prison and you did not look after
me.'

44"They also will answer, 'Lord, when
did we see you hungry or thirsty or a
stranger or needing clothes or sick or in
prison, and did not help you?'

45"He will reply, 'I tell you the
truth, whatever you did not do for one
of the least of these, you did not do for
me.'[i]

46"Then they will go away to eternal
punishment, but the righteous to eternal
life.[j] "[k]

25:34 [y]S Mt 3:2; 5:3,10,19; 19:14; S Ac 20:32; 1Co 15:50; Gal 5:21; Jas 2:5 [z]Heb 4:3; 9:26; Rev 13:8; 17:8
25:35 [a]Job 31:32; Heb 13:2
25:36 [b]Isa 58:7; Eze 18:7; Jas 2:15, 16 [c]Jas 1:27 [d]2Ti 1:16
25:40 [e]S Mt 10:40, 42; Heb 13:2
25:41 [f]S Mt 7:23 [g]Isa 66:24; Mt 3:12; S 5:22; Mk 9:43,48; Lk 3:17; Jude 7 [h]2Pe 2:4
25:45 [i]Pr 14:31; 17:5
25:46 [j]Mt 19:29; Jn 3:15,16,36; 17:2, 3; Ro 2:7; Gal 6:8; 1Jn 1:2; 5:11,13,20 [k]Da 12:2; Jn 5:29; Ac 24:15; Ro 2:7,8; Gal 6:8
26:1 [l]S Mt 7:28
26:2 [m]S Jn 11:55
26:3 [n]Ps 2:2 [o]ver 57; Lk 3:2; Jn 11:47-53; 18:13, 14,24,28; Ac 4:6
26:4 [p]S Mt 12:14
26:5 [q]Mt 27:24
26:6 [r]S Mt 21:17
26:11 [s]Dt 15:11
26:12 [t]Jn 19:40

Chapter 26

The Plot Against Jesus

26:2–5pp — Mk 14:1,2; Lk 22:1,2

WHEN Jesus had finished saying all
these things,[l] he said to his disciples, 2"As you know, the Passover[m] is
two days away—and the Son of Man will
be handed over to be crucified."

3Then the chief priests and the elders
of the people assembled[n] in the palace of
the high priest, whose name was Caiaphas,[o] 4and they plotted to arrest Jesus in
some sly way and kill him.[p] 5"But not
during the Feast," they said, "or there
may be a riot[q] among the people."

Jesus Anointed at Bethany

26:6–13pp — Mk 14:3–9
26:6–13Ref — Lk 7:37,38; Jn 12:1–8

6While Jesus was in Bethany[r] in the
home of a man known as Simon the Leper, 7a woman came to him with an alabaster jar of very expensive perfume, which
she poured on his head as he was reclining at the table.

8When the disciples saw this, they
were indignant. "Why this waste?" they
asked. 9"This perfume could have been
sold at a high price and the money given
to the poor."

10Aware of this, Jesus said to them,
"Why are you bothering this woman? She
has done a beautiful thing to me. 11The
poor you will always have with you,[s] but
you will not always have me. 12When she
poured this perfume on my body, she did
it to prepare me for burial.[t] 13I tell you
the truth, wherever this gospel is
preached throughout the world, what she
has done will also be told, in memory of
her."

Judas Agrees to Betray Jesus

26:14–16pp — Mk 14:10,11; Lk 22:3–6

14Then one of the Twelve—the one

25:37–46 CHRISTIAN ETHICS, Righteousness—Jesus draws our attention to the least of this world (the widows, orphans, aliens, and poor of the Old Testament). Our response to these who have no advocate and are unable to help themselves gives us some indication of the validity of the bond we profess to have with Christ. Jesus virtually says to see Him we must recognize Him in the hungry, thirsty, strangers, sick, and imprisoned around us. If we love Him, would we not go to Him? Then, let us love Him through these oppressed humans. See notes on DISCIPLESHIP, Poor, Hungry, Homeless, Oppressed (Index, p. 1860).

25:46 SALVATION, Eternal Life—Those who have been made right with God through faith in Christ, and who reflect this as they live by God's standards, will live forever with God in heaven. Those who are not and do not will experience the eternal punishment of hell. Eternal life begins here as we live out God's quality of life among those for whom God cares especially. Compare Lk 4:18–19.

26:6–13 JESUS CHRIST, Death—See note on 16:21–23; Jn 12:1–10. Compare Mk 14:3–9; Lk 7:36–38. To honor Christ is not wasteful. Extravagant tribute to the King has its eternal reward. Jesus accepted the woman's tribute as proper preparation for His coming death and burial.

26:6–13 STEWARDSHIP, Service to God—Stewardship involves sensitivity concerning when to use resources and inner freedom to act extravagantly at the proper time. Jesus appreciated the woman's beautiful, extravagant gift because it showed her sensitivity to Him as He faced the cross. His disciples seem to have had good intentions but lacked sensitivity. See note on Ac 4:32—5:11.

26:14–16,25–26 JESUS CHRIST, Death—Compare Mk 14:10–11; Lk 22:3–6. Late Tuesday night or Wednesday of the last week Judas betrayed Jesus. The thirty pieces of silver (Zec 11:12) were the traditional value of a slave. See note on Jn 13:18–30.

26:14–16,23–25,47–49 SIN, Individual Choice—Just as Judas made the fatal choice of betraying Jesus to the authorities, so every person makes the choice for or against the Lord. We cannot shift the blame to another for our sinful acts. When personal goals are not fulfilled, greed often sets in to lead us to

called Judas Iscariot[u]—went to the chief
priests 15and asked, "What are you willing to give me if I hand him over to you?"
So they counted out for him thirty silver
coins.[v] 16From then on Judas watched for
an opportunity to hand him over.

The Lord's Supper

26:17–19pp — Mk 14:12–16; Lk 22:7–13
26:20–24pp — Mk 14:17–21
26:26–29pp — Mk 14:22–25; Lk 22:17–20; 1Co 11:23–25

17On the first day of the Feast of Unleavened Bread,[w] the disciples came to
Jesus and asked, "Where do you want us
to make preparations for you to eat the
Passover?"[x]
18He replied, "Go into the city to a certain man and tell him, 'The Teacher says:
My appointed time[y] is near. I am going
to celebrate the Passover with my disciples at your house.' " 19So the disciples
did as Jesus had directed them and prepared the Passover.
20When evening came, Jesus was reclining at the table with the Twelve.
21And while they were eating, he said, "I
tell you the truth, one of you will betray
me."[z]
22They were very sad and began to say
to him one after the other, "Surely not I,
Lord?"
23Jesus replied, "The one who has
dipped his hand into the bowl with me
will betray me.[a] 24The Son of Man will
go just as it is written about him.[b] But
woe to that man who betrays the Son of
Man! It would be better for him if he had
not been born."
25Then Judas, the one who would betray him,[c] said, "Surely not I, Rabbi?"[d]
Jesus answered, "Yes, it is you."[c]
26While they were eating, Jesus took
bread, gave thanks and broke it,[e] and
gave it to his disciples, saying, "Take and
eat; this is my body."
27Then he took the cup,[f] gave thanks
and offered it to them, saying, "Drink
from it, all of you. 28This is my blood of
the[d] covenant,[g] which is poured out for
many for the forgiveness of sins.[h] 29I tell
you, I will not drink of this fruit of the
vine from now on until that day when I
drink it anew with you[i] in my Father's
kingdom."
30When they had sung a hymn, they
went out to the Mount of Olives.[j]

Jesus Predicts Peter's Denial

26:31–35pp — Mk 14:27–31; Lk 22:31–34

31Then Jesus told them, "This very
night you will all fall away on account of
me,[k] for it is written:

" 'I will strike the shepherd,
and the sheep of the flock will be
scattered.'[e] [l]

32But after I have risen, I will go ahead of
you into Galilee."[m]
33Peter replied, "Even if all fall away
on account of you, I never will."
34"I tell you the truth," Jesus answered, "this very night, before the
rooster crows, you will disown me three
times."[n]
35But Peter declared, "Even if I have to
die with you,[o] I will never disown you."
And all the other disciples said the same.

26:14 [u]ver 25,47; S Mt 10:4
26:15 [v]Ex 21:32; Zec 11:12
26:17 [w]Ex 12:18-20 [x]Dt 16:5-8
26:18 [y]Mk 14:35, 41; Jn 7:6,8,30; 8:20; 12:23; 13:1; 17:1
26:21 [z]Lk 22:21-23; Jn 13:21
26:23 [a]Ps 41:9; Jn 13:18
26:24 [b]ver 31,54, 56; Isa 53; Da 9:26; Mk 9:12; Lk 24:25-27,46; Ac 17:2,3; 26:22, 23; 1Pe 1:10,11
26:25 [c]S Mt 10:4 [d]S Mt 23:7
26:26 [e]S Mt 14:19
26:27 [f]1Co 10:16
26:28 [g]Ex 24:6-8; Zec 9:11; Mal 2:5; Heb 9:20; 10:29; S 13:20 [h]S Mt 20:28; Mk 1:4
26:29 [i]Ac 10:41
26:30 [j]S Mt 21:1
26:31 [k]Mt 11:6; 13:21 [l]Zec 13:7; Jn 16:32
26:32 [m]Mt 28:7, 10,16
26:34 [n]ver 75; Jn 13:38
26:35 [o]Jn 13:37

[c]25 Or *"You yourself have said it"* [d]28 Some manuscripts *the new* [e]31 Zech. 13:7

the wrong, sinful choices. Commitment to those sinful choices destroys life, making it better never to have seen the light of day than to face God's judgment on sinners.

26:17–30 JESUS CHRIST, Death—Compare Mk 14:12–25; Lk 22:7–23; 1 Co 11:23–26. Jesus prepared His disciples for His death through the Passover and Lord's Supper, which would help them realize His death was not an accident but God's appointed will. Jesus looked beyond His death to renewed fellowship in the eternal kingdom.

26:17–30 ORDINANCES, Lord's Supper as New Covenant—Jesus gave the bread and cup to His disciples while they were celebrating the Passover. This makes it clear that He intended this Supper to be a sign of the new covenant as the Passover had been the sign of the old covenant. When He took the bread, He was taking the most basic necessity of daily nourishment for our bodies. His body, offered for us on the cross, symbolized the absolute necessity for our spiritual nourishment as Christian disciples. "Gave thanks" (Greek *eucharistō*) provides the name "Eucharist" by which many Christians designate the Lord's Supper. The cup signifies the "blood of the covenant," a reference to the death of Jesus by which the new covenant was established. "Until that day when I drink it anew with you in my Father's kingdom" draws our attention away from the past references to the Passover and forward to the death, resurrection, and return of Christ. It concentrates on the future when Christ will come in victory and celebrate with His disciples in the Father's kingdom.

26:26–28 REVELATION, Actions—The shared Passover concluded with Jesus's revelations that bread and cup represent His body and blood, symbols of the gift He offered by His willingness to die for all. Connecting His own life and death with the Jewish meal of a sacrificed lamb, Jesus revealed Himself as an offered lamb.

26:26–27 PRAYER, Thanksgiving—See notes on 14:19; Mk 8:6–7. Although the Passover ritual required separate prayers for the elements, the prayers in Mk 8:6–7 indicate that Jesus' attitude was of blessing and gratitude throughout the meal.

26:28 SALVATION, Forgiveness—The wine in the Lord's Supper represents the blood of Christ which was poured out for the forgiveness of sins (Heb 9:22). Christ's death on the cross was an atoning sacrifice for sins and established God's new covenant with His people.

26:30 WORSHIP, Music—See note on 1 Ch 6:31–32.

26:31–32 REVELATION, Jesus Christ—Jesus fulfilled the Scripture (Zec 13:7) and revealed Himself as the Shepherd to be killed. He then proclaimed Himself Lord of the grave, declaring He would rise and go ahead of them to Galilee. The disciples did not understand the mystery of resurrection. They knew the meaning of sacrifice but not power over death. Even Jesus' revelation was not immediately clear to His disciples.

Doctrinal Emphases in the Miracles of Our Lord

MIRACLE	BIBLE PASSAGE				DOCTRINAL EMPHASIS*
Water Turned to Wine				John 2:1-11	Vocabulary in defining miracles
Healings	Matthew 4:23-24	Mark 1:32-34			Christ as the agent of miracles
Healing of a Leper	Matthew 8:1-4	Mark 1:40-42	Luke 5:12-13		Christ as the agent of miracles
Healing of a Roman Centurion's Servant	Matthew 8:5-13		Luke 7:1-10		Faith as the context of miracles
Healing of Peter's Mother-in-law	Matthew 8:14-15	Mark 1:29-31	Luke 4:38-39		Christ as the agent of miracles
Calming of the Storm at Sea	Matthew 8:23-27	Mark 4:35-41	Luke 8:22-25		Nature as the context of miracles
Healing of the Wild Men of Gadara	Matthew 8:28-34	Mark 5:1-15	Luke 8:26-35		Christ as the agent of miracles
Healing of a Paralytic	Matthew 9:1-7	Mark 2:1-12	Luke 5:18-25		Christ as the agent of miracles
Healing of a Woman with a Hemorrhage	Matthew 9:20-22	Mark 5:25-29	Luke 8:43-48		Faith as the context of miracles
Raising of Jairus' Daughter	Matthew 9:23-25	Mark 5:22-42	Luke 8:41-56		Faith as the context of miracles
Healing of Two Blind Men	Matthew 9:27-31				Faith as the context of miracles
Healing of a Demon-possessed Man	Matthew 8:32-33				Revelation as the purpose of miracles
Healing of a Man with a Shriveled Hand	Matthew 12:10-13	Mark 3:1-5	Luke 6:6-10		Redemption as the purpose of miracles
Feeding of 5,000 People	Matthew 14:15-21	Mark 6:35-44	Luke 9:12-17	John 6:1-13	Christ as the agent of miracles
Walking on the Sea	Matthew 14:22-25	Mark 6:47-51		John 6:16-21	Christ as the agent of miracles
Healing of the Syrophoenician's Daughter	Matthew 15:21-28	Mark 7:24-30			Faith as the context of miracles
Feeding of 4,000 People	Matthew 15:32-38	Mark 8:1-9			Christ as the agent of miracles
Healing of a Boy with Seizures	Matthew 17:14-18	Mark 9:14-29	Luke 9:37-43		Faith as the context of miracles
Healing of Two Blind Men at Jericho	Matthew 20:30-34				Faith as the context of miracles
Healing of a Man with an Unclean Spirit		Mark 1:23-26	Luke 4:33-35		Christ as the agent of miracles
Healing of a Deaf, Speechless Man		Mark 7:31-37			Methods in defining miracles
Healing of a Blind Man at Bethsaida		Mark 8:22-26			Christ as the agent of miracles
Healing of Blind Bartimaeus		Mark 10:46-52	Luke 18:35-43		Faith as the context of miracles
A Miraculous Catch of Fish			Luke 5:4-11	John 21:1-11	Nature as the context of miracles
Raising of A Widow's Son			Luke 7:11-15		Christ as the agent of miracles
Healing of an Infirm Woman			Luke 13:11-13		Praise as the purpose of miracles
Healing of a Man with the Dropsy			Luke 14:1-4		Christ as the agent of miracles
Healing of Ten Lepers			Luke 17:11-19		Faith as the context of miracles
Healing of Malchus' Ear			Luke 22:50-51	John 18:3-11	Christ as the agent of miracles
Healing of Official's Son				John 4:46-54	Faith as the context of miracles
Healing of a Lame Man at Bethesda				John 5:1-9	Faith as the context of miracles
Healing of a Blind Man				John 9:1-12	Faith as the context of miracles
Raising of Lazarus				John 11:38-44	Christ as the agent of miracles

*Emphasis of annotation on the Doctrine of Miracle. See annotation at Bible passage and outline of the doctrine of miracle at the Doctrinal Reference Index.

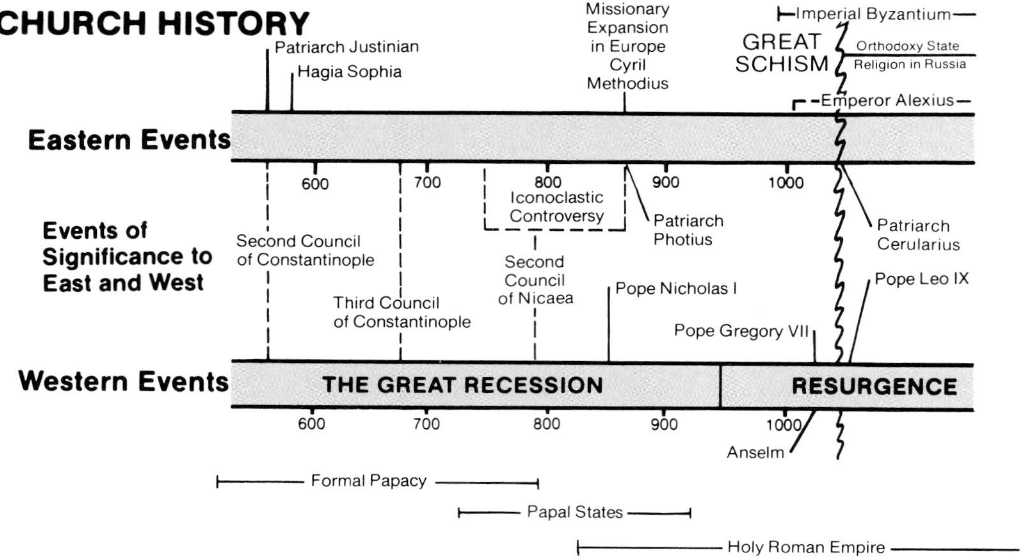
CHURCH HISTORY
Patriarch Justinian
Hagia Sophia
Missionary Expansion in Europe Cyril Methodius
Imperial Byzantium
GREAT SCHISM
Orthodoxy State Religion in Russia
Emperor Alexius
Eastern Events
600
700
800
900
1000
Iconoclastic Controversy
Patriarch Photius
Patriarch Cerularius
Events of Significance to East and West
Second Council of Constantinople
Second Council of Nicaea
Pope Nicholas I
Pope Leo IX
Third Council of Constantinople
Pope Gregory VII
Western Events
THE GREAT RECESSION
RESURGENCE
600
700
800
900
1000
Anselm
Formal Papacy
Papal States
Holy Roman Empire

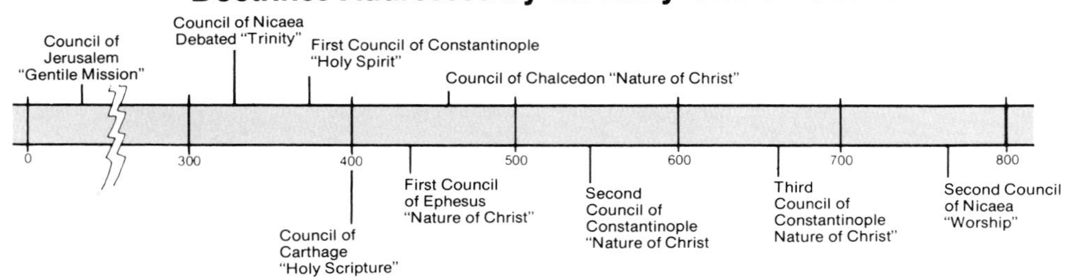
Doctrines Addressed by the Early Church Councils
Council of Jerusalem "Gentile Mission"
Council of Nicaea Debated "Trinity"
First Council of Constantinople "Holy Spirit"
Council of Chalcedon "Nature of Christ"
0
300
400
500
600
700
800
Council of Carthage "Holy Scripture"
First Council of Ephesus "Nature of Christ"
Second Council of Constantinople "Nature of Christ
Third Council of Constantinople Nature of Christ"
Second Council of Nicaea "Worship"

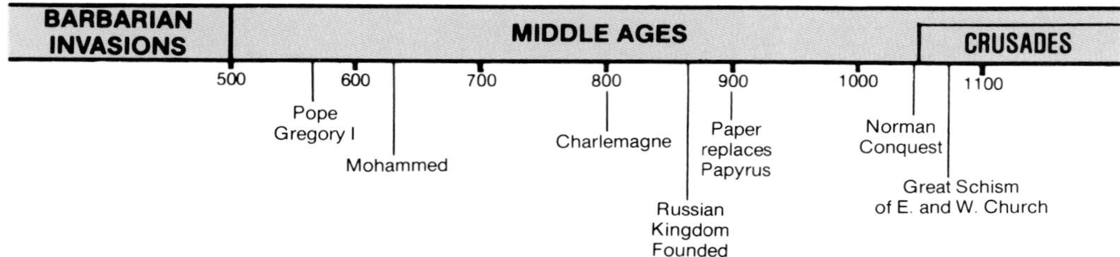
MEDIEVAL HISTORY
WORLD HISTORY
BARBARIAN INVASIONS
MIDDLE AGES
CRUSADES
500
600
700
800
900
1000
1100
Pope Gregory I
Mohammed
Charlemagne
Russian Kingdom Founded
Paper replaces Papyrus
Norman Conquest
Great Schism of E. and W. Church

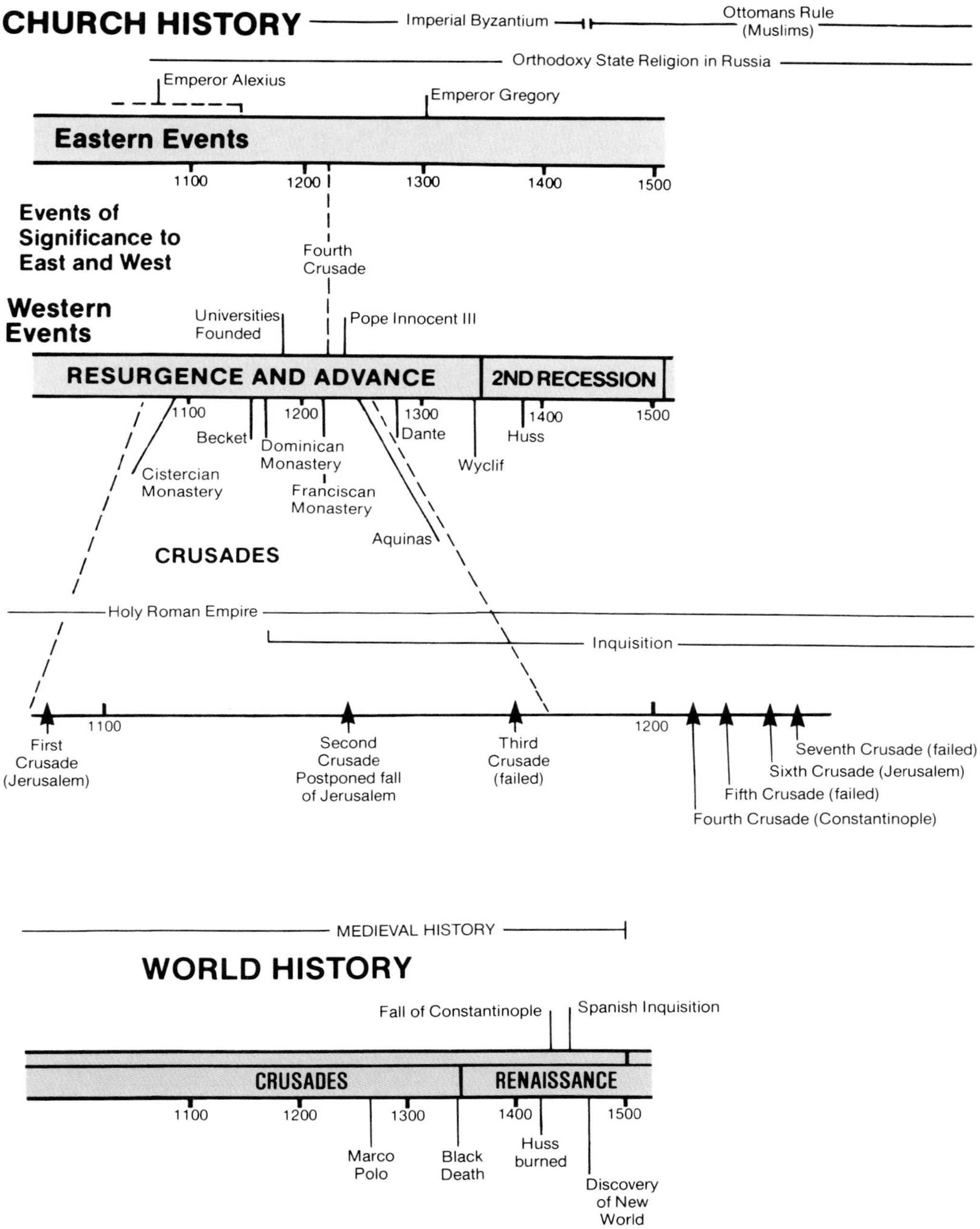

CHURCH HISTORY
Imperial Byzantium
Ottomans Rule (Muslims)
Orthodoxy State Religion in Russia
Emperor Alexius
Emperor Gregory
Eastern Events
1100
1200
1300
1400
1500
Events of Significance to East and West
Fourth Crusade
Western Events
Universities Founded
Pope Innocent III
RESURGENCE AND ADVANCE
2ND RECESSION
1100
1200
1300
1400
1500
Becket
Dominican Monastery
Dante
Huss
Wyclif
Cistercian Monastery
Franciscan Monastery
Aquinas
CRUSADES
Holy Roman Empire
Inquisition
1100
1200
First Crusade (Jerusalem)
Second Crusade Postponed fall of Jerusalem
Third Crusade (failed)
Seventh Crusade (failed)
Sixth Crusade (Jerusalem)
Fifth Crusade (failed)
Fourth Crusade (Constantinople)
MEDIEVAL HISTORY
WORLD HISTORY
Fall of Constantinople
Spanish Inquisition
CRUSADES
RENAISSANCE
1100
1200
1300
1400
1500
Marco Polo
Black Death
Huss burned
Discovery of New World

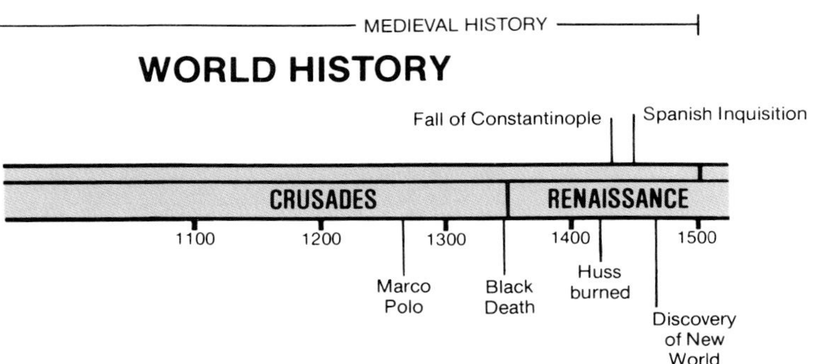

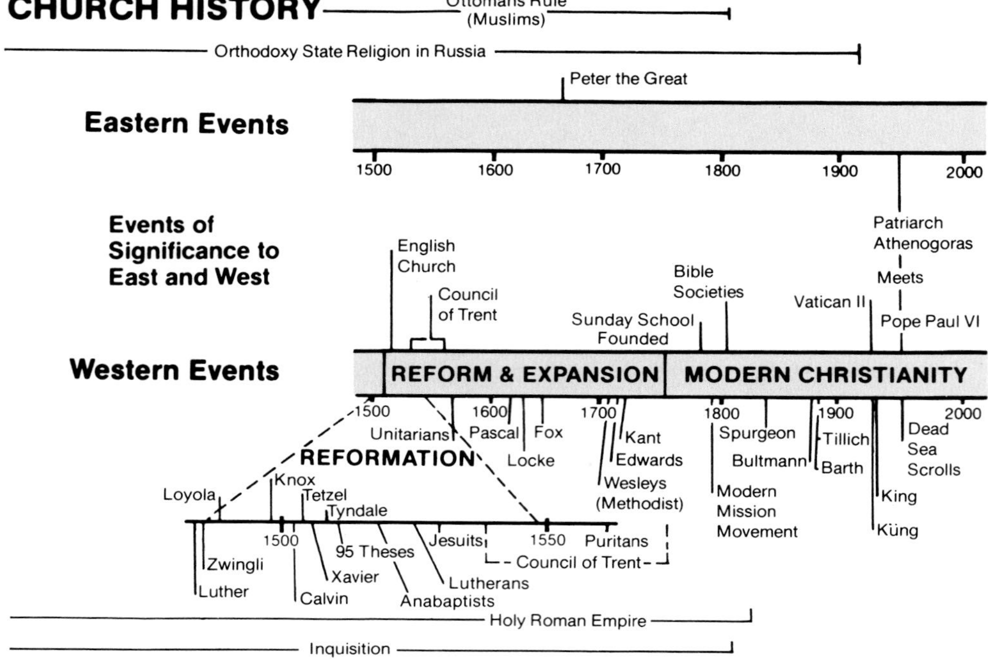
CHURCH HISTORY
Ottomans Rule (Muslims)
Orthodoxy State Religion in Russia
Peter the Great
Eastern Events
1500
1600
1700
1800
1900
2000
Events of Significance to East and West
English Church
Council of Trent
Bible Societies
Sunday School Founded
Vatican II
Patriarch Athenogoras Meets Pope Paul VI
Western Events
REFORM & EXPANSION
MODERN CHRISTIANITY
Unitarians
Pascal
Fox
Locke
Kant
Edwards
Wesleys (Methodist)
Spurgeon
Bultmann
Modern Mission Movement
Tillich
Barth
King
Küng
Dead Sea Scrolls
REFORMATION
Loyola
Knox
Tetzel
Tyndale
1550
Zwingli
Luther
Calvin
95 Theses
Xavier
Anabaptists
Lutherans
Jesuits
Puritans
Council of Trent
Holy Roman Empire
Inquisition

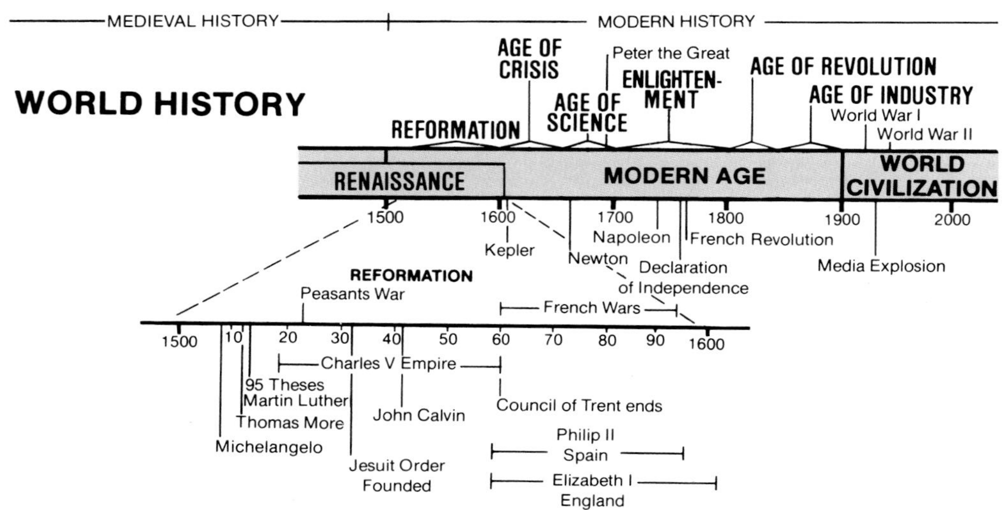
MEDIEVAL HISTORY
MODERN HISTORY
WORLD HISTORY
AGE OF CRISIS
Peter the Great
ENLIGHTEN-MENT
AGE OF REVOLUTION
AGE OF SCIENCE
AGE OF INDUSTRY
REFORMATION
World War I
World War II
RENAISSANCE
MODERN AGE
WORLD CIVILIZATION
1500
1600
1700
1800
1900
2000
Kepler
Newton
Napoleon
French Revolution
Declaration of Independence
Media Explosion
REFORMATION
Peasants War
French Wars
1500
10
20
30
40
50
60
70
80
90
1600
Charles V Empire
95 Theses
Martin Luther
Thomas More
Michelangelo
John Calvin
Jesuit Order Founded
Council of Trent ends
Philip II Spain
Elizabeth I England

Gethsemane

26:36–46pp — Mk 14:32–42; Lk 22:40–46

36 Then Jesus went with his disciples to
a place called Gethsemane, and he said to
them, "Sit here while I go over there and
pray." 37 He took Peter and the two sons
of Zebedee[p] along with him, and he began to be sorrowful and troubled. 38 Then
he said to them, "My soul is overwhelmed with sorrow[q] to the point of
death. Stay here and keep watch with
me."[r]

39 Going a little farther, he fell with his
face to the ground and prayed, "My Father, if it is possible, may this cup[s] be
taken from me. Yet not as I will, but as
you will."[t]

40 Then he returned to his disciples and
found them sleeping. "Could you men
not keep watch with me[u] for one hour?"
he asked Peter. 41 "Watch and pray so
that you will not fall into temptation.[v]
The spirit is willing, but the body is
weak."

42 He went away a second time and
prayed, "My Father, if it is not possible for this cup to be taken away
unless I drink it, may your will be
done."[w]

43 When he came back, he again found
them sleeping, because their eyes were
heavy. 44 So he left them and went away
once more and prayed the third time, saying the same thing.

45 Then he returned to the disciples and
said to them, "Are you still sleeping and
resting? Look, the hour[x] is near, and the
Son of Man is betrayed into the hands of
sinners. 46 Rise, let us go! Here comes my
betrayer!"

26:37 [p]S Mt 4:21
26:38 [q]S Jn 12:27 [r]ver 40,41
26:39 [s]S Mt 20:22 [t]ver 42; Ps 40:6-8; Isa 50:5; Mt 6:10; Jn 4:34; 5:30; 6:38
26:40 [u]ver 38
26:41 [v]Mt 6:13
26:42 [w]S ver 39
26:45 [x]S ver 18
26:47 [y]S Mt 10:4
26:49 [z]ver 25; S Mt 23:7
26:50 [a]Mt 20:13; 22:12
26:51 [b]Lk 22:36,38 [c]Jn 18:10
26:52 [d]Ge 9:6; Ex 21:12; Rev 13:10
26:53 [e]2Ki 6:17; Da 7:10; Mt 4:11
26:54 [f]S ver 24; S Mt 1:22
26:55 [g]Mk 12:35; Lk 21:37; Jn 7:14, 28; 18:20
26:56 [h]S ver 24; S Mt 1:22

Jesus Arrested

26:47–56pp — Mk 14:43–50; Lk 22:47–53

47 While he was still speaking, Judas,[y]
one of the Twelve, arrived. With him was
a large crowd armed with swords and
clubs, sent from the chief priests and the
elders of the people. 48 Now the betrayer
had arranged a signal with them: "The
one I kiss is the man; arrest him." 49 Going at once to Jesus, Judas said, "Greetings, Rabbi!"[z] and kissed him.

50 Jesus replied, "Friend,[a] do what you
came for."[f]

Then the men stepped forward, seized
Jesus and arrested him. 51 With that, one
of Jesus' companions reached for his
sword,[b] drew it out and struck the servant of the high priest, cutting off his
ear.[c]

52 "Put your sword back in its place,"
Jesus said to him, "for all who draw the
sword will die by the sword.[d] 53 Do you
think I cannot call on my Father, and he
will at once put at my disposal more than
twelve legions of angels?[e] 54 But how
then would the Scriptures be fulfilled[f]
that say it must happen in this way?"

55 At that time Jesus said to the crowd,
"Am I leading a rebellion, that you have
come out with swords and clubs to capture me? Every day I sat in the temple
courts teaching,[g] and you did not arrest
me. 56 But this has all taken place that the
writings of the prophets might be fulfilled."[h] Then all the disciples deserted
him and fled.

Before the Sanhedrin

26:57–68pp — Mk 14:53–65; Jn 18:12,13,19–24

57 Those who had arrested Jesus took

[f]50 Or *"Friend, why have you come?"*

26:36–46 JESUS CHRIST, Suffering—As a human, Jesus suffered physical and emotional pain. Gethsemane shows the height of His emotional agony as He struggled in prayer with the Father over the events He faced. Even in agony, He obeyed the Father.

26:36–44 PRAYER, Petition—No prayer in Jesus' life shows the perfection of His humanity better than the Gethsemane prayer. He would not have been human if He had not shrunk from the impending cross. He made no attempt to argue His case. He did not suggest another way. Rather, He simply prayed for God's direction and will, noting His desire for another path if possible. He searched the great cosmic mind of God for some other possibility. There was no other way, so He committed Himself to the Father's will. Prayer voices our human desires but seeks God's perfect will and guidance above all.

26:40–41 PRAYER, Petition—The disciples' deliverance from temptation was important to Christ (6:13; Jn 17:15). He knew their danger and warned them that willingness of spirit was not enough; they needed moral strength, strength of spirit. See note on Lk 22:31–32. Such strength comes from prayer.

26:47–56 JESUS CHRIST, Death—Compare 14:43–52; Lk 22:47–53; Jn 18:2–12. Jesus' arrest was at night, in His place of prayer, in secret, accompanied by Judas' treachery, interrupted by violence, and concluded with the desertion of His disciples. The kiss was a typical way for a student to greet a teacher. Facing death, Jesus refused to use violence or to use supernatural powers or supporters to win His way. See note on 4:1–11. He sought to fulfill Scripture and God's purpose. Political rebellion was not His way of being King of God's people.

26:51–53 CHRISTIAN ETHICS, War and Peace—Jesus and the Father chose to bring in and illustrate the Kingdom by the ways of peace and not war. God had shown many times in Israel's history He has the power and resources to win war and rule over all human powers. In Christ He chose to call people to accept freely the life of peace as peacemakers. See note on 5:9.

26:57—27:26 JESUS CHRIST, Death—Compare Mk 14:53—15:15; Lk 22:54—23:25; Jn 18:12—19:16. The trial of Jesus was a complex and involved process. Jesus was taken to the house of Caiphas and tried before the Sanhedrin (26:57–68). The second trial was before Pilate (27:11–26). Between the two trials are the two travails of Peter and Judas. Peter repented and lived to serve. Judas was remorseful and took his own life. Only Matthew speaks of Pilate's wife and her troubled dreams about Jesus (27:19). Sinless Jesus was sentenced to capital punishment on the evidence of false witnesses quoting Him out of context on religious teaching. Envy, not evidence, led to His death. Pilate the judge gave in to political

him to Caiaphas,[i] the high priest, where
the teachers of the law and the elders had
assembled. 58But Peter followed him at a
distance, right up to the courtyard of the
high priest.[j] He entered and sat down
with the guards[k] to see the outcome.
59The chief priests and the whole Sanhedrin[l] were looking for false evidence
against Jesus so that they could put him to
death. 60But they did not find any, though
many false witnesses[m] came forward.
Finally two[n] came forward 61and declared, "This fellow said, 'I am able to
destroy the temple of God and rebuild it
in three days.' "[o]
62Then the high priest stood up and
said to Jesus, "Are you not going to answer? What is this testimony that these
men are bringing against you?" 63But
Jesus remained silent.[p]
The high priest said to him, "I charge
you under oath[q] by the living God:[r] Tell
us if you are the Christ,[g][s] the Son of
God."[t]
64"Yes, it is as you say,"[u] Jesus replied. "But I say to all of you: In the future you will see the Son of Man sitting at
the right hand of the Mighty One[v] and
coming on the clouds of heaven."[w]
65Then the high priest tore his
clothes[x] and said, "He has spoken blasphemy! Why do we need any more witnesses? Look, now you have heard the
blasphemy. 66What do you think?"
"He is worthy of death,"[y] they answered.
67Then they spit in his face and struck
him with their fists.[z] Others slapped him
68and said, "Prophesy to us, Christ. Who
hit you?"[a]

Peter Disowns Jesus

26:69–75pp — Mk 14:66–72; Lk 22:55–62; Jn 18:16–18,25–27

69Now Peter was sitting out in the
courtyard, and a servant girl came to him.
"You also were with Jesus of Galilee,"
she said.
70But he denied it before them all. "I
don't know what you're talking about,"
he said.
71Then he went out to the gateway,
where another girl saw him and said to
the people there, "This fellow was with
Jesus of Nazareth."
72He denied it again, with an oath: "I
don't know the man!"
73After a little while, those standing
there went up to Peter and said, "Surely
you are one of them, for your accent gives
you away."
74Then he began to call down curses on
himself and he swore to them, "I don't
know the man!"
Immediately a rooster crowed. 75Then
Peter remembered the word Jesus had
spoken: "Before the rooster crows, you
will disown me three times."[b] And he
went outside and wept bitterly.

Chapter 27

Judas Hangs Himself

EARLY in the morning, all the chief
priests and the elders of the people
came to the decision to put Jesus to
death.[c] 2They bound him, led him away
and handed him over[d] to Pilate, the governor.[e]
3When Judas, who had betrayed him,[f]
saw that Jesus was condemned, he was
seized with remorse and returned the
thirty silver coins[g] to the chief priests
and the elders. 4"I have sinned," he said,
"for I have betrayed innocent blood."
"What is that to us?" they replied.
"That's your responsibility."[h]
5So Judas threw the money into the

26:57 [i]S ver 3
26:58 [j]ver 69; Mk 14:66; Lk 22:55; Jn 18:15 [k]Mk 15:16; Lk 11:21; Jn 7:32, 45,46
26:59 [l]S Mt 5:22
26:60 [m]Ps 27:12; 35:11; Ac 6:13 [n]Dt 19:15
26:61 [o]S Jn 2:19
26:63 [p]S Mk 14:61 [q]Lev 5:1 [r]S Mt 16:16 [s]Lk 22:67 [t]S Mt 4:3
26:64 [u]Mt 27:11; Lk 22:70 [v]S Mk 16:19 [w]S Rev 1:7
26:65 [x]S Mk 14:63
26:66 [y]Lev 24:16; Jn 19:7
26:67 [z]S Mt 16:21
26:68 [a]Lk 22:63-65
26:75 [b]ver 34; Jn 13:38
27:1 [c]S Mt 12:14; Mk 15:1; Lk 22:66
27:2 [d]Mt 20:19 [e]Mk 15:1; Lk 13:1; Ac 3:13; 1Ti 6:13
27:3 [f]S Mt 10:4 [g]Mt 26:14,15
27:4 [h]ver 24

[g]63 Or *Messiah*; also in verse 68

pressure rather than carry out justice and release Jesus.

26:64 JESUS CHRIST, Christ—See notes on 13:37–43; Mk 14:53—15:15. Facing death, Jesus accepted messianic titles but did not interpret them.

26:64 LAST THINGS, Return Promises—The victory of Christ involves resurrection and enthronement, as well as future return. Even His enemies will someday see Him as He is, not as a defendant on trial but as a messianic King and sovereign Judge.

26:69–75 SIN, Responsibility—Just as Peter was responsible for his denial of Jesus, so we are each responsible for every sinful act we commit. Overwhelming guilt is the first responsible response to our own sin. Guilt can then be relieved through confession, repentance, and acceptance of God's forgiveness.

27:1–10 JESUS CHRIST, Death—Compare Jer 19:1–13; 32:6–9; Zec 11:12–13. Even the details of Jesus' death can be understood as fulfilling Scripture for those faithful enough to understand Scripture correctly.

27:3–5 *JESUS CHRIST,* Death—See note on Jn 13:18–30.

27:3–5 HUMANITY, Death—Remorse springs from our guilt being exposed in a situation we cannot escape. Repentance is far different. It includes the intention to change. Deep remorse in a hopeless situation makes suicide attractive. The greatest tragedy at such a time is the failure to recognize that God still offers hope. Trust in Him brings hope to every situation. God will forgive whatever we did to cause remorse. The past cannot be rewritten, but in the future we can change.

27:3–10 SIN, Responsibility—A person must accept responsibility for personal sin and turn away from it in repentance. Peter faced his sin with bitter tears of repentance (26:75) and then turned back to Christ for a new commission (Jn 21:15–19; Ac 2). Judas did not repent (Greek *metanoeō*). He was seized with remorse (Greek *metamelomai*). He looked back at his action, saw he had done wrong, and tried to undo it through his own actions. We cannot accept responsibility for sin by trusting our own skills and powers to get rid of it and its results. As with any sinful act, Judas could not stop its destructive results. The proper reaction to sin is to look to God and accept His forgiveness. Judas committed suicide, seeking to escape his responsibility. We cannot escape responsibility. God holds us eternally responsible until we let Christ's blood cover our sins. See notes on 26:14–16,23–25,47–49, 69–75.

temple[i] and left. Then he went away and
hanged himself.[j]
6 The chief priests picked up the coins
and said, "It is against the law to put this
into the treasury, since it is blood money." 7 So they decided to use the money to
buy the potter's field as a burial place for
foreigners. 8 That is why it has been called
the Field of Blood[k] to this day. 9 Then
what was spoken by Jeremiah the prophet was fulfilled:[l] "They took the thirty
silver coins, the price set on him by the
people of Israel, 10 and they used them to
buy the potter's field, as the Lord commanded me."[h] [m]

Jesus Before Pilate

27:11–26pp — Mk 15:2–15; Lk 23:2,3, 18–25; Jn 18:29–19:16

11 Meanwhile Jesus stood before the
governor, and the governor asked him,
"Are you the king of the Jews?"[n]
"Yes, it is as you say," Jesus replied.
12 When he was accused by the chief
priests and the elders, he gave no answer.[o] 13 Then Pilate asked him, "Don't
you hear the testimony they are bringing
against you?"[p] 14 But Jesus made no reply,[q] not even to a single charge—to the
great amazement of the governor.
15 Now it was the governor's custom at
the Feast to release a prisoner[r] chosen
by the crowd. 16 At that time they had a
notorious prisoner, called Barabbas. 17 So
when the crowd had gathered, Pilate
asked them, "Which one do you want me
to release to you: Barabbas, or Jesus who
is called Christ?"[s] 18 For he knew it was
out of envy that they had handed Jesus
over to him.
19 While Pilate was sitting on the
judge's seat,[t] his wife sent him this message: "Don't have anything to do with
that innocent[u] man, for I have suffered a
great deal today in a dream[v] because of
him."
20 But the chief priests and the elders
persuaded the crowd to ask for Barabbas
and to have Jesus executed.[w]
21 "Which of the two do you want me
to release to you?" asked the governor.
"Barabbas," they answered.
22 "What shall I do, then, with Jesus
who is called Christ?"[x] Pilate asked.
They all answered, "Crucify him!"
23 "Why? What crime has he committed?" asked Pilate.
But they shouted all the louder, "Crucify him!"
24 When Pilate saw that he was getting
nowhere, but that instead an uproar[y]
was starting, he took water and washed
his hands[z] in front of the crowd. "I am
innocent of this man's blood,"[a] he said.
"It is your responsibility!"[b]
25 All the people answered, "Let his
blood be on us and on our children!"[c]
26 Then he released Barabbas to them.
But he had Jesus flogged,[d] and handed
him over to be crucified.

The Soldiers Mock Jesus

27:27–31pp — Mk 15:16–20

27 Then the governor's soldiers took
Jesus into the Praetorium[e] and gathered
the whole company of soldiers around
him. 28 They stripped him and put a scarlet robe on him,[f] 29 and then twisted together a crown of thorns and set it on his
head. They put a staff in his right hand
and knelt in front of him and mocked
him. "Hail, king of the Jews!" they said.[g]
30 They spit on him, and took the staff and
struck him on the head again and again.[h]
31 After they had mocked him, they took
off the robe and put his own clothes on
him. Then they led him away to crucify
him.[i]

The Crucifixion

27:33–44pp — Mk 15:22–32; Lk 23:33–43; Jn 19:17–24

32 As they were going out,[j] they met a

27:5 [i]Lk 1:9,21 [j]Ac 1:18
27:8 [k]Ac 1:19
27:9 [l]S Mt 1:22
27:10 [m]Zec 11:12, 13; Jer 32:6-9
27:11 [n]S Mt 2:2
27:12 [o]S Mk 14:61
27:13 [p]Mt 26:62
27:14 [q]S Mk 14:61
27:15 [r]Jn 18:39
27:17 [s]ver 22; Mt 1:16
27:19 [t]Jn 19:13 [u]ver 24 [v]Ge 20:6; Nu 12:6; 1Ki 3:5; Job 33:14-16; Mt 1:20; 2:12,13, 19,22
27:20 [w]Ac 3:14
27:22 [x]Mt 1:16
27:24 [y]Mt 26:5 [z]Ps 26:6 [a]Dt 21:6-8 [b]ver 4
27:25 [c]Jos 2:19; S Ac 5:28
27:26 [d]Isa 53:5; Jn 19:1
27:27 [e]Jn 18:28, 33; 19:9
27:28 [f]Jn 19:2
27:29 [g]Isa 53:3; Jn 19:2,3
27:30 [h]S Mt 16:21
27:31 [i]Isa 53:7
27:32 [j]Heb 13:12

[h] *10* See Zech. 11:12,13; Jer. 19:1-13; 32:6-9.

27:11 JESUS CHRIST, King—Jesus was the King of the Jews, fulfilling the promises to David but only in light of Isa 53. See notes on 25:31–46; 26:64.

27:26–30 JESUS CHRIST, Suffering—Compare Mk 15:16–19; Lk 22:63–65; Jn 19:2–3,5. Jesus suffered as intensely as any human can from physical beating and emotional mockery. The mocking of Jesus took the form of a cruel game revolving about His royal status as king. Jesus did not fit human standards of kingship. He did fit God's. Luke speaks of a mocking before Jesus' trial by Pilate. John speaks of a mocking during the time of the trial. Matthew and Mark tell of the final suffering after the trial in preparation for the crucifixion.

27:32–55 JESUS CHRIST, Death—Refusing to take a painkiller, Jesus faced death fully conscious of His pain and of the actions around Him. Christians read each element of the crucifixion in light of Old Testament expectations (Ex 26:31–33; Dt 21:22–23; Ps 22:1,7,8,18; 28:8; 69:9,21; Isa 53:19). Christ's claim to be King of His people was the central emphasis of the crucifixion. See note on 27:11. He rules by suffering for our sins and serving our deepest needs rather than by setting up a system for others to serve Him. Faith must see Him as King on a cross not as King because He escaped the cross. God had power to rescue Jesus but had love for us that let Jesus suffer for us. Part of the suffering occurred as Jesus felt forsaken by the Father. This feeling let Jesus identify totally with our feelings. This shows how deeply sin penetrated the heart of the Godhead, for the sinless Jesus suffered all the consequences of our sin. Jesus' sense of desertion did not rise because God was in any way displeased with Jesus. Jesus' use of Ps 22 points to deep trust as well as deep sense of being alone. Compare Ps 22:19–31. Christ's death led to the splitting of the Temple veil, showing all Christians have direct access as priests before God. God's holy presence is not limited to religious officials or to special holy festivals. Compare Heb 9:1–28; 10:19–22. The earthquake showed God's powerful presence at the cross. Compare Ex 19:18; Jdg 5:4–5; 2 Sa 22:8. The return to life of some saints symbolized Jesus' victory over death for the righteous, a victory to be completely realized

man from Cyrene,[k] named Simon, and
they forced him to carry the cross.[l]
33 They came to a place called Golgotha
(which means The Place of the Skull).[m]
34 There they offered Jesus wine to drink,
mixed with gall;[n] but after tasting it, he
refused to drink it. 35 When they had crucified him, they divided up his clothes by
casting lots.[i o] 36 And sitting down, they
kept watch[p] over him there. 37 Above his
head they placed the written charge
against him: THIS IS JESUS, THE KING OF
THE JEWS. 38 Two robbers were crucified
with him,[q] one on his right and one
on his left. 39 Those who passed by hurled
insults at him, shaking their heads[r]
40 and saying, "You who are going to
destroy the temple and build it in
three days,[s] save yourself![t] Come down
from the cross, if you are the Son of
God!"[u]

41 In the same way the chief priests, the
teachers of the law and the elders
mocked him. 42 "He saved others," they
said, "but he can't save himself! He's the
King of Israel![v] Let him come down now
from the cross, and we will believe[w] in
him. 43 He trusts in God. Let God rescue
him[x] now if he wants him, for he said, 'I
am the Son of God.' " 44 In the same way
the robbers who were crucified with him
also heaped insults on him.

The Death of Jesus

27:45–56pp — Mk 15:33–41; Lk 23:44–49

45 From the sixth hour until the ninth
hour darkness[y] came over all the land.
46 About the ninth hour Jesus cried out in
a loud voice, ***"Eloi, Eloi,***[j] ***lama sabach-
thani?"***—which means, "My God, my
God, why have you forsaken me?"[k z]

47 When some of those standing there
heard this, they said, "He's calling Elijah."

48 Immediately one of them ran and got
a sponge. He filled it with wine vinegar,[a]
put it on a stick, and offered it to Jesus to
drink. 49 The rest said, "Now leave him
alone. Let's see if Elijah comes to save
him."

50 And when Jesus had cried out again
in a loud voice, he gave up his spirit.[b]

51 At that moment the curtain of the
temple[c] was torn in two from top to bottom. The earth shook and the rocks
split.[d] 52 The tombs broke open and the
bodies of many holy people who had died
were raised to life. 53 They came out of
the tombs, and after Jesus' resurrection

27:32 [k]Ac 2:10; 6:9; 11:20; 13:1 [l]Mk 15:21; Lk 23:26
27:33 [m]Jn 19:17
27:34 [n]ver 48; Ps 69:21
27:35 [o]Ps 22:18
27:36 [p]ver 54
27:38 [q]Isa 53:12
27:39 [r]Ps 22:7; 109:25; La 2:15
27:40 [s]S Jn 2:19 [t]ver 42 [u]Mt 4:3,6
27:42 [v]Jn 1:49; 12:13 [w]S Jn 3:15
27:43 [x]Ps 22:8
27:45 [y]Am 8:9
27:46 [z]Ps 22:1
27:48 [a]ver 34; Ps 69:21
27:50 [b]Jn 19:30
27:51 [c]Ex 26:31-33; Heb 9:3,8; 10:19,20 [d]ver 54

[i]35 A few late manuscripts *lots that the word spoken by the prophet might be fulfilled: "They divided my garments among themselves and cast lots for my clothing"* (Psalm 22:18) [j]46 Some manuscripts *Eli, Eli* [k]46 Psalm 22:1

only when He comes again. These resuscitated saints had not experienced the resurrection. They would die again. The guards' confession of Jesus as Son of God previewed what all people should confess because of the cross. The death of Jesus opened the way to God for all people, not just Jews.

27:42–43 SALVATION, Belief—Compare 4:5–7. Jesus refused to resort to sensationalism to get persons to believe in Him (Mk 15:32). Faith does not result from overwhelming material evidence. Faith comes through person-to-person experience with God.

27:46 GOD, Faithfulness—Care must be taken in interpreting this verse lest we contradict the teaching of the faithfulness of God to those who are faithful to Him. Did God turn His back upon Jesus here, even momentarily, and leave Him in a forsaken condition? Some hold that when Jesus died bearing the sins of the world upon Himself God could not look upon Him since He was laden with our sins. This has the difficulty of one part of the Trinity turning its back upon another part of the Trinity and fails to see that God was in Christ in His death for the sins of the world (2 Co 5:18–19). Further, if God could not look upon sin here, how has He ever looked upon any of us, and how could Jn 3:16 have been written of Him? If Jesus thus felt forsaken, why was His next cry from the cross a cry of commitment into His Father's hands? See Mt 27:50 and the parallel Lk 23:46. If the Father could not look upon Him, how then could the Father receive Him? Jesus' cry of awful agony and loneliness on the cross does not mean that God had in fact turned His back on Jesus. It only shows the very real experience of suffering that Jesus had here in a human life. Do not underestimate Jesus' feeling of agony and despair and forsakenness. His *feeling* forsaken, however, does not mean that He *was* forsaken by God. Notice that Jesus Himself pointed beyond His sense of despair in an expression of great faith and truth. Many feel that the cry of Mt 27:46 is Jesus' way of referencing not just the first verse of Ps 22, from which these words come, but actually calls up the whole of that psalm. Ps 22 is anything but a cry of despair or forsakenness. It is in reality a psalm expressing faith in God and in God's nearness and goodness even in times of great difficulty. It is a psalm expressing victory rather than despair and defeat. Jesus, then, was saying to the mocking multitudes, "You may think that God has forsaken me, (see Mt 27:43 where they were certain God would not deliver Him), but as a matter of fact God has been right here with me through this whole business and will bring triumph and salvation out of my suffering." There is an element of Jesus' suffering agony and loneliness in His experience upon the cross. But He gave witness to His faith in the presence, the blessing, and the victory of God through His suffering. Read the whole of Ps 22 and note the many messianic references in it.

27:46 PRAYER, Petition—This prayer established as real the fact that God had forsaken Him when He became sin (2 Co 5:21). Jesus was in the hell of exile from God for the sake of others who would not need to experience that same exile. Even then Jesus faithfully prayed. No experience separates us from the possibility of prayer.

27:51–53 MIRACLE, Redemption—The miracles of that Friday, redemptive in nature, disturbed all creation. Jesus' death has cosmic significance (Ro 8:18–25). From top to bottom the veil was torn, suggesting God's action, not human action. The veil had separated worshipers from the Holy of Holies. Jesus' death made God's presence accessible to the ordinary worshiper, not only to the High Priest (Heb 10:19–23). The death of the Redeemer had profound meaning for all the dead. Those who rose *after* Jesus' resurrection symbolized the hope all people have because of Christ's resurrection.

27:52 HUMANITY, Death—This miracle demonstrates a new dimension to death. Following Jesus' own death, death itself had been conquered. Resurrection is clearly God's answer to death. Note the distinction here between the resurrection of Jesus and the resuscitation of the others, who would again enter the grave. See 1 Co 15:54–57.

they went into the holy city[e] and appeared to many people.
54When the centurion and those with
him who were guarding[f] Jesus saw the
earthquake and all that had happened,
they were terrified, and exclaimed,
"Surely he was the Son[1] of God!"[g]
55Many women were there, watching
from a distance. They had followed Jesus
from Galilee to care for his needs.[h]
56Among them were Mary Magdalene,
Mary the mother of James and Joses, and
the mother of Zebedee's sons.[i]

The Burial of Jesus

27:57–61pp — Mk 15:42–47; Lk 23:50–56; Jn 19:38–42

57As evening approached, there came a
rich man from Arimathea, named Joseph,
who had himself become a disciple of
Jesus. 58Going to Pilate, he asked for
Jesus' body, and Pilate ordered that it be
given to him. 59Joseph took the body,
wrapped it in a clean linen cloth, 60and
placed it in his own new tomb[j] that he
had cut out of the rock. He rolled a big
stone in front of the entrance to the tomb
and went away. 61Mary Magdalene and
the other Mary were sitting there opposite the tomb.

The Guard at the Tomb

62The next day, the one after Preparation Day, the chief priests and the Pharisees went to Pilate. 63"Sir," they said,
"we remember that while he was still
alive that deceiver said, 'After three days
I will rise again.'[k] 64So give the order for
the tomb to be made secure until the
third day. Otherwise, his disciples may
come and steal the body[l] and tell the
people that he has been raised from the
dead. This last deception will be worse
than the first."
65"Take a guard,"[m] Pilate answered.
"Go, make the tomb as secure as you
know how." 66So they went and made
the tomb secure by putting a seal[n] on the
stone[o] and posting the guard.[p]

Chapter 28

The Resurrection

28:1–8pp — Mk 16:1–8; Lk 24:1–10

AFTER the Sabbath, at dawn on the first
day of the week, Mary Magdalene[q]
and the other Mary[r] went to look at the
tomb.
2There was a violent earthquake,[s] for
an angel[t] of the Lord came down from
heaven and, going to the tomb, rolled
back the stone[u] and sat on it. 3His appearance was like lightning, and his
clothes were white as snow.[v] 4The
guards were so afraid of him that they
shook and became like dead men.
5The angel said to the women, "Do not
be afraid,[w] for I know that you are looking for Jesus, who was crucified. 6He is
not here; he has risen, just as he said.[x]
Come and see the place where he lay.
7Then go quickly and tell his disciples:
'He has risen from the dead and is going
ahead of you into Galilee.[y] There you
will see him.' Now I have told you."
8So the women hurried away from the
tomb, afraid yet filled with joy, and ran to
tell his disciples. 9Suddenly Jesus met
them.[z] "Greetings," he said. They came
to him, clasped his feet and worshiped
him. 10Then Jesus said to them, "Do not
be afraid. Go and tell my brothers[a] to go
to Galilee; there they will see me."

The Guards' Report

11While the women were on their way,
some of the guards[b] went into the city
and reported to the chief priests everything that had happened. 12When the

[1]54 Or *a son*

27:53 [e]S Mt 4:5
27:54 [f]ver 36 [g]S Mt 4:3; 17:5
27:55 [h]Lk 8:2,3
27:56 [i]Mk 15:47; Lk 24:10; Jn 19:25
27:60 [j]Mt 27:66; 28:2; Mk 16:4; Ac 13:29
27:63 [k]S Mt 16:21
27:64 [l]Mt 28:13
27:65 [m]ver 66; Mt 28:11
27:66 [n]Da 6:17 [o]ver 60; Mt 28:2 [p]Mt 28:11
28:1 [q]Lk 8:2 [r]Mt 27:56
28:2 [s]Mt 27:51 [t]Jn 20:12; S Ac 5:19 [u]Mt 27:60
28:3 [v]Da 7:9; 10:6; Mk 9:3; S Jn 20:12
28:5 [w]ver 10; S Mt 14:27
28:6 [x]S Mt 16:21
28:7 [y]ver 10,16; Mt 26:32
28:9 [z]Jn 20:14-18
28:10 [a]Mt 12:50; 25:40; Mk 3:34; Jn 20:17; Ro 8:29; Heb 2:11-13,17
28:11 [b]Mt 27:65, 66

28:1–20 JESUS CHRIST, Resurrection—Compare Mk 16:1–8; Lk 24:1–53; Jn 20:1—21:25. Jesus' resurrection fulfilled God's purpose and Jesus' predictions. See note on Mt 16:21–23. The resurrection gave Christ's followers joy and eagerness to testify. Religious leaders used fake testimony to discount the resurrection just as they used false testimony to convict Jesus and sentence Him to the cross (26:59–61).
28:2 REVELATION, Angels—God used an angel to reveal the news of resurrection to the first witnesses.
28:5–7 HUMANITY, Death—Jesus' resurrection provided the final triumph over human death. We must still endure death and grief, but now physical death is the beginning of a new existence with God. See Mk 16:5–7; Lk 24:4–8.
28:5–7 REVELATION, Jesus Christ—Jesus rose revealing for the first time God's power over death and the certainty of eternal life. The incredible was explained by God's representative, probably to those whose faith and loyalty remained most constant during these awful and awesome days of trial, crucifixion, and death. The resurrected Christ did not return immediately to the heavenly Father but made plans to be seen by His followers in Galilee. He had to prepare them to be messengers of His revelation (vv 19–20).
28:6–7 MISSIONS, Call—Messengers for God must have only one qualification. God's messengers are those who know the crucified and risen Christ by experience. By faith they experience the forgiveness, salvation, and hope that comes from knowing the risen Lord. God calls us whom He saved to share the good news. It is our task—not that of heavenly angels—to share the resurrection story. Only sinners who have known forgiveness in the risen Christ can share the story effectively. For the power of the personal testimony in sharing the gospel, see the experience of the man born blind in Jn 9:1–41.
28:8 SALVATION, Joy—Reverential awe and joy accompany our salvation. Christians have plenty to be happy about—among them Christ's empty tomb. We should want to run and share the good news of Christ's resurrection with others.
28:9 PRAYER, Worship—After the resurrection, the women had no question that Jesus was worthy of praise. Compare Jn 9:38. Proper prayer is always prayer to the resurrected Lord.

chief priests had met with the elders and
devised a plan, they gave the soldiers a
large sum of money, [13]telling them, "You
are to say, 'His disciples came during the
night and stole him away[c] while we
were asleep.' [14]If this report gets to the
governor,[d] we will satisfy him and keep
you out of trouble." [15]So the soldiers took
the money and did as they were instructed. And this story has been widely circulated among the Jews to this very day.

The Great Commission

[16]Then the eleven disciples went to
Galilee, to the mountain where Jesus had
told them to go.[e] [17]When they saw him,
they worshiped him; but some doubted.
[18]Then Jesus came to them and said, "All
authority in heaven and on earth has
been given to me.[f] [19]Therefore go and
make disciples of all nations,[g] baptizing
them in[m] the name of the Father and of
the Son and of the Holy Spirit,[h] [20]and
teaching[i] them to obey everything I have
commanded you. And surely I am with
you[j] always, to the very end of the
age."[k]

28:13 [c]Mt 27:64
28:14 [d]S Mt 27:2
28:16 [e]ver 7,10; Mt 26:32
28:18 [f]Da 7:13,14; Lk 10:22; Jn 3:35; S 13:13; 17:2; 1Co 15:27; Eph 1:20-22; Php 2:9,10
28:19 [g]Isa 49:6; Mk 16:15,16; Lk 24:47; Ac 1:8; 14:21 [h]Ac 1:8; 2:38; 8:16; Ro 6:3,4; Gal 3:27; Col 2:12
28:20 [i]Jn 14:26; Ac 2:42 [j]Dt 31:6; 1Ki 8:57; Hag 1:13; Mt 18:20; Ac 18:10 [k]Mt 13:39; 24:3

[m]*19* Or *into*; see Acts 8:16; 19:5; Romans 6:3; 1 Cor. 1:13; 10:2 and Gal. 3:27.

28:18–20 JESUS CHRIST, Authority—The resurrection underscored Jesus' absolute authority over the universe. The Father gave the Son the authority. The baptismal formula shows Jesus is divine, a member of the Trinity. His authority means that He deserves absolute obedience. His promised presence shows His authority rests on absolute love and care.

28:18–20 EVANGELISM, Call to Evangelize—A call to evangelize was Christ's last message to His disciples. That is our primary calling. This commission involves all the ingredients to the successful work of the church. Christ's authority provides power in the Holy Spirit. Christ sends us to lead others to follow Him. New disciples are to be integrated by baptism into the church so spiritual growth can take place. They are to be taught the Lord's ways. Jesus promised to be involved in the task with us. We are to carry on until the end of the age. When God's people take this passage seriously, world evangelization will flourish.

28:18–20 MISSIONS, Command—The Great Commission provides a fitting climax to the gospel that begins with lineage of Jesus, the King of the Jews, and ends with a kingly command to extend His kingdom to all peoples. The central importance of this teaching can be seen by its repetition. It appears in four different passages (Mk 16:15; Lk 24:47; Jn 20:21; Ac 1:8) and in three locations (Jerusalem, Galilee, and the Mount of Olives). The Great Commission, given to the eleven apostles on a mountain in Galilee (28:7,9,16), is directed to His church and to all Christians. It teaches the power and authority for the church's missionary task. God the Father has given authority to the Son. The authority is valid in heaven and on earth. The authority is to make disciples, baptizing them in the name of the Father, the Son, and the Holy Spirit, and teaching them to obey all of the instructions of Jesus. We must confess God has authoritatively commanded us to take up the missionary task. Only one Greek verb in the Great Commission appears in the imperative or command form: "make disciples." This principal verb shows Christ's intent that Christians should witness with the goal of winning persons to Him. A disciple is a follower of Christ, a learner in the school of Christ. The scope of this command is "all nations." Nations can be used in the sense of modern nations, but it can also be translated as "Gentiles" or the "peoples." Its meaning goes beyond just nations or states and describes discipling the peoples, the tribes, and the families. Witness must not be limited to our familiar cultural circle (Rev 14:6). Baptism represents the new disciple's first opportunity to obey Christ and to witness to others. In baptism we testify of our faith in Christ's death, resurrection, and return (Ro 6:4). We testify of our commitment to walk in the new life (Col 3:1) and of our belief in the Trinity—God the Father, the Son, and the Holy Spirit. By baptizing, the church carries out the missionary command of introducing new disciples into the fellowship of Christ's church. Baptism is not the end of the missionary task. The missionary witness leads new Christians into a continuing growth in discipleship. Converts must receive instruction, training, and nurture in the Christian way. The Christian faith is a way of life; it begins and continues with a relationship with a Person. See Jn 15:5; 14:6; Ac 9:2. The challenge of making disciples from all nations, tribes, and peoples is beyond human capability. Jesus concluded the Great Commission with the promise of His presence. He never promised missionary witness would be easy. He did promise to be with us to give needed power, faith, encouragement, and knowledge (Lk 9:23; Jn 12:24). This promise has no time limit. Christ is with us, His missionary witnesses, until the end of time. The Gospel of Matthew begins (1:23) with the angel informing Joseph of the Messiah's name—Immanuel—which means, "God with us." It ends with His promise to be with His people in all time and all places as we carry out His missionary command.

28:19 GOD, Trinity—This verse is crucially important in our understanding of the Christian doctrine of the Trinity. This one verse emphasizes both the unity and the plurality of God. Keep in mind the fundamental emphasis of the Old Testament concerning there being only one God. Add to that the New Testament recognition that three are recognized as God: God the Father, God the Son, and God the Holy Spirit. Many assertions are made concerning the divine nature of each of the three Persons. Many passages show that the work of one involves the work of one or both of the other two Persons. Here the unity of God—the oneness of God—is shown by the emphasis on baptizing in the name (singular), rather than names (plural) of God the Father, God the Son, and God the Holy Spirit. There is no hierarchy of persons here. The three are named on a coordinate level, apparently. We must be careful that we do not lose either the unity or the diversity in the nature of God. See notes on 3:16–17; 16:16–17,27.

28:19–20 HOLY SPIRIT, Presence of God—The Gospel writer pointed to a trinitarian understanding of God. The association of the Spirit with the Father and the Son in the baptismal formula is an affirmation of the deity of the Spirit. The Spirit is the equal of the Father and the Son and is not to be confused with either the Father or the Son. Jesus' promise to be with the disciples was fulfilled by the Spirit. See Jn 16:16,18; 1 Jn 3:24.

28:19 ORDINANCES, Baptism Commanded—Jesus' Great Commission includes the command to baptize. The sequence of His commands is important. Beginning with a participle (as you are going), Jesus used the imperative "make disciples of all nations." This command is followed immediately by "baptizing them," showing that in this way they were identified to the world as His followers. Then comes the final command, "teaching them," which is the meaning of the word "disciple" (learner). This makes baptism the sign of public confession of Jesus as Savior and Lord, identifying a follower of Jesus. All three Persons of the Godhead are connected with baptism.

Mark

Theological Setting

Is God able to sustain the confessing church in the crisis of persecution and martyrdom? Christians in Rome faced this question as they first heard and read the Gospel of Mark. In AD 64 a devastating fire swept through Rome, threatening to reduce the Eternal City to ash and rubble. Of the fourteen districts of the city, only four were untouched. Three were leveled to the ground. It was persistently rumored that the fire had been ordered by the emperor. He had done so because he intended to construct a new palace in the vicinity of the Great Circus, the precise area where the fire first broke out. It was to distract attention from such popular rumors that Nero shifted the blame for the fire on the Christians of Rome, a group that had become the object of marketplace gossip because of their distinctive practices and life-style.

Recognized Christians were arrested and tortured. On the basis of their information large numbers of others were paraded before Roman magistrates and condemned to death, not for the crime of arson, but because popular prejudice permitted the humiliation of the Christians. That sequence of events created confusion within the house-churches of Rome. Identification as a Christian could lead to a martyr's death.

In the climate of uncertainty created by the emperor's actions, Christians had several options:

1. They could decide that God had abandoned them or was incapable of defending them. The solution would be to deny the lordship of Christ and to affirm openly their loyalty to the emperor and to the gods of the Roman pantheon. This course of action would preserve their lives at the cost of exposing Jesus Christ to public contempt and confirming a pagan society in its unbelief.

2. They could withdraw from the confessing church and seek to conceal their identity by melting into the faceless humanity that made up the mixed population of Rome.

3. They could fall back on a belief in the God of the magic wand who would never permit His people to suffer or to experience humiliation. The result would almost certainly be frustration, embitterment, and despair when persecution and martyrdom continued.

4. They could wait passively for the dreaded knock on the door, arrest, a brief interrogation, and the sentence of death. Each passing day would drain their spirits and intensify their fears. They would finally be reduced to a state of apathy.

5. They could continue to meet together for worship, instruction, and mutual encouragement, boldly accepting the consequences of their commitment to Christ. Such gatherings might center attention on a faithful waiting for God to come in judgment on the present situation.

Among the Christian leaders in Rome was John Mark of Jerusalem. Mark recognized that frightened men and women would need to be strengthened for the testing of their faith. The earliest of our Gospels was his pastoral response to the crisis in Rome. Mark's Gospel was essentially a pamphlet for hard times. The witness Mark bore to Jesus centered on Jesus' commitment to His own followers, even when they failed to understand the significance of rejection, suffering, and death in God's plan for Him, and for them.

Mark wrote to strengthen Christians and to provide them with a basis for faithfulness to Jesus. He demonstrated that a Christian can suffer no form of humiliation that has not been endured already by Jesus, the Lord. Were Christians misrepresented and falsely accused by the authorities in Rome? Jesus *was said to be* deranged by his family (Mk 3:21) and to be demonic by officials from Jerusalem (3:22-30). Were Christians sometimes betrayed to the authorities by their own family and friends? One of Jesus' own disciples was Judas Iscariot, "who betrayed him" (3:19). Would Christians have to stand before a Roman magistrate who possessed the powers of life or death? Jesus stood before Pontius Pilate and was condemned to death by crucifixion (15:1-20). Jesus had not rejected suffering and death. They must not do so either. God's response to the faithful obedience of His Son was sustaining strength for suffering and vindication through resurrection (16:6-7). Jesus' resurrection demonstrated that suffering, humiliation, and death were not the last word for one who trusted God and remained faithful to Him. The solemn pledge that Jesus would gather His scattered disciples in Galilee (14:28; 16:7) served to remind the oppressed

Christians in Rome that Jesus is alive and remains committed to them as well. A suffering Messiah and Servant Lord is made visible in the world through the servant church, which is prepared to respond to Jesus with fidelity. Mere deliverance from crisis is not the answer. The answer is unwavering commitment to Jesus as the anointed Agent of God's salvation and as God's Son.

Theological Outline

Mark: Confession of Jesus as God's Agent and Unique Son

- I. God Has Acted for His People by Sending His Son as His Agent. (1:1-13)
  - A. God fulfilled the words of His prophets. (1:1-3)
  - B. God announced His action through the herald in the wilderness. (1:4-8)
  - C. God's endorsement of Jesus as His beloved Son showed He is the promised Lord. (1:9-11)
  - D. God sustained His Son in the experience of testing in the wilderness. (1:12-13)
- II. The Appearance of God's Son as His Agent Signaled the Presence of the New Age. (1:14-45)
  - A. God's Agent announced the presence of the new age. (1:14-15)
  - B. The call to become fishers of men was a consequence of the presence of the new age. (1:16-20)
  - C. The unique authority of God's Agent demonstrated the presence of the new age. (1:21-28)
  - D. Healing through God's Agent revealed the saving character of the new age. (1:29-34)
  - E. The urgency of preaching was consistent with the presence of the new age. (1:35-39)
  - F. The healing of a leper was evidence of the powers of the new age. (1:40-45)
- III. The Old Order Failed to Recognize God's Agent or the Presence of the new age. (2:1—3:6)
  - A. The old order failed to recognize that Jesus had authority to forgive sins. (2:1-12)
  - B. The old order resented God's Agent for forgiving outcasts and sinners. (2:13-17)
  - C. The old order failed to understand fasting was inappropriate when God's Agent was present. (2:18-22)
  - D. The old order failed to recognize that God's Agent was the Lord of the sabbath. (2:23—3:5)
  - E. The old order displayed hardness of heart when it schemed to destroy God's Agent. (3:6)
- IV. The Presence of God's Agent Provoked a Reaction from Others. (3:7—6:6)
  - A. Crowds followed God's Agent to receive the blessings of the new age. (3:7-10)
  - B. Unclean spirits recognized the threat posed by the presence of God's Agent. (3:11-12)
  - C. God's Agent appointed the twelve to express His unique authority. (3:13-19)
  - D. God's Agent was regarded by His family as deranged. (3:20-21)
  - E. God's Agent was regarded by the old order as demonic. (3:22-30)
  - F. God's Agent identified His true family as those who do God's will in the new age. (3:31-35)
  - G. God's Agent used parables to clarify the character of the new age. (4:1-34)
  - H. When God's Agent subdued the hostile power of the sea, the reaction was awe. (4:35-41)
  - I. When God's Agent extended the salvation of the new age to the Gentiles, the reaction was both terror and gratitude. (5:1-20)
  - J. When God's Agent subdued the powers of disease and death, the reaction was fear and amazement. (5:21-43)
  - K. When God's Agent addressed those who knew Him well, the reaction was contempt and unbelief. (6:1-6)
- V. God's Agent Extended the Blessings of the New Age in Spite of Opposition. (6:7—8:30)
  - A. God's Agent extended the blessings of the new age through the twelve, warning them to expect opposition. (6:7-13)
  - B. The murder of the herald of the new age anticipated the death of God's Agent. (6:14-29)
  - C. God's Agent provided rest in the wilderness as a blessing of the new age. (6:30-44)
  - D. God's Agent provided relief to those who obey Him as a blessing of the new age. (6:45-52)
  - E. God's Agent provided healing for those who seek Him as a blessing of the new age. (6:53-56)
  - F. God's Agent challenged the old order traditions with enduring commandments. (7:1-23)
  - G. God's Agent extended new age blessings to believing Gentiles. (7:24—8:10)
  - H. God's Agent experienced the old order's opposition in their demand for a sign. (8:11-13)
  - I. The twelve failed to understand the significance of the blessings of the new age. (8:14-21)
  - J. God's Agent opened blind eyes as a sign of the new age. (8:22-26)
  - K. Jesus was recognized as God's Agent, the mediator of the blessings of the new age. (8:27-30)
- VI. God's Agent Exhibited the New Age Paradox: Suffering Precedes Vindication. (8:31—10:52)
  - A. God's Agent must experience suffering prior to vindication by resurrection. (8:31-33)
  - B. New age people participate in the paradox: the way to life is through death. (8:34-38)
  - C. The transfiguration provides assurance: vindication will follow suffering. (9:1-8)

D. Both the herald and the Agent of the new age exhibited the pattern of suffering and rejection followed by vindication. (9:9-13)
E. The powers of the new age are released through faith and prayer. (9:14-29)
F. The paradox of the new age that suffering precedes vindication is reaffirmed. (9:30-32)
G. The paradox of the new age is that greatness is expressed through humble service. (9:33-41)
H. The fact of the new age accounts for the stringent requirements of discipleship. (9:42-50)
I. The creation intention of God for marriage is reaffirmed in the new age. (10:1-12)
J. Entrance into the new age is through childlike faith. (10:13-16)
K. Entrance into the new age requires sacrificial commitment. (10:17-31)
L. The paradox of the new age is reaffirmed. (10:32-45)
M. True discipleship responds immediately to the blessings of the new age. (10:46-52)

VII. The Presence of God's Agent in Jerusalem Intensified the Conflict between the Old Order and the New Age. (11:1—12:44)
A. The significance of the entrance of God's Agent into Jerusalem was unrecognized. (11:1-11)
B. The presence of God's Agent in Jerusalem introduced judgment on the old order. (11:12-25)
C. The authority of God's Agent was challenged by representatives of the old order. (11:27-33)
D. God's Agent taught of His transcendent dignity. (12:1-12)
E. The wisdom of God's Agent was challenged by representatives of the old order. (12:13-27)
F. God's Agent was vindicated by His teaching on the greatest commandment. (12:28-34)
G. God's Agent exposed the inability of the old order to understand Scripture. (12:35-37)
H. God's Agent exposed the hypocrisy of the old order. (12:38-40)
I. God's Agent presented a proper response to the presence of the new age. (12:41-44)

VIII. God's Agent Foresaw Impending Distress for Jerusalem and the Old Order. (13:1-37)
A. God's Agent foresaw the impending destruction of the Temple. (13:1-4)
B. God's Agent warned of deception through those who falsely claim to act for God. (13:5-8)
C. God's Agent warned of impending persecution and called for steadfastness. (13:9-13)
D. God's Agent warned of the sacrilege that causes desolation. (13:14-23)
E. God's Agent looked beyond the impending distress to triumph for His people. (13:24-37)

IX. The Old Order Was Unified in Its Action Against God's Agent. (14:1—15:47)
A. Representatives of the old order determined to seize God's Agent. (14:1-2)
B. God's Agent was anointed for His burial. (14:3-9)
C. God's Agent was denied by one of the twelve who agreed to betray Him. (14:10-11)
D. God's Agent announced His betrayal during the Passover meal. (14:12-21)
E. God's Agent provided His own symbol of the new age. (14:22-26)
F. God's Agent foresaw the failure and denial of His own followers. (14:27-31)
G. God's Agent affirmed His submission to the will of God in Gethsemane. (14:32-42)
H. God's Agent experienced betrayal and arrest, fulfilling Scripture. (14:43-52).
I. God's Agent was condemned, mocked, and brutalized by the old order. (14:53-65)
J. The prophecy of Peter's denial was fulfilled. (14:66-72)
K. The old religious order joined the political order to condemn God's Agent. (15:1-20)
L. God's Agent was crucified as King of the Jews. (15:21-37)
M. God's Agent was acknowledged to be the Son of God by a Roman. (15:38-39)
N. The death and burial of God's Agent was witnessed by godly women. (15:40-47)

X. The Resurrection of God's Agent Validated the Presence of the New Age. (16:1-8)

XI. A Later Appendix: Proof of the Vindication of God's Agent. (16:9-20)

Theological Conclusions

The Gospel of Mark brought stability, hope, and identity to a confused and frightened body of Christians by emphasizing five doctrines:

1. the sovereign initiative of God in sending His Son as the Agent of His saving will;
2. the presence of the new age and the reality of its blessings;
3. the paradox of the new age that suffering precedes vindication;
4. the ability of God to sustain the one who is faithful to Him;
5. the importance of the confession of Jesus as God's Agent and Son as the measure of Christian commitment.

Christians in Rome became confused and frightened when they were singled out for arrest and death in the aftermath of the great fire. The Gospel of Mark shows that this development had been foreseen by Jesus. (4:17; 9:49; 10:30; 13:9-13). Jesus had called for a surrender of life to cross-bearing in response to the call of God (8:34-38).

People who openly acknowledged they were Christians when paraded before a Roman magistrate were designated "confessors." Confessing that "Jesus is Lord" or "Jesus is the Son of God," they could not affirm the lordship of Caesar. They sealed their confession with their own blood. In his opening verse Mark declared his readiness to take his place among the ranks of the confessors. Mark brought together two significant early Christian confessions, "Jesus is the Messiah" and "Jesus is the Son of God." "Jesus is the Messiah" affirmed that He was the Agent of God who was sent to accomplish the redemption of God's people and to usher in the promised new age. "Jesus is God's Son" affirmed that He is uniquely qualified to achieve redemption and to mediate the blessings of the new age.

Mark gave his pamphlet a confessional structure. The Gospel falls roughly into two equal halves, and each half is brought to a point of climax with one of these two confessions. The first half of the Gospel (1:1 to 8:30) reaches a climax in 8:29 when Peter, a Jew and a representative of the people of the new age, confesses openly that Jesus is the Messiah. Each of the incidents recorded in the first half of Mark's pamphlet prepared his audience for this moment of recognition and confession. Prior to 8:29 those who responded to Jesus' call did not understand who He was. (4:41)

The popular consensus was that Jesus was a prophet, but there was no agreement whether He was a recent prophet, John the Baptist brought back from the dead, Elijah who had returned to announce the day of restoration, or one of the prophets from Israel's remote past (6:14-16; 8:27,28). Not until Jesus posed the pointed question to the twelve at Caesarea Philippi did he receive the appropriate response, "You are the Christ."

The second half of the Gospel clarifies what it means to confess that Jesus is God's Agent. Each group had their own expectations. Jesus, however, had come from God to fulfill His mission. He could not permit His disciples to fill the designation "messiah" with their own conceptions. He immediately began to define the significance of "messiah" as God intended. He spoke of God's Agent as a suffering, rejected Individual who would be killed and after three days rise again (8:31). Peter's sense of outrage at such a suggestion indicated he had failed to grasp the paradox of the new age that suffering precedes vindication.

Christians participate in this paradox. We are summoned to identify with Jesus, even if this means we will share His suffering and rejection (8:34-38). Three times in the central section of the Gospel, Jesus announced the pattern of suffering that was integral to His mission (8:31; 9:31; 10:33-34). On each occasion the twelve failed to understand (8:32-33; 9:32; 10:35-41), and each time Jesus called them to true discipleship expressed through unwavering loyalty and humble service (8:34-38; 9:33-37; 10:42-45).

The second half of Mark's Gospel is controlled by the theme of Jesus' journey to Jerusalem, where the prophecy of His suffering, death, and resurrection was fulfilled. A full third of the Gospel is centered in Jerusalem, where the conflict between the representatives of the old order and Jesus as the Agent of the new age was intensified. The climax in the account is reached in the confession of the Roman centurion responsible for the crucifixion, "Surely this man was the Son of God!" (15:39). The Roman represented the Gentile world that had been hostile to God. By making the confession of Peter and of the Roman centurion points of climax, Mark emphasized that Jew and Gentile can be led to join their voices in acknowledging the dignity of Jesus as God's Agent and unique Son.

The structure of confession that Mark gave to his Gospel served to call Christians to identify themselves with the confessing church as a bold expression of their Christian commitment. The entire Gospel stands as a witness to God's ability to sustain those who are committed to the accomplishment of His will in spite of opposition. It celebrates the truth that vindication follows suffering.

Contemporary Teaching

The Gospel of Mark centers our attention on Jesus as the Agent of God, whose ministry of the word and power demonstrate His transcendent authority and His absolute claim on our allegiance.

Mark asks us: (1) to take our stand in the confessing church in a society that has become thoroughly secular in its orientation and values; (2) to recognize the fact of the martyr church throughout the world and to identify ourselves with our suffering brothers and sisters; (3) to recognize the cost of discipleship and to refuse to trivialize the call to cross-bearing; (4) to celebrate the ability of God to sustain Christians in circumstances of rejection, suffering, and humiliation; (5) to examine the quality of our commitment to Jesus and to respond to Him with uncompromising loyalty; (6) to acknowledge the authority of Jesus to compel our obedience in every area of life and to respond with integrity; (7) to be prepared for the spiritual conflict that committed discipleship always provokes; (8) to translate Christian devotion into humble service to the people of God; and (9) to display a quality of life that will make Jesus visible to a broken and dying world.

Chapter 1

John the Baptist Prepares the Way

1:2–8pp — Mt 3:1–11; Lk 3:2–16

THE beginning of the gospel about
Jesus Christ, the Son of God.[a] [a]

2 It is written in Isaiah the prophet:

"I will send my messenger ahead of
you,
who will prepare your way"[b] [b] —
3 "a voice of one calling in the desert,
'Prepare the way for the Lord,
make straight paths for him.' "[c] [c]

4 And so John[d] came, baptizing in the
desert region and preaching a baptism of
repentance[e] for the forgiveness of sins.[f]
5 The whole Judean countryside and all
the people of Jerusalem went out to him.
Confessing their sins, they were baptized
by him in the Jordan River. 6 John wore
clothing made of camel's hair, with a
leather belt around his waist,[g] and he ate
locusts[h] and wild honey. 7 And this was
his message: "After me will come one
more powerful than I, the thongs of
whose sandals I am not worthy to stoop
down and untie.[i] 8 I baptize you with[d]
water, but he will baptize you with the
Holy Spirit."[j]

The Baptism and Temptation of Jesus

1:9–11pp — Mt 3:13–17; Lk 3:21,22
1:12,13pp — Mt 4:1–11; Lk 4:1–13

9 At that time Jesus came from Nazareth[k] in Galilee and was baptized by
John[l] in the Jordan. 10 As Jesus was coming up out of the water, he saw heaven
being torn open and the Spirit descending
on him like a dove.[m] 11 And a voice came
from heaven: "You are my Son,[n] whom I
love; with you I am well pleased."[o]
12 At once the Spirit sent him out into
the desert, 13 and he was in the desert forty days,[p] being tempted by Satan.[q] He
was with the wild animals, and angels attended him.

The Calling of the First Disciples

1:16–20pp — Mt 4:18–22; Lk 5:2–11; Jn 1:35–42

14 After John[r] was put in prison, Jesus

1:1 [a]S Mt 4:3
1:2 [b]Mal 3:1; Mt 11:10; Lk 7:27
1:3 [c]Isa 40:3; Jn 1:23
1:4 [d]S Mt 3:1 [e]ver 8; Jn 1:26,33; Ac 1:5,22; 11:36; 13:24; 18:25; 19:3,4 [f]Lk 1:77
1:6 [g]2Ki 1:8 [h]Lev 11:22
1:7 [i]Ac 13:25
1:8 [j]Isa 44:3; Joel 2:28; Jn 1:33; Ac 1:5; 2:4; 11:16; 19:4-6
1:9 [k]S Mt 2:23 [l]S Mt 3:1
1:10 [m]Jn 1:32
1:11 [n]S Mt 3:17 [o]S Mt 3:17
1:13 [p]Ex 24:18; 1Ki 19:8 [q]S Mt 4:10; Heb 4:15
1:14 [r]S Mt 3:1

[a] *1* Some manuscripts do not have *the Son of God.*
[b] *2* Mal. 3:1 [c] *3* Isaiah 40:3 [d] *8* Or *in*

1:1–11 JESUS CHRIST, Authority—John pointed to Christ's superior authority. This, not the birth, was Mark's beginning point for the gospel.

1:1 JESUS CHRIST, Son of God—Some manuscripts of this verse do not have the title Son of God. This title, Son of God, is one of the major ways in which Christians have thought of Jesus. Ancient Near Eastern civilizations thought of their kings as being sons of the gods by some mythical physical propagation. The New Testament speaks of Jesus' sonship to God in an entirely different manner. He was God's Son by virtue of an eternal relationship. The kings of Israel were called sons of God by reason of the covenant. See note on Mt 16:16. Israel, the nation, was also spoken of as a child of God (Hos 11:1). Angelic beings are called the sons of God (Job 1:6) because of their function as members of the heavenly council. Only Jesus is acknowledged as full Son of God by reason of an eternal relationship. Compare Mk 3:11; Mt 14:33; 27:45.

1:1–2 HOLY SCRIPTURE, Gospel—Mark gave the label "Gospel" to the literary form he wrote. A Gospel is a written revelation of Jesus Christ. Gospels begin differently and end differently. Gospels follow the outline of Christ's life, an outline provided by Mark and followed in different ways by Matthew and Luke, who together have over ninety percent of Mark's material. God's inspiration of Scripture included providing Mark as a written source for Matthew and Luke. For Mark, the gospel begins as the fulfillment of Old Testament prophecy. Mark cited Isaiah as the source of his prophetic quotation, then quoted Mal 3:1 before quoting Isa 40:3.

1:4 SALVATION, Forgiveness—John the Baptist preached the forgiveness of sins. Compare Lk 1:77; 3:3.

1:4–11 ORDINANCES, Baptism by John—See note on Mt 3:4–17. Matthew mentioned that John preached repentance and required evidence of it in order to baptize his converts. Mark used the specific phrase "baptism of repentance." "Repent" means to "turn around" in both Hebrew (*shub*) and Greek (*metanoeō*). Thus baptism became for John and for later Christians a sign of turning one's whole life around and directing it toward faith in God.

1:8 HOLY SPIRIT, Promised—See note on Mt 3:11.

1:9–11 JESUS CHRIST, Son of God—See notes on 1:1; Mt 3:13–17.

1:9–10 HOLY SPIRIT, Jesus—See note on Mt 3:16–17.

1:11 GOD, Love—Love which is such a fundamental aspect of God's nature is a two-dimensional love. It reaches out to humans, the creation of God, for whom He feels a parental or fatherly concern. The other dimension is the love shared by the three Persons who make up the Trinity. We might even say love unites the Trinity into the unity we know as God. This passage declares the love of God the Father for the Son. Jesus came into the world as the expression of God's love to the world that is lost. Thus the love of God specifically reaches out from God in heaven to Jesus on earth as the bond that unites them. Love (Greek *agape*) is a self-giving love that seeks to give itself away for the benefit of its object. It is not a self-seeking love, selfishly looking for something in return. It is a wholehearted love, holding nothing back. It expresses more than friendship or attachment. It goes beyond emotion, sentiment, or feeling. It expresses creative purpose. Out of the riches of its own resources, it seeks to meet all the needs and interests of its object. That kind of love flows from the Father to the Son. That kind of love also flowed from the Son to the lost of the world as He gave Himself for their salvation. See note on Mt 3:16–17.

1:11 REVELATION, Jesus Christ—See note on Mt 3:16–17.

1:12–13 JESUS CHRIST, Temptation—The wilderness is the place of temptation, of wanderings, and of wild animals. See note on Mt 4:1–11. Mark indicated the Spirit impelled or drove Jesus into the wilderness. Similarly a scapegoat (Azazel, a goat laden with Israel's sin) was sent into the desert during the Feast of the Tabernacles (Lev 16:21–22).

1:12 HOLY SPIRIT, Jesus—The Spirit led Jesus into the desert to be tested. The verb is a strong one and suggests that the Spirit's leadership of Jesus is a powerful urging or moving. This may be compared to the way the Spirit moved Ezekiel and other prophets. See Eze 3:12; note on Mt 4:1.

1:13 EVIL AND SUFFERING, Satan—See note on Mt 4:1–11.

1:14–15 PROCLAMATION, Gospel—See note on Lk 10:9. Jesus is the supreme pattern of gospel proclamation. Upon the imprisonment of John the Baptist, He stepped into the spotlight to preach. He announced that the kingdom of God was at hand. People were to enter that kingdom through repentance and faith. As Jesus demonstrated, the ministry of proclamation involves the announcement of eternal truth and the call for personal commitment. All true proclamation follows this pattern.

went into Galilee,[s] proclaiming the good
news of God.[t] 15"The time has come,"[u]
he said. "The kingdom of God is near.
Repent and believe[v] the good news!"[w]
16As Jesus walked beside the Sea of
Galilee, he saw Simon and his brother
Andrew casting a net into the lake, for
they were fishermen. 17"Come, follow
me," Jesus said, "and I will make you
fishers of men." 18At once they left their
nets and followed him.[x]
19When he had gone a little farther, he
saw James son of Zebedee and his brother
John in a boat, preparing their nets.
20Without delay he called them, and they
left their father Zebedee in the boat with
the hired men and followed him.

Jesus Drives Out an Evil Spirit

1:21–28pp — Lk 4:31–37

21They went to Capernaum, and when
the Sabbath came, Jesus went into the
synagogue and began to teach.[y] 22The
people were amazed at his teaching, because he taught them as one who had
authority, not as the teachers of the law.[z]
23Just then a man in their synagogue who
was possessed by an evil[e] spirit cried
out, 24"What do you want with us,[a] Jesus
of Nazareth?[b] Have you come to destroy
us? I know who you are—the Holy One
of God!"[c]
25"Be quiet!" said Jesus sternly.
"Come out of him!"[d] 26The evil spirit
shook the man violently and came out of
him with a shriek.[e]
27The people were all so amazed[f] that
they asked each other, "What is this? A
new teaching—and with authority! He
even gives orders to evil spirits and they
obey him." 28News about him spread
quickly over the whole region[g] of Galilee.

Jesus Heals Many

1:29–31pp — Mt 8:14,15; Lk 4:38,39
1:32–34pp — Mt 8:16,17; Lk 4:40,41

29As soon as they left the synagogue,[h]
they went with James and John to the
home of Simon and Andrew. 30Simon's
mother-in-law was in bed with a fever,
and they told Jesus about her. 31So he
went to her, took her hand and helped
her up.[i] The fever left her and she began
to wait on them.
32That evening after sunset the people
brought to Jesus all the sick and demon-
possessed.[j] 33The whole town gathered
at the door, 34and Jesus healed many who
had various diseases.[k] He also drove out
many demons, but he would not let the
demons speak because they knew who he
was.[l]

1:14 [s]Mt 4:12 [t]Mt 4:23
1:15 [u]Ro 5:6; Gal 4:4; Eph 1:10 [v]S Jn 3:15 [w]Ac 20:21
1:18 [x]S Mt 4:19
1:21 [y]ver 39; S Mt 4:23; S Mk 10:1
1:22 [z]S Mt 7:28,29
1:24 [a]S Mt 8:29 [b]Jdg 13:5; S Mt 2:23; Lk 24:19; Jn 1:45,46; Ac 4:10; 24:5 [c]Ps 16:10; Isa 41:14,16,20; Lk 1:35; Jn 6:69; Ac 3:14; 1Jn 2:20
1:25 [d]ver 34
1:26 [e]Mk 9:20
1:27 [f]Mk 10:24,32
1:28 [g]S Mt 9:26
1:29 [h]ver 21,23
1:31 [i]S Lk 7:14
1:32 [j]S Mt 4:24
1:34 [k]S Mt 4:23 [l]Mk 3:12; Ac 16:17,18

[e]23 Greek *unclean;* also in verses 26 and 27

1:15 HISTORY, Kingdom—God's goal is to rule history. In Jesus His kingdom became concretely real on earth as people through Jesus let God rule their lives. Thus Jesus showed the kingdom of heaven has earthly foundations and an earthly history. To enter the kingdom is to know true historical existence rather than to escape from history.
1:15 SALVATION, Belief—Jesus preached that persons should believe the good news about the arrival of God's kingdom in His own life and ministry. Belief centers on whether we accept Jesus' coming as the ultimate good news God has for the world.
1:15 THE CHURCH, God's Kingdom—Mark and Luke, writing mainly for Gentile audiences, freely used the expression, "the kingdom of God." See note on Mt 3:2.
1:16–20 HUMANITY, Work—See Mt 4:18–22; Lk 5:8–11.
1:17–18 EVANGELISM, Call to Evangelize—We are to leave our "nets," whatever they may be, so we will not be deterred from being "fishers of men." See note on Mt 4:19.
1:21–45 JESUS CHRIST, Miracles—Mark is supremely the Gospel of miracles. Basically there are four types of miracles which Jesus performs: physical healing (1:31,34,41–42; 2:12; 3:5; 5:29; 6:56; 7:35; 8:25); exorcism or driving out evil spirits (1:26,34; 5:13; 7:30; 9:26); mighty works demonstrating His power over nature (4:39; 6:41,48; 8:7; 11:21); raising from the dead (5:42). Jesus' miracles showed He was God's Son with God's authority to bring God's kingdom. People were not allowed to proclaim this message until the cross and resurrection made plain what it meant to call and follow Jesus as Son of God. See note on Mt 9:27–34.
1:21–28 MIRACLE, Christ—Miracles support Christ's *teaching authority. The* outburst of confession must have disturbed the synagogue service! Demon-possessed persons appear to have had certain spiritual perceptions. In command of the situation, Jesus spoke authoritatively and healed the man. The crowd was amazed at the authority with which Jesus taught and healed.
1:21–22 EDUCATION, Jesus—Jesus began His public ministry with the activity that became His trademark—teaching. The synogogue was a logical place to do this since instruction was central to all synogogue services. The people were amazed that His interpretations were unique and original, for only rabbis were permitted to teach with the authority conferred upon them by their masters. See note on Mt 7:28–29.
1:22–28 JESUS CHRIST, Authority—See notes on Mt 7:28; 8:5. His authority extended over the powers and representatives of evil. They recognized who He was and obeyed Him.
1:23–24 JESUS CHRIST, Sinless—Compare Lk 4:31–37. The demons recognized that Jesus shared God's moral purity. The Holy One is without sin.
1:25,34 JESUS CHRIST, Secret—Jesus did not want testimony from demons. He kept secret His identity to avoid inciting political action and to let eyes of faith discern who He was. See note on Mt 12:13–21. The messianic secret is a major emphasis of Mark's Gospel (Mk 1:44; 3:12; 4:10–12; 5:43; 7:36; 8:17–21,26,30; 9:9).
1:25 REVELATION, Events—Miracles revealed Christ's authority over the demonic and attracted great interest. They had to be combined with teaching to help people understand the true meaning of Messiah. Even the demons recognized Him as God's Holy One, but intellectual recognition is not sufficient response to revelation.
1:25–27 EDUCATION, Jesus—Although their amazement had been prompted by a healing miracle, the people called it a "new teaching." The healing established the authority of His teaching. What teachers do has a strong bearing on how people respond to what the teachers say.
1:29–34 MIRACLE, Christ—See note on Lk 4:38–41.
1:30 JESUS CHRIST, Miracles—See Mt 8:14; Lk 4:38.

Jesus Prays in a Solitary Place

1:35–38pp — Lk 4:42,43

35Very early in the morning, while it was still dark, Jesus got up, left the house and went off to a solitary place, where he prayed.[m] 36Simon and his companions went to look for him, 37and when they found him, they exclaimed: "Everyone is looking for you!"

38Jesus replied, "Let us go somewhere else—to the nearby villages—so I can preach there also. That is why I have come."[n] 39So he traveled throughout Galilee, preaching in their synagogues[o] and driving out demons.[p]

A Man With Leprosy

1:40–44pp — Mt 8:2–4; Lk 5:12–14

40A man with leprosy[f] came to him and begged him on his knees,[q] "If you are willing, you can make me clean."

41Filled with compassion, Jesus reached out his hand and touched the man. "I am willing," he said. "Be clean!" 42Immediately the leprosy left him and he was cured.

43Jesus sent him away at once with a strong warning: 44"See that you don't tell this to anyone.[r] But go, show yourself to the priest[s] and offer the sacrifices that Moses commanded for your cleansing,[t] as a testimony to them." 45Instead he went out and began to talk freely, spreading the news. As a result, Jesus could no longer enter a town openly but stayed outside in lonely places.[u] Yet the people still came to him from everywhere.[v]

1:35 [m]S Lk 3:21
1:38 [n]Isa 61:1
1:39 [o]S Mt 4:23 [p]S Mt 4:24
1:40 [q]Mk 10:17
1:44 [r]S Mt 8:4 [s]Lev 13:49 [t]Lev 14:1-32
1:45 [u]Lk 5:15,16 [v]Mk 2:13; Lk 5:17; Jn 6:2
2:2 [w]ver 13; Mk 1:45
2:3 [x]S Mt 4:24
2:5 [y]Lk 7:48
2:7 [z]Isa 43:25
2:10 [a]S Mt 8:20

Chapter 2

Jesus Heals a Paralytic

2:3–12pp — Mt 9:2–8; Lk 5:18–26

A few days later, when Jesus again entered Capernaum, the people heard that he had come home. 2So many[w] gathered that there was no room left, not even outside the door, and he preached the word to them. 3Some men came, bringing to him a paralytic,[x] carried by four of them. 4Since they could not get him to Jesus because of the crowd, they made an opening in the roof above Jesus and, after digging through it, lowered the mat the paralyzed man was lying on. 5When Jesus saw their faith, he said to the paralytic, "Son, your sins are forgiven."[y]

6Now some teachers of the law were sitting there, thinking to themselves, 7"Why does this fellow talk like that? He's blaspheming! Who can forgive sins but God alone?"[z]

8Immediately Jesus knew in his spirit that this was what they were thinking in their hearts, and he said to them, "Why are you thinking these things? 9Which is easier: to say to the paralytic, 'Your sins are forgiven,' or to say, 'Get up, take your mat and walk'? 10But that you may know that the Son of Man[a] has authority on earth to forgive sins . . . ." He said to the paralytic, 11"I tell you, get up, take your mat and go home." 12He got up, took his mat and walked out in full view of them all. This amazed everyone and they

f40 The Greek word was used for various diseases affecting the skin—not necessarily leprosy.

1:35 PRAYER, Jesus' Example—Jesus prayed alone. See note on Jn 6:15. If He needed to start the day with God, so do His followers.

1:38–39 REVELATION, Word—Proclaiming the good news of salvation was the center of Jesus' ministry. Healing miracles provided opportunity to preach. Jesus attempted to reach as many people as possible. Preaching continues to be a major means of revealing God's salvation to people who do not know Christ.

1:38–39 PROCLAMATION, Compulsion—See note on 1 Co 9:16–18.

1:40–45 MIRACLE, Christ—See note on Lk 5:12–26.

2:1–5 JESUS CHRIST, Miracles—Compare Mt 9:1–8; Lk 5:18–26. Miracles illustrated different aspects of Jesus' nature, authority, and mission depending upon the context in which Jesus performed them. This miracle showed Jesus' equality with God in having power to forgive sins. That same equality was shown by His ability to know His opponents' thoughts.

2:1–12 MIRACLE, Faith—Miracles prove forgiveness is available for people of faith. The faith of five men was involved, those who bore the paralytic and the victim himself. In response to their faith Jesus forgave the man's sins. Some present cried out "Blasphemy!" Forgiveness is God's occupation. Through the miracle Jesus showed forgiveness was His occupation. This meant He was God. The healing amazed the many witnesses. Some praised God, thus taking a first step of faith. The final act of faith starred the paralytic: he walked away. All need the miracle of forgiveness. Have you experienced it?

2:1–12 EVIL AND SUFFERING, Human Origin—See note on Mt 9:1–8.

2:7 GOD, Trinity—The scholarly critics were exactly right: only God can forgive sin. What they failed to understand, at this point, was the trinitarian nature of God. They did not understand that Jesus is the Son of God, the second Person of the Trinity. What one Person of the Trinity does, the other two are involved in also. The Persons of the Trinity are so distinct from each other that it can properly be said that one or another of them does a particular thing. At the same time, they are so united in the one God that what any one of them does necessarily involves the other two also. For instance, Ge 1:1,2 shows that both God and the Holy Spirit were active in creation. Jn 1:3 declares that the world was created by Jesus, the Word of God. These are not contradictory statements. They are simply statements made from different trinitarian vantage points. Thus when Jesus spoke the word of forgiveness here to the paralytic, He did it in the power of God the Father, not in distinction from Him. Jesus was fully divine while He was here on earth, but His divine nature was working within the limits of the human nature He had voluntarily entered (Jn 1:14; Php 2:5–8; 1 Jn 4:2–3). The mighty works Jesus did while on this earth He did by the power of God the Father working through Him.

2:8–11 REVELATION, Author of Grace—See note on Mt 9:4.

2:10 JESUS CHRIST, Son of Man—Son of man was connected with Christ's divine authority on earth as well as with His humble identity with us as humans. See note on Mt 8:20.

praised God,[b] saying, "We have never
seen anything like this!"[c]

The Calling of Levi

2:14–17pp — Mt 9:9–13; Lk 5:27–32

13Once again Jesus went out beside the
lake. A large crowd came to him,[d] and he
began to teach them. 14As he walked
along, he saw Levi son of Alphaeus sitting
at the tax collector's booth. "Follow
me,"[e] Jesus told him, and Levi got up
and followed him.
15While Jesus was having dinner at
Levi's house, many tax collectors and
"sinners" were eating with him and his
disciples, for there were many who followed him. 16When the teachers of the
law who were Pharisees[f] saw him eating
with the "sinners" and tax collectors,
they asked his disciples: "Why does he
eat with tax collectors and 'sinners'?"[g]
17On hearing this, Jesus said to them,
"It is not the healthy who need a doctor,
but the sick. I have not come to call the
righteous, but sinners."[h]

Jesus Questioned About Fasting

2:18–22pp — Mt 9:14–17; Lk 5:33–38

18Now John's disciples and the Pharisees were fasting.[i] Some people came
and asked Jesus, "How is it that John's
disciples and the disciples of the Pharisees are fasting, but yours are not?"
19Jesus answered, "How can the guests
of the bridegroom fast while he is with
them? They cannot, so long as they have
him with them. 20But the time will come
when the bridegroom will be taken from
them,[j] and on that day they will fast.
21"No one sews a patch of unshrunk
cloth on an old garment. If he does, the
new piece will pull away from the old,
making the tear worse. 22And no one
pours new wine into old wineskins. If he
does, the wine will burst the skins, and
both the wine and the wineskins will be
ruined. No, he pours new wine into new
wineskins."

Lord of the Sabbath

2:23–28pp — Mt 12:1–8; Lk 6:1–5
3:1–6pp — Mt 12:9–14; Lk 6:6–11

23One Sabbath Jesus was going through
the grainfields, and as his disciples
walked along, they began to pick some
heads of grain.[k] 24The Pharisees said to
him, "Look, why are they doing what is
unlawful on the Sabbath?"[l]
25He answered, "Have you never read
what David did when he and his companions were hungry and in need? 26In the
days of Abiathar the high priest,[m] he entered the house of God and ate the consecrated bread, which is lawful only for
priests to eat.[n] And he also gave some to
his companions."[o]
27Then he said to them, "The Sabbath
was made for man,[p] not man for the Sabbath.[q] 28So the Son of Man[r] is Lord even
of the Sabbath."

Chapter 3

ANOTHER time he went into the synagogue,[s] and a man with a shriveled

2:12 [b]S Mt 9:8 [c]Mt 9:33
2:13 [d]Mk 1:45; Lk 5:15; Jn 6:2
2:14 [e]S Mt 4:19
2:16 [f]Ac 23:9 [g]S Mt 9:11
2:17 [h]Lk 19:10; 1Ti 1:15
2:18 [i]S Mt 6:16-18; Ac 13:2
2:20 [j]Lk 17:22
2:23 [k]Dt 23:25
2:24 [l]S Mt 12:2
2:26 [m]1Ch 24:6; 2Sa 8:17 [n]Lev 24:5-9 [o]1Sa 21:1-6
2:27 [p]Ex 23:12; Dt 5:14 [q]Col 2:16
2:28 [r]S Mt 8:20
3:1 [s]S Mt 4:23; Mk 1:21

2:13 EDUCATION, Jesus—Whether in a synogogue, marketplace, or on the shores of a lake, the typical activity of Jesus was teaching. Christian teaching need not be confined to classrooms or to certain hours in the weekly schedule.
2:15–16 SIN, Violation—Who is a sinner? The teachers of the law and the Pharisees had a pat definition. They thought the people who refused to do religion their way were sinners. Such people did not have time to learn the Pharisees' system or desire to do religion by legalistic laws. They would not observe the rituals, refrain from fellowship with people who ignored Pharisaic rules, and interpret each verse of the law with minute regulations. The Pharisees excluded such people from their fellowship. They included Jesus among their sinners because of the people He associated with. The hottest arguments between Jesus and His opponents centered on the definition of sin. They would not let Jesus be Messiah because He was a "sinner" according to their definition. Jesus defined sin differently. He freely associated with the common people who did not have time or interest in escaping the Pharisaic category of sinners. He condemned the hypocrisy of the religious leaders saying they were blind to God's actions through His ministry and blind to the needs of people. Sin was refusing to love God and other people more than a religious system.
2:15–17 EVANGELISM, Lostness—Evangelism helps lost people find a cure for their sin sickness. Self-righteous people are usually the last to acknowledge they are lost. Jesus is the only Physician who can cure sin sickness. He sends His followers not to judge others but to proclaim the good news to all people, even at the risk of being criticized by the self-righteous. Jesus paid special attention to those the religious hypocrites rejected. He calls us to follow Him to love sinners.
2:17 JESUS CHRIST, Mission—The Jewish leaders looked for Messiah to join their religious institutions and establish them as the dominant power on earth. God sent Jesus to people open to repentance (1:15), so He worked outside the power structures with people acknowledging their sin and need.
2:18–20 PRAYER, Lament—See note on Mt 9:14–15.
2:20 JESUS CHRIST, Death—Jesus faced His death from the beginning of His ministry. His disciples' lives centered around Him, not around ritual observances. His presence is reason for joy. His death is the cause for fasting. Jesus' ministry pointing to His death brought a new reality into religion.
2:23–28 JESUS CHRIST, Authority—Jesus did not submit to human legalism. He knew all creation and religion was to help and serve people, whom God gave authority over creation (Ge 1:26–28). He assumed God's power in giving authoritative interpretation of Scripture and in asserting His authority over divinely appointed institutions.
2:27 HUMANITY, Relationship to God—Life becomes livable and enriched when people relate to God through obedience. God's laws are not a restriction upon human freedom. They are a guide to achieving the full potential of human life.
2:27 HOLY SCRIPTURE, Relationship—God's inspired laws were not intended to be rigid rules used to judge others. They direct and guide God's most important creation, human beings, to exercise freedom for the good of creation. Rules are means by which God's purposes are realized in people.
3:1–6 JESUS CHRIST, Miracles—Compare Mt 12:9–14; Lk 6:6–11. This miracle represented Jesus' angry response to His opponents as well as His compassion for the handicapped

hand was there. 2Some of them were
looking for a reason to accuse Jesus, so
they watched him closely[t] to see if he
would heal him on the Sabbath.[u] 3Jesus
said to the man with the shriveled hand,
"Stand up in front of everyone."
4Then Jesus asked them, "Which is
lawful on the Sabbath: to do good or to do
evil, to save life or to kill?" But they remained silent.
5He looked around at them in anger
and, deeply distressed at their stubborn
hearts, said to the man, "Stretch out your
hand." He stretched it out, and his hand
was completely restored. 6Then the Pharisees went out and began to plot with the
Herodians[v] how they might kill Jesus.[w]

Crowds Follow Jesus

3:7–12pp — Mt 12:15,16; Lk 6:17–19

7Jesus withdrew with his disciples to
the lake, and a large crowd from Galilee
followed.[x] 8When they heard all he was
doing, many people came to him from Judea, Jerusalem, Idumea, and the regions
across the Jordan and around Tyre and
Sidon.[y] 9Because of the crowd he told his
disciples to have a small boat ready for
him, to keep the people from crowding
him. 10For he had healed many,[z] so that
those with diseases were pushing forward to touch him.[a] 11Whenever the
evil[g] spirits saw him, they fell down before him and cried out, "You are the Son
of God."[b] 12But he gave them strict orders not to tell who he was.[c]

The Appointing of the Twelve Apostles

3:16–19pp — Mt 10:2–4; Lk 6:14–16; Ac 1:13

13Jesus went up on a mountainside and
called to him those he wanted, and they
came to him.[d] 14He appointed twelve—
designating them apostles[h][e]—that they
might be with him and that he might
send them out to preach 15and to have
authority to drive out demons.[f] 16These
are the twelve he appointed: Simon (to
whom he gave the name Peter);[g] 17James
son of Zebedee and his brother John (to
them he gave the name Boanerges, which
means Sons of Thunder); 18Andrew, Philip, Bartholomew, Matthew, Thomas,
James son of Alphaeus, Thaddaeus, Simon
the Zealot 19and Judas Iscariot, who betrayed him.

Jesus and Beelzebub

3:23–27pp — Mt 12:25–29; Lk 11:17–22

20Then Jesus entered a house, and
again a crowd gathered,[h] so that he and
his disciples were not even able to eat.[i]
21When his family heard about this, they
went to take charge of him, for they said,
"He is out of his mind."[j]
22And the teachers of the law who
came down from Jerusalem[k] said, "He is
possessed by Beelzebub[i]![l] By the prince
of demons he is driving out demons."[m]
23So Jesus called them and spoke to
them in parables:[n] "How can Satan[o]
drive out Satan? 24If a kingdom is divided
against itself, that kingdom cannot stand.
25If a house is divided against itself, that
house cannot stand. 26And if Satan opposes himself and is divided, he cannot
stand; his end has come. 27In fact, no one
can enter a strong man's house and carry
off his possessions unless he first ties up
the strong man. Then he can rob his
house.[p] 28I tell you the truth, all the sins
and blasphemies of men will be forgiven

3:2 [t]S Mt 12:10 [u]Lk 14:1
3:6 [v]Mt 22:16; Mk 12:13 [w]S Mt 12:14
3:7 [x]Mt 4:25
3:8 [y]S Mt 11:21
3:10 [z]S Mt 4:23 [a]S Mt 9:20
3:11 [b]S Mt 4:3; Mk 1:23,24
3:12 [c]S Mt 8:4; Mk 1:24,25,34; Ac 16:17,18
3:13 [d]Mt 5:1
3:14 [e]S Mk 6:30
3:15 [f]S Mt 10:1
3:16 [g]Jn 1:42
3:20 [h]ver 7 [i]Mk 6:31
3:21 [j]Jn 10:20; Ac 26:24
3:22 [k]Mt 15:1 [l]Mt 10:25; 11:18; 12:24; Jn 7:20; 8:48,52; 10:20 [m]Mt 9:34
3:23 [n]Mk 4:2 [o]S Mt 4:10
3:27 [p]Isa 49:24,25

[g]*11* Greek *unclean*; also in verse 30 [h]*14* Some manuscripts do not have *designating them apostles.* [i]*22* Greek *Beezeboul* or *Beelzeboul*

man. Because Jesus broke human tradition to help a person in need, religious leaders joined forces to seek His death.

3:1–6 MIRACLE, Redemption—See note on Mt 12:9–14.

3:11–12 JESUS CHRIST, Secret—See note on 1:25,34.

3:13–14 PROCLAMATION, Call—See note on Jer 1:4–9.

3:20–30 JESUS CHRIST, Son of God—Jesus' actions clearly distinguished Him from all other humans. His own human family and the legal experts recognized that. Only the Son of God in flesh could do what He was doing. See note on Mt 12:23–28.

3:21,31–35 FAMILY, Priorities—Jesus faced interfamily tension because of His commitment to the will of God. Even though Mary had been told that her Son was destined for a particular calling in life, she along with her other children did not understand Jesus. They feared for His mental condition and wanted to take Him home. His brothers even ridiculed Him (7:2–5). Jesus declared all who follow the will of God are His family. He did not reject His mother or family. His tender care for her at the cross indicates this (Jn 19:26–27). He declared that as Son of God all who enter into close relationship with the Father become His family as well.

3:22–30 EVIL AND SUFFERING, Satan—Jesus was able to cast out demons because He was more powerful than Satan or Beelzebub. Beelzebub is the English equivalent of the Latin Vulgate translation. The Greek is *Beelzeboul,* a transliteration from Semitic Baal-zebul, the name of a Canaanite god meaning "Prince Baal" or "Baal the exalted one." Israel made a play on the name, changing it to Baal-Zebub or Lord of the flies. At some point in time the Jews began using the name as a synonym for Satan. As God does not rule alone, but has His heavenly council (Job 1:6), so Satan rules over other demons who carry out his will. Jesus was accused of acting like one of the demons. Jesus' power over the demons was shown in His healing. Such healing demonstrated that Jesus was establishing God's kingdom. Satan does not have complete control of this world. He may cause some illness. He may lead people to fall for his temptation. He may cause evil in our lives and world, but his defeat is sure. Jesus is Lord, not Beelzebub.

3:28–29 SIN, Against God—Ultimately, all sin is against God. Sin against the Holy Spirit is serious because the Holy Spirit is the One who convicts us of sin. Blasphemy against the Holy Spirit cannot be forgiven. Conviction precedes repentance. Without the convicting Spirit, we cannot find forgiveness. Blasphemy against the Spirit is the willful and blatant act of attributing to Satan that which is clearly a work of the Holy Spirit. This terrible sin occurs when a person consciously rejects the truth, believing Satan rather than God. God will not forgive such blatant rebellion. The nature of the problem is

them. 29 But whoever blasphemes against
the Holy Spirit will never be forgiven; he
is guilty of an eternal sin."[q]
30 He said this because they were saying, "He has an evil spirit."

Jesus' Mother and Brothers

3:31–35pp — Mt 12:46–50; Lk 8:19–21

31 Then Jesus' mother and brothers arrived.[r] Standing outside, they sent someone in to call him. 32 A crowd was sitting
around him, and they told him, "Your
mother and brothers are outside looking
for you."
33 "Who are my mother and my brothers?" he asked.
34 Then he looked at those seated in a
circle around him and said, "Here are my
mother and my brothers! 35 Whoever does
God's will is my brother and sister and
mother."

Chapter 4

The Parable of the Sower

4:1–12pp — Mt 13:1–15; Lk 8:4–10
4:13–20pp — Mt 13:18–23; Lk 8:11–15

AGAIN Jesus began to teach by the
lake.[s] The crowd that gathered
around him was so large that he got into a
boat and sat in it out on the lake, while all
the people were along the shore at the
water's edge. 2 He taught them many
things by parables,[t] and in his teaching
said: 3 "Listen! A farmer went out to sow
his seed.[u] 4 As he was scattering the seed,
some fell along the path, and the birds
came and ate it up. 5 Some fell on rocky
places, where it did not have much soil. It
sprang up quickly, because the soil was
shallow. 6 But when the sun came up, the
plants were scorched, and they withered
because they had no root. 7 Other seed fell
among thorns, which grew up and
choked the plants, so that they did not
bear grain. 8 Still other seed fell on good
soil. It came up, grew and produced a
crop, multiplying thirty, sixty, or even a
hundred times."[v]
9 Then Jesus said, "He who has ears to
hear, let him hear."[w]
10 When he was alone, the Twelve and
the others around him asked him about
the parables. 11 He told them, "The secret
of the kingdom of God[x] has been given
to you. But to those on the outside[y] everything is said in parables 12 so that,

" 'they may be ever seeing but never
perceiving,
and ever hearing but never
understanding;
otherwise they might turn and be
forgiven!'[j] "[z]

13 Then Jesus said to them, "Don't you
understand this parable? How then will
you understand any parable? 14 The farmer sows the word.[a] 15 Some people are
like seed along the path, where the word
is sown. As soon as they hear it, Satan[b]
comes and takes away the word that was
sown in them. 16 Others, like seed sown
on rocky places, hear the word and at
once receive it with joy. 17 But since they
have no root, they last only a short time.
When trouble or persecution comes because of the word, they quickly fall away.
18 Still others, like seed sown among
thorns, hear the word; 19 but the worries
of this life, the deceitfulness of wealth[c]
and the desires for other things come in
and choke the word, making it unfruitful.
20 Others, like seed sown on good soil,
hear the word, accept it, and produce a
crop—thirty, sixty or even a hundred
times what was sown."

[j]12 Isaiah 6:9,10

3:29 [q]Mt 12:31,32; Lk 12:10
3:31 [r]ver 21
4:1 [s]Mk 2:13; 3:7
4:2 [t]ver 11; Mk 3:23
4:3 [u]ver 26
4:8 [v]Jn 15:5; Col 1:6
4:9 [w]ver 23; S Mt 11:15
4:11 [x]S Mt 3:2 [y]1Co 5:12,13; Col 4:5; 1Th 4:12; 1Ti 3:7
4:12 [z]Isa 6:9,10; S Mt 13:13-15
4:14 [a]Mk 16:20; Lk 1:2; Ac 4:31; 8:4; 16:6; 17:11; Php 1:14
4:15 [b]S Mt 4:10
4:19 [c]Mt 19:23; 1Ti 6:9,10,17; 1Jn 2:15-17

---

debated. Has the heart become so hardened the person cannot distinguish good from evil or cannot repent? Or does God of His own free choice close the door to any possible repentance? Some have attempted to give a catalog of "unforgiveable" sins, but the New Testament does not list any other sins beyond forgiveness. We must be cautious not to apply the doctrine in the wrong way. People sometimes fear they have "sinned away the day of grace." People who feel such a yearning for salvation may be sure the Spirit continues to work in their lives. Where the Spirit works, grace for forgiveness is available. Some people in desperation or anger shake a fist and complain to God. They are simply repeating the actions of many of the psalmists. They are not guilty of the unforgiveable sin. The doctrine of the unforgiveable sin is a warning against overconfidence and religious blindness, not of temporary wrongdoing.

3:31–35 JESUS CHRIST, Son of God—See note on Mt 12:46–49.

3:33–35 HUMANITY, Relationships—The closest and most precious human relationships are inside the family. Jesus calls us to even dearer relationships—inside His spiritual family. These relationships are formed by total commitment to Jesus' way of life. They may enhance normal family relationships. They may replace family relationships.

3:34 REVELATION, Fellowship—Anyone who follows the purposes and intentions of God is linked with Jesus as a family. Those who perform the same acts and have the same attitudes are the true "blood" kinship of God. Family ties are created by following the Father's words, that is putting His revealed will into practice. The initial and most important step in following God's will is placing faith in Christ for salvation. Compare 1 Jn 3:23.

4:2 EDUCATION, Parables—Parables were powerful teaching tools in the hands of the master Teacher. The parables of Jesus are among the best known stories in the world. Though they are stories about everyday things, they pierce to the very heart of spiritual truths. As teachers, we need to use stories from everyday life to help students see the radical effects Christian faith should have in our lives.

4:11–12,33–34 JESUS CHRIST, Secret—See note on 1:25,34.

4:13–20 ELECTION, Perseverance—The elect of God withstand pressures. Persecutions, problems, and pleasures of the world do not succeed in pulling them away from the kingdom of God. See note on Mt 13:1–43.

A Lamp on a Stand

21He said to them, "Do you bring in a
lamp to put it under a bowl or a bed?
Instead, don't you put it on its stand?[d]
22For whatever is hidden is meant to be
disclosed, and whatever is concealed is
meant to be brought out into the open.[e]
23If anyone has ears to hear, let him
hear."[f]
24"Consider carefully what you hear,"
he continued. "With the measure you
use, it will be measured to you—and
even more.[g] 25Whoever has will be given
more; whoever does not have, even what
he has will be taken from him."[h]

The Parable of the Growing Seed

26He also said, "This is what the kingdom of God is like.[i] A man scatters seed
on the ground. 27Night and day, whether
he sleeps or gets up, the seed sprouts and
grows, though he does not know how.
28All by itself the soil produces grain—
first the stalk, then the head, then the full
kernel in the head. 29As soon as the grain
is ripe, he puts the sickle to it, because
the harvest has come."[j]

The Parable of the Mustard Seed

4:30–32pp — Mt 13:31,32; Lk 13:18,19

30Again he said, "What shall we say
the kingdom of God is like,[k] or what parable shall we use to describe it? 31It is like
a mustard seed, which is the smallest
seed you plant in the ground. 32Yet when
planted, it grows and becomes the largest
of all garden plants, with such big
branches that the birds of the air can
perch in its shade."
33With many similar parables Jesus
spoke the word to them, as much as they
could understand.[l] 34He did not say anything to them without using a parable.[m]

4:21 [d]S Mt 5:15
4:22 [e]Jer 16:17; Mt 10:26; Lk 8:17; 12:2
4:23 [f]ver 9; S Mt 11:15
4:24 [g]S Mt 7:2
4:25 [h]S Mt 25:29
4:26 [i]S Mt 13:24
4:29 [j]Rev 14:15
4:30 [k]S Mt 13:24
4:33 [l]Jn 16:12
4:34 [m]S Jn 16:25
4:36 [n]ver 1; Mk 3:9; 5:2,21; 6:32,45
4:40 [o]Mt 14:31; Mk 16:14
5:2 [p]Mk 4:1 [q]Mk 1:23

But when he was alone with his own disciples, he explained everything.

Jesus Calms the Storm

4:35–41pp — Mt 8:18,23–27; Lk 8:22–25

35That day when evening came, he said
to his disciples, "Let us go over to the
other side." 36Leaving the crowd behind,
they took him along, just as he was, in
the boat.[n] There were also other boats
with him. 37A furious squall came up, and
the waves broke over the boat, so that it
was nearly swamped. 38Jesus was in the
stern, sleeping on a cushion. The disciples woke him and said to him, "Teacher,
don't you care if we drown?"
39He got up, rebuked the wind and said
to the waves, "Quiet! Be still!" Then the
wind died down and it was completely
calm.
40He said to his disciples, "Why are
you so afraid? Do you still have no
faith?"[o]
41They were terrified and asked each
other, "Who is this? Even the wind and
the waves obey him!"

Chapter 5

The Healing of a Demon-possessed Man

5:1–17pp — Mt 8:28–34; Lk 8:26–37
5:18–20pp — Lk 8:38,39

THEY went across the lake to the region of the Gerasenes.[k] 2When Jesus
got out of the boat,[p] a man with an evil[l]
spirit[q] came from the tombs to meet
him. 3This man lived in the tombs, and
no one could bind him any more, not
even with a chain. 4For he had often been
chained hand and foot, but he tore the
chains apart and broke the irons on his
feet. No one was strong enough to sub-

[k] *1* Some manuscripts *Gadarenes*; other manuscripts *Gergesenes* [l] *2* Greek *unclean*; also in verses 8 and 13

4:23–24 REVELATION, Inspiration—God's presence and truth is being spoken and demonstrated all the time by His people. The alert and teachable may hear it while others miss it. We are responsible to respond to what is being revealed.
4:26–32 THE CHURCH, God's Kingdom—God freely offers entrance to the kingdom to those who repent (1:15). Those who enter must work patiently and steadily until God's moment of fulfillment. We cannot bring the fulfillment through human action, planning, or violence. We can have hope because the harvest is sure, but we cannot determine the time or manner of harvest. See notes on Mt 13:24–30, 31–32.
4:26–29 EVANGELISM, Gospel—The gospel is "the power of God for the salvation of everyone who believes" (Ro 1:16). The message of the Kingdom is a small seed, but when planted in an open heart, it produces salvation. Our role is to take the gospel, plant it in lives, and watch God grow it.
4:30–32 REVELATION, History—All revelation, like the arrival of the kingdom of God on earth, appears small and unimportant at first but will grow because of its nature. Jesus was a small Babe, born in an unnoticed town. Thus began God's revelation of His great rule over all the earth.
4:35–41 JESUS CHRIST, Miracles—Compare Mt 8:23–27; Lk 8:22–25. Jesus' power over natural forces pointed minds of faith to see He was divine.
4:35–41 CREATION, Freedom—Jesus, God in human flesh, exercised free control over the elements of nature in whose creation He participated (Jn 1:3). Freedom to control the created world demonstrated His divine nature. See note on Lk 8:22–25.
4:35–41 MIRACLE, Nature—See note on Lk 8:22–25.
4:40 PRAYER, Hindrances—See note on Mt 8:26.
5:1–20 JESUS CHRIST, Son of God—Jesus exercised power over demons, showing He was divine, a fact the demons accepted. See note on 1:22–28.
5:1–20 MIRACLE, Christ—Miracles evidence Christ's supreme power and provide reason for us to witness. From the storm at sea Jesus and His disciples moved into the teeth of another storm—human personality. The demoniac was a hard case: he had shattered both handcuffs and foot fetters. He reigned in the cemetery. As frequently true of demoniacs, he showed spiritual perception in addressing Jesus. Jesus proved stronger than the legion of demons. He healed the man and sent him back as a symbolic and vocal witness to the power of God. See note on Mt 8:28–34.

due him. 5Night and day among the
tombs and in the hills he would cry out
and cut himself with stones.
6When he saw Jesus from a distance,
he ran and fell on his knees in front of
him. 7He shouted at the top of his voice,
"What do you want with me,[r] Jesus, Son
of the Most High God?[s] Swear to God
that you won't torture me!" 8For Jesus
had said to him, "Come out of this man,
you evil spirit!"
9Then Jesus asked him, "What is your
name?"
"My name is Legion,"[t] he replied,
"for we are many." 10And he begged
Jesus again and again not to send them
out of the area.
11A large herd of pigs was feeding on
the nearby hillside. 12The demons begged
Jesus, "Send us among the pigs; allow us
to go into them." 13He gave them permission, and the evil spirits came out and
went into the pigs. The herd, about two
thousand in number, rushed down the
steep bank into the lake and were
drowned.
14Those tending the pigs ran off and
reported this in the town and countryside, and the people went out to see what
had happened. 15When they came to
Jesus, they saw the man who had been
possessed by the legion[u] of demons,[v] sitting there, dressed and in his right mind;
and they were afraid. 16Those who had
seen it told the people what had happened to the demon-possessed man—and
told about the pigs as well. 17Then the
people began to plead with Jesus to leave
their region.
18As Jesus was getting into the boat,
the man who had been demon-possessed
begged to go with him. 19Jesus did not let
him, but said, "Go home to your family
and tell them[w] how much the Lord has
done for you, and how he has had mercy
on you." 20So the man went away and
began to tell in the Decapolis[m][x] how
much Jesus had done for him. And all the
people were amazed.

A Dead Girl and a Sick Woman

5:22–43pp — Mt 9:18–26; Lk 8:41–56

21When Jesus had again crossed over
by boat to the other side of the lake,[y] a
large crowd gathered around him while
he was by the lake.[z] 22Then one of the
synagogue rulers,[a] named Jairus, came
there. Seeing Jesus, he fell at his feet
23and pleaded earnestly with him, "My
little daughter is dying. Please come and
put your hands on[b] her so that she will
be healed and live." 24So Jesus went with
him.
A large crowd followed and pressed
around him. 25And a woman was there
who had been subject to bleeding[c] for
twelve years. 26She had suffered a great
deal under the care of many doctors and
had spent all she had, yet instead of getting better she grew worse. 27When she
heard about Jesus, she came up behind
him in the crowd and touched his cloak,
28because she thought, "If I just touch his
clothes,[d] I will be healed." 29Immediate-
ly her bleeding stopped and she felt in
her body that she was freed from her suffering.[e]
30At once Jesus realized that power[f]
had gone out from him. He turned around
in the crowd and asked, "Who touched
my clothes?"
31"You see the people crowding against
you," his disciples answered, "and yet
you can ask, 'Who touched me?' "
32But Jesus kept looking around to see
who had done it. 33Then the woman,
knowing what had happened to her,
came and fell at his feet and, trembling
with fear, told him the whole truth. 34He
said to her, "Daughter, your faith has
healed you.[g] Go in peace[h] and be freed
from your suffering."
35While Jesus was still speaking, some

5:7 [r]S Mt 8:29 [s]S Mt 4:3; Lk 1:32; 6:35; Ac 16:17; Heb 7:1
5:9 [t]ver 15
5:15 [u]ver 9 [v]ver 16,18; S Mt 4:24
5:19 [w]S Mt 8:4
5:20 [x]Mt 4:25; Mk 7:31
5:21 [y]Mt 9:1 [z]Mk 4:1
5:22 [a]ver 35,36,38; Lk 13:14; Ac 13:15; 18:8,17
5:23 [b]Mt 19:13; Mk 6:5; 7:32; 8:23; 16:18; Lk 4:40; 13:13; S Ac 6:6
5:25 [c]Lev 15:25-30
5:28 [d]S Mt 9:20
5:29 [e]ver 34
5:30 [f]Lk 5:17; 6:19
5:34 [g]S Mt 9:22 [h]S Ac 15:33

[m]*20* That is, the Ten Cities

5:18–19 PRAYER, Hindrances—Some prayers receive an answer of "no." As worthy as the desire to stay with Jesus was, Jesus had a higher purpose for the former demoniac. Prayer leads us to follow God's will to achieve His purposes.

5:19 GOD, Grace—Jesus' miraculous healing of Legion, casting the demons out of him, was a powerful demonstration of the grace of God. Grace is the unmerited blessing, the gift of God's overflowing love to one who does not deserve it and has no grounds for asking for it. Jesus Himself was the instrument of healing for the pathetic, demon-possessed man, but He told him that the blessing that came to him was mercy from the Lord. God's grace is manifested in every good thing that we enjoy in life. See Jas 1:17.

5:19–20 EVANGELISM, In the Home—God saves us and sends us to tell those closest to us about His salvation. Evangelism begins in our homes and with our friends. See Guide to Family Worship, pp. 1801–1802.

5:21–24,35–43 JESUS CHRIST, Miracles—Compare Mt 9:23–26; Lk 8:41–56. The raising of Jairus' daughter was Jesus' first raising from the dead. Power over death pointed believers to see Jesus was the Son of God in flesh.

5:21–43 MIRACLE, Faith—Miracles reward determined faith. Jairus risked his reputation as a religious leader because he trusted Jesus. The desperate woman risked public shame in touching a man because she believed He could heal her. Jesus rewarded the faith of both.

5:23 PRAYER, Sincerity—Prayer cannot be indifferent ritual; Jairus was earnest. God responds to sincere prayer, not to words mouthed to fulfill requirements or impress others. Compare Lk 8:41.

5:25–34 JESUS CHRIST, Miracles—On the way to the raising of Jairus' daughter, Jesus healed the woman with a hemorrhage. Jesus' divine nature is seen in His ability to know healing power had gone out.

5:25–34 PRAYER, Faith—See note on Mt 9:20–22.

5:35–40 HUMANITY, Attitudes to Death—At a time of

men came from the house of Jairus, the
synagogue ruler.[i] "Your daughter is
dead," they said. "Why bother the teacher any more?"
36 Ignoring what they said, Jesus told
the synagogue ruler, "Don't be afraid;
just believe."
37 He did not let anyone follow him except Peter, James and John the brother of
James.[j] 38 When they came to the home
of the synagogue ruler,[k] Jesus saw a commotion, with people crying and wailing
loudly. 39 He went in and said to them,
"Why all this commotion and wailing?
The child is not dead but asleep."[l] 40 But
they laughed at him.
After he put them all out, he took the
child's father and mother and the disciples who were with him, and went in
where the child was. 41 He took her by the
hand[m] and said to her, *"Talitha koum!"*
(which means, "Little girl, I say to you,
get up!"). 42 Immediately the girl stood
up and walked around (she was twelve
years old). At this they were completely
astonished. 43 He gave strict orders not to
let anyone know about this,[o] and told
them to give her something to eat.

Chapter 6

A Prophet Without Honor

6:1–6pp — Mt 13:54–58

JESUS left there and went to his hometown,[p] accompanied by his disciples.
2 When the Sabbath came,[q] he began to
teach in the synagogue,[r] and many who
heard him were amazed.[s]
"Where did this man get these
things?" they asked. "What's this wisdom that has been given him, that he
even does miracles! 3 Isn't this the carpenter? Isn't this Mary's son and the brother
of James, Joseph,[n] Judas and Simon?[t]
Aren't his sisters here with us?" And
they took offense at him.[u]
4 Jesus said to them, "Only in his hometown, among his relatives and in his own
house is a prophet without honor."[v] 5 He
could not do any miracles there, except
lay his hands on[w] a few sick people and
heal them. 6 And he was amazed at their
lack of faith.

Jesus Sends Out the Twelve

6:7–11pp — Mt 10:1,9–14; Lk 9:1,3–5

Then Jesus went around teaching from
village to village.[x] 7 Calling the Twelve to
him,[y] he sent them out two by two[z] and
gave them authority over evil[o] spirits.[a]
8 These were his instructions: "Take
nothing for the journey except a staff—
no bread, no bag, no money in your belts.
9 Wear sandals but not an extra tunic.
10 Whenever you enter a house, stay there
until you leave that town. 11 And if any
place will not welcome you or listen to
you, shake the dust off your feet[b] when
you leave, as a testimony against them."
12 They went out and preached that
people should repent.[c] 13 They drove out
many demons and anointed many sick
people with oil[d] and healed them.

John the Baptist Beheaded

6:14–29pp — Mt 14:1–12
6:14–16pp — Lk 9:7–9

14 King Herod heard about this, for
Jesus' name had become well known.
Some were saying,[p] "John the Baptist[e]
has been raised from the dead, and that is
why miraculous powers are at work in
him."
15 Others said, "He is Elijah."[f]
And still others claimed, "He is a
prophet,[g] like one of the prophets of long
ago."[h]

[n]3 Greek *Joses*, a variant of *Joseph* [o]7 Greek *unclean* [p]14 Some early manuscripts *He was saying*

5:35 [i]S ver 22
5:37 [j]S Mt 4:21
5:38 [k]S ver 22
5:39 [l]S Mt 9:24
5:41 [m]Mk 1:31 [n]S Lk 7:14
5:43 [o]S Mt 8:4
6:1 [p]S Mt 2:23
6:2 [q]Mk 1:21 [r]S Mt 4:23 [s]S Mt 7:28
6:3 [t]S Mt 12:46 [u]Mt 11:6; Jn 6:61
6:4 [v]Lk 4:24; Jn 4:44
6:5 [w]S Mk 5:23
6:6 [x]Mt 9:35; Mk 1:39; Lk 13:22
6:7 [y]Mk 3:13 [z]Dt 17:6; Lk 10:1 [a]S Mt 10:1
6:11 [b]S Mt 10:14
6:12 [c]Lk 9:6
6:13 [d]S Jas 5:14
6:14 [e]S Mt 3:1
6:15 [f]Mal 4:5 [g]S Mt 21:11 [h]Mt 16:14; Mk 8:28

---

death, grief leads people to release their emotions in sobbing and tears. Grief is natural and should not be denied. At the same time, unbelief makes people ridicule the idea that death is not necessarily final. Faith leads people to believe the Lord of the living is also Lord of the dead and will intervene for His own sovereign purposes.

5:41–42 REVELATION, Author of Life—God is in charge of life and death. His Son Jesus has the power and the authority to reverse even death. By delivering people from death, Jesus revealed the nature and power of God.

5:43 JESUS CHRIST, Secret—See note on 1:25,34.

6:1–6 JESUS CHRIST, *Wisdom of God*—Jesus' teaching and miracles clearly marked Him as different from all other inhabitants of earth. Unable to explain Him, the people who knew Him best rejected Him. Their lack of faith inhibited Christ's miracle-working power. Jesus cannot be explained as only a highly gifted man. He was God in flesh.

6:5–6 MIRACLE, Faith—Jesus responded to faith. Where there was no faith, Jesus performed few miracles. God's power is unlimited, but He has chosen to work through people of faith. We must constantly ask if our faith lets God work through us.

6:6–13 JESUS CHRIST, Mission—See note on Mt 10:1–42.

6:6 EDUCATION, Jesus—See notes on 2:13; Mt 4:23.

6:10–11 REVELATION, Actions—God's truth is carried by chosen messengers. His revealed purpose and call to follow is to be taken to each home. People who reject the message need to understand clearly what they have done. Jesus provided a symbolic act to reveal God's rejection of those who rejected His revelation. Sandal shaking was a Hebrew custom for refusal or rejection of hospitality.

6:13 MIRACLE, Nature—The disciples shared in Jesus' ability to calm the fears of the demon-possessed. It is significant that they used oil, an ancient medical ointment, to anoint many of the sick. Modern medicine has worked miracles—and this often in response to faith. God can use human inventions and skills to perform His miracles. The eye of faith sees God at work through human hands.

6:14–16 JESUS CHRIST, John—See note on Mt 14:1.

6:14 MIRACLE, Revelation—See note on Mt 14:2.

16But when Herod heard this, he said,
"John, the man I beheaded, has been
raised from the dead!"
17For Herod himself had given orders
to have John arrested, and he had him
bound and put in prison.[i] He did this
because of Herodias, his brother Philip's
wife, whom he had married. 18For John
had been saying to Herod, "It is not lawful for you to have your brother's wife."[j]
19So Herodias nursed a grudge against
John and wanted to kill him. But she was
not able to, 20because Herod feared John
and protected him, knowing him to be a
righteous and holy man.[k] When Herod
heard John, he was greatly puzzled[q]; yet
he liked to listen to him.
21Finally the opportune time came. On
his birthday Herod gave a banquet[l] for
his high officials and military commanders and the leading men of Galilee.[m]
22When the daughter of Herodias came in
and danced, she pleased Herod and his
dinner guests.

The king said to the girl, "Ask me for
anything you want, and I'll give it to
you." 23And he promised her with an
oath, "Whatever you ask I will give you,
up to half my kingdom."[n]
24She went out and said to her mother,
"What shall I ask for?"

"The head of John the Baptist," she answered.
25At once the girl hurried in to the king
with the request: "I want you to give me
right now the head of John the Baptist on
a platter."
26The king was greatly distressed, but
because of his oaths and his dinner
guests, he did not want to refuse her. 27So
he immediately sent an executioner with
orders to bring John's head. The man
went, beheaded John in the prison, 28and
brought back his head on a platter. He
presented it to the girl, and she gave it to
her mother. 29On hearing of this, John's
disciples came and took his body and laid
it in a tomb.

Jesus Feeds the Five Thousand

6:32–44pp — Mt 14:13–21; Lk 9:10–17; Jn 6:5–13
6:32–44Ref — Mk 8:2–9

30The apostles[o] gathered around Jesus
and reported to him all they had done and
taught.[p] 31Then, because so many people
were coming and going that they did not
even have a chance to eat,[q] he said to
them, "Come with me by yourselves to a
quiet place and get some rest."
32So they went away by themselves in
a boat[r] to a solitary place. 33But many
who saw them leaving recognized them
and ran on foot from all the towns and got
there ahead of them. 34When Jesus landed and saw a large crowd, he had compassion on them, because they were like
sheep without a shepherd.[s] So he began
teaching them many things.
35By this time it was late in the day, so
his disciples came to him. "This is a remote place," they said, "and it's already
very late. 36Send the people away so they
can go to the surrounding countryside
and villages and buy themselves something to eat."
37But he answered, "You give them
something to eat."[t]

They said to him, "That would take
eight months of a man's wages[r]! Are we
to go and spend that much on bread and
give it to them to eat?"
38"How many loaves do you have?" he
asked. "Go and see."

When they found out, they said, "Five
—and two fish."[u]
39Then Jesus directed them to have all
the people sit down in groups on the
green grass. 40So they sat down in groups
of hundreds and fifties. 41Taking the five
loaves and the two fish and looking up to
heaven, he gave thanks and broke the

6:17 [i]Mt 4:12; 11:2; Lk 3:19,20
6:18 [j]Lev 18:16; 20:21
6:20 [k]S Mt 11:9
6:21 [l]Est 1:3; 2:18 [m]Lk 3:1
6:23 [n]Est 5:3,6; 7:2
6:30 [o]Mt 10:2; Lk 9:10; 17:5; 22:14; 24:10; Ac 1:2,26 [p]Lk 9:10
6:31 [q]Mk 3:20
6:32 [r]ver 45; S Mk 4:36
6:34 [s]S Mt 9:36
6:37 [t]2Ki 4:42-44
6:38 [u]Mt 15:34; Mk 8:5

[q]20 Some early manuscripts *he did many things*
[r]37 Greek *take two hundred denarii*

6:17–18 FAMILY, Divorce—Jewish law condemned a man for having sexual relations with his brother's wife (Lev 18:16) and for marrying the wife of his brother (Lev 20:21) while the brother was still living. In addition, divorcing a wife to marry a divorced woman was looked upon with disfavor by the rabbis. John the Baptist condemned Herod for violating both of these regulations of Jewish law. Such actions continue to be sin no matter how strongly society may accept them. John's death contributed to the controversy over divorce between the Pharisees and Jesus. See Mk 10:2–9; note on Mt 19:3–9.

6:26–28 HUMANITY, Moral Consciousness—When a person is more concerned with what people think than with what is right, moral consciousness is dead. Preserving another's life is always more valuable than preserving my own reputation.

6:30–44 JESUS CHRIST, Mission—Jesus ministered to and taught the masses. He also devoted time to withdrawing from the crowds to pray, teach His disciples, and prepare for His forthcoming death. Compare 7:24—8:9; 8:13–30; Mt 14:13–21; 15:21–38; 16:5–20; Lk 9:10–27; Jn 6:1–13. His God-given mission included both public and private times, but the crowds often interrupted His attempts at privacy.

6:30–52 MIRACLE, Christ—See note on Mt 14:13–21. Disciples may not understand miracles. Feeding the hungry points to Christ's divine Messiahship just as strongly as walking on water. Understanding miracles requires faith, not intellectual knowledge.

6:30 CHURCH LEADERS, The Twelve—Messengers cannot consider themselves greater than their message or the One who sent them (Jn 13:16). The apostles had been authorized by Jesus to share in His work and were required to give an account of their work to Him. Apart from Him, they were nothing.

***6:31–32* PRAYER, Jesus' Example**—See note on Mt 14:13–14,23.

6:34 JESUS CHRIST, Miracles—See note on Mt 14:14.

6:41 PRAYER, Thanksgiving—See note on Mt 14:19.

loaves.[v] Then he gave them to his disciples to set before the people. He also divided the two fish among them all.
42They all ate and were satisfied, 43and
the disciples picked up twelve basketfuls
of broken pieces of bread and fish. 44The
number of the men who had eaten was
five thousand.

Jesus Walks on the Water

6:45–51pp — Mt 14:22–32; Jn 6:15–21
6:53–56pp — Mt 14:34–36

45Immediately Jesus made his disciples
get into the boat[w] and go on ahead of him
to Bethsaida,[x] while he dismissed the
crowd. 46After leaving them, he went up
on a mountainside to pray.[y]
47When evening came, the boat was in
the middle of the lake, and he was alone
on land. 48He saw the disciples straining
at the oars, because the wind was against
them. About the fourth watch of the
night he went out to them, walking on
the lake. He was about to pass by them,
49but when they saw him walking on the
lake, they thought he was a ghost.[z] They
cried out, 50because they all saw him and
were terrified.

Immediately he spoke to them and
said, "Take courage! It is I. Don't be
afraid."[a] 51Then he climbed into the
boat[b] with them, and the wind died
down.[c] They were completely amazed,
52for they had not understood about the
loaves; their hearts were hardened.[d]
53When they had crossed over, they
landed at Gennesaret and anchored
there.[e] 54As soon as they got out of the
boat, people recognized Jesus. 55They ran
throughout that whole region and carried
the sick on mats to wherever they heard
he was. 56And wherever he went—into
villages, towns or countryside—they
placed the sick in the marketplaces. They
begged him to let them touch even the
edge of his cloak,[f] and all who touched
him were healed.

Chapter 7

Clean and Unclean

7:1–23pp — Mt 15:1–20

THE Pharisees and some of the teachers
of the law who had come from Jerusalem gathered around Jesus and 2saw
some of his disciples eating food with
hands that were "unclean,"[g] that is, unwashed. 3(The Pharisees and all the Jews
do not eat unless they give their hands a
ceremonial washing, holding to the tradition of the elders.[h] 4When they come
from the marketplace they do not eat unless they wash. And they observe many
other traditions, such as the washing of
cups, pitchers and kettles.[s])[i]
5So the Pharisees and teachers of the
law asked Jesus, "Why don't your disciples live according to the tradition of the
elders[j] instead of eating their food with
'unclean' hands?"
6He replied, "Isaiah was right when he
prophesied about you hypocrites; as it is
written:

" 'These people honor me with their lips,
but their hearts are far from me.
7They worship me in vain;
their teachings are but rules taught by men.'[t] [k]

8You have let go of the commands of God
and are holding on to the traditions of
men."[l]
9And he said to them: "You have a fine
way of setting aside the commands of

6:41 [v]S Mt 14:19
6:45 [w]ver 32 [x]S Mt 11:21
6:46 [y]S Lk 3:21
6:49 [z]Lk 24:37
6:50 [a]S Mt 14:27
6:51 [b]ver 32 [c]Mk 4:39
6:52 [d]Mk 8:17-21
6:53 [e]Jn 6:24,25
6:56 [f]S Mt 9:20
7:2 [g]Ac 10:14,28; 11:8; Ro 14:14
7:3 [h]ver 5,8,9,13; Lk 11:38
7:4 [i]Mt 23:25; Lk 11:39
7:5 [j]S ver 3; Gal 1:14; Col 2:8
7:7 [k]Isa 29:13
7:8 [l]S ver 3

[s]4 Some early manuscripts *pitchers, kettles and dining couches* [t]6,7 Isaiah 29:13

6:45–47 JESUS CHRIST, Miracles—See notes on 4:35–41; Mt 14:25–33. Until after the resurrection, even the disciples did not grasp the meaning of Jesus' miraculous powers.

6:45–46 PRAYER, Jesus' Example—See note on Jn 6:15.

6:56 MIRACLE, Faith—The needy may in faith take the initiative in miracles. Those who came to Him and touched Him were healed. They did not consider this magic. They knew Jesus' power released by their faith brought miracles.

7:1–23 JESUS CHRIST, Teaching—Religion is built on revelation and traditional interpretation of the revelation. As the major source of God's revelation, Jesus opposed human *tradition which* set aside God's intentions to serve human ends.

7:1–22 SIN, Violation—Sin is a matter of attitude before it becomes actions. Jesus had to teach this to His disciples as well as His opponents because the Jewish system had strayed so far and was ingrained so deep. The Pharisees had created a long list of regulations which tightly defined sin. Jesus recognized these as human traditions rather than Word of God. He said sin has more to do with what a person is than what a person does. Sin was not involved in whether a person carried out a proper ceremony or happened to touch a person or object that was defined as "unclean" or that had not participated in a ceremony of cleansing. Sin is a matter of the heart where motivation and attitudes are formed. Sin means thinking about something, planning to do it, and then doing it. Jesus' criticism strikes at the center of the human tendency to hide behind a screen of "proper" morality or religion to escape the direct demand of God and the personal relationship with God which characterize true religion. Sin is knowing God's will and refusing to follow it. See note on 2:15–16.

7:1–23 CHRISTIAN ETHICS, Moral Imperatives—Morality may become human tradition that interprets God's commands to suit human convenience. However, true interpretation must coincide with God's goals of holiness and justice. See note on Mt 15:1–20.

7:6–8 REVELATION, Commitment—True understanding and commitment to God's word brings outward and inward change. Jesus was dismayed and angered that the religious people pretended with outward gestures to believe God but showed no change of heart so that love and forgiveness did not live in them. They pretended to be converted with outward signs only. Pleasing other people by obeying human rites and rules does not please God.

7:9–13 STEWARDSHIP, Care of Family—Providing for

God in order to observe[u] your own traditions![m] 10For Moses said, 'Honor your father and your mother,'[v][n] and, 'Anyone who curses his father or mother must be put to death.'[w][o] 11But you say[p] that if a man says to his father or mother: 'Whatever help you might otherwise have received from me is Corban' (that is, a gift devoted to God), 12then you no longer let him do anything for his father or mother. 13Thus you nullify the word of God[q] by your tradition[r] that you have handed down. And you do many things like that."

14Again Jesus called the crowd to him and said, "Listen to me, everyone, and understand this. 15Nothing outside a man can make him 'unclean' by going into him. Rather, it is what comes out of a man that makes him 'unclean.'[x] "

17After he had left the crowd and entered the house, his disciples asked him[s] about this parable. 18"Are you so dull?" he asked. "Don't you see that nothing that enters a man from the outside can make him 'unclean'? 19For it doesn't go into his heart but into his stomach, and then out of his body." (In saying this, Jesus declared all foods[t] "clean.")[u]

20He went on: "What comes out of a man is what makes him 'unclean.' 21For from within, out of men's hearts, come evil thoughts, sexual immorality, theft, murder, adultery, 22greed,[v] malice, deceit, lewdness, envy, slander, arrogance and folly. 23All these evils come from inside and make a man 'unclean.' "

The Faith of a Syrophoenician Woman

7:24–30pp — Mt 15:21–28

24Jesus left that place and went to the vicinity of Tyre.[y][w] He entered a house and did not want anyone to know it; yet he could not keep his presence secret. 25In fact, as soon as she heard about him, a woman whose little daughter was possessed by an evil[z] spirit[x] came and fell at his feet. 26The woman was a Greek, born in Syrian Phoenicia. She begged Jesus to drive the demon out of her daughter.

27"First let the children eat all they want," he told her, "for it is not right to take the children's bread and toss it to their dogs."

28"Yes, Lord," she replied, "but even the dogs under the table eat the children's crumbs."

29Then he told her, "For such a reply, you may go; the demon has left your daughter."

30She went home and found her child lying on the bed, and the demon gone.

The Healing of a Deaf and Mute Man

7:31–37pp — Mt 15:29–31

31Then Jesus left the vicinity of Tyre[y] and went through Sidon, down to the Sea of Galilee[z] and into the region of the Decapolis.[a][a] 32There some people brought to him a man who was deaf and could hardly talk,[b] and they begged him to place his hand on[c] the man.

33After he took him aside, away from the crowd, Jesus put his fingers into the man's ears. Then he spit[d] and touched the man's tongue. 34He looked up to heaven[e] and with a deep sigh[f] said to him, *"Ephphatha!"* (which means, "Be opened!"). 35At this, the man's ears were opened, his tongue was loosened and he began to speak plainly.[g]

[u]*9* Some manuscripts *set up* [v]*10* Exodus 20:12; Deut. 5:16 [w]*10* Exodus 21:17; Lev. 20:9 [x]*15* Some early manuscripts *'unclean.'* [16]*If anyone has ears to hear, let him hear.* [y]*24* Many early manuscripts *Tyre and Sidon* [z]*25* Greek *unclean* [a]*31* That is, the Ten Cities

7:9 [m]S ver 3
7:10 [n]Ex 20:12; Dt 5:16 [o]Ex 21:17; Lev 20:9
7:11 [p]Mt 23:16,18
7:13 [q]S Heb 4:12 [r]S ver 3
7:17 [s]Mk 9:28
7:19 [t]Ro 14:1-12; Col 2:16; 1Ti 4:3-5 [u]S Ac 10:15
7:22 [v]Mt 20:15
7:24 [w]S Mt 11:21
7:25 [x]S Mt 4:24
7:31 [y]ver 24; S Mt 11:21 [z]S Mt 4:18 [a]Mt 4:25; Mk 5:20
7:32 [b]Mt 9:32; Lk 11:14 [c]S Mk 5:23
7:33 [d]Mk 8:23
7:34 [e]Mk 6:41; Jn 11:41 [f]Mk 8:12
7:35 [g]Isa 35:5,6

---

the physical needs of one's family is as important a part of Christian stewardship as giving to God's work. See note on 1 Ti 5:4,8.

7:9–13 FAMILY, Role Relationships—See note on Mt 15:3–6.

7:14–23 EVIL AND SUFFERING, Human Origin—Evil actions are rooted in an evil heart. Humans enjoy setting up rules, prejudices, taboos, and laws which define what is good and what is evil. The Pharisees had set up a long list of such traditional definitions for the Jews. Jesus reminded them that God, not humans, is the only source for defining what is evil. God defines evil in relation to humans by their desires and intentions. Evil motives make us evil, so that we succumb to Satanic temptation and to our own desires, thus committing evil actions (Jer 17:4–10; Mt 15:10–20).

7:24–30 JESUS CHRIST, Mission—Compare Mt 15:21–28. In healing the Gentile woman's daughter, Jesus went beyond the borders of Israel and ministered to non-Jews. The woman was rewarded for her persistence and determination and possibly for her wit. Jesus knew His mission was to concentrate on Israel, who had preparation from history and Scripture to receive Him. Jesus extended His mission beyond Israel to show God's concern for all people (Ge 12:1–3).

7:24–30 MIRACLE, Faith—See note on Mt 15:21–28.

7:25–30 PRAYER, Persistence—See note on Mt 15:21–28.

7:31–37 JESUS CHRIST, Miracles—See note on 1:25,34. Jesus' miracles created response among the people. Compare Mt 15:29–31.

7:32–37 MIRACLE, Methods—Miracles are performed in many ways. In this instance Jesus put fingers in the man's ears, used spittle, touched the man's tongue, and prayed. Other times people touched Jesus. See note on 6:56. He spoke a word (5:41) or used physical elements (8:6). The methods used are not the primary elements of miracles. One cannot learn secret actions, pat formulas, or magical deceptions to perform miracles. Miracles come from humans with faith when God provides the power. Divine miracles amaze people and send them to testify to God's goodness. The church must minister with various methods to various individual needs to strengthen faith.

7:34 PRAYER, Jesus' Example—Jesus looked to heaven and sighed a prayer as He healed a man. Healing through prayer is a possibility with God. Prayer does not have to be audible.

36Jesus commanded them not to tell
anyone.[h] But the more he did so, the
more they kept talking about it. 37People
were overwhelmed with amazement.
"He has done everything well," they
said. "He even makes the deaf hear and
the mute speak."

Chapter 8

Jesus Feeds the Four Thousand

8:1–9pp — Mt 15:32–39
8:1–9Ref — Mk 6:32–44
8:11–21pp — Mt 16:1–12

DURING those days another large
crowd gathered. Since they had
nothing to eat, Jesus called his disciples to
him and said, 2"I have compassion for
these people;[i] they have already been
with me three days and have nothing to
eat. 3If I send them home hungry, they
will collapse on the way, because some of
them have come a long distance."
4His disciples answered, "But where in
this remote place can anyone get enough
bread to feed them?"
5"How many loaves do you have?"
Jesus asked.
"Seven," they replied.
6He told the crowd to sit down on the
ground. When he had taken the seven
loaves and given thanks, he broke them
and gave them to his disciples to set before the people, and they did so. 7They
had a few small fish as well; he gave
thanks for them also and told the disciples to distribute them.[j] 8The people ate
and were satisfied. Afterward the disciples picked up seven basketfuls of broken
pieces that were left over.[k] 9About four
thousand men were present. And having
sent them away, 10he got into the boat
with his disciples and went to the region
of Dalmanutha.
11The Pharisees came and began to
question Jesus. To test him, they asked
him for a sign from heaven.[l] 12He sighed
deeply[m] and said, "Why does this generation ask for a miraculous sign? I tell you
the truth, no sign will be given to it."
13Then he left them, got back into the
boat and crossed to the other side.

The Yeast of the Pharisees and Herod

14The disciples had forgotten to bring
bread, except for one loaf they had with
them in the boat. 15"Be careful," Jesus
warned them. "Watch out for the yeast[n]
of the Pharisees[o] and that of Herod."[p]
16They discussed this with one another
and said, "It is because we have no
bread."
17Aware of their discussion, Jesus
asked them: "Why are you talking about
having no bread? Do you still not see or
understand? Are your hearts hardened?[q]
18Do you have eyes but fail to see, and
ears but fail to hear? And don't you remember? 19When I broke the five loaves
for the five thousand, how many basketfuls of pieces did you pick up?"
"Twelve,"[r] they replied.
20"And when I broke the seven loaves
for the four thousand, how many basketfuls of pieces did you pick up?"
They answered, "Seven."[s]
21He said to them, "Do you still not
understand?"[t]

The Healing of a Blind Man at Bethsaida

22They came to Bethsaida,[u] and some
people brought a blind man[v] and begged
Jesus to touch him. 23He took the blind
man by the hand and led him outside the
village. When he had spit[w] on the man's
eyes and put his hands on[x] him, Jesus
asked, "Do you see anything?"
24He looked up and said, "I see people;
they look like trees walking around."
25Once more Jesus put his hands on
the man's eyes. Then his eyes were
opened, his sight was restored, and he
saw everything clearly. 26Jesus sent him
home, saying, "Don't go into the village.[b]"

Peter's Confession of Christ

8:27–29pp — Mt 16:13–16; Lk 9:18–20

27Jesus and his disciples went on to the
villages around Caesarea Philippi. On the
way he asked them, "Who do people say I
am?"

[b]*26* Some manuscripts *Don't go and tell anyone in the village*

7:36 [h]S Mt 8:4
8:2 [i]S Mt 9:36
8:7 [j]Mt 14:19
8:8 [k]ver 20
8:11 [l]S Mt 12:38
8:12 [m]Mk 7:34
8:15 [n]1Co 5:6-8 [o]Lk 12:1 [p]S Mt 14:1; Mk 12:13
8:17 [q]Isa 6:9,10; Mk 6:52
8:19 [r]Mt 14:20; Mk 6:41-44; Lk 9:17; Jn 6:13
8:20 [s]ver 6-9; Mt 15:37
8:21 [t]Mk 6:52
8:22 [u]S Mt 11:21 [v]Mk 10:46; Jn 9:1
8:23 [w]Mk 7:33 [x]S Mk 5:23

8:1–9 JESUS CHRIST, Miracles—See notes on Mt 14:14; 16:1–4. No miracle can compel faith from unbelieving hearts.
8:1–10 MIRACLE, Christ—See note on Mt 15:29–39.
8:6–7 PRAYER, Thanksgiving—See note on Mt 14:19. He gave separate thanks for the loaves and the fish.
8:11–13 MIRACLE, Vocabulary—See note on Mt 16:1–4.
8:22–26 JESUS CHRIST, Miracles—This mighty work is found only in Mark. The gradual accomplishment of this miracle paralleled the gradual growth of the disciples' understanding.
8:22–26 MIRACLE, Christ—Miraculous events may become symbolic parables. Jesus healed the blind man in a unique two-step process. As in 7:32–37 Jesus used the power of touch in healing. Unique here is the apparent partial cure after the first "treatment." The larger context depicts the blindness of the disciples. They could not understand the feeding miracle (v 21). Nor could they let the Christ (v 29) suffer and die (vv 31–32). Disciples could be agents of Satan (v 33). This healing serves as a parable to offer them their sight. They must not only make the proper confession with their lips. Then they saw only dimly. They had to understand the Suffering Servant's mission and be ready to follow to the cross (v 34). Then they could truly see. Many persons with normal eyesight are spiritually blind. Many who think they have perfect spiritual vision are agents of Satan.

28They replied, "Some say John the
Baptist;[y] others say Elijah;[z] and still others, one of the prophets."
29"But what about you?" he asked.
"Who do you say I am?"
Peter answered, "You are the
Christ.[c] "[a]
30Jesus warned them not to tell anyone
about him.[b]

Jesus Predicts His Death

8:31 — 9:1pp — Mt 16:21–28; Lk 9:22–27

31He then began to teach them that the
Son of Man[c] must suffer many things[d]
and be rejected by the elders, chief
priests and teachers of the law,[e] and that
he must be killed[f] and after three days[g]
rise again.[h] 32He spoke plainly[i] about
this, and Peter took him aside and began
to rebuke him.
33But when Jesus turned and looked at
his disciples, he rebuked Peter. "Get behind me, Satan!"[j] he said. "You do not
have in mind the things of God, but the
things of men."
34Then he called the crowd to him
along with his disciples and said: "If anyone would come after me, he must deny
himself and take up his cross and follow
me.[k] 35For whoever wants to save his
life[d] will lose it, but whoever loses his
life for me and for the gospel will save
it.[l] 36What good is it for a man to gain
the whole world, yet forfeit his soul? 37Or
what can a man give in exchange for his
soul? 38If anyone is ashamed of me and
my words in this adulterous and sinful
generation, the Son of Man[m] will be
ashamed of him[n] when he comes[o] in his
Father's glory with the holy angels."

Chapter 9

AND he said to them, "I tell you the
truth, some who are standing here
will not taste death before they see the
kingdom of God come[p] with power."[q]

The Transfiguration

9:2–8pp — Lk 9:28–36
9:2–13pp — Mt 17:1–13

2After six days Jesus took Peter, James
and John[r] with him and led them up a
high mountain, where they were all
alone. There he was transfigured before

8:28 [y]S Mt 3:1 [z]Mal 4:5
8:29 [a]Jn 6:69; 11:27
8:30 [b]S Mt 8:4; 16:20; 17:9; Mk 9:9; Lk 9:21
8:31 [c]S Mt 8:20 [d]S Mt 16:21 [e]Mt 27:1,2 [f]Ac 2:23; 3:13 [g]S Mt 16:21 [h]S Mt 16:21
8:32 [i]Jn 18:20
8:33 [j]S Mt 4:10
8:34 [k]Mt 10:38; Lk 14:27
8:35 [l]S Jn 12:25
8:38 [m]S Mt 8:20 [n]Mt 10:33; Lk 12:9 [o]S 1Th 2:19
9:1 [p]Mk 13:30; Lk 22:18 [q]Mt 24:30; 25:31
9:2 [r]S Mt 4:21

[c]*29* Or *Messiah.* "The Christ" (Greek) and "the Messiah" (Hebrew) both mean "the Anointed One."
[d]*35* The Greek word means either *life* or *soul;* also in verse 36.

8:29 JESUS CHRIST, Christ—See note on Mt 16:16.
8:29–30 REVELATION, Jesus Christ—See note on Mt 16:15–17.
8:30 JESUS CHRIST, Secret—See note on 1:25,34.
8:31–32 JESUS CHRIST, Death—See note on Mt 16:21–23.
8:31–38 JESUS CHRIST, Temptation—See note on Mt 16:21–23.
8:31 JESUS CHRIST, Son of Man—Jesus used Son of man often to mean "I." See note on Mt 8:20.
8:31–38 EVIL AND SUFFERING, Endurance—See note on Mt 16:21–27.
8:34–38 CHRISTIAN ETHICS, Character—The Christian life is to be keynoted as a life of surrender. To deny oneself is not a call to a colorless life. Rather, it is a call to deny the baser nature and pursue the higher levels of ethical standards to which Jesus points. This paradox of finding life by losing it is open to the test of experience. Mature Christians attest to its validity.
8:36–37 HUMANITY, Spiritual Nature—Some interpreters see little more to the New Testament concept of soul than was present in the Old Testament understanding, where the *nephesh* was actually the totality of life. It appears that Jesus was heightening this meaning with a fuller understanding that people are made up of both body and soul, with the soul living on after the body has died. The physical nature of a person is localized in physical life. The spiritual nature is established within the soul. Life in its fullness cannot ultimately separate the two. Sin brings spiritual death. Physical death separates body and soul. In the resurrection our full nature as God intended it to be is discovered (Mt 16:26; Lk 9:25).
8:38—9:1 JESUS CHRIST, Son of Man—See note on Mt 13:37–43; 16:27–28.
8:38 SIN, Unbelief—Sin at its deepest level is unbelief in Jesus. Total trust and commitment to Jesus leads us to seek to live the perfect life Jesus led. Our society makes such commitment difficult, for ours is a sinful generation committed to many things and causes opposed to God and godliness. Society makes us feel shame and embarrassment because of our Christian commitment. Christ calls us to witness to that commitment everywhere. Failure to witness grows out of shame and fear when faced by society. Failure to witness reflects unbelief and lack of commitment. That is sin.
8:38 REVELATION, Angels—Angels will accompany Christ at the second coming.
8:38 SALVATION, Definition—God's salvation is glorification. It has to do with the final blessed and abiding state of the redeemed. Future blessedness for those saved is related to their present faithfulness to Jesus Christ.
8:38 LAST THINGS, Encourages Faithfulness—The association of the holy angels with Jesus at His coming suggests the final judgment. See 2 Th 1:7. To be ashamed of Jesus and His words now will have serious consequences then. At the time of judgment, the Son of man will be ashamed of such a one. The very thought of it compels fidelity to Him and glad confession of Him.
9:1 LAST THINGS, Coming Kingdom—Jesus announced the kingdom of God was near as He opened His public ministry in Galilee (1:14–15). Through the casting out of demons, Jesus proclaimed the kingdom of God to have come upon His generation (Mt 12:28). Just prior to His transfiguration, Jesus also promised a future coming of the kingdom. He taught His disciples and us to pray for the kingdom to come (Mt 6:10). The kingdom or rule of God was both active in the ministry of Jesus and promised by Him as a future event to come. The present rule of God in individual lives will at that future event issue in a kingdom as a realm over which God rules through Christ. See Rev 11:15–17; 12:10; 20:4–6.
9:1 THE CHURCH, God's Kingdom—In Jesus, the kingdom of God had already come, although those around Him failed to understand its significance. Yet, the kingdom awaited its fuller manifestation which occurred when Jesus conquered death and sin on the cross. The resurrection and Pentecost (Ac 2) confirmed for believers that Jesus' transfiguration and death revealed the presence of God's kingdom. We still wait for the final coming of the kingdom of God which will take place when Jesus returns triumphantly to the earth.
9:2–13 JESUS CHRIST, Son of God—See notes on 1:1; Mt 17:1–13.

them. 3His clothes became dazzling
white,[s] whiter than anyone in the world
could bleach them. 4And there appeared
before them Elijah and Moses, who were
talking with Jesus.
5Peter said to Jesus, "Rabbi,[t] it is good
for us to be here. Let us put up three
shelters—one for you, one for Moses and
one for Elijah." 6(He did not know what
to say, they were so frightened.)
7Then a cloud appeared and enveloped
them, and a voice came from the cloud:[u]
"This is my Son, whom I love. Listen to
him!"[v]
8Suddenly, when they looked around,
they no longer saw anyone with them except Jesus.
9As they were coming down the mountain, Jesus gave them orders not to tell
anyone[w] what they had seen until the
Son of Man[x] had risen from the dead.
10They kept the matter to themselves,
discussing what "rising from the dead"
meant.
11And they asked him, "Why do the
teachers of the law say that Elijah must
come first?"
12Jesus replied, "To be sure, Elijah
does come first, and restores all things.
Why then is it written that the Son of
Man[y] must suffer much[z] and be rejected?[a] 13But I tell you, Elijah has come,[b]
and they have done to him everything
they wished, just as it is written about
him."

The Healing of a Boy With an Evil Spirit

9:14–28; 30–32pp — Mt 17:14–19; 22,23; Lk 9:37–45

14When they came to the other disciples, they saw a large crowd around them
and the teachers of the law arguing with
them. 15As soon as all the people saw
Jesus, they were overwhelmed with wonder and ran to greet him.
16"What are you arguing with them
about?" he asked.
17A man in the crowd answered,
"Teacher, I brought you my son, who is
possessed by a spirit that has robbed him
of speech. 18Whenever it seizes him, it
throws him to the ground. He foams at
the mouth, gnashes his teeth and becomes rigid. I asked your disciples to
drive out the spirit, but they could not."
19"O unbelieving generation," Jesus
replied, "how long shall I stay with you?
How long shall I put up with you? Bring
the boy to me."
20So they brought him. When the spirit
saw Jesus, it immediately threw the boy
into a convulsion. He fell to the ground
and rolled around, foaming at the
mouth.[c]
21Jesus asked the boy's father, "How
long has he been like this?"
"From childhood," he answered. 22"It
has often thrown him into fire or water to
kill him. But if you can do anything, take
pity on us and help us."
23" 'If you can'?" said Jesus. "Everything is possible for him who believes."[d]
24Immediately the boy's father exclaimed, "I do believe; help me overcome my unbelief!"
25When Jesus saw that a crowd was
running to the scene,[e] he rebuked the
evil[e] spirit. "You deaf and mute spirit,"
he said, "I command you, come out of
him and never enter him again."
26The spirit shrieked, convulsed him
violently and came out. The boy looked
so much like a corpse that many said,
"He's dead." 27But Jesus took him by the
hand and lifted him to his feet, and he
stood up.
28After Jesus had gone indoors, his dis-

9:3 [s]S Mt 28:3
9:5 [t]S Mt 23:7
9:7 [u]Ex 24:16 [v]S Mt 3:17
9:9 [w]S Mk 8:30 [x]S Mt 8:20
9:12 [y]S Mt 8:20 [z]S Mt 16:21 [a]Lk 23:11
9:13 [b]S Mt 11:14
9:20 [c]Mk 1:26
9:23 [d]S Mt 21:21; Mk 11:23; Jn 11:40
9:25 [e]ver 15

[e]25 Greek *unclean*

9:7 GOD, Love—Jesus talked with Elijah and Moses, the two great leaders of the traditions of prophecy and the Law, concerning the death He was to suffer as Savior of the world (Lk 9:31). In the context of the discussion of Jesus' climactic death, God spoke the word of love and approval from heaven. While drawing nearer to the cross, Jesus received the reassurance of God's leadership and God's love to see Him through that ordeal. What Jesus was to do on the cross is intimately bound up with what God had been doing in past ages through the two great religious traditions, the priestly and the prophetic. What Jesus was about to do on the cross was not only the outcome of these two traditions, but was also the result of God's own love. God expressed His love for Jesus who in turn poured out His life as an expression of God's love for lost sinners. See note on 1:11.

9:9–10 JESUS CHRIST, Resurrection—See note on Mt 17:9–13.

9:9–13 HOLY SCRIPTURE, Authoritative—The experts in Scripture were so blind to its true meaning they did not recognize the One to whom all Scripture points. They saw neither John the Baptist as the expected Elijah (Mal 4:5) nor suffering as the predicted life of the Messiah (Isa 53). Only after Christ's death would the disciples be able to understand and proclaim these truths. At times dedicated disciples can understand Scripture only in light of historical events.

9:12–13 JESUS CHRIST, Suffering—The mission Jesus accepted led to physical and emotional suffering. This was the biggest stumbling block to acceptance as Messiah, so it was the point He emphasized repeatedly, interpreting His mission in light of Isa 53.

9:14–29 MIRACLE, Faith—Prayer, not personal power, is essential for miracles. The disciples had the power once to cast out demons. See note on 6:13. They could not take such power for granted. They must pray to God in faith. See Mt 17:14–21.

9:19–29 PRAYER, Hindrances—Human faith is never perfect. The prayer for overcoming unbelief is appropriate for all people. Unbelief is the great hindrance to prayer. Belief makes all things possible (10:27; Job 42:2; Jer 32:27; Mt 19:26; Ro 4:21). See note on Ge 18:14.

9:28–29 JESUS CHRIST, Authority—Jesus attributed His authority to power with God in prayer and invited disciples to share that power. Demonic power can never overcome Jesus' authority. It may overcome Christians' weak faith and lack of

ciples asked him privately,[f] "Why
couldn't we drive it out?"
29He replied, "This kind can come out
only by prayer.[t]"
30They left that place and passed
through Galilee. Jesus did not want anyone to know where they were, 31because
he was teaching his disciples. He said to
them, "The Son of Man[g] is going to be
betrayed into the hands of men. They will
kill him,[h] and after three days[i] he will
rise."[j] 32But they did not understand
what he meant[k] and were afraid to ask
him about it.

Who Is the Greatest?

9:33–37pp — Mt 18:1–5; Lk 9:46–48

33They came to Capernaum.[l] When
he was in the house,[m] he asked them,
"What were you arguing about on the
road?" 34But they kept quiet because on
the way they had argued about who was
the greatest.[n]
35Sitting down, Jesus called the Twelve
and said, "If anyone wants to be first, he
must be the very last, and the servant of
all."[o]
36He took a little child and had him
stand among them. Taking him in his
arms,[p] he said to them, 37"Whoever welcomes one of these little children in my
name welcomes me; and whoever welcomes me does not welcome me but the
one who sent me."[q]

Whoever Is Not Against Us Is for Us

9:38–40pp — Lk 9:49,50

38"Teacher," said John, "we saw a
man driving out demons in your name
and we told him to stop, because he was
not one of us."[r]
39"Do not stop him," Jesus said. "No
one who does a miracle in my name can
in the next moment say anything bad
about me, 40for whoever is not against us
is for us.[s] 41I tell you the truth, anyone
who gives you a cup of water in my name
because you belong to Christ will certainly not lose his reward.[t]

Causing to Sin

42"And if anyone causes one of these
little ones who believe in me to sin,[u] it
would be better for him to be thrown into
the sea with a large millstone tied around
his neck.[v] 43If your hand causes you to
sin,[w] cut it off. It is better for you to enter
life maimed than with two hands to go
into hell,[x] where the fire never goes
out.[g][y] 45And if your foot causes you to
sin,[z] cut it off. It is better for you to enter
life crippled than to have two feet and be
thrown into hell.[h][a] 47And if your eye
causes you to sin,[b] pluck it out. It is better for you to enter the kingdom of God
with one eye than to have two eyes and
be thrown into hell,[c] 48where

" 'their worm does not die,
and the fire is not quenched.'[i][d]

49Everyone will be salted[e] with fire.
50"Salt is good, but if it loses its saltiness, how can you make it salty again?[f]
Have salt in yourselves,[g] and be at peace
with each other."[h]

9:28 [f]Mk 7:17
9:31 [g]S Mt 8:20 [h]ver 12; Ac 2:23; 3:13 [i]S Mt 16:21 [j]S Mt 16:21
9:32 [k]Lk 2:50; 9:45; 18:34; Jn 12:16
9:33 [l]S Mt 4:13 [m]Mk 1:29
9:34 [n]Lk 22:24
9:35 [o]Mt 18:4; Mk 10:43; Lk 22:26
9:36 [p]Mk 10:16
9:37 [q]S Mt 10:40
9:38 [r]Nu 11:27-29
9:40 [s]Mt 12:30; Lk 11:23
9:41 [t]S Mt 10:42
9:42 [u]S Mt 5:29 [v]Mt 18:6; Lk 17:2
9:43 [w]S Mt 5:29 [x]Mt 5:30; 18:8 [y]S Mt 25:41
9:45 [z]S Mt 5:29 [a]Mt 18:8
9:47 [b]S Mt 5:29 [c]Mt 5:29; 18:9
9:48 [d]Isa 66:24; S Mt 25:41
9:49 [e]Lev 2:13
9:50 [f]Mt 5:13; Lk 14:34,35 [g]Col 4:6 [h]Ro 12:18; 2Co 13:11; 1Th 5:13

[t]29 Some manuscripts *prayer and fasting* [g]43 Some manuscripts *out, 44where / " 'their worm does not die, / and the fire is not quenched.'* [h]45 Some manuscripts *hell, 46where / " 'their worm does not die, / and the fire is not quenched.'* [i]48 Isaiah 66:24

prayer. Prayer is the path to power.

9:31 JESUS CHRIST, Death—At least as early as His baptism, Jesus was aware of His messianic role of suffering (2:20; Mt 4:1–10). Just after the transfiguration, He spoke specifically of His betrayal, death, and resurrection. See note on Mt 16:21–23.

9:31–32 REVELATION, Word—Jesus revealed His betrayal, death, and resurrection to His disciples, but they still had no idea of His power to rise and live again. Even those closest to Jesus had difficulty understanding His sacrifice and the sacrifice He expects of His disciples.

9:33–37 HUMANITY, Relationships—Pride disrupts relationships between people. It also hinders the relationship between people and God. When pride is cast aside for an attitude of childlike humility, these relationships can stand. In Christ's kingdom the attitude of the faithful, obedient servant replaces that of the egotistical, self-seeking official. Christ teaches only one office—God's slave. See notes on Mt 18:1–5; Lk 9:46–48.

9:33–37 THE CHURCH, Servants—Greatness in the kingdom is judged by how we receive the weak and powerless. Anyone will accept those who can reward us, but the great ones in the kingdom receive those who cannot give a reward. We live in God's kingdom as we show God's love to those who do not know love. When we seek to build a kingdom of power for ourselves, we have forsaken God's way. See notes on Mt 20:20–28; 23:11.

9:39–41 ELECTION, Righteousness—Identifying the elect of God may be difficult by human standards. Caution should be taken in saying who is or is not elect. One sign of election is ministry of mercy to the elect in the name of Christ. Condemnation is not the task of the elect. The elect should be receptive of and encouraging to any person open to the gospel.

9:41 DISCIPLESHIP, Rewarded—Every act of Christian service will be rewarded by spiritual growth that will qualify the disciple for "a rich welcome" into God's eternal kingdom. See note on 2 Pe 1:10–11.

9:42–50 SIN, Serious—See note on Mt 18:6–9.

9:43–48 LAST THINGS, Hell—Nothing is valuable enough to cause us to miss the future consummation of God's kingdom. The only alternative is hell (Greek *geennan*). See note on Mt 5:22. Surely, the actualization of hell is even worse than the visualization of it.

9:50 CHRISTIAN ETHICS, Character—Salt is marked by its ability to flavor with only a little of its presence. Adding zest to an otherwise dull meal, it was a valuable commodity in the ancient world. It even was used as money. Christians should give the world the gospel flavor.

Chapter 10

Divorce

10:1–12pp — Mt 19:1–9

JESUS then left that place and went into
the region of Judea and across the Jordan.[i] Again crowds of people came to
him, and as was his custom, he taught
them.[j]
2Some Pharisees[k] came and tested him
by asking, "Is it lawful for a man to divorce his wife?"
3"What did Moses command you?" he
replied.
4They said, "Moses permitted a man to
write a certificate of divorce and send her
away."[l]
5"It was because your hearts were
hard[m] that Moses wrote you this law,"
Jesus replied. 6"But at the beginning of
creation God 'made them male and female.'[j][n] 7'For this reason a man will
leave his father and mother and be united
to his wife,[k] 8and the two will become
one flesh.'[l][o] So they are no longer two,
but one. 9Therefore what God has joined
together, let man not separate."
10When they were in the house again,
the disciples asked Jesus about this. 11He
answered, "Anyone who divorces his
wife and marries another woman commits adultery against her.[p] 12And if she
divorces her husband and marries another man, she commits adultery."[q]

The Little Children and Jesus

10:13–16pp — Mt 19:13–15; Lk 18:15–17

13People were bringing little children
to Jesus to have him touch them, but the
disciples rebuked them. 14When Jesus
saw this, he was indignant. He said to
them, "Let the little children come to
me, and do not hinder them, for the kingdom of God belongs to such as these.[r] 15I
tell you the truth, anyone who will not
receive the kingdom of God like a little
child will never enter it."[s] 16And he took
the children in his arms,[t] put his hands
on them and blessed them.

The Rich Young Man

10:17–31pp — Mt 19:16–30; Lk 18:18–30

17As Jesus started on his way, a man
ran up to him and fell on his knees[u] before him. "Good teacher," he asked,
"what must I do to inherit eternal life?"[v]
18"Why do you call me good?" Jesus
answered. "No one is good—except God
alone. 19You know the commandments:
'Do not murder, do not commit adultery,
do not steal, do not give false testimony,
do not defraud, honor your father and
mother.'[m][w]
20"Teacher," he declared, "all these I
have kept since I was a boy."
21Jesus looked at him and loved him.
"One thing you lack," he said. "Go, sell
everything you have and give to the
poor,[x] and you will have treasure in
heaven.[y] Then come, follow me."[z]
22At this the man's face fell. He went
away sad, because he had great wealth.
23Jesus looked around and said to his
disciples, "How hard it is for the rich[a] to
enter the kingdom of God!"

10:1 [i]Mk 1:5; Jn 10:40; 11:7 [j]S Mt 4:23; Mk 2:13; 4:2; 6:6, 34
10:2 [k]Mk 2:16
10:4 [l]Dt 24:1-4; Mt 5:31
10:5 [m]Ps 95:8; Heb 3:15
10:6 [n]Ge 1:27; 5:2
10:8 [o]Ge 2:24; 1Co 6:16
10:11 [p]S Lk 16:18
10:12 [q]Ro 7:3; 1Co 7:10,11
10:14 [r]S Mt 25:34
10:15 [s]Mt 18:3
10:16 [t]Mk 9:36
10:17 [u]Mk 1:40 [v]Lk 10:25; S Ac 20:32
10:19 [w]Ex 20:12-16; Dt 5:16-20
10:21 [x]S Ac 2:45 [y]Mt 6:20; Lk 12:33 [z]S Mt 4:19
10:23 [a]Ps 52:7; 62:10; Mk 4:19; 1Ti 6:9,10,17

[j]6 Gen. 1:27 [k]7 Some early manuscripts do not have *and be united to his wife.* [l]8 Gen. 2:24 [m]19 Exodus 20:12-16; Deut. 5:16-20

10:1–52 JESUS CHRIST, Mission—See note on Mt 10:1–42.
10:1 EDUCATION, Jesus—Teaching was Jesus' customary way of ministering to the crowds that followed Him. See note on 2:13.
10:2–12 FAMILY, Divorce—See note on Mt 19:3–9.
10:13–16 JESUS CHRIST, Mission—Childlike trust and acceptance are the requirements for membership in Christ's kingdom. See note on Mt 19:13–14.
10:13–16 PRAYER, Blessing—See note on Mt 19:13–15.
10:14–15 THE CHURCH, God's Kingdom—See note on Mt 18:1–4.
10:16 SALVATION, Blessing—See note on Mt 19:13–15.
10:17–18 GOD, Goodness—See note on Mt 19:17.
10:17–27 SALVATION, Definition—God's salvation is eternal life, the kind of life which God gives to those who come to Him through the one Mediator between God and persons—Jesus Christ (1 Ti 2:5). Rich persons can be saved. Jesus loves them and wants them to love God supremely and to love their neighbors as themselves.
10:17–27 CHRISTIAN ETHICS, Moral Imperatives—Some interpreters key in on Jesus' instruction to the man to sell all he had as the basis for a "works" salvation, but Jesus showed the need for balance in our understanding of salvation. Salvation comes only through God's graciousness extended toward us, but that salvation issues forth in recognizable acts and attitudes which reflect the ethical dimensions of that salvation. For this man a test of his faith was to do an act of mercy because Christ Himself commanded it and because the doing of it would substantiate any faith claim he might make. Obedience to Christ's teaching is one side of faith in His saving work. See Guide to Applying the Word, pp. 1811–1812.
10:21–23 HUMANITY, Relationships—When people value possessions above God, they have severed their relationships both with God and people. Any degree of spiritual perception indicates such a life is visibly empty and unfulfilling. See Mt 19:21–23; Lk 18:22–25.
10:21 REVELATION, Commitment—Jesus realized the young man's idolatry of his possessions and revealed to him the obstacle God would have him overcome. Christ loved the man but confronted him with God's will for single devotion to God. Revelation contains both gift and demand. The two cannot be separated.
10:21 DISCIPLESHIP, Poor—Disciples who commit their wealth to meet the needs of poor people will have riches in heaven. Such commitment removes wealth as an obstacle to receiving God's eternal blessings. It shows we value our relationship to God above our possessions. Those "disciples" who make worldly wealth their treasure need not expect heavenly reward. They are not following Christ. See Lk 12:34; note on Mt 19:21.
10:23–27 THE CHURCH, God's Kingdom—See note on Mt 19:24–26. Only by the power and grace of God can anyone enter the kingdom of God.

24The disciples were amazed at his
words. But Jesus said again, "Children,
how hard it is[n] to enter the kingdom of
God![b] 25It is easier for a camel to go
through the eye of a needle than for a
rich man to enter the kingdom of God."[c]
26The disciples were even more
amazed, and said to each other, "Who
then can be saved?"
27Jesus looked at them and said, "With
man this is impossible, but not with God;
all things are possible with God."[d]
28Peter said to him, "We have left everything to follow you!"[e]
29"I tell you the truth," Jesus replied,
"no one who has left home or brothers or
sisters or mother or father or children or
fields for me and the gospel 30will fail to
receive a hundred times as much[f] in this
present age (homes, brothers, sisters,
mothers, children and fields—and with
them, persecutions) and in the age to
come,[g] eternal life.[h] 31But many who are
first will be last, and the last first."[i]

Jesus Again Predicts His Death

10:32–34pp — Mt 20:17–19; Lk 18:31–33

32They were on their way up to Jerusalem, with Jesus leading the way, and the
disciples were astonished, while those
who followed were afraid. Again he took
the Twelve[j] aside and told them what
was going to happen to him. 33"We are
going up to Jerusalem,"[k] he said, "and
the Son of Man[l] will be betrayed to the
chief priests and teachers of the law.[m]
They will condemn him to death and will
hand him over to the Gentiles, 34who will
mock him and spit on him, flog him[n] and
kill him.[o] Three days later[p] he will
rise."[q]

The Request of James and John

10:35–45pp — Mt 20:20–28

35Then James and John, the sons of
Zebedee, came to him. "Teacher," they
said, "we want you to do for us whatever
we ask."
36"What do you want me to do for
you?" he asked.
37They replied, "Let one of us sit at
your right and the other at your left in
your glory."[r]
38"You don't know what you are asking,"[s] Jesus said. "Can you drink the
cup[t] I drink or be baptized with the baptism I am baptized with?"[u]
39"We can," they answered.
Jesus said to them, "You will drink the
cup I drink and be baptized with the baptism I am baptized with,[v] 40but to sit at
my right or left is not for me to grant.
These places belong to those for whom
they have been prepared."

10:24 [b]Mt 7:13,14; Jn 3:5
10:25 [c]Lk 12:16-20; 16:19-31
10:27 [d]S Mt 19:26
10:28 [e]S Mt 4:19
10:30 [f]Mt 6:33 [g]S Mt 12:32 [h]S Mt 25:46
10:31 [i]S Mt 19:30
10:32 [j]Mk 3:16-19
10:33 [k]S Lk 9:51 [l]S Mt 8:20 [m]Mt 27:1,2
10:34 [n]S Mt 16:21 [o]Ac 2:23; 3:13 [p]S Mt 16:21 [q]S Mt 16:21
10:37 [r]Mt 19:28
10:38 [s]Job 38:2 [t]S Mt 20:22 [u]Lk 12:50
10:39 [v]Ac 12:2; Rev 1:9

[n]24 Some manuscripts *is for those who trust in riches*

10:27 PRAYER, Faith—See note on 9:19–29.

10:29–31 GOD, Goodness—Jesus did not cheapen the appeal or the demand of the gospel by promising a merit system of rewards for those who earn them. He was quick to promise that those who are faithful to Him and to God in this world will be abundantly blessed in the life that is to come. God's goodness shows itself to us in many ways in the present life, and it will show itself in many more ways in rich blessings in eternity. Such is the loving nature of a good God who is faithful to those who love Him and serve Him.

10:29–31 LAST THINGS, Age to Come—Jesus indicated the existence of two ages. One is the present age of history with its opportunities and rewards. The age to come lies beyond the historical order but can be experienced or entered within the present age. The life of the age to come is eternal life. A believer in Jesus possesses eternal life already (Jn 5:24). In that sense the age to come has broken in upon the present age. Even so, the future will bring full and final enjoyment of eternal life in the coming age. God's evaluation of persons may prove quite different from our earthly expectations. See notes on Mt 12:32; Jn 12:25.

10:29–31 EVANGELISM, Rewards—Seeking God's eternal rewards is not wrong. It is a legitimate motive to evangelize. Serving Christ faithfully often involves sacrifices and self-denial. Our Lord promises that the abundance of the reward will outshine any sacrifice we make to win others to Christ (Ro 8:18). If we do not serve Jesus selflessly, we may be the "first" that shall be "last" as our Lord warned us.

10:32–34 JESUS CHRIST, Death—See note on Mt 16:21–23. In this third prediction the details of His being mocked and mistreated are added.

10:35–45 *THE CHURCH*, Servants—Suffering, humiliation, and humility mark the church. We are no better than Christ, our Master. As He served other people without seeking fame, power, or position, so must we. We cannot demand heavenly rewards. We can only offer earthly service. See notes on 9:33–37; Mt 20:20–28; 23:11.

10:38–39 JESUS CHRIST, Mission—Jesus' reference to baptism, in this passage, refers to His death. The cup (the Lord's Supper) and baptism (the ritual of confession and the symbol of death and resurrection) are the ordinances He gave and which He sealed by His death. Baptism, in this instance, means a baptism of suffering. He knew His mission led to suffering. His disciples could expect the same. Jesus' followers often must suffer for His sake. Tradition says that all of Jesus' first apostles except John died a martyr's death. An old saying goes, "The blood of the martyrs is the seed of the church." Contemporary Christians should not seek martyrdom, but neither should they shun it. Courageous martyrs in all ages have shared Jesus' baptism of blood and live on in our memories as witnesses (Greek *martures*, Ac 1:8) to our Lord. See note on Mt 20:20–23.

10:38–40 ORDINANCES, Baptism as Death—To baptize (Greek *baptizō*) can mean to drown or overwhelm as in a flood. It is clear that Jesus used this word as a metaphor for the suffering and death which would soon "overwhelm" Him on the cross. The "cup" is also the symbol of bitter dregs of suffering. In mentioning baptism and the cup, Jesus connected both of the later Christian ordinances with His death.

10:39–40 ELECTION, God's Servants—Seats or service has been a continuing issue of debate and discussion in the Christian community. The issue has developed into conflict and controversy since the beginning of the church. Jesus cleared up the issue for the elect, yet the controversy persists. Suffering and service with Jesus are the proper positions for those who are the elect of God. See note on Mt 20:23.

10:41–45 DISCIPLESHIP, Nature—Office and power do not make a person great. Service does. To be Christ's disciple is to serve God and other people. The Lord Himself came not to be served but to serve, even unto death on a cross. Disciples do

41When the ten heard about this, they
became indignant with James and John.
42Jesus called them together and said,
"You know that those who are regarded
as rulers of the Gentiles lord it over them,
and their high officials exercise authority
over them. 43Not so with you. Instead,
whoever wants to become great among
you must be your servant,[w] 44and whoever wants to be first must be slave of all.
45For even the Son of Man did not come
to be served, but to serve,[x] and to give
his life as a ransom for many."[y]

Blind Bartimaeus Receives His Sight

10:46–52pp — Mt 20:29–34; Lk 18:35–43

46Then they came to Jericho. As Jesus
and his disciples, together with a large
crowd, were leaving the city, a blind
man, Bartimaeus (that is, the Son of
Timaeus), was sitting by the roadside
begging. 47When he heard that it was
Jesus of Nazareth,[z] he began to shout,
"Jesus, Son of David,[a] have mercy on
me!"
48Many rebuked him and told him
to be quiet, but he shouted all the
more, "Son of David, have mercy on
me!"
49Jesus stopped and said, "Call him."
So they called to the blind
man, "Cheer up! On your feet! He's
calling you." 50Throwing his cloak
aside, he jumped to his feet and came to
Jesus.
51"What do you want me to do for
you?" Jesus asked him.
The blind man said, "Rabbi,[b] I want to
see."
52"Go," said Jesus, "your faith has
healed you."[c] Immediately he received
his sight and followed[d] Jesus along the
road.

10:43 [w]S Mk 9:35
10:45 [x]S Mt 20:28 [y]S Mt 20:28
10:47 [z]S Mk 1:24 [a]S Mt 9:27
10:51 [b]S Mt 23:7
10:52 [c]S Mt 9:22 [d]S Mt 4:19
11:1 [e]S Mt 21:17 [f]S Mt 21:1
11:2 [g]Nu 19:2; Dt 21:3; 1Sa 6:7
11:4 [h]Mk 14:16
11:9 [i]Ps 118:25,26; Mt 23:39
11:10 [j]Lk 2:14
11:11 [k]Mt 21:12, 17

Chapter 11

The Triumphal Entry

11:1–10pp — Mt 21:1–9; Lk 19:29–38
11:7–10pp — Jn 12:12–15

As they approached Jerusalem and came
to Bethphage and Bethany[e] at the
Mount of Olives,[f] Jesus sent two of his
disciples, 2saying to them, "Go to the village ahead of you, and just as you enter it,
you will find a colt tied there, which no
one has ever ridden.[g] Untie it and bring
it here. 3If anyone asks you, 'Why are you
doing this?' tell him, 'The Lord needs it
and will send it back here shortly.' "
4They went and found a colt outside in
the street, tied at a doorway.[h] As they
untied it, 5some people standing there
asked, "What are you doing, untying that
colt?" 6They answered as Jesus had told
them to, and the people let them go.
7When they brought the colt to Jesus and
threw their cloaks over it, he sat on it.
8Many people spread their cloaks on the
road, while others spread branches they
had cut in the fields. 9Those who went
ahead and those who followed shouted,

"Hosanna![o] "
"Blessed is he who comes in the name
of the Lord!"[p] [i]
10"Blessed is the coming kingdom of our
father David!"
"Hosanna in the highest!"[j]

11Jesus entered Jerusalem and went to
the temple. He looked around at everything, but since it was already late, he
went out to Bethany with the Twelve.[k]

[o] *9* A Hebrew expression meaning "Save!" which became an exclamation of praise; also in verse 10
[p] *9* Psalm 118:25,26

---

not search for power and authority. We seek ways to help others. The greatest disciple will be the greatest servant. See note on 1 Co 3:9; Life in Christ: The Disciple's Cross, pp. 1748–1751.

10:45 JESUS CHRIST, Son of Man—The title Son of man is the most frequently used title for Jesus in the Synoptic Gospels. In the Old Testament the term appeared in Ezekiel as a name for the prophet who represented men to God and God to men (Eze 2:1). Daniel refers to a redeemer figure who will establish an everlasting kingdom (Da 7:13). Between the Testaments, the Book of Enoch used the idea of a Messiah coming at the end time on the clouds. It might well be said that Jesus *incorporated all of these ideas* and enlarged them. The distinctive feature that appears in the New Testament is the idea of the Son of man suffering, as in this verse. See notes on Mt 8:20; Jn 8:28. Some scholars have divided the Son of man sayings in the Gospels into three categories: a reference to the self (Mt 8:20); a reference to suffering (Mk 10:45); and a reference to the future, coming Son of man (Mk 14:62).

10:45 JESUS CHRIST, Death—This verse was used by later theologians to assert a ransom theory of Jesus' atonement. It should not be pressed to such an extent that one asks if the "ransom" were paid to the devil, to God's own internal requirements, or to someone else. Jesus' metaphor of ransom speaks of the costliness of His sacrifice. We are so precious to God He was willing to let His Son die to save us from the death penalty of sin. See note on Mt 20:28.

10:46–52 JESUS CHRIST, Son of David—See notes on Mt 1:1; 20:29–34. Bartimaeus did not understand messiahship as did Jesus, but he expressed faith with courage and persistence. Jesus rewarded the faith with healing.

10:46–52 MIRACLE, Faith—Faith seeking God's miraculous help must often overcome a hostile crowd. See note on Mt 20:29–34.

10:51–52 PRAYER, Faith—Prayer for healing depends on faith and on God's purposes (Mt 9:22; 15:28; Lk 17:19).

11:1–11 JESUS CHRIST, Son of David—See note on Mt 21:1–11.

11:9–10 PRAYER, Praise—See note on Mt 21:9.

11:10 THE CHURCH, God's Kingdom—In Jesus, the kingdom is both present and future. God is to be praised because He blessed His people by coming into the world. Jesus fulfilled the promises to David not by reestablishing a political rule in Jerusalem but by serving God's people and bringing God's kingdom near. Some interpreters look for fulfillment of the political promises at the Second Coming.

Jesus Clears the Temple

11:12–14pp — Mt 21:18–22
11:15–18pp — Mt 21:12–16; Lk 19:45–47; Jn 2:13–16

12The next day as they were leaving
Bethany, Jesus was hungry. 13Seeing in
the distance a fig tree in leaf, he went to
find out if it had any fruit. When he
reached it, he found nothing but leaves,
because it was not the season for figs.[l]
14Then he said to the tree, "May no one
ever eat fruit from you again." And his
disciples heard him say it.
15On reaching Jerusalem, Jesus entered
the temple area and began driving out
those who were buying and selling there.
He overturned the tables of the money
changers and the benches of those selling
doves, 16and would not allow anyone to
carry merchandise through the temple
courts. 17And as he taught them, he said,
"Is it not written:

" 'My house will be called
a house of prayer for all nations'[q]?[m]

But you have made it 'a den of robbers.'[r] "[n]
18The chief priests and the teachers of
the law heard this and began looking for a
way to kill him, for they feared him,[o]
because the whole crowd was amazed at
his teaching.[p]
19When evening came, they[s] went out
of the city.[q]

The Withered Fig Tree

11:20–24pp — Mt 21:19–22

20In the morning, as they went along,
they saw the fig tree withered from the
roots. 21Peter remembered and said to
Jesus, "Rabbi,[r] look! The fig tree you
cursed has withered!"
22"Have[t] faith in God," Jesus answered. 23"I tell you the truth, if anyone
says to this mountain, 'Go, throw yourself
into the sea,' and does not doubt in his
heart but believes that what he says will
happen, it will be done for him.[s]
24Therefore I tell you, whatever you ask
for in prayer, believe that you have received it, and it will be yours.[t] 25And
when you stand praying, if you hold anything against anyone, forgive him, so that
your Father in heaven may forgive you
your sins.[u] "[u]

The Authority of Jesus Questioned

11:27–33pp — Mt 21:23–27; Lk 20:1–8

27They arrived again in Jerusalem, and
while Jesus was walking in the temple
courts, the chief priests, the teachers of
the law and the elders came to him.
28"By what authority are you doing these
things?" they asked. "And who gave you
authority to do this?"
29Jesus replied, "I will ask you one
question. Answer me, and I will tell you
by what authority I am doing these
things. 30John's baptism—was it from
heaven, or from men? Tell me!"
31They discussed it among themselves
and said, "If we say, 'From heaven,' he
will ask, 'Then why didn't you believe
him?' 32But if we say, 'From men' . . . ."
(They feared the people, for everyone
held that John really was a prophet.)[v]
33So they answered Jesus, "We don't
know."
Jesus said, "Neither will I tell you by
what authority I am doing these things."

Chapter 12

The Parable of the Tenants

12:1–12pp — Mt 21:33–46; Lk 20:9–19

HE then began to speak to them in parables: "A man planted a vineyard.[w]

11:13 [l]Lk 13:6-9
11:17 [m]Isa 56:7 [n]Jer 7:11
11:18 [o]Mt 21:46; Mk 12:12; Lk 20:19 [p]S Mt 7:28
11:19 [q]Lk 21:37
11:21 [r]S Mt 23:7
11:23 [s]S Mt 21:21
11:24 [t]S Mt 7:7
11:25 [u]S Mt 6:14
11:32 [v]S Mt 11:9
12:1 [w]Isa 5:1-7

[q]17 Isaiah 56:7 [r]17 Jer. 7:11 [s]19 Some early manuscripts *he* [t]22 Some early manuscripts *If you have* [u]25 Some manuscripts *sins.* 26*But if you do not forgive, neither will your Father who is in heaven forgive your sins.*

11:12–31 JESUS CHRIST, Authority—See note on Mt 21:12–16. Compare Lk 19:45–48; Jn 2:13–16. Two events happened on Monday: the cursing of a barren fig tree and the final cleansing of the Temple. The most evident meaning of the tree is that the miracle was to encourage His disciples' faith (Mk 11:23–25) as they saw Jesus' authority over nature and over God's house. The turmoil in the Temple on the previous day and the disruption of Temple business on this day were the final straws for Jesus' opponents. People take action when their finances are affected. Jesus refused to give unbelieving authorities answers about His authority, though believers could not doubt God's authority was at work in Him.
11:17 REVELATION, Actions—See note on Mt 21:13.
11:17 PRAYER, Corporate—God graciously provided the tabernacle and the Temple to give His people access to Him. See notes on 1 Ki 8:22–53; 2 Ch 2:4; Isa 56:7. God's house was being used in a way different from the purpose of its dedication. God's congregation should be more interested in prayer than in economic profits.
11:17 EVANGELISM, Worship—True worship begins when we sincerely seek God. That is why God's house was known to Israel as a "house of prayer." That principle must not be corrupted if evangelism is to be effective in the worship of God's people.
11:25–26 REVELATION, Fellowship—Forgiveness with God is linked with understanding one's relationship to other human beings. Grace enters our life to the extent that we understand and employ God's grace in human relationships.
11:25 PRAYER, Humility—See note on Mt 6:14–15. No one posture is commanded for prayer in the Bible. Standing in God's presence is one posture of prayer (1 Ki 8:14,22; Ne 9:4; Ps 134:1; Mt 6:5). So was kneeling (1 Ki 8:54; Da 6:10; Ac 7:60; 20:36; 21:5; Eph 3:14). Prostration on one's face before God shows intense humility and need (Nu 16:45; Jos 7:6; 2 Sa 12:16; 1 Ki 18:42; Ezr 10:1; Mk 14:35). Bowing the head is another gesture of humility (Ge 24:26; Ex 34:8; 1 Ki 18:42; Ne 8:6).
12:1–12 JESUS CHRIST, Son of God—Jesus was God's only Son, whom He loved dearly. He represented God's final hope to turn Israel to respect and obey Him and His will. Israel rejected Him as they had the prophets. See note on Mt 21:33–44.

He put a wall around it, dug a pit for the
winepress and built a watchtower. Then
he rented the vineyard to some farmers
and went away on a journey. 2At harvest
time he sent a servant to the tenants to
collect from them some of the fruit of the
vineyard. 3But they seized him, beat him
and sent him away empty-handed. 4Then
he sent another servant to them; they
struck this man on the head and treated
him shamefully. 5He sent still another,
and that one they killed. He sent many
others; some of them they beat, others
they killed.
6"He had one left to send, a son, whom
he loved. He sent him last of all,[x] saying,
'They will respect my son.'
7"But the tenants said to one another,
'This is the heir. Come, let's kill him, and
the inheritance will be ours.' 8So they
took him and killed him, and threw him
out of the vineyard.
9"What then will the owner of the
vineyard do? He will come and kill those
tenants and give the vineyard to others.
10Haven't you read this scripture:

" 'The stone the builders rejected
has become the capstone[v]; [y]
11the Lord has done this,
and it is marvelous in our eyes'[w]?"[z]

12Then they looked for a way to arrest
him because they knew he had spoken
the parable against them. But they were
afraid of the crowd;[a] so they left him and
went away.[b]

Paying Taxes to Caesar

12:13–17pp — Mt 22:15–22; Lk 20:20–26

13Later they sent some of the Pharisees
and Herodians[c] to Jesus to catch him[d] in
his words. 14They came to him and said,
"Teacher, we know you are a man of integrity. You aren't swayed by men, because you pay no attention to who they
are; but you teach the way of God in accordance with the truth. Is it right to pay
taxes to Caesar or not? 15Should we pay
or shouldn't we?"
But Jesus knew their hypocrisy. "Why
are you trying to trap me?" he asked.
"Bring me a denarius and let me look at
it." 16They brought the coin, and he
asked them, "Whose portrait is this? And
whose inscription?"
"Caesar's," they replied.
17Then Jesus said to them, "Give to
Caesar what is Caesar's and to God what
is God's."[e]
And they were amazed at him.

Marriage at the Resurrection

12:18–27pp — Mt 22:23–33; Lk 20:27–38

18Then the Sadducees,[f] who say there
is no resurrection,[g] came to him with a
question. 19"Teacher," they said, "Moses
wrote for us that if a man's brother dies
and leaves a wife but no children, the
man must marry the widow and have
children for his brother.[h] 20Now there
were seven brothers. The first one married and died without leaving any children. 21The second one married the widow, but he also died, leaving no child. It
was the same with the third. 22In fact,
none of the seven left any children. Last
of all, the woman died too. 23At the resurrection[x] whose wife will she be, since
the seven were married to her?"
24Jesus replied, "Are you not in error
because you do not know the Scriptures[i]
or the power of God? 25When the dead
rise, they will neither marry nor be given
in marriage; they will be like the angels
in heaven.[j] 26Now about the dead rising
—have you not read in the book of Moses, in the account of the bush, how God
said to him, 'I am the God of Abraham,
the God of Isaac, and the God of Jacob'[y]?[k] 27He is not the God of the dead,
but of the living. You are badly mistak-
en!"

The Greatest Commandment

12:28–34pp — Mt 22:34–40

28One of the teachers of the law[l] came
and heard them debating. Noticing that
Jesus had given them a good answer, he
asked him, "Of all the commandments,
which is the most important?"
29"The most important one," an-

12:6 [x]Heb 1:1-3
12:10 [y]S Ac 4:11
12:11 [z]Ps 118:22, 23
12:12 [a]S Mk 11:18 [b]Mt 22:22
12:13 [c]Mt 22:16; Mk 3:6 [d]S Mt 12:10
12:17 [e]Ro 13:7
12:18 [f]S Ac 4:1 [g]Ac 23:8; 1Co 15:12
12:19 [h]Dt 25:5
12:24 [i]2Ti 3:15-17
12:25 [j]1Co 15:42, 49,52
12:26 [k]Ex 3:6
12:28 [l]Lk 10:25-28; 20:39

[v]*10* Or *cornerstone* [w]*11* Psalm 118:22,23
[x]*23* Some manuscripts *resurrection, when men rise from the dead,* [y]*26* Exodus 3:6

12:13–34 JESUS CHRIST, Teaching—Jesus taught the ultimate truth about God and people without favoritism for anyone. His opponents recognized this. Instead of letting this point them to faith, they played on Jesus' honesty to trap Him. Knowledge of Jesus is not enough to be God's people. Trusting commitment to Jesus is what He seeks. Jesus' divine authority finally silenced His opponents. They could not trap Him.
12:13–17 CHRISTIAN ETHICS, Church and State—See notes on Mt 22:15–22; Ro 13:1–7.
12:13–17 STEWARDSHIP, Taxes—See note on Mt 22:21.
12:14,32 EDUCATION, Jesus—See note on Mt 22:24,36.
12:15–17 HUMANITY, Relationships—See note on Mt 22:18–21.
12:18–27 HUMANITY, Nature of Death—See note on Mt 22:23–33.
12:18–25 LAST THINGS, Heaven—The power of God knows no limits. He will raise the dead. He will also establish a future blessedness in heaven not dependent on earthly relationships for maximum fulfillment and joy. Heaven's relations are to be that which exists among angels. There will be no need for marital union. Happiness will be raised to a higher than earthly level.
12:18–27 FAMILY, Temporal—See note on Mt 22:23–32.

swered Jesus, "is this: 'Hear, O Israel, the
Lord our God, the Lord is one.[z] 30Love
the Lord your God with all your heart and
with all your soul and with all your mind
and with all your strength.'[a][m] 31The second is this: 'Love your neighbor as yourself.'[b][n] There is no commandment greater than these."

32"Well said, teacher," the man replied. "You are right in saying that God is
one and there is no other but him.[o] 33To
love him with all your heart, with all your
understanding and with all your strength,
and to love your neighbor as yourself is
more important than all burnt offerings
and sacrifices."[p]

34When Jesus saw that he had answered wisely, he said to him, "You are
not far from the kingdom of God."[q] And
from then on no one dared ask him any
more questions.[r]

Whose Son Is the Christ?

12:35–37pp — Mt 22:41–46; Lk 20:41–44
12:38–40pp — Mt 23:1–7; Lk 20:45–47

35While Jesus was teaching in the temple courts,[s] he asked, "How is it that the
teachers of the law say that the Christ[c] is
the son of David?[t] 36David himself,
speaking by the Holy Spirit,[u] declared:

" 'The Lord said to my Lord:
"Sit at my right hand
until I put your enemies
under your feet." '[d][v]

37David himself calls him 'Lord.' How
then can he be his son?"

The large crowd[w] listened to him with
delight.

38As he taught, Jesus said, "Watch out
for the teachers of the law. They like to
walk around in flowing robes and be
greeted in the marketplaces, 39and have
the most important seats in the synagogues and the places of honor at banquets.[x] 40They devour widows' houses
and for a show make lengthy prayers.
Such men will be punished most severely."

The Widow's Offering

12:41–44pp — Lk 21:1–4

41Jesus sat down opposite the place
where the offerings were put[y] and
watched the crowd putting their money
into the temple treasury. Many rich people threw in large amounts. 42But a poor
widow came and put in two very small
copper coins,[e] worth only a fraction of a
penny.[f]

43Calling his disciples to him, Jesus
said, "I tell you the truth, this poor
widow has put more into the treasury
than all the others. 44They all gave
out of their wealth; but she, out of her
poverty, put in everything—all she had
to live on."[z]

12:30 [m]Dt 6:4,5
12:31 [n]Lev 19:18; S Mt 5:43
12:32 [o]Dt 4:35,39; Isa 45:6,14; 46:9
12:33 [p]1Sa 15:22; Hos 6:6; Mic 6:6-8; Heb 10:8
12:34 [q]S Mt 3:2 [r]Mt 22:46; Lk 20:40
12:35 [s]S Mt 26:55 [t]S Mt 9:27
12:36 [u]2Sa 23:2 [v]Ps 110:1; S Mt 22:44
12:37 [w]Jn 12:9
12:39 [x]Lk 11:43
12:41 [y]2Ki 12:9; Jn 8:20
12:44 [z]2Co 8:12

[z]*29* Or *the Lord our God is one Lord* [a]*30* Deut. 6:4,5 [b]*31* Lev. 19:18 [c]*35* Or *Messiah* [d]*36* Psalm 110:1 [e]*42* Greek *two lepta* [f]*42* Greek *kodrantes*

12:29–31 GOD, One God—Jesus declared here that the basic religious demand is that we recognize the uniqueness of God as the one true God. Such a recognition of the uniqueness of God carries with it a far reaching demand upon us. Recognizing God for who He is means then that we should love Him with the totality of our being. Knowing and loving God in this unrestricted way means that we should also love our fellow humans with a love that arises from the very depths of our hearts. These are really not two separate commandments growing out of the recognition of God's sovereign authority; they are two phases of one responsibility to love. According to 1 Jn 4:20 we cannot love God without loving our fellow human beings. This two-sided commandment, which Mt 22:40 says is the foundation of all of the law and the prophets, is taken from Dt 6:4 and Lev 19:18. They, thus, are not new commandments in the teaching of Jesus. What is new is Jesus' joining them as a single demand made by the true recognition of the uniqueness of God's holy authority. The unique sovereignty of God is not a neutral piece of information but demands total commitment from us.

12:29–31 HOLY SCRIPTURE, Relationship—See note on Mt 22:37–39.

12:30 SALVATION, Love of God—The saved should love God with their whole being. This is the most important of all the commandments. See note on Mt 22:37–39.

12:34 THE CHURCH, God's Kingdom—Entrance into the kingdom comes through Jesus. The teacher came near when he accepted Jesus' teaching that love is central and recognized that attitude is more important than ritual acts of worship. He still needed to commit his life to that love by following Christ. The kingdom involves more than accepting Jesus' teachings. It means answering Jesus' call to discipleship.

12:35–37 JESUS CHRIST, Son of David—See note on Mt 22:41–46.

12:38–40 DISCIPLESHIP, Oppressed—Jesus had strong words for His enemies. He warned the religious legalists they faced eternal punishment. Why? Because they wanted the chief places in the synagogue and places of honor at social occasions. These legalists lacked the compassion to reach out to the oppressed. Rather, they misused their leadership to take advantage of defenseless people such as widows. These religious leaders prayed long prayers and appeared religious, but they oppressed the defenseless rather than ministering to the oppressed. Disciples gain honor in secret service, not in public display. See notes on Mt 9:36; Heb 13:1–3.

12:38–40 EDUCATION, Scribes and Pharisees—Jesus questioned the motives of certain scribes and teachers of the law who loved to call attention to themselves. Status-seekers make poor teachers of divine revelation. See Lk 20:45–47.

12:40 PRAYER, Sincerity—Jesus denounced insincere show before people, not the length of the prayers. He Himself prayed all night (Lk 6:12). Whether public or private, prayer is conversation with God, not display of piety before people.

12:41–44 STEWARDSHIP, Sacrificial Giving—Stewardship is measured by the sacrifice we make, not by the amount we give. The widow's willingness to give all she had represented better stewardship than the large gifts of the rich who retained abundant resources. The amount left after the gift is a more significant figure than the amount of the gift. Christian stewardship involves sacrificial giving which counts the need rather than the availability of resources for personal use. See note on 2 Co 8:1—9:15.

Chapter 13

Signs of the End of the Age

13:1–37pp — Mt 24:1–51; Lk 21:5–36

As he was leaving the temple, one of his
disciples said to him, "Look, Teacher! What massive stones! What magnificent buildings!"
2"Do you see all these great buildings?" replied Jesus. "Not one stone here
will be left on another; every one will be
thrown down."[a]
3As Jesus was sitting on the Mount of
Olives[b] opposite the temple, Peter,
James, John[c] and Andrew asked him privately, 4"Tell us, when will these things
happen? And what will be the sign that
they are all about to be fulfilled?"
5Jesus said to them: "Watch out that
no one deceives you.[d] 6Many will come
in my name, claiming, 'I am he,' and will
deceive many. 7When you hear of wars
and rumors of wars, do not be alarmed.
Such things must happen, but the end is
still to come. 8Nation will rise against nation, and kingdom against kingdom.
There will be earthquakes in various
places, and famines. These are the beginning of birth pains.
9"You must be on your guard. You will
be handed over to the local councils and
flogged in the synagogues.[e] On account
of me you will stand before governors and
kings as witnesses to them. 10And the
gospel must first be preached to all nations. 11Whenever you are arrested and
brought to trial, do not worry beforehand
about what to say. Just say whatever is
given you at the time, for it is not you
speaking, but the Holy Spirit.[f]
12"Brother will betray brother to death,
and a father his child. Children will rebel
against their parents and have them put
to death.[g] 13All men will hate you because of me,[h] but he who stands firm to
the end will be saved.[i]
14"When you see 'the abomination that
causes desolation'[g][j] standing where it[h]
does not belong—let the reader understand—then let those who are in Judea
flee to the mountains. 15Let no one on the
roof of his house go down or enter the
house to take anything out. 16Let no one
in the field go back to get his cloak.
17How dreadful it will be in those days for
pregnant women and nursing mothers![k]
18Pray that this will not take place in winter, 19because those will be days of distress unequaled from the beginning,
when God created the world,[l] until
now—and never to be equaled again.[m]
20If the Lord had not cut short those days,
no one would survive. But for the sake of
the elect, whom he has chosen, he has
shortened them. 21At that time if anyone
says to you, 'Look, here is the Christ[i]!'
or, 'Look, there he is!' do not believe it.[n]
22For false Christs and false prophets[o]

13:2 [a]Lk 19:44
13:3 [b]S Mt 21:1 [c]S Mt 4:21
13:5 [d]ver 22; Jer 29:8; Eph 5:6; 2Th 2:3,10-12; 1Ti 4:1; 2Ti 3:13; 1Jn 4:6
13:9 [e]S Mt 10:17
13:11 [f]Mt 10:19, 20; Lk 12:11,12
13:12 [g]Mic 7:6; Mt 10:21; Lk 12:51-53
13:13 [h]S Jn 15:21 [i]S Mt 10:22
13:14 [j]Da 9:27; 11:31; 12:11
13:17 [k]Lk 23:29
13:19 [l]Mk 10:6 [m]Da 9:26; 12:1; Joel 2:2
13:21 [n]Lk 17:23; 21:8
13:22 [o]S Mt 7:15

[g]*14* Daniel 9:27; 11:31; 12:11 [h]*14* Or *he;* also in verse 29 [i]*21* Or *Messiah*

13:1–37 JESUS CHRIST, Final Coming—See note on Mt 24:1—25:46.

13:1–37 LAST THINGS, Great Tribulation—Mk 13 is often called the "Little Apocalypse." Revelation is, of course, the fullest apocalyptic book of the New Testament. The point of departure was the destruction of the Temple in Jerusalem. The topic, however, seems to enlarge until Jerusalem's destruction is only a prefiguring of end time tribulation. See note on Da 9:24–27. It is in this light that signs of the end are given (vv 5–8), distress and trouble predicted (vv 9–13), the appearance of an abomination that causes desolation announced (vv 14–20), and false messiahs and false prophets expected (vv 21–23). Then the Son of man will appear (vv 24–31). The unknown hour of His coming demands watchfulness (vv 32–37).

13:6,13 REVELATION, Faithfulness—Strange signs will attend the second appearance of Jesus. False teachers will confuse and lead people in the wrong direction. The pressure and confusion will be great enough that some loved ones will be divided and alienated, but those who endure and believe to the end will be redeemed by the God of faithfulness.

13:9–10 EVANGELISM, Persecution—Christians who tell others of their sin and their need of Jesus Christ as Savior can expect persecution in one form or another. For Jesus' sake we endure, and in the context of sacrifice the gospel will eventually reach the entire world.

13:10 PROCLAMATION, Compulsion—See note on 1 Co 9:16–18.

13:11 HOLY SPIRIT, Protects—Jesus promised that His followers would have the Spirit's help when they were persecuted for being His followers. They could count on the Spirit's provision of the words they needed to testify of Jesus and to defend themselves. See Ac 7:1–58; notes on Mt 10:19–20; Lk 12:11–12.

13:12 FAMILY, Priorities—See note on Lk 12:49–53.

13:13 ELECTION, Perseverance—See note on 4:13–20.

13:14 HOLY SCRIPTURE, Inspired—Jesus picked up the inspired apocalyptic language of Daniel's prophecy. Apparently Jesus pointed to the Roman destruction of the Jewish Temple in AD 70 and beyond that to the second coming, showing Scripture is opened to renewed understanding and fulfillment for different generations. God has new things to reveal from His Word.

13:14–23 LAST THINGS, Great Tribulation—The phrase "abomination that causes desolation" comes verbatim from Da 9:27; 11:31; 12:11. Abomination is a term that described sacrilege, such as the profaning of a holy place. Many believe Daniel's prophecy had immediate reference to the unclean sacrifices in the Jerusalem Temple commanded by Antiochus Epiphanes in 168 BC. The word of Jesus had additional reference to the sacking of the Temple by the Romans in AD 70. Compare Lk 21:20. This had been the point of a direct statement by Jesus in 13:2. Amillennialists interpret the phrase in terms of that past history and do not apply it to the future. Premillennialists often interpret the abomination that causes desolation as a reference to the time of the antichrist immediately before Christ returns (13:24–27). See note on 1 Jn 2:18. Many see this complex set of ongoing interpretations as an illustration of the multiple fulfillment feature of many biblical prophecies. See notes on Eze 38:1—39:29; Da 9:24–27.

13:18 PRAYER, Petition—See note on Mt 24:20.

13:20–23 ELECTION, Eternal Security—See note on Mt 24:10–13.

13:22 MIRACLE, God's Working—See note on Mt 24:24.

13:22 CHURCH LEADERS, False Prophet—False proph-

will appear and perform signs and miracles[p] to deceive the elect—if that were
possible. 23So be on your guard;[q] I have
told you everything ahead of time.
24"But in those days, following that distress,

" 'the sun will be darkened,
and the moon will not give its light;
25the stars will fall from the sky,
and the heavenly bodies will be
shaken.'[j] [r]

26"At that time men will see the Son of
Man coming in clouds[s] with great power
and glory. 27And he will send his angels
and gather his elect from the four winds,
from the ends of the earth to the ends of
the heavens.[t]
28"Now learn this lesson from the fig
tree: As soon as its twigs get tender and
its leaves come out, you know that summer is near. 29Even so, when you see
these things happening, you know that it
is near, right at the door. 30I tell you the
truth, this generation[k][u] will certainly
not pass away until all these things have
happened.[v] 31Heaven and earth will pass
away, but my words will never pass
away.[w]

The Day and Hour Unknown

32"No one knows about that day or
hour, not even the angels in heaven, nor
the Son, but only the Father.[x] 33Be on
guard! Be alert![l][y] You do not know
when that time will come. 34It's like a
man going away: He leaves his house and
puts his servants[z] in charge, each with
his assigned task, and tells the one at the
door to keep watch.
35"Therefore keep watch because you
do not know when the owner of the
house will come back—whether in the
evening, or at midnight, or when the
rooster crows, or at dawn. 36If he comes
suddenly, do not let him find you sleeping. 37What I say to you, I say to everyone: 'Watch!' "[a]

13:22 [p]S Jn 4:48; 2Th 2:9,10
13:23 [q]2Pe 3:17
13:25 [r]Isa 13:10; 34:4; S Mt 24:29
13:26 [s]S Rev 1:7
13:27 [t]Zec 2:6
13:30 [u]Mk 9:1 [v]Lk 17:25
13:31 [w]S Mt 5:18
13:32 [x]Ac 1:7; 1Th 5:1,2
13:33 [y]1Th 5:6
13:34 [z]Mt 25:14
13:37 [a]Lk 12:35-40
14:1 [b]S Jn 11:55 [c]S Mt 12:14
14:3 [d]S Mt 21:17 [e]Lk 7:37-39
14:7 [f]Dt 15:11
14:8 [g]Jn 19:40
14:9 [h]S Mt 24:14; Mk 16:15
14:10 [i]Mk 3:16-19 [j]S Mt 10:4

Chapter 14

Jesus Anointed at Bethany

14:1–11pp — Mt 26:2–16
14:1,2,10,11pp — Lk 22:1–6
14:3–8Ref — Jn 12:1–8

NOW the Passover[b] and the Feast of
Unleavened Bread were only two
days away, and the chief priests and the
teachers of the law were looking for some
sly way to arrest Jesus and kill him.[c]
2"But not during the Feast," they said,
"or the people may riot."
3While he was in Bethany,[d] reclining
at the table in the home of a man known
as Simon the Leper, a woman came with
an alabaster jar of very expensive perfume, made of pure nard. She broke the
jar and poured the perfume on his head.[e]
4Some of those present were saying in-
dignantly to one another, "Why this
waste of perfume? 5It could have been
sold for more than a year's wages[m] and
the money given to the poor." And they
rebuked her harshly.
6"Leave her alone," said Jesus. "Why
are you bothering her? She has done a
beautiful thing to me. 7The poor you will
always have with you, and you can help
them any time you want.[f] But you will
not always have me. 8She did what she
could. She poured perfume on my body
beforehand to prepare for my burial.[g] 9I
tell you the truth, wherever the gospel is
preached throughout the world,[h] what
she has done will also be told, in memory
of her."
10Then Judas Iscariot, one of the
Twelve,[i] went to the chief priests to betray Jesus to them.[j] 11They were delighted to hear this and promised to give him

[j]25 Isaiah 13:10; 34:4 [k]30 Or *race* [l]33 Some manuscripts *alert and pray* [m]5 Greek *than three hundred denarii*

---

ets dare to take the office of prophet on themselves and simulate the prophetic gift to win favor and prestige. They deceive the unwary so that believers must be on constant guard against them. The final days of history will see their number increase, but they will not win the victory.

13:32 GOD, Wisdom—See note on Mt 24:36.

13:32–35 HISTORY, Time—Decisive moments stand out in history as times of crisis and opportunity. The end of chronological history as we know it is such a decisive moment. That moment in time will introduce the final events of judgment and the eternal reign of Christ with His saints. No human has the power or means to determine the date of that decisive moment. God alone determines and knows the time of the end.

14:3–9 JESUS CHRIST, Death—See note on Mt 26:6–13.

14:3–9 STEWARDSHIP, Service to God—See note on *Mt 26:6–13; Ac 4:32–5:11.*

14:10–11 JESUS CHRIST, Death—See note on Mt 26:14–16,25–26.

14:10–11,43–45 SIN, Individual Choice—See note on Mt 26:14–16,23–25,47–49.

14:10–26 ORDINANCES, Observance of Lord's Supper—Mark has almost exactly the same words as Matthew in his account of the Lord's Supper (Mt 26:17–30). In his description of the preparation for the Supper, Mark has several distinctive details found also in Lk 22:1–30: a man carrying a jar of water, a large upper room furnished and ready, a location in the city. For this and other reasons, such as the gathering of the early Christians at the home of John Mark (Ac 12:12), many scholars believe the Last Supper was held in the home of Mark. See notes on Mt 26:17–30; Lk 22:1–30. Mark may have been an eyewitness to some of the details he gives in his Gospel.

14:11 STEWARDSHIP, Attitudes—Loyalty to Christ does not have a price. Judas sold Christ to the priests for four months' pay (Mt 26:15). He valued personal power, political freedom, and financial resources above Jesus and the kingdom of God. The Christian steward must decide if Christ's call to serve God by serving others is more important than worldly values.

money. So he watched for an opportunity
to hand him over.

The Lord's Supper

14:12–26pp — Mt 26:17–30; Lk 22:7–23
14:22–25pp — 1Co 11:23–25

12 On the first day of the Feast of Unleavened Bread, when it was customary
to sacrifice the Passover lamb,[k] Jesus'
disciples asked him, "Where do you want
us to go and make preparations for you to
eat the Passover?"
13 So he sent two of his disciples, telling
them, "Go into the city, and a man carrying a jar of water will meet you. Follow
him. 14 Say to the owner of the house he
enters, 'The Teacher asks: Where is my
guest room, where I may eat the Passover
with my disciples?' 15 He will show you a
large upper room,[l] furnished and ready.
Make preparations for us there."
16 The disciples left, went into the city
and found things just as Jesus had told
them. So they prepared the Passover.
17 When evening came, Jesus arrived
with the Twelve. 18 While they were reclining at the table eating, he said, "I tell
you the truth, one of you will betray me
—one who is eating with me."
19 They were saddened, and one by one
they said to him, "Surely not I?"
20 "It is one of the Twelve," he replied,
"one who dips bread into the bowl with
me.[m] 21 The Son of Man[n] will go just as it
is written about him. But woe to that man
who betrays the Son of Man! It would be
better for him if he had not been born."
22 While they were eating, Jesus took
bread, gave thanks and broke it,[o] and
gave it to his disciples, saying, "Take it;
this is my body."
23 Then he took the cup, gave thanks
and offered it to them, and they all drank
from it.[p]
24 "This is my blood of the[n] covenant,[q]
which is poured out for many," he said to
them. 25 "I tell you the truth, I will not
drink again of the fruit of the vine until
that day when I drink it anew in the kingdom of God."[r]
26 When they had sung a hymn, they
went out to the Mount of Olives.[s]

Jesus Predicts Peter's Denial

14:27–31pp — Mt 26:31–35

27 "You will all fall away," Jesus told
them, "for it is written:

" 'I will strike the shepherd,
and the sheep will be scattered.'[o][t]

28 But after I have risen, I will go ahead of
you into Galilee."[u]
29 Peter declared, "Even if all fall away,
I will not."
30 "I tell you the truth," Jesus answered, "today—yes, tonight—before
the rooster crows twice[p] you yourself
will disown me three times."[v]
31 But Peter insisted emphatically,
"Even if I have to die with you,[w] I will
never disown you." And all the others
said the same.

Gethsemane

14:32–42pp — Mt 26:36–46; Lk 22:40–46

32 They went to a place called Gethsemane, and Jesus said to his disciples, "Sit
here while I pray." 33 He took Peter,
James and John[x] along with him, and he
began to be deeply distressed and troubled. 34 "My soul is overwhelmed with
sorrow to the point of death,"[y] he said to
them. "Stay here and keep watch."
35 Going a little farther, he fell to the
ground and prayed that if possible the
hour[z] might pass from him. 36 "*Abba*,[q]

14:12 [k]Ex 12:1-11; Dt 16:1-4; 1Co 5:7
14:15 [l]Ac 1:13
14:20 [m]Jn 13:18-27
14:21 [n]S Mt 8:20
14:22 [o]S Mt 14:19
14:23 [p]1Co 10:16
14:24 [q]S Mt 26:28
14:25 [r]S Mt 3:2
14:26 [s]S Mt 21:1
14:27 [t]Zec 13:7
14:28 [u]Mk 16:7
14:30 [v]ver 66-72; Lk 22:34; Jn 13:38
14:31 [w]Lk 22:33; Jn 13:37
14:33 [x]S Mt 4:21
14:34 [y]Jn 12:27
14:35 [z]ver 41; S Mt 26:18

[n]24 Some manuscripts *the new* [o]27 Zech. 13:7
[p]30 Some early manuscripts do not have *twice.*
[q]36 Aramaic for *Father*

14:12–26 JESUS CHRIST, Death—See note on Mt 26:17–30.

14:14 EDUCATION, Jesus—The most convincing evidence in the Gospels that Jesus functioned primarily as a teacher is the fact that He referred to Himself as "The Teacher."

14:22 REVELATION, Jesus Christ—See note on Mt 26:26–28.

14:22–23 PRAYER, Thanksgiving—See note on Mt 26:26–27.

14:24 THE CHURCH, Covenant People—Jesus fulfilled the covenant of the Old Testament. His life and ministry tied the covenant people of the Old Testament to God's new work in the church in the New Testament. Jesus came to fulfill the old covenant and to issue in the age of the new covenant. Many people believe that Jesus referred to Jeremiah's message of the new covenant. See note on Jer 31:31–34. What Jeremiah proclaimed as coming in the future, Jesus brought to fulfillment. The names of the two divisions of the Bible get their names from the covenant concept. In the life of Jesus, the grandest hopes of the old covenant and the brightest possibilities of the new covenant came together.

14:26 WORSHIP, Music—See note on 1 Ch 6:31–32.

14:32–42 JESUS CHRIST, Suffering—See note on Mt 26:36–46.

14:32–39 PRAYER, Petition—See notes on 11:25; Ge 17:3,17; Mt 26:36–44. Jesus called God "Abba," the most intimate Aramaic term for "Father." Prayer is an intimate, trusting relationship.

14:36 GOD, Father—Jesus here showed the warmth and intimacy of the relationship to God that He enjoys. In the Aramaic language which Jesus most likely was speaking, He used the term Abba in addressing God. This would be roughly equivalent to our saying Daddy, an intimate term used in a warm family setting. Notice that Jesus not only approached God in that warm, personal, intimate way. He also showed profound respect and obedience. While He prayed for some way other than the awful agony of the cross, He nevertheless expressed His full commitment to doing the will of His Father no matter what the cost to Himself.

14:36 JESUS CHRIST, Son of God—Jesus used a familiar Aramaic word, "Abba," to address His Heavenly Father. The term is not lacking in respect but is full of affection. Compare Ro 8:15; Gal 4:6.

Father,"[a] he said, "everything is possible
for you. Take this cup[b] from me. Yet not
what I will, but what you will."[c]
37Then he returned to his disciples and
found them sleeping. "Simon," he said to
Peter, "are you asleep? Could you not
keep watch for one hour? 38Watch and
pray so that you will not fall into temptation.[d] The spirit is willing, but the body
is weak."[e]
39Once more he went away and prayed
the same thing. 40When he came back, he
again found them sleeping, because their
eyes were heavy. They did not know
what to say to him.
41Returning the third time, he said to
them, "Are you still sleeping and resting?
Enough! The hour[f] has come. Look, the
Son of Man is betrayed into the hands of
sinners. 42Rise! Let us go! Here comes my
betrayer!"

Jesus Arrested

14:43–50pp — Mt 26:47–56; Lk 22:47–50; Jn 18:3–11

43Just as he was speaking, Judas,[g] one
of the Twelve, appeared. With him was a
crowd armed with swords and clubs, sent
from the chief priests, the teachers of the
law, and the elders.
44Now the betrayer had arranged a signal with them: "The one I kiss is the
man; arrest him and lead him away under
guard." 45Going at once to Jesus, Judas
said, "Rabbi!"[h] and kissed him. 46The
men seized Jesus and arrested him.
47Then one of those standing near drew
his sword and struck the servant of the
high priest, cutting off his ear.
48"Am I leading a rebellion," said
Jesus, "that you have come out with
swords and clubs to capture me? 49Every
day I was with you, teaching in the temple courts,[i] and you did not arrest me.
But the Scriptures must be fulfilled."[j]
50Then everyone deserted him and fled.[k]
51A young man, wearing nothing but a
linen garment, was following Jesus.
When they seized him, 52he fled naked,
leaving his garment behind.

Before the Sanhedrin

14:53–65pp — Mt 26:57–68; Jn 18:12,13,19–24
14:61–63pp — Lk 22:67–71

53They took Jesus to the high priest,
and all the chief priests, elders and teachers of the law came together. 54Peter followed him at a distance, right into the
courtyard of the high priest.[l] There he
sat with the guards and warmed himself
at the fire.[m]
55The chief priests and the whole Sanhedrin[n] were looking for evidence
against Jesus so that they could put him to
death, but they did not find any. 56Many
testified falsely against him, but their
statements did not agree.
57Then some stood up and gave this
false testimony against him: 58"We heard
him say, 'I will destroy this man-made
temple and in three days will build another,[o] not made by man.' " 59Yet even then
their testimony did not agree.
60Then the high priest stood up before
them and asked Jesus, "Are you not going
to answer? What is this testimony that
these men are bringing against you?"
61But Jesus remained silent and gave no
answer.[p]
Again the high priest asked him, "Are
you the Christ,[r] the Son of the Blessed
One?"[q]
62"I am," said Jesus. "And you will see
the Son of Man sitting at the right hand of
the Mighty One and coming on the
clouds of heaven."[r]
63The high priest tore his clothes.[s]
"Why do we need any more witnesses?"
he asked. 64"You have heard the blasphemy. What do you think?"
They all condemned him as worthy of
death.[t] 65Then some began to spit at

14:36 [a]Ro 8:15; Gal 4:6 [b]S Mt 20:22 [c]S Mt 26:39
14:38 [d]Mt 6:13 [e]Ro 7:22,23
14:41 [f]ver 35; S Mt 26:18
14:43 [g]S Mt 10:4
14:45 [h]S Mt 23:7
14:49 [i]S Mt 26:55 [j]Isa 53:7-12; S Mt 1:22
14:50 [k]ver 27
14:54 [l]S Mt 26:3 [m]Jn 18:18
14:55 [n]S Mt 5:22
14:58 [o]S Jn 2:19
14:61 [p]Isa 53:7; Mt 27:12,14; Mk 15:5; Lk 23:9; Jn 19:9 [q]Mt 16:16; Jn 4:25,26
14:62 [r]S Rev 1:7
14:63 [s]Lev 10:6; 21:10; Nu 14:6; Ac 14:14
14:64 [t]Lev 24:16

[r]61 Or *Messiah*

14:36 REVELATION, God's Nature—The Son agonized with the Father, struggling from His human side to avoid the maximum price if possible. Yet the fully obedient Lord was prepared to give Himself totally, for He came to fulfill the revealed will of the Father.

14:36 DISCIPLESHIP, Kingdom of God—Jesus' commitment to the will of the Father is to the basic characteristic of the kingdom of God. Such commitment makes the sovereign rule of God a reality in the lives of His people. See note on Mt 6:33.

14:37–38 PRAYER, Petition—See note on Mt 26:40–41.

14:43–52 JESUS CHRIST, Death—See note on Mt 26:47–56. Mark added the account of the disciple who fled naked. His identity is not known, although tradition suggests it was Mark himself.

14:48–49 CHRISTIAN ETHICS, War and Peace—See note on Mt 26:51–53.

14:53—15:15 JESUS CHRIST, Death—See note on Mt 26:57—27:26. Mark identified Barabbas as an insurrectionist. It is the supreme irony that Barabbas means "son of the father." The guilty son went free while the innocent, true Son died in his place. Jesus admitted He was the Messiah, God's Son. He used Greek (*egō eimi*, "I Am"), recalling God's personal name (Ex 3:14) and indicating Christ's divine identity. He shares God's function as final judge. See note on 10:45. The title of Christ or Messiah had political overtones, having been adopted from Israel's kings. Jesus and the early church were eager to disassociate themselves from the political understanding to stress the call to a distinctive relationship with and mission of suffering for God. See note on Gal 1:1.

14:62 LAST THINGS, Return Promises—Jesus' forthright acknowledgment that He was the Messiah brought forth the added assurance that a time would come when He would be seen as such. He promised He would occupy the place and privilege of deity and then return on the clouds of heaven (13:26). Usually, Jesus' promises to return were voiced to His followers as encouragement in hard times and as incentives to faithfulness. Here, spoken in the midst of unbelievers to one who opposed Him, the promise suggests a coming in which He would exercise the power of deity in judgment.

him; they blindfolded him, struck him
with their fists, and said, "Prophesy!"
And the guards took him and beat him.[u]

Peter Disowns Jesus

14:66–72pp — Mt 26:69–75; Lk 22:56–62;
Jn 18:16–18,25–27

66While Peter was below in the courtyard,[v] one of the servant girls of the high
priest came by. 67When she saw Peter
warming himself,[w] she looked closely at
him.

"You also were with that Nazarene,
Jesus,"[x] she said.

68But he denied it. "I don't know or
understand what you're talking about,"[y]
he said, and went out into the entryway.[s]

69When the servant girl saw him there,
she said again to those standing around,
"This fellow is one of them." 70Again he
denied it.[z]

After a little while, those standing near
said to Peter, "Surely you are one of
them, for you are a Galilean."[a]

71He began to call down curses on himself, and he swore to them, "I don't know
this man you're talking about."[b]

72Immediately the rooster crowed the
second time.[t] Then Peter remembered
the word Jesus had spoken to him: "Before the rooster crows twice[u] you will
disown me three times."[c] And he broke
down and wept.

Chapter 15

Jesus Before Pilate

15:2–15pp — Mt 27:11–26; Lk 23:2,3,18–25;
Jn 18:29–19:16

VERY early in the morning, the chief
priests, with the elders, the teachers
of the law[d] and the whole Sanhedrin,[e]
reached a decision. They bound Jesus, led
him away and handed him over to Pilate.[f]

2"Are you the king of the Jews?"[g]
asked Pilate.

"Yes, it is as you say," Jesus replied.

3The chief priests accused him of many
things. 4So again Pilate asked him,
"Aren't you going to answer? See how
many things they are accusing you of."

5But Jesus still made no reply,[h] and Pilate was amazed.

6Now it was the custom at the Feast to
release a prisoner whom the people requested. 7A man called Barabbas was in
prison with the insurrectionists who had
committed murder in the uprising. 8The
crowd came up and asked Pilate to do for
them what he usually did.

9"Do you want me to release to you the
king of the Jews?"[i] asked Pilate, 10know-
ing it was out of envy that the chief
priests had handed Jesus over to him.
11But the chief priests stirred up the
crowd to have Pilate release Barabbas[j]
instead.

12"What shall I do, then, with the one
you call the king of the Jews?" Pilate
asked them.

13"Crucify him!" they shouted.

14"Why? What crime has he committed?" asked Pilate.

But they shouted all the louder, "Crucify him!"

15Wanting to satisfy the crowd, Pilate
released Barabbas to them. He had Jesus
flogged,[k] and handed him over to be crucified.

The Soldiers Mock Jesus

15:16–20pp — Mt 27:27–31

16The soldiers led Jesus away into the
palace[l] (that is, the Praetorium) and
called together the whole company of soldiers. 17They put a purple robe on him,
then twisted together a crown of thorns
and set it on him. 18And they began to
call out to him, "Hail, king of the Jews!"[m]
19Again and again they struck him on the
head with a staff and spit on him. Falling
on their knees, they paid homage to him.
20And when they had mocked him, they
took off the purple robe and put his own
clothes on him. Then they led him out[n]
to crucify him.

The Crucifixion

15:22–32pp — Mt 27:33–44; Lk 23:33–43; Jn 19:17–24

21A certain man from Cyrene,[o] Simon,
the father of Alexander and Rufus,[p] was
passing by on his way in from the country, and they forced him to carry the
cross.[q] 22They brought Jesus to the place
called Golgotha (which means The Place
of the Skull). 23Then they offered him
wine mixed with myrrh,[r] but he did not
take it. 24And they crucified him. Dividing up his clothes, they cast lots[s] to see
what each would get.

[s] 68 Some early manuscripts *entryway and the rooster crowed* [t] 72 Some early manuscripts do not have *the second time.* [u] 72 Some early manuscripts do not have *twice.*

14:65 [u]S Mt 16:21
14:66 [v]ver 54
14:67 [w]ver 54 [x]S Mk 1:24
14:68 [y]ver 30,72
14:70 [z]ver 30,68, 72 [a]Ac 2:7
14:71 [b]ver 30,72
14:72 [c]ver 30,68
15:1 [d]Mt 27:1; Lk 22:66 [e]S Mt 5:22 [f]S Mt 27:2
15:2 [g]ver 9,12,18, 26; S Mt 2:2
15:5 [h]S Mk 14:61
15:9 [i]S ver 2
15:11 [j]Ac 3:14
15:15 [k]Isa 53:6
15:16 [l]Jn 18:28,33; 19:9
15:18 [m]S ver 2
15:20 [n]Heb 13:12
15:21 [o]S Mt 27:32 [p]Ro 16:13 [q]Mt 27:32; Lk 23:26
15:23 [r]ver 36; Ps 69:21; Pr 31:6
15:24 [s]Ps 22:18

14:66–72 SIN, Responsibility—See note on Mt 26:69–75.

15:12–19 JESUS CHRIST, King—See note on Mt 27:11. Jesus' opponents accepted their King only with mockery and injury. They encouraged the death of the Suffering Servant, who died for their sins and ours. They were not the last to mock and hurt the Christ. See note on Mt 27:26–30.

15:21–41 JESUS CHRIST, Death—See note on Mt 27:32–55. Compare Lk 23:26–56; Jn 19:17–37. Even as His life and works fulfilled Old Testament expectations, so also Jesus' death was described in terms of prophetic fulfillment.

25 It was the third hour when they crucified him. 26 The written notice of the
charge against him read: THE KING OF THE
JEWS.[t] 27 They crucified two robbers with
him, one on his right and one on his
left.[v] 29 Those who passed by hurled insults at him, shaking their heads[u] and
saying, "So! You who are going to destroy
the temple and build it in three days,[v]
30 come down from the cross and save
yourself!"
31 In the same way the chief priests and
the teachers of the law mocked him[w]
among themselves. "He saved others,"
they said, "but he can't save himself!
32 Let this Christ,[w][x] this King of Israel,[y]
come down now from the cross, that we
may see and believe." Those crucified
with him also heaped insults on him.

The Death of Jesus

15:33–41pp — Mt 27:45–56; Lk 23:44–49

33 At the sixth hour darkness came over
the whole land until the ninth hour.[z]
34 And at the ninth hour Jesus cried out in
a loud voice, *"Eloi, Eloi, lama sabachtha-
ni?"*—which means, "My God, my God,
why have you forsaken me?"[x][a]
35 When some of those standing near
heard this, they said, "Listen, he's calling
Elijah."
36 One man ran, filled a sponge with
wine vinegar,[b] put it on a stick, and offered it to Jesus to drink. "Now leave him
alone. Let's see if Elijah comes to take
him down," he said.
37 With a loud cry, Jesus breathed his
last.[c]
38 The curtain of the temple was torn in
two from top to bottom.[d] 39 And when
the centurion,[e] who stood there in front
of Jesus, heard his cry and[y] saw how he
died, he said, "Surely this man was the
Son[z] of God!"[f]
40 Some women were watching from a
distance.[g] Among them were Mary Magdalene, Mary the mother of James the
younger and of Joses, and Salome.[h] 41 In
Galilee these women had followed him
and cared for his needs. Many other
women who had come up with him to
Jerusalem were also there.[i]

The Burial of Jesus

15:42–47pp — Mt 27:57–61; Lk 23:50–56; Jn 19:38–42

42 It was Preparation Day (that is, the
day before the Sabbath).[j] So as evening
approached, 43 Joseph of Arimathea, a
prominent member of the Council,[k] who
was himself waiting for the kingdom of
God,[l] went boldly to Pilate and asked for
Jesus' body. 44 Pilate was surprised to hear
that he was already dead. Summoning the
centurion, he asked him if Jesus had already died. 45 When he learned from the
centurion[m] that it was so, he gave the
body to Joseph. 46 So Joseph bought some
linen cloth, took down the body, wrapped
it in the linen, and placed it in a tomb cut
out of rock. Then he rolled a stone against
the entrance of the tomb.[n] 47 Mary Magdalene and Mary the mother of Joses[o]
saw where he was laid.

Chapter 16

The Resurrection

16:1–8pp — Mt 28:1–8; Lk 24:1–10

WHEN the Sabbath was over, Mary
Magdalene, Mary the mother of
James, and Salome bought spices[p] so that
they might go to anoint Jesus' body. 2 Very
early on the first day of the week, just
after sunrise, they were on their way to
the tomb 3 and they asked each other,
"Who will roll the stone away from the
entrance of the tomb?"[q]
4 But when they looked up, they saw
that the stone, which was very large, had
been rolled away. 5 As they entered the
tomb, they saw a young man dressed in a
white robe[r] sitting on the right side, and
they were alarmed.
6 "Don't be alarmed," he said. "You are

15:26 [t]S ver 2
15:29 [u]Ps 22:7; 109:25 [v]S Jn 2:19
15:31 [w]Ps 22:7
15:32 [x]S Mk 14:61 [y]S ver 2
15:33 [z]Am 8:9
15:34 [a]Ps 22:1
15:36 [b]ver 23; Ps 69:21
15:37 [c]Jn 19:30
15:38 [d]Heb 10:19, 20
15:39 [e]ver 45 [f]Mk 1:1,11; 9:7; S Mt 4:3
15:40 [g]Ps 38:11 [h]Mk 16:1; Lk 24:10; Jn 19:25
15:41 [i]Mt 27:55, 56; Lk 8:2,3
15:42 [j]Mt 27:62; Jn 19:31
15:43 [k]S Mt 5:22 [l]S Mt 3:2; Lk 2:25, 38
15:45 [m]ver 39
15:46 [n]Mk 16:3
15:47 [o]ver 40
16:1 [p]Lk 23:56; Jn 19:39,40
16:3 [q]Mk 15:46
16:5 [r]S Jn 20:12

[v]27 Some manuscripts *left,* [28]*and the scripture was fulfilled which says, "He was counted with the lawless ones"* (Isaiah 53:12) [w]32 Or *Messiah* [x]34 Psalm 22:1 [y]39 Some manuscripts do not have *heard his cry and.* [z]39 Or *a son*

15:32 MIRACLE, Faith—Unprecedented miracles do not create faith, for faith is a personal relationship of trust in a personal God. Faith is not reluctant intellectual assent prompted by an overwhelming display of power. At the beginning of His ministry Jesus had resisted the temptation (Mt 4:7) to perform a sign which might attract the multitudes to a spurious faith. Consistent with that earlier decision, He refused to appeal to a shallow faith. He followed God's plan of atoning death and resurrection, not human plans of magical displays of power. The church must follow Christ's humble servant approach to provoke faith, not the world's call for dazzling entertainment.

15:34 PRAYER, Petition—See note on Mt 27:46.

15:37–39 HISTORY, Salvation—The death of an Individual at a specific moment in history at the hands of a human government is the central event of salvation. This is true because the Individual was the Son of God. The crucifixion shows how seriously God takes history as His arena of action rather than limiting Himself to an isolated heavenly world of divine beings.

15:42–47 JESUS CHRIST, Death—A respected Jewish leader witnessed that Jesus died like all humans. The Roman governor sealed the tomb, so the body could not have been stolen (Mt 28:13). The death of Jesus was real. Neither it nor the resurrection can be called a hoax.

16:1–8 JESUS CHRIST, Resurrection—If we follow the earliest manuscripts of Mark, the bewildering news of resurrection ends the Gospel. Hearing of resurrection even from heavenly messengers was not enough to bring faith. The personal appearances of the resurrected Christ produced faith. Compare Jn 20:24–29. See note on Mt 28:1–20.

16:5–7 HUMANITY, Death—See note on Mt 28:5–7.

looking for Jesus the Nazarene,[s] who
was crucified. He has risen! He is not
here. See the place where they laid him.
7But go, tell his disciples and Peter, 'He is
going ahead of you into Galilee. There
you will see him,[t] just as he told
you.' "[u]
8Trembling and bewildered, the wom-
en went out and fled from the tomb. They
said nothing to anyone, because they
were afraid.

[The earliest manuscripts and some other ancient witnesses do not have Mark 16:9-20]

9When Jesus rose early on the first day
of the week, he appeared first to Mary
Magdalene,[v] out of whom he had driven
seven demons. 10She went and told those
who had been with him and who were
mourning and weeping. 11When they
heard that Jesus was alive and that she
had seen him, they did not believe it.[w]
12Afterward Jesus appeared in a different form to two of them while they were
walking in the country.[x] 13These returned and reported it to the rest; but
they did not believe them either.
14Later Jesus appeared to the Eleven as
they were eating; he rebuked them for
their lack of faith and their stubborn refusal to believe those who had seen him
after he had risen.[y]
15He said to them, "Go into all the
world and preach the good news to all
creation.[z] 16Whoever believes and is
baptized will be saved, but whoever does
not believe will be condemned.[a] 17And
these signs[b] will accompany those who
believe: In my name they will drive out
demons;[c] they will speak in new
tongues;[d] 18they will pick up snakes[e]
with their hands; and when they drink
deadly poison, it will not hurt them at all;
they will place their hands on[f] sick people, and they will get well."
19After the Lord Jesus had spoken to
them, he was taken up into heaven[g] and
he sat at the right hand of God.[h] 20Then
the disciples went out and preached everywhere, and the Lord worked with
them and confirmed his word by the
signs[i] that accompanied it.

16:6 [s]S Mk 1:24
16:7 [t]Jn 21:1-23 [u]Mk 14:28
16:9 [v]Mk 15:47; Jn 20:11-18
16:11 [w]ver 13,14; Lk 24:11
16:12 [x]Lk 24:13-32
16:14 [y]Lk 24:36-43
16:15 [z]Mt 28:18-20; Lk 24:47,48; Ac 1:8
16:16 [a]Jn 3:16,18, 36; Ac 16:31
16:17 [b]S Jn 4:48 [c]Mk 9:38; Lk 10:17; Ac 5:16; 8:7; 16:18; 19:13-16 [d]Ac 2:4; 10:46; 19:6; 1Co 12:10,28,30; 13:1; 14:2-39
16:18 [e]Lk 10:19; Ac 28:3-5 [f]S Ac 6:6
16:19 [g]Lk 24:50, 51; Jn 6:62; Ac 1:9-11; 1Ti 3:16 [h]Ps 110:1; Mt 26:64; Ac 2:33; 5:31; Ro 8:34; Col 3:1; Heb 1:3; 12:2
16:20 [i]S Jn 4:48

16:9–20 HOLY SCRIPTURE, Collection—Through the generations dedicated people copied God's inspired Word and produced hundreds of manuscripts of the Bible. With their human freedom and limits, these people copied the text with amazing accuracy. Occasionally, a few differences crept into the text. Mk 16:9–20 is one significant addition present in the manuscript used for King James Version but not in the earliest and most reliable manuscripts. Some manuscripts add a brief missionary commission after v 8. Some manuscripts with vv 9–20 also contain an extensive addition to v 14. Obviously, from the third century on readers thought v 8 was not a satisfactory ending to Mark, particularly because it ended abruptly with a Greek conjunction. The original ending of Mark remains uncertain. Some have thought Mark was prevented from finishing the Gospel. Others accept v 8 as the original ending. Others think the original scroll was damaged or torn. This difference in thought indicates 16:9–20 should not be used as the sole basis of doctrine. The foundation of doctrine is well established from biblical texts that appear in the earliest manuscripts. Compare Jn 7:53—8:11. Conclusions about the doctrine of revelation or Scripture should be based on the clear teachings which appear throughout the Bible. Scripture texts whose proper interpretation is difficult to establish should not form the foundation of doctrine.

Luke

Theological Setting

The world into which Jesus came had numerous forces and powers "harking their wares" to people who were hungry, ill, despondent, blind, lame, enslaved, freed—to identify only a few of the existing conditions. Luke wrote a Gospel to a Christian community whose own beliefs were not unified. What place did Gentiles, outcasts, and women have in the church? What role did the Holy Spirit play? What missionary challenge had Jesus in relationship to Judaism and in relationship to the Roman Empire? What was the kingdom of God? Luke wanted his readers to understand the full significance and implications of Christ's gospel. Dated AD 60-70, Luke's Gospel coexisted with numerous rivals of diverse theological, cultural, and political ideals.

1. Jews and Gentiles alike could have depended upon the Roman government and its power. Rome did many things to benefit her people and offered itself as a god to the people of the first century.

2. They could have worshiped the emperor as the spirit of Rome. What more could a worshiper desire? Freedom of travel, well-maintained roadways, unquestioned peace and protection, emperors who could even claim they fed the slaves and the poor—were these not adequate provisions for anyone? The worship of the emperor was an attempt to embody and personify this spirit, thus meeting the innate need of the human soul to worship and at the same time unifying the empire.

3. The people of Luke's day could have been lured simply to enjoy the contemporary culture and refinement. Greek art, philosophy, literature, and a most expressive language followed the victorious Grecian armies. Cultures were melted and poured into the molds created by Hellenism, the type of life produced by the Greco-Roman world. The Sophists, for example, believed truth to be a matter of individual opinion. Stoics later believed that happiness came by living according to reason. All else was unimportant. To the Epicureans, pleasure brought happiness, while the Skeptic concluded that nothing at all mattered.

4. The readers of this Gospel also faced the influence of the mystery religions. The uniqueness, secrecy, and personal appeal of frenzied rites, lacking stringent personal moral demand, offered great appeal and temptation to many of Luke's readers.

5. Luke's contemporaries also faced the enticement of Judaism. Judaism held forth a much higher moral standard than the other religions of the day. Moreover, Judaism's standards could be checked very simply. One either kept the Jewish law with its scribal interpretations or broke it. Judaism could call on its long tradition as the faith of the fathers.

6. Complete devotion to Christ and service to the world was the Christian option.

Theological Outline

Luke: Christ Is the Savior for All People

I. The Purpose of Luke's Gospel Is to Provide Certainty in Christian Teaching. (1:1-4)

II. Jesus Fulfilled the Expectations of Judaism. (1:5—2:52)

- A. The Spirit-filled forerunner brought many Israelites back to God. (1:5-25).
- B. Virgin-born Jesus is the Son of God who fulfills the promises to David. (1:26-38)
- C. The humble birth of Jesus fulfilled God's promises to the patriarchs. (1:39-56)
- D. The awe-inspiring birth of John showed God fulfills His plan of redemption. (1:57-80)
- E. Jesus' birth in Bethlehem fulfilled messianic expectations. (2:1-7)
- F. God Himself verified Jesus' birth as the messianic fulfillment. (2:8-20)
- G. Jesus fulfilled all Jewish legal requirements. (2:21-24)
- H. Jesus' coming fulfilled God's promises to the devout Jews of His day and provided the salvation promised all people. (2:25-40)
- I. Jesus revealed divine wisdom among Israel's teachers. (2:41-52)

III. Jesus Accepted the Prophets' Messianic Mission But Was Rejected by His Own People. (3:1—4:44)

- A. The prophesied forerunner called for a repentant Israel to look for the coming Messiah. (3:1-20)

B. The Father and the Spirit acknowledged Jesus, the Son of God, at His baptism. (3:21-22)
C. His lineage linked Jesus with David and with the whole created race. (3:23-38)
D. The Son of God overcame Satan and his temptations to follow worldly methods. (4:1-13)
E. Jesus accepted the Spirit's mission, but His own people would not accept Him. (4:14-30)
F. Jesus revealed messianic power and authority in His teaching and healing. (4:31-37)
G. Jesus followed God's agenda to establish His Kingdom. (4:38-44)

IV. Jesus Fulfilled His Mission in God's Way of Faith, Love, and Forgiveness. (5:1—7:50)
A. Jesus shared His mission with persons showing faith. (5:1-16)
B. Jesus proved His divine power to forgive to the religious leaders. (5:17-26)
C. Jesus' mission called acknowledged sinners into the joy of a new age. (5:27-39)
D. Jesus' mission centered on human need, not human regulations. (6:1-11)
E. Jesus' mission called a new Israel to a life of loving action rather than condemning self-righteousness. (6:12-49)
F. Jesus' mission was to persons of faith, whatever their cultural or national identity. (7:1-10)
G. Jesus' mission gained acceptance among the needy multitude. (7:11-17)
H. Jesus' mission mirrored the Spirit's prophetic mission He had announced. (7:18-23)
I. Jesus' mission inaugurated God's kingdom in God's way. (7:24-30)
J. Jesus' divine mission of forgiveness involves those with love. (7:31-50)

V. Jesus' Kingdom Involves Awesome Power But Demands Commitment to Death. (8:1—9:50)
A. God's kingdom gains support from the socially deprived. (8:1-3)
B. God's kingdom seeks persons who will learn and follow the Messiah's teachings. (8:4-21)
C. The Master of the Kingdom controls all threatening forces. (8:22-25)
D. The Master of the Kingdom frees persons from demonic forces and invites them to witness to His mission. (8:26-39)
E. The Master of the Kingdom exercises power over incurable sickness and death. (8:40-56)
F. The Master of the Kingdom empowers His followers to carry out His mission. (9:1-6)
G. Jesus' kingdom power was obvious to the king. (9:7-9)
H. Jesus' kingdom power satisfies human needs. (9:10-17)
I. The Kingdom involves both King and followers in self-sacrificing suffering before the Kingdom is manifest. (9:18-27)
J. Judaism's supreme heroes affirmed Jesus' kingdom authority. (9:28-36)
K. Kingdom power comes from sacrificial commitment to the Kingdom's mission. (9:37-45)
L. Kingdom greatness depends on faith and commitment, not on position. (9:46-50)

VI. Faithful Ministry and Witness Characterize the Growing Kingdom. (9:51—13:21)
A. Jesus' mission had to climax in Jerusalem and could not be deterred. (9:51-56)
B. Kingdom service takes priority over all obligations. (9:57-62)
C. The Kingdom calls for courageous witness in view of approaching judgment. (10:1-16)
D. Joy in participation, not pride in authority, is the goal of the kingdom. (10:17-20)
E. Jesus' revelation of the Father is the event the prophets looked for. (10:21-24)
F. Loving ministry to others, not religious position, marks Kingdom leadership. (10:25-37)
G. Learning the Master's teaching takes precedence over all worldly concerns. (10:38-42)
H. Kingdom members pray for the Kingdom to come, for daily bread, and for forgiveness, assured the heavenly Father will answer with the Holy Spirit. (11:1-13)
I. Jesus' authority over demonic powers shows the Kingdom blessing is near. (11:14-28)
J. As Son of Man, Jesus is the only sign of the Kingdom and brings unprecedented judgment on unbelievers. (11:29-32)
K. The Kingdom brings true light to those who see. (11:33-36)
L. Kingdom members help the needy rather than burdening the pious. (11:37-54)
M. Kingdom members witness openly to the Son of Man, trusting the Holy Spirit rather than fearing persecution. (12:1-12)
N. Kingdom members seek the Kingdom rather than material riches. (12:13-34)
O. Kingdom members serve faithfully, ready for the Master's return. (12:35-48)
P. Jesus' followers must expect opposition and division. (12:49-53)
Q. Now is the time to settle things with the eternal Judge through repentance. (12:54—13:9)
R. The Kingdom frees people from human regulations and satanic domination. (13:10-17)
S. The Kingdom grows in a steady way with surprising results. (13:18-21)

VII. The Kingdom Has Surprising Entrance Requirements. (13:22—19:27)
A. Kingdom entrance is not governed by human admission standards. (13:22-30)

B. King Jesus, not human rulers, ruled His destiny. (13:31-35)
C. Concern for people, not for human reputation, governs conduct in the Kingdom. (14:1-14)
D. Acceptance of Christ's invitation is the only requirement for membership. (14:15-24)
E. Kingdom membership requires total allegiance to His demands. (14:25-35)
F. Repentant sinners find joyful reception in the Kingdom. (15:1-32)
G. Earthly treasures may serve Kingdom purposes but must not be one's master. (16:1-13)
H. The kingdom fulfills the Old Testament but sets higher standards than Judaism. (16:14-31)
I. Kingdom membership involves responsible forgiveness and faithful service. (17:1-10)
J. Faith is the only entrance requirement into the Kingdom. (17:11-19)
K. Kingdom members prepare for the sudden return of the Son of Man. (17:20-37)
L. Kingdom members pray persistently with faith in God's justice. (18:1-8)
M. The Kingdom involves trusting humility, not confident self-righteousness. (18:9-17)
N. Obedient faith, not abundant wealth, qualifies a person for the Kingdom. (18:18-30)
O. Discipleship involves blind allegiance to the Suffering Servant. (18:31-43)
P. Recognition of being lost is the first requirement for Kingdom entrance. (19:1-10)
Q. Kingdom membership involves loyal service and patient waiting for reward. (19:11-27)

VIII. Jesus Exercised Proper Kingdom Authority Which Roused Opposition. (19:28—22:6)
A. The elect people rejected their promised King when He appeared to them. (19:28-44)
B. Jesus exercised authority over God's house. (19:45—20:19)
C. Jesus exercised God's authority, not that of human politics. (20:20-26)
D. Jesus showed theological understanding greater than that of the Sadducees. (20:27-40)
E. Messiah's role is greater than the political role of David. (20:41-44)
F. False religious leaders face severe judgment. (20:45-47)
G. Generosity, not total amount, determines the value of Kingdom stewardship. (21:1-4)
H. The Son of Man, not human authorities or secret religious teaching, controls the future, for which disciples must wait faithfully. (21:5-36)
I. Human betrayal, not popular demand or legal justice, led to Jesus' arrest. (21:37—22:6)

IX. Jesus Died as the True Passover Lamb. (22:7—23:56)
A. Jesus' Passover sacrifice opens the way to Kingdom service and Kingdom rule. (22:7-30)
B. Participation in Christ's Passover brings satanic and human opposition. (22:31-38)
C. Participation in Christ's Passover demands earnest prayer. (22:39-46)
D. Jesus' death did not result from political rebellion but from spiritual darkness. (22:47-53)
E. Refusal to participate in Christ's Passover death brings bitter sorrow. (22:54-62)
F. Religious blindness and pride, not legal justice, led to the Son of Man's crucifixion. (22:63-71)
G. Crowd pleasure, not legal indictments, led the government to sanction Christ's crucifixion. (23:1-25)
H. Christ's crucifixion began judgment for the corrupt religious system. (23:26-31)
I. Jesus responded to His opponents in forgiveness, not vengeance. (23:32-34)
J. Jesus died to bring sinners into His kingdom, not to save Himself. (23:35-43)
K. Jesus exercised sovereign control and faith even in His death. (23:44-46)
L. Jesus died unjustly as a righteous man. (23:47-49)
M. Jesus actually died as shown by His burial. (23:50-56)

X. Christ's Resurrection Is the Doorway to Faith and Mission. (24:1-53)
A. Jesus' resurrection fulfilled prophecy, affirmed His own teaching, and awakened faith in doubting disciples. (24:1-45)
B. Christ's resurrection prepared the way for the church's gospel of forgiveness. (24:46-48)
C. The church needed the Spirit before undertaking its mission. (24:49)
D. Christ's ascension leads the church to worship. (24:50-53)

Theological Conclusions

The Gospel of Luke affirms that Jesus is the Savior of all people and suggests several facts regarding His person and purpose:

1. He is a Servant.
2. He is the Redeemer fulfilling God's purpose.
3. He reveals that God's love is intended for all people.
4. He leads His followers to praise the Father in worship.
5. Jesus shows the central place of the home.
6. He prepares for and points to the importance and works of the Holy Spirit.

7. Jesus was a Man of prayer.
8. He brings joy to His followers.

Jesus is a Servant of divine purpose. The first recorded words of Jesus underscore this prominently (2:49). Jesus' responsibility in God's house was that which He was obligated to do. This indicates His commitment to God even as a twelve-year-old boy. This same sense of obligation to the Father's will is also seen in His commitment to the cross (9:22).

Jesus is the Redeemer. The account of Gabriel's appearance to Mary offers adequate evidence of Jesus' work as Redeemer. His name was to be called Jesus (1:31) meaning *the Lord saves.*

God's love is intended for all persons. Jesus was the fulfillment of God's promise to Abraham and his seed as emphasized in Luke 1:55. He was more. He came to earth to offer Himself as Savior of all people. Luke's genealogy of Jesus does not end at Abraham but continues back to Adam, the first human (3:23-38). Matthew revealed Jesus as the Messiah of the Old Testament. Luke was more interested in showing Jesus to be the Redeemer of the whole world. Therefore, Luke frequently stressed that the Kingdom is available to Samaritans (9:51-56), pagans (2:32; 3:6,38), Jews (1:33), publicans, sinners, and people of ill repute (3:12; 5:27-32; 19:2-10), and people automatically respected because of their identities and positions in life (7:36; 14:1).

Jesus also revealed God's concern for women. The record of the angel's visit to Mary suggests the place of honor which God gave to the young Jewish maiden. Luke tells us of the experiences of Elizabeth, of Anna, of Jesus raising the son of the widow of Nain, and of the woman anointing Jesus' feet in the house of Simon the Pharisee. He further recorded in great vividness the accounts of Mary Magdalene, and Mary and Martha. Women first experienced the resurrection and reported it to the apostles (24:1-10).

Jesus leads His followers to praise the Father. The expression "praising God" occurs more frequently in this Gospel than in all the remainder of the New Testament books combined. The Gospel begins with an emphasis upon praise with Mary's hymn of praise known as the "Magnificat" (1:46-55), Zechariah's "Benedictus" (1:68-79), and the praise of Simeon (2:29-32).

Jesus shows the central place of the home. God's love and provision for humanity are exemplified by Jesus' experiences and the homes in which they occur. John often depicted Jesus in public ceremonies, but Luke more frequently revealed Jesus' activities within the homes. He was a guest in the home of Mary and Martha. Following the call of Levi, Jesus shared His love with a multitude of publicans whom Levi wished to introduce to Jesus. One of the closing accounts of Luke's record is the recalling of Jesus' breaking bread with the disciples of Emmaus. This emphasis is often overlooked but is of untold significance.

Jesus prepared for and pointed to the work of the Holy Spirit. The working and the significance of the Holy Spirit within an individual's life appears repeatedly in this Gospel. From the work of the Holy Spirit in Mary's conception (1:35) to Jesus' reference to "what my Father has promised" (24:49), numerous references to or implications concerning the Holy Spirit and His work are recorded. The Holy Spirit descended upon Jesus at the time of His baptism (3:22). Jesus was "full of the Holy Spirit" (4:1) and was led by the Spirit in the desert to be tempted (4:1*b*-2).

Jesus was a Man of prayer. Luke also revealed the emphasis Jesus placed upon prayer. On seven different occasions Luke is the only Gospel writer indicating that Jesus prayed.

Jesus brings joy to His followers. Luke's Gospel is characterized by joy. The three parables of Luke 15—The Parables of the Lost Sheep, Lost Coin, and Lost Son—reflect the joy that issues from God's deep love for humankind. This love, was reflected for all people. He was concerned about the needs of Jews and Samaritans, the poor and the rich, the "self-righteous" and the lost, the "successful" and the broken individuals. Jesus offers the joy of salvation to every person.

Contemporary Teaching

Described by many as the most beautiful account of the life of Jesus, the Gospel of Luke reminds us of many needed spiritual truths. Luke challenges us: (1) to remember some basic facts of the Christian gospel (1:1-4); (2) to realize he was not a gullible historian (1:3); (3) to remember that the first recorded words of Jesus were words of commitment and that He was a servant of God's purpose; (4) to recall the practical application and eternal nature of His miracles and teachings; (5) to view again the sin and hatred that took Jesus to the cross; (6) to remember that He died for all people, not just for Jews; and (7) to experience again the power and fellowship of this resurrected Jesus and to enjoy the blessings which can be ours in praise, worship, service, and guidance of the Holy Spirit.

Chapter 1

Introduction

1:1–4Ref— Ac 1:1

MANY have undertaken to draw up an
account of the things that have
been fulfilled[a] among us, 2just as they
were handed down to us by those who
from the first[a] were eyewitnesses[b] and
servants of the word.[c] 3Therefore, since I
myself have carefully investigated everything from the beginning, it seemed good
also to me to write an orderly account[d]
for you, most excellent[e] Theophilus,[f]
4so that you may know the certainty of
the things you have been taught.[g]

The Birth of John the Baptist Foretold

5In the time of Herod king of Judea[h]
there was a priest named Zechariah, who
belonged to the priestly division of Abijah;[i] his wife Elizabeth was also a descendant of Aaron. 6Both of them were
upright in the sight of God, observing all
the Lord's commandments and regulations blamelessly.[j] 7But they had no children, because Elizabeth was barren; and
they were both well along in years.
8Once when Zechariah's division was
on duty and he was serving as priest before God,[k] 9he was chosen by lot,[l] according to the custom of the priesthood,
to go into the temple of the Lord and
burn incense.[m] 10And when the time for
the burning of incense came, all the assembled worshipers were praying outside.[n]
11Then an angel[o] of the Lord appeared
to him, standing at the right side of the
altar of incense.[p] 12When Zechariah saw
him, he was startled and was gripped
with fear.[q] 13But the angel said to him:
"Do not be afraid,[r] Zechariah; your
prayer has been heard. Your wife Elizabeth will bear you a son, and you are to
give him the name John.[s] 14He will be a
joy and delight to you, and many will rejoice because of his birth,[t] 15for he will
be great in the sight of the Lord. He is
never to take wine or other fermented
drink,[u] and he will be filled with the
Holy Spirit[v] even from birth.[b][w] 16Many
of the people of Israel will he bring back
to the Lord their God. 17And he will go on
before the Lord,[x] in the spirit and power
of Elijah,[y] to turn the hearts of the fathers to their children[z] and the disobedient to the wisdom of the righteous—to
make ready a people prepared for the
Lord."[a]
18Zechariah asked the angel, "How can
I be sure of this?[b] I am an old man and
my wife is well along in years."[c]
19The angel answered, "I am Gabriel.[d]
I stand in the presence of God, and I have
been sent to speak to you and to tell you
this good news. 20And now you will be
silent and not able to speak[e] until the day
this happens, because you did not believe
my words, which will come true at their
proper time."
21Meanwhile, the people were waiting
for Zechariah and wondering why he
stayed so long in the temple. 22When he
came out, he could not speak to them.
They realized he had seen a vision in the
temple, for he kept making signs[f] to
them but remained unable to speak.

[a]*1* Or *been surely believed* [b]*15* Or *from his mother's womb*

1:2 [a]Mk 1:1; Jn 15:27; Ac 1:21,22 [b]Heb 2:3; 1Pe 5:1; 2Pe 1:16; 1Jn 1:1 [c]S Mk 4:14
1:3 [d]Ac 11:4 [e]Ac 24:3; 26:25 [f]Ac 1:1
1:4 [g]Jn 20:31; Ac 2:42
1:5 [h]Mt 2:1 [i]1Ch 24:10
1:6 [j]Ge 6:9; Dt 5:33; 1Ki 9:4; Lk 2:25
1:8 [k]1Ch 24:19; 2Ch 8:14
1:9 [l]Ac 1:26 [m]Ex 30:7,8; 1Ch 23:13; 2Ch 29:11; Ps 141:2
1:10 [n]Lev 16:17
1:11 [o]S Ac 5:19 [p]Ex 30:1-10
1:12 [q]Jdg 6:22,23; 13:22
1:13 [r]ver 30; S Mt 14:27 [s]ver 60, 63; S Mt 3:1
1:14 [t]ver 58
1:15 [u]Nu 6:3; Lev 10:9; Jdg 13:4; Lk 7:33 [v]ver 41,67; Ac 2:4; 4:8,31; 6:3, 5; 9:17; 11:24; Eph 5:18; S Ac 10:44 [w]Jer 1:5; Gal 1:15
1:17 [x]ver 76 [y]S Mt 11:14 [z]Mal 4:5,6 [a]S Mt 3:3
1:18 [b]Ge 15:8 [c]ver 34; Ge 17:17
1:19 [d]ver 26; Da 8:16; 9:21
1:20 [e]Ex 4:11; Eze 3:26
1:22 [f]ver 62

1:1–4 HUMANITY, Intellectual Nature—Scripture demands full use of our intellect. Luke provides the example for all believers who study the gospel. He went to the proper sources—eyewitnesses, servants of the Word. He used his own skills to investigate the tradition he was given. He placed all he knew into sensible order. Such personal study brings certainty. God's people are expected to use their full intellect to interpret the material He has inspired to be passed on.

1:1–4 HOLY SCRIPTURE, Eyewitnesses—Luke relied on several eyewitnesses and scribes for his record of the events of Jesus' life. Luke used their information to write an orderly record of Jesus' life. Jesus' teachings were collected orally and in writing before Luke wrote. One of Luke's sources—Mark—is also included in inspired Scripture. Other sources used by Luke have not been preserved. God's inspiration and revelation include the direction of Luke in selecting from his sources and also the preservation of Luke's Gospel.

1:5–23 JESUS CHRIST, Lord—John the Baptist fulfilled Isaiah's prophecy (40:3) that God's way would be prepared. For Isaiah, Lord meant God. The angel used Lord to refer to Christ's coming, thus identifying the Lord Jesus as divine. See note on Eph 1:3.

1:10 WORSHIP, Corporate—See note on Ps 42:1–4. Jewish worship had set times. Christian worship follows the same principle. The community needs set times for public worship.

1:10 PRAYER, Corporate—Although only the priest could enter the sanctuary to keep the incense burning, the entire congregation was praying outside when Zechariah's vision occurred. Prayer is every believer's responsibility, not just a preacher's.

1:11–20 REVELATION, Angels—One of God's messengers appeared to Zechariah, a priest performing his annual duty at the Temple. Confronted by angels, people often feel fear and panic. Angels bring reassurance before delivering God's message. See note on Da 10:18—11:1.

1:13 PRAYER, Answer—Their prayer evidently had been made while they were young and persistently repeated. This is an example of an answer to prayer deferred for God's timing.

1:15 CHRISTIAN ETHICS, Alcohol—See notes on Nu 6:3–4,20; Mt 11:18–19.

1:16–17 EVANGELISM, God's Provision—The coming of Christ was God's provision of salvation. That divine act included the coming of the forerunner of our Lord, John the Baptist. In the spirit of Elijah, John came to call people to repentance to prepare them for Jesus' coming. Thus in that sense he becomes something of the pattern of how we are to evangelize today.

1:20 EVIL AND SUFFERING, Punishment—Zechariah was punished for doubting God's plan for the conception of John the Baptist. Appropriately, his punishment made him unable to share his once-in-a-life experience of serving at God's incense altar and to share the experience he had had with God's messenger.

23When his time of service was completed, he returned home. 24After this his
wife Elizabeth became pregnant and for
five months remained in seclusion.
25"The Lord has done this for me," she
said. "In these days he has shown his favor and taken away my disgrace[g] among
the people."

The Birth of Jesus Foretold

26In the sixth month, God sent the angel Gabriel[h] to Nazareth,[i] a town in Galilee, 27to a virgin pledged to be married to
a man named Joseph,[j] a descendant of
David. The virgin's name was Mary.
28The angel went to her and said, "Greetings, you who are highly favored! The
Lord is with you."
29Mary was greatly troubled at his
words and wondered what kind of greeting this might be. 30But the angel said to
her, "Do not be afraid,[k] Mary, you have
found favor with God.[l] 31You will be
with child and give birth to a son, and
you are to give him the name Jesus.[m]
32He will be great and will be called the
Son of the Most High.[n] The Lord God
will give him the throne of his father David,[o] 33and he will reign over the house
of Jacob forever; his kingdom[p] will never
end."[q]
34"How will this be," Mary asked the
angel, "since I am a virgin?"
35The angel answered, "The Holy Spirit will come upon you,[r] and the power of
the Most High[s] will overshadow you. So
the holy one[t] to be born will be called[c]
the Son of God.[u] 36Even Elizabeth your
relative is going to have a child[v] in her
old age, and she who was said to be barren is in her sixth month. 37For nothing is
impossible with God."[w]
38"I am the Lord's servant," Mary answered. "May it be to me as you have
said." Then the angel left her.

Mary Visits Elizabeth

39At that time Mary got ready and hurried to a town in the hill country of Judea,[x] 40where she entered Zechariah's
home and greeted Elizabeth. 41When
Elizabeth heard Mary's greeting, the baby
leaped in her womb, and Elizabeth was
filled with the Holy Spirit.[y] 42In a loud
voice she exclaimed: "Blessed are you
among women,[z] and blessed is the child
you will bear! 43But why am I so favored,
that the mother of my Lord[a] should come

1:25 [g]Ge 30:23; Isa 4:1
1:26 [h]S ver 19 [i]S Mt 2:23
1:27 [j]Mt 1:16,18, 20; Lk 2:4
1:30 [k]ver 13; S Mt 14:27 [l]Ge 6:8
1:31 [m]Isa 7:14; Mt 1:21,25; Lk 2:21
1:32 [n]ver 35,76; S Mk 5:7 [o]S Mt 1:1
1:33 [p]Mt 28:18 [q]2Sa 7:16; Ps 89:3, 4; Isa 9:7; Jer 33:17; Da 2:44; 7:14,27; Mic 4:7; Heb 1:8
1:35 [r]Mt 1:18 [s]ver 32,76; S Mk 5:7 [t]S Mk 1:24 [u]S Mt 4:3
1:36 [v]ver 24
1:37 [w]S Mt 19:26
1:39 [x]ver 65
1:41 [y]S ver 15
1:42 [z]Jdg 5:24
1:43 [a]S Jn 13:13

[c]35 Or *So the child to be born will be called holy,*

1:24–25 FAMILY, Childbearing—See note on Ge 4:1–2 for the significance of childbearing to women.

1:25 HISTORY, Individual—God's saving acts bring new hope to individuals. He works mighty deeds in individual lives as well as in international political affairs.

1:26–38 JESUS CHRIST, Virgin Birth—Jesus' birth showed His unique nature as God and man, the divine living in human flesh accepting human limits. Mary—a woman—and the Holy Spirit—God—cooperated in the birth. The Bible does not tell us how the divine miracle happened. He was "Son of the Most High" but also a helpless human infant nestled in His mother's arms. Only God could make such a birth possible. See note on Mt 1:18.

1:26–29 REVELATION, Angels—See note on 1:11–20. Angels carried God's messages to specially chosen individuals. They did not simply repeat the message. They engaged in conversation with people.

1:30 GOD, Grace—Out of His grace God selected Mary to become the mother of Jesus. God's grace is unmerited favor. His grace operates without regard to our being worthy of His blessing. Virtually all of God's relationships to us are expressions of His grace, in one way or another. Grace, or love, is the very heart of God's existence. Luke emphasized the grace of God throughout this chapter. Notice especially vv 50,54,58, 72,78.

1:31–37 HUMANITY, Birth—Birth is a natural physical process. Natural processes do not seal off God's activity. He can interrupt natural processes or work through natural processes to achieve His will. God worked in a special way to allow the virgin Mary to conceive. He worked in a different, yet still miraculous, way to allow the aged, barren Elizabeth to conceive. He worked through natural processes to allow each to carry and bear her son.

1:32–33 JESUS CHRIST, King—Israel's long-expected King was born to an humble family in alien surroundings. No human ceremony crowned Him King except the mocking ceremony at His trial and crucifixion (Mk 15:16–20,26,32). God pronounced Him King at His birth and will reveal His royal splendor when He returns to rule the world.

1:32–33 LAST THINGS, Coming Kingdom—God fulfilled His promises to David (2 Sa 7) through His Son and David's descendant Jesus. God's eternal purpose was to establish His eternal kingdom with Jesus as King.

1:32–33 THE CHURCH, God's Kingdom—Jesus fulfilled the teaching of the Old Testament concerning the righteous reign of God. David ruled for a few years on a throne in Jerusalem. Jesus reigns forever in the hearts of His followers. He will come again to establish His kingdom fully and openly. See notes on Ps 103:19; Isa 9:7.

1:35 REVELATION, Divine Presence—Mary experienced God's presence in a manner never before revealed. Through the Spirit she became the mother of God's Son. The revelation was both frightening and bewildering, yet caused great celebration (vv 46–56).

1:37 MIRACLE, God's Working—This simple statement furnishes the backdrop for all the miracles of the New Testament. To Mary's surprise (v 34) the angel affirmed God's powers working in her life to accomplish His purpose. God still seeks to surprise us with His unlimited power. He can use you to do anything He wants when you echo Mary's submission (v 38).

1:38,74 SALVATION, Obedience—Mary obeyed the Lord and became the mother of the world's Savior.

1:38 THE CHURCH, Servants—Mary served God because she humbled herself in submission before God. She allowed God to have control of her life. She was willing to accept embarrassing questions and ridicule from people to accomplish God's purposes for her. See note on Da 9:11.

1:39–45 JESUS CHRIST, Birth—This passage is often called the Visitation, which refers to the visit of Mary to Elizabeth to share each other's joy. During this visit, the babe in Elizabeth's womb acknowledged the Messiah to be born of Mary.

1:42 SALVATION, Blessing—Elizabeth, filled with the Holy Spirit, pronounced the virgin Mary and her child blessed. Obeying God and letting Him accomplish His plans through us brings blessing.

to me? 44 As soon as the sound of your
greeting reached my ears, the baby in my
womb leaped for joy. 45 Blessed is she
who has believed that what the Lord has
said to her will be accomplished!"

Mary's Song

1:46–53pp — 1Sa 2:1–10

46 And Mary said:

"My soul glorifies the Lord[b]
47 and my spirit rejoices in God my
Savior,[c]
48 for he has been mindful
of the humble state of his servant.[d]
From now on all generations will call
me blessed,[e]
49 for the Mighty One has done great
things[f] for me—
holy is his name.[g]
50 His mercy extends to those who fear
him,
from generation to generation.[h]
51 He has performed mighty deeds with
his arm;[i]
he has scattered those who are
proud in their inmost
thoughts.[j]
52 He has brought down rulers from their
thrones
but has lifted up the humble.[k]
53 He has filled the hungry with good
things[l]
but has sent the rich away empty.
54 He has helped his servant Israel,
remembering to be merciful[m]
55 to Abraham and his descendants[n]
forever,

1:46 [b]Ps 34:2,3
1:47 [c]Ps 18:46; Isa 17:10; 61:10; Hab 3:18; 1Ti 1:1; 2:3; 4:10
1:48 [d]ver 38; Ps 138:6 [e]Lk 11:27
1:49 [f]Ps 71:19 [g]Ps 111:9
1:50 [h]Ex 20:6; Ps 103:17
1:51 [i]Ps 98:1; Isa 40:10 [j]Ge 11:8; Ex 18:11; 2Sa 22:28; Jer 13:9; 49:16
1:52 [k]S Mt 23:12
1:53 [l]Ps 107:9
1:54 [m]Ps 98:3
1:55 [n]S Gal 3:16
1:59 [o]Ge 17:12; Lev 12:3; Lk 2:21; Php 3:5
1:60 [p]ver 13,63; S Mt 3:1
1:62 [q]ver 22
1:63 [r]ver 13,60; S Mt 3:1
1:64 [s]ver 20; Eze 24:27
1:65 [t]ver 39
1:66 [u]Ge 39:2; Ac 11:21
1:67 [v]S ver 15 [w]Joel 2:28

even as he said to our fathers."

56 Mary stayed with Elizabeth for about
three months and then returned home.

The Birth of John the Baptist

57 When it was time for Elizabeth to
have her baby, she gave birth to a son.
58 Her neighbors and relatives heard that
the Lord had shown her great mercy, and
they shared her joy.

59 On the eighth day they came to circumcise[o] the child, and they were going
to name him after his father Zechariah,
60 but his mother spoke up and said, "No!
He is to be called John."[p]

61 They said to her, "There is no one
among your relatives who has that
name."

62 Then they made signs[q] to his father,
to find out what he would like to name
the child. 63 He asked for a writing tablet,
and to everyone's astonishment he
wrote, "His name is John."[r] 64 Immediately his mouth was opened and his
tongue was loosed, and he began to
speak,[s] praising God. 65 The neighbors
were all filled with awe, and throughout
the hill country of Judea[t] people were
talking about all these things. 66 Everyone
who heard this wondered about it, asking, "What then is this child going to
be?" For the Lord's hand was with him.[u]

Zechariah's Song

67 His father Zechariah was filled with
the Holy Spirit[v] and prophesied:[w]

1:46–55 PRAYER, Praise—This prayer recognized the right order of things. Compare Jn 17. Human praise comes to us only because God chooses to act through us. All praise belongs to God, our personal Savior, who faithfully and mercifully keeps His promises.

1:47 GOD, Savior—Mary praised God as her Savior. She recognized the redemptive nature of God Himself. He not only would send a Savior—Jesus, who would be born of her in the miracle of the virgin birth—but God Himself is Savior. She praised God for His faithfulness to His covenant with Abraham and Israel (vv 54,55,72). This Old Testament theme of the faithfulness of God to His covenant is carried over into the New Testament. God is basically seen as a God of redemptive love. He even named His Son, sent into our world to save lost sinners, Jesus, which means the Lord saves, or Yahweh saves (Mt 1:21). God as Savior is at the very heart of our understanding of God.

1:48 THE CHURCH, Servants—See note on 1:38.

1:50,65 SALVATION, Fear of God—Awe and reverence surround the birth of Jesus and His forerunner, John the Baptist. God extends His mercy to the truly pious. See note on Mt 9:8.

1:53 DISCIPLESHIP, Hungry—Mary spoke prophetically through her song of the blessings under the reign of her Son. The poor will be lifted up, and the hungry will be satisfied with good things. Jesus lived out this type of ministry. See note on 4:18–21. Christ's disciples follow His example in meeting the needs of the poor and hungry.

1:54–55 JESUS CHRIST, Fulfilled—In her "Magnificat," Mary praised God that through Jesus, Israel would be helped and the promises to Abraham (Ge 12:1–7) fulfilled. Jesus is the hope around which the Old Testament centered.

1:54–55 HISTORY, Promise—In Christ, God fulfilled the promises of salvation first given Abraham (Ge 12:1–7). Salvation in Christ thus stands in continuity with God's history of salvation rather than being radically new and different.

1:58 SALVATION, Joy—Joy is God's gift to all who have a part in the salvation Christ brings.

1:59 FAMILY, Accepting Covenant—The Abrahamic covenant (Ge 12:1–3; 17:1–8) demanded circumcision of males as the seal of the covenant (Ge 17:9–14). Naming the child in accord with family lineage was performed at the circumcision ceremony. Thus, the attendants were surprised when the son of Zechariah and Elizabeth was named John rather than a family name. Mary and Joseph fulfilled the same law of covenant in the circumcision of Jesus (Lk 2:21). In this act, the parents accepted covenantal requirements as well as obeying the special instructions of God's revelation to each family.

1:64 PRAYER, Praise—Zechariah's long period of being mute was broken by praise.

1:67–79 JESUS CHRIST, Redeemer—Zechariah's "Benedictus" focused on Jesus as the promised Redeemer as much as on his own son John, who prepared the way. Jesus represented the redemption (Greek *lutrōsis*) of Israel. He set Israel free. Zechariah pointed to political hope of rescue from enemies and spiritual release to serve God. Such salvation can come only through forgiveness of sins.

1:67 HOLY SPIRIT, Revelation—The phrase "filled with the Holy Spirit" is found in the New Testament only in the

68"Praise be to the Lord, the God of
Israel,[x]
because he has come and has
redeemed his people.[y]
69He has raised up a horn[d][z] of salvation
for us
in the house of his servant David[a]
70(as he said through his holy prophets
of long ago),[b]
71salvation from our enemies
and from the hand of all who hate
us—
72to show mercy to our fathers[c]
and to remember his holy
covenant,[d]
73 the oath he swore to our father
Abraham:[e]
74to rescue us from the hand of our
enemies,
and to enable us to serve him[f]
without fear[g]
75 in holiness and righteousness[h]
before him all our days.

76And you, my child, will be called a
prophet[i] of the Most High;[j]
for you will go on before the Lord to
prepare the way for him,[k]
77to give his people the knowledge of
salvation
through the forgiveness of their
sins,[l]
78because of the tender mercy of our
God,
by which the rising sun[m] will come
to us from heaven
79to shine on those living in darkness
and in the shadow of death,[n]
to guide our feet into the path of
peace."[o]

80And the child grew and became
strong in spirit;[p] and he lived in the
desert until he appeared publicly to Israel.

Chapter 2

The Birth of Jesus

IN those days Caesar Augustus[q] issued a
decree that a census should be taken
of the entire Roman world.[r] 2(This was
the first census that took place while Qui-
rinius was governor of Syria.)[s] 3And everyone went to his own town to register.
4So Joseph also went up from the town

[d]69 *Horn* here symbolizes strength.

1:68 [x]Ge 24:27; 1Ki 8:15; Ps 72:18 [y]Ps 111:9; Lk 7:16
1:69 [z]1Sa 2:1,10; 2Sa 22:3; Ps 18:2; 89:17; 132:17; Eze 29:21 [a]S Mt 1:1
1:70 [b]Jer 23:5; Ac 3:21; Ro 1:2
1:72 [c]Mic 7:20 [d]Ps 105:8,9; 106:45; Eze 16:60
1:73 [e]Ge 22:16-18
1:74 [f]Heb 9:14 [g]1Jn 4:18
1:75 [h]Eph 4:24
1:76 [i]S Mt 11:9 [j]ver 32,35; S Mk 5:7 [k]ver 17; S Mt 3:3
1:77 [l]Jer 31:34; Mt 1:21; Mk 1:4
1:78 [m]Mal 4:2
1:79 [n]Ps 107:14; Isa 9:2; 59:9; Mt 4:16; S Ac 26:18 [o]S Lk 2:14
1:80 [p]Lk 2:40,52
2:1 [q]Lk 3:1; Mt 22:17 [r]S Mt 24:14
2:2 [s]Mt 4:24; Ac 15:23,41; 21:3; Gal 1:21

writings of Luke (Luke and Acts) and in a single passage in Paul (Eph 5:18). It also appears in the Old Testament. See Ex 31:3; 35:31. The filling of the Spirit is associated with prophecy. A person was so full of the Spirit that the message overflowed and had to be proclaimed. See Ac 2:4; 4:8; notes on Ac 4:31; 6:1–6; 13:9. In Luke's Gospel three persons are said to have been filled with the Spirit: John the Baptist (1:15), his mother Elizabeth (1:41), and his father Zechariah (1:67). These fillings with the Spirit were clearly prophetic and should be paralleled to the Spirit's work with prophets throughout Israel's history. See note at Zec 7:12. One distinctly new factor was that their messages explicitly concerned Jesus. In the Christian age, the Spirit's work is always to point people to Jesus. See Jn 15:25–26; 16:5–15. The work of the Spirit through John and his parents was a sign of the new age, the age of Jesus Christ. Their ministry (and that of Simeon, see note on Lk 2:25–32) was a bridge between the Spirit's work under the old covenant (testament) and His work under the new covenant.

1:67 REVELATION, Inspiration—Zechariah, indwelt by the Spirit of God, testified in song to the mystery and miracle which occurred in his family. He related God's presence in his family affairs to His intervention to redeem Israel. Personal revelation became an instrument of salvation for the nation and beyond. Personal revelation was the first step in God's inspiring this part of Scripture through the Spirit. How Zechariah's song of joy was preserved, discovered by Luke, and incorporated into the Bible is a part of the miraculous mystery of inspiration.

1:67–75 THE CHURCH, Covenant People—The work of Jesus is consistent with the hope of believers before the coming of the Messiah. Jesus fulfilled what God had been doing through the centuries, creating a people for Himself. God's promises to the patriarchs were fulfilled in Christ. God's expectations of service, worship, holiness, and righteousness continue for New Testament Christians.

1:67–79 PRAYER, Praise—Zechariah's prayer is prophetic of the work of his son John and of the greater work of the Savior for whom John would prepare the way. At the same time, it is a hymn of praise in psalm form for the God of those works. Birth is an appropriate reason to praise God and to dedicate a child to God's purposes.

1:68–69 SALVATION, Redemption—See note on Ex 6:6. The coming of Christ brings redemption to God's people in the fullest and ultimate sense. "Horn" means strength or might. God brought about a mighty salvation through Jesus Christ. In so doing He fulfilled the promises made to David, though in a way unexpected by the Jews. God redeems His people in the way He knows is best, not in the ways we choose. Compare 2 Sa 7.

1:69 JESUS CHRIST, Son of David—See note on Mt 1:1.

1:77 SALVATION, Forgiveness—God expresses salvation in many ways in individual lives—deliverance, refuge, rest, hope, blessing. The basic expression of salvation brought through Jesus is forgiveness, the taking away of our load of guilt and giving us freedom to reach the potential God created in us.

1:78–79 SALVATION, Initiative—Zechariah, the father of John the Baptist, connected the coming of Jesus Christ with the prophecies of Isa 9:2; 11:1. Christ is the Light of the world who delivers His people from the darkness of sin and evil.

2:1–20 JESUS CHRIST, Birth—The cloth strips were used both for infants and for wrapping the bodies of the dead, a deeper symbol in the light of subsequent events. The Gloria of the angels (v 14) is Luke's third Christmas song. "Peace to men" is certainly the intent of God expressed in the birth of Jesus. God has shown His favor on those "on whom His favor rests," that is, those who were both available and willing to hear the word of God in the birth of Jesus Christ. The first witnesses to Christmas were working people who were not afraid to interrupt their usual schedule to participate in God's good news. Mary had much to ponder, much to treasure, and also much to suffer. If some have exaggerated the role of Mary, others have dismissed her great acts of faith and her essential part in the gospel of the Word of God. Our familiarity with Luke's Christmas story is often overladen with latter romantic ideas about Christmas. The reality of suffering and deprivation at His birth was as real as that at His death.

2:1 HISTORY, Linear—Jesus' birth came in the ongoing stream of history. God worked through unbelieving rulers and their political purposes to provide the unrepeatable gift of salvation in Christ.

2:4–7 HUMANITY, Birth—Caring parents prepare for the birth of a child.

of Nazareth in Galilee to Judea, to Bethlehem[t] the town of David, because he belonged to the house and line of David.
5 He went there to register with Mary,
who was pledged to be married to him[u]
and was expecting a child. 6 While they
were there, the time came for the baby to
be born, 7 and she gave birth to her firstborn, a son. She wrapped him in cloths
and placed him in a manger, because
there was no room for them in the inn.

The Shepherds and the Angels

8 And there were shepherds living out
in the fields nearby, keeping watch over
their flocks at night. 9 An angel[v] of the
Lord appeared to them, and the glory of
the Lord shone around them, and they
were terrified. 10 But the angel said to
them, "Do not be afraid.[w] I bring you
good news of great joy that will be for all
the people. 11 Today in the town of David
a Savior[x] has been born to you; he is
Christ[e][y] the Lord.[z] 12 This will be a
sign[a] to you: You will find a baby
wrapped in cloths and lying in a manger."

13 Suddenly a great company of the
heavenly host appeared with the angel,
praising God and saying,

14 "Glory to God in the highest,
and on earth peace[b] to men on
whom his favor rests."

15 When the angels had left them and
gone into heaven, the shepherds said to
one another, "Let's go to Bethlehem and
see this thing that has happened, which
the Lord has told us about."

16 So they hurried off and found Mary
and Joseph, and the baby, who was lying
in the manger.[c] 17 When they had seen
him, they spread the word concerning
what had been told them about this child,
18 and all who heard it were amazed at
what the shepherds said to them. 19 But
Mary treasured up all these things and
pondered them in her heart.[d] 20 The
shepherds returned, glorifying and praising God[e] for all the things they had heard
and seen, which were just as they had
been told.

Jesus Presented in the Temple

21 On the eighth day, when it was time
to circumcise him,[f] he was named Jesus,
the name the angel had given him before
he had been conceived.[g]

2:4 [t]S Jn 7:42
2:5 [u]Lk 1:27
2:9 [v]S Ac 5:19
2:10 [w]S Mt 14:27
2:11 [x]S Mt 1:21; S Jn 3:17; 4:42; Ac 5:31; 13:23; S Ro 11:14; 1Ti 4:10; 1Jn 4:14 [y]Mt 1:16; 16:16, 20; Jn 11:27; Ac 2:36; 3:20; S 9:22 [z]S Jn 13:13
2:12 [a]1Sa 2:34; 10:7; 2Ki 19:29; Ps 86:17; Isa 7:14
2:14 [b]Isa 9:6; 52:7; 53:5; Mic 5:5; Lk 1:79; S Jn 14:27; Ro 5:1; Eph 2:14,17
2:16 [c]ver 7
2:19 [d]ver 51
2:20 [e]S Mt 9:8
2:21 [f]S Lk 1:59 [g]S Lk 1:31

[e] *11* Or *Messiah.* "The Christ" (Greek) and "the Messiah" (Hebrew) both mean "the Anointed One"; also in verse 26.

2:9,14 GOD, Glory—The glory of God is a visible, concentrated manifestation of the nature or person of God. Often the glory of God is associated with "shining." The emphasis is not upon the "shining," or how the manifestation occurs, but on the sense of awe that it produces in those who perceive it. When people "see" the glory of God, they have a heightened, acute awareness of the presence and power, the majesty and authority of the holy God. See notes on Ex 16:7,10; 40:34–38. The cry of "glory to God" is the equivalent of praying that nothing will stand in the way of all people seeing how great God is.

2:11 JESUS CHRIST, Savior—"Savior" (Greek *sōter*) applied to Jesus is an extension of the Old Testament idea of God saving and delivering His people. Salvation applies to all areas of life—physical, psychic, and spiritual. The verb "save" is often used in conjunction with Jesus' acts on behalf of humankind. God is acknowledged as Savior often in the New Testament. Compare 1:47. To call Jesus Savior is to relate Him to God. Jesus is called Savior only here in the Synoptic Gospels, once in John (4:42), once in 1 John (4:14), twice in Acts (5:31; 13:23). The other references are in the Pauline works and 2 Peter. See note on Mt 1:18–25. As Savior, Jesus is the Christ or Messiah. See note on Mt 16:16. He is the Lord. See note on Lk 1:5–23.

2:13 REVELATION, Angels—Angels can appear in groups with an individual representative speaking. Angels praise God and thus encourage people to join their song. God sent angels to the shepherds, people of no social standing in the world's eyes. See note on 1:26–29.

2:13 PRAYER, Praise—Many of the appearances of angels describe them praising God (Isa 6:3; Rev 5:11–12). The praise here contains a benediction for God's people. Prayer is a heavenly occupation as well as an earthly one.

2:14,40 GOD, Grace—The grace of God is active and outgoing. God is not a detached God, uninvolved with what is going on here on earth. V 14 expresses the grace of God as His favor towards people whose redemption He was working out even then. In v 40, His grace was active in the developing life of His Son, Jesus, whom the Father had sent into the world to be the Redeemer of lost people. God's grace is not merely a detached sentiment, but an active quality, expressed in positive, redemptive, creative ways as God pursues His own purposes. Because God is gracious at the core of His being, He sent His Son to save us as the expression of His nature.

2:14 CHRISTIAN ETHICS, War and Peace—The angels welcomed Christ's birth with praise to God and a blessing calling for peace to all those committed to God's grace. Peace will never result from good human intentions. God inaugurated peace by sending Jesus to Mary in Bethlehem. Only persons dedicated to praising Him can be instruments of peace, for He is the only source of peace. See note on Mic 5:2–5.

2:17 EVANGELISM, Personal—When the shepherds saw the Christ child, they went away sharing the grand event. It should be no different with Christians today. The natural reaction to Christ is to tell all we have seen and heard. The gospel is available to all people—even the poorest people, like the shepherds. See Guide to Personal Testimony, pp. 1786–1788.

2:20 PRAYER, Praise—Praise of God surrounds the incarnation of God into human flesh (1:46–55,64,67–79; 2:13–14,28–32,38). The coming of Jesus as Savior is the central reason to praise God. Such praise reflects heavenly activity (2:14).

2:21–38 JESUS CHRIST, Birth—This passage is called the Presentation. After Jesus had been circumcised on the eighth day following His birth, Mary and Joseph presented Him in the Temple (Lev 12:3). This was an important event for firstborn sons (Ex 13:2). The circumcision marked Him as a Jewish male and sealed Him by the sign of the covenant of God with Israel. The pair of birds represented the traditional gift of poor families (Lev 12:8). Simeon, one whom God had promised would see the Messiah, recognized the child as a fulfillment of God's special promise. Simeon's song, the Nunc Dimittis (vv 29–32), is the fourth and final of Luke's Christmas songs. This song, like Zechariah's and Mary's, is flavored with Old Testament references (Ps 119:116; Isa 9:2; 42:6; 49:6; 52:10). The birth of Jesus was bound up with expectations and fulfillment. An aged prophetess Anna also testified to Jesus as the long-awaited Messiah. At Christmas all orders

22When the time of their purification
according to the Law of Moses[h] had been
completed, Joseph and Mary took him to
Jerusalem to present him to the Lord 23(as
it is written in the Law of the Lord, "Every firstborn male is to be consecrated to
the Lord"[f]),[i] 24and to offer a sacrifice in
keeping with what is said in the Law of
the Lord: "a pair of doves or two young
pigeons."[g][j]
25Now there was a man in Jerusalem
called Simeon, who was righteous and devout.[k] He was waiting for the consolation
of Israel,[l] and the Holy Spirit was upon
him. 26It had been revealed to him by the
Holy Spirit that he would not die before
he had seen the Lord's Christ. 27Moved
by the Spirit, he went into the temple
courts. When the parents brought in the
child Jesus to do for him what the custom
of the Law required,[m] 28Simeon took him
in his arms and praised God, saying:

29"Sovereign Lord, as you have
promised,[n]
you now dismiss[h] your servant in
peace.[o]
30For my eyes have seen your
salvation,[p]
31 which you have prepared in the
sight of all people,
32a light for revelation to the Gentiles
and for glory to your people
Israel."[q]

33The child's father and mother marveled at what was said about him. 34Then
Simeon blessed them and said to Mary,
his mother:[r] "This child is destined to
cause the falling[s] and rising of many in
Israel, and to be a sign that will be spoken
against, 35so that the thoughts of many
hearts will be revealed. And a sword will
pierce your own soul too."
36There was also a prophetess,[t] Anna,
the daughter of Phanuel, of the tribe of
Asher. She was very old; she had lived
with her husband seven years after her
marriage, 37and then was a widow until
she was eighty-four.[i][u] She never left the
temple but worshiped night and day, fasting and praying.[v] 38Coming up to them
at that very moment, she gave thanks to
God and spoke about the child to all who
were looking forward to the redemption
of Jerusalem.[w]
39When Joseph and Mary had done everything required by the Law of the Lord,
they returned to Galilee to their own
town of Nazareth.[x] 40And the child grew
and became strong; he was filled with

2:22 [h]Lev 12:2-8
2:23 [i]Ex 13:2,12, 15; Nu 3:13
2:24 [j]Lev 12:8
2:25 [k]Lk 1:6 [l]ver 38; Isa 52:9; Lk 23:51
2:27 [m]ver 22
2:29 [n]ver 26 [o]Ac 2:24
2:30 [p]Isa 40:5; 52:10; Lk 3:6
2:32 [q]Isa 42:6; 49:6; Ac 13:47; 26:23
2:34 [r]S Mt 12:46 [s]Isa 8:14; Mt 21:44; 1Co 1:23; 2Co 2:16; Gal 5:11; 1Pe 2:7,8
2:36 [t]S Ac 21:9
2:37 [u]1Ti 5:9 [v]Ac 13:3; 14:23; 1Ti 5:5
2:38 [w]ver 25; Isa 40:2; 52:9; Lk 1:68; 24:21
2:39 [x]ver 51; S Mt 2:23

[f]*23* Exodus 13:2,12 [g]*24* Lev. 12:8 [h]*29* Or *promised, / now dismiss* [i]*37* Or *widow for eighty-four years*

---

of God's creation were involved: the star; foreign folk (Magi) representing all of the ethnic groups; the great of earth (Herod the King); the wealth of earth (the Magi's gifts); the law (both Roman and Jewish); the prophets (John and Anna); the priesthood (Zechariah); the poor of the earth (shepherds); the angels; and even the animals (by implication from the manger). Jesus' birth is for all the world.

2:22–24 PRAYER, Commitment—The firstborn was spared in the tenth plague of Egypt (Ex 12:12–13); God then required that the firstborn be dedicated to Him (Ex 13:1–2,12–13). The Lord had allowed the tribe of Levi to become a substitute for the firstborn (Nu 3:11–13). The consecration of Jesus is important, for He would become the High Priest (Heb 4:14; 5:4–6). The sacrificial ritual symbolized commitment. Acts of worship can be symbolic prayers even without times and words of prayer.

2:25–32 HOLY SPIRIT, Revelation—The Holy Spirit gave Simeon the gift of prophecy. The Spirit revealed a message to him (v 26) and led him to deliver that message at the right moment (v 27). See note on 1:67.

2:26,29 GOD, Faithfulness—God's promise to Simeon was at long last fulfilled. God does not forget His people, nor does He forget His promises to them. His promises are not always fulfilled in quite the way that we expect, because of our partial understanding; but God always fulfills His promises, sometimes in ways much greater than we had expected.

2:26 REVELATION, Inspiration—God honors devout, righteous people. The Spirit revealed to a humble and devout man that he would see God's Child before he died. The Spirit led Simeon to the right place to find Jesus. Simeon, recognizing Jesus, spontaneously burst out in a celebrative song. Simeon's song is not directly attributed to the Spirit as was Zechariah's, but it was no less inspired. See note on 1:67.

2:28–35 PRAYER, Thanksgiving—Simeon's gratitude, like Zechariah's praise, contained a prophetic note. See note on 1:67–79.

2:30 JESUS CHRIST, Savior—See note on 2:11. As Savior, Jesus provided deliverance from sin for people of all races and nations.

2:30 SALVATION, Definition—Jesus Christ is God's salvation. He embodied God's promised deliverance.

2:30–32 EVANGELISM, Christ the Hope—Salvation resides in the person of Jesus Christ (1 Jn 5:11–12). The fortunate ones who saw Him in the flesh saw God's salvation. We can see Him with the eyes of faith and invite others to join us. He stands as our only hope of eternal life. Every race, color, culture, and language group are welcomed by Christ and His witnesses. Christ has provided salvation. We announce its availability to all people.

2:34–35 JESUS CHRIST, Suffering—Jesus' coming brought decision time. People must accept Him and rise to salvation or reject Him and fall to judgment. He would suffer rejection, which would bring His mother suffering, also.

2:34 PROCLAMATION, Unbelievers—See note on Ac 26:19–29.

2:36–38 PRAYER, Thanksgiving—Anna's recognition and thanksgiving grew out of a life of worship, prayer, and fasting. God calls some people to a special dedication to the life of prayer. He calls all to the ministry of daily prayer (1 Th 5:17).

2:38 JESUS CHRIST, Redeemer—See note on 1:67–79.

2:39 JESUS CHRIST, Fulfilled—Jesus not only fulfilled the messianic hopes of Israel. He fulfilled all the scriptural requirements to be a member of God's covenant people.

2:40–52 JESUS CHRIST, Birth—Whereas the birth of Jesus was marked by supernatural events, His childhood growth was natural for any human being. He increased His capacities in all areas of life. His spiritual growth amazed the religious authorities. Still He remained an obedient child.

2:40 REVELATION, Jesus Christ—The presence of God was uniquely active in this Child, whose will and attitude developed with His body to reach the full potential God had for Him as His Messenger of redemption.

wisdom, and the grace of God was upon
him.[y]

The Boy Jesus at the Temple

41Every year his parents went to Jerusalem for the Feast of the Passover.[z]
42When he was twelve years old, they
went up to the Feast, according to the
custom. 43After the Feast was over, while
his parents were returning home, the boy
Jesus stayed behind in Jerusalem, but
they were unaware of it. 44Thinking he
was in their company, they traveled on
for a day. Then they began looking for
him among their relatives and friends.
45When they did not find him, they went
back to Jerusalem to look for him. 46After
three days they found him in the temple
courts, sitting among the teachers, listening to them and asking them questions.
47Everyone who heard him was amazed[a]
at his understanding and his answers.
48When his parents saw him, they were
astonished. His mother[b] said to him,
"Son, why have you treated us like this?
Your father[c] and I have been anxiously
searching for you."
49"Why were you searching for me?"
he asked. "Didn't you know I had to be in
my Father's house?"[d] 50But they did not
understand what he was saying to
them.[e]
51Then he went down to Nazareth with
them[f] and was obedient to them. But his
mother treasured all these things in her
heart.[g] 52And Jesus grew in wisdom and
stature, and in favor with God and men.[h]

2:40 [y]ver 52; Lk 1:80
2:41 [z]Ex 23:15; Dt 16:1-8; Lk 22:8
2:47 [a]S Mt 7:28
2:48 [b]S Mt 12:46 [c]Lk 3:23; 4:22
2:49 [d]Jn 2:16
2:50 [e]S Mk 9:32
2:51 [f]ver 39; S Mt 2:23 [g]ver 19
2:52 [h]ver 40; 1Sa 2:26; Pr 3:4; Lk 1:80
3:1 [i]S Mt 27:2 [j]S Mt 14:1
3:2 [k]S Mt 26:3 [l]S Mt 3:1 [m]Lk 1:13
3:3 [n]ver 16; S Mk 1:4
3:6 [o]Isa 40:3-5; Ps 98:2; Isa 42:16; 52:10; Lk 2:30
3:7 [p]Mt 12:34; 23:33 [q]S Ro 1:18
3:8 [r]Isa 51:2; Lk 19:9; Jn 8:33,39; Ac 13:26; Ro 4:1, 11,12,16,17; 9:7,8; Gal 3:7

Chapter 3

John the Baptist Prepares the Way

3:2–10pp — Mt 3:1–10; Mk 1:3–5
3:16,17pp — Mt 3:11,12; Mk 1:7,8

IN the fifteenth year of the reign of Ti-
berius Caesar—when Pontius Pilate[i]
was governor of Judea, Herod[j] tetrarch
of Galilee, his brother Philip tetrarch of
Iturea and Traconitis, and Lysanias tetrarch of Abilene— 2during the high
priesthood of Annas and Caiaphas,[k] the
word of God came to John[l] son of Zechariah[m] in the desert. 3He went into all the
country around the Jordan, preaching a
baptism of repentance for the forgiveness
of sins.[n] 4As is written in the book of the
words of Isaiah the prophet:

"A voice of one calling in the desert,
'Prepare the way for the Lord,
make straight paths for him.
5Every valley shall be filled in,
every mountain and hill made low.
The crooked roads shall become
straight,
the rough ways smooth.
6And all mankind will see God's
salvation.' "[j][o]

7John said to the crowds coming out to
be baptized by him, "You brood of vipers![p] Who warned you to flee from the
coming wrath?[q] 8Produce fruit in keeping with repentance. And do not begin to
say to yourselves, 'We have Abraham as
our father.'[r] For I tell you that out of

[j]6 Isaiah 40:3-5

2:41–42 FAMILY, Worship—Joseph and Mary illustrate the devotion to God essential for family life. Each year they traveled to Jerusalem to observe the Passover, a worship experience required of all faithful Jews. See note on Ex 12:3–4. Families need periodic religious observances to cement their growing relationship with God.

2:46 EDUCATION, Questions—Asking and answering questions, one of the most ancient educational methods in the world, played an important role in the religious instruction of first-century Jewish boys. In the Temple scene, Jesus was not "grilling" His teachers, as some suppose, but was asking for information. Question-asking should not be the exclusive prerogative of teachers; it is important for learners to raise questions, too.

2:49 JESUS CHRIST, Son of God—Jesus became aware of His unique status as God's Son at an early age. How or precisely when this occurred the Bible does not say.

2:49–50 REVELATION, Commitment—Jesus at twelve was already committed to the study and understanding of the revealed Law, revealing His commitment to devote time and primary interest to His heavenly Father's will.

3:1–20 JESUS CHRIST, John—In accordance with Scripture (Isa 40:3–5), John prepared the way for Jesus. He showed the need of a Savior and called for repentance in light of the Savior's coming. Fulfillment of God's promises did not belong to a race or a religion. It belonged to a faithful, obedient people. John pointed people away from himself to Jesus as the promised Messiah.

3:1–14 STEWARDSHIP, Life-style—The godly life begins with accepting God's gift of salvation in repentance, a turning from worldly values and personal greed to honesty, generosity, and contentment with what one has. See note on Lk 12:16–31.

3:1–22 ORDINANCES, Baptism by John—See notes on Mt 3:4–17; Mk 1:4–11. Luke carefully located the ministry of John the Baptist in the desert. Compare 1:80. The ruins of the Dead Sea Scrolls community of Qumran contain many cisterns and *mikve* (ritual baptistries). The ruins are very near to and visible from the place where John baptized in the Jordan. While the Qumran community used repeated ritual baths or baptisms in preparation for various religious activities, John baptized his converts only once in the Jordan as a sign of repentance and preparation for the dawning Messianic Age. This also distinguished Christian baptism with the additional significance that converts were being resurrected to a new life in Christ (Ro 6:4).

3:6 SALVATION, Definition—Simeon was not the only one to see God's salvation in Jesus Christ. All persons can now see it. Compare Isa 40:3–5; 52:10.

3:6 EVANGELISM, God's Provision—God alone provides salvation. Redemption is found solely in Jesus Christ. No one else can save.

3:8–9 ELECTION, Israel—Arrogance marked the crowds who came to hear John the Baptist preach. Their superiority complex moved them to believe that biological identity with Abraham gave them immunity from the penalty of sin and guaranteed their election as children of God. John warned that like trees and vineyards destroyed for the lack of good fruit, the process was at work, already cutting them off from election status and promise. From stones God can raise up new children of Abraham to participate in His election purposes. Only true repentance guarantees the blessings of election.

these stones God can raise up children for
Abraham. 9The ax is already at the root of
the trees, and every tree that does not
produce good fruit will be cut down and
thrown into the fire."[s]
10"What should we do then?"[t] the
crowd asked.
11John answered, "The man with two
tunics should share with him who has
none, and the one who has food should
do the same."[u]
12Tax collectors also came to be baptized.[v] "Teacher," they asked, "what
should we do?"
13"Don't collect any more than you are
required to,"[w] he told them.
14Then some soldiers asked him, "And
what should we do?"
He replied, "Don't extort money and
don't accuse people falsely[x]—be content
with your pay."
15The people were waiting expectantly
and were all wondering in their hearts if
John[y] might possibly be the Christ.[k] [z]
16John answered them all, "I baptize you
with[l] water.[a] But one more powerful
than I will come, the thongs of whose
sandals I am not worthy to untie. He will
baptize you with the Holy Spirit and with
fire.[b] 17His winnowing fork[c] is in his
hand to clear his threshing floor and to
gather the wheat into his barn, but he
will burn up the chaff with unquenchable
fire."[d] 18And with many other words
John exhorted the people and preached
the good news to them.
19But when John rebuked Herod[e] the

3:9 [s]S Mt 3:10
3:10 [t]ver 12,14; Ac 2:37; 16:30
3:11 [u]Isa 58:7; Eze 18:7
3:12 [v]Lk 7:29
3:13 [w]Lk 19:8
3:14 [x]Ex 23:1; Lev 19:11
3:15 [y]S Mt 3:1 [z]Jn 1:19,20; Ac 13:25
3:16 [a]ver 3; S Mk 1:4 [b]Jn 1:26, 33; Ac 1:5; 2:3; 11:16; 19:4
3:17 [c]Isa 30:24 [d]Mt 13:30; S 25:41
3:19 [e]ver 1; S Mt 14:1
3:20 [f]S Mt 14:3,4
3:21 [g]Mt 14:23; Mk 1:35; 6:46; Lk 5:16; 6:12; 9:18,28; 11:1
3:22 [h]Isa 42:1; Jn 1:32,33; Ac 10:38 [i]S Mt 3:17 [j]S Mt 3:17
3:23 [k]Mt 4:17; Ac 1:1 [l]Lk 1:27
3:27 [m]Mt 1:12

tetrarch because of Herodias, his brother's wife, and all the other evil things he
had done, 20Herod added this to them all:
He locked John up in prison.[f]

The Baptism and Genealogy of Jesus

3:21,22pp — Mt 3:13–17; Mk 1:9–11
3:23–38pp — Mt 1:1–17

21When all the people were being baptized, Jesus was baptized too. And as he
was praying,[g] heaven was opened 22and
the Holy Spirit descended on him[h] in
bodily form like a dove. And a voice came
from heaven: "You are my Son,[i] whom I
love; with you I am well pleased."[j]
23Now Jesus himself was about thirty
years old when he began his ministry.[k]
He was the son, so it was thought, of Joseph,[l]

the son of Heli, 24the son of Matthat,
the son of Levi, the son of Melki,
the son of Jannai, the son of Joseph,
25the son of Mattathias, the son of
Amos,
the son of Nahum, the son of Esli,
the son of Naggai, 26the son of Ma-
ath,
the son of Mattathias, the son of
Semein,
the son of Josech, the son of Joda,
27the son of Joanan, the son of Rhesa,
the son of Zerubbabel,[m] the son of
Shealtiel,
the son of Neri, 28the son of Melki,
the son of Addi, the son of Cosam,

[k] *15* Or *Messiah* [l] *16* Or *in*

3:11 DISCIPLESHIP, Poor—John the Baptist called on the people to produce evidence of real repentance before he baptized them. The first evidence he suggested was that they should share food and clothing with the poor. If we have truly repented and committed our lives to Christ, the unfortunate members of our society will know it. See 2 Th 1:11; Jas 2:14–26.

3:13–14 CHRISTIAN ETHICS, Property Rights—Accepting pay for work done and value rendered is the reasonable right of every worker. To expect and demand more pay than the value rendered the employer is wrong and should lead to repentance. Being content with fair wages curbs greediness and allows us to turn attention to our ministry for God.

3:16 HOLY SPIRIT, Redemption—See note on Mt 3:11. John seems to have understood baptism with fire to refer to judgment (v 17). When his prophecy was fulfilled at Pentecost, the fire had to do with a gift of prophecy (tongues of fire, Ac 2:3–4). As the church proclaimed the message of Christ, those who accepted it were saved; but those who rejected it were judged. See Ac 5:1–10. The idea of fire and Christ's judgment in human lives is found in Paul's writing (1 Co 3:10–16).

3:18 PROCLAMATION, Exhortation—See note on Ac 14:21–22.

3:21–23 JESUS CHRIST, Servant—See note on Mt 3:13–17.

3:21–22 HOLY SPIRIT, Jesus—See note on Mt 3:16–17. Alone among the Gospel writers, Luke pointed out that Jesus was praying at His baptism (v 21). The association of the Spirit with prayer is surprisingly rare in the Old Testament. In Nu 25:15–18; Jdg 3:8–10; 1 Sa 16:1–2,12–13, God gave His Spirit to individuals after other people prayed. In Ps 51:10–11 David prayed that the Spirit would not be taken away from him. In the New Testament, a closer association is made between prayer and the Spirit. It is not that one must pray to receive the Spirit, for God gives His Spirit freely to His people. People must pray so that they may experience the Spirit's guidance or power in their lives. See Ac 7:35–59; 13:2–3; Ro 8:15,26–27; Php 3:3; Jude 20; notes on Lk 11:13; Ac 4:31; Gal 4:6; Eph 2:18; 3:14–19; 6:18. Prayer concerning the Spirit is opening ourselves to His work in our lives. In this, Jesus set the perfect example at His baptism.

3:21–22 PRAYER, Jesus' Example—Each occurrence of God speaking from heaven to Christ or about Christ occurred while Jesus was praying (9:29; Jn 12:27–29). Prayer marked every part of Christ's ministry.

3:22 GOD, Love—Love is the key element uniting the three Persons of the Trinity. See note on Mk 1:11.

3:22 REVELATION, Actions—God blessed and recognized His Son, revealing His special Presence and purpose in Him through a symbolic dedication (baptism) and through the symbol of the Spirit's presence (dove).

3:23–38 JESUS CHRIST, Son of God—Jesus entered His world-changing ministry with proper credentials. He was physically related to all people through Adam, the father of the human race. He was more than another human. He joined Adam as Son of God. As the second Adam, He would restore creation, removing the sin and its effects which the first Adam had introduced. Compare Ro 5:12–21; 1 Co 15:20–23. To the outside world, Jesus appeared to be a normal son of Joseph. In reality He was the new David (Ps 2:7) and the new Adam, the only true Son of God.

the son of Elmadam, the son of Er,
29 the son of Joshua, the son of Eliezer,
the son of Jorim, the son of Matthat,
the son of Levi, 30 the son of Simeon,
the son of Judah, the son of Joseph,
the son of Jonam, the son of Eliakim,
31 the son of Melea, the son of Menna,
the son of Mattatha, the son of Nathan,[n]
the son of David, 32 the son of Jesse,
the son of Obed, the son of Boaz,
the son of Salmon,[m] the son of Nahshon,
33 the son of Amminadab, the son of Ram,[n]
the son of Hezron, the son of Perez,[o]
the son of Judah, 34 the son of Jacob,
the son of Isaac, the son of Abraham,
the son of Terah, the son of Nahor,[p]
35 the son of Serug, the son of Reu,
the son of Peleg, the son of Eber,
the son of Shelah, 36 the son of Cainan,
the son of Arphaxad,[q] the son of Shem,
the son of Noah, the son of Lamech,[r]
37 the son of Methuselah, the son of Enoch,
the son of Jared, the son of Mahalalel,
the son of Kenan,[s] 38 the son of Enosh,
the son of Seth, the son of Adam,
the son of God.[t]

Chapter 4

The Temptation of Jesus

4:1–13pp — Mt 4:1–11; Mk 1:12,13

JESUS, full of the Holy Spirit,[u] returned
from the Jordan[v] and was led by the
Spirit[w] in the desert, 2 where for forty
days[x] he was tempted by the devil.[y] He
ate nothing during those days, and at the
end of them he was hungry.
3 The devil said to him, "If you are the
Son of God,[z] tell this stone to become
bread."
4 Jesus answered, "It is written: 'Man
does not live on bread alone.'[o] "[a]
5 The devil led him up to a high place
and showed him in an instant all the
kingdoms of the world.[b] 6 And he said to
him, "I will give you all their authority
and splendor, for it has been given to
me,[c] and I can give it to anyone I want
to. 7 So if you worship me, it will all be
yours."
8 Jesus answered, "It is written: 'Worship the Lord your God and serve him
only.'[p] "[d]
9 The devil led him to Jerusalem and
had him stand on the highest point of the
temple. "If you are the Son of God," he
said, "throw yourself down from here.
10 For it is written:

" 'He will command his angels
concerning you
to guard you carefully;
11 they will lift you up in their hands,
so that you will not strike your foot
against a stone.'[q] "[e]

12 Jesus answered, "It says: 'Do not put
the Lord your God to the test.'[r] "[f]
13 When the devil had finished all this
tempting,[g] he left him[h] until an opportune time.

Jesus Rejected at Nazareth

14 Jesus returned to Galilee[i] in the

3:31 [n]2Sa 5:14; 1Ch 3:5
3:33 [o]Ru 4:18-22; 1Ch 2:10-12
3:34 [p]Ge 11:24,26
3:36 [q]Ge 11:12 [r]Ge 5:28-32
3:37 [s]Ge 5:12-25
3:38 [t]Ge 5:1,2,6-9
4:1 [u]ver 14,18; S Lk 1:15,35; 3:16, 22; 10:21 [v]Lk 3:3, 21 [w]Eze 37:1; Lk 2:27
4:2 [x]Ex 34:28; 1Ki 19:8 [y]Heb 4:15
4:3 [z]S Mt 4:3
4:4 [a]Dt 8:3
4:5 [b]S Mt 24:14
4:6 [c]Jn 12:31; 14:30; 1Jn 5:19
4:8 [d]Dt 6:13
4:11 [e]Ps 91:11,12
4:12 [f]Dt 6:16
4:13 [g]Heb 4:15 [h]Jn 14:30
4:14 [i]Mt 4:12

[m]32 Some early manuscripts *Sala* [n]33 Some manuscripts *Amminadab, the son of Admin, the son of Arni;* other manuscripts vary widely. [o]4 Deut. 8:3 [p]8 Deut. 6:13 [q]11 Psalm 91:11,12 [r]12 Deut. 6:16

4:1–13 JESUS CHRIST, Temptation—See note on Mt 4:1–11. In Luke the order is reversed of the temptation in the Temple and the temptation for worldly power, possibly to show that spiritual power and corruption are even worse than misuse of political power. Luke indicated that the tempter left Jesus only for a while. The temptation of Jesus, like ours, was a lifelong process (Lk 22:28). Jesus resisted all pressures and all temptations. The Spirit's presence strengthened Him in resisting. For temptation to be real, Jesus had to be able to sin. For salvation to be secure, He had to resist temptation; and He did.

4:1–13 EVIL AND SUFFERING, Satan—See note on Mt 4:1–11.

4:1–13 SIN, Tempting—Temptation is not sin. To face a situation and consider doing what is wrong is not sin. Jesus faced temptation, but He certainly did not sin. Sin is seeing the sinful opportunity and desiring to participate in it. The Christian response to temptation is to see the situation through the perspective of God's Word and to decide definitely not to participate. God's Word helps us to see the hidden implications of an action, not just the simple act. The act may not be sinful. The motivation for the act or the priority taught by the act may be sinful as seen in the temptation to use miraculous powers for selfish purposes. Some acts such as worshiping Satan are sinful in themselves.

4:3,9 JESUS CHRIST, Son of God—Satan recognized Jesus as Son of God and tempted Him precisely at that point. How would the Son of God reveal Himself to the world? To be Son of God for Jesus meant to be obedient, not to be greedy for power and recognition.

4:4 HOLY SCRIPTURE, Obedience—See note on Mt 4:4–10.

4:8 PRAYER, Worship—See note on Mt 4:10.

4:14–31 JESUS CHRIST, Mission—Jesus' ministry was begun in a context of rejection. He likened His rejection in Nazareth to the rejection of Old Testament prophets (1 Ki 18:4,13; 19:2; 22:8; 2 Ki 2:23). The positive purpose of His mission was taken from Isa 61:1–2. The setting in Isaiah speaks of glowing promises for those whom Messiah delivers. Jesus' purpose in ministry was to preach, to announce freedom, to heal, and to proclaim that God's time is at hand. He was rejected because hometown people could not believe a local product could accomplish so much and because they did not see Messiah in the ministry role. We should give equal attention to those to whom He sought to minister: the poor, prisoners, the blind, and the oppressed. Modern ministers might find it easy to follow Jesus' type of ministry and ignore some of

power of the Spirit, and news about him
spread through the whole countryside.[j]
15He taught in their synagogues,[k] and everyone praised him.

16He went to Nazareth,[l] where he had
been brought up, and on the Sabbath day
he went into the synagogue,[m] as was his
custom. And he stood up to read.[n] 17The
scroll of the prophet Isaiah was handed to
him. Unrolling it, he found the place
where it is written:

18"The Spirit of the Lord is on me,[o]
because he has anointed me
to preach good news[p] to the poor.
He has sent me to proclaim freedom
for the prisoners
and recovery of sight for the blind,
to release the oppressed,
19 to proclaim the year of the Lord's
favor."[s] [q]

20Then he rolled up the scroll, gave it
back to the attendant and sat down.[r] The
eyes of everyone in the synagogue were
fastened on him, 21and he began by saying to them, "Today this scripture is fulfilled[s] in your hearing."

22All spoke well of him and were
amazed at the gracious words that came
from his lips. "Isn't this Joseph's son?"
they asked.[t]

23Jesus said to them, "Surely you will
quote this proverb to me: 'Physician, heal
yourself! Do here in your hometown[u]
what we have heard that you did in Capernaum.' "[v]

24"I tell you the truth," he continued,
"no prophet is accepted in his hometown.[w] 25I assure you that there were
many widows in Israel in Elijah's time,
when the sky was shut for three and a
half years and there was a severe famine
throughout the land.[x] 26Yet Elijah was
not sent to any of them, but to a widow in
Zarephath in the region of Sidon.[y] 27And
there were many in Israel with leprosy[t]
in the time of Elisha the prophet, yet not
one of them was cleansed—only Naaman
the Syrian."[z]

28All the people in the synagogue were
furious when they heard this. 29They got
up, drove him out of the town,[a] and took
him to the brow of the hill on which the
town was built, in order to throw him
down the cliff. 30But he walked right
through the crowd and went on his
way.[b]

Jesus Drives Out an Evil Spirit

4:31–37pp — Mk 1:21–28

31Then he went down to Capernaum,[c]
a town in Galilee, and on the Sabbath began to teach the people. 32They were
amazed at his teaching,[d] because his
message had authority.[e]

33In the synagogue there was a man
possessed by a demon, an evil[u] spirit. He
cried out at the top of his voice, 34"Ha!
What do you want with us,[f] Jesus of Naz-

4:14 [j]S Mt 9:26
4:15 [k]S Mt 4:23
4:16 [l]S Mt 2:23 [m]Mt 13:54 [n]S 1Ti 4:13
4:18 [o]S Jn 3:34 [p]Mk 16:15
4:19 [q]Isa 61:1,2; Lev 25:10; Ps 102:20; 103:6; Isa 42:7; 49:8,9; 58:6
4:20 [r]ver 17; S Mt 26:55
4:21 [s]S Mt 1:22
4:22 [t]Mt 13:54,55; Jn 6:42; 7:15
4:23 [u]ver 16; S Mt 2:23 [v]Mk 1:21-28; 2:1-12
4:24 [w]Mt 13:57; Jn 4:44
4:25 [x]1Ki 17:1; 18:1; Jas 5:17,18; Rev 11:6
4:26 [y]1Ki 17:8-16; S Mt 11:21
4:27 [z]2Ki 5:1-14
4:29 [a]Nu 15:35; Ac 7:58; Heb 13:12
4:30 [b]Jn 8:59; 10:39
4:31 [c]ver 23; S Mt 4:13
4:32 [d]S Mt 7:28 [e]ver 36; Mt 7:29
4:34 [f]S Mt 8:29

[s] *19* Isaiah 61:1,2 [t] *27* The Greek word was used for various diseases affecting the skin—not necessarily leprosy. [u] *33* Greek *unclean;* also in verse 36

those special groups to whom He specifically sought to minister. Those who minister in His name today may expect to face hostility and rejection when they minister in His way and to the special kinds of people to whom His ministry was directed.

4:14 HOLY SPIRIT, Jesus—This is the most general statement in the Gospels concerning the work of the Spirit in the life and ministry of Jesus. Jesus' work in Galilee was empowered by the Spirit. This is similar to the work of the Spirit in the lives of ancient Israel's leaders, especially Saul and David, with whom the Spirit apparently worked over a number of years. Major aspects of Jesus' ministry were preaching, teaching, healing, and exorcism; in the Gospels all of these forms of ministry are attributed at one point or another to the Spirit. Each step of Christ's ministry was led by the Spirit.

4:14–21 PROCLAMATION, Clarity—See note on Isa 61:1–3. Jesus illustrated the simplicity of proclamation. He made His meaning clear so all people could understand. He tied His own ministry to the prophecy of Isa 61:1–3. The proclamation of the gospel should never be obscure. It must always ring with a clear and simple message of eternal truth. Jesus beautifully combined preaching and teaching. Proclamation includes content that teaches. Proclamation explains the meaning of God's Word for the present audience. Proclamation leads to understanding, decision, and commitment.

4:14–15 EDUCATION, Jesus—See note on Mk 1:21–22.

4:15–21 WORSHIP, Proclamation—See note on Jer 26:2–7.

4:16–19 HOLY SPIRIT, Jesus—Jesus' ministry did not meet the Jewish leaders' expectations. It did meet God's. The Spirit directed Jesus' ministry and fulfilled Old Testament expectations of the Messiah. See Isa 61:1–2. Jesus affirmed the Spirit's role in His life by quoting Isaiah.

4:18 EVIL AND SUFFERING, God's Present Help—Jesus' ministry, anticipated in Isa 61:1–2, was addressed to the needs of suffering humanity. He demonstrated what God's kingdom is. The kingdom is not pride in prosperity and power. It is helping the needy enjoy life's necessities. It is not greater wealth for the rich but deserved reward for the faithful. Jesus and His kingdom overcome the injustice and evil of this world. His ministry is the model for ours. Participating in His kingdom by faith now ensures participation in the final victory of His kingdom.

4:18–21 REVELATION, Jesus Christ—God's plan for Jesus was to fulfill the purpose set forth in Isaiah's commission. Jesus declared He was God's fulfillment of that promise and plan. Hometown people who knew Jesus best rejected Him first. Even the supreme revelation of God in Christ was not obvious and compelling. Faith is necessary to recognize revelation.

4:18–21 DISCIPLESHIP, Persons—Jesus announced that His ministry would meet every human need and would fulfill the prophecy of Isaiah. Through the Spirit's power His disciples share His ministry. The way we meet human needs demonstrates whether we truly are His disciples. This commitment will be revealed on judgment day. See notes on 14:12–14; Mt 25:34–46.

4:20–29 MIRACLE, Faith—Cynical unbelief limits the opportunity for miracles. God works where people are ready for His action. The cynical unbelief at Nazareth contrasted sharply with the simple trust of Zarephath's widow and the ultimate obedience of Naaman. See notes on 1 Ki 17:22; 2 Ki 5:1–27.

4:31–32 EDUCATION, Jesus—See note on Mt 7:28–29.

4:33–37 MIRACLE, Christ—See note on Mk 1:21–28.

areth?[g] Have you come to destroy us? I
know who you are[h]—the Holy One of
God!"[i]
35"Be quiet!" Jesus said sternly.[j]
"Come out of him!" Then the demon
threw the man down before them all and
came out without injuring him.
36All the people were amazed[k] and
said to each other, "What is this teaching? With authority[l] and power he gives
orders to evil spirits and they come out!"
37And the news about him spread
throughout the surrounding area.[m]

Jesus Heals Many

4:38–41pp — Mt 8:14–17
4:38–43pp — Mk 1:29–38

38Jesus left the synagogue and went to
the home of Simon. Now Simon's mother-in-law was suffering from a high fever,
and they asked Jesus to help her. 39So he
bent over her and rebuked[n] the fever,
and it left her. She got up at once and
began to wait on them.
40When the sun was setting, the people
brought to Jesus all who had various
kinds of sickness, and laying his hands on
each one,[o] he healed them.[p] 41More-
over, demons came out of many people,
shouting, "You are the Son of God!"[q] But
he rebuked[r] them and would not allow
them to speak,[s] because they knew he
was the Christ.[v]
42At daybreak Jesus went out to a solitary place. The people were looking for
him and when they came to where he
was, they tried to keep him from leaving
them. 43But he said, "I must preach the
good news of the kingdom of God[t] to the
other towns also, because that is why I
was sent." 44And he kept on preaching in
the synagogues of Judea.[w][u]

4:34 [g]S Mk 1:24 [h]Jas 2:19 [i]ver 41; S Mk 1:24
4:35 [j]ver 39,41; Mt 8:26; Lk 8:24
4:36 [k]S Mt 7:28 [l]ver 32; Mt 7:29; S Mt 10:1
4:37 [m]ver 14; S Mt 9:26
4:39 [n]ver 35,41
4:40 [o]S Mk 5:23 [p]S Mt 4:23
4:41 [q]S Mt 4:3 [r]S ver 35 [s]S Mt 8:4
4:43 [t]S Mt 3:2
4:44 [u]S Mt 4:23
5:1 [v]S Mk 4:14; S Heb 4:12
5:3 [w]Mt 13:2
5:4 [x]Jn 21:6
5:5 [y]Lk 8:24,45; 9:33,49; 17:13 [z]Jn 21:3
5:6 [a]Jn 21:11
5:8 [b]Ge 18:27; Job 42:6; Isa 6:5
5:10 [c]S Mt 14:27
5:11 [d]ver 28; S Mt 4:19

Chapter 5

The Calling of the First Disciples

5:1–11pp — Mt 4:18–22; Mk 1:16–20; Jn 1:40–42

ONE day as Jesus was standing by the
Lake of Gennesaret,[x] with the people crowding around him and listening to
the word of God,[v] 2he saw at the water's
edge two boats, left there by the fishermen, who were washing their nets. 3He
got into one of the boats, the one belonging to Simon, and asked him to put out a
little from shore. Then he sat down and
taught the people from the boat.[w]
4When he had finished speaking, he
said to Simon, "Put out into deep water,
and let down[y] the nets for a catch."[x]
5Simon answered, "Master,[y] we've
worked hard all night and haven't caught
anything.[z] But because you say so, I will
let down the nets."
6When they had done so, they caught
such a large number of fish that their nets
began to break.[a] 7So they signaled their
partners in the other boat to come and
help them, and they came and filled both
boats so full that they began to sink.
8When Simon Peter saw this, he fell at
Jesus' knees and said, "Go away from me,
Lord; I am a sinful man!"[b] 9For he and all
his companions were astonished at the
catch of fish they had taken, 10and so
were James and John, the sons of Zebedee, Simon's partners.
Then Jesus said to Simon, "Don't be
afraid;[c] from now on you will catch
men." 11So they pulled their boats up on
shore, left everything and followed him.[d]

v*41* Or *Messiah* w*44* Or *the land of the Jews*; some manuscripts *Galilee* x*1* That is, Sea of Galilee y*4* The Greek verb is plural.

4:38–41 MIRACLE, Christ—Suffering challenged Christ's compassion. He healed persons He knew such as Peter's mother-in-law and the unnamed multitudes. This had been God's purpose all along as the reference in Isaiah underscores. The risen Christ continues to show compassion for the sick and needy.

4:42–43 PRAYER, Jesus' Example—Jesus went alone to pray. See note on Mk 1:35; Jn 6:15.

4:43 REVELATION, Messengers—See note on Mk 1:38–39.

4:43 THE CHURCH, God's Kingdom—The gospel is good news. This gospel must not be limited to small groups. The good news of God's reign in the hearts of human beings must be preached to all the world, following the example of Jesus.

4:43–44 PROCLAMATION, Compulsion—See note on 1 Co 9:16–18.

5:1–26 JESUS CHRIST, Miracles—Jesus was a Proclaimer of God's word (4:43). Miracles occurred in the context of His preaching ministry. "Master" (v 5) is used only by Luke in the New Testament, always as an address to Jesus. The miracle showed Peter that Jesus was holy. Encounter with Jesus led not to death (Ex 33:20) but to mission service. Miracles drew crowds to whom Jesus could preach (v 15). God's power was the necessary ingredient for miracles (v 17). Miracles led the audience to praise and reverence. See note on Mk 2:1–5.

5:1–11 MIRACLE, Nature—Miracles use natural elements in an unexpected way for a spiritual purpose. The fish were there. The miracle came at Jesus' timing and authoritative statement. The immediate result was the astonishment of Peter, James, and John. Jesus could accomplish what professional fishermen could not. They recognized the holy nature of Jesus and their own sinfulness. The ultimate result was their following Jesus. Whatever way God chooses to work in our world to perform miracles, He seeks to lead us to confess our sin and follow Him without reservations. See Jn 21:4–11.

5:8–11 HUMANITY, Relationship to God—Christ's miracle amazed fisherman Peter. He recognized immediately only God could perform such an act. He fell in worship and in the presence of the holy God confessed his sin. The first step in human relationship to God is recognition of His holy purity and our sinfulness. God continues the relationship by accepting our repentance and forgiving us.

5:8–10 REVELATION, Jesus Christ—Miraculous revelation sought to lead people to recognize Jesus as the holy God in person and thus to recognize their own sinfulness. From those who responded with such faith, Jesus picked followers to do what He was doing, become fishers, catching other people for God. See note on Mt 4:19.

The Man With Leprosy

5:12–14pp — Mt 8:2–4; Mk 1:40–44

12While Jesus was in one of the towns,
a man came along who was covered with
leprosy.[z][e] When he saw Jesus, he fell
with his face to the ground and begged
him, "Lord, if you are willing, you can
make me clean."
13Jesus reached out his hand and
touched the man. "I am willing," he said.
"Be clean!" And immediately the leprosy
left him.
14Then Jesus ordered him, "Don't tell
anyone,[f] but go, show yourself to the
priest and offer the sacrifices that Moses
commanded[g] for your cleansing, as a testimony to them."
15Yet the news about him spread all the
more,[h] so that crowds of people came to
hear him and to be healed of their sicknesses. 16But Jesus often withdrew to
lonely places and prayed.[i]

Jesus Heals a Paralytic

5:18–26pp — Mt 9:2–8; Mk 2:3–12

17One day as he was teaching, Pharisees and teachers of the law,[j] who had
come from every village of Galilee and
from Judea and Jerusalem, were sitting
there. And the power of the Lord was
present for him to heal the sick.[k] 18Some
men came carrying a paralytic on a mat
and tried to take him into the house to lay
him before Jesus. 19When they could not
find a way to do this because of the
crowd, they went up on the roof and lowered him on his mat through the tiles into
the middle of the crowd, right in front of
Jesus.
20When Jesus saw their faith, he said,
"Friend, your sins are forgiven."[l]
21The Pharisees and the teachers of the
law began thinking to themselves, "Who
is this fellow who speaks blasphemy?
Who can forgive sins but God alone?"[m]
22Jesus knew what they were thinking
and asked, "Why are you thinking these
things in your hearts? 23Which is easier:
to say, 'Your sins are forgiven,' or to say,
'Get up and walk'? 24But that you may
know that the Son of Man[n] has authority
on earth to forgive sins. . . ." He said to
the paralyzed man, "I tell you, get up,
take your mat and go home." 25Immedi-
ately he stood up in front of them, took
what he had been lying on and went
home praising God. 26Everyone was
amazed and gave praise to God.[o] They
were filled with awe and said, "We have
seen remarkable things today."

The Calling of Levi

5:27–32pp — Mt 9:9–13; Mk 2:14–17

27After this, Jesus went out and saw a
tax collector by the name of Levi sitting at
his tax booth. "Follow me,"[p] Jesus said
to him, 28and Levi got up, left everything
and followed him.[q]
29Then Levi held a great banquet for
Jesus at his house, and a large crowd of
tax collectors[r] and others were eating
with them. 30But the Pharisees and the
teachers of the law who belonged to their
sect[s] complained to his disciples, "Why
do you eat and drink with tax collectors
and 'sinners'?"[t]
31Jesus answered them, "It is not the
healthy who need a doctor, but the sick.
32I have not come to call the righteous,
but sinners to repentance."[u]

Jesus Questioned About Fasting

5:33–39pp — Mt 9:14–17; Mk 2:18–22

33They said to him, "John's disciples[v]

5:12 [e]S Mt 8:2
5:14 [f]S Mt 8:4 [g]Lev 14:2-32
5:15 [h]S Mt 9:26
5:16 [i]S Lk 3:21
5:17 [j]Mt 15:1; Lk 2:46 [k]Mk 5:30; Lk 6:19
5:20 [l]Lk 7:48,49
5:21 [m]Isa 43:25
5:24 [n]S Mt 8:20
5:26 [o]S Mt 9:8
5:27 [p]S Mt 4:19
5:28 [q]ver 11; S Mt 4:19
5:29 [r]Lk 15:1
5:30 [s]Ac 23:9 [t]S Mt 9:11
5:32 [u]S Jn 3:17
5:33 [v]Lk 7:18; Jn 1:35; 3:25,26

[z]12 The Greek word was used for various diseases affecting the skin—not necessarily leprosy.

5:12–26 MIRACLE, Christ—Miracles should help people in their spiritual as well as their physical needs. Christ's miracles taught a great deal about who He is. Leprosy was greatly feared in the ancient world, and authorities had carefully outlined conditions for testing its healing. The leper had no question about the ability of Jesus to heal him—only as to His willingness. He did not know Jesus! Jesus was willing to accept the scandal of being ritually unclean. Helping people came before pleasing public piety. Jesus was not willing to let the public raise false expectations of Him in the use of His power. Thus, He did not let popularity as a healer interfere with His teaching ministry.

5:14 JESUS CHRIST, Secret—See note on Mt 12:13–21.

5:16 PRAYER, Jesus' Example—See note on 4:42–43.

5:17 GOD, Power—The power of God made the healing miracles possible. The mighty power evident in the works of Jesus could only be the power of God. Understanding this helped His disciples and others finally come to know that Jesus was divine. The One who brought about the beginning of all things also has the power to intervene and redirect the course of events in any of His creatures. God usually works through natural law, which is the expression of His will as much as miracles. See Mt 5:45 where the rain and the sunshine in their normal patterns are simply the result of God's orders. God always has the prerogative of working in extraordinary ways.

5:17–26 EVIL AND SUFFERING, Human Origin—The teachers knew only God could forgive sins. When Jesus forgave sins, they rightly implied He was acting as God. Wrongly, they refused to accept the healing as evidence that Jesus was the Son of God. They thus conceived evil thoughts accusing Jesus of evil. When Jesus forgave the man's sins, He did not specifically say the man's disease was due to his sin. See note on Jn 9:1–4.

5:17–26 SALVATION, Healing—See note on Mt 9:1–8.

5:21–24 GOD, Trinity—See note on Mk 2:7.

5:22 REVELATION, Jesus Christ—Christ revealed both that He has the power to forgive (as God) and that God through forgiveness releases captives of body and mind. See note on Mt 9:4.

5:25–26 PRAYER, Praise—Jesus performed this miracle in such a way that God received the glory. The natural response to miracle is to glorify God.

5:29–32 SIN, Violation—See note on Mk 2:15–16.

5:31–32 JESUS CHRIST, Mission—See note on Mk 2:17.

5:33–39 JESUS CHRIST, Death—See note on Mk 2:20.

5:33–35 PRAYER, Lament—See note on Mt 9:14–15.

often fast and pray, and so do the disciples of the Pharisees, but yours go on eating and drinking."
34Jesus answered, "Can you make the
guests of the bridegroom[w] fast while he is
with them? 35But the time will come
when the bridegroom will be taken from
them;[x] in those days they will fast."
36He told them this parable: "No one
tears a patch from a new garment and
sews it on an old one. If he does, he will
have torn the new garment, and the
patch from the new will not match the
old. 37And no one pours new wine into
old wineskins. If he does, the new wine
will burst the skins, the wine will run out
and the wineskins will be ruined. 38No,
new wine must be poured into new wineskins. 39And no one after drinking old
wine wants the new, for he says, 'The old
is better.' "

Chapter 6

Lord of the Sabbath

6:1–11pp — Mt 12:1–14; Mk 2:23–3:6

ONE Sabbath Jesus was going through
the grainfields, and his disciples began to pick some heads of grain, rub them
in their hands and eat the kernels.[y]
2Some of the Pharisees asked, "Why are
you doing what is unlawful on the Sabbath?"[z]
3Jesus answered them, "Have you never read what David did when he and his
companions were hungry?[a] 4He entered
the house of God, and taking the consecrated bread, he ate what is lawful only
for priests to eat.[b] And he also gave some
to his companions." 5Then Jesus said to
them, "The Son of Man[c] is Lord of the
Sabbath."
6On another Sabbath[d] he went into
the synagogue and was teaching, and a
man was there whose right hand was
shriveled. 7The Pharisees and the teachers of the law were looking for a reason to
accuse Jesus, so they watched him closely[e] to see if he would heal on the Sabbath.[f] 8But Jesus knew what they were
thinking[g] and said to the man with the
shriveled hand, "Get up and stand in
front of everyone." So he got up and
stood there.
9Then Jesus said to them, "I ask you,
which is lawful on the Sabbath: to do
good or to do evil, to save life or to destroy it?"
10He looked around at them all, and
then said to the man, "Stretch out your
hand." He did so, and his hand was completely restored. 11But they were furious[h]
and began to discuss with one another
what they might do to Jesus.

The Twelve Apostles

6:13–16pp — Mt 10:2–4; Mk 3:16–19; Ac 1:13

12One of those days Jesus went out to a
mountainside to pray, and spent the night
praying to God.[i] 13When morning came,
he called his disciples to him and chose
twelve of them, whom he also designated
apostles:[j] 14Simon (whom he named Peter), his brother Andrew, James, John,
Philip, Bartholomew, 15Matthew,[k]
Thomas, James son of Alphaeus, Simon
who was called the Zealot, 16Judas son of
James, and Judas Iscariot, who became a
traitor.

Blessings and Woes

6:20–23pp — Mt 5:3–12

17He went down with them and stood
on a level place. A large crowd of his disciples was there and a great number of
people from all over Judea, from Jerusalem, and from the coast of Tyre and Sidon,[l] 18who had come to hear him and
to be healed of their diseases. Those troubled by evil[a] spirits were cured, 19and
the people all tried to touch him,[m] be-

5:34 [w]Jn 3:29
5:35 [x]Lk 9:22; 17:22; Jn 16:5-7
6:1 [y]Dt 23:25
6:2 [z]S Mt 12:2
6:3 [a]1Sa 21:6
6:4 [b]Lev 24:5,9
6:5 [c]S Mt 8:20
6:6 [d]ver 1
6:7 [e]S Mt 12:10 [f]S Mt 12:2
6:8 [g]S Mt 9:4
6:11 [h]Jn 5:18
6:12 [i]S Lk 3:21
6:13 [j]S Mk 6:30
6:15 [k]Mt 9:9
6:17 [l]Mt 4:25; S Mt 11:21; Mk 3:7,8
6:19 [m]S Mt 9:20

[a]*18* Greek *unclean*

6:1–11 JESUS CHRIST, Authority—See note on Mk 2:23–28.

6:12–16 JESUS CHRIST, Mission—Jesus did not work alone in His mission. He called twelve men of varied backgrounds to train to continue His mission. Jesus' calling did not transform these men into saints or slaves. They remained free to follow, deny, or betray. Jesus' mission is to lead people to follow Him freely and gladly.

6:12–13 PRAYER, Jesus' Example—Major decisions in Jesus' life were preceded by prayer. Before He chose the twelve (vv 13–16), He prayed all night. Important decisions should call us to long, extended prayer periods. See Guide to Extended Prayer, pp. 1767–1769.

6:13 CHURCH LEADERS, The Twelve—An apostle is a person commissioned to act with full authority for another. Jesus chose the twelve apostles from His larger group of followers so they could learn His ways and teaching from their closer fellowship with Him. He could then empower them to work in His name and extend His ministry in Israel. They preached His message of the coming of the kingdom and were given the necessary power—authority over demons—to fulfill their task. Because the apostles were His agents, those who responded to the apostles were, in effect, responding to Jesus.

6:17 CHURCH LEADERS, Disciple—Disciples are not limited to the twelve apostles. All Christians are called to be disciples. A disciple is one committed to follow Jesus Christ as Lord regardless of the cost (14:26–33). Disciples are called to a higher righteousness (Mt 5:20) and are called to make others disciples (Mt 28:19). Among His many followers Jesus chose twelve for a special role. Similarly, many disciples of Jesus today are chosen to carry out special functions in the life of the church. Not all can be the head, the eyes, or the ears. Some must be the feet (1 Co 12:12–26), that is, there must be some specialization among the disciples. No disciple is unimportant to the life of the church body. Everyone has an important function. No disciple can claim to be more essential than another.

6:19 JESUS CHRIST, Miracles—See note on 5:1–26.

cause power was coming from him and
healing them all.[n]
20Looking at his disciples, he said:

"Blessed are you who are poor,
for yours is the kingdom of God.[o]
21Blessed are you who hunger now,
for you will be satisfied.[p]
Blessed are you who weep now,
for you will laugh.[q]
22Blessed are you when men hate you,
when they exclude you[r] and insult
you[s]
and reject your name as evil,
because of the Son of Man.[t]

23"Rejoice in that day and leap for
joy,[u] because great is your reward in
heaven. For that is how their fathers
treated the prophets.[v]

24"But woe to you who are rich,[w]
for you have already received your
comfort.[x]
25Woe to you who are well fed now,
for you will go hungry.[y]
Woe to you who laugh now,
for you will mourn and weep.[z]
26Woe to you when all men speak well
of you,
for that is how their fathers treated
the false prophets.[a]

Love for Enemies

6:29,30pp — Mt 5:39–42

27"But I tell you who hear me: Love
your enemies, do good to those who hate
you,[b] 28bless those who curse you, pray

6:19 [n]Mk 5:30; Lk 5:17
6:20 [o]S Mt 25:34
6:21 [p]Isa 55:1,2; Mt 5:6 [q]Isa 61:2,3; Mt 5:4; Rev 7:17
6:22 [r]Jn 9:22; 16:2 [s]Isa 51:7 [t]S Jn 15:21
6:23 [u]S Mt 5:12 [v]S Mt 5:12
6:24 [w]Jas 5:1 [x]Lk 16:25
6:25 [y]Isa 65:13 [z]Pr 14:13
6:26 [a]S Mt 7:15
6:27 [b]ver 35; Mt 5:44; Ro 12:20
6:28 [c]S Mt 5:44
6:30 [d]Dt 15:7,8, 10; Pr 21:26
6:31 [e]Mt 7:12
6:32 [f]Mt 5:46
6:34 [g]Mt 5:42
6:35 [h]ver 27 [i]S Ro 8:14 [j]S Mk 5:7
6:36 [k]Jas 2:13 [l]Mt 5:48; 6:1; Lk 11:2; 12:32; Ro 8:15; Eph 4:6; 1Pe 1:17; 1Jn 1:3; 3:1
6:37 [m]S Mt 7:1 [n]Mt 6:14
6:38 [o]Ps 79:12; Isa 65:6,7 [p]S Mt 7:2

for those who mistreat you.[c] 29If someone strikes you on one cheek, turn to him
the other also. If someone takes your
cloak, do not stop him from taking your
tunic. 30Give to everyone who asks you,
and if anyone takes what belongs to you,
do not demand it back.[d] 31Do to others as
you would have them do to you.[e]
32"If you love those who love you,
what credit is that to you?[f] Even 'sinners' love those who love them. 33And if
you do good to those who are good to
you, what credit is that to you? Even 'sinners' do that. 34And if you lend to those
from whom you expect repayment, what
credit is that to you?[g] Even 'sinners' lend
to 'sinners,' expecting to be repaid in full.
35But love your enemies, do good to
them,[h] and lend to them without expecting to get anything back. Then your reward will be great, and you will be sons[i]
of the Most High,[j] because he is kind to
the ungrateful and wicked. 36Be merciful,[k] just as your Father[l] is merciful.

Judging Others

6:37–42pp — Mt 7:1–5

37"Do not judge, and you will not be
judged.[m] Do not condemn, and you will
not be condemned. Forgive, and you will
be forgiven.[n] 38Give, and it will be given
to you. A good measure, pressed down,
shaken together and running over, will
be poured into your lap.[o] For with the
measure you use, it will be measured to
you."[p]
39He also told them this parable: "Can

6:20–23 JESUS CHRIST, Kingdom of God—Luke's account of the Beatitudes is in the second person—you. Matthew's account is in the third person plural (Mt 5:3–10). Luke gives a corresponding list of woes for those who do not do the requirements of God (vv 24–26; Mt 23). Luke's account does not spiritualize the poor and the hungry (Mt 5:3,6). God's kingdom includes people who depend on God rather than on personal power, talents, and resources. See note on Mt 5:1–12.

6:20–36 EVIL AND SUFFERING, Endurance—See notes on 4:18; Mt 5:10–12, 38–48.

6:20 REVELATION, Commitment—For those who believe and for those who need to, Jesus revealed the character of God not only in His own actions but by interpreting God's heart in statements collected later to teach and direct disciples. Organized for teaching purposes, these sayings, often known as the Sermon on the Plain parallel to Matthew's Sermon on the Mount (5—7), were probably used to instruct new converts in the early church. They call disciples to accept God's revelation and live it in daily life.

6:20 THE CHURCH, God's Kingdom—The kingdom of God belongs to the weak and the outcast of the world rather than to the wealthy and the powerful. The kingdom does not belong to the poor because they are poor. The kingdom belongs to all who humble their spirits before God. See notes on Mt 18:1–4; 19:14.

6:27–36 HUMANITY, Relationships—See note on Mt 5:43–48.

6:27–35 DISCIPLESHIP, Neighbor Love—The Golden Rule is the key to understanding the demands of love of neighbor. For the disciple, neighbor love must include every person, even enemies. Such love is not partial, nor is it se Mercy controls the disciple's life, not justice or greed. disciple asks not what is due me but what can I do for someone else. See note on 10:25–37.

6:28 PRAYER, Intercession—See note on Mt 5:44–45.

6:35–36 THE CHURCH, God's Community—Sons of the Most High must follow in the steps of the Most High, obeying His commands and showing kindness to friends and enemies alike. See note on Mt 5:9.

6:36 GOD, Grace—God is a merciful God, motivated to deal kindly with us out of His deep love. God's fundamental stance towards us is that of mercy, but that mercy makes a stringent demand upon us. If we receive His mercy, He expects us to reproduce that kind of mercy in all our human relationships.

6:36 JESUS CHRIST, Son of God—Jesus, the Son of God, taught His followers to see God as their Father, too.

6:38 STEWARDSHIP, Rewards—Our motives for giving usually determine the rewards we expect. Like a generous merchant who dispenses a heaping measure of grain, God pours out love and blessings to those who exhibit love for others by gracious giving. The greatest reward to the faithful giver is the joy of participating in Christ's ministry and seeing the results. Christ taught that rewards are gifts from God. They cannot be earned and are primarily spiritual rather than material. God may choose to provide material blessings as well as all spiritual blessings, but we have no right or reason to demand or expect material gifts. The lives of Jesus and Paul illustrate this. The wealth of joyous faith and fulfilling life are the greatest rewards possible.

6:39–40 EDUCATION, Example—Learners will be like

a blind man lead a blind man? Will they
not both fall into a pit?[q] 40A student is
not above his teacher, but everyone who
is fully trained will be like his teacher.[r]
41"Why do you look at the speck of
sawdust in your brother's eye and pay no
attention to the plank in your own eye?
42How can you say to your brother,
'Brother, let me take the speck out of
your eye,' when you yourself fail to see
the plank in your own eye? You hypocrite, first take the plank out of your eye,
and then you will see clearly to remove
the speck from your brother's eye.

A Tree and Its Fruit

6:43,44pp — Mt 7:16,18,20

43"No good tree bears bad fruit, nor
does a bad tree bear good fruit. 44Each
tree is recognized by its own fruit.[s] People do not pick figs from thornbushes, or
grapes from briers. 45The good man
brings good things out of the good stored
up in his heart, and the evil man brings
evil things out of the evil stored up in his
heart. For out of the overflow of his heart
his mouth speaks.[t]

The Wise and Foolish Builders

6:47–49pp — Mt 7:24–27

46"Why do you call me, 'Lord, Lord,'[u]
and do not do what I say?[v] 47I will show
you what he is like who comes to me and
hears my words and puts them into practice.[w] 48He is like a man building a
house, who dug down deep and laid the
foundation on rock. When a flood came,
the torrent struck that house but could
not shake it, because it was well built.
49But the one who hears my words and
does not put them into practice is like a
man who built a house on the ground
without a foundation. The moment the
torrent struck that house, it collapsed and
its destruction was complete."

Chapter 7

The Faith of the Centurion

7:1–10pp — Mt 8:5–13

WHEN Jesus had finished saying all
this[x] in the hearing of the people,
he entered Capernaum. 2There a centurion's servant, whom his master valued
highly, was sick and about to die. 3The
centurion heard of Jesus and sent some
elders of the Jews to him, asking him to
come and heal his servant. 4When they
came to Jesus, they pleaded earnestly
with him, "This man deserves to have
you do this, 5because he loves our nation
and has built our synagogue." 6So Jesus
went with them.
He was not far from the house when
the centurion sent friends to say to him:
"Lord, don't trouble yourself, for I do not
deserve to have you come under my roof.
7That is why I did not even consider myself worthy to come to you. But say the
word, and my servant will be healed.[y]
8For I myself am a man under authority,
with soldiers under me. I tell this one,
'Go,' and he goes; and that one, 'Come,'
and he comes. I say to my servant, 'Do
this,' and he does it."
9When Jesus heard this, he was
amazed at him, and turning to the crowd
following him, he said, "I tell you, I have
not found such great faith even in Israel."
10Then the men who had been sent returned to the house and found the servant well.

Jesus Raises a Widow's Son

7:11–16Ref — 1Ki 17:17–24; 2Ki 4:32–37; Mk 5:21–24,35–43; Jn 11:1–44

11Soon afterward, Jesus went to a town

6:39 [q]Mt 15:14
6:40 [r]S Jn 13:16
6:44 [s]Mt 12:33
6:45 [t]Pr 4:23; Mt 12:34,35; Mk 7:20
6:46 [u]S Jn 13:13 [v]Mal 1:6; Mt 7:21
6:47 [w]Lk 8:21; 11:28; Jas 1:22-25
7:1 [x]Mt 7:28
7:7 [y]Ps 107:20

---

their teachers, for better or for worse. Rarely will pupils go beyond their master's level of knowledge or attitude toward the subject matter. Whether the teacher is informed or naive, enthusiastic or dull, the personal example will profoundly influence learners, probably more than the subject matter taught.

6:46 JESUS CHRIST, Lord—Lord is more than a polite title of respect used to talk to or about Jesus. Lord represents Jesus as our Master and calls us to strict obedience. See note on Lk 1:5–23.

6:46–49 ELECTION, Righteousness—The elect have true wisdom because they are obedient persons who hear God's words and practice them. Their lives have secure foundations. Election results in righteous, obedient lives.

6:46–49 DISCIPLESHIP, Lordship of Christ—Discipleship involves *hearing* the words of the Lord as authoritative teaching and *heeding* them as authoritative command. Jesus showed the foolishness of merely claiming Him as Lord and then not being obedient. The implication is that we should stop claiming Jesus is the Lord of our lives if we are not willing to put His teachings into practice. When we make false claims about Christ's lordship in our lives, we are in for a shocking surprise. See note on Ro 6:5–18.

6:47 REVELATION, Faithfulness—True followers are those who receive God's revelation and put the teachings into practice in their daily lives. See note on 6:20.

7:1–10 JESUS CHRIST, Miracles—Jesus' miracles show He is God because in them the unequaled power of God was at work. A Roman officer in charge of 100 soldiers saluted Christ as a servant greets a master. Jesus' nature as God was visible through the miracles but only to people with faith like the centurion's. Compare Mt 8:1–10; Jn 4:46–54.

7:1–10 MIRACLE, Faith—See note on Mt 8:5–13.

7:1–10 EVANGELISM, Results—A foreign soldier displayed great faith, receiving as high a compliment as Jesus gave anyone. Such faith comes by God's grace to those who humbly accept it (Eph 2:8–9). Great faith produces great works.

7:4–10 PRAYER, Humility—See note on Mt 8:10–13. The Jewish elders considered the centurion worthy of Jesus' attention (v 4); he considered himself unworthy (v 6). Interceding for good citizens is a prayer task of believers. When such people are not believers, their salvation becomes the subject of intercession.

7:11–17 JESUS CHRIST, Miracles—Compare 1 Ki 17:17–24; 2 Ki 4:32–37. This mighty work demonstrated Jesus' power over the last enemy, death. The dire circum-

called Nain, and his disciples and a large
crowd went along with him. 12As he approached the town gate, a dead person
was being carried out—the only son of
his mother, and she was a widow. And a
large crowd from the town was with her.
13When the Lord[z] saw her, his heart
went out to her and he said, "Don't cry."
14Then he went up and touched the
coffin, and those carrying it stood still. He
said, "Young man, I say to you, get up!"[a]
15The dead man sat up and began to talk,
and Jesus gave him back to his mother.
16They were all filled with awe[b] and
praised God.[c] "A great prophet[d] has appeared among us," they said. "God has
come to help his people."[e] 17This news
about Jesus spread throughout Judea[b]
and the surrounding country.[f]

Jesus and John the Baptist

7:18–35pp — Mt 11:2–19

18John's[g] disciples[h] told him about all
these things. Calling two of them, 19he
sent them to the Lord to ask, "Are you
the one who was to come, or should we
expect someone else?"
20When the men came to Jesus, they
said, "John the Baptist sent us to you to
ask, 'Are you the one who was to come,
or should we expect someone else?' "
21At that very time Jesus cured many
who had diseases, sicknesses[i] and evil
spirits, and gave sight to many who were
blind. 22So he replied to the messengers,
"Go back and report to John what you
have seen and heard: The blind receive
sight, the lame walk, those who have leprosy[c] are cured, the deaf hear, the dead
are raised, and the good news is preached
to the poor.[j] 23Blessed is the man who
does not fall away on account of me."
24After John's messengers left, Jesus
began to speak to the crowd about John:
"What did you go out into the desert to
see? A reed swayed by the wind? 25If not,
what did you go out to see? A man
dressed in fine clothes? No, those who
wear expensive clothes and indulge in
luxury are in palaces. 26But what did you
go out to see? A prophet?[k] Yes, I tell you,
and more than a prophet. 27This is the
one about whom it is written:

> " 'I will send my messenger ahead of
> you,
> who will prepare your way before
> you.'[d] [l]

28I tell you, among those born of women
there is no one greater than John; yet the
one who is least in the kingdom of God[m]
is greater than he."
29(All the people, even the tax collectors, when they heard Jesus' words, acknowledged that God's way was right, because they had been baptized by John.[n]
30But the Pharisees and experts in the
law[o] rejected God's purpose for themselves, because they had not been baptized by John.)
31"To what, then, can I compare the

7:13 [z]ver 19; Lk 10:1; 13:15; 17:5; 22:61; 24:34; Jn 11:2
7:14 [a]Mt 9:25; Mk 1:31; Lk 8:54; Jn 11:43; Ac 9:40
7:16 [b]Lk 1:65 [c]S Mt 9:8 [d]ver 39; S Mt 21:11 [e]Lk 1:68
7:17 [f]S Mt 9:26
7:18 [g]S Mt 3:1 [h]S Lk 5:33
7:21 [i]S Mt 4:23
7:22 [j]Isa 29:18,19; 35:5,6; 61:1,2; Lk 4:18
7:26 [k]S Mt 11:9
7:27 [l]Mal 3:1; Mt 11:10; Mk 1:2
7:28 [m]S Mt 3:2
7:29 [n]Mt 21:32; Mk 1:5; Lk 3:12
7:30 [o]S Mt 22:35

[b]*17* Or *the land of the Jews* [c]*22* The Greek word was used for various diseases affecting the skin—not necessarily leprosy. [d]*27* Mal. 3:1

stances of the recipient and the deep compassion of Jesus are to be noted. The miracle did not automatically prove Jesus was unique among humans. It showed He was at least one of the prophets God sent to help His people.

7:11–17 MIRACLE, Christ—Miracle flows from God's compassion and shows God helps His people. There is no confession of faith or even request for help. The young man was the widow's only son, and his death left her desolate. Jesus was moved with compassion: His love overflowed. In touching the coffin Jesus became unclean, just as in touching the leper (5:13) He became unclean. Miracles show God's compassionate willingness to overcome all obstacles to help us. They lead us to praise God and acclaim Christ as our Lord, God's greatest Prophet.

7:16 HISTORY, Salvation—Jesus' miracles showed His divine power. In Him God had entered history to redeem His people. The Bible repeatedly underlines the historical nature of salvation.

7:16 SALVATION, Definition—The resurrection of the widow's son in Nain was a sign that God had come in Jesus of Nazareth to deliver His people. Their awe and praise reflected their salvation. See note on Ex 20:20. Faith begins with awe and reverence for God.

7:16 WORSHIP, Reverence—See note on Mt 9:8.

7:16 PRAYER, Praise—See note on 5:25–26. Signs of God's presence among us should lead to praise.

7:18–35 JESUS CHRIST, John—See note on Mt 11:2–19.

7:23 ELECTION, Faith—John's disciples could not understand how John as God's elect could suffer imprisonment. John could not decide how Jesus' ministry filled the role of the promised Messiah. Personal suffering and lack of worldly recognition and power may lead people away from Jesus. The elect trust Jesus even when human logic may point in other directions.

7:28 THE CHURCH, God's Kingdom—Greatness in God's kingdom is determined by humility, faith, and trust. See note on Mt 18:1–4. John exhibited these qualities, but Jesus referred to John the Baptist as the end of an era. John did not live to see the triumph of Jesus over sin and death at the cross. This event marked the beginning of God's reign in a unique way.

7:29–30 ORDINANCES, Baptism by John—The people, even tax collectors, strongly supported the words of Jesus because they had been baptized by John. The Pharisees and experts in the law stood in opposition because they had rejected John's baptism. Thus baptism became the public sign by which followers of John were identified and distinguished from his opponents. In the same way, baptism became the sign by which Christians were identified. Later, in the time of the great Roman persecutions, it could mark them for martyrdom.

7:31–35 SIN, Blindness—Failure to see God at work indicates spiritual blindness. God worked through the ascetic John and through Jesus, who participated in life's normal activities. Jesus' opponents had their own traditions and dogmas about how God must act to fulfill His promises and save His people. These traditions and dogmas blinded them to God's plan of action.

7:31–50 REVELATION, Messengers—See note on Mt 11:18–19. The religious community called John too rigid and sad. They called Jesus' ministry too free and happy. They would not respond to any type invitation (revelation) from God. Often people the religious community rejects respond

people of this generation? What are they
like? 32They are like children sitting in
the marketplace and calling out to each
other:

" 'We played the flute for you,
and you did not dance;
we sang a dirge,
and you did not cry.'

33For John the Baptist came neither eating bread nor drinking wine,[p] and you
say, 'He has a demon.' 34The Son of Man
came eating and drinking, and you say,
'Here is a glutton and a drunkard, a friend
of tax collectors and "sinners." '[q] 35But
wisdom is proved right by all her children."

Jesus Anointed by a Sinful Woman

7:37–39Ref — Mt 26:6–13; Mk 14:3–9; Jn 12:1–8
7:41,42Ref — Mt 18:23–34

36Now one of the Pharisees invited
Jesus to have dinner with him, so he
went to the Pharisee's house and reclined
at the table. 37When a woman who had
lived a sinful life in that town learned that
Jesus was eating at the Pharisee's house,
she brought an alabaster jar of perfume,
38and as she stood behind him at his feet
weeping, she began to wet his feet with
her tears. Then she wiped them with her
hair, kissed them and poured perfume on
them.
39When the Pharisee who had invited
him saw this, he said to himself, "If this
man were a prophet,[r] he would know
who is touching him and what kind of
woman she is—that she is a sinner."
40Jesus answered him, "Simon, I have
something to tell you."
"Tell me, teacher," he said.
41"Two men owed money to a certain
moneylender. One owed him five hundred denarii,[e] and the other fifty. 42Nei-
ther of them had the money to pay him
back, so he canceled the debts of both.
Now which of them will love him more?"
43Simon replied, "I suppose the one
who had the bigger debt canceled."
"You have judged correctly," Jesus
said.
44Then he turned toward the woman
and said to Simon, "Do you see this woman? I came into your house. You did not
give me any water for my feet,[s] but she
wet my feet with her tears and wiped
them with her hair. 45You did not give
me a kiss,[t] but this woman, from the
time I entered, has not stopped kissing
my feet. 46You did not put oil on my
head,[u] but she has poured perfume on
my feet. 47Therefore, I tell you, her many
sins have been forgiven—for she loved
much. But he who has been forgiven little
loves little."
48Then Jesus said to her, "Your sins are
forgiven."[v]
49The other guests began to say among
themselves, "Who is this who even forgives sins?"
50Jesus said to the woman, "Your faith
has saved you;[w] go in peace."[x]

Chapter 8

The Parable of the Sower

8:4–15pp — Mt 13:2–23; Mk 4:1–20

AFTER this, Jesus traveled about from
one town and village to another, proclaiming the good news of the kingdom of
God.[y] The Twelve were with him, 2and
also some women who had been cured of
evil spirits and diseases: Mary (called
Magdalene)[z] from whom seven demons

7:33 [p]Lk 1:15
7:34 [q]Lk 5:29,30; 15:1,2
7:39 [r]ver 16; S Mt 21:11
7:44 [s]Ge 18:4; 19:2; 43:24; Jdg 19:21; Jn 13:4-14; 1Ti 5:10
7:45 [t]Lk 22:47,48; S Ro 16:16
7:46 [u]Ps 23:5; Ecc 9:8
7:48 [v]Mt 9:2
7:50 [w]S Mt 9:22 [x]S Ac 15:33
8:1 [y]S Mt 4:23
8:2 [z]Mt 27:55,56

[e]*41* A denarius was a coin worth about a day's wages.

better to Christ's revelation than do the religious leaders.
7:36–38 JESUS CHRIST, Teaching—See note on Mt 26:6–13. Jesus sought to teach in relationships and parables the value of love. He displayed His own love by accepting persons whom respected society ignored or shunned. He showed His equality with God by forgiving sins. He elicited faith from people and thus gave them salvation. He showed that the greater the debtor, the greater is grace and the greater should be the gratitude for forgiveness.
7:36–50 SALVATION, Love of God—The woman in the house of Simon demonstrated the lavish kind of love Christians should have for Christ their Savior. The point of this account is that one who loves much is forgiven much. Also, one who is forgiven much loves much.
7:39 SIN, Violation—See notes on Mk 2:15–16; 7:1–22.
7:40–50 STEWARDSHIP, Service to God—Forgiveness and salvation are the greatest gifts God gives us. Being forgiven produces gratitude. Gratitude to God is well expressed in giving of self and possessions. See note on Ac 4:32—5:11.
8:1–3 STEWARDSHIP, Service to God—Stewardship involves using our financial means to make it possible for God's called-out people to make ministry their full-time occupation. During Jesus' ministry, these women provided necessities for Him and His disciples. See note on Ac 4:32—5:11.
8:1 THE CHURCH, God's Kingdom—See note on 4:43.
8:1 PROCLAMATION, Authoritative—Jesus' ministry illustrated the nature of proclamation. The Greek uses two verbs to describe Jesus' preaching ministry. Proclaiming (Greek *kērussō*) is the clear and authoritative announcement of news. The proclaimer (Greek *kērux*) or herald was the king's spokesman. His announcement carried royal authority and sought to inform the people of important events and decisions. Most often the herald was a slave of the king. The New Testament uses the noun (*kērux*) only three times (1 Ti 2:7; 2 Ti 1:11; 2 Pe 2:5). The emphasis is on the act of proclamation and its content, not on the person or office. The content focuses on the presence of God's kingdom in Jesus and a reordering of life and the universe under God's rule. To announce the good news (Greek *euangelizō*) is to bring a message of gladness or good news. Whereas the content of Old Testament proclamation often centered on rebuke and judgment, the New Testament message centers on the good news of opportunity for eternal life through the kingdom of God established in the life, death, and resurrection of Christ. See notes on Lk 10:9; Jer 19:14–15. The New Testament calls God's people to follow Jesus in proclaiming with authority the good news of and from our heavenly King.

had come out; 3Joanna the wife of Cuza,
the manager of Herod's[a] household; Su-
sanna; and many others. These women
were helping to support them out of their
own means.
4While a large crowd was gathering
and people were coming to Jesus from
town after town, he told this parable: 5"A
farmer went out to sow his seed. As he
was scattering the seed, some fell along
the path; it was trampled on, and the
birds of the air ate it up. 6Some fell on
rock, and when it came up, the plants
withered because they had no moisture.
7Other seed fell among thorns, which
grew up with it and choked the plants.
8Still other seed fell on good soil. It came
up and yielded a crop, a hundred times
more than was sown."

When he said this, he called out, "He
who has ears to hear, let him hear."[b]
9His disciples asked him what this parable meant. 10He said, "The knowledge of
the secrets of the kingdom of God has
been given to you,[c] but to others I speak
in parables, so that,

" 'though seeing, they may not see;
though hearing, they may not
understand.'[f][d]

11"This is the meaning of the parable:
The seed is the word of God.[e] 12Those
along the path are the ones who hear,
and then the devil comes and takes away
the word from their hearts, so that they
may not believe and be saved. 13Those on
the rock are the ones who receive the
word with joy when they hear it, but they
have no root. They believe for a while,
but in the time of testing they fall away.[f]
14The seed that fell among thorns stands
for those who hear, but as they go on
their way they are choked by life's worries, riches[g] and pleasures, and they do
not mature. 15But the seed on good soil
stands for those with a noble and good
heart, who hear the word, retain it, and
by persevering produce a crop.

A Lamp on a Stand

16"No one lights a lamp and hides it in
a jar or puts it under a bed. Instead, he
puts it on a stand, so that those who come
in can see the light.[h] 17For there is nothing hidden that will not be disclosed, and
nothing concealed that will not be known
or brought out into the open.[i] 18There-
fore consider carefully how you listen.
Whoever has will be given more; whoever does not have, even what he thinks he
has will be taken from him."[j]

Jesus' Mother and Brothers

8:19–21pp — Mt 12:46–50; Mk 3:31–35

19Now Jesus' mother and brothers
came to see him, but they were not able
to get near him because of the crowd.
20Someone told him, "Your mother and
brothers[k] are standing outside, wanting
to see you."
21He replied, "My mother and brothers
are those who hear God's word and put it
into practice."[l]

Jesus Calms the Storm

8:22–25pp — Mt 8:23–27; Mk 4:36–41
8:22–25Ref — Mk 6:47–52; Jn 6:16–21

22One day Jesus said to his disciples,
"Let's go over to the other side of the
lake." So they got into a boat and set out.
23As they sailed, he fell asleep. A squall
came down on the lake, so that the boat
was being swamped, and they were in
great danger.
24The disciples went and woke him,

8:3 [a]S Mt 14:1
8:8 [b]S Mt 11:15
8:10 [c]S Mt 13:11 [d]Isa 6:9; S Mt 13:13,14
8:11 [e]S Heb 4:12
8:13 [f]Mt 11:6
8:14 [g]Mt 19:23; 1Ti 6:9,10,17
8:16 [h]S Mt 5:15
8:17 [i]Mt 10:26; Mk 4:22; Lk 12:2
8:18 [j]S Mt 25:29
8:20 [k]Jn 7:5
8:21 [l]Lk 6:47; 11:28; Jn 14:21

[f]*10* Isaiah 6:9

8:3 JESUS CHRIST, Suffering—Jesus did not accumulate worldly resources (Mt 8:20). He endured the life of poverty supported only by faithful followers.

8:4–18 ELECTION, Perseverance—The parable of the sower explains how those who appear to be the elect will fall away from God, but the elect will persevere and be fruitful. The lamp on a stand portrays the visible and open quality of the life and witness of the elect who realize that election status brings election responsibilities. See note on Mk 4:13–20.

8:10 THE CHURCH, God's Kingdom—See note on Mt 13:10–17.

8:12 EVIL AND SUFFERING, Satan—See note on Mt 13:19.

8:14 CHRISTIAN ETHICS, Property Rights—See note on Mt 13:22.

8:19–21 JESUS CHRIST, Son of God—See note on Mt 12:46–49.

8:20–21 HUMANITY, Relationships—See note on Mt 12:48–50.

8:22–25 JESUS CHRIST, Miracles—See note on Mk 4:35–41.

8:22–25 CREATION, Freedom—Though storms arose and subsided frequently on the Sea of Galilee, this event was more than a coincidence. Jesus, during His earthly ministry, supplemented His teachings and acts of compassion with signs showing that He controlled the elements of nature. God established laws whereby the universe operates, but He remains above them. God is a free, personal Spirit and has assigned all things to the Son. To validate His earthly ministry and prove Himself Lord of everything, including the natural forces, Jesus occasionally gave a personal demonstration of His power. This strengthened the faith of His followers, helping to remove any doubts that arose as they faced indifferent people and even hostile enemies. We need to realize that God does not work a miracle every time we capriciously desire one. If, however, He feels His redemptive program needs one, He has the freedom to act in a supernatural way for us. See note on Mk 4:35–41.

8:22–25 MIRACLE, Nature—Storms yet come up quickly on the Sea of Galilee and as quickly abate. Only God's Son announced when the storm would abate and interpreted it as a sign of God's redemptive love. The disciples were frightened by this storm. Jesus calmed the storm at sea and in their hearts. He showed Himself to have divine power both over the natural elements and over human fears. Such miracles should lead people to recognize Him as God's divine Son and to trust Him for salvation.

saying, "Master, Master,[m] we're going to
drown!"
He got up and rebuked[n] the wind and
the raging waters; the storm subsided,
and all was calm.[o] 25"Where is your
faith?" he asked his disciples.
In fear and amazement they asked one
another, "Who is this? He commands
even the winds and the water, and they
obey him."

The Healing of a Demon-possessed Man

8:26–37pp — Mt 8:28–34
8:26–39pp — Mk 5:1–20

26They sailed to the region of the Gerasenes,[g] which is across the lake from
Galilee. 27When Jesus stepped ashore, he
was met by a demon-possessed man from
the town. For a long time this man had
not worn clothes or lived in a house, but
had lived in the tombs. 28When he saw
Jesus, he cried out and fell at his feet,
shouting at the top of his voice, "What do
you want with me,[p] Jesus, Son of the
Most High God?[q] I beg you, don't torture
me!" 29For Jesus had commanded the
evil[h] spirit to come out of the man. Many
times it had seized him, and though he
was chained hand and foot and kept under guard, he had broken his chains and
had been driven by the demon into solitary places.
30Jesus asked him, "What is your
name?"
"Legion," he replied, because many
demons had gone into him. 31And they
begged him repeatedly not to order them
to go into the Abyss.[r]
32A large herd of pigs was feeding there
on the hillside. The demons begged Jesus
to let them go into them, and he gave
them permission. 33When the demons
came out of the man, they went into the
pigs, and the herd rushed down the steep
bank into the lake[s] and was drowned.
34When those tending the pigs saw
what had happened, they ran off and reported this in the town and countryside,
35and the people went out to see what
had happened. When they came to Jesus,
they found the man from whom the demons had gone out, sitting at Jesus' feet,[t]
dressed and in his right mind; and they
were afraid. 36Those who had seen it told
the people how the demon-possessed[u]
man had been cured. 37Then all the people of the region of the Gerasenes asked
Jesus to leave them,[v] because they were
overcome with fear. So he got into the
boat and left.
38The man from whom the demons had
gone out begged to go with him, but Jesus
sent him away, saying, 39"Return home
and tell how much God has done for
you." So the man went away and told all
over town how much Jesus had done for
him.

A Dead Girl and a Sick Woman

8:40–56pp — Mt 9:18–26; Mk 5:22–43

40Now when Jesus returned, a crowd
welcomed him, for they were all expecting him. 41Then a man named Jairus, a
ruler of the synagogue,[w] came and fell at
Jesus' feet, pleading with him to come to
his house 42because his only daughter, a
girl of about twelve, was dying.
As Jesus was on his way, the crowds
almost crushed him. 43And a woman was
there who had been subject to bleeding[x]
for twelve years,[i] but no one could heal
her. 44She came up behind him and
touched the edge of his cloak,[y] and immediately her bleeding stopped.

8:24 [m]S Lk 5:5 [n]Lk 4:35,39,41 [o]Ps 107:29; Jnh 1:15
8:28 [p]S Mt 8:29 [q]S Mk 5:7
8:31 [r]Rev 9:1,2,11; 11:7; 17:8; 20:1,3
8:33 [s]ver 22,23
8:35 [t]Lk 10:39
8:36 [u]S Mt 4:24
8:37 [v]Ac 16:39
8:41 [w]ver 49; S Mk 5:22
8:43 [x]Lev 15:25-30
8:44 [y]S Mt 9:20

[g]*26* Some manuscripts *Gadarenes*; other manuscripts *Gergesenes*; also in verse 37 [h]*29* Greek *unclean* [i]*43* Many manuscripts *years, and she had spent all she had on doctors*

8:25 PRAYER, Hindrances—See note on Mt 8:26.
8:26–39 JESUS CHRIST, Miracles—See note on Mk 5:1–20.
8:31 LAST THINGS, Intermediate State—The Abyss is a name for the realm of the dead, apparently related to the Old Testament "pit." See note on Jnh 2:2,6. Some interpreters see it as a place of intermediate punishment where the wicked await final judgment and the eternal punishment in Gehenna, or the lake of fire. Evil spirits or demons fear imprisonment in the Abyss (Lk 8:31). Fallen angels, imprisoned there for disobedience (2 Pe 2:4), await judgment and final destiny. Demons, who are under a king called the "angel of the Abyss" (Rev 9:11), emerge from it (Rev 9:1–3). The beast of Rev 17 comes up out of the Abyss to go to his final destruction (v 8). It is the temporary place of confinement for Satan for a thousand years (Rev 20:3) before final consignment to the lake of fire forever (Rev 20:10). For the intermediate state for the righteous, see note on 2 Co 5:1–10.
8:36–37 REVELATION, Events—Jesus Christ used His healing powers to declare God's good news of freedom from all kinds of oppression, including the demonic forces at work in people's bodies. He was careful not to use healing as a main way of attracting believers, for He knew that belief based on supernatural acts holds little faith for the trials and tests of human life. His power revealed brought both awe and fear to the people. They did not know how to respond to His revelation, particularly when it threatened their economic life.
8:36 EVANGELISM, Social Action—The healing of the demon-possessed man so impressed the witnesses that they told all the people what Jesus had done. The meeting of temporal needs often opens the door to an effective witness to our Lord's love and grace.
8:38–39 PRAYER, Hindrances—See note on Mk 5:18–19.
8:39 EVANGELISM, In the Home—See note on Mk 5:19–20.
8:40–56 JESUS CHRIST, Miracles—See notes on Mk 5:21–24,35–43; 5:25–34.
8:41 PRAYER, Humility—See note on Mk 5:23. Jairus symbolized his humility by falling at Jesus' feet.
8:43–48 REVELATION, Jesus Christ—Jesus revealed Himself as God's sensitive Son, who moved in a crowd but immediately detected the touch of despair and pain. Healing could go out from Jesus to a person of faith even when He did not take the initiative. Such healing became a mode of revealing who Jesus is and of showing God's power and compassion.

42Even while the boy was coming, the
demon threw him to the ground in a convulsion. But Jesus rebuked the evil[k] spirit, healed the boy and gave him back to
his father. 43And they were all amazed at
the greatness of God.
While everyone was marveling at all
that Jesus did, he said to his disciples,
44"Listen carefully to what I am about to
tell you: The Son of Man is going to be
betrayed into the hands of men."[x] 45But
they did not understand what this meant.
It was hidden from them, so that they did
not grasp it,[y] and they were afraid to ask
him about it.

Who Will Be the Greatest?

9:46–48pp — Mt 18:1–5
9:46–50pp — Mk 9:33–40

46An argument started among the disciples as to which of them would be the
greatest.[z] 47Jesus, knowing their
thoughts,[a] took a little child and had him
stand beside him. 48Then he said to them,
"Whoever welcomes this little child in
my name welcomes me; and whoever
welcomes me welcomes the one who
sent me.[b] For he who is least among you
all—he is the greatest."[c]
49"Master,"[d] said John, "we saw a
man driving out demons in your name
and we tried to stop him, because he is
not one of us."
50"Do not stop him," Jesus said, "for
whoever is not against you is for you."[e]

Samaritan Opposition

51As the time approached for him to be
taken up to heaven,[f] Jesus resolutely set
out for Jerusalem.[g] 52And he sent messengers on ahead, who went into a Samaritan[h] village to get things ready for
him; 53but the people there did not welcome him, because he was heading for
Jerusalem. 54When the disciples James
and John[i] saw this, they asked, "Lord,
do you want us to call fire down from
heaven to destroy them[l]?"[j] 55But Jesus
turned and rebuked them, 56and[m] they
went to another village.

The Cost of Following Jesus

9:57–60pp — Mt 8:19–22

57As they were walking along the
road,[k] a man said to him, "I will follow
you wherever you go."
58Jesus replied, "Foxes have holes and
birds of the air have nests, but the Son of
Man[l] has no place to lay his head."
59He said to another man, "Follow
me."[m]
But the man replied, "Lord, first let me
go and bury my father."
60Jesus said to him, "Let the dead bury
their own dead, but you go and proclaim
the kingdom of God."[n]
61Still another said, "I will follow you,
Lord; but first let me go back and say
good-by to my family."[o]
62Jesus replied, "No one who puts his

9:44 [x]S ver 22
9:45 [y]S Mk 9:32
9:46 [z]Lk 22:24
9:47 [a]S Mt 9:4
9:48 [b]S Mt 10:40 [c]S Mk 9:35
9:49 [d]S Lk 5:5
9:50 [e]Mt 12:30; Lk 11:23
9:51 [f]S Mk 16:19 [g]Lk 13:22; 17:11; 18:31; 19:28
9:52 [h]S Mt 10:5
9:54 [i]S Mt 4:21 [j]2Ki 1:10,12
9:57 [k]ver 51
9:58 [l]S Mt 8:20
9:59 [m]S Mt 4:19
9:60 [n]S Mt 3:2
9:61 [o]1Ki 19:20

[k]42 Greek *unclean* [l]54 Some manuscripts *them, even as Elijah did* [m]55,56 Some manuscripts *them. And he said, "You do not know what kind of spirit you are of, for the Son of Man did not come to destroy men's lives, but to save them." 56And*

9:43 JESUS CHRIST, Miracles—Jesus' miracles showed the crowds God was at work among them.
9:43 SALVATION, Fear of God—The fear of God is amazement at His greatness. Amazement over the greatness of God is a proper response to Jesus and His works, for Jesus is the Son who shows us the Father.
9:44 JESUS CHRIST, Son of Man—Jesus represents the supreme irony of history. The One sent to establish an eternal kingdom (Da 7:13–14) was given over to human powers. The disciples could not believe the Messiah (v 20) would die without establishing the kingdom. Jesus' mission from God was to be King on the cross.
9:46–48 HUMANITY, Relationships—People looking for recognition seek to associate with those who appear to be important by the world's standards. God desires that His people choose to serve the little and insignificant (by the world's standards). See notes on Mt 18:1–5; Mk 9:33–37.
9:46–50 THE CHURCH, Practice—The church has servants but not rulers. No human official controls the church; all serve Christ through the church. The church practices openness and acceptance toward all people. The child, the weak, the poor, and the powerless belong to God. Those who reject these little ones reject Christ. Those who accept the outcasts show they have accepted Christ. Christ has followers who do not belong to our group. We cannot reject them for not being with us or doing things our way. When they oppose evil and serve Christ, they are part of His church. See note on Mt 20:20–28.
9:49–50 THE CHURCH, Redeemed of All Ages—God's people include all who serve Him and do His will. The people of God are multinational, bearing different gifts and speaking many languages. This great throng of people is united by common allegiance to Jesus Christ as Lord. See note on Jn 10:14–18.
9:51 JESUS CHRIST, Ascension—Jerusalem was not the ultimate goal for Jesus. Death, resurrection, and ascension had been in God's plan from the beginning. His ascension enabled Him to have a universal, eternal mission.
9:57–62 JESUS CHRIST, Kingdom of God—The King had no home. See note on Mt 8:20. His followers were to have no excuses.
9:58–62 CHRISTIAN ETHICS, Character—Inherent in this passage are Jesus' themes of denial of self, the priority of the kingdom of God, and the single-mindedness needed for discipleship. Jesus does not accept excuses. He seeks volunteers who will give their lives for God's kingdom as He did. God's kingdom, not personal fortune or lists of rules, establishes the priorities in Christian ethics.
9:59–60 HUMANITY, Burial—See note on Mt 8:21–22.
9:59–62 FAMILY, Priorities—See note on 12:49–53.
9:60–62 THE CHURCH, God's Kingdom—Work in God's kingdom requires total devotion and absolute attention. Even devotion to family must not keep us from doing God's will.
9:60 PROCLAMATION, Compulsion—Commitment to Christ brings a compulsion to proclaim. Jesus would not accept delays and excuses. He called people to center life on God's kingdom and to announce that kingdom constantly and consistently.

hand to the plow and looks back is fit for
service in the kingdom of God."

Chapter 10

Jesus Sends Out the Seventy-two

10:4–12pp — Lk 9:3–5
10:13–15,21,22pp — Mt 11:21–23,25–27
10:23,24pp — Mt 13:16,17

AFTER this the Lord[p] appointed seventy-two[n] others[q] and sent them two
by two[r] ahead of him to every town and
place where he was about to go.[s] 2He
told them, "The harvest is plentiful, but
the workers are few. Ask the Lord of the
harvest, therefore, to send out workers
into his harvest field.[t] 3Go! I am sending
you out like lambs among wolves.[u] 4Do
not take a purse or bag or sandals; and do
not greet anyone on the road.
5"When you enter a house, first say,
'Peace to this house.' 6If a man of peace is
there, your peace will rest on him; if not,
it will return to you. 7Stay in that house,
eating and drinking whatever they give
you, for the worker deserves his wages.[v]
Do not move around from house to
house.
8"When you enter a town and are welcomed, eat what is set before you.[w] 9Heal
the sick who are there and tell them,
'The kingdom of God[x] is near you.' 10But
when you enter a town and are not welcomed, go into its streets and say, 11'Even
the dust of your town that sticks to our
feet we wipe off against you.[y] Yet be sure
of this: The kingdom of God is near.'[z] 12I
tell you, it will be more bearable on that
day for Sodom[a] than for that town.[b]
13"Woe to you,[c] Korazin! Woe to you,
Bethsaida! For if the miracles that were
performed in you had been performed in
Tyre and Sidon, they would have repented long ago, sitting in sackcloth[d] and
ashes. 14But it will be more bearable for
Tyre and Sidon at the judgment than for
you. 15And you, Capernaum,[e] will you be
lifted up to the skies? No, you will go
down to the depths.[o]
16"He who listens to you listens to me;
he who rejects you rejects me; but he
who rejects me rejects him who sent
me."[f]
17The seventy-two[g] returned with joy

10:1 [p]S Lk 7:13 [q]Lk 9:1,2,51,52 [r]Mk 6:7 [s]Mt 10:1
10:2 [t]Mt 9:37,38; Jn 4:35
10:3 [u]Mt 10:16
10:7 [v]S 1Ti 5:18
10:8 [w]1Co 10:27
10:9 [x]S Mt 3:2
10:11 [y]S Mt 10:14 [z]ver 9
10:12 [a]S Mt 10:15 [b]Mt 11:24
10:13 [c]Lk 6:24-26 [d]S Rev 11:3
10:15 [e]S Mt 4:13
10:16 [f]S Mt 10:40
10:17 [g]ver 1

[n] *1* Some manuscripts *seventy;* also in verse 17
[o] *15* Greek *Hades*

10:1–24 JESUS CHRIST, Mission—See note on Mt 10:1–42. Jesus identified with His disciples on mission and with the Father who sent Him.

10:1–24 EVANGELISM, Call to Evangelize—This important passage presents several principles in Christ's call to evangelize: (1) there is an open field of great need; (2) prayer for God-called workers is vital; (3) Christ's witnesses will experience persecution and pressure; (4) God will provide all of one's needs; (5) Christian service attempts to meet all manner of needs; (6) an evangelistic partner gives strength to witnessing; (7) judgment is certain to those who reject the message of salvation; (8) the Lord identifies with and gives His power to His faithful witnesses; (9) Satan and opposition will be routed before the power of Christ; (10) enlisting people as citizens of heaven is the most important task; (11) effective witnessing brings joy to our Lord; and (12) taking part in God's great work of world evangelization is a privilege. As we use these principles in witnessing to God's grace in Christ, we will be successful.

10:1–18 MISSIONS, Examples—The sending of missionaries in addition to the disciples was intended to prepare people for the actual visit of Jesus. This sending had many similarities to the sending of the twelve (9:1–7). Although the specific assignment was limited, Jesus gave some missionary principles that are valid for His followers in all times: (1) effective witnesses go in obedience to their Lord; (2) God has people willing to respond if His people will go; (3) fellowship in witness gained by going with a partner strengthens the witness; (4) an adequate supply of evangelists, pastors, and missionaries comes in response to prayer; (5) Christian witnesses are often at risk as "lambs among wolves;" (6) God can and will provide for His messengers' needs; (7) God's business is urgent; (8) the impact of our witness can be enhanced by receiving hospitality graciously (v 7); (9) messengers of the gospel deserve support; (10) God's missionaries or "sent ones" represent Him; and (11) following Christ's instructions will bring harvest and joy.

10:2 PRAYER, Command of God—This important prayer command gives a name of God to pray to—"Lord of the harvest." Evangelism and missions should be constant subjects of prayer.

10:9–11 THE CHURCH, God's Kingdom—The gospel of the kingdom must be proclaimed and received. No one is forced to receive it, but all must be encouraged to accept it. The kingdom brings healing and salvation to those who believe but rejection and judgment for those who do not. See note on 4:43.

10:9 PROCLAMATION, Central Theme—The presence of God's kingdom was the central theme Jesus preached (8:1; Mk 1:14–15). He gave His disciples the same theme to preach (Mt 10:7). The kingdom's presence meant God was in Jesus fulfilling His promises and inaugurating His new order of life under His rule. Proclamation was not limited to one place or one time. Both Jesus and the disciples went everywhere proclaiming the gospel. Proclamation was a part of their total ministry, which included healing and other ministries to the deep needs of people. The proclamation of the gospel is one way God establishes and invites participation in His kingdom.

10:13 MIRACLE, Vocabulary—"Miracles" (Greek *dunameis*) may be literally translated "powers." Jesus' contemporaries did not perceive the out-of-the-ordinary powers behind His miracles. They sought only to protect their religious tradition. They could not see God's holy presence and the contrast to their sin. Jesus' powers were so extraordinary Gentiles would repent, but not religion-hardened "people of God."

10:16 SALVATION, Acceptance—See note on Mt 10:40–42. Listening and rejecting are opposites in this text. Compare Jn 18:37.

10:16 THE CHURCH, People of God—The church continues Christ's ministry and receives the same reactions He did. To reject the church's message of God's kingdom in Christ is to reject God and His salvation.

10:17–20 EVIL AND SUFFERING, Satan—Satan is the tempter or accuser who brings charges against people before the heavenly throne (Job 1:6–12; Zec 3:1). Compare Jn 12:31; Rev 12:7–9. His defeat and ouster from heaven became sure when Christ gave His power over satanic forces to His church (Mk 3:15). The church must be intent on defeating Satan and participating in the heavenly kingdom, not on proudly exhibiting its power on earth. The verse is not a call to Christians to test God by opening themselves to danger. It is a call to confess God's power and certain victory over all that opposes Him.

and said, "Lord, even the demons submit
to us in your name."[h]
18He replied, "I saw Satan[i] fall like
lightning from heaven.[j] 19I have given
you authority to trample on snakes[k] and
scorpions and to overcome all the power
of the enemy; nothing will harm you.
20However, do not rejoice that the spirits
submit to you, but rejoice that your
names are written in heaven."[l]
21At that time Jesus, full of joy through
the Holy Spirit, said, "I praise you, Father, Lord of heaven and earth, because
you have hidden these things from the
wise and learned, and revealed them to
little children.[m] Yes, Father, for this was
your good pleasure.
22"All things have been committed to
me by my Father.[n] No one knows who
the Son is except the Father, and no one
knows who the Father is except the Son
and those to whom the Son chooses to
reveal him."[o]
23Then he turned to his disciples and
said privately, "Blessed are the eyes that
see what you see. 24For I tell you that
many prophets and kings wanted to see
what you see but did not see it, and to
hear what you hear but did not hear it."[p]

The Parable of the Good Samaritan

10:25–28pp — Mt 22:34–40; Mk 12:28–31

25On one occasion an expert in the law
stood up to test Jesus. "Teacher," he
asked, "what must I do to inherit eternal
life?"[q]
26"What is written in the Law?" he replied. "How do you read it?"
27He answered: " 'Love the Lord your
God with all your heart and with all your
soul and with all your strength and with
all your mind'[p];[r] and, 'Love your neighbor as yourself.'[q] "[s]
28"You have answered correctly,"
Jesus replied. "Do this and you will
live."[t]
29But he wanted to justify himself,[u] so
he asked Jesus, "And who is my neighbor?"
30In reply Jesus said: "A man was going
down from Jerusalem to Jericho, when he
fell into the hands of robbers. They
stripped him of his clothes, beat him and
went away, leaving him half dead. 31A
priest happened to be going down the

10:17 [h]S Mk 16:17
10:18 [i]S Mt 4:10 [j]Isa 14:12; Rev 9:1; 12:8,9
10:19 [k]Mk 16:18; Ac 28:3-5
10:20 [l]S Rev 20:12
10:21 [m]1Co 1:26-29
10:22 [n]S Mt 28:18 [o]Jn 1:18
10:24 [p]1Pe 1:10-12
10:25 [q]Mt 19:16; Lk 18:18
10:27 [r]Dt 6:5 [s]Lev 19:18; S Mt 5:43
10:28 [t]S Ro 7:10
10:29 [u]Lk 16:15

[p]*27* Deut. 6:5 [q]*27* Lev. 19:18

10:17–20 REVELATION, Divine Presence—Christ's followers found evil was subject to them. This symbolically foreshadowed God's full reign in the world. These signs, revealed through the disciples, teach the nature and purpose of God. He makes good to rule evil and redeems all who submit to His loving and good will. Christ reminded His disciples the greatest miracle is the salvation we as sinners receive, not the power God displays through us.

10:19–20 SALVATION, Initiative—Jesus sent out the seventy-two in twos to minister in His name. Compare 9:1–6. This sending was symbolic of the coming mission to the Gentiles. God took the initiative in salvation for all nations. Jesus gave His sent ones authority to carry out their mission. God's sent ones were to rejoice more that they had received His mercy and forgiveness than in their power over evil spirits.

10:21 GOD, Trinity—The trinitarian relationship of the Father, the Son, and the Holy Spirit is in full view here. Jesus, the Son, prompted by the Holy Spirit, uttered praise to the Father. The Holy Spirit is evidently the common bond that united God in heaven and Jesus on earth. The diversity here is easier to perceive than is the unity, but do not forget the underlying monotheism—the fact that there is only one God—which must always be considered as the background to every verse of the Bible. Jesus praised the sovereignty of God the Father. Jesus called Him Lord of both heaven and earth. Because part of the world is in rebellion against God, some people fail to see that God is Lord of the earth—the world. He always has been and always will be. One day that lordship will be acknowledged by all, even those who now rebel against God.

10:21 HOLY SPIRIT, Jesus—Joy comes from God's Spirit. The Spirit exercises tremendous power in the lives of God's people. Only occasionally does the Old Testament specifically suggest the Spirit gives great joy. David prayed that the Spirit would not be taken from him and that the joy of his salvation would be restored (Ps 51:11–12). The Spirit helped Jesus experience great joy. Jesus' disciples were filled with the joy of the Spirit. See note on Ac 13:52. The fruit of the Spirit is joy (Gal 5:22). See Ro 14:17; 1 Th 1:6. The Spirit also assisted Jesus in His prayer. The Spirit helped the disciples to pray. See Jude 20; notes on Lk 3:21–22; Ro 8:25–27; Eph 2:18; 6:18.

10:21 SALVATION, Joy—God's people should rejoice when His rule is manifested on earth and Satan falls.

10:21–22 PRAYER, Jesus' Example—Jesus praised the Father for the way He worked. His prayers rejoiced in agreement with God the Father. Compare 1 Co 1:27–29. The worldly wise are likely to miss the wisdom of faith.

10:22 JESUS CHRIST, Son of God—Jesus was conscious of a unique relationship to the Father. He alone could introduce people to the Father's true nature, for He alone shared fully in intimate personal relationship with the Father. To know the Father we must know the Son. Compare 22:70; Jn 14:9–11; 17:3.

10:22 ELECTION, In Christ—The elect come to truly know God through the revelation which comes through God's chosen Son. See note on Mt 11:27.

10:25–28 SALVATION, Eternal Life—God's requirement for eternal life is to love Him supremely and to love your neighbor as much as yourself. No one can love in these ways without the help which God gives through faith in Christ. See note on Mk 12:30.

10:25–37 DISCIPLESHIP, Neighbor Love—The lawyer understood what the Law required for eternal life, but he did not understand the full significance of such love. To be valid, such love must be expressed in action. The lawyer sought to limit his neighborliness. He wanted to determine whom he should help. Jesus said he must give unselfish and unlimited assistance to anyone in need, even someone who might hurt his reputation. See note on 6:27–35.

10:26–37 CHRISTIAN ETHICS, Moral Imperatives—Jesus used God's imperatives as the basis of His teaching. To gain eternal life through the law required complete, unselfish devotion to God and others. Despite the lawyer's initial claim, he and all others fell short. Persons cannot "justify" themselves. Faith in Christ's atoning work is necessary. Salvation in Christ sharpens our obligation to devote life to God and neighbor rather than to self and ego-boosting rules.

10:30–37 CHRISTIAN ETHICS, Race Relations—Tensions between two races have never been higher than those between Jews and Samaritans. Jesus told Jews that Samaritans who help in self-giving love make the best neighbors. Self-giving love overcomes racial barriers.

same road, and when he saw the man, he
passed by on the other side.[v] 32So too, a
Levite, when he came to the place and
saw him, passed by on the other side.
33But a Samaritan,[w] as he traveled, came
where the man was; and when he saw
him, he took pity on him. 34He went to
him and bandaged his wounds, pouring
on oil and wine. Then he put the man on
his own donkey, took him to an inn and
took care of him. 35The next day he took
out two silver coins[r] and gave them to
the innkeeper. 'Look after him,' he said,
'and when I return, I will reimburse you
for any extra expense you may have.'

36"Which of these three do you think
was a neighbor to the man who fell into
the hands of robbers?"

37The expert in the law replied, "The
one who had mercy on him."

Jesus told him, "Go and do likewise."

At the Home of Martha and Mary

38As Jesus and his disciples were on
their way, he came to a village where a
woman named Martha[x] opened her
home to him. 39She had a sister called
Mary,[y] who sat at the Lord's feet[z] listening to what he said. 40But Martha was
distracted by all the preparations that had
to be made. She came to him and asked,
"Lord, don't you care[a] that my sister has
left me to do the work by myself? Tell her
to help me!"

41"Martha, Martha," the Lord answered, "you are worried[b] and upset
about many things, 42but only one thing
is needed.[s c] Mary has chosen what is
better, and it will not be taken away from
her."

Chapter 11

Jesus' Teaching on Prayer

11:2–4pp — Mt 6:9–13
11:9–13pp — Mt 7:7–11

ONE day Jesus was praying[d] in a certain place. When he finished, one of
his disciples said to him, "Lord,[e] teach
us to pray, just as John taught his disciples."

2He said to them, "When you pray,
say:

" 'Father,[t]
hallowed be your name,
your kingdom[f] come.[u]
3Give us each day our daily bread.
4Forgive us our sins,
for we also forgive everyone who
sins against us.[v g]
And lead us not into temptation.[w] ' "[h]

5Then he said to them, "Suppose one
of you has a friend, and he goes to him at

10:31 [v]Lev 21:1-3
10:33 [w]S Mt 10:5
10:38 [x]Jn 11:1; 12:2
10:39 [y]Jn 11:1; 12:3 [z]Lk 8:35
10:40 [a]Mk 4:38
10:41 [b]Mt 6:25-34; Lk 12:11,22
10:42 [c]Ps 27:4
11:1 [d]S Lk 3:21 [e]S Jn 13:13
11:2 [f]S Mt 3:2
11:4 [g]Mt 18:35; Mk 11:25 [h]Mt 26:41; Jas 1:13

[r]35 Greek *two denarii* [s]42 Some manuscripts *but few things are needed—or only one* [t]2 Some manuscripts *Our Father in heaven* [u]2 Some manuscripts *come. May your will be done on earth as it is in heaven.* [v]4 Greek *everyone who is indebted to us* [w]4 Some manuscripts *temptation but deliver us from the evil one*

10:38–42 FAMILY, Role Relationships—Jesus did not follow His culture, which limited the role of women. He encouraged women to use their interests and skills for spiritual growth. Several principles emerge from Jesus' relationships with Mary, Martha, and Lazarus (Jn 11:1–44; 12:1–3): (1) contrary to Jewish practice, Jesus taught and accepted a woman as one able to understand the meaning of His message; (2) even though food is necessary to physical life, excessive attention to housework may keep a person from experiencing even more important spiritual food; (3) Jesus found refuge in a home even though conflicting feelings divided the family members; (4) Jesus taught some of His most powerful truths in a family grief experience; and (5) Jesus experienced human sorrow even though He planned to use this experience to teach others about the power of God.

11:1–4 PRAYER, Jesus' Example—The Old Testament had been full of examples of prayer and teaching on prayer. John had taught on prayer, but Jesus' example was unique. It inspired the disciples to ask Him to teach them to pray as He prayed. The Model Prayer as given here is slightly shortened from the version in Mt 6:9–13. The Model Prayer provides a form for unison prayer in public worship but is much more. It illustrates the relationships and subjects of prayer. It encourages us to learn through practice and imitation how to pray openly to the Father for His kingdom purposes.

11:2 GOD, Holy—God is holy. We should acknowledge His holiness when we approach Him in prayer. Holiness is the unique nature of God. It includes His moral purity but is more. Everything God is is included in His holiness, the special *characteristic of God alone. Holiness is the* boundary that marks off God from all else. It speaks of His transcendence, His being high and lifted over us. It is the constant reminder that God is God and humans are but His creatures. When we come before God in prayer, we should be in an attitude of reverence, respect, and awe. God is not unapproachable; but He must be approached in the proper manner. See notes on Ex 3:5–6; 19:10–24; Lev 11:44–45; 2 Co 7:1.

11:2,13 GOD, Father—We pray to God as Father. Out of His fatherly concern for us He hears our prayers and cares for us in our needs. Jesus used the analogy of human parents, imperfect and sinful, who have the best interests of their children at heart, to show that God, who is perfect, certainly has our best interests in His heart and will respond to us in terms of our needs. Jesus invites us to a personal, intimate approach to God, not to a distant and formal relationship to an unapproachable or indifferent, uncaring kind of god.

11:3–4 CHRISTIAN ETHICS, Character—Requests for daily bread and forgiveness of sins come after the address of praise for the holiness of God and the coming of the kingdom. The order is proper: first, a vertical relationship is established from individual below to God above; then, one's relationship to others on a horizontal plane as equals in God's sight builds out of that. Both relationships depend upon our own sense of forgiveness which we receive and extend.

11:4 SIN, Estrangement—See note on Mt 6:14–15.

11:5–8 HUMANITY, Relationships—People expect friends to welcome them and help them in an emergency. Failure may destroy or deny friendship.

11:5–13 PRAYER, Persistence—See note on 18:1–8. Jesus did not intend to indicate reluctance on God's part. The major point of the parable is the value of persistence. It is because of the man's boldness (v 8, literally "shamelessness"), that the friend finally responded. Prayer should not be curtailed by fear, pride, or shame. We can trust God to accept our boldness.

midnight and says, 'Friend, lend me three
loaves of bread, 6because a friend of mine
on a journey has come to me, and I have
nothing to set before him.'
7"Then the one inside answers, 'Don't
bother me. The door is already locked,
and my children are with me in bed. I
can't get up and give you anything.' 8I tell
you, though he will not get up and give
him the bread because he is his friend,
yet because of the man's boldness[x] he
will get up and give him as much as he
needs.[i]
9"So I say to you: Ask and it will be
given to you;[j] seek and you will find;
knock and the door will be opened to
you. 10For everyone who asks receives;
he who seeks finds; and to him who
knocks, the door will be opened.
11"Which of you fathers, if your son
asks for[y] a fish, will give him a snake
instead? 12Or if he asks for an egg, will
give him a scorpion? 13If you then,
though you are evil, know how to give
good gifts to your children, how much
more will your Father in heaven give the
Holy Spirit to those who ask him!"

Jesus and Beelzebub

11:14,15, 17–22, 24–26pp — Mt 12:22,24–29, 43–45
11:17–22pp — Mk 3:23–27

14Jesus was driving out a demon that
was mute. When the demon left, the man
who had been mute spoke, and the crowd
was amazed.[k] 15But some of them said,
"By Beelzebub,[z][l] the prince of demons,
he is driving out demons."[m] 16Others
tested him by asking for a sign from heav-
en.[n]
17Jesus knew their thoughts[o] and said
to them: "Any kingdom divided against
itself will be ruined, and a house divided
against itself will fall. 18If Satan[p] is divided against himself, how can his kingdom
stand? I say this because you claim that I
drive out demons by Beelzebub. 19Now if
I drive out demons by Beelzebub, by
whom do your followers drive them out?
So then, they will be your judges. 20But if
I drive out demons by the finger of God,[q]
then the kingdom of God[r] has come to
you.
21"When a strong man, fully armed,
guards his own house, his possessions are
safe. 22But when someone stronger attacks and overpowers him, he takes away
the armor in which the man trusted and
divides up the spoils.
23"He who is not with me is against
me, and he who does not gather with me,
scatters.[s]
24"When an evil[a] spirit comes out of a
man, it goes through arid places seeking
rest and does not find it. Then it says, 'I
will return to the house I left.' 25When it
arrives, it finds the house swept clean
and put in order. 26Then it goes and takes
seven other spirits more wicked than itself, and they go in and live there. And
the final condition of that man is worse
than the first."[t]
27As Jesus was saying these things, a
woman in the crowd called out, "Blessed
is the mother who gave you birth and
nursed you."[u]
28He replied, "Blessed rather are those
who hear the word of God[v] and obey
it."[w]

The Sign of Jonah

11:29–32pp — Mt 12:39–42

29As the crowds increased, Jesus said,

11:8 [i]Lk 18:1-6
11:9 [j]S Mt 7:7
11:14 [k]Mt 9:32,33
11:15 [l]S Mk 3:22 [m]Mt 9:34
11:16 [n]S Mt 12:38
11:17 [o]S Mt 9:4
11:18 [p]S Mt 4:10
11:20 [q]Ex 8:19 [r]S Mt 3:2
11:23 [s]Mt 12:30; Mk 9:40; Lk 9:50
11:26 [t]2Pe 2:20
11:27 [u]Lk 23:29
11:28 [v]S Heb 4:12 [w]Pr 8:32; Lk 6:47; 8:21; Jn 14:21

[x]8 Or *persistence* [y]11 Some manuscripts *for bread, will give him a stone; or if he asks for* [z]15 Greek *Beezeboul* or *Beelzeboul*; also in verses 18 and 19
[a]24 Greek *unclean*

11:9–12 PRAYER, Faith—See note on Mt 7:7–11. In Matthew, the Father in heaven gives good gifts. Luke emphasized a much greater gift, the Holy Spirit. Luke has a strong emphasis on the Holy Spirit in his gospel. A chief goal in prayer is to be led by God's Spirit.

11:13 HOLY SPIRIT, Promised—The Old Testament promised God would someday give His Spirit to His people. See note on Joel 2:28–32. Jesus announced that the promised gift was available for His followers. All they need to do is ask. For Christ's original disciples to ask for the Spirit was to ask for God's promised age of salvation, thus equivalent to asking for the Kingdom to come (Lk 11:2). This prayer found rich answer at Pentecost (Ac 2). Christ's followers are unique because the Spirit indwells us. See notes on Ro 2:29; 1 Co 12:1–3. In time of need we can call on the Spirit for help. See note on Ro 8:25–27. We can expect God to provide the Spirit's needed presence because God is the perfect Father.

11:14–28 JESUS CHRIST, Kingdom of God—See note on Mt 12:23–28. Jesus' miracles demonstrated the presence of God's kingdom on earth. He defeated Satan rather than aligning Himself with Satan. See note on Mt 4:1–11. Humans show they are participating in God's kingdom by obeying God's Word.

11:14–26 MIRACLE, Revelation—Miracles point to spiritual power. But who is the source? The hardened response of the religious leaders accused Jesus of being in league with the prince of demons because of His power over demons. Logically, Jesus disproved their charge—the prince of demons would hardly attack his subjects! The alternative is clear: by the "finger of God" He cast out demons. See note on Ex 8:19. Miraculous events do not reveal God to us unless we have an inspired interpreter to point us to God. Vv 24–26 underscore the necessity of continual care for those who are healed.

11:14–26 EVIL AND SUFFERING, Satan—See note on Mt 12:22–29.

11:20 THE CHURCH, God's Kingdom—See note on Mt 12:28. The "finger of God" is an Old Testament expression referring to a direct act of God (Ex 19:1; 31:18).

11:23 THE CHURCH, People of God—See note on Mt 12:30.

11:27–28 SALVATION, Blessing—Compare 1:42. Jesus calls blessed those who hear and obey the Word of God. They demonstrate they have experienced God's salvation.

11:28 SALVATION, Obedience—Hearing and obeying the Word of God is more blessed than birthing and nursing the Messiah.

11:29–42 JESUS CHRIST, Miracles—See note on Mt 12:38–42. Jesus is greater than the Old Testament prophets

“This is a wicked generation. It asks for a
miraculous sign,[x] but none will be given
it except the sign of Jonah.[y] 30For as Jonah was a sign to the Ninevites, so also
will the Son of Man be to this generation.
31The Queen of the South will rise at the
judgment with the men of this generation
and condemn them; for she came from
the ends of the earth to listen to Solomon’s wisdom,[z] and now one[b] greater
than Solomon is here. 32The men of Nineveh will stand up at the judgment with
this generation and condemn it; for they
repented at the preaching of Jonah,[a] and
now one greater than Jonah is here.

The Lamp of the Body

11:34,35pp — Mt 6:22,23

33“No one lights a lamp and puts it in a
place where it will be hidden, or under a
bowl. Instead he puts it on its stand, so
that those who come in may see the
light.[b] 34Your eye is the lamp of your
body. When your eyes are good, your
whole body also is full of light. But when
they are bad, your body also is full of
darkness. 35See to it, then, that the light
within you is not darkness. 36Therefore, if
your whole body is full of light, and no
part of it dark, it will be completely lighted, as when the light of a lamp shines on
you.”

Six Woes

**37When Jesus had finished speaking, a
Pharisee invited him to eat with him; so
he went in and reclined at the table.[c]
38But the Pharisee, noticing that Jesus did
not first wash before the meal,[d] was surprised.**
39Then the Lord[e] said to him, “Now
then, you Pharisees clean the outside of
the cup and dish, but inside you are full of
greed and wickedness.[f] 40You foolish
people![g] Did not the one who made the
outside make the inside also? 41But give
what is inside ⌊the dish⌋[c] to the poor,[h]
and everything will be clean for you.[i]
42“Woe to you Pharisees, because you
give God a tenth[j] of your mint, rue and
all other kinds of garden herbs, but you
neglect justice and the love of God.[k] You
should have practiced the latter without
leaving the former undone.[l]
43“Woe to you Pharisees, because you
love the most important seats in the synagogues and greetings in the marketplaces.[m]
44“Woe to you, because you are like
unmarked graves,[n] which men walk over
without knowing it.”
**45One of the experts in the law[o] an-
swered him, “Teacher, when you say
these things, you insult us also.”
46Jesus replied,** “And you experts in
the law, woe to you, because you load
people down with burdens they can hardly carry, and you yourselves will not lift
one finger to help them.[p]
47“Woe to you, because you build
tombs for the prophets, and it was your
forefathers who killed them. 48So you testify that you approve of what your forefathers did; they killed the prophets, and
you build their tombs.[q] 49Because of this,
God in his wisdom[r] said, ‘I will send
them prophets and apostles, some of
whom they will kill and others they will
persecute.’[s] 50Therefore this generation
will be held responsible for the blood of
all the prophets that has been shed since
the beginning of the world, 51from the
blood of Abel[t] to the blood of Zechari-

11:29 [x]ver 16; S Mt 12:38 [y]Jnh 1:17; Mt 16:4
11:31 [z]1Ki 10:1; 2Ch 9:1
11:32 [a]Jnh 3:5
11:33 [b]S Mt 5:15
11:37 [c]Lk 7:36; 14:1
11:38 [d]Mk 7:3,4
11:39 [e]S Lk 7:13 [f]Mt 23:25,26; Mk 7:20-23
11:40 [g]Lk 12:20; 1Co 15:36
11:41 [h]Lk 12:33 [i]S Ac 10:15
11:42 [j]Lk 18:12 [k]Dt 6:5; Mic 6:8 [l]Mt 23:23
11:43 [m]Mt 23:6,7; Lk 14:7; 20:46
11:44 [n]Mt 23:27
11:45 [o]S Mt 22:35
11:46 [p]S Mt 23:4
11:48 [q]Mt 23:29-32; Ac 7:51-53
11:49 [r]1Co 1:24, 30; Col 2:3 [s]Mt 23:34
11:51 [t]Ge 4:8

[b]*31* Or *something*; also in verse 32 [c]*41* Or *what you have*

---

represented by Jonah. All should heed His call to repentance.
11:37–54 JESUS CHRIST, Teaching—Jesus felt no awe for the learned legal experts. He knew His teaching was superior to theirs.
11:37–52 CHRISTIAN ETHICS, Moral Imperatives—In one of His harshest sounding statements Jesus drew a stark contrast between the appearance of religion and true works resulting from a faith relationship with God. True religion is sensitive to the plight of the poor and to justice and love (reciprocal virtues). Christ’s followers build self-esteem through the servant’s way of humility and not through egomania. Following rules without helping people has no place in Christ’s teachings. See note on Mt 25:37–46.
11:41 DISCIPLESHIP, Poor—Willingly giving to meet the needs of the poor indicates a person’s heart is right. When we share in love with the poor, we show Christ, not wealth, rules us. Giving to the poor from greedy hearts hoping to get public recognition or tax benefits does not meet Jesus’ teaching. The Pharisees gave alms to the poor. Christ’s disciples sacrifice to ensure the needs of the poor are met. Modern Pharisees give a pittance to be sure their ego needs are met. See note on Mk 10:21.
11:42–52 SIN, Against God—Attitudes and relationships determine guilt more than specific acts and theological expertise. God does not relate to His people in a legalistic manner, expecting us to know and follow an enormous number of religious rules. Even professional experts cannot remember and obey all the rules. God expects us to let Him change our hearts and revolutionize our attitudes. When love for God, justice, and concern for other people rule our hearts, we will follow the necessary rules. Hypocrisy and contempt for other people are sins which constantly tempt religious people. Such attitudes lead to wrong interpretations of Scripture which lead other people to sin. The ultimate result is that hypocrisy and false interpretations lead people to reject Jesus, the only Way to salvation. See note on Mt 18:6–9.
11:42 SALVATION, Love of God—Tithing should never be substituted for loving God and doing justice. Salvation cannot be bought or earned. Salvation does respond to the needs of others in giving and acting.
11:42 STEWARDSHIP, Tithe—See note on Mt 23:23–24.
11:49–52 REVELATION, Messengers—Jesus charged the religious leaders were ignoring God’s revelation through the prophets and in the laws. Those who saw themselves as helpers of God actually had become hindrances to the revelation of God to His people. Religious leadership begins with personal obedience to God’s revelation.

ah,[u] who was killed between the altar
and the sanctuary. Yes, I tell you, this
generation will be held responsible for it
all.[v]
52"Woe to you experts in the law, because you have taken away the key to
knowledge. You yourselves have not entered, and you have hindered those who
were entering."[w]
53When Jesus left there, the Pharisees
and the teachers of the law began to oppose him fiercely and to besiege him with
questions, 54waiting to catch him in
something he might say.[x]

Chapter 12

Warnings and Encouragements

12:2–9pp — Mt 10:26–33

MEANWHILE, when a crowd of many
thousands had gathered, so that
they were trampling on one another,
Jesus began to speak first to his disciples,
saying: "Be on your guard against the
yeast of the Pharisees, which is hypocrisy.[y] 2There is nothing concealed that will
not be disclosed, or hidden that will not
be made known.[z] 3What you have said in
the dark will be heard in the daylight, and
what you have whispered in the ear in
the inner rooms will be proclaimed from
the roofs.
4"I tell you, my friends,[a] do not be
afraid of those who kill the body and after
that can do no more. 5But I will show you
whom you should fear: Fear him who,
after the killing of the body, has power to
throw you into hell. Yes, I tell you, fear
him.[b] 6Are not five sparrows sold for two
pennies[d]? Yet not one of them is forgotten by God. 7Indeed, the very hairs of
your head are all numbered.[c] Don't be
afraid; you are worth more than many
sparrows.[d]
8"I tell you, whoever acknowledges me
before men, the Son of Man will also acknowledge him before the angels of
God.[e] 9But he who disowns me before
men will be disowned[f] before the angels
of God. 10And everyone who speaks a
word against the Son of Man[g] will be forgiven, but anyone who blasphemes
against the Holy Spirit will not be forgiv-
en.[h]
11"When you are brought before synagogues, rulers and authorities, do not
worry about how you will defend yourselves or what you will say,[i] 12for the
Holy Spirit will teach you at that time
what you should say."[j]

The Parable of the Rich Fool

13Someone in the crowd said to him,
"Teacher, tell my brother to divide the
inheritance with me."
14Jesus replied, "Man, who appointed
me a judge or an arbiter between you?"
15Then he said to them, "Watch out! Be
on your guard against all kinds of greed; a
man's life does not consist in the abundance of his possessions."[k]
16And he told them this parable: "The
ground of a certain rich man produced a
good crop. 17He thought to himself,

11:51 [u]2Ch 24:20,21 [v]Mt 23:35,36
11:52 [w]Mt 23:13
11:54 [x]S Mt 12:10
12:1 [y]Mt 16:6,11,12
12:2 [z]S Mk 4:22
12:4 [a]Jn 15:14,15
12:5 [b]Heb 10:31
12:7 [c]S Mt 10:30 [d]Mt 12:12
12:8 [e]Lk 15:10
12:9 [f]Mk 8:38; 2Ti 2:12
12:10 [g]S Mt 8:20 [h]Mt 12:31,32; S 1Jn 5:16
12:11 [i]Mt 10:17,19; Lk 21:12,14
12:12 [j]Ex 4:12; Mt 10:20; Mk 13:11; Lk 21:15
12:15 [k]Job 20:20; 31:24; Ps 62:10

[d]6 Greek *two assaria*

12:1 SIN, Hypocrisy—Sin is being religiously two-faced, claiming to be righteous while ignoring the attitudes and relationships God expects from us. See note on 11:42–52.

12:1–48 ELECTION, Mission—Election assumes the elect participate in God's mission and ministry. The elect are bold witnesses, sometimes in a hostile environment. The gracious, merciful God provides the kingdom as a free gift to them. The elect are known not by their wealth, power, or large numbers but by the grace of the God who elected them.

12:6–7 HUMANITY, Worth—People and animals are related, but God places far more value on people than on animal life. See note on Ge 2:7. Knowing God places such worth on us, we need not fear the physical or psychological attacks of other people. We need fear only God and be about His business.

12:8–10 JESUS CHRIST, Son of Man—See note on Mt 10:32–42. Those who rejected Jesus in His earthly ministry had an opportunity to respond to the Holy Spirit after Pentecost. Those who reject the Spirit's call to faith in Christ have no hope for forgiveness.

12:11–12 HOLY SPIRIT, Protects—Jesus promised His disciples that when they went on trial for their faith the Spirit would give them prophetic gifts to enable them to testify faithfully and to defend themselves effectively. In John, the Spirit is called a lawyer (Greek *paraclete*) who will defend the disciples on trial (Jn 16:5–15). Paul referred to the Spirit as a seal who guarantees that Christians will be kept to the end (2 Co 2:22; 5:5; Eph 1:13). The Spirit helps Christians guard what has been entrusted to us (2 Ti 1:14). This protective work of the Spirit was especially important to Christians experiencing persecution. It is important for us to know the Spirit will defend us, will assist us to be witnesses, and will seal us safely until the end. See notes on Mt 10:19–20; Mk 13:11.

12:13–34 CHRISTIAN ETHICS, Property Rights—Placing material things over personal relationships has disastrous results. One can become consumed by the bigger is better syndrome. Greed gradually gains control. All energy is expended on material security so that a vision of wealth guides character formation. Life is too short to be centered on the material. God offers so many possibilities for us that it is foolish to spend all our physical and emotional energies on satisfying ego needs to have more than others. Serving God silences our greed and leads to satisfaction with what He supplies. Concern for the need of others replaces worry over personal desires. See note on Mt 6:19–34.

12:13–15 PRAYER, Hindrances—Jesus denounced the petition of the person in the crowd as greed. Wrong motives hinder prayer (Jas 4:1–3).

12:16–31 STEWARDSHIP, Life-style—How we live expresses our Christian faith. Personal life-style is made up of attitudes and values, activities, conduct patterns, goals, and specific uses of material possessions. The world insists that the good life consists of accumulating possessions and indulging in luxuries. Christ showed that life is fulfilling only when we seek to extend His kingdom by loving, serving, and giving to others. Jesus' teachings and His life-style denounced getting wealth as the aim of life. He reminded His followers that owning material riches is temporary; spiritual riches are eternal. Money and possessions are to be used in spiritual serving. See note on 1 Ti 6:6–19.

'What shall I do? I have no place to store
my crops.'

18"Then he said, 'This is what I'll do. I
will tear down my barns and build bigger
ones, and there I will store all my grain
and my goods. 19And I'll say to myself,
"You have plenty of good things laid up
for many years. Take life easy; eat, drink
and be merry." '

20"But God said to him, 'You fool![l]
This very night your life will be demanded from you.[m] Then who will get what
you have prepared for yourself?'[n]

21"This is how it will be with anyone
who stores up things for himself but is
not rich toward God."[o]

Do Not Worry

12:22–31pp — Mt 6:25–33

22Then Jesus said to his disciples:
"Therefore I tell you, do not worry about
your life, what you will eat; or about your
body, what you will wear. 23Life is more
than food, and the body more than
clothes. 24Consider the ravens: They do
not sow or reap, they have no storeroom
or barn; yet God feeds them.[p] And how
much more valuable you are than birds!
25Who of you by worrying can add a single hour to his life[e]? 26Since you cannot
do this very little thing, why do you worry about the rest?

27"Consider how the lilies grow. They
do not labor or spin. Yet I tell you, not
even Solomon in all his splendor[q] was
dressed like one of these. 28If that is how
God clothes the grass of the field, which
is here today, and tomorrow is thrown
into the fire, how much more will he
clothe you, O you of little faith![r] 29And
do not set your heart on what you will eat
or drink; do not worry about it. 30For the
pagan world runs after all such things,
and your Father[s] knows that you need
them.[t] 31But seek his kingdom,[u] and
these things will be given to you as
well.[v]

32"Do not be afraid,[w] little flock, for
your Father has been pleased to give you
the kingdom.[x] 33Sell your possessions
and give to the poor.[y] Provide purses for
yourselves that will not wear out, a treasure in heaven[z] that will not be exhausted, where no thief comes near and no
moth destroys.[a] 34For where your treasure is, there your heart will be also.[b]

Watchfulness

12:35,36pp — Mt 25:1–13; Mk 13:33–37
12:39,40; 42–46pp — Mt 24:43–51

35"Be dressed ready for service and
keep your lamps burning, 36like men
waiting for their master to return from a
wedding banquet, so that when he comes
and knocks they can immediately open
the door for him. 37It will be good for
those servants whose master finds them
watching when he comes.[c] I tell you the
truth, he will dress himself to serve, will
have them recline at the table and will
come and wait on them.[d] 38It will be
good for those servants whose master
finds them ready, even if he comes in the
second or third watch of the night. 39But
understand this: If the owner of the
house had known at what hour the thief[e]
was coming, he would not have let his
house be broken into. 40You also must be
ready,[f] because the Son of Man will
come at an hour when you do not expect
him."

41Peter asked, "Lord, are you telling
this parable to us, or to everyone?"

42The Lord[g] answered, "Who then is
the faithful and wise manager, whom the
master puts in charge of his servants to
give them their food allowance at the
proper time? 43It will be good for that servant whom the master finds doing so
when he returns. 44I tell you the truth, he
will put him in charge of all his possessions. 45But suppose the servant says to
himself, 'My master is taking a long time
in coming,' and he then begins to beat
the menservants and maidservants and to
eat and drink and get drunk. 46The master of that servant will come on a day
when he does not expect him and at an
hour he is not aware of.[h] He will cut him
to pieces and assign him a place with the
unbelievers.

12:20 [l]Jer 17:11; Lk 11:40 [m]Job 27:8 [n]Ps 39:6; 49:10
12:21 [o]ver 33
12:24 [p]Job 38:41; Ps 147:9
12:27 [q]1Ki 10:4-7
12:28 [r]S Mt 6:30
12:30 [s]S Lk 6:36 [t]Mt 6:8
12:31 [u]S Mt 3:2 [v]Mt 19:29
12:32 [w]S Mt 14:27 [x]S Mt 25:34
12:33 [y]S Ac 2:45 [z]S Mt 6:20 [a]S Jas 5:2
12:34 [b]Mt 6:21
12:37 [c]Mt 24:42, 46; 25:13 [d]S Mt 20:28
12:39 [e]Mt 6:19; 1Th 5:2; 2Pe 3:10; Rev 3:3; 16:15
12:40 [f]Mk 13:33; Lk 21:36
12:42 [g]S Lk 7:13
12:46 [h]ver 40

[e]*25* Or *single cubit to his height*

12:19–20 HUMANITY, Life—The present is not permanent. People make plans for the future based on present achievements. Such plans should not be totally self-centered. We need to remember God controls the future. Our plans must include Him, His will, and His work on earth. Our largest building project is His kingdom.

12:22–34 CREATION, Purposeful—Understanding the doctrine of creation does more than add to our intellectual knowledge. It helps us set priorities in life. God created a world that rewards faith. God takes care of the nonhuman realm without His creatures having to experience intense anxiety or excessive striving. He will provide for our needs if we will trust Him. Our Creator wants the best for us. We should participate in His plan for the world by showing this kind of joy in helping others. We demonstrate by our loyalties the kind of world we believe God has made.

12:31 THE CHURCH, God's Kingdom—See note on Mt 13:44–46. The kingdom of God is the greatest gift one can receive and the highest priority in life.

12:32 THE CHURCH, God's Kingdom—God desires that all people receive His gracious gift, the kingdom. The kingdom is not a political power that terrorizes people. It is Christ's rule of love which casts out fear.

12:40 JESUS CHRIST, Son of Man—Jesus as the Son of man will return as Judge. See notes on Mt 25:31–46; Mk 10:45.

12:40 LAST THINGS, Demands Preparedness—See note on Mt 24:36–44.

47“That servant who knows his master’s will and does not get ready or does
not do what his master wants will be
beaten with many blows.[i] 48But the one
who does not know and does things deserving punishment will be beaten with
few blows.[j] From everyone who has
been given much, much will be demanded; and from the one who has been entrusted with much, much more will be
asked.

Not Peace but Division

12:51–53pp — Mt 10:34–36

49“I have come to bring fire on the
earth, and how I wish it were already kindled! 50But I have a baptism[k] to undergo,
and how distressed I am until it is completed![l] 51Do you think I came to bring
peace on earth? No, I tell you, but division. 52From now on there will be five in
one family divided against each other,
three against two and two against three.
53They will be divided, father against son
and son against father, mother against
daughter and daughter against mother,
mother-in-law against daughter-in-law
and daughter-in-law against mother-in-
law.”[m]

Interpreting the Times

54He said to the crowd: “When you see
a cloud rising in the west, immediately
you say, ‘It’s going to rain,’ and it does.[n]
55And when the south wind blows, you
say, ‘It’s going to be hot,’ and it is. 56Hyp-
ocrites! You know how to interpret the
appearance of the earth and the sky. How
is it that you don’t know how to interpret
this present time?[o]
57“Why don’t you judge for yourselves
what is right? 58As you are going with
your adversary to the magistrate, try hard
to be reconciled to him on the way, or he
may drag you off to the judge, and the
judge turn you over to the officer, and the
officer throw you into prison.[p] 59I tell
you, you will not get out until you have
paid the last penny.[f] ”[q]

Chapter 13

Repent or Perish

NOW there were some present at that
time who told Jesus about the Galileans whose blood Pilate[r] had mixed
with their sacrifices. 2Jesus answered,
“Do you think that these Galileans were
worse sinners than all the other Galileans
because they suffered this way?[s] 3I tell
you, no! But unless you repent, you too
will all perish. 4Or those eighteen who
died when the tower in Siloam[t] fell on
them—do you think they were more
guilty than all the others living in Jerusalem? 5I tell you, no! But unless you repent,[u] you too will all perish.”
6Then he told this parable: “A man had
a fig tree, planted in his vineyard, and he
went to look for fruit on it, but did not
find any.[v] 7So he said to the man who
took care of the vineyard, ‘For three years
now I’ve been coming to look for fruit on
this fig tree and haven’t found any. Cut it
down![w] Why should it use up the soil?’
8“ ‘Sir,’ the man replied, ‘leave it alone
for one more year, and I’ll dig around it
and fertilize it. 9If it bears fruit next year,
fine! If not, then cut it down.’ ”

[f]59 Greek *lepton*

12:47 [i]Dt 25:2
12:48 [j]Lev 5:17; Nu 15:27-30
12:50 [k]Mk 10:38 [l]S Jn 19:30
12:53 [m]Mic 7:6; Mt 10:21
12:54 [n]Mt 16:2
12:56 [o]Mt 16:3
12:58 [p]Mt 5:25
12:59 [q]Mt 5:26; Mk 12:42
13:1 [r]S Mt 27:2
13:2 [s]Jn 9:2,3
13:4 [t]Jn 9:7,11
13:5 [u]Mt 3:2; Ac 2:38
13:6 [v]Isa 5:2; Jer 8:13; Mt 21:19
13:7 [w]S Mt 3:10

12:48 LAST THINGS, Judgment—One principle of divine judgment is that of proportional responsibility. Levels of punishment will be fitted to variations of opportunity, thus to degrees of accountability. Premeditated or high-handed sins have always been deserving of greater punishment than unwitting sins (Nu 15:22–31). The result of this principle is that there are to be degrees of punishment and reward.

12:49–53 FAMILY, Priorities—Family relationships are given a high priority in the Bible, but the ultimate loyalty of every believer is to Jesus Christ as Lord. Quoting Mic 7:6, Jesus announced the potential divisions among family members that can occur because of decisions to follow or not follow Him. Each Christian must choose the cross. Ultimate loyalty can be given only to Christ—not to husband, wife, children, or parents. Obviously, Christian commitment includes faithful service to family, but Christ must be supreme.

12:50 JESUS CHRIST, Mission—The Prince of peace brought disruption and division because people could not separate themselves from the comfort of their religious ways to see Him as the true fulfillment of God’s plans and purposes. See notes on Mt 10:32–42; Mk 10:38–39.

12:50 ORDINANCES, Baptism as Death—See note on Mk 10:38–40.

13:1–5 EVIL AND SUFFERING, Punishment—Traditional Jewish belief taught that good people succeeded in life, but the wicked suffered. Catastrophe indicated the victims were wicked. Jesus refused to interpret two contemporary tragedies within this view. He called religious people away from judging other people. He warned the self-righteous to repent before they faced even worse tragedy at the final judgment.

13:1–5 SIN, Death—Humans judge one another. People who suffer extraordinarily tend to be ranked as extraordinary sinners. See the Book of Job. We conclude suffering and persecution is the consequence of intense sin. Jesus refused to grade sinners. He placed all of us in one category. We all deserve death. We will get it if we do not repent and trust Him for salvation. Some sins do have worse consequences in this world than others, but the wages of any sin is death. See note on Ro 6:23.

13:1–5 SALVATION, Repentance—None is excused from repenting. God does not categorize sinners and seek more repayment through suffering and sacrifice from some than from others. All have sinned (Ro 3:23). All must respond to God with repentance.

13:2–5 PRAYER, Repentance—Outer circumstances do not indicate that God is rewarding or punishing an individual. Repentance is a prayer all must pray. Those who repent know they are right with God.

13:6–9 DISCIPLESHIP, Involvement—Christ expects disciples to be fruitful. His patience with fruitless disciples has limits.

A Crippled Woman Healed on the Sabbath

10On a Sabbath Jesus was teaching in
one of the synagogues,[x] 11and a woman
was there who had been crippled by a
spirit for eighteen years.[y] She was bent
over and could not straighten up at all.
12When Jesus saw her, he called her forward and said to her, "Woman, you are
set free from your infirmity." 13Then he
put his hands on her,[z] and immediately
she straightened up and praised God.
14Indignant because Jesus had healed
on the Sabbath,[a] the synagogue ruler[b]
said to the people, "There are six days for
work.[c] So come and be healed on those
days, not on the Sabbath."
15The Lord answered him, "You hypocrites! Doesn't each of you on the Sabbath untie his ox or donkey from the stall
and lead it out to give it water?[d] 16Then
should not this woman, a daughter of
Abraham,[e] whom Satan[f] has kept bound
for eighteen long years, be set free on the
Sabbath day from what bound her?"
17When he said this, all his opponents
were humiliated,[g] but the people were
delighted with all the wonderful things
he was doing.

The Parables of the Mustard Seed and the Yeast

13:18,19pp — Mk 4:30–32
13:18–21pp — Mt 13:31–33

18Then Jesus asked, "What is the kingdom of God[h] like?[i] What shall I compare
it to? 19It is like a mustard seed, which a
man took and planted in his garden. It
grew and became a tree,[j] and the birds
of the air perched in its branches."[k]
20Again he asked, "What shall I compare the kingdom of God to? 21It is like
yeast that a woman took and mixed into a
large amount[g] of flour until it worked all
through the dough."[l]

The Narrow Door

22Then Jesus went through the towns
and villages, teaching as he made his way
to Jerusalem.[m] 23Someone asked him,
"Lord, are only a few people going to be
saved?"
He said to them, 24"Make every effort
to enter through the narrow door,[n] because many, I tell you, will try to enter
and will not be able to. 25Once the owner
of the house gets up and closes the door,
you will stand outside knocking and
pleading, 'Sir, open the door for us.'
"But he will answer, 'I don't know you
or where you come from.'[o]
26"Then you will say, 'We ate and
drank with you, and you taught in our
streets.'
27"But he will reply, 'I don't know you
or where you come from. Away from me,
all you evildoers!'[p]
28"There will be weeping there, and
gnashing of teeth,[q] when you see Abraham, Isaac and Jacob and all the prophets
in the kingdom of God, but you yourselves thrown out. 29People will come
from east and west[r] and north and south,
and will take their places at the feast in
the kingdom of God. 30Indeed there are
those who are last who will be first, and
first who will be last."[s]

Jesus' Sorrow for Jerusalem

13:34,35pp — Mt 23:37–39
13:34,35Ref — Lk 19:41

31At that time some Pharisees came to

13:10 [x]S Mt 4:23
13:11 [y]ver 16
13:13 [z]S Mk 5:23
13:14 [a]S Mt 12:2 [b]S Mk 5:22 [c]Ex 20:9
13:15 [d]Lk 14:5
13:16 [e]S Lk 3:8 [f]S Mt 4:10
13:17 [g]Isa 66:5
13:18 [h]S Mt 3:2 [i]S Mt 13:24
13:19 [j]Lk 17:6 [k]S Mt 13:32
13:21 [l]1Co 5:6
13:22 [m]S Lk 9:51
13:24 [n]Mt 7:13
13:25 [o]Mt 7:23; 25:10-12
13:27 [p]S Mt 7:23
13:28 [q]S Mt 8:12
13:29 [r]S Mt 8:11
13:30 [s]S Mt 19:30

[g]*21* Greek *three satas* (probably about 1/2 bushel or 22 liters)

13:10–17 JESUS CHRIST, Authority—Jesus' miracles brought praise to God and ridicule for Himself, causing division as He had said (12:49–53). Division came because He exercised authority over the legalistic rules of traditional religion.

13:10–17 MIRACLE, Praise—Miracles evoke opposite reactions from people. Healing on the Sabbath aroused the wrath of the religious leaders but praise from the woman who was healed and delight from the crowd. The woman had been "crippled by a spirit," yet the healing action does not mention a demon. He touched her, and she received strength—"set free" on the Sabbath day. Legalism seeks obedience to human interpretations. Christ's followers praise God for every person set free to serve Him.

13:10–16 EVIL AND SUFFERING, Satan—Satan's forces can cause human diseases and disorders (4:33; 8:29; 9:39; 11:14; Mt 8:28; 9:32; 12:22; 17:15–18; Mk 5:2; 7:25; Jn 10:20). Not all disease is to be explained as demon-possession. Our task is not to argue over causes or to find excuses for our inaction. Christ sends us to take up His ministry of healing with all the tools we have—those supplied by modern medicine and knowledge and those supplied by Christ.

13:14–17 CHRISTIAN ETHICS, Moral Imperatives—Would Jesus say the treatment of animals was unimportant? Not at all. Rather His point was that if the humane treatment of animals falls under the shadow of the moral law, how much more does the humane treatment of fellow human beings? Where traditions have become so rigid and forgetful of people, those traditions need to be examined through the looking glass of the Gospels.

13:18–30 ELECTION, Free Will—Election does not answer the question of how many will be saved? Election invites people to enter the door to God's kingdom before time is gone and judgment comes. Associating with religious people is not the identifying mark of the elect. Knowing and obeying Jesus is. Election is not a source of pride for the secure elect. It is a warning to all who hear to be sure not to be thrown out.

13:18–21 THE CHURCH, God's Kingdom—See notes on Mt 13:31–32, 33.

13:22 EDUCATION, Jesus—See note on Mk 2:13.

13:24–30 JESUS CHRIST, Teaching—Compare Mt 25:1–13. The demands of the Kingdom are strict. Entrance into the Kingdom is urgent.

13:31–35 JESUS CHRIST, Death—Facing death, Jesus maintained control of His destiny. The Pharisees were aware of Jesus' danger and the possibility of His death. Jesus had known His peril and His destiny for some time (9:44; Mk 2:20). In this passage He described His sacrificial death in line with the fate of Israel's prophets. Israel's religious leaders in Jerusalem caused the death of the prophets and would cause His own. He tenderly lamented over the city He loved and had tried to

Jesus and said to him, "Leave this place
and go somewhere else. Herod[t] wants to
kill you."
32He replied, "Go tell that fox, 'I will
drive out demons and heal people today
and tomorrow, and on the third day I will
reach my goal.'[u] 33In any case, I must
keep going today and tomorrow and the
next day—for surely no prophet[v] can die
outside Jerusalem!
34"O Jerusalem, Jerusalem, you who
kill the prophets and stone those sent to
you, how often I have longed to gather
your children together, as a hen gathers
her chicks under her wings,[w] but you
were not willing! 35Look, your house is
left to you desolate.[x] I tell you, you will
not see me again until you say, 'Blessed is
he who comes in the name of the
Lord.'[h]"[y]

Chapter 14

Jesus at a Pharisee's House

14:8–10Ref — Pr 25:6,7

ONE Sabbath, when Jesus went to eat
in the house of a prominent Pharisee,[z] he was being carefully watched.[a]
2There in front of him was a man suffering from dropsy. 3Jesus asked the Pharisees and experts in the law,[b] "Is it lawful
to heal on the Sabbath or not?"[c] 4But
they remained silent. So taking hold of
the man, he healed him and sent him
away.
5Then he asked them, "If one of you
has a son[1] or an ox that falls into a well
on the Sabbath day, will you not immediately pull him out?"[d] 6And they had
nothing to say.
7When he noticed how the guests
picked the places of honor at the table,[e]
he told them this parable: 8"When someone invites you to a wedding feast, do not
take the place of honor, for a person more
distinguished than you may have been invited. 9If so, the host who invited both of
you will come and say to you, 'Give this
man your seat.' Then, humiliated, you
will have to take the least important
place. 10But when you are invited, take
the lowest place, so that when your host
comes, he will say to you, 'Friend, move
up to a better place.' Then you will be
honored in the presence of all your fellow
guests. 11For everyone who exalts himself
will be humbled, and he who humbles
himself will be exalted."[f]
12Then Jesus said to his host, "When
you give a luncheon or dinner, do not
invite your friends, your brothers or relatives, or your rich neighbors; if you do,
they may invite you back and so you will
be repaid. 13But when you give a banquet, invite the poor, the crippled, the
lame, the blind,[g] 14and you will be
blessed. Although they cannot repay you,
you will be repaid at the resurrection of
the righteous."[h]

The Parable of the Great Banquet

14:16–24Ref — Mt 22:2–14

15When one of those at the table with
him heard this, he said to Jesus, "Blessed
is the man who will eat at the feast[i] in
the kingdom of God."[j]
16Jesus replied: "A certain man was
preparing a great banquet and invited
many guests. 17At the time of the banquet
he sent his servant to tell those who had
been invited, 'Come, for everything is
now ready.'
18"But they all alike began to make excuses. The first said, 'I have just bought a
field, and I must go and see it. Please excuse me.'
19"Another said, 'I have just bought
five yoke of oxen, and I'm on my way to
try them out. Please excuse me.'
20"Still another said, 'I just got married, so I can't come.'
21"The servant came back and reported
this to his master. Then the owner of the
house became angry and ordered his servant, 'Go out quickly into the streets and
alleys of the town and bring in the poor,

13:31 [t]S Mt 14:1
13:32 [u]S Heb 2:10
13:33 [v]S Mt 21:11
13:34 [w]S Mt 23:37
13:35 [x]Jer 12:17; 22:5 [y]Ps 118:26; Lk 19:38
14:1 [z]Lk 7:36; 11:37 [a]S Mt 12:10
14:3 [b]S Mt 22:35 [c]S Mt 12:2
14:5 [d]Lk 13:15
14:7 [e]S Lk 11:43
14:11 [f]S Mt 23:12
14:13 [g]ver 21
14:14 [h]Ac 24:15
14:15 [i]Isa 25:6; Mt 26:29; Lk 13:29; Rev 19:9 [j]S Mt 3:2

[h]35 Psalm 118:26 [1]5 Some manuscripts *donkey*

minister to. See note on Mt 23:37–39.

13:34 SALVATION, Human Freedom—Jesus wept over those who were unwilling to let Him gather them under His saving wings. Compare 19:41.

13:35 PRAYER, Blessing—See note on Mt 23:39.

14:1–6 JESUS CHRIST, Authority—See note on 13:10–17. Jesus' authority and wisdom silenced the legal experts by demanding their advice before His compassionate action.

14:1–24 ELECTION, Righteousness—God's elect minister in love to the poor, cripple, lame, and blind. At the resurrection of the righteous, they will be blessed and rewarded for their ministry of loving service to the least and the lowest. The self-righteous religious hypocrites will not participate in the Messiah's banquet at the end of time.

14:7–11 CHRISTIAN ETHICS, Character—The many references to humility in Jesus' teachings should give us pause to think about them more seriously. The mark of humility is to think of others more highly. Not a weak-kneed approach to life, rather it gives attention to the great work God is doing in others and the great care He extends to them. They are made in His image, thus deserving of love. See note on Mt 7:1–5,12.

14:12–14 DISCIPLESHIP, Persons—Discipleship is not a social hour we share with our group. Discipleship is using every occasion of life to minister to persons in need. Participation in God's kingdom is our reward, not participation in earthly award ceremonies. See note on Mt 25:34–46.

14:13 DISCIPLESHIP, Handicapped—Jesus told His Pharisee host he should have a banquet for handicapped persons rather than for relatives and rich friends. Then he would receive God's blessings. See note on Mt 25:34–46. The handicapped should participate fully in our programs and fellowship. God welcomes the handicapped with their special gifts into His kingdom.

the crippled, the blind and the lame.'[k]
22" 'Sir,' the servant said, 'what you ordered has been done, but there is still
room.'
23"Then the master told his servant,
'Go out to the roads and country lanes
and make them come in, so that my
house will be full. 24I tell you, not one of
those men who were invited will get a
taste of my banquet.' "[l]

The Cost of Being a Disciple

25Large crowds were traveling with
Jesus, and turning to them he said: 26"If
anyone comes to me and does not hate
his father and mother, his wife and children, his brothers and sisters—yes, even
his own life—he cannot be my disciple.[m]
27And anyone who does not carry his
cross and follow me cannot be my disciple.[n]
28"Suppose one of you wants to build a
tower. Will he not first sit down and estimate the cost to see if he has enough
money to complete it? 29For if he lays the
foundation and is not able to finish it, everyone who sees it will ridicule him,
30saying, 'This fellow began to build and
was not able to finish.'
31"Or suppose a king is about to go to
war against another king. Will he not first
sit down and consider whether he is able
with ten thousand men to oppose the one
coming against him with twenty thousand? 32If he is not able, he will send a
delegation while the other is still a long
way off and will ask for terms of peace.
33In the same way, any of you who does
not give up everything he has cannot be
my disciple.[o]
34"Salt is good, but if it loses its saltiness, how can it be made salty again?[p]
35It is fit neither for the soil nor for the
manure pile; it is thrown out.[q]

14:21 [k]ver 13
14:24 [l]Mt 21:43; Ac 13:46
14:26 [m]Mt 10:37; S Jn 12:25
14:27 [n]Mt 10:38; Lk 9:23
14:33 [o]Php 3:7,8
14:34 [p]Mk 9:50
14:35 [q]Mt 5:13 [r]S Mt 11:15
15:1 [s]Lk 5:29
15:2 [t]S Mt 9:11
15:3 [u]Mt 13:3
15:4 [v]Ps 23; 119:176; Jer 31:10; Eze 34:11-16; Lk 5:32; 19:10
15:6 [w]ver 9
15:7 [x]ver 10
15:9 [y]ver 6
15:10 [z]ver 7
15:11 [a]Mt 21:28

"He who has ears to hear, let him
hear."[r]

Chapter 15

The Parable of the Lost Sheep

15:4–7pp — Mt 18:12–14

NOW the tax collectors[s] and "sinners" were all gathering around to
hear him. 2But the Pharisees and the
teachers of the law muttered, "This man
welcomes sinners and eats with them."[t]
3Then Jesus told them this parable:[u]
4"Suppose one of you has a hundred
sheep and loses one of them. Does he not
leave the ninety-nine in the open country
and go after the lost sheep until he finds
it?[v] 5And when he finds it, he joyfully
puts it on his shoulders 6and goes home.
Then he calls his friends and neighbors
together and says, 'Rejoice with me; I
have found my lost sheep.'[w] 7I tell you
that in the same way there will be more
rejoicing in heaven over one sinner who
repents than over ninety-nine righteous
persons who do not need to repent.[x]

The Parable of the Lost Coin

8"Or suppose a woman has ten silver
coins[j] and loses one. Does she not light a
lamp, sweep the house and search carefully until she finds it? 9And when she
finds it, she calls her friends and neighbors together and says, 'Rejoice with me;
I have found my lost coin.'[y] 10In the
same way, I tell you, there is rejoicing in
the presence of the angels of God over
one sinner who repents."[z]

The Parable of the Lost Son

11Jesus continued: "There was a man
who had two sons.[a] 12The younger one

[j]8 Greek *ten drachmas,* each worth about a day's wages

14:25–27 FAMILY, Priorities—"Hate" here does not refer to emotional or mental dislike of the family members mentioned nor of one's own life. Instead, it indicates a total rejection of anything and anyone who would block our absolute commitment to Jesus as Lord. See note on Mt 10:21,34–39.

14:26 JESUS CHRIST, Son of God—Jesus consciously gathered devoted disciples to create a family of God. Loyalty to God's family takes precedence over all other loyalties. Compare Mt 10:37. Luke's forceful word "hate" needs to be read in light of Matthew's expression.

14:26–33 DISCIPLESHIP, Nature—Discipleship is a full-time job placed before all other priorities and responsibilities. Christian disciples are devoted, obedient followers of Christ. Nothing comes before Christ in the life of a disciple. Disciples voluntarily accept Christ as Master and His teachings as commands. Only one question determines if you are a disciple: Have you in faith given up *everything* for Christ? See note on Mk 10:41–45.

14:28–33 DISCIPLESHIP, Involvement—Being a disciple is a call to total involvement in the work of Christ. To decide to follow Christ with no intention to be involved in His work is as foolish as to decide to build a building without getting a cost estimate.

14:34–35 DISCIPLESHIP, Involvement—Disciples are the salt of the earth. The life of a true disciple flavors and preserves the society. Such saltiness is an essential part of a disciple's character which will endure to the end. For Christian influence to permeate and preserve society, disciples must get involved in the lives and social affairs of our day. Disciples do not withdraw from society to preserve our holiness. Disciples involve themselves in all parts of society to give it a righteous flavor. See note on Mt 5:14–16.

15:1–2 SIN, Violation—See note on Mk 2:15–16.

15:3–32 REVELATION, Author of Love—Luke brought together three stories revealing the depth of God's love and the extent to which He takes initiative to find His own. God loves His children, even to the last one. Jesus is, in fact, a revelation of how far God goes in seeking His misplaced children.

15:6,9–10 SALVATION, Joy—Rejoicing breaks out in heaven when one sinner is saved. In the same way, God's people on earth should rejoice when one lost person turns to Christ.

15:7,10 SALVATION, Repentance—God cares for individuals. Repentance is His goal for every person. He will not be satisfied unless every person repents.

15:11–32 HUMANITY, Family Relationships—Family

said to his father, ‘Father, give me my
share of the estate.’[b] So he divided his
property[c] between them.
13“Not long after that, the younger son
got together all he had, set off for a distant country and there squandered his
wealth[d] in wild living. 14After he had
spent everything, there was a severe famine in that whole country, and he began
to be in need. 15So he went and hired
himself out to a citizen of that country,
who sent him to his fields to feed pigs.[e]
16He longed to fill his stomach with the
pods that the pigs were eating, but no
one gave him anything.
17“When he came to his senses, he
said, ‘How many of my father’s hired men
have food to spare, and here I am starving
to death! 18I will set out and go back to
my father and say to him: Father, I have
sinned[f] against heaven and against you.
19I am no longer worthy to be called your
son; make me like one of your hired
men.’ 20So he got up and went to his father.

“But while he was still a long way off,
his father saw him and was filled with
compassion for him; he ran to his son,
threw his arms around him and kissed
him.[g]
21“The son said to him, ‘Father, I have
sinned against heaven and against you.[h] I
am no longer worthy to be called your
son.[k]’
22“But the father said to his servants,
‘Quick! Bring the best robe[i] and put it
on him. Put a ring on his finger[j] and
sandals on his feet. 23Bring the fattened
calf and kill it. Let’s have a feast and celebrate. 24For this son of mine was dead
and is alive again;[k] he was lost and is
found.’ So they began to celebrate.[l]
25“Meanwhile, the older son was in
the field. When he came near the house,
he heard music and dancing. 26So he
called one of the servants and asked him
what was going on. 27‘Your brother has
come,’ he replied, ‘and your father has

15:12 [b]Dt 21:17 [c]ver 30
15:13 [d]ver 30; Lk 16:1
15:15 [e]Lev 11:7
15:18 [f]Lev 26:40; Mt 3:2
15:20 [g]Ge 45:14, 15; 46:29; Ac 20:37
15:21 [h]Ps 51:4
15:22 [i]Zec 3:4; Rev 6:11 [j]Ge 41:42
15:24 [k]Eph 2:1,5; 5:14; 1Ti 5:6 [l]ver 32
15:28 [m]Jnh 4:1
15:30 [n]ver 12,13 [o]Pr 29:3
15:32 [p]ver 24; Mal 3:17
16:1 [q]Lk 15:13,30

killed the fattened calf because he has
him back safe and sound.’
28“The older brother became angry[m]
and refused to go in. So his father went
out and pleaded with him. 29But he answered his father, ‘Look! All these years
I’ve been slaving for you and never disobeyed your orders. Yet you never gave
me even a young goat so I could celebrate
with my friends. 30But when this son of
yours who has squandered your property[n] with prostitutes[o] comes home, you
kill the fattened calf for him!’
31“ ‘My son,’ the father said, ‘you are
always with me, and everything I have is
yours. 32But we had to celebrate and be
glad, because this brother of yours was
dead and is alive again; he was lost and is
found.’ ”[p]

Chapter 16

The Parable of the Shrewd Manager

JESUS told his disciples: “There was a
rich man whose manager was accused
of wasting his possessions.[q] 2So he called
him in and asked him, ‘What is this I hear
about you? Give an account of your management, because you cannot be manager
any longer.’
3“The manager said to himself, ‘What
shall I do now? My master is taking away
my job. I’m not strong enough to dig, and
I’m ashamed to beg— 4I know what I’ll
do so that, when I lose my job here, people will welcome me into their houses.’
5“So he called in each one of his master’s debtors. He asked the first, ‘How
much do you owe my master?’
6“ ‘Eight hundred gallons[1] of olive oil,’
he replied.
“The manager told him, ‘Take your
bill, sit down quickly, and make it four
hundred.’
7“Then he asked the second, ‘And how
much do you owe?’

[k]*21* Some early manuscripts *son. Make me like one of your hired men.* [l]*6* Greek *one hundred batous* (probably about 3 kiloliters)

relationships become too easily twisted and broken. Only God-like love can keep a family together. Pride and jealousy only isolate members. In God’s family we can always trust the Heavenly Father to be waiting for His repentant children to return. Similarly, we should be ready to accept and forgive members of our physical family and of God’s community of believers.

15:11–32 SALVATION, Initiative—Unsaved persons are lost, as lost as was the prodigal son. God is the loving Father, who like the father of the prodigal son, yearns for all lost prodigals to be saved. Saved persons should want to see lost persons saved as much as God does.

15:11–32 CHRISTIAN ETHICS, Property Rights—The father’s generosity seems whimsical to our contemporary minds. Yet such response to the son both before he left home and after his return typify God’s grace toward us. In turn, unlike the elder brother, we are to extend grace to others because we have been graced. Material goods serve best when they are shared in celebration of the renewal of human lives.

15:20–24 SIN, Against God—The prodigal sinned against his father—wasting resources, betraying confidences, straying into a wicked life-style, and disgracing the family name. He recognized that sin against family is ultimately sin against God, for we miss the target God has set for our lives. A ruined life is not an unforgivable sin against God. The Heavenly Father waits for us to return and repent.

16:1–15 CHRISTIAN ETHICS, Property Rights—Money is a means to other ends and not an end in itself. It should be used to establish relationships with people rather than for the accumulation of things. Its use must display our honesty and trustworthiness. Serving the Master, not money, is the central value of life. Such values go directly opposite to normal human, worldly values, but they win God’s approval.

"'A thousand bushels[m] of wheat,' he
replied.
"He told him, 'Take your bill and make
it eight hundred.'
8 "The master commended the dishonest manager because he had acted
shrewdly. For the people of this world[r]
are more shrewd[s] in dealing with their
own kind than are the people of the
light.[t] 9 I tell you, use worldly wealth[u] to
gain friends for yourselves, so that when
it is gone, you will be welcomed into eternal dwellings.[v]
10 "Whoever can be trusted with very
little can also be trusted with much,[w] and
whoever is dishonest with very little will
also be dishonest with much. 11 So if you
have not been trustworthy in handling
worldly wealth,[x] who will trust you with
true riches? 12 And if you have not been
trustworthy with someone else's property, who will give you property of your
own?
13 "No servant can serve two masters.
Either he will hate the one and love the
other, or he will be devoted to the one
and despise the other. You cannot serve
both God and Money."[y]
14 The Pharisees, who loved money,[z]
heard all this and were sneering at
Jesus.[a] 15 He said to them, "You are the
ones who justify yourselves[b] in the eyes
of men, but God knows your hearts.[c]
What is highly valued among men is detestable in God's sight.

Additional Teachings

16 "The Law and the Prophets were
proclaimed until John.[d] Since that time,
the good news of the kingdom of God is
being preached,[e] and everyone is forcing
his way into it. 17 It is easier for heaven
and earth to disappear than for the least
stroke of a pen to drop out of the Law.[f]
18 "Anyone who divorces his wife and
marries another woman commits adultery, and the man who marries a divorced
woman commits adultery.[g]

The Rich Man and Lazarus

19 "There was a rich man who was
dressed in purple and fine linen and lived
in luxury every day.[h] 20 At his gate was
laid a beggar[i] named Lazarus, covered
with sores 21 and longing to eat what fell
from the rich man's table.[j] Even the
dogs came and licked his sores.
22 "The time came when the beggar
died and the angels carried him to Abraham's side. The rich man also died and
was buried. 23 In hell,[n] where he was in
torment, he looked up and saw Abraham
far away, with Lazarus by his side. 24 So
he called to him, 'Father Abraham,[k] have
pity on me and send Lazarus to dip the tip
of his finger in water and cool my tongue,
because I am in agony in this fire.'[l]
25 "But Abraham replied, 'Son, remember that in your lifetime you received
your good things, while Lazarus received
bad things,[m] but now he is comforted
here and you are in agony.[n] 26 And besides all this, between us and you a great
chasm has been fixed, so that those who
want to go from here to you cannot, nor
can anyone cross over from there to us.'

16:8 [r]Ps 17:14 [s]Ps 18:26 [t]Jn 12:36; Eph 5:8; 1Th 5:5
16:9 [u]ver 11,13 [v]Mt 19:21; Lk 12:33
16:10 [w]Mt 25:21, 23; Lk 19:17
16:11 [x]ver 9,13
16:13 [y]ver 9,11; Mt 6:24
16:14 [z]S 1Ti 3:3 [a]Lk 23:35
16:15 [b]Lk 10:29 [c]S Rev 2:23
16:16 [d]Mt 5:17; 11:12,13 [e]S Mt 4:23
16:17 [f]S Mt 5:18
16:18 [g]Mt 5:31,32; 19:9; Mk 10:11; Ro 7:2,3; 1Co 7:10, 11
16:19 [h]Eze 16:49
16:20 [i]Ac 3:2
16:21 [j]Mt 15:27; Lk 15:16
16:24 [k]ver 30; S Lk 3:8 [l]S Mt 5:22
16:25 [m]Ps 17:14 [n]Lk 6:21,24,25

[m]*7* Greek *one hundred korous* (probably about 35 kiloliters) [n]*23* Greek *Hades*

16:16–17 JESUS CHRIST, Kingdom of God—Jesus' coming marked a new age in God's history with His people. With Jesus the kingdom age dawned, forcing people to respond to or reject the call to repent. "Forcing his way" is difficult to understand. It may mean Satan or human opponents are fighting forcefully against the kingdom or that the crowds are thronging to the kingdom in contrast to earlier response to the prophets. The kingdom did not stand in contrast or opposition to God's earlier work. The kingdom initiated by Jesus will fulfill every promise and demand of the Old Testament.

16:16 THE CHURCH, God's Kingdom—Crowds forced their way to Jesus to learn of His kingdom. The people could not follow the legalistic demands of the Pharisees. See note on 7:28.

16:19–31 EVIL AND SUFFERING, God's Future Help—Although suffering and injustice prevailed for Lazarus in this life, he was rewarded after death. Eternity is the only existence where people do not suffer. Those who do not receive eternal life from God face eternal suffering.

16:19–26 LAST THINGS, Intermediate State—Jesus contrasted the destinies of two persons. One died and entered a condition of blessedness. The other died and entered one of misery. Both were presented by Jesus as entering their future condition immediately following death. The suggestion in Jesus' story is that the spirits of the righteous enter a conscious state of blessedness. Similarly, the spirits of the unrighteous go into a state of conscious torment. See 23:43. Many do not think the account of the rich man and Lazarus was intended as a detailed eschatological picture of the afterlife at the end time. Rather, it is a strong statement that the final judgment will rectify life's seeming injustices. Other interpreters think Jesus gave a literal picture not of the final state but of the intermediate state between death and the resurrection. In either view Jesus taught that righteousness will be rewarded; unrighteousness will be punished. It is implicit in the account that one's attitude toward God, revealed in the actions of this life, determines one's condition in the life to come. Future judgment hinges on the decisions made during this lifetime. The contrast between torment and comfort in the eschatological estate is vividly drawn. "Hell" (Greek *hades*) is often used simply to designate the abode of the departed dead. Compare Ac 2:27, 31. Hades occurs in ten New Testament passages. It never speaks of the destiny of believers and is never directly identified with Gehenna, the place of fiery torment. This passage comes closest to doing so, inasmuch as torment, agony, and fire are associated with it. In addition, it is placed in contrast to the place and condition of blessing. Furthermore, the division between the two is portrayed as absolute and final. Hades may pose a threat (Rev 6:8), but it can never prevail over the church (Mt 16:18). Christ holds power over Hades (Rev 1:18), and will eventually defeat it (Rev 20:13–14). Compare Lk 10:15; Mt 11:23. See note on Rev 20:14.

16:19–29 PRAYER, Hindrances—Death ends the opportunity to confess, repent, and seek salvation. The prayer of the former rich man was unanswerable. It was too late; the gulf was fixed.

27"He answered, 'Then I beg you, father, send Lazarus to my father's house,
28for I have five brothers. Let him warn
them,[o] so that they will not also come to
this place of torment.'
29"Abraham replied, 'They have Moses[p] and the Prophets;[q] let them listen
to them.'
30" 'No, father Abraham,'[r] he said,
'but if someone from the dead goes to
them, they will repent.'
31"He said to him, 'If they do not listen
to Moses and the Prophets, they will not
be convinced even if someone rises from
the dead.' "

Chapter 17

Sin, Faith, Duty

JESUS said to his disciples: "Things that
cause people to sin[s] are bound to
come, but woe to that person through
whom they come.[t] 2It would be better
for him to be thrown into the sea with a
millstone tied around his neck than for
him to cause one of these little ones[u] to
sin.[v] 3So watch yourselves.
"If your brother sins, rebuke him,[w]
and if he repents, forgive him.[x] 4If he
sins against you seven times in a day, and
seven times comes back to you and says,
'I repent,' forgive him."[y]
5The apostles[z] said to the Lord,[a] "Increase our faith!"
6He replied, "If you have faith as small
as a mustard seed,[b] you can say to this
mulberry tree, 'Be uprooted and planted
in the sea,' and it will obey you.[c]
7"Suppose one of you had a servant
plowing or looking after the sheep.
Would he say to the servant when he
comes in from the field, 'Come along now
and sit down to eat'? 8Would he not rather say, 'Prepare my supper, get yourself
ready and wait on me[d] while I eat and
drink; after that you may eat and drink'?
9Would he thank the servant because he
did what he was told to do? 10So you also,
when you have done everything you
were told to do, should say, 'We are unworthy servants; we have only done our
duty.' "[e]

Ten Healed of Leprosy

11Now on his way to Jerusalem,[f] Jesus
traveled along the border between Samaria and Galilee.[g] 12As he was going into a
village, ten men who had leprosy[o][h] met
him. They stood at a distance[i] 13and
called out in a loud voice, "Jesus, Master,[j] have pity on us!"
14When he saw them, he said, "Go,
show yourselves to the priests."[k] And as
they went, they were cleansed.
15One of them, when he saw he was
healed, came back, praising God[l] in a
loud voice. 16He threw himself at Jesus'
feet and thanked him—and he was a Samaritan.[m]
17Jesus asked, "Were not all ten
cleansed? Where are the other nine?
18Was no one found to return and give
praise to God except this foreigner?"
19Then he said to him, "Rise and go; your
faith has made you well."[n]

The Coming of the Kingdom of God

17:26,27pp — Mt 24:37-39

20Once, having been asked by the Pharisees when the kingdom of God would

[o] *12* The Greek word was used for various diseases affecting the skin—not necessarily leprosy.

16:28 [o]Ac 2:40; 20:23; 1Th 4:6
16:29 [p]S Lk 24:27, 44; Jn 1:45; 5:45-47; Ac 15:21 [q]Lk 4:17; 24:27,44; Jn 1:45
16:30 [r]ver 24; S Lk 3:8
17:1 [s]S Mt 5:29 [t]Mt 18:7
17:2 [u]Mk 10:24; Lk 10:21 [v]S Mt 5:29
17:3 [w]S Mt 18:15 [x]Eph 4:32; Col 3:13
17:4 [y]Mt 18:21,22
17:5 [z]S Mk 6:30 [a]S Lk 7:13
17:6 [b]Mt 13:31; 17:20; Lk 13:19 [c]S Mt 21:21; Mk 9:23
17:8 [d]Lk 12:37
17:10 [e]1Co 9:16
17:11 [f]S Lk 9:51 [g]Lk 9:51,52; Jn 4:3, 4
17:12 [h]S Mt 8:2 [i]Lev 13:45,46
17:13 [j]S Lk 5:5
17:14 [k]Lev 14:2; Mt 8:4
17:15 [l]S Mt 9:8
17:16 [m]S Mt 10:5
17:19 [n]S Mt 9:22

16:27–31 EVANGELISM, Judgment—People who persistently reject salvation in Christ face eternal separation from God in hell. There they will realize how vital it is to receive God's forgiveness and life. The rich man, even in hell, was so aware of these truths that he wanted someone to tell his brothers of the eternal fate of those who refuse Christ. The lesson is for Christians. It calls us to love the lost who face such judgment. Our witness can lead people to Christ and away from hell.

16:29–31 HOLY SCRIPTURE, Authoritative—God has revealed the way to life through the Scriptures. Spectacular events and unusual messengers will not convert those who choose to live their own selfish way. Faith is always based on more than objective proof. The majority of Judah's population did not believe Christ's resurrection. See Jn 12:10–11.

16:30 SALVATION, Repentance—Those who refuse to repent upon hearing God's Law and His prophets would not repent if one from the dead went to them. People do not need more evidence to repent. They need faith in God.

17:1–4 SIN, Serious—We must face temptation. It is a part of life. We must not cause temptation. That is grave sin. We should take extreme steps to avoid leading new, immature believers astray. We need to pray for faith to avoid this sin and to forgive those who sin against us. See note on Mt 18:6–9.

17:3–4 SALVATION, Repentance—We are to forgive other believers when they repent.

17:3–4 FAMILY, Forgiveness—Continuing expression of forgiveness is a fundamental factor in Christian family life. Jesus described a fellow disciple rather than an actual brother in the home, but the principle of expressed forgiveness remains the same. God's judgment is promised to those who refuse to express forgiveness even though they desire it for themselves (Mt 18:23–35).

17:5–6 PRAYER, Faith—See note on Mt 21:19–22.

17:7–10 DISCIPLESHIP, Nature—The disciple is a servant at the Master's call. Our service is to be done from gratitude for what Christ did, not in expectation of rewards.

17:11–19 MIRACLE, Faith—Ten lepers, at least one of them a Samaritan, asked for healing. In response to His charge to show themselves to the priest, they went—in faith. All were cleansed. Only one, a Samaritan, returned to thank Jesus. This action expressed greater faith. Miracles should increase our faith and cause us to thank and praise God.

17:16–19 PRAYER, Thanksgiving—Praise and gratitude must be expressed in the same kind of faith as petition. Believers acknowledge God's work in our world and in our lives with thanks. See note on Ps 30:1–12.

17:20–21 REVELATION, Divine Presence—The reign and control of God in our lives does not appear from without. It cannot be forced on us. The kingdom is present within us when the Spirit of God reveals His truth to us and when the human spirit has an open mind and heart to God's activity.

come,[o] **Jesus replied,** "The kingdom of God does not come with your careful observation, 21nor will people say, 'Here it is,' or 'There it is,'[p] because the kingdom of God is within[p] you."

22Then he said to his disciples, "The time is coming when you will long to see one of the days of the Son of Man,[q] but you will not see it.[r] 23Men will tell you, 'There he is!' or 'Here he is!' Do not go running off after them.[s] 24For the Son of Man in his day[q] will be like the lightning,[t] which flashes and lights up the sky from one end to the other. 25But first he must suffer many things[u] and be rejected[v] by this generation.[w]

26"Just as it was in the days of Noah,[x] so also will it be in the days of the Son of Man. 27People were eating, drinking, marrying and being given in marriage up to the day Noah entered the ark. Then the flood came and destroyed them all.

28"It was the same in the days of Lot.[y] People were eating and drinking, buying and selling, planting and building. 29But the day Lot left Sodom, fire and sulfur rained down from heaven and destroyed them all.

30"It will be just like this on the day the Son of Man is revealed.[z] 31On that day no one who is on the roof of his house, with his goods inside, should go down to get them. Likewise, no one in the field should go back for anything.[a] 32Remember Lot's wife![b] 33Whoever tries to keep his life will lose it, and whoever loses his life will preserve it.[c] 34I tell you, on that night two people will be in one bed; one will be taken and the other left. 35Two women will be grinding grain together; one will be taken and the other left.[r] "[d]

37"Where, Lord?" they asked.

He replied, "Where there is a dead body, there the vultures will gather."[e]

Chapter 18

The Parable of the Persistent Widow

THEN Jesus told his disciples a parable to show them that they should always pray and not give up.[f] 2He said: "In a certain town there was a judge who neither feared God nor cared about men. 3And there was a widow in that town who kept coming to him with the plea, 'Grant me justice[g] against my adversary.'

4"For some time he refused. But finally he said to himself, 'Even though I don't fear God or care about men, 5yet because this widow keeps bothering me, I will see that she gets justice, so that she won't eventually wear me out with her coming!' "[h]

6And the Lord[i] said, "Listen to what the unjust judge says. 7And will not God bring about justice for his chosen ones, who cry out[j] to him day and night? Will he keep putting them off? 8I tell you, he will see that they get justice, and quickly. However, when the Son of Man[k] comes,[l] will he find faith on the earth?"

The Parable of the Pharisee and the Tax Collector

9To some who were confident of their own righteousness[m] and looked down on

p*21* Or *among* q*24* Some manuscripts do not have *in his day.* r*35* Some manuscripts *left.* *36Two men will be in the field; one will be taken and the other left.*

17:20 [o]S Mt 3:2
17:21 [p]ver 23
17:22 [q]S Mt 8:20 [r]S Lk 5:35
17:23 [s]Mt 24:23; Lk 21:8
17:24 [t]Mt 24:27
17:25 [u]S Mt 16:21 [v]Lk 9:22; 18:32 [w]Mk 13:30; Lk 21:32
17:26 [x]Ge 6:5-8; 7:6-24
17:28 [y]Ge 19:1-28
17:30 [z]Mt 10:23; S 16:27; 24:3,27, 37,39; 25:31; S 1Co 1:7; S 1Th 2:19; 2Th 1:7; 2:8; 2Pe 3:4; S Rev 1:7
17:31 [a]Mt 24:17, 18
17:32 [b]Ge 19:26
17:33 [c]S Jn 12:25
17:35 [d]Mt 24:41
17:37 [e]Mt 24:28
18:1 [f]Isa 40:31; Lk 11:5-8; S Ac 1:14; S Ro 1:10; 12:12; Eph 6:18; Col 4:2; 1Th 5:17
18:3 [g]Isa 1:17
18:5 [h]Lk 11:8
18:6 [i]S Lk 7:13
18:7 [j]Ex 22:23; Ps 88:1; Rev 6:10
18:8 [k]S Mt 8:20 [l]S Mt 16:27
18:9 [m]Lk 16:15

God's revelation is constantly about us, but it is as our minds and hearts open to His revelation that God can begin the conversation of faith with us.

17:20–21 THE CHURCH, God's Kingdom—In Jesus, the kingdom of God is a present reality. Speculation about the coming of the kingdom may blind us to the presence of the kingdom now. Only those who let Jesus control their lives now are ready for the kingdom to come in its fulfillment. See note on Mt 3:2.

17:22–37 JESUS CHRIST, Judgment—The return of the Son of man will interrupt daily routines unexpectedly. See note on Mt 13:37–43. The Son of man can return because He suffered and died. His return will be clearly revealed to all people. No one will have to fear they missed it. They do need to fear they will not be part of the Son of man's eternal kingdom.

17:22–37 LAST THINGS, Coming Kingdom—Upon the heels of a strong statement about the present reality of the kingdom of God (17:20–21) is an extended explanation about its future coming. That future is truly apocalyptic—it will be brought by no human agency. The Son of man will burst forth with the suddenness of a flash of lightning. In the consummation of the kingdom, God acts directly and sovereignly from heaven. Life going on in its usual pursuits will be interrupted by the revealing of the Son of man. The coming kingdom involves unexpected destruction upon the wicked. The consummation of history and the future coming of God's kingdom are converging events associated with the future revelation of the Son of man.

18:1–8 EVIL AND SUFFERING, God's Present Help—Prayer is the road to justice for the faithful. God knows we suffer and hears our cries for relief. He has an answer for our problems and will help us. His help may not be evident fully until the Son of man returns in judgment. See note on 16:19–31.

18:1–8 PRAYER, Persistence—Persistence proves the reality of faith. God's plan and promise is for a world of justice. We should pray to that end.

18:7 ELECTION, Divine Justice—God is a God of justice. He hears the prayers of the elect who cry day and night. When the Son of man returns, the suffering elect will be present with faith that relies upon the God of justice. Election to the kingdom is one way God provides justice in an unjust society. The elect have faith in God's justice.

18:8 JESUS CHRIST, Son of Man—On His return Christ will be looking for people with persistent faith expressed through insistent prayer.

18:9–14 CHRISTIAN ETHICS, Character—See note on 14:7–11.

18:9–14 PRAYER, Hindrances—Jesus warned about hypocrisy in praying. See note on Mt 6:5–8. He specified that praying for the ears of men gets the reward of men. Pride prevents prayer from achieving its purpose. Humility is the way to open communication with the merciful God.

everybody else,[n] Jesus told this parable:
10"Two men went up to the temple to
pray,[o] one a Pharisee and the other a tax
collector. 11The Pharisee stood up[p] and
prayed about[s] himself: 'God, I thank you
that I am not like other men—robbers,
evildoers, adulterers—or even like this
tax collector. 12I fast[q] twice a week and
give a tenth[r] of all I get.'
13"But the tax collector stood at a distance. He would not even look up to
heaven, but beat his breast[s] and said,
'God, have mercy on me, a sinner.'[t]
14"I tell you that this man, rather than
the other, went home justified before
God. For everyone who exalts himself
will be humbled, and he who humbles
himself will be exalted."[u]

The Little Children and Jesus

18:15–17pp — Mt 19:13–15; Mk 10:13–16

15People were also bringing babies to
Jesus to have him touch them. When the
disciples saw this, they rebuked them.
16But Jesus called the children to him and
said, "Let the little children come to me,
and do not hinder them, for the kingdom
of God belongs to such as these. 17I tell
you the truth, anyone who will not receive the kingdom of God like a little
child[v] will never enter it."

The Rich Ruler

18:18–30pp — Mt 19:16–29; Mk 10:17–30

18A certain ruler asked him, "Good
teacher, what must I do to inherit eternal
life?"[w]
19"Why do you call me good?" Jesus
answered. "No one is good—except God
alone. 20You know the commandments:
'Do not commit adultery, do not murder,
do not steal, do not give false testimony,
honor your father and mother.'[t]"[x]
21"All these I have kept since I was a
boy," he said.
22When Jesus heard this, he said to
him, "You still lack one thing. Sell everything you have and give to the poor,[y] and
you will have treasure in heaven.[z] Then
come, follow me."
23When he heard this, he became very
sad, because he was a man of great
wealth. 24Jesus looked at him and said,
"How hard it is for the rich to enter the
kingdom of God![a] 25Indeed, it is easier
for a camel to go through the eye of a
needle than for a rich man to enter the
kingdom of God."
26Those who heard this asked, "Who
then can be saved?"
27Jesus replied, "What is impossible
with men is possible with God."[b]
28Peter said to him, "We have left all
we had to follow you!"[c]
29"I tell you the truth," Jesus said to
them, "no one who has left home or wife
or brothers or parents or children for the
sake of the kingdom of God 30will fail to
receive many times as much in this age
and, in the age to come,[d] eternal life."[e]

Jesus Again Predicts His Death

18:31–33pp — Mt 20:17–19; Mk 10:32–34

31Jesus took the Twelve aside and told

18:9 [n]Isa 65:5
18:10 [o]Ac 3:1
18:11 [p]Mt 6:5; Mk 11:25
18:12 [q]Isa 58:3; Mt 9:14 [r]Mal 3:8; Lk 11:42
18:13 [s]Isa 66:2; Jer 31:19; Lk 23:48 [t]Lk 5:32; 1Ti 1:15
18:14 [u]S Mt 23:12
18:17 [v]Mt 11:25; 18:3
18:18 [w]Lk 10:25
18:20 [x]Ex 20:12-16; Dt 5:16-20; Ro 13:9
18:22 [y]S Ac 2:45 [z]S Mt 6:20
18:24 [a]Pr 11:28
18:27 [b]S Mt 19:26
18:28 [c]S Mt 4:19
18:30 [d]S Mt 12:32 [e]S Mt 25:46

[s]*11* Or *to* [t]*20* Exodus 20:12-16; Deut. 5:16-20

18:12 STEWARDSHIP, Tithe—Tithing and giving more than the legal requirements can be done for the wrong reasons. A Christ-like spirit of humility and love should accompany giving and, indeed, all aspects of life. See note on Nu 18:21–32.

18:13–14 SALVATION, Confession—See note on Ps 106:6. Confession is asking for God's mercy. Both the actions and words of the publican demonstrated his sense of unworthiness and his total dependence on God. Salvation comes to such humble confessors no matter how sinful their past lives.

18:14 SALVATION, Justification—God justifies the humble who cry for His mercy. God counts humble confession as righteousness.

18:15–17 PRAYER, Blessing—See note on Mt 19:13–15.

18:17 SALVATION, Acceptance—Those who do not accept the rule of God like a little child cannot have citizenship in His kingdom. God wants us to give total acceptance to His reign. See note on Mt 19:13–15.

18:17 THE CHURCH, God's Kingdom—See note on Mt 18:1–4.

18:18–19 JESUS CHRIST, Sinless—The ruler recognized the unique moral quality of Jesus' life. Jesus reminded him that "good" in the absolute sense describes God and no one else. Unconsciously the ruler had correctly seen that Jesus' pure life identified Him as divine.

18:18–30 CHRISTIAN ETHICS, Property Rights—Riches do not absolutely shut the rich out of God's kingdom, but they do blind us to God's values. Riches too often replace God in a person's life. When they do, entry to God's kingdom is blocked. See notes on 16:1–15; Mt 6:19–34.

18:22–24 HUMANITY, Relationships—See note on Mk 10:21–23.

18:22–24 STEWARDSHIP, Care of Needy—See notes on Mt 19:21–26; 1 Jn 3:17.

18:24–25 THE CHURCH, God's Kingdom—See note on Mt 19:24–26.

18:27 GOD, Power—See note on Mt 19:16–26.

18:27 PRAYER, Faith—See note on Mk 9:19–29.

18:29–30 SALVATION, Eternal Life—Eternal life is here identified with the world to come. It is both a present (Jn 5:24) and future reality for those who follow Jesus.

18:31–34 JESUS CHRIST, Death—Compare Mt 20:17–19; Mk 10:32–34. See note on Mt 16:21–23. Jesus understood Isa 53 and other Old Testament passages to point to the necessity of Messiah's death and resurrection. His disciples read the Old Testament in a more traditional way and could not understand the expected King's talk about death rather than victory.

18:31–33 HOLY SCRIPTURE, Redemption—Christ's closest disciples looked for an earthly kingdom (Mk 10:35–37). They expected the prophecies of Messiah as a new David ruling in Jerusalem to be fulfilled literally. Jesus pointed to a different emphasis in the prophets, that of Suffering Servant (Isa 53). He explained that He would be sacrificed after torture, killed, and then rise again. Bewildered, the followers listened without much understanding. Only the resurrection led them to see Christ's interpretation of Scripture was right. Often the correct understanding of revelation comes only after further experience with God.

them, "We are going up to Jerusalem,[f]
and everything that is written by the
prophets[g] about the Son of Man[h] will be
fulfilled. 32 He will be handed over to the
Gentiles.[i] They will mock him, insult
him, spit on him, flog him[j] and kill
him.[k] 33 On the third day[l] he will rise
again."[m]

34 The disciples did not understand any
of this. Its meaning was hidden from
them, and they did not know what he
was talking about.[n]

A Blind Beggar Receives His Sight

18:35–43pp — Mt 20:29–34; Mk 10:46–52

35 As Jesus approached Jericho,[o] a blind
man was sitting by the roadside begging.
36 When he heard the crowd going by, he
asked what was happening. 37 They told
him, "Jesus of Nazareth is passing by."[p]

38 He called out, "Jesus, Son of David,[q]
have mercy[r] on me!"

39 Those who led the way rebuked him
and told him to be quiet, but he shouted
all the more, "Son of David, have mercy
on me!"[s]

40 Jesus stopped and ordered the man to
be brought to him. When he came near,
Jesus asked him, 41 "What do you want
me to do for you?"

"Lord, I want to see," he replied.

42 Jesus said to him, "Receive your
sight; your faith has healed you."[t] 43 Immediately he received his sight and followed Jesus, praising God. When all the
people saw it, they also praised God.[u]

Chapter 19

Zacchaeus the Tax Collector

JESUS entered Jericho[v] and was passing
through. 2 A man was there by the
name of Zacchaeus; he was a chief tax
collector and was wealthy. 3 He wanted to
see who Jesus was, but being a short man
he could not, because of the crowd. 4 So
he ran ahead and climbed a sycamore-
fig[w] tree to see him, since Jesus was coming that way.[x]

5 When Jesus reached the spot, he
looked up and said to him, "Zacchaeus,
come down immediately. I must stay at
your house today." 6 So he came down at
once and welcomed him gladly.

7 All the people saw this and began to
mutter, "He has gone to be the guest of a
'sinner.' "[y]

8 But Zacchaeus stood up and said to
the Lord,[z] "Look, Lord! Here and now I
give half of my possessions to the poor,
and if I have cheated anybody out of anything,[a] I will pay back four times the
amount."[b]

9 Jesus said to him, "Today salvation
has come to this house, because this man,
too, is a son of Abraham.[c] 10 For the Son
of Man came to seek and to save what
was lost."[d]

The Parable of the Ten Minas

19:12–27Ref — Mt 25:14–30

11 While they were listening to this, he
went on to tell them a parable, because
he was near Jerusalem and the people
thought that the kingdom of God[e] was
going to appear at once.[f] 12 He said: "A
man of noble birth went to a distant
country to have himself appointed king
and then to return. 13 So he called ten of
his servants[g] and gave them ten minas.[u]
'Put this money to work,' he said, 'until I
come back.'

[u] *13* A mina was about three months' wages.

18:31 [f]S Lk 9:51 [g]Ps 22; Isa 53 [h]S Mt 8:20
18:32 [i]Lk 23:1 [j]S Mt 16:21 [k]S Ac 2:23
18:33 [l]S Mt 16:21 [m]S Mt 16:21
18:34 [n]S Mk 9:32
18:35 [o]Lk 19:1
18:37 [p]Lk 19:4
18:38 [q]ver 39; S Mt 9:27 [r]Mt 17:15; Lk 18:13
18:39 [s]ver 38
18:42 [t]S Mt 9:22
18:43 [u]S Mt 9:8; Lk 13:17
19:1 [v]Lk 18:35
19:4 [w]1Ki 10:27; 1Ch 27:28; Isa 9:10 [x]Lk 18:37
19:7 [y]S Mt 9:11
19:8 [z]S Lk 7:13 [a]Lk 3:12,13 [b]Ex 22:1; Lev 6:4, 5; Nu 5:7; 2Sa 12:6; Eze 33:14,15
19:9 [c]S Lk 3:8
19:10 [d]Eze 34:12, 16; S Jn 3:17
19:11 [e]S Mt 3:2 [f]Lk 17:20; Ac 1:6
19:13 [g]Mk 13:34

18:35–43 MIRACLE, Praise—Miracles are evangelistic. They can bring the person healed and the crowd observing to praise God. Faith is the necessary ingredient. See note on Mt 20:29–34.

18:38–39 JESUS CHRIST, Son of David—See notes on Mt 1:1; Mk 10:46–52.

18:42–43 PRAYER, Praise—See notes on 5:25–26; Mk 10:51–52. Praise is catching. When we praise God, others join in. See Guide to Praise, p. 1762.

19:1–10 JESUS CHRIST, Sinless—Jesus did not understand moral purity in terms of contamination by other people. He associated with all people, seeking to bring all to a life-converting faith in God.

19:1–10 CHRISTIAN ETHICS, Property Rights—Zacchaeus was willing to restore fraudulently obtained taxes. His act of restitution is a commendable example for us to follow if we have cheated or defrauded someone else. Finding the joy of salvation in Christ leads us to loosen our grip on worldly goods and gain concern for other's needs. See note on 18:18–30.

19:1–8 STEWARDSHIP, Life-style—Restitution is a good sign of a changed life. Zacchaeus exhibited repentance by pledging to make a fourfold return for wrongs committed and giving half of his possessions to the poor. Good stewardship is the result of a new life committed to serve Christ. See note on 12:16–31.

19:7–8 SIN, Responsibility—A totally reformed life witnesses that the person cannot be classified with excluded, rejected sinners. See note on Mk 2:15–16.

19:8 DISCIPLESHIP, Nature—The dramatic change in the life of Zacchaeus indicated true repentance and conversion, the beginning point of discipleship. Discipleship involves service to others, not unjust treatment to amass material wealth.

19:9–10 ELECTION, Remnant—Obedience to Pharisaic laws did not determine the elect remnant of Israel. Salvation came to even a sinner like Zacchaeus, when he repented and committed himself to God. Election does not point to people who have achieved righteousness. In love and through Jesus Christ God elects sinners and saves them from a life-style of sin and alienation.

19:10 JESUS CHRIST, Mission—Jesus' mission was to lead people to a saving relationship with God. Such a relationship delivers from sin and selfishness to service of God and other people.

19:11–27 JESUS CHRIST, King—Jesus did not appear to be a king during His earthly ministry. Jewish leaders refused to accept His way of life as that of God's messianic King. His rule as King will be apparent when He returns to judge people according to their responsible stewardship.

19:11–27 STEWARDSHIP, Management—See notes on Ge 39:2–6; Mt 25:15–30.

14 "But his subjects hated him and sent
a delegation after him to say, 'We don't
want this man to be our king.'
15 "He was made king, however, and
returned home. Then he sent for the servants to whom he had given the money,
in order to find out what they had gained
with it.
16 "The first one came and said, 'Sir,
your mina has earned ten more.'
17 " 'Well done, my good servant!'[h] his
master replied. 'Because you have been
trustworthy in a very small matter, take
charge of ten cities.'[i]
18 "The second came and said, 'Sir,
your mina has earned five more.'
19 "His master answered, 'You take
charge of five cities.'
20 "Then another servant came and
said, 'Sir, here is your mina; I have kept it
laid away in a piece of cloth. 21 I was
afraid of you, because you are a hard man.
You take out what you did not put in and
reap what you did not sow.'[j]
22 "His master replied, 'I will judge you
by your own words,[k] you wicked servant! You knew, did you, that I am a hard
man, taking out what I did not put in, and
reaping what I did not sow?[l] 23 Why then
didn't you put my money on deposit, so
that when I came back, I could have collected it with interest?'
24 "Then he said to those standing by,
'Take his mina away from him and give it
to the one who has ten minas.'
25 " 'Sir,' they said, 'he already has ten!'
26 "He replied, 'I tell you that to everyone who has, more will be given, but as
for the one who has nothing, even what
he has will be taken away.[m] 27 But those
enemies of mine who did not want me to
be king over them—bring them here and
kill them in front of me.' "

The Triumphal Entry

19:29–38pp — Mt 21:1–9; Mk 11:1–10
19:35–38pp — Jn 12:12–15

28 After Jesus had said this, he went on
ahead, going up to Jerusalem.[n] 29 As he
approached Bethphage and Bethany[o] at
the hill called the Mount of Olives,[p] he
sent two of his disciples, saying to them,
30 "Go to the village ahead of you, and as
you enter it, you will find a colt tied
there, which no one has ever ridden. Untie it and bring it here. 31 If anyone asks
you, 'Why are you untying it?' tell him,
'The Lord needs it.' "
32 Those who were sent ahead went
and found it just as he had told them.[q]
33 As they were untying the colt, its owners asked them, "Why are you untying
the colt?"
34 They replied, "The Lord needs it."
35 They brought it to Jesus, threw their
cloaks on the colt and put Jesus on it. 36 As
he went along, people spread their
cloaks[r] on the road.
37 When he came near the place where
the road goes down the Mount of Olives,[s] the whole crowd of disciples began
joyfully to praise God in loud voices for all
the miracles they had seen:
38 "Blessed is the king who comes in the
name of the Lord!"[v] [t]

"Peace in heaven and glory in the
highest!"[u]

39 Some of the Pharisees in the crowd
said to Jesus, "Teacher, rebuke your disciples!"[v]
40 "I tell you," he replied, "if they keep
quiet, the stones will cry out."[w]
41 As he approached Jerusalem and saw
the city, he wept over it[x] 42 and said, "If
you, even you, had only known on this
day what would bring you peace—but
now it is hidden from your eyes. 43 The
days will come upon you when your enemies will build an embankment against
you and encircle you and hem you in on
every side.[y] 44 They will dash you to the
ground, you and the children within your
walls.[z] They will not leave one stone on
another,[a] because you did not recognize
the time of God's coming[b] to you."

Jesus at the Temple

19:45,46pp — Mt 21:12–16; Mk 11:15–18; Jn 2:13–16

45 Then he entered the temple area and

[v] *38* Psalm 118:26

19:17 [h]Pr 27:18 [i]Lk 16:10
19:21 [j]Mt 25:24
19:22 [k]2Sa 1:16; Job 15:6 [l]Mt 25:26
19:26 [m]S Mt 25:29
19:28 [n]Mk 10:32; S Lk 9:51
19:29 [o]S Mt 21:17 [p]S Mt 21:1
19:32 [q]Lk 22:13
19:36 [r]2Ki 9:13
19:37 [s]S Mt 21:1
19:38 [t]Ps 118:26; Lk 13:35 [u]S Lk 2:14
19:39 [v]Mt 21:15, 16
19:40 [w]Hab 2:11
19:41 [x]Isa 22:4; Lk 13:34,35
19:43 [y]Isa 29:3; Jer 6:6; Eze 4:2; 26:8; Lk 21:20
19:44 [z]Ps 137:9 [a]Lk 21:6 [b]1Pe 2:12

19:14,27 GOD, Wrath—Jesus suggested through this parable that we must fear the wrath of God. It is not a light thing to oppose the will of God. Those who reject the will of God will finally receive His wrath in judgment. See note on Jn 3:36.
19:28–44 JESUS CHRIST, King—See note on Mt 21:1–11. Luke related the destruction of Jerusalem to lack of belief in God's Messiah.
19:37–38 MIRACLE, Praise—Miracles show Jesus is King and His kingdom will surely come. The word translated miracles (Greek *dunamis*) means literally "powers or powerful works." They showed Jesus' royal power. His healings resulted in the praise of God. God continues to show His kingdom's power among His people. One day every person will see Jesus is King.
19:37–38 WORSHIP, Corporate—See note on Ps 42:1–4. Corporate worship can occur spontaneously away from a normal place of worship.
19:37–40 PRAYER, Praise—See notes on 18:42–43; Mt 21:9. Jesus knew that His own praise was inevitable. God's purpose is to bring the world to Jesus' feet in praise.
19:41–44 SIN, Judgment—God came to us in the flesh in Jesus. Rejecting Jesus brings God's judgment on us. The Jews of Jesus' day suffered His intervention in the Romans' destruction of Jerusalem in AD 70. One day all people will face Him when He intervenes in history for the last time.
19:41–44 HISTORY, Judgment—Christ's coming did not bring an end to judgment. Rather Israel's rejection of Jesus led to renewed judgment.

began driving out those who were selling.
46"It is written," he said to them, " 'My
house will be a house of prayer'[w];[c] but
you have made it 'a den of robbers.'[x] "[d]

47Every day he was teaching at the
temple.[e] But the chief priests, the teachers of the law and the leaders among the
people were trying to kill him.[f] 48Yet
they could not find any way to do it, because all the people hung on his words.

Chapter 20

The Authority of Jesus Questioned

20:1–8pp — Mt 21:23–27; Mk 11:27–33

ONE day as he was teaching the people
in the temple courts[g] and preaching
the gospel,[h] the chief priests and the
teachers of the law, together with the elders, came up to him. 2"Tell us by what
authority you are doing these things,"
they said. "Who gave you this authority?"[i]

3He replied, "I will also ask you a question. Tell me, 4John's baptism[j]—was it
from heaven, or from men?"

5They discussed it among themselves
and said, "If we say, 'From heaven,' he
will ask, 'Why didn't you believe him?'
6But if we say, 'From men,' all the people[k] will stone us, because they are persuaded that John was a prophet."[l]

7So they answered, "We don't know
where it was from."

8Jesus said, "Neither will I tell you by
what authority I am doing these things."

The Parable of the Tenants

20:9–19pp — Mt 21:33–46; Mk 12:1–12

9He went on to tell the people this parable: "A man planted a vineyard,[m] rented
it to some farmers and went away for a
long time.[n] 10At harvest time he sent a
servant to the tenants so they would give
him some of the fruit of the vineyard. But
the tenants beat him and sent him away
empty-handed. 11He sent another servant, but that one also they beat and
treated shamefully and sent away empty-
handed. 12He sent still a third, and they
wounded him and threw him out.

13"Then the owner of the vineyard
said, 'What shall I do? I will send my son,
whom I love;[o] perhaps they will respect
him.'

14"But when the tenants saw him, they
talked the matter over. 'This is the heir,'
they said. 'Let's kill him, and the inheritance will be ours.' 15So they threw him
out of the vineyard and killed him.

"What then will the owner of the vineyard do to them? 16He will come and kill
those tenants[p] and give the vineyard to
others."

When the people heard this, they said,
"May this never be!"

17Jesus looked directly at them and
asked, "Then what is the meaning of that
which is written:

" 'The stone the builders rejected
has become the capstone[y]'[z]?[q]

18Everyone who falls on that stone will be
broken to pieces, but he on whom it falls
will be crushed."[r]

19The teachers of the law and the chief
priests looked for a way to arrest him[s]
immediately, because they knew he had
spoken this parable against them. But
they were afraid of the people.[t]

Paying Taxes to Caesar

20:20–26pp — Mt 22:15–22; Mk 12:13–17

20Keeping a close watch on him, they
sent spies, who pretended to be honest.
They hoped to catch Jesus in something
he said[u] so that they might hand him
over to the power and authority of the
governor.[v] 21So the spies questioned
him: "Teacher, we know that you speak
and teach what is right, and that you do
not show partiality but teach the way of
God in accordance with the truth.[w] 22Is it
right for us to pay taxes to Caesar or
not?"

23He saw through their duplicity and

19:46 [c]Isa 56:7 [d]Jer 7:11
19:47 [e]S Mt 26:55 [f]S Mt 12:14; Mk 11:18
20:1 [g]S Mt 26:55 [h]Lk 8:1
20:2 [i]Jn 2:18; Ac 4:7; 7:27
20:4 [j]S Mk 1:4
20:6 [k]Lk 7:29 [l]S Mt 11:9
20:9 [m]Isa 5:1-7 [n]Mt 25:14
20:13 [o]S Mt 3:17
20:16 [p]Lk 19:27
20:17 [q]Ps 118:22; S Ac 4:11
20:18 [r]Isa 8:14,15
20:19 [s]Lk 19:47 [t]S Mk 11:18
20:20 [u]S Mt 12:10 [v]Mt 27:2
20:21 [w]Jn 3:2

[w]*46* Isaiah 56:7 [x]*46* Jer. 7:11 [y]*17* Or *cornerstone* [z]*17* Psalm 118:22

19:45—20:8 JESUS CHRIST, Authority—See note on Mk 11:12–31. The people accepted Jesus' authority. The Jewish authorities feared the people. Jesus exercised His authority even over the Temple.

19:46 PRAYER, Church—See note on Mt 21:13.

20:4–7 ORDINANCES, Baptism by John—Jesus confronted the religious leaders with a painful dilemma: was John's baptism from heaven or from men? Now that John was safely dead, they were willing to acknowledge him as a prophet to curry the favor of the people, if for no other reason. They had, however, refused the baptism of John, which was the heavenly sign of the dawning Messianic Age that Jesus was fulfilling. By the very witness of John they should have accepted Jesus. See note on 7:29–30. They were rejecting Jesus as they had rejected John. This blatant contradiction exposed their hypocrisy.

20:9–19 JESUS CHRIST, Son of God—See note on Mk 12:1–12.

20:20–26 CHRISTIAN ETHICS, Citizenship—Jesus provided a timeless principle for dealing with the claims God seeks over our lives as well as the claims of the most powerful temporal force on our lives, the government. The passage does not provide a final, clear resolution to all our questions, whether theological or political. Three things are clear: this is a beginning place to inform our Christian consciences in citizenship matters; it is a reminder that the extension of governmental authority misses no one; and no matter what one's income or social position, paying taxes is a part of the submission to the state. See note on Ro 13:1–7.

20:21,28,39 EDUCATION, Jesus—See note on Mt 22:24,36.

said to them, 24“Show me a denarius.
Whose portrait and inscription are on it?”
25“Caesar’s,” they replied.
He said to them, “Then give to Caesar
what is Caesar’s,[x] and to God what is
God’s.”
26They were unable to trap him in
what he had said there in public. And
astonished by his answer, they became
silent.

The Resurrection and Marriage

20:27–40pp — Mt 22:23–33; Mk 12:18–27

27Some of the Sadducees,[y] who say
there is no resurrection,[z] came to Jesus
with a question. 28“Teacher,” they said,
“Moses wrote for us that if a man’s brother dies and leaves a wife but no children,
the man must marry the widow and have
children for his brother.[a] 29Now there
were seven brothers. The first one married a woman and died childless. 30The
second 31and then the third married her,
and in the same way the seven died, leaving no children. 32Finally, the woman
died too. 33Now then, at the resurrection
whose wife will she be, since the seven
were married to her?”
34Jesus replied, “The people of this age
marry and are given in marriage. 35But
those who are considered worthy of taking part in that age[b] and in the resurrection from the dead will neither marry nor
be given in marriage, 36and they can no
longer die; for they are like the angels.
They are God’s children,[c] since they are
children of the resurrection. 37But in the
account of the bush, even Moses showed
that the dead rise, for he calls the Lord
‘the God of Abraham, and the God of
Isaac, and the God of Jacob.’[a][d] 38He is
not the God of the dead, but of the living,
for to him all are alive.”
39Some of the teachers of the law responded, “Well said, teacher!” 40And no
one dared to ask him any more questions.[e]

Whose Son Is the Christ?

20:41–47pp — Mt 22:41–23:7; Mk 12:35–40

41Then Jesus said to them, “How is it
that they say the Christ[b] is the Son of
David?[f] 42David himself declares in the
Book of Psalms:

“ ‘The Lord said to my Lord:
“Sit at my right hand
43until I make your enemies
a footstool for your feet.” ’[c][g]

44David calls him ‘Lord.’ How then can
he be his son?”
45While all the people were listening,
Jesus said to his disciples, 46“Beware of
the teachers of the law. They like to walk
around in flowing robes and love to be
greeted in the marketplaces and have the
most important seats in the synagogues
and the places of honor at banquets.[h]
47They devour widows’ houses and for a
show make lengthy prayers. Such men
will be punished most severely.”

Chapter 21

The Widow’s Offering

21:1–4pp — Mk 12:41–44

As he looked up, Jesus saw the rich putting their gifts into the temple treasury.[i] 2He also saw a poor widow put in
two very small copper coins.[d] 3“I tell you
the truth,” he said, “this poor widow has
put in more than all the others. 4All these
people gave their gifts out of their wealth;
but she out of her poverty put in all she
had to live on.”[j]

Signs of the End of the Age

21:5–36pp — Mt 24; Mk 13
21:12–17pp — Mt 10:17–22

5Some of his disciples were remarking
about how the temple was adorned with
beautiful stones and with gifts dedicated
to God. But Jesus said, 6“As for what you
see here, the time will come when not
one stone will be left on another;[k] every
one of them will be thrown down.”
7“Teacher,” they asked, “when will
these things happen? And what will be
the sign that they are about to take
place?”
8He replied: “Watch out that you are

[a]37 Exodus 3:6 [b]41 Or *Messiah* [c]43 Psalm 110:1 [d]2 Greek *two lepta*

20:25 [x]Lk 23:2; Ro 13:7
20:27 [y]S Ac 4:1 [z]Ac 23:8; 1Co 15:12
20:28 [a]Dt 25:5
20:35 [b]S Mt 12:32
20:36 [c]S Jn 1:12
20:37 [d]Ex 3:6
20:40 [e]Mt 22:46; Mk 12:34
20:41 [f]S Mt 1:1
20:43 [g]Ps 110:1; S Mt 22:44
20:46 [h]S Lk 11:43
21:1 [i]Mt 27:6; Jn 8:20
21:4 [j]2Co 8:12
21:6 [k]Lk 19:44

20:24–26 HUMANITY, Relationships—The image upon the coin symbolically represented the owner of the coin and the government that issued it. As members of society, Christians are expected to pay government taxes. This underscores the Christian’s relationship to the community. See note on Mt 17:24–27. While the image upon a coin is representative of government authority, the image upon a person is God’s. See note on Ge 1:26–29. People’s basic relationship ought to be in obedience to God. See Mk 12:15–17.

20:27–40 HUMANITY, Nature of Death—See note on Mt 22:23–33.

20:36 THE CHURCH, God’s Community—God’s children live as part of a new community based on faith. Those who live as part of God’s community will never die because their hope rests on the death and resurrection of Jesus. See note on Mt 5:9.

20:41–47 JESUS CHRIST, Son of David—See note on Mt 22:41–46.

20:45–47 PRAYER, Sincerity—See note on Mk 12:40.

20:45–47 EDUCATION, Scribes and Pharisees—See note on Mk 12:38–40.

21:1–4 STEWARDSHIP, Care of Needy—See notes on Mk 12:41–44; 1 Jn 3:17.

21:5–9 JESUS CHRIST, Christ—See note on Mt 24:5, 23–25.

not deceived. For many will come in my
name, claiming, 'I am he,' and, 'The time
is near.' Do not follow them.[l] 9When
you hear of wars and revolutions, do not
be frightened. These things must happen
first, but the end will not come right
away."

10Then he said to them: "Nation will
rise against nation, and kingdom against
kingdom.[m] 11There will be great earthquakes, famines and pestilences in various places, and fearful events and great
signs from heaven.[n]

12"But before all this, they will lay
hands on you and persecute you. They
will deliver you to synagogues and prisons, and you will be brought before kings
and governors, and all on account of my
name. 13This will result in your being witnesses to them.[o] 14But make up your
mind not to worry beforehand how you
will defend yourselves.[p] 15For I will give
you[q] words and wisdom that none of
your adversaries will be able to resist or
contradict. 16You will be betrayed even
by parents, brothers, relatives and
friends,[r] and they will put some of you to
death. 17All men will hate you because of
me.[s] 18But not a hair of your head will
perish.[t] 19By standing firm you will gain
life.[u]

20"When you see Jerusalem being surrounded by armies,[v] you will know that
its desolation is near. 21Then let those
who are in Judea flee to the mountains,
let those in the city get out, and let those
in the country not enter the city.[w] 22For
this is the time of punishment[x] in fulfillment[y] of all that has been written.
23How dreadful it will be in those days for
pregnant women and nursing mothers!
There will be great distress in the land
and wrath against this people. 24They will
fall by the sword and will be taken as prisoners to all the nations. Jerusalem will be
trampled[z] on by the Gentiles until the
times of the Gentiles are fulfilled.

25"There will be signs in the sun,
moon and stars. On the earth, nations
will be in anguish and perplexity at the
roaring and tossing of the sea.[a] 26Men
will faint from terror, apprehensive of
what is coming on the world, for the
heavenly bodies will be shaken.[b] 27At
that time they will see the Son of Man[c]
coming in a cloud[d] with power and great
glory. 28When these things begin to take
place, stand up and lift up your heads,
because your redemption is drawing
near."[e]

29He told them this parable: "Look at
the fig tree and all the trees. 30When they
sprout leaves, you can see for yourselves
and know that summer is near. 31Even so,
when you see these things happening,
you know that the kingdom of God[f] is
near.

32"I tell you the truth, this generation[e][g] will certainly not pass away until
all these things have happened. 33Heaven
and earth will pass away, but my words
will never pass away.[h]

34"Be careful, or your hearts will be
weighed down with dissipation, drunkenness and the anxieties of life,[i] and that
day will close on you unexpectedly[j] like
a trap. 35For it will come upon all those
who live on the face of the whole earth.
36Be always on the watch, and pray[k] that
you may be able to escape all that is about
to happen, and that you may be able to
stand before the Son of Man."

37Each day Jesus was teaching at the
temple,[l] and each evening he went out[m]
to spend the night on the hill called the
Mount of Olives,[n] 38and all the people
came early in the morning to hear him at
the temple.[o]

Chapter 22

Judas Agrees to Betray Jesus

22:1,2pp — Mt 26:2-5; Mk 14:1,2,10,11

NOW the Feast of Unleavened Bread,
called the Passover, was approach-

21:8 [l]Lk 17:23
21:10 [m]2Ch 15:6; Isa 19:2
21:11 [n]Isa 29:6; Joel 2:30
21:13 [o]Php 1:12
21:14 [p]Lk 12:11
21:15 [q]S Lk 12:12
21:16 [r]Lk 12:52,53
21:17 [s]S Jn 15:21
21:18 [t]S Mt 10:30
21:19 [u]S Mt 10:22
21:20 [v]S Lk 19:43
21:21 [w]Lk 17:31
21:22 [x]Isa 63:4; Da 9:24-27; Hos 9:7 [y]S Mt 1:22
21:24 [z]Isa 5:5; 63:18; Da 8:13; Rev 11:2
21:25 [a]2Pe 3:10,12
21:26 [b]S Mt 24:29
21:27 [c]S Mt 8:20 [d]S Rev 1:7
21:28 [e]Lk 18:7
21:31 [f]S Mt 3:2
21:32 [g]Lk 11:50; 17:25
21:33 [h]S Mt 5:18
21:34 [i]Mk 4:19 [j]Lk 12:40,46; 1Th 5:2-7
21:36 [k]Mt 26:41
21:37 [l]S Mt 26:55 [m]Mk 11:19 [n]S Mt 21:1
21:38 [o]Jn 8:2

[e]32 Or *race*

21:13–15 EVANGELISM, Persecution—See note on Mt 10:11–20.

21:15 JESUS CHRIST, Intercession—The risen Christ provides for His persecuted people.

21:18–19 SALVATION, Obedience—Jesus promises to protect those who obey Him. Ultimately His protection is from eternal destruction.

21:27–28 LAST THINGS, Salvation's Completion—The coming of Christ with power and great glory will signal the approaching completion of redemption. Included are the consummation of personal salvation, as well as creation's redemption, the church's honor as Christ's bride, and the end of evil. Premillennialists believe Christ's earthly millennial kingdom will be established at the second coming, while amillennialists believe the event will usher in the new heavens and new earth. "Redemption" is a broad concept in the Bible, ranging from the personal to the cosmic, from the physical to the spiritual, and from the temporal to the eternal. It is associated in all its fullness with the future coming of Christ.

21:28 SALVATION, Glorification—Our salvation is not yet complete. Glorification is the word we use to denote its final completion. That will take place in connection with the second coming of Christ. See notes on Mk 8:38; 1 Co 1:18.

21:28 SALVATION, Redemption—The complete redemption of God's people will take place in the end time when Christ returns. This is the only place the word redemption occurs in the Gospels.

21:33 HOLY SCRIPTURE, Authoritative—See note on Isa 40:8.

21:36 PRAYER, Petition—Special alertness in prayer will be important in the last days. See note on Mt 24:20.

22:1–4,20–23,47–48 SIN, Individual Choice—Satan took over Judas and used him in accomplishing the most devilish act ever committed—crucifying the innocent Son of

ing,[p] 2and the chief priests and the teachers of the law were looking for some way
to get rid of Jesus,[q] for they were afraid
of the people. 3Then Satan[r] entered Judas, called Iscariot,[s] one of the Twelve.
4And Judas went to the chief priests and
the officers of the temple guard[t] and discussed with them how he might betray
Jesus. 5They were delighted and agreed to
give him money.[u] 6He consented, and
watched for an opportunity to hand Jesus
over to them when no crowd was
present.

The Last Supper

22:7–13pp — Mt 26:17–19; Mk 14:12–16
22:17–20pp — Mt 26:26–29; Mk 14:22–25; 1Co 11:23–25
22:21–23pp — Mt 26:21–24; Mk 14:18–21; Jn 13:21–30
22:25–27pp — Mt 20:25–28; Mk 10:42–45
22:33,34pp — Mt 26:33–35; Mk 14:29–31; Jn 13:37,38

7Then came the day of Unleavened
Bread on which the Passover lamb had to
be sacrificed.[v] 8Jesus sent Peter and
John,[w] saying, "Go and make preparations for us to eat the Passover."
9"Where do you want us to prepare for
it?" they asked.
10He replied, "As you enter the city, a
man carrying a jar of water will meet you.
Follow him to the house that he enters,
11and say to the owner of the house, 'The
Teacher asks: Where is the guest room,
where I may eat the Passover with my
disciples?' 12He will show you a large upper room, all furnished. Make preparations there."
13They left and found things just as
Jesus had told them.[x] So they prepared
the Passover.
14When the hour came, Jesus and his
apostles[y] reclined at the table.[z] 15And
he said to them, "I have eagerly desired
to eat this Passover with you before I suffer.[a] 16For I tell you, I will not eat it again
until it finds fulfillment in the kingdom of
God."[b]
17After taking the cup, he gave thanks
and said, "Take this and divide it among
you. 18For I tell you I will not drink again
of the fruit of the vine until the kingdom
of God comes."
19And he took bread, gave thanks and
broke it,[c] and gave it to them, saying,
"This is my body given for you; do this in
remembrance of me."
20In the same way, after the supper he
took the cup, saying, "This cup is the
new covenant[d] in my blood, which is
poured out for you. 21But the hand of him
who is going to betray me is with mine
on the table.[e] 22The Son of Man[f] will go
as it has been decreed,[g] but woe to that
man who betrays him." 23They began to
question among themselves which of
them it might be who would do this.
24Also a dispute arose among them as
to which of them was considered to be
greatest.[h] 25Jesus said to them, "The
kings of the Gentiles lord it over them;
and those who exercise authority over
them call themselves Benefactors. 26But
you are not to be like that. Instead, the

22:1 [p]S Jn 11:55
22:2 [q]S Mt 12:14
22:3 [r]S Mt 4:10 [s]S Mt 10:4
22:4 [t]ver 52; Ac 4:1; 5:24
22:5 [u]Zec 11:12
22:7 [v]Ex 12:18-20; Dt 16:5-8; S Mk 14:12
22:8 [w]Ac 3:1,11; 4:13,19; 8:14
22:13 [x]Lk 19:32
22:14 [y]S Mk 6:30 [z]Mt 26:20; Mk 14:17,18
22:15 [a]S Mt 16:21
22:16 [b]S Lk 14:15
22:19 [c]S Mt 14:19
22:20 [d]Ex 24:8; Isa 42:6; Jer 31:31-34; Zec 9:11; 2Co 3:6; Heb 8:6; 9:15
22:21 [e]Ps 41:9
22:22 [f]S Mt 8:20 [g]Ac 2:23; 4:28
22:24 [h]Mk 9:34; Lk 9:46

God. Judas could not be excused. He chose to be Satan's accomplice. See note on Mt 26:14–16,23–25,47–49.

22:1–30 ORDINANCES, Institution of Lord's Supper—Luke described the institution of the Lord's Supper in the upper room with Jesus' disciples on the night before His death in almost exactly the same words as Matthew and Mark. The only difference was that Luke described a cup before the bread as well as a cup after the bread. Luke was apparently emphasizing the first cup as the cup of the Passover which they were celebrating on this evening, while he distinguished the bread and cup which followed as the new covenant in the body and blood of Jesus. See notes on Mt 26:17–30; Mk 14:10–26.

22:3–6 JESUS CHRIST, Death—See note on Mt 26:14–16,25–26.

22:3 EVIL AND SUFFERING, Satan—Satan's control over Judas did not relieve Judas of guilt. Satan cannot make us do what we do not choose to allow him to do. As did Jesus, so we have the power to resist Satan and temptation if our faith is strong. See note on vv 31–33.

22:7–23 JESUS CHRIST, Death—See note on Mt 26:17–30.

22:11 EDUCATION, Jesus—See note on Mk 14:14.

22:14–16 JESUS CHRIST, Death—Jesus longed to partake of this final Passover with His disciples and anticipated the messianic banquet in the heavenly kingdom.

22:14–16 REVELATION, Events—See note on Mt 26:26–28.

22:19–20 PRAYER, Thanksgiving—See note on Mt 26:26–27.

22:20 JESUS CHRIST, Death—Jesus viewed His death as the fulfillment of the Old Testament promise of a new covenant. See notes on 16:16–17; Jer 31:31–34. He saw His death as a necessary sacrifice for the sins of all people. Compare Ex 24:8.

22:20 SALVATION, Atonement—The cup of wine in the Lord's Supper symbolizes Christ's atonement for our sins on the cross. See notes on Lev 17:11; Eze 16:63; Mt 26:28.

22:20 THE CHURCH, Covenant People—See note on Mk 14:24.

22:24–27 JESUS CHRIST, Servant—As promised King and Messiah, Jesus saw Himself as God's Servant sent to suffer for and serve God's people. By teaching and example, He led followers to adopt the servant role of leadership and ministry.

22:24–30 CHRISTIAN ETHICS, Character—Humility results in a life of servanthood. Serving others in the name of Christ portrays the words we say about humility. Christ did not come to raise hopes for personal fame and power. He came looking for people dedicated to help our world and its needs by serving God and others. See note on 14:7–11.

22:25–26 DISCIPLESHIP, Spiritual Leaders—After the Last Supper, a dispute arose among the apostles over who was considered greatest. Jesus took the opportunity to teach them a new definition of leadership. Gentile political rulers exercised authority over other people and called themselves Benefactors, a title of honor supposedly bestowed for service to the people. Not even the apostles of Jesus were to lord it over others to gain power, prestige, or wealth. Nor should pastors and other spiritual leaders today. Care must be exercised not to confuse leadership with authority. Jesus defined leadership as becoming the least prestigious person and serving tables for the fellowship. Leadership supplies the needs of the community, not the needs of the leader's ego. Leadership imitates the humility of Christ, not the pride of political rulers. See notes on Ac 10:25–26; Heb 13:7,17.

greatest among you should be like the
youngest,[i] and the one who rules like
the one who serves.[j] 27For who is greater, the one who is at the table or the one
who serves? Is it not the one who is at
the table? But I am among you as one
who serves.[k] 28You are those who have
stood by me in my trials. 29And I confer
on you a kingdom,[l] just as my Father
conferred one on me, 30so that you may
eat and drink at my table in my kingdom[m] and sit on thrones, judging the
twelve tribes of Israel.[n]

31"Simon, Simon, Satan has asked[o] to
sift you[f] as wheat.[p] 32But I have prayed
for you,[q] Simon, that your faith may not
fail. And when you have turned back,
strengthen your brothers."[r]

33But he replied, "Lord, I am ready to
go with you to prison and to death."[s]

34Jesus answered, "I tell you, Peter, before the rooster crows today, you will
deny three times that you know me."

35Then Jesus asked them, "When I
sent you without purse, bag or sandals,[t]
did you lack anything?"

"Nothing," they answered.

36He said to them, "But now if you
have a purse, take it, and also a bag; and
if you don't have a sword, sell your cloak
and buy one. 37It is written: 'And he was
numbered with the transgressors'[g];[u]
and I tell you that this must be fulfilled in
me. Yes, what is written about me is
reaching its fulfillment."

38The disciples said, "See, Lord, here
are two swords."

"That is enough," he replied.

22:26 [i]1Pe 5:5 [j]S Mk 9:35
22:27 [k]S Mt 20:28
22:29 [l]S Mt 25:34; 2Ti 2:12
22:30 [m]S Lk 14:15 [n]S Mt 19:28
22:31 [o]Job 1:6-12 [p]Am 9:9
22:32 [q]Jn 17:9,15; S Ro 8:34 [r]Jn 21:15-17
22:33 [s]Jn 11:16
22:35 [t]Mt 10:9,10; Lk 9:3; 10:4
22:37 [u]Isa 53:12
22:39 [v]Lk 21:37 [w]S Mt 21:1
22:40 [x]Mt 6:13
22:41 [y]Lk 18:11
22:42 [z]S Mt 20:22 [a]S Mt 26:39
22:43 [b]Mt 4:11; Mk 1:13
22:46 [c]ver 40
22:49 [d]ver 38

Jesus Prays on the Mount of Olives

22:40–46pp — Mt 26:36–46; Mk 14:32–42

39Jesus went out as usual[v] to the
Mount of Olives,[w] and his disciples followed him. 40On reaching the place, he
said to them, "Pray that you will not fall
into temptation."[x] 41He withdrew about
a stone's throw beyond them, knelt
down[y] and prayed, 42"Father, if you are
willing, take this cup[z] from me; yet not
my will, but yours be done."[a] 43An angel
from heaven appeared to him and
strengthened him.[b] 44And being in anguish, he prayed more earnestly, and his
sweat was like drops of blood falling to
the ground.[h]

45When he rose from prayer and went
back to the disciples, he found them
asleep, exhausted from sorrow. 46"Why
are you sleeping?" he asked them. "Get
up and pray so that you will not fall into
temptation."[c]

Jesus Arrested

22:47–53pp — Mt 26:47–56; Mk 14:43–50; Jn 18:3–11

47While he was still speaking a crowd
came up, and the man who was called
Judas, one of the Twelve, was leading
them. He approached Jesus to kiss him,
48but Jesus asked him, "Judas, are you betraying the Son of Man with a kiss?"

49When Jesus' followers saw what was
going to happen, they said, "Lord, should
we strike with our swords?"[d] 50And one

[f] *31* The Greek is plural. [g] *37* Isaiah 53:12
[h] *44* Some early manuscripts do not have verses 43 and 44.

22:26–27 THE CHURCH, Servants—Jesus calls His ministers to unending service to one another and to God. Jesus set the example of humility and service which we should follow. See notes on Mt 20:20–28; 23:11.

22:28–30 JESUS CHRIST, Kingdom of God—The Father placed Jesus in charge of the kingdom. As He served and suffered, He knew He would one day rule. He encouraged the disciples to have the same faith. He could not promise them the most prominent positions in the coming kingdom (Mk 10:40). He could promise new responsibility in the kingdom for their service and suffering in beginning the new Israel, the church.

22:29–30 THE CHURCH, God's Kingdom—God's kingdom is the kingdom of Christ. He freely grants His people fellowship with Him in His kingdom. As the patriarchs first heard the promises of the covenant (Ge 17:1–21), Jesus made His disciples the first members of His kingdom and promised suitable reward for faithful service. Jesus emphasized humility and service before promising reward and authority.

22:31–33 EVIL AND SUFFERING, Satan—Peter, like all of us, did not realize how treacherous it is to make rash commitments that Satan can use to his advantage. Satan has power over us only when faith fails. Christ prays for us and waits to restore us. We can learn from our failures and use the experience to strengthen others so Satan cannot use them.

22:31–32 PRAYER, Petition—The "you" in v 31 is plural; they would all fall. The "you" in v 32 is singular. Jesus had always taken a special interest in Simon (Mt 16:17–18; Jn 1:42). Simon's impulsive character required special prayer to keep his faith from failing. Jesus' prayers had purpose. He expected His prayer to be answered, and He gave Peter instructions for the time after his strengthening. The courageous stand of Peter before the Sanhedrin (Ac 4:8–13,18–20) was part of the answer to this prayer. Jesus continues to intercede for us (Heb 7:25).

22:36–38 JESUS CHRIST, Fulfilled—Jesus understood His ministry, death, and resurrection as the fulfillment of the Old Testament, especially Isa 53. As He approached the moment of conflict and suffering, He warned His disciples to be prepared for the same. He did not want them to prepare for rebellion and war, just self-protection.

22:39–46 JESUS CHRIST, Suffering—See note on Mt 26:36–46.

22:39–45 PRAYER, Sincerity—See notes on Mt 26:36–44; Mk 14:32–39. The intensity of the trauma is indicated in the sweating of blood, hematidrosis, a phenomenon occurring in intense feeling when the dilation of blood vessels pressing against the sweat glands causes the vessels to burst and the blood seeps through the sweat glands. See note on Heb 5:7.

22:40,46 PRAYER, Petition—See note on Mt 26:40–41.

22:49–51 JESUS CHRIST, Miracles—Compare Mt 26:51; Jn 18:10. Luke emphasized here Jesus' compassionate healing. Even in the midst of His own great dilemma, Jesus thought of others. His mighty works of healing were for all—friend or foe. They were not for selfish gain but to meet human need. They served others, not Himself.

22:49–53 CHRISTIAN ETHICS, War and Peace—See note on Mt 26:51–53.

of them struck the servant of the high
priest, cutting off his right ear.
51But Jesus answered, "No more of
this!" And he touched the man's ear and
healed him.
52Then Jesus said to the chief priests,
the officers of the temple guard,[e] and the
elders, who had come for him, "Am I
leading a rebellion, that you have come
with swords and clubs? 53Every day I was
with you in the temple courts,[f] and you
did not lay a hand on me. But this is your
hour[g]—when darkness reigns."[h]

Peter Disowns Jesus

22:55–62pp — Mt 26:69–75; Mk 14:66–72; Jn 18:16–18,25–27

54Then seizing him, they led him away
and took him into the house of the high
priest.[i] Peter followed at a distance.[j]
55But when they had kindled a fire in the
middle of the courtyard and had sat down
together, Peter sat down with them. 56A
servant girl saw him seated there in the
firelight. She looked closely at him and
said, "This man was with him."
57But he denied it. "Woman, I don't
know him," he said.
58A little later someone else saw him
and said, "You also are one of them."
"Man, I am not!" Peter replied.
59About an hour later another asserted,
"Certainly this fellow was with him, for
he is a Galilean."[k]
60Peter replied, "Man, I don't know
what you're talking about!" Just as he
was speaking, the rooster crowed. 61The
Lord[l] turned and looked straight at Peter. Then Peter remembered the word
the Lord had spoken to him: "Before the
rooster crows today, you will disown me
three times."[m] 62And he went outside
and wept bitterly.

The Guards Mock Jesus

22:63–65pp — Mt 26:67,68; Mk 14:65; Jn 18:22,23

63The men who were guarding Jesus
began mocking and beating him. 64They
blindfolded him and demanded, "Prophesy! Who hit you?" 65And they said many
other insulting things to him.[n]

Jesus Before Pilate and Herod

22:67–71pp — Mt 26:63–66; Mk 14:61–63; Jn 18:19–21
23:2,3pp — Mt 27:11–14; Mk 15:2–5; Jn 18:29–37
23:18–25pp — Mt 27:15–26; Mk 15:6–15; Jn 18:39–19:16

66At daybreak the council[o] of the elders of the people, both the chief priests
and teachers of the law, met together,[p]
and Jesus was led before them. 67"If you
are the Christ,[i]" they said, "tell us."
Jesus answered, "If I tell you, you will
not believe me, 68and if I asked you, you
would not answer.[q] 69But from now on,
the Son of Man will be seated at the right
hand of the mighty God."[r]
70They all asked, "Are you then the
Son of God?"[s]
He replied, "You are right in saying I
am."[t]
71Then they said, "Why do we need
any more testimony? We have heard it
from his own lips."

Chapter 23

THEN the whole assembly rose and led
him off to Pilate.[u] 2And they began
to accuse him, saying, "We have found
this man subverting our nation.[v] He opposes payment of taxes to Caesar[w] and
claims to be Christ,[j] a king."[x]
3So Pilate asked Jesus, "Are you the
king of the Jews?"
"Yes, it is as you say," Jesus replied.
4Then Pilate announced to the chief
priests and the crowd, "I find no basis for
a charge against this man."[y]
5But they insisted, "He stirs up the
people all over Judea[k] by his teaching.
He started in Galilee[z] and has come all
the way here."
6On hearing this, Pilate asked if the
man was a Galilean.[a] 7When he learned
that Jesus was under Herod's jurisdiction,
he sent him to Herod,[b] who was also in
Jerusalem at that time.
8When Herod saw Jesus, he was greatly
pleased, because for a long time he had
been wanting to see him.[c] From what he
had heard about him, he hoped to see

[i]67 Or *Messiah* [j]2 Or *Messiah*; also in verses 35 and 39 [k]5 Or *over the land of the Jews*

22:52 [e]ver 4
22:53 [f]S Mt 26:55 [g]Jn 12:27 [h]Mt 8:12; Jn 1:5; 3:20
22:54 [i]Mt 26:57; Mk 14:53 [j]Mt 26:58; Mk 14:54; Jn 18:15
22:59 [k]Lk 23:6
22:61 [l]S Lk 7:13 [m]ver 34
22:65 [n]S Mt 16:21
22:66 [o]S Mt 5:22 [p]Mt 27:1; Mk 15:1
22:68 [q]Lk 20:3-8
22:69 [r]S Mk 16:19
22:70 [s]S Mt 4:3 [t]Mt 27:11; Lk 23:3
23:1 [u]S Mt 27:2
23:2 [v]ver 14 [w]Lk 20:22 [x]Jn 19:12
23:4 [y]ver 14,22,41; Mt 27:23; Jn 18:38; 1Ti 6:13; S 2Co 5:21
23:5 [z]Mk 1:14
23:6 [a]Lk 22:59
23:7 [b]S Mt 14:1
23:8 [c]Lk 9:9

22:52–53 JESUS CHRIST, Death—See note on Mt 26:47–56. Jesus reigned as King on the cross, winning victory over sin. Still His conviction and crucifixion represented evil's greatest hour, the time when human sin and Satan's power joined to kill God's Messiah. Evil appeared to triumph but in fact simply accomplished God's plan to provide atonement for sin.

22:54–62 SIN, Responsibility—See note on Mt 26:69–75.

22:63–65 JESUS CHRIST, Suffering—See note on Mt 27:26–30.

22:67—23:4 JESUS CHRIST, Christ—See note on Mk 14:53—15:15. Jesus' trial was conducted to trap Him, not to get evidence. The court was predisposed to reject His testimony. They considered His claims to be Messiah, King, Son of man, and Son of God to be blasphemy. Compare Ex 20:7; Lev 24:16. They accused Jesus in the Roman court of political rebellion and treason. See note on 22:52–53. Rome's representative remained unconvinced.

23:5–16 JESUS CHRIST, Teaching—Jesus taught service, loyalty, love, and repentance. The Jews tried to convict Him of teaching sedition, rebellion, and treason. His teachings upset their religious system and security. They claimed He sought to upset Rome's administrative system and peace. Representatives of Romans and Jews found Jesus innocent, but they did not have courage to enact justice.

23:8 MIRACLE, Vocabulary—Miracles are "signs" (Greek *semeion*) which should point people to God. They are

him perform some miracle. 9He plied him
with many questions, but Jesus gave him
no answer.[d] 10The chief priests and the
teachers of the law were standing there,
vehemently accusing him. 11Then Herod
and his soldiers ridiculed and mocked
him. Dressing him in an elegant robe,[e]
they sent him back to Pilate. 12That day
Herod and Pilate became friends[f]—before this they had been enemies.
13Pilate called together the chief
priests, the rulers and the people, 14and
said to them, "You brought me this man
as one who was inciting the people to
rebellion. I have examined him in your
presence and have found no basis for
your charges against him.[g] 15Neither has
Herod, for he sent him back to us; as you
can see, he has done nothing to deserve
death. 16Therefore, I will punish him[h]
and then release him.[l] "
18With one voice they cried out,
"Away with this man! Release Barabbas
to us!"[i] 19(Barabbas had been thrown
into prison for an insurrection in the city,
and for murder.)
20Wanting to release Jesus, Pilate appealed to them again. 21But they kept
shouting, "Crucify him! Crucify him!"
22For the third time he spoke to them:
"Why? What crime has this man committed? I have found in him no grounds for
the death penalty. Therefore I will have
him punished and then release him."[j]
23But with loud shouts they insistently
demanded that he be crucified, and their
shouts prevailed. 24So Pilate decided to
grant their demand. 25He released the
man who had been thrown into prison for
insurrection and murder, the one they
asked for, and surrendered Jesus to their
will.

The Crucifixion

23:33–43pp — Mt 27:33–44; Mk 15:22–32; Jn 19:17–24

26As they led him away, they seized Simon from Cyrene,[k] who was on his way
in from the country, and put the cross on
him and made him carry it behind
Jesus.[l] 27A large number of people followed him, including women who
mourned and wailed[m] for him. 28Jesus
turned and said to them, "Daughters of
Jerusalem, do not weep for me; weep for
yourselves and for your children.[n] 29For
the time will come when you will say,
'Blessed are the barren women, the
wombs that never bore and the breasts
that never nursed!'[o] 30Then

" 'they will say to the mountains, "Fall
on us!"
and to the hills, "Cover us!" '[m][p]

31For if men do these things when the
tree is green, what will happen when it is
dry?"[q]
32Two other men, both criminals, were
also led out with him to be executed.[r]
33When they came to the place called the
Skull, there they crucified him, along
with the criminals—one on his right, the
other on his left. 34Jesus said, "Father,[s]
forgive them, for they do not know what
they are doing."[n][t] And they divided up
his clothes by casting lots.[u]
35The people stood watching, and the
rulers even sneered at him.[v] They said,
"He saved others; let him save himself if
he is the Christ of God, the Chosen
One."[w]
36The soldiers also came up and
mocked him.[x] They offered him wine
vinegar[y] 37and said, "If you are the king
of the Jews,[z] save yourself."
38There was a written notice above
him, which read: THIS IS THE KING OF THE
JEWS.[a]
39One of the criminals who hung there
hurled insults at him: "Aren't you the
Christ? Save yourself and us!"[b]
40But the other criminal rebuked him.
"Don't you fear God," he said, "since

[l]16 Some manuscripts *him.*" [17]*Now he was obliged to release one man to them at the Feast.* [m]30 Hosea 10:8 [n]34 Some early manuscripts do not have this sentence.

23:9 [d]S Mk 14:61
23:11 [e]Mk 15:17-19; Jn 19:2,3
23:12 [f]Ac 4:27
23:14 [g]S ver 4
23:16 [h]ver 22; Mt 27:26; Jn 19:1; Ac 16:37; 2Co 11:23,24
23:18 [i]Ac 3:13,14
23:22 [j]ver 16
23:26 [k]S Mt 27:32 [l]Mk 15:21; Jn 19:17
23:27 [m]Lk 8:52
23:28 [n]Lk 19:41-44; 21:23,24
23:29 [o]Mt 24:19
23:30 [p]Hos 10:8; Isa 2:19; Rev 6:16
23:31 [q]Eze 20:47
23:32 [r]Isa 53:12; Mt 27:38; Mk 15:27; Jn 19:18
23:34 [s]S Mt 11:25 [t]S Mt 5:44 [u]Ps 22:18
23:35 [v]Ps 22:17 [w]Isa 42:1
23:36 [x]Ps 22:7 [y]Ps 69:21; Mt 27:48
23:37 [z]Lk 4:3,9
23:38 [a]S Mt 2:2
23:39 [b]ver 35,37

not sideshows entertaining the curious and doubtful. It is tragic to find the heartless curiosity which characterized Herod. Herod had no faith in Jesus. He only ridiculed Him (v 11). God does not waste His signs on such people.

23:12 SALVATION, Reconciliation—Reconciliation on the human to human level led Herod and Pilate to become friends. When persons are reconciled to God on the divine to human level, they, too, become friends. An unexpected result of Jesus' trial was political and personal reconciliation. An expected result of Jesus' ministry is reconciliation in the church.

23:26–56 JESUS CHRIST, Death—See note on Mt 27:32–55. In His deepest suffering, Jesus expressed loving concern for others—women of Jerusalem and the thieves. He promised the penitent thief a place with Him in paradise, seemingly a parallel expression affirming the thief's plea for participation in Christ's kingdom.

23:34 EVIL AND SUFFERING, Endurance—In His death, Jesus exemplified the forgiving, non-vindictive response to persecution. See notes on Mt 5:10–12, 38–48.

23:34 PRAYER, Intercession—Jesus had taught on forgiving enemies (Mt 6:14–15). This prayer was probably on behalf of the Roman soldiers primarily but also all those involved in executing Jesus. In its widest theological context, the prayer can be applied to all sinners who caused Jesus to go to the cross. He is willing to forgive. We have to ask for and accept His forgiveness. Jesus' first and last words from the cross were a prayer to His Father.

23:35,39 SALVATION, Initiative—Jesus of Nazareth was sent and anointed by God to be the Savior of the world. He refused to save Himself from crucifixion on the cross so He could obey the Father and save us from our sins. Christ voluntarily died on the cross. He proved He was Messiah in obedient love, not in self-centered, flamboyant miracles. Compare 4:9–12.

you are under the same sentence? 41We
are punished justly, for we are getting
what our deeds deserve. But this man has
done nothing wrong."[c]
42Then he said, "Jesus, remember me
when you come into your kingdom.[o]"[d]
43Jesus answered him, "I tell you the
truth, today you will be with me in paradise."[e]

Jesus' Death

23:44–49pp — Mt 27:45–56; Mk 15:33–41

44It was now about the sixth hour, and
darkness came over the whole land until
the ninth hour,[f] 45for the sun stopped
shining. And the curtain of the temple[g]
was torn in two.[h] 46Jesus called out with
a loud voice,[i] "Father, into your hands I
commit my spirit."[j] When he had said
this, he breathed his last.[k]
47The centurion, seeing what had happened, praised God[l] and said, "Surely
this was a righteous man." 48When all
the people who had gathered to witness
this sight saw what took place, they beat
their breasts[m] and went away. 49But all
those who knew him, including the women who had followed him from Galilee,[n]
stood at a distance,[o] watching these
things.

Jesus' Burial

23:50–56pp — Mt 27:57–61; Mk 15:42–47; Jn 19:38–42

50Now there was a man named Joseph,
a member of the Council, a good and upright man, 51who had not consented to
their decision and action. He came from
the Judean town of Arimathea and he was
waiting for the kingdom of God.[p] 52Going to Pilate, he asked for Jesus' body.
53Then he took it down, wrapped it in
linen cloth and placed it in a tomb cut in
the rock, one in which no one had yet
been laid. 54It was Preparation Day,[q] and
the Sabbath was about to begin.
55The women who had come with
Jesus from Galilee[r] followed Joseph and
saw the tomb and how his body was laid
in it. 56Then they went home and prepared spices and perfumes.[s] But they
rested on the Sabbath in obedience to the
commandment.[t]

Chapter 24

The Resurrection

24:1–10pp — Mt 28:1–8; Mk 16:1–8; Jn 20:1–8

ON the first day of the week, very early
in the morning, the women took the
spices they had prepared[u] and went to
the tomb. 2They found the stone rolled
away from the tomb, 3but when they entered, they did not find the body of the
Lord Jesus.[v] 4While they were wondering about this, suddenly two men in
clothes that gleamed like lightning[w]
stood beside them. 5In their fright the
women bowed down with their faces to
the ground, but the men said to them,
"Why do you look for the living among
the dead? 6He is not here; he has risen!

23:41 [c]S ver 4
23:42 [d]S Mt 16:27
23:43 [e]2Co 12:3,4; Rev 2:7
23:44 [f]Am 8:9
23:45 [g]Ex 26:31-33; Heb 9:3,8 [h]Heb 10:19,20
23:46 [i]Mt 27:50 [j]Ps 31:5; 1Pe 2:23 [k]Jn 19:30
23:47 [l]S Mt 9:8
23:48 [m]Lk 18:13
23:49 [n]Lk 8:2 [o]Ps 38:11
23:51 [p]Lk 2:25,38
23:54 [q]Mt 27:62
23:55 [r]ver 49
23:56 [s]Mk 16:1; Lk 24:1 [t]Ex 12:16; 20:10
24:1 [u]Lk 23:56
24:3 [v]ver 23,24
24:4 [w]S Jn 20:12

[o]42 Some manuscripts *come with your kingly power*

23:42–43 PRAYER, Salvation—It is not too late to pray this prayer while the body has breath. The criminal's prayer was answered. You can pray the same prayer in faith and be sure He will answer.
23:43 REVELATION, Jesus Christ—The anointed Child of Bethlehem has the power to declare a man forgiven and safe immediately. Dying on a cross, He revealed God's love at its highest measure: to offer love and compassion when He hurts the most.
23:43 SALVATION, Glorification—Paradise is the place of glorification. It is another word for heaven. God in salvation gives us more than we ask, hope, or think.
23:43 LAST THINGS, Intermediate State—The repentant thief went at death to where Jesus went. Jesus called the place paradise. See note on 2 Co 12:3–4. The term often described a place of beauty and enjoyment. Heaven in the final sense will be established at the end time; the period until then is referred to as the intermediate state. At death we go immediately to be with our Lord.
23:46 PRAYER, Commitment—This is the most trusting prayer any human ever prayed at death. See note on 23:34.
23:47 PRAYER, Praise—Luke the Gentile noted Gentile praise. Jesus received praise at His death as at His birth. See note on 2:20. Compare 7:1–10; Ac 10:45–46.
23:50–56 JESUS CHRIST, Death—See note on Mk 15:42–47.
23:50–51 THE CHURCH, God's Kingdom—Joseph sought the fulfillment of God's kingdom. He wanted God to reign over him. Simeon (Lk 2:25) and Joseph of Arimathea are excellent examples of those who devoted themselves to God's kingdom rather than personal power.
24:1–53 JESUS CHRIST, Resurrection—See notes on Mt 28:1–20; Mk 16:1–8; Jn 20:10–18; 21:1–14. Jesus' death predictions helped His followers understand Him and His mission in light of the resurrection, but the resurrection message remained meaningless even to the disciples without personal experience of the empty tomb and resurrected Christ. See note on Mt 16:21–23. Without the resurrection appearance disciples could point to Jesus only as a powerful prophet who had apparently failed to fulfill their messianic hopes. Jesus could show He was Messiah by explaining the Old Testament Scriptures correctly and by breaking bread, a symbolic reminder of the Lord's Supper. Fellowship with the risen Christ leads to faith in the resurrection.
24:1–49 MIRACLE, Christ—The resurrection of Christ is the supreme miracle. Accept it, and you can accept all the others. It is unique, unlike all other miracles—even the raising of Jairus' daughter, the widow's son, and Lazarus. The evidence for the resurrection miracle here is twofold: the empty tomb and His presence with His doubting friends. The body of Jesus, though recognizable by faith, was not bound by time and space. The two travelers to Emmaus could not recognize Him immediately. He then "disappeared from their sight." From Emmaus they returned to the eleven in Jerusalem, and Jesus appeared suddenly in their midst. The challenge of Jesus to the troubled friends was threefold: (1) touch me; (2) feed me; and (3) hear me. The power of the resurrection continues to strengthen and bless His believing friends. Only Luke (here and in Ac 1:9) cites the ascension, perhaps to assure us that His body is a spiritual body. The appearances evoked worship, joy, and praise (v 52). The resurrection miracle fulfilled Scripture and Jesus' own predictions. It is the strongest evidence Jesus is the Messiah promised Israel and the Savior given the world.
24:4–8 HUMANITY, Death—See note on Mt 28:5–7.

Remember how he told you, while he
was still with you in Galilee:[x] 7'The Son
of Man[y] must be delivered into the
hands of sinful men, be crucified and on
the third day be raised again.' "[z] 8Then
they remembered his words.[a]

9When they came back from the tomb,
they told all these things to the Eleven
and to all the others. 10It was Mary Magdalene, Joanna, Mary the mother of
James, and the others with them[b] who
told this to the apostles.[c] 11But they did
not believe[d] the women, because their
words seemed to them like nonsense.
12Peter, however, got up and ran to the
tomb. Bending over, he saw the strips of
linen lying by themselves,[e] and he went
away,[f] wondering to himself what had
happened.

On the Road to Emmaus

13Now that same day two of them were
going to a village called Emmaus, about
seven miles[p] from Jerusalem.[g] 14They
were talking with each other about everything that had happened. 15As they talked
and discussed these things with each other, Jesus himself came up and walked
along with them;[h] 16but they were kept
from recognizing him.[i]

17He asked them, "What are you discussing together as you walk along?"

They stood still, their faces downcast.
18One of them, named Cleopas,[j] asked
him, "Are you only a visitor to Jerusalem
and do not know the things that have
happened there in these days?"

19"What things?" he asked.

"About Jesus of Nazareth,"[k] they replied. "He was a prophet,[l] powerful in
word and deed before God and all the
people. 20The chief priests and our rulers[m] handed him over to be sentenced to
death, and they crucified him; 21but we
had hoped that he was the one who was
going to redeem Israel.[n] And what is
more, it is the third day[o] since all this
took place. 22In addition, some of our
women amazed us.[p] They went to the
tomb early this morning 23but didn't find
his body. They came and told us that they
had seen a vision of angels, who said he
was alive. 24Then some of our companions went to the tomb and found it just as
the women had said, but him they did not
see."[q]

25He said to them, "How foolish you
are, and how slow of heart to believe all
that the prophets have spoken! 26Did not
the Christ[q] have to suffer these things
and then enter his glory?"[r] 27And beginning with Moses[s] and all the Prophets,[t]
he explained to them what was said in all
the Scriptures concerning himself.[u]

28As they approached the village to
which they were going, Jesus acted as if
he were going farther. 29But they urged
him strongly, "Stay with us, for it is nearly evening; the day is almost over." So he
went in to stay with them.

30When he was at the table with them,
he took bread, gave thanks, broke it[v] and
began to give it to them. 31Then their
eyes were opened and they recognized
him,[w] and he disappeared from their
sight. 32They asked each other, "Were
not our hearts burning within us[x] while
he talked with us on the road and opened
the Scriptures[y] to us?"

33They got up and returned at once to
Jerusalem. There they found the Eleven
and those with them, assembled together
34and saying, "It is true! The Lord[z] has
risen and has appeared to Simon."[a]
35Then the two told what had happened
on the way, and how Jesus was recognized by them when he broke the
bread.[b]

Jesus Appears to the Disciples

36While they were still talking about

24:6 [x]Mt 17:22,23; Lk 9:22; 24:44
24:7 [y]S Mt 8:20 [z]S Mt 16:21
24:8 [a]Jn 2:22
24:10 [b]Lk 8:1-3 [c]S Mk 6:30
24:11 [d]Mk 16:11
24:12 [e]Jn 20:3-7 [f]Jn 20:10
24:13 [g]Mk 16:12
24:15 [h]ver 36
24:16 [i]Jn 20:14; 21:4
24:18 [j]Jn 19:25
24:19 [k]S Mk 1:24 [l]S Mt 21:11
24:20 [m]Lk 23:13
24:21 [n]Lk 1:68; 2:38; 21:28 [o]S Mt 16:21
24:22 [p]ver 1-10
24:24 [q]ver 12
24:26 [r]Heb 2:10; 1Pe 1:11
24:27 [s]Ge 3:15; Nu 21:9; Dt 18:15 [t]Isa 7:14; 9:6; 40:10,11; 53; Eze 34:23; Da 9:24; Mic 7:20; Mal 3:1 [u]Jn 1:45
24:30 [v]S Mt 14:19
24:31 [w]ver 16
24:32 [x]Ps 39:3 [y]ver 27,45
24:34 [z]S Lk 7:13 [a]1Co 15:5
24:35 [b]ver 30,31

[p]13 Greek *sixty stadia* (about 11 kilometers)
[q]26 Or *Messiah*; also in verse 46

24:13–27,45 EDUCATION, Jesus—The teaching ministry of Jesus did not end with His crucifixion. As shown by the post-resurrection encounters on the road to Emmaus and in Jerusalem, He continued to be "The Teacher" among His followers. Even to the present day, the risen Christ continues to illuminate the minds of those who call Him Lord.

24:16,25 REVELATION, Divine Presence—The risen Christ joined the preoccupied travelers and revealed in Scripture and personal presence the reality of God. They did not respond, being too concerned with their grief and fears. God's presence does not bring revelation if we are not open to Him. Only later reflection let the disciples see the revelation in this experience with Jesus. God walks beside us and within us, waiting to be recognized. At times, we have to reflect upon an experience to realize God was present and active with us.

24:25–27,37–41 SALVATION, Belief—Christ wants persons to believe all that the prophets of Israel said about Him. His resurrection from the dead authenticated what the Scriptures had predicted. Suffering, not political power, was the legitimate Old Testament expectation of the Messiah. Compare Isa 52:13—53:12.

24:27 EDUCATION, Scripture Study—The Bible is the textbook of the Christian faith. The Old Testament sheds light on the mission and teaching of Jesus Christ, and the New Testament enlarges our understanding of the message of Israel's prophets. Christian teaching must be based on Scripture, must point to Jesus Christ, and must not contradict Scripture.

24:30 PRAYER, Thanksgiving—After the resurrection, Jesus continued to bless food. See note on Mt 14:19.

24:35 ORDINANCES, Presence in the Lord's Supper—Cleopas and the other unnamed disciple recognized Jesus as He broke the bread during a meal. The action reminded them and calls to our mind the Last Supper. See note on 22:1–30. Luke taught, through this event, that in the Lord's Supper Christian disciples recognized the presence of their Lord. We can be sure of this because "breaking bread" is Luke's regular term for the Lord's Supper (Ac 2:42).

this, Jesus himself stood among them and
said to them, "Peace be with you."[c]
37They were startled and frightened,
thinking they saw a ghost.[d] 38He said to
them, "Why are you troubled, and why
do doubts rise in your minds? 39Look at
my hands and my feet. It is I myself!
Touch me and see;[e] a ghost does not
have flesh and bones, as you see I have."
40When he had said this, he showed
them his hands and feet. 41And while
they still did not believe it because of joy
and amazement, he asked them, "Do you
have anything here to eat?" 42They gave
him a piece of broiled fish, 43and he took
it and ate it in their presence.[f]
44He said to them, "This is what I told
you while I was still with you:[g] Everything must be fulfilled[h] that is written
about me in the Law of Moses,[i] the
Prophets[j] and the Psalms."[k]
45Then he opened their minds so they
could understand the Scriptures. 46He
told them, "This is what is written: The
Christ will suffer[l] and rise from the dead
on the third day,[m] 47and repentance and
forgiveness of sins will be preached in his
name[n] to all nations,[o] beginning at Jerusalem.[p] 48You are witnesses[q] of these
things. 49I am going to send you what my
Father has promised;[r] but stay in the city
until you have been clothed with power
from on high."

The Ascension

50When he had led them out to the vicinity of Bethany,[s] he lifted up his hands
and blessed them. 51While he was blessing them, he left them and was taken up
into heaven.[t] 52Then they worshiped
him and returned to Jerusalem with great
joy. 53And they stayed continually at the
temple,[u] praising God.

24:36 [c]Jn 20:19, 21,26; S 14:27
24:37 [d]Mk 6:49
24:39 [e]Jn 20:27; 1Jn 1:1
24:43 [f]Ac 10:41
24:44 [g]Lk 9:45; 18:34 [h]S Mt 1:22; 16:21; Lk 9:22,44; 18:31-33; 22:37 [i]S ver 27 [j]S ver 27 [k]Ps 2; 16; 22; 69; 72; 110; 118
24:46 [l]S Mt 16:21 [m]S Mt 16:21
24:47 [n]Ac 5:31; 10:43; 13:38 [o]Mt 28:19; Mk 13:10 [p]Isa 2:3
24:48 [q]S Jn 15:27; Ac 1:8; 2:32; 4:20; 5:32; 13:31; 1Pe 5:1
24:49 [r]S Jn 14:16; Ac 1:4
24:50 [s]S Mt 21:17
24:51 [t]2Ki 2:11
24:53 [u]S Ac 2:46

24:44–46 HOLY SCRIPTURE, Authoritative—The basic authority of Scripture is its witness to Jesus Christ, the living Word who became flesh (Jn 1:14). Jesus claimed all the Old Testament writings pointed to Him when rightly interpreted. The task of the church is to interpret Scripture under guidance of the Spirit so that the Bible points people to Jesus. We should expect Bible promises to be fulfilled. We should understand the fulfillment in the light of Jesus' ministry, not in the light of human tradition or selfish interests. The criterion by which the whole Bible is to be interpreted is Jesus. Only as we interpret Scripture in light of what He has done will it lead us into all truth.

24:44–49 MISSIONS, Message—The risen Lord explained to the eleven apostles ("sent ones") the entire Old Testament as relating to Himself and the purpose of His life and ministry. He tied together all of the Old Testament and showed its relation to all of the events leading to His death and resurrection. He showed that the entire intent of the Old Testament and, thus, of His life, ministry, death, and resurrection, pointed to the missionary purpose of the "sent ones"—to proclaim repentance and forgiveness in the name of Jesus Christ to all the peoples of the world, beginning right where they were—in Jerusalem. The conversation has tremendous implications for Christ's church and for Christians of all ages. Missions is not an activity tacked on to the gospel, but reflects the very purpose of God from eternity. Missions is not based on a single passage, like Mt 28:18–20, but on a theme that permeates the Bible. The beginning point for missions is where we are, but our missionary task extends to the end of the world. This passage gives us: (1) the source of missions as the purpose of God; (2) the message as repentance and forgiveness in the name of Jesus; (3) the scope beginning where we are and reaching to the ends of the earth; and (4) the power—the Holy Spirit. The worldwide evangelistic and mission task is too great for human power, but God has provided for our being clothed in the power of the Holy Spirit for the task.

24:45–47 SALVATION, Forgiveness—Christ's Great Commission included the preaching of forgiveness of sins to all peoples from Jerusalem to the ends of the earth. Compare Jn 20:23. Salvation begins in forgiveness.

24:45–49 EVANGELISM, Universality—Evangelism centers on the Scripture-fulfilling work of Christ. He sends His followers to call every person in the world to repentance and forgiveness. The Holy Spirit in us leads us and gives us power and courage to witness. See note on Mt 28:18–20.

24:47 SALVATION, Repentance—Repentance and forgiveness of sins go together. God forgives only those who repent.

24:47 PROCLAMATION, Central Theme—Proclamation is an authoritative invitation to repentance and forgiveness made possible by the suffering, death, and resurrection of Christ. Proclamation is a universal task which fulfills the biblical purpose of God as recorded in Scripture.

24:50–53 JESUS CHRIST, Ascension—Compare Ac 1:9–11. Other gospels show the gospel could be narrated without the story of the ascension. The resurrection marked Jesus' victory over sin and death, assuring the completion of God's saving acts. The ascension is God's final and confirming act on Jesus. Theologians speak of Jesus' humiliation and His exaltation. The wonders of the virgin birth and the ascension bracket Jesus' earthly existence. The ascension is the only logically possible outcome of God's greatest act in Jesus Christ, the resurrection. The purpose of the ascension was to remove the glorified body of Christ out of earthly, physical limitations and to provide the appropriate context for Jesus' homecoming in heaven, God's sphere. There Jesus began His ministry for the church and prepared to return for the final judgment.

24:50–51 PRAYER, Blessing—See notes on Ge 14:18–20; 48:15–20; Mt 19:13–15. Blessing was characteristic of Jesus. His final blessing invoked God's continued power on their daily ministry in His physical absence.

24:52 SALVATION, Joy—God's people can worship His ascended Son and go to every city with the same kind of great joy.

24:52–53 WORSHIP, Buildings—At times New Testament worship included assembling in the building constructed to honor God. Joyful praise was a major component of worship. See note on Ge 28:16–22.

24:52–53 PRAYER, Praise—Praise was the inevitable result of all they had seen. Losing the physical presence of Jesus was not cause for mourning but for joy because the early church knew the resurrected Lord would fulfill His promises.

John

Theological Setting

The Gospel of John explores what it means to confess that Jesus is "the Christ, the Son of God" (20:31). This Gospel was written for a local church that had been closely related to Judaism. When the Jewish community began to take steps to expel those who confessed Jesus, the Christians formed a separate community. As a separate community, the Christians had to define what it meant to confess Jesus. They needed answers for their continuing debate with the Jewish community. They were concerned about those who remained behind in the synagogue, who believed secretly, fearing what would happen if they confessed Christ publicly.

The Gospel of John, therefore, detailed the struggle of various individuals who were confronted both by Jesus and by the Jewish authorities: Nicodemus, the Samaritan woman, the man at the Pool of Bethesda, and the blind man. As these persons moved step-by-step toward faith, the Gospel of John unfolds the meaning of faith and the reasons why some never believe. Repeatedly, the Gospel calls for public confession of one's faith (1:19; 11:27; 12:42).

John used individuals and groups to represent various responses to Jesus and, thereby, to lead readers to the response of faith. Through the response of "the Jews" to Jesus, John explained the reasons for unbelief. Some were not given, called, drawn, or chosen (6:37,39,44,65; 10:3,27). These love darkness rather than light. Their works are evil (3:19). They seek human glory rather than the glory of God (5:44; 12:43). For John, these are the characteristics of unbelief. The Gospel that proclaims God's love for the world should never be interpreted as condoning hatred or persecution of the Jewish people.

The Gospel of John also reflects a struggle to find a better understanding of who Jesus was, for others held differing understandings concerning Jesus. John's church faced several options. Each option contains an element of truth, but did not include the whole truth about Jesus. John wrote to show the total picture of Jesus, who is Truth.

1. *Jesus, the miracle Worker.* Some Christians, like the "super apostles" Paul refuted in 2 Co 10—13, apparently believed Jesus was primarily a miracle Worker. For them, following Jesus meant imitating His miracles with mighty works and glory of their own. John interpreted both Jesus' miracles and His death and resurrection as "signs" that point to a higher, spiritual reality—Jesus as God's incarnate Son.

2. *Jesus, the wisdom Teacher.* Alongside the four Gospels, collections of the sayings and discourses of Jesus circulated in the early church. Those who used only collections of sayings apparently diminished the significance of both Jesus' miracles and His death and resurrection. For them, following Jesus meant living by His teachings, His wisdom. John showed his church that Christianity was more than good ethics. John included large blocks of Jesus' sayings and discourses but used the form of a narrative Gospel with miracles and an account of Jesus' death and resurrection. The Gospel, therefore, centers on the person and work of Jesus, the Son of God.

3. *Jesus, the crucified Messiah.* Mark and Paul, each in his own way, emphasized the suffering, death and resurrection of Jesus. John also emphasized Jesus' death and resurrection. For John, the death of Jesus was His "hour" that glorified His Father. His death on the cross, therefore, was His exaltation, His "lifting up" (3:14; 8:28; 12:32).

4. *Jesus, the divine Revealer.* The Gnostics believed Jesus had come to enlighten our spirits so that we might be delivered from this world and from the prison of our fleshly bodies, since the world of spirit and flesh were opposed to one another. Because flesh was material, and the material world was inherently evil, the Gnostics reasoned, Jesus did not actually become flesh but came as a god striding upon the earth. He imparted a saving knowledge. Being illuminated by His revelation would free persons to ascend to the world above. Evidently, early stages of such teachings threatened John's church. John affirmed Jesus as the eternal, divine Redeemer come from heaven, but he also affirmed that Jesus became flesh (1:14). As such, He performed miracles that were signs to His divine identity and taught His disciples the way

to the Father. John climaxed his Gospel with the death and resurrection of Christ, pointing to the kingship of Jesus. The result is a Gospel that recounted the ministry of Jesus and His miraculous works, contained long sections of dialogues and sayings of Jesus, and climaxed with the crucifixion and resurrection of Jesus.

The Holy Spirit or *Paraclete* had been active in and was working through the writing of the Gospel. The Gospel of John would remind Christians what Jesus had taught and would teach them—things they did not yet understand. As a result, the Gospel writer expected that: (1) the community of believers would be strengthened, (2) secret Jewish believers who remained within Judaism would be encouraged to make a public confession of their faith, (3) followers of John the Baptist would see that he had borne witness to Jesus, and (4) the church would be able to reject false teachings about Jesus.

Theological Outline

John: Jesus, the Revealer of Life from Above

- I. The Arrival of the Revealer (1:1-51)
  - A. Jesus, the Word, the Light of the World (1:1-18)
  - B. Jesus, the Lamb of God, the King of Israel (1:19-51)
- II. The Signs of the Revealer of Life (2:1—12:50)
  - A. Jesus reveals the new life (2:1—4:54)
    1. The first sign: the wine of the new age (2:1-12)
    2. The new temple: Jesus Himself (2:13-25)
    3. The new birth from above (3:1-14)
    4. The new disclosure of God's love (3:15-36)
    5. The water of new life, living water (4:1-42)
    6. The second sign: life that comes by faith (4:43-54)
  - B. The new life on trial: confrontation and fulfillment (5:1—12:50)
    1. The third sign: wholeness and freedom for the afflicted and bound (5:1-47)
       - a. The issues: Sabbath and Sonship (5:1-18)
       - b. The witnesses for Jesus: the Father, John the Baptist, Jesus' works, the Scriptures, and Moses (5:19-47)
    2. The fourth sign: providing the bread of life (6:1-71)
       - a. Bread for the multitudes (6:1-21)
       - b. The true Bread from heaven: Jesus (6:22-50)
       - c. Eating the true Bread (6:51-59)
       - d. Defection and confession (6:60-71)
    3. The Feast of Tabernacles: Israel on trial (7:1—8:59)
       - a. Argument over Jesus' origin and authority (7:1-52)
       - (Forgiveness of the woman taken in adultery 7:53—8:11)
       - b. The true Son and the true children (8:12-59)
    4. Jesus gives sight to those who will see and calls those who will hear. (9:1—10:42)
       - a. The fifth sign: The Light of the world brings sight to the blind and blindness to those who will not see. (9:1-41)
       - b. The good Shepherd, His sheep, and the hirelings (10:1-42)
    5. Jesus: the Resurrection and the Life (11:1—12:50)
       - a. The sixth sign: Jesus reveals His power to give life. (11:1-44)
       - b. Jesus will give life by dying for the children of God. (11:45-57)
       - c. Jesus faces the hour of His death. (12:1-50)
- III. The Exaltation of the Revealer of Life (13:1—20:31)
  - A. Jesus' farewell to "his own" (13:1—17:26)
    1. The meaning of the cross in the washing of feet (13:1-20)
    2. Love and betrayal: the new command to love one another (13:21-38)
    3. The promise of His presence: the place Jesus will prepare for "his own" (14:1-31)
    4. The vine and the branches: a legacy of peace and joy (15:1-27)
    5. Comfort for the "little while" (16:1-33)
    6. Jesus' prayer for "his own": that they be one (17:1-26)
  - B. The Revealer's death (18:1—19:42)
    1. Arrest and trial: Jesus confesses; Peter denies (18:1-27)
    2. Trial before Pilate: the trial of a King (18:28—19:16)
    3. Jesus' death, the enthronement of the Revealer (19:16-37)
    4. Jesus' burial, funeral for a King (19:38-42)

C. The return of the Revealer (20:1-29)
  1. Overcoming death: discovering the resurrection (20:1-18)
  2. Overcoming doubt: seeing and believing (20:19-29)
D. John's purpose in writing: that you may believe and have life (20:30-31)
IV. The Vocation of Those Who Receive Life from Above (21:1-25)
A. Fishing: the missionary task of the church. (21:1-14)
B. Feeding sheep: the pastoral task of the church (21:15-23)
C. The true witness (21:24-25)

Theological Conclusions

The Gospel of John develops the theme that Jesus, as the Revealer of the Father, brought new life to all who would believe in Him. Four of John's doctrines are vital to understanding the life of Jesus:

1. Jesus was the Word (*logos*) of God, God in human flesh.
2. The children of God are led by His Spirit.
3. The church is to be marked by love and unity.
4. The life from above, eternal life, begins now.

Jesus, in whom the eternal Word (*logos*) of God became flesh, revealed to us the character of God as Father. As the unique Son, He made it possible for all who believe in Him to become children of God (1:12). God's children are born from above (3:3,5) and live by means of the living water (4:10,14) and the Bread from heaven (6:51). They are vitally related to Jesus, as sheep to the Shepherd (10:27) or branches to the Vine (15:5). Only those who respond in faith can see that Jesus is the Revealer and Giver of Life. In that sense, we are all born blind—and some choose to remain blind.

The Holy Spirit, Counselor, or *Paraclete* allows the followers of Jesus to continue to experience His presence after His death. Jesus went to prepare a place for His own and promised that He would come again to be with them through the Spirit (14:23). The Spirit reminds us of all that Jesus taught; He teaches all things; He inspires witness and empowers mission. The risen Lord is already with His own through the presence of His Spirit within them.

As the children of God guided by His Spirit, the church is to be recognized by its love and its unity. The oneness of the church was decribed as a unity of spirit. We will be one with one another because we are one with the Father, just as Jesus was One with the Father (17:22). The new community of believers will be persecuted by the world because of its faith. Nevertheless, it will continue the work of God's redemptive revelation by bearing a true witness, gathering other believers, and feeding them with Jesus' Word. This Word, the revelation that came through Jesus, is the living Water and the Bread from heaven that sustains the life of all God's children.

One of John's distinctive teachings is that the hope for the future is already being realized. We do not have to await the coming of Jesus to experience His presence; His Spirit is already within us. We do not have to await the end of time to see God's judgment; judgment is already being determined by our response to the Revealer (3:19-21). We do not have to await the resurrection to experience the new life; eternal life begins when believers are born from above. We have already passed from death into life (5:24). While this was the dominant emphasis of John's teaching about the last things (eschatology), the Gospel still speaks of the future day of judgment (5:28-29; 6:39-40).

John revealed, therefore, how God grants His people the experience of a life that has its origin, its power, and its end in Him. Jesus came to reveal this life and to enable others to share in it. Those who respond in faith to the Word of God in Jesus find the life that Jesus promised.

Contemporary Teaching

In its simplest form, the message of the Gospel of John is this: Jesus revealed the Father so that by living in faithful response to that revelation we may have the Life that comes from God. Therefore, the Gospel of John calls us: (1) to trust that the highest truth about God, ourselves, and the purpose of life has been revealed by Jesus; (2) to confess our faith in Jesus as "the Christ, the Son of God" (20:31) so that we may be born again, from above; (3) to nourish our new life by feeding on the revelation that has come through Jesus; (4) to maintain the new commandment of love for one another, as He loved us (13:34); (5) to share life and worship in community, as sheep in His pasture or branches of His vine; (6) to be sensitive and responsive to the presence of the Holy Spirit within us and among us; and (7) to bear a true and faithful witness to the world that has not yet accepted its blindness. Only by such a response to the love of God, revealed in the life of Jesus, can we experience life that is marked by the abiding Spirit of God. Our present experience of that life, moreover, is only the beginning of eternal life.

Chapter 1

The Word Became Flesh

IN the beginning was the Word,[a] and
the Word was with God,[b] and the
Word was God.[c] 2He was with God in
the beginning.[d]
3Through him all things were made;
without him nothing was made that has
been made.[e] 4In him was life,[f] and that
life was the light[g] of men. 5The light
shines in the darkness,[h] but the darkness
has not understood[a] it.[i]
6There came a man who was sent from
God; his name was John.[j] 7He came as a
witness to testify[k] concerning that light,
so that through him all men might believe.[l] 8He himself was not the light; he
came only as a witness to the light. 9The
true light[m] that gives light to every man[n]
was coming into the world.[b]
10He was in the world, and though the
world was made through him,[o] the
world did not recognize him. 11He came
to that which was his own, but his own
did not receive him.[p] 12Yet to all who
received him, to those who believed[q] in
his name,[r] he gave the right to become
children of God[s]— 13children born not
of natural descent,[c] nor of human decision or a husband's will, but born of
God.[t]
14The Word became flesh[u] and made
his dwelling among us. We have seen his
glory,[v] the glory of the One and Only,[d]
who came from the Father, full of grace[w]
and truth.[x]

1:1 [a]Isa 55:11; Rev 19:13 [b]Jn 17:5; 1Jn 1:2 [c]Php 2:6 **1:2** [d]Ge 1:1; Jn 8:58; 17:5,24; 1Jn 1:1; Rev 1:8 **1:3** [e]ver 10; 1Co 8:6; Col 1:16; Heb 1:2 **1:4** [f]S Jn 5:26; 6:57; 11:25; 14:6; Ac 3:15; Heb 7:16; 1Jn 1:1,2; 5:20; Rev 1:18 [g]Ps 36:9; Jn 3:19; 8:12; 9:5; 12:46 **1:5** [h]Ps 18:28 [i]Jn 3:19 **1:6** [j]S Mt 3:1 **1:7** [k]ver 15,19,32; Jn 3:26; 5:33 [l]ver 12; S Jn 3:15 **1:9** [m]1Jn 2:8 [n]Isa 49:6 **1:10** [o]S ver 3 **1:11** [p]Isa 53:3 **1:12** [q]ver 7; S Jn 3:15 [r]S 1Jn 3:23 [s]Dt 14:1; S Ro 8:14; 8:16,21; Eph 5:1; 1Jn 3:1,2 **1:13** [t]Jn 3:6; Tit 3:5; Jas 1:18; 1Pe 1:23; 1Jn 3:9; 4:7; 5:1,4 **1:14** [u]Gal 4:4; Php 2:7,8; 1Ti 3:16; Heb 2:14; 1Jn 1:1,2; 4:2 [v]Ex 33:18; 40:34 [w]S Ro 3:24 [x]Jn 14:6

[a]5 Or *darkness, and the darkness has not overcome* [b]9 Or *This was the true light that gives light to every man who comes into the world* [c]13 Greek *of bloods* [d]14 Or *the Only Begotten*

1:1–18 JESUS CHRIST, Preexistent—John's account of Jesus' beginnings is an absolute account that stretches back beyond time and into eternity. John contributed an essential understanding to the Gospels' composite picture of Jesus. He affirmed that God's Messiah was in the beginning. "In the beginning" is different from "from the beginning." In the beginning speaks of eternity. From the beginning means as far back as humans have had any experience (8:44). Jesus is identified with the Creator rather than the created. He shares the divine attribute of eternal existence. John's Gospel reveals: (1) Messiah has always been with God; (2) Messiah is called the Word of God; (3) Messiah is God's agent of creation; (4) Messiah is light in contrast to darkness; (5) Messiah is witnessed to by John the Baptist; (6) Messiah is not known by His own; (7) Messiah is the only begotten of the Father—a distinct and exclusively Johannine expression which means unique, one of a kind; (8) Messiah is superior to the authority of Judaism; and (9) Messiah is the only one who has seen God face to face. The actual account of Messiah's birth is in v 14. The term for "made flesh" in Latin is *incarnatus*, from which we derive the word "incarnation." We mean by this term that God entered our history through Jesus Christ in actual human form. We dare not miss the light of Jesus' humanity (v 14) among the deep theological expressions about His unique relationship to God. V 9 may mean that Jesus gives some light to every person who comes into the world, or it may mean that His coming into the world illumines what we really are. Jesus is not only what God is like; He is also what humanity was intended to be. In this sense, we shall be like Him (1 Jn 3:2). That is, we shall become really and fully human in Him and completely so in eternity. John's Christmas story is a vivid visual in black and white, in darkness and light.

1:1 JESUS CHRIST, Word of God—Jesus is explicitly called the Word (Greek *logos*) in this verse and in v 14. The idea of Jesus as Word is one of the most significant insights about Christ in the New Testament. Word of God has roots in the Old Testament word of the Lord revealed to and through the prophets. By the word or speech of God the world was formed and the will of God accomplished (Ge 1). Another Old Testament idea related to word is the notion of wisdom, the personified knowledge of God (Pr 1:20–33; 8:22–26). These Old Testament ideas are given full meaning and substance by John's declaration that the Word became flesh (Jn 1:14). The Greeks tended to associate word (*logos*) with mind, rational thought. They talked of a rational pattern implanted in the universe. John used the term *logos* to build a bridge of understanding between the Greek and Hebrew cultures, uniting all of these ideas in applying them to Jesus. Jesus is God's plan for the world, God's action agent who secures what God wants done, the application of God's wisdom. Christ unites creation and redemption. As the Word became flesh, Jesus was God in human form communicating God's will in all He said and did. He embodied ultimate truth. To communicate or proclaim about God is to point to Jesus. Only in Him can life and the universe be seen as rational and meaningful. Human speech cannot adequately communicate God. The Word become flesh can, did, and does show us the Father.

1:1–4 REVELATION, Jesus Christ—Jesus is the Word of revelation alive in human flesh. His revelation did not begin at birth in Bethlehem. He has been actively revealing God since creation in which He was active. He shows the nature of the life God creates.

1:3 CREATION, The Trinity—All three members of the Trinity were present at the creation. The Father spoke the world into being. The Spirit was hovering over the waters (Ge 1:2). All of it happened, however, through the agency of the Son, the Word made flesh. The world was created in order that its inhabitants might bring glory to the Creator. This can be done only as we give full allegiance to the Son, who was with the Father from the beginning and is the Father's final Word concerning Himself (Heb 1:1–2).

1:4–5 JESUS CHRIST, Light—Life involves conflict between God, who is good, and evil powers. Evil is darkness, shutting out opportunity to see or know good. God is the source of light which exposes evil for what it is. Jesus is that light in person exposing the evil of the world and pointing the way to God. Compare 8:12; 12:46; 1 Jn 2:8.

1:4 JESUS CHRIST, Life—Life is more than physical functioning of the body. Life involves personal relationship and meaning. Full life includes relationship with God. In this sense Jesus is the source of life. He lived the fullest human life ever lived. He is the link to the Creator of life. By His death, He enabled sinners to inherit eternal life. Compare 5:26,40; 10:10; 14:6.

1:6 JESUS CHRIST, John—John represented God but not in the way Jesus did. John was a messenger leading people to believe in Christ.

1:7,12,50–51 SALVATION, Belief—This Gospel has a marked preference for the word "believe." The word is found in almost every chapter in some form. Compare 19:35; 20:29–31. John the Baptist bore witness to Jesus Christ as the Light of the world, that persons might believe in Him. The Jewish people were reluctant to believe in Jesus. Those who did believe in Him, He made sons and daughters of God. Nathaniel believed in Jesus because Jesus saw him under the fig tree. We should believe in Him because He is the way to God and eternal life.

1:7–9 EVANGELISM, Personal—John illustrated person-

15John testifies[y] concerning him. He
cries out, saying, "This was he of whom
I said, 'He who comes after me has
surpassed me because he was
before me.' "[z] 16From the fullness[a] of
his grace[b] we have all received one blessing after another. 17For the law was
given through Moses;[c] grace and truth
came through Jesus Christ.[d] 18No one has
ever seen God,[e] but God the One and
Only,[e f] who is at the Father's side, has
made him known.

John the Baptist Denies Being the Christ

19Now this was John's[g] testimony
when the Jews[h] of Jerusalem sent priests
and Levites to ask him who he was. 20He
did not fail to confess, but confessed freely, "I am not the Christ.[g] "[i]
21They asked him, "Then who are you?
Are you Elijah?"[j]
He said, "I am not."
"Are you the Prophet?"[k]
He answered, "No."
22Finally they said, "Who are you?
Give us an answer to take back to those
who sent us. What do you say about yourself?"
23John replied in the words of Isaiah
the prophet, "I am the voice of one calling in the desert,[l] 'Make straight the
way for the Lord.' "[h m]
24Now some Pharisees who had been
sent 25questioned him, "Why then do
you baptize if you are not the Christ, nor
Elijah, nor the Prophet?"
26"I baptize with[i] water,"[n] John replied, "but among you stands one you do

1:15 [y]ver 7 [z]ver 30; Mt 3:11
1:16 [a]Eph 1:23; Col 1:19; 2:9 [b]S Ro 3:24
1:17 [c]Dt 32:46; Jn 7:19 [d]ver 14
1:18 [e]Ex 33:20; Jn 6:46; Col 1:15; 1Ti 6:16; 1Jn 4:12 [f]Jn 3:16,18; 1Jn 4:9
1:19 [g]S Mt 3:1 [h]Jn 2:18; 5:10,16; 6:41,52; 7:1; 10:24
1:20 [i]Jn 3:28; Lk 3:15,16
1:21 [j]S Mt 11:14 [k]Dt 18:15
1:23 [l]Mt 3:1 [m]Isa 40:3
1:26 [n]S Mk 1:4

[e]18 Or *the Only Begotten* [f]18 Some manuscripts *but the only* (or *only begotten*) *Son* [g]20 Or *Messiah.* "The Christ" (Greek) and "the Messiah" (Hebrew) both mean "the Anointed One"; also in verse 25. [h]23 Isaiah 40:3 [i]26 Or *in*; also in verses 31 and 33

al witnessing. Despite his own power and popularity, he pointed people to Christ and away from himself. He sought to bring people to believe in Christ.

1:9–13 REVELATION, Jesus Christ—Jesus is the genuine Light providing knowledge and salvation that God promised to the world. He was the Creator come to be with His beloved creatures. He brought saving power for all who believe in His nature and purpose (His name). Most people have rejected His revelation. All who believe and respond become part of the family of God adopted in love and grace.

1:10–13 ELECTION, Faith—Jesus, chosen of God, was rejected by His own people. God elected to reject the people who took pride in their election. Those who accepted Jesus in faith became sons and daughters of God. Election is God's decision to accept as His people those who trust Jesus for salvation. The opportunity for faith is a gift of God's grace, not of human achievement.

1:11–12 SALVATION, Acceptance—Those who receive Christ accept Him. Receiving Christ and believing in Him are the same thing.

1:12–13 THE CHURCH, God's Community—To belong to God's redeemed family requires more than natural birth. God's children experience a new spiritual birth through faith in Jesus, the divine Son of God. Only God can give the spiritual power to become God's children.

1:12 EVANGELISM, Call to Salvation—All who receive Christ by repentance and faith (Ac 2:38) become children of God. This call and promise must be declared to all mankind.

1:13 SALVATION, Initiative—God through Christ took the initiative in making persons children of God. We become children of God through believing in the name of the One God sent to us, not through human descent or will.

1:14 JESUS CHRIST, Glory—Glory is the weight or importance of God. It is the shining light in which God confronts humans as His way of visible revelation of the invisible God. It is the radiant power of the Creator appearing in creation. It is that which the human eye cannot see without facing death (Ex 33:17–23). The radiance of God became visible to humans in Jesus Christ.

1:14–18 REVELATION, Jesus Christ—God's presence became a human being and revealed the fullness of God's identity in flesh. The glory of God (Ex 33:22) became visible as grace and truth which all people need. He is a greater revelation than Moses' Law which revealed God's guidelines for life. He shows those guidelines can really be lived out in human flesh on earth. He is God in flesh letting us see what otherwise was impossible to see.

1:14 HISTORY, Salvation—See note on Mt 1:1–17.

1:18 JESUS CHRIST, Son of God—John's Gospel highlights the close and unique connection of Jesus the Son with God as Father. One way of reenforcing this unique relationship is by the term only begotten or One and Only (Greek *monogenes*; 1:14,18; 3:16,18). Another way of expressing this distinctive relationship of God the Father to Jesus the Son of God is to stress the distinctiveness of their inner involvement. Jesus does this in John's Gospel. God sends the Son (3:16–18). God loves the Son (3:35). The Son depends completely on the Father (5:19). The Father, in return, commits everything to the Son (5:19–21). Giving honor to the Son is giving honor to the Father (5:23). Jesus declared Himself to be the Son of God or demonstrated Himself to be so by His works (10:37–38). Father and Son share an eternal glory (17:1). The entire Gospel of John is written that we might believe that Jesus is the Son of God (20:31). The relation of the Father and the Son is extended in 1 John. That brief epistle makes twenty references to Jesus as God's Son.

1:19–34 JESUS CHRIST, John—John's Gospel does not describe the actual baptism of Jesus as do the other three Gospels (Mt 3:13–17; Mk 1:1–11; Lk 3:1–20). Instead, John gave the testimony of John the Baptist. There were still followers of John the Baptist throughout the first century. It is possible that John included elements in his account which de-emphasized the role of John the Baptist and emphasized the significance of Jesus, the Messiah (vv 6–8,19–27). Like Mark and Luke, John recounted the humble place of the Baptist as unworthy to latch the sandals of Messiah. Like all three other Gospels, John quoted Isa 40:3, assigning John the place of the forerunner. John the Baptist claimed that God gave him a sign to identify the Messiah. That sign was the coming and remaining of the Holy Spirit. The rabbis taught that the Spirit of God left the earth with the last of the prophets and would not return until the coming of the Messiah. In the interval, God Himself was thought to intervene by a direct voice from heaven. We can see, then, how Jesus' baptism was a confirmation of His messiahship. The Spirit of God came in the visual symbol of a dove, and the voice of God was heard. Christians today revere Jesus, God's Messiah, through the power of the Spirit. We share in the witness of the New Testament and the Baptist's remarkable claim, "This is the Son of God" (v 34).

1:24–33 ORDINANCES, Baptism by John—One of the main elements in John's message was the announcement of the Messiah (Anointed One) who was coming after him and would be anointed with the Holy Spirit. This great distinction was further emphasized by the difference in their baptisms: John was baptizing in water, but the coming One would baptize with the Holy Spirit. Two additional things are made clear in these verses: (1) John came baptizing in water so that the Messiah might be revealed to Israel; and (2) John recognized

not know. 27He is the one who comes
after me,[o] the thongs of whose sandals I
am not worthy to untie."[p]
28This all happened at Bethany on the
other side of the Jordan,[q] where John
was baptizing.

Jesus the Lamb of God

29The next day John saw Jesus coming
toward him and said, "Look, the Lamb of
God,[r] who takes away the sin of the
world![s] 30This is the one I meant when I
said, 'A man who comes after me has surpassed me because he was before me.'[t]
31I myself did not know him, but the reason I came baptizing with water was that
he might be revealed to Israel."
32Then John gave this testimony: "I
saw the Spirit come down from heaven as
a dove and remain on him.[u] 33I would
not have known him, except that the one
who sent me to baptize with water[v] told
me, 'The man on whom you see the Spirit
come down and remain is he who will
baptize with the Holy Spirit.'[w] 34I have
seen and I testify that this is the Son of
God."[x]

Jesus' First Disciples

1:40–42pp — Mt 4:18–22; Mk 1:16–20; Lk 5:2–11

35The next day John[y] was there again
with two of his disciples. 36When he saw
Jesus passing by, he said, "Look, the
Lamb of God!"[z]
37When the two disciples heard him
say this, they followed Jesus. 38Turning
around, Jesus saw them following and
asked, "What do you want?"
They said, "Rabbi"[a] (which means
Teacher), "where are you staying?"
39"Come," he replied, "and you will
see."
So they went and saw where he was

1:27 [o]ver 15,30 [p]Mk 1:7
1:28 [q]Jn 3:26; 10:40
1:29 [r]ver 36; Ge 22:8; Isa 53:7; 1Pe 1:19; Rev 5:6; 13:8 [s]S Jn 3:17
1:30 [t]ver 15,27
1:32 [u]Mt 3:16
1:33 [v]S Mk 1:4 [w]S Mk 1:8
1:34 [x]ver 49; S Mt 4:3
1:35 [y]S Mt 3:1
1:36 [z]S ver 29
1:38 [a]ver 49; S Mt 23:7
1:41 [b]Jn 4:25
1:42 [c]Ge 17:5,15; 32:28; 35:10 [d]Mt 16:18
1:43 [e]Mt 10:3; Jn 6:5-7; 12:21,22; 14:8,9 [f]S Mt 4:19
1:44 [g]S Mt 11:21
1:45 [h]Jn 21:2 [i]S Lk 24:27 [j]S Lk 24:27 [k]S Mk 1:24 [l]Lk 3:23
1:46 [m]Jn 7:41,42, 52
1:47 [n]Ro 9:4,6 [o]Ps 32:2
1:49 [p]ver 38; S Mt 23:7 [q]ver 34; S Mt 4:3 [r]S Mt 2:2; 27:42; Jn 12:13

staying, and spent that day with him. It
was about the tenth hour.
40Andrew, Simon Peter's brother, was
one of the two who heard what John had
said and who had followed Jesus. 41The
first thing Andrew did was to find his
brother Simon and tell him, "We have
found the Messiah" (that is, the Christ).[b]
42And he brought him to Jesus.
Jesus looked at him and said, "You are
Simon son of John. You will be called[c]
Cephas" (which, when translated, is Peter[j]).[d]

Jesus Calls Philip and Nathanael

43The next day Jesus decided to leave
for Galilee. Finding Philip,[e] he said to
him, "Follow me."[f]
44Philip, like Andrew and Peter, was
from the town of Bethsaida.[g] 45Philip
found Nathanael[h] and told him, "We
have found the one Moses wrote about in
the Law,[i] and about whom the prophets
also wrote[j]—Jesus of Nazareth,[k] the
son of Joseph."[l]
46"Nazareth! Can anything good come
from there?"[m] Nathanael asked.
"Come and see," said Philip.
47When Jesus saw Nathanael approaching, he said of him, "Here is a true Israelite,[n] in whom there is nothing false."[o]
48"How do you know me?" Nathanael
asked.
Jesus answered, "I saw you while you
were still under the fig tree before Philip
called you."
49Then Nathanael declared, "Rabbi,[p]
you are the Son of God;[q] you are the
King of Israel."[r]
50Jesus said, "You believe[k] because I
told you I saw you under the fig tree. You

[j]42 Both *Cephas* (Aramaic) and *Peter* (Greek) mean *rock.* [k]50 Or *Do you believe . . . ?*

---

the Messiah because the Holy Spirit came down like a dove and remained on Him. This is the plainest statement we have as to why John baptized. He was and is a powerful witness to the messiahship of Jesus as the Son of God. See note on Mt 3:4–17.

1:29,36 JESUS CHRIST, Lamb of God—A lamb symbolized the Jewish sacrifices (Ex 12:3–4,21; 13:13; 29:38–41; Lev 4:32; 14:10; Nu 29:7–11). The Suffering Servant was pictured as a sacrificial lamb (Isa 53). Jesus took up all the rich symbolism of Jewish sacrifice on Himself, dying as the Passover Lamb, leading out of slavery to sin, and suffering as the Servant for the sins of many. Through Christ the Lamb atonement is available.

1:29–31 REVELATION, Jesus Christ—God worked out a plan of revelation. He introduced the Old Testament system of sacrifices to help people know their need of salvation and the means to restore right relationship with God. He sent John to prepare the way for Jesus and testify about Him. He sent Jesus to accomplish what the sacrificial system introduced—saving relationship to God.

1:29 SALVATION, Atonement—John the Baptist points to Jesus as God's Lamb, who makes atonement for the world's sin. See note on Lev 1:4.

1:32–33 HOLY SPIRIT, Jesus—See note on Mt 3:11.

1:33 REVELATION, Spirit—God revealed to John that he would see the Spirit come to the Messiah. At Jesus' baptism, the Spirit of God revealed Jesus as the Son of God to John. He then revealed this to others through his testimony. The revelation chain here included private experience with God, the Spirit's testimony, and John's human witness.

1:38 EDUCATION, Jesus—In the Gospels, Jesus is often called "Rabbi." See note on Mt 23:8. Here the writer translated the term for his Gentile readers. It means "Teacher." See Jn 20:16.

1:41 JESUS CHRIST, Christ—See note on Mt 16:16.

1:41 EVANGELISM, Personal—Personal evangelism creates a chain of witnesses. John pointed Andrew to Christ. Andrew brought his brother Simon to Jesus. Andrew used a simple personal testimony to win his brother. We who know the Savior need to tell others and create a chain of witnesses.

1:45 JESUS CHRIST, Fulfilled—Jesus was the goal of the Old Testament. The Scripture points to Him. Compare Lk 24:44–47.

1:49 JESUS CHRIST, King—Jesus fulfilled all Israel's messianic expectations. See note on Mt 27:11.

shall see greater things than that." 51 He
then added, "I tell you[t] the truth, you[t]
shall see heaven open,[s] and the angels of
God ascending and descending[t] on the
Son of Man."[u]

Chapter 2

Jesus Changes Water to Wine

ON the third day a wedding took place
at Cana in Galilee.[v] Jesus' mother[w]
was there, 2 and Jesus and his disciples
had also been invited to the wedding.
3 When the wine was gone, Jesus' mother
said to him, "They have no more wine."
4 "Dear woman,[x] why do you involve
me?"[y] Jesus replied. "My time[z] has not
yet come."
5 His mother said to the servants, "Do
whatever he tells you."[a]
6 Nearby stood six stone water jars, the
kind used by the Jews for ceremonial
washing,[b] each holding from twenty to
thirty gallons.[m]
7 Jesus said to the servants, "Fill the jars
with water"; so they filled them to the
brim.
8 Then he told them, "Now draw some
out and take it to the master of the banquet."
They did so, 9 and the master of the
banquet tasted the water that had been
turned into wine.[c] He did not realize
where it had come from, though the servants who had drawn the water knew.
Then he called the bridegroom aside
10 and said, "Everyone brings out the
choice wine first and then the cheaper
wine after the guests have had too much
to drink; but you have saved the best till
now."
11 This, the first of his miraculous
signs,[d] Jesus performed at Cana in Galilee. He thus revealed his glory,[e] and his
disciples put their faith in him.[f]

Jesus Clears the Temple

2:14–16pp — Mt 21:12,13; Mk 11:15–17; Lk 19:45,46

12 After this he went down to Capernaum[g] with his mother[h] and brothers[i]
and his disciples. There they stayed for a
few days.
13 When it was almost time for the Jewish Passover,[j] Jesus went up to Jerusa-

[l]*51* The Greek is plural. [m]*6* Greek *two to three metretes* (probably about 75 to 115 liters)

1:51 [s]S Mt 3:16 [t]Ge 28:12 [u]S Mt 8:20
2:1 [v]Jn 4:46; 21:2 [w]S Mt 12:46
2:4 [x]Jn 19:26 [y]S Mt 8:29 [z]S Mt 26:18
2:5 [a]Ge 41:55
2:6 [b]Mk 7:3,4; Jn 3:25
2:9 [c]Jn 4:46
2:11 [d]ver 23; Mt 12:38; Jn 3:2; S 4:48; 6:2,14,26, 30; 12:37; 20:30 [e]Jn 1:14 [f]Ex 14:31
2:12 [g]S Mt 4:13 [h]S Mt 12:46 [i]S Mt 12:46
2:13 [j]S Jn 11:55

1:51 JESUS CHRIST, Son of Man—See note on Mk 10:45. Jesus was the ladder connecting heaven and earth and bringing heavenly revelation to earth. Compare Ge 28:12. In His ministry the disciples knew God was present with His people.
2:1–11 JESUS CHRIST, Miracles—There is a notable shift of terms, meaning, and frequency of Jesus' mighty works from the Synoptic Gospels to the Fourth Gospel. In the first three Gospels the miracles are called *dunameis*, mighty works or miracles. Their primary significance is to demonstrate the power of the kingdom of God. Such mighty works occur frequently in the Synoptics. John's designation for the mighty works is sign (Greek *semeion*). Jesus' term is work (Greek *ergon*; 17:4). Even the words of Jesus, in John, are part of His work (14:10). The signs in John are symbolic acts signifying what God will ultimately do for the redeemed. Compare Rev 21:1–8. The signs in John's Gospel are accompanied with discourses or explanations of their meaning. There are only seven signs in John (2:1–11; 4:46–54; 5:1–9; 6:5–13; 6:19–21; 9:1–41; 11:1–44). The signs point readers to faith in Christ so they may participate in eternal life. The first sign shows the water of purification so central to Jewish practice replaced by wine, the symbol of Jesus' blood. Jesus is the only way to purification before God. Ritual will not work. In Jesus, God's kingdom has entered the world revealing God's glory. See note on 1:14.
2:1–11 MIRACLE, Vocabulary—John emphasized Jesus' miracles as signs revealing Jesus' glory, His magnificent divine presence. Such revelation leads disciples to faith. This is the first of seven major signs in John's Gospel prior to the resurrection. See notes on 2:1–11; 4:46–54; 5:1–16; 6:3–15; 6:16–34; 9:1–41; 11:1–44. Such signs were not overwhelming proofs accepted by all people who witnessed them. Some people simply sought further miraculous works for their own selfish needs. Some wanted the sign power used to restore political power and domination to Israel. Some saw the signs as blasphemy and sought to kill Jesus for them. Only faith could recognize Jesus' divine glory in the signs. In His glory we see Him as He is—the only Son from the Father. This glory is not revealed in political power but in the sacrificial death on the cross and in the resurrection. In Jesus we have the best that God can give us. He surpasses all other revelations. Religion which does not center in faith in Christ is false because it ignores God's Best.
2:1–11 CHRISTIAN ETHICS, Alcohol—This incident, the first of Jesus' messianic signs, shows Jesus easily fitting into the enjoyment of the occasion of the Cana wedding. Jesus provides the drink expected at the messianic banquet and replaces the water of purification in the Jewish rituals with the choicest drink of His time. He provides abundantly for the people as was expected in the last days. See notes on Isa 25:6; Am 9:14.
2:4 HISTORY, Time—Jesus had appeared historically in time and space, but His time or hour had not come. This shows the biblical emphasis on time as content-oriented rather than calendar-oriented. Christ's time was the moment of decision, of crisis or opportunity. The time was His crucifixion and resurrection, historical events which revealed to the world God's commitment to history and to people and which set up the time of decision for all people to believe in Christ as Savior or reject Him. Compare 7:6,8,30; 8:20; 12:23; 13:1; 17:1; Mt 26:18; Mk 14:35,41. As God's Son, Jesus lived out His earthly life knowing His hour of sacrifice would come.
2:11,22–25 SALVATION, Belief—This is the first miraculous sign in the fourth Gospel. All the signs were intended to get persons to put their faith in Christ (20:31). John showed various levels of belief in Christ. The disciples trusted Jesus (v 11) but came to deeper understanding in their faith only after the resurrection (v 22). The crowds believed He had Messiah's powers, but they did not have faith which Jesus could trust with His own secrets concerning the nature of Messiah (vv 23–25). Nicodemus recognized Jesus' heavenly mission but still had to be born again (3:2–3). John warned against temporary faith resembling hero worship. He sought life-changing faith ready to feed Christ's sheep and share Christ's death.
2:12–22 JESUS CHRIST, Authority—See note on Mk 11:12–31. The Temple was not the eternal way to God's presence. Jesus Christ is. He established Himself as the authoritative way to God by cleansing the Temple and by predicting His own death and resurrection. The resurrection is the ultimate sign of Jesus as the way to God's presence. See note on Lk 24:1–53.

lem.[k] 14In the temple courts he found
men selling cattle, sheep and doves,[l] and
others sitting at tables exchanging money.[m] 15So he made a whip out of cords,
and drove all from the temple area, both
sheep and cattle; he scattered the coins of
the money changers and overturned their
tables. 16To those who sold doves he said,
"Get these out of here! How dare you
turn my Father's house[n] into a market!"

17His disciples remembered that it is
written: "Zeal for your house will consume me."[n] [o]

18Then the Jews[p] demanded of him,
"What miraculous sign[q] can you show us
to prove your authority to do all this?"[r]

19Jesus answered them, "Destroy this
temple, and I will raise it again in three
days."[s]

20The Jews replied, "It has taken forty-
six years to build this temple, and you are
going to raise it in three days?" 21But the
temple he had spoken of was his body.[t]
22After he was raised from the dead, his
disciples recalled what he had said.[u]
Then they believed the Scripture[v] and
the words that Jesus had spoken.

23Now while he was in Jerusalem at
the Passover Feast,[w] many people saw
the miraculous signs[x] he was doing and
believed[y] in his name.[o] 24But Jesus
would not entrust himself to them, for he
knew all men. 25He did not need man's
testimony about man,[z] for he knew what
was in a man.[a]

Chapter 3

Jesus Teaches Nicodemus

NOW there was a man of the Pharisees
named Nicodemus,[b] a member of
the Jewish ruling council.[c] 2He came to
Jesus at night and said, "Rabbi,[d] we
know[e] you are a teacher who has come
from God. For no one could perform the
miraculous signs[f] you are doing if God
were not with him."[g]

3In reply Jesus declared, "I tell you the
truth, no one can see the kingdom of God
unless he is born again.[p]"[h] [i]

4"How can a man be born when he is
old?" Nicodemus asked. "Surely he cannot enter a second time into his mother's
womb to be born!"

5Jesus answered, "I tell you the truth,
no one can enter the kingdom of God unless he is born of water and the Spirit.[j] [k]

2:13 [k]Dt 16:1-6; Lk 2:41
2:14 [l]Lev 1:14; Dt 14:26 [m]Dt 14:25
2:16 [n]Lk 2:49
2:17 [o]Ps 69:9
2:18 [p]S Jn 1:19 [q]S ver 11 [r]S Mt 12:38
2:19 [s]S Mt 16:21; 26:61; 27:40; Mk 14:58; 15:29; Ac 6:14
2:21 [t]1Co 6:19
2:22 [u]Lk 24:5-8; Jn 12:16; 14:26 [v]Ps 16:10; S Lk 24:27
2:23 [w]ver 13 [x]S ver 11 [y]S Jn 3:15
2:25 [z]Isa 11:3 [a]Dt 31:21; 1Ki 8:39; S Mt 9:4; Jn 6:61,64; 13:11
3:1 [b]Jn 7:50; 19:39 [c]Lk 23:13
3:2 [d]S Mt 23:7 [e]ver 11 [f]S Jn 2:11 [g]Jn 10:38; 14:10, 11; Ac 2:22; 10:38
3:3 [h]S Jn 1:13 [i]S Mt 3:2
3:5 [j]S Ac 22:16 [k]Tit 3:5

[n]*17* Psalm 69:9 [o]*23* Or *and believed in him*
[p]*3* Or *born from above*; also in verse 7

2:23–25 JESUS CHRIST, Miracles—Jesus' miracles showed the crowds He was the true Passover Lamb providing delivery from sin. The faith brought by the signs placed the crowds closer to Jesus than were the spiritually blind people in the Temple. They did not have saving faith, entrusting their lives to Christ. As God's Son, Jesus could see all their thoughts and knew they were attracted to His power, not to His mission which was to reveal God and His salvation.

3:1–15 SALVATION, As New Birth—Nicodemus was exhibit A of the truth of 2:25. He was a real person; yet he represented all people. What Jesus said to him in vv 3,7, He says to all. The only way to enter the kingdom of God is through the new birth. "Born again" means born from above. It is the work of God and not the work of human beings. It is the new birth which the Holy Spirit gives. Being born again is mysterious like the blowing of the wind. It is a miracle after the analogy of the virgin birth of Jesus Christ (Mt 1:18–25; Lk 1:34–35) and that of the first creation (Ge 1:1–2). We get our phrases new birth, second birth, twice-born, regeneration, and born again primarily from this passage. Vv 14–15 are crucial to answering the how of the new birth. They refer to the incident in Nu 21:4–9. The new birth is possible through Christ's sacrificial death on the cross and through faith in Him as God's antidote for the poison of sin (Jn 8:28; 12:32–33). "Eternal life" is another way of referring to the kingdom of God in John's Gospel. The new birth is the door to eternal life. Compare 1:13; Eze 37:1–10; 2 Co 5:17; Eph 2:15; Tit 3:5; 1 Pe 1:3,23; Rev 21:5.

3:2 JESUS CHRIST, Teaching—In the New Testament, Jesus is many times spoken of as teaching. Nicodemus recognized Jesus as a Rabbi, one of the many Jewish interpreters of the Law who gathered disciples and performed authenticating signs. Nicodemus acknowledged that Jesus came from God, responding to Jesus' mighty works. Compare 1:38,49; 3:2,26; 6:25; 20:16. This term implies all the traditional reverence and respect which Judaism had for wisdom and instruction. Jesus was critical of an exaggerated place of teachers who desired compliments more than service (Mt 23:7–8). He knew Nicodemus' respectful form of address did not issue from a heart of saving faith. Jesus must be seen as more than a powerful teacher.

3:2 MIRACLE, Vocabulary—For Nicodemus the signs signified that God was with Jesus and authenticated Jesus as a Teacher of God's truth. Nicodemus did not question the miraculous nature of His works. See note on 2:1–11.

3:3–5 ORDINANCES, Baptism as New Life—The words "born of water and the Spirit" have been a battleground of interpretation. Bible students have seen (1) John's baptism and Jesus'; (2) baptism and Pentecost; (3) a demand for humble submission by a Jewish leader to water baptism before expecting to receive God's Spirit; (4) reception of Christ's word or teaching as well as the Spirit; and (5) spiritual cleansing and the Spirit's power. The immediate context compels us to see the primary contrast between the physical birth (which Nicodemus asked about) and the new birth (or birth from above) which Jesus said is essential in order to see the kingdom of God. There is also a contrast, just two chapters earlier in this same Gospel (1:26,33), between John's water baptism and Jesus' Spirit baptism. That may be in the background of this saying, but it cannot refer to Christian baptism at this point in Jesus' ministry because it had not been given or commanded yet. Because the Greek has no article ("the") with Spirit, it would be ungrammatical to separate water from Spirit. Probably both water and wind (spirit) symbolize the powerful activity of the Holy Spirit in the new birth. The main point is abundantly clear: physical birth is not enough; one must be born again spiritually to enter the kingdom of heaven. The contrast is emphasized in v 6.

3:5–6 HOLY SPIRIT, Regenerates—See note on Eze 37:12–14. Jesus surprised Nicodemus by saying that even religious leaders such as Pharisees must be born again to enter the kingdom of God. He described the new birth as a work of the Spirit (vv 5–6). Other similar ideas include a new age (Col 1:26), a new creation (2 Co 5:17), a new covenant (1 Co 11:25), a new creature (Gal 5:16), a new man (Eph 4:24), and regeneration (Tit 3:5–6). In Christ all things are new (2 Co 5:17). The Spirit as the giver of life is specifically affirmed by John (6:63) and Paul (Ro 8:2).

[6]Flesh gives birth to flesh, but the Spirit[q]
gives birth to spirit.[l] [7]You should not be
surprised at my saying, 'You[r] must be
born again.' [8]The wind blows wherever it
pleases. You hear its sound, but you cannot tell where it comes from or where it
is going. So it is with everyone born of
the Spirit."[m]

[9]"How can this be?"[n] Nicodemus
asked.

[10]"You are Israel's teacher,"[o] said
Jesus, "and do you not understand these
things? [11]I tell you the truth, we speak of
what we know,[p] and we testify to what
we have seen, but still you people do not
accept our testimony.[q] [12]I have spoken to
you of earthly things and you do not believe; how then will you believe if I speak
of heavenly things? [13]No one has ever
gone into heaven[r] except the one who
came from heaven[s]—the Son of Man.[s] [t]
[14]Just as Moses lifted up the snake in the
desert,[u] so the Son of Man must be lifted
up,[v] [15]that everyone who believes[w] in
him may have eternal life.[t] [x]

[16]"For God so loved[y] the world that he
gave[z] his one and only Son,[u] [a] that whoever believes[b] in him shall not perish but
have eternal life.[c] [17]For God did not send
his Son into the world[d] to condemn the
world, but to save the world through
him.[e] [18]Whoever believes in him is not
condemned,[f] but whoever does not believe stands condemned already because
he has not believed in the name of God's
one and only Son.[v] [g] [19]This is the verdict: Light[h] has come into the world, but
men loved darkness instead of light because their deeds were evil.[i] [20]Everyone
who does evil hates the light, and will not
come into the light for fear that his deeds
will be exposed.[j] [21]But whoever lives by
the truth comes into the light, so that it
may be seen plainly that what he has
done has been done through God."[w]

John the Baptist's Testimony About Jesus

[22]After this, Jesus and his disciples

3:6 [l]S Jn 1:13; 1Co 15:50 **3:8** [m]1Co 2:14-16 **3:9** [n]Jn 6:52,60 **3:10** [o]Lk 2:46 **3:11** [p]Jn 1:18; 7:16,17 [q]ver 32 **3:13** [r]Pr 30:4; Ac 2:34; Eph 4:8-10 [s]ver 31; Jn 6:38,42; Heb 4:14; 9:24 [t]S Mt 8:20 **3:14** [u]Nu 21:8,9 [v]S Jn 12:32 **3:15** [w]ver 16,36; Ge 15:6; Nu 14:11; Mt 27:42; Mk 1:15; Jn 1:7,12; 2:23; 5:24; 7:38; 20:29; Ac 13:39; 16:31; Ro 3:22; 10:9,10; 1Jn 5:1,5,10 [x]ver 16,36; S Mt 25:46; Jn 20:31 **3:16** [y]Ro 5:8; Eph 2:4; 1Jn 4:9,10 [z]Isa 9:6; Ro 8:32 [a]Ge 22:12; Jn 1:18 [b]S ver 15 [c]ver 36; Jn 6:29,40; 11:25,26 **3:17** [d]Jn 6:29,57; 10:36; 11:42; 17:8,21; 20:21 [e]Isa 53:11; S Mt 1:21; S Lk 2:11; 19:10; Jn 1:29; 12:47; S Ro 11:14; 1Ti 1:15; 2:5,6; 1Jn 2:2; 3:5

3:18 [f]Jn 5:24 [g]Jn 1:18; 1Jn 4:9 **3:19** [h]S Jn 1:4 [i]Ps 52:3; Jn 7:7 **3:20** [j]Eph 5:11,13

[q]*6* Or *but spirit* [r]*7* The Greek is plural.
[s]*13* Some manuscripts *Man, who is in heaven*
[t]*15* Or *believes may have eternal life in him*
[u]*16* Or *his only begotten Son* [v]*18* Or *God's only begotten Son* [w]*21* Some interpreters end the quotation after verse 15.

3:8 HOLY SPIRIT, Freedom—Jesus affirmed two things about the Spirit here: freedom and mystery. The Spirit (Greek *pneuma*) moves about just as freely as the wind (Greek *pneuma*). No religious group controls Him. No religious doctrine fully defines or confines Him. He is at liberty to move about exactly as He pleases. The Spirit works to regenerate all ungodly people, even pious Pharisees. The reminder is still needed today in the church. The movement of the Spirit is mysterious, like the wind. You cannot see the wind; you can only see the results of its moving, such as the movement of tree branches. You cannot see the Spirit; you can only see the results of His works, such as the changed lives of those who have been born again. Both the freedom and the mystery of the Spirit suggest that He is divine, for only God is utterly free and utterly mysterious.

3:10 EDUCATION, Scribes and Pharisees—Nicodemus, a Pharisee and respected teacher, was schooled in the Old Testament Scriptures. Yet, he did not comprehend Jesus' reference to a new birth, even though the prophet Ezekiel had used similar language. See Eze 36:26. Here is living proof that a teacher may have a comprehensive knowledge of the Scriptures, yet be lacking in spiritual insight.

3:12–16,36 SALVATION, Belief—Nicodemus, a blue-blooded intellectual of Israel, had trouble believing in Jesus. Yet, then and now, whoever believes in Jesus as the Son of God has eternal life. Total commitment to Jesus is the one requirement for salvation.

3:13–15 JESUS CHRIST, Preexistent—See note on Mk 10:45. Jesus' home is heaven, not earth. No other human can say this. He chose to obey the Father, come to earth, and be lifted up on the cross for our sins to give us eternal life.

3:15–16,36 SALVATION, Eternal Life—Eternal life is another term for the kingdom of God and the new birth in the fourth Gospel. It is the present possession, as well as a future hope, for all persons who believe in the Son of God. God loves the world so much that He sent His Son to die on the cross to give eternal life to those who trust in Him. He does not want anyone to perish in sin, but those who reject His Son are already living under the wrath of God. They need to believe and know eternal life. See "How to Accept Christ" pp. 1745–1747.

3:16 GOD, Love—The most profound expression of the love of God for us is the gift of His only Son to be our Savior. The word translated love here is one of special significance, meaning a love that seeks to give itself away in behalf of its object. It is a love that seeks the best interests of its object while seeking nothing for itself in return. Notice that v 17 states the priority of God's purpose to save over judgment or condemnation. For this reason God is declared to be love (1 Jn 4:8,16). See note on Mk 1:11.

3:16–18 JESUS CHRIST, Son of God—See note on 1:18. Jesus is God's salvation gift to the world. His purpose is salvation, not condemnation. He is the only path to full salvation.

3:17–18 SALVATION, Initiative—God loved the world so much that He sent His only begotten Son, the only One of His kind, to save the world and not to condemn it. "World" here means that part of humankind which is in rebellion against God, as well as the physical world.

3:18–21 SIN, Individual Choice—Jesus, the Light (8:12), reveals us for what we are: either of God or not. The Son of God demands that we either believe in Him and come into the light or else reject Him and remain in darkness. No neutral position can be taken. Jesus confronts each one of us with these two choices. We refuse to believe because our depraved lifestyles prefer sin to Jesus. Such depravity comes because we choose evil deeds. Such depravity makes us guilty and fearful. We know our wickedness becomes evident in the presence of Jesus' purity. Even so, we are not beyond hope. Jesus came to save sinners.

3:19 JESUS CHRIST, Light—See note on 1:4–5.

3:19–21 CHRISTIAN ETHICS, Character—Evil character causes people to reject Christ. People are totally devoted in love to the darkness of the world's way, or they are ready to have their lives examined and changed by the Light of the world, Jesus. Persons devoted to evil fear what the Light would reveal in their lives. Persons dedicated to truth in knowledge and in action come to Christ and give evidence that God is at work in Christ's coming.

3:22–26 ORDINANCES, Baptism by Jesus—Only John's Gospel gives an account of Jesus' ministry in Judea, paralleling the ministry of John the Baptist. Jesus' ministry brought two areas of conflict: with the Jews who wanted to interpret John's baptism as some kind of ceremonial washing like they practiced and with John's disciples who were jealous of the re-

went out into the Judean countryside,
where he spent some time with them,
and baptized.[k] 23Now John[l] also was
baptizing at Aenon near Salim, because
there was plenty of water, and people
were constantly coming to be baptized.
24(This was before John was put in prison.)[m] 25An argument developed between
some of John's disciples and a certain
Jew[x] over the matter of ceremonial
washing.[n] 26They came to John and said
to him, "Rabbi,[o] that man who was with
you on the other side of the Jordan—the
one you testified[p] about—well, he is
baptizing, and everyone is going to him."
27To this John replied, "A man can receive only what is given him from heav-
en. 28You yourselves can testify that I
said, 'I am not the Christ[y] but am sent
ahead of him.'[q] 29The bride belongs to
the bridegroom.[r] The friend who attends
the bridegroom waits and listens for him,
and is full of joy when he hears the bridegroom's voice. That joy is mine, and it is
now complete.[s] 30He must become greater; I must become less.

31"The one who comes from above[t] is
above all; the one who is from the earth
belongs to the earth, and speaks as one
from the earth.[u] The one who comes
from heaven is above all. 32He testifies to
what he has seen and heard,[v] but no one
accepts his testimony.[w] 33The man who
has accepted it has certified that God is
truthful. 34For the one whom God has
sent[x] speaks the words of God, for God[z]
gives the Spirit[y] without limit. 35The Father loves the Son and has placed everything in his hands.[z] 36Whoever believes
in the Son has eternal life,[a] but whoever
rejects the Son will not see life, for God's
wrath remains on him."[a]

Chapter 4

Jesus Talks With a Samaritan Woman

THE Pharisees heard that Jesus was
gaining and baptizing more disciples
than John,[b] 2although in fact it was not

3:22 [k]Jn 4:2
3:23 [l]S Mt 3:1
3:24 [m]Mt 4:12; 14:3
3:25 [n]Jn 2:6
3:26 [o]S Mt 23:7 [p]Jn 1:7
3:28 [q]Jn 1:20,23
3:29 [r]Mt 9:15 [s]Jn 16:24; 17:13; Php 2:2; 1Jn 1:4; 2Jn 12
3:31 [t]ver 13 [u]Jn 8:23; 1Jn 4:5
3:32 [v]Jn 8:26; 15:15 [w]ver 11
3:34 [x]S ver 17 [y]Isa 42:1; Mt 12:18; Lk 4:18; Ac 10:38
3:35 [z]S Mt 28:18
3:36 [a]S ver 15; Jn 5:24; 6:47
4:1 [b]Jn 3:22,26

[x]*25* Some manuscripts *and certain Jews* [y]*28* Or *Messiah* [z]*34* Greek *he* [a]*36* Some interpreters end the quotation after verse 30.

sponse to Jesus. John was true to his witness in 1:26–34, rejoicing that Christ the "bridegroom" had come and must become greater. John's baptism was very different from the Levitical rituals of washing. It was the sign of the Messianic Age, which Jesus was bringing to fulfillment in His ministry. See note on 4:1–2.

3:27–30 JESUS CHRIST, John—John promoted Jesus at the cost of his own popularity. See note on 1:19–34.

3:29 SALVATION, Joy—The coming of Christ makes the joy of God's people complete.

3:30 EVANGELISM, Holy Life—The power of a holy life is vital to effective evangelization. Humility is a strong characteristic of such a life. John exemplified that quality. He understood his position in the light of the person and ministry of Jesus. Humility is an honest evaluation of oneself in the light of Christ.

3:31–36 JESUS CHRIST, Son of God—See note on 3:13–15. Jesus is the true source of revelation because only He has had intimate experiences with the Father in heaven. To accept His testimony is to trust God's truthfulness. Jesus' words are from God. In love God has given Jesus all authority. Compare 5:22,26–27; 6:37; 12:49; 17:2,6,8,11–12,22. Belief in Christ as God's divine Son is the standard for eternal judgment.

3:33 GOD, Faithfulness—Jesus testified to God's saving love. A small minority accepted His testimony. By so doing they proclaimed that God is truthful; He does what He says He will do. Despite the control exercised by the Roman government, the Jews should not lose hope. God in sending Jesus had provided the way to eternal life, a way much more desirable than a way to eternal political power. God had been and always will be true to His plans, not to the way we interpret His plans.

3:33 SALVATION, Acceptance—Acceptance of Christ's testimony is certification of God's truthfulness. Christ testifies to God's saving love for all people.

3:34–36 GOD, Trinity—The Father loves the Son and trusts Him with everything. He communicates and empowers Him without limit through the Spirit. He places His entire work of salvation in the hands of the Son. Confidence in God's faithfulness rests on the testimony of the Son. Here we clearly see the close relationship among the three Persons of the Trinity and yet the different spheres of work. While the identity of the Father and the Son is clearly separate, remember that They are nevertheless One. All that Jesus said or did was at the same time the work of the Father through Him. In His human experience here on earth, Jesus subordinated Himself to God the Father. The infinite Jesus humbled Himself to accept the limitations of human life according to Php 2:5–11. See note on Mt 24:36. God the Father was working through Jesus the Son in ways that go beyond any and all human limitations. This is the mystery of the Trinity on the one hand and the mystery of the incarnation on the other hand.

3:34 HOLY SPIRIT, Indwells—The Spirit guided Jesus in His words, just as He guided the prophets before Him. The gift of the Spirit to Jesus was even greater than the gift to the prophets. The prophets received the Spirit only temporarily as they received and proclaimed a specific message, but Jesus had the Spirit without limit, that is, permanently and in everything He did. The generalized wording of the verse may be intentional to indicate that God continues to give His church the Spirit without limit to live out and proclaim the gospel. The church must appropriate the work of the Spirit, following Christ's example. Jesus totally appropriated and followed the Spirit's guidance.

3:36 GOD, Wrath—The wrath of God is as real as His love, even though the priority clearly falls on the love of God as He relates to sinful people. Note vv 16–17. God's wrath is not a fit of uncontrolled anger. It is the inevitable suffering and destruction that we bring upon ourselves when we refuse to let God's love have its way. See notes on Ge 6:5–8; 19:13,24–26. The hand of God which reaches out to bless in love becomes a hand of judgment when we refuse to accept the blessing offered. Wrath comes upon anyone who rejects Jesus, the Savior God sent to give us eternal life.

4:1–43 CHRISTIAN ETHICS, Race Relations—No social barrier is too extreme for the gospel message to cross. The Samaritian woman was an outcast to Jewish society on at least two counts: mixed ethnic lineage and an unacceptable marital situation. Jesus demonstrated by His actions, however, that each person has worth. Social or racial standing never places a person beyond the touch of grace. Contemporary attempts to discriminate, to stereotype, and to paternalize those ethnically different from us find their source in prejudice and a false sense of superiority which in turn stem from our sinful nature.

4:1–2 ORDINANCES, Baptism by Jesus—Only John's Gospel tells us that Jesus carried on a ministry in Judea at the same time as John the Baptist. Nothing is said about Jesus baptizing in the Spirit (1:33). That was to come later. The

Jesus who baptized, but his disciples.
3 When the Lord[c] learned of this, he left
Judea[d] and went back once more to Galilee.
4 Now he had to go through Samaria.[e]
5 So he came to a town in Samaria called
Sychar, near the plot of ground Jacob had
given to his son Joseph.[f] 6 Jacob's well
was there, and Jesus, tired as he was from
the journey, sat down by the well. It was
about the sixth hour.
7 When a Samaritan woman came to
draw water, Jesus said to her, "Will you
give me a drink?"[g] 8 (His disciples had
gone into the town[h] to buy food.)
9 The Samaritan woman said to him,
"You are a Jew and I am a Samaritan[i]
woman. How can you ask me for a
drink?" (For Jews do not associate with
Samaritans.[b])
10 Jesus answered her, "If you knew the
gift of God and who it is that asks you for
a drink, you would have asked him and
he would have given you living water."[j]
11 "Sir," the woman said, "you have
nothing to draw with and the well is
deep. Where can you get this living water? 12 Are you greater than our father Jacob, who gave us the well[k] and drank
from it himself, as did also his sons and
his flocks and herds?"
13 Jesus answered, "Everyone who
drinks this water will be thirsty again,
14 but whoever drinks the water I give
him will never thirst.[l] Indeed, the water
I give him will become in him a spring of
water[m] welling up to eternal life."[n]
15 The woman said to him, "Sir, give
me this water so that I won't get thirsty[o]
and have to keep coming here to draw
water."
16 He told her, "Go, call your husband
and come back."
17 "I have no husband," she replied.
Jesus said to her, "You are right when
you say you have no husband. 18 The fact
is, you have had five husbands, and the
man you now have is not your husband.
What you have just said is quite true."
19 "Sir," the woman said, "I can see
that you are a prophet.[p] 20 Our fathers
worshiped on this mountain,[q] but you
Jews claim that the place where we must
worship is in Jerusalem."[r]
21 Jesus declared, "Believe me, woman,
a time is coming[s] when you will worship
the Father neither on this mountain nor
in Jerusalem.[t] 22 You Samaritans worship
what you do not know;[u] we worship
what we do know, for salvation is from
the Jews.[v] 23 Yet a time is coming and has
now come[w] when the true worshipers
will worship the Father in spirit[x] and
truth, for they are the kind of worshipers
the Father seeks. 24 God is spirit,[y] and his

[b] 9 Or *do not use dishes Samaritans have used*

4:3 [c]S Lk 7:13 [d]Jn 3:22
4:4 [e]S Mt 10:5
4:5 [f]Ge 33:19; Jos 24:32
4:7 [g]Ge 24:17; 1Ki 17:10
4:8 [h]ver 5,39
4:9 [i]S Mt 10:5
4:10 [j]Isa 44:3; 55:1; Jer 2:13; 17:13; Zec 14:8; Jn 7:37,38; Rev 7:17; 21:6; 22:1,17
4:12 [k]ver 6
4:14 [l]Jn 6:35 [m]Isa 12:3; 58:11; Jn 7:38 [n]S Mt 25:46
4:15 [o]Jn 6:34
4:19 [p]S Mt 21:11
4:20 [q]Dt 11:29; Jos 8:33 [r]Lk 9:53
4:21 [s]Jn 5:28; 16:2 [t]Mal 1:11; 1Ti 2:8
4:22 [u]2Ki 17:28-41 [v]Isa 2:3; Ro 3:1,2; 9:4,5; 15:8,9
4:23 [w]Jn 5:25; 16:32 [x]Php 3:3
4:24 [y]Php 3:3

Gospel writer made clear that His disciples actually did the baptizing and not Jesus. Compare 3:22. The water baptism was a sign that identified the disciples of John and the disciples of Jesus. It has continued to be a sign that identifies Christian disciples until this day. That brought the crisis of these verses: word had reached the Pharisees that Jesus was "gaining and baptizing more disciples than John." This phrase meant that the official hostility toward John would be shifted to Jesus and might cut off His ministry before His "hour" had come. That is why Jesus left Judea and went back to Galilee (v 3).

4:1–42 EVANGELISM, Personal—In the Lord's dialog with the Samaritan woman we learn principles of how to do personal evangelism. A witness: (1) is concerned with one individual; (2) begins with felt needs and desires of the lost person; (3) directs the conversation to the person's basic spiritual need; (4) shows the person his or her sin and need of salvation; (5) keeps the conversation from straying from the real issue; (6) points to Jesus as Messiah and Savior; and (7) leads the new convert to witness to others. Today, Christians can follow Jesus' example and principles. See Guide to Counseling New Christians, pp. 1817–1818.

4:10 SALVATION, As Being in Christ—Believers live in Christ much like fish live in water. He is our natural element—the Water of life. Salvation means being "in Christ," asking Him for life, and living out the life available only in Him.

4:12 JESUS CHRIST, Fulfilled—Jesus surpassed all Israel's heroes of faith, even the founding father Jacob, also named Israel (v 6; Ge 32:28).

4:13–14 JESUS CHRIST, Life—See note on 1:4. Jesus quenches human spiritual thirst for meaning and thus represents life at its richest and fullest.

4:14,36 SALVATION, Eternal Life—Jesus is the Giver of eternal life. Eternal life is like an ever-flowing spring of living water. It is the crop which God's reapers are now harvesting, the gathering of the lost into God's kingdom.

4:17–19 JESUS CHRIST, Prophet—Jesus had greater prophetic powers than any of His predecessors, even Moses. Accepting Him as a prophet is not sufficient to gain eternal life.

4:19–24 WORSHIP, Buildings—Buildings are not essential for worship. Worship is not limited to any geographical location. The attitude of the human spirit is the only limiting factor in worship. See notes on Ge 28:16–22; 2 Sa 22:1–51; Mt 4:10.

4:21–23 GOD, One God—The most basic understanding of the Bible is that there is only one God. He is the universal God, the one and only God. He is not like the so-called gods of the nations, immobile and localized because they are chiseled out of stone or wood. With the teaching of Jesus, the understanding of God was broadened so that people would understand that God can be worshiped anywhere, not just in special localities.

4:23 HISTORY, Worship—Human controversies over proper places and times of worship lost their meaning in Jesus' coming. He introduced a new time, a new critical opportunity for decision into history. His coming was the decisive moment in the history of worship, leading all worshipers directly to the Father in spirit rather than material-dominated sacrificial ritual.

4:23–24 PRAYER, Worship—The opposite of spirit is flesh. Worship is not a performance to bring pride to those performing, be they preachers, singers, or laypersons. It is not performed for the sake of the performers or participants. It is an offering to God and must be done in that which is hidden, the spirit. The opposite of truth is falsehood. Worship must be genuine. Prayer pervades true worship seeking fellowship with God.

4:24 GOD, Spirit—God is spirit, not physical or material. He thus exists on a different plane from us and is not subject to the limitations of a physical body. God is deeply personal and can be worshiped only at the most intensely personal level, from our spirit to God as spirit. Worship is not offered to a

worshipers must worship in spirit and in
truth."
25 The woman said, "I know that Messiah" (called Christ)[z] "is coming. When
he comes, he will explain everything to
us."
26 Then Jesus declared, "I who speak to
you am he."[a]

The Disciples Rejoin Jesus

27 Just then his disciples returned[b] and
were surprised to find him talking with a
woman. But no one asked, "What do you
want?" or "Why are you talking with
her?"
28 Then, leaving her water jar, the
woman went back to the town and said to
the people, 29 "Come, see a man who told
me everything I ever did.[c] Could this be
the Christ[c]?"[d] 30 They came out of the
town and made their way toward him.
31 Meanwhile his disciples urged him,
"Rabbi,[e] eat something."
32 But he said to them, "I have food to
eat[f] that you know nothing about."
33 Then his disciples said to each other,
"Could someone have brought him
food?"
34 "My food," said Jesus, "is to do the
will[g] of him who sent me and to finish
his work.[h] 35 Do you not say, 'Four
months more and then the harvest'? I tell
you, open your eyes and look at the fields!
They are ripe for harvest.[i] 36 Even now
the reaper draws his wages, even now he
harvests[j] the crop for eternal life,[k] so
that the sower and the reaper may be
glad together. 37 Thus the saying 'One
sows and another reaps'[l] is true. 38 I sent
you to reap what you have not worked
for. Others have done the hard work, and
you have reaped the benefits of their labor."

Many Samaritans Believe

39 Many of the Samaritans from that
town[m] believed in him because of the
woman's testimony, "He told me everything I ever did."[n] 40 So when the Samaritans came to him, they urged him to stay
with them, and he stayed two days. 41 And
because of his words many more became
believers.
42 They said to the woman, "We no longer believe just because of what you said;
now we have heard for ourselves, and we
know that this man really is the Savior of
the world."[o]

Jesus Heals the Official's Son

43 After the two days[p] he left for Galilee. 44 (Now Jesus himself had pointed out
that a prophet has no honor in his own
country.)[q] 45 When he arrived in Galilee,
the Galileans welcomed him. They had
seen all that he had done in Jerusalem at
the Passover Feast,[r] for they also had
been there.
46 Once more he visited Cana in Galilee, where he had turned the water into
wine.[s] And there was a certain royal official whose son lay sick at Capernaum.
47 When this man heard that Jesus had arrived in Galilee from Judea,[t] he went to
him and begged him to come and heal his
son, who was close to death.
48 "Unless you people see miraculous
signs and wonders,"[u] Jesus told him,
"you will never believe."
49 The royal official said, "Sir, come
down before my child dies."
50 Jesus replied, "You may go. Your son
will live."
The man took Jesus at his word and
departed. 51 While he was still on the way,
his servants met him with the news that
his boy was living. 52 When he inquired as

4:25 [z]Mt 1:16; Jn 1:41
4:26 [a]Jn 8:24; 9:35-37
4:27 [b]ver 8
4:29 [c]ver 17,18 [d]Mt 12:23; Jn 7:26, 31
4:31 [e]S Mt 23:7
4:32 [f]Job 23:12; Mt 4:4; Jn 6:27
4:34 [g]S Mt 26:39 [h]S Jn 19:30
4:35 [i]Mt 9:37; Lk 10:2
4:36 [j]Ro 1:13 [k]S Mt 25:46
4:37 [l]Job 31:8; Mic 6:15
4:39 [m]ver 5 [n]ver 29
4:42 [o]S Lk 2:11
4:43 [p]ver 40
4:44 [q]Mt 13:57; Lk 4:24
4:45 [r]Jn 2:23
4:46 [s]Jn 2:1-11
4:47 [t]ver 3,54
4:48 [u]Da 4:2,3; S Jn 2:11; Ac 2:43; 14:3; Ro 15:19; 2Co 12:12; Heb 2:4

[c]29 Or *Messiah*

---

physical object or in a mechanical way. True worship of God must be in a personal relationship.
4:25–30 JESUS CHRIST, Christ—Even the Samaritans shared the messianic hope of Israel. Jesus used Old Testament language about God in accepting the designation as Messiah. See note on Mk 14:53—15:15. He admitted to Samaritans what He kept secret from Jews. See note on Mk 1:25,34.
4:34 JESUS CHRIST, Mission—Jesus did the Father's work in complete obedience.
4:39–42,48,53 SALVATION, Belief—Here are two contrasting examples of persons who became believers in Christ—Samaritans and a certain royal official. The biblical doctrine of salvation teaches that Jesus is indeed the Savior of the world, the Savior of all persons who believe no matter their background, influence, or personal history. See note on 2:11, 22–25.
4:42 JESUS CHRIST, Savior—Jesus is called Savior, an Old Testament word for God's work (Ps 24:5; Isa 17:10; 43:3; 45:21; 60:16; 62:11; Lk 1:47). Jesus is the source of salvation or deliverance from sin for all the world, even the Samaritans. Compare 1 Jn 4:14; Ac 1:8. See note on Lk 2:11.
4:46–54 JESUS CHRIST, Miracles—Compare Mt 8:5–13; Lk 7:1–10. See note on Jn 2:1–11. Miracles do not bring faith to those seeking spectacular power for selfish purposes. Miracles become a means to saving faith for those open to trust Christ despite all obstacles.
4:46–54 MIRACLE, Faith—Miracles should not be necessary for faith but can serve as an evangelistic tool leading people to faith. Jesus was upset because the people would not believe without miracles. The royal official needed only Christ's word (v 50; Greek *episteusen,* "believed") to believe. He told the story to his household, and all the members believed in Jesus. Compare Mt 8:5–13; Lk 7:1–10. See note on Jn 2:1–11.
4:50–54 REVELATION, Author of Life—Jesus is the Author and Sustainer of life with the Father and has power over life and death. Faith was sufficient to gain the gift of life restored. John arranged his gospel around seven major signs (2:1–11; 4:46–54; 5:1–15; 6:1–15; 6:16–21; 9:1–41; 11:1–57). Each sign reveals a unique feature of Jesus as the Messiah and Savior. Together they seek to lead readers to life-giving faith in Christ (20:30–31).

to the time when his son got better, they
said to him, "The fever left him yesterday
at the seventh hour."
53Then the father realized that this was
the exact time at which Jesus had said to
him, "Your son will live." So he and all
his household[v] believed.
54This was the second miraculous
sign[w] that Jesus performed, having come
from Judea to Galilee.

Chapter 5

The Healing at the Pool

SOME time later, Jesus went up to Jerusalem for a feast of the Jews. 2Now
there is in Jerusalem near the Sheep
Gate[x] a pool, which in Aramaic[y] is
called Bethesda[d] and which is surrounded by five covered colonnades. 3Here a
great number of disabled people used to
lie—the blind, the lame, the paralyzed.[e]
5One who was there had been an invalid
for thirty-eight years. 6When Jesus saw
him lying there and learned that he had
been in this condition for a long time, he
asked him, "Do you want to get well?"
7"Sir," the invalid replied, "I have no
one to help me into the pool when the
water is stirred. While I am trying to get
in, someone else goes down ahead of
me."
8Then Jesus said to him, "Get up! Pick
up your mat and walk."[z] 9At once the
man was cured; he picked up his mat and
walked.
The day on which this took place was a
Sabbath,[a] 10and so the Jews[b] said to the
man who had been healed, "It is the Sabbath; the law forbids you to carry your
mat."[c]
11But he replied, "The man who made
me well said to me, 'Pick up your mat and
walk.' "
12So they asked him, "Who is this fellow who told you to pick it up and walk?"
13The man who was healed had no idea
who it was, for Jesus had slipped away
into the crowd that was there.
14Later Jesus found him at the temple
and said to him, "See, you are well again.
Stop sinning[d] or something worse may
happen to you." 15The man went away
and told the Jews[e] that it was Jesus who
had made him well.

Life Through the Son

16So, because Jesus was doing these
things on the Sabbath, the Jews persecuted him. 17Jesus said to them, "My Father[f] is always at his work[g] to this very
day, and I, too, am working." 18For this

[d]2 Some manuscripts *Bethzatha*; other manuscripts *Bethsaida* [e]3 Some less important manuscripts *paralyzed—and they waited for the moving of the waters. 4From time to time an angel of the Lord would come down and stir up the waters. The first one into the pool after each such disturbance would be cured of whatever disease he had.*

4:53 [v]S Ac 11:14
4:54 [w]S ver 48; S Jn 2:11
5:2 [x]Ne 3:1; 12:39 [y]Jn 19:13,17,20; 20:16; Ac 21:40; 22:2; 26:14
5:8 [z]Mt 9:5,6
5:9 [a]Mt 12:1-14; Jn 9:14
5:10 [b]ver 16 [c]Ne 13:15-22; Jer 17:21; S Mt 12:2
5:14 [d]Mk 2:5; Jn 8:11
5:15 [e]S Jn 1:19
5:17 [f]Lk 2:49 [g]Jn 9:4; 14:10

5:1–15 JESUS CHRIST, Miracles—Compare Mt 9:1–8; Mk 2:1–12; Lk 5:18–26. The impact of Jesus' direct command of healing is that angelic cures and miraculous means are not necessary to the Messiah's power to heal. This sign heralded the beginning of Jesus' tensions with the Jerusalem religious establishment and began their determination to kill Him (v 18).

5:1–16 MIRACLE, Faith—Miracles do not always bring the healed to mature faith. The invalid believed in the healing power of the waters. How long he had waited is not specified, but he had been helpless for thirty-eight years. Jesus challenged his faith, asking if he wanted to be healed and telling him to get up, pick up his pallet, and walk. Imagine—for thirty-eight years he had not walked; now Jesus commanded him to get up and walk. He did just that. Bodily healing came. Spiritual sickness remained (v 14). Healing the body did not bring loyalty and trust. Fear of religious powers (v 15) remained stronger than trust in the Healer's power. We must ask for more than physical healing. We must ask for faith and the power to stop sinning. That is the greater miracle.

5:14 EVIL AND SUFFERING, Repentance—Physical suffering is not the worst thing humans endure. An invalid for 38 years was healed. Then he faced the most difficult decision of his life. How would he act as a well person? Jesus called him to step out in faith, give God the credit, and stop fearing religious leaders and their power structures. Life in fear instead of faith would lead to greater problems than he had ever faced. Freedom from suffering should lead to repentance and faith. See note on 9:1–4.

5:14 SIN, Individual Choice—Sin is not a permanent, *unchangeable characteristic of our lives.* Jesus tells those who would follow Him to quit sinning. That is His expectation. Those who seriously commit life to Him do stop. Sin is no longer the identifying mark of believers. Those who do not choose in Christ to stop sinning face eternal condemnation. This does not mean a person becomes perfect and never sins. It does mean the person does not consciously live continuously in sin. We root out known sin and actively strive for perfection.

5:16–17 CREATION, Continuous—Though God rested after creation (Ge 2:2), He did not cease to be active. Jesus saw His role as continuing the creative work of God by helping people who had pressing needs. Constructive work, designed to help extend God's kingdom with deeds of love and mercy, make the world God created a better place to live. In this way, we become co-creators with Him.

5:17–18 GOD, One God—Jesus' identification of Himself with God appeared blasphemous to the Jews because by this time they clearly perceived that there is only one God. A major problem of the Old Testament was the people's tendency to worship other gods, compromising the uniqueness of the one true God. They learned their lesson well in captivity and now reacted sharply in defense of the one God. In the rest of this chapter, note the many ways Jesus shares the power and authority of His Father in the works that He does. This can only be understood properly in the light of our doctrine of the Trinity, one God known in three Persons. See notes on Mt 3:16–17; 16:16–17,27.

5:17 JESUS CHRIST, Mission—Jesus' mission was the same as God's. Both work ceaselessly to accomplish it. Human legalistic traditions could not prevent Jesus from accomplishing the Father's will.

5:17–19 REVELATION, Actions—Jesus is the means through which God is revealed and works. Since God never rests from doing good, the Son never stops doing good. God revealed His own character through Jesus' actions and words (v 36).

5:18–27 JESUS CHRIST, God—Jesus implied He was equal with God by His intimate reference to God as "My

reason the Jews tried all the harder to kill
him;[h] not only was he breaking the Sabbath, but he was even calling God his
own Father, making himself equal with
God.[i]
19Jesus gave them this answer: "I tell
you the truth, the Son can do nothing by
himself;[j] he can do only what he sees his
Father doing, because whatever the Father does the Son also does. 20For the Father loves the Son[k] and shows him all he
does. Yes, to your amazement he will
show him even greater things than
these.[l] 21For just as the Father raises the
dead and gives them life,[m] even so the
Son gives life[n] to whom he is pleased to
give it. 22Moreover, the Father judges no
one, but has entrusted all judgment to the
Son,[o] 23that all may honor the Son just as
they honor the Father. He who does not
honor the Son does not honor the Father,
who sent him.[p]
24"I tell you the truth, whoever hears
my word and believes him who sent me[q]
has eternal life[r] and will not be condemned;[s] he has crossed over from
death to life.[t] 25I tell you the truth, a
time is coming and has now come[u] when
the dead will hear[v] the voice of the Son
of God and those who hear will live. 26For
as the Father has life in himself, so he has
granted the Son to have life[w] in himself.
27And he has given him authority to
judge[x] because he is the Son of Man.
28"Do not be amazed at this, for a time
is coming[y] when all who are in their
graves will hear his voice 29and come
out—those who have done good will rise
to live, and those who have done evil will
rise to be condemned.[z] 30By myself I can
do nothing;[a] I judge only as I hear, and
my judgment is just,[b] for I seek not to
please myself but him who sent me.[c]

Testimonies About Jesus

31"If I testify about myself, my testimony is not valid.[d] 32There is another who
testifies in my favor,[e] and I know that his
testimony about me is valid.
33"You have sent to John and he has
testified[f] to the truth. 34Not that I accept
human testimony;[g] but I mention it that
you may be saved.[h] 35John was a lamp
that burned and gave light,[i] and you
chose for a time to enjoy his light.
36"I have testimony weightier than
that of John.[j] For the very work that the
Father has given me to finish, and which
I am doing,[k] testifies that the Father has
sent me.[l] 37And the Father who sent me
has himself testified concerning me.[m]
You have never heard his voice nor seen

5:18 [h]S Mt 12:14 [i]Jn 10:30,33; 19:7
5:19 [j]ver 30; S Jn 14:24
5:20 [k]Jn 3:35 [l]Jn 14:12
5:21 [m]Ro 4:17; 8:11; 2Co 1:9; Heb 11:19 [n]Jn 11:25
5:22 [o]ver 27; Ge 18:25; Jdg 11:27; Jn 9:39; S Ac 10:42
5:23 [p]Lk 10:16; S 1Jn 2:23
5:24 [q]S Mt 10:40; S Jn 3:15; S 3:17 [r]S Mt 25:46 [s]Jn 3:18 [t]1Jn 3:14
5:25 [u]Jn 4:23; 16:32 [v]Jn 8:43,47
5:26 [w]Dt 30:20; Job 10:12; 33:4; Ps 36:9; S Jn 1:4
5:27 [x]S ver 22
5:28 [y]Jn 4:21; 16:2
5:29 [z]S Mt 25:46
5:30 [a]ver 19 [b]Isa 28:6; Jn 8:16 [c]S Mt 26:39
5:31 [d]Jn 8:14
5:32 [e]ver 37; Jn 8:18
5:33 [f]S Jn 1:7
5:34 [g]1Jn 5:9 [h]Ac 16:30,31; Eph 2:8; Tit 3:5
5:35 [i]Da 12:3; 2Pe 1:19
5:36 [j]1Jn 5:9 [k]Jn 14:11; 15:24 [l]S Jn 3:17
5:37 [m]Jn 8:18

Father" (v 17) and by claiming a joint mission. Jesus is completely dependent on the Father (3:34; 7:28; 8:26,42; 9:4; 12:49). Jesus can work because the Father in love entrusts work to Him. A major task of the Son is to give eternal life through His resurrection. This makes the Son the standard of judgment and the Judge. Relation to Him determines eternal life or condemnation. The Son deserves all the honor the Father does.

5:21–24 LAST THINGS, Judgment—Jesus claimed to be the unique Son of God the Father and insisted that He was given the same power over death that the Father has (v 21). That power over physical death provides hope to believers to be faithful to their Lord even in the face of persecution by those who can kill the body. This power over death is of crucial importance to a Christian view of death. Among the greater works of Jesus is His power to give spiritual life in the present time, which continues into eternity (v 24). This power is commensurate with Christ's power to raise the dead. Spiritual life begins at the point of conversion and transcends death (v 24). Another of Jesus' greater works is that of judgment (Ac 10:42). The power over physical and spiritual life and the conducting of judgment attest to the divine sonship of Jesus. Resurrection and judgment are closely connected eschatological events. The first of these was foreshadowed in Jesus' earthly ministry by the quickening to life in spiritual birth, as well as in His raising of three persons back to continued earthly life (Jn 11:38–44; Mk 5:35–43; Lk 7:11–17). The future judgment was foreshadowed in Jesus' temporal judgment in the condemnation of the religiously unrighteous and hypocritical in His earthly life (Mt 23).

5:24 SALVATION, Eternal Life—Eternal life is crossing over from death to life, from mere existence to life with a capital L. It is available right now to all those who hear Christ's Word and believe God who sent Him. See Guide to Accepting Christ (pp. 1745–1747).

5:25–29 LAST THINGS, Unbelievers' Resurrection—Hearing the voice of the Son of God brings spiritual life to the spiritually dead. The hour for this possibility arrived in Jesus' first coming. A future time is coming when those who are physically dead will be brought to life again, some to a bodily resurrection "to live," others to a bodily resurrection "to be condemned." This is one of the clearest teachings concerning the future resurrection of unbelievers to the full, bodily experience of eternal condemnation. See notes on Rev 20:4–5, 11–15.

5:27–30 JESUS CHRIST, Judgment—See note on Mk 10:45. Jesus has authority to exercise eternal judgment. Since He pleases God, His judgment is just.

5:31–40 EVANGELISM, Power—Different lines of evidence point to Jesus as the promised Messiah and Savior. Each type of testimony has power to convince. For the believer, Christ's testimony is of top importance, but the unbeliever needs other evidence. John the Baptist provided important human testimony. Human testimony needs God's confirming power to lead people to salvation. Jesus' powerful ministry and miracles showed God's approval. The inspired Scriptures give God's convicting testimony to Jesus; yet study of Scripture does not lead to eternal life unless it leads to Jesus.

5:36–47 JESUS CHRIST, Fulfilled—Rightly understood, the Old Testament testifies to the mission and ministry of Jesus. His mission is precisely what God said He would do in Scripture and what God told Him to do as He ministered. Interpretation of Scripture that does not lead to Jesus is incomplete interpretation. See Guide to Interpreting the Bible, pp. 1769–1772.

5:37–40,45–47 HOLY SCRIPTURE, Redemption—Jesus is the greatest revelation of God, revealed in Scripture and manifested in the flesh (ch 1). Some who claimed to seek and follow God refused to see and believe Jesus. Diligent study of Scripture is fruitless if it does not lead to faith in Christ. Faith, not facts, is the ultimate purpose of Scripture study. Jewish leaders read Moses to determine rules for living and for judging others. If people will not believe God's revelation in human form and in inspired writing, how will they begin to believe in Jesus, who is more than human form, being God in person?

his form,[n] 38nor does his word dwell in
you,[o] for you do not believe[p] the one he
sent.[q] 39You diligently study[f] the Scriptures[r] because you think that by them
you possess eternal life.[s] These are the
Scriptures that testify about me,[t] 40yet
you refuse to come to me[u] to have life.
41"I do not accept praise from men,[v]
42but I know you. I know that you do not
have the love of God in your hearts. 43I
have come in my Father's name, and you
do not accept me; but if someone else
comes in his own name, you will accept
him. 44How can you believe if you accept
praise from one another, yet make no effort to obtain the praise that comes from
the only God[g] ?[w]
45"But do not think I will accuse you
before the Father. Your accuser is Moses,[x] on whom your hopes are set.[y] 46If
you believed Moses, you would believe
me, for he wrote about me.[z] 47But since
you do not believe what he wrote, how
are you going to believe what I say?"[a]

Chapter 6

Jesus Feeds the Five Thousand

6:1–13pp — Mt 14:13–21; Mk 6:32–44; Lk 9:10–17

SOME time after this, Jesus crossed to
the far shore of the Sea of Galilee
(that is, the Sea of Tiberias), 2and a great
crowd of people followed him because
they saw the miraculous signs[b] he had
performed on the sick. 3Then Jesus went
up on a mountainside[c] and sat down
with his disciples. 4The Jewish Passover
Feast[d] was near.
5When Jesus looked up and saw a great
crowd coming toward him, he said to
Philip,[e] "Where shall we buy bread for
these people to eat?" 6He asked this only
to test him, for he already had in mind
what he was going to do.
7Philip answered him, "Eight months'
wages[h] would not buy enough bread for
each one to have a bite!"
8Another of his disciples, Andrew, Simon Peter's brother,[f] spoke up, 9"Here
is a boy with five small barley loaves and
two small fish, but how far will they go
among so many?"[g]
10Jesus said, "Have the people sit
down." There was plenty of grass in that
place, and the men sat down, about five
thousand of them. 11Jesus then took the
loaves, gave thanks,[h] and distributed to
those who were seated as much as they
wanted. He did the same with the fish.
12When they had all had enough to eat,
he said to his disciples, "Gather the
pieces that are left over. Let nothing be
wasted." 13So they gathered them and
filled twelve baskets with the pieces of
the five barley loaves left over by those
who had eaten.
14After the people saw the miraculous
sign[i] that Jesus did, they began to say,
"Surely this is the Prophet who is to
come into the world."[j] 15Jesus, knowing
that they intended to come and make him
king[k] by force, withdrew again to a
mountain by himself.[l]

Jesus Walks on the Water

6:16–21pp — Mt 14:22–33; Mk 6:47–51

16When evening came, his disciples

[f]39 Or *Study diligently* (the imperative) [g]44 Some early manuscripts *the Only One* [h]7 Greek *two hundred denarii*

5:37 [n]Dt 4:12; 1Ti 1:17; S Jn 1:18
5:38 [o]1Jn 1:10; 2:14 [p]Isa 26:10 [q]S Jn 3:17
5:39 [r]Ro 2:17,18 [s]S Mt 25:46 [t]S Lk 24:27,44; Ac 13:27
5:40 [u]Jn 6:44
5:41 [v]ver 44
5:44 [w]S Ro 2:29
5:45 [x]Jn 9:28 [y]Ro 2:17
5:46 [z]Ge 3:15; S Lk 24:27,44; Ac 26:22
5:47 [a]Lk 16:29,31
6:2 [b]S Jn 2:11
6:3 [c]ver 15
6:4 [d]S Jn 11:55
6:5 [e]S Jn 1:43
6:8 [f]Jn 1:40
6:9 [g]2Ki 4:43
6:11 [h]ver 23; S Mt 14:19
6:14 [i]S Jn 2:11 [j]Dt 18:15,18; Mt 11:3; S 21:11
6:15 [k]Jn 18:36 [l]Mt 14:23; Mk 6:46

6:1–15 JESUS CHRIST, King—Compare Mt 14:13–21; Mk 6:32–44; Lk 9:10–17. This sign led the crowds to try to manipulate Jesus' power for their political ambitions. Jesus sought faith, not national fanaticism. He refused to adopt their strategy or be manipulated.
6:2 MIRACLE, Vocabulary—See note on 2:1–11.
6:3–15 MIRACLE, Christ—Miracles are "signs" pointing to God, but they must be correctly interpreted. When the crowd saw the "sign," they confessed Jesus as "the Prophet." They were correct, but they misinterpreted "Prophet" as political ruler. The serious situation caused Jesus to withdraw from the crowd because He saw that they were about to "make him king by force." We need more than miraculous signs which we can use to support our false theology. We need Jesus' teachings, too. See note on Mt 14:13–21. John's unique emphases include the timing at "the Passover Feast," the "testing" of Philip, the presence of the lad with the lunch, and the response of the satisfied crowd.
6:11 PRAYER, Thanksgiving—See note on Mt 14:19.
6:14 JESUS CHRIST, Prophet—In the Old Testament prophets were those who spoke a word on behalf of God. They spoke what they had heard and described what they had seen. The prophets represented God to the people. They foretold the message God gave them and told forth ideas of social justice and practical application of the will of God for their day. Moses was the great prophet and represented the people to God as well as God to the people. He left a promise that a prophet like Moses would come again to lead God's people (Dt 18:15). Early Christians saw the coming of Jesus as a fulfillment of this prophecy (Ac 3:22; 7:37). In the latter history of Israel the Jews felt the Spirit of prophecy had left Israel and would return in the Messianic Age (Joel 2: 28–32). Compare Ac 2. This belief was heightened in the period between the Testaments so that one of the characteristics of the expected Messiah was that He would bring the Spirit and restore prophecy. Jews also expected the return of Elijah (Mal 4:5). Jesus designated John as this prophetic forerunner to the great eschatological Prophet (Mt 17:10–13). Two types of references to Jesus as prophet appear in the New Testament. People impressed by His works put Him in the general class of prophets (9:17; Lk 7:16). People of faith saw that Jesus was the last, great eschatological Prophet (Jn 6:14) like Moses.
6:15 PRAYER, Jesus' Example—Compare Mt 14:23; Mk 6:45–46. Jesus went alone to pray. The Greek text emphasizes solitariness by the use of the phrase, He "withdrew by Himself alone." Jesus wanted fellowship with His Father more than with people seeking purposes opposed to the Father's.
6:16–24 JESUS CHRIST, Miracles—This sign pointed to Jesus as divine. "It is I" translates the linguistic allusion to the divine name (Greek *egō eimi*). See note on Mk 14:53—15:15. His divine nature is shown by His authority over the natural world. "Don't be afraid" reflects Old Testament prophetic language promising salvation.
6:16–34 MIRACLE, Christ—People may benefit from

went down to the lake, 17where they got
into a boat and set off across the lake for
Capernaum. By now it was dark, and
Jesus had not yet joined them. 18A strong
wind was blowing and the waters grew
rough. 19When they had rowed three or
three and a half miles,[i] they saw Jesus
approaching the boat, walking on the water;[m] and they were terrified. 20But he
said to them, "It is I; don't be afraid."[n]
21Then they were willing to take him into
the boat, and immediately the boat
reached the shore where they were heading.

22The next day the crowd that had
stayed on the opposite shore of the lake[o]
realized that only one boat had been
there, and that Jesus had not entered it
with his disciples, but that they had gone
away alone.[p] 23Then some boats from Tiberias[q] landed near the place where the
people had eaten the bread after the Lord
had given thanks.[r] 24Once the crowd realized that neither Jesus nor his disciples
were there, they got into the boats and
went to Capernaum in search of Jesus.

Jesus the Bread of Life

25When they found him on the other
side of the lake, they asked him, "Rabbi,[s] when did you get here?"

26Jesus answered, "I tell you the truth,
you are looking for me,[t] not because you
saw miraculous signs[u] but because you
ate the loaves and had your fill. 27Do not
work for food that spoils, but for food that
endures[v] to eternal life,[w] which the Son
of Man[x] will give you. On him God the
Father has placed his seal[y] of approval."

28Then they asked him, "What must
we do to do the works God requires?"

29Jesus answered, "The work of God is
this: to believe[z] in the one he has
sent."[a]

30So they asked him, "What miraculous sign[b] then will you give that we may
see it and believe you?[c] What will you
do? 31Our forefathers ate the manna[d] in
the desert; as it is written: 'He gave them
bread from heaven to eat.'[j]"[e]

32Jesus said to them, "I tell you the
truth, it is not Moses who has given you
the bread from heaven, but it is my Father who gives you the true bread from
heaven. 33For the bread of God is he who
comes down from heaven[f] and gives life
to the world."

34"Sir," they said, "from now on give
us this bread."[g]

35Then Jesus declared, "I am[h] the
bread of life.[i] He who comes to me will
never go hungry, and he who believes[j]
in me will never be thirsty.[k] 36But as I
told you, you have seen me and still you
do not believe. 37All that the Father gives
me[l] will come to me, and whoever
comes to me I will never drive away.

6:19 [m]Job 9:8
6:20 [n]S Mt 14:27
6:22 [o]ver 2 [p]ver 15-21
6:23 [q]ver 1 [r]ver 11
6:25 [s]S Mt 23:7
6:26 [t]ver 24 [u]ver 30; S Jn 2:11
6:27 [v]Isa 55:2 [w]ver 54; S Mt 25:46 [x]S Mt 8:20 [y]Ro 4:11; 1Co 9:2; 2Co 1:22; Eph 1:13; 4:30; 2Ti 2:19; Rev 7:3
6:29 [z]1Jn 3:23 [a]S Jn 3:17
6:30 [b]S Jn 2:11 [c]S Mt 12:38
6:31 [d]Nu 11:7-9 [e]Ex 16:4,15; Ne 9:15; Ps 78:24; 105:40
6:33 [f]ver 50; Jn 3:13,31
6:34 [g]Jn 4:15
6:35 [h]Ex 3:14; Jn 8:12; 10:7,11; 11:25; 14:6; 15:1 [i]ver 48,51 [j]S Jn 3:15 [k]Jn 4:14
6:37 [l]ver 39; Jn 17:2,6,9,24

[i]19 Greek *rowed twenty-five or thirty stadia* (about 5 or 6 kilometers) [j]31 Exodus 16:4; Neh. 9:15; Psalm 78:24,25

Christ's miracles but never see the "sign" pointing them to believe in Jesus. Jesus knew the crowds were attracted to His signs more than to His truth. They ate the miraculous meal; yet they asked for more signs. They wanted to see something like Moses did in providing the manna. They failed to see that He Himself was the Bread of life. See note on Mt 14:22–33.

6:25–59 JESUS CHRIST, Bread of Life—Signs did not lead the crowds to faith as they should have. See note on 2:1–11. They sought food and power, not faith, thus acquiring new hunger rather than eternal life. They needed to look beyond religious institutions like Passover and beyond miracles like the manna in the wilderness (Ex 16) to God's new sign—Jesus, the provider of eternal life. Believers partake of the Bread of life through faith and strengthen their faith through partaking of the elements of the Lord's Supper. As the Bread of life, Jesus came down from heaven and is eternal in contrast to manna, which perished. See note on 3:13–15.

6:26–27 SALVATION, Acceptance—Acceptance of Christ means accepting Him as the Bread of life. It is accepting the Father's credentials that He is the Son of man and is able to provide life's greatest need—eternal life.

6:27–57 GOD, Sovereignty—Jesus declared that His ministry was the work of God through Him. God is in charge, working in His world, working through His Son. This is not to say that God is simply manipulating people to accept or reject His Son. God is the ultimate cause of what is happening. He works in people in ways that respect their individual freedom. He draws a favorable response from them, rather than coercing them to make a certain response to Jesus. This is another indication of the closeness of the trinitarian relationship; specifically, the work of the Father and the work of the Son are virtually identical. The Father and the Son cannot be truly separated. God is one.

6:27–68 SALVATION, Eternal Life—Jesus Christ is heaven's Bread which satisfies the hunger for God. Those who trust in Him have eternal life now and forever more. Christians eat His body and drink His blood symbolically whenever they partake of the Lord's Supper. Those who have eternal life Christ will raise from the dead on the last day.

6:29 REVELATION, Jesus Christ—The greatest test of belief in God's revelation is whether or not we accept His greatest revelation: Jesus Christ. God sent the Son to reveal the fullness of the Father (1:14). God is the Author of all good things and reveals Himself throughout history in His loving kindness. He, not Moses, gave bread in the wilderness, and He gives the everlasting food from heaven, Jesus Christ as Savior. The Jews took too much pride in the human agent of revelation and so came close to confusing Moses with God. Revelation leads us to look beyond the human agent to God, the true Source of life.

6:33 JESUS CHRIST, Preexistent—Jesus' claim to have come from heaven implies His preexistence with God in heaven.

6:35–70 ELECTION, God's Initiative—The human-centered approach to salvation says persons approach God on the basis of effort and excellence. It reasons that just as human beings make scientific discoveries so they also discover God as they use a multiplicity of approaches. Jesus taught that God draws persons to Himself. The saving faith persons have in Jesus Christ is a gift from the Almighty God. The mystery of election is in the hands of a loving God who desires that none should perish. He guarantees salvation for those who fully trust Him and His way. His way of election is to provide spiritual nourishment and hope through Jesus. People must choose God's way in faith without seeing their faith as a human achievement earning rewards.

38 For I have come down from heaven[m]
not to do my will but to do the will[n] of
him who sent me.[o] 39 And this is the will
of him who sent me, that I shall lose none
of all that he has given me,[p] but raise
them up at the last day.[q] 40 For my Father's will is that everyone who looks to
the Son[r] and believes in him shall have
eternal life,[s] and I will raise him up at
the last day."

41 At this the Jews began to grumble
about him because he said, "I am the
bread that came down from heaven."
42 They said, "Is this not Jesus, the son of
Joseph,[t] whose father and mother we
know?[u] How can he now say, 'I came
down from heaven'?"[v]

43 "Stop grumbling among yourselves,"
Jesus answered. 44 "No one can come to
me unless the Father who sent me draws
him,[w] and I will raise him up at the last
day. 45 It is written in the Prophets: 'They
will all be taught by God.'[k][x] Everyone
who listens to the Father and learns from
him comes to me. 46 No one has seen the
Father except the one who is from God;[y]
only he has seen the Father. 47 I tell you
the truth, he who believes has everlasting
life.[z] 48 I am the bread of life.[a] 49 Your
forefathers ate the manna in the desert,
yet they died.[b] 50 But here is the bread
that comes down from heaven,[c] which a
man may eat and not die. 51 I am the living bread[d] that came down from heav-
en.[e] If anyone eats of this bread, he will
live forever. This bread is my flesh, which
I will give for the life of the world."[f]

52 Then the Jews[g] began to argue
sharply among themselves,[h] "How can
this man give us his flesh to eat?"

53 Jesus said to them, "I tell you the
truth, unless you eat the flesh[i] of the Son
of Man[j] and drink his blood,[k] you have
no life in you. 54 Whoever eats my flesh
and drinks my blood has eternal life, and I
will raise him up at the last day.[l] 55 For
my flesh is real food and my blood is real
drink. 56 Whoever eats my flesh and
drinks my blood remains in me, and I in
him.[m] 57 Just as the living Father sent
me[n] and I live because of the Father, so
the one who feeds on me will live because of me. 58 This is the bread that came
down from heaven. Your forefathers ate
manna and died, but he who feeds on this
bread will live forever."[o] 59 He said this
while teaching in the synagogue in Capernaum.

Many Disciples Desert Jesus

60 On hearing it, many of his disciples[p]
said, "This is a hard teaching. Who can
accept it?"[q]

61 Aware that his disciples were grumbling about this, Jesus said to them,
"Does this offend you?[r] 62 What if you
see the Son of Man[s] ascend to where he
was before![t] 63 The Spirit gives life;[u] the
flesh counts for nothing. The words I
have spoken to you are spirit[1] and they
are life. 64 Yet there are some of you who
do not believe." For Jesus had known[v]
from the beginning which of them did
not believe and who would betray him.[w]
65 He went on to say, "This is why I told
you that no one can come to me unless
the Father has enabled him."[x]

66 From this time many of his disciples[y]
turned back and no longer followed him.

67 "You do not want to leave too, do
you?" Jesus asked the Twelve.[z]

68 Simon Peter answered him,[a] "Lord,
to whom shall we go? You have the words
of eternal life.[b] 69 We believe and know
that you are the Holy One of God."[c]

70 Then Jesus replied, "Have I not chosen you,[d] the Twelve? Yet one of you is a
devil!"[e] 71 (He meant Judas, the son of

[k]45 Isaiah 54:13 [1]63 Or *Spirit*

6:38 [m]Jn 3:13,31 [n]S Mt 26:39 [o]S Jn 3:17
6:39 [p]Isa 27:3; Jer 23:4; Jn 10:28; 17:12; 18:9 [q]ver 40,44,54
6:40 [r]Jn 12:45 [s]S Mt 25:46
6:42 [t]Lk 4:22 [u]Jn 7:27,28 [v]ver 38, 62
6:44 [w]ver 65; Jer 31:3; Jn 12:32
6:45 [x]Isa 54:13; Jer 31:33,34; 1Co 2:13; 1Th 4:9; Heb 8:10,11; 10:16; 1Jn 2:27
6:46 [y]S Jn 1:18; 5:37; 7:29
6:47 [z]S Mt 25:46
6:48 [a]ver 35,51
6:49 [b]ver 31,58
6:50 [c]ver 33
6:51 [d]ver 35,48 [e]ver 41,58 [f]Heb 10:10
6:52 [g]S Jn 1:19 [h]Jn 7:43; 9:16; 10:19
6:53 [i]Mt 26:26 [j]S Mt 8:20 [k]Mt 26:28
6:54 [l]ver 39
6:56 [m]Jn 15:4-7; 1Jn 2:24; 3:24; 4:15
6:57 [n]S Jn 3:17
6:58 [o]ver 49-51; Jn 3:36; 5:24
6:60 [p]ver 66 [q]ver 52
6:61 [r]Mt 13:57
6:62 [s]S Mt 8:20 [t]S Mk 16:19; S Jn 3:13; 17:5
6:63 [u]2Co 3:6
6:64 [v]S Jn 2:25 [w]S Mt 10:4
6:65 [x]ver 37,44; S Mt 13:11
6:66 [y]ver 60
6:67 [z]Mt 10:2
6:68 [a]Mt 16:16 [b]ver 63; S Mt 25:46
6:69 [c]S Mk 1:24; 8:29; Lk 9:20
6:70 [d]Jn 15:16,19 [e]Jn 13:27; 17:12

6:38–40 JESUS CHRIST, Mission—Doing God's will, providing eternal security for believers, and bringing resurrection to eternal life for His followers was God's mission, which Jesus fulfilled.

6:39–54 LAST THINGS, Believers' Resurrection—The possession of eternal life through looking to and believing in Jesus carries with it the additional promise of resurrection at the last day. The response to the drawing of the Father, an inclining of the heart at the initiation of divine impulses, brings one to the hope of bodily resurrection at the last day. Eternal life includes the furnishing of a body designed to house such life by means of resurrection at the last day.

6:46 JESUS CHRIST, Son of God—The Son alone saw God because He was the only inhabitant of heaven sent to live on earth. See note on 3:31–36.

6:47–51 HUMANITY, Death—Even God's love and provision does not exempt His people from the normal experiences of life, including physical death. Belief in Christ brings hope of resurrection from the grave and eternal life.

6:57 GOD, Living—For Jesus, God is not an impersonal, immobile, uncaring, distant God. He is a living God, very much aware of what is going on, very much in control of His world, very much present and active in pursuit of His purposes. As the living God, He is the source of true life for all. See notes on Ex 3:12–16; Nu 14:21,28.

6:58 HUMANITY, Death—See note on 6:47–51.

6:62 JESUS CHRIST, Preexistent—The Son of man not only came down to bring the eternal kingdom (Da 7:13–14). He ascended back to the Father. Early in His ministry Jesus prepared the disciples for His resurrection and ascension.

6:69 JESUS CHRIST, Sinless—Faith sees the holiness, the moral purity of Christ, a purity characterizing God as no one else (Isa 6:3). See note on Mk 1:23–24.

6:70–71 JESUS CHRIST, Death—See note on 13:18–30.

6:70–71 EVIL AND SUFFERING, Satan—Close relationship to God's people and their activities does not guarantee salvation. Even one of Christ's closest followers proved dedicated to Satan rather than to God. See note on Lk 22:3.

6:70 CHURCH LEADERS, The Twelve—Jesus created the circle of twelve disciples to serve His special purposes, not the purposes of the disciples. Like the twelve, we are to serve Jesus' purposes, not those of our own invention.

Simon Iscariot,[f] who, though one of the
Twelve, was later to betray him.)[g]

Chapter 7

Jesus Goes to the Feast of Tabernacles

AFTER this, Jesus went around in Galilee, purposely staying away from Judea because the Jews[h] there were waiting to take his life.[i] 2But when the Jewish Feast of Tabernacles[j] was near,
3Jesus' brothers[k] said to him, "You ought
to leave here and go to Judea, so that your
disciples may see the miracles you do.
4No one who wants to become a public
figure acts in secret. Since you are doing
these things, show yourself to the
world." 5For even his own brothers did
not believe in him.[l]

6Therefore Jesus told them, "The right
time[m] for me has not yet come; for you
any time is right. 7The world cannot hate
you, but it hates me[n] because I testify
that what it does is evil.[o] 8You go to the
Feast. I am not yet[m] going up to this
Feast, because for me the right time[p] has
not yet come." 9Having said this, he
stayed in Galilee.

10However, after his brothers had left
for the Feast, he went also, not publicly,
but in secret. 11Now at the Feast the Jews
were watching for him[q] and asking,
"Where is that man?"

12Among the crowds there was widespread whispering about him. Some said,
"He is a good man."

Others replied, "No, he deceives the
people."[r] 13But no one would say anything publicly about him for fear of the
Jews.[s]

Jesus Teaches at the Feast

14Not until halfway through the Feast
did Jesus go up to the temple courts and
begin to teach.[t] 15The Jews[u] were
amazed and asked, "How did this man
get such learning[v] without having studied?"[w]

16Jesus answered, "My teaching is not
my own. It comes from him who sent
me.[x] 17If anyone chooses to do God's
will, he will find out[y] whether my teaching comes from God or whether I speak
on my own. 18He who speaks on his own
does so to gain honor for himself,[z] but he
who works for the honor of the one who
sent him is a man of truth; there is nothing false about him. 19Has not Moses giv-
en you the law?[a] Yet not one of you
keeps the law. Why are you trying to kill
me?"[b]

20"You are demon-possessed,"[c] the

6:71 [f]S Mt 26:14 [g]S Mt 10:4
7:1 [h]S Jn 1:19 [i]ver 19,25; S Mt 12:14
7:2 [j]Lev 23:34; Dt 16:16
7:3 [k]S Mt 12:46
7:5 [l]Ps 69:8; Mk 3:21
7:6 [m]S Mt 26:18
7:7 [n]Jn 15:18,19 [o]Jn 3:19,20
7:8 [p]ver 6; S Mt 26:18
7:11 [q]Jn 11:56
7:12 [r]ver 40,43
7:13 [s]Jn 9:22; 12:42; 19:38; 20:19
7:14 [t]ver 28; S Mt 26:55
7:15 [u]S Jn 1:19 [v]Ac 26:24 [w]Mt 13:54
7:16 [x]S Jn 14:24
7:17 [y]Ps 25:14
7:18 [z]Jn 5:41; 8:50,54
7:19 [a]Dt 32:46; Jn 1:17 [b]ver 1; S Mt 12:14
7:20 [c]S Mk 3:22

[m]8 Some early manuscripts do not have *yet.*

7:1–10 JESUS CHRIST, Secret—Jesus did not campaign like a public figure. He abided by God's time schedule to accomplish God's purposes. Thus He remained in the relative secrecy of Galilee rather than going to the cosmopolitan Jerusalem and traveled secretly rather than with the festival crowds when He chose to make the trip south. See note on Mk 1:25,34.

7:2–5 FAMILY, Priorities—See note on Mk 3:21,31–35.

7:3–5,31 MIRACLE, Vocabulary—Jesus' own family saw His miracles (v 3; Greek *erga,* "works"). His brothers did not believe on Him. They saw only a person seeking earthly fame and plotted strategy to help Him. Many in the crowd did believe on Him—to them His works became signs (v 31; Greek *semeion*) seeing in Him God's promised Messiah.

7:6–8 HISTORY, Time—Jesus lived not according to religious calendars but according to the Father's time. He followed the Father's plan, seizing the right moments to give new meaning to history and to fulfill God's plan of salvation. He refused to let His appearance stir the crowds to action before the decisive moment God chose to act.

7:6,8,30 ELECTION, Predestination—God's purpose pointed Jesus to the time of the cross. The cross was an event controlled by God and not by human power struggles. God had a right time (Greek *kairos*) when the cross could accomplish God's purpose for it. The right time is God's agenda for establishing His priorities and His will. At the right time Jesus entered into human history. At the right time He was baptized. At the right time He brought His ministry to a conclusion and faced the challenge of Calvary. No one could delay, hurry up, or prevent Jesus from keeping those significant historical appointments which He chose to keep in humble obedience to the Father, thus accomplishing God's election purposes.

7:7 SIN, Depravity—Apart from God, human society is dedicated to evil. Looking to human accomplishments gives no reason for hope. Hope rests only in the saving work of Jesus, whom the world rejected.

7:12 JESUS CHRIST, Sinless—Seeing Jesus as a good, compassionate man who helps people is not enough. Neither is a belief in Him that fears public opinion and will not openly confess Him. Saving faith confesses Jesus as the sinless Son of God.

7:14–24 JESUS CHRIST, Teaching—Jesus' teaching amazed people because He lacked formal education. Christ learned not from human teachers but from His Heavenly Father. People need more than law to gain eternal life, because people do not obey the law. Thus Jesus pointed to the way of faith.

7:16–19 REVELATION, Faithfulness—Jesus was faithful to the message the Father gave Him. Fidelity may be measured by whether one seeks personal honor or God's, personal will or the Father's. Revelation comes through one who speaks and teaches truth, not falsehood. Scripture was revealed not to bring personal pride of achievement but obedience honoring God.

7:16–17 EDUCATION, God—Jesus acknowledged a principle deeply imbedded in the Old Testament concept of education. God is the Teacher of His people. See notes on Job 36:22; Ps 25:4–9. Just as Moses received the Law from God, so Jesus identified God as the Author of His teaching. Note, too, that one can appropriate this teaching only by doing God's will. Learning is putting newly acquired knowledge into action.

7:19 SIN, Universal Nature—Jewish religious leaders prided themselves on their knowledge of and faithfulness to their Scripture. They wanted to kill Jesus because He claimed to be Messiah but did not meet their standards. See note on Mk 7:1–22. Jesus reminded them that not a single one of them met the standards set by Scripture. All have sinned. No one has the right to condemn another.

7:20 EVIL AND SUFFERING, Satan—A strict line separates Jesus and the demonic. Only the spiritually blind can confuse Jesus and satanic powers. We cannot reject Jesus' teaching simply because it goes against our tradition. See note

crowd answered. "Who is trying to kill
you?"
[21]Jesus said to them, "I did one miracle,[d] and you are all astonished. [22]Yet,
because Moses gave you circumcision[e]
(though actually it did not come from Moses, but from the patriarchs),[f] you circumcise a child on the Sabbath. [23]Now if
a child can be circumcised on the Sabbath
so that the law of Moses may not be broken, why are you angry with me for healing the whole man on the Sabbath?
[24]Stop judging by mere appearances, and
make a right judgment."[g]

Is Jesus the Christ?

[25]At that point some of the people of
Jerusalem began to ask, "Isn't this the
man they are trying to kill?[h] [26]Here he is,
speaking publicly, and they are not saying
a word to him. Have the authorities[i]
really concluded that he is the Christ[n]?[j]
[27]But we know where this man is from;[k]
when the Christ comes, no one will know
where he is from."
[28]Then Jesus, still teaching in the temple courts,[l] cried out, "Yes, you know
me, and you know where I am from.[m] I
am not here on my own, but he who sent
me is true.[n] You do not know him, [29]but
I know him[o] because I am from him and
he sent me."[p]
[30]At this they tried to seize him, but no
one laid a hand on him,[q] because his
time had not yet come.[r] [31]Still, many in
the crowd put their faith in him.[s] They
said, "When the Christ comes, will he do
more miraculous signs[t] than this man?"
[32]The Pharisees heard the crowd whispering such things about him. Then the
chief priests and the Pharisees sent temple guards to arrest him.
[33]Jesus said, "I am with you for only a
short time,[u] and then I go to the one
who sent me.[v] [34]You will look for me,
but you will not find me; and where I am,
you cannot come."[w]
[35]The Jews said to one another,
"Where does this man intend to go that
we cannot find him? Will he go where
our people live scattered[x] among the
Greeks,[y] and teach the Greeks? [36]What
did he mean when he said, 'You will look
for me, but you will not find me,' and
'Where I am, you cannot come'?"[z]
[37]On the last and greatest day of the
Feast,[a] Jesus stood and said in a loud
voice, "If anyone is thirsty, let him come
to me and drink.[b] [38]Whoever believes[c]
in me, as[o] the Scripture has said,[d]
streams of living water[e] will flow from
within him."[f] [39]By this he meant the
Spirit,[g] whom those who believed in him
were later to receive.[h] Up to that time
the Spirit had not been given, since Jesus
had not yet been glorified.[i]
[40]On hearing his words, some of the
people said, "Surely this man is the
Prophet."[j]
[41]Others said, "He is the Christ."
Still others asked, "How can the Christ
come from Galilee?[k] [42]Does not the
Scripture say that the Christ will come
from David's family[p][l] and from Bethlehem,[m] the town where David lived?"
[43]Thus the people were divided[n] because
of Jesus. [44]Some wanted to seize him, but
no one laid a hand on him.[o]

Unbelief of the Jewish Leaders

[45]Finally the temple guards went back
to the chief priests and Pharisees, who
asked them, "Why didn't you bring him
in?"
[46]"No one ever spoke the way this man
does,"[p] the guards declared.
[47]"You mean he has deceived you

7:21 [d]ver 23; Jn 5:2-9
7:22 [e]Lev 12:3 [f]Ge 17:10-14
7:24 [g]1Sa 16:7; Isa 11:3,4; Jn 8:15; 2Co 10:7
7:25 [h]ver 1; S Mt 12:14
7:26 [i]ver 48 [j]Jn 4:29
7:27 [k]Mt 13:55; Lk 4:22; Jn 6:42
7:28 [l]ver 14 [m]Jn 8:14 [n]Jn 8:26, 42
7:29 [o]S Mt 11:27 [p]S Jn 3:17
7:30 [q]ver 32,44; Jn 10:39 [r]S Mt 26:18
7:31 [s]Jn 8:30; 10:42; 11:45; 12:11,42 [t]S Jn 2:11
7:33 [u]Jn 12:35; 13:33; 16:16 [v]Jn 16:5,10,17,28
7:34 [w]ver 36; Jn 8:21; 13:33
7:35 [x]S Jas 1:1 [y]Jn 12:20; Ac 17:4; 18:4
7:36 [z]ver 34
7:37 [a]Lev 23:36 [b]Isa 55:1; Rev 22:17
7:38 [c]S Jn 3:15 [d]Isa 58:11 [e]S Jn 4:10 [f]S Jn 4:14
7:39 [g]Joel 2:28; Jn 1:33; Ac 2:17,33 [h]S Jn 20:22 [i]Jn 12:23; 13:31,32
7:40 [j]S Mt 21:11
7:41 [k]ver 52; Jn 1:46
7:42 [l]S Mt 1:1 [m]Mic 5:2; Mt 2:5, 6; Lk 2:4
7:43 [n]Jn 6:52; 9:16; 10:19
7:44 [o]ver 30
7:46 [p]S Mt 7:28

[n]26 Or *Messiah*; also in verses 27, 31, 41 and 42
[o]37,38 Or / *If anyone is thirsty, let him come to me. / And let him drink,* [38]*who believes in me. / As*
[p]42 Greek *seed*

on Mt 12:22–29.

7:25–52 JESUS CHRIST, Christ—The Jews were eager students of Scripture and knew the necessary credentials for Messiah. From their interpretation they did not think Jesus met the credentials. Jesus' basic credential was that God had sent Him. His signs led many to believe in Him. See note on 2:1–11. He showed that Scripture pointed to Him as the source for eternal life. See notes on 6:14; Mt 16:16. Jesus had been born in Bethlehem, fulfilling Micah's prophecy (5:2), but the crowds were not aware of that credential. Compare Lk 2:4.

7:28 GOD, Faithfulness—Not only is God truth, in distinction from falsehood; He is faithful and dependable. He is the foundation upon which all that is good, or true, or desirable rests. In contrast to the pagan gods, God is thoroughly dependable, faithful to Himself and to His people. His character is unchanging, not subject to whims of the moment or the changing of the tides. In His faithfulness to His covenant promises, God sent Jesus, who truly knows God, being the divine Son of God. See notes on Ge 35:3; Nu 26:65.

7:30 HISTORY, Time—God controls time. He will not let His enemies act to bring critical moments of history before they fit His plan for providing salvation. Humans did not control Jesus even when they arrested Him. They could do so only in God's time.

7:37 SALVATION, Acceptance—Accepting Christ means accepting Him as the Water of life. See note on 4:10.

7:39 HOLY SPIRIT, Promised—When Jesus spoke of streams of living water, He referred to the Spirit. Jesus here brought two images together: life (6:63) and water (3:5). Whoever believes in Jesus will be given the Spirit. This teaching is similar to Old Testament promises and to the prophecy of John the Baptist (1:33), but it goes beyond them by specifying that those with faith in Christ will receive the Spirit. This happened at Pentecost (Ac 2). John clarified that the Spirit was not given until after Jesus was glorified, suggesting that the crucified and risen Christ would be in a position to give the Spirit. John later carefully distinguished Christ from the Spirit so that no one will confuse them (Jn 16:7). See note on Lk 11:13.

also?”[q] the Pharisees retorted. 48“Has
any of the rulers or of the Pharisees believed in him?[r] 49No! But this mob that
knows nothing of the law—there is a
curse on them.”
50Nicodemus,[s] who had gone to Jesus
earlier and who was one of their own
number, asked, 51“Does our law condemn anyone without first hearing him to
find out what he is doing?”
52They replied, “Are you from Galilee,
too? Look into it, and you will find that a
prophet[q] does not come out of Galilee.”[t]

[The earliest manuscripts and many other ancient witnesses do not have John 7:53-8:11]

53Then each went to his own home.

Chapter 8

BUT Jesus went to the Mount of Olives.[u] 2At dawn he appeared again in
the temple courts, where all the people
gathered around him, and he sat down to
teach them.[v] 3The teachers of the law
and the Pharisees brought in a woman
caught in adultery. They made her stand
before the group 4and said to Jesus,
“Teacher, this woman was caught in the
act of adultery. 5In the Law Moses commanded us to stone such women.[w] Now
what do you say?” 6They were using this
question as a trap,[x] in order to have a
basis for accusing him.[y]
But Jesus bent down and started to
write on the ground with his finger.
7When they kept on questioning him, he
straightened up and said to them, “If any
one of you is without sin, let him be the
first to throw a stone[z] at her.”[a] 8Again
he stooped down and wrote on the
ground.
9At this, those who heard began to go
away one at a time, the older ones first,
until only Jesus was left, with the woman
still standing there. 10Jesus straightened
up and asked her, “Woman, where are
they? Has no one condemned you?”
11“No one, sir,” she said.
“Then neither do I condemn you,”[b]
Jesus declared. “Go now and leave your
life of sin.”[c]

The Validity of Jesus’ Testimony

12When Jesus spoke again to the people, he said, “I am[d] the light of the
world.[e] Whoever follows me will never
walk in darkness, but will have the light
of life.”[f]
13The Pharisees challenged him, “Here
you are, appearing as your own witness;
your testimony is not valid.”[g]
14Jesus answered, “Even if I testify on
my own behalf, my testimony is valid, for
I know where I came from and where I
am going.[h] But you have no idea where I
come from[i] or where I am going. 15You
judge by human standards;[j] I pass judgment on no one.[k] 16But if I do judge, my
decisions are right, because I am not
alone. I stand with the Father, who sent
me.[l] 17In your own Law it is written that
the testimony of two men is valid.[m] 18I
am one who testifies for myself; my other
witness is the Father, who sent me.”[n]
19Then they asked him, “Where is your
father?”
“You do not know me or my Father,”[o]
Jesus replied. “If you knew me, you
would know my Father also.”[p] 20He
spoke these words while teaching[q] in the
temple area near the place where the offerings were put.[r] Yet no one seized
him, because his time had not yet
come.[s]
21Once more Jesus said to them, “I am
going away, and you will look for me, and
you will die[t] in your sin. Where I go, you
cannot come.”[u]
22This made the Jews ask, “Will he kill
himself? Is that why he says, ‘Where I go,
you cannot come’?”
23But he continued, “You are from below; I am from above. You are of this
world; I am not of this world.[v] 24I told
you that you would die in your sins; if

7:47 [q]ver 12
7:48 [r]Jn 12:42
7:50 [s]Jn 3:1; 19:39
7:52 [t]ver 41
8:1 [u]S Mt 21:1
8:2 [v]ver 20; S Mt 26:55
8:5 [w]Lev 20:10; Dt 22:22; Job 31:11
8:6 [x]Mt 22:15,18 [y]S Mt 12:10
8:7 [z]Dt 17:7; Eze 16:40 [a]Ro 2:1, 22
8:11 [b]Jn 3:17 [c]Jn 5:14
8:12 [d]S Jn 6:35 [e]S Jn 1:4 [f]Pr 4:18; Mt 5:14
8:13 [g]Jn 5:31
8:14 [h]Jn 13:3; 16:28 [i]Jn 7:28; 9:29
8:15 [j]S Jn 7:24 [k]Jn 3:17
8:16 [l]Jn 5:30
8:17 [m]S Mt 18:16
8:18 [n]Jn 5:37
8:19 [o]Jn 16:3 [p]S 1Jn 2:23
8:20 [q]S Mt 26:55 [r]Mk 12:41 [s]S Mt 26:18
8:21 [t]Eze 3:18 [u]Jn 7:34; 13:33
8:23 [v]Jn 3:31; 17:14

[q]*52* Two early manuscripts *the Prophet*

7:53—8:11 HOLY SCRIPTURE, Collection—See note on Mk 16:9–20.
8:12 JESUS CHRIST, Light—See note on 1:4–5.
8:13–30 JESUS CHRIST, Son of God—Jesus is so closely related to the Father in the trinitarian relationship that to know One is to know the Other. Jesus came to earth on God’s mission but remained aware His original and eternal home was with the Father in Heaven. See note on 1:1–18. Jesus continued to use the “I Am” formula identifying Himself with God. See note on Mk 14:53—15:15. Jesus’ true identity became clear only through His death and resurrection. He accomplished His mission and endured human rejection, mockery, and persecution because He was aware of the Father’s constant presence.
8:19,55 SALVATION, Knowledge of God—God makes Himself known through His Son. To know the Son is to know the Father. Compare 15:21; 17:3,25.
8:20 HISTORY, Time—See note on 7:30.
8:20 ELECTION, Predestination—See note on 7:6,8,30.
8:21–24 SIN, Unbelief—One sin determines our eternal fate. To reject Jesus, refusing to believe He is God’s Son who died for our sins, is the sin which forfeits eternal life and leads to death and eternal condemnation.
8:24,30–31,45–46 SALVATION, Belief—Those who believe in Christ will know the truth and be set free from their sins. They will do what Jesus has taught them to do. Failure to

you do not believe that I am ⌊the one I
claim to be⌋,[r][w] you will indeed die in
your sins.”
25“Who are you?” they asked.
“Just what I have been claiming all
along,” Jesus replied. 26“I have much to
say in judgment of you. But he who sent
me is reliable,[x] and what I have heard
from him I tell the world.”[y]
27They did not understand that he was
telling them about his Father. 28So Jesus
said, “When you have lifted up the Son of
Man,[z] then you will know that I am ⌊the
one I claim to be⌋ and that I do nothing on
my own but speak just what the Father
has taught me.[a] 29The one who sent me
is with me; he has not left me alone,[b] for
I always do what pleases him.”[c] 30Even
as he spoke, many put their faith in
him.[d]

The Children of Abraham

31To the Jews who had believed him,
Jesus said, “If you hold to my teaching,[e]
you are really my disciples. 32Then you
will know the truth, and the truth will set
you free.”[f]
33They answered him, “We are Abraham's descendants[s][g] and have never
been slaves of anyone. How can you say
that we shall be set free?”
34Jesus replied, “I tell you the truth,
everyone who sins is a slave to sin.[h]
35Now a slave has no permanent place in
the family, but a son belongs to it forever.[i] 36So if the Son sets you free,[j] you
will be free indeed. 37I know you are
Abraham's descendants. Yet you are
ready to kill me,[k] because you have no
room for my word. 38I am telling you
what I have seen in the Father's presence,[l] and you do what you have heard
from your father.[t] ”[m]
39“Abraham is our father,” they answered.
“If you were Abraham's children,”[n]
said Jesus, “then you would[u] do the
things Abraham did. 40As it is, you are
determined to kill me,[o] a man who has
told you the truth that I heard from
God.[p] Abraham did not do such things.
41You are doing the things your own father does.”[q]
“We are not illegitimate children,”
they protested. “The only Father we have
is God himself.”[r]

The Children of the Devil

42Jesus said to them, “If God were your
Father, you would love me,[s] for I came
from God[t] and now am here. I have not
come on my own;[u] but he sent me.[v]
43Why is my language not clear to you?
Because you are unable to hear what I
say. 44You belong to your father, the devil,[w] and you want to carry out your father's desire.[x] He was a murderer from
the beginning, not holding to the truth,
for there is no truth in him. When he lies,
he speaks his native language, for he is a
liar and the father of lies.[y] 45Yet because
I tell the truth,[z] you do not believe me!
46Can any of you prove me guilty of sin? If
I am telling the truth, why don't you believe me? 47He who belongs to God hears
what God says.[a] The reason you do not

[r]24 Or *I am he*; also in verse 28 [s]33 Greek *seed*; also in verse 37 [t]38 Or *presence. Therefore do what you have heard from the Father.* [u]39 Some early manuscripts *"If you are Abraham's children," said Jesus, "then*

8:24 [w]Jn 4:26; 13:19
8:26 [x]Jn 7:28 [y]Jn 3:32; 15:15
8:28 [z]S Jn 12:32 [a]S Jn 14:24
8:29 [b]ver 16; Jn 16:32 [c]Isa 50:5; Jn 4:34; 5:30; 6:38
8:30 [d]S Jn 7:31
8:31 [e]Jn 15:7; 2Jn 9
8:32 [f]ver 36; Ro 8:2; 2Co 3:17; Gal 5:1,13
8:33 [g]ver 37,39; S Lk 3:8
8:34 [h]S Ro 6:16
8:35 [i]Gal 4:30
8:36 [j]ver 32
8:37 [k]ver 39,40
8:38 [l]Jn 5:19,30; 14:10,24 [m]ver 41, 44
8:39 [n]ver 37; S Lk 3:8
8:40 [o]S Mt 12:14 [p]ver 26
8:41 [q]ver 38,44 [r]Isa 63:16; 64:8
8:42 [s]1Jn 5:1 [t]S Jn 13:3 [u]Jn 7:28 [v]S Jn 3:17
8:44 [w]1Jn 3:8 [x]ver 38,41 [y]Ge 3:4; 4:9; 2Ch 18:21; Ps 5:6; 12:2
8:45 [z]Jn 18:37
8:47 [a]Jn 18:37; 1Jn 4:6

believe Jesus is God who became flesh and solved our sin and guilt problem is to believe Jesus is a fraud and a liar. Believing Jesus was just a good man or great teacher contradicts everything Jesus stood for.

8:24 LAST THINGS, Unbelievers' Death—The death of unbelievers is a death in sins. The failure to believe in Jesus leaves sins unforgiven. Such a death is one of eternal hopelessness.

8:28 JESUS CHRIST, Son of Man—See note on Mk 10:45. In John's Gospel the special emphasis on Son of man is on suffering. The Son of man who descended from heaven must be lifted up to heaven on a cross (Jn 3:14; 8:28). His body is given up to be "eaten" (6:53). By a play on words the lifting up of the Son of man at His crucifixion also describes His glorification (11:4; 12:23; 13:31).

8:31–59 JESUS CHRIST, Mission—Jesus' mission was to communicate eternal truth, the personal reality of God, to all people. Jesus in person and in action was the Truth. To love the Truth is to love Jesus, the Son sent by the Father. Failure to understand this is a sure sign a person does not belong to God and is not saved. Jesus cannot be dismissed as of bad ancestry or of being demon-possessed. Nor was He a self-seeking egotist. He was an obedient Servant of the Father seeking salvation for every person. As such, He is greater than any person who ever lived. Compare 4:12. He is the eternal "I Am." See note on Mk 14:53—15:15.

8:31–59 EVIL AND SUFFERING, Satan—Satan has no moral constraints. Murder and lying are normal for him. Satan confuses people making them think they are following God when actually they are following the devil. We must constantly check our lives by Christ's teachings rather than by human traditions preserved and taught by religious institutions. We must be Christ-pleasers not people-pleasers.

8:31–37 SIN, Slavery—Sin is addictive. It masters everyone who tries it. Sin promises freedom but cannot deliver. Only Jesus Christ can give true freedom—freedom to master sin and reach one's God-given potential.

8:31–47 ELECTION, Remnant—Descendants of Abraham are not automatically children of God. Many of Abraham's descendants did not and do not observe the covenant stipulations that God made with Abraham, nor do they possess faith that parallels the faith Abraham had in God. Abraham's descendants had difficulty in accepting Jesus and His teachings. The elect of God hear and obey the teachings of Jesus. In Christ God is creating the elect remnant.

8:31–41 SALVATION, Initiative—God sent Jesus to tell people the truth that would set them free from their sins. All Jews are natural descendents of Abraham but not necessarily his spiritual offspring (Ro 9:6–8; Gal 3:6–14).

8:42 SALVATION, Love of God—Those who love God the Father will also love God the Son, because the Son is of God.

8:46 JESUS CHRIST, Sinless—No one could list one sin Jesus committed. See note on 6:69. Compare 9:16.

hear is that you do not belong to God."

The Claims of Jesus About Himself

48The Jews answered him, "Aren't we right in saying that you are a Samaritan[b] and demon-possessed?"[c]

49"I am not possessed by a demon," said Jesus, "but I honor my Father and you dishonor me. 50I am not seeking glory for myself;[d] but there is one who seeks it, and he is the judge. 51I tell you the truth, if anyone keeps my word, he will never see death."[e]

52At this the Jews exclaimed, "Now we know that you are demon-possessed![f] Abraham died and so did the prophets, yet you say that if anyone keeps your word, he will never taste death. 53Are you greater than our father Abraham?[g] He died, and so did the prophets. Who do you think you are?"

54Jesus replied, "If I glorify myself,[h] my glory means nothing. My Father, whom you claim as your God, is the one who glorifies me.[i] 55Though you do not know him,[j] I know him.[k] If I said I did not, I would be a liar like you, but I do know him and keep his word.[l] 56Your father Abraham[m] rejoiced at the thought of seeing my day; he saw it[n] and was glad."

57"You are not yet fifty years old," the Jews said to him, "and you have seen Abraham!"

58"I tell you the truth," Jesus answered, "before Abraham was born,[o] I am!"[p] 59At this, they picked up stones to stone him,[q] but Jesus hid himself,[r] slipping away from the temple grounds.

8:48 [b]S Mt 10:5 [c]ver 52; S Mk 3:22
8:50 [d]ver 54; Jn 5:41
8:51 [e]Jn 11:26
8:52 [f]ver 48; S Mk 3:22
8:53 [g]ver 39; Jn 4:12
8:54 [h]ver 50 [i]Jn 16:14; 17:1,5
8:55 [j]ver 19 [k]Jn 7:28,29 [l]Jn 15:10
8:56 [m]ver 37,39; Ge 18:18 [n]S Mt 13:17
8:58 [o]S Jn 1:2 [p]Ex 3:14; 6:3
8:59 [q]Ex 17:4; Lev 24:16; 1Sa 30:6; Jn 10:31; 11:8 [r]Jn 12:36
9:2 [s]S Mt 23:7 [t]ver 34; Lk 13:2; Ac 28:4 [u]Eze 18:20 [v]Ex 20:5; Job 21:19
9:3 [w]Jn 11:4
9:4 [x]Jn 11:9; 12:35
9:5 [y]S Jn 1:4
9:6 [z]Mk 7:33; 8:23
9:7 [a]ver 11; 2Ki 5:10; Lk 13:4 [b]Isa 35:5; Jn 11:37
9:8 [c]Ac 3:2,10
9:11 [d]ver 7

Chapter 9

Jesus Heals a Man Born Blind

As he went along, he saw a man blind from birth. 2His disciples asked him, "Rabbi,[s] who sinned,[t] this man[u] or his parents,[v] that he was born blind?"

3"Neither this man nor his parents sinned," said Jesus, "but this happened so that the work of God might be displayed in his life.[w] 4As long as it is day,[x] we must do the work of him who sent me. Night is coming, when no one can work. 5While I am in the world, I am the light of the world."[y]

6Having said this, he spit[z] on the ground, made some mud with the saliva, and put it on the man's eyes. 7"Go," he told him, "wash in the Pool of Siloam"[a] (this word means Sent). So the man went and washed, and came home seeing.[b]

8His neighbors and those who had formerly seen him begging asked, "Isn't this the same man who used to sit and beg?"[c] 9Some claimed that he was.

Others said, "No, he only looks like him."

But he himself insisted, "I am the man."

10"How then were your eyes opened?" they demanded.

11He replied, "The man they call Jesus made some mud and put it on my eyes. He told me to go to Siloam and wash. So I went and washed, and then I could see."[d]

12"Where is this man?" they asked him.

"I don't know," he said.

8:51–59 HUMANITY, Death—See note on Pr 11:19. Physical and spiritual death are different yet related. Physical death comes to all because we are mortals. Spiritual death can be escaped, however, through obedience to Jesus Christ.
8:51 SALVATION, Eternal Life—Compare 5:24; 6:68. Those who keep Christ's Word will never see spiritual death. They will never lose eternal life.
8:54 JESUS CHRIST, Glory—See note on 1:14.
8:58 JESUS CHRIST, Preexistent—Jesus boldly claimed to have known Abraham as He existed eternally with the Father before Abraham was born.
9:1–41 JESUS CHRIST, Miracles—John's sixth sign, the healing of a blind man, provided the occasion for a long discourse on suffering, the problem of evil, and the cause and intention of affliction. Blindness is not God's will. He wants all to see the Light of salvation available only in Christ. See note on 1:4–5. Jesus' miracles showed His unique, divine power. This confused religious leaders because He did not do religion their way. They acted defensively and barred from worship and membership in their religion anyone who acknowledged Jesus as the Messiah.
9:1–41 MIRACLE, Faith—Miracles do more than restore physical powers. They teach spiritual truth. The healing event became a parable of light and darkness. What faith the blind man acted out in his walk to Siloam! . . . dodging the crowds, with a dirty face, just because a man had placed mud in his eyes. Although the religious leaders sought to discredit the miracle, the man saw more clearly than they—both physically and spiritually. Powerful religious leaders remained in spiritual darkness. The blind man gained physical and spiritual sight (v 38).
9:1–4 EVIL AND SUFFERING, Punishment—Jesus rejected the view that all suffering was due to sin. Because the man was blind, Jesus had the opportunity to reveal God's power. We do not have explanations about the cause of every case of suffering. We can look to see how God can work even through suffering to achieve His purposes. See note on Lk 13:1–5.
9:3–6 REVELATION, Persons—Suffering is not always the result of sin. Some suffering or handicap may be an opportunity for God's grace and healing to be displayed. Jesus felt compelled to be busy being God's light in the world. In sickness or health His followers can reveal His light to the world's darkness.
9:4 HISTORY, Time—Humans have a history, a beginning and an end. So does the created world. So did Christ in His earthly existence. Christ in His ministry and His disciples through the centuries of history must work urgently while their limited life and the world's limited life give opportunity. Christ's death points to the night of judgment when no one can proclaim or accept salvation. Each moment of time thus is filled with content as the opportunity for doing God's work of proclamation.

The Pharisees Investigate the Healing

13 They brought to the Pharisees the man who had been blind. 14 Now the day on which Jesus had made the mud and opened the man's eyes was a Sabbath.[e] 15 Therefore the Pharisees also asked him how he had received his sight.[f] "He put mud on my eyes," the man replied, "and I washed, and now I see."

16 Some of the Pharisees said, "This man is not from God, for he does not keep the Sabbath."[g]

But others asked, "How can a sinner do such miraculous signs?"[h] So they were divided.[i]

17 Finally they turned again to the blind man, "What have you to say about him? It was your eyes he opened."

The man replied, "He is a prophet."[j]

18 The Jews[k] still did not believe that he had been blind and had received his sight until they sent for the man's parents. 19 "Is this your son?" they asked. "Is this the one you say was born blind? How is it that now he can see?"

20 "We know he is our son," the parents answered, "and we know he was born blind. 21 But how he can see now, or who opened his eyes, we don't know. Ask him. He is of age; he will speak for himself." 22 His parents said this because they were afraid of the Jews,[l] for already the Jews had decided that anyone who acknowledged that Jesus was the Christ[v] would be put out[m] of the synagogue.[n] 23 That was why his parents said, "He is of age; ask him."[o]

24 A second time they summoned the man who had been blind. "Give glory to God,[w]"[p] they said. "We know this man is a sinner."[q]

25 He replied, "Whether he is a sinner or not, I don't know. One thing I do know. I was blind but now I see!"

26 Then they asked him, "What did he do to you? How did he open your eyes?"

27 He answered, "I have told you already[r] and you did not listen. Why do you want to hear it again? Do you want to become his disciples, too?"

28 Then they hurled insults at him and said, "You are this fellow's disciple! We are disciples of Moses![s] 29 We know that God spoke to Moses, but as for this fellow, we don't even know where he comes from."[t]

30 The man answered, "Now that is remarkable! You don't know where he comes from, yet he opened my eyes. 31 We know that God does not listen to sinners. He listens to the godly man who does his will.[u] 32 Nobody has ever heard of opening the eyes of a man born blind. 33 If this man were not from God,[v] he could do nothing."

34 To this they replied, "You were steeped in sin at birth;[w] how dare you lecture us!" And they threw him out.[x]

Spiritual Blindness

35 Jesus heard that they had thrown him out, and when he found him, he said, "Do you believe[y] in the Son of Man?"[z]

36 "Who is he, sir?" the man asked. "Tell me so that I may believe in him."[a]

37 Jesus said, "You have now seen him; in fact, he is the one speaking with you."[b]

38 Then the man said, "Lord, I believe," and he worshiped him.[c]

39 Jesus said, "For judgment[d] I have come into this world,[e] so that the blind will see[f] and those who see will become blind."[g]

40 Some Pharisees who were with him heard him say this and asked, "What? Are we blind too?"[h]

41 Jesus said, "If you were blind, you would not be guilty of sin; but now that you claim you can see, your guilt remains.[i]

Chapter 10

The Shepherd and His Flock

"I tell you the truth, the man who does not enter the sheep pen by the gate, but climbs in by some other

9:14 [e]Mt 12:1-14; Jn 5:9
9:15 [f]ver 10
9:16 [g]S Mt 12:2 [h]S Jn 2:11 [i]S Jn 6:52
9:17 [j]S Mt 21:11
9:18 [k]S Jn 1:19
9:22 [l]S Jn 7:13 [m]ver 34; Lk 6:22 [n]Jn 12:42; 16:2
9:23 [o]ver 21
9:24 [p]Jos 7:19 [q]ver 16
9:27 [r]ver 15
9:28 [s]Jn 5:45
9:29 [t]Jn 8:14
9:31 [u]Ge 18:23-32; Ps 34:15,16; 66:18; 145:19,20; Pr 15:29; Isa 1:15; 59:1,2; Jn 15:7; Jas 5:16-18; 1Jn 5:14,15
9:33 [v]ver 16; Jn 3:2
9:34 [w]ver 2 [x]ver 22,35; Isa 66:5
9:35 [y]S Jn 3:15 [z]S Mt 8:20
9:36 [a]Ro 10:14
9:37 [b]Jn 4:26
9:38 [c]Mt 28:9
9:39 [d]S Jn 5:22 [e]Jn 3:19; 12:47 [f]Lk 4:18 [g]Mt 13:13
9:40 [h]Ro 2:19
9:41 [i]Jn 15:22,24

[v]22 Or *Messiah* [w]24 A solemn charge to tell the truth (see Joshua 7:19)

9:16–34 JESUS CHRIST, Sinless—Religious leaders classified Jesus as a sinner because He did not keep their legalistic rules such as sabbath observance. Even some of them had to confess His power showed He was not to be dismissed as belonging to the category of sinful people. The healed man understood Jesus was a godly person sent from God and doing His will.

9:35–41 JESUS CHRIST, Son of Man—Jesus accepted the "Son of Man" title and demanded faith in Him as the way to salvation. Worship is the proper response to the "Son of Man."

9:35–37 REVELATION, Jesus Christ—Avoiding those who resisted believing in Him, Jesus sought to reveal Himself to a humble and teachable person. Jesus was the Son of man revealing God's kingdom to the world.

9:35–38 PRAYER, Faith—Jesus often probed for belief. The faith response to the healing was, properly, worship. The prayer of commitment and faith heals spiritual blindness.

9:36–38 WORSHIP, Individual—See note on Mt 17:1–8. Worship is an activity of believers in positive response to Christ.

9:39 JESUS CHRIST, Judgment—Jesus' presence brought the necessity to believe or reject Him, dividing humanity into two classes—the seeing and blind or the saved and lost.

10:1–21,25–30 JESUS CHRIST, Shepherd—Jesus is the Way to God's pasture and the Shepherd who leads us to His salvation. He sacrificed His own life that we might have eternal life. He enters into intimate personal relationship with each of His people. No human authorities gained power over Jesus. He voluntarily died and was raised according to God's mission for Him.

way, is a thief and a robber.[j] 2The man
who enters by the gate is the shepherd of
his sheep.[k] 3The watchman opens the
gate for him, and the sheep listen to his
voice.[l] He calls his own sheep by name
and leads them out.[m] 4When he has
brought out all his own, he goes on ahead
of them, and his sheep follow him because they know his voice.[n] 5But they
will never follow a stranger; in fact, they
will run away from him because they do
not recognize a stranger's voice." 6**Jesus
used this figure of speech,[o] but they did
not understand what he was telling
them.[p]**

7Therefore Jesus said again, "I tell you
the truth, I am[q] the gate[r] for the sheep.
8All who ever came before me[s] were
thieves and robbers,[t] but the sheep did
not listen to them. 9I am the gate; whoever enters through me will be saved.[x] He
will come in and go out, and find pasture.
10The thief comes only to steal and kill
and destroy; I have come that they may
have life,[u] and have it to the full.[v]

11"I am[w] the good shepherd.[x] The
good shepherd lays down his life for the
sheep.[y] 12The hired hand is not the shepherd who owns the sheep. So when he
sees the wolf coming, he abandons the
sheep and runs away.[z] Then the wolf attacks the flock and scatters it. 13The man
runs away because he is a hired hand and
cares nothing for the sheep.

14"I am the good shepherd;[a] I know
my sheep[b] and my sheep know me—

10:1 [j]ver 8,10
10:2 [k]ver 11,14; Mk 6:34
10:3 [l]ver 4,5,14,16,27 [m]ver 4,5,14,16,27
10:4 [n]S ver 3
10:6 [o]S Jn 16:25 [p]S Mk 9:32
10:7 [q]S Jn 6:35 [r]ver 9
10:8 [s]Jer 23:1,2; Eze 34:2 [t]ver 1
10:10 [u]S Jn 1:4; 3:15,16; 5:40; 20:31 [v]Ps 65:11; Ro 5:17
10:11 [w]S Jn 6:35 [x]ver 14; Ps 23:1; Isa 40:11; Eze 34:11-16,23; Mt 2:6; Lk 12:32; Heb 13:20; 1Pe 2:25; 5:4; Rev 7:17 [y]ver 15, 17,18; Jn 15:13; 1Jn 3:16
10:12 [z]Zec 11:16, 17
10:14 [a]S ver 11 [b]ver 27; Ex 33:12
10:15 [c]Mt 11:27 [d]ver 11,17,18
10:16 [e]Isa 56:8; Ac 10:34,35 [f]Jn 11:52; 17:20, 21; Eph 2:11-19 [g]Eze 34:23; 37:24
10:17 [h]ver 11,15, 18
10:18 [i]Mt 26:53 [j]Jn 15:10; Php 2:8; Heb 5:8
10:19 [k]S Jn 6:52
10:20 [l]S Mk 3:22 [m]2Ki 9:11; Jer 29:26; Mk 3:21
10:21 [n]S Mt 4:24 [o]Ex 4:11; Jn 9:32, 33
10:23 [p]Ac 3:11; 5:12
10:24 [q]S Jn 1:19 [r]Lk 22:67; Jn 16:25,29
10:25 [s]Jn 4:26; 8:58

15just as the Father knows me and I know
the Father[c]—and I lay down my life for
the sheep.[d] 16I have other sheep[e] that
are not of this sheep pen. I must bring
them also. They too will listen to my
voice, and there shall be one flock[f] and
one shepherd.[g] 17The reason my Father
loves me is that I lay down my life[h]—
only to take it up again. 18No one takes it
from me, but I lay it down of my own
accord.[i] I have authority to lay it down
and authority to take it up again. This
command I received from my Father."[j]

**19At these words the Jews were again
divided.[k] 20Many of them said,** "He is
demon-possessed[l] and raving mad.[m]
Why listen to him?"

21But others said, "These are not the
sayings of a man possessed by a demon.[n]
Can a demon open the eyes of the
blind?"[o]

The Unbelief of the Jews

**22Then came the Feast of Dedication[y]
at Jerusalem. It was winter, 23and Jesus
was in the temple area walking in Solomon's Colonnade.[p] 24The Jews[q] gathered around him, saying,** "How long will
you keep us in suspense? If you are the
Christ,[z] tell us plainly."[r]

25Jesus answered, "I did tell you,[s] but
you do not believe. The miracles I do in

[x]*9* Or *kept safe* [y]*22* That is, Hanukkah [z]*24* Or *Messiah*

10:9 SALVATION, Definition—Jesus Christ is the Gate into the fold of God (Ps 28:9). God's salvation is available only through His Son (Ac 4:12). Acceptance of God's grace in Christ is a necessary human response to receive salvation.

10:10,28 SALVATION, Eternal Life—Eternal life is life of a heavenly quality and quantity and can never be lost. These verses teach the eternal security of believers. See note on 8:51.

10:14–15 REVELATION, Author of Love—Christ revealed the heart of God as He identified Himself as the Shepherd-Son whose mind and heart were committed to offer love and life for the sake of His charge. Jesus loved enough to know His sheep personally.

10:14–18 SALVATION, Atonement—Jesus as the Good Shepherd voluntarily laid down His life on the cross to make an atonement for His sheep. Believers in Him all belong to His one flock.

10:14–18 THE CHURCH, Redeemed of All Ages—Jesus is the Shepherd of His sheep—all those who call on the name of Christ. He knows His sheep and calls them by name. The flock of God is not a large, nameless group of people, but individuals known of God and called by Him. God's people include others who are different in race, nationality, and native religion than those to whom the gospel first came. All these belong to God because Jesus laid down His life for the sheep. God's purpose in Christ is to bring all His people together in His service. Spiritual unity under Christ is God's plan for all His people. Church groups maintain separate identities to accomplish a unique mission, but all have a spiritual relationship to Christ's larger family. See note on Lk 9:49–50.

10:17–18 REVELATION, Author of Love—The cross revealed God's supreme love for us and for His Son. The cross did not surprise God. It was part of His plan of revelation, a plan to which Jesus totally committed Himself.

10:19–42 JESUS CHRIST, Christ—See note on Mt 16:16. Jesus' miracles showed He is the Christ. Self-centered religious leaders tried to credit His power to Satan. The miracles showed Jesus was from God, but the leaders saw only a breaking of their rules (Lev 24:16) and wanted to kill Him. Christ calls people to listen to Him and not to human traditions. John used Ps 82:6 to show He was the specially dedicated Son of the Father, uniquely united with the Father in the Trinity.

10:25–38 GOD, Trinity—Near Eastern people could apply the term "gods" to powerful rulers appointed by the high god. Jesus showed the complete distinction between these human rulers and Himself. His actions, particularly His healing miracles, were the actions of God. Thus He was the incarnate Son of God—God appearing on earth in human flesh. The Father and Son were united. This passage builds a firm foundation for the teaching of the Trinity, one God known to us in three distinguishable but inseparable Persons. See note on Mt 3:16–17.

10:25–30 REVELATION, Faithfulness—Jesus' followers are His sheep who know Him well and thus believe His revelation. He offers us life eternal and is faithful to us with His life, so we are never in permanent danger. Unbelievers cannot claim they were cheated of revelation. Their closed minds do not let them respond to revelation. Open minds believe Christ's acts and deeds, seeing that He and the Father are identical in nature.

10:25–29 THE CHURCH, People of God—God's people obey. We follow Christ where He leads. We are secure in His hand and participate in eternal life. No one is more powerful than God, so He offers perfect protection to His obedient people.

my Father's name speak for me,[t] 26but
you do not believe because you are not
my sheep.[u] 27My sheep listen to my
voice; I know them,[v] and they follow
me.[w] 28I give them eternal life,[x] and they
shall never perish;[y] no one can snatch
them out of my hand.[z] 29My Father, who
has given them to me,[a] is greater than
all[a]; [b] no one can snatch them out of my
Father's hand. 30I and the Father are
one."[c]

31Again the Jews picked up stones to
stone him,[d] 32but Jesus said to them, "I
have shown you many great miracles
from the Father. For which of these do
you stone me?"

33"We are not stoning you for any of
these," replied the Jews, "but for blasphemy, because you, a mere man, claim
to be God."[e]

34Jesus answered them, "Is it not written in your Law,[f] 'I have said you are
gods'[b]?[g] 35If he called them 'gods,' to
whom the word of God[h] came—and the
Scripture cannot be broken[i]— 36what
about the one whom the Father set
apart[j] as his very own[k] and sent into the
world?[l] Why then do you accuse me of
blasphemy because I said, 'I am God's
Son'?[m] 37Do not believe me unless I do
what my Father does.[n] 38But if I do it,
even though you do not believe me, believe the miracles, that you may know
and understand that the Father is in me,
and I in the Father."[o] 39Again they tried
to seize him,[p] but he escaped their
grasp.[q]

40Then Jesus went back across the Jordan[r] to the place where John had been
baptizing in the early days. Here he
stayed 41and many people came to him.
They said, "Though John never performed a miraculous sign,[s] all that John
said about this man was true."[t] 42And in
that place many believed in Jesus.[u]

Chapter 11

The Death of Lazarus

NOW a man named Lazarus was sick.
He was from Bethany,[v] the village
of Mary and her sister Martha.[w] 2This
Mary, whose brother Lazarus now lay
sick, was the same one who poured perfume on the Lord and wiped his feet with
her hair.[x] 3So the sisters sent word to
Jesus, "Lord, the one you love[y] is sick."

4When he heard this, Jesus said, "This
sickness will not end in death. No, it is
for God's glory[z] so that God's Son may
be glorified through it." 5Jesus loved Martha and her sister and Lazarus. 6Yet when
he heard that Lazarus was sick, he stayed
where he was two more days.

[a] *29* Many early manuscripts *What my Father has given me is greater than all* [b] *34* Psalm 82:6

10:25 [t]Jn 5:36; 14:11
10:26 [u]Jn 8:47
10:27 [v]ver 14 [w]ver 4
10:28 [x]S Mt 25:46 [y]Isa 66:22 [z]S Jn 6:39
10:29 [a]Jn 17:2,6,24 [b]Jn 14:28
10:30 [c]Dt 6:4; Jn 17:21-23
10:31 [d]S Jn 8:59
10:33 [e]Lev 24:16; Mt 26:63-66; Jn 5:18
10:34 [f]Jn 8:17; 12:34; 15:25; Ro 3:19; 1Co 14:21 [g]Ps 82:6
10:35 [h]S Heb 4:12 [i]S Mt 5:18
10:36 [j]Jer 1:5 [k]Jn 6:69 [l]S Jn 3:17 [m]Jn 5:17,18
10:37 [n]ver 25
10:38 [o]Jn 14:10,11,20; 17:21
10:39 [p]Jn 7:30 [q]Lk 4:30; Jn 8:59
10:40 [r]Jn 1:28
10:41 [s]S Jn 2:11 [t]Jn 1:26,27,30,34
10:42 [u]S Jn 7:31
11:1 [v]S Mt 21:17 [w]Lk 10:38
11:2 [x]Mk 14:3; Lk 7:38; Jn 12:3
11:3 [y]ver 5,36
11:4 [z]ver 40

10:27 DISCIPLESHIP, Lordship of Christ—True disciples hear the Lord's voice and follow Him. They know the security of being united with Him. They neither complain nor rebel. They obey. Simply put, discipleship is total obedience to Christ. See note on Ro 6:5–18.

10:28–29 ELECTION, Eternal Security—The salvation of the elect is secure for time and eternity. This eternal security is because the elect are in God's hands. No one is strong enough to snatch them from God's hand. Eternal security is not payment for human achievement. It is a gift of God's election to give salvation through Christ.

10:36 JESUS CHRIST, I Am—Jesus was what He claimed, the unique Son of God. See notes on 3:31–36; 8:31–59.

11:1–44 JESUS CHRIST, Miracles—The seventh sign was the raising of Lazarus. It became the occasion for the discourse on the resurrection and its life. This concludes the first part of John's Gospel, the book of signs. It serves as a transition to the second half, the book of glory. Lazarus had been dead long enough for the body to begin its decay. Jesus raised him back to earthly existence. The final resurrection of all persons occurs at the last day. We have not yet tasted death, but we have already begun to experience the power of Him who overcomes death. See note on 2:1–11.

11:1–44 MIRACLE, Christ—Miracles provide opportunity to teach spiritual truth, to lead people to faith, and to reveal the person of Christ. Jesus carefully planned His visit to Bethany for the raising of Lazarus. The understanding and faith of the disciples was provoked. The faith of the sisters was challenged. All came through when confronted with the gift of new life. The difficulty of the miracle is underscored in the hopelessness of the sisters and the notation that Lazarus had been in the grave four days . . . already his spirit had departed according to Jewish beliefs. Yet a bit of faith, the size of a grain of mustard seed, prompted such remarks as "if you had been here, my brother would not have died" (v 21). At Jesus' direction they took away the stone. Jesus called to Lazarus, and Lazarus came forth. Again (see ch 9) the religious leaders tried to discredit the miracle (12:10), for many believed on Jesus. Even the religious leaders complained to one another that Jesus did many signs (vv 45–48), but the signs did not point them to God. Miracles do not force us to God. They provide reason and opportunity to believe in Him.

11:1–44 HUMANITY, Death—When physical death comes to a loved one, people naturally feel grief. This was true even of Jesus. At the same time, the power and love of Jesus can restore life. No one, however, ultimately escapes physical death as long as this world endures.

11:1–44 FAMILY, Role Relationships—See note on Lk 10:38–42.

11:3 EVIL AND SUFFERING, God's Present Help—Even those Jesus loves are subject to suffering and death. We should not expect our faith in the Lord to protect us always from affliction. Rather, we should believe that the Lord will one day raise us from the dead, as He did Lazarus. God can help us and teach us through our suffering. See note on 9:1–4.

11:4 GOD, Glory—The glory of God is some event or happening that reveals the person or power of God. In some Old Testament instances, the glory of God was manifested in some visible form, like a shining light. The emphasis, however, is not on the event or means of disclosing the glory of God. The emphasis is on the strong, unmistakable perception of God's person and God's power. In this case the miracle of healing was important, but the way that the healing pointed to God's power was more important. It revealed the glory of God.

11:4 JESUS CHRIST, Glory—Jesus' miracles brought the glorious presence of God in power and led people to acknowledge God as the One with supreme glory. See note on 1:14. Compare 2:11; 7:39; 8:50,54; 11:4,40; 12:16–28,41; 13:31–32; 14:13; 15:8; 16:14; 17:1–10,22–24; 21:19.

7 Then he said to his disciples, "Let us
go back to Judea."[a]
8 "But Rabbi,"[b] they said, "a short
while ago the Jews tried to stone you,[c]
and yet you are going back there?"
9 Jesus answered, "Are there not
twelve hours of daylight? A man who
walks by day will not stumble, for he sees
by this world's light.[d] 10 It is when he
walks by night that he stumbles, for he
has no light."
11 After he had said this, he went on to
tell them, "Our friend[e] Lazarus has fall-
en asleep;[f] but I am going there to wake
him up."
12 His disciples replied, "Lord, if he
sleeps, he will get better." 13 Jesus had
been speaking of his death, but his disciples thought he meant natural sleep.[g]
14 So then he told them plainly, "Lazarus is dead, 15 and for your sake I am glad I
was not there, so that you may believe.
But let us go to him."
16 Then Thomas[h] (called Didymus) said
to the rest of the disciples, "Let us also
go, that we may die with him."

Jesus Comforts the Sisters

17 On his arrival, Jesus found that Lazarus had already been in the tomb for four
days.[i] 18 Bethany[j] was less than two
miles[c] from Jerusalem, 19 and many Jews
had come to Martha and Mary to comfort
them in the loss of their brother.[k]
20 When Martha heard that Jesus was
coming, she went out to meet him, but
Mary stayed at home.[l]
21 "Lord," Martha said to Jesus, "if you
had been here, my brother would not
have died.[m] 22 But I know that even now
God will give you whatever you ask."[n]
23 Jesus said to her, "Your brother will
rise again."
24 Martha answered, "I know he will
rise again in the resurrection[o] at the last
day."[p]
25 Jesus said to her, "I am[q] the resurrection and the life.[r] He who believes[s]
in me will live, even though he dies;
26 and whoever lives and believes[t] in me
will never die.[u] Do you believe this?"
27 "Yes, Lord," she told him, "I believe
that you are the Christ,[d][v] the Son of
God,[w] who was to come into the
world."[x]
28 And after she had said this, she went
back and called her sister Mary aside.
"The Teacher[y] is here," she said, "and is
asking for you." 29 When Mary heard this,
she got up quickly and went to him.
30 Now Jesus had not yet entered the village, but was still at the place where Martha had met him.[z] 31 When the Jews who
had been with Mary in the house, comforting her,[a] noticed how quickly she got
up and went out, they followed her, supposing she was going to the tomb to
mourn there.
32 When Mary reached the place where
Jesus was and saw him, she fell at his feet
and said, "Lord, if you had been here, my
brother would not have died."[b]
33 When Jesus saw her weeping, and
the Jews who had come along with her
also weeping, he was deeply moved[c] in
spirit and troubled.[d] 34 "Where have you
laid him?" he asked.
"Come and see, Lord," they replied.
35 Jesus wept.[e]
36 Then the Jews said, "See how he
loved him!"[f]
37 But some of them said, "Could not he

11:7 [a]Jn 10:40
11:8 [b]S Mt 23:7 [c]Jn 8:59; 10:31
11:9 [d]Jn 9:4; 12:35
11:11 [e]ver 3 [f]S Mt 9:24
11:13 [g]Mt 9:24
11:16 [h]Mt 10:3; Jn 14:5; 20:24-28; 21:2; Ac 1:13
11:17 [i]ver 6,39
11:18 [j]ver 1; S Mt 21:17
11:19 [k]ver 31; Job 2:11
11:20 [l]Lk 10:38-42
11:21 [m]ver 32,37
11:22 [n]ver 41,42
11:24 [o]Da 12:2; Jn 5:28,29; Ac 24:15 [p]Jn 6:39, 40
11:25 [q]S Jn 6:35 [r]S Jn 1:4 [s]S Jn 3:15
11:26 [t]S Jn 3:15 [u]S Mt 25:46
11:27 [v]S Lk 2:11 [w]S Mt 4:3 [x]Jn 6:14
11:28 [y]Mt 26:18; Jn 13:13
11:30 [z]ver 20
11:31 [a]ver 19
11:32 [b]ver 21
11:33 [c]ver 38 [d]S Jn 12:27
11:35 [e]Lk 19:41
11:36 [f]ver 3

[c] *18* Greek *fifteen stadia* (about 3 kilometers)
[d] *27* Or *Messiah*

11:7 JESUS CHRIST, Mission—This crucial event in the life of Jesus marked a turning point in His ministry. With Jesus' return to Judea for the raising of Lazarus, Jesus turned from showing the glory of the Father to the disciples to showing God's glory to all the world through the final events of His ministry, especially the cross.

11:11–13 LAST THINGS, Believers' Death—Although the actual physical death of Lazarus was clearly validated (vv 14,39), Jesus spoke of it as sleep. See note on Ac 7:60. For believers, death is no more sinister than sleep. It is in fact true rest. For the power of God, resurrection from the dead is no more difficult than rousing persons from sleep.

11:15,25–27,40–48 SALVATION, Belief—This is the *sign of signs* in John's Gospel. Jesus raised Lazarus from the dead after he had been dead four days. The sign was intended to evoke faith in those who saw it and heard about it. All those who believe in Jesus will be raised from the dead. He has the power over death and the grave. He did not come to break the power of a political empire. He came to win victory over death.

11:22 PRAYER, Faith—Death is not a barrier for absolute faith. See notes on Mt 21:19–22; Mk 9:19–29.

11:24 LAST THINGS, Believers' Resurrection—While an immediate raising back to life was not in Martha's hope, the prospect of future resurrection was. Jesus is the source of present spiritual life, which is eternal life. He is also the power for future resurrection life at the last day. In Him, present and future merge, as spiritual and physical resurrection find a common source. The present power witnesses to that of the last day, and that of the last day is predicated on that of the present display.

11:25 JESUS CHRIST, Resurrection—Jesus was raised from the dead and thus became the way of resurrection for those who trust Him. As the Resurrection, He gives eternal life.

11:25 REVELATION, Author of Life—Here Jesus made a most important revelation: He is the Author of resurrection and life. Any who believe in Him receive with Him the power to overcome death. Each person's destiny depends on response to this revelation.

11:28 JESUS CHRIST, Teaching—His followers confessed Christ as "Messiah" and "Son of God." They addressed Him as "Teacher" because that was the role He most often filled.

11:28 EDUCATION, Jesus—Friends are most likely to know our true identity. It is significant, therefore, that Martha called Jesus "Teacher" when telling her sister of His arrival in their home at Bethany. See note on 13:13.

11:35–38 JESUS CHRIST, Suffering—Jesus knew the suffering that love brings. He cried like all humans who lose loved ones.

who opened the eyes of the blind man[g] have kept this man from dying?"[h]

Jesus Raises Lazarus From the Dead

38 Jesus, once more deeply moved,[i] came to the tomb. It was a cave with a stone laid across the entrance.[j] 39 "Take away the stone," he said.

"But, Lord," said Martha, the sister of the dead man, "by this time there is a bad odor, for he has been there four days."[k]

40 Then Jesus said, "Did I not tell you that if you believed,[l] you would see the glory of God?"[m]

41 So they took away the stone. Then Jesus looked up[n] and said, "Father,[o] I thank you that you have heard me. 42 I knew that you always hear me, but I said this for the benefit of the people standing here,[p] that they may believe that you sent me."[q]

43 When he had said this, Jesus called in a loud voice, "Lazarus, come out!"[r] 44 The dead man came out, his hands and feet wrapped with strips of linen,[s] and a cloth around his face.[t]

Jesus said to them, "Take off the grave clothes and let him go."

The Plot to Kill Jesus

45 Therefore many of the Jews who had come to visit Mary,[u] and had seen what Jesus did,[v] put their faith in him.[w] 46 But some of them went to the Pharisees and told them what Jesus had done. 47 Then the chief priests and the Pharisees[x] called a meeting[y] of the Sanhedrin.[z]

"What are we accomplishing?" they asked. "Here is this man performing many miraculous signs.[a] 48 If we let him go on like this, everyone will believe in him, and then the Romans will come and take away both our place[e] and our nation."

49 Then one of them, named Caiaphas,[b] who was high priest that year,[c] spoke up, "You know nothing at all! 50 You do not realize that it is better for you that one man die for the people than that the whole nation perish."[d]

51 He did not say this on his own, but as high priest that year he prophesied that Jesus would die for the Jewish nation, 52 and not only for that nation but also for the scattered children of God, to bring them together and make them one.[e] 53 So from that day on they plotted to take his life.[f]

54 Therefore Jesus no longer moved about publicly among the Jews.[g] Instead he withdrew to a region near the desert, to a village called Ephraim, where he stayed with his disciples.

55 When it was almost time for the Jewish Passover,[h] many went up from the country to Jerusalem for their ceremonial cleansing[i] before the Passover. 56 They kept looking for Jesus,[j] and as they stood in the temple area they asked one another, "What do you think? Isn't he coming to the Feast at all?" 57 But the chief priests and Pharisees had given orders that if anyone found out where Jesus was, he should report it so that they might arrest him.

Chapter 12

Jesus Anointed at Bethany

12:1–8Ref — Mt 26:6–13; Mk 14:3–9; Lk 7:37–39

SIX days before the Passover,[k] Jesus arrived at Bethany,[l] where Lazarus lived, whom Jesus had raised from the dead. 2 Here a dinner was given in Jesus' honor. Martha served,[m] while Lazarus was among those reclining at the table

11:37 [g]Jn 9:6,7 [h]ver 21,32
11:38 [i]ver 33 [j]Mt 27:60; Lk 24:2; Jn 20:1
11:39 [k]ver 17
11:40 [l]ver 23-25 [m]ver 4
11:41 [n]Jn 17:1 [o]S Mt 11:25
11:42 [p]Jn 12:30 [q]S Jn 3:17
11:43 [r]S Lk 7:14
11:44 [s]Jn 19:40 [t]Jn 20:7
11:45 [u]ver 19 [v]Jn 2:23 [w]Ex 14:31; S Jn 7:31
11:47 [x]ver 57 [y]Mt 26:3 [z]S Mt 5:22 [a]S Jn 2:11
11:49 [b]S Mt 26:3 [c]ver 51; Jn 18:13, 14
11:50 [d]Jn 18:14
11:52 [e]Isa 49:6; Jn 10:16
11:53 [f]S Mt 12:14
11:54 [g]Jn 7:1
11:55 [h]Ex 12:13, 23,27; Mt 26:1,2; Mk 14:1; Jn 13:1 [i]2Ch 30:17,18
11:56 [j]Jn 7:11
12:1 [k]S Jn 11:55 [l]S Mt 21:17
12:2 [m]Lk 10:38-42

[e]*48* Or *temple*

11:40 JESUS CHRIST, Glory—Giving life to the dead reveals God's glory in Jesus. See note on v 4.

11:40 REVELATION, Events—Jesus assured two very close friends that their belief in Him and His power would allow them to see the fullness of God's will revealed in their brother's recovery from death. God's glory is the full manifestation of His power and presence. See note on Ex 33:18–22.

11:41–42 PRAYER, Answer—See note on Mk 7:34. Jesus' words imply a prayer previously made, probably during the four day wait prior to the journey to Bethany (vv 6,17). Here He acknowledged the Father as His source of healing power. Answered prayer calls forth thanks. Believers need never doubt. God hears and responds to prayer.

11:43–44 LAST THINGS, Believers' Resurrection—The raising of Lazarus back to continued earthly life was a demonstration in time of the end time power of God to effect the resurrection of believers (5:28–29). Lazarus was raised but would die again. Believers will be raised never again to die.

11:51 JESUS CHRIST, Atonement—Even the religious establishment unconsciously and against their own wills acknowledged the atoning work of Christ.

11:51–52 THE CHURCH, Redeemed of All Ages—The church goes beyond all racial and political boundaries. Christ's death offered salvation to all people. The Jewish leaders thought they could escape punishment from the Roman government by letting Jesus die. God's purposes go beyond the Jewish nation to include all people. He works to unite all people under Christ. Churches are local groups, but they are part of the spiritual church and, consequently, are not to live in isolation. Christ's spiritual church includes all people everywhere who follow Jesus as Lord. See notes on 10:14–18; 20:29; Lk 9:49–50.

11:55 JESUS CHRIST, Mission—John's account of the last events in Jesus' ministry speaks of Jesus' journey to Jerusalem and gives a report of Jesus' final teaching in that city. This period of final teaching involves the inclusion of Greek-speaking Jews, symbolic of the ingathering of the Gentiles, and Jesus' references to Old Testament prophecy to anticipate His death (Isa 53:1). His ministry ended where it began—with prophetic insights. Compare Mk 11:1.

12:1–10 JESUS CHRIST, Death—See note on Lk 7:36–38. Christ's healing signs did bring people to faith. A true believer prepared Him for death as religious leaders prepared to kill Him.

12:1–8 STEWARDSHIP, Service to God—See note on Mt 26:6–13.

with him. 3Then Mary took about a pint[f]
of pure nard, an expensive perfume;[n]
she poured it on Jesus' feet and wiped his
feet with her hair.[o] And the house was
filled with the fragrance of the perfume.
4But one of his disciples, Judas Iscariot,
who was later to betray him,[p] objected,
5"Why wasn't this perfume sold and the
money given to the poor? It was worth a
year's wages.[g]" 6He did not say this because he cared about the poor but because he was a thief; as keeper of the
money bag,[q] he used to help himself to
what was put into it.
7"Leave her alone," Jesus replied. "It
was intended that she should save this
perfume for the day of my burial.[r] 8You
will always have the poor among you,[s]
but you will not always have me."
9Meanwhile a large crowd of Jews
found out that Jesus was there and came,
not only because of him but also to see
Lazarus, whom he had raised from the
dead.[t] 10So the chief priests made plans
to kill Lazarus as well, 11for on account of
him[u] many of the Jews were going over
to Jesus and putting their faith in him.[v]

The Triumphal Entry

12:12–15pp — Mt 21:4–9; Mk 11:7–10; Lk 19:35–38

12The next day the great crowd that
had come for the Feast heard that Jesus
was on his way to Jerusalem. 13They took
palm branches[w] and went out to meet
him, shouting,

"Hosanna![h]"

"Blessed is he who comes in the name
of the Lord!"[i] [x]

"Blessed is the King of Israel!"[y]
14Jesus found a young donkey and sat
upon it, as it is written,

15"Do not be afraid, O Daughter of Zion;
see, your king is coming,
seated on a donkey's colt."[j] [z]

16At first his disciples did not understand all this.[a] Only after Jesus was glorified[b] did they realize that these things
had been written about him and that they
had done these things to him.
17Now the crowd that was with him[c]
when he called Lazarus from the tomb
and raised him from the dead continued
to spread the word. 18Many people, because they had heard that he had given
this miraculous sign,[d] went out to meet
him. 19So the Pharisees said to one another, "See, this is getting us nowhere. Look
how the whole world has gone after
him!"[e]

Jesus Predicts His Death

20Now there were some Greeks[f]
among those who went up to worship at
the Feast. 21They came to Philip, who
was from Bethsaida[g] in Galilee, with a
request. "Sir," they said, "we would like
to see Jesus." 22Philip went to tell Andrew; Andrew and Philip in turn told
Jesus.
23Jesus replied, "The hour[h] has come
for the Son of Man to be glorified.[i] 24I
tell you the truth, unless a kernel of

12:3 [n]Mk 14:3 [o]Jn 11:2
12:4 [p]S Mt 10:4
12:6 [q]Jn 13:29
12:7 [r]Jn 19:40
12:8 [s]Dt 15:11
12:9 [t]Jn 11:43,44
12:11 [u]ver 17,18; Jn 11:45 [v]S Jn 7:31
12:13 [w]Lev 23:40 [x]Ps 118:25,26 [y]S Jn 1:49
12:15 [z]Zec 9:9
12:16 [a]S Mk 9:32 [b]ver 23; Jn 2:22; 7:39
12:17 [c]Jn 11:42
12:18 [d]ver 11; Lk 19:37
12:19 [e]Jn 11:47,48
12:20 [f]Jn 7:35; Ac 11:20
12:21 [g]S Mt 11:21
12:23 [h]S Mt 26:18 [i]Jn 13:32; 17:1

[f]*3* Greek *a litra* (probably about 0.5 liter) [g]*5* Greek *three hundred denarii* [h]*13* A Hebrew expression meaning "Save!" which became an exclamation of praise [i]*13* Psalm 118:25, 26 [j]*15* Zech. 9:9

12:4–6 CHRISTIAN ETHICS, Property Rights—Thievery is wrong (Ex 20:15). Thievery in the name of religion and charity shows greed has consumed a life. See notes on Mt 6:19–34; Lk 16:1–15.

12:10–11,35–46 SALVATION, Belief—Those who trust in Jesus trust in the Light. He came to deliver persons from darkness, but not everyone wants to see the glory of God revealed in Christ. Only faith, not miracles, leads to true trust in Christ. Faith leads to public testimony because its goal is not human praise. This rejection of Christ was foretold in Isa 6:10; 53:1. The writer of this Gospel was convinced that in the historical chain of cause and effect every result follows a divine purpose. As it was in the days of Isaiah, so it was in the days of Jesus, and so it is in our day. A divine law teaches that sin causes blindness of the soul and a moral insensibility to spiritual truths.

12:12–19 JESUS CHRIST, King—See note on Lk 19:28–44. The disciples fulfilled Scripture and honored Jesus as the messianic King, but they understood the full meaning of their actions only after the resurrection.

12:13 PRAYER, Praise—See note on Mt 21:9.

12:17–19 EVANGELISM, Testimony—Jesus' miracle works had great power to convince others and bring them to faith. Testimony to Christ and His saving grace is powerful in any age and is a vital part of evangelization. Such testimony disturbs those who oppose the Lord, as it did the Pharisees. God still shows His miraculous power to support His witnessing people.

12:20–33 JESUS CHRIST, Glory—See note on 11:4. Facing death brought troubled emotions to Christ as it would to any human, but He obediently carried out the Father's mission; for only in death could He bring glory to God and salvation to God's chosen.

12:20–50 JESUS CHRIST, Death—The Greeks, either Greek-speaking Jews or Gentiles, asked to see Jesus. Jesus used this meeting as an opportunity to foretell His death by means of the vivid metaphor of a grain of wheat dying, being buried, and reproducing. The divine voice reconfirmed Jesus, as at the baptism (Mk 1:11). Jesus and John speak all through the Gospel of His "hour" or "time," that is the appointed time of His destiny when He should accomplish His messianic task (2:4; 7:30; 8:20; 12:23,27; 13:1; 17:1). Jesus was intensely aware that His hour was involved with Satan (12:31; 14:30; 16:11). Jesus' recourse in His time of crisis was to His Father and to the Scriptures.

12:23–29 REVELATION, Author of Life—Jesus' death was the Father's full revelation of His power over death and thus a revelation of God's glory. Jesus' human reaction was to question the Father's wisdom in asking Jesus to sacrifice His life. The great moment of revelation troubled Christ's heart, but He did not avoid it. He knew God had brought Him to the moment to conquer death and in that event reveal the way to eternal life for us.

12:23–33 HISTORY, Time—See notes on 2:4; 7:6–8. Christ's death is the most significant moment of history, for it allowed Christ and the Father to reveal Their full glory and to

wheat falls to the ground and dies,[j] it
remains only a single seed. But if it dies,
it produces many seeds. 25The man who
loves his life will lose it, while the man
who hates his life in this world will keep
it[k] for eternal life.[l] 26Whoever serves
me must follow me; and where I am, my
servant also will be.[m] My Father will hon-
or the one who serves me.

27"Now my heart is troubled,[n] and
what shall I say? 'Father,[o] save me from
this hour'?[p] No, it was for this very reason I came to this hour. 28Father, glorify
your name!"

Then a voice came from heaven,[q] "I
have glorified it, and will glorify it again."
29The crowd that was there and heard it
said it had thundered; others said an angel had spoken to him.

30Jesus said, "This voice was for your
benefit,[r] not mine. 31Now is the time for
judgment on this world;[s] now the prince
of this world[t] will be driven out. 32But I,
when I am lifted up from the earth,[u] will
draw all men to myself."[v] 33He said this
to show the kind of death he was going to
die.[w]

34The crowd spoke up, "We have
heard from the Law[x] that the Christ[k]
will remain forever,[y] so how can you say,
'The Son of Man[z] must be lifted up'?[a]
Who is this 'Son of Man'?"

35Then Jesus told them, "You are going
to have the light[b] just a little while longer. Walk while you have the light,[c] before darkness overtakes you.[d] The man
who walks in the dark does not know
where he is going. 36Put your trust in the
light while you have it, so that you may
become sons of light."[e] When he had
finished speaking, Jesus left and hid himself from them.[f]

The Jews Continue in Their Unbelief

37Even after Jesus had done all these
miraculous signs[g] in their presence, they
still would not believe in him. 38This was
to fulfill the word of Isaiah the prophet:

"Lord, who has believed our message
and to whom has the arm of the
Lord been revealed?"[l] [h]

39For this reason they could not believe, because, as Isaiah says elsewhere:

40"He has blinded their eyes
and deadened their hearts,
so they can neither see with their
eyes,
nor understand with their hearts,
nor turn—and I would heal
them."[m] [i]

41Isaiah said this because he saw Jesus'
glory[j] and spoke about him.[k]

42Yet at the same time many even
among the leaders believed in him.[l] But
because of the Pharisees[m] they would not
confess their faith for fear they would be
put out of the synagogue;[n] 43for they
loved praise from men[o] more than praise
from God.[p]

44Then Jesus cried out, "When a man

[k] *34* Or *Messiah* [l] *38* Isaiah 53:1 [m] *40* Isaiah 6:10

12:24 [j] 1Co 15:36
12:25 [k] Mt 10:39; Mk 8:35; Lk 14:26; 17:33 [l] S Mt 25:46
12:26 [m] Jn 14:3; 17:24; 2Co 5:8; Php 1:23; 1Th 4:17
12:27 [n] Mt 26:38, 39; Jn 11:33,38; 13:21 [o] S Mt 11:25 [p] ver 23
12:28 [q] S Mt 3:17
12:30 [r] Ex 19:9; Jn 11:42
12:31 [s] Jn 16:11 [t] Jn 14:30; 16:11; 2Co 4:4; Eph 2:2; 1Jn 4:4; 5:19
12:32 [u] ver 34; Isa 11:10; Jn 3:14; 8:28 [v] Jn 6:44
12:33 [w] Jn 18:32; 21:19
12:34 [x] S Jn 10:34 [y] Ps 110:4; Isa 9:7; Eze 37:25; Da 7:14 [z] S Mt 8:20 [a] Jn 3:14
12:35 [b] ver 46 [c] Eph 5:8 [d] 1Jn 1:6; 2:11
12:36 [e] ver 46; S Lk 16:8 [f] Jn 8:59
12:37 [g] S Jn 2:11
12:38 [h] Isa 53:1; Ro 10:16
12:40 [i] Isa 6:10; S Mt 13:13,15
12:41 [j] Isa 6:1-4 [k] Lk 24:27
12:42 [l] ver 11; Jn 7:48 [m] S Jn 7:13 [n] Jn 9:22
12:43 [o] 1Sa 15:30 [p] S Ro 2:29

receive praise acknowledging Their glory. The basic purpose of historical time is to give praise and glory to God. Christ's death spelled Satan's ultimate defeat. It showed no one, not even death, could defeat God and His control of history.

12:23–26 DISCIPLESHIP, Lordship of Christ—Death to self-seeking is the disciple's goal. We seek to kill all selfish goals and ambitions which dominate life without Christ. We love Christ rather than selfish ambition. Those who live under the lordship of Christ have no choice but to follow Him obediently. Disciples come under His lordship voluntarily; once we have chosen Him as Master, we must obey completely. See note on Lk 6:46–49.

12:25 LAST THINGS, Age to Come—Similar to the present age and the age to come are John's words about "this world" and "eternal life." This world is the sphere of Satan's activity. The life of eternity is God's kind of life. He has manifested His life in the coming of Christ (1:4). In receiving Christ, believers receive eternal life (3:16). The life of the age to come is experienced by believers in the present age through the indwelling of the Holy Spirit. See note on Mk 10:29–31.

12:27–28 PRAYER, Will of God—Jesus demonstrated in prayer His determination to do the will of God (4:34; 6:38; 17:4). Prayer commits us to God's will no matter the personal cost. See note on Lk 3:21–22.

12:28 GOD, Glory—God works through human circumstances to reveal His position as the only God so we will honor and worship Him. We are quick to place blame (v 21). God wants us to see reason to praise Him. He allows some things to happen because He plans to use them to display His powerful presence so we will glorify Him. God's glory and the Son's are practically identical here, another basis for the teaching of the Trinity. See note on Mt 3:16–17.

12:32 THE CHURCH, People of God—Jesus died that all people might know His saving power. He commanded the church to proclaim His message to everyone. No people are excluded from the church. They exclude themselves when they refuse to accept Jesus as Lord.

12:33–36 JESUS CHRIST, Death—Jesus controlled His future and faced death with purpose. He corrected the crowd's misinterpretation of Scripture and encouraged them to trust Him as God's Light to salvation. See note on 1:4–5.

12:41 JESUS CHRIST, Fulfilled—The glory of God dazzled Isaiah (Isa 6). The glory of the Father is also the glory of the Son, so Isaiah saw Jesus' glory. Jesus fulfilled the hard message of rejection and the glorious promises of the prophet.

12:42 SALVATION, Confession—Confession is sometimes hindered by fear of what others may do to us. We should seek to build a community which encourages persons to confess their faith in Christ.

12:44–50 GOD, Trinity—This passage illustrates how integral to the New Testament the doctrine of the Trinity is. The work of the Father and the work of the Son flow into one another; indeed, the work One does is the work of the Other. Response in faith to One means response to the Other. Seeing Jesus is seeing the Father, for Jesus is the perfect revelation of the Father. Jesus is not to judge. The Father is, yet Jesus' word is the basis for condemnation. Jesus speaks, but His are the Father's words. The unity of God and the separateness of the Father and the Son must be seen here. To miss either is to miss something important. See note on 10:25–38.

12:44–50 JESUS CHRIST, Son of God—Jesus claimed identity with the Father (10:30,38). To trust One is to trust the

believes in me, he does not believe in me
only, but in the one who sent me.[q]
45When he looks at me, he sees the one
who sent me.[r] 46I have come into the
world as a light,[s] so that no one who
believes in me should stay in darkness.
47"As for the person who hears my
words but does not keep them, I do not
judge him. For I did not come to judge
the world, but to save it.[t] 48There is a
judge for the one who rejects me and
does not accept my words; that very word
which I spoke will condemn him[u] at the
last day. 49For I did not speak of my own
accord, but the Father who sent me commanded me[v] what to say and how to say
it. 50I know that his command leads to
eternal life.[w] So whatever I say is just
what the Father has told me to say."[x]

Chapter 13

Jesus Washes His Disciples' Feet

IT was just before the Passover Feast.[y]
Jesus knew that the time had come[z]
for him to leave this world and go to the
Father.[a] Having loved his own who were
in the world, he now showed them the
full extent of his love.[n]
2The evening meal was being served,
and the devil had already prompted Judas
Iscariot, son of Simon, to betray Jesus.[b]
3Jesus knew that the Father had put all
things under his power,[c] and that he had
come from God[d] and was returning to
God; 4so he got up from the meal, took off
his outer clothing, and wrapped a towel
around his waist.[e] 5After that, he poured
water into a basin and began to wash his
disciples' feet,[f] drying them with the
towel that was wrapped around him.
6He came to Simon Peter, who said to
him, "Lord, are you going to wash my
feet?"
7Jesus replied, "You do not realize now
what I am doing, but later you will understand."[g]
8"No," said Peter, "you shall never
wash my feet."
Jesus answered, "Unless I wash you,
you have no part with me."
9"Then, Lord," Simon Peter replied,
"not just my feet but my hands and my
head as well!"
10Jesus answered, "A person who has
had a bath needs only to wash his feet;
his whole body is clean. And you are
clean,[h] though not every one of you."[i]
11For he knew who was going to betray
him,[j] and that was why he said not every one was clean.
12When he had finished washing their
feet, he put on his clothes and returned
to his place. "Do you understand what I
have done for you?" he asked them.
13"You call me 'Teacher'[k] and 'Lord,'[l]

12:44 [q]S Mt 10:40; Jn 5:24
12:45 [r]S Jn 14:9
12:46 [s]S Jn 1:4
12:47 [t]S Jn 3:17
12:48 [u]Jn 5:45
12:49 [v]Jn 14:31
12:50 [w]S Mt 25:46 [x]S Jn 14:24
13:1 [y]S Jn 11:55 [z]S Mt 26:18 [a]Jn 16:28
13:2 [b]S Mt 10:4
13:3 [c]S Mt 28:18 [d]Jn 8:42; 16:27,28, 30; 17:8
13:4 [e]S Mt 20:28
13:5 [f]S Lk 7:44
13:7 [g]ver 12
13:10 [h]Jn 15:3 [i]ver 18
13:11 [j]S Mt 10:4
13:13 [k]Mt 26:18; Jn 11:28 [l]S Mt 28:18; Lk 1:43; 2:11; 6:46; 11:1; Ac 10:36; Ro 10:9, 12; 14:9; 1Co 12:3; Php 2:11; Col 2:6

[n]1 Or *he loved them to the last*

Other. Christ's mission was salvation, not judgment (8:15). He repeated exactly the Father's words.

12:44–45 JESUS CHRIST, God—Jesus explained that because He revealed the Father, belief in Him was belief in God. Jesus' unity with the Father was so complete that He claimed that to see Him was to see God. See note on 14:9.

12:44–46 REVELATION, Jesus Christ—Jesus revealed His intimacy with the Father. Whoever believes in Him and sees Him also believes in and sees God. Christ is light, making clear who the Father is and lighting the path that leads to Him.

12:48 LAST THINGS, Last Days—"The last day" is to be distinguished from "the last days." Expressed in the plural, the reference is to the entire period which began when Christ came into the world. The time of the Spirit's activity in the earth, for example, is called "the last days" (Ac 2:17). Compare Heb 1:2; 1 Pe 1:20; Jude 18. In the singular, however, the last day speaks of a future time when such things as resurrection (Jn 6:39–40) and judgment (12:48) occur. Compare 1 Jn 2:18.

13:1–20 JESUS CHRIST, Death—In New Testament times footwashing was an elemental courtesy of the host performed by a servant. Jesus washed the disciples' feet as an act of humble service, showing the depth of His love for them. They, busy in disputing who would be greatest (Lk 22:24–30), would not do this simple task of hospitality for one another. Jesus, the Master, showed the true humility of God's Servant and washed their feet. Peter's impetuous protest gave an opportunity to speak of cleanness and to indicate that one among them was unclean.

13:1 HISTORY, Time—Death and resurrection came at the decisive moment God planned. They spelled victory, not defeat, allowing the Son to return to the Father and rule time and history.

13:1–17 DISCIPLESHIP, Lordship of Christ—Discipleship does what pride will not. Discipleship forgets my position, my reputation, my title, my family tradition. Discipleship remembers only Christ's humble example and other people's needs. As Christ's followers we must learn our role is that of humble servants. No task or person is beneath us. We are not too good to do anything that ministers to another in Jesus' name.

13:1–30 ORDINANCES, Lord's Supper as Humility—John presented a long account of the Last Supper of Jesus with His disciples, but never mentioned the institution of the Lord's Supper with the bread and the cup as did the other three Gospel writers. John did mention the piece of bread Jesus dipped in the dish and gave to Judas (v 26) and reported that as soon as Judas had taken the bread he went out into the night. Most of John's description of the Last Supper focuses upon Jesus' washing of the disciples' feet. He did it to demonstrate His role as servant and commanded the disciples to serve one another in this way. Some Christians have taken this footwashing to be an ordinance or sacrament in the same way as baptism and the Lord's Supper. It is clear from the Book of Acts and the rest of the New Testament that the early church did not practice footwashing as a Christian ordinance like baptism and the Lord's Supper. The reason may be that footwashing did not mirror the death and resurrection of Jesus as baptism and the Lord's Supper did. Christians did continue to fulfill the role of servant as Jesus commanded by caring for the sick, feeding the hungry, and probably also by washing dirty feet and bodies. They made it an actual service instead of a ritual.

13:2,27 EVIL AND SUFFERING, Satan—See note on 6:70–71.

13:2 SIN, Individual Choice—Even though Satan may prompt one to sin, the choice to submit is still that of the individual. See notes on Mt 26:14–16,23–25,47–49; Lk 22:1–4,20–23,47–48.

13:13 EDUCATION, Jesus—"Teacher" and "Lord" are not synonymous. As Lord, Jesus is sovereign; as Teacher, He

and rightly so, for that is what I am.
14Now that I, your Lord and Teacher,
have washed your feet, you also should
wash one another's feet.[m] 15I have set
you an example that you should do as I
have done for you.[n] 16I tell you the truth,
no servant is greater than his master,[o]
nor is a messenger greater than the one
who sent him. 17Now that you know
these things, you will be blessed if you do
them.[p]

Jesus Predicts His Betrayal

18"I am not referring to all of you;[q] I
know those I have chosen.[r] But this is to
fulfill the scripture:[s] 'He who shares my
bread[t] has lifted up his heel[u] against
me.'[o][v]
19"I am telling you now before it happens, so that when it does happen you
will believe[w] that I am He.[x] 20I tell you
the truth, whoever accepts anyone I send
accepts me; and whoever accepts me accepts the one who sent me."[y]
21After he had said this, Jesus was troubled in spirit[z] and testified, "I tell you
the truth, one of you is going to betray
me."[a]
22His disciples stared at one another, at
a loss to know which of them he meant.
23One of them, the disciple whom Jesus
loved,[b] was reclining next to him. 24Si-
mon Peter motioned to this disciple and
said, "Ask him which one he means."
25Leaning back against Jesus, he asked
him, "Lord, who is it?"[c]
26Jesus answered, "It is the one to
whom I will give this piece of bread when
I have dipped it in the dish." Then, dipping the piece of bread, he gave it to Judas Iscariot,[d] son of Simon. 27As soon as
Judas took the bread, Satan entered into
him.[e]
"What you are about to do, do quickly," Jesus told him, 28but no one at the
meal understood why Jesus said this to
him. 29Since Judas had charge of the money,[f] some thought Jesus was telling him
to buy what was needed for the Feast,[g]
or to give something to the poor.[h] 30As
soon as Judas had taken the bread, he
went out. And it was night.[i]

Jesus Predicts Peter's Denial

13:37,38pp — Mt 26:33–35; Mk 14:29–31; Lk 22:33,34

31When he was gone, Jesus said, "Now
is the Son of Man[j] glorified[k] and God is
glorified in him.[l] 32If God is glorified in
him,[p] God will glorify the Son in himself,[m] and will glorify him at once.
33"My children, I will be with you only
a little longer. You will look for me, and
just as I told the Jews, so I tell you now:
Where I am going, you cannot come.[n]
34"A new command[o] I give you: Love
one another.[p] As I have loved you, so
you must love one another.[q] 35By this all
men will know that you are my disciples,
if you love one another."[r]
36Simon Peter asked him, "Lord,
where are you going?"[s]
Jesus replied, "Where I am going, you
cannot follow now,[t] but you will follow
later."[u]
37Peter asked, "Lord, why can't I follow you now? I will lay down my life for
you."
38Then Jesus answered, "Will you
really lay down your life for me? I tell you

[o]18 Psalm 41:9 [p]32 Many early manuscripts do not have *If God is glorified in him.*

13:14 [m]1Pe 5:5
13:15 [n]S Mt 11:29; S 1Ti 4:12
13:16 [o]Mt 10:24; Lk 6:40; Jn 15:20
13:17 [p]Mt 7:24, 25; Lk 11:28; Jas 1:25
13:18 [q]ver 10 [r]Jn 15:16,19 [s]S Mt 1:22 [t]Mt 26:23 [u]Jn 6:70 [v]Ps 41:9
13:19 [w]Jn 14:29; 16:4 [x]Jn 4:26; 8:24
13:20 [y]S Mt 10:40
13:21 [z]S Jn 12:27 [a]Mt 26:21
13:23 [b]Jn 19:26; 20:2; 21:7,20
13:25 [c]Mt 26:22; Jn 21:20
13:26 [d]S Mt 10:4
13:27 [e]Lk 22:3
13:29 [f]Jn 12:6 [g]ver 1 [h]Jn 12:5
13:30 [i]Lk 22:53
13:31 [j]S Mt 8:20 [k]Jn 7:39; 12:23 [l]Jn 14:13; 17:4; 1Pe 4:11
13:32 [m]Jn 17:1
13:33 [n]S Jn 7:33, 34
13:34 [o]Jn 15:12; 1Jn 2:7-11; 3:11 [p]Lev 19:18; 1Th 4:9; 1Pe 1:22 [q]Jn 15:12; Eph 5:2; 1Jn 4:10,11
13:35 [r]1Jn 3:14; 4:20
13:36 [s]Jn 16:5 [t]ver 33; Jn 14:2 [u]Jn 21:18,19; 2Pe 1:14

---

leads His disciples into all truth. A Christian is one who not only obeys the Lord, but also learns from the Teacher.

13:14–16 REVELATION, Actions—Christ used an humble act (washing of feet) to declare God's heart and mind concerning how people are to understand each other. Christ is in fact the Master, but He reversed roles with those who serve by serving them. Thus He revealed God's will for His children to be servants of one another in love and commitment to God's way of life.

13:14–15 EDUCATION, Example—By washing His disciples' feet to demonstrate the principle of self-giving service, Jesus taught an unforgettable lesson in servant-leadership. Profound truths are often communicated more dramatically through emotional and sensory experience than through verbal instruction.

13:18–30 JESUS CHRIST, Death—John related the betrayal of Jesus not only to Judas but also to the source of all betrayal, the evil one. John 6:70–71 speaks of Judas as a betrayer from the beginning. Jesus did not choose Judas so that he would betray Him. Jesus had to be betrayed, but Judas did not have to do it. All of the disciples were potential betrayers of Christ (vv 31–38), as are all of His disciples today. The difference between Peter and Judas is that Peter sought forgiveness and Judas did not. Satan entered into Judas (13:2,27) as he does into all willing persons. Judas must be held responsible for his betrayal and we for ours. When Jesus perceived Judas and the high priest's soldiers coming, He looked behind them to the ultimate betrayer, the prince of this world (14:30). John's elaborate explanation about the disciples' misunderstanding as to who was the betrayer explains why Judas could leave freely to complete his betrayal. John's simple phrase "it was night" is intended not so much to tell the time as to tell the status of the soul of the betrayer. John, who was always adding theological insight to historical details, would connect this with the darkness and light motif that runs through this Gospel.

13:19 JESUS CHRIST, I Am—Jesus predicted His betrayal so His disciples would eventually learn He was divine (Greek *egō eimi*). See note on Mk 14:53—15:15.

13:31–32 GOD, Trinity—The close relationship of Jesus and God the Father in the trinitarian understanding of God is illustrated here. To glorify One is to glorify the Other. Such glory came as Jesus faced His atoning death on the cross. See note on Mt 3:16–17.

13:31–32 JESUS CHRIST, Glory—See note on 11:4.

13:34–35 DISCIPLESHIP, Neighbor Love—Disciple love is an important dimension of neighbor love. Jesus said that disciples' love for one another would identifiy them to others as His true disciples. The lack of love for one another raises confusing questions for others about Christian discipleship. Hatred, fighting, jealousy, and snobbery have no place among disciples. Love overcomes such worldly feelings. See notes on Ro 12:10; 13:8.

the truth, before the rooster crows, you
will disown me three times![v]

Chapter 14

Jesus Comforts His Disciples

"DO not let your hearts be troubled.[w] Trust[x] in God[q]; [y] trust
also in me. 2 In my Father's house are
many rooms; if it were not so, I would
have told you. I am going there[z] to prepare a place for you. 3 And if I go and prepare a place for you, I will come back[a]
and take you to be with me that you also
may be where I am.[b] 4 You know the way
to the place where I am going."

Jesus the Way to the Father

5 Thomas[c] said to him, "Lord, we don't
know where you are going, so how can
we know the way?"
6 Jesus answered, "I am[d] the way[e] and
the truth[f] and the life.[g] No one comes
to the Father except through me.[h] 7 If you
really knew me, you would know[r] my
Father as well.[i] From now on, you do
know him and have seen him."
8 Philip[j] said, "Lord, show us the Father and that will be enough for us."
9 Jesus answered: "Don't you know me,
Philip, even after I have been among you
such a long time? Anyone who has seen
me has seen the Father.[k] How can you
say, 'Show us the Father'? 10 Don't you
believe that I am in the Father, and that
the Father is in me?[l] The words I say to
you are not just my own.[m] Rather, it is
the Father, living in me, who is doing his
work. 11 Believe me when I say that I am
in the Father and the Father is in me; or
at least believe on the evidence of the
miracles themselves.[n] 12 I tell you the

[q] 1 Or *You trust in God* [r] 7 Some early manuscripts *If you really have known me, you will know*

13:38 [v] Jn 18:27
14:1 [w] ver 27 [x] S Jn 3:15 [y] Ps 4:5
14:2 [z] Jn 13:33,36; 16:5
14:3 [a] ver 18,28; S Mt 16:27 [b] S Jn 12:26
14:5 [c] S Jn 11:16
14:6 [d] S Jn 6:35 [e] Jn 10:9; Eph 2:18; Heb 10:20 [f] Jn 1:14 [g] S Jn 1:4 [h] Ac 4:12
14:7 [i] Jn 1:18; S 1Jn 2:23
14:8 [j] S Jn 1:43
14:9 [k] Isa 9:6; Jn 1:14; 12:45; 2Co 4:4; Php 2:6; Col 1:15; Heb 1:3
14:10 [l] ver 11,20; Jn 10:38; 17:21 [m] S ver 24
14:11 [n] Jn 5:36; 10:38

14:1,11–14,28 SALVATION, Belief—Compare Mt 21:21–22. Faith in God the Father and in God the Son cannot be separated. Faith leads us to prayer. Prayer gives power to do God's works for His glory. Faith also relieves our anxieties.

14:1–3 LAST THINGS, Heaven—Without using the word "heaven," Jesus nonetheless captured the essence of heaven as a prepared place called His Father's house. He ascended to the Father to prepare for His followers to join Him. The hope of heaven is a cure for troubled hearts. That hope is founded on trust in Christ. The essential joy of heaven will be its abode with the Father and its fellowship with the Son.

14:2 JESUS CHRIST, Ascension—Jesus looked beyond His death to His mission in heaven preparing for His followers an eternal home. He will return to take us home.

14:6–31 GOD, Trinity—To know, to see, or to hear Jesus the Son is to know, to see, or to hear God the Father. They are one in one another. We are able to understand the unity of the two and the difference between the two only in the light of the doctrine of the Trinity, one God known to us in three Persons.

14:6 JESUS CHRIST, I Am—Jesus made several strong claims for Himself and His ministry. Many of the terms He used to describe His work are metaphors that give rise to titles applied to Him and to artistic images related to Christ. He used the forceful I am (*ego eimi*). This could be understood as referring to the personal name of God as it appeared in the Greek translation of the Old Testament (Ex 3:14) or to a claim to be Messiah. See note on Mk 14:53—15:15. This often aroused great opposition to His ministry because His opponents understood this veiled messianic reference. Compare 6:20; 8:24,28,58; 13:19; 18:5. When He referred to Himself as a great item of necessity, He gave titles that persist as marvelous metaphors of His messianic mission. Three of these primary terms are found in this passage. They are the Way, the Truth, the Life. Jesus is the road to God, the accurate understanding of God, and our very existence come from God. Other terms occurring in John which give us provocative messianic titles for Jesus are: water (4:14); bread (6:35); light (8:12); the door (10:7); the good shepherd (10:11); the resurrection and the *life (11:25); the vine (15:5).*

14:6–7 REVELATION, Divine Presence—Jesus is the eternal life God has for us. No one has access to the way of life, the truth about life, or life's meaning outside of God's revelation in Jesus Christ. He leads to eternal life in God's presence. He is preparing our eternal home and will return to lead believers to His eternal home.

14:6–14 SALVATION, Knowledge of God—Those who truly know the Son know the Father also, because Jesus is the way to the Father.

14:9–11 JESUS CHRIST, Son of God—Jesus claimed identity with the Father in the unique trinitarian relationship. See note on 12:44–50.

14:9 JESUS CHRIST, God—Jesus claimed that He was so like the Father that to see Him was to see the Father. See note on 12:44–45.

14:9–12 REVELATION, Jesus Christ—Jesus' words and deeds are one with the Father. To see Jesus at work and to hear Him teach is to experience God. See note on 12:44–46. Intellectual knowledge does not come to this conclusion. God reveals it to people with faith. Jesus promised to let His followers be agents of revelation through the works of the Spirit.

14:11–12 MIRACLE, Instruments—Jesus expected His followers to come to faith through His words and works. Then they would do greater miracles than He had done because He would empower them from His heavenly home with the Father. Miraculous works by His followers have the same purpose as Jesus' signs: to bring glory to God. See note on 2:1–11. Such miraculous work is closely linked to prayer in Jesus' name, in uniting ourselves with Jesus and His will (15:7,16; 16:23–24; Mt 7:7–8; 18:19; 21:22; 1 Jn 3:21–22; 5:14–15). Such teaching gives modern believers reason to believe in God's miracle-working power today when we unite ourselves to God's will, obey Him, and seek to bring glory to Him and not to ourselves.

14:11–12 MISSIONS, Source—The presence of the living Christ in the believer is the source of missionary motivation. Paul pointed out that Christ's love impels or compels us (2 Co 5:14). Jesus made a staggering promise: the one with faith in Him will do what He has been doing—preaching the kingdom, teaching, healing, and expressing His compassionate ministry—and more. See Mt 9:35–38; Lk 4:18–21. Incredible, but true! How is it possible? Because Jesus ascended to the Father. He lives in believers everywhere, working through us. Jesus fed the 5,000. His caring children feed multiplied thousands each year in hunger relief. Limited by space and time, He drew followers to Him in Judea, Galilee, and Samaria. Each year, through the power of the Holy Spirit and in response to the message of His disciples, millions have pledged and continue to pledge allegiance to Him. The source of these works is Jesus Himself.

14:12,15,21 DISCIPLESHIP, Lordship of Christ—Faith does not exist without loving obedience. Faith and love prompt the true disciple of Christ to follow Christ's example and obey His commands. The result is the blessing of a loving relationship with God. Where faith does not produce obedient acts of love, the relationship with God does not exist. We have no right to lessen Christ's definition of discipleship. Letting people meet our standards and feel security as members of our group is not being a disciple under Christ's lordship.

truth, anyone who has faith[o] in me will do what I have been doing.[p] He will do even greater things than these, because I am going to the Father. 13 And I will do whatever you ask[q] in my name, so that the Son may bring glory to the Father. 14 You may ask me for anything in my name, and I will do it.

Jesus Promises the Holy Spirit

15 "If you love me, you will obey what I command.[r] 16 And I will ask the Father, and he will give you another Counselor[s] to be with you forever— 17 the Spirit of truth.[t] The world cannot accept him,[u] because it neither sees him nor knows him. But you know him, for he lives with you and will be[s] in you. 18 I will not leave you as orphans;[v] I will come to you.[w] 19 Before long, the world will not see me anymore, but you will see me.[x] Because I live, you also will live.[y] 20 On that day[z] you will realize that I am in my Father,[a] and you are in me, and I am in you.[b] 21 Whoever has my commands and obeys them, he is the one who loves me.[c] He who loves me will be loved by my Father,[d] and I too will love him and show myself to him."

22 Then Judas[e] (not Judas Iscariot) said, "But, Lord, why do you intend to show yourself to us and not to the world?"[f]

23 Jesus replied, "If anyone loves me, he will obey my teaching.[g] My Father will love him, and we will come to him and make our home with him.[h] 24 He who does not love me will not obey my teaching. These words you hear are not my own; they belong to the Father who sent me.[i]

25 "All this I have spoken while still with you. 26 But the Counselor,[j] the Holy Spirit, whom the Father will send in my name,[k] will teach you all things[l] and will remind you of everything I have said to you.[m] 27 Peace I leave with you; my peace I give you.[n] I do not give to you as

14:12 [o]Mt 21:21 [p]Lk 10:17
14:13 [q]S Mt 7:7
14:15 [r]ver 21,23; Ps 103:18; Jn 15:10; 1Jn 2:3-5; 3:22,24; 5:3; 2Jn 6; Rev 12:17; 14:12
14:16 [s]ver 26; Jn 15:26; 16:7
14:17 [t]Jn 15:26; 16:13; 1Jn 4:6; 5:6 [u]1Co 2:14
14:18 [v]1Ki 6:13 [w]ver 3,28; S Mt 16:27
14:19 [x]Jn 7:33,34; 16:16 [y]Jn 6:57
14:20 [z]Jn 16:23,26 [a]ver 10,11; Jn 10:38; 17:21 [b]S Ro 8:10
14:21 [c]S ver 15 [d]Dt 7:13; Jn 16:27; 1Jn 2:5
14:22 [e]Lk 6:16; Ac 1:13 [f]Ac 10:41
14:23 [g]S ver 15 [h]S Ro 8:10
14:24 [i]ver 10; Dt 18:18; Jn 5:19; 7:16; 8:28; 12:49, 50
14:26 [j]ver 16; Jn 15:26; 16:7 [k]Ac 2:33 [l]Jn 16:13; 1Jn 2:20,27 [m]Jn 2:22
14:27 [n]Nu 6:26; Ps 85:8; Mal 2:6; S Lk 2:14; 24:36; Jn 16:33; Php 4:7; Col 3:15

[s]*17* Some early manuscripts *and is*

14:13–14 PRAYER, In Jesus' Name—Jesus' name is the legal warrant for the prayers of Christians. The use of the name presupposes that the person praying is manifesting the character of Jesus in his or her request and that the request will represent a continuation of the work of Christ. See notes on 15:7, 16; Mk 9:19–29.

14:14–16 JESUS CHRIST, Intercession—The ascended Christ is ready to answer the faithful prayers of His people. He will send the Spirit as God's comforting presence with us.

14:15–21 HOLY SPIRIT, Personal—The Holy Spirit is the personal God present with His people. John 14—16 is a single long sermon by Jesus. He spoke four times of the Holy Spirit. See 14:15–21,25–26; 16:2–16; note on 15:26–27. He said more about the Spirit than is recorded in all the other Gospels together. Jesus referred to the Spirit as *paraclete*, a Greek word referring to any person who helps another. A lawyer may be referred to as a *paraclete.* Part of the Spirit's work resembles that of a defense lawyer (16:5–16). A person who gives comfort, good advice, wise instruction, or moral support of any kind is a *paraclete.* Jesus spoke of the Spirit as another Paraclete (14:16), which means He had been a *paraclete* for His disciples. After Jesus returned to His Father, the help and guidance Jesus provided for His disciples was and is provided by the Spirit until Christ returns. Jesus' earthly ministry was brief. The Spirit's ministry is eternal. Since Christ sent the Spirit from the Father, Christ and the Father will be present with the disciples, too (vv 20,23; compare Mt 28:19–20; 1 Jn 2:24). The Spirit's work is to teach. He is the Spirit of truth (v 17). He helps disciples remember, understand, and live by Jesus' commands to love (vv 15,21). The word *spirit* might seem to suggest that the Spirit is present everywhere, with everyone; but Jesus teaches otherwise. The Spirit is given as Paraclete only to disciples. The world neither knows nor accepts Him (v 17). The divine Counselor lives in disciples.

14:15–17 REVELATION, Divine Presence—The disciples feared Jesus' death would make them spiritual orphans with no one to turn to for help. Jesus revealed a new Presence would be available. God's Spirit fulfills Christ's promise by living in believers and guiding our lives.

14:15,21,23–24,28 SALVATION, Love of God—Those who love Christ will obey His commands and experience the Father's love and presence.

14:16 PRAYER, Holy Spirit Guides—We have the Spirit to guide us in prayer as a direct result of Jesus' prayer.

14:17,20 DISCIPLESHIP, Holy Spirit—When we commit ourselves to God in Christ by faith, God enters into our heart in the person of the Holy Spirit and transforms our nature and disposition. We become new creatures in Christ. The Spirit makes such a radical change in us that our whole personality is set on doing the will of God. The Spirit's daily leadership is the defining characteristic of every disciple. See notes on 16:13–14; 1 Co 6:19–20.

14:19 LAST THINGS, Believers' Resurrection—Jesus spoke of the day of His own resurrection. At that day His disciples would understand His life of oneness and fellowship with the Father. Believers' present experience of eternal (5:24) and abundant (10:10) life, as well as the hope of future resurrection to life, are based on the resurrection of Jesus.

14:23 SALVATION, Obedience—Compare 15:10. Love of Christ leads us to obey His teaching. Love and obedience are two sides of the same reality. They cannot be separated.

14:26 HOLY SPIRIT, Teaches—The Spirit came to the disciples in power only after Jesus had gone. This is one clear way by which the Spirit is distinguished from the Son. The Spirit teaches disciples about Jesus and helps us recall His teaching. He does not take disciples away from Christ but reminds us of Christ. This vital truth is expressed in several ways in the New Testament. At Pentecost the Spirit guided Peter to preach *about Christ* (Ac 2:22). The New Testament refers to the Spirit as "the Spirit of Jesus" (Ac 16:7), "the Spirit of Christ" (Ro 8:9), "the Spirit of his Son" (see note on Gal 4:6), and "the Spirit of Jesus Christ" (Php 1:19). When disciples need a way to test whether the Spirit is at work in someone's life, we are not to use criteria such as enthusiasm or success. The only criterion is faithfulness to Jesus Christ. See 1 Jn 4:2–3; note on 1 Co 12:1–3. The Spirit is always closely related to Jesus Christ. Apart from Jesus, the Spirit is not working, however much power or emotion is displayed. Whenever anyone is committed to Jesus, the Spirit is at work. All Christians have the Spirit, whether they are outwardly powerful or weak people, whether they are emotional or quiet (Ro 8:9).

14:27 EVIL AND SUFFERING, God's Present Help—Jesus promised peace for His disciples, despite the activity of Satan. Peace is not the absence of external conflict. It is the power of internal security. By going to the Father by way of the cross and resurrection, Jesus established salvation from sin and all its consequences. He sent the Holy Spirit to bring comfort and peace in our lives. If your life is fragmented and insecure, God is not at fault. He offers peace even for the sufferer.

26“When the Counselor[g] comes,
whom I will send to you from the Father,[h] the Spirit of truth[i] who goes out
from the Father, he will testify about
me.[j] 27And you also must testify,[k] for
you have been with me from the beginning.[l]

Chapter 16

“ALL this[m] I have told you so that you
will not go astray.[n] 2They will
put you out of the synagogue;[o] in fact, a
time is coming when anyone who kills
you will think he is offering a service to
God.[p] 3They will do such things because
they have not known the Father or me.[q]
4I have told you this, so that when the
time comes you will remember[r] that I
warned you. I did not tell you this at first
because I was with you.[s]

15:26 [g]Jn 14:16
15:26 [h]Jn 14:26; 16:7 [i]S Jn 14:17 [j]1Jn 5:7
15:27 [k]S Lk 24:48; Jn 21:24; 1Jn 1:2; 4:14 [l]S Lk 1:2
16:1 [m]Jn 15:18-27 [n]Mt 11:6
16:2 [o]Jn 9:22; 12:42 [p]Isa 66:5; Ac 26:9,10; Rev 6:9
16:3 [q]Jn 15:21; 17:25; 1Jn 3:1
16:4 [r]Jn 13:19; 14:29 [s]Jn 15:27
16:5 [t]ver 10,17,28; Jn 7:33 [u]Jn 13:36; 14:5
16:6 [v]ver 22
16:7 [w]Jn 14:16,26; 15:26 [x]Jn 7:39; 14:26
16:9 [y]Jn 15:22
16:10 [z]Ac 3:14; 7:52; Ro 1:17; 3:21,22; 1Pe 3:18 [a]S ver 5
16:11 [b]S Jn 12:31
16:12 [c]Mk 4:33; 1Co 3:2

The Work of the Holy Spirit

5“Now I am going to him who sent
me,[t] yet none of you asks me, ‘Where
are you going?’[u] 6Because I have said
these things, you are filled with grief.[v]
7But I tell you the truth: It is for your
good that I am going away. Unless I go
away, the Counselor[w] will not come to
you; but if I go, I will send him to you.[x]
8When he comes, he will convict the
world of guilt[w] in regard to sin and righteousness and judgment: 9in regard to
sin,[y] because men do not believe in me;
10in regard to righteousness,[z] because I
am going to the Father,[a] where you can
see me no longer; 11and in regard to judgment, because the prince of this world[b]
now stands condemned.
12“I have much more to say to you,
more than you can now bear.[c] 13But

[w]*8* Or *will expose the guilt of the world*

---

their gospel, and that was what the Spirit guided them to witness to. The “Spirit of truth” (Jn 14:17; 15:26; 16:13) guided these disciples into “all truth” (16:13). That never means truth which supersedes the truth of Jesus Christ; Jesus is the truth (1:17; 14:6) into whom the Spirit always guides the disciples.

16:1–33 EVIL AND SUFFERING, Rejoicing—Disciples will suffer, but their sorrow will turn into joy. Christians can rejoice in the midst of suffering because Jesus overcame the world. Here “world” is a comprehensive term for all that opposes God. In this sense the world includes religious people who persecute true believers thinking they are defending God. At times disciples must suffer most at the hands of people who also claim to be disciples but really never have met God. The Holy Spirit gives Christ’s followers insight to understand and courage to endure. Thus, while suffering physically, we can rejoice knowing God’s love, peace, and final victory. See note on 1 Jn 2:15–17.

16:5–32 GOD, Trinity—The Father, Son, and Holy Spirit share a common life and do a common work. We see them separately, but they are so related to each other that they cannot be entirely separated from each other. See note on 15:26.

16:5 JESUS CHRIST, Ascension—See note on 14:2. Jesus’ ascension led to another means of revelation able to reach all followers throughout the world. This was the giving of the Spirit.

16:5–7 HOLY SPIRIT, The Twelve—The disciples benefited from Jesus’ departure. Jesus left the *Paraclete,* or Counselor, with them. See note on 14:15–21. He was and is able to guide them even more than the earthly Jesus. Disciples could fan out to the ends of the earth and still be guided and empowered by the Spirit (Mt 28:19–20; see note on Ac 1:8). The gift of the Spirit would help the disciples to overcome their sadness and anxiety about Jesus’ apparent absence. They would not be alone; Jesus would send the Spirit to be with them.

16:7–11 SIN, Unbelief—The Spirit makes a depraved world aware of its sin. He reveals our need to believe in the crucified and risen Lord, who can remove our guilt and set us right with God. A basic sin is failure to believe in Jesus as God’s Son. See note on Mt 12:31–32.

16:8–11 HOLY SPIRIT, Convicts—Jesus’ departure might appear as cause for alarm for the disciples left to face a hostile world. Actually, in leaving the world to return to the Father, Jesus gave the world reason for concern, for He sent the Spirit to judge the world. Such judgment exposed the world to truth and invited its population to decision for or against Jesus. The Spirit exposes the true nature 1) of sin as refusal to have faith in Christ, 2) of righteousness as defined by Christ’s cross which provided salvation and opened the way to eternal life with God, and 3) of judgment as God’s judgment of Satan through Christ’s death on the cross. The judging exposure of the Spirit should lead the world to put their own faith in Christ through the disciples’ witness. See 17:20–21.

16:11 EVIL AND SUFFERING, Satan—Satan may rule the majority of lives and actions in this world. That does not mean he has control of the world. In the cross and resurrection God defeated Satan and all satanic purposes. See note on 14:30. This was not a defeat in one small skirmish. It was eternal judgment on Satan. The world does not know or understand this decision. The Holy Spirit reveals it to us as Christ’s followers. Satan’s eternal defeat is a certain fact.

16:12–15 HOLY SPIRIT, Teaches—The Spirit of truth guides disciples into all truth. He reveals God’s truth even more fully than Jesus Himself had been able to do because Jesus did His teaching before the cross. The Spirit does His teaching after the cross and the resurrection, which is the fullest self-revelation of God. Jesus sometimes spoke in figurative language, but after the resurrection the truth could be expressed in clear language (16:25). The Spirit reveals the meaning of the cross and resurrection and brings glory to Christ.

16:12–14 CREATION, Continuous—The revealing of new truth is a form of continuous creation. Jesus projected this same concept to His disciples. Until the crucifixion and resurrection were historical facts, they could not understand its full meaning. Until the very last minute, they did not even believe He was going to be killed. How could they be aware of atonement and justification? God still works to make His truth known to us. We must, of course, be cautious at this point. The final revelation has come in Jesus Christ. We do not need a new “Messiah,” because He has already come. Our need is to understand fully the revelation that has been made. Even more, we need to obey the demands of Christ’s message once we understand it!

16:13–15 HOLY SCRIPTURE, Spirit—God, the Holy Spirit, is the ultimate Author of Scripture. He is also the only adequate Interpreter of Scripture. No human has full authority to interpret Scripture for another. Each person can rely on the Holy Spirit to guide into truth. That which we gain from the Spirit we should proclaim fervently and live out completely. We cannot force that belief on another, however, for as human interpreters under the Spirit, we remain open to misunderstanding. The Spirit seeks to bring glory to Jesus, so that all true interpretation of Scripture will glorify the Christ. Christ remains the ultimate revelation of God. See note on Lk 24:44–46.

16:13–15 REVELATION, Divine Presence—The Holy Spirit will finish God’s revelation by declaring and interpreting

when he, the Spirit of truth,[d] comes, he will guide you into all truth.[e] He will not speak on his own; he will speak only what he hears, and he will tell you what is yet to come. 14He will bring glory to me by taking from what is mine and making it known to you. 15All that belongs to the Father is mine.[f] That is why I said the Spirit will take from what is mine and make it known to you.

16"In a little while[g] you will see me no more, and then after a little while you will see me."[h]

The Disciples' Grief Will Turn to Joy

17Some of his disciples said to one another, "What does he mean by saying, 'In a little while you will see me no more, and then after a little while you will see me,'[i] and 'Because I am going to the Father'?"[j] 18They kept asking, "What does he mean by 'a little while'? We don't understand what he is saying."

19Jesus saw that they wanted to ask him about this, so he said to them, "Are you asking one another what I meant when I said, 'In a little while you will see me no more, and then after a little while you will see me'? 20I tell you the truth, you will weep and mourn[k] while the world rejoices. You will grieve, but your grief will turn to joy.[l] 21A woman giving birth to a child has pain[m] because her time has come; but when her baby is born she forgets the anguish because of her joy that a child is born into the world. 22So with you: Now is your time of grief,[n] but I will see you again[o] and you will rejoice, and no one will take away your joy.[p] 23In that day[q] you will no longer ask me anything. I tell you the truth, my Father will give you whatever you ask in my name.[r] 24Until now you have not asked for anything in my name. Ask and you will receive,[s] and your joy will be complete.[t]

25"Though I have been speaking figuratively,[u] a time is coming[v] when I will no longer use this kind of language but will tell you plainly about my Father. 26In that day you will ask in my name.[w] I am not saying that I will ask the Father on your behalf. 27No, the Father himself loves you because you have loved me[x] and have believed that I came from God.[y] 28I came from the Father and entered the world; now I am leaving the world and going back to the Father."[z]

29Then Jesus' disciples said, "Now you are speaking clearly and without figures of speech.[a] 30Now we can see that you know all things and that you do not even need to have anyone ask you questions. This makes us believe[b] that you came from God."[c]

31"You believe at last!"[x] Jesus answered. 32"But a time is coming,[d] and has come, when you will be scattered,[e] each to his own home. You will leave me all alone.[f] Yet I am not alone, for my Father is with me.[g]

33"I have told you these things, so that in me you may have peace.[h] In this world you will have trouble.[i] But take heart! I have overcome[j] the world."

16:13 [d]S Jn 14:17 [e]Ps 25:5; Jn 14:26
16:15 [f]Jn 17:10
16:16 [g]S Jn 7:33 [h]ver 22; Jn 14:18-24
16:17 [i]ver 16 [j]ver 5
16:20 [k]Mk 16:10; Lk 23:27 [l]Jn 20:20
16:21 [m]Isa 13:8; 21:3; 26:17; Mic 4:9; 1Th 5:3
16:22 [n]ver 6 [o]ver 16 [p]ver 20; Jer 31:12
16:23 [q]ver 26; Jn 14:20 [r]S Mt 7:7
16:24 [s]S Mt 7:7 [t]S Jn 3:29
16:25 [u]ver 29; Ps 78:2; Eze 20:49; Mt 13:34; Mk 4:33, 34; Jn 10:6 [v]ver 2
16:26 [w]ver 23,24
16:27 [x]Jn 14:21,23 [y]ver 30; S Jn 13:3
16:28 [z]ver 5,10,17; Jn 13:3
16:29 [a]S ver 25
16:30 [b]1Ki 17:24 [c]ver 27; S Jn 13:3
16:32 [d]ver 2,25 [e]Mt 26:31 [f]Mt 26:56 [g]Jn 8:16, 29
16:33 [h]S Jn 14:27 [i]Jn 15:18-21 [j]Ro 8:37; 1Jn 4:4; 5:4; Rev 2:7,11,17, 26; 3:5,12,21; 21:7

[x]31 Or *"Do you now believe?"*

---

all truth to maturing disciples able to understand in light of the resurrection. The Spirit prepares God's people for the future by teaching us Jesus' truth. The Spirit is the indwelling interpreter of God's will. See note on 14:15–17.

16:13–14 DISCIPLESHIP, Holy Spirit—As disciples, we do not know everything we need to know to follow Christ. God knows. He gives us the knowledge we need, when we need it through the Holy Spirit. By the ministry of the Holy Spirit Jesus exercises His lordship over His disciples. Without the daily experience of the Spirit we cannot be disciples. See notes on Gal 5:16; Eph 3:16.

16:13–15 EDUCATION, Spirit—The Holy Spirit is the Teacher in the lives of Christians. Under His guidance, the words of biblical revelation become a living word for each of us. As we study the recorded teachings of Jesus, the Spirit gives insight into their meanings. The Spirit is present at the Christian's study desk and in every Christian study group, leading believers into all truth. See 14:16–17.

16:22,24 SALVATION, Joy—The world cannot give and cannot take away the joy Christ gives. Joy comes as we stay in communication with Christ through prayer.

16:23–24 PRAYER, In Jesus' Name—See note on 14:13–14. The Christian's joy depends on the exercise of prayer privileges. We exercise that privilege by praying to the Father through Christ. Previously, the disciples had relied on Jesus' physical presence. The new experience of asking in the name of the ascended Christ brought new power and joy. Such power and joy remain available for believers.

16:26–27 GOD, Love—Love occupies the central place in the relationship of believers and God. The Father loves believers because they have loved Jesus. Jesus Himself came as the expression of God's love to the lost. See note on 3:16. The key New Testament teaching is the love of God the Father. His love is displayed to the lost, to believers, and to the Son who gave Himself in sacrifice to save the lost. Love, in turn, becomes the foremost characteristic of Christians and is their badge of identification as the people of Jesus Christ. See note on 15:9–14.

16:26–27 PRAYER, Love of God—See note on 14:13–14. An answer is assured because of the love of God.

16:27 EVANGELISM, Results—To love and believe in Jesus Christ lets us experience the special love and grace of God.

16:28 JESUS CHRIST, Preexistent—See note on 6:33.

16:29–30 JESUS CHRIST, Secret—The secret ways of teaching were intended to provide revelation for the disciples. See note on Mk 1:25,34. They finally understood His meaning as He faced the cross.

16:33 CREATION, Evil—The world after the fall (Ge 3) is so constituted that trouble and frustration will come to people who seek to follow God. Jesus has warned us troubles will come when we are faithful to Him. God did not create the world's troubles. He made us free to respond to Him. In our freedom we choose evil or experience the consequences of the evil choices of others, bringing trouble and frustration to the world. Christ has overcome the troubled world.

Chapter 17

Jesus Prays for Himself

AFTER Jesus said this, he looked toward
heaven[k] and prayed:

"Father, the time has come.[l] Glorify your Son, that your Son may glorify you.[m] 2For you granted him authority over all people[n] that he might
give eternal life[o] to all those you
have given him.[p] 3Now this is eternal life: that they may know you,[q]
the only true God, and Jesus Christ,
whom you have sent.[r] 4I have
brought you glory[s] on earth by completing the work you gave me to do.[t]
5And now, Father, glorify me[u] in
your presence with the glory I had
with you[v] before the world began.[w]

Jesus Prays for His Disciples

6"I have revealed you[y][x] to those
whom you gave me[y] out of the
world. They were yours; you gave
them to me and they have obeyed
your word. 7Now they know that everything you have given me comes
from you. 8For I gave them the words
you gave me[z] and they accepted
them. They knew with certainty that
I came from you,[a] and they believed
that you sent me.[b] 9I pray for them.[c]
I am not praying for the world, but
for those you have given me,[d] for
they are yours. 10All I have is yours,
and all you have is mine.[e] And glory
has come to me through them. 11I
will remain in the world no longer,
but they are still in the world,[f] and I
am coming to you.[g] Holy Father, protect them by the power of your
name—the name you gave me—so
that they may be one[h] as we are
one.[i] 12While I was with them, I
protected them and kept them safe
by that name you gave me. None has
been lost[j] except the one doomed to
destruction[k] so that Scripture would
be fulfilled.[l]

13"I am coming to you now,[m] but I
say these things while I am still in
the world, so that they may have the
full measure of my joy[n] within them.
14I have given them your word and
the world has hated them,[o] for they

17:1 [k]Jn 11:41 [l]S Mt 26:18 [m]Jn 12:23; 13:31, 32
17:2 [n]S Mt 28:18 [o]S Mt 25:46 [p]ver 6, 9,24; Da 7:14; Jn 6:37,39
17:3 [q]S Php 3:8 [r]ver 8,18,21,23,25; S Jn 3:17
17:4 [s]Jn 13:31 [t]S Jn 19:30
17:5 [u]ver 1 [v]Php 2:6 [w]S Jn 1:2
17:6 [x]ver 26; Jn 1:18 [y]S ver 2
17:8 [z]ver 14,26; S Jn 14:24 [a]S Jn 13:3 [b]ver 3, 18,21,23,25; S Jn 3:17
17:9 [c]Lk 22:32 [d]S ver 2
17:10 [e]Jn 16:15
17:11 [f]Jn 13:1 [g]ver 13; Jn 7:33 [h]ver 21-23; Ps 133:1 [i]Jn 10:30
17:12 [j]S Jn 6:39 [k]Jn 6:70 [l]S Mt 1:22
17:13 [m]ver 11 [n]S Jn 3:29
17:14 [o]Jn 15:19

[y]6 Greek *your name*; also in verse 26

17:1,4 GOD, Glory—Notice the close relationship between the Father and the Son. Each glorifies the other. Glorifying God is revealing something about the person or nature of God and acknowledging His preeminent place above all other authorities. See notes on 11:4; 12:28.

17:1–5 JESUS CHRIST, Glory—See note on 11:4. The cross and resurrection were the ultimate signs of Christ's divine glory. In them Jesus had authority to provide eternal life to all people of God.

17:1 HISTORY, Time—See note on 12:23–33.

17:1–26 PRAYER, Intercession—In ch 17 He prayed as the Son of God and as the Head of the church. He knew He would die the next day. The exaltation He asked for Himself would place Him above all things with the Father for the sake of His followers. He identified Himself with the Father's glory and deity. He stated lines of identity for His followers that would seem audacious from their lips. They belonged to the Father (v 6); they recognized Jesus' authority (vv 7–8); they brought Him glory (v 10), and have been given divine glory (v 22); and they were not of the world (vv 14,16). Jesus made five specific petitions for His followers: that they be kept (vv 11, 15), sanctified (v 17), in the Father and the Son (v 21), with Him to see His glory (v 24), and that they may all be one (v 21). Christians are not God the Son. Still this prayer gives an example for us from three standpoints: (1) its purposes are spiritual, (2) it is a statement of agreement with God, and (3) the faith of the requests is on a cosmic scale. The prayer assures us Jesus cares for and prays for us His church.

17:2–3 SALVATION, Eternal Life—Christ defined eternal life as intimate personal knowledge of Father and Son. Eternal life is not a possession but an eternal relationship. Christ gives eternal life to all those whom the Father gives Him. The believer's security is anchored in God's faithfulness.

17:5 JESUS CHRIST, Preexistent—Jesus prayed that He might return to the Father and enjoy the honor He had known with the Father before the world began.

17:6–26 JESUS CHRIST, Intercession—Jesus prayed for us as He faced the cross and continues to pray for all believers.

17:6–19 EVIL AND SUFFERING, Rejoicing—Jesus prayed that the Father would protect His disciples in the world. We will not be immune from problems, but we will have joy and a sense of God's presence in our trials. Part of our protection is our unity in the body of Christ. God's protection is not a monastic escape from the world but a secure participation with God in the world.

17:6–9 REVELATION, Jesus Christ—Jesus revealed all that God wished to have known about God. He prayed as the One who stands between the people and God as the link of life. What Jesus revealed came from the Father.

17:9–18 CREATION, Purposeful—Jesus made a distinction between the world and those in it. In John's Gospel, the world is human society organizing itself without God. God loved this world and sent His Son to be its Savior (3:16). At the close of His ministry, however, Jesus prayed for people, not for the world. As the Father had sent Jesus to the world, He was now about to send His followers into the world. They needed the Father's watchcare and guidance in this evil world so they could be effective witnesses for Him.

17:11–12 GOD, Power—A major aspect of God's work for believers is protecting or preserving us through His mighty power. The same power which brought about creation and raised Jesus from the dead is available to guard and preserve the Christian. See Ro 8:28–39.

17:11 THE CHURCH, Redeemed of All Ages—Jesus cares for His people and intercedes on their behalf. God desires that all His redeemed ones be united in Christ Jesus. The unity of the church is personal, not organizational. The church of the ages is united in love and purpose as are God and Jesus. See notes on 10:14–18; 20:29; Lk 9:49–50.

17:12–15 ELECTION, Protection—Christ protected His elect disciples and prayed for God to continue that protection. The protection did not apply to the one who chose to betray Christ in fulfillment of Scripture. Scripture did not force Judas to betray Christ. Scripture (Ps 41:9) anticipated that a friend would betray Him. Judas was in his very nature lost and bound for destruction. He would not hear, trust, and obey Christ. He chose to be the betrayer and suffered the consequences of his choice.

17:13 SALVATION, Joy—Believers can have the same joy Christ had. Christ's prayer is still being answered today.

17:14 REVELATION, Inspiration—Christ gave His followers the words from God, breathing God's revelation into

are not of the world any more than I
am of the world.[p] [15]My prayer is not
that you take them out of the world
but that you protect them from the
evil one.[q] [16]They are not of the
world, even as I am not of it.[r]
[17]Sanctify[z] them by the truth; your
word is truth.[s] [18]As you sent me into
the world,[t] I have sent them into
the world.[u] [19]For them I sanctify myself, that they too may be truly sanctified.[v]

Jesus Prays for All Believers

[20]"My prayer is not for them
alone. I pray also for those who will
believe in me through their message,
[21]that all of them may be one,[w] Father, just as you are in me and I am
in you.[x] May they also be in us so
that the world may believe that you
have sent me.[y] [22]I have given them
the glory that you gave me,[z] that
they may be one as we are one:[a] [23]I
in them and you in me. May they be
brought to complete unity to let the
world know that you sent me[b] and
have loved them[c] even as you have
loved me.

[24]"Father, I want those you have
given me[d] to be with me where I
am,[e] and to see my glory,[f] the glory
you have given me because you loved
me before the creation of the
world.[g]
[25]"Righteous Father, though the
world does not know you,[h] I know
you, and they know that you have
sent me.[i] [26]I have made you known
to them,[j] and will continue to make
you known in order that the love you
have for me may be in them[k] and
that I myself may be in them."

Chapter 18

Jesus Arrested

18:3–11pp — Mt 26:47–56; Mk 14:43–50; Lk 22:47–53

**WHEN he had finished praying, Jesus
left with his disciples and crossed
the Kidron Valley.[l] On the other side
there was an olive grove,[m] and he and his
disciples went into it.[n]
[2]Now Judas, who betrayed him, knew
the place, because Jesus had often met
there with his disciples.[o] [3]So Judas came**

17:14 [p]ver 16; Jn 8:23
17:15 [q]S Mt 5:37
17:16 [r]ver 14
17:17 [s]S Jn 15:3; 2Sa 7:28; 1Ki 17:24
17:18 [t]ver 3,8,21, 23,25; S Jn 3:17 [u]Jn 20:21
17:19 [v]ver 17
17:21 [w]Jer 32:39 [x]ver 11; Jn 10:38 [y]ver 3,8,18,23,25; S Jn 3:17
17:22 [z]Jn 1:14 [a]S Jn 14:20
17:23 [b]ver 3,8,18, 21,25; S Jn 3:17 [c]Jn 16:27
17:24 [d]S ver 2 [e]S Jn 12:26 [f]Jn 1:14 [g]ver 5; S Mt 25:34; S Jn 1:2
17:25 [h]Jn 15:21; 16:3 [i]ver 3,8,18,21, 23; S Jn 3:17; 16:27
17:26 [j]ver 6 [k]Jn 15:9
18:1 [l]2Sa 15:23 [m]ver 26; S Mt 21:1 [n]Mt 26:36
18:2 [o]Lk 21:37; 22:39

[z]*17* Greek *hagiazo (set apart for sacred use* or *make holy)*; also in verse 19

their lives and hearts. Such revelation leads to persecution not power in the world. Revelation gives spiritual power to endure persecution.

17:17 HOLY SCRIPTURE, Purpose—The word of God which Jesus brought (v 14) makes disciples different from the world; it sanctifies them or makes them holy. Thus God's word fulfilled the Old Testament purpose of God (Lev 11:44; 19:1). The sanctifying word also sends disciples into the world on Christ's mission (Jn 17:18). How can disciples be sure they are truly God's people on God's mission? They know because they have God's Word which is truth. It corresponds to the real world, does not lie or deceive, and represents absolute divine revelation. In John's writings word and truth have their primary meaning in Jesus (1:14; 14:6). Secondarily, they refer to the revelation about God present in Jesus and in His teachings (17:14). Scriptures ultimately point to and are to be interpreted in light of Jesus. See note on Lk 24:44–46.

17:17 SALVATION, Sanctification—Jesus prayed that the Father would separate His disciples from worldliness and dedicate and equip them for His service. Disciples are equipped for God's work through the truth, which is the Word of God (Ps 119:142). God's Word, both living and written, is the chief means through which He sanctifies us.

17:18–19 EVANGELISM, Call to Evangelize—The Father sent Jesus to provide salvation. Jesus totally dedicated Himself to the mission, giving up His own life. Jesus, in turn, sends us after the lost. He calls us to the same dedication He showed.

17:20–21 HUMANITY, Commitment—The people of God are expected to have the same kind of loving, committed relationship with each other as the Father and Jesus have with one another. See note on Ge 1:26–29.

17:20–23 THE CHURCH, Redeemed of All Ages—The church was not limited in time. Jesus sought fruitful disciples who would carry on His work after He ascended to the Father. *He prayed for all the church through all ages.* He wanted the expansion of the church to produce a unified people. Divisions of the heart among God's believers are not His will. A united people of God can witness effectively for Him. The continuing presence of Jesus with His church brings unity, displaying God's love to the world. All believers should work for unity of heart and mind with other believers rather than engaging in that which is divisive. Individual identity and mission of individual groups within Christianity must never blind us to the larger unity of the church around the world. See note on v 11.

17:20–23 EVANGELISM, Results—Jesus prayed for the evangelistic work of the church. He expects disciples to lead others to believe and then to incorporate new believers into His church. We can count on the power of Christ's prayer as we testify to others about Him. Only as we remain closely related to God will our lives reflect His love and attract people to Him.

17:24 LAST THINGS, Heaven—Participation in present spiritual union with Christ results eventually in sharing the eternal presence of Christ. Jesus anticipated, longed for, and requested a return to the state of glory He had known with the Father from eternity past. To see that glory is to be where He is. See note on 14:1–3. Heaven will be perception of and participation in the eternal glory of Christ (Ro 8:17–18).

17:25 GOD, Righteous—As He faced His arrest and crucifixion, Jesus specifically addressed God as righteous Father. He thus affirmed that God was doing what is right and fair even as He let Jesus suffer and die. The New Testament puts such strong emphasis on God's love that it is easy to forget His righteousness. Basically, the righteousness of God is a major theme in the Old Testament and is simply assumed in the New. God's righteousness means He always does what is right. He is faithful and true to Himself and to His people in all circumstances. Righteousness is not the opposite of love, nor does it stand in contrast to love. Love and righteousness are perfectly coordinated. Both are a vital part of God's nature. There is no love in God which is not righteous, and there is no righteousness in God which is not loving.

17:26 DISCIPLESHIP, Neighbor Love—Jesus stated that He made God known to His believers in order for the love God has for Him to be in them. Neighbor love in the lives of disciples is the same love the heavenly Father has for His only begotten Son. Disciples are to love redemptively, even as God through Christ loves redemptively. In fact, God loves redemptively through His disciples by the ministry of the Holy Spirit. See 14:15–17; note on 1 Jn 2:3–6.

to the grove, guiding[p] a detachment of
soldiers and some officials from the chief
priests and Pharisees.[q] They were carrying torches, lanterns and weapons.
4 Jesus, knowing all that was going to
happen to him,[r] went out and asked
them, "Who is it you want?"[s]
5 "Jesus of Nazareth,"[t] they replied.
"I am he," Jesus said. (And Judas the
traitor was standing there with them.)
6 When Jesus said, "I am he," they drew
back and fell to the ground.
7 Again he asked them, "Who is it you
want?"[u]
And they said, "Jesus of Nazareth."
8 "I told you that I am he," Jesus answered. "If you are looking for me, then
let these men go." 9 This happened so
that the words he had spoken would be
fulfilled: "I have not lost one of those you
gave me."[a] [v]
10 Then Simon Peter, who had a sword,
drew it and struck the high priest's servant, cutting off his right ear. (The servant's name was Malchus.)
11 Jesus commanded Peter, "Put your
sword away! Shall I not drink the cup[w]
the Father has given me?"

Jesus Taken to Annas

18:12,13pp — Mt 26:57

12 Then the detachment of soldiers with
its commander and the Jewish officials[x]
arrested Jesus. They bound him 13 and
brought him first to Annas, who was the
father-in-law of Caiaphas,[y] the high
priest that year. 14 Caiaphas was the one
who had advised the Jews that it would
be good if one man died for the people.[z]

Peter's First Denial

18:16–18pp — Mt 26:69,70; Mk 14:66–68; Lk 22:55–57

15 Simon Peter and another disciple
were following Jesus. Because this disciple was known to the high priest,[a] he
went with Jesus into the high priest's
courtyard,[b] 16 but Peter had to wait outside at the door. The other disciple, who
was known to the high priest, came back,
spoke to the girl on duty there and
brought Peter in.
17 "You are not one of his disciples, are
you?" the girl at the door asked Peter.
He replied, "I am not."[c]
18 It was cold, and the servants and officials stood around a fire[d] they had made
to keep warm. Peter also was standing
with them, warming himself.[e]

18:3 [p]Ac 1:16 [q]ver 12
18:4 [r]Jn 6:64; 13:1,11 [s]ver 7
18:5 [t]S Mk 1:24
18:7 [u]ver 4
18:9 [v]S Jn 6:39
18:11 [w]S Mt 20:22
18:12 [x]ver 3
18:13 [y]ver 24; S Mt 26:3
18:14 [z]Jn 11:49-51
18:15 [a]S Mt 26:3 [b]Mt 26:58; Mk 14:54; Lk 22:54
18:17 [c]ver 25
18:18 [d]Jn 21:9 [e]Mk 14:54,67
18:20 [f]S Mt 4:23 [g]Mt 26:55 [h]Jn 7:26
18:22 [i]ver 3 [j]Mt 16:21; Jn 19:3
18:23 [k]Mt 5:39; Ac 23:2-5
18:24 [l]ver 13; S Mt 26:3
18:25 [m]ver 18 [n]ver 17
18:26 [o]ver 10 [p]ver 1
18:27 [q]Jn 13:38
18:28 [r]S Mt 27:2 [s]ver 33; Jn 19:9 [t]Jn 11:55

The High Priest Questions Jesus

18:19–24pp — Mt 26:59–68; Mk 14:55–65; Lk 22:63–71

19 Meanwhile, the high priest questioned Jesus about his disciples and his
teaching.
20 "I have spoken openly to the world,"
Jesus replied. "I always taught in synagogues[f] or at the temple,[g] where all the
Jews come together. I said nothing in secret.[h] 21 Why question me? Ask those
who heard me. Surely they know what I
said."
22 When Jesus said this, one of the officials[i] nearby struck him in the face.[j] "Is
this the way you answer the high priest?"
he demanded.
23 "If I said something wrong," Jesus replied, "testify as to what is wrong. But if I
spoke the truth, why did you strike
me?"[k] 24 Then Annas sent him, still
bound, to Caiaphas[l] the high priest.[b]

Peter's Second and Third Denials

18:25–27pp — Mt 26:71–75; Mk 14:69–72; Lk 22:58–62

25 As Simon Peter stood warming himself,[m] he was asked, "You are not one of
his disciples, are you?"
He denied it, saying, "I am not."[n]
26 One of the high priest's servants, a
relative of the man whose ear Peter had
cut off,[o] challenged him, "Didn't I see
you with him in the olive grove?"[p]
27 Again Peter denied it, and at that moment a rooster began to crow.[q]

Jesus Before Pilate

18:29–40pp — Mt 27:11–18,20–23; Mk 15:2–15; Lk 23:2,3,18–25

28 Then the Jews led Jesus from Caiaphas to the palace of the Roman governor.[r] By now it was early morning, and
to avoid ceremonial uncleanness the Jews
did not enter the palace;[s] they wanted to
be able to eat the Passover.[t] 29 So Pilate
came out to them and asked, "What
charges are you bringing against this
man?"
30 "If he were not a criminal," they replied, "we would not have handed him
over to you."
31 Pilate said, "Take him yourselves and
judge him by your own law."
"But we have no right to execute anyone," the Jews objected. 32 This happened

[a] 9 John 6:39 [b] 24 Or *(Now Annas had sent him, still bound, to Caiaphas the high priest.)*

18:5 JESUS CHRIST, I Am—See note on 14:6.

18:11 ELECTION, Sovereignty—Peter attempted to protect Jesus from the bitter cup of suffering. Jesus' suffering was not irrational or unexplained suffering. Jesus' suffering, by God's own decree, was redemptive and saving in nature. God chose the way of suffering, not that of the sword, to establish the kingdom for His elect.

18:15–18,25–27 SIN, Responsibility—See note on Mt 26:69–75.

18:31–32 JESUS CHRIST, Death—The Jews had the power of death by stoning in matters of religious transgression (Ac 7:54–60). It was to their advantage to have Jesus crucified as

so that the words Jesus had spoken indicating the kind of death he was going to
die[u] would be fulfilled.
33Pilate then went back inside the palace,[v] summoned Jesus and asked him,
"Are you the king of the Jews?"[w]
34"Is that your own idea," Jesus asked,
"or did others talk to you about me?"
35"Am I a Jew?" Pilate replied. "It was
your people and your chief priests who
handed you over to me. What is it you
have done?"
36Jesus said, "My kingdom[x] is not of
this world. If it were, my servants would
fight to prevent my arrest by the Jews.[y]
But now my kingdom is from another
place."[z]
37"You are a king, then!" said Pilate.
Jesus answered, "You are right in saying I am a king. In fact, for this reason I
was born, and for this I came into the
world, to testify to the truth.[a] Everyone
on the side of truth listens to me."[b]
38"What is truth?" Pilate asked. With
this he went out again to the Jews and
said, "I find no basis for a charge against
him.[c] 39But it is your custom for me to
release to you one prisoner at the time of
the Passover. Do you want me to release
'the king of the Jews'?"
40They shouted back, "No, not him!
Give us Barabbas!" Now Barabbas had
taken part in a rebellion.[d]

Chapter 19

Jesus Sentenced to be Crucified

19:1–16pp — Mt 27:27–31; Mk 15:16–20

THEN Pilate took Jesus and had him
flogged.[e] 2The soldiers twisted together a crown of thorns and put it on his
head. They clothed him in a purple robe
3and went up to him again and again, saying, "Hail, king of the Jews!"[f] And they
struck him in the face.[g]
4Once more Pilate came out and said to
the Jews, "Look, I am bringing him out[h]
to you to let you know that I find no basis
for a charge against him."[i] 5When Jesus
came out wearing the crown of thorns
and the purple robe,[j] Pilate said to them,
"Here is the man!"
6As soon as the chief priests and their
officials saw him, they shouted, "Crucify!
Crucify!"
But Pilate answered, "You take him
and crucify him.[k] As for me, I find no
basis for a charge against him."[l]
7The Jews insisted, "We have a law,
and according to that law he must die,[m]
because he claimed to be the Son of
God."[n]
8When Pilate heard this, he was even
more afraid, 9and he went back inside the
palace.[o] "Where do you come from?" he
asked Jesus, but Jesus gave him no answer.[p] 10"Do you refuse to speak to
me?" Pilate said. "Don't you realize I
have power either to free you or to crucify you?"
11Jesus answered, "You would have no
power over me if it were not given to you
from above.[q] Therefore the one who
handed me over to you[r] is guilty of a
greater sin."
12From then on, Pilate tried to set Jesus
free, but the Jews kept shouting, "If you
let this man go, you are no friend of Caesar. Anyone who claims to be a king[s]
opposes Caesar."
13When Pilate heard this, he brought
Jesus out and sat down on the judge's
seat[t] at a place known as the Stone Pavement (which in Aramaic[u] is Gabbatha).
14It was the day of Preparation[v] of Passover Week, about the sixth hour.[w]
"Here is your king,"[x] Pilate said to the
Jews.
15But they shouted, "Take him away!
Take him away! Crucify him!"
"Shall I crucify your king?" Pilate
asked.

18:32 [u]Mt 20:19; 26:2; Jn 3:14; 8:28; 12:32,33
18:33 [v]ver 28,29; Jn 19:9 [w]Lk 23:3; S Mt 2:2
18:36 [x]S Mt 3:2 [y]Mt 26:53 [z]Lk 17:21; Jn 6:15
18:37 [a]Jn 3:32 [b]Jn 8:47; 1Jn 4:6
18:38 [c]S Lk 23:4
18:40 [d]Ac 3:14
19:1 [e]Dt 25:3; Isa 50:6; 53:5; Mt 27:26
19:3 [f]Mt 27:29 [g]Jn 18:22
19:4 [h]Jn 18:38 [i]ver 6; S Lk 23:4
19:5 [j]ver 2
19:6 [k]Ac 3:13 [l]ver 4; S Lk 23:4
19:7 [m]Lev 24:16 [n]Mt 26:63-66; Jn 5:18; 10:33
19:9 [o]Jn 18:33 [p]S Mk 14:61
19:11 [q]S Ro 13:1 [r]Jn 18:28-30; Ac 3:13
19:12 [s]Lk 23:2
19:13 [t]Mt 27:19 [u]S Jn 5:2
19:14 [v]Mt 27:62 [w]Mk 15:25 [x]ver 19, 21

a political offender thus nullifying His messianic following, or so they supposed. John knew the crucifixion was an outcome of Jesus' own prophecy as to what type of death He would die.

18:32 REVELATION, Jesus Christ—Jesus revealed His own death. As all inspired predictions, His were fulfilled by God. Compare v 9.

18:33–37 JESUS CHRIST, King—See note on Mt 27:11. Jesus had His own definition of kingship. He did not threaten the Roman government. He threatened the religious rulers. His was not a physical kingdom based on war and violence. His is a spiritual kingdom establishing the truth in the world. Being part of His kingdom is knowing God, who is truth, and whom we know as we know Jesus. Pilate and the Jewish leaders rejected the truth and thus sealed themselves out of God's kingdom.

18:37 SALVATION, Acceptance—Compare with 3:33; Lk 10:16. Acceptance of Christ means listening to Him and obeying Him.

19:1–6 JESUS CHRIST, Suffering—See note on Mt 27:26–30.

19:7 JESUS CHRIST, Son of God—Son of God is the key title in John's Gospel. It represents equality with God. The religious leaders took Jesus' claim to be God's Son as a claim to be divine, which was blasphemy for them (Lev 24:16) but is the heart of the gospel for Christians. The religious leaders had their law right. They had their eyes closed to the light of God's revelation, however, for Jesus' works showed He truly was God in flesh.

19:11 JESUS CHRIST, Authority—The Roman government might claim authority over the greater part of the earth. They had no authority over Jesus. See note on Mt 28:18–20.

19:11 SIN, Responsibility—The darkest sin ever committed was the crucifixion of Jesus Christ. Who was responsible? We cannot blame Pilate entirely. Greater guilt goes to the one who belonged to God's chosen people and should have recognized and believed in the Messiah. The specific reference here may be to either Caiaphas, the high priest, or Judas, the betrayer. In the larger scriptural context the reference is to anyone confronted directly by the claims of Christ who rejects those claims. We are personally responsible for our response to Jesus.

"We have no king but Caesar," the
chief priests answered.
16Finally Pilate handed him over to
them to be crucified.[y]

The Crucifixion

19:17–24pp — Mt 27:33–44; Mk 15:22–32; Lk 23:33–43

So the soldiers took charge of Jesus.
17Carrying his own cross,[z] he went out
to the place of the Skull[a] (which in Aramaic[b] is called Golgotha). 18Here they
crucified him, and with him two others[c]
—one on each side and Jesus in the middle.
19Pilate had a notice prepared and fastened to the cross. It read: JESUS OF NAZA-
RETH,[d] THE KING OF THE JEWS.[e] 20Many of
the Jews read this sign, for the place
where Jesus was crucified was near the
city,[f] and the sign was written in Aramaic, Latin and Greek. 21The chief priests of
the Jews protested to Pilate, "Do not
write 'The King of the Jews,' but that this
man claimed to be king of the Jews."[g]
22Pilate answered, "What I have written, I have written."
23When the soldiers crucified Jesus,
they took his clothes, dividing them into
four shares, one for each of them, with
the undergarment remaining. This garment was seamless, woven in one piece
from top to bottom.
24"Let's not tear it," they said to one
another. "Let's decide by lot who will get
it."
This happened that the scripture might
be fulfilled[h] which said,

"They divided my garments among
them
and cast lots for my clothing."[c] [i]

So this is what the soldiers did.
25Near the cross[j] of Jesus stood his
mother,[k] his mother's sister, Mary the
wife of Clopas, and Mary Magdalene.[l]
26When Jesus saw his mother[m] there, and
the disciple whom he loved[n] standing
nearby, he said to his mother, "Dear
woman, here is your son," 27and to the
disciple, "Here is your mother." From
that time on, this disciple took her into
his home.

The Death of Jesus

19:29,30pp — Mt 27:48,50; Mk 15:36,37; Lk 23:36

28Later, knowing that all was now completed,[o] and so that the Scripture would
be fulfilled,[p] Jesus said, "I am thirsty."
29A jar of wine vinegar[q] was there, so
they soaked a sponge in it, put the sponge
on a stalk of the hyssop plant, and lifted it
to Jesus' lips. 30When he had received the
drink, Jesus said, "It is finished."[r] With
that, he bowed his head and gave up his
spirit.
31Now it was the day of Preparation,[s]
and the next day was to be a special Sabbath. Because the Jews did not want the
bodies left on the crosses[t] during the
Sabbath, they asked Pilate to have the
legs broken and the bodies taken down.
32The soldiers therefore came and broke
the legs of the first man who had been
crucified with Jesus, and then those of
the other.[u] 33But when they came to
Jesus and found that he was already dead,
they did not break his legs. 34Instead, one
of the soldiers pierced[v] Jesus' side with a
spear, bringing a sudden flow of blood
and water.[w] 35The man who saw it[x] has
given testimony, and his testimony is
true.[y] He knows that he tells the truth,
and he testifies so that you also may believe. 36These things happened so that
the scripture would be fulfilled:[z] "Not
one of his bones will be broken,"[d] [a]
37and, as another scripture says, "They
will look on the one they have
pierced."[e] [b]

19:16 [y]Mt 27:26; Mk 15:15; Lk 23:25
19:17 [z]Ge 22:6; Lk 14:27; 23:26 [a]Lk 23:33 [b]S Jn 5:2
19:18 [c]Lk 23:32
19:19 [d]S Mk 1:24 [e]ver 14,21
19:20 [f]Heb 13:12
19:21 [g]ver 14
19:24 [h]ver 28,36,37; S Mt 1:22 [i]Ps 22:18
19:25 [j]Mt 27:55,56 [k]S Mt 12:46 [l]Lk 24:18
19:26 [m]S Mt 12:46 [n]S Jn 13:23
19:28 [o]S ver 30; Jn 13:1 [p]ver 24,36,37; S Mt 1:22
19:29 [q]Ps 69:21
19:30 [r]Lk 12:50; Jn 4:34; 17:4
19:31 [s]ver 14,42 [t]Dt 21:23; Jos 8:29; 10:26,27
19:32 [u]ver 18
19:34 [v]Zec 12:10; Rev 1:7 [w]1Jn 5:6,8
19:35 [x]S Lk 24:48 [y]Jn 15:27; 21:24
19:36 [z]ver 24,28,37; S Mt 1:22 [a]Ex 12:46; Nu 9:12; Ps 34:20
19:37 [b]Zec 12:10; Rev 1:7

[c]*24* Psalm 22:18 [d]*36* Exodus 12:46; Num. 9:12; Psalm 34:20 [e]*37* Zech. 12:10

19:17–22 JESUS CHRIST, King—See note on 18:33–37.
19:23–24 JESUS CHRIST, Fulfilled—Even the actions of pagan soldiers fulfilled God's scriptural plan for Jesus. Compare Ps 22:18.
19:26–27 JESUS CHRIST, Death—As He died, Jesus showed His divine love for His mother. Thus He served other people's needs to the last.
19:30 JESUS CHRIST, Mission—Death appeared to finish a human life. Instead it victoriously completed the saving mission of God's Son. He had given His life for many.
19:30 HUMANITY, Death—Death, the common enemy of all people, came to Jesus Himself. He simply yielded His spirit. The separation of spirit and flesh is the end of life as we know it. See note on Zec 12:1.
19:34–37 JESUS CHRIST, Death—The spear pierced Jesus' heart causing water from the protective sac around the heart to flow. This physical condition represented symbolic spiritual meaning for John as fulfillment of Zec 12:10. People look on Jesus in judgment on their own unbelief or see in His crucifixion the blood of redemption and the water of life. Compare 3:18–21.
19:35–37 HOLY SCRIPTURE, Eyewitnesses—The Gospel writer was an eyewitness to the death and crucifixion of Jesus. He testified in truth. He wrote what he saw so others could read and believe in Christ. His written record of God's revelation was vital to the early church, leading people to faith. The church recognized God's inspiration in it and collected it with other inspired writings as Holy Scripture.
19:35 SALVATION, Belief—This text underscores the intense evangelistic intention of the fourth Gospel. John wanted people to believe in Jesus as the only source of eternal life. Do you accept his testimony? See Guide to Accepting Christ (pp 1745–1747).
19:35 EVANGELISM, Testimony—Eyewitness testimony to Christ's death and resurrection is the basis of evangelism. John's Gospel, as well as the Gospels of Matthew, Mark, and Luke, is based on such testimony. Testimony to Christ is given so people will commit their lives to Him and experience salvation.

The Burial of Jesus

19:38–42pp — Mt 27:57–61; Mk 15:42–47; Lk 23:50–56

38Later, Joseph of Arimathea asked Pilate for the body of Jesus. Now Joseph
was a disciple of Jesus, but secretly because he feared the Jews.[c] With Pilate's
permission, he came and took the body
away. 39He was accompanied by Nicodemus,[d] the man who earlier had visited
Jesus at night. Nicodemus brought a mixture of myrrh and aloes, about seventy-
five pounds.[f] 40Taking Jesus' body, the
two of them wrapped it, with the spices,
in strips of linen.[e] This was in accordance with Jewish burial customs.[f] 41At
the place where Jesus was crucified,
there was a garden, and in the garden a
new tomb, in which no one had ever
been laid. 42Because it was the Jewish day
of Preparation[g] and since the tomb was
nearby,[h] they laid Jesus there.

Chapter 20

The Empty Tomb

20:1–8pp — Mt 28:1–8; Mk 16:1–8; Lk 24:1–10

EARLY on the first day of the week,
while it was still dark, Mary Magdalene[i] went to the tomb and saw that the
stone had been removed from the entrance.[j] 2So she came running to Simon
Peter and the other disciple, the one
Jesus loved,[k] and said, "They have taken
the Lord out of the tomb, and we don't
know where they have put him!"[l]
3So Peter and the other disciple started
for the tomb.[m] 4Both were running, but
the other disciple outran Peter and
reached the tomb first. 5He bent over and
looked in[n] at the strips of linen[o] lying
there but did not go in. 6Then Simon Peter, who was behind him, arrived and
went into the tomb. He saw the strips of
linen lying there, 7as well as the burial
cloth that had been around Jesus' head.[p]
The cloth was folded up by itself, separate
from the linen. 8Finally the other disciple,
who had reached the tomb first,[q] also
went inside. He saw and believed. 9(They
still did not understand from Scripture[r]
that Jesus had to rise from the dead.)[s]

Jesus Appears to Mary Magdalene

10Then the disciples went back to their
homes, 11but Mary stood outside the
tomb crying. As she wept, she bent over
to look into the tomb[t] 12and saw two angels in white,[u] seated where Jesus' body
had been, one at the head and the other
at the foot.
13They asked her, "Woman, why are
you crying?"[v]
"They have taken my Lord away," she
said, "and I don't know where they have
put him."[w] 14At this, she turned around
and saw Jesus standing there,[x] but she
did not realize that it was Jesus.[y]
15"Woman," he said, "why are you
crying?[z] Who is it you are looking for?"
Thinking he was the gardener, she
said, "Sir, if you have carried him away,
tell me where you have put him, and I
will get him."
16Jesus said to her, "Mary."
She turned toward him and cried out in
Aramaic,[a] "Rabboni!"[b] (which means
Teacher).
17Jesus said, "Do not hold on to me, for
I have not yet returned to the Father. Go
instead to my brothers[c] and tell them, 'I
am returning to my Father[d] and your Father, to my God and your God.' "
18Mary Magdalene[e] went to the disciples[f] with the news: "I have seen the
Lord!" And she told them that he had
said these things to her.

Jesus Appears to His Disciples

19On the evening of that first day of the
week, when the disciples were together,
with the doors locked for fear of the
Jews,[g] Jesus came and stood among them

19:38 [c]S Jn 7:13
19:39 [d]Jn 3:1; 7:50
19:40 [e]Lk 24:12; Jn 11:44; 20:5,7 [f]Mt 26:12
19:42 [g]ver 14,31 [h]ver 20,41
20:1 [i]ver 18; Lk 8:2; Jn 19:25 [j]Mt 27:60,66
20:2 [k]S Jn 13:23 [l]ver 13
20:3 [m]Lk 24:12
20:5 [n]ver 11 [o]S Jn 19:40
20:7 [p]Jn 11:44
20:8 [q]ver 4
20:9 [r]Mt 22:29; Jn 2:22 [s]Lk 24:26, 46; Ac 2:24
20:11 [t]ver 5
20:12 [u]Mt 28:2,3; Mk 16:5; Lk 24:4; Ac 1:10; S 5:19; 10:30
20:13 [v]ver 15 [w]ver 2
20:14 [x]Mk 16:9 [y]Lk 24:16; Jn 21:4
20:15 [z]ver 13
20:16 [a]S Jn 5:2 [b]S Mt 23:7
20:17 [c]S Mt 28:10 [d]Jn 7:33
20:18 [e]S ver 1 [f]Lk 24:10,22,23
20:19 [g]S Jn 7:13

[f]39 Greek *a hundred litrai* (about 34 kilograms)

19:38–42 JESUS CHRIST, Death—Jesus' burial was on the same day as His crucifixion as required by Jewish law (Dt 21:22–23). This final indignity of burial as a criminal would give rise to the idea of associating Jesus' death with the "curse of the law" (Gal 3:13; 2 Co 5:21).

20:1–9 JESUS CHRIST, Secret—Christ's resurrection surprised His disciples. Despite thinking they had understood Jesus' teaching (18:29–30), they understood Christ's resurrection only after experiencing the resurrected Christ.

20:8,24–31 SALVATION, Belief—God wants all persons to believe in His Son. Doubting Thomas believed in the end. Seeing the physical presence of Jesus is not necessary for belief. The testimony of the gospel writer can lead you to faith in Christ.

20:10–18 JESUS CHRIST, Resurrection—Meeting the resurrected Christ surprised Mary. Jesus did not want Mary to hold on to Him. She needed to tell the others and to be ready to live with the Spirit, who would come, rather than with Jesus, who was to go to the Father.

20:16 EDUCATION, Jesus—See notes on 1:38; Mt 23:8.

20:17,28 GOD, Trinity—The separate Persons of the Trinity appear clearly here. Jesus must leave earth and return home to the Father. Jesus called the Father, my God. Still, Thomas can call Jesus, "God." The separate Persons form one God in the mystery of the Trinity. See note on Mt 3:16–17.

20:19 LAST THINGS, Resurrection Body—In His resurrection body Jesus clearly transcended time and space. He had power to vanish so as to cease to be seen by others (Lk 24:31). The descriptions of His resurrection body are our best source of information about the nature of resurrection bodies of believers. See note on Php 3:20–21. The recognizability of Jesus in His resurrection body, even to the presentation of the scars of crucifixion (Jn 20:20), suggests visual continuity between the physical bodies and those of resurrection. See note on 1 Co 15:35–49.

and said, "Peace[h] be with you!"[i] 20After
he said this, he showed them his hands
and side.[j] The disciples were overjoyed[k]
when they saw the Lord.
21Again Jesus said, "Peace be with
you![l] As the Father has sent me,[m] I am
sending you."[n] 22And with that he
breathed on them and said, "Receive the
Holy Spirit.[o] 23If you forgive anyone his
sins, they are forgiven; if you do not forgive them, they are not forgiven."[p]

Jesus Appears to Thomas

24Now Thomas[q] (called Didymus), one
of the Twelve, was not with the disciples
when Jesus came. 25So the other disciples
told him, "We have seen the Lord!"
But he said to them, "Unless I see the
nail marks in his hands and put my finger
where the nails were, and put my hand
into his side,[r] I will not believe it."[s]
26A week later his disciples were in the
house again, and Thomas was with them.
Though the doors were locked, Jesus
came and stood among them and said,
"Peace[t] be with you!"[u] 27Then he said
to Thomas, "Put your finger here; see my
hands. Reach out your hand and put it
into my side. Stop doubting and believe."[v]
28Thomas said to him, "My Lord and
my God!"
29Then Jesus told him, "Because you
have seen me, you have believed;[w]
blessed are those who have not seen and
yet have believed."[x]
30Jesus did many other miraculous
signs[y] in the presence of his disciples,
which are not recorded in this book.[z]
31But these are written that you may[g] believe[a] that Jesus is the Christ, the Son of
God,[b] and that by believing you may
have life in his name.[c]

Chapter 21

Jesus and the Miraculous Catch of Fish

AFTERWARD Jesus appeared again to
his disciples,[d] by the Sea of Tiberias.[h][e] It happened this way: 2Simon Pe-

[g]31 Some manuscripts *may continue to* [h]1 That is, Sea of Galilee

20:19 [h]S Jn 14:27 [i]ver 21,26; Lk 24:36-39
20:20 [j]Lk 24:39, 40; Jn 19:34 [k]Jn 16:20,22
20:21 [l]ver 19 [m]S Jn 3:17 [n]Mt 28:19; Jn 17:18
20:22 [o]Jn 7:39; Ac 2:38; 8:15-17; 19:2; Gal 3:2
20:23 [p]Mt 16:19; 18:18
20:24 [q]S Jn 11:16
20:25 [r]ver 20 [s]Mk 16:11
20:26 [t]S Jn 14:27 [u]ver 21
20:27 [v]ver 25; Lk 24:40
20:29 [w]S Jn 3:15 [x]1Pe 1:8
20:30 [y]S Jn 2:11 [z]Jn 21:25
20:31 [a]S Jn 3:15; 19:35 [b]S Mt 4:3 [c]S Mt 25:46
21:1 [d]ver 14; Jn 20:19,26 [e]Jn 6:1

20:20 SALVATION, Joy—Those who saw the crucified Christ as their resurrected Lord were overjoyed. The joy of our salvation is needed to fulfill the Great Commission.

20:21–22 HOLY SPIRIT, Mission—The Spirit allows disciples to take up the mission the Father gave the Son. That mission is to preach forgiveness in Christ's name. Such proclamation is possible only under the Spirit's leadership. All disciples are called to receive the Spirit and testify to the gospel of forgiveness.

20:21–23 EVANGELISM, Call to Evangelize—Jesus sent the church to evangelize the world. The church carries forward the ministry God gave Jesus. The church's witness is possible only as we experience the Holy Spirit's power. In that power our testimony confronts people with salvation in Christ. Those who accept Him find freedom from guilt. Those who reject Him lose the opportunity for forgiveness.

20:21 MISSIONS, Command—Jesus' words are one of five occasions in the Gospels and Acts on which He presents the Great Commission to the disciples, calling them to continue His mission until His return. See note on Mt 28:18–20. This repetition of the Great Commission shows that the world mission of the church was neither an afterthought nor a one-time comment. Missions was central to Jesus' instruction of the disciples and for His commission to His church. This great verse defines the source, the model, and the authority for missions. What Jesus did in His life becomes our model or pattern for missions. What He said becomes our authority for missions. His being sent from the Father and our being sent reveal the source of missions. The model for our mission is that of Jesus. He was sent from the Father; declared the Father's message; and engaged in preaching, teaching, healing, receiving outcasts, unmasking sin, serving, and finally dying for others. The Father sent the Son because God loves the lost world (Jn 3:16). God's purpose was to reconcile the lost world to Himself through Jesus Christ. See 3:17; 2 Co 5:19. He sent Jesus as the God-Man, to walk the dusty roads of everyday experience, speak the human language, understand the people, love them, serve them (Mk 10:40), and declare the Father's message for them. In the same way the Father sent the Son, the risen Lord sent His disciples to a lost and needy world. The mandate is clear. We are to be like Him. Jesus is continuing His mission and His ministry through us, His church. We are sent as the Father sent Him with the same purpose, method, and authority—to be His ambassadors in the power of the Spirit.

20:25–28 JESUS CHRIST, Lord—The disciples recognized Jesus as their Master and as divine. See note on Lk 1:5–23.

20:29 SALVATION, Blessing—Christ gives the blessing of eternal life to all who believe in Him. The ultimate meaning of blessing is to have eternal life in Christ. Without that no other blessings have meaning.

20:29 THE CHURCH, Redeemed of All Ages—The church can be seen from different perspectives, each of which contains part of the meaning of church: (1) a local congregation (the most frequent meaning); (2) believers in a geographical area; (3) believers in a particular time period; and (4) all believers throughout history. Jesus described His small group of followers as believers. At the same time He pointed ahead to the church of all history, the believers who could not see Jesus in the flesh and yet trusted Him for salvation. See note on Mt 12:46–50.

20:30–31 MIRACLE, Vocabulary—Jesus performed "signs" to provoke faith. This was not faith in a magician but faith in Jesus, the Christ, the Son of God. Many of His miracles were not recorded in the Bible, but all were signs to produce faith. Those recorded should lead us to faith in Jesus. Have you seen the signs, believed in Christ, and received eternal life? Or do you read the stories but miss the signs? Are you still spiritually blind?

20:30–31 HOLY SCRIPTURE, Writing—Not all of Jesus' miracles and deeds were recorded. The written Gospels do not claim to be complete biographies (21:25). They are selected events and teachings which reveal the nature and purpose of Christ, thus leading readers to faith. They provide a witness of God's revealed truth to all readers. They show that revelation and inspiration involve a conscious effort to write experiences in a book, an effort involving selection and reflection under divine guidance.

20:31 SALVATION, Eternal Life—John's Gospel, and indeed all Scripture, is written that persons may believe Jesus is the Savior of the world and receive His love gift of eternal life.

20:31 EVANGELISM, Call to Salvation—John wrote his Gospel to lead people to faith in Christ and thus to full, meaningful life. Evangelists today follow the Fourth Evangelist and seek to bring people to confess Jesus as God's promised Christ or Messiah, the very Son of God in whose name is life.

21:1–14 JESUS CHRIST, Resurrection—The resurrected Lord could perform signs just as could Jesus before the cross.

ter, Thomas[f] (called Didymus), Nathanael[g] from Cana in Galilee,[h] the sons of
Zebedee,[i] and two other disciples were
together. 3"I'm going out to fish," Simon
Peter told them, and they said, "We'll go
with you." So they went out and got into
the boat, but that night they caught nothing.[j]
4Early in the morning, Jesus stood on
the shore, but the disciples did not realize
that it was Jesus.[k]
5He called out to them, "Friends,
haven't you any fish?"
"No," they answered.
6He said, "Throw your net on the right
side of the boat and you will find some."
When they did, they were unable to haul
the net in because of the large number of
fish.[l]
7Then the disciple whom Jesus loved[m]
said to Peter, "It is the Lord!" As soon as
Simon Peter heard him say, "It is the
Lord," he wrapped his outer garment
around him (for he had taken it off) and
jumped into the water. 8The other disciples followed in the boat, towing the net
full of fish, for they were not far from
shore, about a hundred yards.[i] 9When
they landed, they saw a fire[n] of burning
coals there with fish on it,[o] and some
bread.
10Jesus said to them, "Bring some of
the fish you have just caught."
11Simon Peter climbed aboard and
dragged the net ashore. It was full of large
fish, 153, but even with so many the net
was not torn. 12Jesus said to them,
"Come and have breakfast." None of the
disciples dared ask him, "Who are you?"
They knew it was the Lord. 13Jesus came,
took the bread and gave it to them, and
did the same with the fish.[p] 14This was
now the third time Jesus appeared to his
disciples[q] after he was raised from the
dead.

Jesus Reinstates Peter

15When they had finished eating, Jesus
said to Simon Peter, "Simon son of John,
do you truly love me more than these?"
"Yes, Lord," he said, "you know that I
love you."[r]
Jesus said, "Feed my lambs."[s]
16Again Jesus said, "Simon son of John,
do you truly love me?"
He answered, "Yes, Lord, you know
that I love you."
Jesus said, "Take care of my sheep."[t]
17The third time he said to him, "Simon son of John, do you love me?"
Peter was hurt because Jesus asked
him the third time, "Do you love me?"[u]
He said, "Lord, you know all things;[v]
you know that I love you."
Jesus said, "Feed my sheep.[w] 18I tell
you the truth, when you were younger
you dressed yourself and went where you
wanted; but when you are old you will
stretch out your hands, and someone else
will dress you and lead you where you do
not want to go." 19Jesus said this to indicate the kind of death[x] by which Peter
would glorify God.[y] Then he said to him,
"Follow me!"[z]
20Peter turned and saw that the disciple whom Jesus loved[a] was following
them. (This was the one who had leaned
back against Jesus at the supper and had
said, "Lord, who is going to betray
you?")[b] 21When Peter saw him, he
asked, "Lord, what about him?"
22Jesus answered, "If I want him to remain alive until I return,[c] what is that to
you? You must follow me."[d] 23Because of

21:2 [f]S Jn 11:16 [g]Jn 1:45 [h]Jn 2:1 [i]S Mt 4:21
21:3 [j]Lk 5:5
21:4 [k]Lk 24:16; Jn 20:14
21:6 [l]Lk 5:4-7
21:7 [m]S Jn 13:23
21:9 [n]Jn 18:18 [o]ver 10,13
21:13 [p]ver 9
21:14 [q]Jn 20:19,26
21:15 [r]Mt 26:33,35; Jn 13:37 [s]Lk 12:32
21:16 [t]2Sa 5:2; Eze 34:2; Mt 2:6; S Jn 10:11; Ac 20:28; 1Pe 5:2,3
21:17 [u]Jn 13:38 [v]Jn 16:30 [w]S ver 16
21:19 [x]Jn 12:33; 18:32 [y]Jn 13:36; 2Pe 1:14 [z]S Mt 4:19
21:20 [a]ver 7; S Jn 13:23 [b]Jn 13:25
21:22 [c]S Mt 16:27 [d]ver 19; S Mt 4:19

i8 Greek *about two hundred cubits* (about 90 meters)

See notes on 2:1–11; 20:25–28. The resurrection appearances helped the disciples understand who Jesus was and to see that He was the fulfillment of Scripture. See note on 20:1–9.

21:6 MIRACLE, Faith—That seasoned fishermen, somewhat disillusioned at the death of Jesus, should willingly obey directions from a "landlubber" suggests the sensitivity of these disciples. The fish were real, almost breaking the net; and the disciples remembered the number—153 (v 11). They believed on Him, and Peter was restored (after his denial) to discipleship. Do you need to see Christ's miracles as signs inviting you to restored fellowship and discipleship? See Lk 5:1–11.

21:13 ORDINANCES, Lord's Supper as Death and Resurrection—Although Jesus gave the disciples bread and fish that He had prepared over a fire beside the sea, the words echo the language of the Lord's Supper. Even more, they recall the commentary of Jesus upon the feeding of the 5,000 in Jn 6, when He said that they must "eat his flesh and drink his blood" (v 53) to have eternal life. While not an explicit observance of the Lord's Supper, these meals provide a background for understanding that just as Jesus was providing physical food and drink for their sustenance, He was, more importantly, providing spiritual food and drink for their souls by His death and resurrection.

21:15–23 SALVATION, Love of God—Saved persons are to love Christ more than anything else in the universe. We are to serve faithfully and follow Christ. We should not expect our fervent love for Christ to prevent our physical death. For the believer physical death leads only to eternal life.

21:15–17 DISCIPLESHIP, Nature—Discipleship has only one requirement. We may be disciples if we love Jesus so deeply we are willing to do what He asks. Each time Simon Peter answered Jesus' question concerning loving Him, the Lord gave him a task to do. When Peter asked what John was to do, Jesus said that should not concern Peter. Love for Jesus leads us to serve other people. Every disciple has a task. My primary concern is to do the task the Lord has given to me because I love Him. The Lord will give others whatever assignment pleases Him. See note on 1 Jn 3:17–18.

21:22–23 LAST THINGS, Return Promises—The return of Jesus is an underlying assumption of His full ministry. The first coming is not complete without the second coming. Jesus could speak almost offhandedly about His return, so certain was its reality. See note on Ac 1:11.

this, the rumor spread among the brothers[e] that this disciple would not die. But
Jesus did not say that he would not die;
he only said, "If I want him to remain
alive until I return, what is that to you?"
24This is the disciple who testifies to
these things[f] and who wrote them
down. We know that his testimony is
true.[g]
25Jesus did many other things as well.[h]
If every one of them were written down,
I suppose that even the whole world
would not have room for the books that
would be written.

21:23 [e]S Ac 1:16
21:24 [f]S Jn 15:27 [g]Jn 19:35
21:25 [h]Jn 20:30

21:24–25 HOLY SCRIPTURE, Eyewitnesses—The disciple was the witness and recorder of all the experiences collected in this book and declared them true as personal witness. Apparently another inspired writer referred to John the eyewitness in third person and testified for the believers to the truth of "his testimony." These believers evidently received and preserved John's Gospel until it was collected with the other Gospels and became part of the New Testament. He revealed further that his recorded experiences are only a partial collection of the many words and deeds of Jesus Christ. See note on 20:30–31.

21:25 JESUS CHRIST, Miracles—John reported miracles to get belief (20:31). Jesus did many things John and the other Gospel writers did not report. No report can be exhaustive. The inspired reports are sufficient to lead us to faith and salvation.

Acts

Theological Setting

"Acts" as a book title may suggest that Luke wrote the book of Acts to give a historical account of what happened to the original apostles whom Jesus called and trained, but after listing the eleven apostles and the new one elected in place of Judas, Luke never mentioned nine of them any more. Luke gave only one sentence about James (Ac 12:2), and only a slight mention of John. After Acts 12, Peter moved off the stage. Even the story of Paul was not complete. In the strict sense, this book does not disclose the "acts of the apostles."

Some suggest that the book should be called "The Acts of the Holy Spirit," since it tells about the coming of the Holy Spirit. Fifty times, Luke specifically referred to the Holy Spirit. However eleven chapters of the book do not mention the Holy Spirit at all. In the section after Acts 21:11, the Holy Spirit is mentioned only once. The entire book, then, is not about the "acts of the Holy Spirit."

Others have suggested that the book was written to reveal the geographic expansion of Christianity. Using Acts 1:8 as an outline of the book, some say that the book of Acts was simply the narrative of the expansion of the church as it spread from Jerusalem eventually to Rome. Christianity was evidently already in Rome before Paul got there, so Luke missed a major part of the story if the geographic expansion of Christianity was his focus.

What then was Luke trying to do? Luke's purpose was to proclaim the expansion of Christianity to all the world "without hindrance" (28:31). The central theme of the book is that God was doing something in the world in Jesus Christ that could not be stopped by anyone or anything. No barriers could prevent the spread of the gospel across the world. Luke wrote the book of Acts to proclaim and explain that truth.

Theological Outline

Acts: The Unhindered Movement of God

- I. God Prepared the Way for Unhindered Mission. (1:1-26)
  - A. Jesus' resurrection appearances prove He rose from the dead. (1:1-3)
  - B. Jesus prepared for the Spirit's coming with power for the task ahead. (1:4-11)
  - C. The church waited and organized itself for its mission. (1:12-26)
- II. Persecution of His People Cannot Hinder God's Purpose. (2:1—8:4)
  - A. The Spirit empowers God's people for their mission. (2:1-4)
  - B. The gospel message overcomes ridicule to form a unified church of repentant believers. (2:5-47)
  - C. The gospel message overcomes imprisonment to add to the church. (3:1—4:4)
  - D. The gospel message overcomes legal rulings and threats to increase the power, unity, and generosity of the church. (4:5-37)
  - E. The Spirit overcomes Satan's attempts to hinder the church through greed and pride. (5:1-16)
  - F. Human jealousy and fear cannot fight successfully against God. (5:17-42)
  - G. Spirit-filled leaders help the church overcome cultural disputes and continue to increase in number. (6:1-7)
  - H. False accusers may bring persecution and death to the church but cannot halt its progress. (6:8—8:4)
- III. God Is Not Hindered by Cultural Barriers. (8:5-40)
  - A. The gospel message brings joy to traditional enemies. (8:5-8)
  - B. The gospel message proves more powerful than magic. (8:9-13)
  - C. The Holy Spirit manifests itself among traditional enemies. (8:14-25)
  - D. The gospel message overcomes physical and racial barriers humans set up. (8:26-40)
- IV. God Is Not Hindered by Organized Opposition. (9:1-31)
  - A. God can convert the strongest persecutors. (9:1-22)
  - B. God can protect His chosen message from opposition inside and outside the church. (9:23-31)

V. God Is Not Hindered by Physical Barriers. (9:32-43)
   A. Physical illness does not stop the gospel. (9:32-34)
   B. Death does not stop the gospel. (9:35-43)
VI. God Is Not Hindered by Racial Barriers. (10:1—11:30)
   A. God does not show favoritism to people because of racial or religious backgrounds. (10:1-48)
   B. The evidence of the Holy Spirit quiets racial prejudice in the church. (11:1-18)
   C. God leads His people to preach to all nationalities. (11:19-26)
   D. Racially diverse converts have a mission to the "mother church." (11:27-30)
VII. God Is Not Hindered by Political Persecution. (12:1-25)
   A. God can rescue His praying people from their persecutors. (12:1-19)
   B. God punishes those who usurp His place. (12:20-23)
   C. Even in persecution God blesses the missionary efforts of His people. (12:24-25)
VIII. God Is Not Hindered by Geographic Boundaries. (13:1—20:12)
   A. The Holy Spirit overcomes sorcery to bless the missionary efforts of the church. (13:1-12)
   B. Missionary work among "pagan races" fulfills the Old Testament expectation. (13:13-52)
   C. Persecution only helps spread the missionary work. (14:1-7)
   D. Missionaries are God's messengers, not gods. (14:8-20)
   E. Missions involves strengthening churches and reporting to the sending church. (14:21-28)
   F. Missionaries preach salvation by grace through faith without ritual burdens. (15:1-35)
   G. God can use disagreement among missionaries to spread the gospel. (15:36-41)
   H. Missionaries do not have to belong to the "mother church" or meet racial requirements. (16:1-5)
   I. God directs His missionaries' paths. (16:6-15)
   J. God can turn persecution into evangelistic opportunities. (16:16-40)
   K. God can use the jealousy of religious people to spread His gospel. (17:1-15)
   L. God can use intellectual argument to lead some people to salvation. (17:16-34)
   M. God encourages His missionaries to preach fearlessly. (18:1-17)
   N. Missionaries must follow God's will in their work. (18:18-23)
   O. Missionary fervor requires accurate understanding, as well as zeal and fervor. (18:24-28)
   P. Missionaries lead people to baptism in Jesus' name and to receive the Spirit from God. (19:1-8)
   Q. God blesses true missionary preaching but disciplines sternly those who try to use Jesus' name for personal gain. (19:9-22)
   R. The gospel upsets those who gain their living through false religion. (19:23-41)
   S. The missionary revisits new Christians to strengthen them. (20:1-12)
IX. God Is Not Hindered by Chains of Human Bondage. (20:13—28:31)
   A. Missionaries testify of Christ, even in the face of danger. (20:13-24)
   B. Missionaries train leaders to carry on their work. (20:25-38)
   C. Missionaries must be willing to die for their faith. (21:1-14)
   D. Missionaries use every opportunity to share their personal testimonies. (21:15—22:21)
   E. Missionaries use political rights to gain further opportunities to witness. (22:22—23:11)
   F. God protects His missionaries against religious enemies. (23:12-35)
   G. Enemies cannot prove their case against God's missionaries. (24:1—25:27)
   H. Imprisonment lets missionaries preach forgiveness. (26:1-32)
   I. God can protect His missionaries against dangers. (27:1—28:10)
   J. God uses fellow Christians to encourage enchained missionaries. (28:11-16)
   K. Even a foreign prison cannot deter God's missionaries from preaching the gospel. (28:17-31)

Theological Conclusions

The book of Acts is by style and approach a historical book. However, doctrinal issues flow through every experience and event. Many of the critical doctrinal issues today are spoken to in the book of Acts. The major theological contribution of this writing relates to the following doctrines:

1. the person of Jesus Christ,
2. the origin and nature of the church,
3. the challenge of missions, and
4. the doctrine of God,

The foundation of the faith of these first disciples was a Person who lived among them and who claimed to be the Son of God. Luke began the book of Acts with some affirmations about Jesus. The risen Christ gave evidence and encouragement to the disciples in facing the task before them (1:1-5). The ascended Christ universalized and vitalized the gospel (1:9). The coming Christ will return to bring to a culmination all that God has done (1:10-11). The sermons included in the book of Acts (2:14-40; 3:12-26; 4:8-12; 5:29-32; 10:34-43; 13:16-41) further developed these themes concerning Jesus Christ and affirmed that all of this happened in fulfillment of the promises God made to the people of Israel. See summary of the Gospel, p. 1663. Luke proclaimed to the people of his day the centrality of Christ.

The book of Acts is most important perhaps because of the insight it gives concerning the origin and nature of the church. In every century, God's people raise the questions: "Who are we?" and "Why are we here?" The definitive answers to those questions are found in the book of Acts.

The practice that provided power for the people of God was prayer (1:12-26). In the coming of the Holy Spirit at Pentecost, the church was empowered for the ministry to which God had called it (2:1-13). Luke outlined the qualities that should characterize God's people in every generation: doctrinal study, fellowship, worship at the Lord's table, prayer, mutual support, and evangelism (2:42-47). In a dramatic story of healing (3:1-10) Luke epitomized the ministry of the church. The ministry of the church is to take the resources available and apply them to the needs of those around us.

The story of the expansion of the church through every barrier standing in the way provides a picture of the mission of the church. The mission of the church was to move out in obedience to the command of Christ (1:8) and be His witnesses in the world to every inhabitant no matter the cost. From the moment when the disciples moved out of the upper room, motivated by the presence and power of the Holy Spirit to proclaim the gospel to the city of Jerusalem, until the book closed with Paul in Rome proclaiming the gospel of Christ to that pivotal city, the book of Acts reminds us that our purpose as God's people is to be on mission for Him.

In Acts 1—7, we see the mission outreach of the church primarily to the Jews in Jerusalem. In Acts 8, the mission outreach of the church gradually expanded to include the Samaritans (8:5,14). In Acts 10, the mission of the church expanded further to include Gentiles. Cornelius (10:1) and the Gentiles in Antioch (11:21) received Christ in response to the preaching of the gospel. Beginning in Acts 13, with the missionary journeys of Paul, the mission venture spread throughout the world known at that time. Luke was explaining to the people of his day the worldwide scope of their mission challenge.

The book of Acts proclaims that God started something in Jesus Christ that cannot be stopped. The focus of the book, therefore, is on God. Primarily in the teachings about the Holy Spirit, Luke gives us a picture of the presence of God in the life of every believer. When the Holy Spirit comes to a believer, He provides power (1:8), boldness (5:29), and character (6:3). "Signs and wonders" is a common phrase that Luke uses throughout the book of Acts (2:19,22,43; 4:30; 5:12; 7:36; 14:3) to indicate the power of God manifest in their lives. Disciples rely on that power in their bold proclamation of the gospel.

The book also clearly focuses on the purpose of God. God's purpose is to provide every person with an opportunity to respond to His love and grace so that they may be redeemed. The picture of God given in the book of Acts is not complete until we also notice what Luke said about the love of God. Peter's classic statement, "I now realize how true it is that God does not show favoritism but accepts men from every nation who fear Him and do what is right" (10:34), is affirmed in every experience described in the book of Acts. All people were created by God and all have equal opportunity to be restored to God through Christ. God's love is for all mankind. Luke was providing for the people of his day a portrait of God and a perception of the church which would inspire and encourage them as they carried out their work.

Contemporary Teaching

The book of Acts focuses our attention on God and what He is doing in our world. Luke reminds us of the roots of our faith, the reason for our existence as the church, and the resources by which we can carry out our work.

In the book of Acts, Luke asks us: (1) to remember who Jesus is and what He has commanded us to do; (2) to understand the essentials of the Gospel and to proclaim that message to the world; (3) to recognize the worldwide dimensions of our mission challenge; (4) to refuse to let barriers and obstacles prevent us from sharing the message of Christ; (5) to reach out to all people in the name of Christ, regardless of race or social status; (6) to recognize that God still wants to perform "signs and wonders" in our midst if we will be open to the Holy Spirit; (7) to examine daily God's Word so that we can be more effective for Him; (8) to deepen our involvement in prayer as the practice by which we can be prepared for our task; and (9) to renew our commitment to be witnesses for Jesus Christ.

Chapter 1

Jesus Taken Up Into Heaven

IN my former book,[a] Theophilus, I
wrote about all that Jesus began to do
and to teach[b] 2until the day he was taken
up to heaven,[c] after giving instructions[d]
through the Holy Spirit to the apostles[e]
he had chosen.[f] 3After his suffering, he
showed himself to these men and gave
many convincing proofs that he was alive.
He appeared to them[g] over a period of
forty days and spoke about the kingdom
of God.[h] 4On one occasion, while he was
eating with them, he gave them this command: "Do not leave Jerusalem, but
wait[i] for the gift my Father promised,
which you have heard me speak about.[j]
5For John baptized with[a] water,[k] but in
a few days you will be baptized with the
Holy Spirit."[l]
6So when they met together, they
asked him, "Lord, are you at this time
going to restore[m] the kingdom to Israel?"
7He said to them: "It is not for you to
know the times or dates the Father has
set by his own authority.[n] 8But you will
receive power when the Holy Spirit
comes on you;[o] and you will be my witnesses[p] in Jerusalem, and in all Judea and
Samaria,[q] and to the ends of the earth."[r]
9After he said this, he was taken up[s]
before their very eyes, and a cloud hid
him from their sight.
10They were looking intently up into
the sky as he was going, when suddenly
two men dressed in white[t] stood beside
them. 11"Men of Galilee,"[u] they said,
"why do you stand here looking into the
sky? This same Jesus, who has been taken
from you into heaven, will come back[v] in

1:1 [a]Lk 1:1-4 [b]Lk 3:23
1:2 [c]ver 9,11; S Mk 16:19 [d]Mt 28:19,20 [e]S Mk 6:30 [f]Jn 13:18; 15:16,19
1:3 [g]Mt 28:17; Lk 24:34,36; Jn 20:19,26; 21:1, 14; 1Co 15:5-7 [h]S Mt 3:2
1:4 [i]Ps 27:14 [j]Lk 24:49; Jn 14:16; Ac 2:33
1:5 [k]S Mk 1:4 [l]S Mk 1:8
1:6 [m]Mt 17:11; Ac 3:21
1:7 [n]Dt 29:29; Ps 102:13; Mt 24:36
1:8 [o]Ac 2:1-4 [p]S Lk 24:48 [q]Ac 8:1-25 [r]S Mt 28:19
1:9 [s]ver 2; S Mk 16:19
1:10 [t]S Jn 20:12
1:11 [u]Ac 2:7 [v]S Mt 16:27

[a]5 Or *in*

1:1–2 HOLY SPIRIT, Jesus—The Spirit guided all Jesus' ministry, both His healing activities and His teaching. The power behind His ministry came to the disciples after the resurrection and ascension (v 8). See note on Lk 4:14.

1:1–4 HOLY SCRIPTURE, Writing—Luke wrote two books to Theophilus (Lk 1:3). The first centered on Christ's acts and teaching. The second (Acts) centered on the work of the Holy Spirit through the apostles to spread the gospel throughout the world of the Roman Empire. Under the Spirit's power, the apostles' preaching continued Christ's revelation.

1:2,16–20 ELECTION, Providence—Judas was numbered with the twelve disciples, having a share in their common ministry. The untimely end of Judas did not surprise God. The worst acts of Judas in betraying Jesus were used by God to bring salvation in the crucifixion and death of Jesus Christ. No matter what evil occurs in the lives of human beings, the election purposes of God finally triumph.

1:2–5 CHURCH LEADERS, The Twelve—After the apostles had failed so miserably when they abandoned Jesus on the cross, the risen Lord reestablished them. He gave them new courage and promised them new power for a new mission. They would continue His work on earth and lay the foundations for His church. The twelve apostles were not appointed by any local church and, therefore, were not tied to any one church. They belonged to the entire church as ambassadors-at-large of the risen Lord.

1:4–5 GOD, Trinity—Jesus was speaking to His followers, reminding them that the Father will send the Holy Spirit upon them. This might lead to the conclusion there are three Gods if we do not keep the unity of the three in mind through the doctrine of the Trinity. The distinctions let us know God as Father, Son, and Holy Spirit, each working for our salvation. Still we must not forget that the three are but one God and are not separable from one another. See notes on Mt 3:16–17; Jn 20:17,28.

1:4–5 ORDINANCES, Baptism by Holy Spirit—The baptism of the Spirit, which John the Baptist had prophesied (Jn 1:33), was about to come. It was a "gift" from the "Father." Both Jesus (Jn 14:16–17) and John had delivered that promise. It would bring the power to witness. The "gift" and the "power" are the Holy Spirit Himself, not something else. He would come upon them and empower them to be witnesses to Jesus, exactly as described in ch 2.

1:5 HOLY SPIRIT, Promised—John's prediction (see Jn 1:33; notes on Mt 3:11; Lk 3:16) was renewed by Jesus and fulfilled at Pentecost (Ac 2).

1:6–8 MISSIONS, Power—Jesus called the disciples to their first priority—being witnesses to Him from their homeland to the very ends of the earth. Christ's final meeting with His apostles on the Mount of Olives (1:12) provided a bridge between Jesus' earthly ministry and what He would do through His Spirit's indwelling of His disciples. In Lk 24:49, He had told the disciples to wait in Jerusalem until God gave them power. As the forty days of resurrection appearances came to a close, Jesus reinforced the Great Commission and promised the power to carry it out. Jesus described three things about power for the world missions task: its need, its nature, and its provision. Jesus promised the power before He described the task. In Mt 28:20, Jesus promised His presence. Here He promised His power through the indwelling Spirit of God. The nature of this power is seen in the word *dunamin*, which supplies the root of English words like dynamic, dynamism, dynamo, and dynamite. This power is a personal power which comes from the Holy Spirit into our lives. It is a power to convict, convert, regenerate, comfort, and keep. Christ's promise was fulfilled in the Spirit's coming to the church in Ac 2:4. The purpose of the power is to equip disciples to be witnesses to the ends of the earth. The emphasis is on being Christ's witnesses. A verbal witness is an integral part of the total witness, but it needs a consistent life to back it up. The word for witnesses is *martures*, transliterated sometimes as "martyr." Christ's disciples are to give witness with life, word, deed, and death, if necessary. These original witnesses had observed Jesus in action, walked beside Him, known the splendor of His life, the compassion of His vicarious death, the glory of His resurrection, and the joy of forgiveness of sin. He began with the disciples where they were—in Jerusalem. Jerusalem was a difficult place to witness, the place of past failure. Peter had denied Him there; others had fled. It was the place of future persecution. Stephen would be stoned there (Ac 7:54–57), but it was a place of future harvest (2:41,47; 4:4; 5:13). Their witness was to reach to "Judea." Judea was the Roman province around Jerusalem. "Judea" describes reaching out beyond our home community in home missions. The outreach of witness must go to Samaria. Because of the Samaritans' diverse cultural and racial background, the Jews had nothing to do with the Samaritans (Jn 4:9). Samaritans represented a blending of Israelites with the foreign people of the land during the Exile. Samaritans were viewed as half-breeds, and Jews generally despised them. Jesus specifically told the disciples that they were to bear witness to Samaria. "Samaria" describes witnessing to those from different ethnic groups, peoples, families, and subcultures. Jesus radically cut across the prejudices of His disciples to state that the gospel was for the Samaritans, too. The mission of the church has not ended until it reaches "the ends of the earth."

1:7 GOD, Sovereignty—Jesus ascribed to God the ultimate authority—only He knows some things. Humans cannot know

the same way you have seen him go into
heaven."

Matthias Chosen to Replace Judas

12 Then they returned to Jerusalem[w]
from the hill called the Mount of Olives,[x]
a Sabbath day's walk[b] from the city.
13 When they arrived, they went upstairs
to the room[y] where they were staying.
Those present were Peter, John, James
and Andrew; Philip and Thomas, Bartholomew and Matthew; James son of Alphaeus and Simon the Zealot, and Judas
son of James.[z] 14 They all joined together
constantly in prayer,[a] along with the
women[b] and Mary the mother of Jesus,
and with his brothers.[c]
15 In those days Peter stood up among
the believers[c] (a group numbering about
a hundred and twenty) 16 and said,
"Brothers,[d] the Scripture had to be fulfilled[e] which the Holy Spirit spoke long
ago through the mouth of David concerning Judas,[f] who served as guide for those
who arrested Jesus— 17 he was one of our
number[g] and shared in this ministry."[h]
18 (With the reward[i] he got for his
wickedness, Judas bought a field;[j] there
he fell headlong, his body burst open and
all his intestines spilled out. 19 Everyone
in Jerusalem heard about this, so they
called that field in their language[k] Akel-
dama, that is, Field of Blood.)
20 "For," said Peter, "it is written in
the book of Psalms,

" 'May his place be deserted;
let there be no one to dwell in
it,'[d] [l]

and,

" 'May another take his place of
leadership.'[e] [m]

21 Therefore it is necessary to choose one
of the men who have been with us the
whole time the Lord Jesus went in and
out among us, 22 beginning from John's
baptism[n] to the time when Jesus was tak-
en up from us. For one of these must become a witness[o] with us of his resurrection."
23 So they proposed two men: Joseph
called Barsabbas (also known as Justus)
and Matthias. 24 Then they prayed,[p]
"Lord, you know everyone's heart.[q]
Show us[r] which of these two you have
chosen 25 to take over this apostolic ministry, which Judas left to go where he belongs." 26 Then they cast lots, and the lot
fell to Matthias; so he was added to the
eleven apostles.[s]

1:12 [w]Lk 24:52 [x]S Mt 21:1
1:13 [y]Ac 9:37; 20:8 [z]Mt 10:2-4; Mk 3:16-19; Lk 6:14-16
1:14 [a]Ac 2:42; 4:24; 6:4; S Lk 18:1; S Ro 1:10 [b]Lk 23:49,55 [c]S Mt 12:46
1:16 [d]Ac 6:3; 11:1, 12,29; 14:2; 18:18, 27; 21:7; S 22:5; S Ro 7:1 [e]ver 20; S Mt 1:22 [f]S Mt 10:4
1:17 [g]Jn 6:70,71 [h]ver 25
1:18 [i]Mt 26:14,15 [j]Mt 27:3-10
1:19 [k]S Jn 5:2
1:20 [l]Ps 69:25 [m]Ps 109:8
1:22 [n]S Mk 1:4 [o]ver 8; S Lk 24:48
1:24 [p]Ac 6:6; 13:3; 14:23 [q]S Rev 2:23 [r]1Sa 14:41
1:26 [s]S Ac 2:14

[b]*12* That is, about 3/4 mile (about 1,100 meters)
[c]*15* Greek *brothers* [d]*20* Psalm 69:25
[e]*20* Psalm 109:8

---

when the end of all things will come. In Mt 24:36 Jesus declared that not even the incarnate Son of God on earth knew the time of His second coming. God is in control of His world with a sovereignty that is not shared with any except by His own will. We do not need this knowledge, so we should not worry about it. We do need the power the Spirit gives to witness, and we need to use our time witnessing.

1:7 HISTORY, Time—See note on Mk 13:32–35.

1:8 HOLY SPIRIT, Mission—Jesus set out a program of outward expansion for the Spirit-empowered church. Throughout the world, the church witnesses to the crucified and risen Lord and to the salvation God has provided through Him. The power of the Spirit can send an ordinary group of people on a world mission and enable them to succeed at it, even in centers of earthly powers.

1:8 EVANGELISM, Call to Evangelize—See note on Lk 24:45–49. Those who make up the church are to become witnesses to God's saving power in His Son. All believers share in this commission, not just church leaders. We are to cross all regional, cultural, and geographical barriers to share Christ's gospel. The Holy Spirit empowers us to testify for Christ to all people.

1:9–12 JESUS CHRIST, Ascension—See note on Lk 24:50–53. Luke in Acts gives the fullest expression of Jesus' ascension. The ascension in Acts is coupled with the mission mandate of the church and the promise of spiritual power and presence (v 8). The earthly existence of Jesus ended with a note of promise about His ultimate coming and His eternal ministry.

1:11 JESUS CHRIST, Final Coming—The messenger from God promised a return of "this same Jesus" in the same fashion in which He went away. That is, He who ascended will descend, come again. See notes on 1 Th 4:13–18; Heb 9:28.

1:11 LAST THINGS, Return Promises—The same promise to return that Jesus had used to encourage His disciples was reaffirmed by two heavenly visitors. See note on Jn 14:1–3. As Jesus was seen to be taken up bodily, so He will return in the same way. As He was hidden by a cloud at His departure, He will be revealed with a cloud at His return. See note on Mt 24:27–28,30.

1:14 PRAYER, Corporate—The text literally says they were continuing with one mind (Greek *homothumadon*). Compare 2:46. They had known the example of Jesus in prayer (Jn 17:22). Corporate prayer unites the church in commitment to God's purposes. Both men and women were included.

1:18–19 SIN, Individual Choice—See note on Mt 26:14–16,23–25,47–49.

1:21–26 ELECTION, Leadership—God used human activities to reveal His choice of leaders for the beginning church. God's election can be revealed in numerous ways through His sovereign grace.

1:21–26 THE CHURCH, Practice—The church works to solve problems in ways which please Christ and the fellowship of believers and which promote the kingdom of God. The early church acted to solve the problem created by the betrayal of Judas by selecting two men who had witnessed the death and resurrection of Jesus. From these two men, the Holy Spirit chose one to serve. The church must ask God's guidance when choosing a person to serve God through a particular ministry. Both the church and the Holy Spirit choose those set apart for ministry.

1:21–22 CHURCH LEADERS, Apostle—The apostles were the eyewitnesses of what Jesus said and did and of His resurrection. The Spirit was given to them to help them remember what Jesus said (Jn 14:26). Their chief function was to proclaim the gospel to others (Ac 2:14–41) and to instruct the church in Christian truth (2:42). The New Testament is the end product of this apostolic witness.

1:24–26 PRAYER, Petition—The prayer was based on God's knowledge of human hearts and the need of the church for God-chosen leadership.

Chapter 2

The Holy Spirit Comes at Pentecost

WHEN the day of Pentecost[t] came,
they were all together[u] in one
place. 2Suddenly a sound like the blowing
of a violent wind came from heaven and
filled the whole house where they were
sitting.[v] 3They saw what seemed to be
tongues of fire that separated and came to
rest on each of them. 4All of them were
filled with the Holy Spirit[w] and began to
speak in other tongues[f][x] as the Spirit
enabled them.
5Now there were staying in Jerusalem
God-fearing[y] Jews from every nation under heaven. 6When they heard this
sound, a crowd came together in bewil-
derment, because each one heard them
speaking in his own language. 7Utterly
amazed,[z] they asked: "Are not all these
men who are speaking Galileans?[a] 8Then
how is it that each of us hears them in his
own native language? 9Parthians, Medes
and Elamites; residents of Mesopotamia,
Judea and Cappadocia,[b] Pontus[c] and
Asia,[d] 10Phrygia[e] and Pamphylia,[f] Egypt
and the parts of Libya near Cyrene;[g] visitors from Rome 11(both Jews and converts
to Judaism); Cretans and Arabs—we hear
them declaring the wonders of God in our
own tongues!" 12Amazed and perplexed,
they asked one another, "What does this
mean?"
13Some, however, made fun of them
and said, "They have had too much
wine.[g]"[h]

Peter Addresses the Crowd

14Then Peter stood up with the Eleven,
raised his voice and addressed the crowd:
"Fellow Jews and all of you who live in
Jerusalem, let me explain this to you; listen carefully to what I say. 15These men
are not drunk, as you suppose. It's only
nine in the morning![i] 16No, this is what
was spoken by the prophet Joel:

17" 'In the last days, God says,

2:1 [t]Lev 23:15,16; Ac 20:16; 1Co 16:8 [u]Ac 1:14
2:2 [v]Ac 4:31
2:4 [w]S Lk 1:15 [x]S Mk 16:17
2:5 [y]Lk 2:25; Ac 8:2
2:7 [z]ver 12 [a]Ac 1:11
2:9 [b]1Pe 1:1 [c]Ac 18:2; 1Pe 1:1 [d]Ac 16:6; 19:10; Ro 16:5; 1Co 16:19; 2Co 1:8; Rev 1:4
2:10 [e]Ac 16:6; 18:23 [f]Ac 13:13; 14:24; 15:38 [g]S Mt 27:32
2:13 [h]1Co 14:23; Eph 5:18
2:15 [i]1Th 5:7

[f]4 Or *languages*; also in verse 11 [g]13 Or *sweet wine*

2:1–4 HOLY SPIRIT, Pentecost—The gift of the Spirit to the church at Pentecost fulfilled Old Testament prophecies concerning the Spirit and Jesus' promises to give the Spirit to His disciples. See notes on Joel 2:28–32; Lk 3:16; 11:13. What God began in the unique Pentecost event has continued throughout the life of the church. All Christians receive the Spirit. See note on Ac 2:38–39. The church received the Spirit at a moment God chose. The church had not become more committed, prayerful, or spiritual. The gift of the Spirit was entirely a matter of grace. The Spirit was given each person in the church, as the tongues of fire separating and resting on each person shows. The Spirit represented a new commitment of God to the covenant relationship summarized in Lev 26:12. Three miraculous signs accompanied the giving of the Spirit: the sound of a wind (Greek *pneuma* means both wind and Spirit); tongues of fire (tongues point to the worldwide mission of the church to preach the gospel); and speaking "in other tongues," which also pointed to the preaching mission. Scholars are divided about how to understand the gift of the Spirit. In Ac 2 (and presumably, therefore, Ac 10; 19) the church apparently spoke foreign languages they had not studied (2:8–11); at Corinth some members of the church uttered "sounds" which no one present could understand (1 Co 14:6–19). The emphasis at Pentecost was that God gave His Spirit to all His people to witness and prophesy; the attending signs were secondary, given to interpret the great gift of the Spirit and enable the widening of the church's witness. The Spirit gives the church the gifts it needs to witness to the world. The church is called to be open to receive the gifts God gives and not to judge one another on the basis of having or not having received certain gifts.

2:1–13 EVANGELISM, Holy Spirit—God gave the Holy Spirit to equip and empower the church for the task of world evangelization. The Spirit is given all believers (v 38). Without this giving and infilling of the Spirit of God upon the church, people are never brought to faith in Jesus Christ. God's people must be dynamically related to the Spirit to be used as His agents to win others. Such relationship may confuse the world, but the Spirit's power to raise questions is necessary for great soul winning (v 41).

2:14–22 HOLY SPIRIT, Revelation—Pentecost was the great revelation of the Spirit. God acted in history to give His Spirit on the day of Pentecost. Everyone, believer or not, could see the results. Revelation of the Spirit was experiential. The church, upon whom God poured out His Spirit, experienced His coming and made a definite personal response. Revelation was verbal. God led Peter to preach and explain the experience. Later God inspired Luke to write the Book of Acts. Verbal revelation without any experience of the Spirit would be dead. An experience without a historical act of God would be shifted away from its Christian base and therefore its Christian meaning. Finally, an act of God without some proclamation of it would be an empty exercise of power without meaning for the church. God's act renders the revelation of the Spirit to be Christian; experience renders the revelation alive; and verbal interpretation renders it intelligible. Peter's sermon shows the nature of the Spirit's revelation. When the Spirit is at work, Christ Jesus is proclaimed. The Spirit led Peter to preach about Jesus, not about the Spirit. The Spirit always leads people to preach about Christ. See 1 Co 12:1–4; notes on Jn 14:26; 15:26–27; 16:12–15; Ac 1:8.

2:16–21 HOLY SCRIPTURE, Authoritative—The early church accepted the Old Testament as authoritative Scripture. They looked for God's actions in their lives. The new revelation in apostolic preaching through the Spirit fulfilled the inspired expectation of Joel 2:28–32.

2:16–21 LAST THINGS, Last Days—Peter applied the prophecy (Joel 2:28–32) concerning Israel in the messianic era to the church of his day. The period following the first advent of Christ began the last days (v 17), the present work of the Holy Spirit being part of the messianic era. The ultimate fulfillment of the apocalyptic upheavals in nature await the consummation phase of the last days, a time associated with great tribulation and the return of Christ. See note on Rev 6:12–17. That final consummation is to be accompanied by a judgment upon the present world order. Out of the cosmic judgment will come the new redeemed order of nature and the world. The last days and their climactic castastrophies will be followed by the "great and glorious day of the Lord" (v 20).

2:17 CHURCH LEADERS, Prophet—Jews in the first century believed the spirit of prophecy departed with Malachi, the last of the Old Testament prophets. Its reappearance was believed to be the sign of the dawning Messianic Age. Peter announced that the same Spirit that had inspired the prophets was poured out on the followers of Jesus at Pentecost. The Spirit ignored age, social, and sex distinctions to empower

I will pour out my Spirit on all
people.[j]
Your sons and daughters will
prophesy,[k]
your young men will see visions,
your old men will dream dreams.
18Even on my servants, both men and
women,
I will pour out my Spirit in those
days,
and they will prophesy.[l]
19I will show wonders in the heaven
above
and signs on the earth below,[m]
blood and fire and billows of smoke.
20The sun will be turned to darkness
and the moon to blood[n]
before the coming of the great and
glorious day of the Lord.
21And everyone who calls
on the name of the Lord[o] will be
saved.'[h] [p]

22"Men of Israel, listen to this: Jesus of
Nazareth[q] was a man accredited by God
to you by miracles, wonders and signs,[r]
which God did among you through him,[s]
as you yourselves know. 23This man was
handed over to you by God's set purpose
and foreknowledge;[t] and you, with the
help of wicked men,[i] put him to death
by nailing him to the cross.[u] 24But God
raised him from the dead,[v] freeing him
from the agony of death, because it was
impossible for death to keep its hold on
him.[w] 25David said about him:

" 'I saw the Lord always before me.
Because he is at my right hand,
I will not be shaken.
26Therefore my heart is glad and my
tongue rejoices;
my body also will live in hope,

2:17 [j]Nu 11:25; Isa 44:3; Eze 39:29; Jn 7:37-39; Ac 10:45 [k]S Ac 21:9
2:18 [l]Ac 21:9-12
2:19 [m]Lk 21:11
2:20 [n]S Mt 24:29
2:21 [o]Ge 4:26; 26:25; Ps 105:1; Ac 9:14; 1Co 1:2; 2Ti 2:22 [p]Joel 2:28-32; Ro 10:13
2:22 [q]S Mk 1:24 [r]S Jn 4:48 [s]S Jn 3:2
2:23 [t]Isa 53:10; Ac 3:18; 4:28 [u]Mt 16:21; Lk 24:20; Ac 3:13
2:24 [v]ver 32; Ac 13:30,33,34,37; 17:31; Ro 6:4; 8:11; 10:9; 1Co 6:14; 15:15; Eph 1:20; Col 2:12; Heb 13:20; 1Pe 1:21 [w]Jn 20:9

[h]*21* Joel 2:28-32 [i]*23* Or *of those not having the law* (that is, Gentiles)

God's people and accomplish His purposes.

2:17–40 EVANGELISM, Work of Christ—In Peter's sermon, as reported by Luke, the whole gospel message is recorded: Jesus was the Messiah. He lived a matchless life, died on the cross, and rose from the dead. He calls all to repentance and faith, promising forgiveness and a new life. This is the message of power, the good news we are to proclaim to all people in all generations everywhere. It clearly centers in Jesus Christ and His work. God by the Holy Spirit uses that message to convert and save the lost. See Gospel Summary, p. 1663.

2:21 SALVATION, As Deliverance—Joel 2:32 was fulfilled in the coming of Christ and through the outpouring of the Holy Spirit. Compare Ro 10:13. Christ's coming let salvation break out of national, geographical, racial, and political barriers to become available to all people.

2:22,33 GOD, Trinity—Both the separateness and the unity of the three Persons is expressed. God the Father is the point of focus: He did the mighty works performed *through* Jesus, and He gave the Spirit to the Son to be poured out on the church. See note on Mt 3:16–17.

2:22 JESUS CHRIST, Miracles—Peter said Jesus was accredited by God through His miracles. Miracles were God's work done through Jesus as God's agent.

2:22 CREATION, Miracles—God created a world that operates predictably through law. He, however, is Lord over nature and can work in ways that may appear to be a suspension of His natural laws. When He wishes to implement His redemptive program for sinful people, God takes whatever steps are necessary.

2:22,43 MIRACLE, Instruments—Miracles are not limited to Jesus and His day. See Jn 14:11–12. Three different words in the miracle vocabulary are used in v 22: powers, wonders, and signs (Greek *dunamis, teras, semeion*). All three are descriptive of Jesus' work and provided illustrations from His ministry for Peter's Pentecost sermon. The Holy Spirit worked in the early church to enable many believers to do wonders and signs (v 43).

2:23–24 GOD, Wisdom—The sovereignty of God was at work even in the death of Jesus. God was in control through all of His suffering and death. Furthermore, the power of God raised Jesus to life from the grave. God's wisdom is shown here in God's foreknowledge of how all of this would turn out. God knew what He was doing through Jesus and accomplished His purpose of salvation for lost people. God's foreknowledge does not mean that He causes everything that happens. It means that He knows in advance what will happen. In His sovereignty and wisdom He can work through what happens to accomplish His purposes. He can even take wicked human deeds and work through those circumstances, which He did not cause, to accomplish His righteous purposes. See note on Ro 8:28.

2:23–36 JESUS CHRIST, Lord—The early church confessed Jesus as Lord. See note on Jn 20:25–28. "Lord" (Greek *kurios*) indicated power and authority as master or ruler. By the time of Jesus the Roman emperor was at times called lord and god. "Lord" came to be used in the Greek translation of the Old Testament in place of the divine personal name (Hebrew *Yahweh*), which the Jews refused to pronounce. Ps 110:1 used "Lord" both in reference to God and to the king, a usage which became understood as referring to Messiah. The New Testament used the Psalm to show Jesus, the Messiah, was Lord or God and superior to David (Mt 22:44–45; Mk 12:35–37; Lk 20:41–44; Heb 1:13). "Lord" could be used as a polite form of address, "Sir" (Jn 4:11,15). For the New Testament writers "Lord" identified Jesus as the authoritative Master of the church, ruler of the world, to whom all powers in the universe are subject (Ro 10:9; 14:9; Eph 1:20–21; Php 2:5–11). He is the one Lord of all (1 Co 8:5–6). Neither the church nor the world gave Jesus this exalted title. God the Father made Him Lord. He did this through purposeful preparation, sending Jesus on a mission to earth. God gave Him the victory through resurrection. Preparation for Jesus to become Lord is revealed in the Scriptures (Ps 16:8–11). The power of the church on Pentecost came because the ascended Lord received the Holy Spirit and gave it to the church as He had promised (Jn 7:39; 14:16).

2:23–33 ELECTION, Foreknowledge—The death of Jesus meant more than a cruel, untimely assassination of a good man that took place without divine action or reaction. God's foreknowledge enabled Him to use the crucifixion for His purposes of redemption. Foreknowledge (Greek *prognōsis*) is knowledge that makes prediction of the future possible. God's nature includes knowledge of the future and plans for the future. Human actions cannot surprise Him or defeat His purposes. God included Christ's crucifixion in His plan and purpose of salvation. Such knowledge does not mean God caused people to act wickedly. Both Jews and Gentiles acted wickedly and must bear responsibility for the physical act of crucifying Christ. Compare Ro 8:29; 11:2; 1 Pe 1:2,20. God's "set purpose" (Greek *boulē*) represents a free decision to act to accomplish plans and purposes. Stress is on the irrevocable decision and will to act. Old Testament quotations show God planned salvation through Christ's death long before Christ's birth. Compare 4:28; 13:36; 20:27; Lk 7:30; 10:22; Eph 1:11; Heb 6:17.

2:24 HUMANITY, Death—The Greek word for agony describes a woman's labor pains. Death is thus understood as pain against which a person struggles. God, in raising Christ, demonstrated that death, like birth, is not an end but a begin-

27because you will not abandon me to
the grave,
nor will you let your Holy One see
decay.[x]
28You have made known to me the paths
of life;
you will fill me with joy in your
presence.'[j] [y]

29"Brothers,[z] I can tell you confidently
that the patriarch[a] David died and was
buried,[b] and his tomb is here[c] to this
day. 30But he was a prophet and knew
that God had promised him on oath that
he would place one of his descendants on
his throne.[d] 31Seeing what was ahead, he
spoke of the resurrection of the Christ,[k]
that he was not abandoned to the grave,
nor did his body see decay.[e] 32God has
raised this Jesus to life,[f] and we are all
witnesses[g] of the fact. 33Exalted[h] to the
right hand of God,[i] he has received from
the Father[j] the promised Holy Spirit[k]
and has poured out[l] what you now see
and hear. 34For David did not ascend to
heaven, and yet he said,

" 'The Lord said to my Lord:
"Sit at my right hand
35until I make your enemies
a footstool for your feet." '[l] [m]

36"Therefore let all Israel be assured of
this: God has made this Jesus, whom you
crucified, both Lord[n] and Christ."[o]
37When the people heard this, they
were cut to the heart and said to Peter
and the other apostles, "Brothers, what
shall we do?"[p]
38Peter replied, "Repent and be baptized,[q] every one of you, in the name of
Jesus Christ for the forgiveness of your
sins.[r] And you will receive the gift of the
Holy Spirit.[s] 39The promise is for you and
your children[t] and for all who are far
off[u]—for all whom the Lord our God will
call."
40With many other words he warned
them; and he pleaded with them, "Save
yourselves from this corrupt generation."[v] 41Those who accepted his message were baptized, and about three thousand were added to their number[w] that
day.

The Fellowship of the Believers

42They devoted themselves to the apos-

2:27 [x]ver 31; Ac 13:35
2:28 [y]Ps 16:8-11
2:29 [z]S Ac 22:5 [a]Ac 7:8,9 [b]Ac 13:36; 1Ki 2:10 [c]Ne 3:16
2:30 [d]S Mt 1:1
2:31 [e]Ps 16:10
2:32 [f]S ver 24 [g]S Lk 24:48
2:33 [h]S Php 2:9 [i]S Mk 16:19 [j]Ac 1:4 [k]Jn 7:39; 14:26; 15:26 [l]Ac 10:45
2:35 [m]Ps 110:1; S Mt 22:44
2:36 [n]S Mt 28:18 [o]S Lk 2:11
2:37 [p]Lk 3:10,12, 14; Ac 16:30
2:38 [q]ver 41; Ac 8:12,16,36,38; 9:18; 10:48; 16:15, 33; 19:5; 22:16; Col 2:12 [r]Jer 36:3; Mk 1:4; S Lk 24:47; Ac 3:19 [s]S Jn 20:22
2:39 [t]Isa 44:3; 65:23 [u]Isa 57:19; Ac 10:45; Eph 2:13
2:40 [v]Dt 32:5; Php 2:15
2:41 [w]ver 47; Ac 4:4; 5:14; 6:1,7; 9:31,35,42; 11:21, 24; 14:1,21; 16:5; 17:12

[j]*28* Psalm 16:8-11 [k]*31* Or *Messiah.* "The Christ" (Greek) and "the Messiah" (Hebrew) both mean "the Anointed One"; also in verse 36. [l]*35* Psalm 110:1

ning, a struggle won by Christ.

2:32–33 HOLY SPIRIT, Transforms—The Spirit changes lives. Peter's audience could not believe their eyes and ears. Uneducated people boldly challenged the entire Jewish religious tradition and system. Peter had one answer. Jesus had poured out God's promised Spirit. Only Jesus Christ has the power to pour God's Spirit into people's lives. The Spirit always appears in specific persons—Christ's people—and never elsewhere. Christians receive the Spirit and call others to accept Christ.

2:36 GOD, Trinity—This verse does not mean that at some prior time Jesus was not Lord and Christ. Jesus did not achieve a new status or position; He did not develop from lower to higher. This verse needs to be understood in the light of our understanding of the Trinity. God openly revealed or established the true, previously hidden, identity of Jesus as Lord and Christ (anointed, Messiah). Ro 1:4 expresses this same idea in slightly different language; here the resurrection of Jesus from the dead dramatically and forcefully demonstrated who He really was. See note on Jn 3:34–36.

2:38–39 HOLY SPIRIT, Indwells—The New Testament is clear about these two things: 1) all Christians receive the Spirit; 2) only Christians receive the Spirit. No Christian is ever without the Spirit, and no one except Christians ever receives the Spirit. The Spirit is a gift of grace fulfilling God's promise. Human effort or achievement cannot gain the Spirit. Repentance can. See note on Lk 11:13.

2:38 SALVATION, Forgiveness—Peter preached repentance for the forgiveness of sins on the day of Pentecost. This message was typical of speeches in the apostolic church (3:19; 5:31; 8:22; 10:43; 13:38; 26:18). Compare Mk 1:4,15.

2:38–41 ORDINANCES, Baptismal Candidate—Peter's sequence is important: first repent, and then be baptized. The answer Peter gave is confirmed by Luke's comment in v 41 that those who received his word were baptized. Baptism was the public act of confession of Christ in whose name they were baptized. Forgiveness of sins was and is the goal. Repentance and confession of Christ's name are the way. Baptism is the outward, public symbol of repentance and confession. With repentance and baptism they received the gift of the Holy Spirit. The promise of the Spirit is for all whom the Lord will call, for them and their children, and for all who are far off. The Spirit anointed Jesus at His baptism (Jn 1:32). Beginning at Pentecost, the gift of the Spirit was associated with the baptism of Christians. The persons baptized must have repented and received the Word. The meaning is that their sins had been forgiven, and they had received the Holy Spirit.

2:38 PROCLAMATION, Central Theme—See notes on 3:11–26; Lk 24:47.

2:41 EVANGELISM, Mass—This verse presents a fine example of effective mass evangelism. We find mass evangelism is possible when the church responds to the challenge (1:6–8), prays (1:14), receives power from the Holy Spirit (2:1–4), proclaims the gospel (2:17–39), and persuades the people (2:40). When these ingredients are present in the ministry of evangelism, great results will emerge. See Guide to Mass Evangelism, pp. 1835–1837.

2:42–46 ORDINANCES, Observance of Lord's Supper—One of the continuing activities of the early Christians was the "breaking of bread" from home to home, accompanied by the apostles' teaching, fellowship, and prayers. Sometimes the phrase "breaking of bread" may refer to a regular fellowship meal, but most often it seems to refer to the Lord's Supper because it is in the context of worship, prayer, and praise to God. Although they seem to have observed the "breaking of bread" frequently, there is no command anywhere in the Bible that specifies how often the Supper should be observed. The only indirect reference is in Jesus' phrase "whenever you drink it, in remembrance of me" (1 Co 11:25). The emphasis is always upon the proper observance and meaning, not upon the frequency.

2:42–47 WORSHIP, Community—See notes on Ge 28:16–22; Dt 11:13; Eph 5:17–20. Early Christian worship included teaching based on the Old Testament and on experiences with Jesus, community fellowship and meals, prayer, and praise. Such worship led to church growth. See note on Ex 16:23–30.

2:42–47 PRAYER, Biblical Characters—Prayer had been prominent in Jesus' life. It was prominent in the early church throughout the Book of Acts. Especially emphasized is unity of

tles' teaching[x] and to the fellowship, to
the breaking of bread[y] and to prayer.[z]
43Everyone was filled with awe, and
many wonders and miraculous signs were
done by the apostles.[a] 44All the believers
were together and had everything in
common.[b] 45Selling their possessions
and goods, they gave to anyone as he had
need.[c] 46Every day they continued to
meet together in the temple courts.[d]
They broke bread[e] in their homes and
ate together with glad and sincere hearts,
47praising God and enjoying the favor of
all the people.[f] And the Lord added to
their number[g] daily those who were being saved.

Chapter 3

Peter Heals the Crippled Beggar

ONE day Peter and John[h] were going
up to the temple[i] at the time of
prayer—at three in the afternoon.[j]
2Now a man crippled from birth[k] was being carried to the temple gate[l] called
Beautiful, where he was put every day to
beg[m] from those going into the temple
courts. 3When he saw Peter and John
about to enter, he asked them for money.
4Peter looked straight at him, as did John.
Then Peter said, "Look at us!" 5So the
man gave them his attention, expecting
to get something from them.
6Then Peter said, "Silver or gold I do
not have, but what I have I give you. In
the name of Jesus Christ of Nazareth,[n]
walk." 7Taking him by the right hand, he
helped him up, and instantly the man's
feet and ankles became strong. 8He
jumped to his feet and began to walk.
Then he went with them into the temple
courts, walking and jumping,[o] and praising God. 9When all the people[p] saw him
walking and praising God, 10they recognized him as the same man who used to
sit begging at the temple gate called Beautiful,[q] and they were filled with wonder
and amazement at what had happened to
him.

Peter Speaks to the Onlookers

11While the beggar held on to Peter
and John,[r] all the people were astonished and came running to them in the
place called Solomon's Colonnade.[s]
12When Peter saw this, he said to them:
"Men of Israel, why does this surprise
you? Why do you stare at us as if by our
own power or godliness we had made
this man walk? 13The God of Abraham,
Isaac and Jacob,[t] the God of our fathers,[u] has glorified his servant Jesus.

2:42 [x]Mt 28:20 [y]S Mt 14:19 [z]S Ac 1:14
2:43 [a]Ac 5:12
2:44 [b]Ac 4:32
2:45 [c]Mt 19:21; Lk 12:33; 18:22; Ac 4:34,35; 6:1
2:46 [d]Lk 24:53; Ac 3:1; 5:21,42 [e]ver 42; S Mt 14:19
2:47 [f]S Ro 14:18 [g]S ver 41
3:1 [h]S Lk 22:8 [i]Ac 2:46 [j]Ps 55:17; Ac 10:30
3:2 [k]Ac 14:8 [l]Lk 16:20 [m]Jn 9:8
3:6 [n]ver 16; S Mk 1:24
3:8 [o]Isa 35:6; Ac 14:10
3:9 [p]Ac 4:16,21
3:10 [q]ver 2
3:11 [r]S Lk 22:8 [s]Jn 10:23; Ac 5:12
3:13 [t]Ex 3:6 [u]Ac 5:30; 7:32; 22:14

mind among the believers. See note on 1:14.

2:42 EDUCATION, Disciples—Teaching is an indispensable function and a continuous process within the community of faith. Teaching is as close to the heartbeat of a congregation as are fellowship, ministry, and prayer.

2:43 SALVATION, Fear of God—See note on Mt 9:8; Lk 9:43. Awe is coupled here with wonders and signs.

2:44–46 EVIL AND SUFFERING, Comfort—The early disciples responded to the suffering of the hungry by sharing their possessions. We are called by God to comfort and help the needy.

2:44–45 CHRISTIAN ETHICS, Property Rights—The gospel message led the first church to ignore personal property claims in the interest of meeting the needs of others.

2:45 STEWARDSHIP, Service to God—Great needs prompt special responses by believers. Early Christians shared their assets as a voluntary response of Christian concern. The believers made their property available for the common good of fellow believers. Christian stewards cannot hoard resources for personal desires when members of the Christian family lack life's basic needs. The Bible shows that putting all resources in a common fund was an unusual and temporary plan for supplying needs of fellow Christians. The Bible also shows that supplying needs of fellow Christians is God's plan for the church. See note on 4:32—5:11.

2:47 EVANGELISM, In the Church—This verse is the culmination of the glorious events on the Day of Pentecost—and the most profound. The church was winning people continually. Evangelism is not one great event (v 41), but a daily ministry for the people of God. See Guide to Church Evangelism, pp. 1833–1835.

3:1–16 MIRACLE, Redemption—It was almost as if Jesus Himself was walking with them. They were going to the Temple; a lame man was begging at the gate, and they healed him. Though he asked only for money, he received a great deal more. Peter lifted him to his feet, and his bones were strong enough that he could walk . . . and jump . . . and praise God. Peter's summary in v 16 emphasized his "complete healing." The healing became a sign for a sermon, and many believed (4:4). A physical life had been redeemed from uselessness. It provided opportunity to redeem many from spiritual uselessness.

3:1–16 EVIL AND SUFFERING, Compassion—The church continues Jesus' healing ministry showing compassion to the suffering. We cannot simply discuss the theology of evil and suffering. We must be actively involved in loving and helping sufferers.

3:1 PRAYER, Ordered—It was the hour of prayer, the second of three daily prayer times, so they were probably enroute to join the body of believers. See note on 2:42–47. Prayer may be said at any moment, but believers also need regular times of prayer.

3:8 WORSHIP, Buildings—See notes on Ge 28:16–22; Lk 24:52–53.

3:11–26 PROCLAMATION, Gospel—The New Testament usually followed the outline of the gospel. This content of proclamation is referred to by the Greek word (*kerygma*) for proclamation (Ro 16:25; 1 Co 2:4; 15:14; 2 Ti 4:17; Tit 1:3). This included: (1) Jesus' descent from David as qualification to be Israel's Messiah; (2) His death, fulfilling Scripture; (3) His resurrection, fulfilling Scripture; (4) His ascension and exaltation to God's right hand, proving He is Lord and Christ or Messiah; (5) His deliverance of sinners to eternal life; (6) a call to repent; and (7) the promise of Christ's return to establish fully the kingdom. Compare Ac 2:14–39; 4:10–12; 5:30–32; 10:36–43; 13:16–41; Ro 1:1–4; 2:16; 8:34; 10:8–9; 1 Co 15:1–7; Gal 1:3–4; 3:1; 4:6; 1 Th 1:10.

3:13 JESUS CHRIST, Servant—Jesus was the Suffering Servant announced by the servant poems in Isaiah (42:1–4; 49:1–7; 50:4–11; 52:13—53:12) Apparently, Israel never directly related these passages to the Messiah. Jesus understood suffering as a necessary part of His ministry predicted by Scripture (Mt 17:12; Mk 8:31; 9:12; Lk 9:22; 22:15; 24:26; Jn 1:36; 2:19; 3:14). Jesus is Lord. See note on 2:23–36. Yet He is God's obedient Servant. He was willing to suffer that we might be saved. Compare Heb 5:8–10.

You handed him over[v] to be killed, and
you disowned him before Pilate,[w] though
he had decided to let him go.[x] 14You disowned the Holy[y] and Righteous One[z]
and asked that a murderer be released to
you.[a] 15You killed the author of life, but
God raised him from the dead.[b] We are
witnesses[c] of this. 16By faith in the name
of Jesus,[d] this man whom you see and
know was made strong. It is Jesus' name
and the faith that comes through him that
has given this complete healing to him, as
you can all see.
17"Now, brothers,[e] I know that you
acted in ignorance,[f] as did your leaders.[g] 18But this is how God fulfilled[h]
what he had foretold[i] through all the
prophets,[j] saying that his Christ[m] would
suffer.[k] 19Repent, then, and turn to God,
so that your sins may be wiped out,[l] that
times of refreshing may come from the
Lord, 20and that he may send the Christ,[m]
who has been appointed for you—even
Jesus. 21He must remain in heaven[n] until
the time comes for God to restore everything,[o] as he promised long ago through
his holy prophets.[p] 22For Moses said,
'The Lord your God will raise up for you a
prophet like me from among your own
people; you must listen to everything he
tells you.[q] 23Anyone who does not listen
to him will be completely cut off from
among his people.'[n] [r]
24"Indeed, all the prophets[s] from Samuel on, as many as have spoken, have
foretold these days. 25And you are heirs[t]
of the prophets and of the covenant[u] God
made with your fathers. He said to Abraham, 'Through your offspring all peoples
on earth will be blessed.'[o] [v] 26When God
raised up[w] his servant, he sent him first[x]
to you to bless you by turning each of you
from your wicked ways."

Chapter 4

Peter and John Before the Sanhedrin

THE priests and the captain of the temple guard[y] and the Sadducees[z] came
up to Peter and John while they were
speaking to the people. 2They were greatly disturbed because the apostles were
teaching the people and proclaiming in
Jesus the resurrection of the dead.[a]

3:13 [v]Ac 2:23 [w]S Mt 27:2 [x]S Lk 23:4
3:14 [y]S Mk 1:24; Ac 4:27 [z]Ac 7:52 [a]Mk 15:11; Lk 23:18-25
3:15 [b]S Ac 2:24 [c]S Lk 24:48
3:16 [d]ver 6
3:17 [e]S Ac 22:5 [f]Lk 23:34 [g]Ac 13:27
3:18 [h]S Mt 1:22 [i]Ac 2:23 [j]S Lk 24:27 [k]Ac 17:2,3; 26:22, 23
3:19 [l]Ps 51:1; Isa 43:25; 44:22; S Ac 2:38
3:20 [m]S Lk 2:11
3:21 [n]Ac 1:11 [o]Mt 17:11; Ac 1:6 [p]Lk 1:70
3:22 [q]Dt 18:15,18; Ac 7:37
3:23 [r]Dt 18:19
3:24 [s]S Lk 24:27
3:25 [t]Ac 2:39 [u]Ro 9:4,5 [v]Ge 12:3; 22:18; 26:4; 28:14
3:26 [w]ver 22; S Ac 2:24 [x]Ac 13:46; Ro 1:16
4:1 [y]Lk 22:4 [z]Mt 3:7; 16:1,6; 22:23,34; Ac 5:17; 23:6-8
4:2 [a]Ac 17:18

[m]*18* Or *Messiah*; also in verse 20 [n]*23* Deut. 18:15,18,19 [o]*25* Gen. 22:18; 26:4

3:14 JESUS CHRIST, Sinless—Jesus was called by titles which belonged to God describing divine moral perfection. Compare Dt 32:4; 2 Ki 19:22; Ps 119:137; Isa 1:4; 5:19; Jer 12:1; Hos 11:9; Zep 3:5. Righteousness characterized the messianic Servant (Isa 53:11).

3:15 JESUS CHRIST, Life—"Author" (Greek *archegos*) means the one who begins something, the ruler, leader, founder. As the first person resurrected from death, Jesus is the Pioneer or Founder of eternal life who leads His followers to know life. See note on Jn 1:4. Compare Heb 2:10; 12:2.

3:15 EVANGELISM, Work of Christ—See note on 2:17–40.

3:16 JESUS CHRIST, Miracles—After His ascension, Jesus' miraculous power continued to work through the church.

3:17–26 REVELATION, Jesus Christ—God revealed Himself powerfully through sermons of chosen preachers. The sermons were based on the Old Testament viewed as authoritative, inspired Scripture. Christ was everything the Old Testament expected and more. He fulfilled the covenant promises to Abraham (Ge 12:1–7), the hope for a prophet like Moses (Dt 18:14–19), and the prophetic visions of the future from Samuel (1 Sa 12) onward. The apostles' sermons called people to accept Jesus as God's fulfillment of their scriptural expectations, to repent and turn from their evil ways, and to trust Jesus for salvation.

3:17–26 ELECTION, Israel—The early apostolic preaching saw the election purposes of God clearly expressed in the crucifixion. Those crucifying Jesus acted in ignorance. They did not recognize they were killing God's Messiah, nor did they know they helped to bring to pass the sacrificial death needed to provide forgiveness for the sins of the world. Resurrection and Pentecost provided the missing knowledge. Many who allowed the crucifixion to take place or who were silent bystanders at the cross faced rejection. They should have reflected on Christ's death in light of Scripture and repented. Helping crucify Christ was not unforgivable. Pentecost represented God's faithfulness to His promise to Israel's patriarchs. To reject the message preached at Pentecost is not forgivable. The elect are people of repentance, not a people of the same race.

3:18 JESUS CHRIST, Fulfilled—Early Christian preaching centered on Jesus as fulfillment of Scripture. See note on Lk 24:1–53.

3:19–21 JESUS CHRIST, Final Coming—Christ's coming is related to repentance and conversion of the lost. Since Peter's audience here was Jewish, some interpreters relate this to a conversion of Jews before Jesus comes. Before He comes again, Jesus lives in heaven with the Father.

3:19–21 HISTORY, Time—History for God's people should be refreshing, meaningful time. Such joy and meaning will be fully realized when Christ returns at the time the Father chooses to fulfill all His promises.

3:19 SALVATION, Renewal—Peter preached that refreshment from God came through repentance of sin. God renews those who get their sins wiped out. See note on 2:38.

3:21 CREATION, Hope—The created world's only hope is the return of Jesus to transform everything and make it once more a paradise as originally brought into existence by God.

3:21 LAST THINGS, Humanity Restored—Christ's return in power will be to establish a new world order free from evil and disobedience. This restoration is to include the redemption of nature and the perfecting of human society under the kingly rule of Christ as God's will is done on earth as it is in heaven. See notes on Ro 8:18–23; 1 Jn 3:2–3.

3:22–23 JESUS CHRIST, Prophet—See note on Jn 6:14.

3:25 THE CHURCH, Covenant People—See notes on Ge 17:1–21; Jer 30:22.

3:25 EVANGELISM, God's Provision—See note on Ge 12:1–7.

3:26 JESUS CHRIST, Servant—Jesus was God's Servant sent to turn Israel from sin. See note on v 13.

3:26 SALVATION, Blessing—The resurrected Lord Jesus was sent first to bless the Jewish people by turning them from their wicked ways.

4:1–4 EDUCATION, Evangelists—Teaching is not just preparation for evangelism or follow-up after evangelism. It is a mainline evangelistic strategy. Beginning with the ministry of Jesus and continued by first-century Christians, educational evangelism has always been in the forefront of the church's efforts to reach a lost world. See 5:21; 17:2; 28:31.

4:1–4 EVANGELISM, Power—The power of the gospel causes self-interest groups to oppose it but brings many unbelievers to faith. Powerful gospel preaching results in great church growth.

3They seized Peter and John, and because it was evening, they put them in jail[b] until the next day. 4But many who heard the message believed, and the number of men grew[c] to about five thousand.

5The next day the rulers,[d] elders and teachers of the law met in Jerusalem. 6Annas the high priest was there, and so were Caiaphas,[e] John, Alexander and the other men of the high priest's family. 7They had Peter and John brought before them and began to question them: "By what power or what name did you do this?"

8Then Peter, filled with the Holy Spirit,[f] said to them: "Rulers and elders of the people![g] 9If we are being called to account today for an act of kindness shown to a cripple[h] and are asked how he was healed, 10then know this, you and all the people of Israel: It is by the name of Jesus Christ of Nazareth,[i] whom you crucified but whom God raised from the dead,[j] that this man stands before you healed. 11He is

> " 'the stone you builders rejected,
> which has become the
> capstone.[p]'[q][k]

12Salvation is found in no one else, for there is no other name under heaven given to men by which we must be saved."[l]

13When they saw the courage of Peter and John[m] and realized that they were unschooled, ordinary men,[n] they were astonished and they took note that these men had been with Jesus.[o] 14But since they could see the man who had been healed standing there with them, there was nothing they could say. 15So they ordered them to withdraw from the Sanhedrin[p] and then conferred together. 16"What are we going to do with these men?"[q] they asked. "Everybody living in Jerusalem knows they have done an outstanding miracle,[r] and we cannot deny it. 17But to stop this thing from spreading any further among the people, we must warn these men to speak no longer to anyone in this name."

18Then they called them in again and commanded them not to speak or teach at all in the name of Jesus.[s] 19But Peter and John replied, "Judge for yourselves whether it is right in God's sight to obey you rather than God.[t] 20For we cannot help speaking[u] about what we have seen and heard."[v]

21After further threats they let them go. They could not decide how to punish them, because all the people[w] were praising God[x] for what had happened. 22For the man who was miraculously healed was over forty years old.

The Believers' Prayer

23On their release, Peter and John went back to their own people and reported all that the chief priests and elders had said to them. 24When they heard this, they raised their voices together in prayer to God.[y] "Sovereign Lord," they said, "you made the heaven and the earth and the sea, and everything in them.[z]

[p]11 Or *cornerstone* [q]11 Psalm 118:22

4:3 [b]Ac 5:18
4:4 [c]S Ac 2:41
4:5 [d]Lk 23:13
4:6 [e]S Mt 26:3
4:8 [f]S Lk 1:15 [g]ver 5; Lk 23:13
4:9 [h]Ac 3:6
4:10 [i]S Mk 1:24 [j]S Ac 2:24
4:11 [k]Ps 118:22; Isa 28:16; Zec 10:4; Mt 21:42; Eph 2:20; 1Pe 2:7
4:12 [l]S Mt 1:21; Jn 14:6; Ac 10:43; S Ro 11:14; 1Ti 2:5
4:13 [m]S Lk 22:8 [n]Mt 11:25 [o]Mk 3:14
4:15 [p]S Mt 5:22
4:16 [q]Jn 11:47 [r]Ac 3:6-10
4:18 [s]Am 7:13; Ac 5:40
4:19 [t]Ac 5:29
4:20 [u]Job 32:18; Jer 20:9; Am 3:8 [v]S Lk 24:48
4:21 [w]Ac 5:26 [x]S Mt 9:8
4:24 [y]S Ac 1:14 [z]Ne 9:6; Job 41:11; Isa 37:16

4:8–10 HOLY SPIRIT, Energizes—While Peter and John were on trial for their faith, the Spirit empowered Peter to preach. Jesus had promised that under these circumstances the Spirit would tell the disciples what to say (Lk 12:11–12; Jn 16:7–11). "Filled" with the Spirit means simply that the Spirit, who had come to live permanently in Peter's life at Pentecost, consciously led Peter to speak. Peter's gift was prophecy, the great gift of the Spirit (1 Co 14:1), when practiced in love as Peter showed here. See 1 Co 13:13. By proclamation the world mission of the church is carried out. All Christian proclamation is about Jesus. The Spirit guides the church in all its proclamation and thereby reminds people of Jesus. See notes on Jn 14:26; 15:26–27; 16:12–15.

4:9–22 MIRACLE, Instruments—Peter and John were quite conscious of their power but knew it to be God's power in them. The lame man, now healed, stood before the religious leaders whole. All they could do they did: they simply ordered silence about the man's healing though he was over forty years old. They pointed from the healing to the Healer. Miracles must be used as opportunities to point people away from people to God.

4:10,30 JESUS CHRIST, Miracles—See note on 3:16.

4:10–20 PROCLAMATION, Gospel—See notes on 3:11–26; 1 Co 2:2; 9:16–18.

4:12 JESUS CHRIST, Savior—Jesus is the only Savior. His salvation is available to all people. See note on Jn 4:42.

4:12 SALVATION, As Being in Christ—Salvation is found in Christ and in Him alone. Compare 2 Ti 2:10.

4:12 EVANGELISM, Work of Christ—See note on 2:17–40. The ministry, death, and resurrection of Jesus made salvation possible. Evangelists must lead people to Christ for salvation because salvation is not available in any other place or through any other person.

4:23–31 GOD, Sovereignty—God is not only addressed here as sovereign, but is described as having been active in accomplishing His purposes. His sovereign acts reach back to creation of everything. His wisdom in knowing beforehand what would happen is also to be seen here. It is a statement of praise and faith to say that God has accomplished His will in all that Jesus did and endured. That is not saying that God *caused* the foul deeds that happened. God in His infinite goodness does not cause evil. He may bring good out of evil circumstances, but we cannot say that God causes evil.

4:24 CREATION, Personal Creator—God showed His personal concern for individuals by delivering Peter and John. The early church responded with grateful praise to the Creator. The Lord of creation is also the personal God of believers. Creation is a basic New Testament teaching as well as an Old Testament doctrine. Compare 17:24–31.

4:24–31 PRAYER, Petition—In this prayer the New Testament church quoted Scripture, acknowledged all things as being in God's control, asked for extraordinary boldness in preaching and witnessing and for powerful signs to confirm their message. They prayed in Jesus' name. See notes on Jn 16:23–24, 26–27. The answer came immediately in the person of the Spirit.

4:25 HOLY SPIRIT, Revelation—The "Spirit of truth" (Jn 14:17) began His work of revealing early in Israel's history (see

25You spoke by the Holy Spirit through
the mouth of your servant, our father David:[a]

" 'Why do the nations rage
and the peoples plot in vain?
26The kings of the earth take their stand
and the rulers gather together
against the Lord
and against his Anointed One.'[r][s][b]

27Indeed Herod[c] and Pontius Pilate[d] met
together with the Gentiles and the people[t] of Israel in this city to conspire
against your holy servant Jesus,[e] whom
you anointed. 28They did what your power and will had decided beforehand
should happen.[f] 29Now, Lord, consider
their threats and enable your servants to
speak your word with great boldness.[g]
30Stretch out your hand to heal and perform miraculous signs and wonders[h]
through the name of your holy servant
Jesus."[i]

31After they prayed, the place where
they were meeting was shaken.[j] And
they were all filled with the Holy Spirit[k]
and spoke the word of God[l] boldly.[m]

The Believers Share Their Possessions

32All the believers were one in heart
and mind. No one claimed that any of his
possessions was his own, but they shared
everything they had.[n] 33With great power the apostles continued to testify[o] to
the resurrection[p] of the Lord Jesus, and
much grace[q] was upon them all. 34There
were no needy persons among them. For
from time to time those who owned lands
or houses sold them,[r] brought the money from the sales 35and put it at the apostles' feet,[s] and it was distributed to anyone as he had need.[t]
36Joseph, a Levite from Cyprus, whom
the apostles called Barnabas[u] (which
means Son of Encouragement), 37sold a
field he owned and brought the money
and put it at the apostles' feet.[v]

4:25 [a]Ac 1:16
4:26 [b]Ps 2:1,2; Da 9:25; Lk 4:18; Ac 10:38; Heb 1:9
4:27 [c]S Mt 14:1 [d]S Mt 27:2; Lk 23:12 [e]ver 30; Ac 3:13,14
4:28 [f]Ac 2:23
4:29 [g]ver 13,31; Ps 138:3; Ac 9:27; 13:46; 14:3; 28:31; Eph 6:19; Php 1:14
4:30 [h]S Jn 4:48 [i]ver 27
4:31 [j]Ac 2:2 [k]S Lk 1:15 [l]S Heb 4:12 [m]S ver 29
4:32 [n]Ac 2:44
4:33 [o]S Lk 24:48 [p]Ac 1:22 [q]S Ro 3:24
4:34 [r]Mt 19:21; Ac 2:45
4:35 [s]ver 37; Ac 5:2 [t]Ac 2:45; 6:1
4:36 [u]Ac 9:27; 11:22,30; 13:2; 1 Co 9:6; Gal 2:1,9, 13
4:37 [v]ver 35; Ac 5:2

[r]*26* That is, Christ or Messiah [s]*26* Psalm 2:1,2
[t]*27* The Greek is plural.

notes on Ge 41:38–39) and has continued it ever since. He has revealed God's truth through prophets and apostles, and especially through Jesus. One aspect of the Spirit's revelatory work was to inspire the writing down of revelations, an activity that led to the creation of the Holy Scriptures. John and Peter referred to this revelatory work when they quoted Ps 2 as the words of David spoken through the Holy Spirit.

4:27 JESUS CHRIST, Servant—See note on 3:13.

4:27–28 HISTORY, Freedom—God's plan for saving a people for Himself included Christ's death. Herod, Pilate, and many other people conspired to cause Christ's physical death. Their historical actions were not forced upon them. They acted in freedom and had to bear responsibility for their sinful acts. God works out His plans in time and history without robbing humans of freedom to act.

4:30 MIRACLE, Instruments—Peter's prayer asked God to empower His church to heal, to perform signs, and to perform wonders through the name of Jesus. This was the experience of the church as described in Acts. They used miracles to praise God and to witness to Jesus.

4:31 HOLY SPIRIT, Church—From the beginning the Spirit was understood to be powerful. His power was expressed in a variety of ways. See notes on Jdg 15:14; Eze 2:1–2; Mk 1:12. At Pentecost three powerful signs were given. See note on Ac 2:1–4. Here yet another sign of power is mentioned, an earthquake. Doubtless it reminded the disciples of the power of God's Spirit in them and gave them strength and courage. The purpose of this powerful sign was not to display a sensational act. It empowered the church to preach God's word with boldness. The Spirit always empowers the church to preach. The message the Spirit gives is always the message about Jesus Christ. The great works of God are done in the world through displays of power, even earthquakes. These are only signs, supporting the preaching of the gospel. God gives these signs whenever it pleases Him, but wise men will not seek them (1 Co 1:22–23). To seek them can even be a form of temptation (Mt 4:1–11). See note on Ac 6:1–6.

4:31 REVELATION, Spirit—Through prayer the disciples continued to receive revelation (Jn 14:16). Revelation came in the form of power from the Spirit.

4:31–33 PROCLAMATION, Anointing—See note on Isa 61:1–3. The Holy Spirit provides power for preaching. The Spirit can give all believers power to proclaim God's Word of salvation.

4:32–37 EVIL AND SUFFERING, Comfort—See note on 2:44–46.

4:32,35,36–37 DISCIPLESHIP, Persons—The early disciples in Jerusalem minimized private ownership and shared everything. They provided the apostles with resources to distribute to those who had need. The generosity of Barnabas provides a good example. Scripture does not set this up as an eternal model for all to follow. It is a model for our concern for the needy. Churches today should make provision for such distribution by benevolence committees. Discipleship must express itself through the church budget which should reflect a greater concern for those outside the church than for ourselves. See note on 20:35.

4:32 CHRISTIAN ETHICS, Property Rights—See note on 2:44–45.

4:32—5:11 STEWARDSHIP, Service to God—Believers, like Barnabas, who give property to meet the needs of the Christian community are praised. Ananias and Sapphira coveted such praise but were unwilling to give the money gained in their sale. Their sin was attempting to deceive God and fellow believers. We may be tempted to seek pride and prestige by deceiving others concerning our ability and willingness to give. Christians serve God by giving to accomplish His purposes. Gifts to meet needs of fellow Christians, build places of worship, support the work of the church, and extend missionary efforts are ways to serve Christ through the use of money.

4:32 THE CHURCH, Local Body—A group of believers serving Christ in one geographical location is a church. The believers in Jerusalem formed a church. Most New Testament passages relating to the church refer to a local body of believers. The local church is not isolated or provincial. The Jerusalem church became the base for the church's mission outreach to Samaria and beyond. The local fellowship must display unity and commitment to minister to one another as the Jerusalem church did here. They must also display Christ's love to the whole world. Besides the local church, the New Testament refers to the church in a more general and expanded sense. See notes on Jn 10:14–18; 20:29.

4:33 GOD, Grace—Grace here is the redemptive blessing of God. The grace of God was active through these maturing believers as they reached out to unbelievers with the gospel. Grace is the redemptive love of God in action, the unmerited favor of God reaching out.

Chapter 5

Ananias and Sapphira

NOW a man named Ananias, together
with his wife Sapphira, also sold a
piece of property. 2With his wife's full
knowledge he kept back part of the money for himself,[w] but brought the rest and
put it at the apostles' feet.[x]
3Then Peter said, "Ananias, how is it
that Satan[y] has so filled your heart[z] that
you have lied to the Holy Spirit[a] and
have kept for yourself some of the money
you received for the land?[b] 4Didn't it belong to you before it was sold? And after
it was sold, wasn't the money at your disposal?[c] What made you think of doing
such a thing? You have not lied to men
but to God."[d]
5When Ananias heard this, he fell
down and died.[e] And great fear[f] seized
all who heard what had happened. 6Then
the young men came forward, wrapped
up his body,[g] and carried him out and
buried him.
7About three hours later his wife came
in, not knowing what had happened. 8Pe-
ter asked her, "Tell me, is this the price
you and Ananias got for the land?"
"Yes," she said, "that is the price."[h]
9Peter said to her, "How could you
agree to test the Spirit of the Lord?[i]
Look! The feet of the men who buried
your husband are at the door, and they
will carry you out also."
10At that moment she fell down at his
feet and died.[j] Then the young men
came in and, finding her dead, carried
her out and buried her beside her husband.[k] 11Great fear[l] seized the whole
church and all who heard about these
events.

The Apostles Heal Many

12The apostles performed many miraculous signs and wonders[m] among the
people. And all the believers used to meet
together[n] in Solomon's Colonnade.[o]
13No one else dared join them, even
though they were highly regarded by the
people.[p] 14Nevertheless, more and more
men and women believed in the Lord and
were added to their number.[q] 15As a result, people brought the sick into the
streets and laid them on beds and mats so
that at least Peter's shadow might fall on
some of them as he passed by.[r] 16Crowds
gathered also from the towns around Jerusalem, bringing their sick and those tormented by evil[u] spirits, and all of them
were healed.[s]

The Apostles Persecuted

17Then the high priest and all his associates, who were members of the party[t]
of the Sadducees,[u] were filled with jeal-

5:2 [w]Jos 7:11 [x]Ac 4:35,37
5:3 [y]S Mt 4:10 [z]Jn 13:2,27 [a]ver 9 [b]Dt 23:21
5:4 [c]Dt 23:22 [d]Lev 6:2
5:5 [e]ver 10; Ps 5:6 [f]ver 11
5:6 [g]Jn 19:40
5:8 [h]ver 2
5:9 [i]ver 3
5:10 [j]ver 5 [k]ver 6
5:11 [l]ver 5; Ac 19:17
5:12 [m]S Jn 4:48; Ac 2:43 [n]Ac 4:32 [o]Jn 10:23; Ac 3:11
5:13 [p]Ac 2:47; 4:21
5:14 [q]S Ac 2:41
5:15 [r]Ac 19:12
5:16 [s]Mt 8:16; S Mk 16:17
5:17 [t]Ac 15:5 [u]S Ac 4:1

[u]*16* Greek *unclean*

5:1–11 MIRACLE, Judgment—Miracles can judge as well as heal. The greed of Ananias and Sapphira produced pre-meditated deception. This is a high-handed sin against the Holy Spirit. Peter himself did not pronounce judgment against Ananias. Ananias and Sapphira died, and the early church interpreted it as God's judgment on their deception. Perhaps they died of shock at the embarrassing scene. This may have been the first death experienced in the church after the resurrection. It shocked the congregation, striking them with holy fear. Exactly how God causes miracles to happen, we do not know. He may use natural laws of life and death. He may intervene directly. The important thing is that God's people have an inspired interpreter who recognizes and interprets God's actions.

5:1–11 SIN, Serious—To use religious acts to gain worldly recognition is a serious sin. Using deception to make the act appear greater than it is compounds the sin. Such an act is not simply a game of deception fooling our friends. It is a lie told to God in the Person of the Spirit. We dare not take lightly our religious acts or promises. God does not take us lightly.

5:1–11 CHRISTIAN ETHICS, Covetousness—Material goods are not the only things we covet. We may more often covet personal attention, praise, and prestige. To gain these through unethical means such as lying or telling half-truths is sinful and merits only God's judgment.

5:1–11 FAMILY, God's Judgment—When families conspire together to deceive God and His people, they bring God's judgment on the individuals in the family. The social unit God designed for intimacy and sharing can become an instrument for evil and destruction.

5:5 REVELATION, Events—Revelation through God's judgment on sin is New Testament teaching as well as Old Testament.

5:11 THE CHURCH, Local Body—The whole church was the local Jerusalem congregation which witnessed these events. Their fear included reverence, respect, and awe before the astounding acts of God. See notes on 4:32; 8:1.

5:12–16 MIRACLE, Faith—The miracle-working ability passed easily from Jesus Himself to His church. Both "signs" and "wonders" bound the community together. So convinced was the populace of apostolic power that many brought their sick to allow Peter's shadow to pass over them. This practice smacks of magic but must be seen in light of v 14. The reputation of the church for spiritual power to heal led to faith which led to more healing. Miracles never depend on or point to the powers of a human being. They depend on faith and point to Christ. Christ calls on the church to exercise faith in His name and witness His power to the world.

5:12–42 EVIL AND SUFFERING, Rejoicing—Despite being persecuted, the disciples rejoiced. To suffer for Christ is a privilege of discipleship.

5:12–14 THE CHURCH, Local Body—The local church assembles for worship and fellowship. "Meet together" includes the meaning in common consent and purpose. Christ wanted His followers to be unified (Jn 17:21–23). Unity remains the church's goal. Unity does not mean exclusiveness. The Jerusalem church continued to evangelize and grow. The faithfulness and unity of the church gained respect and admiration in the community from those without the courage to commit themselves fully to Christ and His church. See notes on 4:32; 8:1; Jn 17:11.

5:12–14 EVANGELISM, Social Action—God gave the early church healing power. This power attracted people and resulted in church growth. The power of ministry to people's physical needs should be a basic part of a church's evangelism program. See note on 4:1–4.

5:15–16 EVIL AND SUFFERING, Compassion—See note on 3:1–16.

ousy. 18They arrested the apostles and put
them in the public jail.[v] 19But during the
night an angel[w] of the Lord opened the
doors of the jail[x] and brought them out.[y]
20"Go, stand in the temple courts," he
said, "and tell the people the full message
of this new life."[z]

21At daybreak they entered the temple
courts, as they had been told, and began
to teach the people.

When the high priest and his associates[a] arrived, they called together the
Sanhedrin[b]—the full assembly of the elders of Israel—and sent to the jail for the
apostles. 22But on arriving at the jail, the
officers did not find them there.[c] So they
went back and reported, 23"We found the
jail securely locked, with the guards
standing at the doors; but when we
opened them, we found no one inside."
24On hearing this report, the captain of
the temple guard and the chief priests[d]
were puzzled, wondering what would
come of this.

25Then someone came and said, "Look!
The men you put in jail are standing in
the temple courts teaching the people."
26At that, the captain went with his officers and brought the apostles. They did
not use force, because they feared that
the people[e] would stone them.

27Having brought the apostles, they
made them appear before the Sanhedrin[f]
to be questioned by the high priest.
28"We gave you strict orders not to teach
in this name,"[g] he said. "Yet you have
filled Jerusalem with your teaching and
are determined to make us guilty of this
man's blood."[h]

29Peter and the other apostles replied:
"We must obey God rather than men![i]
30The God of our fathers[j] raised Jesus
from the dead[k]—whom you had killed
by hanging him on a tree.[l] 31God exalted
him to his own right hand[m] as Prince and
Savior[n] that he might give repentance
and forgiveness of sins to Israel.[o] 32We
are witnesses of these things,[p] and so is
the Holy Spirit,[q] whom God has given to
those who obey him."

33When they heard this, they were furious[r] and wanted to put them to death.
34But a Pharisee named Gamaliel,[s] a
teacher of the law,[t] who was honored by
all the people, stood up in the Sanhedrin
and ordered that the men be put outside
for a little while. 35Then he addressed
them: "Men of Israel, consider carefully
what you intend to do to these men.
36Some time ago Theudas appeared,
claiming to be somebody, and about four
hundred men rallied to him. He was
killed, all his followers were dispersed,
and it all came to nothing. 37After him,
Judas the Galilean appeared in the days of
the census[u] and led a band of people in
revolt. He too was killed, and all his followers were scattered. 38Therefore, in
the present case I advise you: Leave these
men alone! Let them go! For if their purpose or activity is of human origin, it will
fail.[v] 39But if it is from God, you will not
be able to stop these men; you will only
find yourselves fighting against God."[w]

40His speech persuaded them. They
called the apostles in and had them
flogged.[x] Then they ordered them not to
speak in the name of Jesus, and let them
go.

41The apostles left the Sanhedrin, rejoicing[y] because they had been counted
worthy of suffering disgrace for the
Name.[z] 42Day after day, in the temple
courts[a] and from house to house, they

5:18 [v]Ac 4:3
5:19 [w]Ge 16:7; Ex 3:2; Mt 1:20; 2:13,19; 28:2; Lk 1:11; 2:9; S Jn 20:12; Ac 8:26; 10:3; 12:7,23; 27:23 [x]Ac 16:26 [y]Ps 34:7
5:20 [z]Jn 6:63,68
5:21 [a]Ac 4:5,6 [b]ver 27,34,41; S Mt 5:22
5:22 [c]Ac 12:18,19
5:24 [d]Ac 4:1
5:26 [e]Ac 4:21
5:27 [f]S Mt 5:22
5:28 [g]Ac 4:18 [h]Mt 23:35; 27:25; Ac 2:23,36; 3:14,15; 7:52
5:29 [i]Ex 1:17; Ac 4:19
5:30 [j]S Ac 3:13 [k]S Ac 2:24 [l]Ac 10:39; 13:29; Gal 3:13
5:31 [m]S Mk 16:19 [n]S Lk 2:11 [o]S Mt 1:21; Mk 1:4; Lk 24:47; Ac 2:38; 3:19; 10:43
5:32 [p]S Lk 24:48 [q]Jn 15:26
5:33 [r]Ac 2:37; 7:54
5:34 [s]Ac 22:3 [t]Lk 2:46; 5:17
5:37 [u]Lk 2:1,2
5:38 [v]Mt 15:13
5:39 [w]2Ch 13:12; Pr 21:30; Isa 46:10; Ac 7:51; 11:17
5:40 [x]S Mt 10:17
5:41 [y]S Mt 5:12 [z]S Jn 15:21
5:42 [a]S Ac 2:46

5:19 MIRACLE, Instruments—Miracles help the church in crisis. God uses various beings as His messengers to help His people out of desperate circumstances. "Angel" in both Hebrew and Greek can refer either to a heavenly angelic messenger or to a human messenger. Any translator must make a subjective judgment as to which is correct in any particular case. "Angel" is apparently meant here. Compare 7:30; 8:26; 12:7,11. When God uses His messengers to deliver His people, the church must be spiritually alert to recognize His activity and to give Him the glory. God wants us to share the message of His miraculous deliverance so others may come to faith in Him.

5:25–28 EDUCATION, Evangelists—What upset the authorities was that these Christians were teaching the people in the Temple area. This episode attests to the power of "instructional evangelism" as a tool for communicating the gospel. See note on 4:1–4.

5:29,32 SALVATION, Obedience—Whenever we have to choose between obeying God and religious authorities, we should obey God. The Holy Spirit is God's gift to those who obey Him.

5:29–32 PROCLAMATION, Gospel—See notes on 3:11–26; 4:31–33; 1 Co 9:16–18.

5:29–32 EVANGELISM, Holy Spirit—See note on 2:1–13.

5:31 JESUS CHRIST, Savior—The ascended Christ reigns with God as our Savior, providing the possibility for repentance and forgiveness. See note on 4:12.

5:32 HOLY SPIRIT, Convicts—Jesus had promised His disciples that when they were on trial because of their faith, the Spirit would give them words for self-defense (Lk 13:11–12). That promise was fulfilled before the Sanhedrin. See Ac 4:8. The apostles defended themselves simply by preaching Jesus as the crucified and risen Savior (vv 30–31). The Spirit always reminds Christians of Christ and helps them to preach Christ to one another and to the world. The Spirit bears witness concerning Jesus; the church hears His witness and is thereby enabled to give its witness concerning Jesus. All who hear this witness and accept it are given the Spirit, and thus become equipped to proclaim Christ.

5:35–39 HUMANITY, Relationship to God—Opposition to God's servants is opposition to God Himself. No creature can overcome the Creator. In our planning we need to be sure we know God's will.

5:39 GOD, Sovereignty—God controls the growth of His church. If the church resulted from human plans, energies, and manipulations, it would have died long ago. God's church lives and grows because the sovereign God planned it and guides it to accomplish His purposes. Humans may fight the church. In so doing, they fight God's plans. They are destined to lose.

never stopped teaching and proclaiming
the good news[b] that Jesus is the
Christ.[v] [c]

Chapter 6

The Choosing of the Seven

IN those days when the number of disciples was increasing,[d] the Grecian
Jews[e] among them complained against
the Hebraic Jews because their widows[f]
were being overlooked in the daily distribution of food.[g] 2So the Twelve gathered
all the disciples[h] together and said, "It
would not be right for us to neglect the
ministry of the word of God[i] in order to
wait on tables. 3Brothers,[j] choose seven
men from among you who are known to
be full of the Spirit[k] and wisdom. We will
turn this responsibility over to them[l]
4and will give our attention to prayer[m]
and the ministry of the word."

5This proposal pleased the whole
group. They chose Stephen,[n] a man full
of faith and of the Holy Spirit;[o] also Philip,[p] Procorus, Nicanor, Timon, Parme-
nas, and Nicolas from Antioch, a convert
to Judaism. 6They presented these men to
the apostles, who prayed[q] and laid their
hands on them.[r]

7So the word of God spread.[s] The
number of disciples in Jerusalem increased rapidly,[t] and a large number of
priests became obedient to the faith.

Stephen Seized

8Now Stephen, a man full of God's
grace and power, did great wonders and
miraculous signs[u] among the people.
9Opposition arose, however, from members of the Synagogue of the Freedmen
(as it was called)—Jews of Cyrene[v] and

5:42 [b]S Ac 13:32 [c]S Ac 9:22
6:1 [d]S Ac 2:41 [e]Ac 9:29 [f]Ac 9:39, 41; 1Ti 5:3 [g]Ac 4:35
6:2 [h]S Ac 11:26 [i]S Heb 4:12
6:3 [j]S Ac 1:16 [k]S Lk 1:15 [l]Ex 18:21; Ne 13:13
6:4 [m]S Ac 1:14
6:5 [n]ver 8; Ac 7:55-60; 11:19; 22:20 [o]S Lk 1:15 [p]Ac 8:5-40; 21:8
6:6 [q]S Ac 1:24 [r]Nu 8:10; 27:18; Ac 9:17; 19:6; 28:8; 1Ti 4:14; S Mk 5:23
6:7 [s]Ac 12:24; 19:20 [t]S Ac 2:41
6:8 [u]S Jn 4:48
6:9 [v]S Mt 27:32

[v]42 Or *Messiah*

5:42 JESUS CHRIST, Christ—Among Jews the early Christian message centered on Jesus as Messiah.

5:42 PROCLAMATION, Central Theme—See note on Lk 24:47. Jesus as the promised Messiah or Christ of Israel is the central content of New Testament proclamation. To preach Christ is to call for repentance and to offer forgiveness in His name. Proclamation is a daily task to be done wherever a believer is.

5:42 EDUCATION, Christians—The teaching activity of Christians is not limited to particular times or places. It is an unceasing activity which takes place in homes, in the marketplace, and in congregational gatherings. See note on 2:42.

6:1–6 HOLY SPIRIT, Fills—As leaders, the church sought persons filled with the Spirit. The text does not indicate the outward evidence that showed the church which people were so filled. It indicates people distinguished by the leadership of God in their lives and their submission to Him. Wisdom also filled their lives, so rational behavior rather than ecstatic loss of control dominated them. Full of the Spirit, these men were willing to serve tables and administer programs so the apostles could preach and pray. See 2:4; 4:8; 9:17; Lk 1:15,42; Eph 5:19; notes on 4:31; 13:9; Lk 1:67. The entire congregation could be filled (4:31).

6:1–7 DISCIPLESHIP, Laity—The twelve apostles were unable to meet all of the needs of the growing number of disciples in the early church. The apostles needed help as Moses did at the time his father-in-law gave him advice (Ex 18:13–24). They asked the church to choose seven qualified men to help them serve. The laity today, like these seven, must lead the church in ministry to the community's needy and in reaching those outside the church. See note on 1 Co 3:9.

6:1–6 CHURCH LEADERS, Deacon—The seven men chosen to assist the Twelve are not identified as deacons, but the verb "to wait on" (Greek *diakonein*) comes from the same root as the noun (Greek *diakonos*) translated into English as deacon. The selection of the seven grew out of the needs of the apostles in ministering to the congregation. The special responsibilities of the seven involved practical service. Those chosen for this assignment had already demonstrated evidence of the working of the Spirit in their lives and ministry. Following the example of these seven, deacons of today will see their responsibilities as serving with the pastor in ministering to the needs of the church congregation and the community.

6:4 PRAYER, Biblical Characters—Prayer was one of the two great responsibilities of the leaders. Church leaders can minister effectively only when they pray consistently.

6:6 PRAYER, Will of God—Church leaders are chosen and set apart for service under God's leadership gained in prayer.

6:6 CHURCH LEADERS, Ordination—Ordination does not elevate anyone to a superior position in the church, nor does it convey any special rights. The ordained acknowledge in public that they willingly accept the responsibilities for whatever ministry they are called to do. Ordination should take place only after evidence of the Spirit's call and with the concurrence of the congregation. See note on 13:3.

6:7 CHURCH LEADERS, Priest—The priests in Judaism mediated between God and the people by offering sacrifices in the Temple. It was a hereditary office in the family of Levi. Because of the finality of Jesus' sacrifice (Heb 8:1–2), the church no longer needs the office of priest. No office connected to the Temple sacrificial service was continued in the church. Even Jewish priests who joined the church played no priestly role. Each believer had the right to go directly to God in prayer and to apply God's Word. Every believer becomes a responsible priest before God (Heb 8; 1 Pe 2; 1 Jn 1:9).

6:7 EVANGELISM, Power—See notes on 2:17–40; 4:1–4. Even Jewish priests were converted in great numbers and added to the church. The gospel's power can reach all people. The church's evangelistic ministry should not neglect any group of people.

6:8 GOD, Power—Both the grace and power of God are operative in spreading the gospel. Jesus promised His disciples He would be with them. That promise is fulfilled in the power and grace of God working through His people in our efforts to spread the gospel. Grace is the redemptive love of God reaching out to the lost and bringing them to conversion. God gives us grace and power to accomplish His will.

6:8–10 HOLY SPIRIT, Protects—See note on 5:32. The members of the synagogue set out to condemn Stephen but found his defense so strong they were on the defensive. The Spirit protected Stephen by leading him to refute his opponents. Only false testimony led to his conviction. At Stephen's defense was Saul of Tarsus (Ac 8:1), who eventually was convicted and became a proclaimer of what he had first received (1 Co 15:3) from the preaching of people such as Stephen.

6:8 MIRACLE, Instruments—Many church leaders were credited with doing exceptional deeds. Stephen's ministry was short-lived, but he performed both "wonders" and "signs." God's instruments in performing miracles are not limited to any one leadership position in the church. God is free to use any person He chooses to be His miraculous instrument.

6:8—7:60 EVIL AND SUFFERING, Endurance—Stephen responded to persecution by forgiving his enemies. Many early Christians were willing to die for their faith. To be a martyr means literally to be a witness, living or dead, for the gospel.

Alexandria as well as the provinces of Cilicia[w] and Asia.[x] These men began to argue with Stephen, 10 but they could not stand up against his wisdom or the Spirit by whom he spoke.[y]

11 Then they secretly[z] persuaded some men to say, "We have heard Stephen speak words of blasphemy against Moses and against God."[a]

12 So they stirred up the people and the elders and the teachers of the law. They seized Stephen and brought him before the Sanhedrin.[b] 13 They produced false witnesses,[c] who testified, "This fellow never stops speaking against this holy place[d] and against the law. 14 For we have heard him say that this Jesus of Nazareth will destroy this place[e] and change the customs Moses handed down to us."[f]

15 All who were sitting in the Sanhedrin[g] looked intently at Stephen, and they saw that his face was like the face of an angel.

Chapter 7

Stephen's Speech to the Sanhedrin

THEN the high priest asked him, "Are these charges true?"

2 To this he replied: "Brothers and fathers,[h] listen to me! The God of glory[i] appeared to our father Abraham while he was still in Mesopotamia, before he lived in Haran.[j] 3 'Leave your country and your people,' God said, 'and go to the land I will show you.'[w] [k]

4 "So he left the land of the Chaldeans and settled in Haran. After the death of his father, God sent him to this land where you are now living.[l] 5 He gave him no inheritance here,[m] not even a foot of ground. But God promised him that he and his descendants after him would possess the land,[n] even though at that time Abraham had no child. 6 God spoke to him in this way: 'Your descendants will be strangers in a country not their own, and they will be enslaved and mistreated four hundred years.[o] 7 But I will punish the nation they serve as slaves,' God said, 'and afterward they will come out of that country and worship me in this place.'[x] [p] 8 Then he gave Abraham the covenant of circumcision.[q] And Abraham became the father of Isaac and circumcised him eight days after his birth.[r] Later Isaac became the father of Jacob,[s] and Jacob became the father of the twelve patriarchs.[t]

9 "Because the patriarchs were jealous of Joseph,[u] they sold him as a slave into Egypt.[v] But God was with him[w] 10 and rescued him from all his troubles. He gave Joseph wisdom and enabled him to gain the goodwill of Pharaoh king of Egypt; so he made him ruler over Egypt and all his palace.[x]

11 "Then a famine struck all Egypt and Canaan, bringing great suffering, and our fathers could not find food.[y] 12 When Jacob heard that there was grain in Egypt, he sent our fathers on their first visit.[z] 13 On their second visit, Joseph told his brothers who he was,[a] and Pharaoh learned about Joseph's family.[b] 14 After this, Joseph sent for his father Jacob and his whole family,[c] seventy-five in all.[d] 15 Then Jacob went down to Egypt, where he and our fathers died.[e] 16 Their bodies were brought back to Shechem and placed in the tomb that Abraham had bought from the sons of Hamor at Shechem for a certain sum of money.[f]

17 "As the time drew near for God to fulfill his promise to Abraham, the number of our people in Egypt greatly increased.[g] 18 Then another king, who knew nothing about Joseph, became ruler of Egypt.[h] 19 He dealt treacherously with our people and oppressed our forefathers by forcing them to throw out their newborn babies so that they would die.[i]

20 "At that time Moses was born, and he was no ordinary child.[y] For three months he was cared for in his father's house.[j] 21 When he was placed outside, Pharaoh's daughter took him and brought him up as her own son.[k] 22 Moses was educated in all the wisdom of the Egyp-

[w] 3 Gen. 12:1 [x] 7 Gen. 15:13,14 [y] 20 Or *was fair in the sight of God*

6:9 [w]Ac 15:23,41; 22:3; 23:34 [x]S Ac 2:9
6:10 [y]Lk 21:15
6:11 [z]1Ki 21:10 [a]Mt 26:59-61
6:12 [b]S Mt 5:22
6:13 [c]Ex 23:1; Ps 27:12 [d]Mt 24:15; Ac 7:48; 21:28
6:14 [e]S Jn 2:19 [f]Ac 15:1; 21:21; 26:3; 28:17
6:15 [g]S Mt 5:22
7:2 [h]Ac 22:1 [i]Ps 29:3 [j]Ge 11:31; 15:7
7:3 [k]Ge 12:1
7:4 [l]Ge 12:5
7:5 [m]Heb 11:13 [n]Ge 12:7; 17:8; 26:3
7:6 [o]Ex 1:8-11; 12:40
7:7 [p]Ge 15:13,14; Ex 3:12
7:8 [q]Ge 17:9-14 [r]Ge 21:2-4 [s]Ge 25:26 [t]Ge 29:31-35; 30:5-13,17-24; 35:16-18,22-26
7:9 [u]Ge 37:4,11 [v]Ge 37:28; Ps 105:17 [w]Ge 39:2,21,23; Hag 2:4
7:10 [x]Ge 41:37-43; Ps 105:20-22
7:11 [y]Ge 41:54
7:12 [z]Ge 42:1,2
7:13 [a]Ge 45:1-4 [b]Ge 45:16
7:14 [c]Ge 45:9,10 [d]Ge 46:26,27; Ex 1:5; Dt 10:22
7:15 [e]Ge 46:5-7; 49:33; Ex 1:6
7:16 [f]Ge 23:16-20; 33:18,19; 50:13; Jos 24:32
7:17 [g]Ex 1:7; Ps 105:24
7:18 [h]Ex 1:8
7:19 [i]Ex 1:10-22
7:20 [j]Ex 2:2; Heb 11:23
7:21 [k]Ex 2:3-10

6:11 SIN, Lawlessness—Political collusion against religious opponents breaks the laws of God and humanity. To use false testimony to get a court to condemn an innocent person to death is outrageous sin. The Jewish leaders were so anxious to defend their interpretation of religious tradition and, thus, from their viewpoint to defend God that they unmercifully sacrificed an innocent man to protect their cause. So often Christian martyrs have been killed by others in the name of Christ. Taking violent measures to defend religious tradition is sin. It does not serve well the Prince of Peace.

7:1–53 REVELATION, History—New Testament preachers looked on Old Testament history as the arena in which God revealed Himself to His people and prepared for Jesus Christ. They knew that history through the Old Testament, which they accepted as inspired, authoritative Scripture. At least the Law had been revealed through angels as mediators (vv 38,53). History was rejection as well as revelation, for Israel repeatedly rejected the Spirit's revelation and direction. To have authoritative Scripture is not enough. God expects His people to live the life called for by the Scripture.

7:1–53 HISTORY, Confession—Stephen continued Israel's manner of worship by confessing the acts of God in history. He used history to show it as a history of Israel's sin. See note on Ps 106:2. Christ's death represented only the last act in Israel's history of sin.

7:2,55 GOD, Glory—On the one hand, the glory of God is our perception of God. On the other hand, the glory of God is God's revelation of Himself in such a way that we behold Him and are awestruck. In either case, the glory of God results in a sense of awe at the presence of God.

tians[l] and was powerful in speech and
action.
23“When Moses was forty years old, he
decided to visit his fellow Israelites. 24He
saw one of them being mistreated by an
Egyptian, so he went to his defense and
avenged him by killing the Egyptian.
25Moses thought that his own people
would realize that God was using him to
rescue them, but they did not. 26The next
day Moses came upon two Israelites who
were fighting. He tried to reconcile them
by saying, ‘Men, you are brothers; why
do you want to hurt each other?’
27“But the man who was mistreating
the other pushed Moses aside and said,
‘Who made you ruler and judge over us?[m]
28Do you want to kill me as you killed the
Egyptian yesterday?’[z] 29When Moses
heard this, he fled to Midian, where he
settled as a foreigner and had two sons.[n]
30“After forty years had passed, an angel appeared to Moses in the flames of a
burning bush in the desert near Mount
Sinai. 31When he saw this, he was
amazed at the sight. As he went over to
look more closely, he heard the Lord’s
voice:[o] 32‘I am the God of your fathers,[p]
the God of Abraham, Isaac and Jacob.’[a]
Moses trembled with fear and did not
dare to look.[q]
33“Then the Lord said to him, ‘Take off
your sandals; the place where you are
standing is holy ground.[r] 34I have indeed
seen the oppression of my people in
Egypt. I have heard their groaning and
have come down to set them free. Now
come, I will send you back to Egypt.’[b][s]
35“This is the same Moses whom they
had rejected with the words, ‘Who made
you ruler and judge?’[t] He was sent to be
their ruler and deliverer by God himself,
through the angel who appeared to him
in the bush. 36He led them out of Egypt[u]
and did wonders and miraculous signs[v]
in Egypt, at the Red Sea[c][w] and for forty
years in the desert.[x]
37“This is that Moses who told the Israelites, ‘God will send you a prophet like
me from your own people.’[d][y] 38He was
in the assembly in the desert, with the
angel[z] who spoke to him on Mount Sinai, and with our fathers;[a] and he received living words[b] to pass on to us.[c]
39“But our fathers refused to obey him.
Instead, they rejected him and in their
hearts turned back to Egypt.[d] 40They told
Aaron, ‘Make us gods who will go before
us. As for this fellow Moses who led us
out of Egypt—we don’t know what has
happened to him!’[e][e] 41That was the
time they made an idol in the form of a
calf. They brought sacrifices to it and held
a celebration in honor of what their
hands had made.[f] 42But God turned
away[g] and gave them over to the worship of the heavenly bodies.[h] This agrees
with what is written in the book of the
prophets:

“ ‘Did you bring me sacrifices and
offerings
forty years in the desert, O house of
Israel?
43You have lifted up the shrine of
Molech
and the star of your god Rephan,
the idols you made to worship.
Therefore I will send you into exile’[f][i]
beyond Babylon.

44“Our forefathers had the tabernacle
of the Testimony[j] with them in the
desert. It had been made as God directed
Moses, according to the pattern he had
seen.[k] 45Having received the tabernacle,
our fathers under Joshua brought it with
them when they took the land from the
nations God drove out before them.[l] It
remained in the land until the time of
David,[m] 46who enjoyed God’s favor and
asked that he might provide a dwelling
place for the God of Jacob.[g][n] 47But it was
Solomon who built the house for him.[o]
48“However, the Most High[p] does not
live in houses made by men.[q] As the
prophet says:

49“ ‘Heaven is my throne,
and the earth is my footstool.[r]
What kind of house will you build for
me?
says the Lord.
Or where will my resting place be?
50Has not my hand made all these
things?’[h][s]

51“You stiff-necked people,[t] with uncircumcised hearts[u] and ears! You are

7:22 [l]1Ki 4:30; Isa 19:11
7:27 [m]Ge 19:9; Nu 16:13
7:29 [n]Ex 2:11-15
7:31 [o]Ex 3:1-4
7:32 [p]S Ac 3:13 [q]Ex 3:6
7:33 [r]Ex 3:5; Jos 5:15
7:34 [s]Ex 3:7-10
7:35 [t]ver 27
7:36 [u]Ex 12:41; 33:1 [v]Ex 11:10; S Jn 4:48 [w]Ex 14:21 [x]Ex 15:25; 17:5,6
7:37 [y]Dt 18:15,18; Ac 3:22
7:38 [z]ver 53 [a]Ex 19:17; Lev 27:34 [b]Dt 32:45-47; Heb 4:12 [c]Ro 3:2
7:39 [d]Nu 14:3,4
7:40 [e]Ex 32:1,23
7:41 [f]Ex 32:4-6; Ps 106:19,20; Rev 9:20
7:42 [g]Jos 24:20; Isa 63:10 [h]Jer 19:13
7:43 [i]Am 5:25-27
7:44 [j]Ex 38:21; Nu 1:50; 17:7 [k]Ex 25:8,9,40
7:45 [l]Jos 3:14-17; 18:1; 23:9; 24:18; Ps 44:2 [m]2Sa 7:2,6
7:46 [n]2Sa 7:8-16; 1Ki 8:17; Ps 132:1-5
7:47 [o]1Ki 6:1-38
7:48 [p]S Mk 5:7 [q]1Ki 8:27; 2Ch 2:6
7:49 [r]Mt 5:34,35
7:50 [s]Isa 66:1,2
7:51 [t]Ex 32:9; 33:3,5 [u]Lev 26:41; Dt 10:16; Jer 4:4; 9:26

[z]*28* Exodus 2:14 [a]*32* Exodus 3:6 [b]*34* Exodus 3:5,7,8,10 [c]*36* That is, Sea of Reeds [d]*37* Deut. 18:15 [e]*40* Exodus 32:1 [f]*43* Amos 5:25-27 [g]*46* Some early manuscripts *the house of Jacob* [h]*50* Isaiah 66:1,2

7:39–43 GOD, One God—From beginning to end the Bible simply assumes the existence of God, without any attempt to prove He exists. It goes to great lengths to stress that only one God is truly God: all other ideas or images of gods are human creations and as such are worthless. God’s people of every generation must check up on their true devotion and loyalty to the one God. The Jews of Stephen’s day had no idols. Still they resisted the Holy Spirit (v 51).

7:51–53 SIN, Against God—Israel told her history with pride as the history of God’s salvation for an elect people. Stephen told it as a history rejecting God’s leaders and leadership, a history of resisting the Holy Spirit, a history climaxing in the violent rejection of the righteous Messiah. Refusing to follow God’s directions for our lives given us through His Word and His Spirit is resisting the Holy Spirit. See note on Mt 12:31–32.

just like your fathers: You always resist
the Holy Spirit! 52Was there ever a prophet your fathers did not persecute?[v] They
even killed those who predicted the coming of the Righteous One. And now you
have betrayed and murdered him[w]—
53you who have received the law that was
put into effect through angels[x] but have
not obeyed it."

The Stoning of Stephen

54When they heard this, they were furious[y] and gnashed their teeth at him.
55But Stephen, full of the Holy Spirit,[z]
looked up to heaven and saw the glory of
God, and Jesus standing at the right hand
of God.[a] 56"Look," he said, "I see heav-
en open[b] and the Son of Man[c] standing
at the right hand of God."
57At this they covered their ears and,
yelling at the top of their voices, they all
rushed at him, 58dragged him out of the
city[d] and began to stone him.[e] Meanwhile, the witnesses[f] laid their clothes[g]
at the feet of a young man named Saul.[h]
59While they were stoning him, Stephen prayed, "Lord Jesus, receive my
spirit."[i] 60Then he fell on his knees[j]
and cried out, "Lord, do not hold this sin
against them."[k] When he had said this,
he fell asleep.[l]

Chapter 8

AND Saul[m] was there, giving approval
to his death.

The Church Persecuted and Scattered

On that day a great persecution broke
out against the church at Jerusalem, and
all except the apostles were scattered[n]
throughout Judea and Samaria.[o] 2Godly
men buried Stephen and mourned deeply
for him. 3But Saul[p] began to destroy the
church.[q] Going from house to house, he
dragged off men and women and put
them in prison.

Philip in Samaria

4Those who had been scattered[r]
preached the word wherever they
went.[s] 5Philip[t] went down to a city in
Samaria and proclaimed the Christ[1]
there. 6When the crowds heard Philip
and saw the miraculous signs he did, they

7:52 [v]S Mt 5:12 [w]Ac 3:14; 1Th 2:15
7:53 [x]ver 38; Gal 3:19; Heb 2:2
7:54 [y]Ac 5:33
7:55 [z]S Lk 1:15 [a]S Mk 16:19
7:56 [b]S Mt 3:16 [c]S Mt 8:20
7:58 [d]Lk 4:29 [e]Lev 24:14,16 [f]Dt 17:7 [g]Ac 22:20 [h]Ac 8:1
7:59 [i]Ps 31:5; Lk 23:46
7:60 [j]Lk 22:41; Ac 9:40 [k]S Mt 5:44 [l]S Mt 9:24
8:1 [m]Ac 7:58 [n]ver 4; Ac 11:19 [o]Ac 9:31
8:3 [p]Ac 7:58 [q]Ac 9:1,13,21; 22:4,19; 26:10,11; 1Co 15:9; Gal 1:13, 23; Php 3:6; 1Ti 1:13
8:4 [r]ver 1 [s]Ac 15:35
8:5 [t]Ac 6:5; 21:8

[1]5 Or *Messiah*

7:52 JESUS CHRIST, Fulfilled—Jesus fulfilled the prophets' predictions, predictions for which the prophets were persecuted and killed. The prophets pointed to Jesus as the sinless, righteous Messiah (Isa 53:11). See note on 3:14. The Jews treated Jesus as they had the prophets.

7:53 SIN, Transgression—Jewish identity came from the Law and obedience to it. Stephen claimed they had followed their interpretation of the Law. They had not obeyed God. Had they truly obeyed God's laws, they would have followed the prophets and Jesus. Instead, they killed them. The religious are always tempted to devise ways to satisfy God and then to take pride in meeting the standards we set. Following God in truth means one thing: following Jesus to the cross in humility.

7:54–60 JESUS CHRIST, Ascension—Stephen, the first person to be killed because he was a Christian, saw a vision of the ascended Christ with God. He used Jesus' favorite title for Himself, Son of man, to refer to the reigning Christ. The dying Stephen directed his prayer to Christ.

7:55–56 HOLY SPIRIT, Revelation—The Spirit reveals Jesus (Jn 15:26; 16:15; note on Jn 14:26). Usually He did this by reminding the disciples of Jesus and then guiding and empowering them to proclaim Jesus, as He did at Pentecost (Ac 2). In extreme crisis the Spirit gave Stephen a revelation of Jesus in the form of a vision. He saw Jesus in glory, standing beside the Father. The fullness of the Spirit allowed Stephen not only to speak but to see the heavenly vision. Apart from the Spirit, our speech about God is halting and our understanding blurred.

7:55 REVELATION, Visions—God granted Stephen a vision of Father and Son through the power of the Spirit. The vision strengthened Stephen more than providing content for his preaching as did most prophetic visions. See note on Eze 1:1–28.

7:59–60 PRAYER, Jesus' Example—In essence, Stephen prayed Christ's first and last prayers on the cross in reverse order. Compare Lk 23:34,46. Believers can face death in confidence and good conscience by following Christ's example.

7:60 LAST THINGS, Believers' Death—Jesus referred to physical death as sleep on several occasions (Mk 5:39; Jn 11:11). The point was not to teach an idea of "soul sleep," or unconscious existence after death and prior to resurrection. Jesus' other teachings about death disallow this. See notes on Lk 16:19–26; 23:43. Rather, the concern was to teach an idea of death for a believer as something to be no more feared than falling asleep. At death, believers are given quiet rest from life's pains and labors. Paul followed Jesus in the use of the same idea of death for believers as sleep (1 Th 4:13).

8:1 SIN, Evil Desire—We can sin without acting. Saul is not accused of false testimony or violent action against Stephen. He simply sat and did nothing, consenting to what others did. We are judged for what we approve as well as for what we do. Silent acceptance of the wrong others do is sin.

8:1 THE CHURCH, Local Body—The word church (Greek *ekklēsia*) means an assembly. In Greek, this general term was not specifically restricted to religious groups. It often referred to the democratic assembly conducting the political affairs of the city. The earliest Greek translation of the Old Testament—the Septuagint—used *ekklēsia* to refer to God's people assembled in answer to His call. The early Christians narrowed the meaning of the term to a local assembly of Christians and then used it for the collective group. The church is the assembly of believers. It is also the believers as a collective group, whether in one place or including all believers. Early persecution scattered the assembled church, and, in so doing, offered the church new opportunities for evangelism.

8:4–5 PROCLAMATION, Central Theme—The persecuted church scattered and found further evangelistic opportunities to share the good news of the word (Greek *euangelizō*). God's word of good news is the central theme for the herald of the heavenly King. Philip shared the good news by proclaiming Christ. Jesus is the center of God's word, being the Word made flesh (Jn 1:14). See notes on Ac 5:42; Jer 1:4–9; Lk 8:1; 24:47; Ro 10:14–15.

8:4–8 EVANGELISM, Universality—Evangelism among the Samaritans was a major breakthrough for the gospel. Some in Jerusalem believed people outside of Abraham's lineage had to become Jews religiously before they could become Christians. Philip's evangelizing in Samaria proved that belief wrong. He opened the door to those outside the Jewish community. He proved the gospel to have a universal appeal for all people who will hear, heed, and believe.

8:6–24 MIRACLE, Instruments—Both Stephen (see note on 6:8) and Philip, from among the Seven, were credited with

all paid close attention to what he said.
7With shrieks, evil[j] spirits came out of
many,[u] and many paralytics and cripples
were healed.[v] 8So there was great joy in
that city.

Simon the Sorcerer

9Now for some time a man named Simon had practiced sorcery[w] in the city
and amazed all the people of Samaria. He
boasted that he was someone great,[x]
10and all the people, both high and low,
gave him their attention and exclaimed,
"This man is the divine power known as
the Great Power."[y] 11They followed him
because he had amazed them for a long
time with his magic. 12But when they believed Philip as he preached the good
news of the kingdom of God[z] and the
name of Jesus Christ, they were baptized,[a] both men and women. 13Simon
himself believed and was baptized. And
he followed Philip everywhere, astonished by the great signs and miracles[b] he
saw.
14When the apostles in Jerusalem
heard that Samaria[c] had accepted the
word of God,[d] they sent Peter and John[e]
to them. 15When they arrived, they
prayed for them that they might receive
the Holy Spirit,[f] 16because the Holy Spirit had not yet come upon any of them;[g]
they had simply been baptized into[k] the
name of the Lord Jesus.[h] 17Then Peter
and John placed their hands on them,[i]
and they received the Holy Spirit.[j]
18When Simon saw that the Spirit was
given at the laying on of the apostles'
hands, he offered them money 19and said,
"Give me also this ability so that everyone on whom I lay my hands may receive
the Holy Spirit."
20Peter answered: "May your money
perish with you, because you thought you

8:7 [u]S Mk 16:17 [v]S Mt 4:24
8:9 [w]Ac 13:6 [x]Ac 5:36
8:10 [y]Ac 14:11; 28:6
8:12 [z]S Mt 3:2 [a]S Ac 2:38
8:13 [b]ver 6; Ac 19:11
8:14 [c]ver 1 [d]S Heb 4:12 [e]S Lk 22:8
8:15 [f]S Jn 20:22
8:16 [g]S Ac 10:44; 19:2 [h]Mt 28:19; S Ac 2:38
8:17 [i]S Ac 6:6 [j]S Jn 20:22

[j]7 Greek *unclean* [k]16 Or *in*

miracles. Miracles enhanced Philip's preaching mission in Samaria. Seeing the signs, the crowds listened more closely (v 6), believed, and were baptized (v 12). His healing ministry included the demon-possessed, the paralytics, and the crippled. Such miraculous powers impressed the sorcerer, Simon, who recognized Philip's work as superior to his own magic. Peter, John, and the Holy Spirit impressed him more. He decided to buy such miraculous power (vv 18–19). Finally, he asked for prayer (v 24). Miracle power belongs to God not us. He gives it away through the Holy Spirit to whom He chooses. We can obtain it in no other way. Trying to get what God does not choose to give is sin.

8:8 SALVATION, Joy—The preaching of the gospel brings great joy to any city. See note on Ps 149:5.

8:12 THE CHURCH, God's Kingdom—God's kingdom has been established. The coming of Jesus demonstrated the rule of God and provided the means for men and women to submit themselves to that rule. See notes on Mt 3:2; Lk 4:43.

8:12–17 ORDINANCES, Baptism by Holy Spirit—The ones who believed Philip as he preached the gospel of the kingdom and the name of Christ were baptized, but these first converts in Samaria did not immediately receive the Holy Spirit. When Peter and John came from the apostles in Jerusalem to see these new converts, the fact that they prayed for them to receive the Holy Spirit shows they expected them to receive the Spirit at the beginning of their Christian lives. Laying their hands on them was an old biblical sign of the bestowal of the Spirit. At other times the Spirit came while they were preaching, before any baptism or laying on of hands, as at the house of Cornelius (10:44–46). Thus, the Spirit cannot be programmed rigidly, but the coming of the Spirit is closely associated with confession of Christ and baptism throughout the Book of Acts.

8:14–17 HOLY SPIRIT, Mission—Jesus promised to give the Spirit to His disciples, a promise fulfilled at Pentecost. See notes on 1:5, 8; 2:1–4. From Pentecost onward, everyone who became a Christian received the gift of the Spirit (2:38). Anyone who does not have the Spirit is not a follower of Christ (Ro 8:9). The gift of the Spirit was given to people at the time of their conversion in all the recorded stories except this one. There was a delay between when the Samaritans believed the gospel (v 12) and when they received the Spirit at the hands of Peter and John (v 17). It is not to be understood as a second experience, as some say. It is not an ordinary pattern to be duplicated by later generations. It is the exception to the ordinary pattern. Normally the Spirit is given to people when they are converted. The explanation for the delay was that the Samaritans were the first non-Jewish converts to Christian faith. They traced their ancestry back to the mixed peoples who resettled Samaria after it fell to the Assyrians in 722 BC. Many Jews looked with contempt upon Samaritans (Lk 10:30–36; Jn 4:9). At issue here was how the Samaritans could really be Christians. Would God accept them just as He had the Jews? The risen Christ had told the disciples to witness to Samaria (see note on Ac 1:8), but they had not done so until Philip arrived. God had His own way of convincing the Jerusalem church to accept this new phase of the gospel's outreach. Only after the Jerusalem church had sent Peter and John to Samaria did God give His Spirit to the Samaritans. The delay convinced Peter and John that God accepted Samaritans just as He did the Jews, for Peter and John began to preach to Samaritans (v 25). Prayer (v 15) and laying on of hands (v 17) to receive the Spirit are not conditions for all Christians to receive a second blessing, as is sometimes taught. They were part of God's plan to convince Peter and John that He accepted Samaritans as well as Jews.

8:14–17 PRAYER, Intercession—Prayer played an important part in the manifestation of the Holy Spirit to the Samaritan believers. Believers need to intercede for the church that God's power will be manifest in it.

8:18–19 HOLY SPIRIT, Freedom—The Spirit is free and cannot be bought. Simon was a magician (v 9) who misunderstood Peter and John's laying on of hands as magic. He wanted to buy some of their power! Even though he had believed in Jesus (v 13), he was very misguided, perhaps in part by the extraordinary delay in the Spirit's being given to Samaritans. See note on vv 14–17. Peter rebuked him for such sin (vv 21–23), and Simon seems to have repented (v 24). The Spirit is God's free "gift" (v 21) to His people. He cannot be bought by money, religious acts, or good deeds; most certainly, never as a reward. No one could ever deserve the precious presence of God.

8:18–23 CHRISTIAN ETHICS, Property Rights—Spiritual power is not for sale. Only a repentant heart is fit to minister for God. Money's power has limits.

8:18–23 STEWARDSHIP, Attitudes—Simon saw spiritual power as a way to make money. Buying and selling church offices or privileges is a sin appropriately called simony. Christians must not use their faith or church membership to make money or gain prestige. See note on Mt 6:19–33.

8:18–24 PRAYER, Intercession—Simon's mercenary sin required repentance and prayer. He asked the apostles to pray for him. Asking others to intercede for you is proper prayer procedure if it is combined with personal repentance and prayer. Other people cannot pray the prayer of repentance for you.

could buy the gift of God with money![k]
21 You have no part or share[l] in this ministry, because your heart is not right[m] before God. 22 Repent[n] of this wickedness
and pray to the Lord. Perhaps he will forgive you for having such a thought in
your heart. 23 For I see that you are full of
bitterness and captive to sin."
24 Then Simon answered, "Pray to the
Lord for me[o] so that nothing you have
said may happen to me."
25 When they had testified and proclaimed the word of the Lord,[p] Peter and
John returned to Jerusalem, preaching
the gospel in many Samaritan villages.[q]

Philip and the Ethiopian

26 Now an angel[r] of the Lord said to
Philip,[s] "Go south to the road—the
desert road—that goes down from Jerusalem to Gaza." 27 So he started out, and on
his way he met an Ethiopian[l][t] eunuch,[u] an important official in charge of
all the treasury of Candace, queen of the
Ethiopians. This man had gone to Jerusalem to worship,[v] 28 and on his way home
was sitting in his chariot reading the book
of Isaiah the prophet. 29 The Spirit told[w]
Philip, "Go to that chariot and stay near
it."
30 Then Philip ran up to the chariot and
heard the man reading Isaiah the prophet. "Do you understand what you are
reading?" Philip asked.
31 "How can I," he said, "unless someone explains it to me?" So he invited
Philip to come up and sit with him.
32 The eunuch was reading this passage
of Scripture:

"He was led like a sheep to the
slaughter,
and as a lamb before the shearer is
silent,
so he did not open his mouth.
33 In his humiliation he was deprived of
justice.
Who can speak of his descendants?
For his life was taken from the
earth."[m][x]

34 The eunuch asked Philip, "Tell me,
please, who is the prophet talking about,
himself or someone else?" 35 Then Philip
began[y] with that very passage of Scripture[z] and told him the good news[a] about
Jesus.
36 As they traveled along the road, they
came to some water and the eunuch said,
"Look, here is water. Why shouldn't I be
baptized?"[n][b] 38 And he gave orders to
stop the chariot. Then both Philip and the
eunuch went down into the water and
Philip baptized him. 39 When they came

8:20 [k]2Ki 5:16; Da 5:17; Mt 10:8; Ac 2:38
8:21 [l]Ne 2:20 [m]Ps 78:37
8:22 [n]Ac 2:38
8:24 [o]Ex 8:8; Nu 21:7; 1Ki 13:6; Jer 42:2
8:25 [p]S Ac 13:48 [q]ver 40
8:26 [r]S Ac 5:19 [s]Ac 6:5
8:27 [t]Ps 68:31; 87:4; Zep 3:10 [u]Isa 56:3-5 [v]1Ki 8:41-43; Jn 12:20
8:29 [w]Ac 10:19; 11:12; 13:2; 20:23; 21:11
8:33 [x]Isa 53:7,8
8:35 [y]Mt 5:2 [z]Lk 24:27; Ac 17:2; 18:28; 28:23 [a]S Ac 13:32
8:36 [b]S Ac 2:38; 10:47

[l]*27* That is, from the upper Nile region [m]*33* Isaiah 53:7,8 [n]*36* Some late manuscripts *baptized?" 37Philip said, "If you believe with all your heart, you may." The eunuch answered, "I believe that Jesus Christ is the Son of God."*

8:23 SIN, Slavery—The inability or the unwillingness to escape the past, disobedient life is a crucial link in the chain of sin's bondage. Only true repentance can change this situation. See note on Jn 8:31–37.

8:25 EVANGELISM, Universality—Peter and John (8:14) saw the truth that the gospel was for all and began preaching to the Samaritans. See note on vv 4–8.

8:26–27 REVELATION, Angels—Angels are messengers from God who often instruct God's followers on decisions and actions they should take to follow God's will. The messengers appear to be human or divine, for God uses both in the Scriptures to reveal His will to people. Here the angel is an instrument of the Spirit (v 29). See note on Ge 18:1—19:29.

8:26–40 EVANGELISM, Universality—Philip evangelized a Gentile. He first won the Samaritans (partly Jewish people). Then he gave the gospel to a God-fearing Gentile and won him to faith in Jesus Christ. This was another significant breakthrough. Again, it demonstrated that the gospel is for all people of all colors, races, cultures, and religious backgrounds. Notice, in the attempt to witness to the eunuch, Philip preached Christ. It is the message of Jesus that wins. See note on 2:17–40.

8:26–40 MISSIONS, Examples—This passage describes a bridge in missions moving from Samaria toward the ends of the earth as called for in 1:8. Philip had gone to the Samaritans to share Christ. The Samaritans lived at some distance geographically from Judea, but at a great distance culturally, socially, and religiously. See note on 1:6–8. God led Philip into a still wider circle to reach an Ethiopian who was a eunuch and of a different race. The Holy Spirit leads His people into missions in and beyond the home community. Several features in this incident make it most instructive in missions: (1) sometimes the Spirit's call to missions comes in the midst of a fruitful ministry (8:5–8,12,25); (2) God sometimes has prepared plans and people of which we are not aware (v 26); (3) the central message of missions is the good news about Jesus (v 35); and (4) when we are obedient to God's command, He brings results (vv 36–39).

8:30–38 REVELATION, Jesus Christ—Authoritative Scripture's meaning is not always easy to understand, especially for the untrained. Scripture points to Jesus and leads to confession of faith, salvation, and baptism.

8:34–35 EDUCATION, Evangelists—In an ideal teaching situation, an enthusiastic and knowledgeable teacher sits in intimate conversation with a highly motivated learner explaining the meaning of the Word of God. In a sense, all personal evangelism involves such intimacy. See note on 4:1–4.

8:35 PROCLAMATION, Central Theme—See note on 1 Co 2:2.

8:36–39 ORDINANCES, Baptism as Confession—Some late manuscripts of the New Testament (See NIV footnote) include v 37, in which the eunuch confessed Jesus Christ as the Son of God before Philip baptized him. Although earlier manuscripts do not have this confession at this particular point, it is clear throughout the Book of Acts that only those who believed the gospel and confessed Jesus as the Christ, the Son of God, were baptized. The authority for Philip to baptize came not from any earthly organization but directly from Christ through the Holy Spirit. As the church became established more firmly, baptism and the Lord's Supper, the two New Testament ordinances, were observed in the local church. The Spirit commanded Philip to go to the eunuch's chariot and then, after the mission was completed, took him away (8:29,39).

8:39 HOLY SPIRIT, Mission—The Spirit guided the church in a general way to preach Christ. On some special occasions, He also guided people to witness to specific persons or groups. The power of the Spirit led the church in its great world mission. Personal witnessing to individuals is the foundation of that mission. This, too, is the Spirit's work. The Spirit may have taken Philip away in an unusual manner. See

up out of the water, the Spirit of the Lord
suddenly took Philip away,[c] and the eunuch did not see him again, but went on
his way rejoicing. 40 Philip, however, appeared at Azotus and traveled about,
preaching the gospel in all the towns[d]
until he reached Caesarea.[e]

Chapter 9

Saul's Conversion

9:1–19pp — Ac 22:3–16; 26:9–18

MEANWHILE, Saul was still breathing
out murderous threats against the
Lord's disciples.[f] He went to the high
priest 2 and asked him for letters to the
synagogues in Damascus,[g] so that if he
found any there who belonged to the
Way,[h] whether men or women, he might
take them as prisoners to Jerusalem. 3 As
he neared Damascus on his journey, suddenly a light from heaven flashed around
him.[i] 4 He fell to the ground and heard a
voice[j] say to him, "Saul, Saul, why do
you persecute me?"
5 "Who are you, Lord?" Saul asked.
"I am Jesus, whom you are persecuting," he replied. 6 "Now get up and go
into the city, and you will be told what
you must do."[k]
7 The men traveling with Saul stood
there speechless; they heard the sound[l]
but did not see anyone.[m] 8 Saul got up
from the ground, but when he opened his
eyes he could see nothing.[n] So they led
him by the hand into Damascus. 9 For
three days he was blind, and did not eat
or drink anything.
10 In Damascus there was a disciple
named Ananias. The Lord called to him in
a vision,[o] "Ananias!"
"Yes, Lord," he answered.
11 The Lord told him, "Go to the house
of Judas on Straight Street and ask for a
man from Tarsus[p] named Saul, for he is
praying. 12 In a vision he has seen a man
named Ananias come and place his hands
on[q] him to restore his sight."
13 "Lord," Ananias answered, "I have
heard many reports about this man and
all the harm he has done to your saints[r]
in Jerusalem.[s] 14 And he has come here
with authority from the chief priests[t] to
arrest all who call on your name."[u]
15 But the Lord said to Ananias, "Go!
This man is my chosen instrument[v] to
carry my name before the Gentiles[w] and
their kings[x] and before the people of Israel. 16 I will show him how much he
must suffer for my name."[y]
17 Then Ananias went to the house and
entered it. Placing his hands on[z] Saul, he
said, "Brother Saul, the Lord—Jesus,
who appeared to you on the road as you
were coming here—has sent me so that
you may see again and be filled with the
Holy Spirit."[a] 18 Immediately, something
like scales fell from Saul's eyes, and he
could see again. He got up and was baptized,[b] 19 and after taking some food, he
regained his strength.

8:39 [c]1Ki 18:12; 2Ki 2:16; Eze 3:12, 14; 8:3; 11:1,24; 43:5; 2Co 12:2; 1Th 4:17; Rev 12:5
8:40 [d]ver 25 [e]Ac 10:1,24; 12:19; 21:8,16; 23:23,33; 25:1,4,6, 13
9:1 [f]S Ac 8:3
9:2 [g]Isa 17:1; Jer 49:23 [h]Ac 19:9, 23; 22:4; 24:14,22
9:3 [i]1Co 15:8
9:4 [j]Isa 6:8
9:6 [k]ver 16; Eze 3:22
9:7 [l]Jn 12:29 [m]Da 10:7
9:8 [n]ver 18
9:10 [o]Ac 10:3,17, 19; 12:9; 16:9,10; 18:9
9:11 [p]ver 30; Ac 11:25; 21:39; 22:3
9:12 [q]S Mk 5:23
9:13 [r]ver 32; Ac 26:10; Ro 1:7; 15:25,26,31; 16:2, 15; Eph 1:1; Php 1:1 [s]S Ac 8:3
9:14 [t]ver 2,21 [u]S Ac 2:21
9:15 [v]Ac 13:2; Ro 1:1; Gal 1:15; 1Ti 1:12 [w]Ro 11:13; 15:15, 16; Gal 1:16; 2:7,8 [x]Ac 25:22,23; 26:1
9:16 [y]Ac 20:23; 21:11; 2Co 6:4-10; 11:23-27; 2Ti 1:8; 2:3,9
9:17 [z]S Ac 6:6 [a]S Lk 1:15
9:18 [b]S Ac 2:38

---

2 Ki 2:16; Eze 2:2; 3:12,14,24; 11:1,24; 43:5; notes on 1 Ki 18:12; Eze 8:3.

9:1–18 JESUS CHRIST, Ascension—The ascended Christ spoke to Saul of Tarsus converting Him from persecutor to proclaimer. To persecute the church is to persecute Jesus. Christ also directed Ananias to minister to Paul. Jesus is called Lord. See note on 2:23–36.

9:2–31 THE CHURCH, People of God—Both Damascus and Jerusalem had local groups of disciples assembling for worship and fellowship. Both were churches, local representations of the entire church. Persecution made the church cautious. Still God brought new leadership to the church. Any action of persecuting the church is persecuting Jesus (v 5) because the church is Christ's body representing His presence and mission on earth. Whether in Damascus or in other parts of the world, those who serve Christ are the people of God and remain under His caring eye—even in the midst of persecution. One name for the early church was "the Way," a name which showed the church as pointing to Christ and, thus, to the Way of eternal life (Jn 14:6).

9:3–8 REVELATION, Visions—Jesus appeared in a personal vision to lead Saul to salvation. Saul saw what others did not. See note on 7:55.

9:11 PRAYER, Commitment—The Lord reported to Ananias that Paul was praying. It is His nature to know that. Saul was fasting and praying. Committing himself to God after his saving experience, Ananias supplied at least a portion of the answer to Saul's prayer. A saving experience with Christ leads us to prayer.

9:13–14 THE CHURCH, Saints—The saints are people who call on Christ for salvation and direction. See notes on Ro 1:7; 1 Co 1:2.

9:15–16 ELECTION, Mission—The conversion of Saul was for the sake of Gentiles who would become a part of God's elect. God mysteriously used a persecutor of the church to reveal the election of the Gentiles. Such a conversion reveals the depth of God's love and the mystery of election.

9:15 EVANGELISM, Call to Evangelize—When Paul met Jesus Christ, it meant conversion, salvation, and a call to evangelize others. Paul's commission was special because he became the "apostle to the Gentiles" (Ro 11:13). The principle of the call to evangelize is for every believer. Genuine believers are saved so as to carry the gospel message to "Gentiles and their kings and before the people of Israel," i.e., to all people. The call to witness for Christ is a direct result of redemption. No one is exempt.

9:17 HOLY SPIRIT, Fills—See note on 6:1–6.

9:18 MIRACLE, Faith—The sightlessness of Saul after his encounter with the Lord and the blinding light lasted three days (v 9). Under the merciful ministry of Ananias "scales" fell from his eyes, and he could see again. His spiritual sight was even clearer. The transformation from Saul the persecutor to Paul the preacher was a greater miracle than the blinding and healing of Paul. In faith each of us can receive spiritual sight and transformation.

9:18 ORDINANCES, Baptism as Confession—When Ananias came to Saul, the first thing he did was to identify the One who sent him, the Lord Jesus, as the same One whom Saul met on the road to Damascus. Ananias laid his hands on him, and the scales fell from Saul's eyes. Although Saul had been blinded by the encounter with Jesus on the road, he could now see clearly, and was baptized. The movement was from darkness to light. Saul the persecutor was then identified by his baptism as a follower of Jesus.

Saul in Damascus and Jerusalem

Saul spent several days with the disciples[c] in Damascus.[d] 20At once he began
to preach in the synagogues[e] that Jesus is
the Son of God.[f] 21All those who heard
him were astonished and asked, "Isn't he
the man who raised havoc in Jerusalem
among those who call on this name?[g]
And hasn't he come here to take them as
prisoners to the chief priests?"[h] 22Yet
Saul grew more and more powerful and
baffled the Jews living in Damascus by
proving that Jesus is the Christ.[o] [i]
23After many days had gone by, the
Jews conspired to kill him,[j] 24but Saul
learned of their plan.[k] Day and night
they kept close watch on the city gates in
order to kill him. 25But his followers took
him by night and lowered him in a basket
through an opening in the wall.[l]
26When he came to Jerusalem,[m] he
tried to join the disciples, but they were
all afraid of him, not believing that he
really was a disciple. 27But Barnabas[n]
took him and brought him to the apostles.
He told them how Saul on his journey
had seen the Lord and that the Lord had
spoken to him,[o] and how in Damascus
he had preached fearlessly in the name of
Jesus.[p] 28So Saul stayed with them and
moved about freely in Jerusalem, speaking boldly in the name of the Lord. 29He
talked and debated with the Grecian
Jews,[q] but they tried to kill him.[r]
30When the brothers[s] learned of this,
they took him down to Caesarea[t] and
sent him off to Tarsus.[u]
31Then the church throughout Judea,
Galilee and Samaria[v] enjoyed a time of
peace. It was strengthened; and encouraged by the Holy Spirit, it grew in numbers,[w] living in the fear of the Lord.

Aeneas and Dorcas

32As Peter traveled about the country,
he went to visit the saints[x] in Lydda.
33There he found a man named Aeneas, a
paralytic who had been bedridden for
eight years. 34"Aeneas," Peter said to
him, "Jesus Christ heals you.[y] Get up
and take care of your mat." Immediately
Aeneas got up. 35All those who lived in
Lydda and Sharon[z] saw him and turned
to the Lord.[a]
36In Joppa[b] there was a disciple named
Tabitha (which, when translated, is Dorcas[p]), who was always doing good[c] and
helping the poor. 37About that time she
became sick and died, and her body was
washed and placed in an upstairs room.[d]
38Lydda was near Joppa; so when the disciples[e] heard that Peter was in Lydda,
they sent two men to him and urged him,
"Please come at once!"
39Peter went with them, and when he
arrived he was taken upstairs to the
room. All the widows[f] stood around
him, crying and showing him the robes
and other clothing that Dorcas had made
while she was still with them.
40Peter sent them all out of the room;[g]
then he got down on his knees[h] and
prayed. Turning toward the dead woman,
he said, "Tabitha, get up."[i] She opened

9:19 [c]S Ac 11:26 [d]Ac 26:20
9:20 [e]Ac 13:5,14; 14:1; 17:2,10,17; 18:4,19; 19:8 [f]S Mt 4:3
9:21 [g]S Ac 8:3 [h]ver 14
9:22 [i]S Lk 2:11; Ac 5:42; 17:3; 18:5,28
9:23 [j]S Ac 20:3
9:24 [k]Ac 20:3,19; 23:16,30
9:25 [l]1Sa 19:12; 2Co 11:32,33
9:26 [m]Ac 22:17; 26:20; Gal 1:17,18
9:27 [n]S Ac 4:36 [o]ver 3-6 [p]ver 20,22
9:29 [q]Ac 6:1 [r]2Co 11:26
9:30 [s]S Ac 1:16 [t]S Ac 8:40 [u]S ver 11
9:31 [v]Ac 8:1 [w]S Ac 2:41
9:32 [x]S ver 13
9:34 [y]Ac 3:6,16; 4:10
9:35 [z]1Ch 5:16; 27:29; SS 2:1; Isa 33:9; 35:2; 65:10 [a]S Ac 2:41
9:36 [b]Jos 19:46; 2Ch 2:16; Ezr 3:7; Jnh 1:3; Ac 10:5 [c]1Ti 2:10; Tit 3:8
9:37 [d]Ac 1:13; 20:8
9:38 [e]S Ac 11:26
9:39 [f]Ac 6:1; 1Ti 5:3
9:40 [g]Mt 9:25 [h]Lk 22:41; Ac 7:60 [i]S Lk 7:14

[o]22 Or *Messiah* [p]36 Both *Tabitha* (Aramaic) and *Dorcas* (Greek) mean *gazelle.*

9:20 PROCLAMATION, Central Theme—Jesus is the center of Christian preaching. See notes on 3:11–26; 8:4–5.

9:22 JESUS CHRIST, Christ—Early Christian witness to the Jews centered in using Scripture to prove Jesus was Messiah. See note on 5:42.

9:31 HOLY SPIRIT, Church—"Timid" does not belong in the church's vocabulary. The Spirit gives the church strength and courage to accomplish its mission. Before the early church reached out to "God-fearers"—non-Jews who followed all Jewish practices open to uncircumcised people—(10:2), the Spirit gave the church a peaceful time of numerical growth and deepened commitment. The Spirit works with the entire church as well as individual members to provide power and guidance in the astonishing mission to witness to every person on earth. See note on 1:8.

9:31 SALVATION, Fear of God—The early church, living in the fear of the Lord, grew and prospered. Believers who live in the fear of God can count on His blessings. See notes on Pr 1:7,29; Mt 9:8.

9:31 EVANGELISM, Holy Spirit—Church growth depends on God's strength and encouragement provided by the Holy Spirit. The result is a reverent, worshiping, witnessing church. See notes on 4:1–4; 6:7.

9:32–43 MIRACLE, Faith—Miracles lead to church growth. Peter and John had already caused great commotion with the healing of the lame man at the Temple. See note on 3:1–16. Peter's reputation was that of a preacher/healer. Aeneas had been an invalid for eight years—paralyzed. Peter took no credit to himself. Aeneas arose from his bed, and many believed in the Lord. In nearby Joppa, a beloved disciple, Dorcas, died. The Christians sent for Peter, knowing of his healings. The miracle was quickly and unceremoniously accomplished. Many "believed in the Lord." The growth in the number of disciples serves to confirm the church's faith in the miracle-working ministry of church leaders. Such leaders must be careful not to take credit for the church's growth. All praise must go to Christ, the Source of miracles.

9:32 THE CHURCH, Saints—See notes on Ro 1:7; 1 Co 1:2.

9:33 JESUS CHRIST, Miracles—See note on 3:16.

9:35,42 JESUS CHRIST, Lord—Christian conversion centers on Jesus becoming Lord of a person's life. See note on 2:23–36.

9:36–41 THE CHURCH, Saints—Saints let people see God's love as they help the poor and do good. God works through such ministries to bring other people to believe in Christ. Thus the church grows. See notes on Ro 1:7; 1 Co 1:2.

9:36–39 CHURCH LEADERS, Widow—Widows were a recognized group in the church who had a special ministry assigned to them. Their primary responsibilities on behalf of the community were works of charity and prayer. See 1 Ti 5:3–13.

9:40 PRAYER, Petition—The church had prayed (4:30) that "signs and wonders" would be performed. This mighty work of faith was by the same man whom Jesus had reprimanded for his "little faith" in Mt 8:26. Note that he knelt; humility and faith go together. Prayer can lead to healing when it accomplishes His larger purpose (v 42).

her eyes, and seeing Peter she sat up.
41He took her by the hand and helped her
to her feet. Then he called the believers
and the widows and presented her to
them alive. 42This became known all over
Joppa, and many people believed in the
Lord.[j] 43Peter stayed in Joppa for some
time with a tanner named Simon.[k]

Chapter 10

Cornelius Calls for Peter

At Caesarea[l] there was a man named
Cornelius, a centurion in what was
known as the Italian Regiment. 2He and
all his family were devout and God-fearing;[m] he gave generously to those in need
and prayed to God regularly. 3One day at
about three in the afternoon[n] he had a
vision.[o] He distinctly saw an angel[p] of
God, who came to him and said, "Cornelius!"

4Cornelius stared at him in fear. "What
is it, Lord?" he asked.

The angel answered, "Your prayers
and gifts to the poor have come up as a
memorial offering[q] before God.[r] 5Now
send men to Joppa[s] to bring back a man
named Simon who is called Peter. 6He is
staying with Simon the tanner,[t] whose
house is by the sea."

7When the angel who spoke to him had
gone, Cornelius called two of his servants
and a devout soldier who was one of his
attendants. 8He told them everything that
had happened and sent them to Joppa.[u]

Peter's Vision

10:9–32Ref — Ac 11:5–14

9About noon the following day as they
were on their journey and approaching
the city, Peter went up on the roof[v] to
pray. 10He became hungry and wanted
something to eat, and while the meal was
being prepared, he fell into a trance.[w]
11He saw heaven opened[x] and something
like a large sheet being let down to earth
by its four corners. 12It contained all
kinds of four-footed animals, as well as
reptiles of the earth and birds of the air.
13Then a voice told him, "Get up, Peter.
Kill and eat."

14"Surely not, Lord!"[y] Peter replied.
"I have never eaten anything impure or
unclean."[z]

15The voice spoke to him a second
time, "Do not call anything impure that
God has made clean."[a]

16This happened three times, and immediately the sheet was taken back to
heaven.

17While Peter was wondering about
the meaning of the vision,[b] the men sent
by Cornelius[c] found out where Simon's
house was and stopped at the gate.
18They called out, asking if Simon who
was known as Peter was staying there.

19While Peter was still thinking about
the vision,[d] the Spirit said[e] to him, "Simon, three[q] men are looking for you.
20So get up and go downstairs. Do not
hesitate to go with them, for I have sent
them."[f]

21Peter went down and said to the
men, "I'm the one you're looking for.
Why have you come?"

22The men replied, "We have come
from Cornelius the centurion. He is a
righteous and God-fearing man,[g] who is
respected by all the Jewish people. A
holy angel told him to have you come
to his house so that he could hear
what you have to say."[h] 23Then Peter
invited the men into the house to be his
guests.

9:42 [j]S Ac 2:41
9:43 [k]Ac 10:6
10:1 [l]S Ac 8:40
10:2 [m]ver 22,35; Ac 13:16,26
10:3 [n]Ps 55:17; Ac 3:1 [o]S Ac 9:10 [p]S Ac 5:19
10:4 [q]Ps 20:3; S Mt 10:42; 26:13 [r]Rev 8:4
10:5 [s]S Ac 9:36
10:6 [t]Ac 9:43
10:8 [u]S Ac 9:36
10:9 [v]S Mt 24:17
10:10 [w]Ac 22:17
10:11 [x]S Mt 3:16
10:14 [y]Ac 9:5 [z]Lev 11:4-8,13-20; 20:25; Dt 14:3-20; Eze 4:14
10:15 [a]ver 28; Ge 9:3; Mt 15:11; Lk 11:41; Ac 11:9; Ro 14:14,17,20; 1Co 10:25; 1Ti 4:3, 4; Tit 1:15
10:17 [b]S Ac 9:10 [c]ver 7,8
10:19 [d]S Ac 9:10 [e]S Ac 8:29
10:20 [f]Ac 15:7-9
10:22 [g]ver 2 [h]Ac 11:14

[q]*19* One early manuscript *two;* other manuscripts do not have the number.

9:41–42 SALVATION, Belief—The early Christians were called believers. Raising Dorcas from death gave Peter and the church opportunity to share the news of Christ's power and increase the number of believers. Miracles can lead to true belief but do not necessarily do so (Jn 11:45–46).

10:1–48 EVANGELISM, Universality—God leads His people to share the good news with all people. Roman race and employment by the enemy army did not exclude Cornelius from the gospel. God's plan is to bless all peoples through the gospel. He calls us to take an active role in fulfilling the plan. See note on 8:26–40.

10:2–6 PRAYER, Persistence—Cornelius was a Gentile God-fearer. (He had not formally converted to the Jewish faith.) He "prayed regularly." The 3:00 PM hour was the second of three prescribed hours of prayer for the Jews. See note on 3:1. His vision occurred while he was in prayer. The angel indicated his prayers were answered, having been remembered by God. Regular prayer will eventually result in receiving God's answer.

10:3–18 REVELATION, Visions—God declared Himself in a vision interpreted by an angel to Cornelius and put the praying Peter into a trance to receive a vision repeated three times. These visions occurred at a point of spiritual need in both lives. God used the visions to begin the mission outside Judaism.

10:9 PRAYER, Biblical Characters—Peter was a man of prayer (3:1; 9:40). The apostles gave their attention to prayer (6:4). His vision and Cornelius' vision (vv 2–6) occurred while they were in prayer. God uses praying persons to accomplish His will.

10:19 HOLY SPIRIT, Mission—The Spirit sometimes guides the church in specific ways to accomplish its world mission. The Spirit clearly told Peter to go with the three messengers from Cornelius. This event is important in two ways. First, since Pentecost Peter had been the outstanding spokesman for the church, so it was particularly important that the Spirit guide him. Second, Cornelius was the first Gentile to become a Christian, and it was crucially important for the church to realize its mission included Gentiles as well as Jews and Samaritans. The Spirit was leading the church, represented by Peter, over what is perhaps the single most important threshold it would ever have to cross—the racial barrier. The Spirit seeks to break down every barrier which would prevent us from witnessing to any person who does not trust Christ.

Peter at Cornelius' House

The next day Peter started out with
them, and some of the brothers[i] from
Joppa went along.[j] 24The following day
he arrived in Caesarea.[k] Cornelius was
expecting them and had called together
his relatives and close friends. 25As Peter
entered the house, Cornelius met him
and fell at his feet in reverence. 26But Peter made him get up. "Stand up," he said,
"I am only a man myself."[l]

27Talking with him, Peter went inside
and found a large gathering of people.[m]
28He said to them: "You are well aware
that it is against our law for a Jew to associate with a Gentile or visit him.[n] But
God has shown me that I should not call
any man impure or unclean.[o] 29So when
I was sent for, I came without raising any
objection. May I ask why you sent for
me?"

30Cornelius answered: "Four days ago I
was in my house praying at this hour, at
three in the afternoon. Suddenly a man in
shining clothes[p] stood before me 31and
said, 'Cornelius, God has heard your
prayer and remembered your gifts to the
poor. 32Send to Joppa for Simon who is
called Peter. He is a guest in the home of
Simon the tanner, who lives by the sea.'
33So I sent for you immediately, and it
was good of you to come. Now we are all
here in the presence of God to listen to
everything the Lord has commanded you
to tell us."

34Then Peter began to speak: "I now
realize how true it is that God does not
show favoritism[q] 35but accepts men from
every nation who fear him and do what is
right.[r] 36You know the message[s] God
sent to the people of Israel, telling the
good news[t] of peace[u] through Jesus
Christ, who is Lord of all.[v] 37You know
what has happened throughout Judea, beginning in Galilee after the baptism that
John preached— 38how God anointed[w]
Jesus of Nazareth with the Holy Spirit and
power, and how he went around doing
good and healing[x] all who were under
the power of the devil, because God was
with him.[y]

39"We are witnesses[z] of everything he
did in the country of the Jews and in Jerusalem. They killed him by hanging him
on a tree,[a] 40but God raised him from the

10:23 [i]S Ac 1:16 [j]ver 45; Ac 11:12
10:24 [k]S Ac 8:40
10:26 [l]Ac 14:15; Rev 19:10; 22:8,9
10:27 [m]ver 24
10:28 [n]Jn 4:9; 18:28; Ac 11:3 [o]S ver 14,15; Ac 15:8,9
10:30 [p]S Jn 20:12
10:34 [q]Dt 10:17; 2Ch 19:7; Job 34:19; Mk 12:14; Ro 2:11; Gal 2:6; Eph 6:9; Col 3:25; Jas 2:1; 1Pe 1:17
10:35 [r]Ac 15:9
10:36 [s]1Jn 1:5 [t]S Ac 13:32 [u]S Lk 2:14 [v]S Mt 28:18
10:38 [w]S Ac 4:26 [x]S Mt 4:23 [y]S Jn 3:2
10:39 [z]ver 41; S Lk 24:48 [a]S Ac 5:30

10:25–26 DISCIPLESHIP, Spiritual Leaders—Ministry should bring honor and reverence to God, not to human ministers. Peter, one of the apostles, was on a special mission for God when he entered Cornelius' house. He evidently was surprised when Cornelius fell down in reverence before him. Peter wasted no time in letting him know that such an expression was not appropriate. He was just a man and was due no such reverence. He then went on with his ministry. See 14:8–15. Spiritual leaders who perform unusual ministries for Christ today need to make sure they are not honored in inapproriate ways. Spiritual leaders point others to God, not to themselves. See note on Heb 13:7,17.

10:28–35 CHRISTIAN ETHICS, Race Relations—Peter's vision was fresh insight to him. Yet, at root it is the same inclusiveness for God's message of faith finally understood by Jonah. Perhaps no prejudice is more dangerous or difficult to displace than one held in place by religious tradition. Place of birth, cultural tradition, color of skin, sex, race, and nationality seem to separate us. The gospel calls us all together as one family in God's church.

10:30 PRAYER, Ordered—See note on vv 2–6. Cornelius' charity showed the genuineness of his prayers.

10:31 STEWARDSHIP, Rewards—Good stewardship shown in care for the needy demonstrates devotion to God. God rewards such devotion through His presence and attention. Good stewardship does not guarantee God will answer our prayers in the way we want. It does lead to a relationship with God in which we know God listens and answers prayers as He sees best. See notes on Mt 6:2–4; 1 Jn 3:17.

10:34–35 GOD, Righteous—Each person has free access to God, for God has no favorites. He is not a respecter of persons and makes no discrimination among people on the earth. He sees us all as persons He has created, as objects of His loving concern. The racial, class, sex, and cultural barriers we experience are our own creation out of our sinfulness. God created our differences, but He did not intend them to be barriers or walls of division separating people. Indeed, the work of God as a righteous God is to destroy all these artificial barriers in the human family. See Gal 3:28.

10:34–35 SALVATION, Fear of God—God accepts Gentiles who fear Him and do what is right. Accident of birth does not give one extra privilege with God or relieve one of responsibility before God. The call to accept His salvation goes out to all.

10:34–48 EVANGELISM, Call to Salvation—Those who are witnesses to the life, death, and resurrection of Jesus must share that salvation message. This passage has special reference to those who witnessed the resurrection of Jesus. The principle of witnessing lives on to all generations. Every believer through faith is a witness to Christ's glorious resurrection. Christians are to be witnesses to the power of the resurrected Christ in our lives and through our verbal witness. As we tell what Christ did in the first century and what He did in our lives, the Spirit leads people to repentance and forgiveness. See note on 24:10–21.

10:36 JESUS CHRIST, Lord—Jesus rules all. Many people do not acknowledge His lordship. Still He has authority over all the universe. See note on 2:23–36.

10:36–43 PROCLAMATION, Gospel—See note on 3:11–26. Jesus' earthly ministry is part of the message to be proclaimed. Preaching is a direct result of Jesus' command (Mt 28:19–20).

10:37,47–48 ORDINANCES, Baptism in Jesus' Name—The church at Jerusalem challenged Peter's authority to baptize the converts at Caesarea. He had to defend his action to the church. The Holy Spirit came in power upon the people and authorized the baptism in water. No one could challenge the Spirit's authority. Peter ordered them to be baptized "in the name of Jesus Christ," identifying them as belonging to Jesus. See note on 8:36–39.

10:38 JESUS CHRIST, Mission—Jesus was the anointed Messiah working under the Spirit's power helping people and defeating the devil through His miracles.

10:38 HOLY SPIRIT, Jesus—See notes on Mt 3:16–17; Lk 4:14. The Spirit as God's presence with Jesus, the Son of God, proved more powerful than Satan as shown by Jesus' healing powers. The Spirit anointed Jesus as the Christ or "Anointed One."

10:40–42 GOD, Sovereignty—The sovereignty of God operated in the resurrection of Jesus, the choosing of witnesses to the resurrection, and the preaching of the gospel of Jesus. This does not mean that God was simply manipulating the events and persons of history. In an unseen way God was at work in the events surrounding the gospel and its spread. The

dead[b] on the third day and caused him to
be seen. 41He was not seen by all the people,[c] but by witnesses whom God had
already chosen—by us who ate[d] and
drank with him after he rose from the
dead. 42He commanded us to preach to
the people[e] and to testify that he is the
one whom God appointed as judge of the
living and the dead.[f] 43All the prophets
testify about him[g] that everyone[h] who
believes[i] in him receives forgiveness of
sins through his name."[j]
44While Peter was still speaking these
words, the Holy Spirit came on[k] all who
heard the message. 45The circumcised believers who had come with Peter[l] were
astonished that the gift of the Holy Spirit
had been poured out[m] even on the Gentiles.[n] 46For they heard them speaking in
tongues[r][o] and praising God.
Then Peter said, 47"Can anyone keep
these people from being baptized with
water?[p] They have received the Holy
Spirit just as we have."[q] 48So he ordered
that they be baptized in the name of Jesus
Christ.[r] Then they asked Peter to stay
with them for a few days.

Chapter 11

Peter Explains His Actions

THE apostles and the brothers[s]
throughout Judea heard that the Gentiles also had received the word of God.[t]
2So when Peter went up to Jerusalem, the
circumcised believers[u] criticized him
3and said, "You went into the house of
uncircumcised men and ate with
them."[v]
4Peter began and explained everything
to them precisely as it had happened: 5"I
was in the city of Joppa praying, and in a
trance I saw a vision.[w] I saw something
like a large sheet being let down from
heaven by its four corners, and it came
down to where I was. 6I looked into it
and saw four-footed animals of the earth,
wild beasts, reptiles, and birds of the air.
7Then I heard a voice telling me, 'Get up,
Peter. Kill and eat.'
8"I replied, 'Surely not, Lord! Nothing
impure or unclean has ever entered my
mouth.'
9"The voice spoke from heaven a second time, 'Do not call anything impure
that God has made clean.'[x] 10This happened three times, and then it was all
pulled up to heaven again.
11"Right then three men who had been
sent to me from Caesarea[y] stopped at the
house where I was staying. 12The Spirit
told[z] me to have no hesitation about going with them.[a] These six brothers[b] also
went with me, and we entered the man's
house. 13He told us how he had seen an
angel[c] appear in his house and say, 'Send
to Joppa for Simon who is called Peter.
14He will bring you a message[d] through
which you and all your household[e] will
be saved.'
15"As I began to speak, the Holy Spirit

10:40 [b]S Ac 2:24
10:41 [c]Jn 14:17,22 [d]Lk 24:43; Jn 21:13; Ac 1:4
10:42 [e]Mt 28:19,20 [f]S Jn 5:22; Ac 17:31; Ro 14:9; 2Co 5:10; 2Ti 4:1; 1Pe 4:5
10:43 [g]Isa 53:11; Ac 26:22 [h]Ac 15:9 [i]S Jn 3:15 [j]S Lk 24:27
10:44 [k]Ac 8:15,16; 11:15; 15:8; 19:6; S Lk 1:15
10:45 [l]ver 23 [m]Ac 2:33,38 [n]Ac 11:18; 15:8
10:46 [o]S Mk 16:17
10:47 [p]Ac 8:36 [q]S Jn 20:22; Ac 11:17
10:48 [r]S Ac 2:38
11:1 [s]S Ac 1:16 [t]S Heb 4:12
11:2 [u]Ac 10:45
11:3 [v]Ac 10:25,28; Gal 2:12
11:5 [w]Ac 10:9-32; S 9:10
11:9 [x]S Ac 10:15
11:11 [y]S Ac 8:40
11:12 [z]S Ac 8:29 [a]Ac 15:9; Ro 3:22 [b]ver 1,29; S Ac 1:16
11:13 [c]S Ac 5:19
11:14 [d]Ac 10:36 [e]Jn 4:53; Ac 16:15, 31-34; 18:8; 1Co 1:11,16

[r]46 Or *other languages*

sovereignty of God does not overrule human free will but works in it and through it. His sovereignty continues to lead us to witness to Christ and His resurrection.

10:41 JESUS CHRIST, Resurrection—Resurrection appearances were not to the crowds but to God's chosen witnesses so they could testify to Him.

10:41–42 ELECTION, Foreknowledge—Christ's choice of disciples involved God's foreknowledge, planning for witnesses to the resurrection. This made God's election purpose possible through the evangelistic witness of the apostles. The doctrine of election is closely related to evangelism and centers on the resurrection of Jesus.

10:42 JESUS CHRIST, Judgment—Jesus as the ascended Lord judges people and will preside over the final judgment. Thus He fulfills the role of the Son of man (Da 7:13–14). Compare Ac 17:31.

10:42 LAST THINGS, Judgment—See note on Jn 5:21–24.

10:42–48 MISSIONS, Scope—God gave the Roman centurion, Cornelius, a vision to prepare him and to bring Simon Peter from Joppa to share Christ. The event clearly shows that God is interested not only in geographical or numerical growth, but also in people from different racial, ethnic, and language backgrounds. Daring to reach across cultural barriers is a crucial element in expansion of the kingdom of God today. As with Peter, God often must nudge us very hard to reach out to those who are different from us.

10:43 JESUS CHRIST, Fulfilled—See notes on 3:18; 7:52.

10:44–47 HOLY SPIRIT, Indwells—All believers receive the Spirit to live in and direct their lives. Cornelius and the other Gentiles received the Spirit in the same manner with the same signs as the Jewish Christians at Pentecost received Him (ch 2). The milestone in Christian missions so impressed Peter he reported the event enthusiastically to the Jerusalem church (11:1–18; 15:7–11). The Spirit came before baptism and so cannot be connected to baptism in any causal way. See note on 8:14–17.

10:48 JESUS CHRIST, Lord—Jesus' name was pronounced over persons being baptized. This placed persons under Jesus' power and signified Jesus was Lord of their lives and hope of their resurrection. Compare 2:38.

11:5,18 PRAYER, Answer—See note on 1:9. Actions done through God's leadership in answering prayer are right. They may be questioned by the larger community. The community's understanding serves to verify God's leadership. If the community is not convinced the action is God's will, further prayer is needed on both sides. Agreement that God's will is being done leads everyone to praise God.

11:14 SALVATION, Initiative—God took the initiative in saving the non-Jews. Cornelius and his household were the first clear-cut case in the early apostolic church of Gentiles being saved. Other examples of household salvation are 16:15, 31–34; Jn 4:53; and possibly Lk 19:9. A New Testament household included the whole family and possibly slaves and employees also. The sense of corporate identity and solidarity was more visible in the first Christian century than it is in modern Western culture. However, these Scriptural cases of household salvation do not teach infant baptism. Nor do they rule out the necessity of personal faith in each individual believer. They encourage us to try to win whole families to Christ so that individual believers in a household will have a better support system for their growth in Christ. See note on 16:30–31.

11:15–18 ELECTION, Other Nations—Some of the Jew-

came on[f] them as he had come on us at
the beginning.[g] 16Then I remembered
what the Lord had said: 'John baptized
with[s] water,[h] but you will be baptized
with the Holy Spirit.'[i] 17So if God gave
them the same gift[j] as he gave us,[k] who
believed in the Lord Jesus Christ, who
was I to think that I could oppose God?"
18When they heard this, they had no
further objections and praised God, saying, "So then, God has granted even the
Gentiles repentance unto life."[l]

The Church in Antioch

19Now those who had been scattered
by the persecution in connection with
Stephen[m] traveled as far as Phoenicia,
Cyprus and Antioch,[n] telling the message
only to Jews. 20Some of them, however,
men from Cyprus[o] and Cyrene,[p] went to
Antioch[q] and began to speak to Greeks
also, telling them the good news[r] about
the Lord Jesus. 21The Lord's hand was
with them,[s] and a great number of people believed and turned to the Lord.[t]
22News of this reached the ears of the
church at Jerusalem, and they sent Barnabas[u] to Antioch. 23When he arrived and
saw the evidence of the grace of God,[v]
he was glad and encouraged them all to
remain true to the Lord with all their
hearts.[w] 24He was a good man, full of the
Holy Spirit[x] and faith, and a great number of people were brought to the Lord.[y]
25Then Barnabas went to Tarsus[z] to
look for Saul, 26and when he found him,
he brought him to Antioch. So for a
whole year Barnabas and Saul met with
the church and taught great numbers of
people. The disciples[a] were called Christians first[b] at Antioch.
27During this time some prophets[c]
came down from Jerusalem to Antioch.
28One of them, named Agabus,[d] stood up
and through the Spirit predicted that a
severe famine would spread over the entire Roman world.[e] (This happened during the reign of Claudius.)[f] 29The disciples,[g] each according to his ability, decided to provide help[h] for the brothers[i]
living in Judea. 30This they did, sending

11:15 [f]S Ac 10:44 [g]Ac 2:4 **11:16** [h]S Mk 1:4 [i]S Mk 1:8 **11:17** [j]Ac 2:38 [k]Ac 10:45,47 **11:18** [l]Ro 10:12, 13; 2Co 7:10 **11:19** [m]Ac 8:1,4 [n]ver 26,27; Ac 13:1; 14:26; 18:22; Gal 2:11 **11:20** [o]Ac 4:36 [p]S Mt 27:32 [q]S ver 19 [r]S Ac 13:32 **11:21** [s]Lk 1:66 [t]S Ac 2:41 **11:22** [u]S Ac 4:36 **11:23** [v]Ac 13:43; 14:26; 15:40; 20:24 [w]Ac 14:22 **11:24** [x]S Lk 1:15 [y]S Ac 2:41 **11:25** [z]S Ac 9:11 **11:26** [a]ver 29; Ac 6:1,2; 9:19,26, 38; 13:52 [b]Ac 26:28; 1Pe 4:16 **11:27** [c]Ac 13:1; 15:32; 1Co 11:4; 12:28,29; 14:29,32, 37; S Eph 4:11 **11:28** [d]Ac 21:10 [e]S Mt 24:14 [f]Ac 18:2 **11:29** [g]S ver 26 [h]Ro 15:26; 2Co 8:1-4; 9:2 [i]ver 1,12; S Ac 1:16

[s]*16* Or *in*

ish Christians were narrow of mind and heart, continuing the nationalistic religion of their ancestors. The gift of the Spirit to the Gentiles shocked them. The elect cannot predict what God will do next or whom He will favor with spiritual or material blessings. The elect cannot control either God or the Holy Spirit. The Holy Spirit in a life shows the person is one of God's elect.

11:15–16 ORDINANCES, Baptism by Holy Spirit—Peter defended his acceptance and baptism of the Gentile converts in Caesarea by appealing to the promise of Jesus that although John baptized in water, they would be baptized with the Holy Spirit. When the Holy Spirit came in power upon the converts at Caesarea, God was obviously approving them. God and His Spirit are the final authorities as to who should be baptized. Human prejudice and tradition should not prohibit believers from baptism.

11:17 GOD, Sovereignty—Peter here recognized the sovereign will of God and respected it. God gives believers His Spirit regardless of human barriers. We must find the will of God and do it in our lives, lest we be found fighting against God. God's will ought to be seen as the ultimate authority over us. Our opinions and wishes pale into insignificance alongside the will of God. This is the meaning of His being Lord.

11:18 SALVATION, Eternal Life—This is the same kind of life referred to elsewhere in Scripture as eternal life. Eternal life is God's gift to both Gentile and Jewish Christians. Repentance leads to eternal life. See note on 10:34–35.

11:21 JESUS CHRIST, Lord—Jesus was present in a powerful way with the early church, leading to conversions and church growth. See note on 9:35,42.

11:21 EVANGELISM, Power—The great Gentile church at Antioch was born. Out of it later came the first Gentile missionary thrust (13:13). See notes on 4:1–4; 5:12–14.

11:22–25 EVANGELISM, *Power*—An obedient life, faith, and the Holy Spirit provide an evangelist's power.

11:23 GOD, Grace—The evidence of the grace of God referred to here was the salvation of Gentiles. Jesus had specifically commanded the church to take the gospel to all people. Still the early Christians—for the most part Jewish by background—were hesitant to go to the Gentiles. It took special leading from the Holy Spirit for the church to realize fully that the gospel was indeed for all people without distinction. This was implicit from the beginning of God's redemptive work. The covenant with Abraham specifically stated that the covenant community of his descendants was to be a source of blessings to all nations. God has always been gracious to all. His people have been much more hesitant to share God with other people. See note on Ge 12:1–3.

11:24 HOLY SPIRIT, Fills—The Spirit gave Barnabas the gift of preaching, so that many were brought to Christ through his ministry. To be filled with the Spirit is to be equipped to preach the gospel. See note on 6:1–6.

11:26 THE CHURCH, Local Body—A group of believers in one place form God's church there. The Antioch church so displayed the Spirit of Christ they were named Christians after their Master. The church is eager to hear and obey Christ's authoritative teaching. See notes on 4:32; 8:1.

11:26 EDUCATION, Pastors—Teaching is a major pastoral function. As in the case of Barnabas and Saul, the spiritual shepherds of Christian congregations are responsible for communicating the Word of truth faithfully and accurately. See note on Eph 4:11–16.

11:28 HOLY SPIRIT, Protects—The Spirit protects God's people in many ways. He can warn of approaching danger. Agabus, a prophet, predicted a coming famine through knowledge the Spirit gave. The Spirit does not always choose to warn His people of such dangers. At times He gives strength and faith to endure them. Always He is present to help His people in time of danger. See note on 20:22–23.

11:28 HISTORY, Nature—God controls the history of the natural world and can give His prophets insight to predict natural catastrophes.

11:29 STEWARDSHIP, Care of Needy—Giving according to one's ability is an essential part of the Christian giving principle. Christians meet the needs of fellow believers who are hurting even when the believers are not personally known or do not live in the same community. Giving is not the responsibility of a few wealthy members but of all disciples. See notes on Mt 5:42; 1 Co 16:1–4; 1 Jn 3:17.

11:30 CHURCH LEADERS, Elder—Elders, a familiar title in Judaism, was used to designate certain leaders in the early church. They functioned alongside the apostles in Jerusalem. See 15:2,4,6,22,23; 16:4; 21:18. They apparently were part of a pastoral leadership team in the church in Jerusalem, responsible for overseeing the ministry of the congregation. Today churches use various titles for the members of the pastoral

their gift to the elders[j] by Barnabas[k] and
Saul.[l]

Chapter 12

Peter's Miraculous Escape From Prison

IT was about this time that King Herod[m]
arrested some who belonged to the
church, intending to persecute them. 2He
had James, the brother of John,[n] put to
death with the sword.[o] 3When he saw
that this pleased the Jews,[p] he proceeded
to seize Peter also. This happened during
the Feast of Unleavened Bread.[q] 4After
arresting him, he put him in prison,
handing him over to be guarded by four
squads of four soldiers each. Herod intended to bring him out for public trial
after the Passover.[r]
5So Peter was kept in prison, but the
church was earnestly praying to God for
him.[s]
6The night before Herod was to bring
him to trial, Peter was sleeping between
two soldiers, bound with two chains,[t]
and sentries stood guard at the entrance.
7Suddenly an angel[u] of the Lord appeared
and a light shone in the cell. He struck
Peter on the side and woke him up.
"Quick, get up!" he said, and the chains
fell off Peter's wrists.[v]
8Then the angel said to him, "Put on
your clothes and sandals." And Peter did
so. "Wrap your cloak around you and follow me," the angel told him. 9Peter followed him out of the prison, but he had
no idea that what the angel was doing
was really happening; he thought he was
seeing a vision.[w] 10They passed the first
and second guards and came to the iron
gate leading to the city. It opened for
them by itself,[x] and they went through
it. When they had walked the length of
one street, suddenly the angel left him.
11Then Peter came to himself[y] and
said, "Now I know without a doubt that
the Lord sent his angel and rescued me[z]
from Herod's clutches and from everything the Jewish people were anticipat-
ing."
12When this had dawned on him, he
went to the house of Mary the mother of
John, also called Mark,[a] where many
people had gathered and were praying.[b]
13Peter knocked at the outer entrance,
and a servant girl named Rhoda came to
answer the door.[c] 14When she recognized Peter's voice, she was so overjoyed[d] she ran back without opening it
and exclaimed, "Peter is at the door!"
15"You're out of your mind," they told
her. When she kept insisting that it was
so, they said, "It must be his angel."[e]
16But Peter kept on knocking, and
when they opened the door and saw him,
they were astonished. 17Peter motioned
with his hand[f] for them to be quiet and
described how the Lord had brought him
out of prison. "Tell James[g] and the brothers[h] about this," he said, and then he left
for another place.
18In the morning, there was no small
commotion among the soldiers as to what
had become of Peter. 19After Herod had a
thorough search made for him and did
not find him, he cross-examined the
guards and ordered that they be executed.[i]

Herod's Death

Then Herod went from Judea to Caesarea[j] and stayed there a while. 20He had
been quarreling with the people of Tyre
and Sidon;[k] they now joined together
and sought an audience with him. Having
secured the support of Blastus, a trusted
personal servant of the king, they asked
for peace, because they depended on the
king's country for their food supply.[l]
21On the appointed day Herod, wearing his royal robes, sat on his throne and
delivered a public address to the people.
22They shouted, "This is the voice of a
god, not of a man." 23Immediately, be-

11:30 [j]Ac 14:23; 15:2,22; 20:17; 1Ti 5:17; Tit 1:5; Jas 5:14; 1Pe 5:1; 2Jn 1 [k]S Ac 4:36 [l]Ac 12:25
12:1 [m]S Mt 14:1
12:2 [n]S Mt 4:21 [o]Mk 10:39
12:3 [p]Ac 24:27; 25:9 [q]Ex 12:15; 23:15; Ac 20:6
12:4 [r]S Jn 11:55
12:5 [s]S Ac 1:14; Ro 15:30,31; Eph 6:18
12:6 [t]Ac 21:33
12:7 [u]S Ac 5:19 [v]Ps 107:14; Ac 16:26
12:9 [w]S Ac 9:10
12:10 [x]Ac 5:19; 16:26
12:11 [y]Lk 15:17 [z]Ps 34:7; Da 3:28; 6:22; 2Co 1:10; 2Pe 2:9
12:12 [a]ver 25; Ac 13:5,13; 15:37, 39; Col 4:10; 2Ti 4:11; Phm 24; 1Pe 5:13 [b]ver 5
12:13 [c]Jn 18:16,17
12:14 [d]Lk 24:41
12:15 [e]S Mt 18:10
12:17 [f]Ac 13:16; 19:33; 21:40 [g]S Ac 15:13 [h]S Ac 1:16
12:19 [i]Ac 16:27 [j]S Ac 8:40
12:20 [k]S Mt 11:21 [l]1Ki 5:9,11; Eze 27:17

---

leadership team. The New Testament uses titles such as elders, pastors, and bishops for pastoral leaders. See note on 20:17.

12:1–19 EVIL AND SUFFERING, Endurance—Persecution marked the earliest history of the church as Acts repeatedly shows. Jesus had prepared His disciples for this (Mt 5:10–12, 38–48; Jn 15:18–27; 16:1–33). Such persecution pleases God's enemies and may serve selfish, political purposes. Persecution cannot defeat the prayers and faith of God's people. It may provide God opportunity to test and strenghthen His people as we endure persecution.

12:5–17 MIRACLE, Revelation—God reveals Himself through miracles. God sent His messenger to deliver Peter from prison. See note on 5:19. The experience made Peter know without a doubt that God had rescued him. The church learned God answered their prayers. The divine revelation strengthened the church. God's *powerful work in the church always strengthens His people. We need* to pray for the display of His power among us.

12:5–12 PRAYER, Corporate—Troubles of a fellow believer should bring the church to prayer. God at times chooses to respond to the church's intercession in powerful ways. Church prayer needs to be earnest and persistent.

12:20–23 EVIL AND SUFFERING, Punishment—God's punishment for evil and sin is a New Testament teaching as well as an Old Testament one. God's angel killed Herod for his sin. Unlike the Word of God, human claims of divinity and power wither and die.

12:21–23 GOD, Jealous—God takes Himself very seriously and will not share His sovereignty or authority with other gods. He does not permit anyone to usurp His rightful position as Lord. When Herod permitted himself to be praised as a god, God crushed him in wrath. See notes on Eze 16:38; Na 1:2; Mt 3:7–10.

12:23 MIRACLE, Judgment—Opposition to God may bring a miracle of judgment. The Lord works in mysterious ways. How Peter's strange release must have gnawed at Herod! He wanted to be god. He wanted all attention on him, not on Christ and His church. A messenger of the Lord struck him

cause Herod did not give praise to God,
an angel[m] of the Lord struck him down,[n]
and he was eaten by worms and died.
24But the word of God[o] continued to
increase and spread.[p]
25When Barnabas[q] and Saul had finished their mission,[r] they returned
from[t] Jerusalem, taking with them John,
also called Mark.[s]

Chapter 13

Barnabas and Saul Sent Off

IN the church at Antioch[t] there were
prophets[u] and teachers:[v] Barnabas,[w]
Simeon called Niger, Lucius of Cyrene,[x]
Manaen (who had been brought up with
Herod[y] the tetrarch) and Saul. 2While
they were worshiping the Lord and fasting, the Holy Spirit said,[z] "Set apart for
me Barnabas and Saul for the work[a] to
which I have called them."[b] 3So after
they had fasted and prayed, they placed
their hands on them[c] and sent them
off.[d]

On Cyprus

4The two of them, sent on their way by
the Holy Spirit,[e] went down to Seleucia
and sailed from there to Cyprus.[f] 5When
they arrived at Salamis, they proclaimed
the word of God[g] in the Jewish synagogues.[h] John[i] was with them as their
helper.
6They traveled through the whole island until they came to Paphos. There
they met a Jewish sorcerer[j] and false
prophet[k] named Bar-Jesus, 7who was an
attendant of the proconsul,[l] Sergius Pau-
lus. The proconsul, an intelligent man,
sent for Barnabas and Saul because he
wanted to hear the word of God. 8But Ely-

12:23 [m]S Ac 5:19 [n]1Sa 25:38; 2Sa 24:16,17; 2Ki 19:35
12:24 [o]S Heb 4:12 [p]Ac 6:7; 19:20
12:25 [q]S Ac 4:36 [r]Ac 11:30 [s]S ver 12
13:1 [t]S Ac 11:19 [u]S Ac 11:27 [v]S Eph 4:11 [w]S Ac 4:36 [x]S Mt 27:32 [y]S Mt 14:1
13:2 [z]S Ac 8:29 [a]Ac 14:26 [b]Ac 9:15; 22:21
13:3 [c]S Ac 6:6 [d]Ac 14:26
13:4 [e]ver 2,3 [f]Ac 4:36
13:5 [g]S Heb 4:12 [h]S Ac 9:20 [i]S Ac 12:12
13:6 [j]Ac 8:9 [k]S Mt 7:15
13:7 [l]ver 8,12; Ac 18:12; 19:38

[t]25 Some manuscripts *to*

down. Worm-eaten, he died. God can still use His resources to judge human arrogance.

12:24 EVANGELISM, Power—God may use unexpected news in the political sector to empower His church's witness.

13:1–4 HOLY SPIRIT, Leaders—The Spirit calls out leaders for specific tasks in the church's mission. In this instance the Spirit spoke to the church as the church sought God's will by worship and fasting. The Spirit then directed Paul and Barnabus where to go to begin their mission. They did not go independently, however. The church sent them. The Spirit works through the church to send missionary leaders to accomplish the church's mission: proclaiming Jesus to every person in the world.

13:1 THE CHURCH, Local Body—See notes on 4:32; 8:1; 11:26.

13:1 CHURCH LEADERS, Prophet—Prophets received visions from God and declared the divine will for their day. The Holy Spirit spoke through a prophet to lead the church to send out Barnabas and Saul as missionaries to the Mediterranean world. God continues to use various methods and people to reveal His will to His churches.

13:1 EDUCATION, Prophets—Some interpreters believe Luke intended to make no distinction between the prophets and teachers named here. The prophet speaks a fresh word from the Lord; the teacher helps believers deepen their understanding of the word of the Lord, especially in relation to the Scriptures. A prophetic insight often comes in an instructional situation, and the prophetic message frequently serves as a stimulus to learning. By their very nature, prophecy and teaching are companion functions.

13:1–3 EVANGELISM, Call to Evangelize—God started the worldwide mission of the gospel by leading the church to dedicate two experienced evangelists. This is the final significant breakthrough in the New Testament for the spread of the gospel. Paul and Barnabas led the church's active evangelistic efforts among Gentiles "to the ends of the earth" (1:8). See notes on 8:4–8, 25, 26–40; 10:1–48. This monumental missionary movement began in the church using dedicated leaders, who began with worship, prayer, and fasting. Leaders of the movement responded as the Holy Spirit spoke and called. Great missionary evangelism possesses these ingredients.

13:2–3 REVELATION, Spirit—The Spirit of God, active to reveal and interpret God's will, declared that two disciples were to be messengers of the good news to Gentiles. The inspiration of the Spirit enables followers to understand His will in events and plans. Prayer and fasting with reflection and openness prepare people for God's revelation.

13:2–3 WORSHIP, Humility—The early church humbly worshiped God with weeping and fasting. Out of that worship experience God sent the first official missionaries from their group. See note on Jdg 20:26.

13:2–3 PRAYER, Corporate—The Antioch church was given to prayer as was the Jerusalem church. See notes on 1:14, 24–26; 4:24–31. The instruction for the first missionary journey came while they were praying, just as the visions of Cornelius and Peter occurred at times of prayer (10:2–6,9). Prayer allows God to speak to us. The Holy Spirit had already spoken to Saul and Barnabas. The church heard the Lord when they prayed.

13:2–5 MISSIONS, Sending—Antioch is the first church in recorded history to send out foreign missionaries. This church provides a model for missionary-sending churches: (1) God reveals His will to a church that seeks His face in worship, prayer, and fasting; (2) the Holy Spirit speaks to the group sending the missionary, as well as to the individual called (v 2*a*); (3) the Spirit calls individuals to a missions task (v 2*b*); (4) the selection of the missionary by a church, or a board is an awesome responsibility and requires personal dedication and prayer for God's guidance; and (5) sending missionaries calls for support by the home constituency. Two expressions described this enabling process of the church in Antioch—the laying on of hands and the sending on the way. The terms express the blessing, the support, and the encouragement for missionaries. Such support would include prayer (Eph 6:19), finances (Lk 10:7; Ro 10:14) and personal support (Php 1:3–5; 4:10,14–16). Antioch became the sending church with a vision for the world. From there, their missionaries went to Europe and throughout Asia Minor. From here, the spread of the gospel to the ends of the earth continued clear to Rome, the nerve center for reaching the ultimate purpose.

13:3 CHURCH LEADERS, Ordination—The New Testament reports the laying on of hands in a variety of situations. Hands were laid on the sick (9:17; 27:8; Mk 5:23), on converts at baptism (Ac 8:17–19), and as a gesture of blessing on those commissioned for a special work of ministry. The word "ordination" in the technical sense of "ordaining to ministry" does not occur in the New Testament. In this passage, Paul and Barnabas were chosen for a special missionary task but not ordained to a lifetime ministry. Paul insisted that he was an apostle since his conversion and that his apostleship was not of human derivation or authorization (Gal 1:1). The commission came from the Holy Spirit (Ac 13:2), and the church responded by confirming with a public and formal act that God had called them to this particular work. It is not clear who laid hands on them, but perhaps the entire church did. In ordination, the church affirms those who have been chosen by God for special ministry, pledges its wholehearted support, and authorizes them to act in the name of the church.

mas the sorcerer[m] (for that is what his
name means) opposed them and tried to
turn the proconsul[n] from the faith.[o]
9Then Saul, who was also called Paul,
filled with the Holy Spirit,[p] looked
straight at Elymas and said, 10"You are a
child of the devil[q] and an enemy of everything that is right! You are full of all
kinds of deceit and trickery. Will you never stop perverting the right ways of the
Lord?[r] 11Now the hand of the Lord is
against you.[s] You are going to be blind,
and for a time you will be unable to see
the light of the sun."[t]
Immediately mist and darkness came
over him, and he groped about, seeking
someone to lead him by the hand.
12When the proconsul[u] saw what had
happened, he believed, for he was
amazed at the teaching about the Lord.

In Pisidian Antioch

13From Paphos,[v] Paul and his companions sailed to Perga in Pamphylia,[w]
where John[x] left them to return to Jerusalem. 14From Perga they went on to Pi-
sidian Antioch.[y] On the Sabbath[z] they
entered the synagogue[a] and sat down.
15After the reading from the Law[b] and
the Prophets, the synagogue rulers sent
word to them, saying, "Brothers, if you
have a message of encouragement for the
people, please speak."
16Standing up, Paul motioned with his
hand[c] and said: "Men of Israel and you
Gentiles who worship God, listen to me!
17The God of the people of Israel chose
our fathers; he made the people prosper
during their stay in Egypt, with mighty
power he led them out of that country,[d]
18he endured their conduct[u][e] for about
forty years in the desert,[f] 19he overthrew
seven nations in Canaan[g] and gave their
land to his people[h] as their inheritance.[i]
20All this took about 450 years.
"After this, God gave them judges[j] until the time of Samuel the prophet.[k]
21Then the people asked for a king,[l] and
he gave them Saul[m] son of Kish, of the
tribe of Benjamin,[n] who ruled forty
years. 22After removing Saul,[o] he made
David their king.[p] He testified concerning him: 'I have found David son of Jesse
a man after my own heart;[q] he will do
everything I want him to do.'[r]
23"From this man's descendants[s] God
has brought to Israel the Savior[t] Jesus,[u]
as he promised.[v] 24Before the coming of
Jesus, John preached repentance and bap-

13:8 [m]Ac 8:9 [n]S ver 7 [o]Isa 30:11; Ac 6:7
13:9 [p]S Lk 1:15
13:10 [q]Mt 13:38; Jn 8:44 [r]Hos 14:9
13:11 [s]Ex 9:3; 1Sa 5:6,7; Ps 32:4 [t]Ge 19:10,11; 2Ki 6:18
13:12 [u]S ver 7
13:13 [v]ver 6 [w]S Ac 2:10 [x]S Ac 12:12
13:14 [y]Ac 14:19,21 [z]ver 27,42,44; Ac 16:13; 18:4 [a]S Ac 9:20
13:15 [b]Ac 15:21
13:16 [c]S Ac 12:17
13:17 [d]Ex 6:6,7; Dt 7:6-8
13:18 [e]Dt 1:31 [f]Nu 14:33; Ps 95:10; Ac 7:36
13:19 [g]Dt 7:1 [h]Jos 19:51; Ac 7:45 [i]Ps 78:55
13:20 [j]Jdg 2:16 [k]1Sa 3:19,20; Ac 3:24
13:21 [l]1Sa 8:5,19 [m]1Sa 10:1 [n]1Sa 9:1,2
13:22 [o]1Sa 15:23,26 [p]1Sa 16:13; Ps 89:20 [q]1Sa 13:14; Jer 3:15 [r]Isa 44:28
13:23 [s]S Mt 1:1 [t]S Lk 2:11 [u]Mt 1:21 [v]ver 32; 2Sa 7:11; 22:51; Jer 30:9

[u] *18* Some manuscripts *and cared for them*

13:6–17 MIRACLE, Judgment—Not all miracles are examples of healing. Ananias and Sapphira (see note on 5:1–11), Herod (see note on 12:23), and Bar-Jesus experienced the wrath of God as the result of their sin. Bar-Jesus' interference with the Christian witness caused Saul to rebuke him sharply and to pronounce his blindness as the work of the Lord.

13:6–12 EVIL AND SUFFERING, Punishment—Elymas was struck blind for his sin of sorcery and his attempt to prevent others from trusting Christ. See note on 12:20–23.

13:6–12 EVANGELISM, Holy Spirit—As Paul and Barnabas ministered in Paphos, they set the pattern for effective evangelism in the power of the Holy Spirit. The pattern was and always must be: (1) realize there will be problems and confront the opposition; (2) minister in the fullness of the Holy Spirit; (3) bend the opposition in God's power; (4) give the teachings of the Lord clearly and freely; (5) trust God for victory and (6) expect positive results. See Guide to Dealing with Questions and Objections, pp. 1792–1794.

13:9 HOLY SPIRIT, Gifts—God's Spirit equips His chosen leaders to carry out the tasks He has given them. The Spirit called Paul and Barnabas to become missionaries and directed them to Cyprus (vv 1–4). He gave to Paul two gifts for carrying out his ministry. One was the gift of prophecy, of proclaiming Christ, which Paul had been doing for some time. The other was a gift of spiritual discernment which enabled Paul to interpret Elymas's conduct and to pronounce divine judgment upon him (vv 10–11). Paul mentioned this gift of discernment in 1 Co 12:10–11.

13:10 EVIL AND SUFFERING, Satan—Satan works his evil and trickery through people. People who oppose God and His work in the lives of His people are Satan's sons.

13:16–41 REVELATION, History—Paul summarized Israel's history with God and God's intervention and revelation to them over the years. His greatest revelation in history is Jesus Christ and His resurrection. See note on 7:1–53.

13:16–31 HISTORY, Confession—New Testament proclamation continued the Old Testament practice of formulating confessions of faith in narrative form, confessing God's historical acts. New Testament confessions center on the history of Jesus. This confession is a message of salvation available to all peoples—Jews and non-Jews. The confession is not a statement to be memorized and held as a standard of judgment for others. It is a personal formulation of the church's central message.

13:16–41 PROCLAMATION, Gospel—See note on 3:11–26. God's salvation history with Israel is a part of Christian proclamation. Jesus' offer of justification and forgiveness for intentional and unintentional sins through faith is a crucial element of proclamation.

13:16–43 EVANGELISM, Gospel—The evangelistic message shows God's work through all generations to prepare the way for Christ and Christ's work to bring salvation. The resurrection is at the center of the gospel message. The gospel calls on people to repent of sins, experience forgiveness, and believe in Christ for salvation. See note on 2:17–40.

13:17–48 ELECTION, Other Nations—Israel's election promises were fulfilled in Jesus. Most of Abraham's descendants rejected Jesus. Many Gentiles joyously heard and obediently embraced the word of the Lord. In spite of opposition to their accepting the gospel, those elected for salvation were saved. Thank God that the election purposes of God included Gentiles. Thank God for Jewish Christians, small in number, who were "a light to the Gentiles" in carrying salvation to the end of the world that they knew. "Appointed" (v 48; Greek *tasso*) reflects a military term to order troops into battle position. It implies authority of the commander and describes the order or plans established. Salvation of Gentiles was not a historical accident. God planned it and executed orders to bring about the plan. Compare 22:10; Ro 13:1.

13:23 JESUS CHRIST, Savior—Jesus was the hope of Israel, fulfilling the promises to David (2 Sa 7:11–12). He was the Savior for whom Israel waited. Compare Isa 19:20; 62:11; Mic 7:11. See note on Lk 2:11.

13:24 ORDINANCES, Background of Baptism—Jewish proselyte baptism was performed upon Gentiles who converted to Judaism. It was not for Israelites. John's baptism required repentance for everyone, and "all the people of Israel," like everyone else, had to receive baptism. This shows that John's

tism to all the people of Israel.[w] 25 As John
was completing his work,[x] he said: 'Who
do you think I am? I am not that one.[y]
No, but he is coming after me, whose
sandals I am not worthy to untie.'[z]
26 "Brothers,[a] children of Abraham,[b]
and you God-fearing Gentiles, it is to us
that this message of salvation[c] has been
sent. 27 The people of Jerusalem and their
rulers did not recognize Jesus,[d] yet in
condemning him they fulfilled the words
of the prophets[e] that are read every Sabbath. 28 Though they found no proper
ground for a death sentence, they asked
Pilate to have him executed.[f] 29 When
they had carried out all that was written
about him,[g] they took him down from
the tree[h] and laid him in a tomb.[i] 30 But
God raised him from the dead,[j] 31 and for
many days he was seen by those who had
traveled with him from Galilee to Jerusalem.[k] They are now his witnesses[l] to
our people.
32 "We tell you the good news:[m] What
God promised our fathers[n] 33 he has fulfilled for us, their children, by raising up
Jesus.[o] As it is written in the second
Psalm:

" 'You are my Son;
today I have become your
Father.[v]'[w][p]

34 The fact that God raised him from the
dead, never to decay, is stated in these
words:

" 'I will give you the holy and sure
blessings promised to
David.'[x][q]

35 So it is stated elsewhere:

" 'You will not let your Holy One see
decay.'[y][r]

36 "For when David had served God's
purpose in his own generation, he fell
asleep;[s] he was buried with his fathers[t]
and his body decayed. 37 But the one
whom God raised from the dead[u] did not
see decay.
38 "Therefore, my brothers, I want you
to know that through Jesus the forgiveness of sins is proclaimed to you.[v]
39 Through him everyone who believes[w]
is justified from everything you could not
be justified from by the law of Moses.[x]
40 Take care that what the prophets have
said does not happen to you:

41 " 'Look, you scoffers,
wonder and perish,
for I am going to do something in your
days
that you would never believe,
even if someone told you.'[z] "[y]

42 As Paul and Barnabas were leaving
the synagogue,[z] the people invited them
to speak further about these things on the
next Sabbath. 43 When the congregation
was dismissed, many of the Jews and devout converts to Judaism followed Paul
and Barnabas, who talked with them and
urged them to continue in the grace of
God.[a]
44 On the next Sabbath almost the
whole city gathered to hear the word of
the Lord. 45 When the Jews saw the
crowds, they were filled with jealousy
and talked abusively[b] against what Paul
was saying.[c]
46 Then Paul and Barnabas answered
them boldly: "We had to speak the word
of God to you first.[d] Since you reject it
and do not consider yourselves worthy of
eternal life, we now turn to the Gentiles.[e] 47 For this is what the Lord has
commanded us:

13:24 [w]S Mk 1:4
13:25 [x]Ac 20:24 [y]Jn 1:20 [z]Mt 3:11; Jn 1:27
13:26 [a]S Ac 22:5 [b]S Lk 3:8 [c]Ac 4:12; 28:28
13:27 [d]Ac 3:17 [e]S Lk 24:27; S Mt 1:22
13:28 [f]Mt 27:20-25; Ac 3:14
13:29 [g]S Mt 1:22; Lk 18:31 [h]S Ac 5:30 [i]Lk 23:53
13:30 [j]S Mt 16:21; 28:6; S Ac 2:24
13:31 [k]Mt 28:16 [l]S Lk 24:48
13:32 [m]Isa 40:9; 52:7; Ac 5:42; 8:35; 10:36; 14:7, 15,21; 17:18 [n]Ac 26:6; Ro 1:2; 4:13; 9:4
13:33 [o]S Ac 2:24 [p]Ps 2:7; S Mt 3:17
13:34 [q]Isa 55:3
13:35 [r]Ps 16:10; Ac 2:27
13:36 [s]S Mt 9:24 [t]2Sa 7:12; 1Ki 2:10; 2Ch 29:28; Ac 2:29
13:37 [u]S Ac 2:24
13:38 [v]S Lk 24:47; Ac 2:38
13:39 [w]S Jn 3:15 [x]S Ro 3:28
13:41 [y]Hab 1:5
13:42 [z]ver 14
13:43 [a]S Ac 11:23; 14:22; S Ro 3:24
13:45 [b]Ac 18:6; 1Pe 4:4; Jude 10 [c]S 1Th 2:16
13:46 [d]ver 26; Ac 3:26 [e]Mt 21:41; Ac 18:6; 22:21; 26:20; 28:28; Ro 11:11

[v]33 Or *have begotten you* [w]33 Psalm 2:7 [x]34 Isaiah 55:3 [y]35 Psalm 16:10 [z]41 Hab. 1:5

---

baptism, and not Jewish proselyte baptism, is the most direct antecedent to Christian baptism. Proselyte baptism showed that the converts belonged to the covenant people of Israel; Christian baptism showed that the converts belonged to Jesus Christ.

13:26,47 SALVATION, Initiative—These verses and their contexts make it unmistakably clear that God's message of salvation was to Jews and non-Jews. V 47 quotes Isa 49:6. Compare Isa 42:6. Paul's point was that he was fulfilling God's command by offering salvation to the Gentiles.

13:27–41 JESUS CHRIST, Fulfilled—Jesus fulfilled the intention of God's history with Israel and of the Scriptures. He suffered, died, and was resurrected, providing forgiveness and placing believers in right relationship with God.

13:32–35 PROCLAMATION, Gospel—See notes on 3:11–26; 14:21–22. The gospel is good news to those who are not saved. Proclamation in the New Testament is the sharing of the good news of God's salvation through Jesus with the non-Christian world. It is the open and public proclaiming of the redemptive work of God through Jesus Christ. In short, it is evangelistic in nature. Compare 10:36; 11:20; Mk 1:14–15. In the New Testament, preaching does not have to do primarily with the delivery of sermons to the converted. Most often the proclamation of the good news is to the non-Christian world.

13:39 SALVATION, Justification—Paul preached that by faith Jesus justifies persons from everything the Law of Moses could not. The Law of Moses did not claim to deal with anything but unintentional sins (Lev 4:2; Heb 9:7). Paul could not find satisfaction for his sin problem through the Jewish system. He found satisfaction in Christ, who atoned for all his sins and relieved all his guilt. Only the mercy of God can deal with intentional sin. God revealed that mercy fully in Christ.

13:46,48 SALVATION, Eternal Life—See note on 11:18. Faith leads to eternal life. Rejecting Christ forfeits hope for eternal life.

13:46 CHRISTIAN ETHICS, Race Relations—At the risk of losing favor with fellow Christians, Paul and Barnabas still followed the higher plane of taking the gospel to all people.

13:46–48 EVANGELISM, Universality—The missionaries realized that salvation was "first for the Jew" but also for the Greeks or Gentiles (Ro 1:16). It is for all who will respond. Believers of all backgrounds honor God with their changed lives and experience God's joy.

“ ‘I have made you[a] a light for the
Gentiles,[f]
that you[a] may bring salvation to the
ends of the earth.’[b] ”[g]

48 When the Gentiles heard this, they
were glad and honored the word of the
Lord;[h] and all who were appointed for
eternal life believed.
49 The word of the Lord[i] spread
through the whole region. 50 But the Jews
incited the God-fearing women of high
standing and the leading men of the city.
They stirred up persecution against Paul
and Barnabas, and expelled them from
their region.[j] 51 So they shook the dust
from their feet[k] in protest against them
and went to Iconium.[l] 52 And the disciples[m] were filled with joy and with the
Holy Spirit.[n]

Chapter 14

In Iconium

At Iconium[o] Paul and Barnabas went as
usual into the Jewish synagogue.[p]
There they spoke so effectively that a
great number[q] of Jews and Gentiles believed. 2 But the Jews who refused to believe stirred up the Gentiles and poisoned
their minds against the brothers.[r] 3 So
Paul and Barnabas spent considerable
time there, speaking boldly[s] for the Lord,
who confirmed the message of his grace
by enabling them to do miraculous signs
and wonders.[t] 4 The people of the city
were divided; some sided with the Jews,
others with the apostles.[u] 5 There was a
plot afoot among the Gentiles and Jews,[v]
together with their leaders, to mistreat
them and stone them.[w] 6 But they found
out about it and fled[x] to the Lycaonian
cities of Lystra and Derbe and to the surrounding country, 7 where they continued
to preach[y] the good news.[z]

In Lystra and Derbe

8 In Lystra there sat a man crippled in
his feet, who was lame from birth[a] and
had never walked. 9 He listened to Paul as
he was speaking. Paul looked directly at
him, saw that he had faith to be healed[b]
10 and called out, “Stand up on your
feet!”[c] At that, the man jumped up and
began to walk.[d]
11 When the crowd saw what Paul had
done, they shouted in the Lycaonian language, “The gods have come down to us
in human form!”[e] 12 Barnabas they called
Zeus, and Paul they called Hermes because he was the chief speaker.[f] 13 The
priest of Zeus, whose temple was just outside the city, brought bulls and wreaths
to the city gates because he and the
crowd wanted to offer sacrifices to them.
14 But when the apostles Barnabas and
Paul heard of this, they tore their
clothes[g] and rushed out into the crowd,
shouting: 15 “Men, why are you doing
this? We too are only men,[h] human like
you. We are bringing you good news,[i]
telling you to turn from these worthless
things[j] to the living God,[k] who made
heaven and earth[l] and sea and everything in them.[m] 16 In the past, he let[n] all
nations go their own way.[o] 17 Yet he has
not left himself without testimony:[p] He
has shown kindness by giving you rain
from heaven and crops in their seasons;[q]
he provides you with plenty of food and
fills your hearts with joy.”[r] 18 Even with
these words, they had difficulty keeping
the crowd from sacrificing to them.
19 Then some Jews[s] came from Antioch

[a] *47* The Greek is singular. [b] *47* Isaiah 49:6

13:47 [f]S Lk 2:32 [g]Isa 49:6
13:48 [h]ver 49; Ac 8:25; 15:35,36; 19:10,20
13:49 [i]S ver 48
13:50 [j]S 1Th 2:16
13:51 [k]S Mt 10:14 [l]Ac 14:1,19,21; 16:2; 2Ti 3:11
13:52 [m]S Ac 11:26 [n]S Lk 1:15
14:1 [o]S Ac 13:51 [p]S Ac 9:20 [q]S Ac 2:41
14:2 [r]S Ac 1:16
14:3 [s]S Ac 4:29 [t]S Jn 4:48
14:4 [u]Ac 17:4,5; 28:24
14:5 [v]S Ac 20:3 [w]ver 19
14:6 [x]Mt 10:23
14:7 [y]Ac 16:10 [z]ver 15,21; S Ac 13:32
14:8 [a]Ac 3:2
14:9 [b]Mt 9:28,29; 13:58
14:10 [c]Eze 2:1 [d]Ac 3:8
14:11 [e]Ac 8:10; 28:6
14:12 [f]Ex 7:1
14:14 [g]S Mk 14:63
14:15 [h]S Ac 10:26 [i]ver 7,21; S Ac 13:32 [j]1Sa 12:21; 1Th 1:9 [k]S Mt 16:16 [l]Ge 1:1 [m]Ps 146:6; Rev 14:7
14:16 [n]Ac 17:30 [o]Ps 81:12; Mic 4:5
14:17 [p]Ro 1:20 [q]Dt 11:14; Job 5:10; Ps 65:10 [r]Ps 4:7
14:19 [s]Ac 13:45

13:52 HOLY SPIRIT, Fills—See note on 6:1–6. The filling of the Spirit occurs frequently for Christians and may include being filled with courage (see note on 4:31), wisdom (7:3), faith (7:5), ecstasy (7:55), healing (9:17), goodness (see note on 11:24), and discernment (see note on 13:9). In the present passage, it is associated with joy. The congregation of God’s people were all filled with the Spirit.

13:52 SALVATION, Joy—The early disciples were filled with joy as their Lord had prayed they would be. See note on Jn 17:13. Frequently in the New Testament joy and the Holy Spirit are closely linked (Lk 10:21). This same fullness of joy is still available to Christians through the Holy Spirit.

14:1 PROCLAMATION, Unbelievers—See note on 26:19–29.

14:1–2 EVANGELISM, Worship—Paul’s pattern was to begin his witness to Christ in the Jewish synagogues during worship. This was a wise evangelistic strategy because he could begin to get a hearing for the gospel. We are wise to begin our evangelization where we can get an open door and ear. Evangelism is an integral part of public worship.

14:3,26 GOD, *Grace*—*Grace is that unmerited favor of God extended to* people. Usually it is thought of as His blessing in redemption, the foregiveness of sins, and the new life of conversion. It is used in v 26 to describe the blessing of God in keeping and using His servants in proclaiming the gospel of Jesus. In both cases the grace of God is intimately bound up with God’s intention to bring salvation to lost people.

14:3 MIRACLE, Instruments—While Paul and Barnabas preached, the Lord verified the preaching by giving signs and wonders. Here is one of the clearest statements of explanation for the miracles—not to mystify, but to testify.

14:8–10 MIRACLE, Faith—Miracles are available to faith. As Peter and John had healed a lame man (see note on 3:1–16), so Paul healed a man born lame. He listened as Paul preached, and Paul sensed his faith. The lame man obeyed Paul’s command to get up. He jumped up and walked about. The crowd witnessed the healing and immediately arranged to treat Paul and Barnabas as gods. This gave them a chance to preach the gospel.

14:11–15 GOD, Creator—Paul pointed to the one true God, the living Creator of all things. These points are not elaborated here, but they stand in sharp contrast to the ideas of the crowds who were ready to proclaim Paul and Barnabas gods. No human has accomplished what God has, so no human can usurp any part of His authority.

14:15 SALVATION, Repentance—To repent is to turn from the worship of idols to the living God. The opportunity to repent is good news.

and Iconium[t] and won the crowd over.
They stoned Paul[u] and dragged him outside the city, thinking he was dead. 20But
after the disciples[v] had gathered around
him, he got up and went back into the
city. The next day he and Barnabas left
for Derbe.

The Return to Antioch in Syria

21They preached the good news[w] in
that city and won a large number[x] of disciples. Then they returned to Lystra, Iconium[y] and Antioch, 22strengthening the
disciples and encouraging them to remain
true to the faith.[z] "We must go through
many hardships[a] to enter the kingdom of
God," they said. 23Paul and Barnabas appointed elders[c][b] for them in each
church and, with prayer and fasting,[c]
committed them to the Lord,[d] in whom
they had put their trust. 24After going
through Pisidia, they came into Pamphylia,[e] 25and when they had preached the
word in Perga, they went down to Attalia.
26From Attalia they sailed back to Antioch,[f] where they had been committed to
the grace of God[g] for the work they had
now completed.[h] 27On arriving there,
they gathered the church together and reported all that God had done through
them[i] and how he had opened the
door[j] of faith to the Gentiles. 28And they
stayed there a long time with the disciples.[k]

Chapter 15

The Council at Jerusalem

SOME men[l] came down from Judea to
Antioch and were teaching the brothers:[m] "Unless you are circumcised,[n] according to the custom taught by Moses,[o]
you cannot be saved." 2This brought Paul
and Barnabas into sharp dispute and de-

14:19 [t]S Ac 13:51 [u]2Co 11:25; 2Ti 3:11
14:20 [v]ver 22,28; S Ac 11:26
14:21 [w]S Ac 13:32 [x]S Ac 2:41 [y]S Ac 13:51
14:22 [z]Ac 11:23; 13:43 [a]Jn 16:33; 1Th 3:3; 2Ti 3:12
14:23 [b]S Ac 11:30 [c]Ac 13:3 [d]Ac 20:32
14:24 [e]S Ac 2:10
14:26 [f]S Ac 11:19 [g]S Ac 11:23 [h]Ac 13:1,3
14:27 [i]Ac 15:4,12; 21:19 [j]1Co 16:9; 2Co 2:12; Col 4:3; Rev 3:8
14:28 [k]S Ac 11:26
15:1 [l]ver 24; Gal 2:12 [m]S Ac 1:16 [n]ver 5; Gal 5:2,3 [o]S Ac 6:14

[c]23 Or *Barnabas ordained elders*; or *Barnabas had elders elected*

14:21–22 PROCLAMATION, Exhortation—Preaching the gospel strengthens and encourages believers. New believers especially need exhortation to move on in their commitment and faith. Compare Lk 3:18; 1 Th 3:2; 2 Ti 4:2.

14:21–28 EVANGELISM, Follow-up—Evangelism includes helping people come to Christ and helping them grow spiritually in Him. A new convert is a babe in Christ (Heb 5:12–13). Converts need to be guided in the Christian maturation process (1 Pe 2:2). Paul did this as he revisited and established the new converts in the churches he founded. Several principles emerge in this context: New converts need to be strengthened. They face temptations to forsake the faith. They need leadership. They need to be involved in the ministry of the church. They need prayer and the fellowship of believers. See Stages in Spiritual Growth, pp. 1812–1817.

14:22 THE CHURCH, God's Kingdom—The kingdom of God was established by Christ. As the church follows the Master, it represents the kingdom. Still, the kingdom will not be experienced in its fullness until Christ returns. At that time, faithful disciples having followed Christ through the hardships of discipleship will enter the kingdom. Believers must expect a hard time from the world which opposes God. Self-denial and cross-bearing are the way to the kingdom. See note on Lk 9:60–62.

14:23 THE CHURCH, Practice—Churches select leaders and set them apart for Christ's service. The selection is made under God's leadership. "Appointed" originally meant to elect by a show of hands and later came to mean appoint. How Paul and Barnabas selected the leaders is not clear. The church should elect its leaders. To do so, the church must show the seriousness of purpose of the early churches. Prayer and fasting indicates they devoted time to determine God's will and allowed nothing to interfere with their communication with God. If God does not select and lead the church's leaders, the human leaders cannot be effective in spiritual ministry.

14:23 PRAYER, Commitment—This prayer was to commit the elders to the Lord's direction. Fasting often accompanied prayer (13:2).

14:23 CHURCH LEADERS, Elder—In the absence of the apostles, local leaders provided stability and care for a church. In the newly founded churches, Paul and Barnabas appointed converts who had demonstrated spiritual maturity to assume responsibility for the churches they had started. They chose these leaders after prayer and fasting. This reveals that the leading of the Holy Spirit is essential in making such decisions. The early church apostles took initiative in selection of church leaders until the churches became strong enough to select their own leaders under God's guidance.

14:27 CHRISTIAN ETHICS, Race Relations—See note on 13:46.

14:27 THE CHURCH, Local Body—The church at Antioch received the message to send out missionaries. At the conclusion of the first missionary journey, the church gathered to hear how God opened the door of faith to the Gentiles. The local church should be involved in mission work far beyond its location. See notes on 4:32; 11:26.

15:1–31 CHRISTIAN ETHICS, Race Relations—Incredibly, contemporary believers still behave as the Judaizers of the first century, stressing religious traditions for theological principles. There must be those, like Paul and Barnabas, willing to confront these false prophets with true words of testimony. The nature of salvation through Christ is such that all people, no matter the color of skin or socio-economic standing, can avail themselves of it. The church's task is to use its resources to bring every person on earth to accept the gospel. Any extra requirements placed on one group of people reveal only our prejudice. See note on 10:28–35.

15:1–31 CHRISTIAN ETHICS, Moral Imperatives—Much care and encouragement can be extended to young converts with tactful, cordial communication about relevant standards of behavior for Christians. Such standards must not center on traditional rituals but on actions which distinguish a Christian from other religions and from the evil conduct of the world. The intention is to lead people to faith not to burden them with unnecessary guilt.

15:1–35 THE CHURCH, Practice—Questions and problems arise in the fellowship of believers. When difficulties become evident, Christians have an opportunity to demonstrate the power of Christ in their lives. Our response to conflict and to those who disagree with us shows the depth of our Christian character. Conditions and circumstances continually change, causing new questions to arise. Some people in the early church questioned whether salvation rested on legalism—outward acts which others could see—or totally on the grace of God. Many early believers insisted the Gentiles must be circumcised. The early church met this problem swiftly and openly, affirming the work of grace. The council at Jerusalem sent a letter of encouragement to Gentile believers to build their faith. During conflict, churches must exercise compassion, restraint, and concern that God's will be done and that the fellowship of believers be strengthened. Personal experience, the Holy Spirit's witness, the theology of salvation by grace alone, and Bible study provide answers to the church's problems. Churches must deal with problems quickly and effectively, seeking to preserve the truth of the gospel and the unity of the churches. See note on 1:21–26.

bate with them. So Paul and Barnabas
were appointed, along with some other
believers, to go up to Jerusalem[p] to see
the apostles and elders[q] about this question. 3The church sent them on their
way, and as they traveled through Phoenicia[r] and Samaria, they told how the
Gentiles had been converted.[s] This news
made all the brothers very glad. 4When
they came to Jerusalem, they were welcomed by the church and the apostles
and elders, to whom they reported everything God had done through them.[t]

5Then some of the believers who belonged to the party[u] of the Pharisees[v]
stood up and said, "The Gentiles must be
circumcised and required to obey the law
of Moses."[w]

6The apostles and elders met to consider this question. 7After much discussion,
Peter got up and addressed them: "Brothers, you know that some time ago God
made a choice among you that the Gentiles might hear from my lips the message
of the gospel and believe.[x] 8God, who
knows the heart,[y] showed that he accepted them by giving the Holy Spirit to
them,[z] just as he did to us. 9He made no
distinction between us and them,[a] for he
purified their hearts by faith.[b] 10Now
then, why do you try to test God[c] by putting on the necks of the disciples a yoke[d]
that neither we nor our fathers have been
able to bear? 11No! We believe it is
through the grace[e] of our Lord Jesus that
we are saved, just as they are."

12The whole assembly became silent as
they listened to Barnabas and Paul telling
about the miraculous signs and wonders[f]
God had done among the Gentiles
through them.[g] 13When they finished,
James[h] spoke up: "Brothers, listen to
me. 14Simon[d] has described to us how
God at first showed his concern by taking
from the Gentiles a people for himself.[i]
15The words of the prophets are in agreement with this, as it is written:

16" 'After this I will return
and rebuild David's fallen tent.
Its ruins I will rebuild,
and I will restore it,
17that the remnant of men may seek the
Lord,
and all the Gentiles who bear my
name,
says the Lord, who does these
things'[e][j]
18 that have been known for ages.[f][k]

19"It is my judgment, therefore, that
we should not make it difficult for the
Gentiles who are turning to God. 20In-
stead we should write to them, telling
them to abstain from food polluted by
idols,[l] from sexual immorality,[m] from
the meat of strangled animals and from
blood.[n] 21For Moses has been preached
in every city from the earliest times and is
read in the synagogues on every Sabbath."[o]

The Council's Letter to Gentile Believers

22Then the apostles and elders,[p] with
the whole church, decided to choose
some of their own men and send them to
Antioch[q] with Paul and Barnabas. They
chose Judas (called Barsabbas) and Silas,[r]
two men who were leaders among the
brothers. 23With them they sent the following letter:

[d]14 Greek *Simeon*, a variant of *Simon*; that is, Peter
[e]17 Amos 9:11,12 [f]17,18 Some manuscripts
things'— / 18known to the Lord for ages is his work

15:2 [p]Gal 2:2 [q]S Ac 11:30
15:3 [r]Ac 11:19 [s]Ac 14:27
15:4 [t]ver 12; Ac 14:27; 21:19
15:5 [u]Ac 5:17 [v]Mt 3:7 [w]ver 1
15:7 [x]Ac 10:1-48
15:8 [y]S Rev 2:23 [z]S Ac 10:44,47
15:9 [a]Ac 10:28,34; 11:12 [b]Ac 10:43
15:10 [c]Ac 5:9 [d]S Mt 23:4; Gal 5:1
15:11 [e]S Ro 3:24; Gal 2:16; Eph 2:5-8
15:12 [f]S Jn 4:48 [g]ver 4; Ac 14:27; 21:19
15:13 [h]Ac 12:17; 21:18; 1Co 15:7; Gal 1:19; 2:9,12
15:14 [i]2Pe 1:1
15:17 [j]Am 9:11,12
15:18 [k]Isa 45:21
15:20 [l]1Co 8:7-13; 10:14-28; Rev 2:14, 20 [m]1Co 10:7,8; Rev 2:14,20 [n]ver 29; Ge 9:4; Lev 3:17; 7:26; 17:10-13; 19:26; Dt 12:16,23
15:21 [o]Ac 13:15; 2Co 3:14,15
15:22 [p]S Ac 11:30 [q]S Ac 11:19 [r]ver 27,32,40; Ac 16:19,25,29; 2Co 1:19; 1Th 1:1; 2Th 1:1; 1Pe 5:12

15:3–4,22,30 THE CHURCH, Local Body—Local churches need to communicate with one another. Such communication brings mutual encouragement and problem-solving. The local church at Jerusalem played a major role in problem-solving because of its unique situation that the apostles were there. No one local church can exercise authority over another. They can give counsel and encouragement. See notes on 4:32; 8:1.

15:3 EVANGELISM, In the Church—Paul realized he was responsible to the churches in his missionary-evangelism. We are all responsible to the whole body of Christ in our evangelization efforts. This attitude brings joy to all, and the entire cause of Christ is thereby strengthened.

15:7 ELECTION, Other Nations—A few members of the Jerusalem church were dually aligned with the Jewish Pharisees. They wanted all Gentile converts to be circumcised and to obey the Law of Moses. Paul stood his ground against these persons. Peter supported him, saying God had elected him to preach the gospel to the Gentiles (10:1–48). The Holy Spirit validated the conversion experiences of the Gentiles by becoming as personal to them as He was among Jewish Christians.

15:8 GOD, Wisdom—*God knows all things:* He knows what is in the heart of each individual. He knows our true attitude to Him. His knowledge of persons and their various needs, problems, and attitudes is not the detached knowledge of much information gained by study, implication, or some other indirect way. Rather, it is personal knowledge which God gains first-hand in His own observation of and relationship to people. God's knowledge is not disinterested knowledge but has a redemptive purpose. God is always and in all ways seeking to bring His redemptive love to bear upon all individuals. He knows each of us as individuals and seeks to deal with us on the basis of that knowledge. See note on 1 Sa 2:3.

15:11 SALVATION, Grace—The Jerusalem Conference (ch 15) dealt with whether circumcision was required for salvation. Circumcision of the flesh is not required for salvation, but grace is. All people find salvation the same way—through God's grace. Grace (Greek *charis*) is the free decision and gift of God to save sinners who do not deserve salvation. Grace excludes all human achievement in relation to salvation. Grace is accepted with gratitude and surprise at God's goodness in being so gracious.

15:12 MIRACLE, Instruments—Miracles lead to missions. The reports of signs and wonders silenced the foes of Barnabas and Saul. God had allowed the miraculous to reach the Gentile world! Even the conservative, tradition-bound Jerusalem church had to acknowledge that missions was God's plan for the ages. Evidence of God's miracles silences argument from human tradition and reason.

The apostles and elders, your brothers,

To the Gentile believers in Antioch,[s]
Syria[t] and Cilicia:[u]

Greetings.[v]

24We have heard that some went
out from us without our authorization and disturbed you, troubling
your minds by what they said.[w] 25So
we all agreed to choose some men
and send them to you with our dear
friends Barnabas and Paul— 26men
who have risked their lives[x] for the
name of our Lord Jesus Christ.
27Therefore we are sending Judas and
Silas[y] to confirm by word of mouth
what we are writing. 28It seemed
good to the Holy Spirit[z] and to us not
to burden you with anything beyond
the following requirements: 29You
are to abstain from food sacrificed to
idols, from blood, from the meat of
strangled animals and from sexual
immorality.[a] You will do well to
avoid these things.

Farewell.

30The men were sent off and went
down to Antioch, where they gathered
the church together and delivered the letter. 31The people read it and were glad for
its encouraging message. 32Judas and Silas,[b] who themselves were prophets,[c]
said much to encourage and strengthen
the brothers. 33After spending some time
there, they were sent off by the brothers
with the blessing of peace[d] to return to
those who had sent them.[g] 35But Paul
and Barnabas remained in Antioch,
where they and many others taught and
preached[e] the word of the Lord.[f]

15:23 [s]ver 1; S Ac 11:19 [t]S Lk 2:2 [u]ver 41; S Ac 6:9 [v]Ac 23:25, 26; Jas 1:1
15:24 [w]ver 1; Gal 1:7; 5:10
15:26 [x]Ac 9:23-25; 14:19; 1Co 15:30
15:27 [y]S ver 22
15:28 [z]Ac 5:32
15:29 [a]ver 20; Ac 21:25
15:32 [b]S ver 22 [c]S Ac 11:27
15:33 [d]1Sa 1:17; Mk 5:34; Lk 7:50; Ac 16:36; 1Co 16:11
15:35 [e]Ac 8:4 [f]S Ac 13:48
15:36 [g]Ac 13:4,13, 14,51; 14:1,6,24,25 [h]S Ac 13:48
15:37 [i]S Ac 12:12
15:38 [j]Ac 13:13
15:40 [k]S ver 22 [l]S Ac 11:23
15:41 [m]ver 23; S Lk 2:2 [n]S Ac 6:9 [o]Ac 16:5
16:1 [p]Ac 14:6 [q]Ac 17:14; 18:5; 19:22; 20:4; Ro 16:21; 1Co 4:17; 16:10; 2Co 1:1,19; Php 1:1; 2:19; Col 1:1; 1Th 1:1; 3:2,6; 2Th 1:1; 1Ti 1:2,18; 2Ti 1:2, 5,6; Phm 1 [r]2Ti 1:5
16:2 [s]ver 40; S Ac 1:16 [t]S Ac 13:51
16:3 [u]Gal 2:3
16:4 [v]S Ac 11:30 [w]Ac 15:2 [x]Ac 15:28,29
16:5 [y]Ac 9:31; 15:41 [z]S Ac 2:41

Disagreement Between Paul and Barnabas

36Some time later Paul said to Barnabas, "Let us go back and visit the brothers
in all the towns[g] where we preached the
word of the Lord[h] and see how they are
doing." 37Barnabas wanted to take John,
also called Mark,[i] with them, 38but Paul
did not think it wise to take him, because
he had deserted them[j] in Pamphylia and
had not continued with them in the
work. 39They had such a sharp disagreement that they parted company. Barnabas
took Mark and sailed for Cyprus, 40but
Paul chose Silas[k] and left, commended
by the brothers to the grace of the Lord.[l]
41He went through Syria[m] and Cilicia,[n]
strengthening the churches.[o]

Chapter 16

Timothy Joins Paul and Silas

HE came to Derbe and then to Lystra,[p]
where a disciple named Timothy[q]
lived, whose mother was a Jewess and a
believer,[r] but whose father was a Greek.
2The brothers[s] at Lystra and Iconium[t]
spoke well of him. 3Paul wanted to take
him along on the journey, so he circumcised him because of the Jews who lived
in that area, for they all knew that his
father was a Greek.[u] 4As they traveled
from town to town, they delivered the
decisions reached by the apostles and elders[v] in Jerusalem[w] for the people to
obey.[x] 5So the churches were strengthened[y] in the faith and grew daily in numbers.[z]

Paul's Vision of the Man of Macedonia

6Paul and his companions traveled

[g]33 Some manuscripts *them,* [34]*but Silas decided to remain there*

15:28 HOLY SPIRIT, Teaches—The Spirit is the church's great Teacher. The Spirit guides the church to carry out its world missionary task. The council which met at Jerusalem made an important decision concerning the acceptance of Gentiles into the church. The letter from the leaders of the Jerusalem church showed that the Holy Spirit had guided the council in its decision. Christians sometimes make poor decisions. Barnabus disagreed with Paul about John Mark (15:36–40), and Peter failed to be firm in his commitment to Gentile Christians (Gal 2:11–14). The New Testament records quite clearly that the Spirit did teach the church as it made crucial decisions such as that of the Jerusalem council. It is not always easy to be sure about the specific guidance of the Spirit. Presumably mistakes are made today just as in the early church. It is important to seek the Spirit's teaching as the church carries out its world missionary task.

15:35 PROCLAMATION, Instruction—The proclaiming of the gospel (Greek *euangelizō*) includes instruction (Greek *didaskō*) to the believer. The Word of God is written specifically to believers. While proclamation provides instruction in the evangelistic thrust of the gospel, it also instructs in the doctrine and principles which produce a godly life, the only genuinely effective platform from which we can reach the lost. Compare 11:25–26. The ultimate goal for every believer is to be presented "perfect in Christ" (Col 1:28). Faithful proclamation continually guides the believer in the truth of God. Compare 1 Th 4:1–2; 1 Ti 2:1–7.

15:35 EDUCATION, Missionaries—See note on 18:11.

16:4–5 THE CHURCH, Practice—See note on 15:1–35. The elders and apostles met in Jerusalem to discuss circumcision. They sought to strengthen the churches in their faith. The council demonstrated its willingness to ignore secondary issues in order to proclaim the heart of the gospel. The work of the church is to proclaim the gospel of Christ to those apart from Him and to strengthen the saved.

16:5 EVANGELISM, Power—See note on 11:21.

16:6–10 HOLY SPIRIT, Mission—The Spirit can say no. He prevented Paul from entering Asia or Bithynia. "Spirit of Jesus" appears only here in the New Testament. The Spirit is elsewhere referred to as the Spirit of Christ (Ro 8:9; 1 Pe 1:11), the Spirit of Jesus Christ (Php 1:19), and the Spirit of God's Son (see note on Gal 4:6). These phrases all indicate how closely the early church associated the Spirit with Christ. The Spirit was given to all who believed in Christ and only to those who believed in Christ. He always reminded them of Christ; He glorified Christ; He equipped the church to pro-

throughout the region of Phrygia[a] and
Galatia,[b] having been kept by the Holy
Spirit from preaching the word in the
province of Asia.[c] 7When they came to
the border of Mysia, they tried to enter
Bithynia, but the Spirit of Jesus[d] would
not allow them to. 8So they passed by
Mysia and went down to Troas.[e] 9During
the night Paul had a vision[f] of a man of
Macedonia[g] standing and begging him,
"Come over to Macedonia and help us."
10After Paul had seen the vision, we[h] got
ready at once to leave for Macedonia,
concluding that God had called us to
preach the gospel[i] to them.

Lydia's Conversion in Philippi

11From Troas[j] we put out to sea and
sailed straight for Samothrace, and the
next day on to Neapolis. 12From there we
traveled to Philippi,[k] a Roman colony
and the leading city of that district of
Macedonia.[l] And we stayed there several days.

13On the Sabbath[m] we went outside
the city gate to the river, where we expected to find a place of prayer. We sat
down and began to speak to the women
who had gathered there. 14One of those
listening was a woman named Lydia, a
dealer in purple cloth from the city of
Thyatira,[n] who was a worshiper of God.
The Lord opened her heart[o] to respond
to Paul's message. 15When she and the
members of her household[p] were baptized,[q] she invited us to her home. "If
you consider me a believer in the Lord,"
she said, "come and stay at my house."
And she persuaded us.

Paul and Silas in Prison

16Once when we were going to the
place of prayer,[r] we were met by a slave
girl who had a spirit[s] by which she predicted the future. She earned a great deal
of money for her owners by fortune-tell-
ing. 17This girl followed Paul and the rest
of us, shouting, "These men are servants
of the Most High God,[t] who are telling
you the way to be saved." 18She kept this
up for many days. Finally Paul became so
troubled that he turned around and said
to the spirit, "In the name of Jesus Christ
I command you to come out of her!" At
that moment the spirit left her.[u]

19When the owners of the slave girl realized that their hope of making money[v]
was gone, they seized Paul and Silas[w] and
dragged[x] them into the marketplace to
face the authorities. 20They brought them
before the magistrates and said, "These
men are Jews, and are throwing our city
into an uproar[y] 21by advocating customs
unlawful for us Romans[z] to accept or
practice."[a]

22The crowd joined in the attack
against Paul and Silas, and the magistrates
ordered them to be stripped and beaten.[b]
23After they had been severely flogged,
they were thrown into prison, and the
jailer[c] was commanded to guard them
carefully. 24Upon receiving such orders,
he put them in the inner cell and fastened their feet in the stocks.[d]

16:6 [a]Ac 2:10; 18:23 [b]Ac 18:23; Gal 1:2; 3:1 [c]S Ac 2:9
16:7 [d]Ro 8:9; Gal 4:6; Php 1:19; 1Pe 1:11
16:8 [e]ver 11; Ac 20:5; 2Co 2:12; 2Ti 4:13
16:9 [f]S Ac 9:10 [g]Ac 19:21,29; 20:1, 3; Ro 15:26; 1Co 16:5; 1Th 1:7, 8
16:10 [h]ver 10-17; Ac 20:5-15; 21:1-18; 27:1-28:16 [i]Ac 14:7
16:11 [j]S ver 8
16:12 [k]Ac 20:6; Php 1:1; 1Th 2:2 [l]S ver 9
16:13 [m]S Ac 13:14
16:14 [n]Rev 1:11; 2:18,24 [o]Lk 24:45
16:15 [p]S Ac 11:14 [q]S Ac 2:38
16:16 [r]ver 13 [s]Dt 18:11; 1Sa 28:3,7
16:17 [t]S Mk 5:7
16:18 [u]S Mk 16:17
16:19 [v]ver 16; Ac 19:25,26 [w]S Ac 15:22 [x]Ac 8:3; 17:6; 21:30; Jas 2:6
16:20 [y]Ac 17:6
16:21 [z]ver 12 [a]Est 3:8
16:22 [b]2Co 11:25; 1Th 2:2
16:23 [c]ver 27,36
16:24 [d]Job 13:27; 33:11; Jer 20:2,3; 29:26

---

claim Christ. This association with Christ renders the Spirit knowable. He is not a vague, amorphous, pervasive Spirit in the world. He is the definite, recognizable, invasive Spirit who lives with the followers of Jesus of Nazareth. At times He tells us no so He can lead us to a greater ministry for Jesus.

16:9–10 REVELATION, Dreams—God visited Paul in a night vision, calling him to proclaim God's purposes across the border. Revelation includes God's calling and directing individual missionaries to spread His gospel.

16:13 WORSHIP, Buildings—Community worship can be held without buildings. See note on Ge 28:16–22.

16:13 PRAYER, Corporate—The synagogue or the meeting place of the Jews was a "place of prayer," just as the Temple was a "house of prayer" (Mt 21:13). God's people need to meet together for prayer.

16:13–15 EVANGELISM, Worship—Honest worship of God helps make one receptive to the Spirit and is thus a significant context in which to evangelize. See note on 14:1–2.

16:14 SALVATION, Acceptance—Accepting the gospel is not a human achievement. It depends on God opening the heart to make it responsive to the gospel message. Such acceptance was prepared by previous worship experiences.

16:15 ORDINANCES, Baptismal Candidate—The household baptisms in Acts raise the question whether babies or other nonbelievers were baptized. We certainly may suppose that there were babies, small children, slaves, and others in some of these households. Luke is very consistent: in every case he mentions that those who believed, or those who received his word, were baptized. In v 14, the Lord opened Lydia's heart to receive Paul's message; and in v 15, she identified herself as a "believer in the Lord." Baptism is the outward sign of this inward belief in the Lord Jesus. Only believers are proper subjects for baptism. Compare v 31; 18:8; 1 Co 1:16.

16:16–18 MIRACLE, Redemption—Miracles redeem people physically, providing opportunity for useful life. They often do more. The poor afflicted girl was a slave, exploited by her owners. It is widely supposed that she had the ability of ventriloquism (Greek *puthon*) and was emotionally, if not mentally, deranged. Her cries proved troublesome, and Paul commanded the spirit to come out of her. She was healed immediately, freed from her derangement—a redeemed personality. The result: Paul and Silas found they needed to be redeemed from prison. Their imprisonment led to a further miracle and a marvelous witnessing opportunity.

16:16–40 EVIL AND SUFFERING, Endurance—See note on 12:1–19.

16:16–24 CHRISTIAN ETHICS, Property Rights—Greed and love of money may lead to tyranny and oppression of others. Christians seek to free people from such tyranny even when it brings persecution.

16:16 PRAYER, Corporate—See note on v 13.

16:16–17 EVANGELISM, In the Marketplace—Paul seized every opportunity to minister the gospel of Christ and excluded no one from hearing the message. This example of the demon-possessed woman is a classic example of evangelism in the marketplace, that is, witnessing in the daily routine of life. It was costly to Paul. He was thrown in prison. Even that resulted in the conversion of the Philippian jailor and his family. God honors witnessing in the marketplace of life.

25 About midnight[e] Paul and Silas[f]
were praying and singing hymns[g] to
God, and the other prisoners were listening to them. 26 Suddenly there was such a
violent earthquake that the foundations
of the prison were shaken.[h] At once all
the prison doors flew open,[i] and everybody's chains came loose.[j] 27 The jailer
woke up, and when he saw the prison
doors open, he drew his sword and was
about to kill himself because he thought
the prisoners had escaped.[k] 28 But Paul
shouted, "Don't harm yourself! We are
all here!"

29 The jailer called for lights, rushed in
and fell trembling before Paul and Silas.[l]
30 He then brought them out and asked,
"Sirs, what must I do to be saved?"[m]

31 They replied, "Believe[n] in the Lord
Jesus, and you will be saved[o]—you and
your household."[p] 32 Then they spoke the
word of the Lord to him and to all the
others in his house. 33 At that hour of the
night[q] the jailer took them and washed
their wounds; then immediately he and
all his family were baptized.[r] 34 The jailer
brought them into his house and set a
meal before them; he[s] was filled with joy
because he had come to believe in God
—he and his whole family.

35 When it was daylight, the magistrates
sent their officers to the jailer with the
order: "Release those men." 36 The jailer[t] told Paul, "The magistrates have ordered that you and Silas be released. Now
you can leave. Go in peace."[u]

37 But Paul said to the officers: "They
beat us publicly without a trial, even
though we are Roman citizens,[v] and
threw us into prison. And now do they
want to get rid of us quietly? No! Let
them come themselves and escort us
out."

38 The officers reported this to the magistrates, and when they heard that Paul
and Silas were Roman citizens, they were
alarmed.[w] 39 They came to appease them
and escorted them from the prison, re-
questing them to leave the city.[x] 40 After
Paul and Silas came out of the prison,
they went to Lydia's house,[y] where they
met with the brothers[z] and encouraged
them. Then they left.

Chapter 17

In Thessalonica

WHEN they had passed through Am-
phipolis and Apollonia, they came
to Thessalonica,[a] where there was a Jewish synagogue. 2 As his custom was, Paul
went into the synagogue,[b] and on three

16:25 [e]Ps 119:55, 62 [f]S Ac 15:22 [g]S Eph 5:19
16:26 [h]Ac 4:31 [i]Ac 5:19; 12:10 [j]Ac 12:7
16:27 [k]Ac 12:19
16:29 [l]S Ac 15:22
16:30 [m]Ac 2:37
16:31 [n]S Jn 3:15 [o]S Ro 11:14 [p]S Ac 11:14
16:33 [q]ver 25 [r]S Ac 2:38
16:34 [s]S Ac 11:14
16:36 [t]ver 23,27 [u]S Ac 15:33
16:37 [v]Ac 22:25-29
16:38 [w]Ac 22:29
16:39 [x]Mt 8:34; Lk 8:37
16:40 [y]ver 14 [z]ver 2; S Ac 1:16
17:1 [a]ver 11,13; Php 4:16; 1Th 1:1; 2Th 1:1; 2Ti 4:10
17:2 [b]S Ac 9:20

16:25–27 MIRACLE, Methods—God can accomplish the same miraculous result through different methods. This prison release does not refer to a messenger of the Lord. See note on 5:19. An earthquake came while Paul and Silas were praying and singing. The site was probably an underground dungeon. Their feet and hands were bound to hooks anchored in the mortar between the stones. When the foundations began to crumble, the anchors gave way, and the prisoners were freed. The earthquake was God's means of effecting their release. A natural catastrophe had miraculous timing. This led to a greater miracle: salvation for a frightened jailer.

16:25 WORSHIP, Music—See notes on 1 Ch 6:31–32; Ps 42:1–4.

16:25 PRAYER, Praise—Desperate situations do not necessitate desperate petitions. Faith may use the situation for worship and praise. Paul was a man of prayer (20:36; Ro 1:10; Php 1:4). These were not prayers of despair, for the singing demonstrates praise. The subsequent conversion of the jailer may demonstrate the object of their prayers.

16:25–34 EVANGELISM, Persecution—Paul and Silas were in the Philippian dungeon because of their faithful witness to Christ. Evangelization in the Spirit often brings persecution. In the midst of physical suffering, the men had positive spirits. They sang and prayed at midnight. God honors that spirit and attitude. The Lord sent deliverance and conversion as a result. God's people use hard times as God's opportunity for evangelism. Leading people to ask the right questions and directing them to Jesus is the proper procedure. See Guide to Life-style Evangelism, pp. 1831–1832.

16:26 REVELATION, Author of Creation—God used an earthquake to shake the entire jail area and provide opportunity for witness. The power of God can be revealed to a nonbeliever on the basis of events in nature.

16:30–31 SALVATION, Belief—Salvation comes when a person recognizes a personal need for salvation, determines how to be saved, and trusts Jesus Christ for salvation. To believe in Christ is the only answer to the jailer's question. Nothing else is needed. If the jailer needed to believe to be saved, so did each member of his family and each slave in the household. The master's example made it easier for them, but they, too, needed to believe to be saved and then be baptized.

16:31–34 ORDINANCES, Baptismal Candidate—The candidate, or person being baptized, was required to believe in the Lord Jesus Christ. This requirement is stated three different times: (1) you and anyone in your house who believes in the Lord Jesus Christ will be saved; (2) they preached the "word of the Lord" to all who were in his house; (3) the jailer and everyone in his family came to believe in God. It is certain that other family members were not saved because the jailer believed, since that would contradict the explicit preaching of the word of God to each one and the believing of each one in the house.

16:34 SALVATION, Joy—Salvation brings joy to those who believe in Christ. The jailer celebrated the new faith he and his family had found.

16:37–40 CHRISTIAN ETHICS, Church and State—The appeal of Paul and Silas on the grounds of their Roman citizenship provides a good example of making the government watch out for its citizens, part of its God-ordained responsibility on behalf of justice. Governments should establish a system of justice that prevents punishment of people for carrying out religious and evangelistic activities. Free exercise of religion should be every citizen's right. This scriptural standpoint is not shared, however, by systems which do not recognize God. In such societies Christians need to work to change the system while being prepared to endure the legal punishments of the system.

17:1–4 EVANGELISM, Worship—See note on 16:13–15.

17:2–4 JESUS CHRIST, Christ—See note on 9:22.

17:2 EDUCATION, Missionaries—Paul and other early Christian missionaries often went into the synagogues (13:5; 14:1; 17:10; 18:4), just as Jesus had done. There they functioned as teachers, for instruction was the central emphasis in synagogue services. Modern missionaries, too, find that teaching is an effective approach to spread the gospel. See note on

Sabbath[c] days he reasoned with them
from the Scriptures,[d] 3explaining and
proving that the Christ[h] had to suffer[e]
and rise from the dead.[f] "This Jesus I am
proclaiming to you is the Christ,[h]"[g] he
said. 4Some of the Jews were persuaded
and joined Paul and Silas,[h] as did a large
number of God-fearing Greeks and not a
few prominent women.

5But the Jews were jealous; so they
rounded up some bad characters from the
marketplace, formed a mob and started a
riot in the city.[i] They rushed to Jason's[j]
house in search of Paul and Silas in order
to bring them out to the crowd.[i] 6But
when they did not find them, they
dragged[k] Jason and some other brothers[l] before the city officials, shouting:
"These men who have caused trouble all
over the world[m] have now come here,[n]
7and Jason has welcomed them into his
house. They are all defying Caesar's decrees, saying that there is another king,
one called Jesus."[o] 8When they heard
this, the crowd and the city officials were
thrown into turmoil. 9Then they made Jason[p] and the others post bond and let
them go.

In Berea

10As soon as it was night, the brothers
sent Paul and Silas[q] away to Berea.[r] On
arriving there, they went to the Jewish
synagogue.[s] 11Now the Bereans were of
more noble character than the Thessalonians,[t] for they received the message
with great eagerness and examined the
Scriptures[u] every day to see if what Paul
said was true.[v] 12Many of the Jews believed, as did also a number of prominent
Greek women and many Greek men.[w]
13When the Jews in Thessalonica
learned that Paul was preaching the word
of God at Berea,[x] they went there too,
agitating the crowds and stirring them
up. 14The brothers[y] immediately sent
Paul to the coast, but Silas[z] and Timothy[a] stayed at Berea. 15The men who escorted Paul brought him to Athens[b] and
then left with instructions for Silas and
Timothy to join him as soon as possible.[c]

In Athens

16While Paul was waiting for them in
Athens, he was greatly distressed to see
that the city was full of idols. 17So he reasoned in the synagogue[d] with the Jews
and the God-fearing Greeks, as well as in
the marketplace day by day with those
who happened to be there. 18A group of
Epicurean and Stoic philosophers began
to dispute with him. Some of them asked,
"What is this babbler trying to say?" Others remarked, "He seems to be advocating foreign gods." They said this because
Paul was preaching the good news[e]
about Jesus and the resurrection.[f]
19Then they took him and brought him to
a meeting of the Areopagus,[g] where they
said to him, "May we know what this
new teaching[h] is that you are presenting? 20You are bringing some strange
ideas to our ears, and we want to know
what they mean." 21(All the Athenians[i]
and the foreigners who lived there spent
their time doing nothing but talking
about and listening to the latest ideas.)
22Paul then stood up in the meeting of
the Areopagus[j] and said: "Men of Athens! I see that in every way you are very
religious.[k] 23For as I walked around and
looked carefully at your objects of worship, I even found an altar with this inscription: TO AN UNKNOWN GOD. Now
what you worship as something unknown[l] I am going to proclaim to you.
24"The God who made the world and

17:2 [c]S Ac 13:14 [d]Ac 8:35; 18:28
17:3 [e]Lk 24:26; Ac 3:18 [f]Lk 24:46; S Ac 2:24 [g]S Ac 9:22
17:4 [h]S Ac 15:22
17:5 [i]ver 13; S 1Th 2:16 [j]Ro 16:21
17:6 [k]S Ac 16:19 [l]S Ac 1:16 [m]S Mt 24:14 [n]Ac 16:20
17:7 [o]Lk 23:2; Jn 19:12
17:9 [p]ver 5
17:10 [q]S Ac 15:22 [r]ver 13; Ac 20:4 [s]S Ac 9:20
17:11 [t]S ver 1 [u]Lk 16:29; Jn 5:39 [v]Dt 29:29
17:12 [w]S Ac 2:41
17:13 [x]S Heb 4:12
17:14 [y]S Ac 9:30 [z]S Ac 15:22 [a]S Ac 16:1
17:15 [b]ver 16,21,22; Ac 18:1; 1Th 3:1 [c]Ac 18:5
17:17 [d]S Ac 9:20
17:18 [e]S Ac 13:32 [f]ver 31,32; Ac 4:2
17:19 [g]ver 22 [h]Mk 1:27
17:21 [i]S ver 15
17:22 [j]ver 19 [k]ver 16
17:23 [l]Jn 4:22

[h]3 Or *Messiah* [i]5 Or *the assembly of the people*

18:11. Learning about Jesus leads to faith.

17:7 JESUS CHRIST, King—The Jews used the same tactics with Paul they had used with Jesus. They tried to convince Roman authorities Christianity represented allegiance to a new king and thus treason against Rome. See notes on Mt 27:11; Jn 18:33–37.

17:10–12 EVANGELISM, Gospel—When people honestly search the Scriptures, they discover the gospel (Jn 5:39). The Word of God is powerful. It reveals a person's need of Christ (Heb 4:12–13). In Berea, this openness to God's truth resulted in many conversions.

17:11 HOLY SCRIPTURE, Authoritative—Even the preaching of Paul stood under the judgment of Scripture in the hands of the laity. The Scriptures are given to all of God's people to be used to understand God's teachings. Every teaching of human proclaimers must be placed under the light of Scripture and tested. Studying Scripture leads to belief in the gospel. Scripture is our only source of authoritative teaching.

17:16–29 GOD, One God—*People in biblical times had many ideas about gods.* There was no shortage of belief in gods in that time. The problem was to help people see that there is truly only one God. In modern times, our problem may be just the opposite: helping people who live without any idea of God come to believe in the one true God. The point is exactly the same: there is one true God.

17:22–31 EDUCATION, Missionaries—Because he was a skilled teacher, Paul met the Athenian intellectuals on common ground, having demonstrated his knowledge of their poetry, philosophy, and religious lore. From there he led them to the heart of the Christian gospel. Some accepted the gospel and became Christians.

17:24–28 GOD, Creator—God is the Creator of all that exists; in particular, every human being exists only because of the creative power of God who brought us into existence and gives us life. This means that God is Father of all persons inasmuch as Paul described us as the offspring of God, children of God by creation. Further, this Creator-Father is also the sovereign Lord over all things and holds all persons accountable unto Himself (vv 29–31). See notes on Dt 32:6; Mal 2:10; Mt 5:43–48.

***17:24–28* CREATION, Sovereignty**—Paul addressed people who did not have the Jewish background of monotheism, the belief in one God. The Greek philosophers often taught the existence of a supreme being, but most of the

everything in it[m] is the Lord of heaven
and earth[n] and does not live in temples
built by hands.[o] 25And he is not served
by human hands, as if he needed anything, because he himself gives all men
life and breath and everything else.[p]
26From one man he made every nation of
men, that they should inhabit the whole
earth; and he determined the times set
for them and the exact places where they
should live.[q] 27God did this so that men
would seek him and perhaps reach out
for him and find him, though he is not far
from each one of us.[r] 28'For in him we
live and move and have our being.'[s] As
some of your own poets have said, 'We
are his offspring.'

29"Therefore since we are God's offspring, we should not think that the divine being is like gold or silver or stone
—an image made by man's design and
skill.[t] 30In the past God overlooked[u]
such ignorance,[v] but now he commands
all people everywhere to repent.[w] 31For
he has set a day when he will judge[x] the
world with justice[y] by the man he has
appointed.[z] He has given proof of this to
all men by raising him from the dead."[a]

17:24 [m]Isa 42:5; Ac 14:15 [n]Dt 10:14; Isa 66:1, 2; Mt 11:25 [o]1Ki 8:27; Ac 7:48 **17:25** [p]Ps 50:10-12; Isa 42:5 **17:26** [q]Dt 32:8; Job 12:23 **17:27** [r]Dt 4:7; Isa 55:6; Jer 23:23, 24 **17:28** [s]Dt 30:20; Job 12:10; Da 5:23 **17:29** [t]Isa 40:18-20; Ro 1:23 **17:30** [u]Ac 14:16; Ro 3:25 [v]ver 23; 1Pe 1:14 [w]Lk 24:47; Tit 2:11,12 **17:31** [x]S Mt 10:15 [y]Ps 9:8; 96:13; 98:9 [z]S Ac 10:42 [a]S Ac 2:24 **17:32** [b]ver 18,31 **17:34** [c]ver 19,22 **18:1** [d]S Ac 17:15 [e]Ac 19:1; 1Co 1:2; 2Co 1:1,23; 2Ti 4:20 **18:2** [f]ver 19,26; Ro 16:3; 1Co 16:19; 2Ti 4:19 [g]Ac 11:28 **18:3** [h]Ac 20:34; 1Co 4:12; 1Th 2:9; 2Th 3:8 **18:4** [i]S Ac 13:14 [j]S Ac 9:20

32When they heard about the resurrection of the dead,[b] some of them sneered,
but others said, "We want to hear you
again on this subject." 33At that, Paul left
the Council. 34A few men became followers of Paul and believed. Among them
was Dionysius, a member of the Areopagus,[c] also a woman named Damaris, and
a number of others.

Chapter 18

In Corinth

AFTER this, Paul left Athens[d] and went
to Corinth.[e] 2There he met a Jew
named Aquila, a native of Pontus, who
had recently come from Italy with his
wife Priscilla,[f] because Claudius[g] had
ordered all the Jews to leave Rome. Paul
went to see them, 3and because he was a
tentmaker as they were, he stayed and
worked with them.[h] 4Every Sabbath[i] he
reasoned in the synagogue,[j] trying to
persuade Jews and Greeks.
5When Silas[k] and Timothy[l] came
from Macedonia,[m] Paul devoted himself

18:5 [k]S Ac 15:22 [l]S Ac 16:1 [m]S Ac 16:9; 17:14,15

common people believed in many deities, each usually reflecting some value of life, either good or bad. They served their gods by providing food for them, dressing their idols, and moving them to the proper places for worship. Paul tried first to move them to a monotheistic viewpoint. His next step was to show them that the person-like qualities of God have been revealed to the world in Jesus Christ whom God has raised from the dead. Basic is the fact that God should not be conceived of in materialistic terms. He has no needs we might provide. He stands apart from His creation and should be worshiped in spirit not as a glorified physical superman. His creation means all people are related and should relate to the same God. The Creator alone determines the fate of the national and cultural groups He created. Our present generation has difficulty in divorcing material things from worship. We can only do it when we understand the true nature of this world, ourselves, and the Creator. Our whole existence is determined by Him, for the Creator remains actively involved with His creation.

17:24–28 HUMANITY, Relationships—All persons in this world have a basic, fundamental relationship to one another and to the one Creator God. In relating to God we cannot provide goods or services He must have. Rather, He has supplied everything we have. He has provided living space for the different races and cultures. He has guided history through its various periods, determining which nations ruled at different times. Life itself is a gift from and depends on Him. In relating to other people, cultural pride and prejudice should vanish. We should learn from the achievements of one another and should treat all people as members of the Creator's family.

17:24–28 REVELATION, Author of Creation—The Creator planned for human beings to seek and know Him. His loving initiative made it possible for us to seek Him (Ro 3:10; 1 Jn 4:10). God remains available to those who seek. Through the orders of His created world, He reveals Himself to all who search. Our very lives, our existence, and our active movement are grounded in His presence.

17:26 HISTORY, Universal—God controls the history of all peoples, not just believers. He has exercised control since creation and has been concerned with the historical circumstances of all people. Each people has an opportunity to reach out to God.

17:26 CHRISTIAN ETHICS, Race Relations—This verse has been used to defend racism on the grounds that certain ethnic groups should "go back to where they came from" or "stay where they belong." The verse is part of the larger context of Paul's sermon on Mars Hill dealing with the sovereignty of God. Thus, the primary discussion is God-centered or theological and not man-centered or anthropological. Rather than supporting God-ordained racial superiority, this verse portrays the encompassing love of God for all people. From creation onward we share common characteristics as members of God's created family. Creation joins us together rather than separates us.

17:30 SALVATION, Repentance—No one is exempted from the command to repent. Everyone is now called upon to change his or her mind about God, sin, and self. God does not overlook the sins of those who reject Him.

17:31 JESUS CHRIST, Judgment—God, the Creator and Ruler, has given Jesus the position as Judge at the last day. See note on 10:42. The resurrection is the proof of Jesus' right and appointment to rule.

17:31 LAST THINGS, Judgment—Among the truths validated by Jesus' resurrection was the fact of future judgment. The day has been set, and the Judge appointed. God has not revealed the time appointed but has declared the Judge's identity. The Man He has appointed is the same as was raised from the dead, even Christ Jesus. In light of the certainty of judgment, God has commanded repentance on the part of all people everywhere.

17:34 EVANGELISM, Results—Numbers do not measure the evangelist's success. Paul witnessed to individuals (16:31) as well as masses. He endured rejection and persecution (16:22). In sophisticated Athens he succeeded in gaining a hearing. Masses did not accept Christ, but the power of the gospel did work among Athen's intellectual elite. God calls us to witness. He makes the final evaluation of the results.

18:3 HUMANITY, Work—Physical labor is necessary to support both life and ministry. Being servants of God does not exempt people from daily work. Some people feel bivocational ministers or lay ministers provide a second-class ministry. However, a bivocational ministry is clearly biblical.

exclusively to preaching, testifying to the
Jews that Jesus was the Christ.[j] [n] 6But
when the Jews opposed Paul and became
abusive,[o] he shook out his clothes in protest[p] and said to them, "Your blood be
on your own heads![q] I am clear of my
responsibility.[r] From now on I will go to
the Gentiles."[s]

7Then Paul left the synagogue and
went next door to the house of Titius Justus, a worshiper of God.[t] 8Crispus,[u] the
synagogue ruler,[v] and his entire household[w] believed in the Lord; and many of
the Corinthians who heard him believed
and were baptized.

9One night the Lord spoke to Paul in a
vision:[x] "Do not be afraid;[y] keep on
speaking, do not be silent. 10For I am
with you,[z] and no one is going to attack
and harm you, because I have many people in this city." 11So Paul stayed for a
year and a half, teaching them the word
of God.[a]

12While Gallio was proconsul[b] of
Achaia,[c] the Jews made a united attack
on Paul and brought him into court.
13"This man," they charged, "is persuad-
ing the people to worship God in ways
contrary to the law."

14Just as Paul was about to speak, Gallio said to the Jews, "If you Jews were
making a complaint about some misde-
meanor or serious crime, it would be reasonable for me to listen to you. 15But
since it involves questions about words
and names and your own law[d]—settle
the matter yourselves. I will not be a
judge of such things." 16So he had them
ejected from the court. 17Then they all
turned on Sosthenes[e] the synagogue ruler[f] and beat him in front of the court.
But Gallio showed no concern whatever.

Priscilla, Aquila and Apollos

18Paul stayed on in Corinth for some
time. Then he left the brothers[g] and
sailed for Syria,[h] accompanied by Priscilla and Aquila.[i] Before he sailed, he had
his hair cut off at Cenchrea[j] because of a
vow he had taken.[k] 19They arrived at
Ephesus,[l] where Paul left Priscilla and
Aquila. He himself went into the synagogue and reasoned with the Jews.
20When they asked him to spend more
time with them, he declined. 21But as he
left, he promised, "I will come back if it
is God's will."[m] Then he set sail from
Ephesus. 22When he landed at Caesarea,[n] he went up and greeted the church
and then went down to Antioch.[o]

23After spending some time in Antioch,
Paul set out from there and traveled from
place to place throughout the region of
Galatia[p] and Phrygia,[q] strengthening all
the disciples.[r]

24Meanwhile a Jew named Apollos,[s] a
native of Alexandria, came to Ephesus.[t]
He was a learned man, with a thorough
knowledge of the Scriptures. 25He had

18:5 [n]S Ac 9:22
18:6 [o]S Ac 13:45 [p]S Mt 10:14 [q]2Sa 1:16; Eze 33:4 [r]Eze 3:17-19; Ac 20:26 [s]S Ac 13:46
18:7 [t]Ac 16:14
18:8 [u]1Co 1:14 [v]S Mk 5:22 [w]S Ac 11:14
18:9 [x]S Ac 9:10 [y]S Mt 14:27
18:10 [z]S Mt 28:20
18:11 [a]S Heb 4:12
18:12 [b]Ac 13:7,8, 12; 19:38 [c]ver 27; Ro 15:26; 1Co 16:15; 2Co 9:2; 1Th 1:7,8
18:15 [d]Ac 23:29; 25:11,19
18:17 [e]1Co 1:1 [f]ver 8
18:18 [g]ver 27; S Ac 1:16 [h]S Lk 2:2 [i]S ver 2 [j]Ro 16:1 [k]Nu 6:2,5,18; Ac 21:24
18:19 [l]ver 21,24; Ac 19:1,17,26; 1Co 15:32; 16:8; Eph 1:1; 1Ti 1:3; Rev 1:11; 2:1
18:21 [m]Ro 1:10; 15:32; 1Co 4:19; Jas 4:15
18:22 [n]S Ac 8:40 [o]S Ac 11:19
18:23 [p]S Ac 16:6 [q]Ac 2:10; 16:6 [r]Ac 14:22; 15:32, 41
18:24 [s]Ac 19:1; 1Co 1:12; 3:5,6,22; 4:6; 16:12; Tit 3:13 [t]S ver 19

j5 Or *Messiah;* also in verse 28

18:6 EVANGELISM, Confrontation—Paul was obedient to his responsibility to evangelize, even if he was criticized and his gospel message rejected. He clearly spelled out the results of rejection. We must evangelize regardless of the response. Evangelism includes confronting people with the judgment they face without Christ.

18:8 ORDINANCES, Baptismal Candidate—Always the order is absolutely important: first, believe in the Lord; then, be baptized. Baptism was the outward expression of the inward belief. In the case of Crispus, the ruler of the synagogue, his entire household was not baptized because he believed. Rather, as Luke says, he and his entire household believed in the Lord. Because of this belief in Jesus, they were baptized.

18:9–10 JESUS CHRIST, Intercession—The ascended Lord protects those who serve Him. The particular promise to Paul cannot be made a general principle that Jesus will not let harm come to anyone who serves Him. We can know that Jesus knows us, cares for us, and helps us even in troubled times. See note on Ro 8:26–39.

18:9 REVELATION, Dreams—Dream and vision may refer to the same reality. Paul received revelation in a vision at night, probably during a dream. The vision encouraged the apostle to speak the words which God placed in his mind and mouth. See note on 16:9–10.

18:11 EDUCATION, Missionaries—In one of the longest sojourns of his missionary career, Paul remained in Corinth for a year and a half. During that time, teaching was his primary strategy for winning the Corinthians to Christ. See note on 17:2.

18:12–17 CHRISTIAN ETHICS, Church and State—Gallio made an important statement regarding the intrusion of the state into determining theological orthodoxy—the state has no business in settling such matters.

18:18 DISCIPLESHIP, Women—Priscilla's level of leadership is indicated by the fact that she and her husband, Aquila, traveled with Paul in ministry. Christians gathered in Priscilla's homes in Corinth and Ephesus. She was a great encouragement to other leaders. Paul gave her special greetings (1 Ti 4:19). Clearly she was a leader in her own right. It may be significant that her name precedes that of her husband at times. See note on Ro 16:1–3.

18:19 EDUCATION, Missionaries—See note on 17:2.

18:21 GOD, Sovereignty—God is in charge. Christian servants need to follow the leading of God as He works. What we do in Christian service ought not simply be what we think we ought to do, but should be done out of a sense of the leadership of God, the will of God. God will not manipulate us, nor will He coerce us, but He does desire that we follow His leading.

18:22 THE CHURCH, Local Body—See notes on 4:32; 5:12–14.

18:24–26 EDUCATION, Christians—The Apollos episode tells us a great deal about Christian teaching in the early church. His previous instruction "in the way of the Lord" reflected the universal practice during the New Testament period of schooling every convert in the teachings of Jesus. The spontaneous lesson in the home of Priscilla and Aquila showed that the teaching function was not restricted to "official" teachers in the church. He taught with enthusiasm and fervor, convinced of the truth. Apollos learned an important lesson. Even the skilled teacher may be corrected and taught by people with less training and skill.

18:25 ORDINANCES, Baptism by Holy Spirit—Apollos had been instructed in the way of the Lord Jesus. He taught about Jesus accurately, but he knew only John's baptism. For him baptism had been a sign of repentance and expectation. He had to learn that baptism was a symbol of the death and

been instructed in the way of the Lord,
and he spoke with great fervor[k][u] and
taught about Jesus accurately, though he
knew only the baptism of John.[v] 26He began to speak boldly in the synagogue.
When Priscilla and Aquila[w] heard him,
they invited him to their home and explained to him the way of God more adequately.
27When Apollos wanted to go to Achaia,[x] the brothers[y] encouraged him and
wrote to the disciples there to welcome
him. On arriving, he was a great help to
those who by grace had believed. 28For
he vigorously refuted the Jews in public
debate, proving from the Scriptures[z] that
Jesus was the Christ.[a]

Chapter 19

Paul in Ephesus

WHILE Apollos[b] was at Corinth,[c]
Paul took the road through the interior and arrived at Ephesus.[d] There he
found some disciples 2and asked them,
"Did you receive the Holy Spirit[e] when[l]
you believed?"
They answered, "No, we have not
even heard that there is a Holy Spirit."
3So Paul asked, "Then what baptism
did you receive?"
"John's baptism," they replied.
4Paul said, "John's baptism[f] was a
baptism of repentance. He told the people
to believe in the one coming after him,
that is, in Jesus."[g] 5On hearing this, they
were baptized into[m] the name of the Lord
Jesus.[h] 6When Paul placed his hands on
them,[i] the Holy Spirit came on them,[j]
and they spoke in tongues[n][k] and prophesied. 7There were about twelve men in
all.
8Paul entered the synagogue[l] and
spoke boldly there for three months, arguing persuasively about the kingdom of
God.[m] 9But some of them[n] became obstinate; they refused to believe and publicly
maligned the Way.[o] So Paul left them.
He took the disciples[p] with him and had
discussions daily in the lecture hall of Ty-
rannus. 10This went on for two years,[q] so
that all the Jews and Greeks who lived in
the province of Asia[r] heard the word of
the Lord.[s]
11God did extraordinary miracles[t]
through Paul, 12so that even handkerchiefs and aprons that had touched him
were taken to the sick, and their illnesses
were cured[u] and the evil spirits left
them.
13Some Jews who went around driving
out evil spirits[v] tried to invoke the name

18:25 [u]Ro 12:11 [v]S Mk 1:4
18:26 [w]S ver 2
18:27 [x]S ver 12 [y]ver 18; S Ac 1:16
18:28 [z]Ac 8:35; 17:2 [a]ver 5; S Ac 9:22
19:1 [b]S Ac 18:24 [c]S Ac 18:1 [d]S Ac 18:19
19:2 [e]S Jn 20:22
19:4 [f]S Mk 1:4 [g]Jn 1:7
19:5 [h]S Ac 2:38
19:6 [i]S Ac 6:6 [j]S Ac 10:44 [k]S Mk 16:17
19:8 [l]S Ac 9:20 [m]S Mt 3:2; Ac 28:23
19:9 [n]Ac 14:4 [o]ver 23; S Ac 9:2 [p]ver 30; S Ac 11:26
19:10 [q]Ac 20:31 [r]ver 22,26,27; S Ac 2:9 [s]S Ac 13:48
19:11 [t]Ac 8:13
19:12 [u]Ac 5:15
19:13 [v]Mt 12:27

[k]25 Or *with fervor in the Spirit* [l]2 Or *after* [m]5 Or *in* [n]6 Or *other languages*

resurrection of Christ and thus of the believer's new life in Christ.

18:27 SALVATION, Grace—Those among whom Apollos labored in Achaia had believed by grace. God's grace in Jesus Christ enables us to trust Him for our salvation. See note on 15:11.

18:28 JESUS CHRIST, Fulfilled—See note on 13:27–41.

19:1–7 HOLY SPIRIT, Indwells—The disciples to whom Paul spoke at Ephesus were not Christians. They were disciples of John the Baptist, but not of Christ. They had received John's baptism; but they had not, of course, received the Holy Spirit, as the Spirit is given only to Christians. Paul preached to them about Christ; and they were baptized as Christians and received the gift of the Spirit, just as all Christians do. They also were given the gift of speaking in tongues, mentioned for the third and final time in Acts. See 10:46; note on 2:1–4. Since the tongues at Pentecost seem to have been foreign languages (rather than unknown tongues), it is possible that this was the case also of Cornelius at Caesarea and of the twelve disciples of John at Corinth; but the author does not specify that this was so. We need to talk to people about the Spirit to be sure they are Christians. It is easy to believe teachings without having saving faith in Christ. Conscious possession of the Spirit marks the true believer.

19:1–7 ORDINANCES, Baptism in Jesus' Name—Some interpreters have tried to make these twelve disciples at Ephesus *Christians who simply had not* yet received the Holy Spirit. This cannot be the case. They did not even know there was a Holy Spirit, and they had received only John's baptism. This made them disciples of John the Baptist, small groups of whom had continued to exist since the time of John's preaching at the Jordan River. Paul told the people to believe in the One coming after John, that is, in Jesus. By so doing they would follow what John had said. When they believed in Jesus, they were baptized in His name. They became Christians when they believed in Jesus, not when they believed in John. Then Paul laid his hands on them. The Holy Spirit came and gave them power to speak in tongues and prophesy, which means to witness to Jesus, just as the disciples had done at Pentecost. In fact, this is a kind of Gentile Pentecost, fulfilling the promise of Jesus in 1:8: "to the ends of the earth."

19:8 THE CHURCH, God's Kingdom—The kingdom was the center of Christ's proclamation and that of the early church. The church must invite people to repent and join God's kingdom. See notes on Mt 3:2; Lk 10:9–11.

19:8–10 EDUCATION, Missionaries—The greatest teachers do not have perfect success. Teaching the truth often leads to rejection, opposition, and hardship. Teaching success is marked by faithfulness to the task, not by public popularity. See note on 17:2.

19:9–10 EVANGELISM, In the Marketplace—The synagogue excluded Paul. He turned the defeat into new evangelistic strategy. He held public discussions in a famous lecture hall normally used by secular educators. His powerful presentations attracted audiences throughout the province. The gospel spread from the urban center outwards as people reported their experiences with Paul and his Savior.

19:11–12 MIRACLE, Instruments—God was at work. This was the faith of the church and of Luke, the inspired narrator. Earlier (5:15–16) Peter's shadow was sought. Here handkerchiefs and aprons (used by Paul as a tentmaker) became challenges to faith. "Extraordinary miracles" they were, for God healed through them. God's work transforms magic into miracle.

19:13–16 MIRACLE, Instruments—God's name is not magic. Using His name does not automatically bring miracle. The quasi-magic approach to healing in Ephesus resulted in this humorous tale. These Jews are described as professional peripatetic exorcists. From their kind must have come Simon (8:9) and Bar-Jesus (13:6). They respected the "name of Jesus" but appear to have had a secondhand acquaintance with Him "whom Paul preaches." In contrast with the highly successful miracle-working ministry of Paul (see note on 19:11–12), they failed miserably and dangerously. The demon-possessed resist-

of the Lord Jesus over those who were
demon-possessed. They would say, "In
the name of Jesus,[w] whom Paul preaches,
I command you to come out." 14Seven
sons of Sceva, a Jewish chief priest, were
doing this. 15⌊One day⌋ the evil spirit answered them, "Jesus I know, and I know
about Paul, but who are you?" 16Then the
man who had the evil spirit jumped on
them and overpowered them all. He gave
them such a beating that they ran out of
the house naked and bleeding.
17When this became known to the
Jews and Greeks living in Ephesus,[x] they
were all seized with fear,[y] and the name
of the Lord Jesus was held in high honor.
18Many of those who believed now came
and openly confessed their evil deeds. 19A
number who had practiced sorcery
brought their scrolls together and burned
them publicly. When they calculated the
value of the scrolls, the total came to fifty
thousand drachmas.[o] 20In this way the
word of the Lord[z] spread widely and
grew in power.[a]
21After all this had happened, Paul decided to go to Jerusalem,[b] passing
through Macedonia[c] and Achaia.[d] "After I have been there," he said, "I must
visit Rome also."[e] 22He sent two of his
helpers,[f] Timothy[g] and Erastus,[h] to
Macedonia, while he stayed in the province of Asia[i] a little longer.

The Riot in Ephesus

23About that time there arose a great
disturbance about the Way.[j] 24A silversmith named Demetrius, who made silver shrines of Artemis, brought in no little business for the craftsmen. 25He called
them together, along with the workmen
in related trades, and said: "Men, you
know we receive a good income from this
business.[k] 26And you see and hear how
this fellow Paul has convinced and led
astray large numbers of people here in
Ephesus[l] and in practically the whole
province of Asia.[m] He says that man-
made gods are no gods at all.[n] 27There is
danger not only that our trade will lose its
good name, but also that the temple of
the great goddess Artemis will be discredited, and the goddess herself, who is worshiped throughout the province of Asia
and the world, will be robbed of her divine majesty."
28When they heard this, they were furious and began shouting: "Great is Artemis of the Ephesians!"[o] 29Soon the
whole city was in an uproar. The people
seized Gaius[p] and Aristarchus,[q] Paul's
traveling companions from Macedonia,[r]
and rushed as one man into the theater.
30Paul wanted to appear before the
crowd, but the disciples[s] would not let
him. 31Even some of the officials of the
province, friends of Paul, sent him a message begging him not to venture into the
theater.
32The assembly was in confusion:
Some were shouting one thing, some another.[t] Most of the people did not even
know why they were there. 33The Jews
pushed Alexander to the front, and some
of the crowd shouted instructions to him.
He motioned[u] for silence in order to
make a defense before the people. 34But
when they realized he was a Jew, they all
shouted in unison for about two hours:
"Great is Artemis of the Ephesians!"[v]
35The city clerk quieted the crowd and
said: "Men of Ephesus,[w] doesn't all the
world know that the city of Ephesus is
the guardian of the temple of the great
Artemis and of her image, which fell from
heaven? 36Therefore, since these facts are
undeniable, you ought to be quiet and not
do anything rash. 37You have brought
these men here, though they have neither robbed temples[x] nor blasphemed
our goddess. 38If, then, Demetrius and his
fellow craftsmen[y] have a grievance
against anybody, the courts are open and
there are proconsuls.[z] They can press
charges. 39If there is anything further you
want to bring up, it must be settled in a
legal assembly. 40As it is, we are in danger of being charged with rioting because
of today's events. In that case we would
not be able to account for this commotion, since there is no reason for it." 41Af-
ter he had said this, he dismissed the assembly.

Chapter 20

Through Macedonia and Greece

WHEN the uproar had ended, Paul
sent for the disciples[a] and, after
encouraging them, said good-by and set
out for Macedonia.[b] 2He traveled
through that area, speaking many words
of encouragement to the people, and finally arrived in Greece, 3where he stayed
three months. Because the Jews made a
plot against him[c] just as he was about to
sail for Syria,[d] he decided to go back
through Macedonia.[e] 4He was accompa-

19:13 [w]Mk 9:38
19:17 [x]S Ac 18:19 [y]Ac 5:5,11
19:20 [z]S Ac 13:48 [a]Ac 6:7; 12:24
19:21 [b]Ac 20:16, 22; 21:4,12,15; Ro 15:25 [c]S Ac 16:9 [d]S Ac 18:12 [e]Ro 15:24,28
19:22 [f]Ac 13:5 [g]S Ac 16:1 [h]Ro 16:23; 2Ti 4:20 [i]ver 10,26,27; S Ac 2:9
19:23 [j]S Ac 9:2
19:25 [k]Ac 16:16, 19,20
19:26 [l]S Ac 18:19 [m]S Ac 2:9 [n]Dt 4:28; Ps 115:4; Isa 44:10-20; Jer 10:3-5; Ac 17:29; 1Co 8:4; Rev 9:20
19:28 [o]S Ac 18:19
19:29 [p]Ac 20:4; Ro 16:23; 1Co 1:14 [q]Ac 20:4; 27:2; Col 4:10; Phm 24 [r]S Ac 16:9
19:30 [s]S Ac 11:26
19:32 [t]Ac 21:34
19:33 [u]S Ac 12:17
19:34 [v]ver 28
19:35 [w]S Ac 18:19
19:37 [x]Ro 2:22
19:38 [y]ver 24 [z]Ac 13:7,8,12; 18:12
20:1 [a]S Ac 11:26 [b]S Ac 16:9
20:3 [c]ver 19; Ac 9:23,24; 14:5; 23:12,15,30; 25:3; 2Co 11:26; S 1Th 2:16 [d]S Lk 2:2 [e]S Ac 16:9

[o]*19* A drachma was a silver coin worth about a day's wages.

---

ed and attacked them. Jesus' name is powerful only as we commit ourselves to faith in Him.

19:23–41 GOD, One God—Faithfulness to God may cost us business and make us forsake inherited traditions. Not even a tradition about an image falling from heaven can establish another god's right to our worship. See note on 17:16–29.

nied by Sopater son of Pyrrhus from Berea, Aristarchus[f] and Secundus from
Thessalonica,[g] Gaius[h] from Derbe, Timothy[i] also, and Tychicus[j] and Trophimus[k] from the province of Asia.[l] 5These
men went on ahead and waited for us[m] at
Troas.[n] 6But we sailed from Philippi[o] after the Feast of Unleavened Bread, and
five days later joined the others at Troas,[p] where we stayed seven days.

Eutychus Raised From the Dead at Troas

7On the first day of the week[q] we
came together to break bread.[r] Paul
spoke to the people and, because he intended to leave the next day, kept on talking until midnight. 8There were many
lamps in the upstairs room[s] where we
were meeting. 9Seated in a window was a
young man named Eutychus, who was
sinking into a deep sleep as Paul talked
on and on. When he was sound asleep,
he fell to the ground from the third story
and was picked up dead. 10Paul went
down, threw himself on the young man[t]
and put his arms around him. "Don't be
alarmed," he said. "He's alive!"[u] 11Then
he went upstairs again and broke bread[v]
and ate. After talking until daylight,
he left. 12The people took the young
man home alive and were greatly comforted.

Paul's Farewell to the Ephesian Elders

13We went on ahead to the ship and
sailed for Assos, where we were going to
take Paul aboard. He had made this arrangement because he was going there
on foot. 14When he met us at Assos, we
took him aboard and went on to Mityle-
ne. 15The next day we set sail from there
and arrived off Kios. The day after that we
crossed over to Samos, and on the following day arrived at Miletus.[w] 16Paul had
decided to sail past Ephesus[x] to avoid
spending time in the province of Asia,[y]
for he was in a hurry to reach Jerusalem,[z] if possible, by the day of Pentecost.[a]

17From Miletus,[b] Paul sent to Ephesus
for the elders[c] of the church. 18When
they arrived, he said to them: "You know
how I lived the whole time I was with
you,[d] from the first day I came into the
province of Asia.[e] 19I served the Lord
with great humility and with tears,[f] although I was severely tested by the plots
of the Jews.[g] 20You know that I have not
hesitated to preach anything[h] that would
be helpful to you but have taught you
publicly and from house to house. 21I
have declared to both Jews[i] and Greeks
that they must turn to God in repentance[j] and have faith in our Lord Jesus.[k]

22"And now, compelled by the Spirit, I

20:4 [f]S Ac 19:29 [g]S Ac 17:1 [h]S Ac 19:29 [i]S Ac 16:1 [j]Eph 6:21; Col 4:7; Tit 3:12 [k]Ac 21:29; 2Ti 4:20 [l]S Ac 2:9
20:5 [m]S Ac 16:10 [n]S Ac 16:8
20:6 [o]S Ac 16:12 [p]S Ac 16:8
20:7 [q]1Co 16:2; Rev 1:10 [r]S Mt 14:19
20:8 [s]Ac 1:13; 9:37
20:10 [t]1Ki 17:21; 2Ki 4:34 [u]Mt 9:23, 24
20:11 [v]ver 7; S Mt 14:19
20:15 [w]ver 17; 2Ti 4:20
20:16 [x]S Ac 18:19 [y]S Ac 2:9 [z]S Ac 19:21 [a]S Ac 2:1
20:17 [b]ver 15 [c]S Ac 11:30
20:18 [d]Ac 18:19-21; 19:1-41 [e]S Ac 2:9
20:19 [f]Ps 6:6 [g]S ver 3
20:20 [h]ver 27; Ps 40:10; Jer 26:2; 42:4
20:21 [i]Ac 18:5 [j]S Ac 2:38 [k]Ac 24:24; 26:18; Eph 1:15; Col 2:5; Phm 5

20:7–12 MIRACLE, Praise—The hour was late; the sermon long; lamps were heating the room. Eutychus sat in a window, went to sleep, and fell to the ground from the third story. Now everyone was awake and supposed Eutychus to be dead. Paul reassured the crowd, "He's alive." It is not certain Dr. Luke considered this a miracle of restoration to life—perhaps the young man was merely knocked unconscious. Then the miracle was preservation of life. The crowd rejoiced in his well-being. They had seen God at work.

20:7 ORDINANCES, Observance of Lord's Supper—To "break bread" is almost certainly a reference to the Lord's Supper. See note on 2:42–46; Lk 24:35. Because of this verse, many Christians observe the Lord's Supper every Sunday. If properly carried out, such weekly observance may be very appropriate. Yet, this is the only time weekly observance is mentioned. Nowhere is weekly observance commanded or reported, and nowhere is any other frequency commanded. The emphasis is always upon meaning and proper observance, never upon frequency. That question is left open by the indefinite phrase "whenever you drink this cup" (1 Co 11:25).

20:7 WORSHIP, Calendar—See note on Ex 16:23–30. The resurrection changed the worship calendar for Jesus' first followers.

20:17 CHURCH LEADERS, Elder—The elders of the church are the same people described as overseers or bishops in 20:28. The designations as elders, overseers (bishops), and pastors (shepherds) are synonymous titles that refer to the same leadership role. They exercise spiritual care over the local church, protecting the church from false leaders.

20:17–21 EVANGELISM, Call to Salvation—Paul's consistent life, humility, persistent preaching, public teaching, and testimony to Christ were all part of his evangelistic ministry. He called all people to salvation through turning from sin to serve God in total commitment of life to Christ.

20:20–21 WORSHIP, Proclamation—See note on Jer 26:2–7.

20:20–21 PROCLAMATION, Unbelievers—Proclamation helps the church to grow in Christ and invites the unsaved to believe in Christ. Paul did not shrink back from preaching (Greek *anangellō*) what was helpful to the Ephesians. He publicly invited people of all races to accept the gospel. God intends for unbelievers to be brought to repentance and faith through the preaching of the gospel (1 Co 1:21). Proclamation closes with an appeal for repentance and faith, the gift of the Holy Spirit, and the promise of salvation (Eph 1:13–14). New Testament proclamation is primarily the authoritative declaration of the good news, inviting all people to salvation through our Lord Jesus Christ.

20:20–21 EDUCATION, Missionaries—Paul provided an important clue concerning his missionary methods when he bid farewell to the Ephesian elders. He taught the Christian faith in private homes as well as in public gatherings. He was willing to teach all who would listen regardless of race or culture. He sought to bring his pupils to repentance and faith in Christ, not just increase their factual knowledge. He did not refrain from teaching certain truths for fear of opposition. He taught whatever God showed him was helpful for the people.

20:21 SALVATION, Repentance—Jews and Greeks—that is, all people—must turn to God in repentance to be saved. Saving faith includes and implies repentance. The two cannot be separated.

20:22–23 HOLY SPIRIT, Guides—The Spirit guides a Christian even in desperate danger. The Spirit was given to Paul at his conversion, called him to be a missionary, and guided him at various times on his journeys. See notes on 6:1–6; 13:1–4; 16:6–10. The Spirit led Paul to leave the churches he had planted for the last time and go to Jerusalem. The Spirit prepared Paul to suffer there for his faith. The Spirit always guides Christians to bear witness concerning Christ. In some cases, He guides us to do this even though we will be persecuted. Remaining alive is not the Christian's goal. Accomplishing the Spirit's mission for us is.

am going to Jerusalem,[l] not knowing
what will happen to me there. 23I only
know that in every city the Holy Spirit
warns me[m] that prison and hardships are
facing me.[n] 24However, I consider my
life worth nothing to me,[o] if only I may
finish the race[p] and complete the task[q]
the Lord Jesus has given me[r]—the task
of testifying to the gospel of God's
grace.[s]
25"Now I know that none of you
among whom I have gone about preaching the kingdom[t] will ever see me
again.[u] 26Therefore, I declare to you today that I am innocent of the blood of all
men.[v] 27For I have not hesitated to proclaim to you the whole will of God.[w]
28Keep watch over yourselves and all the
flock[x] of which the Holy Spirit has made
you overseers.[p][y] Be shepherds of the
church of God,[q][z] which he bought[a]
with his own blood.[b] 29I know that after I
leave, savage wolves[c] will come in
among you and will not spare the flock.[d]
30Even from your own number men will
arise and distort the truth in order to
draw away disciples[e] after them. 31So be
on your guard! Remember that for three
years[f] I never stopped warning each of
you night and day with tears.[g]
32"Now I commit you to God[h] and to
the word of his grace, which can build
you up and give you an inheritance[i]
among all those who are sanctified.[j] 33I
have not coveted anyone's silver or gold
or clothing.[k] 34You yourselves know that
these hands of mine have supplied my
own needs and the needs of my companions.[l] 35In everything I did, I showed you
that by this kind of hard work we must
help the weak, remembering the words
the Lord Jesus himself said: 'It is more
blessed to give than to receive.'"
36When he had said this, he knelt
down with all of them and prayed.[m]
37They all wept as they embraced him
and kissed him.[n] 38What grieved them
most was his statement that they would
never see his face again.[o] Then they accompanied him to the ship.[p]

Chapter 21

On to Jerusalem

AFTER we[q] had torn ourselves away
from them, we put out to sea and
sailed straight to Cos. The next day we
went to Rhodes and from there to Patara.
2We found a ship crossing over to Phoenicia,[r] went on board and set sail. 3After
sighting Cyprus and passing to the south
of it, we sailed on to Syria.[s] We landed at
Tyre, where our ship was to unload its
cargo. 4Finding the disciples[t] there, we
stayed with them seven days. Through
the Spirit[u] they urged Paul not to go on
to Jerusalem. 5But when our time was up,
we left and continued on our way. All the

[p]28 Traditionally *bishops* [q]28 Many manuscripts *of the Lord*

20:22 [l]ver 16
20:23 [m]S Ac 8:29; 21:4 [n]S Ac 9:16
20:24 [o]Ac 21:13 [p]2Ti 4:7 [q]2Co 4:1 [r]Gal 1:1; Tit 1:3 [s]S Ac 11:23
20:25 [t]S Mt 4:23 [u]ver 38
20:26 [v]Eze 3:17-19; Ac 18:6
20:27 [w]S ver 20
20:28 [x]ver 29; S Jn 21:16 [y]S 1Ti 3:1 [z]S 1Co 10:32 [a]S 1Co 6:20 [b]S Ro 3:25
20:29 [c]Eze 34:5; Mt 7:15 [d]ver 28
20:30 [e]S Ac 11:26
20:31 [f]Ac 19:10 [g]ver 19
20:32 [h]Ac 14:23 [i]S Eph 1:14; S Mt 25:34; Col 1:12; 3:24; Heb 9:15; 1Pe 1:4 [j]Ac 26:18
20:33 [k]1Sa 12:3; 1Co 9:12; 2Co 2:17; 7:2; 11:9; 12:14-17; 1Th 2:5
20:34 [l]S Ac 18:3
20:36 [m]Lk 22:41; Ac 9:40; 21:5
20:37 [n]S Lk 15:20
20:38 [o]ver 25 [p]Ac 21:5
21:1 [q]S Ac 16:10
21:2 [r]Ac 11:19
21:3 [s]S Lk 2:2
21:4 [t]S Ac 11:26 [u]ver 11; Ac 20:23

20:24,32 GOD, Grace—Grace is a beautiful word for the love of God in action providing redemption for lost people. Grace is the unmerited favor God gives to us in the forgiveness of our sins and all of the spiritual resources that build up the new life in Christ. Grace is God's active, creative blessing in the lives of those who respond to Him in faith.

20:24 DISCIPLESHIP, Lordship of Christ—Paul's goal was to complete the task God had given to him, no matter what the cost might be. Such sacrificial living in obedience to the Lord is essential in reaching God's goals.

20:25 THE CHURCH, God's Kingdom—See note on 19:8.

20:28 HOLY SPIRIT, Leaders—The Spirit chooses leaders for the church. Thus the seven Grecian Jewish Christians were all full of the Spirit (6:1–3), and Paul and Barnabus were called to be missionaries by the Spirit (13:1–2). The overseers or pastors of the church of Ephesus were led by the Spirit into their pastoral work.

20:28 SALVATION, Atonement—God purchased or obtained His church with the shed blood of His Son on Calvary. The New Testament doctrine of salvation centers on God's act of atonement at the cross. The church can exist because of God's act to create it.

20:28 THE CHURCH, Local Body—Each believer has the responsibility to strengthen other believers. This is especially true of those who shepherd the flock. Jesus died for the church. Christians must live to strengthen it. See note on Mt 16:18–19.

20:28 CHURCH LEADERS, Pastor and Overseer—This passage indicates that pastors and overseers (or bishops) are identical offices designated by different terms. The same leaders are also called elders (v 17). The person responsible for a church is portrayed under the image of shepherd (pastor) who cares for a flock and under the image of overseer or guardian (bishop) who gives leadership to a particular congregation. This same combination of images is used of Jesus in 1 Pe 2:25. Jesus is the Shepherd and Overseer of our souls. The overseers are not elevated to a rank above the rest of the congregation. They are not dignitaries but servants who see to the worship, evangelism, training, discipline, and administration of the local congregation. They have responsibility for the spiritual welfare of their people as well as authority to supervise and nurture them.

20:32 SALVATION, Sanctification—See notes on 26:18; Jn 17:17. Sanctification is being made holy by His gospel of grace. Sanctification involves a building process in the spiritual and ethical life of the believer. Sanctification leads to participation in Christ's eternal inheritance.

20:35 DISCIPLESHIP, Persons—Paul used his personal example to motivate the Ephesians to work hard and help the weak. He recalled Jesus' teaching that more happiness is found through giving than through getting. That principle should guide every disciple.

20:35 STEWARDSHIP, Care of Needy—Receiving is good; giving is better. Paul believed in working diligently to provide for one's family and to give. Giving to help the weak is an essential part of worship. Such giving brings a Christian joy. Jesus' life of giving is the Christian's model. See note on Mt 5:23–24.

20:36 PRAYER, Blessing—Prayer was used to send Paul away. He had been sent out with prayer from Antioch. See note on 13:2–3. No doubt this prayer also included Paul's blessings on the Ephesian church. Separation from other believers is an important time to pray for one another.

21:5 PRAYER, Biblical Characters—See note on 20:36. Prayer is appropriate anywhere.

disciples and their wives and children accompanied us out of the city, and there
on the beach we knelt to pray.[v] 6After
saying good-by to each other, we went
aboard the ship, and they returned home.
7We continued our voyage from Tyre[w]
and landed at Ptolemais, where we greeted the brothers[x] and stayed with them
for a day. 8Leaving the next day, we
reached Caesarea[y] and stayed at the
house of Philip[z] the evangelist,[a] one of
the Seven. 9He had four unmarried
daughters who prophesied.[b]
10After we had been there a number of
days, a prophet named Agabus[c] came
down from Judea. 11Coming over to us,
he took Paul's belt, tied his own hands
and feet with it and said, "The Holy Spirit
says,[d] 'In this way the Jews of Jerusalem
will bind[e] the owner of this belt and will
hand him over to the Gentiles.' "[f]
12When we heard this, we and the people there pleaded with Paul not to go up
to Jerusalem. 13Then Paul answered,
"Why are you weeping and breaking my
heart? I am ready not only to be bound,
but also to die[g] in Jerusalem for the
name of the Lord Jesus."[h] 14When he
would not be dissuaded, we gave up[i] and
said, "The Lord's will be done."[j]
15After this, we got ready and went up
to Jerusalem.[k] 16Some of the disciples
from Caesarea[l] accompanied us and
brought us to the home of Mnason,
where we were to stay. He was a man
from Cyprus[m] and one of the early disciples.

Paul's Arrival at Jerusalem

17When we arrived at Jerusalem, the
brothers[n] received us warmly.[o] 18The
next day Paul and the rest of us went to
see James,[p] and all the elders[q] were
present. 19Paul greeted them and reported in detail what God had done among
the Gentiles[r] through his ministry.[s]
20When they heard this, they praised
God. Then they said to Paul: "You see,
brother, how many thousands of Jews
have believed, and all of them are zealous[t] for the law.[u] 21They have been informed that you teach all the Jews who
live among the Gentiles to turn away
from Moses,[v] telling them not to circumcise their children[w] or live according to
our customs.[x] 22What shall we do? They
will certainly hear that you have come,
23so do what we tell you. There are four
men with us who have made a vow.[y]
24Take these men, join in their purification rites[z] and pay their expenses, so
that they can have their heads shaved.[a]
Then everybody will know there is no
truth in these reports about you, but that
you yourself are living in obedience to the
law. 25As for the Gentile believers, we
have written to them our decision that
they should abstain from food sacrificed
to idols, from blood, from the meat of
strangled animals and from sexual immorality."[b]
26The next day Paul took the men and
purified himself along with them. Then
he went to the temple to give notice of
the date when the days of purification
would end and the offering would be
made for each of them.[c]

Paul Arrested

27When the seven days were nearly
over, some Jews from the province of
Asia saw Paul at the temple. They stirred
up the whole crowd and seized him,[d]
28shouting, "Men of Israel, help us! This
is the man who teaches all men everywhere against our people and our law and
this place. And besides, he has brought
Greeks into the temple area and defiled
this holy place."[e] 29(They had previously
seen Trophimus[f] the Ephesian[g] in the
city with Paul and assumed that Paul had
brought him into the temple area.)
30The whole city was aroused, and the
people came running from all directions.
Seizing Paul,[h] they dragged him[i] from
the temple, and immediately the gates
were shut. 31While they were trying to
kill him, news reached the commander of

21:5 [v]Lk 22:41; Ac 9:40; 20:36
21:7 [w]Ac 12:20 [x]S Ac 1:16
21:8 [y]S Ac 8:40 [z]Ac 6:5; 8:5-40 [a]Eph 4:11; 2Ti 4:5
21:9 [b]Ex 15:20; Jdg 4:4; Ne 6:14; Lk 2:36; Ac 2:17; 1Co 11:5
21:10 [c]Ac 11:28
21:11 [d]S Ac 8:29 [e]ver 33 [f]1Ki 22:11; Isa 20:2-4; Jer 13:1-11; Mt 20:19
21:13 [g]Ac 20:24 [h]S Jn 15:21; S Ac 9:16
21:14 [i]Ru 1:18 [j]S Mt 26:39
21:15 [k]S Ac 19:21
21:16 [l]S Ac 8:40 [m]ver 3,4
21:17 [n]S Ac 9:30 [o]Ac 15:4
21:18 [p]S Ac 15:13 [q]S Ac 11:30
21:19 [r]Ac 14:27; 15:4,12 [s]Ac 1:17
21:20 [t]Ac 22:3; Ro 10:2; Gal 1:14; Php 3:6 [u]Ac 15:1,5
21:21 [v]ver 28 [w]Ac 15:19-21; 1Co 7:18,19 [x]S Ac 6:14
21:23 [y]Nu 6:2,5, 18; Ac 18:18
21:24 [z]ver 26; Ac 24:18 [a]Ac 18:18
21:25 [b]Ac 15:20, 29
21:26 [c]Nu 6:13-20; Ac 24:18
21:27 [d]Jer 26:8; Ac 24:18; 26:21; S 1Th 2:16
21:28 [e]Mt 24:15; Ac 6:13; 24:5,6
21:29 [f]Ac 20:4; 2Ti 4:20 [g]S Ac 18:19
21:30 [h]Ac 26:21 [i]S Ac 16:19

21:8 CHURCH LEADERS, Evangelist—Philip, the evangelist, is best known for his missionary work in Samaria and with the Ethiopian eunuch (8:5–40). An evangelist brings the good news of salvation to the unconverted and calls them to repentance. Pastors can also do the work of evangelists (2 Ti 4:5). Evangelists are included in the leadership team God has given the church (Eph 4:11).

21:9–11 CHURCH LEADERS, Prophet—The gift of prophecy can be bestowed as God wills upon any Christian (2:17; 19:6; 1 Co 11:5). The community does not install anyone into this office. It simply recognizes that someone has the prophetic gift. Both men and women may prophesy (1 Co 11:4–5). The church is to listen to such proclamation of God's will in an orderly fashion and weigh its meaning (1 Co 14:29–33). The message of a prophet may be quite specific, as in the case of Agabus (Ac 21:10–11).

21:11 HOLY SPIRIT, Revelation—The Spirit uses different means to reveal His will to protect His people. Agabus had been given the gift of prophecy earlier (see note on 11:28) and had predicted a famine. Prediction is an infrequent prophetic work in the New Testament. Agabus continued another prophetic tradition, that of acting out a prophetic oracle. Compare Jer 13:1–11. Ordinarily the gift of prophecy to Christians equipped them to proclaim the gospel, but occasionally it included predictions and oracles direct from God. See note on Ac 20:22–23.

21:12–14 DISCIPLESHIP, Kingdom of God—Personal safety and security do not occupy the disciple's mind. Kingdom business does. Paul demonstrated the same kind of commitment Jesus expressed in His Gethsemane prayer. God's will, not human precautions, determined their actions. See note on Mk 14:36.

the Roman troops that the whole city of
Jerusalem was in an uproar. 32He at once
took some officers and soldiers and ran
down to the crowd. When the rioters saw
the commander and his soldiers, they
stopped beating Paul.[j]
33The commander came up and arrested him and ordered him to be bound[k]
with two[l] chains.[m] Then he asked who
he was and what he had done. 34Some in
the crowd shouted one thing and some
another,[n] and since the commander
could not get at the truth because of the
uproar, he ordered that Paul be taken into
the barracks.[o] 35When Paul reached the
steps,[p] the violence of the mob was so
great he had to be carried by the soldiers.
36The crowd that followed kept shouting,
"Away with him!"[q]

Paul Speaks to the Crowd

22:3–16pp — Ac 9:1–22; 26:9–18

37As the soldiers were about to take
Paul into the barracks,[r] he asked the
commander, "May I say something to
you?"
"Do you speak Greek?" he replied.
38"Aren't you the Egyptian who started a
revolt and led four thousand terrorists out
into the desert[s] some time ago?"[t]
39Paul answered, "I am a Jew, from
Tarsus[u] in Cilicia,[v] a citizen of no ordinary city. Please let me speak to the people."

Chapter 22

40HAVING received the commander's
permission, Paul stood on the steps
and motioned[w] to the crowd. When they
were all silent, he said to them in Aramaic[r]:[x] 1Brothers and fathers,[y] listen now
to my defense."
2When they heard him speak to them
in Aramaic,[z] they became very quiet.
Then Paul said: 3"I am a Jew,[a] born in
Tarsus[b] of Cilicia,[c] but brought up in
this city. Under[d] Gamaliel[e] I was thoroughly trained in the law of our fathers[f]
and was just as zealous[g] for God as any of
you are today. 4I persecuted[h] the followers of this Way[i] to their death, arresting
both men and women and throwing them
into prison,[j] 5as also the high priest and
all the Council[k] can testify. I even obtained letters from them to their brothers[l] in Damascus,[m] and went there to
bring these people as prisoners to Jerusalem to be punished.
6"About noon as I came near Damascus, suddenly a bright light from heaven
flashed around me.[n] 7I fell to the ground
and heard a voice say to me, 'Saul! Saul!
Why do you persecute me?'
8" 'Who are you, Lord?' I asked.
" 'I am Jesus of Nazareth,[o] whom you
are persecuting,' he replied. 9My companions saw the light,[p] but they did not
understand the voice[q] of him who was
speaking to me.
10" 'What shall I do, Lord?' I asked.
" 'Get up,' the Lord said, 'and go into
Damascus. There you will be told all that
you have been assigned to do.'[r] 11My
companions led me by the hand into Damascus, because the brilliance of the light
had blinded me.[s]
12"A man named Ananias came to see
me.[t] He was a devout observer of the
law and highly respected by all the Jews
living there.[u] 13He stood beside me and
said, 'Brother Saul, receive your sight!'
And at that very moment I was able to see
him.
14"Then he said: 'The God of our fathers[v] has chosen you to know his will
and to see[w] the Righteous One[x] and to
hear words from his mouth. 15You will be
his witness[y] to all men of what you have
seen[z] and heard. 16And now what are

21:32 [j]Ac 23:27
21:33 [k]ver 11 [l]Ac 12:6 [m]Ac 20:23; 22:29; Eph 6:20; 2Ti 2:9
21:34 [n]Ac 19:32 [o]ver 37; Ac 22:24; 23:10,16,32
21:35 [p]ver 40
21:36 [q]Lk 23:18; Jn 19:15; Ac 22:22
21:37 [r]S ver 34
21:38 [s]Mt 24:26 [t]Ac 5:36
21:39 [u]S Ac 9:11 [v]S Ac 6:9
22:1 [w]S Ac 12:17 [x]S Jn 5:2 [y]Ac 7:2
22:2 [z]Ac 21:40; S Jn 5:2
22:3 [a]Ac 21:39 [b]S Ac 9:11 [c]S Ac 6:9 [d]Lk 10:39 [e]Ac 5:34 [f]Ac 26:5 [g]1Ki 19:10; S Ac 21:20
22:4 [h]S Ac 8:3 [i]S Ac 9:2 [j]ver 19,20
22:5 [k]Lk 22:66 [l]S Ac 1:16; 2:29; 13:26; 23:1; 28:17, 21; S Ro 7:1; 9:3 [m]Ac 9:2
22:6 [n]Ac 9:3
22:8 [o]S Mk 1:24
22:9 [p]Ac 26:13 [q]Ac 9:7
22:10 [r]Ac 16:30
22:11 [s]Ac 9:8
22:12 [t]Ac 9:17 [u]Ac 10:22
22:14 [v]S Ac 3:13 [w]S 1Co 15:8 [x]Ac 7:52
22:15 [y]Ac 23:11; 26:16 [z]ver 14

[r]40 Or possibly *Hebrew*; also in 22:2

22:1–29 CHRISTIAN ETHICS, Church and State—Paul persecuted Christians as a part of His religious convictions. It may be argued whether a government should have allowed his activities. After his conversion he faced similar persecution. He did not appeal on religious grounds. Because the situation had become a civil matter, it was appropriate for Paul to appeal to the rights of his Roman citizenship to restore some order to the situation.

22:7–11 REVELATION, Visions—See note on 9:3–8. A vision serves as revelation to the recipient. When repeated in personal testimony, it becomes revelation to a wider audience. When written in a book through God's inspiration, it becomes revelation for a still wider audience.

22:14 JESUS CHRIST, Sinless—See note on 3:14.

22:14–16 ELECTION, Predestination—When Paul was arrested in Jerusalem, he boldly spoke of God electing him not only for salvation but for the specific service of sharing the gospel with Gentiles. Election was not the final step. Paul had to activate the benefits of election by praying in faith and obeying God in baptism. "Chosen" (Greek *procheirizō*) means to get something ready for use. In political and military settings it refers to election of leaders. God chose or elected Paul to know Him in salvation and prepared him as a missionary to the Gentiles. Compare 3:20; 26:16.

22:16 SALVATION, As Cleansing—Christian baptism symbolizes the washing away of sin. Salvation centers on getting rid of the sin problem every person faces. Through Christ's death God provided the possibility to repent, believe, and be cleansed of sin.

22:16 ORDINANCES, Baptism in Jesus' Name—In Paul's account of his conversion and the role of Ananias in baptizing him, he recalls a four-step exhortation: (1) get up: meaning to act right now and put it off no longer; (2) be baptized: the visible sign by which he acknowledged Jesus as Lord and Savior; (3) wash your sins away: not that the water could actually wash away sins, but it could be the outward sign of what Jesus did in the heart; and (4) call on Jesus' name: which actually means that Paul was submitting himself to Jesus as Lord. By having the name of Jesus pronounced over him, Paul was identified as belonging to Jesus and being His servant. Paul explains, in his own testimony, what baptism really meant to him and what it should mean to us.

you waiting for? Get up, be baptized[a] and wash your sins away,[b] calling on his name.'[c]

17"When I returned to Jerusalem[d] and was praying at the temple, I fell into a trance[e] 18and saw the Lord speaking. 'Quick!' he said to me. 'Leave Jerusalem immediately, because they will not accept your testimony about me.'

19" 'Lord,' I replied, 'these men know that I went from one synagogue to another to imprison[f] and beat[g] those who believe in you. 20And when the blood of your martyr[s] Stephen was shed, I stood there giving my approval and guarding the clothes of those who were killing him.'[h]

21"Then the Lord said to me, 'Go; I will send you far away to the Gentiles.' "[i]

Paul the Roman Citizen

22The crowd listened to Paul until he said this. Then they raised their voices and shouted, "Rid the earth of him![j] He's not fit to live!"[k]

23As they were shouting and throwing off their cloaks[l] and flinging dust into the air,[m] 24the commander ordered Paul to be taken into the barracks.[n] He directed[o] that he be flogged and questioned in order to find out why the people were shouting at him like this. 25As they stretched him out to flog him, Paul said to the centurion standing there, "Is it legal for you to flog a Roman citizen who hasn't even been found guilty?"[p]

26When the centurion heard this, he went to the commander and reported it. "What are you going to do?" he asked. "This man is a Roman citizen."

27The commander went to Paul and asked, "Tell me, are you a Roman citizen?"

"Yes, I am," he answered.

28Then the commander said, "I had to pay a big price for my citizenship."

"But I was born a citizen," Paul replied.

29Those who were about to question him[q] withdrew immediately. The commander himself was alarmed when he realized that he had put Paul, a Roman citizen,[r] in chains.[s]

Before the Sanhedrin

30The next day, since the commander wanted to find out exactly why Paul was being accused by the Jews,[t] he released him[u] and ordered the chief priests and all the Sanhedrin[v] to assemble. Then he brought Paul and had him stand before them.

Chapter 23

PAUL looked straight at the Sanhedrin[w] and said, "My brothers,[x] I have fulfilled my duty to God in all good conscience[y] to this day." 2At this the high priest Ananias[z] ordered those standing near Paul to strike him on the mouth.[a] 3Then Paul said to him, "God will strike you, you whitewashed wall![b] You sit there to judge me according to the law, yet you yourself violate the law by commanding that I be struck!"[c]

4Those who were standing near Paul said, "You dare to insult God's high priest?"

5Paul replied, "Brothers, I did not realize that he was the high priest; for it is written: 'Do not speak evil about the ruler of your people.'[t] "[d]

6Then Paul, knowing that some of them were Sadducees[e] and the others Pharisees, called out in the Sanhedrin, "My brothers,[f] I am a Pharisee,[g] the son of a Pharisee. I stand on trial because of my hope in the resurrection of the dead."[h] 7When he said this, a dispute broke out between the Pharisees and the Sadducees, and the assembly was divided. 8(The Sadducees say that there is no resurrection,[i] and that there are neither angels nor spirits, but the Pharisees acknowledge them all.)

9There was a great uproar, and some of the teachers of the law who were Pharisees[j] stood up and argued vigorously. "We find nothing wrong with this man,"[k] they said. "What if a spirit or an angel has spoken to him?"[l] 10The dispute became so violent that the commander was afraid Paul would be torn to pieces by them. He ordered the troops to go down and take him away from them by force and bring him into the barracks.[m]

11The following night the Lord stood

22:16 [a]S Ac 2:38 [b]Lev 8:6; Ps 51:2; Eze 36:25; Jn 3:5; 1Co 6:11; Eph 5:26; Tit 3:5; Heb 10:22; 1Pe 3:21 [c]Ro 10:13
22:17 [d]Ac 9:26 [e]Ac 10:10
22:19 [f]ver 4; S Ac 8:3 [g]S Mt 10:17
22:20 [h]Ac 7:57-60; 8:1
22:21 [i]S Ac 9:15; S 13:46
22:22 [j]Ac 21:36 [k]Ac 25:24
22:23 [l]Ac 7:58 [m]2Sa 16:13
22:24 [n]S Ac 21:34 [o]ver 29
22:25 [p]Ac 16:37
22:29 [q]ver 24 [r]ver 24,25; Ac 16:38 [s]S Ac 21:33
22:30 [t]Ac 23:28 [u]Ac 21:33 [v]S Mt 5:22
23:1 [w]Ac 22:30 [x]S Ac 22:5 [y]Ac 24:16; 1Co 4:4; 2Co 1:12; 1Ti 1:5,19; 3:9; 2Ti 1:3; Heb 9:14; 10:22; 13:18; 1Pe 3:16,21
23:2 [z]Ac 24:1 [a]Jn 18:22
23:3 [b]Mt 23:27 [c]Lev 19:15; Dt 25:1,2; Jn 7:51
23:5 [d]Ex 22:28
23:6 [e]ver 7,8; S Ac 4:1 [f]S Ac 22:5 [g]Ac 26:5; Php 3:5 [h]Ac 24:15,21; 26:8
23:8 [i]Mt 22:23; 1Co 15:12
23:9 [j]Mk 2:16 [k]ver 29; Jer 26:16; S Lk 23:4; Ac 25:25; 26:31; 28:18 [l]Ac 22:7,17,18
23:10 [m]S Ac 21:34

[s]20 Or *witness* [t]5 Exodus 22:28

22:17 PRAYER, Instruction—A vision often came in a time of prayer. See notes on 9:11; 10:9. God uses prayer time to guide His people in important decisions of life.

22:20–21 EVANGELISM, Call to Evangelize—Crisis moments call us to God. Paul was not converted by Stephen's preaching. He took up the persecution of the church (8:1–3). The witness of Stephen's martyrdom deeply influenced Paul. It was a first step to his call to witness to Gentiles. God's call leads each of us to a specific evangelistic task. We are responsible to carry out that task. As we do, we are to use every opportunity to share Christ with others.

23:6–8 LAST THINGS, Believers' Resurrection—The hope of the resurrection of the dead is at the heart of authentic, biblical faith. Without it the whole Christian movement ends in hopeless futility (1 Co 15:16–19).

23:11 JESUS CHRIST, Intercession—See note on

near Paul and said, "Take courage![n] As you have testified about me in Jerusalem, so you must also testify in Rome."[o]

The Plot to Kill Paul

12The next morning the Jews formed a conspiracy[p] and bound themselves with an oath not to eat or drink until they had killed Paul.[q] 13More than forty men were involved in this plot. 14They went to the chief priests and elders and said, "We have taken a solemn oath not to eat anything until we have killed Paul.[r] 15Now then, you and the Sanhedrin[s] petition the commander to bring him before you on the pretext of wanting more accurate information about his case. We are ready to kill him before he gets here."

16But when the son of Paul's sister heard of this plot, he went into the barracks[t] and told Paul.

17Then Paul called one of the centurions and said, "Take this young man to the commander; he has something to tell him." 18So he took him to the commander.

The centurion said, "Paul, the prisoner,[u] sent for me and asked me to bring this young man to you because he has something to tell you."

19The commander took the young man by the hand, drew him aside and asked, "What is it you want to tell me?"

20He said: "The Jews have agreed to ask you to bring Paul before the Sanhedrin[v] tomorrow on the pretext of wanting more accurate information about him.[w] 21Don't give in to them, because more than forty[x] of them are waiting in ambush for him. They have taken an oath not to eat or drink until they have killed him.[y] They are ready now, waiting for your consent to their request."

22The commander dismissed the young man and cautioned him, "Don't tell anyone that you have reported this to me."

Paul Transferred to Caesarea

23Then he called two of his centurions and ordered them, "Get ready a detachment of two hundred soldiers, seventy horsemen and two hundred spearmen[u] to go to Caesarea[z] at nine tonight.[a] 24Provide mounts for Paul so that he may be taken safely to Governor Felix."[b]

25He wrote a letter as follows:

26Claudius Lysias,

To His Excellency,[c] Governor Felix:

Greetings.[d]

27This man was seized by the Jews and they were about to kill him,[e] but I came with my troops and rescued him,[f] for I had learned that he is a Roman citizen.[g] 28I wanted to know why they were accusing him, so I brought him to their Sanhedrin.[h] 29I found that the accusation had to do with questions about their law,[i] but there was no charge against him[j] that deserved death or imprisonment. 30When I was informed[k] of a plot[l] to be carried out against the man, I sent him to you at once. I also ordered his accusers[m] to present to you their case against him.

31So the soldiers, carrying out their orders, took Paul with them during the night and brought him as far as Antipatris. 32The next day they let the cavalry[n] go on with him, while they returned to the barracks.[o] 33When the cavalry[p] arrived in Caesarea,[q] they delivered the letter to the governor[r] and handed Paul over to him. 34The governor read the letter and asked what province he was from. Learning that he was from Cilicia,[s] 35he said, "I will hear your case when your accusers[t] get here." Then he ordered that Paul be kept under guard[u] in Herod's palace.

Chapter 24

The Trial Before Felix

FIVE days later the high priest Ananias[v] went down to Caesarea with some of the elders and a lawyer named Tertullus, and they brought their charges[w] against Paul before the governor.[x] 2When Paul was called in, Tertullus presented his case before Felix: "We have enjoyed a long period of peace under you, and your foresight has brought about reforms in this nation. 3Everywhere and in every way, most excellent[y] Felix, we acknowledge this with profound gratitude. 4But in order not to weary you further, I would request that you be kind enough to hear us briefly.

5"We have found this man to be a trou-

23:11 [n]S Mt 14:27 [o]Ac 19:21; 28:23
23:12 [p]S Ac 20:3 [q]ver 14,21,30; Ac 25:3
23:14 [r]ver 12
23:15 [s]ver 1; Ac 22:30
23:16 [t]ver 10; S Ac 21:34
23:18 [u]S Eph 3:1
23:20 [v]ver 1 [w]ver 14,15
23:21 [x]ver 13 [y]ver 12,14
23:23 [z]S Ac 8:40 [a]ver 33
23:24 [b]ver 26,33; Ac 24:1-3,10; 25:14
23:26 [c]Lk 1:3; Ac 24:3; 26:25 [d]Ac 15:23
23:27 [e]Ac 21:32 [f]Ac 21:33 [g]Ac 22:25-29
23:28 [h]Ac 22:30
23:29 [i]Ac 18:15; 25:19 [j]S ver 9
23:30 [k]ver 20,21 [l]S Ac 20:3 [m]ver 35; Ac 24:19; 25:16
23:32 [n]ver 23 [o]S Ac 21:34
23:33 [p]ver 23,24 [q]S Ac 8:40 [r]ver 26
23:34 [s]S Ac 6:9; 21:39
23:35 [t]ver 30; Ac 24:19; 25:16 [u]Ac 24:27
24:1 [v]Ac 23:2 [w]Ac 23:30,35 [x]S Ac 23:24
24:3 [y]Lk 1:3; Ac 23:26; 26:25

[u]23 The meaning of the Greek for this word is uncertain.

18:9–10. The risen Lord gives courage.

23:11 REVELATION, Visions— Circumstances do not limit God's power to reveal Himself through visions. Under arrest, Paul gained God's encouragement and direction. See note on 7:55.

23:11 EVANGELISM, Call to Evangelize—God is with us when we speak for Christ. He gives us courage to do His will. Wherever He leads us, He provides all we need to witness to His salvation. See note on 16:25–34.

24:5 THE CHURCH, People of God—Early Christians were known by several names: "the Way," "Nazarenes," and "Christians." Names, of course, do not adequately describe the

blemaker, stirring up riots[z] among the
Jews[a] all over the world. He is a ringlead-
er of the Nazarene[b] sect[c] 6and even
tried to desecrate the temple;[d] so we
seized him. 8By[v] examining him yourself
you will be able to learn the truth about
all these charges we are bringing against
him."

9The Jews joined in the accusation,[e]
asserting that these things were true.

10When the governor[f] motioned for
him to speak, Paul replied: "I know that
for a number of years you have been a
judge over this nation; so I gladly make
my defense. 11You can easily verify that
no more than twelve days[g] ago I went up
to Jerusalem to worship. 12My accusers
did not find me arguing with anyone at
the temple,[h] or stirring up a crowd[i] in
the synagogues or anywhere else in the
city. 13And they cannot prove to you the
charges they are now making against
me.[j] 14However, I admit that I worship
the God of our fathers[k] as a follower of
the Way,[l] which they call a sect.[m] I believe everything that agrees with the Law
and that is written in the Prophets,[n]
15and I have the same hope in God as
these men, that there will be a resurrection[o] of both the righteous and the wicked.[p] 16So I strive always to keep my conscience clear[q] before God and man.

17"After an absence of several years, I
came to Jerusalem to bring my people
gifts for the poor[r] and to present offerings. 18I was ceremonially clean[s] when
they found me in the temple courts doing
this. There was no crowd with me, nor
was I involved in any disturbance.[t] 19But
there are some Jews from the province of
Asia,[u] who ought to be here before you
and bring charges if they have anything

24:5 [z]Ac 16:20; 17:6 [a]Ac 21:28 [b]S Mk 1:24 [c]ver 14; Ac 26:5; 28:22
24:6 [d]Ac 21:28
24:9 [e]S 1Th 2:16
24:10 [f]S Ac 23:24
24:11 [g]Ac 21:27; ver 1
24:12 [h]Ac 25:8; 28:17 [i]ver 18
24:13 [j]Ac 25:7
24:14 [k]S Ac 3:13 [l]S Ac 9:2 [m]S ver 5 [n]Ac 26:6,22; 28:23
24:15 [o]Ac 23:6; 28:20 [p]S Mt 25:46
24:16 [q]S Ac 23:1
24:17 [r]Ac 11:29, 30; Ro 15:25-28,31; 1Co 16:1-4,15; 2Co 8:1-4; Gal 2:10
24:18 [s]Ac 21:26 [t]ver 12
24:19 [u]S Ac 2:9 [v]Ac 23:30
24:21 [w]Ac 23:6
24:22 [x]S Ac 9:2
24:23 [y]Ac 23:35 [z]Ac 28:16 [a]Ac 23:16; 27:3
24:24 [b]S Ac 20:21
24:25 [c]Gal 5:23; 1Th 5:6; 1Pe 4:7; 5:8; 2Pe 1:6 [d]Ac 10:42 [e]Jer 36:16
24:27 [f]Ac 25:1,4,9, 14 [g]Ac 12:3; 25:9 [h]Ac 23:35; 25:14
25:1 [i]S Ac 24:27

against me.[v] 20Or these who are here
should state what crime they found in me
when I stood before the Sanhedrin—
21unless it was this one thing I shouted as
I stood in their presence: 'It is concerning
the resurrection of the dead that I am on
trial before you today.' "[w]

22Then Felix, who was well acquainted
with the Way,[x] adjourned the proceedings. "When Lysias the commander
comes," he said, "I will decide your
case." 23He ordered the centurion to
keep Paul under guard[y] but to give him
some freedom[z] and permit his friends to
take care of his needs.[a]

24Several days later Felix came with his
wife Drusilla, who was a Jewess. He sent
for Paul and listened to him as he spoke
about faith in Christ Jesus.[b] 25As Paul dis-
coursed on righteousness, self-control[c]
and the judgment[d] to come, Felix was
afraid[e] and said, "That's enough for now!
You may leave. When I find it convenient, I will send for you." 26At the same
time he was hoping that Paul would offer
him a bribe, so he sent for him frequently
and talked with him.

27When two years had passed, Felix
was succeeded by Porcius Festus,[f] but
because Felix wanted to grant a favor to
the Jews,[g] he left Paul in prison.[h]

Chapter 25

The Trial Before Festus

THREE days after arriving in the province, Festus[i] went up from Caesa-

[v]6-8 Some manuscripts *him and wanted to judge him according to our law. 7But the commander, Lysias, came and with the use of much force snatched him from our hands 8and ordered his accusers to come before you. By*

people of God. Whatever names may be used are relatively unimportant as long as God's people obey Him and do His will. Following the Nazarene was heresy in the Roman world and could be legally punished. Early Christians willingly followed Jesus rather than Caesar. See note on 9:2.

24:10–21 EVANGELISM, Testimony—Paul stood before Felix to testify to God's saving grace in his life. He used every opportunity to testify, even in making his defense before the ruler. Several principles of a strong testimony are found in the passage: (1) he complimented the hearer, making a positive impression; (2) he defended his actions as being honest and open; (3) he forthrightly confessed his faith in Christ; (4) he tied his testimony to Scripture; (5) he told of his ministry to others in Christ's service; and (6) he centered his testimony on the resurrected Christ. See Guide to Personal Testimony, pp. 1786–1788.

24:14 THE CHURCH, People of God—Government and/or religious opponents may call Christianity a dangerous, heretical sect. The church sees itself as the fulfillment and continuation of the people of God begun with God's revelation to the fathers—Abraham, Isaac, and Jacob. See note on v 5.

24:14 WORSHIP, Service—See note on Mt 4:10.

24:15 LAST THINGS, Unbelievers' Resurrection—The resurrection of both the righteous and the wicked is clearly affirmed. The judgment of the wicked necessarily implies their bodily resurrection, even though it is not often asserted as forthrightly as here. The biblical emphasis is upon the hope that believers have by virtue of a promised resurrection of the righteous. The fact that the same sentence asserts resurrection for both the righteous and the wicked does not require that both occur simultaneously. The fact can be declared, but the details omitted. Some interpreters believe that other passages suggest an interval between the two. See notes on 1 Co 15:20–23; Rev 20:4–5.

24:17 STEWARDSHIP, Care of Needy—The great Jerusalem offering was important in Paul's ministry. It provides scriptural material for Christians' understanding of stewardship and giving. Christians everywhere should respond to needs among suffering Christians. See notes on 2 Co 8:1—9:15; 1 Jn 3:17.

24:24–25 PROCLAMATION, Unbelievers—See notes on 26:19–29; Heb 4:2.

25:1–12 CHRISTIAN ETHICS, Church and State—Paul's case involved religious charges (23:29). The Jews tried to turn it into a civil case (24:5). Felix knew his court really had no jurisdiction in such matters but feared to oppose the Jews. He wanted Paul to pay a bribe (24:26). Festus, likewise, refused to exercise his legal responsibility (25:9). Civil courts and judges must make decisions in civil cases and leave religious matters to religious bodies. Paul rightly appealed his case to a higher court seeking to get a decision on the civil charge. The

rea[j] to Jerusalem, 2where the chief
priests and Jewish leaders appeared before him and presented the charges
against Paul.[k] 3They urgently requested
Festus, as a favor to them, to have Paul
transferred to Jerusalem, for they were
preparing an ambush to kill him along the
way.[l] 4Festus answered, "Paul is being
held[m] at Caesarea,[n] and I myself am going there soon. 5Let some of your leaders
come with me and press charges against
the man there, if he has done anything
wrong."

6After spending eight or ten days with
them, he went down to Caesarea, and the
next day he convened the court[o] and ordered that Paul be brought before him.[p]
7When Paul appeared, the Jews who had
come down from Jerusalem stood around
him, bringing many serious charges
against him,[q] which they could not
prove.[r]

8Then Paul made his defense: "I have
done nothing wrong against the law of
the Jews or against the temple[s] or
against Caesar."

9Festus, wishing to do the Jews a favor,[t] said to Paul, "Are you willing to go
up to Jerusalem and stand trial before me
there on these charges?"[u]

10Paul answered: "I am now standing
before Caesar's court, where I ought to
be tried. I have not done any wrong to
the Jews,[v] as you yourself know very
well. 11If, however, I am guilty of doing
anything deserving death, I do not refuse
to die. But if the charges brought against
me by these Jews are not true, no one has
the right to hand me over to them. I appeal to Caesar!"[w]

12After Festus had conferred with his
council, he declared: "You have appealed
to Caesar. To Caesar you will go!"

Festus Consults King Agrippa

13A few days later King Agrippa and
Bernice arrived at Caesarea[x] to pay their
respects to Festus. 14Since they were
spending many days there, Festus discussed Paul's case with the king. He said:
"There is a man here whom Felix left as a
prisoner.[y] 15When I went to Jerusalem,
the chief priests and elders of the Jews
brought charges against him[z] and asked
that he be condemned.

16"I told them that it is not the Roman
custom to hand over any man before he
has faced his accusers and has had an opportunity to defend himself against their
charges.[a] 17When they came here with
me, I did not delay the case, but convened the court the next day and ordered
the man to be brought in.[b] 18When his
accusers got up to speak, they did not
charge him with any of the crimes I had
expected. 19Instead, they had some
points of dispute[c] with him about their
own religion[d] and about a dead man
named Jesus who Paul claimed was alive.
20I was at a loss how to investigate such
matters; so I asked if he would be willing
to go to Jerusalem and stand trial there on
these charges.[e] 21When Paul made his
appeal to be held over for the Emperor's
decision, I ordered him held until I could
send him to Caesar."[f]

22Then Agrippa said to Festus, "I
would like to hear this man myself."

He replied, "Tomorrow you will hear
him."[g]

Paul Before Agrippa

26:12–18pp — Ac 9:3–8; 22:6–11

23The next day Agrippa and Bernice[h]
came with great pomp and entered the
audience room with the high ranking officers and the leading men of the city. At
the command of Festus, Paul was brought
in. 24Festus said: "King Agrippa, and all
who are present with us, you see this
man! The whole Jewish community[i] has
petitioned me about him in Jerusalem
and here in Caesarea, shouting that he
ought not to live any longer.[j] 25I found
he had done nothing deserving of death,[k]
but because he made his appeal to the
Emperor[l] I decided to send him to
Rome. 26But I have nothing definite to
write to His Majesty about him. Therefore I have brought him before all of you,
and especially before you, King Agrippa,
so that as a result of this investigation I
may have something to write. 27For I
think it is unreasonable to send on a prisoner without specifying the charges
against him."

Chapter 26

THEN Agrippa said to Paul, "You have
permission to speak for yourself."[m]

So Paul motioned with his hand[n] and
began his defense: 2"King Agrippa, I consider myself fortunate to stand before
you[o] today as I make my defense against

25:1 [j]S Ac 8:40
25:2 [k]ver 15; Ac 24:1
25:3 [l]S Ac 20:3
25:4 [m]Ac 24:23 [n]S Ac 8:40
25:6 [o]ver 17 [p]ver 10
25:7 [q]Mk 15:3; Lk 23:2,10; Ac 24:5,6 [r]Ac 24:13
25:8 [s]Ac 6:13; 24:12; 28:17
25:9 [t]Ac 24:27; 12:3 [u]ver 20
25:10 [v]ver 8
25:11 [w]ver 21,25; Ac 26:32; 28:19
25:13 [x]S Ac 8:40
25:14 [y]Ac 24:27
25:15 [z]ver 2; Ac 24:1
25:16 [a]ver 4,5; Ac 23:30
25:17 [b]ver 6,10
25:19 [c]Ac 18:15; 23:29 [d]Ac 17:22
25:20 [e]ver 9
25:21 [f]ver 11,12
25:22 [g]Ac 9:15
25:23 [h]ver 13; Ac 26:30
25:24 [i]ver 2,3,7 [j]Ac 22:22
25:25 [k]S Ac 23:9 [l]S ver 11
26:1 [m]Ac 9:15; 25:22 [n]S Ac 12:17
26:2 [o]Ps 119:46

legal system needs to protect citizens against false charges and against all attempts to circumvent justice.

26:1–20 EVANGELISM, Testimony—Paul stood in chains before Agrippa just as he stood before Felix to testify to God's grace in his life. See note on 24:10–21. Paul used this difficult situation to share and witness to what God had done in his life through Jesus Christ. Sharing what Jesus means in one's life is always a powerful, persuasive testimony. The apostle urged the powerful King to become a Christian. Through this encounter, all the elements of an effective testimony are seen: (1) tell of Jesus Christ regardless of the difficulties; (2) urge the hearers to receive Christ whether they respond or not; and (3) press on no matter what others think or say. God will honor such a testimony.

all the accusations of the Jews,[p] 3and especially so because you are well acquainted with all the Jewish customs[q] and controversies.[r] Therefore, I beg you to listen
to me patiently.
4"The Jews all know the way I have
lived ever since I was a child,[s] from the
beginning of my life in my own country,
and also in Jerusalem. 5They have known
me for a long time[t] and can testify, if
they are willing, that according to the
strictest sect[u] of our religion, I lived as a
Pharisee.[v] 6And now it is because of my
hope[w] in what God has promised our fathers[x] that I am on trial today. 7This is
the promise our twelve tribes[y] are hoping to see fulfilled as they earnestly serve
God day and night.[z] O king, it is because
of this hope that the Jews are accusing
me.[a] 8Why should any of you consider it
incredible that God raises the dead?[b]
9"I too was convinced[c] that I ought to
do all that was possible to oppose[d] the
name of Jesus of Nazareth.[e] 10And that is
just what I did in Jerusalem. On the authority of the chief priests I put many of
the saints[f] in prison,[g] and when they
were put to death, I cast my vote against
them.[h] 11Many a time I went from one
synagogue to another to have them punished,[i] and I tried to force them to blaspheme. In my obsession against them, I
even went to foreign cities to persecute
them.
12"On one of these journeys I was going to Damascus with the authority and
commission of the chief priests. 13About
noon, O king, as I was on the road, I saw
a light from heaven, brighter than the
sun, blazing around me and my companions. 14We all fell to the ground, and I
heard a voice[j] saying to me in Aramaic,[w][k] 'Saul, Saul, why do you persecute
me? It is hard for you to kick against the
goads.'
15"Then I asked, 'Who are you, Lord?'
" 'I am Jesus, whom you are persecuting,' the Lord replied. 16'Now get up and
stand on your feet.[l] I have appeared to
you to appoint you as a servant and as a
witness of what you have seen of me and
what I will show you.[m] 17I will rescue
you[n] from your own people and from the
Gentiles.[o] I am sending you to them 18to
open their eyes[p] and turn them from
darkness to light,[q] and from the power of
Satan to God, so that they may receive
forgiveness of sins[r] and a place among
those who are sanctified by faith in me.'[s]
19"So then, King Agrippa, I was not disobedient[t] to the vision from heaven.
20First to those in Damascus,[u] then to
those in Jerusalem[v] and in all Judea, and
to the Gentiles[w] also, I preached that
they should repent[x] and turn to God and
prove their repentance by their deeds.[y]
21That is why the Jews seized me[z] in the
temple courts and tried to kill me.[a] 22But
I have had God's help to this very day,
and so I stand here and testify to small
and great alike. I am saying nothing beyond what the prophets and Moses said
would happen[b]— 23that the Christ[x]
would suffer[c] and, as the first to rise
from the dead,[d] would proclaim light to
his own people and to the Gentiles."[e]
24At this point Festus interrupted
Paul's defense. "You are out of your

26:2 [p]Ac 24:1,5; 25:2,7,11
26:3 [q]ver 7; S Ac 6:14 [r]Ac 25:19
26:4 [s]Gal 1:13,14; Php 3:5
26:5 [t]Ac 22:3 [u]S Ac 24:5 [v]Ac 23:6; Php 3:5
26:6 [w]Ac 23:6; 24:15; 28:20 [x]S Ac 13:32; Ro 15:8
26:7 [y]Jas 1:1 [z]1Th 3:10; 1Ti 5:5 [a]ver 2
26:8 [b]Ac 23:6
26:9 [c]1Ti 1:13 [d]Jn 16:2 [e]S Jn 15:21
26:10 [f]S Ac 9:13 [g]S Ac 8:3; 9:2,14, 21 [h]Ac 22:20
26:11 [i]S Mt 10:17
26:14 [j]Ac 9:7 [k]S Jn 5:2
26:16 [l]Eze 2:1; Da 10:11 [m]Ac 22:14,15
26:17 [n]Jer 1:8,19 [o]S Ac 9:15; S 13:46
26:18 [p]Isa 35:5 [q]Ps 18:28; Isa 42:7, 16; Eph 5:8; Col 1:13; 1Pe 2:9 [r]Lk 24:47; Ac 2:38 [s]S Ac 20:21,32
26:19 [t]Isa 50:5
26:20 [u]Ac 9:19-25 [v]Ac 9:26-29; 22:17-20 [w]S Ac 9:15; S 13:46 [x]Ac 3:19 [y]Jer 18:11; 35:15; Mt 3:8; Lk 3:8
26:21 [z]Ac 21:27,30 [a]Ac 21:31
26:22 [b]S Lk 24:27, 44; Ac 10:43; 24:14
26:23 [c]S Mt 16:21 [d]1Co 15:20,23; Col 1:18; Rev 1:5 [e]S Lk 2:32

[w]*14* Or *Hebrew* [x]*23* Or *Messiah*

26:4–23 HISTORY, Confession—See note on 13:16–31. Following the Israelite tradition by confessing faith through reciting history, the New Testament uses personal testimony, the recitation of an individual's history with God to confess faith. See Guide to Personal Testimony, pp. 1786–1788.

26:6 HISTORY, Promise—The Christian message is the fulfillment of the Old Testament promises. Christianity is the fulfillment of God's history with Israel.

26:10 THE CHURCH, Saints—Saints are members of the church. See notes on Ro 1:7; 1 Co 1:2.

26:15–18 ELECTION, Predestination—See note on 22:14–16.

26:16–18 REVELATION, Jesus Christ—God reveals Himself in crucial moments in our lives, when we least expect it, and turns even evil experiences into redemptive opportunities. See note on 22:7–11.

26:16 THE CHURCH, Servants—Paul was an apostle with great respect and influence in the church. He viewed his calling as that of a servant and witness. God calls every believer to serve and witness for Christ. See note on Da 9:11.

26:18 SALVATION, Sanctification—Christian workers should be as concerned as Paul about the sanctification of their converts. Sanctification is by faith in Jesus Christ. Here the emphasis is on the beginning of sanctification at conversion. Sanctification involves forgiveness of sins. Here the emphasis is on a passive state given by God to those actively serving Him. God's power makes the Christian holy. Elsewhere, sanctification is also described as an active process of growing in Christ's image. See notes on 20:32; Gal 5:22–25.

26:19–29 PROCLAMATION, Unbelievers—Proclaiming the gospel brings two responses. Some will accept the gospel with repentance and faith (14:1; Ro 16:25–27). Others will respond with rejection and rebellion (Ac 24:24–25; 2 Th 1:8). This dual reaction is clearly seen in 1 Co 1:18–25. When Simeon spoke of Jesus Christ in the Temple, he pointed out these two results (Lk 2:34). The results belong to God (1 Co 3:1–9)! Our assignment is to preach the gospel so that all people will be brought either to receive Him or reject Him. See note on Ro 10:8–13.

26:20 SALVATION, Repentance—Paul never separated the preaching of repentance from good works. Deeds of Christian love show a person has repented, that is, turned from sin to God. This means repentance is a change of direction in one's life, not simply a statement made once and never acted upon.

26:20 SALVATION, Obedience—Obedience is the proof of repentance.

26:20 DISCIPLESHIP, Conversion—Discipleship is not a word game played to impress other people. It is conversion to a new way of life. Paul preached to everyone, Jew or Gentile, that repentance as well as faith must be proved by deeds. See note on Lk 19:8; How to Accept Christ, pp. 1745–1747.

26:22–23 JESUS CHRIST, Fulfilled—See note on 13:27–41.

mind,[f] Paul!" he shouted. "Your great
learning[g] is driving you insane."
25"I am not insane, most excellent[h]
Festus," Paul replied. "What I am saying
is true and reasonable. 26The king is familiar with these things,[i] and I can
speak freely to him. I am convinced that
none of this has escaped his notice, because it was not done in a corner. 27King
Agrippa, do you believe the prophets? I
know you do."
28Then Agrippa said to Paul, "Do you
think that in such a short time you can
persuade me to be a Christian?"[j]
29Paul replied, "Short time or long—I
pray God that not only you but all who
are listening to me today may become
what I am, except for these chains."[k]
30The king rose, and with him the governor and Bernice[l] and those sitting
with them. 31They left the room, and
while talking with one another, they said,
"This man is not doing anything that deserves death or imprisonment."[m]
32Agrippa said to Festus, "This man
could have been set free[n] if he had not
appealed to Caesar."[o]

Chapter 27

Paul Sails for Rome

WHEN it was decided that we[p] would
sail for Italy,[q] Paul and some other
prisoners were handed over to a centurion named Julius, who belonged to the Imperial Regiment.[r] 2We boarded a ship
from Adramyttium about to sail for ports
along the coast of the province of Asia,[s]
and we put out to sea. Aristarchus,[t] a
Macedonian[u] from Thessalonica,[v] was
with us.
3The next day we landed at Sidon;[w]
and Julius, in kindness to Paul,[x] allowed
him to go to his friends so they might
provide for his needs.[y] 4From there we
put out to sea again and passed to the lee
of Cyprus because the winds were against
us.[z] 5When we had sailed across the
open sea off the coast of Cilicia[a] and
Pamphylia,[b] we landed at Myra in Lycia.
6There the centurion found an Alexandrian ship[c] sailing for Italy[d] and put us
on board. 7We made slow headway for
many days and had difficulty arriving off
Cnidus. When the wind did not allow us
to hold our course,[e] we sailed to the lee
of Crete,[f] opposite Salmone. 8We moved
along the coast with difficulty and came
to a place called Fair Havens, near the
town of Lasea.
9Much time had been lost, and sailing
had already become dangerous because
by now it was after the Fast.[y][g] So Paul
warned them, 10"Men, I can see that our
voyage is going to be disastrous and bring
great loss to ship and cargo, and to our
own lives also."[h] 11But the centurion, instead of listening to what Paul said, followed the advice of the pilot and of the
owner of the ship. 12Since the harbor was
unsuitable to winter in, the majority decided that we should sail on, hoping to
reach Phoenix and winter there. This was
a harbor in Crete,[i] facing both southwest
and northwest.

The Storm

13When a gentle south wind began to
blow, they thought they had obtained
what they wanted; so they weighed anchor and sailed along the shore of Crete.
14Before very long, a wind of hurricane
force,[j] called the "northeaster," swept
down from the island. 15The ship was
caught by the storm and could not head
into the wind; so we gave way to it and
were driven along. 16As we passed to the
lee of a small island called Cauda, we
were hardly able to make the lifeboat[k]
secure. 17When the men had hoisted it
aboard, they passed ropes under the ship
itself to hold it together. Fearing that they
would run aground[l] on the sandbars of
Syrtis, they lowered the sea anchor and
let the ship be driven along. 18We took
such a violent battering from the storm
that the next day they began to throw the
cargo overboard.[m] 19On the third day,
they threw the ship's tackle overboard
with their own hands. 20When neither
sun nor stars appeared for many days and
the storm continued raging, we finally
gave up all hope of being saved.
21After the men had gone a long time
without food, Paul stood up before them
and said: "Men, you should have taken
my advice[n] not to sail from Crete;[o] then
you would have spared yourselves this
damage and loss. 22But now I urge you to
keep up your courage,[p] because not one
of you will be lost; only the ship will be
destroyed. 23Last night an angel[q] of the

[y]9 That is, the Day of Atonement (Yom Kippur)

26:24 [f]S Jn 10:20; S 1Co 4:10 [g]Jn 7:15
26:25 [h]S Ac 23:26
26:26 [i]ver 3
26:28 [j]Ac 11:26
26:29 [k]S Ac 21:33
26:30 [l]Ac 25:23
26:31 [m]S Ac 23:9
26:32 [n]Ac 28:18 [o]S Ac 25:11
27:1 [p]S Ac 16:10 [q]Ac 18:2; 25:12,25 [r]Ac 10:1
27:2 [s]S Ac 2:9 [t]S Ac 19:29 [u]S Ac 16:9 [v]S Ac 17:1
27:3 [w]Mt 11:21 [x]ver 43 [y]Ac 24:23; 28:16
27:4 [z]ver 7
27:5 [a]S Ac 6:9 [b]S Ac 2:10
27:6 [c]Ac 28:11 [d]ver 1; Ac 18:2; 25:12,25
27:7 [e]ver 4 [f]ver 12, 13,21; Tit 1:5
27:9 [g]Lev 16:29-31; 23:27-29; Nu 29:7
27:10 [h]ver 21
27:12 [i]S ver 7
27:14 [j]Mk 4:37
27:16 [k]ver 30
27:17 [l]ver 26,39
27:18 [m]ver 19,38; Jnh 1:5
27:21 [n]ver 10 [o]S ver 7
27:22 [p]ver 25,36
27:23 [q]S Ac 5:19

26:29 PRAYER, Intercession—Paul prayed for everyone to be saved. Intercession for the lost is the responsibility of all believers. See note on 1 Ti 2:1–3.

27:13–44 MIRACLE, Revelation—God can bring miraculous assurance before He performs an event we recognize as miraculous. The severity of the storm contrasted sharply with the calm of Paul's faith. The assurance of Paul in the crisis is striking: an angel of God appeared to him (v 23) promising no one would die. The providential care of God is explicit in the account. The pretense of the sailors, the starvation diet, the breakup of the ship, and the threat of the soldiers—from all they were rescued. No one was lost. That is the miracle. Nothing drastic happened. God's protection is a miracle.

27:23–24 REVELATION, Angels—A messenger of God

God whose I am and whom I serve[r]
stood beside me[s] 24and said, 'Do not be
afraid, Paul. You must stand trial before
Caesar;[t] and God has graciously given
you the lives of all who sail with you.'[u]
25So keep up your courage,[v] men, for I
have faith in God that it will happen just
as he told me.[w] 26Nevertheless, we must
run aground[x] on some island."[y]

The Shipwreck

27On the fourteenth night we were still
being driven across the Adriatic[z] Sea,
when about midnight the sailors sensed
they were approaching land. 28They took
soundings and found that the water was a
hundred and twenty feet[a] deep. A short
time later they took soundings again and
found it was ninety feet[b] deep. 29Fearing
that we would be dashed against the
rocks, they dropped four anchors from
the stern and prayed for daylight. 30In an
attempt to escape from the ship, the sailors let the lifeboat[z] down into the sea,
pretending they were going to lower
some anchors from the bow. 31Then Paul
said to the centurion and the soldiers,
"Unless these men stay with the ship,
you cannot be saved."[a] 32So the soldiers
cut the ropes that held the lifeboat and let
it fall away.
33Just before dawn Paul urged them all
to eat. "For the last fourteen days," he
said, "you have been in constant suspense and have gone without food—you
haven't eaten anything. 34Now I urge you
to take some food. You need it to survive.
Not one of you will lose a single hair from
his head."[b] 35After he said this, he took
some bread and gave thanks to God in
front of them all. Then he broke it[c] and
began to eat. 36They were all encouraged[d] and ate some food themselves.
37Altogether there were 276 of us on
board. 38When they had eaten as much as
they wanted, they lightened the ship by
throwing the grain into the sea.[e]
39When daylight came, they did not
recognize the land, but they saw a bay
with a sandy beach,[f] where they decided

27:23 [r]Ro 1:9 [s]Ac 18:9; 23:11; 2Ti 4:17
27:24 [t]Ac 23:11 [u]ver 44
27:25 [v]ver 22,36 [w]Ro 4:20,21
27:26 [x]ver 17,39 [y]Ac 28:1
27:30 [z]ver 16
27:31 [a]ver 24
27:34 [b]S Mt 10:30
27:35 [c]S Mt 14:19
27:36 [d]ver 22,25
27:38 [e]ver 18; Jnh 1:5
27:39 [f]Ac 28:1
27:40 [g]ver 29
27:41 [h]2Co 11:25
27:43 [i]ver 3
27:44 [j]ver 22,31
28:1 [k]S Ac 16:10 [l]Ac 27:26,39
28:4 [m]Mk 16:18 [n]Lk 13:2,4
28:5 [o]Lk 10:19
28:6 [p]Ac 14:11

to run the ship aground if they could.
40Cutting loose the anchors,[g] they left
them in the sea and at the same time untied the ropes that held the rudders. Then
they hoisted the foresail to the wind and
made for the beach. 41But the ship struck
a sandbar and ran aground. The bow
stuck fast and would not move, and the
stern was broken to pieces by the pounding of the surf.[h]
42The soldiers planned to kill the prisoners to prevent any of them from swim-
ming away and escaping. 43But the centurion wanted to spare Paul's life[i] and kept
them from carrying out their plan. He ordered those who could swim to jump
overboard first and get to land. 44The rest
were to get there on planks or on pieces
of the ship. In this way everyone reached
land in safety.[j]

Chapter 28

Ashore on Malta

ONCE safely on shore, we[k] found out
that the island[l] was called Malta.
2The islanders showed us unusual kindness. They built a fire and welcomed us
all because it was raining and cold. 3Paul
gathered a pile of brushwood and, as he
put it on the fire, a viper, driven out by
the heat, fastened itself on his hand.
4When the islanders saw the snake hanging from his hand,[m] they said to each other, "This man must be a murderer; for
though he escaped from the sea, Justice
has not allowed him to live."[n] 5But Paul
shook the snake off into the fire and suffered no ill effects.[o] 6The people expected him to swell up or suddenly fall dead,
but after waiting a long time and seeing
nothing unusual happen to him, they
changed their minds and said he was a
god.[p]
7There was an estate nearby that belonged to Publius, the chief official of the
island. He welcomed us to his home and

[z]*27* In ancient times the name referred to an area extending well south of Italy. [a]*28* Greek *twenty orguias* (about 37 meters) [b]*28* Greek *fifteen orguias* (about 27 meters)

reassured the representative of God that he and those who traveled with him were safe in God's hands. Paul used the revelation to encourage the ship's pagan crew. See note on 26:16–18.

27:35 PRAYER, Thanksgiving—Paul's great faith was infectious. Faith is shown in gratitude even as it can be in petition. Paul customarily gave thanks for food, just as did Jesus (Mt 14:19; 26:26–27).

28:3–6 MIRACLE, Exception—Miracles may defy natural expectations. Paul's series of crises convinced the islanders of his horrible guilt. They sat back and waited for him to die. When he did not, they decided he was divine. Paul knew God had worked in an exceptional way outside all their previous experiences. God has power to use the nature He created to work His miracles for His people. See note on 16:25–27. He can also work outside what we describe as the laws of nature. Our definitions of miracles must not limit the ways God can act to achieve His purposes for His people. See note on 27:13–44. God's protection is clear—against the elements of nature. Such a miracle is an exceptional event in God's purpose. We cannot presume on God and expect Him to save us from any danger we get ourselves into.

28:7–10 MIRACLE, Instruments—God heals through His human instruments in many ways. The father of their host Publius was ill. Luke diagnosed it as fever and dysentery. Through Paul's ministry of prayer and touch, he was healed. Many others came to be healed. The ministry of prayer and a loving touch proved to be the channel God used for healing. He can still use the same channels to accomplish His healing purposes.

for three days entertained us hospitably.
8His father was sick in bed, suffering from
fever and dysentery. Paul went in to see
him and, after prayer,[q] placed his hands
on him[r] and healed him.[s] 9When this
had happened, the rest of the sick on the
island came and were cured. 10They honored us[t] in many ways and when we
were ready to sail, they furnished us with
the supplies we needed.

Arrival at Rome

11After three months we put out to sea
in a ship that had wintered in the island.
It was an Alexandrian ship[u] with the fig-
urehead of the twin gods Castor and Pol-
lux. 12We put in at Syracuse and stayed
there three days. 13From there we set sail
and arrived at Rhegium. The next day the
south wind came up, and on the following day we reached Puteoli. 14There we
found some brothers[v] who invited us to
spend a week with them. And so we
came to Rome. 15The brothers[w] there had
heard that we were coming, and they
traveled as far as the Forum of Appius and
the Three Taverns to meet us. At the
sight of these men Paul thanked God and
was encouraged. 16When we got to
Rome, Paul was allowed to live by himself, with a soldier to guard him.[x]

Paul Preaches at Rome Under Guard

17Three days later he called together
the leaders of the Jews.[y] When they had
assembled, Paul said to them: "My brothers,[z] although I have done nothing
against our people[a] or against the customs of our ancestors,[b] I was arrested in
Jerusalem and handed over to the Romans. 18They examined me[c] and wanted
to release me,[d] because I was not guilty
of any crime deserving death.[e] 19But
when the Jews objected, I was compelled

28:8 [q]Jas 5:14,15 [r]S Ac 6:6 [s]S Ac 9:40
28:10 [t]Ps 15:4
28:11 [u]Ac 27:6
28:14 [v]S Ac 1:16
28:15 [w]S Ac 1:16
28:16 [x]Ac 24:23; 27:3
28:17 [y]Ac 25:2 [z]S Ac 22:5 [a]S Ac 25:8 [b]S Ac 6:14
28:18 [c]Ac 22:24 [d]Ac 26:31,32 [e]S Ac 23:9
28:19 [f]S Ac 25:11
28:20 [g]Ac 26:6,7 [h]S Ac 21:33
28:21 [i]S Ac 22:5
28:22 [j]S Ac 24:5, 14
28:23 [k]S Mt 3:2; Ac 19:8 [l]Ac 17:3 [m]S Ac 8:35
28:24 [n]Ac 14:4; 17:4,5
28:25 [o]S Heb 3:7
28:27 [p]Ps 119:70

to appeal to Caesar[f]—not that I had any
charge to bring against my own people.
20For this reason I have asked to see you
and talk with you. It is because of the
hope of Israel[g] that I am bound with this
chain."[h]

21They replied, "We have not received
any letters from Judea concerning you,
and none of the brothers[i] who have
come from there has reported or said anything bad about you. 22But we want to
hear what your views are, for we know
that people everywhere are talking
against this sect."[j]

23They arranged to meet Paul on a certain day, and came in even larger numbers to the place where he was staying.
From morning till evening he explained
and declared to them the kingdom of
God[k] and tried to convince them about
Jesus[l] from the Law of Moses and from
the Prophets.[m] 24Some were convinced
by what he said, but others would not
believe.[n] 25They disagreed among themselves and began to leave after Paul had
made this final statement: "The Holy
Spirit spoke the truth to your forefathers
when he said[o] through Isaiah the prophet:

26" 'Go to this people and say,
"You will be ever hearing but never
understanding;
you will be ever seeing but never
perceiving."
27For this people's heart has become
calloused;[p]
they hardly hear with their ears,
and they have closed their eyes.
Otherwise they might see with their
eyes,
hear with their ears,
understand with their hearts

28:8 PRAYER, Petition—Miracles sometimes resulted from the apostles' prayers. See note on 9:40.

28:15 PRAYER, Thanksgiving—Paul was grateful to find Christians in Rome. Gratitude characterized his life (1 Co 1:4; Php 1:3; Col 1:3; 1 Th 1:2). He obeyed his own command to give thanks "in all circumstances" (1 Th 5:18). Christian community and fellowship are reasons for thanksgiving.

28:22 THE CHURCH, People of God—See notes on 24:5; 24:14.

28:23 THE CHURCH, God's Kingdom—The kingdom appeared in Jesus of Nazareth, but it was not absolutely new and unexpected. God's revelation and promises to Israel and God's inspiration producing the Old Testament had prepared for His revelation of the kingdom in Jesus. See notes on Lk 4:43; 10:9–11.

28:23–31 EVANGELISM, Personal—Acts closes with Paul under house arrest. He still welcomed people and personally shared Christ with them. Even if he could no longer preach to the masses, he shared with the few, or even just with the one, who would listen. No circumstance quieted his personal witness for Christ. As a result, some accepted Jesus Christ as Savior; some did not. Thus the Greek text of the Book of Acts ends with a beautiful adverb: "without hindrance" (Greek *akōlutōs*). The gospel went through Paul unhindered even though he was in prison. The gospel continues to go on through the centuries, regardless of problems, persecutions, perversions, and powers—going "without hindrance." It shall be until our Lord returns.

28:25–28 HOLY SPIRIT, Revelation—The Spirit's revelation does not gain automatic acceptance and obedience. It may harden people's hearts. The Spirit worked through prophets to bring God's word to Israel. This revelatory activity included the writing as well as the speaking of the prophets. The Hebrew Bible was the Scripture used by the early church. Paul used Isa 6:9–10 to show that Jewish religious leaders of his day reacted just like those of Isaiah's. They would not accept or follow the Spirit's revelation.

28:25–28 ELECTION, Other Nations—Under Roman guard, Paul fearlessly and confidently informed Jewish leaders and all who would listen that God's salvation had been sent by God to the Gentiles. Paul supported the argument by quoting Isa 6:9–10. Spiritual dullness and insensitivity prevented the Jews from understanding God's election purposes in Jesus. They thus did not act on and receive the blessings of God's election of their people.

and turn, and I would heal them.'[c] [q]

28"Therefore I want you to know that
God's salvation[r] has been sent to the
Gentiles,[s] and they will listen!"[d]

30For two whole years Paul stayed
there in his own rented house and welcomed all who came to see him. 31Bold-
ly[t] and without hindrance he preached
the kingdom of God[u] and taught about
the Lord Jesus Christ.

28:27 [q]Isa 6:9,10; S Mt 13:15
28:28 [r]Lk 2:30 [s]S Ac 13:46
28:31 [t]S Ac 4:29 [u]ver 23; S Mt 4:23

[c]*27* Isaiah 6:9,10 [d]*28* Some manuscripts *listen!" 29After he said this, the Jews left, arguing vigorously among themselves.*

28:31 JESUS CHRIST, Kingdom of God—Preaching about God's kingdom and teaching about Jesus are parallel subjects, virtually the same thing. Compare Mk 1:15.

28:31 THE CHURCH, God's Kingdom—See note on Lk 4:43. The kingdom of God must be proclaimed and taught. People need the good news of God's kingdom. God gives the church the freedom it has to preach the kingdom even under unfavorable circumstances.

28:31 EDUCATION, Missionaries—Paul ended his missionary career just as he had carried it out in previous years, as a teacher. Now under house arrest in Rome, he taught Christ freely to all who came to him. Christ's rule and lordship remained at the center of Paul's proclamation and teaching.

Romans

Theological Setting

How should the salvation God has revealed in Jesus Christ influence the way we live and understand our relationship with God? It was mainly regarding this question that Paul wrote to the church at Rome sometime around AD 55. He was probably in Corinth, the capital of what is now called Greece, during the three months just preceding his visit to Jerusalem (Ac 20:2-3). Paul's plans were to deliver the offerings made by the churches in Macedonia and Achaia to the poor Christians in Jerusalem and then to engage in missionary work in Spain, visiting the Romans on his way (15:25-28). Paul hoped his visit with the Christians in Rome would be mutually beneficial (1:11-13) and that he could journey on to Spain with their support (15:24).

Paul's letter to the Romans had a dual purpose. He sought to introduce himself and his understanding of the gospel to the Romans. He also wanted to deal with some of the problems in the church (14:1-16) and the misunderstanding of his preaching that they had heard (3:8; 6:1-2,15). Romans is not as devoted to and determined by the church's problems as is, for example, 1 Corinthians. For this reason the apostle was free to communicate how he understood what God has done for us in Christ. Romans, thus, mirrors Paul's nearly twenty years of reflection on the gospel and his experience as an apostle among the churches.

Paul knew from his own experience (Ac 9:1-19) that the gospel was "the power of God for . . . salvation" (Ro 1:16) and that he was under obligation to make it clear what salvation should mean in the lives of persons (1:16-17). From his experience with churches, he knew the Romans needed to keep some things firmly in mind if they were to realize the fullest benefits of salvation:

1. *Who needs to be saved?* The Roman church contained both Jews and Gentiles who had become believers in Christ. The Jewish Christians were inclined to feel they were not as sinful as the Gentile Christians because of the high morals they had practiced as Jews. Paul reminded the Jewish Christians they had not fully kept the law (2:1—3:8) and that their sins were so visible as to cause Gentiles to blaspheme God's name (2:24). Gentiles might plead they had no revelation and were less guilty, but Paul affirmed they, too, were without excuse. They should have learned from the creation itself but had rejected such knowledge (1:18-23). Paul concluded that all—both Jews and Greeks—are under sin and that no person has ever been good enough for God to justify him or her apart from Christ (3:10-20).

2. *What can persons do to be saved?* The Jews felt they earned God's favor by doing good works as the law prescribed. The Gentiles generally believed that specified sacrifices caused their gods to favor them. These ideas tended to persist among the Christians with the Jews remembering the law and the promise to Abraham (4:1-24), while the Gentiles remembered how they had been taught that eating certain foods or celebrating special days pleased their gods (14:1-12). Paul summoned the Christians to remember that all persons have only one way of salvation—"justified freely by his grace through the redemption that came by Christ Jesus" (3:24). See How to Accept Christ, pp 1745-1747.

3. *What is the source of salvation?* God saves persons on the basis of trust in Christ, and this trust is focused in what Jesus accomplished in His death. Paul knew the importance of the teachings of Jesus. He applied these teachings in his exhortations (13:8-10). He knew, however, that true Christian faith must focus in and make central the death of Jesus. He reminded the Romans that Christ's death was for us—"the ungodly" (5:6)—and that His death demonstrated God's love (5:8). Christ's dying for us not only allows us to be "justified by His blood" (5:9); but it is also, as Paul wanted the Romans to remember, our basis for a continuing relationship with God in which we shall be "saved through his life" (5:10) and are able to "rejoice in God" (5:11). See also 5:2-5.

4. *What is the practical result of faith in Christians' lives?* Trust in Jesus Christ makes Christians struggle against sin in their lives and provides the resources to overcome sin. Paul knew that all people were vulnerable to sin, which meant they did not achieve the life God intended. Rather, they were trapped in an existence that could be called death (6:23). This death could come from the so-called grosser sins

to which the Gentiles were tempted (13:13-14), through social sins which Jewish law did not prohibit (12:14-18), or through allowing freedom in Christ to decay into rules and practices which destroyed Christian fellowship (14:1—15:13). Knowing that his readers were vulnerable to assaults from all these and other directions which could lead to sin reigning in their lives (6:12-14), Paul forcefully reminded his readers that their having trusted Christ constituted crossing a boundary from death to life (6:5-11). Paul used the symbolism of their baptism to press his point: their baptism pictured their entrance into death to sin through symbolic burial with Christ, and their resurrection with Him to a new life in which "death no longer had dominion" (6:9). The baptism of the Christian portrayed what happened at the moment of trusting Christ when one passed from the dominion of sin (6:14) to that of righteousness (6:18). This experience with Christ summons Christians to accomplish in their own lives what Christ had accomplished for them. They have been set free—they must not be sin's slave (6:15-18); they have become slaves of righteousness—they must yield themselves to God (6:19-22). The struggle with sin is agonizing because of sin's power (7:13-20) and because of the painful realities about one's self that must be faced (7:15-18,21-23). This struggle would lead to despair if one had only his or her own strength to rely on (7:24), but God provides Christians with the "Spirit of life" in Christ Jesus (8:2) so that His children can live in the Spirit (8:9-11) and according to God's will (8:3-8).

5. *As Christians, can we trust God, or must we fear His judgment?* God may be trusted to be merciful and faithful. For the Roman Christian community which contained both Jews and Gentiles, the fact that most Jewish persons did not accept Christ as Messiah was troubling. For the Jewish Christians, it raised the question of God's faithfulness to His promises to Israel as they had understood them (9:4-6). For the Gentile Christians it raised the question of their proper attitude toward Jewish Christians (11:13-32). Paul's stress in Romans 9-11 is that God has been faithful to His promises, properly understood, because His salvation was pledged to the remnant who were faithful (9:6-29) and not to all of Jewish descent as some had believed. God had always saved persons on the basis of their faith (10:1-20); and the disobedience of the Jews (10:21) should not obscure the fact that a remnant of Christian Jews existed, establishing God's faithfulness (11:1-12). Granted this, both Jewish and Gentile Christians needed to understand that salvation was based on God's mercy and that God's promises always rested on this foundation (11:13-32) with the result that all Christians could say, "To him be the glory forever! Amen" (11:36).

Paul stressed the five areas discussed above because he knew faithfulness to God and the full realization of what He offered persons in their salvation in Christ depended on both adequate awareness of what God had done and on strenuous dedication to do what God wanted done.

Theological Outline

Romans: The Revelation of God's Righteousness in Salvation through Jesus Christ for All Persons

- I. Introduction: Qualifications and Reason for Writing. (1:1-15)
  - A. Apostolic calling qualifies the author. (1:1-7)
  - B. Grateful, prayerful concern for the readers motivates the writing. (1:8-15)
- II. Theme: The Power for Salvation and the Righteousness of God Are Revealed. (1:16-17)
- III. All People Need Salvation from the Power of Sin. (1:18—3:20)
  - A. The power of sin rules among the Gentiles. (1:18-32)
    - 1. The Gentiles reject the knowledge of God. (1:18-23)
    - 2. The Gentiles experience the results of rebellion against God. (1:24-32)
  - B. The power of sin rules among the Jews. (2:1—3:8)
    - 1. The Jews demonstrate their disobedience. (2:1-16)
    - 2. The Jews confuse privilege and responsibility. (2:17—3:8)
  - C. All humanity—Jews and Gentiles—stand under the power of sin. (3:9-20)
- IV. God Provides Righteousness through Jesus Christ on the Basis of Faith. (3:21—4:25)
  - A. God manifests His righteousness. (3:21-26)
    - 1. God's righteousness is through faith. (3:21-23)
    - 2. God's righteousness is through the blood of Christ. (3:24-25*a*)
    - 3. God's righteousness is shown in His passing over former sins. (3:25*b*-26)
  - B. Justification is by faith for all persons. (3:27—4:25)
    - 1. Justifying faith excludes all boasting. (3:27-31)
    - 2. The example of Abraham confirms justification by faith. (4:1-25)
- V. Salvation in Christ Results in Victorious New Life. (5:1—8:39)
  - A. Justification results in peace and righteousness. (5:1-21)
    - 1. Peace with God results in rejoicing in all circumstances. (5:1-11)
    - 2. Christ reverses the results of Adam's sin. (5:12-21)

B. Christian life is a victorious struggle with sin. (6:1—7:25)
1. Faith unites believers in dying and rising with Christ. (6:1-11)
2. Believers are not slaves of sin, but of righteousness. (6:12-23)
3. Dying with Christ sets us free from law. (7:1-6)
4. Struggle with sin is defeat without Christ. (7:7-25)
C. The Spirit of Christ is the power of the Christian's life. (8:1-39)
1. The Spirit is the power for freedom from sin. (8:1-4)
2. Life in the Spirit is the opposite of life in the flesh. (8:5-11)
3. The Spirit creates and witnesses to our status as God's children. (8:12-17)
4. The Spirit confers victorious life. (8:18-39)
VI. God Is Faithful in All His Promises. (9:1—11:36)
A. Paul grieves over Israel's rejection of Christ. (9:1-5)
B. God's sovereignty is displayed in His dealings with Israel. (9:6-29)
1. God's sovereignty is illustrated in His elective choices. (9:6-13)
2. God's sovereignty is seen in His mercy. (9:14-18)
3. God has chosen both Jews and Gentiles. (9:19-29)
C. Israel's freedom to choose explains her rejection of Christ. (9:30—10:21)
1. Israel chose works rather than faith. (9:30-33)
2. Israel rejected righteousness based on faith. (10:1-15)
3. Israel refuses to hear and obey. (10:16-21)
D. God's righteousness is displayed in His mercy. (11:1-36)
1. The saved remnant of Jews shows God's mercy. (11:1-6)
2. The salvation extended to the Gentiles shows God's mercy. (11:7-24)
3. All persons—Jews and Gentiles—are dependent on God's mercy. (11:25-32)
4. God deserves praise for His judgments. (11:33-36)
VII. The Saving Mercy of God in Christ Summons Christians to Obedience. (12:1—15:13)
A. Theme of the exhortations: Christians need to be transformed. (12:1-2)
B. Christians must be responsible members of the body of Christ. (12:3-21)
1. Christians need to view themselves and others appropriately. (12:3-5)
2. Christians must express their different gifts in faith. (12:6-13)
3. Christian life demands love in action. (12:14-21)
C. Christians must fulfill their appropriate obligations to the state. (13:1-7)
D. Christians must remember the supremacy of love and the urgency of the times. (13:8-14)
1. Love fulfills the law. (13:8-10)
2. The critical nature of the times calls for radical commitment to Christ. (13:11-14)
E. Christians must seek to edify one another in the fellowship of the church. (14:1—15:13)
1. The strong and the weak in the church must realize that Christ is the Lord of both groups. (14:1-12)
2. Christians should live by their own convictions, pursue harmony, and avoid making others stumble. (14:13-23)
3. Strong Christians are obligated to bear with and live in harmony with the weak. (15:1-6)
4. All Christians are to receive one another as Christ has received them. (15:7-13)
VIII. Conclusion (15:14—16:27)

Theological Conclusions

The Letter to the Romans provides the most extensive discussion in the New Testament of several doctrines that can deepen our theological understanding and Christian commitment. The righteousness of God, the salvation Christ brings, and the work of the Spirit are three important emphases.

The righteousness of God is featured in Paul's statement of the theme of Romans (1:16-17). The righteousness of God means that God will always do what is just. The righteousness of God stresses what God does more than who He is. The righteousness of God revealed in the gospel is that God sets things right in Jesus Christ. This righteousness which God manifests in the gospel events becomes operative in our lives through faith. Trust or faith is essential both to understand and to avail one's self of the revelation in the gospel (3:22). God declares the sinner righteous (justified) on the basis of what He did in Christ (3:21-26); and the justified person yields his or her life as an instrument of righteousness (6:12-14). Therefore, the result of the righteousness of God is making persons righteous through faith (1:17; 5:1-5).

The salvation that the power of God brings in Christ (1:16) has three dimensions in Christian experience. The first dimension of one's experience of salvation comes at the moment one trusts Christ;

this is the past experience of salvation which Paul specifically delineates in 8:24: "For in this hope we were saved." This hope is expressed as a movement from death to life (5:17), from being under the power of sin to being justified (6:3-11), and from being the slave of sin to being the servant of God (6:20-22).

The second dimension of salvation is the operation of the power of the gospel in the current life of the Christian. Christians look back to an experience of salvation, but they also "live a new life" (6:4) that involves a constant struggle with sin (6:12,15-23) and the yielding of self "to God . . . as instruments of righteousness" (6:13). See chs 5—8; 12—15; 1 Co 1:18.

The third dimension of salvation is in the future. Christians not only are experiencing salvation; they also look to the future with confidence that present sufferings are not worth comparing with the glory to be revealed in us (8:18). God is working all things together for our good so we will be "more than conquerors" (8:37), and so our bodies will be redeemed (8:22-23). Paul summed up this future dimension of salvation in 5:9: we shall "be saved from God's wrath through him!"

The discussion of the Holy Spirit in ch 8 is the most extensive in the New Testament and reflects Paul's distinctive stress on the role of the Spirit in the ethical life of the Christian. The emphasis in Romans is that life in the Spirit is a quality of ethical life which is contrasted with life in the flesh (8:9). The contrasts Paul used are dramatic and instructive: the "law of the Spirit of life" is contrasted with the "law of sin and death" (8:2), the conduct "according to the sinful nature" with that "according to the Spirit" (8:4), and the ones who "have their minds set on what that nature desires" with those who "have their minds set on what the Spirit desires" (8:5). Two life-styles—"controlled not by the sinful nature but by the Spirit" (8:9)—represent the human alternatives. A life in the Spirit is life that fulfills God's demand for righteousness (8:4). The person controlled by a sinful nature is not aware that this is his or her realm of life. Life dedicated to selfish and sinful ways without regard for God proves a person is in the flesh. The Christian who lives in the Spirit demonstrates this by dedication to Christ, to righteousness, and to others.

Contemporary Teaching

The specific circumstances of modern life and the complex problems they present for Christians may be different, but the distinctive doctrines of Romans have abiding value.

The righteousness of God, understood as God's love in action setting things right, summons us as Christians to realize that God's intention in declaring us righteous is that we become righteous. To fulfill the will of God and to become righteous is to be actively involved in what God wishes accomplished in our world. Righteousness is not a state of being, allowing the Christian to be a spectator of life's circumstances; righteousness is the activity in which Christians should be engaged. Righteousness means doing what God wants done in our lives and in our world. To be Christian means to be at work in the task of sharing the gospel (1:14-15), using gifts of service in the church (12:3-8), and demonstrating a life-style that is contrary to the world's by seeking to treat others as Christ's example portrays.

The salvation that the power of God brought to the Romans is also operative in the world today. This salvation provides Christians with a foundation of assurance, confidence, and hope in a world dominated by insecurity and hopelessness. Christians know because of past experience with Christ that the highest priority is commitment to a life set free from sin. The logical and intended outcome of trusting Christ is that lives are dedicated to God and lived out in the confidence that there is no ultimate terror in the universe for those who have trusted Christ.

Finally, the doctrine of the Holy Spirit in Romans summons us to a Christian life centered in a declaration of war on sin in our lives and an unending struggle to achieve righteousness in terms of doing what God wants done. To be a Christian is not to achieve a certain level of morality coupled to faithful attendance at church services, but to go far beyond this; to be a Christian is to be in the struggle with the sin in one's life. Christians realize that the struggle is with sin in two of its basic manifestations—sin as activity which is rebellion against God's will and commandments, and sin as existing in those things in our lives which keep us from doing the things God would have us do. The tragedy so many Christians experience is that they have not really enjoyed the fullness of their salvation. The reason is they have failed to recognize that sin is not limited to doing what is forbidden. The most crippling and common sin among many Christians is that they are giving their fiercest energies, prime time, and most creative thought to enterprises that they really know are not life's most crucial priorities. The Spirit of life in Christ calls us to live, to develop our life-styles, and to set our minds on what God desires to have us do in our world. The Spirit leads us to be concerned about this with commitment so that we pray "Your will be done on earth as it is in heaven" (Mt 6:10) and then set ourselves to the task of trying to do it.

Chapter 1

PAUL, a servant of Christ Jesus, called
to be an apostle[a] and set apart[b] for
the gospel of God[c]— 2the gospel he
promised beforehand[d] through his
prophets[e] in the Holy Scriptures[f] 3re-
garding his Son, who as to his human nature[g] was a descendant of David,[h] 4and
who through the Spirit[a] of holiness was
declared with power to be the Son of
God[b][i] by his resurrection from the
dead:[j] Jesus Christ our Lord.[k] 5Through
him and for his name's sake, we received
grace[l] and apostleship to call people
from among all the Gentiles[m] to the obedience that comes from faith.[n] 6And you
also are among those who are called to
belong to Jesus Christ.[o]

7To all in Rome who are loved by God[p]
and called to be saints:[q]

Grace and peace to you from God our
Father and from the Lord Jesus Christ.[r]

1:1 [a]S 1Co 1:1 [b]S Ac 9:15 [c]Ro 15:16; S 2Co 2:12; 11:7; 1Th 2:8,9; 1Pe 4:17 **1:2** [d]S Ac 13:32; Tit 1:2 [e]Lk 1:70; Ro 3:21 [f]Gal 3:8 **1:3** [g]S Jn 1:14; Ro 9:5 [h]S Mt 1:1 **1:4** [i]S Mt 4:3 [j]S Ac 2:24 [k]1Co 1:2 **1:5** [l]1Ti 1:14 [m]S Ac 9:15 [n]Ac 6:7; Ro 16:26 **1:6** [o]Jude 1; Rev 17:14 **1:7** [p]Ro 8:39; 1Th 1:4 [q]S Ac 9:13 [r]1Co 1:3; Eph 1:2; 1Ti 1:2; Tit 1:4; 1Pe 1:2 **1:8** [s]1Co 1:4; Eph 1:16; 1Th 2:13; 2Th 1:3; 2Ti 1:3 [t]S Ro 10:18; 16:19 **1:9** [u]2Ti 1:3 [v]Job 16:19; Jer 42:5; 2Co 1:23; Gal 1:20; Php 1:8; 1Th 2:5,10 **1:10** [w]1Sa 12:23; S Lk 18:1;

Paul's Longing to Visit Rome

8First, I thank my God through Jesus
Christ for all of you,[s] because your faith
is being reported all over the world.[t]
9God, whom I serve[u] with my whole
heart in preaching the gospel of his Son,
is my witness[v] how constantly I remember you 10in my prayers at all times;[w] and
I pray that now at last by God's will[x] the
way may be opened for me to come to
you.[y]

11I long to see you[z] so that I may impart to you some spiritual gift[a] to make
you strong— 12that is, that you and I may
be mutually encouraged by each other's
faith. 13I do not want you to be un-

S Ac 1:14; Eph 1:16; Php 1:4; Col 1:9; 2Th 1:11; 2Ti 1:3; Phm 4 [x]S Ac 18:21 [y]ver 13; Ro 15:32 **1:11** [z]Ro 15:23 [a]1Co 1:7; 12:1-31

[a]4 Or *who as to his spirit* [b]4 Or *was appointed to be the Son of God with power*

1:1–4 HOLY SPIRIT, Trinity—In this trinitarian passage the Spirit is said to have disclosed Christ's divine sonship by raising Christ from the dead. The Spirit is always associated with life and breath. See note on Eze 37:12–14. The Gospels do not explicitly associate the Spirit with the resurrection of Christ. Paul did associate the Spirit with the resurrection of Christ (Ro 8:11; 1 Ti 3:16; 1 Pe 3:18).

1:1 THE CHURCH, Servants—Paul and other Christians called themselves servants or slaves (Greek *doulos*) of Jesus Christ. A bondslave owed his life to his master. By using the term slave, Christians testify that Jesus is the Lord of our lives. He is the Master, and His followers do His will. In contrast to those trapped in the human institution of slavery, Christians voluntarily and joyfully submit to the Master, who lovingly guides us through life.

1:1–5 PROCLAMATION, Gospel—See note on Ac 3:11–26. Proclamation is a call to faith which produces obedience.

1:1 CHURCH LEADERS, Apostle—Paul's apostleship was often challenged by his opponents because he was not one of the original twelve apostles. He asserted, nevertheless, that he, too, had been called an apostle by the risen Christ, who commissioned him to preach to the Gentiles (11:13; Gal 1:16; 2:8). He considered this to be a grace given to him (Eph 3:7) that was not based on his personal merit. He was a witness of the resurrection of Christ and had received his gospel directly from Him (Gal 1:11–12). He performed the signs of an apostle (2 Co 12:12). The churches he founded were a seal of his apostleship (1 Co 9:2). He bore in his body the marks of Jesus (Gal 6:17) from his apostolic sufferings (1 Co 15:10). Paul confessed that he was the least of the apostles (1 Co 15:9). Paul did not hand his apostleship down to one of his younger preachers. It was a unique office for eyewitnesses of Christ.

1:3–4 JESUS CHRIST, Son of God—The gospel centers on the Son of God, who was both human, born in the line of David, and divine, as demonstrated by the resurrection. The resurrection was not a point of time when Jesus became Son of God. He has been Son of God eternally (Jn 1:1–18). The resurrection gave proof to the world of Jesus' position as did the work of the Holy Spirit in making believers holy. The resurrected Son of God is thus our Lord. See notes on Mk 1:1; Ac 2:23–36.

1:3 JESUS CHRIST, Son of David—See note on Mt 1:1.

1:5–7 GOD, Grace—Grace is the redemptive love of God in action reaching out to people who do not deserve it but are loved by God anyhow. Grace sums up the totality of what the gospel is about.

1:5–6 ELECTION, Faith—By God's matchless grace, faith was granted to the Gentiles to be obedient as the elect of God. The call went out to all Gentiles. The evidence of faith led Paul to assure the Roman Christians they were among the elect even though he did not know them personally. "Called" (Greek *kletos*) is to speak to another person to create or enrich a personal relationship. Election is Christ's calling into personal relationship with Him and His church. The calling may be rejected (Mt 22:14). Compare 1:1,7; 8:28; 1 Co 1:2,24.

1:5 SALVATION, Obedience—Obedience to Christ is the product of faith. Compare Ac 26:20.

1:7 THE CHURCH, Saints—Saints (Greek *hagioi*) means the holy ones of God set apart for His service. In the Old Testament, Israel, as the covenant people, formed a holy nation set apart for God's service. The nation was consecrated as a peculiar possession of God, the unique and sole Source of holiness. See note on Ex 19:4–8. The term "saints" designates the Christian community as recipients of the covenant promises of God. The holiness of Christians results from the call of God and His work in our lives. In the New Testament, "saints" describes all Christians, for all believers are called to minister and serve in Christ's name. Saints are not a select group with greater holiness than others. Saints cannot share their holiness to make others holy. Saints are living believers, not dead revered ones. The saints were members of the various churches addressed in the New Testament (1 Co 1:2; 2 Co 1:1; Eph 1:1; Php 1:1; Col 1:2). "Saints" is equivalent to "Christians" (Ac 9:13,32; 26:10; Heb 13:24; Rev 5:8).

1:7 PRAYER, Blessing—Paul's greetings were prayers. Near the beginnings of his letters Paul invariably prayed for grace and peace (1 Co 1:3; 2 Co 1:2; Gal 1:3; Eph 1:2; Php 1:2; Col 1:2; 1 Th 1:1; 2 Th 1:2; 1 Ti 1:2; 2 Ti 1:2; Tit 1:4; Phm 3). Sincere written prayers encourage other believers as well as calling God's blessing on them. See note on Ro 15:33.

1:8 PRAYER, Thanksgiving—See note on Ac 28:15. Paul took a normal form of Greek letters and transformed it into Christian prayer. Correspondence expressing gratitude to God for the recipients encourages them, cements relationships, and joins separated people in worship of God. Christian thanks goes to God through Jesus, our greatest reason for gratitude. See note on Php 1:3.

1:9–10 PRAYER, Kingdom Growth—Virtually all Paul's recorded prayers are for the purpose of advancing God's work and kingdom. See note on Mt 6:9–13. Even his petition to go to Rome, personal as it seems, had spiritual purposes in view.

1:13–17 EVANGELISM, Holy Life—Paul described three elements of his life which gave power to his evangelistic efforts: a sense of obligation, eagerness, and pride instead of shame in the gospel. Christ's death for him put Paul in debt,

aware,[b] brothers,[c] that I planned many
times to come to you (but have been prevented from doing so until now)[d] in order that I might have a harvest among
you, just as I have had among the other
Gentiles.
14I am obligated[e] both to Greeks and
non-Greeks, both to the wise and the
foolish. 15That is why I am so eager to
preach the gospel also to you who are at
Rome.[f]
16I am not ashamed of the gospel,[g] because it is the power of God[h] for the salvation of everyone who believes:[i] first
for the Jew,[j] then for the Gentile.[k] 17For
in the gospel a righteousness from God is
revealed,[l] a righteousness that is by
faith[m] from first to last,[c] just as it is written: "The righteous will live by faith."[d] [n]

God's Wrath Against Mankind

18The wrath of God[o] is being revealed
from heaven against all the godlessness
and wickedness of men who suppress the
truth by their wickedness, 19since what
may be known about God is plain to
them, because God has made it plain to
them.[p] 20For since the creation of the
world God's invisible qualities—his eternal power and divine nature—have been
clearly seen, being understood from what
has been made,[q] so that men are without
excuse.[r]
21For although they knew God, they
neither glorified him as God nor gave
thanks to him, but their thinking became
futile and their foolish hearts were darkened.[s] 22Although they claimed to be
wise, they became fools[t] 23and exchanged the glory of the immortal God
for images[u] made to look like mortal man
and birds and animals and reptiles.

1:13 [b]S Ro 11:25 [c]S Ro 7:1 [d]Ro 15:22,23
1:14 [e]1Co 9:16
1:15 [f]Ro 15:20
1:16 [g]2Ti 1:8 [h]1Co 1:18 [i]S Jn 3:15 [j]Ac 3:26; 13:46 [k]S Ac 13:46; Ro 2:9,10
1:17 [l]Ro 3:21; Php 3:9 [m]S Ro 9:30 [n]Hab 2:4; Gal 3:11; Heb 10:38
1:18 [o]Jn 3:36; Ro 5:9; Eph 5:6; Col 3:6; 1Th 1:10; Rev 19:15
1:19 [p]Ac 14:17
1:20 [q]Ps 19:1-6 [r]Ro 2:1
1:21 [s]Ge 8:21; Jer 2:5; 17:9; Eph 4:17,18
1:22 [t]1Co 1:20,27; 3:18,19
1:23 [u]Dt 4:16,17; Ps 106:20; Jer 2:11; Ac 17:29

[c]*17* Or *is from faith to faith* [d]*17* Hab. 2:4

---

under obligation to witness. The sense of obligation made him eager to pay the debt and preach to all people. He was on fire for the gospel. Thus he took pride in the gospel and could find no reason to be ashamed of it. His life centered on the gospel (Greek *euangelion,* the root of the English word evangelism). The gospel was powerful good news putting people in right relationship with Christ and thus providing salvation. This produced a righteous life dedicated to sharing the gospel with others.

1:16–17 SALVATION, Justification—The gospel declares that God puts persons right with Him through faith in Christ. See note on Hab 2:4. God does not wait for humans to achieve righteousness, that is, to do what is right. God acted in Christ to give us righteousness. The gift of righteousness is at the same time a call to be righteous, not by rigidly following a legalistic list of rules and traditions, but by letting trust in God control every action of life.

1:16–17 SALVATION, Initiative—The gospel which we preach is God's gospel, not ours (Mk 1:14). It is the good news that God's reign has arrived in Jesus of Nazareth. Those who turn from sin and trust themselves to Christ will be saved (Mk 1:15). That gospel has the power to save those who believe, whether Jew or Gentile. The gospel reveals that persons are made right with God through faith or faithfulness (Hab 2:4). According to Paul elsewhere (Gal 3:8), this gospel was announced in advance to Abraham. Compare Ge 12:2–3.

1:17 GOD, Righteous—The gospel is not only about the forgiving love of God in the provision of new life for dying sinners. It is also about the righteousness of God brought to Christian converts. In salvation God seeks to replace our unrighteousness with a righteousness that He develops in us. The righteousness of God means more than that He opposes evil. It means primarily that God does what is right and seeks to create right ways of living, right ways of doing, right ways of thinking in the lives and hearts of His people.

1:18 GOD, Wrath—God's wrath is His response to persistent sin and unrighteousness. Wrath is what results from one's refusing to let God's love have its way. See note on Mt 3:7–10.

1:18–32 CREATION, Evil—Evil is not an integral part of creation. Evil results from human sin. Sin is possible in God's creation because God chose to make people with free wills capable of choosing to obey or rebel. Creation shows an orderly God of infinite power. Humans choose to make their own gods and follow foolish moral choices. God allows them to follow their evil desires and face the ultimate result. The Creator's wrath against the evil that has contaminated His work is not His anger bursting forth to destroy. Rather, it is the love of God functioning in the world He made to assure the righteous that they will be vindicated. God's wrath operates continually but will be climaxed at the final judgment. A moral order exists in this world. The person who violates it will suffer the consequences of his or her actions. Righteousness will eventually triumph, and evil will suffer. This fact was built by God into the very structures of the universe He created. Belief in an all-powerful Creator is only one part of biblical faith. Saving faith must go further, establishing personal trust in the Creator as Savior. With such faith, we can endure the evil that harasses us, knowing we will be vindicated by God's moral law which is an expression of His own character.

1:18–32 EVIL AND SUFFERING, Human Origin—Human refusal to acknowledge and worship the self-evident God is at the root of much of what we call evil in this world. Such rebellion against God is rebellion against the truth. Refusal to accept the truth brings intellectual and moral darkness leading to human wickedness. One evident sign of such wickedness is the immense variety of false worship and false religion humans create. Another sign is sexual immorality. Evil actions are not God's plan for the world or a sign of God's weakness. They result from the misused human freedom God created. We invent ways of doing evil. God endures human sin but punishes it in two ways. We suffer the natural consequences of our sinful acts, thus missing the fullness of life God intended, and we face the eternal judgment of death.

1:18–25 SIN, Universal Nature—Can God in justice condemn those who have never heard the gospel? Paul faced this issue head on as he introduced his good news of justification by faith to the church in Rome. His inspired understanding shows that all people have brought condemnation on themselves. No one responds properly to the revelation God gives of Himself through the natural yearning for God placed in the human heart and through the witness to God set in the created order of the universe. God's wrath against all creatures is justified. No one has a satisfactory excuse. No one has become what God intended. We are guilty of (1) lack of gratitude and worship of God; (2) foolish false worship; and (3) sinful desires, especially wrong sexual desires. Our problem is not justifying God's wrath. It is helping people understand the nature of their sin and guilt and then pointing them toward faith in Christ as the universal solution to the universal problem.

1:18–20 REVELATION, Author of Creation—Atheists have no excuse. Open-minded attention to the nature of creation makes the existence of God evident. Pagans have no excuse. The eternal power of God is evident in creation. Nothing made by human hands or included as part of the created order is powerful enough to be God. All people have enough revelation in creation to point them to worship the invisible God. Any person who does not stands under God's righteous judgment.

24Therefore God gave them over[v] in
the sinful desires of their hearts to sexual
impurity for the degrading of their bodies
with one another.[w] 25They exchanged
the truth of God for a lie,[x] and worshiped
and served created things[y] rather than
the Creator—who is forever praised.[z]
Amen.[a]

26Because of this, God gave them
over[b] to shameful lusts.[c] Even their
women exchanged natural relations for
unnatural ones.[d] 27In the same way the
men also abandoned natural relations
with women and were inflamed with lust
for one another. Men committed indecent acts with other men, and received in
themselves the due penalty for their perversion.[e]

28Furthermore, since they did not
think it worthwhile to retain the knowledge of God, he gave them over[f] to a
depraved mind, to do what ought not to
be done. 29They have become filled with
every kind of wickedness, evil, greed and
depravity. They are full of envy, murder,
strife, deceit and malice. They are gossips,[g] 30slanderers, God-haters, insolent,
arrogant and boastful; they invent ways of
doing evil; they disobey their parents;[h]
31they are senseless, faithless, heartless,[i]
ruthless. 32Although they know God's
righteous decree that those who do such
things deserve death,[j] they not only continue to do these very things but also approve[k] of those who practice them.

Chapter 2

God's Righteous Judgment

YOU, therefore, have no excuse,[l] you
who pass judgment on someone else,
for at whatever point you judge the other,
you are condemning yourself, because
you who pass judgment do the same
things.[m] 2Now we know that God's judgment against those who do such things is

1:24 [v]ver 26,28; Ps 81:12; Eph 4:19 [w]1Pe 4:3
1:25 [x]Isa 44:20 [y]Jer 10:14; 13:25; 16:19,20 [z]Ro 9:5; 2Co 11:31 [a]S Ro 11:36
1:26 [b]ver 24,28 [c]Eph 4:19; 1Th 4:5 [d]Lev 18:22,23
1:27 [e]Lev 18:22; 20:13; 1Co 6:18
1:28 [f]ver 24,26
1:29 [g]2Co 12:20; 1Ti 5:13; Jas 3:2; 3Jn 10
1:30 [h]2Ti 3:2
1:31 [i]2Ti 3:3
1:32 [j]S Ro 6:23 [k]Ps 50:18; Lk 11:48; Ac 8:1; 22:20
2:1 [l]Ro 1:20 [m]2Sa 12:5-7; S Mt 7:1,2

1:21–23 HUMANITY, Intellectual Nature—Pride in human intellect can lead people to become foolish. The natural order reveals God to us. Human pride leads us to worship objects we create instead of the Creator. Nothing could be more foolish.

1:21 SALVATION, Knowledge of God—Salvation comes to a person when the person responds in faith to the knowledge of God in Christ. Intellectual knowledge about God can come to people through observation of and reflection on the natural created order. With only that knowledge people do not respond in a personal relationship to God. Only by hearing the gospel and entering into a personal faith relationship with Jesus do people have saving knowledge of God. Then they gain deeper understanding of the revelation available through the natural world.

1:21 PRAYER, Command of God—Sinful unbelievers fail to acknowledge God as source of all possessions and joy. Thanksgiving is an integral part of relationship with God. Creation itself should turn people to give thanks.

1:24–27 HUMANITY, Relationships—People following their own folly instead of God's will may pervert the natural sexual relations God provided for His people. Adulterous relationships, some in the name of worship (fertility cults), as well as homosexual relationships, pervert God's intent. See note on 1:21–23.

1:26–32 SIN, Depravity—All people need the gospel because of the moral depravity of our world. Depravity occurs as people choose to follow sinful desires rather than the knowledge of God revealed to them. God does not hold on to sinful people and force them to do His will. He gives them or delivers them (note same verb in 8:32) to their own desires. God lets us be free to sin. He does not give up on us. Sin should lead to guilt and then to a search to be rid of guilt. Christ is the end of the search. God lets us go our own ways to bring us back to serve Christ freely. The moral depravity we choose over the knowledge of God has many manifestations. Homosexuality most obviously reverses the order God intended. Greed, envy, murder, gossiping, and all the rest of Paul's list just as surely reverse God's order and reveal our depravity. That depravity affects our thoughts, desires, will, and actions. Depravity deserves death. We know this and march on into death's arms. Truly we have no excuse.

1:26–28 FAMILY, Sexual Sin—One consequence of human rejection of God's plan for life is homosexual activity. The biblical revelation uniformly declares heterosexual relationships to be God's intended form of sexual interaction and condemns homosexual acts (Lev 18:22; 20:13). A homosexual life-style is contrary to the gospel (1 Co 6:9; 1 Ti 1:10). Even though rejecting homosexual acts, the New Testament offers forgiveness and a new life orientation to homosexuals (1 Co 6:11) as well as to other sinners.

1:28–32 HUMANITY, Intellectual Nature—The term *depraved* normally describes something that does not measure up to a standard. When applied to the human mind, this refers to a mind that does not measure up to God's standards. The human mind makes the free choice to ignore God and follow its own wisdom. In so doing, it lets fleshly lust dominate rather than the spiritual drive to know God. Such an intellect leads people astray, causing the rejection of God Himself and leading to wholly irresponsible behavior. God gives people freedom to choose. We know what is right and choose what is wrong. We encourage others to do the same. Sin dominates our life. This is human moral and intellectual depravity. We need help. Our wisdom is not sufficient.

1:28–32 CHRISTIAN ETHICS, Moral Limits—Humans rebel against moral limits. God responds to continued rebellion by letting people carry their moral freedom of choice to absurd limits. Evil becomes standard operating procedure for such people. Even in the face of death resulting from their rebellion, they continue devoting themselves to immorality. They lose the ability to distinguish right and wrong, being deaf to God's voice.

2:1–11 EVIL AND SUFFERING, Punishment—God judges Jews and Gentiles fairly and shows no favoritism. All will be punished for their sins. Judgment is God's business, not ours. God decides who receives eternal wrath and who receives eternal life. The just final judgment of God is the answer to questions of injustice and unfairness.

2:2 GOD, Judge—As the Creator-Lord who brought us into existence, God holds us accountable unto Himself for what we do with our lives. Every person must answer to God, who judges us all. The One who judges us is also known to us as the Heavenly Father, who expresses His deep and abiding interest in us. That loving nature of God will not be compromised or manipulated. He who is Father to us will also act as Judge over us. Sometimes this judgment is exercised in the end of time, or in eternity. At other times, His judgment may be exercised on us in this life. How and when God sits in judgment upon us is His business and not ours, for He is the sovereign Lord of us all. He may withhold His judgment, or delay His judgment when He wishes, when He sees that it is in our best interest as He seeks to accomplish His purposes in us. His judgment may be tempered in mercy if we have responded to Him in faith. But no one deserves whatever mercy He may show, for we are without excuse in our sins.

based on truth. 3So when you, a mere
man, pass judgment on them and yet do
the same things, do you think you will
escape God's judgment? 4Or do you show
contempt for the riches[n] of his kindness,[o] tolerance[p] and patience,[q] not realizing that God's kindness leads you toward repentance?[r]

5But because of your stubbornness and
your unrepentant heart, you are storing
up wrath against yourself for the day of
God's wrath[s], when his righteous judgment[t] will be revealed. 6God "will give
to each person according to what he has
done."[e u] 7To those who by persistence
in doing good seek glory, honor[v] and immortality,[w] he will give eternal life.[x]
8But for those who are self-seeking and
who reject the truth and follow evil,[y]
there will be wrath and anger.[z] 9There
will be trouble and distress for every human being who does evil:[a] first for the
Jew, then for the Gentile;[b] 10but glory,
honor and peace for everyone who does
good: first for the Jew, then for the Gentile.[c] 11For God does not show favoritism.[d]

12All who sin apart from the law will
also perish apart from the law, and all
who sin under the law[e] will be judged by
the law. 13For it is not those who hear the
law who are righteous in God's sight, but
it is those who obey[f] the law who will be
declared righteous. 14(Indeed, when Gentiles, who do not have the law, do by nature things required by the law,[g] they
are a law for themselves, even though
they do not have the law, 15since they
show that the requirements of the law
are written on their hearts, their consciences also bearing witness, and their
thoughts now accusing, now even defending them.) 16This will take place on
the day when God will judge men's secrets[h] through Jesus Christ,[i] as my gospel[j] declares.

The Jews and the Law

17Now you, if you call yourself a Jew; if
you rely on the law and brag about your
relationship to God;[k] 18if you know his
will and approve of what is superior because you are instructed by the law; 19if
you are convinced that you are a guide for

2:4 [n]Ro 9:23; 11:33; Eph 1:7,18; 2:7; 3:8,16; Col 2:2 [o]Ro 11:22 [p]Ro 3:25 [q]Ex 34:6; Ro 9:22; 1Ti 1:16; 1Pe 3:20; 2Pe 3:15 [r]2Pe 3:9
2:5 [s]Ps 110:5; Rev 6:17 [t]Jude 6
2:6 [u]Ps 62:12; S Mt 16:27
2:7 [v]ver 10 [w]1Co 15:53,54; 2Ti 1:10 [x]S Mt 25:46
2:8 [y]2Th 2:12 [z]Eze 22:31
2:9 [a]Ps 32:10 [b]ver 10; Ro 1:16
2:10 [c]ver 9; Ro 1:16
2:11 [d]S Ac 10:34
2:12 [e]Ro 3:19; 6:14; 1Co 9:20,21; Gal 4:21; 5:18; S Ro 7:4
2:13 [f]Jas 1:22,23,25
2:14 [g]Ac 10:35
2:16 [h]Ecc 12:14; 1Co 4:5 [i]Ac 10:42 [j]Ro 16:25; 2Ti 2:8
2:17 [k]ver 23; Jer 8:8; Mic 3:11; Jn 5:45; Ro 9:4

[e]6 Psalm 62:12; Prov. 24:12

2:4 GOD, Grace—We have received abundant grace from God as He has sought in a variety of ways to bring us to repentance and faith.
2:4 SALVATION, Repentance—God's kindness leads persons to repentance. In His love God is kind and patient and does not judge and punish people immediately for sins. His kindness is not softness towards sin but love for sinners seeking to provide time to change.
2:5–9 GOD, Wrath—When God's gracious love cannot have its way in bringing us to repentance and faith, He has no alternative left but wrath. That wrath will ultimately be revealed on the final judgment day. We may escape temporarily, but we cannot escape His wrath forever unless we devote our lives to Him.
2:5 HUMANITY, Human Nature—Human nature is turned toward rebellion against God. A stubborn persistence, a single-minded hardness towards things spiritual makes us refuse to turn away from the existing patterns of life and leads us to reject God's will. See note on 8:5–8.
2:5–16 LAST THINGS, Judgment—God judges human beings according to their conduct. Divine judgment is an ongoing reality in the present time. There are temporal judgments and punishments for evil. However, the "day of God's wrath" (v 5), will be a future, final judgment. See note on Rev 20:11–15. Evil conduct can cause a storing up of divine wrath. God carries out judgment, both present and future, on the basis of underlying principles. Judgment will be on an individual basis, rather than a national one as was often the case in the Old Testament. It will be conducted on the basis of works, as the true inner character is revealed through conduct. Divine judgment will be without partiality. It will be based on response to the knowledge and understanding of God that an individual has (vv 12–15). Even the secrets of human hearts will be judged.
2:6–9 SALVATION, Eternal Life—At first reading these verses appear to teach salvation by works instead of by faith. Paul was showing the Jews their laws and legalistic system did not provide salvation. Any person with or without the law will be rewarded for persistently doing good. Any person with or without the law who does evil will perish. Paul's final conclusion (3:23) is that no one does good. All do evil. All need justification by faith. Eternal life is the free gift of God based on faith in Christ and cannot be earned by Jew or Gentile through good works. See note on Eph 2:4–5,7–10.
2:11 GOD, Righteous—See note on Ac 10:34–35.
2:12–16 HUMANITY, Moral Consciousness—No one can plead ignorance before God. He judges us on the moral knowledge we have. Those who know the teachings of God's Word face judgment on that basis. Others have through creation a sense to do right. They are judged on this basis. None can plead innocent. All have sinned consciously against what they knew to be right. Right knowledge is not the criterion. Right action is.
2:12 SIN, Universal Nature—Whether a person has knowledge of the law does not alone determine moral accountability before God. Many have sinned without knowledge of the law. Everyone has some internal code or law that acts as a standard of behavior. The apostle's point is that no one can keep a code without fault, whether that code is written or unwritten, from God or from man. Sin is the deification of self which is a rebellion against divine restraint.
2:13 SIN, Disobeying—An expert in God's Word is still a sinner. God does not evaluate us on our knowledge of His will. He judges us because we disobey. We do not do what we know to do.
2:13 SALVATION, Obedience—God reckons as righteous those who do the law and not those who merely hear it with their ears. Jewish pride in their law profited nothing because it did not lead to obedience. See note on 2:6–9.
2:16 JESUS CHRIST, Judgment—Jesus is God's Agent to judge all people at the end of time. See note on Ac 17:31.
2:16 PROCLAMATION, Gospel—See note on Ac 3:11–26. The final judgment is part of gospel proclamation.
2:17–29 ELECTION, Israel—The elect of God are made righteous with God by faith. This applies to Jew and Gentile. Jews are not assured of election by physical acts, legal obedience, or documented genealogies. A heart of faith changed by God's Spirit is the true sign of election.
2:19–24 EDUCATION, Example—Those who were schooled in the Law were potential teachers of the blind, the wayward, and the young. Their failure to be obedient to the Law nullified that potential. Likewise, we cannot teach effectively what we do not practice. Belief includes action as well as factual knowledge. A thief or adulterer makes a poor instructor

the blind, a light for those who are in the
dark, 20an instructor of the foolish, a
teacher of infants, because you have in
the law the embodiment of knowledge
and truth— 21you, then, who teach others, do you not teach yourself? You who
preach against stealing, do you steal?[l]
22You who say that people should not
commit adultery, do you commit adultery? You who abhor idols, do you rob
temples?[m] 23You who brag about the
law,[n] do you dishonor God by breaking
the law? 24As it is written: "God's name
is blasphemed among the Gentiles because of you."[f] [o]
25Circumcision has value if you observe the law,[p] but if you break the law,
you have become as though you had not
been circumcised.[q] 26If those who are
not circumcised keep the law's requirements,[r] will they not be regarded as
though they were circumcised?[s] 27The
one who is not circumcised physically
and yet obeys the law will condemn you[t]
who, even though you have the[g] written
code and circumcision, are a lawbreaker.
28A man is not a Jew if he is only one
outwardly,[u] nor is circumcision merely
outward and physical.[v] 29No, a man is a
Jew if he is one inwardly; and circumci-

2:21 [l]Mt 23:3,4
2:22 [m]Ac 19:37
2:23 [n]S ver 17
2:24 [o]Isa 52:5; Eze 36:22; 2Pe 2:2
2:25 [p]ver 13,27; Gal 5:3 [q]Jer 4:4; 9:25,26
2:26 [r]Ro 8:4 [s]S 1Co 7:19
2:27 [t]Mt 12:41,42
2:28 [u]Mt 3:9; Jn 8:39; Ro 9:6,7 [v]Gal 6:15
2:29 [w]Dt 30:6 [x]Php 3:3; Col 2:11 [y]Ro 7:6; 2Co 3:6 [z]Jn 5:44; 12:43; 1Co 4:5; 2Co 10:18; Gal 1:10; 1Th 2:4; 1Pe 3:4
3:2 [a]Ro 9:4,5 [b]Dt 4:8; Ps 147:19; Ac 7:38
3:3 [c]Ro 10:16; Heb 4:2 [d]2Ti 2:13
3:4 [e]Jn 3:33 [f]Ps 116:11 [g]Ps 51:4
3:5 [h]Ro 5:8 [i]Ro 6:19; Gal 3:15
3:6 [j]Ge 18:25; Ro 2:16

sion is circumcision of the heart,[w] by the
Spirit,[x] not by the written code.[y] Such a
man's praise is not from men, but from
God.[z]

Chapter 3

God's Faithfulness

WHAT advantage, then, is there in being a Jew, or what value is there in
circumcision? 2Much in every way![a] First
of all, they have been entrusted with the
very words of God.[b]
3What if some did not have faith?[c]
Will their lack of faith nullify God's faithfulness?[d] 4Not at all! Let God be true,[e]
and every man a liar.[f] As it is written:

"So that you may be proved right
when you speak
and prevail when you judge."[h] [g]

5But if our unrighteousness brings out
God's righteousness more clearly,[h] what
shall we say? That God is unjust in bringing his wrath on us? (I am using a human
argument.)[i] 6Certainly not! If that were
so, how could God judge the world?[j]
7Someone might argue, "If my falsehood

[f] *24* Isaiah 52:5; Ezek. 36:22 [g] *27* Or *who, by means of a* [h] *4* Psalm 51:4

in morals. A teacher should provide light for those in moral and intellectual darkness. This is impossible when the intellectually superior teacher lives in moral darkness.

2:28–29 CREATION, New Creation—The Creator's new creation in Christ contains many implications for doctrine and discipleship. Israel was God's chosen people for one purpose. They were His instrument through whom salvation would come to the world. The Messiah came and fulfilled Israel's distinctive mission. Those who accepted Christ as Lord and Savior became a new community, the "Israel of God" (Gal 6:16). Circumcision had become religiously meaningless, unable to guarantee inclusion in or exclusion from the people of God. All that mattered was whether or not one had become a new person through Jesus Christ (Gal 6:15). We can be certain today that God loves all people because He is the Creator of all the world. He has no special favorites. Jesus came to seek and save people of every race. He wants to see His "new creation" increase in His world.

2:29 HOLY SPIRIT, Indwells—Circumcision was the sign of the covenant between God and Israel. The gift of the Spirit to Christians is a sign of the new covenant between God and the church. Outward obedience may win human praise. The indwelling of the Spirit is the only way to receive God's praise.

3:1–20 ELECTION, Condemnation—Because of wickedness and disobedience, humankind rejects the invitation of the God who elects. Human rejection suffers the penalty of God's wrath. Jews had an advantage in having God's inspired teachings, but their unrighteousness brought deserved condemnation. Condemnation of faithless Jews does not nullify God's justice or faithfulness. God remains the righteous Judge with the right to condemn all unrighteousness and faithlessness.

3:3–4 GOD, Faithfulness—Paul's opponents argued against his doctrine of wrath and judgment: if God is absolutely faithful to His human creations, then He must save all of them ultimately. Otherwise, it was not fair for Him to create them. If He elected the Jews to be His people, then He must save every one of them to be faithful to His elect. Paul proved them wrong. The Jews can rightfully point with pride to their place in God's work of salvation. They cannot thereby avoid personal responsibility (Am 3:2). God is gracious to provide a way of salvation at all. No person deserves salvation, can demand salvation, or accuse God of unfaithfulness in not providing salvation. God gave us freedom to return or reject His love. When we reject it, as we all do, we deserve His wrath. His faithfulness to His purposes demands He let us experience His wrath. His grace in offering salvation gives us an escape from wrath if we accept it.

3:5–26 GOD, Righteous—God's action in bringing mercy, forgiveness, and salvation to lost sinners is perfectly in keeping with His justice and righteousness. Humans have proved their inability to be righteous by meeting legal standards. So God in Christ has provided a way for us to be right with Him apart from legal standards. The death of Jesus as an atoning sacrifice is God's expression of His displeasure with sin, of His judgment upon sin, and of His love for sinners. God's righteousness results in His doing what is just in offering salvation to us. Some hold that God's love motivates Him to be merciful and forgiving while His righteousness demands that He punish the sinner, but God's love and righteousness are perfectly coordinated, seeking the same results.

3:5–8 EVIL AND SUFFERING, Providence—Although God can bring good out of an evil situation, disciples should not do evil in order that God can do more good. We cannot justify our evil behavior through twisted theological or philosophical arguments. Neither can we condemn God or escape the reality of His just judgment. Divine providence not human reason rules our universe.

3:5–6 LAST THINGS, Judgment—God is righteous and thus will judge the world fairly. See notes on 2 Co 5:10; Rev 20:11–15.

3:6 GOD, Judge—One of God's activities in presiding over the world as its sovereign Creator is to judge all people. God created all people and holds them all responsible to Him for what they do with their lives. They are created with a sense of responsibility, and they must finally give answer to the One who created them. If we try to use human logic to argue away the wrath of God, then we must take away God's role as world Judge. The inspired Bible will not let us do that.

enhances God's truthfulness and so increases his glory,[k] why am I still condemned as a sinner?"[l] 8Why not say—as
we are being slanderously reported as
saying and as some claim that we say—
"Let us do evil that good may result"?[m]
Their condemnation is deserved.

No One Is Righteous

9What shall we conclude then? Are we
any better[i]?[n] Not at all! We have already
made the charge that Jews and Gentiles
alike are all under sin.[o] 10As it is written:

"There is no one righteous, not even
one;
11 there is no one who understands,
no one who seeks God.
12All have turned away,
they have together become
worthless;
there is no one who does good,
not even one."[j] [p]
13"Their throats are open graves;
their tongues practice deceit."[k] [q]
"The poison of vipers is on their
lips."[l] [r]
14 "Their mouths are full of cursing
and bitterness."[m] [s]
15"Their feet are swift to shed blood;
16 ruin and misery mark their ways,
17and the way of peace they do not
know."[n] [t]
18 "There is no fear of God before their
eyes."[o] [u]

19Now we know that whatever the law
says,[v] it says to those who are under the
law,[w] so that every mouth may be silenced[x] and the whole world held accountable to God.[y] 20Therefore no one
will be declared righteous in his sight by
observing the law;[z] rather, through the
law we become conscious of sin.[a]

Righteousness Through Faith

21But now a righteousness from God,[b]
apart from law, has been made known, to
which the Law and the Prophets testify.[c]
22This righteousness from God[d] comes
through faith[e] in Jesus Christ[f] to all who
believe.[g] There is no difference,[h] 23for
all have sinned[i] and fall short of the glory of God, 24and are justified[j] freely by
his grace[k] through the redemption[l] that
came by Christ Jesus. 25God presented
him as a sacrifice of atonement,[p] [m]

3:7 [k]ver 4 [l]Ro 9:19 **3:8** [m]Ro 6:1 **3:9** [n]ver 1 [o]ver 19, 23; 1Ki 8:46; 2Ch 6:36; Ps 106:6; Ro 5:12; 11:32; Gal 3:22 **3:12** [p]Ps 14:1-3; 53:1-3; Ecc 7:20 **3:13** [q]Ps 5:9 [r]Ps 140:3 **3:14** [s]Ps 10:7 **3:17** [t]Isa 59:7,8 **3:18** [u]Ps 36:1 **3:19** [v]S Jn 10:34 [w]S Ro 2:12 [x]Ps 63:11; 107:42; Eze 16:63 [y]ver 9 **3:20** [z]Ac 13:39; Gal 2:16 [a]S Ro 4:15 **3:21** [b]Isa 46:13; Jer 23:6; Ro 1:17; 9:30 [c]Ac 10:43; Ro 1:2 **3:22** [d]Ro 1:17 [e]S Ro 9:30 [f]Gal 2:16; 3:22 [g]S Jn 3:15; Ro 4:11; 10:4 [h]Ro 10:12; Gal 3:28; Col 3:11 **3:23** [i]S ver 9 **3:24** [j]S Ro 4:25 [k]Jn 1:14,16,17; Ro 4:16; 5:21; 6:14; 11:5; 2Co 12:9; Eph 2:8; 4:7; Tit 2:11; Heb 4:16 [l]Ps 130:7; 1Co 1:30; Gal 4:5; Eph 1:7,14; Col 1:14; Heb 9:12 **3:25** [m]Ex 25:17; Lev 16:10; Ps 65:3; Heb 2:17; 9:28; 1Jn 4:10

[i] *9* Or *worse* [j] *12* Psalms 14:1-3; 53:1-3; Eccles. 7:20 [k] *13* Psalm 5:9 [l] *13* Psalm 140:3 [m] *14* Psalm 10:7 [n] *17* Isaiah 59:7,8 [o] *18* Psalm 36:1 [p] *25* Or *as the one who would turn aside his wrath, taking away sin*

3:7–8 SIN, Against God—Human sin provides God an opportunity to show His mercy and faithfulness. In response to sin, God provides a way of salvation and reveals more about His own righteousness. Sinners can argue that sin has a good purpose. Such false reasoning says we should go on sinning so God can go on proving how true and faithful He is. Paul disagreed. Sin is evil and never justified. Sin is against God, not for Him. God does good because of who He is, not because of our evil.

3:9–18 HUMANITY, Spiritual Nature—Scripture, as well as human experience, point to the universality of sin. All people of all cultures turn away from God, toward selfishness, and against fellow humans. See center column for Paul's Scripture sources. No evidence points to the goodness and growing perfection of human beings. All evidence points to our sinful nature. Guilt plagues us all. We know we are accountable to our Creator.

3:9–23 SIN, Universal Nature—With or without God's written revelation, Jew or non-Jew—we all sin and stand condemned under God's wrath. No one can claim innocence from experience or by logic. Only Jesus, of all people who have ever or will ever live, was sinless.

3:19–20 CHRISTIAN ETHICS, Moral Imperatives—Law does not lead to salvation. Law makes us aware of our duty to God and our inability to fulfill that duty. Law lets us know we have failed God's expectations and deserve the penalty—death. Without imperatives showing God's expectations, we would not be aware of our failures and would not understand our separation from God. See note on 7:1–25.

3:20 SIN, Lawlessness—The law of God does not provide a way to righteousness. It provides a mirror to reveal our sin. The more law we know the more we are conscious of what we have done wrong, not of what we have done right. Obeying laws will never lead to salvation—trusting Christ will.

3:21–31 SALVATION, Justification—Christ has made known fully the righteousness which God demands and approves. He did not make it known in a law book but in a completely human Life. All persons, whoever they are, need this righteousness. The only way they can get it is through faith in Christ. God has made it possible for all persons to be put right with Him through the sacrifice of His Son on the cross. The cross is the demonstration of the awfulness of sin and of the justice of God.

3:23 GOD, Glory—The glory of God is the open disclosure of the true nature of God as holy, righteous, loving, and powerful. His glory is His right to all prestige and honor. We "see" the glory of God when we have a deep perception of who God is and how great He is. Our sins stand in awful contrast to the glory of God. They make us stand in need of His redemption.

3:24–25 JESUS CHRIST, Atonement—Salvation from sin is available because Jesus died to set us free from guilt and death.

3:24 SALVATION, Redemption—Our new standing with God comes through redemption in Christ. Here redemption means Christ's act of ransoming us from sin. This redemption means nothing less than our freedom and emancipation from the guilt, power, and consequences of our sins.

3:24 SALVATION, Grace—Jesus Christ redeems us and puts us right with God by the free gift of His grace, not by any good we have done. Compare 2:6–11.

3:25 GOD, Grace—God's grace is dramatically demonstrated through His offering His own Son as an atoning sacrifice for our sins, thus leaving us unpunished for our sins when we accept His grace. What greater love could God show than this? See note on Jn 3:16.

3:25 SALVATION, Atonement—God presented Jesus Christ publicly as an atoning sacrifice on the cross, (Greek *hilasterion*, probably referring to the atonement cover or mercy seat). The mercy seat was the covering of the ark in the tabernacle (Ex 25:17–22; Heb 9:5). It was the place of propitiation, or the place where God's forgiving mercy was shown. The text teaches us that now the cross of Christ is the place where God's saving mercy is revealed. The word also refers to the averting of the results of God's anger. In the cross God took upon Himself the punishment for sin. This shows the depth of His love and grace.

through faith in his blood.[n] He did this to
demonstrate his justice, because in his
forbearance he had left the sins committed beforehand unpunished[o]— 26he did
it to demonstrate his justice at the
present time, so as to be just and the one
who justifies those who have faith in
Jesus.
27Where, then, is boasting?[p] It is excluded. On what principle? On that of observing the law? No, but on that of faith.
28For we maintain that a man is justified
by faith apart from observing the law.[q]
29Is God the God of Jews only? Is he not
the God of Gentiles too? Yes, of Gentiles
too,[r] 30since there is only one God, who
will justify the circumcised by faith and
the uncircumcised through that same
faith.[s] 31Do we, then, nullify the law by
this faith? Not at all! Rather, we uphold
the law.

Chapter 4

Abraham Justified by Faith

WHAT then shall we say[t] that Abraham, our forefather,[u] discovered
in this matter? 2If, in fact, Abraham was
justified by works, he had something to
boast about—but not before God.[v]
3What does the Scripture say? "Abraham
believed God, and it was credited to him
as righteousness."[q] [w]
4Now when a man works, his wages
are not credited to him as a gift,[x] but as
an obligation. 5However, to the man who
does not work but trusts God who justifies the wicked, his faith is credited as
righteousness.[y] 6David says the same
thing when he speaks of the blessedness
of the man to whom God credits righteousness apart from works:

7"Blessed are they
whose transgressions are forgiven,
whose sins are covered.
8Blessed is the man
whose sin the Lord will never count
against him."[r] [z]

9Is this blessedness only for the circumcised, or also for the uncircumcised?[a]
We have been saying that Abraham's
faith was credited to him as righteousness.[b] 10Under what circumstances was
it credited? Was it after he was circumcised, or before? It was not after, but before! 11And he received the sign of circumcision, a seal of the righteousness
that he had by faith while he was still
uncircumcised.[c] So then, he is the father[d] of all who believe[e] but have not
been circumcised, in order that righteousness might be credited to them.
12And he is also the father of the circumcised who not only are circumcised but
who also walk in the footsteps of the faith
that our father Abraham had before he
was circumcised.
13It was not through law that Abraham
and his offspring received the promise[f]
that he would be heir of the world,[g] but
through the righteousness that comes by
faith.[h] 14For if those who live by law are
heirs, faith has no value and the promise
is worthless,[i] 15because law brings
wrath.[j] And where there is no law there
is no transgression.[k]
16Therefore, the promise comes by
faith, so that it may be by grace[l] and may
be guaranteed[m] to all Abraham's offspring—not only to those who are of the
law but also to those who are of the faith
of Abraham. He is the father of us all.[n]
17As it is written: "I have made you a
father of many nations."[s] [o] He is our father in the sight of God, in whom he believed—the God who gives life[p] to the

3:25 [n]Ac 20:28; Ro 5:9; Eph 1:7; Heb 9:12,14; 13:12; 1Pe 1:19; Rev 1:5 [o]Ac 14:16; 17:30
3:27 [p]Ro 2:17,23; 4:2; 1Co 1:29-31; Eph 2:9
3:28 [q]ver 20,21; Ac 13:39; Gal 2:16; 3:11; Eph 2:9; Jas 2:20,24,26
3:29 [r]Ac 10:34,35; Ro 9:24; 10:12; 15:9; Gal 3:28
3:30 [s]S Ro 4:11,12; Gal 3:8
4:1 [t]S Ro 8:31 [u]S Lk 3:8
4:2 [v]1Co 1:31
4:3 [w]ver 5,9,22; Ge 15:6; Gal 3:6; Jas 2:23
4:4 [x]Ro 11:6
4:5 [y]ver 3,9,22; S Ro 9:30
4:8 [z]Ps 32:1,2; 103:12; 2Co 5:19
4:9 [a]Ro 3:30 [b]S ver 3
4:11 [c]Ge 17:10,11 [d]ver 16,17; S Lk 3:8 [e]S Ro 3:22
4:13 [f]S Ac 13:32; Gal 3:16,29 [g]Ge 17:4-6 [h]S Ro 9:30
4:14 [i]Gal 3:18
4:15 [j]Ro 7:7-25; 1Co 15:56; 2Co 3:7; Gal 3:10; S Ro 7:12 [k]Ro 3:20; 5:13; 7:7
4:16 [l]S Ro 3:24 [m]Ro 15:8 [n]ver 11; S Lk 3:8; S Gal 3:16
4:17 [o]Ge 17:5 [p]S Jn 5:21

[q]*3* Gen. 15:6; also in verse 22 [r]*8* Psalm 32:1,2 [s]*17* Gen. 17:5

3:29–30 GOD, One God—Despite the Old Testament commission to be a blessing to the nations (Ge 12:3) and a kingdom of priests (Ex 19:6), the Jews isolated themselves from the world and wanted God to be the God for one nation. Paul used their basic teaching—only one God exists—to convince them God was just in admitting non-Jews to salvation. We must join God in inviting all people to salvation by faith.

3:29–31 EVANGELISM, Universality—Paul's statements ended his argument that righteousness, that is, a right standing before God, comes not by works of the law, but by faith in Jesus Christ. He reached the climax by declaring the gospel is for all, Jew and Gentile alike. God calls all people to Himself. All must be saved by faith, whether they have the law or not. Why? Because God is Lord of all. He justifies any and all who will believe in Jesus Christ (5:1–2).

4:1–25 SALVATION, Justification—Abraham, the father of all the faithful, *was justified by faith and not by law.* God *credited him* as righteous because of his faith. Persons are not justified by the religious rite of circumcision or any other rite but by faith in Christ crucified and raised from the dead.

4:7–8 SALVATION, Forgiveness—Paul used the quotation from Ps 32:1–2 to teach justification by faith and God's free forgiveness of sins. Those whose sins are covered are blessed.

4:9 SALVATION, Blessing—Justification by faith is God's supreme blessing. It is available to all people no matter what their religious heritage and tradition. The blessedness of God's justification by faith is to both circumcised Jews and uncircumcised Gentiles.

4:17 GOD, Creator—God showed His creative power in Abraham's life by causing Sarah, a woman long past child-bearing age, to conceive Isaac. God was thus able to create something from nothing according to human standards. Paul wanted His readers to see that God had again demonstrated this creative power in creating the resurrection life for Jesus. As Creator, then, God brings all things into existence and can even bring the dead back to life. From the standpoint of our Christian faith, His greatest work is the miracle of the new birth, new life for spiritually dead people through Christ.

dead and calls[q] things that are not[r] as
though they were.
[18]Against all hope, Abraham in hope
believed and so became the father of
many nations,[s] just as it had been said to
him, "So shall your offspring be."[t] [t]
[19]Without weakening in his faith, he
faced the fact that his body was as good as
dead[u]—since he was about a hundred
years old[v]—and that Sarah's womb was
also dead.[w] [20]Yet he did not waver
through unbelief regarding the promise of
God, but was strengthened[x] in his faith
and gave glory to God,[y] [21]being fully persuaded that God had power to do what he
had promised.[z] [22]This is why "it was
credited to him as righteousness."[a]
[23]The words "it was credited to him"
were written not for him alone, [24]but also
for us,[b] to whom God will credit righteousness—for us who believe in him[c]
who raised Jesus our Lord from the
dead.[d] [25]He was delivered over to death
for our sins[e] and was raised to life for our
justification.[f]

4:17 [q]Isa 48:13 [r]1Co 1:28
4:18 [s]ver 17 [t]Ge 15:5
4:19 [u]Heb 11:11,12 [v]Ge 17:17 [w]Ge 18:11
4:20 [x]1Sa 30:6 [y]S Mt 9:8
4:21 [z]Ge 18:14; S Mt 19:26
4:22 [a]S ver 3
4:24 [b]Ps 102:18; Hab 2:2; Ro 15:4; 1Co 9:10; 10:11; 2Ti 3:16,17 [c]Ro 10:9; 1Pe 1:21 [d]S Ac 2:24
4:25 [e]Isa 53:5,6; Ro 5:6,8; 8:32; 2Co 5:21 [f]Isa 53:11; Ro 3:24; 5:1,9,16,18; 8:30; 1Co 6:11; 2Co 5:15
5:1 [g]S Ro 4:25 [h]S Ro 3:28 [i]S Lk 2:14 [j]ver 10
5:2 [k]Eph 2:18; 3:12 [l]1Co 15:1 [m]S Heb 3:6
5:3 [n]S Mt 5:12 [o]S Heb 10:36
5:5 [p]Php 1:20; S Heb 3:6; 1Jn 3:2,3 [q]ver 8; Jn 3:16; Ro 8:39 [r]Ac 2:33; 10:45; Tit 3:5,6

Chapter 5

Peace and Joy

THEREFORE, since we have been justified[g] through faith,[h] we[u] have
peace[i] with God through our Lord Jesus
Christ,[j] [2]through whom we have gained
access[k] by faith into this grace in which
we now stand.[l] And we[u] rejoice in the
hope[m] of the glory of God. [3]Not only so,
but we[u] also rejoice in our sufferings,[n]
because we know that suffering produces
perseverance;[o] [4]perseverance, character;
and character, hope. [5]And hope[p] does
not disappoint us, because God has
poured out his love[q] into our hearts by
the Holy Spirit,[r] whom he has given us.
[6]You see, at just the right time,[s] when
we were still powerless,[t] Christ died for
the ungodly.[u] [7]Very rarely will anyone
die for a righteous man, though for a good
man someone might possibly dare to die.
[8]But God demonstrates his own love for

5:6 [s]Mk 1:15; Gal 4:4; Eph 1:10 [t]ver 8,10; [u]Ro 4:25

[t]*18* Gen. 15:5 [u]*1,2,3* Or *let us*

4:21 GOD, Power—Abraham had every reason to doubt God's power to fulfill the promise of a son. Abraham never doubted. So we should never doubt God's power to fulfill the promises He has given us in Christ.

4:23–25 JESUS CHRIST, Atonement—Our freedom from guilt and death is possible because God gave Jesus into the power of sinful people and let Him die for us. We stand in right relationship with God, no longer held accountable for our forgiven sins, because God raised Jesus from the dead.

4:25 SALVATION, Initiative—Christ died for our sins on the cross and was raised to life on the third day to put us right with God (2 Co 5:21; 1 Pe 2:24). God Himself provided the Lamb for the sacrifice for our sins (Ge 22:7–8,13–18; Isa 53:7; Jn 1:36).

5:1–11 JESUS CHRIST, Death—The death of Christ made possible for the Christian: peace, grace, joy, hope amid suffering, right relationship with God, salvation from judgment, reconciliation with God, and a life experiencing God's salvation daily. Christ's death for ungodly sinners is certainly more than sufficient proof God loves us.

5:1–5 HOLY SPIRIT, Security—The Spirit provides the believer's guarantee. Paul wrote of the past ("we have been justified"), the present ("we have peace"), and the future ("the hope of the glory of God") aspects of salvation. The gift of the Spirit to Christians is an assurance that in the future our hopes will be fulfilled. Through the Spirit, God pours His love into our hearts. God demonstrated His love by the cross (v 8), and so the pouring of His love into Christians' hearts through the Spirit includes the Spirit's continuing witness to Christ (Jn 15:26). The Spirit, by His presence, gives us the assurance we are loved by God. Through the Spirit, God provides Christians with the love which they are to mediate to others, for the fruit of the Spirit is love (Gal 5:22). This hope in love guaranteeing our future with God does not protect us from suffering. It provides courage to endure present problems in face of future reward.

5:1–18 SALVATION, Justification—In 1:18—4:25 Paul answered the question: Why do persons need salvation? In 5:1—8:39 he addressed the question: What are the benefits of salvation? One of the benefits is that persons justified by faith have peace with God. They are delivered from the wrath and condemnation of God and given eternal life.

5:2 GOD, Glory—God has consistently let His people see evidence of His glorious presence and power among them. One day we will see Him in all His glory. Until that day we live motivated by the hope of seeing that glory. Thus even in suffering we can rejoice and praise God.

5:2,17 SALVATION, Grace—God so abundantly supplies us with sufficient grace that we have a place to stand and something great for which to live. Grace is not simply a one-time gift we receive. It is a state in which we live. Life itself is a continuing experience of God's salvation, an experience made possible by God's continuing grace. Salvation is never something we can lay claim to as a possession earned. It is always a gift received in grace.

5:2 LAST THINGS, Humanity Restored—Restoration to the divine intention, likeness, and fellowship is the hope of glory. "Glory" speaks of a manifestation of God's true nature, presence, or likeness. He is glorified when He is allowed to be seen as He really is. To be where God is will be glory. To be what God intended will be glory. To do what God purposed will be glory.

5:3–5 EVIL AND SUFFERING, Rejoicing—Because Paul recognized that sufferings could have several good consequences, he rejoiced in sufferings. He did not deny the pain of the suffering but saw past its immediate circumstances to its final results in his life. Suffering teaches us to continue trying rather than quitting. This strengthens and matures our basic character as persons. In maturity we gain a new perspective even as we suffer, looking on life with hope rather than despair, a hope based on enduring experience with God and growing faith in God's promises as enforced in our life by the Holy Spirit.

5:5–8 GOD, Trinity—The love of God is the root from which comes all of the redemptive grace of God, both in giving His Son to die for sinners and in giving His Holy Spirit to dwell within believers, thus creating hope in us. The Father, the Son, and the Holy Spirit are all included in this redemptive love of God. All three are a part of the process of bringing lost persons into the new life of salvation. It is the action of the trinitarian God which saves us, not the work of any one member of the Trinity in distinction from the other two.

5:6 HISTORY, Salvation—Salvation, being put in right relationship with God, is not based on theological theories or human stories. It is based on the historical act of Christ's sacrificial death.

5:8 EVANGELISM, Work of Christ—See note on Ac 4:12. Christ's death demonstrated God's absolute love for us. God made the ultimate sacrifice so you could have salvation.

us in this: While we were still sinners,
Christ died for us.[v]
9 Since we have now been justified[w] by
his blood,[x] how much more shall we be
saved from God's wrath[y] through him!
10 For if, when we were God's enemies,[z]
we were reconciled[a] to him through the
death of his Son, how much more, having
been reconciled, shall we be saved
through his life![b] 11 Not only is this so,
but we also rejoice in God through our
Lord Jesus Christ, through whom we
have now received reconciliation.[c]

Death Through Adam, Life Through Christ

12 Therefore, just as sin entered the
world through one man,[d] and death
through sin,[e] and in this way death came
to all men, because all sinned[f]— 13 for
before the law was given, sin was in the
world. But sin is not taken into account
when there is no law.[g] 14 Nevertheless,
death reigned from the time of Adam to
the time of Moses, even over those who
did not sin by breaking a command, as
did Adam,[h] who was a pattern of the one
to come.[i]
15 But the gift is not like the trespass.
For if the many died by the trespass of the
one man,[j] how much more did God's
grace and the gift that came by the grace
of the one man, Jesus Christ,[k] overflow
to the many! 16 Again, the gift of God is
not like the result of the one man's sin:
The judgment followed one sin and
brought condemnation, but the gift followed many trespasses and brought justification. 17 For if, by the trespass of the
one man, death[l] reigned through that
one man, how much more will those who
receive God's abundant provision of
grace and of the gift of righteousness

5:8 [v]Jn 3:16; 15:13; 1Pe 3:18; 1Jn 3:16; 4:10
5:9 [w]S Ro 4:25 [x]S Ro 3:25 [y]S Ro 1:18
5:10 [z]Ro 11:28; Col 1:21 [a]ver 11; Ro 11:15; 2Co 5:18,19; Col 1:20,22 [b]Ro 8:34; Heb 7:25
5:11 [c]S ver 10
5:12 [d]ver 15,16,17; Ge 3:1-7; 1Co 15:21,22 [e]ver 14,18; Ge 2:17; 3:19; S Ro 6:23 [f]S Ro 3:9
5:13 [g]S Ro 4:15
5:14 [h]Ge 3:11,12 [i]1Co 15:22,45
5:15 [j]ver 12,18,19 [k]Ac 15:11
5:17 [l]S ver 12

5:9 GOD, Wrath—Sin has brought us all under God's wrath. We deserve to die (3:23). Christ's atoning death has justified us, removing our status as sinners under wrath. This means we are saved from God's wrath. We do not have to fear the final judgment. See note on 1:18.

5:9–10,15–21 SALVATION, Initiative—God initiates our deliverance from sin through the death of Christ on the cross. The redemptive work of Christ makes us God's friends. Adam by his disobedience involved all persons in guilt, bondage, and death. Christ by His obedience even unto death involves all believers in the blessings of salvation.

5:9 LAST THINGS, Judgment—God's judgment upon the unrighteous is a matter of divine wrath. See note on 2:5–16. Being saved from His future wrath is a major aspect of salvation. Experiencing that wrath in judgment is eternal destruction. See note on 2 Th 1:7–10.

5:10–11 SALVATION, Reconciliation—See note on 2 Co 5:18–21. Sin makes the righteous God angry. Sinners become God's enemies. Jesus in His death restored the relationship between us as sinners and God in His grace. This is reconciliation (Greek *katallassō*), "put into friendship with." Reconciliation comes through God's initiative. It is His accomplishment and His gift. Salvation is spoken of here as future, referring to final salvation in the final judgment when the living Christ completes His work of intercession for us by presenting us to the Father. Then salvation will be complete in our experience as well as in God's provision.

5:11 SALVATION, Joy—The reconciled to God through Christ rejoice in God.

5:12–21 HUMANITY, Death and Sin—God has begun twice—the old creation in Adam and the new creation in Christ. Adam chose to become like God rather than serve God. Adam thus separated the human race from God, creating a race serving itself rather than God. Through the first sin, each person became inclined toward sin. This does not mean sin is biologically transmitted from one generation to the next. Rather sin sits on the throne ruling the world. Each person follows the course set by Adam and encouraged by the sinful environment chooses to rebel against God. Thus all humans sin and deserve to die. Christ offers the new way of God's grace and human obedience. With grace on the throne we can be set right with God and participate in eternal life.

5:12–21 SIN, Universal Nature—This passage is about as close to a philosophical understanding of sin as can be found in the New Testament. Paul did not set forth an elaborate scheme describing sin's *origin and dissemination.* Instead, he gave a practical theological rationale for the problem of sin. Sin entered the world through the first person, Adam, but it soon infested the human race. Paul did not excuse everyone else but Adam from blame. He said all have sinned. I must bear individual responsibility for my sinful actions. The result of sin is both physical and spiritual death. The Bible does not give us reason to speak in specifics as to how sin causes death. It generalizes: death is the by-product of sin. The text clearly places responsibility for sin's entrance in the world squarely on Adam and teaches that somehow Adam's posterity ever since has inherited both an environment in which sin is easy and a nature which is inclined toward sin. The practical outcome of our sinful nature is that we enter the world acting selfishly and sinfully. God does not hold us accountable for our sinful actions until we are able spiritually and intellectually to be aware of and sense guilt for our sins. The Bible does not indicate how the sinful nature is passed on from one generation to the next. At least since Augustine in the fifth century, this passage has been used to say sin is passed from one generation to another through the sexual act. Paul did not say that. He said all people sinned whether with specific legal commands or not. See note on 1:18–25. Legal commands only increase the range of conscious sinning. All people are conscious of sin and guilt even without laws. We may argue the hows of our relationship to Adam's sin. We cannot argue the fact we have sinned individually and must accept responsibility for our sin.

5:12–21 FAMILY, New Selfhood—Christ's death demonstrates God's love for human beings who reject God's will and become enemies of grace. When we accept that love, we experience reconciliation with God. New selfhood begins (Eph 4:22–44). The one gospel of grace brings both men and women into a new relationship with God, self, and others. The gospel creates a new equality between man and woman based upon the new selfhood in Christ. See note on Gal 3:26–29. This is a spiritual equality that provides a foundation for man and woman to relate to each other in home and society on a more equal basis.

5:15–21 GOD, Grace—The sin of Adam was devastating in its effect upon all people, involving them in sin also. Adam's sin brought God's wrath and judgment into the world. The grace of God loosed through Jesus Christ was even greater in its impact upon mankind. Undeserved salvation became available to all people. Jesus showed that God's grace is greater than all human sin.

5:15–21 JESUS CHRIST, Life—Jesus is God's gift of grace providing eternal life as an alternative to the death and judgment brought by Adam.

5:15,20–21 SALVATION, Grace—Grace is not limited to a select few. God, in providing salvation through Jesus, offers grace to all sinners in abundance (v 17). The supply of grace is far greater than all human capacity to sin. In God's plan grace will ultimately rule the world.

reign in life[m] through the one man, Jesus
Christ.
18Consequently, just as the result of
one trespass was condemnation for all
men,[n] so also the result of one act of
righteousness was justification[o] that
brings life[p] for all men. 19For just as
through the disobedience of the one
man[q] the many were made sinners,[r]
so also through the obedience[s] of the
one man the many will be made righteous.
20The law was added so that the trespass might increase.[t] But where sin increased, grace increased all the more,[u]
21so that, just as sin reigned in death,[v] so
also grace[w] might reign through righteousness to bring eternal life[x] through
Jesus Christ our Lord.

Chapter 6

Dead to Sin, Alive in Christ

WHAT shall we say, then?[y] Shall we
go on sinning so that grace may increase?[z] 2By no means! We died to sin;[a]
how can we live in it any longer? 3Or
don't you know that all of us who were
baptized[b] into Christ Jesus were baptized
into his death? 4We were therefore buried with him through baptism into
death[c] in order that, just as Christ was
raised from the dead[d] through the glory
of the Father, we too may live a new
life.[e]
5If we have been united with him like
this in his death, we will certainly also be
united with him in his resurrection.[f]
6For we know that our old self[g] was crucified with him[h] so that the body of sin[i]
might be done away with,[v] that we
should no longer be slaves to sin[j]— 7be-
cause anyone who has died has been
freed from sin.[k]
8Now if we died with Christ, we believe that we will also live with him.[l]
9For we know that since Christ was
raised from the dead,[m] he cannot die
again; death no longer has mastery over
him.[n] 10The death he died, he died to

5:17 [m]Jn 10:10 **5:18** [n]S ver 12 [o]S Ro 4:25 [p]Isa 53:11 **5:19** [q]ver 12 [r]S Ro 3:9 [s]S Php 2:8 **5:20** [t]Ro 3:20; 7:7, 8; Gal 3:19 [u]Ro 6:1; 1Ti 1:13, 14 **5:21** [v]ver 12,14; S Ro 6:16 [w]S Ro 3:24 [x]S Mt 25:46 **6:1** [y]S Ro 8:31 [z]ver 15; Ro 3:5,8 **6:2** [a]S ver 6; ver 10,11; S ver 18; Ro 8:13; Col 3:3,5; 1Pe 2:24 **6:3** [b]S Mt 28:19 **6:4** [c]S ver 6 [d]S Ac 2:24 [e]Ro 7:6; S 2Co 5:17; Eph 4:22-24; Col 3:10 **6:5** [f]ver 4,8; Ro 8:11; 2Co 4:10; Eph 2:6; Php 3:10, 11; Col 2:12; 3:1; 2Ti 2:11 **6:6** [g]S Gal 5:24; Eph 4:22; Col 3:9 [h]S ver 2; ver 3-8; 2Co 4:10; Gal 2:20; 5:24; 6:14; Php 3:10; Col 2:12, 20; 3:3 [i]Ro 7:24 [j]S ver 16 **6:7** [k]S ver 18 **6:8** [l]S ver 5 **6:9** [m]ver 4; S Ac 2:24 [n]Rev 1:18

[v]6 Or *be rendered powerless*

5:15–21 CHRISTIAN ETHICS, Righteousness—See note on 8:4,10.

5:18,21 SALVATION, Eternal Life—The contrast here is between Adam and Christ. Through Adam we are all condemned, but through Christ and His sacrificial death all believers are made right with God and receive eternal life. Eternal life is available to all people, but people retain the freedom to reject God's gift.

5:19–21 HUMANITY, Death—Jesus' victory over sin gives us victory over death. This includes the immediate victory over spiritual death and the ultimate victory over physical death. Eternal life is granted immediately and resurrection in the future.

6:1 SIN, Against God—See note on 3:7–8.

6:1–23 CHRISTIAN ETHICS, Character—Grace that saves us is not a license to sin or live in any manner we please. The grace that frees us from sin is also the resource to live a life of obedient love to the call of God.

6:3–4 ORDINANCES, Form of Baptism—The graphic language of Paul assumes immersion baptism, the picture of burial and resurrection with Christ. The literal meaning of the Greek word *baptizō* is to immerse. Paul was arguing that the form of baptism carries its meaning. One must be buried through baptism into death, not literally but spiritually. Just as Christ was raised from the dead, so the new Christian must be raised to live a new life. This is the primary reason for preserving the original New Testament form of baptism: immersion under water. Burial and resurrection of the Christian believer in immersion baptism bears witness to Christ's death and resurrection, declares the believer's death to an old sinful nature and resurrection to a new life, and points to the coming day when believers will be raised from the dead to live forever with the Lord. Paul's primary argument in this passage is that because we have died to an old sinful nature we cannot go on living in sin as some were trying to do. To go on in the same old sinful life would make a mockery of the meaning of baptism.

6:5–7 HUMANITY, Spiritual Nature—The spiritual nature of people is transformed through the death and resurrection of Jesus, who offers eternal life. Accepting Him, we die to the power of sin in our lives, letting His power control our choices. As Jesus, we must face physical death. His resurrection promises us victory over death's power. See note on 5:19–21.

6:5–22 SIN, Slavery—Humans are depraved. That means our entire personalities and beings are trapped in slavery to sin. The Christian identifies with Christ's crucifixion, accepting His death as victory over sin. As symbolized in baptism, the old depraved self is dead for the Christian, who becomes a slave to Christ rather than a slave to sin. God accepts the Christian and forgives sin because of Christ's death and His grace. The Christian continues to struggle with sin, repenting and seeking forgiveness for sins committed; but the direction of life is obedience to Christ and death of sin. The resurrection is the sure proof that God has power over death and sin. To live in slavery to sin means to deny the power of Christ's resurrection. We have earned sin's wages and deserve to die. In His love and grace, God has given us eternal life through Jesus Christ. When the power of His resurrection works in our life, we conquer sin and its temptations, living for God's righteousness. We will sin, but we must not easily excuse sin. God has provided the power to live for Him and not to be enslaved to sin. We must let that power rule our lives.

6:5–18 DISCIPLESHIP, Lordship of Christ—Who or what you obey is your master. By nature we obey sin. The Christian is dead to sin and alive to God. Sin is no longer our master, for we are under grace. We have voluntarily become obedient from the heart to a new Master. See note on Lk 6:46–49.

6:5 LAST THINGS, Believers' Resurrection—Believers' resurrection will be like that of Christ. He was the first to experience resurrection unto eternal life. Those whom He raised during his public ministry were only raised to continued earthly life. Believers will be raised as Christ was and thus share with Him the experience of being raised bodily from the dead.

6:8–14 HUMANITY, Spiritual Nature—A clear distinction exists between natural mortality and eternal life. With the salvation experience, people receive a life which allows victory over sin itself. The body, however, is still mortal. That will not be transformed until the resurrection. Since Christ lives in us, we must constantly let Him win the victory over sin in us.

6:9–10 JESUS CHRIST, Resurrection—Resurrection freed Jesus from the possibility of death, both physical and spiritual. The saving results of His death and resurrection are sure forever. Christ's victory has been accomplished once for all.

sin[o] once for all;[p] but the life he lives,
he lives to God.
11In the same way, count yourselves
dead to sin[q] but alive to God in Christ
Jesus. 12Therefore do not let sin reign[r] in
your mortal body so that you obey its evil
desires. 13Do not offer the parts of your
body to sin, as instruments of wickedness,[s] but rather offer yourselves to God,
as those who have been brought from
death to life; and offer the parts of your
body to him as instruments of righteousness.[t] 14For sin shall not be your master,[u] because you are not under law,[v]
but under grace.[w]

Slaves to Righteousness

15What then? Shall we sin because we
are not under law but under grace?[x] By
no means! 16Don't you know that when
you offer yourselves to someone to obey
him as slaves, you are slaves to the one
whom you obey[y]—whether you are
slaves to sin,[z] which leads to death,[a] or
to obedience, which leads to righteousness? 17But thanks be to God[b] that,
though you used to be slaves to sin,[c] you
wholeheartedly obeyed the form of teaching[d] to which you were entrusted. 18You
have been set free from sin[e] and have
become slaves to righteousness.[f]
19I put this in human terms[g] because
you are weak in your natural selves. Just
as you used to offer the parts of your body
in slavery to impurity and to ever-increasing wickedness, so now offer them in
slavery to righteousness[h] leading to holiness. 20When you were slaves to sin,[i]
you were free from the control of righteousness.[j] 21What benefit did you reap
at that time from the things you are now
ashamed of? Those things result in
death![k] 22But now that you have been set
free from sin[l] and have become slaves to
God,[m] the benefit you reap leads to holiness, and the result is eternal life.[n] 23For
the wages of sin is death,[o] but the gift of
God is eternal life[p] in[w] Christ Jesus our
Lord.

Chapter 7

An Illustration From Marriage

DO you not know, brothers[q]—for I am
speaking to men who know the law
—that the law has authority over a man
only as long as he lives? 2For example, by
law a married woman is bound to her
husband as long as he is alive, but if her
husband dies, she is released from the
law of marriage.[r] 3So then, if she marries
another man while her husband is still
alive, she is called an adulteress.[s] But if
her husband dies, she is released from
that law and is not an adulteress, even
though she marries another man.
4So, my brothers, you also died to the

6:10 [o]S ver 2 [p]S Heb 7:27 **6:11** [q]S ver 2 **6:12** [r]ver 16 **6:13** [s]ver 16,19; Ro 7:5 [t]Ro 12:1; 2Co 5:14,15; 1Pe 2:24 **6:14** [u]S ver 16 [v]S Ro 2:12 [w]S Ro 3:24 **6:15** [x]ver 1,14 **6:16** [y]2Pe 2:19 [z]ver 6,12,14,17,20; Ge 4:7; Ps 51:5; 119:133; Jn 8:34; Ro 5:21; 7:14,23, 25; 8:2; 2Pe 2:19 [a]S ver 23 **6:17** [b]Ro 1:8; S 2Co 2:14 [c]S ver 16 [d]2Ti 1:13 **6:18** [e]S ver 2; ver 7,22; Ro 8:2; 1Pe 4:1; S ver 16 [f]S ver 22 **6:19** [g]Ro 3:5; Gal 3:15 [h]S ver 13; S ver 22 **6:20** [i]S ver 16 [j]ver 16 **6:21** [k]S ver 23 **6:22** [l]S ver 18 [m]ver 18,19; Ro 7:25; 1Co 7:22; Eph 6:6; 1Pe 2:16 [n]S Mt 25:46 **6:23** [o]ver 16,21; Ge 2:17; Pr 10:16; Eze 18:4; Ro 1:32; S 5:12; 7:5,13; 8:6, 13; Gal 6:7,8; Jas 1:15 [p]S Mt 25:46 **7:1** [q]S Ac 1:16; S 22:5; Ro 1:13; 1Co 1:10; 5:11; 6:6; 14:20,26; Gal 3:15; 6:18 **7:2** [r]1Co 7:39 **7:3** [s]S Lk 16:18

[w]23 Or *through*

6:14–18 SALVATION, Grace—Sin is no longer the master of the saved, because we are under grace and not law. That does not give us reason to ignore God's laws and see how much we can sin so God can provide more grace. Believers commit themselves as slaves to God's righteousness and, thus, fight against sin and its temptations.

6:15–22 CHRISTIAN ETHICS, Righteousness—Through Christ's righteous act we are transformed, devoting our lives to the righteous way of life He pioneered. Thus our lives mirror God's holiness, and we receive eternal life as God's gracious wage. See notes on Lev 19:1–18; Gal 5:5; Eph 4:24.

6:22–23 SALVATION, Eternal Life—Jesus Christ liberates persons from sin and gives them eternal life. Holiness becomes the life-style for God's people.

6:23 SIN, Death—Sin pays us what we earn—death. God gives us what we need—eternal life. Which do you want? Thus Paul summarized his first six chapters. We have a choice: serve sin and die, or serve Christ and live forever.

6:23 EVANGELISM, Lostness—Sin pays fair wages—eternal death. God in love gives what is not earned—eternal life. You must decide whether to be content with your wages or accept God's gift. Until you accept God's gift, you are lost.

7:1–25 SIN, Slavery—Sin is more than an act. It is a power which controls us and leads us to death. We learn to sin when we rebel against God's laws that set limits for our lives. The limits are good and necessary for us. Without them society could not exist. God's Law shows the limits people are to accept to be His people. We do not receive the Law that way. We rebel against limits. We reverse the Law's purpose. Instead of letting Law lead us to life with God and away from the danger zone of death, *we let Law rouse our selfishness and jealousy. We do* exactly what the Law forbids. We sin in not trusting God to show us the nature of true life. We sin in doing what God forbids. We sin in letting sin control life rather than God. We cannot blame God for giving us the Law, nor can we blame the Law. God was good to show us the nature of true life. The Law is good in outlining for us the proper limits to life. Sin as a power ruling our lives turns the good law into an instrument to serve evil purposes by using it to arouse our selfish desires to be god. Here we see sin's power to take something good and use it for bad. Humans are depraved in themselves. We cannot overcome the power of sin. Rather we serve sin, letting it be our master. Even though we know what is right, we do not have the power in ourselves to do it. Life is a war between our desires to do good and our enslavement to sin, with sin more powerful and winning the war. The outlook brings total despair until we turn to Jesus. He has won the victory over sin. His Spirit gives us power to defeat sin and serve Christ. Life is meant to be lived in the freedom of the Spirit, not in legalism under the law and sin.

7:1–25 CHRISTIAN ETHICS, Moral Imperatives—God's moral imperatives are good and holy directing us to life at its best. Our sinful nature rebels at the call to give up any freedom and leads us to do precisely what the law forbids. Law defines good and bad for us. Under sin's leadership we choose the bad. The choice of bad is sin and deserves death. Thus I become aware of the nature of sin. Now the choice faces me—sin or Christ. To choose Christ is to choose salvation by grace rather than by law. The call to obey remains, but now the power of the Spirit is available to lead me to obedience. The Spirit enables me to do what I wanted all along but was not able to because I was controlled by sin. See note on 3:19–20. Struggle with sin is a sign of God's presence battling sin for us. Such a struggle assures us the Christian life is real.

7:4–6 HUMANITY, Human Nature—Human life may be dominated by either legalism or God's Spirit. Legalism leads us to test the law and follow the impulses of our flesh. See NIV footnote. The flesh represents our basic human nature domi-

law[t] through the body of Christ,[u] that
you might belong to another,[v] to him
who was raised from the dead, in order
that we might bear fruit to God. 5For
when we were controlled by the sinful
nature,[x w] the sinful passions aroused by
the law[x] were at work in our bodies,[y] so
that we bore fruit for death.[z] 6But now,
by dying to what once bound us, we have
been released from the law[a] so that we
serve in the new way of the Spirit, and
not in the old way of the written code.[b]

Struggling With Sin

7What shall we say, then?[c] Is the law
sin? Certainly not![d] Indeed I would not
have known what sin was except through
the law.[e] For I would not have known
what coveting really was if the law had
not said, "Do not covet."[y f] 8But sin,
seizing the opportunity afforded by the
commandment,[g] produced in me every
kind of covetous desire. For apart from
law, sin is dead.[h] 9Once I was alive apart
from law; but when the commandment
came, sin sprang to life and I died. 10I
found that the very commandment that
was intended to bring life[i] actually
brought death. 11For sin, seizing the opportunity afforded by the commandment,[j] deceived me,[k] and through the
commandment put me to death. 12So
then, the law is holy, and the commandment is holy, righteous and good.[l]
13Did that which is good, then, become
death to me? By no means! But in order
that sin might be recognized as sin, it produced death in me[m] through what was
good,[n] so that through the commandment sin might become utterly sinful.
14We know that the law is spiritual;
but I am unspiritual,[o] sold[p] as a slave to
sin.[q] 15I do not understand what I do. For
what I want to do I do not do, but what I
hate I do.[r] 16And if I do what I do not
want to do, I agree that the law is good.[s]
17As it is, it is no longer I myself who do
it, but it is sin living in me.[t] 18I know
that nothing good lives in me, that is, in
my sinful nature.[z u] For I have the desire
to do what is good, but I cannot carry it
out. 19For what I do is not the good I want
to do; no, the evil I do not want to do—
this I keep on doing.[v] 20Now if I do what
I do not want to do, it is no longer I who
do it, but it is sin living in me that does
it.[w]
21So I find this law at work:[x] When I
want to do good, evil is right there with
me. 22For in my inner being[y] I delight in
God's law;[z] 23but I see another law at
work in the members of my body, waging
war[a] against the law of my mind and
making me a prisoner of the law of sin[b]
at work within my members. 24What a
wretched man I am! Who will rescue me
from this body of death?[c] 25Thanks be to
God—through Jesus Christ our Lord![d]
So then, I myself in my mind am a
slave to God's law,[e] but in the sinful nature a slave to the law of sin.[f]

Chapter 8

Life Through the Spirit

THEREFORE, there is now no condemnation[g] for those who are in Christ

7:4 [t]ver 6; S Ro 6:6; 8:2; Gal 2:19; 3:23-25; 4:31; 5:1 [u]Col 1:22 [v]Gal 2:19,20
7:5 [w]S Gal 5:24 [x]Ro 7:7-11 [y]Ro 6:13 [z]S Ro 6:23
7:6 [a]S ver 4 [b]Ro 2:29; 2Co 3:6
7:7 [c]S Ro 8:31 [d]S ver 12 [e]S Ro 4:15 [f]Ex 20:17; Dt 5:21
7:8 [g]ver 11 [h]S Ro 4:15
7:10 [i]Lev 18:5; Lk 10:26-28; S Ro 10:5; Gal 3:12
7:11 [j]ver 8 [k]Ge 3:13
7:12 [l]ver 7,13,14,16; Ro 8:4; Gal 3:21; 1Ti 1:8; S Ro 4:15
7:13 [m]S Ro 6:23 [n]S ver 12
7:14 [o]1Co 3:1 [p]1Ki 21:20,25; 2Ki 17:17 [q]S Ro 6:16
7:15 [r]ver 19; Gal 5:17
7:16 [s]S ver 12
7:17 [t]ver 20
7:18 [u]ver 25; S Gal 5:24
7:19 [v]ver 15
7:20 [w]ver 17
7:21 [x]ver 23,25
7:22 [y]Eph 3:16 [z]Ps 1:2; 40:8
7:23 [a]Gal 5:17; Jas 4:1; 1Pe 2:11 [b]S Ro 6:16
7:24 [c]Ro 6:6; 8:2
7:25 [d]S 2Co 2:14 [e]S Ro 6:22 [f]S Ro 6:16
8:1 [g]ver 34

[x]5 Or *the flesh*; also in verse 25 [y]7 Exodus 20:17; Deut. 5:21 [z]18 Or *my flesh*

nated by worldly desires rather than spiritual goals. Following the flesh, we deserve and receive death. Christ frees us from the domination of sinful nature and lets us follow the guidance of God's Spirit away from death to eternal life. See Jas 1:14–15.

7:6 HOLY SPIRIT, Transforms—Obeying God is not a dreaded, impossible duty but a natural result of the Spirit in us. Paul contrasted the old way of life with the new way Christ established. Since the old way was dominated by the law, he could be understood as saying Christ's way is not a way of moral obedience. To prevent this misunderstanding, he affirmed that Christians are set free from (attempting to be justified by) the law, just so we will be free to serve Christ by serving other people. Paul called this kind of service "the new way of the Spirit." The Spirit is not a passive observer of the lives of Christians. He is actively at work in all believers to transform us into the kinds of persons God wants us to be. This means new service in a new freedom with a fuller understanding (Jn 15:15). The Spirit is not given for our enjoyment but to change us so we will be of service to Christ.

7:14–25 HUMANITY, Human Nature—Life is war. We commit ourselves to Christ but still seek to please the world. The person whose spiritual nature has been reborn through Jesus experiences a constant conflict between the spiritual and the human natures. We know what is right but desire to do what is wrong. This conflict can lead to an inner wretchedness and a struggle for peace. The only deliverance comes through Jesus. Following Him brings inner peace and eternal life. See Gal 6:17.

7:24–25 SALVATION, As Deliverance—Jesus Christ the Lord rescues us from the body of death, that is, the old sinful nature. He makes us victorious in the struggle against sin. He leads from despair to joy.

7:25 PRAYER, Thanksgiving—Paul could not answer the question he had just asked without gratitude. Thanks overwhelmed him at the thought of salvation in Christ. See note on Ac 28:15.

8:1–17 HOLY SPIRIT, Obeyed—The Spirit is not a possession we hold on to but a person we love and obey. People must choose between the way of the flesh or sinful nature and the way of the Spirit. We should choose "the Spirit of life" (v 2), "the Spirit" (v 4), "the Spirit of Christ" (v 9), "the Spirit of Him who raised Jesus" (God, v 11), "the Spirit of God" (v 14), and "the Spirit of sonship" (v 15). The Spirit gives life (v 2), peace (v 6), freedom (v 9), leadership (v 14), assurance (v 16), hope (vv 23–24), and help (v 26). The Spirit is with all Christians (vv 9,14). The Spirit makes Christians God's children and able to say "Father" when we pray (v 15). The Spirit assures us that we are in fact God's children (v 16), and that, even though we pass through much suffering, we will eventually share in the glory of Christ (v 17). With all this we remain free. We must choose to follow the Spirit, to live according to the Spirit (v 5), to set our minds on what the Spirit desires (v 5), to be controlled by the Spirit (v 9), to put to death the old way of life (v

Jesus,[a][h] 2because through Christ Jesus[i]
the law of the Spirit of life[j] set me free[k]
from the law of sin[l] and death. 3For what
the law was powerless[m] to do in that it
was weakened by the sinful nature,[b][n]
God did by sending his own Son in the
likeness of sinful man[o] to be a sin offering.[c][p] And so he condemned sin in sinful man,[d] 4in order that the righteous requirements[q] of the law might be fully
met in us, who do not live according to
the sinful nature but according to the
Spirit.[r]

5Those who live according to the sinful
nature have their minds set on what that
nature desires;[s] but those who live in
accordance with the Spirit have their
minds set on what the Spirit desires.[t]
6The mind of sinful man[e] is death,[u] but
the mind controlled by the Spirit is life[v]
and peace; 7the sinful mind[f] is hostile to
God.[w] It does not submit to God's law,
nor can it do so. 8Those controlled by the
sinful nature[x] cannot please God.

9You, however, are controlled not by
the sinful nature[y] but by the Spirit, if the
Spirit of God lives in you.[z] And if anyone
does not have the Spirit of Christ,[a] he
does not belong to Christ. 10But if Christ
is in you,[b] your body is dead because of
sin, yet your spirit is alive because of
righteousness. 11And if the Spirit of him
who raised Jesus from the dead[c] is living
in you, he who raised Christ from
the dead will also give life to your mortal
bodies[d] through his Spirit, who lives in
you.

12Therefore, brothers, we have an obligation—but it is not to the sinful nature,
to live according to it.[e] 13For if you live
according to the sinful nature, you will
die;[f] but if by the Spirit you put to death
the misdeeds of the body,[g] you will
live,[h] 14because those who are led by the

8:1 [h]ver 39; S Ro 16:3 **8:2** [i]Ro 7:25 [j]1Co 15:45 [k]Jn 8:32,36; S Ro 6:18 [l]S Ro 6:16; S 7:4 **8:3** [m]Heb 7:18; 10:1-4 [n]Ro 7:18,19; S Gal 5:24 [o]S Php 2:7 [p]Heb 2:14,17 **8:4** [q]Ro 2:26 [r]S Gal 5:16 **8:5** [s]Gal 5:19-21 [t]Gal 5:22-25 **8:6** [u]S Ro 6:23 [v]ver 13; Gal 6:8 **8:7** [w]Jas 4:4 **8:8** [x]S Gal 5:24 **8:9** [y]S Gal 5:24 [z]ver 11; 1Co 6:19; 2Ti 1:14 [a]Jn 14:17; S Ac 16:7; 1Jn 4:13 **8:10** [b]ver 9; Ex 29:45; Jn 14:20, 23; 2Co 13:5; Gal 2:20; Eph 3:17; Col 1:27; Rev 3:20 **8:11** [c]S Ac 2:24 [d]Jn 5:21; S Ro 6:5 **8:12** [e]ver 4; S Gal 5:24 **8:13** [f]S Ro 6:23 [g]S Ro 6:2 [h]ver 6; Gal 6:8

a *1* Some later manuscripts *Jesus, who do not live according to the sinful nature but according to the Spirit,* **b** *3* Or *the flesh*; also in verses 4, 5, 8, 9, 12 and 13 **c** *3* Or *man, for sin* **d** *3* Or *in the flesh* **e** *6* Or *mind set on the flesh* **f** *7* Or *the mind set on the flesh*

13), and to be led by the Spirit (v 18). These phrases all refer to a serious commitment to live as Christians with the help of God's Spirit. This includes high moral standards (v 4) and more. Obeying the Spirit means a personal loyalty and obedience to Christ which expresses itself by following the leadership of the Spirit in all life's decisions. This is active cooperation as well as passive yielding. The Spirit's work is not irresistible. The Spirit prefers to wait and allow us to obey His leadership freely. Paul's call to obey the Spirit makes no sense at all if the Spirit is only an impersonal power or force. The Spirit is personal, and this leads to the commands to respond to the Spirit in a fully personal manner.

8:1–17 SIN, Against God—Life is dominated either by sin or by God's Spirit. Christ gave the death sentence to sin, which had given us the death sentence. He gave us a choice. Center life on Him or on sin. Choose life or death. Be at peace with God or at war with Him. Live in the Spirit to please God, or live in sin to please death.

8:1–3,9–10 SALVATION, As Being in Christ—In Christ is a favorite phrase of Paul's to describe the multifaceted meaning of salvation. Those in Christ are set free from condemnation caused by sin. Life is life in the Spirit rather than life in the old sinful nature dominated by physical desires. We must still face physical death because of our sin, but we can count on resurrection and eternal life because God has made us right or justified (Greek *dikaiosunē*).

8:1 SALVATION, Initiative—To be in Christ is to be saved and safe forevermore, beyond any condemnation for the sin God has washed away and forgiven.

8:3 JESUS CHRIST, Sinless—Jesus was fully human in every way we are but one. He was in our likeness, a likeness that was originally the likeness or image of God (Ge 1:26). But unlike Adam and every other descendant of Adam (Ro 3:23), Jesus did not sin. His sinless life made Him different from us, thus making Him a suitable sacrifice before God to bring forgiveness for our sins.

8:3–4 HUMANITY, Spiritual Nature—In many instances, the biblical concept of flesh focuses less on our physical nature and more on our sinful nature. Our selfish, sinful tendencies exercise strong control. Psychology, sociology, and technology may help us understand our guilt and our desires. They cannot change them. Only God's Spirit can. The redeemed are given a spiritual nature which will ultimately be victorious over the sinful nature through our obedience to the power of God's Spirit.

8:4,10 CHRISTIAN ETHICS, Justice—Christianity turns religion's center of interest from the law and its interpretation to the Spirit and His direction of our lives. Rightly understood law and Spirit do not contradict. They both point us to righteousness (Greek *dikaiosunē*), a word meaning both righteousness and justification. God's acts in Christ have made us right with Him, conferring on us the status of being justified. This status is more than a name or category given us. It is a new way of life to be lived out in the power of God's Spirit. Righteousness is not something we strive after or claim rewards for achieving. It is God's gift in Christ through the Spirit for people of faith. See note on Php 3:9.

8:5–8 HUMANITY, Human Nature—The end result of following the bent of human nature is physical and spiritual death. People who yield their behavior to the sinful nature will never be pleasing to God.

8:10 HUMANITY, Spiritual Nature—Sin resulting in death is not the only choice. In Christ God acted in grace. When we in faith allow Jesus to become Lord of life, His indwelling presence brings life to the spiritual nature. We must still undergo physical death, but we can enjoy spiritual life even before we die.

8:12–18 EVIL AND SUFFERING, Endurance—Suffering with Christ is a natural part of being a child of God. We do not fear suffering but endure it knowing our future is not determined by how the world treats us but by the heavenly inheritance God has promised. Our suffering is infinitely small compared to the glorious inheritance God has for us.

8:12–17 HUMANITY, Relationship to God—The Greek term for "sonship" refers to being adopted into God's family and becoming His children. Thus, the relationship of Creator-creature is uplifted to one of Parent-child. The relationship of terrified slave becomes loving child. The new relationship does not guarantee freedom from suffering, but it does promise a glorious future.

8:12–17 THE CHURCH, God's Community—God's children are characterized by the leadership of His Spirit. Christians rejoice in being called the sons of God. Slaves and hirelings may cringe before the master, but children serve with joy and without fear. As sons of God, Christians are heirs of the Father, sharing Christ's inheritance. This means we will share in the suffering of rejection with Him but will also share the glory of eternal life with Him. We are confident of being God's children because His Spirit lives in us, leads us to pray to God, and assures us we belong to God.

Spirit of God[i] are sons of God.[j] 15For
you did not receive a spirit[k] that makes
you a slave again to fear,[l] but you received the Spirit of sonship.[g] And by him
we cry, *"Abba,*[h] Father."[m] 16The Spirit
himself testifies with our spirit[n] that we
are God's children.[o] 17Now if we are
children, then we are heirs[p]—heirs of
God and co-heirs with Christ, if indeed
we share in his sufferings[q] in order that
we may also share in his glory.[r]

Future Glory

18I consider that our present sufferings
are not worth comparing with the glory
that will be revealed in us.[s] 19The creation waits in eager expectation for the
sons of God[t] to be revealed. 20For the
creation was subjected to frustration, not
by its own choice, but by the will of the
one who subjected it,[u] in hope 21that[i]
the creation itself will be liberated from
its bondage to decay[v] and brought into
the glorious freedom of the children of
God.[w]
22We know that the whole creation has
been groaning[x] as in the pains of childbirth right up to the present time. 23Not
only so, but we ourselves, who have the
firstfruits of the Spirit,[y] groan[z] inwardly
as we wait eagerly[a] for our adoption as
sons, the redemption of our bodies.[b]
24For in this hope we were saved.[c] But
hope that is seen is no hope at all.[d] Who
hopes for what he already has? 25But if
we hope for what we do not yet have, we
wait for it patiently.[e]
26In the same way, the Spirit helps us
in our weakness. We do not know what
we ought to pray for, but the Spirit[f] him-

8:14 [i]S Gal 5:18 [j]ver 19; Hos 1:10; Mal 3:17; Mt 5:9; S Jn 1:12; Gal 3:26; 4:5; Eph 1:5; Rev 21:7 **8:15** [k]S Jn 20:22 [l]S 2Ti 1:7 [m]Mk 14:36; Gal 4:5,6 **8:16** [n]2Co 1:22; Eph 1:13 [o]S ver 14; S Jn 1:12 **8:17** [p]S Ac 20:32; Gal 3:29; 4:7; Eph 3:6; Tit 3:7 [q]S 2Co 1:5 [r]2Ti 2:12; 1Pe 4:13 **8:18** [s]2Co 4:17; 1Pe 4:13; 5:1 **8:19** [t]S ver 14 **8:20** [u]Ge 3:17-19; 5:29 **8:21** [v]Ac 3:21; 2Pe 3:13; Rev 21:1 [w]S Jn 1:12 **8:22** [x]Jer 12:4 **8:23** [y]S 2Co 5:5 [z]2Co 5:2,4 [a]ver 19; Gal 5:5 [b]ver 11; Php 3:21 **8:24** [c]1Th 5:8; Tit 3:7 [d]S 2Co 4:18 **8:25** [e]Ps 37:7 **8:26** [f]ver 15,16

[g]*15* Or *adoption* [h]*15* Aramaic for *Father* [i]*20,21* Or *subjected it in hope. 21For*

8:15,23 SALVATION, As Adoption—God's salvation is expressed in terms of adoption as His sons. Sonship and adoption are synonymous. The Holy Spirit is the Spirit of adoption who makes us children of God. He enables us to call God our Father. "Abba" is the Aramaic word meaning "Father" or "Daddy." God becomes the Father of the saved in a real and intimate sense. Adopted children are no less children of their parents than are their naturally born offspring. Compare Gal 4:5–6; Eph 1:5. V 23 reveals a future dimension to adoption into God's family, which we call glorification. See notes on Mk 8:38; 1 Co 1:18. The presence of God's Spirit assures us we belong to Him.

8:15 PRAYER, Holy Spirit Helps—By an operation of the Holy Spirit the Christian cries to God in the closest possible intimacy (Mk 14:36). The Fatherhood of God is made real by the "Spirit of sonship." Complete confidence that prayer is an intimate conversation between an open, trusting child and a loving, concerned Father is one of the New Testament's greatest contributions to the doctrine of prayer.

8:17 LAST THINGS, Heaven—Heaven means being glorified with Christ and sharing the eternal inheritance that is His from the Father. As God's children, we can expect earthly suffering and rejection before we receive our glorious inheritance. See note on Jn 14:1–3.

8:18–25 CREATION, New Creation—Sin will never have the last word. God made the earth as a habitation for His people. The presence of sin brought on decay and frustration of purposes (Ge 3:17–19). Along with His people, the earth will be redeemed by the Creator. Paul personified the elements of nature as looking forward to deliverance the same way that Christians anticipate our glorified resurrection body. The same Holy Spirit that brooded over the waters in creation (Ge 1:2) has been given to Christians as a foretaste and guarantee of the glorious hope that awaits us. We can live with joy, confident that we have a wonderful hope awaiting us. That hope includes a new, redeemed world, which will again pass God's examination as "very good" (Ge 1:31).

8:18–25 EVIL AND SUFFERING, God's Future Help—Present sufferings for humanity and all of creation will end when God guides history to its climax.

8:18–23 LAST THINGS, Creation's Redemption—God's eschatological salvation will include the whole created order. Just as the created order was affected by the advent of human sin, so it will be by future human redemption. A cosmic liberation from decay awaits the final, full redemption of the children of God. The redemption of nature is to be associated with that of believers' bodies. Three statements underlie the eager expectation of creation: because of human sin, God subjected the created order to frustration (Ge 3:17–19); the created order is presently in bondage to decay; and it has been and yet continues to groan with birth pains. The analogy of travail suggests the coming to be of something new. Creation is not what it should be due to human sin. It cannot serve its true function of glorifying God. It decays and thus goes nowhere. It is temporary rather than eternal. It suffers pain rather than being the arena of peace. It can look forward to a new glory when God creates a new earth.

8:19–21 THE CHURCH, God's Community—God's plan for His people includes the renewal of His creation from the curse brought by human sin (Ge 3:17–18). When God brings this final redemption, He will reveal the members of His family in the full freedom of the relationship of the covenant formula. Only then will we know all that is meant by belonging to God's family. See notes on 8:12–17; Jer 30:22; Mt 5:9.

8:20 EVIL AND SUFFERING, Natural Origin—The created world order, the environment of human life, is not perfect as it was created (Ge 1). It is a frustrated order cursed because of human sin (Ge 3). God's ultimate salvation includes hope for the created order. What we refer to as natural evil will one day vanish. Storms and catastrophes will no longer threaten us. Pain and laborious work seeking to make the earth fertile will cease. The enmity between the human and animal world will vanish.

8:23 HOLY SPIRIT, Security—The Spirit is the firstfruits of heaven. Since we have the Spirit now, we know a little of what heaven will be like and are assured of our final destiny. God's gift of the Spirit to the church is an event in the present which foreshadows the future union of God and His people in eternity. The ground of the Christian hope is the risen Christ and the descended Spirit. If Christ is raised (and He is), then God will raise His people up (1 Co 15:20–28). Similarly, if the Spirit has been given to God's people (and He has), then we may await our final destiny without fear (Ro 8:15), with assurance (v 16), and with eagerness and hope (vv 23–25). See Jn 16:5–11; 2 Co 1:22; note on Eph 1:13–14.

8:25–27 HOLY SPIRIT, Intercedes—The Spirit assists us in our prayers. The Spirit within the church makes us children of God, able to pray to God as *Abba*, Father (8:15; note on Gal 4:6). When we pray, we sometimes experience a profound sense of need. We realize how little we know, how ill-equipped we are even to pray properly. We cannot express adequately our love for God, our worship of Him, our sense of repentance, or even our requests to Him. We may be without words for our prayers, expressing our deepest desires with groans rather than words. Those groans, like the prayer *Abba*, are the work of the Spirit within us, assisting us in our prayers, praying within us and for us. We may be sure God will answer these prayers. God knows what those inarticulate groans mean. He knows they

self intercedes for us[g] with groans that
words cannot express. 27And he who
searches our hearts[h] knows the mind of
the Spirit, because the Spirit intercedes[i]
for the saints in accordance with God's
will.

More Than Conquerors

28And we know that in all things God
works for the good[j] of those who love
him,[j] who[k] have been called[k] according to his purpose.[l] 29For those God foreknew[m] he also predestined[n] to be conformed to the likeness of his Son,[o] that
he might be the firstborn[p] among many
brothers. 30And those he predestined,[q]
he also called;[r] those he called, he also
justified;[s] those he justified, he also glorified.[t]
31What, then, shall we say in response
to this?[u] If God is for us,[v] who can be
against us?[w] 32He who did not spare his
own Son,[x] but gave him up for us all—
how will he not also, along with him, graciously give us all things? 33Who will
bring any charge[y] against those whom
God has chosen? It is God who justifies.
34Who is he that condemns?[z] Christ
Jesus, who died[a]—more than that, who
was raised to life[b]—is at the right hand
of God[c] and is also interceding for us.[d]
35Who shall separate us from the love of
Christ?[e] Shall trouble or hardship or persecution or famine or nakedness or danger or sword?[f] 36As it is written:

> "For your sake we face death all day long;

8:26 [g]Eph 6:18 **8:27** [h]S Rev 2:23 [i]S ver 34 **8:28** [j]Ge 50:20; Isa 38:17; Jer 29:11 [k]ver 30; Ro 11:29; 1Co 1:9; Gal 1:6, 15; Eph 4:1,4; 1Th 2:12; 2Ti 1:9; Heb 9:15; 1Pe 2:9; 2Pe 1:10 [l]Eph 1:11; 3:11; Heb 6:17 **8:29** [m]Ro 11:2; 1Pe 1:2 [n]Eph 1:5, 11 [o]1Co 15:49; 2Co 3:18; Php 3:21; 1Jn 3:2 [p]S Col 1:18 **8:30** [q]Eph 1:5,11 [r]S ver 28 [s]S Ro 4:25 [t]Ro 9:23 **8:31** [u]Ro 4:1; 6:1; 7:7; 9:14,30 [v]Ex 3:12; Isa 41:10; Hag 1:13 [w]Ps 56:9; 118:6; Isa 8:10; Jer 20:11; Heb 13:6 **8:32** [x]Ge 22:13; Mal 3:17; Jn 3:16; Ro 5:8 **8:33** [y]Isa 50:8,9 **8:34** [z]ver 1 [a]Ro 5:6-8 [b]S Ac 2:24 [c]S Mk 16:19 [d]ver 27; Job 16:20; Isa 53:12; Heb 7:25; 9:24; 1Jn 2:1 **8:35** [e]ver 37-39 [f]1Co 4:11; 2Co 11:26,27

[j]28 Some manuscripts *And we know that all things work together for good to those who love God*
[k]28 Or *works together with those who love him to bring about what is good—with those who*

are prayers aligned with His great will and purpose, which is to create a family for Himself. Prayer not only goes to God; in some sense, it comes from God. The Spirit in the church enables us to pray and prays for us. The Spirit talks to God from within the church. The implications of this for understanding the Spirit are important. This means the Spirit definitely is personal; only a person can pray; a force or a power cannot. It means the Spirit is in some means distinguishable from the Father, for He prays to the Father. On the other hand, the Spirit is very closely related to God, who understands fully the meaning of the Spirit's prayers. This is the mystery of the Trinity.

8:26–39 JESUS CHRIST, Intercession—In this great Trinitarian intercessory passage Paul wrote of the Spirit who interprets, of the Father who knows the mind of the Spirit, and of the risen Christ at the right hand of God who intercedes for us. The whole idea of intercession is to have someone in the position of influence and power pleading your cause. Such is Jesus on behalf of humankind.

8:26–27 PRAYER, Holy Spirit Helps—"Helps" (Greek *sunantilambanomai*) means "to take hold with another" and implies joint sharing in the same work. It is the word used by Martha asking for Mary's help in the kitchen (Lk 10:40). The intercession of the Spirit is on a communicative level above the level of words. Within the Trinity, where communication is perfectly expressed and perfectly understood above any level of or type of communication known on earth, the awkward prayers of Christians are translated into the high and noble level of God Himself.

8:28 GOD, Goodness—The sovereign God works through all things to bring good to His people. This verse does not say, as some have wrongfully held, that God causes all things that happen. God is a good, righteous, faithful God who does not cause evil and suffering. In His sovereignty He does permit them. Nor does the verse teach that all things are good. The Bible constantly describes sinful, satanic evil in this world. This verse does teach us that when evil events do occur, God can work through those tragic circumstances to bring a blessing to His people. God may chastise His people on occasion, but we should not draw the hasty conclusion that every instance of calamity or suffering is God's attempt to chastise us. The misuse of human freedom or the working of natural law may be the cause of the calamaties that befall us. The point here is that our loving Heavenly Father can even work in these circumstances to sustain and bless us. We may suffer. We need not lose faith or despair.

8:28–39 EVIL AND SUFFERING, Providence—God works in every situation for the good of His people. No suffering can cut God's people off from His love. We must evaluate suffering in terms of its effect on our long-term goal. Our goal is to participate in the salvation made possible by God's love proven and displayed in the cross and resurrection of Christ. No type of evil and suffering can keep us from participating in that salvation. Only failure to trust Christ separates us from His saving love.

8:28–35 ELECTION, Predestination—Paul described a chain of events in election which guaranteed Christian hope even in dire earthly circumstances. Hope is defined as faith that all circumstances work to deepen our relationship with Christ and reconfirm our salvation. This applies to the elect who have been called, foreknown, and predestined. (1) Called means to have received an invitation from God to fulfill and be a part of His election purpose. See note on 1:5–6. (2) Foreknown (Greek *proginōskō*) is to be known intimately in personal relationship even before creation (Eph 1:4; 2 Ti 1:9). Foreknowledge is possible because God knows past, present, and future. His purpose of individual election and salvation began before the earth did. Humans maintain the freedom to reject relationship with God and refuse to accept His invitation to salvation. See note on Ac 2:23–33. (3) Predestined (Greek *proorizō*) is to determine beforehand. God determined the goal of election to be creating a people fully in His image like Christ. Predestination is thus a decision to create a holy people (Ex 19:3–6). Predestination is the term theologians use to affirm the eternal initiative, continuity, grace, and faithfulness of God in creating a people for Himself. The plan of God results in victory for His people since no one can oppose God and successfully accuse His elect.

8:28 SALVATION, Love of God—Those who love God can expect Him to work in all things for our good. The verse does not say that all things automatically work together for good or that only good things will happen. God's love controls history of the race and of individuals. No matter what happens, His love can transform the event to achieve His purposes.

8:29 HUMANITY, Relationship to God—God adopts us as Jesus' brother. Our lives no longer conform to the world's definition of living. God works in us to conform us to Christ.

8:29–30 LAST THINGS, Humanity Restored—Paul listed a chain of five certainties leading to our assurance of glory. Ultimate glorification is conformity to the likeness of Christ. This is the ultimate restoration of humanity, both in an individual sense and the collective sense of the whole group of the called becoming like his Son (Eph 4:13).

8:30 SALVATION, Glorification—God is in control of salvation all the way—from planning it to providing final rewards in glory. Salvation is a process in which God chooses to save, calls people to salvation, works in Christ to provide salvation, and then gives the eternal rewards of salvation. The

we are considered as sheep to be
slaughtered."[l] [g]

37No, in all these things we are more than
conquerors[h] through him who loved
us.[i] 38For I am convinced that neither
death nor life, neither angels nor demons,[m] neither the present nor the future,[j] nor any powers,[k] 39neither height
nor depth, nor anything else in all creation, will be able to separate us from the
love of God[l] that is in Christ Jesus our
Lord.[m]

Chapter 9

God's Sovereign Choice

I speak the truth in Christ—I am not
lying,[n] my conscience confirms[o] it in
the Holy Spirit— 2I have great sorrow
and unceasing anguish in my heart. 3For I
could wish that I myself[p] were cursed[q]
and cut off from Christ for the sake of my
brothers,[r] those of my own race,[s] 4the
people of Israel.[t] Theirs is the adoption
as sons;[u] theirs the divine glory,[v] the
covenants,[w] the receiving of the law,[x]
the temple worship[y] and the promises.[z]
5Theirs are the patriarchs,[a] and from
them is traced the human ancestry of
Christ,[b] who is God over all,[c] forever
praised![n] [d] Amen.
6It is not as though God's word[e] had
failed. For not all who are descended
from Israel are Israel.[f] 7Nor because they
are his descendants are they all Abraham's children. On the contrary, "It is
through Isaac that your offspring will be

8:36 [g]Ps 44:22; 1Co 4:9; 15:30,31; 2Co 4:11; 6:9; 11:23 **8:37** [h]1Co 15:57 [i]Ro 5:8; Gal 2:20; Eph 5:2; Rev 1:5; 3:9 **8:38** [j]1Co 3:22 [k]Eph 1:21; Col 1:16; 1Pe 3:22 **8:39** [l]S Ro 5:8 [m]ver 1; S Ro 16:3 **9:1** [n]Ps 15:2; 2Co 11:10; Gal 1:20; 1Ti 2:7 [o]S Ro 1:9 **9:3** [p]Ex 32:32 [q]1Co 12:3; 16:22 [r]S Ac 22:5 [s]Ro 11:14 **9:4** [t]ver 6 [u]Ex 4:22; 6:7; Dt 7:6 [v]Heb 9:5 [w]Ge 17:2; Dt 4:13; Ac 3:25; Eph 2:12 [x]Ps 147:19 [y]Heb 9:1 [z]S Ac 13:32; S Gal 3:16 **9:5** [a]Ro 11:28 [b]Mt 1:1-16; Ro 1:3 [c]Jn 1:1; Col 2:9 [d]Ro 1:25; 2Co 11:31 **9:6** [e]S Heb 4:12 [f]Ro 2:28,29; Gal 6:16

[l]*36* Psalm 44:22 [m]*38* Or *nor heavenly rulers* [n]*5* Or *Christ, who is over all. God be forever praised!* Or *Christ. God who is over all be forever praised!*

entire process is certain because it is God's process, so it can all be described in past tense.

8:31–39 GOD, Love—The sovereign power of God's love can protect and preserve God's people to the uttermost. God has shown the strength and depth of His love by sacrificing even His own Son for us. Nothing can break the bond of love established between believers and God through Jesus Christ. That bond of love is maintained as Jesus prays for us. God the Father, Jesus the Son, and the Holy Spirit are all involved intimately with the believer. The work of these three is distinct, yet all three are so involved that no clear line can be drawn between what any One of them does in distinction from the other two Persons who make up the Trinity.

8:34 PROCLAMATION, Gospel—See note on Ac 3:11–26. Christ's intercession for believers is a part of the gospel we proclaim.

8:34 PRAYER, Intercession—Three New Testament writers state that Christ as High Priest is interceding with God on behalf of the saints. See notes on Heb 7:25; 9:24–25; 1 Jn 2:1. That He is at the right hand of God indicates that He is very near to, intimate with, and has access to the ear of God, as well as sharing God's authority. The Holy Spirit is the Intercessor with the saint on earth (v 26). Christ is the Intercessor with God in heaven. These facts are bases for confidence in prayer.

8:38–39 HUMANITY, Relationship to God—The new relationship to God, established by His love through the redemptive act of Jesus, can never be brought to an end. Many forces work to destroy the relationship, but none can succeed. The Father's love is too strong.

8:38–39 LAST THINGS, Inspires Hope—Believers have a secure future hope because we have experienced God's love in Christ Jesus. Within this relationship neither the crisis of death nor the calamities of life, neither spirit beings that are good nor those that are evil, neither anything in time nor in space, in fact, nothing in all the created order can interrupt or sever the believer's ties with God forged by His redeeming love.

9:1 HOLY SPIRIT, Teaches—The Spirit guides the Christian conscience in knowledge and emotion. Paul felt a great anguish because most Jews were not accepting Christ. He feared his readers would see his anguished claims as self-serving and not reflecting his true feelings. He took an oath that his conscience confirmed his anguish. Conscience may mislead, for some people have consciences which have been seared as with a hot iron. See 1 Ti 4:2. Paul's conscience was trustworthy because he submitted it to the Holy Spirit. The Spirit provided Paul's conscience with very definite guidance. It affirmed what he wrote was true and what he felt was right. Our conscience can guide us when we live in the Spirit.

9:1–3 EVANGELISM, Love—Paul was so burdened for the conversion of the Jewish people that he was willing to be separated from Christ if that would in some way effect their salvation. That is like the spirit of Moses (Ex 32:31–32). That is love—love so deep it brings sorrow and anguish. Such love motivates to effective evangelism (2 Co 5:14–21).

9:3–33 ELECTION, Remnant—God's mercy, not human effort or ethnic designation, makes the election choice of those whom God calls His people. Human reason does not understand the depth of God's wisdom utilized in His act of election. Israel's rejection is not God's failure but the working out of His sovereign purpose to save Jews and Gentiles by faith. From Isaac onward, God has chosen a part or remnant of Abraham's seed to accomplish His purposes. Election includes God's freedom to accomplish His purposes in the way He chooses. Neither history nor doctrine can command what God must do or what is just for God to do. Only God can determine what is merciful and just over the long run of history. Everything He does lets people see His power and wrath so that they may recognize His glory, His unique nature and reputation deserving human praise and service.

9:3 PRAYER, Sincerity—"Wish" (Greek *euchomai*) is literally "pray." Paul knew God could not grant his wish. He used hyperbole to indicate the intensity of his yearning for his Jewish brothers. Such intensity marks Christian faith and prayer.

9:4–6 REVELATION, Events—God's choice of Israel, His revelation in personal manifestations (glory), giving of laws, covenants, promises, and the Temple worship set Israel apart as recipients of God's revelation. Jesus Christ is God's greatest and most significant revelation. He also was designed to communicate the truth to Israel. None of God's attempts to reveal Himself have failed. They will be used in history not only for the Jew, but also for the Gentile (vv 23–24).

9:4–9 THE CHURCH, Covenant People—Tradition and family cannot make us part of God's family. The Israelites had received God's call to the patriarchs (Ge 17:1–21), His glorious revelation to Moses; His covenant (Ex 19—24); His Law, instructing in the way of life with Him; His Temple, signifying His presence with them; and His promises, especially those of the Messiah. Still they rebelled against Him and did not accept His Messiah. Thus, they did not become the true Israel and could not be called God's children. God desires that all people know Christ, including those to whom He first revealed Himself.

9:5 JESUS CHRIST, God—Christ's human ancestry is traced to the patriarchs while His divine ancestry is equated with God. Some translators punctuate this verse so that the last phrase is a doxology praising God (see NIV note) rather than a

reckoned."[o][g] 8In other words, it is not
the natural children who are God's children,[h] but it is the children of the promise who are regarded as Abraham's offspring.[i] 9For this was how the promise
was stated: "At the appointed time I will
return, and Sarah will have a son."[p][j]

10Not only that, but Rebekah's children
had one and the same father, our father
Isaac.[k] 11Yet, before the twins were born
or had done anything good or bad[l] —in
order that God's purpose[m] in election
might stand: 12not by works but by him
who calls—she was told, "The older will
serve the younger."[q][n] 13Just as it is written: "Jacob I loved, but Esau I hated."[r][o]

14What then shall we say?[p] Is God unjust? Not at all![q] 15For he says to Moses,

"I will have mercy on whom I have
mercy,
and I will have compassion on
whom I have compassion."[s][r]

16It does not, therefore, depend on man's
desire or effort, but on God's mercy.[s]
17For the Scripture says to Pharaoh: "I
raised you up for this very purpose, that I
might display my power in you and that
my name might be proclaimed in all the
earth."[t][t] 18Therefore God has mercy on
whom he wants to have mercy, and he
hardens whom he wants to harden.[u]

19One of you will say to me:[v] "Then
why does God still blame us?[w] For who
resists his will?"[x] 20But who are you, O
man, to talk back to God?[y] "Shall what is
formed say to him who formed it,[z] 'Why
did you make me like this?'"[u][a] 21Does
not the potter have the right to make out
of the same lump of clay some pottery for
noble purposes and some for common
use?[b]

22What if God, choosing to show his
wrath and make his power known, bore
with great patience[c] the objects of his
wrath—prepared for destruction?[d]
23What if he did this to make the riches of
his glory[e] known to the objects of his
mercy, whom he prepared in advance for
glory[f]— 24even us, whom he also
called,[g] not only from the Jews but also
from the Gentiles?[h] 25As he says in Hosea:

"I will call them 'my people' who are
not my people;
and I will call her 'my loved one'
who is not my loved one,"[v][i]

26and,

"It will happen that in the very place
where it was said to them,
'You are not my people,'
they will be called 'sons of the living
God.'"[w][j]

27Isaiah cries out concerning Israel:

"Though the number of the Israelites
be like the sand by the sea,[k]
only the remnant will be saved.[l]
28For the Lord will carry out
his sentence on earth with speed
and finality."[x][m]

29It is just as Isaiah said previously:

"Unless the Lord Almighty[n]
had left us descendants,

9:7 [g]Ge 21:12; Heb 11:18
9:8 [h]S Ro 8:14 [i]S Gal 3:16
9:9 [j]Ge 18:10,14
9:10 [k]Ge 25:21
9:11 [l]ver 16 [m]Ro 8:28
9:12 [n]Ge 25:23
9:13 [o]Mal 1:2,3
9:14 [p]S Ro 8:31 [q]2Ch 19:7
9:15 [r]Ex 33:19
9:16 [s]Eph 2:8; Tit 3:5
9:17 [t]Ex 9:16; 14:4; Ps 76:10
9:18 [u]Ex 4:21; 7:3; 14:4,17; Dt 2:30; Jos 11:20; Ro 11:25
9:19 [v]Ro 11:19; 1Co 15:35; Jas 2:18 [w]Ro 3:7 [x]2Sa 16:10; 2Ch 20:6; Da 4:35
9:20 [y]Job 1:22; 9:12; 40:2 [z]Isa 64:8; Jer 18:6 [a]Isa 29:16; 45:9; 10:15
9:21 [b]2Ti 2:20
9:22 [c]S Ro 2:4 [d]Pr 16:4
9:23 [e]S Ro 2:4 [f]Ro 8:30
9:24 [g]S Ro 8:28 [h]S Ro 3:29
9:25 [i]Hos 2:23; 1Pe 2:10
9:26 [j]Hos 1:10; S Mt 16:16; S Ro 8:14
9:27 [k]Ge 22:17; Hos 1:10 [l]2Ki 19:4; Jer 44:14; 50:20; Joel 2:32; Ro 11:5
9:28 [m]Isa 10:22,23
9:29 [n]Jas 5:4

[o]*7* Gen. 21:12 [p]*9* Gen. 18:10,14 [q]*12* Gen. 25:23 [r]*13* Mal. 1:2,3 [s]*15* Exodus 33:19 [t]*17* Exodus 9:16 [u]*20* Isaiah 29:16; 45:9 [v]*25* Hosea 2:23 [w]*26* Hosea 1:10 [x]*28* Isaiah 10:22,23

statement of Christ's equality with God.

9:10–13,25–26 GOD, Love—Human arguments can try to prove God unjust because He chooses to save some but not all. Only through a selfish attitude on our part could we complain about how God has shown His love and mercy. God's sovereign love is the explanation for His choice of Jacob over Esau in earlier times and for what He was doing in Paul's time to develop a people for Himself. As sovereign Lord, Creator of all things, He has the perfect right to plan and work in His world according to His own purposes. His purpose could be one of total destruction. Instead, He chose in love to work out a way to save those who believe. See note on Mt 20:1–16 where Jesus dealt with virtually the same theme.

9:14 GOD, Justice—Paul was quick to defend the sovereign will of God from any charges of injustice in bestowing His love and mercy on unworthy people. God is a faithful God who always is true to His own character and keeps His promises. His actions are always right, just. We can charge God with being unjust only out of our ignorance and our self-seeking sinfulness.

9:15–21 GOD, Sovereignty—We cannot understand why God chose Israel in the first place, nor why He has now broadened the scope of His chosen people in a way that seemingly leaves Israel in a much less favorable position. The sovereignty of God stands behind His work of salvation. In His sovereign free will He developed a method to achieve His saving purposes in this world. We may not be able to understand His reasons. We can affirm God is Lord of all and is free to work as He chooses in pursuit of His own purposes. This He does in a way that is both just (v 14) and merciful (vv 15,16, 23). God's wrath is used to let His chosen people recognize His mercy and glory.

9:20 HUMANITY, Relationship to God—Our basic relationship with God is Creator-creature. As finite mortals we dare not argue with God or sit in judgment over our Creator.

9:22–23 THE CHURCH, God's Community—God's community of people is composed of people from all racial and cultural backgrounds. The only qualification is to receive Christ in faith commitment, knowing human activities and morality cannot qualify us. This means God can accept people who many religious people tend to reject. It also means God is free to reject people who try to earn His favor rather than trust God's grace. See notes on Eze 36:28; Hos 1:10–11.

9:27–29 THE CHURCH, Remnant—The Old Testament remnant doctrine applies to the church. Just as God had reduced Israel to a remnant under Assyria, Babylon, and Persia, so God again reduced His people to those who followed Jesus, Israel's Messiah. God added to His Israelite faithful remnant those Gentiles or non-Jews who trusted Jesus for salvation. The church is God's remnant seeking to lead all people—Jews and Gentiles—to Christ. See note on Isa 1:7–9.

we would have become like Sodom,
we would have been like
Gomorrah."[y] [o]

Israel's Unbelief

30What then shall we say?[p] That the
Gentiles, who did not pursue righteousness, have obtained it, a righteousness
that is by faith;[q] 31but Israel, who pursued a law of righteousness,[r] has not attained it.[s] 32Why not? Because they pursued it not by faith but as if it were by
works. They stumbled over the "stumbling stone."[t] 33As it is written:

"See, I lay in Zion a stone that causes
men to stumble
and a rock that makes them fall,
and the one who trusts in him will
never be put to shame."[z] [u]

Chapter 10

BROTHERS, my heart's desire[v] and
prayer to God for the Israelites is that
they may be saved. 2For I can testify
about them that they are zealous[w] for
God, but their zeal is not based on knowledge. 3Since they did not know the righteousness that comes from God and
sought to establish their own, they did
not submit to God's righteousness.[x]
4Christ is the end of the law[y] so that
there may be righteousness for everyone
who believes.[z]

5Moses describes in this way the righteousness that is by the law: "The man
who does these things will live by
them."[a] [a] 6But the righteousness that is
by faith[b] says: "Do not say in your heart,
'Who will ascend into heaven?'[b]"[c] (that
is, to bring Christ down) 7"or 'Who will
descend into the deep?'[c]"[d] (that is, to
bring Christ up from the dead).[e] 8But
what does it say? "The word is near you;
it is in your mouth and in your heart,"[d] [f]
that is, the word of faith we are proclaiming: 9That if you confess[g] with your
mouth, "Jesus is Lord,"[h] and believe[i] in
your heart that God raised him from the
dead,[j] you will be saved.[k] 10For it is
with your heart that you believe and are
justified, and it is with your mouth that
you confess and are saved. 11As the Scrip-

9:29 [o]Isa 1:9; Ge 19:24-29; Dt 29:23; Isa 13:19; Jer 50:40
9:30 [p]S Ro 8:31 [q]Ro 1:17; 3:22; 4:5,13; 10:6; Gal 2:16; Php 3:9; Heb 11:7
9:31 [r]Dt 6:25; Isa 51:1; Ro 10:2,3; 11:7 [s]Gal 5:4
9:32 [t]1Pe 2:8
9:33 [u]Isa 8:14; 28:16; Ro 10:11; 1Pe 2:6,8
10:1 [v]Ps 20:4
10:2 [w]S Ac 21:20
10:3 [x]Ro 1:17; S 9:31
10:4 [y]Gal 3:24; Ro 7:1-4 [z]S Ro 3:22
10:5 [a]Lev 18:5; Dt 4:1; 6:24; Ne 9:29; Pr 19:16; Isa 55:3; Eze 20:11, 13,21; S Ro 7:10
10:6 [b]S Ro 9:30 [c]Dt 30:12
10:7 [d]Dt 30:13 [e]S Ac 2:24
10:8 [f]Dt 30:14
10:9 [g]Mt 10:32 [h]S Jn 13:13 [i]S Jn 3:15 [j]S Ac 2:24 [k]S Ro 11:14

[y] *29* Isaiah 1:9 [z] *33* Isaiah 8:14; 28:16
[a] *5* Lev. 18:5 [b] *6* Deut. 30:12 [c] *7* Deut. 30:13
[d] *8* Deut. 30:14

10:1–21 ELECTION, God's Purpose—God does not intend for any person to be lost. Continuously God seeks the salvation of humankind. Humans face a free choice in response to His invitation to become members of the elect. The proper choice is to surrender all claims to earn or deserve salvation and to accept faith in Christ as a gift of God's grace. People who refuse to accept Christ as God's way of salvation give up the privilege of election.

10:1–11 CHRISTIAN ETHICS, Justice—God's people cannot achieve a just society simply through human zeal and enthusiasm. We must receive righteousness from God through faith. Proclaiming the gospel should lead to a transformed people who can thus be a transformed society. Without evangelism the call for a new, just society is hollow. See notes on 8:4,10; Php 3:9.

10:1 PRAYER, Sincerity—See note on 9:3. Earnest prayer for the lost is the believer's constant task.

10:1 EVANGELISM, Love—See note on 9:1–3.

10:3–4 GOD, Righteous—Righteousness does not come by human actions in following commandments, whether human or divine (v 5). Righteousness comes from God Himself. We experience righteousness by a faith relationship to God through Jesus Christ (vv 9–10). God's righteousness, then, is the source and cause of any righteousness in people.

10:4 JESUS CHRIST, Fulfilled—Jesus fulfilled the law of Moses. In Him the law reached its goal. He has thus opened the way to God through trust in Him rather than through observance of legal requirements.

10:4–17 SALVATION, Belief—Faith comes from hearing the message of the gospel. Those who hear and believe will be saved. The same message is offered to both Jews and Gentiles. Compare Heb 4:2–3. Jews cannot rely on their zeal for the law. They must believe in the resurrected Christ and confess Him openly. No human achievement can gain salvation. Making Jesus Lord of life is the way of salvation. Humans remain free to reject the gospel message, and, sadly, most Jews did reject it.

10:4 CHRISTIAN ETHICS, Moral Imperatives—Our model for living and source of willpower for living is Christ Himself. He did all the law required. He was a perfect, sinless human being. He fulfilled the law's requirements for atonement. We trust in Him to make us right with God and to lead us in the right direction toward God.

10:8–9 REVELATION, Inspiration—People do not have to search for revelation or force God to give it. The revelation of God is available and near to every human being. The gospel message of what Jesus has done for us is all the revelation we need to know God in salvation. See Gospel summary, p. 1663.

10:8–10 SALVATION, Confession—Confession and belief belong together like a hand and glove. Those who confess Jesus as Lord will be saved. The oldest creed of the church is, "Jesus is Lord." A believer will confess Christ publicly. Believing and confessing are not two stages in a process but two parts of one action.

10:8–13 PROCLAMATION, Faith—The ultimate goal of preaching the gospel is to lead individuals to faith in Jesus Christ. This faith will be revealed by the act of repentance leading to a change of life (Ac 26:20; 1 Co 15:1–5). Faith centers on the lordship of the resurrected Christ. When Christians proclaim (Greek *kerusso*) the gospel, unbelievers will likely respond in faith. See note on Ac 3:11–26.

10:9–12 JESUS CHRIST, Lord—Jesus' authority is not limited racially. He rules all people. "Jesus is Lord" was the earliest confession of faith by which Christians proclaimed to each other and the world their submission to Christ's rule in their lives. See note on Ac 10:36.

10:10–15 MISSIONS, Means—This great salvation passage is also a key missions passage. Salvation comes through Christ to the believer regardless of race, status, or nationality (v 13). Vv 12–13 show the need and the right of everyone to hear the good news. The lost cannot hear the message without someone to share it. Missionaries cannot go unless they are sent. The people of God, therefore, have the joy and the responsibility to send them. Sending others as missionaries is no substitute for our own witness responsibility. We are to go and share Christ as far as we can. Then we are to join hands with other Christians in order that Christ's message might reach to the ends of the earth. See Guide to Missions Ministries, pp. 1837–1840.

10:11–13 GOD, One God—We misunderstand God when we think He limits His interest to one particular kind of people. The one true God has a true interest in all people. He is not identified with one race or class. He is the universal God, from whom all persons have come. He has a deep, fatherly

ture says, "Anyone who trusts in him will
never be put to shame."[e] [l] 12 For there is
no difference between Jew and Gentile[m]
—the same Lord is Lord of all[n] and richly
blesses all who call on him, 13 for, "Everyone who calls on the name of the Lord[o]
will be saved."[f] [p]

14 How, then, can they call on the one
they have not believed in? And how can
they believe in the one of whom they
have not heard? And how can they hear
without someone preaching to them?
15 And how can they preach unless they
are sent? As it is written, "How beautiful
are the feet of those who bring good
news!"[g] [q]

16 But not all the Israelites accepted the
good news.[r] For Isaiah says, "Lord, who
has believed our message?"[h] [s] 17 Consequently, faith comes from hearing the
message,[t] and the message is heard
through the word of Christ.[u] 18 But I ask:
Did they not hear? Of course they did:

> "Their voice has gone out into all the
> earth,
> their words to the ends of the
> world."[i] [v]

19 Again I ask: Did Israel not understand?
First, Moses says,

> "I will make you envious[w] by those
> who are not a nation;
> I will make you angry by a nation
> that has no understanding."[j] [x]

20 And Isaiah boldly says,

> "I was found by those who did not
> seek me;
> I revealed myself to those who did
> not ask for me."[k] [y]

21 But concerning Israel he says,

> "All day long I have held out my hands
> to a disobedient and obstinate
> people."[l] [z]

Chapter 11

The Remnant of Israel

I ask then: Did God reject his people?
By no means![a] I am an Israelite myself, a descendant of Abraham,[b] from the
tribe of Benjamin.[c] 2 God did not reject
his people,[d] whom he foreknew.[e] Don't
you know what the Scripture says in the
passage about Elijah—how he appealed
to God against Israel: 3 "Lord, they have
killed your prophets and torn down your
altars; I am the only one left, and they are
trying to kill me"[m]?[f] 4 And what was
God's answer to him? "I have reserved

10:11 [l]Isa 28:16; Ro 9:33
10:12 [m]S Ro 3:22, 29 [n]S Mt 28:18
10:13 [o]S Ac 2:21 [p]Joel 2:32
10:15 [q]Isa 52:7; Na 1:15
10:16 [r]Heb 4:2 [s]Isa 53:1; Jn 12:38
10:17 [t]Gal 3:2,5 [u]Col 3:16
10:18 [v]Ps 19:4; S Mt 24:14; Ro 1:8; Col 1:6,23; 1Th 1:8
10:19 [w]Ro 11:11, 14 [x]Dt 32:21
10:20 [y]Isa 65:1; Ro 9:30
10:21 [z]Isa 65:2; Jer 35:17
11:1 [a]Lev 26:44; 1Sa 12:22; Ps 94:14; Jer 31:37; 33:24-26 [b]2Co 11:22 [c]Php 3:5
11:2 [d]S ver 1 [e]S Ro 8:29
11:3 [f]1Ki 19:10,14

[e] *11* Isaiah 28:16 [f] *13* Joel 2:32 [g] *15* Isaiah 52:7 [h] *16* Isaiah 53:1 [i] *18* Psalm 19:4 [j] *19* Deut. 32:21 [k] *20* Isaiah 65:1 [l] *21* Isaiah 65:2 [m] *3* 1 Kings 19:10,14

interest in offering salvation to all persons.

10:12 SALVATION, Blessing—God is Lord over both Jew and Gentile. He richly blesses all who call on Him.

10:12–15 EVANGELISM, Universality—"Everyone who calls on the name of the Lord will be saved." This truth is for all people of all classes, colors, cultures, and countries. Anyone who turns to Jesus Christ will be saved. He is rich to all who call upon Him. That should encourage our sharing the gospel with everyone. People are lost until they hear the gospel and believe it. Many may not hear if you do not obey God's call and witness to the gospel.

10:14–15 PROCLAMATION, Call—The exciting thing about proclamation is that it is done by individuals like us. From Old Testament times God has set apart certain individuals to be proclaimers of His truth. See note on Jer 1:4–9. While Jeremiah was willing to proclaim God's Word, Jonah was reluctant. God used them both. In New Testament times this pattern continued until every believer became a proclaimer of the gospel (Ac 8:4–5). Proclaiming the gospel is the privilege of every believer. God still calls some to stand in a pulpit to "preach" regularly. He expects all to find a place where people need to hear. There they can proclaim the gospel. Through that proclamation many will be saved.

10:16–21 REVELATION, Messengers—The message of God's freedom and salvation is not accepted by all, as Isa 53:1 states. Revelation requires a faith response to Jesus Christ who delivered God's revelation in Person. Not all who see and witness God's manifestation respond in faith and belief, as the Old Testament repeatedly witnesses.

10:16 SALVATION, Acceptance—See note on Mt 19:16–30.

11:1–36 GOD, Wisdom—The fate of His own people—the Jews—plagued Paul. How could the chosen people not accept Christ and not participate in salvation through Him? Paul answered with the themes of the wisdom and the grace of God. In His wisdom, God foreknew Israel: what she was, what she would do, and what she would ultimately become. He has not rejected Israel and is not through with Israel (v 2). Rather, God has broadened the focus of His grace and has brought the Gentiles into the covenant community (vv 11,25). The true Israelites will yet believe and be grafted back into the believing community (v 23). This reflects Paul's earlier statement that not everyone who is a blood descendant of Abraham is a true Israelite (9:6,8), but only those who are the children of Abraham in faith. These believing Israelites are the remnant (v 5) that God cultivated and preserved. God also included Gentiles in a new community of faith, continuing what He started out to do from the beginning. Through His sovereign grace He is extending His mercy to all people by offering them salvation (10:9–13; 11:33–36). Paul's fervent hope was that Jews who did not yet believe would come to see that God's purpose is to create a spiritual community and that they would join it in true faith (v 23).

11:1–36 ELECTION, Remnant—Among Jews and Gentiles are persons who constitute the elect of God. Among Israel is a remnant that is faithful to the election requirements of God. The salvation of the Gentiles is an act of grace which will move a remnant of Israel to realize the passionate depth of God's invitation. Election does not mean God has rejected anyone. He has elected all who will follow in faith. Election gives neither Jew nor Gentile reason to boast. It is a call to mission to all people to fulfill God's eternal purpose of creating a people of faith to whom He can show His mercy. The mercy of God is for all persons. The mystery of God's wisdom and knowledge cannot be fully grasped intellectually by humankind. The blessing of election is solely from, through, and to the honor, praise, and glory of the God of election. God's gift of election is based on God's love for the disobedient. The beauty of election is not human merit but the matchless mercy of God.

11:2 PRAYER, Fellowship with God—See note on 1 Ki 19:8–18.

11:4–5 THE CHURCH, Remnant—See notes on

for myself seven thousand who have not
bowed the knee to Baal."[n][g] 5 So too, at
the present time there is a remnant[h] chosen by grace.[i] 6 And if by grace, then it is
no longer by works;[j] if it were, grace
would no longer be grace.[o]
7 What then? What Israel sought so earnestly it did not obtain,[k] but the elect
did. The others were hardened,[l] 8 as it is
written:

"God gave them a spirit of stupor,
eyes so that they could not see
and ears so that they could not
hear,[m]
to this very day."[p][n]

9 And David says:

"May their table become a snare and a
trap,
a stumbling block and a retribution
for them.
10 May their eyes be darkened so they
cannot see,[o]
and their backs be bent forever."[q][p]

Ingrafted Branches

11 Again I ask: Did they stumble so as to
fall beyond recovery? Not at all![q] Rather,
because of their transgression, salvation
has come to the Gentiles[r] to make Israel
envious.[s] 12 But if their transgression
means riches for the world, and their loss
means riches for the Gentiles,[t] how
much greater riches will their fullness
bring!
13 I am talking to you Gentiles. Inasmuch as I am the apostle to the Gentiles,[u] I make much of my ministry 14 in
the hope that I may somehow arouse my
own people to envy[v] and save[w] some of
them. 15 For if their rejection is the reconciliation[x] of the world, what will their
acceptance be but life from the dead?[y]
16 If the part of the dough offered as firstfruits[z] is holy, then the whole batch is
holy; if the root is holy, so are the
branches.
17 If some of the branches have been
broken off,[a] and you, though a wild olive
shoot, have been grafted in among the
others[b] and now share in the nourishing
sap from the olive root, 18 do not boast
over those branches. If you do, consider
this: You do not support the root, but the
root supports you.[c] 19 You will say then,
"Branches were broken off so that I could
be grafted in." 20 Granted. But they were
broken off because of unbelief, and you
stand by faith.[d] Do not be arrogant,[e] but
be afraid.[f] 21 For if God did not spare the
natural branches, he will not spare you
either.
22 Consider therefore the kindness[g]
and sternness of God: sternness to those
who fell, but kindness to you, provided
that you continue[h] in his kindness. Otherwise, you also will be cut off.[i] 23 And if
they do not persist in unbelief, they will
be grafted in, for God is able to graft them
in again.[j] 24 After all, if you were cut out
of an olive tree that is wild by nature, and
contrary to nature were grafted into a cultivated olive tree,[k] how much more
readily will these, the natural branches,
be grafted into their own olive tree!

All Israel Will Be Saved

25 I do not want you to be ignorant[l] of
this mystery,[m] brothers, so that you may
not be conceited:[n] Israel has experienced a hardening[o] in part until the full
number of the Gentiles has come in.[p]
26 And so all Israel will be saved,[q] as it is
written:

11:4 [g]1Ki 19:18
11:5 [h]S Ro 9:27 [i]S Ro 3:24
11:6 [j]Ro 4:4
11:7 [k]Ro 9:31 [l]ver 25; S Ro 9:18
11:8 [m]S Mt 13:13-15 [n]Dt 29:4; Isa 29:10
11:10 [o]ver 8 [p]Ps 69:22,23
11:11 [q]ver 1 [r]S Ac 13:46 [s]ver 14; Ro 10:19
11:12 [t]ver 25
11:13 [u]S Ac 9:15
11:14 [v]ver 11; Ro 10:19; 1Co 10:33; 1Th 2:16 [w]S Mt 1:21; S Lk 2:11; S Jn 3:17; Ac 4:12; 16:31; 1Co 1:21; 1Ti 2:4; Tit 3:5
11:15 [x]S Ro 5:10 [y]Lk 15:24,32
11:16 [z]Lev 23:10, 17; Nu 15:18-21
11:17 [a]Jer 11:16; Jn 15:2 [b]Ac 2:39; Eph 2:11-13
11:18 [c]Jn 4:22
11:20 [d]1Co 10:12; 2Co 1:24 [e]1Ti 6:17 [f]1Pe 1:17
11:22 [g]Ro 2:4 [h]1Co 15:2; Col 1:23; Heb 3:6 [i]Jn 15:2
11:23 [j]2Co 3:16
11:24 [k]Jer 11:16
11:25 [l]Ro 1:13; 1Co 10:1; 12:1; 2Co 1:8; 1Th 4:13 [m]S Ro 16:25 [n]Ro 12:16 [o]ver 7; S Ro 9:18 [p]Lk 21:24
11:26 [q]Isa 45:17; Jer 31:34

[n]4 1 Kings 19:18 [o]6 Some manuscripts *by grace. But if by works, then it is no longer grace; if it were, work would no longer be work.* [p]8 Deut. 29:4; Isaiah 29:10 [q]10 Psalm 69:22,23

9:27–29; 11:26–28; Zec 13:9. Paul asserted God's intention to preserve for Himself a remnant from the nation Israel. God brought believing Gentiles into the church along with the people of Israel who accepted Christ. Therefore, those who trust Christ from every nation make up Christ's body, God's true remnant.

11:5–6 SALVATION, Grace—Israel always had a faithful remnant who did not forsake God's covenant. In Paul's time the remnant was the church. That remnant had always been chosen by God's grace and not by their good works. The Jewish believers were evidence God had not rejected His promise or people. Salvation by grace showed God had never changed His plan or method. No person of any race has ever earned salvation through obeying rules. See note on 16:19,26.

11:15 SALVATION, Reconciliation—In ch 9—11, Paul addressed the question: What about those who refuse the gospel? Regarding the Jews, he concluded that if their rejection of Christ meant the reconciliation of the world to God, their acceptance of Christ will be nothing short of life from the dead. All persons, including the Jews, have hope to be reconciled to God through Christ. See note on 2 Co 5:18–21.

11:25–27 LAST THINGS, Return Purposes—Christ's final return will show that God has faithfully accomplished His covenant with Israel, a covenant which promised blessing to the nations (Ge 12:3). This passage has led to differing interpretations of "all Israel": (1) universal salvation for all people, Jews and Gentiles, a view opposed by Paul's strong insistence on judgment on sinners and salvation by faith alone; (2) the church as spiritual Israel, a view perhaps opposed by the contrast between Gentiles and Israel and by the use of Zion and Jacob; (3) believing Jews led to belief by the Gentiles' example and showing God has been faithful to His covenant, a view opposed by the historical sequence Israel, Gentiles, Israel; (4) the conversion to faith of the Jewish generation living when Jesus returns, a view which may be the best solution to a difficult problem. That generation will recognize in the returning deliverer the one who had been all along their promised Messiah. Thus Christ's return will accomplish God's covenant promise to take away Israel's sins. This achievement is coordinate with the gathering of the full number of the Gentiles into God's redemptive plan.

11:26–28 THE CHURCH, Covenant People—God is faithful to His covenant and promises to save Israel in fulfillment of His promises to the patriarchs.

"The deliverer will come from Zion;
he will turn godlessness away from
Jacob.
27And this is[r] my covenant with them
when I take away their sins."[s r]

28As far as the gospel is concerned,
they are enemies[s] on your account; but
as far as election is concerned, they are
loved on account of the patriarchs,[t] 29for
God's gifts and his call[u] are irrevocable.[v]
30Just as you who were at one time disobedient[w] to God have now received
mercy as a result of their disobedience,
31so they too have now become disobedient in order that they too may now[t] receive mercy as a result of God's mercy to
you. 32For God has bound all men over to
disobedience[x] so that he may have mercy on them all.

Doxology

33Oh, the depth of the riches[y] of the
wisdom and[u] knowledge of
God![z]
How unsearchable his judgments,
and his paths beyond tracing out![a]
34"Who has known the mind of the
Lord?
Or who has been his counselor?"[v b]
35"Who has ever given to God,
that God should repay him?"[w c]
36For from him and through him and to
him are all things.[d]
To him be the glory forever!
Amen.[e]

Chapter 12

Living Sacrifices

THEREFORE, I urge you,[f] brothers, in
view of God's mercy, to offer your
bodies as living sacrifices,[g] holy and
pleasing to God—this is your spiritual[x]
act of worship. 2Do not conform[h] any
longer to the pattern of this world,[i] but
be transformed by the renewing of your
mind.[j] Then you will be able to test and
approve what God's will is[k]—his good,
pleasing[l] and perfect will.

3For by the grace given me[m] I say to
every one of you: Do not think of yourself
more highly than you ought, but rather
think of yourself with sober judgment, in
accordance with the measure of faith God
has given you. 4Just as each of us has one
body with many members, and these

11:27 [r]Isa 59:20, 21; 27:9; Heb 8:10, 12
11:28 [s]Ro 5:10 [t]Dt 7:8; 10:15; Ro 9:5
11:29 [u]S Ro 8:28 [v]S Heb 7:21
11:30 [w]S Eph 2:2
11:32 [x]S Ro 3:9
11:33 [y]S Ro 2:4 [z]Ps 92:5; Eph 3:10; Col 2:3 [a]Job 5:9; 11:7; Ps 139:6; Ecc 8:17; Isa 40:28
11:34 [b]Isa 40:13, 14; Job 15:8; 36:22; Jer 23:18; 1Co 2:16
11:35 [c]Job 41:11; 35:7
11:36 [d]1Co 8:6; 11:12; Col 1:16; Heb 2:10 [e]Ro 16:27; Eph 3:21; 1Ti 1:17; 1Pe 5:11; Jude 25; Rev 5:13; 7:12
12:1 [f]Eph 4:1; 1Pe 2:11 [g]Ro 6:13, 16,19; 1Co 6:20; 1Pe 2:5
12:2 [h]1Pe 1:14 [i]1Co 1:20; 2Co 10:2; 1Jn 2:15 [j]Eph 4:23 [k]S Eph 5:17 [l]S 1Ti 5:4
12:3 [m]Ro 15:15; 1Co 15:10; Gal 2:9; Eph 3:7; 4:7; 1Pe 4:10,11

[r]*27* Or *will be* [s]*27* Isaiah 59:20,21; 27:9; Jer. 31:33,34 [t]*31* Some manuscripts do not have *now.* [u]*33* Or *riches and the wisdom and the* [v]*34* Isaiah 40:13 [w]*35* Job 41:11 [x]*1* Or *reasonable*

12:1 GOD, Grace—Salvation is free, in the sense we do not deserve it and cannot earn it. Because of God's free gift of mercy to us, we owe to God everything we have and are. If we properly understand what becoming a Christian is, salvation costs us everything. Paul here asked for total commitment of believers to God.

12:1–5 DISCIPLESHIP, Nature—Christian discipleship involves complete consecration to Christ and to His cause. Paul based his appeal to sacrificial service on the mercy of God which every Christian has experienced. He did not command nor require; he appealed. He called for a living sacrifice. No longer can God be pleased with a slain beast or mere material things on the altar. He wants lives sacrificed on the altar to Him. He does not want us to die for Him; He wants us to live for Him. Holy living pleases God. Most of the problems we find in trying to live the Christian life probably arise from trying to half live it. Complete commitment to Christ on the part of those who make up the body of Christ brings true unity in the church. That unity will be experienced when members function as the Lord leads and realize that we really belong to Christ's body and not to self. (1 Co 6:19). Discipleship is never practiced in isolation but in relations with others.

12:1–3 CHRISTIAN ETHICS, Worship—Worship is more than feeling good about God. Worship includes the matter of applying faith to everyday life. We worship as we pattern a life after God's ways and not the world's. This is possible when God changes our mindstyle. That is, God's Spirit works in us so we can test and judge to determine God's will.

12:1–8 STEWARDSHIP, Sacrificial Giving—Christian stewardship means sacrificing our lives as acts of worship to God. Time, energy, and resources cannot be divided between God's percent and my percent. God owns all. He gave us all we have. We are to use all we have and are for Him in His work. We are to determine the gift(s) God has given us and use them, confident God will bless our efforts in His way. One gift is the ability to contribute to the needs of others. We should use this gift to be generous with our resources to help those who have no resources. See note on 2 Co 8:1—9:15.

12:1–2 WORSHIP, Sacrifice—The New Testament shows the need of the giving of ourselves and all we are to God as an act of worship. Christ's death on the cross fulfilled the Old Testament requirement to make animal sacrifices. That aspect of worship is now expressed in the giving of our lives completely to the Lord and faithful giving of our possessions. See notes on Lev 7:35–38; 1 Sa 15:22–23; 2 Co 8:1–8. Such self-giving is a basic attitude of worship. See note on 2 Sa 22:1–51.

12:1 PRAYER, Worship—Humans usually serve sin. Voluntary presentation of self to God for His purposes is a spiritual act of worship. See notes on Jn 4:23–24; Heb 13:15–16.

12:2 EDUCATION, Spiritual Renewal—The key to living a transformed life is cultivating a renewed mind. The Christian who is too lazy mentally to drink deeply from God's revealed Word or to think courageously about the meaning of personal faith will tend to be shaped by institutionalized values and socially acceptable modes of thought. The teacher may become the lazy person's god. The teacher must remain an instrument though whom God can work to challenge learners to think, question, and change. The Christian must find God's will personally and individually. No teacher can find God's will for me. Spiritual transformation through learning is a continuing process, not a once-for-all accomplishment. See note on 1 Co 1:18–31.

12:3–8 CHURCH LEADERS, Authority—Leadership authority is based on God's grace and His gifts. Humans do not deserve or earn leadership roles. God does not give every gift to each church member. Members are to serve in accordance with the gifts they possess and are not to run after other people's gifts. The key is for various members to use their gifts cooperatively and to give place to others when they exercise a different gift. No one may attempt to monopolize all the gifts. Paul listed several leadership functions needed in the church and for which God gave gifts to His people. These do not exhaust the leadership gifts God gave the church. God continues to give leadership gifts according to the needs of His churches. Note the gift of service (Greek *diakonia*) is related to the work of the deacon but is given to the whole church.

12:4–8 THE CHURCH, Body of Christ—The church

members do not all have the same function,[n] 5so in Christ we who are many
form one body,[o] and each member belongs to all the others. 6We have different
gifts,[p] according to the grace given us. If
a man's gift is prophesying,[q] let him use
it in proportion to his[y] faith.[r] 7If it is
serving, let him serve; if it is teaching, let
him teach;[s] 8if it is encouraging, let him
encourage;[t] if it is contributing to the
needs of others, let him give generously;[u] if it is leadership, let him govern diligently; if it is showing mercy, let him do
it cheerfully.

Love

9Love must be sincere.[v] Hate what is
evil; cling to what is good.[w] 10Be devoted
to one another in brotherly love.[x] Honor
one another above yourselves.[y] 11Never
be lacking in zeal, but keep your spiritual
fervor,[z] serving the Lord. 12Be joyful in
hope,[a] patient in affliction,[b] faithful in
prayer.[c] 13Share with God's people who
are in need.[d] Practice hospitality.[e]

14Bless those who persecute you;[f]
bless and do not curse. 15Rejoice with
those who rejoice; mourn with those
who mourn.[g] 16Live in harmony with
one another.[h] Do not be proud, but be
willing to associate with people of low position.[z] Do not be conceited.[i]

17Do not repay anyone evil for evil.[j]
Be careful to do what is right in the eyes
of everybody.[k] 18If it is possible, as far as
it depends on you, live at peace with everyone.[l] 19Do not take revenge,[m] my
friends, but leave room for God's wrath,
for it is written: "It is mine to avenge; I
will repay,"[a] [n] says the Lord. 20On the
contrary:

"If your enemy is hungry, feed him;
if he is thirsty, give him something
to drink.
In doing this, you will heap burning
coals on his head."[b] [o]

21Do not be overcome by evil, but overcome evil with good.

Chapter 13

Submission to the Authorities

EVERYONE must submit himself to the
governing authorities,[p] for there is
no authority except that which God has

12:4 [n]1Co 12:12-14; Eph 4:16 **12:5** [o]1Co 6:15; 10:17; 12:12,20, 27; Eph 2:16; 4:4, 25; 5:30; Col 3:15 **12:6** [p]1Co 7:7; 12:4,8-10 [q]S Eph 4:11 [r]1Pe 4:10,11 **12:7** [s]S Eph 4:11 **12:8** [t]Ac 11:23; 13:15; 15:32 [u]2Co 8:2; 9:5-13 **12:9** [v]2Co 6:6; 1Ti 1:5 [w]Ps 97:10; Am 5:15; 1Th 5:21, 22 **12:10** [x]Ps 133:1; 1Th 4:9; Heb 13:1; 1Pe 1:22 [y]Php 2:3 **12:11** [z]Ac 18:25 **12:12** [a]Ro 5:2 [b]Heb 10:32,36 [c]S Lk 18:1 **12:13** [d]S Ac 24:17 [e]2Ki 4:10; Job 31:32; 1Ti 3:2; 5:10; Heb 13:2; 1Pe 4:9 **12:14** [f]S Mt 5:44 **12:15** [g]Job 30:25 **12:16** [h]S Ro 15:5 [i]ver 3; Ps 131:1; Isa 5:21; Jer 45:5; Ro 11:25 **12:17** [j]ver 19; Pr 20:22; 24:29 [k]2Co 8:21 **12:18** [l]S Mk 9:50; S Ro 14:19 **12:19** [m]ver 17; Lev 19:18; Pr 20:22; 24:29 [n]Dt 32:35; Ge 50:19; 1Sa 26:10; Ps 94:1; Jer 51:36 **12:20** [o]Pr 25:21,22; Ex 23:4; Mt 5:44; Lk 6:27 **13:1** [p]Tit 3:1; 1Pe 2:13,14

[y]6 Or *in agreement with the* [z]16 Or *willing to do menial work* [a]19 Deut. 32:35 [b]20 Prov. 25:21,22

forms the body of Christ. The body serves as a beautiful picture of the life of the church. An individual's body has many parts serving various functions. The church consists of people serving Christ in many ways according to the different gifts Christ has given. The church as the body of Christ emphasizes the diversity of gifts which come together to serve one purpose. As members of Christ's church, we must love one another as we love ourselves. The emphasis is not on uniformity but on a diversity which Christ brings together and uses for His purpose. The unity of the church results not from everyone thinking alike but from Christ bringing the various parts together in service to Him.

12:9–21 CHRISTIAN ETHICS, Character—To do the will of God involves a disciplined application of our will in the matters of life. This begins with a goal of doing good rather than evil to other persons no matter how they treat us. See note on Mt 7:1–5,12. It rests on an attitude of love and respect for others. It involves personal humility. See note on Mt 18:1–10. Enthusiasm for God's work fuels our will to do His will. Faithful prayer enables us to endure the dark hours of life. Then we can share with others in need. Humility allows us to do God's will rather than center life on pride in personal achievements. Humility lets us seek to please others and live without fighting or quarreling.

12:9 FAMILY, Authentic Love—"Sincere" (Greek *anupokritos*) means authentic or undisguised. In a world where much that looks real is not real, love in the family must be the real thing expressed in action, not merely in words. Paul gave examples of loving behavior (1 Co 13:4–7) and described his own ministry as one of sincere love (2 Co 6:6). Peter encouraged such love among the fellowship of faith as a demonstration of true conversion (1 Pe 1:22).

12:10 DISCIPLESHIP, Neighbor Love—Disciples love one another as brothers and sisters in Christ. We seek the well-being of one another even at the cost of personal self-interest. See note on Mt 22:37–40.

12:10 FAMILY, Mutual Respect—To honor one another is to show respect for the other's personhood. Such respect is essential to Christian home relationships as well as to life in the church. Husbands are to treat their wives with respect (1 Pe 3:7); wives are to respect their husbands (Eph 5:33); children are to respect parents (Eph 6:1–3); and parents are to discipline children while still showing respect and sensitivity for the child's emotional and spiritual needs (Eph 6:4).

12:12 PRAYER, Persistence—"Faithful" (Greek *proskartereō*) implies intensification of strength and persistent devotion. We are to be strong in our devotion to prayer, making it a priority nothing can dislodge.

12:13 THE CHURCH, Saints—See notes on 15:26; 16:2.

12:13 FAMILY, Social Concern—Christian servanthood expresses itself in concern for the welfare of others and can be demonstrated by families. Paul encouraged Christians to pursue the grace of hospitality, a quality of caring which families can practice through their homes. In Galatians, he instructed Christians not to become weary in their social concern but to continue to do good to others (6:9–10).

12:14–21 EVIL AND SUFFERING, Vindication—Disciples should not retaliate against oppressors. See note on Mt 5:38–48. Instead, we should identify with those who suffer. We should leave vindication and punishment to God. In living the Christian life, peace is our goal, not justice, as we deal with our enemies. Seeking peace may involve submission to political authorities whose views stand in stark contrast to ours (13:1–17).

12:20 DISCIPLESHIP, Hungry—Compassionate ministry to the hungry should include even enemies. Such compassionate care may cause them to repent and change their ways. Disciples do not set up qualifications people must meet to deserve our ministry. We find people in need and show them Christ's love.

13:1 GOD, Sovereignty—God is the ultimate authority, the sovereign Lord over the universe. Any human authority is a qualified authority, an authority subject to the higher authority of God. In this case, governmental authorities are seen as a part of the will of God for governing the ordinary life of people on the earth. It is God's will that human life be governed or

established.[q] The authorities that exist
have been established by God. 2Conse-
quently, he who rebels against the authority is rebelling against what God has
instituted,[r] and those who do so will
bring judgment on themselves. 3For rulers hold no terror for those who do right,
but for those who do wrong. Do you want
to be free from fear of the one in authority? Then do what is right and he will
commend you.[s] 4For he is God's servant
to do you good. But if you do wrong, be
afraid, for he does not bear the sword for
nothing. He is God's servant, an agent of
wrath to bring punishment on the wrong-
doer.[t] 5Therefore, it is necessary to submit to the authorities, not only because of
possible punishment but also because of
conscience.[u]

6This is also why you pay taxes,[v] for
the authorities are God's servants, who
give their full time to governing. 7Give
everyone what you owe him: If you owe
taxes, pay taxes;[w] if revenue, then revenue; if respect, then respect; if honor,
then honor.

13:1 [q]Da 2:21; 4:17; Jn 19:11
13:2 [r]Ex 16:8
13:3 [s]1Pe 2:14
13:4 [t]1Th 4:6
13:5 [u]Pr 24:21,22
13:6 [v]Mt 22:17
13:7 [w]Mt 17:25; 22:17,21; Lk 23:2
13:8 [x]ver 10; S Mt 5:43; Jn 13:34; Col 3:14
13:9 [y]Ex 20:13-15, 17; Dt 5:17-19,21 [z]Mt 7:12 [a]Lev 19:18; S Mt 5:43
13:10 [b]S ver 8; ver 9
13:11 [c]1Co 7:29-31; 10:11; Jas 5:8; 1Pe 4:7; 1Jn 2:18; Rev 22:10 [d]Eph 5:14; 1Th 5:5, 6
13:12 [e]Heb 10:25; 1Jn 2:8 [f]Eph 5:11 [g]Eph 6:11,13; 1Th 5:8
13:13 [h]S Eph 5:18

Love, for the Day Is Near

8Let no debt remain outstanding, except the continuing debt to love one another, for he who loves his fellowman has
fulfilled the law.[x] 9The commandments,
"Do not commit adultery," "Do not murder," "Do not steal," "Do not covet,"[c] [y]
and whatever other commandment there
may be, are summed up[z] in this one
rule: "Love your neighbor as yourself."[d] [a] 10Love does no harm to its
neighbor. Therefore love is the fulfillment of the law.[b]

11And do this, understanding the
present time. The hour has come[c] for
you to wake up from your slumber,[d] because our salvation is nearer now than
when we first believed. 12The night is
nearly over; the day is almost here.[e] So
let us put aside the deeds of darkness[f]
and put on the armor[g] of light. 13Let us
behave decently, as in the daytime, not in
orgies and drunkenness,[h] not in sexual

[c]9 Exodus 20:13-15,17; Deut. 5:17-19,21 [d]9 Lev. 19:18

---

directed in an orderly, just way. A government, or an official, may do things that are most displeasing to God, but the function of government grows out of the will of God and is based upon the sovereign authority of God Himself.

13:1–7 CREATION, Order—Though God, as divine Creator, possesses complete authority, He recognizes the need for practical order in the lives of human beings in today's world. Because all people, at present, do not submit to His claim on their lives, He cannot rule the world as a theocracy. He, therefore, recognizes the validity and function of earthly governments in the world He made. They are necessary for people to live together in a form of harmony, though this method of preserving order falls far short of His eventual goal for His created beings.

13:1–7 CHRISTIAN ETHICS, Church and State—This passage is Paul's most concise summary of Christians' relationships to the state. He based his argument on the order of creation. God has ordained order rather than disorder. Thus He has established the principle of government. Paul did not describe any particular system of government as God's choice. Remember he lived under the rule of the Roman empire and could argue that even the Caesars and their appointees were deserving of honor. They were acting on behalf of the principle of government and justice which stands for order out of chaos. Government officials are, in fact, ministers for the cause of justice. They are not to be feared unless laws have been broken, for they have been given the sword of authority to keep justice. Paul did not want the fledgling Christian movement to be lost in potentially self-destructive revolutions. Rather, pay the appropriate taxes and duties. In return we expect a system working for the well-being of the whole society. Paul left some room for difference with a government as he considered those who deserve honor and those who do not. The conclusion is that the burden of proof is on one who does not submit to the principle of civil government in his or her life.

13:8 DISCIPLESHIP, Neighbor Love—Loving others is a debt we never can pay in full. Christ has given us so much love we are eternally in debt. This is the only debt we have the right to maintain continuously. All other debts should be paid on schedule. See note on Jn 13:34–35.

13:8–14 CHRISTIAN ETHICS, Moral Imperatives—Christian ethics can be briefly summarized. Love people, and be willing to do for them whatever you would do for yourself. Carried out perfectly, such love fulfills all the rest of the law. Live in light of Christ's immediate return. Do not put off until later any changes needed to be made or any actions needed to be taken. Do everything as if it could be seen by every person in broad daylight. Have no actions you want to hide. Seek to please Christ and not self. Live as He would live.

13:8 CHRISTIAN ETHICS, Property Rights—In a sense everyone to whom we owe a monetary debt owns a part of our allegiance. Such allegiances can be so burdensome as to draw us from our first love of Jesus Christ. Paul's advice is timely for everyone who will risk ruining the work of the gospel in their own lives because of feeding their own greed.

13:8 STEWARDSHIP, Attitudes—Responsible Christians avoid becoming so indebted they limit the personal freedom necessary to serve Christ. In biblical days, anyone failing to pay a debt could become a slave. Credit abuse is a form of slavery or addiction that threatens many today. Christian stewards manage their finances and control spending to meet their obligations.

13:11 SALVATION, Glorification—This text shows the dynamic nature of salvation. The Roman Christians were asleep, not living the dynamic Christian life. They needed to live life in daily expectation and joy of Christ's return. We as Christians are not yet what we will become in the end time but need to be all we can be in Christ in the present.

13:11–12 LAST THINGS, Salvation's Completion—All that Christ will complete at His return constitutes the meaning of salvation in this passage. In its future completion, salvation is nearer to every believer now than it was when we first believed. This should lead us to live as God desires not according to the world's darkness.

13:13 CHRISTIAN ETHICS, Alcohol—In the first century the alcoholic content of wine was lower than many of the contemporary alcoholic beverages. One could get drunk on such content, however, though it might take longer. Paul's strong warnings about drunkenness stem from addressing the attitudes among those who would be so intemperate as to drink so long they were drunk and not in control of themselves. Too, he, no doubt, was concerned that drunk Christians would be seen as no different from some of the cults of that time. As well, for the sake of the Christian community and its gospel, the churches should shun those who might hinder the gospel (as drunkards would). Christians should be willing to abstain from drunkenness to preserve our Christian witness to a world looking for reasons to criticize us.

immorality and debauchery, not in dissension and jealousy.[i] 14Rather, clothe
yourselves with the Lord Jesus Christ,[j]
and do not think about how to gratify the
desires of the sinful nature.[e] [k]

Chapter 14

The Weak and the Strong

ACCEPT him whose faith is weak,[l]
without passing judgment on disput-
able matters. 2One man's faith allows him
to eat everything, but another man,
whose faith is weak, eats only vegetables.[m] 3The man who eats everything
must not look down on[n] him who does
not, and the man who does not eat everything must not condemn[o] the man who
does, for God has accepted him. 4Who are
you to judge someone else's servant?[p] To
his own master he stands or falls. And he
will stand, for the Lord is able to make
him stand.

5One man considers one day more sacred than another;[q] another man considers every day alike. Each one should be
fully convinced in his own mind. 6He
who regards one day as special, does so to
the Lord. He who eats meat, eats to the
Lord, for he gives thanks to God;[r] and he
who abstains, does so to the Lord and
gives thanks to God. 7For none of us lives
to himself alone[s] and none of us dies to
himself alone. 8If we live, we live to the
Lord; and if we die, we die to the Lord.
So, whether we live or die, we belong to
the Lord.[t]

9For this very reason, Christ died and
returned to life[u] so that he might be the
Lord of both the dead and the living.[v]
10You, then, why do you judge your
brother? Or why do you look down on[w]
your brother? For we will all stand before
God's judgment seat.[x] 11It is written:

" 'As surely as I live,'[y] says the Lord,
'every knee will bow before me;
every tongue will confess to
God.' "[f] [z]

12So then, each of us will give an account
of himself to God.[a]

13Therefore let us stop passing judgment[b] on one another. Instead, make up
your mind not to put any stumbling block
or obstacle in your brother's way.[c] 14As
one who is in the Lord Jesus, I am fully
convinced that no food[g] is unclean in itself.[d] But if anyone regards something as
unclean, then for him it is unclean.[e] 15If
your brother is distressed because of
what you eat, you are no longer acting in
love.[f] Do not by your eating destroy your
brother for whom Christ died.[g] 16Do not
allow what you consider good to be spoken of as evil.[h] 17For the kingdom of God
is not a matter of eating and drinking,[i]

[e]14 Or *the flesh* [f]11 Isaiah 45:23 [g]14 Or *that nothing*

13:13 [i]Lk 21:34; Gal 5:20,21; Eph 5:18; 1Pe 4:3
13:14 [j]Gal 3:27; Eph 4:24; Col 3:10, 12 [k]S Gal 5:24
14:1 [l]Ro 15:1; 1Co 8:9-12; 9:22
14:2 [m]ver 14
14:3 [n]ver 10; Lk 18:9 [o]ver 10,13; Col 2:16
14:4 [p]S Mt 7:1
14:5 [q]Gal 4:10; Col 2:16
14:6 [r]S Mt 14:19; 1Co 10:30,31; 1Ti 4:3,4
14:7 [s]2Co 5:15; Gal 2:20
14:8 [t]Php 1:20
14:9 [u]Rev 1:18; 2:8 [v]S Ac 10:42; 2Co 5:15
14:10 [w]ver 3; S Mt 7:1 [x]S 2Co 5:10
14:11 [y]Isa 49:18 [z]Isa 45:23; Php 2:10,11
14:12 [a]Mt 12:36; 1Pe 4:5
14:13 [b]ver 1; S Mt 7:1 [c]S 2Co 6:3
14:14 [d]ver 20; S Ac 10:15 [e]1Co 8:7
14:15 [f]Eph 5:2 [g]ver 20; 1Co 8:11
14:16 [h]1Co 10:30
14:17 [i]1Co 8:8

13:14 HUMANITY, Spiritual Nature—The spiritual nature is described as a person putting on a new garment, Jesus Himself. When clothed with Him, people should seek to live according to His guidance rather than by following the old nature of the flesh. See Gal 3:27; Eph 6:11–18.

14:1–23 HUMANITY, Relationships—Fellowship should be a fundamental concern to all Christians. We should live in the sensitive awareness of the weaknesses of others so we do not lead another into sin. Christians need to know that behavior can have destructive consequences on fellow believers. Further, we should accept other Christians without passing judgment upon the centralities of their faith. We can still love one another even while disagreeing so as not to give Satan a foothold through division.

14:4–9 JESUS CHRIST, Lord—As Lord, Jesus Christ not only rules over us. He provides needed strength for our weaknesses. Life is lived in relationship to the risen Lord and His will for us, not in relationship to the opinions and judgments of other people. Only He earned the right to be our Lord through death and resurrection. See note on 10:9–12.

14:5–6 WORSHIP, Calendar—See note on Ex 16:23–30.

14:6 PRAYER, Thanksgiving—Regardless of the conviction, virtue is a result of gratitude to God as source of everything we receive.

14:10–12 GOD, Judge—The freedom God has given to us comes with the price tag of responsibility and accountability. As sovereign Lord and Creator of the world and all its people, God is also the Judge before whom we all must stand. Every person must give account to God. In a sense, judgment comes daily as God interacts with our lives. But we also face a final judgment in the end time. This judgment poses no threat to the Christian, so far as our eternal destiny is concerned. We have already been pronounced forgiven through the saving work of Jesus. Each of us may still expect to give an account to God for what we have done with our lives. The judgment does remind us not to usurp God's authority and judge others. See note on 2:2.

14:10–12 LAST THINGS, Judgment—Humans are not authorized to judge others. The fact that all of us must stand before God's judgment seat is sobering. Paul wrote to other Christians that there is judgment for believers as well as unbelievers. For believers, the nature of the judgment is not the determination of eternal destiny but rather the assignment of rewards. See note on 2 Co 5:10. The quotation from Isa 45:23 is used to lead to the conclusion that each person must appear before God in judgment.

14:14 SALVATION, As Being in Christ—Being in Christ gives us insight into moral problems and makes us sensitive to personal relationships.

14:15 JESUS CHRIST, Death—Christ's death for all people gives value to every person so that our decisions are to be made in light of their effect on people for whom Christ died.

14:17–18 HOLY SPIRIT, Transforms—Joy is the customary way of life of those who have received the Spirit. See Gal 5:22; note on Ac 13:52. The Spirit transforms those in whom He lives. We may have lived without joy, or only with the kind of joy which comes from having selfish desires fulfilled. The Spirit transforms us into people who have joy because we have found our true destiny. The joy we have, not the legalistic rules we follow, shows we are Christ's.

14:17 SALVATION, Joy—The kingdom of God means joy in the Holy Spirit. All who belong to God's rule have that joy as a fruit of the Spirit (Gal 5:22).

14:17 THE CHURCH, God's Kingdom—The value of the kingdom of God cannot be compared to earthly treasures. God's kingdom produces the spiritual—and enduring—treasures of righteousness (right living among people), peace (well-being in all relationships), and joy. These spiritual trea-

but of righteousness, peace[j] and joy in
the Holy Spirit,[k] 18because anyone who
serves Christ in this way is pleasing to
God and approved by men.[l]
19Let us therefore make every effort to
do what leads to peace[m] and to mutual
edification.[n] 20Do not destroy the work
of God for the sake of food.[o] All food is
clean,[p] but it is wrong for a man to eat
anything that causes someone else to
stumble.[q] 21It is better not to eat meat or
drink wine or to do anything else that
will cause your brother to fall.[r]
22So whatever you believe about these
things keep between yourself and God.
Blessed is the man who does not condemn[s] himself by what he approves.
23But the man who has doubts[t] is condemned if he eats, because his eating is
not from faith; and everything that does
not come from faith is sin.

Chapter 15

WE who are strong ought to bear with
the failings of the weak[u] and not to
please ourselves. 2Each of us should
please his neighbor for his good,[v] to
build him up.[w] 3For even Christ did not
please himself[x] but, as it is written: "The
insults of those who insult you have fallen
on me."[h][y] 4For everything that was
written in the past was written to teach
us,[z] so that through endurance and the
encouragement of the Scriptures we
might have hope.
5May the God who gives endurance
and encouragement give you a spirit of
unity[a] among yourselves as you follow
Christ Jesus, 6so that with one heart and
mouth you may glorify[b] the God and Father[c] of our Lord Jesus Christ.
7Accept one another,[d] then, just as
Christ accepted you, in order to bring
praise to God. 8For I tell you that Christ
has become a servant of the Jews[i][e] on
behalf of God's truth, to confirm the
promises[f] made to the patriarchs 9so that
the Gentiles[g] may glorify God[h] for his
mercy, as it is written:

> "Therefore I will praise you among the
> Gentiles;
> I will sing hymns to your name."[j][i]

10Again, it says,

> "Rejoice, O Gentiles, with his
> people."[k][j]

11And again,

> "Praise the Lord, all you Gentiles,
> and sing praises to him, all you
> peoples."[l][k]

12And again, Isaiah says,

> "The Root of Jesse[l] will spring up,
> one who will arise to rule over the
> nations;
> the Gentiles will hope in him."[m][m]

13May the God of hope fill you with all

[h] *3* Psalm 69:9 [i] *8* Greek *circumcision*
[j] *9* 2 Samuel 22:50; Psalm 18:49 [k] *10* Deut. 32:43
[l] *11* Psalm 117:1 [m] *12* Isaiah 11:10

14:17 [j]Isa 32:17 [k]Ro 15:13; Gal 5:22
14:18 [l]Lk 2:52; Ac 24:16; 2Co 8:21
14:19 [m]Ps 34:14; Ro 12:18; 1Co 7:15; 2Ti 2:22; Heb 12:14 [n]Ro 15:2; 1Co 14:3-5,12,17, 26; 2Co 12:19; Eph 4:12,29
14:20 [o]ver 15 [p]ver 14; S Ac 10:15 [q]ver 13; 1Co 8:9-12
14:21 [r]S Mt 5:29
14:22 [s]1Jn 3:21
14:23 [t]ver 5
15:1 [u]Ro 14:1; 1Th 5:14
15:2 [v]S 1Co 10:24 [w]S Ro 14:19
15:3 [x]2Co 8:9 [y]Ps 69:9
15:4 [z]S Ro 4:23,24
15:5 [a]Ro 12:16; 1Co 1:10; 2Co 13:11; Eph 4:3; Php 2:2; Col 3:14; 1Pe 3:8
15:6 [b]Ps 34:3 [c]Rev 1:6
15:7 [d]Ro 14:1
15:8 [e]Mt 15:24; Ac 3:25,26 [f]2Co 1:20
15:9 [g]S Ro 3:29 [h]S Mt 9:8 [i]2Sa 22:50; Ps 18:49
15:10 [j]Dt 32:43; Isa 66:10
15:11 [k]Ps 117:1
15:12 [l]S Rev 5:5 [m]Isa 11:10; Mt 12:21

---

sures should not be traded for earthly riches which soon pass away. Our relationships with other people should show our love for them and our concentration on spiritual treasures rather than on earthly pleasures. Compare Mt 6:33.

14:19–23 CHRISTIAN ETHICS, Moral Limits—Paul's teaching here is of supreme importance as one of the building blocks for a consistent approach to Christian decision-making. Though Paul claimed his freedom in Christ, he still (1 Co 9:1,19; 10:25–33) highlighted the need to be sensitive to others' consciences. Our conscience may not be violated by a particular action, but such an action may be perceived as immoral by other individuals living out of another level of ethical maturity. For them moral confusion may set in. Does one live life, then, continually bending to the dictates of others' consciences? Yes, when the motivation is to nurture others in the understanding of the kingdom of God and to bring honor to God. No, when the bending limits or alters our own sense of maturity in God. A fragile balance results, and constant vigilance to such a tension is necessary. We must avoid an attitude of condemnation and a feeling of guilt. We must seek to mature and help others mature. Above all, we must seek to avoid quarrels and divisions in God's church. Church unity is more important than my freedom.

15:3 JESUS CHRIST, Suffering—Jesus was not self-centered, doing what He pleased. He suffered insult and persecution for our sake, showing us the way to deal with other people for their good.

15:4 HOLY SCRIPTURE, Hope—We gain hope from Scripture. Through it we find strength to endure life's disappointments, crises, and hardships. Scripture encourages us to hope in Christ in spite of life's circumstances. Scripture does not merely provide information about the past. It is not designed for us to read selectively, choosing parts to obey and discarding the rest. We read Scripture to discover Jesus Christ, to learn more about Him, and to grow as His disciples.

15:5–7 THE CHURCH, Local Body—God desires unity among His people. The church should be one in Christ Jesus. Holding grudges and resenting other members of the body separates us from the will of Christ. Christians should accept one another as Christ accepted us. See note on Jn 17:11.

15:7–8 JESUS CHRIST, Servant—Jesus accepted us for fellowship with Him even though our faith and morals were not as strong as His. Thus we have no reason not to accept other Christians who may not agree with us (14:1). Jesus did not take advantage of His strength but accepted the role of service (Greek *diakonos*) to fulfill God's mission set forth in Scripture.

15:7 SALVATION, Acceptance—God's people are to accept one another as Christ has accepted them. This is part of true worship.

15:7–12 EVANGELISM, Universality—Jesus, a Jew by human lineage, confirmed that the Jewish nation would be a channel of blessing for the Gentile world. In turn, the Gentiles would glorify God for His limitless mercy. Salvation is a great source of rejoicing for all. This is certainly a reason to evangelize everyone. See note on 10:12–15.

15:8–12 ELECTION, God's Promise—Jews and Gentiles should accept one another just as Christ has accepted both of them. On behalf of God, Jesus became a servant of the Jews, *thereby keeping* God's election promises to their mothers and fathers. Enabling the Gentiles to glorify God and become a part of God's elect people was part of the original promise (Ge 12:1–3).

15:13 HOLY SPIRIT, Transforms—The Holy Spirit trans-

joy and peace[n] as you trust in him, so
that you may overflow with hope by the
power of the Holy Spirit.[o]

Paul the Minister to the Gentiles

14 I myself am convinced, my brothers,
that you yourselves are full of goodness,[p]
complete in knowledge[q] and competent
to instruct one another. 15 I have written
you quite boldly on some points, as if to
remind you of them again, because of the
grace God gave me[r] 16 to be a minister of
Christ Jesus to the Gentiles[s] with the
priestly duty of proclaiming the gospel of
God,[t] so that the Gentiles might become
an offering[u] acceptable to God, sanctified
by the Holy Spirit.
17 Therefore I glory in Christ Jesus[v] in
my service to God.[w] 18 I will not venture
to speak of anything except what Christ
has accomplished through me in leading
the Gentiles[x] to obey God[y] by what I
have said and done— 19 by the power of
signs and miracles,[z] through the power
of the Spirit.[a] So from Jerusalem[b] all the
way around to Illyricum, I have fully proclaimed the gospel of Christ.[c] 20 It has always been my ambition to preach the
gospel[d] where Christ was not known, so
that I would not be building on someone
else's foundation.[e] 21 Rather, as it is written:

"Those who were not told about him
will see,
and those who have not heard will
understand."[n][f]

22 This is why I have often been hindered
from coming to you.[g]

Paul's Plan to Visit Rome

23 But now that there is no more place
for me to work in these regions, and
since I have been longing for many years
to see you,[h] 24 I plan to do so when I go to
Spain.[i] I hope to visit you while passing
through and to have you assist[j] me on
my journey there, after I have enjoyed
your company for a while. 25 Now, however, I am on my way to Jerusalem[k] in the
service[l] of the saints[m] there. 26 For Macedonia[n] and Achaia[o] were pleased to
make a contribution for the poor among
the saints in Jerusalem.[p] 27 They were
pleased to do it, and indeed they owe it to
them. For if the Gentiles have shared in

15:13 [n]Ro 14:17 [o]ver 19; 1Co 2:4; 4:20; 1Th 1:5
15:14 [p]Eph 5:9 [q]S 2Co 8:7; 2Pe 1:12
15:15 [r]S Ro 12:3
15:16 [s]S Ac 9:15 [t]ver 19; S Ro 1:1 [u]Isa 66:20
15:17 [v]Php 3:3 [w]Heb 2:17
15:18 [x]Ac 15:12; 21:19; Ro 1:5 [y]Ro 16:26
15:19 [z]S Jn 4:48; Ac 19:11 [a]S ver 13 [b]Ac 22:17-21 [c]S 2Co 2:12
15:20 [d]Ro 1:15 [e]2Co 10:15,16
15:21 [f]Isa 52:15
15:22 [g]Ro 1:13
15:23 [h]Ac 19:21; Ro 1:10,11
15:24 [i]ver 28 [j]1Co 16:6; Tit 3:13
15:25 [k]S Ac 19:21 [l]S Ac 24:17 [m]S Ac 9:13
15:26 [n]S Ac 16:9 [o]S Ac 18:12 [p]S Ac 24:17

n21 Isaiah 52:15

---

forms the lives of God's people. He uses His great power to do this, yet He does not overwhelm us. People who do not know Christ are without God and therefore without hope (Eph 2:12). Christ through the Spirit brings us hope when we accept Him. That hope must be nurtured and cared for, especially in the face of persecution. To possess a steady hope that you will ultimately share in God's glory is a source of great joy (Ro 5:2). Christians may nurture hope; but ultimately only the Spirit keeps hope alive. We should pray that God will help us to overflow with hope by the power of the Spirit.

15:14 THE CHURCH, People of God—In Christ all people are one. No one lords it over others; no one exercises absolute or dictatorial powers. Those who are first in the kingdom of God are those who serve Christ and His church. All are brothers and sisters in Christ because all are indebted to the work of Christ, who created for Himself a redeemed people. We can learn from every other Christian.

15:14 EDUCATION, Christians—Christians should be able to teach one another. This practice requires that we be authentic persons whose lives are marked by genuine goodness. It also requires that we have enough understanding of our faith to teach it intelligently. The preparation of Christian teachers should focus on who they are, not just on techniques of instruction.

15:15 HOLY SCRIPTURE, Collection—Paul wrote God's truth under the power of God's grace and direction. Commissioned to be a minister and proclaimer of God's revelation to the Gentiles, Paul also used letter writing to communicate God's message. Individual letters written to meet individual church needs became accepted by the churches as authoritative Scripture, inspired by the will and plan of God. Churches then collected other letters of Paul and learned God's Word from them. Eventually under God's direction the inspired letters were collected together. The collection process did not include every letter Paul wrote but all those God's Spirit led to be included as Scripture.

15:15–22 PROCLAMATION, Call—See note on Jer 1:4–9. The call to preach is based on God's grace, not on human merit or achievement. A special task of proclamation is to speak to those who have not heard.

15:16 HOLY SPIRIT, Transforms—The Spirit transforms sinners into holy people acceptable to God (Lev 11:44). That transforming action is not limited to one race of people with one set of religious traditions and worship rituals. Paul devoted his life to ministry serving Jesus, the High Priest. The only ritual was in proclaiming the gospel and bringing the Gentile converts to Him. The Holy Spirit in the life of these non-Jewish believers showed God accepted Gentile converts without their participation in Jewish Temple rituals. Every Christian needs to be made holy by the Spirit and to bring new converts as an offering to God.

15:18 JESUS CHRIST, Ascension—The ascended Christ expanded the ministry of the earthly Christ by leading the Gentiles to salvation. Human ministry is the work of the risen Christ through the human servant.

15:18–19 MIRACLE, Instruments—Paul insisted that his effectiveness as a Christian witness depended not on himself but on Christ. The signs and wonders and the ever-present Spirit of God empowered him for his mission. Miracles are not performed for their own sake. They lead to proclamation and belief.

15:18 EVANGELISM, Results—Evangelism leads people to obedience. Paul would not brag of his accomplishments. He simply obeyed Christ and led others to obey Him. Obedience among Christians causes others to obey the gospel and be saved.

15:26–27 STEWARDSHIP, Care of Needy—The Christian life is always spiritual in nature and claims material things to serve spiritual ends. Christians are to serve God and fellow Christians by properly using material possessions. The Gentile Christians knew they owed their opportunity for salvation to the missionary efforts of the Jews. They were willing to cross geographical and racial lines to help the Jews in their physical needs. Christian love places no limits on who can be helped by our sacrificial gifts to God's work. See notes on Dt 8:7–9,10–14,18; Ac 24:17.

15:26 THE CHURCH, Saints—"Saints" is used often in association with the love which Christians have for one another. The context of this verse concerns the offering which Gentile saints made for the poorer and more persecuted saints of Jerusalem. To be a saint, a member of Christ's church, is to love and help others. See notes on 1:7; 16:2.

the Jews' spiritual blessings, they owe it
to the Jews to share with them their material blessings.[q] 28 So after I have completed this task and have made sure that
they have received this fruit, I will go to
Spain[r] and visit you on the way. 29 I
know that when I come to you,[s] I will
come in the full measure of the blessing
of Christ.
30 I urge you, brothers, by our Lord
Jesus Christ and by the love of the Spirit,[t] to join me in my struggle by praying
to God for me.[u] 31 Pray that I may be rescued[v] from the unbelievers in Judea and
that my service[w] in Jerusalem may be acceptable to the saints[x] there, 32 so that by
God's will[y] I may come to you[z] with joy
and together with you be refreshed.[a]
33 The God of peace[b] be with you all.
Amen.

Chapter 16

Personal Greetings

I commend[c] to you our sister Phoebe, a
servant[o] of the church in Cenchrea.[d]
2 I ask you to receive her in the Lord[e] in a
way worthy of the saints[f] and to give her
any help she may need from you, for she
has been a great help to many people,
including me.
3 Greet Priscilla[p] and Aquila,[g] my fellow
workers[h] in Christ Jesus.[i] 4 They
risked their lives for me. Not only I
but all the churches of the Gentiles
are grateful to them.
5 Greet also the church that meets at
their house.[j]
Greet my dear friend Epenetus, who
was the first convert[k] to Christ in
the province of Asia.[l]
6 Greet Mary, who worked very hard for
you.
7 Greet Andronicus and Junias, my relatives[m] who have been in prison
with me.[n] They are outstanding
among the apostles, and they were
in Christ[o] before I was.
8 Greet Ampliatus, whom I love in the
Lord.
9 Greet Urbanus, our fellow worker in
Christ,[p] and my dear friend Sta-
chys.
10 Greet Apelles, tested and approved in
Christ.[q]

15:27 [q]1Co 9:11
15:28 [r]ver 24
15:29 [s]Ro 1:10,11
15:30 [t]Gal 5:22; Col 1:8 [u]2Co 1:11; Col 4:12
15:31 [v]2Co 1:10; 2Th 3:2; 2Ti 3:11; 2Pe 2:9 [w]ver 25; S Ac 24:17 [x]S Ac 9:13
15:32 [y]S Ac 18:21 [z]Ro 1:10,13 [a]1Co 16:18; Phm 7
15:33 [b]Ro 16:20; 2Co 13:11; Php 4:9; 1Th 5:23; 2Th 3:16; Heb 13:20
16:1 [c]S 2Co 3:1 [d]Ac 18:18
16:2 [e]Php 2:29 [f]S Ac 9:13
16:3 [g]S Ac 18:2 [h]S Php 2:25 [i]ver 7, 9,10; Ro 8:1,39; 1Co 1:30; 2Co 5:17; Gal 1:22; 5:6; Eph 1:13
16:5 [j]1Co 16:19; Col 4:15; Phm 2 [k]1Co 16:15 [l]S Ac 2:9
16:7 [m]ver 11,21 [n]Col 4:10; Phm 23 [o]S ver 3
16:9 [p]S ver 3
16:10 [q]S ver 3

[o]*1* Or *deaconess* [p]*3* Greek *Prisca,* a variant of *Priscilla*

15:29 SALVATION, Blessing—Paul knew that he would go to preach the gospel in Rome with the fullness of Christ's blessing. Christ blesses those who do His will.

15:30 HOLY SPIRIT, Transforms—The Spirit pours God's love into Christians' hearts (5:5). The Spirit produces the fruit of love in the lives of Christians (Gal 5:22). Such love would lead the Roman Christians to join Paul in prayer for his struggles to go to Rome. The Spirit's love bonds Christians into God's family, leading us to pray for one another.

15:30–32 PRAYER, Intercession—Prayer may be a struggle, a work. The word (Greek *sunagōnisasthai*) Paul used in urging the Romans to pray is the word from which English "agonize" is derived. He expected God's will to be accomplished through prayer, but he knew he faced physical agony and wanted fellow Christians to bear part of the spiritual agony through prayer. True intercessory prayer involves suffering spiritual pain for others. See note on 2 Th 3:1–5. See Guide to Intercession, pp. 1800–1801.

15:33 PRAYER, Blessing—Paul regularly ended letters with a benediction (1 Co 16:23; 2 Co 13:11,14; Gal 6:18; Eph 6:23–24; Php 4:9,23; Col 4:18; 1 Th 5:28; 2 Th 3:16; 1 Ti 6:21; 2 Ti 4:22; Tit 3:15; Phm 25). Paul could challenge his readers to change their way of living and oppose false teachers and teachings, but he closed in prayer seeking God's continuing and eternal direction of his readers' daily lives. Blessing on God's people should be a part of the daily prayer life of each believer. See note on Ro 1:7.

16:1–3 DISCIPLESHIP, Women—All Christian disciples, whether women or men, serve under the lordship of Christ. All have the same access to God in Christ. Women have always had a distinctive part in the ministry of Christian churches since the earliest days. In this passage Paul commended Phoebe as a servant of the church. "Servant" (Greek *diakonos*) could refer to any kind of service, but it can be translated "deacon" (NIV note). She served the church in a specific way, possibly as a woman deacon or deaconess. Paul referred to her in a quite different way than to Priscilla and Aquila, *who were* his fellow workers *(v 3). See note on Ac 18:18.* Compare notes *on Church Leaders, Deacon* (Index, p. 1868). Some Bible students think Phoebe carried Paul's letter to Rome. Paul certainly appreciated her ministry and told the church at Rome to help her in any way possible. Bible scholars debate Phoebe's role and other references to women as deacons. Every ministry mentioned in the New Testament is referred to by a derivative of the word for deacon, which actually means "servant." Did Phoebe hold the office of deacon, or did she otherwise serve in a manner distinctive enough to be referred to as a deaconess? If she held the office of deacon, were her duties the same as those of a male deacon? Different opinions are held among Bible students regarding the role of women, but no doubt exists as to any woman's responsibility to seek God's will for her life. Women and men equally are priests under the lordship of Christ.

16:1–2 CHURCH LEADERS, Deacon—Phoebe probably delivered the letter to Rome. Paul commended her to them as a sister in Christ and a servant (Greek *diakonos*) of the church in Cenchrea. Since the feminine form of servant is not used in the Greek, two interpretations are possible. She could have been a deaconess. See note on 1 Ti 3:8–12. Deaconesses are mentioned in Christian writings after the New Testament. This also could be a general reference to her service in the church. See note on Ro 12:3–8. In the New Testament, the distinction between full-time and volunteer or part-time ministry was not clearly made. Every Christian was to be a servant of Christ in the church. In this strategic seaport, Phoebe had been able to render particular service to Paul and many others. If deaconess was an official leadership position in the early church, its function is not clear. Some Bible students think they performed the same duties as male deacons. Others think they ministered only to women. Still others do not think women served officially as deacons at all.

16:2 THE CHURCH, Saints—Christians demonstrate practical service toward each other. Paul described all Christians as saints—male or female, Jew or Gentile. To be a Christian is to be ready to help any other Christian in any way possible. See note on 1:7.

16:4 THE CHURCH, Local Body—See note on Ac 4:32.

16:5 THE CHURCH, Local Body—The church is not a building. It is an assembly of believers in Christ who have been called by Him and redeemed through His blood. The church consists of believers in Christ, not of bricks and mortar. See note on Ac 8:1.

Greet those who belong to the household[r] of Aristobulus.
11Greet Herodion, my relative.[s]
Greet those in the household[t] of Narcissus who are in the Lord.
12Greet Tryphena and Tryphosa, those women who work hard in the Lord.
Greet my dear friend Persis, another woman who has worked very hard in the Lord.
13Greet Rufus,[u] chosen[v] in the Lord, and his mother, who has been a mother to me, too.
14Greet Asyncritus, Phlegon, Hermes, Patrobas, Hermas and the brothers with them.
15Greet Philologus, Julia, Nereus and his sister, and Olympas and all the saints[w] with them.[x]
16Greet one another with a holy kiss.[y]
All the churches of Christ send greetings.

17I urge you, brothers, to watch out for
those who cause divisions and put obstacles in your way that are contrary to the
teaching you have learned.[z] Keep away
from them.[a] 18For such people are not
serving our Lord Christ,[b] but their own
appetites.[c] By smooth talk and flattery
they deceive[d] the minds of naive people.
19Everyone has heard[e] about your obedience, so I am full of joy over you; but I
want you to be wise about what is good,
and innocent about what is evil.[f]
20The God of peace[g] will soon crush[h]
Satan[i] under your feet.
The grace of our Lord Jesus be with you.[j]
21Timothy,[k] my fellow worker, sends
his greetings to you, as do Lucius,[l] Jason[m] and Sosipater, my relatives.[n]
22I, Tertius, who wrote down this letter, greet you in the Lord.
23Gaius,[o] whose hospitality I and the
whole church here enjoy, sends you his
greetings.
Erastus,[p] who is the city's director of
public works, and our brother Quartus
send you their greetings.[q]
25Now to him who is able[q] to establish
you by my gospel[r] and the proclamation
of Jesus Christ, according to the revelation of the mystery[s] hidden for long ages
past, 26but now revealed and made
known through the prophetic writings[t]
by the command of the eternal God, so
that all nations might believe and obey[u]
him— 27to the only wise God be glory
forever through Jesus Christ! Amen.[v]

16:10 [r]S Ac 11:14
16:11 [s]ver 7,21 [t]S Ac 11:14
16:13 [u]Mk 15:21 [v]S 2Jn 1
16:15 [w]ver 2; S Ac 9:13 [x]ver 14
16:16 [y]1Co 16:20; 2Co 13:12; 1Th 5:26; 1Pe 5:14
16:17 [z]Gal 1:8,9; 1Ti 1:3; 6:3 [a]Mt 18:15-17; 1Co 5:11; 2Th 3:6, 14; 2Ti 3:5; Tit 3:10; 2Jn 10
16:18 [b]Ro 14:18 [c]Php 3:19 [d]2Sa 15:6; Ps 12:2; Isa 30:10; Col 2:4
16:19 [e]Ro 1:8 [f]S 1Co 14:20
16:20 [g]S Ro 15:33 [h]Ge 3:15 [i]S Mt 4:10 [j]2Co 13:14; S Gal 6:18; 1Th 5:28; Rev 22:21
16:21 [k]S Ac 16:1 [l]Ac 13:1 [m]Ac 17:5 [n]ver 7,11
16:23 [o]S Ac 19:29 [p]Ac 19:22; 2Ti 4:20
16:25 [q]2Co 9:8; Eph 3:20; Jude 24 [r]Ro 2:16; 2Ti 2:8 [s]Isa 48:6; Eph 1:9; 3:3-6,9; Col 1:26, 27; 2:2; 1Ti 3:16
16:26 [t]Ro 1:2 [u]Ro 1:5
16:27 [v]S Ro 11:36

[q]23 Some manuscripts *their greetings.* 24*May the grace of our Lord Jesus Christ be with all of you. Amen.*

16:13 ELECTION, Personal—Rufus, a member of the church in Rome, occupied a warm place in Paul's heart. His mother was like a mother to Paul. Rufus was chosen to be a member of God's elect. See note on 1:5–6. Election applies to individuals in their relationship to God as well as to communities of faith.

16:15 THE CHURCH, Saints—See note on 1 Co 1:2.

16:16 THE CHURCH, Local Body—See note on Ac 4:32.

16:17–19 CHRISTIAN ETHICS, Character—Innocence and wisdom can go together. One must be alert to the dragging down effects of those whose purposes are alien to the gospel. Once these purposes are recognized and it is obvious such people cannot be won to the gospel, they should be avoided.

16:17–18 THE CHURCH, Local Body—The church on earth is not perfect. Some members sinfully serve selfish desires instead of Christ. They divide the church and obstruct its work. Christians must not use such people as models. Rather we must turn away from them to work with God's faithful leaders. See note on 15:5–7.

16:19,26 SALVATION, Obedience—God wanted all nations to believe and obey Him as did the Christians in Rome. Obedience is a partner of faith.

16:23 THE CHURCH, Local Body—See note on Ac 8:1.

16:25–27 GOD, Eternal—God is eternal, without beginning and without ending. See note on Ge 1:1. Thus His commands have eternal authority. The eternal God's revelation of His salvation for all people through Christ calls us to glorify Him.

16:25–26 HOLY SCRIPTURE, Redemption—Paul affirmed the revelation of God in Jesus Christ as a mystery unveiled through His preaching the gospel to the Gentiles. The mystery of God's plan for all persons to find salvation in Christ fulfilled the prophet's writing but was not properly understood until Christ came. Thus, Paul showed that Christ gave new meaning to the Old Testament, all of which must be read in light of His ministry, death, and resurrection. Paul's doxology praising God (vv 25–27) appears in important early New Testament manuscripts at different places in the text of Romans. Some manuscripts have it both here and after 14:23. Others place it only after 14:23. A papyrus manuscript from AD 200 has the doxology after 15:33.

16:25–27 PROCLAMATION, Gospel—See notes on Ac 3:11–26; 26:19–29. Proclamation seeks to bring all people of all races to trust Christ for salvation.

16:25–27 PRAYER, Praise—Paul wrote to correct and challenge churches, but he let them know the ultimate goal was to bring glory to God. Thus he frequently included in his letters doxologies, or statements of praise to God's glory (Greek *doxa*). Compare 11:36; Gal 1:5; Eph 3:21; 2 Ti 4:18; Heb 13:21; 1 Pe 4:11; 2 Pe 3:18). Doxology is a form of prayer exalting and praising the essential nature of God.

16:26 EVANGELISM, Universality—See note on 10:12–15.

1 Corinthians

Theological Setting

The church at Corinth existed in a secular and sensual city. The people were preoccupied with pleasure, athletics, and commercial and personal affluence. How could a church function in such an environment? First Corinthians is written to show us the answer to that concern. The answer is important because churches today exist in a similar world.

The city of Corinth was strategically located on the narrow neck of land (an isthmus) that connected mainland Greece and the Peloponnesus. It provided a natural stop-over for those enroute between Rome and the East. In addition, many trade routes converged on Corinth, and much cargo was transported overland through the city to avoid the long trip around the Peloponnesus. Old Corinth was destroyed in 146 BC by the Roman, L. Mummius Achaicus. Reconstructed in 44 BC by Julius Caesar, the city was given the status of a Roman colony. Shortly after its reconstruction, Corinth regained its commercial status and became one of the leading cities in all of Greece. Corinth enjoyed great wealth and prosperity during this period. It was the capital of the Roman province of Achaia.

This city was a melting pot of many nationalities. Old Corinth had been synonymous with debauchery and gross immorality. New Corinth soon took on the same characteristics. The vitally important city was intellectually proud, materially affluent, and morally corrupt. The prevailing philosophy in Corinth encouraged its people to indulge their desires, whatever they might be. Greed, dishonesty, drunkenness, impurity, lust, and selfishness of every kind flourished in Corinth. The Corinthians recognized no law but their own lusts and desires and no god but themselves.

When Paul came to Corinth, he stayed in the home of Aquila and Priscilla, Jews who had been expelled from Rome by the Emperor Claudius. They worked together through the week at the craft of tentmaking, and Paul preached in the synagogue every sabbath (Ac 18:4). Soon, however, legalistic Jews refused to allow Paul to teach in the synagogue, so he moved next door to the house of Justus and continued to preach the gospel (Ac 18:7).

Paul remained in Corinth for about a year and a half, and established a growing church (Ac 18:8,10). Apparently, the new congregation faced little threat of persecution. The membership was as cosmopolitan as the city itself and included some Jews (Ac 18:8,10), though the church was basically Gentile and ex-pagan in nature. Socially, the membership ranged from the very affluent city treasurer (Ro 16:23) to Jewish refugees (Ac 18:2) and former criminals (1 Co 6:9-11).

The completely anti-Christian religious and social environment created a great instability in the church. These new believers had little knowledge of the Old Testament and its preparation for the Christian gospel. For that reason, Paul went to great lengths to teach this group of infant believers. After Paul left Corinth, there was a strong attempt to undermine his authority. Pagan influences and practices engulfed the whole life of the church.

Paul's letter to the Corinthian church was written about AD 55 from Ephesus, during his third missionary journey. The immediate occasion for the letter was correspondence which the apostle Paul had received from Corinth (1 Co 7:1). He answered questions that had been asked in that letter about marriage and celibacy, food offered to idols, proper dress and responsibilities for women, public worship, spiritual gifts, and the resurrection of the dead. Paul endeavored to resolve the difficulties which these issues had caused in the church. See Introduction to 2 Corinthians.

Apart from the letter from the church in Corinth, Paul had other concerns. He also had received reports of disturbing behavior on the part of some of the believers in Corinth and of growing divisions in the church itself (1:11). Factions were forming. A hostile and quarrelsome spirit had developed. Some members of the church had actually taken civil matters to the pagan courts against other believers. Gross sexual impurity was common and condoned. The basic purpose of this letter was to correct the conduct and attitudes of many of these believers.

The pagan setting, out of which the members had come, offered and revealed little understanding of the Christian concept of the family. The Christian ideal and pagan permissiveness were in constant conflict. Should a Christian woman dress in the popular fashion which identified her with the immoral "Corinthian" women, or should she refuse to conform to social pressure? Should capable women take part in leading services of worship? The services of worship were sometimes disrupted by uncontrolled speaking in other "tongues." What guidelines should be followed in this matter? The concept of the resurrection of the dead was Jewish and foreign to the Greek mind, which had a notion of immortality but not the resurrection of the body. Who was right, Paul or Plato? As in the society around them, believers struggled with loyalties divided between gifted leaders. This often caused the rise of factions and groups within the fellowship of the church. How could this issue be resolved?

The big temptation was for each of these problems to be viewed in the secular and social setting. A strong word from the Lord was needed. First Corinthians is that strong and authoritative Word. Guidelines and principles are given that can direct us today in dealing with these same problems.

The apostle Paul had been the leader in the early days of the church at Corinth. He held a deep sense of responsibility for its members. He wanted to direct them away from pagan solutions and toward facing their problems in a godly and uniquely Christian manner. His call was for them to break completely with the pagan responses and reactions, and realize that Christ lived within them, that their bodies were a special temple of the Holy Spirit. Having pointed them toward distinctively Christian behavior, he instructed them in matters of doctrine so they would not fall into error.

Theological Outline

I. Salutation (1:1-3)
II. Thanksgiving for the Church's Testimony and Gifts and for God's Grace and Faithfulness (1:4-9)
III. A Call to Church Unity (1:10—4:21)
   A. The fact of divisions: Loyalty to human leaders rather than Christ (1:10-17)
   B. The causes of the divisions (1:18—4:5)
      1. Misconception of the Spirit's "foolish" message of the cross (1:18—3:4)
      2. Misconception of the ministry: No more boasting about humans (3:5—4:5)
   C. Personal application and conclusion: Imitate the "fools for Christ" (4:6-21)
IV. Incest (5:1-13)
   A. The problem (5:1)
   B. The lack of church discipline (5:2-8)
   C. Reminder of previous instruction: Do not associate with immoral persons (5:9-12)
   D. Final admonition: Expel the wicked (5:13)
V. Lawsuits before Pagans (6:1-11)
   A. The problem and the public shame (6:1-8)
   B. Sanctified heirs of the Kingdom are not immoral. (6:9-11)
VI. Fornication (6:12-20)
   A. Freedom is not my master. (6:12-14)
   B. Sanctity of believers' bodies as members of Christ (6:15-20)
VII. Marriage (7:1-40)
   A. Value of celibacy and marriage (7:1-9)
   B. Circumstances of marriage and divorce (7:10-16)
   C. Continuing in one's call (7:17-24)
   D. Celibacy superior for some (7:25-38)
   E. Advice to widows (7:39-40)
VIII. The Weaker Brother (8:1—11:1)
   A. General principle: Do not let your freedom cause others to stumble. (8:1-13)
   B. Flexibility and discipline needed to reach the lost (9:1-27)
   C. Application of the principles (10:1—11:1)
      1. Learn from history to overcome temptation. (10:1-13)
      2. The Lord's Supper separates Christians from idols. (10:14-22)
      3. Seek the good of others and the glory of God. (10:23—11:1)
IX. Conduct in Worship (11:2-16)
   A. Theological reason: Traditional teaching and the principle of the head (11:2-3)
   B. Biblical reason: The order of creation (11:4-12)
   C. Physical reason: Disregarding the natural way brings disgrace. (11:13-16)
X. The Abuse of the Lord's Supper (11:17-34)

A. Paul's indignation: Theological and social divisions bring no praise. (11:17-22)
B. Institution of the Lord's Supper (11:23-26)
C. Application to Corinthian Christians: Improper observance brings judgment. (11:27-34)

XI. The Abuse of Spiritual Gifts (12:1—14:40)
A. The validity and unity of the gifts to honor Christ and serve the common goal (12:1-11)
B. The diversity of spiritual gifts within the body (12:12-31*a*)
C. The gifts to be exercised in love (12:31*b*—13:13)
D. The proper use of gifts in public worship (14:1-36)
E. Conclusion: Let worship be orderly. (14:37-40)

XII. Heresy Concerning the Resurrection (15:1-58)
A. The resurrection of Christ (15:1-34)
1. The integral part of Christian faith (15:1-11)
2. Guarantee of believers' resurrection (15:12-34)
B. The nature of the resurrection body (15:35-57)
C. Concluding appeal: Remain faithful in God's work. (15:58)

XIII. Collection for the Poor (16:1-4)

XIV. Paul's Plans (16:5-12)

XV. Final Exhortation for Faithfulness and Courage (16:13-24)

Theological Conclusions

1. Christian faith calls for thoroughly Christian conduct by believers.
2. Gifted leaders should never be followed in such a way as to divide the church.
3. Our bodies are a special dwelling-place for the Holy Spirit. We should always recognize that truth and live consistently with His presence within us.
4. Marriage is a sacred relationship, and great care should be taken to maintain its strength.
5. Spiritual gifts are God's gracious provision for the church and are always to be exercised cooperatively in love.
6. One of the indispensable Christian distinctives is the hope of the resurrection of the dead.
7. Church discipline must be clearly understood and properly carried out by the church.

Contemporary Teaching

While this letter was designed to deal with specific needs in the church at Corinth, it has tremendous value for us. The hearts of people have not changed, and neither have the principles by which God works. Paul dealt with practical problems in such a way that we have strong principles and guidelines by which we can measure our lives and conduct and with which we can deal with difficulties facing us in a modern world. We face the same essential issues today, and we need the same sure word from God.

We have the same tendency to build factions around gifted leaders. This is a danger and temptation to avoid. With radio and television bringing so many leaders into our homes and with pastors and teachers receiving so much public exposure, this is a relevant problem. We dare not glorify humans. We should magnify only the cross of our Lord (1:17-31).

Our own very pagan and carnal society continually influences our lives. We should emphasize again the spiritual nature of our faith and be constantly reminded of the demands of the gospel for holy conduct and behavior by believers. Our bodies are sacred temples in which the Holy Spirit dwells.

Tremendous pressure is being brought against the home today. Immorality and unfaithfulness are commonplace. Serial marriages are becoming accepted as normal, and the prospects for the future seem to indicate a continuing lack of support for the Christian family. The teachings of 1 Corinthians concerning marriage and morality and the guidelines given by Paul need great emphasis in our society today.

One of the significant problems we face today is the abuse of spiritual gifts. This abuse threatens great harm to the church. Paul dealt openly and specifically with this area and gave strong direction that can protect the church and ensure maximum good from the use of these gifts in the church.

Paul's doctrinal teaching reminds us of the need for doctrinal purity in all ages. The great doctrines such as the resurrection of the dead are basic to every age. Proper understanding of doctrinal truth will keep us on the path of ministry and service to which God has called us and will keep us from becoming victims of cultic influences.

One of the great applications to us today is in the area of church discipline. High standards should be set and maintained for church membership. Certainly a high standard for membership must be a reality if we are to expect healthy church life and renewal in our day.

Chapter 1

PAUL, called to be an apostle[a] of Christ
Jesus by the will of God,[b] and our
brother Sosthenes,[c]

2 To the church of God[d] in Corinth,[e]
to those sanctified in Christ Jesus and
called[f] to be holy, together with all those
everywhere who call on the name[g] of
our Lord Jesus Christ—their Lord and
ours:

3 Grace and peace to you from God our
Father and the Lord Jesus Christ.[h]

Thanksgiving

4 I always thank God for you[i] because
of his grace given you in Christ Jesus.
5 For in him you have been enriched[j] in
every way—in all your speaking and in
all your knowledge[k]— 6 because our testimony[l] about Christ was confirmed in
you. 7 Therefore you do not lack any spiritual gift[m] as you eagerly wait for our Lord
Jesus Christ to be revealed.[n] 8 He will
keep you strong to the end, so that you
will be blameless[o] on the day of our Lord
Jesus Christ.[p] 9 God, who has called you[q]
into fellowship with his Son Jesus Christ
our Lord,[r] is faithful.[s]

Divisions in the Church

10 I appeal to you, brothers,[t] in the
name of our Lord Jesus Christ, that all of
you agree with one another so that there
may be no divisions among you[u] and that
you may be perfectly united[v] in mind
and thought. 11 My brothers, some from
Chloe's household[w] have informed me
that there are quarrels among you.
12 What I mean is this: One of you says, "I
follow Paul";[x] another, "I follow Apollos";[y] another, "I follow Cephas[a]";[z]
still another, "I follow Christ."

13 Is Christ divided? Was Paul crucified
for you? Were you baptized into[b] the
name of Paul?[a] 14 I am thankful that I did
not baptize any of you except Crispus[b]
and Gaius,[c] 15 so no one can say that you
were baptized into my name. 16 (Yes, I
also baptized the household[d] of Stephanas;[e] beyond that, I don't remember if I
baptized anyone else.) 17 For Christ did

1:1 [a]Ro 1:1; Eph 1:1; 2Ti 1:1 [b]S 2Co 1:1 [c]Ac 18:17 **1:2** [d]S 1Co 10:32 [e]S Ac 18:1 [f]Ro 1:7 [g]S Ac 2:21 **1:3** [h]S Ro 1:7 **1:4** [i]S Ro 1:8 **1:5** [j]2Co 9:11 [k]S 2Co 8:7 **1:6** [l]2Th 1:10; 1Ti 2:6; Rev 1:2 **1:7** [m]Ro 1:11; 1Co 12:1-31 [n]S Mt 16:27; S Lk 17:30; 1Th 1:10; S 2:19; Tit 2:13; Jas 5:7,8; 1Pe 1:13; 2Pe 3:12; S Rev 1:7 **1:8** [o]S 1Th 3:13 [p]Am 5:18; 1Co 5:5; Php 1:6,10; 2:16; 1Th 5:2 **1:9** [q]S Ro 8:28 [r]1Jn 1:3 [s]Dt 7:9; Isa 49:7; 1Co 10:13; 1Th 5:24; 2Th 3:3; 2Ti 2:13; Heb 10:23; 11:11 **1:10** [t]S Ro 7:1 [u]1Co 11:18 [v]S Ro 15:5 **1:11** [w]S Ac 11:14 **1:12** [x]1Co 3:4,22 [y]S Ac 18:24 [z]Jn 1:42; 1Co 3:22; 9:5 **1:13** [a]S Mt 28:19 **1:14** [b]Ac 18:8 [c]S Ac 19:29 **1:16** [d]S Ac 11:14 [e]1Co 16:15

[a] *12* That is, Peter [b] *13* Or *in*; also in verse 15

1:1 JESUS CHRIST, Lord—The risen Lord makes His church holy. See note on Ac 2:23–36.

1:2 THE CHURCH, Saints—The church consists of those who have been called out to serve Christ. "Church" usually designates a local body of believers. Geographically, this church was located in Corinth. Spiritually, the church is of God. For Paul, the church had its sole foundation in Christ who began His church and is its only Lord. Morally, the church is holy because members have been made holy by Christ and live pure lives for Him. Thus, church members are saints or holy ones. That saints are not super Christians in a separate category from others is clearly shown here. Paul addressed the Corinthians as holy or saints, then dealt with all their moral and spiritual problems. Saints are all Christians in all churches in every place. See note on Ro 1:7.

1:2 PRAYER, In Jesus' Name—Prayer history was born when, at the birth of Enosh, men began to "call on the name of the Lord." See note on Ge 4:26. In the New Testament, Christians call on the name of the Lord Jesus Christ. That prayer distinctively separates Christians from all other religious people.

1:3,4,9 GOD, Trinity—The references here to God the Father and to Jesus the Son might lead you to believe they are two separate divine persons, and thus two gods. We must read this and all Bible texts in the context of the trinitarian understanding: one God is made known to us in three Persons. We must retain both the unity and the plurality in our understanding of God. See note on Mt 3:16–17.

1:3–4 PRAYER, Blessing—See notes on Ac 28:15; Ro 1:7.

1:5,30 SALVATION, As Being in Christ—Those who are in Christ find Him to be their all in all, their everything. Every aspect of life is changed for those in Christ.

1:6 EVANGELISM, Testimony—One's testimony needs to be confirmed by the Holy Spirit and the fruit of actual conversions to attest to its validity.

1:7–8 JESUS CHRIST, Final Coming—The last days will reveal the full glory of Jesus, who keeps us strong as we wait for Him.

1:7–8 LAST THINGS, Return Attitudes—Paul stressed an eager waiting for the Lord's return as the attitude of Christians. As we wait, we are to be faithful ministers, using our gifts in God's service. The quality and enthusiasm of Christian service is greatly enhanced by a vital, personal anticipation of Christ's return. "The day of our Lord Jesus Christ" is a reference to His revelation at the second coming. See note on Zep 1:14—2:3.

1:9 GOD, Faithfulness—The gods of the nations in biblical times were fickle, undependable, changeable, and moody. In sharp contrast, the biblical writers picture God's faithfulness to His promises and to His people. God has given His people the spiritual gifts they need to endure faithfully to the end. We can count on God to continue to supply our needs and to bring the final victory He promised.

1:9–10 THE CHURCH, Fellowship—Fellowship with Jesus Christ is the church's distinctive mark. Fellowship (Greek *koinōnia*) describes partners who share a close unity or fellowship. The church has this unity created by Christ through the Spirit. The fellowship led church members to help one another in spiritual and economic difficulties. Fellowship does not represent an organization or a group. It represents the relationship between the believer and God and among believers. Such relationships are not possible through human achievements. God transforms Christians and makes fellowship possible. Fellowship in Christ should produce perfect unity among church members. See note on Ro 15:5–7.

1:13–17 ORDINANCES, Baptism as Unity—The church members in Corinth were splitting into factions and claiming Paul, or Cephas, or Apollos, or even Christ as their leader. In so doing they were actually trying to divide the body of Christ. Paul appealed to the fact that all of them had been baptized in the name of Christ to demonstrate their unity. The name pronounced over them in baptism meant that they belonged to Jesus, not to some earthly leader. In a shocking comment, Paul expressed thanks that he did not baptize many of them lest they use this to claim a special status of being in Paul's party. Paul even declared that Christ did not send him to baptize but to preach the gospel. Paul did baptize and approved baptism, but only as a secondary step. The primary importance belonged to preaching and believing the gospel of Jesus Christ, because, without that, baptism would be meaningless.

1:17 JESUS CHRIST, Ascension—The ascended Lord directs the work of His ministering people.

1:17 HUMANITY, Intellectual Nature—The biblical revelation places a major emphasis upon the proper value and use

not send me to baptize,[f] but to preach
the gospel—not with words of human
wisdom,[g] lest the cross of Christ be emptied of its power.

Christ the Wisdom and Power of God

18For the message of the cross is foolishness[h] to those who are perishing,[i]
but to us who are being saved[j] it is the
power of God.[k] 19For it is written:

"I will destroy the wisdom of the wise;
the intelligence of the intelligent I
will frustrate."[c] [l]

20Where is the wise man?[m] Where is
the scholar? Where is the philosopher of
this age?[n] Has not God made foolish[o]
the wisdom of the world? 21For since in
the wisdom of God the world[p] through
its wisdom did not know him, God was
pleased through the foolishness of what
was preached to save[q] those who believe.[r] 22Jews demand miraculous signs[s]
and Greeks look for wisdom, 23but we
preach Christ crucified:[t] a stumbling
block[u] to Jews and foolishness[v] to Gentiles, 24but to those whom God has
called,[w] both Jews and Greeks, Christ the
power of God[x] and the wisdom of God.[y]
25For the foolishness[z] of God is wiser
than man's wisdom, and the weakness[a]
of God is stronger than man's strength.
26Brothers, think of what you were
when you were called.[b] Not many of you
were wise[c] by human standards; not
many were influential; not many were of
noble birth. 27But God chose[d] the foolish[e] things of the world to shame the
wise; God chose the weak things of the
world to shame the strong. 28He chose
the lowly things of this world and the de-

1:17 [f]Jn 4:2; S Ac 2:38 [g]1Co 2:1,4,13
1:18 [h]ver 21,23,25; 1Co 2:14 [i]2Co 2:15; 4:3; 2Th 2:10 [j]Ac 2:47 [k]ver 24; Ro 1:16
1:19 [l]Isa 29:14
1:20 [m]Isa 19:11,12 [n]1Co 2:6,8; 3:18; 2Co 4:4; Gal 1:4 [o]ver 27; Job 12:17; Isa 44:25; Jer 8:9; Ro 1:22; 1Co 3:18,19
1:21 [p]ver 27,28; 1Co 6:2; 11:32 [q]S Ro 11:14 [r]S Ro 3:22
1:22 [s]S Mt 12:38; S Jn 2:11; S 4:48
1:23 [t]1Co 2:2; Gal 3:1 [u]S Lk 2:34 [v]S ver 18
1:24 [w]S Ro 8:28 [x]ver 18; Ro 1:16 [y]ver 30; S Col 2:3
1:25 [z]S ver 18 [a]2Co 13:4
1:26 [b]S Ro 8:28 [c]ver 20
1:27 [d]Jas 2:5 [e]ver 20; Ro 1:22; 1Co 3:18,19

[c]*19* Isaiah 29:14

---

of human wisdom. Fundamentally, however, the gospel is most effectively communicated as a spiritual truth, recognizing the limitations of human intellect.

1:17–18 PROCLAMATION, Call—See notes on 2:1–5; Jer 1:4–9; Heb 4:2. The call to proclaim is a call to depend on God, not to show off human wisdom in pride.

1:18–25 GOD, Power—We can measure the power of God in many ways. Some ways are biblical; others are not. Faith recognizes that the greatest demonstration of God's power is in the salvation He brought to us. Only God's power can transform a broken, sinful life into a rich and full life patterned after the very life of Christ. Only His power can guarantee eternal life which death cannot touch. To talk of power in such ways sounds foolish to unbelievers. Only God's revelation lets us recognize Christ's atoning death as the epitome of power.

1:18–19 HUMANITY, Intellectual Nature—Human wisdom is limited when it comes to understanding the ways of God. To the unaided human intellect, God's provision of salvation is utter folly.

1:18 SALVATION, Definition—Salvation is God's atonement for sin through the cross of Christ (15:3). That message is the dynamite (Greek *dunamis*) of God which transforms those who are being saved. Paul spoke here of salvation in the present tense. God's salvation is past (justification), present (sanctification), and future (glorification). God has acted to save us, and we have accepted salvation through faith in the past. We are experiencing salvation daily through the power of the Spirit in the present. We will know the fullness of salvation at the resurrection.

1:18–25 PROCLAMATION, Unbelievers—See notes on Ac 20:20–21; 26:19–29.

1:18–31 EDUCATION, Spiritual Renewal—One kind of preaching, teaching, and learning emphasizes elegant language and scintillating ideas but is devoid of spiritual energy. It can be entertaining or boringly dull. In either case, it fails to transform lives. Authentic Christian teaching does not bypass the intellect. It is predicated upon the assumption that a rational understanding of the faith must be infused with the spiritual power that reaches to the roots of personality and causes the Word to become flesh. See note on Ro 12:2. The preaching of the gospel is "foolishness" only in the sense that unredeemed people regard it so. Paul neither confessed to foolishness nor advocated it. He certainly was not arguing for an uneducated ministry. Nor was he denouncing education in general. Human knowledge is not opposed to the wisdom of God. It simply falls short of the spiritual understanding that comes through Jesus Christ.

1:20–25 HUMANITY, Intellectual Nature—Some people praise human intellect and exalt themselves because of accomplishments. Others look for supernatural signs to point to the way of God. But divine wisdom is from another nature than the human intellect and cannot be comprehended without divine aid.

1:21–30 GOD, Wisdom—The wisdom of God goes beyond the highest point of human wisdom. Human philosophies would never have thought up the Christian gospel of salvation through Jesus Christ. Those persons who have been saved by the grace of God have seen that true wisdom which comes from God. God Himself is not known by human wisdom, nor is He found at the end of an argument. God is known only when He reveals Himself and we respond to that revelation in faith. Christ is the outward expression of the wisdom of God. See Isa 55:8–9.

1:21 REVELATION, Word—God communicates Himself and His purposes in many ways to a world which does not know Him. God did not use human wisdom as His major means of revelation. He chose what appears to the world to be foolish announcements to save those who humbly believe. Ironically in a sophisticated world which worships wisdom, God uses simple and seemingly foolish ways to reveal the greatest wisdom of all to all who will see and respond (2:7).

1:21 SALVATION, Definition—God's salvation comes to the world through preaching the message of Christ crucified on the cross for our sins. That Christ-centered message is the wisdom of God. Those who believe it in their hearts will be saved. Salvation, then, comes through hearing good news about Christ and committing oneself to the message (Ro 10:9).

1:21–25 EVANGELISM, Gospel—Christian preaching has a basic content summarizing the gospel. The Greek word *kērygma* is used to indicate this basic core of what is preached. It centers on Jesus Christ. The *kērygma* has several vital elements: (1) Jesus is the Messiah; (2) He lived a marvelous, victorious, sinless life doing good; (3) He died on the cross in our place to pay the penalty of our sins; (4) He was bodily raised from the dead; (5) He is coming again to end this present evil age; (6) He calls all people to repentance and faith; and (7) He promises forgiveness, redemption, the gift of the Holy Spirit, and eternal life. The world calls the *kērygma* foolishness. Believers know it is God's wise way leading to salvation. See note on Ac 2:17–40.

1:22 MIRACLE, Vocabulary—Jews always sought for signs during the ministry of Jesus—signs that God was at work, signs to prove relationship with God. They refused, however, to let Christ's miraculous signs point them to God. In contrast Paul, though having performed signs himself, insisted that preaching Christ was more important. Miracles are without purpose if they do not lead to faith commitment to Christ.

1:23 JESUS CHRIST, Death—Christ's death as the way to salvation does not fit a logical system of human argument. It

spised things—and the things that are
not[f]—to nullify the things that are, 29so
that no one may boast before him.[g] 30It is
because of him that you are in Christ
Jesus,[h] who has become for us wisdom
from God—that is, our righteousness,[i]
holiness[j] and redemption.[k] 31Therefore,
as it is written: "Let him who boasts
boast in the Lord."[d] [l]

Chapter 2

WHEN I came to you, brothers, I did
not come with eloquence or superior wisdom[m] as I proclaimed to you the
testimony about God.[e] 2For I resolved to
know nothing while I was with you except Jesus Christ and him crucified.[n] 3I
came to you[o] in weakness[p] and fear, and
with much trembling.[q] 4My message and
my preaching were not with wise and
persuasive words,[r] but with a demonstration of the Spirit's power,[s] 5so that
your faith might not rest on men's wisdom, but on God's power.[t]

Wisdom From the Spirit

6We do, however, speak a message of
wisdom among the mature,[u] but not the
wisdom of this age[v] or of the rulers of
this age, who are coming to nothing.[w]
7No, we speak of God's secret wisdom, a
wisdom[x] that has been hidden[y] and that
God destined for our glory before time
began. 8None of the rulers of this age[z]
understood it, for if they had, they would
not have crucified the Lord of glory.[a]
9However, as it is written:

"No eye has seen,
  no ear has heard,
 no mind has conceived

1:28 [f]Ro 4:17 **1:29** [g]Eph 2:9 **1:30** [h]S Ro 16:3 [i]Jer 23:5,6; 33:16; 2Co 5:21; Php 3:9 [j]1Co 1:2 [k]S Ro 3:24 **1:31** [l]Jer 9:23,24; Ps 34:2; 44:8; 2Co 10:17 **2:1** [m]ver 4,13; 1Co 1:17 **2:2** [n]Gal 6:14; 1Co 1:23 **2:3** [o]Ac 18:1-18 [p]1Co 4:10; 9:22; 2Co 11:29,30; 12:5,9,10; 13:9 [q]S 2Co 7:15 **2:4** [r]ver 1 [s]S Ro 15:13 **2:5** [t]2Co 4:7; 6:7 **2:6** [u]Eph 4:13; Php 3:15; Col 4:12; Heb 5:14; 6:1; Jas 1:4 [v]ver 8; S 1Co 1:20 [w]Ps 146:4 **2:7** [x]ver 1 [y]Ro 16:25 **2:8** [z]ver 6; S 1Co 1:20 [a]Ps 24:7; Ac 7:2; Jas 2:1

[d]*31* Jer. 9:24 [e]*1* Some manuscripts *as I proclaimed to you God's mystery*

represents God's wise way of reaching all people for salvation without requiring human accomplishments.

1:26–30 HUMANITY, Potentiality—God surprises us. He works through people without worldly qualifications. No one can boast of attaining or deserving a position with God. Still God takes us in His service and works through us to amaze those who claim proper credentials for success.

1:27–29 ELECTION, Righteousness—Election is not by human standards. God chose the foolish things of this world to shame the wise and accomplish His purpose. The weak and despised are chosen by God to receive righteousness, holiness, and redemption in Jesus Christ. The goal of election remains a holy, obedient people.

1:30 JESUS CHRIST, Wisdom of God—God's wisdom is not seen in human argument but in a person—Jesus Christ. What He has done cannot be argued away. He has made it possible for us to be seen as morally pure, set free from sin, and in right relationship with God.

1:30 SALVATION, Redemption—Christ Jesus became our redemption. He paid the penalty for our sins on the cross and released us from our slavery to sin. In Christ we are accounted righteous by God, just as if we had never sinned. We are viewed as holy just as God is holy. These words describe our present state in Christ.

2:1–5 PROCLAMATION, Clarity—See note on Ac 3:11–26. Proclamation should be simple and transparent. The desired result of preaching is repentance and faith. The message is not to be obscured with eloquent words and confusing rhetoric. Paul refused to use clever language or to manipulate God's Word. He presented the gospel with a simple and open statement of truth (2 Co 4:1–6). He depended on the Spirit's power to change lives. This dramatic change in the heart and life of the individual, which comes when one is saved, does not come about by the emotional power of enticing words but by the simple, straightforward presentation of the gospel in all its clarity and power. Attention must be focused on the Word, not on the proclaimer. Compare 1 Co 1:17–18; Gal 1:6–12; Eph 3:8–9.

2:2 PROCLAMATION, Central Theme—The heart of the gospel is Jesus Christ. Everything we preach centers in Him. The focal point of His ministry is His substitutionary death on the cross (Ro 5:8; Gal 3:13; 1 Ti 2:6). The lost have no other way to be saved (Ac 4:12), so the proclaimer must always seek to magnify and lift up the Lord Jesus Christ. Only in Jesus Christ can saved individuals be united. People are not saved by accepting a system of theological propositions, but by receiving Jesus Christ as Lord and Savior. He must always be the central theme of our proclamation (Ac 8:35; 1 Ti 3:16; 2 Ti 1:8–11; 2 Pe 1:16–21).

2:4–5 GOD, Power—The wisdom and the power of the gospel that changes people's lives comes from above, from God, not from humans. The implication of this is that we must be careful not to try to substitute human wisdom and power for the authentic power of God. See note on 1:21–30.

2:4–5 HOLY SPIRIT, Mission—The Spirit empowers God's people to carry out the world missionary task. Paul and all other evangelists do this work, not with the persuasive power of words as men of the world use, but with the power of the Spirit. This power of the Spirit, which is in fact the power of God (v 10), consists precisely in the content of the message about Christ, for the gospel is the power of God (Ro 1:16). By reminding the church of our Lord Jesus Christ, the Spirit empowers the church to do evangelistic work.

2:6–16 GOD, Trinity—The Father-Creator in His eternal wisdom planned salvation before time began. Christ the Lord was crucified to provide that salvation. The Spirit is present among us to teach us the wisdom of God's salvation and how to communicate this to others. He gives us the mind of Christ. The three Persons who make up the godhead are so intertwined in the work of salvation we cannot really separate them, except in theory. Both the unity—the oneness of God—and the diversity or plurality of the three Persons who make up our understanding of God must be kept in view. To lose either side of this polarity of one-yet-three is to lose the distinctively Christian understanding of God. See note on Mt 3:16–17.

2:7 HISTORY, Time—Humanity and the world are not eternal. Time itself has a beginning. Time is not meaningless repetition or unending emptiness. Time is the arena of God's actions to reveal His glory and bring us to our eternal salvation.

2:8 JESUS CHRIST, Glory—"Lord of glory" combines two titles normally associated with God and applies them to Christ. See notes on Jn 11:4; Ac 2:23–36. Human wisdom led to condemning to death the One who in His personal presence revealed God in all His glory.

2:9–14 HOLY SPIRIT, Revelation—Before Christ came, no one knew God's great purpose. It was a secret, hidden from everyone. This meant that the meaning of life and history were utterly mysterious. God has revealed His purposes through Jesus, who was crucified and raised by God (v 2). That purpose was to gather together a great family of God made up of all kinds of people with Christ as head (Eph 1:9–10). The Spirit takes the message of Christ and makes it come alive for the church, revealing the hidden purpose of God. The Spirit is able to reveal God's purpose because He is the One who knows God's thoughts. The Spirit is not with the world, so the world does not know God's purpose at all. It seems foolish to the world that God would allow His Son to die to bring together

what God has prepared for those
who love him"[f] [b]—

10but God has revealed[c] it to us by his
Spirit.[d]
The Spirit searches all things, even the
deep things of God. 11For who among
men knows the thoughts of a man[e] except the man's spirit[f] within him? In the
same way no one knows the thoughts of
God except the Spirit of God. 12We have
not received the spirit[g] of the world[h] but
the Spirit who is from God, that we may
understand what God has freely given us.
13This is what we speak, not in words
taught us by human wisdom[i] but in
words taught by the Spirit, expressing
spiritual truths in spiritual words.[g] 14The
man without the Spirit does not accept
the things that come from the Spirit of
God,[j] for they are foolishness[k] to him,
and he cannot understand them, because
they are spiritually discerned. 15The spiritual[l] man makes judgments about all
things, but he himself is not subject to
any man's judgment:

16"For who has known the mind of the Lord
that he may instruct him?"[h] [m]

But we have the mind of Christ.[n]

2:9 [b]Isa 64:4; 65:17
2:10 [c]S Mt 13:11; 2Co 12:1,7; Gal 1:12; 2:2; Eph 3:3,5 [d]Jn 14:26
2:11 [e]Jer 17:9 [f]Pr 20:27
2:12 [g]Ro 8:15 [h]1Co 1:20,27; Jas 2:5
2:13 [i]ver 1,4; 1Co 1:17
2:14 [j]Jn 14:17 [k]S 1Co 1:18
2:15 [l]1Co 3:1; Gal 6:1
2:16 [m]Isa 40:13; S Ro 11:34 [n]Jn 15:15
3:1 [o]1Co 2:15 [p]Ro 7:14; 1Co 2:14 [q]1Co 14:20
3:2 [r]Heb 5:12-14; 1Pe 2:2 [s]Jn 16:12
3:3 [t]Ro 13:13; 1Co 1:11; Gal 5:20
3:4 [u]1Co 1:12
3:5 [v]S Ac 18:24 [w]1Co 4:1; 2Co 6:4; Eph 3:7; Col 1:23, 25
3:6 [x]Ac 18:4-11; 1Co 4:15; 9:1; 15:1
3:8 [y]ver 14; Ps 18:20; 62:12; Mt 25:21; 1Co 9:17
3:9 [z]Mk 16:20; 2Co 6:1; 1Th 3:2 [a]Isa 61:3 [b]Eph 2:20-22; 1Pe 2:5
3:10 [c]S Ro 12:3

Chapter 3

On Divisions in the Church

BROTHERS, I could not address you as
spiritual[o] but as worldly[p]—mere infants[q] in Christ. 2I gave you milk, not
solid food,[r] for you were not yet ready
for it.[s] Indeed, you are still not ready.
3You are still worldly. For since there is
jealousy and quarreling[t] among you, are
you not worldly? Are you not acting like
mere men? 4For when one says, "I follow
Paul," and another, "I follow Apollos,"[u]
are you not mere men?
5What, after all, is Apollos?[v] And what
is Paul? Only servants,[w] through whom
you came to believe—as the Lord has assigned to each his task. 6I planted the
seed,[x] Apollos watered it, but God made
it grow. 7So neither he who plants nor he
who waters is anything, but only God,
who makes things grow. 8The man who
plants and the man who waters have one
purpose, and each will be rewarded according to his own labor.[y] 9For we are
God's fellow workers;[z] you are God's
field,[a] God's building.[b]
10By the grace God has given me,[c] I

[f] *9* Isaiah 64:4 [g] *13* Or *Spirit, interpreting spiritual truths to spiritual men* [h] *16* Isaiah 40:13

Jews and Gentiles to be His people. The church knows this mystery and speaks about it with a language the world calls foolish, but which the Spirit reveals as the truth of God. God gave the Spirit to the church to do this revealing work. It consists especially of reminding the church about the crucified and risen Lord and helping the church to trace out the implications of Christ's life, death, and resurrection. The revealing activity of the Spirit within the church does not consist so much of dreams (as for Joseph), visions (Ezekiel), or oracles (Micah) as it does of keeping the church's attention focused on Christ and raising the consciousness of the church concerning the ultimacy and completeness of the divine revelation given in Christ.

2:9–12 REVELATION, Spirit—The Spirit of God is vital in all revelation. He works in the deeper things of life and understands the depths of human existence as no one else can. As the human spirit within us understands us better than anyone else can, so the Holy Spirit knows and understands the thoughts and mind of God as no one else. The free and awesome gift of God is His Spirit in us, that we might understand the truth and being of God and know His ways.

2:9 SALVATION, Love of God—Compare Isa 64:4. Those who love Christ can count on a storehouse of wonderful surprises because God loves us.

2:13–16 HUMANITY, Spiritual Nature—The spiritual nature responds to God's revelation rather than to the human intellect. Human intellect may grow and develop upon the foundation of the Spirit, but the spiritual nature develops only as God's Spirit lives and works in us. Unspiritual people laugh at our "foolishness" because they do not have the Spirit.

2:16 JESUS CHRIST, Wisdom of God—Humans cannot know everything God knows and plans. Christians can have the Spirit to reveal Christ's mind in a specific decision. The ascended Lord continues to help His followers have the proper point of view toward life.

3:1–9 PROCLAMATION, Proclaimer—*See notes on Ac 26:19–29; Col 1:3–6;* 2 Ti 3:14–17. The proclaimer must proclaim what the audience needs and is able to understand. Paul could preach only about the basics of the faith in Corinth because of their immaturity in the faith. Each proclaimer must find the task for which God has provided gifts and opportunity. Proclaimers are not in competition with one another.

3:5–6 ELECTION, Leadership—Because the elect are in Christ, they are unified. Unity is built on Christ. God's elected leaders each have an assigned task. No leader has reason for personal boasting.

3:5 EVANGELISM, Involves—Christians are to accept their position in evangelism. We have no power in ourselves to save anyone. We are only servants, called to share the message and ministry of evangelization so people will look to Christ and be saved (4:1–2).

3:9 DISCIPLESHIP, Laity—All Christian disciples are God's fellow workers. None is left out, and all are needed. The abilities and the expertise of the laity are needed in the ministry of the church today. Not all serve in the same way, but all are called to serve in some way. Paul pictured the church as a body with many members and with every member having a distinct and distinctive task. See Ro 12:4–5; 1 Co 12:27–31. A witnessing and serving laity is essential to a functioning and growing church. The challenges are great. Too few workers produce too many burnt-out ministers. Shared ministry was the answer for Moses' busy days (Ex 18:13–24), for Jesus' growing ministry (Mk 3:13–15), for the growing needs of the early church (Ac 6:1–7), and for the busy pastor in a changing culture today. Christ still is the Head of the church. He still can and will use all of His disciples in His extended ministry. See notes on Mk 10:41–45; Ro 16:1–3; Personal Spiritual Inventory, pp. 1751–1753.

3:10 GOD, Grace—Effectiveness in Christian work is due more to God's work through us than to our own efforts. Paul had every reason to boast of his missionary, evangelistic work. Instead he proclaimed God's grace given him to lay a foundation on which others will build.

3:10–15 THE CHURCH, People of God—Church growth is a team effort which should not produce jealousy. Paul began Christian work at Corinth (Ac 18:1–11). Apollos and others led in the church's development (1 Co 3:1–9). Glory belonged only to Christ, who made the church possible.

laid a foundation[d] as an expert builder,
and someone else is building on it. But
each one should be careful how he
builds. 11For no one can lay any foundation other than the one already laid,
which is Jesus Christ.[e] 12If any man
builds on this foundation using gold, silver, costly stones, wood, hay or straw,
13his work will be shown for what it is,[f]
because the Day[g] will bring it to light. It
will be revealed with fire, and the fire
will test the quality of each man's work.[h]
14If what he has built survives, he will
receive his reward.[i] 15If it is burned up,
he will suffer loss; he himself will be
saved, but only as one escaping through
the flames.[j]

16Don't you know that you yourselves
are God's temple[k] and that God's Spirit
lives in you?[l] 17If anyone destroys God's
temple, God will destroy him; for God's
temple is sacred, and you are that temple.

18Do not deceive yourselves. If any one
of you thinks he is wise[m] by the standards of this age,[n] he should become a
"fool" so that he may become wise. 19For
the wisdom of this world is foolishness[o]
in God's sight. As it is written: "He
catches the wise in their craftiness"[i];[p]
20and again, "The Lord knows that the
thoughts of the wise are futile."[j][q] 21So
then, no more boasting about men![r] All
things are yours,[s] 22whether Paul or
Apollos[t] or Cephas[k][u] or the world or
life or death or the present or the future[v]—all are yours, 23and you are of
Christ,[w] and Christ is of God.

Chapter 4

Apostles of Christ

So then, men ought to regard us as servants[x] of Christ and as those entrusted[y] with the secret things[z] of God.
2Now it is required that those who have
been given a trust must prove faithful. 3I
care very little if I am judged by you or by
any human court; indeed, I do not even
judge myself. 4My conscience[a] is clear,
but that does not make me innocent.[b] It
is the Lord who judges me.[c] 5Therefore
judge nothing[d] before the appointed
time; wait till the Lord comes.[e] He will
bring to light[f] what is hidden in darkness and will expose the motives of

[i] *19* Job 5:13 [j] *20* Psalm 94:11 [k] *22* That is, Peter

3:10 [d]Ro 15:20; S Eph 2:20
3:11 [e]Isa 28:16; Eph 2:20
3:13 [f]1Co 4:5 [g]S 1Co 1:8; 2Th 1:7-10; 2Ti 1:12,18; 4:8 [h]Nu 31:22,23; Jer 23:28,29; Mal 3:3; S 2Th 1:7
3:14 [i]S ver 8
3:15 [j]Jude 23
3:16 [k]1Co 6:19; 2Co 6:16; Eph 2:21, 22; Heb 3:6 [l]S Ro 8:9
3:18 [m]Isa 5:21; 1Co 8:2; Gal 6:3 [n]S 1Co 1:20
3:19 [o]ver 18; Ro 1:22; 1Co 1:20, 27 [p]Job 5:13
3:20 [q]Ps 94:11
3:21 [r]1Co 4:6 [s]Ro 8:32
3:22 [t]ver 5,6 [u]S 1Co 1:12 [v]Ro 8:38
3:23 [w]1Co 15:23; 2Co 10:7; Gal 3:29
4:1 [x]S 1Co 3:5 [y]1Co 9:17; Tit 1:7 [z]S Ro 16:25
4:4 [a]S Ac 23:1 [b]Ro 2:13 [c]2Co 10:18
4:5 [d]S Mt 7:1,2 [e]S 1Th 2:19 [f]Job 12:22; Ps 90:8; 1Co 3:13

God gives churches different leaders with different gifts. Christian leaders must not compete with one another but work together to serve Christ. Christ will reward leaders whose work stands His test. All other work faces destruction.

3:11 JESUS CHRIST, Savior—Jesus in His death and resurrection did all that was necessary to make salvation available. We can add nothing to what He did. We need simply to trust Him for salvation. See note on Ac 13:23.

3:12–15 LAST THINGS, Judgment—The "day" in view is that described in 1 Co 1:8 as the second coming of Christ. His coming includes judgment, and here the plain statement is that the works of believers will be tested. The basis for testing is the quality of the work, not its quantity. Reward is promised those whose service is of enduring quality. The loss in view is that of rewards, not of salvation or one's soul. The nature of the reward itself is not specified.

3:15–17 ELECTION, Condemnation—God's Spirit dwells in the elect, God's temple. The elect must preserve their sacredness as God's temple to escape the wrath of God's destruction.

3:15 SALVATION, Definition—God's salvation is without end. Those Christians who do not build wisely upon the foundation of Jesus Christ will not be rewarded for their flimsy works, but they will indeed be saved. This text teaches the eternal security of the believer. It also encourages cooperation within the church to build as well as possible for God.

3:16 HOLY SPIRIT, Church—Solomon built the first Temple as a house for God. God's cloud showed He was present in it (1 Ki 8:10–13). Yet Israel always recognized that in some sense God's presence is elusive. God does not dwell in houses made with hands. He lives in the highest heaven and yet also in humble hearts (Isa 57:15). The early church continued to worship at the Temple in Jerusalem (Ac 3:1), yet they knew that in a true sense God did not dwell there, but in the hearts of His people. His people—the church—form the temple of God. The pronouns in 1 Co 3:16 are plural referring to the church, not to an individual. See 6:19. In His church God is always present as Holy Spirit. The one Spirit builds one church. Leaders who would divide the church oppose the Spirit.

3:16–17 SIN, Discipline—Paul described the church as God's Temple and reminded his readers that undermining the work of God in His church is a grevious sin. God intervenes to protect His church.

3:16–17 THE CHURCH, People of God—The church as a collective group of believers can be called God's temple. This applies the Old Testament experience of the Temple as the place where God lived and met His people to the New Testament church, a group of believers with various geographical locations. God cannot be located geographically, but He can be represented personally by a member in whom the Spirit lives. Members have a sacred duty to live as God directs and protect the unity of God's temple. Members who sow dissension and discord in the church must take seriously God's threat of destruction.

4:4 GOD, Judge—Thinking I am innocent does not make me so. God is the only Judge. We should not worry about how people judge us, nor should we appoint ourselves judges over others. We should seek to be ready for the day of His judgment.

4:4–5 JESUS CHRIST, Judgment—Christ is the final Judge who will reveal human motives. He has not called us to be judges of any other person.

4:4 HUMANITY, Moral Consciousness—The human conscience is not as sensitive to sin as God is. The Greek text literally says, "nothing against myself I know." Our moral consciousness may reveal sin and evoke guilt. If our conscience does not convict us of sin, we cannot claim innocence. We need to tune our consciousness to God's wave length concerning sin.

4:5 HISTORY, Judgment—God has a time for final judgment, a time begun by Christ's return. Humans do not have a time to be judges. That is God's role.

4:5 LAST THINGS, Judgment—Final judgment awaits the Lord's return. Accurate judgment requires the ability to know and take into account that which has been done in secrecy from human eyes. It requires that motives behind the outward acts be taken into consideration. The positive aspect of final judgment is that praise will be given the worthy just as condemnation will be given the unworthy. The warning is clear that motives for service and ministry will be clear to God and a major factor in His judgment.

men's hearts. At that time each will receive his praise from God.[g]
6Now, brothers, I have applied these
things to myself and Apollos for your benefit, so that you may learn from us the
meaning of the saying, "Do not go beyond what is written."[h] Then you will
not take pride in one man over against
another.[i] 7For who makes you different
from anyone else? What do you have that
you did not receive?[j] And if you did receive it, why do you boast as though you
did not?

8Already you have all you want! Already you have become rich![k] You have
become kings—and that without us! How
I wish that you really had become kings
so that we might be kings with you! 9For
it seems to me that God has put us apostles on display at the end of the procession, like men condemned to die[l] in the
arena. We have been made a spectacle[m]
to the whole universe, to angels as well as
to men. 10We are fools for Christ,[n] but
you are so wise in Christ![o] We are weak,
but you are strong![p] You are honored, we
are dishonored! 11To this very hour we go
hungry and thirsty, we are in rags, we are
brutally treated, we are homeless.[q] 12We
work hard with our own hands.[r] When
we are cursed, we bless;[s] when we are
persecuted,[t] we endure it; 13when we
are slandered, we answer kindly. Up to
this moment we have become the scum
of the earth, the refuse[u] of the world.

14I am not writing this to shame you,[v]
but to warn you, as my dear children.[w]
15Even though you have ten thousand
guardians in Christ, you do not have
many fathers, for in Christ Jesus I became
your father[x] through the gospel.[y]
16Therefore I urge you to imitate me.[z]
17For this reason I am sending to you[a]
Timothy,[b] my son[c] whom I love, who is
faithful in the Lord. He will remind you of
my way of life in Christ Jesus, which
agrees with what I teach everywhere in
every church.[d]
18Some of you have become arrogant,[e]
as if I were not coming to you.[f] 19But I
will come to you very soon,[g] if the Lord
is willing,[h] and then I will find out not
only how these arrogant people are talking, but what power they have. 20For the
kingdom of God is not a matter of[i] talk
but of power.[j] 21What do you prefer?
Shall I come to you with a whip,[k] or in
love and with a gentle spirit?

Chapter 5

Expel the Immoral Brother!

IT is actually reported that there is sexual immorality among you, and of a kind
that does not occur even among pagans:
A man has his father's wife.[l] 2And you
are proud! Shouldn't you rather have
been filled with grief[m] and have put out
of your fellowship[n] the man who did
this? 3Even though I am not physically
present, I am with you in spirit.[o] And I
have already passed judgment on the one
who did this, just as if I were present.
4When you are assembled in the name of
our Lord Jesus[p] and I am with you in
spirit, and the power of our Lord Jesus is
present, 5hand this man over[q] to Satan,[r]

4:5 [g]S Ro 2:29
4:6 [h]1Co 1:19,31; 3:19,20 [i]1Co 1:12; 3:4
4:7 [j]Jn 3:27; Ro 12:3,6
4:8 [k]Rev 3:17,18
4:9 [l]S Ro 8:36 [m]Ps 71:7; Heb 10:33
4:10 [n]S 1Co 1:18; Ac 17:18; 26:24 [o]1Co 3:18; 2Co 11:19 [p]S 1Co 2:3
4:11 [q]Ro 8:35; 2Co 11:23-27
4:12 [r]S Ac 18:3 [s]Ro 12:14; 1Pe 3:9 [t]S Mt 5:44
4:13 [u]Jer 20:18; La 3:45
4:14 [v]1Co 6:5; 15:34; 2Th 3:14 [w]S 1Th 2:11
4:15 [x]S ver 14 [y]1Co 9:12,14,18, 23; 15:1
4:16 [z]1Co 11:1; Php 3:17; 4:9; 1Th 1:6; 2Th 3:7,9
4:17 [a]1Co 16:10 [b]S Ac 16:1 [c]S 1Ti 1:2 [d]S 1Co 7:17
4:18 [e]Jer 43:2 [f]ver 21
4:19 [g]1Co 16:5,6; 2Co 1:15,16 [h]S Ac 18:21
4:20 [i]Ro 14:17 [j]S Ro 15:13
4:21 [k]2Co 1:23; 2:1; 13:2,10
5:1 [l]Lev 18:8; Dt 22:30; 27:20
5:2 [m]2Co 7:7-11 [n]ver 13
5:3 [o]Col 2:5; 1Th 2:17
5:4 [p]2Th 3:6
5:5 [q]1Ti 1:20 [r]S Mt 4:10

4:6–7 HUMANITY, Human Nature—Our common humanity leads us to become proud about our abilities and attainments. Yet every possession comes as a gift from God who eliminates any basis for pride.

4:12–13 EVIL AND SUFFERING, Endurance—See note on Ro 12:14–21.

4:14 HOLY SCRIPTURE, Relationship—Paul explained his attitude and love as he revealed God's will in writing to the congregation at Corinth. He wrote as a spiritual father and revealed God's love as a warning signal against deception and self-destruction in the church. See note on Ro 15:15.

4:15–16 THE CHURCH, Practice—The church needs respected, faithful leaders whom other members may imitate confidently. Too many guardians or teachers (Greek *paidagogos*) lead people to jealousy and quarreling (3:2) instead of to Christ.

4:17 EDUCATION, Example—A part of Timothy's curriculum, as he taught the Corinthians, would be drawn directly from the life of Paul. How many Christian teachers would dare say, "My life is the book from which I want you to learn?" How many can say, "My life agrees with my teaching"?

4:20 THE CHURCH, God's Kingdom—To a church beset with divisions and problems, Paul exhorted the fellowship to hear his word and to follow it. The kingdom of God is the rule of God and, therefore, the power of God. The church must follow God's will. People who talk eloquently about the kingdom may be troublemakers. The test is whether their lives demonstrate God's power.

5:1–5 THE CHURCH, Discipline—See notes on Ac 1:21–26; 15:1–35; 1 Co 4:15–16. The church must protect its power to proclaim the gospel of Christ. The church must accept those outside the fellowship with compassion but never accept the practices of the world. Decisions affecting the fellowship of the church should be made by the assembled church under the guidance of the Holy Spirit.

5:1–5 FAMILY, Sexual Sin—The church's silence encourages sexual immorality. A church member was having sexual relations with his stepmother. Whether his father was still living or whether the member was married to her is not known. Interpreters assume the woman was not a Christian (v 12) since Paul passed no judgment on her. Hebrew (Lev 18:8) and Roman law prohibited such incest. For the Christian fellowship not to take action was unthinkable because of the influence such behavior would have on others. Separation from the fellowship was intended to lead to repentance and reconciliation. Apparently the church took action, and the incestuous member repented of his transgression (2 Co 2:5–11; 7:8–13). Paul encouraged forgiveness and reaffirmation of love for the sinner. The church must actively oppose sexual immorality which threatens the church and family life. The church must work to restore the repentant sinner.

5:5 EVIL AND SUFFERING, Satan—God can use Satan's treatment of a person to discipline the person, leading that individual to repentance and restoration with God's people. Satan does not intend to help a person towards salvation. Anyone outside the fellowship of the church is under Satan's power. A believer cannot live under such conditions and will eventually return to God or die. Spiritual exclusion may lead to

so that the sinful nature[l] may be destroyed and his spirit saved on the day of
the Lord.[s]
6 Your boasting is not good.[t] Don't you
know that a little yeast[u] works through
the whole batch of dough?[v] 7 Get rid of
the old yeast that you may be a new batch
without yeast—as you really are. For
Christ, our Passover lamb, has been sacrificed.[w] 8 Therefore let us keep the Festival, not with the old yeast, the yeast of
malice and wickedness, but with bread
without yeast,[x] the bread of sincerity and
truth.
9 I have written you in my letter not to
associate[y] with sexually immoral people— 10 not at all meaning the people of
this world[z] who are immoral, or the
greedy and swindlers, or idolaters. In that
case you would have to leave this world.
11 But now I am writing you that you must
not associate with anyone who calls himself a brother[a] but is sexually immoral or
greedy, an idolater[b] or a slanderer, a
drunkard or a swindler. With such a man
do not even eat.[c]
12 What business is it of mine to judge
those outside[d] the church? Are you not
to judge those inside?[e] 13 God will judge
those outside. "Expel the wicked man
from among you."[m][f]

Chapter 6

Lawsuits Among Believers

IF any of you has a dispute with another,
dare he take it before the ungodly for
judgment instead of before the saints?[g]
2 Do you not know that the saints will
judge the world?[h] And if you are to judge
the world, are you not competent to
judge trivial cases? 3 Do you not know that

[l] 5 Or *that his body;* or *that the flesh* [m] 13 Deut. 17:7; 19:19; 21:21; 22:21,24; 24:7

5:5 [s]S 1Co 1:8
5:6 [t]Jas 4:16 [u]Mt 16:6,12 [v]Gal 5:9
5:7 [w]Ex 12:3-6,21; Mk 14:12; 1Pe 1:19
5:8 [x]Ex 12:14,15; Dt 16:3
5:9 [y]Eph 5:11; 2Th 3:6,14
5:10 [z]1Co 10:27
5:11 [a]S Ro 7:1 [b]1Co 10:7,14 [c]S Ro 16:17
5:12 [d]S Mk 4:11 [e]ver 3-5; 1Co 6:1-4
5:13 [f]Dt 13:5; 17:7; 19:19; 22:21,24; 24:7; Jdg 20:13
6:1 [g]Mt 18:17
6:2 [h]Mt 19:28; Lk 22:30; 1Co 5:12

physical death but not to damnation.

5:5 HUMANITY, Physical Nature—The Greek is literally "the flesh," clearly referring to the physical nature of a person. In most of the New Testament this expression refers to that part of our nature which is in rebellion against God. When our physical nature leads us astray, it is better that the body should perish and our soul (spiritual nature) be delivered.

5:5 SALVATION, Definition—Believers do sin, and sometimes grievously as was the case here. Paul counseled that this offending Christian be expelled from the church in order to deal with his fleshly nature. We have no way of knowing whether the man had been dealt with according to the disciplinary procedures of Mt 18:15–17. Satan is the ruler of the forces of evil. Paul's thinking seemed to be that by expelling the man from the fellowship of the church he would be in the realm controlled by Satan—the world. In that realm of sickness and death he would die, but his spirit would be saved in the day of the Lord. Others think destruction refers not to death, but to the realm outside God's spiritual protection. The object would be to cause repentance. Spirit here does not mean some invisible real essence alive apart from a body. It refers to the spiritual being saved by receiving a resurrection body. Whatever unresolved questions we may have about this incident, we should remember that Paul's ultimate objective was to save the man. That objective should govern all church discipline.

5:7 JESUS CHRIST, Lamb of God—Jesus celebrated the Passover with His disciples and then was crucified. Passover celebrated redemption from Egyptian slavery through the blood of the sacrificial lamb placed on Israelite doorposts. On the cross Jesus freed us from slavery to sin, meaning our moral behavior should be different. See note on Ex 12:46.

5:7 SALVATION, Atonement—Often in the Bible yeast or leaven symbolizes sin and evil. Believers are a new batch of unleavened dough without evil because Christ, the Passover Lamb, has been sacrificed to atone for our sin.

5:9–13 THE CHURCH, Discipline—The church lives and ministers in a hostile world. To carry out the commission of Christ, the church must remain in the world showing the power of Christ by living by His standards. When church members reflect the practices of those who refuse to repent, we lose the power to proclaim the gospel. The local church must maintain moral discipline within its membership. See note on vv 1–5.

5:11 CHRISTIAN ETHICS, Alcohol—See note on Ro 13:13.

5:11 CHRISTIAN ETHICS, Property Rights—Greed is contagious. Associating with greedy people willing to swindle others brings the growing temptation to reach their financial class and use their methods. Greed and swindling are as evil as sexual immorality, drunkenness, slander, and idolatry.

5:12 LAST THINGS, Judgment—Those outside the circle of saving faith are judged by God Himself. See note on Rev 20:11–15. The church needs to keep its own fellowship pure and to refrain from assuming God's role as Judge of the world. The command not to judge one another (Ro 14:10–12) is not to be construed so as to allow immorality and wickedness to remain within the church.

5:12–13 THE CHURCH, Local Body—See note on Mt 18:15–20.

5:13 GOD, Judge—God is not only Judge over Christians (4:4), but He is also Judge over those who are not Christians. As sovereign Lord He is Judge of all persons. As individuals we do not presume to judge anyone. As a Christian church, we must judge flagrant violators within the church to protect the church's witness.

6:1–8 CHRISTIAN ETHICS, Church and State—Paul was distressed that the Corinthians had so quickly fallen back on the civil courts. Such a development indicated not that problems cannot develop between fellow Christians but that they had been so immature to let conflict resolution get beyond the power of Christian love, forgiveness, and reconciliation to act. Paul had been forced to appeal his case to civil authorities (Ac 25:11), but his was not a dispute among Christians. The church should be able to find people and processes to settle disputes among members without going to civil court.

6:1–6 THE CHURCH, Discipline—God gave Christians guidelines to settle disputes and strengthen the fellowship of believers. See note on Mt 18:15–20. Each member must accept the authority of Christ and desire to overcome differences with little damage to the church. Conflicts will continue unless believers are willing to discuss differences and change hostile attitudes. The Holy Spirit will guide the church concerning differences. To resolve conflict, believers must rely on the Spirit's power and prefer others above self. If mediation is needed, other Christians should provide it. The church should not need secular processes conducted by unbelievers to settle its disputes.

6:2–3 LAST THINGS, Judgment—Believers are in some way to participate in judging the world. Because of spiritual union with Christ, to whom God has committed all judgment, believers share His work with Him. See note on Jn 5:21–24. Furthermore, there is to be participation in judging angels. Most likely the reference is to disobedient angels, such as are mentioned in Jude 6. Compare 2 Pe 2:4. Amillennialists, post-millennialists, and historical premillennialists generally interpret this judging to come about through the power of Christ-like living, which will judge and convict evil. Dispensational

we will judge angels? How much more
the things of this life! 4Therefore, if you
have disputes about such matters, appoint as judges even men of little account
in the church![n] 5I say this to shame
you.[i] Is it possible that there is nobody
among you wise enough to judge a dispute between believers?[j] 6But instead,
one brother[k] goes to law against another
—and this in front of unbelievers![l]

7The very fact that you have lawsuits
among you means you have been completely defeated already. Why not rather
be wronged? Why not rather be cheated?[m] 8Instead, you yourselves cheat and
do wrong, and you do this to your brothers.[n]

9Do you not know that the wicked will
not inherit the kingdom of God?[o] Do not
be deceived:[p] Neither the sexually immoral nor idolaters nor adulterers[q] nor
male prostitutes nor homosexual offenders[r] 10nor thieves nor the greedy nor
drunkards nor slanderers nor swindlers[s]
will inherit the kingdom of God. 11And
that is what some of you were.[t] But you
were washed,[u] you were sanctified,[v]
you were justified[w] in the name of the
Lord Jesus Christ and by the Spirit of our
God.

Sexual Immorality

12"Everything is permissible for me"
—but not everything is beneficial.[x] "Everything is permissible for me"—but I
will not be mastered by anything.
13"Food for the stomach and the stomach
for food"—but God will destroy them
both.[y] The body is not meant for sexual
immorality, but for the Lord,[z] and the
Lord for the body. 14By his power God
raised the Lord from the dead,[a] and he
will raise us also.[b] 15Do you not know
that your bodies are members of Christ
himself?[c] Shall I then take the members
of Christ and unite them with a prostitute? Never! 16Do you not know that he
who unites himself with a prostitute is
one with her in body? For it is said, "The
two will become one flesh."[o][d] 17But he
who unites himself with the Lord is one
with him in spirit.[e]

18Flee from sexual immorality.[f] All
other sins a man commits are outside his
body, but he who sins sexually sins
against his own body.[g] 19Do you not
know that your body is a temple[h] of the
Holy Spirit, who is in you, whom you
have received from God? You are not

[n]4 Or *matters, do you appoint as judges men of little account in the church?* [o]16 Gen. 2:24

6:5 [i]S 1Co 4:14 [j]Ac 1:15
6:6 [k]S Ro 7:1 [l]2Co 6:14,15; 1Ti 5:8
6:7 [m]Mt 5:39,40
6:8 [n]1Th 4:6
6:9 [o]S Mt 25:34 [p]Job 13:9; 1Co 15:33; Gal 6:7; Jas 1:16 [q]Lev 18:20; Dt 22:22 [r]Lev 18:22
6:10 [s]1Ti 1:10; Rev 21:8; 22:15
6:11 [t]S Eph 2:2 [u]S Ac 22:16 [v]1Co 1:2 [w]S Ro 4:25
6:12 [x]1Co 10:23
6:13 [y]Col 2:22 [z]ver 15,19; Ro 12:1
6:14 [a]S Ac 2:24 [b]S Ro 6:5; Eph 1:19,20; 1Th 4:16
6:15 [c]S Ro 12:5
6:16 [d]Ge 2:24; Mt 19:5; Eph 5:31
6:17 [e]Jn 17:21-23; Ro 8:9-11; Gal 2:20
6:18 [f]ver 9; 1Co 5:1; 2Co 12:21; Gal 5:19; Eph 5:3; 1Th 4:3,4; Heb 13:4 [g]Ro 6:12
6:19 [h]Jn 2:21

---

premillennialists generally believe the reference applies to the end time in various ways.

6:10 CHRISTIAN ETHICS, Alcohol—Being a drunkard or alcoholic is not the unforgiveable sin. It does involve sin of which one must repent to be part of God's kingdom just as we must repent of all other sin. Sinful habits are not part of the Christian life. See note on Ro 13:13.

6:11 GOD, Trinity—Note the interrelatedness of the work of the three Persons of the Trinity in salvation. See note on Mt 3:16–17.

6:12–20 SIN, Depravity—Christians cannot justify sexual sin in any way. Because Christians' bodies are part of Christ (v 15), their bodily sins (Greek *porneia*) are, therefore, not only sins against Christ, but also against themselves. By linking bodily behavior with the presence of the Holy Spirit, the apostle made it impossible for believers to separate their sexual practices from their relationship with the Lord. Christians cannot put themselves above the moral and ethical standards given by the Spirit without attempting to deny the Spirit within them.

6:12–20 CHRISTIAN ETHICS, Character—Integrity of character involves respect for our physical bodies. Our bodies are to represent Christ and do nothing which would bring shame on His name. Addiction to alcohol, food, or drugs shows that we have let something other than Christ be our Master.

6:14 GOD, Power—The power of God raised Jesus from the dead. The same power of God will raise us from the dead in the resurrection. This same power of God operates in us in conversion, or the new birth. This is why the gospel is more than a philosophy: it brings the power of God into the life of the believer.

6:14 JESUS CHRIST, Resurrection—Jesus' resurrection is the guarantee for our resurrection.

6:14 LAST THINGS, Believers' Resurrection—The bodies of believers are destined for resurrection. The assurance of this is found in the fact of Christ's resurrection. The power to accomplish it will be God's.

6:15–17 THE CHURCH, Body of Christ—Paul used the imagery of the church as the body of Christ in different ways in various contexts. Here he used the imagery to prohibit sexual immorality. Apparently one Corinthian Christian used his freedom in Christ as a license for immorality, and some of the church approved. These people misunderstood the meaning of grace and the nature of the Christ-life. Paul reminded the people that they were the body of Christ. Each person was a member of Christ and, as such, could not be united with immorality. Since God owns us by the power of Christ's death on the cross, all our actions must be subjected to Him. Christ defines and determines all our relationships and actions.

6:15–17 FAMILY, One Flesh—Sexual union is God's plan to create physical and emotional unity in the marriage relationship. Such unity is the foundation of the family. Participation in such union outside the marriage commitment destroys family and betrays our commitment to Christ to whose body we belong and to whom we are united in spiritual union as His bride. Sexual activity is not a right and/or need for every individual to be satisfied the easiest way possible. Sexual activity is demonstration of commitment and unity within the family. See note on Ge 2:24.

6:18–20 HOLY SPIRIT, Obeyed—The Holy Spirit lives in holy people. God gave the Spirit to Christians, and He lives in each member of the church as in a temple. See note on 3:16 for the whole church as God's temple. The Christian as a temple indwelt by the Spirit must not do anything that would be unthinkable in public worship. It is unspeakably wrong for a Christian to commit sexual immorality (vv 12–18).

6:19–20 SALVATION, Redemption—We were slaves to sin, but God bought us with the death of His Son on the cross (1 Ti 2:6; Tit 2:14). Thus, we belong to God and should serve Him.

6:19–20 DISCIPLESHIP, Holy Spirit—God lives in you. Is He comfortable there, or do your actions cause Him problems? The body of the Christian disciple is the temple of God—the dwelling place of God. God bought and paid for you on the cross. You belong to God. You, the disciple, must serve the God who purchased and indwells you. You have a heavy responsibility to keep your body as the temple of God, fit for His dwelling.

your own;[i] 20you were bought at a
price.[j] Therefore honor God with your
body.[k]

Chapter 7

Marriage

NOW for the matters you wrote about:
It is good for a man not to marry.[p] [l]
2But since there is so much immorality,
each man should have his own wife, and
each woman her own husband. 3The husband should fulfill his marital duty to his
wife,[m] and likewise the wife to her husband. 4The wife's body does not belong to
her alone but also to her husband. In the
same way, the husband's body does not
belong to him alone but also to his wife.
5Do not deprive each other except by mutual consent and for a time,[n] so that you
may devote yourselves to prayer. Then
come together again so that Satan[o] will
not tempt you[p] because of your lack of
self-control. 6I say this as a concession,
not as a command.[q] 7I wish that all men
were as I am.[r] But each man has his own
gift from God; one has this gift, another
has that.[s]

8Now to the unmarried and the widows I say: It is good for them to stay unmarried, as I am.[t] 9But if they cannot
control themselves, they should marry,[u]
for it is better to marry than to burn with
passion.

10To the married I give this command
(not I, but the Lord): A wife must not
separate from her husband.[v] 11But if she
does, she must remain unmarried or else
be reconciled to her husband.[w] And a
husband must not divorce his wife.

12To the rest I say this (I, not the
Lord):[x] If any brother has a wife who is
not a believer and she is willing to live
with him, he must not divorce her. 13And
if a woman has a husband who is not a
believer and he is willing to live with her,
she must not divorce him. 14For the unbelieving husband has been sanctified
through his wife, and the unbelieving
wife has been sanctified through her believing husband. Otherwise your children
would be unclean, but as it is, they are
holy.[y]

6:19 [i]Ro 14:7,8
6:20 [j]Ps 74:2; S Mt 20:28; Ac 20:28; 1Co 7:23; Rev 5:9; 14:4 [k]Php 1:20
7:1 [l]ver 8,26
7:3 [m]Ex 21:10; 1Pe 3:7
7:5 [n]Ex 19:15; 1Sa 21:4,5 [o]S Mt 4:10 [p]1Th 3:5
7:6 [q]2Co 8:8
7:7 [r]ver 8; 1Co 9:5 [s]Mt 19:11,12; Ro 12:6; 1Co 12:4,11
7:8 [t]ver 1,26
7:9 [u]1Ti 5:14
7:10 [v]Mal 2:14-16; S Lk 16:18
7:11 [w]ver 39; Ro 7:2,3
7:12 [x]ver 6,10; 2Co 11:17
7:14 [y]Mal 2:15

[p]*1* Or "*It is good for a man not to have sexual relations with a woman.*"

7:1–9 EVIL AND SUFFERING, Satan—Satan tempts people to sexual sin by using the lack of self-control to lead them to immorality. Satan can take the good gift of God and lead people to use it in sinful ways.

7:1–5 HUMANITY, Marriage—Human commitments in marriage can distract a person's commitment to Christ. For some it is better not to marry than to get their lives so involved. On the other hand, because of the nature of human sexuality and its compelling force, marriage offers an opportunity to serve God as well.

7:1,7–9 FAMILY, Single—Remaining single offers extra time for special service to God. It was Paul's choice of life-style based on a God-given gift to live it. Most people do not have this gift. Thus, marriage is the more common life-style for God's people. The single person must be able to avoid temptations to sexual immorality. See note on Mt 19:10–12.

7:2–7 FAMILY, Need Fulfillment—Husband and wife share mutual responsibility for the sexual fulfillment of the marriage partner. Christians cannot claim private possession of their own bodies since in the one-flesh relationship husband and wife belong to each other. This is a distinct advance over the older concept of the wife as property rather than partner or the wife as only satisfying the husband's needs. Sexual needs are part of human nature created by God. The marriage relationship is the only relationship in which sexual needs can be truly satisfied.

7:5 PRAYER, Family—Paul expected married people to pray together. 1 Pe 3:7 implies that the prayer of a husband and wife is important.

7:6,10,12,25,40 HOLY SCRIPTURE, Inspired—Paul made a distinction between his own personal views and those which he perceived as coming directly from Jesus and His teaching. He declared what he thought when he had no certain word from God. He explained in regard to marriage what was revealed to him from Christ and what was his best personal opinion (9:8). Paul was convinced God's Spirit was leading him to make his judgments. The early church confirmed his conviction the Spirit had inspired him by following God's direction and including this passage in the collection of inspired Scriptures.

7:8–9 HUMANITY, Celibacy—Celibacy is one manner of life for a Christian in God's service. It is not acceptable when human passion becomes overwhelming and uncontrolled.

7:8,25–28,32–40 FAMILY, Priorities—The question of priorities was basic in Paul's advice to widows and other unmarried persons to remain single if they were not subject to intensive sexual desire. Paul favored singleness as a religious commitment freeing persons to give full time to preparing people for Christ's coming, whereas marriage naturally placed other demands on time. Paul did not have a negative attitude toward marriage, but vocationally he believed singleness was preferable during the crisis times ahead. He instructed younger widows to marry rather than become dependent on the church for support (1 Ti 5:11–14). Vocational priorities and personal gifts thus should determine a person's decision to marry.

7:10–11 FAMILY, Divorce—Marriage is designed for permanence. Divorce must not be seen as an easy option to escape problems. Christians married to one another should commit themselves to each other and to working out problems in the relationship. To do otherwise goes against God's Word. See note on Mt 19:3–9.

7:12–16 FAMILY, Intermarriage—Marriage to a non-Christian is not grounds for divorce. Such marriage provides Christian influence for the children and hope to lead the unbeliever to salvation in Christ. Such a marriage is acceptable in God's sight. Divorce should not occur unless the unbelieving partner desires it. See notes on Dt 7:3–4; Ne 10:28–30, 13:23–27; 2 Co 6:14–18.

7:14 SALVATION, Sanctification—Most interpreters think Paul is treating the idea of holiness in a physical or material way rather than thinking of the moral influence of persons on each other. That interpretation would account better for their children being holy. However, it is evident that Paul was not saying holiness shared in marriage saves the unbelieving partner or the children. See note on Mt 19:13–15. The clue to Paul's meaning may be that these were spouses who became Christians after their marriage. Godliness has more power than ungodliness. The believing spouse does sanctify the unbelieving spouse in the sense of making marriage acceptable to God, and in the sense of blessing it. God will bless that marriage and the children of it because of the sanctified spouse. Salvation makes such a difference in a person's ethical life and attitudes that those nearby become better people and are influenced to follow Christ.

15But if the unbeliever leaves, let him
do so. A believing man or woman is not
bound in such circumstances; God has
called us to live in peace.[z] 16How do
you know, wife, whether you will save[a]
your husband?[b] Or, how do you know,
husband, whether you will save your
wife?

17Nevertheless, each one should retain
the place in life that the Lord assigned to
him and to which God has called him.[c]
This is the rule I lay down in all the
churches.[d] 18Was a man already circumcised when he was called? He should not
become uncircumcised. Was a man uncircumcised when he was called? He should
not be circumcised.[e] 19Circumcision is
nothing and uncircumcision is nothing.[f]
Keeping God's commands is what counts.
20Each one should remain in the situation
which he was in when God called him.[g]
21Were you a slave when you were
called? Don't let it trouble you—although
if you can gain your freedom, do so. 22For
he who was a slave when he was called
by the Lord is the Lord's freedman;[h] similarly, he who was a free man when he
was called is Christ's slave.[i] 23You were
bought at a price;[j] do not become slaves
of men. 24Brothers, each man, as responsible to God, should remain in the situation God called him to.[k]

25Now about virgins: I have no command from the Lord,[l] but I give a judgment as one who by the Lord's mercy[m] is
trustworthy. 26Because of the present crisis, I think that it is good for you to remain as you are.[n] 27Are you married? Do
not seek a divorce. Are you unmarried?
Do not look for a wife.[o] 28But if you do
marry, you have not sinned;[p] and if a
virgin marries, she has not sinned. But
those who marry will face many troubles
in this life, and I want to spare you
this.

29What I mean, brothers, is that the
time is short.[q] From now on those who
have wives should live as if they had
none; 30those who mourn, as if they did
not; those who are happy, as if they
were not; those who buy something,
as if it were not theirs to keep; 31those
who use the things of the world, as
if not engrossed in them. For this
world in its present form is passing
away.[r]

32I would like you to be free from concern. An unmarried man is concerned
about the Lord's affairs[s]—how he can
please the Lord. 33But a married man is
concerned about the affairs of this world
—how he can please his wife— 34and his
interests are divided. An unmarried woman or virgin is concerned about the Lord's
affairs: Her aim is to be devoted to the
Lord in both body and spirit.[t] But a married woman is concerned about the affairs
of this world—how she can please her
husband. 35I am saying this for your own
good, not to restrict you, but that you may
live in a right way in undivided[u] devotion to the Lord.

36If anyone thinks he is acting improperly toward the virgin he is engaged to,
and if she is getting along in years and he
feels he ought to marry, he should do as
he wants. He is not sinning.[v] They
should get married. 37But the man who
has settled the matter in his own mind,
who is under no compulsion but has control over his own will, and who has made
up his mind not to marry the virgin—this
man also does the right thing. 38So then,
he who marries the virgin does right,[w]

7:15 [z]S Ro 14:19; 1Co 14:33
7:16 [a]S Ro 11:14 [b]1Pe 3:1
7:17 [c]Ro 12:3 [d]1Co 4:17; 14:33; 2Co 8:18; 11:28
7:18 [e]Ac 15:1,2
7:19 [f]Ro 2:25-27; Gal 5:6; 6:15; Col 3:11
7:20 [g]ver 24
7:22 [h]Jn 8:32,36 [i]S Ro 6:22
7:23 [j]S 1Co 6:20
7:24 [k]ver 20
7:25 [l]ver 6; 2Co 8:8 [m]2Co 4:1; 1Ti 1:13,16
7:26 [n]ver 1,8
7:27 [o]ver 20,21
7:28 [p]ver 36
7:29 [q]ver 31; S Ro 13:11,12
7:31 [r]ver 29; S Heb 12:27
7:32 [s]1Ti 5:5
7:34 [t]Lk 2:37
7:35 [u]Ps 86:11
7:36 [v]ver 28
7:38 [w]Heb 13:4

7:18–20 EVANGELISM, Universality—One need not become a Jew and keep the law of circumcision or any other ritual requirement to be a Christian. The gospel is free and is for all. We need only respond to that divine call to salvation in repentance and faith. See note on Ac 20:17–21.

7:23 SALVATION, Redemption—See note on 6:19–20. The price of salvation was too high for Christians ever again to become slaves to anyone or anything.

7:25–35 HUMANITY, Marriage—In critical times, marriage may become a distraction to service. Yet, it must be clearly understood that neither celibacy nor marriage is necessarily better than the other as a life-style for serving God. A person's situation and needs provide criteria for determining whether to marry. The ultimate criterion is the ability to serve God.

7:29–31 LAST THINGS, Age to Come—Some interpreters believe Paul referred to the time until the second coming. Thus Paul would have meant that the necessary prelude for the age to come is the passing away of the world in its present form. In its place will dawn the new age. Each generation must live in the conviction that time is short. Whether the point of termination be death or Christ's return, *the time is short* for all persons. See note on Mt 12:32. Others believe Paul saw an immediate threat of severe persecution and recommended waiting until the "crisis" (v 26) passed to participate in life's normal activities.

7:31 CREATION, Purposeful—God made a world that will give way shortly to a different approach to life. Paul lived as though the world was about to come to an end. Our individual lives are always precarious. We do not know when they will pass away. The physical world is decaying and waiting to be redeemed. See note on Ro 8:18–25. Paul felt that the present has much more to offer than gratification of the fleshly desires. God's people need to learn the true nature of meaningful values in God's world.

7:36–38 FAMILY, Priorities—The NIV and the NIV footnote offer different interpretations of the Greek original by biblical translators. In the footnote the text assumes a father's decision concerning giving his daughter in marriage. The NIV text describes a couple who either are engaged and trying to decide about getting married or a couple who have determined to live together in a spiritual relationship without sexual intercourse. The NIV assumes the engaged couple is meant and that Paul was giving permission to marry if sexual desire is becoming too strong. He still encouraged singleness in light of the times but approved marriage as right if it is desired. The woman's needs are an important criteria here. All priorities must be taken into account as a couple considers marriage. The needs of both partners deserve equal consideration.

but he who does not marry her does even
better.[q]
39A woman is bound to her husband as
long as he lives.[x] But if her husband dies,
she is free to marry anyone she wishes,
but he must belong to the Lord.[y] 40In my
judgment,[z] she is happier if she stays as
she is—and I think that I too have the
Spirit of God.

Chapter 8

Food Sacrificed to Idols

NOW about food sacrificed to idols:[a]
We know that we all possess knowledge.[r][b] Knowledge puffs up, but love
builds up. 2The man who thinks he
knows something[c] does not yet know as
he ought to know.[d] 3But the man who
loves God is known by God.[e]
4So then, about eating food sacrificed
to idols:[f] We know that an idol is nothing at all in the world[g] and that there is
no God but one.[h] 5For even if there are
so-called gods,[i] whether in heaven or on
earth (as indeed there are many "gods"
and many "lords"), 6yet for us there is
but one God,[j] the Father,[k] from whom
all things came[l] and for whom we live;
and there is but one Lord,[m] Jesus Christ,
through whom all things came[n] and
through whom we live.
7But not everyone knows this.[o] Some
people are still so accustomed to idols
that when they eat such food they think
of it as having been sacrificed to an idol,

7:39 [x]Ro 7:2,3 [y]2Co 6:14
7:40 [z]ver 25
8:1 [a]ver 4,7,10; Ac 15:20 [b]Ro 15:14
8:2 [c]1Co 3:18 [d]1Co 13:8,9,12; 1Ti 6:4
8:3 [e]Jer 1:5; Ro 8:29; Gal 4:9
8:4 [f]ver 1,7,10; Ex 34:15 [g]Ac 14:15; 1Co 10:19; Gal 4:8 [h]ver 6; Dt 6:4; Ps 86:10; Eph 4:6; 1Ti 2:5
8:5 [i]2Th 2:4
8:6 [j]S ver 4 [k]Mal 2:10 [l]S Ro 11:36 [m]Eph 4:5 [n]S Jn 1:3
8:7 [o]ver 1 [p]Ro 14:14; 1Co 10:28
8:8 [q]Ro 14:17
8:9 [r]S 2Co 6:3; Gal 5:13 [s]Ro 14:1
8:10 [t]ver 1,4,7
8:11 [u]Ro 14:15,20
8:12 [v]Mt 18:6 [w]Mt 25:40,45
8:13 [x]S Mt 5:29
9:1 [y]ver 19 [z]S 1Co 1:1; 2Co 12:12 [a]S 1Co 15:8

and since their conscience is weak,[p] it is
defiled. 8But food does not bring us near
to God;[q] we are no worse if we do not
eat, and no better if we do.
9Be careful, however, that the exercise
of your freedom does not become a stumbling block[r] to the weak.[s] 10For if anyone with a weak conscience sees you
who have this knowledge eating in an
idol's temple, won't he be emboldened to
eat what has been sacrificed to idols?[t]
11So this weak brother, for whom Christ
died, is destroyed[u] by your knowledge.
12When you sin against your brothers[v] in
this way and wound their weak conscience, you sin against Christ.[w] 13There-
fore, if what I eat causes my brother to
fall into sin, I will never eat meat again,
so that I will not cause him to fall.[x]

Chapter 9

The Rights of an Apostle

AM I not free?[y] Am I not an apostle?[z]
Have I not seen Jesus our Lord?[a]
Are you not the result of my work in the

[q]*36-38* Or *36If anyone thinks he is not treating his daughter properly, and if she is getting along in years, and he feels she ought to marry, he should do as he wants. He is not sinning. He should let her get married. 37But the man who has settled the matter in his own mind, who is under no compulsion but has control over his own will, and who has made up his mind to keep the virgin unmarried—this man also does the right thing. 38So then, he who gives his virgin in marriage does right, but he who does not give her in marriage does even better.* [r]*1* Or *"We all possess knowledge," as you say*

7:40 HOLY SPIRIT, Revelation—In this chapter Paul gave guidance concerning marriage and family life. Some of what he said repeated the teachings of Jesus which are, of course, authoritative for the church (v 10). Elsewhere he gave guidance on matters about which Jesus had not spoken (v 12). He acknowledged these teachings as his own opinion, but he believed they came from the Spirit. In including the teachings in its Scripture, the church has confessed its agreement with Paul that the Spirit inspired his writing.

8:1–8 GOD, One God—Early Christians lived in a polytheistic world, where people believed in many gods. The teaching here is that these gods are only empty ideas, the creation of sinful human imagination. There is only one God, whom we know as the Father of our Lord Jesus Christ.

8:1–3 HUMANITY, Intellectual Nature—Undisciplined human intellect can lead to pride and self-exaltation. When the love of God tempers human knowledge, we can know and serve God and experience true knowledge and life.

8:1–13 CHRISTIAN ETHICS, Character—Character reveals itself in humble concern for other people rather than in proud display of superior knowledge. Theological understanding may give us freedom, but Christian character will lead us to limit freedom out of love for a person with differing theological understanding.

8:3 SALVATION, Love of God—God knows those who love Him.

8:4–6 GOD, Trinity—God the Father is the Creator who controls our lives in His sovereign rule over the world. Jesus Christ is the Lord and Master, the agent through whom the world was created and through whom we live. We can easily conclude this speaks of two Gods, Jesus and the Father. That obviously is a contradiction of v 4: there is only one God. Here we face the glorious mystery of God's unity in three Persons. See note on Mt 3:16–17.

8:4–6 JESUS CHRIST, Lord—Christians serve and seek to please only one Lord, Jesus. He was the agent or Word through whom God created our world (Jn 1:3,10). Compare Pr 3:19–20; 8:22–31. Jesus is the source of redemption, too, giving us eternal life. See note on Ac 2:23–36.

8:7 HUMANITY, Moral Consciousness—When a person's moral consciousness is weak or underdeveloped, innocent acts can appear wrong. If such a person commits that act, it has become a sin for that person and he or she is guilty. The act although innocent to others, was done with the belief that it was wrong and, thus, was an act of rebellion or disobedience against the conscience. However, it does not follow that an act disobedient to Scripture is justifiable whether or not anyone believes it to be correct. Christians must accept one another's moral feelings, study Scripture together to determine God's teachings, and tolerate differences in love.

8:12 SIN, Estrangement—There is always the possibility of wounding the conscience of a brother or sister in Christ. This wounding does not mean offending another's feelings, but inducing someone into an act the person believes is wrong. Although the act is not sinful as such, a possible result is a faith burdened with excessive and damaging guilt. The sin against one's fellow Christian is against Christ because His Spirit indwells His people.

9:1–15 CHURCH LEADERS, Authority—Vocational church leaders have the right to be paid as do people in any other vocation. They do not have a right to demand payment or do anything that would "hinder the gospel of Christ" (v 12). Paul often worked as a tentmaker (Ac 18:3) to avoid burdening the churches, but he also accepted a monetary gift gratefully

Lord?[b] 2Even though I may not be an apostle to others, surely I am to you! For you are the seal[c] of my apostleship in the Lord.

3This is my defense to those who sit in judgment on me. 4Don't we have the right to food and drink?[d] 5Don't we have the right to take a believing wife[e] along with us, as do the other apostles and the Lord's brothers[f] and Cephas[s]?[g] 6Or is it only I and Barnabas[h] who must work for a living?

7Who serves as a soldier[i] at his own expense? Who plants a vineyard[j] and does not eat of its grapes? Who tends a flock and does not drink of the milk? 8Do I say this merely from a human point of view? Doesn't the Law say the same thing? 9For it is written in the Law of Moses: "Do not muzzle an ox while it is treading out the grain."[t][k] Is it about oxen that God is concerned?[l] 10Surely he says this for us, doesn't he? Yes, this was written for us,[m] because when the plowman plows and the thresher threshes, they ought to do so in the hope of sharing in the harvest.[n] 11If we have sown spiritual seed among you, is it too much if we reap a material harvest from you?[o] 12If others have this right of support from you, shouldn't we have it all the more?

But we did not use this right.[p] On the contrary, we put up with anything rather than hinder[q] the gospel of Christ. 13Don't you know that those who work in the temple get their food from the temple, and those who serve at the altar share in what is offered on the altar?[r] 14In the same way, the Lord has commanded that those who preach the gospel should receive their living from the gospel.[s]

15But I have not used any of these rights.[t] And I am not writing this in the hope that you will do such things for me. I would rather die than have anyone deprive me of this boast.[u] 16Yet when I preach the gospel, I cannot boast, for I am compelled to preach.[v] Woe to me if I do not preach the gospel! 17If I preach voluntarily, I have a reward;[w] if not voluntarily, I am simply discharging the trust committed to me.[x] 18What then is my reward? Just this: that in preaching the gospel I may offer it free of charge,[y] and so not make use of my rights[z] in preaching it.

19Though I am free[a] and belong to no man, I make myself a slave to everyone,[b] to win as many as possible.[c] 20To the Jews I became like a Jew, to win the Jews.[d] To those under the law I became like one under the law (though I myself am not under the law),[e] so as to win those under the law. 21To those not having the law I became like one not having the law[f] (though I am not free from God's law but am under Christ's law),[g] so as to win those not having the law. 22To the weak I became weak, to win the weak.[h] I have become all things to all men[i] so that by all possible means I might save some.[j] 23I do all this for the sake of the gospel, that I may share in its blessings.

24Do you not know that in a race all the runners run, but only one gets the prize?[k] Run[l] in such a way as to get the prize. 25Everyone who competes in the games goes into strict training. They do it to get a crown[m] that will not last; but we do it to get a crown that will last forever.[n] 26Therefore I do not run like a man running aimlessly;[o] I do not fight like a man beating the air.[p] 27No, I beat my body[q] and make it my slave so that after I have preached to others, I myself will not be disqualified for the prize.[r]

[s]5 That is, Peter [t]9 Deut. 25:4

9:1 [b]1Co 3:6; 4:15
9:2 [c]2Co 3:2,3
9:4 [d]ver 14; S Ac 18:3
9:5 [e]1Co 7:7,8 [f]S Mt 12:46 [g]S 1Co 1:12
9:6 [h]S Ac 4:36
9:7 [i]2Ti 2:3,4 [j]Dt 20:6; Pr 27:18; 1Co 3:6,8
9:9 [k]Dt 25:4; 1Ti 5:18 [l]Dt 22:1-4; Pr 12:10
9:10 [m]S Ro 4:23,24 [n]Pr 11:25; 2Ti 2:6
9:11 [o]ver 14; Ro 15:27; Gal 6:6
9:12 [p]ver 15,18; S Ac 18:3 [q]2Co 6:3; 11:7-12
9:13 [r]Lev 6:16,26; Dt 18:1
9:14 [s]S 1Ti 5:18
9:15 [t]ver 12,18; S Ac 18:3 [u]2Co 11:9,10
9:16 [v]Ro 1:14; Ac 9:15; 26:16-18
9:17 [w]1Co 3:8,14 [x]1Co 4:1; Gal 2:7; Col 1:25
9:18 [y]2Co 11:7; 12:13 [z]ver 12,15
9:19 [a]ver 1 [b]2Co 4:5; Gal 5:13 [c]Mt 18:15; 1Pe 3:1
9:20 [d]Ac 16:3; 21:20-26; Ro 11:14 [e]S Ro 2:12
9:21 [f]Ro 2:12,14 [g]Gal 6:2
9:22 [h]S Ro 14:1; S 1Co 2:3 [i]1Co 10:33 [j]S Ro 11:14
9:24 [k]Php 3:14; Col 2:18 [l]ver 25,26; Gal 2:2; 5:7; Php 2:16; 2Ti 4:7; Heb 12:1
9:25 [m]2Ti 2:5 [n]2Ti 4:8; Jas 1:12; 1Pe 5:4; Rev 2:10; 3:11
9:26 [o]S ver 24 [p]1Ti 6:12
9:27 [q]Ro 8:13 [r]ver 24

(Php 4:10–19). Compare Ac 20:34; 1 Th 2:9; 2 Th 3:7–10; 1 Ti 5:18.

9:16–18 PROCLAMATION, Compulsion—Proclamation is not an achievement leading us to brag. It is a compulsion bringing its own reward. Two compelling reasons motivate us to proclaim the gospel: (1) people are lost without Christ and need to be saved; (2) we need to obey God. The gospel requires urgency of proclamation. Every person who is not saved is destined for eternal separation from God (Mt 25:46; Rev 20:11–15). God desires all to be saved (Mt 24:14; 2 Pe 3:9). God's love and His Spirit live in the believer, compelling every believer to proclaim the gospel. This sense of urgency rested on Jesus (Mk 1:38–39; Lk 4:43–44). That same compulsion moved the hearts of the early believers (Mk 13:10; Ac 4:17–20). The compulsion to proclaim the gospel is rooted in the awareness that God has assigned us that task as believers (2 Co 5:17–21).

9:19–23 EVANGELISM, Personal—Many sacrificial demands are necessary to evangelize effectively. Although we have freedom in Christ, love for the lost world constrains us to assume the servant role and be willing to become all things to all people to win them to Christ. We serve their needs rather than asserting our rights. We must identify with people, sacrifice our own pleasure, and pour ourselves out to them if we are to point them to Jesus Christ. See Guide to Relational Evangelism, pp. 1784–1786.

9:23 SALVATION, Blessing—Paul became all things to all persons in order to share in the blessings of the gospel. We do not evangelize in order to feather our own nests. We evangelize because the good news impels us to. We know the end result of suffering for the gospel is the promised blessing of God.

9:24–27 LAST THINGS, Judgment—The awarding of a prize for successful running following strict training indicates the judgment in view has to do with service and rewards, rather than salvation or lostness. Salvation is a gift of grace, but rewards are earned. The symbolism of reward for Christians is the victor's crown. It is possible to be disqualified from receiving rewards. Failure to remain disciplined and faithful courts disqualification (2 Jn 8).

Chapter 10

Warnings From Israel's History

FOR I do not want you to be ignorant[s]
of the fact, brothers, that our forefathers were all under the cloud[t] and that
they all passed through the sea.[u] 2They
were all baptized into[v] Moses in the
cloud and in the sea. 3They all ate the
same spiritual food[w] 4and drank the same
spiritual drink; for they drank from the
spiritual rock[x] that accompanied them,
and that rock was Christ. 5Nevertheless,
God was not pleased with most of them;
their bodies were scattered over the
desert.[y]
6Now these things occurred as examples[u][z] to keep us from setting our hearts
on evil things as they did. 7Do not be idolaters,[a] as some of them were; as it is
written: "The people sat down to eat and
drink and got up to indulge in pagan revelry."[v][b] 8We should not commit sexual
immorality, as some of them did—and in
one day twenty-three thousand of them
died.[c] 9We should not test the Lord,[d] as
some of them did—and were killed by
snakes.[e] 10And do not grumble, as some
of them did[f]—and were killed[g] by the
destroying angel.[h]
11These things happened to them as
examples[i] and were written down as
warnings for us,[j] on whom the fulfillment of the ages has come.[k] 12So, if you
think you are standing firm,[l] be careful
that you don't fall! 13No temptation has
seized you except what is common to
man. And God is faithful;[m] he will not let
you be tempted beyond what you can
bear.[n] But when you are tempted, he will
also provide a way out so that you can
stand up under it.

Idol Feasts and the Lord's Supper

14Therefore, my dear friends,[o] flee
from idolatry.[p] 15I speak to sensible people; judge for yourselves what I say. 16Is
not the cup of thanksgiving for which we
give thanks a participation in the blood of
Christ? And is not the bread that we
break[q] a participation in the body of

10:1 [s]S Ro 11:25 [t]Ex 13:21; Ps 105:39 [u]Ex 14:22,29; Ps 66:6
10:2 [v]Ro 6:3
10:3 [w]S Jn 6:31
10:4 [x]Ex 17:6; Nu 20:11; Ps 78:15; 105:41
10:5 [y]Nu 14:29; Heb 3:17; Jude 5
10:6 [z]ver 11
10:7 [a]ver 14 [b]Ex 32:4,6,19
10:8 [c]Nu 25:1-9
10:9 [d]Ex 17:2; Ps 78:18; 95:9; 106:14 [e]Nu 21:5,6
10:10 [f]Nu 16:41; 17:5,10 [g]Nu 16:49 [h]Ex 12:23; 1Ch 21:15; Heb 11:28
10:11 [i]ver 6 [j]S Ro 4:24 [k]S Ro 13:11
10:12 [l]Ro 11:20; 2Co 1:24
10:13 [m]S 1Co 1:9 [n]2Pe 2:9
10:14 [o]Heb 6:9; 1Pe 2:11; 1Jn 2:7; Jude 3 [p]ver 7; 1Jn 5:21
10:16 [q]S Mt 14:19

[u]6 Or *types*; also in verse 11 [v]7 Exodus 32:6

10:2 ORDINANCES, Background of Baptism—Baptism pictures the great redemptive act of God in the death and resurrection of Jesus. The great redemptive act of God in the Old Testament was the Exodus and the crossing of the Red Sea (Ex 14:1—15:18). This event was seen by Christians as a preview of the new Passover and the new covenant which would come in Jesus. Paul drew a parallel between the crossing of the sea and Christian baptism. The "cloud" was the cloud of God's glory, representing the divine presence that surrounded them as the waters of baptism surround the Christian believer. Passing through the sea was like passing through the waters of baptism to the new life in Christ. God has one plan of redemption. What the people of the old covenant experienced in the Exodus was pointing to the fulfillment in Jesus Christ, the new Moses, who sealed the new covenant with His death and resurrection.

10:3–4 ORDINANCES, Background of Lord's Supper—Just as baptism was the fulfillment of the meaning of the cloud and the sea of the old covenant, so the Lord's Supper fulfills the meaning of God's provision of the manna and the water in the wilderness (Nu 16:1—17:7). The bread and cup are spiritual food and drink in the new covenant, as the manna and water from the rock were in the old covenant. When Christ is called the "spiritual rock," it simply means that the rock which gave them living water is a symbol of Christ who gives life to those who depend upon Him. Paul meant that Christ would always be present to nourish His people wherever and whenever we call upon Him.

10:6–13 SIN, Transgression—Paul outlined four aspects of the evil things Israel practiced in the wilderness: idolatry (v 7), fornication (v 8), testing the Lord (v 9), and grumbling (v 10). These sins have a universal nature that is not limited to the situations either in the wilderness or at Corinth. It would be foolish, if not arrogant, for modern believers to scoff and think we cannot succumb to the same behavior. The apostle's words continue to admonish and warn Christians. We will face temptation. Temptation is not sin. God wants to help us through temptation to victory.

10:7–20 GOD, One God—Here is a warning to remain true to the one and only God and not become involved in any way with false, substitute gods. Such activity involves us in the demonic realm.

10:9–11,22 GOD, Jealous—God is jealous to protect His purity and that of His people. We must take seriously our responsibilities to God. If we are flagrantly unfaithful to Him, we can expect to suffer punishment, His wrath. Our only hope then would be to be stronger than God.

10:11 HISTORY, Time—The time of Jesus on earth is the central moment of history. History has meaning through Christ's saving work. He fulfilled all hopes raised in the past and provided concrete hope for the future.

10:13 GOD, Faithfulness—Our heavenly Father is faithful to us in all the circumstances of life. His faithfulness is not like ours, running hot and cold. We can depend upon Him to watch over us and to help us in all the times where we need Him. He expects right actions and right attitudes from us at all times, but understands the strength of temptation. He gives us power to overcome temptation. When we succumb to temptation, we cannot blame Him. We did not take the help available to us from our faithful God.

10:14–22 EVIL AND SUFFERING, Satan—Anything that we cling to and trust in our hearts that is not God is an idol and, therefore, demonic. Christians must choose to worship God alone. Any participation in ceremonies identified with false gods and false worship is forbidden to us. The Corinthians wanted to please everyone by participating in idol worship and Christian worship. Paul warned them against such evil.

10:15 HUMANITY, Intellectual Nature—God's people are expected to be able to consider and to evaluate what is communicated. We are responsible under God to gather evidence and decide under God's leadership what we believe and how we should act. No other person has authority to tell us. Such serious judgment must be founded upon the primary relationship with God. See Heb 5:14.

10:15–22 ORDINANCES, Lord's Supper as Humility—The cup of thanksgiving is so-called because Jesus gave thanks over the bread and cup at the Last Supper and because Christians were giving thanks for the body and blood of Christ offered for them. Paul was emphasizing the one cup and the one loaf by which Christians participate symbolically in the one body of Christ. Paul used this powerful argument for unity in two ways: it means that Christians must not be divided into factions because they are members of the one body of Christ, and Christians must not participate in sacrificial meals in idol temples because that demonstrates participation symbolically with idols. It would be a foolish contradiction to participate in both the "Lord's table and the table of demons."

Christ?[r] 17Because there is one loaf, we, who are many, are one body,[s] for we all partake of the one loaf.

18Consider the people of Israel: Do not those who eat the sacrifices[t] participate in the altar? 19Do I mean then that a sacrifice offered to an idol is anything, or that an idol is anything?[u] 20No, but the sacrifices of pagans are offered to demons,[v] not to God, and I do not want you to be participants with demons. 21You cannot drink the cup of the Lord and the cup of demons too; you cannot have a part in both the Lord's table and the table of demons.[w] 22Are we trying to arouse the Lord's jealousy?[x] Are we stronger than he?[y]

The Believer's Freedom

23"Everything is permissible"—but not everything is beneficial.[z] "Everything is permissible"—but not everything is constructive. 24Nobody should seek his own good, but the good of others.[a]

25Eat anything sold in the meat market without raising questions of conscience,[b] 26for, "The earth is the Lord's, and everything in it."[w] [c]

27If some unbeliever invites you to a meal and you want to go, eat whatever is put before you[d] without raising questions of conscience. 28But if anyone says to you, "This has been offered in sacrifice," then do not eat it, both for the sake of the man who told you and for conscience' sake[x] [e]— 29the other man's conscience, I mean, not yours. For why should my freedom[f] be judged by another's conscience? 30If I take part in the meal with thankfulness, why am I denounced because of something I thank God for?[g]

31So whether you eat or drink or whatever you do, do it all for the glory of God.[h] 32Do not cause anyone to stumble,[i] whether Jews, Greeks or the church of God[j]— 33even as I try to please everybody in every way.[k] For I am not seeking my own good but the good of many,[l] so that they may be saved.[m] 1Follow my example,[n] as I follow the example of Christ.[o]

Chapter 11

Propriety in Worship

2I praise you[p] for remembering me in everything[q] and for holding to the teachings,[y] just as I passed them on to you.[r]

3Now I want you to realize that the head of every man is Christ,[s] and the head of the woman is man,[t] and the head of Christ is God.[u] 4Every man who prays or prophesies[v] with his head covered dishonors his head. 5And every woman who prays or prophesies[w] with her head uncovered dishonors her head—it is just as though her head were shaved.[x] 6If a woman does not cover her head, she should have her hair cut off; and if it is a disgrace for a woman to have her hair cut or shaved off, she should cover her head. 7A man ought not to cover

10:16 [r]Mt 26:26-28; 1Co 11:23-25
10:17 [s]S Ro 12:5
10:18 [t]Lev 7:6,14,15
10:19 [u]S 1Co 8:4
10:20 [v]Lev 17:7; Dt 32:17; Ps 106:37; Rev 9:20
10:21 [w]2Co 6:15,16
10:22 [x]Dt 32:16,21; 1Ki 14:22; Ps 78:58; Jer 44:8 [y]Ecc 6:10; Isa 45:9
10:23 [z]1Co 6:12
10:24 [a]ver 33; S Ro 15:1,2; 1Co 13:5; Php 2:4,21
10:25 [b]S Ac 10:15; 1Co 8:7
10:26 [c]Ps 24:1; Ex 9:29; 19:5; Job 41:11; Ps 50:12; 1Ti 4:4
10:27 [d]Lk 10:7
10:28 [e]1Co 8:7,10-12
10:29 [f]1Co 9:1,19
10:30 [g]S Ro 14:6
10:31 [h]Zec 14:21; Col 3:17; 1Pe 4:11
10:32 [i]S Mt 5:29; Ac 24:16; S 2Co 6:3 [j]Ac 20:28; 1Co 1:2; 11:16,22; 15:9; 1Ti 3:5,15
10:33 [k]Ro 15:2; 1Co 9:22 [l]S ver 24 [m]S Ro 11:14
11:1 [n]S 1Co 4:16 [o]Ro 15:3; 1Pe 2:21
11:2 [p]ver 17,22 [q]1Co 4:17 [r]ver 23; 1Co 15:2,3; 2Th 2:15; 3:6
11:3 [s]S Eph 1:22 [t]Ge 3:16; Eph 5:23 [u]1Co 3:23
11:4 [v]S Ac 11:27
11:5 [w]S Ac 21:9 [x]Dt 21:12

[w]26 Psalm 24:1 [x]28 Some manuscripts *conscience' sake, for "the earth is the Lord's and everything in it"* [y]2 Or *traditions*

10:22 HUMANITY, Relationship to God—No creature is as powerful as the Creator. To participate in pagan worship is to claim our judgment is superior to God's.

10:23–24 DISCIPLESHIP, Neighbor Love—Christ frees us from sin. Such freedom does not sell us to the slavery of selfish indulgence. Other people and their best interests set limits on my behavior. Christian disciples look after our neighbors' welfare rather than our own.

10:25–31 STEWARDSHIP, God's Ownership—Material things belong to God and are entrusted to us for our use. We may misuse things, but this does not take them away from God's ownership. The evil is in the user, not in the material thing itself. Paul explained that the ritual defilement of meat by pagans in sacrifices did not make the meat evil. It was God's before they took it, and it remained His. Christians use material things in ways that show concern for fellow believers. We are to use all things to the glory of God. See note on Ps 24:1.

10:30 PRAYER, Thanksgiving—See note on Ro 14:6. Food does not determine whether a meal is pleasing to God. The dedication of the meal to Him through a prayer of thanks does.

10:31–33 HUMANITY, Relationships—If I act in a way I know will offend a fellow disciple, I have done wrong. Relating positively to others to bring glory to God is my first responsibility. We must live so as to encourage others rather than offend them.

10:31–33 CHRISTIAN ETHICS, Character—See note on 8:1–13.

10:31–33 EVANGELISM, Glory to God—The highest motive in Christian evangelization is to bring glory to God. This motivation will so affect our life-style that we will never cause anyone to stumble because of our actions or ambitions. It will move us to self-giving for God's glory and the good of all people. The best good we bring to all people is to help them accept Jesus as Savior and thus find life. See note on 9:19–23.

10:32 THE CHURCH, People of God—God's people, the church, are free from legalistic rules to live under the Spirit's guidance and Scripture's teaching. With such freedom we still have responsibility for other people. We must do nothing which would influence any other person to turn away from Christ. In love, we give up our freedom to help other people. See note on 3:16–17.

11:3 JESUS CHRIST, Authority—Jesus the Son is divine yet submitted to the Father's will. This is the mystery of the Trinity.

11:4–5 PRAYER, Humility—In Paul's day humility was indicated in different ways for men and women. The men prayed with their heads uncovered to indicate reverence and respect. Women covered their heads to demonstrate modesty. Immodest women were immoral. The important factor in either case was humility. In public prayer people need to demonstrate humility before God.

his head,[z] since he is the image[y] and
glory of God; but the woman is the glory
of man. 8For man did not come from
woman, but woman from man;[z] 9neither
was man created for woman, but woman
for man.[a] 10For this reason, and because
of the angels, the woman ought to have a
sign of authority on her head.
11In the Lord, however, woman is not
independent of man, nor is man independent of woman. 12For as woman came
from man, so also man is born of woman.
But everything comes from God.[b]
13Judge for yourselves: Is it proper for a
woman to pray to God with her head uncovered? 14Does not the very nature of
things teach you that if a man has long
hair, it is a disgrace to him, 15but that if a
woman has long hair, it is her glory? For
long hair is given to her as a covering. 16If
anyone wants to be contentious about
this, we have no other practice—nor do
the churches of God.[c]

The Lord's Supper

11:23–25pp — Mt 26:26–28; Mk 14:22–24; Lk 22:17–20

17In the following directives I have no
praise for you,[d] for your meetings do
more harm than good. 18In the first place,
I hear that when you come together as a
church, there are divisions[e] among you,
and to some extent I believe it. 19No
doubt there have to be differences among
you to show which of you have God's approval.[f] 20When you come together, it is
not the Lord's Supper you eat, 21for as
you eat, each of you goes ahead without
waiting for anybody else.[g] One remains
hungry, another gets drunk. 22Don't you
have homes to eat and drink in? Or do
you despise the church of God[h] and humiliate those who have nothing?[i] What
shall I say to you? Shall I praise you[j] for
this? Certainly not!
23For I received from the Lord[k] what I
also passed on to you:[l] The Lord Jesus,
on the night he was betrayed, took bread,
24and when he had given thanks, he

11:7 [y]Ge 1:26; 5:1; 9:6; Jas 3:9
11:8 [z]Ge 2:21-23; 1Ti 2:13
11:9 [a]Ge 2:18
11:12 [b]S Ro 11:36
11:16 [c]S 1Co 7:17; S 10:32
11:17 [d]ver 2,22
11:18 [e]1Co 1:10-12; 3:3
11:19 [f]1Jn 2:19
11:21 [g]2Pe 2:13; Jude 12
11:22 [h]S 1Co 10:32 [i]Jas 2:6 [j]ver 2,17
11:23 [k]Gal 1:12 [l]S ver 2

[z]4-7 Or *4Every man who prays or prophesies with long hair dishonors his head. 5And every woman who prays or prophesies with no covering ⌊of hair⌋ on her head dishonors her head—she is just like one of the "shorn women." 6If a woman has no covering, let her be for now with short hair, but since it is a disgrace for a woman to have her hair shorn or shaved, she should grow it again. 7A man ought not to have long hair*

11:10–11 REVELATION, Angels—Paul tried to convince people of the awesome responsibility of worship and the need for submission to the authority and presence of God. The veiled woman indicates such humble posture. The angels who veil themselves before God with wings (Isa 6:2; Eze 1:11) are symbols of submission in God's presence.

11:11–12 HUMANITY, Marriage—The fulfillment of man and woman in each other is probably based upon Ge 2:20*b*–25. The ideal relationship within a marriage is one where each partner finds fulfillment in relating to the other. Neither male nor female can claim priority over the other.

11:12 GOD, Sovereignty—Man and woman live in a relationship of mutual interdependence, but that relationship must not become primary in life. Beyond all human relationships, beyond all earthly relationships, stands God's ultimate authority. Everything has come from God, and we all owe ultimate allegiance to God to whom we are held accountable.

11:13 PRAYER, Humility—See note on 11:4–5.

11:16 THE CHURCH, Local Body—Paul wrote local churches and used experiences of other local churches to help them. Local churches must not be isolated. They need to cooperate and benefit from other churches' experiences. See note on Ac 4:32.

11:17–34 ORDINANCES, Observance of Lord's Supper—Out of the oral teaching which Paul received from Jesus (v 23), probably through Peter, John, or James (see Ac 15:2; Gal 1:18–19), Paul gave the fullest, and probably the earliest account we have of the Last Supper. He condemned the abuse of the Lord's Supper by the Corinthians and, thereby, gave us more insight about the proper observance of the Supper than any other New Testament writer. Several distinctive points should be noted. (1) When they came together as a church, but had divisions among them, their eating and drinking could not really be a true observance of the Lord's Supper; they had to be unified in the Lord to observe the Lord's Supper properly. (2) Some plunged ahead with their eating and drinking, not waiting for anyone else, leaving some hungry while others got drunk. This shows that they were eating an *agape* or "love-feast" meal in connection with their effort to observe the Lord's Supper. Paul condemned their gluttony and their insensitivity to others. (3) Paul connected the eating of the bread and the drinking of the cup with proclaiming "the Lord's death until he comes," meaning that every proper observance of the Supper points back to the death of Christ and forward to the second coming of Christ. (4) Finally, Paul pronounced the severe judgment that those who eat and drink the body and blood of the Lord "in an unworthy manner" were actually sinning against the body and blood of the Lord. The consequences were serious. Because of this outrageous abuse of the Lord's Supper many of the Corinthians were weak and sick, and some had died. This exhortation calls us to serious and thoughtful observance of the Lord's Supper, being sensitive to the needs of other people and especially concentrating upon the Lord's atoning death on Calvary and His coming again in glory.

11:18–19 THE CHURCH, Local Body—The church is not the building but the assembly of the people of God, joining in fellowship and worship of God. See note on Ro 16:5. Oneness is the common goal. Confession, forgiveness, and acceptance must be practiced for the church to be what Jesus intended. Differences of opinion are normal among God's people. Each member must seek God's will in the issues the church faces. Ugly disharmony is not normal. It reveals that the wrong attitude prevails and that God does not approve.

11:21–22 DISCIPLESHIP, Hungry—Division of goods, not division in rival parties, characterizes disciples. We share with the needy. The church in Corinth was divided into groups of privileged and underprivileged. When they met to eat their potluck feasts, some had more than was needed; others had little to eat and were humiliated because they had nothing. The factions and lack of concern for one another revealed their discipleship was lacking even as they prepared for the sacred worship experience of the Lord's Supper. Paul had no praise for them. Their love for one another should have caused them to share. See notes on Lk 6:27–35; Ro 12:20; 13:8.

11:22 THE CHURCH, Fellowship—See notes on 11:18–19; Ro 16:5. Eating and drinking while assembled as the people of God is not prohibited. However, without the fellowship of the body which includes love and concern for every member, eating and drinking should be excluded as part of the worship of God. See note on 1 Co 1:9–10.

11:23 REVELATION, Jesus Christ—Paul explained the mystery and content of the Lord's Supper. He received its interpretation from Jesus Himself. Such a personal revelation is

broke it and said, "This is my body,[m]
which is for you; do this in remembrance
of me." 25 In the same way, after supper
he took the cup, saying, "This cup is the
new covenant[n] in my blood;[o] do this,
whenever you drink it, in remembrance
of me." 26 For whenever you eat this
bread and drink this cup, you proclaim
the Lord's death until he comes.[p]
27 Therefore, whoever eats the bread or
drinks the cup of the Lord in an unworthy
manner will be guilty of sinning against
the body and blood of the Lord.[q] 28 A man
ought to examine himself[r] before he eats
of the bread and drinks of the cup. 29 For
anyone who eats and drinks without recognizing the body of the Lord eats and
drinks judgment on himself. 30 That is
why many among you are weak and sick,
and a number of you have fallen asleep.[s]
31 But if we judged ourselves, we would
not come under judgment.[t] 32 When we
are judged by the Lord, we are being disciplined[u] so that we will not be condemned with the world.[v]
33 So then, my brothers, when you
come together to eat, wait for each other.
34 If anyone is hungry,[w] he should eat at
home,[x] so that when you meet together
it may not result in judgment.

And when I come[y] I will give further
directions.

Chapter 12

Spiritual Gifts

NOW about spiritual gifts,[z] brothers, I
do not want you to be ignorant.[a]
2 You know that when you were pagans,[b]
somehow or other you were influenced
and led astray to mute idols.[c] 3 Therefore
I tell you that no one who is speaking by
the Spirit of God says, "Jesus be
cursed,"[d] and no one can say, "Jesus is
Lord,"[e] except by the Holy Spirit.[f]
4 There are different kinds of gifts, but

11:24 [m]1Co 10:16
11:25 [n]S Lk 22:20 [o]1Co 10:16
11:26 [p]S 1Co 1:7
11:27 [q]Heb 10:29
11:28 [r]2Co 13:5
11:30 [s]S Mt 9:24
11:31 [t]Ps 32:5; 1Jn 1:9
11:32 [u]Ps 94:12; 118:18; Pr 3:11,12; Heb 12:7-10; Rev 3:19 [v]Jn 15:18, 19
11:34 [w]ver 21 [x]ver 22 [y]S 1Co 4:19
12:1 [z]Ro 1:11; 1Co 1:7; 14:1,37 [a]S Ro 11:25
12:2 [b]S Eph 2:2 [c]Ps 115:5; Jer 10:5; Hab 2:18,19
12:3 [d]Ro 9:3; 1Co 16:22 [e]S Jn 13:13 [f]1Jn 4:2,3

---

unique to an apostle who did not know Christ prior to His crucifixion. A vision or dream is most likely the means of such revelation, although Paul may have learned the meaning from other apostles or through the oral teaching of the church. How Paul received revelation is not important. Christ as the source of revelation is. Compare 7:1–40.

11:24 PRAYER, Thanksgiving—See note on Mt 26:26–27.

11:26 LAST THINGS, Return Promises—The second coming of Christ is a pervasive, underlying assumption of many New Testament passages. Even the backward-looking memorialization of the death of Jesus by the Lord's Supper carries a promise of His future return.

11:27–32 SIN, Against God—The Lord's Supper may be your invitation to sin. Participation in this central act of worship is sinful if we make it a social occasion or participate without committing ourselves to Christ's call to life leading to the cross. Divine discipline will fall on the sinner who brings dishonor to Christ and His death for us.

11:31–32 GOD, Judge—God is Judge of every person. There is a final judgment when we shall all give account to God. There is also an ongoing judgment in life where God watches our actions, judging or blessing as is appropriate. He chastises us as an expression of His Fatherly interest in us, and that for a redemptive purpose. His judgment is to bring us into conformity to His will and save us from more severe judgment and the calamities that we bring upon ourselves.

12:1–6 GOD, Trinity—Spiritual gifts enable God's people to do His work. The Holy Spirit reveals Himself in each life through the person's particular gift. God the Father is the ultimate source of each gift. Each gift helps us testify of Christ. Thus the three Persons who make up the one God in Christian faith are very closely identified in providing spiritual gifts and in guiding their work. See note on Mt 3:16–17.

12:1–3 HOLY SPIRIT, Indwells—God poured out His Spirit on all the Christians at Pentecost. See note on Ac 2:1–4. From that time all new believers in Christ have received the Spirit (Ac 2:38; Ro 8:9). Only the indwelling Spirit can lead you to confess Christ as Lord. In Corinth some Christians were unclear about this. Some church members spoke in unknown tongues (1 Co 14:2) and claimed this gift showed they had the Spirit. In their view Christians who did not speak in tongues did not have the Spirit. Paul disagreed strongly. One sign shows the Spirit's presence. The Spirit is present with those who sincerely confess that Jesus is Lord. He is never present with anyone who says that Jesus is cursed. The Spirit is present with all Christians and with no one else. The Spirit is always working to build up the people of God, never to tear them apart; and He is always working to extend the gospel message, never to muzzle that message. The criteria for the Spirit: (1) He is present when people confess that Jesus is Lord; (2) He is working in a church which follows the way of love; and (3) He is active when the church uses His gifts of prophecy to proclaim the gospel. See 1 Jn 4:1–3.

12:3,5 JESUS CHRIST, Lord—See notes on 8:4–6; Ac 2:23–36.

12:4–11 HOLY SPIRIT, Gifts—God gives His Holy Spirit to His people, so the Spirit Himself is the ultimate spiritual gift (Ac 2:38). The background of the New Testament teaching about the Spirit and His gifts is the work of the Spirit in the Old Testament. There His most characteristic work was to give a selected individual a gift (or gifts) with which to serve God by serving the people. See note on Zec 4:6. In the church, the Spirit is present with each of God's people, not just with selected leaders. Every Christian is a gifted person (1 Co 12:7). The Spirit always brings one or more spiritual gifts to a Christian's life. These gifts are talents—spiritual endowments which equip the person to serve Christ. See 7:7; 12—14; Ro 12:1–8; Eph 4:1–13; 1 Pe 4:10. Gifts vary from person to person. This led to the problem at Corinth. God intends for His people to have a variety of gifts, but there is only one God, one Christ, one Spirit. Diversity of gifts should not cause a division in the church (vv 4–6). The various gifts should unite the church. The variety of gifts is for the good of all. Christians are given gifts so they can serve each other (1 Pe 4:10). Anyone who uses a gift to create disunity among God's people is misguided. Gifts are for building up the entire church, not for making one person feel proud and another feel left out. Paul listed several gifts, but there is no reason to suppose these lists are comprehensive. He did not mention gifts which are widely recognized today, such as gifts of music, of youth work, or of counseling. Whatever skill you have which can be used to serve Christ and His people is a gift of the Spirit. Gifts may be given suddenly or developed slowly. Paul recognized both miraculous powers (1 Co 12:10) and leadership (Ro 12:8). The sovereign Spirit gives whatever gifts He decides. Christians should receive them with thanks and use them responsibly. The ultimate gift of the Spirit is the one gift available to all Christians: the gift of love (1 Co 13). To have all other gifts and lack love is to have nothing; to lack all other gifts and have love is to have everything (13:1–3). All other gifts should be used in a spirit of love (14:1). Next to the gift of love, Paul valued prophecy most highly (1 Co 14:1). This gift enabled the church to carry out its task of world evangelism. All gifts come from the Spirit to individuals for the church's good. Each can show that the Spirit is working in a believer's life, but no one of them

the same Spirit.[g] 5There are different
kinds of service, but the same Lord.
6There are different kinds of working, but
the same God[h] works all of them in all
men.[i]

7Now to each one the manifestation of
the Spirit is given for the common good.[j]
8To one there is given through the Spirit
the message of wisdom,[k] to another the
message of knowledge[l] by means of the
same Spirit, 9to another faith[m] by the
same Spirit, to another gifts of healing[n]
by that one Spirit, 10to another miraculous powers,[o] to another prophecy,[p] to
another distinguishing between spirits,[q]
to another speaking in different kinds of
tongues,[a r] and to still another the interpretation of tongues.[a] 11All these are the
work of one and the same Spirit,[s] and he
gives them to each one, just as he determines.

One Body, Many Parts

12The body is a unit, though it is made
up of many parts; and though all its parts
are many, they form one body.[t] So it is
with Christ.[u] 13For we were all baptized[v] by[b] one Spirit[w] into one body—
whether Jews or Greeks, slave or free[x]
—and we were all given the one Spirit to
drink.[y]
14Now the body is not made up of one
part but of many.[z] 15If the foot should
say, "Because I am not a hand, I do not
belong to the body," it would not for that
reason cease to be part of the body. 16And
if the ear should say, "Because I am not
an eye, I do not belong to the body," it
would not for that reason cease to be part
of the body. 17If the whole body were an
eye, where would the sense of hearing
be? If the whole body were an ear, where
would the sense of smell be? 18But in fact
God has arranged[a] the parts in the body,
every one of them, just as he wanted
them to be.[b] 19If they were all one part,
where would the body be? 20As it is,
there are many parts, but one body.[c]

21The eye cannot say to the hand, "I
don't need you!" And the head cannot
say to the feet, "I don't need you!" 22On
the contrary, those parts of the body that
seem to be weaker are indispensable,
23and the parts that we think are less honorable we treat with special honor. And
the parts that are unpresentable are treated with special modesty, 24while our pre-
sentable parts need no special treatment.
But God has combined the members of
the body and has given greater honor to
the parts that lacked it, 25so that there
should be no division in the body, but
that its parts should have equal concern
for each other. 26If one part suffers, every
part suffers with it; if one part is honored,
every part rejoices with it.

27Now you are the body of Christ,[d]
and each one of you is a part of it.[e] 28And
in the church[f] God has appointed first of
all apostles,[g] second prophets,[h] third
teachers, then workers of miracles, also
those having gifts of healing,[i] those able
to help others, those with gifts of administration,[j] and those speaking in different kinds of tongues.[k] 29Are all apostles?

12:4 [g]ver 8-11; Ro 12:4-8; Eph 4:11; Heb 2:4
12:6 [h]Eph 4:6 [i]S Php 2:13
12:7 [j]1Co 14:12; Eph 4:12
12:8 [k]1Co 2:6 [l]S 2Co 8:7
12:9 [m]Mt 17:19, 20; 1Co 13:2 [n]ver 28,30; Mt 10:1
12:10 [o]ver 28-30; Gal 3:5 [p]S Eph 4:11 [q]1Jn 4:1 [r]S Mk 16:17
12:11 [s]S ver 4
12:12 [t]S Ro 12:5 [u]ver 27
12:13 [v]S Mk 1:8 [w]Eph 2:18 [x]Gal 3:28; Col 3:11 [y]Jn 7:37-39
12:14 [z]ver 12,20
12:18 [a]ver 28 [b]ver 11
12:20 [c]ver 12,14; S Ro 12:5
12:27 [d]Eph 1:23; 4:12; Col 1:18,24 [e]S Ro 12:5
12:28 [f]S 1Co 10:32 [g]S Eph 4:11 [h]S Eph 4:11 [i]ver 9 [j]Ro 12:6-8 [k]ver 10; S Mk 16:17

[a] *10* Or *languages*; also in verse 28 [b] *13* Or *with*; or *in*

is to be used as a test of a believer's spirituality as long as love uses the gift in ministry. See Guide to Discovering Your Spiritual Gifts, pp. 1796–1799.

12:9-10 MIRACLE, Instruments—God gives some of His people special gifts to carry on His healing ministry. To others He gives the gift of miracles or powerful works. Both of these gifts are described in general terms so that specific definition is difficult. God has not taken His power away from His church. The gifts are to testify to Jesus, be acknowledged as the work of God's Spirit, be accepted as part of the gifts given the church, be used for the common good of the church rather than for the prestige and ego needs of an individual member. Christians "eagerly desire spiritual gifts" (14:1), while letting the Spirit determine the gifts we need and can best use. Each gift is given as God determines. People are only instruments God uses for His purposes. The church needs all the gifts God gives. The gifts of healing and miraculous powers must bring unity to Christ's body. Such gifts may include the God-given skills of modern physicians, scientists, and counselors. We must not limit these gifts to such skills. God gives the gifts as He determines. We must not try to limit what He chooses to do.

12:12–31 THE CHURCH, Body of Christ—Each church member plays a significant and important part in the church's life. The church needs every member. The church's unity is expressed through the diverse gifts God gives its members. Gifts present no reason to boast of oneself or despise another. God gave the gifts to build up the church. We should thank God for all the church's gifts. We should seek to mature and be able to exercise new gifts God may give us. All gifts must be exercised in faith, hope, and love (ch 13). See note on Ro 12:4–8.

12:28 GOD, Trinity—Christ is the head of His body, the church. The Holy Spirit is usually thought of as giving spiritual gifts to believers (vv 3,7). God Himself directs the church and its life. He provides human leaders for it but remains the unqualified sovereign authority of the church.

12:28–29 CHURCH LEADERS, Prophet—The function of prophets is to announce and interpret revelation from God that they have received, to reveal spiritual insight which is hidden to others, and to foretell the future to warn and encourage their hearers. The combination of proclamation (forthtelling) and prediction (foretelling) distinguishes the prophet from someone who merely prognosticates the future. The authority of prophets derives from the inspiration of the Holy Spirit. As a gift of the Spirit, prophecy may be given to and exercised by any of God's people. See note on Ac 2:17.

12:28–29 CHURCH LEADERS, Teacher—The teachers are the guardians and interpreters of the Christian tradition and give religious instruction to the converted. As Jesus taught those who responded to His preaching, so teachers are to explain the mysteries, nature, and principles of the Kingdom and to make clear the meaning of the Scriptures to the congregation. They also instruct in the moral duties of the Christian life. An individual becomes a teacher only if the person has been endowed with the spiritual gift of teaching. The teacher may have another office in the church such as overseer or pastor (1 Ti 3:2; 5:17; Tit 1:9).

Are all prophets? Are all teachers? Do all work miracles? 30Do all have gifts of healing? Do all speak in tongues[c]?[l] Do all interpret? 31But eagerly desire[d][m] the greater gifts.

Love

And now I will show you the most excellent way.

Chapter 13

If I speak in the tongues[e][n] of men and of angels, but have not love, I am only a resounding gong or a clanging cymbal. 2If I have the gift of prophecy[o] and can fathom all mysteries[p] and all knowledge,[q] and if I have a faith[r] that can move mountains,[s] but have not love, I am nothing. 3If I give all I possess to the poor[t] and surrender my body to the flames,[f][u] but have not love, I gain nothing.

4Love is patient,[v] love is kind. It does not envy, it does not boast, it is not proud.[w] 5It is not rude, it is not self-seeking,[x] it is not easily angered,[y] it keeps no record of wrongs.[z] 6Love does not delight in evil[a] but rejoices with the truth.[b] 7It always protects, always trusts, always hopes, always perseveres.[c]

8Love never fails. But where there are prophecies,[d] they will cease; where there are tongues,[e] they will be stilled; where there is knowledge, it will pass away. 9For we know in part[f] and we prophesy in part, 10but when perfection comes,[g] the imperfect disappears. 11When I was a child, I talked like a child, I thought like a child, I reasoned like a child. When I became a man, I put childish ways[h] behind me. 12Now we see but a poor reflection as in a mirror;[i] then we shall see face to face.[j] Now I know in part; then I shall know fully, even as I am fully known.[k]

13And now these three remain: faith, hope and love.[l] But the greatest of these is love.[m]

Chapter 14

Gifts of Prophecy and Tongues

Follow the way of love[n] and eagerly desire[o] spiritual gifts,[p] especially the gift of prophecy.[q] 2For anyone who speaks in a tongue[g][r] does not speak to men but to God. Indeed, no one understands him;[s] he utters mysteries[t] with his spirit.[h] 3But everyone who prophesies speaks to men for their strengthening,[u] encouragement[v] and comfort. 4He who speaks in a tongue[w] edifies[x] himself, but he who prophesies[y] edifies the church. 5I would like every one of you to speak in tongues,[i] but I would rather have you prophesy.[z] He who prophesies is greater than one who speaks in tongues,[i] unless he interprets, so that the church may be edified.[a]

6Now, brothers, if I come to you and speak in tongues, what good will I be to you, unless I bring you some revelation[b] or knowledge[c] or prophecy or word of instruction?[d] 7Even in the case of lifeless things that make sounds, such as the flute or harp, how will anyone know what tune is being played unless there is a distinction in the notes? 8Again, if the trumpet does not sound a clear call, who will get ready for battle?[e] 9So it is with you. Unless you speak intelligible words with your tongue, how will anyone know what you are saying? You will just be speaking into the air. 10Undoubtedly there are all sorts of languages in the world, yet none of them is without meaning. 11If then I do not grasp the meaning of what someone

[c]30 Or *other languages* [d]31 Or *But you are eagerly desiring* [e]1 Or *languages* [f]3 Some early manuscripts *body that I may boast* [g]2 Or *another language*; also in verses 4, 13, 14, 19, 26 and 27 [h]2 Or *by the Spirit* [i]5 Or *other languages*; also in verses 6, 18, 22, 23 and 39

12:30 [l]ver 10
12:31 [m]1Co 14:1, 39
13:1 [n]ver 8; S Mk 16:17
13:2 [o]ver 8; S Eph 4:11; S Ac 11:27 [p]1Co 14:2 [q]S 2Co 8:7 [r]1Co 12:9 [s]Mt 17:20; 21:21
13:3 [t]Lk 19:8; S Ac 2:45 [u]Da 3:28
13:4 [v]1Th 5:14 [w]1Co 5:2
13:5 [x]S 1Co 10:24 [y]S Mt 5:22 [z]Job 14:16,17; Pr 10:12; 17:9; 1Pe 4:8
13:6 [a]2Th 2:12 [b]2Jn 4; 3Jn 3,4
13:7 [c]ver 8,13
13:8 [d]ver 2 [e]ver 1
13:9 [f]ver 12; S 1Co 8:2
13:10 [g]Php 3:12
13:11 [h]Ps 131:2
13:12 [i]Job 26:14; 36:26 [j]Ge 32:30; Job 19:26; 1Jn 3:2 [k]1Co 8:3; Gal 4:9
13:13 [l]Ro 5:2-5; Gal 5:5,6; Eph 4:2-5; Col 1:4, 5; 1Th 1:3; 5:8; Heb 6:10-12 [m]Mt 22:37-40; 1Co 16:14; Gal 5:6; 1Jn 4:7-12,16
14:1 [n]1Co 16:14 [o]ver 39; 1Co 12:31 [p]S 1Co 12:1 [q]ver 39; S Eph 4:11
14:2 [r]S Mk 16:17 [s]ver 6-11,16 [t]1Co 13:2
14:3 [u]ver 4,5,12, 17,26; S Ro 14:19 [v]ver 31
14:4 [w]S Mk 16:17 [x]S ver 3 [y]S 1Co 13:2
14:5 [z]Nu 11:29 [a]S ver 3
14:6 [b]ver 26; Eph 1:17 [c]S 2Co 8:7 [d]Ro 6:17
14:8 [e]Nu 10:9; Jer 4:19

13:1–12 REVELATION, Author of Love—Tongue-speaking and preaching skills are means of revelation but secondary in the Christian life to God's love being active in one's life. Intellectual ability (the wisdom often worshiped by Paul's readers) and powerful faith that can perform miracles do not compare to love that reveals God's own heart. Our ability to understand or know God's truth is still limited as human beings, but one day we shall see God's truth and love face-to-face.

13:1–13 CHRISTIAN ETHICS, Character—In these verses Paul provided the most well-rounded yet concise definition of love (Greek *agape*) in the New Testament. He enumerated the results of such love rather than specific strategies to have these results. This should not be considered an omission on Paul's part. Love cannot be expressed simply by following a legalistic pattern. That love which seeks the positive results named by Paul will also work out methods which are inspired by the same love. Programs, processes, and actions mean nothing if love does not motivate them. Love is a consistent attitude of personal humility and devotion to the good of others. We can love because God loved us (1 Jn 4:19). We seek to have love become our identifying characteristic as it is God's (1 Jn 4:16). Christian ethics is a God-centered ethic of love.

14:1–39 HOLY SPIRIT, Gifts—See note on Ac 2:1–4.

14:1–19 PRAYER, Corporate—Speaking in tongues, at least in this passage, was to God. Prophesying was to people. In corporate prayer, all should participate, but they cannot if the prayer is unintelligible. Praying which pleases God is neither spiritless mind nor mindless spirit, but prayer in which the mind is tuned to the frequency of the Holy Spirit. Praying in tongues needs interpretation for the mind of the person praying to be actively involved and also for the congregation to be actively involved in worship.

14:3–5 CHURCH LEADERS, Prophet—The prophet proclaims God's message to build up, exhort, and encourage the community. Prophecy is Spirit-inspired speech from God that is intelligible and convicts the hearts of the hearers. Prophets edify the church and not simply themselves. For this reason, Paul preferred the gift of prophecy over that of tongues. Prophecy is to be exercised in a spirit of order and not tumult.

is saying, I am a foreigner to the speaker, and he is a foreigner to me.[f] 12So it is with you. Since you are eager to have spiritual gifts,[g] try to excel in gifts that build up[h] the church.

13For this reason anyone who speaks in a tongue should pray that he may interpret what he says.[i] 14For if I pray in a tongue, my spirit prays,[j] but my mind is unfruitful. 15So what shall I do? I will pray with my spirit,[k] but I will also pray with my mind; I will sing[l] with my spirit, but I will also sing with my mind. 16If you are praising God with your spirit, how can one who finds himself among those who do not understand[j] say "Amen"[m] to your thanksgiving,[n] since he does not know what you are saying? 17You may be giving thanks well enough, but the other man is not edified.[o]

18I thank God that I speak in tongues more than all of you. 19But in the church I would rather speak five intelligible words to instruct others than ten thousand words in a tongue.[p]

20Brothers, stop thinking like children.[q] In regard to evil be infants,[r] but in your thinking be adults. 21In the Law[s] it is written:

"Through men of strange tongues
and through the lips of foreigners
I will speak to this people,
but even then they will not listen to me,"[k] [t]
says the Lord.

22Tongues, then, are a sign, not for believers but for unbelievers; prophecy,[u] however, is for believers, not for unbelievers. 23So if the whole church comes together and everyone speaks in tongues, and some who do not understand[l] or some unbelievers come in, will they not say that you are out of your mind?[v] 24But if an unbeliever or someone who does not understand[m] comes in while everybody is prophesying, he will be convinced by all that he is a sinner and will be judged by all, 25and the secrets[w] of his heart will be laid bare. So he will fall down and worship God, exclaiming, "God is really among you!"[x]

Orderly Worship

26What then shall we say, brothers?[y] When you come together, everyone[z] has a hymn,[a] or a word of instruction,[b] a revelation, a tongue[c] or an interpretation.[d] All of these must be done for the strengthening[e] of the church. 27If anyone speaks in a tongue, two—or at the most three—should speak, one at a time, and someone must interpret. 28If there is no interpreter, the speaker should keep quiet in the church and speak to himself and God.

29Two or three prophets[f] should speak, and the others should weigh carefully what is said.[g] 30And if a revelation comes to someone who is sitting down, the first speaker should stop. 31For you can all prophesy in turn so that everyone may be instructed and encouraged. 32The spirits of prophets are subject to the control of prophets.[h] 33For God is not a God of disorder[i] but of peace.[j]

As in all the congregations[k] of the saints,[l] 34women should remain silent in

14:11 fGe 11:7
14:12 gS 1Co 12:1 hS ver 3
14:13 iver 5
14:14 jver 2
14:15 kver 2,14 lS Eph 5:19
14:16 mDt 27:15-26; 1Ch 16:36; Ne 8:6; Ps 106:48; Rev 5:14; 7:12 nS Mt 14:19; 1Co 11:24
14:17 oS ver 3
14:19 pver 6
14:20 q1Co 3:11; Eph 4:14; Heb 5:12, 13; 1Pe 2:2 rJer 4:22; Mt 10:16; Ro 16:19
14:21 sver 34; S Jn 10:34 tDt 28:49; Isa 28:11,12
14:22 uver 1
14:23 vAc 2:13
14:25 wRo 2:16 xIsa 45:14; Zec 8:23
14:26 yS Ro 7:1 z1Co 12:7-10 aS Eph 5:19 bver 6 cver 2 d1Co 12:10 eS Ro 14:19
14:29 fver 32,37; S 1Co 13:2 g1Co 12:10
14:32 h1Jn 4:1
14:33 iver 40 jS Ro 15:33 kS 1Co 7:17; S 10:32 lS Ac 9:13

j*16* Or *among the inquirers* k*21* Isaiah 28:11,12
l*23* Or *some inquirers* m*24* Or *or some inquirer*

14:19 EDUCATION, Instruction—Christian teaching and learning are illuminated by the Spirit, but they do not circumvent the mind. The substance of the Christian faith is intelligible, and the communication of the Christian faith must be rational. The study desk and the prayer closet are both essential to Christian teaching and learning. Teaching is an attempt to communicate, not to display personal spiritual powers or gifts. Teachers serve learners' needs rather than satisfy personal ego problems.

14:20 CREATION, Evil—God's good world has been infiltrated by those who seek to harm good people and good causes. God allows good and evil to exist side by side, but gives specific instructions as to how His people shall deal with evil. By dealing with it properly, we can become stronger in character.

14:26–40 REVELATION, Inspiration—Inspiration seeks to strengthen the church, provide instruction for life and faith, encourage God's people, and promote peace. God uses every means to make Himself known in order to accomplish these goals. Insight into God's revealed teaching many come to any faithful believer at any moment. Worship is a setting God uses to teach His people. God's revealed will should be shared with the church in orderly fashion. Anyone sharing God's revealed insights should do so to help the church and not to gain personal power or prestige. Revelation begins with God, not humans. He gives all gifts of revelation and ministry.

14:26–33 WORSHIP, Corporate—See note on Ps 42:1–4. Corporate worship in the early church included several elements. Worship sought to interpret God's will clearly to His people and to strengthen the church.

14:33 GOD, Father—God the Father is a purposive, orderly God working for good ends. His actions are not random and erratic, and His purposes are not everchanging. When worship becomes chaotic and out of control, it no longer reflects the God of peace.

14:34–37 HOLY SCRIPTURE, Authoritative—Paul wrote with conscious authority from God. He expected the church to follow his teaching. No person has a monopoly on revelation. All claims to inspired truth must be tested against the written revelation God's Spirit inspired. Paul accepted women prophets (11:5) but insisted they maintain order and not do anything in their cultural setting which might bring disgrace on the church.

14:34 THE CHURCH, Local Body—See notes on 11:22; Ac 16:4–5; Ro 15:5–7. The problems at Corinth called for local solutions to the particular difficulties in the church. At Corinth, eating and drinking took place in private, not at the church. At Corinth, women spoke at home, not while in church. Prostitution, associated with pagan religion at Corinth, and other difficulties probably necessitated Paul's words. In other contexts, women prayed, prophesied, and advanced the kingdom of God in the New Testament (1 Co 11:5; Ac 16:14–15; 18:26). The church should solve fellowship problems quickly to avoid hindering the cause of Christ.

the churches. They are not allowed to
speak,[m] but must be in submission,[n] as
the Law[o] says. 35If they want to inquire
about something, they should ask their
own husbands at home; for it is disgraceful for a woman to speak in the church.
36Did the word of God[p] originate with
you? Or are you the only people it has
reached? 37If anybody thinks he is a
prophet[q] or spiritually gifted,[r] let him
acknowledge that what I am writing to
you is the Lord's command.[s] 38If he ignores this, he himself will be ignored.[n]
39Therefore, my brothers, be eager[t] to
prophesy,[u] and do not forbid speaking in
tongues. 40But everything should be done
in a fitting and orderly[v] way.

Chapter 15

The Resurrection of Christ

NOW, brothers, I want to remind you
of the gospel[w] I preached to you,[x]
which you received and on which you
have taken your stand. 2By this gospel
you are saved,[y] if you hold firmly[z] to the
word I preached to you. Otherwise, you
have believed in vain.
3For what I received[a] I passed on to
you[b] as of first importance[o]: that Christ
died for our sins[c] according to the Scriptures,[d] 4that he was buried,[e] that he was
raised[f] on the third day[g] according to
the Scriptures,[h] 5and that he appeared to
Peter,[p][i] and then to the Twelve.[j] 6After
that, he appeared to more than five hundred of the brothers at the same time,
most of whom are still living, though
some have fallen asleep.[k] 7Then he appeared to James,[l] then to all the apostles,[m] 8and last of all he appeared to me
also,[n] as to one abnormally born.
9For I am the least of the apostles[o] and
do not even deserve to be called an apostle, because I persecuted[p] the church of
God.[q] 10But by the grace[r] of God I am
what I am, and his grace to me[s] was not
without effect. No, I worked harder than
all of them[t]—yet not I, but the grace of
God that was with me.[u] 11Whether,
then, it was I or they,[v] this is what we
preach, and this is what you believed.

The Resurrection of the Dead

12But if it is preached that Christ has

14:34 [m]1Co 11:5, 13 [n]S Eph 5:22; 1Ti 2:11,12 [o]ver 21; Ge 3:16 **14:36** [p]S Heb 4:12 **14:37** [q]S Ac 11:27; 1Co 13:2; 2Co 10:7 [r]1Co 2:15; S 12:1 [s]1Jn 4:6 **14:39** [t]ver 1; 1Co 12:31 [u]ver 1; S Eph 4:11 **14:40** [v]ver 33; Col 2:5 **15:1** [w]Isa 40:9; Ro 2:16 [x]S 1Co 3:6; S Gal 1:8 **15:2** [y]Ro 1:16 [z]S Ro 11:22 **15:3** [a]Gal 1:12 [b]S 1Co 11:2 [c]Isa 53:5; Jn 1:29; S Gal 1:4; 1Pe 2:24 [d]S Mt 26:24; S Lk 24:27; S 24:44; Ac 17:2; 26:22,23 **15:4** [e]Mt 27:59,60 [f]S Ac 2:24 [g]S Mt 16:21 [h]Jn 2:21,22; Ac 2:25,30,31 **15:5** [i]Lk 24:34 [j]Mk 16:14; Lk 24:36-43 **15:6** [k]ver 18,20; S Mt 9:24 **15:7** [l]S Ac 15:13 [m]Lk 24:33,36,37; Ac 1:3,4 **15:8** [n]Ac 9:3-6,17; 1Co 9:1; Gal 1:16 **15:9** [o]2Co 12:11; Eph 3:8; 1Ti 1:15 [p]S Ac 8:3 [q]S 1Co 10:32 **15:10** [r]S Ro 3:24 [s]S Ro 12:3 [t]2Co 11:23; Col 1:29 [u]S Php 2:13 **15:11** [v]Gal 2:6

[n]38 Some manuscripts *If he is ignorant of this, let him be ignorant* [o]3 Or *you at the first* [p]5 Greek *Cephas*

15:1–7 PROCLAMATION, Gospel—See notes on Ac 3:11–26; Ro 10:8–13. These verses give the most concise definition of the content of the gospel to be found anywhere in Scripture. Christ's death, burial, and resurrection are said to have been "according to the Scriptures." These events not only happened at the time, place, and in the manner described in Scripture but also for the purpose and with the results described in Scripture. He died in our place, satisfying the demands of God's holiness. He rose bodily from the grave. Through personal faith in Him, we can be delivered from eternal punishment in hell and live eternally in His presence. The content of our proclamation is the Word of God (2 Ti 3:14—4:2).

15:2 ELECTION, Righteousness—Profession of faith in Christ demands obedience to the election calling. The gospel must be professed and practiced.

15:3–8 JESUS CHRIST, Death—This brief summary of the gospel may well be the first written account of the gospel. The gospel centers on Christ fulfilling Scripture through His death, burial, resurrection, and resurrection appearances. Paul connected the death of Jesus and our sins. Latter theories of atonement developed Paul's ideas of Christ's death for us along the lines of substitutionary, moral influence, and representation explanations. See History of Doctrine of Jesus Christ, p. 1704; History of Doctrine of Salvation, p. 1716.

15:3 HOLY SCRIPTURE, Redemption—Revelation centers on the life and work of Christ as fulfillment of all revealed truth. The Christ-centered content of revelation was first preached at Pentecost (Ac 2), then passed orally through preaching and teaching. Paul received it orally, used it as the center of his preaching, and then wrote it down here, where it became written revelation. Paul witnessed to his call to pass the story of redemption on to his audiences, both Jews and Gentiles. His revelation of redemption includes the death of Christ as gift to redeem all people of their sins, the Scriptures as direct revelation of God's truth and love, and resurrection as revealed by Scripture and confirmed by many disciples.

15:3 EDUCATION, Tradition—Like a flaming Olympic torch passed from one runner to another, the gospel tradition had been passed from faithful believers to Paul. Through careful instruction, he communicated that message to his children in the faith. See 4:14. Each generation of Christians must raise up faithful teachers who will pass the torch to the next generation of believers. The faith is always one generation away from oblivion. The church depends on dedicated teachers for its continued existence.

15:6–8 JESUS CHRIST, Resurrection—This earliest written statement of the Christian message tells of five appearances of the resurrected Christ: to Peter; to the apostles; to 500 (possibly the same as the ascension appearance in Ac 1:1–11); the appearance to James; and to Paul (Ac 9:1–6). Interestingly, the appearances to women at the tomb are not listed, showing Paul's list is not supposed to be complete.

15:7–9 CHURCH LEADERS, Apostle—The office of apostle was unique. Christ directly commissioned the apostles to bear witness to Him. They could not transfer this office to another and could not be replaced by another generation of apostles. Paul considered himself to be the last to receive this commission from the risen Lord. The literary fruit of their work is their witness to Jesus contained in the New Testament.

15:9 THE CHURCH, Local Body—See notes on Ac 8:1; 9:2–31.

15:10 GOD, Grace—God's grace comes to us not only in the free gift of salvation, but also in the unfolding development of the Christian life and in our service in the church. We must put forth our very best efforts to grow and serve God. At the same time we know we have unseen spiritual resources enabling us to serve. The grace of God provides these resources. We have not earned them, nor should we be jealous or proud of them. We should be humbly grateful for the grace God gives us to do His work.

15:12–19 JESUS CHRIST, Resurrection—Jesus' resurrection proves resurrection is possible, forms the center of gospel preaching, is the foundation of our faith, and gives hope for departed loved ones and us to be raised from death.

15:12–19 LAST THINGS, Believers' Death—To live as a Christian is to be in Christ (Jn 15:5). To die as a Christian is to fall asleep in Him. See note on Ac 7:60. The text presents the

been raised from the dead,[w] how can
some of you say that there is no resurrection[x] of the dead?[y] 13If there is no resurrection of the dead, then not even Christ
has been raised. 14And if Christ has not
been raised,[z] our preaching is useless
and so is your faith. 15More than that, we
are then found to be false witnesses about
God, for we have testified about God that
he raised Christ from the dead.[a] But he
did not raise him if in fact the dead are
not raised. 16For if the dead are not
raised, then Christ has not been raised
either. 17And if Christ has not been
raised, your faith is futile; you are still in
your sins.[b] 18Then those also who have
fallen asleep[c] in Christ are lost. 19If only
for this life we have hope in Christ, we
are to be pitied more than all men.[d]

20But Christ has indeed been raised
from the dead,[e] the firstfruits[f] of those
who have fallen asleep.[g] 21For since
death came through a man,[h] the resurrection of the dead[i] comes also through
a man. 22For as in Adam all die, so in
Christ all will be made alive.[j] 23But each
in his own turn: Christ, the firstfruits;[k]
then, when he comes,[l] those who belong to him.[m] 24Then the end will come,
when he hands over the kingdom[n] to
God the Father after he has destroyed all
dominion, authority and power.[o] 25For
he must reign[p] until he has put all his
enemies under his feet.[q] 26The last enemy to be destroyed is death.[r] 27For he
"has put everything under his feet."[q][s]
Now when it says that "everything" has
been put under him, it is clear that this
does not include God himself, who put
everything under Christ.[t] 28When he has
done this, then the Son himself will be
made subject to him who put everything
under him,[u] so that God may be all in
all.[v]

29Now if there is no resurrection, what

15:12 [w]ver 4 [x]S Jn 11:24 [y]Ac 17:32; 23:8; 2Ti 2:18 **15:14** [z]1Th 4:14 **15:15** [a]S Ac 2:24 **15:17** [b]S Ro 4:25 **15:18** [c]ver 6,20; S Mt 9:24 **15:19** [d]S 1Co 4:9 **15:20** [e]1Pe 1:3 [f]ver 23; S Ac 26:23 [g]ver 6,18; S Mt 9:24 **15:21** [h]S Ro 5:12 [i]ver 12 **15:22** [j]Ro 5:14-18; S 1Co 6:14 **15:23** [k]ver 20 [l]ver 52; S 1Th 2:19 [m]S 1Co 3:23 **15:24** [n]Da 2:44; 7:14,27; 2Pe 1:11 [o]Ro 8:38 **15:25** [p]Isa 9:7; 52:7 [q]ver 27; S Mt 22:44 **15:26** [r]2Ti 1:10; Rev 20:14; 21:4 **15:27** [s]ver 25; Ps 8:6; S Mt 22:44 [t]S Mt 28:18 **15:28** [u]Php 3:21 [v]1Co 3:23

[q]*27* Psalm 8:6

---

logical reasoning that if Christ had not risen from the dead, then death would be the end for all, even believers. Here the resurrection is asserted as one of the most crucial of all doctrines, so much so that if Christ did not arise, our lives are hopeless. The resurrection of Christ insures that those fallen asleep in Him are not lost.

15:14 PROCLAMATION, Gospel—Without Christ's resurrection we have nothing to preach. The bodily resurrection of Christ is the source for our resurrection hope and thus for our preaching. See note on Ac 3:11–26.

15:19 HUMANITY, Death—Most people throughout the Old Testament era and some people in the New Testament era did not believe in life after death. With the resurrection of Jesus and the preaching of the gospel, we have a new hope—life after death. Without such hope, life loses meaning. See note on Mt 22:23–33.

15:19,22 SALVATION, As Being in Christ—Our hope in Christ is for this world and the next. Being in Christ is union with Christ through faith. In Christ we suffer the world's ridicule and persecution, but we look forward to eternal life.

15:20–28 JESUS CHRIST, Final Coming—This passage is the heart of Paul's affirmations about the last things. This resurrection chapter details the witnesses to Jesus' resurrection, including himself (vv 1–11); points out the centrality of Jesus' resurrection as a basis for the gospel (vv 12–19); appeals to the pagan custom of baptizing for the dead as proof that even pagans affirm resurrection (v 29); suggests that Paul put his own life and ministry on the line for the sake of belief in resurrection (vv 30–34); gives analogies by which to express resurrection (vv 35–49); and concludes with a glorious tribute to the work of Christ, who overcame death, the last enemy (vv 50–57). As always, Paul added an ethical injunction to Christians to continue their work for God in the light of these great realities. The basic facts of the last things are: (1) Christ is the firstfruits of the resurrection and appropriately so. Since a man (Adam) had occasioned death, the man, Jesus, brought the only satisfactory resolution of death—resurrection. (2) At Christ's coming those who belong to Him are raised. (3) At the end Christ turns over the Kingdom to the Father that "God may be all in all." Christ's turning over the Kingdom to God should not be seen as an essential subordination of the Son to the Father. Rather it is a functional subordination that characterizes trinitarian relationships. The Father delights in the Son; the Son gives honor to the Father; the Spirit bears witness to the Son. See note on Mt 24:1—25:46; History of the Doctrine of God, p. 1703.

15:20–23 LAST THINGS, Believers' Resurrection—The order of resurrection begins with Christ followed by that of believers at the time of His coming. Christ's resurrection—the firstfruits of the new covenant—is God's guarantee that His followers will rise too. Being made alive is an accomplishment possible only in Christ. All people are descendants of Adam; thus all people face eternal death. But as Adam ushered in an era of death, Christ ushered in an era of life; and that life is possible only through Christ. For the resurrection of unbelievers, see note on Rev 20:4–5.

15:21–22 HUMANITY, Death—Some Corinthians denied the human body would be resurrected (v 12). Paul pointed to Jesus' resurrection as the primary and only necessary evidence for resurrection. Jesus' resurrection has changed the course of human history. The first human being sinned and brought death into the world, a pattern followed by all humans. Jesus did not sin. He brought resurrection and promised the ultimate destruction of death. This did not change the mortal nature of humans. It did give hope to those who belong to Christ.

15:24,27–28 GOD, Trinity—God's plan to save the world works towards its climax. Through the resurrection God the Father has placed His kingdom in the Son's hands. When Christ reigns fully, having done away with all enemies—even death—then He will hand the kingdom back to the Father. Thus in all things, even in the relationships among the three Persons of the Trinity, the Father reigns supreme.

15:24–28 LAST THINGS, Kingdom Established—As God's rule in human hearts, the kingdom of God was inaugurated at Christ's first coming (Mk 1:14–15). Those who receive Him as Lord come under the rule of God in their lives. In its present sense, the kingdom has come to every person who accepts the rule of God in faith. The kingdom of God will be fully established only in the future. What Jesus inaugurated at His first coming, He will consummate at His second coming. The established, consummated kingdom is to be handed over by the victorious Christ to God the Father. Such final establishment requires the conquest of all enemies under the rule of God. The final enemy is death. The ultimate goal is the glory of God in the final and total establishment of His rule.

15:29 ORDINANCES, Baptism as Confession—The basic meaning here is clear if details of interpretation are not. Since baptism pictures resurrection of the dead, it would be a mockery to practice baptism if we do not believe in the resurrection of the dead. Only confessing believers are to be baptized. No support is given "proxy" baptism of one person in place of another. Paul argued that if we do not believe in the resurrection of the dead, baptism is meaningless. Some inter-

will those do who are baptized for the dead? If the dead are not raised at all, why are people baptized for them? 30And as for us, why do we endanger ourselves every hour?[w] 31I die every day[x]—I mean that, brothers—just as surely as I glory over you in Christ Jesus our Lord. 32If I fought wild beasts[y] in Ephesus[z] for merely human reasons, what have I gained? If the dead are not raised,

"Let us eat and drink,
for tomorrow we die."[r] [a]

33Do not be misled:[b] "Bad company corrupts good character."[c] 34Come back to your senses as you ought, and stop sinning; for there are some who are ignorant of God[d]—I say this to your shame.[e]

The Resurrection Body

35But someone may ask,[f] "How are the dead raised? With what kind of body will they come?"[g] 36How foolish![h] What you sow does not come to life unless it dies.[i] 37When you sow, you do not plant the body that will be, but just a seed, perhaps of wheat or of something else. 38But God gives it a body as he has determined, and to each kind of seed he gives its own body.[j] 39All flesh is not the same: Men have one kind of flesh, animals have another, birds another and fish another. 40There are also heavenly bodies and there are earthly bodies; but the splendor of the heavenly bodies is one kind, and the splendor of the earthly bodies is another. 41The sun has one kind of splendor,[k] the moon another and the stars another;[l] and star differs from star in splendor.

42So will it be[m] with the resurrection of the dead.[n] The body that is sown is perishable, it is raised imperishable;[o] 43it is sown in dishonor, it is raised in glory;[p] it is sown in weakness, it is raised in power; 44it is sown a natural body, it is raised a spiritual body.[q]

If there is a natural body, there is also a spiritual body. 45So it is written: "The first man Adam became a living being"[s];[r] the last Adam,[s] a life-giving spirit.[t] 46The spiritual did not come first, but the natural, and after that the spiritual.[u] 47The first man was of the dust of the earth,[v] the second man from heaven.[w] 48As was the earthly man, so are those who are of the earth; and as is the man from heaven, so also are those who are of heaven.[x] 49And just as we have borne the likeness of the earthly man,[y] so shall we[t] bear the likeness of the man from heaven.[z]

50I declare to you, brothers, that flesh and blood[a] cannot inherit the kingdom of God,[b] nor does the perishable inherit the imperishable.[c] 51Listen, I tell you a mys-

[r]32 Isaiah 22:13 [s]45 Gen. 2:7 [t]49 Some early manuscripts *so let us*

15:30 [w]2Co 11:26
15:31 [x]S Ro 8:36
15:32 [y]2Co 1:8 [z]S Ac 18:19 [a]Isa 22:13; Lk 12:19
15:33 [b]S 1Co 6:9 [c]Pr 22:24,25
15:34 [d]S Gal 4:8 [e]S 1Co 4:14
15:35 [f]Ro 9:19 [g]Eze 37:3
15:36 [h]Lk 11:40; 12:20 [i]Jn 12:24
15:38 [j]Ge 1:11
15:41 [k]Ps 19:4-6 [l]Ps 8:1,3
15:42 [m]Da 12:3; Mt 13:43 [n]ver 12 [o]ver 50,53,54
15:43 [p]Php 3:21; Col 3:4
15:44 [q]ver 50
15:45 [r]Ge 2:7 [s]Ro 5:14 [t]Jn 5:21; 6:57,58; Ro 8:2
15:46 [u]ver 44
15:47 [v]Ge 2:7; 3:19; Ps 90:3 [w]Jn 3:13,31
15:48 [x]Php 3:20,21
15:49 [y]Ge 5:3 [z]S Ro 8:29
15:50 [a]Eph 6:12; Heb 2:14 [b]S Mt 25:34 [c]ver 42,53,54

preters think the baptism "for the dead" is simply a play on words, in which the believer acts out the picture of his death and resurrection, appearing to be "dead" and then alive again. In Corinth and other places people may have been baptized on behalf of loved ones who had died before there was ever any opportunity to hear the gospel of Christ, to believe, and to be baptized. Nowhere does Paul give any approval to such a practice, but it may be that he turned that practice right back upon the Corinthians, arguing that they were inconsistent if they practiced vicarious baptism, or any baptism, and still did not believe in the resurrection. Others see the "dead" as dead believers whose baptism and Christian lives should serve as an incentive or witness to Christian hope and restore confidence in the belief in resurrection. The witness of their lives would make it difficult to think they were baptized and lived for Christ in vain.

15:34 SIN, Unbelief—Resurrection faith is central to Christianity. Denying Christ's resurrection separates one from the Christian faith. The Christian gospel is a call to believe, to stop sinning through unbelief.

15:34 SALVATION, Knowledge of God—Those who keep on in their old life-style of sin have no saving knowledge of God even though they have been baptized and are on the roll of members of a local church.

15:35–49 LAST THINGS, Resurrection Body—The resurrection body will be of a nature corresponding to the eternal order. The principle is that God has always provided bodies suitable to the sphere of life assigned. Our resurrection bodies will have both continuity and difference in relation to our present bodies. Nature illustrates this. There is continuity between what is planted and what sprouts, grows, and is harvested. Physical bodies are perishable, subject to dishonor (by disease, aging, and death), weak, and natural. Resurrection bodies will be spiritual, knowing imperishability, glory, and power. The prototype for resurrection bodies of believers is Jesus' body following His resurrection. Resurrection bodies will bear the likeness of this Man from heaven. See note on Php 3:20–21.

15:38–57 HUMANITY, Life—The nature of the resurrection is first death and then life. The resurrection gives life only after what has been physical dies. We are given a spiritual body only after the death of our earthly bodies. Resurrection hope appears foolish to natural logic. Human bodies are buried and decay. How can they be raised? Paul says you must look at the processes God has created in our natural order. A plant dies and leaves seeds. They produce a plant quite different from the seed but according to God's plan. Bodily flesh is not the same for all creatures. Not all parts of creation have the same glorious appearance. Thus God can use the dead physical body as the seed to produce the glorious spiritual body with its own type of outer covering and its own appearance. The promise is that God will give those who trust in Christ a body like the resurrected Christ had, one that will last throughout eternity, will have no ugliness or weakness, and will not be subject to the processes that weaken and destroy the natural, physical body. Apparently, the spiritual body's appearance will have sufficient continuity with that of the natural body that persons will be recognizable.

15:50–57 LAST THINGS, Believers' Resurrection—The future resurrection of believers is a mystery in the sense of being a revealed truth that otherwise could not be known. The time will be the return of Christ, signaled by the last trumpet. Compare Rev 10:5–7; 11:15. The event will be instantaneous, as the blinking of the eyes. The result will be bodies imperishable and immortal. The purpose will be to inherit the eternal kingdom of God, which requires imperishable bodies. See note on 1 Th 4:14–18.

tery:[d] We will not all sleep,[e] but we will
all be changed[f]— 52in a flash, in the
twinkling of an eye, at the last trumpet.
For the trumpet will sound,[g] the dead[h]
will be raised imperishable, and we will
be changed. 53For the perishable[i] must
clothe itself with the imperishable,[j] and
the mortal with immortality. 54When the
perishable has been clothed with the imperishable, and the mortal with immortality, then the saying that is written will
come true: "Death has been swallowed
up in victory."[u] [k]

55"Where, O death, is your victory?
Where, O death, is your sting?"[v] [l]

56The sting of death is sin,[m] and the power of sin is the law.[n] 57But thanks be to
God![o] He gives us the victory through
our Lord Jesus Christ.[p]
58Therefore, my dear brothers, stand
firm. Let nothing move you. Always give
yourselves fully to the work of the Lord,[q]
because you know that your labor in the
Lord is not in vain.[r]

Chapter 16

The Collection for God's People

NOW about the collection[s] for God's
people:[t] Do what I told the Galatian[u] churches to do. 2On the first day of
every week,[v] each one of you should set
aside a sum of money in keeping with his
income, saving it up, so that when I come
no collections will have to be made.[w]
3Then, when I arrive, I will give letters of
introduction to the men you approve[x]
and send them with your gift to Jerusalem. 4If it seems advisable for me to go
also, they will accompany me.

Personal Requests

5After I go through Macedonia, I will
come to you[y]—for I will be going
through Macedonia.[z] 6Perhaps I will stay
with you awhile, or even spend the winter, so that you can help me on my journey,[a] wherever I go. 7I do not want to
see you now and make only a passing visit; I hope to spend some time with you, if
the Lord permits.[b] 8But I will stay on at
Ephesus[c] until Pentecost,[d] 9because a
great door for effective work has opened
to me,[e] and there are many who oppose
me.
10If Timothy[f] comes, see to it that he
has nothing to fear while he is with you,
for he is carrying on the work of the
Lord,[g] just as I am. 11No one, then,
should refuse to accept him.[h] Send him
on his way[i] in peace[j] so that he may
return to me. I am expecting him along
with the brothers.
12Now about our brother Apollos:[k] I
strongly urged him to go to you with the
brothers. He was quite unwilling to go
now, but he will go when he has the opportunity.
13Be on your guard; stand firm[l] in the
faith; be men of courage; be strong.[m]
14Do everything in love.[n]
15You know that the household of
Stephanas[o] were the first converts[p] in
Achaia,[q] and they have devoted themselves to the service[r] of the saints.[s] I
urge you, brothers, 16to submit[t] to such
as these and to everyone who joins in the
work, and labors at it. 17I was glad when
Stephanas, Fortunatus and Achaicus arrived, because they have supplied what
was lacking from you.[u] 18For they refreshed[v] my spirit and yours also. Such
men deserve recognition.[w]

Final Greetings

19The churches in the province of
Asia[x] send you greetings. Aquila and

15:51 [d]1Co 13:2; 14:2 [e]S Mt 9:24 [f]2Co 5:4; Php 3:21
15:52 [g]S Mt 24:31 [h]Jn 5:25
15:53 [i]ver 42,50,54 [j]2Co 5:2,4
15:54 [k]Isa 25:8; Heb 2:14; Rev 20:14
15:55 [l]Hos 13:14
15:56 [m]S Ro 5:12 [n]S Ro 4:15
15:57 [o]S 2Co 2:14 [p]Ro 8:37; Heb 2:14,15
15:58 [q]1Co 16:10 [r]Isa 65:23
16:1 [s]S Ac 24:17 [t]S Ac 9:13 [u]S Ac 16:6
16:2 [v]Ac 20:7 [w]2Co 9:4,5
16:3 [x]2Co 3:1; 8:18,19
16:5 [y]S 1Co 4:19 [z]S Ac 16:9
16:6 [a]Ro 15:24; Tit 3:13
16:7 [b]S Ac 18:21
16:8 [c]S Ac 18:19 [d]S Ac 2:1
16:9 [e]S Ac 14:27
16:10 [f]S Ac 16:1 [g]1Co 15:58
16:11 [h]1Ti 4:12 [i]2Co 1:16; 3Jn 6 [j]S Ac 15:33
16:12 [k]S Ac 18:24
16:13 [l]1Co 1:8; 2Co 1:21; Gal 5:1; Php 1:27; 1Th 3:8; S Tit 1:9 [m]S Eph 6:10
16:14 [n]1Co 14:1
16:15 [o]1Co 1:16 [p]Ro 16:5 [q]S Ac 18:12 [r]S Ac 24:17 [s]S Ac 9:13
16:16 [t]1Th 5:12; Heb 13:17
16:17 [u]2Co 11:9; Php 2:30
16:18 [v]Ro 15:32; Phm 7 [w]Php 2:29
16:19 [x]S Ac 2:9

[u]*54* Isaiah 25:8 [v]*55* Hosea 13:14

15:57 JESUS CHRIST, Resurrection—Christians rejoice because God has provided victory over death through Christ's resurrection.

15:57 PRAYER, Thanksgiving—Of the innumerable blessings God gives, the greatest is our victory over death through Christ. That blessing deserves the greatest gratitude.

15:58 CHRISTIAN ETHICS, Character—Hold on, persevere, be faithful to the trust put in you, have courage—these entail Paul's directive as surely for our day as for the Corinthians. In this firmness of intent for the Lord's work, one can be sure God's blessings will come.

15:58 LAST THINGS, Encourages Faithfulness—Hope concerning the future victory of Christ, with the abolishing of death and the establishing of God's kingdom, encourages faithfulness. Such hope makes possible unmovable steadfastness of character and joyful abandon to the work of the Lord. After all, faithful labor has promise of eternal reward.

16:1–4 STEWARDSHIP, Management—A good plan can assure that one's commitment to give is fulfilled. Paul urged the Corinthians to fulfill their pledge to the Jerusalem offering and suggested a three-point plan: (1) be regular—set aside money each week; (2) be worshipful—make the offering a part of the Lord's Day worship; and (3) be worthy in the amount given—give according to the amount earned. These guidelines fit the spiritual needs of Christians for growth in giving. See note on 2 Co 8:1—9:15.

16:1 THE CHURCH, Saints—See notes on Ro 1:7; 15:26.

16:2 WORSHIP, Calendar—See note on Ac 20:7.

16:13–14 DISCIPLESHIP, Neighbor Love—God needs courageous disciples with strong convictions. Love should motivate where and how we take courageous stands. As we differ with others, we must relate to them in love. See note on 1 Jn 3:17–18.

16:13–14 CHRISTIAN ETHICS, Character—Christians are strong, courageous, and persistent. They are not abrasive and hardheaded. Standing firm should be in loving care not in proud dogmatism.

16:15–18 THE CHURCH, Practice—See note on 4:15–16.

16:19 THE CHURCH, Local Body—See notes on Ac 4:32; 8:1.

Priscilla[w y] greet you warmly in the Lord,
and so does the church that meets at
their house.[z] 20All the brothers here
send you greetings. Greet one another
with a holy kiss.[a]
21I, Paul, write this greeting in my own
hand.[b]
22If anyone does not love the Lord[c] —a
curse[d] be on him. Come, O Lord[x]![e]
23The grace of the Lord Jesus be with
you.[f]
24My love to all of you in Christ Jesus.
Amen.[y]

16:19 [y]S Ac 18:2 [z]S Ro 16:5
16:20 [a]S Ro 16:16
16:21 [b]Gal 6:11; Col 4:18; 2Th 3:17; Phm 19
16:22 [c]Eph 6:24 [d]Ro 9:3 [e]Rev 22:20
16:23 [f]S Ro 16:20

[w] *19* Greek *Prisca*, a variant of *Priscilla*
[x] *22* In Aramaic the expression *Come, O Lord* is *Marana tha.*
[y] *24* Some manuscripts do not have *Amen.*

16:22 LAST THINGS, Return Attitudes—"Come, O Lord" (Greek *maranatha*) is a transliteration of an Aramaic word. The word could mean, "Our Lord is come" and thus be a confession of the incarnation. However, the preceding context of warning suggests the word expresses a desire for the second coming. As such, it expresses the deep longing for Christ's return but a sad recognition that His coming will mean eternal judgment for unbelievers.

16:22–24 PRAYER, Blessing—See note on Ro 15:33; Rev 22:20–21. Paul placed everyone who did not love (Greek *phileo*) Christ under curse (Greek *anathema*). This meant they should be placed under sacred ban and totally destroyed. Paul was not talking about pagan unbelievers. He wrote to the church. Devotion to Christ calls for intense love. Anything else is destructive for the church (Rev 3:15–16).

2 Corinthians

Theological Setting

Paul wrote 2 Corinthians in response to serious problems that had developed in the church at Corinth. These problems manifested themselves in attacks upon Paul and his apostolic ministry. Divisions within the church and their attacks upon Paul denied the very essence of the gospel (5:19). The problems at Corinth had been developing for some time. The formation of groups attached to their favorite preachers indicated less than full support for Paul. In 2 Corinthians, especially in chapters 10—13, opposition to Paul had developed into open hostility and rebellion. This opposition included rejection of his ministry and his gospel. Paul's first ministry in Corinth was on his second missionary journey (Ac 18:1-18). See Introduction to 1 Corinthians.

Ephesus was Paul's center for ministry on his third missionary journey (Ac 19:1—20:1). While there, Paul's evangelistic efforts seem to have been highly successful. His ministry in Ephesus continued for two years and was so successful that "all the Jews and Greeks who lived in the province of Asia heard the word of the Lord" (Ac 19:10). As Paul's ministry at Ephesus was flourishing, trouble brewed at Corinth. Both Ephesus and Corinth were coastal cities, separated only by the Aegean Sea. Communication between the two cities was easy. Contacts between Paul and the Corinthians were frequent, and the reports became increasingly disturbing as hostility to Paul increased. During Paul's early ministry in Ephesus, a party spirit developed in Corinth. Church members became self-centered rather than Christ-centered. Hostile teachers may have come into Corinth and promoted the problem. In 2 Co 11:20 Paul reminded the Corinthians they had been led astray by leaders who took advantage of them in order to exalt themselves. Reports of trouble came to him by "Chloe's *people*" (1 Co 1:11) and others. Because of these reports and in response to a letter from the Corinthian church, Paul wrote 1 Corinthians in which he warned of the dangers of the self-centered life instead of the Christ-centered life of love.

Paul already had written them a letter that warned against association with immoral people (1 Co 5:9). All of this letter has been lost, unless a fragment has been preserved in 2 Co 6:14—7:1. First Corinthians, therefore, was Paul's second attempt to deal by letter with their problems. Paul urged Apollos, who had returned from Corinth, to go back to Corinth. Apollos refused (1 Co 16:12). Paul then sent Timothy (1 Co 4:17). Timothy failed to solve the problems and was again with Paul when he wrote 2 Corinthians (1:1). During this period, Paul made a brief visit to Corinth. Although not recorded in Acts, this visit appears in three references in 2 Corinthians (2:1; 12:14; 13:1). Having been a painful visit (2:1), it must have failed to produce reconciliation. Paul sent a letter of such strong rebuke that he regretted sending it. Later he rejoiced because the letter had made them sorrowful unto repentance (7:8-10). Titus probably was the bearer of this letter (8:6, 16-17). It was not preserved unless all or part of it survives in 2 Co 10—13.

Sometime after Titus left for Corinth, Paul left Ephesus. He stopped at Troas, where he found an open door for missionary work; but his heart was not in it (2:12-13). Paul had longed for Titus to return with news that the problems had been solved in Corinth. When Titus failed to meet him, he feared that all had been lost in Corinth. Titus finally met Paul in Macedonia (7:6-7). He brought the good news that attitudes in Corinth had improved. Paul then wrote 2 Corinthians, promising an early visit to them. In the most autobiographical of his letters, Paul revealed much about himself, his calling, and his ministry. Among Paul's other letters, only Galatians comes close to 2 Corinthians in what it reveals about Paul.

This epistle well could be termed a document on the minister and ministry. As Paul defended his own character and ministry, he enunciated those principles that should characterize every person who has been called to minister in Christ's name. Although the apostles were the leaders, ministry was not limited to them. The whole congregation has a responsibility for ministry. Just as God "reconciled us to himself through Christ," He has given to "us the ministry of reconciliation" (5:18).

This letter was not written as a theological treatise. It was written to deal with specific problems in a local situation. Nevertheless, in confronting these problems, Paul has given insight into rich theological truths for all Christians. Second Corinthians, therefore, is always contemporary for those who would understand better the meaning of ministry in the name of Christ.

Theological Outline

Second Corinthians: The Nature of Apostolic Ministry

I. Salutation (1:1-2)

II. Apostolic Ministry Defined in Light of the Minister's Relations with the Church (1:3—2:17)

- A. Apostolic ministry includes both affliction and comfort. (1:3-11)
  - 1. God comforts His ministers so they may minister to others. (1:3-6)
  - 2. The minister is comforted by the concern of those to whom he ministers. (1:7-11)
- B. The minister acts with integrity under God's guidance. (1:12—2:4)
  - 1. The minister's change of plans is due to God's guidance, not human fickleness. (1:12-24)
  - 2. The minister's harsh discipline comes out of his abundant love for the church. (2:1-4)
- C. The ministry of the church should reflect redemptive love and forgiveness in dealing with offenders. (2:5-11)
- D. God leads His ministers to spread His Word with sincere motives, not greedy ones. (2:12-17)

III. Apostolic Ministry Defined in Light of its Glory and Shame (3:1—7:16)

- A. The true minister has no need for self-commendation. (3:1-6)
- B. Apostolic ministers are ministers of a new and greater covenant. (3:7—4:6)
- C. Even as the apostolic minister suffers persecution, weakness, and death, life in Jesus is being manifested. (4:7-12)
- D. The suffering and weakness of this mortal life will be swallowed up by the glory of that which is to come. (4:13—5:10)
  - 1. Present trials are great, but they will pass away. (4:13-18)
  - 2. The Spirit is the pledge of immortality. (5:1-10)
- E. God's ministers are controlled by the love of Christ. (5:11-15)
- F. The apostolic message is that God was in Christ reconciling the world unto Himself. (5:16-21)
- G. Faithfulness in proclaiming this message involves suffering, privation, endurance, righteous living, and a spirit of rejoicing. (6:1-10)
- H. Christ's ambassador calls church members to openness, trust, and a separated life. (6:11—7:4)
- I. The restoration of broken fellowship brings comfort and joy. (7:5-16)

IV. Apostolic Ministry Defined in Terms of Social Concerns (8:1—9:15)
(Note: See 1 Corinthians 16:1-4 for reference to this offering.)

- A. The example of the Macedonian churches: They gave liberally, first having given themselves. (8:1-4)
- B. The self-giving of Jesus challenges Christians to be faithful in giving to those in need. (8:5-15)
- C. The care with which the offering would be handled encouraged faithful giving. (8:16—9:5)
- D. In giving, we reap as we sow, whether sparingly or bountifully. (9:6-15)

V. Apostolic Ministry Defined in Light of Personal Defense (10:1—13:10)

- A. Paul answered the allegations made against him. (10:1-18)
- B. In irony, Paul used the foolishness of boasting to defend his ministry. (11:1—12:13)
  - 1. He boasted of his jealousy for them lest they be led astray. (11:1-6)
  - 2. He boasted that he had preached the gospel to them without charge. (11:7-12)
  - 3. He could not boast of having boldness to exploit the Corinthians. (11:13-21*a*)
  - 4. He could boast of experiencing both suffering and God's deliverance. (11:21*b*-33)
  - 5. He boasted of visions, his ministry, and the sufficiency of God's grace. (12:1-13)
- C. In spite of attacks made upon his ministry, Paul anticipated a third visit. (12:14-21)
- D. Paul warned that he would deal with them forthrightly when he came. (13:1-10)

VI. Farewell (13:11-14)

Theological Conclusions

Second Corinthians is both theological and practical. Paul used theological truth as a basis for dealing with the problems at Corinth. The following theological conclusions are reflected:

1. The Father and the Son act in unity in redemptive reconciliation. God the Father was not absent while His Son endured the agony of redeeming a lost humanity. God was active in His Son (5:19). The Son was not seeking to change God. Both the Son and the Father were seeking to change attitudes toward God, a change from rebellion to trust.

2. Not only does God in Christ reconcile us to Himself, He commits us to a ministry of reconciliation. God reconciles lost people unto Himself because He loves them, wants them to escape the destructiveness of sin, and desires eternal fellowship with them. He also desires that the redeemed ones share in the redeeming of others. This ministry of reconciliation has both vertical and horizontal dimensions. It involves first of all the reconciliation of the individual to God. It involves also the reconciling of persons to persons. Those who participate in the ministry of reconciliation must be reconciled to each other. This is why the problems in the church at Corinth were so devastating. Christians who exhibit envy and jealousy among themselves are ill-equipped to bear testimony to the reconciling power of God. Others cannot be convinced that God can bring peace to their lives if they can see no peace among the members of the church.

3. Ministering in Christ's name involves suffering as well as victory. Paul's references to his own sufferings show that even the most faithful followers of Christ endure sufferings. He suffered both because of his own physical infirmities and because of persecution. Paul suffered personal attacks from false teachers and even from the Corinthians who had been led astray by these teachers.

Although He sustains the Christian who suffers, God does not always deliver the Christian from suffering. Even Paul, through whom God had worked miracles of healing, did not always get the deliverance he sought. His "thorn in the flesh" was not taken away (12:7-10). However, God gave the grace necessary to sustain Paul.

Through the frailty and suffering of His messengers, God effects that which is good. His power is manifested as He works through the limitations of His servants. (4:7). God's power was perfected in Paul's weakness (12:7-9). God also uses our sufferings and human limitations to remind us that our strength is in Him and not in ourselves. Paul saw God as using his "thorn in the flesh" to keep him in a spirit of humility (12:7). Suffering also aids us in relating to and revealing the sufferings of Jesus (4:10).

4. Prayer has an important place in the Christian's life. Prominent in the life of a Christian should be prayers of thanksgiving. Even as Paul dealt with the problems at Corinth, he offered prayers of thanksgiving. He praised God for the comfort that he received even amid troubles (1:3-4). He thanked God for leading in triumph as the Word was being preached (2:14-17). Paul thanked God for putting concern and care for the Corinthians in the heart of Titus (8:16). He thanked God for His "indescribable gift," evidently the gift of His Son that inspires Christian giving (9:15). The prayer life of a Christian should include petitions for self. Paul's emphasis on his praying concerning his "thorn in the flesh" reveals that Paul prayed concerning his own needs. Only one who prays concerning his own needs, including God's guidance, will know how to pray for others. Second Corinthians also teaches the importance of intercessory prayer (2 Co 1:11). The Corinthians had helped Paul through their prayers. Paul prayed for the Corinthians to do no wrong, but to do right. He also prayed that they might be perfect (13:7-9).

5. Serving Christ involves ministering to the total person. Paul always made the proclamation of the gospel the foundation of his ministry. He recognized, however, that God's love for us includes concern for the total person. Our ministry, therefore, should be to the total person. Nowhere is Paul's recognition of this truth more evident than in his leading the churches to make an offering for the needy Christians in Jerusalem. Our ministry should be broad enough to deal with any need that hinders us from living the abundant life intended by God. All ministry in Christ's name is spiritual ministry.

Contemporary Teaching

Second Corinthians challenges us to give ourselves to the ministry of healing broken relationships. This ministry is grounded in the fact that God has reconciled us to Himself and given us a ministry of reconciliation (5:19). This task has to do primarily with the reconciling of people to God, but it includes the reconciling of people to one another. All Christians are to give themselves to this ministry.

Divisions within destroy the ministry of the church to the world. Christians, therefore, are to minister to one another in a spirit of love and mutual forgiveness. Only a church whose members are reconciled to one another can carry on a ministry of reconciliation.

We should reflect the redemptive love and forgiveness of God in all areas of our ministry. Even as the church at Corinth dealt with an offender in their midst, Paul admonished the people to forgive and comfort the offender (2:7). Our function is not to overwhelm others with harsh condemnation, but to lead them to repentance and to acceptance of God's forgiveness.

Those who lead in ministry need the concern and support of those they lead. Even Paul, the great apostle, was heartbroken and discouraged because of problems among the Corinthians and their failure to give him their confidence and support. At Troas, therefore, he was unable to preach even though a door was open to him (2:12-13).

Chapter 1

PAUL, an apostle[a] of Christ Jesus by
the will of God,[b] and Timothy[c] our
brother,

To the church of God[d] in Corinth,[e]
together with all the saints throughout
Achaia:[f]

2Grace and peace to you from God our
Father and the Lord Jesus Christ.[g]

The God of All Comfort

3Praise be to the God and Father of our
Lord Jesus Christ,[h] the Father of compassion and the God of all comfort, 4who
comforts us[i] in all our troubles, so that
we can comfort those in any trouble with
the comfort we ourselves have received
from God. 5For just as the sufferings of
Christ flow over into our lives,[j] so also
through Christ our comfort overflows. 6If
we are distressed, it is for your comfort
and salvation;[k] if we are comforted, it is
for your comfort, which produces in you
patient endurance of the same sufferings
we suffer. 7And our hope for you is firm,
because we know that just as you share in
our sufferings,[l] so also you share in our
comfort.

8We do not want you to be unin-
formed,[m] brothers, about the hardships
we suffered[n] in the province of Asia.[o]
We were under great pressure, far beyond our ability to endure, so that we despaired even of life. 9Indeed, in our
hearts we felt the sentence of death. But
this happened that we might not rely on
ourselves but on God,[p] who raises the
dead.[q] 10He has delivered us from such a
deadly peril,[r] and he will deliver us. On
him we have set our hope[s] that he will
continue to deliver us, 11as you help us by
your prayers.[t] Then many will give
thanks[u] on our[a] behalf for the gracious
favor granted us in answer to the prayers
of many.

Paul's Change of Plans

12Now this is our boast: Our conscience[v] testifies that we have conducted
ourselves in the world, and especially in
our relations with you, in the holiness[w]
and sincerity[x] that are from God. We
have done so not according to worldly
wisdom[y] but according to God's grace.
13For we do not write you anything you
cannot read or understand. And I hope
that, 14as you have understood us in part,
you will come to understand fully that
you can boast of us just as we will boast of
you in the day of the Lord Jesus.[z]

15Because I was confident of this, I
planned to visit you[a] first so that you
might benefit twice.[b] 16I planned to visit
you on my way[c] to Macedonia[d] and to
come back to you from Macedonia, and
then to have you send me on my way[e] to
Judea.[f] 17When I planned this, did I do it
lightly? Or do I make my plans in a worldly manner[g] so that in the same breath I
say, "Yes, yes" and "No, no"?

18But as surely as God is faithful,[h] our
message to you is not "Yes" and "No."
19For the Son of God,[i] Jesus Christ, who
was preached among you by me and Si-

1:1 [a]S 1Co 1:1 [b]1Co 1:1; Eph 1:1; Col 1:1; 2Ti 1:1 [c]S Ac 16:1 [d]S 1Co 10:32 [e]S Ac 18:1 [f]S Ac 18:12
1:2 [g]S Ro 1:7
1:3 [h]Eph 1:3; 1Pe 1:3
1:4 [i]Isa 49:13; 51:12; 66:13; 2Co 7:6,7,13
1:5 [j]Ro 8:17; 2Co 4:10; Gal 6:17; Php 3:10; Col 1:24; 1Pe 4:13
1:6 [k]2Co 4:15
1:7 [l]S ver 5
1:8 [m]S Ro 11:25 [n]1Co 15:32 [o]S Ac 2:9
1:9 [p]Jer 17:5,7 [q]S Jn 5:21
1:10 [r]S Ro 15:31 [s]1Ti 4:10
1:11 [t]Ro 15:30; Php 1:19 [u]2Co 4:15; 9:11
1:12 [v]S Ac 23:1 [w]1Th 2:10 [x]2Co 2:17 [y]1Co 1:17; 2:1,4,13
1:14 [z]S 1Co 1:8
1:15 [a]S 1Co 4:19 [b]Ro 1:11,13; 15:29
1:16 [c]1Co 16:5-7 [d]S Ac 16:9 [e]1Co 16:11; 3Jn 6 [f]Ac 19:21
1:17 [g]2Co 10:2,3; 11:18
1:18 [h]S 1Co 1:9
1:19 [i]S Mt 4:3

[a] *11* Many manuscripts *your*

1:1 THE CHURCH, Saints—See note on 1 Co 1:2.

1:2–7 GOD, Trinity—Father and Son join in giving grace—unmerited accepting love—to the church. The Father gives comfort and compassion to the troubled church. This points up the purpose of God's grace to us: that we might be good ministers of His grace to others, comforting one another even as we suffer together for Christ's sake. For all this we praise the Father of our Lord Jesus.

1:2 PRAYER, Blessing—See note on Ro 1:7.

1:3–11 EVIL AND SUFFERING, Comfort—Because God has comforted us, we can comfort others in their suffering. Comfort involves encouraging and strengthening the afflicted. We may comfort others by witnessing to our own troubles and how God has helped us in them. Christian comfort does not make us comfortable. It gives us strength to endure as Christians in a world set against Christ. As Christ suffered, so must we. As we suffer, we receive comfort and strength from God and from Christian prayer partners. See note on 7:2–16.

1:3 PRAYER, Praise—See note on Ro 16:25–27.

1:5 JESUS CHRIST, Suffering—Jews looked to a time of suffering before Messiah came. The New Testament emphasizes instead the sufferings the Messiah endured. Paul and the church had to suffer as Jesus suffered. In a sense Jesus continues to suffer as His body suffers. Christ brings more than suffering. He brings comfort in suffering.

1:10–11 PRAYER, Corporate—Paul considered his helpers in prayer to be real partners. Their prayers helped deliver him from persecution and trouble. Prayer partners participate not only in intercession but also in thanksgiving.

1:13–14 HOLY SCRIPTURE, Authoritative—Paul had to defend himself. He wrote what God revealed to him in these letters in readable, understandable language. He suggested that a partial insight would give way to a clearer understanding of him and his ministry.

1:14 LAST THINGS, Return Promises—The day of the Lord Jesus is the day of His second coming. See note on 1 Co 1:7–8.

1:17–24 PROCLAMATION, Authoritative—See note on Jer 1:4–9. Proclamation sounds a certain, positive tone because Jesus is the clear fulfillment of all God's promises.

1:18–22 GOD, Faithfulness—Paul had to defend himself for having confused the Corinthians by changing his travel plans. He claimed his intention was trustworthy and clear just as God is faithful, constant, and unchanging. Nothing is unclear about what Christ did for us. He gave us God's final "yes," providing perfect salvation. Thus God has shown Himself to be faithful to His promises and to His people. He has placed the seal of His ownership upon us, guaranteeing our final eternal salvation. He has been faithful from first to last in gracefully providing salvation.

1:18–24 ELECTION, Eternal Security—No matter how numerous are God's promises, the elect can trust God to keep His word. Jesus represents the fulfillment of all God's promises. God gives eternal security to His people by keeping them firmly in the faith through the presence of His Spirit. Eternal security provides no reason for pride or boasting. It is another reason to praise God.

las[b] [j] and Timothy,[k] was not "Yes" and
"No," but in him it has always[l] been
"Yes." 20For no matter how many promises[m] God has made, they are "Yes" in
Christ. And so through him the
"Amen"[n] is spoken by us to the glory of
God.[o] 21Now it is God who makes both
us and you stand firm[p] in Christ. He
anointed[q] us, 22set his seal[r] of ownership on us, and put his Spirit in our hearts
as a deposit, guaranteeing what is to
come.[s]

Chapter 2

23I call God as my witness[t] that it was in
order to spare you[u] that I did not return
to Corinth. 24Not that we lord it over[v]
your faith, but we work with you for your
joy, because it is by faith you stand firm.[w]
1So I made up my mind that I would not
make another painful visit to you.[x] 2For if I
grieve you,[y] who is left to make me glad
but you whom I have grieved? 3I wrote as
I did[z] so that when I came I should not be
distressed[a] by those who ought to make
me rejoice. I had confidence[b] in all of you,
that you would all share my joy. 4For I
wrote you[c] out of great distress and anguish of heart and with many tears, not to
grieve you but to let you know the depth of
my love for you.

Forgiveness for the Sinner

5If anyone has caused grief,[d] he has
not so much grieved me as he has grieved
all of you, to some extent—not to put it
too severely. 6The punishment[e] inflicted
on him by the majority is sufficient for
him. 7Now instead, you ought to forgive
and comfort him,[f] so that he will not be
overwhelmed by excessive sorrow. 8I
urge you, therefore, to reaffirm your love
for him. 9The reason I wrote you[g] was to
see if you would stand the test and be
obedient in everything.[h] 10If you forgive
anyone, I also forgive him. And what I
have forgiven—if there was anything to
forgive—I have forgiven in the sight of
Christ for your sake, 11in order that Satan[i] might not outwit us. For we are not
unaware of his schemes.[j]

Ministers of the New Covenant

12Now when I went to Troas[k] to
preach the gospel of Christ[l] and found
that the Lord had opened a door[m] for me,
13I still had no peace of mind,[n] because I
did not find my brother Titus[o] there. So I

1:19 [j]S Ac 15:22 [k]S Ac 16:1 [l]Heb 13:8 **1:20** [m]Ro 15:8 [n]S 1Co 14:16 [o]Ro 15:9 **1:21** [p]S 1Co 16:13 [q]1Jn 2:20,27 **1:22** [r]Ge 38:18; Eze 9:4; Hag 2:23 [s]S 2Co 5:5 **1:23** [t]S Ro 1:9 [u]1Co 4:21; 2Co 2:1,3; 13:2,10 **1:24** [v]1Pe 5:3 [w]Ro 11:20; 1Co 15:1 **2:1** [x]S 2Co 1:23 **2:2** [y]2Co 7:8 **2:3** [z]ver 4,9; 2Co 7:8,12 [a]2Co 12:21 [b]2Co 7:16; 8:22; Gal 5:10; 2Th 3:4; Phm 21 **2:4** [c]ver 3,9; 2Co 7:8,12 **2:5** [d]1Co 5:1,2 **2:6** [e]1Co 5:4,5; 2Co 7:11 **2:7** [f]Gal 6:1; Eph 4:32; Col 3:13 **2:9** [g]ver 3,4; 2Co 7:8,12 [h]2Co 7:15; 10:6 **2:11** [i]S Mt 4:10 [j]Lk 22:31; 2Co 4:4; 1Pe 5:8,9 **2:12** [k]S Ac 16:8 [l]S Ro 1:1; 2Co 4:3,4; 8:18; 9:13; 1Th 3:2 [m]S Ac 14:27 **2:13** [n]2Co 7:5 [o]2Co 7:6,13; 8:6,16,23; 12:18; Gal 2:1,3; Tit 1:4

[b] *19* Greek *Silvanus,* a variant of *Silas*

1:20 JESUS CHRIST, Fulfilled—Jesus, God's Son, is the center of Christian preaching. The message is clear. In Jesus all Old Testament promises find their fulfillment. In Him God saves His people and gives us security.

1:20–21 SALVATION, As Being in Christ—Christ fulfills the promises given to Israel in the Old Testament. Those in Christ are inheritors of all the promises of God. God has put His guarantee on us in Christ. No one can doubt our saving relationship with Him.

1:21–22 HOLY SPIRIT, Security—The Spirit is a seal which protects Christians, giving us security and assurance. The Spirit is a guarantee or down payment on a future eternal life in the presence of God. See notes on Ro 5:1–5; Eph 1:13–14.

1:24 CHURCH LEADERS, Authority—Leaders are not to deal with their charges in a high-handed manner by trying to impose their will or their doctrine on them. Even the apostle Paul could not dictate to a congregation. Leaders must understand that they are not lords. They are always to work *with* the congregation and not work over them or work them over. Leaders are to lead the members to a stronger faith.

2:1–11 EVIL AND SUFFERING, Human Origin—Human relationships can cause pain and suffering. Honest confrontation is painful to all parties concerned but is necessary to restore relationships. Paul's relationships with the Corinthians included great distress as he tried to lead them to Christ's way of humble, self-giving love. Relationship problems within the church cause the whole church, not just individuals, to suffer. A combination of discipline and forgiveness is needed to restore the relationships.

2:3 HOLY SCRIPTURE, Inspired—Paul wrote the church in response to some of the problems he had with the congregation. This shows his writing was prompted by particular concerns and his need to call the church to responsible discipleship (v 9). The writing God inspired for a local situation was recognized as inspired for the general church as God led in the collection and formation of the New Testament. See note on 1:13–14.

2:5–11 DISCIPLESHIP, The Fallen—Discipline should be backed with forgiveness. Church discipline may be appropriate when serious offense is involved, but Christians never are free to withhold forgiveness when a person evidences repentance. Undue punishment may cause overwhelming discouragement and grief unless Christian love is reaffirmed. Redemptive love and real forgiveness are essential in maintaining a strong fellowship in a church. Such qualities should be in good supply in any church. Discipline and punishment should never be the dominating note in a church's life. See note on Gal 6:1–2; Guide to Counseling for Laity, pp. 1826–1831.

2:5–11 THE CHURCH, Discipline—The church disciplines members in love to bring them to repentance. When a disciplined member repents, the church must accept and forgive. Such discipline is carried out by the majority of the local church. See note on 1 Co 5:1–5.

2:5–11 FAMILY, Sexual Sin—See note on 1 Co 5:1–5.

2:11 EVIL AND SUFFERING, Satan—Satan is involved in church relationships seeking to bring hurt and divisions. When love and forgiveness do not characterize the church, Satan wins. We must never underestimate his deceptive resourcefulness.

2:12–14 JESUS CHRIST, Ascension—The ascended Christ still leads the lives of His people, opening doors of ministry. Paul called Christ's leadership a "triumphal procession" celebrating the gospel's victories in people's lives.

2:12 HUMANITY, Moral Consciousness—Paul's conscience would not let him carry out his plans. A person's conscience, while not naturally trustworthy (1 Co 4:4), can be trusted when it is led not merely by human wisdom but by the revelatory gift from God.

2:12–13 EVANGELISM, Holy Spirit—Paul constantly stressed that doors for evangelism are opened by the Holy Spirit alone (Ac 4:31). To go ahead of God or lag behind will thwart the work of the Holy Spirit in opening people to receive our testimony. We must walk with God in the fullness of the Holy Spirit to be effective witnesses.

said good-by to them and went on to Macedonia.[p]
14 But thanks be to God,[q] who always
leads us in triumphal procession in Christ
and through us spreads everywhere the
fragrance[r] of the knowledge[s] of him.
15 For we are to God the aroma[t] of Christ
among those who are being saved and
those who are perishing.[u] 16 To the one
we are the smell of death;[v] to the other,
the fragrance of life. And who is equal to
such a task?[w] 17 Unlike so many, we do
not peddle the word of God for profit.[x]
On the contrary, in Christ we speak before God with sincerity,[y] like men sent
from God.[z]

Chapter 3

ARE we beginning to commend ourselves[a] again? Or do we need, like
some people, letters of recommendation[b]
to you or from you? 2 You yourselves are
our letter, written on our hearts, known
and read by everybody.[c] 3 You show that
you are a letter from Christ, the result of
our ministry, written not with ink but
with the Spirit of the living God,[d] not on
tablets of stone[e] but on tablets of human
hearts.[f]
4 Such confidence[g] as this is ours
through Christ before God. 5 Not that we
are competent in ourselves[h] to claim anything for ourselves, but our competence
comes from God.[i] 6 He has made us competent as ministers of a new covenant[j]—not of the letter[k] but of the
Spirit; for the letter kills, but the Spirit
gives life.[l]

The Glory of the New Covenant

7 Now if the ministry that brought
death,[m] which was engraved in letters on
stone, came with glory, so that the Israelites could not look steadily at the face of
Moses because of its glory,[n] fading
though it was, 8 will not the ministry of
the Spirit be even more glorious? 9 If the
ministry that condemns men[o] is glorious,
how much more glorious is the ministry
that brings righteousness![p] 10 For what
was glorious has no glory now in comparison with the surpassing glory. 11 And if
what was fading away came with glory,
how much greater is the glory of that
which lasts!
12 Therefore, since we have such a
hope,[q] we are very bold.[r] 13 We are not
like Moses, who would put a veil over his

2:13 [p]S Ac 16:9
2:14 [q]Ro 6:17; 7:25; 1Co 15:57; 2Co 9:15 [r]Eze 20:41; Eph 5:2; Php 4:18 [s]S 2Co 8:7
2:15 [t]S ver 14; Ge 8:21; Ex 29:18; Nu 15:3 [u]S 1Co 1:18
2:16 [v]S Lk 2:34; Jn 3:36 [w]2Co 3:5,6
2:17 [x]S Ac 20:33; 2Co 4:2; 1Th 2:5 [y]1Co 5:8 [z]2Co 1:12; 12:19
3:1 [a]Ro 16:1; 2Co 5:12; 10:12, 18; 12:11 [b]Ac 18:27; Ro 16:1; 1Co 16:3
3:2 [c]1Co 9:2
3:3 [d]S Mt 16:16 [e]ver 7; Ex 24:12; 31:18; 32:15,16 [f]Pr 3:3; 7:3; Jer 31:33; Eze 36:26
3:4 [g]S Eph 3:12
3:5 [h]2Co 2:16 [i]1Co 15:10
3:6 [j]S Lk 22:20 [k]Ro 2:29; 7:6 [l]Jn 6:63
3:7 [m]ver 9; S Ro 4:15 [n]ver 13; Ex 34:29-35; Isa 42:21
3:9 [o]ver 7; Dt 27:26 [p]Ro 1:17; 3:21,22
3:12 [q]Ro 5:4,5; 8:24,25 [r]S Ac 4:29

2:14 PRAYER, Thanksgiving—Paul was in the habit of breaking into frequent thanksgiving for God's presence in his ministry. Four other times in this letter he breaks into thanksgiving or is concerned with offering thanksgiving (1:11; 4:15; 8:16; 9:11). See note on Ac 28:15. The results of Paul's missionary ministry gave reason to thank and praise God, not exalt Paul.

2:14–16 EVANGELISM, Involves—What a profound responsibility Paul placed on believers! We are an aroma to the world of life or death. How essential for us to spread the fragrance of the knowledge of Christ in such a way as to bring life. We have God's promise of victory—He leads us in His triumphal procession. We are utterly unequal to the task, but Christ gives us grace and power to evangelize with effect.

3:2–3 THE CHURCH, People of God—God's people are His new creation, working, witnessing, and living to help change the world for Christ. Christian workers need no better recommendation than the lives of those whom we have influenced to live for Christ. The result of our ministry should be persons following the Spirit's leadership.

3:3–11 HOLY SPIRIT, Leaders—The Holy Spirit alone rewards our ministry. God gave Moses the glorious task of presenting the covenant to Israel in the form of the Ten Commandments written on stones (Ex 20:1–17; Dt 5:1–21). He gave to Paul the even more glorious privilege of presenting the new covenant to the world in the form of the Holy Spirit written on the hearts of God's people. The presence of the Spirit gives life to God's people and creates a community of righteousness which surpasses in glory national Israel and its Law. The church and its glory will never fade away. The churches Paul started and the presence of the Spirit with them were the only commendations Paul had or desired to have (v 1). Congratulations and symbols of success from other Christians were unnecessary. Paul's concern was for the church's welfare.

3:6 THE CHURCH, Covenant People—We can minister because of the gift of God. He prepares us and makes possible our ministry on His behalf. Our ministry is in the name of Jesus, who gave Himself to establish a new covenant based on forgiveness of sin. Our ministry is not a legalistic call to follow regulations but a joyful invitation to let God's Spirit fill and direct our lives. See note on Jer 31:31–34.

3:7–18 GOD, Glory—Faith in Christ is more glorious than faith in Moses. Both came with glory, but certainly the ever-present Spirit in us brings more glory, a stronger experience of God's overwhelming presence, than did the writing on stone tablets housed in the ark. The law shows us we are condemned sinners. Christ makes us right with God. Through Moses only veiled glory was seen. In Christ the full glorious presence of God becomes visible. Belonging to Christ, we reflect His glory to the world. As we grow in Christ, we more fully reflect His glory, because we become more like Him. In all this the trinitarian God—Father, Son, and Spirit—are at work.

3:7–18 REVELATION, Divine Presence—Paul sheds light on the hiddenness of Old Testament revelation, speaking of Moses' laws and their revelation as manifesting the glory of God behind a veil (partly seen and understood). See note on Ex 34:29–35. People maintain that same partial, veiled understanding of God when they remain in the light of the Old Testament and do not see the full revelation of God in the person of Jesus Christ. Christ and the Spirit are the same, that is both are divine members of the Trinity. Compare Ac 16:6–7; Ro 8:9. Freedom appears to those who experience God's Spirit in their lives. Those who experience the presence of the Spirit also are being transformed into the likeness of the full presence of God within them.

3:7–18 THE CHURCH, People of God—The church is the people of God. The covenant people of God began with Abraham and Moses—the old covenant—and is completed in Christ with the new covenant. Christ provides new boldness to approach God, new revelation and understanding of God's nature and purpose, and new freedom in the Spirit compared to the school teacher function of the law. The Spirit is changing the people of God—Christ's church—to be like Him and show the world His greatness and hope. Thus, the church of the new covenant is far greater and more glorious than the people of God formed through Old Testament revelation.

3:13–18 JESUS CHRIST, Fulfilled—Jesus Christ fulfills the Old Testament hope of entering the presence of God without fear and knowing plainly the meaning of God's Word.

face[s] to keep the Israelites from gazing at
it while the radiance was fading away.
14But their minds were made dull,[t] for to
this day the same veil remains when the
old covenant[u] is read.[v] It has not been
removed, because only in Christ is it tak-
en away. 15Even to this day when Moses
is read, a veil covers their hearts. 16But
whenever anyone turns to the Lord,[w] the
veil is taken away.[x] 17Now the Lord is
the Spirit,[y] and where the Spirit of the
Lord is, there is freedom.[z] 18And we,
who with unveiled faces all reflect[c][a] the
Lord's glory,[b] are being transformed into
his likeness[c] with ever-increasing glory,
which comes from the Lord, who is the
Spirit.

Chapter 4

Treasures in Jars of Clay

THEREFORE, since through God's mercy[d] we have this ministry, we do not
lose heart.[e] 2Rather, we have renounced
secret and shameful ways;[f] we do not
use deception, nor do we distort the word
of God.[g] On the contrary, by setting forth
the truth plainly we commend ourselves
to every man's conscience[h] in the sight
of God. 3And even if our gospel[i] is
veiled,[j] it is veiled to those who are perishing.[k] 4The god[l] of this age[m] has
blinded[n] the minds of unbelievers, so
that they cannot see the light of the gospel of the glory of Christ,[o] who is the
image of God.[p] 5For we do not preach
ourselves,[q] but Jesus Christ as Lord,[r]
and ourselves as your servants[s] for Jesus'
sake. 6For God, who said, "Let light shine
out of darkness,"[d][t] made his light shine
in our hearts[u] to give us the light of the
knowledge of the glory of God in the face
of Christ.[v]

3:13 [s]ver 7; Ex 34:33 **3:14** [t]Ro 11:7,8; 2Co 4:4 [u]Ac 13:15; 15:21 [v]ver 6 **3:16** [w]Ro 11:23 [x]Ex 34:34; Isa 25:7 **3:17** [y]Isa 61:1,2; Gal 4:6,7 [z]S Jn 8:32 **3:18** [a]1Co 13:12 [b]Jn 17:22,24; 2Co 4:4,6 [c]S Ro 8:29 **4:1** [d]1Co 7:25; 1Ti 1:13,16 [e]ver 16; Ps 18:45; Isa 40:31 **4:2** [f]Ro 6:21; S 1Co 4:5 [g]2Co 2:17; S Heb 4:12 [h]2Co 5:11 **4:3** [i]S 2Co 2:12 [j]2Co 3:14 [k]S 1Co 1:18 **4:4** [l]S Jn 12:31 [m]S 1Co 1:20 [n]2Co 3:14 [o]ver 6 [p]S Jn 14:9 **4:5** [q]1Co 1:13 [r]1Co 1:23 [s]1Co 9:19 **4:6** [t]Ge 1:3; Ps 18:28 [u]2Pe 1:19 [v]ver 4

[c] *18* Or *contemplate* [d] *6* Gen. 1:3

The experience of Christ makes believers reflect His, and thus God's, radiant glory.

3:17–18 HOLY SPIRIT, Transforms—To turn to Christ and the way of faith is to have the Spirit. To know Christ is to know the Spirit. To have Christ is to have the Spirit. Salvation and the gift of the Spirit are inseparable expressions of grace. By His gifts of life and freedom, the Spirit transforms Christians into the kind of person Jesus was. We share the glorious life of Jesus, who never was enslaved by the law but served God freely and in love. That glory of Christ increases in Christians as we progress in the experience of freedom and life which is given by Christ and by the Spirit. Being freed from the law could suggest lack of concern about moral character. This is the opposite of the truth. Paul felt morality could not come by the law, but only as a gift of the Spirit to one who lives in freedom from the law. The gospel alone brings righteousness (v 9). The Spirit works to transform Christians, who share in Christ's life of freedom, into good persons who bear fruit such as love, joy, and peace (Gal 5:22). See "Life in Christ: The Disciple's Cross," pp. 1748–1751.

3:18 SALVATION, Glorification—Saved persons are being transformed into the likeness of Christ. Our transformation will become complete at the resurrection. "Transformed" (Greek *metamorphomai*) is the same word used of Christ's transfiguration (Mt 17:2; Mk 9:2).

4:1–6 PROCLAMATION, Clarity—See note on 1 Co 2:1–5. Proclamation is not deceptive selling trying to gain followers at any cost. Proclamation is clear explanation of God's Word centering on Jesus.

4:2 CHURCH LEADERS, Authority—The authority of any leader in the church derives from the leader's own devotion to live out God's Word. Leaders must plainly teach God's truth rather than human theories. Teaching must be backed by noble character. Christ gave us the example to follow (Jn 13:1–17).

4:4,6 GOD, One God—V 4 refers to the god of this age, Satan, who as a false god has wielded enormous influence for evil in this world. It is not an admission that he is a god. That would be polytheism, the belief in more than one god. Often Satan demands and people give him worship due only God. We treat him as though he were God. The Bible teaches pointedly that there is only one God, revealed to us most clearly as the Father of our Lord Jesus Christ. All other "gods" are but pretenders, deceivers, worthless ideas. We see God not in Satan but in Christ.

4:4 JESUS CHRIST, God—See note on Col 1:15.

4:4 EVIL AND SUFFERING, Satan—Satan is the god of this age. That is, he is the evil of this world in person. People may not consciously worship Satan; yet by acting as he desires they make him god. Calling Satan god in this sense does not give him any of the qualities and characteristics of the one, unique God. It does not lead to a dualistic world with a good God and bad god competing on an equal basis. Calling Satan god recognizes what the majority of the world is doing. Satan's major work is blinding people to the meaning of Jesus Christ and His gospel.

4:4 HUMANITY, Image of God—The original image of God was stamped upon people in creation but was distorted by sin. God's image can be clearly seen in Jesus. See Ge 1:26–28; Jn 14:7–9.

4:5 JESUS CHRIST, Lord—See notes on Ac 2:23–36; 1 Co 8:4–6.

4:5 THE CHURCH, Servants—Christ is the subject of Christian proclamation. The human preacher, even an apostle, is simply a slave of Christ. See note on Ro 1:1.

4:5 CHURCH LEADERS, Pastor and Overseer—The aim of all pastors is to see that Jesus Christ is the Lord of the church. They are to overcome the temptation to be self-promoting or self-serving. Pastors possess spiritual gifts to serve the church for Jesus.

4:6 GOD, Glory—God sent Jesus so we may see His glory, how much greater He is than all other beings in the universe. Only in Christ can we find salvation. See note on 3:7–18.

4:6 JESUS CHRIST, Light—The Creator of light placed the light of salvation in our lives by introducing us to Jesus, who revealed God's glory. See notes on Jn 1:4–5; 11:4.

4:6 CREATION, New Creation—Paul combined two familiar concepts: creation and salvation. The creation story in Genesis taught plainly that a personal Creator brought the world into existence. The same thing, in a spiritual sense, had happened in his own life. His transformation from the cold legalism of his former religion to the warmth of Christ's loving presence in his heart was as much a miracle as the original creation. The center of his life became the very Person whom he had sought to destroy. The glory of His presence illuminated Paul so completely that the system by which he had previously sought to find acceptance with God seemed as the original darkness (Ge 1:2). The coming of Christ is like the glorious creation of light (Ge 1:3), bringing new life and promise for happy days.

4:6 SALVATION, Knowledge of God—The quotation is from Ge 1:3. Paul may be thinking about the brilliant light which he saw at his conversion on the Damascus road (Ac 9:3; 22:6; 26:13). God illuminates His people through the light of Christ shining in their hearts. God the Creator and God the Savior are one and the same. To have knowledge of God's glory is to have seen God (Ex 33:18–20). We can see God by

7But we have this treasure in jars of
clay[w] to show that this all-surpassing
power is from God[x] and not from us.
8We are hard pressed on every side,[y] but
not crushed; perplexed,[z] but not in despair; 9persecuted,[a] but not abandoned;[b] struck down, but not destroyed.[c] 10We always carry around in
our body the death of Jesus,[d] so that the
life of Jesus may also be revealed in our
body.[e] 11For we who are alive are always
being given over to death for Jesus'
sake,[f] so that his life may be revealed
in our mortal body. 12So then, death
is at work in us, but life is at work in
you.[g]
13It is written: "I believed; therefore I
have spoken."[e][h] With that same spirit of
faith[i] we also believe and therefore
speak, 14because we know that the one
who raised the Lord Jesus from the dead[j]
will also raise us with Jesus[k] and present
us with you in his presence.[l] 15All this is
for your benefit, so that the grace that is
reaching more and more people may
cause thanksgiving[m] to overflow to the
glory of God.
16Therefore we do not lose heart.[n]
Though outwardly we are wasting away,
yet inwardly[o] we are being renewed[p]
day by day. 17For our light and momentary troubles are achieving for us an eternal glory that far outweighs them all.[q]
18So we fix our eyes not on what is seen,
but on what is unseen.[r] For what is seen
is temporary, but what is unseen is eternal.

Chapter 5

Our Heavenly Dwelling

NOW we know that if the earthly[s]
tent[t] we live in is destroyed, we
have a building from God, an eternal
house in heaven, not built by human
hands. 2Meanwhile we groan,[u] longing
to be clothed with our heavenly dwelling,[v] 3because when we are clothed, we
will not be found naked. 4For while we
are in this tent, we groan[w] and are burdened, because we do not wish to be unclothed but to be clothed with our heavenly dwelling,[x] so that what is mortal
may be swallowed up by life. 5Now it is
God who has made us for this very pur-

[e] *13* Psalm 116:10

4:7 [w]Job 4:19; Isa 64:8; 2Ti 2:20 [x]Jdg 7:2; 1Co 2:5; 2Co 6:7
4:8 [y]2Co 7:5 [z]Gal 4:20
4:9 [a]Jn 15:20; Ro 8:35 [b]Heb 13:5 [c]Ps 37:24; Pr 24:16
4:10 [d]S Ro 6:6; S 2Co 1:5 [e]S Ro 6:5
4:11 [f]Ro 8:36
4:12 [g]2Co 13:9
4:13 [h]Ps 116:10 [i]1Co 12:9
4:14 [j]S Ac 2:24 [k]1Th 4:14 [l]Eph 5:27; Col 1:22; Jude 24
4:15 [m]2Co 1:11; 9:11
4:16 [n]ver 1; Ps 18:45 [o]Ro 7:22 [p]Ps 103:5; Isa 40:31; Col 3:10
4:17 [q]Ps 30:5; Ro 8:18; 1Pe 1:6,7
4:18 [r]2Co 5:7; Ro 8:24; Heb 11:1
5:1 [s]1Co 15:47 [t]Isa 38:12; 2Pe 1:13,14
5:2 [u]ver 4; Ro 8:23 [v]ver 4; 1Co 15:53, 54
5:4 [w]ver 2; Ro 8:23 [x]ver 2; 1Co 15:53, 54

looking at Jesus.

4:7–12 HUMANITY, Life—The human being is frail and weak, in the process of dying. We live under pressure, perplexity, persecution, and pain. This is part of human existence. Despite all these problems, we know Christ is alive and working through us. This gives us confidence to face life's threats and problems.

4:8–18 EVIL AND SUFFERING, Endurance—Although frequently mistreated, Paul was encouraged by his faith in God, who raised Jesus from the dead. We cannot expect a world without problems, sorrows, and pains. Our Lord endured the same kind of world. Our troubles last but a moment compared to the eternal glory God has for us. Meanwhile, in our sufferings we represent Christ to the world. See notes on Ro 5:3–5; 8:12–18, 28–39.

4:10–11 REVELATION, Persons—To live in discipleship with God is to experience the presence of the Spirit of God, whose fullness makes our lives reveal the death and the life of Christ. As followers indwelt by the Spirit of God, we are living witnesses of Jesus' sacrifice and love and also of His power for eternal life.

4:14 JESUS CHRIST, Resurrection—See note on 1 Co 15:12–19.

4:14–18 LAST THINGS, Believers' Resurrection—Paul faced opposition in Corinth and had to endure the weakness of his gradually dying body. Still he emphasized thanksgiving because he had confidence God would raise him and his fellow believers just as He raised Jesus. The temporary troubles of life fade in light of the eternal glory that waits for us. God is the Author of resurrection. Resurrection will introduce believers to Christ's eternal presence. Even in troubled times, we find hope by fixing our gaze on the invisible, eternal world rather than the material, temporary world.

4:15 SALVATION, Grace—God's grace was reaching more and more persons in Corinth and elsewhere during the Apostolic Age. His grace is behind the growth and expansion of the Christian faith. We should overflow with thanks and praise as God causes His church to grow.

4:15 PRAYER, Thanksgiving—Paul was deeply concerned to credit God properly. See notes on 2:14; Col 2:7.

5:1–6 HOLY SPIRIT, Security—See notes on 1:21–22; Ro 5:1–5; Eph 1:13–14.

5:1–5 EVIL AND SUFFERING, God's Future Help—Present suffering will eventually be eliminated. See note on Ro 8:18–25.

5:1–10 LAST THINGS, Intermediate State—The state of believers between death and Christ's return has been greatly debated. This passage is central in determining one's belief about the intermediate state. Alternative viewpoints include: (1) Soul sleep—the body decays, and the soul is unconscious until the Lord returns. See note on Ac 7:60. (2) Immediate resurrection—the believer is immediately at home worshiping with Jesus in the heavenly Temple. The age to come is already a reality in eternity which is not conscious of passing time as we are. (3) Disembodied state—a person exists as an unclothed spirit without a body until the resurrection body is received at the resurrection of the dead, but the disembodied spirit is with the Lord and is conscious. See notes on Isa 14:9; Lk 16:19–26; 1 Co 15:20–23; Php 1:21–24. Basic issues involved are (1) the Hebrew understanding of humans as unified beings rather than as two- (body and soul) or three-part (body, soul, and spirit) beings; (2) the relationship between time in this age and eternity in the next; (3) the symbolic or literal nature of the description of thirst, tongue, finger, and seeing in Lk 16:24; (4) the meaning of "eternal house in heaven" (resurrection body or heavenly Temple of worship), "naked" (disembodied, or without grace and righteousness at the judgment), "away from the body" (disembodied or dead and thus in the resurrected body); and (5) the relationship among 1 Co 15; 2 Co 5; and Php 1:23. Those who believe this text refers to an intermediate state point to "meanwhile" (v 2) and the references to "naked" and "unclothed" (vv 2–3). Others suggest that Paul used "meanwhile" in reference to his time on earth. In any view, interpreters agree Paul comforted his readers, assuring them that death simply translates us into the Lord's presence. He also warned that we must face Christ as Judge.

5:5 GOD, Creator—Why were we created? Was it just to suffer through life until death releases us? No! God had a marvelous purpose. He created people for eternal life with Him. We know this because His Spirit works in our life, giving us present experience with God as a down payment on what we will receive.

pose and has given us the Spirit as a deposit, guaranteeing what is to come.[y]
6Therefore we are always confident
and know that as long as we are at home
in the body we are away from the Lord.
7We live by faith, not by sight.[z] 8We are
confident, I say, and would prefer to be
away from the body and at home with the
Lord.[a] 9So we make it our goal to please
him,[b] whether we are at home in the
body or away from it. 10For we must all
appear before the judgment seat of
Christ, that each one may receive what is
due him[c] for the things done while in
the body, whether good or bad.

The Ministry of Reconciliation

11Since, then, we know what it is to
fear the Lord,[d] we try to persuade men.
What we are is plain to God, and I hope it
is also plain to your conscience.[e] 12We
are not trying to commend ourselves to
you again,[f] but are giving you an opportunity to take pride in us,[g] so that you
can answer those who take pride in what
is seen rather than in what is in the
heart. 13If we are out of our mind,[h] it is
for the sake of God; if we are in our right
mind, it is for you. 14For Christ's love
compels us, because we are convinced
that one died for all, and therefore all
died.[i] 15And he died for all, that those
who live should no longer live for themselves[j] but for him who died for them[k]
and was raised again.

16So from now on we regard no one
from a worldly[l] point of view. Though
we once regarded Christ in this way, we
do so no longer. 17Therefore, if anyone is
in Christ,[m] he is a new creation;[n] the old
has gone, the new has come![o] 18All this
is from God,[p] who reconciled us to himself through Christ[q] and gave us the ministry of reconciliation: 19that God was rec-

5:5 [y]Ro 8:23; 2Co 1:22; Eph 1:13,14
5:7 [z]1Co 13:12; S 2Co 4:18
5:8 [a]S Jn 12:26
5:9 [b]Ro 14:18; Eph 5:10; Col 1:10; 1Th 4:1
5:10 [c]S Mt 16:27; Ac 10:42; Ro 2:16; 14:10; Eph 6:8
5:11 [d]Job 23:15; Heb 10:31; 12:29; Jude 23 [e]2Co 4:2
5:12 [f]S 2Co 3:1 [g]2Co 1:14
5:13 [h]2Co 11:1,16,17; 12:11
5:14 [i]Ro 6:6,7; Gal 2:20; Col 3:3
5:15 [j]Ro 14:7-9 [k]Ro 4:25
5:16 [l]2Co 10:4; 11:18
5:17 [m]S Ro 16:3 [n]S Jn 1:13; S Ro 6:4; Gal 6:15 [o]Isa 65:17; Rev 21:4,5
5:18 [p]S Ro 11:36 [q]S Ro 5:10

5:8 LAST THINGS, Intermediate State—To be away from the body through death is for believers to be at home with the Lord. Rather than an interval of soul sleep or lethargic semiconsciousness, the time following death and prior to Jesus' return is a time of being with the Lord.

5:10 JESUS CHRIST, Judgment—Every person who ever lives must keep an appointment with Christ at the final judgment. Believers will be rewarded. Others will be punished eternally.

5:10 LAST THINGS, Judgment—An important aspect of future judgment is the assignment of rewards. While salvation itself is a gift of grace, rewards must be earned by faithful living and serving. Often in Scripture the rewards for faithfulness are described as crowns (1 Co 9:25; 2 Ti 4:8; Jas 1:12). Rewards can be lost, whereas salvation is secure (1 Co 3:15; 2 Jn 8). Some hold to a single, future, general judgment for all persons, while others expect several separate judgments. This passage refers only to the rewarding of believers, whichever interpretation is followed. For judgment upon unbelievers, see note on Rev 20:11–15.

5:11 GOD, Wisdom—Paul had to defend his leadership position for the Corinthians. His evidence: God knew his intentions. God, in His infinite wisdom, knows us better than we know ourselves. We may even deceive ourselves as to what we really are, but not God.

5:11 SALVATION, Fear of God—Knowledge that we must face God in judgment brings reverence and awe into our lives. The fear of the Lord is an important motive in seeking to persuade others to become Christians. The doctrine of salvation supports world evangelization.

5:14–15 JESUS CHRIST, Death—Jesus died for the salvation of all. Believers receive that salvation and forsake self-centered living for Christ-centered living.

5:14–15,21 SALVATION, Atonement—Christ died as a representative of the human race. God made Him a sin offering for us that we might live for Him and not for ourselves. Atonement is potentially universal, available to all people. It becomes an active reality only in the lives of those who commit themselves to Christ.

5:14 EVANGELISM, Love—Love for the lost constrains us to share Christ with them. Christians love the lost because they are in great need; they are without God; they will spend eternity in hell. We lovingly move them to Jesus, their only hope.

5:17 GOD, Creator—In salvation God has done a new work of creation, in contrast to, or in completion of, the first creation of humans. God first brought persons into physical existence out of nothingness; now, He brings persons from spiritual death, or nothingness, to spiritual life.

5:17–21 SALVATION, As Being in Christ—To be in Christ is to be a new creation. The first part of v 19 is the best summary sentence of the gospel in the Bible. God and Christ cannot be pitted against each other. Those in Christ can become godlike in their character and conduct.

5:17–19 LAST THINGS, Creation's Redemption—The inclusion of the world (Greek *kosmos*) in the message and ministry of reconciliation lifts the thought beyond only individualistic reconciliation. Clearly, individual believers, being by faith "in Christ," are new creations, reconciled to God through Christ. This, however, is part of the larger cosmic reconciliation that happens "in Christ." The final expression of creation's future share in redemption is the new heavens and new earth which emerge after the first heaven and first earth have passed away. See note on Rev 21:1. The light of revelation enables believers to look for such cosmic newness (2 Pe 3:13). The work of transformation has begun in Christ. Creation, human history, and salvation will finally converge in the consummation of all things in the advent of the eternal order.

5:17–21 PROCLAMATION, Compulsion—See note on 1 Co 9:16–18.

5:18–21 GOD, Grace—Without God's grace salvation would not be possible. God is the Redeemer. The whole work of salvation from start to finish is God's work. In its entirety salvation is the work of God the Father who was reconciling a rebellious world to Himself.

5:18–21 JESUS CHRIST, Redeemer—Jesus in His death suffered the punishment for our sin and restored the relationship between us and God. God no longer inputs sin on our record. Rather He counts us as ministers leading others to Jesus and thus to reconciliation with God.

5:18–21 SALVATION, Reconciliation—Salvation is reconciliation to God so that He no longer charges our sins against our account. God has done everything necessary for us to be reconciled to Him. We must give up our hostility to Him and accept His reconciliation. Reconciliation here means bringing God and human beings together or making them friends. See note on Ro 5:10–11. God takes the initiative in bringing back alienated strangers to Himself. His initiative is through Christ and Christ's ambassadors, such as Paul. The ministry of reconciliation is given to all saved persons. None is excluded, though Christ has called and gifted some Christians to be His special ambassadors (Eph 4:11–14).

5:18 SALVATION, Grace—The new creation, wherein God makes us new persons in Christ, is a gift from God's gracious hands. The ministry of reconciliation is another of God's gifts.

5:18–20 DISCIPLESHIP, Involvement—Involvement in society's life is crucial for discipleship. Just as God did not

onciling the world to himself in Christ,
not counting men's sins against them.[r]
And he has committed to us the message
of reconciliation. 20We are therefore
Christ's ambassadors,[s] as though God
were making his appeal through us.[t] We
implore you on Christ's behalf: Be reconciled to God.[u] 21God made him who had
no sin[v] to be sin[f] for us, so that in him
we might become the righteousness of
God.[w]

Chapter 6

AS God's fellow workers[x] we urge you
not to receive God's grace in vain.[y]
2For he says,

> "In the time of my favor I heard you,
> and in the day of salvation I helped
> you."[g] [z]

I tell you, now is the time of God's favor,
now is the day of salvation.

Paul's Hardships

3We put no stumbling block in anyone's path,[a] so that our ministry will not
be discredited. 4Rather, as servants of
God we commend ourselves in every
way: in great endurance; in troubles,
hardships and distresses; 5in beatings,
imprisonments[b] and riots; in hard work,
sleepless nights and hunger;[c] 6in purity,
understanding, patience and kindness; in
the Holy Spirit[d] and in sincere love;[e] 7in
truthful speech[f] and in the power of
God;[g] with weapons of righteousness[h]
in the right hand and in the left; 8through
glory and dishonor,[i] bad report[j] and
good report; genuine, yet regarded as impostors;[k] 9known, yet regarded as unknown; dying,[l] and yet we live on;[m]
beaten, and yet not killed; 10sorrowful,
yet always rejoicing;[n] poor, yet making
many rich;[o] having nothing,[p] and yet
possessing everything.[q]
11We have spoken freely to you, Corinthians, and opened wide our hearts to
you.[r] 12We are not withholding our affection from you, but you are withholding
yours from us. 13As a fair exchange—I
speak as to my children[s]—open wide
your hearts[t] also.

Do Not Be Yoked With Unbelievers

14Do not be yoked together[u] with unbelievers.[v] For what do righteousness
and wickedness have in common? Or
what fellowship can light have with darkness?[w] 15What harmony is there between
Christ and Belial[h]?[x] What does a believer[y] have in common with an unbeliever?[z] 16What agreement is there between
the temple of God and idols?[a] For we are
the temple[b] of the living God.[c] As God
has said: "I will live with them and walk
among them, and I will be their God, and
they will be my people."[i] [d]

5:19 [r]S Ro 4:8
5:20 [s]2Co 6:1; Eph 6:20 [t]ver 18 [u]Isa 27:5
5:21 [v]Heb 4:15; 7:26; 1Pe 2:22,24; 1Jn 3:5 [w]S Ro 1:17; S 1Co 1:30
6:1 [x]S 1Co 3:9; 2Co 5:20 [y]1Co 15:2
6:2 [z]Isa 49:8; Ps 69:13; Isa 55:6
6:3 [a]S Mt 5:29; Ro 14:13,20; 1Co 8:9,13; 9:12; 10:32
6:5 [b]Ac 16:23; 2Co 11:23-25 [c]1Co 4:11
6:6 [d]1Co 2:4; 1Th 1:5 [e]Ro 12:9; 1Ti 1:5
6:7 [f]2Co 4:2 [g]2Co 4:7 [h]Ro 13:12; 2Co 10:4; Eph 6:10-18
6:8 [i]1Co 4:10 [j]1Co 4:13 [k]Mt 27:63
6:9 [l]S Ro 8:36 [m]2Co 1:8-10; 4:10, 11
6:10 [n]S Mt 5:12; 2Co 7:4; Php 2:17; 4:4; Col 1:24; 1Th 1:6 [o]2Co 8:9 [p]Ac 3:6 [q]Ro 8:32; 1Co 3:21
6:11 [r]2Co 7:3
6:13 [s]S 1Th 2:11 [t]2Co 7:2
6:14 [u]Ge 24:3; Dt 22:10; 1Co 5:9, 10 [v]1Co 6:6 [w]Eph 5:7,11; 1Jn 1:6
6:15 [x]1Co 10:21 [y]Ac 5:14 [z]1Co 6:6
6:16 [a]1Co 10:21 [b]S 1Co 3:16 [c]S Mt 16:16 [d]Lev 26:12; Jer 32:38; Eze 37:27; Rev 21:3

[f]*21* Or *be a sin offering* [g]*2* Isaiah 49:8
[h]*15* Greek *Beliar*, a variant of *Belial*
[i]*16* Lev. 26:12; Jer. 32:38; Ezek. 37:27

---

retreat from a sinful, rebellious world, so Christians do not turn away from the non-Christian world. Reconciliation is God's goal for the world. He made reconciliation possible through Christ. He sends us to the hurting, isolated people separated from Christ by their sin. We are ministers showing the path to reconciliation with God through Christ. See Guide to Seeking Reconciliation, pp. 1782–1784.

5:19 SALVATION, Forgiveness—See note on Ps 130:3–4. Jesus Christ made it possible for our sins to be blotted out.

5:20 EVANGELISM, Involves—We are Christ's representatives on earth. We speak for the King of heaven, or rather let Him speak through us. Our message is clear: be reconciled to God through faith in Jesus Christ! Evangelism is not an option; it is our primary role as Christians.

5:21 JESUS CHRIST, Sinless—Jesus did not sin. He chose to die on the cross and accept the punishment of our sin. Jesus has given us His righteousness, which includes moral rightness and right relationship with God.

5:21 CHRISTIAN ETHICS, Justice—Righteous people gain their right standing with God and their new righteous nature through God's act of declaring us righteous in Christ. See notes on Ro 8:4,10; Php 3:9.

6:1–10 EVIL AND SUFFERING, Rejoicing—Despite much suffering, Paul could rejoice because of his faith in God. Paul's troubles were part of his witness and ministry.

6:1 ELECTION, Free Will—God calls the elect to understand the high cost of discipleship. Anything less than obedience to God, who has revealed Himself to us in Jesus Christ, is cheap grace. Failure to live and suffer for Christ is failure to understand election, salvation, and grace.

6:1–2 EVANGELISM, Call to Salvation—The call to all people is: now is the time of God's favor. The call concerning the grace of God comes through faithful witnesses—God's fellow workers. That is what we are to be. When we are faithful to the grace of God, He will use us to enable others to receive that saving grace.

6:2 HISTORY, Time—Every day has become a time full of opportunity and at the same time a moment of crisis, for God offers salvation through Christ. This day provides opportunity to accept that offer. Tomorrow may not.

6:2 SALVATION, Initiative—The verse is a quotation from, and a commentary on, Isa 49:8. The divine initiative makes salvation available to us right now. We do not have to wait for it. God's salvation is available to us today.

6:4 THE CHURCH, Servants—The church's servant does not have an easy life, as Paul's experiences demonstrated. God seeks leaders committed to His gospel and willing to pay any price necessary to proclaim it. Leaders who refuse to be servants cause members to stumble and their own ministry to lose credibility. See notes on 4:5; Mt 20:20–28; Ro 1:1.

6:14–18 FAMILY, Intermarriage—A Christian should marry a Christian. Since Christ through the Holy Spirit dwells within the believer, Christians are not to marry unbelievers and participate in their false worship. Marriage should strengthen Christian faith. See notes on Dt 7:3–4; 1 Co 6:15–17; 7:12–16.

6:16–17 THE CHURCH, People of God—The new covenant church is called to avoid all worldly actions. See note on Jer 30:22. Through His Spirit, God lives in the believers, who are God's Temple. See note on 1 Co 3:16–17. We cannot participate in worship and practices of other religions and/or philosophies because these would dishonor God. Believers honor Christ and Him alone.

17"Therefore come out from them[e]
and be separate,
says the Lord.
Touch no unclean thing,
and I will receive you."[j] [f]
18"I will be a Father to you,
and you will be my sons and
daughters,[g]
says the Lord Almighty."[k] [h]

Chapter 7

SINCE we have these promises,[i] dear
friends,[j] let us purify ourselves from
everything that contaminates body and
spirit, perfecting holiness[k] out of reverence for God.

Paul's Joy

2Make room for us in your hearts.[l] We
have wronged no one, we have corrupted
no one, we have exploited no one. 3I do
not say this to condemn you; I have said
before that you have such a place in our
hearts[m] that we would live or die with
you. 4I have great confidence in you; I
take great pride in you.[n] I am greatly encouraged;[o] in all our troubles my joy
knows no bounds.[p]
5For when we came into Macedonia,[q]
this body of ours had no rest, but we
were harassed at every turn[r]—conflicts
on the outside, fears within.[s] 6But God,
who comforts the downcast,[t] comforted
us by the coming of Titus,[u] 7and not only
by his coming but also by the comfort you
had given him. He told us about your
longing for me, your deep sorrow, your
ardent concern for me, so that my joy was
greater than ever.
8Even if I caused you sorrow by my letter,[v] I do not regret it. Though I did regret it—I see that my letter hurt you, but
only for a little while— 9yet now I am
happy, not because you were made sorry,
but because your sorrow led you to repentance. For you became sorrowful as
God intended and so were not harmed in
any way by us. 10Godly sorrow brings repentance that leads to salvation[w] and
leaves no regret, but worldly sorrow
brings death. 11See what this godly sorrow has produced in you: what earnestness, what eagerness to clear yourselves,
what indignation, what alarm, what longing, what concern,[x] what readiness to
see justice done. At every point you have
proved yourselves to be innocent in this
matter. 12So even though I wrote to
you,[y] it was not on account of the one
who did the wrong[z] or of the injured party, but rather that before God you could
see for yourselves how devoted to us you
are. 13By all this we are encouraged.
In addition to our own encouragement,
we were especially delighted to see how
happy Titus[a] was, because his spirit has
been refreshed by all of you. 14I had
boasted to him about you,[b] and you have
not embarrassed me. But just as everything we said to you was true, so our
boasting about you to Titus[c] has proved
to be true as well. 15And his affection for
you is all the greater when he remembers
that you were all obedient,[d] receiving
him with fear and trembling.[e] 16I am glad
I can have complete confidence in you.[f]

Chapter 8

Generosity Encouraged

AND now, brothers, we want you to
know about the grace that God has

[j] *17* Isaiah 52:11; Ezek. 20:34,41
[k] *18* 2 Samuel 7:14; 7:8

6:17 [e]Rev 18:4 [f]Isa 52:11; Eze 20:34,41
6:18 [g]Ex 4:22; 2Sa 7:14; 1Ch 17:13; Isa 43:6; S Ro 8:14 [h]2Sa 7:8
7:1 [i]2Co 6:17,18 [j]S 1Co 10:14 [k]1Th 4:7; 1Pe 1:15, 16
7:2 [l]2Co 6:12,13
7:3 [m]2Co 6:11,12; Php 1:7
7:4 [n]ver 14; 2Co 8:24 [o]ver 13 [p]S 2Co 6:10
7:5 [q]2Co 2:13; S Ac 16:9 [r]2Co 4:8 [s]Dt 32:25
7:6 [t]2Co 1:3,4 [u]ver 13; S 2Co 2:13
7:8 [v]2Co 2:2,4
7:10 [w]Ac 11:18
7:11 [x]ver 7
7:12 [y]ver 8; 2Co 2:3,9 [z]1Co 5:1,2
7:13 [a]ver 6; S 2Co 2:13
7:14 [b]ver 4 [c]ver 6
7:15 [d]2Co 2:9; 10:6 [e]Ps 55:5; 1Co 2:3; Php 2:12
7:16 [f]S 2Co 2:3

7:1 GOD, Holy—The holiness of God demands holiness on our part. In the strict sense, holiness belongs only to God. Christians should grow in a vital relationship with God so that His holiness becomes evident in our lives. We cannot truly reverence God apart from being marked by His holiness. To reverence Him means to submit ourselves to His holy and sovereign authority, forsaking our sin and self-centeredness.

7:2–16 EVIL AND SUFFERING, Comfort—Fears, conflicts, and broken relationships cause suffering for the Christian. Help comes from God's presence, assistance and comfort of Christian friends, remembrances and gifts sent by others, and good news. Sorrow may be good when it causes changed actions and attitudes or renewed relationships. God works through our Christian relationships to heal hurts and comfort us in hardship and distress.

7:9–10 SALVATION, Repentance—Godly sorrow and worldly sorrow are here contrasted. The Corinthian Christians are examples of godly sorrow. Repentance and salvation are the fruit of godly sorrow over our sins. This grief that leaves no regret is the kind salvation teaches.

7:10–11 CHRISTIAN ETHICS, Justice—True repentance is known by several characteristics. One, which modern Christianity has not always honored, is that of the concern for justice and the eagerness to act on that concern.

8:1 GOD, Grace—Our power to act like God comes from the grace—unearned and undeserved love—God gives us. In this instance, God's grace developed a spirit of generosity in the Macedonian churches. We need that same grace of generosity to help people in need.

8:1—9:15 STEWARDSHIP, Sacrificial Giving—Christian giving is a grace. That means giving is the power of God's love at work in the Christian life to do God's work. Paul described the nature of Christian stewardship as he described the example of the Macedonians and encouraged the Corinthians in their stewardship. Stewardship means: (1) severe testing can result in overflowing joy; (2) extreme poverty can bring abundant generosity; (3) Christian giving goes beyond apparent economic ability to show total devotion to Christ; (4) stewards give voluntarily rather than under outside compulsion; (5) self must be dedicated to God before money can truly represent Christian stewardship; (6) Christians should not be content until we excel in giving; (7) giving shows the sincerity of love; (8) giving can never match but should seek to imitate Christ's gracious love in giving Himself for our salvation; (9) promises must be followed by actions; (10) giving is measured by our resources, not someone else's; (11) giving should result in the needs of all the Christian family being equally met; (12) a church's stewardship depends on enthusiastic leaders; (13)

given the Macedonian[g] churches. 2Out
of the most severe trial, their overflowing
joy and their extreme poverty welled up
in rich generosity.[h] 3For I testify that
they gave as much as they were able,[i]
and even beyond their ability. Entirely on
their own, 4they urgently pleaded with us
for the privilege of sharing[j] in this service[k] to the saints.[l] 5And they did not
do as we expected, but they gave themselves first to the Lord and then to us in
keeping with God's will. 6So we urged[m]
Titus,[n] since he had earlier made a beginning, to bring also to completion[o] this
act of grace on your part. 7But just as you
excel in everything[p]—in faith, in
speech, in knowledge,[q] in complete earnestness and in your love for us[1] —see
that you also excel in this grace of giving.

8I am not commanding you,[r] but I
want to test the sincerity of your love by
comparing it with the earnestness of others. 9For you know the grace[s] of our Lord
Jesus Christ,[t] that though he was rich,
yet for your sakes he became poor,[u] so
that you through his poverty might become rich.[v]

10And here is my advice[w] about what
is best for you in this matter: Last year
you were the first not only to give but
also to have the desire to do so.[x] 11Now
finish the work, so that your eager willingness[y] to do it may be matched by your
completion of it, according to your
means. 12For if the willingness is there,
the gift is acceptable according to what
one has,[z] not according to what he does
not have.

13Our desire is not that others might be
relieved while you are hard pressed, but
that there might be equality. 14At the
present time your plenty will supply what
they need,[a] so that in turn their plenty
will supply what you need. Then there
will be equality, 15as it is written: "He
who gathered much did not have too
much, and he who gathered little did not
have too little."[m][b]

Titus Sent to Corinth

16I thank God,[c] who put into the
heart[d] of Titus[e] the same concern I have
for you. 17For Titus not only welcomed
our appeal, but he is coming to you with
much enthusiasm and on his own initiative.[f] 18And we are sending along with
him the brother[g] who is praised by all
the churches[h] for his service to the gospel.[i] 19What is more, he was chosen by
the churches to accompany us[j] as we
carry the offering, which we administer
in order to honor the Lord himself and to
show our eagerness to help.[k] 20We want
to avoid any criticism of the way we administer this liberal gift. 21For we are taking pains to do what is right, not only in
the eyes of the Lord but also in the eyes
of men.[l]

22In addition, we are sending with
them our brother who has often proved
to us in many ways that he is zealous, and
now even more so because of his great
confidence in you. 23As for Titus,[m] he is
my partner[n] and fellow worker[o] among
you; as for our brothers,[p] they are representatives of the churches and an honor
to Christ. 24Therefore show these men
the proof of your love and the reason for
our pride in you,[q] so that the churches
can see it.

Chapter 9

THERE is no need[r] for me to write to
you about this service[s] to the

8:1 [g]S Ac 16:9
8:2 [h]Ex 36:5; 2Co 9:11
8:3 [i]1Co 16:2
8:4 [j]ver 1 [k]S Ac 24:17 [l]S Ac 9:13
8:6 [m]ver 17; 2Co 12:18 [n]ver 16, 23; S 2Co 2:13 [o]ver 10,11
8:7 [p]2Co 9:8 [q]Ro 15:14; 1Co 1:5; 12:8; 13:1,2; 14:6
8:8 [r]1Co 7:6
8:9 [s]S Ro 3:24 [t]2Co 13:14 [u]Mt 20:28; Php 2:6-8 [v]2Co 6:10
8:10 [w]1Co 7:25,40 [x]1Co 16:2,3; 2Co 9:2
8:11 [y]ver 12,19; Ex 25:2; 2Co 9:2
8:12 [z]Mk 12:43, 44; 2Co 9:7
8:14 [a]Ac 4:34; 2Co 9:12
8:15 [b]Ex 16:18
8:16 [c]S 2Co 2:14 [d]Rev 17:17 [e]S 2Co 2:13
8:17 [f]ver 6
8:18 [g]2Co 12:18 [h]S 1Co 7:17 [i]S 2Co 2:12
8:19 [j]Ac 14:23; 1Co 16:3,4 [k]ver 11, 12
8:21 [l]Ro 12:17; S 14:18; S Tit 2:14
8:23 [m]S 2Co 2:13 [n]Phm 17 [o]S Php 2:25 [p]ver 18,22
8:24 [q]2Co 7:4,14; 9:2
9:1 [r]1Th 4:9 [s]S Ac 24:17

[1] *7* Some manuscripts *in our love for you*
[m] *15* Exodus 16:18

stewardship demands trustworthy administrators; (14) our stewardship can set an enthusiastic example which others will follow; (15) stewardship involves willing, cheerful generosity, not grudging gifts; (16) generosity brings God's blessings to meet our economic and spiritual needs; (17) generous giving should bring gratitude to God rather than to people; (18) our giving generates praise for God in other places from unknown people; (19) our giving leads the people benefiting from our gifts to pray for us; and (20) God is the greatest Giver responsible for all we have and especially for our salvation in Christ.

8:1–8 WORSHIP, Sacrifice—The churches in Macedonia provide an example of worship involving the giving of themselves as well as their material wealth to the Lord. See notes on Lev 7:35–38; Ro 12:1–2.

8:3–4 THE CHURCH, Saints—See note on Ro 15:26.

8:9 JESUS CHRIST, Preexistent—Christ became "poor" in that He laid aside His existence with the Father to be born for our salvation.

8:9 JESUS CHRIST, Suffering—Jesus gave up the glories of heaven to experience earth's poverty, including suffering on the cross so we can have the riches of His salvation.

8:9 SALVATION, Blessing—Jesus became poor, giving up the riches of heaven, that we might be made rich with His blessings.

8:9 SALVATION, Grace—Jesus graphically showed us the meaning of grace. For no reason but His love for us and His obedience to the Father, He left the glory of heaven to take up the poverty of a wandering Galilean preacher and suffered death on the cross.

8:16 PRAYER, Thanksgiving—See note on 2:14. Fellow ministers in the gospel are cause for thanks not jealousy.

8:18–24 THE CHURCH, Local Body—Local churches cooperate together to meet the needs of other churches whether far or near. By collecting and delivering the offering from the various mission churches to the church in Jerusalem, Paul built a spirit of cooperation and a sense of unity among all the churches. Thereby, Christ was honored. Paul assured proper administration of the offering by letting the churches choose trusted representatives to assist in administering the offering. The church is not a dictatorship administered by one person but a group of Christ's servants who choose their own representatives and leaders. Paul's method shows the important place of proper administration, efforts at unity, mutual support, and cooperation. See notes on Mk 9:33–37; Ac 4:32.

9:1 THE CHURCH, Saints—See note on Ro 15:26.

saints.[t] 2For I know your eagerness to
help,[u] and I have been boasting[v] about it
to the Macedonians, telling them that
since last year[w] you in Achaia[x] were
ready to give; and your enthusiasm has
stirred most of them to action. 3But I am
sending the brothers[y] in order that our
boasting about you in this matter should
not prove hollow, but that you may be
ready, as I said you would be.[z] 4For if any
Macedonians[a] come with me and find
you unprepared, we—not to say anything
about you—would be ashamed of having
been so confident. 5So I thought it necessary to urge the brothers[b] to visit you in
advance and finish the arrangements for
the generous gift you had promised. Then
it will be ready as a generous gift,[c] not as
one grudgingly given.[d]

Sowing Generously

6Remember this: Whoever sows sparingly will also reap sparingly, and whoever sows generously will also reap generously.[e] 7Each man should give what he
has decided in his heart to give,[f] not re-
luctantly or under compulsion,[g] for God
loves a cheerful giver.[h] 8And God is
able[i] to make all grace abound to you, so
that in all things at all times, having all
that you need,[j] you will abound in every
good work. 9As it is written:

"He has scattered abroad his gifts[k] to
the poor;
his righteousness endures
forever."[n] [l]

10Now he who supplies seed to the sower
and bread for food[m] will also supply and
increase your store of seed and will enlarge the harvest of your righteousness.[n]
11You will be made rich[o] in every way so
that you can be generous[p] on every occasion, and through us your generosity will
result in thanksgiving to God.[q]
12This service that you perform is not
only supplying the needs[r] of God's people but is also overflowing in many expressions of thanks to God.[s] 13Because of
the service[t] by which you have proved
yourselves, men will praise God[u] for the
obedience that accompanies your confession[v] of the gospel of Christ,[w] and for
your generosity[x] in sharing with them
and with everyone else. 14And in their
prayers for you their hearts will go out to
you, because of the surpassing grace God
has given you. 15Thanks be to God[y] for
his indescribable gift![z]

9:1 [t]S Ac 9:13
9:2 [u]2Co 8:11,12, 19 [v]2Co 7:4,14; 8:24 [w]2Co 8:10 [x]S Ac 18:12
9:3 [y]2Co 8:23 [z]1Co 16:2
9:4 [a]Ro 15:26
9:5 [b]ver 3 [c]Php 4:17 [d]2Co 12:17,18
9:6 [e]Pr 11:24,25; 22:9; Gal 6:7,9
9:7 [f]Ex 25:2; 2Co 8:12 [g]Dt 15:10 [h]Ro 12:8
9:8 [i]Eph 3:20 [j]Php 4:19
9:9 [k]Mal 3:10 [l]Ps 112:9
9:10 [m]Isa 55:10 [n]Hos 10:12
9:11 [o]1Co 1:5 [p]ver 5 [q]2Co 1:11; 4:15
9:12 [r]2Co 8:14 [s]S 2Co 1:11
9:13 [t]S 2Co 8:4 [u]S Mt 9:8 [v]S Heb 3:1 [w]S 2Co 2:12 [x]ver 5
9:15 [y]S 2Co 2:14 [z]Ro 5:15,16
10:1 [a]Mt 11:29 [b]Gal 5:2; Eph 3:1
10:2 [c]S 1Co 4:21 [d]Ro 12:2
10:3 [e]ver 2
10:4 [f]S 2Co 6:7 [g]1Co 2:5 [h]ver 8; Jer 1:10; 23:29; 2Co 13:10
10:5 [i]Isa 2:11,12; 1Co 1:19 [j]2Co 9:13
10:6 [k]2Co 2:9; 7:15
10:7 [l]S Jn 7:24; 2Co 5:12 [m]1Co 1:12; S 3:23; 14:37 [n]2Co 11:23
10:8 [o]ver 13,15 [p]ver 4; Jer 1:10; 2Co 13:10

Chapter 10

Paul's Defense of His Ministry

BY the meekness and gentleness[a] of
Christ, I appeal to you—I, Paul,[b]
who am "timid" when face to face with
you, but "bold" when away! 2I beg you
that when I come I may not have to be as
bold[c] as I expect to be toward some people who think that we live by the standards of this world.[d] 3For though we live
in the world, we do not wage war as the
world does.[e] 4The weapons we fight
with[f] are not the weapons of the world.
On the contrary, they have divine power[g] to demolish strongholds.[h] 5We demolish arguments and every pretension
that sets itself up against the knowledge
of God,[i] and we take captive every
thought to make it obedient[j] to Christ.
6And we will be ready to punish every act
of disobedience, once your obedience is
complete.[k]
7You are looking only on the surface of
things.[o] [l] If anyone is confident that he
belongs to Christ,[m] he should consider
again that we belong to Christ just as
much as he.[n] 8For even if I boast somewhat freely about the authority the Lord
gave us[o] for building you up rather than
pulling you down,[p] I will not be ashamed

[n]9 Psalm 112:9 [o]7 Or *Look at the obvious facts*

9:8,14 GOD, Grace—See note on 8:1.
9:9–10 CHRISTIAN ETHICS, Justice—Paul reminded the Corinthians of God's sufficiency of grace and of His justice. The conclusion shown for believers is that our justice and righteousness are to correspond to God's. We are to give to the poor. Giving is a part of our righteousness. Righteousness is thus expressed outwardly in meeting the needs of other people. Such acts of righteousness bring a harvest so we can give even more. Justice is thus based on willingness to give to others, not on demand for rights.
9:11 PRAYER, Thanksgiving—See note on 2:14. Generous, unselfish giving leads to generous reasons for generous thanks and a growing richness of generosity.
9:12–15 DISCIPLESHIP, Persons—Why do you as a disciple obediently serve God by sharing resources with other people? It is so other people may see God's grace in your life and praise God. Disciples should be so devoted to God that all praise is directed toward Him. See note on Mt 5:14–16.
9:13 SALVATION, Confession—Confessing the good news about Christ should be accompanied with such obedience that it causes others to praise God. Obedience here was liberal participation in the collection for the poor saints in Jerusalem.
10:2–6 CHRISTIAN ETHICS, Character—Christians are involved in a battle of principles, philosophies, and world views. Paul's battle plan and confirmation of his relationship to Christ resided in his determination to wage this battle for people's minds by spiritual means, which transcend the ways of the world.
10:5 SALVATION, Knowledge of God—The world scorns the gospel and proudly sets up clever arguments against it. God's people destroy such arguments knowing that true knowledge of God comes only through faith, not through human reason. We should bring every thought into relation to Christ. All of our thinking should have a consistent unity which comes from having Christ at the center. Salvation is based not on hidden or philosophical knowledge, but on relational and personal knowledge of God which comes through Jesus Christ and the Holy Spirit.

of it. 9I do not want to seem to be trying
to frighten you with my letters. 10For
some say, "His letters are weighty and
forceful, but in person he is unim-
pressive[q] and his speaking amounts to
nothing."[r] 11Such people should realize
that what we are in our letters when we
are absent, we will be in our actions
when we are present.
12We do not dare to classify or compare
ourselves with some who commend
themselves.[s] When they measure themselves by themselves and compare themselves with themselves, they are not
wise. 13We, however, will not boast beyond proper limits, but will confine our
boasting to the field God has assigned to
us,[t] a field that reaches even to you.
14We are not going too far in our boasting, as would be the case if we had not
come to you, for we did get as far as you[u]
with the gospel of Christ.[v] 15Neither do
we go beyond our limits[w] by boasting of
work done by others.[p][x] Our hope is
that, as your faith continues to grow,[y]
our area of activity among you will greatly
expand, 16so that we can preach the gospel[z] in the regions beyond you.[a] For we
do not want to boast about work already
done in another man's territory. 17But,
"Let him who boasts boast in the
Lord."[q][b] 18For it is not the one who
commends himself[c] who is approved,
but the one whom the Lord commends.[d]

Chapter 11

Paul and the False Apostles

I hope you will put up with[e] a little of
my foolishness;[f] but you are already
doing that. 2I am jealous for you with a
godly jealousy. I promised you to one husband,[g] to Christ, so that I might present
you[h] as a pure virgin to him. 3But I am
afraid that just as Eve was deceived by the
serpent's cunning,[i] your minds may
somehow be led astray from your sincere
and pure devotion to Christ. 4For if someone comes to you and preaches a Jesus
other than the Jesus we preached,[j] or if
you receive a different spirit[k] from the
one you received, or a different gospel[l]
from the one you accepted, you put up
with it[m] easily enough. 5But I do not
think I am in the least inferior to those
"super-apostles."[n] 6I may not be a
trained speaker,[o] but I do have knowledge.[p] We have made this perfectly clear
to you in every way.
7Was it a sin[q] for me to lower myself
in order to elevate you by preaching the
gospel of God[r] to you free of charge?[s] 8I
robbed other churches by receiving support from them[t] so as to serve you. 9And
when I was with you and needed something, I was not a burden to anyone, for
the brothers who came from Macedonia
supplied what I needed.[u] I have kept myself from being a burden to you[v] in any
way, and will continue to do so. 10As
surely as the truth of Christ is in me,[w]
nobody in the regions of Achaia[x] will
stop this boasting[y] of mine. 11Why? Because I do not love you? God knows[z] I
do![a] 12And I will keep on doing what I
am doing in order to cut the ground from
under those who want an opportunity to
be considered equal with us in the things
they boast about.
13For such men are false apostles,[b] deceitful[c] workmen, masquerading as apos-

10:10 [q]ver 1; 1Co 2:3; Gal 4:13, 14 [r]1Co 1:17; 2Co 11:6
10:12 [s]ver 18; S 2Co 3:1
10:13 [t]ver 15,16; S Ro 12:3
10:14 [u]S 1Co 3:6 [v]S 2Co 2:12
10:15 [w]ver 13 [x]Ro 15:20 [y]2Th 1:3
10:16 [z]S Ro 1:1; S 2Co 2:12 [a]S Ac 19:21
10:17 [b]Jer 9:24; Ps 34:2; 44:8; 1Co 1:31
10:18 [c]ver 12 [d]S Ro 2:29
11:1 [e]ver 4,19,20; Mt 17:17 [f]ver 16, 17,21; 2Co 5:13
11:2 [g]Hos 2:19; Eph 5:26,27 [h]S 2Co 4:14
11:3 [i]Ge 3:1-6,13; 1Ti 2:14; Rev 12:9
11:4 [j]1Co 3:11 [k]Ro 8:15 [l]Gal 1:6-9 [m]S ver 1
11:5 [n]2Co 12:11; Gal 2:6
11:6 [o]S 1Co 1:17 [p]S 2Co 8:7; Eph 3:4
11:7 [q]2Co 12:13 [r]S Ro 1:1 [s]1Co 9:18
11:8 [t]Php 4:15,18
11:9 [u]Php 4:15,18 [v]2Co 12:13,14,16
11:10 [w]S Ro 9:1 [x]S Ac 18:12 [y]1Co 9:15
11:11 [z]ver 31; S Ro 1:9 [a]2Co 12:15
11:13 [b]S Mt 7:15 [c]Tit 1:10

[p] *13-15* Or *13We, however, will not boast about things that cannot be measured, but we will boast according to the standard of measurement that the God of measure has assigned us—a measurement that relates even to you. 14 . . . . 15Neither do we boast about things that cannot be measured in regard to the work done by others.* [q] *17* Jer. 9:24

10:12–18 EVANGELISM, Involves—Everyone has his or her ministry given by the grace and wisdom of God (Ro 12:3–8). Therefore, it is not wise to compare ourselves with others of God's people. We do not commend ourselves or boast beyond our called position and service in Christ. We do not intrude into someone else's ministry or claim credit for it. Our only boast is in Jesus Christ and His great work through us (Gal 6:14). This is the spirit that will bring the Lord's commendation and approval. This attitude will make our evangelistic effort effective and spread it to regions beyond.

10:13 ELECTION, Leadership—The elect are humble and faithful in carrying out the mission God has chosen for them. Arrogance, superiority attitudes, and self-righteous behavior are not in harmony with the gratitude that comes from accepting salvation from God's grace. Being elected is to walk humbly, faithfully, and obediently with God.

11:1–3 THE CHURCH, Bride—See note on Rev 21:2. As the bride of Christ, the church must serve Him with sincere and pure devotion.

11:2 FAMILY, Symbolic Nature—*Symbolizing* the church as the bride of Christ is found in Paul's writings as well as in Rev 21:2,9, where the New Jerusalem represents the body of believers in Christ.

11:4 JESUS CHRIST, Redeemer—Paul preached Jesus as Lord and suffering Redeemer. Others tried to interpret Jesus as a Jewish teacher of legalism or as a teacher of secret knowledge for salvation. We know Jesus through the inspired Scriptures. The temptation is to see Jesus in our image.

11:8–16 STEWARDSHIP, Support Ministry—In Old Testament life, the Temple tithe and offerings primarily supported the Levites or priests (Nu 18:20–24; Eze 44:28–30). Both Christ and Paul affirmed that supporting God-called ministers is the duty of the Christian church. Paul was anxious to assure the Corinthians that he was not after their money but desired that they know Christ. Paul apologized for permitting them to be "inferior" to other churches by not supporting his ministry. His self-support was for their good and was not an example to be followed in all churches. See note on 1 Ti 5:18.

11:13 CHURCH LEADERS, False Apostle—False apostles preach a different gospel (13:4) based on human achievement. They demand payment for their services. See note on 1 Co 9:1–15. They boast in their status and claim a superiority over their fellow Christians. They seek their own success and win influence over Christians by treachery and deceit. The church needs leaders who serve the church by proclaiming the lordship of Christ (4:5).

tles of Christ.[d] 14And no wonder, for Satan[e] himself masquerades as an angel of
light. 15It is not surprising, then, if his
servants masquerade as servants of righteousness. Their end will be what their
actions deserve.[f]

Paul Boasts About His Sufferings

16I repeat: Let no one take me for a
fool.[g] But if you do, then receive me just
as you would a fool, so that I may do a
little boasting. 17In this self-confident
boasting I am not talking as the Lord
would,[h] but as a fool.[i] 18Since many are
boasting in the way the world does,[j] I
too will boast.[k] 19You gladly put up
with[l] fools since you are so wise![m] 20In
fact, you even put up with[n] anyone who
enslaves you[o] or exploits you or takes advantage of you or pushes himself forward
or slaps you in the face. 21To my shame I
admit that we were too weak[p] for that!
What anyone else dares to boast about
—I am speaking as a fool—I also dare to
boast about.[q] 22Are they Hebrews? So am
I.[r] Are they Israelites? So am I.[s] Are
they Abraham's descendants? So am I.[t]
23Are they servants of Christ?[u] (I am out
of my mind to talk like this.) I am more. I
have worked much harder,[v] been in prison more frequently,[w] been flogged more
severely,[x] and been exposed to death
again and again.[y] 24Five times I received
from the Jews the forty lashes[z] minus
one. 25Three times I was beaten with
rods,[a] once I was stoned,[b] three times I
was shipwrecked,[c] I spent a night and a
day in the open sea, 26I have been constantly on the move. I have been in danger from rivers, in danger from bandits,
in danger from my own countrymen,[d] in
danger from Gentiles; in danger in the
city,[e] in danger in the country, in danger
at sea; and in danger from false brothers.[f] 27I have labored and toiled[g] and
have often gone without sleep; I have
known hunger and thirst and have often
gone without food;[h] I have been cold and
naked. 28Besides everything else, I face
daily the pressure of my concern for all
the churches.[i] 29Who is weak, and I do
not feel weak?[j] Who is led into sin,[k] and
I do not inwardly burn?
30If I must boast, I will boast[l] of the
things that show my weakness.[m] 31The
God and Father of the Lord Jesus, who is
to be praised forever,[n] knows[o] that I am
not lying. 32In Damascus the governor under King Aretas had the city of the Dama-
scenes guarded in order to arrest me.[p]
33But I was lowered in a basket from a
window in the wall and slipped through
his hands.[q]

Chapter 12

Paul's Vision and His Thorn

I must go on boasting.[r] Although there
is nothing to be gained, I will go on to
visions and revelations[s] from the Lord. 2I
know a man in Christ[t] who fourteen
years ago was caught up[u] to the third
heaven.[v] Whether it was in the body or
out of the body I do not know—God
knows.[w] 3And I know that this man—
whether in the body or apart from the
body I do not know, but God knows—
4was caught up[x] to paradise.[y] He heard

11:13 [d]Rev 2:2
11:14 [e]S Mt 4:10
11:15 [f]S Mt 16:27; Php 3:19
11:16 [g]ver 1
11:17 [h]1Co 7:12, 25 [i]ver 21
11:18 [j]2Co 5:16; 10:4 [k]ver 21; Php 3:3,4
11:19 [l]S ver 1 [m]1Co 4:10
11:20 [n]S ver 1 [o]Gal 2:4; 4:9; 5:1
11:21 [p]2Co 10:1, 10 [q]ver 17,18; Php 3:4
11:22 [r]Php 3:5 [s]Ro 9:4; 11:1 [t]S Lk 3:8; Ro 11:1
11:23 [u]S 1Co 3:5 [v]S 1Co 15:10 [w]Ac 16:23; 2Co 6:4,5 [x]Ac 16:23; 2Co 6:4, 5 [y]S Ro 8:36
11:24 [z]Dt 25:3
11:25 [a]Ac 16:22 [b]Ac 14:19 [c]Ac 27:1-44
11:26 [d]S Ac 20:3 [e]Ac 21:31 [f]Gal 2:4
11:27 [g]S Ac 18:3; Col 1:29 [h]1Co 4:11,12; 2Co 6:5
11:28 [i]S 1Co 7:17
11:29 [j]S Ro 14:1; S 1Co 2:3 [k]S Mt 5:29
11:30 [l]ver 16; Gal 6:14; 2Co 12:5, 9 [m]S 1Co 2:3
11:31 [n]Ro 1:25; 9:5 [o]ver 11; S Ro 1:9
11:32 [p]Ac 9:24
11:33 [q]Ac 9:25
12:1 [r]ver 5,9; 2Co 11:16,30 [s]ver 7; S 1Co 2:10
12:2 [t]S Ro 16:3 [u]ver 4; S Ac 8:39 [v]Eph 4:10 [w]2Co 11:11
12:4 [x]ver 2 [y]Lk 23:43; Rev 2:7

11:14–15 EVIL AND SUFFERING, Satan—Satan is deceptive. The Jews knew traditions of Satan assuming the form of an angel to deceive people. Only spiritual maturity and insight can protect us from the master of deceit. He uses people in church offices to deceive God's people. Paul knew false apostles who misled the churches he worked with. Such agents or instruments of Satan have no part in Christian hope. See note on Eph 6:10–20.

11:23 THE CHURCH, Servants—See notes on Mt 20:20–28; Ro 1:1.

11:28 THE CHURCH, Local Body—See note on Ac 4:32.

11:31 PRAYER, Praise—Paul inserted a brief doxology to reinforce his oath that he told the truth. See note on Ro 16:25–27.

12:1–10 EVIL AND SUFFERING, Testing—Paul's thorn in the flesh was a "messenger of Satan," but God used it to remind Paul of His grace and power. Paul prayed for relief from the suffering, but the suffering remained; his faith was strengthened. The thorn may have been a physical illness (Gal 4:13), but Paul here did not define the thorn. We cannot escape suffering through prayer or piety. Only God can give relief. At times He chooses not to help, knowing suffering can help us. Suffering can humble us, making us depend on God rather than ourselves.

12:1–5 REVELATION, Visions—Visions revealing God may strengthen personal faith but they do not make one Christian superior to another. Paul noted two possible types of visions: (1) in the body wherein the person is transported by divine powers to be with God; (2) out of the body in which a person has a spiritual experience with God with the body remaining on earth. Paul viewed the secrets of God's heavenly dwelling, but God did not allow him to share the secrets. Paul thus showed the manner of vision and the contents of vision are not to be used as measuring devices to determine spiritual heroes. Humble service is the measure of a Christian. Paul spoke from personal experience. He did not say if other Christians might have similar visions.

12:3–4 LAST THINGS, Heaven—Paul humbly described his own vision of "paradise," a word borrowed by the Jews from the Persian language, meaning "enclosure, garden, park" (Ne 2:8; Ecc 2:5; SS 4:13). The early Greek translation of the Old Testament used paradise for the garden of Eden in Ge 2—3 or of God (Ge 13:10; Isa 51:3; Eze 28:13; 31:8). In the period between the Testaments at least some Jewish groups developed the idea of paradise as the resting place of righteous souls before the final resurrection. In the New Testament paradise is (1) where the repentant thief would join Jesus "today" after the crucifixion, (2) a renewed garden of Eden promised to the faithful (Rev 2:7), (3) and the place to which Paul was caught up (2 Co 12:4). It was apparently the same as the "third heaven" (12:2). Paul could not describe paradise. Neither was he certain whether he had been transported bodily or whether he had had a vision or his soul had left his body. Which he meant depends on whether Paul believed in the traditional Hebrew understanding of the unity of body and soul or whether he was influenced by Greek thought and separated body and soul. Paradise is, at least, the place where departed righteous dead are present with God. See note on 5:1–10.

inexpressible things, things that man is
not permitted to tell. 5I will boast about a
man like that, but I will not boast about
myself, except about my weaknesses.[z]
6Even if I should choose to boast,[a] I
would not be a fool,[b] because I would be
speaking the truth. But I refrain, so no
one will think more of me than is war-
ranted by what I do or say.

7To keep me from becoming conceited
because of these surpassingly great revelations,[c] there was given me a thorn in
my flesh,[d] a messenger of Satan,[e] to torment me. 8Three times I pleaded with the
Lord to take it away from me.[f] 9But he
said to me, "My grace[g] is sufficient for
you, for my power[h] is made perfect in
weakness.[i]"[j] Therefore I will boast all
the more gladly about my weaknesses, so
that Christ's power may rest on me.
10That is why, for Christ's sake, I delight[k] in weaknesses, in insults, in hardships,[l] in persecutions,[m] in difficulties.
For when I am weak, then I am strong.[n]

Paul's Concern for the Corinthians

11I have made a fool of myself,[o] but
you drove me to it. I ought to have been
commended by you, for I am not in the
least inferior to the "super-apostles,"[p]
even though I am nothing.[q] 12The things
that mark an apostle—signs, wonders
and miracles[r]—were done among you
with great perseverance. 13How were you
inferior to the other churches, except
that I was never a burden to you?[s] Forgive me this wrong![t]

14Now I am ready to visit you for the
third time,[u] and I will not be a burden to
you, because what I want is not your possessions but you. After all, children
should not have to save up for their parents,[v] but parents for their children.[w]
15So I will very gladly spend for you everything I have and expend myself as
well.[x] If I love you more,[y] will you love
me less? 16Be that as it may, I have not
been a burden to you.[z] Yet, crafty fellow
that I am, I caught you by trickery! 17Did I
exploit you through any of the men I sent
you? 18I urged[a] Titus[b] to go to you and I
sent our brother[c] with him. Titus did
not exploit you, did he? Did we not act
in the same spirit and follow the same
course?

19Have you been thinking all along that
we have been defending ourselves to
you? We have been speaking in the sight
of God[d] as those in Christ; and everything we do, dear friends,[e] is for your
strengthening.[f] 20For I am afraid that
when I come[g] I may not find you as I
want you to be, and you may not find me
as you want me to be.[h] I fear that there
may be quarreling,[i] jealousy, outbursts
of anger, factions,[j] slander,[k] gossip,[l] arrogance[m] and disorder.[n] 21I am afraid
that when I come again my God will
humble me before you, and I will be
grieved[o] over many who have sinned
earlier[p] and have not repented of the im-

12:5 [z]ver 9,10; S 1Co 2:3
12:6 [a]2Co 10:8 [b]ver 11; 2Co 11:16
12:7 [c]ver 1; S 1Co 2:10 [d]Nu 33:55 [e]S Mt 4:10
12:8 [f]Mt 26:39,44
12:9 [g]S Ro 3:24 [h]S Php 4:13 [i]S 1Co 2:3 [j]1Ki 19:12
12:10 [k]S Mt 5:12 [l]2Co 6:4 [m]2Th 1:4 [n]2Co 13:4
12:11 [o]2Co 11:1 [p]2Co 11:5 [q]1Co 15:9,10
12:12 [r]S Jn 4:48
12:13 [s]ver 14; 1Co 9:12,18 [t]2Co 11:7
12:14 [u]2Co 13:1 [v]1Co 4:14,15 [w]Pr 19:14
12:15 [x]Php 2:17; 1Th 2:8 [y]2Co 11:11
12:16 [z]2Co 11:9
12:18 [a]2Co 8:6,16 [b]S 2Co 2:13 [c]2Co 8:18
12:19 [d]Ro 9:1 [e]S 1Co 10:14 [f]S Ro 14:19; 2Co 10:8
12:20 [g]2Co 2:1-4 [h]1Co 4:21 [i]1Co 1:11; 3:3 [j]Gal 5:20 [k]Ro 1:30 [l]S Ro 1:29 [m]1Co 4:18 [n]1Co 14:33
12:21 [o]2Co 2:1,4 [p]2Co 13:2

12:7 EVIL AND SUFFERING, Satan—Satan, not God, is the immediate cause of physical and emotional suffering. Satan gave Paul the thorn to torment him and divert him from faith and ministry. God allowed Satan to torment Paul and then used Satan's instrument of torment to increase Paul's faith.
12:8–10 GOD, Grace—God's grace is shown in many ways in our lives. In this instance, God's grace was the power to endure a heavy burden or difficult problem. This particular hardship was a blessing in disguise, in one sense, for it produced strength of character. See Ja 1:2–4. It also made Paul learn to rely upon God's help in carrying this burden or thorn in the flesh. God's powerful grace is made more real to us when we are faced with our limitations and weaknesses.
12:8–9 PRAYER, Answer—This is one of the rare cases in the Bible where God explains an answer of "no" to a prayer. God's glory is not shown in human strength. Paul had such impressive struggles that God's glory was best demonstrated by working through the unexpected—human weakness. God's "no's" work to use us better to accomplish His perfect purposes.
12:9 JESUS CHRIST, Intercession—The ascended Christ encourages His people when they are troubled.
12:12 MIRACLE, Vocabulary—In this defense of his apostleship Paul confirmed the attitude of the church at Corinth: they expected him to prove his apostleship by his miraculous actions. God worked through him; they had seen the evidence. Three words are used: "signs," "wonders," and "powers." These are the most commonly used words in the New Testament for miracles. *See note on Ac 2:22,43. God* gave the apostles miraculous powers to confirm their ministries over against false preachers to whom He did not give such powers. He continues to give miraculous powers to His church when we need them to fulfill His purposes.
12:12 MIRACLE, Instruments—The three most frequently used words, "signs, wonders, and miracles" refer here to the work of apostles in the early church. Although these acts characterized early church leaders, miracles were performed by others. It is true that when performed by evil men they appear as magic: the exorcisms of Acts 19 were not effective though the work of Simon (Acts 8:9ff) and the work of Elymas (Acts 13:8) mystified many. Stories abound of miracles beyond the biblical accounts in the life of the early church. God's actions were not exhausted in the years covered by the Bible.
12:13 THE CHURCH, Local Body—The local church has the responsibility to provide financial support for its pastoral leaders. See note on Ac 4:32.
12:14 FAMILY, Economic Support—Paul gave insight into his understanding of parental responsibility for children as he reminded the Corinthians of his deep care for them. Parents are to provide for their children. Adult children do have personal financial responsibility for aged parents (1 Ti 5:4,8,16). Economic support is still a primary function of the family even though governmental support systems are often necessary and can be used legitimately.
12:19 SALVATION, As Being in Christ—Those in Christ speak in a certain way. We speak the truth in love. Our speech strengthens others rather than defending ourselves and giving us reason for pride.
12:20–21 SIN, Estrangement—Sin characterizes the world. It threatens the church. Christians can feel too secure in Christ or too free from the slavery of sin. Paul feared he would feel estranged from some Corinthian church members and they from one another because of the sin which had invaded the church. The only answer to sin is repentance.

purity, sexual sin and debauchery[q] in
which they have indulged.

Chapter 13

Final Warnings

THIS will be my third visit to you.[r]
"Every matter must be established
by the testimony of two or three witnesses."[rs] 2I already gave you a warning
when I was with you the second time. I
now repeat it while absent:[t] On my return I will not spare[u] those who sinned
earlier[v] or any of the others, 3since you
are demanding proof that Christ is speaking through me.[w] He is not weak in dealing with you, but is powerful among you.
4For to be sure, he was crucified in weakness,[x] yet he lives by God's power.[y]
Likewise, we are weak[z] in him, yet by
God's power we will live with him[a] to
serve you.
5Examine yourselves[b] to see whether
you are in the faith; test yourselves.[c] Do
you not realize that Christ Jesus is in
you[d]—unless, of course, you fail the
test? 6And I trust that you will discover
that we have not failed the test. 7Now we

12:21 [q]S 1Co 6:18
13:1 [r]2Co 12:14 [s]Dt 19:15; S Mt 18:16
13:2 [t]ver 10 [u]2Co 1:23 [v]2Co 12:21
13:3 [w]Mt 10:20; 1Co 5:4
13:4 [x]1Co 1:25; Php 2:7,8; 1Pe 3:18 [y]Ro 1:4; 6:4; 1Co 6:14 [z]ver 9; S 1Co 2:3 [a]S Ro 6:5
13:5 [b]1Co 11:28 [c]La 3:40; Jn 6:6 [d]S Ro 8:10
13:9 [e]S 1Co 2:3 [f]2Co 4:12 [g]ver 11; Eph 4:13
13:10 [h]S 2Co 1:23 [i]2Co 10:8
13:11 [j]1Th 4:1; 2Th 3:1 [k]S Mk 9:50 [l]1Jn 4:16 [m]S Ro 15:33; Eph 6:23
13:12 [n]S Ro 16:16
13:13 [o]Php 4:22
13:14 [p]S Ro 16:20; 2Co 8:9 [q]Ro 5:5; Jude 21 [r]Php 2:1

pray to God that you will not do anything
wrong. Not that people will see that we
have stood the test but that you will do
what is right even though we may seem
to have failed. 8For we cannot do anything against the truth, but only for the
truth. 9We are glad whenever we are
weak[e] but you are strong;[f] and our
prayer is for your perfection.[g] 10This is
why I write these things when I am absent, that when I come I may not have to
be harsh[h] in my use of authority—the
authority the Lord gave me for building
you up, not for tearing you down.[i]

Final Greetings

11Finally, brothers,[j] good-by. Aim for
perfection, listen to my appeal, be of one
mind, live in peace.[k] And the God of
love[l] and peace[m] will be with you.
12Greet one another with a holy kiss.[n]
13All the saints send their greetings.[o]
14May the grace of the Lord Jesus
Christ,[p] and the love of God,[q] and the
fellowship of the Holy Spirit[r] be with you
all.

[r]*1* Deut. 19:15

13:1–12 CHRISTIAN ETHICS, Character—Paul's invitation to the Corinthians to test the validity of their discipleship is the same test he applied to himself and which we can apply to ourselves. The dimensions of the test are ethical in nature. That is, one who is in the faith will be marked by the presence of truth, peace, and love. Paul did not call for a minimum passing grade. He asked for perfection.

13:1–10 THE CHURCH, Discipline—Church discipline is not a matter of settling one individual's desires. Other witnesses must provide evidence before the church exercises discipline against a member. Pastoral leadership such as Paul's may be needed to guide a church in disciplining members. Each individual should check personally to see what personal changes are needed. We should pray for one another that we will not act improperly. Discipline is not carried out for personal advantage but for the cause of God's truth. See note on 2:5–11.

13:4 GOD, Trinity—On earth Jesus the Son lived and died in weakness. He truly experienced human life—otherwise He could not have died. But He was brought back from the dead by the power of God, the same power that now sustains us. While the separateness of the Father and the Son here is plain, do not forget the underlying unity they have in the one God.

13:4 JESUS CHRIST, Death—By obeying the Father and submitting to the humiliation of death on the cross, Jesus appeared weak to the world. God showed Jesus was not weak by raising Him from death. The power that raised Jesus is available to Christians who serve God and one another through the powerful Lord who reigns in heaven.

13:7 PRAYER, Intercession—Paul had been severe with the Corinthian church. He prayed that they would do no further wrong. Prayer is a proper action toward people with whom we disagree.

13:10 CHURCH LEADERS, Apostle—The authority of the apostle came directly from Christ. It was conveyed as Christ spoke through the apostle and brought the community of faith into being. His conduct confirmed his apostleship (1 Th 2:1–12) which was used only for the well-being of the community (2 Co 10:8).

13:11,14 PRAYER, Blessing—Unique among the closing benedictions of Paul's letters, this prayer invoked the full work of the Trinity in the life of the church at Corinth. See note on Ro 15:33.

13:13 THE CHURCH, Saints—See notes on Ro 1:7; 1 Co 1:2.

13:14 HOLY SPIRIT, Fellowship—God's great purpose is to create a community of free people and to bind them to Himself in a covenant characterized by the words, "I will . . . be your God, and you will be my people" (Lev 26:12). In the Old Testament God's family was the nation of Israel. In the New Testament it is the Christian church. In the church the Spirit initiates (by regeneration) new believers into the church, begins to transform them into persons who love, seals them so that they will not be lost, gives them gifts by which they may serve the church and so serve Christ, guides and empowers the church on its world mission, fosters worship in the church, and always reminds the church about Christ. In all of this, the Spirit is creating the church, a community of faith who share a common life. That is what Paul referred to here as the fellowship created by the Spirit. Paul's benediction here is a prayer that the Corinthians may share together in the community of love, faith, and hope made possible by God's giving His Spirit to the followers of His Son. The common life of Christians is the life of the Spirit, the life shared originally by Father and Son and which Christians have come to share in, as in a family (1 Jn 1:3).

Galatians

Theological Setting

Paul's letter to the churches of Galatia answers two major questions.

Question One: Are people justified simply by faith in Christ or is justification earned by following certain rituals or rules?

This was an important question for the first century Christians. People were accustomed to religions in which they earned their salvation through following rituals, ceremonies, or laws. Even these provided only the assurance of a temporary relationship with God. Persons continually had to fulfill the rituals and rules, and that could not be done perfectly. Therefore, one mistake, one lapse, and the whole relationship was in jeopardy. Into this culture, however, came the gospel of Christ which proclaimed that a relationship with God was possible based only on faith. People were asked to believe simply that Christ died on the cross for their sins. No rituals, laws, or ceremonies were required. Even more astounding, this good news about Jesus promised justification to the believer. That is, believers were treated by God as if they had never sinned. What assurance, security, and freedom it gave believers in their relationship with Christ.

Question Two: If people are justified simply by faith in Christ, how should they live their lives?

People accustomed to a religion of "dos and don'ts," rituals, and practices experienced a great liberty in Christ. How were they to live in this new freedom? Was this freedom to be a license for living in the flesh? "No!" Paul answered forcefully. They were to serve one another by love (5:13), for their faith worked by love (5:6). They were to live and walk by the Spirit (5:16,25). This life in the Spirit was witnessed by the fruit of the Spirit (5:22-23). As a result, the believer became a new creation who sowed and reaped of the Spirit rather than of the flesh (6:8-9).

Paul needed to address these questions because he had enthusiastically, powerfully, and clearly proclaimed the gospel to these churches in the central part of Asia Minor. The people had heard and accepted the message of justification by faith in Christ with its privileges and responsibilities. Evidently, however, following Paul's departure, others had come to the Galatian churches and proclaimed a "slightly different" gospel. They maintained that believers must be circumcised and observe certain rules if they wished assurance of a right relationship with God.

While Paul never named these opponents, a character sketch may be built through the comments Paul made directly and by implication. Directly, they were characterized as troublers, distorters (1:7), twice condemned (1:8,9), hinderers (5:7), trying to make a good showing in the flesh, and avoiding persecution for the cross of Christ (6:12). By implication, they were people-pleasers (1:10), false brothers (2:4), the party of the circumcised (2:12), bewitchers (3:1), and born of the flesh, fit to be cast out (4:29-30). Little wonder then that Paul wished they would even "emasculate themselves" (5:12), and that he withheld the benediction of peace and mercy from them (6:16).

This vigorous treatment of the opponents by Paul is paralleled by an equally vigorous defense of the gospel. Even the leaders in the Jerusalem church did not push for the Gentiles to be circumcised. To affirm justification by the law actually made a mockery of Christ's crucifixion (1:11—2:21). Paul started with Abraham and built a logical treatise that justification is by faith alone (3:6-25).

Any deviations in the gospel were seen as a mockery of Christ and His ministry, crucifixion, and resurrection. Paul loved the Galatian believers as his own children (4:19). He desired to see Christ formed in them. On one hand he chastized them for deserting the gospel so soon (1:6). On the other hand, they were still family—brothers in Christ (1:11; 4:12,28,31; 5:13; 6:1,18) and sons of God (4:6,12). They were born of the Spirit and set free by Christ (5:1). Paul did not want to see them enslaved again.

Thus, in Galatians Paul concisely and dramatically affirmed God's plan of salvation. Persons are justified by faith in Christ with privileges and responsibilities.

Theological Outline

Galatians: Justification by Faith: Its Privileges and Responsibilities

I. The Players (1:1-5)
   A. Paul's credentials came not from humans but from the risen Christ. (1:1)
   B. The churches of Galatia receive grace and peace. (1:2)
   C. Christ gave Himself for our sins. (1:3-5)
II. The Problem: The Nature of the Gospel. (1:6-10)
   A. People who follow a different gospel desert God. (1:6)
   B. People who advocate another gospel confuse the church. (1:7)
   C. People who preach another gospel are condemned eternally. (1:8-9)
   D. The minister of the true gospel pleases God, not people. (1:10)
III. The Answer, Part I: Believers Are Justified Simply by Faith in Christ. (1:11—5:12)
   A. Personal example proves faith is the only requirement to be right with God. (1:11—2:21)
      1. The gospel comes from Christ, not people. (1:11-24)
      2. The gospel of grace has apostolic endorsement. (2:1-10)
      3. Whoever adds to the gospel of grace is a hypocrite. (2:11-14)
      4. Faith in Christ saves, but legalism cannot save. (2:15-21)
   B. To return to legalism is to accept slavery instead of sonship. (3:1—5:12)
      1. Faith in the crucified Christ, not legalism, brings the indwelling Spirit. (3:1-5)
      2. Abraham's inheritance comes through faith to both Jews and non-Jews. (3:6-9)
      3. Christ has provided redemption for all who believe. (3:10-14)
      4. Christ is the true heir of Abraham. (3:15-16)
      5. The Law cannot annul the justification by faith promised to Abraham. (3:17-22)
      6. The Law was used as a tutor to bring believers to Christ. (3:23-25)
      7. Faith in and baptism into Christ make us one in Christ. (3:26-29)
      8. The Law acted as guardian until believers became full sons of God through Christ's redemption. (4:1-7)
      9. Return to legalism from faith is a son's return to slavery. (4:8-11)
      10. Zeal must be directed to the source of your joy—Christ. (4:12-19)
      11. Interpretation of Scripture shows legalism leads to slavery, while Christ leads to the promised freedom of sons. (4:20—5:1)
      12. Return to legalism is to fall away from the grace of Christ, which expresses itself in love. (5:2-12)
IV. The Answer, Part 2: Believers Are Justified Simply by Faith in Christ to Serve Freely in the Spirit through Love. (5:13—6:10)
   A. Scripture shows love fulfills the whole law. (5:13-15)
   B. Life in the Spirit overcomes the weakness of the law. (5:16-24)
      1. Life under the law stands in direct conflict with life in the Spirit. (5:16-18)
      2. Sinners will not inherit God's kingdom. (5:19-21)
      3. The fruit of the Spirit fulfills the intention of the law. (5:22-23)
      4. Life in Christ crucifies fleshly desires. (5:24)
   C. Believers should live and walk by the Spirit. (5:25—6:10)
      1. Life in the Spirit leaves no room for pride and envy. (5:25-26)
      2. Life in the Spirit leads us to help one another, even one who is wayward. (6:1-2)
      3. Life in the Spirit leads to a realistic self-appraisal. (6:3-5).
      4. Life in the Spirit leads to sharing with Christian teachers. (6:6)
      5. Sowing to physical pleasure reaps destruction, while sowing to please the Spirit reaps eternal life. (6:7-9)
      6. Life in the Spirit does good to all people, especially Christians. (6:10)
V. Conclusion: Boast Only that You Are New Creations in Christ. (6:11-18)
   A. Summary (6:11-17)
      1. Legalism is not true to its own claims. (6:11-13)
         a. Legalism seeks to impress others, not God. (6:11-12*a*)
         b. Legalism wants to avoid persecution for the cross of Christ. (6:12*b*)
         c. Legalists boast of controlling others rather than keeping the law themselves. (6:13)
      2. Christ recreates us to meet God's claims. (6:14-17)
         a. Christians glory in the cross of Christ through which worldly values are crucified. (6:14)
         b. In Christ legal requirements are unimportant, for the believer has new values and desires. (6:15)

c. New creatures in Christ form the true Israel of God. (6:16)
d. Personal experience shows the teaching to be trustworthy. (6:17)

B. Farewell: May Christ's grace be with the Christian family. (6:18)

Theological Conclusions

Two major doctrinal issues are emphasized brilliantly in Galatians:

1. Justification by faith in Christ; and
2. Justification in Christ enables believers to serve God, others, and themselves with love in the Spirit.

Both doctrines are connected intricately with Christ's crucifixion.

Justification by faith in Christ is the heart of the gospel message. This doctrine clearly testifies to the effectiveness of Christ's death on the cross. His crucifixion did deal with the human sin problem completely. Believers can have perfect assurance of sins forgiven. Indeed, believers are new creations because of the cross of Jesus. All of this is available to anyone. Persons must simply believe that Christ died for their sins. Little wonder that this doctrine is seen by Paul as worth such a vigorous defense to the Galatians.

Justification in Christ sets the believer free to serve God, others, and themselves in the Spirit by love. Pronounced justified before God, believers are freed to be new creations. As new creations, they naturally produce the fruit of the Spirit. This fruit serves as the enabling quality for believers to restore others, examine themselves, and care for their teachers and communities. Thus, the believer sows and reaps in the Spirit. Again it is little wonder that Paul argued so fiercely that believers should not become enslaved again to the keeping of the Law. Christ's death on the cross set believers free in the Spirit.

In addition to these two major doctrines, Paul presented items of theological significance concerning the defense and advancement of the gospel.

A believer should love people even when they are caught in trespass. This effort defends the gospel because the believers are modeling service in love. The gospel does not negate confrontation but rather necessitates it. Such confrontation is done with humility and in love.

A believer must seek diligently to understand the truth and to see what truths are fundamental. Paul chose to defend major truths which centered on the worth of the crucifixion of Christ. God helps the discerning believer to concentrate on major items not minor ones.

A believer is to speak up vigorously for the truth. This means that all the training and resources the believer has are to be marshalled in the defense of truth and in efforts to resist false teaching. Such a defense is to be scriptural, logical, and concise and will aid other believers in understanding the truth and defeating the false.

Contemporary Teaching

The church today faces struggles similar to those of the Galatian churches. People still find it difficult to accept salvation as a free gift. They want to earn it, so they develop a code or ritual to justify themselves. Even more sadly, they fall prey to cults and sects which have an "aura of holiness" about them because they emphasize some kind of legal regimen which requires discipline. We must reaffirm soundly that we are justified simply by faith in Christ Jesus. It is His crucifixion that sets us free to serve Him in love—not anything we have done, are doing, or will do. Immediately with justification we receive those same privileges that Paul declared to the Galatians: freedom, liberty, sonship, the spirit of promise, and a new creation.

However with the privileges come responsibilities. We are to stay in the freedom which Christ gives to break the yoke of legalism. What do you let bind you? Cast it off with Christ's help. We are to serve through love. Service to God, others, and ourselves is done not from compulsion but from love. How are you serving God, others, and yourself? Live and walk in the Spirit. The fruit of the Spirit is a natural part of the believer's life (5:22-23). Thus, believers have a checklist to examine how well they are living in the Spirit. How do you measure up? We are not to give up on others, but actively, vigorously seek their restoration. That is loving service. Who are you helping to restore? Know yourself (6:3-5). This is fundamental for our growth in responsibility for ourselves and others. To use the fruit of the Spirit as a checklist in our lives is to do self-examination. Restoration of others is hindered if not blocked by an unrealistic appraisal of one's own abilities. Enlist the help of prayer and an honest friend to evaluate yourself! We get exactly what we sow. We cannot reap in the Spirit if we sow the flesh. God help us to live and walk by the Spirit. What are you sowing in the Spirit?

Chapter 1

PAUL, an apostle[a]—sent not from men
nor by man,[b] but by Jesus Christ[c]
and God the Father,[d] who raised him
from the dead[e]— 2 and all the brothers
with me,[f]

To the churches in Galatia:[g]

3 Grace and peace to you from God our
Father and the Lord Jesus Christ,[h] 4 who
gave himself for our sins[i] to rescue us
from the present evil age,[j] according to
the will of our God and Father,[k] 5 to
whom be glory for ever and ever.
Amen.[l]

No Other Gospel

6 I am astonished that you are so quickly deserting the one who called[m] you by
the grace of Christ and are turning to a
different gospel[n]— 7 which is really no
gospel at all. Evidently some people are
throwing you into confusion[o] and are trying to pervert[p] the gospel of Christ. 8 But
even if we or an angel from heaven
should preach a gospel other than the one
we preached to you,[q] let him be eternally
condemned![r] 9 As we have already said,
so now I say again: If anybody is preaching to you a gospel other than what you
accepted,[s] let him be eternally condemned!

10 Am I now trying to win the approval
of men, or of God? Or am I trying to
please men?[t] If I were still trying to
please men, I would not be a servant of
Christ.

Paul Called by God

11 I want you to know, brothers,[u] that
the gospel I preached[v] is not something
that man made up. 12 I did not receive it
from any man,[w] nor was I taught it; rather, I received it by revelation[x] from Jesus
Christ.[y]

1:1 [a]S 1Co 1:1 [b]ver 11,12 [c]ver 15,16; S Ac 9:15; 20:24 [d]ver 15,16; S Ac 9:15; 20:24 [e]S Ac 2:24
1:2 [f]Php 4:21 [g]S Ac 16:6
1:3 [h]S Ro 1:7
1:4 [i]S Mt 20:28; S Ro 4:25; S 1Co 15:3; Gal 2:20 [j]S 1Co 1:20 [k]S Php 4:20
1:5 [l]S Ro 11:36
1:6 [m]ver 15; S Ro 8:28 [n]2Co 11:4
1:7 [o]Ac 15:24; Gal 5:10 [p]Jer 23:16, 36
1:8 [q]ver 11,16; 1Co 15:1; 2Co 11:4; Gal 2:2 [r]Ro 9:3
1:9 [s]Ro 16:17
1:10 [t]S Ro 2:29
1:11 [u]1Co 15:1 [v]S ver 8
1:12 [w]ver 1 [x]ver 16; S 1Co 2:10 [y]1Co 11:23; 15:3

1:1,3–4 GOD, Trinity—The Father and the Son made Paul an apostle. They shared this work together. God the Father made and carried out the plan to provide salvation through Christ. God the Son came to earth and died for our sins. The Father raised the Son. Each has His individual identity, but they also share a common life in the one godhead. See note on Mt 3:16–17.

1:1 JESUS CHRIST, Christ—See note on Mt 16:16. Paul, an apostle of Jesus Christ, used the term Christ (Messiah) almost as a part of the proper name of Jesus. Early believers, especially Paul, came to identify Jesus alone as the long-awaited Messiah of God. In Israel's history, any anointed king or priest could be referred to as messiah (Lev 4:3,16; 6:15; 1 Sa 24:7; 2 Sa 1:14; 19:22; Ps 16:6; 89:39; Isa 45:1). Jesus removed political overtones from the title and showed its true meaning as God's Suffering Servant/Redeemer.

1:2 THE CHURCH, Local Body—Each local congregation of believers is a church. Paul wrote this letter to several congregations or churches in Galatia. See notes on Ac 4:32; 1 Co 1:2.

1:3–12 PROCLAMATION, Gospel—See notes on Ac 3:11–26; 1 Co 2:1–5; 2 Ti 3:14–17. Proclamation has only one message, salvation through faith in Christ. Any other message, requiring anything but faith from people, is a false gospel.

1:3–5 PRAYER, Blessing—See notes on Ro 1:7; 16:25–27. This blessing closes with a doxology.

1:4 JESUS CHRIST, Atonement—Jesus' basic identification for the Christian is as the One who died for my sins, rescuing me from the evil and death of this world to experience eternal life. Jesus has completed the rescue effort. We need to trust Him for salvation.

1:4 CREATION, Evil—Rather than immediately destroying evil when it followed human sin into the world He created, God set into motion a plan to redeem the world. Though God delivers us from sin through Christ's atonement, He does not immediately remove us from living in this evil world. He delivers us from the guilt of sin, as far as He is concerned, in our original encounter with His Son as our Savior. He progressively delivers us from the power of sin in our lives as we grow in grace and knowledge of Him. At the Lord's coming, He will remove His children from the evil world. Our task today is to show to our wicked world what a God-rescued and Christ-controlled life can mean in a corrupt society.

1:4 EVIL AND SUFFERING, Natural Origin—The world we live in is evil. It is not the very good world God created (Ge 1). Human sin has corrupted the world and brought God's curse on it (Ge 3). This does not mean the world is totally corrupt and beyond hope. In Christ, God has brought hope. Christ's church is the leaven of good seeking to change the world. Even in the evil world, revelation of God shines through (Ro 1).

1:4 HISTORY, Time—Christians live in history dominated by self-interest and Satan's actions. Christ's saving acts place Christians in the age of eternity where evil cannot threaten. The Christian life is a way to live the life of eternity in the realm of history.

1:4–12 ELECTION, In Christ—Jesus Christ has made possible our election by giving Himself to rescue us from this evil age. He has made possible the forgiveness of sins. Through Jesus Christ, God chooses some to serve as preachers, teachers, evangelists, missionaries, helpers, and servants.

1:6–8 SALVATION, Grace—God's call into His kingdom is by the grace of Christ. A gospel not of grace, whether of law or of some other substance, is not the apostolic gospel. Without grace there is no good news worth hearing or sharing. People who deceive others by changing the gospel to include human achievement and pride deserve eternal condemnation.

1:10 THE CHURCH, Servants—A slave works to please only one person—the master. Believers concentrate all efforts on satisfying our Master—Jesus Christ. See note on Ro 1:1.

1:11–17 REVELATION, Visions—Christ and no one else revealed the nature and content of the gospel Paul preached. That gave Paul his claim to be an apostle and authenticated his preaching over against his opponents. His vision of Jesus transformed his life. See notes on Ac 7:55; 22:7–11; 26:16–18. Individual experiences with Christ stand behind the true minister of the gospel.

1:11—2:15 EVANGELISM, Work of Christ—The work of Christ with no additions is the center of the gospel. Paul placed his ministry on the line to defend his understanding of the gospel. He showed the Galatians why his definition of the gospel is correct. He received the truth by direct revelation from Jesus Christ (1:11). This implies those who preached something else did not get it from God. God in His grace revealed Jesus Christ to him so he could preach the truth to the Gentiles (1:15–16). He had the church evaluate and judge his gospel understanding, and the leaders in the Jerusalem church concurred with him (2:1–10; Ac 15). He confronted church leaders who did not act on the gospel truth and showed the consistency of his life and teaching (2:11–13). The gospel must be maintained in its purity, because through the clear and correct proclamation of the gospel, people are saved. "A different gospel" (1:6) leaves people in their lost state. Evangelists are commanded to call people to faith in the crucified and risen Lord. Nothing else can be added and still have the gospel.

13For you have heard of my previous
way of life in Judaism,[z] how intensely I
persecuted the church of God[a] and tried
to destroy it.[b] 14I was advancing in Judaism beyond many Jews of my own age
and was extremely zealous[c] for the traditions of my fathers.[d] 15But when God,
who set me apart from birth[a][e] and called
me[f] by his grace, was pleased 16to reveal
his Son in me so that I might preach him
among the Gentiles,[g] I did not consult
any man,[h] 17nor did I go up to Jerusalem
to see those who were apostles before I
was, but I went immediately into Arabia
and later returned to Damascus.[i]
18Then after three years,[j] I went up to
Jerusalem[k] to get acquainted with Peter[b]
and stayed with him fifteen days. 19I saw
none of the other apostles—only James,[l]
the Lord's brother. 20I assure you before
God[m] that what I am writing you is no
lie.[n] 21Later I went to Syria[o] and Cilicia.[p] 22I was personally unknown to the
churches of Judea[q] that are in Christ.[r]
23They only heard the report: "The man
who formerly persecuted us is now
preaching the faith[s] he once tried to destroy."[t] 24And they praised God[u] because of me.

Chapter 2

Paul Accepted by the Apostles

FOURTEEN years later I went up again
to Jerusalem,[v] this time with Barnabas.[w] I took Titus[x] along also. 2I went in
response to a revelation[y] and set before
them the gospel that I preach among the
Gentiles.[z] But I did this privately to
those who seemed to be leaders, for fear
that I was running or had run my race[a]
in vain. 3Yet not even Titus,[b] who was
with me, was compelled to be circumcised, even though he was a Greek.[c]
4⌞This matter arose⌟ because some false
brothers[d] had infiltrated our ranks to spy
on[e] the freedom[f] we have in Christ
Jesus and to make us slaves. 5We did not
give in to them for a moment, so that the
truth of the gospel[g] might remain with
you.
6As for those who seemed to be important[h]—whatever they were makes no
difference to me; God does not judge by
external appearance[i]—those men added
nothing to my message.[j] 7On the contrary, they saw that I had been entrusted
with the task[k] of preaching the gospel to
the Gentiles,[c][l] just as Peter[m] had been
to the Jews.[d] 8For God, who was at work
in the ministry of Peter as an apostle[n] to
the Jews, was also at work in my ministry
as an apostle[o] to the Gentiles. 9James,[p]
Peter[e][q] and John, those reputed to be
pillars,[r] gave me and Barnabas[s] the right
hand of fellowship when they recognized
the grace given to me.[t] They agreed that
we should go to the Gentiles,[u] and they

1:13 [z]Ac 26:4,5 [a]S 1Co 10:32 [b]S Ac 8:3 **1:14** [c]S Ac 21:20 [d]Mt 15:2 **1:15** [e]Isa 49:1,5; Jer 1:5 [f]S Ac 9:15; S Ro 8:28 **1:16** [g]S Ac 9:15; Gal 2:9 [h]Mt 16:17 **1:17** [i]Ac 9:2,19-22 **1:18** [j]Ac 9:22,23 [k]Ac 9:26,27 **1:19** [l]Mt 13:55; S Ac 15:13 **1:20** [m]S Ro 1:9 [n]S Ro 9:1 **1:21** [o]S Lk 2:2 [p]S Ac 6:9 **1:22** [q]1Th 2:14 [r]S Ro 16:3 **1:23** [s]Ac 6:7 [t]S Ac 8:3 **1:24** [u]S Mt 9:8 **2:1** [v]Ac 15:2 [w]S Ac 4:36 [x]S 2Co 2:13 **2:2** [y]S 1Co 2:10 [z]Ac 15:4,12 [a]S 1Co 9:24 **2:3** [b]ver 1; S 2Co 2:13 [c]Ac 16:3; 1Co 9:21 **2:4** [d]S Ac 1:16; 2Co 11:26 [e]Jude 4 [f]Gal 5:1,13 **2:5** [g]ver 14 **2:6** [h]ver 2 [i]S Ac 10:34; S Rev 2:23 [j]1Co 15:11 **2:7** [k]1Th 2:4; 1Ti 1:11 [l]S Ac 9:15 [m]ver 9,11,14 **2:8** [n]Ac 1:25 [o]S 1Co 1:1 **2:9** [p]S Ac 15:13 [q]ver 7,11,14 [r]1Ti 3:15; Rev 3:12 [s]ver 1; S Ac 4:36 [t]S Ro 12:3 [u]S Ac 9:15

[a] *15* Or *from my mother's womb* [b] *18* Greek *Cephas* [c] *7* Greek *uncircumcised* [d] *7* Greek *circumcised*; also in verses 8 and 9 [e] *9* Greek *Cephas*; also in verses 11 and 14

1:15 GOD, Sovereignty—Paul found that his life had meaning because God had chosen him from birth and had prepared him through grace to be a chosen instrument in Christian service. God is a God who plans and pursues His purposes through history. His grace bestowed on individuals is more than individual acts of kindness. His grace, His redeeming and nurturing power, is bestowed on people for the purpose of using them in the pursuit of His overall purpose in the world. This does not mean that God manipulates us in spite of our freedom of choice. God respects our free will and works with us to secure our willing submission to His will for us. No one who finds and does the will of God feels manipulated or coerced. Rather, we feel singly blessed by the grace of God.

1:22 SALVATION, As Being in Christ—Christian churches, as well as individual Christians, are in Christ. He controls their lives.

1:22 THE CHURCH, Local Body—See note on v 2; Ac 4:32.

2:1–14 THE CHURCH, Practice—The early church faced serious questions concerning Gentiles. Did Christ intend for the gospel to extend to Gentiles as well as Jews? Should believing Gentiles be circumcised and required to accept Jewish dietary laws? Could believing Jews eat with believing Gentiles who ate "unclean" food? Paul asserted the power of Christ in his life and encouraged the acceptance of Gentile believers. He even opposed the apostle Peter. No person no matter how respected and experienced should be followed when their direction opposes Christ's. In every dispute or question, the church must yield to the authority of Christ. Personal prejudices and long-held traditions must not supplant the word of Christ to His church. See note on Ac 1:21–26.

2:2 REVELATION, Visions—Paul's dealing with other apostles was directed by a vision from God, not by commands from human leaders. The apostles confirmed Paul's commission to preach and his mission to the Gentiles (v 9). Revelation directs the lives of God's people. Such revelation received by an individual is subject to the test of conforming to the revelation of Scripture and to the wider experience of the church.

2:3–21 CHRISTIAN ETHICS, Moral Imperatives—God's imperatives must be consistently applied in all situations. Public opinion should not be the cause of obedience or disobedience. We should not attempt to change back and forth from legalism to grace. We have a responsibility to confront the church anytime it leads us in any ethical direction which departs from the love of Christ.

2:4 SALVATION, Human Freedom—Jesus Christ gives freedom. He releases persons from bondage such as religious legalism. Human systems exercise control over others. Jesus sets people free to attain full potential.

2:6 GOD, Judge—God does not judge persons from a superficial, external point of view. God judges from the viewpoint of His unlimited wisdom. He sees persons and situations as they really are. We can trust God to be a faithful, righteous judge, never unfair or wrong or deceived.

2:6 CHURCH LEADERS, Authority—Leaders in the church are not to be followed simply because they are the leaders, no matter how distinguished or successful. Human reputations, appearances, and rank do not impress God. The key to authority is whether or not the leaders uphold the truth of the gospel. If they do not, they are discredited.

2:8 CHURCH LEADERS, Apostle—Apostles had different roles in the early church. Peter led the mission to Jews. Paul spearheaded church building among non-Jews. Both acknowledged the other's calling and ministry.

to the Jews. 10All they asked was that we
should continue to remember the poor,[v]
the very thing I was eager to do.

Paul Opposes Peter

11When Peter[w] came to Antioch,[x] I
opposed him to his face, because he was
clearly in the wrong. 12Before certain
men came from James,[y] he used to eat
with the Gentiles.[z] But when they arrived, he began to draw back and separate himself from the Gentiles because he
was afraid of those who belonged to the
circumcision group.[a] 13The other Jews
joined him in his hypocrisy, so that by
their hypocrisy even Barnabas[b] was led
astray.
14When I saw that they were not acting
in line with the truth of the gospel,[c] I
said to Peter[d] in front of them all, "You
are a Jew, yet you live like a Gentile and
not like a Jew.[e] How is it, then, that you
force Gentiles to follow Jewish customs?[f]
15"We who are Jews by birth[g] and not
'Gentile sinners'[h] 16know that a man is
not justified by observing the law,[i] but
by faith in Jesus Christ.[j] So we, too, have
put our faith in Christ Jesus that we may
be justified by faith in Christ and not by
observing the law, because by observing
the law no one will be justified.[k]
17"If, while we seek to be justified in
Christ, it becomes evident that we ourselves are sinners,[l] does that mean that
Christ promotes sin? Absolutely not![m] 18If
I rebuild what I destroyed, I prove that I

2:10 [v]S Ac 24:17
2:11 [w]ver 7,9,14 [x]S Ac 11:19
2:12 [y]S Ac 15:13 [z]Ac 11:3 [a]Ac 10:45; 11:2
2:13 [b]ver 1; S Ac 4:36
2:14 [c]ver 5 [d]ver 7, 9,11 [e]Ac 10:28 [f]ver 12
2:15 [g]Php 3:4,5 [h]1Sa 15:18; Lk 24:7
2:16 [i]S Ro 3:28 [j]S Ro 9:30 [k]S Ro 3:28; S 4:25
2:17 [l]ver 15 [m]Gal 3:21
2:19 [n]S Ro 7:4 [o]Ro 6:10,11,14; 2Co 5:15
2:20 [p]S Ro 6:6 [q]S Ro 8:10; 1Pe 4:2 [r]S Mt 4:3 [s]S Ro 8:37 [t]S Gal 1:4
2:21 [u]Gal 3:21
3:1 [v]Lk 24:25 [w]S Ac 16:6 [x]Gal 5:7 [y]1Co 1:23
3:2 [z]S Jn 20:22 [a]ver 5,10; Gal 2:16 [b]Ro 10:17; Heb 4:2
3:5 [c]1Co 12:10 [d]ver 2,10; Gal 2:16
3:6 [e]Ge 15:6; S Ro 4:3
3:7 [f]ver 9 [g]S Lk 3:8

am a lawbreaker. 19For through the law I
died to the law[n] so that I might live for
God.[o] 20I have been crucified with
Christ[p] and I no longer live, but Christ
lives in me.[q] The life I live in the body, I
live by faith in the Son of God,[r] who
loved me[s] and gave himself for me.[t] 21I
do not set aside the grace of God, for if
righteousness could be gained through
the law,[u] Christ died for nothing!"[f]

Chapter 3

Faith or Observance of the Law

YOU foolish[v] Galatians![w] Who has be-
witched you?[x] Before your very eyes
Jesus Christ was clearly portrayed as crucified.[y] 2I would like to learn just one
thing from you: Did you receive the Spirit[z] by observing the law,[a] or by believing what you heard?[b] 3Are you so foolish? After beginning with the Spirit, are
you now trying to attain your goal by human effort? 4Have you suffered so much
for nothing—if it really was for nothing?
5Does God give you his Spirit and work
miracles[c] among you because you observe the law, or because you believe
what you heard?[d]
6Consider Abraham: "He believed
God, and it was credited to him as righteousness."[g][e] 7Understand, then, that
those who believe[f] are children of Abraham.[g] 8The Scripture foresaw that God

[f]21 Some interpreters end the quotation after verse 14.
[g]6 Gen. 15:6

2:17 SIN, Against God—See note on Ro 3:7–8.

2:20–21 JESUS CHRIST, Atonement—See note on 1:4. Christ's love was the motivating factor behind His atoning death. His death, not human merit or achievement, is the only way to right relationship with God.

2:20 SALVATION, As Being in Christ—The best commentary on this text may be Jn 15:1–17. Being in Christ is tied inseparably and mystically to our radical identification with Christ in His death and resurrection. It is a life lived by faith in the Son of God. We let Christ direct our thoughts and actions. We bury selfish interests in the interest of Christ.

2:21 GOD, Grace—God's grace does what no human achievement ever could. Salvation, including forgiveness and regeneration, could never come through human effort, neither by keeping the law nor through any heroic act. Only the grace of God can save sinners from death, transform our lives here and now, and give us eternal life.

2:21 CHRISTIAN ETHICS, Justice—See note on Ro 10:1–11; Php 3:9.

3:1–5 HOLY SPIRIT, Indwells—How does a person receive the indwelling Spirit? God always gives His Spirit graciously. No one can purchase, earn, or deserve this gift (Ac 8:9–25). The Spirit is not given because people pray, repent, commit themselves, or somehow become more spiritual or deserving. The Spirit is given because God is generous and gracious. He freely chooses to give His Spirit to those who hear and believe the gospel of His Son. You can have the Spirit if you commit yourself in faith to Christ.

3:1 PROCLAMATION, Gospel—See notes on 1:3–12; Ac 3:11–26.

3:3–8 REVELATION, Spirit—Using Scripture to reveal the work of the Spirit, Paul explained the role of the Law and the Holy Spirit in revelation. Rules by themselves without God's Spirit are of little help. The Law was designed to reveal the Spirit of God, which affects the believer by producing the faith required for salvation. Works or legal behavior do not save. People are saved by faith responding to the Spirit of God.

3:5 MIRACLE, Faith—Powerful deeds were not performed among the Galatians (Derbe, Lystra, Iconium—Ac 14) because of their good works or obedience to the law. They were given by God in response to the faith of the people. God confirmed the gospel of faith not the religion of legalism with His miracles.

3:6–25 THE CHURCH, Covenant People—God's work in Christ is consistent with His eternal purpose—to bring all people unto Him. Through Abraham the promise came. See note on Ge 17:1–21. Abraham received the promise in faith. Others outside the people of Israel receive the promise in the same way. They show God's call to Abraham to bring blessing to the nations is being realized. God's promises are sure. All He has done has prepared the way for Christ, who fulfilled the promise to Abraham and His plan of justification by faith for all people. See note on Ro 9:22–23.

3:7 HISTORY, Intentions—God's intentions have always been to justify all who would have faith. The history of Israel is the history of God seeking to fulfill this intention. God's intentions do not change through history. Our understanding of His intentions does change.

3:8–14 EVANGELISM, God's Provision—See note on Ge 12:1–7.

3:8 MISSIONS, Scope—Paul refers to and quotes Ge 12:3 to show that the Scriptures foresaw that God would justify all people, not just Jews, by faith in Christ. God had revealed this world-embracing good news to Abraham when He first called him to bless the nation. See note on Ge 12:1–3. Thus, from

would justify the Gentiles by faith, and
announced the gospel in advance to Abraham: "All nations will be blessed through
you."[h] [h] 9So those who have faith[i] are
blessed along with Abraham, the man of
faith.[j]
10All who rely on observing the law[k]
are under a curse,[l] for it is written:
"Cursed is everyone who does not continue to do everything written in the
Book of the Law."[i] [m] 11Clearly no one is
justified before God by the law,[n] because, "The righteous will live by
faith."[j] [o] 12The law is not based on faith;
on the contrary, "The man who does
these things will live by them."[k] [p]
13Christ redeemed us from the curse of
the law[q] by becoming a curse for us, for
it is written: "Cursed is everyone who is
hung on a tree."[l] [r] 14He redeemed us in
order that the blessing given to Abraham
might come to the Gentiles through
Christ Jesus,[s] so that by faith we might
receive the promise of the Spirit.[t]

The Law and the Promise

15Brothers,[u] let me take an example
from everyday life. Just as no one can set
aside or add to a human covenant that
has been duly established, so it is in this
case. 16The promises were spoken to
Abraham and to his seed.[v] The Scripture
does not say "and to seeds," meaning
many people, but "and to your seed,"[m] [w]
meaning one person, who is Christ.
17What I mean is this: The law, introduced 430 years[x] later, does not set
aside the covenant previously established
by God and thus do away with the promise. 18For if the inheritance depends on
the law, then it no longer depends on a
promise;[y] but God in his grace gave it to
Abraham through a promise.
19What, then, was the purpose of the
law? It was added because of transgressions[z] until the Seed[a] to whom the
promise referred had come. The law was
put into effect through angels[b] by a mediator.[c] 20A mediator,[d] however, does not
represent just one party; but God is one.
21Is the law, therefore, opposed to the
promises of God? Absolutely not![e] For if
a law had been given that could impart
life, then righteousness would certainly
have come by the law.[f] 22But the Scripture declares that the whole world is a
prisoner of sin,[g] so that what was promised, being given through faith in Jesus
Christ, might be given to those who believe.
23Before this faith came, we were held
prisoners[h] by the law, locked up until
faith should be revealed.[i] 24So the law
was put in charge to lead us to Christ[n] [j]

[h] *8* Gen. 12:3; 18:18; 22:18 [i] *10* Deut. 27:26 [j] *11* Hab. 2:4 [k] *12* Lev. 18:5 [l] *13* Deut. 21:23 [m] *16* Gen. 12:7; 13:15; 24:7 [n] *24* Or *charge until Christ came*

3:8 [h]Ge 12:3; 18:18; 22:18; 26:4; Ac 3:25
3:9 [i]ver 7; Ro 4:16 [j]Ro 4:18-22
3:10 [k]ver 2,5; Gal 2:16 [l]ver 13; S Ro 4:15 [m]Dt 27:26; Jer 11:3
3:11 [n]S Ro 3:28 [o]Hab 2:4; S Ro 9:30; Heb 10:38
3:12 [p]Lev 18:5; S Ro 10:5
3:13 [q]Gal 4:5 [r]Dt 21:23; S Ac 5:30
3:14 [s]Ro 4:9,16 [t]ver 2; Joel 2:28; S Jn 20:22; S Ac 2:33
3:15 [u]S Ro 7:1
3:16 [v]Ge 17:19; Ps 132:11; Mic 7:20; Lk 1:55; Ro 4:13,16; 9:4,8; Gal 3:29; 4:28 [w]Ge 12:7; 13:15; 17:7,8,10; 24:7
3:17 [x]Ge 15:13,14; Ex 12:40; Ac 7:6
3:18 [y]Ro 4:14
3:19 [z]Ro 5:20 [a]ver 16 [b]Dt 33:2; Ac 7:53 [c]Ex 20:19; Dt 5:5
3:20 [d]1Ti 2:5; Heb 8:6; 9:15; 12:24
3:21 [e]Gal 2:17; S Ro 7:12 [f]Gal 2:21
3:22 [g]Ro 3:9-19; 11:32
3:23 [h]Ro 11:32 [i]ver 25
3:24 [j]ver 19; Ro 10:4; S 4:15

first to last, the Bible sets the scope of the missionary task as the whole world. All people are invited to walk the path of faith to Christ.

3:10–25 SALVATION, Justification—See note on Ro 4:1–25. The Law of Moses cannot impart life, but faith can and does. The role of the Law is to lead us to Christ, but it cannot justify us. Christ became a curse for us on the cross in order to bring the blessing of Abraham to all persons. We walk with Christ in the freedom of faith to fulfill the intention of the Law and to be the kind of people God has been working to create since He first created people.

3:13–14 JESUS CHRIST, Redeemer—All people face death because they sin, disobeying God's law and coming under its curses (Dt 27:14–26). Christ was treated as a criminal under curse (Dt 21:23), lifted the curse from us, and opened salvation to all people according to God's original intention as revealed to Abraham (Ge 12:1–3). His redeeming action on the cross lets us live in the power of the Spirit.

3:13–14 SALVATION, Redemption—Christ became our substitute on the cross. He took our place. The text uses the language of substitution (2 Co 5:21). This means that God Himself bore the consequences of our sin in Christ. It does not mean that Christ is a third party who comes between God and persons to absorb all the blows God can inflict. We see in this text the high cost of God's salvation. Christ's redemption is the fulfillment of God's promise to Abraham (Ge 12:2–3).

3:14 GOD, Trinity—The Father redeemed us so all persons—Jews and non-Jews—might find salvation in Christ. This results in the living experience of the Spirit. Each Person of the Trinity has a part in the redemptive work of the one true God.

3:14 HOLY SPIRIT, Promised—The gift of the Spirit through faith in Christ fulfills, not contradicts, the Old Testament promises. Christ died so the blessings God had promised Israel might be given to the Gentiles, too. The Old Testament looked to the time all people would receive the Spirit. See Nu 11:29–30; notes on Isa 32:14–18; 44:1–4; Eze 36:24–30; 37:12–14; Joel 2:28–32. The promise was fulfilled for Jewish followers of Christ at Pentecost (Ac 2) and for Gentile followers of Christ beginning with Cornelius (Ac 10:1–48). See note on Gal 3:1–5.

3:15–29 SALVATION, Initiative—God's salvation history began with the choice of one man, Abraham. Salvation history refers to the series of events in the life and history of Israel which led to the coming of Christ the Savior. Both Old and New Testaments bear witness to the story of God's saving actions. Ge 12:1–3, God's call and promise to Abraham, is the link between Ge 1—11 and the rest of the Bible. God overcame the rebellion of Ge 11:1–9 through Abraham and his seed. The Law which God gave to the nation Israel did not set aside His covenant with Abraham. The Law's purpose was to help the world know what sin was until God fulfilled His promise to Abraham in Christ.

3:16 JESUS CHRIST, Fulfilled—Jesus is the ultimate focus and fulfillment of the promise of blessing to the nations through Abraham (Ge 12:1–3).

3:22 SIN, Universal Nature—The Law was intended not only to lead us to Christ (v 24), but also to convict us of our sins so that we might look to the promise of God for salvation. Our attempts to keep the Law only show that we are *all* incapable of keeping it perfectly, as the Law itself demands. As sinners, we all have the opportunity to believe in Christ.

3:22–24 HOLY SCRIPTURE, Redemption—The inspired Old Testament reveals that all people live isolated from God and in sin. It lets people know their need for salvation and thus leads to Christ. Jesus Christ is the promise and power of redemption from sin and is available to all who believe in Him. Christ's Spirit leads us to obey God in love without trying to follow a legalistic system.

that we might be justified by faith.[k]
25Now that faith has come, we are no longer under the supervision of the law.[l]

Sons of God

26You are all sons of God[m] through
faith in Christ Jesus, 27for all of you who
were baptized into Christ[n] have clothed
yourselves with Christ.[o] 28There is neither Jew nor Greek, slave nor free,[p] male
nor female,[q] for you are all one in Christ
Jesus.[r] 29If you belong to Christ,[s] then
you are Abraham's seed,[t] and heirs[u] according to the promise.[v]

Chapter 4

WHAT I am saying is that as long as
the heir is a child, he is no different from a slave, although he owns the
whole estate. 2He is subject to guardians
and trustees until the time set by his father. 3So also, when we were children,
we were in slavery[w] under the basic principles of the world.[x] 4But when the time
had fully come,[y] God sent his Son,[z] born
of a woman,[a] born under law,[b] 5to redeem[c] those under law, that we might
receive the full rights[d] of sons.[e] 6Be-
cause you are sons, God sent the Spirit of
his Son[f] into our hearts,[g] the Spirit who
calls out, *"Abba,*[o] Father."[h] 7So you are
no longer a slave, but a son; and since
you are a son, God has made you also an
heir.[i]

Paul's Concern for the Galatians

8Formerly, when you did not know
God,[j] you were slaves[k] to those who by
nature are not gods.[l] 9But now that you
know God—or rather are known by
God[m]—how is it that you are turning
back to those weak and miserable principles? Do you wish to be enslaved[n] by
them all over again?[o] 10You are observing
special days and months and seasons and

3:24 [k]Gal 2:16 **3:25** [l]S Ro 7:4 **3:26** [m]S Ro 8:14 **3:27** [n]S Mt 28:19 [o]S Ro 13:14 **3:28** [p]1Co 12:13; Col 3:11 [q]Ge 1:27; 5:2; Joel 2:29 [r]Jn 10:16; 17:11; Eph 2:14,15 **3:29** [s]S 1Co 3:23 [t]ver 16; S Lk 3:8 [u]S Ro 8:17 [v]ver 16 **4:3** [w]ver 8,9,24,25; Gal 2:4 [x]Col 2:8,20 **4:4** [y]Mk 1:15; Ro 5:6; Eph 1:10 [z]S Jn 3:17 [a]S Jn 1:14 [b]Lk 2:27 **4:5** [c]S Ro 3:24 [d]Jn 1:12 [e]S Ro 8:14 **4:6** [f]S Ac 16:7 [g]Ro 5:5 [h]Ro 8:15, 16 **4:7** [i]S Ro 8:17 **4:8** [j]Ro 1:28; 1Co 1:21; 15:34; 1Th 4:5; 2Th 1:8 [k]S ver 3 [l]2Ch 13:9; Isa 37:19; Jer 2:11; 5:7; 16:20; 1Co 8:4,5 **4:9** [m]1Co 8:3 [n]S ver 3 [o]Col 2:20

[o]6 Aramaic for *Father*

3:26 GOD, Father—Believers are sons of God by adoption, by regeneration (Jn 1:12). This is in distinction to the way in which Jesus is the Son of God by incarnation. It is also in distinction to the relationship that all persons have as children of God by virtue of their creation by God. See note on Mt 5:43–48.

3:26–29 HUMANITY, Human Nature—Racial, social, and sexual differences are insignificant to people united in Christ. This does not mean that these differences are physically eliminated. Gentiles remain Gentiles, and men remain men. Jesus has abolished the significance of these differences which had stood as barriers between people. All have equal access to God through Jesus.

3:26–29 THE CHURCH, God's Community—The church is a community of God's people blind to all distinctions which normally separate and segregate people. We share faith in Christ and find unity in Him. Thus, we can ignore all other traits, classifications, and characteristics. We celebrate together in God's family and look forward to receiving our full inheritance. See notes on Jn 1:12–13; Ro 15:14.

3:26–29 FAMILY, New Selfhood—Christ brought new identity to believers, joining them in His body and obliterating concern for differences which previously separated them. Equality of male and female provides a basis for the Christian family. See note on Ro 5:12–21.

3:27 ORDINANCES, Baptism in Jesus' Name—Being baptized "into the name of Christ" means being incorporated into the personal presence or "body" of Christ. People are often identified by the group they belong to: Jew or Greek, slave or free, male or female. Being baptized into Christ is like being clothed with Christ, putting on a new kind of human nature—Christian human nature. The new order of humanity in Christ transcends all the old divisions between Jew and Greek, slave and free, male and female. The important new reality is that we are all one new redeemed humanity in Christ and members of His one body. In the Bible there is no word for "person." "Name" is used for "person." Therefore, having the name of Christ pronounced over one in baptism means that one belongs to Christ and that the personality of Christ must be expressed in that life.

4:1–7 SALVATION, As Adoption—As God's creatures and as sinners purchased back by God, we deserve only to be His slaves without personal freedom. In grace He has made us His adopted sons with full inheritance rights and full freedom. The Spirit leads us to know God as our "father" and as the Father. See note on Ro 8:15,23.

4:4–6 GOD, Trinity—See note on 3:14.

4:4 JESUS CHRIST, Son of God—Jesus was both God and man. See note on Lk 1:26–38. His earthly birth fulfilled God's plan, coming at the right time and fulfilling all requirements of inspired Law (Lk 2:21–39). He was thus qualified to redeem humans who broke the Law and were slaves to sin. Jesus through the Spirit made us adopted children of God and taught us to speak intimately to our Heavenly Father. See note on Mk 14:36.

4:4 HISTORY, Time—See note on 1 Co 10:11. God worked at the proper time in history through normal human means to provide salvation. He went so far as to let His eternal Son enter history as a human being with His own history of birth and death.

4:4–7 THE CHURCH, God's Community—We may be called the sons of God because of God's grace. He adopted us, not because of our merit but because of His desire to make for Himself a people. See notes on Jn 1:12–13; Ro 8:12–17.

4:5 SALVATION, Redemption—Christ's redemption brings freedom to all who are in bondage to religious law.

4:6 HOLY SPIRIT, Intercedes—Jesus regularly addressed God as *Abba,* an Aramaic word meaning Father or Papa. He taught His followers to begin their prayers with the words *Our Father* (Mt 6:9). The Spirit, whom God has given His children, teaches us to pray *Abba,* Father, reminding us of Jesus' own teaching on this subject (Jn 14:26). This implies three things. First, we are assured of the Father's love and protection, sealed by the Spirit. See note on Eph 1:13–14. Second, the Spirit reveals the deep things of God (1 Co 2:9–10). Third, the Spirit fosters worship and prayer, the activities at the center of the shared life (fellowship) of the church. The phrase "Spirit of his Son" appears nowhere else in the New Testament (compare Ac 8:39; 16:7; Ro 8:9; 1 Pe 1:11). The Spirit is called the Spirit of Christ because He is given only to those who have faith in Christ and because He always works to remind us of Christ and His teachings and gospel. See note on Ro 8:25–27.

4:6 PRAYER, Holy Spirit Helps—See note on Ro 8:15.

4:8–11 ELECTION, Personal—The elect are those persons known by God in intimate personal relationship. Under the slavery of sin, persons are not aware of God's knowledge and love. God sends the Spirit of His Son into the hearts of the elect so they become aware of God and His love for them. The elect should move ever forward, never to return again to live as slaves of sin.

4:9 SALVATION, Knowledge of God—Those who know God have been freed from all masters but Christ. Salvation begins with God's knowledge of us, rather than our knowledge of Him.

years![p] 11 I fear for you, that somehow I have wasted my efforts on you.[q]

12 I plead with you, brothers,[r] become like me, for I became like you. You have done me no wrong. 13 As you know, it was because of an illness[s] that I first preached the gospel to you. 14 Even though my illness was a trial to you, you did not treat me with contempt or scorn. Instead, you welcomed me as if I were an angel of God, as if I were Christ Jesus himself.[t] 15 What has happened to all your joy? I can testify that, if you could have done so, you would have torn out your eyes and given them to me. 16 Have I now become your enemy by telling you the truth?[u]

17 Those people are zealous to win you over, but for no good. What they want is to alienate you ⌞from us⌟, so that you may be zealous for them.[v] 18 It is fine to be zealous, provided the purpose is good, and to be so always and not just when I am with you.[w] 19 My dear children,[x] for whom I am again in the pains of childbirth until Christ is formed in you,[y] 20 how I wish I could be with you now and change my tone, because I am perplexed about you!

Hagar and Sarah

21 Tell me, you who want to be under the law,[z] are you not aware of what the law says? 22 For it is written that Abraham had two sons, one by the slave woman[a] and the other by the free woman.[b] 23 His son by the slave woman was born in the ordinary way;[c] but his son by the free woman was born as the result of a promise.[d]

24 These things may be taken figuratively, for the women represent two covenants. One covenant is from Mount Sinai and bears children who are to be slaves: This is Hagar. 25 Now Hagar stands for Mount Sinai in Arabia and corresponds to the present city of Jerusalem, because she is in slavery with her children. 26 But the Jerusalem that is above[e] is free, and she is our mother. 27 For it is written:

> "Be glad, O barren woman,
> who bears no children;
> break forth and cry aloud,
> you who have no labor pains;
> because more are the children of the desolate woman
> than of her who has a husband."[p] [f]

28 Now you, brothers, like Isaac, are children of promise.[g] 29 At that time the son born in the ordinary way[h] persecuted the son born by the power of the Spirit.[i] It is the same now. 30 But what does the Scripture say? "Get rid of the slave woman and her son, for the slave woman's son will never share in the inheritance with the free woman's son."[q] [j] 31 Therefore, brothers, we are not children of the slave woman,[k] but of the free woman.[l]

Chapter 5

Freedom in Christ

It is for freedom that Christ has set us free.[m] Stand firm,[n] then, and do not let yourselves be burdened again by a yoke of slavery.[o]

2 Mark my words! I, Paul, tell you that if you let yourselves be circumcised,[p] Christ will be of no value to you at all. 3 Again I declare to every man who lets himself be circumcised that he is obligat-

4:10 [p]Ro 14:5; Col 2:16
4:11 [q]1Th 3:5
4:12 [r]S Ro 7:1; Gal 6:18
4:13 [s]1Co 2:3
4:14 [t]Mt 10:40
4:16 [u]Am 5:10
4:17 [v]Gal 2:4,12
4:18 [w]ver 13,14
4:19 [x]S 1Th 2:11 [y]Ro 8:29; Eph 4:13
4:21 [z]S Ro 2:12
4:22 [a]Ge 16:15 [b]Ge 21:2
4:23 [c]ver 28,29; Ro 9:7,8 [d]Ge 17:16-21; 18:10-14; 21:1; Heb 11:11
4:26 [e]Heb 12:22; Rev 3:12; 21:2,10
4:27 [f]Isa 54:1
4:28 [g]ver 23; S Gal 3:16
4:29 [h]ver 23 [i]Ge 21:9
4:30 [j]Ge 21:10
4:31 [k]S Ro 7:4 [l]ver 22
5:1 [m]ver 13; Jn 8:32; Gal 2:4; S Ro 7:4 [n]S 1Co 16:13 [o]S Mt 23:4; Gal 2:4
5:2 [p]ver 3,6,11,12; Ac 15:1

[p]*27* Isaiah 54:1 [q]*30* Gen. 21:10

4:12–20 EVANGELISM, Work of Christ—The purity of the gospel rests on Christ's work and not on any human achievement. Deeds done for self-satisfaction are not part of the gospel. Personal zeal does not prove one's preaching is correct. See note on 1:11—2:15.

4:13–14 EVIL AND SUFFERING, Endurance—Illness is not enjoyable for the sufferer or those who wait on the sick. Illness may change our plans into God's opportunity. Illness forced Paul to stop his journey and stay in Galatia. There he preached the gospel. Despite the burden of caring for Paul, the Galatians treated him as God's messenger. In sickness we need to be aware of opportunities God gives us to minister to others.

4:18 CHRISTIAN ETHICS, Character—Enthusiasm adds spice to life. Taken to an extreme, however, or done as an end in itself, it can become counterproductive to the purposes of the Gospel. Enthusiasm must be a real, ongoing part of character, not a temporary act to impress other people.

4:19 SALVATION, As Being in Christ—We should be like a woman giving birth to a child in wanting to see Christ formed in our converts. To be saved is to have Christ in us, as well as for us to be *in Him.*

4:21–31 HOLY SCRIPTURE, Relationship—Paul explained symbolically the meaning of Abraham's two sons and the two kinds of covenants God made with His people. The first is a covenant of slavery, the second a covenant of freedom. God intends for His children to be free, and the promise is made real by the Spirit of God, who reveals freedom through Christ. The heart of Old Testament teaching thus points to the way of Christ, not the way of legalism.

4:26—5:13 SALVATION, Human Freedom—This is Paul's conclusion to his argument in chs 3—4. Law is not, never was, and never can be God's way of salvation for humankind. Believers are called to be free. They are to stand fast in the liberty given them by Christ, but should never abuse or misuse their freedom. Trying to follow legalistic religious rules is slavery. Serving our own fleshly desires because we refuse to discipline ourselves is also slavery. Obeying Christ in faith and love is true freedom to achieve our potential. See note on 2:4.

5:1–21 ELECTION, In Christ—Election is God's plan to save persons and create a people for Himself. He chose to create the people in Christ Jesus and through no other way. Faith, not works, is the only way to be included in the elect. God's grace, not human obedience to law, is the creative force behind election. Faith becomes visible in acts and relationships of love. Election in Christ is freedom from an obligation to earn salvation through human effort. It is a call to be free from sin. It is the opposite of freedom to sin. The free life is possible only through the indwelling Spirit. Sin is slavery, not freedom.

ed to obey the whole law.[q] 4You who are
trying to be justified by law[r] have been
alienated from Christ; you have fallen
away from grace.[s] 5But by faith we eagerly await through the Spirit the righteousness for which we hope.[t] 6For in Christ
Jesus[u] neither circumcision nor uncircumcision has any value.[v] The only thing
that counts is faith expressing itself
through love.[w]

7You were running a good race.[x] Who
cut in on you[y] and kept you from obeying
the truth? 8That kind of persuasion does
not come from the one who calls you.[z]
9"A little yeast works through the whole
batch of dough."[a] 10I am confident[b] in
the Lord that you will take no other
view.[c] The one who is throwing you into
confusion[d] will pay the penalty, whoever
he may be. 11Brothers, if I am still preaching circumcision, why am I still being
persecuted?[e] In that case the offense[f] of
the cross has been abolished. 12As for
those agitators,[g] I wish they would go
the whole way and emasculate themselves!

13You, my brothers, were called to be
free.[h] But do not use your freedom to
indulge the sinful nature[r];[i] rather, serve
one another[j] in love. 14The entire law is
summed up in a single command: "Love
your neighbor as yourself."[s][k] 15If you
keep on biting and devouring each other,
watch out or you will be destroyed by
each other.

Life by the Spirit

16So I say, live by the Spirit,[l] and you
will not gratify the desires of the sinful
nature.[m] 17For the sinful nature desires
what is contrary to the Spirit, and the
Spirit what is contrary to the sinful nature.[n] They are in conflict with each other, so that you do not do what you want.[o]
18But if you are led by the Spirit,[p] you are
not under law.[q]

19The acts of the sinful nature are obvious: sexual immorality,[r] impurity and
debauchery; 20idolatry and witchcraft; hatred, discord, jealousy, fits of rage, selfish
ambition, dissensions, factions 21and
envy; drunkenness, orgies, and the like.[s]
I warn you, as I did before, that those
who live like this will not inherit the
kingdom of God.[t]

22But the fruit[u] of the Spirit is love,[v]

5:3 [q]Ro 2:25; Gal 3:10; Jas 2:10 **5:4** [r]S Ro 3:28 [s]Heb 12:15; 2Pe 3:17 **5:5** [t]Ro 8:23,24 **5:6** [u]S Ro 16:3 [v]S 1Co 7:19 [w]1Th 1:3; Jas 2:22 **5:7** [x]S 1Co 9:24 [y]Gal 3:1 **5:8** [z]S Ro 8:28 **5:9** [a]1Co 5:6 **5:10** [b]S 2Co 2:3 [c]Php 3:15 [d]ver 12; Gal 1:7 **5:11** [e]Gal 4:29; 6:12 [f]S Lk 2:34 **5:12** [g]ver 10 **5:13** [h]S ver 1 [i]S ver 24; 1Co 8:9; 1Pe 2:16 [j]1Co 9:19; 2Co 4:5; Eph 5:21 **5:14** [k]Lev 19:18; S Mt 5:43; Gal 6:2 **5:16** [l]ver 18,25; Ro 8:2,4-6,9,14; S 2Co 5:17 [m]S ver 24 **5:17** [n]Ro 8:5-8 [o]Ro 7:15-23 **5:18** [p]S ver 16 [q]S Ro 2:12; 1Ti 1:9 **5:19** [r]S 1Co 6:18 **5:21** [s]Mt 15:19; Ro 13:13 [t]S Mt 25:34 **5:22** [u]Mt 7:16-20; Eph 5:9 [v]Col 3:12-15

[r] *13* Or *the flesh;* also in verses 16, 17, 19 and 24
[s] *14* Lev. 19:18

5:5 HOLY SPIRIT, Security—Christians are forgiven people who have begun to be changed by the Spirit into people of love and goodness (Gal 5:22) but who realize we are far from perfect (Php 3:12–14). Thus, we hope for a time when we shall be fully transformed into people of righteousness and love. We are confident our hopes will be fulfilled (Php 1:6), for the very presence of the Spirit within us is a guarantee we shall arrive at our true destiny. See notes on 2 Co 1:21–22; Eph 1:13–14.

5:5 CHRISTIAN ETHICS, Justice—The just, righteous society represents hope, not reality. Only righteous people can create a righteous society. In Christ, God began creating the new, just society. His church lives out righteousness in faith through the Spirit. In God's chosen time, God will bring a new earth, and our hope for justice will be fully realized. See note on Ro 8:4,10.

5:6 SALVATION, As Being in Christ—Circumcision or any other religious ritual has no saving value to those in Christ. The thing which matters most to Christians is faith working through love.

5:6–15 CHRISTIAN ETHICS, Character—See note on 1 Co 8:1–13.

5:13–26 HUMANITY, Spiritual Nature—Christians experience internal warfare. We remain humans with all the fleshly desires and temptations. We have God's Spirit in us to free us and empower us to overcome temptation and fleshly desires. We have the freedom to conquer, but we may not have the will to "keep in step with the Spirit." We must constantly give the Spirit control of our wills so His fruits will grow in our lives.

5:16–18 HOLY SPIRIT, Obeyed—The Spirit leads away from sin. The Spirit does not overwhelm Christians and force us to do God's will. Rather, He offers His gifts, power, and guidance and then expects us to follow Him. He gives new life in Christ. Naturally we should walk in His life (v 25) of love, joy, peace, and the like (v 22). The Christian life is a mystery. It is given completely by God. God provides the standards of love. God gives the Spirit who alone can enable Christians to live up to the standards (v 22). The life of a Christian is all of God, all done by His Spirit within. However, the Christian must cooperate. We must live the life to which we are called. We must trust God and His Spirit rather than ourselves. The metaphor of love as a fruit (v 22) captures the paradox in a single phrase. The Christian must bear the fruit, but only the Spirit can produce it. See note on Ro 8:1–17.

5:16–21 SIN, Depravity—Sin is an ever-present threat even for the Christian (v 13). This list of sinful acts describes behavior we are all capable of performing if we do not walk with the Spirit who dwells within us. Christians, therefore, should not assume they are immune from committing the most immoral acts. When we trust ourselves, sin rules our lives and leads us to unimaginable actions. Only when we totally trust Christ does the threat of sin disappear.

5:16 DISCIPLESHIP, Holy Spirit—Two alternatives face you! You may follow God's Spirit or self-centered desires. The Holy Spirit makes it possible for Christians to overcome our lower nature and serve God according to His will. See note on Eph 3:16.

5:16–26 CHRISTIAN ETHICS, Character—Paul contrasted the observable effects and patterns of a life apart from God with the outworking of the Holy Spirit in one's life. On one hand is evil and negative orientation. On the other is a positive, outward, and caring orientation. The energy and motivation for the positive dimensions are found in the Spirit. The Spirit of God is recognized in the New Testament as the abiding Sustainer of the Christian in discovering and practicing the ethical facets of the gospel.

5:18 CHRISTIAN ETHICS, Moral Imperatives—The ritual law has been transcended by the work of Christ. The moral law remains in place. These standards are meant for our good. Their pull draws us to true freedom. To return to a ritualistic expression of the law would enslave us to a lower level of maturity in God. The Holy Spirit will guide us in the path of love to fulfill the law. See note on Ro 7:1–25.

5:22–26 HOLY SPIRIT, Transforms—The Spirit of God is the Holy Spirit. Not only is He holy, one of His activities is to sanctify others, to make us holy. See Ro 15:16; 1 Co 6:11; 2 Th 2:13; 1 Pe 1:2. An agricultural metaphor describes this sanctifying work of the Spirit. The Spirit produces fruit in a Christian's life. For the Christian's role in this, see note on

joy, peace,[w] patience, kindness, goodness, faithfulness, 23gentleness and self-
control.[x] Against such things there is no
law.[y] 24Those who belong to Christ Jesus
have crucified the sinful nature[z] with its
passions and desires.[a] 25Since we live by
the Spirit,[b] let us keep in step with the
Spirit. 26Let us not become conceited,[c]
provoking and envying each other.

Chapter 6

Doing Good to All

BROTHERS, if someone is caught in a
sin, you who are spiritual[d] should restore[e] him gently. But watch yourself, or
you also may be tempted. 2Carry each
other's burdens, and in this way you will
fulfill the law of Christ.[f] 3If anyone
thinks he is something[g] when he is nothing, he deceives himself.[h] 4Each one
should test his own actions. Then he can
take pride in himself,[i] without comparing himself to somebody else,[j] 5for each
one should carry his own load.[k]
6Anyone who receives instruction in
the word must share all good things with
his instructor.[l]
7Do not be deceived:[m] God cannot be
mocked. A man reaps what he sows.[n]
8The one who sows to please his sinful
nature,[o] from that nature[t] will reap destruction;[p] the one who sows to please
the Spirit, from the Spirit will reap eternal life.[q] 9Let us not become weary in
doing good,[r] for at the proper time we
will reap a harvest if we do not give up.[s]
10Therefore, as we have opportunity, let
us do good[t] to all people, especially to
those who belong to the family[u] of believers.

Not Circumcision but a New Creation

11See what large letters I use as I write
to you with my own hand![v]

5:22 [w]Mal 2:6 **5:23** [x]S Ac 24:25 [y]ver 18 **5:24** [z]ver 13,16-21; S Ro 6:6; 7:5,18; 8:3-5,8,9,12,13; 13:14; Gal 6:8; Col 2:11 [a]ver 16,17 **5:25** [b]S ver 16 **5:26** [c]Php 2:3 **6:1** [d]1Co 2:15; 3:1 [e]S Mt 18:15; S 2Co 2:7 **6:2** [f]1Co 9:21; Jas 2:8 **6:3** [g]Ro 12:3; 1Co 8:2 [h]1Co 3:18 **6:4** [i]2Co 13:5 [j]2Co 10:12 **6:5** [k]ver 2; Jer 31:30 **6:6** [l]1Co 9:11,14; 1Ti 5:17,18 **6:7** [m]S 1Co 6:9 [n]Pr 22:8; Jer 34:17; Hos 10:12,13; 2Co 9:6 **6:8** [o]S Gal 5:24 [p]Job 4:8; Hos 8:7; S Ro 6:23 [q]Jas 3:18 **6:9** [r]1Co 15:58; 2Co 4:1 [s]Job 42:12; Ps 126:5; Heb 12:3; Rev 2:10 **6:10** [t]Pr 3:27; S Tit 2:14 [u]Eph 2:19; 1Pe 4:17 **6:11** [v]S 1Co 16:21

[t]8 Or *his flesh, from the flesh*

5:16–18. Sanctification is the work of God which begins when a person becomes a Christian and continues throughout life on earth. It is completed only in the life to come (Php 1:6). The Spirit does not force us to be holy. He exerts His influence on us. The Spirit is present in our lives, reminds us of Christ and our call to discipleship, creates the community of faith known as the church, guides us in our study of inspired Scripture, assures us we have been accepted by God, and guides the church in its decisions. In all this, the Spirit exercises a transforming influence upon each Christian. See note on 1 Co 12:4–11.

5:22–25 SALVATION, Sanctification—Sanctification is life in the Spirit. The sanctified person bears the fruit of the Spirit and crucifies his or her old sinful nature (vv 19–21). This does not mean that saved persons are without sin. It does mean we constantly fight against sin and yield ourselves to the Spirit.

6:1–2 DISCIPLESHIP, The Fallen—Redemptive love reaches out to lift up the fallen and restore them to fellowship. This love involves discipline offered gently but firmly, exercising care not to fall into the same temptation. Vindication, glee, and a sense of superiority have no place in discipline. Christian disciples also demonstrate redemptive love by helping others bear their burdens. Such sharing is clear evidence of the love which Jesus says fulfills all of the law. See notes on Mt 22:37–40; 2 Co 2:5–11.

6:2 CHRISTIAN ETHICS, Moral Imperatives—In faith, Christians accept Christ's teachings as the law needed to guide life's moral decisions. This law leads us in one basic direction —helping people in need. The church's unique mark before the world is our concern for and devotion to one another.

6:3–5 CHRISTIAN ETHICS, Character—See note on 2 Co 13:1–12.

6:6 CHURCH LEADERS, Teacher—Teachers are very important to the life of the believer and the church. They pass on and interpret the faith of the church. The church must have people with the gift and calling of teaching. Those who become the professional teachers of the church deserve financial support. See notes on 1 Co 9:1–15; 12:28–29.

6:6 EDUCATION, Christians—Teachers and learners in the church should engage in mutual support of one another, sharing personal and spiritual resources, bearing one another's loads. See v 2. The word "share" comes *from the Greek koinonia (usually translated "fellowship") which* denotes mutual participation in a cause. Taken seriously, this biblical concept can foster a genuine team spirit among teachers and learners in Christian congregations. In a real sense we are all teachers of one another, and we all learn from one another.

6:7–10 GOD, Sovereignty—God governs this world in such a way that we are rewarded or punished according to what we have put into this life. God is in complete charge, knows us fully and clearly, and holds us accountable to Himself. On the one hand, He is quick to bless those who are faithful to Him. On the other hand, He is ready and able to bring to judgment those who do not take their responsibilities to Him seriously. God will not be manipulated, bought off, or fooled. The grace of God given to us as forgiveness and salvation does not free us from the necessity of responsible, faithful living. Grace increases our responsibility rather than lessening it.

6:7–8 EVIL AND SUFFERING, Deserved—Paul affirmed the traditional view that actions have sure consequences. Punishment for sin will certainly come in this world or the next. See note on Pr 1:10–19.

6:7–10 HUMANITY, Spiritual Nature—The spiritual harvest principle works, but Christians may get weary waiting for the harvest. Persons follow either the fleshly desires and reap destruction, or they follow God's Spirit and reap eternal life. While still in the flesh, we must choose to follow the Spirit. We retain the possibility of following sinful desires. God has regenerated us without making robots of us. See 5:13–26.

6:8 SALVATION, Eternal Life—Compare Jn 4:36. Eternal life is God's gift to those who sow to please the Spirit instead of their own selfish, sinful nature.

6:9–10 CHRISTIAN ETHICS, Character—The application of doing good is broad. We should do good to those like us, but also to those different from us. The motivation for doing good is many fold: because God expects it of us; because human creatures made in the image of God need good and not bad; because doing good provides a basis for further witness of the gospel's redemptive power.

6:9–10 FAMILY, Social Concern—See note on Ro 12:13.

6:10 THE CHURCH, People of God—God's people make up the family of believers or the household of faith. In other passages the church is described similarly as the house of God (Heb 3:6; 1 Pe 2:5–10) and as the household of God (1 Ti 3:15). The imagery obviously refers to the people of God in the Old Testament. The church fulfills Old Testament expectations for the covenant people and looks forward to the complete fulfillment. As God's family, the church cares for one another in all personal needs as well as doing what is right and good for nonbelievers. The people were chosen to serve God.

12 Those who want to make a good impression outwardly[w] are trying to compel
you to be circumcised.[x] The only reason
they do this is to avoid being persecuted[y]
for the cross of Christ. 13 Not even those
who are circumcised obey the law,[z] yet
they want you to be circumcised that they
may boast about your flesh.[a] 14 May I never boast except in the cross of our Lord
Jesus Christ,[b] through which[u] the world
has been crucified to me, and I to the
world.[c] 15 Neither circumcision nor uncircumcision means anything;[d] what
counts is a new creation.[e] 16 Peace and
mercy to all who follow this rule, even to
the Israel of God.

17 Finally, let no one cause me trouble,
for I bear on my body the marks[f] of
Jesus.

18 The grace of our Lord Jesus Christ[g]
be with your spirit,[h] brothers. Amen.

6:12 [w]Mt 23:25,26 [x]Ac 15:1 [y]Gal 5:11
6:13 [z]Ro 2:25 [a]Php 3:3
6:14 [b]1Co 2:2 [c]S Ro 6:2,6
6:15 [d]S 1Co 7:19 [e]S 2Co 5:17
6:17 [f]Isa 44:5; S 2Co 1:5; 11:23
6:18 [g]S Ro 16:20 [h]Php 4:23; 2Ti 4:22; Phm 25

[u] *14* Or *whom*

6:12 EVIL AND SUFFERING, Endurance—Emphasizing relatively minor points of doctrine can be an attempt to evade larger, more threatening issues. Paul's Judaizing opponents insisted Christians remain tied to Jewish practices to avoid persecution from Jewish religious leaders and possibly to maintain the church as a part of Judaism and thus avoid persecution by the Roman government which recognized Judaism.

6:15 SALVATION, Definition—God's salvation produces a new creation in Christ (Ro 8:19–23; 2 Co 5:17; Eph 2:15; Rev 21:5). Through Christ, God is making new persons, a new race of the new birth, a new community, a new city, and a new creation. See note on Ps 53:6.

6:16 THE CHURCH, True Israel—The church is the true Israel. All people come to God by faith, both the Jew and the Gentile. See note on 3:6–25. Paul used Israel as an image for the church. All Israel will be saved; however, this Israel is not the Israel of the flesh but those who receive the promise by faith. See notes on Ro 9:4–9; 11:26–28.

6:18 PRAYER, Blessing—See note on Ro 15:33.

Ephesians

Theological Setting

How do you find victory in Christ? This question becomes especially acute when problems become evident in the church. A number of common problems plagued the churches of Asia Minor, including the church at Ephesus. First, the heathen religions had to be reckoned with as powerful and growing forces. These groups were making bold claims of power and supremacy while offering enticements to the human nature in the name of religion. For example, the religious rites involving prostitution exercised in connection with the temple of Diana in Ephesus were famous and alluring.

Second, internal bickering threatened the church itself. The Christians with Jewish backgrounds felt their previous, historical heritage gave them an advantage over Gentiles. This view caused hard feelings within the body of believers.

Third, the allure of the world attempted to claim the allegiance of believers because their vocational and financial success often was wrapped up in how they related to the secular world. Therefore, the believers in Asia Minor faced some very difficult options. (1) They could try to "fit in" in both worlds. This attempt would mean compromise in the areas of both integrity and morality. It would bring them into conflict with the Spirit of God residing in their lives and with all they had been taught by Paul and other teachers sent from God. It would mean the deadening of their consciences. (2) They could choose to withdraw from all the battles of life and to live a monastic existence, avoiding the pain and agony of "taking a stand." (3) They could maintain their commitment to the cause of Christ at all cost and run all the risks inherent in that kind of decision. The risks might include public humiliation, loss of earning power, and even physical persecution. To follow this direction they would need to be dependent upon the lordship of Christ and to keep unity in the body of believers.

In writing Ephesians Paul was encouraging the believers in Asia Minor to opt for the latter life-style and was informing them not only of the ingredients of this life-style but of the difficulties of that decision. His readers could have reacted to the letter with indifference, except for several factors. First, Paul bore in his own body the marks of a life of commitment. It was common knowledge that Paul had suffered great persecution because of his unwavering faith in Jesus Christ and of his zeal for the cause of Christ. At the time this letter was written Paul was confined to prison in Rome (3:1,13). He did not ask the recipients of this letter to live by any standard he had not already set for himself. If necessary, he could point to his own life as a model to be followed. It is difficult to take exception to that kind of life statement.

Second, Paul's letter commanded great authority because of his relationship to the recipients. The lengthy and tedious process of founding the church at Ephesus was begun during a brief stay at Ephesus on his second missionary journey (Ac 18:18-21). He was on his way from Greece to Syria with Aquila and Priscilla. While there he taught in the synagogue, and "refuted the Jews in public debate" (18:28). His stay was brief, but it is obvious that the time was spent effectively. He had made his way into their hearts, because they tried to persuade him to stay. He declined their offer but left Aquila and Priscilla with them, promising to return, "God willing." He did return on his third missionary journey and remained there over two years (Ac 19:10; 20:31), reasoning with the Jews and teaching the new converts.

Serious students of the Bible generally agree the book of Ephesians reaches the pinnacle of Pauline literature. It has been called by many the "queen of the epistles." The letter has inspired and transformed the lives of countless readers since its writing in the first century.

It is a widely held belief that the words of Paul in this writing were meant for a wider audience than just the believers in Ephesus. The only reference to the Ephesians is found in (1:1), and this phrase, "to the saints in Ephesus," is not found in the two oldest Greek manuscripts. The letter was probably a "circular letter" sent to many churches and assemblies of believers in Asia Minor. As the letter was delivered from church to church, each one could insert its own name in (1:1) because it was applicable to such a broad range of believers. This fact adds to its relevance to every Christian today.

The letter is one of Paul's finest because he was not dealing with any one particular issue, nor was he defending the gospel against any one heresy or group teaching heresy. Rather, he intended to let the recipients know who they were in Christ, all that was available to them in Christ, and the importance of oneness within the body of Christ in the struggle of life. He was doing a masterful job of discipling the believers for the years to come when he would not be with them in person. He knew the opposition they would be facing in a society turned against them. He desired for them a strong faith that would produce confidence and boldness, out of which would come victory.

Theological Outline

Ephesians: Unity in Christ

- I. The Apostle Sends Greetings to the Church. (1:1-2)
- II. Believers Who Make Up the Church Have a Great Potential in Christ. (1:3—3:21)
  - A. God has chosen believers to be His children. (1:3-6)
  - B. Christ in His death and resurrection has provided believers an inheritance that includes forgiveness and eternal life. (1:7-12)
  - C. The Holy Spirit has sealed the believers' inheritance. (1:13-14)
  - D. The apostle prays for the believers' full understanding of the power of Christ and their inheritance in Him. (1:15-23)
  - E. By grace believers have been delivered from death in trespasses and sin and have been given life. (2:1-10)
  - F. In Christ all believers are one, reconciled to both God and other persons. (2:11-22)
  - G. The grace of God is broad enough for Gentiles as well as Jews. (3:1-13)
  - H. The apostle prays for the believers to be strengthened spiritually. (3:14-19)
  - I. The apostle praises God and calls for the church through the ages to glorify Him. (3:20-21)
- III. Believers Need to Practice Their Faith. (4:1—6:20)
  - A. Believers should humbly seek unity. (4:1-3)
  - B. Unity involves one body, spirit, hope, Lord, faith, baptism, and Father. (4:4-6)
  - C. God provided differing gifts to build the church in unity and maturity. (4:7-16)
  - D. A holy and separated life is necessary in Christ. (4:17-21)
  - E. Christ transforms the believers' attitudes and actions. (4:22—5:17)
  - F. Spirit-filled believers do God's will and worship together with joy, thanksgiving, and mutual respect. (5:18-20)
  - G. Husbands and wives should live in love and respect. (5:21-33)
  - H. Parents should teach their children about God, while children obey. (6:1-4)
  - I. On-the-job relationships and attitudes are governed by the believers' relationship to Christ. (6:5-9)
  - J. Christ equips believers for spiritual warfare. (6:10-17)
  - K. Believers are encouraged to pray for boldness. (6:18-20)
- IV. The Apostle Concludes His Letter with a Personal Word of Encouragement. (6:21-24)

Theological Conclusions

Ephesians may be considered a manual of Christian living. It pulls together much of the material of the other letters of the New Testament, but in a more concise form. Ephesians gives some practical advice for spiritual growth and development.

Ephesians contains many theological implications, but five stand out as being most important. First, believers have position in Christ. We might not be growing as rapidly in the faith as we would like, but we have certain inherent qualities because we are the adopted children of God. This fact should give us confidence in the face of threats from an alien world.

Second, believers have a new nature as seen in 2:1-10. This new nature opens to believers all kinds of possibilities we never had before. Even though the "old person" is still present, the potential is there for unbelievable growth. "We are God's workmanship, created in Christ Jesus to do good works" (2:10).

Third, closely related to that potential seen in the "new person" is now the possibility for real unity in the "body of Christ," the church. All barriers between people within the body have been broken down by Christ. Nothing that separates us within the body is beyond reconciliation. This offers the church unlimited potential. All barriers between believers are potential stepping-stones to harmony and accord.

Fourth, Ephesians points out the importance of a holy, separated life. It speaks to the issue of living in a world out of which believers have been called. Such living can only be done successfully if certain elements are present. According to the apostle, believers are responsible to see that our life is open to the filling of the Spirit of God constantly and consistently. Without this consistent infilling the flesh dominates the believers' lives. To live the holy and separated life, we must not only recognize we are in a battle, but we must give careful emphasis to the armor we are provided. The apostle evidently took his concept of the armor from the Roman soldier who was daily by his side. Without this armor believers are defenseless.

Finally, Ephesians teaches that family life and vocational life are spiritual issues. Believers often separate family and vocational life from the commitments of the Christian faith too easily. These commitments are inseparable for Paul. Believers have a responsibility both as church members and as family members. We have responsibility to our vocation, whether as employees or employers. No part of life is isolated from expressions of our faith.

Contemporary Teaching

Ephesians contains some basic lessons and valuable applications for believers of every generation, including the present generation of Christians.

1. We need to live from a positive perspective. We can do this only as we recognize our position in Christ. The Lord has lost none of His power to sustain His children. As we live from a positive perspective, we have greater opportunity to impact our society. Our lives demonstrate desirable characteristics that draw others to Christ.

2. We need to maintain unity within the Christian fellowship at the expense of personal prejudices, but stop short of spiritual compromise. Many of the issues that divide believers and harm Christian witness are of little eternal impact.

3. A life of holiness and separation from the world needs to be a continuing Christian distinctive. The apostle's admonition to a holy life follows Christ's own command to His followers when He said, "But seek first his kingdom and his righteousness, and all these things will be given to you as well" (Mt 6:33). This command is always a current mandate for the believer.

4. We need to carry our faith over into all the relationships of life and especially into those relationships involving family and vocation, since they consume the greatest part of our time and energy. The believer's witness will be the most crucial in these two areas of life. The home will be our greatest sphere of influence.

The church today faces many of the same decisions the churches in Asia Minor faced when they received Paul's letter. Our options are similar to the ones they had, and the impact of our life directions will be as crucial, perhaps even more crucial.

Chapter 1

PAUL, an apostle[a] of Christ Jesus by
the will of God,[b]

To the saints[c] in Ephesus,[a][d] the faithful[b][e] in Christ Jesus:

2Grace and peace to you from God our
Father and the Lord Jesus Christ.[f]

Spiritual Blessings in Christ

3Praise be to the God and Father of our
Lord Jesus Christ,[g] who has blessed us in
the heavenly realms[h] with every spiritual
blessing in Christ. 4For he chose us[i] in
him before the creation of the world[j] to
be holy and blameless[k] in his sight. In
love[l] 5he[c] predestined[m] us to be adopted as his sons[n] through Jesus Christ, in
accordance with his pleasure[o] and will—
6to the praise of his glorious grace,[p]
which he has freely given us in the One
he loves.[q] 7In him we have redemption[r]
through his blood,[s] the forgiveness of
sins, in accordance with the riches[t] of
God's grace 8that he lavished on us with
all wisdom and understanding. 9And he[d]
made known to us the mystery[u] of his
will according to his good pleasure,
which he purposed[v] in Christ, 10to be
put into effect when the times will have
reached their fulfillment[w]—to bring all
things in heaven and on earth together
under one head, even Christ.[x]
11In him we were also chosen,[e] having
been predestined[y] according to the plan
of him who works out everything in conformity with the purpose[z] of his will,
12in order that we, who were the first to
hope in Christ, might be for the praise of

1:1 [a]S 1Co 1:1 [b]S 2Co 1:1 [c]S Ac 9:13 [d]S Ac 18:19 [e]Col 1:2 **1:2** [f]S Ro 1:7 **1:3** [g]2Co 1:3; 1Pe 1:3 [h]ver 20; Eph 2:6; 3:10; 6:12 **1:4** [i]2Th 2:13 [j]S Mt 25:34 [k]Lev 11:44; 20:7; 2Sa 22:24; Ps 15:2; Eph 5:27; Col 1:22 [l]Eph 4:2,15,16 **1:5** [m]ver 11; Ro 8:29,30 [n]S Ro 8:14,15 [o]Lk 12:32; 1Co 1:21; Col 1:19 **1:6** [p]ver 12,14 [q]Mt 3:17 **1:7** [r]ver 14; S Ro 3:24 [s]S Ro 3:25 [t]S Ro 2:4 **1:9** [u]S Ro 16:25 [v]S ver 11 **1:10** [w]Mk 1:15; Ro 5:6; Gal 4:4 [x]Col 1:20 **1:11** [y]ver 5; Ro 8:29,30 [z]ver 9; Ro 8:28; Eph 3:11; Heb 6:17

[a] *1* Some early manuscripts do not have *in Ephesus.*
[b] *1* Or *believers who are* [c] *4,5* Or *sight in love. 5He*
[d] *8,9* Or *us. With all wisdom and understanding, 9he*
[e] *11* Or *were made heirs*

1:1–14 ELECTION, In Christ—Election in Christ was not God's last resort after all other plans failed. From before the foundation of the world God chose the elect in Christ for holy and blameless living. In Christ He has richly lavished the blessings of redemption, forgiveness, wisdom, and understanding upon the elect. God's will has always been to provide salvation and create His people through Christ's blood. At the proper moment in history He revealed His plan in the ministry, death, and resurrection of Christ. The guarantee of election is the Holy Spirit, who is an installment on the inheritance of all who are God's treasure and elect. See note on Ro 8:28–35.

1:1,5,13 SALVATION, As Being in Christ—Those in Christ are saints. They are God's children through their adoption in Christ. All who hear and believe the gospel are included in Christ's people. The Holy Spirit in us marks us as being in Christ.

1:1 THE CHURCH, Saints—Christians are saints because they are in Christ Jesus. The Christian's holiness is a gift to be used in the service of Christ. See note on Ro 1:7.

1:2 PRAYER, Blessing—See note on Ro 1:7.

1:3–23 GOD, Sovereignty—We praise the sovereign God because He has planned and worked since before He created our world. Every effort was directed to our salvation. God is at work, approaching us as heavenly Father, crucified Son, and indwelling Holy Spirit, that He might save and develop our lives into spiritual maturity. This shows the total grace of God in all His sovereign work and rule. His grace appears again as He gives His authority to Christ to rule the kingdom.

1:3 JESUS CHRIST, Lord—See notes on Jn 20:25–28; Ac 2:23–36. Lord (Greek *kurios*) is the most frequently used title for Jesus in the New Testament. Different contexts gave different meanings. In the Roman court, it showed respect for nobility and particularly for the Caesars. The New Testament does not contain an example of this. It is probable that early Christians were persecuted or even killed because they would not say Caesar is Lord. Christians used the term in an absolute sense to refer to God. This came from the Jewish custom of using Lord (Hebrew *adonai*) to refer to God instead of using the divine name (Hebrew *Yahweh*). Lord was Paul's favorite designation for Jesus, and for Paul the rabbi to refer to Christ as Lord is evidence Paul viewed Jesus as divine. Paul frequently designated himself a slave (Greek *doulos*). Since Jesus Christ is Lord, Paul was servant. The first missionary apostle provided the premier relationship for Jesus and His people—Lord and servants.

1:3 SALVATION, Blessing—God blesses us with everything we need in Christ. His blessings are in heavenly things more than earthly things.

1:3–14 PRAYER, Praise—See note on Ro 16:25–27. Paul gave a trinitarian doxology—to the Father (v 3), Son (v 12), and the Holy Spirit (v 14).

1:4 GOD, Love—Love is the underlying motive for all that God does. It is His eternal characteristic which led to His developing a plan to save people even before He created the world.

1:5 THE CHURCH, God's Community—See notes on Jn 1:12–13; Gal 4:4–7.

1:6–8 SALVATION, Grace—God's glorious grace is cause for praise. He lavishes upon us the riches of His grace through His beloved Son. We have everything we need in the One whom He loves (1 Co 1:30).

1:7–10 JESUS CHRIST, Redeemer—By pouring out His blood on the cross, Jesus redeemed us from slavery to sin, forgave our sins, lavished God's grace on us, revealed the nature of God's wisdom, and previewed His ultimate purpose to unite the universe under His rule.

1:7,14 SALVATION, Redemption—The cross of Christ is the ground of forgiveness. It is the focal point of God's plan for dealing with sin. The Holy Spirit is the guarantee of the believer's future inheritance (2 Co 1:21–22). He is a downpayment and foretaste of the salvation which is yet to come.

1:7 SALVATION, Forgiveness—Forgiveness of sins is in Christ who redeemed us through His death on the cross. Compare Col 1:14; 2:13.

1:8 GOD, Wisdom—Grace is not an emotional act separated from intelligence and purpose. God is wise as He distributes His grace to us. He clearly is accomplishing a predetermined plan as He reaches out to us in His saving love. God is a purposive God whose wisdom informs and guides His every action.

1:9–10 REVELATION, History—God has a purpose for history and is accomplishing it. In Christ the church knows God's purpose, Christ ruling all creation. As with all revealed promises and purposes of God, this, too, will be fulfilled.

1:10 HISTORY, Time—See note on Gal 4:4.

1:10 LAST THINGS, History's Goal—The purposes of God are to be brought to their intended goal. These purposes are centered in Christ and come to fruition in association with Him. "All things" is an all-embracing phrase for the whole of creation, the times of human history, and the totality of redeemed humanity. All will be headed up in Christ, and therein final harmony and God's eternally intended purpose will be realized.

1:12–17 GOD, Glory—God worked to save us so we would recognize the marvelous greatness of His glory and praise Him.

his glory.[a] 13 And you also were included
in Christ[b] when you heard the word of
truth,[c] the gospel of your salvation. Having believed, you were marked in him
with a seal,[d] the promised Holy Spirit,[e]
14 who is a deposit guaranteeing our inheritance[f] until the redemption[g] of
those who are God's possession—to the
praise of his glory.[h]

Thanksgiving and Prayer

15 For this reason, ever since I heard
about your faith in the Lord Jesus[i] and
your love for all the saints,[j] 16 I have not
stopped giving thanks for you,[k] remembering you in my prayers.[l] 17 I keep asking that the God of our Lord Jesus Christ,
the glorious Father,[m] may give you the
Spirit[f] of wisdom[n] and revelation, so
that you may know him better. 18 I pray
also that the eyes of your heart may be
enlightened[o] in order that you may know
the hope to which he has called[p] you,
the riches[q] of his glorious inheritance[r]
in the saints,[s] 19 and his incomparably
great power for us who believe. That
power[t] is like the working of his mighty
strength,[u] 20 which he exerted in Christ
when he raised him from the dead[v] and
seated him at his right hand[w] in the heavenly realms,[x] 21 far above all rule and authority, power and dominion,[y] and every
title[z] that can be given, not only in the
present age but also in the one to come.[a]
22 And God placed all things under his
feet[b] and appointed him to be head[c]
over everything for the church, 23 which
is his body,[d] the fullness of him[e] who
fills everything in every way.[f]

Chapter 2

Made Alive in Christ

As for you, you were dead in your transgressions and sins,[g] 2 in which you

1:12 [a]ver 6,14 **1:13** [b]S Ro 16:3 [c]Eph 4:21; Col 1:5 [d]Eph 4:30 [e]Jn 14:16,17 **1:14** [f]S Ac 20:32; S 2Co 5:5 [g]ver 7; S Ro 3:24 [h]ver 6,12 **1:15** [i]S Ac 20:21 [j]S Col 1:4 **1:16** [k]S Ro 1:8 [l]S Ro 1:10 **1:17** [m]Jn 20:17; Ro 15:6; Rev 1:6 [n]Ex 28:3; Isa 11:2; Php 1:9; Col 1:9 **1:18** [o]Job 42:5; 2Co 4:6; Heb 6:4 [p]S Ro 8:28 [q]ver 7; S Ro 2:4 [r]ver 11 [s]Col 1:12 **1:19** [t]Eph 3:7; Col 1:29 [u]Isa 40:26; Eph 6:10 **1:20** [v]S Ac 2:24 [w]S Mk 16:19 [x]S ver 3 **1:21** [y]Eph 3:10; Col 1:16 [z]Php 2:9, 10 [a]S Mt 12:32 **1:22** [b]S Mt 22:44; S 28:18 [c]1Co 11:3; Eph 4:15; 5:23; Col 1:18; 2:19 **1:23** [d]S 1Co 12:27 [e]S Jn 1:16; Eph 3:19 [f]Eph 4:10 **2:1** [g]ver 5; Col 2:13

[f]17 Or *a spirit*

1:13–14 HOLY SPIRIT, Security—An important work of the Spirit clearly is to protect God's people. See notes on Mk 13:11; Jn 16:8–11; Ac 4:8–10; 5:32; 6:8–10. The metaphor of a seal meant that the contents of the document under it were protected by the power of the official who placed the seal and identified as belonging to the official. Christians are protected by the power of the God and identified as His because He put His Spirit on them as a seal. This security is a great source of assurance for Christians. Those who live with such security and assurance, quite understandably, experience boldness, joy, and peace as a result. See Ac 13:42; Gal 5:22; notes on Ac 4:31; 9:31. The Spirit is also a deposit or down payment. A deposit is simply the first payment. The remainder will come later. The gift of the Spirit is God's first payment to His people. The remainder of His blessings will be given later, in the life to come. The Spirit's presence with us is a foretaste of the life to come. See notes on Ro 8:23; Gal 5:5.

1:14 LAST THINGS, Humanity Restored—God will redeem or fully restore believers in Christ so we perfectly conform to His will. Until then the Spirit in our lives guarantees we will be redeemed. See notes on Ro 8:18–23; 1 Jn 3:2–3.

1:15 THE CHURCH, Saints—Love "does" more than it "feels." God's people love one another. Others come to know about this love through the deeds of love we do for each other. Such loving action brings joy and thanksgiving to God's people. Saints are holy ones because Christ's love impels us to action. See note on Ro 16:2.

1:15–19 PRAYER, Intercession—Intercession reaches its highest authority and power when it is for spiritual purposes. Paul prayed the Ephesians would know God better and experience His strength. Paul's deep concern for his churches is shown by his frequent prayers for them (2 Co 13:7; Php 1:4; Col 1:3; 2:1; 1 Th 1:2; 2 Th 1:11).

1:17 GOD, Trinity—Separate activities of the three Persons of the Trinity appear clearly here. The Father of Christ hears prayers and sends the Spirit, who reveals God to us. Jesus is the Lord whom we serve as slaves.

1:17 JESUS CHRIST, God—See Eph 1:3. "God of our Lord Jesus Christ" is a title showing the unique relationship of the divine Person to Jesus Christ.

1:17 HOLY SPIRIT, Revelation—The Spirit reveals Christ and guides the church to proclaim Christ. He also reveals to Christians the kind of lives we are to live (Ro 8:6–16; Gal 5:22). He continues to help the church to understand God better (1 Co 2:9–12). The Spirit's revelation is not a past event already finished. It is a growing awareness and appreciation of God and His glorious love and purposes which the Spirit assists the church to come to. We should join Paul and pray that the Spirit will help us to know God and His purposes, activities, and character better. The church will never have a comprehensive understanding of God, but the Spirit will always help those who are willing to grow in their understanding.

1:17 HUMANITY, Relationship to God—Those who truly "know" God experience Him in daily life. This is made possible by His own revelation and not by human discovery.

1:17 REVELATION, Spirit—Revelation has one purpose—to let us know God better. Such knowledge means relationship to a Person, not accumulation of facts. The Holy Spirit is the immediate source of such revelation. The Spirit leads us to relationship with Christ.

1:17 SALVATION, Knowledge of God—The Holy Spirit is given to us as God's people to help us know God better. He is a teaching Spirit imparting wisdom and divine truth.

1:19–20 GOD, Power—The redeeming grace of God is as much a disclosure of His power as it is of His love. The same power that brought Jesus from the dead—could there be a greater display of power?—is available to the believer in Christ, both in time and in eternity. What God does in transforming human lives in this world and what He does in giving them eternal life in the next world are both examples of His mighty power.

1:20–23 JESUS CHRIST, Ascension—Jesus' resurrection and ascension revealed God's unsurpassed power and established Jesus as supreme ruler over all heavenly and earthly powers for eternity.

1:21 LAST THINGS, Age to Come—Believers participate in two ages, the present age and the one to come. See note on Mt 12:32. The exalted authority of Christ spans both ages. He brings the powers of the age to come into the present age.

1:22–23 THE CHURCH, Body of Christ—The church exists because of Jesus Christ, the risen Lord ruling in the heavens (v 20). Using the imagery of the body, Christ is the head which directs the actions of all other parts of the body. The church is connected directly to its Head and, thus, represents Christ's presence in the world. See notes on Ro 12:4–8; 1 Co 12:12–31.

2:1–10 HUMANITY, Spiritual Nature—Sin brings death. Paul called many people who were physically alive dead because sin and Satan ruled their lives. Following natural desires of the flesh brings God's wrath on us. God gives us an option—the way of His love and grace. We can know the true quality life—eternal life—God intended us to have. This life provided

my insight[k] into the mystery of Christ,
5which was not made known to men in
other generations as it has now been revealed by the Spirit to God's holy apostles
and prophets.[l] 6This mystery is that
through the gospel the Gentiles are
heirs[m] together with Israel, members together of one body,[n] and sharers together in the promise in Christ Jesus.[o]
7I became a servant of this gospel[p] by
the gift of God's grace given me[q] through
the working of his power.[r] 8Although I
am less than the least of all God's people,[s] this grace was given me: to preach
to the Gentiles[t] the unsearchable riches
of Christ,[u] 9and to make plain to everyone the administration of this mystery,[v]
which for ages past was kept hidden in
God, who created all things. 10His intent
was that now, through the church, the
manifold wisdom of God[w] should be
made known[x] to the rulers and authorities[y] in the heavenly realms,[z] 11accord-
ing to his eternal purpose[a] which he accomplished in Christ Jesus our Lord. 12In
him and through faith in him we may approach God[b] with freedom and confidence.[c] 13I ask you, therefore, not to be
discouraged because of my sufferings for
you, which are your glory.

A Prayer for the Ephesians

14For this reason I kneel[d] before the
Father, 15from whom his whole family[h]
in heaven and on earth derives its name.
16I pray that out of his glorious riches[e] he
may strengthen you with power[f]
through his Spirit in your inner being,[g]
17so that Christ may dwell in your
hearts[h] through faith. And I pray that
you, being rooted[i] and established in
love, 18may have power, together with all

3:4 [k]2Co 11:6
3:5 [l]Ro 16:26; S Eph 4:11
3:6 [m]S Ro 8:17 [n]Eph 2:15,16 [o]Eze 47:22
3:7 [p]S 1Co 3:5 [q]S Ro 12:3 [r]Eph 1:19; Col 1:29
3:8 [s]S 1Co 15:9 [t]S Ac 9:15 [u]S Ro 2:4
3:9 [v]S Ro 16:25
3:10 [w]S Ro 11:33; 1Co 2:7 [x]1Pe 1:12 [y]Eph 1:21; 6:12; Col 2:10,15 [z]S Eph 1:3
3:11 [a]S Eph 1:11
3:12 [b]Eph 2:18 [c]2Co 3:4; Heb 3:14; 4:16; 10:19,35; 1Jn 2:28; 3:21; 4:17
3:14 [d]Php 2:10
3:16 [e]ver 8; S Ro 2:4 [f]S Php 4:13 [g]Ro 7:22
3:17 [h]S Ro 8:10 [i]Col 2:7

[h] *15* Or *whom all fatherhood*

non-Israelites into God's people. Paul did not claim a monopoly on such revelation. Apostles and other preachers also received it. Revelation came at God's time to people God chose to accomplish God's eternal purposes.

3:5 HISTORY, Knowledge—Knowledge of God did not come all at once. God worked through history to reveal His will as people were prepared to accept it. Before Christ's birth, God worked in many ways to prepare His people to know and follow Christ. He gave the apostles special understanding of His history with His people so they could understand Christ's work in light of all God's history of salvation.

3:5 CHURCH LEADERS, Prophet—Prophets are closely associated with apostles. See 2:20; 4:11. Prophets and apostles received and made known the mysteries of God, that is the gospel of Christ which made salvation available to all people, not just Jews. The authority of the prophet resides in the revelation received through the Spirit. The gift of prophecy belongs to the church as a whole (Ac 2) but manifests itself in certain individuals. Potentially, then, every Christian can be a prophet; but, like apostles, prophets are not selected by the church. They are selected by the Spirit who inspires them with a message for His people.

3:6 THE CHURCH, Body of Christ—The church unites all believers from all races and locations in a common ministry in Christ and a common hope for Christ's return. The inclusion of Gentiles in God's purposes remained mysteriously unclear under the old covenant. It became clear in Christ. See notes on Ro 12:4–8; 1 Co 12:12–31; Eph 1:22–23.

3:6 EVANGELISM, Results—Paul often speaks of the "mystery" of redemption. The "mystery" is that God is calling out the Gentiles and making them heirs with Israel, molding them into one body in Jesus Christ. In this way God is building the kingdom. This was seen as a mystery because neither the Jews nor Gentiles realized before Christ came all God had in store for the entirety of humanity. Now the mystery is revealed (Col 1:26). All peoples can come to Christ. That is the result of God's great redemptive work in Christ. We should urge all to receive Him as Lord and Savior.

3:6 MISSIONS, Scope—In a lyric manner, Ephesians speaks in cosmic terms—Christ as Lord of the whole universe (1:20–22). Equally, the letter speaks to God's purpose for the world, of His love plan, and of His selecting of persons to be channels of His grace to the world (1:4–11). This wonderful cosmic work of God is a mystery. "Mystery" does not mean a continuing puzzle. It means that which was hidden but has now been revealed. The curtain has been drawn back and the wonderful treasure exposed. The mystery is that God receives persons from every race, tribe, color, and language who come to Him through Christ Jesus. Those who trust Christ become heirs together with Israel of the promises of God. Both the Jews and the nations must come to God not through the law, but by faith in Jesus Christ (2:16). The impact of this doctrine is incalculable because it means that from all eternity God has loved the peoples of the world and has planned to send His Son that believing they might become His people. This building of the family of God out of former enemies shows Christ's ability to bring His peace and reconciliation (2:14).

3:7,20 GOD, Power—God's power is clearly demonstrated in what He does in saving and transforming sinners. The same mighty power which created the universe and brought Jesus back from the dead, also operates in us who are believers, making us witnesses to His gospel. See note on 1:19–20.

3:7 THE CHURCH, Servants—The Greek word for servant in this passage is *diakonos*, the term from which we get the word deacon. Here, the word implies a function rather than an office. Paul affirmed his service to Christ as a minister or servant of Christ, a service which God granted by His grace. Rather than laborious servitude, ministry for Christ brings joyful freedom. Every Christian should be a servant of Christ. Ministry is not confined to certain officers of the church but is commanded for every believer.

3:8–13 ELECTION, God's Purpose—God accomplished His eternal purpose in and through Jesus Christ. God's continuing intention is that the church should unveil to the world His manifold wisdom and matchless love. This is to be done through the preaching of the unsearchable riches of Jesus Christ. Election in Christ makes it possible for us to enter God's presence in confidence. He will accept us.

3:8–11 THE CHURCH, People of God—God's purpose is that all people may know Him. God has given the church the task of proclaiming the good news of Jesus to all the world. All the people of God must involve themselves in this great work. The church here refers to all believers not to the local congregation.

3:8–9 PROCLAMATION, Call—See notes on Jer 1:4–9; 1 Co 2:1–5.

3:8 EVANGELISM, Call to Evangelize—Paul always reveled in his call to reach the lost for Christ. In principle, that call comes to every believer. We thus should revel in the fact we can share the gospel and help others to our Lord. We are not worthy; it all comes through grace.

3:8 MISSIONS, Scope—Ephesians is a missionary letter to Christians in Ephesus and surrounding regions. Paul gloried in the fact that he was an apostle to the Gentiles. His message to the Gentiles or the nations was to be the "unsearchable riches of Christ." Paul's mission was to reveal to all people that the way to God was open to all peoples in Christ Jesus. Once Paul knew that the gospel was meant for all peoples, he was driven

the saints,[j] to grasp how wide and long
and high and deep[k] is the love of Christ,
19and to know this love that surpasses
knowledge[l]—that you may be filled[m] to
the measure of all the fullness of God.[n]
20Now to him who is able[o] to do immeasurably more than all we ask[p] or
imagine, according to his power[q] that is
at work within us, 21to him be glory in
the church and in Christ Jesus throughout all generations, for ever and ever!
Amen.[r]

Chapter 4

Unity in the Body of Christ

As a prisoner[s] for the Lord, then, I urge
you to live a life worthy[t] of the calling[u] you have received. 2Be completely
humble and gentle; be patient, bearing
with one another[v] in love.[w] 3Make every
effort to keep the unity[x] of the Spirit
through the bond of peace.[y] 4There is
one body[z] and one Spirit[a]— just as you
were called to one hope when you were
called[b]— 5one Lord,[c] one faith, one
baptism; 6one God and Father of all,[d]
who is over all and through all and in
all.[e]
7But to each one of us[f] grace[g] has
been given[h] as Christ apportioned it.
8This is why it[i] says:

"When he ascended on high,
he led captives[i] in his train
and gave gifts to men."[j] [j]

9(What does "he ascended" mean except
that he also descended to the lower,
earthly regions[k]? 10He who descended is
the very one who ascended[k] higher than
all the heavens, in order to fill the whole

[i]8 Or *God* [j]8 Psalm 68:18 [k]9 Or *the depths of the earth*

3:18 [j]Eph 1:15 [k]Job 11:8,9; Ps 103:11
3:19 [l]Php 4:7 [m]Col 2:10 [n]Eph 1:23
3:20 [o]Ro 16:25; 2Co 9:8 [p]1Ki 3:13 [q]ver 7
3:21 [r]S Ro 11:36
4:1 [s]S Eph 3:1 [t]Php 1:27; Col 1:10; 1Th 2:12 [u]S Ro 8:28
4:2 [v]Col 3:12,13 [w]ver 15,16; Eph 1:4
4:3 [x]S Ro 15:5 [y]Col 3:15
4:4 [z]S Ro 12:5 [a]1Co 12:13; Eph 2:18 [b]S Ro 8:28
4:5 [c]1Co 8:6
4:6 [d]Dt 6:4; Zec 14:9 [e]S Ro 11:36
4:7 [f]1Co 12:7,11 [g]S Ro 3:24 [h]S Ro 12:3
4:8 [i]Col 2:15 [j]Ps 68:18
4:10 [k]Pr 30:1-4

---

to share it. Since as Christians today we understand both that the gospel is for all peoples and that two-thirds of our world does not even claim to follow Jesus, we find a tremendous impetus to reach from our home community to the ends of the earth with the good news of Jesus.

3:11–12 JESUS CHRIST, Mission—God's long history with Israel was not a failure. God accomplished His eternal purpose of reuniting creation under His rule. Jesus' ministry, death, and resurrection assured that even the evil spiritual powers that appear to dominate the world would recognize His right to rule the universe. In so doing Christ gives every person freedom to approach God.

3:12 SALVATION, Human Freedom—All persons may confidently and freely approach God through Christ. We do not have to pass any human requirements.

3:12 PRAYER, In Christ—See notes on 2:18; Heb 4:15–16. Prayer is done in freedom and confidence because we are in Christ.

3:14–19 HOLY SPIRIT, Revelation—The Spirit gives revelation so we may have power to understand and act. Paul prayed that the Ephesians would be given power, not power to act but power to understand the extent of God's love. Only the Spirit could reveal this. That limitless and gracious love is revealed ultimately in Jesus and His sacrifice. The Spirit always works to help the church remember Jesus and His gospel (see note on Jn 14:26), appreciate the love of God demonstrated at the cross (Ro 5:8), and understand the purpose of God being carried out there. See note on Eph 3:2–6. When we begin to comprehend this love, the Spirit gives us power to act in this love.

3:14–19 PRAYER, Intercession—See note on 1:15–19. Paul prayed for knowledge on a scale too great for human words. He asked that they know that which surpasses knowledge. The result of that knowledge will be the experience of the fullness of God. Prayer knows no limits in the spiritual blessings desired for others. Such blessings come through the trinitarian God—the Spirit in your inner being, Christ in your heart, filled with God's fullness.

3:16 DISCIPLESHIP, Enabling Power—Inner moral power is necessary for obedient discipleship. The Holy Spirit provides the dynamic power we need for living victoriously. See Gal 5:16; note on 1 Pe 4:11.

3:18–19 JESUS CHRIST, Love—Jesus loves us more than we can ever know and wants us to progress in understanding His love and in loving as He loved.

3:20–21 GOD, Glory—One purpose of the church is to praise God, ascribing magnificence and glory to Him for what He did in Christ. See note on Ro 3:23.

3:20–21 PRAYER, Praise—See note on Ro 16:25–27. The human mind cannot grasp all that God can do. It is immeasurable, yet He works in and through us.

4:1–6 GOD, One God—These verses make the strongest possible declaration of and call for the unity of Christians, the unity of the church, and the unity of the work of the Holy Spirit among us. Lord in verse 5 probably refers to Christ—our Savior. All of this unity flows out from the oneness of God, the one and only true God. The one Father is Father of all, over all. The stress is on the universal nature and authority of God the Father. See notes on Mt 3:16–17; 5:43–48.

4:1–7 ELECTION, Responsibility—Election is a calling to live up to, not a possession to cherish. Election calls the church to unity and cooperative ministry with the gifts given each member.

4:1–3 CHRISTIAN ETHICS, Character—The call to serve Christ is a high honor. It should bring humility and devotion. Devotion to Christ expresses itself in loving behavior. Only such behavior shows we are worthy of the high calling.

4:1–6 THE CHURCH, Body of Christ—As God is One so is the church. To serve Christ the church must maintain its unity. Each member must serve in gentle, humble love, seeking peace and unity with every other member. The one Spirit in our lives leads us to be one church, not a church with divisions and splits. The one hope in Christ is greater reason for unity than any disagreements which might separate us. Our commitment to the one Lord and His church made in baptism should lead to unity despite all temptations to divide. See notes on 1:22–23; Ro 12:4–8; 1 Co 12:12–31.

4:3–6 HOLY SPIRIT, Fellowship—God's purpose is to create a great family of free persons to be His own people. When people trust Christ as their Savior, God pours His Spirit into their hearts. The Spirit incorporates us into the common life of the Christian community. Christians should live with humility, patience, and especially love, so that the common life of the community will not be broken. Jesus had prayed that His followers would be as united with each other as He was with the Father (Jn 17:20–23). See note on 2 Co 13:14.

4:5 ORDINANCES, Baptism as Unity—Baptism emphasizes the unity of Christian believers because they are baptized into one body, through one Spirit, by one faith, in the one Lord Jesus Christ. Baptism does not guarantee this unity, but baptism signifies this unity in the one Lord. That is why Paul exhorted the Ephesians to "keep the unity of the Spirit through the bond of peace" (v 3). If we do not keep the unity of the Spirit with our fellow believers in the body of Christ, we are contradicting what we confessed in our baptism. See note on Gal 3:27.

4:6 GOD, Sovereignty—God is superior to and has power

universe.)[l] 11It was he who gave[m] some
to be apostles,[n] some to be prophets,[o]
some to be evangelists,[p] and some to be
pastors and teachers,[q] 12to prepare God's
people for works of service, so that the
body of Christ[r] may be built up[s] 13until
we all reach unity[t] in the faith and in the
knowledge of the Son of God[u] and become mature,[v] attaining to the whole
measure of the fullness of Christ.[w]
14Then we will no longer be infants,[x]
tossed back and forth by the waves,[y] and
blown here and there by every wind of
teaching and by the cunning and craftiness of men in their deceitful scheming.[z]
15Instead, speaking the truth in love,[a] we
will in all things grow up into him who is
the Head,[b] that is, Christ. 16From him
the whole body, joined and held together
by every supporting ligament, grows[c]
and builds itself up[d] in love,[e] as each
part does its work.

4:10 [l]Eph 1:23
4:11 [m]ver 8
[n]1Co 12:28; Eph 2:20; 3:5; 2Pe 3:2; Jude 17
[o]S Ac 11:27; Ro 12:6; 1Co 12:10,28; 13:2,8; 14:1,39; Eph 2:20; 3:5; 2Pe 3:2 [p]Ac 21:8; 2Ti 4:5 [q]Ac 13:1; Ro 2:21; 12:7; 1Co 12:28; 14:26; 1Ti 1:7; Jas 3:1
4:12 [r]S 1Co 12:27 [s]S Ro 14:19
4:13 [t]ver 3,5 [u]S Php 3:8 [v]S 1Co 2:6; Col 1:28 [w]Jn 1:16; Eph 1:23; 3:19
4:14 [x]S 1Co 14:20 [y]Isa 57:20; Jas 1:6 [z]Eph 6:11
4:15 [a]ver 2,16; Eph 1:4 [b]S Eph 1:22
4:16 [c]Col 2:19 [d]1Co 12:7 [e]ver 2, 15; Eph 1:4
4:17 [f]Eph 2:2 [g]Ro 1:21

Living as Children of Light

17So I tell you this, and insist on it in
the Lord, that you must no longer[f] live as
the Gentiles do, in the futility of their
thinking.[g] 18They are darkened in their
understanding[h] and separated from the
life of God[i] because of the ignorance that
is in them due to the hardening of their
hearts.[j] 19Having lost all sensitivity,[k]
they have given themselves over[l] to sensuality[m] so as to indulge in every kind of
impurity, with a continual lust for more.
20You, however, did not come to know
Christ that way. 21Surely you heard of
him and were taught in him in accordance with the truth that is in Jesus.
22You were taught, with regard to your
former way of life, to put off[n] your old
self,[o] which is being corrupted by its de-

4:18 [h]Dt 29:4; Ro 1:21 [i]Eph 2:12 [j]2Co 3:14 4:19 [k]1Ti 4:2 [l]Ro 1:24 [m]Col 3:5; 1Pe 4:3 4:22 [n]ver 25,31; Col 3:5,8,9; Jas 1:21; 1Pe 2:1 [o]S Ro 6:6

---

and authority over all persons and things in the universe.

4:7–12 JESUS CHRIST, Ascension—The ascended Lord did not forget the people He left behind. He sent the Spirit with gifts to equip His church for ministry. Jesus is the one who came from heaven to earth, ascended back to heaven with the resurrection victory capturing all evil powers, and then sent the Spirit back to earth.

4:11–16 SALVATION, Sanctification—Salvation as sanctification is growth toward maturity by the measure of the fully grown Christ. God does not want us to remain childish and immature in our faith. His gifts to the church are intended to help His body grow internally and in missionary outreach.

4:11–16 THE CHURCH, Body of Christ—See notes on 1:22–23; Ro 12:4–8; 1 Co 12:12–31. Christ gives gifts to His church for a purpose—to equip believers to do the work of ministry and by so doing to build up the church. Every Christian is called to do the work of ministry and to build up the body of Christ. The goal of Christ is that such equipping, ministering, and building up will go on until complete maturity is achieved. Every Christian has the responsibility to help every other member of the body of Christ to grow in faith. Maturity leads a Christian to be discerning in what to believe as true. Teachers with wrong motives should not deceive mature Christians. The church grows spiritually and numerically when each part of the body lives under Christ's control.

4:11–13 WORSHIP, Priesthood—The New Testament teaches that God ordained leaders in the church. Their purpose is to equip each individual believer to be a priest. See note on 1 Ch 6:48–49. This great doctrine of the priesthood of the believer means that every individual Christian has direct access to God through Christ, the one Mediator between God and us (1 Ti 2:5). We need no human mediator between us and God. Jesus Christ gives us direct access to God (Heb 4:14–16).

4:11–12 CHURCH LEADERS, Authority—God's gifts to the church are persons, not formal offices. God is concerned about ordering the church but not about establishing orders of ministry. These persons have been given the ability to fulfill a variety of duties that enable the church to be and do what God intended it to be and do. Together they function to guide the church in faith, knowledge, and truth, and to preserve it from being swept away by error or by division. These leaders are not given to the church to do everything. The church member would then simply become a consumer of the leaders' spiritual gifts. Leaders are given to the church to equip the members so that all might do the work of ministry together and so build up the body of Christ. All Christians do not have the same calling or function, but all Christians have the same responsibility to be ministers (Ro 15:27; Phm 13). The persons who perform the duties of the listed offices function as equippers who prepare the rest of the members for their work for Christ. All Christians are called to use their own gifts in ministry.

4:11 CHURCH LEADERS, Teacher—Teachers build up the life and thought of the church by interpreting the revelation in Jesus Christ and applying it to daily life. They are to teach all things whatsoever Christ commanded (Mt 28:20). They give instruction in doctrine and required moral standards for believers.

4:11–16 EDUCATION, Pastors—Christ has given a variety of ministers of the Word to the church for the purpose of preparing God's people for service, building up the body of Christ, and fostering spiritual maturity in the members. Among these "gifts" are pastor-teachers. (Many interpreters agree that "pastors" and "teachers" refer to the same persons, since the two words share a common article in Greek.) Contemporary Christians tend to lose sight of the pastor's teaching function. For example, pastors are often called "preacher" but rarely "teacher." The educational function of the pastor remains an indispensable part of Christ's design for His church.

4:11–16 EVANGELISM, Involves—All God's people have spiritual gifts. God gives His gifted people as His gift to the church so the work of the church—the ministry—can be carried on. This implies that we need to discover our ministry gift, develop our gift, and use our gift in ministry and service as God enables us and leads us. This is the key to effective Christian service and evangelization. Ministry and witness go hand in hand. The ultimate goal of evangelism is to develop mature Christians, not simply to multiply spiritual infants. See Guide to Discovering Your Spiritual Gifts, pp. 1796–1799.

4:13 LAST THINGS, Humanity Restored—Christ exhibits in His person the divine intention for human beings. In God's new creation we will be made into the likeness of Christ. That will be the glory of redeemed humanity. The restoration to the image of God involves both a present process and a future accomplishment (1 Jn 3:2).

4:15 JESUS CHRIST, Lord—The ascended Christ is the Head of the church and the mature Example for all Christians to imitate. See note on 1:3.

4:15,25,29–31 FAMILY, Communication—Even though addressed to the church as the family of God, these verses apply equally well to family relationships in the home. Honesty and helpfulness are encouraged, whereas lying, slander, and rage are condemned. See note on Col 3:8–10. The word structure in v 30 suggests that unwholesome language grieves the Holy Spirit, who is present in the church or home at all times.

4:17–19 SIN, Depravity—Living apart from grace blinds one to the nature and will of God. Human reason can defend any life-style because sin controls reason. Sin hardens our

ceitful desires; [p] 23 to be made new in the
attitude of your minds; [q] 24 and to put on [r]
the new self, [s] created to be like God in
true righteousness and holiness. [t]

25 Therefore each of you must put off
falsehood and speak truthfully [u] to his
neighbor, for we are all members of one
body. [v] 26 "In your anger do not sin"[1] : [w]
Do not let the sun go down while you are
still angry, 27 and do not give the devil a
foothold. [x] 28 He who has been stealing
must steal no longer, but must work, [y]
doing something useful with his own
hands, [z] that he may have something to
share with those in need. [a]

29 Do not let any unwholesome talk
come out of your mouths, [b] but only what
is helpful for building others up [c] according to their needs, that it may benefit
those who listen. 30 And do not grieve the
Holy Spirit of God, [d] with whom you
were sealed [e] for the day of redemption. [f]
31 Get rid of [g] all bitterness, rage and anger, brawling and slander, along with every form of malice. [h] 32 Be kind and compassionate to one another, [i] forgiving
each other, just as in Christ God forgave
you. [j]

Chapter 5

BE imitators of God, [k] therefore, as
dearly loved children [l] 2 and live a life
of love, just as Christ loved us [m] and gave
himself up for us [n] as a fragrant offering
and sacrifice to God. [o]

3 But among you there must not be
even a hint of sexual immorality, [p] or of
any kind of impurity, or of greed, [q] because these are improper for God's holy
people. 4 Nor should there be obscenity,
foolish talk [r] or coarse joking, which are

4:22 [p]Jer 17:9; Heb 3:13 **4:23** [q]Ro 12:2; Col 3:10 **4:24** [r]S Ro 13:14 [s]S Ro 6:4 [t]Eph 2:10 **4:25** [u]Ps 15:2; Lev 19:11; Zec 8:16; Col 3:9 [v]S Ro 12:5 **4:26** [w]Ps 4:4; S Mt 5:22 **4:27** [x]2Co 2:10,11 **4:28** [y]Ac 20:35 [z]1Th 4:11 [a]Gal 6:10 **4:29** [b]Mt 12:36; Eph 5:4; Col 3:8 [c]S Ro 14:19 **4:30** [d]Isa 63:10; 1Th 5:19 [e]2Co 1:22; 5:5; Eph 1:13 [f]Ro 8:23 **4:31** [g]S ver 22 [h]Col 3:8; 1Pe 2:1 **4:32** [i]1Pe 3:8 [j]Mt 6:14,15; Col 3:12,13 **5:1** [k]Mt 5:48; Lk 6:36 [l]S Jn 1:12 **5:2** [m]S Jn 13:34 [n]ver 25; S Gal 1:4; 2:20 [o]Heb 7:27

5:3 [p]S 1Co 6:18 [q]Col 3:5 **5:4** [r]Eph 4:29

[1] *26* Psalm 4:4

---

intellectual capacities and leads us away from the life God wants us to live. Sin gives us a consuming desire to do what is wrong. By letting human intellect control our lives, we ignore grace and choose a life that may lead to depravity.

4:17–32 CHRISTIAN ETHICS, Character—Paul contrasted the way of the Gentiles and that of Christians as the difference of darkness and light. He put particular emphasis on the change of attitudes caused by the indwelling of Christ. Christ in us evokes changed actions, particularly verbal ones noted here. Rather than giving vent to our natural drives when confronted by opposing parties, Paul says to begin and to continue relationships from a position of forgiveness. Such an approach more nearly assures smoothness and longevity of relationships.

4:20 SALVATION, Knowledge of God—The Christ whom believers know teaches them to put off the old self of sin which characterized their former life.

4:22–24 FAMILY, New Selfhood—See note on Ro 5:12–21.

4:24 CHRISTIAN ETHICS, Justice—Note the active choice of putting on righteousness. Typical of Paul's imperative style, he commanded those who know a higher ethical level of living to choose it and to live it out. The product of evangelism is a new person in right standing with God who lives the life of righteousness and reflects God's holiness. See notes on Lev 19:1–18; Ro 10:1–11.

4:25,29 CHRISTIAN ETHICS, Language—Lying has no place among God's people. Neither does nagging criticism that seeks to divide God's church. Words that do not strengthen church fellowship should never be uttered. See note on Col 4:6.

4:25 THE CHURCH, Body of Christ—Christian unity in Christ's body develops as we trust one another with the truth rather than trying to compliment, appease, flatter, or fool one another. The love of Christ leads us to love and trust one another, seeking to mature together in Christ. See note on vv 11–16.

4:26–27 FAMILY, Conflict Resolution—Anger is a response to disappointment, frustration, blocked plans, or personal putdowns that happen from time to time in most Christian homes. Anger can either be buried inside oneself or expressed in attacking the one toward whom anger is directed. Neither of these approaches is a Christian way of handling anger. The positive approach is to resolve anger so that it will not build up to an explosion or poison the inner being by becoming resentment. Thus, Paul advised Christians to recognize their anger, deal with the issues that cause it, and resolve it before going to bed. When anger is internalized and stored up, it becomes resentment which gives opportunity for the devil to work in one's heart. Prayer to God and open communication with other people help us resolve anger.

4:28 HUMANITY, Work—God's grace incorporates even thieves into His church. Thieves seek to gain financial resources without working. God calls them to do honorable work and use the proceeds to help the needy. Human work is not simply a way to gain personal riches. It is a way to help the community as a whole, including the poor.

4:28 DISCIPLESHIP, God's Purposes—Disciples ought not to be lazy or dishonest. We work hard to earn a living and to have resources to help those who cannot earn a living. In this way our work serves God's purposes.

4:28 CHRISTIAN ETHICS, Property Rights—The Christian calling includes the imperative of seeking honest ways of making a living. The goals in our work are to project a witness for Christ as well as to share of one's earnings with those who have little of this world's material goods. Stealing is wrong, but the thief can be forgiven and restored. See note on Ex 20:15.

4:29–32 SIN, Against God—Sin aimed at other people—criticism, slander, anger—grieves God's Spirit and so is sin against God. Since the Spirit lives in us, our actions which are not under His control bring anguish to Him.

4:30 HOLY SPIRIT, Personal—The Bible uses various kinds of language to speak about the mysterious Spirit of God. Some of that language is nonpersonal. The Spirit is like a wind which blows (Jn 3:8) or like water which is poured out (Ac 2:33). The language of the Spirit is usually very personal. Christians are not to grieve the Spirit. The Spirit is a Person who is sensitive and is hurt by the immoral behavior of those in whose hearts He lives (Isa 63:10). When Paul said not to quench the Spirit (1 Th 5:19), the language is nonpersonal (the Spirit is like a fire); but it should be interpreted as personal. It means the same thing as not grieving the Spirit. Not to grieve the Spirit and not to quench the Spirit both refer to commitment to the way of life into which the Spirit leads the church. The church should be in communion (see note on 2 Co 13:14) with the Spirit, personally responsive to His leadership. We should make a free personal, moral response to the personal Spirit of God. He is with us and is grieved when we sin. On the seal of the Spirit, see note on Eph 1:13–14.

4:30 SALVATION, Redemption—Compare 1:13. The Holy Spirit is the seal of redemption. Seals were used in the ancient world to designate possession by an owner. Brands and tattoos were used to denote ownership of cattle and slaves. Christians, in similar fashion, are marked by the Spirit. He is the sign that persons belong to Christ. The seal of the Spirit is the basis for Christian assurance now and in the future (2 Ti 2:19). The cross and resurrection completed God's act of redemption. Only the second coming and day of resurrection

out of place, but rather thanksgiving.[s]
5For of this you can be sure: No immoral,
impure or greedy person—such a man is
an idolater[t]—has any inheritance[u] in
the kingdom of Christ and of God.[m v] 6Let
no one deceive you[w] with empty words,
for because of such things God's wrath[x]
comes on those who are disobedient.[y]
7Therefore do not be partners with them.
8For you were once[z] darkness, but
now you are light in the Lord. Live as
children of light[a] 9(for the fruit[b] of the
light consists in all goodness,[c] righteousness and truth) 10and find out what
pleases the Lord.[d] 11Have nothing to do
with the fruitless deeds of darkness,[e] but
rather expose them. 12For it is shameful
even to mention what the disobedient do
in secret. 13But everything exposed by
the light[f] becomes visible, 14for it is light
that makes everything visible. This is
why it is said:

"Wake up, O sleeper,[g]
rise from the dead,[h]
and Christ will shine on you."[i]

15Be very careful, then, how you live[j]
—not as unwise but as wise, 16making
the most of every opportunity,[k] because
the days are evil.[l] 17Therefore do not be
foolish, but understand what the Lord's
will is.[m] 18Do not get drunk on wine,[n]
which leads to debauchery. Instead, be
filled with the Spirit.[o] 19Speak to one another with psalms, hymns and spiritual
songs.[p] Sing and make music in your
heart to the Lord, 20always giving
thanks[q] to God the Father for everything,
in the name of our Lord Jesus Christ.
21Submit to one another[r] out of reverence for Christ.

5:4 [s]S ver 20 **5:5** [t]Col 3:5 [u]S Ac 20:32 [v]S Mt 25:34 **5:6** [w]S Mk 13:5 [x]S Ro 1:18 [y]Eph 2:2 **5:8** [z]S Eph 2:2 [a]Jn 8:12; S Lk 16:8; S Ac 26:18 **5:9** [b]Mt 7:16-20; Gal 5:22 [c]Ro 15:14 **5:10** [d]S 1Ti 5:4 **5:11** [e]Ro 13:12; 2Co 6:14 **5:13** [f]Jn 3:20,21 **5:14** [g]Ro 13:11 [h]Isa 26:19; Jn 5:25 [i]Isa 60:1; Mal 4:2 **5:15** [j]ver 2 **5:16** [k]Col 4:5 [l]Eph 6:13 **5:17** [m]Ro 12:2; Col 1:9; 1Th 4:3 **5:18** [n]Lev 10:9; Pr 20:1; Isa 28:7; Ro 13:13 [o]S Lk 1:15 **5:19** [p]Ps 27:6; 95:2; Ac 16:25; 1Co 14:15,26; Col 3:16 **5:20** [q]ver 4; Job 1:21; Ps 34:1; Col 3:17; Heb 13:15 **5:21** [r]Gal 5:13; 1Pe 5:5

[m]5 Or *kingdom of the Christ and God*

will complete our experience of redemption.

4:30 LAST THINGS, Salvation's Completion—The day of redemption is the future time of salvation's completion. The Spirit's indwelling is the seal or guarantee to believers of such a day. See note on 1:14.

4:32 GOD, Grace—The forgiving grace of God which we have received puts us under obligation to treat others just as God has treated us. Grace has not truly done its work in us until we respond in grace to others about us.

4:32 SALVATION, Forgiveness—Christians are to forgive each other as God in Christ has forgiven them. See note on Mt 18:21–35. Compare Col 3:13.

5:1–2 GOD, Love—God's purpose in creation and salvation is to lead a people to imitate His life in ours. We should live in the same pure, self-giving manner that God does, practicing a totally self-sacrificing love for one another. We learn this love from Christ's example on the cross.

5:1–21 CHRISTIAN ETHICS, Character—The Christian should present a life-style to the world which projects a stark contrast to the world's ways. A life that exhibits thanksgiving and peace is desired. An inclination to find and share the truth, as opposed to the world's ways which lead to darkness of mind and soul, is a natural part of the Christian's way. Finally, an important overarching principle for interpersonal relationships is that of mutual submission. This ideal runs throughout the New Testament. Inherent in this idea are the virtues of humility, forgiveness, and servanthood.

5:2 JESUS CHRIST, Love—Christ's love is our example, a love which led Him to sacrifice His life for us on the cross.

5:2,25–27 SALVATION, Atonement—Christ sacrificed Himself for the church because He loves her and wants to make her holy and blameless. Believing husbands and wives and all Christians are to love each other with the same kind of sacrifical love.

5:4 CHRISTIAN ETHICS, Language—Language and speech are good gifts of God. Rather than foolish use of these gifts or using our speech to injure others, Christians are admonished to use their speech as a means of communicating their gratitude to God for His gifts of life to us. We never have reason to use obscene language or jokes. We must find better ways to satisfy our ego needs for importance. Being righteous is much more important than being coarsely funny.

5:4 PRAYER, Thanksgiving—Christians should consider carefully the content of their talk. Thanksgiving credits God and is a proper topic for conversation.

5:5 GOD, Wrath—God stands totally opposed to sin. His willingness to forgive sin does not at all mean His laxity towards those who practice sinning. His forgiveness only follows our repentance, our turning from the practice of sin. If we do not turn from our sins, we will face God's wrath. No trickery with words by any preacher or teacher can change that.

5:17–20 WORSHIP, Community—See note on 1 Ch 16:4. Instructions and descriptions of worship in the New Testament are few and vague. Simplicity is the best word to describe early church worship services. Those services featured praise, thanksgiving, singing, prayer, Scripture reading, exposition, instruction in Christ's teaching, the Lord's Supper, and fellowship. Compare Ac 2:42–47; Col 3:16.

5:18–20 HOLY SPIRIT, Fills—See note on Ac 6:1–6. The present passage is unique in calling for people to cooperate with the Spirit to be filled. Paul addressed the entire community, not merely individuals. The command is plural. The filling of the Spirit is contrasted with drunkenness (Ac 2:13). Both wine and the Spirit do their work deep in the human psyche. They affect people below the level of consciousness, down at the foundations of personality. The Spirit is not merely with God's people but in them. The meaning of the present text is: let all the church, therefore, cooperate with the Spirit who lives down deep in their hearts so they will spontaneously overflow with orderly and joyous worship of God.

5:18 CHRISTIAN ETHICS, Alcohol—A recurring theme for Paul was to avoid drunkenness, for all sorts of other evils could follow. Rather than being deceived about being euphoric through wine, Paul exhorts us to know true euphoria through a life fulfilled by the Holy Spirit. See note on 1 Sa 1:14–15.

5:19–20 WORSHIP, Music—Music played a strong role in the worship of the early church. Praise and thanksgiving were expressed through music. The early church learned to worship God with thanksgiving for everything. A grateful heart is necessary for worship. See notes on Ex 15:1–21; 1 Ch 6:31–32; 16:4.

5:19–20 PRAYER, Thanksgiving—Not all prayer is spoken; singing is a high communication to the Lord and should be done from the heart. V 20 is the first of two Pauline injunctions to thank God in all things. See note on 1 Th 5:17–18.

5:21 FAMILY, Role Relationships—Mutual submission based upon shared reverence for Christ as Lord is one of three evidences of the Spirit-filled life (vv 18–21). The others are joyful singing (v 19) and thanksgiving for God's blessings (v 20). The theme of mutual submission introduced Paul's discussion both of family and master-slave relationships. Christians in Ephesus were concerned how Christians were to deal with authority in these social institutions. Paul's position was that authentic faith in Christ will enable believers to be in submission to one another even though social custom expected submission only of women, children, and slaves.

Wives and Husbands

5:22–6:9pp — Col 3:18–4:1

22 Wives, submit to your husbands[s] as
to the Lord.[t] 23 For the husband is the
head of the wife as Christ is the head of
the church,[u] his body, of which he is the
Savior. 24 Now as the church submits to
Christ, so also wives should submit to
their husbands[v] in everything.
25 Husbands, love your wives,[w] just as
Christ loved the church and gave himself
up for her[x] 26 to make her holy,[y] cleansing[n] her by the washing[z] with water
through the word, 27 and to present her to
himself[a] as a radiant church, without
stain or wrinkle or any other blemish, but
holy and blameless.[b] 28 In this same way,
husbands ought to love their wives[c] as
their own bodies. He who loves his wife
loves himself. 29 After all, no one ever hated his own body, but he feeds and cares
for it, just as Christ does the church—
30 for we are members of his body.[d]
31 "For this reason a man will leave his
father and mother and be united to his
wife, and the two will become one
flesh."[o][e] 32 This is a profound mystery
—but I am talking about Christ and the
church. 33 However, each one of you also
must love his wife[f] as he loves himself,
and the wife must respect her husband.

5:22 [s]Ge 3:16; 1Co 14:34; Col 3:18; 1Ti 2:12; Tit 2:5; 1Pe 3:1,5,6 [t]Eph 6:5
5:23 [u]S Eph 1:22
5:24 [v]S ver 22
5:25 [w]ver 28,33; Col 3:19 [x]S ver 2
5:26 [y]Jn 17:19; Heb 2:11; 10:10, 14; 13:12 [z]S Ac 22:16
5:27 [a]S 2Co 4:14 [b]Eph 1:4
5:28 [c]ver 25
5:30 [d]S Ro 12:5; S 1Co 12:27
5:31 [e]Ge 2:24; Mt 19:5; 1Co 6:16
5:33 [f]ver 25
6:1 [g]Pr 6:20; Col 3:20
6:3 [h]Ex 20:12; Dt 5:16
6:4 [i]Col 3:21 [j]Ge 18:19; Dt 6:7; Pr 13:24; 22:6
6:5 [k]1Ti 6:1; Tit 2:9; 1Pe 2:18 [l]Col 3:22 [m]Eph 5:22
6:6 [n]S Ro 6:22

Chapter 6

Children and Parents

CHILDREN, obey your parents in the
Lord, for this is right.[g] 2 "Honor
your father and mother"—which is the
first commandment with a promise—
3 "that it may go well with you and that
you may enjoy long life on the earth."[p][h]
4 Fathers, do not exasperate your children;[i] instead, bring them up in the
training and instruction of the Lord.[j]

Slaves and Masters

5 Slaves, obey your earthly masters with
respect[k] and fear, and with sincerity of
heart,[l] just as you would obey Christ.[m]
6 Obey them not only to win their favor
when their eye is on you, but like slaves
of Christ,[n] doing the will of God from
your heart. 7 Serve wholeheartedly, as if

[n] *26* Or *having cleansed* [o] *31* Gen. 2:24
[p] *3* Deut. 5:16

5:22 JESUS CHRIST, Lord—See note on 4:15.

5:22—6:4 FAMILY, Role Relationships—Paul applied the concept of mutual submission to Christian family relationships: husband-wife, parent-child. In each case self-giving of one to the other is described. For the wife it is voluntary yielding in love to her husband's headship in the home. The husband is to yield himself to his wife in the same spirit that Christ yielded Himself to the cross to establish the church. Children are to submit themselves to their parents in obedience, and fathers are to give themselves to the task of guidance and discipline for their children (Col 3:18–21). Mutual submission does not define how individual families will determine role responsibilities in the home. It affirms a new attitude of voluntary submission in love from each family member based upon Christian faith. Submission as a Christian attitude is basic to social life in the gospel (Ro 13:1–7; Tit 3:1; Heb 13:7; 1 Pe 2:13—3:7). It refuses to use other people as objects, and it understands authority as servanthood (Mt 20:25–28; Lk 22:24–27).

5:23–24 THE CHURCH, Body of Christ—Christ is the loving, sacrificing Head of the church. The church is the obedient, grateful body which serves its Savior.

5:25–32 JESUS CHRIST, Love—The object of Jesus' love is His bride, the church. He showed His love in His death, which purified His people. He continues to show His love through constant care for us.

5:25–27 LAST THINGS, Church's Consummation—Although individual members stand justified before God, the church as a body looks toward a consummation in which imperfection gives way to perfection. As a bride in beauty and human perfections joins her beloved for marriage, the church in radiant spotlessness will be presented to the heavenly Bridegroom. Complete salvation has a corporate element as well as an individual one.

5:25–32 THE CHURCH, Body of Christ—The church responds to Christ as a loving wife responds to a loving and kind husband. Christ gave Himself on the cross for His church to set the church apart as His unique people living in service to Him. He is now cleansing the church that it might be presented to Him as a purified body. Because we are members of His body, we must live in ways pleasing to Him.

5:26 SALVATION, As Cleansing—See note on Ac 22:16. Compare 1 Co 6:11. "Word" may be a reference to the formula said over persons being baptized or to their confession of faith. The doctrine of salvation is closely linked with the church ordinances of baptism and the Lord's Supper.

5:26 ORDINANCES, Baptism as Cleansing—Just as husbands took a public vow to be faithful to their wives, setting them apart from their relation to all others ("setting apart" is the root meaning of the word "holy"), so Christians are "set apart" by Christ through the public act of baptism to be His faithful bride. The metaphor of marriage is used as a powerful illustration of the covenant relationship of God to His people from the time of the Old Testament prophets right on through the New Testament. "Washing with water through the word" is clearly a reference to baptism, but it is not the literal washing with water that cleanses and sets apart the Christian. It is "through the word," the convicting, cleansing power of the Word of God (made flesh in Jesus Christ and written in the Bible), that we are saved and sanctified (made holy) as the bride of Christ. See notes on Jn 3:3–5; Tit 3:5.

6:4 EDUCATION, Parents—Responsibility for nurturing children in the faith is fixed squarely on the shoulders of Christian fathers. Obviously, mothers will have much to do with the nurture and training of children (see note on Pr 1:8–9); but fathers who relinquish this duty entirely to their wives do so in clear violation of New Testament teaching. "Training" is the Greek word, *paideia,* which denotes a combination of instruction, discipline, and personal guidance. Fathers are also warned against engendering anger and frustration in their children, since this will negate much of their positive teaching.

6:5–8 DISCIPLESHIP, Rewarded—Personal justice is not the goal of discipleship. My task is not to make sure I get justice. I must be more concerned that I act justly and fight for justice for others. Paul called on slaves to accept their unjust status and serve their masters in love and loyalty. Whatever our social or employment status, we know our ultimate supervisor is God. Every action we take, every job we do, we do to please Him. Earthly managers pay only earthly wages. When we face our true Master, He will reward us for faithfulness to Him. Earthly status and position will play no role. All are slaves of God. See notes on Mt 25:34–46; 2 Pe 1:10–11.

you were serving the Lord, not men,[o]
8because you know that the Lord will reward everyone for whatever good he
does,[p] whether he is slave or free.
9And masters, treat your slaves in the
same way. Do not threaten them, since
you know that he who is both their Master and yours[q] is in heaven, and there is
no favoritism[r] with him.

The Armor of God

10Finally, be strong in the Lord[s] and in
his mighty power.[t] 11Put on the full armor of God[u] so that you can take your
stand against the devil's schemes. 12For
our struggle is not against flesh and
blood,[v] but against the rulers, against the
authorities,[w] against the powers[x] of this
dark world and against the spiritual forces
of evil in the heavenly realms.[y] 13There-
fore put on the full armor of God,[z] so
that when the day of evil comes, you may
be able to stand your ground, and after
you have done everything, to stand.
14Stand firm then, with the belt of truth
buckled around your waist,[a] with the
breastplate of righteousness in place,[b]
15and with your feet fitted with the readiness that comes from the gospel of
peace.[c] 16In addition to all this, take up
the shield of faith,[d] with which you can
extinguish all the flaming arrows of the
evil one.[e] 17Take the helmet of salvation[f] and the sword of the Spirit,[g] which
is the word of God.[h] 18And pray in the
Spirit[i] on all occasions[j] with all kinds of
prayers and requests.[k] With this in mind,
be alert and always keep on praying[l] for
all the saints.
19Pray also for me,[m] that whenever I
open my mouth, words may be given me
so that I will fearlessly[n] make known the
mystery[o] of the gospel, 20for which I am
an ambassador[p] in chains.[q] Pray that I
may declare it fearlessly, as I should.

Final Greetings

21Tychicus,[r] the dear brother and
faithful servant in the Lord, will tell you
everything, so that you also may know
how I am and what I am doing. 22I am
sending him to you for this very purpose,
that you may know how we are,[s] and
that he may encourage you.[t]
23Peace[u] to the brothers, and love with
faith from God the Father and the Lord
Jesus Christ. 24Grace to all who love our
Lord Jesus Christ with an undying love.

6:7 [o]Col 3:23
6:8 [p]S Mt 16:27; Col 3:24
6:9 [q]Job 31:13,14 [r]S Ac 10:34
6:10 [s]2Sa 10:12; Ps 27:14; Hag 2:4; 1Co 16:13; 2Ti 2:1 [t]Eph 1:19
6:11 [u]ver 13; Ro 13:12; 1Th 5:8
6:12 [v]1Co 15:50; Heb 2:14 [w]Eph 1:21; 3:10 [x]Ro 8:38 [y]S Eph 1:3
6:13 [z]ver 11; S 2Co 6:7
6:14 [a]Isa 11:5 [b]Ps 132:9; Isa 59:17; 1Th 5:8
6:15 [c]Isa 52:7; Ro 10:15
6:16 [d]1Jn 5:4 [e]S Mt 5:37
6:17 [f]Isa 59:17 [g]Isa 49:2 [h]S Heb 4:12
6:18 [i]Ro 8:26,27 [j]S Lk 18:1 [k]Mt 26:41; Php 1:4; 4:6 [l]S Ac 1:14; Col 1:3
6:19 [m]S 1Th 5:25 [n]S Ac 4:29 [o]S Ro 16:25
6:20 [p]2Co 5:20 [q]S Ac 21:33
6:21 [r]S Ac 20:4
6:22 [s]Col 4:7-9 [t]Col 2:2; 4:8
6:23 [u]Gal 6:16; 2Th 3:16; 1Pe 5:14

6:8 LAST THINGS, Judgment—The aspect of judgment that applies to believers is that of the determination of rewards. Good will be rewarded regardless of earthly status. See note on 2 Co 5:10.

6:9 GOD, Justice—We should be just in our dealings with people we supervise and work with because we expect God to deal justly with us. We will ultimately face a just God.

6:10–20 EVIL AND SUFFERING, Satan—Disciples must struggle with superhuman forms of evil, including Satan. God's spiritual armor will help the disciple in these struggles (1 Pe 5:8–9). The enemy causing the evil we face is not a human force we have a chance to defeat in our own power. The enemy is an evil spiritual force led by Satan. The enemy includes rulers and authorities, angelic forces created by God through Christ (Col 1:16) who have rebelled against God and exercise temporary power in our universe. Compare Eph 1:21; 3:10; Col 2:15. Powers may be pagan gods connected with sun worship who cannot bring light to the evil darkness we must endure. Evil is not a problem limited to life on earth. Spiritual forces represent Satan's followers who oppose God on His heavenly territory. Will God or Satan exercise ultimate control of the universe? The Bible assures us God's victory is guaranteed (Eph 1:3,10,14,20–22; 2:6; 3:10; 4:10). We can participate in God's victory by identifying with Him and living according to His will (5:7–20).

6:13 HISTORY, Time—God's history of salvation does not mean history progressively becomes better. God's people still face evil and must look forward to even greater struggle before final salvation comes.

6:14 CHRISTIAN ETHICS, Righteousness—Righteousness is protection against evil temptations. Unless we are slaves to righteousness, we will be slaves to Satan and sin (Ro 6:15–22). Righteousness is also a visible witness to those around us that life in God does not avoid the spiritual perils of this world but rather engages them and defeats them.

6:17 HOLY SPIRIT, Revelation—Paul's metaphor of Christians as soldiers includes only one offensive weapon: the Word of God the Spirit gives to God's people. The Word of God is the gospel message about Jesus Christ proclaimed by Christians (Php 1:14; Col 1:25; 1 Th 2:13). It is called the Spirit's sword for three reasons: (1) the Spirit always works to remind Christians about Jesus; (2) the Spirit guides and empowers the church as it proclaims the Word of God about Jesus; and (3) the Spirit uses the truth of the Word of God to protect Christians. See notes on Mk 13:11; Jn 16:8–11. The message about Jesus is found not only in oral but in written form, that is, as Scripture. Therefore, the Bible is also the Word of God and the Sword of the Spirit (2 Ti 3:14–17).

6:18 HOLY SPIRIT, Intercedes—The Spirit guides the church in its prayers. See note on Ro 8:25–27. The church is to continue praying, and the Spirit will assist the church through it all.

6:18–20 PRAYER, Intercession—Paul went from the general to the specific. He first urged all kinds of prayer for all saints. Prayer should characterize the life of the Christian. Then he asked prayer for his special circumstances. See note on 2 Th 3:1–5. He was in prison (3:1) and needed fearlessness. Intercession should make specific requests which lead to the spread of the gospel.

6:21 THE CHURCH, Servants—See note on 3:7. Every Christian is a minister of the Lord and a beloved brother.

6:23–24 PRAYER, Blessing—See note on Ro 15:33.

Philippians

Theological Setting

The gospel creates partnerships. One such partnership resulted in the letter of the apostle Paul to the church in Philippi.

Located in eastern Macedonia, ten miles inland from the Aegean Sea, Philippi took its name from Philip II, Alexander the Great's father. Just west of the town near the Gangites River, Antony and Octavian (later called Augustus) defeated Cassius and Brutus in 42 BC. In 30 BC, Octavian made the town a Roman colony for retired soldiers and bestowed upon Philippi the full privileges of Roman citizenship, to which Paul made an oblique reference in the letter (3:20). Philippi was located on the Via Egnata, a major Roman road that transversed Macedonia and facilitated the apostle's missionary efforts in the area.

On his second missionary journey he had answered a visionary call from a man in Macedonia saying, "Come over . . . and help us" (Ac 16:9-10). In response to that vision he traveled to Philippi and established the first church in Macedonia (Ac 16). He visited the church on at least one other occasion (Ac 20). Through intervening years a deep affection grew between the apostle and the Philippian church. On several occasions they sent him financial help (2 Co 11:7; Php 4:15-16), and also contributed to the poor in Jerusalem (2 Co 8).

Then, from a Roman prison he wrote a letter to them in response to another gift they sent to him by the hand of Epaphroditus. He penned a love letter which was full of personal insights into the character of Paul, the character of the Philippian church, and the character of their partnership in the gospel.

From the soil of mutual love between an embattled apostle and a beloved congregation grew a partnership that is instructive to the Christian church today. It was a partnership of mutual encouragement, support, prayer, and suffering.

The Philippian church, unlike several others of the New Testament, was not plagued by doctrinal controversy, leadership crises, or internal conflict. Though it did have some problems, this church seemed to require little correction in comparison to other congregations to which Paul wrote. Therefore, stinging rebukes or harsh admonitions do not characterize the letter. Rather, expressions of love and appreciation set the tone.

This personal letter celebrates a partnership between a missionary apostle and a concerned congregation and presents some of the most profound insights in the New Testament. In the context of partnership, the Holy Spirit inspired instruction about the person of Christ, the nature of Christian joy, the process of sanctification, the sufficiency of grace, the redemptive value of suffering, and much more.

Theological Outline

Philippians: The Gospel Makes Us Partners

I. Salutation (1:1-2)
II. Introduction (1:3-26)
  A. Thanksgiving prayer (1:3-11)
    1. Thanksgiving for partnership in the gospel which God will complete (1:3-6)
    2. Affection for partners who share God's grace (1:7-8)
    3. Petition that the partners' love may lead to insight and righteousness (1:9-11)
  B. Adverse personal circumstances may advance the gospel. (1:12-26)
    1. Imprisonment can cause others to witness. (1:12-18)
    2. Life is Christ, and death is eternal life with Christ. (1:19-24)
    3. Beyond prison lies hope for new joy in partnership. (1:25-26)
III. Pastoral Admonitions (1:27—2:18)
  A. Admonition to consistency (1:27)
  B. Admonition to courage (1:28-30)
  C. Admonition to unity (2:1-11)

1. Union with Christ is the basis of unity. (2:1-2)
2. The way to unity is humility. (2:3-4)
3. Jesus, the Suffering Servant, is the example of humility. (2:5-11)

D. Admonition to responsibility and obedience (2:12-13)
E. Admonition to a blameless life of rejoicing (2:14-18)

IV. Pastoral Concerns (2:19-30)
A. Pastoral concern for the church's welfare (2:19-24)
B. Pastoral concern for a distressed minister (2:25-30)

V. Pastoral Warning and Encouragement (3:1—4:1)
A. Warning against legalistic zealots: Glory only in Christ. (3:1-3)
B. Warning against confidence in the flesh: Place confidence only in Christ and the resurrection hope. (3:4-11)
C. Warning against satisfaction with the past: Press onward to the heavenly prize. (3:12-16)
D. Warning against enemies of the cross: Stand firm as citizens of heaven. (3:17—4:1)

VI. Final Exhortation (4:2-9)
A. To personal reconciliation (4:2-3)
B. To joy and gentleness (4:4-5)
C. To peace of mind (4:6-7)
D. To noble thoughts (4:8-9)

VII. Conclusion (4:10-23)
A. The apostle's contentment in Christ's strength (4:10-13)
B. The apostle's appreciation for the church's stewardship (4:14-20)
C. The apostle's final greetings and benediction (4:21-23)

Theological Conclusions

Even though Paul wrote this letter from prison, Christian joy provides the underlying theme. In the midst of suffering and conflict the apostle rejoiced. He rejoiced in the partnership he had with the Philippian Christians (1:4), in the fact the gospel was being preached as a result of his imprisonment (1:14), at the prospect of seeing the Philippians again (1:26), in the unity of believers (2:2), in spite of suffering (2:17), and because of the gift he had received at the hand of Epaphroditus (4:18). Because of his own joy, he frequently encouraged the Philippians to rejoice (2:14,18,29; 3:1; 4:4).

The joy of partnership in the gospel rests on strong theological foundations:

1. fellowship with Christ,
2. commitment to the gospel,
3. understanding of life as stewardship,
4. imitation of the Suffering Servant,
5. the unity of the church, and
6. the hope of resurrection.

From salutation (1:1) to benediction (4:23) the letter testifies to Christ as the basis of human life and eternal hope. The joy of the Lord is not dependent on circumstances or people. It comes from within, the result of deep and abiding fellowship with Jesus Christ. Life's goal, and also death's, is to exalt Christ (1:19-25). Cultural roots and past history are not so important as the desire to know Christ in fuller and deeper ways (3:1-11). "I can do everything through him who gives me strength" (4:13).

Nothing should deter or distract the follower of Christ. Courageous commitment to the gospel will result in a life consistent with the gospel (1:6-7), a boldness in the work of the gospel (1:27-28), an acceptance of suffering for the gospel (1:28-29), a willingness to die for the gospel (2:17), and a contentment because of the gospel (4:11).

The church's financial gift occasioned the Philippian letter (4:10-17). Such giving came only because the church had learned to live as stewards of Christ. They did not greedily gather material goods. Rather they shared in Paul's troubles. Why? Because they were partners in the gospel (1:5). They "share[d] in God's grace" (1:7). They prayed for an imprisoned brother (1:19). They looked to the interests of others (2:4). Life as stewardship meant not to rest on past achievements (3:12) but "to work out your salvation with fear and trembling" (2:12).

In 2:6-11 Paul used a hymn to describe in exalted terms the humiliation of Christ which serves as an example for all believers. Jesus was and is the eternal God. Yet he willingly emptied Himself to become a servant of God's sinful human creatures (2:6-7). Jesus, the universal King, obeyed His Father and suffered the excruciating and demeaning death on the cross. What is the result? God the Father exalted His obedient Son (2:9). This exaltation is past, present, and future. Jesus *was* raised from the grave and exalted, raised up, to His Father's right hand. *Now* He occupies the preeminent place in the eternal order. *One day* He *will* return to the earth. He *will* be acknowledged as Lord and King by the entire universe. Why did God inspire Paul to write such a sublime description of the Suffering Servant? "Your attitude should be the same as that of Christ Jesus" (2:5).

Apparently the Philippian church did not have serious problems to divide their efforts. Paul knew the potential was there, especially since he was in prison. Paul appealed for unity by asking the Philippians to have the same humility and self-emptying attitude Jesus exhibited. Believers are united with Christ and in fellowship with the Spirit (2:1). This bond should make us like-minded, with the same love and purpose. This fellowship demands humility, considering others better than ourselves (2:2-3). Only such unified people can act as one person fighting for the faith of the gospel (1:27). Such a united church can be partners with apostles and with Christ in the gospel of suffering.

Paul did not discuss the second coming for the Philippians. He pointed to its certainty as the basis of both his own circumstances and of his pastoral warning and encouragement. Death held no fear. It represented the gain of eternal life (1:21-23). It represented imitation of Christ and hope to be exalted to be with Him (1:23; 2:8-9). It pointed to a time he could boast of his labor in the gospel (2:16). Resurrection hope gave power to life, fellowship in suffering, and a goal for personal existence (3:7-14). When that day finally comes, enemies will be destroyed, and we will finally enjoy our heavenly citizenship in bodies Christ has transformed to be like His "glorious body" (3:18-21).

Contemporary Teaching

The book of Philippians is a fresh reminder to the contemporary church of some essential Christian virtues. It is instructive for practical living and congregational effectiveness. Today, more than ever, we need to hear and apply the truths of Philippians.

1. Partnership and fellowship in the gospel needs to be rediscovered in a day when individuals often see themselves as isolated disciples of Jesus Christ and the churches see themselves as competing with each other. Because we have a common experience with the gospel, we should pray for one another, encourage one another, and support one another in time of need with our resources, as did Paul and the Philippians.

2. Unity between Christians is closely related to the idea of partnership. It is described as "being like-minded, having the same love, being one in spirit and purpose" (2:2). Christians ought to strive for unity in a spirit of humility and unselfishness. Personal and petty differences should be submerged in the greater purposes of the gospel. Selfish ambition and competing attitudes ought to be rejected and replaced by a Christlike humility. A fragmented and polarized world can receive no greater witness than the unity of believers.

3. The joy of the Lord is one of the true marks of a Christian. It is contagious. It conquers circumstances. It communicates contentment. It comes from God Himself. Joy is not a superficial happiness or a sentimental feeling. Joy is an abiding confidence in God. Joy is an exuberance for life and an anticipation of God's triumph. Joy is a celebration of Christ's power and presence. Joy reflects a genuine excitement for the gospel.

4. Single-minded commitment to Jesus Christ identifies a disciple. The very purpose of life is to know Christ and to make Him known. All other achievements and accomplishments pale into insignificance by comparison. It is the highest of all privileges to have fellowship with Jesus Christ, to share Him with others, to bear suffering on His account, to reflect His character, and to honor His name.

It is the greatest of all responsibilities to be committed to Jesus Christ. It ought to be the highest priority of life. It is an ever increasing demand and a never-ending pilgrimage. The result of such a relationship is to experience His complete sufficiency and absolute supply. Jesus is Lord.

Chapter 1

PAUL and Timothy,[a] servants of Christ
Jesus,

To all the saints[b] in Christ Jesus at Philippi,[c] together with the overseers[a] [d]
and deacons:[e]

2 Grace and peace to you from God our
Father and the Lord Jesus Christ.[f]

Thanksgiving and Prayer

3 I thank my God every time I remember you.[g] 4 In all my prayers for all of you,
I always pray[h] with joy 5 because of your
partnership[i] in the gospel from the first
day[j] until now, 6 being confident of this,
that he who began a good work in you
will carry it on to completion[k] until the
day of Christ Jesus.[l]

7 It is right[m] for me to feel this way
about all of you, since I have you in my
heart;[n] for whether I am in chains[o] or
defending[p] and confirming the gospel, all
of you share in God's grace with me.
8 God can testify[q] how I long for all of you
with the affection of Christ Jesus.

9 And this is my prayer: that your love[r]
may abound more and more in knowledge and depth of insight,[s] 10 so that you
may be able to discern what is best and
may be pure and blameless until the day
of Christ,[t] 11 filled with the fruit of righteousness[u] that comes through Jesus
Christ—to the glory and praise of God.

Paul's Chains Advance the Gospel

12 Now I want you to know, brothers,
that what has happened to me has really
served to advance the gospel. 13 As a result, it has become clear throughout the
whole palace guard[b] and to everyone
else that I am in chains[v] for Christ. 14 Because of my chains,[w] most of the brothers
in the Lord have been encouraged to
speak the word of God more courageously
and fearlessly.[x]

15 It is true that some preach Christ out
of envy and rivalry, but others out of

[a] *1* Traditionally *bishops* [b] *13* Or *whole palace*

1:1 [a] S Ac 16:1; 2Co 1:1 [b] S Ac 9:13 [c] S Ac 16:12 [d] S 1Ti 3:1 [e] 1Ti 3:8
1:2 [f] S Ro 1:7
1:3 [g] S Ro 1:8
1:4 [h] S Ro 1:10
1:5 [i] Ac 2:42; Php 4:15 [j] Ac 16:12-40
1:6 [k] Ps 138:8 [l] ver 10; S 1Co 1:8
1:7 [m] 2Pe 1:13 [n] 2Co 7:3 [o] ver 13, 14,17; S Ac 21:33 [p] ver 16
1:8 [q] S Ro 1:9
1:9 [r] 1Th 3:12 [s] S Eph 1:17
1:10 [t] ver 6; S 1Co 1:8
1:11 [u] S Jas 3:18
1:13 [v] ver 7,14,17; S Ac 21:33
1:14 [w] ver 7,13,17; S Ac 21:33 [x] S Ac 4:29

1:1 THE CHURCH, Servants—See note on Ro 1:1.

1:1 THE CHURCH, Saints—The saints made up the local church at Philippi. See notes on Ro 1:7; Eph 1:1.

1:1 CHURCH LEADERS, Pastor and Overseer—This is the only passage where Paul specifically greeted by title certain officers of a church. He mentioned these church leaders only after he addressed the congregation as a whole. Therefore, he did not regard them as being more important than the congregation, although they did have oversight. The function of oversight and protective care was intended to serve the spiritual welfare of the community. By identifying himself and Timothy as servants, Paul indicated that the spiritual leadership of a community must be exercised with humility. The use of the plural indicates that the church was not governed by one monarchical bishop. Rather, the church at Philippi had several overseers or bishops. These with the deacons formed the pastoral leadership team of the church. See notes on Ac 11:30; 1 Ti 3:1–7.

1:1 CHURCH LEADERS, Deacon—The basic meaning of deacon (Greek *diakonos*) is servant. Elsewhere in the New Testament the Greek word is translated servant or minister (2 Co 6:4; 11:23; Eph 6:21; Col 1:23; 4:7; 1 Ti 4:6). As church leadership roles developed, the term deacon was increasingly used for those who worked in coordination with the overseer and voluntarily performed necessary services to enhance the welfare of the congregation. They embodied the kind of sacrificial service that Jesus commended to his disciples (Mt 23:11–12; Mk 10:42–45; Jn 13:14–17).

1:2–23 GOD, Trinity—The Persons of the Trinity work together and individually for Christians. The Father and Son provide grace and peace which make the Christian life possible. We pray to the Father (v 3). In answer to prayer the Spirit of Jesus Christ provides help (v 19). God begins and carries to completion His work of salvation, which becomes fully complete on the day of Christ (v 6). God's grace has allowed us to have the loving affection of Christ (v 8). Christ has made us right with God and filled our lives with righteousness, so we will praise the Father. Our righteous lives then exalt Christ (v 20) and provide joy in Christ for others (v 26). We speak the word of God, which means to preach Christ (vv 14–15). Living is Christ (v 21) and dying is being with Christ (v 23).

1:2 PRAYER, Blessing—See note on Ro 1:7.

1:3 PRAYER, Thanksgiving—The Philippian church brought special joy to Paul. See notes on Ac 28:15; Ro 1:8; 2 Co 2:14. Compare 1 Co 1:4; 2 Co 1:11; Eph 1:16; Col 1:3; 1 Th 1:2; 2 Th 1:3; 1 Ti 1:12; 2 Ti 1:3; Phm 4.

1:4–11 PRAYER, Intercession—Paul prayed for his churches. See notes on Eph 1:15–19; 3:14–19. Paul prayed his fellow believers would have love leading both to spiritual insight and moral purity.

1:6 GOD, Faithfulness—Salvation is not temporary. We can depend upon God to complete what He started. Our faithful God will not forget us along the way or grow weary and give up. See note on 1 Co 1:9.

1:6 LAST THINGS, Salvation's Completion—God's faithfulness guarantees the completion of what He begins. He begins a good work of salvation in each believer at the time of conversion. He watches over its development and progression. The completion of the good work of grace will occur in the day Jesus returns in victory. See note on 1 Jn 3:2–3.

1:8 JESUS CHRIST, Love—See note on Eph 3:18–19.

1:9–10 CHRISTIAN ETHICS, Character—Love will act in discernment based on knowledge which broadens and deepens. This is different from an emotion passing for love which acts impulsively and shallowly. Christian character shows itself in making the best decisions for all concerned. Only Christ's love can lead to such decisions.

1:9–11 FAMILY, Continuing Growth—Paul prayed for the disciples to grow in love, knowledge, insight, and fruitbearing (1 Co 13:11–12; Eph 4:14–15; Col 1:9–12). Since the family and the church are described in similar terms, family members also are to grow in all of these needs as they give respect and honor to each other. Spiritual growth is essential for the Christian family.

1:11 CHRISTIAN ETHICS, Righteousness—See notes on 3:9; Ro 8:4,10.

1:12–18 EVIL AND SUFFERING, Providence—Although in prison, Paul saw good emerging from his suffering as others preached the gospel. God can use our troubles and suffering to spread His gospel. The content of the gospel, not the life or work of the preacher, provides salvation. This gives us reason to rejoice even as we suffer.

1:14 REVELATION, Events—Paul's imprisonment and pain become the inspiration for his co-laborers to speak God's revelation to people throughout the regions Paul had visited. The Spirit of God uses difficult events as opportunities to reveal His strength.

1:14–18 PROCLAMATION, Anointing—See note on Isa 61:1–3. We do not stand in judgment over the motives of others. We rejoice that people hear the gospel.

goodwill. 16The latter do so in love,
knowing that I am put here for the defense of the gospel.[y] 17The former preach
Christ out of selfish ambition,[z] not sincerely, supposing that they can stir up
trouble for me while I am in chains.[c] [a]
18But what does it matter? The important
thing is that in every way, whether from
false motives or true, Christ is preached.
And because of this I rejoice.

Yes, and I will continue to rejoice, 19for
I know that through your prayers[b] and
the help given by the Spirit of Jesus
Christ,[c] what has happened to me will
turn out for my deliverance.[d] [d] 20I eagerly expect[e] and hope that I will in no way
be ashamed, but will have sufficient courage[f] so that now as always Christ will be
exalted in my body,[g] whether by life or
by death.[h] 21For to me, to live is Christ[i]
and to die is gain. 22If I am to go on living
in the body, this will mean fruitful labor
for me. Yet what shall I choose? I do not
know! 23I am torn between the two: I
desire to depart[j] and be with Christ,[k]
which is better by far; 24but it is more
necessary for you that I remain in the
body. 25Convinced of this, I know that I
will remain, and I will continue with all
of you for your progress and joy in the
faith, 26so that through my being with
you again your joy in Christ Jesus will
overflow on account of me.

27Whatever happens, conduct yourselves in a manner worthy[l] of the gospel
of Christ. Then, whether I come and see
you or only hear about you in my absence, I will know that you stand firm[m] in
one spirit, contending[n] as one man for
the faith of the gospel 28without being
frightened in any way by those who oppose you. This is a sign to them that they
will be destroyed, but that you will be
saved—and that by God. 29For it has
been granted to you[o] on behalf of Christ
not only to believe on him, but also to
suffer[p] for him, 30since you are going
through the same struggle[q] you saw[r] I
had, and now hear[s] that I still have.

Chapter 2

Imitating Christ's Humility

If you have any encouragement from being united with Christ, if any comfort
from his love, if any fellowship with the
Spirit,[t] if any tenderness and compassion,[u] 2then make my joy complete[v] by

1:16 [y]ver 7,12
1:17 [z]Php 2:3 [a]ver 7,13,14; S Ac 21:33
1:19 [b]2Co 1:11 [c]S Ac 16:7 [d]Phm 22
1:20 [e]Ro 8:19 [f]ver 14 [g]1Co 6:20 [h]Ro 14:8
1:21 [i]Gal 2:20
1:23 [j]2Ti 4:6 [k]S Jn 12:26
1:27 [l]S Eph 4:1 [m]S 1Co 16:13 [n]Jude 3
1:29 [o]Mt 5:11,12; Ac 5:41 [p]S Ac 14:22
1:30 [q]1Th 2:2; Heb 10:32 [r]Ac 16:19-40 [s]ver 13
2:1 [t]2Co 13:14 [u]Col 3:12
2:2 [v]S Jn 3:29

[c] *16,17* Some late manuscripts have verses 16 and 17 in reverse order. [d] *19* Or *salvation*

1:18–20 HOLY SPIRIT, Protects—The Spirit is called "the Spirit of Jesus Christ" because Christ gave the Spirit to His followers and also because the Spirit always works to remind the church of Jesus Christ. Paul was under arrest when he wrote Philippians, but his greatest hope was not that he would be freed but that, free or not, he would boldly proclaim Christ. He urged the church to pray that he would, and he was confident that the Spirit would help him do this (v 19). The Spirit's protection enables us to accomplish God's plans for proclamation, not our plans for personal security.

1:19 PRAYER, Intercession—Paul expected that his deliverance from prison would result from their prayers. Compare vv 24–25.

1:20–27 CHRISTIAN ETHICS, Character—Christian courage is not necessarily fearless. It acts in faith. Based on Christ's steadfastness, such courage recognizes the importance of this life as a means of advancing the gospel but knows its passing nature, too. Paul's plea for conduct worthy of the gospel is another of his many patterns of appeal for right living. See note on Eph 4:1–3.

1:21–24 LAST THINGS, Believers' Death—To live as Christians is a matter of having Christ and living in spiritual union with Him. To die as Christians is to gain even more. It is to be with Christ where He is. Death is a departure for eternal fellowship with Christ in heaven. See note on Lk 23:43. The limitations of time, a sinful nature, and a body of flesh will be laid aside. The gain thereby is incalculable. As with 2 Co 5:1–10, this passage plays a key role in understanding the intermediate state. The key question is what the opposite state is of "remain in the body." It may be a disembodied state of the soul waiting for resurrection, or an immediate state of bodily resurrection with Christ overcoming in eternity the earthly time gap, or it may be a statement of faith concerning the ongoing fellowship with Christ without attempting to answer the questions about the nature of intermediate existence. See note on 2 Co 5:1–10. He consistently emphasized the importance of the coming of Christ and the bodily resurrection.

1:27–30 EVIL AND SUFFERING, Endurance—See note on Col 1:24. We are not the only ones who suffer. We can gain courage to endure from others' examples. Our calling is not to avoid suffering but to stand firm and faithful as we suffer.

1:27–30 PROCLAMATION, Faith—The proclamation of the gospel is primarily for the purpose of reaching the lost. Of course, there are also benefits for the believer. Indeed, the close relation between preaching and teaching (see note on Jer 19:14–15) make proclamation an inevitable blessing and strength for the believer. Note this beautiful result in Ac 14:21–22. Proclamation is also used as a strong tool of instruction to believers (Col 1:28; 1 Th 4:1–2,8; 2 Ti 1:11). It is used of God to bring reproof and rebuke to believers (2 Ti 4:2). The proclamation of the gospel is a strong stimulant for growth, maturity, and perseverance (Col 1:5–6; Lk 8:9–21).

2:1–2 HOLY SPIRIT, Fellowship—The church is not basically a building or an organization, but a family of persons who share a common life (fellowship). That common life is a gift of the Spirit who gives life (Eze 37:1–14) by regeneration (Jn 3:5–7; Ti 3:5–6). It is a life of love and trust. It is the life of the eternal God shared with His people (2 Pe 1:4; 1 Jn 1:3). Although a gift of God, this fellowship must be nurtured by the church, as Paul urged the Philippians to do. Since you have been initiated by the Spirit into the life shared together by God and His church, then live in love, humility, and service to one another.

2:1 SALVATION, As Being in Christ—To be in Christ is to be united with Him. The text tells us some of the benefits of being in Christ.

2:1–18 CHRISTIAN ETHICS, Character—A graphic portrayal of Christ's life of humility which will issue in ultimate exaltation is Paul's centerpiece argument for Christian unity. Imitation of such humility in interpersonal relationships will produce a life of purity with one another. Choose and cultivate this approach, said Paul, knowing God is undergirding your efforts in this direction.

2:1–2 THE CHURCH, People of God—The united people of God gain courage and comfort from Christ, live in fellowship with the Spirit, and reflect the church's unity through love, compassion, and common attitudes and goals. See note on Ac 5:12–14.

being like-minded,[w] having the same
love, being one[x] in spirit and purpose.
3Do nothing out of selfish ambition or
vain conceit,[y] but in humility consider
others better than yourselves.[z] 4Each of
you should look not only to your own interests, but also to the interests of others.[a]
5Your attitude should be the same as
that of Christ Jesus:[b]

6Who, being in very nature[e] God,[c]
did not consider equality with God[d]
something to be grasped,
7but made himself nothing,[e]
taking the very nature[f] of a
servant,[f]
being made in human likeness.[g]
8And being found in appearance as a
man,
he humbled himself
and became obedient to death[h]—
even death on a cross![i]
9Therefore God exalted him[j] to the
highest place
and gave him the name that is above
every name,[k]
10that at the name of Jesus every knee
should bow,[l]
in heaven and on earth and under
the earth,[m]
11and every tongue confess that Jesus
Christ is Lord,[n]
to the glory of God the Father.

Shining as Stars

12Therefore, my dear friends, as you
have always obeyed—not only in my
presence, but now much more in my absence—continue to work out your salvation with fear and trembling,[o] 13for it is
God who works in you[p] to will and to act
according to his good purpose.[q]
14Do everything without complaining[r]
or arguing, 15so that you may become
blameless[s] and pure, children of God[t]
without fault in a crooked and depraved
generation,[u] in which you shine like
stars in the universe 16as you hold out[g]
the word of life—in order that I may
boast on the day of Christ[v] that I did not
run[w] or labor for nothing.[x] 17But even if

2:2 [w]Php 4:2 [x]S Ro 15:5
2:3 [y]Gal 5:26 [z]Ro 12:10; 1Pe 5:5
2:4 [a]S 1Co 10:24
2:5 [b]S Mt 11:29
2:6 [c]Jn 1:1; S 14:9 [d]Jn 5:18
2:7 [e]2Co 8:9 [f]S Mt 20:28 [g]S Jn 1:14; Ro 8:3; Heb 2:17
2:8 [h]S Mt 26:39; Jn 10:18; Ro 5:19; Heb 5:8 [i]S 1Co 1:23
2:9 [j]Isa 52:13; 53:12; Da 7:14; Ac 2:33; Heb 2:9 [k]Eph 1:20,21
2:10 [l]Ps 95:6; Isa 45:23; Ro 14:11 [m]Mt 28:18; Eph 1:10; Col 1:20
2:11 [n]S Jn 13:13
2:12 [o]S 2Co 7:15
2:13 [p]Ezr 1:5; 1Co 12:6; 15:10; Gal 2:8; Heb 13:21 [q]Eph 1:5
2:14 [r]1Co 10:10; 1Pe 4:9
2:15 [s]S 1Th 3:13 [t]Mt 5:45,48; Eph 5:1 [u]Ac 2:40
2:16 [v]S 1Co 1:8 [w]S 1Co 9:24 [x]1Th 2:19

[e]6 Or *in the form of* [f]7 Or *the form* [g]16 Or *hold on to*

2:4 DISCIPLESHIP, Persons—Discipleship focuses on other people—their needs and hopes—not on my selfish purposes. Christian disciples imitate the humility of Christ by overcoming selfish ambition and giving priority to the interests of others. See note on 2 Co 9:12–15.

2:5–11 JESUS CHRIST, Servant—Jesus is the supreme example of humility. He is divine by nature but did not selfishly demand His divine rights. Instead He gave up the glory of heaven to become a human. Even then He did not seek royal treatment but took the servant's role. Humble service was not the end of His humility. He obeyed the Father's plan and died for our sins. Through His humble service, Jesus pleased the Father, who made Him Ruler of the universe. See note on Eph 1:3.

2:6 GOD, Trinity—The foundation for understanding the one God as trinitarian—three Persons in One—is built on this verse. Jesus existed as God. His very form—the essential nature and character—identified Him as God. In every way He was and is God. As such, He did not defensively latch onto His Godness, nor did He aggressively exploit the powers of being God. Instead, He revealed the true essence of being God—self-giving love. All this means the Son cannot be placed in any category below or less than God. He, the Father, and the Spirit share Godness. This is clear. Our difficulty comes when we try to use human logic to define how the three Persons we know and experience as God can form one God. That is the glorious mystery of Trinity. See note on Mt 3:16–17.

2:7 JESUS CHRIST, Preexistent—*Kenosis* is the Greek word translated "made Himself nothing." It literally means poured Himself out. Paul speaks of the preexistent Christ who limits Himself to become human like us. That Christ took the role of a servant assumes that He forsook another role, His preexistent life with God.

2:11 GOD, Trinity—Our understanding of God is trinitarian. Knowing Jesus the Son and the Holy Spirit helps us know God the Father better. Confessing who Jesus really is brings glory, honor, and ultimate recognition to God the Father. There is no competition among members of the Trinity. They are unified as One in purpose. See note on Mt 3:16–17.

2:11 SALVATION, Confession—See note on Ro 10:8–10. God wants every tongue to confess Jesus as Lord. Confession includes thanksgiving, praise, and commitment.

2:12–13 SALVATION, Definition—Compare Eph 2:4–10. This text focuses upon the present tense of salvation. See note on 1 Co 1:18. Paul did not say salvation is uncertain or that we should be fearful of losing our salvation. On the contrary, he wanted to emphasize the security of believers. He called on the church to work on her spiritual health, continuing the obedient pattern of life she had known until spiritual disease no longer plagued Christ's body. The enormity of such a task calls for humility expressed by "fear and trembling" before the task. The church can accomplish the task and grow to spiritual health because God is at work to help the church. God's energy can change the church's will and change our actions until we accomplish His purpose. This is the present tense of salvation.

2:13 ELECTION, God's Purpose—God works in the elect to actualize His good purpose. No obstruction impedes or impairs the work of the elect who have the same attitude of humility that was in Jesus Christ.

2:14–18 EVIL AND SUFFERING, Rejoicing—Paul rejoiced in his suffering and encouraged other disciples to join his rejoicing. Suffering in persecution caused by our Christian faith must not lead to complaining or arguing with other Christians. As we suffer, our lives must be clearly different from those of non-Christians.

2:15 CREATION, Evil—Paul never allowed his idealism to blind him to the true facts of life. He recognized that the good world God created had become infiltrated by sin. He also knew, however, that the Savior wanted His followers to help change that condition.

2:15 HUMANITY, Relationship to God—Those who have been redeemed by Jesus have been brought into a relationship with God best understood as that of Parent-child. As such, we trust the Father rather than complaining, and we live to please the Father rather than imitate the sinful world around us which refuses to follow God. See note on Ro 8:12–17.

2:15 THE CHURCH, God's Community—As part of God's community, His children should display characteristics of the Father. The Christian community must be the salt of the earth, the light of the world, and the instrument for peace. See note on Mt 5:9.

2:17–18 SALVATION, Joy—Joy keynotes Philippians. Christians can rejoice even when they are being poured out like a drink offering to Christ. See note on Mt 5:12.

I am being poured out like a drink offering[y] on the sacrifice[z] and service coming from your faith, I am glad and rejoice
with all of you.[a] 18So you too should be
glad and rejoice with me.

Timothy and Epaphroditus

19I hope in the Lord Jesus to send Timothy[b] to you soon,[c] that I also may be
cheered when I receive news about you.
20I have no one else like him,[d] who takes
a genuine interest in your welfare. 21For
everyone looks out for his own interests,[e] not those of Jesus Christ. 22But you
know that Timothy has proved himself,
because as a son with his father[f] he has
served with me in the work of the gospel.
23I hope, therefore, to send him as soon
as I see how things go with me.[g] 24And I
am confident[h] in the Lord that I myself
will come soon.
25But I think it is necessary to send
back to you Epaphroditus, my brother,
fellow worker[i] and fellow soldier,[j] who
is also your messenger, whom you sent to
take care of my needs.[k] 26For he longs for
all of you[l] and is distressed because you
heard he was ill. 27Indeed he was ill, and
almost died. But God had mercy on him,
and not on him only but also on me, to
spare me sorrow upon sorrow. 28There-
fore I am all the more eager to send
him,[m] so that when you see him again
you may be glad and I may have less anxiety. 29Welcome him in the Lord with
great joy, and honor men like him,[n] 30be-
cause he almost died for the work of
Christ, risking his life to make up for the
help you could not give me.[o]

Chapter 3

No Confidence in the Flesh

FINALLY, my brothers, rejoice in the
Lord! It is no trouble for me to write
the same things to you again,[p] and it is a
safeguard for you.
2Watch out for those dogs,[q] those men
who do evil, those mutilators of the flesh.
3For it is we who are the circumcision,[r]
we who worship by the Spirit of God,
who glory in Christ Jesus,[s] and who put
no confidence in the flesh— 4though I
myself have reasons for such confidence.[t]
If anyone else thinks he has reasons to
put confidence in the flesh, I have more:
5circumcised[u] on the eighth day, of the
people of Israel,[v] of the tribe of Benjamin,[w] a Hebrew of Hebrews; in regard to
the law, a Pharisee;[x] 6as for zeal,[y] persecuting the church;[z] as for legalistic righteousness,[a] faultless.
7But whatever was to my profit I now
consider loss[b] for the sake of Christ.
8What is more, I consider everything a
loss compared to the surpassing greatness
of knowing[c] Christ Jesus my Lord, for
whose sake I have lost all things. I consider them rubbish, that I may gain Christ[d]
9and be found in him, not having a righteousness of my own that comes from the

2:17 [y]2Co 12:15; 2Ti 4:6 [z]Ro 15:16 [a]S 2Co 6:10
2:19 [b]S Ac 16:1 [c]ver 23
2:20 [d]1Co 16:10
2:21 [e]S 1Co 10:24
2:22 [f]1Co 4:17; 1Ti 1:2
2:23 [g]ver 19
2:24 [h]Php 1:25
2:25 [i]Ro 16:3,9,21; 2Co 8:23; Php 4:3; Col 4:11; Phm 1 [j]Phm 2 [k]Php 4:18
2:26 [l]Php 1:8
2:28 [m]ver 25
2:29 [n]1Co 16:18; 1Ti 5:17
2:30 [o]1Co 16:17
3:1 [p]Php 2:18
3:2 [q]Ps 22:16,20; Rev 22:15
3:3 [r]Ro 2:28,29; Gal 6:15; Col 2:11 [s]Ro 15:17; Gal 6:14
3:4 [t]2Co 11:21
3:5 [u]S Lk 1:59 [v]2Co 11:22 [w]Ro 11:1 [x]Ac 23:6
3:6 [y]S Ac 21:20 [z]S Ac 8:3 [a]ver 9; Ro 10:5
3:7 [b]Mt 13:44; Lk 14:33
3:8 [c]ver 10; Jer 9:23,24; Jn 17:3; Eph 4:13; S 2Pe 1:2 [d]Ps 73:25

2:25 CHURCH LEADERS, Apostle—"Messenger" (Greek *apostolos*) is used here in the non-technical sense of messenger or representative of a church. Churches may send their appointed messengers to work with other churches, but only Jesus appointed the apostles (2 Co 8:23).

3:1–4 HOLY SPIRIT, Church—Circumcision was the sign of the covenant between God and His people (Ge 17:1–27). Paul contrasted Spirit with flesh. The sign of the covenant cannot be circumcision, which is of the flesh, but rather is the gift of the Spirit (Lev 26:41; Dt 10:16; 30:6; Jer 4:4; 9:25–26). The contrast between flesh and Spirit appears in Jn 3:6; Ro 8:1–13. The flesh produces legalistic worship centered in ceremonies and rules. The church is those who worship God with the help of the Spirit and who glory in Jesus Christ. Only those who have faith in Jesus have the Spirit to assist them to worship God. God sends forth His Spirit into His people, and the worship of His people comes back to Him in heartfelt praise and thanksgiving.

3:1 HOLY SCRIPTURE, Writing—The content of revelation repeats itself. People forget or do not obey. God then inspired His servant to repeat previous instructions to guard believers from false teachings and other temptations. To write again may indicate a previous letter to the Philippians which was not preserved. God's inspiration and revelation included leading the church to preserve only the inspired writings He intended to be part of Scripture. See note on Ro 15:15.

3:1–11 SALVATION, Definition—God's salvation is the righteousness that comes from God through faith in Christ. It does not come through human merit or the keeping of a legal code. If so, Saul of Tarsus, who became Paul the apostle to the Gentiles, would not have counted all such things as nothing for the sake of Christ. Salvation is personal knowledge of Jesus Christ through daily relationship and commitment. Such knowledge is powerful enough to change a life, for it means the resurrected Christ will be at work in the life. This present power produces hope of attaining the Christian goal of personal resurrection. See note on Ps 22:5,8.

3:1 SALVATION, Joy—Rejoicing in the Lord should be a dominant theme among believers. See note on 2:17–18; compare 4:4.

3:1–11 CHRISTIAN ETHICS, Character—In spite of trials and sufferings, Paul's relationship with Christ provided him joy. He called Christians to the same sense of rejoicing. Rather than dwelling on the past which cannot be changed, Paul exhorted Christians to keep their eyes on the forward pull of Christ.

3:1 PRAYER, Praise—This is a command. See notes on Lev 23:40; Dt 12:7,12. Prayer is a time of joy.

3:3 WORSHIP, Service—See note on Mt 4:10.

3:7–11 EVIL AND SUFFERING, Endurance—Christians should share in Christ's suffering, being willing even to die as martyrs. Knowing Christ gives a different perspective on life and its possessions. Health is not as valuable as faithfulness to Christ and sharing in His resurrection. A Christian is ready to endure anything for Christ and the resurrection. See note on Col 1:24.

3:8 SALVATION, Knowledge of God—Knowing Jesus Christ as one's Lord is worth losing everything.

3:9 CHRISTIAN ETHICS, Righteousness—Our righteousness comes through our faith in Christ. God, as the sinless Suffering Servant, counts His righteousness as ours. This righteousness, like that portrayed in the Old Testament, is not static but is known for its application to personal and social behavior. Such faith and righteousness are difficult to separate since they

law,[e] but that which is through faith in
Christ—the righteousness[f] that comes
from God and is by faith.[g] 10I want to
know[h] Christ and the power of his resurrection and the fellowship of sharing in
his sufferings,[i] becoming like him in his
death,[j] 11and so, somehow, to attain to
the resurrection[k] from the dead.

Pressing on Toward the Goal

12Not that I have already obtained all
this, or have already been made perfect,[l]
but I press on to take hold[m] of that for
which Christ Jesus took hold of me.[n]
13Brothers, I do not consider myself yet to
have taken hold of it. But one thing I do:
Forgetting what is behind[o] and straining
toward what is ahead, 14I press on[p] toward the goal to win the prize[q] for which
God has called[r] me heavenward in
Christ Jesus.

15All of us who are mature[s] should
take such a view of things.[t] And if on
some point you think differently, that too
God will make clear to you.[u] 16Only let
us live up to what we have already attained.

17Join with others in following my example,[v] brothers, and take note of those
who live according to the pattern we gave
you.[w] 18For, as I have often told you before and now say again even with tears,[x]
many live as enemies of the cross of
Christ.[y] 19Their destiny[z] is destruction,
their god is their stomach,[a] and their glory is in their shame.[b] Their mind is on
earthly things.[c] 20But our citizenship[d] is
in heaven.[e] And we eagerly await a Savior from there, the Lord Jesus Christ,[f]
21who, by the power[g] that enables him
to bring everything under his control,
will transform our lowly bodies[h] so that
they will be like his glorious body.[i]

Chapter 4

THEREFORE, my brothers, you whom I
love and long for,[j] my joy and
crown, that is how you should stand
firm[k] in the Lord, dear friends!

Exhortations

2I plead with Euodia and I plead with
Syntyche to agree with each other[l] in
the Lord. 3Yes, and I ask you, loyal yoke-
fellow,[h] help these women who have
contended at my side in the cause of the
gospel, along with Clement and the rest
of my fellow workers,[m] whose names are
in the book of life.[n]
4Rejoice in the Lord always. I will say it
again: Rejoice![o] 5Let your gentleness be
evident to all. The Lord is near.[p] 6Do not
be anxious about anything,[q] but in everything, by prayer and petition, with
thanksgiving, present your requests to
God.[r] 7And the peace of God,[s] which
transcends all understanding,[t] will guard
your hearts and your minds in Christ
Jesus.
8Finally, brothers, whatever is true,

[h]3 Or *loyal Syzygus*

3:9 [e]ver 6; Ro 10:5 [f]Jer 33:16 [g]S Ro 9:30
3:10 [h]S ver 8 [i]S 2Co 1:5 [j]S Ro 6:3-5
3:11 [k]S Jn 11:24; S Ro 6:5; Rev 20:5, 6
3:12 [l]1Co 13:10 [m]1Ti 6:12 [n]Ac 9:5, 6
3:13 [o]Lk 9:62
3:14 [p]Heb 6:1 [q]1Co 9:24 [r]S Ro 8:28
3:15 [s]S 1Co 2:6 [t]Gal 5:10 [u]Eph 1:17; 1Th 4:9
3:17 [v]S 1Co 4:16 [w]S 1Ti 4:12
3:18 [x]Ac 20:31 [y]Gal 6:12
3:19 [z]Ps 73:17 [a]Ro 16:18 [b]Ro 6:21; Jude 13 [c]Ro 8:5,6; Col 3:2
3:20 [d]Eph 2:19 [e]Col 3:1; Heb 12:22 [f]S 1Co 1:7
3:21 [g]Eph 1:19 [h]1Co 15:43-53 [i]Ro 8:29; Col 3:4
4:1 [j]Php 1:8 [k]S 1Co 16:13
4:2 [l]Php 2:2
4:3 [m]S Php 2:25 [n]S Rev 20:12
4:4 [o]Ps 85:6; 97:12; Hab 3:18; S Mt 5:12; Ro 12:12; Php 3:1
4:5 [p]Ps 119:151; 145:18; Heb 10:37; Jas 5:8,9
4:6 [q]Mt 6:25-34 [r]Eph 6:18; 1Ti 2:1
4:7 [s]Isa 26:3; S Jn 14:27 [t]Eph 3:19

move together in observable life-style and conscious choices. We cannot be righteous in our own efforts apart from Christ. We cannot receive righteousness from Christ without faith. We cannot be counted as righteous in Christ without the desire to let the Spirit create a life of righteous acts in us. See notes on Hos 2:19–20; Hab 2:4; Ro 8:4,10.

3:11 LAST THINGS, Believers' Resurrection—The resurrection from the dead here is that which awaits believers who know Christ and share fellowship in His sufferings in this life. In Greek the verse is an "if" clause reading literally, "If somehow I might attain." The whole "if" clause is a statement of humility, rather than one of uncertainty. Believers' resurrection is as certain as the fact Christ was raised. See notes on 1 Co 6:14; 2 Co 4:14–18. The only possible uncertainty for believers is whether they will have died by the return of Christ (and thereby participate in the resurrection of the dead) or whether they will be still alive when He comes (and thereby receive transformed bodies in association with being caught up to meet Him in the air). See note on 1 Th 4:14–18.

3:20–21 JESUS CHRIST, Final Coming—Jesus will come from heaven as our Savior. He will use the power which makes Him Lord of the universe to give us a heavenly body like His resurrected body.

3:20–21 LAST THINGS, Resurrection Body—The time of receiving the resurrection body is associated with the future return of Christ. The power that produces bodily resurrection will be that of Christ. The accompaniment of this resurrection will be a transformation (literally, a metamorphosis). The result will be a resurrection body like that of the resurrected, ascended Lord. As He in His raised body could pass from earth to heaven, so the resurrection bodies of believers outfits them for heavenly dwelling. See note on 1 Co 15:35–49.

3:20 THE CHURCH, People of God—Christian citizenship is in heaven, not on earth. As citizens of God's kingdom, we must daily conduct our lives by the standards of His kingdom. We serve the true King alone, and we await the final coming of His reign over the world.

3:21 HUMANITY, Spiritual Nature—See 1 Co 15.

4:2–3 CHURCH LEADERS, Authority—Even though Paul was an apostle, he worked in cooperation with others. He called both men and women his fellow workers. They did not work "under" him but "side by side" with him. He pleaded and requested cooperation. See 2:25; Ro 16:21; 2 Co 8:23.

4:4–7 CHRISTIAN ETHICS, Character—Rejoice in God; be full of thanksgiving toward Him. Such attitudes bring the sense of fulfillment and joy in God that affects all of our relationships. This is God's peace, a peace so wonderful the human mind cannot fully understand it. This peace can be a present reality for the person who gently and kindly lives life by letting God take care of anxieties. Prayer is the lifeline to peace. See note on Jn 14:27.

4:4 WORSHIP, Rejoicing—This entire letter of Paul's is a call to rejoicing. Here we are specifically commanded to rejoice, a vital part of our worship of the Lord. See note on Ezr 3:10–11.

4:4 PRAYER, Praise—See note on 3:1.

4:6 PRAYER, Petition—The antidote to anxiety is thanksgiving. Thanksgiving acknowledges God as source. That is the attitude with which we should make our requests. See note on Col 4:2–4; Guide to Petition, pp. 1765–1767.

4:8–9 CHRISTIAN ETHICS, Character—To identify what is the will of God, Christians need consciously to think on the positive dimensions of life. Being confident of his own standing with Christ, Paul was able to suggest they imitate his

whatever is noble, whatever is right,
whatever is pure, whatever is lovely,
whatever is admirable—if anything is excellent or praiseworthy—think about
such things. 9 Whatever you have learned
or received or heard from me, or seen in
me—put it into practice.[u] And the God
of peace[v] will be with you.

Thanks for Their Gifts

10 I rejoice greatly in the Lord that at
last you have renewed your concern for
me.[w] Indeed, you have been concerned,
but you had no opportunity to show it. 11 I
am not saying this because I am in need,
for I have learned to be content[x] whatever the circumstances. 12 I know what it is
to be in need, and I know what it is to
have plenty. I have learned the secret of
being content in any and every situation,
whether well fed or hungry,[y] whether
living in plenty or in want.[z] 13 I can do
everything through him who gives me
strength.[a]
14 Yet it was good of you to share[b] in
my troubles. 15 Moreover, as you Philippians know, in the early days[c] of your acquaintance with the gospel, when I set
out from Macedonia,[d] not one church
shared with me in the matter of giving
and receiving, except you only;[e] 16 for
even when I was in Thessalonica,[f] you
sent me aid again and again when I was
in need.[g] 17 Not that I am looking for a
gift, but I am looking for what may be
credited to your account.[h] 18 I have received full payment and even more; I am
amply supplied, now that I have received
from Epaphroditus[i] the gifts you sent.
They are a fragrant[j] offering, an acceptable sacrifice, pleasing to God. 19 And my
God will meet all your needs[k] according
to his glorious riches[l] in Christ Jesus.
20 To our God and Father[m] be glory for
ever and ever. Amen.[n]

Final Greetings

21 Greet all the saints in Christ Jesus.
The brothers who are with me[o] send
greetings. 22 All the saints[p] send you
greetings, especially those who belong to
Caesar's household.
23 The grace of the Lord Jesus Christ[q]
be with your spirit.[r] Amen.[i]

4:9 [u]S 1Co 4:16 [v]S Ro 15:33
4:10 [w]2Co 11:9
4:11 [x]1Ti 6:6,8; Heb 13:5
4:12 [y]S 1Co 4:11 [z]2Co 11:9
4:13 [a]2Co 12:9; Eph 3:16; Col 1:11; 1Ti 1:12; 2Ti 4:17
4:14 [b]Php 1:7
4:15 [c]Php 1:5 [d]S Ac 16:9 [e]2Co 11:8,9
4:16 [f]S Ac 17:1 [g]1Th 2:9
4:17 [h]1Co 9:11,12
4:18 [i]Php 2:25 [j]S 2Co 2:14
4:19 [k]Ps 23:1; 2Co 9:8 [l]S Ro 2:4
4:20 [m]Gal 1:4; 1Th 1:3; 3:11,13 [n]S Ro 11:36
4:21 [o]Gal 1:2
4:22 [p]S Ac 9:13
4:23 [q]S Ro 16:20 [r]S Gal 6:18

[i]23 Some manuscripts do not have *Amen.*

---

life-style. What they had seen, they should do. His suggestions of acting on what we know of the will of God—and thus gaining more light—continues to be a valid principle.

4:8–9 EDUCATION, Participation—Modern educators speak of the learner's active participation in the educational process. That is what Paul advocated here. The Greek word (*logizesthe*) underlying "think" means, "to calculate," "to reckon carefully." To think then is to weigh seriously the cost of incorporating the virtues listed in verse 8 into one's daily life. Thus, the Christian is to grapple with these concepts, not just reflect on them passively.

4:9 REVELATION, Messengers—Encouraging his beloved congregation, Paul directed them to pay notice to what he had said, written, taught, and lived before them. To obey and follow these directives from God would bring them God's peace and inner harmony. Revelation is given for obedience not just for mental knowledge. God's chosen messenger of revelation communicates it in action as well as in words.

4:10–13 DISCIPLESHIP, Enabling Power—Discipleship does not depend on our situation. Material resources do not provide the power a disciple needs. Only Christ can provide the strength needed to do everything God wants done. Paul was able to face all kinds of circumstances with contentment because he expected Christ to provide the strength required. Such strong faith qualifies a disciple for big and difficult tasks. See note on Eph 3:16.

4:10–20 STEWARDSHIP, Support Ministry—Paul graciously acknowledged the Philippians' gifts given to help in his ministry. He demonstrated the minister's responsibility to be satisfied in ministry and not become a burden to the church. He also demonstrated that the church benefits by financially supporting the minister. See note on 2 Co 11:8–16.

4:13–20 GOD, Father—God the Father is faithful to meet our needs as we serve Him. He has the power to give us all the strength we need in life's problem hours. Still, we also appreciate human help. Note the close relationship of Father and Son in dealing with the believer. We know we can count on God because of what He has done for us in Christ.

4:18 PRAYER, Worship—The gifts to Paul, the man of God, were a gift of worship and praise to God Himself.

4:19 CHRISTIAN ETHICS, Property Rights—The world's richest person was Jesus, who had no place to sleep (Mt 8:20). He shared the Heavenly Father's unlimited resources. We can, too, if we dedicate all we have to Him.

4:19 PRAYER, Faithfulness of God—This is a promise to be appropriated in prayer.

4:20 PRAYER, Praise—See note on Ro 16:25–27.

4:21–22 THE CHURCH, Saints—See note on 1 Co 1:2

4:23 PRAYER, Blessing—See note on Ro 15:33.

Colossians

Theological Setting

What place does Jesus occupy in relation to the creation and the church? Who can find salvation in Him, and how can they find it? These two central issues emerge in the letter to the Colossians.

Colosse was a major textile center located in western Asia Minor in the Lycus River valley. The city was especially prosperous during the Persian period (sixth to fourth centuries BC), but its influence as a commercial center had waned somewhat by the first century AD. Apparently, Paul did not establish the church at Colosse. Perhaps his converts from nearby cities did.

False teachers were at work in the church at Colosse (2:4,8). Their teachings removed Jesus from His central place in revelation and salvation. They also perverted the gospel teaching about how people could be redeemed. They regarded their teaching as a philosophy, but Paul called it "human tradition" and an empty deceit (2:8). He did not actually describe their views; he assumed the readers knew them. Rather, he responded to the false teachers. We can only infer their views by studying his answers. For Paul, these false teachers represented a threat:

1. *To the centrality of Jesus.* Paul described Jesus in exalted terms, both in His relationship to the creation (1:15-17,20) and to the church (1:18-19,21-22). We can imply from Paul's statements that the false teachers were belittling the all-sufficiency of Christ and removing Him from the supreme and central place in Christian faith.

As Redeemer—Since Paul began and ended his exalted description of Christ with reference to His work of redemption (1:13-14) and reconciliation (1:20-22), we can infer that the false teachers did not see Jesus' death as fully sufficient to deliver people. To faith in Christ, they added the worship of other spiritual beings (2:18-19), religious rituals (2:16-17), and legal practices (2:20-23). Apparently, the false teachers borrowed and combined Jewish and pagan ideas with Christian teachings. Gentile paganism conceived of a number of deities, some of whom dwelt on the stars, moon, planets, and other heavenly bodies and controlled people's fates. Perhaps they were thinking of Jesus as one among many divine or semidivine beings coming from the supreme God. Such beings supposedly controlled access to salvation. In 1:16 and 2:10, Paul stressed that Jesus is supreme over all spiritual powers, not merely one among many.

As Creator—Evidently the Colossian teachers saw Christ as only one among a number of divine beings involved in the creation (2:11-17, 20-23). They said Christ was not the only one who exercised rule over the creation. Paul answered, "all things" were made in and through Christ. Jesus is Lord over all of creation, not just part of it (1:16-17).

As Revealer—The false teachers did not see Jesus as the only Revealer of God. They were claiming secret revelations and visions, some of which came from the other spiritual powers (2:18). Paul responded that Jesus was "the image of the invisible God" (1:15). He had all wisdom and knowledge (2:3). At the heart of the error at Colosse was a denial of Jesus' real humanity. He may be one of the divine beings, they taught, but not the only divine Son of God and surely not truly human. (See Paul's answers in 1:19 and 2:9. Note the stress on humanness in 1:22.) If the fullness of God's nature is dispersed among a number of lesser divine beings, then no Christian is complete who does not seek to know them all. Paul's answer is in 2:10.

2. *To the equality and unity of believers.* The error at Colosse created a sense of elitism. Some saw themselves as superior because of secret knowledge gained from the powers and because of unique spiritual experiences. See 2:10,16-19 for Paul's responses. The Colossian teachers may have made distinctions among those who could progress to maturity and those doomed to a mediocre level of growth. Paul's stress on "all" in 1:28 hints at this. They may even have taught that some were not included in God's saving purpose. Note Paul's stress on "all" in 1:20. Such elitism would divide the church. Paul stressed the opposite, that Christ's death and the gospel unify (1:20-22; 2:2-3,5; 3:11,14-15).

Theological Outline

Colossians: The All-Sufficiency of Christ

I. Greeting, Thanksgiving, and Prayer (1:1-14)
   A. Paul and Timothy greet the Colossians as saints and faithful brothers in Christ and pray that they will have grace and peace. (1:1-2)
   B. Paul gives thanks to God for the Colossians' mature response to the gospel as reported to him by a Colossian named Epaphras. (1:3-8)
   C. Paul prays that his readers will come to a full knowledge of God's person and will live a life of good works empowered by God's Spirit in joy and endurance. (1:9-11)
   D. Paul offers thanks to God for the Christian inheritance, especially for deliverance from sin and for forgiveness. (1:12-14)

II. Christ Is Supreme in the Universe and in the Church. (1:15—2:5)
   A. Christ is supreme in the universe. (1:15-17)
      1. He is the image of the unseen God. (1:15)
      2. God created all the world through Christ; Christ is Lord over all, and all the creation is united in Him. (1:16-17)
   B. Christ is supreme in the church because He embodies God's fullness and has reconciled all the creation to God. (1:18-20)
   C. Believers have experienced Christ's supremacy in the saving power of the gospel. (1:21-23)
   D. Christ's supremacy, as the One who fulfills God's eternal saving purpose for all people, is revealed in the gospel. (1:24-29)
   E. Christians should have full confidence in Christ's supremacy and sufficiency as their Savior. (2:1-5)

III. False Teachings Deceive Believers into Practices that Do Not Free from Sin. (2:6—3:4)
   A. Believers must not allow elemental human traditions to move them from their faith in Christ as an all-sufficient Savior. (2:6-8)
   B. Christ's fullness is available by faith. (2:9-10)
   C. Legal practices, like circumcision, do not enhance the power of Christ's cross to deliver from sin. (2:11-15)
   D. Keeping rules about diet, observing religious rituals, and suppressing normal physical needs do not add to Christ's ability to deliver from sin's power. (2:16-23)
   E. Believers should devote themselves to receiving more of the fullness of their new life in Christ. (3:1-4)

IV. The Nature of the New Life in Christ and Its Demands Upon the Believers. (3:5—4:6)
   A. Believers must allow Christ to cleanse their lives of old practices. (3:5-11)
   B. Believers must find in Christ and in life with their fellow believers the power for unity, mutual love, and forgiveness. (3:12-14)
   C. Church life should include teaching, mutual encouragement, and worship—all in Christ's name. (3:15-17)
   D. Christians should be faithful and compassionate in family relationships. (3:18—4:1)
   E. Believers should be faithful in prayer and live so that they will attract outsiders to Christ. (4:2-6)

V. Closing Greetings and Blessings (4:7-18)

Theological Conclusions

Colossians encourages and strengthens Christians by stressing four theological themes:

1. Christ's supremacy and sufficiency,
2. becoming and being a Christian,
3. the nature of the church, and
4. the ethical demands of the Christian life.

God created all the universe through Christ, who is Lord over and unifies all creation (1:15-17). The eternal Son of God became a real human being in Jesus Christ. He embodies all God's fullness (1:19; 2:9) and is the fullest revelation of the unseen God (1:15; 2:8). His death and resurrection are fully sufficient to reconcile and deliver all people and the creation itself (1:20-23; 2:13-15). Because of His triumph over sin, death, and the powers of darkness, God has established Jesus as Lord of the church and the creation (1:13-18; 2:14-15; 3:1).

Christ embodies God's *fullness*, and His saving work accomplishes our deliverance and forgiveness. Therefore, we can claim His fullness and His salvation only by faith (1:4,6,22-23; 2:5-7,9-10). No amount of rule-keeping, ritual, or austere living can bring any more of Christ's presence and power into our lives or enlarge our freedom from sin (2:11-23). Being Christian continues on the same basis as we began, faith in Christ. He reveals Himself to us, changes us, delivers us, and leads us only in response to our continued trust. Our response is to answer His love and faithfulness with our own.

The church is Christ's body, and He is its Head (1:18). Individual Christians have their identities determined by the larger community, the church. Each of us is a unique individual, but we are whole only in relation to the rest of the body. A nose separate from the head is still a nose but has no real identity or purpose apart from the rest of the face. Also, a face without a nose is less than complete. The body of Christ carries on His work in the world and shares His rejection (1:24-29).

The Christian life expresses itself in loving acceptance of others, in loving service and witness, and personal moral purity. How Christ loves and forgives us obligates us to treat others in the same way (3:12-15). Our love for others must be more than sentiment or tolerance. Compassion leads to action. Love expresses itself in service (1:4,9-10). Love also reaches out to the unsaved in speech and in actions that reveal Christ (1:28-29; 4:3-6).

Contemporary Teaching

The letter to Colosse speaks with real penetration to several modern, but not necessarily new, concerns.

1. We must be aware of systems of thought that devalue Christ's centrality as Revealer, Lord, and Savior. Astrology, cults with books that attempt to stand level with the Bible's authority, and teachings that blend human effort with faith to achieve freedom from sin must be avoided.

2. We must maintain grace and faith as the only bases for growing toward maturity. If a faith commitment is the only way to begin the Christian life, then it is the only way to go forward. Keeping rules, worshiping in certain ways, or having certain experiences do not earn us a larger share of Christ's fullness. See How to Accept Christ, pp. 1745-1747.

3. Extreme individualism destroys life together in the church. Our individual goals, preferences, and needs must be subordinated to those of the larger fellowship. Pride, preoccupation with self-centered concerns, and aggressive anger disrupt the unity of the church. We can best adopt the servant role in concert with others.

4. Christ gives us absolute standards of moral conduct. Impurity of thought, speech, and action; unforgiveness and hostility; unfaithfulness to Christ; deceit and greed always are destructive and wrong. Love, purity, acts of mercy, gentleness, faithfulness, and forgiveness always are edifying and right. We are enabled to live a new life as we receive of Christ's fullness by faith.

5. We must beware of a naive blending of elements of other faiths with Christianity. We may profit from dialogue with Buddhism, Hinduism, Judaism, and other world religions; but many elements of those faiths are not compatible with our own. Many elements of astrology and occultism are very similar to the errors at Colosse. Horoscopes do not reveal God's will. Only Christ does.

Chapter 1

PAUL, an apostle[a] of Christ Jesus by
the will of God,[b] and Timothy[c] our
brother,

2To the holy and faithful[a] brothers in
Christ at Colosse:

Grace[d] and peace to you from God our
Father.[b] [e]

Thanksgiving and Prayer

3We always thank God,[f] the Father of
our Lord Jesus Christ, when we pray for
you, 4because we have heard of your faith
in Christ Jesus and of the love[g] you have
for all the saints[h]— 5the faith and love
that spring from the hope[i] that is stored
up for you in heaven[j] and that you have
already heard about in the word of
truth,[k] the gospel 6that has come to you.
All over the world[l] this gospel is bearing
fruit[m] and growing, just as it has been
doing among you since the day you heard
it and understood God's grace in all its
truth. 7You learned it from Epaphras,[n]
our dear fellow servant, who is a faithful
minister[o] of Christ on our[c] behalf, 8and
who also told us of your love in the Spirit.[p]

9For this reason, since the day we
heard about you,[q] we have not stopped
praying for you[r] and asking God to fill
you with the knowledge of his will[s]
through all spiritual wisdom and understanding.[t] 10And we pray this in order
that you may live a life worthy[u] of the
Lord and may please him[v] in every way:
bearing fruit in every good work, growing
in the knowledge of God,[w] 11being
strengthened with all power[x] according
to his glorious might so that you may
have great endurance and patience,[y] and
joyfully 12giving thanks to the Father,[z]
who has qualified you[d] to share in the
inheritance[a] of the saints in the kingdom
of light.[b] 13For he has rescued us from
the dominion of darkness[c] and brought

1:1 [a]S 1Co 1:1 [b]S 2Co 1:1 [c]S Ac 16:1
1:2 [d]Col 4:18 [e]S Ro 1:7
1:3 [f]S Ro 1:8
1:4 [g]Gal 5:6 [h]S Ac 9:13; Eph 1:15; Phm 5
1:5 [i]ver 23; 1Th 5:8; Tit 1:2 [j]1Pe 1:4 [k]S 2Ti 2:15
1:6 [l]ver 23; S Ro 10:18 [m]Jn 15:16
1:7 [n]Col 4:12; Phm 23 [o]Col 4:7
1:8 [p]Ro 15:30
1:9 [q]ver 4; Eph 1:15 [r]S Ro 1:10 [s]S Eph 5:17 [t]S Eph 1:17
1:10 [u]S Eph 4:1 [v]S 2Co 5:9 [w]ver 6
1:11 [x]S Php 4:13 [y]Eph 4:2
1:12 [z]Eph 5:20 [a]S Ac 20:32 [b]S Ac 26:18
1:13 [c]S Ac 26:18

[a]2 Or *believing* [b]2 Some manuscripts *Father and the Lord Jesus Christ* [c]7 Some manuscripts *your* [d]12 Some manuscripts *us*

1:2 THE CHURCH, Saints—See notes on Ro 1:7; Eph 1:1.

1:2 PRAYER, Blessing—See note on Ro 1:7.

1:3–14 GOD, Trinity—This passage is essential for us to develop an understanding of the nature of the one God known in three Persons. We pray and give thanks to the Father. His grace in providing salvation is the heart of the gospel (v 6). He fills us with spiritual wisdom to know and do His will. We grow in His knowledge and gain strength from His power. Even though we may not be Jews, God gives us the necessary qualifications to be His heirs, participating in the kingdom, which belongs to the beloved Son. God has rescued us and reconciled us through Christ. Christ is the Father's Son in whom we have faith and whose ministers we are. We seek to live lives worthy of His example so we may fully please Him. He is the agent of our redemption and forgiveness. The Spirit is the source of the love which characterizes God's church.

1:3–6 PROCLAMATION, Growth—The ultimate purpose of the gospel is to bring people to faith in Jesus Christ and lead them to grow and mature in that relationship (1 Pe 2:1–3). God's concern is not only for the salvation of the lost but also for the regular spiritual growth of the saved. The failure to grow spiritually often produces theological and moral heresy (1 Co 3:1–3). The proclamation of the gospel is God's safeguard for believers intended to encourage us in spiritual growth and perseverance.

1:3 PRAYER, Thanksgiving—See note on Php 1:3.

1:4–5 THE CHURCH, Saints—Heavenly hope is the basis for saintly service. See notes on Ro 16:2; Eph 1:15.

1:5–7 REVELATION, Word—The revelation of God's truth produces growth and response to grace and redemption. Preaching the gospel of hope and love is one means of God's revelation.

1:5 LAST THINGS, Inspires Hope—Hope that is anchored in the glories of heaven inspires faith and love for present living. The basis of future, heavenly hope is the good news of the Word of truth.

1:6 GOD, Grace—Salvation involves understanding that God is on our side because He has chosen to show us grace rather than absolute justice.

1:6 EVANGELISM, Results—The gospel of grace is the power of God unto salvation (Ro 1:16). As the gospel goes all over the world, it breaks down all barriers: religious, cultural, and racial. This glorious reality brings people to faith in Christ and bears fruit for God's glory.

1:7–8 HOLY SPIRIT, Transforms—God gives His Spirit to those who have faith in His Son Jesus (v 4). The Spirit exercises a personal, moral, transforming influence upon us, so we become people of love. This is God's ultimate purpose for us (Mt 22:34–40; 1 Co 13) because it makes possible the common, covenant life (fellowship) shared by God and His people. See note on Php 2:1–2. Love is the firstfruit of the Spirit (Gal 5:22).

1:7 THE CHURCH, Servants—Paul called Epaphras a fellow slave and a faithful servant (*diakonos*) of Christ Jesus. All Christians are ministers of Christ; all who minister in His name are highly esteemed. The greatest in the kingdom is the one who stoops to help others. See notes on Mt 20:20–28; Ro 1:1; Eph 3:7.

1:7 CHURCH LEADERS, Deacon—Epaphras was a minister (Greek *diakonos*) of Christ. (Compare 4:7; Eph 6:21; 1 Th 3:2.) Deacon originally meant table waiters or servants (Jn 2:5,9). The early church leaders saw themselves as servants of the new covenant (2 Co 3:6), of Christ (2 Co 11:23), of God (2 Co 6:4), of the gospel (Eph 3:7), or of the church (Col 1:25). These leaders followed Christ's call for greatness by becoming servants (Mk 10:43; Greek *diakonos*). Eventually deacons became one of the two major leadership positions in the church along with the pastors, who could be called overseers or bishops and elders. See note on Php 1:1.

1:9–12 PRAYER, Intercession—See note on Php 1:4–11. Being filled with the knowledge of God results in the life described in vv 10–12. See Guide to Intercession, pp. 1800–1801.

1:10 CHRISTIAN ETHICS, Character—See note on Eph 4:1–3.

1:11,29 GOD, Power—To live the Christian life we must receive God's strength. He has all power so we need not worry the supply will run dry. In troubled times His strength provides the patience we need to continue growing in Christ rather than giving up.

1:13–14 JESUS CHRIST, Kingdom of God—The kingdom of God is the kingdom of Jesus. Those who have received His redemption and forgiveness are members of the kingdom.

1:13–14 SALVATION, Definition—See note on Jdg 3:9. Humans normally live under the power or tyranny of evil and sin. Satan rules life. God has defeated the dark powers and led us away to a new homeland—the kingdom where His beloved Son rules. There we experience the freedom of His redemption and of forgiveness from sin and guilt. Salvation is thus a present experience of new living conditions.

us into the kingdom[d] of the Son he
loves,[e] 14in whom we have redemption,[e][f] the forgiveness of sins.[g]

The Supremacy of Christ

15He is the image[h] of the invisible
God,[i] the firstborn[j] over all creation.
16For by him all things were created:[k]
things in heaven and on earth, visible and
invisible, whether thrones or powers or
rulers or authorities;[l] all things were
created by him and for him.[m] 17He is before all things,[n] and in him all things
hold together. 18And he is the head[o] of
the body, the church;[p] he is the beginning and the firstborn[q] from among the
dead,[r] so that in everything he might
have the supremacy. 19For God was
pleased[s] to have all his fullness[t] dwell in
him, 20and through him to reconcile[u] to
himself all things, whether things on
earth or things in heaven,[v] by making
peace[w] through his blood,[x] shed on the
cross.

21Once you were alienated from God
and were enemies[y] in your minds[z] because of[f] your evil behavior. 22But now
he has reconciled[a] you by Christ's physical body[b] through death to present you[c]
holy in his sight, without blemish and
free from accusation[d]— 23if you continue[e] in your faith, established[f] and firm,
not moved from the hope[g] held out in
the gospel. This is the gospel that you
heard and that has been proclaimed to
every creature under heaven,[h] and of
which I, Paul, have become a servant.[i]

Paul's Labor for the Church

24Now I rejoice[j] in what was suffered

1:13 [d]2Pe 1:11 [e]Mt 3:17 **1:14** [f]S Ro 3:24 [g]Eph 1:7 **1:15** [h]S Jn 14:9 [i]S Jn 1:18; 1Ti 1:17; Heb 11:27 [j]S ver 18 **1:16** [k]S Jn 1:3 [l]Eph 1:20,21 [m]S Ro 11:36 **1:17** [n]S Jn 1:2 **1:18** [o]S Eph 1:22 [p]ver 24; S 1Co 12:27 [q]ver 15; Ps 89:27; Ro 8:29; Heb 1:6 [r]Ac 26:23; Rev 1:5 **1:19** [s]S Eph 1:5 [t]S Jn 1:16 **1:20** [u]S Ro 5:10 [v]Eph 1:10 [w]S Lk 2:14 [x]Eph 2:13 **1:21** [y]Ro 5:10 [z]Eph 2:3 **1:22** [a]ver 20; S Ro 5:10 [b]Ro 7:4 [c]S 2Co 4:14 [d]Eph 1:4; 5:27 **1:23** [e]S Ro 11:22 [f]Eph 3:17 [g]ver 5 [h]ver 6; S Ro 10:18 [i]ver 25; S 1Co 3:5 **1:24** [j]S 2Co 6:10

[e] *14* A few late manuscripts *redemption through his blood* [f] *21* Or *minds, as shown by*

1:15–20 JESUS CHRIST, God—Jesus is superior in every realm of life. He is the perfect image or representation of God, unlike sinful humans created in that image but marring it through rebellion (Ge 1:26–27). To see the visible Jesus is to see the invisible God. He has inheritance rights and supreme authority over all creation because He is God's Son. He participated in creation. See note on Jn 1:1–18. He thus has authority over all created beings, even the invisible demonic powers. Compare note on Eph 1:20–23. Creation was for Him, having as its goal His glory and rule. Nothing existed before Him, and thus nothing and no one can claim authority over Him. What He created, He held together in a meaningful pattern, so all meaning in life and the universe has its source in Christ. That meaning is revealed to the world through the church of which Christ is the Head. He is Head because He was the first to be resurrected from the dead. God chose to let the fullness or total being of God dwell in the Son. On this basis the church confesses Jesus is God in flesh who restored the broken relationship between us and God by dying on the cross.

1:15–17 JESUS CHRIST, Preexistent—Jesus is the "firstborn" or prior to all creation. He is the Agent of creation both on earth and heaven and has superiority over all things.

1:15 JESUS CHRIST, God—In contrast to male and female who were created "in the image of God" (Ge 1:27), Christ "is the image of the invisible God." Jesus Christ is the perfect and complete revelation of God to humanity.

1:15–17 CREATION, Jesus Christ—Many interpreters see in the background of this passage a heresy similar to an eclectic viewpoint known as gnosticism. In this view matter was essentially evil. The pure Christ could not be contaminated by an "evil" material body in this understanding. Christ came as merely an emanation from the Father and not as a true human being. Paul showed neither matter nor human bodies are inherently evil. God did not create evil things. His creation was very good. Christ existed as coequal and coexistent with the Father. He indeed was the personal Creator by whom the world came into being. Everything that was created originated with Him. The world that has become marred and divided will be restored to a unity only as it finds its center in Christ. He is the Source and, therefore, has authority over all creation.

1:16–18 STEWARDSHIP, Purpose of Possessions—Christ is the source of creation and the power that sustains it. He gives purpose and stability to the material order. This provides the basis for the Christian view of the material world. This view contrasts sharply with non-Christian views that either say material things are evil and valueless or think the material world is all that exists and so is all-important. Christians view material things as good and valuable if used to fulfill God's holy purposes for money and possessions and to reach the lost world. See note on Ge 1:26–31.

1:18 THE CHURCH, Body of Christ—The church has only one position of honor, which is permanently filled by Christ. See note on Eph 1:22–23.

1:19–20 CHRISTIAN ETHICS, War and Peace—Sin and guilt separate us from God, the source of peace. Reconciliation bringing peace and order into creation has been performed through Jesus' act of redemption. True peace with God is found through Him.

1:20–22 JESUS CHRIST, Redeemer—The Christ who created, maintains, and rules the cosmos came to earth to die for us so He could let us be at peace with God and make us morally holy in God's sight.

1:20–23 SALVATION, Reconciliation—See notes on 2 Co 5:18–21; Eph 2:16–18. God's reconciliation through Christ is all inclusive. It is vertical, reconciliation between persons and God; and horizontal, reconciliation between persons and persons and between nature and God. As all humankind and all nature descended from good in the fall of Adam, so all persons and nature itself are restored in the saving work of Christ (Ro 8:19–23).

1:20 SALVATION, Atonement—Christ's death on the cross makes it possible for all things to be reconciled to God. It brings peace or wholeness back to God's creation. His atonement has a cosmic dimension.

1:21–22 HUMANITY, Relationship to God—The relationship with God, which had been broken by human rebellion and sinfulness, has now been restored by God through the death of Christ. God's aim has always been to create a holy, pure people (Lev 11:44). Christ's death covered our sins. Christ will present us to the Father as His people with no one to accuse us. Having this assurance in Christ, we must live the life of holiness.

1:21 SIN, Alienation—Sin sets up a barrier between the sinner and God, making us God's enemies. Christ provides a way to destroy the sin barrier and reconcile enemies.

1:23 THE CHURCH, Servants—See note on Eph 3:7.

1:23–29 EVANGELISM, Call to Evangelize—The call to witness makes us servants of the gospel, not its masters. As we preach the gospel, we must obey it. Serving the gospel means sharing it with other people wherever we are. Serving means laboring with all the energy God gives to bring Christ's eternal hope to all people.

1:24 EVIL AND SUFFERING, Rejoicing—Christ's suffering adequately atoned for sin. The church continues to suffer so all the world may know of and benefit from Christ's atonement. Christians must continue the ministry and, therefore, the suffering of Jesus until He returns. Knowing the ultimate purpose of our suffering allows us to rejoice in it. We do not

for you, and I fill up in my flesh what is
still lacking in regard to Christ's afflictions,[k] for the sake of his body, which is
the church.[l] 25I have become its servant[m] by the commission God gave me[n]
to present to you the word of God[o] in its
fullness— 26the mystery[p] that has been
kept hidden for ages and generations, but
is now disclosed to the saints. 27To them
God has chosen to make known[q] among
the Gentiles the glorious riches[r] of this
mystery, which is Christ in you,[s] the
hope of glory.
28We proclaim him, admonishing[t] and
teaching everyone with all wisdom,[u] so
that we may present everyone perfect[v]
in Christ. 29To this end I labor,[w] struggling[x] with all his energy, which so powerfully works in me.[y]

Chapter 2

I want you to know how much I am
struggling[z] for you and for those at Laodicea,[a] and for all who have not met me
personally. 2My purpose is that they may
be encouraged in heart[b] and united in
love, so that they may have the full riches
of complete understanding, in order that
they may know the mystery[c] of God,
namely, Christ, 3in whom are hidden all
the treasures of wisdom and knowledge.[d] 4I tell you this so that no one may
deceive you by fine-sounding arguments.[e] 5For though I am absent from
you in body, I am present with you in
spirit[f] and delight to see how orderly[g]
you are and how firm[h] your faith in
Christ[i] is.

Freedom From Human Regulations Through Life With Christ

6So then, just as you received Christ
Jesus as Lord,[j] continue to live in him,
7rooted[k] and built up in him, strengthened in the faith as you were taught,[l]
and overflowing with thankfulness.
8See to it that no one takes you captive
through hollow and deceptive philosophy,[m] which depends on human tradition
and the basic principles of this world[n]
rather than on Christ.
9For in Christ all the fullness[o] of the
Deity lives in bodily form, 10and you have
been given fullness in Christ, who is the
head[p] over every power and authority.[q]
11In him you were also circumcised,[r] in
the putting off of the sinful nature,[g][s] not
with a circumcision done by the hands of
men but with the circumcision done by
Christ, 12having been buried with him in
baptism[t] and raised with him[u] through

[g] 11 Or *the flesh*

1:24 [k]S 2Co 1:5 [l]S 1Co 12:27
1:25 [m]ver 23; S 1Co 3:5 [n]Eph 3:2 [o]S Heb 4:12
1:26 [p]S Ro 16:25
1:27 [q]S Mt 13:11 [r]S Ro 2:4 [s]S Ro 8:10
1:28 [t]Col 3:16 [u]1Co 2:6,7 [v]Mt 5:48; Eph 5:27
1:29 [w]1Co 15:10; 2Co 11:23 [x]Col 2:1 [y]Eph 1:19; 3:7
2:1 [z]Col 1:29; 4:12 [a]Col 4:13,15,16; Rev 1:11; 3:14
2:2 [b]Eph 6:22; Col 4:8 [c]S Ro 16:25
2:3 [d]Isa 11:2; Jer 23:5; Ro 11:33; 1Co 1:24,30
2:4 [e]S Ro 16:18
2:5 [f]1Co 5:4; 1Th 2:17 [g]1Co 14:40 [h]1Pe 5:9 [i]S Ac 20:21
2:6 [j]S Jn 13:13; Col 1:10
2:7 [k]Eph 3:17 [l]Eph 4:21
2:8 [m]1Ti 6:20 [n]ver 20; Gal 4:3
2:9 [o]S Jn 1:16
2:10 [p]S Eph 1:22 [q]S Mt 28:18
2:11 [r]Ro 2:29; Php 3:3 [s]S Gal 5:24
2:12 [t]S Mt 28:19 [u]S Ro 6:5

suffer for ourselves or for some mysterious evil force we do not understand. We suffer for Christ and His church.

1:24 THE CHURCH, Body of Christ—See note on Eph 1:22–23.

1:25–27 REVELATION, Word—Revelation serves God's church, calling people to proclaim God's word to all people. The word brings hope of eternal life in Christ.

1:25 THE CHURCH, Servants—Paul's servanthood came by divine call so the gospel might be proclaimed to all people. He was servant (Greek *diakonos*) not only of Christ but also of the church. Christ's called-out servants do not seek to use the church for personal advantage. They are the church's slaves for Christ's advantage. See note on Eph 3:7.

1:25 PROCLAMATION, Call—See notes on Jer 1:4–9; 1 Co 1:17–18.

1:26–27 THE CHURCH, Saints—See notes on 1 Co 1:2; Eph 3:6.

1:27 JESUS CHRIST, Hope—Our hope for life in glory beyond death rests in the saving work of Jesus. We have this hope because Jesus now lives in our lives.

1:27 SALVATION, As Being in Christ—To be in Christ is to have Christ in you. Communion with Christ is our hope of eternal life here and hereafter. Life in Christ is the goal toward which God pointed creation from the beginning.

1:28 PROCLAMATION, Instruction—See note on Ac 15:35. Proclamation seeks to instruct believers to avoid and to resist temptation and to grow into Christian maturity. Such proclamation centers on Christ, not on human abilities and achievements.

2:1 PRAYER, Sincerity—Paul labored in prayer. See note on Ro 15:30–32.

2:2–3,9 GOD, Trinity—See note on Mt 3:16–17.

2:3 JESUS CHRIST, Secret—Jesus is God's secret, an open secret for saving all the world. All of God's treasures are hidden in Jesus. God's secret is expanded to include us, since we are to be in union with Christ (v 6).

2:6–8 EDUCATION, Correction—In the absence of sound teaching, distortions of truth will always rush in to fill the vacuum. Paul expressed the hope that his teaching of the believers at Philippi would establish them in the faith firmly enough to enable them to distinguish between Christian doctrine and human philosophies parading as religious teachings. Today, no less than in the first century, Christian education stands as a bulwark against false teaching. Such education must be grounded in Christ as Lord of life not on faith in deceptive human teachers.

2:7 PRAYER, Thanksgiving—Perhaps the dominant note in Paul's teaching on prayer is the importance of thanksgiving. No matter the physical circumstances, thanks for salvation floods over out of the Christian life. See note on 2 Co 2:14.

2:9–15 JESUS CHRIST, God—V 9 is perhaps the fullest affirmation of Christ's deity in Scripture. In Jesus of Nazareth, God was uniquely and bodily among us. Since the power of God rested in Jesus Christ, Christ overcomes all other powers. Jesus' mark is not physical circumcision. Rather, Jesus' circumcision is a symbolic expression to describe the excising of humanity's lower nature to bring the renewal of being in Christ. Baptism is the outward sign of this renewal. Paul employed a series of metaphors to describe this cosmic Christ.

2:9–10 JESUS CHRIST, Son of God—See note on 1:15–20.

2:9 JESUS CHRIST, God—To counter the heresy in Colosse of substituting inferior beings for Christ (2:8,16–17), Paul boasted of Christ's superiority in that the very essence of God dwells in Christ.

2:12 GOD, Power—Salvation for people comes as much from the power of God as it does from the love of God. God's grace, as we experience it, is the combination of His love and His power focused upon our needs. The greatest display of God's power was in His raising Christ from the dead. That same power raises us to new life in Christ. We must trust God to use His power to save us.

2:12,20 ORDINANCES, Baptism as New Life—Baptism pictures the believer's death and resurrection with Christ "through your faith in the power of God." It is the power of God working through the faith of the believer which actually

your faith in the power of God, who
raised him from the dead.[v]
13When you were dead in your sins[w]
and in the uncircumcision of your sinful
nature,[h] God made you[i] alive[x] with
Christ. He forgave us all our sins,[y] 14hav-
ing canceled the written code, with its
regulations,[z] that was against us and that
stood opposed to us; he took it away, nailing it to the cross.[a] 15And having disarmed the powers and authorities,[b] he
made a public spectacle of them, triumphing over them[c] by the cross.[j]
16Therefore do not let anyone judge
you[d] by what you eat or drink,[e] or with
regard to a religious festival,[f] a New
Moon celebration[g] or a Sabbath day.[h]
17These are a shadow of the things that
were to come;[i] the reality, however, is
found in Christ. 18Do not let anyone who
delights in false humility[j] and the worship of angels disqualify you for the
prize.[k] Such a person goes into great detail about what he has seen, and his unspiritual mind puffs him up with idle notions. 19He has lost connection with the
Head,[l] from whom the whole body,[m]
supported and held together by its liga-
ments and sinews, grows as God causes it
to grow.[n]
20Since you died with Christ[o] to the
basic principles of this world,[p] why, as
though you still belonged to it, do you
submit to its rules:[q] 21"Do not handle!
Do not taste! Do not touch!"? 22These are
all destined to perish[r] with use, because
they are based on human commands and
teachings.[s] 23Such regulations indeed
have an appearance of wisdom, with their
self-imposed worship, their false humility[t] and their harsh treatment of the
body, but they lack any value in restraining sensual indulgence.

Chapter 3

Rules for Holy Living

SINCE, then, you have been raised with
Christ,[u] set your hearts on things
above, where Christ is seated at the right
hand of God.[v] 2Set your minds on things
above, not on earthly things.[w] 3For you
died,[x] and your life is now hidden with
Christ in God. 4When Christ, who is

2:12 [v]S Ac 2:24
2:13 [w]Eph 2:1,5 [x]Eph 2:5 [y]Eph 4:32
2:14 [z]Eph 2:15 [a]1Pe 2:24
2:15 [b]ver 10; Eph 6:12 [c]Mt 12:29; Lk 10:18; Jn 12:31
2:16 [d]Ro 14:3,4 [e]Mk 7:19; Ro 14:17 [f]Lev 23:2; Ro 14:5 [g]1Ch 23:31 [h]Mk 2:27,28; Gal 4:10
2:17 [i]Heb 8:5; 10:1
2:18 [j]ver 23 [k]1Co 9:24; Php 3:14
2:19 [l]S Eph 1:22 [m]S 1Co 12:27 [n]Eph 4:16
2:20 [o]S Ro 6:6 [p]ver 8; Gal 4:3,9 [q]ver 14,16
2:22 [r]1Co 6:13 [s]Isa 29:13; Mt 15:9; Tit 1:14
2:23 [t]ver 18
3:1 [u]S Ro 6:5 [v]S Mk 16:19
3:2 [w]Php 3:19,20
3:3 [x]S Ro 6:2; 2Co 5:14

[h] *13* Or *your flesh* [i] *13* Some manuscripts *us* [j] *15* Or *them in him*

brings about this spiritual death and resurrection, but baptism is the outward sign of it. Because we as Christians have died to the old way of life, we must not any longer be controlled by "the basic principles of this world." These principles are the worldly values and powerful forces which control and influence human lives in contradiction to the purposes of God. Such worldly principles include lust, wealth, political power, Satanic temptations. Since Christians have died with Christ to their old sinful natures and risen to a new life in Christ, as pictured in baptism, we should not any longer be controlled by the old powers which dominated our lives before we became Christians. See note on Ro 6:3–4.

2:13–15 JESUS CHRIST, Death—Christ's death for us brought eternal victory over all forces—human and demonic—which claim power or authority over us and our world. Our failure to meet legal regulations is not held against us. We are forgiven in Christ's death.

2:13 SIN, Death—Like the Jews who viewed the uncircumcised as outside the covenant promises of God, so Paul understood those outside of Christ. To be outside of Christ is to be spiritually dead.

2:13–23 CHRISTIAN ETHICS, Character—Paul contrasted the development of character as proposed by the pagan world with the Christian approach. Mottos are not enough. Religious rituals and prohibitions do not develop character. Personal character grows as a part of the church—Christ's body. Only as we are directly connected with Christ do we grow. Such growth leads us away from self indulgence of worldly desires to be like Christ.

2:15 EVIL AND SUFFERING, Satan—In Jesus, God triumphed over superhuman evil (1:16; Eph 6:12). Evil is only temporary. The cross has sealed its doom.

2:16–17 JESUS CHRIST, Fulfilled—Jesus fulfilled the Jewish regulations and celebrations by achieving perfectly the intentions they achieved only partially.

2:17 ELECTION, In Christ—The ritualistic and ceremonial trappings of religion, the esoteric doctrinal extremes of cults, and the deceptive philosophies of secular faiths are not the essence of true faith. The reality is to be found only in Jesus Christ. The elect, therefore, are committed to the basic principles of Christ and not to the false values of society.

2:18–19 SIN, Alienation—Sin infects even the "spiritually minded" when their speculations separate them from union with the rest of the body of Christ. Religious knowledge and spiritual experiences can be occasions for sin when they lead us to pride. Pride makes us concentrate on ourselves and our desires rather than on Christ and the needs of His church.

2:19 THE CHURCH, Body of Christ—See note on Eph 1:22–23.

2:20–23 WORSHIP, False—See note on Ex 22:20.

3:1–4 JESUS CHRIST, Ascension—Christ is with the Father. Christians also die in Christ to be raised in Christ.

3:1 ORDINANCES, Baptism as New Life—Most of Paul's references to baptism as death and resurrection emphasize the old sins which are left behind, the death of the old nature which has been buried with Christ. Here he emphasized the new life in Christ, being raised with Him. This new life is characterized by setting our hearts on things above. In the old life we were controlled by the values and powers of the sinful world. Now we are to be controlled by the vision of Christ, seated at the right hand of God (which means He is exercising the power of God in the world through our lives). Others around us may be controlled by the worldly values, but we as Christians are to be controlled by the values of Christ. See notes on 2:12,20; Ro 6:3–4.

3:4 JESUS CHRIST, Life—Jesus the ascended Lord is the source of life now and the hope for eternal glory when He returns.

3:4 SALVATION, As Being in Christ—Christ is the very life of Christians. Compare 2 Ti 1:1. The Christian believer will be one with Christ in the end, as in the beginning of the Christian journey. The resurrected Christ is at the center of everything the Christian does and is the indwelling power behind each accomplishment of the Christian. This is our guarantee of knowing Him when He returns to complete the establishment of His kingdom.

3:4 LAST THINGS, Humanity Restored—Restoration to glory for fallen humanity awaits the return of Christ for its full realization. Moral and spiritual restoration begins with forgiveness, conversion, and new birth, as we die to sin and live with Christ (v 3). See How To Accept Christ, pp. 1745–1747. It continues with sanctification or spiritual growth. It climaxes at the appearance of Christ, when restored humanity shares His glory. Such is the personal hope of each individual Christian.

your[k] life,[y] appears,[z] then you also will
appear with him in glory.[a]
5Put to death,[b] therefore, whatever belongs to your earthly nature:[c] sexual immorality,[d] impurity, lust, evil desires and
greed,[e] which is idolatry.[f] 6Because of
these, the wrath of God[g] is coming.[l]
7You used to walk in these ways, in the
life you once lived.[h] 8But now you must
rid yourselves[i] of all such things as
these: anger, rage, malice, slander,[j] and
filthy language from your lips.[k] 9Do not
lie to each other,[l] since you have taken
off your old self[m] with its practices 10and
have put on the new self,[n] which is being renewed[o] in knowledge in the image
of its Creator.[p] 11Here there is no Greek
or Jew,[q] circumcised or uncircumcised,[r]
barbarian, Scythian, slave or free,[s] but
Christ is all,[t] and is in all.
12Therefore, as God's chosen people,
holy and dearly loved, clothe yourselves[u]
with compassion, kindness, humility,[v]
gentleness and patience.[w] 13Bear with
each other[x] and forgive whatever griev-
ances you may have against one another.
Forgive as the Lord forgave you.[y] 14And
over all these virtues put on love,[z] which
binds them all together in perfect unity.[a]
15Let the peace of Christ[b] rule in your
hearts, since as members of one body[c]
you were called to peace.[d] And be thankful. 16Let the word of Christ[e] dwell in
you richly as you teach and admonish one
another with all wisdom,[f] and as you
sing psalms,[g] hymns and spiritual songs
with gratitude in your hearts to God.[h]
17And whatever you do,[i] whether in
word or deed, do it all in the name of the
Lord Jesus, giving thanks[j] to God the Father through him.

Rules for Christian Households

3:18–4:1pp — Eph 5:22–6:9

18Wives, submit to your husbands,[k] as
is fitting in the Lord.
19Husbands, love your wives and do
not be harsh with them.
20Children, obey your parents in everything, for this pleases the Lord.

3:4 [y]Gal 2:20 [z]1Co 1:7 [a]1Pe 1:13; 1Jn 3:2 **3:5** [b]S Ro 6:2; S Eph 4:22 [c]S Gal 5:24 [d]S 1Co 6:18 [e]Eph 5:3 [f]Gal 5:19-21; Eph 5:5 **3:6** [g]S Ro 1:18 **3:7** [h]S Eph 2:2 **3:8** [i]S Eph 4:22 [j]Eph 4:31 [k]Eph 4:29 **3:9** [l]S Eph 4:22,25 [m]S Ro 6:6 **3:10** [n]S Ro 6:4; S 13:14 [o]Ro 12:2; S 2Co 4:16; Eph 4:23 [p]Eph 2:10 **3:11** [q]Ro 10:12; 1Co 12:13 [r]S 1Co 7:19 [s]Gal 3:28 [t]Eph 1:23 **3:12** [u]ver 10 [v]Php 2:3 [w]2Co 6:6; Gal 5:22,23; Eph 4:2 **3:13** [x]Eph 4:2 [y]Eph 4:32 **3:14** [z]1Co 13:1-13 [a]S Ro 15:5 **3:15** [b]S Jn 14:27 [c]S Ro 12:5 [d]S Ro 14:19 **3:16** [e]Ro 10:17 [f]Col 1:28 [g]Ps 47:7 [h]S Eph 5:19 **3:17** [i]1Co 10:31 [j]S Eph 5:20 **3:18** [k]S Eph 5:22

[k]4 Some manuscripts *our* [l]6 Some early manuscripts *coming on those who are disobedient*

3:5–8 SIN, Depravity—See note on Gal 5:16–21.
3:5–17 CHRISTIAN ETHICS, Character—One pattern of ethical living is to put off the negative and put on the positive. Positive Christian attitudes turn attention away from personal desires and achievements to relations with and needs of others. Love is the center from which all other Christian attitudes flow. See note on 1 Co 13:1–13.
3:5 CHRISTIAN ETHICS, Property Rights—Greed is a form of idolatry, making what is material take the place of God. See note on 1 Co 5:11.
3:6 GOD, Wrath—The wrath of God is just as real as the love of God. Wrath is necessary because human sin is real. The threat of God's wrath should lead us to forsake sin. See notes on Mt 3:7–10; Jn 3:36; Ro 1:18.
3:8–9 CHRISTIAN ETHICS, Language—A person ruled by Christ and led by the Spirit will put away speech patterns reflecting anger and defamation of others' character. Language which is less than clean and pure in tone and content should not come from a Christian's mouth.
3:8–10 FAMILY, Communication—See note on Eph 4:15,25,29–31.
3:9–11 HUMANITY, Image of God—The image of God which had been marred by human sin is being renewed through Christ Jesus, who is the image of God (1:15). In salvation we are becoming like Christ. This new image is renewed in the knowledge which God gives rather than in a rebellious search for knowledge which He did not reveal. This new image overcomes those things such as race or religious rites which have separated us from one another. Christ becomes the only focus of attention. All else is forgotten. See notes on Ge 1:26–29; 5:1–3; 33:1–10; 2 Co 4:4; Gal 3:26–29; Jas 3:9.
3:10 GOD, Creator—The spiritual work of God in human hearts is the climactic phase of what God began to do in creating the physical universe and bringing life into existence on earth.
3:10 SALVATION, Renewal—Salvation changes a person from an old self to a new self. The new self is a self recreated in the image of God to be as He originally created us (Ge 1:27). Christ is the model, for He is the image of God (Col 1:15). We grow daily to know Christ better and to be more like Him. We know His will and are determined to do it.
3:11 THE CHURCH, People of God—See note on Gal 3:26–29. Those who have put on the new nature should not be burdened with the old distinctions.
3:11 EVANGELISM, Results—We are all one in Christ. He has melded us all together in His great love. See note on Eph 3:6.
3:12 ELECTION, Responsibility—The doctrine of Jesus' resurrection and the doctrine of election interface in determining the principles needed for the practice of Christian ethics. The elect are persons who have put to death the greed and evil desires of the flesh to arise in the newness of holy living with Jesus Christ. God's elect are bound to each other by the virtues of love, forgiveness, unity, compassion, kindness, humility, gentleness, and patience. The elect do everything in the name of Jesus Christ, for the glory and honor of God.
3:15 THE CHURCH, Body of Christ—In Christ, the church seeks to bring wholeness and peaceful acceptance of others. Disputes and fights should never characterize the body of the Prince of Peace. See notes on Eph 1:22–23; 4:1–6.
3:15 PRAYER, Thanksgiving—See note on 2:7.
3:16–17 HOLY SCRIPTURE, Authoritative—The revelation of God in the words and life of Jesus is to be the guiding set of principles by which all believers live. Wisdom, uplifting songs, hymns, and worship actions which elevate the believer are to be used regularly. Thanksgiving is to be a daily attitude. Paul assumed the church knew Christ's teachings even though written Gospels were not yet available. Christ's teachings had become authoritative for the church as they were preserved, passed on, preached, and interpreted in oral form. They remain authoritative for the church in the inspired written Bible.
3:16 WORSHIP, Music—See note on Eph 5:19–20. Music and teaching played vital roles in New Testament worship.
3:16 PRAYER, Praise—See note on Eph 5:19–20. Praise and thanksgiving come from lives filled with God's Word.
3:16 EDUCATION, Christians—Ideally, in a congregation of Christians, every person is a teacher, and every person a learner. Each of us has something to share out of our personal experiences with God. Each of us has something to learn from brothers and sisters in Christ. This will happen only where the word of Christ dwells within the hearts of the people. As we sing hymns of worship and praise with grateful hearts, we teach one another.
3:18–21 FAMILY, Role Relationships—See note on Eph 5:22—6:4.

21Fathers, do not embitter your children, or they will become discouraged.
22Slaves, obey your earthly masters in
everything; and do it, not only when
their eye is on you and to win their favor,
but with sincerity of heart and reverence
for the Lord. 23Whatever you do, work at
it with all your heart, as working for the
Lord, not for men, 24since you know that
you will receive an inheritance[l] from the
Lord as a reward.[m] It is the Lord Christ
you are serving. 25Anyone who does
wrong will be repaid for his wrong, and
there is no favoritism.[n]

Chapter 4

MASTERS, provide your slaves with
what is right and fair,[o] because
you know that you also have a Master in
heaven.

Further Instructions

2Devote yourselves to prayer,[p] being
watchful and thankful. 3And pray for us,
too, that God may open a door[q] for our
message, so that we may proclaim the
mystery[r] of Christ, for which I am in
chains.[s] 4Pray that I may proclaim it
clearly, as I should. 5Be wise[t] in the way
you act toward outsiders;[u] make the
most of every opportunity.[v] 6Let your
conversation be always full of grace,[w]
seasoned with salt,[x] so that you may
know how to answer everyone.[y]

Final Greetings

7Tychicus[z] will tell you all the news
about me. He is a dear brother, a faithful
minister and fellow servant[a] in the Lord.

3:24 [l]S Ac 20:32 [m]S Mt 16:27
3:25 [n]S Ac 10:34
4:1 [o]Lev 25:43,53
4:2 [p]S Lk 18:1
4:3 [q]S Ac 14:27 [r]S Ro 16:25 [s]S Ac 21:33
4:5 [t]Eph 5:15 [u]S Mk 4:11 [v]Eph 5:16
4:6 [w]Eph 4:29 [x]Mk 9:50 [y]1Pe 3:15
4:7 [z]S Ac 20:4 [a]Eph 6:21,22; Col 1:7
4:8 [b]Eph 6:21,22; Col 2:2
4:9 [c]Phm 10 [d]ver 12
4:10 [e]S Ac 19:29 [f]S Ac 12:12 [g]S Ac 4:36
4:11 [h]S Php 2:25
4:12 [i]Col 1:7; Phm 23 [j]ver 9 [k]S Ro 15:30 [l]S 1Co 2:6
4:13 [m]S Col 2:1
4:14 [n]2Ti 4:11; Phm 24 [o]2Ti 4:10; Phm 24
4:15 [p]S Col 2:1 [q]S Ro 16:5
4:16 [r]2Th 3:14; S 1Ti 4:13
4:17 [s]Phm 2 [t]2Ti 4:5
4:18 [u]S 1Co 16:21 [v]Heb 13:3 [w]S Ac 21:33 [x]1Ti 6:21; 2Ti 4:22; Tit 3:15; Heb 13:25

8I am sending him to you for the express
purpose that you may know about our[m]
circumstances and that he may encourage
your hearts.[b] 9He is coming with Onesimus,[c] our faithful and dear brother, who
is one of you.[d] They will tell you everything that is happening here.
10My fellow prisoner Aristarchus[e]
sends you his greetings, as does Mark,[f]
the cousin of Barnabas.[g] (You have received instructions about him; if he
comes to you, welcome him.) 11Jesus,
who is called Justus, also sends greetings.
These are the only Jews among my fellow
workers[h] for the kingdom of God, and
they have proved a comfort to me. 12Epa-
phras,[i] who is one of you[j] and a servant
of Christ Jesus, sends greetings. He is always wrestling in prayer for you,[k] that
you may stand firm in all the will of God,
mature[l] and fully assured. 13I vouch for
him that he is working hard for you and
for those at Laodicea[m] and Hierapolis.
14Our dear friend Luke,[n] the doctor, and
Demas[o] send greetings. 15Give my greetings to the brothers at Laodicea,[p] and to
Nympha and the church in her house.[q]
16After this letter has been read to you,
see that it is also read[r] in the church of
the Laodiceans and that you in turn read
the letter from Laodicea.
17Tell Archippus:[s] "See to it that you
complete the work you have received in
the Lord."[t]
18I, Paul, write this greeting in my own
hand.[u] Remember[v] my chains.[w] Grace
be with you.[x]

[m]8 Some manuscripts *that he may know about your*

3:22—4:1 DISCIPLESHIP, Rewarded—See note on Eph 6:5–8.
3:24 THE CHURCH, Servants—The highest motive for right attitudes and actions is ministry for the Lord Jesus. See notes on Mt 20:20–28; Ro 1:1.
3:25—4:1 GOD, Justice—God is a righteous God. He has no favorites and will not allow sin to go unpunished. See notes on Gal 6:7–10; Eph 6:9.
4:2–4 PRAYER, Intercession—See note on Ro 12:12. We are to be strong in prayer. Paul made specific prayer requests that related to his immediate situation in prison, but he looked to the ultimate goal of clear proclamation of the gospel. See note on 2 Th 3:1–5.
4:5–6 EVANGELISM, Testimony—A godly life leaves a clear testimony for Jesus Christ that will open doors of opportunity to share the gospel of Christ. We should so live and seize those witnessing opportunities. See Guide to Relational Evangelism, pp. 1784–1786.
4:6 CHRISTIAN ETHICS, Language—Take the high road for your conversation, says Paul. Everyone is edified, and such a route indicates the quality of your relationship with God. Gracious language shows more care for others than for self. Seasoned language is mature, thoughtful, and helpful.
4:7 THE CHURCH, Servants—See note on Eph 6:21.
4:11 THE CHURCH, God's Kingdom—See note on Ac 28:31. Work for the church is kingdom work.
4:12 THE CHURCH, Servants—A servant of Christ prays continually for others. See note on Ro 1:1.
4:12 PRAYER, Intercession—Intercession is a wrestling match, not because we must fight against God but because we are joining God in the fight against evil. Prayer is not superficial talk but emotional involvement in the struggles of God's people in a hostile world. See notes on 2:1; Ro 15:30–32.
4:15 THE CHURCH, Local Body—A church is a local group of believers who may meet at any location for worship, instruction, and fellowship. Many New Testament churches met in private homes. See notes on Ro 16:5; 1 Co 1:2.
4:16 HOLY SCRIPTURE, Collection—Paul instructed the congregation to read the letter caringly and to pass it on for other churches, while receiving from them other letters, which obviously were already seen as bearing God's wisdom and direction for practical living. The custom mentioned here initiated the gathering of these letters into collections, which were soon recognized as bearing the revelation of God in them. Thus Paul's letters became regarded as authoritative Scripture soon after they were written. The letter to Laodicea has not been preserved. Compare 1 Co 5:9. God did not lead the church to preserve all Paul's writings. See note on Php 3:1.
4:18 PRAYER, Blessing—See note on Ro 15:33.

1 Thessalonians

Theological Setting

On Paul's second missionary journey the Holy Spirit had a surprise for Paul. He guided Paul to Troas and thence to Philippi in Macedonia (Ac 16:6-12). This was either late AD 49 or early AD 50. As the result of a fruitful ministry there, Paul and Silas were illegally beaten and imprisoned. Eventually they left that city for Thessalonica, the principal and capital city of the Roman province of Macedonia.

Thessalonica was located on the Thermaic Gulf, having an excellent harbor. The Egnatian Way, an international highway connecting Europe and Asia, ran through the city. These, plus rich natural resources in the region, made Thessalonica a great trade center. The city had a strong colony of Jews with political influence. As was his custom, Paul began his work there by preaching and interpreting the Old Testament Scriptures in the synagogue (Ac 17:2). He had to leave Thessalonica because of mob action instigated by the Jewish leaders (Ac 17:5-10). Paul and his company had a brief but successful ministry in Berea. Again he left there due to trouble caused by Thessalonian Jews (Ac 17:10-13).

From Berea Paul went to Athens, leaving Silas and Timothy in Berea. Upon his arrival in the university city he sent word for them to join him there (Ac 17:14-15). Though he longed to keep Timothy with him, Paul sent him back to Thessalonica to ascertain the state of the Christians there (1 Th 3:1-2,5). It is obvious that he assumed they also were being persecuted. Later, Timothy joined Paul in Corinth to report that despite hardships they remained true to the faith (1 Th 3:6-8).

Then, probably in late AD 50, Paul wrote 1 Thessalonians. He rejoiced in their steadfastness and exhorted them to continue to witness for Christ by both word and deed. He dealt with their problems concerning the Lord's return. In all likelihood 1 Thessalonians is Paul's first epistle. It may be the first New Testament book to be written. This precious letter gives us an inside view of life in the early church. Even so early, the church faced pressing questions.

1. When would Christ return? Had those believers who had died missed the blessings of His return?
2. What should they expect from a minister? Who could they trust as a true spiritual leader?
3. What is the place of daily work in the life of Christians waiting for the second coming?

Paul answered these questions in love and concern for his beloved church.

Theological Outline

1 Thessalonians: Our Destiny in a Hostile World

I. The Church Is Founded on Past Faithfulness. (1:1-10)
- A. Signature, address, and greeting (1:1)
- B. Past faith, love, and hope inspire thanksgiving. (1:2-3)
- C. Election, power, conviction, and the Spirit brought the gospel. (1:4-5)
- D. Model Christian living resulted from the gospel. (1:6-7)
- E. Zealous witness and far-reaching Christian influence spread the gospel. (1:8-9)
- F. Earnest hope in the resurrection marked the church's life. (1:10)

II. Opposition and Persecution Cannot Halt the Gospel. (2:1-20)
- A. Suffering and insult do not deter Christian witness. (2:1-2)
- B. Sincerity of method and purpose stand behind gospel witness. (2:3-6*a*)
- C. Love, not personal greed, motivates witness. (2:6*b*-12)
- D. Steadfastness and endurance mark Christian converts. (2:13-16)
- E. The gospel creates enduring fellowship and love. (2:17-18)
- F. A new church becomes the reward for a Christian witness. (2:19-20)

III. Concern for the Church Dominates the Minister's Heart. (3:1—4:12)
- A. Sacrificial love leads the minister to show concern even under personal persecution. (3:1-5)
- B. The church's faithfulness gives the minister encouragement and joy. (3:6-10)
- C. The concerned minister prays for the church's future. (3:11-13)

D. The concerned minister teaches the church righteous living. (4:1-8)
E. The concerned minister leads the church to grow in brotherly love. (4:9-12)

IV. Problems Related to the Lord's Return. (4:13—5:11)
A. Living and deceased believers have equal hope. (4:13-18)
B. The time is uncertain. (5:1-3)
C. The church needs to be alert. (5:4-8)
D. Believers have assurance. (5:9-11)

V. Concluding Exhortations (5:12-28)
A. Respect Christian leaders. (5:12-13)
B. Care for fellow-Christians. (5:14-15)
C. Always be thankful. (5:16-18)
D. Test prophetic utterances to God. (5:19-22)
E. Commit yourself to God, who is faithful. (5:23-24)
F. Closing requests and benediction (5:25-28)

Theological Conclusions

In testifying to the life of an early church and answering the questions of that church, 1 Thessalonians provides vital doctrinal teaching for today's church. We learn of:

1. the mission of the church,
2. the role of the minister,
3. the nature of the Christian life,
4. the Christian reaction to death, and
5. the nature of the second coming.

Christianity is ever a missionary faith, and its field is the entire world. In Thessalonica Paul preached the gospel not as mere words, but as a message empowered by the Holy Spirit (1:5-6). Without the Spirit's power the gospel is merely words. It is He who convicts those who hear and enables them to respond positively to the gospel's appeal. Happy is that church today whose name is synonymous with missions and evangelism.

Paul was a living example of the fact that opposition to the gospel is no reason to stop proclaiming it (2:1-2). Instead, having established a church in one place, he moved on to do the same elsewhere. The minister today is a church planter led by God's Spirit and not by personal gain. Though the apostle Paul was a missionary with a worldwide vision, he never ceased to have a pastor's heart (3:1-8). His body might be in Athens or Corinth, but his heart remained in Thessalonica. He got to the point where he "could stand it no longer" and "sent to find out about your faith" (3:5). From the minister's heart, Paul refused to accept salary for his work so as not to burden the church (2:6,9). He constantly prayed for the church (3:10). The minister's role, then, is to help the church at whatever personal cost necessary.

The Christian life is a pilgrimage wherein believers grow into the likeness of Christ. Skeptics may argue against the believer's logic, but they cannot refute the evidence of personal experience in the Lord. If the world does not see Jesus in His people, it is not likely to look for Him elsewhere. First Thessalonians challenges Christians to remain faithful witnesses even under persecution and faithful moral examples even under severe temptation. We are to love each other and attend to the work God gives us.

Christians are not immune to bereavement (4:13-18). We need not fear death. Death does not rob us of any benefit of Christ's second coming. We sorrow but with the assurance that death for a believer is only being "away from the body and at home with the Lord" (2 Co 5:8). In God's own time we will all be together eternally in the glorious family of God . . . "and so we will be with the Lord forever" (1 Th 4:17). It is idle exercise trying to figure out the time of the Lord's return (5:1). We should be busy getting people ready for the event when it occurs.

Contemporary Teaching

The Book of 1 Thessalonians teaches many things which are as true today as they were in the first century. Among them are: (1) People are saved by obeying the Spirit-empowered gospel and are debtors to share it with all people everywhere. (2) We should not be deterred by opposition, but should see it as evidence of the great need for the gospel. (3) Christians should be concerned about the problems faced by others in the fellowship of believers. (4) Our lives bear testimony to the power of God to meet human need; failure to live for Him becomes a stumbling block to those who would seek Him. (5) The fact of the Lord's return is certain. The time for it is indefinite but will be sudden. Christians should live every moment so as to be pleasing to Him when He comes.

Chapter 1

PAUL, Silas[a][a] and Timothy,[b]
To the church of the Thessalonians[c]
in God the Father and the Lord Jesus
Christ:

Grace and peace to you.[b][d]

Thanksgiving for the Thessalonians' Faith

2We always thank God for all of you,[e]
mentioning you in our prayers.[f] 3We
continually remember before our God
and Father[g] your work produced by
faith,[h] your labor prompted by love,[i]
and your endurance inspired by hope[j] in
our Lord Jesus Christ.
4For we know, brothers loved by
God,[k] that he has chosen you, 5because
our gospel[l] came to you not simply with
words, but also with power,[m] with the
Holy Spirit and with deep conviction. You
know[n] how we lived among you for your
sake. 6You became imitators of us[o] and of
the Lord; in spite of severe suffering,[p]
you welcomed the message with the joy[q]
given by the Holy Spirit.[r] 7And so you
became a model[s] to all the believers in
Macedonia[t] and Achaia.[u] 8The Lord's
message[v] rang out from you not only in
Macedonia and Achaia—your faith in
God has become known everywhere.[w]
Therefore we do not need to say anything
about it, 9for they themselves report what
kind of reception you gave us. They tell
how you turned[x] to God from idols[y] to
serve the living and true God,[z] 10and to
wait for his Son from heaven,[a] whom he
raised from the dead[b]—Jesus, who rescues us from the coming wrath.[c]

Chapter 2

Paul's Ministry in Thessalonica

YOU know, brothers, that our visit to
you[d] was not a failure.[e] 2We had
previously suffered[f] and been insulted in
Philippi,[g] as you know, but with the help
of our God we dared to tell you his gospel
in spite of strong opposition.[h] 3For the
appeal we make does not spring from error or impure motives,[i] nor are we trying to trick you.[j] 4On the contrary, we
speak as men approved by God to be en-

1:1 [a]S Ac 15:22 [b]S Ac 16:1; 2Th 1:1 [c]S Ac 17:1 [d]S Ro 1:7
1:2 [e]S Ro 1:8; Eph 5:20 [f]S Ro 1:10
1:3 [g]S Php 4:20 [h]Gal 5:6; 2Th 1:11; Jas 2:14-26 [i]1Th 3:6; 2Th 1:3; S 1Co 13:13 [j]Ro 8:25
1:4 [k]Col 3:12; 2Th 2:13
1:5 [l]S 2Co 2:12; 2Th 2:14 [m]Ro 1:16; S Ro 15:13 [n]1Th 2:10
1:6 [o]S 1Co 4:16 [p]Ac 17:5-10 [q]S 2Co 6:10 [r]Ac 13:52
1:7 [s]S 1Ti 4:12 [t]S Ac 16:9 [u]S Ac 18:12
1:8 [v]2Th 3:1 [w]Ro 1:8
1:9 [x]Ac 14:15 [y]1Co 12:2; Gal 4:8 [z]S Mt 16:16
1:10 [a]S 1Co 1:7 [b]S Ac 2:24 [c]S Ro 1:18
2:1 [d]1Th 1:5,9 [e]2Th 1:10
2:2 [f]Ac 14:19; 16:22; Php 1:30 [g]S Ac 16:12 [h]Ac 17:1-9
2:3 [i]2Co 2:17 [j]2Co 4:2

[a] *1* Greek *Silvanus,* a variant of *Silas* [b] *1* Some early manuscripts *you from God our Father and the Lord Jesus Christ*

1:1 THE CHURCH, Local Body—See note on 1 Co 1:2.
1:1 PRAYER, Blessing—See note on Ro 1:7.
1:2–3 PRAYER, Thanksgiving—See note on Php 1:3.
1:3 DISCIPLESHIP, Nature—Disciples should not stand lazily by waiting for the judgment day. Trust in God and in His saving purposes leads us to work for Him. Love for God and His creatures prompts us to act in love for others. Hope in Christ's promise of eternal life inspires us to continue working patiently until the promises are completely fulfilled.
1:4 GOD, Love—Without God's love there would be no gospel. The whole Bible is, in a sense, the unfolding story of God's love.
1:4–6 HOLY SPIRIT, Regenerates—When Paul preached the gospel for the first time in the Greek city of Thessalonica, a number of Jews and Gentiles put their faith in Christ (Ac 17:1–9). The Spirit had made the church's testimony to the gospel possible (Jn 15:26), called Paul to preach it (Ac 13:2–4), guided Paul on his travels, (Ac 16:6–7), and was responsible for its being heard by the Thessalonians. When they believed the gospel, they experienced the power and joy of the new life the Spirit gives. Thus the Spirit convicts, regenerates, and gives joy to us as we enter God's new life of eternal salvation.
1:4–5 PROCLAMATION, Anointing—See note on Isa 61:1–3.
1:5–6 HOLY SCRIPTURE, Inspired—The words of Paul are the inspired revelation of God at work, communicating the good news of Jesus Christ with deep impact and belief (2:13). The Holy Spirit gave power to Paul's words, elicited deep commitment from the audience, and gave them great joy.
1:5 EVANGELISM, Holy Spirit—The gospel possesses great power to convert because the Holy Spirit uses it as His sword to bring deep conviction and, thereby, save the hearers. The power of human eloquence is not enough. Only God's power leads to salvation. We can witness with genuine power from heaven. See note on Ro 1:13–17.
1:6 SALVATION, Joy—Suffering does not cut off the joy the Spirit gives. See note on Php 2:17–18.
1:6–8 EVANGELISM, Testimony—The Thessalonians had a marvelous testimony of Christ. It rang out far and wide because they had learned well to live and witness through Paul's example. God calls witnesses to be examples to others even in suffering. See note on Col 4:5–6.
1:8 MISSIONS, Examples—No better example of the church discharging its missionary responsibility appears in the New Testament. The faith of the church at Thessalonica had spread through the surrounding region of Macedonia just as the faith of the church in Rome had spread throughout the world (Ro 1:8). What a challenge for contemporary churches to become models for missions in the surrounding territory! Their faith spread beyond their own province or state (Macedonia) and to the next province, Achaia. But their interest in missionary outreach became known far beyond even those regions. Their central testimony concerned the change in their lives Jesus had brought about and their confidence in His return (vv 9–10).
1:9 GOD, Living—The God of Christianity stands in sharp contrast to the gods of the nations of the ancient world. The God revealed to us in the mighty events of the Bible is a living God, not an empty idea or a human creation set up as an idol. As such, God enters into personal relationships with His people, hears our prayers, moves to help us, and cares for us individually.
1:10 GOD, Wrath—God will reveal His furious wrath on the judgment day. Only one way of escape is possible. We can trust in Jesus. Otherwise we suffer His wrath.
1:10 JESUS CHRIST, Final Coming—Judgment and wrath lie ahead for the world. Christians have no reason to fear. Jesus, the resurrected One, is coming again to rescue us.
1:10 SALVATION, As Deliverance—Jesus rescues us from the wrath of God which at the end of time will express itself finally against all sin.
1:10 PROCLAMATION, Gospel—See note on Ac 3:11–26.
2:1–9 EVANGELISM, Personal—Paul outlined his method of evangelism and gave us an example to follow: he ministered despite hardship and persecution; he ministered with pure motives; he ministered the true gospel of Christ; he ministered for God's glory; he ministered selflessly; he ministered in humility; he ministered with care and sacrificial love; and he ministered long and laboriously. Little wonder Paul could say "our visit to you was not a failure" (v 1).

trusted with the gospel.[k] We are not trying to please men[l] but God, who tests our hearts.[m] 5You know we never used flattery, nor did we put on a mask to cover up greed[n]—God is our witness.[o] 6We were not looking for praise from men,[p] not from you or anyone else.

As apostles[q] of Christ we could have been a burden to you,[r] 7but we were gentle among you, like a mother caring for her little children.[s] 8We loved you so much that we were delighted to share with you not only the gospel of God[t] but our lives as well,[u] because you had become so dear to us. 9Surely you remember, brothers, our toil and hardship; we worked[v] night and day in order not to be a burden to anyone[w] while we preached the gospel of God to you.

10You are witnesses,[x] and so is God,[y] of how holy,[z] righteous and blameless we were among you who believed. 11For you know that we dealt with each of you as a father deals with his own children,[a] 12encouraging, comforting and urging you to live lives worthy[b] of God, who calls[c] you into his kingdom and glory.

13And we also thank God continually[d] because, when you received the word of God,[e] which you heard from us, you accepted it not as the word of men, but as it actually is, the word of God, which is at work in you who believe. 14For you, brothers, became imitators[f] of God's churches in Judea,[g] which are in Christ Jesus: You suffered from your own countrymen[h] the same things those churches suffered from the Jews, 15who killed the Lord Jesus[i] and the prophets[j] and also drove us out. They displease God and are hostile to all men 16in their effort to keep us from speaking to the Gentiles[k] so that they may be saved. In this way they always heap up their sins to the limit.[l] The wrath of God has come upon them at last.[c]

Paul's Longing to See the Thessalonians

17But, brothers, when we were torn away from you for a short time (in person, not in thought),[m] out of our intense longing we made every effort to see you.[n] 18For we wanted to come to you—certainly I, Paul, did, again and again—but Satan[o] stopped us.[p] 19For what is our hope, our joy, or the crown[q] in which we will glory[r] in the presence of our Lord Jesus when he comes?[s] Is it not you? 20Indeed, you are our glory[t] and joy.

Chapter 3

So when we could stand it no longer,[u] we thought it best to be left by ourselves in Athens.[v] 2We sent Timothy,[w]

2:4 [k]Gal 2:7; 1Ti 1:11 [l]S Ro 2:29 [m]S Rev 2:23
2:5 [n]S Ac 20:33 [o]ver 10; S Ro 1:9
2:6 [p]Jn 5:41,44 [q]1Co 9:1,2 [r]2Co 11:7-11
2:7 [s]S ver 11
2:8 [t]S Ro 1:1 [u]2Co 12:15; 1Jn 3:16
2:9 [v]S Ac 18:3 [w]S 2Co 11:9; 2Th 3:8
2:10 [x]1Th 1:5 [y]ver 5; S Ro 1:9 [z]2Co 1:12
2:11 [a]ver 7; 1Co 4:14; Gal 4:19; S 1Ti 1:2; Phm 10; S 1Jn 2:1
2:12 [b]S Eph 4:1 [c]S Ro 8:28
2:13 [d]1Th 1:2; S Ro 1:8 [e]S Heb 4:12
2:14 [f]1Th 1:6 [g]Gal 1:22 [h]Ac 17:5; 2Th 1:4
2:15 [i]Lk 24:20; Ac 2:23 [j]S Mt 5:12
2:16 [k]Ac 13:45,50; 17:5; S 20:3; 21:27; 24:9 [l]Mt 23:32
2:17 [m]1Co 5:3; Col 2:5 [n]1Th 3:10
2:18 [o]S Mt 4:10 [p]Ro 1:13; 15:22
2:19 [q]Isa 62:3; Php 4:1 [r]2Co 1:14 [s]S Mt 16:27; S Lk 17:30; S 1Co 1:7; 4:5; 1Th 3:13; 2Th 1:8-10; 1Pe 1:7; 1Jn 2:28; S Rev 1:7
2:20 [t]2Co 1:14
3:1 [u]ver 5 [v]S Ac 17:15 3:2 [w]S Ac 16:1

[c]16 Or *them fully*

2:12 THE CHURCH, God's Kingdom—The kingdom belongs to God. He calls us to enter His kingdom by His grace. Those who submit to the rule of God and join in the fellowship of the kingdom accept a new life-style which shows God's power and rule. The early church consisted of born-again people who had not attained perfection. These ordinary people struggled to live a life pleasing to God. They were members of His kingdom.

2:13 HOLY SCRIPTURE, Inspired—Paul preached the gospel of Christ to the Thessalonians (Ac 17:1–4). They recognized the words they heard as being more than human words expressing human reasoning and arguments. The gospel message was and is God's word of salvation, working in believing hearts to create obedience to the gospel. The gospel message is now preserved in Holy Scripture. Scripture is words physically produced by humans but also miraculously inspired by God. Scripture works in the heart of believers creating their faith and leading them to obey the gospel.

2:13 SALVATION, Acceptance—God's people recognize divine revelation through faith. We accept His Word as His Word and not as the word of a human being. Acceptance means more than hearing and affirming. It means obeying.

2:13 PRAYER, Thanksgiving—See notes on Ac 28:15; 2 Co 2:14. Acceptance of and dedication to God's Word leading to personal salvation is a prime reason for thanksgiving.

2:14–16 EVIL AND SUFFERING, Human Origin—Christians suffer for Christ because humans do not want to give up their power and position. Just as Jewish religious leaders opposed Jesus and initiated proceedings which led to His crucifixion, so people of every generation oppose the spread of the gospel. We may suffer for Christ. We know we are pleasing Him. Those who persecute God's people do not please God.

2:14 THE CHURCH, Local Body—See notes on Ac 4:32; 8:1. Plural churches mean a church is local.

2:15–16 SIN, Disobeying—Stopping the mission of God's church is sin. Religious pride and racial prejudice lead us to make the church do things our way. God's love leads us to witness to all people, leading them to salvation in Christ.

2:15–16 EVANGELISM, Persecution—Suffering is an inevitable result of standing for Christ and sharing the gospel, but God will care for His people and judge the persecutors. To resist the gospel is bad enough; to persecute those who do embrace and propagate its truth is tragic beyond words.

2:16 GOD, Wrath—This difficult passage shows a past aspect of God's wrath in comparison to the future aspect of 1:10. Persons who heap up sins trying to prevent the preaching of the gospel find God can act in their lives to protect His witnesses. What actual event Paul had in mind as evidence of God's wrath having come we do not know.

2:18 EVIL AND SUFFERING, Satan—Satan interfered with Paul's plans to visit the church at Thessalonica. Part of Satan's strategy is to change or delay the church's missionary efforts.

2:19 JESUS CHRIST, Final Coming—See note on Mt 24:1—25:46. From the believer's perspective, the greatest part of Christ's final coming will be people led to Christ through our testimony.

2:19–20 EVANGELISM, Results—Saved people are the fruit and reward of faithful evangelism. Seeing people saved is the joy and glory of those who faithfully witness—in this life and the next.

3:1–5 EVIL AND SUFFERING, Satan—Satan's temptations did not end with Jesus (Mt 4:1–11). He tempts the church to give up faith and ministry in the face of suffering. The church must expect to suffer because the world is opposed to our ministry. Our steadfast faith gives strength and courage to leaders who must suffer for the faith.

who is our brother and God's fellow worker[d][x] in spreading the gospel of Christ,[y] to strengthen and encourage you in your faith, 3so that no one would be unsettled by these trials.[z] You know quite well that we were destined for them.[a] 4In fact, when we were with you, we kept telling you that we would be persecuted. And it turned out that way, as you well know.[b] 5For this reason, when I could stand it no longer,[c] I sent to find out about your faith.[d] I was afraid that in some way the tempter[e] might have tempted you and our efforts might have been useless.[f]

Timothy's Encouraging Report

6But Timothy[g] has just now come to us from you[h] and has brought good news about your faith and love.[i] He has told us that you always have pleasant memories of us and that you long to see us, just as we also long to see you.[j] 7Therefore, brothers, in all our distress and persecution we were encouraged about you because of your faith. 8For now we really live, since you are standing firm[k] in the Lord. 9How can we thank God enough for you[l] in return for all the joy we have in the presence of our God because of you?[m] 10Night and day we pray[n] most earnestly that we may see you again[o] and supply what is lacking in your faith.

11Now may our God and Father[p] himself and our Lord Jesus clear the way for us to come to you. 12May the Lord make your love increase and overflow for each other[q] and for everyone else, just as ours does for you. 13May he strengthen your hearts so that you will be blameless[r] and holy in the presence of our God and Father[s] when our Lord Jesus comes[t] with all his holy ones.[u]

Chapter 4

Living to Please God

FINALLY, brothers,[v] we instructed you how to live[w] in order to please God,[x] as in fact you are living. Now we ask you and urge you in the Lord Jesus to do this more and more. 2For you know what instructions we gave you by the authority of the Lord Jesus.

3It is God's will[y] that you should be sanctified: that you should avoid sexual immorality;[z] 4that each of you should learn to control his own body[e][a] in a way that is holy and honorable, 5not in passionate lust[b] like the heathen,[c] who do not know God;[d] 6and that in this matter no one should wrong his brother or take advantage of him.[e] The Lord will punish men[f] for all such sins,[g] as we have already told you and warned you. 7For God did not call us to be impure, but to live a holy life.[h] 8Therefore, he who rejects this instruction does not reject man but God, who gives you his Holy Spirit.[i]

9Now about brotherly love[j] we do not need to write to you,[k] for you yourselves

3:2 [x]S 1Co 3:9 [y]S 2Co 2:12
3:3 [z]Mk 4:17; Jn 16:33; Ro 5:3; 2Co 1:4; 4:17; 2Ti 3:12 [a]S Ac 9:16; 14:22
3:4 [b]1Th 2:14
3:5 [c]ver 1 [d]ver 2 [e]Mt 4:3 [f]Gal 2:2; Php 2:16
3:6 [g]S Ac 16:1 [h]Ac 18:5 [i]1Th 1:3 [j]1Th 2:17,18
3:8 [k]S 1Co 16:13
3:9 [l]1Th 1:2 [m]1Th 2:19,20
3:10 [n]2Ti 1:3 [o]1Th 2:17
3:11 [p]ver 13; S Php 4:20
3:12 [q]Php 1:9; 1Th 4:9,10; 2Th 1:3
3:13 [r]Ps 15:2; 1Co 1:8; Php 2:15; 1Th 5:23; 1Ti 6:14; 2Pe 3:14 [s]ver 11; S Php 4:20 [t]S 1Th 2:19 [u]Mt 25:31; 2Th 1:7
4:1 [v]2Co 13:11; 2Th 3:1 [w]S Eph 4:1 [x]S 2Co 5:9
4:3 [y]S Eph 5:17 [z]S 1Co 6:18
4:4 [a]1Co 7:2,9
4:5 [b]Ro 1:26 [c]Eph 4:17 [d]S Gal 4:8
4:6 [e]Lev 25:17; 1Co 6:8 [f]Dt 32:35; Ps 94:1; Ro 2:5-11; 12:19; Heb 10:30,31 [g]Heb 13:4
4:7 [h]Lev 11:44; 1Pe 1:15
4:8 [i]Eze 36:27; Ro 5:5; 2Co 1:22; Gal 4:6; 1Jn 3:24
4:9 [j]S Ro 12:10 [k]1Th 5:1

[d]2 Some manuscripts *brother and fellow worker*; other manuscripts *brother and God's servant* [e]4 Or *learn to live with his own wife*; or *learn to acquire a wife*

3:2 PROCLAMATION, Exhortation—See note on Ac 14:21–22.

3:2 EVANGELISM, Follow-up—New Christians need encouragement, especially when they experience trouble. Timothy was sent to encourage the church by God's power. His presence strengthened the believers to share in the ministry of the gospel. The church always needs such leaders who will encourage the believers to witness for Christ.

3:6–10 EVIL AND SUFFERING, Comfort—Paul was encouraged by the faith of the Thessalonians. See note on 3:1–5.

3:9 SALVATION, Joy—God's joy sometimes comes to us because of other Christians and their faithfulness to Christ.

3:9 PRAYER, Thanksgiving—See note on 2:13. Knowing others have responded to God and remain faithful due to our ministry leads us to give thanks.

3:10–11 PRAYER, Persistence—Continual prayer shows our intense dedication to a project for God. While God waits for the best time to act, we continue praying. Compare 5:17.

3:11 GOD, Trinity—The Father and Son needed to work together to enable Paul to visit the Thessalonians. The Bible shows both activities of joint action and of separate actions by the three Persons of the Trinity.

3:12–13 PRAYER, Intercession —Paul's recorded prayers are for spiritual purposes. See note on Eph 1:15–19. Love in the congregation and personal moral purity are related to regular intercessory prayer.

3:13 JESUS CHRIST, Final Coming—Jesus will not come alone. "Holy ones" will be with Him. These may be angels as *in other descriptions of God coming to His people* (Dt 33:2; Ps 68:17; Da 7:10; Zec 14:5; Mk 8:38; 13:27; Rev 19:14). The "holy ones" may be resurrected believers (1 Th 4:14; 2 Th 1:10). Important is, Jesus is coming.

4:1–12 CHRISTIAN ETHICS, Character—Paul appealed to two motivations for the Thessalonians to live up to high ethical standards. One was to please God. The other was to live so as to win the respect of those outside the gospel. If persons knew only these two guidelines, they would be enough to begin and continue the journey of growing toward mature Christian character. The Christian call is always to improve on what we are already doing.

4:1–2 PROCLAMATION, Instruction—See notes on Ac 15:35; Col 1:28.

4:2, 8–9 REVELATION, Jesus Christ—The words of instruction and care Paul offered were not his alone. They came directly from Jesus Christ, as revealed to the apostle. Rejecting the Bible's instructions is a rejection of God and a refusal to follow the Holy Spirit's presence in your life. Love of neighbor is a central Scriptural teaching the Thessalonians knew without Paul teaching them.

4:3–8 SIN, Depravity—A Christian who commits sexual immorality becomes guilty of not only fornication but also of rejecting inspired authority and the Holy Spirit. Sexual sin is not only wrong in itself but harms other people. God punishes the sexually immoral members of His church. See note on Gal 5:16–21.

4:5 SALVATION, Knowledge of God—Those who know God do not live like the heathen.

4:8 HOLY SPIRIT, Resisted—Paul's concern throughout this passage (4:3–8) was that the church avoid sexual immorality. *Holy* living is required by God who gives His *Holy* Spirit to His people. God gives His Spirit to all His people to help us resist sin. To choose to sin is to resist God's Spirit.

have been taught by God[l] to love each
other.[m] 10And in fact, you do love all the
brothers throughout Macedonia.[n] Yet we
urge you, brothers, to do so more and
more.[o]
11Make it your ambition to lead a quiet
life, to mind your own business and to
work with your hands,[p] just as we told
you, 12so that your daily life may win the
respect of outsiders[q] and so that you will
not be dependent on anybody.

The Coming of the Lord

13Brothers, we do not want you to be
ignorant[r] about those who fall asleep,[s]
or to grieve like the rest of men, who
have no hope.[t] 14We believe that Jesus
died and rose again[u] and so we believe
that God will bring with Jesus those who
have fallen asleep in him.[v] 15According
to the Lord's own word, we tell you that
we who are still alive, who are left till the
coming of the Lord,[w] will certainly not
precede those who have fallen asleep.[x]
16For the Lord himself will come down
from heaven,[y] with a loud command,
with the voice of the archangel[z] and
with the trumpet call of God,[a] and the
dead in Christ will rise first.[b] 17After
that, we who are still alive and are left[c]
will be caught up together with them in
the clouds[d] to meet the Lord in the air.
And so we will be with the Lord[e] forever. 18Therefore encourage each other[f]
with these words.

Chapter 5

NOW, brothers, about times and
dates[g] we do not need to write to
you,[h] 2for you know very well that the
day of the Lord[i] will come like a thief in
the night.[j] 3While people are saying,
"Peace and safety,"[k] destruction will
come on them suddenly,[l] as labor pains
on a pregnant woman, and they will not
escape.[m]
4But you, brothers, are not in darkness[n] so that this day should surprise you
like a thief.[o] 5You are all sons of the
light[p] and sons of the day. We do not
belong to the night or to the darkness.
6So then, let us not be like others, who
are asleep,[q] but let us be alert[r] and self-
controlled.[s] 7For those who sleep, sleep
at night, and those who get drunk, get
drunk at night.[t] 8But since we belong to
the day,[u] let us be self-controlled, putting
on faith and love as a breastplate,[v] and
the hope of salvation[w] as a helmet.[x] 9For
God did not appoint us to suffer wrath[y]
but to receive salvation through our Lord
Jesus Christ.[z] 10He died for us so that,
whether we are awake or asleep, we may
live together with him.[a] 11Therefore en-

4:9 [l]S Jn 6:45 [m]S Jn 13:34 **4:10** [n]S Ac 16:9 [o]S 1Th 3:12 **4:11** [p]Eph 4:28; 2Th 3:10-12 **4:12** [q]S Mk 4:11 **4:13** [r]S Ro 11:25 [s]S Mt 9:24 [t]Eph 2:12 **4:14** [u]Ro 14:9; 1Co 15:3,4; 2Co 5:15 [v]1Co 15:18 **4:15** [w]S 1Co 1:7 [x]1Co 15:52 **4:16** [y]S Mt 16:27 [z]Jude 9 [a]S Mt 24:31 [b]1Co 15:23; 2Th 2:1; Rev 14:13 **4:17** [c]1Co 15:52 [d]Ac 1:9; S Ac 8:39; S Rev 1:7; 11:12 [e]S Jn 12:26 **4:18** [f]1Th 5:11 **5:1** [g]Ac 1:7 [h]1Th 4:9 **5:2** [i]S 1Co 1:8 [j]S Lk 12:39 **5:3** [k]Jer 4:10; 6:14; Eze 13:10 [l]Job 15:21; Ps 35:8; 55:15; Isa 29:5; 47:9,11 [m]2Th 1:9 **5:4** [n]S Ac 26:18; 1Jn 2:8 [o]ver 2 **5:5** [p]S Lk 16:8 **5:6** [q]Ro 13:11 [r]S Mt 25:13 [s]S Ac 24:25 **5:7** [t]Ac 2:15; Ro 13:13; 2Pe 2:13 **5:8** [u]ver 5 [v]S Eph 6:14 [w]Ro 8:24 [x]Isa 59:17; Eph 6:17 **5:9** [y]1Th 1:10 [z]2Th 2:13,14 **5:10** [a]Ro 14:9; 2Co 5:15

4:13–18 JESUS CHRIST, Final Coming—In his first written expression about the Lord's coming, Paul listed the following plan: (1) Christians should not grieve for the dead hopelessly as unbelievers do. (2) Those who die as Christians God will bring to life as He did Jesus. (3) Those who are alive at Jesus' coming will be preceded in the resurrection by the righteous dead. (4) The Christians who are alive at Jesus' coming will be gathered with the resurrected believers. Jesus and they will remain together for eternity. (5) This plan of God is a great comfort to believers who grieve for dead loved ones. See note on 1 Co 15:20–28. Compare 1 Th 2:19; 3:13; 5:23; 2 Th 2:1,8.

4:14 HUMANITY, Nature of Death—Death is often likened to sleep. For the Christian, the idea of sleeping in the arms of Jesus carries a beautiful image of safety and comfort. Even greater hope comes knowing death is not the end. We have hope of resurrection in Jesus.

4:14–18 LAST THINGS, Rapture—Believers who die before Christ comes will not be cheated. In fact, they will be raised first before the believers still alive are caught up to be with Christ. "Caught up" (translated *rapere* in the Latin Vulgate) gave rise in the nineteenth century to the word "rapture" among dispensationalists. The rapture refers to the church being caught up to be with Christ at the beginning of the seven-year tribulation period (and thus seven years before Christ returns to earth). Other views use the word more loosely to refer to believers being caught up to meet Christ when He returns. Historical premillennialists believe the church will go through a literal tribulation period and that the rapture will occur at the same time that Christ comes in His glorious return. See note on Rev 20:4–5. Some amillennialists equate the catching up here with a general resurrection and judgment without reference to a specific end time tribulation period. Other amillennialists and most postmillennialists believe the church will go through the tribulation period before being raptured. Variations of opinion arise out of the fact that the Bible does not clearly relate the catching up of living believers in sequence of time to Christ's return. See notes on Da 9:24–27; Mt 24:21–22. The important teaching here is that Jesus' resurrection guarantees eternal life for all believers, both those who die and those alive when He returns. See note on 1 Co 15:50–57.

5:1–3 LAST THINGS, Day of the Lord—The return of Christ and the future day of the Lord are intertwined concepts. Both are held forth in Scripture as events that will overtake the world suddenly and without warning as the breaking in of a thief in the night. The majority of people will not be looking for coming judgment and destruction. Too often we expect peace and safety to be achieved by human effort. The element of surprise is consistently predicted to be attached to the coming day of the Lord.

5:4–8 CHRISTIAN ETHICS, Character—Self-control is a primary ingredient of Christian character. A Christian has responsibility to choose to will to do the right and to reject the wrong. The Bible gives no hint of a "devil made me do it" theology. We can choose to reject a licentious approach to life as faith, hope, and love become active ingredients of our character.

5:4–11 LAST THINGS, Purity—The very unknown time of the arrival of the day of the Lord should serve to promote purity of life. Believers are informed through Scripture about the fact of the Lord's coming. Living in the light of the promise, none should be taken by surprise. Alertness and self-control should flow out of living in the light of the promises. Faith, love, and hope are proper qualities of those who dwell in the light and who expect to live together with Christ when He comes. We can be confident God has appointed us to enjoy final salvation, not eternal wrath.

5:9–10 JESUS CHRIST, Savior—Believers need not fear death or the final judgment. Jesus came and died as our Savior, assuring us of eternal salvation.

courage one another[b] and build each other up,[c] just as in fact you are doing.

Final Instructions

12Now we ask you, brothers, to respect
those who work hard[d] among you, who
are over you in the Lord[e] and who admonish you. 13Hold them in the highest
regard in love because of their work. Live
in peace with each other.[f] 14And we
urge you, brothers, warn those who are
idle,[g] encourage the timid, help the
weak,[h] be patient with everyone. 15Make
sure that nobody pays back wrong for
wrong,[i] but always try to be kind to each
other[j] and to everyone else.

16Be joyful always;[k] 17pray continually;[l] 18give thanks in all circumstances,[m]
for this is God's will for you in Christ
Jesus.

19Do not put out the Spirit's fire;[n] 20do
not treat prophecies[o] with contempt.
21Test everything.[p] Hold on to the
good.[q] 22Avoid every kind of evil.

23May God himself, the God of peace,[r]
sanctify you through and through. May
your whole spirit, soul[s] and body be kept
blameless[t] at the coming of our Lord
Jesus Christ.[u] 24The one who calls[v] you
is faithful[w] and he will do it.[x]

25Brothers, pray for us.[y] 26Greet all the
brothers with a holy kiss.[z] 27I charge you
before the Lord to have this letter read to
all the brothers.[a]

28The grace of our Lord Jesus Christ be
with you.[b]

5:11 [b]1Th 4:18 [c]Eph 4:29 **5:12** [d]Ro 16:6,12; 1Co 15:10 [e]1Ti 5:17; Heb 13:17 **5:13** [f]S Mk 9:50 **5:14** [g]2Th 3:6,7,11 [h]Ro 14:1; 1Co 8:7-12 **5:15** [i]Ro 12:17; 1Pe 3:9 [j]Eph 4:32 **5:16** [k]Php 4:4 **5:17** [l]S Lk 18:1 **5:18** [m]S Eph 5:20 **5:19** [n]Eph 4:30 **5:20** [o]1Co 14:1-40 **5:21** [p]1Co 14:29; 1Jn 4:1 [q]Ro 12:9 **5:23** [r]S Ro 15:33 [s]Heb 4:12 [t]S 1Th 3:13 [u]S 1Th 2:19 **5:24** [v]S Ro 8:28 [w]S 1Co 1:9 [x]Nu 23:19; Php 1:6 **5:25** [y]Eph 6:19; Col 4:3; 2Th 3:1; Heb 13:18 **5:26** [z]S Ro 16:16 **5:27** [a]2Th 3:14; S 1Ti 4:13 **5:28** [b]S Ro 16:20

5:12–13 THE CHURCH, Practice—Christians should respect leaders called of Christ to do specific works of ministry. Leaders earn respect, honor, and love through their work for Christ. Leaders must work for peace in the church.

5:12–15 CHURCH LEADERS, Authority—Formalized ministry was just beginning to develop in the church. Church leaders either did not have specific titles for their offices, or those titles were considered unimportant. Today leaders who direct the activity of the church are to be treated with respect and gratitude because they give themselves to labor among the congregation. One of the key requirements for leadership is readiness to work for the welfare of the congregation. The congregation as a whole, however, has the shared responsibility of admonishing the disorderly, encouraging the timid, and helping the weak in faith.

5:16–22 HOLY SPIRIT, Resisted—The Spirit burns in a Christian's life and must not be put out. John the Baptist first associated the Spirit with fire. See note on Lk 3:16. The Spirit's fire was visible at Pentecost. See note on Ac 2:1–4. Fire suggests great power; the *tongues* of fire at Pentecost suggest speech, powerful speech. In this text Paul was thinking along the same lines. The Spirit, like fire, is not to be quenched or put out; specifically, His gifts of speech, either for prayer (v 17) or for proclamation (v 19) are to be accepted and used. They must not be neglected and silenced. The Spirit does not overwhelm the church with the gifts of speech. The church must cooperate if the gifts are to be fully used. The Spirit helps the church to pray (Ro 8:15,26–27). He gives some the gift of prophecy (1 Co 12:28–31; 14:1). In the present text, Paul simply reminded the Thessalonian church to be open to the Spirit's leadership in prayer and proclamation. But how can the church be sure that a sermon is really from God? We are to test prophetic messages. Here Paul did not specify what criteria are to be used for the testing. The criteria are found in 1 Co 12—14. See note on 1 Co 12:1–3.

5:17–18 PRAYER, Persistence—This is a command. See notes on 3:12–13; Eph 5:19–20. God's will is that we gratefully acknowledge His hand in all circumstances, not for all circumstances. Circumstances change; God does not. The Christian has an obligation to remain aware of God's goodness regardless of appearances. Continuous prayer involves an attitude of openness to God in all situations and a practice of talking to God about all situations.

5:20 CHURCH LEADERS, Prophet—The prophetic task is susceptible to misuse. False prophets may seek to lead the church astray. Nevertheless, it is not to be undervalued, resented, or ignored. We must not hamper the guidance of the Spirit in the community.

5:22 EVIL AND SUFFERING, Endurance—Disciples should avoid evil. Evil may come in the form of temptation by the devil. Activities or ideas initiated by other people may lead us to evil. Our own wrong desires and attitudes may open the door to evil. We must say no to all these.

5:23–24 GOD, Faithfulness—Christians must be made holy so that we may stand innocent before Christ when He comes. We cannot achieve this in our own power and wisdom. God must sanctify us. We know He called us to salvation. We know He is faithful and fulfills His promises. Thus we know He will sanctify us so we have no need to fear the judgment.

5:23 JESUS CHRIST, Final Coming—Paul united ethics (behavior) and eschatology (Christ's final coming). He prayed that the Thessalonians would be kept pure until Christ's coming.

5:23 SALVATION, Sanctification—God's sanctification is for our total being, outward and inward. He wants to make us wholly holy. Sanctification is salvation presently at work in us leading us to obey Him and preparing us for the final judgment.

5:23–28 PRAYER, Blessing—Unlike Paul's usual benediction at the close of his letters, this one is in two parts (vv 23,28). See notes on Ro 15:33; 2 Th 3:1–5.

2 Thessalonians

Theological Setting

The exact date of Paul's mission to Thessalonica is not known, and the same is true of his letters to the very young church there. Most scholars agree that 2 Thessalonians must have been written not more than a year or two after Paul and Silas left the city. The church was apparently enthusiastic, but clearly the believers had not as yet matured in their faith. Paul wrote to committed Christians who had not progressed very far in the Christian life. See introduction to 1 Thessalonians.

The Greeks of the first century were not a stolid race. We see their enthusiasm and excitement expressed in the riots when the first Christian preachers visited them. Such a riot broke out in Thessalonica (Ac 17:5-8,13). Those who became Christians during this time did so with verve and enthusiasm. However, they had not yet had the time to come to grips with all that being a Christian meant.

The opening salutation spoke of grace and peace as coming from God the Father and the Lord Jesus Christ (1:2). Throughout the whole letter Christ is seen as in the closest relationship to the Father. This is indicated by the fact that we are sometimes uncertain whether "Lord" means the Father or the Son, as in the expression "the Lord of peace" (3:16). The greatness of Christ is seen in the description of His majestic return with the angels when He comes in judgment (1:7-10). There is not a great deal in this letter about the salvation Christ has wrought, though there are references to the gospel (1:8; 2:14), to salvation (2:13), and to the "testimony" of the preachers (1:10). It is plain enough that Paul had preached the good news of the salvation Christ had brought about by His death for sinners, and that the Thessalonians were so clear on this that Paul had no need to go over it again.

They were not allowed to study the meaning of their new faith in peace and quietness (1:4). While they exulted in what the new relationship to God meant, they apparently did not take seriously enough the demands of Christian teaching, particularly in two areas. These areas included the second coming of our Lord and that of daily living. Some of them had come to believe that "the coming of our Lord" was at hand, or had even begun (2:2). Some of them had given up working for their living (3:6-13), perhaps because they held the view that the Lord's coming was so close that there was no point in it. Paul wrote to settle them down a little, while not restraining their enthusiasm.

Theological Outline

2 Thessalonians: The Demands of Christian Teaching

I. Salvation (1:1-2)
II. Church Leaders Pray for the Church. (1:3-12)
    A. Growth in Christian faith, love, and perseverance inspire thanksgiving. (1:3-4)
    B. God is just and will help His people who suffer injustice. (1:5-7*a*)
    C. Christ's return will provide ultimate justice. (1:7*b*-10)
    D. Prayer helps God's people fulfill their purposes and glorify Christ. (1:11-12)
III. Christ's Return Will Defeat Satanic Forces. (2:1-12)
    A. Despite deceptive reports, Christ has not returned. (2:1-2)
    B. The man of lawlessness must appear before Christ returns. (2:3-8)
    C. Deceived followers of lawlessness will perish. (2:9-12)
IV. Election Leads to Thanksgiving. (2:13-17)
    A. God chose us to share Christ's glory. (2:13-14)
    B. God calls you to firm commitment to His teachings. (2:15)
    C. Encouragement and hope comes from God's grace. (2:16-17)
V. God Is Faithful. (3:1-5)
    A. God's evangelists need our prayers. (3:1-2)
    B. God is faithful to protect His people. (3:3)
    C. God's people are faithful to follow His will. (3:4-5)

VI. God Disciplines His People. (3:6-15)
   A. God's people must not become lazy busybodies. (3:6-13)
   B. Disobedient people must receive brotherly discipline. (3:14-15)
VII. Concluding Greetings. (3:16-18)

Theological Conclusions

The letter is not a long one and does not give us a definitive outline of the whole Christian faith. Paul wrote to meet a present need, and the arrangement of his letter focuses on local circumstances.

Perhaps we can say that there are four great teachings in this letter:

1. the greatness of God,
2. the wonder of salvation in Christ,
3. the Second Coming, and
4. the importance of life and work each day.

God loves people like the Thessalonians and has brought them into the church (1:4). He has elected them (2:13), called them (1:11; 2:14), and saved them. His purposes last through to the end when they will be brought to their climax with the return of Christ and judgment of all. It is interesting to see so clearly expressed in this early letter these great doctrines of election and call, which meant so much to Paul. We may see also his doctrine of justification behind the references to God counting the believers worthy (1:5,11) and, of course, in his teaching on faith (1:3; 4:11; 2:13; 3:2).

Salvation in Christ is proclaimed in the gospel and will be consummated when Christ comes again to overthrow all evil and bring rest and glory to His own. This great God loves His people and has given them comfort and hope, two important qualities for persecuted people (2:16). The apostle prayed that the hearts of his converts would be directed into "the love of God" (3:5), which may mean God's love for them or their love for God. Probably it is God's love for them that is the primary thought, but Paul also notes an answering love from the new believers. There are repeated references to revelation (1:7; 2:6,8). While the term is not used in quite the same way as in some other places, it reminds us that God has not left us to our own devices. He has revealed what is necessary and has further revelations for the last days.

The Second Coming is seen here in terms of the overthrow of all evil, especially the man of lawlessness. Paul made it clear that Christ's coming will be majestic, that it will mean punishment for people who refuse to know God and who reject the gospel, and that it will bring rest and glory to believers (1:7-10). In the end it is God and good that will be triumphant, not evil.

In view of God's love issuing in election and call, it is interesting to see Paul's stress on God's judgment. He spoke of God's righteous judgment (1:5) and felt that God will in due course punish those who persecute the believers and will give the believers rest (1:6-7). But others than the persecutors will suffer in the judgment. Those who refuse to know God and those who reject the gospel will receive the consequences of their actions (1:8-9). Eternal issues are involved when the gospel is preached, and Paul would not allow the Thessalonians to miss these.

But when would it all take place? From 2:2 we see that some of the converts had misunderstood either a "spirit" (i.e., a prophecy or a revelation) or a "word" (oral communication) or a letter (which may mean a genuine letter from Paul that was not understood correctly, or a letter that claimed to be from Paul and was not), with the result that they thought it would all take place very soon. In fact, they thought Christ had already returned. Of course, the glorious appearing of Christ had not taken place yet, but "the day of the Lord" was a complex event, with quite a number of features. They evidently felt "the day" had dawned, the events had begun to unfold, and all that the coming of Christ involved would very soon be accomplished.

Paul made it clear that that was not so. There were several things that must happen first; for example, "the rebellion" that occurs and the revelation of "the man of lawlessness" (2:3). He did not explain either. He was probably referring to what he had told the Thessalonians while he had been among them. Unfortunately, we do not know what he said then, so we are left to do some guessing. That a rebellion against the faith will precede the Lord's return is clearly a well-known part of Christian teaching (Mt 24:10ff.; 1 Ti 4:1-3; 2 Ti 3:1-9; 4:3-4). Some manuscripts read "man of sin" (instead of "lawlessness"), but there is no real difference in meaning for "sin is lawlessness" (1 Jn 3:4). The Bible does not use the term "man of lawlessness" elsewhere, but clearly he is the same as the one called "antichrist" (1 Jn 2:18). Paul was saying that in the end time one will appear who will do the work of Satan in a special way. *He will oppose the true God and claim divine honors for himself* (2:4).

Paul spoke of that which restrains (2:6) and He who restrains (2:7), and that which will be removed before the man of lawlessness is revealed. We do not have enough information to know precisely what is meant, and many suggestions have been made. Perhaps the best is the rule of law which may be personified in the ruler. It could be illustrated in the Roman Empire (personified in its emperor) and in other states. When this is finally removed, the time of the lawless one will come. But Paul's important point is that believers should not be rushing into premature expectations. In due course these things will take place, and God will do away with all the forces of evil (2:8-10).

Paul had a good deal to say about people he calls "disorderly" and who appear to be idle, not working at all (3:6-12). This may have been because they thought the Lord's coming was so close there was no point in it, or perhaps they were so "spiritual minded" that they concentrated on higher things and let other people provide for their needs. Paul counseled all to work for their living (3:12). No doctrinal emphasis, not even that of Christ's return, should lead Christians away from work. People able to work should earn their daily bread. Believers are to work for their living and not grow weary in doing good.

Contemporary Teaching

What does this letter have to say to modern Christians with very different situations and problems? First, it tells of the greatness of Christ and of His connection with the Father. There is a tendency to see Jesus as simply a wise religious teacher, a great man, but no more. He was, of course, a great Man and a great Teacher, but Paul would not let the Thessalonians think He was no more. Jesus is to be seen as especially close to the Father, as One who is intimately involved in bringing us salvation, who will return in due course to bring relief to those who suffer for Him, and who will punish those set on evil courses.

Second, Paul warned us to be careful with speculations about the second coming of Christ. All through the centuries some people have been certain that the return of Christ would take place during their lives. They have too often allowed that to shape their thinking. Of course, in time one generation will be correct in that view. But this letter makes clear the dangers of being too convinced about matters that God has not revealed to His people. In the meantime, Christians must remain firm in the truth that Christ will come again. That is an important part of Christian teaching. Let us also remember—of that day and hour no one knows (Mk 13:32).

Third, we must see the importance of our daily work. For many of us it is unspectacular, even humdrum. However, it is important that we work and do our work well. Paul could appeal to his own example. While in our society it is not wise to draw attention to ourselves, we must live so that if others were to follow our example they would be led closer to Christ.

Chapter 1

PAUL, Silas[a] [a] and Timothy,[b]
To the church of the Thessalonians[c]
in God our Father and the Lord Jesus
Christ:

2Grace and peace to you from God the
Father and the Lord Jesus Christ.[d]

Thanksgiving and Prayer

3We ought always to thank God for
you,[e] brothers, and rightly so, because
your faith is growing more and more, and
the love every one of you has for each
other is increasing.[f] 4Therefore, among
God's churches we boast[g] about your
perseverance and faith[h] in all the persecutions and trials you are enduring.[i]
5All this is evidence[j] that God's judgment is right, and as a result you will be
counted worthy[k] of the kingdom of God,
for which you are suffering. 6God is
just:[l] He will pay back trouble to those
who trouble you[m] 7and give relief to you
who are troubled, and to us as well. This
will happen when the Lord Jesus is revealed from heaven[n] in blazing fire[o]
with his powerful angels.[p] 8He will punish[q] those who do not know God[r] and
do not obey the gospel of our Lord
Jesus.[s] 9They will be punished with everlasting destruction[t] and shut out from
the presence of the Lord[u] and from the
majesty of his power[v] 10on the day[w] he
comes to be glorified[x] in his holy people
and to be marveled at among all those
who have believed. This includes you, because you believed our testimony to
you.[y]
11With this in mind, we constantly
pray for you,[z] that our God may count
you worthy[a] of his calling,[b] and that by
his power he may fulfill every good purpose[c] of yours and every act prompted by
your faith.[d] 12We pray this so that the
name of our Lord Jesus may be glorified
in you,[e] and you in him, according to the
grace of our God and the Lord Jesus
Christ.[b]

Chapter 2

The Man of Lawlessness

CONCERNING the coming of our Lord
Jesus Christ[f] and our being gathered to him,[g] we ask you, brothers, 2not

[a] *1* Greek *Silvanus,* a variant of *Silas* [b] *12* Or *God and Lord, Jesus Christ*

1:1 [a]S Ac 15:22 [b]S Ac 16:1; 1Th 1:1 [c]S Ac 17:1
1:2 [d]S Ro 1:7
1:3 [e]S Ro 1:8; Eph 5:20 [f]S 1Th 3:12
1:4 [g]2Co 7:14 [h]1Th 1:3 [i]1Th 1:6; 2:14; S 3:3
1:5 [j]Php 1:28 [k]Lk 20:35
1:6 [l]Lk 18:7,8 [m]Ro 12:19; Col 3:25; S Rev 6:10
1:7 [n]S Lk 17:30 [o]Heb 10:27; S 12:29; 2Pe 3:7; S Rev 1:14 [p]Jude 14
1:8 [q]Ps 79:6; Isa 66:15; Jer 10:25 [r]S Gal 4:8 [s]Ro 2:8; S 2Co 2:12
1:9 [t]Php 3:19; 1Th 5:3; 2Pe 3:7 [u]2Ki 17:18 [v]Isa 2:10,19; 2Th 2:8
1:10 [w]1Co 3:13 [x]Jn 17:10 [y]1Co 1:6
1:11 [z]S Ro 1:10 [a]ver 5 [b]S Ro 8:28 [c]Ro 15:14 [d]1Th 1:3
1:12 [e]Isa 24:15; Php 2:9-11
2:1 [f]S 1Th 2:19 [g]Mk 13:27; 1Th 4:15-17

1:1 THE CHURCH, Local Body—See note on 1 Co 1:2.
1:2 PRAYER, Blessing—See note on Ro 1:7.
1:3 PRAYER, Thanksgiving—Thanksgiving is a duty. Paul here names two works of God for which he is grateful—the congregation's love for each other and faith in God. See note on Php 1:3.
1:4–10 EVIL AND SUFFERING, Vindication—Although we suffer now, Christians are assured of God's eternal judgment on our oppressors. God's justice may not be apparent in this life. We may suffer innocently throughout our years on earth. Suffering for God and His kingdom will ultimately prove the right choice.
1:4 THE CHURCH, Local Body—See note on Ac 4:32.
1:5–9 GOD, Justice—God, as sovereign Lord over the universe, is the just Judge who holds all persons accountable to Himself. Suffering, especially religious persecution, may cause us to doubt God's justice. When we look back, we can see how God has worked to allow us to grow in endurance and faith. This gives evidence of His justice. Further evidence comes as we realize God will ultimately punish the unjust persecutors.
1:7–10 JESUS CHRIST, Final Coming—Jesus will come to pronounce judgment on unbelievers. He will receive praise from all believers.
1:7–8 SALVATION, Obedience—God will punish those who do not obey the gospel of Christ. This will happen in connection with Christ's second coming. Salvation includes creating a new self which obeys God (Col 1:13–14; 3:4,10).
1:7–10 LAST THINGS, Hell—The prospect of punishment upon the unbelieving and disobedient will accompany the revealing of Christ at His second coming. The punishment will be everlasting in nature. In substance it will involve separation from God. Such a display of divine power will be a marvel to believers, even as His coming will mean glory for the people of God. Punishment of unbelievers is based on God's justice (v 6).
1:8 PROCLAMATION, Unbelievers—See notes on Ac 26:19–29; Heb 4:2.
1:10 THE CHURCH, Saints—Believers in Christ and saints or "holy people" are names for Christians, those who have committed their lives to Jesus Christ. Christians await the day when Jesus returns to the earth. Believers give glory to Christ, who died to forgive their sins. See note on 1 Co 1:2.
1:10 EVANGELISM, Results—Jesus will be glorified on the day of His glorious return in and through those who believe and are saved. Some will take part because of our testimony.
1:11 DISCIPLESHIP, Conversion—God fulfills His purposes through deeds in the life of a disciple who is prompted by faith. Through such fulfillment the Lord indicates the disciple's worthiness. In answer to authentic faith God takes the initiative in accomplishing His purposes. See note on 1 Th 1:3. The second coming of Christ (v 10) casts its bright light over all Christian actions, so that we do everything to bring glory to Christ. Our enduring faith issues in faithful acts to fulfill good purposes He has given us. Such active faith based on hope proves worthy of His call to discipleship and to heaven.
1:11–12 PRAYER, Intercession—Paul prayed constantly for spiritual purposes. See notes on Eph 1:15–19; 1 Th 3:10–11.
2:1–12 JESUS CHRIST, Final Coming—Paul set to rest rumors the Lord had already come. When Jesus returns, everyone will know it. Jesus will destroy all opposition when He comes.
2:1–12 LAST THINGS, Great Tribulation—Despite reports in Paul's day and throughout history, the day of the Lord has not come. Amillennialists interpret the man of lawlessness to be representative of those enemies of Christ who appear throughout history, the phrase being used on the same order of 1 Jn 2:18 (antichrists). Premillennialists believe that the eschatological day of the Lord awaits a time of rebellion and the appearing of a unique man of lawlessness. While lawlessness as a principle is already at work (v 7), the personification of it in a person of lawlessness remains restrained. Such events are to be associated with a future time of intense tribulation, involving religious and political rebellion and persecution. See notes on Mt 24:21–22; Rev 13:1–10. Premillennialists believe this future uprising of evil is consistently described in Scripture as the backdrop of the return of Christ. He will ultimately put down evil and establish His kingdom. The man of lawlessness will be revealed (Greek *apokaluptō*). He will have a coming (Greek *parousia*). The New Testament uses these terms to

to become easily unsettled or alarmed by
some prophecy, report or letter[h] supposed to have come from us, saying that
the day of the Lord[i] has already come.[j]
3Don't let anyone deceive you[k] in any
way, for ⌊that day will not come⌋ until the
rebellion[l] occurs and the man of lawlessness[c] is revealed,[m] the man doomed to
destruction. 4He will oppose and will exalt himself over everything that is called
God[n] or is worshiped, so that he sets
himself up in God's temple, proclaiming
himself to be God.[o]
5Don't you remember that when I was
with you I used to tell you these things?[p]
6And now you know what is holding him
back,[q] so that he may be revealed at the
proper time. 7For the secret power of lawlessness is already at work; but the one
who now holds it back[r] will continue to
do so till he is taken out of the way. 8And
then the lawless one will be revealed,[s]
whom the Lord Jesus will overthrow with
the breath of his mouth[t] and destroy by
the splendor of his coming.[u] 9The coming of the lawless one will be in accordance with the work of Satan[v] displayed
in all kinds of counterfeit miracles, signs
and wonders,[w] 10and in every sort of evil
that deceives those who are perishing.[x]
They perish because they refused to love
the truth and so be saved.[y] 11For this reason God sends them[z] a powerful delusion[a] so that they will believe the lie[b]
12and so that all will be condemned who
have not believed the truth but have delighted in wickedness.[c]

Stand Firm

13But we ought always to thank God for
you,[d] brothers loved by the Lord, because from the beginning God chose
you[d e] to be saved[f] through the sanctifying work of the Spirit[g] and through belief
in the truth. 14He called you[h] to this
through our gospel,[i] that you might
share in the glory of our Lord Jesus
Christ. 15So then, brothers, stand firm[j]
and hold to the teachings[e] we passed on
to you,[k] whether by word of mouth or by
letter.

2:2 [h]ver 15; 2Th 3:17 [i]S 1Co 1:8 [j]2Ti 2:18
2:3 [k]S Mk 13:5 [l]Mt 24:10-12 [m]ver 8; Da 7:25; 8:25; 11:36; Rev 13:5,6
2:4 [n]1Co 8:5 [o]Isa 14:13,14; Eze 28:2
2:5 [p]1Th 3:4
2:6 [q]ver 7
2:7 [r]ver 6
2:8 [s]S ver 3 [t]Isa 11:4; Rev 2:16; 19:15 [u]S Lk 17:30
2:9 [v]S Mt 4:10 [w]Mt 24:24; Rev 13:13; S Jn 4:48
2:10 [x]S 1Co 1:18 [y]Pr 4:6; Jn 3:17-19
2:11 [z]Ro 1:28 [a]Mt 24:5; S Mk 13:5 [b]Ro 1:25
2:12 [c]Ro 1:32; 2:8
2:13 [d]S Ro 1:8 [e]Eph 1:4 [f]1Th 5:9 [g]1Pe 1:2
2:14 [h]S Ro 8:28; S 11:29 [i]1Th 1:5
2:15 [j]S 1Co 16:13 [k]S 1Co 11:2

[c]3 Some manuscripts *sin* [d]13 Some manuscripts *because God chose you as his firstfruits* [e]15 Or *traditions*

describe Christ's second coming. See note on 1 Ti 6:14–15. Thus the man of lawlessness apparently will imitate the return of Christ, but he will be an agent of Satan, not of God. He will try to rule over God's kingdom from God's place of worship, pretending to be God. Compare Da 11:36–37. The victory belongs to Christ and those who follow Him. Those who reject Christ face condemnation with the man of lawlessness.

2:2,15 HOLY SCRIPTURE, Authoritative—Paul warned the young congregation not to be easily misled by a prophecy, report, or letter which might be false. Not all prophetic comment is from God. Not all reports or letters are inspired. The best advice is to turn to the established and clearly inspired letters and words. All teaching about which we have questions can be measured in light of clear Scriptural teachings. Obviously the day of the Lord's return has not occurred. Paul considered his oral and written instructions authoritative. The oral instructions were not preserved. His writing to the Thessalonians became part of Scripture. See note on Col 4:16.

2:3–10 EVIL AND SUFFERING, Satan—Satan's power will not be curbed until the end time. At that time a "man of lawlessness" will lead Satan's forces against God and His people. He will personify evil—exalting self over God, claiming to be God, displaying supernatural powers and signs, and deceiving people. This final show of force by Satan and his cohorts will not succeed. The "man of lawlessness" will be destroyed by Christ's second coming.

2:9–12 CREATION, Evil—Paul told the Thessalonians of a coming foe that would resemble Satan in many of his deeds. He would exploit those who were not able to distinguish his source. Sinful people in all ages lose the ability to recognize evil in false teachers. The problem of wickedness in God's good world baffles us all, but we must accept it as a fact. The way to be certain we can be spared the destruction Paul spoke of is to love and serve the holy God in faith. When we grow in fellowship with God, neither Satan nor his representatives on earth can trick us into believing his falsehoods.

2:9–10 MIRACLE, Evil—God does not have a monopoly on miracles. Satan can enable his followers to perform deceptive works. This will occur in a special way in the last days. The words are right: "miracles, signs, and wonders," but they will be counterfeit because they are the work of Satan. From the time of the magicians in Pharaoh's court, through the ministry of the early church, Satan's servants deceived the people with their sleight-of-hand magic tricks. Satan remains in the deception business. We must beware his powers. God's miracles point us to love. Thus we can recognize them.

2:10,13 SALVATION, Definition—Persons are free to accept or reject God's salvation. God takes the initiative in choosing His people. These verses contradict the notion that all persons will be finally saved by God whatever they do or leave undone. People who refuse to accept Christ's truth and God's love face eternal judgment. Saved persons commit themselves to God's truth and let the Spirit make them holy. See note on Ps 132:16; 1 Th 5:23.

2:11–12 EVIL AND SUFFERING, Divine Origin—The one sovereign God controls the fate of all persons. He has allowed evil to exist as a judgment on human sin and a test of human freedom. People who love lawlessness rather than God and follow lies rather than God's truth have chosen condemnation rather than eternal life. God will allow the man of lawlessness to deceive them and lead them to eternal death. God has chosen to let evil triumph over those who choose evil and reject Him.

2:13–15 HOLY SPIRIT, Transforms—Salvation includes a life sanctified or made holy by the Holy Spirit. The Spirit enables us to remember and practice the inspired teachings of God's Word. See note on Gal 5:22–26.

2:13—14 CREATION, Sovereignty—Salvation has its roots in creation and its goal in Christ's glorious return. The sovereign Creator who chose His people for salvation before creation also determined when Christ would return to earth. The God who made the world knows when to send His Son to transform it and free it from the curse under which it now lies because of sin.

2:13 PRAYER, Thanksgiving—See notes on 1:3; Col 2:7.

2:15 CHURCH LEADERS, Teacher—The teacher passes on the traditions of the faith as they relate to the life and teachings of Jesus and to Christian doctrine and practice. This experience gives the church stability so that it will not run adrift from its dogmatic moorings. A danger exists that teaching will degenerate into the traditions of men (Mk 7:8; Col 2:8) and exercise a stranglehold on the faith. To prevent this, traditions must be continuously validated by the Holy Spirit in the life of the church according to the standard of Christ and the gospel. See 1 Co 12:1–3; 14:29; Gal 1:6–9; Col 2:6–8; 2 Th 2:2; 1 Jn 4:1–3.

16May our Lord Jesus Christ himself
and God our Father,[l] who loved us[m] and
by his grace gave us eternal encouragement and good hope, 17encourage[n] your
hearts and strengthen[o] you in every good
deed and word.

Chapter 3

Request for Prayer

FINALLY, brothers,[p] pray for us[q] that
the message of the Lord[r] may spread
rapidly and be honored, just as it was
with you.[s] 2And pray that we may be
delivered from wicked and evil men,[t] for
not everyone has faith. 3But the Lord is
faithful,[u] and he will strengthen and protect you from the evil one.[v] 4We have
confidence[w] in the Lord that you are doing and will continue to do the things we
command. 5May the Lord direct your
hearts[x] into God's love and Christ's perseverance.

Warning Against Idleness

6In the name of the Lord Jesus Christ,[y]
we command you, brothers, to keep away
from[z] every brother who is idle[a] and
does not live according to the teaching[f]
you received from us.[b] 7For you yourselves know how you ought to follow our
example.[c] We were not idle when we
were with you, 8nor did we eat anyone's
food without paying for it. On the contrary, we worked[d] night and day, laboring and toiling so that we would not be a
burden to any of you. 9We did this, not
because we do not have the right to such
help,[e] but in order to make ourselves a
model for you to follow.[f] 10For even
when we were with you,[g] we gave you
this rule: "If a man will not work,[h] he
shall not eat."

11We hear that some among you are
idle. They are not busy; they are busybodies.[i] 12Such people we command and
urge in the Lord Jesus Christ[j] to settle
down and earn the bread they eat.[k]
13And as for you, brothers, never tire of
doing what is right.[l]

14If anyone does not obey our instruction in this letter, take special note of
him. Do not associate with him,[m] in order that he may feel ashamed.[n] 15Yet do
not regard him as an enemy, but warn
him as a brother.[o]

Final Greetings

16Now may the Lord of peace[p] himself
give you peace at all times and in every
way. The Lord be with all of you.[q]

17I, Paul, write this greeting in my own
hand,[r] which is the distinguishing mark
in all my letters. This is how I write.

18The grace of our Lord Jesus Christ be
with you all.[s]

2:16 [l]S Php 4:20 [m]S Jn 3:16
2:17 [n]1Th 3:2 [o]2Th 3:3
3:1 [p]1Th 4:1 [q]S 1Th 5:25 [r]1Th 1:8 [s]1Th 2:13
3:2 [t]S Ro 15:31
3:3 [u]S 1Co 1:9 [v]S Mt 5:37
3:4 [w]S 2Co 2:3
3:5 [x]1Ch 29:18
3:6 [y]1Co 5:4 [z]ver 14; S Ro 16:17 [a]ver 7,11 [b]S 1Co 11:2
3:7 [c]ver 9; S 1Co 4:16
3:8 [d]S Ac 18:3; Eph 4:28
3:9 [e]1Co 9:4-14 [f]ver 7; S 1Co 4:16
3:10 [g]1Th 3:4 [h]1Th 4:11
3:11 [i]ver 6,7; 1Ti 5:13
3:12 [j]1Th 4:1 [k]1Th 4:11; Eph 4:28
3:13 [l]Gal 6:9
3:14 [m]ver 6; S Ro 16:17 [n]S 1Co 4:14
3:15 [o]Gal 6:1; 1Th 5:14; Phm 16
3:16 [p]S Ro 15:33 [q]Ru 2:4
3:17 [r]S 1Co 16:21
3:18 [s]S Ro 16:20

[f]6 Or *tradition*

2:16–17 PRAYER, Blessing—Prayer can speak a blessing. Blessing includes the power to act right for God as well as daily physical needs. The eternal encouragement came by the initiative of God. Paul prayed for the continuation of what God initiated. See note on Nu 6:22–27.

3:1–5 EVIL AND SUFFERING, God's Present Help—God will protect disciples from the evil one. Wicked people try to lead us to follow Satan. God has power to protect us from both sources of evil if we choose to let Him.

3:1–5 PRAYER, Intercession—Paul often asked for prayer. Three of his requests were on behalf of the proclamation of the gospel (Eph 6:19; Col 4:3). Two of them were for preservation in danger (Ro 15:31; 1 Th 5:25). As he asked for intercession for himself, he interceded for others. See note on 2 Th 1:11–12.

3:1 EVANGELISM, Prayer—Paul well realized the power of prayer in the spread of the gospel. Without prayer our witness has little power. Those who pray much are used mightily of God to help others to Christ. May God give us the spirit of prayer for effective evangelism. See Guide to Intercession, pp. 1800–1801.

3:2–3 SALVATION, As Deliverance—God's salvation is deliverance from His enemies and ours. We should pray for God to deliver His servants from the enemies of the Christian faith (Php 1:19). "The evil one" is the devil.

3:3 GOD, Faithfulness—Persecution may make us ask where God is. The inspired Word promises us He is faithful. He will protect us from Satan who lies behind our persecutions. We should thus continue to serve Him obediently.

3:6,14 HOLY SCRIPTURE, Authoritative—Those who did not follow and keep the rules Paul gave were to be isolated, for they were ignoring the teachings of Jesus Christ as revealed to the apostle. Such teachings were handed down orally by Christian teachers and regarded as authoritative long before achieving written form. The church believed the letter reflected accurately Christ's teaching and the early church's preaching. Thus the letter written by human hands could be accepted as God's truth and thus as Scripture. See note on Col 3:16–17.

3:6–13 STEWARDSHIP, Work—Work is honorable and necessary. Honest industry serves both human needs and the ministries of Christ. Work is not a punishment for our sin. Sin does cause labor to be toilsome, often a struggle against circumstances (Ge 3). Labor is an essential part of our role as caretaker of God's world. To work is to be a steward of God's world.

3:6 EDUCATION, Moral Purity—First-century Christians called themselves "followers of the Way" (Ac 9:2). This was not purely an abstract notion. A part of the Christian way was a code of conduct by which believers were expected to live. This moral tradition was taught to the new Christian generation. Today, as in early churches, one of the primary purposes of teaching is to help members of the household of faith live redeemed lives.

3:14–15 THE CHURCH, Discipline—See notes on 1 Co 5:1–5, 9–13; 2 Co 2:5–11.

3:16–18 PRAYER, Blessing—See note on Ro 15:33. God's presence in our lives is the ultimate blessing.

1 Timothy

Theological Setting

Paul had left Timothy in a difficult situation. He had left him in charge of the work in Ephesus (1:3). Paul had continued his journey to Macedonia, and from there he wrote this letter of encouragement and instruction to Timothy, the pastoral leader.

The younger pastoral leader faced a number of problems in Ephesus. The church was having doctrinal problems. Teachers had brought in a mixture of Jewish errors with ideas that would later develop into gnosticism. The very character of the gospel was threatened.

The church also faced relational problems. What role were women to have in the church? Evidently, the new freedom that women were given in Christ was creating stress in fellowship. Questions rose, especially about their role in public worship. Members also surfaced questions about how the spiritual leaders should relate to different age groups within the church.

Timothy faced ministerial problems. Evidently, Timothy found himself unprepared for the daily stress of the pastoral ministry. How could he maintain his spiritual balance under the stress? How was he supposed to relate to the different pressures that he encountered?

The church had financial challenges. Some of the spiritual leaders were too interested in the profit they could realize from their ministry. What should be the attitude of a minister toward money?

This list of problems has a contemporary sound to it. Even though the world has undergone dramatic changes since the first century, the challenges of sincere church members have not changed that much. We are still struggling with the challenge of knowing how to behave in the house of God (3:15).

Paul's letters to Titus and Timothy have been called "pastoral letters" because they were addressed to pastors to help them understand how they were to do their ministry. While the instructions reflect the historical setting of Ephesus and the letter to Timothy, the principles have an abiding value to the persons involved in the pastoral ministry in any age.

It is impossible to put a specific date on the writing of this letter. When it is related to the other events in the life of Paul which can be dated, we conclude that it was probably written after AD 62 and before AD 67. He was ministering in Macedonia at the time of the writing (1:3). The letter probably came out of the period not covered in any detail in the Acts. It may have been written on a missionary journey taken by Paul after being released from his first Roman imprisonment.

The epistle will leave spiritual leaders with unanswered questions about the form their work is to take. However, it will give them clear guidance about the kind of persons they are to be and some principles they can use in building relationships within the church.

Theological Outline

1 Timothy: Instructions for Church Leaders

- I. Salutation: The Instructions for Church Leaders are from One who has Authority from the Lord Himself. (1:1-12)
- II. Spiritual Leaders of the Church Are Stewards of the Gospel. (1:3-20)
  - A. Stewards must face the threat of false teachers. (1:3-11)
  - B. Stewards have experienced the gospel in their personal lives. (1:12-17)
  - C. Stewards must defend the gospel from false teachers. (1:18-20)
- III. Spiritual Leaders Must Lead the Church in Worship. (2:1-15)
  - A. The worship should give priority to prayer. (2:1-8)
  - B. The worship should observe proper order. (2:9-15)
- IV. Spiritual Leaders Must Meet High Qualifications. (3:1-16)
  - A. The personal life of the pastor must be exemplary. (3:1-7)
  - B. The personal life of the deacon must be exemplary. (3:8-13)
  - C. The nature of the church demands these high qualifications. (3:14-15)

D. The message of the church demands these high qualifications. (3:16)

V. Spiritual Leaders Must Conduct Their Ministries with Integrity. (4:1-16)
  A. They must keep the people of God sensitive to false teachers. (4:1-5)
  B. They must maintain proper discipline in their spiritual lives. (4:6-8)
  C. They must endure the hardships that come from serving the Lord God. (4:9-10)
  D. They must carefully guard their daily walk. (4:11-16)

VI. Spiritual Leaders Must Show Concern for the Welfare of the Whole Church. (5:1—6:2)
  A. They are to cultivate healthy relationships with different age groups. (5:1-2)
  B. They are to guide the church to support the widows in the congregation. (5:3-16)
    (1) The support of the church should not replace the family. (5:3-4)
    (2) The support of the church should not encourage idleness. (5:5-7)
    (3) The support of the church should enable ministry. (5:8-16)
  C. They are to encourage the church to support the ministers of the congregation. (5:17-18)
  D. They are to be impartial in all of their relationships in the church. (5:19-25)
  E. They are to encourage healthy relationships between servants and masters. (6:1-2)

VII. Spiritual Leaders Are to Be Careful of Their Relationship to Material Things. (6:3-21)
  A. Spiritual leaders who use the ministry for financial profit are false teachers. (6:3-5)
  B. Spiritual leaders should be content with what they have. (6:6-8)
  C. Spiritual leaders who love money will fall into other sins. (6:9-10)
  D. Spiritual leaders build protection from the allurement of the material when they give proper priority to their calling. (6:11-16)
  E. Spiritual leaders must help the rich in the congregation to use their wealth wisely. (6:17-19)
  F. Spiritual leaders are the stewards of the greater treasure of the gospel. (6:20-21)

Theological Conclusions

The letter is primarily a practical letter. Paul did not intend to offer profound theological conclusions as he did in Romans. He did build practical ministry on theological foundations.

We can see an emphasis here upon the supreme value of the gospel, the demonic character of the corruption of the gospel, the high calling of the church, and the qualifications for spiritual leaders. This epistle provides us with a composite picture of good spiritual leaders. The emphasis is upon the kind of person they should be rather than how they do their work. These leaders have been enriched by their experiences in the grace of God (1:14). They find strength for their ministry in the grace of the Lord (1:12). They keep a good conscience (1:19). They are self-controlled in every respect (3:1-3). They have healthy relationships with their families (3:4). They live godly lives (4:8). They are persons of faith (3:13). They are impartial in their judgments (5:17-25). They are free from the love of money (3:3; 6:10). They have hearts attuned to holy lives (6:11). They have a firm commitment to their callings (6:13-14).

Timothy was to embody these things in his own life and was to seek others who would walk this high road. This action was to be taken in the morally and religiously corrupt society of Ephesus. The church in any community is to follow the same pattern. The church is to seek as leaders persons ready to walk the high road spiritually and morally.

This epistle also gives us needed insight into the true teaching of the church. Without giving a full statement of faith, Paul does provide us with helpful insights into the character of faith. The church's true teachings aim for members to have love which grows out of a pure heart (1:5). They are according to the "glorious gospel of the blessed God" (1:11). They are healthy (1:10). They do not give attention to fables, endless genealogies, and doctrines of demons (1:4,6; 4:1-7). They are built on great doctrinal truths (1:15; 2:4,5; 3:16; 4:10). They give proper place to the church (3:15). They always encourage godly living (6:3). They make much of the words of Jesus (6:3).

True teachings are important for teachers. Spiritual leaders will effect both their own lives and the lives of those they minister to by the teachings that they share (4:16).

Contemporary Teaching

This epistle requires spiritual leaders to take a serious look at their lives and ministries. The apostle calls on us: (1) to keep the gospel of Jesus Christ pure and free from any corruption from false teachings that would weaken its saving power, (2) to give priority to prayer for those who are in places of responsibility, (3) to choose persons for spiritual leadership who represent the best that the gospel can produce, (4) to keep our lives under discipline, (5) to give attention to all segments of the church family, (6) to cultivate a life of contentment, and (7) to be faithful to our calling in Christ Jesus regardless of what life may bring.

Chapter 1

PAUL, an apostle of Christ Jesus by the
command of God[a] our Savior[b] and
of Christ Jesus our hope,[c]

2To Timothy[d] my true son[e] in the
faith:

Grace, mercy and peace from God the
Father and Christ Jesus our Lord.[f]

Warning Against False Teachers of the Law

3As I urged you when I went into Macedonia,[g] stay there in Ephesus[h] so that
you may command certain men not to
teach false doctrines[i] any longer 4nor to
devote themselves to myths[j] and endless
genealogies.[k] These promote controversies[l] rather than God's work—which is
by faith. 5The goal of this command is
love, which comes from a pure heart[m]
and a good conscience[n] and a sincere
faith.[o] 6Some have wandered away from
these and turned to meaningless talk.
7They want to be teachers[p] of the law,
but they do not know what they are talking about or what they so confidently affirm.[q]
8We know that the law is good[r] if one
uses it properly. 9We also know that law[a]
is made not for the righteous[s] but for
lawbreakers and rebels,[t] the ungodly
and sinful, the unholy and irreligious; for
those who kill their fathers or mothers,
for murderers, 10for adulterers and perverts, for slave traders and liars and perjurers—and for whatever else is contrary
to the sound doctrine[u] 11that conforms to
the glorious gospel of the blessed God,
which he entrusted to me.[v]

The Lord's Grace to Paul

12I thank Christ Jesus our Lord, who
has given me strength,[w] that he considered me faithful, appointing me to his service.[x] 13Even though I was once a blasphemer and a persecutor[y] and a violent
man, I was shown mercy[z] because I acted in ignorance and unbelief.[a] 14The
grace of our Lord was poured out on me
abundantly,[b] along with the faith and
love that are in Christ Jesus.[c]
15Here is a trustworthy saying[d] that
deserves full acceptance: Christ Jesus
came into the world to save sinners[e]—of
whom I am the worst. 16But for that very
reason I was shown mercy[f] so that in
me, the worst of sinners, Christ Jesus
might display his unlimited patience[g] as
an example for those who would believe[h] on him and receive eternal life.[i]
17Now to the King[j] eternal, immortal,[k]
invisible,[l] the only God,[m] be honor and
glory for ever and ever. Amen.[n]
18Timothy, my son,[o] I give you this instruction in keeping with the prophecies
once made about you,[p] so that by follow-

1:1 [a]S 2Co 1:1; Tit 1:3 [b]S Lk 1:47 [c]Col 1:27
1:2 [d]S Ac 16:1 [e]ver 18; 1Co 4:17; S 1Th 2:11; 2Ti 1:2; Tit 1:4 [f]S Ro 1:7
1:3 [g]S Ac 16:9 [h]S Ac 18:19 [i]Gal 1:6,7; 1Ti 6:3
1:4 [j]1Ti 4:7; 2Ti 4:4; Tit 1:14 [k]Tit 3:9 [l]S 2Ti 2:14
1:5 [m]2Ti 2:22 [n]S Ac 23:1; 1Ti 4:2 [o]Gal 5:6; 2Ti 1:5
1:7 [p]S Eph 4:11 [q]Job 38:2
1:8 [r]Ro 7:12
1:9 [s]Gal 5:23 [t]Gal 3:19
1:10 [u]1Ti 6:3; 2Ti 1:13; 4:3; Tit 1:9; 2:1
1:11 [v]Gal 2:7; 1Th 2:4; Tit 1:3
1:12 [w]S Php 4:13 [x]S Ac 9:15
1:13 [y]S Ac 8:3 [z]ver 16 [a]Ac 26:9
1:14 [b]2Co 4:15 [c]2Ti 1:13; S 1Th 1:3
1:15 [d]1Ti 3:1; 4:9; 2Ti 2:11; Tit 3:8 [e]Mk 2:17; S Jn 3:17
1:16 [f]ver 13 [g]S Ro 2:4 [h]S Jn 3:15 [i]S Mt 25:46
1:17 [j]Rev 15:3 [k]1Ti 6:16 [l]S Col 1:15 [m]Jude 25 [n]S Ro 11:36
1:18 [o]S ver 2 [p]1Ti 4:14

[a]9 Or *that the law*

1:1 GOD, Savior—Here God is called Savior, a term we normally apply to Jesus. Jesus came to earth and died for our sins. The Father chose to save us and worked out His salvation plans through Jesus. This again shows the close relationship between the three Persons of the Trinity, God the Father, Jesus the Son, and the Holy Spirit. Each Person, and what each Person does, is inseparably connected to the other two Persons and what they do. The very root idea of God is that He is a saving kind of God.
1:2 PRAYER, Blessing—See note on Ro 1:7.
1:3–7 HUMANITY, Relationships—The ideal relationship between people is that of self-giving love. This love is founded upon a proper relationship with God and with oneself. Relationships are destroyed by proud teachers seeking to gain self-glory by promoting controversy.
1:3–7 EDUCATION, False Teachers—Ephesus was a hotbed of pagan religions, Jewish tradition, and bizarre philosophical teachings. Some persons were trying to combine these into a strange conglomeration of doctrine. The church's greatest danger comes not from those who oppose Christianity, but from those who want to modify Christian beliefs to suit cultural values, political doctrines, and popular superstitions. Another challenge to the integrity of the church is the presence of numbers of unqualified persons who pose as teachers. They promote conflict and controversy rather than love, which is the goal of Christian teaching. See note on Col 2:6–8.
1:12–13 PRAYER, Thanksgiving—See note on Php 1:3. Thanks was usually for the recipients. Here it was for God's action in his life enabling him to serve Christ.
1:13–16 SALVATION, Grace—Saul of Tarsus, who became Paul the apostle to the Gentiles, is exhibit A of God's grace in Christ Jesus. The grace which saved Paul can save us all. No person is too evil to be saved through God's grace.
1:15 JESUS CHRIST, Mission—Jesus' basic mission was to gain salvation for sinners. He thus made salvation available to each of us.
1:15 HOLY SCRIPTURE, Authoritative—Paul knew his teaching had proven true in life and could be trusted. The "worst of sinners" could teach absolute truth (3:1; 4:9; 2 Ti 2:11; Tit 3:8). The church agreed that Paul's teaching was trustworthy. Thus they collected his personal letters to young pastors as part of Holy Scripture. Not just the verses Paul indicated are trustworthy. All Scripture is trustworthy. Following its teachings leads us to salvation in Christ, to responsible service in His church, and to faithful spiritual discipline as His disciples.
1:15 SALVATION, Definition—God's salvation is from sin and for sinners (Mt 1:21). A proper human response to salvation is the confession of sin.
1:16 SALVATION, Eternal Life—All who commit themselves to Christ in faith receive eternal life. All sinners still have a chance if they will repent and believe.
1:17 GOD, One God—Paul used His own prayer of praise to teach Timothy the basic nature of the Father. He is the one and only true God, who rules the earth. He is immortal, not subject to death. He is invisible, letting us see evidence of His glory but never permitting us to make an image which would supposedly represent Him. He has always been and will always be. Invisible and immortal refer to His existence as spirit rather than as physical being.
1:18–20 EVIL AND SUFFERING, Satan—God lets Satan punish us at times to lead us away from wicked behavior and back to Him. See note on 1 Co 5:5.
1:18–20 ELECTION, Perseverance—Paul gave encouragement to Timothy to continue in the faith. He informed Timothy that it was possible to shipwreck his faith and have to be handed to Satan for discipline.

ing them you may fight the good fight,[q]
19holding on to faith and a good conscience.[r] Some have rejected these and
so have shipwrecked their faith.[s]
20Among them are Hymenaeus[t] and Alexander,[u] whom I have handed over to
Satan[v] to be taught not to blaspheme.

Chapter 2

Instructions on Worship

I urge, then, first of all, that requests,
prayers,[w] intercession and thanksgiving be made for everyone— 2for kings
and all those in authority,[x] that we may
live peaceful and quiet lives in all godliness[y] and holiness. 3This is good, and
pleases[z] God our Savior,[a] 4who wants[b]
all men[c] to be saved[d] and to come to a
knowledge of the truth.[e] 5For there is
one God[f] and one mediator[g] between
God and men, the man Christ Jesus,[h]
6who gave himself as a ransom[i] for all
men—the testimony[j] given in its proper
time.[k] 7And for this purpose I was appointed a herald and an apostle—I am
telling the truth, I am not lying[l]—and a
teacher[m] of the true faith to the Gentiles.[n]
8I want men everywhere to lift up holy
hands[o] in prayer, without anger or disputing.
9I also want women to dress modestly,
with decency and propriety, not with
braided hair or gold or pearls or expensive clothes,[p] 10but with good deeds,[q]
appropriate for women who profess to
worship God.
11A woman should learn in quietness
and full submission.[r] 12I do not permit a
woman to teach or to have authority over
a man; she must be silent.[s] 13For Adam
was formed first, then Eve.[t] 14And Adam
was not the one deceived; it was the
woman who was deceived and became a
sinner.[u] 15But women[b] will be saved[c]
through childbearing—if they continue

1:18 [q]1Ti 6:12; 2Ti 2:3; 4:7 **1:19** [r]ver 5; S Ac 23:1 [s]1Ti 6:21; 2Ti 2:18 **1:20** [t]2Ti 2:17 [u]2Ti 4:14 [v]1Co 5:5 **2:1** [w]Eph 6:18 **2:2** [x]Ezr 6:10; Ro 13:1 [y]1Ti 3:16; 4:7,8; 6:3,5,6,11; 2Ti 3:5; Tit 1:1 **2:3** [z]S 1Ti 5:4 [a]S Lk 1:47 **2:4** [b]Eze 18:23,32; 33:11 [c]1Ti 4:10; Tit 2:11; 2Pe 3:9 [d]S Jn 3:17; S Ro 11:14 [e]2Ti 2:25; Tit 1:1; Heb 10:26 **2:5** [f]Dt 6:4; Ro 3:29,30; 10:12 [g]S Gal 3:20 [h]Ro 1:3 **2:6** [i]S Mt 20:28 [j]S 1Co 1:6 [k]1Ti 6:15; Tit 1:3 **2:7** [l]S Ro 9:1 [m]2Ti 1:11 [n]S Ac 9:15 **2:8** [o]Ps 24:4; 63:4; 134:2; 141:2; Lk 24:50 **2:9** [p]1Pe 3:3 **2:10** [q]Pr 31:13 **2:11** [r]1Pe 3:3,4 **2:12** [s]S Eph 5:22 **2:13** [t]Ge 2:7,22; 1Co 11:8 **2:14** [u]Ge 3:1-6,13; 2Co 11:3

[b]*15* Greek *she* [c]*15* Or *restored*

2:1–2 CHRISTIAN ETHICS, Citizenship—To the question, "Where does one begin in citizenship responsibilities as a Christian?" comes Paul's response: pray. Citizenship concerns, particularly those involving the persons in leadership, are worthy of intense prayer attention. Such prayer can serve as the channels through which God provides opportunities for government officials to perceive Christians as among those who are good citizens. Thus, the result is more opportunity for Christian witness and greater influence in decision-making circles.

2:1–3 PRAYER, Intercession—This key passage gives the content of public prayers in the churches of Paul's day. Paul named four kinds of prayers. (1) Requests (Greek *deēsis*) relate to what is lacking in a person's life and thus what one intensely asks for. Prayer is for specific things to meet real needs (Lk 5:12; 9:38). Such prayer can be asked for oneself or in intercession for another (Ac 8:24; Ro 10:1). (2) Prayers (Greek *proseuchē*) is a general term covering all types of communication with God. The root meaning is to make confident statements about oneself. (3) Intercession (Greek *enteuxis*) is an appeal or official petition for someone. It describes the Spirit's work (Ro 8:26–27). (4) Thanksgiving (Greek *eucharistia*) is related to joy and grace. It is an attitude expressed by showing gratitude or thanks to another. It is an essential element of prayer (Eph 5:20; Col 2:7; 3:7; 4:2; 1 Th 5:18). As a technical term, it referred to the blessing before a meal (Lk 22:17; 1 Co 11:24). The term became the general name for the Lord's Supper. Such prayers go outside the church to raise up political leaders before God. Authorities are important to the church, and prayers affect thrones. Paul had purpose in this injunction: the church will be able to function peacefully, and godliness and holiness can flourish if God directs thrones and authorities according to the prayers of Christians.

2:3 GOD, Savior—See note on 1:1.

2:5 GOD, Trinity—God is one. Yet He uses as His mediator between Himself and us His Son Jesus. Jesus is the image of God (Col 1:15), equal with God (Php 2:6). Only the wonderful mystery of the Trinity can explain this separation of work and yet identity as one God.

2:5–6 JESUS CHRIST, Redeemer—Jesus is the only mediator between us and God. He is both human and divine, but here the human nature is emphasized to show He can identify with us. Jesus brought peace between humanity and God by dying for us, paying the price to free us from sin. He opened the way for all people of every nation and race to find salvation through faith in Him.

2:5 DISCIPLESHIP, Priesthood—Religion has traditionally employed holy men to act as priests who serve as mediators or go-betweens to maintain proper relationships between God and humans. Such holy priests prayed, taught, and offered sacrifices on behalf of the larger community. God taught Israel how to do this in a way which would please Him until the appropriate time came for Him to send Christ. Christ offered sacrifice of Himself, totally pleasing God. No other sacrifice was needed. This made Him the perfect Mediator, speaking to God continually on our behalf. His perfect teachings are given all people, not just the initiated scribes and leaders. This means Christ has opened a new and living way for us to go to God. We do not have to pray to, confess to, or depend on the offerings of other humans. We have the priestly rights and rites for ourselves. We have the privilege and responsibility to pray directly to Christ, to confess sins directly to Christ, to study, interpret, and follow Christ's teachings for ourselves, and to depend on Christ's sacrifice and nothing else for our salvation. No one can do our religion for us, no matter how much we pay them. We must deal with Christ directly and with Him alone. See notes on Heb 10:19–22; 1 Pe 2:5,9–10.

2:5 WORSHIP, Priesthood—Human priests are no longer needed to represent God's people in His presence. Believers have direct access to Jesus Christ, who alone is the Mediator between God and us. See note on Eph 4:11–13.

2:7 PROCLAMATION, Call—See notes on Jer 1:4–9; Lk 8:1; Ac 15:35. Proclaiming the gospel is a task done in response to divine appointment. God compels us to preach.

2:7 EVANGELISM, Teaching—Paul saw himself as a teacher of the gospel, as did our Lord Jesus Christ. Teaching the gospel is vital along with the proclamation of the preacher.

2:8 PRAYER, Command of God—Prayerful people should be in perfect control of their temperament. Praying together makes it difficult to argue against one another. The church is to seek God's will, not prove our personal opinion.

2:15 SALVATION, As Deliverance—God's salvation includes women as well as men. Compare 4:10. God saves them. Their childbearing does not. See note on Eph 2:4–5,7–10. This text contradicted an early non-biblical idea that women had to become males in order to be saved or that sexual relationships and birth are evil, part of the world's way instead of God's. The literal translation is "she will be saved through the childbearing." This may be a reference to the birth of Christ as glorifying womanhood. If the meaning is woman's physical

in faith, love[v] and holiness with propriety.

Chapter 3

Overseers and Deacons

HERE is a trustworthy saying:[w] If anyone sets his heart on being an overseer,[dx] he desires a noble task. 2Now
the overseer must be above reproach,[y]
the husband of but one wife,[z] temperate,[a] self-controlled, respectable, hospitable,[b] able to teach,[c] 3not given to drunkenness,[d] not violent but gentle, not quarrelsome,[e] not a lover of money.[f] 4He
must manage his own family well and see
that his children obey him with proper
respect.[g] 5(If anyone does not know how
to manage his own family, how can he
take care of God's church?)[h] 6He must
not be a recent convert, or he may become conceited[i] and fall under the same
judgment[j] as the devil. 7He must also
have a good reputation with outsiders,[k]
so that he will not fall into disgrace and
into the devil's trap.[l]
8Deacons,[m] likewise, are to be men
worthy of respect, sincere, not indulging
in much wine,[n] and not pursuing dishonest gain. 9They must keep hold of the
deep truths of the faith with a clear conscience.[o] 10They must first be tested;[p]
and then if there is nothing against them,
let them serve as deacons.
11In the same way, their wives[e] are to
be women worthy of respect, not malicious talkers[q] but temperate[r] and trustworthy in everything.
12A deacon must be the husband of but
one wife[s] and must manage his children
and his household well.[t] 13Those who
have served well gain an excellent standing and great assurance in their faith in
Christ Jesus.
14Although I hope to come to you soon,
I am writing you these instructions so
that, 15if I am delayed, you will know how
people ought to conduct themselves in
God's household, which is the church[u]
of the living God,[v] the pillar and foundation of the truth. 16Beyond all question,
the mystery[w] of godliness[x] is great:

2:15 [v]1Ti 1:14
3:1 [w]S 1Ti 1:15 [x]Ac 20:28; Php 1:1; Tit 1:7
3:2 [y]Tit 1:6-8 [z]ver 12 [a]ver 11; Tit 2:2 [b]S Ro 12:13 [c]2Ti 2:24
3:3 [d]Tit 1:7 [e]2Ti 2:24 [f]Lk 16:14; 1Ti 6:10; 2Ti 3:2; Heb 13:5; 1Pe 5:2
3:4 [g]ver 12; Tit 1:6
3:5 [h]S 1Co 10:32
3:6 [i]1Ti 6:4; 2Ti 3:4 [j]S 2Pe 2:4
3:7 [k]S Mk 4:11 [l]2Ti 2:26
3:8 [m]Php 1:1 [n]1Ti 5:23; Tit 1:7; 2:3
3:9 [o]S Ac 23:1
3:10 [p]1Ti 5:22
3:11 [q]2Ti 3:3; Tit 2:3 [r]ver 2
3:12 [s]ver 2 [t]ver 4
3:15 [u]ver 5; S 1Co 10:32 [v]S Mt 16:16
3:16 [w]S Ro 16:25 [x]S 1Ti 2:2

[d] *1* Traditionally *bishop;* also in verse 2 [e] *11* Or *way, deaconesses*

---

safety in childbearing, the reference should be interpreted against the background of Ge 3:16. If the meaning is the birth of Christ by the virgin Mary, the phrase should be interpreted as a fulfillment of the prophecy in Ge 3:15 about Eve's seed bruising the head of the serpent-tempter. The preposition here translated *through* does not mean *by means of.* See 1 Co 3:16 for a similar use of *saved* and *through,* where the meaning is to come safely through the fire. Woman's physical safekeeping in childbirth is the most likely meaning.

3:1 HOLY SCRIPTURE, Authoritative—See note on 1:15.

3:1–7 CHURCH LEADERS, Pastor and Overseer—Those who are chosen to watch over the spiritual welfare of a local church must possess the highest personal and moral qualities. First, as representatives of the church to the community and as examples to church members, they must be above reproach in their life-styles. They must not be given to pride or greed, and must be faithful in marriage. Second, since they are responsible for teaching and preaching, they should possess the gifts necessary for fulfilling these functions. They must be well trained and well grounded in the faith (not a new convert) to be able to impart sound doctrine and to guard the church from error. Third, since they are charged with exercising oversight, they should show evidence of a gift for personal relationships. They should not be violent or quarrelsome, overbearing or quick tempered (Tit 1:7). As leaders of the church family, they should model a well-ordered family life in their own homes. They must also be hospitable to receive traveling Christians, as well as the poor, as guests.

3:3–4 CHRISTIAN ETHICS, Alcohol—Church leaders must set examples for others to follow. Getting drunk is not excusable for a church leader. See note on Ro 13:13.

3:8–12 CHURCH LEADERS, Deacon—The deacon is to meet the same spiritual standards as the overseers with the exception of the gift for teaching. These standards are expected of all Christians, but those chosen for special leadership roles in the church must be carefully screened by the congregation to see if they demonstrate suitability for office. Deacons must give evidence of a Christian life-style. They should have a sound knowledge of the faith and lead pure and sincere lives. Nothing is said of their specific duties because these depend on the church situation. The "women" (v 11) may refer to the wives of deacons or to women who serve as deacons (NIV footnote). In either case they must meet moral qualifications and perform church tasks "in the same way." See note on Ro 16:1–2.

3:11 DISCIPLESHIP, Women—The context may make use of the word "wives" appropriate, but the Greek word (*gunaikas*) means simply "women." Since vv 12 and 13 refer to deacons again, some feel that the women referred to should be viewed as wives of deacons. Others insist that "the women" could refer to deaconesses or female deacons. No matter how "the women" may be viewed, these women were active in ministry. Their qualifications are similar to those given for deacons. Women have continued to be active in Christian ministry. Paul stressed the manner of behavior that is appropriate for them. See note on Ro 16:1–3.

3:14–15 HOLY SCRIPTURE, Writing—Written revelation occurred as God directed the personal lives of His messengers. Paul would have preferred instructing Timothy in person. Facing delay in meeting Timothy, he wrote the instructions instead. Thus writings directed to specific life needs became part of inspired Scripture.

3:15–16 GOD, One God—How do you explain God in a simple statement? That is the problem faced here. He goes beyond our human understanding. He towers so far beyond us in every way that He is shrouded in mystery except for the ways He has stooped to reveal Himself to us. Even where He has revealed Himself to us, as in the incarnation of His Son Jesus Christ, we are yet confronted with profound mystery (Isa 55:8–9). The height of sinful human ego may be thinking we understand all of the mystery about God.

3:15 THE CHURCH, People of God—God's household is the church, a family trying to live in obedience to God. The church knows and teaches the truth because it serves the One who is Truth (Jn 14:6). See note on Gal 6:10.

3:16 JESUS CHRIST, Mission—The mission of Christ summarized in this hymn is the center of the Christian confession of faith. Jesus' mission included incarnation—becoming human; resurrection—God's Spirit showing Christ, and not His enemies, was right in God's sight; victory—angels witnessed His power over all spiritual forces; proclamation—His gospel broke the barriers of race and religion to reach all nations; acceptance—people around the world believed in Him for salvation; and ascension—He was taken into glory.

3:16 PROCLAMATION, Central Theme—See note on 1 Co 2:2.

He[f] appeared in a body,[g y]
was vindicated by the Spirit,
was seen by angels,
was preached among the nations,[z]
was believed on in the world,
was taken up in glory.[a]

Chapter 4

Instructions to Timothy

THE Spirit[b] clearly says that in later
times[c] some will abandon the faith
and follow deceiving spirits[d] and things
taught by demons. 2Such teachings come
through hypocritical liars, whose consciences have been seared as with a hot
iron.[e] 3They forbid people to marry[f] and
order them to abstain from certain
foods,[g] which God created[h] to be received with thanksgiving[i] by those who
believe and who know the truth. 4For everything God created is good,[j] and nothing is to be rejected[k] if it is received with
thanksgiving, 5because it is consecrated
by the word of God[l] and prayer.
6If you point these things out to the
brothers, you will be a good minister of
Christ Jesus, brought up in the truths of
the faith[m] and of the good teaching that
you have followed.[n] 7Have nothing to do
with godless myths and old wives' tales;[o]
rather, train yourself to be godly.[p] 8For
physical training is of some value, but
godliness has value for all things,[q] holding promise for both the present life[r] and
the life to come.[s]
9This is a trustworthy saying[t] that deserves full acceptance 10(and for this we
labor and strive), that we have put our
hope in the living God,[u] who is the Savior of all men,[v] and especially of those
who believe.
11Command and teach these things.[w]
12Don't let anyone look down on you[x]
because you are young, but set an example[y] for the believers in speech, in life, in
love, in faith[z] and in purity. 13Until I
come,[a] devote yourself to the public
reading of Scripture,[b] to preaching and to
teaching. 14Do not neglect your gift,
which was given you through a prophetic

3:16 [y]S Jn 1:14 [z]Ps 9:11; Col 1:23 [a]S Mk 16:19
4:1 [b]Jn 16:13; S Ac 8:29; 1Co 2:10 [c]2Ti 3:1; 2Pe 3:3 [d]S Mk 13:5
4:2 [e]Eph 4:19
4:3 [f]Heb 13:4 [g]Col 2:16 [h]Ge 1:29; 9:3 [i]ver 4; Ro 14:6; 1Co 10:30
4:4 [j]Ge 1:10,12,18, 21,25,31; Mk 7:18, 19; Ro 14:14-18 [k]S Ac 10:15
4:5 [l]S Heb 4:12
4:6 [m]1Ti 1:10 [n]2Ti 3:15
4:7 [o]1Ti 1:4; 2Ti 2:16 [p]S 1Ti 2:2
4:8 [q]1Ti 6:6 [r]Ps 37:9,11; Pr 22:4; Mt 6:33; Mk 10:29,30 [s]Mk 10:29,30
4:9 [t]S 1Ti 1:15
4:10 [u]S Mt 16:16 [v]S Lk 1:47; S 2:11
4:11 [w]1Ti 5:7; 6:2
4:12 [x]S 2Ti 1:7; Tit 2:15 [y]Php 3:17; 1Th 1:7; 2Th 3:9; Tit 2:7; 1Pe 5:3 [z]1Ti 1:14
4:13 [a]1Ti 3:14 [b]Lk 4:16; Ac 13:14-16; Col 4:16; 1Th 5:27

[f]*16* Some manuscripts *God* [g]*16* Or *in the flesh*

4:1 HOLY SPIRIT, Revelation—The Holy Spirit is the church's primary source of revelation. He worked through inspired writers over many centuries to give us the Bible. How the Spirit spoke in this instance to Paul is not clear. It may have been through Old Testament prophecy, the teaching of Jesus, prophets in the church, or direct revelation. The revelation is a prediction concerning the end times. We can depend on revelation from the Spirit. We must be on guard, however, for demonic powers seek to deceive us. All that claims to be the Spirit's revelation is not. The true record of the Spirit's revelation is the Bible. The Bible becomes revelation in our lives as we study it under the Spirit's guidance.

4:1 ELECTION, Perseverance—See note on 1:18–20.

4:1–3 LAST THINGS, Last Days—The last days preceding the return of Christ and the judgment of the wicked are to be marked by signs. Among these are an abandonment of the faith or a departure from revealed truth; the influence of deceiving and demonic spirits; the presence of false teachers who in hypocrisy and untruth forbid marriage and seek to impose food restrictions.

4:1–2 EDUCATION, False Teachers—Demonic teachings threaten the church when its teachers are deceptive hypocrites and liars. Such teachers try to set laws and legal systems in place of truth and love.

4:2 HUMANITY, Moral Consciousness—The Greek word for "seared" carries the idea of having been branded with a branding iron. The demonic teachers' consciences were so branded by evil that they lost all moral sensitivity and were no longer able to distinguish between right and wrong. This can happen to any person whose life has lost its foundation of faith.

4:3 CHRISTIAN ETHICS, Moral Imperatives—False teachers trouble the church with false rules. God's rules are good for us and bring joy and thanksgiving into our lives. A key to determining if an action is right is its ability to make us praise and thank God.

4:3–5 FAMILY, Creation—Marriage is part of God's purpose in creation and should not be forbidden. See note on Ge 2:18–24.

4:4 CREATION, Good—Material things are not by nature evil. Neither the healthy sexual relationships of marriage nor certain foods are sinful in themselves. God ordained marriage and procreation at creation (Ge 1:28; 2:24–25). Everything He created was "very good" (Ge 1:26). We are to use the personal relationships and material things God gives us, thanking Him for them and dedicating them to His purposes.

4:4–5 PRAYER, Sovereignty of God—Holiness does not depend on legal specifications, but on relationship with God. In prayerful fellowship with God, gratefully acknowledging Him as invariable source, Christians hallow everything we touch.

4:6 EDUCATION, Parents—Timothy's early training under the guidance of a godly mother and grandmother was a precious heritage. See 2 Ti 1:5. This training made him a good minister or servant (Greek *diakonos*) of Jesus and His church. It molded not only Timothy's thinking but his life.

4:9 HOLY SCRIPTURE, Authoritative—See note on 1:15.

4:10 GOD, Personal—God is a living, personal God who knows His people and responds to their needs. He is not a fixed principle like gravity. He is a Heavenly Father who relates to us in personal relationships. He knows our needs, especially our need for salvation, and works to supply our needs. We must trust Him.

4:10 SALVATION, Definition—God has made salvation available to all people but has left people free to reject it if they choose. Only those who believe share in salvation. See note on 2 Th 2:10,13.

4:13 HOLY SCRIPTURE, Unity—The New Testament church sought God's revelation by reading Old Testament Scripture, preaching it in light of Christ, and teaching it.

4:14 CHURCH LEADERS, Ordination—The laying on of hands does not confer a divine gift. In this instance, the laying on of hands accompanied the gift which only God can bestow. Nothing can compensate for the lack of a divine gift for ministry. By laying on their hands, the leaders of the church recognized and affirmed the presence of spiritual gifts in Timothy. Paul either participated in this ceremony as one of the elders, or Timothy had hands laid on him twice (2 Ti 1:6). The question remains open whether Timothy entered an official leadership position in the church through ordination or whether he had his gifts affirmed and was commissioned for a specific mission.

4:14 CHURCH LEADERS, Elder—The early church had a pastoral leadership team with several elders or pastors (Ac 20:17, 28). Elders (Greek *presbuteros*) may represent a term taken over from Judaism. The special Greek term here (*presbuterion*) refers to a council or body of elders. The term was used for members of the Jewish Sanhedrin (Mt 26:3; Mk

message[c] when the body of elders[d] laid
their hands on you.[e]

15Be diligent in these matters; give
yourself wholly to them, so that everyone
may see your progress. 16Watch your life
and doctrine closely. Persevere in them,
because if you do, you will save[f] both
yourself and your hearers.

Chapter 5

Advice About Widows, Elders and Slaves

Do not rebuke an older man[g] harshly,[h] but exhort him as if he were
your father. Treat younger men[i] as
brothers, 2older women as mothers, and
younger women as sisters, with absolute
purity.

3Give proper recognition to those widows who are really in need.[j] 4But if a
widow has children or grandchildren,
these should learn first of all to put their
religion into practice by caring for their
own family and so repaying their parents
and grandparents,[k] for this is pleasing to
God.[l] 5The widow who is really in
need[m] and left all alone puts her hope in
God[n] and continues night and day to
pray[o] and to ask God for help. 6But the
widow who lives for pleasure is dead
even while she lives.[p] 7Give the people
these instructions,[q] too, so that no one
may be open to blame. 8If anyone does
not provide for his relatives, and especially for his immediate family, he has denied[r] the faith and is worse than an unbeliever.

9No widow may be put on the list of
widows unless she is over sixty, has been
faithful to her husband,[h] 10and is well
known for her good deeds,[s] such as
bringing up children, showing hospitality,[t] washing the feet[u] of the saints, helping those in trouble[v] and devoting herself to all kinds of good deeds.

11As for younger widows, do not put
them on such a list. For when their sensual desires overcome their dedication to
Christ, they want to marry. 12Thus they
bring judgment on themselves, because
they have broken their first pledge. 13Be-
sides, they get into the habit of being idle
and going about from house to house.
And not only do they become idlers, but
also gossips[w] and busybodies,[x] saying
things they ought not to. 14So I counsel
younger widows to marry,[y] to have children, to manage their homes and to give
the enemy no opportunity for slander.[z]
15Some have in fact already turned away
to follow Satan.[a]

16If any woman who is a believer has
widows in her family, she should help
them and not let the church be burdened
with them, so that the church can help
those widows who are really in need.[b]

17The elders[c] who direct the affairs of
the church well are worthy of double
honor,[d] especially those whose work is
preaching and teaching. 18For the Scrip-

4:14 [c] 1Ti 1:18 [d] S Ac 11:30 [e] S Ac 6:6; 2Ti 1:6
4:16 [f] S Ro 11:14
5:1 [g] Tit 2:2 [h] Lev 19:32 [i] Tit 2:6
5:3 [j] ver 5,16
5:4 [k] ver 8; Eph 6:1, 2 [l] Ro 12:2; Eph 5:10; 1Ti 2:3
5:5 [m] ver 3,16 [n] 1Co 7:34; 1Pe 3:5 [o] Lk 2:37; S Ro 1:10
5:6 [p] S Lk 15:24
5:7 [q] 1Ti 4:11; 6:2
5:8 [r] 2Pe 2:1; Jude 4
5:10 [s] Ac 9:36; 1Ti 6:18; 1Pe 2:12 [t] S Ro 12:13 [u] S Lk 7:44 [v] ver 16
5:13 [w] S Ro 1:29 [x] 2Th 3:11
5:14 [y] 1Co 7:9 [z] 1Ti 6:1
5:15 [a] S Mt 4:10
5:16 [b] ver 3-5
5:17 [c] S Ac 11:30 [d] Php 2:29; 1Th 5:12

[h] 9 Or *has had but one husband*

8:31). In the early church elders took up pastoral leadership roles, one of which apparently was ordination.

5:1–2 CHRISTIAN ETHICS, Character—Relationships with older people as described by Paul are consistent with the message in Ex 20:12: honor your parents. Relationships with men and women of one's own age are described as to be on a familial level. Such relationships should not be ruined by improper sexual overtones but be typified by mutual respect.

5:4,8 STEWARDSHIP, Care of Family—Biblical faith places a high priority on the family. Meeting the physical needs of one's family is a part of Christian stewardship. Christians should manage personal resources in a responsible way to care for family needs.

5:5 PRAYER, Kingdom Growth—The church is to mirror the God we pray to in care for the needy. The continuous prayer of a godly widow is important to the church; the church should care for her.

5:8 SIN, Disobeying—To fail to fulfill family responsibilities is sin, marking one as untrue to the commitment of faith in Christ. Even non-believers provide necessities of life for their families.

5:9–15 CHURCH LEADERS, Widow—Those who were enrolled as widows had devoted themselves to service in the church and were distinguished from other widows who were cared for by the church (5:3–4). The responsibilities of the office of widow involved administering charity and hospitality to those in distress and engaging in intercessory prayer. Paul insisted that they be over the age of sixty, have been faithful in marriage or had only one husband (NIV footnote), and have a reputation for good works.

5:14–15 EVIL AND SUFFERING, Satan—Satan uses the good, natural desires God created to tempt us to lose self-control. Following sexual desires outside marriage is following Satan. See note on 1 Co 7:1–9.

5:17 THE CHURCH, Practice—See note on 1 Th 5:12–13.

5:17–18 CHURCH LEADERS, Elder—Leaders of the church may divide among themselves the various tasks such as preaching, teaching, and administration according to their spiritual gifts. The structure may be adjusted to expand the effectiveness of the leaders. The church should respect and honor its leaders. Financial support is one way to show honor. See note on 1 Co 9:1–15.

5:17 EDUCATION, Qualified Teachers—Not all the elders in the church served as teachers and preachers. Some persons have the gift of teaching; others do not. The church should seek qualified persons for this important task. See note on 2 Ti 2:2.

5:18–21 HOLY SCRIPTURE, Authoritative—Paul quoted Dt 25:4 and Lk 10:7 as Scripture, showing the growth of the teaching of Jesus in standard form people could identify. Paul could use this authoritative teaching to illustrate his point. Because of his apostolic authority, he could expect obedience to his teaching. He could invoke Christ, the Father, and the angels as witnesses that his own instructions were to be obeyed. God led the church to recognize His inspiration behind Paul's authority and to include the letter in the canon of Holy Scripture.

5:18 STEWARDSHIP, Support Ministry—Paul tried not to burden churches financially and so supported himself as far as possible. He set an example for bi-vocational ministers. He did not set up his example as the only right one. He encouraged churches to provide the necessary resources for church leaders so they could be as productive as possible. Churches should

ture says, "Do not muzzle the ox while it
is treading out the grain,"[i][e] and "The
worker deserves his wages."[j][f] 19 Do not
entertain an accusation against an elder[g]
unless it is brought by two or three witnesses.[h] 20 Those who sin are to be rebuked[i] publicly, so that the others may
take warning.[j]
21 I charge you, in the sight of God and
Christ Jesus[k] and the elect angels, to
keep these instructions without partiality,
and to do nothing out of favoritism.
22 Do not be hasty in the laying on of
hands,[l] and do not share in the sins of
others.[m] Keep yourself pure.[n]
23 Stop drinking only water, and use a
little wine[o] because of your stomach and
your frequent illnesses.
24 The sins of some men are obvious,
reaching the place of judgment ahead of
them; the sins of others trail behind
them. 25 In the same way, good deeds are
obvious, and even those that are not cannot be hidden.

Chapter 6

6 ALL who are under the yoke of slavery
should consider their masters worthy of full respect,[p] so that God's name
and our teaching may not be slandered.[q]
2 Those who have believing masters are
not to show less respect for them because
they are brothers.[r] Instead, they are to
serve them even better, because those
who benefit from their service are believers, and dear to them. These are the
things you are to teach and urge on
them.[s]

Love of Money

3 If anyone teaches false doctrines[t] and
does not agree to the sound instruction[u]
of our Lord Jesus Christ and to godly
teaching, 4 he is conceited[v] and understands nothing. He has an unhealthy interest in controversies and quarrels about
words[w] that result in envy, strife, malicious talk, evil suspicions 5 and constant
friction between men of corrupt mind,
who have been robbed of the truth[x] and
who think that godliness is a means to
financial gain.
6 But godliness with contentment[y] is
great gain.[z] 7 For we brought nothing into
the world, and we can take nothing out of
it.[a] 8 But if we have food and clothing, we
will be content with that.[b] 9 People who
want to get rich[c] fall into temptation and
a trap[d] and into many foolish and harmful desires that plunge men into ruin and
destruction. 10 For the love of money[e] is a
root of all kinds of evil. Some people, eager for money, have wandered from the
faith[f] and pierced themselves with many
griefs.[g]

Paul's Charge to Timothy

11 But you, man of God,[h] flee from all
this, and pursue righteousness, godliness,[i] faith, love,[j] endurance and gentleness. 12 Fight the good fight[k] of the
faith. Take hold of[l] the eternal life[m] to

5:18 [e]Dt 25:4; 1Co 9:7-9 [f]Lk 10:7; Lev 19:13; Dt 24:14,15; Mt 10:10; 1Co 9:14
5:19 [g]S Ac 11:30 [h]S Mt 18:16
5:20 [i]2Ti 4:2; Tit 1:13; 2:15 [j]Dt 13:11
5:21 [k]1Ti 6:13; 2Ti 4:1
5:22 [l]S Ac 6:6 [m]Eph 5:11 [n]Ps 18:26
5:23 [o]1Ti 3:8
6:1 [p]S Eph 6:5 [q]1Ti 5:14; Tit 2:5,8
6:2 [r]Phm 16 [s]1Ti 4:11
6:3 [t]1Ti 1:3 [u]S 1Ti 1:10
6:4 [v]1Ti 3:6; 2Ti 3:4 [w]S 2Ti 2:14
6:5 [x]2Ti 3:8; Tit 1:15
6:6 [y]Php 4:11; Heb 13:5 [z]1Ti 4:8
6:7 [a]Job 1:21; Ps 49:17; Ecc 5:15
6:8 [b]Pr 30:8; Heb 13:5
6:9 [c]Pr 15:27; 28:20 [d]1Ti 3:7
6:10 [e]S 1Ti 3:3 [f]ver 21; Jas 5:19 [g]Jos 7:21
6:11 [h]2Ti 3:17 [i]ver 3,5,6; S 1Ti 2:2 [j]1Ti 1:14; 2Ti 2:22; 3:10
6:12 [k]1Co 9:25,26; S 1Ti 1:18 [l]ver 19; Php 3:12 [m]S Mt 25:46

[i]18 Deut. 25:4 [j]18 Luke 10:7

---

make every effort to provide for the physical needs of their leaders. See note on Php 4:10–20.

5:20 THE CHURCH, Discipline—The church is not a society of the perfect. Members sin. Each church has the responsibility to develop ways to rebuke, warn, and exhort members who continue in sin. In this way the church family encourages each other in Christian faithfulness and maturity. See notes on 1 Co 5:1–5, 9–13; 2 Co 2:5–11.

5:22 CHURCH LEADERS, Ordination—The church bears responsibility for those it ordains; therefore, it should do this with great care. Only those of proven character and who clearly possess spiritual gifts for their ministry should be ordained. The church should give the person time to give evidence of spiritual gifts before ordination.

5:23 CHRISTIAN ETHICS, Alcohol—Timothy's maladies are not elaborated upon. Evidently, a mix of water and wine helped his condition and could be prescribed by Paul from the common medicinal understanding of the day. Many contemporary prescriptions contain some percentage of alcohol content. Thus, its medicinal value, properly administered, may be beneficial. The Scripture does not give us license to prescribe alcoholic drinks for our own health.

6:3–10 CHRISTIAN ETHICS, Property Rights—Many who consider themselves wise in money matters cannot or will not count the costs involved in pursuing money as an end in itself. Once entered, the trap of greed is a difficult one from which to escape. Too often money becomes the chief goal of religious teachers who become willing to teach any kind of false doctrine and stir up trouble in churches simply to make money. They need to make godly living a chief goal, finding personal contentment and satisfaction therein. Such a life leads to eternal goals. Riches do not. Love of money leads away from God to grief.

6:3–6 EDUCATION, False Teachers—Some false teachers are not avowed enemies of truth. They stray from the gospel because they are infatuated with novelty, like those Athenians who "spent their time doing nothing but talking about and listening to the latest ideas" (Ac 17:21). Personal pride and conceit stand behind such infatuation. This conduct leads to controversies, suspicions, and quarrels rather than to peace and cooperation. Christian teaching is more than wrangling over trivialities disguised as religious thoughts. See note on 2 Ti 2:15–18.

6:6–10 SIN, Evil Desire—Money can become God. Loving money and devoting all life's energies to attain it or what it can buy is sin. Making money god leads to a series of sins and may even lead one to ignore Christian commitment. The road to money's temple is paved with grief.

6:6–19 STEWARDSHIP, Life-style—Wealth threatens our spiritual life. Persons caught up in the get-rich drive find that, while money itself is not evil, the love of money brings many evils. Such love often makes money into god. Accumulating wealth gets top priority. Money is seen as the only source of security. Godly contentment is the desired alternative. Three guidelines help Christians seek contentment and keep money in its place: (1) we brought nothing into this world and will take nothing out; (2) God gives the power to acquire money, and; (3) money should be used to serve God and others. See note on Lk 12:16–31.

6:12 SALVATION, Eternal Life—Persons are called to eternal life by God. One way they can own that calling is by publicly confessing Jesus Christ as Lord. This confession gives

which you were called when you made
your good confession[n] in the presence of
many witnesses. 13In the sight of God,
who gives life to everything, and of Christ
Jesus, who while testifying before Pontius
Pilate[o] made the good confession,[p] I
charge you[q] 14to keep this command
without spot or blame[r] until the appearing of our Lord Jesus Christ,[s] 15which
God will bring about in his own time[t] —
God, the blessed[u] and only Ruler,[v] the
King of kings and Lord of lords,[w] 16who
alone is immortal[x] and who lives in unapproachable light,[y] whom no one has
seen or can see.[z] To him be honor and
might forever. Amen.[a]

17Command those who are rich[b] in
this present world not to be arrogant nor
to put their hope in wealth,[c] which is so
uncertain, but to put their hope in God,[d]
who richly provides us with everything
for our enjoyment.[e] 18Command them to
do good, to be rich in good deeds,[f] and
to be generous and willing to share.[g] 19In
this way they will lay up treasure for
themselves[h] as a firm foundation for the
coming age, so that they may take hold
of[i] the life that is truly life.

20Timothy, guard what has been
entrusted[j] to your care. Turn away
from godless chatter[k] and the opposing
ideas of what is falsely called knowledge, 21which some have professed and
in so doing have wandered from the
faith.[l]

Grace be with you.[m]

6:12 [n]S Heb 3:1 **6:13** [o]Jn 18:33-37 [p]ver 12 [q]1Ti 5:21; 2Ti 4:1 **6:14** [r]S 1Th 3:13 [s]S 1Co 1:7; 2Ti 1:10; 4:1,8 **6:15** [t]1Ti 2:6; Tit 1:3 [u]1Ti 1:11 [v]1Ti 1:17 [w]Dt 10:17; Ps 136:3; Da 2:47; Rev 1:5; 17:14; 19:16 **6:16** [x]1Ti 1:17 [y]Ps 104:2; 1Jn 1:7 [z]S Jn 1:18 [a]S Ro 11:36 **6:17** [b]ver 9 [c]Ps 62:10; Jer 49:4; Lk 12:20,21 [d]1Ti 4:10 [e]Ac 14:17 **6:18** [f]S 1Ti 5:10 [g]Ro 12:8,13; Eph 4:28 **6:19** [h]S Mt 6:20 [i]ver 12; Php 3:12 **6:20** [j]2Ti 1:12,14 [k]2Ti 2:16 **6:21** [l]ver 10; 2Ti 2:18 [m]S Col 4:18

---

them something to hold on to as they engage in the good fight of faith. Eternal life is a present reality for all believers. We realize that quality of life in differing degrees according to our commitment to Christ.

6:13 GOD, Sovereignty—God, in His sovereignty, shows His creative power in giving life. This may also be a reference to His being Savior, giving new life in the place of spiritual death.

6:14–15 JESUS CHRIST, Final Coming—Christ's second coming encourages believers to maintain a high level of ethical behavior. See note on 1 Th 5:23. We do not know when Christ will come. His coming will complete God's purposes and plans.

6:14–15 LAST THINGS, Return Promises—The time of Christ's return lies in the sovereign decision of God. The promise is secure. The Lord will come. Sometimes it is described as an "appearing" (Greek *epiphaneia*) as in this passage. This stresses the return of Christ as a manifestation (2 Ti 1:10; 4:1,8; Tit 2:13). Elsewhere the return is called a revelation or unveiling (Greek *apokalupsis*), stressing God's act (1 Co 1:7; 2 Th 1:7; 1 Pe 1:7,13; 4:13). The most common term is coming (Greek *parousia*), which emphasizes the presence or arrival of the one who returns (1 Co 15:23; 2 Th 2:8; 2 Pe 3:4, 1 Jn 2:28).

6:15–16 GOD, Holy—The unique, sovereign God is the one and only true God. He is exalted above all else. He will never die. The reference to His dwelling in light is a reference to His holiness. The original idea of holiness was separateness or shining, a reference to the special sphere of God's existence, separate, apart from, above all else. Sinful humans cannot approach the holy God. See note on 1:17.

6:15 HISTORY, Eternal—History on earth will end when Jesus appears again to establish the eternal kingdom. God has plans for history until the time He has planned for the full inbreak of eternity. Only God can bring the end of time and the full revelation of eternity.

6:17–19 CHRISTIAN ETHICS, Property Rights—People rich in material goods should not be declared guilty of greed because of association. Not everyone is called to a life of poverty. How would the Kingdom advance sometimes without the necessary funds? Those entrusted with riches are warned to make sure their priorities do not shift away from primary loyalty to God to primary loyalty to money. They need to check their attitude towards other people, their generosity with the needy, and the richness of their actions in light of God's will. See note on Lk 18:18–30.

6:21 PRAYER, Blessing—See note on Ro 15:33.

2 Timothy

Theological Setting

Second Timothy is a precious treasure to the Bible student because it contains the last recorded words of the great apostle Paul. This last letter of the old missionary may have been written in late summer of 67 AD, almost thirty-five years after his conversion to Christ on the Damascus road, and twenty years since he had embarked on his first missionary journey. Now he was in a prison in Rome awaiting his final trial and, ultimately, execution.

From his prison cell Paul wrote this pastoral letter to encourage Timothy to exercise his pastoral office faithfully in spite of opposition from within and without the church.

1. From the outside, persecution of Christianity was increasing. Emperor Nero accused Christians of being incendiaries and terrorists and blamed them for the burning of Rome. Timothy was encouraged to follow the example of Paul, who was not ashamed to suffer for Christ and endured all things for the elect's sake.

2. Facing the enemies from within, Timothy was urged to resist the efforts of false teachers through "sound teaching" (1:13), and to train others to hand on the teaching (2:2). The false teachers claimed the final resurrection had already occurred (2:18). They taught with fancy words which pleased people but were far from God's truth (2:16,23; 4:4).

3. In his own personal life, Timothy was instructed to flee youthful desires, to keep himself pure, to avoid strife, and to make full proof of his ministry.

Theological Outline

2 Timothy: The Faithful Pastor

- I. Remembrance of Timothy (1:1-5)
  - A. Greeting to Timothy (1:1-2)
  - B. Thanksgiving to God (1:3*a*)
  - C. Remembering Timothy (1:3*b*-5)
- II. Encouragement in Tribulation (1:6-18)
  - A. Stir up the gift. (1:6)
  - B. Do not be fearful. (1:7)
  - C. Endure suffering. (1:8-10)
  - D. Do not be ashamed of Christ. (1:11-12)
  - E. Hold steadfast. (1:13-18)
- III. Instruction in Ministry (2:1-26)
  - A. Be strong in Christ's grace. (2:1-6)
  - B. Endure all things. (2:7-13)
  - C. Endeavor to please the Lord. (2:14-18)
  - D. Turn from wickedness. (2:19-22)
  - E. Avoid arguments. (2:23-26)
- IV. Explanation of Persecution (3:1-13)
  - A. Terrible times shall come. (3:1-9)
  - B. The godly shall suffer persecution. (3:10-13)
- V. Challenge to Perseverence (3:14—4:5)
  - A. Stay by the Holy Scriptures. (3:14-17)
  - B. Remember the account we must give. (4:1)
  - C. Prove your ministry. (4:2-5)
- VI. *Farewell from a Faithful Servant* (4:6-22)
  - A. Ready to be offered (4:6-7)
  - B. Reward to be received (4:8)

C. Requests of Timothy (4:9-15)
D. Remembrance of the trial (4:16-18*a*)
E. Remarks about friends (4:19-21)
F. Final benediction (4:22)

Theological Conclusions

Paul encouraged Timothy to faithfulness in ministry in the midst of doctrinal error and dangerous times. He charged Timothy to remember: (1) the salvation and calling of the Christian are by the grace of God and not by human works; (2) the security of the believer is in Christ; (3) the empowering of the believer is by the Lord; (4) all the writing of the Bible is inspired of God, and (5) the source of Christian doctrine; (6) true doctrine requires proper interpretation of God's Word; (7) all Scripture is profitable for instruction in righteousness that the believer may become mature in faith and works; (8) all who will live godly in Christ Jesus shall suffer persecution, but (9) the Lord will stand with Christians during times of trouble and preserve them unto His heavenly kingdom; (10) pastoral duty includes preaching the Word, encouraging the believers, enduring hardship, and doing the work of an evangelist.

Contemporary Teaching

1. Sound doctrine and godly living are both requirements of the Christian life. Christians ought to believe and behave.

2. Since there are more false teachings and strange cults today than ever before, Christians should preserve the doctrine of God once delivered to the saints and recorded in the Holy Scriptures.

3. True doctrine comes from a proper interpretation of the Word of God. The believer must "cut straight" the Word of truth rather than "patching" passages together out of context.

4. Corrupt minds encourage wickedness. A pleasure-mad society promotes love of self more than love of God.

5. In contrast, the disciple of Jesus Christ should run from lust; depart from iniquity; be purged of impurity; and follow after righteousness, faith, love, and peace.

6. Godly living does not mean exemption from tribulation and persecution. The Christian is encouraged to endure suffering, to be strong in grace, and to endeavor to please the Lord.

7. Jesus Christ is able to keep that which we have committed unto Him, and God will always stand with us and strengthen us.

8. Our Savior Jesus Christ has been raised from the dead, has abolished death, and has brought life and immortality to all who trust in Him.

9. A crown of righteousness awaits those who love the appearing of the Lord.

10. Since a person cannot know the hour of departure from this life, each one should be ready to meet the Lord.

Chapter 1

PAUL, an apostle[a] of Christ Jesus by
the will of God,[b] according to the
promise of life that is in Christ Jesus,[c]

2 To Timothy,[d] my dear son:[e]

Grace, mercy and peace from God the
Father and Christ Jesus our Lord.[f]

Encouragement to Be Faithful

3 I thank God,[g] whom I serve, as my
forefathers did, with a clear conscience,[h]
as night and day I constantly remember
you in my prayers.[i] 4 Recalling your
tears,[j] I long to see you,[k] so that I may
be filled with joy. 5 I have been reminded
of your sincere faith,[l] which first lived in
your grandmother Lois and in your mother Eunice[m] and, I am persuaded, now
lives in you also. 6 For this reason I remind you to fan into flame the gift of God,
which is in you through the laying on of
my hands.[n] 7 For God did not give us a
spirit of timidity,[o] but a spirit of power,[p]
of love and of self-discipline.

8 So do not be ashamed[q] to testify
about our Lord, or ashamed of me his
prisoner.[r] But join with me in suffering
for the gospel,[s] by the power of God,
9 who has saved[t] us and called[u] us to a
holy life—not because of anything we
have done[v] but because of his own purpose and grace. This grace was given us
in Christ Jesus before the beginning of
time, 10 but it has now been revealed[w]
through the appearing of our Savior,
Christ Jesus,[x] who has destroyed death[y]
and has brought life and immortality to
light through the gospel. 11 And of this
gospel[z] I was appointed[a] a herald and an
apostle and a teacher.[b] 12 That is why I
am suffering as I am. Yet I am not
ashamed,[c] because I know whom I have
believed, and am convinced that he is
able to guard[d] what I have entrusted to
him for that day.[e]

13 What you heard from me,[f] keep[g] as
the pattern[h] of sound teaching,[i] with
faith and love in Christ Jesus.[j] 14 Guard[k]

1:1 [a]S 1Co 1:1 [b]S 2Co 1:1 [c]Eph 3:6; Tit 1:2; 1Ti 6:19
1:2 [d]S Ac 16:1 [e]S 1Ti 1:2 [f]S Ro 1:7
1:3 [g]S Ro 1:8 [h]S Ac 23:1 [i]S Ro 1:10
1:4 [j]Ac 20:37 [k]2Ti 4:9
1:5 [l]1Ti 1:5 [m]Ac 16:1; 2Ti 3:15
1:6 [n]S Ac 6:6; 1Ti 4:14
1:7 [o]Jer 42:11; Ro 8:15; 1Co 16:10,11; 1Ti 4:12; Heb 2:15 [p]Isa 11:2
1:8 [q]ver 12,16; Mk 8:38 [r]S Eph 3:1 [s]2Ti 2:3,9; 4:5
1:9 [t]S Ro 11:14 [u]S Ro 8:28 [v]S Eph 2:9
1:10 [w]Eph 1:9 [x]S 1Ti 6:14 [y]1Co 15:26,54
1:11 [z]ver 8 [a]S Ac 9:15 [b]1Ti 2:7
1:12 [c]ver 8,16; Mk 8:38 [d]ver 14; 1Ti 6:20 [e]ver 18; S 1Co 1:8; 2Ti 4:8
1:13 [f]2Ti 2:2 [g]S Tit 1:9 [h]Ro 6:17 [i]S 1Ti 1:10 [j]S 1Th 1:3; 1Ti 1:14
1:14 [k]ver 12

1:2 PRAYER, Blessing—See note on Ro 1:7.

1:3 HUMANITY, Moral Consciousness—The Greek expression is literally "clean conscience." Paul joined himself to his Jewish ancestors as serving God without a sense of guilt. Following Christ did not make a Jew feel guilty. Neither should it make Timothy, son of a Greek father, feel guilty. The conscience can confirm our moral and religious decisions if it has been cleansed by Christ. The sense of right or wrong may not always be trustworthy, however. See note on Tit 1:15.

1:3 WORSHIP, Service—See note on Mt 4:10.

1:3 PRAYER, Persistence—See notes on Php 1:3; 1 Th 3:12–13; 5:17–18. Regular prayer, including asking for forgiveness, praying for enemies, and thanking God, helps us have a clear conscience.

1:8 EVIL AND SUFFERING, Endurance—See note on Col 1:24.

1:8–11 PROCLAMATION, Call—See notes on Jer 1:4–9; Lk 8:1; 1 Co 2:2. The call to proclamation may be a call to persecution and pain.

1:8 EVANGELISM, Personal—One should never be ashamed to share the gospel of Christ nor fail to stand by those who do. See note on Ro 1:13–17.

1:9–10 GOD, Grace—Grace is central to our idea of God, and to our idea of the gospel and Christianity. The grace of God, God's redemptive blessing through Jesus for those who do not deserve it, originated in eternity, before the beginning of time. This means grace is an essential, vital part of God's nature. Grace is not a back-up plan God instituted when all else failed. God fully revealed His plan of grace through Jesus, who came to earth as the incarnate Son to die for our sins. Grace is God's planning and acting. Humans can never earn it or claim any right to it.

1:9–10 JESUS CHRIST, Mission—Christ's revelation of God's grace was planned in eternity before the world began. Christ appeared in the time God planned to save us from sin and death. His resurrection destroyed death by giving believers the possibility to live forever through their own resurrection.

1:9–10 SALVATION, Definition—God's salvation is His call to a holy life, a life characterized by incorruptibility and light. It is a response to His election in Christ before time began. It results from His grace. Its fullness became visible through Christ's work on the cross. Its result is eternal life. Immortality literally means life without death, a life available through Christ at the resurrection. It does not let Christians avoid physical death. See notes on Ps 132:16; Eph 2:4–5,7–10.

1:9 SALVATION, Grace—God calls us and saves us because of His purpose and grace, not because we deserve His salvation. His grace toward us is embodied in Jesus Christ.

1:10 HUMANITY, Death—The Christian no longer must fear death as the end of life and hope. Christ's resurrection shows death's power is dead. See notes on 1 Co 15:19, 21–22, 38–57.

1:10 REVELATION, Author of Grace—Grace and forgiveness have been evident in God's work forever, but especially clear in the revelation of God through Jesus Christ, God's greatest gift of grace for His people.

1:11–12 EVIL AND SUFFERING, Endurance—See note on Col 1:24.

1:11 EDUCATION, Missionaries—Paul saw both preaching and teaching as essential to his calling as an apostle and missionary for Christ. Proclaiming the gospel and instructing converts in the faith always go hand in hand. See note on Ac 17:2.

1:12 ELECTION, Eternal Security—Paul had great assurance in the permanence and security of his salvation. He knew whom he had believed and was convinced that Jesus Christ would guard what he entrusted to Him. Nevertheless, he encouraged Timothy to guard his deposit of faith with the aid of the Holy Spirit.

1:12 SALVATION, Belief—"Have believed" is in the perfect tense in the Greek, which indicates action begun and completed in the past with its effects continued in the present. Our faith is tested belief or trust. We can stake our whole life on the trustworthiness of God in Christ. The judgment day will prove our faith to be vindicated.

1:13–14 HOLY SCRIPTURE, Inspired—God-inspired teachings are to be kept and used in faith and love. Protecting these teachings from misunderstanding and improper use, the faithful disciple had as an aid the presence and power of the Spirit of God within him. The Spirit both guards and empowers the true revelations of God by prompting the human mind and heart and by strengthening the keeper of His words.

1:13–14 EDUCATION, Pastors—The pastor-teacher has a two-pronged responsibility: (1) to teach correct doctrine; (2) to teach it in love. Only the Holy Spirit living in the pastor-teacher can ensure that sound doctrinal tradition is maintained and passed on. Sometimes, doctrinal "correctness" becomes an excuse for behaving in unloving ways. See Eph 4:15.

1:14 HOLY SPIRIT, Indwells—The Spirit helps our memo-

the good deposit that was entrusted to
you—guard it with the help of the Holy
Spirit who lives in us.[l]
15You know that everyone in the province of Asia[m] has deserted me,[n] including Phygelus and Hermogenes.
16May the Lord show mercy to the
household of Onesiphorus,[o] because he
often refreshed me and was not
ashamed[p] of my chains.[q] 17On the contrary, when he was in Rome, he searched
hard for me until he found me. 18May the
Lord grant that he will find mercy from
the Lord on that day![r] You know very
well in how many ways he helped me[s] in
Ephesus.[t]

Chapter 2

YOU then, my son,[u] be strong[v] in the
grace that is in Christ Jesus. 2And the
things you have heard me say[w] in the
presence of many witnesses[x] entrust to
reliable men who will also be qualified to
teach others. 3Endure hardship with us[y]
like a good soldier[z] of Christ Jesus. 4No
one serving as a soldier gets involved in
civilian affairs—he wants to please his
commanding officer. 5Similarly, if anyone
competes as an athlete, he does not receive the victor's crown[a] unless he competes according to the rules. 6The hard-
working farmer should be the first to receive a share of the crops.[b] 7Reflect on
what I am saying, for the Lord will give
you insight into all this.
8Remember Jesus Christ, raised from
the dead,[c] descended from David.[d] This
is my gospel,[e] 9for which I am suffering[f]
even to the point of being chained[g] like a
criminal. But God's word[h] is not
chained. 10Therefore I endure everything[i] for the sake of the elect,[j] that
they too may obtain the salvation[k] that is
in Christ Jesus, with eternal glory.[l]
11Here is a trustworthy saying:[m]

If we died with him,
  we will also live with him;[n]
12if we endure,
  we will also reign with him.[o]
If we disown him,
  he will also disown us;[p]
13if we are faithful,
  he will remain faithful,[q]
  for he cannot disown himself.

A Workman Approved by God

14Keep reminding them of these
things. Warn them before God against

1:14 [l]S Ro 8:9
1:15 [m]S Ac 2:9 [n]2Ti 4:10,11,16
1:16 [o]2Ti 4:19 [p]ver 8,12; Mk 8:38 [q]S Ac 21:33
1:18 [r]S ver 12 [s]Heb 6:10 [t]S Ac 18:19
2:1 [u]S 1Ti 1:2 [v]S Eph 6:10
2:2 [w]2Ti 1:13 [x]1Ti 6:12
2:3 [y]ver 9; 2Ti 1:8; 4:5 [z]S 1Ti 1:18
2:5 [a]S 1Co 9:25
2:6 [b]1Co 9:10
2:8 [c]S Ac 2:24 [d]S Mt 1:1 [e]Ro 2:16; 16:25
2:9 [f]S Ac 9:16 [g]S Ac 21:33 [h]S Heb 4:12
2:10 [i]Col 1:24 [j]Tit 1:1 [k]2Co 1:6 [l]2Co 4:17; 1Pe 5:10
2:11 [m]S 1Ti 1:15 [n]Ro 6:2-11
2:12 [o]Ro 8:17; 1Pe 4:13 [p]Mt 10:33
2:13 [q]Ro 3:3; S 1Co 1:9

ry. By living in us, He always reminds us about Jesus. That is what Jesus had said He would do. See Jn 15:26; 16:15; note on Jn 14:26. The church must not become so innovative and up-to-date that we forget our foundation. The church must carefully guard the message it has inherited concerning Christ. The Spirit's basic work is to keep us obedient to the gospel of Christ.

1:16–18 PRAYER, Intercession—Paul prayed for God's mercy and eternal salvation for one who befriended him. Intercession for friends is a regular part of prayer.

2:1 SALVATION, Grace—Grace also means God's power in some instances, as in this text. His unmerited favor carries with it an enabling power. Trusting in His grace rather than in our power we can overcome temptations and enemies. See note on Isa 33:2.

2:2 REVELATION, Persons—The words of truth are entrusted to steady teachers, who pass on the message and become instruments of God revealing His will to disciples.

2:2 EDUCATION, Qualified Teachers—The pastor is responsible to learn sound teaching and teach it to reliable members who will teach others. The pastor cannot monopolize the teaching function. God gives the gift of teaching to whom He will. Any church member who has the gift of teaching is responsible under God to learn from other teachers but also to study God's Word personally. Such personal study should let God's Word critique teachings learned from others. See note on 1 Ti 5:17.

2:2 EVANGELISM, In the Church—As a leader, Timothy was to instruct faithful Christians, who then, in turn, could teach others also. This principle is most important in the development of an evangelistic church. To share Christ is not the duty of just one or two leaders. They are to teach others how to evangelize who will then teach others until all in the body of Christ are instructed in sharing their faith. This is how the entire world can come to hear the gospel. See Guide to Church Evangelism, pp. 1833–1835.

2:3–7 EVIL AND SUFFERING, Endurance—To illustrate the necessity of enduring suffering, Paul used three illustrations: a soldier, an athlete, and a farmer. The point of all three images is that Christians are to please the Lord above all else and not serve secondary ends.

2:8–13 JESUS CHRIST, Son of David—As a human Son of David, Jesus fulfilled all God's promises to Israel. As the One raised from death, He gave us reason to endure all the world's suffering and persecution, knowing we will live with Him now and forever. On the cross He put away our old way of life and introduced us to enduring faithfulness which will lead us to reign with Him in heaven. He is always faithful to His character and His promises.

2:8–13 EVIL AND SUFFERING, Endurance—Concern for Christ and His church dominates the life of the Christian. We are willing to endure whatever suffering we must so people may hear the gospel, accept Christ, and participate in His salvation. We would not want anyone to miss the opportunity for salvation because we refused to suffer. Suffering tests our enduring faithfulness to the faithful One. See note on Php 1:12–18.

2:8–9 HOLY SCRIPTURE, Powerful—The Word of God, alive and unchained, cannot be contained by human effort. Even though the messenger is imprisoned, the message is never imprisoned.

2:10–26 ELECTION, Eternal Security—God knows those who are His. Yet God's elect must behave with righteous intentions, seeking to achieve God's noble purposes. The elect often endure hardness as good soldiers of Jesus Christ. Such endurance is motivated by love for God's elect church.

2:11–13 HOLY SCRIPTURE, Writing—Paul apparently used an early church hymn to reinforce his point. Revelation and inspiration included taking material from other sources and incorporating it as part of the inspired text. See note on 1 Ti 1:15.

2:11 ORDINANCES, Baptism as New Life—This is a part of an early Christian hymn which Paul quoted. The first two lines express the theology which Paul proclaimed about baptism as dying and rising with Christ. See notes on Ro 6:3–4; Col 2:12,20. Paul may have written the hymn originally, or he may be recalling a hymn that Timothy already knew. It was probably a hymn used at baptism, interpreting the inward spiritual meaning of the outward act of baptism.

quarreling about words;[r] it is of no value, and only ruins those who listen. 15Do
your best to present yourself to God as
one approved, a workman who does not
need to be ashamed and who correctly
handles the word of truth.[s] 16Avoid godless chatter,[t] because those who indulge
in it will become more and more ungodly.
17Their teaching will spread like gangrene. Among them are Hymenaeus[u] and
Philetus, 18who have wandered away
from the truth. They say that the resurrection has already taken place,[v] and
they destroy the faith of some.[w] 19Never-
theless, God's solid foundation stands
firm,[x] sealed with this inscription: "The
Lord knows those who are his,"[a][y] and,
"Everyone who confesses the name of
the Lord[z] must turn away from wickedness."

20In a large house there are articles not
only of gold and silver, but also of wood
and clay; some are for noble purposes and
some for ignoble.[a] 21If a man cleanses
himself from the latter, he will be an instrument for noble purposes, made holy,
useful to the Master and prepared to do
any good work.[b]

22Flee the evil desires of youth, and
pursue righteousness, faith, love[c] and
peace, along with those who call on the
Lord[d] out of a pure heart.[e] 23Don't have
anything to do with foolish and stupid arguments, because you know they produce
quarrels.[f] 24And the Lord's servant must
not quarrel; instead, he must be kind to
everyone, able to teach, not resentful.[g]
25Those who oppose him he must gently
instruct, in the hope that God will grant
them repentance leading them to a
knowledge of the truth,[h] 26and that they
will come to their senses and escape from
the trap of the devil,[i] who has taken
them captive to do his will.

Chapter 3

Godlessness in the Last Days

BUT mark this: There will be terrible
times in the last days.[j] 2People will
be lovers of themselves, lovers of money,[k] boastful, proud,[l] abusive,[m] disobedient to their parents,[n] ungrateful, unholy, 3without love, unforgiving, slanderous, without self-control, brutal, not
lovers of the good, 4treacherous,[o] rash,
conceited,[p] lovers of pleasure rather than
lovers of God— 5having a form of godliness[q] but denying its power. Have nothing to do with them.[r]

6They are the kind who worm their
ways[s] into homes and gain control over
weak-willed women, who are loaded
down with sins and are swayed by all
kinds of evil desires, 7always learning but
never able to acknowledge the truth.[t]
8Just as Jannes and Jambres opposed Moses,[u] so also these men oppose[v] the
truth—men of depraved minds,[w] who, as

2:14 [r]ver 23; 1Ti 1:4; 6:4; Tit 3:9
2:15 [s]Eph 1:13; Col 1:5; Jas 1:18
2:16 [t]Tit 3:9; 1Ti 6:20
2:17 [u]1Ti 1:20
2:18 [v]2Th 2:2 [w]1Ti 1:19; 6:21
2:19 [x]Isa 28:16 [y]Ex 33:12; Nu 16:5; Jn 10:14; 1Co 8:3; Gal 4:9 [z]1Co 1:2
2:20 [a]Ro 9:21
2:21 [b]2Co 9:8; Eph 2:10; 2Ti 3:17
2:22 [c]1Ti 1:14; 6:11 [d]S Ac 2:21 [e]1Ti 1:5
2:23 [f]S ver 14
2:24 [g]1Ti 3:2,3
2:25 [h]S 1Ti 2:4
2:26 [i]1Ti 3:7
3:1 [j]1Ti 4:1; 2Pe 3:3
3:2 [k]S 1Ti 3:3 [l]Ro 1:30 [m]2Pe 2:10-12 [n]Ro 1:30
3:4 [o]Ps 25:3 [p]1Ti 3:6; 6:4
3:5 [q]S 1Ti 2:2 [r]S Ro 16:17
3:6 [s]Jude 4
3:7 [t]S 1Ti 2:4
3:8 [u]Ex 7:11 [v]Ac 13:8 [w]1Ti 6:5

[a] *19* Num. 16:5 (see Septuagint)

2:15 REVELATION, Messengers—Carriers of the truth of God are to represent that truth and the God of truth well enough that we need never apologize for ourselves. God wants His people to be well prepared in the interpretation of God's truth. The messenger who interprets God's truth for others is an agent of His revelation.

2:15 CHURCH LEADERS, Teacher—The teacher is one who correctly handles the Word of truth. The image is that of laying out a road. The teacher is to lay out a clearly marked pathway for others to walk. This effort requires study. Teachers are those who have been gifted by the Spirit and have devoted their minds to God so that they might impart His wisdom to His people.

2:15–18 EDUCATION, False Teachers—The Word of God can be abused as well as used. It is always in danger of being distorted by teachers who handle it casually. The only effective way to prevent distortion of the Word of truth is diligent preparation at the study desk. Where teachers and learners are lax in their study of the Scriptures, Bible classes are often filled with godless chatter and vain babblings. Instead of becoming mature in the faith, members and teachers become ungodly. Yet they claim success because their teaching becomes so popular, spreading "like gangrene." See note on 1 Ti 6:3–6.

2:16 SIN, Moral Insensitivity—When persons continually engage in sin, they will reap the consequences. Foolish chatter occupies our minds with unworthy thoughts which eventually emerge as unworthy actions. Soon we no longer realize the sins we are committing. We become morally inept, unable to do what is right.

2:19 SALVATION, Confession—See notes on Ro 10:8–10; Php 2:11. Genuine confession will be accompanied by forsaking wickedness.

2:23–26 EVIL AND SUFFERING, Satan—The devil uses church arguments and divisions to capture people. Patient teachers who refuse to argue can lead people to repentance and truth. Resentment is the tool of Satan.

2:23–26 EDUCATION, Qualified Teachers—Qualified Christian teachers will not be drawn into senseless quarrels about various religious notions. They will depend upon gentle, positive instruction to correct deviations from the truth. Their kind spirit will lead more people to repentance and truth than any amount of fighting and quarreling.

2:24–25 THE CHURCH, Servants—Servants of God kindly help other believers without seeking arguments or reasons for resentment.

3:1–9 SIN, Depravity—This passage stands as a warning against utopian idealism that believes human society, through its own exertions, will continue to improve itself. Although material progress scarcely can be denied, humanity will continue to be driven by a destructive self-motivation and in many ways will decline morally and spiritually through neglect. Self-love and materialism head the list of sins leading to depravity. Religious practices are a part of these depraved people's lives, but the power of God plays no part in directing their lives. The depraved person learns much but never puts learning into practice and never gives homage to the Source of truth. Such people cannot be counted as believers.

3:1–17 CHRISTIAN ETHICS, Moral Imperatives—Certain attitudes and actions are wrong and always will be. Paul provided a long list. The bad life centers on self and sensuality, not on God and others. Evil people manipulate and abuse the needy and weak instead of helping them. God's people must continually study God's inspired Word and let it correct and change us.

far as the faith is concerned, are rejected.
9But they will not get very far because, as
in the case of those men,[x] their folly will
be clear to everyone.

Paul's Charge to Timothy

10You, however, know all about my
teaching,[y] my way of life, my purpose,
faith, patience, love, endurance, 11perse-
cutions, sufferings—what kinds of things
happened to me in Antioch,[z] Iconium[a]
and Lystra,[b] the persecutions I endured.[c] Yet the Lord rescued[d] me from
all of them.[e] 12In fact, everyone who
wants to live a godly life in Christ Jesus
will be persecuted,[f] 13while evil men
and impostors will go from bad to
worse,[g] deceiving and being deceived.[h]
14But as for you, continue in what you
have learned and have become convinced
of, because you know those from whom
you learned it,[i] 15and how from infancy[j]
you have known the holy Scriptures,[k]
which are able to make you wise[l] for
salvation through faith in Christ Jesus.
16All Scripture is God-breathed[m] and is
useful for teaching,[n] rebuking, correcting
and training in righteousness,[o] 17so that
the man of God[p] may be thoroughly
equipped for every good work.[q]

Chapter 4

IN the presence of God and of Christ
Jesus, who will judge the living and
the dead,[r] and in view of his appearing[s]
and his kingdom, I give you this charge:[t]
2Preach[u] the Word;[v] be prepared in season and out of season; correct, rebuke[w]
and encourage[x]—with great patience
and careful instruction. 3For the time will
come when men will not put up with
sound doctrine.[y] Instead, to suit their
own desires, they will gather around
them a great number of teachers to say
what their itching ears want to hear.[z]
4They will turn their ears away from the
truth and turn aside to myths.[a] 5But you,

3:9 [x]Ex 7:12; 8:18; 9:11
3:10 [y]1Ti 4:6
3:11 [z]Ac 13:14,50 [a]S Ac 13:51 [b]Ac 14:6 [c]2Co 11:23-27 [d]S Ro 15:31 [e]Ps 34:19
3:12 [f]Jn 15:20; S Ac 14:22
3:13 [g]2Ti 2:16 [h]S Mk 13:5
3:14 [i]2Ti 1:13
3:15 [j]2Ti 1:5 [k]Jn 5:39 [l]Dt 4:6; Ps 119:98,99
3:16 [m]2Pe 1:20,21 [n]S Ro 4:23,24 [o]Dt 29:29
3:17 [p]1Ti 6:11 [q]2Ti 2:21
4:1 [r]S Ac 10:42 [s]ver 8; S 1Ti 6:14 [t]1Ti 5:21; 6:13
4:2 [u]1Ti 4:13 [v]Gal 6:6 [w]1Ti 5:20; Tit 1:13; 2:15 [x]Tit 2:15
4:3 [y]S 1Ti 1:10 [z]Isa 30:10
4:4 [a]S 1Ti 1:4

3:10–13 EVIL AND SUFFERING, Endurance—See note on Mt 5:10–12.

3:10 EDUCATION, Example—Paul reminded Timothy that his teaching and his way of life were cut from the same cloth. In fact, the way he lived attested to the authenticity of what he taught. See note on 1 Co 4:17.

3:14–17 HOLY SCRIPTURE, Authoritative—The instruction of Christian leaders, the authority of the Scriptures, and the authority of Jesus Christ combine to make a person wise and prepared for salvation by belief in Jesus. Scripture is God-breathed and thus authoritative in all areas of ministry —instructing in proper doctrine, rebuking sinful behavior, correcting false doctrine, and training in right living. All of these contributions equip the person God has called to be skilled and capable in doing good for God. Every passage of Scripture has God as its ultimate Author and salvation, doctrine, and Christlike life as its purpose.

3:14–17 PROCLAMATION, Reproof—See note on 1 Co 15:1–7. The purpose of reproof or rebuke is to correct the erring one. The proclamation of the gospel will point out the error in the lives of the hearers and will point them to the right way. This is a clear responsibility of preaching (2 Ti 4:2). Paul rebuked the church at Galatia because they had moved away from the true gospel to embrace heresy (Gal 1:6–12). Paul also devoted much of his first letter to the church at Corinth to rebuking the actions and attitudes of the believers there (1 Co 3:1–9; 5:1–13).

3:14–17 EDUCATION, Scripture Study—The Bible is the textbook of the Christian faith. The Scriptures are the source of religious instruction of both children and adults, pointing the way to salvation, clarifying understandings of the gospel, and providing guidance for living in daily life. All doctrine must be formed on the basis of the Bible text. Church history, contemporary church experience, and the leadership of God's Spirit will help each generation of Christian teachers find words to communicate true doctrinal teaching, but every teaching must ultimately rest on Scripture. All biblical teaching will lead people to salvation through faith in Jesus Christ. See note on Lk 24:27.

3:15 SALVATION, Belief—The sacred Scriptures make persons wise to the salvation which Christ gives. They teach us that salvation comes through faith in Christ. True wisdom leads to trust in Christ's strength to save, not to confidence in our intelligence.

4:1,8 GOD, Judge—In His sovereignty over the world, God will judge all persons. We must each give answer to God for our lives. God is a just Judge who has already forgiven our sins, if we have accepted His grace through Jesus Christ. For the responsible, faithful Christian, judgment is not a threat but a time of blessing. Notice Jesus is the Judge in this passage.

4:1 JESUS CHRIST, Final Coming—See note on 1 Ti 6:14–15.

4:1 LAST THINGS, Encourages Faithfulness—Awareness of life being lived in the full gaze and knowledge of God, who will at the last be Judge, is strong encouragement to faithful living and serving. The anticipation of Christ's return and the coming of God's kingdom also motivate us to be faithful. Judgment will involve all people—those dead at Christ's coming and those still living.

4:1–2 PROCLAMATION, Authoritative—Proclamation involves an authoritative, public declaration of the truth of the gospel. God speaks through His messengers. Paul's admonition to Timothy makes this clear. Proclamation is a command for the proclaimer God calls. Declaring the gospel brings God's authority to bear on the needs of God's people for correction and for encouragement. Proclamation is a strong stimulant for growth, maturity, and perseverance (Lk 8:15; Col 1:5–6). Proclamation is to be done when it is convenient and when it is inconvenient, when people respond and even when they do not respond. Scripture reveals that proclamation of His Word is both a human responsibility and an incomparable privilege. See notes on 2 Ti 3:14–17; Lk 8:1; Ac 14:21–22. The source of our gospel message is the Word of God. Jesus Christ is adequately and completely revealed through the pages of our Bible. What we preach must be consistent with the Word of God; for when we preach, we deliver God's message (1 Pe 4:11). The gospel preacher must always stand with open Bible in hand to declare, "Thus says the Lord."

4:2–4 EDUCATION, False Teachers—False teachers are not always doctrinal deviationists. They sometimes prostitute truth for their need to be popular and say what people want to hear by selling their consciences in exchange for compliments. Standing against popular prejudices requires more courage than defending hallowed doctrines.

4:3 CHURCH LEADERS, Teacher—Paul warned that the task of teaching could fall into unworthy hands. This was because people would prefer teachers who fit their views and who taught only what their audience wanted to hear. Self-appointed teachers would arise who deceived others with shallow teaching (1 Ti 1:6–7) or who expounded the doctrines of men as if they were the teaching of God (Col 2:22). Others, motivated by greed, might simply want to exploit their listeners (2 Pe 2:1–3). See Guide to Teaching the Word, pp. 1806–1809.

keep your head in all situations, endure
hardship,[b] do the work of an evangelist,[c] discharge all the duties of your ministry.
6 For I am already being poured out like
a drink offering,[d] and the time has come
for my departure.[e] 7 I have fought the
good fight,[f] I have finished the race,[g] I
have kept the faith. 8 Now there is in store
for me[h] the crown of righteousness,[i]
which the Lord, the righteous Judge, will
award to me on that day[j]—and not only
to me, but also to all who have longed for
his appearing.[k]

Personal Remarks

9 Do your best to come to me quickly,[l]
10 for Demas,[m] because he loved this
world,[n] has deserted me and has gone to
Thessalonica.[o] Crescens has gone to Galatia,[p] and Titus[q] to Dalmatia. 11 Only
Luke[r] is with me.[s] Get Mark[t] and bring
him with you, because he is helpful to me
in my ministry. 12 I sent Tychicus[u] to
Ephesus.[v] 13 When you come, bring the
cloak that I left with Carpus at Troas,[w]
and my scrolls, especially the parch-
ments.
14 Alexander[x] the metalworker did me
a great deal of harm. The Lord will repay
him for what he has done.[y] 15 You too
should be on your guard against him, because he strongly opposed our message.
16 At my first defense, no one came to
my support, but everyone deserted me.
May it not be held against them.[z] 17 But
the Lord stood at my side[a] and gave me
strength,[b] so that through me the message might be fully proclaimed and all the
Gentiles might hear it.[c] And I was delivered from the lion's mouth.[d] 18 The Lord
will rescue me from every evil attack[e]
and will bring me safely to his heavenly
kingdom.[f] To him be glory for ever and
ever. Amen.[g]

Final Greetings

19 Greet Priscilla[b] and Aquila[h] and the
household of Onesiphorus.[i] 20 Erastus[j]
stayed in Corinth, and I left Trophimus[k]
sick in Miletus.[l] 21 Do your best to get
here before winter.[m] Eubulus greets you,
and so do Pudens, Linus, Claudia and all
the brothers.
22 The Lord be with your spirit.[n] Grace
be with you.[o]

4:5 [b]2Ti 1:8; 2:3,9 [c]Ac 21:8; Eph 4:11 **4:6** [d]Nu 15:1-12; 28:7,24; Php 2:17 [e]Php 1:23 **4:7** [f]S 1Ti 1:18 [g]S 1Co 9:24; Ac 20:24 **4:8** [h]Col 1:5; 1Pe 1:4 [i]S 1Co 9:25 [j]S 2Ti 1:12 [k]S 1Ti 6:14 **4:9** [l]ver 21; Tit 3:12 **4:10** [m]Col 4:14; Phm 24 [n]1Jn 2:15 [o]S Ac 17:1 [p]S Ac 16:6 [q]S 2Co 2:13 **4:11** [r]Col 4:14; Phm 24 [s]2Ti 1:15 [t]S Ac 12:12 **4:12** [u]S Ac 20:4 [v]S Ac 18:19 **4:13** [w]S Ac 16:8 **4:14** [x]Ac 19:33; 1Ti 1:20 [y]Ps 28:4; 109:20; Ro 2:6; 12:19 **4:16** [z]Ac 7:60 **4:17** [a]Ac 23:11 [b]S Php 4:13 [c]S Ac 9:15 [d]1Sa 17:37; Ps 22:21; Da 6:22; 1Co 15:32 **4:18** [e]Ps 121:7; 2Pe 2:9 [f]ver 1 [g]S Ro 11:36 **4:19** [h]S Ac 18:2 [i]2Ti 1:16 **4:20** [j]Ac 19:22 [k]Ac 20:4; 21:29 [l]Ac 20:15,17 **4:21** [m]ver 9; Tit 3:12 **4:22** [n]S Gal 6:18 [o]S Col 4:18

[b]19 Greek *Prisca,* a variant of *Priscilla*

4:5 CHURCH LEADERS, Evangelist—The work of an evangelist is to declare to the world the gospel, God's judgment on sin, and His offer of grace and salvation. It is an important aspect of Christian ministry. The task is to awaken faith and make disciples for Christ. Though some persons are specially gifted as evangelists, all have the responsibility to witness. The writers of the gospels were called evangelists at a later time.

4:5 EVANGELISM, Obedience—Although Timothy did not have the itinerant evangelistic ministry as did his mentor Paul, he was nevertheless to do the work of the evangelist where he was as God led him. It was the only way Timothy could discharge all the duties of his ministry. Because all God's people are ministers (Eph 4:11–12), the principle applies to all. All are to do the work of an evangelist, that is, share Christ as we have opportunity.

4:6–10 ELECTION, Perseverance—Demas had deserted the faith. He loved the world more than Jesus Christ. Paul remained faithful until the very end. Persecutions, sufferings, or an inadequate understanding of Scripture may lead people to reject the faith. Students of sound doctrine look in faith and hope to the coming day when Jesus will judge the living and the dead. They look to receive a crown of righteousness, for they keep their election legacy.

4:6–8 LAST THINGS, Believers' Death—Death for believers may be described as a departure to be with Christ and to receive rewards. It is also described as the putting down of a temporary tent in order to take up a building of God that is eternal. For the intermediate state, see notes on Ac 7:60; 2 Co 5:1–10.

4:8 JESUS CHRIST, Judgment—Christ's final judgment will include rewards for all who have centered life on Him and His promises.

4:8 LAST THINGS, Return Attitudes—The expectation of the Lord's appearing with its subsequent rewards is the subject of eager longing on the part of those who have lived faithfully in Christ Jesus. One's approach to death is filled with hope by the thought of Christ's return.

4:16–18 EVIL AND SUFFERING, God's Present Help—Although in jail, Paul was confident of God's strength (2 Th 3:3). God's presence can be so strong that even betrayal by trusted friends will not shake a believer's faith and endurance. God can rescue us from any earthly dangers if He chooses to do so. He will bring us safely to our heavenly reward. We do not rely on earthly, human help. God is our source of help.

4:16 PRAYER, Jesus' Example—Paul prayed for deserting friends. Christ had taught that enemies should be prayed for (Mt 5:44).

4:16–17 EVANGELISM, Power—Even if all people desert us, God will stand by us and strengthen us for the task of sharing Christ. He is able to deliver us and make our witness for Christ effectual in winning people to our Lord.

4:17–18 JESUS CHRIST, Ascension—The ascended Lord stands by His people in our times of need. He will protect us until He gives us our eternal reward.

4:17 REVELATION, Divine Presence—God is present when everyone else deserts us. Paul experienced God's strength as he stood alone to face a pagan judge and to make the gospel known under very difficult circumstances.

4:17 PROCLAMATION, Anointing—See notes on Isa 61:1–3; Ac 3:11–26.

4:22 PRAYER, Blessing—See note on Ro 15:33.

Titus

Theological Setting

Paul wrote this pastoral letter to his close friend and associate in ministry, Titus, to remind Titus of his task in Crete: to "straighten out what was left unfinished," to "appoint elders in every town," and to put to silence "the commands of those who reject the truth" (1:5,14). Titus was one of the younger men whom Paul had won to Christ and enlisted to help in his ministry—Timothy and Epaphroditus were others (Php 2:19-30).

Records are incomplete regarding Paul's visit(s) to Crete. So far as we know, Paul did not found the church there; but it is clear that he went to Crete to organize and to strengthen the churches and to put them on a sound doctrinal foundation. Titus, who had accompanied Paul, was left behind to complete the task Paul had begun. Titus had become a personal representative of this special apostle Paul.

Although Acts did not mention Titus in its accounts of Paul's missionary voyages, Paul's epistles clearly showed that Titus was a companion and trusted associate of Paul. Galatians 2:3 tells us Paul refused to require Titus to be circumcised, even though the Judaizers insisted that Gentiles had to be circumcised before they could become Christians. Paul had deep regard for Titus (2 Co 2:12-14; 7:5-7). They ministered in partnership together (2 Co 8:16-23).

The last time Titus is mentioned in the New Testament is in 2 Ti 4:10, where Paul wrote that Titus had gone to Dalmatia—apparently on another assignment. Whether Paul and Titus ever met in Nicopolis as planned (Tit 3:12), we do not know because the records are incomplete.

An active and committed group was following Paul around seeking to lead churches back to Jewish customs. These Judaizers taught that before Gentiles could become Christians they had to become Jews by being circumcized. The apostle had to refute their error and to encourage Christians to stand firm in the grace for which Christ set them free. Others enjoyed arguing and debating about philosophies, genealogies, and controversies. Paul had to address these problems as well.

Some persons in Crete were tempted to take the low road of deceit, immorality, and ungodliness. In this letter to Titus, Paul wrote of this situation and set forth clearly his purpose: to help the church grow in faith and in "knowledge of the truth" so they could lead more godly lives (1:1).

Paul knew Titus faced the common enemies of all Christians—the world, the flesh, and the devil—but Paul had taught Titus the demands of discipleship. He entrusted his young associate with the task of bringing the churches in Crete in line with the Christian faith.

Theological Outline

Titus: The Minister's Guide

I. Introduction and Salutation (1:1-4)

II. The Minister's Primary Task (1:5-9)
- A. His task is to set in order everything that was lacking. (1:5)
- B. To help accomplish this task, elders are needed in every town. (1:5)
- C. The qualifications for elders are specified. (1:6-9)

III. Ministers Unmask False Teachers and Correct False Teaching. (1:10-16)
- A. False teachers must be silenced. (1:10-12)
- B. False teachers must be rebuked and corrected. (1:13-16)

IV. Ministers Must Train Other Leaders. (2:1-15)
- A. Ministers must teach in accord with sound doctrine. (2:1)
- B. Older men have a role in the church. (2:1)
- C. Older women must meet personal standards of conduct. (2:3)
- D. Older women are to teach the younger women. (2:4-5)
- E. Young men should exercise self-control. (2:6)
- F. A minister is to be an example in life and teaching. (2:7-8)

G. Slaves have Christian duties. (2:9-10)
H. Moral demands and glorious hope grow out of the salvation Christ provided. (2:11-14)
I. God's minister is to encourage and to rebuke with authority. (2:15)

V. Followers of Christ Have Moral and Civic Responsibilities. (3:1-11)
A. Believers are to submit to their rulers and government authorities. (3:1)
B. Believers are to be ready to do any good work. (3:1)
C. Believers are to be considerate, peaceable, and humble. (3:2)
D. Hatred and slavery to passions mark the non-Christian life. (3:3)
E. Salvation comes through God's mercy, not human works. (3:4-5*a*)
F. Salvation comes through the work of the Holy Spirit. (3:5*b*-6)
G. Salvation provides the hope of eternal life. (3:7)
H. Christians are to devote themselves to doing what is good. (3:8)
I. Christians are to avoid foolish controversies and arguments. (3:9)
J. Two warnings are sufficient for persons who seek to divide God's church. (3:10-11)

VI. Closing Remarks and Benediction (3:12-15)

Theological Conclusions

The life of a church and its minister must rest on strong theological foundations. Paul delineated these for Titus and for us. He centered his attention on:

1. Jesus Christ,
2. salvation,
3. the Christian life, and
4. church leaders.

Jesus is God and Savior whose expected return is the Christian's hope (2:13). He is the Redeemer, who gave His life for us so we might be a holy people (2:14). Jesus poured out the Holy Spirit on believers making us heirs of eternal life (3:5-7).

Salvation comes to unrighteous people (3:3) through the grace (2:11), kindness, love, and mercy of God (3:4-5). Human acts play no part in gaining salvation (3:5). The Holy Trinity provides salvation. God, who is Father, Son, and Spirit, planned for it, promised it, and brought it forth, through proclamation of His Word (1:2-3). Jesus gave Himself for our salvation (2:13-14) and was the Agent through whom God gave us His Spirit (3:5-7). The Holy Spirit brought about the cleansing of our lives as symbolized in baptism, and He brought about our rebirth to be His heirs (3:7). Salvation changes ungodly lives (1:1-2, 11-12; 3:8) and gives us an eternal hope (1:2; 2:13; 3:7).

The Christian life is of utmost concern for Titus as it should be for us. The young minister needed to remember the pastor's primary duty—teaching. Such teaching must reflect sound doctrine (2:1) and be suited to the particular needs of each age group and social class in the church (2:2-10). Christians must not live as nonbelievers, who oppose their teaching (1:10-11). Christians must say "no" to worldly passions, live upright lives, and be the pure people Christ came to create (2:11-14). They must be good, supportive citizens of the state seeking peace and acting humbly (3:1-2). In summary, the Christian life is devoted to doing good (3:8,14).

Christ is Lord of His church; still the church needs human leaders. Two types of people exercise leadership. First, there are those rebellious, deceiving, greedy leaders who seek only personal gain. They ruin the church with false teachings (1:10-16). They lead the church into controversies and quarrels which are useless and divisive (3:9-10). Such leaders must be silenced because their actions reveal they do not even know God (1:11,16). There are those true leaders appointed within the church (1:5). Such pastoral leaders must meet high standards (1:6-9) and be able to give leadership against false teachers. They must lead the church to maturity in Christ, doing what is good (3:14).

Contemporary Teaching

Persons in this generation may be tempted to believe that they are saved by works. This book refutes that error and declares salvation to be by God's grace (3:5).

Many persons express no hope in life beyond death. The Letter to Titus offers "eternal life, which God, who does not lie, promised before the beginning of time" (1:2).

Church leaders need to be instructed in sound doctrine, in godly living, and in doing good—virtues that do not come automatically (1:7-9). Church members need to honor and to follow their appointed pastors and church leaders (3:1). All persons need to learn the standard of Christian living for their age groups and avoid controversies and quarrels. The people of God must give themselves to doing good.

Chapter 1

PAUL, a servant of God[a] and an apostle[b] of Jesus Christ for the faith of
God's elect and the knowledge of the
truth[c] that leads to godliness[d]— 2a faith
and knowledge resting on the hope of
eternal life,[e] which God, who does not
lie,[f] promised before the beginning of
time,[g] 3and at his appointed season[h] he
brought his word to light[i] through the
preaching entrusted to me[j] by the command of God[k] our Savior,[l]

4To Titus,[m] my true son[n] in our common faith:

Grace and peace from God the Father
and Christ Jesus our Savior.[o]

Titus' Task on Crete

1:6–8Ref — 1Ti 3:2–4

5The reason I left you in Crete[p] was
that you might straighten out what was
left unfinished and appoint[a] elders[q] in
every town, as I directed you. 6An elder
must be blameless,[r] the husband of but
one wife, a man whose children believe
and are not open to the charge of being
wild and disobedient. 7Since an overseer[b][s] is entrusted with God's work,[t]
he must be blameless—not overbearing,
not quick-tempered, not given to drunkenness, not violent, not pursuing dishonest gain.[u] 8Rather he must be hospitable,[v] one who loves what is good,[w] who
is self-controlled,[x] upright, holy and disciplined. 9He must hold firmly[y] to the
trustworthy message as it has been
taught, so that he can encourage others
by sound doctrine[z] and refute those who
oppose it.
10For there are many rebellious people,
mere talkers[a] and deceivers, especially
those of the circumcision group.[b] 11They
must be silenced, because they are ruining whole households[c] by teaching
things they ought not to teach—and that
for the sake of dishonest gain. 12Even one
of their own prophets[d] has said, "Cretans[e] are always liars, evil brutes, lazy
gluttons." 13This testimony is true.
Therefore, rebuke[f] them sharply, so that
they will be sound in the faith[g] 14and will
pay no attention to Jewish myths[h] or to
the commands[i] of those who reject the
truth.[j] 15To the pure, all things are
pure,[k] but to those who are corrupted
and do not believe, nothing is pure.[l] In
fact, both their minds and consciences
are corrupted.[m] 16They claim to know
God, but by their actions they deny
him.[n] They are detestable, disobedient
and unfit for doing anything good.[o]

Chapter 2

What Must Be Taught to Various Groups

YOU must teach what is in accord with
sound doctrine.[p] 2Teach the older
men[q] to be temperate,[r] worthy of re-

a5 Or *ordain* b7 Traditionally *bishop*

1:1 aRo 1:1; Jas 1:1 bS 1Co 1:1 cS 1Ti 2:4 dS 1Ti 2:2
1:2 eTit 3:7; 2Ti 1:1 fNu 23:19; Heb 6:18 g2Ti 1:9
1:3 h1Ti 2:6; 6:15 i2Ti 1:10 jS 1Ti 1:11 kS 2Co 1:1; 1Ti 1:1 lS Lk 1:47
1:4 mS 2Co 2:13 nS 1Ti 1:2 oS Ro 1:7
1:5 pAc 27:7 qS Ac 11:30
1:6 rS 1Th 3:13; 1Ti 3:2
1:7 sS 1Ti 3:1 t1Co 4:1 uS 1Ti 3:3,8
1:8 vS Ro 12:13 w2Ti 3:3 xTit 2:2,5,6,12
1:9 yS 1Co 16:13; 1Ti 1:19; 2Ti 1:13; 3:14 zS 1Ti 1:10
1:10 a1Ti 1:6 bAc 10:45; 11:2
1:11 c1Ti 5:13
1:12 dAc 17:28 eAc 2:11
1:13 fS 1Ti 5:20 gTit 2:2
1:14 hS 1Ti 1:4 iS Col 2:22 j2Ti 4:4
1:15 kPs 18:26; Mt 15:10,11; Mk 7:14-19; Ac 10:9-16,28; Col 2:20-22 lRo 14:14,23 m1Ti 6:5
1:16 nJer 5:2; 12:2; 1Jn 2:4 oHos 8:2,3
2:1 pS 1Ti 1:10
2:2 q1Ti 5:1 r1Ti 3:2

1:2–3 REVELATION, Inspiration—God never breaks a promise. His eternal purpose before creation was to provide eternal life for His elect people. He fulfilled this in Jesus Christ, a fulfillment revealed to the world in Paul's preaching. Such preaching came at God's command, not from human pride. Revelation comes in God's way at God's time for God's purposes through God's chosen proclaimers.

1:2 SALVATION, Eternal Life—Eternal life is a hope from God promised before time began. Compare 1 Pe 1:10–11.

1:3 PROCLAMATION, Gospel—See note on Ac 3:11–26.

1:4 PRAYER, Blessing—See note on Ro 1:7.

1:5 THE CHURCH, Practice—Elders and bishops serve as pastors or shepherds of the churches, teaching and preaching the gospel of the kingdom.

1:5–9 CHURCH LEADERS, Pastor and Overseer—A main function of an overseer or bishop is teaching and preaching. Therefore, overseers or bishops must be adequately trained in Scripture and doctrine. There is no indication that an overseer supervised office holders in other churches. Overseer and elder are apparently used interchangeably in this passage to refer to the same office. Timothy seemed to exercise unique authority in the historical situation of the young church to appoint leaders for the church. Such leaders had to meet strict requirements. See 1 Ti 2:24–26; 2 Ti 2:24–26; notes on Ac 14:23; 20:17, 28; 1 Ti 3:1–7; 4:14.

1:7 CHRISTIAN ETHICS, Alcohol—See note on 1 Ti 3:3–4.

1:9–16 EDUCATION, Correction—In his role as teacher, the bishop or pastor is to communicate sound doctrine, on one hand, and refute those who oppose it, on the other. "Sound doctrine" is not one individual's private interpretation. It is the body of truth taught by Jesus, passed on by the apostles, interpreted by Paul and other New Testament writers, and authenticated by the larger community of Christians. Sometimes, heretical teaching becomes so rampant within a congregation that it must be stopped by decisive action on the part of church leaders. The Bible is the source for church leaders to use in opposing false doctrine. See v 11.

1:10–11 CHRISTIAN ETHICS, Property Rights—Some of the slickest hucksters in the world are those who prey on unsuspecting people by means of a religious message for a price. Such practices call us to remember the gospel is free. Truth remains the same no matter the price offered by adherents of false doctrine. See note on 1 Ti 6:3–10.

1:15 HUMANITY, Moral Consciousness—Greed for money can corrupt Christian teachers. True believers do not have to seek out secret teachings about eating and living habits. The Christian is free to enjoy all God's good creation without worrying about ritualistic laws of cleanliness. Only corrupt teachers need such laws because they have lost all moral sensitivity. The spiritual state of a person affects the sensitivity of the moral consciousness. The conscience cannot always be a trustworthy guide.

1:15–16 SIN, Depravity—Those who continually engage in sin will become morally bankrupt. Their minds and consciences become so corrupted they have no moral values. Religious people are included among the morally bankrupt. Such a lack of true faith becomes readily apparent through sinful actions.

2:2–10 FAMILY, Role Relationships—Home relationships should honor the lordship of Christ over the home and demonstrate to the outside world the power of the Word of God. The love shown in a Christian home should overcome non-Christians' arguments against Christianity. In Paul's instructions to Titus concerning family relationships, the familiar

spect, self-controlled,[s] and sound in
faith,[t] in love and in endurance.
3Likewise, teach the older women to
be reverent in the way they live, not to be
slanderers[u] or addicted to much wine,[v]
but to teach what is good. 4Then they can
train the younger women[w] to love their
husbands and children, 5to be self-controlled[x] and pure, to be busy at home,[y]
to be kind, and to be subject to their husbands,[z] so that no one will malign the
word of God.[a]
6Similarly, encourage the young men[b]
to be self-controlled.[c] 7In everything set
them an example[d] by doing what is
good.[e] In your teaching show integrity,
seriousness 8and soundness of speech
that cannot be condemned, so that those
who oppose you may be ashamed because
they have nothing bad to say about us.[f]
9Teach slaves to be subject to their
masters in everything,[g] to try to please
them, not to talk back to them, 10and not
to steal from them, but to show that they
can be fully trusted, so that in every way
they will make the teaching about God
our Savior[h] attractive.[i]
11For the grace[j] of God that brings salvation has appeared[k] to all men.[l] 12It
teaches us to say "No" to ungodliness
and worldly passions,[m] and to live self-
controlled,[n] upright and godly lives[o] in
this present age, 13while we wait for the
blessed hope—the glorious appearing[p] of
our great God and Savior, Jesus Christ,[q]
14who gave himself for us[r] to redeem us
from all wickedness[s] and to purify[t] for
himself a people that are his very own,[u]
eager to do what is good.[v]
15These, then, are the things you
should teach. Encourage and rebuke with
all authority. Do not let anyone despise
you.

Chapter 3

Doing What Is Good

REMIND the people to be subject to
rulers and authorities,[w] to be obedient, to be ready to do whatever is good,[x]
2to slander no one,[y] to be peaceable and
considerate, and to show true humility toward all men.
3At one time[z] we too were foolish, disobedient, deceived and enslaved by all
kinds of passions and pleasures. We lived

2:2 [s]ver 5,6,12; Tit 1:8 [t]Tit 1:13
2:3 [u]1Ti 3:11 [v]1Ti 3:8
2:4 [w]1Ti 5:2
2:5 [x]ver 2,6,12; Tit 1:8 [y]1Ti 5:14 [z]S Eph 5:22 [a]1Ti 6:1; S Heb 4:12
2:6 [b]1Ti 5:1 [c]ver 2, 5,12; Tit 1:8
2:7 [d]S 1Ti 4:12 [e]S ver 14
2:8 [f]S 1Pe 2:12
2:9 [g]S Eph 6:5
2:10 [h]S Lk 1:47 [i]Mt 5:16
2:11 [j]S Ro 3:24 [k]2Ti 1:10 [l]S 1Ti 2:4
2:12 [m]Tit 3:3 [n]ver 2,5,6; Tit 1:8 [o]2Ti 3:12
2:13 [p]S 1Co 1:7; S 1Ti 6:14 [q]2Pe 1:1
2:14 [r]S Mt 20:28 [s]S Mt 1:21 [t]Heb 1:3; 1Jn 1:7 [u]Ex 19:5; Dt 4:20; 14:2; Ps 135:4; Mal 3:17; 1Pe 2:9 [v]ver 7; Pr 16:7; Mt 5:16; 2Co 8:21; Eph 2:10; Tit 3:1,8, 14; 1Pe 2:12,15; 3:13
3:1 [w]Ro 13:1; 1Pe 2:13,14 [x]S 2Ti 2:21; S Tit 2:14
3:2 [y]Eph 4:31
3:3 [z]S Eph 2:2

"household duties" pattern of Eph 5:21—6:4 and Col 3:18—4:1 is evident. In Titus, however, stronger emphasis is given to the importance of personal self-control and self-giving in order that outsiders may not be able to criticize the behavior of Christians. Men are to exemplify self-control; older women are to demonstrate reverent submission to Christ; younger women are to honor their husbands through yieldedness in love to their headship in the home. Slaves are to be honest and submissive to their masters. God's Word is exalted by all believers through practicing a life of respect for social custom. Mutual submission to one another in faith demonstrates submission to the lordship of Christ and provides an authentic witness of faith to the world.

2:3 CHRISTIAN ETHICS, Alcohol—Older women play an influential role in the Christian community and must teach by good example as well as words. Women's substance abuse can have deadly effect on a new generation. See note on 1 Ti 3:3–4.

2:7 EDUCATION, Qualified Teachers—Integrity is a quality found in teachers whose motives are pure. See Mt 5:8. Some teach out of a need for status or self-gratification. The Christian teacher should be motivated by love for people and love for truth. Teachers must not give reason for criticism of their teaching or of their conduct.

2:11–12 GOD, Grace—God's grace provides salvation. His grace became visible to us in the ministry, death, and resurrection of Christ. His grace changes our lives, teaching us to say, "No," to temptation and to live like God wants us to while we wait for Christ to come again.

2:11–14 JESUS CHRIST, Final Coming—See note on 1 Ti 6:14–15.

2:11–12 SALVATION, Grace—God's grace which brings salvation is unveiled to all in Jesus Christ. It teaches how to avoid worldly temptations and live disciplined lives. See note on 2 Ti 1:9.

2:11–13 LAST THINGS, Return Attitudes—For believers Christ's return is a cause for hope. Only believers have real hope because we alone have accepted His redemption. Our hope comes from the grace of God, who provides salvation. The forgiveness of sins coupled with living a godly life eliminates all dread over the return of Christ and transforms the prospect into a blessed hope.

2:13 GOD, Trinity—Translation is uncertain here. Apparently Jesus is called God and Savior. This would be an explicit reference to Jesus as God. His coming again is the central reason Christians have hope. As God, Jesus is one of the three Persons of the Trinity. God is known to us in three Persons who have their own identity but are not totally separable. See note on Mt 3:16–17.

2:14 JESUS CHRIST, Redeemer—Jesus' redeeming work was intended to make us able to live moral, obedient lives.

2:14 SALVATION, Redemption—See note on 1 Co 6:19–20. Good works are not the root of salvation, but they are the fruit of salvation. Redemption means freedom from a life of wickedness and to a life of obedience and purity. Christ died to provide us this redemption.

2:14 SALVATION, As Cleansing—Redemption and purification are two ways of expressing the meaning of salvation. God is concerned about the life-styles of His people. He looks for eager obedience and active doing of good.

2:14 THE CHURCH, People of God—Christians are the people of God because of the work of Christ. The response of Christians to Christ's work of redemption and purification is a life dedicated to Him and filled with good deeds. See note on Eph 2:10.

3:1–2 CHRISTIAN ETHICS, Citizenship—Obedience to governmental law is a basic duty of Christian citizens. Government may enforce laws which a disciple seeking to follow God's law of love cannot in good conscience obey. Then protests may be in order. Protests within a society should be made only from a stance of cooperative citizenship. See notes on Lk 20:20–26; Ro 13:1–7; 1 Ti 2:1–2.

3:3–7 HOLY SPIRIT, Regenerates—To be given God's Spirit is to receive a new life, a cleansing, and a new standing before God. The Spirit's indwelling power changes foolish, disobedient people dominated by hatred into kind, loving people with eternal hope. Salvation involves this washing and renewal, this transformation and regeneration of life by the Spirit. Every person who truly receives Christ as Lord and Savior at the same time receives the life-changing Spirit. We do not grow to a place where we deserve the Spirit. We do not add the Spirit as a next and advanced stage of discipleship. The Spirit regenerates the life of every Christian. Salvation does not occur without the work of the Spirit in our lives.

in malice and envy, being hated and hating one another. 4But when the kindness[a] and love of God our Savior[b] appeared,[c] 5he saved us,[d] not because of
righteous things we had done,[e] but because of his mercy.[f] He saved us through
the washing[g] of rebirth and renewal[h] by
the Holy Spirit, 6whom he poured out on
us[i] generously through Jesus Christ our
Savior, 7so that, having been justified by
his grace,[j] we might become heirs[k] having the hope[l] of eternal life.[m] 8This is a
trustworthy saying.[n] And I want you to
stress these things, so that those who
have trusted in God may be careful to devote themselves to doing what is good.[o]
These things are excellent and profitable
for everyone.

9But avoid[p] foolish controversies and
genealogies and arguments and quarrels[q]
about the law,[r] because these are unprofitable and useless.[s] 10Warn a divisive
person once, and then warn him a second
time. After that, have nothing to do with
him.[t] 11You may be sure that such a man
is warped and sinful; he is self-con-
demned.

Final Remarks

12As soon as I send Artemas or Tychicus[u] to you, do your best to come to me
at Nicopolis, because I have decided to
winter there.[v] 13Do everything you can
to help Zenas the lawyer and Apollos[w] on
their way and see that they have everything they need. 14Our people must learn
to devote themselves to doing what is
good,[x] in order that they may provide for
daily necessities and not live unproductive lives.

15Everyone with me sends you greetings. Greet those who love us in the
faith.[y]

Grace be with you all.[z]

3:4 [a]Eph 2:7 [b]S Lk 1:47 [c]Tit 2:11
3:5 [d]S Ro 11:14 [e]S Eph 2:9 [f]1Pe 1:3 [g]S Ac 22:16 [h]Ro 12:2
3:6 [i]S Ro 5:5
3:7 [j]S Ro 3:24 [k]S Ro 8:17 [l]Ro 8:24 [m]S Mt 25:46; Tit 1:2
3:8 [n]S 1Ti 1:15 [o]S Tit 2:14
3:9 [p]2Ti 2:16 [q]S 2Ti 2:14 [r]Tit 1:10-16 [s]2Ti 2:14
3:10 [t]S Ro 16:17
3:12 [u]S Ac 20:4 [v]2Ti 4:9,21
3:13 [w]S Ac 18:24
3:14 [x]S Tit 2:14
3:15 [y]1Ti 1:2 [z]S Col 4:18

3:3 SIN, Slavery—Paul's statement to Titus affirmed that the person in sin is enslaved to the passions of sin. Hatred rules our relationships. The only power which can break the bondage of sin is the power of God in Christ. See note on Ro 6:5–22.

3:4–6 GOD, Trinity—All three Persons who make up the one being of God share in the work of saving sinful persons. God is our Savior. His love appeared in the person of Jesus, the Son. Salvation includes the work of the Spirit in renewing and purifying our lives. Jesus our Savior poured out the Spirit on us. We must not try to compartmentalize the one God. He is too big and complex for human formulas. While the three Persons are distinguishable, with characteristic works they perform, they nevertheless have an inner relationship with each other, and all share in what each does. This is part of the mystery of the trinitarian understanding of God. See note on Mt 3:16–17.

3:4 GOD, Love—God's love is the love of a Savior who delivers us from destruction because He desires to have mercy rather than pure justice. That love replaces the hatred which dominates life without Christ.

3:4–7 JESUS CHRIST, Love—By coming to earth, Jesus revealed God's love (Greek *philanthrōpia*). His mercy is the motive behind our salvation. Jesus poured the Spirit upon us to give us hope of eternal life and to encourage us to live morally pure lives.

3:5 SALVATION, Renewal—God's salvation is accomplished through renewal by the Holy Spirit. The Spirit of the first creation (Ge 1:2) is the same Spirit of the new creation.

3:5 SALVATION, Grace—God's mercy and grace are synonymous. His mercy is extended because of His nature and not because of our righteousness.

3:5 ORDINANCES, Baptism as Cleansing—The "washing of rebirth" and the renewal by the Holy Spirit connects new birth and the Spirit in the same way they are connected in Jn 3:5. See note on Jn 3:3–5. Baptism does not literally wash away sins, but baptism would have no meaning if the Holy Spirit did not bring about a new birth and a renewal of the life of the Christian believer. Baptism must declare outwardly and visibly this inward and spiritual rebirth. Even the Jewish proselyte baptismal formula spoke of one coming from the baptismal waters as a "newborn babe." The Christians proclaimed that the Holy Spirit brought about this new birth. They confessed it publicly through baptism.

3:7 SALVATION, Justification—Persons are set right with God by the grace of Jesus Christ, that is His grace shown us in His death on the cross.

3:7 SALVATION, Eternal Life—The hope of eternal life is made real for us through the saving work of Christ. Eternal life is a quality of obedient life now and a hope for full realization of that life in the future.

3:8 HOLY SCRIPTURE, Authoritative—See note on 1 Ti 1:15.

3:9 CHRISTIAN ETHICS, Moral Imperatives—Time is too short and important to be wasted in arguments about details. People are too important to be hurt and rejected because they do not agree with us on a matter of interpretation. The major points of God's expectations are clear and should be followed. Otherwise, we need to agree to disagree.

3:10–11 SIN, Depravity—The practice of sin will warp the minds of persons until they become depraved in attitudes and motives. The depraved person argues about unimportant matters and seeks to bring divisions in the church.

3:10 THE CHURCH, Discipline—The church has responsibility to exercise discipline among its members. People who try to divide the church and thus divert it from its ministry create a special danger to the church. They must be warned and encouraged to stop their divisive activities. If they refuse to stop, the church may have to separate itself from the divisive person to maintain the church's ministry and unity. Such action is not routine for the church, occurring only in extreme circumstances. See notes on 1 Co 5:1–5, 9–13; 2 Co 2:5–11.

3:15 PRAYER, Blessing—See note on Ro 15:33.

Philemon

Theological Setting

The letter to Philemon is the shortest of all Paul's writings. It contains only 335 words in the original Greek. Philemon's chief contribution to the New Testament comes from the insight which this letter provides into Paul's methods of dealing with the practice of slavery.

The appearance of such words as "prisoner" (vv 1,9) and "chains" (v 10) suggest Paul wrote the letter from prison. Paul had led Onesimus to Christ (v 10) during his imprisonment. Such an opportunity for preaching the gospel in prison was available to Paul during his confinement in Rome (Ac 28:16,30-31). Most New Testament scholars feel that Paul wrote Philemon from Rome in the early AD 60s.

The letter to Philemon lacks a specific geographical destination, but the names of Mark, Aristarchus, Epaphras, Demas, and Luke appear in both the letter to the Colossians and to Philemon (Col 4:10,12,14; Phm 23-24). This fact, together with the information that both Archippus (Col 4:17) and Onesimus (Col 4:9) were from Colosse, suggests that this was also Philemon's hometown.

Paul was also in prison when he wrote Colossians (Col 4:3). Upon completion of the Colossian letter, Paul gave the completed letter to Tychicus to carry to its destination (Col 4:7-9). As Tychicus brought both the letters of Colossians and Philemon, he also brought the former slave Onesimus back to his master. He probably carried the letter to Ephesus at the same time (Eph 6:21,22).

Philemon was a slaveowner who also hosted a church in his home (vv. 2,10-12). The commitment, love, and faith of Philemon provided great joy and encouragement for Paul (vv. 4-7). Although one cannot be certain, it is likely that Apphia (v. 2) was Philemon's wife, and that Archippus was his son.

Paul mentioned that the Colossian readers had never seen him face to face (Col 2:1). He had apparently never visited Colosse, but had spent over two years in Ephesus one hundred miles away (Ac 19:8-10; 20:31). During the time of Paul's ministry in Ephesus, Philemon had likely journeyed to the city, had heard Paul's preaching, and became a Christian (v 19).

The following events apparently led to the writing of this letter:

1. The slave Onesimus robbed his master Philemon and ran away (vv 11,18).

2. As a runaway slave Onesimus made his way to Rome and eventually met Paul (v 10). It is not clear how or why Onesimus came into contact with Paul. He could have wanted economic help, or he could have had a guilty conscience concerning his escape.

3. Onesimus became a Christian through Paul's work and performed some services for him (vv 10,13).

4. Onesimus was still the legal property of Philemon, and Paul wrote to smooth the way for his return to his master (vv 14-15).

5. Paul wanted Philemon to accept Onesimus as a brother in Christ and not merely as a slave (vv 16-17).

Theological Outline

Philemon: Your Slave Is Your Brother

I. Greetings (1-3)
  A. The writer: Paul (1*a*)
  B. The readers: Philemon, Apphia, Archippus, the house church (1*b*-2)
  C. The wish: Grace and peace (3)
II. A Commendation for Philemon (4-7)
  A. Gratitude to God for the love and faith of Philemon (4-6)
  B. Joy and encouragement to others from the ministry of Philemon (7)
III. A Plea for Onesimus (8-22)
  A. *The basis of the plea* (8-9)
    1. Not an absolute command (8)
    2. But a loving request (9)

B. The reason for the plea (10-16)
   1. The conversion of Onesimus (10)
   2. The unprofitable past service of Onesimus (11)
   3. Philemon's ownership of Onesimus (12)
   4. Paul's use of Onesimus as a helper (13)
   5. Paul's desire to obtain Philemon's permission (14)
   6. Paul's wish that Onesimus might receive a new status (15-16)

C. An appeal to secure the request (17-20)
   1. An appeal based on friendship (17)
   2. Including a promise to repay losses (18-19)
   3. An urge to perform spiritual duty (20)

D. An expression of confidence about the request (21-22)
   1. The expected answer (21)
   2. A coming visit (22)

IV. A Closing Salutation (23-25)
   A. A greeting from friends (23-24)
   B. A wish from Paul (25)

Theological Conclusions

The writers of the New Testament did not attack the essential elements of slavery, but what they said revolutionized the thinking of Christians on the subject. Paul had warned slaveowners that they had a responsibility towards their slaves (Col 4:1). Paul addressed slaves as responsible moral beings who were to fear God (Col 3:22). In Philemon, Paul did not condemn slavery, but he presented Onesimus as a Christian brother instead of a slave (v 16). When an owner can refer to a slave as a brother, the slave has reached a position in which the legal title of slave is meaningless.

The early church did not attack slavery directly, but it laid the foundation for a new relationship between owner and slave. Paul attempted to unite both Philemon and Onesimus with Christian love so that emancipation would become a necessity. The owner and the slave were to conduct their relationships in the light of belonging to the same Lord. After exposure to the light of the gospel, the institution of slavery could only shrivel and die.

Contemporary Teaching

Employers, political leaders, corporation executives, and parents can follow the spirit of Paul's teaching by treating Christian employees, co-workers, and family members as members of Christ's body. Christians in modern society must not view their helpers as stepping-stones to help them achieve their ambitions but as Christian brothers and sisters who must receive gracious treatment. In addition, all Christian leaders must recognize that God holds them accountable for the treatment of those who work for them, whether the helpers are Christians or not. They must eventually answer to God for their actions (Col 4:1).

PAUL, a prisoner[a] of Christ Jesus, and
Timothy[b] our brother,[c]

To Philemon our dear friend and fellow
worker,[d] 2to Apphia our sister, to Archippus[e] our fellow soldier[f] and to the
church that meets in your home:[g]

3Grace to you and peace from God our
Father and the Lord Jesus Christ.[h]

Thanksgiving and Prayer

4I always thank my God[i] as I remember you in my prayers,[j] 5because I hear
about your faith in the Lord Jesus[k] and
your love for all the saints.[l] 6I pray that
you may be active in sharing your faith,
so that you will have a full understanding
of every good thing we have in Christ.
7Your love has given me great joy and encouragement,[m] because you, brother,
have refreshed[n] the hearts of the saints.

Paul's Plea for Onesimus

8Therefore, although in Christ I could
be bold and order you to do what you
ought to do, 9yet I appeal to you[o] on the
basis of love. I then, as Paul—an old man
and now also a prisoner[p] of Christ
Jesus— 10I appeal to you for my son[q]
Onesimus,[a][r] who became my son while
I was in chains.[s] 11Formerly he was useless to you, but now he has become useful both to you and to me.

12I am sending him—who is my very
heart—back to you. 13I would have liked
to keep him with me so that he could
take your place in helping me while I am
in chains[t] for the gospel. 14But I did not
want to do anything without your consent, so that any favor you do will be
spontaneous and not forced.[u] 15Perhaps
the reason he was separated from you for
a little while was that you might have
him back for good— 16no longer as a
slave,[v] but better than a slave, as a dear
brother.[w] He is very dear to me but even
dearer to you, both as a man and as a
brother in the Lord.

17So if you consider me a partner,[x]
welcome him as you would welcome me.
18If he has done you any wrong or owes
you anything, charge it to me.[y] 19I, Paul,
am writing this with my own hand.[z] I
will pay it back—not to mention that you
owe me your very self. 20I do wish, brother, that I may have some benefit from you
in the Lord; refresh[a] my heart in Christ.
21Confident[b] of your obedience, I write
to you, knowing that you will do even
more than I ask.

22And one thing more: Prepare a guest
room for me, because I hope to be[c] restored to you in answer to your prayers.[d]

23Epaphras,[e] my fellow prisoner[f] in
Christ Jesus, sends you greetings. 24And
so do Mark,[g] Aristarchus,[h] Demas[i] and
Luke, my fellow workers.[j]

25The grace of the Lord Jesus Christ be
with your spirit.[k]

1:1 [a]ver 9,23; S Eph 3:1 [b]S Ac 16:1 [c]2Co 1:1 [d]S Php 2:25
1:2 [e]Col 4:17 [f]Php 2:25 [g]S Ro 16:5
1:3 [h]S Ro 1:7
1:4 [i]S Ro 1:8 [j]S Ro 1:10
1:5 [k]S Ac 20:21 [l]S Col 1:4; 1Th 3:6
1:7 [m]2Co 7:4,13 [n]ver 20; Ro 15:32; 1Co 16:18
1:9 [o]1Co 1:10 [p]ver 1,23; S Eph 3:1
1:10 [q]S 1Th 2:11 [r]Col 4:9 [s]S Ac 21:33
1:13 [t]ver 10; S Ac 21:33
1:14 [u]2Co 9:7; 1Pe 5:2
1:16 [v]1Co 7:22 [w]Mt 23:8; S Ac 1:16; 1Ti 6:2
1:17 [x]2Co 8:23
1:18 [y]Ge 43:9
1:19 [z]S 1Co 16:21
1:20 [a]ver 7; 1Co 16:18
1:21 [b]S 2Co 2:3
1:22 [c]Php 1:25; 2:24; Heb 13:19 [d]2Co 1:11; Php 1:19
1:23 [e]Col 1:7 [f]ver 1; Ro 16:7; Col 4:10
1:24 [g]S Ac 12:12 [h]S Ac 19:29 [i]Col 4:14; 2Ti 4:10 [j]ver 1
1:25 [k]S Gal 6:18

[a]*10 Onesimus* means *useful.*

---

1 CHURCH LEADERS, Minister—Paul mentions many workers in the church without giving any official title except fellow worker. See Ro 16:3,9,21; 2 Co 8:23; Col 4:11; notes on Php 2:25; 4:2–3. They are not Paul's assistants, but they share with Paul the task of ministry, commissioned by God to proclaim the gospel.

2 THE CHURCH, Local Body—See notes on Ro 16:5; 1 Co 1:2; Col 4:15.

3 PRAYER, Blessing—See note on Ro 1:7.

4–7 DISCIPLESHIP, Neighbor Love—Life, even that of discipleship, needs refreshment. Other disciples can provide needed refreshment for us. Christian love is strong encouragement to others. It refreshes the hearts of brothers and sisters in Christ. See note on Ro 12:10.

4–5 PRAYER, Thanksgiving—See note on Php 1:3.

6 PRAYER, Intercession—Paul often prayed for the communication of the gospel. See note on 2 Th 3:1–5.

6 EVANGELISM, Personal—Paul wanted Philemon to be active in sharing his faith. In that way he would mature in the faith and deepen as a believer. To do personal evangelism is a great strength to one's own personal faith as well as a means to lead others into the faith.

8–22 THE CHURCH, Practice—Christian love and brotherhood helps solve problems and disputes among believers in the church. Paul could have commanded Philemon to accept back his runaway slave Onesimus, but he chose to appeal to Philemon as a brother in Christ. This serves as a model for settling disputes in the church. One party who loves Christ and loves both parties involved enters the dispute in love to help the church, the people involved, and the cause of Christ. See note on Mt 18:15–20.

15–17 CHRISTIAN ETHICS, Social Relationships—Business relationships often categorize and separate people. Christian love joins all people in the Christian family. Paul did not comment on the rightness or wrongness of the institution of slavery. Instead he provided a basis for overcoming the social barriers of business relationships and ultimately of doing away with slavery. To treat another person as a brother makes owning a person as a slave imposible.

22 PRAYER, Answer—Paul was fond of his spiritual children and his Christian friends. He had hoped to be restored to the Romans (Ro 15:32). Philemon was praying for him while he was in prison. Paul expected the prayers to be answered. Believers should pray with expectancy, trusting God to answer our prayers.

25 PRAYER, Blessing—See note on Ro 15:33.

Hebrews

Theological Setting

The Book of Hebrews is more like a sermon than a letter. Compare the opening verses of Hebrews with the beginning verses of the letters of Paul, James, and Peter—all of which reflect the format of a typical first-century letter. By contrast, the author of Hebrews launched right into his subject. He never mentioned his name or the name of the group to whom he was writing. Only the final verses sound anything like a letter (13:17-25).

The author probably was a pastor or some other leader of the church to which he wrote. He asked his readers to pray that he might soon be restored to them (13:18-19). He referred to his writing as an exhortation (13:22), another word for a sermon. Hebrews, therefore, was probably a sermon that an absent leader wrote and sent to his congregation.

The first followers of Jesus were Jews; but as the years passed, an increasing number of Gentiles became committed followers. In time, Gentile believers became the majority; eventually, the overwhelming majority. The Book of Acts tells how this happened. The Book of Hebrews reflects the period when large numbers of Jews had professed faith in Jesus as the Christ, but some had not yet come to grips with the uniqueness of Christian faith and the full meaning of following Jesus. One of their temptations was to cling to the relative security of traditional beliefs and practices. The author challenged his readers to leave the old ways behind and move toward full maturity in Christ.

Like several other New Testament books, Hebrews reflects a time when Christians were persecuted for their faith. The church had already passed through one period of trouble. They had been subject to public abuse. Some had had their property plundered, and some had been imprisoned (10:32-34). No one had yet died for the faith, but the author seems to have expected that the faithful might eventually be called on to lay down their lives (12:4).

The grim reality of persecution was a deep concern of the author of Hebrews, and it was the setting in which the congregation read what he wrote. This is also the perspective from which we should read and study Hebrews.

Theological Outline

Hebrews: Jesus, The Perfect Way

I. Jesus Is God's Ultimate Revelation. (1:1—2:4)
  - A. Jesus, God in person, fulfills and surpasses the prophetic word. (1:1-3)
  - B. Jesus is superior to angels. (1:4-14)
  - C. Jesus provides salvation which we dare not ignore. (2:1-4)

II. Jesus Is God's Son and Our Brother. (2:5-18)
  - A. The world is subjected to Jesus, the crucified Lord, who died for us. (2:5-9)
  - B. Jesus is our brother and the Author of our salvation. (2:10-13)
  - C. Jesus died to conquer Satan and free us from the fear of death. (2:14-15)
  - D. Jesus, our High Priest, atoned for our sins and helps us overcome temptation. (2:16-18)

III. Jesus Provides a Way of Faith That Assures and Perseveres. (3:1—4:13)
  - A. Believers must focus on Jesus, the High Priest, who is more faithful than Moses. (3:1-6)
  - B. Believers must be aware of the danger of disbelief. (3:7-19)
  - C. Believers must claim God's promised rest in faith. (4:1-11)
  - D. God, through His Word, is the only Judge. (4:12-13)

IV. Jesus, the Sinless High Priest, Is the Only Source of Salvation. (4:14—5:10)
  - A. Through the sinless High Priest we can approach God in confidence. (4:14-16)
  - B. The obedient High Priest met all the qualifications and became the Source of eternal salvation. (5:1-10)

V. Jesus, the Eternal High Priest, Calls His Followers to Christian Maturity. (5:11—6:20)

A. Believers need to mature in Christ. (5:11—6:3)
B. Believers must show their faith is genuine and persevere in Christ. (6:4-12)
C. God's faithful promises provide secure hope. (6:13-20)

VI. Jesus, the Perfect Sacrifice, Is the Only Priest Believers Need. (7:1—10:39)
A. Jesus is the promised, permanent Priest who offers a better covenant and complete salvation. (7:1-25)
B. Jesus is the perfect Priest who meets our need. (7:26-28)
C. Jesus' ministry in the heavenly worship place is superior to all other priests. (8:1-13)
D. Jesus' sacrifice of His own blood provides eternal redemption from sin in a new covenant. (9:1-22)
E. Jesus' sacrifice was once for all and pointed to His return to bring eternal salvation. (9:23-28)
F. Jesus' sacrifice provided perfect forgiveness and made all other sacrifices unnecessary. (10:1-18)
G. Jesus' sacrifice calls for His followers to live faithfully, even under persecution. (10:19-39)

VII. Jesus Inspires Us to a Life of Faith. (11:1-40)
A. Faith lays claim to the unseen realities of God and His purpose. (11:1-7)
B. Faith presses on even when some of God's promises remain unfulfilled. (11:8-22)
C. Faith risks everything for God and His purpose. (11:23-31)
D. Faith endures even when earthly deliverance does not come. (11:32-40)

VIII. Jesus, the Perfect Example of Faith, Inspires Believers to Persevere. (12:1-29)
A. Jesus' example of suffering encourages perseverance in the face of difficulties. (12:1-6)
B. Suffering should be seen as the Father's discipline. (12:7-13)
C. To see Jesus, believers must live holy lives. (12:14-17)
D. Believers listen to God's warnings and worship in gratitude before the divine Judge. (12:18-29)

IX. Jesus, the Unchanging Savior, Expects His Followers to Live a Life of Love. (13:1-25)
A. Christian love includes all people. (13:1-3)
B. Christian love leads to pure marriage. (13:4)
C. Christian love does not love money. (13:5-6)
D. Christian love imitates worthy leaders. (13:7)
E. Christian love centers on the unchanging Christ. (13:8)
F. Christian love does not follow strange teachings. (13:9-10)
G. Christian love endures isolation and persecution. (13:11-14)
H. Christian love praises God and shares with others. (13:15-16)
I. Christian love obeys and prays for Christian leaders. (13:17-19)
J. Christian love does God's will. (13:20-21)

X. Conclusion (13:22-25)

Theological Conclusions

Hebrews focuses our attention on Jesus Christ and His saving work for us. From Christ's faithful work, Hebrews draws strong conclusions for persons who need to persevere in faith. Hebrews focuses on:

1. Christ as High Priest and sacrifice,
2. Christ as author of our salvation,
3. assurance of and perseverance in salvation, and
4. the way of the cross.

Only Hebrews fully develops the concept of Christ's priestly work. Jesus is our perfect High Priest and sacrifice. This presentation builds on Old Testament teachings and is consistent with the rest of the New Testament. Jesus Christ is the ultimate High Priest who fulfilled and brought to an end the priests and sacrifices of the old covenant. He is a one-of-a-kind Priest, like Melchizedek, not one of the many levitical priests. The levitical priests were sinful; Jesus was sinless. The levitical priests were mortal; therefore, a priest could serve only during his lifetime. Our resurrected High Priest has established an eternal priesthood. The Jewish high priest offered sacrifices for himself and for the people. The sinless Jesus needed no sacrifice for Himself; instead, He offered Himself as the sacrifice for others. His self-giving death was the once-for-all, all-sufficient sacrifice for human sin. How can a sinful person dare to presume to approach the holy God? God Himself through Jesus opened the way for us to receive forgiveness of sins and to come boldly to God's throne of grace. Sin is serious. Forgiveness is costly, but God in Christ has borne the cost so that we may have access to God.

The Book of Hebrews refers to Jesus as the Author of our salvation. He is the One who opens the way into unknown regions so that others may follow. Jesus is leading many sons to glory. He is able to help us because He has already successfully passed this way. The Book of Hebrews emphasizes the human experience of the Son of God as the basis for the help He provides. One of the roles of a priest was to empathize with the needs of fellow human beings. Although Jesus is the sinless, eternal High Priest, He fully shared in our humanity. No New Testament book gives any stronger emphasis to the full humanity as well as the full deity of Jesus. He prayed. He was tempted. He suffered. He died. Jesus, therefore, is able to sympathize with us and to help us in similar circumstances. He teaches us to pray, helps us ovecome temptation, enables us to endure suffering, and delivers us from the fear of death.

Assurance and perseverance are two biblical doctrines that should be considered side by side; otherwise, the biblical view may be distorted. Assurance without perseverance can degenerate into presumption; and perseverance without assurance can become salvation by human effort, not God's grace. One of the problems of interpretation is that these doctrines are not always presented side by side in the same passage. The Bible writers were dealing with real-life situations; therefore, they emphasized what their readers needed to hear. Some situations called for words of comfort and assurance; other situations called for words of conviction and warning. The Book of Hebrews includes some words of assurance, but the emphasis is on the need for perseverance. The author apparently was dealing with a situation that called for an emphasis on faithfulness and endurance. His readers had professed faith in Christ, but many of them were failing to press on in the faith. The author apparently feared what some of them would do under the pressure of a life-or-death persecution. He, therefore, warned against presuming on a profession of faith that was not resulting in a forward movement in faith and faithfulness.

Some interpret Hebrews as teaching a doctrine of apostasy from the Christian faith by people of genuine faith. More likely, the author was emphasizing that true faith perseveres. True faith is not perfect faith, but it does continually call us to move forward for the Lord. The idea of perseverance is not confined to Hebrews. Jesus spoke of perseverance as a quality of saving faith (Mt 10:22; 24:13). He emphasized that the test of true discipleship is doing God's will; professed disciples who do not do God's will show that they never really knew Christ (Mt 7:21-23). In Jesus' parable of the soils, some of the seed fell on shallow, rocky soil. This represents people who profess faith but turn aside under pressure because the Word of God has not taken root in their lives (Mk 4:16-17). Paul emphasized the grace of God as the basis for our salvation and assurance, but he also made it clear that saving faith bears good fruit. We are not saved by works, but we are saved unto good works (Eph 2:8-10). At times when Paul was faced with circumstances similar to those in Hebrews, Paul used similar language (1 Co 10:1-13; 2 Co 13:5).

The Book of Hebrews emphasizes three important aspects of Christ's death for us: (1) We have access to God through Christ. (2) We can trust Christ to help us through life's dark valleys because He passed this way before us. (3) We should live and die with the same courageous, self-giving commitment that Jesus showed in His life and death.

The Gospels record how Jesus called people to follow Him in self-denial and crossbearing (Mt 16:24-25; Mk 8:34-38; Lk 9:23). Crossbearing is not an optional feature of Christian living; it is the heart of following Jesus Christ. It means that we must be willing to lay down our lives by dying for Him, but it also means that we must be willing to lay down our lives by living for Him. Within our own strength we cannot do this, but Christ's Spirit abides with us to enable us to live for Christ by serving others. This is what Paul meant by being crucified and risen with Christ (Ro 6:3-4; 2 Co 5:14-15; Gal 2:20; Col 3:1-3). Christ, who died and was raised from death, lives in us to enable us to die to self and to live for God and others.

Contemporary Teaching

Hebrews is among the least read, least studied, and least preached from books of the New Testament. Modern readers have problems with its descriptions of ancient religious practices. Readers in every century have been confused and disturbed by its harsh warnings. However, those who dig into Hebrews discover that it has much to say to us today.

Above all, Hebrews challenges us to be faithful to Christ, no matter what the cost. Fair-weather Christianity finds no comfort in the Book of Hebrews. Our lukewarm complacency is shattered by its words of warning, and our faith is stirred by its words of challenge. We are warned against becoming too comfortable with this world and its values. We are reminded that we are pilgrims on the way to glory and that we are to live in light of the values of that eternal kingdom.

As we walk this pilgrim way, Christ is fully adequate to meet our needs. Through Him, we have access to God in prayer and worship, and we have a fellowship of mutual encouragement with others who are marching to Zion. Christ has passed this way Himself; therefore, He helps and encourages us as we encounter various trials and temptations.

Chapter 1

The Son Superior to Angels

IN the past God spoke[a] to our forefathers through the prophets[b] at many
times and in various ways,[c] 2but in these
last days[d] he has spoken to us by his
Son,[e] whom he appointed heir[f] of all
things, and through whom[g] he made the
universe.[h] 3The Son is the radiance of
God's glory[i] and the exact representation of his being,[j] sustaining all things[k]
by his powerful word. After he had provided purification for sins,[l] he sat down
at the right hand of the Majesty in heav-
en.[m] 4So he became as much superior to
the angels as the name he has inherited is
superior to theirs.[n]
5For to which of the angels did God
ever say,

> "You are my Son;
> today I have become your
> Father[a]"[b]?[o]

Or again,

> "I will be his Father,
> and he will be my Son"[c]?[p]

6And again, when God brings his firstborn[q] into the world,[r] he says,

> "Let all God's angels worship him."[d][s]

7In speaking of the angels he says,

> "He makes his angels winds,
> his servants flames of fire."[e][t]

8But about the Son he says,

> "Your throne, O God, will last for ever
> and ever,[u]
> and righteousness will be the
> scepter of your kingdom.
> 9You have loved righteousness and
> hated wickedness;
> therefore God, your God, has set you
> above your companions[v]
> by anointing you with the oil[w] of
> joy."[f][x]

10He also says,

> "In the beginning, O Lord, you laid the
> foundations of the earth,

1:1 [a]Jn 9:29; Heb 2:2,3; 4:8; 12:25 [b]Lk 1:70; Ac 2:30 [c]Nu 12:6,8
1:2 [d]Dt 4:30; Heb 9:26; 1Pe 1:20 [e]ver 5; S Mt 3:17; Heb 3:6; 5:8; 7:28 [f]Ps 2:8; Mt 11:27; S 28:18 [g]S Jn 1:3 [h]Heb 11:3
1:3 [i]Jn 1:14 [j]S Jn 14:9 [k]Col 1:17 [l]Tit 2:14; Heb 7:27; 9:11-14 [m]S Mk 16:19
1:4 [n]Eph 1:21; Php 2:9,10; Heb 8:6
1:5 [o]Ps 2:7; S Mt 3:17 [p]2Sa 7:14
1:6 [q]Jn 3:16; S Col 1:18 [r]Heb 10:5 [s]Dt 32:43 (LXX and DSS) Ps 97:7
1:7 [t]Ps 104:4
1:8 [u]S Lk 1:33
1:9 [v]Php 2:9 [w]Isa 61:1,3 [x]Ps 45:6,7

[a]5 Or *have begotten you* [b]5 Psalm 2:7 [c]5 2 Samuel 7:14; 1 Chron. 17:13 [d]6 Deut. 32:43 (see Dead Sea Scrolls and Septuagint) [e]7 Psalm 104:4 [f]9 Psalm 45:6,7

1:1–14 GOD, Trinity—The one God has worked in various ways. Primarily, God the Father has revealed Himself through His Son, Jesus Christ, who is exactly like God (v 3). See note on Mt 3:16–17.

1:1–13 JESUS CHRIST, God—Jesus is the supreme revelation of God, completing and surpassing all other revelation God gave. He was the agent in creation, which He continues to sustain. See note on Jn 1:1–18. He has inheritance rights on the universe. He radiates God's glory, so that to see Him is to see God. Compare Ex 33:18–23. He is the exact representation (Greek *charakter*) or the engraving or stamp of God. To see Jesus is to see the innermost being of God. His death fulfilled the intention of the Jewish sacrificial system and purified us from our sins. He is the reigning King over the universe, superior to the angels as shown by Old Testament messianic passages.

1:1–3 CREATION, Progressive—God has been and still is active in the affairs of the world He created. He created and sustains the heavens and earth through Jesus. Compare Jn 1:3. God continues to deal progressively with His creation. He revealed himself in the Old Testament as the people were able to comprehend His message. This does not imply a limitation on God's part but rather that people were unable to grasp His fullness because of their sin and consequent blindness to divine truth. This same truth applies in the physical realm. He continues to create through the processes He has ordained. Also, He creates anew by allowing us to penetrate, through study, His principles that hold the world together. The more we live in the light of His spiritual truth, the better qualified we are to understand His secrets in the physical realm. See note on Jn 16:12–14.

1:1–2 HOLY SCRIPTURE, Purpose—Holy Scripture is a record of God's speaking to His people through many centuries. Scripture shows many ways in which God has communicated with His people. See notes on the doctrine of Revelation (Index, pp. 1854-1855). The climax of and fulfillment of all Scripture is the appearance of Jesus, who in person represented God Himself in all His glory. Thus all Scripture must be read and intepreted in light of the One to whom it points us. See note on Lk 24:44–46.

1:1–2 REVELATION, Jesus Christ—God used many different people in history to reveal Himself and His truth to His people. The climactic revelation fulfilling the intention of all others came in the Son, who not only was a participant in Creation (Jn 1:3) but is also the Heir of all that exists, Ruler of all, and the Agent of creation. See note on Jn 1:1–4.

1:1–2 HISTORY, Knowledge—See note on Eph 3:5.

1:2 JESUS CHRIST, Preexistent—See note on Col 1:15–17.

1:2,10–12 CREATION, Jesus Christ—See note on Jn 1:3. Jesus had a prominent part in the world's creation. God made the world by Him (Jn 1:3) and for Him. God maintains the world through Him. God's redemptive program in Jesus Christ is His way of bringing the fragmented world back to the One for whom it was created (Eph 1:9–10). Since the world is the work of the Son's hand, He is superior to it. Only He has the dynamic resources to unite it and restore it to where it was before sin entered. Though a time will come when the world will be destroyed (2 Pe 3:10), a new heaven and new earth will be formed (Rev 21:1–2) where Jesus Christ will continue to be the Lord. The present world is temporary, subject to the Creator who endures forever.

1:3 GOD, Glory—God's glory is the revelation of who He is and what He is like. Jesus is God and so in His earthly life revealed to us precisely what God is like.

1:3 SALVATION, As Cleansing—The Son of God provided purification for sins in His death on the cross. See note on Tit 2:14.

1:5 GOD, Trinity—Jesus is the eternal Son of God. Hebrews quotes Ps 2:7 to support the deity of the Messiah. It does not point to a time when Jesus did not exist or to a time when He was not God. It points to the intimate relationship within the Trinity. God is the Father of Jesus the Son and gives to the Son all honor and authority.

1:10–12 CREATION, The Trinity—In Ps 102:25–27, these words are applied to God. In this passage, however, the writer refers to the divine Son. The world came into being through a personal Creator known as Father and as Son. Both this passage and the psalm emphasize the Creator's supremacy over His creation. He initiated creation. He will end it and renew it. See note on Ro 8:18–25.

and the heavens are the work of
your hands.[y]
11They will perish, but you remain;
they will all wear out like a
garment.[z]
12You will roll them up like a robe;
like a garment they will be changed.
But you remain the same,[a]
and your years will never end."[g] [b]

13To which of the angels did God ever
say,

"Sit at my right hand[c]
until I make your enemies
a footstool[d] for your feet"[h]?[e]

14Are not all angels ministering spirits[f]
sent to serve those who will inherit[g] salvation?[h]

Chapter 2

Warning to Pay Attention

WE must pay more careful attention,
therefore, to what we have heard,
so that we do not drift away.[i] 2For if the
message spoken[j] by angels[k] was binding, and every violation and disobedience
received its just punishment,[l] 3how shall
we escape if we ignore such a great salvation?[m] This salvation, which was first announced by the Lord,[n] was confirmed to
us by those who heard him.[o] 4God also
testified to it by signs, wonders and various miracles,[p] and gifts of the Holy Spirit[q] distributed according to his will.[r]

Jesus Made Like His Brothers

5It is not to angels that he has subjected the world to come, about which we
are speaking. 6But there is a place where
someone[s] has testified:

"What is man that you are mindful of
him,
the son of man that you care for
him?[t]
7You made him a little[i] lower than the
angels;
you crowned him with glory and
honor
8 and put everything under his
feet."[j] [u]

In putting everything under him, God left
nothing that is not subject to him. Yet at
present we do not see everything subject
to him. 9But we see Jesus, who was made

1:10 [y]Ps 8:6; Zec 12:1
1:11 [z]Isa 34:4; 51:6; S Heb 12:27
1:12 [a]Heb 13:8 [b]Ps 102:25-27
1:13 [c]ver 3; S Mk 16:19 [d]Jos 10:24; Heb 10:13 [e]Ps 110:1; S Mt 22:44
1:14 [f]Ps 91:11; 103:20; Da 7:10 [g]Mt 25:34; Mk 10:17; S Ac 20:32 [h]S Ro 11:14; Heb 2:3; 5:9; 9:28
2:1 [i]S Ro 11:22
2:2 [j]S Heb 1:1 [k]Dt 33:2; Ac 7:53; Gal 3:19 [l]Heb 10:28
2:3 [m]Heb 10:29; 12:25 [n]Heb 1:2 [o]S Lk 1:2
2:4 [p]Mk 16:20; S Jn 4:48 [q]S 1Co 12:4 [r]S Eph 1:5
2:6 [s]Heb 4:4 [t]Job 7:17; Ps 144:3
2:8 [u]Ps 8:4-6; S Mt 22:44

[g]*12* Psalm 102:25-27 [h]*13* Psalm 110:1 [i]*7* Or *him for a little while*; also in verse 9 [j]*8* Psalm 8:4-6

1:12 GOD, Eternal—The idea of the eternity of God is important. If God had a beginning, who caused it? If God has an end, then what? The emphasis of the Bible is that God stands outside time and brought about the beginning of all things. In this sense, the being of God is shrouded in mystery that we cannot penetrate.
1:14 SALVATION, Initiative—God's initiative in human salvation includes creating and sending angels to minister to those whom He has called to salvation.
2:1 ELECTION, Perseverance—The elect of God are encouraged to avoid complacency and self-righteousness. Careful attention to the spoken message helps believers not drift away from God's way. Election calls on the elect to persevere in faith and godly living.
2:1 SALVATION, Obedience—God wants His people to pay such close attention to what He has spoken through His Son (1:2) that they do not drift away. Perhaps these words were originally written to warn Hebrew Christians against the possibility of stagnation in their Christian growth. The text does not teach that believers can lose their faith.
2:3–4 HOLY SPIRIT, Gifts—The gifts of the Spirit to the church are one kind of confirmation that Jesus has truly provided salvation. The Lord Jesus preached the message of salvation, and God confirmed His message by pouring out the Spirit and His gifts. These gifts included the miracles the church experienced. They also included the personal gifts members received and used. God continues to give the church the Spirit's gifts and, thus, confirms His work among us.
2:3–4 REVELATION, Signs—Rejection of so many revelations leads to inevitable rejection of the way of salvation. God has revealed His fantastic love and saving plan through Christ. He has also manifested Himself in signs, wondrous events, and miraculous activities. Now He expresses Himself in a present Spirit who provides special gifts in keeping with God's will. He has used every means possible to convince people to trust Him and nothing else for salvation.
2:3,10 SALVATION, Initiative—Salvation and creation are here linked together. God Himself speaks through Jesus, His words, His deeds, His life, His death, and His resurrection. Christ, the incarnate and suffering Son of God, became the Author of our salvation. To ignore salvation God has provided is foolish and utterly dangerous.
2:4 MIRACLE, Redemption—Age of tradition does not testify to truth. Judaism is much older than Christianity. In Jesus' day some Jewish leaders had perverted God's plan, changing grace to law. God showed Jesus' way was true by performing miracles. By signs, wonders, various miracles, and gifts of the Holy Spirit God's salvation in Jesus was confirmed. The ultimate purpose was salvation for all who will believe. Do you know that salvation?
2:5–9 JESUS CHRIST, King—The entire world is subject to Jesus' rule. That is not apparent now, for ungodly human rulers and evil forces appear to exercise control. We can see Jesus. We know He obediently gave up the heavenly throne to come to earth and die for us. We know God's scriptural promises for His Messiah. Thus we know His rule as King will one day be visible to all people.
2:8 CREATION, Purposeful—God's greatness consists not only in His creative power to bring something out of nothing. His greatness lies also in His ability to realize His purpose. His plan is to establish His kingdom with Jesus ruling all creation. In the cross and resurrection Jesus gained victory over sin and death, clearly revealing His right to rule. One day His rule will be obvious to all people. Then creation's purpose will become full reality. The world will be redeemed from its rebellious state and the curse this has brought to it (Ro 8:18–22).
2:9–18 EVIL AND SUFFERING, Redemptive—Jesus' suffering and death are essential for our salvation. Jesus identified with the human situation, including temptation and death, and can help people today (4:14–16; 5:7–9).
2:9,17 SALVATION, Atonement—Compare 2 Co 5:14. Jesus, as the merciful and faithful High Priest of God's people, made atonement for our sins. He offered Himself as that atonement on the cross (Heb 7:27). His atonement had all people in view. See note on 1 Ti 4:10.
2:9 SALVATION, Grace—Jesus, by the grace of God, represented all of humankind in His death on the cross. No one is excluded from God's grace until we choose to exclude ourselves.

a little lower than the angels, now
crowned with glory and honor[v] because
he suffered death,[w] so that by the grace
of God he might taste death for everyone.[x]

10 In bringing many sons to glory, it was
fitting that God, for whom and through
whom everything exists,[y] should make
the author of their salvation perfect
through suffering.[z] 11 Both the one who
makes men holy[a] and those who are
made holy[b] are of the same family. So
Jesus is not ashamed to call them brothers.[c] 12 He says,

> "I will declare your name to my
> brothers;
> in the presence of the congregation I
> will sing your praises."[k] [d]

13 And again,

> "I will put my trust in him."[l] [e]

And again he says,

> "Here am I, and the children God has
> given me."[m] [f]

14 Since the children have flesh and
blood,[g] he too shared in their humanity[h]
so that by his death he might destroy[i]
him who holds the power of death—that
is, the devil[j]— 15 and free those who all
their lives were held in slavery by their
fear[k] of death. 16 For surely it is not an-

2:9 [v]ver 7; Ac 3:13; S Php 2:9 [w]Php 2:7-9 [x]2Co 5:15
2:10 [y]S Ro 11:36 [z]Lk 24:26; Heb 5:8, 9; 7:28
2:11 [a]Heb 13:12 [b]S Eph 5:26 [c]S Mt 28:10
2:12 [d]Ps 22:22; 68:26
2:13 [e]Isa 8:17 [f]Isa 8:18; Jn 10:29
2:14 [g]1Co 15:50; Eph 6:12 [h]S Jn 1:14 [i]Ge 3:15; 1Co 15:54-57; 2Ti 1:10 [j]1Jn 3:8
2:15 [k]S 2Ti 1:7
2:16 [l]S Lk 3:8
2:17 [m]ver 14; S Php 2:7 [n]Heb 5:2 [o]Heb 3:1; 4:14,15; 5:5,10; 7:26,28; 8:1,3; 9:11 [p]Heb 5:1 [q]S Ro 3:25
2:18 [r]Heb 4:15
3:1 [s]Heb 2:11 [t]S Ro 8:28 [u]S Heb 2:17 [v]1Ti 6:12; Heb 4:14; 10:23; 2Co 9:13
3:2 [w]ver 5; Nu 12:7
3:3 [x]Dt 34:12
3:4 [y]Ge 1:1
3:5 [z]Ex 14:31 [a]ver 2; Nu 12:7
3:6 [b]S Heb 1:2 [c]S 1Co 3:16; 1Ti 3:15

gels he helps, but Abraham's descendants.[l] 17 For this reason he had to be
made like his brothers[m] in every way, in
order that he might become a merciful[n]
and faithful high priest[o] in service to
God,[p] and that he might make atonement for[n] the sins of the people.[q] 18 Because he himself suffered when he was
tempted, he is able to help those who are
being tempted.[r]

Chapter 3

Jesus Greater Than Moses

THEREFORE, holy brothers,[s] who
share in the heavenly calling,[t] fix
your thoughts on Jesus, the apostle and
high priest[u] whom we confess.[v] 2 He was
faithful to the one who appointed him,
just as Moses was faithful in all God's
house.[w] 3 Jesus has been found worthy of
greater honor than Moses,[x] just as the
builder of a house has greater honor than
the house itself. 4 For every house is built
by someone, but God is the builder of
everything.[y] 5 Moses was faithful as a servant[z] in all God's house,[a] testifying to
what would be said in the future. 6 But
Christ is faithful as a son[b] over God's
house. And we are his house,[c] if we hold

[k] *12* Psalm 22:22 [l] *13* Isaiah 8:17
[m] *13* Isaiah 8:18 [n] *17* Or *and that he might turn aside God's wrath, taking away*

2:10 GOD, Sovereignty—God brought all things into existence. They continue to exist for His purposes. In His sovereign power with the capability to do anything He chose, God elected to bring salvation by letting His own Son, our Savior, suffer and die.

2:10–18 JESUS CHRIST, Suffering—Jesus provides the way to salvation for all God's children. He is the Author or Leader (Greek *archēgos*) of salvation. See note on Ac 3:15. He can lead humans to salvation because He is the perfect or complete human. His suffering showed His perfection. He was completely what He ought to be as a human. He endured suffering more intense than endured by any other human. As a human He died. In so doing He defeated all Satan's plans. See note on Mt 4:1–11. He freed us from the fear of death. He suffered temptation as we do; thus He, the Victor over temptation, can identify with us and help us when we are tempted. He showed us that to be human is to be tempted but to be human does not mean to sin.

2:11–12 THE CHURCH, God's Community—God has always sought a holy people who reflect His holiness (Lev 11:44–45; 19:2; 20:7–8,26; 21:8,15; 22:9,16,32–33). As the divine Son, Jesus is holy. Sacrificing Himself, He atoned for our sins and thus made us holy. Jesus admits us into His family (Mt 12:49–50; Mk 3:33–35; Lk 8:21; Ro 8:29). Holiness must be more than an idea. It must be the life-style of the church made possible by the indwelling Holy Spirit. See notes on Jn 1:12–13; Gal 4:4–7.

2:14 JESUS CHRIST, Ascension—Jesus' ascension to heaven showed He had access not to the earthly Most Holy Place where the high priest could go once a year (Lev 16:2, 29–34) but to the heavenly eternal dwelling of God. Thus our atonement is sure.

2:14 HUMANITY, Death—Death, the product of sin, is a testimony of the power of Satan. The victory of Jesus over death is also a victory over Satan. People can thus be freed from the fear of death, sin, and Satan. So freed, we become eager to obey Christ and do good.

2:15 SALVATION, Human Freedom—Christ came into the world to free those who are held in slavery to the fear of death. Salvation includes freedom from human anxiety and promise of life and meaning beyond physical death.

2:17–18 JESUS CHRIST, Priest—As a human, Jesus could fulfill perfectly the high priest's role as our representative before God and as the perfect atonement for sin.

3:1–6 JESUS CHRIST, Son of God—Jesus is the culmination of Old Testament faith, embodying its intentions in Himself and worthy of more honor than any of its heroes. He is worthy because He was the obedient, faithful Son of God.

3:1 SALVATION, Confession—Compare with Php 2:11; Ro 10:8–10; Mt 16:16. We are to confess that Jesus Christ is God's Sent One and our High Priest. Such confession places total trust in Him to deal with our sin problem and to carry our fears and worries to God.

3:1 THE CHURCH, God's Community—Sharing in the community of God means sharing joys and sorrows with one another. Christians share the call of God to serve Him. To be "holy" means to be set apart for service. Therefore, Christians are holy family members. We live out that holiness only as we concentrate our attention on Jesus. See note on 2:11–12.

3:6–19 ELECTION, Perseverance—The Bible encourages believers to be steadfast in clinging to courage and hope in Christ. As Christ was a faithful Son, so believers are to be faithful under Christ, who is over them. Sin seeks to deceive people and lead them away from Christ. The elect give one another courage to remain faithful to Christ. Steadfast faith marks the elect.

3:6 THE CHURCH, People of God—God's people make up the house of God. Christians must be strong in faith and continue in service for God. Persistence and hope characterize members of God's family.

on[d] to our courage and the hope[e] of
which we boast.

Warning Against Unbelief

7So, as the Holy Spirit says:[f]

"Today, if you hear his voice,
8 do not harden your hearts[g]
as you did in the rebellion,
during the time of testing in the
desert,
9where your fathers tested and tried me
and for forty years saw what I did.[h]
10That is why I was angry with that
generation,
and I said, 'Their hearts are always
going astray,
and they have not known my ways.'
11So I declared on oath in my anger,[i]
'They shall never enter my
rest.'[j]"[o][k]

12See to it, brothers, that none of you
has a sinful, unbelieving heart that turns
away from the living God.[l] 13But encourage one another daily,[m] as long as it is
called Today, so that none of you may be
hardened by sin's deceitfulness.[n] 14We
have come to share in Christ if we hold
firmly[o] till the end the confidence[p] we
had at first. 15As has just been said:

3:6 [d]ver 14; S Ro 11:22; Heb 4:14 [e]Ro 5:2; Heb 6:11,18,19; 7:19; 11:1
3:7 [f]Ac 28:25; Heb 9:8; 10:15
3:8 [g]ver 15; Heb 4:7
3:9 [h]Nu 14:33; Dt 1:3; Ac 7:36
3:11 [i]Dt 1:34,35 [j]Heb 4:3,5 [k]Ps 95:7-11
3:12 [l]S Mt 16:16
3:13 [m]Heb 10:24,25 [n]Jer 17:9; Eph 4:22
3:14 [o]ver 6 [p]S Eph 3:12
3:15 [q]ver 7,8; Ps 95:7,8; Heb 4:7
3:16 [r]Nu 14:2
3:17 [s]Nu 14:29; Ps 106:26; 1Co 10:5
3:18 [t]Nu 14:20-23; Dt 1:34,35 [u]Heb 4:6
3:19 [v]Ps 78:22; 106:24; Jn 3:36
4:1 [w]Heb 12:15
4:2 [x]1Th 2:13

"Today, if you hear his voice,
do not harden your hearts
as you did in the rebellion."[p][q]

16Who were they who heard and rebelled? Were they not all those Moses led
out of Egypt?[r] 17And with whom was he
angry for forty years? Was it not with
those who sinned, whose bodies fell in
the desert?[s] 18And to whom did God
swear that they would never enter his
rest[t] if not to those who disobeyed[q]?[u]
19So we see that they were not able to
enter, because of their unbelief.[v]

Chapter 4

A Sabbath-Rest for the People of God

THEREFORE, since the promise of entering his rest still stands, let us be
careful that none of you be found to have
fallen short of it.[w] 2For we also have had
the gospel preached to us, just as they
did; but the message they heard was of
no value to them, because those who
heard did not combine it with faith.[r][x]
3Now we who have believed enter that
rest, just as God has said,

[o] *11* Psalm 95:7-11 [p] *15* Psalm 95:7,8 [q] *18* Or *disbelieved* [r] *2* Many manuscripts *because they did not share in the faith of those who obeyed*

3:7–19 SIN, Rebellion—The author of Hebrews quoted from Ps 95:7*b*–11 to enforce his point to his readers that they should shun the sin of rebellion and accept God's leadership. The reference in the Psalm passage is to the wilderness wanderings recorded in Exodus and Numbers. The Israelites rebelled against God and Moses. Hebrews encourages us to accept God's leadership rather than rebelling against it. Rebellion turns us away from God's grace in search for another way of salvation.
3:12 GOD, Living—God is the living God. He is aware of what we do. We dare not disobey Him.
3:14 SALVATION, As Being in Christ—Being in Christ is sharing in Him, being a partaker of Him. Those who persevere in their Christian life know that they have come to share in the life Christ gives. Believers who are once in Christ continue to be in Christ. Faith does not come and go. It stays firmly fixed on Christ.
4:1–2 SIN, Lack of Faith—The rebellious generation did not enter into the Promised Land because of a lack of faith. The inspired writer of Hebrews perceived a parallel between his generation and the generation of rebellious Israelites. Lack of faith which was manifesting itself among them could cause them to forfeit some of God's blessings. We must be aware that a lack of faith in the promises of God can lead to disastrous consequences in our lives. We forfeit the blessings of God if we do not exercise faith.
4:1–14 ELECTION, Faith—Faith in Christ is the key to election. The elect claim and participate in God's promises through faith. Steadfastness and earnest efforts to serve God characterize the elect. This is not salvation by works but by living, active, obedient trust in the God who keeps His promises.
4:1–11 SALVATION, As Rest—Rest as the end of work and labor describes God's salvation. It was the goal God reached on the seventh day of creation (Ge 2:2–3). It was Israel's goal after possessing the Promised Land (Jos 21:44; 23:1). It represents satisfied enjoyment of what God has planned and accomplished. This is one definition of salvation. We enter rest by faith in the gospel, giving up our works as the way to salvation. The opportunity to enter His rest remains open. This salvation rest will be fully realized only in the resurrection life. Life's greatest failure is the failure to enter the rest God provided for us.
4:1–11 LAST THINGS, Heaven—The Promised Land was a land of rest in comparison to the slavery of Egypt and the rigors of wilderness wandering. As the sabbath day was eagerly anticipated during the six days of work, so the wandering Israelites anticipated the "day of rest" in the Promised Land. The analogy to heaven is similar. Heaven is a rest for God's people from the persecution and suffering the church faces in the world. To enter that "Sabbath-rest" people must have an enduring faith. Obedience in life is necessary for reaching heaven, because genuine faith is obeying and enduring faith.
4:2 PROCLAMATION, Rejection—The gospel proclamation requires a response. Neutrality is not a valid response. The hearer will either receive the message with repentance and faith or will reject it in unbelief. Proclamation confronts the mystery of human free will. God forces no one to be saved. The proclaimer of God's Word is not a coercer of people. Salvation comes when the individual chooses to receive God's offer through Jesus Christ (Jn 1:12; Rev 22:17). Salvation is rejected when the individual chooses not to receive God's offer (Ac 24:24–25; 1 Co 1:18; 2 Th 1:8).
4:3–4 CREATION, Continuous—The first six days of creation were marked by the refrain "evening . . . morning." After the seventh, the writer merely says that God rested. This does not imply idleness but completion of a job, the end of a remarkable whole. Nothing could be or needed to be added to the creation, for it was good and pleasing to the Creator. In another sense, of course, creation is not static, but rather through God's power, the world is dynamically continuing to renew itself. Thus we live in a finished unfinished world. God completed it but endowed it with the ability to move forward "fresh every morning." This type of world is ideally suited to the people God created. We are to continue daily discovering new frontiers of growth and development, as we wait for our work to be complete so we can enter His rest.

"So I declared on oath in my anger,
'They shall never enter my
rest.'"[s] [y]

And yet his work has been finished since
the creation of the world. 4For somewhere he has spoken about the seventh
day in these words: "And on the seventh
day God rested from all his work."[t] [z]
5And again in the passage above he says,
"They shall never enter my rest."[a]
6It still remains that some will enter
that rest, and those who formerly had the
gospel preached to them did not go in,
because of their disobedience.[b] 7There-
fore God again set a certain day, calling it
Today, when a long time later he spoke
through David, as was said before:

"Today, if you hear his voice,
do not harden your hearts."[u] [c]

8For if Joshua had given them rest,[d] God
would not have spoken[e] later about another day. 9There remains, then, a Sabbath-rest for the people of God; 10for anyone who enters God's rest also rests from
his own work,[f] just as God did from
his.[g] 11Let us, therefore, make every effort to enter that rest, so that no one will
fall by following their example of disobedience.[h]
12For the word of God[i] is living[j] and
active.[k] Sharper than any double-edged
sword,[l] it penetrates even to dividing
soul and spirit, joints and marrow; it
judges the thoughts and attitudes of the
heart.[m] 13Nothing in all creation is hidden from God's sight.[n] Everything is uncovered and laid bare before the eyes of
him to whom we must give account.

Jesus the Great High Priest

14Therefore, since we have a great high
priest[o] who has gone through the heavens,[v] [p] Jesus the Son of God,[q] let us hold
firmly to the faith we profess.[r] 15For we
do not have a high priest[s] who is unable
to sympathize with our weaknesses, but
we have one who has been tempted in
every way, just as we are[t]—yet was
without sin.[u] 16Let us then approach[v]
the throne of grace with confidence,[w] so
that we may receive mercy and find grace
to help us in our time of need.

Chapter 5

EVERY high priest is selected from
among men and is appointed to represent them in matters related to God,[x]
to offer gifts and sacrifices[y] for sins.[z]
2He is able to deal gently with those who
are ignorant and are going astray,[a] since
he himself is subject to weakness.[b] 3This
is why he has to offer sacrifices for his
own sins, as well as for the sins of the
people.[c]
4No one takes this honor upon himself;
he must be called by God, just as Aaron
was.[d] 5So Christ also did not take upon
himself the glory[e] of becoming a high
priest.[f] But God said[g] to him,

[s]3 Psalm 95:11; also in verse 5 [t]4 Gen. 2:2 [u]7 Psalm 95:7,8 [v]14 Or *gone into heaven*

4:3 [y]Ps 95:11; Dt 1:34,35; Heb 3:11
4:4 [z]Ge 2:2,3; Ex 20:11
4:5 [a]Ps 95:11; S ver 3
4:6 [b]ver 11; Heb 3:18
4:7 [c]Ps 95:7,8; Heb 3:7,8,15
4:8 [d]Jos 22:4 [e]S Heb 1:1
4:10 [f]Lev 23:3; Rev 14:13 [g]ver 4
4:11 [h]ver 6; Heb 3:18
4:12 [i]S Mk 4:14; Lk 5:1; 11:28; Jn 10:35; Ac 12:24; 1Th 2:13; 2Ti 2:9; 1Pe 1:23; 1Jn 2:14; Rev 1:2,9 [j]Ac 7:38; 1Pe 1:23 [k]Isa 55:11; Jer 23:29; 1Th 2:13 [l]Eph 6:17; S Rev 1:16 [m]1Co 14:24,25
4:13 [n]Ps 33:13-15; Pr 5:21; Jer 16:17; 23:24; Da 2:22
4:14 [o]S Heb 2:17 [p]Heb 6:20; 8:1; 9:24 [q]S Mt 4:3 [r]S Heb 3:1
4:15 [s]S Heb 2:17 [t]Heb 2:18 [u]S 2Co 5:21
4:16 [v]S Heb 7:19 [w]S Eph 3:12
5:1 [x]Heb 2:17 [y]Heb 8:3; 9:9 [z]Heb 7:27
5:2 [a]Isa 29:24; Heb 2:18; 4:15 [b]Heb 7:28
5:3 [c]Lev 9:7; 16:6; Heb 7:27; 9:7
5:4 [d]Ex 28:1; Nu 14:40; 18:7
5:5 [e]Jn 8:54 [f]S Heb 2:17 [g]S Heb 1:1

4:12 HOLY SCRIPTURE, Powerful—God's word was preached in verbal form, lived out in person by Jesus, and finally placed in stable, written form. In every form it is more efficient than any human tool. It is a dynamic, active power, constantly at work in human lives, cutting to the deepest area of personality. God's inspired Word reveals all a person is and can become. It judges every person in relationship to God's will and way. The judgment centers on potential, plans, and attitudes, not simply on individual acts.

4:13 GOD, Wisdom—God's sharp Word shows us where we are wrong not only in what we do, but in how we think and feel. We would like to hide our guilt. We cannot. God has perfect knowledge of what is going on in His world, even to the point of knowing the very thoughts of our hearts. This calls us to repent before we have to face the final judgment.

4:13 HUMANITY, Relationship to God—We must give a personal account to God for what we have said and done in our own lives. A personal relationship to God requires personal responsibility. See note on Rev 20:12–13.

4:13 LAST THINGS, Judgment—Future judgment will be based on God's full and accurate knowledge of us. Everyone, including believers, must render an account to God for the life lived on earth. This should motivate us to obedience realizing nothing can be concealed from Him.

4:14–15 JESUS CHRIST, Sinless—Jesus was thoroughly and completely tempted, yet He did not sin. See note on Mt 4:1–11. To be tempted is not sinful. To yield to temptation is sinful. Jesus was completely human. See note on 2:10–18; Jn 1:1–18. To say Jesus was tempted in every way we are means that He was thoroughly tested at all points wherein He as an individual could be tested. Humans have different temptations according to their own personalities. We need not assert that Jesus had every wicked and distorted thought and desire known to humanity in order to affirm the thoroughness of His temptation or the reality of His sinlessness. His sinlessness was a marvelous quality He brought to His saviorhood. We are not yet sinless, but we do have the resources of a sinless Savior. God through Christ has offered to help us in our temptations (2:18; 1 Co 10:13).

4:14–16 EVIL AND SUFFERING, Redemptive—See note on 2:9–18.

4:14–16 WORSHIP, Priesthood—See note on Eph 4:11–13.

4:15–16 PRAYER, In Christ—If Christ had never become human, an approach to His throne would be either intimidating or insolent. Our High Priest understands the human situation totally. He has taken part in our nature and, therefore, understands every aspect of that nature from within. He is not hostile to humanity but is one of us. He wants to help each of us be the kind of human being He was, and He knows how to help. When we come close to Him, we approach a nature like His. Therefore, we dare to approach with boldness and confidence.

5:5–10 JESUS CHRIST, Priest—Jesus is our High Priest representing us before God because God chose His Son to be our eternal Priest. Interpretation and application of the Old Testament in light of Christ proves this. His prayer life of submission to the Father during His earthly ministry showed He is an effective Priest. His atoning death brought an end to the priests' role in atonement, giving us eternal salvation. His prayer life and His suffering highlight His full humanity in absolute submission to the Father.

"You are my Son;
today I have become your
Father.[w] "[x] [h]

6And he says in another place,

"You are a priest forever,
in the order of Melchizedek.[i] "[y] [j]

7During the days of Jesus' life on earth,
he offered up prayers and petitions[k] with
loud cries and tears[l] to the one who
could save him from death, and he was
heard[m] because of his reverent submission.[n] 8Although he was a son,[o] he
learned obedience from what he suffered[p] 9and, once made perfect,[q] he became the source of eternal salvation for
all who obey him 10and was designated
by God to be high priest[r] in the order of
Melchizedek.[s]

Warning Against Falling Away

6:4–6Ref — Heb 10:26–31

11We have much to say about this, but
it is hard to explain because you are slow
to learn. 12In fact, though by this time you
ought to be teachers, you need someone
to teach you the elementary truths[t] of
God's word all over again. You need milk,
not solid food![u] 13Anyone who lives on
milk, being still an infant,[v] is not acquainted with the teaching about righteousness. 14But solid food is for the mature,[w] who by constant use have trained
themselves to distinguish good from
evil.[x]

Chapter 6

THEREFORE let us leave[y] the elementary teachings[z] about Christ and go
on to maturity, not laying again the foundation of repentance from acts that lead
to death,[z] [a] and of faith in God, 2instruc-
tion about baptisms,[b] the laying on of
hands,[c] the resurrection of the dead,[d]
and eternal judgment. 3And God permitting,[e] we will do so.
4It is impossible for those who have
once been enlightened,[f] who have tasted the heavenly gift,[g] who have shared
in the Holy Spirit,[h] 5who have tasted the
goodness[i] of the word of God[j] and the
powers of the coming age,[6]if they fall

5:5 [h]Ps 2:7; S Mt 3:17
5:6 [i]ver 10; Ge 14:18; Heb 6:20; 7:1-22 [j]Ps 110:4; Heb 7:17,21
5:7 [k]Lk 22:41-44 [l]Mt 27:46,50; Lk 23:46 [m]Ps 22:24 [n]Mk 14:36
5:8 [o]S Heb 1:2 [p]S Php 2:8
5:9 [q]S Heb 2:10
5:10 [r]ver 5; S Heb 2:17 [s]S ver 6
5:12 [t]Heb 6:1 [u]1Co 3:2; 1Pe 2:2
5:13 [v]S 1Co 14:20
5:14 [w]S 1Co 2:6 [x]Isa 7:15
6:1 [y]Php 3:12-14 [z]Heb 5:12 [a]Heb 9:14
6:2 [b]Jn 3:25 [c]S Ac 6:6 [d]S Ac 2:24; Ac 17:18,32
6:3 [e]Ac 18:21
6:4 [f]Heb 10:32 [g]Eph 2:8 [h]Gal 3:2
6:5 [i]Ps 34:8 [j]S Heb 4:12

[w]5 Or *have begotten you* [x]5 Psalm 2:7
[y]6 Psalm 110:4 [z]1 Or *from useless rituals*

5:7 GOD, Sovereignty—In His sovereign authority, God the Father could have saved His Son from the agony of the cross. However, Jesus' suffering and death were part of the Father's plan to provide salvation for lost people. God was with Him through His suffering and death and restored Him to life. See note on Mt 27:46.

5:7 PRAYER, Jesus' Example—Prayer, for Jesus, involved intense emotional energy. Prayer demonstrated His obedient submission to God. Our prayers should be like His, deeply personal, emotional conversation to the loving Father to whom we willingly submit our lives.

5:8–9 SALVATION, Obedience—Jesus Christ is the source of eternal salvation for all who obey Him. Obedience involves commitment of every aspect of life to Him.

5:12—6:3 EDUCATION, Qualified Teachers—Not all church members are qualified to be teachers. Many are immature in the faith. They have not learned to live righteous lives or discuss mature questions. All Christians need to mature in the faith so they can distinguish good from evil. Maturity comes from constant study and practice of the faith. Perhaps the shortage of qualified teachers in many churches today is related to a failure to grow in Christian knowledge. As leaders look in vain for persons capable of teaching others, they can only find babes in Christ, fixated in the kindergarten stages of faith development. Each Christian with teaching gifts should exercise those gifts at the present stage of maturity while seeking constantly for greater knowledge and maturity.

6:1–6 SIN, Guilt—Christians are not exempt from sin, and when Christians sin they bring guilt upon themselves. The serious nature of this problem is highlighted in the text by the figures of speech the author uses to describe the sin and consequent guilt. Christians cannot be content with being elementary school believers, always testing out the ABC's of the faith. We must repent of sins, commit ourselves wholly to Christ, and live godly lives which testify to the power of God in us. Failure to mature is serious sin.

6:2 LAST THINGS, Judgment—The future bodily resurrection of the dead followed by judgment belongs to the elementary truths of Christian faith.

6:2 ORDINANCES, Baptism as Cleansing—Because the writer used the plural *baptisms* and also used the general Greek word for washing (*baptismos*) rather than the special word for Christian baptism (*baptisma*), he was probably including other ritual washings which these people had received or were arguing about. There were, after all, John's baptism, Jewish proselyte baptisms, Levitical washings for religious ceremonies, and numerous ritual baptisms in the mystery religions being practiced at that time. The teaching is that we must get beyond these elementary debates and press on toward maturity (v 1). All the "washings" in the world will not suffice if we do not grow toward maturity in Christ. There is only one baptism in the authority and name of Christ. It does not need to be repeated if it is properly performed upon a genuine believer. It is only the beginning of the Christian journey; one must go on toward maturity in Christ.

6:4 HOLY SPIRIT, Convicts—The Holy Spirit works to convict sinners and lead them to repentance and faith. He also works in the lives of Christians to convict us of sin and to lead us to spiritual growth and maturity. Biblical students are not agreed on which is meant here. At issue is the biblical doctrine of the perseverance of the saints. *Hebrews* apparently addresses Jewish people who have been intimately connected with the church, possibly becoming church members, and yet have not committed themselves totally in faith to Christ. The message for them is that they cannot stand still. They must decide for or against Christ. Otherwise, they will fall away from Christ, back into Judaism, and they will not have a second chance to respond to the Spirit's conviction. If addressed to Christians, the text uses strong language to gain attention so as to lead the Christians from lingering doubts to committed faith.

6:4–12 ELECTION, Perseverance—The crucifying of the Son of God takes place when the elect in spiritual immaturity fail to move away from that behavior which subjects Jesus Christ to public disgrace. Diligence, patience, and persistence in the faith are required of God's elect. People who humbly love and serve God and His people can be confident of sharing God's promised inheritance, for God is just.

6:5 LAST THINGS, Age to Come—The present experience of salvation involves a foretaste of the powers of the age to come. Aspects of the eschatological future have been brought into time. Eternal life is a present reality (Jn 5:24); the kingdom of God has come near (Mk 1:14–15); and the age to come has overlapped this present age through the coming of Christ and the powers and provisions He brings to believers.

away, to be brought back to repentance,[k]
because[a] to their loss they are crucifying
the Son of God[l] all over again and sub-
jecting him to public disgrace.
7Land that drinks in the rain often falling on it and that produces a crop useful
to those for whom it is farmed receives
the blessing of God. 8But land that produces thorns and thistles is worthless and
is in danger of being cursed.[m] In the end
it will be burned.
9Even though we speak like this, dear
friends,[n] we are confident of better
things in your case—things that accompany salvation. 10God is not unjust; he
will not forget your work and the love
you have shown him as you have helped
his people and continue to help them.[o]
11We want each of you to show this same
diligence to the very end, in order to
make your hope[p] sure. 12We do not want
you to become lazy, but to imitate[q] those
who through faith and patience[r] inherit
what has been promised.[s]

The Certainty of God's Promise

13When God made his promise to Abraham, since there was no one greater for
him to swear by, he swore by himself,[t]
14saying, "I will surely bless you and give
you many descendants."[b][u] 15And so after waiting patiently, Abraham received
what was promised.[v]
16Men swear by someone greater than
themselves, and the oath confirms what
is said and puts an end to all argument.[w]
17Because God wanted to make the unchanging[x] nature of his purpose very
clear to the heirs of what was promised,[y]
he confirmed it with an oath. 18God did
this so that, by two unchangeable things
in which it is impossible for God to lie,[z]
we who have fled to take hold of the
hope[a] offered to us may be greatly encouraged. 19We have this hope as an anchor for the soul, firm and secure. It enters the inner sanctuary behind the curtain,[b] 20where Jesus, who went before
us, has entered on our behalf.[c] He has
become a high priest[d] forever, in the order of Melchizedek.[e]

6:6 [k]2Pe 2:21; 1Jn 5:16 [l]S Mt 4:3
6:8 [m]Ge 3:17,18; Isa 5:6; 27:4
6:9 [n]S 1Co 10:14
6:10 [o]S Mt 10:40, 42; 1Th 1:3
6:11 [p]S Heb 3:6
6:12 [q]Heb 13:7 [r]2Th 1:4; Jas 1:3; Rev 13:10; 14:12 [s]Heb 10:36
6:13 [t]Ge 22:16; Lk 1:73
6:14 [u]Ge 22:17
6:15 [v]Ge 21:5
6:16 [w]Ex 22:11
6:17 [x]ver 18; Ps 110:4 [y]Ro 4:16; Heb 11:9
6:18 [z]Nu 23:19; Tit 1:2 [a]S Heb 3:6
6:19 [b]Lev 16:2; Heb 9:2,3,7
6:20 [c]S Heb 4:14 [d]S Heb 2:17 [e]S Heb 5:6
7:1 [f]Ps 76:2 [g]S Mk 5:7 [h]ver 6; Ge 14:18-20
7:3 [i]ver 6 [j]S Mt 4:3
7:4 [k]Ac 2:29 [l]Ge 14:20
7:5 [m]Nu 18:21,26
7:6 [n]Ge 14:19,20 [o]Ro 4:13
7:8 [p]Heb 5:6; 6:20
7:11 [q]ver 18,19; Heb 8:7 [r]Heb 10:1 [s]ver 17; S Heb 5:6
7:13 [t]ver 11 [u]ver 14
7:14 [v]Isa 11:1; Mt 1:3; 2:6; Lk 3:33; Rev 5:5

Chapter 7

Melchizedek the Priest

THIS Melchizedek was king of Salem[f]
and priest of God Most High.[g] He
met Abraham returning from the defeat
of the kings and blessed him,[h] 2and Abraham gave him a tenth of everything. First,
his name means "king of righteousness";
then also, "king of Salem" means "king
of peace." 3Without father or mother,
without genealogy,[i] without beginning
of days or end of life, like the Son of
God[j] he remains a priest forever.
4Just think how great he was: Even the
patriarch[k] Abraham gave him a tenth of
the plunder![l] 5Now the law requires the
descendants of Levi who become priests
to collect a tenth from the people[m]—that
is, their brothers—even though their
brothers are descended from Abraham.
6This man, however, did not trace his descent from Levi, yet he collected a tenth
from Abraham and blessed[n] him who
had the promises.[o] 7And without doubt
the lesser person is blessed by the greater. 8In the one case, the tenth is collected
by men who die; but in the other case, by
him who is declared to be living.[p] 9One
might even say that Levi, who collects the
tenth, paid the tenth through Abraham,
10because when Melchizedek met Abraham, Levi was still in the body of his ancestor.

Jesus Like Melchizedek

11If perfection could have been attained through the Levitical priesthood
(for on the basis of it the law was given to
the people),[q] why was there still need for
another priest to come[r]—one in the order of Melchizedek,[s] not in the order of
Aaron? 12For when there is a change of
the priesthood, there must also be a
change of the law. 13He of whom these
things are said belonged to a different
tribe,[t] and no one from that tribe has
ever served at the altar.[u] 14For it is clear
that our Lord descended from Judah,[v]
and in regard to that tribe Moses said

[a]6 Or *repentance while* [b]14 Gen. 22:17

6:7–10 DISCIPLESHIP, Neighbor Love—Christian disciples are to produce good crops. We are to produce abundant fruits of love by continuing to help God's people. Such works of love accompany authentic salvation. See 1 Co 16:14.
6:10 GOD, Justice—Hebrews uses strong language to warn readers of the dangers of not trusting Christ, but it also assures us that God is just and will not forget His people who faithfully serve Him and His church in love and trust. God's justice is a warning to the fake Christian but a rock of hope for the faithful.
6:10 THE CHURCH, Saints—"His people" can be translated literally *"the saints."* See note on Ro 16:2.
7:1–28 JESUS CHRIST, Priest—This chapter is the basic source for understanding Jesus as priest. The Old Testament background for the notion of Jesus' eternal priesthood comes from Melchizedek (Ge 14:18–24) and the connection of Melchizedek in the messianic Ps 110:4. Jesus' priesthood is like that of Melchizedek in that it is a direct appointment of God and is eternal. Even more than Melchizedek, Jesus was perfectly obedient and sinless. A priest represents people to God. Jesus has done that for us as no one else could or does. He has no successor, for He lives and serves forever as our High Priest, praying to the Father on our behalf. His one sacrifice of Himself serves forever as the way to salvation.
7:1–10 STEWARDSHIP, Tithe—The tithe illustrated how Christ's priesthood is superior to that of the Levites. The Old Testament practice of supporting the ministry of the priest with tithes is affirmed. See note on Nu 18:21–32.

nothing about priests. [15]And what we have said is even more clear if another priest like Melchizedek appears, [16]one who has become a priest not on the basis of a regulation as to his ancestry but on the basis of the power of an indestructible life. [17]For it is declared:

"You are a priest forever,
in the order of Melchizedek."[c] [w]

[18]The former regulation is set aside because it was weak and useless[x] [19](for the law made nothing perfect),[y] and a better hope[z] is introduced, by which we draw near to God.[a]

[20]And it was not without an oath! Others became priests without any oath, [21]but he became a priest with an oath when God said to him:

"The Lord has sworn
and will not change his mind:[b]
'You are a priest forever.' "[c] [c]

[22]Because of this oath, Jesus has become the guarantee of a better covenant.[d]

[23]Now there have been many of those priests, since death prevented them from continuing in office; [24]but because Jesus lives forever, he has a permanent priesthood.[e] [25]Therefore he is able to save[f] completely[d] those who come to God[g] through him, because he always lives to intercede for them.[h]

[26]Such a high priest[i] meets our need—one who is holy, blameless, pure, set apart from sinners,[j] exalted above the heavens.[k] [27]Unlike the other high priests, he does not need to offer sacrifices[l] day after day, first for his own sins,[m] and then for the sins of the people. He sacrificed for their sins once for all[n] when he offered himself.[o] [28]For the law appoints as high priests men who are weak;[p] but the oath, which came after the law, appointed the Son,[q] who has been made perfect[r] forever.

7:17 [w]Ps 110:4; ver 21; S Heb 5:6
7:18 [x]Ro 8:3
7:19 [y]ver 11; Ro 3:20; 7:7,8; Gal 3:21; Heb 9:9; 10:1 [z]S Heb 3:6 [a]ver 25; Heb 4:16; 10:1,22; Jas 4:8
7:21 [b]Nu 23:19; 1Sa 15:29; Mal 3:6; Ro 11:29 [c]Ps 110:4; S Heb 5:6
7:22 [d]S Lk 22:20
7:24 [e]ver 28
7:25 [f]S Ro 11:14 [g]S ver 19 [h]S Ro 8:34
7:26 [i]S Heb 2:17 [j]S 2Co 5:21 [k]S Heb 4:14
7:27 [l]Heb 5:1 [m]S Heb 5:3 [n]Ro 6:10; Heb 9:12,26,28; 10:10; 1Pe 3:18 [o]Eph 5:2; Heb 9:14, 28
7:28 [p]Heb 5:2 [q]S Heb 1:2 [r]S Heb 2:10
8:1 [s]S Heb 2:17 [t]S Mk 16:19; S Heb 4:14
8:2 [u]Heb 9:11,24
8:3 [v]S Heb 2:17 [w]Heb 5:1; 9:9 [x]Heb 9:14
8:4 [y]Heb 5:1; 9:9
8:5 [z]Heb 9:23 [a]Col 2:17; Heb 10:1 [b]Heb 11:7; 12:25 [c]Ex 25:40
8:6 [d]ver 8,13; S Lk 22:20 [e]S Gal 3:20
8:7 [f]Heb 7:11,18; 10:1
8:8 [g]ver 6,13; S Lk 22:20

Chapter 8

The High Priest of a New Covenant

THE point of what we are saying is this: We do have such a high priest,[s] who sat down at the right hand of the throne of the Majesty in heaven,[t] [2]and who serves in the sanctuary, the true tabernacle[u] set up by the Lord, not by man.

[3]Every high priest[v] is appointed to offer both gifts and sacrifices,[w] and so it was necessary for this one also to have something to offer.[x] [4]If he were on earth, he would not be a priest, for there are already men who offer the gifts prescribed by the law.[y] [5]They serve at a sanctuary that is a copy[z] and shadow[a] of what is in heaven. This is why Moses was warned[b] when he was about to build the tabernacle: "See to it that you make everything according to the pattern shown you on the mountain."[e] [c] [6]But the ministry Jesus has received is as superior to theirs as the covenant[d] of which he is mediator[e] is superior to the old one, and it is founded on better promises.

[7]For if there had been nothing wrong with that first covenant, no place would have been sought for another.[f] [8]But God found fault with the people and said[f]:

"The time is coming, declares the Lord,
when I will make a new covenant[g]
with the house of Israel
and with the house of Judah.

[c]*17,21* Psalm 110:4 [d]*25* Or *forever* [e]*5* Exodus 25:40 [f]*8* Some manuscripts may be translated *fault and said to the people.*

7:19 PRAYER, In Christ—See note on 4:15–16.

7:22 THE CHURCH, Covenant People—The church can have complete confidence in the new covenant. It is based on Jesus, the superior revelation of God and the superior Mediator of God's covenant. As God who became flesh, Jesus can guarantee forgiveness is available from God for those who trust Jesus. As the only human who fulfilled completely the obligations of the old covenant, Jesus can guarantee His followers are acceptable to God. Because God has sworn to accept Jesus as the eternal Priest, we can be sure He is presenting our petitions to God and is able to save us. Jesus Christ thus guarantees that the new covenant in His blood (Lk 22:20) is superior to all other covenants. It is the Way to God.

7:25 JESUS CHRIST, Intercession—This verse is the crowning jewel of Hebrews. The basic theme of all of Hebrews is that Jesus is uniquely prepared to be a go-between for us with the Father. He is divine and therefore can interpret God to us. He became human so that He can represent us to God.

7:25 PRAYER, In Christ—Christians have a permanent, never-failing Representative in heaven who is favorable to us and presents our case perfectly. See note on Ro 8:34.

7:26–27 SALVATION, Atonement—Christ's atonement for sins was unlike other high priests in that: (1) He was without sin (4:15); (2) He offered Himself as the sacrifice; and (3) His sacrifice was once for all, never again to be repeated. His sacrifice meets every requirement to provide salvation for you.

8:1—9:28 JESUS CHRIST, Fulfilled—Covenant is the central Old Testament theme. The new covenant (Jer 31:31–34) is the central Old Testament promise. Jesus fulfilled these by becoming the perfect Priest in God's heavenly worship place. By giving His life, Jesus instituted the new covenant (Lk 22:20). His sacrifice once for all obtained eternal salvation and allowed us to serve God obediently from our conscience rather than through efforts to obey legalistic rules. Jesus fulfilled the old covenant requirements by pouring out His own blood on the cross.

8:6—9:28 THE CHURCH, Covenant People—Jesus is the superior High Priest. The new covenant of which He is Mediator is superior to the old covenant. The old covenant promised to make Israel the people of God. It did not provide the power necessary for Israel to keep the covenant. Israel broke the covenant by disobeying. Under the new covenant, Christ provided the means for the covenant to be eternally instituted—through the blood of His perfect sacrifice. Christ then cleanses our hearts, putting right moral desires in our hearts so we can serve Him in holiness. See notes on 7:22; Jer 31:31–34.

9It will not be like the covenant
I made with their forefathers[h]
when I took them by the hand
to lead them out of Egypt,
because they did not remain faithful to
my covenant,
and I turned away from them,
declares the Lord.
10This is the covenant[i] I will make with
the house of Israel
after that time, declares the Lord.
I will put my laws in their minds
and write them on their hearts.[j]
I will be their God,
and they will be my people.[k]
11No longer will a man teach his
neighbor,
or a man his brother, saying, 'Know
the Lord,'
because they will all know me,[l]
from the least of them to the
greatest.
12For I will forgive their wickedness
and will remember their sins no
more.[m]"[g] [n]

13By calling this covenant "new,"[o] he
has made the first one obsolete;[p] and
what is obsolete and aging will soon disappear.

Chapter 9

Worship in the Earthly Tabernacle

NOW the first covenant had regulations for worship and also an earthly
sanctuary.[q] 2A tabernacle[r] was set up. In
its first room were the lampstand,[s] the
table[t] and the consecrated bread;[u] this
was called the Holy Place.[v] 3Behind the
second curtain was a room called the
Most Holy Place,[w] 4which had the golden
altar of incense[x] and the gold-covered
ark of the covenant.[y] This ark contained
the gold jar of manna,[z] Aaron's staff that
had budded,[a] and the stone tablets of the
covenant.[b] 5Above the ark were the
cherubim of the Glory,[c] overshadowing
the atonement cover.[h] [d] But we cannot
discuss these things in detail now.
6When everything had been arranged
like this, the priests entered regularly[e]
into the outer room to carry on their ministry. 7But only the high priest entered[f]
the inner room,[g] and that only once a
year,[h] and never without blood,[i] which
he offered for himself[j] and for the sins
the people had committed in ignorance.[k]
8The Holy Spirit was showing[l] by this
that the way[m] into the Most Holy Place
had not yet been disclosed as long as the
first tabernacle was still standing. 9This is
an illustration[n] for the present time, indicating that the gifts and sacrifices being
offered[o] were not able to clear the conscience[p] of the worshiper. 10They are
only a matter of food[q] and drink[r] and
various ceremonial washings[s] —external
regulations[t] applying until the time of
the new order.

The Blood of Christ

11When Christ came as high priest[u] of
the good things that are already here,[i] [v]
he went through the greater and more
perfect tabernacle[w] that is not man-
made,[x] that is to say, not a part of this
creation. 12He did not enter by means of
the blood of goats and calves;[y] but he
entered the Most Holy Place[z] once for
all[a] by his own blood,[b] having obtained
eternal redemption. 13The blood of goats
and bulls[c] and the ashes of a heifer[d]
sprinkled on those who are ceremonially
unclean sanctify them so that they are
outwardly clean. 14How much more,
then, will the blood of Christ, who

8:9 [h]Ex 19:5,6; 20:1-17
8:10 [i]Ro 11:27 [j]2Co 3:3; Heb 10:16 [k]Eze 11:20; Zec 8:8
8:11 [l]Isa 54:13; S Jn 6:45
8:12 [m]Heb 10:17 [n]Jer 31:31-34
8:13 [o]ver 6,8; S Lk 22:20 [p]2Co 5:17
9:1 [q]Ex 25:8
9:2 [r]Ex 25:8,9 [s]Ex 25:31-39 [t]Ex 25:23-29 [u]Ex 25:30; Lev 24:5-8 [v]Ex 26:33,34
9:3 [w]Ex 26:31-33
9:4 [x]Ex 30:1-5 [y]Ex 25:10-22 [z]Ex 16:32,33 [a]Nu 17:10 [b]Ex 31:18; 32:15
9:5 [c]Ex 25:17-19 [d]Ex 25:20-22; 26:34
9:6 [e]Nu 28:3
9:7 [f]Lev 16:11-19 [g]ver 2,3 [h]Lev 16:34 [i]Lev 16:11,14 [j]Lev 16:11; Heb 5:2,3 [k]Heb 5:2,3
9:8 [l]S Heb 3:7 [m]Jn 14:6; Heb 10:19,20
9:9 [n]Heb 10:1 [o]Heb 5:1; 8:3 [p]S Heb 7:19
9:10 [q]Lev 11:2-23 [r]Nu 6:3; Col 2:16 [s]Lev 11:25,28,40 [t]Heb 7:16
9:11 [u]S Heb 2:17 [v]Heb 10:1 [w]ver 24; Heb 8:2 [x]S Jn 2:19
9:12 [y]ver 19; Lev 16:6,15; Heb 10:4 [z]ver 24 [a]ver 26,28; S Heb 7:27 [b]ver 14; S Ro 3:25
9:13 [c]Heb 10:4 [d]Nu 19:9,17,18

[g] *12* Jer. 31:31-34 [h] *5* Traditionally *the mercy seat*
[i] *11* Some early manuscripts *are to come*

8:10 GOD, One God—The major emphasis of God from the beginning of time has been establishing Himself as the one true God in the hearts of the people whom He has created. God wants every person to know Him as a loving Heavenly Father through a faith relationship with Him. He already is the sovereign Lord over every individual, whether that lordship is respected and honored or not. God wants the more intimate relationship where His authority is honored and He is loved as Father.

8:12 SALVATION, Forgiveness—God's new covenant (Jer 31:34) includes the forgiveness of sins. Forgiveness means total forgetfulness. Forgiven sins never again become a barrier between you and God.

9:5–28 SALVATION, Atonement—See notes on Lev 9:7; 17:11; Ro 3:25. The atonement cover was traditionally called the mercy seat. Blood for atonement was sprinkled on it (Lev 16:14). Jesus Christ, the eternal High Priest, made Himself an eternal sacrifice for sin once for all time and eternity. His sacrifice covered all sins, not just those done unintentionally or in ignorance. He did not act in earthly ritual but in the heavenly presence of the Father. His sacrifice is able to clear our consciences and eliminate our guilt. He redeemed us or set us free for eternal life to serve God. His sacrifice of His own blood met all the law's requirements.

9:9 HUMANITY, Moral Consciousness—For Old Testament worshipers, repeated ritual sacrifices cleansed a person's guilt for a while, but it had to be repeated. Christ's once-for-all sacrifice can remove guilt and thus cleanse our conscience forever.

9:12,15 SALVATION, Redemption—Through Christ's death believers share an eternal redemption. His death was a ransom from sin. Ransom is an image which has to do with a slave or prison. It comes from ancient economic life and means payment of a price. Persons lost their freedom. They forfeited their lives and could not free themselves. Someone came along and paid the price to redeem them. A ransom was provided. That is the context in which Christ should be seen as Redeemer. He delivers His people from bondage to sin and all other masters. He paid the price of His own life in the crucifixion to make possible our freedom to live life as God created and intended it.

9:14 GOD, Trinity—The three Persons of the Trinity participated in providing salvation. Christ poured out His blood as a perfect sacrifice. The Spirit empowered Him to do so. The

through the eternal Spirit[e] offered himself[f] unblemished to God, cleanse our
consciences[g] from acts that lead to
death,[j] [h] so that we may serve the living
God![i]

15For this reason Christ is the mediator[j] of a new covenant,[k] that those who
are called[l] may receive the promised[m]
eternal inheritance[n]—now that he has
died as a ransom to set them free from
the sins committed under the first covenant.[o]

16In the case of a will,[k] it is necessary
to prove the death of the one who made
it, 17because a will is in force only when
somebody has died; it never takes effect
while the one who made it is living.
18This is why even the first covenant was
not put into effect without blood.[p]
19When Moses had proclaimed[q] every
commandment of the law to all the people, he took the blood of calves,[r] together with water, scarlet wool and branches
of hyssop, and sprinkled the scroll and all
the people.[s] 20He said, "This is the blood
of the covenant, which God has commanded you to keep."[l] [t] 21In the same
way, he sprinkled with the blood both the
tabernacle and everything used in its ceremonies. 22In fact, the law requires that
nearly everything be cleansed with
blood,[u] and without the shedding of
blood there is no forgiveness.[v]

23It was necessary, then, for the copies[w] of the heavenly things to be purified
with these sacrifices, but the heavenly
things themselves with better sacrifices
than these. 24For Christ did not enter a
man-made sanctuary that was only a copy
of the true one;[x] he entered heaven itself,[y] now to appear for us in God's presence.[z] 25Nor did he enter heaven to offer
himself again and again, the way the high
priest enters the Most Holy Place[a] every
year with blood that is not his own.[b]
26Then Christ would have had to suffer
many times since the creation of the
world.[c] But now he has appeared[d] once
for all[e] at the end of the ages to do away
with sin by the sacrifice of himself.[f]
27Just as man is destined to die once,[g]
and after that to face judgment,[h] 28so
Christ was sacrificed once[i] to take away
the sins of many people; and he will appear a second time,[j] not to bear sin,[k]
but to bring salvation[l] to those who are
waiting for him.[m]

Chapter 10

Christ's Sacrifice Once for All

THE law is only a shadow[n] of the good
things[o] that are coming—not the realities themselves.[p] For this reason it can
never, by the same sacrifices repeated
endlessly year after year, make perfect[q]
those who draw near to worship.[r] 2If it
could, would they not have stopped being
offered? For the worshipers would have
been cleansed once for all, and would no

9:14 [e]1Pe 3:18 [f]S Eph 5:2 [g]Ps 51:2; 65:3; Jer 33:8; Zec 13:1; S Tit 2:14; Heb 10:2,22 [h]Heb 6:1 [i]S Mt 16:16
9:15 [j]S Gal 3:20 [k]S Lk 22:20 [l]S Ro 8:28; S 11:29 [m]Heb 6:15; 10:36 [n]S Ac 20:32 [o]Heb 7:22
9:18 [p]Ex 24:6-8
9:19 [q]Heb 1:1 [r]ver 12 [s]Ex 24:6-8
9:20 [t]Ex 24:8; S Mt 26:28
9:22 [u]Ex 29:21; Lev 8:15 [v]Lev 17:11
9:23 [w]Heb 8:5
9:24 [x]Heb 8:2 [y]ver 12; S Heb 4:14 [z]S Ro 8:34
9:25 [a]Heb 10:19 [b]ver 7,8
9:26 [c]Heb 4:3 [d]1Jn 3:5 [e]ver 12, 28; S Heb 7:27 [f]ver 12
9:27 [g]Ge 3:19 [h]2Co 5:10
9:28 [i]ver 12,26; S Heb 7:27 [j]S Mt 16:27 [k]1Pe 2:24 [l]Heb 5:9 [m]S 1Co 1:7
10:1 [n]Col 2:17; Heb 8:5 [o]Heb 9:11 [p]Heb 9:23 [q]ver 4, 11; S Heb 7:19 [r]S Heb 7:19

[j]*14* Or *from useless rituals* [k]*16* Same Greek word as *covenant;* also in verse 17 [l]*20* Exodus 24:8

living Father accepted the sacrifice and accepts us as we trust Christ's atoning death and serve God. In their separate roles, Father, Son, and Spirit remain one God. See note on Mt 3:16–17.

9:14 HOLY SPIRIT, Jesus—The Spirit empowered and guided Jesus to offer His life as a sacrifice to God to take away our sins. The Spirit guided and empowered Jesus throughout His public ministry. See note on Lk 4:14. The author of Hebrews indicated that the Spirit even helped Jesus up to the point of His self-sacrifice. The phrase "eternal Spirit" occurs only here in the Bible. This identifies the Spirit as God, who alone is eternal. All else is created.

9:14 SALVATION, As Cleansing—The death of Christ on the cross cleanses our consciences from dead works. The wrong way to salvation and the guilt blocking us from God are removed.

9:22 SALVATION, Forgiveness—There was no forgiveness of sins under the Law without the shedding of blood. Christ fulfilled the Law by shedding His blood. See note on Lev 17:11.

9:24–25 PRAYER, In Christ—See notes on 4:15–16; 7:25. The true sanctuary of God is heaven itself. The atmosphere is holy. Christ, who is perfectly holy (1 Pe 1:19), can rightfully enter that atmosphere. At the same time He is favorably disposed toward us.

9:26 HISTORY, Salvation—See notes on Ro 5:6; 1 Co 10:11. Christ's salvation is not based on a religious cycle in which rituals must be repeated at prescribed intervals to ensure salvation. Christ provided salvation in a one-time historical act which cannot and need not ever be repeated. His act separated time itself into the age of promise and the age of salvation.

9:27–28 HUMANITY, Death—As long as life as we know it endures, physical death shall be a part of its basic experience. We need not fear death because Christ has been raised from the dead and will return to give us eternal salvation.

9:27–28 LAST THINGS, Return Promises—Several events and truths attach to the return of Christ. Judgment follows death. A time of evaluation for determining rewards awaits all believers. See note on 2 Co 5:10. A time of eternal punishment awaits unbelievers. See note on Rev 20:11–15. The completion of salvation awaits Christ's return.

9:28 JESUS CHRIST, Final Coming—This verse gives rise to the term second coming of Christ. He will come to bring salvation to those who have accepted His solution to our sin problem. This is a firm and fast promise of our Lord's final appearing. Compare Mt 16:27; Ac 1:11; 1 Th 4:16.

9:28 SALVATION, Eternal Life—Salvation is a past event provided by Christ's sacrifice and experienced in individual lives through faith. It is a present reality of life in Christ. It remains a future event fully realized in the second coming by those who have believed, are experiencing salvation, and are awaiting the completion of our salvation.

9:28 LAST THINGS, Return Purposes—The common expression "the second coming of Christ" is not found in the Bible. This verse contains the nearest expression to such a phrase. The purpose for Christ appearing a second time is to bring salvation to those waiting for Him. The future completion of salvation is associated both with His return and our bodily resurrection (Ro 8:23).

10:1–18 JESUS CHRIST, Atonement—Jesus' atoning sacrifice came willfully in obedience to God and should free us to obey Him. His sacrifice brought forgiveness forever. No other ritual is needed to secure forgiveness.

longer have felt guilty for their sins.[s]
3But those sacrifices are an annual reminder of sins,[t] 4because it is impossible
for the blood of bulls and goats[u] to take
away sins.[v]
5Therefore, when Christ came into the
world,[w] he said:

"Sacrifice and offering you did not
desire,
but a body you prepared for me;[x]
6with burnt offerings and sin offerings
you were not pleased.
7Then I said, 'Here I am—it is written
about me in the scroll[y]—
I have come to do your will,
O God.' "[m] [z]

8First he said, "Sacrifices and offerings,
burnt offerings and sin offerings you did
not desire, nor were you pleased with
them"[a] (although the law required them
to be made). 9Then he said, "Here I am, I
have come to do your will."[b] He sets
aside the first to establish the second.
10And by that will, we have been made
holy[c] through the sacrifice of the body[d]
of Jesus Christ once for all.[e]
11Day after day every priest stands and
performs his religious duties; again and
again he offers the same sacrifices,[f]
which can never take away sins.[g] 12But
when this priest had offered for all time
one sacrifice for sins,[h] he sat down at the
right hand of God.[i] 13Since that time he
waits for his enemies to be made his footstool,[j] 14because by one sacrifice he has
made perfect[k] forever those who are being made holy.[l]
15The Holy Spirit also testifies[m] to us
about this. First he says:

16"This is the covenant I will make with
them
after that time, says the Lord.
I will put my laws in their hearts,
and I will write them on their
minds."[n] [n]

17Then he adds:

"Their sins and lawless acts
I will remember no more."[o] [o]

18And where these have been forgiven,
there is no longer any sacrifice for sin.

A Call to Persevere

19Therefore, brothers, since we have
confidence[p] to enter the Most Holy
Place[q] by the blood of Jesus, 20by a new
and living way[r] opened for us through
the curtain,[s] that is, his body, 21and
since we have a great priest[t] over the
house of God,[u] 22let us draw near to
God[v] with a sincere heart in full assurance of faith,[w] having our hearts sprinkled to cleanse us from a guilty conscience[x] and having our bodies washed

10:2 [s]Heb 9:9
10:3 [t]Lev 16:34; Heb 9:7
10:4 [u]Heb 9:12,13 [v]ver 1,11
10:5 [w]Heb 1:6 [x]Heb 2:14; 1Pe 2:24
10:7 [y]Ezr 6:2; Jer 36:2 [z]Ps 40:6-8; S Mt 26:39
10:8 [a]ver 5,6; S Mk 12:33
10:9 [b]ver 7
10:10 [c]ver 14; S Eph 5:26 [d]Heb 2:14; 1Pe 2:24 [e]S Heb 7:27
10:11 [f]Heb 5:1 [g]ver 1,4
10:12 [h]Heb 5:1 [i]S Mk 16:19
10:13 [j]Jos 10:24; Heb 1:13
10:14 [k]ver 1 [l]ver 10; S Eph 5:26
10:15 [m]S Heb 3:7
10:16 [n]Jer 31:33; Heb 8:10
10:17 [o]Jer 31:34; Heb 8:12
10:19 [p]S Eph 3:12 [q]Lev 16:2; Eph 2:18; Heb 9:8, 12,25
10:20 [r]Heb 9:8 [s]Heb 6:19; 9:3
10:21 [t]S Heb 2:17 [u]S Heb 3:6
10:22 [v]ver 1; S Heb 7:19 [w]Eph 3:12 [x]Eze 36:25; Heb 9:14; 12:24; 1Pe 1:2

[m]*7* Psalm 40:6-8 (see Septuagint) [n]*16* Jer. 31:33 [o]*17* Jer. 31:34

10:10–39 ELECTION, Perseverance—In Christ redemption is accomplished and election assured. His once-for-all sacrifice provides forgiveness for the elect. No additional sin sacrifice is needed. The elect claim Christ's sacrifice in faith and change from life dominated by sin to life marked by steadfast faith. All God's provisions for salvation through Christ must be appropriated by faith.

10:10–19 SALVATION, Atonement—God's will is that we be made holy by the once-for-all sacrifice of the body of Jesus Christ. "Perfect" in v 14 means perfectly adequate. It does not mean that believers are without sin. Christ has provided all we need for forgiveness and salvation. No other sacrifice for sin can now be made or will ever need to be made than the one Christ made. His sacrifice on the cross opened up the Most Holy Place to all persons.

10:10 THE CHURCH, People of God—By the once and for all sacrifice of Jesus Christ on the cross, all people may know new life and the forgiveness of sins. Through Christ, we may become the people He wants us to be. His death and resurrection established the church, the new covenant people of God.

10:15 HOLY SPIRIT, Revelation—The Spirit reveals God by inspiring the writing of Scripture. See 3:7; 9:8. It is equally appropriate to say that He revealed, past tense (9:8), or that He reveals, present tense (here, 3:7); for the Spirit who first led people to write the Scriptures (2 Pe 2:21) continues to guide God's people to understand them, as Hebrews shows clearly. The Spirit is the Inspirer of Scriptures and the constant Teacher of Scriptures for us.

10:16–17 THE CHURCH, Covenant People—Forgiveness is the key element of Christ's new covenant. Because He guarantees forgiveness, no new or repeated sacrifice is needed. See notes on 8:6—9:28; Jer 31:31–34.

10:17–18 SALVATION, Forgiveness —See note on 8:12.

10:19–22 DISCIPLESHIP, Priesthood—All disciples have access to God and are encouraged to persevere because of sure hope in God's faithfulness. Each disciple is encouraged to minister to others by encouraging them in a life of neighbor love expressed in good deeds. Every disciple has a priestly responsibility in relation to others. See note on 1 Ti 2:5.

10:19–25 WORSHIP, Importance—The Bible admonishes us to approach God in confident worship. The reminder of the need for individual worship is followed by a call to corporate worship. Worship always involves individuals and God. It is not the experience of a spectator. Worship means personal involvement. We do not watch worship; we worship. No greater privilege exists today in the church. See note on Ps 42:1–4.

10:19–22 PRAYER, In Christ—See note on 4:15–16. These verses are the Christian's guarantee of access to God. The High Priest is Himself a living way into God's presence. His sacrifice has cleansed us from sin that would prohibit our entering God's holy presence. We are required only to have sincerity and faith. Then we can say whatever we desire to God, knowing Christ is on our side.

10:22 ORDINANCES, Baptism as Cleansing—All of Hebrews uses the worship practices of the Old Testament as a picture of Christian life and worship. The priests had to be washed with pure water before they exercised their religious duties. See note on Lev 8:6. Christians are all priests and ministers of God. Baptism is similar to the washing of the Levitical priests in that it publicly symbolizes cleansing and dedication for service. Having their "hearts sprinkled" and their bodies "washed" is a parallelism such as we have throughout the Bible, showing that both the inward cleansing (heart) and the outward washing (of the body) must take place in valid Christian baptism. Only full immersion can be called "having our body washed."

with pure water.[y] 23Let us hold unswervingly to the hope[z] we profess,[a] for he
who promised is faithful.[b] 24And let us
consider how we may spur one another
on toward love and good deeds.[c] 25Let us
not give up meeting together,[d] as some
are in the habit of doing, but let us encourage one another[e]—and all the more
as you see the Day approaching.[f]

26If we deliberately keep on sinning[g]
after we have received the knowledge of
the truth,[h] no sacrifice for sins is left,
27but only a fearful expectation of judgment and of raging fire[i] that will consume the enemies of God. 28Anyone who
rejected the law of Moses died without
mercy on the testimony of two or three
witnesses.[j] 29How much more severely
do you think a man deserves to be punished who has trampled the Son of God[k]
under foot,[l] who has treated as an unholy thing the blood of the covenant[m] that
sanctified him,[n] and who has insulted
the Spirit[o] of grace?[p] 30For we know him
who said, "It is mine to avenge; I will
repay,"[p][q] and again, "The Lord will
judge his people."[q][r] 31It is a dreadful
thing[s] to fall into the hands[t] of the living God.[u]

32Remember those earlier days after
you had received the light,[v] when you
stood your ground in a great contest in
the face of suffering.[w] 33Sometimes you
were publicly exposed to insult and persecution;[x] at other times you stood side
by side with those who were so treated.[y]
34You sympathized with those in prison[z]
and joyfully accepted the confiscation of
your property, because you knew that
you yourselves had better and lasting possessions.[a]

35So do not throw away your confidence;[b] it will be richly rewarded. 36You
need to persevere[c] so that when you
have done the will of God, you will receive what he has promised.[d] 37For in
just a very little while,

"He who is coming[e] will come and
will not delay.[f]
38 But my righteous one[r] will live by
faith.[g]
And if he shrinks back,
I will not be pleased with him."[s] [h]

39But we are not of those who shrink
back and are destroyed, but of those who
believe and are saved.

Chapter 11

By Faith

NOW faith is being sure of what we
hope for[i] and certain of what we do

10:22 [y]S Ac 22:16 **10:23** [z]S Heb 3:6 [a]S Heb 3:1 [b]S 1Co 1:9 **10:24** [c]S Tit 2:14 **10:25** [d]Ac 2:42 [e]Heb 3:13 [f]S 1Co 3:13 **10:26** [g]Ex 21:14; Nu 15:30; Heb 5:2; 6:4-8; 2Pe 2:20 [h]S 1Ti 2:4 **10:27** [i]Isa 26:11; 2Th 1:7; Heb 9:27; 12:29 **10:28** [j]Dt 17:6,7; S Mt 18:16; Heb 2:2 **10:29** [k]S Mt 4:3 [l]Heb 6:6 [m]S Mt 26:28 [n]1Co 6:11; Rev 1:5 [o]Eph 4:30; Heb 6:4 [p]Heb 2:3; 12:25 **10:30** [q]Dt 32:35; Ro 12:19 [r]Dt 32:36; Ps 135:14 **10:31** [s]S 2Co 5:11 [t]Isa 19:16 [u]S Mt 16:16 **10:32** [v]Heb 6:4 [w]Php 1:29,30 **10:33** [x]1Co 4:9 [y]Php 4:14; 1Th 2:14 **10:34** [z]Heb 13:3 [a]Heb 11:16; 1Pe 1:4,5 **10:35** [b]S Eph 3:12 **10:36** [c]Ro 5:3; Heb 12:1; Jas 1:3,4, 12; 5:11; 2Pe 1:6 [d]Heb 6:15; 9:15 **10:37** [e]Mt 11:3 [f]Rev 22:20 **10:38** [g]Ro 1:17; Gal 3:11 [h]Hab 2:3,4 **11:1** [i]S Heb 3:6

[p]*30* Deut. 32:35 [q]*30* Deut. 32:36; Psalm 135:14
[r]*38* One early manuscript *But the righteous*
[s]*38* Hab. 2:3,4

10:24–25 DISCIPLESHIP, Neighbor Love—Isolation and individualism are opposed to Christ. Christ brings us together as a family. Christians seek ways to encourage one another to express love through good deeds. Communal worship is one way we gain strength and motivation from other disciples. See note on Ro 12:10.

10:25 LAST THINGS, Encourages Faithfulness—The end time is spoken of as the "day of the Lord" or simply "the Day." See note on Joel 2:28–32. Its certain approach is an encouragement to faithful assembly of believers. The coming day of judgment upon evil and of reward for good is cause for continued personal faithfulness as well as of encouraging others to be faithful.

10:26–31 GOD, Living—Church members need to fear the living Judge as well as do unbelievers outside the church. Hebrews constantly calls church members to check the authenticity of their confession. God's judgment is not based on membership lists. It is based on dedication to Christ. Those who pretend to belong to God face the most severe judgment.

10:26–29 SIN, Judgment—Sin that is continual and deliberate always will produce the judgment of God. This text is closely related to 6:4–6,17–20 in which the terrible sin of falling away from Christ is stated in the strongest terms, followed by a promise of assurance based on the promise of God and the sacrifice of Christ. Here the same terrible sin is asserted in vv 26–31, followed by an appeal to recall "the former days" (vv 32–34), followed again by a statement of hope (vv 35–39). Perhaps v 39 holds the key to this text; it asserts that the soul that truly believes (has genuinely been saved) will not "shrink back" and be "destroyed." See note on 6:1–6.

10:26–31 LAST THINGS, Judgment—Persistent, willful sin shall incur God's wrath in judgment. The punishment of fire is associated with that judgment (Mt 25:41). God will take justified vengeance on human sinfulness. This text refers specifically to those who have been confronted by the truth about Christ and have willfully and continuously scorned that truth. Humans cannot judge the point at which God will act to judge such people. Our responsibility is to continue to witness to them. To meet the avenging God will be dreadful. The threat should cause people to think twice about continuing in sin and ignoring God's offer of salvation in Christ.

10:32–39 EVIL AND SUFFERING, Endurance—Suffering because we are Christians may tempt us to forsake our faith. Memory of past experiences can give us courage to face present persecution. Christian endurance is never complete until our Master returns. We can trust Him. His reward justifies all the suffering we must endure.

10:32–34 LAST THINGS, Encourages Faithfulness—The knowledge of eternal reward encourages faithful endurance of opposition and persecution. Personal suffering and public shame, sympathy with others who suffer, and loss of possessions are bearable when set against the bright prospect of the heavenly possessions awaiting those who are faithful.

11:1—12:1 REVELATION, History—History is the story of God's saving presence leading people to faith and providing testimony which encourages us to persevere in our faith.

11:1–40 HISTORY, Faith—Faith involves absolute confidence in God's historical saving acts. The nature of faith leads to deep involvement in the historical world not isolation and escape into a life of meditation.

11:1–40 SALVATION, Belief—The roll call of faith illustrates the nature of belief in God. Faith is action based on certainty without physical evidence. Faith pleases God. Knowledge of God comes only through faith, since God is invisible. Faith is the human action which God counts as righteousness to wipe out all sin charged against us. Faith trusts God's promises even when they appear impossible. Faith reaches out to the eternal reward God has promised. Faith obeys God even when the divine demand appears unreasonable. Faith fears no human, only God. Faith identifies with God's people no matter how disadvantaged they are. Faith perseveres even when no reward is in sight. The faith of all Israel's heroes found its goal

not see.[j] 2This is what the ancients were commended for.[k]

3By faith we understand that the universe was formed at God's command,[l] so that what is seen was not made out of what was visible.

4By faith Abel offered God a better sacrifice than Cain did. By faith he was commended[m] as a righteous man, when God spoke well of his offerings.[n] And by faith he still speaks, even though he is dead.[o]

5By faith Enoch was taken from this life, so that he did not experience death; he could not be found, because God had taken him away.[p] For before he was taken, he was commended as one who pleased God. 6And without faith it is impossible to please God, because anyone who comes to him[q] must believe that he exists and that he rewards those who earnestly seek him.

7By faith Noah, when warned about things not yet seen,[r] in holy fear built an ark[s] to save his family.[t] By his faith he condemned the world and became heir of the righteousness that comes by faith.[u]

8By faith Abraham, when called to go to a place he would later receive as his inheritance,[v] obeyed and went,[w] even though he did not know where he was going. 9By faith he made his home in the promised land[x] like a stranger in a foreign country; he lived in tents,[y] as did Isaac and Jacob, who were heirs with him of the same promise.[z] 10For he was looking forward to the city[a] with foundations,[b] whose architect and builder is God.[c]

11By faith Abraham, even though he was past age—and Sarah herself was barren[d]—was enabled to become a father[e] because he[t] considered him faithful[f] who had made the promise. 12And so from this one man, and he as good as dead,[g] came descendants as numerous as the stars in the sky and as countless as the sand on the seashore.[h]

13All these people were still living by faith when they died. They did not receive the things promised;[i] they only saw them and welcomed them from a distance.[j] And they admitted that they were aliens and strangers on earth.[k] 14People who say such things show that they are looking for a country of their own. 15If they had been thinking of the country they had left, they would have had opportunity to return.[l] 16Instead, they were longing for a better country—a heavenly one.[m] Therefore God is not ashamed[n] to be called their God,[o] for he has prepared a city[p] for them.

17By faith Abraham, when God tested him, offered Isaac as a sacrifice.[q] He who had received the promises was about to sacrifice his one and only son, 18even though God had said to him, "It is through Isaac that your offspring[u] will be reckoned."[v][r] 19Abraham reasoned that God could raise the dead,[s] and figuratively speaking, he did receive Isaac back from death.

20By faith Isaac blessed Jacob and Esau in regard to their future.[t]

21By faith Jacob, when he was dying, blessed each of Joseph's sons,[u] and worshiped as he leaned on the top of his staff.

22By faith Joseph, when his end was near, spoke about the exodus of the Israelites from Egypt and gave instructions about his bones.[v]

23By faith Moses' parents hid him for three months after he was born,[w] because they saw he was no ordinary child, and they were not afraid of the king's edict.[x]

24By faith Moses, when he had grown up, refused to be known as the son of Pharaoh's daughter.[y] 25He chose to be mistreated[z] along with the people of God rather than to enjoy the pleasures of sin for a short time. 26He regarded disgrace[a] for the sake of Christ[b] as of greater value than the treasures of Egypt, because he was looking ahead to his reward.[c] 27By

[t] *11* Or *By faith even Sarah, who was past age, was enabled to bear children because she* [u] *18* Greek *seed* [v] *18* Gen. 21:12

11:1 [j]S 2Co 4:18
11:2 [k]ver 4,39
11:3 [l]Ge 1; Jn 1:3; Heb 1:2; 2Pe 3:5
11:4 [m]ver 2,39 [n]Ge 4:4; 1Jn 3:12 [o]Heb 12:24
11:5 [p]Ge 5:21-24
11:6 [q]Heb 7:19
11:7 [r]S ver 1 [s]Ge 6:13-22 [t]1Pe 3:20 [u]Ge 6:9; Eze 14:14,20; S Ro 9:30
11:8 [v]Ge 12:7 [w]Ge 12:1-4; Ac 7:2-4
11:9 [x]Ac 7:5 [y]Ge 12:8; 18:1,9 [z]Heb 6:17
11:10 [a]Heb 12:22; 13:14 [b]Rev 21:2,14 [c]ver 16
11:11 [d]Ge 17:17-19; 18:11-14 [e]Ge 21:2 [f]S 1Co 1:9
11:12 [g]Ro 4:19 [h]Ge 22:17
11:13 [i]ver 39 [j]S Mt 13:17 [k]Ge 23:4; Lev 25:23; Php 3:20; 1Pe 1:17; 2:11
11:15 [l]Ge 24:6-8
11:16 [m]2Ti 4:18 [n]Mk 8:38 [o]Ge 26:24; 28:13; Ex 3:6,15 [p]ver 10; Heb 13:14
11:17 [q]Ge 22:1-10; Jas 2:21
11:18 [r]Ge 21:12; Ro 9:7
11:19 [s]Ro 4:21; S Jn 5:21
11:20 [t]Ge 27:27-29,39,40
11:21 [u]Ge 48:1, 8-22
11:22 [v]Ge 50:24, 25; Ex 13:19; Jos 24:32
11:23 [w]Ex 2:2 [x]Ex 1:16,22
11:24 [y]Ex 2:10,11
11:25 [z]ver 37
11:26 [a]Heb 13:13 [b]Lk 14:33 [c]Heb 10:35

and reward in Christ and His atoning work.

11:3 CREATION, Personal Creator—The world had a beginning point when out of nothing God created an ordered universe. The Christian experience of faith begins by accepting a personal Creator as the foundation for life. We do not prove a divine Creator through human logic but come by faith to our conviction that God created the world by His word.

11:6 GOD, One God—Christian life begins by affirming, "God exists." It leads to confession, "He exists for me." Such statements do not come automatically. We must hear the gospel message, experience the Holy Spirit in our lives, and give up self-centered thinking.

11:7 SALVATION, Fear of God—Noah's holy fear caused him to build the ark. Such obedient reverence of God comes from faith.

11:8 SALVATION, Obedience—By faith Abraham obeyed God even without knowing his destination. The Christian life is an Abrahamic journey of obedient faith.

11:13–16 LAST THINGS, Heaven—Those who lived as faithful servants of God before Christ came had the disadvantage of not knowing the kingdom covenant which Christ brought. They will share in the heavenly home, as do those who live by faith in Christ. Compare 13:14; Jn 14:2; Rev 21:2–4. When citizenship in heaven is our goal, God claims us as His own.

11:25–28 EVIL AND SUFFERING, Endurance—Disciples need to follow Moses' example in choosing suffering rather than the pleasures of sin.

11:27 GOD, Presence—God is present in the world with His people. Moses "saw" the invisible God, whose presence was very real to him. Confident of God's presence, Moses carried out the task God had given him. As Heavenly Father,

faith he left Egypt,[d] not fearing the king's
anger; he persevered because he saw him
who is invisible. 28By faith he kept the
Passover and the sprinkling of blood, so
that the destroyer[e] of the firstborn would
not touch the firstborn of Israel.[f]
29By faith the people passed through
the Red Sea[w] as on dry land; but when
the Egyptians tried to do so, they were
drowned.[g]
30By faith the walls of Jericho fell, after
the people had marched around them for
seven days.[h]
31By faith the prostitute Rahab, because
she welcomed the spies, was not killed
with those who were disobedient.[x] [i]
32And what more shall I say? I do not
have time to tell about Gideon,[j] Barak,[k]
Samson,[l] Jephthah,[m] David,[n] Samuel[o]
and the prophets, 33who through faith
conquered kingdoms,[p] administered justice, and gained what was promised; who
shut the mouths of lions,[q] 34quenched
the fury of the flames,[r] and escaped the
edge of the sword;[s] whose weakness was
turned to strength;[t] and who became
powerful in battle and routed foreign armies.[u] 35Women received back their
dead, raised to life again.[v] Others were
tortured and refused to be released, so
that they might gain a better resurrection. 36Some faced jeers and flogging,[w]
while still others were chained and put in
prison.[x] 37They were stoned[y];[y] they
were sawed in two; they were put to
death by the sword.[z] They went about in
sheepskins and goatskins,[a] destitute, persecuted and mistreated— 38the world
was not worthy of them. They wandered
in deserts and mountains, and in caves[b]
and holes in the ground.
39These were all commended[c] for
their faith, yet none of them received
what had been promised.[d] 40God had
planned something better for us so that
only together with us[e] would they be
made perfect.[f]

11:27 [d]Ex 12:50, 51
11:28 [e]1Co 10:10 [f]Ex 12:21-23
11:29 [g]Ex 14:21-31
11:30 [h]Jos 6:12-20
11:31 [i]Jos 2:1,9-14; 6:22-25; Jas 2:25
11:32 [j]Jdg 6-8 [k]Jdg 4-5 [l]Jdg 13-16 [m]Jdg 11-12 [n]1Sa 16:1,13 [o]1Sa 1:20
11:33 [p]2Sa 8:1-3 [q]Da 6:22
11:34 [r]Da 3:19-27 [s]Ex 18:4 [t]2Ki 20:7 [u]Jdg 15:8
11:35 [v]1Ki 17:22, 23; 2Ki 4:36,37
11:36 [w]Jer 20:2; 37:15 [x]Ge 39:20
11:37 [y]2Ch 24:21 [z]1Ki 19:10; Jer 26:23 [a]2Ki 1:8
11:38 [b]1Ki 18:4; 19:9
11:39 [c]ver 2,4 [d]ver 13; Heb 10:36
11:40 [e]Rev 6:11 [f]S Heb 2:10
12:1 [g]S 1Co 9:24 [h]S Heb 10:36
12:2 [i]Ps 25:15 [j]Heb 2:10 [k]Php 2:8, 9; Heb 2:9 [l]Heb 13:13 [m]S Mk 16:19
12:3 [n]Gal 6:9; Rev 2:3
12:4 [o]Heb 10:32-34; 13:13
12:5 [p]ver 3
12:6 [q]Ps 94:12; 119:75; Rev 3:19 [r]Pr 3:11,12
12:7 [s]Dt 8:5; 2Sa 7:14; Pr 13:24
12:8 [t]1Pe 5:9
12:9 [u]Nu 16:22; 27:16; Rev 22:6 [v]Isa 38:16

Chapter 12

God Disciplines His Sons

THEREFORE, since we are surrounded
by such a great cloud of witnesses,
let us throw off everything that hinders
and the sin that so easily entangles, and
let us run[g] with perseverance[h] the race
marked out for us. 2Let us fix our eyes on
Jesus,[i] the author[j] and perfecter of our
faith, who for the joy set before him endured the cross,[k] scorning its shame,[l]
and sat down at the right hand of the
throne of God.[m] 3Consider him who endured such opposition from sinful men,
so that you will not grow weary[n] and lose
heart.
4In your struggle against sin, you have
not yet resisted to the point of shedding
your blood.[o] 5And you have forgotten
that word of encouragement that addresses you as sons:

"My son, do not make light of the
Lord's discipline,
and do not lose heart[p] when he
rebukes you,
6because the Lord disciplines those he
loves,[q]
and he punishes everyone he
accepts as a son."[z] [r]

7Endure hardship as discipline; God is
treating you as sons.[s] For what son is not
disciplined by his father? 8If you are not
disciplined (and everyone undergoes discipline),[t] then you are illegitimate children and not true sons. 9Moreover, we
have all had human fathers who disciplined us and we respected them for it.
How much more should we submit to the
Father of our spirits[u] and live![v] 10Our
fathers disciplined us for a little while as
they thought best; but God disciplines us
for our good, that we may share in his

[w]29 That is, Sea of Reeds [x]31 Or *unbelieving*
[y]37 Some early manuscripts *stoned; they were put to the test;* [z]6 Prov. 3:11,12

God does not forsake His people. He is always accessible to them. Through His presence, we overcome all obstacles to accomplish His mission. See note on Mt 6:1–34.

11:32–39 EVIL AND SUFFERING, Endurance—Earlier heroes of the faith faced suffering courageously. Some experienced deliverance from suffering in this life, but others died for their faith. Christ's resurrection gives us even more reason to remain faithful in suffering and wait for our reward.

12:1–3 JESUS CHRIST, Suffering—In persecution and trouble Jesus becomes our example. If He could endure the cross, what suffering is too great for us? He is our leader, the "author" (Greek *archēgos*) of our faith. See note on 2:10–18.

12:1–11 EVIL AND SUFFERING, Testing—Jesus set the example by His suffering and death. Christians should see our suffering as a divine discipline similar to a father's discipline of a child. Parental discipline grows from love not hate. God shows His love for us by disciplining us to lead us back to Him and to encourage us to endure life's suffering in faithfulness to Him.

12:2 SALVATION, Joy—Jesus is our example in suffering. He endured the cross, knowing the joy His suffering would bring to the world. The agony of suffering love always produces the ecstasy of holy joy.

12:4–11 THE CHURCH, God's Community—Discipline is a mark of sonship. The church as a community, and each member individually, struggles against temptation and sin. God helps in the struggle by rebuking and disciplining us. Receiving His discipline means we are His beloved sons. We can be sure God's discipline is good for us. It should lead us to reverence and worship Him and to live more faithful lives. See note on Hos 1:10–11.

12:5–12 GOD, Father—As a Father who is both righteous and loving, God disciplines His children. His discipline is not just a venting of wrath, "giving us what we deserve." His punishment of us has purpose—it is part of the necessary process of bringing us to responsible maturity, making us His holy people. It is God's sign of love and care, leading us to Him and away from the final judgment.

holiness.[w] 11No discipline seems pleasant
at the time, but painful. Later on, however, it produces a harvest of righteousness
and peace[x] for those who have been
trained by it.
12Therefore, strengthen your feeble
arms and weak knees.[y] 13"Make level
paths for your feet,"[a][z] so that the lame
may not be disabled, but rather healed.[a]

Warning Against Refusing God

14Make every effort to live in peace
with all men[b] and to be holy;[c] without
holiness no one will see the Lord.[d] 15See
to it that no one misses the grace of God[e]
and that no bitter root[f] grows up to
cause trouble and defile many. 16See that
no one is sexually immoral,[g] or is godless
like Esau, who for a single meal sold his
inheritance rights as the oldest son.[h]
17Afterward, as you know, when he wanted to inherit this blessing, he was rejected. He could bring about no change of
mind, though he sought the blessing with
tears.[i]
18You have not come to a mountain
that can be touched and that is burning
with fire; to darkness, gloom and storm;[j]
19to a trumpet blast[k] or to such a voice
speaking words[l] that those who heard it
begged that no further word be spoken to
them,[m] 20because they could not bear
what was commanded: "If even an animal touches the mountain, it must be
stoned."[b][n] 21The sight was so terrifying
that Moses said, "I am trembling with
fear."[c][o]
22But you have come to Mount Zion,[p]
to the heavenly Jerusalem,[q] the city[r] of
the living God.[s] You have come to thousands upon thousands of angels in joyful
assembly, 23to the church of the firstborn,[t] whose names are written in heav-
en.[u] You have come to God, the judge of
all men,[v] to the spirits of righteous men
made perfect,[w] 24to Jesus the mediator[x]
of a new covenant, and to the sprinkled
blood[y] that speaks a better word than the
blood of Abel.[z]
25See to it that you do not refuse[a] him
who speaks.[b] If they did not escape
when they refused him who warned[c]
them on earth, how much less will we, if
we turn away from him who warns us
from heaven?[d] 26At that time his voice
shook the earth,[e] but now he has promised, "Once more I will shake not only
the earth but also the heavens."[d][f] 27The
words "once more" indicate the removing of what can be shaken[g]—that is, created things—so that what cannot be
shaken may remain.
28Therefore, since we are receiving a
kingdom that cannot be shaken,[h] let us
be thankful, and so worship God acceptably with reverence and awe,[i] 29for our
"God is a consuming fire."[e][j]

Chapter 13

Concluding Exhortations

KEEP on loving each other as brothers.[k] 2Do not forget to entertain

[a] *13* Prov. 4:26 [b] *20* Exodus 19:12,13 [c] *21* Deut. 9:19 [d] *26* Haggai 2:6 [e] *29* Deut. 4:24

12:10 [w]S 2Pe 1:4
12:11 [x]Isa 32:17; Jas 3:17,18
12:12 [y]Isa 35:3
12:13 [z]Pr 4:26 [a]Gal 6:1
12:14 [b]S Ro 14:19 [c]Ro 6:22 [d]S Mt 5:8
12:15 [e]Gal 5:4; Heb 3:12; 4:1 [f]Dt 29:18
12:16 [g]S 1Co 6:18 [h]Ge 25:29-34
12:17 [i]Ge 27:30-40
12:18 [j]Ex 19:12-22; 20:18; Dt 4:11
12:19 [k]Ex 20:18 [l]Dt 4:12 [m]Ex 20:19; Dt 5:5, 25; 18:16
12:20 [n]Ex 19:12, 13
12:21 [o]Dt 9:19
12:22 [p]Isa 24:23; 60:14; Rev 14:1 [q]S Gal 4:26 [r]Heb 11:10; 13:14 [s]S Mt 16:16
12:23 [t]Ex 4:22 [u]S Rev 20:12 [v]Ge 18:25; Ps 94:2 [w]Php 3:12
12:24 [x]S Gal 3:20 [y]Heb 9:19; 10:22; 1Pe 1:2 [z]Ge 4:10; Heb 11:4
12:25 [a]Heb 3:12 [b]S Heb 1:1 [c]Heb 8:5; 11:7 [d]Dt 18:19; Heb 2:2, 3; 10:29
12:26 [e]Ex 19:18 [f]Hag 2:6
12:27 [g]Isa 34:4; 54:10; 1Co 7:31; Heb 1:11,12; 2Pe 3:10; 1Jn 2:17
12:28 [h]Ps 15:5; Da 2:44 [i]Mal 2:5; 4:2; Heb 13:15
12:29 [j]Ex 24:17; Dt 4:24; 9:3; Ps 97:3; Isa 33:14; S 2Th 1:7
13:1 [k]S Ro 12:10

12:14–17 CHRISTIAN ETHICS, Character—The life of peace characterized by a spirit of forgiveness and reconciliation is to be a distinguishing facet of the Christian's life-style. This peace can be recognized by its application to prevent boiling over of quarrels into fullscale breakdowns in relationships and by its continual presence in all day-to-day activities.

12:15–16 SIN, Unbelief—Hebrews addressed an audience wanting to face two directions at once—the security of a Jewish legal system and the freedom as a slave of Christ. The inspired writer urged them to face full forward toward Christ and forget legalism. The gravest sin they could commit would be to try to earn salvation through the law and miss the way of grace. Any system that encourages us to accomplish something to be saved leads to the sin of unbelief in the grace of Christ and in the sufficiency of His saving work through the cross and resurrection. The other side is that grace does not give unlimited moral freedom. It frees us from slavery to sin so we may follow Christ in the ways of peace, holiness, and purity.

12:22–24 LAST THINGS, Encourages Faithfulness—The gospel brings one to an awesome experience of the new covenant promises as opposed to old covenant fear (Ex 19:10–25; 20:18–21). Seeing the glorious company we keep and the awesome reality of the one universal Judge, we should eagerly obey the gospel and let the blood of Christ cover our sins. To refuse the gospel is to face the Judge for punishment.

12:24 SALVATION, Atonement—See note on Eze 16:63. Christ is the Mediator of the new covenant which God made with His people. His atonement for our sins makes it possible for us to participate in His new covenant.

12:24 THE CHURCH, Covenant People—People such as Abel (Ge 4:8) died unjustly. Their faithfulness sets a fine example for us, but what they did cannot compare with the atoning death of Christ, which established the new covenant (Lk 22:20). See note on Heb 7:22.

12:25–29 LAST THINGS, Coming Kingdom—The judgment of God upon the present world order will be as a shaking of the heavens and the earth. The purpose is to reveal the durable or eternal things that cannot be shaken. Chief among these is the coming kingdom of God. It will be eternal. The thought of the coming kingdom should lead people to grateful, reverent worship.

12:26–28 CREATION, Purposeful—The writer saw many things around him crumbling. One thing gave him confidence. He knew God had created a world with moral and spiritual values in it that would endure even if the external things about him dissolved. Chief among the things that "cannot be shaken" is God's kingdom of love and righteousness, an integral part of the world He brought into being through His creative powers. The material universe is not eternal. God's kingdom is.

12:28 WORSHIP, Thanksgiving—As we are "thankful," so we shall worship the Lord. See notes on Lev 9:23–24; 2 Sa 22:1–51; 1 Ch 16:4.

12:28–29 PRAYER, Worship—See note on Ro 12:1. The inheritance that belongs to Christians and the awesomeness of God make worship and grateful prayer logical actions.

13:1–3 DISCIPLESHIP, Neighbor Love—Christian love has no limits. It reaches out to everyone in need . . . strangers, brothers, prisoners, sufferers. Christians should keep on loving one another as brothers and sisters in Christ. See note on Ro

strangers,[l] for by so doing some people
have entertained angels without knowing
it.[m] 3Remember those in prison[n] as if
you were their fellow prisoners, and
those who are mistreated as if you yourselves were suffering.
4Marriage should be honored by all,[o]
and the marriage bed kept pure, for God
will judge the adulterer and all the sexually immoral.[p] 5Keep your lives free from
the love of money[q] and be content with
what you have,[r] because God has said,

"Never will I leave you;
never will I forsake you."[f] [s]

6So we say with confidence,

"The Lord is my helper; I will not be
afraid.
What can man do to me?"[g] [t]

7Remember your leaders,[u] who spoke
the word of God[v] to you. Consider the
outcome of their way of life and imitate[w]
their faith. 8Jesus Christ is the same yesterday and today and forever.[x]
9Do not be carried away by all kinds of
strange teachings.[y] It is good for our
hearts to be strengthened[z] by grace, not
by ceremonial foods,[a] which are of no
value to those who eat them.[b] 10We have
an altar from which those who minister
at the tabernacle[c] have no right to eat.[d]
11The high priest carries the blood of
animals into the Most Holy Place as a sin
offering,[e] but the bodies are burned outside the camp.[f] 12And so Jesus also suffered outside the city gate[g] to make the
people holy[h] through his own blood.[i]
13Let us, then, go to him[j] outside the
camp, bearing the disgrace he bore.[k]
14For here we do not have an enduring
city,[l] but we are looking for the city that
is to come.[m]
15Through Jesus, therefore, let us continually offer to God a sacrifice[n] of
praise—the fruit of lips[o] that confess his
name. 16And do not forget to do good and
to share with others,[p] for with such sacrifices[q] God is pleased.
17Obey your leaders[r] and submit to

13:2 [l]Job 31:32; Mt 25:35; S Ro 12:13 [m]Ge 18:1-33; 19:1-3 **13:3** [n]Mt 25:36; Col 4:18; Heb 10:34 **13:4** [o]Mal 2:15; 1Co 7:38; 1Ti 4:3 [p]Dt 22:22; 1Co 6:9; Rev 22:15 **13:5** [q]S 1Ti 3:3 [r]Php 4:11; 1Ti 6:6, 8 [s]Dt 31:6,8; Jos 1:5 **13:6** [t]Ps 118:6,7 **13:7** [u]ver 17,24; 1Co 16:16 [v]S Heb 4:12 [w]Heb 6:12 **13:8** [x]Ps 102:27; Heb 1:12 **13:9** [y]Eph 4:14 [z]Col 2:7 [a]Col 2:16 [b]Heb 9:10 **13:10** [c]Heb 8:5 [d]1Co 9:13; 10:18 **13:11** [e]Lev 16:15 [f]Ex 29:14; Lev 4:12,21; 9:11; 16:27 **13:12** [g]Jn 19:17 [h]S Eph 5:26 [i]S Ro 3:25 **13:13** [j]Lk 9:23 [k]Heb 11:26 **13:14** [l]Heb 12:27 [m]Php 3:20; Heb 11:10,27; 12:22 **13:15** [n]1Pe 2:5 [o]Isa 57:19; Hos 14:2 **13:16** [p]Ro 12:13 [q]Php 4:18 **13:17** [r]ver 7,24

[f]5 Deut. 31:6 [g]6 Psalm 118:6,7

12:10; 13:8.

13:2 REVELATION, Angels—See note on Ge 18:1—19:29.

13:3 PRAYER, Sincerity—An important principle of prayer is to make the cause you are praying for your own. Christ identified with the disciples He prayed for. See note on Jn 17:1–26.

13:4 FAMILY, Sexual Fulfillment—Marriage vows must not be taken lightly. Marriage means fidelity and commitment to one's spouse. Sexual activity outside marriage is sin which faces God's judgment. Only as partners honor marriage can sexual union bring its intended fulfillment. See notes on Pr 5:15–23; 1 Co 7:2–7.

13:5 CHRISTIAN ETHICS, Property Rights—See notes on 1 Ti 6:3–10, 17–19.

13:7,17 DISCIPLESHIP, Spiritual Leaders—All disciples are responsible to God for all they do. Those called to be spiritual leaders such as pastors and teachers (Eph 4:11) are responsible in a special way for the spiritual welfare of all whom they serve. They are God's special messengers, and their lives become models to be imitated by those who follow their leadership. All disciples are responsible for the way they submit to their spiritual leaders. Spiritual leaders should be supported with love and respect so their ministries will be both joyful and successful. That will be beneficial to all. Spiritual leaders exercise authority in love in the church. Such leaders are not dictators, but they do deserve respectful obedience as they seek to keep order and purpose in the church. Such leaders should stay on the alert to prevent harm to God's people. They should exercise authority carefully, knowing they are responsible to God. Proper spiritual leadership is a real advantage for God's people. Both improper leadership and improper followship are burdensome for the leader and the church. No leader has the authority to rob any member of the right and responsibility to exercise individual priesthood before God. See note on 1 Ti 2:5.

13:7 CHURCH LEADERS, Authority—Leaders of the church are to be faithful in instructing their charges in the Word of God and to lead by example. The testimony of their lives for good or ill will continue to instruct the church even after they have died.

13:8 JESUS CHRIST, Savior—We have no excuse to return to inferior ethics or religion. Our Savior is eternal and consistent. We can always count on Him for salvation and need turn to no other savior or religion.

13:11–14 EVIL AND SUFFERING, Endurance—Christians should expect to suffer the type of abuse endured by a criminal taken outside the city gate for execution. In so doing we will suffer as Christ did. Disgrace in the world's eyes can be the mark of Christian endurance.

13:15–16 DISCIPLESHIP, Involvement—Praise and practice work together as proper offerings. The writer of Hebrews wrote powerful, deep theological truths to lead his Jewish readers outside the Jewish camp to Jesus, the only High Priest. He showed that worship which truly pleases God centers not on ritual but on Jesus. Such worship is authenticated by good works of love for other people. This too is proper worship, pleasing God. Only as Christian love involves us in the lives of needy, hurting people are we Christ's disciples. See note on Lk 14:34–35.

13:15–16 PRAYER, Praise—The Old Testament required offerings and sacrifices of animals. In the New Testament a number of offerings and sacrifices are described as acceptable—the body as a "living sacrifice" (not a dead animal) (Ro 12:1); a gift to a servant of God (Php 4:18); and here, the "fruit of lips that confess his name" and doing good and sharing with others. Actions in line with God's purposes represent one form of worship and praise.

13:17 THE CHURCH, Practice—See note on 1 Th 5:12–13.

13:17 CHURCH LEADERS, Authority—The leaders in the church are to be respected and followed to prevent disorder and confusion. Effective leadership requires effective following. It is assumed here that the leaders are trustworthy and that they do not exercise their authority in an authoritarian manner. The congregation is to respond to their leadership cooperatively and should not create a hostile environment in which their leaders must grimly toil. This does not mean that the congregation owes their leaders blind obedience, however; the Christian is accountable to Christ alone. Leaders are not to dominate others by exercising dictatorial control. Their office is a function within the church, not over it. The church is gathered only under Christ and is to be controlled only by the Spirit. Those who lead the church are therefore to imitate Christ in a willingness to serve tirelessly and sacrificially in their watchcare over others. They carry out their calling in obedience to

their authority. They keep watch over
you[s] as men who must give an account.
Obey them so that their work will be a
joy, not a burden, for that would be of no
advantage to you.
18Pray for us.[t] We are sure that we
have a clear conscience[u] and desire to
live honorably in every way. 19I particularly urge you to pray so that I may be
restored to you soon.[v]
20May the God of peace,[w] who through
the blood of the eternal covenant[x]
brought back from the dead[y] our Lord
Jesus, that great Shepherd of the sheep,[z]
21equip you with everything good for doing his will,[a] and may he work in us[b]
what is pleasing to him,[c] through Jesus
Christ, to whom be glory for ever and
ever. Amen.[d]
22Brothers, I urge you to bear with my
word of exhortation, for I have written
you only a short letter.[e]
23I want you to know that our brother
Timothy[f] has been released. If he arrives
soon, I will come with him to see you.
24Greet all your leaders[g] and all God's
people. Those from Italy[h] send you their
greetings.
25Grace be with you all.[i]

13:17 [s]Isa 62:6; Ac 20:28
13:18 [t]S 1Th 5:25 [u]S Ac 23:1
13:19 [v]Phm 22
13:20 [w]S Ro 15:33 [x]Ge 9:16; 17:7,13, 19; Isa 55:3; 61:8; Eze 37:26; S Mt 26:28 [y]S Ac 2:24 [z]S Jn 10:11
13:21 [a]2Co 9:8 [b]S Php 2:13 [c]1Jn 3:22 [d]S Ro 11:36
13:22 [e]1Pe 5:12
13:23 [f]S Ac 16:1
13:24 [g]ver 7,17 [h]Ac 18:2
13:25 [i]S Col 4:18

Christ and may wield only the power of love. They also must give an account to God.

13:18–19 PRAYER, Intercession—Prayer requests are legitimate. Paul often requested prayer. See notes on 2 Th 3:1–5; 2 Ti 1:3.

13:20 JESUS CHRIST, Shepherd—The resurrected Christ cares for and guides us, His flock, so that we can obey His will.

13:20 ELECTION, Righteousness—The Lord Jesus, who shed His blood of the eternal covenant, is able to equip the elect to keep the will of God, faithfully observing His election requirements.

13:20 THE CHURCH, Covenant People—The new covenant in Christ differs from the old covenant because it is eternal. No other covenant will ever replace it. It alone leads to peace with God, ministry, obedience, and resurrection. See note on 8:6—9:28.

13:20–21 PRAYER, Blessing—A closing prayer appropriate for this letter is addressed to Hebrews familiar with the Old Covenant but now in the New Covenant. Prayer should ultimately equip us to do God's will and to please Him. See note on Ro 15:33.

13:25 PRAYER, Blessing—The writer closed with a blessing on the recipients of the letter, typical of a first century Christian letter. See note on Ro 15:33.

James

Theological Setting

Only a person with genuine salvation could withstand what the early Christians faced: Persecution by pagans, heresy by false teachers, and disillusionment over the way some church members behaved. Therefore in this pastoral letter James set forth the nature of true religion.

Synthetic salvation, no doubt, had its appeal. It promised worldly pleasure without fear of divine punishment, belief without any requirements for moral behavior, and ritual without the demand for righteous living. James warned about the dangers of false religion. The persons to whom the sermon-letter was directed were learning to live the Christian life in the midst of a pagan world. Many possessed woefully inadequate views of matters such as faith, wisdom, morality, and prayer. James provided inspired truth.

The early Christians often suffered persecution. Both Jewish and pagan religions viewed suffering as punishment for wrongdoing. Wealth and ease were looked on as rewards for virtuous living. Thus, the suffering of the early Christians was not only painful, it was also embarrassing and bewildering. James addressed the problem of suffering. Wealth also presented a problem in the early churches. Out of fear or habit the poorer Christians tended to treat the wealthier ones with special favors. James wrote concerning the right attitude toward wealth and the wealthy.

In summary, the object of the sermon-letter was to instruct the reader-listeners about the nature of genuine salvation, to motivate them to follow the precepts of true religion, to warn them about false belief and immoral conduct, and to encourage them to follow God's wisdom and morality.

Theological Outline

James: The Nature of True Religion

- I. Salutation (1:1)
- II. True Religion Is Developed by Trials and Testing (1:2-15)
  - A. Joy is the correct response to times of testing. (1:2)
  - B. The testing of faith can result in steadfastness which, when mature, enables us to be perfect, complete, and lacking in nothing. (1:3-4)
  - C. True wisdom comes from God and is available to those who ask in faith, not doubting. (1:5-8)
  - D. Wealth may be a test of faith, not a proof of faith. (1:9-11)
  - E. Perseverance under trial leads to blessing. (1:12)
  - F. Temptation comes from within, not from God, and is to be resisted. (1:13-15)
- III. True Religion Is Initiated by Faith (1:16—2:26)
  - A. Salvation by faith is a gift from God, as are all good gifts. (1:16-17)
  - B. Salvation as an expression of God's will is related to God's Word. (1:18-27)
    - 1. We are to receive God's Word. (1:18-21)
    - 2. We are to do God's Word, not just hear it. (1:22-25)
  - C. Saving faith does not show favoritism but shows love to all. (2:1-13)
  - D. Saving faith issues in godly attitudes and actions. (2:14-26)
    - 1. Faith without action is dead. (2:14-17)
    - 2. Belief is not enough; even the demons believe in God. (2:18-20)
    - 3. Faith and works go together inseparably. (2:21-26)
- IV. True Religion Is Guided by Wisdom (3:1-18)
  - A. The wise person controls the tongue. (3:1-12)
  - B. Earthly wisdom is characterized by evil attitudes and actions. (3:13-16)
  - C. The wise person's life is characterized by moral behavior. (3:17-18)
- V. True Religion Is Demonstrated by Works (4:1—5:12)
  - A. Avoid acting selfishly instead of asking God. (4:1-3)
  - B. Avoid being friendly with the world. (4:4-5)

C. Possess the proper attitude toward self—being humble, not proud or presumptuous. (4:6-10)
D. Avoid speaking against or judging other Christians. (4:11-12)
E. Avoid presuming on God's time. (4:13-16)
F. Do not fail to do what you know is right. (4:17)
G. Avoid depending on wealth. (5:1-3)
H. Avoid treating persons unjustly. (5:4-6)
I. Do not be impatient, for the Lord is coming. (5:7-11)
J. Do not take oaths. (5:12)

VI. True Religion Is Expressed in Prayer (5:13-20)
A. Prayer, including intercession, is a significant part of true religion. (5:13-16)
1. Prayer is a proper response to suffering and illness. (5:13-14)
2. Prayers are to be offered in faith, with right motives. (5:15)
3. Prayer includes confession of sins. (5:16*a*)
B. The righteousness of the person praying is related to the effectiveness of the prayer. (5:16*b*)
C. All humans can pray and be heard. (5:17-18)
D. Intercession for sinners is an important Christian responsibility. (5:19-20)

Theological Conclusions

God inspired James to provide us with certain theological teachings about the Christian life with special emphasis on patiently enduring tribulation, steadfastly seeking God's wisdom, consistently putting faith into action by doing what is right and abstaining from what is wrong, and persistently praying for oneself and for others. His message is practical, dealing with issues of daily life such as control of the tongue, relation to others—especially the wealthy—and helping persons in need. James shows that religion and morality, evangelism and ethics, doctrine and righteousness, belief and behavior, faith and works go together in the Christian life.

The major doctrinal contribution of James deals with the relation of faith and works. The letter clarifies the meaning of the two terms. Salvation, James taught, is a gift from God received by faith; a person cannot be saved by works. Yet, a person who is genuinely saved will demonstrate his or her faith by works of love and ministry. James highlighted faith and works in a way to give added insight into Paul's more elaborate discussions in his letters. Paul, as a missionary-evangelist, stressed that grace and faith, not the law and works, bring salvation. James, as a pastor-teacher, emphasized that the Christian life is a blend of faith and works, that genuine salvation results in ministry and morality.

Contemporary Teaching

Churches today ought to heed and teach the doctrines presented in James. Many of the false beliefs and practices common in the first century are still found today. For example, some persons come to Christ looking for success, wealth, and power. Others come expecting freedom from troubles. In contrast, James warned about the dangers of wealth, and he promised no easy life for believers in Christ. James' message was not gloomy or pessimistic; he spoke of the possibility of joy in the midst of trials. Currently some persons proclaim a false gospel, calling for belief without corresponding behavior. Content with a religion of unproductive belief and religious ritual apart from godly living, they are denied the joy and reward of genuine salvation. Churches ought to teach the whole counsel of God, not just a part, and proclaim all of the Bible, not just selected portions.

James presents a number of basic lessons we should learn:

1. We should seek God's wisdom, not the wisdom of the world.
2. Faith is essential to salvation.
3. Genuine salvation ushers us into a life of obedience to God's will and of ministry to our neighbor, into a life of piety, prayer, purity, humility, ministry, and self-control—especially of the tongue.
4. Trials and tribulations of the Christian when met with joy and steadfastness can strengthen our life in Christ.
5. Failing to do the good we know to do is sin.
6. Attitudes, as well as actions, are important; attitudes lead to action.
7. Wealth presents special problems for Christians, including giving preferential treatment to the wealthy in churches.
8. The devil and the pull of the world to accept its standards can be successfully resisted.
9. Christ's return provides strong motivation to follow Him patiently and faithfully.
10. Turning sinners from the errors of their ways is a vital part of the Christian life.

Chapter 1

JAMES,[a] a servant of God[b] and of the
Lord Jesus Christ,

To the twelve tribes[c] scattered[d]
among the nations:

Greetings.[e]

Trials and Temptations

2Consider it pure joy, my brothers,
whenever you face trials of many kinds,[f]
3because you know that the testing of
your faith[g] develops perseverance.[h]
4Perseverance must finish its work so
that you may be mature[i] and complete,
not lacking anything. 5If any of you lacks
wisdom, he should ask God,[j] who gives
generously to all without finding fault,
and it will be given to him.[k] 6But when
he asks, he must believe and not doubt,[l]
because he who doubts is like a wave of
the sea, blown and tossed by the wind.
7That man should not think he will receive anything from the Lord; 8he is a
double-minded man,[m] unstable[n] in all he
does.
9The brother in humble circumstances
ought to take pride in his high position.[o]
10But the one who is rich should take
pride in his low position, because he will
pass away like a wild flower.[p] 11For the
sun rises with scorching heat[q] and withers[r] the plant; its blossom falls and its
beauty is destroyed.[s] In the same way,
the rich man will fade away even while
he goes about his business.
12Blessed is the man who perseveres
under trial,[t] because when he has stood
the test, he will receive the crown of
life[u] that God has promised to those who
love him.[v]
13When tempted, no one should say,
"God is tempting me." For God cannot
be tempted by evil, nor does he tempt
anyone; 14but each one is tempted when,
by his own[w] evil desire, he is dragged
away and enticed. 15Then, after desire
has conceived, it gives birth to sin;[x] and
sin, when it is full-grown, gives birth to
death.[y]
16Don't be deceived,[z] my dear brothers.[a] 17Every good and perfect gift is from

1:1 aS Ac 15:13 bRo 1:1; Tit 1:1 cAc 26:7 dDt 32:26; Jn 7:35; 1Pe 1:1 eAc 15:23
1:2 fver 12; S Mt 5:12; Heb 10:34; 12:11
1:3 g1Pe 1:7 hS Heb 10:36
1:4 iS 1Co 2:6
1:5 j1Ki 3:9,10; Pr 2:3-6 kPs 51:6; Da 1:17; 2:21; S Mt 7:7
1:6 lS Mt 21:21; Mk 11:24
1:8 mPs 119:113; Jas 4:8 n2Pe 2:14; 3:16
1:9 oS Mt 23:12
1:10 pJob 14:2; Ps 103:15,16; Isa 40:6,7; 1Co 7:31; 1Pe 1:24
1:11 qMt 20:12 rPs 102:4,11 sIsa 40:6-8
1:12 tver 2; Ge 22:1; Jas 5:11; 1Pe 3:14 uS 1Co 9:25 vEx 20:6; 1Co 2:9; 8:3; Jas 2:5
1:14 wPr 19:3
1:15 xGe 3:6; Job 15:35; Ps 7:14; Isa 59:4 yS Ro 6:23 **1:16** zS 1Co 6:9 aver 19; Jas 2:5

1:2–4 EVIL AND SUFFERING, Testing—Disciples can rejoice at their suffering as they realize it is a testing or trying of their faith, helping faith to mature.

1:3–4,12 ELECTION, Testing—Testing develops perseverance. Perseverance is victory over trial. Victory over trial presents the elect with the crown of life which God promises the elect who love Him.

1:5–8 SIN, Lack of Faith—Sin is not just an overt act. The Bible writers acknowledged overt actions as sin, but they went much deeper than that. Lack of faith in God's goodness and promises is also recognized as sin. The doubter is tempted to fall back on human experience that denies God and His power. Human wisdom based on experience is not sufficient to meet life's storms. Believers trust God to provide the needed wisdom.

1:5–8 PRAYER, Faith—God wants to supply what we lack. We should confidently ask Him. Doubts hinder our prayers from being answered. We cannot expect to get things through the world's way and through God's. Total dependence on God is the way of prayer.

1:5 EDUCATION, God—Wisdom differs from the modern technical knowledge people prize. True wisdom enables us to do the right thing in the face of moral dilemmas and to interpret life experiences in light of eternal values. God is the source of this wisdom (Pr 1:7), and it is acquired through prayerful communion with Him. See 3:17.

1:9–11 CHRISTIAN ETHICS, Property Rights—People pursue material goods as ends in themselves, but these things have nothing of the eternally permanent about them. Humility is the only attitude proper for the rich.

1:12 GOD, Judge—Judgment does not always mean punishment. God is the just Judge who will reward the faithful. We should love the Judge.

1:12–18 EVIL AND SUFFERING, Human Origin—God does not tempt us to do evil. While evil can be traced to human desire, only good can come from God. Desire is not sin but the beginning point that can lead to sin if we allow it to. We can blame no one for the evil we do but ourselves.

1:12,25 SALVATION, Blessing—Those who hear and do God's law as taught by Christ are blessed. Those who prove faithful through all life's trials are also blessed. They receive God's rewards. Compare Lk 11:27–28; Jn 13:17.

1:12 SALVATION, Love of God—God promises a crown of life to those who love Him. The crown was a wreath awarded to the victor in athletic games. It symbolized victory and recognized an achievement built upon rigorous discipline. Love of God leads to perseverance for God even under the most difficult circumstances.

1:13–14 GOD, Justice—God is a just God. He neither does evil, causes evil, nor tempts anyone to do evil. Righteousness is such a part of God that He will not tempt any person to do wrong. His desire is to bring every person to do what is right. We must accept responsibility for our sin. God did not make us do it.

1:13–15 SIN, Individual Choice—God is not the author of sin. A person must accept responsibility for personal sinful acts. Someone cannot evade responsibility for sinful acts by saying, "God made me that way. I cannot help myself." Similarly, no one can blame a sin problem on Satan. Satan tempts us to do evil, but we make the choice to sin and must accept the responsibility for our evil choices. Physical, emotional, and psychological desires lead to sinful acts. There is no invisible force that makes persons sin against their wills. Sin is a consciously-chosen path, not an outwardly determined reflex.

1:15 HUMANITY, Death and Sin—Sin and death are tied together throughout the Bible. Ge 3 shows how sin entered the world and brought death by arousing false hopes. The physical death process for humanity has come through human sin. Spiritual death is far more tragic and is the immediate offspring of human sin. See notes on Ge 2:17; Pr 11:19.

1:17 GOD, Goodness—God's goodness can always be depended upon. He wants to give us what is good for us. He is not moody like the gods of the ancient world who had to be placated or humored. He does not run hot and cold. He is not changeable, unpredictable, leading us in one way today and another way tomorrow.

1:17–18 CREATION, Purposeful—Rather than sending temptation to discourage and even thwart the growth of His new creations, God gives good things to help them grow. Persons living out His image through trust in Christ represent God's accomplished purpose for creation. The gifts He conveys are in both the physical or material and the spiritual realm. God would never entice His born again creatures to destroy themselves in sin. He rather wishes them to grow and has provided resources to make this possible.

above,[b] coming down from the Father of
the heavenly lights,[c] who does not
change[d] like shifting shadows. 18 He
chose to give us birth[e] through the word
of truth,[f] that we might be a kind of firstfruits[g] of all he created.

Listening and Doing

19 My dear brothers,[h] take note of this:
Everyone should be quick to listen, slow
to speak[i] and slow to become angry,
20 for man's anger[j] does not bring about
the righteous life that God desires.
21 Therefore, get rid of[k] all moral filth and
the evil that is so prevalent and humbly
accept the word planted in you,[l] which
can save you.
22 Do not merely listen to the word, and
so deceive yourselves. Do what it says.[m]
23 Anyone who listens to the word but
does not do what it says is like a man who
looks at his face in a mirror 24 and, after
looking at himself, goes away and immediately forgets what he looks like. 25 But
the man who looks intently into the perfect law that gives freedom,[n] and continues to do this, not forgetting what he has
heard, but doing it—he will be blessed in
what he does.[o]
26 If anyone considers himself religious
and yet does not keep a tight rein on his
tongue,[p] he deceives himself and his religion is worthless. 27 Religion that God our
Father accepts as pure and faultless is
this: to look after[q] orphans and widows[r]
in their distress and to keep oneself from
being polluted by the world.[s]

Chapter 2

Favoritism Forbidden

MY brothers, as believers in our glorious[t] Lord Jesus Christ, don't show
favoritism.[u] 2 Suppose a man comes into
your meeting wearing a gold ring and fine
clothes, and a poor man in shabby clothes
also comes in. 3 If you show special attention to the man wearing fine clothes and
say, "Here's a good seat for you," but say
to the poor man, "You stand there" or
"Sit on the floor by my feet," 4 have you
not discriminated among yourselves and
become judges[v] with evil thoughts?
5 Listen, my dear brothers:[w] Has not
God chosen those who are poor in the
eyes of the world[x] to be rich in faith[y]
and to inherit the kingdom[z] he promised
those who love him?[a] 6 But you have insulted the poor.[b] Is it not the rich who
are exploiting you? Are they not the ones
who are dragging you into court?[c] 7 Are
they not the ones who are slandering the
noble name of him to whom you belong?
8 If you really keep the royal law found

1:17 [b]Ps 85:12; Jn 3:27; Jas 3:15,17 [c]Ge 1:16; Ps 136:7; Da 2:22; 1Jn 1:5 [d]Nu 23:19; Ps 102:27; Mal 3:6
1:18 [e]S Jn 1:13 [f]S 2Ti 2:15 [g]Jer 2:3; Rev 14:4
1:19 [h]ver 16; Jas 2:5 [i]Pr 10:19; Jas 3:3-12
1:20 [j]S Mt 5:22
1:21 [k]S Eph 4:22 [l]Eph 1:13
1:22 [m]S Mt 7:21; Jas 2:14-20
1:25 [n]Ps 19:7; Jn 8:32; Gal 2:4; Jas 2:12 [o]S Jn 13:17
1:26 [p]Ps 34:13; 39:1; 141:3; Jas 3:2-12; 1Pe 3:10
1:27 [q]Mt 25:36 [r]Dt 14:29; Job 31:16,17,21; Ps 146:9; Isa 1:17, 23 [s]Ro 12:2; Jas 4:4; 2Pe 1:4; 2:20
2:1 [t]Ac 7:2; 1Co 2:8 [u]ver 9; Dt 1:17; Lev 19:15; Pr 24:23; S Ac 10:34
2:4 [v]S Jn 7:24
2:5 [w]Jas 1:16,19 [x]Job 34:19; 1Co 1:26-28 [y]Lk 12:21; Rev 2:9 [z]S Mt 25:34 [a]S Jas 1:12
2:6 [b]1Co 11:22 [c]Ac 8:3; 16:19

1:18 REVELATION, Author of Life—God chose to give us life. He provided true spiritual life by the revelation of purpose and life in the gospel. He wants us to become the finest offering to God, models of life as God intended it (v 21).

1:19–25 SIN, Moral Insensitivity—It is not enough to know or even choose the right act; it must be done. Intellectual assent to God's law is possible without practicing it. This assent gives the person a false sense of faithfulness. God does not seek righteous knowledge. He seeks righteous lives.

1:19–21 CHRISTIAN ETHICS, Character—Losing control affects our whole being. Gaining control of one's anger can provide a key to the maturing expression of more positive virtues in one's character.

1:22–25 SALVATION, Obedience—God's Word requires listeners to be doers. See note on Ro 2:13.

1:23–25 REVELATION, Commitment—Revelation calls people to commitment. True understanding of God's Word produces new behavior and attitudes. Without such commitment we have no personal identity. To know the Word and fail to do it is to deceive oneself about personal security and relationship to God.

1:25 CHRISTIAN ETHICS, Moral Imperatives—God intends for us to have freedom. Lack of imperatives is not freedom. Lack of law is confusion and lack of direction. God's people find direction by studying God's inspired Word, learning it, and putting it into continual daily practice. Only such a life-style brings happiness.

1:26 CHRISTIAN ETHICS, Language—Speech belies true character. Words can quickly destroy any Christian witness if they are not Christlike.

2:1–14 SIN, Estrangement—Favoritism along socioeconomic lines is sinful because it defines a person in terms apart from God's grace. Love demands seeing people as God sees them: needing to be lifted up. This love is the real basis of God's law. To reject love is to be guilty of the whole law. The moral law of God is not a collection of separate pieces from which we pick and choose. It is a whole glued together by love. Refusal to love leads to disobeying one commandment, but it also leads to sinning against the motivation and purpose of the whole. Lack of love and mercy leading to acts of compassion is the basis of immorality. It brings estrangement and distrust among humans and between God and us.

2:1–9 DISCIPLESHIP, Poor—Christian disciples are not to show partiality. Favoritism in relating to others is sin. It breaks the law of neighbor love, which James called the "royal law." James focused on the tendency to be partial toward the rich. Such favoritism results in being manipulated by the rich and also insults the poor. Churches today may reveal a need for this word from James. See note on Lk 10:25–37.

2:1–18 CHRISTIAN ETHICS, Property Rights—The poor suffer oppression, injustice, and ridicule at the hands of the rich. Still the poor even in church do everything possible to impress and please the rich. We are to treat the rich with love due any other person, but favoritism shown for the rich is a sin God judges. James pressed his case so far as to say that the credibility of one's relationship with God can be perceived through one's treatment of the poor. In fact, a faith that does not produce loving treatment of others leaves some doubt as to whether it has been a faith leading to salvation.

2:2 THE CHURCH, Practice—Regular meetings for worship and Bible study are central to church life. Such meetings are open to all people with favoritism shown to none.

2:5 SALVATION, Love of God—God has promised His kingdom to those who love Him (Mt 5:3; Lk 6:20).

2:8–13 CHRISTIAN ETHICS, Moral Imperatives—The moral law has integrity built into it which links the various guidelines given in the Bible. The integrity comes because the one, perfect God inspired the whole law. The integrity is such that one can do wrong by overdoing a right. Too, one who is consistent at some points but inconsistent at others comes under the judgment of the whole law. The purpose of the law is to bring mercy and compassion into the world, not legalism. Life without mercy faces judgment. Life lived in love and mercy has no fear of God's judgment.

in Scripture, "Love your neighbor as
yourself,"[a][d] you are doing right. 9But if
you show favoritism,[e] you sin and are
convicted by the law as lawbreakers.[f]
10For whoever keeps the whole law and
yet stumbles[g] at just one point is guilty of
breaking all of it.[h] 11For he who said,
"Do not commit adultery,"[b][i] also said,
"Do not murder."[c][j] If you do not commit adultery but do commit murder, you
have become a lawbreaker.

12Speak and act as those who are going
to be judged[k] by the law that gives freedom,[l] 13because judgment without mercy will be shown to anyone who has not
been merciful.[m] Mercy triumphs over
judgment!

Faith and Deeds

14What good is it, my brothers, if a man
claims to have faith but has no deeds?[n]
Can such faith save him? 15Suppose a
brother or sister is without clothes and
daily food.[o] 16If one of you says to him,
"Go, I wish you well; keep warm and
well fed," but does nothing about his
physical needs, what good is it?[p] 17In the
same way, faith by itself, if it is not accompanied by action, is dead.[q]

18But someone will say, "You have
faith; I have deeds."

Show me your faith without deeds,[r]
and I will show you my faith[s] by what I
do.[t] 19You believe that there is one
God.[u] Good! Even the demons believe
that[v]—and shudder.

20You foolish man, do you want evidence that faith without deeds is useless[d]?[w] 21Was not our ancestor Abraham

2:8 [d]Lev 19:18; S Mt 5:43
2:9 [e]ver 1 [f]Dt 1:17
2:10 [g]Jas 3:2 [h]Mt 5:19; Gal 3:10; 5:3
2:11 [i]Ex 20:14; Dt 5:18 [j]Ex 20:13; Dt 5:17
2:12 [k]S Mt 16:27 [l]S Jas 1:25
2:13 [m]Mt 5:7; 9:13; 12:7; 18:32-35; Lk 6:37
2:14 [n]Mt 7:26; Jas 1:22-25
2:15 [o]Mt 25:35,36
2:16 [p]Lk 3:11; 1Jn 3:17,18
2:17 [q]ver 20,26; Gal 5:6
2:18 [r]Ro 3:28 [s]Heb 11 [t]Mt 7:16, 17; Jas 3:13
2:19 [u]Dt 6:4; Mk 12:29; 1Co 8:4-6 [v]Mt 8:29; Lk 4:34
2:20 [w]ver 17,26
2:21 [x]Ge 22:9,12
2:22 [y]Heb 11:17 [z]1Th 1:3
2:23 [a]Ge 15:6; S Ro 4:3 [b]2Ch 20:7; Isa 41:8
2:25 [c]S Heb 11:31
2:26 [d]ver 17,20
3:1 [e]S Eph 4:11 [f]S Mt 7:1 [g]Ro 2:21
3:2 [h]1Ki 8:46; Ro 3:9-20; Jas 2:10; 1Jn 1:8 [i]Ps 39:1; Pr 10:19; 1Pe 3:10 [j]S Mt 12:37 [k]Jas 1:26
3:3 [l]Ps 32:9

considered righteous for what he did
when he offered his son Isaac on the altar?[x] 22You see that his faith and his actions were working together,[y] and his
faith was made complete by what he
did.[z] 23And the scripture was fulfilled
that says, "Abraham believed God, and it
was credited to him as righteousness,"[e][a] and he was called God's
friend.[b] 24You see that a person is justified by what he does and not by faith
alone.

25In the same way, was not even Rahab
the prostitute considered righteous for
what she did when she gave lodging to
the spies and sent them off in a different
direction?[c] 26As the body without the
spirit is dead, so faith without deeds is
dead.[d]

Chapter 3

Taming the Tongue

NOT many of you should presume to
be teachers,[e] my brothers, because
you know that we who teach will be
judged[f] more strictly.[g] 2We all stumble[h]
in many ways. If anyone is never at fault
in what he says,[i] he is a perfect man,[j]
able to keep his whole body in check.[k]

3When we put bits into the mouths of
horses to make them obey us, we can
turn the whole animal.[l] 4Or take ships as
an example. Although they are so large
and are driven by strong winds, they are
steered by a very small rudder wherever

[a]*8* Lev. 19:18 [b]*11* Exodus 20:14; Deut. 5:18 [c]*11* Exodus 20:13; Deut. 5:17 [d]*20* Some early manuscripts *dead* [e]*23* Gen. 15:6

2:14–26 SALVATION, Justification—Christians as devoted as Martin Luther have been troubled by this passage when comparing it to Paul's teaching of justification by faith alone. See note on Ro 1:16–17. James argued against a false definition of faith, a definition with intellectual content but no consequences for practical daily life. Faith is not repeating words even demons can repeat (Mk 1:24; 5:7). Faith is commitment to Christ, depending on Him and not on human achievement for salvation, but also serving Him as directed by His Spirit. Paul and James agreed. They simply emphasized different points in the salvation experience and different components of Christian faith. See note on Eph 2:4–5,7–10. Good deeds do not earn salvation one does not have. They do provide evidence of salvation received in faith.

2:14–26 DISCIPLESHIP, Conversion—Mere profession of faith accomplishes nothing. Faith is completed and attested by the actions it prompts. Faith without such actions is dead, and no one can be saved to life in Christ by a dead faith. A Christian is saved and justified before God by faith, but it is a live faith through which God accomplishes His purposes by good works. See note on Eph 2:8–10.

3:1–13 SIN, Hypocrisy—Words control our relationships with people. All of us use words unwisely and hurt others. We are not perfect. We are sinners. We cannot extinguish the fires of hatred, doubt, jealousy, and anger our tongues start. We must be careful to control our words so they do not discredit our Christian confession before the world. To use the tongue to praise God and to spread evil is vile hypocrisy, pretense to be what we are not. Once a word is spoken and heard, it cannot be retrieved; its effect will irresistably run its often destructive course. James singled out teachers because of their potential to influence a number of people. Because impulses take the shape of words, control of the tongue is an indication of a disciplined life.

3:1–12 CHRISTIAN ETHICS, Language—Words need to please God, not impress other people. We can ruin our reputations and our contribution to other people with a few ill-chosen words. Satan delights in controlling our tongue. Then he does not have to control anything else. We have no power over the tongue unless we submit it totally to God. Partial control of the tongue will not do. Nothing should escape our mouths that is not praise to God in some way.

3:1 CHURCH LEADERS, Teacher—Some may want to serve in the church for all too human reasons such as pride and a desire for status. James warned that not many should become teachers. Teachers are responsible and will be held strictly accountable for their teaching and its effects on believers. Therefore, they will be subject to greater condemnation in the judgment. This holds true for anyone who assumes responsibility for the spiritual welfare of the congregation. Teachers should be characterized by wisdom (Col 1:28) and should be humble and not argumentative (Jas 3:13–18). Their teaching must be both sound and godly (1 Ti 1:13; 6:2–3). Their life-styles must conform to what they profess (1 Ti 4:2; 2 Ti 3:10).

the pilot wants to go. 5Likewise the
tongue is a small part of the body, but it
makes great boasts.[m] Consider what a
great forest is set on fire by a small spark.
6The tongue also is a fire,[n] a world of evil
among the parts of the body. It corrupts
the whole person,[o] sets the whole course
of his life on fire, and is itself set on fire
by hell.[p]
7All kinds of animals, birds, reptiles
and creatures of the sea are being tamed
and have been tamed by man, 8but no
man can tame the tongue. It is a restless
evil, full of deadly poison.[q]
9With the tongue we praise our Lord
and Father, and with it we curse men,
who have been made in God's likeness.[r]
10Out of the same mouth come praise and
cursing. My brothers, this should not be.
11Can both fresh water and salt[f] water
flow from the same spring? 12My brothers, can a fig tree bear olives, or a grapevine bear figs?[s] Neither can a salt spring
produce fresh water.

Two Kinds of Wisdom

13Who is wise and understanding
among you? Let him show it[t] by his good
life, by deeds[u] done in the humility that
comes from wisdom. 14But if you harbor
bitter envy and selfish ambition[v] in your
hearts, do not boast about it or deny the
truth.[w] 15Such "wisdom" does not come
down from heaven[x] but is earthly, unspiritual, of the devil.[y] 16For where you
have envy and selfish ambition,[z] there
you find disorder and every evil practice.
17But the wisdom that comes from
heaven[a] is first of all pure; then peace-
loving,[b] considerate, submissive, full of
mercy[c] and good fruit, impartial and sincere.[d] 18Peacemakers[e] who sow in
peace raise a harvest of righteousness.[f]

3:5 [m]Ps 12:3,4; 73:8,9
3:6 [n]Pr 16:27 [o]Mt 15:11,18,19 [p]S Mt 5:22
3:8 [q]Ps 140:3; Ro 3:13
3:9 [r]Ge 1:26,27; 1Co 11:7
3:12 [s]Mt 7:16
3:13 [t]Jas 2:18 [u]S 1Pe 2:12
3:14 [v]ver 16; 2Co 12:20 [w]Jas 5:19
3:15 [x]ver 17; Jas 1:17 [y]1Ti 4:1
3:16 [z]ver 14; Gal 5:20,21
3:17 [a]1Co 2:6; Jas 1:17 [b]Heb 12:11 [c]Lk 6:36 [d]Ro 12:9
3:18 [e]Mt 5:9; S Ro 14:19 [f]Pr 11:18; Isa 32:17; Hos 10:12; Php 1:11
4:1 [g]Tit 3:9 [h]S Ro 7:23
4:2 [i]Mt 5:21,22; Jas 5:6; 1Jn 3:15
4:3 [j]Ps 18:41; S Mt 7:7 [k]Ps 66:18; 1Jn 3:22; 5:14
4:4 [l]Isa 54:5; Jer 3:20; Hos 2:2-5; 3:1; 9:1 [m]S Jas 1:27 [n]Ro 8:7; 1Jn 2:15 [o]Jn 15:19
4:5 [p]1Co 6:19
4:6 [q]Pr 3:34; S Mt 23:12
4:7 [r]Eph 4:27; 6:11; 1Pe 5:6-9
4:8 [s]Ps 73:28; Zec 1:3; Mal 3:7; Heb 7:19 [t]Isa 1:16 [u]Ps 24:4; Jer 4:14 [v]Ps 119:113; Jas 1:8
4:9 [w]Lk 6:25
4:10 [x]ver 6; Job 5:11; 1Pe 5:6
4:11 [y]Ro 1:30; 2Co 12:20; 1Pe 2:1 [z]S Mt 7:1

Chapter 4

Submit Yourselves to God

WHAT causes fights and quarrels[g]
among you? Don't they come from
your desires that battle[h] within you?
2You want something but don't get it. You
kill[i] and covet, but you cannot have
what you want. You quarrel and fight.
You do not have, because you do not ask
God. 3When you ask, you do not receive,[j] because you ask with wrong motives,[k] that you may spend what you get
on your pleasures.
4You adulterous[l] people, don't you
know that friendship with the world[m] is
hatred toward God?[n] Anyone who
chooses to be a friend of the world becomes an enemy of God.[o] 5Or do you
think Scripture says without reason that
the spirit he caused to live in us[p] envies
intensely?[g] 6But he gives us more grace.
That is why Scripture says:

"God opposes the proud
but gives grace to the humble."[h] [q]

7Submit yourselves, then, to God. Resist the devil,[r] and he will flee from you.
8Come near to God and he will come
near to you.[s] Wash your hands,[t] you
sinners, and purify your hearts,[u] you
double-minded.[v] 9Grieve, mourn and
wail. Change your laughter to mourning
and your joy to gloom.[w] 10Humble yourselves before the Lord, and he will lift you
up.[x]
11Brothers, do not slander one another.[y] Anyone who speaks against his
brother or judges him[z] speaks against the

[f]*11* Greek *bitter* (see also verse 14) [g]*5* Or *that God jealously longs for the spirit that he made to live in us;* or *that the Spirit he caused to live in us longs jealously* [h]*6* Prov. 3:34

3:9 HUMANITY, Image of God—People have been created in God's image and represent God on earth. Even as sinners, we continue to bear God's image. To curse a human being is to curse God's image and deserve punishment. See notes on Ge 1:26–29; 9:1–6.

3:13–18 CHRISTIAN ETHICS, Character—James contrasted traits of earthly and heavenly wisdom. Through dedication to God one can live a good, humble life; this is the picture of wisdom. Wisdom is God's will in action, not human knowledge in competition.

3:17–18 EDUCATION, Wisdom—God's wisdom saturates life with qualities which cement good relationships with other people. See note on 1:5.

4:1–12 SIN, Individual Choice—Christians fight. Why? Because we do not control our self-centered desires. We use improper methods to get what we want. We trust our skills and our strength. We need to ask God; but we need to ask with motives of love and service, not motives of selfish power, envy, and pleasure. Sin originates then in selfish desire and lack of humility.

4:2–3 PRAYER, Hindrances—James gave a clear indication why some prayers are not answered. The object of the request would not glorify God or advance His kingdom; it would be spent on personal pleasure. We try the world's way of fighting and covetousness rather than God's way of asking the Father in trust and submission.

4:5–6 HOLY SCRIPTURE, Authoritative—James' quotation of the Old Testament shows that he regarded the Old Testament as God's authoritative Word. He cited it to support the authority of his own inspired word. He did not quote any text word for word. Rather, he stated the meaning of several Old Testament texts much as disciples do today in conversation. He may have interrupted his thought before citing the Greek translation of Pr 3:34 in v 6.

4:7 EVIL AND SUFFERING, Satan—Satan flees stiff resistance because he is not only a liar but a coward as well. We cannot alibi that Satan made us do it, for we can resist him if we choose with God's help to do so.

4:8–10 SALVATION, Acceptance—Acceptance of God means coming near Him in repentance and with deep grief over our sins. The washing called for here is ethical rather than ceremonial. God wants us to accept Him with an undivided heart. He wants us to humble ourselves before Him like the penitent publican (Lk 18:13).

4:8 PRAYER, Command of God—An invitation from God is a command. Effective prayer depends on purity of life and singleness of motive.

law[a] and judges it. When you judge the
law, you are not keeping it,[b] but sitting
in judgment on it. 12There is only one
Lawgiver and Judge,[c] the one who is able
to save and destroy.[d] But you—who are
you to judge your neighbor?[e]

Boasting About Tomorrow

13Now listen,[f] you who say, "Today or
tomorrow we will go to this or that city,
spend a year there, carry on business and
make money."[g] 14Why, you do not even
know what will happen tomorrow. What
is your life? You are a mist that appears
for a little while and then vanishes.[h] 15In-
stead, you ought to say, "If it is the Lord's
will,[i] we will live and do this or that."
16As it is, you boast and brag. All such
boasting is evil.[j] 17Anyone, then, who
knows the good he ought to do and
doesn't do it, sins.[k]

Chapter 5

Warning to Rich Oppressors

NOW listen,[l] you rich people,[m] weep
and wail[n] because of the misery
that is coming upon you. 2Your wealth
has rotted, and moths have eaten your
clothes.[o] 3Your gold and silver are cor-
roded. Their corrosion will testify against
you and eat your flesh like fire. You have
hoarded wealth in the last days.[p] 4Look!
The wages you failed to pay the workmen[q] who mowed your fields are crying
out against you. The cries[r] of the harvesters have reached the ears of the Lord
Almighty.[s] 5You have lived on earth in
luxury and self-indulgence. You have fattened yourselves[t] in the day of slaughter.[i][u] 6You have condemned and murdered[v] innocent men,[w] who were not
opposing you.

Patience in Suffering

7Be patient, then, brothers, until the
Lord's coming.[x] See how the farmer
waits for the land to yield its valuable
crop and how patient he is[y] for the autumn and spring rains.[z] 8You too, be patient and stand firm, because the Lord's
coming[a] is near.[b] 9Don't grumble
against each other, brothers,[c] or you will
be judged. The Judge[d] is standing at the
door![e]

10Brothers, as an example of patience
in the face of suffering, take the prophets[f] who spoke in the name of the Lord.
11As you know, we consider blessed[g]
those who have persevered. You have
heard of Job's perseverance[h] and have
seen what the Lord finally brought
about.[i] The Lord is full of compassion
and mercy.[j]

12Above all, my brothers, do not swear
—not by heaven or by earth or by anything else. Let your "Yes" be yes, and
your "No," no, or you will be condemned.[k]

The Prayer of Faith

13Is any one of you in trouble? He
should pray.[l] Is anyone happy? Let him
sing songs of praise.[m] 14Is any one of you

[i] 5 Or *yourselves as in a day of feasting*

4:11 [a]Jas 2:8 [b]Jas 1:22
4:12 [c]Isa 33:22; S Jas 5:9 [d]Mt 10:28 [e]S Mt 7:1
4:13 [f]Jas 5:1 [g]Pr 27:1; Lk 12:18-20
4:14 [h]Job 7:7; Ps 39:5; 102:3; 144:4; Isa 2:22
4:15 [i]S Ac 18:21
4:16 [j]1Co 5:6
4:17 [k]Lk 12:47; Jn 9:41
5:1 [l]Jas 4:13 [m]Lk 6:24; 1Ti 6:9; Jas 2:2-6 [n]Isa 13:6; Eze 30:2
5:2 [o]Job 13:28; Ps 39:11; Isa 50:9; Mt 6:19,20
5:3 [p]ver 7,8
5:4 [q]Lev 19:13; Jer 22:13; Mal 3:5 [r]Dt 24:15 [s]Ro 9:29
5:5 [t]Eze 16:49; Am 6:1; Lk 16:19 [u]Jer 12:3; 25:34
5:6 [v]Jas 4:2 [w]Heb 10:38
5:7 [x]S 1Co 1:7 [y]Gal 6:9 [z]Dt 11:14; Jer 5:24; Joel 2:23
5:8 [a]S 1Co 1:7 [b]S Ro 13:11
5:9 [c]Jas 4:11 [d]Ps 94:2; 1Co 4:5; Jas 4:12; 1Pe 4:5 [e]Mt 24:33
5:10 [f]S Mt 5:12
5:11 [g]Mt 5:10 [h]Job 1:21,22; 2:10; S Heb 10:36 [i]Job 42:10,12-17 [j]Ex 34:6; Nu 14:18; Ps 103:8
5:12 [k]Mt 5:34-37
5:13 [l]Ps 50:15 [m]Col 3:16

4:13–15 HUMANITY, Life—Life is as temporary as fog, which quickly and silently disappears. A person's life is utterly dependent upon the sustaining power of God. We cannot be proud and boast of future plans and accomplishments. We must live day by day seeking His will and making plans as He leads. Knowing His will, we must commit ourselves to do it.

4:17 SIN, Self-centeredness—Refraining from doing what one knows is good is sin just as surely as is doing the wrong thing. This is commonly called the "sin of omission." We do not act rightly because we think it is not in our own interests to do so. Such self-centeredness is the root of all sins.

5:1–6 SIN, Unrighteousness—The rich face ruin. Why? Because wealth is sin? No! Because wealth becomes god, the expected source of security for eternity. Commitment to wealth breeds injustice, causing inhumane and uncaring treatment of the poor for whom God has special concern. To place top priority on wealth is sin. To gain wealth at the expense of other human beings is sin. To trust wealth instead of God is sin. Sinners face the judgment.

5:4 PRAYER, Mercy of God—The Bible emphasizes repeatedly God's openness to the cry of the oppressed. See note on Ex 2:23–24. Their cry may condemn our self-satisfied religion.

5:7–8 JESUS CHRIST, Final Coming—James, like Paul, used Christ's final coming as an exhortation to patience. James expected the coming of Christ soon. Christians in every age must expect the imminent return of her Lord and not fight one another about it. See notes on 1 Th 4:13–18; 2 Th 1:7–10.

5:7–11 EVIL AND SUFFERING, Endurance—Disciples need patience to persevere in the face of suffering. Christian endurance is not our instinctive response but a learned way of life. Studying the examples of heroes of perseverance like Job and the prophets can help us be patient as we wait for God to show His mercy to us.

5:7–9 LAST THINGS, Return Promises—The coming of the Lord will mean vindication for the faithful. Righteousness will be rewarded, and evil punished. The prospect of that coming offers motivation for patience, in the sense of steadfastness or endurance. On the other hand, the coming of the Lord will mean judgment for some. Those who oppress others are known by the Lord Almighty (vv 1–6). Not only these, but even the faithful who fail to remain strong can expect judgment.

5:11 GOD, Grace—Suffering tempts us to question God's care for us. James called for perserverance, trusting God's love, mercy, and compassion.

5:13–15 EVIL AND SUFFERING, Prayer—A basic Christian response to suffering is to pray. God may relieve the suffering, or, as in Paul's case (2 Co 12:7–10), He may strengthen the sufferer in the suffering. Healing the sick is part of the church's ministry as it was of Christ's. See note on Lk 4:18.

5:13–14 THE CHURCH, Practice—The church needs to find practical ways to help the troubled and sick experience God's presence.

5:13–14 PRAYER, Command of God—All situations call for prayer of some kind—whether we are troubled, happy, or sick. In sickness, the prayer of faith calls forth the divine work.

5:14–16 DISCIPLESHIP, Sick—Christians have no exemption from the natural laws of God's universe. We do get

sick? He should call the elders[n] of the
church to pray over him and anoint him
with oil[o] in the name of the Lord. 15And
the prayer offered in faith[p] will make the
sick person well; the Lord will raise him
up. If he has sinned, he will be forgiven.
16Therefore confess your sins[q] to each
other and pray for each other so that you
may be healed.[r] The prayer of a righteous man is powerful and effective.[s]
17Elijah was a man just like us.[t] He
prayed earnestly that it would not rain,
and it did not rain on the land for three
and a half years.[u] 18Again he prayed, and
the heavens gave rain, and the earth produced its crops.[v]
19My brothers, if one of you should
wander from the truth[w] and someone
should bring him back,[x] 20remember
this: Whoever turns a sinner from the error of his way will save[y] him from death
and cover over a multitude of sins.[z]

5:14 [n]S Ac 11:30 [o]Ps 23:5; Isa 1:6; Mk 6:13; 16:18; Lk 10:34 **5:15** [p]Jas 1:6 **5:16** [q]Mt 3:6; Ac 19:18 [r]Heb 12:13; 1Pe 2:24 [s]S Mt 7:7; S Jn 9:31 **5:17** [t]Ac 14:15 [u]1Ki 17:1; Lk 4:25 **5:18** [v]1Ki 18:41-45 **5:19** [w]Jas 3:14 [x]S Mt 18:15 **5:20** [y]S Ro 11:14 [z]1Pe 4:8

sick. We do have a mission to heal the sick. James described the use of oil, a medical remedy in his day as well as a symbol of God's powerful presence. Christians should pray for the sick and use all resources available to effect healing. Ultimately we must leave the healing to God. Faith in God should not be lost if the sick person is not healed. Prayer never is a device by which God can be manipulated into doing my will. Faithful disciples accept God's answer to prayer whatever it may be. We do know from personal experience the great power prayer has in our ministry to the sick. See note on Lk 9:1–6.

5:14 CHURCH LEADERS, Elder—Elders have responsibility for pastoral oversight and visitation of the sick, orphans, and widows (1:27). Their physical presence with the sick best demonstrates the love and support of the church and fosters hope for God's power to be manifested in healing. See note on 1 Pe 5:1–5.

5:15 SALVATION, Forgiveness—The prayer of faith will bring forgiveness of sin. This text may need to be interpreted against the general belief that sickness is due to sin (Jn 9:2). Even so, God's healing is wholistic, involving the total person.

5:16 PRAYER, Corporate—Christians should pray for one another's known sins. This passage does not give license to share publicly that which might do harm to innocent people, but it does require that Christians be open in areas of need for prayer. We are commanded not to judge (Mt 7:1), while at the same time we pray for the weaknesses of fellow Christians. We need the power of the prayers of others. Confession and intercession are the tasks of all Christians. They are not limited to a professional priesthood. See Guide to Intercession, pp. 1800–1801.

5:17–18 PRAYER, Sincerity—We should not stand in awe of other people who have power in prayer. We should imitate their earnestness. Our prayers can be as powerful and effective as anyone's.

5:19–20 EVANGELISM, Results—Two marvelous results occur when one turns to God. First, that person is saved from death. Secondly, a multitude of sins are covered by the blood of Christ. In this light, to present the truth of our Lord to those who would turn from God is a vital and essential task.

5:20 SALVATION, Initiative—Compare 1 Pe 4:8. God wants the saved to warn sinners about their errors, because the wages of sin is death (Ge 3:3; Ro 6:23). One of the ways God takes the initiative in salvation is by providing saved persons who warn the lost. Some interpreters take the sins covered to be those of the warner, but this has no basis in other Scriptures.

1 Peter

Theological Setting

In the early decades Christians often felt they were exiles and strangers on earth. Usually a spiritual concept, such isolation often became a physical reality as well. The predominantly Gentile group to whom Peter wrote must have felt this way. They lived in lightly populated regions of the Roman Empire. Their alienation from those about them was intensified by the differences in their new life-style brought about by faithfulness to Jesus Christ. Opposition and persecution eventually resulted. Four references to persecution appear in this brief letter. The persecution did not seem to have been organized by the government. Rather, it was mob violence. The letter sought to encourage the readers, in the face of such oppression, to faithfulness and to a proper manner of life before the world.

Theological Outline

1 Peter: Faithfulness under Oppression

I. The Relation of Believers to God (1:1-2)
II. God's Work in Us (1:3-12)
  A. A new birth (1:3-5)
  B. Rejoicing in trial (1:6-9)
  C. Announced by prophets (1:10-12)
III. A Call to Pure Living (1:13—2:10)
  A. The basis of purity (1:13-21)
  B. Born anew to love (1:22-25)
  C. Growing up to salvation (2:1-3)
  D. The living stone (2:4-8)
  E. Being God's people (2:9-10)
IV. The Ethical Principle for Living (2:11—3:12)
  A. Statement of the principle: Live so others will glorify God (2:11-12)
  B. With reference to the government (2:13-17)
  C. With reference to servants (2:18-20)
  D. The example of Christ (2:21-25)
  E. With reference to wives (3:1-6)
  F. With reference to husbands (3:7)
  G. General application (3:8-12)
V. The Proper Attitude Toward Suffering (3:13—4:6)
  A. Suffering for doing right (3:13-17)
  B. The example of Christ (3:18-22)
  C. Living by the will of God (4:1-2)
  D. Judgment of the wicked (4:3-5)
  E. The purpose of the gospel (4:6)
VI. The End of All Things (4:7-19)
  A. Facing the end (4:7-9)
  B. Using God's gifts (4:10-11)
  C. Rejoicing in suffering (4:12-19)
VII. Instructions for Life (5:1-11)
  A. To the elders (5:1-4)
  B. To the younger (5:5)
  C. To all (5:6-9)
  D. Benediction (5:10-11)
VIII. Closing Greetings (5:12-14)

Theological Conclusions

The readers of this letter were chosen by God and sanctified by the Spirit unto obedience to Jesus Christ. The resurrection of Christ had brought a new birth unto a hope that was alive and to a salvation that God had prepared. This hope brought joy even in the midst of trial. Many of the Old Testament titles for God's people were applied to the readers. This new relationship to God came through faith rather than physical birth.

The relationship to God determines the pattern of life. Written to people who came out of an environment with low ethical standards, the inspired Book issued a call to a life worthy of people who bear the name of God. The people were to develop the qualities of God Himself, especially love for one another. Such a life meant they would become a "spiritual house" in God's service (2:5). The relationship to God affected every area of life. The attitude toward the government was to be positive. Servants were to submit to their earthly masters. Wives and husbands had mutual responsibilities. Such conduct might lead to suffering. Non-Christian neighbors might respond in a negative manner to the conduct of believers. However, they should feel no shame in suffering for what was right. Jesus is the example for the believer faced with suffering and oppression. His death had redemptive qualities. Believers could face suffering assured of the final victory and dominion of God in Christ.

Contemporary Teaching

First Peter calls us to a close relationship with God and a manner of life which demonstrates that relationship. In the midst of a non-Christian world, believers must show a godly style of life that differs dramatically from those around us. We are chosen by Him for obedience to Jesus Christ.

We are called upon to appreciate what the death and resurrection of Christ means to us. We are to look to Him as an example of faith and righteous living, even in the midst of trials and suffering. Our lives should reflect the qualities of God as we are made holy. We are to show love and humility in our relations with one another. We are to give evidence of a submissive nature toward government and within the home. Our relationship to Christ should positively affect employer-employee relations. If and when opposition arises, we are to be ready to give a reason for our faith and to act with gentleness and reverence. We are to use the gifts that God gives us in service for Him in our relation to those about us. We are to fulfill our responsibilities with joy and eagerness, seeking to honor Him rather than seeking reward and honor for ourselves.

Chapter 1

PETER, an apostle of Jesus Christ,[a]
To God's elect,[b] strangers in the
world,[c] scattered[d] throughout Pontus,[e]
Galatia,[f] Cappadocia, Asia and Bithynia,[g] 2who have been chosen according to
the foreknowledge[h] of God the Father,
through the sanctifying work of the Spirit,[i] for obedience[j] to Jesus Christ and
sprinkling by his blood:[k]

Grace and peace be yours in abundance.[l]

Praise to God for a Living Hope

3Praise be to the God and Father of our
Lord Jesus Christ![m] In his great mercy[n]
he has given us new birth[o] into a living
hope[p] through the resurrection of Jesus
Christ from the dead,[q] 4and into an inheritance[r] that can never perish, spoil or
fade[s]—kept in heaven for you,[t] 5who
through faith are shielded by God's power[u] until the coming of the salvation[v]
that is ready to be revealed[w] in the last
time. 6In this you greatly rejoice,[x]
though now for a little while[y] you may
have had to suffer grief in all kinds of trials.[z] 7These have come so that your
faith—of greater worth than gold, which
perishes even though refined by fire[a]—
may be proved genuine[b] and may result
in praise, glory and honor[c] when Jesus
Christ is revealed.[d] 8Though you have
not seen him, you love him; and even
though you do not see him now, you believe in him[e] and are filled with an inexpressible and glorious joy, 9for you are receiving the goal of your faith, the salvation of your souls.[f]
10Concerning this salvation, the prophets, who spoke[g] of the grace that was to

1:1 [a]2Pe 1:1 [b]Mt 24:22 [c]S Heb 11:13 [d]S Jas 1:1 [e]Ac 2:9; 18:2 [f]S Ac 16:6 [g]Ac 16:7 **1:2** [h]Ro 8:29 [i]2Th 2:13 [j]ver 14, 22 [k]Heb 10:22; 12:24 [l]S Ro 1:7 **1:3** [m]2Co 1:3; Eph 1:3 [n]Tit 3:5 [o]ver 23; S Jn 1:13 [p]ver 13,21; S Heb 3:6 [q]1Co 15:20; 1Pe 3:21 **1:4** [r]S Ac 20:32; S Ro 8:17 [s]1Pe 5:4 [t]Col 1:5; 2Ti 4:8 **1:5** [u]1Sa 2:9; Jn 10:28 [v]S Ro 11:14 [w]S Ro 8:18 **1:6** [x]Ro 5:2 [y]1Pe 5:10 [z]Jas 1:2; 1Pe 4:12 **1:7** [a]Job 23:10; Ps 66:10; Pr 17:3; Isa 48:10 [b]Jas 1:3 [c]2Co 4:17 [d]ver 13; S 1Th 2:19; 1Pe 4:13

1:8 [e]Jn 20:29 **1:9** [f]Ro 6:22 **1:10** [g]S Mt 26:24

1:1–2 HOLY SPIRIT, Trinity—The Father planned salvation; Jesus died as a sacrifice to provide salvation; and the Spirit works to transform those who are saved into godly people. The Spirit is holy and works to lead us to obey Jesus. See note on Gal 5:22–26.

1:2–3,17–21 GOD, Trinity—Salvation comes through the three Persons of the Trinity. God in His wisdom chose to save both Jews and non-Jews by raising Jesus from death. Jesus sacrificed Himself on the cross. The Holy Spirit works in the lives of believers to make us holy and pure servants, obeying Christ and His teaching. Thus we have faith and hope in the one God. See note on Mt 3:16–17.

1:2 GOD, Wisdom—God knew from the beginning what He would do across the ages of time. He has that perfect wisdom which enables Him to know ahead of time what will happen in any or all circumstances. On this basis He has proceeded to develop His work in the world. This does not mean, however, that God simply causes all things to happen. There are many things that happen in this world that God does not cause and is not pleased with. His foreknowledge is real, genuine, but it is not causative.

1:2,22 SALVATION, Obedience—God's people are chosen for obedience to Christ. The Holy Spirit lives in believers and sanctifies them; that is, the Spirit makes them holy and acceptable to God. The Spirit leads us to obey all Christ taught us. Obeying the truth brings purity into our lives, a purity expressed in love to others.

1:2 SALVATION, Sanctification—Compare 2 Th 2:13. No human achievement is involved in salvation. God took the initiative to choose to save us. Through Christ's blood He saved us. Through the Holy Spirit He works in our lives to sanctify us or make us holy, obedient to Christ.

1:2 CHRISTIAN ETHICS, Obedience—Christians are elected by God for salvation through grace to be sanctified by the Spirit so they will obey Christ. Such obedience is the disciple's identifying mark.

1:2–3 PRAYER, Praise—See notes on Ro 1:7; 16:25–27. The salvation and hope we have in Christ move us to praise God.

1:3–4 JESUS CHRIST, Hope—The resurrection of Christ shows our salvation is secure. We can wait confidently for Christ to come with final salvation.

1:3–7 ELECTION, Eternal Security—The goal of faith is eternal salvation. Through the resurrection of Jesus Christ, the mercy of God presents the elect with a certain inheritance. The faith of the elect is a shield through which God's power preserves the elect until full salvation is revealed in the end time. God's power, not human works, assures eternal security for believers.

1:3–23 SALVATION, Definition—God's salvation is the new birth which brings hope for God's promised inheritance. See note on Jn 3:1–15. The hope will be realized fully only when we are resurrected as was Christ. In that sense salvation is future. See note on 1 Co 1:18. Salvation is certain because we know God's power protects us from temptation which would lead us away from Him. Salvation brings joy even in suffering, which refines our faith. Faith is commitment to the invisible God in expectation of final salvation. Faith leads to holy, obedient living in the present. Faith is centered on Christ's redeeming work on the cross. We learn of Christ's work and expectations through God's trustworthy Word.

1:3–5 LAST THINGS, Heaven—Believers have been born into both a living hope and an eternal inheritance. The inheritance will never perish, spoil, or fade. The object of the hope is heaven, which is also the location of the inheritance. God guards our future inheritance. It is secure.

1:6–7 EVIL AND SUFFERING, Testing—Believers are encouraged to rejoice in the midst of suffering because suffering is a testing of faith similar to the refining of gold. The rewards revealed at Christ's coming make the testing worthwhile.

1:7–9 LAST THINGS, Salvation's Completion—The future revealing of Christ will be a time for testing the faith of believers to reveal that which is genuine. The coming of Christ will also mean the realization of faith's goal, the completing of salvation. The doctrine of last things includes the forward-looking anticipation that what has begun as salvation and which presently continues will reach completion.

1:8 SALVATION, Love of God—We do not have to see Jesus in the flesh to love Him (Jn 20:29; 1 Jn 4:20).

1:8 SALVATION, Joy—Those who believe in Christ are filled with unutterable and exalted joy. Such joy is the portion of the saints.

1:10–12 HOLY SPIRIT, Revelation—The Spirit worked both in the Old Testament prophets such as Isaiah who predicted Christ's sufferings and in Christians who preach the gospel. In both cases His work is revelatory. In both cases what the Spirit reveals is Jesus Christ. In that sense, He truly is "the Spirit of Christ." Christians are privileged to be able to understand that what the Spirit reveals is Christ. The prophets who predicted Christ's suffering and glory did not understand it fully (v 10), and even angels strain to understand it (v 12). God has revealed the meaning of Christ in a special way to the church. See note on 1 Co 2:9–14.

1:10–13 SALVATION, Grace—See note on 2 Ti 2:1. Salvation and grace are used almost interchangeably in v 10. These verses show the dynamic nature of grace. Its use in v 13 refers to the second coming of Christ. Salvation is of grace from

come to you,[h] searched intently and with
the greatest care,[i] 11trying to find out the
time and circumstances to which the
Spirit of Christ[j] in them was pointing
when he predicted[k] the sufferings of
Christ and the glories that would follow.
12It was revealed to them that they were
not serving themselves but you,[l] when
they spoke of the things that have now
been told you by those who have
preached the gospel to you[m] by the Holy
Spirit sent from heaven.[n] Even angels
long to look into these things.

Be Holy

13Therefore, prepare your minds for action; be self-controlled;[o] set your hope[p]
fully on the grace to be given you[q] when
Jesus Christ is revealed.[r] 14As obedient[s]
children, do not conform[t] to the evil desires you had when you lived in ignorance.[u] 15But just as he who called you is
holy, so be holy in all you do;[v] 16for it is
written: "Be holy, because I am holy."[a] [w]
17Since you call on a Father[x] who
judges each man's work[y] impartially,[z]
live your lives as strangers[a] here in reverent fear.[b] 18For you know that it was
not with perishable things such as silver
or gold that you were redeemed[c] from
the empty way of life[d] handed down to
you from your forefathers, 19but with the
precious blood[e] of Christ, a lamb[f] without blemish or defect.[g] 20He was chosen

1:10 [h]ver 13 [i]S Mt 13:17 **1:11** [j]S Ac 16:7; 2Pe 1:21 [k]S Mt 26:24 **1:12** [l]S Ro 4:24 [m]ver 25 [n]S Lk 24:49 **1:13** [o]S Ac 24:25 [p]ver 3,21; S Heb 3:6 [q]ver 10 [r]ver 7; S 1Co 1:7 **1:14** [s]ver 2,22 [t]Ro 12:2 [u]Eph 4:18 **1:15** [v]Isa 35:8; 1Th 4:7; 1Jn 3:3 **1:16** [w]Lev 11:44, 45; 19:2; 20:7 **1:17** [x]S Mt 6:9 [y]S Mt 16:27 [z]S Ac 10:34 [a]S Heb 11:13 [b]Heb 12:28 **1:18** [c]S Mt 20:28; S 1Co 6:20 [d]Gal 4:3 **1:19** [e]S Ro 3:25 [f]S Jn 1:29 [g]Ex 12:5 **1:20** [h]Eph 1:4; S Mt 25:34 [i]Heb 9:26 **1:21** [j]Ro 4:24; 10:9 [k]S Ac 2:24 [l]Php 2:7-9; Heb 2:9 [m]ver 3,13; S Heb 3:6 **1:22** [n]Jas 4:8 [o]ver 2,14 [p]S Jn 13:34; S Ro 12:10 **1:23** [q]ver 3; S Jn 1:13 [r]Jn 1:13 [s]S Heb 4:12 **1:25** [t]Isa 40:6-8; S Jas 1:10,11 **2:1** [u]S Eph 4:22 [v]S Jas 4:11 **2:2** [w]1Co 3:2; Heb 5:12,13 [x]Eph 4:15,16 **2:3** [y]Ps 34:8; Heb 6:5

before the creation of the world,[h] but
was revealed in these last times[i] for your
sake. 21Through him you believe in
God,[j] who raised him from the dead[k]
and glorified him,[l] and so your faith and
hope[m] are in God.
22Now that you have purified[n] yourselves by obeying[o] the truth so that you
have sincere love for your brothers, love
one another deeply,[p] from the heart.[b]
23For you have been born again,[q] not of
perishable seed, but of imperishable,[r]
through the living and enduring word of
God.[s] 24For,

"All men are like grass,
and all their glory is like the flowers
of the field;
the grass withers and the flowers fall,
25 but the word of the Lord stands
forever."[c] [t]

And this is the word that was preached to
you.

Chapter 2

THEREFORE, rid yourselves[u] of all malice and all deceit, hypocrisy, envy,
and slander[v] of every kind. 2Like newborn babies, crave pure spiritual milk,[w]
so that by it you may grow up[x] in your
salvation, 3now that you have tasted that
the Lord is good.[y]

[a]16 Lev. 11:44,45; 19:2; 20:7 [b]22 Some early manuscripts *from a pure heart* [c]25 Isaiah 40:6-8

start to finish.

1:13 LAST THINGS, Return Promises—The full scope of Jesus' power, purpose, and personhood will be revealed when He returns. His second coming will bring the consummation of God's redemptive grace. This fact becomes the anchor for hope and holy obedience.

1:15–16 GOD, Holy—God alone is holy. Objects or persons can be classed as holy only by participation in His holiness. When we are brought into relationship with God, His holiness creates holiness in us in a purifying, sanctifying action. God's holiness makes a stringent demand upon us: we must humble ourselves before Him and become marked with the qualities that mark His own life.

1:17 GOD, Father—The ideas of God as both Father and Judge are perfectly compatible. The idea of God as Father sets forth His loving, compassionate nature, but that does not mean that God is lax with us in what He expects of us. Neither does the idea of His being Judge mean that He is a harsh despot with no mercy, as some might picture Him. He is the perfect combination of just Judge and loving Father.

1:17 SALVATION, Fear of God—Reverent fear of God is the proper stance for Christians in the face of potential danger and suffering and in face of the judgment.

1:17 PRAYER, Faithfulness of God—Prayer is a "calling on" God. Prayer history began that way. See notes on Ge 4:26; 1 Co 1:2. Although we call on Him as Father, we should do it reverently, without forgetting that He is also an unbiased Judge, faithful to His own character. Prayer is an awesome responsibility that should not be taken lightly.

1:18–21 JESUS CHRIST, Death—Jesus' death redeemed *us from empty, meaningless life. The sinless Jesus sacrificed* Himself according to God's eternal plan. His death provides our hope for living.

1:18–19 SALVATION, Redemption—See note on Heb 9:12,15. God did not purchase our redemption with perishable things such as silver or gold. Money cannot buy salvation. It is free to all, but it is not cheap. It cost God the death of His beloved Son.

1:20 REVELATION, Jesus Christ—Before He created the world, God had chosen Jesus as His full revelation to all human beings and had prepared Christ, only to reveal Him later in history, at the right time for such manifestation.

1:22–25 HOLY SCRIPTURE, Powerful—The world is made of things which do not last, but the truth revealed and expressed by God lasts without interruption or fear of destruction. When at work in a person's life, God's Word brings new birth.

1:22 SALVATION, As Cleansing—Only Christ's blood can cleanse from sin and provide salvation. Through the Spirit's sanctifying work (1:2), we can purify ourselves by obeying the truth of the gospel. Obedience should show itself in loving our brothers and sisters from a pure heart. Such pure works demonstrate Christ has cleansed and saved us (Jas 1:14–26). Jews expected religious acts or ceremonies to cleanse them. Such rites have no effect, only loving actions.

1:22 CHRISTIAN ETHICS, Social Relationships—Christian purity comes through the truth of faith in Christ. It expresses itself in love for others.

1:23–24 HUMANITY, Life—Without Christ life is as certain as grass. See note on Isa 40:6–7. Born again in Christ, life is eternal. God's eternal Word promises this.

2:1–2 CHRISTIAN ETHICS, Moral Imperatives—God's election (1:1–2) leads to responsibility to heed God's moral imperatives, thus to maturity in Christ.

2:2 SALVATION, Definition—Christians are not born fully grown. They are like newborn babies who need to grow and mature (Php 2:12). See note on Ps 132:16.

2:3 GOD, Goodness—God Himself is the standard of good-

Atonement

BIBLICAL TEACHINGS		HISTORICAL THEORIES		
Old Testament	**New Testament**	***Objective**	****Subjective**	**Both Objective and Subjective**
Sacrifice—One purpose of the sacrificial system described in the Old Testament was to remove the effects of sin. Atonement in the Old Testament is often associated with the death of a victim (Ex 29:36, Lev 4:20, Lev 16:9) but may also refer to a live offering (Lev 16:10) or a money (Ex 30:16) or prayer (Ex 32:30) offering. Old Testament sacrifices were generally given to remove the barrier sin had raised against God. **Suffering Servant**—The servant poems in Isaiah describe atonement in terms of redemptive suffering that is vicarious (done in place of and for the good of another) and sacrificial (given freely at personal cost) [See Isa 42:1-4; 49:1-6; 50:4-9; 52:13 to 53:12].	**Vicarious Atonement**—Christ died for us, that is on our behalf or for our benefit (Ro 5:8, 8:32; 1 Co 15:3; 2 Co 5:14; Gal 2:20). **Sacrificial Atonement**—Christ died instead of us to cover or remove our sins (Ro 3:25; 1 Co 5:7; Eph 5:2). **Representative Atonement**—Christ represented us on the cross by drawing us into His sacrifice for us so that we die with Him (Ro 6:6,8; 2 Co 5:14; Gal 2:20). **Suffering Servant**—Christ suffered with and for us to reconcile us to God (Lk 22:37, Mk 8:31, 9:31, 10:33, Jn 12:38; Ac 3:13, 4:30; 8:26-40; 1 Pe 2:21-25). **Substitutionary Atonement**—Christ's death satisfies God's wrath over humanity's sin. (Heb 2:17; 1 Jn 2:1-2) **Redemption**—The death of Christ removes or covers our sins so that we can be reconciled or redeemed (Ro 3:24; Co 1:14; Eph 1:7; Heb 9:12). **Ransom**—Christ's purpose was to set us free from our bondage to sin by giving his life (Mk 10:45; 1 Ti 2:6; Tit 2:14) **Bought**—Christ's death was the payment of the price that makes us God's own. (1 Co 6:20, 7:23; Gal 3:13, 4:5)	**Satisfaction Theory**—Introduced by Anselm (1033-1109), this theory holds that God was so dishonored by human sin that He had to take drastic action to reconcile sinners to Him. Like a feudal Lord who demanded satisfaction when he was wronged, God demanded satisfaction for our offense. Christ's death satisfied God's offended honor. This view is based on legal argument. Recognizes God's honor and seriousness of sin. Minimizes God as love. **Penal Substitution**—Introduced by the Reformers (1490-1560) when feudalism was giving way to jurisprudence, this theory holds that God cannot allow His law to be violated, so punishment, not satisfaction is required. Christ was the substitute, suffering the death penalty for us. This view sees atonement as a legal device. Recognizes seriousness of sin. May minimize God's love and forgiveness.	**Moral Influence Theory**—Introduced by Abelard (1079-1142), this theory holds that Christ died for sinful humanity out of love and with the intent of leading humanity to repentance. Thus, Christ's death did not change God's attitude toward humanity but rather, humanity's attitude toward God. Recognizes God as love. Minimizes seriousness of sin and God's response to sin. **Example Theory**—Introduced by Socinus (1539-1604), this theory holds that Christ died rather than yield what he believed to be His duty to God and man. Christ showed us by example how to live and our salvation is in following His example. Recognizes significance of Christ's example. Denies deity of Christ and the necessity of His saving work to our salvation.	**Ransom Theory**—Introduced by the early church fathers (ca. 180) and held as dominant for over a thousand years, this theory holds that Christ's death was the price paid to set us free from bondage to sin. Some (Origen) believed the price was paid to Satan. Takes seriously sin and Christ's work. Wrongly suggests power of Satan over God or an alliance of God and Satan. **Classic View**—Introduced by Gustof Aulen (ca. 1930), this view is an expanded version of the ransom theory. The view holds that Christ engaged all the powers of darkness, sin, death and the devil, and on the cross won the victory for those who believe in Him.

***Objective theories stress that Christ's death changes the attitude of God toward sinners.**
****Subjective theories stress that Christ's death changes human attitudes toward God and sin.**

Doctrinal Emphases in the Letters of Paul

Paul's Letters	Purpose	Major Doctrine(s)	Key Passage	Other Key Doctrines	Influence of the Letter
Romans	To express the nature, of the gospel, its relation to the OT and Jewish law, and its transforming power	Salvation	Ro 3:21-26	God Humanity The Church	Martin Luther (1515), through preparing lectures on Romans, felt himself "to be reborn."
1 Corinthians	To respond to questions about marriage, idol food, public worship; to discourage factions, to instruct on resurrection	The Church	1 Co 12:12-31	God Humanity Jesus Christ	The hymn on love in Chapter 13 is among the most familiar and loved chapters in Paul's writings.
2 Corinthians	To prepare readers for Paul's third visit and to defend Paul and the gospel he taught against false teachers	The Church Jesus Christ Salvation	2 Co 5:11-6:2	God	Called by C.K. Barrett "the fullest and most passionate account of what Paul meant by apostleship."
Galatians	To stress freedom in Christ against Jewish legalism while avoiding moral license	Salvation	Gal 2:15-21	Christian Ethics The Church Election	A sermon on the book of Galatians brought peace of heart to John Wesley. "I felt I did trust Christ alone for salvation."
Ephesians	To explain God's eternal purpose and grace and the goals God has for the church	Jesus Christ	Eph 3:14-21	The Church Salvation God	Called by Samuel Taylor Coleridge "one of the divinest of compositions."
Philippians	To commend Epaphroditus; to affirm generosity; to encourage unity, humility, and faithfulness even to death	Prayer	Php 1:3-11	Christian Ethics Salvation Church	Bengel (1850) described as "Summa epistlae, gaudes, gaudete" which means "The sum of the epistles is 'I rejoice; rejoice ye.'"
Colossians	To oppose false teachings related to a matter and spirit dualism and to stress the complete adequacy of Christ	Jesus Christ	Col 1:15-23	The Church Prayer God	Arius of Alex. (318) used Col. 1:15, from a hymn on the supremacy of Christ, to undermine Christ's deity. Arianism pronounced heretical at Councils of Nicea (325) and Constantinople (381).

Doctrinal Emphases in the Letters of Paul

Paul's Letters	Purpose	Major Doctrine(s)	Key Passage	Other Key Doctrines	Influence of the Letter
1 Thessalonians	To encourage new converts during persecution; to instruct them in Christian living and to assure them concerning the Second Coming	Last Things	1 Th 4:13-18	Evangelism Prayer God	Every chapter of 1 Thessalonians ends with a reference to the second coming.
2 Thessalonians	To encourage new converts in persecution and to correct misunderstandings about the Lord's return	Last Things	2 Th 1:3-12	Prayer The Church Evil & Suffering	With only three chapters, the letter is one of Paul's shortest yet because of 2:3-10 one of the most extensively studied.
1 Timothy	To encourage Timothy as minister, to refute false doctrine, and to instruct about church organization and leadership	Church Leaders	1 Ti 3:1-15	God Christian Ethics Salvation	Known as a "pastoral epistle" since the early part of the 18th century, Thomas Aquinas (d.1274) described 1 Timothy as a "pastoral textbook."
2 Timothy	To encourage Christians in the face of persecution and false doctrine	Education	2 Ti 2:14-19	Evil and Suffering Jesus Christ Prayer	Used by Augustine (d.430) in book four on *Christian Doctrine* to support the importance of Christian teachers.
Titus	To instruct church leaders, to advise about groups in the church, and to teach Christian ethics	Salvation	Tit 2:11-14	God Christian Ethics The Church Sin	Called the "Magna Charta" of Christian liberty.
Philemon	To effect reconciliation between a runaway slave and his Christian master	Christian Ethics	Phm 8-16	Prayer The Church Discipleship	Called by Emil Brunner (d.1965) a classic testimony to what is meant by Christian conservatism in regards to justice.

Biblical Prayers and Related Doctrines

Type of Prayer	Meaning	Old Testament Example	New Testament Example	Jesus' Teaching	Related Doctrines
Confession	Acknowledging sin and helplessness and seeking God's mercy	Psalm 51	Luke 18:13	Luke 15:11-24 Luke 18:10-24	EVIL AND SUFFERING, Repentance; GOD, Grace, Mercy; HOLY SCRIPTURE, Redemption; HUMANITY, Death and Sin; JESUS CHRIST; SALVATION, Grace, Redemption, Confession; SIN
Praise	Adoring God for who He is	1 Chronicles 29:10-13	Luke 1:46-55	Matthew 6:9	CREATION, Praise; GOD, Sovereignty; MIRACLES, Praise; SALVATION, Love of God; STEWARDSHIP, God's Ownership; WORSHIP, Praise
Thanksgiving	Expressing gratitude to God for what He has done	Psalm 105:1-7	1 Thessalonians 5:16-18	Luke 17:11-19	CREATION, Good; GOD, Goodness; STEWARDSHIP, Attitudes; WORSHIP, Thanksgiving
Petition	Making personal request of God	Genesis 24:12-14	Acts 1:24-26	Matthew 7:7-12	EVIL AND SUFFERING, Prayer; HOLY SPIRIT, Gifts; GOD, Father; STEWARDSHIP, God's Ownership
Intercession	Making request of God on behalf of another	Exodus 32:11-13, 31-32	Philippians 1:9-11	John 17:9, 20-21	EVANGELISM, Prayer; HOLY SPIRIT, Intercedes; JESUS CHRIST, Intercession
Commitment	Expressing loyalty to God and His work	1 Kings 8:56-61	Acts 4:24-30	Matthew 6:10 Luke 6:46-49	HOLY SCRIPTURE, Commitment; HOLY SPIRIT, Regenerates; STEWARDSHIP, Rewards
Forgiveness	Seeking mercy for personal sin or the sin of others	Daniel 9:4-19	Acts 7:60	Matthew 6:12 Luke 6:27-36	ELECTION, Forgiveness; FAMILY, Forgiveness; GOD, Grace, Mercy; HOLY SCRIPTURE, Redemption; HUMANITY, Death and Sin; JESUS CHRIST; SALVATION, Forgiveness; SIN, Forgiveness
Confidence	Affirming God's all-sufficiency and the believer's security in His love	Psalm 23	Luke 2:29-32	Matthew 6:5-15, 7:11	CREATION, Confidence; ELECTION, Faithfulness, Eternal Security; GOD, Faithfulness; HOLY SPIRIT, Security; REVELATION, Faithfulness
Benediction	A request for God's blessing	Numbers 6:24-26	Jude 24	Luke 11:5-13	EDUCATION, Happiness; ELECTION, Love; GOD, Love; HOLY SPIRIT, Protects; JESUS CHRIST, Love; LAST THINGS, Hope

eager to do good?[x] 14But even if you
should suffer for what is right, you are
blessed.[y] "Do not fear what they fear[j];
do not be frightened."[k z] 15But in your
hearts set apart Christ as Lord. Always be
prepared to give an answer[a] to everyone
who asks you to give the reason for the
hope[b] that you have. But do this with
gentleness and respect, 16keeping a clear
conscience,[c] so that those who speak
maliciously against your good behavior in
Christ may be ashamed of their slander.[d]
17It is better, if it is God's will,[e] to suffer
for doing good[f] than for doing evil. 18For
Christ died for sins[g] once for all,[h] the
righteous for the unrighteous, to bring
you to God.[i] He was put to death in the
body[j] but made alive by the Spirit,[k]
19through whom[l] also he went and
preached to the spirits in prison[l] 20who
disobeyed long ago when God waited patiently[m] in the days of Noah while the ark
was being built.[n] In it only a few people,
eight in all,[o] were saved[p] through water,
21and this water symbolizes baptism that
now saves you[q] also—not the removal of
dirt from the body but the pledge[m] of a
good conscience[r] toward God. It saves
you by the resurrection of Jesus Christ,[s]
22who has gone into heaven[t] and is
at God's right hand[u]—with angels, authorities and powers in submission to
him.[v]

3:13 [x]S Tit 2:14
3:14 [y]ver 17; 1Pe 2:19,20; 4:15,16 [z]Isa 8:12,13
3:15 [a]Col 4:6 [b]S Heb 3:6
3:16 [c]ver 21; S Ac 23:1 [d]1Pe 2:12,15
3:17 [e]1Pe 2:15; 4:19 [f]1Pe 2:20; 4:15,16
3:18 [g]1Pe 2:21; 4:1,13 [h]S Heb 7:27 [i]S Ro 5:2 [j]Col 1:22; 1Pe 4:1 [k]1Pe 4:6
3:19 [l]1Pe 4:6
3:20 [m]S Ro 2:4 [n]Ge 6:3,5,13,14 [o]Ge 8:18 [p]Heb 11:7
3:21 [q]S Ac 22:16 [r]ver 16; S Ac 23:1 [s]1Pe 1:3
3:22 [t]S Heb 4:14 [u]S Mk 16:19 [v]S Mt 28:18; S Ro 8:38
4:1 [w]S 1Pe 2:21 [x]S Ro 6:18
4:2 [y]Ro 6:2; 1Pe 1:14
4:3 [z]S Eph 2:2 [a]S Ro 13:13
4:4 [b]1Pe 3:16
4:5 [c]S Ac 10:42
4:6 [d]1Pe 3:19
4:7 [e]S Ro 13:11 [f]S Ac 24:25
4:8 [g]S 1Pe 1:22 [h]Pr 10:12; Jas 5:20

Chapter 4

Living for God

THEREFORE, since Christ suffered in
his body,[w] arm yourselves also with
the same attitude, because he who has
suffered in his body is done with sin.[x]
2As a result, he does not live the rest of
his earthly life for evil human desires,[y]
but rather for the will of God. 3For you
have spent enough time in the past[z] doing what pagans choose to do—living in
debauchery, lust, drunkenness, orgies,
carousing and detestable idolatry.[a] 4They
think it strange that you do not plunge
with them into the same flood of dissipation, and they heap abuse on you.[b] 5But
they will have to give account to him who
is ready to judge the living and the
dead.[c] 6For this is the reason the gospel
was preached even to those who are now
dead,[d] so that they might be judged according to men in regard to the body, but
live according to God in regard to the
spirit.
7The end of all things is near.[e] Therefore be clear minded and self-controlled[f]
so that you can pray. 8Above all, love
each other deeply,[g] because love covers
over a multitude of sins.[h] 9Offer hospital-

[j]14 Or *not fear their threats* [k]14 Isaiah 8:12
[l]18,19 Or *alive in the spirit,* 19*through which*
[m]21 Or *response*

3:15–22 JESUS CHRIST, Atonement—Christ's atonement enables and motivates us to moral living. He is Lord over our lives. See note on Eph 1:3. Our sins are cleansed and buried by His once-for-all death on the cross. The death of the Righteous One enabled forgiven sinners to enter God's holy presence. The Spirit raised Him from death and enabled Him to enter even Satan's realm to reveal the gospel to the most disobedient generation in history, that of Noah. Before He ascended to the heights of God's exaltation, He descended to the lowest depths, knowing what even the most wicked of humans ultimately face. Thus He completely overcame sin once and for all.

3:15 EDUCATION, Effective Witnessing—Christians who expect to be effective witnesses for Christ in a largely secular world must speak with up-to-date knowledge backed by experience. A major purpose of the church's educational function is to enable believers to articulate their faith in the marketplace.

3:16 HUMANITY, Moral Consciousness—The Greek word is literally a "good conscience," with the emphasis upon moral goodness. The moral consciousness is not always pure (1 Ti 4:2). Christians in daily witnessing and living must continuously treat other people in such a way enemies will have no evidence to talk against us. Rather, enemies will be ashamed because of our good behavior. Life in this vein keeps the conscience clear.

3:18–19 HOLY SPIRIT, Trinity—The Bible speaks of the Spirit raising Jesus from the dead (Ro 2:1–4; 8:11; 1 Ti 3:16), God raising Jesus (Ac 2:24), and Jesus rising (Mk 8:31). The meaning is the same in each case. The resurrection of Jesus is a work of the triune God. To bring people to God, Jesus died, and the Spirit raised Him to life. The Spirit also empowered Jesus' ministry among the dead. The meaning of this ministry is quite unclear. The text affirms Christ's activity but gives neither the reason for it nor its results.

4:2–5 CHRISTIAN ETHICS, Character—Christian character centers on knowing and doing the will of God, not on giving in to fleshly lusts or worldly pressures to conform. See Knowing and Experiencing the Will of God, pp. 1794–1796.

4:5 GOD, Judge—Multitudes will be shocked. They have gone merrily along sampling the world's pleasures, laughing at Christians who do not. One day they will face God the Father, who will judge the world. Death is no escape. God will judge everyone who ever lived.

4:7 LAST THINGS, History's Goal—God is moving this present world order to an end. He has a goal for history. Included is the inauguration of the eternal order. The nearness which Peter saw shows how closely Jesus' first coming is associated with His second; in God's time the end became near with the life, death, and resurrection of Jesus Christ. See note on Eph 1:10. Associated with the end is God's judgment before which everyone must give an account (v 5).

4:7 PRAYER, Persistence—Prayer requires common sense and watchful alertness.

4:8–10 CHRISTIAN ETHICS, Social Relationships—See note on 1:22.

4:9–11 DISCIPLESHIP, Priesthood—Christian disciples are to be priests, channels through which God's grace can meet the needs of others. See note on 2 Co 9:12–15. No class of professional ministers can lay claim to a monopoly on God's grace or on the power to determine who receives grace. Each disciple receives spiritual gift(s) (Greek *charisma*) from God. We are to use these gifts to serve (Greek *diakoneō*) other people. Such service reflects the grace (Greek *charis*) we have received from God and shows our skills in finding various ways and forms to introduce other people to this grace. Such grace is not a concrete object we give out. It is undeserved love we have received and share. Such grace takes concrete form in our acts of love for others. Such acts bring praise for Christ, not for us. Every Christian has received grace and is responsible for exercising priestly service to administer grace to others. See Guide to Service in Christ's Name, pp. 1823–1826.

ity[i] to one another without grumbling.[j]
10Each one should use whatever gift he
has received to serve others,[k] faithfully[l]
administering God's grace in its various
forms. 11If anyone speaks, he should do it
as one speaking the very words of God.[m]
If anyone serves, he should do it with the
strength God provides,[n] so that in all
things God may be praised[o] through
Jesus Christ. To him be the glory and the
power for ever and ever. Amen.[p]

Suffering for Being a Christian

12Dear friends, do not be surprised at
the painful trial you are suffering,[q] as
though something strange were happening to you. 13But rejoice[r] that you participate in the sufferings of Christ,[s] so that
you may be overjoyed when his glory is
revealed.[t] 14If you are insulted because
of the name of Christ,[u] you are blessed,[v]
for the Spirit of glory and of God rests on
you. 15If you suffer, it should not be as a
murderer or thief or any other kind of
criminal, or even as a meddler. 16Howev-
er, if you suffer as a Christian, do not be
ashamed, but praise God that you bear
that name.[w] 17For it is time for judgment
to begin with the family of God;[x] and if it
begins with us, what will the outcome be
for those who do not obey the gospel of
God?[y] 18And,

> "If it is hard for the righteous to be
> saved,
> what will become of the ungodly
> and the sinner?"[n] [z]

19So then, those who suffer according
to God's will[a] should commit themselves
to their faithful Creator and continue to
do good.

Chapter 5

To Elders and Young Men

TO the elders among you, I appeal as a
fellow elder,[b] a witness[c] of Christ's
sufferings and one who also will share in
the glory to be revealed:[d] 2Be shepherds
of God's flock[e] that is under your care,
serving as overseers—not because you
must, but because you are willing, as God
wants you to be;[f] not greedy for money,[g] but eager to serve; 3not lording it
over[h] those entrusted to you, but being
examples[i] to the flock. 4And when the

4:9 [i]S Ro 12:13 [j]Php 2:14
4:10 [k]Ro 12:6,7 [l]1Co 4:2
4:11 [m]1Th 2:4 [n]Eph 6:10 [o]1Co 10:31 [p]S Ro 11:36
4:12 [q]1Pe 1:6,7
4:13 [r]S Mt 5:12 [s]S 2Co 1:5 [t]Ro 8:17; 1Pe 1:7; 5:1
4:14 [u]S Jn 15:21 [v]Mt 5:11
4:16 [w]Ac 5:41
4:17 [x]Jer 25:29; Eze 9:6; Am 3:2; 1Ti 3:15 [y]2Th 1:8
4:18 [z]Pr 11:31; Lk 23:31
4:19 [a]1Pe 2:15; 3:17
5:1 [b]S Ac 11:30 [c]S Lk 24:48 [d]1Pe 1:5,7; 4:13; Rev 1:9
5:2 [e]S Jn 21:16 [f]2Co 9:7; Phm 14 [g]S 1Ti 3:3
5:3 [h]Eze 34:4; Mt 20:25-28 [i]S 1Ti 4:12

[n] *18* Prov. 11:31

4:11 DISCIPLESHIP, Enabling Power—Disciples serve by the enabling power God provides. The good deeds in our lives are God's deeds, and He gets the glory. See Mt 5:16; note on Php 4:10–13.

4:12–19 EVIL AND SUFFERING, Endurance—Suffering should not surprise Christians. Suffering can be an occasion for the testing of faith and for sharing in Christ's sufferings. Rejoicing and praise are the proper responses to suffering. See note on Col 1:24.

4:14–17 HOLY SPIRIT, Protects—God gave His Spirit to protect His people during times of persecution and suffering. Jesus promised He would do this (Mk 15:11). He said the Spirit is a Lawyer (*paraklētos*) who will shield His followers from false charges (Jn 16:7–11). Many early Christians suffered for their faith. The attitude they took towards persecution was remarkable. They reasoned that since their Lord had suffered, they were privileged to experience what He had experienced. The Spirit protects Christians from persecution; but when it comes, He is "the Spirit of glory" who abides with us during persecution. Certainly He does not desert us. He honors us for sacrifice and suffering, just as He glorified Christ by raising Him from the dead (1 Pe 3:18).

4:16 PRAYER, Praise—Even persecution can be a reason for praise, as it was in Peter's own life (Ac 5:41).

4:18 SIN, Alienation—This question contained in an Old Testament quotation implies that the judgment of God upon sin results in total separation from God in the life to come.

4:19 GOD, Creator—The Creator permitted suffering in His world when people sinned. Now sufferers tend to feel suffering indicates God has forsaken them. Peter teaches us God is true to Himself, to His people, and to His promises. Suffering simply calls us to new commitment to Him and His way of life.

4:19 CREATION, Evil—Though God made a good world, evil has become a part of it because of sin. The works of wicked people sometimes cause good people to suffer. Peter instructed his suffering readers to refrain from doubting God's interest in or His ability to help them. A willingness to do God's will, whatever the cost, is the only ultimate way to face the problem of unexplained suffering. That will is not something new. It is the Creator's eternal purpose.

5:1 JESUS CHRIST, Final Coming—Jesus will reveal (Greek *apokaluptō*) God's heavenly glory and salvation (1:5) for us at Christ's final revelation (Greek *apokalupsis*; 1:7,13; 4:13). Revelation is a technical term for Christ's final coming. Literature such as Daniel and Revelation which center attention on the final kingdom is called apocalyptic literature. Compare Lk 17:30; Ro 8:18; 1 Co 1:7; 3:13; Ga 3:23; 2 Th 1:7; 2:3,6,8; Rev 1:1.

5:1 LAST THINGS, Return Promises—Peter was certain that he would share in the glory to come. Sufferings in the present time are made more bearable by the prospect of sharing in the consummation of Christ's return (4:13). The joy of the future will more than compensate for the brief sufferings of this life (5:4). The return of Christ will mean a crown of unfading, or eternal glory. This glory is the goal of the Christian calling.

5:1–5 CHURCH LEADERS, Pastor and Overseer—The care of the church has been entrusted to those who are designated by different terms—elders, overseers (bishops), and pastors—but who all have the same function. Peter addressed the leaders as elders but used the imagery of shepherding (pastor) and overseeing (overseer, bishop) to portray their responsibilities. The most prevalent term used today for this office is pastor. The flock has been committed to the pastor, who serves under the chief Shepherd. Pastors are not hirelings who care nothing for the sheep. They are to tend the flock assigned to them out of devotion to God not to gratify their personal ambitions. They are not to serve for personal gain whether it be for financial reward, popular acclaim, or reputation. They are not to be domineering or authoritarian in their leadership. Their ministry is to be characterized by selfless service and humility, not arrogance. Peter himself embodied this humility. He did not consider himself to be exalted over the rest of the leaders of the church. Instead, he referred to himself as a fellow elder who had been called by God to the same service of bearing witness to Christ's sufferings and leading His people. See Jn 21:15–19. What he said to them applied also to himself.

5:4 JESUS CHRIST, Final Coming—Ministers of God are likened to shepherds of sheep and are encouraged to be faithful. Those who do will receive their reward when the chief Shepherd appears.

Chief Shepherd[j] appears, you will receive the crown of glory[k] that will never
fade away.[l]

5 Young men, in the same way be submissive[m] to those who are older. All of
you, clothe yourselves with humility[n] toward one another, because,

"God opposes the proud
but gives grace to the humble."[o] [o]

6 Humble yourselves, therefore, under
God's mighty hand, that he may lift you
up in due time.[p] 7 Cast all your anxiety on
him[q] because he cares for you.[r]

8 Be self-controlled[s] and alert. Your enemy the devil prowls around[t] like a roaring lion[u] looking for someone to devour.
9 Resist him,[v] standing firm in the faith,[w]
because you know that your brothers
throughout the world are undergoing the
same kind of sufferings.[x]

10 And the God of all grace, who called
you[y] to his eternal glory[z] in Christ, after
you have suffered a little while,[a] will
himself restore you and make you
strong,[b] firm and steadfast. 11 To him be
the power for ever and ever. Amen.[c]

Final Greetings

12 With the help of Silas,[p][d] whom I regard as a faithful brother, I have written
to you briefly,[e] encouraging you and testifying that this is the true grace of God.
Stand fast in it.[f]

13 She who is in Babylon, chosen together with you, sends you her greetings,
and so does my son Mark.[g] 14 Greet one
another with a kiss of love.[h]

Peace[i] to all of you who are in Christ.

5:4 [j]S Jn 10:11 [k]S 1Co 9:25 [l]1Pe 1:4
5:5 [m]Eph 5:21 [n]1Pe 3:8 [o]Pr 3:34; S Mt 23:12
5:6 [p]Job 5:11; Jas 4:10
5:7 [q]Ps 37:5; Mt 6:25 [r]Ps 55:22; Heb 13:5
5:8 [s]S Ac 24:25 [t]Job 1:7 [u]2Ti 4:17
5:9 [v]S Jas 4:7 [w]Col 2:5 [x]S Ac 14:22
5:10 [y]S Ro 8:28 [z]2Co 4:17; 2Ti 2:10 [a]1Pe 1:6 [b]Ps 18:32; 2Th 2:17
5:11 [c]S Ro 11:36
5:12 [d]S Ac 15:22 [e]Heb 13:22 [f]S 1Co 16:13
5:13 [g]S Ac 12:12
5:14 [h]S Ro 16:16 [i]S Eph 6:23

[o] *5* Prov. 3:34 [p] *12* Greek *Silvanus,* a variant of *Silas*

5:5–8 CHRISTIAN ETHICS, Character—Respect for others, humility, freedom from anxiety, and self-control are Christian character traits.

5:6–11 EVIL AND SUFFERING, God's Present Help—Suffering is temporary. God's people know we will eventually receive His help and relief. Suffering is an opportunity for Satan, who uses our hard times to create fear, anxiety, and doubt. We must humbly trust God and exercise self-control while we wait for God's help. We gain courage by knowing we are not the only ones who must suffer.

5:7 GOD, Love—Love is the most basic word we have concerning what God is like. Because He loves, we can trust Him with anything that worries us.

5:7 PRAYER, Mercy of God—We are not alone. We matter to God, and He can bear our anxieties with more insight than we. Once our worries are deposited with God, we leave them there.

5:9 ELECTION, Perseverance—Though the enemy of the elect is active in seeking their destruction, the elect are called to be alert and vigilant, knowing that the God of grace will make them steadfast and victorious in keeping their election commitments.

5:10,12 GOD, Grace—The grace of God is not a detached sentiment that God has somewhere within His heart. It is an active power through which He seeks to bless us in saving us from sin and death and developing us in Christian growth. Grace is God's love and power working for our benefit, though we do not deserve it. When the world looks dark, we can trust His promise to restore and strengthen us.

5:11 PRAYER, Praise—Some praise is ascription. We use human language to ascribe to Him the glorious characteristics of His nature. This is a way of praising Him. See note on Ro 16:25–27.

5:12 HOLY SCRIPTURE, Writing—The author wrote by the grace and direction of God. He encouraged his readers to believe and to follow the truths revealed in the written message. This is the initial recognition of letters which become Scripture as time, experience, and the inspiration of their wisdom confirmed God's revelation in them.

5:13 THE CHURCH, Local Body—A local church is a group of believers chosen by God. Peter sent greetings from a local church. Babylon stood for evil, so here it probably represents the church living in an evil location, possibly Rome. See notes on Ac 4:32; 8:1.

5:14 PRAYER, Blessing—See note on Heb 13:25.

2 Peter

Theological Setting

Within a generation of the death and resurrection of Jesus, false teachers appeared within the church. These teachers claimed to be true Christians and sought to lead other believers to follow them. The delay in the return of Christ was one of the factors on which they fixed great attention. In the early church, Christians had looked forward to the return of Christ. Some expected Him to return in the immediate future. They made no effort to say when He might return, but they lived in expectation of it at any time. As the years passed and this event did not take place, some claimed it would not occur at all. This attitude cast doubt upon all the promises of God.

Second Peter was written to meet such a situation. The readers knew the truth, but they needed to be reminded of it because false teachers were seeking to persuade them to turn aside from it. The doctrines of the false teachers were far from the truth, and their lives were characterized by immoral conduct. They claimed freedom, but it led people away from God. The readers were urged to reject the appeals of the false teachers and to remain loyal to Christ.

Theological Outline

2 Peter: The Word of Authority

- I. Opening Greeting to Those of Faith (1:1-2)
- II. The Work of God's Power (1:3-4)
  - A. Through knowledge of Him (1:3)
  - B. Partakers of the divine nature (1:4)
- III. The Work of the Believer (1:5-15)
  - A. Effort toward growth (1:5-7)
  - B. The effect of growth (1:8-9)
  - C. The need of zeal (1:10-11)
  - D. A reminder of the truth (1:12-13)
- IV. The Inspiration of Scripture (1:16-21)
- V. The Danger of False Teachers (2:1-22)
  - A. Errors of the false teachers (2:1-3)
  - B. Judgment of the false teachers (2:4-6)
  - C. Rescue of the righteous (2:7-10)
  - D. Moral failures of the false teachers (2:11-22)
- VI. The Delay of the Return of Christ (3:1-13)
  - A. Denial of the return of Christ (3:1-4)
  - B. Destruction by the flood (3:5-7)
  - C. God's reason for delay (3:8-9)
  - D. Promise of destruction by fire (3:10)
  - E. Awaiting new heavens and a new earth (3:11-13)
- VII. Warning to Purity and Steadfastness (3:14-18)

Theological Conclusions

Second Peter stressed the true knowledge that comes from God. False teachers stand condemned. True teaching centers in four areas:

1. Christian maturity,
2. true authority,
3. the return of Christ, and
4. the inspiration of Scripture.

God's power has provided everything the Christian needs (1:3). The Christian must not participate in the world's corrupting evil. Rather, the Christian strives to mature in Christian virtues (1:4-7). Such growth results in a productive Christian life, leading to eternal life in Christ's kingdom. Even proper understanding of Christ's return leads to growth and maturity in Christian conduct (3:14-15,17-18).

Freedom in Christ is a marvelous Christian truth that is easily misunderstood. It can turn people to fulfill selfish desires, reject God's authority, and deny the authority of God's servants in the church. Human greed can lead false teachers to invent stories to gain power and authority. Such authorities stand harshly condemned (2:1-22). Only those who speak on authority of prophets and apostles have true authority (3:1-2).

The false teachers denied the return of Christ. They insisted that the promise of His return had not been realized and would not be in the future. The letter assures the readers that the scoffers were wrong. God has always kept His promises, even the promise of destruction of the world by a flood. God does not count time as humans do. A long time to us is a day in God's sight (3:8). The delay of the return of Christ is an evidence of God's mercy. It provides opportunity for people to repent and receive salvation (3:9). Yet the return of the Lord is certain, and it will lead to the destruction of the heavens and the earth by fire (3:12). But that is not the end. A new heaven and a new earth characterized by righteousness are promised (3:13).

The importance and reliability of Scripture are stressed. At every turn 2 Peter used Old Testament language as the authoritative base for New Testament truths. Old Testament writers served New Testament Christians as they wrote (1:19).

The Bible came into being as men were moved by the Spirit of God. It is God's message and must be heeded, even when it is difficult to understand. The gospel message is not a story of human invention. Understanding of Scripture comes through the same Spirit who inspired its writing. One of the strongest statements in the Bible about its own reliability and inspiration is found in 1:20-21.

Contemporary Teaching

This letter warns us not to be led astray by false teaching and doctrine. In every generation teachers appear who seek to lead the faithful away from God. We need to be reminded of God's truth so we may resist such false teaching.

We are to grow as Christians. This action requires effort on our part. Faith leads to love and to full obedience. We are to be aware of those who by their conduct show that they have departed from God's truth and follow their own desires. The emphasis upon the inspiration of Scripture is important. The nature and value of the Bible are often questioned. The statement on the inspiration of Scripture in this letter referred originally to the Old Testament, but it is proper for us to apply it to all the Bible (1:21). This writing cautions us that God does not follow our timetable. He has a plan, and He will complete it when it pleases Him. The delay in the end provides opportunity for Him to demonstrate His mercy. He will rescue the righteous and punish the wicked.

Chapter 1

SIMON Peter, a servant[a] and apostle of
Jesus Christ,[b]

To those who through the righteousness[c] of our God and Savior Jesus
Christ[d] have received a faith as precious
as ours:

2Grace and peace be yours in abundance[e] through the knowledge of God
and of Jesus our Lord.[f]

Making One's Calling and Election Sure

3His divine power[g] has given us everything we need for life and godliness
through our knowledge of him[h] who
called us[i] by his own glory and goodness. 4Through these he has given us his
very great and precious promises,[j] so
that through them you may participate in
the divine nature[k] and escape the corruption in the world caused by evil desires.[l]
5For this very reason, make every effort
to add to your faith goodness; and to
goodness, knowledge;[m] 6and to knowledge, self-control;[n] and to self-control,
perseverance;[o] and to perseverance, godliness;[p] 7and to godliness, brotherly kindness; and to brotherly kindness, love.[q]
8For if you possess these qualities in increasing measure, they will keep you
from being ineffective and unproductive[r]
in your knowledge of our Lord Jesus
Christ.[s] 9But if anyone does not have
them, he is nearsighted and blind,[t] and
has forgotten that he has been cleansed
from his past sins.[u]
10Therefore, my brothers, be all the
more eager to make your calling[v] and
election sure. For if you do these things,
you will never fall,[w] 11and you will receive a rich welcome into the eternal
kingdom[x] of our Lord and Savior Jesus
Christ.[y]

Prophecy of Scripture

12So I will always remind you of these
things,[z] even though you know them
and are firmly established in the truth[a]
you now have. 13I think it is right to refresh your memory[b] as long as I live in
the tent of this body,[c] 14because I know
that I will soon put it aside,[d] as our Lord
Jesus Christ has made clear to me.[e]
15And I will make every effort to see that
after my departure[f] you will always be
able to remember these things.
16We did not follow cleverly invented
stories when we told you about the pow-

1:1 [a]Ro 1:1 [b]1Pe 1:1 [c]Ro 3:21-26 [d]Tit 2:13
1:2 [e]S Ro 1:7 [f]ver 3,8; 2Pe 2:20; 3:18; S Php 3:8
1:3 [g]1Pe 1:5 [h]S ver 2 [i]S Ro 8:28
1:4 [j]2Co 7:1 [k]Eph 4:24; Heb 12:10; 1Jn 3:2 [l]Jas 1:27; 2Pe 2:18-20
1:5 [m]S ver 2; Col 2:3
1:6 [n]S Ac 24:25 [o]S Heb 10:36 [p]ver 3
1:7 [q]S Ro 12:10; 1Th 3:12
1:8 [r]Jn 15:2; Col 1:10; Tit 3:14 [s]S ver 2
1:9 [t]1Jn 2:11 [u]Eph 5:26; S Mt 1:21
1:10 [v]S Ro 8:28 [w]Ps 15:5; 2Pe 3:17; Jude 24
1:11 [x]Ps 145:13; 2Ti 4:18 [y]2Pe 2:20; 3:18
1:12 [z]Php 3:1; 1Jn 2:21; Jude 5 [a]2Jn 2
1:13 [b]2Pe 3:1 [c]Isa 38:12; 2Co 5:1,4
1:14 [d]2Ti 4:6 [e]Jn 13:36; 21:18,19
1:15 [f]Lk 9:31

1:1 GOD, Righteous—We often connect salvation with the love of God. Here it is connected with the righteousness of God. God's righteousness and love are not separate qualities but are two aspects of the one great God. Salvation is God's fair and right way of dealing with His sinful creatures, offering hope to all who will trust Him. Righteousness characterizes both the Father and the Son.

1:2–3 SALVATION, Knowledge of God—Peter chose a special Greek term (*epignōsis*) to describe the personal knowledge and relationship a person has of Jesus in the conversion experience. This intimate personal knowledge is the foundation of life in Christ. It provides all the benefits of salvation and the power we need to live for Him. Compare v 8; 2:20–21. To know God's salvation is to know Jesus Christ person to person.

1:3–4 GOD, Power—The new life of our salvation comes from the power of God. It is an extension, or conclusion, of the power of God displayed in creation. It provides everything we need.

1:3–11 ELECTION, Eternal Security—God's power provides the resources for the godly life needed to maintain election commitments. God has called us, given rich promises of eternal life, and prepared a rich welcome into His kingdom for us. Salvation is secured by Him. This does not relieve us of responsibility. Rather it increases our calling to make use of His moral resources, to grow spiritually, not to fall away from His way, and thus give objective evidence of our election. Throughout the Bible election is both a promise of eternal security through God's grace and a call to moral righteousness in God's power.

1:3–9 CHRISTIAN ETHICS, Character—Salvation leads to "godliness" (v 3). This finds concrete expression in conscious effort to incorporate Christian characteristics into the disciple's life. These include goodness, knowledge, self-control, perseverance, brotherly kindness, and love. Such character traits lead to a productive life for Christ.

1:4 CREATION, Evil—The evil in the world makes it difficult for us to cope in daily living. To remedy this deficiency, God introduced a new element into His world. He puts a divine nature within us through a new creation. In this way, we have strength to resist the evil and serve Him in the Spirit. The Spirit's work is to create us anew so we will not give in to evil desires.

1:4 SIN, Depravity—Simply defined, depravity is corruption that results from evil desires. God through the work of Christ and the presence of the Holy Spirit provides us a way that is not corrupt and depraved.

1:4 PRAYER, Faithfulness of God—God's promises are vital to a praying Christian. The character of God is utterly reliable.

1:9 SALVATION, As Cleansing—Christian virtues in our life (vv 5–7) help us know we have been cleansed from past sins.

1:10–11 DISCIPLESHIP, Rewarded—Peter encouraged his readers to cultivate qualities of true discipleship (vv 5–8) and, thereby, to grow spiritually. As reward for such discipleship, disciples will be warmly welcomed to inherit eternal life in God's kingdom. See note on Mt 25:34–46.

1:10–11 LAST THINGS, Coming Kingdom—The kingdom of God in its future aspects awaits with rich welcome those who live and die within the certainty of divine calling and election. Unfaithfulness generates a sense of uncertainty, while a productive life based on Christ's standards enlarges one's confidence in Christ's eternal kingdom.

1:11,16–18 JESUS CHRIST, Final Coming—Peter's experience as eyewitness of the transfiguration gives certainty to Christ's final coming. See note on Mt 17:1–13.

1:13–15 HUMANITY, Physical Nature—People's physical nature is actually no more permanent than a tent that is packed up as a camp moves on. The body is put aside, but our life continues in Christ through resurrection. The brief time in this life should leave behind memories of what God has done and taught through us.

1:13–15 LAST THINGS, Believers' Death—Death is the putting off of the body. Viewed as a tent or temporary dwelling, the present physical body must be laid aside for the permanent house not made with hands. See note on 2 Co 5:1–10. Death will be a departure to be with the Lord. See note on Php 1:21–24.

er and coming of our Lord Jesus Christ,[g]
but we were eyewitnesses of his majesty.[h] 17For he received honor and glory
from God the Father when the voice
came to him from the Majestic Glory, saying, "This is my Son, whom I love; with
him I am well pleased."[a][i] 18We ourselves heard this voice that came from
heaven when we were with him on the
sacred mountain.[j]
19And we have the word of the prophets made more certain,[k] and you will do
well to pay attention to it, as to a light[l]
shining in a dark place, until the day
dawns[m] and the morning star[n] rises in
your hearts.[o] 20Above all, you must understand[p] that no prophecy of Scripture
came about by the prophet's own interpretation. 21For prophecy never had its
origin in the will of man, but men spoke
from God[q] as they were carried along by
the Holy Spirit.[r]

Chapter 2

False Teachers and Their Destruction

BUT there were also false prophets[s]
among the people, just as there will
be false teachers among you.[t] They will
secretly introduce destructive heresies,
even denying the sovereign Lord[u] who
bought them[v]—bringing swift destruction on themselves. 2Many will follow
their shameful ways[w] and will bring the
way of truth into disrepute. 3In their
greed[x] these teachers will exploit you[y]
with stories they have made up. Their
condemnation has long been hanging
over them, and their destruction has not
been sleeping.
4For if God did not spare angels when
they sinned,[z] but sent them to hell,[b]
putting them into gloomy dungeons[c] to
be held for judgment;[a] 5if he did not
spare the ancient world[b] when he
brought the flood on its ungodly people,[c]
but protected Noah, a preacher of righteousness, and seven others;[d] 6if he condemned the cities of Sodom and Gomorrah by burning them to ashes,[e] and made
them an example[f] of what is going to
happen to the ungodly;[g] 7and if he rescued Lot,[h] a righteous man, who was distressed by the filthy lives of lawless men[i]
8(for that righteous man,[j] living among
them day after day, was tormented in his
righteous soul by the lawless deeds he
saw and heard)— 9if this is so, then the
Lord knows how to rescue godly men
from trials[k] and to hold the unrighteous
for the day of judgment,[l] while continuing their punishment.[d] 10This is especial-

1:16 [g]Mk 13:26; 14:62 [h]Mt 17:1-8
1:17 [i]S Mt 3:17
1:18 [j]Mt 17:6
1:19 [k]1Pe 1:10,11 [l]Ps 119:105 [m]Lk 1:78 [n]Rev 22:16 [o]2Co 4:6
1:20 [p]2Pe 3:3
1:21 [q]2Ti 3:16 [r]2Sa 23:2; Ac 1:16; 3:18; 1Pe 1:11
2:1 [s]Dt 13:1-3; Jer 6:13; S Mt 7:15 [t]1Ti 4:1 [u]Jude 4 [v]S 1Co 6:20
2:2 [w]Jude 4
2:3 [x]ver 14 [y]2Co 2:17; 1Th 2:5
2:4 [z]Ge 6:1-4 [a]1Ti 3:6; Jude 6; Rev 20:1,2
2:5 [b]2Pe 3:6 [c]Ge 6:5-8:19 [d]Heb 11:7; 1Pe 3:20
2:6 [e]Ge 19:24,25 [f]Nu 26:10; Jude 7 [g]Mt 10:15; 11:23, 24; Ro 9:29
2:7 [h]Ge 19:16 [i]2Pe 3:17
2:8 [j]Heb 11:4
2:9 [k]Ps 37:33; S Ro 15:31; Rev 3:10 [l]S Mt 10:15

[a]*17* Matt. 17:5; Mark 9:7; Luke 9:35 [b]*4* Greek *Tartarus* [c]*4* Some manuscripts *into chains of darkness* [d]*9* Or *unrighteous for punishment until the day of judgment*

1:16–18 HOLY SCRIPTURE, Eyewitnesses—The gospel message rests on eyewitness accounts. The early church had to contend with charges they invented the stories about Jesus. Peter pointed to God's personal revelation at Christ's baptism and transfiguration.

1:16–19 LAST THINGS, Return Promises—The promise of Christ's return is no clever invention of human imagination. It is based on the transfiguration (Mt 17:1–13) as a foreshadowing of Christ in His true majesty as will be seen at His second coming. Eyewitnesses were given a preview of that coming eschatological day of the Lord. The full light of revelation to dawn at Christ's coming will replace the lamp of prophecy.

1:16–21 PROCLAMATION, Central Theme—Proclamation is built on eyewitness testimony and personal experience with Jesus, not on fictitious stories.

1:17 GOD, Father—See note on Mk 9:7.

1:19–21 HOLY SCRIPTURE, Authoritative—Prophets spoke not from their own wisdom but from God's. Their testimony was confirmed and made clear by Christ's coming. Sacred writings have God as their source and are God-breathed (inspired by the presence of the Holy Spirit). Scripture is the truth of God put to writing in exactly the way God wanted it.

1:20–21 HOLY SPIRIT, Revelation—One of the Spirit's great works is to reveal God. In Israel the primary way He did that was to give oracles to prophets. See note on Zec 7:12. Both in their speaking and in their writing, the prophets were guided by the Spirit of God. The Bible is the inspired result of God's plan and purpose. Prophets spoke in the vernacular of their day, but they spoke what God's Spirit wanted them to say.

2:1–3 CHURCH LEADERS, False Prophet—Just as Israel suffered from influential false prophets and false teaching, so will the church. False prophets and false teachers seek popularity, promise what the people desire, slyly undermine the tenets of the faith, live immoral life-styles, and covet financial rewards. They counterfeit the Spirit and lure others astray with enchanting new doctrines.

2:1–3 EDUCATION, False Teachers—One of the crucially important functions of the teaching ministry of the church is to enable Christians to recognize destructive heresies when they see them. Such heresies are based on fabricated stories rather than on Scripture. This false teaching attracts great crowds, destroys the public reputation of the church, and leads its followers to destruction rather than salvation. The motivation for such teaching is personal ambition and greed. See note on Col 2:6–8.

2:3–22 EVIL AND SUFFERING, Punishment—False teachers who claim to follow Christ but lead His people astray face sure and horrible punishment. God's history with angels and with His people provide all the necessary evidence. History also shows God's ability and action in rescuing His faithful people from difficult situations.

2:4 EVIL AND SUFFERING, Satan—Satan's realm includes imprisoned angels who rebelled against God and were condemned to hell. Peter did not describe the fallen angels' sin.

2:4–9 LAST THINGS, Hell—Hell is not the intended abode of human beings. It was designed out of necessity for the devil and his associates (Rev 20:7–10). It is the place of confinement for sinning angels awaiting future judgment (Jude 6). "Hell" here translates the Greek *tartarus,* not Gehenna. See note on Mt 5:22. *Tartarus* appears only here in the New Testament. This term was commonly used in Greek thought to refer to the abode of the wicked dead. The place of this angelic imprisonment is one of gloomy, dense darkness. Through a series of illustrations Peter emphasized that God will make no mistakes in separating the faithful from the wicked. The fate of the wicked is more fully described. The fiery destruction of Sodom and Gomorrah serves as an example of the punishment of the wicked following the day of judgment.

2:5 PROCLAMATION, Exhortation—See note on Lk 8:1. Noah exemplifies God's proclaimers who exhort an audience to make the right decisions in the face of coming catastrophe.

ly true of those who follow the corrupt
desire[m] of the sinful nature[e] and despise
authority.

Bold and arrogant, these men are not
afraid to slander celestial beings;[n] 11 yet
even angels, although they are stronger
and more powerful, do not bring slanderous accusations against such beings in the
presence of the Lord.[o] 12 But these men
blaspheme in matters they do not understand. They are like brute beasts, creatures of instinct, born only to be caught
and destroyed, and like beasts they too
will perish.[p]

13 They will be paid back with harm for
the harm they have done. Their idea of
pleasure is to carouse in broad daylight.[q]
They are blots and blemishes, reveling in
their pleasures while they feast with
you.[f r] 14 With eyes full of adultery, they
never stop sinning; they seduce[s] the unstable;[t] they are experts in greed[u]—an
accursed brood![v] 15 They have left the
straight way and wandered off to follow
the way of Balaam[w] son of Beor, who
loved the wages of wickedness. 16 But he
was rebuked for his wrongdoing by a donkey—a beast without speech—who
spoke with a man's voice and restrained
the prophet's madness.[x]

17 These men are springs without water[y] and mists driven by a storm. Blackest darkness is reserved for them.[z] 18 For
they mouth empty, boastful words[a] and,
by appealing to the lustful desires of sinful human nature, they entice people
who are just escaping[b] from those who
live in error. 19 They promise them freedom, while they themselves are slaves of
depravity—for a man is a slave to whatever has mastered him.[c] 20 If they have
escaped the corruption of the world by
knowing[d] our Lord and Savior Jesus
Christ[e] and are again entangled in it and
overcome, they are worse off at the end
than they were at the beginning.[f] 21 It
would have been better for them not to
have known the way of righteousness,
than to have known it and then to turn
their backs on the sacred command that
was passed on to them.[g] 22 Of them
the proverbs are true: "A dog returns
to its vomit,"[g h] and, "A sow that is
washed goes back to her wallowing in
the mud."

Chapter 3

The Day of the Lord

DEAR friends,[i] this is now my second
letter to you. I have written both of
them as reminders[j] to stimulate you to
wholesome thinking. 2 I want you to recall
the words spoken in the past by the holy
prophets[k] and the command given by
our Lord and Savior through your apostles.[l]

3 First of all, you must understand that

2:10 [m]2Pe 3:3; Jude 16,18 [n]Jude 8
2:11 [o]Jude 9
2:12 [p]Ps 49:12; Jude 10
2:13 [q]S Ro 13:13; 1Th 5:7 [r]1Co 11:20,21; Jude 12
2:14 [s]ver 18 [t]Jas 1:8; 2Pe 3:16 [u]ver 3 [v]Eph 2:3
2:15 [w]Nu 22:4-20; 31:16; Dt 23:4; Jude 11; Rev 2:14
2:16 [x]Nu 22:21-30
2:17 [y]Jude 12 [z]Jude 13
2:18 [a]Jude 16 [b]ver 20; 2Pe 1:4
2:19 [c]S Ro 6:16
2:20 [d]S 2Pe 1:2 [e]2Pe 1:11; 3:18 [f]Mt 12:45
2:21 [g]Eze 18:24; Heb 6:4-6; 10:26,27
2:22 [h]Pr 26:11
3:1 [i]S 1Co 10:14 [j]2Pe 1:13
3:2 [k]Lk 1:70; Ac 3:21 [l]S Eph 4:11

[e] *10* Or *the flesh* [f] *13* Some manuscripts *in their love feasts* [g] *22* Prov. 26:11

2:10–22 HUMANITY, Human Nature—Undisciplined human nature is like an animal who seeks to satisfy every basic urge with neither thought nor care for consequences. Such animal behavior is a sure sign a person is not a Christian. Sadly, such people pose as Christian teachers and lead others astray, promising freedom but leading to addiction and slavery to sin.

2:10 SIN, Self-centeredness—Sin is yielding to our corrupt, depraved, self-centered desires. Sin leads us to make our desires the highest authority in life and to despise and reject all other authorities, including God. Sin will be judged.

2:12–19 SIN, Depravity—Depravity is following animal instincts like beasts rather than accepting the responsibility of humans created in God's image. Depravity applies to false religious leaders belonging to the community of faith (v 1). Depravity is not a momentary state but a continual sin binge. Depravity claims to offer total freedom but produces absolute slavery, making instinctual beasts out of spiritual persons. Depravity leads to the bitterest condemnation and judgment.

2:20–21 ELECTION, Free Will—The elect walk in an intimate fellowship with the God of election. He rescues the elect from the presence, penalty, and power of sin, while reserving the ungodly to the day of judgment for punishment. Election does not rob the elect of free will. We may be introduced to Christ and reject Him, as Israel repeatedly rejected God's prophets. To reject Christ leads to the most horrible condition a person can know.

3:1–2 HOLY SCRIPTURE, Unity—Prophets and Jesus Christ are holy messengers, Jesus Himself being the final and complete revelation. The words of the prophets and the commands of Christ through the apostles are affirmed as God's revelation to His followers. Peter's own inspired writing sought to stimulate wholesome thinking, that is, to bring to mind Christ's teachings and lead to ways of applying His truths to daily life.

3:3–11 CREATION, Personal Creator—When people become too proud in their sophistication or too corrupt in their moral actions, they forget a simple fact. God created the world and in the days of Noah poured out judgment on this world. By faith, we understand that the world was made by the command of God (Heb 11:3). The "ultimate origin" goes back to the simple will of God, implemented through His spoken command. We accept the fact of creation on faith. When we do this, all other things fall into place, are easily understood, and appear consistently logical. The "sameness" of daily life in the universe may seem to point to an eternal universe without a creator. The flood experience and God's coming day of judgment show the world is not eternal. Only God is. The world continues to exist only through God's patience. Its certain destruction calls us to holy living.

3:3–4 LAST THINGS, Return Attitudes—Some scoff at the teaching of a future return of Christ. Peter observed such scoffing in his day, and more was promised as a characteristic of the last days. Such scoffing may be due to ignorance of God's former teaching (Jude 10,18), or it may be deliberate disdain (2 Pe 3:5). Some scoffing may be due to the delayed fulfillment of the promises about Christ's return, especially when the delay is seen as slowness or a sign that Christ is not going to return. Disciples know the delay is due to patient grace to allow everyone opportunity to repent. Against all scoffing resounds the strong affirmation, "The day of the Lord will come" (2 Pe 3:10).

3:4,12 JESUS CHRIST, Final Coming—Courage and patience are enjoined in the face of scoffers who bait Christians about the delay in Christ's final coming. Compare 1:16. Ethical

in the last days[m] scoffers will come, scoffing and following their own evil desires.[n]
4They will say, "Where is this 'coming'
he promised?[o] Ever since our fathers
died, everything goes on as it has since
the beginning of creation."[p] 5But they
deliberately forget that long ago by God's
word[q] the heavens existed and the earth
was formed out of water and by water.[r]
6By these waters also the world of that
time[s] was deluged and destroyed.[t] 7By
the same word the present heavens and
earth are reserved for fire,[u] being kept
for the day of judgment[v] and destruction
of ungodly men.

8But do not forget this one thing, dear
friends: With the Lord a day is like a
thousand years, and a thousand years are
like a day.[w] 9The Lord is not slow in
keeping his promise,[x] as some understand slowness. He is patient[y] with you,
not wanting anyone to perish, but everyone to come to repentance.[z]

10But the day of the Lord will come like
a thief.[a] The heavens will disappear with
a roar;[b] the elements will be destroyed
by fire,[c] and the earth and everything in
it will be laid bare.[h] [d]

3:3 [m]1Ti 4:1; 2Ti 3:1 [n]2Pe 2:10; Jude 18
3:4 [o]Isa 5:19; Eze 12:22; Mt 24:48; S Lk 17:30 [p]Mk 10:6
3:5 [q]Ge 1:6,9; Heb 11:3 [r]Ps 24:2
3:6 [s]2Pe 2:5 [t]Ge 7:21,22
3:7 [u]ver 10,12; S 2Th 1:7 [v]S Mt 10:15
3:8 [w]Ps 90:4
3:9 [x]Hab 2:3; Heb 10:37 [y]S Ro 2:4 [z]S 1Ti 2:4; Rev 2:21
3:10 [a]S Lk 12:39 [b]Isa 34:4 [c]ver 7,12; S 2Th 1:7 [d]Mt 24:35; S Heb 12:27; Rev 21:1
3:12 [e]S 1Co 1:7 [f]Ps 50:3 [g]ver 10
3:13 [h]Isa 65:17; 66:22; Rev 21:1
3:14 [i]S 1Th 3:13
3:15 [j]S Ro 2:4

11Since everything will be destroyed in
this way, what kind of people ought you
to be? You ought to live holy and godly
lives 12as you look forward[e] to the day of
God and speed its coming.[i] [f] That day
will bring about the destruction of the
heavens by fire, and the elements will
melt in the heat.[g] 13But in keeping with
his promise we are looking forward to a
new heaven and a new earth,[h] the home
of righteousness.

14So then, dear friends, since you are
looking forward to this, make every effort
to be found spotless, blameless[i] and at
peace with him. 15Bear in mind that our
Lord's patience[j] means salvation,[k] just
as our dear brother Paul also wrote you
with the wisdom that God gave him.[l]
16He writes the same way in all his letters, speaking in them of these matters.
His letters contain some things that are
hard to understand, which ignorant and
unstable[m] people distort,[n] as they do the
other Scriptures,[o] to their own destruction.

[k]ver 9 [l]Eph 3:3 **3:16** [m]Jas 1:8; 2Pe 2:14 [n]Ps 56:5; Jer 23:36 [o]ver 2

---

behavior is the Christian's answer to the world's skepticism. The "day of God" is an equivalent of the "day of Jesus Christ" or a reference to the final coming of Christ.

3:4 HISTORY, Promise—Christians live in the face of promise even though the central event of history—Christ's death and resurrection—has occurred. Scoffers dismiss Christian hope as false promise. They look to history as eternal and meaning as dependent on human effort. God's historical acts from creation onward give a firm basis to the Christian hope that God will fulfill all His promises.

3:7 LAST THINGS, Creation's Redemption—A necessary prelude to the new heavens and new earth will be the divine judgment upon the present heavens and earth. See note on Rev 21:1. A bond exists between humanity and the created order. From creation it was so. Human sin reverberated in the creation, so the day of judgment for the ungodly will involve a fiery judgment that will reach to the very elements of the universe (2 Pe 3:10). The destruction of the present order prepares for the emergence of the new one.

3:8 HISTORY, Time—Chronology does not affect God. He deals with eternity. This does not mean daily life is unimportant to God. The entire Bible testifies to God's deep involvement in daily life. It does mean by nature God is not limited by time as He acts to achieve His purposes. He will not die and so does not face a time limit on His actions. He knows all of time not just a brief part of it. Thus He knows the most opportune time to fulfill His promises.

3:9 GOD, Love—Why has Christ not returned? Has God forgotten His promises? Certainly not! The same love of God that moved Him to send His Son Jesus to become our Savior also prompts Him to be patient in trying to reach every person possible before the end of time. God's patience and forbearance have been shown in many ways across the ages.

3:9 SALVATION, Repentance—God wants everyone to repent. If anyone does not repent of his or her sins, that will be contrary to the loving Father's will and lead to judgment.

3:10 LAST THINGS, Evil's End—The future day of the Lord will bring a cataclysmic end to the heavens and the earth. It will spell the end of the present reign of evil. Nothing will escape through concealment. All will be exposed to a judgment of fire.

3:11–12,14 CHRISTIAN ETHICS, Character—Eschatology, or the doctrine of last things, encourages us to develop a holy character like God's. See notes on Da 9:24; 11:32–35.

3:11–18 LAST THINGS, Purity—What kind of persons ought people to be in view of the events of the end time? The answer is holy and godly, spotless and blameless, guarded and growing. Since God is holy, to be Godlike is to be holy. To be holy is to be distinct from the ordinary and worldly. Moral blamelessness must be maintained. The influence of error and evil demands persons who are on guard. The prospect of meeting the Lord encourages growth in grace and knowledge of Christ. The sincere expectation of the Lord's coming promotes personal purity.

3:15 HUMANITY, Intellectual Nature—Paul used wisdom to write Scripture. His wisdom used all the intellectual skills he had and all the education he had received, but the most important element of his wisdom was the gift given by God teaching Paul what to write.

3:15–16 HOLY SCRIPTURE, Canonization—The writer referred to several of Paul's letters as Scripture. He indicated that Paul's writings are at times hard to understand and that unwise and mischievous people had sought to distort their meaning. The collection of Paul's letters probably marked the first step in collecting New Testament writings into a canon or authoritative group of New Testament writings. The church soon recognized need for authoritative written teachings concerning Christ parallel to the Old Testament canon. God led in the collection of the canon.

3:16 EDUCATION, Correction—The truth is not always easy to understand. Mature teachers are needed. Sadly, too often untrained and unstable persons readily accept teaching positions and lead conscientious followers of Christ astray, bringing destruction on both teacher and follower. See note on 2:1–3.

[17]Therefore, dear friends, since you already know this, be on your guard[p] so that you may not be carried away by the error[q] of lawless men[r] and fall from your secure position.[s] [18]But grow in the grace[t] and knowledge[u] of our Lord and Savior Jesus Christ.[v] To him be glory both now and forever! Amen.[w]

3:17 [p]1Co 10:12 [q]2Pe 2:18 [r]2Pe 2:7 [s]Rev 2:5
3:18 [t]S Ro 3:24 [u]S 2Pe 1:2 [v]2Pe 1:11; 2:20 [w]S Ro 11:36

[h]10 Some manuscripts *be burned up* [i]12 Or *as you wait eagerly for the day of God to come*

3:17–18 ELECTION, Perseverance—The elect make every effort to be spotless, blameless, and at peace with God. We strive to be spiritually alert persons who grow continuously in grace and in the knowledge of Jesus Christ, our Lord and Savior. False teachers seek to lead us away from sound biblical teachings. We are responsible to maintain sound moral foundations and persevere in and with Christ.

3:18 PRAYER, Praise—The letter ends with a doxology. See note on Ro 16:25–27. Christ had claimed the divine glory as His own (Jn 17:5); this ascription is proper.

1 John

Theological Setting

A "teacher" or a group of "teachers" had come denying that Jesus Christ had come in the flesh. The first letter of John was written to counter this kind of false teaching within the community of early Christians. Already a group of people had left their midst to follow the false teachers and their nefarious doctrine (2:19). John, therefore, was admonishing the remainder of the community to continue firm in their commitment to sound Christian doctrine. By commitment to Jesus as God's Son come in the flesh they could have assurance of eternal life (5:13).

By the time John wrote this letter, the Christian community was being confronted by a variety of false teachings. Many of those who were teaching false doctrine were presenting themselves as spiritually superior. Also, they were presenting their false teachings as an advancement in the spiritual teachings of Christianity. The particular group of teachers John confronted in this letter claimed to have a special insight relative to the incarnation of Jesus. They claimed that Jesus did not come in the flesh (4:2-3). For them, all matter was inherently evil; and since flesh consisted of matter, it, too, was inherently evil. The "flip" side of their spiritual coin was that spirit is inherently good. Therefore, Jesus the Christ could not have come in the flesh, for He was the representative of God who was all Spirit. Had He become flesh, they argued, He necessarily would have partaken of the sinful nature of the flesh.

Beyond this, they claimed to have other special insights into the character and person of God that were not available to ordinary people. These special insights, they taught, were necessary to achieve a right relationship with God (2:19-27). The first readers of this document might have been attracted to this teaching because it promised them a secret or hidden knowledge about God which would set them apart from the masses of humanity. Thus, they would become a part of the spiritually elite who had special insights into the character of God, the person of Christ, and the spiritual world.

In the face of such a challenge, the first readers of this letter had several options:

1. They could accept the doctrines of these false teachers as true and depart from the mainstream of Christianity. Apparently some of their number had already done so.

2. They could accept John's letter as the true apostolic voice in this matter and remain true to revealed Christianity. This certainly was what John hoped for when he wrote this letter.

3. Beyond this, they could expose these false teachers by putting them to the test concerning their view of the person of Christ (4:1-3).

4. They could have remained neutral in the matter, thus allowing the false teachers to gain a platform within their community. Of all the options, this one probably would have been the least attractive to John.

John, the beloved apostle, sustained a special relationship with the Christian community. Whether or not he was the group's founder cannot be ascertained with any certainty. What can be said, however, is that he was their apostolic voice at this particular time. He was more than a pastor to them. He was their spiritual mentor who was seeking to prevent them from falling prey to false spiritual teachings. He had every reason to expect that the first readers of his letters would accept his advice as an apostolic injunction. He certainly had hopes of rescuing them from heretical teaching by presenting to them the truth about Jesus Christ.

Theological Outline

1 John: A Polemic Against False Teachers

I. Establishing a Theological Beachhead (1:1-4)

 A. An assertion concerning the person of Christ (1:1)

  1. He was not a created being. (1:1*a*)

  2. He could be experienced by the senses—hearing, seeing, touching. (1:1*b*)

 B. An assertion concerning the author of the letter (1:2-4)

  1. He was an eyewitness to the Christ event. (1:2)

2. He was a proclaimer of what he had witnessed. (1:3)
3. He was writing to effect a mutual joy. (1:4)

II. The Christian's Life-style (1:5—2:14)
  A. This includes fellowship with God. (1:5-7)
  B. This involves the confession of sin. (1:8-10)
  C. This means obeying the commands of Christ. (2:1-6)
  D. This calls for maintaining a right relationship with other Christians. (2:7-14)

III. The Christian's Relationship to the World (2:15-29)
  A. The Christian cannot love the world. (2:15-17)
  B. The Christian must beware of antichrists. (2:18-27)

IV. A Message for God's Children (2:28—4:21)
  A. All of God's children will one day be like Christ. (2:28—3:3)
  B. God's children are not to continue in sin. (3:4-6)
  C. God's children must guard against being led astray by the forces of evil. (3:7-10)
  D. God's children are to love one another. (3:11-24)
  E. God's children are to "test the spirits." (4:1-3)
  F. God's children are to overcome the world. (4:4-6)
  G. God's children are to reflect God's character. (4:7-21)

V. Final Exhortations. (5:1-21)
  A. Concerning faith: Obedient love is faith's proof. (5:1-5)
  B. Concerning Jesus: Jesus gives us eternal life. (5:6-12)
  C. Concerning assurance: Believers are assured of eternal life. (5:13-15)
  D. Concerning sin: God's children do not continue to sin. (5:16-21)

Theological Conclusions

The first epistle of John represents a major New Testament statement concerning the person and work of Christ. The epistle also contains definitive ethical teachings for the Christian. The following doctrinal emphases may be noted:

1. The uniqueness of the person of Christ.
2. The truth of the genuine incarnation of Christ.
3. The definitive nature of the atonement.
4. A person's relationship to God is reflected in his/her dealings with other persons.
5. The Christian cannot claim sinlessness but must not reflect a life-style of sin.
6. The Christian is to be an overcomer in relation to the world.
7. God is love.

The Christian community to whom John wrote was in danger of succumbing to false teachings concerning the doctrine of Christ, as well as the doctrine of God. These two cornerstone doctrines of Christianity were being undermined by the false teachers. They denied the interest of God in humans and in the created world. They denied the true incarnation of Jesus, and they taught that He was less than the divine Son of God.

Under the leadership of the Holy Spirit, John responded with a resounding assertion of assurance for believers. There is no sham in the Godhead. God is light or good, and in Him there is no darkness or evil at all. God is personified as love. These are the primary affirmations concerning God the Father. Jesus came in the flesh, and anyone who will not affirm this fact is of the devil and is an antichrist. The eternal, immortal, invisible, preexistent Word truly became a man. As a man, He died on the cross, thus making atonement for the sins of all persons. Because of what God in Christ has done, the Christian is to have faith in God and love others. In so doing the believer knows eternal life.

Contemporary Teaching

The first epistle of John challenges modern Christians in several areas of life. John challenges us: (1) to have a proper view of the person and work of Christ. He is the eternal, sinless Son of God who became perfect man in every sense of the word and was the atoning sacrifice for human sin. (2) To understand that we cannot live above sin; but, on the other hand, we are to live a life that is not marred by the continual practice of sin. (3) To be properly related to other persons in an atmosphere of love, trust, and forgiveness. (4) To keep the revelation of God to His people precious and to guard against those who would prevent this sacred trust.

Chapter 1

The Word of Life

THAT which was from the beginning,[a]
which we have heard, which we
have seen with our eyes,[b] which we
have looked at and our hands have
touched[c]—this we proclaim concerning
the Word of life. 2The life appeared;[d] we
have seen it and testify to it,[e] and we
proclaim to you the eternal life,[f] which
was with the Father and has appeared to
us. 3We proclaim to you what we have
seen and heard,[g] so that you also may
have fellowship with us. And our fellowship is with the Father and with his Son,
Jesus Christ.[h] 4We write this[i] to make
our[a] joy complete.[j]

Walking in the Light

5This is the message we have heard[k]
from him and declare to you: God is
light;[l] in him there is no darkness at all.
6If we claim to have fellowship with him
yet walk in the darkness,[m] we lie and do
not live by the truth.[n] 7But if we walk in
the light,[o] as he is in the light, we have
fellowship with one another, and the
blood of Jesus, his Son, purifies us from
all[b] sin.[p]
8If we claim to be without sin,[q] we
deceive ourselves and the truth is not in
us.[r] 9If we confess our sins, he is faithful
and just and will forgive us our sins[s] and
purify us from all unrighteousness.[t] 10If
we claim we have not sinned,[u] we make
him out to be a liar[v] and his word has no
place in our lives.[w]

Chapter 2

MY dear children,[x] I write this to you
so that you will not sin. But if anybody does sin, we have one who speaks
to the Father in our defense[y]—Jesus
Christ, the Righteous One. 2He is the
atoning sacrifice for our sins,[z] and not
only for ours but also for[c] the sins of the
whole world.[a]
3We know[b] that we have come to
know him[c] if we obey his commands.[d]

1:1 [a]S Jn 1:2 [b]S Lk 24:48; Jn 1:14; 19:35; Ac 4:20; 2Pe 1:16; 1Jn 4:14 [c]Jn 20:27 **1:2** [d]Jn 1:1-4; 11:25; 14:6; 1Ti 3:16; 1Pe 1:20; 1Jn 3:5,8 [e]S Jn 15:27 [f]S Mt 25:46 **1:3** [g]S ver 1 [h]1Co 1:9 **1:4** [i]1Jn 2:1 [j]S Jn 3:29 **1:5** [k]1Jn 3:11 [l]1Ti 6:16 **1:6** [m]Jn 3:19-21; 8:12; 2Co 6:14; Eph 5:8; 1Jn 2:11 [n]Jn 3:19-21; 1Jn 2:4; 4:20 **1:7** [o]Isa 2:5 [p]Heb 9:14; Rev 1:5; 7:14 **1:8** [q]Pr 20:9; Jer 2:35; Ro 3:9-19; Jas 3:2 [r]Jn 8:44; 1Jn 2:4 **1:9** [s]Ps 32:5; 51:2; Pr 28:13 [t]ver 7; Mic 7:18-20; Heb 10:22 **1:10** [u]ver 8 [v]1Jn 5:10 [w]Jn 5:38; 1Jn 2:14 **2:1** [x]ver 12,13,28; 1Jn 3:7,18; 4:4; 5:21; S 1Th 2:11 [y]S Ro 8:34; 1Ti 2:5 **2:2** [z]Ro 3:25; 1Jn 4:10 [a]S Mt 1:21; S Jn 3:17 **2:3** [b]ver 5; 1Jn 3:24; 4:13; 5:2 [c]S ver 4 [d]S Jn 14:15

[a]4 Some manuscripts *your* [b]7 Or *every* [c]2 Or *He is the one who turns aside God's wrath, taking away our sins, and not only ours but also*

1:1–3 REVELATION, Word—The revelation of God occurs to the ears, eyes, and touch. It appeared most fully in the living Word with the Father at creation and revealed in the flesh in Jesus. See note on Jn 1:1–4. John's ministry was oral proclamation of his personal, eyewitness testimony of Jesus. He put this in writing to complete the fellowship of his audience with him and with the Father and Son. That complete fellowship completed John's joy.

1:1–4 EVANGELISM, Christ the Hope—Christian hope centers on the reality of the Lord Jesus Christ. We continue to proclaim Christ on the basis of inspired eyewitnesses. See note on 2 Pe 1:16.

1:3 PRAYER, Fellowship with God—Fellowship with God is exercised in prayer. Fellowship implies commonalities. The new creature in Christ (2 Co 5:17) shares a nature, albeit derivative, with God. God shares with the Christian His own holiness and eternality. Every Christian should walk with God.

1:5–7 GOD, Righteous—The darkness of sin has no part in God's existence. His own character sets the standard for what is right. He hates what is evil. His primary purpose as He works in the world is to overcome every sign of evil with His righteousness. We must realize that we cannot be in fellowship with God when we are doing or thinking those things that are evil.

1:6–7 SALVATION, Definition—See note on Eze 36:24–28. Mysteriously and miraculously, the sacrifice of Jesus on the cross is the source of our cleansing from sin. Salvation brings fellowship with other Christians and ethical living in the light of Christ's truth.

1:6 PRAYER, Fellowship with God—See note on 1:3. To claim to walk with God and in darkness is a contradiction in terms.

1:7,9 SALVATION, As Cleansing—See note on Heb 1:3. God's purification awaits our confession of sins.

1:8,10 SIN, Universal Nature—Every person without exception sins. Without this warning, believers may be tempted to embrace a perfectionism that takes the power of sin too lightly and leads to stubborn, spiritual pride. The biblical call is to confess and repent of sin, not to deny sin.

1:8–10 SALVATION, Confession—God promises forgiveness of sins and purification from all unrighteousness to those who confess their sins. To hide, ignore, or claim we do not have sin is to deceive ourselves and lie to God. Such deception denies the truth of God's Word and thus calls God a liar.

1:9 GOD, Faithfulness—John's readers evidently claimed to be above sin and would not confess sin in their lives. John taught that God wants us to confess sin. Then God can show He is faithful to His promises to save us by forgiving our sin. He can show He is the just Judge by taking away our sin and letting us share in His righteousness. God's justice does not force Him to condemn every sinner. His justice has established a way He can forgive sinners.

2:1,22–24 GOD, Trinity—The Son not only died for our sin. He now intercedes for us with the Father. As the only Person ever to live without sin, He is qualified to do this. This means the believer must trust both Father and Son. Belief in the trinitarian nature of God is essential to biblical faith. To deny that Jesus is the divine Messiah is to deny God as our Savior. Without allegiance to the Son, we cannot claim allegiance to the Father.

2:1–2 JESUS CHRIST, Intercession—Jesus died for our sins to lift us above sin. Still believers do sin. The ascended Christ prays for us to the Father so our sins can be forgiven. We need no earthly priest to deal with our sins. We have Jesus Christ. See Guide to Confession, pp. 1763–1765.

2:1,7–8,12–14 HOLY SCRIPTURE, Purpose—Written revelation accomplished several purposes. It helped readers avoid sin and follow the old commandment of love given new expression in Christ's life and the fellowship of the church. It spoke to all age groups with assurance of forgiveness and relationship with God.

2:1 PRAYER, In Christ—Christ is the Christian's "lawyer" in heaven. See notes on Ro 8:34; Heb 7:25.

2:3–28 ELECTION, In Christ—The elect are persons who walk in the light as Jesus did. The antichrists are contrary in their walk, which leads them out from the elect because they never belonged to the elect in the first place. The Holy Spirit's anointing of the elect enables them to be genuine about their election commitment. False teachers tempt the elect away from truth, love, and morality. Salvation in Christ leads us to eternal life.

2:3–6,17,29 SALVATION, Obedience—See note on Jn 14:23. Christ's word, commands, and teaching are the same

4The man who says, "I know him,"[e] but
does not do what he commands is a liar,
and the truth is not in him.[f] 5But if anyone obeys his word,[g] God's love[d] is truly
made complete in him.[h] This is how
we know[i] we are in him: 6Whoever
claims to live in him must walk as Jesus
did.[j]
7Dear friends,[k] I am not writing you a
new command but an old one, which you
have had since the beginning.[l] This old
command is the message you have heard.
8Yet I am writing you a new command;[m]
its truth is seen in him and you, because
the darkness is passing[n] and the true
light[o] is already shining.[p]
9Anyone who claims to be in the light
but hates his brother[q] is still in the darkness.[r] 10Whoever loves his brother lives
in the light,[s] and there is nothing in
him[e] to make him stumble.[t] 11But whoever hates his brother[u] is in the darkness and walks around in the darkness;[v]
he does not know where he is
going, because the darkness has blinded
him.[w]

12I write to you, dear children,[x]
because your sins have been
forgiven on account of his
name.[y]
13I write to you, fathers,
because you have known him who is
from the beginning.[z]
I write to you, young men,
because you have overcome[a] the
evil one.[b]
I write to you, dear children,[c]
because you have known the Father.
14I write to you, fathers,
because you have known him who is
from the beginning.[d]
I write to you, young men,
because you are strong,[e]
and the word of God[f] lives in you,[g]
and you have overcome the evil
one.[h]

Do Not Love the World

15Do not love the world or anything in
the world.[i] If anyone loves the world,
the love of the Father is not in him.[j]
16For everything in the world—the cravings of sinful man,[k] the lust of his eyes[l]
and the boasting of what he has and
does—comes not from the Father but
from the world. 17The world and its desires pass away,[m] but the man who does
the will of God[n] lives forever.

Warning Against Antichrists

18Dear children, this is the last hour;[o]

2:4 [e]ver 3; Tit 1:16; 1Jn 3:6; 4:7,8 [f]1Jn 1:6,8
2:5 [g]S Jn 14:15 [h]1Jn 4:12 [i]S ver 3
2:6 [j]S Mt 11:29
2:7 [k]S 1Co 10:14 [l]ver 24; 1Jn 3:11, 23; 4:21; 2Jn 5,6
2:8 [m]S Jn 13:34 [n]Ro 13:12; Heb 10:25 [o]Jn 1:9 [p]Eph 5:8; 1Th 5:5
2:9 [q]ver 11; Lev 19:17; 1Jn 3:10,15,16; 4:20,21 [r]1Jn 1:5
2:10 [s]1Jn 3:14 [t]ver 11; Ps 119:165
2:11 [u]S ver 9 [v]S 1Jn 1:6 [w]Jn 11:9; 12:35
2:12 [x]S ver 1 [y]S 1Jn 3:23
2:13 [z]S Jn 1:1 [a]S Jn 16:33 [b]ver 14; S Mt 5:37 [c]S ver 1
2:14 [d]S Jn 1:1 [e]Eph 6:10 [f]S Heb 4:12 [g]Jn 5:38; 1Jn 1:10 [h]S ver 13
2:15 [i]Ro 12:2 [j]Jas 4:4
2:16 [k]Ge 3:6; Ro 13:14; Eph 2:3 [l]Pr 27:20
2:17 [m]S Heb 12:27 [n]Mt 12:50
2:18 [o]S Ro 13:11

[d]5 Or *word, love for God* [e]10 Or *it*

---

thing. God wants born-again persons to imitate Jesus in character and conduct. Not to obey is to show we are not Christ's. To obey is to show we have eternal life. See note on Jn 3:1–15.

2:3,13–14 SALVATION, Knowledge of God—We can be sure we know Christ if we obey Him. All members of God's family know Him. Through knowledge of God, we overcome the devil. See note on 2 Pe 1:2–3.

2:3–6 DISCIPLESHIP, Neighbor Love—God's love is made complete in the life of the one who obeys God's commands. The life of the obedient disciple becomes a channel for God to express His redemptive love for others. If we do not obey God's commands, we can hardly have confidence we know God through faith in Christ. In fact, John says bluntly that the person who claims to know God but does not obey His commands is making a false claim. See note on 3:17–18.

2:3–6 CHRISTIAN ETHICS, Obedience—Obedience gives assurance of salvation. Disciples seek to live like Jesus did.

2:5 GOD, Love—God's love is both creative and purposive. He bestows His love upon us for the purpose of creating loving obedience and righteousness in us. His love seeks to draw us into faith and service.

2:9–27 SALVATION, Definition—Love for our brothers and sisters and confession of Jesus as the Messiah are positive proofs of salvation. Love of the world, its values, and its ways shows we have not trusted God and do not belong to Him. Maintaining our confession proves we have eternal life.

2:9–11 CHRISTIAN ETHICS, Social Relationships—Consistent hatred of others is not the trait of a disciple. Love should characterize the disciple's relationships with other people.

2:12 SALVATION, Forgiveness—Our sins are forgiven on account of the name of Jesus Christ. His name saves (Mt 1:21; Ac 4:12). See note on Da 9:19.

2:13–14 EVIL AND SUFFERING, Satan—God is all powerful. Satan is not. Christians can and do overcome the evil one. We can let God's Word lead us to resist temptation. See note on 4:1–4.

2:15–17 EVIL AND SUFFERING, Natural Origin—The "world" does not refer to the physical creation but to all aspects of reality that are opposed to and separated from God. To get carried away by worldly lust is to move further from God and become a part of that which opposes Him. The environment in which we live leads us away from God to evil. God's Spirit leads us away from the world to Christ.

2:15–17 CHRISTIAN ETHICS, Covetousness—God's love motivates Christian ethics (4:7–12, 16–17). Love of the world and desire for its things and ways stands totally opposed to God's love. Proper love leads one to do God's will. See note on 1 Pe 4:2–5.

2:15 STEWARDSHIP, Attitudes—Christian stewards are to care lovingly for God's world. We must not give our first love to the world and its material goods. The steward's supreme love is for God only. When the world becomes the object of our loving devotion, we show we do not love God. See note on Mt 6:19–33.

2:16–17 CREATION, Evil—God created a wondrous world of beautiful things. Every part bears the impress of His finger. The "world" has, however, another meaning. The world refers to the things in God's creation that pull us away from our divine Creator's holiness and, thus, from living in fellowship with Him. "World" in this context is an evil system totally under the grip of the devil. This becomes concrete in wicked desire or base appetite for things forbidden by the holy Creator. The world of sin in the moral realm has left its toll on the natural realm. Evil will eventually be conquered by Christ and removed from the world God created. Implicitly, it has already been defeated in His death and resurrection. When, at His second coming He destroys it completely, God's created world will once more have its original beauty.

2:17,25 SALVATION, Eternal Life—See notes on Jn 10:10,28; Tit 1:2. Eternal life is God's promise to those who do His will.

2:18–23 CREATION, Evil—Evil is already present in an intense form. God's good world which He created for people is continually harassed by those who are against Christ. These opponents of Christ sometimes are found even in the profess-

and as you have heard that the antichrist
is coming,[p] even now many antichrists
have come.[q] This is how we know it is
the last hour. 19They went out from us,[r]
but they did not really belong to us. For if
they had belonged to us, they would have
remained with us; but their going
showed that none of them belonged to
us.[s]
20But you have an anointing[t] from the
Holy One,[u] and all of you know the
truth.[f][v] 21I do not write to you because
you do not know the truth, but because
you do know it[w] and because no lie
comes from the truth. 22Who is the liar?
It is the man who denies that Jesus is the
Christ. Such a man is the antichrist—he
denies the Father and the Son.[x] 23No one
who denies the Son has the Father; whoever acknowledges the Son has the Father also.[y]
24See that what you have heard from
the beginning[z] remains in you. If it does,
you also will remain in the Son and in the
Father.[a] 25And this is what he promised
us—even eternal life.[b]
26I am writing these things to you
about those who are trying to lead you
astray.[c] 27As for you, the anointing[d] you
received from him remains in you, and
you do not need anyone to teach you. But
as his anointing teaches you about all
things[e] and as that anointing is real, not
counterfeit—just as it has taught you, remain in him.[f]

Children of God

28And now, dear children,[g] continue
in him, so that when he appears[h] we
may be confident[i] and unashamed before him at his coming.[j]
29If you know that he is righteous,[k]
you know that everyone who does what
is right has been born of him.[l]

Chapter 3

HOW great is the love[m] the Father has
lavished on us, that we should be
called children of God![n] And that is what
we are! The reason the world does not
know us is that it did not know him.[o]
2Dear friends,[p] now we are children of

2:18 [p]ver 22; 1Jn 4:3; 2Jn 7 [q]1Jn 4:1
2:19 [r]Ac 20:30 [s]1Co 11:19
2:20 [t]ver 27; 2Co 1:21 [u]S Mk 1:24 [v]Jer 31:34; Mt 13:11; Jn 14:26
2:21 [w]2Pe 1:12; Jude 5
2:22 [x]1Jn 4:3; 2Jn 7
2:23 [y]Jn 8:19; 14:7; 1Jn 4:15; 5:1; 2Jn 9
2:24 [z]S ver 7 [a]Jn 14:23; 15:4; 1Jn 1:3; 2Jn 9
2:25 [b]S Mt 25:46
2:26 [c]1Jn 3:7
2:27 [d]ver 20 [e]1Co 2:12 [f]Jn 15:4
2:28 [g]S ver 1 [h]Col 3:4; 1Jn 3:2 [i]S Eph 3:12 [j]S 1Th 2:19
2:29 [k]1Jn 3:7 [l]S Jn 1:13
3:1 [m]S Jn 3:16 [n]ver 2,10; S Jn 1:12 [o]Jn 15:21; 16:3
3:2 [p]S 1Co 10:14

[f]*20* Some manuscripts *and you know all things*

---

ing Christian community. Rather than focus on some distant "antichrist," John warned the people to be concerned about the present evil pretenders who would lead them astray. In every generation evil infiltrates society. We can easily become excited about the future trauma of this world and neglect the present moral and ethical issues.

2:18 LAST THINGS, Last Days—The reference to antichrist has both historical and eschatological significance. The spirit of antichrist (1 Jn 4:3) refers to demonic influences which cause and promote anti-Christian or false doctrines and conduct. Such a spirit has been manifested throughout history. Those who are the possessors of an anti-Christian spirit have been and are many in number. This plurality of antichrists is characteristic of the "last hour." The last hour carries a similar significance to that of the last days. See note on Jn 12:48. In their broadest sweep the last days embrace the time following Christ's first coming and prior to His second coming. This present age is conceived of as the last hour. It is characterized throughout by multiple anti-Christian persons, movements, and influences. Amillennialists believe the reference to antichrists refers only to those who appear throughout the present age. Premillennialists believe that this text and others also point to a final, supreme antichrist yet to come. The final and consummate embodiment of evil opposition to Christ is variously referred to: man of lawlessness (2 Th 2:3–4), beast out of the sea (Rev 13:1–10), and the abomination that causes desolation (Mk 13:14).

2:20 GOD, Holy—See note on 2 Co 7:1.

2:21 HOLY SCRIPTURE, Purpose—The occasion for the letter was not to reveal new truth, since the hearers already knew the truth of God. John affirmed their faith and reminded them their lives could not lie or deny God's deepest revelation, Jesus Christ. Revelation is not proved by new, secret knowledge which John's opponents claimed to have. It is proved by confirming and being consistent with the basic gospel truth of Jesus.

2:22–23 JESUS CHRIST, Son of God—Jesus is the promised Messiah of Israel fulfilling all God's promises. To deny this is to oppose the deity of Jesus as the Son of God, thus to be on Satan's side. The Bible teaches both the real humanity of Jesus and His real deity as God's Son. Faith holds the two together without explaining how this can be true.

2:28 JESUS CHRIST, Final Coming—John warned against false christs or messiahs and against those who deny Jesus is the messianic Son of God. He looked to Christ's appearance (*phaneroō*) and His coming (*parousia*), both technical terms referring to the final coming. See note on Mt 24:1—25:46. Like Paul (1 Th 3:13), James (5:7–8), and Peter (2 Pe 3:11–12), John connected the final coming with his call to continued faithfulness. Faith that Christ will come again calls us to obey Him until that day.

2:28 LAST THINGS, Inspires Hope—Confidence before the Lord at His return is the result of a life lived in union or fellowship with Him. The goal of Christian living should be that of being able to meet the Lord without shame.

2:29 GOD, Righteous—God is righteous, meaning that He not only opposes what is evil but is the source of what is right. He actively seeks to make His people righteous. Righteous lives show God at work. Compare 3:10.

2:29 CHRISTIAN ETHICS, Righteousness—God is the standard of righteousness. Disciples are His born-again children who imitate His actions by doing right. See 3:7.

3:1 GOD, Love—God loved us so much He adopted us as children. This distinguishes us from all people who do not follow Christ. See note on Jn 3:16.

3:1–2 THE CHURCH, God's Community—God's children are characterized by love for one another. We wait for the final realization of what we shall be through the work of Christ Jesus.

3:2 JESUS CHRIST, Final Coming—When Jesus appears, His followers will be like Him. We can never be exactly the same as He is. It will be enough to be like Him. We can never know the fullness of this promise until we see Him and are like Him.

3:2 REVELATION, Fellowship—As children of God, we belong in the same family. God has not yet revealed what we will become. We do know when Christ appears we shall be with Him, know Him in His true nature, and become like Him, thus renewing the image of God. That is a secure and comforting revelation.

3:2–3 LAST THINGS, Purity—The prospect of seeing Christ at His return is a purifying hope. To see Him is to become like Him at last. Since He is pure, purity is required to be like Him. The goal for believers is to become increasingly Christlike.

God,[q] and what we will be has not yet been made known. But we know that when he appears,[g] [r] we shall be like him,[s] for we shall see him as he is.[t] 3 Everyone who has this hope in him purifies himself,[u] just as he is pure.[v]

4 Everyone who sins breaks the law; in fact, sin is lawlessness.[w] 5 But you know that he appeared so that he might take away our sins.[x] And in him is no sin.[y] 6 No one who lives in him keeps on sinning.[z] No one who continues to sin has either seen him[a] or known him.[b]

7 Dear children,[c] do not let anyone lead you astray.[d] He who does what is right is righteous, just as he is righteous.[e] 8 He who does what is sinful is of the devil,[f] because the devil has been sinning from the beginning. The reason the Son of God[g] appeared was to destroy the devil's work.[h] 9 No one who is born of God[i] will continue to sin,[j] because God's seed[k] remains in him; he cannot go on sinning, because he has been born of God. 10 This is how we know who the children of God[l] are and who the children of the devil[m] are: Anyone who does not do what is right is not a child of God; nor is anyone who does not love[n] his brother.[o]

Love One Another

11 This is the message you heard[p] from the beginning:[q] We should love one another.[r] 12 Do not be like Cain, who belonged to the evil one[s] and murdered his brother.[t] And why did he murder him? Because his own actions were evil and his brother's were righteous.[u] 13 Do not be surprised, my brothers, if the world hates you.[v] 14 We know that we have passed from death to life,[w] because we love our brothers. Anyone who does not love remains in death.[x] 15 Anyone who hates his brother[y] is a murderer,[z] and you know that no murderer has eternal life in him.[a]

16 This is how we know what love is: Jesus Christ laid down his life for us.[b] And we ought to lay down our lives for our brothers.[c] 17 If anyone has material possessions and sees his brother in need but has no pity on him,[d] how can the love of God be in him?[e] 18 Dear children,[f] let us not love with words or tongue but with actions and in truth.[g] 19 This then is how we know that we belong to the truth, and how we set our hearts at rest in his presence 20 whenever our hearts condemn us. For God is great-

3:2 [q]ver 1,10; S Jn 1:12 [r]Col 3:4; 1Jn 2:28 [s]Ro 8:29; 2Pe 1:4 [t]Ps 17:15; Jn 17:24; 2Co 3:18
3:3 [u]2Co 7:1; 2Pe 3:13,14 [v]Ps 18:26
3:4 [w]1Jn 5:17
3:5 [x]ver 8; S Jn 3:17 [y]S 2Co 5:21
3:6 [z]ver 9; 1Jn 5:18 [a]3Jn 11 [b]S 1Jn 2:4
3:7 [c]S 1Jn 2:1 [d]1Jn 2:26 [e]1Jn 2:29
3:8 [f]ver 10; Jn 8:44 [g]S Mt 4:3 [h]Heb 2:14
3:9 [i]S Jn 1:13 [j]ver 6; Ps 119:3; 1Jn 5:18 [k]1Pe 1:23
3:10 [l]ver 1,2; S Jn 1:12 [m]ver 8 [n]1Jn 4:8 [o]S 1Jn 2:9
3:11 [p]1Jn 1:5 [q]S 1Jn 2:7 [r]Jn 13:34,35; 15:12; 1Jn 4:7,11, 21; 2Jn 5
3:12 [s]S Mt 5:37 [t]Ge 4:8 [u]Ps 38:20; Pr 29:10
3:13 [v]Jn 15:18,19; 17:14
3:14 [w]Jn 5:24 [x]S 1Jn 2:9
3:15 [y]S 1Jn 2:9 [z]Mt 5:21,22; Jn 8:44 [a]Gal 5:20, 21; Rev 21:8
3:16 [b]Jn 10:11 [c]Jn 15:13; Php 2:17; 1Th 2:8
3:17 [d]Dt 15:7,8; Jas 2:15,16 [e]1Jn 4:20 **3:18** [f]S 1Jn 2:1 [g]Eze 33:31; Ro 12:9

[g]2 Or *when it is made known*

3:3 GOD, Holy—The plea for purity in God's people is based upon the holiness of God. See notes on Lev 11:44–45; 2 Co 7:1; 1 Pe 1:15–16.

3:4 SIN, Lawlessness—One definition for sin in both the Old and New Testaments is lawlessness. Though sin is more than just breaking the law, that certainly is part of it. Law may refer to Old Testament commandments, or to New Testament moral teachings of Jesus. It represents a willing rejection of God's right to direct our lives. Sin is following the law of human and satanic desire rather than following Christ in the way of God.

3:5–24 ELECTION, Righteousness—The nonelect continue in the paths of sin. Repentance has no meaning for them. The elect are passed from death unto life as shown by love for fellow believers. The righteous life is an identifying mark of the elect.

3:5–8 JESUS CHRIST, Mission—Jesus came from heaven to earth to destroy everything Satan has accomplished and to deal with our sin problem. He was qualified to deal with sin because He was without sin.

3:8–10 EVIL AND SUFFERING, Satan—Habitual sinners are under Satan's control and are his children. Satan's existence is and always has been characterized by sin, rebellion against God.

3:10 DISCIPLESHIP, Conversion—Conversion makes us disciples and changes our lives. A person who will not do what is right is a child of the devil, not of God. Love expressed in concrete acts for others reveals our converted lives. See note on 4:19–21.

3:10 THE CHURCH, God's Community—The children of God are characterized by right actions and by love one for another. See note on vv 1–2.

3:11–15 CHRISTIAN ETHICS, Murder—For the disciple murder is an attitude. It arises from guilt and envy and goes on to hatred. Harboring hatred is murder even if no physical act is committed. We avoid murderous hatred through letting Christ's love live in us.

3:14 HUMANITY, Relationships—Love is evidence that people have been delivered from spiritual death to spiritual life. Love within the church is the best evidence members are experiencing eternal life. See Jn 13:34.

3:15 SALVATION, Eternal Life—Those who hate their brothers are murderers like Cain (Ge 4:8–16). They do not possess eternal life, because one evidence of eternal life is that we love our brothers (1 Jn 2:9–10).

3:16 JESUS CHRIST, Love—The sacrificial death of Christ defines what love is. Love can be defined only in action.

3:16 SALVATION, Atonement—See note on Eph 5:2, 25–27. The supreme expression of love is the death of Christ on the cross. We should imitate His love.

3:17–18 DISCIPLESHIP, Neighbor Love—Neighbor love appears in acts better than in words. God's love can hardly be at work in and through the life of a person who is not moved with compassion for those in need. A Christian disciple should love in truth and in deeds. See notes on Jn 17:26; Jas 2:14–26.

3:17–18 CHRISTIAN ETHICS, Property Rights—Our attitude to and actions with property reflects our love for and relationship with Christ. True love acts to help the one in need.

3:17 STEWARDSHIP, Care of Needy—God's love within a person expresses itself in caring for those in need. Helping others is the business of the people of God. The Bible repeatedly places great value on gifts to the poor. Jesus emphasized giving as He spoke of the Good Samaritan (Lk 10:30–37) and of giving a cup of water in His name (Mt 10:42). Christian love expresses itself in action, not in pious words.

3:19–20 GOD, Wisdom—Humility and reverence may make us fear the holy presence of God. We may see Him as always judging our sin and wish He did not know everything. God's knowledge should reassure us. He knows our expressions of love in word and deed. Our consciousness of sin should be set at ease by our realization of His love controlling our lives. Then we have no reason to fear in His presence. See note on 4:7–21.

er than our hearts, and he knows everything.
21 Dear friends,[h] if our hearts do not
condemn us, we have confidence before
God[i] 22 and receive from him anything
we ask,[j] because we obey his commands[k] and do what pleases him.[l]
23 And this is his command: to believe[m] in
the name of his Son, Jesus Christ,[n] and to
love one another as he commanded us.[o]
24 Those who obey his commands[p] live in
him,[q] and he in them. And this is how
we know that he lives in us: We know it
by the Spirit he gave us.[r]

Chapter 4

Test the Spirits

DEAR friends,[s] do not believe every
spirit,[t] but test the spirits to see
whether they are from God, because
many false prophets have gone out into
the world.[u] 2 This is how you can recognize the Spirit of God: Every spirit that
acknowledges that Jesus Christ has come
in the flesh[v] is from God,[w] 3 but every
spirit that does not acknowledge Jesus is
not from God. This is the spirit of the
antichrist,[x] which you have heard is
coming and even now is already in the
world.[y]
4 You, dear children,[z] are from God
and have overcome them,[a] because the
one who is in you[b] is greater than the
one who is in the world.[c] 5 They are from
the world[d] and therefore speak from the
viewpoint of the world, and the world listens to them. 6 We are from God, and
whoever knows God listens to us; but
whoever is not from God does not listen
to us.[e] This is how we recognize the
Spirit[h] of truth[f] and the spirit of falsehood.[g]

God's Love and Ours

7 Dear friends, let us love one another,[h] for love comes from God. Everyone
who loves has been born of God[i] and
knows God.[j] 8 Whoever does not love
does not know God, because God is
love.[k] 9 This is how God showed his love
among us: He sent his one and only
Son[i][l] into the world that we might live
through him.[m] 10 This is love: not that we

3:21 [h]S 1Co 10:14 [i]S Eph 3:12; 1Jn 5:14
3:22 [j]S Mt 7:7 [k]S Jn 14:15 [l]Jn 8:29; Heb 13:21
3:23 [m]Jn 6:29 [n]S Lk 24:47; Jn 1:12; 3:18; 20:31; 1Co 6:11; 1Jn 5:13 [o]S Jn 13:34
3:24 [p]1Jn 2:3 [q]1Jn 2:6; 4:15 [r]1Th 4:8; 1Jn 4:13
4:1 [s]S 1Co 10:14 [t]Jer 29:8; 1Co 12:10; 2Th 2:2 [u]S Mt 7:15; 1Jn 2:18
4:2 [v]S Jn 1:14; 1Jn 2:23 [w]1Co 12:3
4:3 [x]1Jn 2:22; 2Jn 7 [y]1Jn 2:18
4:4 [z]S 1Jn 2:1 [a]S Jn 16:33 [b]Ro 8:31 [c]2Ki 6:16; S Jn 12:31
4:5 [d]Jn 15:19; 17:14,16
4:6 [e]Jn 8:47 [f]S Jn 14:17 [g]S Mk 13:5
4:7 [h]S 1Jn 3:11 [i]S Jn 1:13 [j]S 1Jn 2:4
4:8 [k]ver 7,16
4:9 [l]Jn 1:18 [m]Jn 3:16,17; 1Jn 5:11

[h]6 Or *spirit* [i]9 Or *his only begotten Son*

3:21–22 PRAYER, Will of God—A condition of prayer is that the petitioner be obedient to the known will of God. The purpose of prayer is to accomplish the will of God on earth. See note on 5:14–15.

3:23 SALVATION, Belief—God's command is that we believe in His Son. This brings salvation and leads us to love as He loved (vv 16–19).

3:24—4:3,13–16 HOLY SPIRIT, Indwells—John here presented a circular argument of great importance for understanding the Spirit. I can know Christ is with me by the fact the Spirit is with me. But how can I be sure it is truly God's Spirit who is speaking through another person? God's Spirit leads people to confess that Jesus Christ has come in the flesh. The presence of Christ is validated by the presence of the Spirit, whose authenticity is validated by the confession of faith in Christ. John's particular concern was the false teachers who denied that Christ was fully human, or that He had a physical body. John's principle was wider than this particular controversy. The criterion for recognizing the presence of the Spirit is faith in Christ. Paul presented the same criterion in 1 Co 12:1–3. Paul added a second criterion for ascertaining the Spirit's presence, the criterion of love which builds up the body of Christ. See note on 1 Co 12:1–3. It is possible that John did the same thing in 1 Jn 4:6–8,16. Our theology, our profession, and our life must agree as witnesses to Christ.

4:1–4 EVIL AND SUFFERING, Satan—Satan is not alone. Evil spirits do his work. These deceive God's people by leading us to think the Holy Spirit is inspiring a teacher or preacher when the message comes from the lying spirits of Satan (1 Ki 22:22–23). Satan's spirits are antichrists (1 Jn 2:22) opposing Christ and denying that in Jesus God has come in the flesh. Such spirits are not strong enough to overcome God's faithful people, for the Holy Spirit lives in us. See note on 5:18–19.

4:1 CHURCH LEADERS, Prophet—The spirit of error can infiltrate the church leadership. False prophets claim to possess revelation from God. John warns that not everyone who claims to speak under the guidance of the Spirit is to be believed. Even though they may be inspiring speakers, they must be tested to avoid heresy and division. For Jesus, the test was moral (Mt 7:16,20). Here the test concerns their belief about Christ. 1 Jn 4:7 adds the moral test.

4:2–3 GOD, Trinity—Revelation involves all three Persons of the Trinity. The Father sends revelation through the Spirit. The Spirit testifies that Jesus is the incarnate, truly human Son of God.

4:2–3 JESUS CHRIST, Son of God—See note on 2:22–23.

4:4–18 ELECTION, Righteousness—God's love initiated election and made it secure in Christ. The elect in the Spirit's power reflect God's love in the world. Godly love characterizes the elect and saves us from fear and concern about eternal punishment.

4:6–8 SALVATION, Knowledge of God—Those who hear and heed the ones sent by God know God. Loving one another is proof we know God. See note on 2:3,13–14.

4:7–21 GOD, Love—This passage may be the strongest single passage in the Bible concerning the love of God. The basic message is simple: God is love. The word used here for love is *agapē,* which means a self-giving love that seeks the best interests of its object and is not selfish or self-seeking. God's love creates a response of love in us (v 19). We can know if we truly belong to God by checking to see if love controls our lives. Such love drives out any fear we might have of God's judgment.

4:7–16 GOD, Trinity—The three Persons of the Trinity work together to produce the Christian life in us. Love is the identifying characteristic of the Christian life and comes from God, who is love. God showed us His love by sending His Son to minister and die for us. We know we are living the Christian life because we are aware of the Holy Spirit living in us. That awareness comes as the Spirit leads us to testify about God's love in sending Jesus as our Savior.

4:7–21 CHRISTIAN ETHICS, Social Relationships—See note on 1 Pe 1:22. Relationships not rules are at the heart of Christian ethics. Love is the root of right relationships. Love is not something we manufacture. Love is the central characteristic of God Himself and thus is a gift we receive from Him. Love is defined not by words but by the act of God in giving His Son to die on the cross for us. That love compels us to love others. When we do, we show we belong to God and He lives in us.

4:9 JESUS CHRIST, Life—Jesus is interested in more than our future reward in heaven. He came to give us God's quality of life. We can live fully because God loves us.

loved God, but that he loved us[n] and sent
his Son as an atoning sacrifice for[j] our
sins.[o] 11Dear friends,[p] since God so
loved us,[q] we also ought to love one another.[r] 12No one has ever seen God;[s]
but if we love one another, God lives in
us and his love is made complete in us.[t]

13We know[u] that we live in him and
he in us, because he has given us of his
Spirit.[v] 14And we have seen and testify[w]
that the Father has sent his Son to be the
Savior of the world.[x] 15If anyone acknowledges that Jesus is the Son of God,[y]
God lives in him and he in God.[z] 16And
so we know and rely on the love God has
for us.

God is love.[a] Whoever lives in love
lives in God, and God in him.[b] 17In this
way, love is made complete[c] among us
so that we will have confidence[d] on the
day of judgment,[e] because in this world
we are like him. 18There is no fear in
love. But perfect love drives out fear,[f]
because fear has to do with punishment.
The one who fears is not made perfect in
love.

19We love because he first loved us.[g]
20If anyone says, "I love God," yet hates
his brother,[h] he is a liar.[i] For anyone
who does not love his brother, whom he
has seen,[j] cannot love God, whom he
has not seen.[k] 21And he has given us this
command:[l] Whoever loves God must
also love his brother.[m]

4:10 [n]Ro 5:8,10 [o]S Ro 3:25
4:11 [p]S 1Co 10:14 [q]S Jn 3:16 [r]Jn 15:12; S 1Jn 3:11
4:12 [s]S Jn 1:18 [t]ver 17; 1Jn 2:5
4:13 [u]S 1Jn 2:3 [v]1Jn 3:24
4:14 [w]S Jn 15:27 [x]S Lk 2:11; S Jn 3:17
4:15 [y]S 1Jn 2:23; 5:5 [z]1Jn 3:24
4:16 [a]ver 8 [b]ver 12,13; 1Jn 3:24
4:17 [c]ver 12; 1Jn 2:5 [d]S Eph 3:12 [e]S Mt 10:15
4:18 [f]Ro 8:15
4:19 [g]ver 10
4:20 [h]S 1Jn 2:9 [i]S 1Jn 1:6; 2:4 [j]1Jn 3:17 [k]ver 12; S Jn 1:18
4:21 [l]1Jn 2:7 [m]S Mt 5:43; S 1Jn 2:9
5:1 [n]S Jn 3:15 [o]1Jn 2:22; 4:2,15 [p]S Jn 1:13; S 1Jn 2:23 [q]Jn 8:42
5:2 [r]S 1Jn 2:3 [s]1Jn 3:14
5:3 [t]S Jn 14:15 [u]Mt 11:30; 23:4
5:4 [v]S Jn 1:13 [w]S Jn 16:33
5:5 [x]ver 1; S 1Jn 2:23
5:6 [y]Jn 19:34 [z]S Jn 14:17
5:7 [a]S Mt 18:16
5:9 [b]Jn 5:34 [c]Mt 3:16,17; Jn 5:32,37; 8:17,18

Chapter 5

Faith in the Son of God

EVERYONE who believes[n] that Jesus is
the Christ[o] is born of God,[p] and everyone who loves the father loves his
child as well.[q] 2This is how we know[r]
that we love the children of God:[s] by
loving God and carrying out his commands. 3This is love for God: to obey his
commands.[t] And his commands are not
burdensome,[u] 4for everyone born of
God[v] overcomes[w] the world. This is the
victory that has overcome the world,
even our faith. 5Who is it that overcomes
the world? Only he who believes that
Jesus is the Son of God.[x]

6This is the one who came by water
and blood[y]—Jesus Christ. He did not
come by water only, but by water and
blood. And it is the Spirit who testifies,
because the Spirit is the truth.[z] 7For
there are three[a] that testify: 8the[k] Spirit,
the water and the blood; and the three
are in agreement. 9We accept man's testimony,[b] but God's testimony is greater
because it is the testimony of God,[c]
which he has given about his Son. 10Any-
one who believes in the Son of God has

[j]10 Or *as the one who would turn aside his wrath, taking away* [k]7,8 Late manuscripts of the Vulgate *testify in heaven: the Father, the Word and the Holy Spirit, and these three are one. 8And there are three that testify on earth: the* (not found in any Greek manuscript before the sixteenth century)

4:13–16 SALVATION, As Being in Christ—Those in Christ know they live in God and He lives in them because of the gift of the Holy Spirit. We as Christians are the ones who bear witness that God sent Jesus Christ as the world's Savior and who confess that Jesus is the Son of God. We who are focused on Christ live in love because we live in God who is love. We know and rely on God's love revealed in His Son. To be in Christ, then, is to be in God and to live a life-style characterized by divine love.

4:14 JESUS CHRIST, Savior—Jesus came to earth to save us from our sins (Mt 1:21).

4:19–21 SALVATION, Love of God—God's love is the source of our love. Those who say they love God whom they have not seen, but hate their brothers whom they have seen, are liars. One of God's commands is that those who love Him love their brothers also.

4:19–21 DISCIPLESHIP, Conversion—A liar says he loves God while hating another person. A person who loves God loves other people. Those are John's blunt, inspired conclusions. Every professing Christian needs to hear and consider them. Christian conversion leads us to love others.

5:1–20 GOD, Trinity—See notes on 2:1,22–24; 4:7–16.

5:1–5 THE CHURCH, God's Community—The church is a community of people who believe in Jesus Christ as God's promised Messiah and our Savior. The church gives evidence of this belief by obeying God's commands. Such obedience overcomes the temptations thrust at us by the non-Christian world to live by its standards. We can obey only as we place faith in Christ and not ourselves. The motivation for obedience is love of God. Such love extends then to all other children of God. Obedience, faith, and love thus unite the church into a true community.

5:6 JESUS CHRIST, Son of God—Two major points in Jesus' life reveal Him as Son of God: His baptism by water (Mk 1:11) and His death, where He sacrificed His blood (Mk 15:39). Throughout His ministry Jesus remained the same person—the Son of God come in human flesh. Jesus did not become God's Son at any point in His earthly life. He was God's Son from eternity past and remains God's Son to eternity future. At no point did He surrender His divine nature and become only human.

5:6–8 HOLY SPIRIT, Jesus—God provided three distinct witnesses to validate that Jesus is His Son. The witnesses are the water (Jesus' baptism, together with the Father's words to Christ at that time), the blood (the cross, together with the resurrection), and the Spirit (who was given to Jesus in a special way at His baptism and who guided Jesus throughout His ministry). The Spirit is the Spirit of truth (Jn 14:17; 15:26; 16:13) who reveals God and His truth to us. The Spirit continues to testify to us about Jesus.

5:6–13 REVELATION, Jesus Christ—God has provided three witnesses (Nu 35:30; Dt 17:6; 19:15) to identify Jesus: His baptism, His death, and the Holy Spirit. We have no reason to question such testimony, especially since it comes from God, the Source of all truth. Faith in Christ makes us join the witnesses to Christ. If we do not believe, we say God is a liar. Faith relationship with the Son brings eternal life, the only genuine quality of life.

5:6 ORDINANCES, Baptism by Holy Spirit—Jesus came by "water and blood," meaning that His ministry began with His baptism and culminated in His death. When the spear pierced Jesus' side, blood and water came forth (Jn 19:34). The Spirit testifies through these two signs which were celebrated by early Christians as baptism and the Lord's Supper. When we practice baptism and the Lord's Supper, it is not the physical act alone but the testimony of the Holy Spirit through them which declares the saving power of the death and resurrection of Jesus.

5:10 EVANGELISM, Gospel—The gospel is truth—dis-

this testimony in his heart.[d] Anyone who
does not believe God has made him out
to be a liar,[e] because he has not believed
the testimony God has given about his
Son. 11And this is the testimony: God has
given us eternal life,[f] and this life is in
his Son.[g] 12He who has the Son has life;
he who does not have the Son of God
does not have life.[h]

Concluding Remarks

13I write these things to you who believe in the name of the Son of God[i] so
that you may know that you have eternal
life.[j] 14This is the confidence[k] we have
in approaching God: that if we ask anything according to his will, he hears us.[l]
15And if we know that he hears us—
whatever we ask—we know[m] that we
have what we asked of him.[n]
16If anyone sees his brother commit a
sin that does not lead to death, he should
pray and God will give him life.[o] I refer
to those whose sin does not lead to death.
There is a sin that leads to death.[p] I am
not saying that he should pray about
that.[q] 17All wrongdoing is sin,[r] and
there is sin that does not lead to death.[s]
18We know that anyone born of God[t]
does not continue to sin; the one who
was born of God keeps him safe, and the
evil one[u] cannot harm him.[v] 19We know
that we are children of God,[w] and that
the whole world is under the control of
the evil one.[x] 20We know also that the
Son of God has come[y] and has given us
understanding,[z] so that we may know
him who is true.[a] And we are in him
who is true—even in his Son Jesus
Christ. He is the true God and eternal
life.[b]
21Dear children,[c] keep yourselves
from idols.[d]

5:10 [d]Ro 8:16; Gal 4:6 [e]Jn 3:33; 1Jn 1:10
5:11 [f]S Mt 25:46 [g]S Jn 1:4
5:12 [h]Jn 3:15,16, 36
5:13 [i]S 1Jn 3:23 [j]ver 11; S Mt 25:46
5:14 [k]S Eph 3:12; 1Jn 3:21 [l]S Mt 7:7
5:15 [m]ver 18,19,20 [n]1Ki 3:12
5:16 [o]Jas 5:15 [p]Ex 23:21; Heb 6:4-6; 10:26 [q]Jer 7:16; 14:11
5:17 [r]1Jn 3:4 [s]ver 16; 1Jn 2:1
5:18 [t]S Jn 1:13 [u]S Mt 5:37 [v]Jn 14:30
5:19 [w]1Jn 4:6 [x]Jn 12:31; 14:30; 17:15
5:20 [y]ver 5 [z]Lk 24:45 [a]Jn 17:3 [b]ver 11; S Mt 25:46
5:21 [c]S 1Jn 2:1 [d]1Co 10:14; 1Th 1:9

---

turbing truth. It becomes a divider of people. Those who believe in Christ have the testimony in their hearts that God's Word concerning His Son is true. Those who refuse to believe accuse God of lying. How wise to believe and then share that message of the gospel.

5:11–13 SALVATION, Eternal Life—We can know we have eternal life if we believe in the Son of God. Eternal life is available only through Jesus Christ because it is only God's to give. If you do not know Jesus, you have no hope for eternal life.

5:14–15 PRAYER, Will of God—John named obedience as a condition of prayer (3:21–22). Here the confidence in knowing God's will stands in contrast to the youthful mistake John made in Mk 10:37. Before the bestowal of the Holy Spirit, guidance was from without. Since Pentecost, all believers have the guidance of the Holy Spirit within. God will answer when the Christian asks according to His will.

5:16–17 SIN, Death—Sin and death are vitally connected (Ro 6:23). Sin leads to death both physically and spiritually. In this text we must ask if physical or spiritual death is meant. Good Bible students have answered in both ways. The probable meaning is that the sin that leads to eternal spiritual death is the sin of unbelief and rejection of God. The sin that mars the life of the believer and is confessed and covered by Christ's atonement does not lead to eternal spiritual death. We are to pray with believers that they may have the power of the Spirit in their lives and not fall into a habit of sin.

5:16–17 PRAYER, Intercession—The meaning of the sin which does not lead to death is unclear, although the original recipients of this letter must have understood it in the context of their lives. There is a sin so serious and aggravating that it is beyond the reach even of prayer. Nevertheless, Christians are to pray for sinners and should continue to do so as long as it is in any way feasible. This does not rule out the express leadership of God to stop praying. Jeremiah was commanded not to pray for Israel (14:11), but this was direct revelation.

5:18–19 EVIL AND SUFFERING, Satan—Satan cannot bring eternal harm to God's children. Jesus protects us from him. We are not part of the world Satan controls. Not even Satan can separate us from Christ. See note on 2:15–17.

5:20 JESUS CHRIST, Truth—Only believers know the truth, for truth is not abstract knowledge. Truth is personal and is revealed only in the person of Jesus Christ.

2 John

Theological Setting

Before the apostolic writings which became our New Testament were circulated, the early Christians had no standard by which to judge the doctrines taught by traveling missionaries who might come into their community. Evidently quite a number of these teachers traveled among the churches. Some opposed apostolic teaching or claimed their teaching was an advancement to apostolic doctrine or perhaps a new revelation. Such teachers presented the early church a multiplicity of erroneous teachings. Most of our New Testament documents were written as correctives to one or more of these false teachings.

The second epistle of John responded vigorously to an erroneous teaching. John left no doubt concerning his reaction to those who taught that Jesus had not come in the flesh. See introduction to 1 John. "The chosen lady and her children" probably refers to a Christian community (v 1) for whom John had a deep and abiding love.

Theological Outline

Second John: Responding to False Teachers

I. The Salutation of Love for Those Who Know the Truth (1-2)

II. The Blessings of Grace, Mercy, and Peace (3)

III. Love Is the Identifying Mark for Christians. (4-6)
- A. Living by the truth follows God's command and brings joy to Christians and their leaders. (4)
- B. The love commandment continues God's tradition with His people. (5)
- C. To love is to obey God. (6)

IV. Believers Face Deceivers. (7-11)
- A. Those who do not acknowledge that Jesus Christ came in the flesh are deceivers. (7)
- B. Succumbing to this false teaching brings great loss. (8-9)
- C. Receiving false teachers means sharing their wickedness. (10-11)

V. Personal Conclusion (12-13)

Theological Conclusions

This epistle expresses joy and concern. The joy is in the fact that some are living by the truth. Christian truth is summarized in one word—love, the center of the apostolic message concerning Christ and His commands. The expression of concern has to do with the many deceivers circulating among the Christian communities. To accept their teachings as true and follow them is wicked and dangerous. Anyone who has fellowship with these false teachers shares in their false teaching. The central point of issue is the humanity of Christ. Jesus is the incarnate Son whose teaching must be followed. His Sonship is not understood properly if His full humanity is denied or neglected.

Contemporary Teaching

Though the second epistle of John is brief, it has a poignant message for contemporary Christians. The letter has two main thrusts: (1) Be sure that you conduct your life-style according to the truth of the message of Christ (v 6). Contemporary Christians should interpret the injunction in relation to the entire scriptural revelation as found in our New Testament. We must study God's Word and live according to its teachings. The center of its teaching is the commandment to love. (2) Be on guard against those who would pervert the plain message concerning the incarnation of Jesus Christ (v 7). Some first century teachers claimed to have an advanced revelation which denied that Jesus was truly human. For the contemporary Christian this is especially relevant. Many times we accept the idea that Jesus was a man, but we refuse to allow Him to function as true man. The two heresies about Jesus which must be avoided at all cost are: that Jesus *was only a man*, and that He was not true man. Both of these ideas destroy the true identity of Jesus, who was true man and true God.

THE elder,[a]

To the chosen[b] lady and her children, whom I love in the truth[c]—and
not I only, but also all who know the
truth[d]— 2because of the truth,[e] which
lives in us[f] and will be with us forever:

3Grace, mercy and peace from God the
Father and from Jesus Christ,[g] the Father's Son, will be with us in truth and
love.

4It has given me great joy to find some
of your children walking in the truth,[h]
just as the Father commanded us. 5And
now, dear lady, I am not writing you a
new command but one we have had from
the beginning.[i] I ask that we love one
another. 6And this is love:[j] that we walk
in obedience to his commands.[k] As you
have heard from the beginning,[l] his
command is that you walk in love.
7Many deceivers, who do not acknowledge Jesus Christ[m] as coming in the
flesh,[n] have gone out into the world.[o]
Any such person is the deceiver and the
antichrist.[p] 8Watch out that you do not
lose what you have worked for, but that
you may be rewarded fully.[q] 9Anyone
who runs ahead and does not continue in
the teaching of Christ[r] does not have
God; whoever continues in the teaching
has both the Father and the Son.[s] 10If
anyone comes to you and does not bring
this teaching, do not take him into your
house or welcome him.[t] 11Anyone who
welcomes him shares[u] in his wicked
work.

12I have much to write to you, but I do
not want to use paper and ink. Instead, I
hope to visit you and talk with you face to
face,[v] so that our joy may be complete.[w]

13The children of your chosen[x] sister
send their greetings.

1:1 [a]S Ac 11:30; 3Jn 1 [b]ver 13; Ro 16:13; 1Pe 5:13 [c]ver 3 [d]Jn 8:32; 1Ti 2:4
1:2 [e]2Pe 1:12 [f]Jn 14:17; 1Jn 1:8
1:3 [g]S Ro 1:7
1:4 [h]3Jn 3,4
1:5 [i]S 1Jn 2:7
1:6 [j]1Jn 2:5 [k]S Jn 14:15 [l]S 1Jn 2:7
1:7 [m]1Jn 2:22; 4:2, 3 [n]S Jn 1:14 [o]1Jn 4:1 [p]S 1Jn 2:18
1:8 [q]S Mt 10:42; Mk 10:29,30; 1Co 3:8; Heb 10:35,36; 11:26
1:9 [r]Jn 8:31 [s]S 1Jn 2:23
1:10 [t]S Ro 16:17
1:11 [u]1Ti 5:22
1:12 [v]3Jn 13,14 [w]S Jn 3:29
1:13 [x]ver 1

1 CHURCH LEADERS, Elder—Some have suggested the use of the title "elder" suggests that John was not one elder among many but a superintendent with responsibility for a group of churches in different communities. This interpretation says John could speak on behalf of the churches and had the duty of preventing the spread of error among the churches. He would have been responsible for church discipline (vv 9–10) and the authoritative transmission of the tradition (v 5). A more likely interpretation is that elder did not refer to an office John held but to a respectful title used by Christians to refer to their leader and father in the faith. He had authority not because of his office but because of the wisdom he had shown, the love he had earned, and the power of the Spirit he had displayed.
2–8 ELECTION, Perseverance—Jesus introduces us to truth. Greedy teachers introduce falsehood to lead us away from Christ. In love for Christ and one another, the elect obey Christ and ignore false teachers.
3,9 GOD, Trinity—See note on 1 Jn 5:1–20.
3 PRAYER, Blessing—See note on Ro 1:7.
4–6 CHRISTIAN ETHICS, Social Relationships—See note on 1 Jn 4:7–21.
5 HOLY SCRIPTURE, Canonization—The confirmation of Christ's truth and Old Testament truth are two of the reasons writings became recognized as inspired and thus were considered Scripture. See note on 1 Jn 2:21.
7 JESUS CHRIST, Son of God—See note on 1 Jn 5:6.
7–11 CREATION, Evil—See note on 1 Jn 2:18–23. John warned against having anything to do with these evil workers. Anyone who shows them gracious hospitality encourages their false teachings.
7 LAST THINGS, Great Tribulation—"The antichrist" describes anyone who denies the truth about Christ and seeks to deceive others concerning Him. See notes on 1 Jn 2:18; Rev 13:1–10.
8 LAST THINGS, Encourages Faithfulness—John issued an earnest plea that Christians guard themselves against sin and the consequent loss of rewards. The fact that rewards worked for can be lost promotes faithfulness. Continuance in the faith and in obedience to Christ's commands gains a full reward. See note on 2 Co 5:10.
9 JESUS CHRIST, Teaching—Christ's teaching continues to be authoritative for His followers. Salvation is more than a rite or a future event. It is an ongoing relationship. Salvation changes a life. To belong to God is to do what Christ taught.
10–11 EDUCATION, False Teachers—The insidious influence of false teachers should be taken seriously. Christians should not aid their cause in the name of religious toleration or hospitality. Too easily we tolerate first what we later accept.
12 REVELATION, Messengers—The instrument of God's revelation was both a writer of Scripture and a proclaimer of God's word. Both are inspired ways (God-breathed) of communicating God's truth to His people (3 Jn 13). John found face-to-face communication more effective than writing. God led Him to write, however, thus producing inspired letters the early church recognized as inspired Scripture.

3 John

Theological Setting

Third John is a brief but practical note addressed to a Christian leader named Gaius. The author identified himself only as the elder (v 1). Undoubtedly this is the same person—John, the apostle—who wrote the two previous letters. The doctrinal climate again was one that was charged with tension, dissension, and debate.

The key issue was what relationship Christians should have with visiting Christian teachers. Gaius had been faithful to receive the emissaries of the elder (v 5). Demetrius (v 12) also had been faithful in this regard, but Diotrephes had not (vv 9). Perhaps these were pastors or leaders of three distinct Christian congregations. Diotrephes was not in good standing with the elder (v. 9,10). This possibly was because he had accepted the teaching that Jesus did not come in the flesh. At any rate, he was unwilling to receive the teacher-emissaries from the elder.

The elder, undoubtedly, was the apostolic voice for those who are mentioned in the letter. This fact, however, did not keep Diotrephes from going his own way. He not only refused hospitality to the elder's emissaries; he also was spreading malicious gossip about him. Undoubtedly the elder hoped to keep Gaius and Demetrius safely within the bounds of apostolic Christianity. Just what action he intended to take against Diotrephes is not clear from the letter (v 10). Probably he intended to bring some disciplinary action against him when he visited the community.

Theological Outline

3 John: The Value of Christian Hospitality

I. The Address (1)
II. The Blessing of Good Health and Welfare for a Faithful Spiritual Leader (2-4)
III. Believers Should Show Hospitality and Support for Visiting Believers. (5-8)
IV. Pride, Gossiping, and Lack of Hospitality Bring Condemnation. (9-10)
V. Imitate Good Leaders But Not Wicked Ones. (11-12)
VI. Concluding Remarks (13-14)

Theological Conclusions

The primary teaching of this brief epistle is the value of Christian hospitality. Gaius and Demetrius are positive examples, but Diotrephes is a negative one.

It can be understood from this brief note that apostolic authority was not always accepted by early Christian leaders. Diotrephes had chosen to go his own way. He was not impressed with the elder's credentials as an apostolic voice.

Contemporary Teaching

Several things suggested in this letter are of value to Christians today.

1. Faithfulness to the truth of the gospel message is of paramount importance.
2. Christian hospitality is a valuable commodity.
3. Malicious gossip has no place in the Christian community.
4. Church "bosses" can cause a great deal of havoc.
5. The apostolic truth of Scripture is to be obeyed.

THE elder,[a]

To my dear friend Gaius, whom I
love in the truth.

2Dear friend, I pray that you may enjoy
good health and that all may go well with
you, even as your soul is getting along
well. 3It gave me great joy to have some
brothers[b] come and tell about your faithfulness to the truth and how you continue
to walk in the truth.[c] 4I have no greater
joy than to hear that my children[d] are
walking in the truth.[e]
5Dear friend, you are faithful in what
you are doing for the brothers,[f] even
though they are strangers to you.[g] 6They
have told the church about your love. You
will do well to send them on their way[h]
in a manner worthy[i] of God. 7It was for
the sake of the Name[j] that they went
out, receiving no help from the pagans.[k]
8We ought therefore to show hospitality
to such men so that we may work together for the truth.

9I wrote to the church, but Diotrephes,
who loves to be first, will have nothing to
do with us. 10So if I come,[l] I will call
attention to what he is doing, gossiping
maliciously about us. Not satisfied with
that, he refuses to welcome the brothers.[m] He also stops those who want to do
so and puts them out of the church.[n]
11Dear friend, do not imitate what is
evil but what is good.[o] Anyone who does
what is good is from God.[p] Anyone who
does what is evil has not seen God.[q]
12Demetrius is well spoken of by everyone[r]—and even by the truth itself. We
also speak well of him, and you know that
our testimony is true.[s]
13I have much to write you, but I do
not want to do so with pen and ink. 14I
hope to see you soon, and we will talk
face to face.[t]

Peace to you.[u] The friends here send
their greetings. Greet the friends there by
name.[v]

1:1 [a]S Ac 11:30; 2Jn 1
1:3 [b]ver 5,10; S Ac 1:16 [c]2Jn 4
1:4 [d]S 1Jn 2:1 [e]ver 3
1:5 [f]S ver 3 [g]Ro 12:13; Heb 13:2
1:6 [h]1Co 16:11; 2Co 1:16 [i]S Eph 4:1
1:7 [j]S Jn 15:21 [k]Ac 20:33,35
1:10 [l]ver 14; 2Jn 12 [m]ver 5 [n]Jn 9:22,34
1:11 [o]Ps 34:14; 37:27 [p]1Jn 2:29 [q]1Jn 3:6,9,10
1:12 [r]1Ti 3:7 [s]Jn 19:35; 21:24
1:14 [t]2Jn 12 [u]S Ro 1:7; S Eph 6:23 [v]Jn 10:3

2 PRAYER, Intercession—The elder wrote an affectionate prayer for Gaius, who had been rejected by Diotrephes (v 9). Prayer for the physical and spiritual well-being of Christian friends is a part of our Christian responsibility.

9–10 THE CHURCH, Discipline—Egotistical, self-centered church members cause disputes in the church. They try to destroy the reputation of other church members and destroy Christian fellowship. They assume power and dictate matters in the church such as who may be a member. John set the pattern for the church by dealing with the dispute head-on rather than trying to hide and deny it. The authority and love of Christ must guide attempts to settle disputes. See note on Mt 18:15–20.

9 THE CHURCH, Local Body—See notes on Ac 8:1; 1 Co 1:2; 2 Co 8:18–24.

9–10 CHURCH LEADERS, Authority—Leaders in the church are not to seek preeminence over others nor to malign other leaders in order to win greater influence.

10 CHRISTIAN ETHICS, Language—Gossip seeks to destroy another person to gain power, position, prestige, or personal attention. Gossip stands in sharp contrast to the love and hospitality which mark the disciple's life.

11 GOD, Righteous—God's righteousness creates righteousness in those who come into relationship with Him. Being in relationship with God is more than an empty formality. If righteousness is not produced in the life of one who claims to be a believer, that is a sign the one is not in true relationship with God. See Jas 2:14–26.

11–12 EVIL AND SUFFERING, Human Origin—Evil can be applied to the realm of spirits (1 Jn 4:1–4), to the person Satan (1 Jn 5:18–19), to humans without Christ (Mt 12:35), and to a period of history (Am 5:13). Most often evil refers to specific actions of human beings. We cause much of the world's evil by imitating evil actions and evil people rather than by imitating God who is good (Mt 19:17).

11 CHRISTIAN ETHICS, Righteousness—Ethics centers on knowing and doing the good. Human standards cannot define the good. Good is a personal characteristic of God which disciples imitate in their actions.

13 REVELATION, Messengers—See note on 2 Jn 12.

Jude

Theological Setting

The first century world was largely antagonistic toward the church. The New Testament is replete with accounts of Christians being persecuted (Ac 8:1; 19:23-41), stoned (Ac 7:57-60; 14:19), imprisoned (Ac 16:19-40), intimidated (Ac 4:18), and even murdered (Ac 12:1-2). This type of opposition came mainly from political, commercial, and religious special interest groups. These groups were intent either upon destroying the Christian movement altogether or severely restricting its growing influence.

The most serious threat to the gospel, however, did not originate in pagan society. It came from within the Christian community itself. For in a world permeated with so many religious and philosophical traditions, Christians were frequently tempted to ignore the exclusiveness of the gospel and to blend their new faith with older, more traditional religious beliefs and practices. This situation gave rise to many false teachers who proclaimed their compromised gospels within the Christian community. The results of such heretical teachings were always the same, regardless of the nature of the heresy—the true gospel was perverted; churches were divided; the Christian mission was imperiled; and the faith of genuine Christians was weakened.

How were first century Christians to protect themselves and the integrity of their gospel from the dangerous threat of heresy? Jude is one of several New Testament letters which answered this question as were Galatians, Colossians, 2 Peter, and 1, 2, 3 John. This particular letter addressed the problem of pseudo-Christian teachers who were preaching heresy in some unnamed location.

These teachers were members of the Christian community (v 4). The exact nature of their heresy is obscure. It does, however, resemble gnostic beliefs current in the first century. These teachers apparently denied the historicity of Jesus (v 4). They claimed to have had special visions and believed themselves to be above the angelic powers which, they supposed, dominated the created world (v 8). Consequently, they transformed God's grace into immorality (v 4), which simply means the heretics rejected the moral and ethical demands of the gospel.

This heretical stance resulted in a variety of scandalous behaviors. They gave expression to ungodly lusts (vv 16,18), practiced gluttony and selfishness (v 12), complained about divine providence (v 16), and behaved in a manner designed to use and manipulate other persons (v 16). Both their beliefs and behaviors became a divisive element in the Christian community addressed by Jude (v 19).

The first readers of Jude were encouraged to struggle for the integrity of their faith (v 3). This was their only appropriate response to heresy. But what did this struggle entail? It involved a deeper understanding of God's displeasure with heresy. Toward this end, Jude contains a description of the heretics' ungodly behavior and warns of God's certain judgment (v 11).

The struggle for integrity of the faith also involved continuous spiritual growth on the part of genuine Christians. Then, as now, practicing the faith was the most viable way of defending the faith. Thus, Jude contains an exhortation for Christians to build up their faith and to implement the gospel in their daily lives (vv 20-21). Particularly, he urged Christians to show redemptive love toward the heretics (vv 22-23).

Theological Outline

Jude: Struggling for Integrity of the Faith

- I. Introduction (1-2)
- II. An Appeal to Struggle for the Faith (3-4)
  - A. Authentic Christians contend for the true faith. (3)
  - B. Pseudo-Christians live immoral lives and deny Christ. (4)
- III. The Certainty of Divine Judgment (5-7)
  - A. Hebrew history shows the certainty of judgment. (5)
  - B. Fallen angels show the certainty of judgment. (6)
  - C. Immoral Sodom and Gomorrah show the certainty of judgment. (7)

IV. A Description of Heretics (8-19)
  A. They defile the body. (8*a*)
  B. They flaunt authority. (8*b*-11)
  C. They practice immoralities. (12-16)
  D. They follow ungodly lusts. (17-19)
V. An Exhortation to the Faithful (20-23)
  A. Grow in the faith. (20*a*)
  B. Pray in the Holy Spirit. (20*b*)
  C. Remain in the love of God. (21*a*)
  D. Anticipate the coming of Jesus. (21*b*)
  E. Minister to erring Christians. (22-23)
VI. Conclusion: Praise for the Only God and Savior (24-25)

Theological Conclusions

The letter of Jude encourages Christians to maintain the integrity of their faith by emphasizing three basic doctrines:

1. the ultimate authority of God,
2. the preeminence of Jesus, and
3. authentic faith issues in godly behavior.

The recipients of Jude were struggling with a theological crisis precipitated by some heretical teachers. This crisis raised doubts about the authority and validity of the gospel. Should Christians accept the instruction of the false teachers, or should they continue following the gospel originally proclaimed to them? Members of the Christian community were divided among themselves about what to believe and how to behave (v 19).

Jude addressed this critical situation by affirming the validity of the faith as it was originally presented. This faith was "once for all" given to Christians (v 3). Thus, it was not to be altered or embellished in any way. Christians were exhorted to maintain its integrity. Why? Because the orthodox faith rested upon divine authority rather than on human reason. God takes the initiative in calling people to the faith (v 1). The faith is His gracious gift offered to all humankind (vv 3-4). Consequently, all persons must account to God for their response to His grace (vv 5-9), 14-15). Of all the gods that people serve, only God the Father is truly the Savior (v 25). Only God the Father has eternal wisdom, majesty, and sovereignty (v 25). The Christian gospel is trustworthy because it rests upon the ultimate authority of God.

The historical Jesus was insignificant to the first century false teachers. They denied His actual humanity, claiming that He only appeared to be a man. Some of these teachers spontaneously exclaimed, "Jesus be cursed" in worship services (1 Co 12:3), and some rejected Jesus' lordship (Jude 4). Clearly, their teaching rejected Jesus' importance in salvation. This is why Jude countered their beliefs by focusing upon Jesus' preeminence. All Christians are called by God and are kept secure for Jesus (v 1). Jesus is to be obeyed as both Sovereign and Lord (v 4). The apostolic message bore Jesus' authority (v 17). Jesus will appear as victorious Lord at the end of history (v 21). God saves persons only through Jesus (v 25). According to Jude, Jesus is more than some insignificant figure in the drama of salvation. He is, in fact, the most central Person in the Christian faith.

Jude indicted the false teachers for the inadequacy of their beliefs and the ungodly character of their behavior. In doing this, Jude emphasized the inseparable relationship between faith and practice. What one really believes shapes how one lives. The false teachers faced God's judgment simply because they denied Jesus' lordship and lived in a manner contrary to the gospel (vv 4,8-19). This was the essence of their heresy. Genuine Christians, however, were encouraged to maintain the gospel's integrity and to live consistently with its demands (vv 20-23). Authentic faith always issues in godly behavior.

Contemporary Teaching

Jude focuses our attention upon the integrity of the Christian faith. That integrity is constantly threatened by heresy. Maintaining Christian integrity is the responsibility of Christians in every generation. The church continually must be sensitive to the subtle differences between orthodoxy and heterodoxy. Toward that end, Jude urges Christians to: (1) protect and defend the gospel vigorously; (2) accept the lordship of Jesus; (3) recognize the danger of heresy in both beliefs and behavior; (4) practice the faith in everyday living; and (5) express redemptive love toward those who deny Jesus and doubt the true faith. The letter of Jude stresses that the most effective defense of the faith is a Christian community that practices the faith.

JUDE,[a] a servant of Jesus Christ[b] and a
brother of James,

To those who have been called,[c] who
are loved by God the Father and kept by[a]
Jesus Christ:[d]

2Mercy, peace[e] and love be yours in
abundance.[f]

The Sin and Doom of Godless Men

3Dear friends,[g] although I was very eager to write to you about the salvation we
share,[h] I felt I had to write and urge you
to contend[i] for the faith[j] that was once
for all entrusted to the saints.[k] 4For certain men whose condemnation was written about[b] long ago have secretly slipped
in among you.[l] They are godless men,
who change the grace of our God into a
license for immorality and deny Jesus
Christ our only Sovereign and Lord.[m]

5Though you already know all this,[n] I
want to remind you[o] that the Lord[c] delivered his people out of Egypt, but later
destroyed those who did not believe.[p]
6And the angels who did not keep their
positions of authority but abandoned
their own home—these he has kept in
darkness, bound with everlasting chains
for judgment on the great Day.[q] 7In a
similar way, Sodom and Gomorrah[r] and
the surrounding towns[s] gave themselves
up to sexual immorality and perversion.
They serve as an example of those who
suffer the punishment of eternal fire.[t]

8In the very same way, these dreamers
pollute their own bodies, reject authority
and slander celestial beings.[u] 9But even
the archangel[v] Michael,[w] when he was
disputing with the devil about the body of
Moses,[x] did not dare to bring a slanderous accusation against him, but said,
"The Lord rebuke you!"[y] 10Yet these
men speak abusively against whatever
they do not understand; and what things
they do understand by instinct, like un-
reasoning animals—these are the very
things that destroy them.[z]

11Woe to them! They have taken the
way of Cain;[a] they have rushed for profit
into Balaam's error;[b] they have been destroyed in Korah's rebellion.[c]

12These men are blemishes at your love
feasts,[d] eating with you without the
slightest qualm—shepherds who feed
only themselves.[e] They are clouds without rain,[f] blown along by the wind;[g] autumn trees, without fruit and uprooted[h]
—twice dead. 13They are wild waves of
the sea,[i] foaming up their shame;[j] wandering stars, for whom blackest darkness
has been reserved forever.[k]

14Enoch,[l] the seventh from Adam,
prophesied about these men: "See, the
Lord is coming[m] with thousands upon

1:1 [a]Mt 13:55; Jn 14:22; Ac 1:13 [b]Ro 1:1 [c]Ro 1:6,7 [d]Jn 17:12
1:2 [e]Gal 6:16; 1Ti 1:2 [f]S Ro 1:7
1:3 [g]S 1Co 10:14 [h]Tit 1:4 [i]1Ti 6:12 [j]ver 20; Ac 6:7 [k]S Ac 9:13
1:4 [l]Gal 2:4 [m]Tit 1:16; 2Pe 2:1; 1Jn 2:22
1:5 [n]S 1Jn 2:20 [o]2Pe 1:12,13; 3:1,2 [p]Nu 14:29; Dt 1:32; 2:15; Ps 106:26; 1Co 10:1-5; Heb 3:16,17
1:6 [q]S 2Pe 2:4,9
1:7 [r]S Mt 10:15 [s]Dt 29:23 [t]S Mt 25:41; 2Pe 3:7
1:8 [u]2Pe 2:10
1:9 [v]1Th 4:16 [w]Da 10:13,21; 12:1; Rev 12:7 [x]Dt 34:6 [y]Zec 3:2
1:10 [z]2Pe 2:12
1:11 [a]Ge 4:3-8; Heb 11:4; 1Jn 3:12 [b]S 2Pe 2:15 [c]Nu 16:1-3,31-35
1:12 [d]2Pe 2:13; 1Co 11:20-22 [e]Eze 34:2,8,10 [f]Pr 25:14; 2Pe 2:17 [g]Eph 4:14 [h]Mt 15:13
1:13 [i]Isa 57:20 [j]Php 3:19 [k]2Pe 2:17
1:14 [l]Ge 5:18, 21-24 [m]S Mt 16:27

[a] *1* Or *for*; or *in* [b] *4* Or *men who were marked out for condemnation* [c] *5* Some early manuscripts *Jesus*

1,4,25 GOD, Trinity—Notice how closely related the Father and the Son are in these verses. No clear distinction can be made between them. In the doctrine of the Trinity we understand there is only one God, yet we know Him in three distinct Persons. Thus, anything we say of one of the three necessarily involves the other two, for they are inseparable. God is called Savior, a term usually applied to Jesus. Jesus is called Sovereign, a term usually applied to God the Father. See note on Mt 3:16–17.

1 THE CHURCH, Servants—See note on Ro 1:1.

2 PRAYER, Blessing—Personal letters in the New Testament usually open with prayer for the recipients. See note on Ro 1:7.

3 HOLY SCRIPTURE, Purpose—God's initiative stood behind the two motives that prompted the writing of this letter: the author's interest in sharing his belief about salvation and his concern for the possible weakening of the witness to that revelation among his readers. Jude was afraid his readers were losing their faith foundation. Inspired Scripture leads us to salvation and leads us back to our foundation when false teachers seek to lead us astray.

4 SIN, Depravity—Continual sin results in a depraved attitude toward others and will cause those who are caught up in it even to deny the grace of God. False Christian teachers do not directly deny the grace of God, but they do so indirectly by changing definitions of God's actions toward and expectations of His people. They take God's grace to mean all sins will automatically be forgiven. They say sin gives more opportunity for God to reveal His grace. This would mean Jesus is not Lord and Master of our morals. His teachings would have no authority over us. Immorality under any theological disguise is still sin. Refusing to live like Jesus is depravity.

5–6 LAST THINGS, Judgment—The certainty of God's final judgment of evildoers underlies biblical revelation. Neither unbelievers in the Exodus generation nor sinful angels could escape God's judgment. How much less members of the human family. God's power keeps the wicked beyond death to the final judgment. The "great day" expresses thought similar to that of the future "day of the Lord." See notes on Am 5:18–20; Zep 1:14–2:3.

6 EVIL AND SUFFERING, Satan—See note on 2 Pe 2:4.

7 LAST THINGS, Hell—The destruction of Sodom and Gomorrah is an example of the punishment in a hell of eternal fire. See note on 2 Pe 2:4–9.

8–13 DISCIPLESHIP, Neighbor Love—Love for others should be most prominent at the Lord's Supper when we celebrate God's love for us. Jude portrayed false teachers as blemishes at the charity feasts that early Christians connected with the Lord's Supper. The wealthier disciples contributed provisions for the love feasts. Both rich and poor were free to partake, and food was sent to absent and sick members. Some churches today do a similar thing by receiving an offering for benevolent purposes after observance of the Lord's Supper. The godless false teachers were as shepherds who fed only themselves. They were as fruitless trees and rainless clouds. See note on 1 Jn 3:17–18.

11–13 WORSHIP, False—False worship often centers on self. It leads to eternal punishment. See note on Ex 22:20.

14 LAST THINGS, Judgment—Many interpreters believe that Jude was quoting from 1 Enoch 1:9, a writing of the period between the Old and New Testaments written under the name of the hero of faith in Ge 5:24. Jude used the quotation to support his argument that false teachers face eternal judgment. Though the Book of 1 Enoch was not inspired, this truth apparently was, for Jude was led by the Holy Spirit to include it in his epistle. People who claim to be Christian leaders but teach false doctrine and live immoral lives face judgment, not rewards, when Christ returns with His angels.

thousands of his holy ones[n] 15to judge[o]
everyone, and to convict all the ungodly
of all the ungodly acts they have done in
the ungodly way, and of all the harsh
words ungodly sinners have spoken
against him."[p] 16These men are grumblers[q] and faultfinders; they follow their
own evil desires;[r] they boast[s] about
themselves and flatter others for their
own advantage.

A Call to Persevere

17But, dear friends, remember what
the apostles[t] of our Lord Jesus Christ
foretold.[u] 18They said to you, "In the last
times[v] there will be scoffers who will follow their own ungodly desires."[w]
19These are the men who divide you,
who follow mere natural instincts and do
not have the Spirit.[x]
20But you, dear friends, build yourselves up[y] in your most holy faith[z] and
pray in the Holy Spirit.[a] 21Keep yourselves in God's love as you wait[b] for the
mercy of our Lord Jesus Christ to bring
you to eternal life.[c]

22Be merciful to those who doubt;
23snatch others from the fire and save
them;[d] to others show mercy, mixed
with fear—hating even the clothing
stained by corrupted flesh.[e]

Doxology

24To him who is able[f] to keep you
from falling and to present you before his
glorious presence[g] without fault[h] and
with great joy— 25to the only God[i] our
Savior be glory, majesty, power and authority, through Jesus Christ our Lord, before all ages, now and forevermore![j]
Amen.[k]

1:14 [n]Dt 33:2; Da 7:10; Zec 14:5; Heb 12:22
1:15 [o]2Pe 2:6-9 [p]1Ti 1:9
1:16 [q]1Co 10:10 [r]ver 18; 2Pe 2:10 [s]2Pe 2:18
1:17 [t]S Eph 4:11 [u]Heb 2:3; 2Pe 3:2
1:18 [v]1Ti 4:1; 2Ti 3:1; 2Pe 3:3 [w]ver 16; 2Pe 2:1; 3:3
1:19 [x]1Co 2:14,15
1:20 [y]Col 2:7; 1Th 5:11 [z]ver 3 [a]Eph 6:18
1:21 [b]Tit 2:13; Heb 9:28; 2Pe 3:12 [c]S Mt 25:46
1:23 [d]Am 4:11; Zec 3:2-5; 1Co 3:15 [e]Rev 3:4
1:24 [f]S Ro 16:25 [g]S 2Co 4:14 [h]Col 1:22
1:25 [i]Jn 5:44; 1Ti 1:17 [j]Heb 13:8 [k]S Ro 11:36

17–21 HOLY SPIRIT, Fellowship—The Spirit gives new life to those who put their faith in Christ. This new life is the life of God, and all Christians share it with one another. This is the fellowship of the Spirit. It is a single, undivided fellowship. The Spirit gives gifts which help to strengthen the unity of God's family. The greatest of these gifts is, of course, love. People who work for the unity of the fellowship are guided by the Spirit. See note on 1 Co 12:1–3. Those who undermine that unity are not guided by the Spirit but are following the natural human instinct for alienation. Christians should cooperate in building up the unity of God's people. Jude suggested three things which help: pray in the Spirit, remain in the love of God, and wait for the mercy of Christ. Compare Paul's blessing in 2 Co 13:14. The Spirit leads the Christian fellowship in its great work of worship. In particular, He helps Christians to pray. What we cannot put into words, He offers to God on our behalf. He prays for us. See note on Ro 8:25–27.

17–18 LAST THINGS, Last Days—See note on 2 Pe 3:3–4.

20–21 PRAYER, Holy Spirit Guides—Pray submissive to, filled with, attentive to, and utilizing the power of the Holy Spirit. Jude had just described people devoid of the Spirit. See note on Ro 8:26–27.

21 SALVATION, Eternal Life—Eternal life is future-oriented in this text. The mercy of our Lord Jesus Christ brings it to us. In the meantime, God's loving vigilance should be matched by ours.

21–23 EVANGELISM, Obedience—Amid persecution and ridicule, evangelism is still the order of the day. We have cogent reasons not only to persevere in faith but also to call others to the gospel: (1) obedience keeps us in the love of God; (2) we are sharing the message of eternal life people need to hear; (3) we display mercy for the lost; and (4) people are saved from the eternal flame (Mt 25:41). We are to do this great work in fear and holy living, hating all things spotted by the sinful flesh. To be obedient to our Lord, we must share our faith.

24 SALVATION, Joy—God's mercy and power are able to keep us safe and to fill us with triumphant joy on judgment day.

24–25 PRAYER, Praise—Jude praised God's work for Christians and then ascribed to Him glory, majesty, power, and authority. See note on Ro 16:25–27.

Revelation

Theological Setting

What provides hope for a Christian in the midst of trouble and suffering? John the Apostle was a prisoner of the government on the island of Patmos (1:9). He sought to strengthen the resolve of embattled Christians in the churches in Asia, who suffered persecution from Domitian, the Roman emperor, because they refused to worship him. Their refusal thwarted Domitian's goal of being worshiped so the Roman empire would have a spiritual basis of unity. For Christians, only Jesus deserved the title Lord, while the emperor wanted recognition as lord. Christians said God controlled history, while the emperor claimed to hold the world's fate in his hands. The church was quickly settling into a second- and third-generation existence with most of the apostles and eyewitnesses of Christ having died. Initial enthusiasm and fervor tended to fade. Expectation of Christ's return did not burn so brightly. Faith in God as more powerful than Rome was called in question. False teachers and false doctrines tempted the church to compromise its moral integrity and to serve both Rome and God.

The churches in Asia Minor to whom John wrote faced several temptations in face of false teaching and government persecution: (1) the faint-hearted were tempted to forsake Christ and His church to avoid suffering; (2) they could continue meeting with the church but also bow down to the emperor's image; (3) they had allowed false teachings and claims of secret knowledge into their midst, compromising the true gospel message; and (4) they had allowed their fervor for Christ in some areas to become lukewarm. Christ's revelation called them to commit themselves wholeheartedly to Christ and to serve His church with evangelistic fervor even though they might be sentenced to death. Four ways to interpret Revelation are described under "Contemporary Teaching" (p. 1633), which perhaps should be read before studying the outline. The outline reflects the view called "historical premillennialism."

Theological Outline

Revelation: A Call to a Blessed Hope for Persecuted Believers As Jesus Reveals the Victorious Future

I. Introduction: Jesus' Revelation Was Given Through John by Jesus Christ Himself. (1:1-20)
- A. The revelation of Jesus Christ (1:1-3)
  - 1. Was given by God to John for Christ's servants to show the future (1:1-2)
  - 2. Was given to be studied, understood, and obeyed (1:3)
- B. The trinitarian God addressed the Seven Churches of Asia. (1:4-7)
  - 1. Grace comes from the eternal trinitarian God. (1:4-5)
  - 2. Christ has made believers to be priests in His kingdom. (1:6)
  - 3. Christ's second coming will be known worldwide. (1:7)
- C. Only the Lord God is eternal and almighty. (1:8)
- D. Revelation was written at Christ's command by a faithful sharer in persecution. (1:9-11)
- E. Jesus, who holds the keys to the future, is magnificent in power and splendor. (1:12-20)

II. Jesus Knows His Churches and Commands, Encourages, and Judges Them. (2:1—3:22)
- A. A good, persevering, faithful, doctrinally-strong church may lose its ardor. (2:1-7)
- B. A suffering church should remember that faithful believers will receive a crown of life. (2:8-11)
- C. A faithful church may slip into an easy tolerance of false teachings. (2:12-17)
- D. A church must join its faithful service with the rejection of false teachers and of claims to secret knowledge, and must hold a steadfast hope to share in Christ's eternal rule. (2:18-29)
- E. Christ knows a church's true works and the faithfulness and unfaithfulness of members. (3:1-6)
- F. A church that faithfully perseveres can anticipate honor and reward. (3:7-13)
- G. A lukewarm church must repent or face Christ's judgment. (3:14-22)

III. The Sovereign God Sits Enthroned. (4:1-11)
- A. God controls *and can reveal* the future. (4:1)
- B. The indescribable God sits on His heavenly throne, surrounded by thrones of the earthly founders of the Old Israel and the New Israel. (4:2-5)

C. God is transcendent, all powerful, all wise, eternal, and absolute sovereign over all. (4:6-9)
D. God is Creator and Sustainer of the universe and so is immensely worthy of praise. (4:10-11)

IV. The Redeeming Divine Christ Is Worthy of Praise. (5:1-14)
A. Jesus Christ is the key to understanding the meaning of history. (5:1-5)
B. The divine Christ came to redeem mankind and create a kingdom of believer priests. (5:6-10)
C. Christ is praised by all the hordes in heaven for His redemption. (5:11-14)

V. Disasters Will Continue, and God Will Come in Judgment. (6:1—7:17)
A. Earthly conquerors, war, famine, and death continue through history. (6:1-8)
B. Faithful martyrs of all ages cry out for vindication and are consoled by the faithful God. (6:9-11)
C. At the end time, God will shake the heavens and earth in judgment. (6:12-17)
D. God will protect His people from the judgment. (7:1-12)
E. The redeemed will spend a praise-filled eternity in heaven with God and the Lamb. (7:13-17)

VI. God Will Send Judgment and Woes to the Earth in a Period of Great Tribulation. (8:1—9:21) (Amillennialists interpret the events chapters 8—18 as continuing throughout history rather than at the end time. Dispensationalists believe the church will be taken from the earth before they occur; historical premillennialists believe the church will remain on earth during the tribulation.)
A. Prayer is a vital force in the work of God's kingdom. (8:1-6)
B. God will call the world to repent through four enormous natural disasters. (8:7-12)
C. In the end time, Satan's forces will attack the world, causing great suffering without bringing repentance; God's sealed people will be protected. (8:13—9:21)

VII. God's Message of Redemption and Judgment Will Be Heard. (10:1—11:19)
A. The gospel is to be proclaimed faithfully to rebellious people. (10:1-11)
B. In the end time, two powerful witnesses will proclaim God's message and will be martyred, but their resurrection will result in the conversion of a multitude of people or of Israel. (11:1-14)
C. History will climax in the revelation of God's eternal kingdom. (11:15-19)

VIII. Satan's Desperate War Against Christ and His Church Is Fierce but Will Fail. (12:1—13:18)
A. Christ's incarnation brought Satan's desperate attempt to kill Jesus; having failed, he pursues Christ's church through history and will persecute them even more intensively in the great tribulation. (12:1-17)
B. In the end time an antichrist will arise with Satan's backing and enlist the support of a great many people through deception. (13:1-18)

IX. Salvation and Judgment Are Proclaimed from Heaven. (14:1-20)
A. The faithful redeemed are assured of eternal bliss. (14:1-5)
B. The unredeemed worshipers of the Beast are assured of eternal torment. (14:6-11)
C. Believers are called to perseverance and are promised eternal rest. (14:12-13)
D. Christ will come to claim believers and force vengeance on unbelievers. (14:14-20)

X. The Last Tribulation or Judgment Will Evidence God's Justice. (15:1—16:21)
A. Victory is as sure as the Exodus for God's people. (15:1-4)
B. Judgment represents the covenant law executed by God against human rebels. (15:5-8)
C. Followers of the antichrist face total judgment which witnesses to God's justice. (16:1-7)
D. Judgment calls for repentance, but followers of the antichrist refuse. (16:8-11)
E. Efforts by the antichrist to conquer the earth will be defeated. (16:12-21)

XI. God's Judgment on the Political Power Which Supports the Antichrist Will Be Complete and Just. (17:1—19:5)
A. The evil Babylon power oppresses believers. (17:1-6)
B. The Babylon power includes a complex of many nations and people. (17:7-18)
C. The destruction of the Babylon power will be complete and for just cause. (18:1-24)
D. God's judgment on the Babylon power will bring great rejoicing in heaven. (19:1-5)

XII. Christ Will Come to Consummate History and Create a New Heaven and Earth. (19:6—22:21)
A. He will call His faithful church to a great marriage banquet. (19:6-10)
B. Christ Jesus will return in great victory and power. (19:11-16)
C. The satanic power will gather forces for an assault on the victorious Jesus in the battle of Armageddon (see 16:16), but they will be instantaneously defeated. (19:17-21)
D. Satan will be bound, and Christ will establish His millennial kingdom. (20:1-6)
E. At the end of the millennium, Satan will be defeated and condemned eternally. (20:7-10)
F. At the end of time, all people who ever lived will face judgment. (20:11-15)
G. The old world will pass away, and the new heavens and earth will be established, to which the faithful will be admitted and from which the unredeemed will be barred. (21:1-14)

H. Eternal heaven will be a place of indescribable bliss. (21:15—22:5)
I. Jesus' revelation which He gave to John is certain and should be taken seriously by everyone; believers should be faithful and unbelievers should respond to His invitation. (22:6-21)

Theological Conclusions

The outline shows the theological richness of Revelation despite its complex symbolism. The book represents crucial doctrinal insights for God's people. These center around the teachings on: (1) the sovereignty of God; (2) Jesus as the suffering, atoning, ascended, and returning Messiah; (3) the Holy Spirit; (4) the kingdom of Christ and thus of God; (5) Christian hope; (6) heaven; (7) hell; (8) judgment; (9) sin; (10) Satan; (11) humanity; (12) history; (13) the Christian life; (14) priesthood of believers; (15) church; (16) biblical inspiration; and (17) angels. Perseverance is a continued emphasis throughout the book.

The entire book repeatedly witnesses to God's sovereignty over all human history and activities and over all human institutions. Neither Satan nor his representations in human rulers or religious leaders can overcome God's purposes. In fact, God works out His purposes even through their evil (17:17). The sovereignty of God is the foundation for hope and the promise of victory in the midst of persecution and suffering.

Jesus Christ is the book's central figure. He gives the revelation (1:1) and is the only One able to clarify history's meaning by opening the mysterious scroll (5:5). He is worthy to do so because of His redemptive death and resurrection (5:5-14). He is closely identified with God's Spirit (5:6-7) and is Israel's expected Messiah or Christ (5:5). He is divine, worthy to receive the glory due to God (5:12). The theme of Revelation is the ultimate victory of Christ in His second coming (1:7; 19:11-21; 22:7,12,17,20). He will establish God's kingdom in which He and the Father will rule with the saints (21:1—22:5). He will reign in the millennium (20:4), and He will marry His bride, the church, eternally (19:7-9).

References to the Holy Spirit provide the basis for a doctrine of the Trinity. Individual believers have the Spirit's presence (1:10). The Spirit speaks a word of hope to the churches (2:7,11,17,29; 3:6,13,22; 14:13). The Spirit was an agent in revealing Holy Scripture to John (21:10) and is active in calling for Christ's return and for people to come to Christ (22:17).

Christ's kingdom is presented both as His eternal rule and as His present rule over His churches (chs 2—3). The church represents God's people of the New Covenant in historical existence. Locally, individual churches exist (1:4; 2:1—3:22). Christ is the Head of the church and has authority over it (2:1). The local church teaches good doctrine and disciplines false teachers (2:2-23), proclaims and testifies to the gospel in evangelistic missionary outreach (2:13), and supports other churches.

The picture of the kingdom shows how God's saints respond to His rule: with singing, service, and praise (5:9-13; 7:4-17; 14:2-3; 15:2-4; 19:6). Suffering saints on earth can count on the power of their prayers to the heavenly King on His throne (8:3-5). At the end time Christ's kingdom will be consumated in all its glory, and His reign will be absolute (11:15-19). Christ's kingdom is the goal toward which Christian hope is aimed. In Christ's death and resurrection, Satan *already* has been defeated (12:1-17). Those who reject the gospel for the false security of material wealth and physical safety do so at eternal peril (18:1-24). The faithful are the ones whose future is secure (4:4,10).

The glories of heaven are beyond human imagination. God's presence permeates all of heaven (21:22). Absolutely no evil will be there (21:27; 22:3). Believers can be certain of entering heaven, for our names are written in the book of life (3:5). The Lamb marks His own (22:4). The certainty of heaven does not eliminate the need to urge faithfulness, for a call to faithfulness permeates Revelation.

Those not in the book of life face eternal punishment or hell. This is described as the bottomless pit or Abyss (9:2; 11:7; 17:8; 20:3), the home of demons, evil spirits, and the eternally dead. It is where the satanic beast comes from (13:11). It is a place of eternal torment (14:10-11; 19:3,20; 20:10,15; 21:8). Hell is the result of judgment on evil and evil ones, a necessary partner to Christ's victory over evil and revenge for His saints (16:5-7). Christ will defeat the satanic beast and his supporters (17:13-14). Judgment shows that God is just and true to Himself or trustworthy (15:3; 16:4-7). Judgment through historical punishment calls for repentance (16:8-11; 9:20-21). Judgment completed leaves no hope.

Sin appears in many forms in the world: sexual sins (9:21; 21:8; 22:15), worship of false gods (9:20; 13:4; 8,14-16; 14:11; 21:8; 22:15), involvement in the occult (9:20-21; 18:23; 21:8; 22:15), murder (9:21; 21:8; 22:15), theft (9:21), killing believers (17:6; 18:24), slave-trading (18:13), lying (21:27; 22:15), economic sins (18:3,11-19), political sins (17:2,4,7-13), and cowardice (21:8), which probably refers to those who professed the faith but did not endure. Basically, sin for Revelation is trust in the satanic forces of political and false religious leaders rather than trust in the King of kings.

Satan is clearly depicted as the author of sin. He has the key to the Abyss (9:1-2). He attacks God's witnesses (11:7-10). He sought to destroy Christ (12:1-6) but lost the battle (12:7-11). Ever since he has feverishly attacked Christ's disciples (12:12—13:1). He will marshall forces against God (16:13-14; 19:19) but will be defeated (19:20-21). Christ will bind them in the Abyss (20:1-3), but Satan will gain freedom and again attack God but without success (20:7-10).

Revelation shows an understanding of the destructive capabilities of humanity as well as the evil of Satan. Some humans respond to God's grace and are saved, faithfully serving God (6:9-11), while others obstinately refuse to repent (9:20-21; 16:8-11). Clearly, perseverance is a clear indicator of genuine faith (1:9; 22:7). Satan attacks believers constantly (12:17), requiring believers to remain faithful (1:3; 13:10; 14:12; 21:7; 22:14). Faithfulness involves not betraying Christ in worship or morality by remaining dedicated to truth and purity (14:3-5).

The strength to remain faithful rests on a special type of relationship with God through Christ known as the priesthood of all believers. (1:6; 5:10). God revealed His covenant identity to His people on Sinai (Ex 19:6). Revelation affirms this identity for the church. All citizens of God's kingdom, not just political or religious officials, are to mediate God's salvation to the nations, approach God for themselves, and accept responsibility for personal holiness before God.

The Book of Revelation shows us important points in the teaching about the Bible. Revelation is a direct product of Jesus revealing His word to John (Rev 1:1). It was written down immediately (1:10-11). He did not receive permission to write everything he heard (10:2-4). The writing had a definite purpose (1:1) and was expected to be read and obeyed (1:3; 22:9-10). The trustworthiness of the revelation is asserted (22:6). Its authority is recognized immediately, so that nothing should be added or taken away (22:18-19). The inspired book had words of immediate application to specific congregations (2:1—3:22), has continuing meaning, and has an end time meaning.

Angels appear more in Revelation than in most biblical books. Each church has an angel (1:20), but the exact interpretation here is disputed: pastors, guardian angel, or heavenly counterpart of the earthly church. Angels serve as heavenly heralds (5:2), heavenly messengers on earth to protect God's people (7:1-3), messengers delivering human prayers to God (8:3-5), musicians announcing and introducing God's judgment (8:6—9:13; 18:1-2), agents inflicting divine judgment (9:14-15; 14:19; 15:1—16:71), agents of divine revelation (10:1-11; 14:6-9; 21:9-17; 22:6), messengers of communication in heaven (14:14-18), keepers of the heavenly altar (14:18). Angels may have great authority (18:1), even holding the key to hell (20:1) and being able to introduce people to God's secrets (21:9-10). Still, angels are not to receive human worship (22:8-9). They are worshipers of God (5:11; 7:11). Some angels are not faithful to God, for they follow Satan (12:7-9).

Essentially, Revelation is about history; it reveals its meaning and reveals Christ's final victory at its end. Ceasar and Rome appeared to control history, rather than God controlling it, but He will be ultimately victorious. God's kingdom will be established. The suffering of God's people will be avenged. The satanic forces will suffer eternally. Jesus is coming.

Contemporary Teaching

Many different contemporary teachings have been drawn from the Book of Revelation because of the different ways used to interpret it. Revelation has the form of a letter from John to the churches (1:4; 22:21). The language of apocalyptic literature of the two centuries before and the two centuries after Christ is used. Such literature is filled with figurative and symbolic language. Often it is placed in the mouth of an ancient biblical hero, so we have books from the period entitled 1 Enoch, The Testament of Moses, 2 Baruch, and the Apocalypse of Abraham. Apocalyptic writings sought to lead people through the ages of history to reveal the work of God in the future and give assurance to tormented saints. Obviously, Revelation stands apart from such literature, plainly naming a contemporary figure, John, as the author. Still, it uses symbolism and deals with history in ways similar to apocalyptic writings. The biblical student must use careful judgment in comparing Revelation to this literature.

The student must face several major issues: (1) How does one relate the Old and New Testaments and their interpretation? (2) How does one determine that which is literal and that which is symbolic? (3) What events did the writer see as having already occurred, and what events did he intend to describe as future? (4) Which events still lie in the future? (5) Do the chapters represent a chronological order of different events, or are symbolic pictures drawn to describe the meaning of the same events in different symbols for different emphases? This last question is particularly important for Revelation. Do the seals (ch 6), trumpets (chs 8-9), and bowls (chs 15-16) reflect a chronological sequence of successive events? Or does each section repeat the same event(s) from different perspectives? Or do the three sections have some overlap of events while each adds additional events? These questions and others have led to major differences in understanding the interpretation of Revelation.

1. Postmillennialism says the world will be won to Christ through aggressive evangelism and missions. Christians will grow more Christlike until He will rule the world through His people in this gradually-developed millennial kingdom. Then Christ will return bodily to establish a new heaven and a new earth. This view gave major impetus to the modern mission movement and has recently reappeared in modified interpretations.

2. Amillennialism interprets Revelation symbolically to apply to the constant battle between God and Satan, good and evil, and the church and the world until Christ returns bodily at the end of time. The millennial kingdom (ch 20) applies to the rule of God in believers' hearts throughout history. The tribulation period (7:14; chs 8—9) refers to the troubles God's people pass through because evil people and forces persecute the church. This view accepts that the seals, trumpets, and vials recapitulate the continuing warfare between God and Satan. See Series in Revelation Chart.

3. Premillennialism has developed two distinct forms.

(a) Dispensational premillennialism sees in chapters 2—3 the division of history into seven identifiable church ages, the last age representing the present time, that of apostasy. The church is "raptured" at the end of chapter 3. Chapters 4—22 represent the end time after the rapture of the church, that is the deliverance of the church from the great tribulation. The seals judgment (ch 6) occurs during the first half of the tribulation period during which time 144,000 Jewish converts will be saved by joining the kingdom (rather than by grace though faith; the dispensation of grace will be over). The trumpets judgment (chs 8-9) also occurs during the tribulation. During the great tribulation, the raptured church will be with Christ receiving assignments of millennial rule after the tribulation. During the millennium the Israelite Temple and sacrificial system will have been reestablished.

(b) Historical premillennialism applies chapters 1—3 to the church of the first century and more generally to later centuries without separating history into different ages, just as other Scripture applies to all ages. Chapters 4—22 deal with events from Christ's crucifixion to His return and into eternity. The rapture (which to them refers to meeting Christ in the air) occurs at the beginning of the millennium at which time Christ returns to earth. The seals judgment (ch 6) depicts general historical trends leading up to the end. The 144,000 refers to the church on the threshold of the tribulation. (Some say to old Israel.) The trumpets judgment (chs 8—9) refers to a tribulation period in which the church is on earth. Jews will be used by God during the tribulation, but they will be saved by grace through faith just as all previous believers.

Both premillennial views believe a literal antichrist will appear, and both believe in a literal battle of Armageddon. Christ will rule in a literal millennial kingdom. The two views differ on the details of the millennial kingdom, the number and nature of the resurrection(s) and judgment(s), and on the meaning of the New Jerusalem.

The fact of Revelation's complexities and even more the widely and intensively held differing modern viewpoints have robbed many Christians of the tremendous truths of the Book of Revelation, truths which every disciple should learn and practice. The certainty that God acts in history and is moving this world with a sure hand to a destiny He long ago planned for it should motivate Christians to faithful living. God's uniquely all-encompassing and all-surpassing knowledge and power, along with His presence with us wherever we may be, should cause us to feel good about yielding life to God's will, letting Him become King of life right now. The marvelous pictures of Jesus as victorious King, atoning Lamb, and eternal Lord and Judge should reinforce evangelism with the absolute conviction that Jesus is the only way to salvation. The catalog of sins, the depiction of human nature, and the role of Satan should alert Christians to the need for a separate life and for evaluating the extent of sin in the business and political worlds in which we live. The theme of judgment should convince believers and nonbelievers that a day of judgment is coming for everyone. This judgment should call each of us to review our personal relationships with God and prepare to meet Him in the judgment.

The constant refrain which connects reward with persistence and judgment with actions should caution believers against teaching a way of salvation which is cheap and easy. It should urge each of us to forsake any person, institution, or practice which might lead us to be unfaithful to or unfruitful for Christ. Revelation should lead us to hold high the message that salvation includes yielding to Christ as Lord and that faithfulness means loyalty to Jesus even in the face of persecution and death. Having learned Revelation's lessons, we should have new courage and new hope to face a world of trouble and suffering in the confidence that faith in Christ leads to rule with Him.

Millennial Perspectives On Revelation

	Amillennial	Historical Premillennial	Dispensational Premillennial
	Viewpoint that the present age of Christ's rule in the church is the millennium; Holds to one resurrection and judgment marking the end of history as we know it and the beginning of life eternal	Viewpoint that Christ will reign on earth for 1000 years following His Second Coming; Saints will be resurrected at the beginning of the millennium, nonbelievers at the end, followed by judgment	Viewpoint that after the battle of Armageddon, Christ will rule through the Jews for a literal 1000 years accompanied by two resurrections and at least three judgments
Book of Revelation	Current history written in code to confound enemies and encourage Asian Christians; message applies to all Christians	Immediate application to Asian Christians; applies to all Christians throughout the ages, but the visions also apply to a great future event	"Unveiling" of theme of Christ among churches in present dispensation, also as Judge and King in dispensations to come
Seven candlesticks (1:13)	Churches		Churches, plus end-time application
Seven stars (1:16,20)	Pastors	Symbolizes heavenly or supernatural character of the church (some believe refers to pastors)	Pastors or saints
Churches addressed (chaps. 2-3)	Specific historical situations, truths apply to churches throughout the ages; do not represent periods of church history		Specific historical situations and to all churches throughout the ages; shows progress of churches' spiritual state until end of church age
Twenty-four elders (4:4,10; 5:8,14)	Twelve patriarchs and twelve apostles; together symbolize all the redeemed	Company of angels who help execute God's rule (or elders represent twenty-four priestly and Levitical orders)	The rewarded church; also represents twelve patriarchs and twelve apostles

	Amillennial	Historical Premillennial	Dispensational Premillennial
Sealed book (5:1-9)	Scroll of history; shows God carrying out His redemptive purpose in history	Contains prophecy of end events of chapters 7-22	Title deed to the world
144,000 (7:4-8)	Redeemed on earth who will be protected against God's wrath	Church on threshold of great tribulation	Jewish converts of tribulation period who witness to Gentiles (same as 14:1)
Great Multitude (7:9-10)	Uncountable multitude in heaven praising God for their salvation	Church, having gone through great tribulation, seen in heaven	Gentiles redeemed during tribulation period through witness of 144,000
Great tribulation (first reference in 7:14)	Persecution faced by Asian Christians of John's time; symbolic of tribulation that occurs throughout history	Period at end-time of unexplained trouble, before Christ's return; church will go through it; begins with seventh seal (18:1) which includes trumpets 1-6 (8:2 to 14:20)	Period at end-time of unexplained trouble referred to in 7:14 and described in chapters 11-18; lasts three-and-one-half years, the latter half of seven-year period between rapture and millennium
"Star" (9:4)	Personified evil	Represents an angelic figure divinely commissioned to carry out God's purpose	The leader of apostasy during the great tribulation
Forty-two months (11:2); 1,260 days (11:3)	Indefinite duration of pagan desolation	A symbolic number representing period of evil with reference to last days of age	Half of seven-year tribulation period
Two witnesses (11:3-10)	Spread of gospel in first century	Two actual historical persons at end of time who witness to Israel	A witnessing remnant of Jews in Jerusalem testifying to the coming kingdom and calling Israel to repent

***Postmillennialism—Viewpoint that Christ's reign on earth is spiritual not physical. Christ returns after the millennium that is established by gospel preaching.**

Millennial Perspectives On Revelation

	Amillennial	Historical Premillennial	Dispensational Premillennial
Sodom and Egypt (11:8)	Rome as seat of Empire	Earthly Jerusalem	Earthly Jerusalem
Woman (12:1-6)	True people of God under Old and New Covenants (true Israel)		Indicates Israel, not church; key is comparison with Genesis 37:9
Great red dragon (12:3)	All views identify as Satan		
Manchild (12:4-5)	Christ at His birth, life events, and crucifixion, whom Satan sought to kill	Christ, whose work Satan seeks to destroy	Christ but also the church (head and body); caught up on throne indicates rapture of church
1,260 days (12:6)	Indefinite time	Symbolic number representing period of evil with special reference to last days of age	First half of great tribulation after church is raptured
Sea beast (13:1)	Emperor Domitian, personification of Roman Empire (same as in chap. 17)	Antichrist, here shown as embodiment of the four beasts in Daniel 7	A new Rome, satanic federation of nations that come out of old Roman Empire
Seven heads (13:1)	Roman emperors	Great power, shows kinship with dragon	Seven stages of Roman Empire; sixth was imperial Rome (John's day); last will be federation of nations
Ten horns (13:1)	Symbolize power	Kings, represent limited crowns (ten) against Christ's many	Ten powers that will combine to make the federation of nations of new Rome
Earth beast (13:11)	*Concilia*, Roman body in cities responsible for emperor worship	Organized religion as servant of first beast during great tribulation period; headed by a false prophet	Antichrist, who will head apostate religion, a Jewish leader described in Daniel 11:36-45 (some identify as assistant to the Antichrist)

	Amillennial	Historical Premillennial	Dispensational Premillennial
666 (13:18)	Imperfection, evil; personified as Domitian	Symbolic of evil, short of 777; if a personage meant, he is unknown but will be known at the proper time	Not known, but will be known when time comes
144,000 on Mount Zion (14:1)	Total body of redeemed in heaven		Redeemed Jews gathered in earthly Jerusalem during millennial kingdom
River of blood (14:20)	Symbol of infinite punishment for the wicked	Means God's radical judgment crushes evil thoroughly	Scene of wrath and carnage that will occur in Palestine
Babylon (woman—17:5)	Historical Rome	Capital city of future Antichrist	Apostate church of the future
Beast	Domitian	Antichrist	Head of satanic federation of nations of revived Roman Empire; linked with apostate church (seventh head)
Seven mountains (17:9)	Pagan Rome, which was built on seven hills	Indicate power, so here means a succession of empires, last of which is end-time Babylon	Rome, revived at end-time
Seven heads (17:7) and seven kings (17:10)	Roman emperors from Augustus to Titus, excluding three brief rules	Five past godless kingdoms; sixth was Rome; seventh would arise in end-time	Five distinct forms of Roman government prior to John; sixth was imperial Rome; seventh will be revived Roman Empire
Ten horns (17:7) and ten kings (17:12)	Vassal kings who ruled with Rome's permission	Symbolic of earthly powers that will be subservient to Antichrist	Ten kingdoms arising in future out of revived Roman Empire

Millennial Perspectives On Revelation

	Amillennial	Historical Premillennial	Dispensational Premillennial
Waters (17:15)	People ruled by Roman Empire	Indicates complex civilization	People dominated by apostate church
Bride, wife (19:7)	Total of all the redeemed		The church; does not include Old Testament saints or tribulation saints
Marriage supper (19:9)	Climax of the age; symbolizes complete union of Christ with His people	Union of Christ with His people at His Coming	Union of Christ with His church accompanied by Old Testament saints and tribulation saints
One on white horse (19:11-16)	Vision of Christ's victory over pagan Rome; return of Christ occurs in connection with events of 20:7-10	Second coming of Christ	
Battle of Armageddon (19:19-21; see 16:16)	Not literally at end of time but symbolizes power of God's word overcoming evil; principle applies to all ages	Literal event of some kind at end-time but not literal battle with military weapons; occurs at Christ's return at beginning of millennium	Literal bloody battle at Armageddon (valley of Megiddo) at end of great tribulation between kings of the East and federation of nations of new Rome; they are all defeated by blast from Christ's mouth and then millennium begins
Great supper (19:17)	Stands in contrast to marriage supper		Concludes series of judgments and opens way for kingdom to be established
Binding of Satan (20:2)	Symbolic of Christ's resurrection victory over Satan	Curbing of Satan's power during the millennium	
Millennium (20:2-6)	Symbolic reference to period from Christ's first coming to His second	A historical event, though length of one thousand years may be symbolic, after Armageddon during which Christ rules with His people	A literal one thousand year period after the church age during which Christ rules with His people but especially through the Jews
Those on thrones (20:4)	Martyrs in heaven, their presence with God is a judgment on those who killed them	Saints and martyrs who rule with Christ in the millennium	The redeemed ruling with Christ, appearing and disappearing on earth at will to oversee life on earth
First resurrection (20:5-6)	The spiritual presence with Christ of the redeemed that occurs after physical death	Resurrection of saints at beginning of millennium when Christ returns	Includes three groups: (1) those raptured with church (4:1); (2) Jewish tribulation saints during tribulation (11:11); (3) other Jewish believers at beginning of millennium (20:5-6)
Second death (20:6)	Spiritual death, eternal separation from God		
Second resurrection (implied)	All persons, lost and redeemed, rise when Christ returns in only resurrection that takes place	Nonbelievers, resurrected at end of millennium	
New heavens and earth (21:1)	A new order; redeemed earth		
New Jerusalem (21:2-5)	God dwelling with His saints (the church) in the new age after all other end-time events		
New Jerusalem (21:10-22:5)	Same as 21:2-5		Millennial Jerusalem from which the world will be ruled; the bride as well as the home of the saints.

Series in Revelation

	Amillennial	Historical Premillennial	Dispensational Premillennial
Seal 1 (6:1-2)	Earthly conqueror	Proclamation of gospel; others believe is earthly conqueror	Man's last effort to bring order to earth while rejecting Christ
Seals 2-4 (6:3-8)	Also with seal 1, suffering that must be endured throughout history	Constant problems of war, scarcity, and death	Sequence of disasters brought about by evil rule
Seal 5 (6:9-11)	Assurance for faithful (all ages) that God will judge evil		Jewish martyrs of tribulation period
Seal 6 (6:12-17)	End of time; God's final judgment	Real cosmic catastrophe at end of age	Symbolic description of breakup of society as a result of evil
Seal 7 (8:1)	The seven trumpets to follow		
Trumpets 1-4 (chap. 8)	Fall of Roman Empire through natural calamities	God's wrath falls on a civilization that gives allegiance to Antichrist when choice is very clear; first four trumpets involve natural catastrophes	(1) Judgment on people who refuse gospel; (2) judgment on great world-church; (3) judgment on apostate church leader of great influence; (4) judgment on people who reject Christ and follow cults
Locusts, fifth trumpet (9:3-4)	Internal decay bringing fall of Roman Empire	Symbolic of actual demonic forces released during great tribulation, inflict torture	Predicts disastrous results that will come through demonically-led people following apostate religious leader during great tribulation
Army from East, sixth trumpet (9:13-19)	External attack bringing fall of Roman Empire	Symbolic of actual divine judgment on corrupt civilization, inflicts death	Literal invasion of West by army from East
Seventh trumpet (11:15)	God will one day claim His victory	Announces victorious outcome	Announces arrival of millennial kingdom

	Amillennial	Historical Premillennial	Dispensational Premillennial
First vial (16:2)	Judgment on adherents of false religion, including Domitian worshipers	Inflicted specifically on followers of Antichrist	Spiritual plague as great an annoyance as physical suffering
Second vial (16:3)	Destruction of sources of physical sustenance	Death of everything in sea	Death and desolation, whether literal or symbolic
Third vial (16:4-7)	Those who shed blood of saints will receive a curse of blood	Affects fresh water	Destroys the sources of life
Fourth vial (16:8-9)	Even when people recognize that source of all life fights against them for God, they blaspheme and refuse to repent	God overrules processes of nature to bring judgment, but people still refuse to repent	The primary source of humanity's comfort becomes a curse instead
Fifth vial (16:10-11)	God's judgment on seat of beast's authority; darkness indicates confused and evil plotting	Directed against the demonic civilization of end-time	Great federation of nations of new Rome is attacked at its center; darkness brought about by demonical delusions; symbolic
Sixth vial (16:12-16)	Forces against God will ultimately be destroyed; here refers specifically to Parthians	Serves as preparation for great battle of end-time; a coalition of demonically-inspired rulers	Refers to great world conflict of many nations at Armageddon in Palestine
Seventh vial (16:17-21)	Poured in the air all must breathe; strikes note of final judgment on Roman Empire	Describes fall of end-time Babylon (dealt with more fully later)	Utter destruction of every spiritual and religious institution built without God; the overthrow of civilization

Chapter 1

Prologue

THE revelation of Jesus Christ, which
God gave[a] him to show his servants
what must soon take place.[b] He made it
known by sending his angel[c] to his servant John,[d] 2who testifies to everything
he saw—that is, the word of God[e] and
the testimony of Jesus Christ.[f] 3Blessed
is the one who reads the words of this
prophecy, and blessed are those who hear
it and take to heart what is written in it,[g]
because the time is near.[h]

Greetings and Doxology

4John,

To the seven churches[i] in the province of Asia:

Grace and peace to you[j] from him
who is, and who was, and who is to
come,[k] and from the seven spirits[a][l] before his throne, 5and from Jesus Christ,
who is the faithful witness,[m] the firstborn
from the dead,[n] and the ruler of the
kings of the earth.[o]

To him who loves us[p] and has freed us
from our sins by his blood,[q] 6and has
made us to be a kingdom and priests[r] to
serve his God and Father[s]—to him be
glory and power for ever and ever!
Amen.[t]

7Look, he is coming with the clouds,[u]
and every eye will see him,
even those who pierced him;[v]
and all the peoples of the earth will
mourn[w] because of him.
So shall it be! Amen.

8"I am the Alpha and the Omega,"[x]
says the Lord God, "who is, and who
was, and who is to come,[y] the Almighty."[z]

One Like a Son of Man

9I, John,[a] your brother and companion
in the suffering[b] and kingdom[c] and patient endurance[d] that are ours in Jesus,
was on the island of Patmos because of

1:1 [a]Jn 12:49; 17:8 [b]ver 19; Da 2:28, 29; Rev 22:6 [c]Rev 22:16 [d]ver 4, 9; Rev 22:8 **1:2** [e]ver 9; S Heb 4:12 [f]ver 9; 1Co 1:6; Rev 6:9; 12:17; 19:10 **1:3** [g]Lk 11:28; Rev 22:7 [h]S Ro 13:11 **1:4** [i]ver 11,20 [j]S Ro 1:7 [k]ver 8; Rev 4:8; 11:17; 16:5 [l]Isa 11:2; Rev 3:1; 4:5; 5:6 **1:5** [m]Isa 55:4; Jn 18:37; Rev 3:14 [n]Ps 89:27; Col 1:18 [o]S 1Ti 6:15 [p]S Ro 8:37 [q]S Ro 3:25 **1:6** [r]S 1Pe 2:5; Rev 5:10; 20:6 [s]Ro 15:6 [t]S Ro 11:36 **1:7** [u]Da 7:13; S Mt 16:27; 24:30; 26:64; S Lk 17:30; S 1Co 1:7; S 1Th 2:19; 4:16,17 [v]Jn 19:34,37 [w]Zec 12:10; Mt 24:30 **1:8** [x]S ver 17; Rev 21:6; 22:13 [y]S ver 4 [z]Rev 4:8; 15:3; 19:6 **1:9** [a]ver 1 [b]S Ac 14:22; 2Co 1:7; Php 4:14 [c]ver 6 [d]2Ti 2:12

[a]4 Or *the sevenfold Spirit*

1:1 GOD, Sovereignty—The whole Book of Revelation is a message about the sovereignty of God who holds the future in His hands. The whole book also has a strongly trinitarian tone.
1:1 JESUS CHRIST, Ascension—The ascended Christ cares for His people by revealing to them helpful information about events "soon to take place."
1:1–3 HOLY SCRIPTURE, Writing—John wrote what Jesus gave him through an angel. Angelic revelation is one of many features marking Revelation as an apocalyptic work like Daniel. The words had immediate meaning to the original readers dealing with things near at hand. At the same time the apocalyptic language pointed to the second coming. The writing is not simply an angel's testimony. It is a direct revelation of Jesus. John understood what he wrote as prophecy, both a proclamation of God's word for the present and a prediction of God's work in the future. His audience was to take to heart the message and change their lives, as the following letters to the churches indicate. John's emphasis was not on secret knowledge and schemes but on moral living in preparation of Christ's coming. Compare v 19.
1:4,8 GOD, Eternal—God has no beginning and no ending. Thus He has authority and knowledge to warn the churches and describe the future hope. See note on Ge 1:1.
1:4–6 ELECTION, God's Purpose—God loves His elect. He has freed us from sin and forgiven us so we will fulfill His election purpose of serving as a kingdom of servants and priests. Compare Ex 19:3–6.
1:4 THE CHURCH, Local Body—See notes on Ac 4:32; 8:1.
1:4–6 PRAYER, Blessing—Christian letters normally included an opening blessing and a closing doxology. Compare Jude 2, 24–25. See notes on Ro 1:7; 16:25–27.
1:5–6 JESUS CHRIST, King—Jesus the resurrected One rules all earthly rulers. He loves us, has redeemed us by His blood, and formed us to be what God has always intended His people to be—a kingdom of priests representing God to the nations (Ex 19:6).
1:6 THE CHURCH, People of God—From the very beginning, God intended to make for Himself a people. See note on Ex 19:4–8. In Christ, God has made for Himself a people who serve Him and obey His will. This obedient people is the believing church, God's kingdom on earth waiting for the day of fulfillment. See note on 1 Pe 2:4–10.
1:7 LAST THINGS, Return Promises—See note on 1 Th 4:14–18. The return of Christ from heaven with clouds will be a reversal of the manner of His departure (Ac 1:9). His coming will have universal impact. Every eye shall see Him. Dispensationalists teach a "secret rapture" of the church that will occur seven years before this appearing; this event is what they call the second phase of the second coming. (The first phase, the "rapture," is the catching up of living believers and the raising up of those already dead. After an interval of tribulation, according to this view, Christ will return visibly and in great glory for all to see.) Historical premillennialists place the one return of Christ at the end of the time of tribulation. They see Christ as coming back, catching up the church to meet Him in the air, and then continuing His return accompanied by His saints. They believe the church must endure the tribulation with disciples facing martyrdom. It is this unitary event of coming that will be universally apparent. Amillennialists and postmillennialists apply this text to Christ's return. Many of these see no literal tribulation period preceding it or a literal millennial kingdom following it. A basic issue is how one deals with the Bible's teaching on the unexpectedness of Christ's return. A related issue is what one expects to learn from the symbol-filled language of apocalyptic writing. For many alive at the time, Christ's return will be a dreadful event. It will be worthy of mourning and weeping due to the recognition that He is indeed Lord and they have rejected Him. For these, only judgment and eternal punishment will remain.
1:9–19 JESUS CHRIST, Resurrection—This is a triumphant appearance of the Risen Lord. Jesus is Lord of all His churches. He stands in their midst confirming their faithfulness, as Judge of their witness, and as Comforter in affliction. As the resurrected One, He holds the keys to death and the realm of the dead.
1:9 EVIL AND SUFFERING, Endurance—John and other disciples needed courage and endurance to face persecution and suffering. Some would experience martyrdom when they persisted in faith.
1:9 THE CHURCH, God's Kingdom—The kingdom of God must be shared with other believers. Believers belong to the kingdom because of their submission to God through Christ Jesus. Life in the kingdom involves patient suffering waiting for the King to return.

the word of God[e] and the testimony of
Jesus.[f] 10 On the Lord's Day[g] I was in the
Spirit,[h] and I heard behind me a loud
voice like a trumpet,[i] 11 which said:
"Write on a scroll what you see[j] and
send it to the seven churches:[k] to Ephesus,[l] Smyrna,[m] Pergamum,[n] Thyatira,[o]
Sardis,[p] Philadelphia[q] and Laodicea."[r]
12 I turned around to see the voice that
was speaking to me. And when I turned I
saw seven golden lampstands,[s] 13 and
among the lampstands[t] was someone
"like a son of man,"[b][u] dressed in a robe
reaching down to his feet[v] and with a
golden sash around his chest.[w] 14 His
head and hair were white like wool, as
white as snow, and his eyes were like
blazing fire.[x] 15 His feet were like bronze
glowing in a furnace,[y] and his voice was
like the sound of rushing waters.[z] 16 In
his right hand he held seven stars,[a] and
out of his mouth came a sharp double-
edged sword.[b] His face was like the sun[c]
shining in all its brilliance.
17 When I saw him, I fell at his feet[d] as
though dead. Then he placed his right
hand on me[e] and said: "Do not be
afraid.[f] I am the First and the Last.[g] 18 I
am the Living One; I was dead,[h] and behold I am alive for ever and ever![i] And I
hold the keys of death and Hades.[j]
19 "Write, therefore, what you have
seen,[k] what is now and what will take
place later. 20 The mystery of the seven
stars that you saw in my right hand[l] and
of the seven golden lampstands[m] is this:
The seven stars are the angels[c] of the
seven churches,[n] and the seven lampstands are the seven churches.[o]

Chapter 2

To the Church in Ephesus

"TO the angel[d] of the church in Ephesus[p] write:
These are the words of him who
holds the seven stars in his right
hand[q] and walks among the seven
golden lampstands:[r] 2 I know your
deeds,[s] your hard work and your
perseverance. I know that you cannot
tolerate wicked men, that you have
tested[t] those who claim to be apostles but are not, and have found them
false.[u] 3 You have persevered and
have endured hardships for my
name,[v] and have not grown weary.
4 Yet I hold this against you: You
have forsaken your first love.[w] 5 Remember the height from which you
have fallen! Repent[x] and do the
things you did at first. If you do not
repent, I will come to you and remove your lampstand[y] from its
place. 6 But you have this in your favor: You hate the practices of the
Nicolaitans,[z] which I also hate.
7 He who has an ear, let him hear[a]

1:9 [e]ver 2; S Heb 4:12 [f]S ver 2 **1:10** [g]Ac 20:7 [h]Rev 4:2; 17:3; 21:10 [i]Ex 20:18; Rev 4:1 **1:11** [j]ver 19 [k]ver 4, 20 [l]S Ac 18:19 [m]Rev 2:8 [n]Rev 2:12 [o]Ac 16:14; Rev 2:18,24 [p]Rev 3:1 [q]Rev 3:7 [r]S Col 2:1; Rev 3:14 **1:12** [s]ver 20; Ex 25:31-40; Zec 4:2; Rev 2:1 **1:13** [t]Rev 2:1 [u]Eze 1:26; Da 7:13; 10:16; Rev 14:14 [v]Isa 6:1 [w]Da 10:5; Rev 15:6 **1:14** [x]Da 7:9; 10:6; Rev 2:18; 19:12 **1:15** [y]Eze 1:7; Da 10:6; Rev 2:18 [z]Eze 43:2; Rev 14:2; 19:6 **1:16** [a]ver 20; Rev 2:1; 3:1 [b]Isa 1:20; 49:2; Heb 4:12; Rev 2:12, 16; 19:15,21 [c]Jdg 5:31; Mt 17:2 **1:17** [d]Eze 1:28; Da 8:17,18 [e]Da 8:18 [f]S Mt 14:27 [g]Isa 41:4; 44:6; 48:12; Rev 2:8; 22:13 **1:18** [h]Ro 6:9; Rev 2:8 [i]Dt 32:40; Da 4:34; 12:7; Rev 4:9,10; 10:6; 15:7 [j]Rev 9:1; 20:1 **1:19** [k]ver 11; Hab 2:2 **1:20** [l]S ver 16 [m]S ver 12 [n]ver 4,11 [o]Mt 5:14, 15 **2:1** [p]S Ac 18:19 [q]Rev 1:16 [r]Rev 1:12,13

2:2 [s]ver 19; Rev 3:1,8,15 [t]1Jn 4:1 [u]2Co 11:13 **2:3** [v]S Jn 15:21 **2:4** [w]Jer 2:2; Mt 24:12 **2:5** [x]ver 16,22; Rev 3:3,19 [y]Rev 1:20 **2:6** [z]ver 15 **2:7** [a]S Mt 11:15; ver 11, 17,29; Rev 3:6,13,22; 13:9

[b] *13* Daniel 7:13 [c] *20* Or *messengers* [d] *1* Or *messenger*; also in verses 8, 12 and 18

1:10 HOLY SPIRIT, Revelation—The Holy Spirit led John to write the letters which make up Rev 2:1—3:22. He did so while John worshiped on the Lord's Day, the first day of the week celebrating Christ's resurrection. The Spirit gave John the precise wording of the letters. See 2:1,8,12,18; 3:1,7,14.
1:10 WORSHIP, Calendar—See note on Ac 20:7.
1:10 PRAYER, Holy Spirit Guides—See note on Jude 20–21.
1:18 HUMANITY, Death—Jesus Christ is Lord both of life and death. We have no reason to fear death or the afterlife if we trust and follow Him.
1:18 LAST THINGS, Intermediate State—See notes on Isa 14:9; Lk 8:31; 16:19–26. Hades is the New Testament counterpart to *Sheol* in the Old Testament. Some interpreters believe Hades refers to the general realm of the dead. They believe the statement is that Christ holds the keys to death itself and to the realm of the dead. All people will appear before the great white throne, the only judgment, at which both believers and unbelievers will be judged. Death does not hold the last word about human existence. When it has closed its doors upon a life, Christ still holds the keys to death and opens the way for believers into paradise. For believers, it is comforting to know Christ has the final word. Some say Hades here refers to the intermediate state for unbelievers, corresponding in this view to paradise for believers. Hades will yield to the authority of Christ and deliver up the dead therein to the judgment of the great white throne (Rev 20:13). According to this view, the Great White Throne is a judgment only for unbelievers (Rev 20:11). Mt 25:31–33; 2 Co 5:10; and Rev 20:4 are thought to describe separate and different judgments.
1:20 THE CHURCH, Local Body—See notes on Ac 4:32; 8:1.
2:1 REVELATION, Angels—Each church had an angel. This was either a heavenly representative before God's throne or the pastor of the church viewed as God's messenger to the church.
2:1—3:22 LAST THINGS, Church Age—Dispensationalists hold that the letters have a message for all churches of all ages, but they interpret the letters of the seven churches as dividing the "church age" into seven periods. The letters would represent God's message to the church age, while ch 4 would begin His message to those on earth after the rapture. See note on 1:7. In this view Revelation primarily describes the time of tribulation. All other interpreters, whether amillennialists, postmillennialists, or historical premillennialists, insist that nothing in the text indicates such an interpretation and accept the two chapters on face value.
2:1 THE CHURCH, Local Body—See notes on Ac 4:32; 1 Co 1:2.
2:2–3 EVIL AND SUFFERING, Endurance—See note on 1:9.
2:7 HOLY SPIRIT, Revelation—An important activity of the Spirit is to reveal God and His purposes to God's people. He did this through prophets and other inspired persons in Israel, and He does it in the church as well (1 Co 2:9–12). He also does it through Scripture (2 Pe 1:21). Here and elsewhere in Revelation He revealed God's will by giving prophetic oracles to the churches through John. See Rev 2:11,17,29; 3:6,13,22.
2:7 REVELATION, Spirit—The Spirit of God was at work revealing the future of specific churches. Everyone should listen carefully to the Spirit's disclosure of God's plan for the future and His expectations of the people. Compare 2:11,17,

what the Spirit says to the churches.
To him who overcomes,[b] I will give
the right to eat from the tree of life,[c]
which is in the paradise[d] of God.

To the Church in Smyrna

8“To the angel of the church in Smyrna[e]
write:

These are the words of him who is
the First and the Last,[f] who died and
came to life again.[g] 9I know your afflictions and your poverty—yet you
are rich![h] I know the slander of
those who say they are Jews and are
not,[i] but are a synagogue of Satan.[j]
10Do not be afraid of what you are
about to suffer. I tell you, the devil
will put some of you in prison to test
you,[k] and you will suffer persecution
for ten days.[l] Be faithful,[m] even to
the point of death, and I will give you
the crown of life.[n]
11He who has an ear, let him
hear[o] what the Spirit says to the
churches. He who overcomes will
not be hurt at all by the second
death.[p]

To the Church in Pergamum

12“To the angel of the church in Pergamum[q] write:

These are the words of him who
has the sharp, double-edged sword.[r]
13I know where you live—where Satan has his throne. Yet you remain
true to my name. You did not renounce your faith in me,[s] even in
the days of Antipas, my faithful witness,[t] who was put to death in your
city—where Satan lives.[u]
14Nevertheless, I have a few things
against you:[v] You have people there
who hold to the teaching of Balaam,[w]
who taught Balak to entice the Israelites to sin by eating food sacrificed to
idols[x] and by committing sexual immorality.[y] 15Likewise you also have
those who hold to the teaching of the
Nicolaitans.[z] 16Repent[a] therefore!
Otherwise, I will soon come to you
and will fight against them with the
sword of my mouth.[b]
17He who has an ear, let him
hear[c] what the Spirit says to the
churches. To him who overcomes,[d] I
will give some of the hidden manna.[e] I will also give him a white
stone with a new name[f] written on
it, known only to him who receives
it.[g]

To the Church in Thyatira

18“To the angel of the church in Thyatira[h] write:

These are the words of the Son of
God,[i] whose eyes are like blazing
fire and whose feet are like burnished bronze.[j] 19I know your
deeds,[k] your love and faith, your service and perseverance, and that you
are now doing more than you did at
first.
20Nevertheless, I have this against
you: You tolerate that woman Jeze-

2:7 [b]S Jn 16:33 [c]Ge 2:9; 3:22-24; Rev 22:2,14,19 [d]Lk 23:43
2:8 [e]Rev 1:11 [f]S Rev 1:17 [g]Rev 1:18
2:9 [h]2Co 6:10; Jas 2:5 [i]Rev 3:9 [j]ver 13,24; S Mt 4:10
2:10 [k]Rev 3:10 [l]Da 1:12,14 [m]ver 13; Rev 17:14 [n]S Mt 10:22; S 1Co 9:25
2:11 [o]S ver 7 [p]Rev 20:6,14; 21:8
2:12 [q]Rev 1:11 [r]ver 16; S Rev 1:16
2:13 [s]Rev 14:12 [t]Rev 1:5; 11:3 [u]ver 9,24; S Mt 4:10
2:14 [v]ver 20 [w]S 2Pe 2:15 [x]S Ac 15:20 [y]1Co 6:13
2:15 [z]ver 6
2:16 [a]S ver 5 [b]2Th 2:8; S Rev 1:16
2:17 [c]S ver 7 [d]S Jn 16:33 [e]Jn 6:49,50 [f]Isa 56:5; 62:2; 65:15 [g]Rev 19:12
2:18 [h]ver 24; Ac 16:14; Rev 1:11 [i]S Mt 4:3 [j]S Rev 1:14,15
2:19 [k]S ver 2

29; 3:6,13,22.
2:8–29 ELECTION, Testing—God punishes the disobedient. The faithful often face tests such as persecution and immorality. God promises a crown of life to persecuted believers who are faithful unto death.
2:8 THE CHURCH, Local Body—See notes on Ac 4:32; 1 Co 1:2.
2:9–10 EVIL AND SUFFERING, Satan—The Christians at Smyrna knew their real opposition was inspired by Satan. If they were faithful, they would be rewarded. Those who opposed them in the name of religion were actually serving Satan though they said they were worshiping God. Religious zeal must always be tested by the ethical teachings of Scripture to ensure it is not Satan's instrument.
2:9 CHRISTIAN ETHICS, Property Rights—Wealth cannot be measured in material terms. People under persecution and poverty are rich if they hold fast to faith in Christ.
2:11 THE CHURCH, Local Body—See note on Ac 4:32. Churches are local, autonomous bodies which determine individual directions. All, however, come under the lordship of Christ. Each congregation must obey the word of the Spirit and the teaching of Scripture.
2:12 THE CHURCH, Local Body—See notes on Ac 4:32; 8:1; 1 Co 1:2.
2:13 EVIL AND SUFFERING, Satan—See note on 2:9–10. Satan can work through political rulers who oppose God and His people. Living in such circumstances calls for total devotion and faith.
2:13 EVANGELISM, Persecution—The church at Pergamum remained true despite severe persecution. The phrase "where Satan has his throne" could refer to the huge pagan temple given to the worship of Asclepius. More likely the reference was to Pergamum's reputation as a center where the Roman emperor was worshiped as a god. God's people were under pressure, but they kept their testimony alive and thus won many to Christ. Real evangelism always sparks pressure and problems, but the Lord will always sustain His faithful ones.
2:14 SIN, Depravity—The plague that struck Israel while in Shittim (Nu 25:1–8) was blamed on Balaam, who lured the Midianite women to entice the Israelite men (Nu 31:16). In a similar manner, Christians can also be enticed to accept local standards of religiosity that contradict the gospel. Religion that encourages immorality and lawlessness is sin.
2:16,21,22 SALVATION, Repentance—The church in Pergamum and Thyatira were called to repent. Neither churches nor Christians are exempt from repentance (3:3,19).
2:18,27–29 GOD, Trinity—Divine revelation has a trinitarian basis. Jesus the Son of God gave God's revelation to the church at Thyatira. He assumed the role of Judge of the church. He promised authority to His faithful servants, authority He received from the Father. All of this is what the Spirit says to the churches. Again we see one of the three Persons of the Trinity does not work apart from the others. See note on Mt 3:16–17.
2:18 THE CHURCH, Local Body—See notes on Ac 4:32; 8:1; 1 Co 1:2.
2:19 EVIL AND SUFFERING, Endurance—See note on 1:9.
2:20 SIN, Depravity—Jezebel (see note on 2 Ki 9:22) was

bel,[l] who calls herself a prophetess. By her teaching she misleads my servants into sexual immorality and the eating of food sacrificed to idols.[m] 21I have given her time[n] to repent of her immorality, but she is unwilling.[o] 22So I will cast her on a bed of suffering, and I will make those who commit adultery[p] with her suffer intensely, unless they repent of her ways. 23I will strike her children dead. Then all the churches will know that I am he who searches hearts and minds,[q] and I will repay each of you according to your deeds.[r] 24Now I say to the rest of you in Thyatira, to you who do not hold to her teaching and have not learned Satan's so-called deep secrets (I will not impose any other burden on you):[s] 25Only hold on to what you have[t] until I come.[u]

26To him who overcomes[v] and does my will to the end,[w] I will give authority over the nations[x] —

27'He will rule them with an iron scepter;[y]
he will dash them to pieces like pottery'[e] [z] —

just as I have received authority from my Father. 28I will also give him the morning star.[a] 29He who has an ear, let him hear[b] what the Spirit says to the churches.

Chapter 3

To the Church in Sardis

"TO the angel[f] of the church in Sardis[c] write:

These are the words of him who holds the seven spirits[g] [d] of God and the seven stars.[e] I know your deeds;[f] you have a reputation of being alive, but you are dead.[g] 2Wake up! Strengthen what remains and is about to die, for I have not found your deeds complete in the sight of my God. 3Remember, therefore, what you have received and heard; obey it, and repent.[h] But if you do not wake up, I will come like a thief,[i] and you will not know at what time[j] I will come to you.

4Yet you have a few people in Sardis who have not soiled their clothes.[k] They will walk with me, dressed in white,[l] for they are worthy. 5He who overcomes[m] will, like them, be dressed in white.[n] I will never blot out his name from the book of life,[o] but will acknowledge his name before my Father[p] and his

2:20 [l]1Ki 16:31; 21:25; 2Ki 9:7 [m]ver 14; S Ac 15:20
2:21 [n]Ro 2:4; 2Pe 3:9 [o]Ro 2:5; Rev 9:20; 16:9,11
2:22 [p]Rev 17:2; 18:9
2:23 [q]1Sa 16:7; 1Ki 8:39; Ps 139:1, 2,23; Pr 21:2; Jer 17:10; Lk 16:15; Ro 8:27; 1Th 2:4 [r]S Mt 16:27
2:24 [s]Ac 15:28
2:25 [t]Rev 3:11 [u]S Mt 16:27
2:26 [v]S Jn 16:33 [w]Mt 10:22 [x]Ps 2:8; Rev 3:21
2:27 [y]Rev 12:5; 19:15 [z]Ps 2:9; Isa 30:14; Jer 19:11
2:28 [a]Rev 22:16
2:29 [b]S ver 7
3:1 [c]Rev 1:11 [d]S Rev 1:4 [e]S Rev 1:16 [f]S Rev 2:2 [g]1Ti 5:6
3:3 [h]S Rev 2:5 [i]S Lk 12:39 [j]Lk 12:39
3:4 [k]Jude 23 [l]ver 5, 18; Rev 4:4; 6:11; 7:9,13,14; 19:14
3:5 [m]S Jn 16:33 [n]S ver 4 [o]S Rev 20:12 [p]Mt 10:32

[e]*27* Psalm 2:9 [f]*1* Or *messenger*; also in verses 7 and 14 [g]*1* Or *the sevenfold Spirit*

one of the most notorious queens in Israel, who led the nation into the immoral practices of Baal worship. The Christians in Thyatira had a similar problem with a woman in the congregation who led God's people to sin. Religious office does not protect from sin. Often it tempts one to misuse power. See note on 2:14.

2:20 EDUCATION, False Teachers—The woman called Jezebel stands as a reminder of the insidious influence of false teachers tolerated by the members of a church. Through her seductive teaching, she had somehow convinced Christians at Thyatira that idolatry and fornication were acceptable. Heresy flourishes where sound Christian teaching lags. See 2:14–15.

2:22 EVIL AND SUFFERING, Punishment—The New Testament clearly warns people who do not repent of evil that they will be punished. Physical and emotional suffering are means God uses to punish such people.

2:23 GOD, Judge—God the Son is pictured here as the Judge who acts out of His perfect wisdom and pure righteousness. His righteousness is expressed as wrath against evil. He knows persons and activities which threaten His church, and He acts to protect His church.

2:23 THE CHURCH, Local Body—See note on 2:11. Churches as well as individual Christians stand under the direction and judgment of God.

2:24 EVIL AND SUFFERING, Satan—See note on 2:9–10. A wicked woman in the church can appear brilliant by teaching secret knowledge others have never heard. Such teaching must be tested by the doctrinal and ethical teachings of Scripture. Too often enticing secrets come from Satan, not God. God's people never become holy enough to be able to participate in Satan's activities without harm.

2:26 CHRISTIAN ETHICS, Character—Apocalyptic literature centers on last things with the intention of encouraging readers to do God's will steadfastly. See notes on Da 9:24; 11:32–35; 2 Pe 3:11–12,14.

2:27 JESUS CHRIST, Authority—The Father has given the Son authority over all the universe. Compare Mt 28:18.

3:1 HUMANITY, Death—Not only individuals, but churches and other groups can be spiritually dead. Physical life and activity do not necessarily imply the presence of spiritual life. Only persons and groups directed by God's Spirit can claim spiritual life.

3:1–22 ELECTION, Testing—False confidence, tribulation, indifference, and materialism test God's people. God rebukes the elect when we stray and calls us to repent. Such rebukes are signs of His love. Those who endure the testing will receive God's promised rewards in eternity.

3:1 THE CHURCH, Local Body—See notes on Ac 4:32; 8:1; 1 Co 1:2.

3:3 CHRISTIAN ETHICS, Obedience—The reality of the world's end and God's judgment call us to obedience and repentance. See note on 2:26.

3:3,11 LAST THINGS, Return Promises—Christ's last direct word to the churches contains His personal promise to return. His return holds promise of reward to those who are faithful. It will also mean rescue from the hour of eschatological trial, either by removing the faithful from the earth before it comes (dispensationalism) or by supplying sufficient strength for us to endure while undergoing tribulation (historical premillennialism, amillennialism, and postmillennialism). See note on 1 Th 4:14–18. Christ's promise to return is also a call to repent and obey the gospel. See note on 1:18.

3:5,21–22 GOD, Trinity—The Son has authority over the book of life, yet must report to the Father. Likewise, the Son has authority to let faithful believers join Him on the throne just as He sat on His Father's throne. All this is the Spirit's revelation for the churches. See note on 2:18,27–29.

3:5 JESUS CHRIST, Judgment—In judgment Jesus will identify His faithful followers before the Father, and they will be rewarded.

angels. 6He who has an ear, let him
hear[q] what the Spirit says to the
churches.

To the Church in Philadelphia

7"To the angel of the church in Philadelphia[r] write:

These are the words of him who is
holy[s] and true,[t] who holds the key
of David.[u] What he opens no one
can shut, and what he shuts no one
can open. 8I know your deeds.[v] See,
I have placed before you an open
door[w] that no one can shut. I know
that you have little strength, yet you
have kept my word and have not denied my name.[x] 9I will make those
who are of the synagogue of Satan,[y]
who claim to be Jews though they are
not,[z] but are liars—I will make them
come and fall down at your feet[a] and
acknowledge that I have loved you.[b]
10Since you have kept my command
to endure patiently, I will also keep
you[c] from the hour of trial that is
going to come upon the whole
world[d] to test[e] those who live on
the earth.[f]

11I am coming soon.[g] Hold on to
what you have,[h] so that no one will
take your crown.[i] 12Him who overcomes[j] I will make a pillar[k] in the
temple of my God. Never again will
he leave it. I will write on him the
name of my God[l] and the name of
the city of my God,[m] the new Jerusalem,[n] which is coming down out of
heaven from my God; and I will also
write on him my new name. 13He
who has an ear, let him hear[o] what
the Spirit says to the churches.

To the Church in Laodicea

14"To the angel of the church in Laodicea[p] write:

These are the words of the Amen,
the faithful and true witness,[q] the
ruler of God's creation.[r] 15I know
your deeds,[s] that you are neither
cold nor hot.[t] I wish you were either
one or the other! 16So, because you
are lukewarm—neither hot nor cold
—I am about to spit you out of my
mouth. 17You say, 'I am rich; I have
acquired wealth and do not need a
thing.'[u] But you do not realize that
you are wretched, pitiful, poor, blind
and naked.[v] 18I counsel you to buy
from me gold refined in the fire,[w] so
you can become rich; and white
clothes[x] to wear, so you can cover
your shameful nakedness;[y] and salve
to put on your eyes, so you can see.
19Those whom I love I rebuke and
discipline.[z] So be earnest, and repent.[a] 20Here I am! I stand at the
door[b] and knock. If anyone hears my
voice and opens the door,[c] I will
come in[d] and eat with him, and he
with me.

21To him who overcomes,[e] I will
give the right to sit with me on my
throne,[f] just as I overcame[g] and sat
down with my Father on his throne.
22He who has an ear, let him hear[h]
what the Spirit says to the
churches."

Chapter 4

The Throne in Heaven

AFTER this I looked, and there before
me was a door standing open[i] in
heaven. And the voice I had first heard
speaking to me like a trumpet[j] said,
"Come up here,[k] and I will show you
what must take place after this."[l] 2At
once I was in the Spirit,[m] and there before me was a throne in heaven[n] with
someone sitting on it. 3And the one who
sat there had the appearance of jasper[o]
and carnelian.[p] A rainbow,[q] resembling
an emerald,[r] encircled the throne. 4Sur-
rounding the throne were twenty-four
other thrones, and seated on them were
twenty-four elders.[s] They were dressed

3:6 [q]S Rev 2:7
3:7 [r]Rev 1:11 [s]S Mk 1:24 [t]1Jn 5:20; Rev 6:10; 19:11 [u]Isa 22:22; Mt 16:19
3:8 [v]S Rev 2:2 [w]S Ac 14:27 [x]Rev 2:13
3:9 [y]Rev 2:9 [z]Rev 2:9 [a]Isa 49:23 [b]Isa 43:4; S Ro 8:37
3:10 [c]2Pe 2:9 [d]S Mt 24:14 [e]Rev 2:10 [f]Rev 6:10; 8:13; 11:10; 13:8,14; 17:8
3:11 [g]S Mt 16:27 [h]Rev 2:25 [i]S 1Co 9:25
3:12 [j]S Jn 16:33 [k]Gal 2:9 [l]Rev 14:1; 22:4 [m]Eze 48:35 [n]Gal 4:26; Rev 21:2,10
3:13 [o]S Rev 2:7
3:14 [p]S Col 2:1; Rev 1:11 [q]Jn 18:37; Rev 1:5 [r]Pr 8:22; Jn 1:3; Col 1:16,18
3:15 [s]S Rev 2:2 [t]Ro 12:11
3:17 [u]Hos 12:8; 1Co 4:8 [v]Pr 13:7
3:18 [w]S 1Pe 1:7 [x]S ver 4 [y]Rev 16:15
3:19 [z]Dt 8:5; Pr 3:12; 1Co 11:32; Heb 12:5,6 [a]S Rev 2:5
3:20 [b]Mt 24:33; Jas 5:9 [c]Lk 12:36 [d]S Ro 8:10
3:21 [e]S Jn 16:33 [f]S Mt 19:28 [g]Rev 5:5
3:22 [h]S Rev 2:7
4:1 [i]S Mt 3:16 [j]Rev 1:10 [k]Rev 11:12 [l]Rev 1:19; 22:6
4:2 [m]S Rev 1:10 [n]ver 9,10; 1Ki 22:19; Isa 6:1; Eze 1:26-28; Da 7:9; Rev 20:11
4:3 [o]Rev 21:11 [p]Rev 21:20 [q]Eze 1:28; Rev 10:1 [r]Rev 21:19
4:4 [s]ver 10; Rev 5:6,8,14; 11:16; 19:4

3:7 JESUS CHRIST, Kingdom of God—As the Davidic Messiah, Jesus holds the power to let people in the eternal kingdom or shut them out. He shares God's qualities of being holy and faithful.
3:7 THE CHURCH, Local Body—See notes on Ac 4:32; 8:1; 1 Co 1:2.
3:9 EVIL AND SUFFERING, Satan—See note on 2:9–10.
3:10 EVIL AND SUFFERING, Endurance—See note on 1:9.
3:14 JESUS CHRIST, Authority—See note on 2:27.
3:14 THE CHURCH, Local Body—See notes on Ac 4:32; 8:1; 1 Co 1:2.
3:17–18 CHRISTIAN ETHICS, Property Rights—Wealth is deceiving. We may not have what we think we possess. God is the only source of true wealth.
3:19–21 JESUS CHRIST, Ascension—The ascended Christ disciplines His church, calls to repentance and renewed fellowship, and invites the faithful to join Him in ruling God's kingdom.
3:20 SALVATION, Acceptance—Those who accept Christ will open their lives to Him and will invite Him to be their honored guest. The exalted Christ stands outside the door of hearts closed to Him and gently knocks, asking for entrance.
4:1–11 GOD, Sovereignty—In heaven all inhabitants testify to God's sovereignty as Creator and Ruler of the universe. God is the eternal holy One distinct from all who reside in heaven. Praise and worship is the language of heaven. The sovereign God knows the outcome of history. He sits on heaven's throne guiding the course of history and receiving the praise of all who surround Him. They attest to His holy purity in contrast to their own beings. They know He alone has always existed and always will. Even those who wear crowns of authority in heaven throw them down before the sovereign God. He rules over all.

in white[t] and had crowns of gold on their heads. 5From the throne came flashes of lightning, rumblings and peals of thunder.[u] Before the throne, seven lamps[v] were blazing. These are the seven spirits[h][w] of God. 6Also before the throne there was what looked like a sea of glass,[x] clear as crystal.

In the center, around the throne, were four living creatures,[y] and they were covered with eyes, in front and in back.[z] 7The first living creature was like a lion, the second was like an ox, the third had a face like a man, the fourth was like a flying eagle.[a] 8Each of the four living creatures[b] had six wings[c] and was covered with eyes all around,[d] even under his wings. Day and night[e] they never stop saying:

"Holy, holy, holy
is the Lord God Almighty,[f]
who was, and is, and is to come."[g]

9Whenever the living creatures give glory, honor and thanks to him who sits on the throne[h] and who lives for ever and ever,[i] 10the twenty-four elders[j] fall down before him[k] who sits on the throne,[l] and worship him who lives for ever and ever. They lay their crowns before the throne and say:

11"You are worthy, our Lord and God,
to receive glory and honor and power,[m]
for you created all things,
and by your will they were created
and have their being."[n]

Chapter 5

The Scroll and the Lamb

THEN I saw in the right hand of him who sat on the throne[o] a scroll with writing on both sides[p] and sealed[q] with seven seals. 2And I saw a mighty angel[r] proclaiming in a loud voice, "Who is worthy to break the seals and open the scroll?" 3But no one in heaven or on earth or under the earth could open the scroll or even look inside it. 4I wept and wept because no one was found who was worthy to open the scroll or look inside. 5Then one of the elders said to me, "Do not weep! See, the Lion[s] of the tribe of Judah,[t] the Root of David,[u] has triumphed. He is able to open the scroll and its seven seals."

6Then I saw a Lamb,[v] looking as if it had been slain, standing in the center of the throne, encircled by the four living creatures[w] and the elders.[x] He had seven horns and seven eyes,[y] which are the seven spirits[h][z] of God sent out into all the earth. 7He came and took the scroll from the right hand of him who sat on the throne.[a] 8And when he had taken it, the four living creatures[b] and the twenty-four elders[c] fell down before the Lamb. Each one had a harp[d] and they were holding golden bowls full of incense, which are the prayers[e] of the saints. 9And they sang a new song:[f]

"You are worthy[g] to take the scroll
and to open its seals,
because you were slain,
and with your blood[h] you
purchased[i] men for God
from every tribe and language and
people and nation.[j]
10You have made them to be a kingdom
and priests[k] to serve our God,
and they will reign on the earth."[l]

11Then I looked and heard the voice of many angels, numbering thousands upon thousands, and ten thousand times ten thousand.[m] They encircled the throne and the living creatures[n] and the elders.[o] 12In a loud voice they sang:

"Worthy is the Lamb,[p] who was
slain,[q]
to receive power and wealth and
wisdom and strength
and honor and glory and praise!"[r]

13Then I heard every creature in heaven and on earth and under the earth[s]

4:4 [t]S Rev 3:4,5
4:5 [u]Ex 19:16; Rev 8:5; 11:19; 16:18 [v]Zec 4:2 [w]S Rev 1:4
4:6 [x]Rev 15:2 [y]ver 8,9; Eze 1:5; Rev 5:6; 6:1; 7:11; 14:3; 15:7; 19:4 [z]Eze 1:18; 10:12
4:7 [a]Eze 1:10; 10:14
4:8 [b]S ver 6 [c]Isa 6:2 [d]Eze 1:18 [e]Rev 14:11 [f]Isa 6:3; S Rev 1:8 [g]S Rev 1:4
4:9 [h]ver 2; Ps 47:8; S Rev 5:1 [i]S Rev 1:18
4:10 [j]S ver 4 [k]Dt 33:3; Rev 5:8, 14; 7:11; 11:16 [l]S ver 2
4:11 [m]Rev 1:6; 5:12 [n]Ac 14:15; Rev 10:6
5:1 [o]ver 7,13; Rev 4:2,9; 6:16 [p]Eze 2:9,10 [q]Isa 29:11; Da 12:4
5:2 [r]Rev 10:1
5:5 [s]Ge 49:9 [t]S Heb 7:14 [u]Isa 11:1,10; Ro 15:12; Rev 22:16
5:6 [v]ver 8,9,12,13; S Jn 1:29 [w]S Rev 4:6 [x]S Rev 4:4 [y]Zec 4:10 [z]S Rev 1:4
5:7 [a]S ver 1
5:8 [b]S Rev 4:6 [c]S Rev 4:4 [d]Rev 14:2; 15:2 [e]Ps 141:2; Rev 8:3, 4
5:9 [f]Ps 40:3; 98:1; 149:1; Isa 42:10; Rev 14:3,4 [g]Rev 4:11 [h]Heb 9:12 [i]S 1Co 6:20 [j]S Rev 13:7
5:10 [k]S 1Pe 2:5 [l]Rev 3:21; 20:4
5:11 [m]Da 7:10; Heb 12:22; Jude 14 [n]S Rev 4:6 [o]S Rev 4:4
5:12 [p]ver 13 [q]ver 9 [r]Rev 1:6; 4:11
5:13 [s]ver 3; Php 2:10

[h]5,6 Or *the sevenfold Spirit*

4:5 HISTORY, Future—God knows and controls the immediate and long-range future. He has revealed that part of the future which His people need to know to live courageously and faithfully in the present.
5:1–14 JESUS CHRIST, Lamb of God—God's sacrificed Lamb is the only Being able and worthy to open God's scroll and know divine plans for the future. The Lamb is worthy of worship and thus is divine.
5:8–14 PRAYER, Worship—This section contains three songs of worth and praise—first by the dignitaries of heaven after the Lamb was declared worthy to open the scroll, then by the angels who echoed the song with attributions of glory, and finally by every living celestial and earthly creature. Most of the praise through the Bible is for God as Creator, for God's dealings with people, or for those of His attributes which are propitious toward man, such as mercy or grace. There is relatively little praise for what He is in Himself. See note on Ps 93:1–5. This situation reverses in Revelation. After the great day of God's wrath has come and after Revelation 4, the praise may be said to be celestial in nature. God is praised for His own intrinsic worth. In v 8, the golden bowls of the elders were filled with incense, an agelong symbol of prayer. See note on Ex 30:1,7. The prayers of the saints are enormously valuable in heaven. The elders are mentioned as falling down repeatedly in this book (4:10; 5:8,14; 7:11; 11:16; 19:4). See note on Ge 17:3,17.
5:10 THE CHURCH, People of God—The church serves as priests in God's kingdom waiting for the day God will fully establish the kingdom. See note on 1:6.

and on the sea, and all that is in them,
singing:

"To him who sits on the throne[t] and
to the Lamb[u]
be praise and honor and glory and
power,
for ever and ever!"[v]

14The four living creatures[w] said,
"Amen,"[x] and the elders[y] fell down and
worshiped.[z]

Chapter 6

The Seals

I watched as the Lamb[a] opened the
first of the seven seals.[b] Then I heard
one of the four living creatures[c] say in a
voice like thunder,[d] "Come!" 2I looked,
and there before me was a white horse![e]
Its rider held a bow, and he was given a
crown,[f] and he rode out as a conqueror
bent on conquest.[g]
3When the Lamb opened the second
seal, I heard the second living creature[h]
say, "Come!" 4Then another horse came
out, a fiery red one.[i] Its rider was given
power to take peace from the earth[j] and
to make men slay each other. To him was
given a large sword.
5When the Lamb opened the third seal,
I heard the third living creature[k] say,
"Come!" I looked, and there before me
was a black horse![l] Its rider was holding
a pair of scales in his hand. 6Then I heard
what sounded like a voice among the four
living creatures,[m] saying, "A quart[i] of
wheat for a day's wages,[j] and three
quarts of barley for a day's wages,[j][n] and
do not damage[o] the oil and the wine!"
7When the Lamb opened the fourth
seal, I heard the voice of the fourth living
creature[p] say, "Come!" 8I looked, and
there before me was a pale horse![q] Its
rider was named Death, and Hades[r] was
following close behind him. They were
given power over a fourth of the earth to
kill by sword, famine and plague, and by
the wild beasts of the earth.[s]
9When he opened the fifth seal, I saw
under[t] the altar[u] the souls of those who
had been slain[v] because of the word of
God[w] and the testimony they had maintained. 10They called out in a loud voice,
"How long,[x] Sovereign Lord,[y] holy and
true,[z] until you judge the inhabitants of
the earth[a] and avenge our blood?"[b]
11Then each of them was given a white
robe,[c] and they were told to wait a little
longer, until the number of their fellow
servants and brothers who were to be
killed as they had been was completed.[d]
12I watched as he opened the sixth

[i]6 Greek *a choinix* (probably about a liter) [j]6 Greek *a denarius*

5:13 [t]S ver 1,7 [u]ver 6; Rev 6:16; 7:10 [v]1Ch 29:11; Mal 1:6; 2:2; S Ro 11:36
5:14 [w]S Rev 4:6 [x]Rev 4:9 [y]S Rev 4:4 [z]Rev 4:10
6:1 [a]S Rev 5:6 [b]Rev 5:1 [c]S Rev 4:6,7 [d]Rev 14:2; 19:6
6:2 [e]Zec 1:8; 6:3; Rev 19:11 [f]Zec 6:11; Rev 14:14; 19:12 [g]Ps 45:4
6:3 [h]Rev 4:7
6:4 [i]Zec 1:8; 6:2 [j]Mt 10:34
6:5 [k]Rev 4:7 [l]Zec 6:2
6:6 [m]S Rev 4:6,7 [n]Eze 4:16 [o]Rev 7:1, 3; 9:4
6:7 [p]Rev 4:7
6:8 [q]Zec 6:3 [r]Hos 13:14; Rev 1:18; 20:13,14 [s]Jer 15:2,3; 24:10; Eze 5:12,17
6:9 [t]Ex 29:12; Lev 4:7 [u]Rev 14:18; 16:7 [v]Rev 20:4 [w]Ro 1:2; S Heb 4:12
6:10 [x]Ps 119:84; Zec 1:12 [y]Lk 2:29; 2Pe 2:1 [z]S Rev 3:7 [a]S Rev 3:10 [b]Dt 32:43; 2Ki 9:7; Ps 79:10; Rev 16:6; 18:20; 19:2
6:11 [c]S Rev 3:4 [d]Heb 11:40

6:1—19:21 LAST THINGS, Great Tribulation—Dispensationalists interpret these chapters differently than others. They believe the chapters describe the great tribulation (7:14; Mk 13:14–19), a seven-year period of intense persecution which, however, the church will not go through. See note on Da 9:24–27. In this view Christians will be "raptured" to meet Christ in the air at the beginning of the tribulation period and will, during the seven years, be judged by Christ and assigned places of rulership for the millennial kingdom to be established at the end of the period. See notes on Rev 20:4–5; 2 Co 5:10. The dispensation of grace ends with the rapture, and a new dispensation of the kingdom begins, in which people are saved by joining the kingdom whose prototype was the Old Testament kingdom of Israel. Many dispensationalists see the tribulation as the final years of the Old Testament age. They expect the Jerusalem Temple worship to be restored and the antichrist to proclaim himself god in the Temple. Amillennialists and postmillennialists point out that Christians in the latter part of the first century faced great persecution and that throughout history there have been times of great tribulation through which the church has passed. They believe these events are apocalyptically described in the text (chs 4—19). A historical premillennial view of these chapters finds a prophetic reference to a period of great tribulation associated with end time events, but insists that Scripture does not support the idea that the church will escape it. Salvation by grace through faith is considered to be God's final plan of salvation. They do not expect a return to the Old Testament kingdom and its law, and whatever place God has for Jews at the end time, they will become God's people only by grace through faith in Christ Jesus. This view also understands these chapters to refer to first century experiences of the church and the recurring tribulation of the church throughout its history.

6:1–8 LAST THINGS, Great Tribulation—Popularly referred to as "the four horsemen of the apocalypse," this vision describes four destructive attacks on the earth. Amillennialists and postmillennialists believe the vision applies to all periods of history; premillennialists believe the vision refers particularly to the end time. The white horse and rider represent political might; the red horse represents warfare; the black horse represents famine; and the pale horse represents death. Some see the first rider as a symbol of the church or of Christ. Compare 19:11–16. Dispensationalists usually teach that the first rider is the antichrist. See note on 2 Th 2:1–12. All can see that expanding political power often leads to war, which leads to shortages of staple goods and results in widespread death.

6:8 HUMANITY, Death—Persecution may bring war, famine, and death to God's people. Still, survivors must not give in to fear. God alone grants persecutors their power. All who oppose God's people may do so only as long as God permits. Ultimately, they face greater suffering than they have caused, and God's people face eternal life with the resurrected Christ.

6:9–11 EVIL AND SUFFERING, Endurance—The deaths of Christian martyrs are precious enough to be likened to holy sacrifices. That a person has to die for faith in Christ is an evil caused by wicked persons who do not know the truth and who oppose God. They face eternal punishment, but the faithful martyrs will be rewarded. See note on 1:9.

6:9–11 PRAYER, Lament—God is especially tuned to the cry of the persecuted. See note on Ex 2:23–24. The answer here is a delay, not in blessedness but in revealing the justice of their cause.

6:9 EVANGELISM, Persecution—It costs to be faithful to our gospel witness and testimony. True evangelism brings persecution. See note on 2:13.

6:10 GOD, Judge—The sovereign and holy God will exercise His authority to judge. The picture of God developed all through this book is that of the God of supreme authority and power, who holds all persons accountable to Himself, finally accomplishing His own purposes in the end. He will avenge the martyrs in His judgment, because He is true and faithful.

6:12–17 LAST THINGS, Great Tribulation—The as-

seal. There was a great earthquake.[e] The
sun turned black[f] like sackcloth[g] made
of goat hair, the whole moon turned
blood red, 13and the stars in the sky fell to
earth,[h] as late figs drop from a fig tree[i]
when shaken by a strong wind. 14The sky
receded like a scroll, rolling up,[j] and every mountain and island was removed
from its place.[k]
15Then the kings of the earth, the
princes, the generals, the rich, the
mighty, and every slave and every free
man[l] hid in caves and among the rocks
of the mountains.[m] 16They called to the
mountains and the rocks, "Fall on us[n]
and hide us from the face of him who sits
on the throne[o] and from the wrath of the
Lamb! 17For the great day[p] of their wrath
has come, and who can stand?"[q]

Chapter 7

144,000 Sealed

AFTER this I saw four angels standing at
the four corners[r] of the earth, holding back the four winds[s] of the earth to
prevent[t] any wind from blowing on the
land or on the sea or on any tree. 2Then I
saw another angel coming up from the
east, having the seal[u] of the living God.[v]
He called out in a loud voice to the four
angels who had been given power to
harm the land and the sea:[w] 3"Do not
harm[x] the land or the sea or the trees
until we put a seal on the foreheads[y] of
the servants of our God." 4Then I heard
the number[z] of those who were sealed:
144,000[a] from all the tribes of Israel.

5From the tribe of Judah 12,000 were
sealed,
from the tribe of Reuben 12,000,
from the tribe of Gad 12,000,
6from the tribe of Asher 12,000,
from the tribe of Naphtali 12,000,
from the tribe of Manasseh 12,000,
7from the tribe of Simeon 12,000,
from the tribe of Levi 12,000,
from the tribe of Issachar 12,000,
8from the tribe of Zebulun 12,000,
from the tribe of Joseph 12,000,
from the tribe of Benjamin 12,000.

The Great Multitude in White Robes

9After this I looked and there before
me was a great multitude that no one
could count, from every nation, tribe,
people and language,[b] standing before
the throne[c] and in front of the Lamb.
They were wearing white robes[d] and
were holding palm branches in their
hands. 10And they cried out in a loud
voice:

6:12 [e]Ps 97:4; Isa 29:6; Eze 38:19; Rev 8:5; 11:13; 16:18 [f]S Mt 24:29 [g]Isa 50:3
6:13 [h]S Mt 24:29; Rev 8:10; 9:1 [i]Isa 34:4
6:14 [j]S 2Pe 3:10; Rev 20:11; 21:1 [k]Ps 46:2; Isa 54:10; Jer 4:24; Eze 38:20; Na 1:5; Rev 16:20; 21:1
6:15 [l]Rev 19:18 [m]Isa 2:10,19,21
6:16 [n]Hos 10:8; Lk 23:30 [o]S Rev 5:1
6:17 [p]Joel 1:15; 2:1,2,11,31; Zep 1:14,15; Rev 16:14 [q]Ps 76:7; Na 1:6; Mal 3:2
7:1 [r]Isa 11:12 [s]Jer 49:36; Eze 37:9; Da 7:2; Zec 6:5; Mt 24:31 [t]S Rev 6:6
7:2 [u]Rev 9:4 [v]S Mt 16:16 [w]ver 1
7:3 [x]S Rev 6:6 [y]Eze 9:4; Rev 9:4; 14:1; 22:4
7:4 [z]Rev 9:16 [a]Rev 14:1,3
7:9 [b]S Rev 13:7 [c]ver 15 [d]S Rev 3:4

---

sociation of celestial disturbances with the day of the Lord was made by Joel (2:28–32) and Isaiah (13:6–10). Literal happenings like these have not occurred, so far as historical records reveal. Jesus spoke of similar disturbances (Mt 24:29) but related them to a period following a time of distress or tribulation. This passage is the first of several times in Revelation that such disturbances in the heavens are described (8:8—9:2; 16:8,17–21). These cosmic happenings are associated with God's direct intervention in wrath and judgment. If they are literal events, these occurrences belong to a future tribulation period, referred to by many as the Great Tribulation. Interpreters do not agree as to how literally apocalyptic language is to be understood. Some interpreters see the language here as a literary effort using familiar symbols to prepare people for the awesome finality of Christ's coming. Others argue that direct nonapocalyptic biblical warnings about future, intense, unparalleled tribulations upon the earth make it reasonable to take the celestial disturbances passages to be referring to a literal time of the future wrath of God upon the earth. In either case, God's Word contains a powerful warning about the severity of God's wrath against wickedness.

6:16 JESUS CHRIST, Judgment—Jesus shares the Father's just anger at sin and will execute punishment on unbelievers.

7:1–17 LAST THINGS, Heaven—The 144,000 and the great multitude are identified in accordance with the various millennial views. The 144,000 (12 x 12 x 1000) refers to Israel of the Old Testament or the Israel of the end time. Some believe the numbers symbolize all the Old Testament saints. Others believe the numbers represent all believers as spiritual Israel. Yet others take the 144,000 as a literal number of Jews called to faith in Christ and to a unique ministry of witnessing during the end times. There is no basis here for a belief that only 144,000 will ever be saved. The great multitude refers to the believers in Christ. Much discussion surrounds the precise reference of vv 15–17 whether to saints out of a literal tribulation period at the end time, martyrs, or whether in a general way to all who enter heaven. In either case, the scene is a heavenly one. Those in heaven in some way serve God continually while enjoying unending, direct fellowship with God (21:3). Hunger and thirst are fully satisfied. Discomforts from nature's elements are not experienced. Christ nourishes those in heaven. All tears are wiped away by God Himself. Heaven can be described in terms of what will not be present, as well as of what will be there. See note on Rev 21:9—22:15.

7:2 GOD, Living—God is the living God, not an inanimate object or an impersonal force or principle like gravity. Living also suggests personal, with the particular characteristic of awareness of what is going on in the lives of His people who are enduring suffering.

7:3–17 ELECTION, Protection—God has promised to protect His elect.

7:9–12 PRAYER, Worship—See note on 5:8–14. The praise here is ascription for God's intrinsic worth. The second song is noteworthy in that it begins and ends with "Amen."

7:9 EVANGELISM, Universality—The gospel is for all. Here is the consummation of the grand truth that all peoples can taste of salvation through Jesus Christ. He died and rose again for all. He will clothe all who come to Him in repentance and faith with the white robe of righteousness and give them the palm branch of eternal peace and rest. Tell all people that, for that is our evangelistic responsibility.

7:9 MISSIONS, Results—This wonderful apocalyptic vision of worshipers before the throne of God gives us a deep abiding sense of gratitude and praise. Although the worshipers are from every nation, tribe, language, and people, they are not wearing the typical clothes of the various lands. Their white robes identify them as belonging to God. God desires that men, women, and children from every nation belong to Him. But the contemporary churches must be faithful to the missionary vision for God's plan to be carried out (22:17).

7:10 GOD, Trinity—Salvation is the point of focus for God the Father and the Lamb, Jesus the Son. Salvation comes only from God's throne. This expresses the unity of the Father and the Son in the trinitarian understanding of God. See note on Mt 3:16–17. It also stresses that God is Savior. Calling God Savior tells us what kind of God He is.

"Salvation belongs to our God,[e]
who sits on the throne,[f]
and to the Lamb."

11All the angels were standing around the
throne and around the elders[g] and the
four living creatures.[h] They fell down on
their faces[i] before the throne and worshiped God, 12saying:

"Amen!
Praise and glory
and wisdom and thanks and honor
and power and strength
be to our God for ever and ever.
Amen!"[j]

13Then one of the elders asked me,
"These in white robes[k]—who are they,
and where did they come from?"
14I answered, "Sir, you know."
And he said, "These are they who have
come out of the great tribulation; they
have washed their robes[l] and made
them white in the blood of the Lamb.[m]
15Therefore,

"they are before the throne of God[n]
and serve him[o] day and night in his
temple;[p]
and he who sits on the throne[q] will
spread his tent over them.[r]
16Never again will they hunger;
never again will they thirst.[s]
The sun will not beat upon them,
nor any scorching heat.[t]
17For the Lamb at the center of the
throne will be their
shepherd;[u]
he will lead them to springs of living
water.[v]
And God will wipe away every tear
from their eyes."[w]

Chapter 8

The Seventh Seal and the Golden Censer

WHEN he opened the seventh seal,[x]
there was silence in heaven for
about half an hour.
2And I saw the seven angels[y] who
stand before God, and to them were giv-
en seven trumpets.[z]
3Another angel,[a] who had a golden
censer, came and stood at the altar. He
was given much incense to offer, with the
prayers of all the saints,[b] on the golden
altar[c] before the throne. 4The smoke of
the incense, together with the prayers of
the saints, went up before God[d] from the
angel's hand. 5Then the angel took the
censer, filled it with fire from the altar,[e]
and hurled it on the earth; and there
came peals of thunder,[f] rumblings,
flashes of lightning and an earthquake.[g]

The Trumpets

6Then the seven angels who had the
seven trumpets[h] prepared to sound
them.
7The first angel[i] sounded his trumpet,
and there came hail and fire[j] mixed with
blood, and it was hurled down upon the
earth. A third[k] of the earth was burned
up, a third of the trees were burned up,
and all the green grass was burned up.[l]
8The second angel sounded his trumpet, and something like a huge mountain,[m] all ablaze, was thrown into the sea.
A third[n] of the sea turned into blood,[o] 9a
third[p] of the living creatures in the sea
died, and a third of the ships were destroyed.
10The third angel sounded his trumpet,
and a great star, blazing like a torch, fell
from the sky[q] on a third of the rivers and
on the springs of water[r]—11the name of
the star is Wormwood.[k] A third[s] of the
waters turned bitter, and many people
died from the waters that had become bitter.[t]
12The fourth angel sounded his trumpet, and a third of the sun was struck, a
third of the moon, and a third of the stars,
so that a third[u] of them turned dark.[v] A
third of the day was without light, and
also a third of the night.[w]
13As I watched, I heard an eagle that
was flying in midair[x] call out in a loud
voice: "Woe! Woe! Woe[y] to the inhabitants of the earth,[z] because of the trumpet blasts about to be sounded by the other three angels!"

Chapter 9

THE fifth angel sounded his trumpet,
and I saw a star that had fallen from
the sky to the earth.[a] The star was given
the key[b] to the shaft of the Abyss.[c]
2When he opened the Abyss, smoke rose
from it like the smoke from a gigantic furnace.[d] The sun and sky were darkened[e]
by the smoke from the Abyss.[f] 3And out
of the smoke locusts[g] came down upon
the earth and were given power like that
of scorpions[h] of the earth. 4They were
told not to harm[i] the grass of the earth
or any plant or tree,[j] but only those peo-

[k]*11* That is, Bitterness

7:10 [e]Ps 3:8; Rev 12:10; 19:1 [f]S Rev 5:1
7:11 [g]S Rev 4:4 [h]S Rev 4:6 [i]S Rev 4:10
7:12 [j]S Ro 11:36; Rev 5:12-14
7:13 [k]S Rev 3:4
7:14 [l]Rev 22:14 [m]Heb 9:14; 1Jn 1:7; Rev 12:11
7:15 [n]ver 9 [o]Rev 22:3 [p]Rev 11:19 [q]S Rev 5:1 [r]Isa 4:5, 6; Rev 21:3
7:16 [s]Jn 6:35 [t]Isa 49:10
7:17 [u]S Jn 10:11 [v]S Jn 4:10 [w]Isa 25:8; 35:10; 51:11; 65:19; Rev 21:4
8:1 [x]Rev 6:1
8:2 [y]ver 6-13; Rev 9:1,13; 11:15 [z]S Mt 24:31
8:3 [a]Rev 7:2 [b]Rev 5:8 [c]ver 5; Ex 30:1-6; Heb 9:4; Rev 9:13
8:4 [d]Ps 141:2
8:5 [e]Lev 16:12,13 [f]S Rev 4:5 [g]S Rev 6:12
8:6 [h]S ver 2
8:7 [i]S ver 2 [j]Eze 38:22 [k]ver 7-12; Rev 9:15, 18; 12:4 [l]Rev 9:4
8:8 [m]Jer 51:25 [n]S ver 7 [o]Rev 16:3
8:9 [p]S ver 7
8:10 [q]Isa 14:12; Rev 6:13; 9:1 [r]Rev 14:7; 16:4
8:11 [s]S ver 7 [t]Jer 9:15; 23:15
8:12 [u]S ver 7 [v]Ex 10:21-23; Rev 6:12,13 [w]Eze 32:7
8:13 [x]Rev 14:6; 19:17 [y]Rev 9:12; 11:14; 12:12 [z]S Rev 3:10
9:1 [a]Rev 8:10 [b]Rev 1:18 [c]ver 2, 11; S Lk 8:31
9:2 [d]Ge 19:28; Ex 19:18 [e]Joel 2:2, 10 [f]ver 1,11; S Lk 8:31
9:3 [g]Ex 10:12-15 [h]ver 5,10
9:4 [i]S Rev 6:6 [j]Rev 8:7

7:11–17 WORSHIP, Praise—True worship moves from praise for God to service for God. See note on Isa 6:1–8.
7:13–17 EVIL AND SUFFERING, God's Future Help—Martyrs are assured their suffering will be eliminated in the new world. See note on 6:9–11.
7:17 JESUS CHRIST, Shepherd—Jesus will be the Shepherd King protecting and directing God's faithful who "come out of the great tribulation" (v 14).
8:8—9:2 LAST THINGS, Judgment—See note on 6:12–17.

ple who did not have the seal of God on
their foreheads.[k] 5They were not given
power to kill them, but only to torture
them for five months.[l] And the agony
they suffered was like that of the sting of
a scorpion[m] when it strikes a man. 6Dur-
ing those days men will seek death, but
will not find it; they will long to die, but
death will elude them.[n]
7The locusts looked like horses prepared for battle.[o] On their heads they
wore something like crowns of gold, and
their faces resembled human faces.[p]
8Their hair was like women's hair, and
their teeth were like lions' teeth.[q] 9They
had breastplates like breastplates of iron,
and the sound of their wings was like the
thundering of many horses and chariots
rushing into battle.[r] 10They had tails and
stings like scorpions, and in their tails
they had power to torment people for five
months.[s] 11They had as king over them
the angel of the Abyss,[t] whose name in
Hebrew[u] is Abaddon,[v] and in Greek,
Apollyon.[1]
12The first woe is past; two other woes
are yet to come.[w]
13The sixth angel sounded his trumpet,
and I heard a voice coming from the
horns[m][x] of the golden altar that is before
God.[y] 14It said to the sixth angel who
had the trumpet, "Release the four angels[z] who are bound at the great river
Euphrates."[a] 15And the four angels who
had been kept ready for this very hour
and day and month and year were released[b] to kill a third[c] of mankind.[d]
16The number of the mounted troops was
two hundred million. I heard their number.[e]
17The horses and riders I saw in my
vision looked like this: Their breastplates
were fiery red, dark blue, and yellow as
sulfur. The heads of the horses resembled
the heads of lions, and out of their
mouths[f] came fire, smoke and sulfur.[g]
18A third[h] of mankind was killed[i] by the
three plagues of fire, smoke and sulfur[j]
that came out of their mouths. 19The
power of the horses was in their mouths
and in their tails; for their tails were like
snakes, having heads with which they inflict injury.

9:4 [k]S Rev 7:2,3
9:5 [l]ver 10 [m]ver 3
9:6 [n]Job 3:21; 7:15; Jer 8:3; Rev 6:16
9:7 [o]Joel 2:4 [p]Da 7:8
9:8 [q]Joel 1:6
9:9 [r]Joel 2:5
9:10 [s]ver 3,5,19
9:11 [t]ver 1,2; S Lk 8:31 [u]Rev 16:16 [v]Job 26:6; 28:22; 31:12; Ps 88:11
9:12 [w]S Rev 8:13
9:13 [x]Ex 30:1-3 [y]Rev 8:3
9:14 [z]Rev 7:1 [a]Ge 15:18; Dt 1:7; Jos 1:4; Isa 11:15; Rev 16:12
9:15 [b]Rev 20:7 [c]S Rev 8:7 [d]ver 18
9:16 [e]Rev 5:11; 7:4
9:17 [f]Rev 11:5 [g]ver 18; Ps 11:6; Isa 30:33; Eze 38:22; Rev 14:10; 19:20; 20:10; 21:8
9:18 [h]S Rev 8:7 [i]ver 15 [j]S ver 17
9:20 [k]S Rev 2:21 [l]Dt 4:28; 31:29; Jer 1:16; Mic 5:13; Ac 7:41 [m]S 1Co 10:20 [n]Ps 115:4-7; 135:15-17; Da 5:23
9:21 [o]S Rev 2:21 [p]Isa 47:9,12; Rev 18:23 [q]Rev 17:2,5
10:1 [r]Rev 5:2 [s]Rev 18:1; 20:1 [t]Eze 1:28; Rev 4:3 [u]Mt 17:2; Rev 1:16 [v]Rev 1:15
10:2 [w]ver 8-10; Rev 5:1 [x]ver 5,8
10:3 [y]Hos 11:10 [z]Rev 4:5
10:4 [a]Rev 1:11,19 [b]ver 8 [c]Da 8:26; 12:4,9; Rev 22:10
10:5 [d]ver 1,2 [e]Dt 32:40; Da 12:7
10:6 [f]Ge 14:22; Ex 6:8; Nu 14:30 [g]S Rev 1:18 [h]Ps 115:15; 146:6; Rev 4:11; 14:7 [i]Rev 16:17
10:7 [j]S Mt 24:31 [k]S Ro 16:25 [l]Am 3:7
10:8 [m]ver 4 [n]ver 2
10:9 [o]Jer 15:16; Eze 2:8-3:3

20The rest of mankind that were not
killed by these plagues still did not repent[k] of the work of their hands;[l] they
did not stop worshiping demons,[m] and
idols of gold, silver, bronze, stone and
wood—idols that cannot see or hear or
walk.[n] 21Nor did they repent[o] of their
murders, their magic arts,[p] their sexual
immorality[q] or their thefts.

Chapter 10

The Angel and the Little Scroll

THEN I saw another mighty angel[r]
coming down from heaven.[s] He was
robed in a cloud, with a rainbow[t] above
his head; his face was like the sun,[u] and
his legs were like fiery pillars.[v] 2He was
holding a little scroll,[w] which lay open in
his hand. He planted his right foot on the
sea and his left foot on the land,[x] 3and he
gave a loud shout like the roar of a lion.[y]
When he shouted, the voices of the seven
thunders[z] spoke. 4And when the seven
thunders spoke, I was about to write;[a]
but I heard a voice from heaven[b] say,
"Seal up what the seven thunders have
said and do not write it down."[c]
5Then the angel I had seen standing on
the sea and on the land[d] raised his right
hand to heaven.[e] 6And he swore[f] by
him who lives for ever and ever,[g] who
created the heavens and all that is in
them, the earth and all that is in it, and
the sea and all that is in it,[h] and said,
"There will be no more delay![i] 7But in
the days when the seventh angel is about
to sound his trumpet,[j] the mystery[k] of
God will be accomplished, just as he announced to his servants the prophets."[l]
8Then the voice that I had heard from
heaven[m] spoke to me once more: "Go,
take the scroll[n] that lies open in the hand
of the angel who is standing on the sea
and on the land."
9So I went to the angel and asked him
to give me the little scroll. He said to me,
"Take it and eat it. It will turn your stomach sour, but in your mouth it will be as
sweet as honey."[o] 10I took the little
scroll from the angel's hand and ate it. It

[1] *11 Abaddon* and *Apollyon* mean *Destroyer.*
[m] *13* That is, projections

9:6 HUMANITY, Death—God's judgment on the world will be so severe people will desire death over life. Death is not the worst experience humans face. At times life can be worse. God's people know He has sealed us from His final judgment. The experiences of life can become so unbearable that people will long for death. Death, however, does not come just because people want it. Obviously, suicide can be seen as a way out, but this passage does not refer to that.

9:20 GOD, One God—The one true God stands in sharp contrast to the demons and idols being worshiped by the sinners of this world. Worshiping false gods leads to doing sinful acts in the name of worship.

9:21 CHRISTIAN ETHICS, Murder—The end time calls us to repent. Gross murder and immorality are two signs of the last days. See note on 2:26.

10:6 GOD, Creator—God is the eternal Creator who brought everything into existence. Both of these ideas suggest His sovereignty, the theme of the whole book. The sovereign God controls the destiny of the universe. He decides when the great day of judgment will come.

10:7 GOD, Faithfulness—God does not forget His promises. He is faithful to the end. What He first spoke through His prophets in past ages will come to pass. God's people can depend upon God. Delay does not mean forgotten.

tasted as sweet as honey in my mouth,[p]
but when I had eaten it, my stomach
turned sour. 11Then I was told, "You
must prophesy[q] again about many peoples, nations, languages and kings."[r]

Chapter 11

The Two Witnesses

I was given a reed like a measuring
rod[s] and was told, "Go and measure
the temple of God and the altar, and
count the worshipers there. 2But exclude
the outer court;[t] do not measure it, because it has been given to the Gentiles.[u]
They will trample on the holy city[v] for
42 months.[w] 3And I will give power to
my two witnesses,[x] and they will prophesy for 1,260 days,[y] clothed in sackcloth."[z] 4These are the two olive trees[a]
and the two lampstands that stand before
the Lord of the earth.[b] 5If anyone tries to
harm them, fire comes from their mouths
and devours their enemies.[c] This is how
anyone who wants to harm them must
die.[d] 6These men have power to shut up
the sky[e] so that it will not rain during the
time they are prophesying;[f] and they
have power to turn the waters into
blood[g] and to strike the earth with every
kind of plague as often as they want.

7Now when they have finished their
testimony, the beast[h] that comes up from
the Abyss[i] will attack them,[j] and overpower and kill them. 8Their bodies will
lie in the street of the great city,[k] which
is figuratively called Sodom[l] and Egypt,
where also their Lord was crucified.[m]
9For three and a half days men from every
people, tribe, language and nation[n] will
gaze on their bodies and refuse them
burial.[o] 10The inhabitants of the earth[p]
will gloat over them and will celebrate by
sending each other gifts,[q] because these
two prophets had tormented those who
live on the earth.

11But after the three and a half days[r] a
breath of life from God entered them,[s]
and they stood on their feet, and terror
struck those who saw them. 12Then they
heard a loud voice from heaven saying to
them, "Come up here."[t] And they went
up to heaven in a cloud,[u] while their enemies looked on.

13At that very hour there was a severe
earthquake[v] and a tenth of the city collapsed. Seven thousand people were
killed in the earthquake, and the survivors were terrified and gave glory[w] to the
God of heaven.[x]

14The second woe has passed; the third
woe is coming soon.[y]

The Seventh Trumpet

15The seventh angel sounded his trumpet,[z] and there were loud voices[a] in
heaven, which said:

"The kingdom of the world has
become the kingdom of our
Lord and of his Christ,[b]
and he will reign for ever and
ever."[c]

16And the twenty-four elders,[d] who were
seated on their thrones before God, fell
on their faces[e] and worshiped God,
17saying:

"We give thanks[f] to you, Lord God
Almighty,[g]
the One who is and who was,[h]
because you have taken your great
power
and have begun to reign.[i]
18The nations were angry;[j]
and your wrath has come.
The time has come for judging the
dead,[k]
and for rewarding your servants the
prophets[l]
and your saints and those who
reverence your name,
both small and great[m]—
and for destroying those who destroy
the earth."

19Then God's temple[n] in heaven was
opened, and within his temple was seen
the ark of his covenant.[o] And there came

10:10 [p]S ver 9
10:11 [q]Eze 37:4,9 [r]Da 3:4; S Rev 13:7
11:1 [s]Eze 40:3; Rev 21:15
11:2 [t]Eze 40:17,20 [u]Lk 21:24 [v]S Rev 21:2 [w]ver 3; Da 7:25; 12:7; Rev 12:6,14; 13:5
11:3 [x]Rev 1:5; 2:13 [y]S ver 2 [z]Ge 37:34; 2Sa 3:31; Ne 9:1; Jnh 3:5
11:4 [a]Ps 52:8; Jer 11:16; Zec 4:3, 11 [b]Zec 4:14
11:5 [c]2Sa 22:9; 2Ki 1:10; Jer 5:14; Rev 9:17,18 [d]Nu 16:29,35
11:6 [e]S Lk 4:25 [f]ver 3 [g]Ex 7:17,19; Rev 8:8
11:7 [h]Rev 13:1-4 [i]S Lk 8:31 [j]Da 7:21; Rev 13:7
11:8 [k]Rev 16:19 [l]Isa 1:9; Jer 23:14; Eze 16:46 [m]Heb 13:12
11:9 [n]S Rev 13:7 [o]Ps 79:2,3
11:10 [p]S Rev 3:10 [q]Ne 8:10,12; Est 9:19,22
11:11 [r]ver 9 [s]Eze 37:5,9,10,14
11:12 [t]Rev 4:1 [u]2Ki 2:11; Ac 1:9
11:13 [v]S Rev 6:12 [w]Rev 14:7; 16:9; 19:7 [x]Rev 16:11
11:14 [y]S Rev 8:13
11:15 [z]S Mt 24:31 [a]Rev 16:17; 19:1 [b]Rev 12:10 [c]Ps 145:13; Da 2:44; 7:14,27; Mic 4:7; Zec 14:9; Lk 1:33
11:16 [d]S Rev 4:4 [e]S Rev 4:10
11:17 [f]Ps 30:12 [g]S Rev 1:8 [h]S Rev 1:4 [i]Rev 19:6
11:18 [j]Ps 2:1 [k]Rev 20:12 [l]Rev 10:7 [m]S Rev 19:5
11:19 [n]Rev 15:5,8 [o]Ex 25:10-22; 2Ch 5:7; Heb 9:4

11:2–3 LAST THINGS, Great Tribulation—The holy city of Jerusalem is said to be trampled on by Gentiles for 42 months. This same period of time is mentioned in 13:5. It is a period equal to the 1,260 days in v 3 and in 12:6. Calculated as three and a half years, it is similar to the period of 12:14, "a time, times, and half a time." Dispensationalists apply these numbers to one-half of the seven-year tribulation period prophesied in Daniel. See note on Da 9:24–27. There is not total agreement among such interpreters as to which half of the tribulation period is being described. The only general agreement is that the last three and a half years will see the antichrist in power and the tribulations so intense as to earn for the latter half of the period the designation the Great Tribulation. Amillennialists see the passage and numbers as symbolic of God's protection of His witnessing church and of the danger of persecution the church faces. Whatever the details mean, the passage calls believers to witness for Christ and to know victory is ultimately His.

11:15–18 GOD, Sovereignty—Earthly rulers have temporary power. Evil in this world is temporary. God's sovereign authority and power are eternal, and thus His victory will be everlasting. This means persecution and suffering for Christians are also temporary. God will judge evil, reward faithfulness, and rule the world forever.

11:15 JESUS CHRIST, Kingdom of God—The final victory will see Jesus rule openly and eternally over all creation.

11:15 LAST THINGS, Kingdom Established—The declaration of loud voices in heaven announces an establishing of God's kingdom through conquest of the kingdom of the world. The world will ultimately come under the universal government of Christ, who will reign eternally. Compare Isa 9:6–7.

flashes of lightning, rumblings, peals of
thunder,[p] an earthquake and a great hailstorm.[q]

Chapter 12

The Woman and the Dragon

A great and wondrous sign[r] appeared
in heaven:[s] a woman clothed with
the sun, with the moon under her feet
and a crown of twelve stars[t] on her
head. 2She was pregnant and cried out in
pain[u] as she was about to give birth.
3Then another sign appeared in heaven:[v]
an enormous red dragon[w] with seven
heads[x] and ten horns[y] and seven
crowns[z] on his heads. 4His tail swept a
third[a] of the stars out of the sky and
flung them to the earth.[b] The dragon
stood in front of the woman who was
about to give birth, so that he might devour her child[c] the moment it was born.
5She gave birth to a son, a male child,
who will rule all the nations with an iron
scepter.[d] And her child was snatched
up[e] to God and to his throne. 6The woman fled into the desert to a place prepared
for her by God, where she might be taken
care of for 1,260 days.[f]

7And there was war in heaven. Michael[g] and his angels fought against the
dragon,[h] and the dragon and his angels[i]
fought back. 8But he was not strong
enough, and they lost their place in heav-
en. 9The great dragon was hurled down
—that ancient serpent[j] called the devil,[k] or Satan,[l] who leads the whole
world astray.[m] He was hurled to the
earth,[n] and his angels with him.

10Then I heard a loud voice in heaven[o]
say:

"Now have come the salvation[p] and
the power and the kingdom of
our God,
and the authority of his Christ.
For the accuser of our brothers,[q]
who accuses them before our God
day and night,
has been hurled down.
11They overcame[r] him
by the blood of the Lamb[s]
and by the word of their
testimony;[t]
they did not love their lives so
much
as to shrink from death.[u]
12Therefore rejoice, you heavens[v]
and you who dwell in them!
But woe[w] to the earth and the
sea,[x]
because the devil has gone down to
you!
He is filled with fury,
because he knows that his time is
short."

13When the dragon[y] saw that he had
been hurled to the earth, he pursued the
woman who had given birth to the male
child.[z] 14The woman was given the two
wings of a great eagle,[a] so that she might
fly to the place prepared for her in the
desert, where she would be taken care of
for a time, times and half a time,[b] out of
the serpent's reach. 15Then from his
mouth the serpent[c] spewed water like a
river, to overtake the woman and sweep
her away with the torrent. 16But the earth
helped the woman by opening its mouth
and swallowing the river that the dragon
had spewed out of his mouth. 17Then the
dragon was enraged at the woman and
went off to make war[d] against the rest of
her offspring[e]—those who obey God's
commandments[f] and hold to the testimony of Jesus.[g] 1And the dragon[n] stood
on the shore of the sea.

[n] *1* Some late manuscripts *And I*

11:19 [p]S Rev 4:5 [q]Rev 16:21
12:1 [r]ver 3 [s]Rev 11:19 [t]Ge 37:9
12:2 [u]Isa 26:17; Gal 4:19
12:3 [v]ver 1; Rev 15:1 [w]ver 9,13, 16,17; Rev 13:1 [x]Rev 13:1; 17:3,7,9 [y]Da 7:7,20; Rev 13:1; 17:3,7, 12,16 [z]Rev 19:12
12:4 [a]S Rev 8:7 [b]Da 8:10 [c]Mt 2:16
12:5 [d]Ps 2:9; Rev 2:27; 19:15 [e]S Ac 8:39
12:6 [f]S Rev 11:2
12:7 [g]S Jude 9 [h]ver 3 [i]Mt 25:41
12:9 [j]ver 15; Ge 3:1-7 [k]Mt 25:41; Rev 20:2 [l]S Mt 4:10 [m]Rev 20:3,8,10 [n]Lk 10:18; Jn 12:31
12:10 [o]Rev 11:15 [p]Rev 7:10 [q]Job 1:9-11; Zec 3:1; 1Pe 5:8
12:11 [r]S Jn 16:33; Rev 15:2 [s]S Rev 7:14 [t]Rev 6:9 [u]Lk 14:26; Rev 2:10
12:12 [v]Ps 96:11; Isa 44:23; 49:13; Rev 18:20 [w]S Rev 8:13 [x]Rev 10:6
12:13 [y]ver 3 [z]ver 5
12:14 [a]Ex 19:4 [b]S Rev 11:2
12:15 [c]ver 9
12:17 [d]Rev 11:7; 13:7 [e]Ge 3:15 [f]S Jn 14:15 [g]S Rev 1:2

12:3–17 EVIL AND SUFFERING, Satan—Satan, the accuser, no longer has access to the heavenly throne. See note on Job 1:6–12. Christ was born of woman, suffered, died, was raised, and ascended to heaven. Satan, the dragon, lost the heavenly battle and was cast down to earth. Christ's victory is sure. He reigns in heaven. Christians must still endure suffering because Satan is still loose on earth and enraged against Christ's followers because Satan knows his time is short.

12:5 JESUS CHRIST, Ascension—Jesus was a human born of a woman. Unlike other humans, He was resurrected and taken up to God. In His redemption on the cross came power to overcome Satan and establish God's eternal kingdom under Christ's authority.

12:10–12 GOD, Sovereignty—Even Satan recognizes the authority and power of God. Christ has overcome Him. In relation to eternity he has only a brief time to do his evil work. Victory rests with God and with God's people.

12:11 SALVATION, Atonement—God's people can overcome the devil through the atoning death of Christ on the cross. If we can testify that Christ has covered our sins, we can overcome all evil, sin, and darkness.

12:11 EVANGELISM, Testimony—Our testimony for Christ not only strengthens others and wins people to our Lord, it even defeats Satan, "the accuser of our brothers" (v 10). In the power of Christ's death on the cross, Satan was disarmed. Now we can defeat him through Christ's victory and by the word of our testimony if we will totally give our lives to our Lord, even unto death.

12:12 PRAYER, Worship—The heavenly rejoicing is because the devil's time is short. Heaven is a place of joy in prayer.

12:17 CHRISTIAN ETHICS, Obedience—In the face of the coming end of history, God's people are called to a new commitment to obedience, for only the obedient will be able to stand against the evil dragon.

12:17 EVANGELISM, Persecution—Those who stand for Christ and bear a strong testimony will be persecuted; yet, the Lord promises victory to His faithful witnesses. See note on 2:13.

13:1–18 EVIL AND SUFFERING, Satan—Satan often works through earthly authority. When he uses human rulers, they generally manifest great pride and even claim to be God.

Chapter 13

The Beast out of the Sea

AND I saw a beast coming out of the
sea.[h] He had ten horns and seven
heads,[i] with ten crowns on his horns,
and on each head a blasphemous name.[j]
2The beast I saw resembled a leopard,[k]
but had feet like those of a bear[l] and a
mouth like that of a lion.[m] The dragon
gave the beast his power and his throne
and great authority.[n] 3One of the heads
of the beast seemed to have had a fatal
wound, but the fatal wound had been
healed.[o] The whole world was astonished[p] and followed the beast. 4Men
worshiped the dragon because he had
given authority to the beast, and they also
worshiped the beast and asked, "Who is
like[q] the beast? Who can make war
against him?"

5The beast was given a mouth to utter
proud words and blasphemies[r] and to exercise his authority for forty-two
months.[s] 6He opened his mouth to blaspheme God, and to slander his name and
his dwelling place and those who live in
heaven.[t] 7He was given power to make
war[u] against the saints and to conquer
them. And he was given authority over
every tribe, people, language and nation.[v] 8All inhabitants of the earth[w] will
worship the beast—all whose names
have not been written in the book of life[x]
belonging to the Lamb[y] that was slain
from the creation of the world.[o] [z]

9He who has an ear, let him hear.[a]

10If anyone is to go into captivity,
into captivity he will go.
If anyone is to be killed[p] with the
sword,
with the sword he will be killed.[b]

This calls for patient endurance and faithfulness[c] on the part of the saints.[d]

The Beast out of the Earth

11Then I saw another beast, coming out
of the earth.[e] He had two horns like a
lamb, but he spoke like a dragon.[f] 12He
exercised all the authority[g] of the first
beast on his behalf,[h] and made the earth
and its inhabitants worship the first
beast,[i] whose fatal wound had been
healed.[j] 13And he performed great and
miraculous signs,[k] even causing fire to
come down from heaven[l] to earth in full
view of men. 14Because of the signs[m] he
was given power to do on behalf of the
first beast, he deceived[n] the inhabitants
of the earth.[o] He ordered them to set up
an image in honor of the beast who was
wounded by the sword and yet lived.[p]
15He was given power to give breath to
the image of the first beast, so that it
could speak and cause all who refused to
worship[q] the image to be killed.[r] 16He
also forced everyone, small and great,[s]
rich and poor, free and slave, to receive a
mark on his right hand or on his forehead,[t] 17so that no one could buy or sell
unless he had the mark,[u] which is the
name of the beast or the number of his
name.[v]

13:1 [h]Da 7:1-6; Rev 15:2; 16:13 [i]S Rev 12:3 [j]Da 11:36; Rev 17:3
13:2 [k]Da 7:6 [l]Da 7:5 [m]Da 7:4 [n]Rev 2:13; 16:10
13:3 [o]ver 12,14 [p]Rev 17:8
13:4 [q]Ex 15:11
13:5 [r]Da 7:8,11,20, 25; 11:36; 2Th 2:4 [s]S Rev 11:2
13:6 [t]Rev 12:12
13:7 [u]Da 7:21; Rev 11:7 [v]Rev 5:9; 7:9; 10:11; 17:15
13:8 [w]ver 12,14; S Rev 3:10 [x]S Rev 20:12 [y]S Jn 1:29 [z]S Mt 25:34
13:9 [a]S Rev 2:7
13:10 [b]Jer 15:2; 43:11 [c]S Heb 6:12 [d]Rev 14:12
13:11 [e]ver 1,2 [f]Rev 16:13
13:12 [g]ver 4 [h]ver 14; Rev 19:20 [i]ver 15; Rev 14:9, 11; 16:2; 19:20; 20:4 [j]ver 3
13:13 [k]S Mt 24:24 [l]1Ki 18:38; 2Ki 1:10; Lk 9:54; Rev 20:9
13:14 [m]2Th 2:9,10 [n]Rev 12:9 [o]S Rev 3:10 [p]ver 3, 12
13:15 [q]S ver 12 [r]Da 3:3-6
13:16 [s]S Rev 19:5 [t]Rev 7:3; 14:9; 20:4
13:17 [u]Rev 14:9 [v]ver 18; Rev 14:11; 15:2

[o]8 Or *written from the creation of the world in the book of life belonging to the Lamb that was slain*
[p]10 Some manuscripts *anyone kills*

To worship such human authorities—political or religious—is to worship Satan and to face eternal punishment. To refuse to obey such earthly powers is to face economic loss and persecution, but it is also to gain eternal rewards. God's people must endure such evil leadership in faith and patience. Evil powers may amaze with their authority and signs. Eventually they lose all power. John used symbols and number systems known to his readers to identify the specific beast to whom he referred. We do not have a sure key to his identification system.

13:1–10 CHRISTIAN ETHICS, Church and State—Political powers may blasphemously usurp power over governments. In so doing they oppose God and will eventually submit to His authority. Political power is not sufficient reason for a person to be worshiped. Patient endurance may be the disciple's only course of action when government authorities exercise beastly power under Satan's control.

13:1–10 LAST THINGS, Great Tribulation—The beast rising out of the sea is often identified as the antichrist of 1 John and 2 John and the man of lawlessness of 2 Thessalonians. See notes on 2 Th 2:1–12; 1 Jn 2:18. The dragon of Rev 12 is identified as Satan (v 9) and in this passage as the one giving power and authority to the beast (v 2). The final uprising of evil finds consummate expression in the figure who is referred to by a variety of terminology and imagery. The beast out of the sea has a second beast (13:11–17) who promotes it as the object of worship by the use of oppressive measures. The middle figure of the trio of dragon, beast from the sea, and beast from the earth corresponds to antichrist. Dispensationalists generally identify the ten horns and seven heads as various world rulers who come together in support of the beast. Historical premillennialists generally withhold judgment as to their end time identity, believing this will be clear at the proper time. Amillennialists interpret the text figuratively to refer to worldly and Satanic powers that threaten the church in all ages. John used the animal symbolism of Da 7 to describe powers threatening the church and to call for patient endurance. Worship belongs to God and to no other power.

13:5–10 HISTORY, Judgment—God allows the evil forces of Satan to exercise control and inflict judgment, but their time of power has been limited by Him long before they gain power. God controls time and eternity. Satan does not. God's saints must endure such difficult times with patience and faith.

13:8 JESUS CHRIST, Lamb of God—Jesus' sacrificial death was part of God's eternal plan to create His faithful people who would not worship Satan.

13:13–16 MIRACLE, Evil—The evil beast in John's vision was enabled to perform signs for deceptive purposes. Satan himself is reckoned as the source of the power. The sign was not of redemption but of destruction—fire from heaven. The life given to the image was evil life—enabled to destroy those who refused to worship the beast. See note on 2 Th 2:9–10.

13:18 LAST THINGS, Great Tribulation—"The beast" refers to the same personage as the antichrist, a figure frequently associated with a future great tribulation time. See notes on 1 Jn 2:18; 2 Jn 7. A symbolic number, 666, refers to this personage. Many have sought the meaning or identity by assigning numerical values to the letters of the alphabet to find a name or title which totals 666. Names in Hebrew, Greek, and

18This calls for wisdom.[w] If anyone has
insight, let him calculate the number of
the beast, for it is man's number.[x] His
number is 666.

Chapter 14

The Lamb and the 144,000

THEN I looked, and there before me
was the Lamb,[y] standing on Mount
Zion,[z] and with him 144,000[a] who had
his name and his Father's name[b] written
on their foreheads.[c] 2And I heard a
sound from heaven like the roar of rushing waters[d] and like a loud peal of thunder.[e] The sound I heard was like that of
harpists playing their harps.[f] 3And they
sang a new song[g] before the throne and
before the four living creatures[h] and the
elders.[i] No one could learn the song except the 144,000[j] who had been redeemed from the earth. 4These are those
who did not defile themselves with wom-
en, for they kept themselves pure.[k] They
follow the Lamb wherever he goes.[l]
They were purchased from among men[m]
and offered as firstfruits[n] to God and the
Lamb. 5No lie was found in their
mouths;[o] they are blameless.[p]

The Three Angels

6Then I saw another angel flying in
midair,[q] and he had the eternal gospel to
proclaim to those who live on the earth[r]
—to every nation, tribe, language and
people.[s] 7He said in a loud voice, "Fear
God[t] and give him glory,[u] because the
hour of his judgment has come. Worship
him who made[v] the heavens, the earth,
the sea and the springs of water."[w]
8A second angel followed and said,
"Fallen! Fallen is Babylon the Great,[x]
which made all the nations drink the
maddening wine of her adulteries."[y]
9A third angel followed them and said
in a loud voice: "If anyone worships the
beast[z] and his image[a] and receives his
mark on the forehead[b] or on the hand,
10he, too, will drink of the wine of God's
fury,[c] which has been poured full
strength into the cup of his wrath.[d] He
will be tormented with burning sulfur[e]
in the presence of the holy angels and of
the Lamb. 11And the smoke of their torment rises for ever and ever.[f] There is
no rest day or night[g] for those who worship the beast and his image,[h] or for anyone who receives the mark of his
name."[i] 12This calls for patient endurance[j] on the part of the saints[k] who
obey God's commandments[l] and remain
faithful to Jesus.
13Then I heard a voice from heaven

13:18 [w]Rev 17:9 [x]Rev 15:2; 21:17
14:1 [y]S Rev 5:6 [z]Ps 2:6; Heb 12:22 [a]ver 3; Rev 7:4 [b]Rev 3:12; 22:4 [c]S Rev 7:3
14:2 [d]S Rev 1:15 [e]Rev 6:1 [f]Rev 5:8; 15:2
14:3 [g]S Rev 5:9 [h]S Rev 4:6 [i]S Rev 4:4 [j]ver 1
14:4 [k]2Co 11:2; Rev 3:4 [l]Rev 7:17 [m]Rev 5:9 [n]Jer 2:3; Jas 1:18
14:5 [o]Ps 32:2; Zep 3:13; Jn 1:47; 1Pe 2:22 [p]Eph 5:27
14:6 [q]Rev 8:13; 19:17 [r]S Rev 3:10 [s]S Rev 13:7
14:7 [t]Ps 34:9; Rev 15:4 [u]S Rev 11:13 [v]S Rev 10:6 [w]Rev 8:10; 16:4
14:8 [x]Isa 21:9; Jer 51:8; Rev 16:19; 17:5; 18:2,10 [y]Rev 17:2,4; 18:3,9
14:9 [z]S Rev 13:12 [a]Rev 13:14 [b]S Rev 13:16
14:10 [c]Isa 51:17; Jer 25:15 [d]Jer 51:7; Rev 18:6 [e]S Rev 9:17
14:11 [f]Isa 34:10; Rev 19:3 [g]Rev 4:8 [h]ver 9; S Rev 13:12 [i]Rev 13:17
14:12 [j]S Heb 6:12 [k]Rev 13:10 [l]S Jn 14:15

Latin have all been used in this quest. Others are less specific in their search, allowing a more general symbolism by which six represents fallen humanity raised to the third power, hence, a person of ultimate wickedness. Still others seek meaning along the lines of a trinity of sixes, corresponding to Satan, the beast out of the sea, and the beast out of the earth (Rev 13:1–10,11–17), an unholy trinity of ultimate evil.

14:1,4 GOD, Righteous—Those who are associated with God and the Lamb are pure; for God is holy, righteous, and has nothing to do with evil. His righteousness has a purifying effect on those who come into contact with Him. Those who are not pure cannot claim to be in relationship to God.

14:1–12 ELECTION, Perseverance—God's judgment brings the painful punishment of God's wrath to the ungodly. Until judgment comes, the faithful suffer and are called to faithful, obedient, and patient perseverance.

14:3–4 SALVATION, Redemption—Twenty-eight times this book calls Jesus the Lamb of God. Undergirding that image is the idea of Christ as a sacrifice on the cross for sin. In this passage, the Lamb stands on Mount Zion and receives the praise of all the redeemed. God's great redemption through Christ is worthy of all praise from all His creatures.

14:3 PRAYER, Worship—Worship is often expressed by song. This is a new song, reserved for certain saints.

14:5 CHRISTIAN ETHICS, Honesty—Purity and honesty will mark God's saints in the last days. This should set an example for all disciples in our day.

14:6 EVANGELISM, Gospel—The gospel means "good news." It has a definite content. See note on Ac 2:17–40. It is eternal truth that is the power of God unto eternal salvation (Ro 1:16) for all people from all parts of the world if they will believe.

14:7 GOD, Sovereignty—God's mighty authority is shown by His power to judge and to create. His authority strikes fear into the hearts of people.

14:7 SALVATION, Fear of God—The eternal gospel calls for all persons everywhere to fear God and worship Him. God the Redeemer is also the Creator and Judge. There is an awesomeness about salvation which we dare not overlook.

14:7 WORSHIP, Reverence—The approaching judgment should lead all people to reverent worship and faith. See note on Lev 9:23–24.

14:7 PRAYER, Worship—The heavenly messenger proclaimed an awesome moment. Fear should produce a glorifying of God in such a moment. All are called upon to worship God as Creator.

14:9–20 GOD, Wrath—The wrath of God is shown here as an expression of the mighty power of the sovereign God. This is both a warning to the godless and an encouragement to God's faithful, suffering people. God will act in justice at the right time. Meanwhile, we must patiently obey Him.

14:9–12 EVIL AND SUFFERING, Endurance—See notes on 1:9; 13:1–18.

14:9–11 LAST THINGS, Judgment—The wrath of God in future judgment will be with full strength—unmixed and undiluted. Until final judgment, the manifestations of divine wrath have been tempered with redemptive intent. See Ro 2:5–11. God's wrath in human history is always with a view to securing repentance. The future wrath will not be mixed with redemptive hope. In its full strength, a fierceness of wrath never yet seen, God's wrath will result in eternal torment for the wicked. Compare Rev 15:7.

14:12 CHRISTIAN ETHICS, Obedience—See note on 3:3.

14:13 HUMANITY, Death—Physical death is the avenue of a glorious reunion between believers and our Lord, a time of great happiness. Earthly fears, persecutions, and labor will end. God's enemies will be judged. God's people will enjoy Christ's victory.

14:13 SALVATION, As Rest—God's salvation includes a final resting place for the dead in Christ—heaven (21:1—22:5). "Rest" here probably means final release from sufferings, tortures, and death, as well as cessation of physical work and toil. This is the second of seven beatitudes in Revelation given to comfort those facing the prospect of martyrdom because they confessed their Lord (1:3).

say, "Write: Blessed are the dead who die
in the Lord[m] from now on."
"Yes," says the Spirit,[n] "they will rest
from their labor, for their deeds will follow them."

The Harvest of the Earth

14I looked, and there before me was a
white cloud,[o] and seated on the cloud
was one "like a son of man"[q][p] with a
crown[q] of gold on his head and a sharp
sickle in his hand. 15Then another angel
came out of the temple[r] and called in a
loud voice to him who was sitting on the
cloud, "Take your sickle[s] and reap, because the time to reap has come, for the
harvest[t] of the earth is ripe." 16So he
who was seated on the cloud swung his
sickle over the earth, and the earth was
harvested.
17Another angel came out of the temple in heaven, and he too had a sharp
sickle.[u] 18Still another angel, who had
charge of the fire, came from the altar[v]
and called in a loud voice to him who had
the sharp sickle, "Take your sharp sickle[w] and gather the clusters of grapes from
the earth's vine, because its grapes are
ripe." 19The angel swung his sickle on
the earth, gathered its grapes and threw
them into the great winepress of God's
wrath.[x] 20They were trampled in the
winepress[y] outside the city,[z] and
blood[a] flowed out of the press, rising as
high as the horses' bridles for a distance
of 1,600 stadia.[r]

Chapter 15

Seven Angels With Seven Plagues

I saw in heaven another great and marvelous sign:[b] seven angels[c] with the
seven last plagues[d]—last, because with
them God's wrath is completed. 2And I
saw what looked like a sea of glass[e]
mixed with fire and, standing beside the
sea, those who had been victorious[f] over
the beast[g] and his image[h] and over the
number of his name.[i] They held harps[j]
given them by God 3and sang the song of

14:13 [m]1Co 15:18; 1Th 4:16 [n]Rev 2:7; 22:17
14:14 [o]Mt 17:5 [p]Da 7:13; S Rev 1:13 [q]S Rev 6:2
14:15 [r]ver 17; Rev 11:19 [s]ver 18; Joel 3:13; Mk 4:29 [t]Jer 51:33
14:17 [u]S ver 15
14:18 [v]Rev 6:9; 8:5; 16:7 [w]S ver 15
14:19 [x]Rev 19:15
14:20 [y]ver 19; Isa 63:3; Joel 3:13; Rev 19:15 [z]Heb 13:12; Rev 11:8 [a]Ge 49:11; Dt 32:14
15:1 [b]Rev 12:1,3 [c]ver 6-8; Rev 16:1; 17:1; 21:9 [d]Lev 26:21; Rev 9:20
15:2 [e]Rev 4:6 [f]Rev 12:11 [g]Rev 13:1 [h]Rev 13:14 [i]Rev 13:17 [j]Rev 5:8; 14:2
15:3 [k]Ex 15:1 [l]Jos 1:1 [m]S Rev 5:9 [n]Ps 111:2 [o]S Rev 1:8 [p]Ps 145:17
15:4 [q]Jer 10:7 [r]Ps 86:9 [s]Isa 66:23 [t]Rev 19:8
15:5 [u]Rev 11:19 [v]Ex 38:21; Nu 1:50 [w]S Mt 3:16
15:6 [x]Rev 14:15 [y]S ver 1 [z]Eze 9:2; Da 10:5 [a]Rev 1:13
15:7 [b]S Rev 4:6 [c]S ver 1 [d]S Rev 1:18
15:8 [e]Isa 6:4 [f]Ex 40:34,35; 1Ki 8:10,11; 2Ch 5:13,14
16:1 [g]Rev 11:19 [h]S Rev 15:1 [i]ver 2-21; Ps 79:6; Zep 3:8
16:2 [j]Rev 8:7 [k]ver 11; Ex 9:9-11; Dt 28:35 [l]Rev 13:15-17; 14:9
16:3 [m]Ex 7:17-21; Rev 8:8,9; Rev 11:6

Moses[k] the servant of God[l] and the song
of the Lamb:[m]

"Great and marvelous are your
deeds,[n]
Lord God Almighty.[o]
Just and true are your ways,[p]
King of the ages.
4Who will not fear you, O Lord,[q]
and bring glory to your name?[r]
For you alone are holy.
All nations will come
and worship before you,[s]
for your righteous acts[t] have been
revealed."

5After this I looked and in heaven the
temple,[u] that is, the tabernacle of the
Testimony,[v] was opened.[w] 6Out of the
temple[x] came the seven angels with the
seven plagues.[y] They were dressed in
clean, shining linen[z] and wore golden
sashes around their chests.[a] 7Then one
of the four living creatures[b] gave to the
seven angels[c] seven golden bowls filled
with the wrath of God, who lives for ever
and ever.[d] 8And the temple was filled
with smoke[e] from the glory of God and
from his power, and no one could enter
the temple[f] until the seven plagues of
the seven angels were completed.

Chapter 16

The Seven Bowls of God's Wrath

THEN I heard a loud voice from the
temple[g] saying to the seven angels,[h]
"Go, pour out the seven bowls of God's
wrath on the earth."[i]
2The first angel went and poured out
his bowl on the land,[j] and ugly and painful sores[k] broke out on the people who
had the mark of the beast and worshiped
his image.[l]
3The second angel poured out his bowl
on the sea, and it turned into blood like
that of a dead man, and every living thing
in the sea died.[m]
4The third angel poured out his bowl

[q]*14* Daniel 7:13 [r]*20* That is, about 180 miles (about 300 kilometers)

14:13 SALVATION, Blessing—The dead who die in the Lord are blessed. God's salvation blesses His people from the cradle to the grave, and indeed from before time to after time.

14:13 LAST THINGS, Believers' Death—This strangest of all beatitudes pronounces blessedness upon believers at death. Rest from labors and reward for faithfulness join the prospect of immediate fellowship with Christ to constitute the blessedness. Compare 1:3; 16:15; 19:9; 20:6; 22:7,14.

15:1–4 GOD, Justice—God is a just God. His righteousness is ever true. He will not let the right fail. Nor will He let evil continue. He is faithful to His own righteous nature and will set all things right in the end. We should fall down in worship and gratitude.

15:2 THE CHURCH, People of God—God's people, living in faith and obedience, conquer evil through the power of Christ. The ultimate victory belongs to Christ and those who follow Him.

15:4 EVANGELISM, Universality—The gospel is for all, and all nations and races will find among them those who will respond. We are, therefore, to evangelize all people regardless of who or where they are.

16:1–21 GOD, Wrath—This whole chapter sets forth the wrath of God in vivid, dramatic fashion. The sovereign power of God is shown punishing the evil forces of this world. God is clearly in control. Christians who may wonder at times can take courage from this picture of God's vengeance upon evil. Evil is an ugly reality in our world. One day God will surprise all forces of evil and destroy them. Until then we must be waiting expectantly for Him to come.

on the rivers and springs of water,[n] and
they became blood.[o] 5Then I heard the
angel in charge of the waters say:

"You are just in these judgments,[p]
you who are and who were,[q] the
Holy One,[r]
because you have so judged;[s]
6for they have shed the blood of your
saints and prophets,[t]
and you have given them blood to
drink[u] as they deserve."

7And I heard the altar[v] respond:

"Yes, Lord God Almighty,[w]
true and just are your judgments."[x]

8The fourth angel[y] poured out his
bowl on the sun,[z] and the sun was given
power to scorch people with fire.[a] 9They
were seared by the intense heat and they
cursed the name of God,[b] who had control over these plagues, but they refused
to repent[c] and glorify him.[d]
10The fifth angel poured out his bowl
on the throne of the beast,[e] and his kingdom was plunged into darkness.[f] Men
gnawed their tongues in agony 11and
cursed[g] the God of heaven[h] because of
their pains and their sores,[i] but they
refused to repent of what they had
done.[j]
12The sixth angel poured out his bowl
on the great river Euphrates,[k] and its water was dried up to prepare the way[l] for
the kings from the East.[m] 13Then I saw
three evil[s] spirits[n] that looked like
frogs;[o] they came out of the mouth of the
dragon,[p] out of the mouth of the beast[q]
and out of the mouth of the false prophet.[r] 14They are spirits of demons[s] performing miraculous signs,[t] and they go
out to the kings of the whole world,[u] to
gather them for the battle[v] on the great
day[w] of God Almighty.
15"Behold, I come like a thief![x]
Blessed is he who stays awake[y] and
keeps his clothes with him, so that he
may not go naked and be shamefully exposed."[z]
16Then they gathered the kings together[a] to the place that in Hebrew[b] is called
Armageddon.[c]

16:4 [n]Rev 8:10 [o]Ex 7:17-21 **16:5** [p]Rev 15:3 [q]S Rev 1:4 [r]Rev 15:4 [s]Rev 6:10 **16:6** [t]Lk 11:49-51 [u]Isa 49:26; Rev 17:6; 18:24 **16:7** [v]Rev 6:9; 14:18 [w]S Rev 1:8 [x]Rev 15:3; 19:2 **16:8** [y]Rev 8:12 [z]Rev 6:12 [a]Rev 14:18 **16:9** [b]ver 11,21 [c]S Rev 2:21 [d]S Rev 11:13 **16:10** [e]Rev 13:2 [f]Ex 10:21-23; Isa 8:22; Rev 8:12; 9:2 **16:11** [g]ver 9,21 [h]Rev 11:13 [i]ver 2 [j]S Rev 2:21 **16:12** [k]S Rev 9:14 [l]Isa 11:15,16 [m]Isa 41:2; 46:11 **16:13** [n]Rev 18:2 [o]Ex 8:6 [p]S Rev 12:3 [q]S Rev 13:1 [r]Rev 19:20; 20:10 **16:14** [s]1Ti 4:1 [t]S Mt 24:24 [u]S Mt 24:14 [v]Rev 17:14; 19:19; 20:8 [w]S Rev 6:17 **16:15** [x]S Lk 12:39 [y]Lk 12:37 [z]Rev 3:18 **16:16** [a]ver 14 [b]Rev 9:11 [c]Jdg 5:19; 2Ki 23:29,30; Zec 12:11 **16:17** [d]Eph 2:2 [e]Rev 14:15 [f]Rev 11:15 [g]Rev 21:6 **16:18** [h]S Rev 4:5 [i]S Rev 6:12 [j]Da 12:1; Mt 24:21 **16:19** [k]S Rev 17:18 [l]Rev 18:5 [m]S Rev 14:8 [n]Rev 14:10 **16:20** [o]S Rev 6:14 **16:21** [p]Eze 13:13; 38:22; Rev 8:7; 11:19 [q]ver 9,11 [r]Ex 9:23-25 **17:1** [s]S Rev 15:1 [t]Rev 15:7 [u]Rev 16:19 [v]ver 5, 15,16; Isa 23:17; Rev 19:2 [w]Jer 51:13 **17:2** [x]S Rev 14:8 **17:3** [y]S Rev 1:10 [z]Rev 12:6,14 [a]Rev 18:12,16 [b]Rev 13:1 [c]S Rev 12:3 **17:4** [d]Eze 28:13; Rev 18:16 [e]Jer 51:7; Rev 18:6 [f]ver 2; S Rev 14:8 **17:5** [g]ver 7 [h]S Rev 14:8 [i]ver 1,2

17The seventh angel poured out his
bowl into the air,[d] and out of the temple[e] came a loud voice[f] from the throne,
saying, "It is done!"[g] 18Then there came
flashes of lightning, rumblings, peals of
thunder[h] and a severe earthquake.[i] No
earthquake like it has ever occurred since
man has been on earth,[j] so tremendous
was the quake. 19The great city[k] split
into three parts, and the cities of the nations collapsed. God remembered[l] Babylon the Great[m] and gave her the cup
filled with the wine of the fury of his
wrath.[n] 20Every island fled away and the
mountains could not be found.[o] 21From
the sky huge hailstones[p] of about a hundred pounds each fell upon men. And
they cursed God[q] on account of the
plague of hail,[r] because the plague was
so terrible.

Chapter 17

The Woman on the Beast

ONE of the seven angels[s] who had the
seven bowls[t] came and said to me,
"Come, I will show you the punishment[u]
of the great prostitute,[v] who sits on
many waters.[w] 2With her the kings of the
earth committed adultery and the inhabitants of the earth were intoxicated with
the wine of her adulteries."[x]
3Then the angel carried me away in the
Spirit[y] into a desert.[z] There I saw a
woman sitting on a scarlet[a] beast that
was covered with blasphemous names[b]
and had seven heads and ten horns.[c]
4The woman was dressed in purple and
scarlet, and was glittering with gold, precious stones and pearls.[d] She held a gold-
en cup[e] in her hand, filled with abominable things and the filth of her adulteries.[f]
5This title was written on her forehead:

MYSTERY[g]
BABYLON THE GREAT[h]
THE MOTHER OF PROSTITUTES[i]
AND OF THE ABOMINATIONS OF THE EARTH.

[s]13 Greek *unclean*

16:7 PRAYER, Worship—In 8:3–5, the altar was associated with the prayers of the saints. As terrible as the judgments described, God is true and just.
16:9,11 CHRISTIAN ETHICS, Language—End time tribulations will lead many to blasphemy rather than repentance. See note on 3:3.
16:14,21 MIRACLE, Evil—Spirits of demons were enabled to do signs. Their purpose was to enlist forces to oppose God. Punishment and defeat were certain. This was symbolized by a destructive hail storm. Satanic power causes great suffering; God's power effects redemption. See note on 13:13–16.
17:3 HOLY SPIRIT, Revelation—The Holy Spirit moved people around in the Old Testament. See note on 1 Ki 18:12. One instance of this occurs in the New Testament (Ac 8:39). The person to whom this happened most frequently was Ezekiel. See note on Eze 2:1–2. John's experiences (Rev 21:10) were remarkably similar to those of Ezekiel. The purpose of the moving was to give the prophet a vision. This revelation he then wrote down for his own and future generations. The prophetic vision was one of the Spirit's methods of revelation. See note on 1:10.
17:6 EVIL AND SUFFERING, Endurance—See note on 6:9–11.
17:6 EVANGELISM, Persecution—Pressure comes to the faithful. The evil of this world delight in that, but a true and faithful testimony for Christ will win in the end. We are to bear

6I saw that the woman was drunk
with the blood of the saints,[j] the
blood of those who bore testimony to
Jesus.

When I saw her, I was greatly astonished. 7Then the angel said to me: "Why
are you astonished? I will explain to you
the mystery[k] of the woman and of the
beast she rides, which has the seven
heads and ten horns.[l] 8The beast, which
you saw, once was, now is not, and will
come up out of the Abyss[m] and go to his
destruction.[n] The inhabitants of the
earth[o] whose names have not been written in the book of life[p] from the creation
of the world will be astonished[q] when
they see the beast, because he once was,
now is not, and yet will come.

9"This calls for a mind with wisdom.[r]
The seven heads[s] are seven hills on
which the woman sits. 10They are also
seven kings. Five have fallen, one is, the
other has not yet come; but when he
does come, he must remain for a little
while. 11The beast who once was, and
now is not,[t] is an eighth king. He belongs to the seven and is going to his destruction.

12"The ten horns[u] you saw are ten
kings who have not yet received a kingdom, but who for one hour[v] will receive
authority as kings along with the beast.
13They have one purpose and will give
their power and authority to the beast.[w]
14They will make war[x] against the Lamb,
but the Lamb will overcome[y] them
because he is Lord of lords and
King of kings[z]—and with him will
be his called, chosen[a] and faithful
followers."

15Then the angel said to me, "The waters[b] you saw, where the prostitute sits,
are peoples, multitudes, nations and languages.[c] 16The beast and the ten horns[d]
you saw will hate the prostitute.[e] They
will bring her to ruin[f] and leave her naked;[g] they will eat her flesh[h] and burn
her with fire.[i] 17For God has put it into
their hearts[j] to accomplish his purpose
by agreeing to give the beast their power
to rule,[k] until God's words are fulfilled.[l]
18The woman you saw is the great
city[m] that rules over the kings of the
earth."

17:6 [j]Rev 16:6; 18:24
17:7 [k]ver 5 [l]ver 3; S Rev 12:3
17:8 [m]S Lk 8:31 [n]Rev 13:10 [o]S Rev 3:10 [p]S Rev 20:12 [q]Rev 13:3
17:9 [r]Rev 13:18 [s]ver 3
17:11 [t]ver 8
17:12 [u]S Rev 12:3 [v]Rev 18:10,17,19
17:13 [w]ver 17
17:14 [x]S Rev 16:14 [y]S Jn 16:33 [z]S 1Ti 6:15 [a]Mt 22:14
17:15 [b]ver 1; Isa 8:7; Jer 47:2 [c]S Rev 13:7
17:16 [d]S Rev 12:3 [e]ver 1 [f]Rev 18:17, 19 [g]Eze 16:37,39 [h]Rev 19:18 [i]Rev 18:8
17:17 [j]2Co 8:16 [k]ver 13 [l]Jer 39:16; Rev 10:7
17:18 [m]Rev 16:19; 18:10,18,19,21
18:1 [n]Rev 17:1 [o]Rev 10:1; 20:1 [p]Eze 43:2
18:2 [q]S Rev 14:8 [r]Rev 16:13 [s]Isa 13:21,22; 34:11,13-15; Jer 50:39; 51:37; Zep 2:14,15
18:3 [t]S Rev 14:8 [u]Rev 17:2 [v]ver 11, 15,23; Eze 27:9-25 [w]ver 7,9
18:4 [x]Isa 48:20; Jer 50:8; 51:6,9,45; 2Co 6:17 [y]Ge 19:15
18:5 [z]2Ch 28:9; Ezr 9:6; Jer 51:9 [a]Rev 16:19
18:6 [b]Ps 137:8; Jer 50:15,29 [c]Isa 40:2 [d]Rev 14:10; 16:19; 17:4
18:7 [e]Eze 28:2-8 [f]Ps 10:6; Isa 47:7,8; Zep 2:15
18:8 [g]ver 10; Isa 9:14; 47:9; Jer 50:31,32 [h]Rev 17:16
18:9 [i]ver 3; Rev 14:8; 17:2,4 [j]ver 3,7

Chapter 18

The Fall of Babylon

AFTER this I saw another angel[n] coming down from heaven.[o] He had
great authority, and the earth was illuminated by his splendor.[p] 2With a mighty
voice he shouted:

"Fallen! Fallen is Babylon the Great![q]
She has become a home for demons
and a haunt for every evil[t] spirit,[r]
a haunt for every unclean and
detestable bird.[s]
3For all the nations have drunk
the maddening wine of her
adulteries.[t]
The kings of the earth committed
adultery with her,[u]
and the merchants of the earth grew
rich[v] from her excessive
luxuries."[w]

4Then I heard another voice from heav-
en say:

"Come out of her, my people,[x]
so that you will not share in her
sins,
so that you will not receive any of
her plagues;[y]
5for her sins are piled up to heaven,[z]
and God has remembered[a] her
crimes.
6Give back to her as she has given;
pay her back[b] double[c] for what she
has done.
Mix her a double portion from her
own cup.[d]
7Give her as much torture and grief
as the glory and luxury she gave
herself.[e]
In her heart she boasts,
'I sit as queen; I am not a widow,
and I will never mourn.'[f]
8Therefore in one day[g] her plagues will
overtake her:
death, mourning and famine.
She will be consumed by fire,[h]
for mighty is the Lord God who
judges her.

9"When the kings of the earth who
committed adultery with her[i] and shared
her luxury[j] see the smoke of her burn-

[t]2 Greek *unclean*

our witness with courage. See note on 2:13.
17:14 JESUS CHRIST, King—No human political or military power has a chance against Christ. He will ultimately defeat all opposing forces and rule with His followers.
17:17 HISTORY, Judgment—See note on 13:5–10.
18:1–24 GOD, Judge—The judgment of God upon the wicked is certain. No nation, no matter how proud and powerful, can stand. God's people will yet be vindicated in their struggle with evil forces.
18:1–8 EVIL AND SUFFERING, Punishment—Evil empires which pride themselves in wealth, power, and luxury last only for a short time. God's people must not be deceived and seek to profit from or take pleasure in wicked, worldly power structures. God is mightier than all earthly powers. See note on 13:1–18.
18:9–20 CHRISTIAN ETHICS, Property Rights—The last days will reveal the nature of true wealth, leaving many in mourning because earthly treasures were the only wealth they knew. See note on 3:17–18.

ing,[k] they will weep and mourn over
her.[l] 10Terrified at her torment, they will
stand far off[m] and cry:

"'Woe! Woe, O great city,[n]
O Babylon, city of power!
In one hour[o] your doom has come!'

11"The merchants[p] of the earth will
weep and mourn[q] over her because no
one buys their cargoes any more[r] —
12cargoes of gold, silver, precious stones
and pearls; fine linen, purple, silk and
scarlet cloth; every sort of citron wood,
and articles of every kind made of ivory,
costly wood, bronze, iron and marble;[s]
13cargoes of cinnamon and spice, of incense, myrrh and frankincense, of wine
and olive oil, of fine flour and wheat; cattle and sheep; horses and carriages; and
bodies and souls of men.[t]
14"They will say, 'The fruit you longed
for is gone from you. All your riches and
splendor have vanished, never to be recovered.' 15The merchants who sold
these things and gained their wealth from
her[u] will stand far off,[v] terrified at her
torment. They will weep and mourn[w]
16and cry out:

"'Woe! Woe, O great city,[x]
dressed in fine linen, purple and
scarlet,
and glittering with gold, precious
stones and pearls![y]
17In one hour[z] such great wealth has
been brought to ruin!'[a]

"Every sea captain, and all who travel
by ship, the sailors, and all who earn their
living from the sea,[b] will stand far off.[c]
18When they see the smoke of her burning,[d] they will exclaim, 'Was there ever a
city like this great city[e]?'[f] 19They will
throw dust on their heads,[g] and with
weeping and mourning[h] cry out:

"'Woe! Woe, O great city,[i]
where all who had ships on the sea
became rich through her wealth!
In one hour she has been brought to
ruin![j]
20Rejoice over her, O heaven![k]
Rejoice, saints and apostles and
prophets!
God has judged her for the way she
treated you.'"[l]

21Then a mighty angel[m] picked up a
boulder the size of a large millstone and
threw it into the sea,[n] and said:

18:9 [k]ver 18; Rev 14:11; 19:3 [l]Jer 51:8; Eze 26:17,18
18:10 [m]ver 15,17 [n]ver 16,19 [o]ver 17; Rev 17:12
18:11 [p]Eze 27:27 [q]ver 15,19; Eze 27:31 [r]S ver 3
18:12 [s]Eze 27:12-22; Rev 17:4
18:13 [t]Eze 27:13; 1Ti 1:10
18:15 [u]S ver 3 [v]ver 10,17 [w]ver 11, 19; Eze 27:31
18:16 [x]ver 10,19 [y]Rev 17:4
18:17 [z]ver 10; Rev 17:12 [a]Rev 17:16 [b]Eze 27:28-30 [c]ver 10,15
18:18 [d]ver 9; Rev 19:3 [e]S Rev 17:18 [f]Eze 27:32; Rev 13:4
18:19 [g]Jos 7:6; La 2:10; Eze 27:30 [h]ver 11,15; Eze 27:31 [i]ver 10, 16; Rev 17:18 [j]Rev 17:16
18:20 [k]Jer 51:48; S Rev 12:12 [l]Rev 19:2
18:21 [m]Rev 5:2; 10:1 [n]Jer 51:63 [o]S Rev 17:18
18:22 [p]Isa 24:8; Eze 26:13 [q]Jer 25:10
18:23 [r]Jer 7:34; 16:9; 25:10 [s]ver 3; Isa 23:8 [t]Na 3:4
18:24 [u]Rev 16:6; 17:6 [v]Jer 51:49; Mt 23:35
19:1 [w]ver 6; Rev 11:15 [x]ver 3,4, 6 [y]Rev 7:10; 12:10 [z]Rev 4:11; 7:12
19:2 [a]Rev 16:7 [b]S Rev 17:1 [c]S Rev 6:10
19:3 [d]ver 1,4,6 [e]Isa 34:10; Rev 14:11
19:4 [f]S Rev 4:4 [g]S Rev 4:6 [h]S Rev 4:10 [i]ver 1, 3,6
19:5 [j]Ps 134:1 [k]ver 18; Ps 115:13; Rev 11:18; 13:16; 20:12

"With such violence
the great city[o] of Babylon will be
thrown down,
never to be found again.
22The music of harpists and musicians,
flute players and trumpeters,
will never be heard in you again.[p]
No workman of any trade
will ever be found in you again.
The sound of a millstone
will never be heard in you again.[q]
23The light of a lamp
will never shine in you again.
The voice of bridegroom and bride
will never be heard in you again.[r]
Your merchants were the world's great
men.[s]
By your magic spell[t] all the nations
were led astray.
24In her was found the blood of prophets
and of the saints,[u]
and of all who have been killed on
the earth."[v]

Chapter 19

Hallelujah!

AFTER this I heard what sounded like
the roar of a great multitude[w] in
heaven shouting:

"Hallelujah![x]
Salvation[y] and glory and power[z]
belong to our God,
2 for true and just are his judgments.[a]
He has condemned the great
prostitute[b]
who corrupted the earth by her
adulteries.
He has avenged on her the blood of his
servants."[c]

3And again they shouted:

"Hallelujah![d]
The smoke from her goes up for ever
and ever."[e]

4The twenty-four elders[f] and the four
living creatures[g] fell down[h] and worshiped God, who was seated on the
throne. And they cried:

"Amen, Hallelujah!"[i]

5Then a voice came from the throne,
saying:

"Praise our God,
all you his servants,[j]
you who fear him,
both small and great!"[k]

18:20 SALVATION, Joy—Keeping God with us brings victory over all our foes. All of God's people can rejoice that no power in earth or heaven can overcome Him, or us in Him (Mt 28:18). God and His people will win in the end.

19:1–8 GOD, Sovereignty—God's sovereignty brings forth our praise because He will make Himself known by saving His people and pouring out His wrath on His enemies. All of this brings glory to God. Glory is the true disclosure, or recognition, of what He is.

6Then I heard what sounded like a great multitude,[l] like the roar of rushing waters[m] and like loud peals of thunder, shouting:

"Hallelujah![n]
For our Lord God Almighty[o]
reigns.[p]
7Let us rejoice and be glad
and give him glory![q]
For the wedding of the Lamb[r] has
come,
and his bride[s] has made herself
ready.
8Fine linen,[t] bright and clean,
was given her to wear."

(Fine linen stands for the righteous acts[u] of the saints.)

9Then the angel said to me,[v] "Write:[w] 'Blessed are those who are invited to the wedding supper of the Lamb!'"[x] And he added, "These are the true words of God."[y]

10At this I fell at his feet to worship him.[z] But he said to me, "Do not do it! I am a fellow servant with you and with your brothers who hold to the testimony of Jesus. Worship God![a] For the testimony of Jesus[b] is the spirit of prophecy."

The Rider on the White Horse

11I saw heaven standing open[c] and there before me was a white horse, whose rider[d] is called Faithful and True.[e] With justice he judges and makes war.[f] 12His eyes are like blazing fire,[g] and on his head are many crowns.[h] He has a name written on him[i] that no one knows but he himself.[j] 13He is dressed in a robe dipped in blood,[k] and his name is the Word of God.[l] 14The armies of heaven were following him, riding on white horses and dressed in fine linen,[m] white[n] and clean. 15Out of his mouth comes a sharp sword[o] with which to strike down[p] the nations. "He will rule them with an iron scepter."[u][q] He treads the winepress[r] of the fury of the wrath of God Almighty. 16On his robe and on his thigh he has this name written:[s]

KING OF KINGS AND LORD OF LORDS.[t]

17And I saw an angel standing in the sun, who cried in a loud voice to all the birds[u] flying in midair,[v] "Come,[w] gather together for the great supper of God,[x] 18so that you may eat the flesh of kings, generals, and mighty men, of horses and their riders, and the flesh of all people,[y] free and slave,[z] small and great."[a]

19Then I saw the beast[b] and the kings of the earth[c] and their armies gathered together to make war against the rider on the horse[d] and his army. 20But the beast was captured, and with him the false prophet[e] who had performed the miraculous signs[f] on his behalf.[g] With these signs he had deluded[h] those who had received the mark of the beast[i] and worshiped his image.[j] The two of them were thrown alive into the fiery lake[k] of burning sulfur.[l] 21The rest of them were killed with the sword[m] that came out of the mouth of the rider on the horse,[n] and all the birds[o] gorged themselves on their flesh.

19:6 [l]ver 1; Rev 11:15 [m]S Rev 1:15 [n]ver 1,3,4 [o]S Rev 1:8 [p]Rev 11:15 **19:7** [q]S Rev 11:13 [r]ver 9; Mt 22:2; 25:10; Eph 5:32 [s]Rev 21:2,9; 22:17 **19:8** [t]ver 14; Rev 15:6 [u]Isa 61:10; Eze 44:17; Zec 3:4; Rev 15:4 **19:9** [v]ver 10 [w]Rev 1:19 [x]Lk 14:15 [y]Rev 21:5; 22:6 **19:10** [z]Rev 22:8 [a]Ac 10:25,26; Rev 22:9 [b]S Rev 1:2 **19:11** [c]S Mt 3:16 [d]ver 19,21; Rev 6:2 [e]Rev 3:14 [f]Ex 15:3; Ps 96:13; Isa 11:4 **19:12** [g]S Rev 1:14 [h]Rev 6:2; 12:3 [i]ver 16 [j]S Rev 2:17 **19:13** [k]Isa 63:2,3 [l]Jn 1:1 **19:14** [m]ver 8 [n]S Rev 3:4 **19:15** [o]ver 21; S Rev 1:16 [p]Isa 11:4; 2Th 2:8 [q]Ps 2:9; Rev 2:27; 12:5 [r]S Rev 14:20 **19:16** [s]ver 12 [t]S 1Ti 6:15 **19:17** [u]ver 21 [v]Rev 8:13; 14:6 [w]Jer 12:9; Eze 39:17 [x]Isa 34:6; Jer 46:10 **19:18** [y]Eze 39:18-20 [z]Rev 6:15 [a]S ver 5 **19:19** [b]S Rev 13:1 [c]Rev 16:14,16 [d]ver 11,21 **19:20** [e]Rev 16:13 [f]S Mt 24:24 [g]Rev 13:12 [h]Rev 13:14 [i]Rev 13:16 [j]Rev 13:15 [k]Da 7:11; Rev 20:10,14,15; 21:8 [l]S Rev 9:17 **19:21** [m]ver 15; S Rev 1:16 [n]ver 11,19 [o]ver 17

[u]*15* Psalm 2:9

19:6–9 LAST THINGS, Church's Consummation—The figure of marriage is used in both Testaments to describe God's relation to His people (Hos 2:19–21; Eph 5:25–27). The consummation of the church as the bride of Christ will involve the completion of individual salvation and resultant corporate righteousness of the body, the church. Eternal union with Christ is the church's destiny and hope.

19:7–9 THE CHURCH, Bride—See note on 21:2. The marital relationship is sharply focused to describe the church. The bride makes herself ready for the coming of the Lamb (Christ) for the marriage. The church prepares for the wedding by witnessing, by right living, and by those actions which please the Lamb. The church must remain morally pure as it waits for the bridegroom's appearance.

19:9–10 REVELATION, Angels—The messengers of God revealed the true words of God about the future. They declared as fortunate all those who are invited to Christ's wedding supper (salvation feast). The early church was very confused about the disclosures of this book, unsure as to whether the predictions referred to the immediate situation in Israel then and the fall of Jerusalem which took place in AD 70, or whether the description was for the end of all time. Scholars still differ on which passages reveal which. One thing is certain: the revelation affirms that God is in control over all and that His children, as believers, are to be saved into life eternal by the power of Jesus Christ. Only God deserves worship. Angels do not.

19:10 PRAYER, Worship—Worship belongs only to God. None of the heavenly hosts deserve worship, nor can they mediate our prayers. We pray to God alone, and He hears our prayers.

19:10 EVANGELISM, Testimony—We are mere human beings, deserving no reverence. Nor do angels themselves deserve such. We worship and revere God alone and bear testimony to Him and His holy glory and redemptive grace. Yet that testimony of Jesus and His power to save glorifies God and goes out to a needy world as the real spirit of proclamation. Share it for God's glory and the salvation of others.

19:11—22:21 JESUS CHRIST, Final Coming—The concluding part of the Bible speaks of the concluding events of our world. This last section of the Bible uses previous biblical language to describe Christ's final victory. Christ will ride to victory, punishing His enemies and finally establishing His rule over all creation. Satan will be finally defeated. Jesus will rule with His faithful people and will judge the dead. Unbelievers will be punished, while believers will live eternally in the New Jerusalem. God's church can depend on God's promise. Jesus Christ will come soon. The pure and the faithful will receive His rewards.

19:20 MIRACLE, Evil—Not all "signs" are healing symbols. Here a false prophet had performed and interpreted signs. He had "deluded" the worshipers of the beast. The signs were not indications of redemption, but of destruction. See note on 16:14,21.

Chapter 20

The Thousand Years

AND I saw an angel coming down out of
heaven,[p] having the key[q] to the
Abyss[r] and holding in his hand a great
chain. 2He seized the dragon, that ancient
serpent, who is the devil, or Satan,[s] and
bound him for a thousand years.[t] 3He
threw him into the Abyss,[u] and locked
and sealed[v] it over him, to keep him
from deceiving the nations[w] anymore until the thousand years were ended. After
that, he must be set free for a short time.
4I saw thrones[x] on which were seated
those who had been given authority to
judge.[y] And I saw the souls of those who
had been beheaded[z] because of their testimony for Jesus[a] and because of the
word of God.[b] They had not worshiped
the beast[c] or his image and had not received his mark on their foreheads or
their hands.[d] They came to life and
reigned[e] with Christ a thousand years.
5(The rest of the dead did not come to life
until the thousand years were ended.)
This is the first resurrection.[f] 6Blessed[g]
and holy are those who have part in the
first resurrection. The second death[h] has
no power over them, but they will be
priests[i] of God and of Christ and will
reign with him[j] for a thousand years.

Satan's Doom

7When the thousand years are over,[k]
Satan will be released from his prison
8and will go out to deceive the nations[l]
in the four corners of the earth[m]—Gog
and Magog[n]—to gather them for battle.[o]
In number they are like the sand on the
seashore.[p] 9They marched across the
breadth of the earth and surrounded[q] the
camp of God's people, the city he loves.[r]
But fire came down from heaven[s] and
devoured them. 10And the devil, who deceived them,[t] was thrown into the lake
of burning sulfur,[u] where the beast[v] and

20:1 [p]Rev 10:1; 18:1 [q]Rev 1:18 [r]S Lk 8:31 **20:2** [s]S Mt 4:10 [t]Isa 24:22; S 2Pe 2:4 **20:3** [u]ver 1 [v]Da 6:17; Mt 27:66 [w]ver 8,10; Rev 12:9 **20:4** [x]Da 7:9 [y]Mt 19:28; Rev 3:21 [z]Rev 6:9 [a]S Rev 1:2 [b]S Heb 4:12 [c]S Rev 13:12 [d]S Rev 13:16 [e]ver 6; Rev 22:5 **20:5** [f]ver 6; Lk 14:14; Php 3:11; 1Th 4:16 **20:6** [g]Rev 14:13 [h]S Rev 2:11 [i]S 1Pe 2:5 [j]ver 4; Rev 22:5 **20:7** [k]ver 2 **20:8** [l]ver 3,10; Rev 12:9 [m]Isa 11:12; Eze 7:2; Rev 7:1 [n]Eze 38:2; 39:1 [o]S Rev 16:14 [p]Eze 38:9,15; Heb 11:12 **20:9** [q]Eze 38:9,16 [r]Ps 87:2 [s]Eze 38:22; 39:6; S Rev 13:13

20:10 [t]ver 3,8; Rev 12:9; 19:20 [u]S Rev 9:17 [v]Rev 16:13

20:1–10 EVIL AND SUFFERING, Satan—At the climax of history Satan will be defeated and eternally punished. Satan is a loser whom no one should be foolish enough to follow. Those who do not follow Satan and his beastly forces can look forward to special rewards.

20:1–6 LAST THINGS, Millennium—By way of Latin the term millennium has been employed to refer to the thousand years mentioned five times in this passage and once in the verse following it. The meaning of the thousand years and their relation to Christ's second coming have given rise to various millennial views. The details of these views reach far beyond the mere interpretation of this passage. See Introduction to Revelation, pp. 1630–1634; Chart of Millennial Views, facing p. 1634. Four millennial views have been espoused in recent times—amillennialism, postmillennialism, dispensational premillennialism, and historic premillennialism. Each represents a system of biblical interpretation that involves more than end time events. These views represent varying ways of interpreting Scripture. The prefixes suggest the general stance of each position as it relates to the doctrine of last things. Amillennialism avoids literalism in interpreting the thousand years by seeing it as a symbolic expression that refers either to the spiritual blessedness of present believers or the heavenly blessedness of those who through death are in heaven awaiting Christ's return. It points to one resurrection when all people will be judged, marking the end of history. Postmillennialism understands the Bible to teach the gradual growth of the gospel which will cause the world to become increasingly better until the present order merges into a kingdom of righteousness over which Christ will then return to rule. Thus the return of Christ occurs after (post-) the millennial kingdom established by gospel preaching (Mt 24:14). Premillennialism takes the millennium to be a literal future period during which Christ, following His second coming, will reign with the church on the earth. It will be a time of peace and righteousness with Satan bound and powerless to interfere. This general view takes two distinct forms. Dispensational premillennialism understands the millennium to be literally one thousand years in duration. It is preceded by a seven-year period of tribulation, at the end of which Christ will return in glory with His saints to usher in the millennium after decisively defeating the antichrist and binding Satan. Historic premillennialism holds to a literal tribulation period and millennium, but some allow symbolism in the number of years associated with each. Two major differences with dispensationalism are: (1) Christ's return is not seen to occur in two phases, (a rapture and then a return), but in a single occurrence which follows the tribulation and results in the establishment of the millennial reign; (2) Some dispensationalists believe Christ intended to establish the millennial kingdom at His first coming but could not because of unbelief, at which time He instituted the church age. All dispensationalists believe that after the rapture of the church and the tribulation Christ will establish that kingdom by force. Historical premillennialists insist that Christ's death, resurrection, and establishment of the church, along with salvation by grace through faith, has always been God's primary plan, and the future kingdom will not revert back to the Old Testament form with its legalism. They do not believe Old Testament prophecies about the Jewish nation are related to the millennium. Variations of opinion arise from different ways of interpreting key biblical texts. Each view is held by people who believe the Bible and seek to follow its teachings. We may not settle these differences of interpretation until Christ returns.

20:4–5 LAST THINGS, Believers' Resurrection—This is a basic passage for the discussion of two resurrections as held by some premillennial interpretations. It may point to a special privilege for believers who sacrifice their lives for Christ (martyrs) and participate in the millennial reign. It may be a symbolic assurance that Christ's victory is greater than the brief triumphs of worldly powers who kill believers. It may point to a first resurrection of believers before the millennium and a second resurrection of unbelievers afterwards. See note on Jn 5:25–29.

20:4 EVANGELISM, Persecution—Persecution comes. We may even be called to surrender our lives for Jesus' sake as we faithfully bear our testimony. In the final accounting the faithful will reign with Christ (Ro 8:18). To bear up and keep one's testimony alive for Jesus will result in glory and also in the salvation of others. See note on 2:13.

20:7–10 LAST THINGS, Satan's Defeat—The age-long adversary of humanity faces eschatological defeat. The principle of defeat was accomplished at the cross (Heb 2:14). The preliminary manifestation of the defeat is seen in the binding of Satan for one thousand years (Rev 20:2–3). The final establishment of the eternal order is preceded by the endless confinement and torment of Satan in the lake of fire. Such an end was announced in embryonic form in the prophetic word of Ge 3:15 and reaffirmed by Jesus in Jn 12:31. Those interpreters who look for a literal thousand year reign find here a description of international rebellion led by Satan against the political kingdom of Christ. Some would identify this period of temptation with the tribulation.

the false prophet[w] had been thrown.
They will be tormented day and night for
ever and ever.[x]

The Dead Are Judged

11Then I saw a great white throne[y]
and him who was seated on it. Earth and
sky fled from his presence,[z] and there
was no place for them. 12And I saw the
dead, great and small,[a] standing before
the throne, and books were opened.[b] Another book was opened, which is the
book of life.[c] The dead were judged[d] according to what they had done[e] as recorded in the books. 13The sea gave up
the dead that were in it, and death and
Hades[f] gave up the dead[g] that were in
them, and each person was judged according to what he had done.[h] 14Then
death[i] and Hades[j] were thrown into the
lake of fire.[k] The lake of fire is the second death.[l] 15If anyone's name was not
found written in the book of life,[m] he was
thrown into the lake of fire.

20:10 [w]Rev 16:13 [x]Rev 14:10,11
20:11 [y]S Rev 4:2 [z]S Rev 6:14
20:12 [a]S Rev 19:5 [b]Da 7:10 [c]ver 15; Ex 32:32; Dt 29:20; Da 12:1; Mal 3:16; Lk 10:20; Rev 3:5; 21:27 [d]Rev 11:18 [e]Jer 17:10; S Mt 16:27
20:13 [f]Rev 1:18; 6:8 [g]Isa 26:19 [h]S Mt 16:27
20:14 [i]1Co 15:26 [j]ver 13 [k]S Rev 19:20 [l]S Rev 2:11
20:15 [m]S ver 12
21:1 [n]S 2Pe 3:13 [o]S Rev 6:14
21:2 [p]ver 10; Ne 11:18; Isa 52:1; Rev 11:2; 22:19 [q]ver 10; Heb 11:10; 12:22; Rev 3:12 [r]S Rev 19:7
21:3 [s]Ex 25:8; 2Ch 6:18; Eze 48:35; Zec 2:10 [t]S 2Co 6:16
21:4 [u]S Rev 7:17 [v]Isa 25:8; 1Co 15:26; Rev 20:14

Chapter 21

The New Jerusalem

THEN I saw a new heaven and a new
earth,[n] for the first heaven and the
first earth had passed away,[o] and there
was no longer any sea. 2I saw the Holy
City,[p] the new Jerusalem, coming down
out of heaven from God,[q] prepared as a
bride[r] beautifully dressed for her husband. 3And I heard a loud voice from the
throne saying, "Now the dwelling of God
is with men, and he will live with them.[s]
They will be his people, and God himself
will be with them and be their God.[t] 4He
will wipe every tear from their eyes.[u]
There will be no more death[v] or mourn-

20:11 CHRISTIAN ETHICS, Righteousness—The last judgment will reveal our true righteousness. All our deeds will lay open before God as He judges us.

20:11–15 LAST THINGS, Unbelievers' Resurrection—Many interpreters believe Scripture teaches only one general judgment of all persons, while dispensationalists see evidences for separate judgments for the righteous and the unrighteous, with this passage referring to the second of these. See notes on Mt 25:31–46; 2 Co 5:10. One's interpretation of this passage is based partly on whether Hades is seen to refer to the general realm of the dead or the realm of the wicked dead and whether the book of life is seen to imply the presence of believers, who alone would be found in it, or suggests a sort of double verification of the eternal punishment meted out to unbelievers, whose names are absent from it. All interpreters agree that all persons will be judged. See notes on Rev 20:4–5; Jn 5:25–29.

20:12–13 HUMANITY, Death—God has revealed that physical death is not the end of life. All the dead shall be called before God to give an account of their lives on earth. Death itself will be destroyed, but those not belonging to God's people will suffer the horrors of death forever, the second death.

20:12 REVELATION, Author of Life—God will reveal Himself to all people in the judgment. The dead will appear before God on His throne to give account of their actions. Deeds, recorded throughout their lives, will be revealed. All will be judged according to the records of their daily living, known always to God.

20:14 LAST THINGS, Hell—The second death is identified with the lake of fire. It is thus a synonym for hell. It is second death in that it involves a final separation from God. All people die once. The wicked die a second time with no hope. See notes on Mt 25:31–46; Heb 9:27–28.

21:1–3 CREATION, New Creation—God originally created the earth to be home for humans. Sin, however, entered and changed it into a place of rebellion and alienation from God. The Bible tells how God has been working throughout history to effect a total reversal of this terrible consequence sin brought. With the first coming of Christ, sin was defeated through the atonement and resurrection. At His second coming, the new creation will be revealed. We are to work for the world's improvement, but the task will never be completed until God intervenes miraculously to transform the earth into a heavenly place. Whether God eliminates completely the old or renovates it to form the new is debated by Bible students. The hope for our present created world is that God will make it a new one where He can and will dwell forever with His creation.

21:1–8 EVIL AND SUFFERING, God's Future Help—In the new heaven and earth God will eliminate all suffering (7:16). The limitations and problems of this life will disappear in the new order.

21:1–4 HISTORY, Eternal—History on this earth will end. That is God's plan. A new arena of existence with God will be fully revealed. The sorrows and frustrations of historical life as we know it will vanish, replaced by God's personal, loving presence.

21:1–5 LAST THINGS, Heaven—Out of the new heaven comes a new city, the eternal abode of the redeemed, where God lives with His saints. Heaven will erase five of the sad aspects of human experience: tears, death, mourning, crying, and pain. See note on 6:1—19:21. All things will be made new.

21:1 LAST THINGS, Creation's Redemption—The final vision of the age to come is told in terms of a new heaven and a new earth. Newness is the ultimate expression of the full accomplishment of redemption. As applied to heaven and earth, the newness means total liberation from the bondage to sin and decay. Whether this is correctly interpreted as being a cosmological change, a spiritual change, or both, the new heaven and earth express an eschatological newness that will be accomplished only by the victory of Christ. The new creation is God's environmental provision for the final redemption of humans. See note on Ro 8:18–23.

21:2 THE CHURCH, Bride—Several New Testament writers use the marital relationship as a figure of the relationship between Christ and His church. Most of these occurrences appear in Revelation (19:7,9; 21:9; 22:17). Ephesians 5:24–33 and 2 Co 11:1–6 also refer to the image of the church as the bride of Christ. John the Baptist identified the Messiah with the bridegroom (Jn 3:29). The Book of Revelation contains the highest conception of the church as the bride. The bride is associated with the new Jerusalem which comes from heaven. The imagery of the bride suggests purity and faithfulness, as well as eager longing for the wedding day.

21:3–7 GOD, Father—These gentle, tender words set forth God's nature as Father. He has planned the day when He can be with us personally and remove every reason for tears. That will be a new day. This picture of God stands in sharp contrast to the picture of the sovereign God shown moving in furious wrath in the preceding chapters. Both are true pictures of God. God is a gentle, loving Father to those who will accept Him in faith. He is also a mighty Destroyer to those who oppose Him. Remember that God Himself says He prefers to be gracious and merciful rather than harsh (Ex 20:4–6), for the deepest word that is said about God is that He is love. See notes on Jn 3:16; 1 Jn 4:7–21.

21:3 THE CHURCH, Covenant People—God's covenant

ing or crying or pain,[w] for the old order of
things has passed away."[x]
5He who was seated on the throne[y]
said, "I am making everything
new!"[z] Then he said, "Write this down,
for these words are trustworthy and
true."[a]
6He said to me: "It is done.[b] I am the
Alpha and the Omega,[c] the Beginning
and the End. To him who is thirsty I will
give to drink without cost[d] from the
spring of the water of life.[e] 7He who
overcomes[f] will inherit all this, and I
will be his God and he will be my son.[g]
8But the cowardly, the unbelieving, the
vile, the murderers, the sexually immoral, those who practice magic arts, the
idolaters and all liars[h]—their place will
be in the fiery lake of burning sulfur.[i]
This is the second death."[j]
9One of the seven angels who had the
seven bowls full of the seven last
plagues[k] came and said to me, "Come, I
will show you the bride,[l] the wife of the
Lamb." 10And he carried me away[m] in
the Spirit[n] to a mountain great and high,
and showed me the Holy City, Jerusalem,
coming down out of heaven from God.[o]
11It shone with the glory of God,[p] and its
brilliance was like that of a very precious
jewel, like a jasper,[q] clear as crystal.[r]
12It had a great, high wall with twelve
gates,[s] and with twelve angels at the
gates. On the gates were written the
names of the twelve tribes of Israel.[t]
13There were three gates on the east,
three on the north, three on the south
and three on the west. 14The wall of the
city had twelve foundations,[u] and on
them were the names of the twelve apostles[v] of the Lamb.
15The angel who talked with me had a
measuring rod[w] of gold to measure the
city, its gates[x] and its walls. 16The city
was laid out like a square, as long as it
was wide. He measured the city with the
rod and found it to be 12,000 stadia[v] in
length, and as wide and high as it is long.
17He measured its wall and it was 144
cubits[w] thick,[x] by man's[y] measurement,
which the angel was using. 18The wall
was made of jasper,[z] and the city of pure
gold, as pure as glass.[a] 19The foundations
of the city walls were decorated with every kind of precious stone.[b] The first
foundation was jasper,[c] the second sapphire, the third chalcedony, the fourth
emerald, 20the fifth sardonyx, the sixth
carnelian,[d] the seventh chrysolite, the
eighth beryl, the ninth topaz, the tenth
chrysoprase, the eleventh jacinth, and
the twelfth amethyst.[y] 21The twelve
gates[e] were twelve pearls,[f] each gate
made of a single pearl. The great street of
the city was of pure gold, like transparent
glass.[g]
22I did not see a temple[h] in the city,
because the Lord God Almighty[i] and the
Lamb[j] are its temple. 23The city does not
need the sun or the moon to shine on it,
for the glory of God[k] gives it light,[l] and
the Lamb[m] is its lamp. 24The nations will
walk by its light, and the kings of the
earth will bring their splendor into it.[n]

21:4 [w]Isa 35:10; 65:19 [x]S 2Co 5:17
21:5 [y]Rev 4:9; 20:11 [z]ver 4 [a]Rev 19:9; 22:6
21:6 [b]Rev 16:17 [c]Rev 1:8; 22:13 [d]Isa 55:1 [e]S Jn 4:10
21:7 [f]S Jn 16:33 [g]ver 3; 2Sa 7:14; 2Co 6:16; S Ro 8:14
21:8 [h]ver 27; Ps 5:6; 1Co 6:9; Heb 12:14; Rev 22:15 [i]S Rev 9:17 [j]S Rev 2:11
21:9 [k]S Rev 15:1,6,7 [l]S Rev 19:7
21:10 [m]Eze 40:2; Rev 17:3 [n]S Rev 1:10 [o]S ver 2
21:11 [p]ver 23; Isa 60:1,2; Eze 43:2; Rev 15:8; 22:5 [q]ver 18,19; Rev 4:3 [r]Rev 4:6
21:12 [s]ver 15,21,25; Rev 22:14 [t]Eze 48:30-34
21:14 [u]S Eph 2:20; Heb 11:10 [v]Ac 1:26; Eph 2:20
21:15 [w]Eze 40:3; Rev 11:1 [x]S ver 12
21:17 [y]Rev 13:18
21:18 [z]S ver 11 [a]ver 21
21:19 [b]Ex 28:17-20; Isa 54:11,12; Eze 28:13 [c]S ver 11
21:20 [d]Rev 4:3
21:21 [e]S ver 12 [f]Isa 54:12 [g]ver 18
21:22 [h]Jn 4:21,23 [i]S Rev 1:8 [j]S Rev 5:6
21:23 [k]S ver 11 [l]Isa 24:23; 60:19,20; Rev 22:5 [m]S Rev 5:6
21:24 [n]ver 26; Isa 60:3,5

[v] *16* That is, about 1,400 miles (about 2,200 kilometers) [w] *17* That is, about 200 feet (about 65 meters) [x] *17* Or *high* [y] *20* The precise identification of some of these precious stones is uncertain.

purpose will be fulfilled one day. He will be God for His people without any competitors. They will be absolutely committed to Him. God's presence will be fully known. See note on Jer 30:22.

21:4 HUMANITY, Death—Death, begun by the sin of humanity, will be fully and completely defeated by God. This is the result of God's redemptive activity through Jesus Christ. With the passing of death, there shall also be the passing of grief and sorrow. The redeemed will finally have become what God intends for His people.

21:6 GOD, Sovereignty—The eternal God has always and will always have ultimate control over our world. He wants to use His power to meet our basic needs, not to destroy us. The precious promise of salvation rests on God's sovereign authority and power.

21:6 SALVATION, Definition—God our Savior is the beginning and the end of our salvation. He continues to offer His salvation freely to all who thirst for the water of eternal life.

21:7 THE CHURCH, Covenant People—The Christian church is an enduring, overcoming people. One day problems and persecution will be behind. The true Father-child relationship will be a reality. God's enduring people will receive their inheritance. See note on Eze 36:28.

21:8 CHRISTIAN ETHICS, Murder—Murder leads to eternal judgment, punishment, and separation from God. So do lying and immorality. At the judgment God looks for obedient ones.

21:8 LAST THINGS, Hell—Amid the blessings of heaven is a reminder of the horrors of hell. The horror consists in the types of sinners to be found there, the torment of fire and brimstone, and the final or second death from which there is no escape to life. See note on 20:14.

21:9—22:15 LAST THINGS, Heaven—The city of God possesses the glory of God. Its beauties and perfections are described in symbolic language such as defies total translation into prosaic literalness. The force of this passage is perhaps found more in its overall impact and impression than in its details, though each detail can be seen to have a precious meaning. The centrality of Christ the Lamb is unmistakable. The purity of heaven is guaranteed by the prohibition against anything entering that would defile its holiness.

21:9 THE CHURCH, Bride—See note on 21:2.

21:10 REVELATION, Visions—The King of life took His messenger and showed the future of life in the full reign and control of God. John was allowed to witness a new creation, made perfect by God, designed and working as He intended life and community to be, redeemed from imperfection and sin, and subject to Him. God revealed to His prophet the quality of eternal life and its nature.

21:11,23 GOD, Glory—The glory of God is the expression, or the perception, of what God is, and who God is. Glory represents the shining radiance which makes all other sources of light totally dark in comparison. In the Holy City to come, God will be fully disclosed to His people who shall know Him in the full radiance of His glory.

25On no day will its gates[o] ever be shut,[p]
for there will be no night there.[q] 26The
glory and honor of the nations will be
brought into it.[r] 27Nothing impure will
ever enter it, nor will anyone who does
what is shameful or deceitful,[s] but only
those whose names are written in the
Lamb's book of life.[t]

Chapter 22

The River of Life

THEN the angel showed me the river[u]
of the water of life,[v] as clear as crystal,[w] flowing[x] from the throne of God
and of the Lamb 2down the middle of the
great street of the city. On each side of
the river stood the tree of life,[y] bearing
twelve crops of fruit, yielding its fruit every month. And the leaves of the tree are
for the healing of the nations.[z] 3No longer will there be any curse.[a] The throne
of God and of the Lamb will be in the
city, and his servants will serve him.[b]
4They will see his face,[c] and his name
will be on their foreheads.[d] 5There will
be no more night.[e] They will not need
the light of a lamp or the light of the sun,
for the Lord God will give them light.[f]
And they will reign for ever and ever.[g]
6The angel said to me,[h] "These words
are trustworthy and true.[i] The Lord, the
God of the spirits of the prophets,[j] sent
his angel[k] to show his servants the
things that must soon take place."

Jesus Is Coming

7"Behold, I am coming soon![l]
Blessed[m] is he who keeps the words of
the prophecy in this book."[n]

8I, John, am the one who heard and
saw these things.[o] And when I had heard
and seen them, I fell down to worship at
the feet[p] of the angel who had been
showing them to me. 9But he said to me,
"Do not do it! I am a fellow servant with
you and with your brothers the prophets
and of all who keep the words of this
book.[q] Worship God!"[r]

10Then he told me, "Do not seal up[s]
the words of the prophecy of this book,[t]
because the time is near.[u] 11Let him who
does wrong continue to do wrong; let
him who is vile continue to be vile; let
him who does right continue to do right;
and let him who is holy continue to be
holy."[v]

12"Behold, I am coming soon![w] My reward is with me,[x] and I will give to everyone according to what he has done.[y]
13I am the Alpha and the Omega,[z] the
First and the Last,[a] the Beginning and
the End.[b]

14"Blessed are those who wash their
robes,[c] that they may have the right to
the tree of life[d] and may go through the
gates[e] into the city.[f] 15Outside[g] are the
dogs,[h] those who practice magic arts, the
sexually immoral, the murderers, the
idolaters and everyone who loves and
practices falsehood.

16"I, Jesus,[i] have sent my angel[j] to
give you[z] this testimony for the
churches.[k] I am the Root[l] and the Offspring of David,[m] and the bright Morning
Star."[n]

17The Spirit[o] and the bride[p] say,
"Come!" And let him who hears say,

21:25 [o]S ver 12 [p]Isa 60:11 [q]Zec 14:7; Rev 22:5 **21:26** [r]ver 24 **21:27** [s]Isa 52:1; Joel 3:17; Rev 22:14,15 [t]S Rev 20:12 **22:1** [u]Ps 36:8; 46:4 [v]ver 17; S Jn 4:10 [w]Rev 4:6 [x]Eze 47:1; Zec 14:8 **22:2** [y]S Rev 2:7 [z]Eze 47:12 **22:3** [a]Zec 14:11 [b]Rev 7:15 **22:4** [c]S Mt 5:8 [d]S Rev 7:3 **22:5** [e]Rev 21:25; Zec 14:7 [f]Isa 60:19, 20; Rev 21:23 [g]Da 7:27; Rev 20:4 **22:6** [h]Rev 1:1 [i]Rev 21:5 [j]1Co 14:32; Heb 12:9 [k]ver 16; Rev 1:1 **22:7** [l]ver 12,20; S Mt 16:27 [m]Rev 1:3; 16:15 [n]ver 10,18,19 **22:8** [o]S Rev 1:1 [p]Rev 19:10 **22:9** [q]ver 10,18,19 [r]Rev 19:10 **22:10** [s]Da 8:26; Rev 10:4 [t]ver 7,18, 19 [u]S Ro 13:11 **22:11** [v]Eze 3:27; Da 12:10 **22:12** [w]ver 7,20; S Mt 16:27 [x]Isa 40:10; 62:11 [y]S Mt 16:27 **22:13** [z]Rev 1:8 [a]S Rev 1:17 [b]Rev 21:6 **22:14** [c]Rev 7:14 [d]S Rev 2:7 [e]S Rev 21:12 [f]S Rev 21:27 **22:15** [g]Dt 23:18; 1Co 6:9,10; Gal 5:19-21; Col 3:5,6; Rev 21:8 [h]Php 3:2 **22:16** [i]Rev 1:1 [j]ver 6 [k]Rev 1:4 [l]S Rev 5:5 [m]S Mt 1:1 [n]2Pe 1:19; Rev 2:28 **22:17** [o]Rev 2:7; 14:13 [p]S Rev 19:7

[z] *16* The Greek is plural.

21:27 SALVATION, Obedience—Only those who do the will of God will enter into the city of God, the new Jerusalem.
22:1 GOD, Sovereignty—The throne of God and of the Lamb speaks of the unchallenged sovereignty of God in the Holy City to come.
22:2 SALVATION, Healing—The leaves of the tree of life in the new Jerusalem are for the healing of the nations. Compare Eze 47:12. The healing ministry of the golden city will be adequate for every human hurt.
22:3 WORSHIP, Service—Worship and service are closely related. "His servants will serve him" could readily be translated "His servants will worship him." See notes on Mic 6:6–8; Mt 4:10.
22:6–7 HOLY SCRIPTURE, Authoritative—The messenger of God declared the revelations to be true and coming from God. Christ declared He would appear soon. Those who follow His revelations in this book are fortunate, for Christ is to appear to bring about all things. The sense of urgency in this comment, and Christ's subsequent delay, leaves readers aware that the Lord of life wants His children alert at all times and that time is different in God's mind and plans. See note on 1:1–3.
22:7,12,20 LAST THINGS, Return Promises—How fitting that the last chapter of Revelation should draw the inspired Scriptures to conclusion with a triple promise of Christ's return! Blessedness and reward attach to His coming. The record of God's redemptive revelation leaves the reader with the ringing announcement of the long hoped for return of Jesus.
22:8–9 PRAYER, Worship—See note on 19:10.
22:9 ELECTION, Worship—The elect are not to worship any supernatural being. Only God is worthy of honor, power, and majesty. No spiritual being in heaven can take the place of God. Only worship God. That will be the eternal privilege of the elect in heaven.
22:11 CHRISTIAN ETHICS, Righteousness—The call to repentance will one day cease. Human intentions to change will never have another chance to become reality. Thus apocalyptic calls us to repent and become holy like God before that day comes. In that day people will not suddenly become righteous. The holy will "continue to be holy."
22:13 JESUS CHRIST, God—While the claim "I am the Alpha and Omega" has come from God alone (1:8; 21:6), the close association of the Lamb (Jesus Christ) with God allows Christ to make such a claim.
22:16 JESUS CHRIST, Ascension—See note on 1:1.
22:16 THE CHURCH, Local Body—See notes 2:11; Ac 4:32.
22:17 HOLY SPIRIT, Intercedes—The church lives in expectancy. Jesus is coming soon (v 12). The Spirit joins the church (the bride) in praying to Jesus to come. It is a remarkable form of the Spirit's constantly reminding the church of Jesus that He prays and helps the church to pray for the return of the Lord. See note on Ro 8:25–27.

"Come!" Whoever is thirsty, let him
come; and whoever wishes, let him take
the free gift of the water of life.[q]

18 I warn everyone who hears the
words of the prophecy of this book:[r] If
anyone adds anything to them,[s] God will
add to him the plagues described in this
book.[t] 19 And if anyone takes words
away[u] from this book of prophecy,[v] God
will take away from him his share in the
tree of life[w] and in the holy city, which
are described in this book.

20 He who testifies to these things[x]
says, "Yes, I am coming soon."[y]

Amen. Come, Lord Jesus.[z]

21 The grace of the Lord Jesus be with
God's people.[a] Amen.

22:17 [q] S Jn 4:10
22:18 [r] ver 7,10,19 [s] Dt 4:2; 12:32; Pr 30:6 [t] Rev 15:6-16:21
22:19 [u] Dt 4:2; 12:32; Pr 30:6 [v] ver 7,10,18 [w] S Rev 2:7
22:20 [x] Rev 1:2 [y] ver 7,12; S Mt 16:27 [z] 1Co 16:22
22:21 [a] S Ro 16:20

22:17 THE CHURCH, Bride—See note on 21:2. The bride invites those who thirst to the water of life.

22:17 EVANGELISM, Call to Salvation—"Come" has been called God's favorite word. All in the Godhead—Father, Son, and Holy Spirit—urge people to come to salvation through Jesus Christ. We who have responded and have become Christians join in the divine invitation and cry to all, "Come." We thus engage in and with God Himself in the grand enterprise of world evangelization. What a glorious opportunity! What a wonderful challenge! What a divine work! Can we give it less than our very best?

22:17 MISSIONS, Nature—The missionary note running through the entire Bible appears also in this last chapter of Revelation. The short verse is a gold mine of information on the nature of missions. This message comes from the risen Christ, who is coming again soon (v 12). The center of the message is from the eternal One (v 13). The Holy Spirit's role in missions is crucial and extensive (Ac 1:8; 2:4; 3:8; 5:32; 6:10; 13:2; 16:6–7). Here His role is to draw people to Christ. He joins in issuing the invitation. This work is in keeping with the role of the Counselor Jesus described (Jn 14:13–16). On countless occasions when the missionary or the evangelist preaches Christ and shares the Word, the Holy Spirit comes and prepares the heart so that the Word bears fruit, and unsaved persons are converted. The church, Christ's bride, is also to join in the invitation. To be faithful to its calling, the church must go into the world to share Christ's invitation with people. The Spirit and the church are to invite people to Christ. When we hear and accept the message of Christ we become part of the church, so we also invite others to Christ. Our personal witness of what Christ has done in us is a powerful means of evangelism and missions. People who hear the missionary invitation must meet three conditions to receive God's gracious offer of salvation. They must recognize their need, symbolized by thirst; be willing to repent of sins; and turn to Christ (Ac 3:19–20). The old story is still good news. The invitation is open to everyone.

22:18–19 HOLY SCRIPTURE, Inspired—The God who breathed into each of His messengers the words of revelation declared that no one is to add to or take from the words of God. They are subject to God's intervention if they do. The revelation of God is not to be altered, tampered with, or distorted, for it is an extension of God Himself, even as Jesus Christ is the Word made flesh. The Book of Revelation is thus consciously presented as sacred Scripture (Dt 4:2; 12:32).

22:20–21 PRAYER, Petition—The last two verses in the Bible are prayers. The Christian church lives with the expectant prayer that the great hopes of Revelation will come to pass soon. The Bible's last words bless God's people of all ages with Christ's grace.

22:21 THE CHURCH, Saints—God's people are the saints. God's grace rests on us while we wait for God's final victory. See 1 Co 1:2.

STUDY HELPS

Table of Weights and Measures

WEIGHTS

BIBLICAL UNIT		APPROXIMATE AMERICAN EQUIVALENT		APPROXIMATE METRIC EQUIVALENT	
talent	*(60 minas)*	75	pounds	34	kilograms
mina	*(50 shekels)*	1 1/4	pounds	0.6	kilogram
shekel	*(2 bekas)*	2/5	ounce	11.5	grams
pim	*(2/3 shekel)*	1/3	ounce	7.6	grams
beka	*(10 gerahs)*	1/5	ounce	5.5	grams
gerah		1/50	ounce	0.6	gram

LENGTH

cubit		18	inches	0.5	meter
span		9	inches	23	centimeters
handbreadth		3	inches	8	centimeters

CAPACITY

Dry Measure

cor [homer]	*(10 ephahs)*	6	bushels	220	liters
lethek	*(5 ephahs)*	3	bushels	110	liters
ephah	*(10 omers)*	3/5	bushel	22	liters
seah	*(1/3 ephah)*	7	quarts	7.3	liters
omer	*(1/10 ephah)*	2	quarts	2	liters
cab	*(1/18 ephah)*	1	quart	1	liter

Liquid Measure

bath	*(1 ephah)*	6	gallons	22	liters
hin	*(1/6 bath)*	4	quarts	4	liters
log	*(1/72 bath)*	1/3	quart	0.3	liter

The figures of the table are calculated on the basis of a shekel equaling 11.5 grams, a cubit equaling 18 inches and an ephah equaling 22 liters. The quart referred to is either a dry quart (slightly larger than a liter) or a liquid quart (slightly smaller than a liter), whichever is applicable. The ton referred to in the footnotes is the American ton of 2,000 pounds.

This table is based upon the best available information, but it is not intended to be mathematically precise; like the measurement equivalents in the footnotes, it merely gives approximate amounts and distances. Weights and measures differed somewhat at various times and places in the ancient world. There is uncertainty particularly about the ephah and the bath; further discoveries may give more light on these units of capacity.

Doctrinal Study Helps

of God as Father is shown in His personal concern for all people, His protective watchcare over His people, and in redemption, nurture, and discipline in the lives of Christians.

God has distinctive qualities or attributes. Five of these attributes summarize what God is like: righteousness, love, wisdom, power, and presence.

God's righteousness expresses itself in many ways. He is the ultimate standard of right and wrong. He is faithful, constant, and unchanging in His character. He works for the right, seeking to extend righteousness and justice in the world. He defends the defenseless, helpless, the victimized, the oppressed. He opposes evil in expressions of wrath, anger, judgment, punishment, and jealousy. He sits in judgment on those who do evil.

God's love expresses itself in many ways. His love is coordinated perfectly with His righteousness. God's love is always righteous, and His righteousness is always marked by love. His love is the primary motivation of His being revealed in His actions (Jn 3:16; 1 Jn 4:8,16). God's love is expressed as His mercy in forgiving sinners and in rescuing or blessing those who do not deserve His attention. His love is expressed in grace, the love and power of God reaching to those who do not deserve His blessing. God's grace is shown in forgiveness, conversion, blessing, nurturing, and chastising of individual persons. God's grace creates a response of love, faith, and obedience in the hearts of people whom He is trying to reach. His grace also works in and through His servants to give them guidance and power as they seek to carry out His will.

The wisdom of God is His perfect awareness of what is happening in all of His creation at any given moment. It is also His knowledge of the final outcome of His creation and of how He will work from beginning to ending of human history. Sometimes this is called His omniscience.

The power of God is seen as His ability to accomplish His purposes and carry out His will in the world. He can do what needs to be done in any circumstances. This is sometimes called His omnipotence.

The presence of God in the world is such that He is not separated from any part of His creation. As spirit, God has the perfect capability of being present everywhere in His world at once. For this reason Jesus could promise His disciples He would be with them as they carried out the Great Commission (Mt 28:18-20). God's presence in the world is sometimes called His omnipresence.

God's adequacy to meet the needs of His people and accomplish His will is the underlying thought of the three attributes of wisdom, power, and presence. God is without external limit; that is, He has no limits except those He has set for Himself.

God works in His world. First, God is Creator. He brought the world and everything in it into existence. This is an expression of His sovereignty, wisdom, and power. It leaves us in awe at God's mighty act in creation.

Second, God is Redeemer. He makes salvation possible. He is a God of love, a saving kind of God. He sent forth His Son in the incarnation to complete His plan of redemption. God's work in redemption is related very closely to His work in creation. Salvation completes creation in carrying out the purposes of God and also leaves us in awe.

A third work of God in His world is His continuing involvement in the unfolding of human history. This is an expression of the sovereignty of God, His lordship over the world, sometimes called providence. God has not predetermined all of the events of history. He does work in human history, in ways that we do not necessarily see or understand, to accomplish His purposes. In doing this He fully respects the free will of people, coaxing rather than coercing them to do His will.

The consummation, or completion, of all things in human history and in the will of God is the fourth expression of the work of God. God will one day bring His purposes to fulfillment, bringing history to a close and ushering in eternity. Because God is sovereign, absolute Lord, He will accomplish His will in His world.

Summary of the Doctrine of Jesus Christ

Jesus Christ is the Messiah. He fulfilled God's promises and purposes for His people. Christ (Greek *christos*) translates Messiah (Hebrew *messias*). Messiah speaks of the expectations of the Hebrew Scripture that God would restore the fortunes of His people. John the Baptist was the new Elijah preaching in the wilderness and preparing the way for the Lord's Messiah. He pointed to Jesus as the expected Messiah (Mt 3:14; Jn 1:29-34). Properly interpreted, the Old Testament pointed to Jesus (Lk 24:45-47). God the Father testified to His Son (Lk 3:22; Jn 5:31-40). He was what God's people should have expected Messiah to be. He did what Scripture said Messiah would do. He was the Prophet like Moses (Dt 18:15-18; Jn 1:21; Ac 3:22; 7:37).

Jesus was a human led by the Spirit. He was born to a human mother through the Spirit (Mt 1:18; Lk 1:35). His human ancestry reached back to David, Abraham, and Adam (Mt 1:1-17; Lk 3:23-38). He grew and learned as a human, obeying His human parents (Lk 2:51-52). He knew human hunger, thirst, and pain. Led by the Spirit, He endured Satan's temptation (Lk 4:1-13). He died and was buried like all humans (Lk 23:44-56). He did not simply die a natural death. He was the victim of a ritual murder carried out by the authorities of Rome, engineered by the pious religious leaders of Jerusalem, but made necessary by the sins of all who ever lived. Jesus' humanity, including His sacrificial death, was a major stumbling block for Israel; but it was the way God determined to fulfill His eternal purpose of salvation and blessing.

Jesus was God in human flesh. Even the disciples had difficulty understanding who Jesus was. They had to look and remember back through the resurrection before they could confess fully who Jesus was. Then they understood the virgin birth in Bethlehem was not the beginning. He was God become flesh (Jn 1:14). He had existed before creation. Eternity began His story (Jn 1:1). The Son was eternal God just like the Father. Confessing Jesus' preexistence unites Him with God and with what God had been doing through Israel (Mt 1:1-17). It unites Him with the human race reaching back to Adam, the direct son of God (Lk 3:23-38). The deity of Christ is seen in His moral perfection, His holiness (Lk 4:1-13; Heb 4:15); in His unique miracles (Mk 1:21-45; in the divine authority of His teaching, (Mk 7:29; 9:6; 28:18; Lk 4:32). Jesus was thus the only true Son of God, a title connected to Jewish kings and messianic hopes (Ps 2) but used by Jesus to refer to His intimate personal relationship to the Father in total harmony and obedience (Mt 11:27; Jn 10:30; 14:9). The Son pleased the Father (Mk 1:11). The Son used the intimate family expression *Abba* to talk to the Father (Mk 14:36; Ro 8:15; Gal 4:6). The relationship of Father and Son is so intimate and close, Jesus can be called God (Jn 1:1; 20:28; Tit 2:13; 2 Pe 1:1). The Son is God's image and shares His characteristics (2 Co 4:4; Col 1:15-20; Heb 1:1-14). Believing hearts affirm Jesus is the clearest picture of God the world has ever seen. Christians see in this one proper name, Jesus, a conjunction of God and man. The preexistent heavenly Christ emptied Himself and became like us for our sake (Php 2:1-18). He is Immanuel, "God with us" (Mt 1:23).

The earliest Christian confession was "Jesus is Lord" (Ro 10:9). Lord (Hebrew *adonai*; Greek *kurios*) was the term used in reverence to address God when Jews quit pronouncing the holy name Yahweh. Lord shows Jesus' worth as equal to God. It shows our relationship to Him as His devoted servants. Why is He Lord? Because God exalted Him in the resurrection (Php 2:6-11). The fact of Jesus' resurrection grasped the early believers and helped them begin to understand the person of Christ. No other experience in any other religious movement is so well validated historically. No other religion can duplicate the powerful experience of the resurrection. It claimed the Christians' attention in an unforgettable way. No person before or since has seen an individual bring God's resurrection life to bear on humanity's most pressing problem—death. The resurrection of Jesus Christ is the event that unites all aspects of the Christian gospel, and Jesus Christ provides its firm foundation.

Jesus fulfilled God's purposes. Uniquely God and human, Jesus lived out God's saving will in human flesh. He performed the miracles of God's kingdom in our time and space. He healed all kinds of persons, a token of God's ultimate healing. He raised some from the dead, a token that He would bring God's resurrection life to all who would receive it. He cast out evil spirits as a preview of God's final shutting away of the evil one (Rev 20). He was Lord over wind, sea, and all of nature, indicating that by His power God was already beginning to create a new heaven and a new earth (Rev 21:1). The spectacular impact of His mighty works reinforced and called to mind the power of His teachings.

"No one ever spoke the way this man does" (Jn 7:46). His teachings were about the Father, what He wanted, what He was like, what He would do for His creation. Jesus' teachings required absolute obedience and love to God and the kingdom of God, which began in Jesus' ministry, but would not be culminated until Christ's final coming. Until that coming, Christians were to live in the world by the ethical injunctions He gave (Mt 5—7) and in the kind of love He had shown and commanded (Jn 14—16). To help earthly people understand heavenly things, He spoke in parables. These parables were from realistic, real-life settings. They were about the kingdom of God—what it was like, what was required to live in it, what was the meaning of life according to its teachings, and what the kingdom promised.

Jesus practiced what He preached. He was God's Suffering Servant (Isa 53) giving His life for His friends. The Jews looked for a political king to bring political freedom and power. They were surprised by a Servant who brought spiritual freedom and the way to eternal life. He lived up to His name, Jesus, which meant "he will save his people from their sins" (Mt 1:21). The Gospels tell the message of the Son of Man, He who was humbled, who suffered, who will come again. He embodied life's necessities and invites us to find in Him water (Jn 4:14); bread (Jn 6:41); light (Jn 8:12); life's gate (Jn 10:7); truth (Jn 14:6); resurrection and life (Jn 11:25). Thus He showed us the meaning of God's love by obediently walking the road to the cross to lay down His life according to the Father's will, thus completing the Father's eternal purpose of salvation.

Jesus provides salvation. Christ is the way to God. His way of being in the world was a way of obedience, faithfulness, and service. The earliest Christians saw who He was in what He did. In the great deed of the cross they saw the salvation of the world. The holy, perfect life placed Him in dramatic conflict with the evil all humanity has done. God gave Him over to death (Jn 3:16) but saved Him from physical decay (Ac 2:27). By this act Jesus became our Redeemer (Eph 1:7,14; Col 1:14; Tit 2:14; Heb 9:12), Savior (Jn 4:42; Ac 13:23; Eph 5:23; 1 Jn 4:14), the Lamb of God taking away our sins (Jn 1:29; Ac 8:32; 1 Co 5:7; 1 Pe 1:19; Rev 21:23,27). He is God's great and final High Priest, who both offers and is the sacrifice (Heb 7:1—8:13). Thus He makes atonement for our sins through His blood and puts us at one with God (Ro 3:25; Heb 2:17). Accepting His atoning work in repentance and faith gives us hope for meaningful life in this age and eternal life in the age to come (Ro 8:20-25; 1 Co 15:19; Col 1:27; Heb 6:19; 1 Jn 3:3).

Jesus continues to minister for us. Jesus' resurrection did not separate Him from us. He ascended to be with the Father (Ac 1:9) so that He could send the Holy Spirit to be with each of us (Jn 16:5-16). He sat down at the Father's right hand as our Priest and Intercessor (Ro 8:34; Heb 7:25). In all our troubles believers have an advocate pleading for us with the Father (1 Jn 2:1). This will be true until He returns to reign eternally.

Jesus is the eternal King. Messianic hopes centered on a son of David to be king. Jesus was a Son of David (Mt 1:1-17) to whom even David looked as Lord (Mt 22:43-45). He in God's way fulfilled the Old Testament expectations of a new king (Isa 9:2-7; 11:1-9; 52:13—53:12; Eze 34:23-24; Da 7:13-14; Mic 5:1-5; Zec 2:10-13). In Him God's kingdom was present (Mk 1:14-15). On the cross the nature of His kingly rule was fully revealed. When He comes again the kingdom will be fully established. The final coming of Christ will fulfill divine promise and prediction. Its time is unknown, but it should not surprise God's people

(1 Th 5:1-4). We are to be ready for Him to come to us. The same Jesus who ascended will return (Ac 1:11). His return will bring an end to the struggle of good and evil, the battles among the kingdoms of this world that must become the kingdom of our God and of His Christ (Rev 11:15). Meanwhile, His followers must unite eschatology and ethics in a fashion that will share the gospel with all the world. His people must endure tribulation until the King comes. We must join the chorus praising the humble Son of Man, who is also the final Judge and King. We must prepare to join in the chorus of hallelujahs that will mark His triumphant return (Rev 19:1-7).

Summary of the Doctrine of the Holy Spirit

The Holy Spirit is revealed as the third Person of the Trinity. The one true God has revealed Himself to His people as Father, Son, and Holy Spirit. Within the inner life of the one God exists a mystery, a richness of love and fellowship among three divine persons.

The biblical revelation of the Spirit occurred over many centuries. The Spirit was active in creation (Ge 1:2) and was known as early as the time of Joseph (Ge 41:38). The full revelation of the Spirit did not come until the Day of Pentecost (Ac 2), when the Spirit was poured out on all the followers of Christ.

The biblical language for the Spirit is revealing. The Hebrew word *ruach* may be translated either wind, breath, or Spirit. The same is true of the Greek *pneuma*. In each case, the context indicates the best translation. In the Old Testament the Spirit usually is called the Spirit of the Lord, the Spirit of God, or simply the Spirit; only rarely is He called the Holy Spirit. In the New Testament He is called the Spirit, the Spirit of God, the Holy Spirit, and sometimes the Spirit of Christ, the Spirit of Jesus Christ, and the Spirit of Jesus. Biblical symbols for the Spirit include the dove, wind, fire, and water.

The Holy Spirit works for God's purposes. In the Old Testament, the Spirit is sometimes associated with creation. He is more frequently associated with life. His most representative work was to come into the life of a selected leader of Israel and to give that person a gift or gifts with which to serve God by serving His people. The Spirit usually came to Israel's leaders temporarily, not permanently. His gifts were varied and included the ability to interpret dreams, craftsmanship, military skills, physical strength, leadership skills, and visions. By far the most frequent gift was the gift of prophecy, a gift of speech by which God's word was communicated to His people through the prophet. In all of this the Spirit was understood as God's powerful Spirit present with Israel's leaders. Finally, the Old Testament contains several prophecies of a coming new age in which God would pour out His Spirit on all His people. These prophecies were not fulfilled in the Old Testament history.

The New Testament revelation of the Spirit begins with Jesus. Jesus did not teach much about the Spirit, but He was the unique bearer of the Spirit. The Spirit was involved in Jesus' conception and was given to Jesus in the form of a dove at His baptism. Jesus was guided and empowered by the Spirit to carry out His public ministry. Jesus promised His disciples that the Spirit would be with them to protect them and to help them testify when they were taken into court for being His disciples. In John's Gospel Jesus spoke of the Spirit providing new birth for people. He said that the Spirit would one day be given to His disciples and would act as their Paraclete, which means Counselor, Helper, or even Lawyer. The Paraclete would be with the disciples forever. His main work would be to remind them of Jesus and His teaching and to glorify Jesus.

The Holy Spirit empowers God's people. The prophecies of the Old Testament and the promises of Jesus concerning the Spirit were fulfilled on the Day of Pentecost. At that time God poured out His Spirit on all the disciples. The Spirit formed the disciples into the church and, by giving them prophetic gifts, enabled them to begin their world mission task of preaching the gospel. Acts records the story of the Spirit's guiding to Jerusalem, to Judea, to Samaria, and to the uttermost parts of the earth.

The Holy Spirit leads individuals. The Epistles tell about the Spirit in the life of the church. In a sense, it is the story of Pentecost continued. That is, the Spirit guides the church to proclaim the gospel of Christ. When people accept the gospel, the Spirit comes into their lives and brings them new life. He is present in the life of each Christian as a permanent gift from Christ. He seals Christians and protects them. He gives them gifts by which they serve God by serving His people, just as Israel's leaders had done. He gives wisdom to the church and power for its work. He even assists the church in its prayers and worship. He works to transform Christians into persons of love, joy, peace, patience, gentleness, goodness, faithfulness, humility, and self-control. He gives them boldness, freedom, and life. The Spirit creates a new family of God, a new common life, a new fellowship called the church. The church must be attentive to the guidance of the Spirit. They trust Him and obey His leadership. God's people are warned not to grieve Him by moral disobedience or quench His fire in their lives.

The Spirit is God. When the entire biblical revelation of the Spirit is taken together, a remarkable picture emerges. The Spirit is not a vague, indefinite power, as the English word *Spirit* might suggest. The Spirit revealed in the Bible is quite definite. He is not found everywhere, in general. He is specifically the Spirit of God and more specifically the Spirit of Christ. He is to be found among Christ's people. He is an invasive Spirit, not a pervasive one.

The question that perplexes people about the Spirit is: How do you know where the Spirit is present? The biblical criteria for the Spirit's presence are different than some expect. The Spirit is not identified by the presence of enthusiasm, institutional success, or proper theology. The Spirit is identified by sincere faith in Christ. When Jesus is not Lord, the Spirit is not at work; when Jesus is Lord, the Spirit is at work. The major work of the Spirit is to pour God's love into the hearts of people so that they begin to love God and love one another. As they learn to love, the church is truly edified and is bound together by the Spirit.

The Spirit is very powerful, but it is a mistake to suppose that He is an impersonal power. He is rather a powerful person. It is true that the Bible uses nonpersonal language about the Spirit, just as it does about God. In the case of the Spirit, just as in the case of God, the impersonal language should be interpreted in light of the personal language. The Spirit can be grieved; He provides wisdom, creates fellowship, instills love. These are not descriptions of the working of an impersonal power. The Spirit is a person.

The Spirit is divine. The Bible never suggests that the Spirit is a created person, either an angel or a human being. Those into whose lives the Spirit has come are quite aware that God is personally present with them. The Spirit is, therefore, the divine third person of the Trinity. The mystery of the Trinity is the mystery of the inner life of the one true and living God, and the Spirit is part of that mystery.

The World

Summary of the Doctrine of Creation

The divine Agent of creation. Any approach to the world's beginning must start with the fact of a personal Creator. The Bible does not debate the point but merely assumes His existence. Most, perhaps all, cultures have their origin stories. The Hebrew account, however, stands in striking contrast to those of other civilizations. The latter spoke of many gods and pictured them as fighting, committing adultery, and often identified as part of their own creation. To the Old Testament writers, however, both in Genesis and elsewhere in the Bible, God stands apart as separate from His creation. He is the source of the world's existence but is not to be viewed as mingled with it. Only God is not created. Theologians speak of this as the "transcendence" of God.

Divine transcendence does not mean God is so removed from the world as to be out of touch with it. He is immanent or subjectively involved with both the physical universe and those who inhabit it. These two facts about the divine Creator assure a proper balance, preventing wrong or extreme thinking in either direction.

Why God creates. One overwhelming truth gripped the Bible writers. The world came into existence through choice, not chance, by a Creator who is a free, personal Spirit. Of His own volition, He produced a good world and a proper dwelling place for all His creation.

God continues to sustain His creation. God's creative work includes more than bringing the world into existence and putting human beings on it. Neither the earth nor its inhabitants are self-sustaining. Unless God stood constantly in the shadows keeping watch, the world would soon lapse back into primeval chaos. If He had not early initiated a redemptive program for the humans, they would have deteriorated quickly into an animal-like existence.

In the ultimate context of divine activity, all concepts related to life's reality are a part of the Creator's continuing labor. God's greatest work, surpassing even creation of the world, however, is His redemptive program conceived before the foundation of the world. A close examination of Hebrew Scriptures shows the writers thought first of redemption and praised God for it even before they glorified Him as Creator of the world. They said much more of the God who provides salvation than of the "maker of heaven and earth, the sea, and everything in them" (Ps 146:6).

God cannot be blamed for evil. Did God create evil? The Christian conscience immediately resists such a possibility. Equally unacceptable is a dualism that resembles Eastern mystery cult theology. God's first two created people, given freedom of choice, deliberately violated God's command and introduced wrongdoing into the world. Original sin today, however, should not be regarded as a biological taint, but as a spiritual contagion. In some inexplicable way, the tendency to sin is passed on through biological generation. Yet God does not charge this sin against people until they assent and allow it to dominate their whole being.

Creation finds its goal in Christ. To affirm God as Creator means to confess God's goodness. His essential goodness means creation is good, and history, therefore, has meaning. In Jesus Christ, the agent of creation, He reaffirmed His lordship of all that happens in the human drama. If we regard the first couple as the crown of creation, we should speak of new life in Christ as the climax of creation. The same Spirit that brooded over the waters (Ge 1:2) works regeneration in the human heart. God glorified Himself in His initial creation, but even more so in His Son whom He appointed heir of all things.

Creation will be renewed. A glorious future awaits God's creation. The prophets spoke often about "the day of the Lord," a time when God would act in history to judge evil. Scholars speak of "eschatology" or the doctrine of last things. More than futurology, it is a way of referring to the fact that God will, in final judgment, vindicate His creative acts. Though such interventions into history have occurred periodically, the final event will declare that the One who began history will consummate it to His glory. Nature and redeemed people alike will receive a deliverance from the captivity that has limited their potentialities.

To the contemporary Christian, creation deserves more than a debate concerning methods or dates involved. This glorious doctrine declares that in our present world, which often seems confused and chaotic, a divine Absolute speaks. Holiness and mercy combine to assure us of both God's moral demand and His compassion. He made people for Himself, and they will never find fulfillment until they experience His presence in their lives. Creation and creatures know meaning and hope only as they know and trust the Creator.

Summary of the Doctrine of Miracle

Miracles are evidence of God's working. Miracles may be understood as a part of God's continuing work in His creation. If we are to believe in God as having created the world, we have two simple options: (1) God wound up the entire system and went off into a corner somewhere to await its running down; or (2) God is continually involved in the process of creation. The Genesis story avows that God rested on the seventh day. This is more an avowal of the completion of God's creation than a description of God's having ceased all activity in His creation. The biblical evidence for miracles attests the presence and power of God continuing the work of creation.

Many of the problems modern people have in identifying and understanding miracles spring from their difficulty in understanding the nature and activity of God. God is love. Since the human fall, He has been actively involved in human redemption. Most of the miracles in both the Old and New Testaments may be described as redemptive in nature.

If we can explain a miracle, if we are able to fit it into our scheme of things, then it is no longer a miracle. Miracles are by definition exceptions to our rules and to what we understand as the nature of the universe. Miracles reveal the mystery of God at work in ways we cannot define or explain. The biblical vocabulary shows miracles are evidence of God's power, which brings forth human wonder and amazement. They are signs pointing to God's presence in His universe.

Miracles defy human skill to imitate. They trouble human minds to explain. We do not attempt to confine God to nature. Miracles are comprehensive of, but not contrary to, nature. They are beyond it, or even beside it.

Miracles serve different purposes. They continue God's work in creation, renewing and maintaining the world. They provide redemption and deliverance for God's people as in the Exodus and in the cross. They reveal God's active presence, calling forth faith and praise. They exercise God's judgment on all that opposes Him. They demonstrate God's continuing, unmatched power in His world.

Miracles are worked in the context of faith. Jesus' miraculous signs "are written that you may believe" (Jn 20:31); yet Jesus resisted the temptation to work miracles in order to provoke faith (Mt 4:1-11). He worked miracles in response to faith, not doubt. Saving faith must involve trusting personal relationship, not simply acceptance of Jesus' power to do the unexpected. Miracles become signs leading to saving faith when they cause people to trust Jesus as the Son of God for eternal life. Miracles then illustrate the power of the faith that Jesus provoked. They are more than mere stories of healings. Redemptive in nature, they were always related to the faith of the witnesses.

Miracles are inseparable from the one performing them. In both the Old and the New Testaments miracles were performed by human instruments of divine power. In the persons of Moses, Elijah, and Elisha, God's power made a special entry into human lives. Even demonic powers can do the unexpected with power, but the results of their works show the evil source.

In Christ is the clearest attestation of God's power. The resurrection is the supreme miracle—the vindication of the incarnation of Jesus becoming flesh to fulfill God's purpose. The miracles cannot be separated from Jesus Himself. Sometimes they emphasize the authority of Jesus. Sometimes they emphasize His compassion. Sometimes they emphasize the faith and obedience of the person involved. They show the Creator God completing His work in creation in the unique redemptive work of Christ.

Summary of the Doctrine of Evil and Suffering

The origin of evil and suffering. Evil refers to anyone or anything that disrupts the harmony and unity of God's good creation. Suffering refers to negative experiences that human beings interpret as evil. Understood in light of divine providence, suffering may not always be evil.

God is ultimately responsible for everything that happens in the world. God allows Satan to cause some evil and suffering, but Satan is not equal to God in power or authority. God allows human beings to misuse their freedom, causing some evil and suffering. The physical world is good as created by God, but disturbances in nature can produce human suffering.

Types of evil and suffering. The Bible distinguishes several types of evil and suffering. When God punishes sinners, suffering is deserved. Some suffering is innocent, a testing of the believer's faith. God may allow Satan or human beings to be the direct causes of this type of suffering as in Job's experience. Some suffering is innocent and redemptive. Jesus suffered vicariously for the sins of others.

God's relation to evil and suffering. God punishes sinners. The suffering may occur in this life or after death. The suffering may be the direct action of God or the apparently natural consequence of an action. The Bible generally stresses individual responsibility for sins, but some passages highlight the social dimension of sin and punishment. Not all suffering can be explained as punishment for sin (Job; Ecc; Lk 13:1-5; Jn 9:1-5).

Providence is God's guidance of history and nature according to His redemptive purpose. Evil is contrary to His will, but God can bring ultimate good out of temporary evil (Ge 50:20; Ro 8:28).

God is compassionate, identifying with human suffering. Like a parent, He grieves over the sinfulness of His children.

God responds to human suffering with both present and future help. In the present God may eliminate the suffering or provide divine strength and encouragement in the midst of the suffering (2 Co 12:7-10). In the future God will eliminate suffering for the righteous.

The Christian response to evil and suffering. Depending on the type of suffering, Christians should respond in various ways. If the suffering is punishment for sins, the sufferer should repent.

If suffering is a testing of faith or redemptive, Christians should endure it as part of the cost of commitment and rejoice. Christians should not retaliate against injustice or seek revenge.

Christians can express compassion and comfort to suffering people. Compassion is identification with the sufferer. Comfort includes anything that will help strengthen the sufferer, such as prayer and humanitarian actions.

Christians should be humble in relation to evil and suffering because human knowledge is limited in this life.

Summary of the Doctrine of Humanity

God's creation of humanity. People are the crown of God's creative activity, the most significant of His creatures. Throughout the Bible, God and people are the chief characters. The world is the stage upon which they confront and relate to one another. As we might expect, one of the major teachings of the Bible is the understanding of humanity.

Human beings are created in God's image (Ge 1:26-28). The primary emphasis appears to be spiritual. This image was marred by sin. It can be seen clearly in Jesus (Jn 14:7-9) and is being recreated in Christians (Col 3:9-11). A part of the image of God is seen in human responsibility for the world and all that is in it. We must use the world and our own gifts in accord with God's will. Thus we are ultimately responsible to Him for our acts and for our choices.

Something about the nature of God is also revealed in the loving commitment of a husband and wife, for it was the pair that were first created (Ge 1:26-28). The same thing is to be seen in the love of God's new people in His kingdom (Jn 17:20-23).

The commands of God and people's choices to obey or not to obey further expand our understanding of the image of God (Ge 2:17). Humanity's freedom of choice is a reflection of God's absolute freedom. The sense of right and wrong within the human conscience is also such a reflection (Ro 2:12-16).

A further reflection of the divine image lies in the great potential that people possess (Ge 11:1-9). The value of this potential can be seen in the way people use it (Ge 4:17-22). At its highest, however, it is still limited (Job 28).

The reflection of God in human personality ultimately places value on people (Mt 16:26). The final evaluation of human worth is seen in the price God paid for humanity's redemption (Jn 3:16). God's love places ultimate worth on His human creatures.

Nature of God's human creation. Human nature is precisely what God gave to His people, and this nature pleased Him (Ge 1:26-28,31). No basis for pride exists in this, for often we act more like animals than intelligent humans (Job 4:18-21; 2 Pe 2:10-22).

God created a physical body for humans from the dust of the earth (Ge 2:7). Similarly He created animals from the ground (Ge 2:19). Both have flesh and are living creatures (Ge 1:24; 2:7). The body is God's gift, and its parts are intended to work together (1 Co 12:18-26). Ultimately, however, the physical body is not eternal (2 Pe 1:13-15). Resurrected humans will receive a resurrected body.

A part of humanity's nature is the spiritual nature, the part that reaches out and responds to God (Ge 32:1-30; 35:1). When that nature has been redeemed, people are assured that their spiritual natures ultimately will be victorious over sin.

The Bible clearly states that people have been given minds and are expected to use them (Job 32:8). However, human wisdom at best is quite limited. The ultimate foundation for wisdom is found in God's Word (Pr 1:1-7).

People also are endowed by God with feelings and emotions (Ps 73:21-22). This allows us to rise above the physical, to share in the joys and sorrows of one another, as well as to develop attachments and commitments.

Experiences of human life. Life is also the gift of God, the result of His direct creative act (Ge 2:7). At its best, life is a joyful experience in God's presence and in the presence of others. At its worst, it is utterly unbearable, so that death is desired (Job 7:16).

Birth is the avenue by which life is passed on from generation to generation. While viewed as a natural process of marriage and love, it is also clearly seen as God's gift (Ge 18:10-14).

Children of godly parents are blessed by their early dedication to the Lord (1 Sa 1:21-28). All children are loved and cared for by Jesus (Mt 19:14). As they grow, children become youth on the way to adulthood. There they experience the hopes and dreams of adolescence (Ge 37:2-11). This is the time of great expectations. At the same time, it is the period of immaturity, where strengths and abilities are tried out (Jer 1:6-7).

Marriage is intended by God to meet the basic human need of love and companionship (Ge 2:18). It is the basis of joy and celebration (Ge 2:21-25) but can become a source of heartbreak through infidelity and strife (Hos 3:1-3; Mt 5:31-32).

On the other hand, celibacy is an acceptable life-style when it is based on the desire to find the best means of service to God (1 Co 7:32-38). It needs to be entered into with the full awareness of its difficulties (1 Co 7:8-9).

One normal expectation of marriage is to have children, although this is not always possible. When people become parents, they are responsible for the proper guidance and training of their children (Pr 23:13-14).

Human work is a part of God's intent for people (Ge 2:15). We are expected to do our best and to bring our labor to a good conclusion (2 Ch 32:30). Work is a necessity to support both life and ministry (Ac 18:3).

The last stage of the life process is age (Job 5:26). With the coming of age, life-styles change, and a life founded on service to God still can find avenues of service (Ecc 12:1-7; 2 Sa 19:32-37).

Termination of human life. From the beginning, death has been understood as the consequence of human rebellion (Ge 2:17). This includes both physical as well as spiritual death. The Bible contains a growing revelation that death is not the ultimate end of life, for through Jesus Christ we have hope of a final victory over both spiritual death through redemption and physical death through resurrection (Ro 5:19-21; 1 Co 15:19,21-22,51-57).

In our present state, death is viewed as the natural end of life, something to be accepted like any other part of life (2 Sa 14:14). No achievement or capacity on the part of a person allows an escape from death until this world is transformed (Eze 32:17-32). For the Christian, death is not to be feared because of Jesus' resurrection (1 Co 15:51-57).

The death process was begun by human sin (Ge 2:17). It is continued in each of us through our own personal rebellion against God (Jer 31:29-30). Spiritual death is the result of personal sin (Ro 5:12).

As a natural part of life, death is to be accepted. Grief over the loss of a loved one is natural (2 Sa 1:19-27). Such grief is not an expression of a lack of faith in God but is the natural outcome of life.

Throughout most of the Bible, proper burial was considered to be of extreme importance (Ge 23:3-20). On the other hand, Jesus called His followers to a service to those who are alive, which is more important than their service to the dead (Mt 8:21-22).

Interactions of human life. Each person in this world lives in relationship to those round about. We are involved in personal relationships with our families, our friends, our communities, our world, and God.

The primary human relationship is that with God. We are His creatures. He is the Creator (Ge 1:26-28; 2:7). Creatures are at all times subservient to the Creator, whether they acknowledge this or not.

At the same time, God grants to humanity the power of choice (Ge 3:12-13). At the moment of choice, people are free to obey or to rebel. Each person is responsible for such choices and must face the consequences of them (Ex 20:2-11).

Through God's acts of redemption, people are brought into a new relationship with Him (Col 1:21-22). This new relationship is everlasting, as we have been brought into God's family through adoption (Ro 8:29).

Every person is also related to the community. Our acts affect those around us, and we are affected by theirs (Jos 7:1). This not only calls for purity in life, it also calls for our compassionate response to others' needs (Jnh 1:12-13).

The basis for a stable society is a stable family (Ex 20:12). Family relationships can be and should be used to aid one another in the service of God (Ex 4:14-15). Family ties should be maintained by bonds of love (Lk 15:31-32).

A direct relationship exists between human obedience to God and a wholesome relation to God's creation (Lev 26:3-8). The proper use of the world's resources offers opportunity for God's abundance for all (Pr 14:4).

Summary of the Doctrine of Sin

Definition of sin. The Bible gives no formal definition of sin but describes sin in a number of ways. Sin basically is rebellion against God. From the very beginning humankind has wanted to run the show. Adam and Eve both demonstrated their rebellious natures by seeking to become like God. This malady has infected every person since.

Origin of sin. The Bible teaches that all persons without exception are under the dominion of sin, but the Bible has little to say philosophically about the origin of sin. The Bible *does not* teach that God is the originator of sin. Satan introduced its long and melancholy reign into human history when he beguiled Eve (Ge 3). Since that time, sin has been like a malignant cancer upon the face of human history, distorting and disfiguring the relationship of humanity to God.

Throughout the Old and New Testaments, the sinful state of humanity is recognized to be the result of individual choice. Just as Eve chose and then Adam, so every person after them has made this fateful choice to embrace sin.

Some statements in both the Old and New Testaments can be interpreted to mean that humanity's sinful nature is inherited. Humans are born with a natural tendency to sin and live in an environment of persons and opportunities that make sinning easy. The Jewish mind had no problem in admitting two mutually exclusive ideas into the same system of thought. Any idea that humanity inherits a sinful nature must be coupled with the corollary that every person is indeed responsible for choosing to sin.

The biblical understanding of the corporateness and solidarity of the human race also must be considered to understand sin's origin. When Adam sinned in rebellion, he incorporated all of his descendants in his action. (Heb 7:9-10 uses a similar analogy.) This interpretation does not remove the necessity for each person to accept full responsibility for sinful actions and attitudes.

Adam and Eve set the stage by rebelling against the explicit command of God. Every person who has lived since has followed their example. Whatever else we may say about the origin of sin, we can be sure that the Bible teaches this.

Characteristics of sin. The Bible uses a number of picturesque analogies to describe various aspects of sin. Bible writers speak of transgression of God's Law as one aspect of sin. God made a covenant with Israel and revealed His Law to Moses as conditions of the covenant. This code became the standard for right living. Any violation of this code was considered sin. Disobeying the known will of God is sin.

God revealed His character to Israel as righteous and holy. He commanded Israel to be holy even as He was holy (Lev 11:44). Any action that violates the righteous character of God is sin. Any desire that does not conform to the righteous character of God is an evil desire, and thus to hold on to such a desire is sinful.

God created man and woman and ordered them to multiply and populate the earth so that He might have fellowship with His creation. When any person breaches this fellowship, the action is looked upon as sinful.

In the Bible sin is also seen as unbelief directed toward God. God's truthfulness is not to be questioned, for God does not lie. Unbelief basically questions the truthfulness of God. Thus it is sin. To demonstrate a lack of faith in God's promises or commands is sin.

Biblical vocabulary characterizes sin in a number of interesting ways. Sin is "missing the mark." As a marksman might aim at a target and miss it with an arrow, so a person who sins is missing the mark established by God for righteousness. God has established a standard for righteousness. When a person violates this standard, it is sin. This is known as "stepping across the line" or transgressing the commands of God. Lawlessness is another characterization for sin. The lawless person has no regard for the laws of God.

The basic sin of the Bible is that of rebellion. When one knows the will of God and refuses to conform to it, this is rebellion. This is a grievous sin.

Consequences of sin. Nothing in the Bible is considered to be any more serious than sin in any of its many forms. Primarily sin is so serious because it is basically against God. Though the action may be directed against another person, ultimately it is against God, who created all things.

Sin also is serious because it brings alienation from God. The disastrous results of the sin of Adam and Eve in being cast from the garden certainly illustrate the alienation sin causes from God.

Sin brings about God's intervention in human affairs. This intervention adds weight to the seriousness of sin.

The consequences of sin as set forth in the Bible are varied and many. When a person follows a sinful course consistently, that person will become enslaved to sin (Ro 6). The consistent practice of sin will lead to slavery to sin.

Sin also results in personal depravity. Some certainly will say that depravity is the cause of sin. This surely is a valid argument. A continuance in sin adds to this personal depravity. Depravity can be defined as crooked, perverse, or corrupt. Each of these is an apt characterization of the person whose life has been marred by the constant practice of sin.

Another consequence of sin is spiritual blindness. This is a self-imposed blindness, but it is real and detrimental nonetheless. The adage holds true: "There are none so blind as those who refuse to see." Spiritual truths simply are not visible to that person who has been blinded by sin.

Moral insensitivity is a devastating consequence of sin. The more a person practices sin, the more inept that person becomes in the moral sphere. Such a person reaches the point where the distinction between right and wrong is blurred because of sin.

A person brings guilt upon himself or herself by sin. Personal problems cannot rightly be blamed on another person. Each person must accept the guilt of personal sin (Eze 18:4).

Sin and death are corollaries in the Scripture. One of the by-products of sin is death. This does not mean that every person's death is a result of some sin committed by that person, though there are instances where this is true. Death entered the world because of sin, so we may say that the sin principle and the death principle are vitally related. Continual sinning will bring spiritual death to that person who has not come to repentance and faith in Jesus Christ for spiritual salvation (Rev 20:14).

One of the most devastating consequences of sin for the individual is that sin produces separation from God both in this life and in the life to come. The separation in this life need not be permanent if one repents of sin and turns in faith to Jesus for salvation. For the person who refuses to repent in this life, separation from God becomes final and permanent.

Sin not only has devastating consequences for a person's relation to God, there also are consequences as far as human relations are concerned. Sin produces estrangement from others in this life. When one person wrongs another person, the logical consequence is alienation. Again this relationship need not be permanent, but it is real and can be devastating to good interpersonal relationships.

God's intervention. God does not ignore sin. He seeks through the Bible, His servants, and life's experiences to warn people of sin's consequences. He acts in judgment to discipline His people, seeking to lead them to Him. He ultimately gives unrepentant sinners over to final judgment. That is not His will. He calls all people to repentance and offers forgiveness freely to those who confess and turn from sin.

Knowledge of God

Summary of the Doctrine of Holy Scripture

What Scripture is. The Bible is God's Word of revelation to His human creatures. All Christian teachings are based on the Bible. All doctrinal beliefs and statements must be judged by the Bible.

God is the Author of Scripture. God, the Holy Spirit, worked through humans to produce the authoritative Word of God. Human minds and human language are inadequate to explain the mystery of God's working through humans to produce His trustworthy Word. Humans do not have to understand the process to trust the product.

How God communicated His message. Scripture itself shows various ways God worked to provide us with His written revelation. He directed some human writers to write words immediately (Ex 24:4). He led people to learn and preserve orally some teachings for years before He led persons to write them down (Genesis; Jesus' teachings). He guided teachers, families, and wise men to formulate and memorize proverbial wisdom for generations before directing Solomon (Pr 1:1), the men of Hezekiah (Pr 25:1), and others (Pr 22:17; 24:23; 30:1; 31:1) to collect them into the form He wanted to instruct His people. He inspired poets to compose prayers and worship songs to communicate with and praise Him. He then led as His worshiping people studied and collected these psalms to learn God's word from them. He gave visions to prophets and led apostles like Paul to write letters dealing with specific situations and needs of specific local churches. God, the Author of Scripture, thus used persons He chose to interpret His actions and teachings in the history of His people. He led as humans learned, remembered, delivered, and preserved His Word. The persons God used in this process are heroes of the faith whether we know their names or not. They allowed God to use them and their skills to produce His Word.

How Scripture came to us. The Bible began as individual stories about patriarchs, commandments, psalms, prophecies, proverbs, sayings of Jesus, and letters as well as other individual pieces of literature. The many words of God eventually were collected together into the one Word of God. The process of collection was an important part of God's direction to provide His written revelation. He did not choose to preserve all of Israel's literature as part of His holy Word (Nu 21:14; 2 Sa 1:18; 1 Ch 9:1; 27:24; Lk 1:1-4). He preserved some material twice (2 Sa 22; Ps 18; Isa 2:1-4; Mic 4:1-3; Ex 20; Dt 5; Mt 6:9-13; Lk 11:2-4). He led a prophet to remember and write down his sermons long after they were preached (Jer 36) and then gradually add other sermons (36:32). Apostolic letters were exchanged among churches; copies were made; and a collection of letters was gathered (Col 4:16). Through many centuries and various human processes, God led to ensure His Word was properly remembered, preserved, collected, and joined with other divine words to bring together His written revelation.

Scripture assumed a final written form under God's leadership, though various parts of Scripture took written form at different times. Part of Scripture was first delivered orally, memorized, and taught for long periods before being written down. Some parts of Scripture were written down immediately. Some inspired writers used written sources. Chronicles used much of Samuel and Kings, while Matthew and Luke apparently were familiar with Mark's Gospel. Scribes and secretaries played important roles in writing the words of inspired spokespersons (Jer 36; Rom 16:22; 1 Cor 16:21; Col 4:18). Eventually the Temple and the church communities gathered the various inspired writings into the larger collections and ultimately into the one Book. The long centuries of praying, preaching, singing, teaching, collecting, and writing climaxed in the church having God's holy Word to direct our lives under Him.

The authority of Scripture. Scripture's truth and authority is self-evident to those who believe in Jesus Christ for salvation. Believers follow Jesus in citing Scripture as the authoritative, trustworthy Word of God. Truth never contradicts Scripture (Jn 17:17). Through Scripture, temptation is defeated (Mt 4:1-11). The Bible clearly teaches the way of salvation in Christ. From Scripture the church learns its doctrines, its actions, and its mission. The Scriptures rebuke us when we sin, encourage us under trial, mature us in our faith, proclaim the good news of the gospel to and through us, and correct our doctrine (Ps 19:7-10; Mt 22:20; 1 Ti 3:15—4:3). The result of Scripture study is hope (Ro 15:4).

The authority of Scripture is not limited to a period of history. It "stands forever" (Isa 40:8; Mt 5:18; 1 Pe 1:25). It is God's eternal witness to His saving work, a work climaxed in Jesus Christ, the Word who "became flesh" (Jn 1:14). Any interpretation of Scripture that does not point to Jesus is inadequate (Jn 5:39). Any interpretation of Scripture that turns a person away from Jesus' clear teachings is inadequate. Any interpretation that leads to a division of His church is inadequate (Jn 10:16; 17:11,20-23). The authoritative Scriptures must be interpreted in light of the person, message, and mission of Jesus Christ. The Holy Spirit guides each of God's people as we interpret and obey Scripture (Jn 16:13-15). All biblical teaching thus affirms the complete authority of Scripture, but Scripture only exercises that authority in an individual life when it is read, learned, meditated on, and obeyed (Dt 17:18-20; Ps 119; Ac 17:11).

Why we have Scripture. Biblical testimony and pious research reveal the many people and long centuries God used to provide our Bible. They testify that the Bible is the product of something greater than its many human authors. Holy Scripture is above all the product of the work of God the Holy Spirit. We confess trust in Scripture and submit our lives to its authority because God's Spirit produced it. Neither we nor the Bible attempts to describe the mysterious process by which God worked through humans. We join Scripture in testifying that biblical speakers, collectors, writers, and copiers combined through the centuries to preserve and produce precisely what God chose to teach His people. Scripture is not a product of human will. It is a product of God's Holy Spirit (2 Pe 1:19-21). He inspired or breathed out the words of Scripture (2 Ti 3:16). Therefore, we believe it, accept its offer of salvation, obey it, let it judge our lives, and put our final hope in the Christ to whom it points us.

Summary of the Doctrine of Revelation

God takes the initiative. Revelation refers to God's initiative in disclosing Himself and His will to His creation. Christian teaching on revelation is based on several critical assumptions: (1) God is personal and reveals Himself in ways that allow us to relate to Him as persons; (2) only God, the Creator and Sustainer of life, knows the purposes and plans for all the created order; (3) knowledge of God is not an automatic part of the world or of human existence but is possible only because God chooses to reveal Himself to His children; (4) God uses many different ways to reveal Himself; (5) humans never know all about God, His hiddenness and mystery being aspects that help develop faith in the believer and preserve the uniqueness of God; (6) God's revelation is designed to communicate the full truth about God and the full truth about humans; (7) God's greatest purpose in revelation is to redeem humans from self-centered, sinful existence; and (8) human understanding of revelation is based on Holy Scripture.

Scripture illustrates and teaches that God has taken the initiative to reveal Himself so He can create a people for Himself (Ex 19:3-6). He appeared in special events to individuals

(Ge 12:1-3; Ex 3:1-12) and to the nation (Ex 14; Jos 3—4; 1 Ki 18). Such events might be labeled as political events or as normal events of nature. People of faith saw much more. They saw the miraculous power of God at work. He appeared as a divine presence personally experienced by His people. He is not withdrawn, isolated, unaccessible in the heavens. He comes to be with His people (Ge 26:3,24; 31:3; 35:3; 48:21; Ex 3:12; Mt 28:20; Ac 18:10). The prayer that characterizes God's people is a priestly blessing seeking God's presence (Nu 6:24-27). God led His people to establish a worship place where His name would be present with His people (Ex 25:8; 29:45; Lev 26:11-12; Dt 12:1-28; 26:2; 1 Ki 8; 2 Co 6:16). A major purpose for revelation is to establish a sense of God's presence with His people. The Old Testament often expressed presence in terms of God's glory (Ex 15:11; 24:16; 33:18; 40:34; Dt 5:24; Ps 8:1; 26:8; 72:19; Isa 6:3; Lk 2:9). The New Testament saw God's presence in flesh and blood in Jesus Christ (Jn 1:14), a presence extended after Christ's ascension by the Holy Spirit (Jn 14:16-17).

God tells us who He is. God's self-disclosure reveals important characteristics of God. He is loving, takes initiative toward His children, seeks to guide us and to help us understand for what we are created. He is gracious, purposive, and redemptive, the Author of life and hope. In telling us who He is, God also intends that we develop characteristics like His, thus imaging Him in the world. We are to show love, give hope, and be a people of grace. We are to create fellowship with others, resembling the close fellowship He creates with us. We are to mirror His faithfulness by faithfully following His presence and will. We are to reflect commitment to Him as He has revealed His commitment in sending His Son. We are to see, in His saving actions of self-giving, examples for us to follow as we live for others in His name.

God discloses Himself through different means. God did not limit Himself to one method of revealing Himself. He used events in history (Ex 14; Jos 3—4; Isa 37:36-37; 43:1-13). He sent angelic messengers (Ge 18:1-2; 19:1; 32:24; Ex 3:2; Jos 5:13; Lk 2:9; Ac 5:19) and prophetic messengers. His created world order and beauty show forth His power, majesty, glory, and order to eyes of faith (Ps 8; 19:1-6; 50:6; 148); but full understanding does not result from creation's revelation (Ro 1:18-23). Jesus Christ is the only way to know a saving relationship with God (Jn 14:6). Other means of revelation include symbolic actions (Isa 20; Jer 13; Eze 4), intimate personal relationships (Hos 1—3), natural phenomena (Jnh 1), dreams (Ge 20:3; 37:5-10; Nu 12:6; Mt 1:20; Ac 2:17), signs (Ge 4:15; 9:12; Ex 3:12; 13:16; Nu 17:10; Jos 4:6; Isa 7:11; Mk 13:4; Jn 20:30), and oracles or messages (2 Sa 23:1; Pr 16:10; 31:1; Isa 13:1; 30:6; Jer 23:33; Hab 1:1; Zec 9:1). In each of these ways God let His people know something about His nature, His intentions, and His actions. The revelation was achieved completely, however, only in the incarnation of Jesus Christ, who revealed the face and character of God in human form (Jn 14:7).

Revelation adds to previous revelation. The people of God do not always understand all that God reveals. In revealing Himself, God has chosen to present revelation in relationship to human capability to understand and integrate revelation. This means new generations learn more from God. This does not mean revelation is to be understood as a constantly increasing store of knowledge. Some generations refuse to receive and incorporate new revelation into their understanding of and relationship with God (Isa 7:12-13; Am 6:1-7). Some generations of God's people have to learn over and again the elemental truths of the faith (1 Co 3:1-3; Heb 1—6:2). God worked long generations to prepare His people to receive the Messiah; but even then when Christ came, they could not understand or accept Him, not understanding the meaning of the Scriptures (Jn 7:42).

Revelation thus has a history. The history of revelation is a story of God's patient and persistent manifestation of His love, mercy, and steadfast commitment to His children. Revelation shows God's desire that all people have opportunity to know His good news of salvation and that all believers become instruments of revelation, sharing God's good news of salvation in Jesus Christ.

Our basic source of revelation is Holy Scriptures, which provide God's Word as a trustworthy record of God's saving revelation through the centuries. The Holy Spirit brings us God's presence and leads us to understand the written revelation. The written revelation points us to the holy Maker of life, to the reasons for our life, to the nature of our Maker, and to a saving relationship with Him through Christ.

Summary of the Doctrine of History

History and God. The Bible's teaching on history separates biblical religion from all other religious systems and experience. History makes a startling difference in the biblical understanding of creation, revelation, salvation, worship, and eschatology. These distinctions all arise because of the true God's unique relationship to history. This relationship was uniquely evident in the historical Son, Jesus. The God of Israel revealed His unique characteristics by His actions in Israel's history. Israel's neighbors credited their gods with helping them, or more specifically their king, in historical events, particularly battles. Israel's God controlled all of history. No other god rivaled Yahweh, the God of Israel, as He worked out His purposes for His people. God thus showed His providence and sovereignty through His use of Israel and the other nations for His will. Directing history, God created a people for Himself through Abraham long after human history began. He directed the people on mission as He protected them in the changing fortunes of historical existence. He rescued them from Egypt, the leading military power of the day. He provided a homeland for His homeless people. He chose spiritual and political leaders for them. He gave them a national capital and chose a place where they could worship Him and know He was present with them in national and individual history. Thus His people learned concretely of God's love for them, His election, His salvation, His power, and His presence. God used the historical form of international treaty or covenant to express His unique relationship with Israel. This relationship showed Him to be personal, wanting loyal commitment in personal relationship with His people. It showed Him to be faithful in keeping His commitment to His people. It showed Him to be holy and morally pure in expecting holiness from His people. Israel learned of God's holiness in a different way. Through His prophets, He announced judgment on a disobedient, unholy people. He then used foreign nations as His instruments to judge and discipline His people. God's justice became evident when God, in turn, announced judgment on the foreign nations and brought destruction on them. This proved, also, His claim to be the only true God, not a product of human hands or a fantasy of human wishes.

History and creation. Biblical religion joined the tribes of the world in believing the world was a divine creation. Uniquely, Israel limited creation to the sphere of human history. Creation was not a war or a love affair in the heavens producing a pantheon of gods and establishing the divine power structure. Creation was not a selfish divine act to ensure the gods would be worshiped, housed, cared for, and fed. Creation was the historical beginning point of God's gracious acts to create a people for personal relationship and salvation with Him. Creation showed God's sovereign control and His personal nature, His determination to have a creature in His image with whom to relate. Creation showed God was not a passive God in heaven but an active, working God willing to labor over His creation on earth.

History and revelation. Cultic worship and dramatic enactment of myth were the means of revelation for the religions of biblical days. Cult specialists learned techniques to discover the divine will through observing movement in the heavens or formations of animal parts. Historical events only rarely were interpreted as the work of God and revelation of His will. Israel uniquely learned to teach about God by telling of the acts of God in the nation's history. To confess faith in God was to recite the credo or list of His saving works for the forefathers. Prophetic revelation came not from the stars or reading animal entrails but from God's word about history. Revelation was couched in terms of promises and threats relating to the future. Revelation was not a natural result of viewing history. The inspired interpreter was necessary. All history was not automatically revelation. The specific chain of events linked by God's promises and threats and interpreted through the inspired spokespersons was the part of history that became part of God's unique revelation.

History and worship. The agricultural year, seen as reflecting activities in the world of the gods, gave content to worship for Israel's neighbors. Cultic acts imitated the divine acts to ensure fertility and the necessary continuation of the seasons. Israel transformed agricultural festivals into celebrations of God's historical acts. The Exodus, the conquest, and the historical choice of David as king and Zion as the place of worship became the central elements of content in Israel's worship. In a real sense, the books of law and history along with many of the psalms represent a development of Israel's worship practice of reciting God's acts in history as the center of praise, lament, thanksgiving, petition, and confession. The New Testament continued making historical acts the central content of worship. Christ's life, death, burial, and resurrection became the focal point for Christian worship.

History and salvation. Historical rescue and deliverance is the root of the biblical understanding of salvation. Salvation is not a human achievement through moral living. Salvation is not escape from earthly existence through meditation or rising above the material world. Salvation is God's action in the historical realm to rescue His nation or individuals from the desperate crises of life. Salvation is understood as deliverance in famine, plague, or battle. The Exodus became Israel's focal point for understanding salvation. It became Israel's symbol for looking forward to new salvation acts of God. The New Testament defined salvation in terms of the historical acts of Jesus. Through His atoning act on the cross of Calvary, salvation from sin and to eternal life became available.

History and Jesus. Jesus gives ultimate meaning to human history. In Him God showed how seriously He takes history. God did not choose a wondrous act from heaven to reveal salvation. He chose to enter human history the way all people do—in the form of a flesh and blood baby. Jesus thus showed that God's kingdom, the kingdom of heaven, has earthly dimensions. Only as persons repent and begin life in the kingdom now on earth can they hope to participate in His kingdom. Jesus' suffering and ministry gave new meaning to historical individual life. He showed the saving possibilities of human suffering and trouble. Above all, Jesus' death, burial, and resurrection revealed the supreme love of God and His total commitment to saving humans.

History and hope. History will end. History is not a continuing series of cycles, constantly repeating itself. History is not a meaningless path leading nowhere. History is not an evil, materialistic existence to be escaped through a series of reincarnations, denial, or forgetfulness. History is the beginning point of meaningful life with God pointing beyond itself to a fulfillment in which God through resurrection will establish justice, reward righteousness, punish evil, and establish His eternal kingdom. That kingdom is not a separate realm unrelated to history. It is the climax of history's relationships, values, and commitments.

God's Saving Purpose

Summary of the Doctrine of Election

Definition. Election has been defined in two basic ways. The traditional definition avers that election is God's act of choosing some persons for salvation and other persons for damnation. This tradition is narrow in emphasis because its focus is on the eternal salvation or damnation of the soul. A more inclusive definition of election seeks to incorporate all dimensions of the biblical teaching. This definition centers on God's grace in choosing to make salvation possible and in establishing a covenant relationship. This definition centers on God's initiative, God's purposes, His promises, and Christ's provision of salvation rather than on human destiny.

God's eternal purposes include establishing a free relationship of love with committed people. When the human race showed its choice to rebel against God, He chose to provide blessing for the nations through a covenant with Abraham, with Israel, and with David. Israel's rebellion led to the election of a new covenant way, the way fulfilled by Christ.

Election and God. The doctrine of election centers on God, not on people. God's mysterious providence allows Him to guide human history to accomplish His purposes even when allowing human freedom and human sin. Election affirms the Creator is personally involved in our history. Election thus is based on the personal presence of God among His creation to accomplish His saving will. Election depends on God's sovereignty, that is, His power to achieve His saving purposes despite all opposition and rebellion. Election confesses God's freedom to act as He chooses in His love and wisdom apart from human desires, rules, and logic. Humans cannot put restraints on the way God chooses to effect His saving purposes. Election emphasizes the loving nature of God, which means His electing purposes are just and best. The ultimate fulfillment of election can be believed because God is faithful. He completes what He promises. Election is another way of talking of God's foreknowledge. He knows the future and cannot be surprised by future events or decisions. Such foreknowledge does not cause the future, but it ensures God's faithful accomplishment of His saving purposes.

Election and communities. Election is basically a community relationship. In grace God chose to create a holy people for Himself. He worked through elect Israel to achieve His universal election purposes. He promised blessings to other nations. He elected non-godly and oppressive nations like Assyria, Babylon, and Persia to be His arm of discipline and judgment. In Christ He formed the elect community of the church, revealing His mystery of salvation for all peoples (Eph 1:9; 3:2-6; Col 1:26-27). Election calls for elect communities of faith to respond to God appropriately. The elect of the New Testament are a community called by God's unmerited favor to be persons of the new covenant. They do not view the privilege of being the elect as grounds for pride and self-righteousness. They strive to live obedient, disciplined, and joyous lives, seeing election as a call to salvation, service, and suffering. The elect understand apostasy as the refusal to be the elect and thus the acceptance of punishment as the just reward. They trust faithfulness in perseverance will be rewarded with a crown of life. Worship, being God's servants, responsibility, mission, and testing fill the life of the elect community. Leadership is supplied by God's election from among His elect servants. The elect community sees itself as the faithful remnant protected by God.

Election and individuals. The elect remnant community is composed of elect individuals. They understand their election as predestination, a sovereign, free choice by God of people to use for His purposes (Ro 8:28-35). Predestination assures that believers understand salvation as God's initiative and God's continuing faithful work totally undeserved and unearned by human achievement. Predestination must be understood in light of human free will. Election does not cause a person to choose or reject the salvation God has determined to provide for and offer to humans. People remain totally free to respond to God and are totally responsible for their decisions (Eph 4:1-7; 2 Pe 2:20-21). Righteousness, committed faith, and prayer characterize the life of the elect. Election is never an excuse for self-satisfaction and moral or spiritual laxity. It is a call to perseverance in the faith (Heb 2:1; 3:6-19; 6:4-12; 10:10-39; 2 Pe 3:17-18).

Election and judgment. Judgment holds no fear for the elect. God is faithful and able to provide eternal security for believers. Eternal security means that as believers seek to persevere in faith, we do not depend on our accomplishments. The elect depend not on human works but on the power of the Holy Spirit to protect and preserve our calling until the day dawns that the wicked shall cease from evil and the weary shall be at rest. Then the elect will be gathered into the presence of the Almighty in the New Jerusalem (2 Pe 1:3-11). Election takes seriously God's total opposition to sin. He exercises justice as He condemns unbelievers to eternal punishment (Ro 3:1-20) and as He forgives believers who confess sin (Lk 18:7).

Election represents an ultimate confession of Christ. Jesus Christ is the Elect of God. His redemptive sacrifice has provided us with the promises of the new covenant. In Christ God reconciled the world to Himself. Christ's body is the church. The church is the elected body of Christ's physical presence in the world, endeavoring to carry out God's ministry of calling an unreconciled world to God. The doctrine of election informs us God has a purpose, plan, people, and presence in this world. Through election God remains the sovereign Lord of history and of His church.

Summary of the Doctrine of Salvation

Definition of salvation. Salvation is the work of God whereby He delivers His people from bondage to all evil powers. Viewed negatively, God's deliverance is rescue from such evil powers as sin, selfish and corrupt rulers, Satan, death, the grave, and hell. Viewed positively, His deliverance is into life, light, love, health, wholeness, safety, peace, joy, freedom, and heaven. Salvation is from the worship of idols to the worship of the one true and holy God, the covenant God of Israel who is the God and Father of our Lord Jesus Christ.

Divine provision of salvation. God saves, and He alone saves. Others whom the Bible calls "saviors," such as judges or kings, saved God's people only because God the Savior anointed them and gave them the power to deliver in His name. True provision for salvation came when God sent His only Son as the Savior of the world.

Divine preparation for our salvation began before God created the universe. The first gospel is His promise that the seed of the woman will crush the head of the serpent-tempter (Ge 3:15). We can behold the Lord's preparation for the coming of Christ in the history of Israel, God's part of which is salvation history. Messianic prophecies given to Israel through divinely inspired prophets have their ultimate fulfillment in the person and work of Jesus Christ. The institutions and rites of Israel found true meaning in Christ.

The initiative in salvation is taken by God. He gave His covenant name to Moses at Sinai and revealed His plan to deliver the Hebrews from their Egyptian bondage. When Israel rejected and stood condemned under the old covenant, God initiated the new covenant (Jer 31:31-34). The gospel is essentially God's good news wrapped up in Jesus Christ.

God's grace is behind, before, beneath, and operating in salvation. Were it not for the freely given and unmerited favor of God, all hope of salvation would be lost. God lavishes the riches of His grace on us through Jesus Christ.

Multifaceted meaning of salvation. The salvation God provides is like a prism reflecting the light of His grace. Salvation is adoption into the family of God (Ro 8:12-25; Eph 1:5). We are made children of God through faith in Christ and the work of the Holy Spirit. God becomes the Father of the saved in a real and intimate sense.

Atonement is one of the great biblical words used to describe the taking away of sin. God makes us at one with Him through Jesus Christ. The historical Jesus atoned for our sins on the cross as the loving Suffering Servant of God (Ro 3:25; Heb 2:17).

Being in Christ is another way the Bible describes salvation (Ro 8:1; 1 Co 1:30; 2 Co 5:17). Christ is the natural element of the believer, somewhat comparable to water being the natural element of fish. Those in Christ are in union with Him. He makes it possible for us to become godlike in our character and conduct.

God's salvation is His blessing (Ge 12:1-3; Ps 1:1; Mt 5:3-11). Believers are beneficiaries of God's promised blessing to Abraham and his seed. God blesses us with everything we need in Jesus Christ.

Cleansing, or purging, is another facet of salvation (Isa 35:8; Jn 13:10; 15:3; Heb 9:14; 10:22). When God saves us, He purges away our dross and impurities. He makes us holy. The death of Christ cleanses us from all sin.

Salvation is God's deliverance of His people from their foes, fears, and troubles (Ps 34:17; Mt 6:13). God frees us from every bondage, except voluntary bondage to Christ.

The Bible describes salvation as eternal life (Mt 25:46; Jn 3:16). Eternal life is God's free gift to those who forsake everything and follow Jesus. It is both a present possession and a future reality.

An important facet of salvation is forgiveness (Eph 4:32; Col 2:13). God blots our sins out through the sacrifice of Christ. We are to forgive others as God in Christ forgives us (Mt 6:12-15).

Glorification is the culmination of salvation (Eph 1:13-14; Tit 2:11-14). This refers to salvation as the final blessed and abiding state of the redeemed.

Healing is a biblical meaning of salvation (Jer 17:14; 1 Pe 2:24). There is no wound God cannot heal through the cross of His Son.

A great deal is said about salvation as joy in Scripture (Ps 4:7; Lk 2:10; Jn 15:11). Those who believe in Christ are filled with unutterable and exalted joy. Suffering does not cut off the joy the Spirit gives.

Justification is an indispensable meaning of salvation (Ge 15:6; Ro 4:25; Gal 2:16). The gospel declares that God puts persons in right relationship with Him when they repent and believe in Christ.

New birth, or regeneration, is one of the multifaceted meanings of salvation in God's Word (Jn 3:1-16). Entrance into the kingdom of God is through the new birth. The new birth is possible through Christ's sacrificial death on Calvary and faith in Him as God's antidote for the poison of sin.

Reconciliation is another biblical meaning of salvation (Mt 5:24; Eph 2:16; 2 Co 5:18-20). This means the restoration of a broken relationship. God was in Christ reconciling the world to Himself. That is the essence of the gospel of salvation.

Salvation involves redemption (Ex 6:6; Ps 31:5; Ro 3:24). Redemption means to deliver or set free by paying a price. Christ became our substitute on the cross. This means that God Himself bore the consequences of our sin in Christ.

Salvation provides refuge (Ps 34:8; 73:28; Joel 3:16). God is a safe refuge for all who trust in Him. Salvation as refuge in the Old Testament foreshadows salvation as rest and as eternal life in the New Testament.

Salvation includes remembrance (Ex 3:15; 6:5; Ps 78:35-39; Lk 24:8; 1 Co 11:2). God's remembrance of His people and their remembrance of Him bring about their restoration.

Salvation is renewal or restoration (Ps 103:5; 119:25-40,149—156; Isa 40:31; Tit 3:5). When God renews His people, it is as though they sprout wings like eagles. The restoration of Israel previews the new creation in Christ.

Salvation is rest from life's labors and frustrations (Ex 33:14; Dt 3:20; 12:10; Jos 1:13; 21:44; 22:4; 23:1; Ps 116:7; Isa 28:12; 32:18; La 1:3; Mt 11:28; Heb 4:1-11). Christ offers rest to believers in this life and in the afterlife.

Believers are not born fully grown. They need to grow in grace and progress in holiness. This process by which the believer is separated from sin and set apart to God's service through the Holy Spirit the Bible calls sanctification (Jn 17:17-19; Ac 26:18; Ro 15:16; 1 Pe 1:2).

Faithful students of Scripture should note the meaning of salvation as vindication (Pss 26:1; 135:14; Jer 51:10; 1 Ti 3:16). Vengeance belongs to God. Ultimately, God vindicates all persons who believe in Christ.

Salvation and human freedom. God's sovereignty and human freedom exist side by side in the biblical teaching on salvation. God never violates human freedom in saving persons. We are truly free to choose between life and death. Choosing to serve God brings true freedom. If the Son sets us free, we shall be free indeed (Jn 8:36).

Human response to salvation. Acceptance is a proper human response to God's salvation (Ac 2:41). We are free to accept or reject God's acceptance of us. Those who accept Christ listen to Him and obey Him. We manifest our acceptance of God's Son by our acceptance of His children (Ro 15:7).

Belief, or trust, is an appropriate human response to God's salvation (Ps 4:5; Jn 2:11,22-25; Ac 16:31; Ro 10:9). Trusting God is putting our confidence in Him and leaning on Him with our whole weight. We can stake our whole life on the trustworthiness of God in Christ.

Confession is a desirable human response to God's salvation (Jer 3:13, 22-25; Ro 10:9-10; Php 2:11). Confession is taking responsibility for our sins and acknowledging our guilt. It is also public testimony about our relationship to God. Whoever confesses Jesus is Lord will be saved.

Fear or reverential awe and respect for God is a fitting human response to His salvation (Ge 22:12; Ex 20:20; Isa 33:5-6; Mt 9:8). The path to salvation begins with the proper fear of God.

Knowledge of God is an appropriate response to His salvation (Ex 6:7; Eze 6:7-14; Hos 4:1; Mic 6:5; Ro 1:28; 2 Pe 1:5). The covenant that Christ mediates makes possible a universal knowledge of God. Knowing Jesus Christ as one's Lord and Savior is worth losing everything.

Love of God is a proper human response to His salvation (Dt 6:5; Mt 22:37). God wants His people to love Him supremely and to love neighbor as self.

Our salvation should result in our obedience to God, come what may, woe or weal (Jer 15:17; Jn 14:15-24; Ac 5:29-32; Ro 12:1-2). Saved persons will seek to obey God's Word and do His will. What God wants in our response is actual obedience, not lip service.

Last, but by no means least, repentance is a proper human response to God's salvation (Dt 30:1-10; 2 Ch 30:6; Isa 30:15; Mk 1:15; Ac 17:30). Repentance is a genuine turning from sin toward God.

God's salvation is something to sing and shout about. It is available to every person who will accept it in repentance and faith in Christ.

Summary of the Doctrine of Discipleship

Nature of and preparation for discipleship. Obedient service is the basic expression of discipleship. Such service is voluntary but never optional for the people of God. Christian conversion is the first step in discipleship. Mere profession of faith in words accomplishes nothing. True confession is conversion, converting a sinner into a servant of Christ. Faith is completed by actions it prompts (Jas 2:14-26). Christians are saved to serve (Eph 2:8-10). Humans cannot achieve or deserve conversion or discipleship. People become Christians on Christ's initiative and have no reason to boast (Jn 15:16). Conversion leads to discipleship, the living out of God's will. God provides enabling power for His people to do His will (1 Sa 30:3-8; Hag 2:4-5). Christians need the inner moral power necessary for living victoriously as obedient disciples (Eph 3:16; 1 Pe 4:11). Family and church have responsibilities to train young disciples toward maturity in Christ (Lk 9:2; 2 Ti 3:14-17).

Disciples become part of God's holy priesthood as promised by Moses (Ex 19:6) and fulfilled in the church, the ideal Israel (1 Pe 2:9). All Christian disciples are brothers and sisters with free access to God (Mt 23:1-11) through Christ, our High Priest (1 Ti 2:5; Heb

10:19-22). We need no other Mediator. We have the responsibility to go to God and learn from God directly through Christ rather than depending on human intermediaries.

All Christian disciples are God's fellow workers. None is left out. All are needed. A witnessing and serving laity is essential to a functioning and growing church, as Acts illustrates. Women played an important part in the work of God in the past and should continue today (Ex 15:20-21; Jdg 4—5; Pr 31; 2 Ki 22:11-20; Mt 28:1-10; Lk 8:2-3; Ro 16:1-3).

Guidelines for discipleship. Discipleship occurs only under God's leadership. He has provided leadership in the lives and affairs of His people throughout human history (Ge 12:1-5; 24:1-67; Ex 14:15-16). He provided basic guidelines for disciples through His covenant (Ex 19—24) in which He sought to establish His kingdom. Under the old covenant God made His will known by laws and prophets. Under the new covenant He makes His will known by His Son (Heb 1:1-2). Jesus said the only ones who will enter the kingdom of heaven are those who do "the will of my Father who is in heaven" (Mt 7:21). To be a Christian disciple demands a willingness to give up everything to experience the reality of the kingdom of God through the immediacy of Christ's ruling authority. Being part of the kingdom means a life-evidencing repentance (Mt 3:2; 4:17).

Discipleship is living out the confession, Jesus is Lord. Disciples of Jesus extend the ministry He began by doing obediently what He commands. Discipleship involves hearing the teachings of Jesus as authoritative and following His commands (Lk 6:46; Ro 6:16). Christ exercises His lordship in the lives of disciples through the ministry of the Holy Spirit (Jn 14:17,20; 1 Co 6:19-20; Gal 5:16). When a person repents and makes a personal commitment to Christ by faith, Christ enters the heart in the person of the Holy Spirit and becomes guide, energizer, and enabler in the Christian life (Jn 16:13-14). Disciples also need human role models and spiritual leaders. Disciples do not seek out leadership positions but answer God's call to them (Heb 13:7-17).

Purpose for discipleship. The first priority in a Christian's life is to seek, find, and follow the will of God. That is the way the kingdom of God, His sovereign rule in His creation, is advanced (Mt 6:33). God's purpose is that Christians will bear fruit. Bearing fruit is not a religious obligation; it is a natural result of conversion, submitting to Christ's lordship, and following the Spirit's leadership (Mt 7:16-20). Discipleship centers on love for God and for neighbor (Mt 22:37-40; Lk 6:27-35; Jn 17:26). Discipleship is a responsible stewardship of personal influence on other persons and on society (Mt 5:14-16). Discipleship is more than passive adoration of God. It is active involvement in God's creation and Christ's ministry (Lk 14:34-35; 2 Co 5:18-20). Discipleship does not seek out deserved rewards. Discipleship means doing all for God's glory. Christians share with Christ in meeting needs of other people. The commendation of the Master is the most desired reward (Mt 25:21) God has promised to reward faithful servants (Eph 6:5-8; 2 Pe 1:10-11).

Focus of discipleship. Discipleship focuses on personal spiritual disciplines, such as Bible study, prayer, and worship, to train for service. At heart discipleship is the believer in action for God. God's will for Christian service is as broad as human need. Discipleship involves evangelism and missions as described in separate articles. God wants all material needs met for every person He creates. The Bible describes ministry to the poor and needy (Mt 19:21; Mk 10:21; Lk 11:41); hungry (Lk 1:53; 9:12-17; Ro 12:20); homeless (Ex 22:21; 23:9; Lev 19:33-34; Nu 15:15-16); oppressed (Mt 9:36; Mk 12:38-40); sick (Mt 10:8; Lk 9:1-6; Jas 5:14-16); handicapped (Mt 15:30-31; Lk 14:13); and the fallen (Jn 4:1-42; 2 Co 2:5-11; Gal 6:1-2). In principle discipleship involves creatively meeting any need another person has (Lev 19:1-2,9-19; Lk 4:18-21).

The importance of ministry to human needs was made clear when Jesus said it would indicate qualification for blessing or rejection on the day of judgment and the great separation (Mt 25:31-46).

Summary of the Doctrine of Christian Ethics

Personal character in society. Christian ethics seeks to apply Christian discipleship in the larger society in which Christians live. It involves individual character, social values, and special application of Christian principles. Society is part of the created order of God. God intends for each individual in society to live a life reflecting godly attitudes, intentions, and motivations. These form the individual's Christian character. One's doing portrays one's being. This integrity of character can be noted in both positive and negative fashion.

The New Testament Christian is related to God in a faith relationship that begins the work of righteousness (right standing and good character). Out of this attitudinal perspective the Christian pursues obedience to God's ethical standards. Such a person will consider the virtues of truth and trustworthiness as duties and goals in relationships with others. Respect for the reputation and worth of others will be expressed by discipline of one's tongue, for the power of words carries the effects of life and death. Respect for God and for others will lead Christians away from desiring or coveting what others have or are. Christian character is not a human achievement. It depends on a right relationship with God, a commitment to obey God, and communion with God in prayer.

Social values. Individuals are important in the Bible, but extreme individualism is considered a detriment to the orientation of the Christian community and of society as a whole. Self-love is emphasized, but its tendency toward egocentrism must be avoided. Virtues appropriate to loving our neighbor are to become functional parts of our lives as we put our sense of love into action. Society's good, not personal good, dominates Christian ethics. Christians love others as they love themselves.

God builds into society some sense of order, without which there would be anarchy and chaos. This order finds concrete expression in a covenant relationship. He expects people in a covenant relationship with Him to work within moral boundaries. These boundaries find expression in God's moral commandments. Rather than bringing great restrictiveness to one's life in society, these boundaries provide one with a sense of moral limits and responsibilities. The Christian who accepts these limits and lives within them finds a paradox. These moral imperatives and ordinances from God provide much freedom for the development of one's character and the character of society.

The Christian in society is expected to live a life on behalf of justice. This justice (the balance or fairness God brings into circumstances) is a complex interlinking of peace, mercy, lovingkindness, and righteousness. Thus, the pattern of God's character and nature is to be repeated in the lives of those called by God's name. This pattern will identify issues of oppression and injustice. The Christian will apply the pattern of justice to personal life, seeking not to cause oppression of others through unjust use of personal property or power. Ownership and authority are seen as trusts given by God for which we are responsible to God. Seeking justice, the Christian will identify those in need and those guilty of oppression. Justice will call for help for the needy and accountability on the part of those who are shaping society away from the values projected in the Bible. In all these relationships the Christian will seek to ensure that love of God and neighbor are the controlling motives. Devotion to justice and love of neighbor are not automatic for the Christian. They are developed in corporate worship where we renew commitments to God, learn from God's Word, and gain strength from the worshiping community.

Social problems. Social problems have many causes. Some ethical problems center around the lack of peace and reconciliation; thus, conflict between differing groups is a reality. Such conflict finds many unethical solutions. Murder denies the sacredness of life. War may be murder on a larger scale. Technology may advance life, but it may also intensify conflicts and capacity to harm life. Matters of personhood will be affected as theft takes place. Theft can occur by overt breaking and entering with material goods removed. Covert theft may occur as all manner of dishonest schemes are implemented to manipulate the unsuspecting away from their material goods. Such actions may leave victims alive but violate their personhood. Private practices also may threaten one's own God-given personhood and that of others. Alcohol and drug abuse rob an individual of freedom to control personal actions and may result in physical or mental abuse of others.

Areas of application. Christian ethics calls us to address two problems. One is the tendency to reduce the Christian life only to reflection about the Christian life in study and meditation. The consequences are enormous for evangelism and mission enterprises. Reflection without consequent action reduces the field of vision. Character development lags when one does not implement one's theological reflection. The gospel is inherently theological and ethical. Good theology leads to good ethical application. Christians must apply their reflections as citizens in the world.

The other problem is the tendency to reduce the Christian life to dealing with only personal issues of life. Nowhere does the Bible describe the perfect Christian economic or political system. Some will argue, therefore, that Christians have no place in these large, social arenas. One who does a careful reading of the Bible will come away with the overwhelming conclusion that though we are not of this world, we are to engage and challenge its value systems. Thus, we are to be on a journey of engagement as light and leaven with a global vision.

Places for application of biblical values abound: the need for honesty and justice in citizenship concerns; the properly delineated loyalties in church-state matters; a sense of co-creatorship in environmental issues; the physical and mental well-being of society; racial prejudice, which consists of socioeconomic prejudice; and the need to confront local, national, and international conflict that typifies so much of our existence with the vision of peace.

The vision for society is shaped by what God would have society be. Changes conforming to that vision come as Christians, individually and corporately, apply their sense of godly character and energy to society.

Summary of the Doctrine of Stewardship

God's plan of stewardship. Stewardship is a way of living that involves one's daily activities, values and goals for life, and the use of all possessions. It begins with God and His plans for creation and purposes for humankind. The steward is God's responsible representative and manager of all creation.

In the Creator's design, individuals are given a godlikeness (Ge 1:26-31) that includes the capacity for acting responsibly and intelligently. The steward is free to make decisions but accountable to God for the decisions made and actions taken.

As God's stewards, persons are given delegated authority (Ge 1:28). They are in charge of the material world—an authority that is real but secondary to God's final authority. Personal ownership is permitted but, again, secondary to God's ultimate ownership.

The Bible speaks of the steward as a manager or house overseer. The biblical vocabulary carries the idea of one who is in charge of the management of a household. In the New Testament this role is given added significance by the individual's relationship to the church family. The household manager or steward (Greek *oikonomos*) must exercise responsible stewardship (*oikonomia*) within the church family (Greek *oikos*).

Fundamental to Christian stewardship is a unique Christian view of material order. All things were created by Christ, for Christ, and are held together in Christ (Col 1:15-17). Christ's lordship is the organizing principle of life in which all things fit together to serve their purpose.

The practice of Christian stewardship requires that we allow this unique Christian view to shape our understanding of ownership, life-style, how to earn and spend money—the total use of material things. Non-Christian views insist that material things are either evil, valueless, or the only reality and the priority of life. One cannot be a Christian steward and live by non-Christian views and values!

The New Testament gives clear teachings on the use of material things. We are to use possessions to care for our families (1 Ti 5:4), help the needy (Mt 25:34-40; Lk 10:30-37), and to support the work of the church, ministers, and worldwide mission (1 Co 9:4-18).

A giving God expects a giving people. The Christian steward is a joyous giver. Just as God is a giving Being and Christ a self-giving Savior, so His followers give to express their new nature and life in Christ and to provide the means for fulfilling Christian purposes. They give of both self and possessions.

How much is one to give? The Old Testament tithe law required ten percent of animal and agricultural produce. The giving of alms, firstfruits, sacrifices, and vow and freewill offerings was also prominent in the Old Testament.

Giving reaches its noblest expression, however, in the life that centers in Christ, following the spirit of giving that He taught and exemplified. As one guiding principle, Paul called for giving measured by how one has prospered (1 Co 16:1-3). Certainly the Old Testament guideline is the minimum. The New Testament calls for giving that is regular, generous, worshipful, and growing as one grows in Christian love and grace.

Summary of the Doctrine of Last Things

Last things is often referred to as eschatology (Greek *eschaton*). The doctrine of last things inquires into the final completion or consummation of God's redemptive plan. In this sense, eschatology is about the future. In the biblical revelation this involves a climactic intervention of God into the historical process.

Teachings about last things touch three levels of human hope. In terms of the individual, the doctrine involves death, intermediate state, resurrection, judgment, rewards, and final destiny in heaven or hell. In terms of the church as a community of faith, the doctrine touches subjects like rapture of the church, great tribulation, millennium, and coming kingdom. On the cosmic level the doctrine embraces the renewal of all things, creation's redemption, new heavens and new earth, and the eternal order. In short, the full doctrine of last things requires the consideration of individual, communal, and cosmic eschatologies.

Shape of the future. The doctrine of last things sets the mind looking toward end-time events. Among the major expressions of eschatological hope are the day of the Lord, the kingdom of God, the age to come, and the last days. The day of the Lord was seen by the Old Testament prophets as a time when the Lord alone would be exalted (Isa 2:17) and a time of direct divine intervention into human affairs. Such a day could bring God's judgment through natural phenomena (Am 8:9-14) and human instruments (Zec 14:1-2). Likewise, the day could be associated with salvation for the faithful (Am 9:11-15) and peace among the nations (Isa 2:1-5).

The prophets frequently used an element of surprise, announcing a day of judgment to people expecting salvation (Am 5:18-20). The New Testament continued to look forward to the surprise of the day of the Lord (2 Pe 2:10-12) and called for holy lives to be ready for it. The day can be called the day of Jesus Christ (1 Co 1:8; 2 Co 1:14; Php 1:6,10). No one knows its date (Mt 24:36; 1 Th 5:1). The most important theme in the New Testament to speak of divine intervention into human affairs is the kingdom of God. The phrase refers to the dynamic rule of God. The emphasis ranges from an abstract idea of kingly sovereignty to a future realm over which Christ rules.

In one sense, the rule of God is a present reality among those in whom He reigns as Lord. In this sense, Jesus announced the kingdom to be near in His first coming (Mt 4:17). On an individual basis, the kingdom of God has been inaugurated. On the other hand, Jesus taught His followers to pray for a future coming of the kingdom (Mt 6:10). The future establishment of God's rule involves the second coming of Christ (Rev 19:6-16), His millennial reign (Rev 20:1-6), and the new heavens and new earth (Rev 21:1-5).

Jesus referred to two ages, "this age" and "the age to come" (Mt 12:32). The present age is characterized as evil and one from which Jesus came to effect deliverance (Gal 1:4). Satan is referred to as the god of this age (2 Co 4:4). There is a wisdom that belongs to this age but does not understand God's ways (1 Co 2:6-8).

The victory of Christ through death, resurrection, and exaltation spans both ages (Eph 1:19-21). The church is to be the display of divine grace in the coming ages (Eph 2:7). Believers already have tasted the "powers of the coming age" (Heb 6:5). This age will end and the age to come appear in fullness when Christ returns.

The early church saw the last days as a time of increasing evil. A description of those terrible days has a remarkably contemporary ring (2 Ti 3:1-5). The last days are to be characterized by scoffers possessing evil desires (2 Pe 3:3-4), who would deny the Lord's coming and bring division among believers (Jude 17-19), threatening their faith. Persecution and Satan's forces will bring tribulation on the church (2 Th 2:1-12; 1 Jn 2:18).

Death and resurrection. The individual dimensions of last things calls for consideration of death, the intermediate state, and resurrection.

Death for believers is described as falling asleep (1 Th 4:13), taking a rest (Rev 14:13), or departing to be with the Lord (2 Ti 4:6-8). For unbelievers, death is an enemy to be feared.

The period following death and prior to the resurrection of the body constitutes the intermediate state. Some see this as a period of embodied existence with either an interim body or the resurrection body received at death. Others see the biblical evidence pointing to a disembodied condition until resurrection (2 Co 5:1-5). Others do not think the dead in Christ will be conscious of a time interval between death and the final resurrection (Lk 16:22). This may be explained as the distinction between time consciousness in time and in eternity. The intermediate state for believers in any case is a time of being consciously present with the Lord (Php 1:23-24). For unbelievers, it is to be a time of conscious misery in separation from God (Lk 16:19-26).

The resurrection of believers will occur at the time of Jesus' return (1 Co 15:50-57). The hope for it is grounded on the historical fact of His resurrection. Unbelievers also will be resurrected, but it will be unto condemnation (Jn 5:25-29).

The Bible clearly points to final judgment. Some Bible students see biblical indication of separate judgments, hence separate resurrections, for believers and unbelievers. The interval between the two often is called the millennium (Rev 20:1-6). Many, however, see the biblical revelation pointing toward one general resurrection and judgment (Mt 25:31-46).

Jesus' resurrection body (Jn 20:20—21:14) furnishes the prototype for our resurrection body. He apparently was able to transcend time and space. While details are not given, the indication is there will be both continuity and change in relation to earthly bodies (1 Co 15:35-49). The fact of continuity implies the ability to recognize one another in heaven.

Return of Christ. The central, catalytic event of eschatology will be the return of Christ. From the announcement of the angels at the time of His ascension (Ac 1:11) to the Bible's last chapter (Rev 22:7,12,20) the promise is given.

Jesus spoke of signs preceding His return. He named such things as the appearance of false messiahs, famines and earthquakes, abating love and abounding iniquity, and worldwide proclamation of the gospel (Mt 24:3-14). However, speculation about precise date-setting is disallowed.

More important than when it is to occur are the attitudes held toward the return.

These range from scoffing to eager expectation (2 Pe 3:3-4; Php 3:20). Faith says, "Even so, come, Lord Jesus." Unbelief asks, "Where is the promise of His coming?"

The purpose for Christ's return is to complete what was begun at His first coming. The completion of personal salvation, as well as the presentation of the church as glorious, awaits Jesus' return. The overthrow of evil and the balancing work of a just judgment also await His return.

Several end-time events are connected closely with the return of Christ. What is commonly called the rapture of the church is one. Sincere believers may differ as to the time of occurrence, but all anticipate the catching up of living believers when He returns (1 Th 4:14-18). Many passages speak of a future period of tribulation and persecution for the earth. It will be a time of outpoured wrath. Many see the major portion of Revelation to be speaking of a future tribulation time (chs 4—19). Others are not so confident about such a futuristic and literal application of the apocalyptic language of Revelation. The matter of a millennial period has been the subject of Christian discussion through the centuries. The thousand years of Revelation 20:1-6 can be assigned symbolic meaning. The result is a message about the present spiritual reign of Christ in resurrection and ascension victory. On the other hand, the passage allows for the expectation of a literal, earthly millennial reign of Christ. Whichever interpretation is accepted, Christ's rule as King over creation is the central hope of believers. Judgment and resultant destinies of heaven or hell are prominent themes in discussions of last things. While reverent students may differ on details, everyone expects evil and evil workers to be judged and the righteous and righteous deeds to be rewarded. The ultimate expression of judgment of evil is hell and that of righteousness is heaven. Eternal punishment and eternal blessedness are parallel truths (Jn 5:29).

Implications for today's living. What difference does it make if one has a healthy, balanced, and biblical view of last things? It inspires hope (Col 1:5) and moral purity (1 Jn 3:3). Faithfulness is encouraged by the knowledge that eternal rewards are waiting and by the reminder that the future is secured by sheer grace (1 Co 15:58). The fact that the end includes judgment and separation between the faithful and the unbelieving demands personal preparedness (Mt 25:1-13).

Significance. It would be difficult to overstate the place of eschatology in the whole of biblical teaching. Almost every doctrine has a forward-looking dimension. Each other doctrine stands in the shadow of eschatology.

Creation longs for the consummation of redemption. Affected by the fall, the created order anticipates a liberation from the bondage of decay (Ro 8:18-21).

History as biblically understood is moving toward consummation. It moves toward a summation of "all things in heaven and on earth together under one head, even Christ" (Eph 1:10).

Humanity finds hope in the final restoration of all things. The defeat of Satan and the end of evil, coupled with the newness of a resurrection body and the attainment of full-grown likeness to Christ, will mean paradise regained, the ultimate restoration of grace (Eph 1:10-14).

The kingdom of God, inaugurated by Christ, finds final establishment in the events of the end time. The return of Christ, the overthrow of Satan and evil, and the redemption of believing humanity and the created order will result in the delivering up of the kingdom to God (1 Co 15:24).

The church locates its ultimate destiny and perfection in the eschatological end time. As a bride to be presented to her bridegroom, a body to become full-grown, and a building to be made a holy temple in which God resides, the church moves toward its blessed hope (Rev 19:7-9).

Satan, the archenemy of God, of His purposes, and of His people, will be overcome in the final triumph of Christ and His kingdom. With the defeat of Satan, evil faces its final, losing struggle with righteousness (Rev 20:1-6).

Salvation, initiated within history, finds ultimate realization in end-time events and the eternal order. It encompasses the redemption of individuals, the glorification of the church, and the liberation of the created universe from sin's binding effects (Rev 21:1-7).

God's People

Summary of the Doctrine of The Church

Old Testament concepts. From the beginning, God purposed to create for Himself a people who would live in service and in relationship to Him. God chose Abraham and revealed Himself to Abraham and his descendents.

By initiating a covenant with Abraham, God indicated His desire to establish a relationship with the people whom He created. Covenants had particular meaning in the ancient Near East. Covenants defined relationships between countries, kings, or individuals. For Noah, Abraham, Israel, David, and others with whom God entered into covenant, the covenant described God's promises to His people based on His unswerving love. The covenant established and defined the relationship between God and His people. God initiated the relationship, seeking out a people to serve Him and to do His will.

God's people depend on Him, seeking His guidance for all of life. People in relationship with God obey His commands. God gives directions for living that allow the best possible life.

The kingdom of God in the Old Testament was closely associated with the kingdom of Israel. This association, of course, had great validity. God created the people of Israel and intended for them to obey His commands and to follow His will. However, God's people did not always follow His ways. Many people in Israel rebelled against God, worshiping other gods exclusively or worshiping the Lord along with other gods. Because of this disobedience, the kingdom of Israel cannot be precisely equated with the kingdom of God. The kingdom of God is God's rule over the world. Those who obey God make up His kingdom; those who rebel against God, refusing to follow His way, have no part in the kingdom of God.

The doctrine of the remnant helped to solve the theological problem resulting from the people's disobedience and God's judgment. How could God's people suffer defeat at the hands of approaching armies? Would God abandon the people whom He had chosen and with whom He had entered into covenant? God does judge His people when they rebel against Him. However, God does not abandon even a rebellious people. Judgment has a redemptive purpose. The Lord promised to restore a remnant of faithful people to carry on His work in the world. God's purpose to make for Himself a people remained constant. The people of God survived because God remained faithful to His people. In every age and in the midst of the darkest tragedies of life, the Lord is with His people.

Though the kingdom of Israel did not survive, God's kingdom is everlasting. Jesus proclaimed the fulfillment of the kingdom of God. Those who heard and responded to His work entered God's kingdom. Jesus emphasized the necessity of repentance. All who would become part of the kingdom of God must turn from sin and obey the will of the King.

The kingdom of God was present in the person of Jesus Christ. At the same time the kingdom of God awaits its ultimate fulfillment in the coming again of our Lord. Jesus spoke *of the kingdom of God as present when* people responded to Him in faith and obedience. He also spoke of the kingdom in terms of a future fulfillment.

New Testament concepts. The New Testament writers appear to have drawn from the emphasis of the people of God in the Old Testament as they spoke of the church. Drawing from the aspects of covenant, community, kingdom, and remnant, they believed that God continued to work among His people. God had not forsaken His people in times of trouble in the past. People of faith knew that He would continue to bless His people in the times ahead.

While the idea of the church builds on the work of God in former times, the concept took on greater significance when God appeared in the flesh to seek and to save those who are lost. Jesus began the church. He built it on His own great work and on the response of faith to that work. The church is described by many images. Two of the most comprehensive refer to the church as the bride of Christ and as the body of Christ. The image of the church as the bride of Christ emphasizes the devotion, fidelity, and purity of the church. As the bridegroom, Christ showed His joy and love for the church, even to the point of dying for the church. The church is also the body of Christ. Christ is the head of the church, indicating authority and control. The church is the body of Christ, obeying His commands.

Purpose of the church. Jesus charged the church with unique stewardship responsibilities. He entrusted the church with work that could not be done by any other organization. Jesus gave the church the keys to the kingdom of heaven. As the church proclaims the good news of the kingdom, accepting those whom others reject, forgiveness can be experienced. If the church spurns its obligations of preaching, teaching, and accepting, many people will not know God's forgiveness.

The church is Christ's. It follows Him in obedience and faith. The church practices love and proclaims salvation through Jesus Christ. Every believer follows Christ and is part of the church, ministering in His name and building up the body of Christ.

Functioning of the church. The church is a fellowship. Through the fellowship of the church, love is demonstrated. Jesus left instructions for Christians to love one another and gave guidelines which, if followed, help to restore broken relationships in the fellowship.

All who trust Christ make up the church. Jesus accepts all who accept Him. Jesus' ministry was a ministry of inclusion. Those whom others rejected, Jesus accepted. With these people Jesus built His church. While accepting everyone—the rich and the powerful as well as the poor and weak—Jesus made everyone servants of the great King. Those who make up the church are servants of Christ and others. Those who live for power and glory are frustrated in the church. Jesus made servanthood His criterion for greatness.

People become part of the church as they commit themselves to the person of Jesus Christ, proclaiming Him as their Lord. No one enters into the fellowship of the church apart from Jesus. Those who trust Christ are called saints as well as servants. The term *saints* designates all who trust Christ, not just exceptional Christians. Saints are those who have been set apart for service to God. All Christians are ministers, serving God, His people, and His world.

Form of the church. The church is primarily local in its expression. Yet believers of all ages are part of the kingdom of God. Jesus prayed for those who one day would believe (Jn 17:20). He blessed those who could believe even though they had not seen the mighty miracles of the New Testament era.

As a local body of believers, the church preaches the gospel of the kingdom and demonstrates the new humanity created by the blood of Jesus Christ. Although the church often meets in a building, the church is not a building. The church is the body of believers meeting together in a partnership or fellowship of labor for Jesus Christ. Because the church is local, local problems often are treated in ways that fit the needs of the local congregation. The local congregation deals with problems of fellowship or doctrine according to the teachings of the Scripture, the leading of the Holy Spirit, and methods that promote fellowship and obedience to the commands of Christ.

The church practices according to the commands of Christ. This polity involves the unique relationship of the church with Christ. The church must include rather than exclude people. All who trust Christ are part of His church. Each church differs on certain practices but agrees on the essentials of the faith. As an autonomous body of believers, the church obeys the commands of Christ and follows His leading. No one in the church should "lord it over" other members. Nor should those outside the fellowship control the work of the church. The church proclaims the gospel as it observes the ordinances of the church. Baptism and the Lord's Supper magnify the One who gave His life for the church. These practices look backward to the resurrection of Jesus and point forward to His coming again.

Summary of the Doctrine of Ordinances

Background. As a religious term, ordinances refers to anything that has been ordained or established as a commandment, a worship ritual, or an institution. Specifically it has come to designate baptism and the Lord's Supper as divinely ordained rituals that carry important significance for the Christian church. The background of the ordinances of baptism and the Lord's Supper can be found in the prophetic symbols that appear throughout the Old Testament. Even though the prophets used the power of the word, both spoken and written, to convey their divine message, they often used a sign, a symbol, or a prophetic act to undergird and reinforce the word. Whether we recall the staff of Moses (Ex 4:1-5; 14:16), the prophet Isaiah walking stripped and haggard like a war refugee in Jerusalem (Isa 20), or Ezekiel digging a hole in the side of his house to carry out a few belongings (Eze 12:1-9), we get the divine message of judgment more clearly than words alone could ever convey.

When the action is seen as an action of God to deliver His people, then the symbol carries a special power to re-create the event for the believing community, both in covenant Israel and in the early church. The Exodus and crossing of the Red Sea was a powerful redemptive event that became enshrined in the worship of Israel in the annual Passover celebration (Ex 12—14). In the Lord's Supper, early Christians celebrated in a similar way their redemption through the body and blood of Jesus and their conviction that they would share in the coming messianic banquet in the Father's kingdom.

Meaning. The meaning of the ordinances lies exactly in their power to re-create the redemptive acts of God in history and to give the worshiper an opportunity to participate spiritually in those events. When John baptized in Jordan, he was announcing the inbreaking reign of the Messiah and calling people to repent and prepare for the coming kingdom. When early Christians baptized in Jesus' name, they were identifying with Him in His death and resurrection, repenting of their sins, and confessing Him as Lord and Savior of their lives.

The Lord's Supper provided the opportunity to re-create in a dramatic way the events that occurred in the passion of Jesus and to celebrate His presence with them through the Holy Spirit. It pointed back to the great redemptive act of God in the Exodus of the Old Testament as Jesus became the Passover Lamb of God offered for the sins of the world. It pointed forward to the time when He was coming again to establish His kingdom and gather all the redeemed to the messianic table.

Practice. Most of the conflicts over the ordinances have come over matters of administration and observance: what is the proper form of baptism and the proper elements of the Supper, or who is the authorized administrator and the qualified recipient of the ordinance?

On all these questions, the Bible focuses on the *meaning* of the ordinances. Because baptism means burial and resurrection with Jesus, the burial and resurrection of the Christian believer is pictured in the powerful symbol of baptism as the new believer is buried in and rises from the water. Because baptism in the name of Jesus means confessing Him as Lord, the Bible insists that only one who truly is believing in Jesus can be baptized with that meaning. Jesus is the source and authority for the administration of baptism. He commanded

limited only by their gifts of ministry. Proclamation, teaching, and evangelism roles may be filled by deacons.

Prophets continue the ministry of the apostle. They are not appointed to office by the deliberation of any human body. Prophets have a direct vision of the divine will for their day and proclaim it. Their authority derives from their inspiration alone. Because the New Testament warns that many false prophets will arise, the church has the responsibility of testing them to see if they are genuinely inspired by God.

Teachers are the guardians and interpreters of the Christian tradition. They instruct the church in its moral duties and doctrine. Whereas prophets keep the church from becoming petrified in its tradition, teachers keep the church from fanatical excesses.

The term *evangelist* appears only infrequently in the New Testament. Nevertheless, evangelistic work is mentioned frequently. Evangelists declare the Word of God to those who have never heard in order to awaken faith.

All church leaders have responsibility to God and to the church to be high examples of Christian love and morality as they serve God and His church.

Summary of the Doctrine of Education

Why education? Had the Scriptures been written without reference to education, the nature of biblical revelation would have been radically altered. For the religion of the Bible is a teaching religion, and the God of the Bible is a teaching God (Job 36:22).

Teachers in the Bible. Teaching was woven into the warp and woof of Israel's religious experience. To Israel, the essence of religion was knowing and keeping the law of God. Moses, the great lawgiver, also became Israel's great teacher (Dt 4:5-6). To keep the Law faithfully, they must study its precepts diligently (Dt 5:31). It was no coincidence that the Law came to be called "Torah," a word that also meant "instruction."

The priests and Levites were not mere custodians of the sacrificial system; from the outset, they were charged with the task of instructing the people (Lev 10:11). In post-Exilic times, the priests played an especially important role as teachers of Israel (Ne 8:1-10). Beginning with Samuel (1 Sa 12:23), the prophets also functioned as teachers.

The most important center of education during the Old Testament period was the home. Again and again, parents were urged to tell their children about the mighty acts of God (Ex 12:26-27; 13:14) and were exhorted to instruct them in God's commandments (Dt 6:1-10). In the time of the wisdom writers, fathers and mothers shared this responsibility (Pr 1:8-9).

In the New Testament era, teaching took on new significance in the ministry of Jesus. Teaching was His most typical function (Mt 5:1-2; Lk 4:14-15), and "Teacher" was His primary identity. Disciples (Mk 4:38), opponents (Mt 8:19), and friends (Jn 11:28) all called Him "Teacher." On repeated occasions, Jesus referred to Himself as "Teacher" (Mt 23:10; Mk 14:14; Lk 22:11; Jn 1:13-14).

In the Great Commission (Mt 28:19-20) Jesus commanded His followers to make disciples (learners) and to instruct them in His teachings. Early Christians took this educational mandate seriously, devoting themselves to the teaching of the apostles (Ac 2:42) and instructing one another (Ac 18:26).

Teaching was a mainline evangelistic strategy in the New Testament era. Immediately after Pentecost, Christian disciples taught in the Temple area (Ac 5:42) on a daily basis. Christian missionaries moved into Asia and Europe, teaching the gospel wherever they went (Ac 15:35; 18:11; 28:31). Teaching and proclaiming were separate but closely related activities. Wherever new churches were founded, Christian teachers were there (Ro 12:7; 1 Co

12:28; Gal 6:6; 1 Ti 5:17; Tit 2:3). In Christian homes, the religious instruction of children was as important as it had been in ancient Israel (Eph 6:4).

Aims of education. Christian education has basic aims to achieve. These may be listed as: leading Christians to wisdom, guidance in daily living, happiness, correction of sin and error, influence of the social order, spiritual renewal, moral purity, learning and preserving Christian tradition and teaching, training in effective Christian witnessing, and self-preservation in a society opposed to Christian teachings.

The Bible teaches and illustrates several methods of teaching. These include: discipline, personal example, instruction, object lessons, parables, questioning, Bible study, symbolic actions, repetition, group participation, and obedience.

Today, education remains close to the heartbeat of vital, aggressive Christianity. Those who would live out the teachings of Jesus in a secularized culture must understand their meaning. Those who would share the gospel with a lost world must have an intelligent comprehension of its saving message. This is the task of Christian education.

Summary of the Doctrine of Family

God's preparation for family. Marriage and family are God's idea. From the first chapters of Genesis through virtually all of the New Testament, insights come from God's revelation, assisting couples and families to live creatively and happily together. God designed marriage as an answer to the nature of human life as He purposed it. Family is obviously the result of God's plan for human reproduction, but God's purpose for sexuality is more than procreation. It is also one aspect of the human desire for companionship (Ge 2).

God's purposes for marriage and family. In addition to meeting the human need for companionship, sexual union, and children, family also is the setting within which religious faith is nurtured through parental example and teachings. Family is used as a symbol of God's relationship to His children as Father as well as a symbol of the church in its relationship to Jesus Christ. Both positive and negative illustrations of Hebrew and Christian responses to God are symbolized in family terms. Choosing to remain single is affirmed by the Bible for those who can thus serve God better.

Human failure to fulfill God's plan. Very early in the Bible, man and woman failed to fulfill God's purposes for their lives. Sin affected their relationship to each other as well as to their Creator. Disobedience, female subordination, parental failure, children's rebellion, multiple wives, and broken marriages became a reality among God's people because of sin. God's covenant offer of forgiveness and renewal is continually accepted and quickly neglected. Biblical writers pictured God's judgment on families as well as on the nation in graphic terms.

Human fulfillment of God's plan. The gospel offers new life to men and women through faith in Jesus Christ. New life in Christ restores God's original purpose for family life. The one flesh union becomes a symbolic way of describing the essential unity of marriage partners, while retaining and honoring their individuality. Marriage permanence is taught by Jesus. Fulfilling family relationships is encouraged by the New Testament writers. Centering the home in Christ is the foundation for mutual submission to one another in love.

Qualities of maturity. Marriage and family have high priority, but loyalty to Christ is the supreme loyalty for Christians. Faith is expressed in the home through love and service to one another. This gives testimony to one's acceptance of the lordship of Christ. Religious zeal cannot be substituted for meeting home needs when basic loyalties are not involved.

Essential factors in strong families. Strong family relationships are not maintained automatically. They must be nurtured through Bible study, family worship, communication, conflict resolution, and developing friendships outside the family.

The Church and the World

Summary of the Doctrine of Evangelism

Meaning of evangelism. Evangelism can be defined as a concerted effort to confront unbelievers with the truth about and the claims of Jesus Christ with a view to leading them into repentance toward God and faith in our Lord Jesus Christ and thus into the fellowship of the church. This is our Lord's call when He said, "You will be my witnesses" (Ac 1:8).

The Bible makes it crystal clear that God intends *all* His people to be engaged, one way or another, in the grand task. To be a faithful Christian demands faithful witnessing.

Motives of evangelism. Evangelism brings glory to God, which believers seek to do in all of life. Evangelism flows naturally from believers' love of people. Evangelism represents loving obedience to Christ's commands. These motives lead believers to share the gospel with those who do not know Jesus as Savior.

Reasons for evangelism. Evangelism is necessary because people are lost without Christ, humanity's only hope. Evangelism leads to salvation of people in Christ and thus fulfills God's eternal purpose to create a holy people for Himself. In evangelism, God uses His people, and they get involved in His work.

Theology of evangelism. Evangelism has deep theological roots in God's eternal purpose and love. The ministry, death, resurrection, and return of Christ give content to evangelistic testimony as well as being the theological basis for evangelistic work. We are evangelists because Christ died for us and instilled the resurrection hope in us. God's judgment on sin provides the theological reason for evangelism. All people need to know sinners face judgment eternally without Christ. The alternative is the biblical call to salvation in repentance and faith. The reality of salvation through faith inspires evangelism. The results of salvation in the believer's life give a theological base for personal witness to those who do not know salvation and the new life it brings.

Examples of evangelism. Evangelism occurs in many places in many ways. The Bible tells of mass evangelism, personal evangelism, evangelism through social action, small-group evangelism, and evangelism through teaching.

Practicalities of evangelism. The Bible illustrates the practical work of evangelism. It is a gift of God (Eph 4:11) to be practiced through the church in all areas of society—home, marketplace, and so forth. Evangelism may bring immediate decisions or may be a work of cultivation resulting in long-term results. At times direct confrontation is necessary.

Power of evangelism. Human power is not adequate for the evangelistic task. The indwelling Holy Spirit combines with the power of God in the gospel message to produce effective evangelism. Added power comes from the power of the witness's holy life, a holiness made possible in God's power. The power of the Holy Spirit, the gospel, and the holy life give energy to gospel proclamation done for evangelistic purposes.

Study of and commitment to evangelism will thrust us into the arena of spiritual battles and enable us to see great victories through our witness as people come to Christ.

Summary of the Doctrine of Missions

Missions has its ultimate source in God. In simple definition mission is a sending. In biblical sense it refers to God's eternal plan to reach all people of all ages with His offer of salvation. Missions, in plural, means the organized effort of God's people to carry God's good news to all peoples everywhere and thus fulfill God's eternal mission. Missions was born in the heart of God. His love plan for the world was expressed in His call of Abraham (Ge 12:1-3). The mission of blessing thus was assigned to one people, but its scope has always been all people. This divine concern for all peoples is woven into the entire fabric of the Old Testament (Ps 67:3-4; Isa 42:6-10; 49:6; 66:19).

The scope of missions is all people, nations, and tongues. Missions is a central doctrine running like a golden thread from Genesis to Revelation. It means God sends His people in His authority to carry a message of salvation. Missions is the extension of evangelism to include Christian outreach to every person on earth. Missions calls us to responsibility for all people, especially those we will never see or know.

Missions reveals God's initiative in redeeming the lost. Missions is not a natural human idea or action. It is God's love plan to redeem sinners. This love plan centers on the work of Jesus Christ and offers forgiveness of sin to all people through His name (Lk 24:45-48). God not only took the initiative in providing salvation, but also He took initiative in sending His people out to share the story of salvation. Jesus' Great Commission to missions provides the climax of His ministry and the beginning of Christian missions (Mt 28:18-20; Lk 24:47-48; Jn 20:21; Ac 1:8). Thus God calls His church and its individual members to missions in general and to specific missionary tasks in particular. The command to missions and the call to mission tasks are based on the comprehensive authority of Christ (Mt 28:18). The mission task is an evangelistic one, finding and implementing ways to inform and confront each member of the world's population with the call to salvation through the life, death, and resurrection of Christ. He makes it possible for all peoples to become heirs of God's promises first made to Israel (Ro 1:16; Eph 3:6; Col 1:27). The worldwide missionary effort is possible only because the Holy Spirit empowers it.

God uses human instruments in missions. Missions works through missionaries, people God chooses from local churches and sends across the city or around the world on His mission. Missionaries go because they are filled with God's love and with the desire to glorify Him. Missionaries are not forced to go. They go in free response to God's loving call, following the examples of New Testament missionaries such as Paul and Barnabas (Ac 13:1-5). They go as representatives of the church with the support of the church. Missions is thus a cooperative effort involving God's election, the dedication and support of the church, the individual's free choice and commitment, and the reception by the people whom God prepares for the missionary's coming. The missionary becomes God's ambassador among a new people proclaiming the gospel; ministering to people's needs; sharing God's love in concrete, personal ways; creating fellowship in Christian love; and reconciling people to one another and to God through Jesus Christ.

Missions produces results in history and in eternity. Missions brings new people to join God's kingdom in repentance and faith. It produces changes in people's lives and thus in the life of a society. The fruits of missions will only be known in eternity. Missions is not optional for the Christian or the church today. To be obedient to God is to be missionary. Many persons are not believers because they have never heard the gospel (Ro 10:14-15). To see that they hear is our responsibility as members of the body of Christ.

Histories of the Major Doctrines

Christians rely on God's Word as the source of their beliefs or doctrines. Throughout the history of the Christian church, believers have sought to understand the doctrines of Holy Scripture and communicate those understandings to other believers and the world at large. Seeing how Christian doctrines have been understood through the history of Christ's church helps contemporary disciples better understand the issues involved in each doctrine. Such historical study brings a deepened appreciation for the power and truth of God's holy Word. The histories that follow reveal how Christian thinkers have understood and misunderstood biblical doctrine. Note that some teachings are not valid biblical doctrine and that suggested readings do not always represent the viewpoints of the writer of the article or of the editorial staff.

The Trinitarian God

History of the Doctrine of God

The foundational doctrine for Christianity is its doctrine of God. Proper understanding of the Christian God involves recognizing the nature and character of His Being.

The cardinal tenet of the Jewish concept of God was a strict monotheism. The Shema (Dt 6:4-9) commences with, "Hear, O Israel: The LORD our God, the LORD is one." When early Christians began to describe the impact of Jesus of Nazareth on their lives and to experience the reality of the Holy Spirit, a new formulation describing the nature of God was required. It took several centuries and much disputing for the church to formulate a clear doctrine of the Trinity.

The watershed for the trinitarian debate was the Council of Nicaea, convened in 325 by the Emperor Constantine. The Council addressed the Arian controversy, which derived its name from Arius, a presbyter of Alexandria. Arius suggested a formula of relationship between the Son and the Father that was ultimately rejected. He maintained that: (1) there is only one unbegotten God, one unoriginated Being, without any beginning of existence; (2) the Son was generated by the Father, created out of nothing before the world was called into being, becoming the greatest and first of all created beings; and, (3) for that reason, the Son is of different essence (*heteroousios*) from the Father.

Arius was opposed by Athanasius, archdeacon of Alexandria. Athanasius contended that: (1) the Son was eternally generated by the Father; (2) He is of the same essence (*homoousios*) as the Father; and (3) while there is no division or separation in the essential Being of God, the Son remains a distinct person from the Father.

Constantine's decision to side with Athanasius secured the victory for that position. The Council of Nicaea adopted the statement which became the bedrock Christian declaration regarding the nature of Christ: "We believe in one God, the Father Almighty, Maker of things visible and invisible. And in one Lord Jesus Christ, . . . begotten not made, of one substance (*homoousios*) with the Father . . . ."

The Holy Spirit received only a brief line of treatment at Nicaea: "And (we believe) in the Holy Spirit." The Council of Constantinople in 381, reflecting the influence of the Cappadocian Fathers (Gregory of Nyssa, Gregory of Nazianzus, Basil), endorsed the consubstantiality (same substance) of the Holy Spirit with the Father and the Son. The essence of their doctrine was that the one Godhead exists simultaneously in three modes of being, or hypostases ("one *ousia* in three *hupostaseis*").

Augustine gave the Western tradition its most mature statement on the Trinity in his *De Trinitate.* Between the three hypostases a relation exists of mutual interpenetration and interdwelling. The divine persons are not three separate individuals in the same way as three human beings who belong to the same genus. Each is identical with the others or with the divine Substance itself. Their distinctiveness results from their mutual relations. The Father is distinguished in that He begets the Son, the Spirit in that He is bestowed by the Father and Son.

Development of a doctrine of God bereft of revelational moorings results in a drifting away from traditional Christian understandings of His nature. Philosophical approaches have yielded a variety of unacceptable alternatives of who or what God is, ranging from deism (a Creator who, once finished with the creative process, allows the universe to run itself without personal interference), to pantheism (in which God is identified with the universe in a completely immanental fashion), to process thought (a panentheism where God is in the universe but not exhausted by it), even to the God-is-dead movement (in which God no longer retains viability for modern life and understanding).

Attempts to develop a doctrine of God which elevate one or a group of divine attributes to primary influence have proven inadequate to convey the full spectrum of the biblical revelation regarding the nature of God. Love that champions over holiness or righteousness is not the biblical concept of divine love. Rather, the Bible presents a God whose love is informed by His other divine attributes.

Reggie McNeal

Suggested Reading: Gonzales, Justo L. *A History of Christian Thought,* Vols. 1 and 2. Nashville, Tn: Abingdon Press, 1975. Hocking, David L. *The Nature of God in Plain Language.* Waco, Tx: Word Books, 1984. Ward, Wayne E. *The Holy Spirit.* Nashville, Tn: Broadman Press, 1987.

History of the Doctrine of Jesus Christ

Christology is the branch of theology that deals with the person of Jesus Christ. Any distinction between the person and work of Jesus Christ is strictly for emphasis, for who Jesus Christ was relates to what He did.

In early Christianity some held that Jesus Christ had not come in the flesh and that He only seemed to be human (Docetism), for He would be sinful if He were material or fleshly (gnosticism, ca. 150). Some, primarily of a Jewish background, held that He was only human (Ebionism, ca. 120). Between these two extremes mainstream Christians affirmed both the humanity and the divinity of Jesus Christ.

Mainstream Christians faced views advanced by other Christians known as Monarchians because of their emphasis on one God. Some held that Jesus was merely a good man whom God adopted as His Son (adoptionism). The adoption was usually dated at Jesus' baptism. God then gave to His Son (by adoption, not by nature) a unique power which Jesus employed to perform miracles (dynamism, ca. 200). Others held that the one God successively manifested Himself in three modes as Father, Son, and Spirit, and that Jesus Christ was really this one God in the mode of Son (Modalism, ca. 220). In reaction Tertullian of Carthage argued that God is one substance in three persons and that Jesus Christ was the incarnate Son of God, one person in two natures.

Around 320-325 Arius, presbyter of Alexandria, taught that the Son is not eternal, that He was the first created being and God's agent in the rest of creation. Thus, according to Arius, there is no eternal Son of God; there was a time when He was not, and He came into being from nothing, just as did the rest of creation. The Nicene Council of 325 condemned Arianism and taught that God's Son is eternal, that His essence or substance is the same as that of God the Father, and that the purpose of the incarnation of God's Son was and is humanity's salvation. Thus, mainstream Christianity resolved questions about the Son's relation to the Father (doctrine of Trinity) in such a way as to insist on the divinity of the Son.

Between 370 and 681 Christianity rejected many explanations of Jesus Christ which, while affirming the doctrine of the Trinity, failed to protect the Son's full incarnation. Among unacceptable views were these: (1) Jesus Christ had a human body and a human psyche (soul), but the eternal Logos (Jn 1:1) replaced the human mind, thus denying incarnation at the center of human decision-making (Apollinarianism, 381). (2) Jesus Christ had both a divine nature and a human nature, but each nature had its own person; He was therefore two persons (Nestorianism, 431). (3) Jesus Christ was a single person in two natures, but His human nature was a generic, pre-fall, non-sinful nature different from the nature of all other human beings (Cyrillism, 430). (4) There were two natures, divine and human, before the incarnation of God's Son, but in the incarnation there was only one nature, the human nature being absorbed by the divine nature (Eutychianism, 448; later Monophysitism). (5) Though Jesus Christ was one Person in two natures, He was under the control of only one energy (divine) and one will (Monothelitism, 681).

In 451 the Council of Chalcedon defined what has become known as orthodox Christology—namely, that the incarnate Son of God is "recognized in two natures, without confusion, without change, without division, without separation." The Third Council of Constantinople (681) taught that in Jesus Christ were two natural wills and two natural energies.

Most modern Christian denominations (Anglican, Baptist, Catholic, Congregational, Eastern Orthodox, Lutheran, Methodist, Presbyterian, Reformed, etc.) affirm orthodox Christology; a few espouse Monophysitism which affirms the divine nature, and a few espouse some form of unitarianism which affirms only the human nature. Theologians continue to offer explanations of the relationship between the divine and human natures of Jesus Christ, some emphasizing the divine nature, some emphasizing the human nature, but most emphasizing both natures.

G. Hugh Wamble

Suggested Reading: Hendricks, William L. *Who is Jesus Christ?* Vol. 2 of *Layman's Library of Christian Doctrine.* Nashville, Tn: Broadman Press, 1986. Wells, David F. *The Person of Christ.* Westchester, Ill: Crossway Books, 1984.

History of the Doctrine of the Holy Spirit

Early trinitarian debate focused on the person of Christ, with little emphasis given to the Holy Spirit. At the famous Council of Nicaea in 325, Athanasius prevailed in securing a statement concerning the relationship between the Father and Son that has become Christian dogma. He contended that: (1) the Son was eternally generated by the Father; (2) He is of the same essence (*homoousios*) as the Father; and, (3) while there is no division or separation in the essential Being of God, the Son remains a distinct person from the Father. The Council adopted a statement incorporating these elements, appending only one brief line of treatment regarding the Holy Spirit: "And (we believe) in the Holy Spirit."

After Nicaea, interest was heightened in defining the relationship of the Spirit to the Father and Son. Some claimed that the Spirit was of a different essence from that of the Father and the Son, insisting that the Spirit was a high order of created being. A leading spokesman for this group was Macedonius, bishop of Constantinople, whose followers became known as Macedonians or Pneumatomachians (from *pneuma,* spirit, and *machomai,* to speak evil against).

Athanasius vigorously asserted that the Spirit was also *homoousion* (same essence) with the Father and the Son. He was joined by the Cappadocian fathers—Basil, Gregory of Nyssa, and Gregory of Nazianzus—who argued that the Spirit was consubstantial (same substance) with the other two Persons of the Godhead. At the Council of Alexandria in 362 the proposition was accepted that the Spirit is not a creature but is of the same substance, and is inseparable from, the Father and the Son.

In 381 the general Council of Constantinople promulgated the following formula under the guidance of Gregory of Nazianzus: "And we believe in the Holy Spirit, the Lord, the Life-giving, who proceeds from the Father, who is to be glorified with the Father and the Son, and who speaks through the prophets." Though *homoousion* was not used in the formula, it was clearly understood that consubstantiality had been unequivocally affirmed. This has remained the primary Christian affirmation about the person of the Holy Spirit.

The statement by the Council raised a question regarding the relation of the Holy Spirit to the other members of the Trinity. The Holy Spirit was said to proceed from the Father, while it was neither denied nor affirmed that He also proceeds from the Son. The equivocal nature of the formula reflected the lack of agreement on this point. To say that the Holy Spirit proceeds from the Father only looked like a denial of the essential unity of the Father with the Son; on the other hand, to say that He also proceeds from the Son seemed to place the Spirit in a more dependent position than the Son, thereby circumscribing His deity.

Western theologians generally held to the procession of the Holy Spirit from both the Father and the Son. At the Council of Toledo in 589 the Nicaeno-Constantinopolitan creed was altered to read that the Spirit proceeds from the Father "and the Son." This became known as the famous "*filioque*" (son), receiving its name from the inserted Latin phrase, *procedit ex patre filioque,* proceeds from the Father and the Son.

Eastern theologians rejected the doctrine of double procession, preferring instead to say that the Spirit proceeds from the Father through the Son. This difference became the major dividing issue over which the East and West split.

The Reformers' theological interest in the Holy Spirit concerned mainly the Spirit's role in inspiration and interpretation of the Scripture. Their battlecry of the priesthood of all believers reflected their exalted view of the work of the Spirit both in the believer's individual life and in his or her corporate life with other Christians in the church. Subsequent Protestant development has expanded on these themes.

The modern Pentecostal movement has led to theological discussion over the nature of the sanctifying work of the Spirit in the believer's life and the proper expression of the gifts of the Spirit in the church.

Reggie McNeal

Suggested Reading: Gonzales, Justo L. *A History of Christian Thought, Vols. 1 and 2.* Nashville, Tn: Abingdon Press, 1975. Hocking, David L. *The Nature of God in Plain Language.* Waco, Tx: Word Books, 1984. Ward, Wayne E. *The Holy Spirit.* Nashville, Tn: Broadman Press, 1987.

The World

History of the Doctrine of Creation

Very soon after the New Testament era, ideas denying that the Father of Jesus Christ could have created the world arose in the Christian church. Gnosticism (see glossary) attempted to absolve God from the responsibility of having made the world with its matter and "imperfections." It proposed a long series of ages that stood between the supreme deity and the error from which the world was originated. This was the reason that Marcion (second century) distinguished between the God and Father of Jesus Christ and the Creator of the world. Over against Marcion, Irenaeus affirmed that the God of salvation is the same as the God of creation.

A second issue involved the notion that God created the world out of pre-existing matter and ideas. Basilides and Valentinus (second century) advanced a dualism which held to two self-existent principles—God and matter. These are distinct from and coeternal with each other. Historically, the church has responded with a denial of all forms of ultimate dualism. God creates *ex nihilo* (out of nothing).

Syrian Gnostics (e.g., Satornilus of Antioch and Tatian of Assyria of the second century) theorized that the universe is of the same substance with God and is the product of successive emanations from His being. Pantheism (belief that everything is divine) was early recognized as the ultimate result of such a stance.

Origen (third century) regarded creation as an act of God in eternity past. He affirmed that, God being eternal Creator, creation itself must be eternal. Against Origen, Methodius of Olympus asserted the independence of God in relation to His creation. Augustine introduced the doctrine that time was created *with* the world, thus God eternally *precedes* all that exists.

The Reformers brought the doctrine of creation to the forefront of theological discussion. Luther focused his faith on the fact that "God has created me and all that exists." According to Emil Brunner, creation is the direct and central point of reference for all Calvin's theological statements. Human free will and responsibility were threatened by the Reformers' strong emphasis on divine sovereignty and transcendence.

Enlightenment, heavily influenced by deism (belief that God created but no longer interferes with His creation), showed the opposing tendency of the Reformation: an emphasis on creaturely independence to the neglect of dependence upon God. During this period, Old Testament criticism emerged as a viable avenue for exegesis of the Genesis story of creation. The question arose whether a believer was forced to choose between science and religion as sources for developing a doctrine of creation.

Fresh treatment of the doctrine of creation has appeared in recent systematic theologies. The mood among some theologians (e.g., Barth, Brunner, and Gilkey) is that science and religion are concerned with two different areas of reality. They propose that Scriptures do not attempt to describe the "how" of creation, but Scriptures do affirm the "who" of Creation as the trinitarian God. Other theologians espouse scientific creationism. They believe that Scripture is scientifically valid, and thus accurately details the "how" of creation. For most Christian theologians, the first article of the *Apostles' Creed* continues to be true: "I believe in God, the Father Almighty, maker of heaven and earth."

Mark DeVine

Suggested Reading: Barth, Karl, *The Doctrine of Creation: The Work of Creation.* Vol III, part 1 of *Church Dogmatics Series.* trans. by G. W. Bromiley. ed. by G. W. Bromiley and T. F. Torrance. Edinburgh: T. and T. Clark, 1936-61. Brunner, Emil. *The Christian Doctrine of Creation and Redemption.* Vol. II of *Dogmatic Series.* trans. by Olive Wyon. Philadelphia, Pa: Westminster Press, 1979. Flaming, Peter James. *God and Creation.* Vol. 5, of *Layman's Library of Christian Doctrine.* Nashville, Tn: Broadman Press, 1985. Gilkey, Langdon. *Maker of Heaven and Earth.* Maryland: University Press of America, 1986. Strong, A. H. *Outlines of Systematic Theology.* Philadelphia, Pa: American Baptist Publication Society, 1908.

History of the Doctrine of Miracles

An inquiry into the reality and nature of miracles raises the question of one's understanding of the universe. The people of the Bible never faced the modern problem of miracle. The contemporary tension between the natural and the miraculous may be seen as a by-product of a naturalism that has squeezed out the realm of the supernatural.

Miracles of healing occur throughout the Scripture, clustering around Elijah, Elisha, Jesus, the early disciples and apostles. The writings of early church fathers contain numerous instances of miracles and healings, even though the popular conception is that these occurrences died off. Justin, Minucius Felix, Origen, and Augustine all attest to miracles during their day. Miracles have continued to be reported throughout Christian history from all traditions—Roman Catholic, Eastern Orthodox, and Protestant—particularly during times of persecution and pioneering of the gospel under dangerous conditions. The Pentecostal, charismatic, and neo-charismatic movements of this century have emphasized the miraculous as a normal part of the Christian experience.

Christian theologians have responded in different ways to the question of how miracles relate to the natural order. Some hold that miracles are not contrary to nature. Others contend that they stand outside the order of nature. The former view is sometimes referred to as the harmony view; the latter, the intervention view.

Augustine maintained that miracles are not contrary to the order of nature, for nature reflects nothing but the will of God. Nature includes not merely the observed order of things, but also whatever God does in the universe. Any event in the visible world is natural. Augustine concluded that miracles violate not nature itself, but what we know about nature.The contemporary scholar, C. S. Lewis, echoed some of Augustine's same sentiments when he asserted that miracles do not break the law of nature. What appears to deviate from the order to which we are accustomed is in reality a higher law, the law of eternity, being temporarily put into effect.

Like Augustine, Thomas Aquinas did not consider a miracle to be a violation of the laws of nature. He arrived at this conclusion from a different perspective, however. Unlike Augustine, Aquinas contended that a miracle is outside the laws of nature. Since only God can operate outside nature, only God can perform a miracle.

It becomes apparent that one's view of miracle is related to one's view of the natural world. A mechanistic perspective, holding that the world is controlled by universal laws which cannot be altered, cannot allow for the possibility of miracle.

Benedict Spinoza and David Hume are probably the best known opponents of miracles in the modern period. They both subscribed to the naturalistic mechanistic view of nature that discounts the validity of miracles. Their skepticism was based on the firm conviction that natural laws are established by firm and unalterable experience. If this is true, then there must be a uniform experience against every miraculous event. Contemporary arguments against the possibility of the miraculous build upon their views.

Christians in every century have refused to have their universe so limited. Instead, they have affirmed the miraculous work of God. On the other hand, over-concentration on the miraculous can blind people to the everyday work and presence of God in "non-miraculous" ways. Growing Christians learn to see Him in every aspect of existence.

Reggie McNeal

Suggested Reading: Lewis, C. S. *Miracles.* New York: Macmillan Publishing Co., Inc., 1960. Mallone, George. *Those Controversial Gifts.* Downers Grove, Ill: InterVarsity Press, 1983.

History of the Doctrine of Evil and Suffering

The problem of evil and suffering can arguably be viewed as the single greatest intellectual challenge to Christianity. For the unbeliever for whom no transcendent reality exists, evil can be explained as part of the natural order. One who does not believe in God does not share the Christian predicament of explaining how God can allow evil and suffering to afflict His creation.

Two cardinal attributes of the Christian God are that He is omnipotent (all-powerful) and completely good. The presence of evil challenges this understanding of God. The problem can be stated as follows: Either God cannot or will not prevent evil. If God cannot, then He is limited in power. If He will not, then He is limited in goodness. If God is not limited in either power or goodness, why is there evil in the world? Various approaches to the philosophical and intellectual problems raised by the presence of pain and suffering focus on altering the traditional concepts of God's power and His benevolence or goodness.

Some theologians have reordered the classical position on God's power by suggesting that it is limited. Because they reject the concept of an infinite God, their position is called theistic finitism. One example of such thought is process theology. Following the lead of the mathematician Alfred North Whitehead, process thinkers have applied the dynamics of evolutionary development and Hegelian dialectic (thesis and antithesis yield a new synthesis) to the nature of the universe and God. God is growing along with the universe. He is in process. In this system, God faces situations that He did not foresee. Each new experience expands Him. His existence is contingent upon the universe. He is limited.

Approaches to the problem of evil and suffering that qualify the goodness of God have never been very attractive. Alternatives to a good God degenerate into fatalism (whatever God does is good and cannot be altered by human effort), pessimism (the world is essentially evil), and nihilism (no meaning or purpose remains).

Classic Christianity has not viewed the presence of evil and suffering as sufficient grounds for reordering the biblical notion of a God who is omnipotent and completely good. Christian theodicy is the attempt to justify belief in a perfectly good, all-powerful God in spite of the presence of evil in the world. Various theodicies have developed over the centuries. Representative cases demonstrate the different approaches that have been taken in dealing with the issue.

One approach has addressed the issue by seeking to relieve God of responsibility for the existence of evil. Augustine helped to develop this position. In his early years he had ascribed to Manichaean philosophy, which posited evil and good as eternally coexistent. Augustine correctly saw this view as a threat to the Christian concept of God and creation in which God alone is eternally self-existent. Augustine held that evil results from the absence of good, having no ontological (being) status of its own. Evil resulted from a misuse of something good. Augustine saw humanity as culpable due to the abuse of God-given freedom. Evil was occasioned by the willful misuse of human freedom in rebellion against God.

Irenaean theodicies seek to find a place for evil within the overall good purposes of God. This viewpoint is named after Irenaeus, an early Eastern Father of the church. Irenaeus regarded Adam as having been created by God in an innocent rather than perfect state. He was immature, but had the potential to grow in the likeness of Christ. Irenaeus saw the world acting as an environment for "soul-making."

Those who hold this perspective, such as John Hick in contemporary philosophy, accept the fact that God is responsible for evil. God did not have to create. He acted freely in fashioning a world where He knew that evil would arise. Hick and others assume that there must have been a good reason for God to have created a universe in which evil would exist. They suggest that the world, with its "imperfections," provides the essential environment for humanity's "soul-making" process. Evil and suffering offer challenges to stretch humanity to mature. God will ultimately bring eternal good out of the temporal process.

The Bible does not leave the problem of evil and suffering in intellectual terms. The Christian God understands the issue, for He Himself has been touched by pain, paying the price of evil in immeasurable ways. Into an evil world God sent His only Son. Because God is good, evil cannot ultimately win out. Because of His power, God secures the Christian hope that He can transform evil into triumph.

Reggie McNeal

Suggested Reading: McWilliams, Warren. *When You Walk Through the Fire.* Nashville: Broadman Press, 1986. Murphree, JonTal. *A Loving God and a Suffering World.* Downers Grove, Ill: InterVarsity Press, 1981.

History of the Doctrine of Humanity

The Christian doctrine of humanity or theological anthropology is the attempt by the Christian church to answer the question—what is a human being in light of God's revelation in Holy Scripture? Here theological anthropology differs markedly from secular anthropologies that may study humanity from purely biological, economic, or sociological standpoints.

The doctrine of humanity may be traced historically along two interrelated strands of development. First, humanity may be understood in itself without reference to sin and the fall. Second, the impact of sin upon fallen humanity must be appropriated with respect to God's saving work in Jesus Christ (soteriology).

The early church fathers inherited the anthropology of the Old and New Testaments. The Bible emphasizes the moral and spiritual values of human personality, a deep sense of dependence upon God for all good, the superior worth of human beings in creation, and the covenant relationship between human beings and the heavenly Father.

The influence of Platonism on the early church fathers threatened the Hebraic understanding of the unity of soul (or spirit) and body in dynamic relationship. The Platonic idea of the immortal soul found acceptance in the theologies of Irenaeus (second century) and Tertullian (third century). Even the great Augustine (354-430) insisted that "each person is a soul using a body."

Again in the thirteenth century, Thomas Aquinas taught that the soul was naturally immortal and retained individuality apart from the body. At the Fifth Lateran Council in 1513 the Roman church made the natural immortality of the soul official dogma. However, John Calvin, the sixteenth century Protestant reformer, citing Irenaeus, denied the *natural* immortality of the soul: "Let us learn by experience that we have endurance for eternity through his (God's) goodness, and not from our nature." For Calvin, the immortality of the human soul is always "sustained by his (God's) hand and blessing."

Further implications of theological anthropology for soteriology emerged from the attempt to understand the creation of humanity in the image of God (*imago Dei,* Ge 1:27). Augustine identified the *imago Dei* in human beings as memory, understanding, and will, corresponding to the Holy Trinity in God. Thomas Aquinas identified the *imago Dei* with the reason of the immortal soul. Luther, however, identified the *imago Dei* with the original righteousness of Adam before the fall.

After the fall, according to Lutheran theology following Augustine, Adam transmitted the taint of original sin to his offspring. The human soul was inherited from parents (traducianism). John Calvin, while rejecting traducianism, nevertheless insisted that the fall obliterates the *imago Dei.* In the twentieth century, Karl Barth and Emil Brunner heatedly debated the state and potential of the *imago Dei* after the fall. For Brunner, the *imago Dei* provides a "point of contact" for the Word of God, while Barth insisted that only the gift of faith opens humanity to the Word.

Here, the soteriological implications of the *imago Dei* became acute. How are human beings, if born in bondage to sin, still responsible before God? Do human beings since Adam possess free will? Is salvation grounded in God's gracious election or in meritorious deeds accomplished through free will? Does saving faith function as a gift or a work? The discussion continues in the church.

The decision reached by Augustine, followed by Luther/Calvin and reasserted by Barth, emphasizes human bondage to sin and the need for grace through the gift of saving faith. This consensus is typified in the Westminster Confession of 1646:

> Man by his fall into a state of sin, hath wholly lost all ability of will to any spiritual good accompanying salvation; so as a natural being altogether averse from that good, and dead in sin, is not able by his own strength, to convert himself; or to prepare himself thereunto.

Any adequate Christian doctrine of humanity emphasizes God's saving act in Jesus Christ without ignoring the corresponding human response to that act.

Mark DeVine

Suggested Reading: Berkouwer, G. C., *Man: the Image of God.* Vol. 8 of *Studies in Dogmatics: Theology.* Grand Rapids, Mi: Eerdmans, 1952. Elmore, Vernon O. *Man as God's Creation.* Vol. 6 of *Layman's Library of Christian Doctrine.* Nashville, Tn: Broadman Press, 1986. Robinson, H. Wheeler. *The Christian Doctrine of Man.* Philadelphia, Pa: Fortress Press, 1958.

History of the Doctrine of Sin

The early years of theological formulation by the church were characterized by comparatively little development of the doctrine of sin. Concerns over Christology, the doctrine of the Trinity, and gnosticism dominated the arena of theological argument and thought. As early as the second century, however, Justin Martyr affirmed the universality of sin. Tatian (second century) developed a theory of sin, according to which the fall of Adam resulted in humanity's loss of ability to do good, though not to the point that humans lost moral freedom. Irenaeus (second century) regarded the fall not so much as the occasion for the loss of perfection as an interruption of humanity's progress toward perfection. Tertullian (second-third century) fostered the idea of traducianism: sin is transmitted by procreation.

The founder of the classical doctrine of sin was Augustine of Hippo (fourth-fifth century). The African bishop argued, against Pelagius and his follower, Celestius, for the universality and totality of sin, that unredeemed humanity is unable not to sin, that humanity is unable to acquire merit in God's sight, and that the redemption of humanity by Jesus Christ is concerned first of all with the removal of guilt.

For Augustine, humility was the basic virtue of the Christian life, and therefore pride was the cardinal sin. However, in punishment for Adam's pride the lives of his progeny became suffused with lust, which Augustine narrowed to mean "lust for sexual excitement." In the history of the church, these two conceptions of sin—sin as desire and sin as pride—have, alternately and conjointly, played a large role. Disregarding the danger of oversimplification, one could say that eastern views of sin have been concerned with sensuality, while the western views of sin have focused on the aspect of pride.

The Reformers viewed sin essentially as unbelief, disobedience, and rebellion against God. For the Reformation, sin was the "wrong kind of personal existence." Like Augustine, the Reformers emphasized the universality and totality of sin, humanity's inability not to sin, the impossibility of acquiring merit, and the centrality of guilt in redemption. The third of these emphases—the impossibility of acquiring merit—became the basis for philosophical determinism, or predestination. Humanity's inability to acquire merit because of sin caused the Reformers to reduce humans to purely passive beings, instead of ones who actively *receive* the gift of God.

F. E. D. Schleiermacher (eighteenth-nineteenth century), conceived of sin as a necessary element in humanity's progress toward God-consciousness. Sin results from the war of humanity's lower nature (the flesh) against humanity's higher nature (the spirit). The experience of this conflict leads persons to a knowledge of sin, which indicates how far along they are on the developmental path toward God-consciousness. Without sin, humans could not come into experiential relation with God.

Soren Kierkegaard (nineteenth century) brought sin out of a strictly historical context, that is, sin follows from the fall, and into the present. For Kierkegaard, sin was the result of humanity using personal freedom to find security in some human finite thing rather than relying totally on God. The possibilities of human freedom leave humankind unstable and indecisive, a state from which humans retreat to a sinful and creaturely security.

In recent theology, the accentual difference between the eastern emphasis on desire and the western emphasis on pride have become less important. Karl Barth developed the doctrine of sin by viewing it from three perspectives: sin as pride, sloth, and falsehood. His discussion of sin under the topic of reconciliation is indicative of the theological movement from sin as a substance that can be located in a particular part of humans to sin as a breach in humanity's relationship to God. As late as 1941, however, Reinhold Niebuhr was still advocating a distinction between the old accents: "Biblical and Christian thought has maintained with a fair degree of consistency that pride is more basic than sensuality and that the latter is, in some way, derived from the former."

Walter Draughon, III

Suggested Reading: Barth, Karl. *The Church of Reconciliation.* Vol IV, part 1 and 2 of *Church Dogmatics Series.* trans. by G. W. Bromiley. ed. by G. W. Bromiley and T. F. Torrance. Edinburgh: T. and T. Clark, 1936-61. Brunner, Emil. *The Christian Doctrine of Creation and Redemption.* Vol. II of *Dogmatic Series,* trans. by Olive Wyon. Philadelphia, Pa: Westminster, 1979. McClanahan, John H. *Man as Sinner.* Vol. 7 of *Layman's Library of Christian Doctrine.* Nashville, Tn: Broadman Press, 1987. Niebuhr, Reinhold. *The Nature and Destiny of Man.* Vols. 1 and 2. New York, NY: Macmillan Publishing Co., Inc., 1980. Telfer, William. *The Forgiveness of Sins: An Essay in the History of Christian Doctrine and Practice.* Philadelphia: Muhlenberg Press, 1960.

Knowledge of God

History of the Doctrine of Holy Scripture

The first major issue in the history of the doctrine of Holy Scripture involved determining what was to be included in the Bible and what was to be left out. The Christian church accepted without question the Old Testament as Holy Scripture from the beginning of its existence (2 Ti 3:16; 2 Pe 1:20-21). Soon the church came to regard certain of its own writings as of equal authority and inspiration to those inherited from the Jewish tradition. Thus the letters of Paul are referred to alongside "the other Scriptures" (2 Pe 3:16).

During the second century, the extent of the canon (those books rightly belonging in the Bible) became a burning issue when a heretical teacher named Marcion made a radical proposal. He wanted to eliminate the entire Old Testament as unworthy of the religion of Jesus. He proposed to keep only the Gospel of Luke and some of Paul's letters, and these in a highly censored version, as the only books acceptable to the Christian church. In response to Marcion the church decided that the integrity of creation and redemption required the retention of both Old and New Testaments.

The Montanist movement introduced another factor in the issue regarding canonization of the Bible. With their visions of the second coming and their emphasis on the immediacy of the Spirit, the Montanists produced many visions and sacred texts which bid for inclusion among the more established corpus of Christian writings. Whereas Marcion wanted to restrict the canon severely, the Montanists tried to expand it with little restriction. Many Montanist documents are excluded in the Muratorian canon, the oldest extant list of New Testament writings (ca. 180). St. Athanasius gave the first exact listing of the twenty-seven books of our present New Testament in his *Festal Letter* in 367.

The Bible served along with the rule of faith and the organized ministry as an organ of consolidation in the early church. Readings from both Testaments became a standard part of Sunday worship. The Bible also served as the basis of instruction for the catechumen who desired membership in the church. In addition, the Bible became increasingly appealed to as a primary source and standard for doctrine. For example, the bishops at the Council of Nicaea (325) defended their decision on the nature of Christ by appealing to "what we have learned from the divine Scriptures."

Several important traditions of biblical interpretation developed in the early Christian centuries. A school of allegorical exegesis flourished at Alexandria, while a rival school at Antioch emphasized typology. In the West, St. Augustine's famous treatise on biblical hermeneutics, *On Christian Doctrine*, set forth the ground rules for the subsequent study of the Bible. During the Middle Ages, this tradition crystallized into the *quadriga*, the standard form of the fourfold sense of Scripture—literal, allegorical, tropological (moral), and anagogical (spiritual). Scholastic theologians such as St. Thomas Aquinas strongly affirmed the inspiration and authority of the Bible, although its meaning was often obscured because of excessive allegorizing. In the Late Middle Ages, the relative authority of Scripture and tradition became a pressing issue.

The phrase *sola Scriptura*, "by Scripture alone," has been called the formal principle of the Reformation. While humanist Reformers such as Erasmus of Rotterdam appealed to the Bible in their critique of moral abuses in the church, Luther, Zwingli, Calvin, and the other mainline Reformers challenged the prevailing theology by the norm of Holy Scripture. They did not wish to start new churches, but rather to reform the one true church on the basis of the Word of God. For Luther *sola Scriptura* meant that ecclesiastical tradition, the decrees of popes and church councils, were subject to the written Word of God in the Bible. The Swiss Reformed tradition, led by Huldrych Zwingli, set forth an even stronger statement of this principle in the "Ten Conclusions of Berne" (1528): "The Church of Christ makes no laws or commandments apart from the Word of God; hence all human traditions are not binding upon us except so far as they are grounded upon or prescribed in the Word of God."

While all of the Reformers agreed on primacy of Scripture over tradition, they placed different emphases on its meaning and application. Luther stressed the Christocentric character of the Bible. He likened the words of the Bible to the straw in the manger which nestled the Christ child. This principle led him to question the authority of certain biblical books such as James which, to his mind, spoke more of law and works than of gospel and grace. Calvin's doctrine of Scripture is marked by his insistence on the inner witness of the Holy Spirit. Since God alone is a sufficient witness unto Himself, the same Spirit who inspired the original prophets and apostles must authenticate their message by illuminating the mind of the reader of Holy Writ. Among the radical Reformers, many tried to hold a balance between Word and Spirit, but others subordinated the objective Word in Scripture to one's personal, subjective experience.

In modern times the rise of the historical-critical method of studying the Bible has led many to question traditional views of the inspiration and authority of Holy Scripture. However, not everyone who uses this method has succumbed to its destructive potential. For example, Karl Barth and G. K. Berkouwer have set forth high doctrines of Scripture while also using certain critical methodologies. Other theologians such as Benjamin B. Warfield have defended the authority of the Scriptures in terms of a precise definition of inerrancy. The most definitive formulation of this position thus far is the "Chicago Statement on Biblical Inerrancy" (1979).

Timothy George

Suggested Reading: Grant, Robert M. *A Short History of the Interpretation of the Bible.* New York, NY: Macmillan Publishing Co., Inc., 1972. Lewis, John M. *Revelation, Inspiration, Scripture.* Vol. 3 of *Layman's Library of Christian Doctrine.* Nashville, Tn: Broadman Press, 1985.

History of the Doctrine of Revelation

Revelation is the unveiling (Greek *apokalypsis*) or disclosure of God's redemptive purpose toward humankind. While many religions posit a human search for the divine, the Judeo-Christian tradition affirms that God has taken the initiative to make Himself known (Am 3:7; Heb 1:1-3). The precise scope and nature of God's revelation is a major theme in Christian history.

Most Christian teachers have acknowledged that God is generally knowable throughout all nature and history. Some early Church Fathers such as Justin Martyr believed that the Greek philosophers had approximated the insights of Christianity through the mediation of the *Logos* (human reason informed by Divine reason) even before the incarnation. St. Augustine thought that traces of the Holy Trinity could be discovered in the human faculties of memory, understanding, and will. In the Middle Ages, it was generally believed that God had revealed enough of Himself in the created order for His existence to be proved by natural reason. St. Thomas Aquinas set forth his famous "five ways" by which he argued for the existence of God from certain observable effects in the sensible world such as motion, causation, order, and design. He held that reason was in perfect harmony with God's special revelation, although only through the latter could truths about the Trinity or the incarnation be known.

The Reformers of the sixteenth century also distinguished between general and special revelation. John Calvin set forth the classic Protestant understanding of revelation in his *Institutes of the Christian Religion.* He made a clear distinction between the knowledge of God as Creator and the knowledge of God as Redeemer. The "natural" knowledge of God in nature and in the conscience serves only to render human beings inexcusable before God (Ro 1—2). The knowledge of God as Redeemer is made known through the special acts of God in salvation history, especially in the person and work of Jesus Christ, in the Holy Scriptures, and in the ministry of the church. From this perspective it is the task of theology to offer a faithful exposition of the oracles of God's special revelation. In faith, revelation becomes a matter of inner certitude and assurance.

Another important theme in the history of the doctrine of revelation is the relation between Word and Spirit. Revelation does not isolate God's objective disclosure from humanity's subjective appropriation of that disclosure. Rather, revelation speaks of the coming together of both disclosure and appropriation in an event of encounter. Theologians have spoken of the co-inherence, that is, the mutual relation of Word and Spirit to describe this revelational event. There have been periods in the history of theology, perhaps among certain Protestant Scholastics, when the Word was stressed in isolation from the Spirit; there have been other periods, perhaps among certain Anabaptists and Pietists, when the Spirit overshadowed the Word. Word and Spirit may be distinguished, but they must not be divorced. The same Holy Spirit who originally inspired the apostles and prophets to write the Bible must be present to illuminate the mind of the hearer or reader of Scripture today.

Since the time of Schleiermacher, modern theology has given prominence to the subjective role of human beings as recipients of revelation. The loss of confidence in objective revelation has led some thinkers, notably Feuerbach and Freud, to reduce religion to the projections of the human psyche. Karl Barth and Carl F. H. Henry, though differing as to the form of revelation, have both stressed the objectivity and divine initiative of God's self-disclosure, without neglecting the experience of the believing community in appropriating the salvation God has provided.

Timothy George

Suggested Reading: Barth, Karl. *The Doctrine of the Word of God.* Vol 1, part 1 of *Church Dogmatics Series.* trans. by G. W. Bromiley. ed. by G. W. Bromiley and T. F. Torrance. Edinburgh: T. and T. Clark, 1936-62. Cunliffe-Jones, Hubert and Drewery, Benjamin, eds. *A History of Christian Doctrine.* Philadelphia, Pa: Fortress Press, 1980. Henry, Carl F. H. *God, Revelation, and Authority.* Vols. 1–6. Waco, Tx: Word Books, 1976.

History of the Doctrine of History

Although it is a gross simplification, it is still useful to think of ancient views of history as mythical and cyclical. Just as the year followed patterns of seasons, so too, life was an eternally recurring series of events. To the pagans, even the gods were ultimately in the hands of fate.

By contrast, in Judaism the concept of time was linear. God was seen as the Agent of creation, who was shepherding the movement of people and events through time, and would eventually bring all things to fulfillment. The Hebrews introduced a startling particularity to history. They believed God was Creator of all, and at the same time the God of Moses and the Exodus, the God of Abraham, Isaac, and Jacob. History was viewed as a vehicle by which God was revealing Himself in a very real way—not just revealing moral maxims.

Christians found the mystery of God's plan of redemption to be focused on the life, death, and resurrection of Jesus of Nazareth. God's self-revelation was made so complete in this one Man that Christians called Him "Immanuel," meaning God with us or the Word made flesh. The development of Christian doctrine has been an attempt to comprehend this event.

At first many Christians lived with an expectation of the immediate return of Christ. Worldly events were irrelevant since history was about to come to an end. Some Christians maintained an isolationist identity. Others began to look upon the history of pagan culture as part of the divine preparation for the gospel to the Gentiles, just as the law had been the preparation for the Jews.

Christian historians have approached their task with different purposes in mind. Eusebius of Caesarea (260-339) wrote apologetic works. He wanted to show the continuity of the "true" church as opposed to heterodox (contrary to established Christian belief) groups which used the name of Christ but in terms not concerned with history's mythical theologies. Augustine of Hippo (354-430), drawing upon the parable of the wheat and the weeds (Mt 13:24-30), developed a philosophy of history. The City of God (founded on the love of God) and the City of Man (founded on love of self) existed together until the full number of the elect were gathered. Others like Joachim of Fiore (1135-1202) used mystical numerology taken from various parts of Scripture to foretell the future.

When empire and church were unified, history was seen as the outworking of a single divine plan (often patterned after the history of the nation of Israel). Eventually nationalism began to fragment the empire, and the Reformation divided the church. With each nation or church writing its own version of events the question of historical relativism came to the foreground. Was history simply a matter of propaganda, or did it have an intellectual autonomy?

Much of the focus on history shifted to methodology. The ideal was for the historian to be an observer interested only in the facts. Reacting against mere authoritarianism and drawing on developments in the natural sciences, some writers defined history as a science with its own laws and a commitment to truth apart from any creed. Often divine providence was rejected as a matter of faith, not science, but just as often secular philosophies of history were substituted. The problem with the scientific model was that one could not recreate historical events in the laboratory. Others therefore have attempted to see history as a type of detective work, a skill in which one sifts evidence to make the most logical deduction. Some have simply denied the possibility of truly objective history because it would require a perspective of all time and all events available to God alone.

A Christian view of history is not absorbed in legitimizing its antecedents, predicting the future, or proclaiming any particular movement of the present as the "will of God." Rather it prays, "Father . . . your will be done on earth as it is in heaven" (Mt 6:9*a*, 10). It honors truth wherever it may be found. It acknowledges the God who is Creator *and* Lord of history. It seeks to constantly renew and broaden its understanding of the central mystery of history, Immanuel—God with us.

Mark Fountain

Suggested Reading: McIntire, C. T. ed. *God, History and Historians*. New York: Oxford University Press, 1977.

History of the Doctrine of Election

"Election" in the Bible means "choice." In the Old Testament, Israel was God's elect nation, chosen for the specific purpose of blessing the nations (Ex 19:3-6; Dt 7:6-7). In the New

Testament, Jesus Christ was God's elect Son, chosen to redeem mankind from sin (Mt 12:18; Lk 9:35; 1 Pe 1:20). Following Jesus' death and resurrection, the church became the elect people, chosen for the purpose of glorifying God (Eph 1:4; 1 Pe 2:9). Biblically speaking, then, election refers to God's sure choice of a person or persons to fulfill a divinely appointed purpose.

In the early church, however, the doctrine of election was recast in the speculative context of determinism versus free will. Consequently, the doctrine of predestination eventually eclipsed that of election. Predestination, by definition, relates God's purpose of salvation to the human experience of salvation. This relation has been alternatively viewed as absolute or relative, eternal or temporal, conditional or unconditional. In this context, predestination has two corollaries: election, which is predestination to eternal life, and reprobation, which is predestination to eternal death.

The traditional doctrine of predestination originated with Augustine of Hippo (354-430). Most future variations of the classic doctrine were little more than modifications of his original ideas. The starting point for Augustine was original sin. Adam introduced sin into the world, and the entire human race has been corrupted by his sin and deserves eternal damnation. God, however, determined before creation that certain persons would be saved from this fate. This eternal, absolute, irresistible choice of persons over others for eternal salvation is called divine predestination. Augustine believed that God's choice was so unconditional that the elect constituted a fixed number which could be neither increased nor diminished. Because Augustine claimed that God chose some out of the fallen human race for salvation and merely passed over the rest of mankind, his doctrine is usually called *single predestination*: God chose one group for salvation and simply allowed the rest to suffer for Adam's sin.

Augustine's doctrine of predestination derived from his overwhelming conviction of the sovereignty and priority of God's grace in human salvation. Unfortunately, he took this single truth and elevated it to the neglect of other equally important biblical truths such as human freedom and divine self-limitation. By filtering obvious biblical paradoxes through his own rigid logic, he maintained a consistent theological system, but in so doing he erected a system built on a half-truth.

The doctrine of predestination underwent little alteration during the next thousand years. It was revived to its former Augustinian glory, however, during the Protestant Reformation. John Calvin (1509-1564) immortalized the doctrine in his legendary *Institutes of the Christian Religion*. He followed Augustine at almost every point in his treatment of the topic, but he went beyond Augustine at two points. First, he popularized the notion that God's eternal decision of predestination was in essence an absolute *decree* which was unconditional, immutable, and eternal. By an act of His free will, God decreed before creation who would be elected to salvation and who would be reprobated to damnation. This leads to the second difference between Calvin and Augustine: Calvin explicitly taught *double predestination*. He believed that God not only predestined some to heaven but also predestined some to hell. For Calvin, God did not merely pass over those whom He did not elect; He actively predestined them to condemnation.

This view of predestination provoked immediate debate. The most noted opponent was Jacobus Arminius (1560-1609), who rejected the hyper-Calvinism of some of Calvin's overzealous followers such as Theodore Beza (1519-1605) and Franz Gomarus (1563-1641). Arminius believed that predestination was dependent on human response to God's grace. In Arminius' view God decreed that Christ would be the Savior and that whoever would freely choose to accept God's grace in Christ is elect and whoever would freely reject that offer is reprobate. Both election and reprobation, then, are conditioned upon human free choice, which is foreknown but not determined by God from all eternity. The Calvinistic view prevailed over that of Arminius, however, at the controversial Synod of Dort (1618), which affirmed that both election and reprobation were absolute, irresistible decrees foreordained by God from eternity.

The Calvinist-Arminian debate continued for three centuries until Karl Barth (1886-1968) revolutionized the doctrine of predestination by recasting it in terms of election in Christ, of Christ, and by Christ. Barth claimed that Jesus Christ is the subject of election inasmuch as He is divine. In fact, He is the electing God. This assertion allowed Barth to reject the Calvinistic idea of a hidden, mysterious decree of God which occurred in eternity. Jesus Christ is not only the subject of election as electing God but also the object of election as the elected Person. He elected Himself to suffer and die for the sins of humanity. For Barth, then, double predestination means that Jesus Christ chose rejection for Himself in order that humanity might be elected to salvation. Although he denied espousing universal salvation, Barth often implied that conclusion.

Barth's doctrine of election is first and foremost Christ-centered. This is a necessary corrective to the traditional doctrine of predestination in which Jesus was virtually unrelated to God's eternal decree. However, Barth failed to do full justice to the biblical emphasis on human freedom to reject God's grace.

Paul Baseden

Suggested Reading: Augustine. *On the Predestination of the Saints.* Vol. 1 of *Basic Works of Saint Augustine.* ed. by Whitney L. Oates. New York, NY: Random House, 1948. Barth, Karl. *The Doctrine of God.* Vol. 2 of *Church Dogmatics Series.* trans. by G. W. Bromiley. ed. by G. W. Bromiley and T. F. Torrance. Edinburgh: T. and T. Clark, 1936-61. Calvin, John. *Institutes of the Christian Religion.* 2 vols. in *The Library of Christian Classics.* ed. by John T. McNeill. trans. and indexed by Ford Lewis Battles. Philadelphia, Pa: Westminster Press, 1960.

History of the Doctrine of Salvation

The doctrine of salvation, or soteriology, encompasses the entire range of God's redeeming activity toward humankind. As it has developed in the history of Christian thought, the doctrine of salvation is related to a number of other important theological concerns such as election (which anchors God's salvific purpose in His eternal decree), atonement (the objective, historical procurement of salvation), justification, regeneration, and sanctification (the experiential appropriation of the work of Christ), and glorification (the final completion of God's saving purpose). Already in the New Testament salvation was spoken of as past, present, and future (2 Co 1:10). This perspective continues to inform the development of the doctrine of salvation throughout the history of the church.

The early church fathers were concerned primarily with the objective pole (external events) of salvation. For example, over against certain gnostic and docetic (from the Greek, *dokein*, to seem or appear) teachers who denied the full reality of the incarnation, Ignatius of Antioch declared that Jesus Christ had been "really born of a virgin," that He had "really died, really been buried and really raised from the dead." Many of the early debates about Christ centered on the effectiveness of His life and death for salvation. For example, the fourth-century heretic Apollinarius denied that the incarnate Christ had possessed a true human soul or mind. Apollinarius was condemned at the First Council of Constantinople (381) on the grounds that "what has not been assumed cannot be redeemed." The soteriological motive was also paramount in the formulation of the doctrine of the Trinity. The Nicene Creed declared Jesus Christ, "who for us men and our salvation came down and was incarnate," to be one in essence (*homoousios*) with the Father.

The subjective (internal experience) appropriation of salvation became a major concern in the West during the early fifth century. Earlier church fathers such as Tertullian and Cyprian had stressed the importance of baptism and a rigorous Christian life-style along with repentance and faith as essential components of salvation. The proper balance between divine grace and human responsibility was debated by St. Augustine and his opponent Pelagius. Pelagius believed that it was possible for human beings to earn salvation by observing the law, obeying the Ten Commandments, and following the example of Jesus. For Pelagius grace was merely the natural endowments given to all human beings at birth. St. Augustine, on the other hand, stressed the utter inability of human beings to save themselves apart from the special bestowal of God's grace. He became convinced by reading 1 Co 4:7 ("What do you have that you did not receive?") that even faith itself was a gift of God.

The Pelagian doctrine of salvation was condemned by the church, but St. Augustine's views did not prevail completely. During the Middle Ages, the theology of salvation became tied even more closely to the organized church and the sacramental system. The concept of achieving status with God through the earning of merits was reinforced by the practices of popular piety such as indulgences, pilgrimages, the rosary, etc.

The Reformers of the sixteenth century rediscovered the Augustinian principles of the priority of God's grace in salvation. Martin Luther's struggle to find a gracious God led him to formulate the doctrine of justification by faith alone. He understood faith not only as intellectual assent but also as confident trust, reliance, and commitment. Huldrych Zwingli and John Calvin also stressed both the objective work of Christ's atonement and the personal appropriation of it through repentance and faith.

An excellent summary of Protestant soteriology is found in the first question and answer of the Heidelberg Catechism (1563):

> Q:"What is your only comfort in life and death?"
> A:"That I belong, body and soul, not to myself but to my faithful Savior Jesus Christ who at the cost of His own blood has fully paid for all my sins and has completely freed me from the dominion of the devil, that he protects me so well that without the will of my Father in heaven, not a hair can fall from my head; indeed, that everything must fit his purpose for my salvation. Therefore by his Holy Spirit he also assures me of eternal life and makes me wholeheartedly willing and ready from now on to live for him."

After the Reformation, the experiential aspect of salvation came into prominence in the Pietist movement and the Evangelical Awakenings, as in John Wesley's famous "heart-warming" conversion at Aldersgate in 1736. Some revivalists such as Charles Finney emphasized the intrinsic connection between personal conversion and social reform. In recent times these two concerns have been seen by some as polar opposites rather than mutually related themes. A more holistic doctrine of salvation will not neglect any dimension of God's redeeming purpose in this life, nor will it fail to place the realization of salvation here and now in the context of the consummation of all things at the second coming of Jesus Christ.

Timothy George

Suggested Reading: George, Timothy. *Theology of the Reformers.* Nashville, Tn: Broadman Press, 1987. Lohse, Bernhard. *A Short History of Christian Doctrine.* trans. by Ernest Stoeffer. Philadelphia, Pa: Fortress Press, 1978. Turner, H. E. W. *The Patristic Doctrine of Redemption.* London: Mowbray, 1952.

History of the Doctrine of Discipleship

Christian discipleship has always been understood as faithful obedience to Christ. But after His death and resurrection He was physically removed, and it was difficult for His followers to decide what faithful obedience implied in the new situations they faced. Since the New Testament was not yet in general circulation, early Christians had to rely on the apostolic tradition or "The Rule of Faith" to follow Christ and to teach the Christian faith and responsibilities to others. The churches established by the apostles were seen as the reliable repositories of the faith taught by Christ. In such communities, persons could hear the faith taught and see it lived in faithful discipleship. In the second and third centuries, catechesis (oral instruction) began to develop as a means of preparing converts for baptism. This process of instruction in Christian discipleship could last for up to three years. Augustine's *On the Catechizing of the Uninstructed* (400) and *Enchiridion* (421) give valuable insight into what disciples were taught in the fifth century.

Christianity remained an illegal religion in the Roman Empire until the beginning of the fourth century, and many Christians were persecuted for their faith. Some even sought martyrdom actively as the ultimate proof of their commitment to Christ. They displayed an amazing depth of care for one another, and viewed a life of the highest moral and ethical purity as absolutely essential. A major turning point in the history of the church came with the conversion of Emperor Constantine in 313, and the subsequent legalization of Christianity. A flood of new converts entered the church, and the previously high moral and ethical standards were eroded. In the face of this spiritual laxity, some Christians sought new ways of obeying Christ. Desiring a life devoted to prayer and fellowship with Christ in His sufferings, some hermits had already withdrawn from the world and had undertaken feats of great physical endurance. They were soon joined by numerous followers, from whom the monastic movement blossomed. Athanasius' *Life of Antony* (ca. 360) offers a contemporary glimpse into the early years of the movement. An unfortunate result of monasticism was that it effectively divided Christians into two classes: the spiritual elite who joined monastic communities, and a far larger number of other Christians who became satisfied with a less rigorous commitment. For most of the Middle Ages, it was left to the monks to exemplify (with widely varying degrees of integrity) the life of genuine discipleship.

The monasteries displayed a consistent pattern of healthy beginnings and rapid lapses into luxury and various abuses. Toward the end of the Middle Ages there was a renewed emphasis on faithfulness to Christ, evidenced in various radical reform movements and certain mendicant (begging) monastic orders, like that of Francis of Assisi. The Brethren of the Common Life, whose emphases are represented in *The Imitation of Christ* (ascribed to Thomas à Kempis, d. 1471), stressed that discipleship was the responsibility of all Christians.

The Reformation of the sixteenth century placed renewed emphasis on the importance of personal devotion to Christ and spawned a large number of catechisms for the instruction of believers in matters of faith and practice. Notable among these were Luther's *Small Catechism* and *Large Catechism* (1529), and Calvin's *Catechism of the Church of Geneva* (1545), and *Institutes of the Christian Religion* (various editions from 1536 to 1559). The post-Reformation decline into a sterile, lifeless Christianity was challenged by Pietism in Germany, which produced Philipp Spener and his *Pia Desideria* (1675) and by Puritanism and Methodism (especially John Wesley) in England. Similarly, Soren Kierkegaard's *Training in Christianity* (1850) and *Attack Upon 'Christendom'* (1854-5) sought to shake the Danish state church of the mid-nineteenth century out of its spiritual apathy. *The Journal of John Woolman* (1774) is a moving account of one Quaker's commitment to the personal implications of the lordship of Christ. In our century the incomparable work on discipleship is *The Cost of Discipleship* (1937) by Dietrich Bonhoeffer, who was martyred in Nazi Germany in 1944. Walter Rauschenbusch has offered a challenging statement of the relevance of responsible discipleship to social concerns in *Christianity and the Social Crisis* (1907), and *Christianizing the Social Order* (1912).

A recent trend in the personal spiritual growth of disciples has been the recovery of the ancient practice of placing oneself under a spiritual director or mentor. This is discussed in Kenneth Leech's *Soul Friend* (1977), and Tilden Edwards' *Spiritual Friend* (1980). In the face of today's widespread apathy, there are encouraging signs that many Christians are again searching for a genuine and meaningful spirituality.

Donald L. Morcom

Suggested Reading: Bonhoeffer, Dietrich. *The Cost of Discipleship.* New York, NY: Macmillan Publishing Co., Inc., 1963. Brown, Lavonn D. *The Life of the Church. Layman's Library of Christian Doctrine.* Nashville, Tn: Broadman Press, 1987.

History of the Doctrine of Christian Ethics

With Clement of Alexandria in the late second and the early third centuries, Christian morality became a subject of systematic reflection. Clement was among the first who attempted to bring together the Christian moral principles and Hellenistic philosophical ethics. He conceived the ideal Christian life as a process of two stages. In the preliminary stage, believers follow the church discipline out of hope of reward and fear of punishment. In the higher way, however, they strive to live the pure Christian life out of the love and knowledge of God.

Augustine developed an ethical position which was basically eudaemonist—happiness as the highest good. All human action arises from a quest for happiness, differing only in directions, but happiness can be found only through faith in God and obedience to His commands. For Augustine the fundamental ethical problem was that of the relationship to God. Thus, he stressed the priority of love for God, saying "Love God and do as you please."

During the Middle Ages, Aquinas developed the first full-fledged systematization of Christian ethics. Aquinas's ethics stemmed from the synthesis of biblical teaching and Aristotelianism. His ethical system can be characterized as teleological (end-oriented) in the sense that it emphasized the natural human desire for the perfect good, that is, God as their ultimate goal. For Aquinas the moral life consisted in the best possible use of one's rational powers, and in keeping one's emotions and bodily activities under the control of right reason. He had high regard for the natural law and believed that from it human laws could be derived. The Aristotelianism in Aquinas was strongly rejected by the Reformers, but it continued to prevail in Roman Catholic moral theology.

In the sixteenth century, faithful to his Christocentrism, Luther opposed the work-righteousness morality inherent in medieval theology. He believed that there was no way from self-love to love of God and neighbor except through a radical change of direction. Only faith in the divine initiative of grace could create one anew, and thus Christian ethics was to be based upon faith working through and active in love. His doctrine of "two realms" distinguished the kingdom of God from the human kingdom, while insisting upon God's rule of both realms.

John Calvin, another significant figure in the Reformation, grounded his ethics in God's grace and grateful human obedience. He stressed both the discipline of individual life ruled by personal devotion, and not by legalism, and the creation of sanctified society. It is said that his uncompromising view of the absolute sovereignty of God and insistence upon the limited authority of state under God provided the potential basis for the democratic ideas.

Dissenting from both Protestantism and Catholicism, Anabaptists believed that it was not possible to separate faith from works. Justification by faith meant for them both faith and obedience. They attempted to use exclusively the ethical commands in the Bible as their pattern for living, resulting in an ethical radicalism. They stressed the "community of faith" as the context of ethical decision-making. Their ethical views are still alive in the Mennonites today.

In the modern period, Christian ethics has been shaped and reshaped in many ways. Under the influence of Kant, many theologians, like Schleiermacher and Ritschl, turned their attention to the human and the moral elements in theology. The social gospel of Walter Rauschenbusch stressed the progressive achievement of positive social values and sought the embodiment of Christian values in all social orders. Reinhold Niebuhr, however, criticized the optimism associated with the social gospel movement and insisted upon the necessity of finding proximate Christian solutions to the ultimately insoluble problem of corporate injustice.

In continental Protestantism, Karl Barth turned to the theology of the Word and rejected natural morality. He based Christian ethics upon the doctrine of God's commands and stressed the priority of the divine will rather than rules or principles. The more recent trend in Christian ethics today is concerned with the development of an ethic of virtue and character.

Joon-Sik Park

Suggested Reading: Beach, Waldo and Niebuhr, H. Richard, eds. *Christian Ethics. Sources of The Living Tradition.* New York, NY: Random House, 1973. Childress, James F. and Macquarrie, John, eds. *The Westminster Dictionary of Christian Ethics.* Philadelphia, Pa: Westminster, 1986. Long, E. L., Jr. *A Survey of Christian Ethics.* New York, NY: Oxford University Press, 1967.

History of the Doctrine of Stewardship

Stewardship describes the response of Christians to God's gracious gift of life and love. The word *stewardship* comes from the Greek compound word meaning "house manager." The concept implies trusteeship, responsibility, and partnership. Throughout history, Christians have practiced stewardship from a variety of motives and in a variety of ways.

While biblical stewardship is broader than the practice of giving money to the church, much of the history of the discussion of stewardship centers on money. The earliest Christians gave money to relieve the sick, poor, and widowed and to support apostles, missionaries, and evangelists. Further offerings were made to maintain the practice of public worship. Giving during this early period in the church was motivated primarily by a sense of gratitude for God's gracious act of salvation through Jesus Christ. Little mention is made in the New Testament of how early Christians practiced stewardship of time and talents except for Paul's observation that the Macedonians gave not only of their money, but of themselves first (2 Co 8:5).

The early church fathers addressed stewardship in their writings. These men stressed giving as a Christian duty that should be practiced joyfully. Ireneaus (d. 200) encouraged believers to give at least the tithe joyfully and freely because of the hope Christians have in Jesus Christ. Clement of Alexandria (d. 215) also believed that the Mosaic law concerning tithes was binding on Christians. Origen (d. 254) wrote of the indecency of those who worship God but fail to tithe. Cyprian (d. 258) sought to dissuade a presbyter from accepting outside work. He viewed such as a distraction from divine duties which should be supported by the tithes of believers.

The writings of Augustine (d. 430) and Ambrose (d. 397) reflect a change in the motivation for giving. Both viewed tithing as essential for the Christian but suggested that tithing secured remission of sins. Ambrose taught that those who fail to tithe neither fear God nor know true penitence and confession.

While some writers still stressed joyful tithing or even selling all and giving to the poor [Jerome (d. 420), Gregory the Great (d. 604)], the motivation for Christian giving became increasingly more to earn God's favor as the church became more institutionalized. By the fourth century, when Constantine had legalized Christianity, salvation on merit was the primary motivation for giving to the church.

The moral and religious custom of paying tithes was given stronger impetus by the sanctioning of councils such as the Council of Tours (567), the Second Council of Macon (585), the Council of Rouen (650), and the Council of Metz (756). As early as 585, the tithe had been made the law of the church. Charlemagne, as the Roman Emperor (800-814), made tithing the law of the state as well. From this, tithe as public law extended over Western Christendom.

Mandatory giving and the concept of earning God's favor by tithing so influenced the church that by the eleventh century, Pope Urban II promised indulgences (use of the excess good deeds of saints to excuse one from punishment and penance for small sins) to everyone who would participate in the First Crusade. By the twelfth century, payment for masses (payment for spiritual favors such as communion, penance, prayers for the dead) was a common practice in the church. By the middle of the fifteenth century, many churches had so many paid contracts for masses that they could not fulfill them. In 1428 the Abbot of Cluny was advised by papal commissioners to increase the number of monks to keep up with the paid contracts for masses.

Under the papacy of Leo X, commissioners were appointed to sell indulgences throughout Catholic Europe to pay off the debt he had incurred in building the church of St. Peter in Rome. Albert, the Archbishop of Mainz, was awarded the contract of selling indulgences in Germany. Johann Tetzel was named the collector for Saxony. To insure the largest possible returns, Tetzel sold the indulgences as "the most precious and noble of God's gifts." Tetzel stressed the effectiveness of indulgences for both sins committed and sins intended. He even suggested that people could pay off the sins of deceased parents with his famous line: "Soon as the groschen in the casket rings, the soul from purgatory springs."

The purchase of indulgences and the heavy financial demands the church placed on its members led to the Reformation. Martin Luther, unable to convince area bishops that Tetzel's money collecting was unbiblical, challenged this and other church practices in his ninety-five theses which he nailed to the door of Wittenberg University. Soon after the Reformation began, a growing number of people protested compulsory tithing.

Luther argued that the financial support for the church should be voluntary, but because of economic conditions in Germany felt compelled to rely on secular authorities to protect the church. Anabaptists and later Quakers were the strongest voices in opposing mandatory tithing as a violation of Christian principles. Wanting to remain true to the separation of church and state, they stressed voluntary support of ministry.

Colonial America faced a conflict between compulsory church support in the royal colonies and the voluntary church support of the Pilgrims. By 1650, most churches in New England depended on public taxation and later pew rents, subscription lists, lotteries, and meager voluntary offerings for monetary support.

Following the Revolutionary War in America, voluntary support of the clergy and the church became the norm. Some emphasis on stewardship was stressed, but the tithe was not elevated as the mode of Christian giving at this time.

The Modern Missions Movement underway in England in 1792, called for giving beyond meeting the needs of local congregations. Emphasis on giving was increased, but it was not until the close of the nineteenth century and the beginning of the twentieth century that tithing was stressed as a vital means of performing stewardship. Several significant movements such as the "The Churchman's Tithe Club" (1896), "The Tenth Legion" (1896), and "The Twentieth Century Tithers Association of America" (1904) linked missions and stewardship in America and brought a renewed support to both.

The practice of freewill giving based on an annual pledge did not become a common practice in American Protestant churches until after World War I. The effort to construct and maintain church building space, to support mission causes, and to support a professional ministry challenged churches to develop ways to encourage members to give generously. The campaigns developed to encourage Christian giving in this century have been varied in approach. Stewardship has been seen as a fund-raising activity that either stresses the tithe as an integral part of the Christian life or that rejects the tithe as legalism. Stewardship has been emphasized as either our loving response to a gracious God or as a means of receiving blessings in return.

With the growing awareness that the world's resources are being depleted, stewardship in recent years has been broadened in emphasis to include humanity's proper stewardship of nature. World leaders of the stewardship movement such as Stoughton and Limouze have sought to expand the concept of stewardship beyond fund raising to its rightful place as vital Christian faith in action—the response of Christians to God's gracious gift of life and love.

Candace C. Morris

Suggested Reading: Fisher, Wallace E. *A New Climate for Stewardship.* Nashville, Tn: Abingdon Press, 1976. Hendricks, William L. *Resource Unlimited.* Nashville, Tn: Stewardship Commission of The Southern Baptist Convention, 1972.

History of the Doctrine of Last Things

From its inception, Christianity was marked by an intense expectation of the end of this present age and the inbreaking of God's final rule. Jesus's first sermon declared the kingdom of heaven "is near" (Mt 4:17). The early Christians greeted one another with the word "Maranatha," "O Lord, come!" The post-apostolic church universally affirmed the Second Advent of Jesus Christ. This article of belief was incorporated into the Apostles' Creed: "he shall come again to judge the quick and the dead."

The history of the doctrine of last things has developed along two lines. The first is *personal eschatology*, the teaching about the ultimate destiny of individuals. The second is *corporate eschatology*, the teaching about God's purposes for humankind as a whole and the consummation of all things.

Discussion about the "intermediate state" between death and the resurrection had already begun in New Testament times (1 Th 4:13-18). In the second century Justin Martyr said, "The souls of the pious are in a better place, those of the unjust and wicked in a worse, waiting for the time of judgment." Tertullian believed that only martyrs who had died for the faith were admitted immediately into heaven; other Christians remained in a provisional waiting place. Eventually this idea developed into the concept of purgatory, a place of fiery preparation for the final state of blessedness. Gregory the Great has been called "the inventor of purgatory" because of his stress on it. Dante gave the most vivid elaboration of it in *The Divine Comedy.* All of the Protestant Reformers rejected the doctrine of purgatory. The Thirty-Nine Articles of the Church of England refer to it as "a fond thing vainly invented, and grounded upon no warranty of Scripture."

Most Christians have believed that the soul is alive and aware between death and the resurrection, but some have held that the soul is asleep or even dead in this interval. During the Reformation, some form of soul sleep doctrine was advanced by Luther and many radical Reformers. However, Calvin's first theological treatise, *Psychopannychia* (1534), was a refutation of this idea. The doctrine of conditional immortality or the belief that immortality is a gift from God, not natural endowment for all, has been affirmed by recent religious groups such as Seventh Day Adventists and Jehovah's Witnesses.

Perhaps the most controversial aspect of the doctrine of last things has been the interpretation of the millennium, or thousand year reign of Christ, referred to in Revelation 20. (See Millennial Perspectives Charts.) Three divergent views of the millennium have been set forth in the history of the church. Early church fathers such as Papias, Irenaeus, Tertullian, and Lactantius interpreted Revelation 20 to refer to a literal, 1,000 year reign of Christ on earth. This view called *chiliasm* (from the Greek *chilia*, a thousand) or *premillennialism* was the dominant eschatological belief during the period of martyrdom and persecution. St. Augustine offered an allegorical interpretation of the 1,000 years which equated the millennium with the present age of the church. The position that there will be no literal reign of Christ on earth either before or after His second coming is known as *amillennialism.* A third alternative, *postmillennialism,* claims that the return of Christ will occur only after the kingdom of God has been established by the church. This view has been represented by such diverse figures as John Wesley, Jonathan Edwards, and B. H. Carroll.

The doctrine of last things has generated lively interest in recent years. A variant of premillennialism known as dispensationalism has gained wide acceptance in contemporary evangelical circles. J. N. Darby (d. 1882) in England and the *Scofield Reference Bible* in America have done much to popularize this perspective. At the turn of the century, Albert Schweitzer pointed to the radical eschatological context of Jesus' message. More recently, theologians such as Wolfhart Pannenberg and Jurgen Moltmann have emphasized the future as a major theological category. However the details of the end of time are understood, the personal return of Jesus Christ, the resurrection and final judgment, and the ultimacy of heaven and hell belong to the very foundation of biblical faith.

Timothy George

Suggested Reading: Ashcraft, Morris. *The Christian Hope.* Vol. 15 of *Layman's Library of Christian Doctrine.* Nashville, Tn: Broadman Press, 1988. Clouse, Robert G. ed. *The Meaning of the Millenium.* Downers Grove, Ill: InterVarsity Press, 1977. Erickson, Millard J. *Contemporary Options in Eschatology.* Ada, Mi: Baker Book, 1977. Ladd, George E. *Jesus and the Kingdom.* New York, NY: Harper and Row, 1964.

God's People

History of the Doctrine of the Church

Christians speak often of "church." Sometimes they intend to refer only to the Sunday morning worship service. Other times the organizational structure may be meant. Still other times "church" may mean an entire denomination, or even all Christians everywhere. What is the church? Unlike the doctrines of Christology or the atonement, the doctrine of the church has rarely been the center of a major theological controversy. Usually such controversies have erupted over essential parts of the church's ministry—baptism and the Lord's Supper—or the structure of the church.

During its first three hundred years, the church was often an illegal organization. The persecution of Christians, while not constant, was always a threatening possibility, and occasionally an intense reality. During this period the church evolved into a loosely *hierarchical* structure. A hierarchy is an organizational structure in which authority is entrusted to a few individuals for the good of the whole. By the early second century, many of the *episcopoi* (bishops, or church overseers) in larger cities began to exercise authority over the churches in outlying areas. These bishops were often asked to establish what was *true* apostolic doctrine and practice. The bishops were seen as the successors to the apostles and therefore as the only certain guardians of the true teachings of Christ.

After his conversion to Christianity in 312, the Roman Emperor Constantine made Christianity the official religion of the empire. For the next three hundred years, as the structures of the Roman government disintegrated, the church took on many of the obligations and privileges of the state. In the Donatist controversy of the fourth century, Augustine (354-430) defended the diminishing purity of the church by speaking of the *invisible* church composed of those believers in all places who are truly Christians. By this, Augustine admitted the faults in the *visible* church which were so apparent to the Donatists. During this period a series of outstanding bishops of the church at Rome [culminating in Gregory the Great (540-604)] began to claim the exclusive right to the title "papa" or "pope" which was formerly used of all bishops. The hierarchy itself increasingly became identified as the institution which Christ had left on this earth to mediate His salvation to people through its seven sacraments.

This understanding of the church was radically challenged by the Reformation in the early sixteenth century. As Luther, Zwingli, Calvin, and others preached that salvation came through God's gracious gift of faith, rather than through the sacraments of the church, the church came to be understood differently. The Lutheran tradition stressed worship through the sacraments and the hearing of the Word. The Reformed tradition of Zwingli and Calvin taught that the church was marked by the administration of the sacraments, the preaching of the Word, and the exercise of church discipline. Unlike the magisterial Reformers, the Anabaptists, stressing the separation of the church from the world, held that the biblical model for the church was one in which only believers were to be members. This effectively ended the parish system—the assignment of a certain geographical area to a specific local church.

The rise of denominations as we know them today is a fairly new phenomenon. As the idea of separation of church and state slowly took hold in the American colonies from 1630 to 1790, most of the colonies lifted restrictions on religious groups and stopped using local taxes to support one designated church. This allowed for various denominations—Baptist, Roman Catholic, Quaker, Presbyterian—to exist peacefully in the same area. The nineteenth century saw the rise of extreme denominationalism on the American frontier. Much of the cooperation between evangelical denominations so common in the early part of the nineteenth century ceased due to movements such as Landmarkism. Landmarkism denied the existence of a universal church, saying that the only biblical usage of the word "church" is to refer to a local body. Another innovation concerning the doctrine of the church was promulgated around the turn of this century by C. I. Scofield and other dispensationalists. They taught that the church was simply a parenthesis in history, interrupting God's dealings with His primary concern—the nation of Israel. The twentieth century has seen the birth of many parachurch movements. Parachurch movements are those which work *alongside* the church.

The church is the body of those people who have been called out of the world by God's grace, and who have been called together to glorify Him by serving Him in His world. Despite all of the church's faults locally and globally, we know that, ultimately, the church is to be a radiant church, "without stain or wrinkle or any other blemish, but holy and blameless" (Eph 5:27).

Mark E. Dever

Suggested Reading: Kelly, J. N. D. *Early Christian Doctrines.* San Francisco, Ca: Harper and Row, 1978. Leonard, Bill J. *The Nature of the Church.* Nashville, Tn: Broadman Press, 1986. Martin, Ralph P. *Worship in the Early Church.* Grand Rapids, Mi: Eerdmans, 1964.

History of the Doctrine of Ordinances

In Christian history the terms "sacraments," "mysteries," and "ordinances" have referred to certain rites, the chief being baptism and the Lord's Supper or Eucharist (lit., thanksgiving). "Sacrament" focuses on sacredness inhering in the rite; "ordinance," on the divine authority which ordered or ordained it; "mystery," on the difference between the outward rite and the spiritual reality.

Baptism and the Lord's Supper gained special status in Christian practice, as indicated by *Didache* (ca. 110-120) and Justin's *First Apology* (ca. 150). By 200 Latin Christians were referring to these rites as sacraments. In time other rites were regarded as sacraments.

The first controversy over the validity of sacraments arose in the fourth century. Donatists viewed the administrator's character as crucial to a sacrament's validity. Catholic Christians believed that validity derives from God's ordering of a sacrament. Augustine (354-430) viewed sacraments as visible means of invisible grace.

For centuries Christians differed over the number of sacraments—whether six (Pseudo-Dionysius), five (Abelard and Hugo of St. Victor), or ten (Bernard of Clairvaux). Peter Lombard (d. ca. 1160) contended for seven sacraments. Later scholastics, chief of whom was Thomas Aquinas (d. 1274), settled on seven sacraments. At the Council of Ferrara (1439) the pope dogmatized the seven sacraments, relying largely on Aquinas' theology. In time, Eastern Orthdoxy, which previously accepted only baptism and the Lord's Supper as sacraments, accepted these seven sacraments.

Since the Middle Ages Roman Catholicism has observed seven sacraments: (1) baptism, with infant baptism being normative, to wash away the stain of original sin and bring one into the church where other sacraments or means of grace are available; (2) confirmation to complete baptism and give strength for growth; (3) penance to remove the guilt (but not the penalty) of actual sins; (4) the Eucharist to provide spiritual food of bread and wine changed into Christ's actual body and blood (transubstantiation); (5) unction to cover sins not previously remitted by penance and to prepare one for death; (6) ordination to change one from layman to priest and to confer power to administer sacraments; and (7) marriage to remove concupiscence and to unite husband and wife for the procreation of children.

Protestants denied that sacraments are means of grace and rejected Catholicism's seven sacraments. They viewed sacraments as visible signs and seals of invisible grace already available. They used various terms to express this view: "signs and testimonies of the will of God towards us" (Lutheran Augsburg Confession, article 13); mystical symbols or outward signs and seals of inward grace (Reformed Second Helvetic Confession, chapter 19); "sure witnesses, and effectual signs of grace, and God's good will towards us" (Anglican Thirty-Nine Articles, article 25); "holy signs and seals of the covenant of grace" (Presbyterian Westminster Confession, chapter 27:1).

Most Protestants retained infant baptism as the New Testament successor to circumcision (Ge 17), the sign and seal of God's covenant. Swiss and German brethren, odiously called Anabaptists but now known as Mennonites, and Baptists of England rejected infant baptism and recognized baptism based on repentance and faith only. The Particular Baptists' Confession of 1644 called baptism a sign of the full washing of a believer in Christ's blood, or the believer's interest in His death, burial, and resurrection, and of the Christian's hope in the future resurrection of believers.

Protestants explained the Lord's Supper in various ways: as Christ's physical presence with but not in bread and wine (Lutheran consubstantiation), as merely a remembrance or memorial of Jesus Christ's once-for-all sacrifice (Zwinglian memorialism), and as Christ's spiritual presence with His believers when they partake in faith (Calvinist real presence).

A few Christian groups (e.g., Quakers) reject all outward rites as unnecessary, even harmful, when one already has the inward reality to which they attest.

G. Hugh Wamble

Suggested Reading: Reumann, John. *The Supper of the Lord.* Philadelphia, Pa: Fortress Press, 1985. Smith, B. F. *Christian Baptism.* Nashville, Tn: Broadman Press, 1970.

History of the Doctrine of Worship

The English word "worship" is derived from the Anglo-Saxon "weorthscipe" or worth-ship. Worship is the ordered response of the believing community to the revelation of Almighty God, who alone is worthy of our devotion, praise, prayers, and thanksgiving. Christian worship combined the pattern of devotion set forth in the Old Testament with the understanding that the God of Israel had made Himself known fully and finally in Jesus Christ.

From New Testament times on, the Christian community engaged in the solemn and joyous worship of God as a central focus of its life together. The shift from the Jewish Sabbath to the "Lord's Day," understood as the "eighth day" of the new creation, established a pattern of weekly corporate worship (*Epistle of Barnabas* 15:8,9). By the fourth century the development of the church year was well under way. This involved an annual liturgical reenactment of the great events of Jesus' life and ministry represented by the seasons of Advent, Christmas, Epiphany, Lent, Easter, and Pentecost.

The various liturgies of the early church reveal certain standard features of Christian worship. The public reading of Holy Scripture in both Old and New Testaments followed by a homily or sermon was an integral part of the divine service. Prayers offered in the name of Jesus and hymns sung in His honor allowed the whole assembly to participate in the common worship. The earliest secular description of Christian worship comes from the Roman Pliny who noted that it was the practice of Christians to "sing hymns to Christ as if he were God." The weekly celebration of the Lord's Supper was a high moment in worship for those baptized Christians who appropriated the power and efficacy of Christ's death and resurrection through this dramatic liturgical meal (*Didache* 10). Baptism, too, was a serious act of worship involving renunciation of the devil, confession of faith, the laying on of hands, and the celebration of first communion.

An important aspect of the doctrine of worship is the way it has decisively shaped the development of theology. For example, the Council of Nicaea's (325) description of Jesus Christ as "of the same essence as the Father" was motivated in part by the universal practice of worship and prayer directed to Jesus. Similarly, the placement of the Holy Spirit alongside the Father and the Son in the doxology and in baptism helped to secure full recognition of the Holy Spirit as also "of the same essence" with the Son and the Father. This principle was expressed by the early church in the saying: *lex orandi est lex credendi*, the rule of prayer is the rule of faith.

During the Middle Ages, worship came to be centered in the sacraments of the church, especially the mass which was declared by the Fourth Lateran Council (1215) to be the repeated sacrifice of the transubstantiated body and blood of Christ. The Protestant Reformers restored the priority of the spoken and preached Word to the worship of the church. Luther introduced hymn singing to congregational worship, but retained more of the medieval liturgical tradition than Zwingli or Calvin. In England, these two tendencies were represented by the Anglicans whose *Book of Common Prayer* embodied a kind of reformed Catholicism, and the Puritans, who advocated a simpler, less ornate form of worship. Some of the radical Puritans such as John Bunyan disavowed all forms of "stinted prayers," including the Lord's Prayer, because they felt such devices hindered the free moving of the Spirit.

In recent years there has been a revival of interest in worship among many Christian groups. The "Dogmatic Constitution on the Sacred Liturgy" at Vatican Council II emphasized the importance of the liturgy of the Word and congregational participation in Roman Catholic worship. At the same time, many Protestants have discovered the power of frequent communion and the observance of the church year. Charismatic Christians, among both Catholics and Protestants, have raised the issues of spontaneity and Spirit-filled praise in worship.

All Christians should take care that our common worship issues in the genuine glory of God, while we recognize the great variety of styles and forms believing men and women have used to reach this goal throughout the history of the church.

Timothy George

Suggested Reading: Martin, Ralph P. *Worship in the Early Church.* Grand Rapids, Mi: Eerdmans, 1975. Maxwell, W. D. *An Outline of Christian Worship.* London: Oxford University Press, 1936. Old, Hughes O. *Worship.* in *Guides to the Reformed Tradition.* Leith, John H. and Kuykendall, John W., eds. Atlanta, Ga: John Knox, 1984.

History of the Doctrine of Proclamation

The New Testament refers to the act of proclamation as *kerygma*, the message declared by a herald (1 Co 2:4). This message was believed to be effective unto salvation (1 Co 1:21) and so it became the central act of the Christian missionary outreach. Many early Christian sermons, such as those of St. Paul, were delivered in Jewish synagogues. As the church moved into the Roman world, the gospel was proclaimed in different settings by the martyrs who won many converts by their witness unto death.

From the earliest times proclamation took place not only as a missionary activity, but also in the context of the assembled congregation. Justin Martyr (d. 165) has left an account of regular Sunday worship which involved a sermon along with the celebration of the Lord's Supper. Two of the greatest preachers of the early church were St. Augustine, whose treatise *On Christian Doctrine* set forth the basic principles of homiletics, and St. John Chrysostom (the "golden-mouth"), who combined rhetorical eloquence and prophetic passion in his sermons.

During the Middle Ages, homilies (from the Latin *hjomila*, "a conversation") became a standard part of the monastic liturgy. In the thirteenth century there was a great revival of preaching when the Dominicans and the Franciscans began to carry the message directly to the common people. Some of the great forerunners of the Reformation such as John Huss in Bohemia and Savonarola in Florence, Italy, stirred the masses by their inspired preaching.

The Protestant Reformers reclaimed the centrality of the sermon in Christian worship. The Lutheran Augsburg Confession (1530) declared that the true church was marked by the proper preaching of the Word and the correct administration of the sacraments. For Luther the proclamation of the Word assumed an almost sacramental quality since by it the living voice of the gospel was heard. To improve the quality of preaching, he issued collections of his own sermons (*Postils*) and distributed them to unlearned clergy.

Zwingli and Calvin were great expository preachers whose sermons skillfully combined biblical insight and contemporary application. The great confidence they invested in the office of preaching is reflected in the statement of Heinrich Bullinger, Zwingli's successor, that "the preaching of the word of God is the Word of God." In England, the Puritans emphasized the lively exposition of the Bible and criticized their Anglican counterparts for their "bare reading ministry." The Puritan theologian William Perkins published the *Art of Prophesying* (1592), a popular handbook on preaching.

In the centuries after the Reformation the ministry of preaching was at the center of the successive renewals and awakenings. The Pietists in eighteenth-century Germany stressed the importance of sincere, heart-felt preaching. One of the leading Pietists, August Hermann Francke, was converted during his own sermon! In England, John Wesley and George Whitefield introduced field preaching as a means of reaching the unchurched masses. In New England, Jonathan Edwards was known for his sermon, "Sinners in the Hands of an Angry God," although the Great Awakening broke out while he was preaching a series of expository sermons on the Letter of Paul to the Romans.

One important development of the doctrine of proclamation related to the extent of its outreach. Strong anti-missions leaders held that since the apostles had fulfilled the Great Commission in their own day, it was useless to proclaim the gospel to the heathen today. Andrew Fuller published a book against such thought entitled *The Gospel Worthy of All Acceptance* (1785). William Carey, Adoniram Judson, and others led in the advance of the Modern Missionary Movement.

The nineteenth century produced many notable preachers (e.g., Charles H. Spurgeon, John Henry Newman, Henry Ward Beecher), but the doctrine of proclamation came to prominence again in the theology of Karl Barth in the early twentieth century. The inadequacy of liberal theology evoked a crisis in Barth's pastoral ministry which led him to formulate the task of theology in terms of its service in the proclamation of the Word.

Timothy George

Suggested Reading: Brilioth, Y. *A Brief History of Preaching.* trans. by Karl E. Mattson. Philadelphia, Pa: Fortress Press, 1965. Dargan, E. C. *A History of Preaching.* New York, NY: Burt Franklin, 1965. George, Timothy. *Theology of the Reformers.* Nashville, Tn: Broadman Press, 1987.

History of the Doctrine of Prayer

Tertullian's *On Prayer* (204) is the oldest surviving postbiblical Christian treatise on prayer. Like Origen's more lengthy *On Prayer* (ca. 233) and Cyprian's *On the Lord's Prayer* (252), Tertullian's work is a commentary on the Lord's Prayer. Christians prayed to God during persecution, and by the fourth century, apostles, the Virgin Mary, and martyrs began to be invoked as well as God. The solitaries and the monks sought a life of prayer. By the fourth century prayer was being offered for the deceased. Liturgical development in the church resulted in the loss of spontaneity in prayer. More than a dozen other church fathers wrote treatises on prayer.

In the history of Christian prayer the struggle between the "prophetic" and the "mystical," the one leading to communion with God and the other to absorptive union with the divine, has been paramount (Friedrich Heiler, *Prayer*, chs. 6-9). This was true especially during the medieval period. Augustine of Hippo had attempted a synthesis of the two, and Thomas Aquinas sought to maintain that synthesis, but twelfth-century mystics such as Hugo of St. Victor and sixteenth-century mystics such as Teresa of Avila and John of the Cross gave the mystical or contemplative the preeminence. Prayer to the Virgin Mary and to the saints and for the souls in purgatory was encouraged and widely practiced.

The Protestant Reformation brought about a renewal of prophetic prayer. According to Martin Luther, John Calvin, Philip Melanchthon, and the *Heidelberg Catechism*, prayer is dependent upon the intercession of Jesus Christ and is the privilege and duty of all Christians amid their vocations. Prophetic prayer tended to prevail among the Anabaptists, the Puritans, and the Pietists, whereas the Quakers extended the mystical tradition. A Roman Catholic controversy on prayer between Francois Fénelon and Jacques Bossuet, which led to the papal condemnation (1699) of Fénelon, centered in the proper motive of prayer, whether one's disinterested love of God (Fénelon) or the love for God that pertains to human salvation (Bossuet).

Immanuel Kant anticipated the modern denial of the reality of prayer, but prayers of confession of sin marked the great awakenings in modern Protestantism, and intercessory prayer was the matrix in which the Modern Protestant Missionary Movement was born. The social gospel directed prayer toward societal reform. Philosophical naturalism has argued the impossibility of prayer, especially petitionary prayer, and pantheism (all is divine) has found prayer to a personal [illegible] be contrary to its doctrine of allness. From psychology and philosophy arose the objections that [illegible] is autosuggestion (self-suggestion) or the projection of human wishes. Christians have faced difficulties related to unanswered petitions and intercessions, prayer and God's will, prayer and modern [illegible]d prayer and bodily healing. Important twentieth-century books on prayer include those by [illegible]yth, James Hastings, A. L. Lilley, Friedrich Heiler, O. Hallesby, George A. Buttrick, H. Tre[illegible] Georgia Harkness, Joachim Jeremias, Fred L. Fisher, Donald Coggan, and Thomas Merton.

"The history of the Christian Church is, more than we know, the history of [illegible]yer" (Nels F. S. Ferre, *A Theology for Christian Prayer*, p. 9).

Ja[illegible]

Suggested Reading: Davis, Earl C. *Life in the Spirit*. Vol II. Nashville, Tn: Broadman Press, 1986. [illegible] A. *Prayer*. Nashville, Tn: Abingdon Press, 1942. Hunt, T. W. *The Doctrine of Prayer*. Nashville[illegible] Press, 1986.

History of the Doctrine of Church Leaders

The proper backdrop for understanding the nature and role of church leaders is the doctrine of the priesthood of all believers. Both the Old and New Testaments teach th[illegible] corporate people of God are to serve Him as priests. In Exodus 19:6 God commissioned Israel to [illegible] a kingdom of priests. In 1 Peter 2:9 the apostle taught that this position has been transferred to Christians. In Revelation 5:10 John indicated that this responsibility of serving God as priests has been given once and for all. To help the church accomplish its task, God has always called out leaders from among the royal priesthood to perform various functions. This leadership has assumed different forms throughout Christian history.

Judaism heavily influenced early Christianity. Evidence of this can be seen in church leadership structures. In the local synagogues a council of elders governed the assembly. From among this group a president was chosen who had teaching responsibilities, particularly if there were no trained rabbis available. The early church adopted this approach, with the apostles serving as the elders of the first Jerusalem church. Paul's correspondence indicates that the first mission churches also followed this pattern.

During the thirty years of church history recorded in Acts there began to be some changes. The early simple organization developed into a wider range of leaders. Pastors and bishops (overseers), elders, teachers, and deacons exercised leadership in local churches, while apostles, evangelists, missionaries, and others moved about from congregation to congregation performing their ministries.

Leadership in the early church was based on giftedness. Congregations recognized the gifts given different ones by the Holy Spirit. The leaders' authority came from the ratification by the local congregation of the individual's gifts, ability, spiritual maturity, and doctrinal integrity. The practice of ordination grew out of the simple laying on of hands that signaled a public setting aside of leadership from the church to fulfill certain tasks.

The teachings of Cyprian, bishop of Carthage, (third century) marked an important stage in the development of leadership divisions in the church. Cyprian identified the Eucharist as the sacrament of the sacrifice of the Lord and gave the bishop power to offer this sacrament. By elevating the Lord's Supper to the level of a sacrifice and placing its performance in the hands of a special group, Cyprian inaugurated a process that eclipsed the concept of the universal priesthood of all Christians and initiated the rise of the sacerdotalism (priests as mediators) that characterized the church for a thousand years.

From this point the priesthood came to be identified with a certain class of clerical officers who were regarded increasingly as me...tors between God and the believer.

To assume that Ma... Luther was the first to protest against the state of the Catholic Church ignores the voices of ma...eople raised throughout Christian history. Luther did, it seems, supply the requisite dynamic; and ...as, in part, his teaching about the priesthood of all believers that helped to bring about the R...ation. Luther drew a fundamental distinction between one's calling (vocation) and office (minis... Christians receive the same calling as a result of their experience with Christ: to live a life i...ce to God's purposes. The office one fills in the church rests on the gifts given by the Spiri...er ministry one performs, the calling remains the same.

Th...ntal distinction between Roman Catholics and Protestants concerning the derivation of the ...inistry is status or privilege versus function or service. The Protestant Reformation did ...d to the clergy-laity division, nor did it devalue the importance of ministerial leadership. Rather, the Reformers more clearly defined that ministry belonged to the whole people ...he clergy being responsible for the organization and functioning of that ministry. In this ...ught to restore the notion of universal priesthood.

...essful performance of the church's mission in the world comes as members of the body of ...ognize their leadership functions as priests and as they fulfill that responsibility.

Reggie McNeal

...ed Reading: Edge, Findley. *The Greening of the Church.* Waco, Tx: Word Books, 1971. Snyder, Howard ...*mmunity of the King.* Downers Grove, Ill: InterVarsity Press, 1977.

History of the Doctrine of Education

Every religion has valued religious education for its members. Even religions which preceded Christianity, including the religions of the Chinese, the Assyrians, the Babylonians, the Egyptians, and the Greeks, had systems for instructing their converts. Wherever an active belief exists, there follows the necessity to educate converts in the doctrine of the faith and provide religious instruction for the young. Instruction in faith which was imperative for the pagan convert was likewise important for understanding and growth in the belief of the true and living God.

The Jewish faith was an educational faith from the beginning. It was the responsibility of the patriarchs, though meager and limited in scope, to instruct the young members of the clan or tribe in faith and fellowship that had been established between humanity and God. Teaching was the way the promises of the Word of God were passed on from one generation to another. Though scant and simplistically informal, education was carried on effectively.

Through Moses, the Lawgiver, the fabric of the content for education became more pronounced. Moses received the written content which would form the basis of the curriculum for the instruction of the Hebrew people up to and beyond the ministry of Christ. Throughout the entire period from Moses to Christ, the people followed the commandment of God to train the people in the faith and the doctrine of the Law. This one doctrine, the doctrine of education, was faithfully obeyed.

Judaism had a great deal of influence on the educational philosophy of Christianity. Soon after churches were founded, teaching children became the prime duty of parents. All through the New Testament the process of teaching is emphasized. It was essential to the understanding of preaching. Without instruction in the doctrines of Christ, the preaching of the gospel would have been lost. As a part of the Great Commission, teaching took its rightful place alongside evangelism and proclamation as a vehicle to propagate the message of the early church.

Paul used speaking, writing, and teaching as the means of insuring the truth of the gospel in the lives of the people. Teaching became the important activity in the early church as believers progressed from one learning grade to another. Schools were soon established which went beyond the study of the doctrine and matters of faith to include classical studies in Greek, literature, history, dialectic, and the sciences. Such training proved to be disastrous to Christianity as an educational attempt was made to make the gospel consistent with Greek philosophy.

Christian education during the Middle Ages was deplorable at best. The curriculum of these

our purpose to know God; (3) the gracious action of God in Christ to atone for our sins; and (4) the call to repent and trust in the Savior, Jesus Christ. Our evangelism is the *means* which the Holy Spirit uses to convert the lost.

The early centuries of the church were times of great evangelism. It is estimated that by 300 over ten percent of the world's population professed Christianity. In the Middle Ages, the "conversion" of pagan tribes was often accomplished by conquering them. The Great Awakening of the eighteenth century saw the rise of "evangelists" as we think of them today— John Wesley, George Whitefield, Howel Harris, and Gilbert Tennent. The nineteenth century brought another "awakening" in America which included the evangelistic work of Timothy Dwight, Asahel Nettleton, C. G. Finney, and later in the century, D. L. Moody. It was during this period, through the work of Finney and others, that the popular evangelistic tools of "revival meetings" and "invitationals" were first introduced. The twentieth century has seen innovations in evangelism that have aided the growth of the church; among them are Church Growth theory, Evangelism-in-Depth, and Evangelism Explosion. Music and drama groups have been used to communicate the gospel to modern entertainment-oriented culture. Parachurch organizations have been established to reach particular groups, notably recent international conferences on evangelism include Berlin (1966), and Lausanne (1974).

Two crucial questions for evangelism historically and in our day are *who should be evangelized,* and *how should it be done?*

Some throughout the history of the church have taken the position that all would eventually be saved. This position is known as "universalism." Origen was one of the first theologians to express universalism in his writings. Universalism became most pronounced in America in the eighteenth century. James Murray and Hosea Ballou were two of the earliest and most prominent American universalists. While the universalists in America formed their own denomination, universalist teachings have not been limited to its members. Karl Barth, perhaps the most prominent theologian of this century, is thought by some to have expressed a kind of universalism in which all are understood as being both reprobated and elected in Christ. For universalists the Christian call to bear witness to the good news is usually seen as a call to proclaim to people that they *are already* reconciled to God.

Among those Christians who reject universalism as unbiblical, there is still some question concerning how evangelism is to be done. Our proclamation of the gospel and call for response must be consistent with a biblical understanding of the spiritual death of fallen humanity (Eph 2:1-10). Many contemporary evangelistic methods seem to deny this biblical truth. With his background as a lawyer C. G. Finney, the noted nineteenth-century evangelist, "argued" the gospel with the lost sinner. As the sinner was convinced of the truth of the gospel, he or she was told simply to "decide" for Christ. Yet the adoption of this understanding of salvation has caused much modern evangelism to become emotionally manipulative, seeking simply to cause a momentary decision of the sinner's will, yet neglecting the biblical idea that conversion is the supernatural, gracious act of God toward the sinner. The Christian call to evangelism is a call not simply to persuade people to make decisions, but rather to proclaim to them the good news of salvation in Christ, to call them to repentance, and to give God the glory for regeneration and conversion. We do not fail in our evangelism if we faithfully tell the gospel and yet the person is not converted; we fail only if we do not faithfully tell the gospel at all.

Mark E. Dever

Suggested Reading: Packer, J. I. *Evangelism and the Sovereignty of God.* Downers Grove, Ill: InterVarsity Press, 1961. Metzger, Will. *Tell the Truth.* Downers Grove, Ill: InterVarsity Press, 1981. Green, Michael. *Evangelism in the Early Church.* Philadelphia, Pa: Eerdmans, 1970. J. D. Douglas, ed. *Let the Earth Hear His Voice.* Minneapolis, Mn: World Wide Publications, 1975.

History of the Doctrine of Missions

Commissioned on the mount (Mt 28:19-20) and empowered in the upper room (Ac 1:8), the early disciples were witnesses unto Christ, beginning at Jerusalem. Through the proclamation of the crucified and risen Lord, through the gathering of churches in new areas, and through individual witness even unto death by men and women, youthful converts and aged leaders, the Christian message was carried to the farthest extent of the Roman Empire and even beyond it.

The Church began with a mandate for missions. The history of its continued concern for that mandate can be considered as response, regression, renewal, and reflection.

With Constantine came mass conversions that weakened the fervor of the church and doctrinal controversies that ruptured its fellowship. But even with the rupture, the Copts of Egypt spread the good news to the Sudan and Ethiopia; while the Nestorians found refuge in Persia and from there spread the word to India, Central Asia, and China. In the West, monasteries became training grounds for missionaries to central and western Europe and to the British Isles. Though chieftains and monarchs too often found coercion a tool for the propagation of the faith, western Europe became known as Christian.

When the explorers of Portugal and Spain found new worlds, missionaries as well as merchants followed them. The church was committed to convert the heathen of all lands. When Luther and other Reformers protested against growing abuses in the church, the mission mandate was forgotten for almost two centuries by their followers. While the Roman Catholic Church continued to spread the faith both westward and eastward through their religious orders, many of the Protestants decided the Great Commission no longer applied. It had been fulfilled by the apostles. Their energies turned inward with the struggle to survive.

It took a further inward turning to revive the missionary impulse among Protestants. The Pietists of Germany, revolting against barren orthodoxy and dead formalism, were the key to renewal. Their University of Halle, founded in 1694, trained missionaries in the midst of much protest. The Moravian community at Herrnhut accepted the evangelization of the world as their most pressing obligation, sending out entire families to witness in other countries. Their influence spread to England with the Great Awakening.

Though British mission societies had been formed earlier to meet the needs of the colonists and Indians in America, it was primarily William Carey who awakened Christians of his country to the task of converting persons in other lands. Under his urging, the Baptist Missionary Society was founded in 1792 and became the first of many denominational and interdenominational mission societies.

Though some churches resisted the missionary movement as a human institution, believing God needed no help to save His elect, the nineteenth century became the "Great Century" (Latourette) of Christian world missions with an unprecedented Protestant outreach and a vigorous Catholic work. The modern ecumenical movement had its roots in this mission concern.

Missionaries were often unwanted. Many suffered great deprivations. But they were sustained by the belief that without Christ, people had no hope for salvation. They spared no pains to take the message to them. Yet the missionary presence remained closely associated with colonialism in the minds of many whom they sought to serve.

With the twentieth century came a reassessment of the missionary enterprise. The rise of the third world nations saw the rejection of colonialism and a move toward indigenous leadership and ecclesiastical independence. Missionaries discovered a new role of partner rather than leader. Short terms abroad and summer projects were added to the traditional image. But the greatest challenge was the reassessment of the relation of Christianity to other faiths. Out of a study of comparative religions came a drive to recognize other faiths on a par with Christianity and to strive to cooperate with them for the good of humanity. But such a view was rejected by evangelical Christians who, without neglecting humanitarian service, continue to recognize the uniqueness of the work and revelation of God in Christ.

Barbara Bruce

Suggested Reading: Fletcher, Jesse. *The Mission of the Church.* Vol. 14 of *Layman's Library of Christian Doctrine.* Nashville, Tn: Broadman Press, 1988. Kraemer, Hendrik. *The Christian Message in a Non-Christian World.* New York, NY: International Missionary Council, 1938. Latourette, K. S. *A History of the Expansion of Christianity.* 7 vols. Grand Rapids, Mi: Zondervan, 1937-45. Neill, Stephen. *A History of Christian Missions.* Middlesex, England: Penguin Books Ltd., 1964.

GLOSSARY OF THEOLOGICAL TERMS

Adoption God's loving action making people who receive *salvation* His children and heirs. Ro 8:15,23; Gal 4:5; Eph 1:4.

Advent Christ's coming (1) through the virgin birth to minister and provide salvation; Mt 1:18-25; Lk 2:6-20; Jn 1:1-18; (2) in the clouds for final judgment; Mt 24:30; 1 Co 15:23; 1 Th 4:15-16. See *Parousia; Second Coming.*

Angel A messenger from God, either heavenly (Heb 1:14) or human (2 Sa 19:27), who delivers God's message of instruction, warning, or *hope.*

Antichrist The opponent(s) of Christ who face ultimate defeat but tempt God's people. They are especially associated with end time. 1 Jn 2:18-20; 4:3; 2 Jn 7; Rev 13:1-18; compare Mt 24:5,23-24; Mk 13:21-22.

Apocalyptic (1) A revealing of the future; (2) Jewish and Christian writings such as Daniel and Revelation reflecting persecution of God's people; (3) symbolic language reflecting belief in two opposing universal powers (*God* and *Satan*); two ages of universal history (present age dominated by evil and Satan and age to come under God's rule); and a future judgment giving rewards to the people of God and eternal punishment to the wicked. See Introductions to Daniel; Revelation.

Asceticism Self-denial and personal discipline used by some Christians, especially during the Middle Ages, to try to avoid worldliness and to show devotion to Christ.

Atonement God's way of overcoming sin through Christ's obedience and death to restore believers to a right relationship with God. Lev 16; Mt 26:28; Ro 5:6-11; 1 Th 5:9; Heb 9:12-15; 1 Pe 3:18. See chart at p. 1602.

Baptism A church ordinance or observance that represents the believer's death to sin and resurrection to a new life in Christ. Jn 3:5; Ac 8:36; Ro 6:3-5.

Bible See *Scripture.*

Bishop A church leader: literally, overseer or supervisor; known as pastor in some denominations and as a distinct supervisory office in others. Php 1:1; 1 Ti 3:2; Tit 1:7; 1 Pe 2:25.

Christology The technical term describing a study of the nature and work of Jesus Christ.

Canon The collection of Holy Scripture; the Bible as the authoritative standard by which all doctrine and practice is judged.

Church The community of those who believe in and follow Jesus Christ. Used to designate a congregation, a denomination, or all Christians. Mt 16:18; Ac 8:1; 1 Co 1:1; Eph 1:22-23; 1 Ti 3:15; Heb 12:23.

Church fathers The Christian writers and thinkers from about 90 to about 500 AD who influenced the systematic statements of Christian teaching. See *Doctrine.*

Circumcision The removal of foreskin of the penis as a sign of inclusion among the covenant people of Israel (Ge 17:13). Demanded by some Jewish church members as necessary for salvation, a demand Paul opposed as heresy (Gal 5:1-6).

Communion See *Lord's Supper.*

Confession (1) A statement of personal beliefs; (2) the Christian acknowledgement that Jesus is Lord (Mt 10:32); (3) admission of personal *sin* and seeking *forgiveness* from others (Lk 17:4; Jas 6:16) and from God (1 Jn 1:9).

Consecration Setting apart for God's use.

Consubstantiation The belief in the Lutheran tradition that the body and blood of Christ are mystically and invisibly present in the Lord's supper but are not materially identified with the bread and wine. See *Transubstantiation.*

Conversion God's act of changing a person's life in response to the person's turning to Christ in *repentance* and *faith* from some other belief or from no belief. Ac 15:3; Ro 16:5; 1 Co 16:15.

Covenant A contract or agreement expressing God's gracious promises to His people and their consequent relationship to Him.

Words in italics within definitions are defined in this glossary as a separate entity.

Ge 9:8-17; 17:1-22; Ex 24:1-8; Jer 31:31-34; 1 Co 11:23-26.

Creation God's bringing the world and everything in it into existence from nothing. Ge 1—2; Ps 148:5; Isa 42:5; 43:1; Mal 2:10; Mk 13:19; Jn 1:1-3; 17:24; Ro 8:19-39.

Creed Formal statement of belief accepted as authoritative by the people adopting it.

Cross Two wooden beams shaped as a letter *t* or *x* used as an instrument to kill criminals by the Roman government; the wooden beams on which Jesus was killed and thus a symbol of Christian faith and responsibility. Mt 10:38; 16:24; 27:1-54; Gal 6:14.

Crucifixion A form of execution by affixing a victim to a cross to die; Jesus' death on the cross for sinners. Jn 19:16-37; Ro 6:6; Gal 2:20.

Day of the Lord (1) God's time of decisive intervention in history (La 1:21; Am 5:18-20; Zep 1:7-18; 3:8); (2) the final day of judgment in end time (Lk 17:24; 1 Co 1:8; Rev 16:14).

Deacon An office in the church that involves ministry and service. Php 1:1; 1 Ti 3:8-12.

Demons Evil spirits that serve *Satan.* Mt 12:22-29; 25:41; Lk 11:19; Ro 8:38; 1 Co 10:20.

Denomination An organization of congregations of similar beliefs, church polity (government), and practice. See chart at p. 98.

Devil See *Satan.*

Didache (1) Greek word of teaching in New Testment; (2) a writing of Christian teachings from shortly after AD 100.

Dispensation A distinct period in the history of salvation. For dispensational viewpoints see Introduction to Revelation; chart.

Disciple A follower and learner of Jesus Christ. Jn 8:31; 13:35; Ac 11:26.

Doctrine (1) Carefully formulated statements of teachings on a certain theme; (2) statements of an individual's or a group's beliefs about the Christian gospel based on the teachings of the Bible. See chart at p. 34.

Dogma A fixed and inflexible system of beliefs authorized by group of believers.

Eastern church (1) The early Greek-speaking churches at the Eastern end of the Mediterranean centered in Constantinople that sought to be independent of the Roman church. (2) modern *Orthodox churches* which have developed out of the Eastern tradition. See time line at pp. 1186, 1218.

Ecclesiastical Having to do with the church (Greek *ekklesia*).

Ecumenical (1) Having to do with the unity of all Christians or at least a cooperative spirit among Christians; (2) a term used to describe early church councils that sought to deal with controversy and heresy.

Elder (1) In the Old Testament those who by virtue of age and experience were qualified to give counsel and rule, especially in the local government; Ex 3:16; 24:9; Nu 11:16; Dt 21:2-18; Jdg 8:14-16; 2 Ki 6:32; 23:1; (2) in the New Testament, leaders in the early church (Ac 11:30; 14:23; 1 Ti 4:14; Jas 5:14); (3) in modern churches interpreted by some as the pastors and in others as a separate office.

Election God's gracious action in choosing people to follow Him and obey His commandments. Mt 24:22; Ro 9:11; 11:7, 28; 2 Ti 2:10; 2 Pe 1:10.

Episcopal A form of church government led by bishops (Greek *episkopoi*) characteristic of the Anglican or Protestant Episcopal Church.

Epistemology The study of how we know and of the sources of knowledge. See chart at p.1634.

Epistles New Testament letters by Paul, James, John, Peter, and Jude.

Eschatology The study of last things or end time when Christ returns. See chart at p. 1634.

Eternal life (1) The quality of life Jesus gives His disciples; Jn 3:36; (2) unending life with God given to those who believe in Jesus Christ as Savior and Lord; Tit 1:2; Jude 21.

Ethics The study of morality and moral decisions that guide human conduct.

Eucharist See *Lord's Supper.*

Evangelism The central element of the church's *mission* involving telling others the *gospel* of *salvation* with the goal of leading them to *repentance* and *faith* in Christ.

Evil Anyone or anything that opposes the plan of God.

Exegesis Literally, getting out the meaning; the process by which Bible students interpret *Scripture.* See *Hermeneutics.*

Exile (1) Life in a foreign land away from one's homeland as a result of military defeat or political actions; (2) Israel's life in the Assyrian kingdom after 722 BC; 2 Ki 17; (3) Judah's life in Babylon after 587 BC; 2 Ki 25; Ezra; Nehemiah; Esther.

The Exodus The most important act of national deliverance in the Old Testament when God enabled the Israelites to escape Egypt; Ex 12—15.

Expiation An action directed towards nullifying the effects of sin which breaks the relationship between a person and God; emphasizes the saving event of the atonement of Christ rather than the penalty or punishment endured. Lev 17:11; Dt 21:1-9; Lk 18:13; Heb 2:17; 8:12; 1 Jn 2:2; 4:10. Compare *Propitiation.*

Faith Belief in and personal commitment to Jesus Christ for eternal salvation. Mt 9:22,29; 17:20; Mk 11:22; Lk 17:6; Jn 14:12; Ac 6:7; 20:21; Ro 1:17; 3:22-31; Gal 2:16; Eph 2:8.

Fall The result of the first human sin which marred the *image of God* in humans and created an enviroment for and a tendency towards sin for all people. Ge 2—3.

Fasting Going without food as a sign of repentance, grief, or devotion to God; often connected with devotion to prayer.

Fellowship Shared encouragement and support among Christians. Ac 2:42; 2 Co 6:14; Php 3:10; 1 Jn 1:3-7.

Foreknowledge God's eternal knowledge of the future. Ro 8:29; 11:2; 1 Pe 1:2, 20.

Foreordain See *Predestination.*

Forgiveness (1) Pardon and release from penalty for wrongdoing; (2) God's delivery from sin's wages (Ro 6:23) for those who repent and express faith in Christ; Ac 2:38; 2 Co 2:10; (3) the Christian act of freeing from guilt and blame those by whom one has suffered wrong; Mt 6:14; 2 Co 2:7; Col 3:13.

Free Will The freedom God gives people to make decisions without the decisions being predetermined; the human freedom to reject God's will or to choose to obey God.

Glorification God's action in the lives of believers making them able to share the glory and reward of heaven. Ro 8:17,32.

Gnosticism A view fully developed after 100 AD that stressed salvation through a secret knowledge (Greek *gnosis*) and a dualistic world view with equal powers of good and evil.

Godhead The unity of the triune God: Father, Son, Holy Spirit.

Gospel The good news of the redeeming work of God through the life, death, and resurrection of Jesus Christ. See Summary of Gospel (p 1663).

Gospels The four New Testament accounts of the life of Jesus Christ. Matthew, Mark, and Luke are called Synoptic Gospels because they relate many of the same events and teachings of Jesus. John is the Fourth Gospel and tends to be more theological in nature, telling events and teachings not in the Synoptics.

Grace The unmerited favor of God that provides our salvation. Eph 2:8.

Hades The abode of the dead thought by some to be distinguishable from hell, the final state of the wicked. Mt 16:18; Rev 1:18; 20:13.

Heaven The eternal dwelling place of God and the redeemed. Jn 1:32; 3:13; 2 Co 5:1; Rev 19:11.

Hell The place of everlasting punishment for the lost. Mt 5:22-30; 2 Pe 2:4.

Hellenism The Greek culture spread by Alexander the Great (323 BC) that dominated the biblical world during New Testament times and afterwards.

Heresy Teaching that undermines or denies central Christian belief.

Hermeneutics The study of the principles of interpreting the Bible. See Guide to Interpreting the Bible (p. 1769).

High Priest The chief religious official for Israel and Judaism appointed as the only person allowed to enter the Holy of Holies and offer *sacrifice* on the Day of Atonement (Lev 16); applied to Jesus (Heb 4:13—5:10).

Holy (1) God's distinguishing characteristic that separates Him from all creation; 1 Sa 2:2; Isa 5:16; (2) His distinct ethical purity. Lev 19:2; Rev 4:8; (3) the moral ideal for Christians as they seek to reflect the character of God as known in Christ Jesus. 1 Pe 1:15-16.

Holy of Holies The innermost and most sacred area of the Tabernacle and Temple, where God was present and where on the Day of Atonement sacrifices were made by the *high priest.*

Holy Spirit The third person of the Trinity; the presence of God promised by Christ and sent to His disciples at Pentecost representing God's active presence in the believer, the church, and the world. Lk 12;12; Ac 2:4; Ro 15:13; 1 Th 1:6; 2 Pe 1:21.

Homiletics The art and study of preaching.

Hope The assurance that God grants *eternal life* to those who have trusted Jesus Christ as Lord and Savior. Ro 5:2-5; 8:20-25; 1 Co 15:19; Col 1:27.

Icon An image used in the Orthodox churches as windows into a spiritual world.

Idolatry The worship of that which is not God. Ex 20:4; Isa 45:16-20; 1 Co 10:14; Col 3:5.

Image of God That in human nature which reflected God at creation but was marred in the *fall* by sin and is being restored as Christians are molded into the image of Christ. Ge 1:26-27; 9:6; 1 Co 11:7; 2 Co 4:4; Col 3:10.

Immanence God's presence in His creation; shown most clearly by the *incarnation* in Jesus Christ. Compare *Transcendence.*

Immortality (1) a characteristic of God alone; (2) the Greek belief in the eternal, undying nature of the human soul; often contrasted with biblical belief in resurrection. Ro 1:23; 2:7; 1 Co 15:53; 1 Ti 6:16. Compare *eternal life.*

Incarnation The act of the divine Son Jesus becoming human and enduring all the experiences which tempt us and cause us to suffer. Jn 1:1-18; Php 2:1-11; He 4:15.

Inerrancy The quality of the Bible being without mistakes of fact or interpretation.

Infallibility (1) The trustworthiness of the Bible in what it teaches and promises. (2) Used by Roman Catholics to describe the church and/or the pope in his teaching function, a claim not accepted by non-Catholics.

Inspiration The breathing of God's Spirit on human speech and writing producing the inspired text of the Bible. 2 Ti 3:16-17; 2 Pe 1:21.

Intercession A prayer presenting one person's needs to another as Christians presenting the needs of others to God (1 Ti 2:1) or as Christ (Heb 7:25) or the Holy Spirit (Ro 8:26-27) representing believers before God.

Interpretation The human effort to understand the Bible with the guidance of the Holy Spirit and to apply its meaning to contemporary life. See *Hermeneutics.*

Jesus Christ The eternal Son of God; the Lord and Savior; the second Person of the *Trinity.* Php 2:5-11.

Joy The inner attitude of rejoicing in one's salvation regardless of outward circumstances. Php 1:25-26.

Judgment God's work at the end time involving condemnation for unbelievers and assignment of rewards for believers. Mt 24; Ro 2:3; 14:10; 2 Co 5:10; Heb 9:27.

Justification A believer's righteousness or right relationship to God based on faith in Jesus Christ. Ro 3:20-31. See *Faith.*

Kerygma The Greek word for the content of Christian preaching. See Summary of the Gospel (p. 1663).

Kingdom of God God's sovereign rule in the universe and in the hearts of Christians.

Kingdom of heaven See *Kingdom of God.*

Koinonia Greek word for *fellowship.* See *Fellowship.*

Laity The people of God (Greek *laos*). Ac 15:14; Ro 9:25; 1 Pe 2:10. Often used to refer to Christians who are not ordained ministers or ministers by profession.

Lamb of God A title for Jesus that highlights His sacrifice for our sins and His victory over death. Jn 1:29; 1 Pe 1:19.

Law God's instruction to His people about how to love Him and others. When used with definite article "the" may refer to the Old Testament as a whole but usually to the *Pentateuch* (Genesis—Deuteronomy). Used by Paul and others in New Testament to refer to oral interpretations of the law by Jewish rabbis developed into a system seen as necessary for salvation, a development condemned by the New Testament. Ro 3:20; Gal 2:16. See *Legalism.*

Laying on of hands Setting apart or consecrating a person to God's service through placing hands on the head of the person being dedicated. Ac 8:18; 1 Ti 5:22; 2 Ti 1:6.

Legalism The belief that a person to have salvation must keep God's law (as interpreted by professional teachers) as well as have faith in Christ. See *Law.*

Logos Greek word meaning "word" used to describe the eternal ministry of Christ in creation and His appearance as the Son of God who became flesh. Jn 1:1-18.

Lord A title for God in the Old Testament; also used for Jesus in the New Testament; means Owner or Master worthy of obedience.

Lord's Day The first day of the week (Sunday) on which most Christians have worshiped since Christ's resurrection on the first day of the week. Jn 20:19; Ac 20:7; 1 Co 16:2.

Lord's Supper A church ordinance or observance with breaking of bread and drinking of wine helping Christians (1) remember the last meal Jesus ate and His death on the cross making salvation possible, (2) examine their own lives in light of Christ's demands, and (3) anticipate Christ's return. Mk 14:22-25; 1 Co 11:23-26.

Love (1) God's essential quality (1 Jn 4:8) that seeks the best interests of others regardless of the others' actions; (2) commanded of believers (Jn 15:12).

Lutheran Churches that developed under the influence of Martin Luther and accept the Augsburg Confession as their basic statement of beliefs; noted for emphasis on justification by faith alone and for *consubstantiation* view of Lord's Supper. See *consubstantiation.*

Martyr One who bears witness to Jesus Christ and consequently suffers or dies rather than deny Christ. Ac 7.

Mass The term used by Roman Catholics to describe the worship service centered on the Lord's Supper.

Mediator (1) One who seeks to settle disputes between other persons; (2) Jesus as the One who brought together God and believers through His death and resurrection. See 1 Ti 2:5; Heb 8:6; 9:15; 12:24.

Meditation A prayer form involving silent concentration.

Messiah (1) Literally, the anointed one in reference to an action in the king's inauguration; 1 Sam 16:13; (2) the coming king promised by the prophets; Isa 9; 11; (3) Jesus Christ who fulfilled the prophetic promises; Jn 1:41; (Christ represents the Greek translation of the Hebrew word "messiah.")

Methodist Christian churches that developed under the influence of John and Charles Wesley.

Millennium A thousand year period (Rev 20:3-4) when the righteous will reign on earth.

Minister (1) the loving service of Christians to each other and to those outside the church in the name of Jesus; (2) designation for persons who serve Jesus; (3) used to designate persons ordained to or engaged in ministry as a profession.

Miracle An act of God beyond human understanding that inspires wonder, displays God's greatness, and leads people to recognize God at work in the world.

Mission The God-given responsibility of the church and each believer to bring God's love and the Christian gospel to all people through evangelism, education, and ministry. Missions is used especially to refer to work done by Christians outside their own culture.

Monotheism Belief in only one God; basic to Christianity, Judaism, and Islam.

Morality Right personal actions and character. See *Ethics.*

New birth God's work in the believer at *conversion* to create a new person empowered by the Holy Spirit. Jn 3:3.

Obedience Hearing and following instructions and directions from God; expected of believers. Jn 14:23; Heb 5:9.

Omnipotent God's unlimited power to do that which is within His *holy* and *righteous* character.

Omnipresence God's unlimited presence in all places at all times.

Omniscience God's unlimited knowing.

Ontological Having to do with the essential nature of things or beings; used to argue God's existence as the One with perfect existence.

Ordinances The two symbolic acts Jesus commanded the church to observe: the *Lord's Supper* and *baptism;* referred to by some church groups as sacraments.

Ordination A commissioning to a particular form of ministry; enacted by the church through a ceremony usually involving examination of the candidate's life and beliefs and by the *laying on of hands.*

Original sin The disobedience of Adam and Eve that plunged humankind into sin and has been followed by every person (except Jesus Christ) choosing to sin. See *Fall.*

Orthodoxy Right belief as opposed to *heresy.*

Orthodox church Christian churches including Greek, Russian, Armenian, and Coptic that developed out of the *Eastern church;* stress on tradition, liturgy, and continuity with the doctrine of the *ecumenical* councils. See time line at pp. 1186, 1218.

Pacifism The belief that war is never justifiable.

Parable A short story taken from everyday life to make a spiritual point; Jesus' favorite form of teaching.

Paraclete Greek word for Helper and Counselor (Jn 14:16,26) as promised by Jesus looking to coming of *Holy Spirit.*

Parousia Greek word meaning coming or presence used to refer to Christ's coming, especially the *second coming.* 1 Co 1:8; 15:23; 2 Th 2:8; 2 Pe 1:16.

Passion The suffering of Christ during His time of trial and death on the cross.

Passover The Jewish feast celebrating the Exodus from Egypt (Ex 12); celebrated by Jesus and His disciples at the Last Supper.

Pentecost The fiftieth day after *Passover* celebrated by Jews as the culmination of the Feast of Weeks and by Christians as the anniversary of the coming of the *Holy Spirit.* Ac 2.

Perseverance of the saints A doctrine affirming God's assurance that one who truly believes in Christ as Lord and Savior is securely saved and will persist in exercising faith in Christ. Jn 10:27-29.

Polytheism Belief in more than one god; heresy prevalent in biblical times.

Prayer Communication with God. See Discipline of Prayer (p. 1761).

Preach To declare the good news of Jesus Christ. See Guide to Proclaiming the Word (p. 1809).

Predestination God's eternal plan to provide salvation for His sinful creatures and establish His *kingdom.* Ac 4:27-28; Ro 8:29; 1 Co 2:7; Eph 1:5.

Preeminence Christ's place of priority in God's plan for the universe. Col 1:18.

Preexistence Existing always and before the creation of the universe; a characteristic of the trinitarian God alone. Ge 1:1-2; Jn 1:1-3; Col 1:16.

Presbyter Transliteration of Greek word for *elder.* See *Elder.*

Presbyterian Christian churches led by *presbyters,* growing out of the work of John Calvin and John Knox; accept the 1645 Westminister Confession of Faith.

Priesthood (1) The body of those who represent God and give His instructions to people as well as interceding with God and offering sacrifices to Him; (2) all believers for whom Christ has opened the way for personal intercession with God and responsibility to represent God to the world. Ex 19:6; 1 Pe 2:5; Rev 1:6.

Priesthood of believers The belief that every Christian has direct access to God through Christ without a human *mediator* and that every Christian is to serve as a priest on behalf of others. See *Priesthood.*

Prophet One who speaks for God.

Propitiation An action directed towards God seeking to change God's wrath to favor; one way of explaining Christ's atonement. See *Atonement*; *Expiation.*

Proselyte (1) A person converted to Judaism from another religion; (2) currently used to describe one who changes from one denomination to another.

Protestants Christians who protested against the practices of the Roman Catholic church and developed as separate denominations beginning with the Protestant Reformation initiated by Luther, Zwingli, and Calvin; emphasize the authority of Scripture above the church, justification by faith alone, and the priesthood of believers.

Providence God's care for and guidance of His creation against all opposition.

Ransom Payment offered to secure someone else's release. See *Atonement,* chart at p. 1602.

Rapture The carrying away of believers alive at Christ's return, a view based on an interpretation of 1 Th 4:17. See notes on LAST THINGS, Rapture (Index, p. 1863).

Reconciliation The bringing together of alienated persons; the saving work of Christ and a ministry given believers. 2 Co 5:18-21.

Regeneration See *new birth.*

Repentance A change of heart and mind resulting in a turning from sin to God that allows *conversion* and is expressed through *faith.* Ac 3:19; 8:22; 17:30; 2 Co 7:10.

Resurrection (1) The raising of Jesus from the dead to eternal life; Lk 24:1-12; 1 Co 15; (2) the raising of believers for eternal life with Christ; 2 Co 4:14; (3) the raising of unbelievers to eternal punishment; Mt 25:31-46.

Retribution Punishment of evil for the sake of justice.

Revelation (1) Making known that which has been hidden; God making known His nature and purpose through the natural world, history, prophets, and most completely through Jesus Christ; (2) the last book of the Bible; (3) the Bible as the basic source of knowledge about God, His purpose, and His will.

Righteousness The quality or condition of being in right relationship with God; living out the relationship with God in right relationships with other persons. See *Justification.*

Ritual A symbolic action that points to a spiritual truth.

Roman Catholic The name of the largest group of churches in today's world, centered in Rome and offering allegience to the pope as the earthly head of the church, a claim disputed by other Christian groups. See *Infallible.*

Sabbath The seventh day of the week corresponding to the seventh day of creation when people in the Old Testament were called on to rest from work and reflect on God; Ge 2:2-3; Dt 5:12-15; observed on Saturday by contemporary Jews, Adventists, and others. Most Christian groups celebrate the *Lord's Day.*

Sacrifice (1) According to Mosaic law an offering to God in repentance for sin or as an expression of thanksgiving; (2) Christ as the ultimate Sacrifice for sin. Lev 1—7; 1 Co 5:7; Heb 10:12; 1 Jn 2:2.

Saints Those holy or set apart to God; any person in Christ. Ro 16:2.

Salvation (1) Deliverance from trouble or evil; (2) the process by which God redeems His creation, completed through the life, death, and resurrection of His Son Jesus Christ. See *Regeneration, Sanctification, Glorification.*

Sanctification The process in salvation by which God conforms the believer's life and character to the life and character of Jesus Christ through the Holy Spirit. Ac 26:18; Ro 15:16; 1 Co 6:11; 1 Pe 1:2.

Satan The personalized evil one who leads forces opposed to God and tempts people.

Savior Jesus Christ who brings *salvation.* Lk 2:11; Tit 2:13.

Schism, Great The division between the Western and Eastern churches finalized in 1054. See time line at p. 1218.

Scribe A Jewish teacher of the law, who studied and copied Scripture.

Scripture The Bible, the divinely-inspired record of God's revelation of Himself and the authoritative source for Christian doctrine and teaching. 2 Ti 3:16-17.

Second Coming Christ's return in power and glory to consummate His work of redemption.

Security of the Believer The doctrine that true believers are eternally saved and, therefore, secure in salvation. See *Perseverance of the saints.*

Septuagint Translation of the Hebrew Old Testament into Greek made in third century BC.

Shalom Hebrew word for peace and wholeness meaning fullness of life through God-given harmony with God, the world, others, and oneself.

Sin The universal human condition of broken relationship with God involving missing the mark or falling short of God's intention for human life and breaking God's instructions for life; remedied by belief in Jesus Christ as Savior from sin and Lord of life.

Son of God Title for Jesus stressing His divinity as co-existent with the Father.

Son of Man Title Jesus most frequently used for Himself stressing both His divinity as the prophesied One in the Old Testament and His identification with humans. Da 7:13; 8:17; Mt 8:20.

Soteriology The doctrine of *salvation.*

Soul The whole person as dependent upon God for life's physical, emotional, and spiritual needs.

Sovereignty God's freedom from outward restraint; His unlimited rule of and control over His creation. See *Omnipotent.*

Speaking in tongues Use of language previously unknown to speaker to praise God or to reveal God's message to hearers; a gift of the Holy Spirit. Ac 2:4; 10:46; 1 Co 12:10.

Spirit (1) The quality, power, or force within persons that makes them open to relationship with God; (2) the Spirit of God.

Stewardship Human responsibility to manage resources God has placed in one's care.

Symbolic presence Belief of many evangelical Christians that the bread and wine of the Lord's Supper symbolize Christ's presence but that they do not actually contain His body and blood in any real way. See *Consubstantiation*; *Transubstantiation.*

Systematic Theology The study and organization of Christian doctrines by their individual meanings and in their relationships to each other within the whole doctrinal system. See chart at p. 34.

Temptation The pull toward sin which all humans experience (Heb 4:15); from Satan not God (Jas 1:13-15).

Testament Literally, covenant. See *Covenant.*

Testimony Description of a personal experience of salvation with Christ and of how Jesus Christ influences one's life. See Discipline of Witnessing (p. 1786).

Theodicy An explanation of how evil exists in a world where God is all-good and all-powerful. See Introductions to Job, Habakkuk.

Theology The study of God; the human effort to organize and explain the teachings or doctrines of Scripture.

Tithe One tenth of a person's income and belongings given to God through the church.

Total Depravity The condition of humanity after the fall including involvement of each member of the human race in sin.

Transcendence God's quality of being above or beyond His creation. See *immanence.*

Transfiguration Jesus's appearance in full glory to Peter, James, and John. Mk 9:2-8.

Transubstantiation The belief of the Roman Catholic church that the bread and wine used in *mass* miraculously becomes the actual body and blood of Jesus.

Tribulation Severe affliction or oppression experienced by God's people interpreted by some scholars as a period of persecution and suffering immediately before the *second coming.* See *Rapture.*

Trinity God's revelation of Himself as Father, Son, and Holy Spirit unified as one in the *Godhead* and yet distinct in person and function.

Truth That which is real and reliable; opposite of faleshood and error; descriptive of the divine Father, Son, and Spirit as the full revelation of the one true God. Jn 14:6,17.

Universalism The unbiblical belief that all people will ultimately experience salvation.

Unpardonable sin Persistence in refusing to accept Christ as Lord and Savior which prevents one from receiving God's forgiveness; blasphemy that reflects such a condition. Mk 3:29-30; 2 Th 1:8-9; Heb 6:4-6; 10:26-31; 1 Jn 5:10-17.

Vicarious An act experienced or done for the good of another. See *Atonement,* chart at p. 1602.

Virgin birth The miraculous birth of Christ in which Mary remained a virgin as she conceived and bore Jesus through the intervention of the Holy Spirit. Mt 1:18-25.

Witness Declaring belief in Jesus Christ and the gospel message to unbelievers. See Discipline of Witnessing (p. 1786).

Word of God (1) The Bible, God's inspired written revelation; see *Scripture*; (2) God's message in oral form revealed through prophetic or angelic speakers; Eze 3; Lk 1:11-20; (3) Jesus Christ, God's eternal Word in human flesh; see *Logos*.

Worship Reverence, honor, praise, and service shown to God.

Wrath of God God's consistent response opposing and punishing sin.

Yahweh The Hebrew personal name of God revealed to Moses; came to be thought too holy to pronounce by Jews; often translated LORD or Jehovah. Ex 3:13-15; 6:2-3.

LIFE HELPS: RELATING DOCTRINE TO LIFE

LIFE HELPS: RELATING DOCTRINE TO LIFE

Table of Contents

LIFE HELPS: RELATING DOCTRINE TO LIFE

Discipleship includes learning the Bible's teachings and living out those teachings in daily life. As you begin growing in your life as a disciple, questions naturally will arise concerning the biblical teaching about certain areas of life. The Life Helps which follow assist you as a disciple of Jesus to learn, practice, and improve discipleship skills.

Discipleship is a personal discipline of deepening relationship with God as well as a personal and community ministry of kingdom outreach into the non-Christian world. These helps will lead you to grow in the Christian disciplines of worship, prayer, Bible study, and witness. They will draw you toward involvement in the Christian ministries of worship and intercession, teaching or preaching, evangelism, nurture, service, and missions.

Christian discipline and ministry have meaning for persons who already have accepted Jesus Christ as personal Savior and Lord. The first section calls for you to review how to accept Jesus as Savior to be sure that you have received salvation as His free gift to you.

Becoming a Disciple

HOW TO ACCEPT CHRIST

Do You Know For Certain That You Have Eternal Life and That You Will Go to Heaven When You Die?

God wants you to be sure. The Bible says, "I write these things to you who believe in the name of the Son of God so that you may know that you have eternal life" (1 Jn 5:13). Suppose you were standing before God right now and He asked you, "Why should I let you into heaven?" What do you think you would say? You may not know what to reply. But you do know God loves us and has a purpose for our lives. The Bible states it this way, "For God so loved the world that he gave his one and only Son, that whoever believes in him shall not perish but have eternal life" (Jn 3:16).

God's Purpose Is That You Have Eternal Life.

You can receive eternal life as a free gift. "The gift of God is eternal life in Christ Jesus our Lord" (Ro 6:23*b*).

You can live a full and meaningful life right now. Jesus said, "I have come that they may have life, and have it to the full" (Jn 10:10*b*).

You can spend eternity with Jesus in Heaven, for He promised, "And if I go and prepare a place for you, I will come back and take you to be with me that you also may be where I am" (Jn 14:3).

Our Need Is to Understand Our Problem.

God's purpose is that we have meaning in life as we direct our lives and hearts toward Him. Then why is it that people seldom find true meaning in life? Our sinful nature keeps us from fulfilling God's purpose for our lives.

• *We are all sinners by nature and by choice.* "For all have sinned and fall short of the glory of God" (Ro 3:23).

• *We cannot save ourselves.* "Not by works, so that no one can boast" (Eph 2:9).

• *We deserve death and hell.* "For the wages of sin is death" (Ro 6:23*a*).

• *We can receive what we do not deserve.* God is holy and just and must punish sin, yet He loves us and has provided forgiveness for our sin. Jesus said, "I am the way and the truth and the life. No one comes to the Father except through me" (Jn 14:6).

The good news is. . **God's Provision Is Jesus Christ.** Becoming aware of our sinfulness, we may desire a remedy. God offers that remedy in His Son, Jesus Christ, who became like us to show us how we might become like Him.

• *Jesus is God and became human.* "In the beginning was the Word, and the Word was with God, and the Word was God. . .The Word became flesh and made his dwelling among us" (Jn 1:1,14*a*).

• *Jesus died for us on the cross.* "For Christ died for sins once for all, the righteous for the unrighteous, to bring you to God" (1 Pe 3:18*a*).

• *Jesus was resurrected from the dead.* "He was delivered over to death for our sins and was raised to life for our justification" (Ro 4:25).

The only way Jesus can affect our lives is for us to receive Him. The Bible says, "To all who received him, to those who believed in his name, he gave the right to become children of God" (Jn 1:12).

How We Receive Jesus

Realizing that Jesus is the solution to our rebellion against God, we may desire to establish a relationship with Him. To do so the Bible says:

• *We must repent of our sin.* "Repent, then, and turn to God, so that your sins may be wiped out" (Ac 3:19*a*).

Repentance is not just feeling sorry for our sin. "They should repent and turn to God and prove their repentance by their deeds (Ac 26:20*b*). Repentance is turning away from our sin and turning to God through Jesus. It's like making a U-turn.

• *We must place our faith in Jesus.* "For it is by grace you have been saved, through faith—and this not from yourselves, it is the gift of God" (Eph 2:8). Faith is not just believing facts about Jesus. "You believe that there is one God. Good! Even the demons believe that—and shudder" (Jas 2:19). Faith is trusting in Jesus.

To Trust Totally in Jesus:

• *We must surrender to Jesus as Lord or Master.* "That if you confess with your mouth, 'Jesus is Lord,' and believe in your heart that God raised him from the dead, you will be saved. For . . .it is with your mouth that you confess and are saved" (Ro 10:9-10).

Surrendering to Jesus as Lord is not just words we repeat. Jesus warned, "Not everyone who says to me, 'Lord, Lord,' will enter the kingdom of heaven, but only he who does the will of my Father who is in heaven" (Mt 7:21). Surrendering to Jesus as Lord is giving Jesus control of our lives.

To give Jesus control of our lives is like driving down the highway with another person. As long as you are driving, you are in control. If, at some point, you realize you do not know the way, but the other person does, and you say, "You take the wheel and drive," then the other person is in control. The two of you will take the route that person chooses.

As evidence of giving Jesus control, you will want to identify with Him. The New Testament way is to confess Jesus publicly (Mt 10:32-33) and to follow Him in baptism and church membership (Ac 2:41).

Three Important Questions

- "Does what you have been reading make sense to you?"
- Is there any reason why you would not be willing to receive God's gift of eternal life?"
- "Are you willing to turn from your sin and place your faith in Jesus right now?"

The Bible says, "Everyone who calls on the name of the Lord will be saved" (Ro 10:13). Please read this prayer and see if you want to say something like this to God.

Dear Lord, I believe you are the Son of God and that you died on the cross and were raised from the dead. I know I have sinned and need forgiveness. I turn from my sins and receive you as my Savior and Lord. Thank you for saving me.

Call upon the Lord in repentance, faith, and total trust using these or similar words of your own. Jesus will become your Savior and Lord.

Welcome to the family of God. You have just made the most important decision of your life. You can be sure you are saved and have eternal life. Begin your Christian growth by reading the Scripture passages and annotations on JESUS CHRIST, Savior and SALVATION, Definition (Index, pp. 1847, 1858).

WELCOME TO GOD'S FAMILY

"The Spirit himself testifies with our spirit that we are God's children" (Ro 8:16). As a newborn babe in God's family, you will find assurance and direction from the following truths as you begin to grow in Christ.

1. **You entered God's family by a SPIRITUAL BIRTH.** Jesus taught, "Flesh gives birth to flesh, but the Spirit gives birth to spirit. You should not be surprised at my saying, 'You must be born again' " (Jn 3:6-7).

You can be certain you have eternal life:

- Because birth in Christ is a onetime experience (2 Co 5:17).
- Because of your commitment
  - —You repented of your sins (Ac 3:19).
  - —You placed your faith in Christ (Eph 2:8-9).
  - —You committed your life to the Lord Jesus Christ (Ro 10:9-10).
  - —You prayed asking Jesus to forgive and save you.
- Because of God's record (1 Jn 5:11-13).
- Because of God's nature (1 Jn 5:1-9).
- Because of God's promise (Jn 5:24).

I have assurance I am a Christian and have eternal life because on ________, I
(date)
committed my life to Christ. ________
(signed)

To gain further assurance and confidence, read the Scripture passages and annotations on ELECTION, Eternal Security (Index, p. 1858).

2. **GOD'S WORD is essential for spiritual growth just as food is for physical growth.** "Like newborn babies, crave pure spiritual milk, so that by it you may grow up in your salvation, now that you have tasted that the Lord is good" (1 Pe 2:2-3).

- God's Word will help you grow: READ IT DAILY.
- God's Word will guide you: HEAR IT TAUGHT AND PREACHED.
- God's Word will keep you from sin: MEMORIZE AND OBEY IT.
- God's Word will teach you how to live: STUDY IT.
- God's Word will inspire you: MEDITATE ON IT.
- God's Word will work: PRACTICE IT.

My best time to read God's Word each day is ______________________.

To understand the power of God's Word, read Scripture passages and annotations on HOLY SCRIPTURE, Powerful (Index, p. 1854).

3. **PRAYER is essential to spiritual growth just as breath is to physical growth.**

Praying is like breathing:

- As you exhale, talk to God.
- As you inhale, listen to God.

Talk to Him anytime:

- You want to worship Him.
- You need help.
- You feel lonely.
- You need strength.
- You want guidance.
- You are tempted.
- You sin or fail.

"If we confess our sins, he is faithful and just and will forgive us our sins and purify us from all unrighteousness" (1 Jn 1:9).

Read Scripture passages and annotations on PRAYER, Forgiveness (Index, p. 1867).

4. **THE CHURCH is essential to spiritual growth just as the home is to a baby's growth.** What a good home and family are to a baby, the church is to a new Christian.

God's people, the church, are your new family.

- They will rejoice that you have been born again.
- They will accept you and love you.
- They will encourage you and give you support.
- They will teach you and train you how to live.
- They will worship God with you.

You will want to read the Scripture passages and annotations on CHURCH, Body of Christ (Index, p. 1863).

You declare your acceptance of Christ and your new family by being baptized. "Those who accepted his message were baptized, and. . . the Lord added to their number daily those who were being saved" (Ac 2:41,47*b*). Baptism is a symbolic witness of your faith in the death, burial, and resurrection of Jesus Christ. It does not save you, but it shows your obedience to the example and teachings of Christ. Jesus walked sixty miles to be baptized. Since He placed that much importance on it, will you request baptism? Baptism is the first physical act you can do to show your gratefulness and obedience to God. Before you are baptized, you will want to read Scripture passages and annotations on Ordinances, Baptism as Confession (Index, p. 1864).

5. **COMMUNICATING YOUR FAITH to others is just as important as a baby's learning to talk.**

As a baby tries to communicate, he learns and grows. You will grow as you share your new life with others. Who would be the happiest person to know about your new birth?

Write that person's name. ______________________

Who else could you tell that needs to have this same experience?

Write that person's name. ______________________

You can learn to communicate your faith by reading the article, "Guide to Giving Your Personal Testimony" (pp. 1786–1788) and the Scripture passages and annotations on EVANGELISM, Lostness.

Summary: Steps to Growth

1. Feed on God's Word Daily.
2. Breathe a Prayer Regularly.
3. Join Your New Church Family Sunday.
4. Communicate Your Faith Soon.

LIFE IN CHRIST: THE DISCIPLE'S CROSS

Discipleship may be defined as abiding in Christ. To understand more fully your opportunity and responsibility as a disciple of Jesus, you can work through the simple exercise that

MINISTRY OF WORSHIP/INTERCESSION

PRAYER

Ministry of Service

MINISTRY OF EVANGELISM

Witness CHRIST Fellowship

MINISTRY OF NURTURE

WORD

DENY Luke 9:23
CROSS Luke 14:27
FOLLOW Matthew 4:19

MINISTRY OF TEACHING/PREACHING

follows. You can then lead another person through the exercise to increase your understanding and to help them abide more fully in Christ. Use a blank, unlined sheet of paper to do this exercise. Refer to the Disciple's Cross illustration above to check yourself as you do the exercise. Look up each of the Scripture passages in the Bible as you write them down on the exercise sheet.

A disciple of Christ is one who makes Christ the Lord of his or her life. In the upper right hand corner of your paper, write *Deny* Luke 9:23. Notice in this verse Jesus said we are to do three things: deny ourselves, take up our crosses daily, and follow Christ.

The first commitment of a disciple is to deny oneself. That does not mean to reject your identity but to renounce the self-centered life. In the center of your page represent your life by drawing a circle. The empty circle represents clearing out all of self for Christ. You cannot be a disciple of Christ if you are not willing to deny self. Now read Luke 14:26. This verse simply means nothing can be more important to you than Christ. To commit yourself to self-denial, you will need to understand the lordship of Jesus. Read the Scripture passages and annotations on DISCIPLESHIP, Lordship of Christ.

The Circle: Abiding in Christ

If this circle represents your life, Christ should fill the entire circle. Write the word *Christ* in the circle. That means He is to have the priority in everything. The Christian life is simply Christ living in you. Write *John 15:5* under the word *Christ* in the circle. Read or quote from memory John 15:5. What can you do without abiding in Christ? Nothing! Christ said He is the vine, and we are the branches. The branches are part of the vine. You are a part of Christ. He wants to live His life through you. Is this the kind of life you would like to have?

God has provided a way for Christ to be at the center of your life. This requires a second commitment. Jesus said everyone must "take up his cross daily" (Lk 9:23). To "deny" yourself is the negative side of becoming a disciple; to take up your cross is the positive side. Taking up your cross puts Christ in the center of your life. Write *cross* under *deny* in the right-hand corner. Write *Luke 14:27* beside *cross*. Read or quote the verse. Illustrate this point by drawing a large cross around the circle. Draw the outline of the cross so that the circle is in the center of the cross.

Jesus said you are to bear your cross daily (Lk 9:23). What is involved in bearing the cross? You move beyond denying yourself to taking up a redemptive ministry. The cross for Jesus meant giving Himself to redeem the world. You enter into His ministry by taking up your cross. Bearing your cross and serving others requires discipline. The cross is our analogy to illustrate the disciplines Jesus said a disciple should have to abide in Him and serve Him.

The Lower Part of the Vertical Bar: Word

The way to have Christ living in you is to have His Word in you. (Write *word* on the lower part of the vertical bar of the cross.) Write *John 8:31-32* on the lower part of the vertical bar of the cross. The Word is food for you. You cannot grow unless you have a regular intake of the Word. You receive the Word in many ways: by listening to someone preach it, by reading it, by studying it, by memorizing it, by meditating on it, and by applying it. Making Christ Lord means that you want to study and meditate on the Word regularly. "To continue in the Word" also means to obey it. Write *John 15:10* in the circle as you quote the verse. To abide in Christ means to obey Him. Read the introductory summary on HOLY SCRIPTURE (p. 1677).

The Upper Part of the Vertical Bar: Prayer

A part of living in Christ is living in prayer. Write *prayer* on the upper part of the vertical bar of the cross. Write *John 15:7* on the upper part of the vertical bar of the cross as you read the verse. If you abide in Christ and His Word abides in you, you can ask what you will and God will do it.

Notice the vertical bar of the cross points to the relationship between God and humans and the basic ways one communicates with God and He communicates with you. For further help, read the introductory summary to PRAYER (p. 1697).

The Right Part of the Crossbar: Fellowship

Living in Christ means that you will try to live in fellowship with your brothers and sisters in Christ. Write *fellowship* on the right crossbar. Write *John 13:34-35* at the right on the crossbar as you read it. Jesus said that the way to show you are His disciple is to love one another. God has provided the ideal place for you to grow—His church. The church is not a building or an organization, although it uses both of these. A church is a body of baptized believers who have covenanted together to carry out Christ's ministry in the world. A committed Christian will stay in fellowship with a local body of believers. The church is the body of Christ. If you are living in Christ, you realize it is important to live in His body, the church. Read the introductory summary on THE CHURCH (p. 1692).

The Left Crossbar: Witness

Living in Christ includes witnessing to others. Write *witness* on the left crossbar. Witnessing is sharing Christ with others. Write *John 15:8* at the left on the crossbar as you read the verse. Jesus said that the way to show that you are His disciple is to bear much fruit. This always includes witnessing. Witnessing is the natural outgrowth of living in Christ. If you are living daily in the Word, praying in faith, and fellowshipping with God's people, it becomes natural and normal to share with others the Christ who is living in your heart. Write *Matthew 4:19* beside *follow* in the upper right-hand corner under *deny* and *cross*. Read the introductory summary on EVANGELISM (p. 1701).

From Abiding in Christ to Fruit Bearing

If you live in Christ, you eventually will bear fruit. Fruit does not necessarily grow quickly; but it grows continually and bears in season. Fruit bearing is the normal, natural result of a life that has Christ at the center. Our lives in Christ should continue to grow and expand. Fruit bearing includes the fruit of the Spirit: love, joy, peace, patience, kindness, goodness, faithfulness, gentleness, and self-control (Gal 5:22-23). As the fruit of the Spirit grows in your life, you reach out to others through ministry and service of all kinds. Read the introductory summary on the Holy Spirit (p. 1668).

Add pointed arrows to the ends of the crossbars. They symbolize that our fruit bearing should express itself in ministries. Living in the Word leads to a ministry of teaching or preaching. Write *Ministry of Teaching or Preaching* at the bottom of the cross. Read the introductory summaries on EDUCATION (p. 1699) and on PROCLAMATION (p. 1696). Praying in faith will lead to a ministry of worship or intercession. Write *Ministry of Worship or Intercession* above the cross. Fellowshipping with believers leads to a ministry of nurture to members of the church. Write *Ministry of Nurture* to the right of the cross. Witnessing to the world leads to a ministry of evangelism. Write *Ministry of Evangelism* to the left of the cross. Our witness and our fellowship involves Christian service to other people. Write *Ministry of Service*, John 15:13, above the horizontal bar. These five ministry areas comprise the ministry of a disciple and of Christ's church. Read the introductory summary on DISCIPLESHIP (p. 1688).

The goal in discipleship is expressed in 2 Timothy 2:21. You need to grow in all spiritual disciplines and ministries to master life and to be prepared for the Master's use. If you develop all of these disciplines, your life will be balanced and fruitful.

One way to remember this illustration is:

One Lord as the first priority of your life.

Two relationships: The vertical relationship with God and the horizontal relationship with mankind.

Three commitments: Deny self, take up your cross, and follow Christ daily.

Four disciplines: Living in the Word, praying in faith, fellowshipping with believers, and witnessing to the world.

Five ministry areas: A ministry of teaching/preaching, a ministry of nurture, a ministry of worship/intercession, a ministry of evangelism, and a ministry of service.

PERSONAL SPIRITUAL INVENTORY

Discipleship involves growth in spiritual disciplines and in Christian ministries. Disciples need periodically to measure their growth and determine where further growth needs to take place. The following chart will help you evaluate where you feel you are in your Christian life. It is for your private use and not for comparing with anyone else. It is not a test. No one is expected to make a perfect score. Your score reflects how you *feel* about your life of discipleship as much if not more than it reflects what you are doing as a disciple. You should ask God to help you see where you are now and where He wants you to be as a disciple. Before you complete this exercise, refresh your understanding of discipleship by reading the Scripture passages and annotations on DISCIPLESHIP, Nature, and DISCIPLESHIP, Priesthood (Index, p. 1859).

Read each item below. Place an *x* in the column that most nearly represents your evaluation of your discipleship in this area.

	Always	Usually	Sometimes	Seldom	Never
Discipline of Individual Worship •I have a daily quiet time.					
•I try to make Christ Lord of my life.					
•I feel close to the Lord throughout the day.					
•I try to be aware of God's presence.					
•I am aware that the Lord disciplines me.					
Discipline of Bible Study •I read my Bible daily.					
•I study my Bible each week.					
•I memorize a verse of Scripture each week.					
•I take notes at least once a week as I hear, read, or study the Bible to apply it to my life.					
Discipline of Prayer •I keep a prayer list and pray for the persons and concerns on the list.					
•I have experienced a specific answer to prayer during the past month.					
•Each day my prayers include praise, thanksgiving, confession, petition, intercession.					
Discipline of Fellowshiping with Believers •I seek to live in peace with Christians.					
•I seek reconciliation with those who have a problem with me or with whom I have a problem.					
•Others know I am a Christian by the way I love God's people.					
•I live in harmony with my family.					
Discipline of Witnessing •I pray regularly for lost persons by name.					
•I share my testimony with others when there is an appropriate opportunity.					
•I share the plan of salvation with those who are open to hear it.					
•I witness for Christ each week.					
•I follow up and encourage persons I have won to Christ.					
Ministering to Others. •I serve Christ through a job in my church.					
•I give at least a tithe through my church.					
•At least once a month I do kind deeds for persons less fortunate than myself.					
•I keep goals for my life clearly in mind.					
Subtotals	__x 4	__x 3	__x 2	__x 1	__x 0
Total Score ________ *Totals*					

When you have finished checking each item, add each column. Each check in "Always" column is worth 4 points; the "Usually" column, 3 points; the "Sometimes" column, 2 points; the "Seldom" column, 1 point. Add these four totals together to get your overall score out of a possible 100.

Complete the following statements.

1. I feel that my score (does, does not) adequately reflect my life of discipleship because ____

2. Other things that should be taken into account that are not reflected in the inventory above and how I feel about them are ____

3. My personal overall evaluation of my discipleship is ____________

4. I will begin this week to seek to grow in the following area(s) of discipleship: ____________

Disciplines of Discipleship

DISCIPLINE OF WORSHIP

How to Have a Quiet Time

As a disciple, you realize that Christ must be the center of the Christian life. Spending time with Christ will help keep Him at the center of your life. This time is known as "the quiet time" or "personal devotions." Many Christians testify that nothing else has been as important to them as the daily quiet time.

Set aside at least fifteen minutes each morning for a quiet time. The quiet time is an appointment to begin the day with Jesus Christ, the center of your life. Follow the suggestions below to develop a consistent quiet time.

1. Make a personal quiet time the first *priority* of your day. Select a time to spend with God that fits your schedule. The morning hours are usually preferable, but you may want to set aside your quiet time with the Lord at some other time of the day.

2. Make *preparation* the night before. Set the alarm earlier to allow the time you will devote to your quiet time. If it is difficult for you to wake up in the morning, you may plan to exercise, bathe, or dress before beginning your quiet time. Select a place where you can be alone the entire time without interruption. The night before, gather needed materials—Bible, notebook, prayer list, and pen or pencil.

3. Develop a balanced *plan* of Bible reading and prayer. The quiet time helps you practice spiritual disciplines noted on the vertical bar of the disciple's cross (p. 1749). You may begin your quiet time by examining the nature of prayer. Choose one subhead under PRAYER (p. 1866). Read one or more passages under the subhead each day along with the notes on the subject. As other disciplines and ministries become important in your life, choose those subjects for your quiet time study. Studying passages on God, Jesus Christ, and the Holy Spirit are good ways to help you abide in Christ during your quiet time.

The following suggestions are designed to help you abide in Christ by living in the Word and praying in faith. The suggestions should help you participate in the disciplines of discipleship.

a. Prepare to Communicate with the Master.

• Praise God for being your Lord.

• Deny yourself by confessing your sins and surrendering your will, mind, and emotions to the Master.

• Take up your cross by committing yourself to serve the Master today and asking Him to show you how.

• In your notebook, list questions for which you need answers, matters for which you need guidance, weaknesses for which you need strength, and any other life concerns about which you wish to communicate with God.

• Expect God to speak to you about matters on which He places priority and about which He is ready to reveal His will.

b. Listen to God Speak to You as You Read His Word.

• Read the introductory summary on REVELATION (p. 1678).

• Read the Bible systematically. Choose a doctrine or teaching you want to know more about. Look in the doctrinal index. Find a subhead under the doctrine. Each day read a passage(s) listed in the index. Read the notes at the bottom of the page of Scripture text to help you understand and apply the teaching to your life. Realize that the Scripture text is God's inspired Word speaking to you. The notes are human interpretations best used to help you apply God's Word to your life.

• This approach will help balance your study of the Word. Be sure to read different doctrines. Notice the different types of writing in the Bible—devotional material (Psalms), wisdom teaching (Proverbs, Ecclesiastes), historical writing (Joshua), biographical writing (1 Samuel, the Gospels), narrative material (Ruth, Jonah, Acts), doctrinal writing (Romans), personal letters (Philemon), and apocalyptic writing (Daniel, Revelation).

• Listen to God speak in one of the four areas for which the Bible states it is to be used (2 Ti 3:16-17): (a) teaching—teaching the faith; (b) rebuking—correcting error; (c) correcting—resetting the direction of a person's life; (d) training—training a person in right living. As you read the Bible, review these four areas until it becomes automatic to look for teaching you have not learned, rebuking of an error in your life, correction of a direction in your life, and instruction leading to positive righteousness.

• Mark words, phrases, and verses that speak to you. In the margin place an *M* beside verses you want to memorize; a *T* beside verses with significant teachings for your life; a *C* for correction of life's course, an *R* for training in right living, and a *W* beside a verse to use in witnessing. Some days you may want to go back and review verses you have marked in a particular category.

• Summarize what you believe God has said to you today through the Scripture. Review what you have marked. See if any pattern emerges. Has a particular word or verse spoken to you? Write what God has said to you. What specific response do you need to make to be a better disciple?

c. Pray about what God has said to you.

• Add a heading in your notebook "What God said to me." Write your prayer on the basis of what He said.

• If it is a teaching, repeat that teaching to God as you pray. Thank Him for it. Ask Him to help you apply it to your life. Ask what else He has to say to you. Praise Him.

• If it is a rebuke, confess your sin or failure. Repent of it. Thank God for forgiving you. Commit yourself to learn from His rebuke and not repeat your error.

• If it is a correction, tell God you recognize and accept His guidance. Ask His help in changing your behavior or attitude. Thank Him for His new direction.

• If it is training, promise God you will do as instructed with His help. Describe one new action you will take today because of the instruction.

• Write in your notebook what you have said to God. Check each day to see if you have maintained your previous commitment to Him. This will help you check your growth in discipleship.

Use this plan for a few weeks. It will then become second nature to you as you begin talking with God on the same channel. Often Christians talk to God but do not listen to His response. It is as if you were talking on one channel and God on another. This study method creates interactive communication with God so you are both talking about the same things. It also will give you a basis for sharing with others what God has been saying to you. Later, in reviewing your notes, you will see patterns of what God has been communicating to you over a period of time as well as things that you have been concerned about.

Another plan would be to read through a book of the Bible each week or month.

d. Be persistent until you are consistent. Aim for consistency rather than for length of time spent. Consider having a quiet time for a few minutes every day rather than having long devotional time periods every other day. You are laying a foundation for a lifelong habit. Expect interruptions. More than any other one thing, Satan will try to prevent your spending time with God. He fears the weakest Christian on his or her knees. Do not get frustrated at the persons or events that interrupt your quiet time. Have your quiet time when you will not be interrupted, and plan around interruptions to your quiet time rather than becoming frustrated by them.

e. Focus on the Person you are meeting rather than on the habit of the quiet time. If you were meeting your country's leader at that time, you would not let anything stand in your way. What about meeting God? Your fellowship with God is important to Him as well as to you. He created you with a capacity for fellowship with Him; and He saved you to restore that fellowship. Read the introductory summary on GOD (p. 1664).

f. Keep your notebook daily. You may want to use the following form:

Day of the week ________________ Date ________________

Scripture Passage ________________ Doctrinal Subject ________________

What God said to me: ________________

____

a. Teaching ________________

b. Rebuking ________________

c. Correcting ________________

d. Training ________________

What I said to God: ________________

____

a. Petition ________________

b. Commitment ________________

c. Confession of sin ________________

d. New direction ________________

e. Promise to live right ________________

Verse to memorize: ________________

Meditating on the Word

Meditation has been called reflective thinking with a view to application. It involves musing, pondering, and thinking on the Word of God in such a specific way that the message of the Scriptures is connected to a specific need in your life. One of the great promises in the Word of God deals with the relationship between God's blessings and meditation on His Word. Read Joshua 1:8 and Psalm 1:2-3. Silently reflect on the strength and hope you can gain from God's Word. Reflect on your need for courage, strength, and hope.

Develop a notebook to record your meditations. Begin by meditating on one verse or a brief passage every day for a week. In your notebook, write:

Date ________ Verse Reference ________________

Parameter of the verse (its context): ________________

____

Paraphrase of the verse: ________________

____

Pulverizing the verse for detailed meaning ________________

____

Key words for your heart: ________________

____

Questions about key words:

Why? ________________ When? ________________

Where? ________________ Who? ________________

What? ________________ How? ________________

The verse personalized for me ________________

____

The verse prayed back to God ________________

____

Parallel verses (Cross Reference) summarized

Problems in the verse ______________________________
Possibilities of helping others through the verse ______________________________
____
Protracted study notes, ideas, and outlines ______________________________
____

Look under HOLY SCRIPTURE, Inspired, in the Index. Select a verse for meditation. Pray for wisdom to apply the Word of God to your life (Jas 1:5). Remember, obedience is the key to receiving greater revelation from God and His Word. Do the following exercise in your notebook using the preceding format.

1. Determine the context by reading the verses before and after the selected verse. Learn the setting and theme of the passage. Summarize the teaching of the total context.

2. Paraphrase the verse. Rewrite it in your own words.

3. To find detailed meaning in the verse is to use three exciting ways to assimilate and digest its truths. (a) Read the verse aloud several times, each time emphasizing a different word. Write two or three words you find very important. (b) Contrast the verse: write down the opposite meaning so you will understand what the verse is teaching. (c) Ask questions and seek answers about the two or three important words. Use the question words What?, Why?, When?, Where?, Who?, and How? to relate the words to your own needs. If you choose Philippians 4:13, you might ask: What are some things I can do through Christ? Why have I been failing to do these things? How can I begin doing all things through Christ?

4. Personalize the verse by letting the Spirit lead you to see a need, a challenge, an opportunity, or a failure in your life. Let the Spirit make the verse come alive for you as you digest it and assimilate it into your life. Write something you will do in response to this verse. Be specific.

5. Pray the verse back to God, making it personal for your life. For example, you might pray from Philippians 4:13, Lord, you say I can do all things through Christ. I've been having a tremendous problem with my attitude. I find it difficult to forgive and be positive. I thank You that I can be positive because of Your promises and that I can meet every problem today in Your strength. I claim your strength now for all things today.

6. Use the cross reference system in the center column of your Bible to look up parallel passages which deal with the same content or theme. See the doctrinal notes at the bottom of the page related to your passage. Look up this doctrinal theme in the index to find parallel passages. Summarize the teaching of these verses. Let these verses strengthen the impact of the verse in your life.

7. List problems in the verse, that is, thoughts or ideas you do not understand immediately. Discuss these with a Christian friend or church leader. From Philippians 4:13 you might ask, "How is Christ's strength made available to me to do all things?" When you find an answer, pray about it with God and write it in your notebook.

8. The discipline of meditation should lead you to ministry to others. Write the possibilities you see to use the verse in ministering to others—a relative, a friend, a business associate. Ask, "How can the truth of this verse be transmitted to someone else through me?" Write an action you can take this week.

9. Meditative study is done without study helps and tools. It should lead to protracted or further study. Write thoughts, ideas, outlines, applications, or plans which should lead you to further study. Determine which doctrinal emphasis of the verse is important for your discipleship at this time. Plan a time to study that doctrine through the Scriptures with the help of the index. Use methods of study discussed in the section on Discipline of Living in the Word, p. 1769.

Guide to Individual Worship

Your quiet time and meditation times should lead you to worship God. You can worship Him all alone. "How?" you ask. "Don't I have to go to church and let a minister lead in worship?" Scripture teaches the importance of worship in community, as you will see in another article

Bible Reading Record

When you have read a doctrine from a Bible Book, mark a diagonal line through the square. Use a different color when you have read the doctrine a second time.

Old Testament Doctrines

	Doctrines	Genesis	Exodus	Leviticus	Numbers	Deuteronomy	Joshua	Judges	Ruth	1 Samuel	2 Samuel	1 Kings	2 Kings	1 Chronicles	2 Chronicles	Ezra	Nehemiah	Esther	Job	Psalms	Proverbs	Ecclesiastes	Song of Songs	Isaiah	Jeremiah	Lamentations	Ezekiel	Daniel	Hosea	Joel	Amos	Obadiah	Jonah	Micah	Nahum	Habakkuk	Zephaniah	Haggai	Zechariah	Malachi
	God	●	●	●	●	●	●	●	●	●	●	●	●	●	●	●	●	●	●	●	●	●		●	●	●	●	●	●	●	●	●	●	●	●	●	●	●	●	●
The Trinitarian God	Jesus	●	●		●	●								●					●	●	●			●	●		●	●	●				●	●					●	●
	Holy Spirit	●	●		●	●		●		●	●	●	●	●	●		●		●	●				●			●	●		●				●				●	●	
	Creation	●		●		●								●			●		●	●	●	●		●	●		●		●		●		●							●
	Miracle	●	●				●	●		●		●	●				●		●	●				●	●			●		●			●	●						
The World	Evil and Suffering	●	●	●		●	●	●	●	●	●	●	●	●	●	●	●	●	●	●	●	●		●	●	●	●	●	●	●	●		●	●		●		●	●	●
	Humanity	●	●	●	●	●	●	●	●	●	●	●	●	●	●	●	●		●	●	●	●	●	●	●	●	●	●	●	●	●	●	●	●	●	●			●	●
	Sin	●	●	●	●	●	●	●		●	●	●	●	●	●	●	●		●	●	●	●		●	●	●	●	●	●		●		●	●	●	●	●	●	●	●
	Holy Scripture		●	●		●	●				●	●	●	●	●	●	●			●	●	●		●	●	●	●	●	●					●	●	●	●		●	●
Knowledge of God	Revelation	●	●	●	●	●	●	●	●	●	●	●	●	●	●	●	●	●	●	●	●	●		●	●	●	●	●	●	●	●	●	●	●	●	●	●	●	●	●
	History	●	●	●	●	●	●	●	●	●	●	●	●	●	●	●	●	●		●	●	●		●	●		●	●	●	●	●		●	●	●	●	●	●	●	
	Election	●	●	●	●	●	●	●		●	●	●	●	●	●	●	●			●				●	●	●	●	●	●	●	●		●	●			●	●	●	●
	Salvation	●	●	●	●	●	●	●	●	●	●	●		●	●	●	●		●	●	●	●		●	●	●	●	●	●	●	●		●	●	●	●	●	●	●	●
God's Saving Purpose	Discipleship	●	●	●	●	●		●		●	●		●	●							●			●	●					●	●			●				●		
	Christian Ethics	●	●	●	●	●	●	●		●	●	●	●	●	●	●	●		●	●	●	●		●	●	●	●	●	●		●	●		●	●	●	●	●	●	●
	Stewardship	●	●	●	●	●					●		●	●	●	●	●			●	●	●					●				●			●						●
	Last Things	●	●							●	●	●		●	●				●	●	●	●		●			●	●	●	●	●		●				●			●
	The Church	●	●	●	●	●	●	●			●	●	●	●	●	●	●		●	●				●	●	●	●	●	●	●	●			●			●	●	●	●
	Ordinances			●									●																											
	Worship	●	●	●	●	●		●		●	●	●	●	●	●	●	●			●		●		●	●		●		●	●	●			●			●	●	●	●
God's People	Proclamation					●																		●	●				●	●	●		●	●	●	●			●	
	Prayer	●	●	●	●	●	●	●	●	●	●	●	●	●	●	●	●	●	●	●	●	●		●	●	●	●	●	●	●	●		●	●		●			●	●
	Church Leaders				●																																			
	Education	●	●	●		●	●						●		●		●		●	●	●			●	●		●		●					●				●		●
	Family	●	●	●	●	●	●	●	●	●	●	●		●	●	●	●	●	●	●	●		●	●	●		●		●					●						●
God's People and the World	Evangelism	●	●					●	●	●		●	●		●					●				●	●		●	●			●		●	●		●	●		●	●
	Missions	●	●												●					●				●									●							

New Testament Doctrines

	Doctrines	Matthew	Mark	Luke	John	Acts	Romans	1 Corinthians	2 Corinthians	Galatians	Ephesians	Philippians	Colossians	1 Thessalonians	2 Thessalonians	1 Timothy	2 Timothy	Titus	Philemon	Hebrews	James	1 Peter	2 Peter	1 John	2 John	3 John	Jude	Revelation
The Trinitarian God	God	•	•	•	•	•	•	•	•	•	•	•	•	•	•	•	•	•		•	•	•	•	•	•	•	•	•
	Jesus	•	•	•	•	•	•	•	•	•	•	•	•	•	•	•	•	•		•	•	•	•	•	•			•
	Holy Spirit	•	•	•	•	•	•	•	•	•	•	•	•	•	•	•	•	•		•		•	•	•			•	•
The World	Creation	•	•	•	•	•	•	•	•	•		•	•		•	•				•	•	•	•	•	•			•
	Miracle	•	•	•	•	•	•	•	•	•					•					•								•
	Evil and Suffering	•	•	•	•	•	•	•	•	•	•	•	•	•	•	•	•			•	•	•	•	•		•	•	•
	Humanity	•	•	•	•	•	•	•	•	•	•	•	•	•		•	•	•		•	•	•	•	•				•
	Sin	•	•	•	•	•	•	•	•	•	•		•	•		•	•	•		•	•	•	•	•			•	•
Knowledge of God	Holy Scripture	•	•	•	•	•	•	•	•	•		•	•	•	•	•	•			•	•	•	•	•	•		•	•
	Revelation	•	•	•	•	•	•	•	•	•	•	•	•	•			•	•		•	•	•		•	•	•		•
	History	•	•	•	•	•	•	•	•	•	•					•				•			•					•
God's Saving Purpose	Election	•	•	•	•	•	•	•	•	•		•	•			•	•			•	•	•	•	•	•			•
	Salvation	•	•	•	•	•	•	•	•	•	•	•	•	•	•	•	•	•		•	•	•	•	•			•	•
	Discipleship	•	•	•	•	•	•	•	•	•	•	•	•	•	•	•			•	•	•	•	•	•			•	
	Christian Ethics	•	•	•	•	•	•	•	•	•	•	•	•	•		•	•	•	•	•	•	•	•	•	•	•		•
	Stewardship	•	•	•	•	•	•	•	•			•	•		•	•				•				•				
	Last Things	•	•	•	•	•	•	•	•		•	•	•	•	•	•	•	•		•	•	•	•	•	•		•	•
God's People	The Church	•	•	•	•	•	•	•	•	•	•	•	•	•	•	•		•	•	•		•		•		•	•	•
	Ordinances	•	•	•	•	•	•	•		•	•		•				•	•		•				•				
	Worship	•	•	•	•	•	•	•	•		•	•	•			•	•			•		•					•	•
	Proclamation	•	•	•		•	•	•	•	•	•	•	•	•	•	•	•	•		•			•					
	Prayer	•	•	•	•	•	•	•	•	•	•	•	•	•	•	•	•	•	•	•	•	•	•	•	•	•	•	•
	Church Leaders	•	•	•	•	•	•	•	•	•	•	•	•	•	•	•	•	•	•	•	•	•	•	•	•	•		
	Education	•	•	•	•	•	•	•		•	•	•	•		•	•	•	•		•	•	•	•		•			•
	Family	•	•	•	•	•	•	•	•	•	•	•	•			•		•		•		•						
God's People and the World	Evangelism	•	•	•	•	•	•	•	•	•	•		•	•	•	•	•		•		•	•	•	•			•	•
	Missions	•		•	•	•	•			•	•			•														•

(p. 1802), but it also emphasizes the human need for private worship. You will want to read the Scripture and notes on WORSHIP, Individual, and WORSHIP, Reverence.

Since God first created the world and the original humans, people have stood in awe of creation's attributes. Properly this should lead us to worship the Creator. Too often we worship the creation. The mystery of the sun, moon, and stars prompted worship for some. The animal kingdom with its myriads of sizes and shapes has had its worshipers. Finding no intimacy and help from the created order, people became guilty of creating their own gods and falling down before the work of their own hands (Isa 2:8,20; 46:6). This was not a temporary trend. It is a hard fact of sinful human nature (Ro 1:21-25).

As you study God's Word and turn to worship, you need to be aware of the gods you are tempted to substitute for the true God. One may be your own newfound skills and knowledge of the Bible. Worship of the true God in daily individual worship will help you escape the temptation to make substitutes for God.

Our adversary, the devil, does not want us to worship God. His climactic attempt at destroying the life and ministry of Jesus was his effort to get Jesus to turn His worship away from the living God (Mt 4:9). The enemy still does not want us to worship. He knows the significance of worship in the life of the Christian. He will spare no effort to distract, deceive, and distort to keep us from true worship. Expect struggle and resistance as you worship the living God. Here you may want to read Scripture and notes on EVIL AND SUFFERING, Satan.

Jesus visited with a woman who was confused about worship (Jn 4). Because worship is so important to an individual's spiritual growth, Jesus gave her some teachings to clear up her problem. Her confusion was over the place of worship. The Jews taught that Jerusalem was the place. Her people, the Samaritans, taught that Gerizim was the place. Jesus taught her that worship is not limited to a specific place. God is Spirit and is not therefore limited to one location. True worship takes place in our spirits. Therefore, worship can take place anywhere at any time. See the Scripture and notes on GOD, Presence (Index, p. 1845).

The most pure worship we may ever experience in this life takes place when a sinner bows before Christ's greatness to receive the gift of eternal life. This simple but profound experience is a good model for our personal worship experiences. Our needs will vary from time to time. The same urgency and intensity may not be felt. Nevertheless, when we bring our needy lives before His mighty presence, we find acceptance and help. As you come alone to face God in honest worship, five simple points should help you.

1. Definition of worship.—Worship is a dynamic confrontation with the living God. It is dynamic because His power is experienced. It is a confrontation because worship brings us face to face with God. This definition helps us to understand why almost all individual experiences of worship recorded in the Bible indicate that people bowed to the ground or fell to the ground. We must not think that a particular physical position will automatically produce worship, but we may certainly expect that true worship will bring feelings of repentance, reverence, and humility. See the Scripture and notes on WORSHIP, Humility.

2. Encouragement to individual worship.—The Scriptures tell us that we may come boldly before God's throne to receive mercy and help (Heb 4:16). We are commanded to " seek the LORD while he may be found" (Isa 55:6). Worship is a desirable and profitable experience. It is a time of confidence and joy. It is a necessary discipline for Christ's disciples.

3. Hindrances to individual worship.—You will encounter several hindrances as you fellowship with and worship God. See the Scriptures and notes on PRAYER, Hindrances.

a. Distractions. Worship requires total concentration upon the One you worship. Shut out and ignore all distractions. Make worship your only priority.

b. Feelings. Worship is in "spirit" but not necessarily in the emotions. Failure to feel is not necessarily a failure to worship. Many things affect our feeling—the weather, our health, our circumstances. None of these change God's willingness and our need to come together in worship.

c. Ignorance. Worship involves personal relationship with God. We must know the one we worship. Ignorance of His grace, greatness, promises, actions, and other attributes dilutes our worship. Those who know the Lord and His Word best will find it the most natural and easiest to worship. You will want to read the Scripture and notes on GOD, Holiness, and GOD, Trinity.

4. Helps to individual worship.—God has provided all the resources you need to worship. Consider the following.

a. Spirit. The Holy Spirit lives in every true disciple. He acts as a Helper to our prayers, worship, witness, and work. He will make our sins known to us so that we may confess them. He will make us know God's presence. He will strengthen us in our felt weakness. He will comfort our troubled hearts. Read Scripture and notes on HOLY SPIRIT, Presence of God, and HOLY SPIRIT, Intercedes.

b. Truth. Worship must be in spirit and truth (Jn 4:24). Since the Word of God is truth, the Bible is a major aid to worship. It reveals the nature, attributes, and expectations of the One the Christian worships. The promises of God found in Scripture form the basis for approaching Him and adoring Him. Bible truth builds us up spiritually. Reading Bible truths is a part of worship, leading us to commit our lives to the God of truth.

c. Faith. Faith enables us to enjoy God's presence. Faith pleases God. Faith counts on the presence of God, the promise of God, and the power of God to be at work now. Such reality prompts worship.

d. Prayer and Praise. Prayer and praise are the expressions of need, adoration, and gratitude. They are the most natural parts of individual worship. They come naturally as we meditate on the blessings of God. Such meditation may be done in reading the Bible (Ps 119:97-99) or in reflecting on God's activity in your own life. Prayer and praise are not artificial efforts to say the proper words acceptable and pleasing to God. They are honest communications of your life before God in words that are most natural and true to you.

5. Components of individual worship.—As you seek to worship God personally and individually, include the following actions in your worship.

a. Establish a time for worship. Individual worship can occur spontaneously any time you experience God's presence in your life and respond to it. Regular times scheduled for worship provide spiritual discipline for your life and ensure that you take all of life before God, not just the moments of spontaneous joy or rapture. Each day set aside a regular time to have dynamic confrontation with the living God.

b. Read God's Word. Let God's Word speak to you, interact with your life, and provide reason to respond to God. Look for reasons to praise, confess, commit, intercede, and rejoice before God.

c. Sing to God. Music communicates truth in a mode that is easily received. It makes us feel good. It motivates us to worship as well as to express our worship. In individual worship you do not have to be conscious of musical shortcomings. You can freely make your joyful sounds before God.

d. Praise God. The heart of worship is praise. Find truths from Bible passages, from the doctrinal notes in this Bible, and especially from experiences of your own daily life which are reasons to praise God. Express that praise freely to God in your own words. If you do not feel free to praise or cannot find words to praise, read passages from the Psalms or 1 Corinthians 13; Philippians 2; Colossians 1.

e. Remain silent. Experience the presence of God. Concentrate on Him. Let the awareness of Him dominate your consciousness. Do not even let your own voice detract from concentration on His love surrounding your life.

f. Thank God. List specific reasons from your daily experience to thank God. Thanksgiving is response to a specific act of God. Make yourself aware of what He is doing for you. Read the Psalms of thanksgiving and the opening of Paul's letters to generate ideas as you express gratitude to God.

g. Confess your faith and your sins. As your study of Bible teachings with the *Disciple's Study Bible* leads you to deeper understanding of God and of your beliefs, share with God your own convictions. Confess your beliefs as an act of worship and praise. Read the Scripture and notes on HISTORY, Confession. Confess your weaknesses to God and seek His strength. Confess your sins and seek His forgiveness.

h. Commit your day to God. Conclude your worship with an act of personal commitment, promising God to follow His leadership during the day and asking God for a strong sense of His leading presence throughout the day. Put this in action through the day with brief moments of renewed commitment and petition.

DISCIPLINE OF PRAYER

The discipline of prayer is the foundation of all spiritual disciplines. It is a central component in worship, the atmosphere surrounding effective Bible study, and the power behind witnessing. Delving into the depths of prayer life is essential to growth in discipleship. Such growth involves extended content, extended variety, extended time, and extended intimacy in prayer. To expand the content of your prayer life, study the Bible's teachings on prayers. To do this read the summary on PRAYER, the history of the doctrine of prayer, and Scriptures and notes on various aspects of prayer such as PRAYER, Importance of PRAYER, Examples of PRAYER, Will of God PRAYER, In Christ or PRAYER, Growth of God's People.

To have variety in your prayer experiences, you need to learn various types of prayer. Look at the index (p. 1866) to find sample prayers to read expressing confession, worship, praise, inquiry into God's will, thanksgiving, blessing, commitment, lament, petition, curse, intercession, desire for forgiveness, plea for repentance, and request for salvation. Then read the following guides to prayer.

To extend the time of your prayers, study the Scriptures and notes on PRAYER, Persistence, and PRAYER, Ordered (Index, p. 1868). Then read the article below on "Extended Time in Prayer."

To extend the intimacy of your prayers, read the Scriptures and notes on PRAYER, Holy Spirit Helps; PRAYER, Love of God; and PRAYER, In Jesus' Name. Then carefully work through the article below on conversational prayer.

The study should help you understand the nature of and possibilities in prayer. Your prayer life will be extended in all areas as you pray regularly and develop your own list of prayer concerns.

You can find no better model for your personal prayers than the model of the Master (Mt 6:9-13). Here we see prayer as intimate conversation with our Father but also respectful, reverent conversation with the One in heaven. Prayer acknowledges God's holiness, praising Him for it and recognizing the distinction between Him and us. Prayer submits and commits to God's purpose—the establishment of His kingdom and thus the accomplishment of His will on earth. Prayer petitions God for physical needs, expresses personal need for forgiveness, and commits to a life of forgiving. Prayer recognizes the power of temptation and the tempter but confesses faith in and desire for God's power to overcome evil. Each of these elements should be a part of your prayers and should be personalized to meet your individual situation. Take the model prayer (Mt 6:9-13) and personalize it for your situation now:

My Father who has shown me Fatherly love through ______________________________
You have shown my need to be reverent through ______________________________
You have revealed Your holiness to me by ______________________________
I became a member of Your kingdom on ______________________________
and am ministering in ______________________________
to work for the coming of Your kingdom. I need for Your will to be done in __________
and commit myself to doing what You reveal Your will to be.

My basic needs today are ______________________________
I trust you to supply them and will not waste my energy worrying about them. I have forgiven ______________________________
and want to forgive anyone who has wronged me. I ask You to forgive me for __________
Today I face temptations to ______________, ______________, and to ______________. I know Satan's strong power in luring me to do what is wrong. I trust Your much stronger power to lead me away from temptation, and so I commit myself now to follow Your leadership.

Learn to use this model to fit your situation each day. Deepen your prayer life as you deepen your study of biblical prayer.

Guide to Praise

Prayer's basic purpose is to give God glory (Ps 29:1; 34:3; 69:30; 86:12; 96:3; Da 4:37; Ro 15:6). Praise and thanksgiving are two types of prayer which give glory to God. Each has a different focus. Praise adores God for who He is—His person, character, attributes. Thanksgiving expresses gratitude to God for what He has done—His actions in the distant and immediate past. We usually find it easier to give thanks than to praise, but praising God for Himself is a greater act of worship than thanking Him for what He has done. Thanksgiving leads to praise. We should thank God in everything and praise Him continually. Reading Scripture and notes on PRAYER, Praise (Index, p. 1866) can motivate and teach you to pray prayers of praise.

Three questions rise as we try to praise God: Why? How? What?

Why should I praise the Lord?

1. God's character is worthy of praise (Dt 10:21; 2 Sa 22:4; 1 Ch 16:25; Ps 22:3).
2. Praise is our gift or sacrifice to God (Heb 13:15).
3. God saved us to glorify Him (Ps 50:23; Isa 43:21).
4. God commands us to praise Him (1 Ch 16:28-29; Ps 147:1,20; 148:1-14).
5. Praise follows Jesus' example (Jn 12:28; 17:1).
6. Praise prepares us for what we will do in heaven (Rev 5:9-14; 7:9-17).

How should I praise the Lord?

1. Use words expressing honor, greatness, and joy which are most natural to you. Meditate on God's goodness and greatness and share your immediate feelings with Him.
2. Use scriptural prayers you read aloud thoughtfully and with proper emphasis and feeling.
3. Use Psalms, hymns, and spiritual songs to sing or play praises to God.
4. Use instruments such as piano, guitar, drums, trumpets, and harp (Ps 150).
5. Recite the great savings acts of God in the past to remind you of His greatness and to express your praise (Ps 105).
6. List God's attributes and describe His character. You may need to read the summary on GOD or review the list of God's attributes in the index under GOD.

What should I say when I praise the Lord?

1. Read aloud as your own prayers of praise and adoration from Scripture.
   a. To glorify God's person, character, and attributes (Pss 8; 19; 24; 65; 92; 104; 139).
   b. To praise God's goodness (Ex 15: 1-21; 1 Sa 2:1-10; 1 Ch 29:10-19; Pss 9; 30; 108; 138; Lk 1:46-55).
   c. To invite others to praise God (Pss 147—150; Lk 19:37-38; Eph 3:20-21; 1 Ti 1:17; Jude 25; Rev 5:9-14; 7:9-12; 15:3-4; 19:1-7).
2. Use words of praise such as worship, exalt, extol, adore, magnify, glorify, bless, laud, honor. As you read biblical prayers and hear other Christians pray, learn new words of praise for God.
3. Use exclamations which express your deepest feelings. You may be able to use biblical praise exclamations such as Hallelujah!, or Hosanna!, or praise God! You may prefer to use expressions which have deeply personal meanings for you.

Having learned why to praise, how to praise, and what to say, you need to remember three simple truths. The when of praise is continually, the where of praise is everywhere, and the who of praise is everyone who has breath. Praise is not limited to designated times and places. It should become the natural expression of life in God's presence.

Guide to Thanksgiving

Giving thanks to God is the sublime form of prayer that lays the foundation for other forms of prayer. The following principles will give you guidelines to make thanksgiving a part of every prayer. You will want to read Scripture and notes on PRAYER, Thanks.

1. The source of thanksgiving is grace. Several Hebrew and Greek words translated

"thanksgiving" in our English Bible come from the root words for grace. See Scripture and notes on GOD, Grace. Thanks is our reaction when we realize all we have, receive, and are, is a gift of God's grace. Thanks is rejoicing at what God has given when we were undeserving. True gratitude registers surprise that God could be so good to us when we deserve nothing. Prayer thus begins with praise followed by thanksgiving, acknowledging God's grace (Ac 27:35; 28:15; Ro 6:17; 1 Co 1:4; Col 1:12; Rev 11:17).

2. The condition of thanksgiving is agreement. Thanksgiving means you agree with God. You accept and appreciate what He has chosen to give you or let come into your life. Thus the Bible encourages us to give thanks in all circumstances (1 Th 5:18) and to pray about the things that concern us most by making our petitions with thanksgiving (Php 4:6). In your prayer, agree with God that anything that has come into your life, He has allowed. Express your faith in God by agreeing that He works for our good in all things (Ro 8:28).

3. The response of thanksgiving is worship. Thanksgiving responds to specific actions of God. Praise and thanks are thus natural partners in worship (Ps 100:4; Heb 13:15). An offering to God is a part of thanksgiving worship (Ps 50:14; 107:22). In Old Testament worship petition for help in time of trouble often included a vow or promise to offer praise and thank offerings (Ps 7:17; 28:7; 35:28; 43:4; 51:18-19; 54:6). Concrete actions represent one way of expressing thanks to God, carrying our prayer life over into our daily walk. Then our prayers and our lives worship our Creator. When you thank God, you enter His presence, worship Him, and offer an offering to Him. This pleases Him.

4. The occasion for thanksgiving is everything. Read the following Scriptures and list in your notebook reasons for thanking God (Ge 12:1-6; Ps 21:1-13; 75:1; Jn 6:11; Ro 6:17; 14:6-7; 2 Co 9:11; Eph 5:20; 1 Th 5:18; 2 Th 1:3; 1 Ti 2:1; 4:3-4).

Nothing should escape our thanksgiving. God is active in every area of our lives. He can show us His direction even in the darkest hour. Paul, who suffered so for Christ, most often urged us to thank God for everything. Thanking God frees Him to work in our lives through those very circumstances. The easiest way to pray is to find something in every condition for which to thank God.

5. The reward of thanksgiving is the enjoyment of God's blessings. Through thanksgiving we find peace, joy, growth, worship, and the blessing of life in Christ. Giving thanks generates more reasons for giving thanks. If you have trouble giving thanks under any circumstances, ask the Spirit to fill you (Eph 5:18-20).

Guide to Confession

Do your prayers seem to go unanswered? God desires close communication with His children. We can damage our communication with God by creating barriers between ourselves and God. When you feel a barrier separating you from God, use this guide to help you discover and confess any sin that may be blocking your fellowship with Him. God wants you to walk in the light and have fellowship with Him and other Christians (1 Jn 1:5-10). As you seek renewed, deepened fellowship with God, read Scripture and notes on PRAYER, Confession.

1. Ask the Holy Spirit to convict you of sin (Jn 16:8-11). Conviction is the work of God, not of human self-criticism. Let God search your heart, thoughts, and ways (Ps 139). Do not get in the habit of condemning yourself. Let God's Word applied by the Spirit reveal how God views your heart (Ro 8:26-27; Heb 4:12-13). Read your Bible daily. As you feel the need, read the Ten Commandments (Ex 20:1-17), the Sermon on the Mount (Mt 5—7), and other special passages (Ro 3; 12; Eph 4:17-32; Col 4). Read Scripture and notes on HOLY SPIRIT, Convicts.

2. Agree with God about the seriousness of your sin. Do not try to excuse your behavior. Accept what God convicts you of (1 Jn 1:8-10). Walk in the light of His holiness. Do not compare yourself to someone else to see if or what you need to confess. Compare yourself to the holy God. Confess where you do not live up to His standard. Be honest with God and with yourself. God cannot be deceived, and you gain nothing by fooling yourself. Take your sins and His offer of forgiveness seriously. Confess. Read Scriptures and notes on SIN, Against God.

3. Acknowledge Christ as your only way to forgiveness and as your only advocate before God (1 Jn 2:1-2). Express your sorrow and repentance to God (Ps 51). Ask for forgiveness based on the blood of Christ which purifies us from all sin (1 Jn 1:7). Do not base your request on righteous acts you have done in the past or plan to do in the future (Tit 3:5). Trust only God's mercy. Turn your sins over honestly to Jesus. He will represent you and gain forgiveness for you before the Father (Heb 4:14,16; 7:25; 10:19-22). Do not worry about your sins again. God has forgiven you. Those sins are past history. Read Scripture and notes on JESUS CHRIST, Atonement.

4. Confess your sins to God openly. Seek forgiveness for specific sins, not for sin in general, as a way of your dealing seriously with your behavior and with your relationship with Him. It will help you identify, acknowledge, and correct specific sins in your life. Confess only your sin, not the sin of someone else. Do not blame anyone for your sin. Accept responsibility for what you have done. Let other people deal with their own sins. Read Scripture and notes on SALVATION, Confession.

5. Walk in the light with other Christians. Be honest with other Christians about your sins. Do not claim to be something you are not. Confess your sins to other understanding Christians, and pray for one another (Jas 5:16). This is part of the priesthood of believers. You will want to read Scripture and notes on DISCIPLESHIP, Priesthood. The forgiving attitude of trusted Christians may help you realize that God has forgiven you. Confession may be expressed during prayer together. Confess only to and with those who can help bear your burden before God in the spirit of humility (Gal 6:1). They should be people who will keep your confidence and help you overcome temptation. If your sin is known or affects the church, ask them to forgive you as God has. Do this in a context of prayer. If your sin is against an individual, ask the offended person's forgiveness (Mt 5:23-24). If you cannot accept God's forgiveness and forgive yourself, make an appointment with your pastor or with a trained Christian counselor. This person can help you deal with your guilt feelings.

6. Renounce your sin and make restitution if you feel it is necessary and possible (Lk 19:8). Restitution is not a good work which earns favor with God. It cannot pay for or guarantee forgiveness. Restitution cannot ease your guilt feelings—Christ does that. Restitution restores what you have taken from another person. It may become a witness to that person. It shows you take seriously the consequences of your sin. Read Scripture and notes on SALVATION, Repentance.

7. Walk in the light with Christ. Do not let sin become the controlling guide of your life. Let Christ be your Master. When you do sin again, confess it immediately and accept God's forgiveness. If you continually repeat the same sin, do not give up. Satan will try to convince you that God will not forgive you for sins you repeat. Jesus died for all our sins. Genuine repentance and turning from sin are necessary for you to receive forgiveness. If in genuine repentance you seek forgiveness, God will forgive you again. Surely He will do as much as Jesus asked Peter to do (Lk 17:4). Do not let sin become a game with God, however. Do not sin because you know you can be forgiven. God will not play games. If you willfully sin, you treat lightly Christ's sacrifice for you. If you continually commit the same sin without being freed from it, counsel with your pastor or with a trained Christian counselor. Christ can and wants to overcome any sin. Be assured sin in the life of the Christian does not change our relationship as a child of God. It does create a barrier to fellowship with God. Read Scripture and notes on SALVATION, Obedience.

The guide to confession may be briefly summarized. Forgiveness is the free gift of God. You cannot earn it. Confession and repentance are the God-ordained way to forgiveness. He will free us from the penalty, the presence, and the power of sin. We will never reach perfection in this world but through Jesus Christ we can walk continually in the light with our Holy God.

Guide to Petition

Petition is a form of prayer in which you make requests of God. In petition you seek to know God's will in a particular decision or situation. Then you seek to pray and live in ways that are consistent with His will in the matters about which you are praying. Life's greatest joys come as we make decisions and live in situations according to God's will. To do this you must know what God's will is in your life. You can know only by asking. Read Scripture and notes on PRAYER, Will of God and GOD, Goodness.

How do you find God's will? You study His Word, rely on His Spirit, and pray in faith. The prayer of petition involves letting God communicate truth to you and communicating your faith and situation to Him. As you read the following, follow the instructions to develop a form in your notebook for praying in faith. Read Scripture and notes on PRAYER, Petition.

1. God communicates truth to you. Accept the fact that God can and will work in every situation for your good and for His glory (Ro 8:28). Write, *What is the problem?* Ask God to help you define your problem. Write down the definition. Acknowledge that God has allowed this need to come into your life. Ask God to show you how He can work through your problem for His glory. Write, *God could use my problem as:*

☐ A platform to demonstrate His power.
☐ A source of blessing for which I have not asked.
☐ An opportunity to develop my faith, love, patience, or other character trait.
☐ An opportunity for me to develop a more effective prayer life.
☐ An opportunity to minister to other people.
☐ Other ____
____

Mark the way or ways you think God is working out His will in your problem.

Now write the problem in the form of a question for God to answer. A focused question will make it easier for you to discover an answer in Scripture. Be sure your question asks what His will is instead of telling Him what you want.

Write, *I am committed to God's will in this situation.* ______*Yes* ______*No.* If you must mark No, write the priority or desire which for the moment has become more important than God's will. Return to the guide for confession and confess this to God, asking forgiveness and new direction.

Remember, the all-powerful God loves you and knows all about your circumstances. He could have stopped them or changed them. For some good reason He did not prevent them from happening. He may not have caused the events to happen, but He has not yet intervened. Read Scripture and notes on EVIL AND SUFFERING, Redemptive. Ask the Spirit to fill you and lead you to know and do God's will. List the different possible solutions you now see to the problem. After each, list the pros and cons of each alternative.

Turn to God's Word first for your solution. Begin by reading Ps 27:13-14. Look in the index and find the Scriptures which relate to your problem. Read these systematically. Quote Scriptures you have memorized which relate to your problem. Be careful not to manipulate Scripture to make it say what you want to hear. Allow the Holy Spirit to illuminate a Scripture and apply it to your problem. If you need assurance, read Scripture and notes on HOLY SPIRIT, Teaches, Guides, Intercedes. Read especially Jn 16:13-15. The Spirit's leadership is essential if we are to learn God's answer to our questions through His Word. Continue reading and studying until the Spirit impresses you with a Scripture relating to your problem. Do not expect or demand an immediate answer. Read and pray until the answer comes. Write the Scripture reference with your answer.

Test your interpretation and application of the Scripture by the following questions? Write these in your notebook.

____Is the interpretation consistent with and not contrary to the rest of the Bible?
____Is it consistent with God's character?
____Is it consistent with the immediate context of the passage?
____Does it violate the original meaning of the passage?
____Does the Spirit continue to bear witness as to the interpretation's validity as I continue to pray about it?

As you consider each question, pray for the Spirit's help and write your answer.

2. You communicate your faith to God in three ways:

a. Asking according to His revealed will.

b. Accepting the Word by faith.

c. Acting on the basis of God's Word to you.

First, ask God to answer your petition. Write, *My specific request of God is* ______ Write the request in concrete terms so you can know when God has answered.

Next, accept God's Word in faith (1 Jn 5:14-15). Read Scripture and notes on PRAYER, Faith. Memorize at least one verse of the passage from which you have received an answer. Write, *I believe God will* ______ *for me in this situation.* Trust what God has told you in His Word rather than relying on your feelings or hopes. Write, *I trust God to fulfill His promise and act in this situation for me* ______ *Yes* ______ *No.* If you must answer No at this moment, read Scripture and notes on GOD, Faithfulness. Read again the answer He has given you in Scripture for this problem. Ask the Spirit to pray for you. Continue struggling with God in prayer until you can honestly mark Yes.

3. Act on the basis of God's Word to you. Read Ps 119:57-64. Remember Jesus often instructed persons to do something as evidence of their faith before He answered their requests (Mt 8:8-13; Lk 17:11-14). Read Scripture and notes on SALVATION, Obedience. Write, *Based on the Word of God, I will take the following actions:* ______

Write, *On* ______ *(date), I completed the actions I promised God I would take.*

God delights in answering the prayers of His faithful servants. He often responds to our faithful acts with actions of His own in our lives. When you become aware of God's acts in your life, write, *On* ______ *(date) God answered my prayer of faith by* ______.

Praise and thank God for His action.

What if you do not find a Scripture that gives you direct guidance on a problem or need? Continue to read your Bible and pray until an answer comes (Mt 7:7-11). What if you have to make a decision before you get an answer? Be sure the decision must be made immediately before rushing to rely on your own reason (Pr 3:5-6). If circumstances should force you to make a decision before you get a specific word from God, submit yourself to the will of God and make the decision in light of the total biblical revelation and of the Spirit's leading.

In summary, make your petitions to God and remain open to His leading. If the answer is obvious, write it down and give Him praise and glory. If the answer is long in coming, be faithful in believing prayer. If the answer is not given, go through the petition process again for further guidance. When events prove God has answered the prayer differently from your requests, accept His way and try to discover what He wants to teach you from the experience. Keep a record of God's answers to your prayers. Watch your faith grow.

Do not use these guidelines mechanically. Use them to help you sort out yours and God's responsibilities in believing prayer based on His Word. His Word is more authoritative than any other source of guidance. His Spirit is more sensitive to the Father's will than any person's. Use God's Word and depend on His Spirit to test all other factors that enter into finding God's will in your situation. Be prepared for God to reveal something that you do not request (2 Co 12:7-10).

Should you go through these steps in finding God's will in every decision you make? No! The average person makes over four hundred decisions a day. Use this exercise in the major decisions and problems you face. Get in the habit of living in the Word, abiding in Christ, and praying in faith every day. This will help you make decisions automatically through the direct leading of the Spirit as He brings Scripture verses and biblical principles to mind. As He shapes your life and mind to be like Christ, you can learn to walk in the Spirit. On important issues and problems, you will want to use this process as you seek God's will.

Guide to Extended Prayer

Most persons greatly used of God spend extended times in prayer. Abraham prayed long and often on his journeys. Moses spent long days on the mountain with God in prayer (Ex 24:18). David wrote and prayed many of the Psalms, some of which are quite lengthy. The disciples prayed constantly between the ascension and Pentecost (Ac 1:14). The Bible and church history offer hundreds of examples of extended prayer.

You can join these prayer warriors. Spend an extended time of several hours in prayer at least once a week, or spend a half day in prayer once each month. In times of specific need or at least once a year, you may want to extend your prayer time to one or more days. Use these extended times to evaluate where you are in fulfilling God's purpose for your life and to determine your future goals. To help you understand the need for the practice of extended prayer, read the Scripture and notes on PRAYER, Persistence.

Jesus is our perfect Model in extended prayer. He often sought solitary places to spend extended times with the Father. Jesus bathed His life and ministry in prayer. Jesus taught us that we are not heard because we utter many words (Mt 6:7). An extended time with God is not necessarily better simply because it is extended. Length of prayer gives us no reason to boast. God calls us to pray in secret (Mt 6:6). Great things happen through prayer. Jesus spent much time in extended prayer. We should follow His example. Jesus prayed for extended periods of time:

1. When He was busy. He got up early in the morning to pray (Mk 1:35). He did not let crowds keep Him from praying, though they stayed until late at night and returned early the next day. He put prayer first and found time for extended prayer.

2. When He was tired. Once after a full day of ministry, Jesus asked His disciples to go to the other side of the sea. Then He sent the people away and went up on a mountain to pray (Mt 14:23). He stayed there most of the night. At a time when He was probably tired, Jesus prayed.

3. When He had a decision to make. Before He chose the twelve apostles, Jesus spent the entire night in prayer (Lk 6:12). Before making important decisions, Jesus spent time with the Father.

4. When He prepared to launch His ministry. After His baptism, Jesus followed the Spirit's leading into the wilderness to spend forty days and nights fasting so He could communicate with the Father (Lk 4:1-2). When facing ministry decisions, Jesus spent time in prayer. Such prayer prepared Him for Satan's temptations as well as for His decison-making.

5. When He faced the cross. In Gethsemane Jesus prayed three hours before He went to His trial and crucifixion (Mt 26:39-44). He had already prayed a long intercessory prayer for His disciples (Jn 17). The extended time of prayer prepared Him for the cross, revealed the Father's will, and gave fellowship with the Father.

Occasions for Extended Prayer

Like Jesus, Christians benefit from spending time with the Father. Consider these situations as appropriate ones for extended prayer.

1. You want to glorify God and express your love to Him. Follow the Guide to Praise (p. 1762). Extended praise extends your sense of God's powerful presence with you.

2. You need fellowship with God. The more time you spend with God, the more you want to have uninterrupted times of fellowship with Him.

3. You need guidance. Extended prayer enables you to see things from God's perspective. Prayer clears your mind of selfish interests and lets you receive His Word and direction.

4. You need strength. Times of trial and temptation call God's people to pray. When you are weak, He is strong (2 Co 12:9).

5. You face a critical or new phase of ministry. God wants you in ministry. Read "Ministries in Discipleship" (pp. 1794–1840). He may lead you into a new ministry or a change of direction in ministry. Extended prayer is the proper response.

6. You need spiritual awakening. Personal, church, national, and international revival waits on the prayers of God's people. Claim His promise (2 Ch 7:14).

7. Others need your prayers. You are a priest because you are a believer. Read Scripture and notes on DISCIPLESHIP, Priesthood. Extended prayer interceding for other people is part of your priestly role.

8. The Lord's will does not seem to be happening on earth. Pray that His kingdom will come (Mt 6:10).

9. Laborers are needed in the harvest. Jesus commanded us to pray that God would send out workers (Lk 10:23). The harvest fields wait on Christians to pray.

Practical Suggestions for Extended Prayer

Extended prayer time may be unexplored territory for you. Questions naturally arise. Others have asked and found answers to the same questions. The following practical suggestions in answer to common questions should help you as you enter the exciting field of extended prayer.

1. Why pray for extended periods?
   a. To have uninterrupted fellowship with God;
   b. to evaluate what God has been doing in your life;
   c. to hear what God is saying to you;
   d. to solidify Christ's lordship over all aspects of your life;
   e. to receive guidance for future plans or ministries;
   f. to concentrate with God on a major concern or problem you face;
   g. to intercede for others.
2. What tools can I use during extended prayer?
   a. The Disciple's Study Bible;
   b. prayer lists;
   c. devotional guides;
   d. notepaper with pen or pencil;
   e. Scripture memory cards;
   f. hymnal;
   g. book of meditations and prayers.
3. How can I pray for an extended period?
   a. Use biblical prayers as your own, particularly Psalms.
   b. Listen to God and His Word as much as you talk to Him.
   c. Use prayer tools listed above to listen and talk to God.
   d. Use all the guides to prayer provided in this Study Bible.
   e. Speak honestly and earnestly with God about your concerns, hopes, and goals.
   f. Develop a prayer list of concerns for friends, church members, your community, nation, and world problems.
   g. Meditate on what God has said and is saying to you to determine His will and develop strategies in facing your situation.
   h. Confess your sins and seek God's presence until you are assured of forgiveness.
   i. Review what you have learned from sermons, Bible study groups, and personal Bible study, and commit yourself to incorporate what you have learned into your life.
   j. Advance beyond introspective, self-centered prayer to pray for other people and for larger issues.
4. What schedule should I follow?
   a. Remain flexible, letting God's Spirit direct your time.
   b. Begin with the following sequence of prayer:

• Commitment of prayer time to God	• Bible reading or quotation from memory
• Praise	• Silent listening to God
• Thanksgiving	• Writing of God's answers
• Confession	• Commitment to God's directions
• Petition	• Thanksgiving for God's presence.
• Intercession	

c. A *brief* nap will often refresh you during a long prayer time and give God time to speak through your subconscious.

d. If the time is a community prayer period, spend some time in community prayer.

e. Remain open to impressions from God's Spirit.

5. What can I do when I keep thinking of other things?

a. Pray about the things which come to mind; they may be your true current concerns placed in your mind by God.

b. Write a "to do" list of things you will accomplish later so you won't keep thinking about them during prayer time.

c. List things that continue to come to mind; ask God why.

6. How can I stay alert and awake?

a. Prepare with adequate sleep and physical conditioning.

b. Pray aloud.

c. Vary your physical position and your prayer activities, changing to a new element of your prayer schedule.

d. Walk, stand, kneel, sit, jog as you pray.

e. Pray with your eyes open.

7. How can I make my prayer time meaningful?

a. Keep a written log of your prayer experiences, making entries each ten or fifteen minutes to see where God has been leading you.

b. Study notes of previous extended prayer times to determine continuing prayer needs and to balance your prayer activities among various kinds of prayers and God-centered, self-centered, and other-centered prayers.

c. Concentrate on fellowship with God and getting to know Him better.

d. Express your deepest feelings, showing and deepening your trust in God.

e. Build on and deepen your personal relationship with your Heavenly Father.

Extended prayer leads to extended growth as a Christian. You can experience its joys and peace when you commit yourself to it and practice it. Look upon your extended prayer times as preparation for the activities of heaven.

DISCIPLINE OF LIVING IN THE WORD

Guide to Interpreting the Bible

Reading involves trying to understand the original meaning of the writer. This principle applies to any document you may read from the daily newspaper to the Bible. Certain guidelines can assist you as you sincerely study God's Word. These guides or principles of interpretation help you to be objective, fair, open, and teachable. Then let the Bible say and mean what God seeks to say and mean in your life, not what you might want the Bible to say to fit any preconceived ideas. As you enter the discipline of Bible study, you will want to understand what the Bible says about itself. Read Scripture and notes on HOLY SCRIPTURE, Word, and HOLY SCRIPTURE, Inspired.

The Principle of Preparation

A person should do at least three things to prepare to study the Bible.

1. Make spiritual preparation. Pray for God's leadership in your study and for personal receptivity and humility. Confess sins and review your spiritual condition to see if hidden or known sins might prevent you from hearing and obeying God's truth. Look for your own prejudices and opinions which you will be tempted to find as Bible study conclusions. Ask God to give you wisdom to avoid canonizing your own interpretation and thus making it equal to the Bible. This means you need to pray for the freedom to grant others the right to interpret and to arrive at different understandings from your own. Remember your sinful limitations and ask the Spirit to lead you to His teachings.

2. Make physical preparation. Select a quiet, well-lighted area, preferably with a table or desk. Set a regular time for study, allowing only true emergencies to interfere. Gather resources you need—*Disciple's Study Bible*, other translations, a Bible dictionary, a complete or exhaustive concordance, commentary(ies), etc. Have a notebook to record your results systematically. Being rested and alert helps both the brain and the spirit.

3. Make mental preparation. Understand that all English translations are attempts to express the meaning of God's Word, which was written originally in Hebrew, Aramaic, and Greek. English words may express in slightly different terminology what the translators understand the underlying passages to mean. Thus translation involves interpretation. A comparison of several English translations may be helpful, especially in understanding difficult passages. A Bible dictionary informs you about people and places that are not well-known and helps you define key words. The index of this study Bible indicates where the Bible gives teachings on various doctrines. The notes it references will help you understand those teachings. A concordance will show you verses using the same word as appears in the verse you are studying. An exhaustive concordance can help you see if the same word appears in all verses in the original language, or if the original used different words with slightly different meanings. A trusted and loved pastor or teacher can help you find a commentary which will help you understand the context and meaning of a passage. Mental preparation means committing yourself to the use of good, valid intellectual guidelines so you will be honest in your interpretation of the Bible. The following guidelines help you know and use these valid principles.

The Linguistic Principle

The linguistic or grammatical principle calls on you to pay close attention to the words and kind of literature used by the author. Analyze the subject, verb, and object. Notice their relationship to one another and the tense of the verb, which shows whether the author is speaking about the past, present, or future. Compare several translations to see if differences of opinion are possible about these relationships.

Look for literary devices such as similes, metaphors, hyperbole, parables, apocalyptic language, allegories, etc. These will indicate the kind of literature you are reading. Are you reading poetry, history, law, theological teaching, or apocalyptic assurances? Realize that different kinds of literature are written in different ways and for different reasons. A poet may soar in feeling and imagination in a way a historian would not. Failure to recognize a simile or metaphor may lead to literal interpretation which causes you to misunderstand the passage.

The Historical Principle

The historical principle calls on you to seek to know when the author lived and to understand something about the culture in which the writer and original readers lived. Moses lived under Egyptian dominance, while Amos spoke in the midst of an Assyrian crisis. Paul wrote under Roman power and often from Roman prisons. To ignore the historical circumstances is to remain ignorant of the questions and issues the writers faced. Study carefully the historical application, meaning, and teaching to the original hearers or readers *before* trying to make an application to our own day. If not, you will fall in the trap of "spiritualizing" or allegorizing.

The Contextual Principle

The contextual principle calls on us to determine the teaching of the larger context of a passage before identifying the meaning of a verse or word. Taking a single verse of Scripture out of its context and ignoring the subject being discussed in the larger passage is a dangerous practice. The contextual principle has five dimensions or realms which must be considered.

1. The immediate context contains the verses occurring before and after the verse you are studying. The lessons you draw from the verse must be consistent with the teachings of this immediate context.

2. The book context means the interpretation must conform to the teaching of the entire biblical book in which a verse is located. As you interpret a letter of Paul, you need to ask

how the particular verse fits in the thought structure and theological teaching of the entire letter. Your interpretation must make sense within the argument advanced in the entire book.

3. The author's context means you must interpret the verse in light of all other Scripture passages on the same subject by the same author. For example, when you interpret what Paul had to say about women, their role or place, you should read all Paul had to say in all his writings about women and not simply base your interpretation on one single verse, ignoring everything else Paul said.

4. The Testament context means you should ask how the particular passage or verse fits in with other passages by other authors within the Testament you are reading—Old or New. Understand the verse in light of the inspired revelation in the era in which the verse was written.

5. The biblical context is the final and ultimate one. It calls on us to read the entire Bible, isolate its total teaching on a subject, and compare our interpretation of a verse to the larger biblical teaching. Here the index of this Study Bible and its theological notes can be particularly helpful. Follow a subject all the way through the Bible before deciding on the meaning of one difficult verse. The Bible seldom reveals its total truth about a subject in one single reference. It usually gives us the great, rich truths of God in many passages from different historical circumstances and different writers' perspectives. The contextual principle helps us arrive at a holistic understanding of biblical teachings and protects us from isolated proof text reading which is prone to mirror our own viewpoints and prejudices.

The Practical Principle

The practical principle asks us to leave the world of intellectual and theoretical teaching to apply biblical teaching to our own lives. Are you willing to ask what you should do or believe or become as a result of understanding the meaning of the passage you study? The Bible's inspired purpose is not simply to inform the curious mind. God gave us the Bible to produce faith, commitment, and action.

The Literal Principle

The literal principle prohibits us from looking for a deeper meaning before we take the words exactly as they appear on the surface. The obvious, apparent meaning of Scripture is the intended meaning. For example, the number seven can be the actual number, or it can stand as a symbol for "fullness" or "completeness" as it does in Mt 18:22, where Jesus told Peter to forgive his brother seventy-seven times. The contextual principle can help us decide whether the literal principle should be applied in a specific passage. As a rule of thumb, apply the literal principle unless you have good reason from the context to believe the meaning is figurative.

The Figurative Principle

The figurative principle is the other side of the literal principle and calls on us to believe from the application of the linguistic principle, the historical principle, the contextual principle, and the literal principle that an inspired author intended a deeper or a symbolic meaning rather than a literal one in using a particular word, phrase, or verse. Jesus often used metaphors to describe Himself and His audience. He called people "salt" and "light" and called them to take up "crosses." He did not limit His teaching to the literal words, but meant for us to understand their symbolic value and apply the teachings to all areas of our own lives.

The Allegorical Principle

The allegorical principle extends the figurative principle to every detail of a text by saying that each detail has a figurative meaning. Jesus' parables most often teach one central truth rather than each detail having a deeper symbolic meaning. The Parable of the Sower (Mt 13:1-23) includes Jesus' own allegorical application of the parable, however. Jesus interpreted the different kinds of soil as standing for different kinds of people.

The question naturally arises, how do we know if an author intended a figurative or allegorical interpretation? The other principles help us answer the question. Does the context of the previous verses clue us that the author was using language in a figurative or allegorical way? Does the historical context, the form of literature, or the grammatical structure point away from literal teaching to symbolic language? We need clues from the Bible itself. The rule of thumb is to take the meaning to be literal unless we have reason to believe the author intended a figurative or allegorical meaning.

Conclusion

Thoughtful Bible students may want to secure a book or two on how to study the Bible. You will certainly want to study the following articles in this section of *The Disciple's Study Bible*. Ask a trusted pastor to recommend a good guide on how to study the Bible. As you use a guide and begin to develop your own habits and method of Bible study, consider the following suggestions for sincere Bible students:

1. Do not work out a system so detailed and complex that you will not or cannot use it on a continuing basis.
2. Do not be such a perfectionist that you become impatient with yourself or with others. Bible study takes a lifetime.
3. Plan to read the Bible completely through each year without stopping to study each passage in great detail. Few things will help you more in interpreting the Bible than reading the whole Bible and understanding the verses in light of your reading of the whole.
4. Do not absolutize or canonize your interpretation so as to judge or condemn all others who may differ with you. Continue to be open, teachable, humble, and willing to grow.
5. Seek to apply what you learn to your daily living.
6. Pray to be Christlike in spirit and in love.

Guide to Studying a Theme or Doctrine

A Bible doctrine refers to a specific, essential truth built into the framework of your faith. Doctrine or theme refers to a subject woven throughout the fabric of Scripture. You cannot understand God's teachings on a subject by reading only one or two passages. Read the section on "The Contextual Principle" (p. 1770). The basic intention of *The Disciple's Study Bible* is to help you study biblical doctrine in the entire biblical context. The following words should help you understand what a doctrine is and how to determine your beliefs about a biblical doctrine.

A theme study will generally encompass a broad spectrum of Scripture. For instance, the theme, "God's Love" may be traced from Genesis to Revelation. See GOD, Love. The purpose of a theme study is to hold up the subject like a diamond and turn it so that all of its different facets may be seen. In studying a Bible doctrine, your goal is to uncover all the Scripture has to say on a particular subject. From this study you will draw certain conclusions. Your conclusions should be supported by the weight of the Scripture, consistent with all of the Scripture, and stated within the parameter of the Scripture. For this reason, the study of a theme or doctrine requires dedication to the task. You will want to follow three basic steps.

1. Collect your information.

a. Look up every passage relative to the doctrine. *The Disciple's Study Bible* is intended to help you accomplish this formidable task. Use its index to locate all passages on the theme you are studying. Read the annotations on those passages to see how they relate to the theme. Look for "See" references in the annotations to locate related passages. Look at center-column references related to the passage to locate still other related verses and translation information. Try to be as comprehensive as possible. Do not omit parallel passages relating the same event from a different perspective in a different literary context.

b. Trace the doctrine from Genesis through Revelation in order. Do you see a progression or development in understanding and teaching? Does the theme function different ways in different types of literature? Does historical context provide perspective from which to understand the particular emphasis of a passage? Read The Historical Principle (p. 1770). Do you gain a more complex, richer, deeper understanding by reading all passages in their context rather than depending on only a few references?

2. Analyze your information.

Divide your information into the following categories:

a. the place of the subject in the Old Testament
b. the emphasis Jesus placed on the subject
c. the understanding of the subject by Paul
d. the perspective given by other New Testament writers
e. the place of the doctrine in the Bible's description of past events of history, its teaching of ongoing Christian living, and its relation to eternity and eternal life.

Ask the following questions:

a. Is the theme isolated to one historical period?
b. Is the theme isolated to one form of literature?
c. Is the theme isolated to one biblical writer?
d. Is the theme a major theme with sub-themes comprising it, or is it a sub-theme of a larger doctrine? The index in this study Bible will help you determine this information.
e. What passages give the clearest statements on the doctrine, and which need further study to understand them? The notes on the passages in this study Bible will help you answer this question.

3. Reach your conclusion. Doctrinal conclusions must be based on Scripture rather than being drawn from human experiences or judgments. For example, God's Word clearly teaches salvation by grace through faith. Human reason challenges such an idea, insisting on works as a prerequisite rather than a result and response of faith. The believer must side with God's Word. Conclusions should reflect clear Bible teaching rather than resting on tentative interpretations of vague or obscure passages. Conclusions should remain open to be informed by further study.

You will want to outline the results of your study. The summary statements of the major doctrines involved (pp. 1664-1702) will help you as you summarize and outline your conclusions. Be sure the conclusions result from your study of the Scripture passages themselves. Only Scripture is inspired and authoritative. Study notes, subheads, sermons, and commentaries may show you other people's understanding. They should not determine your conclusions. God's Spirit speaking through Scripture should lead you to your doctrinal beliefs. You will want to include in your results outline:

a. definition of important terms
b. important Scripture references
c. relation to other themes and sub-themes
d. a one- or two-sentence summary of the doctrine
e. optional interpretations of the doctrine
f. practical application of the subject to your life.

Guide to Studying a Book of the Bible

A book is the basic unit of Bible study. Individual verses and passages can be understood only in the context of the entire book. Study of a Bible book involves:

1. Determining the goal of your study.

You may study a Bible book for several reasons: historical information, literary appreciation, doctrinal teaching, or practical application, to name a few. Choosing one major goal as you read a book will help you focus your study.

2. Reading the book

a. Read continuously. Read the book through without interruption. A short book like Jude will require no more than five minutes. You can complete Ephesians in about thirty minutes. Isaiah or Luke may require an hour or two. Observe how the plot or the purpose of the book develops. Such observations can be made only through continuous, uninterrupted reading.

b. Read independently. As you begin to study a Bible book, avoid the use of commentaries, the notes in this study Bible, or other outside helps. Try to understand the Bible for yourself. Remember the principles of Bible interpretation as you read the book. See above. Gain confidence in your ability to understand and interpret the Bible.

c. Read repeatedly. During a first reading, skim the book quickly to get a general idea of content and teaching. Look for the chief emphases of the writer. A first reading of First Peter will reveal suffering mentioned in each chapter. Obviously, Peter wrote to persecuted Christians. Reading Hebrews, you will realize the writer emphasized the superiority and significance of Christ. Take notes in your first reading of the subjects you see reappearing and the verse references for them. After your reading, write two sentences on what you think the writer was attempting to accomplish by writing the book. You may want to check this by reading the introduction to the Bible book in this study Bible. Did the writer of the introduction find the same emphases you find. Such findings should lead to repeated readings of the Bible book. Look for further clues which show the purpose of the writer. Note repeated words or phrases and summary statements in the Bible text. Underline these in your Bible. Find structural phrases used to introduce new sections or topics or to summarize and conclude a section. Compare for instance 1 Co 7:1; 8:1; 12:1; 16:1. Note how Paul used "Therefore" in Ro 12:1 to summarize his conclusion based on chapters 1—11. Compare Eph 4:1 to this. Read the book repeatedly until you feel familiar with what the author is saying. You may want to read from different translations. One reading should be from a paragraphed edition to help you understand the structure of the book, but read for yourself, remembering paragraph divisions are modern interpretations and not part of the original text.

3. Summarizing the book

In your last reading, prepare your own interpretation of the book in a notebook. After you have summarized the content of each paragraph, summarize its teaching. Learn to distinguish between the narrative content telling what happened to whom and the teaching of the inspired book telling how the beliefs and actions of the reader should change or be more deeply confirmed.

4. Outlining the book

Use your summaries to outline the book. Content summaries will lead to content or historical outlines such as birth of Christ, childhood of Christ, ministry of John, baptism and temptation of Christ, Galilean ministry, Judean Ministry, and the death and resurrection of Christ. Teaching summaries should lead to doctrinal or practical application outlines. For an example of these, see the introductions to the Bible books in this study Bible. Sometimes the content of a paragraph can become a point in an outline. At other times, you can combine several paragraph summaries to form a point of your outline. You can make the outlines as detailed as you wish.

5. Applying the book

List the doctrines of the book which are most meaningful for your life now. List the practical applications of the book which could strengthen your Christian discipleship. List questions which your study of the book has raised. Choose one doctrinal teaching of the book which you want to study further. Use the index (pp. 1843–1871) to follow the doctrine through the Bible. Read all Scripture passages listed and the notes related to them. Choose one practical application of the book. Put this on your prayer list. Ask God to help you make this application of biblical truth to your life. Be alert for opportunities to put the biblical truth into action.

6. Illustrating the Method

Study the short book of Philemon. Choose a historical goal. Read the book through quickly and write your understanding of the historical situation. Name the people involved, the setting described, and the problems described. What was Paul's goal in writing?

Begin reading again. Use the grammatical principle (p. 1770) to determine which acts are past, which are present, and which are hoped for as future. What is the literary form used? Is it a personal letter? Use the historical principle to describe all you know about Paul, Philemon, and Onesimus. Can you determine where Philemon lived? Paul did not give a geographical address. Use the center-column references to find other passages in which Mark, Aristarchus, Epaphras, Demas, and Luke appear in Scripture. You may want to use a concordance or Bible dictionary to get more complete information. Note that all appear in the letter to the Colossians and in Philemon. Your study should show that both Archippus and Onesimus were from Colosse. See Col 4:9, 17. Does this lead to the likely conclusion that Philemon was from Colosse?

of His Word as it has been passed from generation to generation. The generations do not, however, protect language from change. Human language is dynamic. Each new generation attaches slightly varying definitions to words. Charity, for example, may have been a suitable translation in a past generation for the Greek word *agape* in 1 Co 13. Today, however, we understand that word more correctly in terms of our word *love*.

The serious student of the Bible will want to uncover the most accurate meaning of its words so as to discern, obey, and convey the true message of God. Ultimately, this is the task of the professional Bible scholar, but with the right helps and procedure, you can deepen your insight into the meaning of the words God used to give us His Word.

The following steps will enable you to grasp a deeper understanding of a Bible word. Write information in your notebook.

1. Ask the following questions.

a. What different translations can I find of the word?

b. What is the word in its original language?

c. Where does the word occur elsewhere in Scripture?

d. How many definitions and translations of the original word can I find?

e. What is the derivation of the word?

f. What grammatical and syntactical information can I find to help me understand the meaning in this passage?

g. What possible meanings of the word do not fit the text I am studying?

h. What possible meanings of the word do fit the text?

i. Which English word or words appear to translate the original word most appropriately in this text?

j. What meanings of the original word are left out in the chosen translation?

k. What meanings of the English translation are not part of the meaning of the original word?

l. Did the word have special religious meanings in the cultural environment in which it was used?

2. Use resource tools to answer your questions.

Many books are available for people without scholarly training to use in checking out the meaning of biblical words. As possible, you will want to place the following in your Bible library.

a. The *Disciple's Study Bible*—The notes on the passage you are studying may give definitions of key words or even note the original language word and its meaning. The center-column reference system may refer you to other verses with the word under study. The note will give you a major doctrine as heading. The index of doctrines (pp. 1843–1871) will lead you to further references to study.

b. A concordance—This study Bible contains a useful concordance listing words alphabetically and showing major occurrences of the word in the Bible. You may choose to study further. Find a concordance keyed to the translation you are using. For the NIV, consult the *NIV Complete Concordance* (1981); for KJV, *Strong's Exhaustive Concordance of the Bible* (Holman); and for NASB, *New American Standard Exhaustive Concordance* (1981). The latter two provide a numbering system referring you to original language terms in the back. With them you can determine the word used in the original language manuscripts.

c. Bible dictionary—Dictionaries provide a general definition, derivation in the original language, the most important passages where each word is used, and synonyms used to express the same or similar meanings. A dictionary such as the *Layman's Bible Dictionary* (Holman, 1989) will give you the basic theological significance of the word.

d. Commentaries—Biblical scholars give the results of the author's study of the biblical word. You may want to begin with *Layman's Bible Book Commentary*, go to *Broadman Bible Commentary* and others.

e. Word study books—These tools give specific information about the theological meaning of major biblical terms. Specifically related to doctrine are more advanced sources,

A Dictionary of Doctrinal Terms (Broadman, 1983), *Word Pictures in the New Testament*, *The New International Dictionary of New Testament Theology* (3 vols.), and *Theological Wordbook of the Old Testament* (2 vols.).

f. Lexicons—The ultimate resources for word study, lexicons are ordered according to the original language. They provide cognate words in related languages, the varying definitions of the same word, and an exhaustive list of Scripture references. Refer to *A Concise Hebrew and Aramaic Lexicon of the Old Testament* (1971) and *Thayer's Greek-English Lexicon of the New Testament*.

g. Translations—Different translations give insight into biblical word meanings by showing the various translation possibilities seen by different translators and translation committees. You should have copies of these Bible translations available: New International Version, King James Version, Revised Standard Version, New American Standard Bible, Today's English Version, *The Amplified Bible*, and *The New Testament in the Language of the People* by Charles B. Williams.

3. Answer your questions.

Write in your notebook an answer to each of the questions you have written. If you have found differing answers, note this.

4. Complete your definition of the word.

After gathering information about the word, prayerfully consider how it is used in the text. Write your own definition making sure it is consistent with what you have found in your study of resources. Note other meanings of the word in other contexts. Do these other meanings give depth to the meaning of the text you are studying?

5. Apply your study to life.

Meditate on the ways your new understanding of the word can be applied to your life. Does it enrich your belief system, deepen your faith, provide new assurance and hope, compel new action, call for confession and renewal? Find ways this week to make the new knowledge part of your life in practical ways.

The Word of God is "more precious than gold, than much pure gold" (Ps 19:10). Studying a Bible word is a rich experience which will give fresh insight into the Scripture as well as increase awareness of the richness of Scripture texts joined by the same word or theme. Surely, if people will spend their lives digging in the recesses of the earth in search of gold, we should count it a privilege to search diligently for that which is far better than gold.

Guide to Studying a Bible Character

God operates in our lives on the basis of principle. He shares His principles with us in the Bible. Have you ever wondered why God did not simply give us a precise, compact listing of all the principles He wants us to follow rather than give us sixty-six books in one? We find the principles of God appearing as way markers in the unfolding drama of history. The few lists of principles such as the Ten Commandments or Beatitudes are revealed in the life struggles of real people making real choices of faith in a real world of trials. Why did God choose to share His Word in this fashion?

In His wisdom God knows how we learn best. He teaches us by illustration as well as by precept. Thus, we can gain much by studying a Bible character. Bible characters show us God's principles worked out in human experience. Their lives reveal the result of choices, both right and wrong. Studying a Bible character encourages us to apply God's principles to our lives. Through such a study we move beyond the mere intellectual comprehension of truth to apprehend the principle as we identify with the Bible character. The following suggestions should assist you as you study Bible characters.

1. Gather basic information about the Bible character.

List in your notebook passages that give insight into the personality of the Bible character. You should include:

a. Genealogy—What environment shaped the person's formative years? What does the person's name mean? What can you discover about the character of the person's parents?

b. Geography—Where was the person born? Where did the person travel? How did geographical and climate factors influence the person's life? Where did the character die?

c. Events—What significant historical events occurred during the person's life? What were the significant personal events which shaped the person's character?

d. Responses—How did the person respond to the events? to other persons? to God?

e. Contemporaries—What other Bible characters were contemporaries of the person you are studying? How did they influence this person? How would you describe their relationship?

f. Statements—What significant statements did the character make? Did others make significant statements to the character? What do these statements reveal about this person?

g. Testimonies—What did other people in the Bible say about this person? You will want to use a concordance to avoid missing statements such as New Testament testimonies about Old Testament characters. Pay attention to the center-column references in your Bible.

h. Divine Witness—Did God go on record regarding the individual? Was a covenant established? a judgment pronounced? a promise made?

i. Influence—What does the Scripture reveal about the impact of this person's life on others? on later biblical history and personalities?

j. Strengths and Weaknesses—List these as the Bible reveals them and as you come to recognize them. How are these manifested? Do you see a change in regard to these during the person's life?

k. Spiritual Discipline—What evidence do you find of the person's devotion or lack of it to the Lord? How did the person express the devotion? How did the devotion influence the person's life?

2. Establish a lifeline chart for your Bible character.

A lifeline chart is simply a straight line upon which you indicate the earliest known fact about the person and continue listing facts chronologically until the last known fact. This is usually from birth to death. Mark significant events with Scripture references. Above the line write events or statements which reveal positive or spiritual contributions and attributes. Below the line write events or statements which reveal weak or negative traits. Indicate major turning points in the individual's life with an asterisk (*).

3. Relate principles from Scripture to the events in the life of your character.

Often a clear scriptural principle will explain why a particular action brought a particular response or result. The Book of Proverbs will be especially helpful here. You may want to study Scripture and notes on CHRISTIAN ETHICS, Moral Imperatives (Index, p. 1861). This exercise will serve to reinforce the authority of God's Word as a guide for your faith and practice. Write the references for these scriptural principles at the bottom of your lifeline chart under the particular event it describes.

4. Write down biblical principles you learn from the character's life.

Read in one sitting all the Bible has to say about the character. See if the Bible draws explicit lessons from the person's life. Write these down. Then prayerfully determine what principles the Scripture teaches through the illustration of the person's life. Note what elements are repeated in describing the person and events. Notice the introduction and conclusion to the person's life. These should give clues as to the major lessons to be learned.

5. Apply the teaching to your life.

Here your study begins to develop character in your life! At the top of your lifeline chart or on a separate page if necessary indicate how you identify with specific character traits of the individual. You may want to note specific events in your life that parallel those of the Bible character. What strengths and weaknesses do you share with the person? What temptations do you also face? What principles do you need to learn? What promises can you count on as having proved true for the Bible character and remaining true for you? Ask God to help you incorporate the truths you have learned from this Bible character to make you a better disciple.

Guide to Memorizing Scripture

Life's situations often do not allow time for Bible study. You need help and direction immediately. Then the lessons of Bible study you have applied to life become operative and important. Then you often need something more. You need reassurance from God. That can come from claiming promises or following directions of Scripture you can quote because they are stored in your memory. Scripture memory provides immediate access to God's Word for daily situations. You can memorize Scripture and gain resources for daily living through the following suggestions:

1. Establish a list of verses to memorize.

In your notebook set up a section of verses to memorize. Add to the list continually. Choose verses which speak to a personal need, verses to be used in witnessing, verses on whose meaning you want to meditate, verses with doctrinal teachings you want to remember, verses you can use in prayer. Always have a list to challenge you to memorize, and always make the list meaningful for your life.

2. Locate the verse in your Bible.

Underline the verse, and read it aloud. Visualize its place on the Bible page.

3. Understand the verse.

Read the verse in relation to its context. Do a word study of significant words in the verse. See pp. 1776–1778. Understanding lets you rightly apply the verse when life needs it.

4. Write the verse on a card.

Record verses to memorize on small 2″ x 3″ cards you can carry in your pocket or purse. Include the Scripture reference and the topic to which it relates. Be sure you have copied correctly.

5. Place the memory card in a prominent place.

Have cards where you shave or make up, snack, talk on the phone, watch TV, work at a hobby. Wherever you do physical tasks which allow concentration on something else, have a Scripture card to review. Use spare moments to review Scripture.

6. Commit the verse to memory.

Divide the verse into natural, meaningful phrases. Learn each phrase word for word. Gain confidence you know the verse word perfect.

7. Record memory verses on a cassette tape.

Leave a space after each verse so you can practice quoting it. Record the verse a second time so you can review it after you have quoted it.

8. Review the memorized verse regularly.

This is the most important secret of Scripture memorization. You should review a new verse at least once a day for six weeks. Review the verse weekly for the next six weeks and then monthly for the rest of your life. Repeat the verse to another person to be sure you are word perfect.

9. File the verse cards systematically.

Take cards of verses you are reviewing once a week and file them under the day of the week to be reviewed. Take other verses and file under topics. You may want to use the topics in the index. Then you will have ready access to verses when you need them.

10. Make Bible memory a regular practice.

Scripture memory can be fun by making a game of remembering verses with your family or friends. Set a goal for the number of verses you will memorize each week. Be sure you cite the topic first, then the Scripture reference, then the verse word for word without prompting, and then the Scripture reference again. Work on the week's new verses and on review verses at the same time each day. Then find other times when you can work on verses while performing other activities. Let God's Word saturate your life.

The Disciple's Study Bible memory plan will give you a balanced beginning for your lifetime task of Scripture memory. If you memorize two verses a week, you can complete this plan in four months. As you study Scripture, you will add other verses to memorize to your file. Find a place in the following outline for those verses, or use the index (pp. 1843–1871) to extend the outline. Remember, the secret to Scripture memory is REVIEW.

I. Becoming a Disciple
  a. God's Purpose—Ro 6:23
  b. Our Need—Ro 3:23
  c. God's Way in Christ—1 Pe 3:18
  d. Our Need to Repent—Ac 3:19
  e. God's Gift of Grace—Eph 2:8-9
  f. Our Salvation through Faith—Ro 10:9-10
II. Life in Christ
  a. Denying Self—Lk 9:23
  b. Living in the Word—Jn 8:31-32
  c. Praying in Faith—Jn 15:7
  d. Fellowshipping with Believers—Jn 13:34-35
  e. Witnessing to the World—Jn 15:8
  f. Ministering to Others—Jn 15:13
III. Discipline of Worship
  a. False Worship—Ro 1:21-25
  b. God Wants Our Worship—Jn 5:23-24
  c. Worship with Confidence—Heb 4:16
IV. Discipline of Prayer
  a. Praise—Rev 4:11
  b. Thanksgiving—1 Th 5:16-18
  c. Worship—Ps 27:1
  d. Petition—Mt 7:7-8
  e. Intercession—Eph 6:18
  f. Promises—Eph 3:20-21
V. Discipline of Bible Study
  a. Hearing the Word—Ro 10:17
  b. Examining the Word—Rev 1:3
  c. Analyzing the Word—Ac 17:10
  d. Remembering the Word—Ps 119:9,11
  e. Thinking on the Word—Ps 1:2-3
  f. Applying the Word—Jas 1:22
VI. Discipline of Witnessing
  a. Christ's Command—Mt 28:19-20
  b. Spirit's Power—Ac 1:8
  c. Witness' Message—Jn 3:15
  d. Witness' Question—Jn 11:26
  e. Witness Results—Psa 126:5-6
  f. Witness Promise—Jn 15:16
VII. Call to Ministry
  a. All Called—Eph 4:1
  b. All Gifted—1 Pe 4:10
  c. All to be Equipped—Eph 4:11-12
  d. All Sent—Jn 20:21
  e. All Empowered—Ac 1:8
  f. All Special—1 Pe 2:9
VIII. Ministry of Service
  a. The Lost—2 Co 5:20
  b. The Poor—1 Jn 3:17
  c. The Hungry—Isa 58:10
  d. The Brokenhearted—Isa 61:1
  e. Widows and Orphans—Jas 1:27
  f. To All Persons—Gal 6:10
IX. Discipline of Fellowship

a. Loving One Another—1 Jn 4:7
b. Build Up One Another—Ro 14:19
c. Bear One Another's Burdens—Gal 6:2
d. Forgive One Another—Col 3:13
e. Exhort One Another—Heb 10:24-25
f. Promote Unity—Jn 17:20-21

DISCIPLINE OF FELLOWSHIP

Guide to Conversational Prayer

Conversational prayer is two or more persons talking with God together. Many people feel embarrassment, fear, and discomfort when they first participate in group prayer. Practice brings excitement and spiritual growth. An ideal number for a prayer group is three to five persons, though the group may be larger. Conversational prayer is much like other conversations. One person says a few sentences on a topic which sparks replies from other group members. Earnest conversational prayer can encourage you to enter into prayer with God on topics which you have never prayed about. Read Scripture and notes on PRAYER, Fellowship with God. As you and your group of Christian friends pray, follow these guidelines;

1. Thank God for the group and your opportunity to be a part of it.
2. Pray about one subject at a time. Allow everyone to speak to God about each subject before changing subjects. Begin praying about a new subject after a significant pause.
3. Begin conversational prayer with praise and worship. Be sure attention is centered on God and not on group action.
4. Pray about matters of mutual interest. Group prayer should center attention on matters about which all members are informed and concerned so all may be involved.
5. Pray brief prayers. One or two sentences are usually enough on one subject at a time. If you want to add something after others have had an opportunity, feel free to do so. Conversational prayer is group participation, rather than going one time around the circle in individual prayers.
6. Use the first person singular pronoun whenever possible. Use I or my instead of we or us.
7. Do not use formal terms of address as each person begins or formal endings such as *Amen* at the end of each short prayer. Remember conversational prayer is all one prayer. It is just being prayed by a group. Use *Amen* only when the group is finished with all prayer subjects.
8. As the group grows in trust and in spiritual maturity, you may be able to handle more personal types of prayer together such as confession of sin and personal requests. As you do, learn to make these specific rather than general, so that you can deal with real concerns before God and find spiritual support from the group.
9. Feel free to change your physical position; open your eyes; or move about.
10. Spend your time in prayer, not, in listing items to pray about.
11. Accept silence as a natural part of prayer. Do not fear moments without sound. Let God use the silence to speak to you.
12. Allow conversational prayer to continue as long as the group desires or time allows.

Guide to Seeking Reconciliation

Christian discipleship is a relationship with God that leads to trusting relationships with fellow believers. Unity among His people was Jesus' prayer for His church (Jn 17:11,21-23). Resentment and an unforgiving spirit represent serious obstacles to God's work and to the unity of His children. They call God's people to reconciliation. Separation from other Christians has burdened many otherwise faithful disciples for years. Here is a way to lift the burden and find reconciliation. The Bible gives clear commands and instructions on how to be reconciled. Follow this guide to Christian reconciliation. God will guide you to reconciliation as you study His Word. Read notes and Scripture on THE CHURCH, Fellowship; HUMANITY, Relationships; SALVATION, Reconciliation.

1. Acknowledge God's intentions.

a. Forgiveness is God's gift to you and His intention for you. He has forgiven each disciple of all confessed sins. His forgiving compassion inspires Christians to forgive others and gives us the freedom to do so. Those not experiencing the grace, love, and joy of God's salvation may have greater difficulty forgiving (Mt 18:23-35).

b. Fellowship with God is His intention for you. God wants disciples to walk openly and honestly with Him as Jesus did. We have no reason to hide anything from God. Similarly, He wants us to walk openly and honestly with others in His light. This calls us to confess our sins to other believers as well as to God (Jas 5:16). Confessing sins to God opens the way to unhindered relationship with Him. Confessing sins to other disciples opens the way to relationship with them.

c. The Holy Spirit guides disciples to confess and find reconciliation. When the Holy Spirit impresses you with the need for reconciliation, you may be sure He will also work in the other person to lead to reconciliation and acceptance. He may use you to help the other person become aware of God's intentions concerning reconciliation.

2. Understand the disciple's responsibility. Your responsibility is to seek peace with all people (Heb 12:14). This calls you to act responsibly in:

a. seeking reconciliation with those you dislike, have offended, or have not forgiven;

b. seeking reconciliation with those who have something against you whether or not you are wrong;

c. seeking reconciliation with those who have wronged you;

d. seeking to maintain peace among and with all disciples;

e. seeking personal cleansing from God before you attempt to be reconciled with another person;

f. seeking pure relationships with others lest they fail to experience God's grace and be forgiven (Heb 12:15);

g. seeking diligently for opportunities to make peace rather than spread gossip or otherwise harm another person;

h. seeking to prevent bitterness and resentment among God's people.

3. Seek reconciliation. Follow these steps:

a. Attempt reconciliation privately. Talk together alone and uninterrupted.

b. Confess your shortcomings without qualifications. You may want to say the following: "I have been thinking a lot about our relationship. The Lord has convicted me of my __(wrong attitude)__ toward you and (if it applies) what I have done when I __(wrong action)__. He has answered my prayer and forgiven me. I would like to ask you to forgive me."

c. Remember the wrong attitudes include an unforgiving spirit, bitterness, resentment, pride, judgmental attitude, and hatred.

d. Remember wrong actions include ignoring, avoiding, talking about, criticizing, arguing unnecessarily, seeking to destroy reputations, embarrassing, teasing, provoking, and tempting other people.

e. Do not qualify or minimize your fault or invite the other person to do so. God has dealt with your sin and forgiven it. The Holy Spirit has convicted you of it. Reconciliation demands dealing with it honestly with the offended party rather than compounding the sin by manipulating the other person. The other person may have wronged you. If you reacted wrongly in attitude or in action, you should confess your sin and let the Holy Spirit take care of convicting the other person.

f. Use the word forgive, and urge the other person to say, "I forgive you." If the person will not forgive you, explain how important forgiveness is to you and to Christian fellowship.

If the person refuses to forgive you, say, "I am sorry for what I have done. I truly want to be reconciled with you and have full Christian fellowship with you. I hope someday you can and will forgive me."

4. If you are not convicted of sin and do not know what the problem separating you from another person is, ask the person if you have offended in any way.

a. If the person says yes, then ask for a description of the offense. Listen carefully seeking to understand the other person's point of view. If you think the assessment is accurate, ask the person to forgive you.

b. If the person's understanding of the situation does not match your understanding, explain the situation as objectively as you can. Seek common understanding of what happened and seek acceptance and/or forgiveness for attitudes or actions which prompted the misunderstanding. Clear up misunderstandings about motives behind actions. Promise to be more careful about actions in the future. Seek to reach an agreement to talk with one another if future misunderstandings arise.

c. If the person says no, ask what has brought obstacles in your relationships. Identify clearly why you have thought your relationship was marred or what led you to believe you had offended the other person.

d. If the person honestly feels no problem exists, accept the opinion; and pledge to love and help each other.

e. Attempt to close the conversation in prayer together.

5. If another Christian has sinned against you, express your feelings to that one in a spirit of love (Mt 18:15-17; Gal 6:1). By facing the problem, you may help the other person seek God's forgiveness. The other person may not be aware of the problem or may not know you are aware of it.

a. Seek to solve the problem through personal consultation (Steps 3 and 4 above).

b. If private appeal does not result in reconciliation, ask two or more understanding, mature, compassionate Christians to help you seek reconciliation. Seek persons the other person trusts, not just your best friends. Let the Christian associates hear both sides of the case. Let them direct the process. Show your willingness to do everything possible to bring reconciliation. Do not become defensive. Be repenting, confessing, accepting. Listen to the other person rather than asserting your rights or viewpoints.

c. If the matter still cannot be resolved, ask your pastor how the local congregation can best deal with the problem. Let the pastor and church leaders take responsibility and leadership. Do not demand that your process be followed. Should this final effort fail, let the congregation decide its actions without your promptings. Continue on your part to demonstrate concern, love, and a desire for reconciliation. Be sure you are not the obstacle to reconciliation. Reconciliation—not justification or vindication—is your goal as a disciple.

6. Through the process of reconciliation, bathe your actions in prayer. Conclude all conversations with offended people with prayer that God will help you both walk together as disciples in His love.

DISCIPLINE OF WITNESSING

Guide to Relational Evangelism

Relational evangelism involves communicating the good news of salvation through relationships. Relational evangelism requires a strong effort on your part to cultivate lost persons through demonstrating the love of Christ in personal relationships. These relationships become the channels through which you share the gospel of Christ. As you prepare for relational evangelism, you will want to read notes and Scripture on EVANGELISM, Cultivation, Holy Life.

1. Realize the need for relational evangelism. Millions of lost people live in our country, yet many disciples and even many churches cannot name one. Develop a sensitivity to the spiritual condition of people you know and meet. Develop a list of lost people for whom you pray daily. Know that each of them shares the basic human need for personal relationships with people who care, share, and give. Join the many disciples and churches who are using relationships to build the interpersonal trust that legitimizes Christian witness.

2. Select persons with whom you can and will develop a relationship. Relational evangelism should include all your acquaintances. Begin with your closest relationships, and move to include those who may only be casual acquaintances. Then look for opportunities to begin cultivating relationships with persons who may be unknown to you at present. Build relationships with nonbelievers in your immediate family, among relatives, with close friends, business associates, neighbors, casual acquaintances, and persons with whom you initiate new relationships.

3. Understand the person's receptivity. Relational evangelism begins with people where they are spiritually. You need to make a kind of "receptivity check." Using relationships to lead lost persons to Christ involves an awareness of the person's attitude toward Christ and toward conversion. The following receptivity scale shows progressive levels of receptivity to the gospel. As a person approaches the top of the scale, the person becomes more open to responding positively to the gospel and to your witness to Christ. Evaluate the receptivity of the persons to whom you are witnessing so that you will select an approach that will best meet their needs, understanding, and attitudes.

Receptivity Scale

a. A person ready to receive Christ.
b. A person open to advice and counsel.
c. A person open to discuss spiritual needs.
d. A person open to sharing feelings and emotions.
e. A person open to sharing intellectual and theological ideas.
f. A person open to casual conversation on light subjects.
g. A casual acquaintance.
h. A person known by sight but with whom no relationship has been established.
i. A person unknown to the witness.

Many people see relational evangelism as a method of moving people up this scale. Relational evangelism begins with a relationship, but it must also be a method of winning people to Christ if it is truly relational evangelism.

4. Build relationships. Loving God also involves loving those whom He created in His image. One of the best ways to build relationships is to begin by expressing Christlike love toward others. A ministry of service may open the door to ongoing relationships which can lead to the salvation of a lost person. Relational evangelists have love for people and get involved in their lives because of that love (Jn 15:12).

Relational evangelism requires that you enjoy relationships with people who do not know Christ. Spend quality time at various types of functions with unbelievers as Jesus did. Join in their celebrations, and be with them in times of crisis. Develop a reservoir of shared experiences as the basis for conversation, the foundation of understanding, and the starting points of trust. To build your relationship with the person:

a. Discover the person's needs and interests. Find concrete ways to show interest in the activities and ideas the person enjoys.

b. Show your love by trying to meet the person's needs. Be a Christian servant to the person not a superior master.

c. Be patient with your friend, encouraging appropriate life-style changes without assuming a holier than thou attitude. Remember, only the transformation that comes through Christ can make your friend a new creature desiring a new life.

d. Mend broken relationships by seeking forgiveness if you have wronged the person. If restitution needs to be made, do so. If you have been wronged, offer forgiveness readily.

e. Include the person in the special activities of your life. Relationship involvement must be a two-way street.

f. Remember special occasions by sending cards or making phone calls.

g. Demonstrate honesty and openness. Prove you can be trusted.

h. Listen to your friend. The listening ear brings comfort.

i. Pray that God will help you build a deep relationship with the person that will encourage the person to seek Christ.

5. Share the gospel. As your relationship deepens, your friend will probably move up the scale of receptivity. Watch for natural opportunities for planting the seed of the gospel. Long before you can use a direct approach to witnessing, you will have the opportunity to let your friend know Christ is the only answer to the longing of the human hearts evoked by its deepest needs.

Depend on the Holy Spirit to prepare the heart of your friend for an openness to the gospel. Watch for the right opportunity to share the gospel with your friend. One of the best ways to witness to a friend is through a personal testimony. "See "Guide to Giving Your Personal Testimony (pp. 1786). Be sure you have prepared a concise, clear presentation of your testimony. Use the "Guide to Using a Marked New Testament" and "Guide to Leading to Commitment" (pp. 1788–1792) to lead the friend to accept Christ.

Once your friend accepts Christ, continue your friendship. Help the new disciple grow spiritually and become an evangelist.

Guide to Giving Your Personal Testimony

A disciple has an experience to share with others. Sharing your experience is the first step in your discipline of witnessing. This section will help you take the facts of your life and write them in a clear, concise way so you can give your personal testimony to a non-Christian. Writing your testimony will help you clarify your experience in your own mind, provide a form others can help you sharpen and make more effective, give you confidence that you have a testimony and can share it with others, and provide a beginning point from which you can depart according to the reactions of the person(s) with whom you share. Read "How to Accept Christ" (pp. 1745–1747) and Scripture and notes on EVANGELISM, Testimony.

God commissioned Christians to share the knowledge of His love with others (Mt 28:18–20). As Christians, we benefit from thinking through our experience with Jesus Christ so we can share with others in a clear, concise way. Consider the following suggestions for preparing a personal testimony:

1. Write your testimony in about 250-500 words. Write in a conversational style which resembles the way you talk with a friend.

2. Write in first person. Use "I" and "me". Emphasize that this is your personal experience, your story, not a sales presentation someone else has written for all people to use.

3. Choose the approach most fitting your experience.

a. The chronological approach emphasizes what happened before and after conversion. This approach is most appropriate if, prior to your conversion, you had significant experiences with which your audience can easily identify. The chronological approach allows you to center on the drama of your conversion experience.

The chronological approach begins at a significant point of your life prior to conversion, tells the conversion experience, and then tells its effects on life up to the present. (See illustration.)

b. The thematic approach is most appropriate for those saved as children, those who recall few events prior to conversion, or those who cannot remember the exact sequence of events in their conversion experience. The thematic approach focuses on an experience, problem, issue, or feeling with which the other person may identify and stresses how salvation has influenced that concern. Your concern may be fear of death, desire for success and happiness, an addiction, relationship problems, a character flaw, a search for identity, or a crisis experience. Conversation with the person may reveal a concern evident in your life and of present concern to the other person. Your theme may be ignorance of any need or problem until you met Jesus. You may begin with testimony to your current situation, such as:

____I have discovered how not to worry.

____I have found a purpose for living.

____I am so happy because ________________________

TWO KINDS OF TESTIMONY OUTLINES

CHRONOLOGICAL

Before → Conversion → After → Now

(Begin here with life story.)

THEMATIC

(Begin here with a common problem.)

Conversion → After → Now

(Before is not discussed.)

Use the flashback techniques to tell how you solved your problem. Bridge the theme to your conversation by saying: "I had a problem similar to yours. If it had not been for an experience I had several years ago, I could not have solved it. May I tell you about it?" This allows you to discuss a problem which arose even after conversion and can take the place of telling your experiences before conversion. You do not have to tell when something happened. Tell how you came to your present situation. You can build your testimony around the four facts of the gospel—sin, sin's penalty, Christ's payment, and receiving Christ. You may say, "Although I did not realize everything that was taking place at the time, I later discovered that . . . ." Work in the four facts with your personal experience.

4. Consider the following outline as a form to use in developing your testimony.

INTRODUCTION

(Interesting life-related event or fact identifying with the other person's situation)

I. Before I Met Christ
   - A. Chronological Approach: My Life and Attitudes Before Conversion
   - B. Thematic Approach: Problem or Need Conversion Solved

II. How I Realized My Need for Christ

III. How I Became a Christian
   - A. Realized my sin
   - B. Knew sin's penalty
   - C. Learned of Christ's payment for sin
   - D. Received Christ by repenting of sin, putting faith in Christ, and surrendering to Jesus as Lord of life.

IV. What Being a Christian Means to Me Now.

V. Closing Question or Invitation.

Begin your testimony with an interesting introduction that helps the person see you as a real person. Give a few, brief facts about your life before you became a Christian. Use only details of interest to the person. If possible, relate details to the other person's situation.

Highlight the events that led to your salvation. Sum up the events that led you to realize your need for Christ. Avoid using specific places, names of churches or people, or dates unless the person hearing your testimony has the same background. If you keep these facts general, more people will be able to identify with you. Do not use religious jargon or church words that might not be understood by those with little religious training or with different religious backgrounds.

Summarize the facts of salvation and how you became a Christian. Tell how you became aware that you were living an "I-controlled life." State how you felt when you realized the nature of sin and the penalty of sin. Tell your joy when you learned Christ paid the penalty for your sin. Summarize how you received Christ. Be sure to emphasize repentance or turning from sin and faith in Christ as the way to salvation. You will want to use some of the information and Scriptures in "How to Accept Christ" (pp. 1745–1747).

Share what knowing Christ as Lord and Savior has meant to you. Summarize specific differences Christ has made in your life. Mention continuing struggles and how Christ helps you daily. Maintain focus on Christ and salvation, not on present problems. The non-Christian can best identify with the need for and experience of salvation through Christ.

Close your testimony so that further conversation focuses on salvation. Use questions as a transition device from your talking to your listening to the other person. Ask: "Has anything like that every happened to you? Does that make any sense to you? Have you ever wanted such an experience? Have you ever made the wonderful discovery of knowing Jesus as your personal Savior?"

5. Check your written testimony to see if the story line is clear, if the important issues have been covered adequately, and if an invitation to know more about Christ has been extended. Is the tone right for conversation with a friend? Have you concluded with a bridge question to involve the other person in talking about salvation? Is your testimony true? You may discover a need to talk with God about your own experience and gain new assurance of your own salvation.

6. Practice giving your testimony to Christians before sharing it with non-Christians. Ask them to help you sharpen it so you can communicate more powerfully to non-Christians.

7. Give your testimony to a non-Christian. Do not worry about memorizing the testimony. Adjust to the situation. Your writing will have helped you clarify your testimony so the Holy Spirit can use it more effectively.

8. Ask God to give you opportunities to give your testimony to others.

9. Your responsibility is to share your testimony and pray for the salvation of others. The Holy Spirit's task is to convict sinners and convert them.

10. Remember the goal is to lead a person to know Christ in salvation. Telling your experience is not the end. Engaging in conversation that gives the other person opportunity to accept Christ is the final step.

Guide to Using a Marked New Testament

Sharing your personal testimony means telling briefly and simply what Christ has done and is doing for you. Presenting the plan of salvation is using the Bible to explain to a non-Christian how to receive Jesus as Savior and Lord. These two—personal testimony and plan of salvation—are powerful and effective tools for leading persons to Christ. Every disciple should know how to use them both. As you learn how to mark and use your New Testament in witnessing, review Scripture and notes on EVANGELISM, Salvation.

To present God's plan of salvation you need to know:

1. How to Mark Your New Testament

You will be more effective and confident as a witness as you develop your ability to use a series of basic Scripture verses to present the plan of salvation. The following verses have been used effectively by many persons. You will want to mark them in your New Testament and use them to witness to others.

Begin at the inside of the front cover of your New Testament. Write a list of the Scriptures given below. The first reference is Ro 3:23. Turn to this verse and find what page number it is on. On the inside front cover, write, *Turn to p. 000*, inserting the page number of Ro 3:23. Proceed to write the caption given below with each reference at the top of the page on which the reference occurs. Underline the reference in your New Testament. Then at the bottom of the page, write, *Turn to p. 000*, with the proper page number for the next reference in the sequence. Thus on the page where Ro 3:23 occurs, you would write, *All people have rebelled against God* at the top of the page, underline Ro 3:23, and then write, *Turn to p. 000*, using the page where Ro 6:23, the second reference, occurs. Continue this process until you have written all the phrases, underlined verses, and written directions for proceeding to the next verse(es) for each of the seven references. Turn to the last page of your New Testament. Find a blank place there or on the inside cover. Write, *Are you ready to receive God's free gift?* Then write the following prayer, *Lord Jesus, I know I am a sinner and need your forgiveness. I know you died on the cross for me. I now turn from my sins and ask You to forgive me. I now invite You into my heart and life. I now trust You as Savior and follow You as Lord. Thank You for saving me. Amen.*

You may get a marked New Testament in your bookstore. *The Great Commission New Testament* (Holman) uses the verses given here and can be given to the person to whom you witness.

2. Basic Scripture Verses

You should have these verses memorized. "See Guide to Memorizing Scripture" (pp. 1780–1782). Look the verses up and mark your New Testament now.

a. All have sinned (rebelled) and fall short of the glory of God.—Ro 3:23.

b. The price of rebellion (sin) is high.—Ro 6:23.

c. God loves us in spite of our rebellion (sin).—Ro 5:8.

d. Repent, then, and turn to God, so that your sins may be wiped out.—Ac 3:19.

e. By God's generosity (grace) you receive His free gift (eternal life) through faith which is also from God.—Eph 2:8.

f. Confess Jesus and believe that He was raised from the dead by God.—Ro 10:9-10.

g. Call on (pray to) the Lord and be saved.—Ro 10:13.

3. How to Present the Plan of Salvation

Presenting the plan of salvation involves knowing what to say and do and how to say and do it. Exactly how you present the plan of salvation to another person depends on your personality and the particular way you relate best to other persons. Use the following procedure as a model. Adapt it to suit your style and the needs of the one to whom you are witnessing. Be sure your presentation remains a conversation between two people showing care for one another.

a. Get acquainted, and establish as much trust as possible.

b. Share your personal testimony. Review "Guide to Personal Testimony" (pp. 1786–1788). Conclude by asking, "Has this ever happened to you?" Listen to the other person's testimony of salvation or admission of never having been saved. If the person is not a Christian, say, "I would like to show you in God's Word how my life has been changed."

c. Give the marked New Testament to the person. Help the person locate and read Ro 3:23. Read the phrase you have written at the top of the page. Give any additional brief explanation that may be needed for a clear understanding. Then do the same with Ro. 6:23.

d. Move quickly from one passage to the next, reading the Scripture and then the phrase. Pace your presentation to ensure the non-Christian can understand but that you do not get so involved in details you lose sight of your witnessing purpose.

e. When you have completed the last Scripture (Ro 10:13), ask, "Does this make sense to you?" Clarify any passages or points which remain unclear.

f. Ask, "Have you experienced the full and meaningful life available through faith in Jesus Christ?" If the person says yes, ask them to share their testimony with you. If they say no or are not sure, ask, "Will you ever consider asking Jesus Christ to come into your life and give you life?" If they agree or do not reply, continue by saying, "Let me share with you what you can do now to receive Jesus into your life."

g. Say, "Let's read again the last Scripture." Read together Ro 10:13. Explain, this simply means that if you pray for Jesus to come into your life, He will come in at this very moment.

h. Turn to the last page of the New Testament and read the question you have written at the top of the page: Are you ready to receive God's free gift? Say, "If you are ready to receive God's free gift, you need to call on Him in prayer. You may pray your own prayer, or you may pray the prayer written here." Read the prayer you have written on the page. Ask, "Will you pray this prayer aloud after me and ask Jesus to come into your life and take control?" Lead the person to pray the prayer.

Say, "Do you understand what you have done? Did you ask Jesus to forgive your sins? Did you ask Him to save you? Did you give Jesus control of your life?" When the person answers the questions affirmatively, shake hands warmly and say with genuine enthusiasm and love, "Welcome to God's family." See p. 1747. Pray a prayer of thanksgiving with the new Christian.

4. How to Help the New Christian

After praying together with the new Christian, you will want to introduce the first steps in Christian discipleship. Do that immediately, if appropriate, or arrange a time to do it. Use your *Disciple's Study Bible* in this discussion. Underline the following verses in your study Bible. You will want to discuss and give directions in four areas:

a. God wants Christians to have assurance of salvation. Read the following Scriptures and make the points indicated. You may want to review Scripture and notes on SALVATION, Sanctification, and SALVATION, Eternal Life.

Say, "You now have eternal life because you were born again (Jn 3:3; 2 Co 5:17), committed yourself to God (Ro 10:13), and claimed God's promises (1 Jn 5:11-13; Jn 5:24)." Remember you have not and can never do anything to earn eternal life. It is God's everlasting gift to you (Eph 2:8-9).

b. You want to give evidence that you have given Jesus control of your life. You will want to prepare to discuss this by reading Scripture and notes on ORDINANCES, Baptism as Confession; CHURCH, Local Body; and CHURCH, Fellowship. Say, "God wants new Christians to confess Him publicly and follow Him in baptism and church membership. The first Christians who received God's word were baptized and added to the church (Ac 2:41-47). Let me introduce you to my church. I think you would like to show your new commitment to God by joining our fellowship. There you can be baptized."

c. God wants new Christians to grow into strong, faithful disciples. To discuss this you will want to read Scripture and notes on DISCIPLESHIP, Lordship of Christ, and DISCIPLESHIP, Nature. Say, "Let's read 1 Pe 2:2 together. Here we see that Christian growth results from:

• Food—God's Word, the Bible, provides spiritual food. To gain spiritual strength and nourishment, you will want to read it, study it, memorize it, practice it, and hear it taught and preached. You will want to get your own copy of a good study Bible to help you in your study. I would like to recommend the study Bible I use designed especially for growth in discipleship.

• Breath—Spiritual breath is prayer. As a new-born child of God, you will want to spend time every day talking to God about your life, your needs, your problems, your dreams, your decisions, and your love for Him. You will want to know God's prayer promise. Let's read Mt 21:22.

• Exercise—Spiritual exercise is helping others, witnessing, and giving time and energy to do God's work. As you exercise spiritually, you become a living testimony to the world. Look at Ro 12:1-2 with me.

• Rest—Spiritual rest comes in congregational worship and individual meditation with God. These give you time to be aware of God's presence with you. Spiritual rest provides inner renewal and strength.

d. God wants disciples to experience victory in our lives. Read 1 Jn 5:4 with me. You will want to remember some things as you look for God's victory in your life:

• Life is a series of battles. You may think you are losing some battles, but you can be absolutely confident of victory. Read 1 Jn 4:4 with me.

• Assured victory does not prevent failure. You are still human and will fail at times. Do not quit because you fail. Ask God to help you fight. Look at Eph 6:10-18.

• God has provided a means by which you can be cleansed of daily sins. Admit sins to Him and ask forgiveness. Let's read 1 Jn 1:9. Make a practice of closing each day with God and gaining His forgiveness and renewal for the next day."

Guide to Leading to Commitment

Your witnessing ministry involves giving your personal testimony and using the New Testament to present the plan of salvation. (See preceding articles.) A presentation of the gospel is incomplete unless hearers are challenged to accept the Christ of the gospel. You need to learn to make a deliberate effort to lead lost people to accept Christ as Savior and Lord. Jesus gave this kind of invitation to individuals (Mt 4:19; 9:9; Jn 1:45-49). Christ's good news offers salvation, forgiveness of sin, and eternal fellowship with God. Everyone who hears such an offer must decide to accept or reject it. You can encourage people to accept it. If a lost person is not helped to understand how to accept Christ and encouraged to say yes, he then virtually has been helped to say no. God intends for Christians to carry the gospel and an invitation to the world—not wait for the world to come to a church building. Sharing the gospel and failing to provide an opportunity for commitment frustrates those who hear the gospel. It can deepen them in their habit of delaying this important decision and result in final rejection.

Humans naturally move slow spiritually. We need encouragement to respond to the offer of the gospel (2 Co 5:11). A favorable impression made by the gospel may die quickly if lost persons do not act on deep impulses which they feel. We encourage a great tragedy when we let a person remain uncommitted or lost when our appeal for a decision to accept Christ would lead to a decision.

The following suggestions may be helpful as you lead people to commit their lives to Jesus Christ:

1. Know exactly what you are going to say. Both you and the lost person feel tense as a decision with eternal significance is made. The lost person needs clear instructions showing exactly what needs to be done. You want to be precise as you outline how to accept Christ as Savior. Clarity helps eliminate tension.

2. Give your testimony briefly, and present the plan of salvation with a marked New Testament. Be sure the person hears gospel content and personal affirmation from you before being asked to make a decision. (See the preceding articles in this study Bible.)

3. Ask leading questions to ensure the lost person understands the gospel offer of salvation. Ask questions like, "Does what we have talked about make sense to you? Do you have any questions about how God has shown His love for you?" These questions lead the listener to make a definite response to your presentation. If the person has no questions, move to point 4 below. If the person has questions, deal with them honestly. See the "Guide to Dealing with Objections and Questions" (pp. 1792–1794).

4. Ask, "Is there any reason you would not be willing to receive God's free gift of salvation?" This is a negative commitment question. It deals with the lost person's willingness to receive God's offer of salvation. This question speaks to a person at the point of will. Again, if the lost person has any questions or excuses at this point, deal with them honestly, openly, and positively.

5. Ask, "Are you willing to turn from your sins and place your faith in Christ right now?" If the lost person says yes, clarify the three things the person needs to do:
   a. Repent of personal sin.
   b. Place faith in Jesus.
   c. Make Jesus Lord of the rest of life.

6. Ask, "Do you want to repent, place your faith in Jesus, and make Him Lord of your life?" If the person agrees, say, "Let's pray together."

   a. You pray a prayer for understanding such as, "Father, I pray that your Holy Spirit will draw Bob to you. Help him turn from his sin and give him faith to believe in Jesus for salvation. Amen."

   b. Ask the person to pray a prayer of commitment such as you have marked on the last page of your New Testament, or let the person express his or her own thoughts. Invite prayer by saying, "If you truly want the Lord to give you eternal life, tell Him out loud."

7. Welcome the person into God's family warmly and enthusiastically. Say, "Welcome to God's family. You have just made the most important decision of your life. You can now be

sure you have salvation and eternal life. I am sure you would like to join me in thanking God for saving you." Say something like, "Father, I thank you for hearing Bob's prayer and saving him. I pray that the Holy Spirit will give him assurance that his sin is forgiven and that he has eternal life. In Jesus' name I pray. Amen."

8. Commit yourself to help the Christian grow. See the previous section, "How to Help the New Christian," (p. 1790.)

9. Be prepared to deal with a negative response. You are responsible for witness. The Holy Spirit convicts of sin and leads to salvation. Some people will not respond even to the Spirit's conviction. You can work as the Spirit leads you to deal with people who refuse to accept God's free gift. Review Scripture and notes on HOLY SPIRIT, Convicts.

A lost person's "no" may be a confused invitation for more information or another invitation. Such a situation calls for sensitivity to God's Spirit and to the person's feelings. Relate Christ's salvation directly to the situation of the person's life. Show that God's love can overcome any obstacle in a person's life. No one would decide if we waited until the perfect moment. We can trust God to accept us as we are and to give strength to solve problems and conflicts.

A witness should never insult, question the integrity of, or emotionally wear down the person to whom you are witnessing. The lost person must make the decision. You cannot. Do not fail to show love for the person and ask for a decision as long as the Holy Spirit is leading you.

When you are convinced the lost person has decided not to accept Christ, you may follow these steps:

a. Have a list of people for whom you are praying. Take the list from your Bible, turn to the page you have written it in your Bible, or take it from your notebook. Say, "I believe the time will soon come when you will want to become a Christian. I want you to know I really care for you. I promise that I will pray every day that God will help you make this great decision for Him."

b. Leave a gospel tract with the person, or give the person a marked New Testament. Encourage the person to read the tract or review the plan of salvation in the Testament. Remind the person that one can accept Christ at any time and in any place. Say, "If you do accept Christ, will you please give me a call just as soon as possible. I want to rejoice with you. My name, address, and phone number are here on this tract (New Testament). Let me know any time I can help you." Make a specific date to eat together, go to a social event, or, especially, go to church together.

c. Close the visit in prayer. Thank God for the opportunity to meet this person, for the time you spent together, and for the good things you know about the person. Leave the person in an amiable mood. Express appreciation for the time spent together.

Guide to Dealing with Questions and Objections

Dealing with objections and questions is an important part of the witnessing process. This is why a witness must have a knowledge background founded in Bible doctrine as well as practical skills. Daily study of the Scriptures and notes in the *Disciple's Study Bible* will prepare you to meet questions and objections as you witness. As you witness, you will inevitably face questions. The following comments may help you deal with them honestly and openly.

1. Trust the Holy Spirit. He empowers the witnessing experience and will use your knowledge and skills to help the other person.

2. Avoid unnecessary questions. Some objections and questions can be answered before they are openly stated. A concise, clear presentation of your testimony and the plan of salvation will answer many questions. See previous article, "Guide to Leading to Commitment," (pp. 1791–1792). If a person interrupts your presentation, you may simply say, "That is a good (or important) question. I think we will deal with it from God's Word as we get further into our discussion." You may want to rearrange your discussion to deal with the issue as smoothly and as quickly as possible. Be sure you deal with the question. Do not leave yourself open to the charge of manipulation or falsehood.

3. Maintain a proper spirit and attitude. Some questions and objections are really reac-

tions against the spirit and attitude of the person trying to witness. Your attitude of love and personal interest can avoid such questions.

4. Negotiate rather than argue. You are not trying to win an argument. You do not want a win/lose outcome. You seek to negotiate a win/win situation. Deal with questions so that you and the lost person are both satisfied with the solution reached.

5. Avoid emotional confrontation. People often become emotional when the conversation turns to personal faith in Christ. Do not fear emotional reactions. Share your emotional feelings. Accept the other person's. Keep your control no matter how the other person reacts. Make every effort to calm the situation and maintain a friendly relationship with the person. Be an example of what the other person would like to be. Show the strength of Christian love.

6. Accept the other person as an equal. Lost persons often think church people are "goody-goody" or self-righteous. Lost people may expect you to look down on them and condemn them. Lost persons tend to feel insecure about their spiritual well-being and sensitive to the attitude of the disciple witnessing for Christ. Treat the lost person as you want to be treated, as a brother or sister created by God.

7. Exercise gentleness. Avoid negative reactions to your forcefulness. If the lost person feels forced to do something, the reaction will be marked by resentment and bitterness. Gentleness and respect avoid such negative reactions.

8. Check your motivation. Motivation often determines attitude and approach to others. Love is the only motive that will adequately express Christ's mind. Seek solutions that communicate love for people.

9. Change objections to questions. Affirm the person for the thought, honesty, and courage reflected by raising the objection. Admit that you may never agree on the solution to the objection. Use the objection to raise a question on which you can agree. Say, "We might argue over that for the next fifty years, but let's assume the answer is this. If that is true, then what do you think that means for the subject we were discussing?" Let the person answer the question you want to raise related to your presentation of the plan of salvation. Always steer the discussion back to your presentation. Help the person see that misconceptions about the Bible, God, and salvation are not true and are not what you believe. Emphasize what we know for sure, not what we must speculate about.

10. Know the following frequently-raised questions and objections. Learn how to deal with them through use of Scripture as illustrated. Write your own response to these problems.

a. I do not know enough to become a Christian. God does not expect us to know everything about being a Christian. A few basic truths must be known before a person becomes a Christian. These are presented in the personal testimony and plan of salvation. They are easily understood and accepted by faith. Salvation is not a matter of education but a matter of willingness to acknowledge and confess sin and to repent and commit oneself to Jesus Christ. Review with this person the simple steps involved in salvation and call for action based on this knowledge. Read Scripture and notes on SALVATION, Grace, and SALVATION, Knowledge of God. Read Jn 8:32; 1 Co 8:1,11; 13:2,8; Eph 2:8-9.

b. I do not feel like it; I do not have any feeling. Many use this excuse because they equate spiritual conviction and salvation with an emotional feeling they have seen someone else demonstrate or heard someone describe in a testimony. Read Jn 16:8. "Convict" means that the Holy Spirit will help one understand about sin, righteousness, and judgment. Knowledge of personal sin demonstrates a person has been convicted by the Spirit and needs to come to Christ for salvation. Feelings fluctuate from day to day and are experienced differently by different people. Feeling does not constitute truth. Faith in Jesus Christ and repentance of sin are the essentials for salvation. These can be experienced under many emotional states. Read Scripture and notes on HOLY SPIRIT, Convicts, and HOLY SPIRIT, Resisted.

c. I had too much religion as a child. Many children are forced to do things they do not want to do. What they are compelled to do may be right and helpful. Parents tell children to go to bed, eat meals, take baths, go to school, etc. Children resent these things. When we become adults, we continue to do them because they prove beneficial. Those who had a bad experience as children should not let that prevent their experiencing the joy and freedom found in Jesus Christ. Read Pr 22:6; 2 Ti 3:15; Eph 6:1-4. Review Scripture and notes on FAMILY, Education.

d. I am not ready—not now; I have plenty of time. Even if people could be sure of salvation at a future time, they and those around them would be forever poorer for having waited. They would miss so much time of joy in God's salvation. Ask such a person, "What would it take for you to get ready? What real reason do you have not to accept Jesus as Lord and Savior now? What do you expect to have that is better than salvation in Christ?" Delay is always dangerous. Not to be saved now is disobedience to God's call (2 Co 6:2). It leads to hardened hearts (Heb 4:7). You have no guarantee of tomorrow (Pr 27:1; Jas 4:13-15). Read Scripture and notes on SIN, Unbelief; SIN, Alienation; EVANGELISM, Call to Salvation.

e. I have always been a Christian. Physical birth into the most religious family is not a substitute for spiritual birth (Jn 3:1-16). Actions and rites by other people cannot make you a Christian. You have sinned (Ro 3:23) and deserve death (Ro 6:23). You must deal with your sin problem before God personally. Becoming a Christian involves receiving Jesus Christ by a direct act of the will (Jn 1:12-13). No one else can exercise faith for you. Ask the person, "When have you personally exercised faith, repented of sin, and committed your life to Jesus as Lord?" Review the plan of salvation with the person. For yourself, review Scripture and notes on Sin, Individual Choice; SALVATION, Acceptance; and FAMILY, Environment.

As long as disciples witness to the lost, we will be confronted with excuses. Witnessing is much more than answering questions. Excuse answering must always be secondary to sharing God's love with others. Use objections and questions as opportunities to introduce another invitation to a person to become a disciple of Jesus Christ.

Ministries in Discipleship

Disciplines lead to ministry, to using the spiritual strength and insight gained from discipline to nourish and help other people in Christ's name. The following guides should assist you to find your place of ministry as Christ's disciple and to exercise that ministry in competence and love. To gain the necessary knowledge base for practical ministry, you will want to review "Life in Christ: The Disciple's Cross" (pp. 1748–1751) and a selection of subjects under the doctrine of DISCIPLESHIP.

KNOWING AND EXPERIENCING THE WILL OF GOD

To *know* God's will and to *experience* Him working in and through our lives to carry out His will is the desire of every Christian's heart! This desire to know God's will is present in each of us because when God saves us He works in us to cause us to *want* to do His will and to enable us to *do* His will (Php 2:13). Therefore, even in *wanting* to do His will, we are responding to His activity of love in our lives. A review of the Bible reveals how God helps us to know His will in very practical ways! Review Scripture and notes on PRAYER, Will of God, and GOD, Father.

From Genesis to Revelation we can see that God always takes the initiative to come to His people. Without Him, we would all go our own way (Ro 3:10-12) and lack understanding. God therefore takes the initiative and comes to us. God's desire is to reveal Himself and His activities or purposes. When we speak of doing God's will, we mean we know what He is doing or about to do and how He would accomplish His will through us. When we know what He is about to do where we are, we will then know how we must adjust our lives so He can accomplish His will through us. This was true of many Bible characters—Noah (Ge 6:9-14), Abram (Ge 12:1-4), and Moses (Ex 3:7-10). With *all* those God used in the Old Testament, the pattern was the same. (1) He came to them; (2) He revealed His planned activity; (3) They believed Him and adjusted their lives to Him; (4) They obeyed Him; and (5) They experienced God doing His will through them. This was also true of the disciples (Mk 1:16-18, Jn 15:16), Paul (Ac 26:13-19) and all those He used in the New Testament. It is just as true today in each of our lives! Since Jesus is our pattern, it is instructive to remember that even He did not take His own initiative, but responded to the Father's activity. The Father loved the Son and showed Him all He was doing (Jn 5:17,20), so Jesus could know the Father's will and experience the Father accomplishing His will through Him (Jn 14:9-11). He saw where the Father was working and joined Him.

Every time God revealed His purposes and plans (His will) to a person, that revelation was at the same time His invitation to adjust their life to Him. They learned what they were to do. Such an invitation brought about a major adjustment of their lives with God. Look again at the lives of Noah, Abraham, Moses, the prophets, the disciples, and others in the Bible. None of these could remain where they were and go with God at the same time. Their lives could never again be "business as usual!" To know what God was going to do and to be a part of His activity always meant adjustment and change. Adjustment, however, made them available to God with a readiness for God to do His work, and accomplish His purposes through them.

Following the 'adjustment to God,' obedience to what God said next was crucial. To obey, led to experiencing God at work through them, accomplishing His will just as He has revealed to them. It is in the doing of His revealed will we know (experience) Him and His will unfolding through us (Mt 7:21-29; Jn 7:17; 8:29-32). This activity of God that follows our obedience brings clear affirmation in our lives that we are doing His will.

Thus, living as a Christian is living in relationship with a Person—hearing Him, obeying Him, and following Him. To know God's will, it is important to know when He is speaking. If we do not know when God is speaking to us, we are in trouble at the heart of the Christian life.

How will we know, then, when God is speaking to us? God spoke in many ways and in many times and places (Heb 1:1). The key was not how He spoke, but: 1. *that* He spoke, 2. that they *knew* it was God, and 3. that they knew *clearly* and specifically what He said.

Those to whom He spoke would then bear witness to what God said, and the activity of God that followed was the evidence it was God who spoke. When God "spoke," He *always* guaranteed that He Himself would bring what He said to pass (1 Ki 8:56; Isa 46:11*b*).

God "speaks" as the Holy Spirit guides. He (a) teaches all things (Jn 14:26); (b) brings all things to our remembrance (Jn 16:13); (c) glorifies Christ—receiving from Christ and revealing to us (Jn 16:14). Without the Holy Spirit helping us, we will not seek God or understand anything from God (Ro 3:10-11; 1 Co 2:9-16). He enables us to know the mind of Christ (1 Co 2:16) and know all things that are freely given to us of God (1 Co 2:14). Without Him, we cannot know or understand (1 Co 2:14). The "sword" the Spirit uses is the Word of God (Eph 6:17).

The Holy Spirit is our infallible Guide. When He guides us (speaks to us), we know what God is saying and doing and how He would have us adjust our lives to Him so He can accomplish His will through us. How does the Holy Spirit speak to us? The Holy Spirit speaks to us through:

1. *The Bible*—He is the Author. While we read and study it, He is present to open our understanding and reveal truth (God's activity) to us (Jn 16:13). When truth becomes clear to us, this does not lead us to God. This *is* the encounter with God, for He alone can reveal truth. Truth is not "discovered." It is *revealed*, as in the Old Testament and Gospels. We then must adjust our lives to Him as He is revealing Himself to us and obey Him in all areas of our lives.

2. *Prayer*—As we pray, the Holy Spirit is present to guide us, so we can *know* the will of God (Ro 8:26-27). He will again use the Word of God as we pray, thus confirming further, in addition to the Bible, His will. Only the Holy Spirit can reveal God's will through God's Word as we pray! This does not *lead* to an encounter with God. It *is* the encounter. He is the only One who can let us meet and hear God. When such an encounter occurs, it is His activity, not ours.

3. *Circumstances*—In the midst of our lives, the Holy Spirit of God is present to guide us and help us understand the mind of God (Ro 8:14-17). Again He uses the Word of God in circumstances to reveal the activity of God, so we can adjust our lives and responses to Him. A caution: if we stand in our circumstances and look through them to God, we will get a distorted picture of God. But if we go alone with God and look at our circumstances with God and from His perspective, we see as He does and now know how to respond to Him in our circumstances.

4. *The Church*—The Holy Spirit works through each of the members of the church family, who together are a living body of Christ, to give each of us a full perspective on the mind of God (Eph 4:1-16; 1 Co 12). "To each one the manifestation of the Spirit is given for the common good" (1 Co 12:7). God stands in the midst of His people to provide the resources we need to know His mind, His heart, and His will.

When the Holy Spirit is consistently revealing the *same* thing through the Bible, prayer, circumstances, and the church, we can proceed with confidence to do what He is "saying", assured that He *has* revealed to us the will of God. For the Holy Spirit is the only One who can do this. When this occurs, it is His activity, and we can proceed confident by knowing that He has spoken to us.

The will of God is God coming to us in His Word, in prayer, in circumstances, and in His church, revealing what He is doing and purposing, so we can adjust our lives to Him, so He can do His will through us. When we obey Him, we experience Him working in us, around us, and through us.

GUIDE TO DISCOVERING YOUR SPIRITUAL GIFTS

Ministering as a disciple calls for us to know the will of God and to know our own interests, resources, and skills. See "Personal Spiritual Inventory" (pp. 1751–1753). Such knowledge can be helped by human tests and analyses, but it is basically a spiritual knowledge revealed by God, the Creator and Giver of personal skills. As you read this article, you will want to study Scripture and notes on HOLY SPIRIT, Gifts; HUMANITY, Image of God; HUMANITY, Potentiality.

1. Five Basic Principles about Spiritual Gifts

a. Every child of God has a spiritual gift or gifts (1 Co 12:7, Eph 4:7-8). Each Christian has been given some manifestation of the Spirit. In God's family of grace no one is left out. Everyone is important. Each has been gifted to accomplish some necessary ministry. If you look down on yourself as being unable to do anything significant for the Lord, you are not being humble. Instead, you are undiscerning and perhaps ungrateful. Therefore, a Christian should never say, "I'm a nobody." Instead, you should say, "I am a child of God. I have received spiritual gifts; therefore I will exercise my gifts in ministry."

b. The gifts of the Spirit are varied and different. Just as many notes are needed to make harmony and many colors to make a painting, so many gifts are essential for the functioning of the body of Christ. Paul put it, "Now the body is not made up of one part but of many" (1 Co 12:14).

More than once Paul used the analogy of the human body with its many members—eyes, ears, hands, feet, to illustrate the varied gifts in the church. "Now you are the body of Christ, and each one of you is a part of it" (1 Co 12:27). The gifts God has given to us determine where we are placed in the body of Christ.

c. The Holy Spirit determines who gets what gifts. We do not choose what gifts we have. The sovereign Holy Spirit assigns to every believer individually as He wills (1 Co 12:11; Eph 4:7). "God has arranged the parts in the body (the church), every one of them, just as he wanted them to be" (1 Co 12:18). Therefore, no one should boast about having certain spiritual gifts. The gifts of the Spirit are just that—gifts. Because we do not earn them or work for them or merit them, we have no grounds for bragging about our gifts.

d. Spiritual gifts are given to individuals to be used for the good of all members of the body. Spiritual gifts are given us to build up one another and to enable us to serve and glorify Christ together. The eye needs the ear; the head needs the foot. If all were hands, how would we walk? Each part or the body is needed to serve the whole. The exercise of our gift(s) is needed to strengthen other saints. We, in turn, will be helped toward maturity through the gifts of others.

Gifts are for the common good, not individual glory (1 Co 12:7). These spiritual gifts are for the benefit of others, for the building up of the church.

e. God wants every disciple to know what his or her spiritual gift(s) is and to use it in ministry. Paul said, "Now about spiritual gifts, brothers, I do not want you to be ignorant" (1 Co 12:1). This being so, it is our responsibility to discover and develop our gifts. None of us is excused. God says we are to know what our gifts are and to put them to use.

The parable of the talents (Mt 25:14-30) uses financial investments as an illustration and teaches that we shall be held responsible for all our gifts. In the day of judgment we will not be praised for our wealth, our possessions, or our fame. We will be praised if we can properly respond to the question, "Did you faithfully use the gifts I gave you?"

Therefore, "Each one should use whatever gift he has received to serve others, faithfully administering God's grace in its various forms" (1 Pe 4:10).

2. Spiritual Gifts Defined

People today often speak of certain individuals as having "charisma" or as being "charismatic." By this they mean that a person has a certain charm, magnetism, or exceptional personality.

Actually, the word *charismatic* comes from the Greek word *charis*, translated *grace* in the New Testament. See Scripture and notes on GOD, Grace. The term "gifts" in 1 Co 12:4 is the Greek word *charisma*, which literally means "gifts of grace." Therefore, we can see that spiritual gifts are rooted in the grace of God. Grace is that which God has done for us in Christ but which we do not deserve. This is true in regard to the matter of our salvation. It is also true when it comes to our spiritual gifts.

A spiritual gift has been described as a special qualification granted by the Spirit to every believer to empower him or her to serve within the framework of the body of Christ. A spiritual gift is a divinely ordained spiritual ability through which Christ enables His church to carry out its task on earth. A short, simple definition might be: A spiritual gift is a Spirit-given ability for Christian service.

3. What spiritual gifts are not

a. Spiritual gifts are not natural talents. Non-Christians have talents, but only Christians have spiritual gifts. Talents have to do with techniques and methods; gifts have to do with spiritual abilities. Talents depend on natural instincts; gifts on spiritual endowment. Talents inspire, or entertain on a natural level; gifts relate to the building up of the church. Something supernatural happens in the one who is ministering when a gift is being exercised. The differences appear in the following chart:

	Talent	Gift
Source	Common grace of Spirit	Special grace of Spirit
Time Given	Present from natural birth	Present from spiritual birth
Nature	Natural ability	Spiritual endowment
Purpose	Instruction, entertainment, inspiration on a natural level	Spiritual growth of believers; Christian service.

Talents are just as much God-given as are spiritual gifts. Nevertheless, we must not forget that they are not the same. A Christian may have good musical ability. If so, this should be recognized as a divinely imparted talent. A disciple should develop that talent to the fullest extent possible. At the same time, we should realize that musical ability is not a spiritual gift. It is highly probable that this person may have the gift of encouragement or evangelism which may be exercised through the medium of music.

b. Spiritual gifts are not offices. The New Testament mentions many offices—apostle, prophet, pastor, teacher, evangelist, and deacon. See Scripture and notes on CHURCH LEADERS. These offices belong to the church to provide organized leadership. Gifts relate to the endowments given the person by the Spirit, empowering the person to serve in the office. The offices and gifts to serve in offices are Christ's gifts to the church to equip the gifted saints (Eph 4:11-12).

Hopefully, a person holding a particular office has a spiritual gift pertaining to that office; otherwise the office would be in name only. A divinely-appointed prophet would have the gift of prophecy, a teacher the gift of teaching, an evangelist the gift of evangelism. However, a person could have a spiritual gift belonging to an office without having that office. A believer could have the spiritual gift of teaching without having the office of teacher. A person could have the gift of evangelism without being an official evangelist. A believer should not hold a divinely-appointed office without possessing the corresponding gift.

c. Spiritual gifts are not the same as the fruit of the Spirit. The gifts of the Spirit differ from the fruit of the Spirit in many ways:

Gifts	**Fruit**
Have to do with service	Have to do with character (Gal 5:22-23)
Are the means to an end	Is the end
What a person has	What a person is
Given from without	Produced from within
All gifts not possessed by every believer	Every variety of fruit should be in every believer

Possession of gifts does not indicate the goodness of a person's life. Samson continued to perform feats long after he was out of touch with God. Judas, likely one of the 70 who cast out demons, became a betrayer. Though the Corinthians excelled in gifts, their church was riddled with problems including divisions, fornication, and drunkenness at the Lord's Supper. It is possible for a church to have a great abundance of gifts, yet at the same time to be full of envy, carnality, and discord.

Because it is better to be godly than gifted, Paul positioned his love chapter (1 Co 13) right in the middle of his long section dealing with spiritual gifts (chs 12—14). Without love, the gifts of the Spirit are but sounding brass, tinkling cymbal, profitless, nothing (1 Co 13:1-3).

d. Spiritual gifts are not the same as roles all Christians are to perform. Many spiritual gifts operate in the area of clear-cut commands. For example, every Christian is commanded to be liberal in giving. Because a believer does not have the gift of contributing is not reason to say, "I don't need to tithe, nor even give, for I do not have that gift." All believers are instructed by the New Testament to support the Lord's work financially. Though some may be given a special ability to donate generously to the Lord's work, all are to share.

All are commanded to witness. Because a believer does not possess the gift of evangelism is no excuse for failure to spread the good news that Jesus saves. Though not all have a spiritual gift in the area of evangelism, the Lord Jesus has commissioned every one of His followers to be a witness for Him.

Commands cover almost every area of gifts. In fact, it is as we do service by obedience to commands that we begin to discover special abilities in certain areas. Moreover, it is our responsibility both to discover and develop whatever our gifts may be. Even if we do not have a divine ability in a particular area, we are still obligated to obey commands as we experience God's leading.

4. What spiritual gifts are.

Now that we have examined what spiritual gifts are not, we shall consider by way of a broad overview what the gifts of the Spirit are. In three different chapters and in three separate letters Paul listed spiritual gifts.

Romans 12:3-8	1 Cor 12:8-10, 28-30		Ephesians 4:11
Prophesying	Wisdom	Tongues	Apostleship
Serving	Knowledge	Interpretation	Prophecy
Teaching	Faith	Apostleship	Evangelism
Encouraging	Healing	Teaching	Pastoring-Teaching
Contribution	Miraculous Powers	Serving	
Leadership	Prophecy	Administration	
Showing Mercy	Distinguishing Spirits		

The different lists indicate that perhaps no list is exhaustive. Perhaps there are other gifts not listed that are given for particular times. With the coming of the Holy Spirit, the body of Christ—the church—has been given abilities and ministries to show others a continuing expression of Christ's love for people. These abilities and ministries are called spiritual gifts. These are the avenues through which God has chosen to express His life and love today. Such gifts are given to every Christian by the Holy Spirit.

The apostle Paul likened the functioning of spiritual gifts to the functioning of the various organs of our physical bodies. Just as all body organs are not alike, neither are all spiritual gifts alike. Nevertheless, the various organs are necessary for a body to be healthy and growing. Spiritual gifts are necessary for the body of Christ to continue to show the world Christ's love and life. The contemporary application happens best when Christians discover, develop, and exercise spiritual gifts.

The spiritual gifts that God has given His children are instruments to reveal God's love. When discovered and put to use, these gifts are effective in showing the nature of our loving Heavenly Father. Unfortunately, many Christians are not exercising their spiritual gifts. As a result, God's grace and love remain unknown and unclaimed by a lost world.

5. How to know your gift.

As a disciple you want to "unwrap" your gift and to begin putting it to use for God's glory. Here are six ways by which you can know what your gifts are:

a. Believe you are gifted. You must not view spiritual gifts as special rewards for the spiritual elite. Spiritual gifts are given to every believer.

b. Pray. "You do not have, because you do not ask God" (Jas 4:2*b*). Ask God to show you what spiritual gifts He has given you.

c. Become aware of the gifts available to you. Study the Bible passages listed above, and be sensitive as you see these gifts becoming operative in your life.

d. Accept responsibility. Many commands in the New Testament operate in the area of spiritual gifts. Everyone, gifted in the area or not, is commanded to evangelize, show mercy, encourage, give, and help. As we begin to obey in these and other areas, the Holy Spirit unveils certain gifts.

e. Consider your desires. What do you enjoy doing? To what are you drawn? What seems to come "naturally" to you? Desire for a gift may well be God's way of showing you that you possess that gift.

f. Accept the confirmation of others. What do others say about you? In what areas do people look up to you? What have you done in the past for which you were genuinely complimented. As we are doing Christian service in obedience to the commands of Christ, others may see a gift in us long before we are aware of it. Therefore, it is imperative for those of us who discern a gift in a fellow believer to encourage that person in the development of that gift.

Many Christians live in spiritual poverty, unaware of the potential that God has given them. They are unaware of the gifts of the Holy Spirit that they have. Their gifts lie like unwrapped presents, unused and neglected. Their potential for Christian ministry is squandered. The needs of our world are too great for us to allow any spiritual gift to be wasted. Unwrap your gifts and dedicate them and yourselves to the ministries God has given you.

MINISTRY OF WORSHIP AND INTERCESSION

Worship is more than an individual discipline in which a disciple praises and gives thanks to God in solitude. See "Discipline of Worship," (pp. 1753–1761). Worship is a corporate ministry of the church in which the body of Christ joins in praise, thanksgiving, intercession, and proclamation. Corporate worship affords an opportunity for the gathered church to witness to and fellowship with unbelievers who come searching for truth, fellowship, and salvation. Review Scripture and notes on WORSHIP.

Guide to Intercession

Intercession is the ministry of the disciple and/or the community of faith in bringing the needs of the church and the world to God. This ministry can be done by any disciple willing to learn how and to devote time to it. It can result in changed lives, changed churches, and a changed world. Read Scripture and notes on PRAYER, Intercession.

A. Begin a ministry of intercession by following these suggestions:

1. Make intercession first priority in your ministry. Use daily quiet time, group Bible study prayer time, congregational worship, and other times of prayer as opportunities for intercession. Direct as much of your prayer time as possible outward rather than inward.

2. Use all phases of prayer in your intercessions (1 Ti 2:1). Combine requests, prayers of praise, intercession, and thanksgiving as you seek to bring needs before God. Request God to act in a specific way to meet the needs. Praise Him because His character and nature lead Him to meet human needs. Boldly state the problems of other people as the central concern of your prayers. Thank God for hearing your intercessions, for blessing the people for whom you pray, and for giving answers not yet received or understood.

3. Intercede for all people. Intercession is not confined to concerns of a select circle of disciples or friends. Intercession encompasses all people. People in authority making important decisions especially need our intercessory prayers even though we may not know them personally and they may not be believers (1 Ti 2:2). Unbelievers should top our intercession list. God wants all persons to be saved, and so should we. Pray for them (1 Ti 2:4).

4. Intercede with an all-embracing purpose. Intercession is not limited to specific life needs and crises. Intercession should seek salvation, peace, godliness, quiet, and holiness for all people (1 Ti 2:2). God's life-style for the world should be the subject of much of our intercession.

5. Pray in unity with other disciples. Sin, anger, disputes separate us from others. Intercession unites us. We should never find reason not to pray with others. We should constantly seek opportunity to join in holy prayer together (1 Ti 2:8).

6. Pray on the basis of God's character. God is good (Ge 18:25), merciful (Ps 25:6), universal (2 Ki 19:19), and a Giver and Keeper of promises (Ex 32:13). Call on His powerful name for your concerns for others.

7. Stand before God in place of the person in need, ready to sacrifice yourself to have the need met as Moses (Ex 32:32), Paul (Ro 9:2-3), and Jesus have done (Mt 26:42; Jn 10:15).

8. Persevere until you prevail. Follow the example of Epaphras (Col 4:12), Christ's parable (Lk 11:5-10), and Abraham (Ge 18:22—19:13).

9. Remember the Lord Himself is your Partner in intercession. Jesus is at God's right hand interceding for us (Jn 17; Ro 8:34). The Holy Spirit groans our prayers to God when words cannot express our desires (Ro 8:26-27). Intercession is not a work you must accomplish alone. It is God's work in which He has made you a partner.

10. Remain confident, for the promise of intercession is sure (Mt 7:7; Jas 5:16).

B. Strengthen your ministry of intercession through these practical actions:

1. Keep a prayer notebook. Note the date you begin praying for a particular need and the date your prayer is answered. Then transfer the need from the intercession column to a thanksgiving column.

2. Join with a prayer partner in intercession. Two or three disciples praying for the same concern gain strength and courage from one another and share the promise of God's presence (Mt 18:19-20).

3. Dedicate a specific time each day to intercessory prayer. Establish a special time each month for a prolonged period of intercession.

4. Have a support group praying for your ministry of intercession. Let a Bible study group,

a woman's or men's group, or another circle of Christian friends know of your dedication to intercession. Ask them as they gather together to pray for you. Also ask them to share prayer concerns with you so the concerns may be included in your intercessory ministry.

5. Be alert to intercessory needs. Constantly add to your intercession list. Keep your notebook close at hand when you talk on the phone, attend church meetings, visit friends, call on hospital patients, or simply chat at work. Write down specific names with specific needs.

6. Pray in specific terms to God. Name names, dates, needs, and expectations. Say, O God, you know Jill Jamaca is concerned about her meeting with her boss this afternoon at 2 PM. She needs to get the promotion they have discussed. Give her peace of mind and strength of will as she talks with Mrs. Smithson. Give her the promotion and let her use the opportunity in greater ministry for you.

7. Pray in God's will. Know that intercession does not force God's hand. It combines your prayer strength with others to call God's presence to bear in a definite situation. Thank God for His actions in the situation even though they do not match your hopes and expectations.

8. Thank God daily for victories. Be ever more sensitive to what God is doing in response to prayer, and praise Him.

Guide to Family Worship

Your family is a major part of your ministry. A call to minister for God as His disciple does not call you to sacrifice your family. It calls you to minister to the circle of people closest to you. Family worship is a major form that ministry can take. As you prepare to strengthen your family's worship, you will want to read Scripture and notes on FAMILY, Bible Study.

To begin family worship or to strengthen it, you will want to answer the following questions:

1. Why should my family have family worship?

a. God commands it. Read Dt 6:6-9. God urged families to keep His commands constantly before them. One way to do this is through instruction in the home or family worship.

b. Experience proves it. Families through the centuries have testified that worship in their homes has strengthened and enriched their family life. Ask the strong Christian families you know the secret of their success. Note how many name family worship.

2. Who should lead family worship?

a. Successful family worship depends on a leader or sponsor who recognizes the value of this practice and is committed to maintaining it faithfully in spite of obstacles.

b. Almost any believing youth or adult could fill this role. The husband should usually accept this responsibility (Eph 6:4). Father's refusal should not prevent a family from participating in family worship.

c. The family member to whom God has revealed the need for worship should take the lead and seek to gain the rest of the family's commitment to worship.

d. The person who initiates and encourages family worship does not need to lead every session. All members of the family from youngest to oldest should be encouraged to take turns in leading the worship experience.

3. When should we hold family worship?

a. A fixed time for worship is as important for a family as it is for a congregation. This allows each busy family member to schedule worship and avoid conflicts.

b. The exact time will vary with different families. Early morning, mealtime, or late evening are all possible times.

c. Each family should find a time which meets its own routine. Having set a time, the family needs to ensure that each member is committed to reserving the time for worship.

d. Worship time need not be rigid and inflexible. Many families find they need to vary the time of worship periodically.

4. Where should we hold family worship?

a. A family needs a specific, regular spot for family worship.

b. The worship place should be where the family is least likely to be interrupted by telephone, television, or other distractions.

c. Resources for family worship should be placed in the selected place always ready for immediate use.

5. What resources do we need for family worship?

a. Resources vary with the needs and abilities of family members. A Bible for each family member is essential.

b. A family with small children will want to use at least part of family worship reading Bible stories from a children's Bible. The *Read-to-Me Bible* provides Bible stories carefully selected for children and told in language children can understand.

c. A family with teenagers will want to devote some family worship time to their concerns. Devotionals for teenagers are available in the *Encounter* Bible.

d. This *Disciple's Study Bible* represents an excellent resource for family worship. Choose a topic such as FAMILY. Read one passage and the notes on it each day. When you have completed one topic, read the summary on the topic together. Discuss together what your family can learn together to strengthen your family life. Let family members choose topics of interest.

e. Whatever resources you choose, center attention on the Bible. Do not let human resources become substitutes for Bible reading.

6. What should we do in family worship?

a. Begin with God's Word. Let someone read a passage aloud. Select the passage from the resources mentioned above or from a devotional magazine or book.

b. Read study Bible notes on the passage if you are using doctrines from the *Disciple's Study Bible* as your resource. Read the children's Bible story from *Read-to-Me*, the *Encounter Bible* devotional, or the devotional from the devotional resource you are using.

c. Encourage each family member to comment on what the Bible passage means or how it helps direct life.

d. Learn or review a memory verse together. See "Guide to Memorizing Scripture" (pp. 1780–1782).

e. Sing hymns together or listen to recorded religious music if you choose.

f. Share experiences and expectations of the day. Help one another recognize God's activity in your experiences. Let each member note prayer concerns.

g. Pray together, letting each person pray. Pray for specific family needs. Also thank God for His presence with, guidance of, and activity for your family. Emphasize prayers of praise and adoration. Your family may want to study Scripture and notes on PRAYER, Biblical Characters or PRAYER, Worship.

7. What can I expect in family worship?

a. Family worship is not easy. Interruptions, distractions, and disappointments are sure to come.

b. God rewards those families who faithfully honor Him in worship despite the obstacles.

c. Claim and be aware of God's promised presence (Mt 18:19-20).

d. Take time to reflect on personal growth and family strength which comes from family worship.

Guide to Worshiping Together as a Church

Worship with a church family brings multiplied blessings (Heb 10:25). External and internal pressures threatened to pull the early believers away from their church and their faith. Regular worship was God's answer to that danger. The first Christians gathered in large groups in the Temple and in small groups in private houses (Ac 2:42, 46). In spite of hardships, opposition, and lack of facilities, they made the effort to join in corporate worship.

The ultimate significance of corporate worship is meeting God in dynamic confrontation. Such a meeting results in enriched lives, wholesome attitudes, and dynamic ministries by the church and by individual worshipers. Encountering other disciples may help us. Meeting God changes us. Worship changes us from glory unto glory as God's Spirit works in us (2 Co 3:18).

To give new meaning and understanding to your worship, you will want to read Scripture and notes on WORSHIP, Importance, and WORSHIP, Corporate. You will want to worship with fellow disciples regularly, at least weekly. This is part of your corporate ministry. You may find your gift and calling in the area of planning and/or leading corporate worship. The following information and guidelines should help you as you minister in worship.

1. Worshiping together benefits individuals and the church. The Bible commands and gives models for corporate worship.

a. Worship unites our voices and lives in praise. Hearing others praise God encourages us to praise Him and gives more power to our praise. The praise of a united church forms a tremendous offering to the Lord. Praise directs attention from the helplessness of the human predicament to the One who is Lord over every circumstance.

b. United prayer has the guarantee of God's presence (Mt 18:19-20).

c. Congregational worship gives support to our prayers. Burdens shared in prayer seem to be spread through the group so no person bears the full brunt of life's hardships.

d. Worshiping together creates unity in God's family. The family feeling of God's people develops around united prayer.

e. Worshiping together feeds us. In public worship called and trained disciples minister to us, instructing us in God's Word and teaching us through hymns, prayers, and sermons. See "Guide to Hearing the Word," pp. 1805–1806.

f. Worshiping in the community of faith encourages God's people. Seeing and hearing about God's work in the lives of others encourages faith. The commitment of fellow worshipers empowers our commitment.

2. Barriers may prevent corporate worship.

a. Too much attention to the mechanics of a worship service will hinder worship. Worrying about how worship is or is not being done takes our attention away from God, the central focus of worship.

b. Too much predictability about a worship service breeds ritual and routine. Excitement and interest die when we can predict everything we will see or hear.

c. Too much showmanship and performance on the part of worship leaders draws attention to them more than to the Lord.

d. Rigidity about musical tastes and sermonic styles will hinder the worship experience of many. As you worship, do not demand every worship leader do things your way. Appreciate the individuality, creativity, and fresh challenge others bring to worship.

e. Individual differences and distractions form barriers to our worship. For worship to mean the most to us, we must become flexible and learn to concentrate on God rather than on human actions, achievements, or differences of taste. The benefits of worship certainly justify the effort to cross the barriers.

3. You can make the most of the opportunity to worship.

a. Be expectant. Approach every worship service with high expectations. You will not be able to anticipate the particular blessing that God will give, but you can expect to meet and commune with God. Worship potential increases if you hunger for the time with God.

b. Pay attention. Overcome barriers to worship by self-discipline. Follow the words of the hymn as the choir sings. Pay attention to the words you sing. Let people lead you in prayer as they pray publicly. Take notes on the sermon. Write what you feel God saying to you through the various activities of worship. Thank God for the opportunity to worship. Be an active participant in worship not a judge of other people's appearances and actions.

c. Help others worship. Worship as a corporate experience calls on you to focus concern on others rather than approach worship selfishly. Sing hymns enthusiastically and joyfully. Use your skills and gifts in worship when the opportunity arises. Sing, pray, testify, show love to others, share your financial resources. Pray for others to receive a blessing from the worship. Pray for God's powerful leadership for the worship leaders.

d. Express gratitude for the worship experience. Praise God for letting you worship and for being the kind of God you want to worship. Thank the worship leaders for helping you worship. Find specific details to mention in thanking others. Express appreciation to fellow disciples sitting near you in worship for their participation with you.

e. Commit yourself to detailed action resulting from the instruction and worship experience. Let worship be the springboard and power station leading you to renewed ministry and spiritual discipline.

f. Share your suggestions for creative, meaningful ways of worship with the worship planners of your church. Encourage them as they seek to overcome barriers to worship and provide challenging opportunities for public worship.

4. Learn to be a worship leader. Leading worship is a ministry to which God calls His people and for which He gives spiritual gifts and skills. He may provide opportunities for you to lead small or larger groups in worship. You will want to be prepared. Read Scripture and notes on WORSHIP, Service; WORSHIP, Pattern; and CHURCH LEADERS, Minister.

a. Worship leaders encourage fellowship between God and believers. They have the awesome responsibility of assisting disciples as we seek God. Worship leaders need to bring God and worshipers together and then step back to let the worship experience happen.

b. Congregations assist worship leaders by praying for them and by affording them the opportunities they need to develop skills in leading corporate worship.

c. To lead worship a person must be in fellowship with God and be worshiping God. You cannot lead a person to do effectively what you have not done and are not doing.

d. The first worship leaders were called apostles. Their successors occupied the position of elder, bishop, or pastor. See these under CHURCH LEADERS. Teaching Scripture was the chief ministry of these early leaders of the church. See EDUCATION, Pastors, and EDUCATION, Christians. The early church did not limit worship leading to professional ministers. Every Christian had opportunity to contribute to worship leadership. God continues to call people to lead in worship. Skills in drama, music, art, and many other areas can be used to direct God's people to adore Him. Any Christian may be used of God to lead others in worship.

5. Develop goals for worship. Participants and leaders of worship should know its goals. If you are a worship leader or planner, you should lead in developing specific goals for each worship service.

a. The objective of a worship leader is to inspire, enable, guide, and enrich the congregation in the experience of God's presence.

b. Promotion of church activities, acclaim and career advancement of gifted singers or speakers, and social fellowship among members are not the goals of worship.

c. Focusing on bringing disciples into fellowship with God will lead to other goals such as evangelism, nurturing of believers, and Christian fellowship being accomplished.

d. Focus on work the congregation should do outside the worship hour reverses priorities. Worship needs to precede work. Work by people who do not genuinely worship will usually be poorly motivated and poorly done.

e. Leading the lost to Christ should be the focus of some worship services. Such passion for the lost should be balanced by a passion for adoring God. Successful worship is not measured by the reaction of others but by the depth of the congregation's communication with God.

f. Certain services may major on Christian fellowship; however, worship leaders and worshipers must remember fellowship between believers is not worship. Worship is the fellowship of a believer with God.

6. Know the dynamics of worship.

a. Worship is initiated by God, centered on God, offered to God, and made acceptable by God. The worship leader must resist the temptation to become the center of attention. Likewise, worshipers must not use their dress, location, or activities to shift attention to themselves.

b. Preaching, teaching, praying, and singing are the major actions of worship. They are designed to lead us to God and give Him glory, not to impress other people.

c. Worship is more than intellectual stimulation. Worship experiences should minister to the whole person. Many activities stir emotions or stimulate the intellect. Worship is more. Worship involves a proper balance of intellect, emotions, and spiritual insight leading the worshiper to praise God with body, soul, and mind.

d. The congregation, worship leaders, and God all have special roles in worship. Humans are in supporting roles in worship. Attention is focused on God, who is the center of this fellowship of love.

e. Ultimately all worship takes place within individuals. Group worship provides benefits not available in the discipline of individual worship, but groups as such do not worship. Each individual comes before God in praise, petition, thanksgiving, intercession, and learning. Without individual relationship with God all worship practices are weak and meaningless.

f. God's freedom must be protected in worship. Who can fathom God's ways? God may want more to happen in worship than you can plan. Worship leaders and worshipers must remain sensitive to things that occur spontaneously in worship.

The most important commandment is to love God (Mk 12:30). This action involves worship and communication. If God is to be first in our loyalty and allegiance, worship must become a major priority of life. A ministry of worship is a high calling for one of God's disciples.

Guide to Hearing the Word

Hearing God's Word effectively is a major part of the ministry of worship. Whether one preaches the Word, teaches the Word, or hears another preach or teach it, every person in worship has the responsibility to hear God's Word. Still, we spend little time learning how to hear God's Word. Reading Scripture and notes on PROCLAMATION will prepare you to learn how to hear God's Word. The following guide will provide suggestions you can use to be a better listener as God speaks.

1. Prepare to hear God's Word.

a. On the basis of Mt 13:3-23 and Jas 1:22-25 evaluate what kind of a hearer you are.

- apathetic, hearing but not prepared to receive, understand, and obey the Word;
- superficial, receiving the Word temporarily but not letting it take root in the heart;
- preoccupied, receiving the Word but letting the worries of this world and desire for worldly things choke out the Word from personal application;
- reproducing hearer, receiving the Word, understanding it, bearing fruit, and bringing forth results.

b. Expect a Word from God. You will seldom receive what you do not expect. In worship, be alert to God rather than to people.

c. Find forgiveness for sin and pride in your heart so the Word may be planted there (Jas 1:21).

d. Prepare a "Hearing the Word" notebook to help you concentrate on God's Word and conserve the message of His Word for you. A sample page might look like the following but with space left to fill out each section.

Date ____________ Place ____________ Speaker ____________
Bible Text ____________ Message Title ____________
Message
1. Introduction ____________
2. Major points ____________
3. Illustration(s) ____________
4. Application ____________
5. Conclusion ____________

1. Main thing God wants me to do, be, or feel as result of hearing. ____________
2. How does my life measure up to this Word? ____________
3. What specific actions will I take to measure up? ____________
4. What questions are raised in my mind by this message? ____________
5. What doctrinal truth will I need to study further? ____________

e. Sit in a place where you can easily hear and will not be easily distracted.

2. Pray for the speaker and for yourself, asking God to speak to you and to others through the message.

3. Listen actively.

a. Encourage the speaker with your attention, facial expressions, and note taking.

b. Outline the message, using the form given or one you design.

c. List points the Spirit raises in your mind from reading the Bible text of the message and from hearing the message.

d. Write down how you will measure your response to the message? At what time will you check to see concrete actions have resulted?

4. Do God's Word. Check yourself several times in the days following the message to see if you have acted concretely on the message and begun to incorporate it in your life.

5. File the message. Develop a topical system and a book of the Bible system to file your notes for further study of the subject.

6. Do further study. Follow the subject of the message through the notes in this study Bible and through this Bible's center column reference system. Memorize Scriptures used in the message to help you remember the message and act on God's Word.

MINISTRY OF TEACHING OR PREACHING

Guide to Teaching the Word

Few people are self-taught. Most of us, however, know how to do the things we do because someone guided us through a process by which we came to understand or to develop the skills needed for these accomplishments. To teach the Bible to ourselves and to others, we need to go through a similar learning process. This guide will help you start that process. As you begin, read the Summary, Scripture, and notes on EDUCATION.

1. Learn the importance of teaching. An effective teaching ministry rises from a sense of the importance of teaching and a confidence of having the gift of teaching. See "Guide to Discovering Your Spiritual Gifts" (p. 1796). If teaching has not been a part of our experience, the things we could not do would overwhelm us. Progress would be slow indeed. Some people face slow progress in Bible study. You can help them make faster progress through a ministry of teaching.

Teaching is important to society, industry, and life. It is vital to the Christian faith. Study Scripture and notes on EDUCATION, Commanded, and EDUCATION, Wholeness. God commanded Moses to teach the Hebrews His commandments so they would be prepared to enter the Promised Land (Dt 4:14). Later God's people were called upon to recount, through teaching, the powerful memories of God's loving deliverance (Jos 4:20-24). Ezra read from the Book of the Law, and the Levites helped the people understand its meaning, leading to their recommitment to God's Law (Neh 8).

We learn most about how to teach the truths of God from the model of our Lord. Jesus taught out of His knowledge of Scripture and from His own personal knowledge of God. Paul continued the teaching ministry modeled by Jesus and urged Christians to share truth through teaching (Col 3:16).

To be a teacher of God's truth—whether from the pulpit or from the classroom—surely is one of the highest of all Christian callings. Your teaching ministry is important.

2. The textbook of Christian teaching is the Bible. Unashamedly, unapologetically, the Bible is the subject of Christian teaching in Sunday School and in other gatherings of believers. Good resources improve teaching. A good environment makes teaching easier. All these are supportive to teaching the truths of Scripture.

To teach the Bible effectively, lay persons require strong curriculum resources, but those curriculum materials are not what we teach. The Bible is the textbook in any Christian study endeavor, especially in Sunday School and in Bible study groups. Regardless of the skill of the teacher or the wisdom of the Bible study leader or of the group members, the point is to teach

God's Word, not simply to share human opinions. We teach not ourselves but Jesus Christ. The aim is to lead persons to trust Jesus Christ as Savior and to follow Him as Lord. To accomplish this, the Bible must be the textbook.

3. Bible teaching leads persons to life-changing encounters. To know Bible facts, Bible history, and Bible stories is important, even crucial for Christians. You cannot overemphasize the need for content knowledge. Without it, we cannot understand the Bible. By itself, however, factual knowledge is not sufficient. Christian Bible teaching is a spiritual undertaking with spiritual purposes. We teach the Bible so persons through its truth used by the Holy Spirit may meet God in a life-changing encounter. We teach so unsaved persons will come to know Christ as Savior. We teach so Christians will mature in their faith and ministry. The Bible has a saving word. It has the answer to despair and fear (Ac 3:10). It carries the promise of victory for the believer (Jn 16:33). Thus we teach the Bible to:

a. Win the lost.
b. Change lives.
c. Nurture Christians.
d. Give hope in despair.
e. Obey Christ's Great Commission (Mt 28:18-20).

4. Much is required of a Bible teacher. Seeking to help someone else find what God is saying to them through Scripture is an awesome responsibility. This is, however, God's plan (Mt 28:18-20).

To recognize that in and of yourself you are not worthy to teach Scripture may be the beginning point for your becoming an effective teacher. It may give proper humility of spirit to approach the teaching task throughout your ministry. It is not a reason for not teaching. God leads people to the teaching ministry. We do not have the right to say He is wrong and refuse to enter the ministry He gives us.

Much is required of the teacher (Lk 12:48). As a dedicated Bible teacher, you will strive prayerfully to model your life after Jesus, to live out of a servant role, and to embody in your life the truth taught. You will remain convinced that Bible teaching is the best way for persons to encounter God, shape ideas, bring change, and influence persons.

A Bible teacher must be spiritually prepared. The foundation is a deep and abiding personal faith in God and in Jesus Christ as Savior. Reliance on the Holy Spirit's presence and commitment to the Bible as the inspired, perfectly authoritative Word of God are essential for teaching. Teachers are most effective when they have daily prayer and Bible study for personal growth as well as for preparation to teach.

Intellectual preparation is necessary along with spiritual preparation. Bible teachers need knowledge of the Bible message, seeing how one passage fits into the whole message of God. They need to know the basic Bible content and history. They need to be committed to learning Bible doctrine through use of a resource like the *Disciple's Study Bible*. They need to know basic principles of Bible interpretation as outlined in "Guide to Interpreting the Bible" (pp. 1769–1772).

Teachers also need a basic knowledge of human nature, especially the characteristics of the persons they teach. A basic love of persons is vital in building relationships necessary for good teaching experiences. An effective Bible teacher will care deeply about the total life of the persons being taught.

When a teacher of deep faith combined with intellectual preparation is joined by the pervading presence of the Holy Spirit, the study of God's Word results in changed lives.

5. Effective teaching follows a tested process. The test of teaching is whether pupils are being transformed into the likeness of Jesus Christ. Human knowledge, activities, and processes cannot guarantee this. The Holy Spirit transforms lives. The Spirit does call on us to use the most effective teaching processes possible to maintain the interest and deepen the experiences of our pupils.

a. Teaching is more than telling. Teaching involves telling our experiences with Jesus Christ. It involves telling what we have learned in studying God's Word. Teaching must be more. When you teach, you not only tell what you have learned but also you guide the learners to make discoveries for themselves. You lead them to feel and know what God is saying to them. To both tell and guide is to follow the model of the master Teacher. Jesus encouraged people to think. He asked searching, probing questions (Mk 8:29) and answered questions from His learners (Lk 10:29-37). He stressed activity (Lk 9:1-6, 10; 10:1-20). He gave object lessons (Mk 11; 14:22-25). He used stories, shocking statements, demonstrations, and group interaction. When you teach, remember that Jesus never ignored the importance of the learner's involvement in the learning process.

b. Teaching the Bible involves studying so much that you teach from the overflow. Saturate yourself in the Scripture passage to be taught. A competent Bible teacher must first be a committed and concerned Bible student. The Bible will not be the central focus of the teaching session unless it has been the central focus of your life and study during the week. You will not want to just tell your experiences and your long-held opinions. You will want to tell what you have learned and become convicted of from the Bible this week. Then you will be an available helper as the Holy Spirit encounters people and changes lives.

Having saturated yourself in the Scripture through several prayerful readings in several translations, you are ready to learn other people's opinions. Turn to curriculum resources provided by your church, to commentaries and Bible dictionaries, and to the Doctrinal Index of this study Bible. Run the cross references found in the center-column reference system of this Bible. Learn as much as time will allow about the passage. Involve yourself in teacher training sessions at your church. If your church does not provide such weekly sessions, talk with church leaders about initiating them. Find a forum to discuss your ideas and the biblical truths as they relate to the members' needs in your church, in your age group, in your class.

c. Teaching requires a plan. A teaching plan has four basic parts. Learning readiness invites learner participation by illustrating the relevance of the Scripture teaching for current life needs. Ask yourself, What story, activity, or statement can I use to raise learners' interest and demonstrate the need to study this lesson? Purposeful Bible study directs learners to Scripture and seeks to find answers to questions learners are asking out of their daily lives. Opportunity for response calls on learners to raise their questions openly and to testify from their experiences as to the meaning and validity of the Bible teachings. The challenge to apply closes the Bible teaching session with a call to learners to practice in concrete ways what they have learned in the session.

To implement the four-point plan, a teacher needs: (1) to develop a personal conviction about the Bible truth; (2) to decide what class members should learn from the passage; (3) to pray about the class members individually, their particular needs, and the application of the lesson to their lives; (4) to know what must be done to help learners see the truth of the passage and want to respond to it.

6. Teaching involves selection of appropriate methods. If you are going to do more than just tell what the Bible says to you, you must explore the methods you will build into your teaching plan. Every session should employ some methods that will cause the learners to interact with the Bible passage, with you, and with fellow learners. The methods you choose will depend upon the central truth of the passage to be taught, the needs and interests of the learners, the aim of the lesson, and the age group you teach. In selecting methods for your teaching session, ask these questions:

a. Does this method emphasize the purpose of this lesson?

b. Does this method encourage the learner to think, feel, know, or be able to do what the lesson is stressing?

c. Does this method bring enthusiastic participation from class members?

d. Does the method complement the learner's stage of development?

e. Does the method encourage the use of available and appropriate resources?

f. Does the method require appropriate guidance from the teacher?

Almost all teaching methods fall into eight basic categories: art, drama, learning games, guided study, listening, music, writing, and verbal methods. Out of this bank you draw those that best suit your leadership style, the developmental stage and learning style of your group, and the purpose of the lesson(s) you are trying to teach. Involvement methods are needed but should not be overly sophisticated and complicated. Study the teaching style of Jesus, and you will find some simple methods that will lead to exciting learning. Study teaching methods suggested in curriculum materials and teacher training materials provided by your church. Discuss teaching methods with other teachers at weekly teachers meetings in your church. Look at EDUCATION for teaching methods used by teachers in the Bible. Be sure you use a new method each month or each quarter. Soon you will have a bank of your own methods that you find comfortable and that your students enjoy.

Caution, love, and the preservation of the dignity of the learners should be your guiding principles as you select and use teaching methods. Teaching plans should never call for overuse of any method. Remember, lecture is only one among many available methods. Whatever methods you choose should be used to stress the Scripture and the learning experience more than the presentation being developed. The method should never stand above the message.

7. Teaching is an experience of ministry in which God will use your gifts.

The time finally comes when you enter the classroom, ready or not. When you do, know:

a. God has gone before you.

b. You teach His Word.

c. The Holy Spirit is present to convict and to draw persons to faith in Christ.

d. God's wisdom through His Spirit will guide you.

e. God's love working through you can lead to learning and to encountering God.

f. Your love of God in Jesus Christ, your commitment to and love of Scripture, and your learners' awareness of your personal concern will warm hearts and make your teaching successful.

g. You do not have to know all the answers, for learning is a process of discovery among you, your pupils, and the Holy Spirit.

Guide to Proclaiming the Word

Proclaiming the Word of God in a devotional, sermon, speech, or lecture involves sharing with others what you have felt or discovered through personal Bible study. When you proclaim the Word, you have a different communication situation than when you teach the Word. Thus you need to follow a different procedure for proclaiming from that of teaching. As opportunity comes to proclaim God's Word, you will want to study the doctrine of PROCLAMATION and its Summary (p. 1696). To prepare for the actual proclamation opportunity, follow this guide:

1. Prepare a "Proclaiming the Word" form for your notebook. Leave space for completing each section. A sample form will resemble the following with spaces left:

Date ____________ Place ____________ Occasion ____________
Group ____________ Scripture Text ____________ Key Idea ____________
Goal ____________ Title ____________
Outline

1. *Introduction*
   a. Attention-getter
   b. Life needs answered
2. *Body of message*
   a. Exposition (Outline by points of Scripture passage)
   b. Topical (Outline by logical points of topic)
   c. Under each point include summary of:
      1). Bible explanation
      2). Illustrations
      3). Practical applications.
3. *Conclusion*
   a. Concrete life response expected
   b. Specific steps to be taken
   c. Immediate act of public or private commitment called for.

2. Select a Scripture passage that has proved meaningful in your life as a disciple. Pray for God's guidance in finding the passage. Study it using the "Guide to Biblical Interpretation" (p. 1769), the "Guide to Studying a Bible Passage" (p. 1775), and the Scripture and notes related to your topic. Be sure you understand the circumstances to which the biblical passage was first addressed and the response it expected. You can find some of this information in the Introduction to the biblical books in this study Bible.

3. Summarize the passage in one sentence. Use this concise statement as the key idea around which you will build your message.

4. State a specific objective or goal for your message:

a. What new idea will the hearers learn?

b. What new encounter will they be encouraged to seek?

c. What new life commitment will they make?

d. What new goals will they set?

e. What specific actions should they plan to take?

Write the objective in precise, personal, and concrete terms. Example: I want my hearers to seek reconciliation before Wednesday with a person with whom they have a problem. State each of the following in one sentence:

- I want them to understand . . . .
- I want them to feel . . . .
- I want them to do . . . .

5. Choose a title that describes what you will talk about or the objective you will aim for. Make the title brief enough to be printed on one line and interesting enough to be remembered. Avoid catchy titles that do not describe content.

6. Decide if the message can best be presented by following scriptural order and making points in succeeding verses or by presenting a central topic coming out of Scripture and presenting points in logical order of the topic.

7. Outline your message. A message of Bible exposition will have points following the order of Bible verses. A topical message will have logical points growing out of the topic but based on truths in the Scripture. Be sure the outline grows from Scripture truth more than from your need to be creative. Note how the biblical writer divided and developed thoughts. Your key idea statement should give you contents for your outline. Your specific objective may give you the concluding point(s) for your outline. Stay true to the key idea, the Scripture text, and your objective as you develop the outline. Seek God's leadership as you write your message. Choose a method of intertwining biblical explanation, practical illustration, and personal application to make your points. Be logical and warmly personal. State outline points in present tense to insure you have relevant truths for the present day.

8. Present your message in a personal way to maintain interest. Use conversational tones. Ask questions for hearers to supply answers for themselves. Invite listeners to relate the message and illustrations to their own experiences. Provide brief periods of silence for them to reflect on such experiences. Invite hearers to jot down key outline points. Maintain as much audience involvement as possible even though you are the only one talking.

a. Introduce your message with a statement, illustration, or question that catches the hearers' attention immediately. Lead them to think, I want to hear this. It affects me. Use a startling statement, an interesting illustration, a striking question, an interesting Bible fact, a case history, or narrative of a life situation. Present the need or ask the question that your message is to answer. This should relate directly to the objective you established.

b. Follow your outline clearly in presenting the body of your message. State the point, explain the biblical basis of your point, illustrate the point, and apply it to personal life. Anticipate questions the listener will raise. Use illustrations to clarify and encourage. Do not leave listeners with abstract theories. Give concrete examples they can apply to their lives.

c. Conclude your message with a concrete life response expected from the hearer, *concrete steps to be* taken to achieve the response, and the initial public or private commitment expected at this moment in this service to ensure the response is made. The goal of your presentation is personal response, changed understanding, new goals, different actions. Make the goal clear to the audience and call for the indicated response. People will not respond if they are not invited.

As God gives gifts and opportunities, proclaim His Word in season and out of season (2 Ti 4:2).

Guide to Applying the Word

Teaching and proclaiming the Word should be founded in a life of applying God's Word. Applying God's Word is the ministry of all who listen to the Word proclaimed and participate in Bible teaching groups. Every disciple of Jesus is obligated to learn how to apply God's Word to daily life. This is what the doctrine of DISCIPLESHIP is all about. It is CHRISTIAN ETHICS in life. Study the Scripture and notes on these doctrines as you work through the following guide.

1. Applying God's Word depends on a foundation of attitude and skills.

Anyone who enters a school must meet certain academic requirements before being admitted for study at the level of the school. You need certain requirements before you can apply God's Word.

a. Be eager to receive and apply God's message. Get rid of hindrances (Jas 1:19-21). Commit yourself to "do what it says" (Jas 1:22). Follow the eager example of Cornelius and his companions (Ac 10:30-33). You will apply God's message only when you want to.

b. Develop a teachable attitude. Be willing to see changes you need to make. Be willing to learn from and obey God's Word.

c. Develop the skill to see a Bible passage's full potential. Recognize the many areas of life in which a passage can help to change you. Scripture can help us know what to believe and how to act (2 Tim 3:16-17). We can defend ourselves against temptation by using the Bible (Mt 4:1-11). Scripture can give us spiritual power (Heb 4:12). Scripture may direct our lives in a wholly unexpected direction as God's promise and call did for Abraham (Ge 12:1-3). Read Scripture and notes on HOLY SCRIPTURE, Powerful.

2. Applying God's Word involves using basic principles.
Review the "Guide to Interpreting the Bible" (pp. 1769–1772).

a. Apply a passage in accordance with the writer's meaning. Read 1 Th 5:17. How can you "Pray continually"? Did Paul mean you should make prayer such a priority that you feel guilty even for eating, sleeping, and studying? Or did he want the Thessalonians and us to be surrounded by an attitude of dependence upon the Lord? Knowing the original meaning encourages further enthusiastic Bible study and wise and joyous Bible application.

b. Apply the passage to present-day culture and situations. Some Bible commands and promises are strongly linked with the Bible's cultural setting. Sometimes commands from the biblical period must be made meaningful to our age. When Paul urged readers to greet one another with a "holy kiss" (2 Co 13:12), he was not writing to create a scandal in the church or embarrassment among members. The eastern culture of the Bible has long used the kiss as a common means of showing affection or respect, especially between members of the same sex. Following the cultural custom of the biblical command could well cause difficulty in our culture. Can we preserve the intent of the command by changing the form of application? What Paul called for was an expression of respect, not a demonstration of sexual attraction. You can find a form of greeting which shows such respect to the people with whom you worship and serve God. This principle calls for care in application. It never gives reason to refuse to obey Bible commands. It does call us to be sensitive to the biblical intention rather than trying to justify ourselves by literally following biblical culture.

c. When appropriate, apply the spirit of a command rather than the exact deed. Jesus washed His disciples' feet and told them they should wash one another's feet (Jn 13:14). He used the practice of His culture of washing the feet of dinner guests to stress the importance of serving one another.

d. View the Bible as a collection of general guidelines, not as a collection of detailed rules. If the Bible were too specific, it would be wedded to one time and culture, losing universal application. As people found new ways to sin, the Bible would no longer be relevant. If the

Bible were merely a book of rules, Christians could obey the letter of the rules, congratulate themselves, and miss the spirit of full commitment. You learn the principles of spiritual growth only as you struggle to apply God's message to the situations in which you live. Jesus told His disciples to give to any person who asks or wants to borrow from you. Does this make you an easy target for every flimflam artist? The spirit of Jesus' command calls for us to develop a way of life characterized by love and generosity. He also wants us to learn how to express Christian love and generosity to best help people in need. The need to learn mature work habits may override the need to have bread. Then the call is to help people find work rather than continually supply bread.

e. Learn how to apply the promises of the Bible. Some promises are universal and timeless. They apply to all persons or to all Christians at all times. Other promises are directed to specific people rather than to everyone. Still other promises have conditions that we must meet before we can expect to realize the promise. Observe these differences as you study God's Word and anticipate His promises.

f. Avoid complacency and overconfidence in applying Scripture. Spiritual health, like physical health, comes from a lifetime of experiences with God and His Word. Always be eager to apply God's Word to your life. If you become complacent, you may stop making progress in the Christian life. If you develop overconfidence, you may become a legalist full of pride and become blind to your own sins.

3. Applying God's Word calls for application of a consistent system. The word *map* can be used as an acrostic to remind you of the system: meditate, area application, practice. We will use Eph 4:32 to illustrate the system.

a. Meditation involves thinking about what the passage is saying with the goal of applying it to your life. Determine the basic intention of the writer for the original audience. Ask God to help you see the central meaning of the passage and to discover its application for your situation. Meditation on Eph 4:32 may show a new meaning of forgiveness for you. You are to forgive other people because God has forgiven you.

b. Area application is the attempt to define the area(s) in your experience in which the biblical intention needs to be applied. In regard to forgiveness, think of all the relationships in which you need to apply forgiveness. Area application demands that you consider all the possible areas in which you can use the teaching of the passage.

c. Practice the principle you learned. Begin with a simple statement of intention: I will forgive the people who have wronged me. State your intentions as concretely as possible. Include names, dates, and specific actions you will take. Pray God will enable you to practice the principle as you live out each day.

MINISTRY OF NURTURE

Christian ministry seeks to mature and train other Christians as well as reach out to the unbelieving world. God gives gifts to some of His people to enable them to counsel and train the Christian family along the stages of spiritual growth. The following guides seek to help you minister to other Christians as God leads you into a ministry of nurture. You will want to study the doctrine of DISCIPLESHIP as you enter this Christian ministry.

Stages in Spiritual Growth

Physical life develops from baby to senior adult. Similarly, spiritual life is a development from first commitment to Christ to full partner in Christian ministry. Disciples grow at different times and rates. Each person's progress varies. Surges of growth are followed by plateaus. Backsliding to a previous level is possible in spiritual development.

Spiritual growth does not occur alone. Christians help other persons grow. As a disciple, you should be aware of your opportunity and responsibility to nurture other people. You can learn to see beyond the outer appearance of persons to their ultimate potential for Christ. Jesus saw past the shifting sands of Simon and called a man Peter, a rock. Barnabas saw beyond the quitter, John Mark, and dedicated his ministry to develop a young man who became the writer of the Gospel of Mark.

You can minister to disciples, leading them through the stages of growth you have experienced. To do so, you need to be aware of the nature of spiritual growth by reading Scripture and notes on SALVATION, Sanctification, and DISCIPLESHIP, Training and by studying the following chart. The chart shows the stages in spiritual development and the commitments a disciple must make to move to the next stage. It also shows the tasks, the roles, and the responsibility levels of the discipler wanting to nurture another person's growth at each stage of spiritual development.

This chart on the stages in spiritual growth seeks to make the following points:

1. The complex nature of spiritual growth includes five basic stages of development: *unbeliever, spiritual babe, spiritual disciple, multiplying leader,* and *co-laborer.* (Read 1 Co 1–4).

a. The *unbeliever* has never made a commitment to Jesus as Savior and Lord. The disciple's role is to be a witness. The task is evangelism. Read "Guide to Giving Your Personal Testimony" and "Guide to Leading to Commitment" (pp. 1786–1788; 1791–1792).

In the ministry of nurture with the unbeliever, a disciple needs to establish a commitment of friendship with the unbeliever. This establishes a relationship in which neither is willing to manipulate the other. Through the verbal and nonverbal witness in friendship the disciple seeks to demonstrate conclusively the reality of Christianity so the unbelieving friend will accept Jesus Christ and salvation. Impatience and loss of interest in the person as friend are the dangers the disciple must overcome in this relationship. Commitment, prayer, and caring mark the discipler's ministry to the unbeliever.

b. The *spiritual babe* has made a commitment to Jesus Christ but has just begun to grow spiritually. The discipler's role to nurture the spiritual babe is to be a parent giving milk to the baby (1 Th 2:7). The task is follow-up. The discipler helps the spiritual babe understand the processes and actions of spiritual growth and leads the babe to allow Christ to become Lord in all areas of life. Without such spiritual nurture, the new Christian can remain a spiritual babe as long as life continues (1 Co 3:1-3).

The traits of spiritual babes include: worldliness, jealousy, quarreling (1 Co 3:3); slowness in learning, having to be taught the elementary truths of God's Word repeatedly, needing teaching about righteousness to be able to distinguish between good and evil (Heb 5:11-14); instability, being easily influenced, susceptible to deceivers (Eph 4:14); lacking Christian virtues, ineffectiveness, unproductivity, spiritual blindness, and forgetfulness (2 Pe 1:5-9).

Abandonment is the pitfall for both discipler and disciple at this stage. If you have led someone to Christ, you should never abandon the responsibility, even when they grow to be leaders (1 Co 4:14-16). Disciplers should always be ready to help disciples benefit from their ministry and that of other co-laborers. This develops churchmanship, commitment to the whole body of Christ, not just to isolated individuals whom we have helped disciple.

In the ministry of nurture with a spiritual babe, the discipler seeks to establish a joint commitment to the lordship of Christ with the spiritual infant. This is the foundation of relationship which will lead the two disciples—discipler and infant—to grow together. The discipler feeds the babe when the babe will drink. One person cannot force growth on another. The discipler can only love the baby and concentrate on developing the new Christian towards the full God-given potential. The beginning point of nurture with the spiritual infant is to ensure the conversion experience and commitment is real. Walking through the exercise with a marked New Testament (p. 1788) can give such reassurance and offer a starting point for growth. Practically, the discipler can use the *Disciple's Study Bible* to introduce the spiritual babe to the spiritual disciplines (worship, prayer, Bible study, Scripture memorization, and witnessing) and the basic doctrines of GOD, Father, Love, Presence, Savior, Sovereignty; JESUS CHRIST, Christ, Son of God, Lord, God, Savior, Atonement, Intercession; and SALVATION, Definition, Justification, Reconciliation, Belief, Confession, Repentance, Eternal Life.

Lack of commitment, frustration, and feelings of superiority are the dangers the discipler

Stages Involved in the Spiritual Development of Disciples

	DISCIPLER			DISCIPLE		
	Discipler's Role	**Discipler's Tasks**	**Discipler's Responsibility**	**Disciple's Responsibility**	**Disciple's Commitment**	**Disciple's Development**
Stage 1	Witness (1 Cor 1:18; 2:1-5)	Evangelism	(Scale of 1-10) 10 (greatest) 9	(Scale of 1-10) 1 (least) 2	*Friendship* that leads to claiming Christ's *Lordship*	From *unbeliever* to *spiritual babe*
Stage 2	Parent (1 Cor 3:1-3)	Follow-up	8 7	3 4	Claiming Christ's *Lordship* that leads to *discipleship*	From *spiritual babe* to *spiritual disciple*
Stage 3	Servant (1 Cor 3:5-6)	Training	6 5	5 6	*Discipleship* that leads to *leadership*	From *spiritual disciple* to *multiplying leader*
Stage 4	Steward (1 Cor 4:1; 3:10-16)	Equipping	4 3	7 8	*Leadership* that leads to *partnership*	From *multiplying leader* to *co-laborer*
Stage 5	Encourager (1 Cor 3:7-9; 4:16, 17)	Supporting	2 1 (least)	9 10 (greatest)	*Partnership* that leads to *churchmanship*	From *co-laborer* to *discipler*

must overcome in the relationship. The discipler's ministry to the spiritual babe should be marked by joint spiritual growth, deepened commitment to the lordship of Christ, and renewed devotion to spiritual disciplines: worship, prayer, Bible study, Scripture memorization, and witnessing. The spiritual babe will become a disciplined disciple only through engaging in the spiritual disciplines with the concerned discipler.

c. The *spiritual disciple* is one committed to training in discipleship and to making Jesus Lord of every area of life. At this stage the discipler's role is to be a servant of Christ and of the spiritual disciple. The discipler should not have a self-image of an authoritative dictator or of a superior disciple. The discipler serves the spiritual needs of the spiritual disciple. Thus the discipler's task is training. At this stage more than one discipler may become involved in the discipling process. No one is seeking to take credit for the spiritual disciple's growth, for God is the One who causes the growth in disciples. The emphasis at this stage is cultivation. One person cannot cause the growth of another; but one person can cultivate the environment so that the other can grow. A discipler seeks to create the right situations for growth, to surround the disciple with opportunities for growth, and to provide models of spiritual disciples from which the emerging spiritual disciple can imitate and learn.

In the ministry of nurture with a spiritual disciple, the discipler seeks to establish a joint commitment to discipleship, continuing the growth of discipler and disciple together in Christ toward spiritual maturity. The beginning point of nurture with the spiritual disciple is the Christian life. Work through DISCIPLESHIP, Lordship of Christ, Spiritual leaders, Neighbor Love, and Persons, and CHRISTIAN ETHICS, Character, Obedience, Righteousness, Justice, Moral Imperatives, Social Relationships in this Bible with the spiritual disciple. Study the summaries of the doctrines of DISCIPLESHIP and CHRISTIAN ETHICS together (pp. 1688–1691). Challenge the spiritual disciple to choose one area of personal ministry and concentrate training together on that area. Study the guide to the area of ministry in these helps. Read the doctrinal notes on the ministry. Establish a practical opportunity to engage in the ministry together. To help choose the area of ministry, the spiritual disciple may want to study carefully the "Personal Spiritual Inventory" (pp. 1751). Enroll the spiritual disciple in a discipleship training course in your local church.

At the end of this stage of growth, the disciple should be evidencing spiritual maturity, bearing fruit, and living a holy life under the Holy Spirit. Most disciples do not consider themselves to be fully mature, but maturity is the goal (Col 1:28; 2 Ti 3:10-17).

Taking God's place in the life of the spiritual disciple is the danger the discipler faces. Ministry to the spiritual disciple should be marked by continuing growth in the spiritual disciplines, growing sensitivity in the areas of Christian ethics and concern for people, and involvement in Christian ministry.

d. The *multiplying leader* is a disciple committed to training other disciples in Christian growth, discipline, and ministry. To nurture a multiplying leader, a discipler assumes the role of steward. In Bible times the steward had the responsibility to oversee an entire household for the owner. As steward, the discipler knows that God is the owner and ruler of the kingdom. The steward does not try to usurp God's authority or position. Rather, the steward seeks to multiply the resources available to extend the Owner's kingdom. Thus the steward's task is equipping the multiplying leader to adopt a self-image of leadership. The disciple must be weaned away from the discipler to become an independent discipler, training other disciples in spiritual growth. A spiritual disciple training under a discipler's leadership is not the goal in spiritual growth. Unfortunately, too few disciples grow to become multiplying leaders. Each spiritual disciple should be led through the spiritual growth process to make a commitment to being equipped for spiritual leadership. Only then is the disciple ready to stand the test of God's refining judgment (1 Co 3:13). The multiplying leader will build life out of the permanent values of God's Word and will help others build lives that will stand the test of eternity. The multiplying leader must have high personal standards and high standards for those to be trained.

Ministering to a multiplying leader, the discipler seeks to give up the reins of leadership, sharing them with the disciple. The goal is to work toward a relationship of partnership. The disciple should be training others in the spiritual disciplines rather than learning discipline from the discipler. The multiplying leader should be established in personal ministry and begin to train others in that ministry. The discipler stands by to give needed advice or direction, to point to new resources, and to guide into the depths of Bible study, Christian decision-making, and doctrine. The multiplying leader should be involved in an advanced discipleship training course in the local church and should be doing individual study in the *Disciple's Study Bible* in doctrines which interest and pertain to the chosen area of ministry. Independence should gradually become evident as the multiplying leader leans less and less on the discipler. Spiritual discipline, ministry, and discipling of others should characterize the multiplying leader's life.

Refusing to allow the disciple independence is the temptation for the discipler at this stage. The discipler's ministry becomes more that of adviser and partner than of trainer. Mutual dependence on and service to one another should mark the growing relationship of the two as they become partners in ministry.

e. A *co-laborer* is the final stage of Christian growth but not the end of the growing process. Discipler and disciple become equal partners in ministry as did Paul with Apollos (1 Co 3:7-9) and with Timothy (4:6,17). The discipler becomes an encourager for the new partner in ministry. The task of the discipler at this stage blends with that of the disciple as the discipler supports, encourages, and becomes a proponent of the other person's ministry. God desires many co-laborers in the church. Together they can produce multiplying leaders. No one can accomplish the tasks of the Kingdom alone. That is why the local church is the best environment for making disciples and for disciple-makers. The supporting task may involve encouraging the new partner in ministry to seek advanced training in denominational training programs, Bible schools, lay institutes, colleges, and seminaries. Seminary extension classes may meet the disciple's need for updated, in-depth training for ministry.

In the new role of partners in ministry, the discipler and the disciple enter a new commitment to partnership. This is not a withdrawal from one another but a deepened commitment to the independent ministry of each. The discipler and disciple both know the other is there when needed even if the more frequent contact of discipler and disciple may disappear. The *Disciple's Study Bible* will become a constant source of reference for each as new Bible study questions, doctrinal discussions, ministry opportunities, and challenges to witness and train arise.

2. Spiritual growth is a process of assuming more responsibility for personal spiritual discipline and ministry.

At first the discipler takes almost all the responsibility to witness to the unbeliever, to lead in spiritual disciplines, and to minister. (Note the responsibility level column on the preceding chart). The unbeliever's only responsibilities are to join in a commitment of friendship and respond to the discipler's gospel witness. The spiritual babe assumes the responsibility to make Christ Lord in growing areas of life and to enter upon personal spiritual disciplines. The discipler still maintains major responsibility to lead the babe's growth through constant feeding. At the spiritual disciple stage, disciple and discipler share an equal responsibility for growth, as the spiritual disciple begins to assume major responsibility for personal spiritual discipline and to enter into ministry responsibilities. When the disciple becomes a multiplying leader, the discipler shifts major responsibilities to the disciple. The multiplying leader not only takes responsibility for personal discipline and ministry but also begins to assume responsibility for training other growing disciples. Finally, the person who grows to the co-laborer stage is now a mature discipler who goes to the other co-laborers for help in solving problems and for direction to new resources, methods, and training opportunities.

3. Guidelines help people pass through the stages of growth and disciple others.

a. Passing on what has been learned is the best way to really learn for oneself. As you pass through a spiritual stage, begin to help people entering that stage. Thus the tasks and commitments of the stage become integral parts of your life.

b. Each disciple has the responsibility to disciple persons at every stage that has been completed personally. A disciple should be helping different people at each stage simultaneously, although one's main ministry may be focused on people in only one of the stages.

Disciplers are the models for the persons they are training. Their discipline and ministry habits will be copied by the disciples.

c. The discipler is not the only determining factor in the process of spiritual growth of disciples. The Holy Spirit working in a person's life and the disciple's response to the Spirit are the major factors. Discipleship materials used such as these in the *Disciple's Study Bible* play vital roles. The home and social environments are extremely important, so that a new disciple should be encouraged and helped in discipling in the home and in participating in social activities with Christian friends. A discipler, thus, should not claim credit for "success" nor assume complete responsibility for the disciple's growth or failure to grow.

d. As a discipler, you need a vision of what God wants to and can accomplish through your discipling ministry and through the ministries of those you train. The need is great. The world's population abounds in unbelievers and spiritual babes. God's vision is to convert unbelievers to spiritual babes and to grow spiritual babes into multiplying leaders and co-laborers. Do you share His vision?

e. As disciples show more interest, give them more time and help. The natural tendency is to neglect growing persons to help others who are not growing. Focusing on one who is growing produces multipliers and co-laborers to help with those who are not growing.

f. Do not work alone. Work with other co-laborers to help people become all God intends them to become.

g. Whatever ministry you focus upon, remember the ultimate goal is to gain new disciples, grow them spiritually, and multiply disciples and disciplers.

4. Spiritual growth involves evaluating where you are and planning where you will go.

a. Take stock of where you are and how you got there. Are you growing spiritually? Are you ready for the next stage of development? Do you have a discipler who can help you in that stage?

b. Are you helping persons at all stages you have passed through already? If so, you are exhibiting the appropriate attitudes of the discipler relative to those stages? Are you letting the persons you disciple assume the proper amount of responsibility?

c. As you examine what you have done, set new goals for the next six months or year. Commit yourself to advance to a new stage of growth. Determine commitments you can make with persons for whom you can become a discipler. Determine areas of personal growth and ways to achieve that growth. Be reasonable but challenging in your expectations of yourself. Ask God to make you a growing Christian disciple involved in discipling others.

Guide to Counseling New Christians

"Make disciples" is the central command of Jesus (Mt 28:19-20). To make disciples Christians need to go, baptize, and teach obedience. Evangelism with integrity means the task of the church and thus of the disciple is not completed until the convert has been baptized, taught, and trained to do the work of winning, teaching, and training others. Care for new converts demonstrates our love for Christ (Jn 21:15-17).

Nurture ministry begins with care of new converts. This ministry opens the door to spiritual growth. Here disciplers take individual responsibility for new converts and make the commitment of Lordship with them. See the "Stages of Spiritual Growth" (pp. 1812–1817). Nurture and follow-up of the new convert must continue until the convert has been established in discipleship programs of the church and has made the personal commitment to grow in Christ's lordship. Consider these steps for follow-up activities with new Christians.

1. Follow-up counseling includes at least four actions.

a. Protect the new convert from devastating temptations (1 Co 10:13; 1 Pe 5:8).

b. Teach the convert the basics of Christian commitment (Col 2:6-7). See "Welcome to God's Family" (pp. 1747–1748).

c. Be a role model for the convert so spiritual discipline will begin and be carried through (Php 4:9).

d. Work with the spiritual babe until signs of a spiritual disciple begin to appear (Col 1:28-29).

2. Follow-up counseling patterns itself after Christ's example.

a. Jesus explained truth (Mt 5—7). He explained how His disciples should live as they followed Him. New Christians need to be counseled on how to live the Christian life.

b. Jesus exampled the truth, living without sin (2 Co 5:21; Heb 4:15; 1 Pe 2:21-22). He modeled what he taught others. New Christians need our example of the Christian life pointing them to Christ.

c. Jesus encouraged the disciples to experiment, applying truths to life situations. He watched them as they did so, encouraging, correcting, and guiding them (Lk 10:1-24). New Christians need to be challenged to experiment in using their skills in witnessing and ministry.

d. Jesus taught the disciples to extend the truth by discipling others (Ac 1;8). The disciples used His pattern and began to teach others as He had taught them (Ac 2:41-42). As we conclude our initial counseling with new Christians, we need to teach them to witness, accompany them as they witness, and show them how to give initial counseling to the new converts they bring to Christ.

3. Follow-up counseling meets the new convert's needs.

a. Tell the convert why. Converts need to know what to do to begin the Christian way. They also will ask why they should do it that way. Point them to texts like 2 Ti 2:2. Show them by example how to find answers to their questions in Scripture. The *Disciple's Study Bible* concordance, center-column references, and Index will be helpful at this point.

b. Show the person how. Demonstrate the meaning of Php 4:9. Counseling a new Christian will surprise you at how much you know and can do. Let the new convert see you study the Bible, pray, worship, witness, and minister. The convert will catch more from your practice of ministry than from your teaching of ministry.

c. Help the person get started. Follow the command of Ac 20:32. Help the person set spiritual goals and stick to them. Make a covenant of discipleship training with the new convert. Set a time to study the Bible together, pray, and discuss questions and temptations which rise in the convert's life. Enroll the new convert in a discipleship training course for new Christians at your church.

d. Help the person keep going. Lead the new convert to memorize and use 1 Pe 1:13-16 as a personal goal in the early days of membership in God's family. Encourage the person to be accountable by checking on progress toward spiritual goals together.

e. Provide resources for the new convert to grow. You, personally, or your church may want to provide a new Bible like the *Disciple's Study Bible* for each new convert. Show the new convert how to use the Bible in beginning a life of spiritual disciplines and Christian ministry.

f. Involve the new convert in witnessing and ministry. Help the new convert begin to fulfill Christ's call in Jn 15:16. Give assignments in ministry, and accompany the new convert in ministry.

Biblical Foundations for Care and Counseling

Since Christian life and ministry is based on the nature of God revealed in the Bible, particularly in Jesus Christ, guidelines for the ministry of caring for persons is grounded in God's nature. His compassion, guidance, comfort, and forgiveness, as well as His confrontation with people in their stubbornness or sin, serve as theological foundations for care and counseling.

Among several illustrations of care and counseling in the Bible, the images of shepherd and father are most popular. The shepherd knows, guides, feeds, and heals his flock; while the father teaches, nurtures, disciplines, and guides his children. Jesus Christ is described as the true Shepherd who best symbolizes the care of the Heavenly Father. Those who follow Him in ministry are to shepherd the flock with His love and care. Throughout the Old and New Testaments, the picture of God as Father gives substance to His care of persons.

Jesus placed love for others on a par with love for God when asked about the greatest commandment (Mk 12:28-31). Caring for persons is therefore essential to Christian faith and becomes one way to demonstrate the reality of one's faith in Jesus Christ as Lord. Every Christian has responsibility to put love for neighbor into practice by seeking ways to be a caregiver or a counseling friend to those who are in need. In this sense, pastoral care is the care given by the members of the Christian fellowship to one another. Many times Christian love realizes a problem is too complex and personal skills are not sufficiently developed for a disciple to handle a counseling situation. Then the proper action is to refer the troubled person to a trained Christian counselor.

God gave gifts through the Holy Spirit to members of the church for specific functions designed to build up the body of Christ. Through the centuries since the writing of the New Testament, vocational specialities exercising God's gifts have expanded in the church. Counseling is one of these ministries. Pastors and other staff members receive training for counseling as part of their educational preparation for ministry.

The calling to counseling ministry as a life vocation has also developed in the church. Men and women trained in the disciplines of human development and interpersonal relationships assist others in a ministry of renewal and redirection. Whether in private practice or on a church staff, Christian counselors understand their task as a ministry which is part of God's redeeming and renewing purpose for human life in the world.

Guide to Counseling for Commitment

Disciples witnessing for Christ often meet persons struggling with decisions related to assurance of salvation, baptism, church membership, reaffirmation of Christ's lordship, commitment to church vocations, or need for growth in Christian maturity. The following guide can be used to counsel those who need to make a decision concerning their relationship to Jesus Christ in these areas. This counseling guide assumes the user is a spiritual disciple and is familiar with basic doctrines of SALVATION; JESUS CHRIST; ORDINANCES; CHURCH; and DISCIPLESHIP.

Counseling should always begin by making sure the other person has had a genuine experience with Jesus Christ and has made a personal commitment to Jesus as Savior and Lord. See "How to Accept Christ" and "Welcome to God's Family" (pp. 1745–1748).

1. Use a standard method of counseling with six steps.

a. State *the question* concisely and clearly. Be sure you and the other person are seeking an answer to the same question.

b. Explore *God's purpose* in relation to the key issue at stake in the question. Ensure the other person sees the basic issue involved and God's commitment in that issue.

c. Determine the *human need* in relation to the issue. What event or relationship or personal need has given rise to the question? Be ready to share your personal experiences with the question.

d. Find *God's provision* in the situation. Show how inspired Scripture provides insight into God's work.

e. Determine our *proper response* to God's provision. Help the person understand the need to respond personally in light of what God has done for us.

f. Formulate a *personal commitment* to God in respect to the basic question and proper response. Help the other person determine what personal commitment needs to be made and what language the person is willing to use to express the commitment as concretely as possible.

2. Doubting one's salvation is not uncommon among Christians. Each individual needs help in finding assurance of salvation. A study of SALVATION, Eternal Life will prepare you to counsel people with such doubts.

a. *God's purpose.* God intends for us to be sure we have eternal life. The Bible gives us that assurance in 1 Jn 5:12-13. God's purpose is that we have joy in salvation not that we be plagued with doubts (Jn 15:10-11).

b. *Our need.* Like you, great heroes of the Bible struggled with assurance of salvation. After an experience of sin, David pleaded for cleansing and restoration of salvation (Ps 51:12). See the index on PRAYER, Petition for other examples. Consider the following questions:

- Why are you experiencing doubt with regard to your salvation?
- Has sin or disobedience caused you to doubt your salvation?

• Has Satan placed doubts in your mind (Ge 3:1; Mt 4:1-11). You may want to work through the index on EVIL AND SUFFERING, Satan, or SIN, Satan, Tempting.

• Have you neglected prayer, Bible study, worship, and witness? You may need to help the person begin working through the above sections under "Disciplines of Discipleship" (pp. 1753–1794).

• Do you have unanswered questions about God or about daily experiences in life? Working through GOD, Personal, Faithfulness; or EVIL AND SUFFERING, Deserved, Redemptive, Present Help, Endurance may provide help.

c. *God's provision.* God has promised to complete His work of salvation in us (Php 1:6). Jesus assured us that all believers already possess eternal life (Jn 5:24). No one can take us out of Jesus' hand (Jn 10:28). The indwelling Holy Spirit tells us we are God's children (Ro 8:16).

d. *Our response.* Having believed in Christ, claim the promises that assure your salvation. Christians are not to trust only our feelings (2 Co 5:7). Receive God's assurance by faith, and express your faith through obedience (1 Jn 2:3-5). If sin is involved in the problem, confess your sin (1 Jn 1:9). Commit yourself anew to Christ's lordship (Ro 10:9-10).

e. *My commitment.* Formulate a commitment concretely expressing the person's understanding of the doubts, asking God to help in the struggle with the doubts, outlining concrete steps to take in dealing with the doubts, committing life to God despite the doubts, and expressing confidence, assurance, and gratitude to God for salvation.

3. Understanding and submitting to the biblical ordinance of baptism is a stumbling block for many people after they have made a personal confession of faith. To counsel such people, you will need to study ORDINANCES, Baptism.

a. *The question.* Why should I be baptized since I . . .? People need to formulate the question in concrete relation to their own circumstances and their own understanding.

b. *God's purpose.* Once a person accepts Jesus Christ as Savior and Lord, he or she will want to be baptized as a response of obedience to Jesus (Mt 28:18-20; Ac 2:38,41). Through the public testimony of baptism we:

• demonstrate our recognition of the lordship of Christ over every aspect of our lives;

• declare our new life in Christ (Ac 8:35-38; 16:25-34);

• portray to onlookers the essentials of the gospel—the death, burial, and resurrection of Christ (1 Co 15:1-4);

• confess the believer's own spiritual death, burial, and resurrection (Ro 6:3-4).

c. *Our need.* Baptism meets the new Christian's need:

• to confess Christ publicly (Mt 10:32);

• to follow Christ's example (Mt 3:13-15);

• to obey Christ's command (Mt 28:18-20);

• to join the fellowship of the church family (Ac 2:41).

d. *God's provision.* Read ORDINANCES, Baptism Commanded, In Jesus' Name, As Confession. Following Jesus' command (Mt 28:18-20), the first local churches made baptism of new converts a regular practice (Ac 8:12,36-38; 9:18; 10:48; 16:15,33). Modern disciples should follow the New Testament example and participate in the ordinance God provided.

e. *Our response.* If you have not done so,

• ask for membership in a local church;

• request the local church to baptize you as in the New Testament;

• be baptized in obedience to Christ and as a testimony of your faith;

• be an example to others through your baptism.

f. *My commitment.* Lead the person to write a concrete commitment such as: *Father, I want to obey You and let others know that I have a new life in Jesus Christ. Bless me as I join ____________church and follow Jesus obediently in baptism. May my baptism be a positive influence on ____________________who has not confessed you as Savior and Lord or followed you in baptism.*

4. Church membership raises question in the minds of many new Christians.

a. *The question.* Why should I join the church since I can pray and study my Bible without being involved with a group of people I do not know? People need to express their own doubts, frustrations, and complaints about church membership and establish a clear goal in joining a church fellowship.

b. *God's purpose.* Those who have accepted Jesus Christ as Savior and Lord benefit from becoming an active part of a local church of dedicated disciples. Jesus built the church (Mt 16:18) and gave Himself for the church's benefit (Eph 5:25). See CHURCH, Body of Christ, Intention of Christ, Fellowship, Local Body, for further understanding of the nature and value of the church. The church is made up of God's people who seek to reach the world for Jesus Christ. The church is important for the disciple, for through the church we become:

- a part of God's work (Ro 12:5);
- part of a worshiping community (Eph 5:19-20; Heb 10:25).
- share our faith to strengthen or evangelize others (Ac 1:8; 2 Co 5:18-20);
- learn how to become the kind of people God wants us to be (2 Pe 3:18);
- minister to one another (1 Co 12:12-26).

c. *Our need.* The Christian life is not a lonely pilgrimage but a family experience. Christians need the fellowship, direction, and support of other Christians (1 Jn 1:3). We need the public identity of church membership. We need strength and courage for daily living gained in fellowship with other believers (Heb 3:13). We need the opportunity for training and ministry provided only by the local church (Ro 12:4-8). The church provides the outlet for us to use the talents and spiritual gifts God has given.

d. *God's provision.* God established the church as the body of Christ (Eph 4:4; Col 1:18). He provides for church membership through the invitation of the local church, which echoes His call to all people (Rev 22:17). God encourages every Christian to participate in church membership (Heb 10:25). Christ set the example through His regular synagogue attendance (Lk 4:16).

e. *Our response.* You may become a member of a local church fellowship in a variety of ways. If you have made a commitment of your life to Jesus Christ as Savior and Lord, you should be a church member. Pray about your decision. Discuss with trusted Christian friends the opportunities for you to serve Christ through various churches. Visit different churches. Discover one in which you can practice spiritual disciplines—worship, prayer, Bible study, and witness—and exercise your spiritual gifts in ministry. Talk with the pastor of the church. Ask how you can become a member. Discuss opportunities for training and ministry the church will involve you in. Follow the pastor's directions, and join the church fellowship.

f. *My commitment.* Write and pray a prayer such as the following expressing your firm commitment to join a local church by a certain date and to serve God faithfully in the church: *Dear Lord, Thank You for Your church. Lead me to a church where I can best serve You. I will join Your church before ______(date)______. Help me to become a faithful church member and support my church family while worshiping You, growing spiritually, and ministering in Your name.*

5. Rededication of life to Jesus Christ concerns many disciples at some point in their Christian life.

a. *The question.* Since life is not going right and I am not being the Christian I know I should be, what can I do? People with guilt, people facing problems, and people experiencing a new plateau or new crisis in spiritual growth often seek counsel as to how to reaffirm or rededicate themselves to Christ as Lord. They need to express their situation concretely and list the alternatives they understand before listening to counsel.

b. *God's purpose.* At times Christians who have claimed that Jesus is Lord of their lives allow other commitments to challenge that priority. They need to ask, "Is Jesus truly Lord of my life? Why do I not feel as close to Him as I once did? "They need to learn:

- God wants to reclaim your life and restore joy (Jn 15:10-11).
- Christ wants to be Lord of all your life (Lk 6:46).
- God is ready to forgive and cleanse you from sin (1 Jn 1:9).
- Other Christians are ready to forgive and restore you (Gal 6:1).

• God wants you to live in fellowship with Him now (1 Jn 1:7).
• God wants you to be filled with His Spirit (Eph 5:18).
• God will make you acceptable for His ministry (2 Ti 4:11).

Reading Scripture and notes on SALVATION, Grace, Justification, Sanctification, Reconciliation, Forgiveness, and Renewal will help a person counsel another or deal with personal concerns about rededication.

c. *Our need.* Rededication is a personal action arising out of very personal concerns. A person needs to talk about these concerns and have someone listen in love. Much of the concern may be on the level of feelings and self-image, levels which need to be dealt with carefully. You may soon face the need to refer the person to someone with professional Christian counseling experience. You need to listen carefully to distinguish what the person feels and what God's inspired Word says. In this situation a person often feels:

• Unjust treatment;
• Guilt;
• Isolation;
• Separation from God;
• Frustration with life;
• Honest doubt about salvation;
• Desire to repent and restore relationship with God. The person's basic need then is to review the basic gospel message, gain reassurance of salvation or confess that salvation was never experienced, and make a new commitment or a recommitment of life to Christ.

d. *God's provision.* God has in Christ done everything necessary to provide salvation, renew Christians, give assurance, and restore the joy of salvation.

• God is ready to forgive and restore you (1 Jn 1:9).
• The blood of Jesus will cover every sin (1 Jn 1:7).
• The Spirit helps in all our weakness and intercedes for us with the Father (Ro 8:26-27).
• God is love and has lavished His love on us so that we are beloved children (1 Jn 3:1,16; 4:7-21).

e. *Our response.* The person's response will depend on the personal situation which originally surfaced the need for recommitment or new commitment. The person will generally need to deal with the questions of confidence in God, forgiveness of sin, and affirmation of personal potential under God. Then the person needs to make a strong commitment to Jesus Christ and be given strong affirmation in this commitment.

• Confess your sins (Pr 28:13).
• Recommit yourself to the lordship of Jesus Christ (Ac 2:36).
• Yield yourself daily to Jesus (Ro 6:12-13; Gal 2:20).
• Be prepared to make necessary personal sacrifices to serve Jesus (Lk 9:23).
• So commit yourself that your reaffirmation of faith will have a lasting significance. Such commitment includes commitment to the Christian disciplines—prayer, Bible study, worship, and witnessing—and to personal ministry.

f. *My commitment.* Make a commitment listing the need for commitment and the experience of renewal. Write this in the form of a prayer including statements like the following: *Lord Jesus, I want to acknowledge my sin and recommit myself to You as Lord. I trust you to provide the strength for me to live for You the rest of my life.*

6. Commitment to church vocation is a serious decision young people and many middle-aged adults face.

a. *The question.* What does God want me to do with my life? Every Christian faces the question at important junctures of life. Many struggle to determine if God is leading them to vocational service in the church. To counsel with such people, you will need to read CHURCH LEADERS; ELECTION, Leadership Responsibility, Mission; and DISCIPLESHIP, God's Leadership.

b. *God's purpose.* You can be certain about God's purpose in the following areas:

• God wants you to know His will (Eph 5:17).
• God promises to help you discover His will (Ro 12:1).

- Every Christian is called to discipleship and service (Eph 4:1).
- God gives us spiritual gifts to minister to others (Ro 12:6; 1 Pe 4:10).
- God gives leaders to the church to equip people for ministry (Eph 4:11-12).

c. *Our need.* Our need as Christians is to determine our gifts and then employ them in Christian service. We share the following needs with all Christians:

- We need to be laborers in the fields white unto harvest (Lk 10:2).
- We need to win the world to Christ because people are lost (Mt 7:13-14).
- We need to do the will of God (Php 2:13).
- We need to train others for service (Eph 4:11-12).

d. *God's provision.* God has provided for all His people to exercise ministry and priesthood. Some He calls to minister in full-time church vocations, others bivocational church vocations, and others as dedicated church workers earning a living through other vocational means. He provides the needs of each. For those who feel led to explore church-related vocations, God's provision means:

- He will only ask you to do what He equips you to do (Ac 1:8; Php 4:13).
- He promises to be with you and help you (Ex 4:12; Jos 1:9).
- Anything He leads you to do is possible in His strength (Php 4:13).
- He calls us to surrender completely to Christ as Lord (Ro 12:1-2).
- He leads us to counsel with leaders of His people (1 Sa 3:1-10).
- He leads us to people and to opportunities for service that reveal our gifts and help us grow to understand His plan for our lives, including His vocational plans.

d. *Our response.* As you seek God's vocational direction, be willing to do God's will now (Ac 9:6). Do not be anxious, but pray for leadership (Php 4:6). Respond to each step as He reveals it, acting in faith. Do not expect God to reveal more than you need to know at the present moment.

e. *My commitment.* Formulate a commitment reviewing the steps by which God has led the person to consider church-related vocations, the questions the person now has, and the commitment to present service the person is willing to make. Conclude with something like: *Thank You for providing a perfect plan for my life. I commit myself today to do Your will as You reveal it to me.* Review "Life in Christ: The Disciple's Cross," p. 1748.

MINISTRY OF SERVICE

Christ summarized His way of life in two commands: love God and love your neighbor (Mt 22:34-40). He taught and demonstrated that greatness comes through serving others (Mk 10:35-45). Service to other people is the characteristic mark of Christian disciples. Every disciple will find ways to serve other people. As you seek your ministry of service, you will want to study DISCIPLESHIP, Persons, Neighbor Love, and CHURCH, Servants. You will want to study the Summaries and Histories on Discipleship and on Christian Ethics as well as scanning the index under these two topics for specific ministry focus possibilities. When you understand the nature of Christian ministry, you can sense God's leadership to ministry, and you can minister more effectively.

Guide to Service in Christ's Name

Service involves self-sacrifice, the investing of oneself and one's resources in behalf of another person, an ideal, or a cause at personal expense. A true service is that done by a servant for a master without thought of recognition or reward. Service in Christ's name means I am the servant and Christ the Master. It implies participation in God's mission in the world He created and loves. Service in Christ's name addresses concrete realities of crucial human need.

Service for Christ gives concrete expression to Christian redemption in a world enslaved to sin. The way of the true believer is practicing justice in business and politics, showing mercy to debtors and needy individuals, and living humbly before God with family and neighbors (Mic 6:6-8). Awareness of the majesty and mission of God leads to humble service for our Lord, whose example we follow and whose character we seek to imitate.

Too often religious people have lives not characterized by goodness, faith without justice, and worship without humaneness. Their lives with God are compartmentalized at church on Sunday, being kept separate from their daily relationships and responsibilities. They preoccupy themselves with external expressions of religion but refuse to practice compassion in real life settings. We still need the impatience and courage of Amos who decried Israel's assemblies and deplored her offerings, seeking instead that people hate evil, love good, practice justice, and seek righteousness (5:14-24). Religious people are called to ministry as well as meditation. Ministry that matters must occur in communities where we live, in relationships where we share, in responsibilities that we assume, and in daily decisions we make.

God demonstrated the true meaning of service in His Son. Rather than write a creed for persons to recite, He set before us the life of Jesus, who came in the form of a servant. We may argue statements of theology, but we can only obey God's ultimate statement about service—the life, death, and resurrection of His Son. Jesus demonstrated humble caring without controlling the outcome. Such is the vulnerability of true compassion. The cross dramatizes a great reversal of human ambition showing in its shame and scandal God's ultimate gesture of love for wayward, lost humanity.

Jesus' imagery of the vine and branches in Jn 15 reminds us that the direction of the Christian life comes from within and moves outward. Nurtured in God's self-giving love (Greek *agape*), disciples naturally express care for each other and for all people, because Christ died for all sinners. Christ expects disciples to express this kind of love He demonstrated to us (Jn 13:34-35). The love Christ demonstrated and commands is inclusive. It includes the poor, the handicapped, the socially outcast, both sexes, and all races. It is based on respect for human personality created in the image of God. It is impartial, embracing all ages, classes, and conditions of persons.

Service for all people in Christ's self-sacrificing love is the task of a disciple. How can you become involved and develop this humble spirit? The following guide is a starting point.

1. Commit yourself to get involved.

Servants are not born. They develop as they commit themselves to service and as they serve. What begins as willingness to help with a person, project, or cause often leads to intense involvement in which the life of service demonstrates faith.

2. Develop a caring image of yourself. Ask God to help you truly love all people as your neighbors. Healthy caregivers are basically secure, though not naive, people. Servant people believe their world will be a better place because they have been a part of it. They do not lose their way despite the awesome darkness of personal pain and social trauma. Carers recognize their own limits and seek mutually satisfying and constructive relationships with other people.

3. Develop basic goals for serving others. Such aims include striving to:

a. Free people from human bondage, insecurity, and evil.

b. Relieve pain and restore human functions in illness, accident, or disaster.

c. Enable persons to rely on available care networks.

d. Change social structures that are damaging to persons.

e. Heal, sustain, guide, and reconcile persons to life.

f. Create opportunities for persons to live useful lives.

4. Understand the nature of service as illustrated by Jesus in Mt 25:

a. Service is done as a natural part of the Christian life, not as a special action to which special attention is called and for which special reward is expected.

b. Opportunities for service come in the everyday experiences and needs of ordinary people—feeding the hungry, providing drink for the thirsty, hosting strangers, sharing clothing, *and visiting prisoners.*

c. Care is an intentional, conscious spirit and act. To care is to pay attention to people and their needs in a spirit of love and in concrete actions.

does your situation seem to be?", listening intently to the answer in which the other person recounts personal difficulties and problems being faced, and then asking (2) "What do you think you should do about it?" This method lets the other person examine the situation and discover possible solutions. Many people's problems can be solved by this method. Often, if this method does not work, time for referral to a more experienced counselor is in order.

b. Questions should make the counselee feel the importance of the now, provoking a sense that this is a special moment.

c. Open questions invite the counselee to express ideas on a variety of subjects through the use of six key words: *what, why, when, how, where,* and *who*. You might ask, "How do you think your husband should go about handling this problem? What have you done about getting this matter under control? Why is this relationship so important to you? When do you plan to put your plan into action? How do your daughter's attitudes look to you?"

d. The best questions focus on feelings rather than on facts. They help people verbalize emotional reactions, opinions, and ideas. Never ask a question that can be answered simply yes or no unless you have a follow-up question ready. Instead of "Do you like . . .?", ask "How do you feel about . . .?" This may evoke feelings and ideas, thus stimulating further discussion. Stimulate conversation by asking: "Have you any ideas on the subject? Would you explain this to me? What is your reaction? What is your opinion?"

3. Questions should have a purpose. Questions should encourage the counselee to examine the troubled situation from all angles and search for workable solutions. To ask purposeful, effective questions;

a. Take every possible chance to ask a searching question; then keep quiet, and listen to the response carefully.

b. Questions that come close to the other person's interest get the best answers, provided the questioner's interested listening encourages the answer.

c. Be prepared to wait. Sometimes a long silence can be more rewarding than another question.

d. The quality of an answer depends on the quality of the attention given by the questioner.

e. Questions that deal with a person's feelings are more provocative than those that deal with facts.

4. A Ten-Step Plan can be used effectively for more complex counseling situations. An important questions propels each step of the plan. Most counseling situations the average disciple becomes involved in are brief counseling sessions involving only one meeting. The session may appear to bog down. The Ten Step Plan is designed to keep the interview moving in a progressive step-by-step order. Slavishly following the guide is not necessary. Some of the steps and questions will not be necessary or applicable to certain cases. Adapt the plan to each situation.

a. Where can we talk? and How long do we have?

If the session is to get off to a good start, both parties need to have some understanding about the direction of the counseling and how long the session is going to last. Biblical wise men met people in the city gate, the heart of commerce and activity. This shows specially prepared settings are not essential for counseling. The special setting is one of the least significant aspects of a counseling experience, though some privacy is desirable. The time agreement should help prevent either party from appearing anxious about previous commitments. Extension of time should be made only if both parties are comfortable with it. Otherwise, another session should be scheduled. Untrained disciples should not become involved in long-term, several-session counseling without calling in the assistance of a pastor or other trained Christian counselor.

b. Why don't you tell me about it?

Rapport is essential to a counseling relationship. It may be defined as a comfortable and unconstrained relationship of mutual confidence that comes to exist between two people. Rapport can be built through the capacity to listen, to give assurance of confidentiality, and to make personal interest and concern clearly understood. As an individual relates personal history

WiseCounsel Course Map

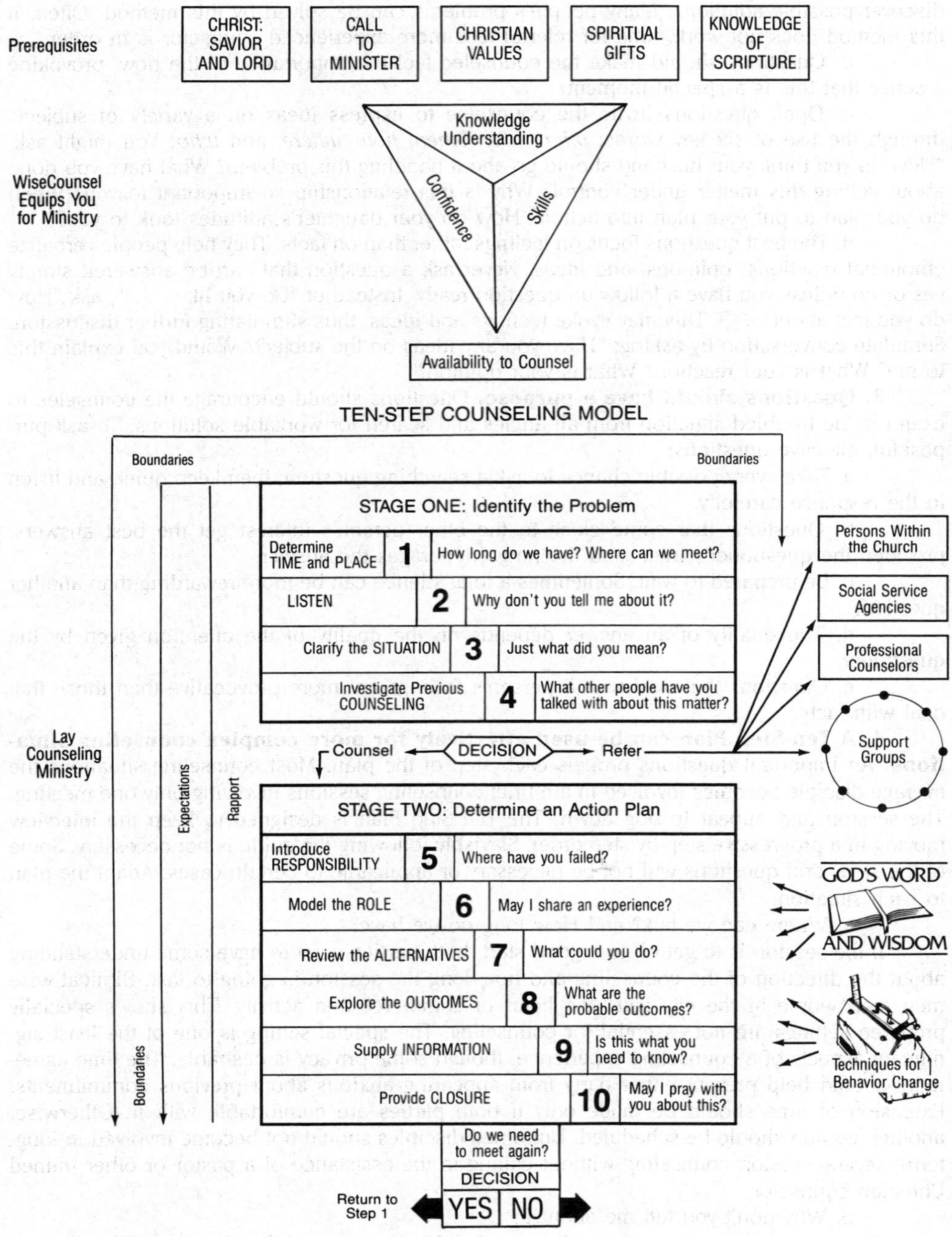

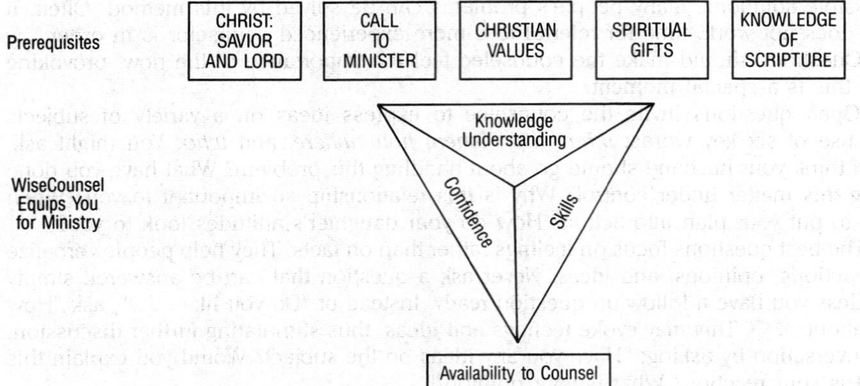

TEN-STEP COUNSELING MODEL

Boundaries — Expectations — Rapport — Boundaries

Lay Counseling Ministry

STAGE ONE: Identify the Problem

Determine TIME and PLACE	1	How long do we have? Where can we meet?
LISTEN	2	Why don't you tell me about it?
Clarify the SITUATION	3	Just what did you mean?
Investigate Previous COUNSELING	4	What other people have you talked with about this matter?

Counsel ⟵ DECISION ⟶ Refer

Refer: Persons Within the Church; Social Service Agencies; Professional Counselors; Support Groups

STAGE TWO: Determine an Action Plan

Introduce RESPONSIBILITY	5	Where have you failed?
Model the ROLE	6	May I share an experience?
Review the ALTERNATIVES	7	What could you do?
Explore the OUTCOMES	8	What are the probable outcomes?
Supply INFORMATION	9	Is this what you need to know?
Provide CLOSURE	10	May I pray with you about this?

GOD'S WORD AND WISDOM

Techniques for Behavior Change

Do we need to meet again?

DECISION

Return to Step 1 ⟵ YES | NO ⟶

and you listen intently, the person has the feeling you are no longer just another individual but an insider with whom confidence can be shared. Jesus continually emphasized the importance of listening (Mk 4:9; 8:18). Certain techniques and actions assure the other person of your personal interest and concern:

• Smile. If you are going to build strong relationships with persons you counsel, you need to begin with a smile.

• Open posture. Your posture conveys strong messages non-verbally to people you counsel. Crossed arms indicate defense, defiance, and withdrawal. Crossed legs and/or a swinging foot indicate boredom. To show you are open-minded and receptive to what the other person wants to say, sit in a relaxed and attentive manner which directs all attention to the other person.

• Lean forward. Leaning back in a chair with both hands clasped behind the back of your neck communicates that you feel superior to the other person. Do everything possible to avoid communicating the wrong message. Lean toward the other person in an attitude of interest.

• Touch. Touch conveys a message that cannot be verbalized. Many people feel they are outcasts from our society just as did the lepers of Jesus' day. His concerned touch reassured the lepers of inclusion in Jesus' larger family. Your touch will show the person you counsel your acceptance and sense of family relationship under God.

• Eye contact. Attention is the great reward we humans can give each other. Attention begins with looking. Fix your eyes on the other person in an interested coaxing manner that helps the person respond, but do not give the impression you are staring.

• Nod. A slight movement of the head has awesome possibilities. A counselor who sits like a bump on a log will not accomplish very much. You must move. A nodding head is a valuable asset for building a relationship with another person.

These techniques help you build rapport. Building rapport through listening, creating confidence, and expressing personal interest is the heart of the counseling process. It helps the other person break out of isolation, put perplexing troubles into words, express emotions, and develop a warm feeling toward you, a fellow-disciple.

c. What do you mean?

A major aim of counseling is to bring clarity to the troubled situation. The person who seeks counseling may be under extreme stress. Stressed people often experience great difficulty in expressing themselves. They stumble around trying to find how to describe their difficulty (ies). They often utter a confused stream of language which may prove coherent but not logically clear. As a counselor, you need to ask gently but firmly, "Will you please explain what you mean when you say you want to get out of it," or "Will you please explain what this relationship has to do with your wife's brother?"

d. Where else have you sought counseling?

Counseling seeks to control the spread of information and the keeping of confidence. The counselor must know how psychologically sophisticated the other person is and how many persons are involved in dealing with the problem(s). If the other person has talked with psychologists, social workers, and psychiatrists, exercise great caution. Discussions may have developed beyond your ability to help. Encourage the person to let one trained counselor be the leader of the counseling process and to let that leader involve and direct any other team members needed in the counseling process. Openly admit that you as an amateur are not trained to work in such a process where professional, trained counselors are already involved.

If the person has not talked with other persons, this may be a golden opportunity for you to provide the counseling assistance of which you are capable.

e. Where have you failed?

Many individuals in trouble blame other people for their problems. They feel circumstances control their actions and have caused their lives to be bad. No matter how unfortunate the circumstances, blaming others cannot change the situation. Steps to vital solutions come only when troubled persons feel they can take positive actions to change their situation. The Christian gospel offers hope, saying every person has sinned and fallen short of God's glory

(Ro 3:23). All people need to acknowledge personal failures before they can really know the experience of salvation through Christ. One way of helping troubled people at this point is to say, "Supposing the other person is 90 percent wrong, could you be 10 percent wrong?" Most people will accept the 10 percent responsibility. Then you can say, Let us talk about your 10 percent. We may well be able to take some action there. When individuals become responsible and work on their irresponsibilities, they move down a pathway toward mature living. This long sentence of two letter words provides a trustworthy guideline: If it is to be, it is up to me to do it.

f. May I share an experience?

People need role models, particularly when they face troubles. Jesus showed us an ethic of imitation as He washed His disciples' feet (Jn 13:1-17). He called us to follow His example. As we learn from Jesus' example, so other people will learn from our actions and experiences. Sharing your experiences of dealing with trouble can demonstrate how you want the other person to deal with problems. Often you will want to share biblical examples.

g. What could you do?

Stress, crises, depression, and anxiety confuse and overwhelm people. They find it difficult to see any options for action. They experience tunnel vision and see only one possible line of action, a line they usually do not like. The counselor's task is to highlight the various options available. This is best done if you can help the other person discover the options. Later the person often confesses, "At the time I felt hedged in with only one way to go."

Of great importance here is to discover the responsibility of a Christian. Help the person ask, "What does the Bible say about this matter?" Together study the scriptural teaching on the subject. The index in the *Disciple's Study Bible* can help you at this point. This is the distinctive work of Christian counseling. The Bible often will show what the person needs to do in the situation or will open possible alternative actions.

h. What will probably happen?

Once you have listed possible alternative actions, guide the other person to identify what will probably happen if each action is taken. You may need to provide an objective and unbiased viewpoint as you brainstorm outcomes with the person. The person must be ready to choose a plan of action and accept responsibliity for its outcome.

i. Is this what you need to know?

Counseling is not the pooling of ignorance. Good decisions on the right course of action come from good information. You will want to be prepared to help the person find the information needed to decide how to act. Provide pamphlets, books, articles. If you do not have these or know where to get them, put the person in touch with a professional in the proper field who does have such information. Your pastor may help you in finding proper information.

j. Will we need to meet again?

The final step for the counselor is in many ways the most important. The counseling session(s) must be closed and the person left responsible to act responsibly. Avoid two traps. Do not dismiss a person needing further help. Do not openly or unconsciously invite the person to become dependent on you and seek your help in every situation that arises. The sweetest word to a counselor's ears should be, "Thank you so much for your help. I feel I can handle this matter now." As you hear these words, leave the door open so the person does not feel cut off or abandoned.

k. May I pray with you about this?

You have the opportunity to invoke the blessing of the great Counselor. Close a counseling session with a brief word of prayer following this pattern:

"Our Heavenly Father, we commend our discussion into your hands and pray that your Holy Spirit will guide ______(name)______ into making the best decision. Give ______ (name)______ strength to take the actions that will bring glory to your name and blessing into his/her life. Through Jesus Christ our Lord we pray. Amen."

As you develop counseling skills, you may find this is the focus of your ministry as a disciple. You may sense that you are fulfilling the commands of Christ, who is the "Wonderful Counselor" (Isa 9:6). Your counseling ministry will always be dependent on Him and will lead you to other people who are part of God's team of counselors, able to help in cases you are not equipped to handle.

MINISTRY OF EVANGELISM AND MISSIONS

Witnessing is a personal discipline for every Christian. Evangelism is a ministry to which some Christians are called, for which they are gifted, and in which they serve Christ and His church. This ministry is exercised in different forms such as life-style, relationships, church outreach, small groups, church programs and services, and mass evangelism efforts. Each of these forms of evangelistic ministry builds on the Christian doctrine of evangelism. As you plan a ministry of evangelism, you will want to study the summary on Evangelism along with the notes and Scripture on EVANGELISM, Gospel, God's Provision, Call to Evangelism, Love, Call to Salvation. A general understanding of the evangelist's commitment can be gained by studying STEWARDSHIP, God's Ownership.

Guide to Life-Style Evangelism

Life-style evangelism involves sharing the good news of Jesus Christ with people who do not know Him as Lord and Savior by living a Christian life which will attract the lost person's attention. Christians who share their testimony by the life they lead have experienced Christ as Savior of their lives and wish for others to have that same experience. They make an intentional effort to live out Christ's grace and love before a lost world.

The characteristics of a life-style evangelist include:

1. An experiential knowledge of Jesus Christ as Savior. The disciple knows Jesus has forgiven personal sins and is constantly delivering from the power of sin. Thus Jesus is invited to and allowed to rule as Master of life for the evangelist.

2. Submission to God. To live is Christ (Php 1:21; Gal 2:20). By allowing the holy God to act through human personality, the life-style evangelist seeks to be holy as God is holy (1 Pe 1:16). Life is no longer seen as a possession for self but as a gift from God.

3. Demonstration of sanctification. See notes and Scripture on SALVATION, Sanctification. Holiness implies that the inward life known totally only to God is clean. As a life-style evangelist, you must submit all of life—inward thoughts and attitudes as well as outward expressions and actions to God for cleansing. When your life demonstrates God's victory over sin, witnessing opportunities come to you.

4. Confidence in the significance and truth of the Bible. The life-style evangelist exercises personal discipline in studying the Bible and living by its truth. Practical truths of the Bible applied to personal life become a part of the life-style evangelist's witness. Lived-out, fleshed-out biblical truth will demonstrate to the lost their need of a Savior. They will give you opportunity to verbalize your witness as Christ meets their needs through your life-style witness.

5. Knowledge of the gospel. See Summary of the gospel (p. 00). Life-style evangelism is possible only for one who deeply knows and lives the gospel of Jesus Christ which says all are lost and can be saved through faith in Christ (Lk 19:10; Jn 3:36). Belief in the truth of the gospel causes the believer to have confidence that any person who has faith in Christ will have all sins forgiven and be provided with eternal life (Jn 3:16). Such confidence prepares the life-style evangelist to share verbal witness and personal testimony at the proper time.

6. Commitment to prayer. The life-style evangelist regularly prays: confessing sins and asking forgiveness and cleansing, interceding for lost people, and petitioning God to save people who have not believed in Christ. Ask God to direct your life in developing relationships with people who need Christ. Seek God's guidance in doing and saying the right things when relating to unbelievers. Ask for sensitivity to the needs of all people to whom you relate.

7. Abounding love. Christian love is the unique distinguishing mark of a Christian. Such love will constantly motivate you to witness to the lost. Love cannot bear the thought of a friend or of any other persons perishing in hell. Such love attracts people. When love for Christ is strong, appropriate acts of kindness follow. Nothing causes others to hunger for Christ like love. Does your Christian love shine through as a light creating good works which point people to Christ? (Mt 5:16).

8. Willingness to witness. Life-style evangelism leads other people to recognize a quality in your life missing in theirs. Their questions provide opportunity for your witness. Share with them what Christ has done for you in your salvation. Tell them the gospel story, emphasizing the cross and resurrection of Christ. Invite the lost to repent and receive Christ through faith. Take them to church. When they have received Christ, ask them to confess Him publicly and to follow Him in baptism. Become a counselor for the new Christian, or direct the babe in Christ to your church's program for new believers. Help the new disciple become a life-style evangelist.

Guide to Small Group Evangelism

Small group evangelism involves discovering and/or forming small groups of people with similar interests to share the gospel of Christ. Such groups may be pre-existing groups gathered for various purposes, or study groups searching for religious truth. The disciple becomes involved in such groups both to share the common interest of the group and to provide a Christian witness for the group. Study of notes and Scripture on EVANGELISM, Small Group will prepare you to work as a small group evangelist with understanding of biblical examples and principles. The following guide will help you in the practical exercise of small group evangelism.

1. Small groups share special needs or interests (Ac 17:16-33). The gospel can be presented in many different ways. When the group shares common interests, the manner of presentation can reach the largest percentage of the people.

2. Small groups meet in a place most comfortable for the group, not the place most familiar or convenient for the evangelist.

3. The beliefs and interests of the group form the starting point for the evangelist's presentation. The method is a positive presentation of the gospel as applied to those interests, not a harsh criticism of the group's current beliefs or actions. As Paul on Mars Hill found a common point of agreement with the small group of philosophers, so we need to emphasize points of common agreement and lead naturally to the gospel's relationship to that common agreement.

4. The evangelist may have to overcome personal prejudice to witness to some groups, as Peter did in witnessing to Cornelius and his household (Ac 10:1-48). Sharing what one has learned from experience with the group is a good way of beginning a gospel presentation. Let the group know your purpose is to learn from them as well as to share your viewpoint and convictions with them.

5. A home is an excellent place to form a small group (Ac 10:1-48; 16:32). The small numbers in a home group enhance the interchange of ideas and promote serious dialogue. The informality of the home and its hospitality help make this form of evangelism successful. The first disciples used homes for many purposes: Christian fellowship (Ac 21:7), prayer meetings (Ac 12:12), the Lord's Supper (Ac 2:46), evangelistic gatherings (Ac 16:32), a planned meeting to hear the gospel (Ac 10:22), and follow-up with seekers (Ac 18:26).

6. Small group evangelism requires a tolerant cultural climate. The group must not involve mutual antagonism which prevents presentation of different opinions. It should promote acceptance of persons even when opinions differ widely. The goal of the group should be to search for truth not to gain a victory over other group members.

7. A small group evangelist must be aware of the emotional climate of the group. Recent experiences such as that of Cornelius in Ac 10 may determine the group's openness to the gospel message. The small group evangelist should be sensitive to the group's receptivity for the gospel and ready to introduce the gospel message and invitation to accept Christ at the proper time.

8. Small group evangelism involves contextualizing the way the good news is presented. The evangelist must consider carefully the religious background and experiences of the group. A purely emotional appeal which does not address directly the group's needs is inadequate. Effective evangelism shows the people how the gospel applies to their needs and interests.

9. Small group evangelism is more than participating in a group with common interests. The evangelist must find opportunity within the group discussion to present clearly the gospel of the crucified and resurrected Christ.

10. Forming a Bible study group is one of the best ways to do small group evangelism. Existing study groups such as Sunday School classes should be used for evangelism. The teacher should present the gospel clearly while teaching the Bible lesson, and all class members should share the gospel in informal meetings and visits with other class participants. Other Bible study groups should be formed to meet the needs of those unwilling or unable to participate in the church's regular Bible study program. Participants in such groups should have common bonds such as age level, occupation, life experiences, or needs. The group could be a woman's Bible study group, a youth group, a divorcees' support group, senior citizens group, or group for ethnics or internationals.

11. Small group evangelism may deal with tightly organized groups which meet regularly or with an informal group together only for a one-time meeting. A group of friends at school; friends gathered for coffee; parents gathered to discuss common parenting problems; or a visit to a hospital, jail, or retirement home may offer opportunity for small group evangelism. Small group evangelism could and should take place in the homes of believing parents as they share the love of God with their children, other family members, and guests.

12. The evangelist must establish good social relationships with those who need to hear the gospel. When Jesus went to the Samaritan woman, He crossed several social barriers but succeeded in winning her to faith. Christians are separated from the world and its ways, but disciples must not be isolated from the people of the world.

13. The evangelist must live a consistent Christian life within the group. People will be attracted to the gospel only if the evangelist demonstrates faith in action as well as words. The evangelist acts in love toward those with whom the gospel is shared, presents the gospel facts without personal condemnation of the group members, and allows the Holy Spirit to convict the listeners of their sins and of their need of the gospel.

14. Small group evangelism rests on the relevance of Christ and the gospel. Christ should be presented as the One who give purpose to life, conquers death, gives peace, cures loneliness, gives control and freedom, and finally prepares a place for us in heaven.

Guide to Church Evangelism

Evangelism was the heart of Jesus' ministry (Lk 19:10), the reason the church was established (Mt 16:13-20), and the commission Christ left with the church before He ascended to the Father (Mt 28:18-20). The church must preach the gospel to all nations before the end comes (Mt 24:14). The church as Christ's body and each member of the local church must concentrate on the evangelistic task of the church. As you seek to be a part of your church's evangelism program and to challenge your church to be evangelistic, you will need the theological foundation provided by notes and Scripture on EVANGELISM, In the Church, In the Marketplace.

God chose the church to take His message of salvation to all people. The church has the responsibility to develop a complete program of ensuring that every person in its range of influence hears the gospel message. The following guidelines will help the church as it prepares to reach out in its community to share the gospel.

1. The message of salvation should cross all racial, social, and cultural barriers. The church should accept no excuse for not reaching people. The church is responsible for all people and needs to develop strategies to reach every segment of the population. Analyze your church and its ministry. How limited is your membership to one group of alike people? What service ministries, small group evangelistic ministries, and personal witnessing ministries are needed to reach the varied population groups of your community? What members of your church have easiest access to the groups not being reached? What training do those people need to reach out effectively to racial, social, cultural, and economic groups your church is

not reaching? Enlist the people. Train them. Develop a strategy for reaching specific target groups. Plan specific reporting sessions to determine how to improve the program and to celebrate the program's success.

2. Prayer is a vital part of the church's evangelistic efforts. Confession of the church's failures in evangelism, petition for laborers for the evangelistic ministry of the church, intercession for the evangelistic workers of the church, and thanksgiving for the evangelistic results of the church are all part of the evangelistic prayer ministry of the church. All members should participate in this prayer task. Establish prayer groups to pray specifically for the evangelistic ministry and for lost persons. Give homebound people specific prayer responsibilities. Organize the prayer ministry of the church for evangelistic needs.

3. God has given evangelistic gifts to members of the church. (Eph 4:11-16). The church needs to recognize these gifts and encourage those with the gifts to lead the church in its evangelistic ministry.

4. God has called all disciples to a discipline of witnessing. The church should provide training for each member to learn to use a marked New Testament, develop a personal testimony presentation, and guide people to commit themselves to Christ. The church should celebrate evangelistic victories with the witnessing disciples. The church should instill confidence, not guilt, in its members as it calls people to witness.

5. Evangelism requires unique training. The church should use its gifted evangelists to train other disciples in evangelism. Evangelism training is training by doing. The church should provide opportunities for experienced witnesses to accompany witnesses in training on personal witness assignments. Evangelistic training shows people how to use the New Testament, their own testimony, and an understanding of common questions and objections to reach other people for Christ. Training assures prospective witnesses that God saves the lost by using His Word and His messenger, that God is present with the person who witnesses for Him, and that God is responsible to bring conviction leading to repentance and salvation. Training is not accomplished in a one-night lecture or an extended training program. Evangelistic training must be continuous, as witnesses share their experiences and learn from one another, always incorporating new disciples into the training program.

6. The church must use the basic church programs to accomplish the evangelistic task. Bible study groups, women's groups, youth groups, and service ministries should be carried out with evangelistic goals. Group leaders should be trained in evangelism. Group programs should include specific evangelistic emphases. The church must use every means at its disposal to present Christ to unbelievers. Programs and activities should be purposefully evangelistic, not just hopefully evangelistic.

7. Worship services ought to be planned and conducted to present the gospel to the lost. The central purpose of the service is to lead participants to worship God. Such services should be attractive and exciting. They should contain an element which clearly presents the gospel and Christ's invitation to salvation. They should provide concrete ways for persons to respond to Christ and accept His salvation. The atmosphere of worship should attract persons to Christ.

8. The evangelistic church has a plan to identify lost people and relate to them personally. Church members should show loving concern and Christian ministry to such people. They should be invited to enroll in Bible study program or in a special evangelistic small group Bible study. The church should plan a strategy to present personal testimonies and the gospel message to every lost person in the community. Such strategy should not rely on the hope that persons will see and respond to mass media presentations. They should entail detailed plans for personal presentations to specific people, until everyone has heard and had a chance to respond.

9. The church should conduct special evangelistic events that will attract the lost. These may be outdoor crusades, church revivals, special features for community groups, special Bible studies, or evangelistic participation in community activities planned by other groups. The interests and needs of the community should guide the planning of the special evangelistic efforts.

10. The church needs evangelistic confidence. Churches who search for lost people can find them. Every church member should be encouraged to help the church discover lost people.

Files should be developed to identify such people and to develop strategies to reach these people. It is inadequate simply to know and admit that millions of people in our country, hundreds of thousands in our state, and hundreds in our community are unsaved and thus lost for eternity. The lost who are not now related to the churches must be located and won to Christ. They must be identified, cultivated, visited, given testimonies, told the gospel, and invited to become disciples of Jesus Christ.

11. Churches must send disciples where the lost are, not expect the lost to come to the churches. Most of the lost are not in church services and will not be unless they are found and invited.

12. The church must develop an attractive reputation. The lost should view the church as a place of love, concern, and ministry, a people of cooperation, helpfulness, and self-giving. The life-style of individual members and of the church as a whole should attract nonbelievers to the church. The services, ministries, and activities of the church should be planned around the interests and needs of the lost community rather than around the traditions of the church or the selfish interests of the members.

13. Something can be done to attract the attention of the lost. Sometimes a direct approach such as visiting homes, mail or telephone solicitation, or direct response advertising may be used. You may succeed with handouts at malls, youth car washes, or booths at country fairs. You may use community religious surveys, census methods inside the church family, telephone census of the community, or newcomer utility services as ways to locate lost people in your community.

14. Cultivation is an essential part of church evangelism. Almost all people who receive Christ have been through a time of cultivation before they accept Him. Unreached people may be at any one of several levels of readiness to relate to the church and its members or to receive Christ. Some may respond positively to an invitation to attend Sunday School or worship services. They may even be ready to receive Christ as Savior immediately. Others may be willing to attend special events or activities of the church but not to attend regular, ongoing activities. Others may not be willing to attend any obviously religious activities but will go with Christian friends to entertainment gatherings or other activities. Some people are rebellious toward Christ and do not wish to be with Christians under any circumstances. Even these can be cultivated through personal one-on-one friendship. The purpose of cultivation is to move people from one stage of readiness in their attitudes to another until they are ready to receive Christ. To cultivate people requires a loving, friendly approach. The cultivation process should develop good will toward Christ, Christians, and the church; show Christian love and interest for the lost person; develop an awareness of needs, and begin to meet the needs of the lost person; and encourage the person to become involved in activities with church people. This may be accomplished best through small group participation rather than seeking immediate enrollment in larger ongoing groups.

15. The Sunday School or other regular Bible study program of the church offers one of the best ways to reach the lost. Small classes can be personal and allow members to know one another's needs. Here persons experience Christian friendship, love, and ministry. Bible teaching regularly leads participants to evaluate their relationship to Christ, teaches the way to salvation, and invites people to accept Christ for salvation. Most people who enroll in Sunday School and attend regularly are eventually won to Christ.

16. In every community people live without knowing Jesus as Savior. These unreached people are the church's greatest responsibility and most glorious opportunity. God has told all disciples to be witnesses for Him. All saved people in the church need to be concerned that those who do not know Christ are lost. Each church member ought to love God enough to desire that the lost be saved and to be willing to be equipped as a witness. The church remains the chief means that God has for reaching the lost.

Guide to Mass Evangelism

Persons must accept salvation one by one as individuals. This does not mean the gospel can only be presented to one person at a time. Since Peter preached at Pentecost, the church has used various ways to present the gospel to masses of people. Mass evangelism is usually understood to refer to preaching the gospel to a gathering of people in a church building or in a crusade setting such as a stadium. Thus mass evangelism has often been associated with revivals. Recently mass evangelism has expanded its scope to include electronic media. Each church needs to seek ways to present the gospel to the masses. As you help your church explore such ways, you will want to study notes and Scripture on EVANGELISM, Mass.

1. Mass evangelism is preaching the gospel of Christ to the lost. The early church openly proclaimed Christ as the Messiah even though they did not have church buildings where masses might gather. They sought out gatherings of people and used every opportunity to proclaim the gospel.

2. The message proclaimed in New Testament mass evangelism presented the seriousness of sin and called for repentance. See the summary of The Gospel.

3. Mass evangelism has a history in the modern church. It came primarily from revivals or awakenings in the early 1700's both in Europe and America. John Wesley and George Whitefield led mass evangelism efforts. Their method of gathering crowds and preaching Christ both in church buildings and in other places has survived as a very important way to practice evangelism.

a. The early evangelists emphasized a heartfelt religion, the priesthood of the believer, and the importance of the common person. Personal testimonies were an important part of these early gatherings, giving rise to lay involvement in leading worship.

b. Late eighteenth century camp meetings became popular ways to preach the gospel and reach the people in a special setting. The nation was filled with social problems and immorality in the years following the War of Revolution. Religious leaders set up campsites on the frontier and preached at a series of services lasting for weeks at a time. Spirited singing and powerful preaching marked the meetings. Strong appeals were made to sinners to repent and turn to Christ.

c. Spontaneous prayer meetings marked the revival of 1857-58. Meetings for mass evangelism broke out in schools and other public places. This revival lasted through the War Between the States and resulted in a new revivalism that lasted from about 1890 to 1945. Outdoor crusades and revivals proved an effective means of winning the lost. Wilbur Chapmen, Dwight L. Moody, and Billy Sunday led mass meetings during this period. The great modern crusades are an outgrowth of the efforts and results of these men. Church revivals of today also grew out of these past movements.

4. Effective mass evangelism depends primarily on the movement of God's Holy Spirit among those who are presenting and those who listen to the gospel. Whether in the New Testament era or at other times in history, the awakening that accompanies mass evangelism success is always founded on prayer and the work of the Spirit.

5. The church is God's chosen instrument to communicate the gospel of Christ. Advances in communication technology influence the methods the church chooses to use to proclaim Christ's good news.

a. Many churches and evangelists use television to preach Christ to the lost. Television is the primary source of information for a large percentage of the population. Since television is not primarily a response-related media, evangelists usually use an accompanying method to insure one-to-one personal communication. Telephone counselors and written correspondence are two ways used to follow-up television evangelism. Television use is not limited to evangelistic crusades and preaching. Worship services, music presentations, special programs, brief messages, public service announcements, paid advertising, talk shows, listener call-in shows, and many other formats may be used to communicate the gospel through television. The church continues to learn how to use this media effectively to reach the millions of lost people.

b. Church and evangelists have much longer experience using radio to tell the good news. Many of the principles mentioned in relation to television also apply to radio. Because radio audiences tend to be highly selective and to concentrate on a few stations featuring their favorite format or type of music, evangelistic radio programming should be aimed at the particular radio station's primary audience. The type of program format, music, features, and proclamation should be selected with the specific audience in mind.

c. Newspapers offer opportunities for mass evangelism. News stories of special church events, paid advertisements, special editorial features, and even comments on the international Sunday School lessons may be welcomed by editors. Newspaper reporters should be invited to cover revivals, historical celebrations, music presentations, and other special events of the church. Church leaders should be available to local newspapers and other media personnel for interviews on contemporary issues in which the church has an interest.

d. Outdoor advertising on billboards or church signs can also deliver brief evangelistic messages or teaser lines to encourage people to seek out the church for help.

e. Direct mail has been used effectively in mass evangelism. This includes letters explaining the way of salvation, tracts dealing with contemporary issues and leading to a call for commitment to Christ and His life-style, brochures describing church ministries and programs, and other creative means of catching the eye of people and relating to their felt needs.

f. The telephone is another tool of media evangelism. The telephone can be used to locate the lost for a follow-up visit, to invite persons to evangelistic events, or to witness directly to the lost.

6. Planning and prayer are the keys to successful mass evangelism efforts in the local church.

a. Prayer preparation must be begun and continued for long periods prior to a scheduled event. Prayer planning should be begun a year prior to the event. Individuals should be committed to specific evangelistic prayer support for at least six months prior to the meeting. Group prayer support should begin in regular church meetings at the same time. Specially organized prayer groups should begin meeting soon thereafter. Prayer for mass evangelism should not be limited to specific meetings, however. Part of the church's ongoing program should include regular, organized prayer support for God's Spirit to come in power upon the church and bring mass evangelism results within the church's ongoing program of proclamation and witness.

b. Church planning should regularly include great attention to mass evangelism both as an ongoing effort and as a concentrated event. Long-range planning should incorporate major events into the calendar from two to five years ahead of time. Persons featured in the event should be contracted at this time as should meeting facilities if these are to include sites outside the church's property. Short-term planning should be done at least a year prior to the meeting and should include a detailed preparation schedule, lining up of church program leaders, committees, and special planning groups for their involvement in planning and carrying out the meeting. A schedule of activities and planning meetings for the year should be drawn up.

c. Special planning should be carried out to involve the church in mass media evangelism. Careful goals should be set for each mass media effort. Ways of measuring the effectiveness of the effort in achieving the goals should be devised and implemented. Regular meetings should evaluate the mass media efforts and implement changes to bring greater effectiveness.

7. Mass evangelism can never be separated from personal evangelism. Though the gospel is presented to the masses, the response to God is personal. All mass evangelism should be done with people and their needs and interests in mind.

Guide to Missions Ministries

What is mission?

Who is a missionary?

How can I participate in the church's mission task?

These are three practical questions each disciple needs to ask and to answer. The answer to the first question is found from Ge 1 through Rev 22. A missions teacher of another era asked his classes, "What is the Bible all about? Is it ALL about anything?" His answer, a resounding Yes! It is all about God's mission of redemption for all persons and all things. He sent His one and only Son to show us clearly His love and purpose (Jn 3:16). His death and resurrection made two things clear: 1) salvation comes only through Him (Ac 4:12); and 2) the Holy Spirit would empower believers to be witnesses of Jesus Christ to the ends of the earth (Ac 1:8). The mission of God is to redeem all things to Himself. The church was created to be a tool in God's hand for His mission. As you seek to find your place in God's mission, you will need to understand fully the biblical teaching about missions. Read the notes and Scripture on MISSIONS. Then study this following "Guide to Missions Ministries."

1. A missionary is someone sent especially to tell others about Jesus (Ac 13:3). Missionaries cross some kind of line or barrier such as race, language, culture, or religion. All Christians are witnesses for Christ wherever they are, but not all Christians are missionaries by the definition above. God's mission requires, however, that we all participate in missions with our various gifts, skills, and calling. Both the missionary sent out to plant a life and believers going temporarily to share their witness are vital to global evangelization.

2. No nation or people is closed to God's presence and activity. We read about resistant areas and responsive areas, open places and "closed" places. At some point in time, a citizen of one country may encounter problems seeking to enter another country to represent Christ, but all churches and believers must join heart and hand in seeking ways for all people to hear God's good news.

3. Vocational missionaries are sent by some sponsoring body in answer to God's call to plant their lives in a continuing witness among another people or on behalf of another people. This complex world calls for at least two approaches to the vocational missionary expression.

a. Resident missionaries can still gain permission to enter foreign countries for the purpose of religious endeavors. These career missionaries devote their lives to:

• introducing persons to Christ;

• starting churches;

• working through the ministries of existing churches;

• training leaders in formal, professional theological studies, informal or extension training, lay institutes, or other types of teaching ministries;

• ministering to youth or to other specific age groups;

• ministering through media ministries such as book and tract production, video production, cassette production;

• serving in health care ministries both in healing and preventative medicine;

• developing whole-person ministries such as goodwill centers, long range development programs, meeting acute hunger needs, disaster ministries, or other ministries called for by the needs of the country and culture. These ministries are part of larger strategies of the whole church reaching out to the whole person.

• Bible translation.

b. Non-resident missionaries must live outside the country of focal ministry and work catalytically to build bridges for witness. World realities often force missionaries to seek means of missionary service outside the traditional role of resident missionary. Non-resident missionaries devote their lives to:

• traveling to identify where the church and Christians exist to lend encouragement, brief personal help, and prayer support;

• researching to discover Christian groups who have any kind of contact with a targeted non-Christian population;

• building awareness networks by taking every appropriate initiative to encourage every available approach by all Great Commission Christians;

• co-ordinating work of a mission organization with an area of work where resources other than personnel may be shared with local Christians to strengthen work in the country where missionary personnel cannot enter;

• secunding or sharing one's spiritual gifts and expertise across organizational and territorial lines to strengthen mission work in many places. Persons with technical expertise are especially effective in such mission work. The non-resident missionary is a new category for most mission organizations, so this list represents only a few possible approaches to a new way of working in global evangelization.

4. Bivocational missionaries are usually resident missionaries sent by a business or-

ganization but encouraged and supported in all ways possible by a Christian missionary organization. The bivocational missionary may receive primary financial support from the business organization or from the missionary organization. A few categories of bivocational missions includes:

a. Coordinated services: Churches, denominations, and interdenominational agencies and institutions provide opportunities for those with skills in education, health care, management, technical areas, and many other fields to meet specific needs defined by a host country. Such host countries may not ask for or allow vocational missionaries but will welcome committed Christian personnel who can help undergird development in a specific area of need defined by the country's government or institutions.

b. Laity abroad: Large corporations and institutions often assign employees to work in foreign countries. An employee may take the initiative in asking for a specific foreign assignment, knowing opportunities for Christian service are available in that country. An employee taking such an assignment may be motivated primarily by a desire to spread the faith in that part of the world.

c. Students abroad: Increasingly, Christian students have opportunities to do both undergraduate and graduate studies in an international setting. To be in resident study abroad not only expands educational experience but also provides an effective way to plant a Christian witness. In such a global village, discipleship calls many more students to study abroad with a missionary motive.

5. A-vocational missionary opportunities challenge many persons whose calling and vocation is to work in their own home and culture. They can dedicate significant blocks of time to cross-cultural missions by fulfilling a narrowly-defined task. Vacation days and other designated times can be used to share expertise and witness in home or overseas missions. Options include:

a. Auxiliary mission service involves one or two years of service in an English language assignment. The permanent missionary force would define a specific skill needed to reinforce their service ministries. Almost any area of endeavor one would engage in at home can be utilized in a mission setting, including church-related work, education, medical receptorships for medical students, and other opportunities for university students.

b. Temporary mission service involves one week to several months' commitment. Special evangelistic campaigns, choral tours, athletic events with witnessing opportunities, construction work, and relief for vocational missionaries comprise a few of the doors open to witness.

c. Vacation tours may be made with a missionary purpose. Rather than sight-seeing alone, many disciples travel with a view of learning more about God's mission throughout the world and to sharing their witness as they do so. Every serious Kingdom citizen should have a valid passport in hand, ready to go anywhere at anytime to tell God's good news in places of great need, and to lend encouragement to believers who desperately need it.

6. All believers can participate in mission ministry even while they remain at home. Mission ministry depends upon personnel, prayer, and financial support from home. Local churches need to educate people about mission opportunities and invite members to listen for God's call to mission work. Individuals and churches need to include substantial mission support funds in their budgets. Churches and each disciple need to devote much time and energy to missionary praying. Our Lord laid on His followers the imperative to pray for laborers for the harvest (Mt 9:37-38). We should also intercede for the laborers once they are working in the harvest. We need to pray that proclaimers will have courage and boldness even as Paul asked for himself (Eph 6:18-20). We are to pray for the lost peoples of the world that they will come to know Jesus as Savior and thus know eternal life.

7. Disciples need to make practical missionary decisions and act on them. They need to determine their role in God's missionary enterprise. They need to become involved in mission efforts sponsored by their local church. They need to set aside specific time periods for missionary prayer. They need to seek God's will about personal involvement in mission ministries.

They need to gain information from pastor, other church staff, denominational mission agencies, or other mission agencies about particular mission service opportunities. Should God open the door and direct, they should enter the process to become vocational, bivocational, or a-vocational missionaries.

Doctrinal Reference Index
NIV Concordance
Maps

DOCTRINAL REFERENCE INDEX

To use the Doctrinal Reference Index, locate the doctrine of interest under its appropriate category (see chart, p. xii). For example, locate GOD, which appears under the category, THE TRINITARIAN GOD. Then locate a particular point about the doctrine that you wish to investigate, for example, God's constant nature. Note that the word *Nature* in point **I.A. "He is Constant in *Nature*"** is italicized. The italicized word or words under each doctrine tells you how the annotation will be labeled. The annotations about God's constant nature will be labeled **GOD** (the doctrine title), **Nature** (the italicized word). Beneath point **I.A. "He is Constant in *Nature*"** note that the six Scripture references are given. Look up any of these six Bible passages in the Bible text, and you will find at the bottom of the page an annotation referenced to the passage and entitled **GOD, Nature.**

THE TRINITARIAN GOD

GOD

I. GOD IS UNIQUE IN NATURE

A. He is Constant in *Nature*

Nu 23:19; Dt 32:3; 2 Ch 2:6; Ps 18:25-31; 40:10; Jer 9:24

B. He is the *One* true *God*

Ge 31:30-35; 35:2; Ex 6:2-3; 8:10; 12:12; 15:1-18; 20:1-7; 32:1; Nu 27:15-16; Dt 3:24; 4:27-40; 5:7-15; 6:4-9; 12:2-7; 29:18-21; Jos 4:24; 22:10-34; 24:14-24; Jdg 8:27,33; 10:6-9; 1 Sa 5:1-5; 7:3-4; 1 Ki 9:6-9; 11:9-13,29-39; 15:12-13; 18:24,27,36-39; 2 Ki 1:2-6; 10:18-27; 11:18; 1 Ch 16:8-36; 2 Ch 2:5; 7:19-22; 13:9-10; 14:11; 15:10-18; 32:13-21; 33:4-13; 34:3-7,32; Ne 1:5; Est 3:2; Ps 81:9-10; Isa 2:8,18,20; 10:10-11; 36:1—37:38; 40:18-20,25; 41:7,22-29; 42:8,17; 43:10-15; 44:6-28; 45:5,14-24; 46:1-13; 48:5,14; 57:1-13; 64:4; 66:18-21; Jer 1:16; 2:5-13,26-28; 5:7-13; 7:18; 10:1-16; 19:4-6; 44:3,8,15-29; 50:2,38,44; 51:15-19; Eze 6:3-7; 11:21; 14:1-11; 20:1-44; 28:1-10; 30:13; Da 2:11,47; Hos 2:2-23; 8:4-6; 10:5-8; Joel 2:27; Am 2:4; Jnh 1:6,14-16; 2:8-9; Mic 1:7; 4:5,13; 5:12-15; 7:14-20; Na 1:14; Hab 2:18-20; Zep 1:4-6; Zec 13:9; Mal 1:11; 2:11-12; Mk 12:29-31; Jn 4:21-23; 5:17-18; Ac 7:39-43; 17:16-29; 19:23-41; Ro 3:29-30; 10:11-13; 1 Co 8:1-8; 10:7-20; 2 Co 4:4,6; Eph 4:1-6; 1 Ti 1:17; 3:15-16; Heb 8:10; 11:6; Rev 9:20

C. He is *Holy*

Ge 32:30; Ex 3:5-6; 19:10-24; 25:1—31:18; 40:9-16; Lev 11:44-45; Nu 1:51; 20:6-13; Dt 23:18; Jos 3:4; 5:15; Jdg 6:20-23; 13:22; 1 Sa 6:19-20; 2 Sa 6:1-7; 1 Ki 6:16; 2 Ki 11:15; 1 Ch 13:10-12; 15:11-15; 16:10,29,35; 2 Ch 3:8,10; 5:7-9; 8:11; 20:21; 23:14,19; 35:13; Ezr 9:2; Job 13:16; Ps 16:3; 22:3; 28:2; 43:3; 46:4; 89:18,35; 93:5; 98:1; 99:3,5,9; 103:1; 105:3,42; 111:9; Pr 9:10; Isa 1:4; 5:16,19,24; 6:3; 8:13; 10:17-20; 30:11-12,15; 31:1; 35:8; 41:14,16,20; 43:3,14,15; 60:9,14; 62:12; Jer 2:3; Eze 20:12,14,40,41; 22:26-31; 36:20-23; 38:1—39:29; 42:13,14,20; 43:7,12; 44:8-9,23; 45:1,3,4; 48:12,18; Da 4:4-23; 9:16,20,24; 12:7; Am 2:7; 4:2; Hab 1:12-13; 2:20; Zep 3:11; Zec 2:12-13; 8:3; 14:20-21; Mal 2:13-16; Lk 11:2; 2 Co 7:1; 1 Ti 6:15-16; 1 Pe 1:15-16; 1 Jn 2:20; 3:3

D. He is *Transcendent*

Job 25:1-6; 37:1-24; Ps 148:13; Isa 40:15-17,21-24; 55:6-13

E. He is *Immanent*

Ps 68:16; 139:7-10

F. He is *Eternal*

Ge 1:1; 21:33; 1 Ch 29:10; Ps 55:19; 93:2; 102:12; 102:25; 132:14; 135:13; La 5:19; Da 6:26; 7:9,14,22,27; Hab 1:12; Ro 16:25-27; Heb 1:12; Rev 1:4,8

G. He is *Spirit*
Jn 4:24

H. He is One in three, *Trinity*
Mt 3:16-17; 16:16-17,27; 20:23; 24:36; 28:19; Mk 2:7; Lk 5:21-24; 10:21; Jn 3:34-36; 10:25-38; 12:44-50; 13:31-32; 14:6-31; 15:26; 16:5-32; 20:17,28; Ac 1:4-5; 2:22,33; 2:36; Ro 5:5-8; 1 Co 1:3,4,9; 2:6-16; 6:11; 8:4-6; 12:1-6; 12:28; 15:24,27-28; 2 Co 1:2-7; 13:4; Gal 1:1,3-4; 3:14; 4:4-6; Eph 1:17; 2:14-22; Php 1:2-23; 2:6; 2:11; Col 1:3-14; 2:2-3,9; 1 Th 3:11; 1 Ti 2:5; Tit 2:13; 3:4-6; Heb 1:1-14; 1:5; 9:14; 1 Pe 1:2-3,17-21; 1 Jn 2:1,22-24; 4:2-3; 4:7-16; 5:1-20; 2 Jn 3,9; Jude 1,4,25; Rev 2:18,27-29; 3:5,21-22; 7:10

I. He reveals Himself in *Glory*
Ex 16:7,10; 40:34-38; 1 Sa 4:5-7,21-22; 1 Ki 8:11; 1 Ch 29:11; 2 Ch 5:14; Ps 8:1,9; 26:8; 29:1-3,9; 57:5,11; 63:2-3; 66:2; 79:9; 85:9; 86:9; 96:3,6-8; 106:20; 108:5; 113:4; 115:1; 138:5; Isa 6:3; 24:15; 26:10,15; 35:2; 58:8; 60:1-2; 66:18-19; Jer 2:11; 13:16; Eze 1:28; 3:12,23; 8:4; 10:4,18-19; 28:22; 39:13,21; 43:2,4-5; 44:4; Hos 4:7; Hab 2:14; Hag 2:7,9; Zec 2:5; Lk 2:9,14; Jn 11:4; 12:28; 17:1,4; Ac 7:2,55; Ro 3:23; 5:2; 2 Co 3:7-18; 4:6; Eph 1:12-17; 3:20-21; Heb 1:3; Rev 21:11,23

II. GOD IS INTIMATE

A. He is *Living*
Nu 14:21,28; Jos 3:10-13; 1 Sa 17:26,36; 1 Ki 17:1,12; Ps 42:2; Isa 37:4,19; Jer 10:9-10; Eze 14:16,18,20; Da 6:20,26-27; Jn 6:57; 1 Th 1:9; Heb 3:12; 10:26-31; Rev 7:2

B. He is *Personal*
Ge 9:8-17; Ex 3:12-16; Ps 86:1-7; 116:1-2; 120:1; 121:3-8; 143:10; Isa 25:1,9; 41:10-13; Jer 30:22; 31:33; Eze 34:24,30-31; 43:7; Hos 2:23; Am 5:14; Jnh 2:6; Zec 2:10-13; 1 Ti 4:10

C. He is *Jealous*
Ex 34:14; Dt 6:10-25; 7:1-6; 1 Ki 14:9-16,22; 16:13; 2 Ki 17:11-41; Ps 79:5; Isa 9:7; 26:11; 30:22; 37:32; Eze 16:38; 23:25; 36:5-6; Joel 2:18; Na 1:2; Zep 1:18; 3:8; Zec 1:14; 8:2; Ac 12:21-23; 1 Co 10:9-11,22

III. GOD RELATES TO US AND TO HIS WORLD

A. He is *Creator*
Ge 1:3—2:25; Ne 9:5-37; Ps 19:1-4; 24:1-2,7-10; 33:6-9; 65:6; 86:9; 93:1; 95:3-7; 96:4-6; 100:3; 115:15; 121:2; 124:8; 134:3; 136:4-9; 146:6; 149:2; Isa 17:7; 37:16; 42:5; 43:1-21; 44:2,21,24; 45:7-9,11-12,18; 48:12-13; 54:5,16; 65:17; Jer 5:22-25; 10:12-16; 27:5-22; 31:35-37; 33:2; Am 4:13; 5:8-9; 9:5-6; Jnh 1:9; Zec 10:1; 12:1-9; Ac 14:11-15; 17:24-28; Ro 4:17; 2 Co 5:5; 5:17; Col 3:10; 1 Pe 4:19; Rev 10:6

B. He is *Judge*
Ge 3:8-24; Ps 1:6; 9:4-9; 50:4,6,16-23; 54:1,4; 75:2,7; 76:8-9; 96:10-13; 98:9; Eze 20:35-38; 21:3-5; 38:22; Da 7:9-10,22,26; Joel 3:2,12; Mic 6:1-16; Ro 2:2; 3:6; 14:10-12; 1 Co 4:4; 5:13; 11:31-32; Gal 2:6; 2 Ti 4:1,8; Jas 1:12; 1 Pe 4:5; Rev 2:23; 6:10; 18:1-24

C. He is *Father*
Dt 1:31; 8:1-5; 14:1-29; 32:6; 2 Sa 7:14; 1 Ch 17:13; 22:10; Ps 68:5; 89:26; 103:8,13; Pr 3:11-12; Isa 43:1-7; 45:10-11; 63:8,16; 64:8; Jer 3:4,19; 31:9,20; Hos 11:1-11; Mal 1:6; 2:10; Mt 5:43-48; 6:1-34; 7:11; 11:25-27; 23:9; Mk 14:36; Lk 11:2,13; 1 Co 14:33; Gal 3:26; Php 4:13-20; Heb 12:5-12; 1 Pe 1:17; 2 Pe 1:17; Rev 21:3-7

IV. GOD HAS DISTINCTIVE QUALITIES

A. He is *Love*
Ex 3:7; 6:5; 15:26; 34:5-7; Dt 7:7-8,12-13; 11:10-15; 30:1-10; 30:11-16; 32:10-12,36; 2 Sa 12:24-25; 1 Ki 8:23; 10:9; 1 Ch 16:34,41; 2 Ch 5:13; 20:21; Ne 1:5; 9:17-19; Ps 13:5; 25:6-10; 26:3; 31:7,16,19,21; 33:5,22; 36:5,7,10; 37:28; 44:3,26; 51:1; 52:8; 62:11-12; 69:13,16; 86:5,13,15; 89:1-49; 90:13-17; 98:2-3; 103:4,8,11,17; 106:1,45; 107:1,8,15,21,31,43; 109:21,26; 118:1-4,29; 119:41,64,76,88,124,149,156,159; 130:7; 136:1-26; 138:2,8; 145:8-9,17; 147:11; Isa 5:1-4; 16:5; 38:17; 40:11; 54:7-10; 55:3; 56:3-8; 60:10; 60:15-16; Jer 12:7,14-17; 13:14,17; 30:18; La 3:22-33; Eze 16:1-63; Da 9:4; Hos 2:1-23; 3:1; 11:1-4,8; 14:1-8; Jnh 3:9; 4:2; Zec 10:3,6; Mt 10:29-31; 18:10-14; Mk 1:11; 9:7; Lk 3:22; Jn 3:16; 15:9-14; 16:26-27; Ro 8:31-39; 9:10-13,25-26; Eph 1:4; 5:1-2; 1 Th 1:4; Tit 3:4; 1 Pe 5:7; 2 Pe 3:9; 1 Jn 2:5; 3:1; 4:7-21

B. He relates in *Mercy*
Ps 143:1

C. He saves in *Grace*
Ge 2:8-24; 19:12-19,29; 22:14; 32:10; 39:21-23; 45:5-9; Ex 1:20-21; Lev 10:11; 23:22; 26:3-13; Ru 2:20; 1 Sa 1:5,19-20; 2:20-21; 2 Sa 9:3; 14:14; 1 Ki 3:6,10-14; 2 Ki 13:23; 1 Ch 29:14-16; 2 Ch 1:8; 29:36; 30:9,18-20; 36:15; Ezr 7:28; 8:22-23; 9:8-15; Ne 2:8,18; 9:17,25,28,31,35; Job 42:10-17; Ps 3:1-8; 5:7-8; 6:2,9; 23:1-6; 57:1; 67:1; 102:13-17; 111:4; 119:132; 123:2-3; 124:1-8; 135:14; 140:6; 147:2-3; Pr 14:31; Ecc 5:18-20; Isa 14:1; 26:10; 43:25; 49:10,13-18; 51:3,12; 57:15; Jer 3:12,14; 16:5,13; Eze 20:17; 33:11; 36:8-12; 39:25; Am 5:15; 7:1-9; Jnh 4:6; 4:11; Hab 3:2; Zec 1:16; 8:15; Mal 3:10; Mt 20:1-16; Mk 5:19; Lk 1:30; 2:14,40; 6:36; Ac 4:33; 11:23; 14:3,26; 20:24,32; Ro 1:5-7; 2:4; 3:25; 5:15-21; 12:1; 1 Co 3:10; 15:10; 2 Co 5:18-21; 8:1; 9:8,14; 12:8-10; Gal 2:21; Eph 2:4-5; 3:1-11; 4:32; Col 1:6; 2 Ti 1:9-10; Tit 2:11-12; Jas 5:11; 1 Pe 5:10,12

D. He is *Righteous*
Ex 2:23-25; 9:27; Lev 1:1; Jos 23:1-16; 2 Sa 10:12; 2 Ch 19:7; Ezr 9:15; Ne 9:8; Job 4:17; Ps 4:1; 5:8; 7:9,11,17; 25:8-9; 31:1; 35:24; 36:6,10; 40:9-11; 48:10; 65:5; 71:2-3,15-19; 89:14; 92:15; 97:2,6; 103:17; 111:3; 119:40,75,137,142; 129:4; 145:17; Pr 17:5; Isa 24:16; 41:10; 45:21,24; 46:13; 51:5,7-8; 63:1; Jer 11:20; 12:1-17; 23:6; Da 9:7,14,16; Jnh

3:8; Zep 3:5; Mal 2:17—3:5; Jn 17:25; Ac 10:34-35; Ro 1:17; 2:11; 3:5-26; 10:3-4; 2 Pe 1:1; 1 Jn 1:5-7; 2:29; 3 Jn 11; Rev 14:1,4

E. His *Goodness* is unequalled
Ezr 3:11; Ps 73:1; 84:11; 106:1; 107:1; 118:1,29; 119:68; Jer 33:11,26; La 3:25; Na 1:7; Mt 19:17; Mk 10:17-18; 10:29-31; Ro 8:28; Jas 1:17; 1 Pe 2:3

F. His *Faithfulness* can be trusted
Ge 8:1; 35:3; Ex 13:5,11; Nu 26:65; Dt 10:11,22; Jos 1:6; 14:6-15; Jdg 2:2-3,10-14; 1 Sa 15:29; 1 Ki 2:4,24,27; 4:20; 8:15,20,23-24,26,56; 9:5; 15:4; 2 Ki 4:44; 8:19; 9:25-26,36-37; 10:10,17,30; 24:2,13; 1 Ch 19:13; 28:20; 2 Ch 6:4,10,14-17,42; 15:2-7; 36:21-23; Ezr 1:1; Ps 4:3; 5:3; 6:4; 9:10; 32:10; 33:4; 37:33; 57:3,10; 71:5-6,15-22; 77:8; 85:10-13; 89:1-49; 92:2; 100:5; 108:4; 119:75-76,86,90,138,160; 138:2; Jer 33:14-26; 39:16-17; 40:1-6; La 3:22; Eze 12:25-28; 14:6-9; Hos 6:3; Zep 3:5; Zec 8:8; Mal 3:6; Mt 27:46; Lk 2:26,29; Jn 3:33; 7:28; Ro 3:3-4; 1 Co 1:9; 10:13; 2 Co 1:18-22; Php 1:6; 1 Th 5:23-24; 2 Th 3:3; 1 Jn 1:9; Rev 10:7

G. His *Justice* is impartial and fair
Ge 18:20-33; 20:4-6; Ex 6:1-8; 2 Ch 12:6; Job 5:8-16; 8:3-20; 13:3—14:17; 15:17-35; 18:3-21; 20:4-29; 23:13-16; 24:1,12; 27:2,11-23; 31:35-37; 34:10-17; 36:3-12; 40:8; 41:11; 42:7-9; Ps 7:6,8,11; 33:5; 72:1; 94:1-2,22-23; 101:1; Isa 5:16; 26:9; 30:18-19; Jer 30:11; Eze 18:25-32; 33:17-20; Da 4:37; Ob 8-14; Hab 1:2-11; 2:16; Zec 1:6; Ro 9:14; Eph 6:9; Col 3:25—4:1; 2 Th 1:5-9; Heb 6:10; Jas 1:13-14; Rev 15:1-4

H. He reacts to sin in *Wrath*
Ge 6:5-8; 17:14; 19:13,24-26; Ex 4:14,24; 22:22-24; 32:10,12,34-35; 33:3; Lev 7:20,21,25,26,27; 26:14-45; Dt 8:19-20; 9:4-6; 11:16-21; 17:1-7,12; Jos 7:1,25-26; 11:20; Jdg 1:7; 1 Sa 3:12-14; 15:1-3; 28:15; 2 Sa 11:27—12:17; 1 Ki 13:4,26; 15:27-30; 16:2,7,13,26,33; 21:21-22; 2 Ki 9:7-10; 13:3; 22:13-17; 24:20; 1 Ch 21:7-15; 2 Ch 12:5-12; 16:7-9; 19:2,10; 21:12-19; 24:18-25; 26:20; 28:5-13,19,24-25; 29:3-10; 32:25; 33:6; 34:21; 36:16; Ezr 5:11-17; 9:7,14; 10:13-14; Ne 13:18; Ps 6:1; 18:7-15; 27:9; 30:5; 37:28; 38:1-3; 44:23; 56:7; 69:24; 74:1; 76:7,10-11; 78:1-72; 80:4; 88:15-18; 90:7-11; 95:10-11; 102:10; 103:8-10; 106:29,32,40; 110:5; 145:8; Pr 24:17-18; Ecc 5:4-7; Isa 5:5-7; 5:25; 9:12-21; 10:4-6,25; 13:3-13; 26:20-21; 28:1-4,16-22; 30:27-33; 34:2,5-15; 47:1-15; 51:17-23; 57:16-18; 59:17-18; 63:3; 64:5,9; 66:5-6,14-16,24; Jer 3:5,12; 4:4,8,26; 6:10-11; 7:20,29; 8:14-17; 10:10,24-25; 17:4,13; 21:4-7,12; 23:19-20; 25:1-38; 30:23-24; 32:29,37; 36:7; 42:18; 44:3,6,8; 51:45,56; La 1:12; 2:1-4,21; 3:1,43; 4:1-22; Eze 5:8-17; 7:8,12-14,19; 8:17-18; 9:3-11; 13:13-16; 16:23,35-42; 21:14-17,28-32; 22:20-31; 24:13; 25:14,17; 36:1-38; 38:18-19; Da 9:16; Hos 1:6—2:1; 5:1-15; 9:10-17; 12:14; Joel 2:13-14; Am 1:3-15; 4:1-13; 8:11-14; Jnh 3:9; Mic 1:3-16; 2:1-5; Na 1:2-6; 2:13; Hab 3:2-17; Zep 1:2-18; Zec 1:2-17; 7:1-14; 8:14-17; Mal 2:1-9; Mt 3:7-10; 18:32-35; Lk 19:14,27; Jn 3:36; Ro 1:18; 2:5-9; 5:9; Eph 2:3-5; 5:5; Col 3:6; 1 Th 1:10; 2:16; Rev 14:9-20; 16:1-21

I. He has perfect *Wisdom*
Dt 31:21; 1 Sa 2:3; 1 Ch 12:17; 28:9; 2 Ch 16:9; Job 11:4-12; 12:13; 28:1-28; Ps 44:21; 73:11; 94:10-11; 139:1-18; 147:5; Pr 3:19-20; 8:12-31; 15:3,11; 30:2-4; Ecc 8:16-17; Isa 28:29; 29:13-21; 31:2; Jer 16:17; 51:15; Eze 8:12; Hos 5:3; Am 5:12; Mk 13:32; Ac 2:23-24; 15:8; Ro 11:1-36; 1 Co 1:21-30; 2 Co 5:11; Eph 1:8; Heb 4:13; 1 Pe 1:2; 1 Jn 3:19-20

J. He has all *Power*
Nu 11:23; Dt 30:1-4; Jos 2:11; Jdg 7:22; 1 Ki 18:36-39; 2 Ch 14:11-13; Job 36:22-33; Ps 21:1,13; 28:1-8; 46:1; 50:1; 59:9,16-17; 66:3,7; 68:28-35; Isa 1:24; 19:1; 40:10,26,28-31; 59:1-20; Jer 10:6; 16:19-21; Eze 37:1-14; Da 3:1-30; Mt 19:16-26; Lk 5:17; 18:27; Jn 17:11-12; Ac 6:8; Ro 4:21; 1 Co 1:18-25; 2:4-5; 6:14; Eph 1:19-20; 3:7,20; Col 1:11,29; 2:12; 2 Pe 1:3-4

K. His *Presence* is always, everywhere available
Ge 16:13; Dt 4:7; Mic 3:4; Hag 1:13; 2:1-9; Heb 11:27

V. GOD WORKS IN HIS WORLD

A. He redeems as *Savior*
Ge 12:1-3; 2 Sa 22:1-51; Ps 7:1; 17:7; 18:1-48; 25:5; 27:1,9; 28:6-9; 35:3; 38:22; 42:5-6,11; 49:15; 51:14; 60:5-12; 62:1-2,6-8; 67:2; 68:19-20; 69:1-36; 80:2-3,7,19; 85:1-7; 88:1; 91:1-16; 98:1-3; 106:4,8,10,21; 138:7; 144:2; Isa 12:1-3; 17:10; 25:9; 38:17,20; 45:15,21; 48:17; 49:7,26; 51:5-6,22; 63:1-16; Jer 14:8-9; 42:11-12; 50:34; Eze 34:1-30; 36:24; Da 3:16-18,28-30; 6:27; Hos 7:13; Am 5:4-6; 9:11-15; Mic 2:12-13; 7:7; Zep 3:17; Zec 8:7-8; Lk 1:47; 1 Ti 1:1; 2:3

B. He fulfills His purposes in *Sovereignty*
Ge 15:13-16; 18:14; 24:3,7,50; 28:3; 41:16,25,28,32; 43:23; Ex 4:21; 7:3-5,13,22; 19:1-6; 20:12-17; 33:19; Dt 1:10; 2:5,9,24-25,30,36; 3:1-11,21-22; 5:32-33; 10:14-21; 26:16; 28:1-68; Jdg 9:23-24,56-57; Ru 1:13,20-21; 4:13; 1 Sa 2:6-10; 12:16-25; 17:45-47; 25:39; 2 Sa 7:22-28; 17:14; 1 Ki 4:29; 8:27,39,50; 11:14-40; 12:15,24; 19:15-18; 22:19; 2 Ki 15:5; 19:20-36; 1 Ch 14:11-17; 17:7-8,24; 18:6,13; 29:11-12; 2 Ch 20:6,15,17,29; 22:7; 25:8-9,20; 36:17-23; Ezr 5:5; Ne 4:14; 9:10; Job 1:21-22; 2:10; 9:2-35; 12:10—14:22; 19:21; 26:6-14; 34:1-30; 38:1—39:30; 42:2-6; Ps 2:4-6; 5:1-2; 10:16; 11:1,4; 22:26-31; 29:10-11; 33:10-21; 44:4; 46:6,10; 47:2-9; 59:5,13; 97:1,5,9; 99:1-2; 104:1-35; 113:4-9; 135:6; 146:7-10; Pr 16:33; 19:21; 20:24; 21:1,30; Ecc 3:11-14; 5:2; 7:13-14; 11:3-5; Isa 14:1-2; 14:26-27; 23:9; 30:1-7; 33:5,10,21-22; 37:16,22-29; 42:24; 45:1-3,11-

14:12-26; 14:43-52; 14:53—15:15; 15:21-41; 15:42-47; Lk 5:33-39; 9:21-27; 13:31-35; 18:31-34; 22:3-6; 22:7-23; 22:14-16; 22:20; 22:52-53; 23:26-56; 23:50-56; Jn 6:70-71; 12:1-10; 12:20-50; 12:33-36; 13:1-20; 13:18-30; 14:30; 18:31-32; 19:26-27; 19:34-37; 19:38-42; Ro 5:1-11; 14:15; 1 Co 1:23; 15:3-8; 2 Co 5:14-15; 13:4; Eph 2:13; Col 2:13-15; 1 Pe 1:18-21; 2:21-24

IV. JESUS FULFILLED GOD'S PURPOSES

A. In His *Teaching*
Mt 5:1-12; 5:8; 6:1-34; 7:1-27; 21:33-44; 23:8-10; Mk 7:1-23; 12:13-34; Lk 7:36-38; 11:37-54; 13:24-30; 23:5-16; Jn 3:2; 7:14-24; 11:28; 2 Jn 9

B. As God's *Servant*
Isa 42:1-16; 49:1-7; 50:4-11; 52:13—53:12; Mt 3:13-17; Lk 3:21-23; 22:24-27; Ac 3:13; 3:26; 4:27; Ro 15:7-8; Php 2:5-11

C. As God's *Shepherd*
Jn 10:1-21,25-30; Heb 13:20; Rev 7:17

D. In His *Glory*
Jn 1:14; 8:54; 11:4; 11:40; 12:20-33; 13:31-32; 17:1-5; 1 Co 2:8

E. As the *Truth* of God
1 Jn 5:20

F. As the *Light* to God
Jn 1:4-5; 3:19; 8:12; 2 Co 4:6

G. By completing His *Mission*
Mt 10:1-42; 19:13-14; Mk 2:17; 6:6-13; 6:30-44; 7:24-30; 10:1-52; 10:13-16; 10:38-39; Lk 4:14-31; 5:31-32; 6:12-16; 9:1-6; 9:10-17; 10:1-24; 12:50; 19:10; Jn 4:34; 5:17; 6:38-40; 8:31-59; 11:7; 11:55; 19:30; Ac 10:38; Eph 3:11-12; 1 Ti 1:15; 3:16; 2 Ti 1:9-10; 1 Jn 3:5-8

H. As the *Bread of Life*
Jn 6:25-59

I. In His *Love*
Eph 3:18-19; 5:2; 5:25-32; Php 1:8; Tit 3:4-7; 1 Jn 3:16

J. As the *Cornerstone*
Eph 2:20; 1 Pe 2:6

V. JESUS PROVIDES SALVATION

A. As *Redeemer*
Mt 20:28; Lk 1:67-79; 2:38; 2 Co 5:18-21; 11:4; Gal 3:13-14; Eph 1:7-10; Col 1:20-22; 1 Ti 2:5-6; Tit 2:14

B. As *Savior*
Mt 1:18-25; Lk 2:11; 2:30; Jn 4:42; Ac 4:12; 5:31; 13:23; 1 Co 3:11; 1 Th 5:9-10; Heb 13:8; 1 Jn 4:14

C. As *Lamb of God*
Jn 1:29,36; 1 Co 5:7; Rev 5:1-14; 13:8

D. As the *Life*
Jn 1:4; 4:13-14; Ac 3:15; Ro 5:15-21; Eph 2:10; Col 3:4; 1 Jn 4:9

E. As our *Priest*
Ge 14:17-24; Heb 2:17-18; 5:5-10; 7:1-28

F. In His *Atonement* for us
Jn 11:51; Ro 3:24-25; 4:23-25; Gal 1:4; 2:20-21; Heb 10:1-18; 1 Pe 3:15-22

G. As our *Hope*
Col 1:27; 1 Pe 1:3-4

VI. JESUS CONTINUES TO MINISTER FOR US

A. In heaven after His *Ascension*
Lk 9:51; 24:50-53; Jn 14:2; 16:5; Ac 1:9-12; 7:54-60; 9:1-18; Ro 15:18; 1 Co 1:17; 2 Co 2:12-14; Eph 1:20-23; 4:7-12; Col 3:1-4; 2 Ti 4:17-18; Heb 2:14; Rev 1:1; 3:19-21; 12:5; 22:16

B. Through *Intercession* for us
Lk 21:15; Jn 14:14-16; 17:6-26; Ac 18:9-10; 23:11; Ro 8:26-39; 2 Co 12:9; Heb 7:25; 1 Jn 2:1-2

VII. JESUS IS THE ETERNAL KING

A. He was *Preexistent*
Jn 1:1-18; 3:13-15; 6:33; 6:62; 8:58; 16:28; 17:5; 2 Co 8:9; Php 2:7; Col 1:15-17; Heb 1:2

B. He is the *Son of David*
Mt 1:1; 12:23-28; 15:22; 21:1-11; 22:41-46; Mk 10:46-52; 11:1-11; 12:35-37; Lk 1:69; 18:38-39; 20:41-47; Ro 1:3; 2 Ti 2:8-13

C. He introduced the *Kingdom of God*
Mt 4:17; 20:20-23; 22:1-14; Lk 6:20-23; 9:57-62; 11:14-28; 16:16-17; 22:28-30; Ac 28:31; Col 1:13-14; Rev 3:7; 11:15

D. We await His *Final Coming*
Mt 23:37-39; 24:1—25:46; 24:25-44; Mk 13:1-37; Ac 1:11; 3:19-21; 1 Co 1:7-8; 15:20-28; Php 3:20-21; 1 Th 1:10; 2:19; 3:13; 4:13-18; 5:23; 2 Th 1:7-10; 2:1-12; 1 Ti 6:14-15; 2 Ti 4:1; Tit 2:11-14; Heb 9:28; Jas 5:7-8; 1 Pe 5:1; 5:4; 2 Pe 1:11,16-18; 3:4,12; 1 Jn 2:28; 3:2; Rev 19:11—22:21

E. He is the Judge in final *Judgment*
Mt 3:11; 10:32-42; 25:31-46; Lk 17:22-37; Jn 5:27-30; 9:39; Ac 10:42; 17:31; Ro 2:16; 1 Co 4:4-5; 2 Co 5:10; 2 Ti 4:8; Rev 3:5; 6:16

F. Misunderstanding made the messianic *Secret* necessary
Mt 12:13-21; 13:10-17,34-35; Mk 1:25,34; 3:11-12; 4:11-12,33-34; 5:43; 8:30; Lk 5:14; Jn 7:1-10; 16:29-30; 20:1-9; Col 2:3

G. He is the expected *King*
Mt 2:1-12; 27:11; Mk 15:12-19; Lk 1:32-33; 19:11-27; 19:28-44; Jn 1:49; 6:1-15; 12:12-19; 18:33-37; 19:17-22; Ac 17:7; Heb 2:5-9; Rev 1:5-6; 17:14

HOLY SPIRIT

I. THE HOLY SPIRIT IS REVEALED

A. *Promised* by God
Mt 3:11; Mk 1:8; Lk 11:13; Jn 7:39; Ac 1:5; Gal 3:14

B. Revealed at *Pentecost*
Ac 2:1-4

C. Described by specific *Vocabulary*
Ex 14:21

II. THE HOLY SPIRIT WORKS FOR GOD'S PURPOSES

A. In *Creation*
Ge 1:1-2; Job 33:1-4

B. In *Redemption*
Lk 3:16

C. In Messianic *Hope*
Isa 11:1-2; 32:14-18; 42:1-2; 44:1-4; 59:21; 61:1-3; Eze 37:12-14; 39:29; Joel 2:28-32; Mt 12:15-21
D. In *Jesus*
Mt 1:18-20; 3:16-17; 4:1; 12:28; Mk 1:9-10; 1:12; Lk 3:21-22; 4:14; 4:16-19; 10:21; Jn 1:32-33; Ac 1:1-2; 10:38; Heb 9:14; 1 Jn 5:6-8
E. In *The Twelve*
Jn 16:5-7
F. In *Revelation*
Nu 11:25-29; 1 Sa 10:5-13; 2 Sa 23:1-4; 1 Ch 12:18; 2 Ch 15:1-2; 24:20; Ne 9:20,30; Eze 8:3; Da 4:9; Mic 3:8; Zec 7:12; Mt 22:43; Lk 1:67; 2:25-32; Ac 2:14-22; 4:25; 7:55-56; 21:11; 28:25-28; 1 Co 2:9-14; 7:40; Eph 1:17; 3:2-6; 3:14-19; 6:17; 1 Ti 4:1; Heb 10:15; 1 Pe 1:10-12; 2 Pe 1:20-21; Rev 1:10; 2:7; 17:3

III. THE HOLY SPIRIT EMPOWERS GOD'S PEOPLE
A. Undergirds the *Church*
Ac 4:31; 9:31; 1 Co 3:16; Php 3:1-4
B. Unites a *Fellowship*
2 Co 13:14; Eph 4:3-6; Php 2:1-2; Jude 17-21
C. *Energizes* for mission
Ac 4:8-10
D. Guides in *Mission*
Hag 2:4-5; Zec 4:6; Jn 15:26-27; 20:21-22; Ac 1:8; 8:14-17; 8:39; 10:19; 16:6-10; 1 Co 2:4-5
E. Calls and equips *Leaders*
Ge 41:38-39; Nu 11:16-17; 24:2; 27:15-21; Dt 34:9; Jdg 3:9-10; 6:34-35; 11:29; 13:24-25; 14:6,19; 15:14; 1 Sa 11:6-7; 2 Ki 2:1-18; 1 Ch 28:11-19; Eze 2:1-2; Ac 13:1-4; 20:28; 2 Co 3:3-11
F. *Teaches* His people
Jn 14:26; 16:12-15; Ac 15:28; Ro 9:1

IV. THE HOLY SPIRIT LEADS INDIVIDUALS
A. *Fills* Christians
Ac 6:1-6; 9:17; 11:24; 13:52; Eph 5:18-20
B. *Convicts* sinners
Jn 16:8-11; Ac 5:32; Heb 6:4
C. *Regenerates* believers
Jn 3:5-6; 1 Th 1:4-6; Tit 3:3-7
D. Permanently *Indwells* the saved
Ps 51:10-12; Eze 36:24-30; Jn 3:34; Ac 2:38-39; 10:44-47; 19:1-7; Ro 2:29; 1 Co 12:1-3; Gal 3:1-5; Eph 2:22; 2 Ti 1:14; 1 Jn 3:24—4:3,13-16
E. *Protects* the endangered
1 Sa 19:18-24; Mt 10:19-20; Mk 13:11; Lk 12:11-12; Ac 6:8-10; 11:28; Php 1:18-20; 1 Pe 4:14-17
F. Gives *Security*
Ro 5:1-5; 8:23; 2 Co 1:21-22; 5:1-6; Gal 5:5; Eph 1:13-14
G. Gives *Gifts* to every believer
Ex 31:1-11; Ac 13:9; 1 Co 12:4-11; 14:1-39; Heb 2:3-4
H. *Transforms* the faithful
Ac 2:32-33; Ro 7:6; 14:17-18; 15:13; 15:16; 15:30; 2 Co 3:17-18; Gal 5:22-26; Col 1:7-8; 2 Th 2:13-15
I. May be *Resisted*
1 Sa 16:13-14; Ps 106:32-33; Isa 63:10-14; 1 Th 4:8; 5:16-22
J. *Guides* the believer
Ac 20:22-23
K. Must be *Obeyed*
Ro 8:1-17; 1 Co 6:18-20; Gal 5:16-18
L. *Intercedes* in prayer for the believer
Ro 8:25-27; Gal 4:6; Eph 6:18; Rev 22:17

V. THE SPIRIT IS GOD
A. *Presence of God*
Ps 139:7; Mt 28:19-20
B. *Personal*
Jn 14:15-21; Eph 4:30
C. Acts in divine *Freedom*
1 Ki 18:12; Jn 3:8; Ac 8:18-19
D. Third of the *Trinity*
Ro 1:1-4; Eph 2:18; 1 Pe 1:1-2; 3:18-19

THE WORLD

CREATION

I. THE DIVINE AGENT OF CREATION
A. *Personal Creator*
Ge 1:1; Ne 9:6; Isa 42:5; 64:8-12; Am 4:13; 5:8-9; 9:5-6; Ac 4:24; Heb 11:3; 2 Pe 3:3-11
B. *Jesus Christ*
Col 1:15-17; Heb 1:2,10-12
C. *The Trinity*
Jn 1:3; Heb 1:10-12

II. WHY GOD CREATES
A. For *Praise*
Ps 148:1-14
B. For *Covenant* Relationship
Mal 2:10
C. For *Redemption*
Dt 32:6; Ps 51:10; Isa 41:17-20; Mt 25:34

III. HOW GOD CREATES
A. In *Sovereignty* as Lord
Dt 4:16-19; Ps 24:1-5; 102:18; Ecc 3:14; Isa 29:14-16; 40:12-31; 45:5-13; Eze 21:30; Ac 17:24-28; 2 Th 2:13—14
B. In *Freedom*
Job 14:5; Ps 135:5-7; Isa 5:1-7; 29:5-8; 51:3; Jer 18:5-12; 51:1-16; Eze 34:25-31; Hos 2:9-13; Mk 4:35-41; Lk 8:22-25
C. In *Love*
Ps 136:4-26
D. With *Purposeful* intent
Job 38:4; 38:31-33; 38:39—39:30; Ps 8:1-9; Pr 3:19-20; 8:22-31; Ecc 3:1-8; 3:9-14; 12:1; Isa 45:18; Lk 12:22-34; Jn 17:9-18; 1 Co 7:31; Heb 2:8; 12:26-28; Jas 1:17-18
E. With *Power*
Ps 89:9-13; Jnh 1:9
F. For *Order*
Ro 13:1-7
G. In *Progressive* manner
Ge 1:3—2:1; Isa 43:14-21; 48:6-7; Heb 1:1-3
H. In *Continuous* work
Jn 5:16-17; 16:12-14; Heb 4:3-4

IV. WHAT GOD CREATES
A. *Earth*
Ge 1:2
B. *Persons*
Ps 139:13-16
C. *Nature*
Ps 104:5-30; Jer 14:22; Hos 4:1-3; Am 8:9; Mt 24:35
D. *Miracles*
Dt 4:32; Job 5:9; 9:4-10; Jer 21:2; Ac 2:22
E. Moral Limitations leading to *Judgment*
Ge 3:14-19; 7:15,22; Job 1:16
F. *Justice* Through Freedom
Job 40:1—41:34; Pr 22:2
G. *New Creation*
Ro 2:28-29; 8:18-25; 2 Co 4:6; Rev 21:1-3

V. OUTCOMES OF GOD'S CREATION
A. It is *Good*
Ge 1:12,18,21,25,31; Pr 14:31; 17:5; 1 Ti 4:4
B. Freedom allows *Sin*
Eze 28:12-15
C. *Evil* exists
Ecc 7:13-14; Isa 54:11-17; 57:1-2; Eze 18:25; 20:1-44; Mt 5:45; Jn 16:33; Ro 1:18-32; 1 Co 14:20; Gal 1:4; Php 2:15; 2 Th 2:9-12; 1 Pe 4:19; 2 Pe 1:4; 1 Jn 2:16-17; 2:18-23; 2 Jn 7-11
D. *Confidence* in humans
1 Ch 16:30; Ps 85:10-13; Isa 43:1-7
E. *Hope*
Ge 8:22; 9:8-17; Lev 26:6-13; Job 12:7-15; Ps 65:5-13; Isa 4:5; 11:6-9; 30:19-26; 34:4; 35:1-10; 40:4; 51:6; 57:14-21; 65:17-25; Ac 3:21

MIRACLE

I. DEFINITION OF MIRACLE
A. *God's Working*
Ge 32:22-32; Jdg 6:17; Job 5:9-16; 9:10; Mt 24:24; Mk 13:22; Lk 1:37
B. *Exception* to ordinary experience
Da 3:1-30; Ac 28:3-6
C. Biblical *Vocabulary* of Miracles
Ne 9:10,17; Mt 11:20-24; 12:38-42; 16:1-4; Mk 8:11-13; Lk 10:13; 23:8; Jn 2:1-11; 3:2; 6:2; 7:3-5,31; 20:30-31; 1 Co 1:22; 2 Co 12:12
D. Worked through various *Methods*
Mk 7:32-37; Ac 16:25-27

II. PURPOSE OF MIRACLES
A. God's work of *Continual Creation*
Ge 11:1-9; 2 Ki 2:19-22
B. *Redemption* of God's People
Ge 7:1—9:17; 19:23-29; Ex 14:21; Ps 78:13-72; Joel 2:18-31; Jnh 1:1—2:10; Mt 12:9-14; 27:51-53; Mk 3:1-6; Ac 3:1-16; 16:16-18; Heb 2:4
C. *Revelation* of God
Ge 28:10-22; Ex 7:8-13; 8:19; Jos 3:1-17; Mt 9:32-34; 12:22-24; 14:2; Mk 6:14; Lk 11:14-26; Jn 15:24; Ac 12:5-17; 27:13-44
D. Elicit *Praise*
Lk 13:10-17; 18:35-43; 19:37-38; Ac 20:7-12
E. Execute God's *Judgment*
2 Ki 2:23-25; Ac 5:1-11; 12:23; 13:6-17
F. Show God's *Power*
Jos 6:20; 2 Ki 6:1-6; Isa 29:14

III. CONTEXT OF MIRACLES
A. World of *Nature*
Ge 37:5-11; Ex 3:2; 16:13; 17:6-7; Jdg 14:6; 1 Sa 7:10; 1 Ki 18:16-39; 2 Ki 20:1-11; Ps 65:8; Mt 2:2,9; 8:23-27; Mk 4:35-41; 6:13; Lk 5:1-11; 8:22-25
B. Response of *Faith*
Ge 22:9-14; Jos 8:10-23; 2 Ki 2:14; 4:1-7; 5:1-27; Ps 74:9; Jer 21:2; 32:17-23; Mic 7:15; Mt 8:5-13; 9:18-26; 9:27-31; 13:58; 15:21-28; 17:14-21; 20:29-34; 21:18-22; Mk 2:1-12; 5:21-43; 6:5-6; 6:56; 7:24-30; 9:14-29; 10:46-52; 15:32; Lk 4:20-29; 7:1-10; 17:11-19; Jn 4:46-54; 5:1-16; 9:1-41; 21:6; Ac 5:12-16; 9:18; 9:32-43; 14:8-10; Gal 3:5

IV. AGENTS OF MIRACLES
A. Humans as *Instruments*
Jos 11:8; 1 Sa 10:9; 1 Ki 17:22; 2 Ki 2:11; 4:8-37; Mt 1:18-25; 7:22; Jn 14:11-12; Ac 2:22,43; 4:9-22; 4:30; 5:19; 6:8; 8:6-24; 14:3; 15:12; 19:11-12; 19:13-16; 28:7-10; Ro 15:18-19; 1 Co 12:9-10; 2 Co 12:12
B. Jesus *Christ*
Mt 4:23-25; 8:3; 8:14-17; 8:28-34; 9:1-8; 12:15-21; 14:13-21; 14:22-33; 15:29-39; Mk 1:21-28; 1:29-34; 1:40-45; 5:1-20; 6:30-52; 8:1-10; 8:22-26; Lk 4:33-37; 4:38-41; 5:12-26; 7:11-17; 9:12-17; 24:1-49; Jn 6:3-15; 6:16-34; 11:1-44
C. The *Evil* One
2 Th 2:9-10; Rev 13:13-16; 16:14,21; 19:20

EVIL AND SUFFERING

I. THE ORIGIN OF EVIL AND SUFFERING
A. The *Divine Origin*
Ge 1:1-3; 2:18; Ex 5:1-23; Ru 1:11-21; 1 Sa 1:5; 16:13-23; 18:10; 1 Ki 17:1; 17:7-24; 22:19-28; 2 Ch 18:18-27; Job 1:16-22; 9:13; 16:6-14; 19:1-22; 30:11-31; 41:1; Ps 90:1-17; Ecc 6:1-2; 7:14; Isa 45:7; 2 Th 2:11-12
B. *Satan* as originator
2 Sa 24:1; 1 Ch 21:1; Job 26:12-13; Ps 89:9-10; Isa 14:3-23; 27:1; Zec 3:1-2; Mt 4:1-11; 5:37; 6:13; 12:22-29; 13:19; 13:38-42; Mk 1:13; 3:22-30; Lk 4:1-13; 8:12; 10:17-20; 11:14-26; 13:10-16; 22:3; 22:31-33; Jn 6:70-71; 7:20; 8:31-59; 13:2,27; 14:30; 16:11; Ac 13:10; 1 Co 5:5; 7:1-9; 10:14-22; 2 Co 2:11; 4:4; 11:14-15; 12:7; Eph 2:2; 6:10-20; Col 2:15; 1 Th 2:18; 3:1-5; 2 Th 2:3-10; 1 Ti 1:18-20; 5:14-15; 2 Ti 2:23-26; Jas 4:7; 2 Pe 2:4; 1 Jn 2:13-14; 3:8-10; 4:1-4; 5:18-19; Jude 6; Rev 2:9-10; 2:13; 2:24; 3:9; 12:3-17; 13:1-18; 20:1-10
C. *Human Origin*
Ge 2:16-17; 3:1-13; 6:5; Ex 1:8-14; 1 Sa 12:13-25; 2 Sa 4:4; 1 Ki 8:33-40; Ps 75:1-10; Pr 31:1-9; Jer 17:9-10; Hab 1:12-17; Mt 2:16-18; 9:1-8; 15:10-20; Mk 2:1-12; 7:14-23; Lk 5:17-26;

Ro 1:18-32; 2 Co 2:1-11; 1 Th 2:14-16; Jas 1:12-18; 3 Jn 11-12

D. *Natural Origin*
Ge 8:21-22; Jnh 1:4-17; Ro 8:20; Gal 1:4; 1 Jn 2:15-17

II. TYPES OF EVIL AND SUFFERING

A. *Deserved*
Ex 15:26; 20:5-6; Lev 26:1-45; Nu 12:1-15; 16:1-50; Dt 4:25-31; 5:9-10; 7:12-16; 9:7-29; 11:26-27; 24:16; 28:1-68; 30:1-20; 31:14—32:49; Jos 23:6-16; Jdg 2:10-23; 2 Ki 14:5-6; Ps 1:1-6; 7:1-17; 19:7-14; 36:1-12; 50:1-23; 112:1-10; Pr 1:1-33; 1:20-33; 2:1-22; 3:1-35; 4:1-27; 5:1-23; 6:1-35; 7:1-27; 9:1-18; 10:1—22:16; 30:10-33; Ecc 1:1-11; 3:16-22; 5:10-17; 7:15-18; 8:9-15; Isa 3:8-17; Jer 31:29-30; La 5:7; Eze 18:1-32; 33:1-20; Gal 6:7-8

B. *Testing*
Ge 22:1-18; Ex 16:1-36; Dt 8:1-5; 13:1-5; Job 1:6-12; 2:1-10; 5:17-27; 7:17-21; 33:12-30; 42:1-15; Ps 6:1-10; 66:1-20; 119:65-72; Isa 48:8-10; Jer 5:1-6; 7:28; Am 4:6-12; 2 Co 12:1-10; Heb 12:1-11; Jas 1:2-4; 1 Pe 1:6-7

C. *Redemptive*
Lev 16:1-34; 1 Ki 8:46-53; Isa 52:13—53:12; Hos 2:1-23; Heb 2:9-18; 4:14-16

III. GOD'S RELATION TO EVIL AND SUFFERING

A. *Punishment*
Ge 3:14-24; 4:10-12; 6:6-13; 18:16—19:29; 38:6-10; Lev 10:1-3; Nu 14:26-35; 20:12; Dt 8:11-20; 32:51; Jos 7:10-26; Jdg 9:23; 1 Sa 2:12-36; 13:13-14; 15:10-29; 19:9; 28:15-19; 2 Sa 12:1-14; 2 Ki 5:19-27; 15:5; 17:7-23; 1 Ch 22:5-10; 28:3; 2 Ch 6:24-31; 6:36-39; 26:16-21; 36:15-21; Ne 9:1-37; Job 4:7-8; 7:1-16; 8:1-6; 8:20; 9:14-35; 13:13-27; 31:1-40; Ps 78:1-22; 82:1-8; 92:1-15; 95:7-11; Pr 1:10-19; Isa 47:11; 51:17-23; Jer 16:1-18; 19:1-15; 44:1-30; La 1:5; Eze 9:9-10; 28:1-10; Da 4:19-33; 5:17-30; Hos 4:9; 8:7; Am 1:2—2:16; 7:1—9:15; Mic 2:1-5; 3:11-12; Hag 1:2-11; Mal 2:17—3:5; 3:13-18; Lk 1:20; 13:1-5; Jn 9:1-4; Ac 12:20-23; 13:6-12; Ro 2:1-11; 2 Pe 2:3-22; Rev 2:22; 18:1-8

B. *Providence*
Ge 41:1-32; 45:4-11; 50:20; Hab 1:5-11; Ro 3:5-8; 8:28-39; Php 1:12-18

C. *God's Compassion*
Ge 16:11; 21:8-20; Ex 2:23-25; 2 Sa 24:25; Job 36:1-26; Ps 103:1-22; Hos 11:1-11

D. *God's Present Help*
Ex 3:7-10; 6:1-8; 15:1-21; Nu 11:4-17; Dt 26:5-11; Jdg 6:11-40; 1 Sa 2:1-10; 7:10-12; 2 Sa 22:1-51; 2 Ki 4:1-37; 20:1-11; Est 4:14; Job 38:1—41:34; Ps 18:1-50; 20:1-9; 21:1-13; 23:1-6; 30:1-12; 34:1-22; 42:1—43:5; 68:1-35; 91:1-16; 107:1-43; 113:1-9; 116:1-19; 118:1-29; 121:1-8; 124:1-8; 136:1-26; 144:1-15; 146:1-10; 147:1-20; Isa 30:7; 38:1-22; 43:2; Da 6:19-24; Mt 11:28-30; Lk 4:18; 18:1-8; Jn 11:3; 14:27; 2 Th 3:1-5; 2 Ti 4:16-18; 1 Pe 5:6-11

E. *God's Future Help*
Job 14:1-22; 16:18-21; 19:23-29; Ps 16:1-11; 37:1-40; 59:1-17; 73:1-28; Da 12:2; Lk 16:19-31; Ro 8:18-25; 2 Co 5:1-5; Rev 7:13-17; 21:1-8

IV. CHRISTIAN RESPONSE TO EVIL AND SUFFERING

A. *Repentance*
Nu 21:4-9; Ezr 9:1-15; Ps 32:1-11; 38:1-22; 51:1-19; 106:1-48; Jer 15:10-21; 18:1-17; La 1:18; 3:1-66; Joel 2:10-14; Jnh 3:1—4:11; Jn 5:14

B. *Rejoicing*
Ecc 9:1-18; 11:9—12:8; Jn 16:1-33; 17:6-19; Ac 5:12-42; Ro 5:3-5; 2 Co 6:1-10; Php 2:14-18; Col 1:24

C. *Endurance*
Ge 50:15-19; Ex 21:23-25; Dt 1:34-40; 1 Sa 24:1-22; 26:1-25; Job 3:1-26; 5:7; 6:1-30; Ps 12:1-8; 13:1-6; 14:1-7; 25:1-22; 27:1-14; 53:1-6; 56:1-13; 57:1-11; 61:1-8; 62:1-12; 64:1-10; 69:1-36; 70:1-5; 71:1-24; 74:1-23; 77:1-20; 79:1-13; 85:1-13; 94:1-23; 120:1-7; 123:1-4; 125:1-5; 126:1-6; 129:1-8; 130:1-8; 140:1-13; 142:1-7; 143:1-12; Ecc 2:17-26; 3:1-9; Jer 20:14-18; Da 3:16-18; Mt 5:10-12; 5:38-48; 10:5-42; 16:21-27; Mk 8:31-38; Lk 6:20-36; 9:18-26; 23:34; Jn 15:18-27; Ac 6:8—7:60; 12:1-19; 16:16-40; Ro 8:12-18; 1 Co 4:12-13; 2 Co 4:8-18; Gal 4:13-14; 6:12; Php 1:27-30; 3:7-11; 1 Th 5:22; 2 Ti 1:8; 1:11-12; 2:3-7; 2:8-13; 3:10-13; Heb 10:32-39; 11:25-28; 11:32-39; 13:11-14; Jas 5:7-11; 1 Pe 2:18-25; 4:12-19; Rev 1:9; 2:2-3; 2:19; 3:10; 6:9-11; 14:9-12; 17:6

D. *Compassion*
Job 12:1—13:12; Ac 3:1-16; 5:15-16

E. *Humility*
Job 11:1-20; 15:1-35; 28:12-28; Ecc 8:16-17; 11:1-8; Isa 58:1-14; Hab 2:4; 3:16-19

F. *Comfort*
Ex 18:17-26; 22:22-27; Dt 14:28-29; 15:7-11; 26:12-15; Job 2:11-13; 16:1-5; Mt 25:31-46; Ac 2:44-46; 4:32-37; 2 Co 1:3-11; 7:2-16; 1 Th 3:6-10

G. *Worship*
Ecc 12:13-14

H. *Prayer*
Ps 3:1-8; 4:1-8; 5:1-12; 9:1—10:18; 11:1-7; 17:1-15; 22:1-31; 26:1-12; 28:1-9; 31:1-24; 39:1-13; 40:1-17; 44:1-26; 54:1-7; 55:1-23; 60:1-12; 63:1-11; 80:1-19; 86:1-17; 88:1-18; 102:1-28; 139:1-24; 141:1-10; Jer 17:14-18; Hab 1:2-4; Jas 5:13-15

I. *Vindication*
Ps 35:1-28; 41:1-13; 52:1-9; 58:1-11; 109:1-31; 137:1-9; Jer 11:18—12:6; 18:18-23; 20:7-12; Ro 12:14-21; 2 Th 1:4-10; 1 Pe 3:8-17

HUMANITY

I. GOD'S CREATION OF HUMANITY

A. The *Image of God*
Ge 1:26-29; 5:1-3; 33:1-10; 2 Co 4:4; Col 3:9-11; Jas 3:9

B. For *Responsibility*
Ge 9:1-6; Ezr 6:14; Eze 3:16-21; 33:1-20; Mt 25:14-30

C. With *Moral Consciousness*
Ge 2:16-17; Lev 21:1-4; Job 42:4-6; Ps 1:1; Mt 14:9-11; Mk 6:26-28; Ro 2:12-16; 1 Co 4:4; 8:7; 2 Co 2:12; 1 Ti 4:2; 2 Ti 1:3; Tit 1:15; Heb 9:9; 1 Pe 3:16

D. With *Potentiality*
Ge 4:17-22; 11:1-9; Ex 4:10-12; 36:1-2; Job 2:3; 28:1-28; Jer 12:5; 1 Co 1:26-30

E. With *Worth*
Lev 27:1-8; Ps 49:7-10; 116:15; 144:3-4; Mt 10:26-31; 16:26; Lk 9:25; 12:6-7

II. NATURE OF GOD'S HUMAN CREATION

A. *Human Nature*
Ge 3:20-24; Jdg 11:1-7; 1 Sa 8:19-20; 28:5-25; Job 4:18-21; 9:2-3; 10:5; 25:4-6; 33:4-7; 33:6; Ps 8:3-8; 22:6; 51:5; 52:1-4; 115:16; Pr 12:23; 14:12; 16:25; Ecc 3:13; Isa 40:6-7; 51:12; 57:14-19; Jer 51:17; Eze 11:18-21; 36:26; Mt 18:1-5; Ro 2:5; 7:4-6; 7:14-25; 8:5-8; 1 Co 4:6-7; Gal 3:26-29; 2 Pe 2:10-22

B. *Physical Nature*
Ge 2:7; 1 Sa 10:23-24; 16:7; 2 Ki 9:30; 1 Ch 12:2; 12:8-15; Job 10:8-12; 12:3; 14:1-2; 14:5; Ps 10:18; 107:18; Isa 2:22; 31:3; Da 1:4; 1:12-16; Am 2:14-16; 1 Co 5:5; 2 Pe 1:13-15

C. *Spiritual Nature*
Ge 28:10-22; 32:1-30; 35:1; Ex 32:1; Ps 32:1-5; 42:1-2; 42:6; 50:7-15; 50:22-23; Pr 14:27; Zec 12:1; Mk 8:36-37; Ro 3:9-18; 6:5-7; 6:8-14; 8:3-4; 8:10; 13:14; 1 Co 2:13-16; Gal 5:13-26; 6:7-10; Eph 2:1-10; Php 3:21

D. *Intellectual Nature*
Dt 29:3-4; 1 Ki 4:29-34; 2 Ch 1:12; Job 1:8; 13:2; 32:8; 38:2; 38:17-18; Ps 90:12; 94:11; 107:43; 111:10; 119:66; 119:97-104; Pr 1:1-7; 1:20-33; 2:1-6; 2:9-11; 8:1—9:16; 10:13; 14:8; 14:15; 14:33; 15:33; 16:16; 17:28; 19:8; 19:20; 21:11; 24:3-4; 24:14; 24:32; 26:12; 27:17; Ecc 1:12-18; 2:26; 7:11-12; 7:23-25; 8:1; 8:16-17; 9:15-18; Isa 29:13-14; 47:10; Jer 8:8-9; 10:7-8; 49:7-8; Eze 28:1-10; Da 2:27-28; 5:7-9; 5:12; 9:22; 12:10; Hos 14:9; Ob 8; Mic 4:11-12; Lk 1:1-4; Ro 1:21-23; 1:28-32; 1 Co 1:17; 1:18-19; 1:20-25; 8:1-3; 10:15

E. *Psychological Nature*
Ps 73:21-22; Pr 15:15; 17:22; 18:14; Eze 3:15

III. EXPERIENCES OF HUMAN LIFE

A. *Life*
Ge 11:10-26; Ex 6:14-25; Lev 17:11; 1 Ch 29:15; Job 7:1-6; 7:16; 12:10; 15:7-9; 27:3; 34:14-15; 40:7—42:3; Ps 13:3; 31:15; 37:2; 39:4-6; 62:9; 78:39; 86:13; 90:5-6; 90:9-10; 91:16; 94:17; 103:13-18; 107:20; 118:17-18; 139:1-24; Pr 25:16-17; 27:20; 30:24-28; Ecc 3:1-8; 3:18-21; 5:18-20; 8:11-13; Isa 38:1-6; Jer 21:8-10; Eze 18:30-32; 37:1-14; Mt 25:1-5; Lk 12:19-20; 1 Co 15:38-57; 2 Co 4:7-12; Jas 4:13-15; 1 Pe 1:23-24

B. *Birth*
Ge 4:1-2; 18:10-14; 25:21; 29:31; 1 Sa 1:19-20; Job 31:15; Jer 1:5; Lk 1:31-37; 2:4-7

C. *Childhood and Youth*
Ge 37:2-11; 1 Sa 1:21-28; Ps 88:15; Ecc 11:9-10; Jer 1:6-7

D. *Marriage*
Ge 2:18; 2:21-25; 24:62-67; 29:18-21; SS 2:16; Jer 44:19; La 1:1; Hos 3:1-3; Mt 5:31-32; 19:1-6; 1 Co 7:1-5; 7:25-35; 11:11-12

E. *Celibacy*
Mt 19:10-12; 1 Co 7:8-9

F. *Parenthood*
Ge 25:27-28; Jdg 13:6-14; Pr 17:25; 23:13-16

G. *Work*
Ge 2:15; 3:17-19; Dt 16:17; Jos 17:14-18; Jdg 4:4-10; 1 Sa 18:5; 18:30; 1 Ki 7:1-12; 1 Ch 25:8; 2 Ch 1:14-17; 8:1-6; 24:13; 26:15; 32:30; Ne 2:20; Ps 104:23; 127:1-2; Pr 6:6-8; 10:5; 12:11; 12:24; 12:27; 13:4; 14:1; 14:23; 16:26; 18:9; 19:15; 20:4; 20:13; 22:13; 24:30-34; 26:13-16; 28:19; 31:10-31; Ecc 3:22; 11:6; Da 1:19-20; 6:1-2; Mt 4:18-22; 9:9; 20:1-16; Mk 1:16-20; Ac 18:3; Eph 4:28

H. *Age*
Jos 13:1-7; 14:6-14; 2 Sa 19:32-37; 1 Ki 2:1-9; Job 5:26; Ecc 12:1-7

IV. TERMINATION OF HUMAN LIFE

A. *Death*
Ge 2:17; 15:15; Jos 23:14; 1 Sa 28:3; 2 Sa 17:23; 2 Ki 4:18-37; 20:1-11; 1 Ch 29:28; 2 Ch 9:31; 34:28; Job 21:23-26; Ps 68:20; Pr 12:28; Ecc 1:11; 2:1-16; 9:1-6; Isa 14:9-21; 25:7-8; 26:13-14; 26:19; 28:15; 28:18; 38:9-19; Jer 8:3; 20:14-18; Eze 28:8-9; Da 12:2; Hos 13:14; Hab 2:5; Zec 1:5; Mt 27:3-5; 27:52; 28:5-7; Mk 16:5-7; Lk 24:4-8; Jn 6:47-51; 6:58; 8:51-59; 11:1-44; 19:30; Ac 2:24; Ro 5:19-21; 1 Co 15:19; 15:21-22; 2 Ti 1:10; Heb 2:14; 9:27-28; Rev 1:18; 3:1; 6:8; 9:6; 14:13; 20:12-13; 21:4

B. *Nature of Death*
2 Sa 14:14; Job 7:7-10; 10:21-22; 14:10-22; 26:6; 30:23; Ps 6:5; 18:4-5; 22:15; 31:11-12; 49:10-17; 49:18-19; 55:15; 88:3-5; 88:10-12; 89:47-48; 115:17; 143:7; Pr 11:7; Jer 9:21; Eze 26:19-21; 32:17-32; Mt 22:23-33; Mk 12:18-27; Lk 20:27-40; 1 Th 4:14

C. *Death and Sin*
Lev 10:1-2; Nu 19:11-22; Dt 24:16; 1 Ki 16:18-19; 1 Ch 10:13-14; 2 Ch 25:4; Ps 1:6; Pr 5:3-6; 5:22-23; 7:10-27; 9:18; 11:19; 13:9; Isa 6:5; 57:1-2; Jer 28:16-17; 31:29-30; Eze 18:1-32; Ro 5:12-21; Jas 1:15

D. *Attitudes to Death*
Ge 23:1-2; 37:34-35; 42:38; 50:1-3; 50:26; Nu 20:28-29; 1 Sa 31:10-12; 2 Sa 1:19-27; 12:18-23; 18:33; 2 Ch 21:18-20; 32:33; Job 3:1-26; 19:23-27; 21:27-33; Ps 55:4; Ecc 2:18-19;

5:15; 7:1-2; Jer 22:18-19; Joel 1:8; Am 8:10; Jnh 4:8; Na 3:19; Mk 5:35-40

E. *Burial*
Ge 23:3-20; 25:7-11; 35:29; 47:29-30; 49:29-33; 50:12-14; Jos 24:29; 1 Ch 10:11-12; 2 Ch 16:13-14; 24:15; 26:23; 28:27; Ps 79:3-4; Ecc 6:3-6; Jer 7:32—8:2; Mt 8:21-22; Lk 9:59-60

V. INTERACTIONS OF HUMAN LIFE

A. *Relationships*
Dt 5:6-21; Ru 4:13-22; 1 Sa 18:1-4; 18:9; 18:28-29; 19:1—20:42; 2 Sa 3:22-39; 9:1—10:2; 19:24-30; 1 Ch 1:1-54; 11:15-19; 12:17-18; 2 Ch 9:1-28; Ezr 9:1-2; Job 19:13-20; 42:11; Ps 44:22; 55:12-14; Pr 12:26; 13:10; 15:22; 17:17; 18:1; 18:19; 18:24; 20:18; 27:9-10; Ecc 4:9-12; Jer 9:4-6; 17:5-7; Eze 34:17-20; Da 2:14; 5:14; 12:3; Mic 7:5-6; Mal 2:10; Mt 2:13; 5:21-22; 5:43-48; 12:48-50; 17:24-27; 19:21-23; 22:18-21; 22:37-40; Mk 3:33-35; 9:33-37; 10:21-23; 12:15-17; Lk 6:27-36; 8:20-21; 9:46-48; 11:5-8; 18:22-24; 20:24-26; Ac 17:24-28; Ro 1:24-27; 14:1-23; 1 Co 10:31-33; Eph 2:11-22; 1 Ti 1:3-7; 1 Jn 3:14

B. *Relationship to God*
Ge 3:12-13; 24:40-42; Ex 20:2-11; Nu 14:1-4; Dt 2:7; 8:17-18; 10:12-13; 26:14; 32:48-52; Jos 1:7-9; 24:12-15; 1 Sa 26:23-24; 2 Sa 5:10; 1 Ki 2:2-4; 2 Ki 16:10-12; 18:7; 1 Ch 11:9; 2 Ch 27:6; Job 7:17-21; Ps 1:2-3; 7:3-5; 9:13; 25:14; 33:13-19; 48:14; 73:27-28; 78:32-42; 119:73; Pr 15:26; Isa 42:5; 45:9-13; Jer 9:23-24; 18:6; 33:3; Eze 18:23; Da 1:17; 2:30; Hab 3:17-18; Mk 2:27; Lk 5:8-11; Ac 5:35-39; Ro 8:12-17; 8:29; 8:38-39; 9:20; 1 Co 10:22; Eph 1:17; Php 2:15; Col 1:21-22; Heb 4:13

C. *Community Relationships*
Ex 20:13-17; Lev 19:9-10; 19:13-18; Nu 1:3; 32:1-42; Dt 24:19; Jos 7:1; 22:8; Jdg 2:10; 21:25; Ru 2:17-18; 1 Sa 18:14-16; 2 Sa 2:4-7; 1 Ki 4:21-28; 9:15—10:29; 1 Ch 5:1-2; Job 2:11-13; 6:14-16; 12:4-5; Jer 11:21; Am 1:9; Jnh 1:4-11; 1:12-13; Mic 2:8-9; 3:1-3; Zec 3:10

D. *Family Relationships*
Ge 27:1-40; 27:41; 44:18-33; Ex 2:1-10; 4:14-15; 20:12; Nu 27:3-4; Jos 7:20-25; Ps 68:6; 133:1; Pr 19:13; Jer 12:6; 32:18; La 5:7; Ob 10-12; Lk 15:11-32

E. *Relationship to Nature*
Lev 26:3-8; Pr 14:4

F. *Commitment* in Relationships
1 Sa 1:8; Jn 17:20-21

SIN

I. DEFINITION OF SIN

A. *Transgression* of Law
Ex 16:20; 20:1-17; Lev 10:1-2; 1 Sa 14:32-34; 1 Ki 12:26-33; 13:1-32; 13:33-34; 14:8-9; 14:22-24; 15:3; 15:26; 15:29-30; 15:34; 16:1-7; 16:8-13; 16:25-26; 16:30-33; 18:18; 22:52-53; 2 Ki 3:2-3; 8:18; 8:27; 9:22; 10:18-36; 13:2; 13:6; 13:11; 14:23-29; 15:9; 15:18; 15:24; 15:28; 16:2-4; 17:2; 17:19; 17:24-41; 21:20-22; 23:32; 23:37; 2 Ch 12:1-2; 12:14; 13:1-20; 20:33; 21:6-7; 21:10; 21:11; 22:3-6; 24:7; 25:14-15; 28:1-4; 28:6; 28:22-25; 33:2-17; 33:22-23; 36:5; 36:9; 36:12-14; Ezr 9:1-2; 10:10; Isa 1:12-16; 43:22-24; Jer 1:16; 16:10-11; 17:1-4; 23:9-15; 35:14-15; La 1:8; Eze 5:6-7; Hos 8:11-14; 13:1-3; Hab 2:18-20; Mal 2:9; Ac 7:53; 1 Co 10:6-13

B. *Covenant Breach*
Dt 4:23-26; Jos 7:11; Jdg 2:20; 3:7; 3:12; 4:1; 6:1; 8:33-35; 13:1; Ne 9:5-37; 13:15-18; Ps 119:53; Jer 11:8-13; 22:8-9; Hos 8:1-10; Mal 2:10-11

C. *Violation* of God's Character
Jos 7:1; Mk 2:15-16; 7:1-22; Lk 5:29-32; 7:39; 15:1-2

D. *Unbelief*
Nu 20:11-12; 27:14; Isa 5:11-12; 17:10; 22:11-14; 30:1-3; 50:1; Eze 39:23-24; Mk 8:38; Jn 8:21-24; 16:7-11; 1 Co 15:34; Heb 12:15-16

E. *Missing the Mark*
Ne 1:6-7

F. *Against God*
Ex 23:24; 23:33; Dt 4:15-19; Jos 7:20; Jdg 2:10-12; 2:17-20; 1 Sa 2:29; 8:7-8; 10:19; 12:9-18; 12:17; 12:20-25; 17:26; 2 Sa 24:1-10; Job 13:23; 31:24-28; Isa 42:24; 63:10; Jer 2:1—3:5; 3:6-10; 15:6; Eze 8:1-18; 16:15-34; Hos 1:2; 2:7-8; 9:1; 10:5-15; Mic 1:5; Zep 2:10; Hag 1:9; Mt 12:31-32; Mk 3:28-29; Lk 11:42-52; 15:20-24; Ac 7:51-53; Ro 3:7-8; 6:1; 8:1-17; 1 Co 11:27-32; Gal 2:17; Eph 4:29-32

G. *Self-centeredness*
Jas 4:17; 2 Pe 2:10

H. *Unfaithfulness*
1 Ch 10:13

II. ORIGIN OF SIN

A. *Universal Nature*
1 Ki 8:27-53; 17:18; 2 Ch 6:36; Job 15:14-16; Ps 14:3-4; 51:5; 119:176; Pr 20:9; Ecc 7:20; Isa 24:5-6; 53:6; Jer 17:9; Am 1:1—2:16; Zep 1:17; Jn 7:19; Ro 1:18-25; 2:12; 3:9-23; 5:12-21; Gal 3:22; 1 Jn 1:8,10

B. Result of *Individual Choice*
Ge 3:6; 4:6-12; Nu 16:22; Mt 26:14-16,23-25,47-49; Mk 14:10-11,43-45; Lk 22:1-4,20-23,47-48; Jn 3:18-21; 5:14; 13:2; Ac 1:18-19; Jas 1:13-15; 4:1-12

C. *Satan*
Job 1:8-10

III. CHARACTERISTICS OF SIN

A. *Disobeying* God
Ex 15:24; 32:7-9; 2 Ch 34:19-28; Ezr 9:11-13; Ro 2:13; 1 Th 2:15-16; 1 Ti 5:8

B. *Lawlessness*
Eze 22:2-16; Hos 4:1-2; Hab 2:4-17; Ac 6:11; Ro 3:20; 1 Jn 3:4

C. *Unrighteousness*
Dt 9:4-6; Isa 3:14-15; 58:1-9; Eze 22:23-29; Hos 4:6-19; Am 6:1-8; Mic 3:1-4; 3:8-11; Jas 5:1-6

D. *Lack of Faith*
Ex 14:11-12; Nu 16:41; 32:1-13; Eze 15:6-8; Heb 4:1-2; Jas 1:5-8

E. *Evil Desire*
Ac 8:1; 1 Ti 6:6-10
F. *Rebellion*
Ge 11:4; Ex 9:34; 17:2-3; Lev 26:14-15; Nu 14:1-38; 17:5; 20:2-5; 21:4-5; Dt 1:26-43; 8:10-20; 9:7—10:11; 31:27; 32:5; Jos 22:16-31; 24:19-20; Jdg 2:2; 2:19; 1 Ch 5:25; 9:1; 2 Ch 11:14-16; 24:17-26; 35:20-24; Ne 9:16-18; Isa 1:2-4; 1:28-29; 30:8-14; 48:1-9; 65:1-7; Jer 3:20-22; 5:7-13; 9:14; 18:15; La 1:18-22; Eze 2:3-4; 2:7; 3:7; 3:16-21; 7:1-27; 12:2; 20:1-38; 21:23-25; 44:6-9; Da 9:4-19; Hos 9:15; Jnh 1:3; Zec 7:11-12; Heb 3:7-19
G. *Hypocrisy*
Lk 12:1; Jas 3:1-13
H. *Violence*
Eze 12:19
I. *Pride*
Nu 12:11; 2 Ch 26:16-21; 32:25
J. *Responsibility*
Ge 39:9; Ex 32:21-24; 34:9; Lev 4:1—5:19; 6:1-3; 24:13-16; Nu 5:6; 9:13; 15:22-31; 27:3; 32:23; Dt 23:21-22; 24:16; 2 Ch 25:1-4; Ps 79:8; 89:30-32; 119:10; Ecc 5:4-6; Eze 7:16-19; 9:9-10; 14:7-10; 18:1-32; 23:35-41; 33:1-20; Hos 13:16; Mt 26:69-75; 27:3-10; Mk 14:66-72; Lk 19:7-8; 22:54-62; Jn 15:22-25; 18:15-18,25-27; 19:11
K. *Serious* in Nature
Lev 16:29-34; Nu 31:5-18; Ps 78:1-72; Eze 4:4-8; Mt 18:6-9; Mk 9:42-50; Lk 17:1-4; Ac 5:1-11
L. *Tempting*
Lk 4:1-13

IV. CONSEQUENCES OF SIN
A. *Slavery* to Sin
Ps 119:133; Pr 5:21-23; 29:6; Jn 8:31-37; Ac 8:23; Ro 6:5-22; 7:1-25; Tit 3:3
B. Personal *Depravity*
Ge 4:23-24; 6:5; 8:21; 2 Ch 30:7-12; 36:16; Ps 10:1-18; 14:1; 36:1-4; 53:1; 73:1-28; 119:70; Isa 2:6-9; 3:8-9; 59:2-15; Jer 13:22-25; 14:10; Eze 16:44-52; Zep 3:1-4; Mt 12:33-37; 23:32; Jn 7:7; Ro 1:26-32; 1 Co 6:12-20; Gal 5:16-21; Eph 4:17-19; Col 3:5-8; 1 Th 4:3-8; 2 Ti 3:1-9; Tit 1:15-16; 3:10-11; 2 Pe 1:4; 2:12-19; Jude 4; Rev 2:14; 2:20
C. Spiritual *Blindness*
Nu 14:44; Jdg 8:22-27; 17:1—21:25; 2 Ki 12:1-3; 14:4; 15:4; 15:35; 2 Ch 27:2; Isa 5:18-24; 42:18-20; Jer 5:21-31; 6:12-15; 8:12-14; 9:3-6; Hos 7:1-16; 11:1-7; Mal 1:6—2:9; Lk 7:31-35
D. *Moral Insensitivity*
Ge 13:13; 1 Sa 2:12-17; 8:3; Am 8:4-6; Mic 2:1-2,8-9; 2 Ti 2:16; Jas 1:19-25
E. *Guilt*
Nu 14:40; 2 Ch 28:9-13; Ps 51:1-19; Isa 6:5; Heb 6:1-6
F. *Death*
Ge 3:4-24; Nu 18:22; Ps 109:1-31; Pr 6:12-19; Lk 13:1-5; Ro 6:23; Eph 2:1-3; Col 2:13; 1 Jn 5:16-17

G. *Alienation* from God
Nu 11:1; 14:43; Dt 20:16-20; 24:4; 32:20; Jdg 10:11-14; 1 Sa 15:1-35; 1 Ki 11:1-13; 2 Ki 22:13; 22:17; 23:4-20; 24:1-4; 24:19-20; 2 Ch 29:6-7; Ezr 9:15; Ne 13:26; Ps 5:4-6; 119:118; Jer 7:16-19; 50:6-7; Hos 5:1-15; Mt 9:13; 13:41-42; Col 1:21; 2:18-19; 1 Pe 4:18
H. *Estrangement* from Others
Ge 5:29; 27:41-45; 31:36; 1 Sa 26:21; 2 Sa 13:1—14:33; Ps 120:2-3; Mt 6:14-15; 18:15-20; Lk 11:4; 1 Co 8:12; 2 Co 12:20-21; Jas 2:1-14
I. *Shame*
Ezr 9:6-7

V. GOD'S INTERVENTION
A. *Judgment*
Ge 20:1-9; 2 Ch 21:12-19; 24:20; Ps 68:21; 94:23; 95:8-11; 112:10; Isa 1:20; 13:9-11; 26:21; Jer 13:9-10; 15:1; 36:31; Hos 10:1-2; 12:14; Mic 6:9-13; Mal 3:5; Lk 19:41-44; Heb 10:26-29
B. *Punishment*
Ge 12:10-20; Nu 16:26; 25:1-3; 1 Sa 2:22-25; 3:13; 12:25; 1 Ki 11:26-39; 16:34; Jer 4:17-18; 5:19; 6:18-20; 7:26-31; 16:16-18; 28:16; 30:10-17; La 1:10-16; 3:39-42; Eze 11:1-12; Hos 2:13; 6:4-5; Na 1:3
C. *Discipline*
Nu 14:23; 2 Sa 12:1-25; 2 Ki 17:7-23; 21:2-17; 24:8-17; 25:1-21; 1 Ch 21:1-8; 2 Ch 25:19-20; Isa 64:4-7; 66:1-4; Jer 19:1-15; 32:29-35; 40:3; 52:2-3; La 1:5; Eze 5:8-17; Da 9:14; Hos 9:7-9; Am 3:1-14; Zep 1:4-13; Zec 8:14-17; 1 Co 3:16-17
D. *Forgiveness*
1 Ki 21:21-28; 2 Ch 28:19; Ps 106:6-46

KNOWLEDGE OF GOD

HOLY SCRIPTURE

I. WHAT SCRIPTURE IS
A. God's *Word*
Ps 12:6; 78:1-6; 145:4-7; Pr 1:20; Isa 1:2-3; Jer 4:3-6; Eze 17:1-6,9
B. *God's Initiative*
2 Ch 36:22-23; Ps 108:7
C. *Inspired* by God
Ex 24:4; Lev 27:34; 2 Sa 22:31; 23:1-3; Pr 30:1-4; 31:1; Isa 39:5-6; Jer 23:9-40; Mic 3:8; Mt 2:18; Mk 13:14; 1 Co 7:6,10,12,25,40; 2 Co 2:3; 1 Th 1:5-6; 2:13; 2 Ti 1:13-14; Rev 22:18-19
D. Communicates God's *Purpose*
Dt 17:18-20; 2 Ch 34:21; Jer 15:16; Jn 17:17; Heb 1:1-2; 1 Jn 2:1,7-8,12-14; 2:21; Jude 3

II. HOW GOD COMMUNICATES HIS MESSAGE
A. *Visions*
Pr 29:18; Da 7:1; Na 1:1
B. *Oracle*
Isa 13:1; Am 1:3; Hab 1:1

C. *Gospel*
Mk 1:1-2
D. Through the *Spirit*
Jn 16:13-15
E. Through *Eyewitnesses*
Lk 1:1-4; Jn 19:35-37; 21:24-25; 2 Pe 1:16-18

III. HOW SCRIPTURE CAME TO US
A. *Writing*
Ex 31:18; 34:27-28; Lev 1:1; Dt 31:12-15; Jos 8:30-35; 10:12-13; 24:25-26; 1 Ki 11:41; 14:19,29; 15:7,23,31; 16:14,20,27; 22:39,45; 2 Ki 1:16-18; 8:23; 10:34; 12:14,15,18,28; 12:19; 13:8,12; 15:6,11,15,21,26,31,36; 16:19; 20:20; 21:17,25; 23:28; 24:5; 1 Ch 28:11-20; 29:29; 2 Ch 9;29; 12:15; 13:22; 26:22; 33:19; Ezr 1:1; Ne 10:36; Ps 102:18-20; Pr 1:1-5; 7:1-3; Ecc 12:9-14; Isa 36:1—39:8; Jer 6:12-15; 6:22-24; 8:10-12; 10:12-16; 16:14-15; 23:5-6; 23:7-8; 23:19-20; 25:13; 30:1-11; 30:23-24; 33:15-16; 46:27-28; 50:41-43; 51:15-19; Eze 43:11; Da 2:4; Hos 8:12; Hab 2:1-3; 3:1-19; Zec 7:11-13; Mal 3:16-17; Jn 20:30-31; Ac 1:1-4; Php 3:1; 1 Ti 3:14-15; 2 Ti 2:11-13; 1 Pe 5:12; Rev 1:1-3
B. *Collection*
2 Sa 22:1-51; 1 Ch 17:16-27; Ps 9:20; 41:13; 72:18-19; 89:52; 106:48; 115:1-18; 116:1-19; 150:6; Pr 25:1; Isa 2:1-4; 8:16; Jer 27:20-22; 33:14-26; 39:3-14; 46:1; 48:45-47; 51:60; 51:64; Mic 4:1-2; Mt 5:3; Mk 16:9-20; Jn 7:53—8:11; Ro 15:15; Col 4:16
C. *Canonization*
Dt 4:2; Jos 23:6; 2 Ki 22:16-20; Ezr 7:6; Ne 8:1-3; 13:1-3; Pr 30:5-6; Mal 4:4; 2 Pe 3:15-16; 2 Jn 5

IV. SCRIPTURE IS *AUTHORITATIVE*
Isa 34:16; 40:8; Mt 5:17-47; 12:17-21; 12:39-41; 13:13-15; 13:33-35; 15:7-9; 21:42; 22:29; Mk 9:9-13; Lk 16:29-31; 21:33; 24:44-46; Ac 2:16-21; 17:11; 1 Co 14:34-37; 2 Co 1:13-14; Col 3:16-17; 2 Th 2:2,15; 3:6,14; 1 Ti 1:15; 3:1; 4:9; 5:18-21; 2 Ti 3:14-17; Tit 3:8; Jas 4:5-6; 2 Pe 1:19-21; Rev 22:6-7

V. WHY WE HAVE SCRIPTURE
A. *Redemption*
2 Ki 23:21-25; Da 12:4-9; Lk 18:31-33; Jn 5:37-40,45-47; Ro 16:25-26; 1 Co 15:3; Gal 3:22-24
B. *Hope*
Ne 1:8-9; La 5:21-22; Ro 15:4
C. *Commitment*
Ps 119:1-176
D. *Inspiration*
Ps 73:16-28; Pr 2:1-22; Jer 36:1-32
E. *Obedience*
Jos 1:5-9; Ps 19:7-10; Pr 3:1-4; 4:1; 5:1; 6:1; Mt 4:4-10; Lk 4:4
F. Right *Relationship* with God and others
Mt 22:37-39; Mk 2:27; 12:29-31; 1 Co 4:14; Gal 4:21-31
G. *Unity*
1 Ti 4:13; 2 Pe 3:1-2
H. *Powerful*
2 Ti 2:8-9; Heb 4:12; 1 Pe 1:22-25

REVELATION

I. GOD TAKES THE INITIATIVE
A. In Specific *Events*
Ge 45:5; Ex 3:2-6; 8:1-2; 16:3-8; 40:34-38; Nu 16:1-50; Dt 1:42; 7:17-24; Jos 3:7-17; 4:20-24; 1 Sa 5:1-3,9,10; 9:15-16; 23:14-28; 1 Ki 5:3-4; 2 Ki 5:1-27; 7:1-7; 1 Ch 5:20-22,25-26; 22:18-19; Ezr 8:21-23; Ne 2:8,18; Ps 34:7-18; 64:9; 76:1; 92:4-7; 106:1-47; 107:1-43; 147:1-20; Ecc 1:12-14; Jer 17:15; La 2:17; 3:22-23; Da 4:2-28; 6:27; Hag 1:3-9; 2:7; Mt 24:9-14; Mk 1:25; Lk 8:36-37; 22:14-16; Jn 11:40; Ac 5:5; Ro 9:4-6; Php 1:14
B. Through *Divine Presence*
Ge 3:8-13; 50:25; Ex 4:10-12; 13:21-22; 25:1—30:38; 33:1-17; 33:18-22; 34:4-12; 34:29-35; Lev 22:31-33; 26:11-13; Nu 4:7; 22:18-20; 35:34; Dt 4:7; 23:14; Jos 7:11-12; 1 Sa 4:1-22; 18:12-14; 2 Sa 6:2-19; 7:4-11; 1 Ki 8:1-21; 8:27-30; 20:13-28; 2 Ki 6:8-17; 1 Ch 23:25; 2 Ch 6:1-2,18-21; 15:1-4; Ezr 7:11-28; Ne 7:5-73; Job 9:9-11; 42:5; Ps 11:4-7; 13:1; 23:4; 26:8; 46:4-11; 118:1-29; Pr 25:2; Ecc 3:11-17; Isa 4:5-6; 6:5-8; 41:10; Jer 52:3; Eze 9:1-11; 10:3-5; 43:6-7; Joel 2:17; Am 5:17; Hab 2:19-20; Zep 3:14-17; Hag 1:13-15; 2:4-5; Zec 2:10-11; Mt 24:44; Lk 1:35; 10:17-20; 17:20-21; 24:16,25; Jn 14:6-7; 14:15-17; 16:13-15; 2 Co 3:7-18; 2 Ti 4:17
C. In *Jesus Christ*
Mt 1:23; 3:16-17; 9:4; 11:18-19; 11:25-27; 16:4; 16:15-17; 20:26-28; 21:13; 23:37; 26:31-32; 28:5-7; Mk 1:11; 8:29-30; 14:22; Lk 2:40; 4:18-21; 5:8-10; 5:22; 8:43-48; 23:43; Jn 1:1-4; 1:9-13; 1:14-18; 1:29-31; 6:29; 9:35-37; 12:44-46; 14:9-12; 15:15-16; 17:6-9; 18:32; Ac 3:17-26; 8:30-38; 26:16-18; 1 Co 11:23; 1 Th 4:2, 8-9; Heb 1:1-2; 1 Pe 1:20; 1 Jn 5:6-13
D. By the Holy *Spirit*
Nu 11:16-30; 1 Ki 22:6-28; 2 Ch 18:5-7; Ne 9:30; Isa 42:1-4; 59:21; Joel 2:28-29; Jn 1:33; Ac 4:31; 13:2-3; 1 Co 2:9-12; Gal 3:3-8; Eph 1:17; Rev 2:7
E. Through His *Word*
Ge 17:1-8; 25:22-23; Ex 24:1-11; Nu 7:89; 12:1-8; 23:1-12; Dt 5:4,23-27; 18:15-19; 18:21-22; 1 Sa 3:1-10; 2 Sa 24:11-13; 1 Ki 11:9-13; 16:34; 19:9-18; Ps 16:7-11; Pr 20:12; Isa 18:4; 28:14-21; Jer 5:12-17; 6:10-11; 42:7-11; 45:1; Eze 6:1-2; 23:1-49; Hos 1:1-2; Mic 2:6-7; Mt 2:5-6; Mk 1:38-39; 9:31-32; 1 Co 1:21; Col 1:5-7; 1:25-27; 1 Jn 1:1-3
F. Through *Persons*
Isa 45:11-13; Hag 2:23; Mt 10:6-8; Jn 9:3-6; 2 Co 4:10-11; 2 Ti 2:2
G. Through His *Messengers*
Ge 18:1—19:29; 32:24-30; Ex 19:17-27; Jos 5:13-15; Jdg 6:11-24; 1 Sa 10:6-13; 2 Ki 3:10-27; 6:1; Isa 30:6-11; 44:24-28; Jer 1:4-9;

1:17-19; 14:14-16; 15:16-18; 25:3-4; 26:1-19; 26:20-23; 35:15; La 2:9,14; Eze 3:8-17; 13:1-23; 22:28; 33:21-25; Da 2:30; 9:9-16; Hos 6:5; Am 1:1,3; 3:7-8; 7:12-17; Ob 1; Jnh 1:1-2; 3:1; Mic 1:1-3; 3:5-7; Zep 1:1,12; Hag 1:1-2; Mal 2:7-8; 3:1-2; Mt 3:2-5; Lk 4:43; 7:31-50; 11:49-52; Ro 10:16-21; Php 4:9; 2 Ti 2:15; 2 Jn 12; 3 Jn 13

H. Through His *Angels*
Ge 32:1-2; Ex 23:20-31; Jdg 2:1-3; 13:3-23; 1 Ki 19:5-8; 2 Ki 1:3-15; Isa 6:2; Eze 10:1-22; Da 10:18—11:1; 12:1; Zec 2:3-5; 4:1; 6:1-8; 12:8; Mt 1:20-21; 2:13; 24:31; 28:2; Mk 8:38; Lk 1:11-20; 1:26-29; 2:13; Ac 8:26-27; 27:23-24; 1 Co 11:10-11; Heb 13:2; Rev 2:1; 19:9-10

I. Through *Dreams*
Ge 28:11-13; Jdg 7:13; 1 Ki 3:4-5; 1 Ch 17:15; Isa 22:1-19; Da 2:25-28; Mt 2:19-23; Ac 16:9-10; 18:9

J. Through *Inspiration*
Mk 4:23-24; Lk 1:67; 2:26; Jn 17:14; Ro 10:8-9; 1 Co 14:26-40; Eph 3:3-9; Tit 1:2-3

K. Through *Visions*
Nu 24:1-25; Jer 1:11-16; Eze 1:1-28; 8:1-18; 40:2-5; Da 10:1-19; Am 9:1-4; Zec 1:7; Ac 7:55; 9:3-8; 10:3-18; 22:7-11; 23:11; 2 Co 12:1-5; Gal 1:11-17; 2:2; Rev 21:10

L. Through *Oracles*
Lev 19:31; 20:6,27; Nu 27:18-21; Dt 18:9-14; Jos 18:6-8; Jdg 1:1-2; 20:18; 1 Sa 10:17-25; 28:6-25; Ps 60:6; 85:7-8; Jer 29:1-32; Zep 1:6-7; Hag 2:11-12

M. Through *Signs*
Jdg 6:36-40; Da 5:2-5; 5:25-28; Heb 2:3-4

N. Through *History*
Ex 14:1—15:18; Dt 1:5—3:29; 8:2-5; 26:5-11; 1 Ch 22:1-19; Ne 9:6-37; Ps 40:5; 44:1-8; 77:1-20; 105:1-45; 114:1-8; 143:5-7; Isa 59:1-20; Jer 29:10; Eze 11:7-12; 16:1-63; 20:1-44; 36:22-28; Hos 12:10-14; Am 2:9-12; Hab 1:5-7; Zec 10:9,12; 12:1-14; 14:6-9; Mk 4:30-32; Ac 7:1-53; 13:16-41; Eph 1:9-10; Heb 11:1—12:1

O. In *Worship*
2 Ch 7:10; Ps 9:1

P. *In Nature*
1 Ki 17:1-7; 18:16-46

II. GOD TELLS US WHO HE IS

A. As *Author of Creation*
Ge 1:2; Ru 1:6; Job 37:14—39:30; Ps 8:3-6; 19:1-6; 29:3-9; 102:25-28; 104:1-35; Eze 34:25-31; Joel 1:1-20; 2:21-24; 3:17-18; Am 4:12-13; 5:8; 9:5; Jnh 1:4-7; 4:6-10; Mt 2:9,12; Ac 16:26; 17:24-28; Ro 1:18-20

B. As *Author of Life*
Ge 1:26-28; Nu 1:1-2; Mk 5:41-42; Jn 4:50-54; 11:25; 12:23-29; 15:1-2; Jas 1:18; Rev 20:12

C. As *Author of Hope*
Ge 22:1-18; Ru 2:19-20; 1 Ch 4:9-10; 2 Ch 6:32-33; Est 4:14; Job 1:1—42:17; Ps 3:4; 42:8-11; 51:11; 126:1-6; Ecc 7:14; 9:1-10; Isa 29:22; Eze 36:8-12

D. As *Author of Grace*
Ge 9:12-16; Lev 9:6,23-24; 25:42,55; 1 Ki 3:8,9; Ps 4:6-7; 103:1-14; Hos 6:1-2; Mk 2:8-11; 2 Ti 1:10

E. As *Author of Love*
Lk 15:3-32; Jn 10:14-15; 10:17-18; 1 Co 13:1-12

F. In the essence of *God's Nature*
Ps 62:11; Pr 11:1; 12:2,22; 15:25-27; Mk 14:36

G. In His *Actions*
Ex 13:1; Lev 19:1-2; Nu 8:17; 15:37-41; 2 Sa 5:10; 1 Ki 17:13-14; Job 33:13-22; Ps 50:1-23; Pr 16:1-7; Isa 7:14; 8:1-4; 8:18-20; 20:2; Jer 32:6-15; Eze 3:1-3; 4:1—5:17; 6:11; 12:1-6; 12:17-20; 24:15-24; Hos 1:2—3:5; Mic 2:12-13; Mt 13:29-30; 21:1-11; 26:26-28; Mk 6:10-11; 11:17; Lk 3:22; Jn 5:17-19; 13:14-16

III. GOD REVEALS HIS INTENTIONS AND PURPOSES

A. *Fellowship* with His people
Lev 20:22-26; Dt 12:4-7; Ps 27:4-9; Ecc 2:24-26; La 3:44-50; Mt 12:48-49; Mk 3:34; 11:25-26; 1 Jn 3:2

B. *Faithfulness* among His people
Ge 15:7-16; 16:1-2; 1 Sa 15:1-26; 1 Ch 10:13-14; 2 Ch 1:2-12; Ps 18:1-50; 119:151; 136:1; Jer 44:1-30; Eze 2:1-10; 14:7-8; Hos 2:19-20; 4:1-3; Mal 2:4-6; Mt 15:17-19; Mk 13:6,13; Lk 6:47; Jn 7:16-19; 10:25-30

C. *Commitment* from His people
Ge 12:1-2; Ex 6:1-5; 19:2-3; 20:1-17; 1 Ki 9:2-3; 2 Ki 17:34-40; 2 Ch 7:11-22; Ps 81:1-14; Pr 14:27; Isa 48:17-19; Mt 4:19; 8:13; 13:8-9; 13:44-46; Mk 7:6-8; 10:21; Lk 2:49-50; 6:20; Jas 1:23-25

HISTORY

I. TIME AND ETERNITY

A. God acts in human *Time*
Ex 12:1-28; 31:12-17; 35:1-3; Lev 23:3; 23:4-43; 25:1-55; Nu 9:1-14; 28:16—29:39; Dt 1:3; Ecc 3:1-8; Mk 13:32-35; Jn 2:4; 7:6-8; 7:30; 8:20; 9:4; 12:23-33; 13:1; 17:1; Ac 1:7; 3:19-21; 1 Co 2:7; 10:11; 2 Co 6:2; Gal 1:4; 4:4; Eph 1:10; 6:13; 2 Pe 3:8

B. Time is *Linear,* not cyclical
Ge 2:4; 2:10-14; 3:20; 5:1-32; 6:9; 9:7; 9:18-19; 11:10,27; 25:19; 37:2; 46:8-27; Nu 33:1-50; Jdg 2:16-23; 1 Ch 1:1—2:17; Lk 2:1

C. God knows and directs the *Future*
Da 8:26; Rev 4:5

D. History's time is not *Eternal*
Isa 66:17-24; Eze 38:1—39:29; Da 2:36-45; 12:13; 1 Ti 6:15; Rev 21:1-4

II. GOD AND POLITICAL HISTORY

A. *God's People* stand in history's center
Ge 23:17-20; 29:1-30; 49:1-28; Ex 19:4; Nu 32:1-42; Jos 1:12-18; 22:1-34; 1 Ki 8:51; 1 Ch 9:3; 17:20-22; 2 Ch 11:4

B. God concentrated on *National* history
Isa 1:24-26; 10:24-27; 41:8-16; 43:1-7; Jer 25:8-14; 32:42; Eze 11:1-21; 17:1-24; 20:1-44; 36:1-38; Hos 11:1-11

C. God is active in international *Politics*
Ge 17:6; Nu 1:1-46; 20:20-21; 21:21-35; Dt 20:1-20; Jos 5:1; 10:1-43; 11:1; 2 Sa 8:1-14; 10:12; 2 Ki 15:37; 18:9-12; Ps 46:8-10

D. God's *Deliverance* is part of history
Ge 14:1-24; Ex 12:29-42; Nu 21:1-3; Jos 3:1-17; 8:1-29; 1 Sa 14:6-23; 17:37-54; 24:8-21; 26:23; 2 Sa 1:15-16; 5:17-25; 7:1; 16:12; 18:31; 2 Ki 22:15-20; 1 Ch 11:14; 2 Ch 13:1-18; 14:8-17; 20:15-30; 32:20-23; Ezr 2:1-70; 8:1-14; 8:31-32; Ne 1:5-11; 4:13-23; 7:4-73; Ps 44:1-8; 64:5-9; 68:21; 76:1-10; 126:1-3; Isa 11:10-16; Jer 23:7-8; Am 9:7; Mic 7:15; Zec 9:16; 10:6-12

E. God's *Kingdom* is first revealed in history
Ob 21; Mk 1:15

F. God's concern is *Universal* history
Ge 10:1-32; 17:20; 20:17-18; 21:13; 22:20-24; 25:1-18; 25:23; 36:1,9; 47:5-6; 48:17-20; Ex 7:5; 9:16; 9:20; 14:4,18; Nu 14:13-16; 22:1—24:25; Dt 23:3-8; Jos 2:10-11; 4:24; 9:1-27; 2 Ki 19:1-37; 2 Ch 6:32-33; Ezr 1:1; 6:22; 7:27; Ne 6:15-16; Ps 86:8-10; Isa 7:17; 10:5-19; 13:1—23:18; 34:1-17; 40:15-17; 41:2-4; 45:1-7; 47:1-15; Jer 46:1—51:64; 51:20-26; Eze 25:1—32:32; 35:1-15; Da 4:25; 5:25-31; 7:15-27; 11:36-45; Joel 3:1-21; Jnh 1:1—4:11; Na 1:1—3:19; Hab 1:5-11; Zec 1:18-21; Ac 17:26

III. HISTORY AND MEANING

A. *Faith* gains understanding of meaning
Ex 14:29-31; Nu 13:1—14:12; 20:12; Jdg 8:33-35; 1 Ch 5:18-26; 2 Ch 16:7-9; 19:2-3; 25:5-12; 26:5; 30:6-9; 31:21; Jer 37:4-10; Hos 12:1-14; Heb 11:1-40

B. God's *Promise* gives history meaning
Ge 4:15-26; 8:22; 15:1-21; 22:15-18; 24:7; 26:2,24; 27:1-40; 28:4; 28:13-15; 29:31—30:24; 46:3-4; 47:26-27; 48:4; 49:26-27; 50:24-25; Ex 1:1-7; 3:16-22; 5:19—6:12; 11:3; 23:20-33; 32:13-14,34-35; 33:1-6,12-17; 34:8-16; Nu 26:1-65; Dt 9:1-3; Jos 11:23; 14:6-15; 21:43-45; 23:1; 1 Ki 8:15-21; 2 Ki 7:1-20; 14:25; 17:3-23; 2 Ch 6:4-6,14-17; 9:26; 14:6-7; 15:15; 21:7; 36:21-23; Lk 1:54-55; Ac 26:6; 2 Pe 3:4

C. History's *Moral* foundation gives meaning
Ge 9:20-27; 18:19; Lev 11:45; 14:33-57; 18:3; Nu 25:1-18; Jos 23:1-16; Jdg 19:1—21:25; 2 Sa 11:27; Hos 10:1-15; Am 1:3—2:16

D. History involves divine *Judgment*
Ge 19:1-29; Lev 26:1-45; Nu 14:17-38; 31:1-24; Dt 8:2-5; 24:9,18; 29:2-29; Jos 7:1-26; Jdg 2:1-15; 10:11-16; 1 Sa 6:1-20; 28:16-19; 1 Ki 9:9; 22:53; 2 Ki 13:1-3; 21:1-15; 23:26-27; 24:2-3; 24:8-17; *25:21; 1 Ch 21:7;* 2 Ch 7:22; 12:1-12; 15:6; 21:12-19; 24:17-25; 25:13-24; 26:16-21; 28:1-8; 28:9-15; 32:24-26; 33:9-13; 33:23-24; 34:26-28; 36:11-21; Isa 30:1-5; 31:1-3; Jer 1:14-19; 2:1—3:5; 4:13-31; 5:15-17; 6:1-30; 11:1-14; 21:1-10; 32:16-25; 34:1-7; Eze 6:1-14; 7:1-27; 12:1-28; 13:1-23; 14:12-23; 15:6-8; 21:1-27; 22:15-16; 23:1-49; 33:23-33; Hos 9:10-17; Am 4:6-12; 6:13-14; Zec 1:2-6; Lk 19:41-44; 1 Co 4:5; Rev 13:5-10; 17:17

E. History points to *Hope*
1 Ch 3:1-24; Ps 74:9-23; 80:1-19; Isa 24:1—27:13; 46:8-13; 49:14-23; Jer 16:10-18; 52:31-34; Hag 2:20-23

F. *Geography* does not limit God
Nu 34:1-29; Jos 13:1—19:51; 18:8-9

IV. HISTORY AND HUMANITY

A. God works in *Individual* history
2 Sa 12:1-19; Ps 92:4; 143:5-6; Pr 27:1; Lk 1:25

B. God gives and limits *Freedom*
Nu 10:11-32; 33:50-56; Jos 15:63; 17:14-18; 19:47; Jdg 18:1,47; Est 4:12-15; Ac 4:27-28

C. God works through *God's Leaders*
Dt 34:10-12; Jos 1:1-11; Jdg 17:6; Ru 4:13-22; 1 Sa 2:27-36; 10:17-19; 15:10-29; 25:32; 2 Sa 5:1-5; 23:8-39; 1 Ki 11:1-39; 2 Ki 1:1-17; 9:1-37; 1 Ch 9:22; 2 Ch 9:8; 35:25

V. HISTORY AND WORSHIP

A. History leads to *Praise*
Ps 66:5-7; 98:1-3; 135:5-18; 136:1-26; 145:1-21

B. *Worship* celebrates God's acts in history
Ge 21:22-34; 26:1-33; Ex 13:1-16; 15:1-21; 29:44-46; 32:2-8; 34:18-28; Lev 9:24; 10:1-2; 16:2; Dt 10:21-22; 16:1-17; Jos 24:1-27; 2 Sa 22:1-51; 2 Ki 10:28-31; 1 Ch 22:1; 2 Ch 2:6-7,13; 5:10; Ezr 1:5-11; Ps 81:5; Jn 4:23

C. *Confession* of belief recites history
Ex 10:1-2; Dt 6:20-25; 26:1-11; Jos 4:1-24; 1 Ki 12:28-30; 1 Ch 16:8-36; 2 Ch 20:5-13; Ps 26:7; 71:14-18; 77:11-20; 105:1-45; 107:2; Eze 16:1-63; 19:1-14; Mic 6:3-5; Hab 3:2-19; Ac 7:1-53; 13:16-31; 26:4-23

D. *Narrative* teaches history
Ge 13:1-13; 33:18—34:31; Dt 1:3—3:29; 2 Ki 14:23-29; 1 Ch 29:29-30; 2 Ch 9:29; Est 1:1—10:3; Zep 1:1

VI. HISTORY AND GOD

A. *God* is active in history
Ge 11:9; 39:2-6; Ex 14:13; Dt 3:21-24; 4:3; 4:32-40; 13:1-11; 33:26-29; Jdg 16:23-24; 1 Sa 4:1-11; 2 Ki 13:23; 18:31-35; Ezr 5:4; Ne 9:5-37; Ps 72:18; 103:7; 106:2; Isa 40:18-24; 41:21-29; 45:18-22; Hos 13:4-13; Zep 1:12; Zec 8:14-15

B. *God's Will* is revealed in history
Nu 16:28-35; Dt 11:2-7; 1 Ch 19:13; Ne 13:26-27; Ps 78:1-72; Jer 7:22-29; 34:13

C. God's *Intentions,* not human ones, guide history
Ge 45:5-7; 50:19-21; Ex 1:8—2:10; 1 Sa 12:6-25; 2 Sa 17:14; 2 Ki 18:25; Gal 3:7

D. God's *Presence* is known in history
Nu 9:15-23; Dt 33:2; Jdg 5:1-31; 1 Sa 18:14; 30:6; 1 Ki 20:13; 1 Ch 22:18; Ps 114:1-8; Isa 8:10; Eze 40:1—48:35; Hag 2:4-5

B. *Acceptance*
Eze 20:40; Mt 10:40-42; Lk 10:16; 18:17; Jn 1:11-12; 3:33; 6:26-27; 7:37; 18:37; Ac 16:14; Ro 10:16; 15:7; 1 Th 2:13; Jas 4:8-10; Rev 3:20

C. *Belief*
Ps 4:5; 9:10; 13:5; 22:5,8; 32:10; 56:3-4,11; 112:7; Pr 3:5-6; Isa 10:20; 26:3; 43:10; Jer 17:7; La 4:12-13; Eze 33:13; Da 3:18,28; Hos 2:20; Jnh 3:5; Hab 2:4; Zep 3:12; Mt 8:5-13,26; 9:1-8,22,28-30; 13:58; 21:21-22; 27:42-43; Mk 1:15; Lk 24:25-27,37-41; Jn 1:7,12,50-51; 2:11,22-25; 3:12-16,36; 4:39-42,48,53; 8:24,30-31,45-46; 11:15,25-27,40-48; 12:10-11,35-46; 14:1,11-14,28; 19:35; 20:8,24-31; Ac 9:41-42; 16:30-31; Ro 10:4-17; 2 Ti 1:12; 3:15; Heb 11:1-40; 1 Jn 3:23

D. *Confession*
Ps 38:18; 106:6; Pr 28:13; Isa 44:5; Jer 3:13,22-25; Hos 4:1; Mic 7:9; Mt 3:6; 10:32-33; 16:17-19; Lk 18:13-14; Jn 12:42; Ro 10:8-10; 2 Co 9:13; Php 2:11; 2 Ti 2:19; Heb 3:1; 1 Jn 1:8-10

E. *Fear of God*
Ge 22:12; Ex 20:20; Dt 6:2,13,24; 10:12,20; Jos 24:14; 1 Ki 8:40,43; Job 1:1,8; Ps 15:4; 34:8-10; 85:9; 112:1; Pr 1:7,29; Isa 8:13-14; 11:2-3; 33:5-6; Jer 26:19; Da 6:26; Zep 3:7; Hag 1:12; Mal 2:5; Mt 9:8; Lk 1:50,65; 9:43; Ac 2:43; 9:31; 10:34-35; 2 Co 5:11; Heb 11:7; 1 Pe 1:17; Rev 14:7

F. *Knowledge of God*
Isa 1:3; 11:9; Jer 22:16; 31:34; Jn 8:19,55; 14:6-14; Ro 1:21; 1 Co 15:34; 2 Co 4:6; 10:5; Gal 4:9; Eph 1:17; 4:20; Php 3:8; 1 Th 4:5; 2 Pe 1:2-3; 1 Jn 2:3,13-14; 4:6-8

G. *Love of God*
Da 9:4; Mk 12:30; Lk 7:36-50; 11:42; Jn 8:42; 14:15,21,23-24,28; 21:15-23; Ro 8:28; 1 Co 2:9; 8:3; Jas 1:12; 2:5; 1 Pe 1:8; 1 Jn 4:19-21

H. *Obedience*
Job 1:1—2:10; 16:17; Ps 119:145; Ecc 12:13; Isa 2:3; Jer 15:17; Eze 11:18-21; Da 9:4,10-11; Hos 6:6; Jnh 3:3-5; Zep 2:3; Hag 1:1-14; Zec 7:9-10; Mt 8:18-22; 21:28-32; 22:37-39; 25:1-13; Lk 1:38,74; 11:28; 21:18-19; Jn 14:23; Ac 5:29,32; 26:20; Ro 1:5; 2:13; 16:19,26; 2 Th 1:7-8; Heb 2:1; 5:8-9; 11:8; Jas 1:22-25; 1 Pe 1:2,22; 1 Jn 2:3-6,17,29; Rev 21:27

I. *Repentance*
Dt 30:1-10; 2 Ch 30:6; Ezr 9:3-7; Ne 1:9; 9:2-3; Job 22:21-26; 40:4-5; Ps 51:1-9; Isa 30:15; 55:6-7; Jer 3:6-18; 5:3; 24:7; La 3:40; Eze 18:21-32; Da 4:27; 9:13; Hos 14:1-2; Joel 2:12-14; Am 4:6-11; Jnh 3:8; Mt 3:1,8,11; 4:17; 18:3; Lk 13:1-5; 15:7,10; 16:30; 17:3-4; 24:47; Ac 14:15; 17:30; 20:21; 26:20; Ro 2:4; 2 Co 7:9-10; 2 Pe 3:9; Rev 2:16,21,22

J. *Remembrance*
Jer 31:20; Eze 6:9; 16:43; Zec 10:9

VI. BENEFITS OF SALVATION

A. *Blessing*
Ge 1:22,28; 12:1-3; Lev 25:21; Nu 6:22-27; Dt 2:7; 24:19; Ru 2:12; 2 Sa 7:9,29; Job 1:3,10; 42:10,12; Ps 1:1; 2:12; 33:11-12; 67:1-2,6-7; 106:3; 119:1-2; 128:1; Pr 3:13,33; Isa 61:9; Jer 4:2; Eze 34:17-31; Hos 1:10; Mt 5:1-12; 16:17; 25:34; Mk 10:16; Lk 1:42; 11:27-28; Jn 20:29; Ac 3:26; Ro 4:9; 10:12; 15:29; 1 Co 9:23; 2 Co 8:9; Eph 1:3; Jas 1:12,25; 1 Pe 3:9; Rev 14:13

B. *Eternal Life*
Mt 19:16-30; 25:46; Lk 10:25-28; 18:29-30; Jn 3:15-16,36; 4:14,36; 5:24; 6:27-68; 8:51; 10:10,28; 17:2-3; 20:31; Ac 11:18; 13:46,48; Ro 2:6-9; 5:18,21; 6:22-23; Gal 6:8; 1 Ti 1:16; 6:12; Tit 1:2; 3:7; Heb 9:28; 1 Jn 2:17,25; 3:15; 5:11-13; Jude 21

C. *Forgiveness*
Ge 50:17-21; Ex 10:17-18; 34:6-9; Lev 4:13-35; 16:30; Jos 24:19; 2 Sa 12:13-14; 2 Ch 7:14; Ps 25:7,11,18; 51:1-9; 99:8; 103:3,10,12; 130:3-4; Isa 2:9; 38:17; 44:22; Da 9:19; Mic 7:18-19; Zec 5:5-11; Mt 6:12,14-15; 9:1-8; 12:31-32; 18:21-35; 26:28; Mk 1:4; Lk 1:77; 24:45-47; Ac 2:38; Ro 4:7-8; 2 Co 5:19; Eph 1:7; 4:32; Heb 8:12; 9:22; 10:17-18; Jas 5:15; 1 Jn 2:12

D. *Healing*
Ps 103:3; Jer 8:22; 17:14; La 2:13; Hos 5:13; 6:1-3; 7:1; 14:1-4; Mt 4:23-24; Lk 5:17-26; Rev 22:2

E. *Joy*
Ps 4:7; 5:11; 16:11; 30:11; 43:4; 51:8,12; 92:4; 149:5; Pr 10:28; Isa 9:3; 12:3; 35:10; 51:3,11; 55:12; 65:18; La 5:15; Joel 1:12; Hab 3:18; Zec 8:18-19; 9:9; 10:7; Mt 5:12; 13:44; 28:8; Lk 1:58; 10:21; 15:6,9-10; 24:52; Jn 3:29; 15:11; 16:22,24; 17:13; 20:20; Ac 8:8; 13:52; 16:34; Ro 5:11; 14:17; Php 2:17-18; 3:1; 1 Th 1:6; 3:9; Heb 12:2; 1 Pe 1:8; Jude 24; Rev 18:20

F. *Renewal*
Isa 1:26; 40:31; 49:8; Jer 30:3,18; 32:15,37,42-44; 50:19; La 5:21; Eze 11:17-21; 37:11-14; 47:7-23; Hos 6:2; Ac 3:19; Col 3:10; Tit 3:5

DISCIPLESHIP

I. *NATURE* OF DISCIPLESHIP
Isa 8:16; Mk 10:41-45; Lk 14:26-33; 17:7-10; 19:8; Jn 15:16-17; 21:15-17; Ro 12:1-5; 1 Th 1:3

II. PREPARATION FOR DISCIPLESHIP

A. Christian *Conversion*
Ac 26:20; Eph 2:8-10; 2 Th 1:11; Jas 2:14-26; 1 Jn 3:10; 4:19-21

B. *Enabling power*
1 Sa 30:3-8; Isa 40:29-31; Hag 2:4-5; Eph 3:16; Php 4:10-13; 1 Pe 4:11

C. *Training*
Mt 10:1; Lk 9:2

D. *Priesthood* of believers
Ex 19:5-8; Mt 23:1-11; 1 Ti 2:5; Heb 10:19-22; 1 Pe 2:5,9-10; 4:9-11

E. Ministry of the *Laity*
Ex 18:13-24; Ac 6:1-7; 1 Co 3:9

F. *Women* in ministry
Jdg 4:4; Pr 31:1; Ac 18:18; Ro 16:1-3; 1 Ti 3:11

III. GUIDELINES FOR DISCIPLESHIP

A. *God's leadership*
Ge 12:1-5; 24:1-67; 45:5; 48:15-16,21; Ex 13:21; 14:15-16; 15:13,18; 17:1-7; Nu 9:15-23; Dt 1:33; 2 Ki 18:5-6

B. *Covenant* agreement
Ex 19:5

C. *Kingdom of God*
Mt 3:2; 4:17; 6:10; 6:33; Mk 14:36; Ac 21:12-14

D. *Lordship of Christ*
Lk 6:46-49; 9:23; Jn 10:27; 12:23-26; 13:1-17; 14:12,15,21; 15:9-12; Ac 20:24; Ro 6:5-18

E. Guidance of the *Holy Spirit*
Jn 14:17,20; 16:13-14; 1 Co 6:19-20; Gal 5:16

F. Assisted by *Spiritual Leaders*
Ex 28:29-30; 32:30-34; 33:12-16; Lev 10:10-11; Nu 10:1-7; 14:1-44; 27:1-11; Dt 18:15; 31:1-8; Jos 24:31-33; 1 Sa 9:13-25; 11:6-7; 2 Sa 6:12-18; 12:1-15; 15:2; Ezr 10:9-17; Joel 2:17; Am 2:6-7; 3:7; Lk 22:25-26; Ac 10:25-26; Heb 13:7,17

IV. PURPOSE FOR DISCIPLESHIP

A. *God's Purposes*
Eph 4:28

B. *Neighbor Love*
Ex 20:13-17; Mt 22:37-40; Lk 6:27-35; 10:25-37; Jn 13:34-35; 17:26; Ro 12:10; 13:8; 1 Co 10:23-24; 16:13-14; Phm 4-7; Heb 6:7-10; 10:24-25; 13:1-3; 1 Jn 2:3-6; 3:17-18; Jude 8-13

C. *Influence*
Mt 5:14-16

D. Active *Involvement*
Isa 42:1-4; Am 5:14-15; 5:21-24; Mic 6:6-8; Lk 13:6-9; 14:28-33; 14:34-35; 2 Co 5:18-20; Heb 13:15-16

E. Service *Rewarded*
Mt 6:1-4; 25:34-46; Mk 9:41; Eph 6:5-8; Col 3:22—4:1; 2 Pe 1:10-11

V. FOCUS OF DISCIPLESHIP

A. Needs of *Persons*
Lev 19:1-2,9-19; Dt 24:17-22; Lk 4:18-21; 14:12-14; Ac 4:32,35,36-37; 20:35; 2 Co 9:12-15; Php 2:4

B. The *Poor*
Ex 22:25-27; 23:6; Lev 23:22; 25:8-13; 25:35-37,39-43; Dt 15:4-11; 24:6,10-15; Isa 3:14-15; 58:6-7; Jer 20:13; 22:15-17; Mt 19:21; Mk 10:21; Lk 3:11; 11:41; Jas 2:1-9

C. The *Hungry*
Lk 1:53; 9:12-17; Ro 12:20; 1 Co 11:21-22

D. The *Homeless*
Ex 22:21; 23:9; Lev 19:33-34; Nu 15:15-16,29; Dt 10:17-19; 12:19

E. The *Oppressed*
Isa 10:1-3; Am 4:1-2; Mt 9:36; Mk 12:38-40

F. The *Sick*
Mt 10:8; Lk 9:1-6; Jas 5:14-16

G. The *Handicapped*
Lev 19:14; Dt 27:18; Mt 15:30-31; Lk 14:13

H. *The Fallen*
2 Co 2:5-11; Gal 6:1-2

CHRISTIAN ETHICS

I. PERSONAL CHARACTER IN SOCIETY

A. Integrity of *Character* through relationship with God
Ge 27:1—28:9; Dt 6:24-25; 13:4; 26:16; Jos 1:7; 1 Sa 12:1-3; Job 31:1-40; Ps 1:1-11; 26:1-12; 37:1-8; 97:10-12; 139:23-24; 141:4; Pr 3:3-4; 10:9; 10:12; 12:15-16; 14:29-31; 16:18-19; 17:1; 17:9; 17:17; 20:22; Isa 2:11-18; 33:14-16; 51:7; 57:15; Jer 7:9; 32:39; Eze 3:20; 18:1-32; Da 6:4-5; Ob 3; Mic 7:1-7; Mt 5:1—7:27; 5:1—7:27; 5:38-48; 6:25-34; 7:1-5,12; 18:1-10; 18:21-25; 19:16-30; 22:34-40; Mk 8:34-38; 9:50; Lk 9:23-27; 9:58-62; 11:3-4; 14:7-11; 18:9-14; 22:24-30; Jn 3:19-21; Ro 6:1-23; 12:9-21; 16:17-19; 1 Co 6:12-20; 8:1-13; 10:31-33; 13:1-13; 15:58; 16:13-14; 2 Co 10:2-6; 13:1-12; Gal 4:18; 5:6-15; 5:16-26; 6:3-5; 6:9-10; Eph 4:1-3; 4:17-32; 5:1-21; Php 1:9-10; 1:20-27; 2:1-18; 3:1-11; 4:4-7; 4:8-9; Col 1:10; 2:13-23; 3:5-17; 1 Th 4:1-12; 5:4-8; 1 Ti 5:1-2; Heb 12:14-17; Jas 1:19-21; 3:13-18; 1 Pe 3:8; 4:2-5; 5:5-8; 2 Pe 1:3-9; 3:11-12,14; Rev 2:26

B. *Covetousness* lies at the heart of idolatry
Ex 20:17; Ac 5:1-11; 1 Jn 2:15-17

C. Truth and trustworthiness yields *Honesty*
Lev 19:35-36; Pr 20:10,23; Rev 14:5

D. *Language* reflects character
Ex 20:7; 20:16; 22:28; 23:1-2; Lev 6:3; 19:11; 24:10-16,23; Dt 5:11; 5:20; 2 Ki 19:22-23; Job 27:4; Ps 34:11-14; 50:16-21; 69:22-28; Pr 6:1-5; 11:11-13; 12:13-24; 13:2-3; 14:23; 15:1-2; 17:4; 17:20,27; 18:13; 18:20-21; 20:14-15; 20:25; 22:11; 24:26; 24:28-29; 25:11; 25:13-14; 25:18; 26:2; 26:4-5; 26:18-19; 26:20; 26:24-28; 28:23; 29:20; Ecc 6:11; 10:20; Jer 7:28; 9:3-8; Mt 5:33-36; 23:16-22; Eph 4:25,29; 5:4; Col 3:8-9; 4:6; Jas 1:26; 3:1-12; 1 Pe 3:9-12; 3 Jn 10; Rev 16:9,11

E. God requires *Obedience*
Ge 17:1,10; 26:5; Ps 112:1; Da 9:4-18; 1 Pe 1:2; 2:12; 1 Jn 2:3-6; Rev 3:3; 12:17; 14:12

F. *Righteousness* involves right relationship with God
Pr 4:18; 10:2,24-25,29-32; 11:5-11,18,21,23,28,30-31; 12:3,5,7,10,21,28; 13:5-6; 14:11,19,32,34; 15:9; 16:31; 24:15-16; 25:4-5; 28:1,10,12,28; 29:2,6,7,27; Isa 1:21-27; 3:10-11; 9:7; 26:1-11; 32:1; 45:8; 48:18-19; 51:1-3; 54:14; 56:1; 60:17; 61:1-11; 62:1-2; Jer 33:15-16; Da 9:24; 12:3,10; Hos 10:12-13; 14:9; Mt 3:15; 9:13; 10:41; 13:43; 23:28,35; 25:37-46; Ro 5:15-21; 6:15-22; Eph 6:14; Php 1:11; 3:9; 1 Jn 2:29; 3 Jn 11; Rev 20:11; 22:11

G. *Prayer* shapes character
1 Ki 8:25,58; 1 Ch 29:18-19

II. SOCIAL VALUES

A. Christians have a *Covenant* with God
2 Ki 18:9-12; 21:1-9; 23:3; 2 Ch 34:31-33; Ne 1:5; Ps 78:5-8; Da 11:32-35

B. God's *Justice* involves personal and social accountability
Ex 2:11-15; Lev 6:2-5; 19:15; 24:17-22; Nu 9:14; 15:15,29; 27:1-11; 35:6-34; 36:1-13; Dt

1:16-17; 4:41-43; 16:18-20; 17:8-13; 19:1-13; 19:14; 19:15-21; 21:1-9; 21:15-17; 23:15-16; 23:19-20; 24:10-22; 24:16; 25:1-3; 25:13-16; 26:13; Jos 20:1-9; 1 Sa 30:1-25; 2 Sa 15:3-6; 1 Ki 3:7-9,16-28; 21:1-19; 2 Ki 14:5-6; 2 Ch 10:1-19; 19:5-11; Job 5:3-7,16; 29:12-17; 31:13-14,21-23; Ps 33:5; 35:10-16; 37:6,25,35-36; 64:1-10; 72:1-14; 82:2-4; 94:1-23; 103:6-7; 109:1-31; 112:1-10; 119:121; 140:12-13; 142:7; 146:5-9; Pr 17:15,23,26; 21:25-26; Ecc 3:16-17; 7:15-16; 8:11-14; Isa 5:7-8; 11:3-5; 42:1-4; 51:4-8; Jer 5:1; 7:5-7; 21:11-12; 22:2-3,13; La 3:32-36; Eze 9:9-10; 13:17-23; 22:1-31; 45:9-12; Da 4:27; Hos 2:19-20; 12:6; Am 1:3—2:16; 5:7-24; 6:12; 8:4-6; Mic 2:1-7; 3:1-12; 6:6-8; Na 1:3-4; Hab 2:4; Zep 2:3; Zec 7:8-10; 8:16; Mal 2:17; Mt 5:6,10,20; 23:23; Ro 8:4,10; 10:1-11; 2 Co 5:21; 7:10-11; 9:9-10; Gal 2:21; 5:5; Eph 4:24

C. God expresses His will through *Moral Imperatives*

Ge 6:9,22; 7:1,5; 18:19; 22:1-19; Ex 12:1—13:16; 15:26; 16:4; 18:20; 19:3-8; 20:8-12; 34:11-26,32; Lev 10:11; Nu 1:54; Dt 5:1; 12:28; 16:12; 28:7; 28:25; Jos 22:5; 23:6; 24:14-15; 1 Sa 12:14-15,20-24; 28:18; 1 Ki 3:3,14; 9:4-5; 11:29-40; 15:1-5; 2 Ki 17:13-23; 1 Ch 22:12-13; 28:6-10; 2 Ch 7:17; 14:2-6; 33:8; Ne 9:13,29; Job 23:12; Ps 34:14; 94:12; Pr 2:20-22; Jer 8:7; 31:33; Eze 20:11-26; Am 5:14-15; Mt 12:1-14; 15:1-20; 23:3; Mk 7:1-23; 10:17-27; Lk 10:26-37; 11:37-52; 13:14-17; Ac 15:1-31; Ro 3:19-20; 7:1-25; 10:4; 13:8-14; Gal 2:3-21; 5:18; 6:2; Eph 2:8-10; 1 Ti 4:3; 2 Ti 3:1-17; Tit 3:9; Jas 1:25; 2:8-13; 1 Pe 2:1-2

D. God expresses His will through *Moral Limits*

Ge 2:16-17; 9:4-11; 31:1-55; Ex 18:16; 20:6; 20:22—23:19; Lev 18:3-30; 18:24-28; 22:9; 23:14; 23:26-32; Nu 15:37-41; Dt 5:32-33; 11:1; 12:23-25; 27:15-26; 2 Ki 17:15-17; Pr 1:10-19; Eze 9:3-11; Hab 2:12,17; Ro 1:28-32; 14:19-23

E. God expects stewardship of *Property Rights*

Dt 27:17; Job 1:9-22; 36:18; Ps 34:9-10; 37:16-17; 39:6; 49:10-19; 112:1-3; 144:12-15; Pr 3:13-18; 8:10-21; 10:4; 11:1; 11:4,16,18,28; 13:8; 15:27; 19:4,7; 22:7,9,26-27; 23:1-8; 27:20; 28:6,22,25,27; 30:8; Ecc 2:4-11; 4:4-8; 5:18-20; Isa 5:8-10; Jer 5:26-29; 17:11; 22:11-17; La 4:1-2; Eze 22:12,27-29; 33:31; Am 6:4-7; 8:4-6; Hag 1:4-11; 2:7-8; Mt 4:8-9; 6:19-34; 13:22; Lk 3:13-14; 8:14; 9:25; 12:13-34; 15:11-32; 16:1-15; 18:18-30; 19:1-10; Jn 12:4-6; Ac 2:44-45; 4:32; 8:18-23; 16:16-24; Ro 13:8; 1 Co 5:11; Eph 4:28; Php 4:19; Col 3:5; 1 Ti 6:3-10; 6:17-19; Tit 1:10-11; Heb 13:5; Jas 1:9-11; 2:1-18; 1 Jn 3:17-18; Rev 2:9; 3:17-18; 18:9-20

F. Chaos exists without *Social Order*

Lev 20:1-27; 23:21; 23:41; 24:3; 25:18-19; 26:3-45; Nu 30:1-16; Dt 4:1-8; 6:17-18; 7:11; 8:1-2,6; 10:12-13; 11:8-9; 11:32; 12:1; 15:5-6; 22:1-4; 27:10; 28:1; 28:1-68; 28:13; 30:11

G. Love of Neighbor should dictate *Social Relationships*

Lev 19:1-18; 19:37; 22:31-33; 2 Sa 12:7-14; Phm 15-17; 1 Pe 1:22; 4:8-10; 1 Jn 2:9-11; 4:7-21; 2 Jn 4-6

H. Corporate *Worship* yields positive social values

Ex 24:3,7; Dt 10:12-13; Ne 10:29; Ps 15:1-5; 24:3-6; Pr 21:3; Ro 12:1-3

III. SOCIAL PROBLEMS

A. *Murder* denies sacredness of human life

Ex 20:13; 21:12-14; Dt 5:17; 27:24-25; Jdg 8:10-21; 9:5; 2 Sa 2:8—4:12; 11:1—12:14; 13:23-33; 20:8-10; 1 Ki 1:1—2:46; 16:10-13; 2 Ki 8:15; 11:15-16; 12:20-21; 15:25,30; 21:23-24; 23:19-20; 2 Ch 15:13; 21:4; 24:20-22; 28:5-11; 33:24-25; Pr 29:10; Mt 5:21-22; 1 Jn 3:11-15; Rev 9:21; 21:8

B. *Theft* contradicts right to property

Ex 20:15; Lev 6:1-5; 19:11; Dt 5:19

C. *Alcohol* abuse affects character and relationships

Ge 9:21; 19:32-35; Lev 10:9; Nu 6:3-4,20; Dt 21:20; Jdg 13:4; 1 Sa 1:14-15; Ps 104:14-15; Pr 20:1; 23:20,29-35; 31:4-7; Isa 5:11-12,22; 25:6; Am 4:1; 6:6; 9:14; Hab 2:15; Mt 11:18-19; Lk 1:15; Jn 2:1-11; Ro 13:13; 1 Co 5:11; 6:10; Eph 5:18; 1 Ti 3:3-4; 5:23; Tit 1:7; 2:3

IV. AREAS OF APPLICATION

A. Christians have *Citizenship* in the world

Ne 5:1-18; Lk 20:20-26; 1 Ti 2:1-2; Tit 3:1-2; 1 Pe 2:13-14

B. Both *Church and State* have claims on Christians

1 Sa 22:1-23; Ezr 7:24; Mt 22:15-22; Mk 12:13-17; Ac 16:37-40; 18:12-17; 22:1-29; 25:1-12; Ro 13:1-7; 1 Co 6:1-8; Rev 13:1-10

C. *Ecology* issues concern Christians

Hos 4:1-3

D. Christians care about the people's *Health*

Ex 22:31; Dt 23:9-14; Da 1:8-16

E. Prejudice in *Race Relations* challenges the church

Lk 10:30-37; Jn 4:1-43; Ac 10:28-35; 13:46; 14:27; 15:1-31; 17:26

F. God created *The State*

Ge 17:6,16

G. *War* calls for the application of *Peace*

Ge 13:7-12; 14:1-16; 26:18-23; 34:1-31; 49:5-7; Ex 14:1—15:18; 17:8-16; 23:22-33; 33:14; Nu 10:9; 21:1-3; 21:23-35; 31:1-54; Dt 1:30; 2:9-23; 2:19—3:11; 3:22; 7:1-26; 12:9-10; 20:1-20; 21:10-14; 23:3-8; 24:5; 25:19; Jos 6:1-27; 7:1—8:29; 10:1-43; 11:1-23; 21:43-45; Jdg 1:1-36; 2:1—3:6; 3:7—16:31; 5:8; 7:1-25; 10:17—11:32; 20:8-48; 1 Sa 4:1-10; 7:7-14; 11:1-11; 15:7-35; 17:1-58; 28:16-19; 2 Sa 5:17-25; 7:1,11; 8:1-14; 1 Ki 5:4; 8:33-49; 8:56; 2 Ki 3:4-27; 6:8-23; 9:1—10:33; 17:1-6; 18:9—19:37; 24:1-4; 25:1-21; 1 Ch 5:18-22; 10:1-12; 2 Ch 11:2-4; 14:1—15:19; 16:1-10; 20:1-30; 26:6-22; Ne 4:1-23; Ps 18:30-50;

D. *Return Purposes*
Mt 16:27; Ro 11:25-27; Heb 9:28
E. Events surrounding
1. *Rapture* of Church
1 Th 4:14-18
2. *Great Tribulation*
Eze 38:1—39:29; Da 9:24-27; 12:1; Mt 24:21-22; Mk 13:1-37; 13:14-23; 2 Th 2:1-12; 2 Jn 7; Rev 6:1—19:21; 6:1-8; 6:12-17; 11:2-3; 13:1-10; 13:18
3. *Millennium*
Rev 20:1-6

IV. THE ETERNAL STATE
A. *Judgment*
Ecc 9:1-6; 11:9; 12:14; Mt 3:11-12; 25:31-46; Lk 12:48; Jn 5:21-24; Ac 10:42; 17:31; Ro 2:5-16; 3:5-6; 5:9; 14:10-12; 1 Co 3:12-15; 4:5; 5:12; 6:2-3; 9:24-27; 2 Co 5:10; Eph 6:8; Heb 4:13; 6:2; 10:26-31; Jude 5-6; 14; Rev 8:8—9:2; 14:9-11
B. *Heaven*
2 Sa 12:23; Ps 42:5,11; Mt 5:11-12; Mk 12:18-25; Jn 14:1-3; 17:24; Ro 8:17; 2 Co 12:3-4; Heb 4:1-11; 11:13-16; 1 Pe 1:3-5; Rev 7:1-17; 21:1-5; 21:9—22:15
C. *Hell*
Ps 37:9-13; Jnh 2:2,6; Mt 5:22; 18:8-9; 24:51; 25:30; Mk 9:43-48; 2 Th 1:7-10; 2 Pe 2:4-9; Jude 7; Rev 20:14; 21:8

V. THE SIGNIFICANCE
A. *History's Goal*
Isa 65:17-25; Eph 1:10; 1 Pe 4:7
B. *Creation's Redemption*
Mt 19:28; Ro 8:18-23; 2 Co 5:17-19; 2 Pe 3:7; Rev 21:1
C. *Salvation's Completion*
Isa 51:4-8; Lk 21:27-28; Ro 13:11-12; Eph 4:30; Php 1:6; 1 Pe 1:7-9
D. *Church's Consummation*
Eph 5:25-27; Rev 19:6-9
E. *Evil's End*
2 Pe 3:10
F. *Humanity Restored*
Ac 3:21; Ro 5:2; 8:29-30; Eph 1:14; 4:13; Col 3:4
G. *Satan's Defeat*
Ge 3:15; Isa 27:1; Rev 20:7-10
H. God's *Kingdom Established*
2 Ch 13:8; Isa 9:6-7; Da 4:3; 4:34; 6:26; 7:14,18,27; 1 Co 15:24-28; Rev 11:15

VI. IMPLICATIONS FOR TODAY'S LIVING
A. *Inspires Hope*
Job 13:15; Ro 8:38-39; Col 1:5; 1 Jn 2:28
B. *Purity*
1 Th 5:4-11; 2 Pe 3:11-18; 1 Jn 3:2-3
C. *Encourages Faithfulness*
Mt 25:14-30; Mk 8:38; 1 Co 15:58; 2 Ti 4:1; Heb 10:25; 10:32-34; 12:22-24; 2 Jn 8
D. *Demands Preparedness*
Mt 24:36-44; 25:1-13; Lk 12:40

GOD'S PEOPLE

THE CHURCH

I. OLD TESTAMENT CONCEPTS
A. *Covenant People*
Ge 6:18; 9:8-17; 12:1-3; 14:13; 15:18; 17:1-21; Ex 2:24; 6:4-5; 19:4-8; 24:1-11; 31:16-17; 34:10-28; Lev 2:13; 24:8; 26:9; 26:15-17; 26:25; 26:40-45; Nu 18:19; 25:10-13; Dt 4:13; 4:23; 4:31; 5:2-3; 7:6-8; 7:9-10; 7:12-13; 8:18; 9:9-15; 17:2; 29:1-15; 29:16-28; 31:16-19; 31:20; 33:9; Jos 5:2-9; 7:11-15; 23:16; 24:25-27; Jdg 2:1-3; 2:20-21; 2 Sa 7:1-17; 23:5; 1 Ki 8:9; 8:21; 8:23; 19:10,14; 2 Ki 11:12,17; 13:23; 17:15; 17:35-39; 18:11-12; 23:2-3; 1 Ch 16:15-17; 2 Ch 5:10; 6:11; 6:14; 7:17-22; 13:1-20; 15:12; 21:7; 23:11; 23:16; 29:10; 34:31-32; Ezr 10:2-5; Ne 1:5; 9:7-8; 9:32-37; 9:38; 10:29; 13:29-30; Ps 25:10; 25:14; 50:5,16; 74:20; 78:10,37; 89:3,28-37; 89:39; 103:17-18; 105:8-11; 106:45; 111:1-10; 132:11-12; Isa 28:15-18; 42:6-7; 49:8; 54:9-10; 55:3; 56:4-8; 59:20-21; 61:8; Jer 2:1-3; 7:23; 11:1-8; 13:11; 14:20-21; 22:8-9; 24:7; 30:22; 31:1; 31:31-34; 32:36-41; 33:17-18; 33:19-22; 34:12-20; 36:30; 50:4-5; Eze 11:17-20; 14:11; 16:1-8; 16:59-63; 17:19; 20:5; 34:25-31; 36:26; 36:28; 37:23; 37:24-28; 44:7; Da 9:4; 11:28-35; 11:32; 12:1-13; Hos 1:8-9; 2:1; 2:14-23; 8:1; Hag 2:4-5; Zec 9:9-13; 11:1-17; 13:9; Mal 1:2-5; 2:4-8; 2:10; 3:1; Mk 14:24; Lk 1:67-75; 22:20; Ac 3:25; Ro 9:4-9; 11:26-28; 2 Co 3:6; Gal 3:6-25; Eph 2:11-18; Heb 7:22; 8:6—9:28; 10:16-17; 12:24; 13:20; Rev 21:3; 21:7
B. *Remnant*
2 Ch 34:9; 34:21; Ezr 1:4; 9:8; 9:13-15; Ne 1:2; Isa 1:7-9; 4:2-6; 6:13; 7:3; 7:18-25; 10:20-23; 11:1-16; 17:4-6; 27:12-13; 28:5-6; 37:4; 37:31-32; 46:3-4; 65:8-10; Jer 3:11-18; 6:9; 23:1-4; 30:11; 30:18-22; 31:1-14; 40:11-12; 42:1-3; 44:7-30; 50:20; La 2:22; Eze 6:8-10; 9:8-10; 11:13; 12:16; 14:22-23; 20:32-38; Joel 2:32; Am 3:12; 5:3; 5:15; Mic 2:12; 4:6-7; 5:7-8; 7:18; Zep 2:6-11; 3:6-13; 3:19-20; Hag 1:12-15; 2:1-5; Zec 8:1-12; 9:7; 9:11-16; 13:8-9; Ro 9:27-29; 11:4-5
C. *God's Community*
Ps 100:3; Isa 64:8-9; Eze 34:1-24; Hos 1:10-11; 11:10; Mt 5:9; 5:43-45; Lk 6:35-36; 20:36; Jn 1:12-13; Ro 8:12-17; 8:19-21; 9:22-23; Gal 3:26-29; 4:4-7; Eph 1:5; Php 2:15; Heb 2:11-12; 3:1; 12:4-11; 1 Jn 3:1-2; 3:10; 5:1-5

II. NEW TESTAMENT CONCEPTS
A. *Body of Christ*
Ro 12:4-8; 1 Co 6:15-17; 12:12-31; Eph 1:22-23; 3:6; 4:1-6; 4:11-16; 4:25; 5:23-24; 5:25-32; Col 1:18; 1:24; 2:19; 3:15
B. Images
1. The *Bride* of Christ
2 Co 11:1-3; Rev 19:7-9; 21:2; 21:9; 22:17

2. The *True Israel*
Gal 6:16

III. PURPOSE OF THE CHURCH
A. Bring about *God's Kingdom*
Ps 103:19; 145:10-13; Isa 9:7; 32:1-8; Da 7:18-27; Mt 3:2; 4:17; 5:1; 5:3; 10:7; 12:28; 13:10-17; 13:19; 13:24-30; 13:31-32; 13:33; 13:36-43; 13:44-46; 13:47-50; 13:52; 18:1-4; 18:23-35; 19:12; 19:14; 19:24-26; 20:1-16; 21:31-32; 22:1-14; 25:1-13; Mk 1:15; 4:26-32; 9:1; 10:14-15; 10:23-27; 11:10; 12:34; Lk 1:32-33; 4:43; 6:20; 7:28; 8:1; 8:10; 9:11; 9:60-62; 10:9-11; 11:20; 12:31; 12:32; 13:18-21; 16:16; 17:20-21; 18:17; 18:24-25; 22:29-30; 23:50-51; Ac 8:12; 14:22; 19:8; 20:25; 28:23; 28:31; Ro 14:17; 1 Co 4:20; Col 4:11; 1 Th 2:12; Rev 1:9
B. *Intention of Christ*
Mt 16:18-19

IV. FUNCTIONING OF THE CHURCH
A. *Discipline*
Mt 18:15-20; 1 Co 5:1-5; 5:9-13; 6:1-6; 2 Co 2:5-11; 13:1-10; 2 Th 3:14-15; 1 Ti 5:20; Tit 3:10; 3 Jn 9-10
B. *Fellowship*
1 Co 1:9-10; 11:22
C. *Practice*
Ezr 10:7-17; Lk 9:46-50; Ac 1:21-26; 14:23; 15:1-35; 16:4-5; 1 Co 4:15-16; 16:15-18; Gal 2:1-14; 1 Th 5:12-13; 1 Ti 5:17; Tit 1:5; Phm 8-22; Heb 13:17; Jas 2:2; 5:13-14
D. *Covenant* keeping
Ps 44:17
E. *Servant*hood
Job 1:8; 2:3; Ps 27:9; 31:16; 34:22; Isa 22:20-25; 37:35; 41:8-9; 42:1-4; 42:18-22; 43:10; 44:1; 44:21; 45:4; 48:20; 49:1-7; 50:4-11; 52:13—53:12; 54:17; 65:13-16; Jer 43:10; 46:28; Da 9:11; 9:17-19; Joel 2:29; Hag 2:23; Zec 3:8; Mt 20:20-28; 23:11; Mk 9:33-37; 10:35-45; Lk 1:38; 1:48; 22:26-27; Jn 15:14-15; Ac 26:16; Ro 1:1; 2 Co 4:5; 6:4; 11:23; Gal 1:10; Eph 3:7; 6:21; Php 1:1; Col 1:7; 1:23; 1:25; 3:24; 4:7; 4:12; 2 Ti 2:24-25; Jude 1
F. *Saints*
Ac 9:13-14; 9:32; 9:36-41; 26:10; Ro 1:7; 12:13; 15:26; 16:2; 16:15; 1 Co 1:2; 16:1; 2 Co 1:1; 8:3-4; 9:1; 13:13; Eph 1:1; 1:15; Php 1:1; 4:21-22; Col 1:2; 1:4-5; 1:26-27; 2 Th 1:10; Heb 6:10; Rev 22:21

V. FORM OF THE CHURCH
A. *Redeemed of All Ages*
Lk 9:49-50; Jn 10:14-18; 11:51-52; 17:11; 17:20-23; 20:29
B. *People of God*
Mt 12:30; 12:46-50; Lk 10:16; 11:23; Jn 10:25-29; 12:32; 15:1-8; Ac 9:2-31; 24:5; 24:14; 28:22; Ro 15:14; 1 Co 3:10-15; 3:16-17; 10:32; 2 Co 3:2-3; 3:7-18; 6:16-17; Gal 6:10; Eph 2:10; 2:19-22; 3:8-11; Php 2:1-2; 3:20; Col 3:11; 1 Ti 3:15; Tit 2:14; Heb 3:6; 10:10; 1 Pe 2:4-10; 2:17; Rev 1:6; 5:10; 15:2
C. *Local Body*
Ac 4:32; 5:11; 5:12-14; 8:1; 11:26; 13:1; 14:27; 15:3-4,22,30; 18:22; 20:28; Ro 15:5-7; 16:4; 16:5; 16:16; 16:17-18; 16:23; 1 Co 5:12-13; 11:16; 11:18-19; 14:34; 15:9; 16:19; 2 Co 8:18-24; 11:28; 12:13; Gal 1:2; 1:22; Col 4:15; 1 Th 1:1; 2:14; 2 Th 1:1; 1:4; Phm 2; 1 Pe 5:13; 3 Jn 9; Rev 1:4; 1:20; 2:1; 2:8; 2:11; 2:12; 2:18; 2:23; 3:1; 3:7; 3:14; 22:16

ORDINANCES

I. BAPTISM
A. *Background of Baptism*
Lev 8:6; Ac 13:24; 1 Co 10:2
B. Meaning
1. *Baptism as Cleansing*
Eph 5:26; Tit 3:5; Heb 6:2; 10:22
2. *Baptism as Unity*
1 Co 1:13-17; Eph 4:5
3. *Baptism as Death*
Mk 10:38-40; Lk 12:50
4. *Baptism as New Life*
Jn 3:3-5; Col 2:12,20; 3:1; 2 Ti 2:11
C. *Form of Baptism*
2 Ki 5:14; Ro 6:3-4
D. *Baptismal Candidate*
Ac 2:38-41; 16:15; 16:31-34; 18:8
E. Administrator
1. *Baptism by John*
Mt 3:4-17; Mk 1:4-11; Lk 3:1-22; 7:29-30; 20:4-7; Jn 1:24-33
2. *Baptism by Jesus*
Jn 3:22-26; 4:1-2
3. *Baptism by Holy Spirit*
Ac 1:4-5; 8:12-17; 11:15-16; 18:25; 1 Jn 5:6
F. Authority for Baptism
1. *Baptism Commanded*
Mt 28:19
2. *Baptism in Jesus' Name*
Ac 10:37,47-48; 19:1-7; 22:16; Gal 3:27
3. *Baptism as Confession*
Ac 8:36-39; 9:18; 1 Co 15:29

II. LORD'S SUPPER
A. *Background of Lord's Supper*
1 Co 10:3-4
B. *Institution of Lord's Supper*
Lk 22:1-30
C. Meaning
1. *Lord's Supper as New Covenant*
Mt 26:17-30
2. *Lord's Supper as Humility*
Jn 13:1-30; 1 Co 10:15-22
3. *Lord's Supper as Death and Resurrection*
Jn 21:13
4. *Presence in the Lord's Supper*
Lk 24:35
D. *Observance of Lord's Supper*
Mk 14:10-26; Ac 2:42-46; 20:7; 1 Co 11:17-34

WORSHIP

I. THE ESSENCE OF WORSHIP

A. *Praise*
Ex 15:1-21; Isa 12:1-6; 44:23; Eze 3:12; Rev 7:11-17

B. *Service*
Dt 11:13; Mic 6:6-8; Mt 4:10; Ac 24:14; Php 3:3; 2 Ti 1:3; Rev 22:3

II. THE *IMPORTANCE* OF WORSHIP

Heb 10:19-25

III. WARNINGS ABOUT *FALSE* WORSHIP

Ex 22:20; Dt 29:18; 1 Sa 13:9-13; 2 Ki 17:25-41; Isa 1:10-17; Am 5:21-27; Zep 1:4-9; Zec 7:4-10; Col 2:20-23; Jude 11-13

IV. THE COMPONENTS OF WORSHIP

A. Attitudes

1. *Reverence*, awe, and adoration
Lev 9:23-24; Jdg 13:19-23; 2 Sa 22:1-51; 1 Ch 29:10-13; 2 Ch 20:18; Ps 5:7; 96:9; Isa 6:1-8; Mt 9:8; Lk 7:16; Rev 14:7

2. *Humility*, weeping, and fasting
Jdg 20:26; Joel 1:13-14; Ac 13:2-3

3. Faith, submission, and *Obedience*
1 Sa 1:9-28; 15:22-23; Ps 61:8; Hos 6:6; Mal 2:13-14

4. *Thanksgiving*
1 Ch 16:4; 2 Ch 7:3; Ps 100:4; Heb 12:28

5. *Rejoicing*
Ezr 3:10-11; Php 4:4

B. Practice

1. *Sacrifice*
Ex 20:24-26; Lev 7:35-38; Dt 26:1-15; 2 Sa 24:21-25; Ro 12:1-2; 2 Co 8:1-8

2. Sacred *Buildings*
Ge 28:16-22; Ex 3:12-18; Dt 12:4-14; 1 Sa 7:15-17; 9:12; 10:3-17; 1 Ki 8:1-66; 1 Ch 22:1-19; Ps 26:8; 134:1-3; Ecc 5:1-7; Hag 1:2-15; 2:3-9; Lk 24:52-53; Jn 4:19-24; Ac 3:8; 16:13

3. *Priesthood*
1 Ch 6:48-49; 15:25-28; 2 Ch 8:12-16; 29:25-36; Zec 3:7; Mal 1:6-14; 2:1-9; 3:3-4; Eph 4:11-13; 1 Ti 2:5; Heb 4:14-16; 1 Pe 2:9

4. *Calendar*
Ex 12:1—13:16; 16:23-30; 23:14-32; 30:10; 34:18-26; Lev 16:1-34; 23:4-38; 25:9; Nu 28:16—29:39; Dt 16:1-17; Ac 20:7; Ro 14:5-6; 1 Co 16:2; Rev 1:10

5. *Prayer*
Ge 12:6-8; 13:4; Ex 34:8-9; 1 Ch 21:26; Ezr 9:5-15; Ne 1:4-11; 9:1-38; Ps 1:1—150:6

6. *Proclamation* of God's Word
Ne 8:1-6; Isa 61:1-2; 63:7; Jer 26:2-7; 44:20-29; Lk 4:15-21; Ac 20:20-21

7. *Music*
Jdg 5:1-31; 2 Sa 6:5; 1 Ch 6:31-32; 25:1-31; 2 Ch 20:28; Isa 38:20; Mt 26:30; Mk 14:26; Ac 16:25; Eph 5:19-20; Col 3:16

8. Sense of *Community*
Ac 2:42-47; Eph 5:17-20

C. Participation

1. *Corporate*
1 Ch 29:20; Ps 42:1-4; Lk 1:10; 19:37-38; 1 Co 14:26-33

2. *Individual*
Ge 4:3-7; 24:26; Ex 33:9-11; 1 Ki 1:47-48; Mt 17:1-8; Jn 9:36-38

PROCLAMATION

I. CONTENT OF PROCLAMATION

A. Definition of *Gospel*
Mt 4:17; Mk 1:14-15; Ac 3:11-26; 4:10-20; 5:29-32; 10:36-43; 13:16-41; 13:32-35; Ro 1:1-5; 2:16; 8:34; 16:25-27; 1 Co 15:1-7; 15:14; Gal 1:3-12; 3:1; 1 Th 1:10; Tit 1:3

B. Simplicity and *Clarity* of the Gospel
Lk 4:14-21; 1 Co 2:1-5; 2 Co 4:1-6

C. *Central Theme* of the Gospel
Mt 10:7; Lk 10:9; 24:47; Ac 2:38; 5:42; 8:4-5; 8:35; 9:20; 1 Co 2:2; 1 Ti 3:16; 2 Pe 1:16-21

D. *Divine Source* of the Gospel
Dt 30:12-13; Zec 1:14,17

II. NATURE OF PROCLAMATION

A. *Authoritative* declaration
Dt 18:9-22; Hos 5:9; Joel 3:9; Am 3:7-10; Mic 1:2; Lk 8:1; 2 Co 1:17-24; 2 Ti 4:1-2

B. Declared by God's Chosen *Proclaimer*
Na 1:15; 1 Co 3:1-9

C. Qualities of the Proclaimer

1. *Call*ed by God
Isa 6:1-13; 40:1-8; Jer 1:4-9; Am 7:12-17; Jnh 1:2; 3:2-4; Hab 1:2-4; Mk 3:13-14; Lk 9:1-2; Ro 10:14-15; 15:15-22; 1 Co 1:17-18; Eph 3:8-9; Col 1:25; 1 Ti 2:7; 2 Ti 1:8-11

2. *Compulsion*
Mt 24:14; Mk 1:38-39; 13:10; Lk 4:43-44; 9:60; 1 Co 9:16-18; 2 Co 5:17-21

3. *Anointing*
Isa 61:1-3; Mic 3:8; Ac 4:31-33; Php 1:14-18; 1 Th 1:4-5; 2 Ti 4:17

4. *Fearless*
Jer 2:2; 19:14-15; Mic 3:5-6; Mt 10:26-28

III. RESULTS OF PROCLAMATION

A. Brings *Unbelievers* to God
Lk 2:34; Ac 14:1; 20:20-21; 24:24-25; 26:19-29; 1 Co 1:18-25; 2 Th 1:8

B. Leads to *Faith*
Ro 10:8-13; Php 1:27-30

C. *Rejection* is possible
Heb 4:2

D. Benefits Believers

1. *Instruction*
Ac 15:35; Col 1:28; 1 Th 4:1-2

2. *Reproof*
2 Ti 3:14-17

3. *Exhortation* and encouragement
Lk 3:18; Ac 14:21-22; 1 Th 3:2; 2 Pe 2:5

4. *Growth* and perseverance
Col 1:3-6

PRAYER

I. THE FOUNDATION OF PRAYER

A. *Universality of* Prayer
1 Ki 5:7; 10:1-9; 2 Ch 9:8; Ezr 6:10,12; Isa 56:7; Jnh 1:14-16; Mt 2:2

B. Prayer and the nature of God

1. *Holiness of God*
Ex 19:10-11; 29:7; Lev 4:1-35; 5:14-19; 8:1-36; Jos 5:15

2. *Mercy of God*
Ex 2:23-24; 3:9; 14:10; 22:22-23; 25:17-22; Nu 16:22; 20:16; 1 Sa 9:16; Mic 7:7; 7:14-20; Jas 5:4; 1 Pe 5:7

3. *Love of God*
Dt 4:7; Ps 23:1-6; Jn 16:26-27

4. *Sovereignty of God*
Ge 18:14; Ex 4:10-13; 2 Sa 7:18-29; 24:25; 1 Ki 17:1; 18:36-39; 18:41-46; 2 Ki 19:14-19; 1 Ch 17:16-27; 2 Ch 14:11; 32:20-21; Ezr 7:27-28; Ps 47:1-9; 58:1-11; 76:1-12; 90:1-17; 146:1-10; Isa 37:14-20; Jer 7:16; 11:14; 29:12-14; Mic 3:4; 1 Ti 4:4-5

5. *Faithfulness of God*
Ge 32:9-12; 2 Ki 22:19; 2 Ch 6:13-42; 7:13-16; 12:7,12; 15:12-15; 16:7-9; 34:27; Pr 15:29; Isa 65:24; Jer 33:3; Zec 10:6; 13:9; Php 4:19; 1 Pe 1:17; 2 Pe 1:4

6. *Honor of God*
Jos 7:7-9

7. *Righteousness of God*
2 Ki 19:4

C. Importance of prayer

1. *Command of God*
1 Ch 23:13; 2 Ch 15:2; 34:3; Isa 62:6-7; Jer 29:7; 31:7; La 2:19; Eze 22:30; Mt 6:9-13; Lk 10:2; Ro 1:21; 1 Ti 2:8; Jas 4:8; 5:13-14

2. *Biblical Characters*
Ac 2:42-47; 6:4; 10:9; 21:5

3. *Jesus' Example*
Mt 11:25-26; 14:13-14,23; Mk 1:35; 6:31-32; 6:45-46; 7:34; Lk 3:21-22; 4:42-43; 5:16; 6:12-13; 9:18; 9:28-29; 10:21-22; 11:1-4; Jn 6:15; Ac 7:59-60; 2 Ti 4:16; Heb 5:7

II. PURPOSE OF PRAYER

A. *Fellowship with God*
Ge 5:24; 6:9; Nu 10:35-36; 1 Ki 19:8-18; Ps 16:1-11; 84:1-12; Ro 11:2; 1 Jn 1:3; 1:6

B. Ascertain and do *Will of God*
Ge 27:27-29; 28:3-4; Ex 8:30-31; 9:33; 28:30; Nu 7:89; 22:1—24:25; Jdg 6:11-24; 6:36-40; 20:9; 1 Sa 1:20; 13:9,13; 14:8-10; 15:11-35; 16:2; 2 Sa 2:1; Mt 12:39; Jn 12:27-28; Ac 6:6; 1 Jn 3:21-22; 5:14-15

C. Experience *God's Presence*
Ge 19:27; Ex 34:34-35; Ps 7:1-17; 48:1-14; 122:1-9; 133:1-3

D. Spiritual *Growth*
1 Sa 30:6

E. To receive God's *Answer*
1 Ki 9:3-9; 2 Ki 19:20-36; 20:9-11; 1 Ch 4:10; 5:20; 21:26; 2 Ch 13:14-18; 18:31; Ezr 8:21-23; Ps 6:1-10; Isa 7:10-14; 30:19-21; 37:21-29; 37:30-32; 58:9; Jer 12:1-6; 42:2—43:4; Lk 1:13; Jn 11:41-42; Ac 11:5,18; 2 Co 12:8-9; Phm 22

F. To receive *Instruction*
Ps 14:1-7; 15:1-5; 36:1-12; 37:4; 53:1-6; 78:1-72; 119:1-176; 127:1-5; 128:1-6; Ac 22:17

G. To receive *Salvation*
Lk 23:42-43

H. To advance God's *Kingdom Growth*
Ro 1:9-10; 1 Ti 5:5

I. To *Inquire* of God
2 Ch 34:21-22

J. To Intercede in *Politics*
Ps 72:1-20; 132:1-18

III. HELPS IN PRAYER

A. *Holy Spirit Helps* in prayer
Ro 8:15; 8:26-27; Gal 4:6

B. *Holy Spirit Guides* in Prayer
Nu 27:15-19; Jn 14:16; Jude 20-21; Rev 1:10

C. Prayer *In Christ* our Advocate
Eph 2:18; 3:12; Heb 4:15-16; 7:19; 7:25; 9:24-25; 10:19-22; 1 Jn 2:1

IV. TYPES OF PRAYER

A. *Confession*
Nu 21:7; Jdg 2:4-5; 2 Sa 24:10; Ezr 9:1-15; 10:1-17; Ne 1:4-11; 9:1-37; Job 5:8; Ps 32:1-11; 51:1-19; 106:1-48; Isa 59:12-15; La 3:40-42; Da 9:3-19

B. *Praise*
Ex 15:1-18; 15:21; 18:10-11; Nu 21:17-18,27-30; Dt 8:10; Jdg 5:1-31; Ru 4:14-15; 1 Sa 2:2-10; 25:32-34; 25:39; 2 Sa 22:1-51; 1 Ch 23:5; 25:3; 2 Ch 5:12-14; 20:18-22; 20:26-28; 23:13-21; Ps 8:1-9; 9:1-20; 21:1-13; 29:1-11; 33:1-22; 66:1-20; 72:18-20; 92:1-15; 93:1-5; 95:1-11; 96:1-13; 97:1-12; 98:1-9; 99:1-9; 100:1-5; 103:1-22; 104:1-35; 108:1-13; 111:1-10; 112:1-10; 113:1-9; 115:1-18; 117:1-3; 124:1-8; 134:1-3; 135:1-21; 145:1-21; 147:1-20; 148:1-14; 149:1-9; 150:1-6; Isa 26:1-21; Da 2:20-23; Mt 21:9; Mk 11:9-10; Lk 1:46-55; 1:64; 1:67-79; 2:13; 2:20; 5:25-26; 7:16; 18:42-43; 19:37-40; 23:47; 24:52-53; Jn 12:13; Ac 16:25; Ro 16:25-27; 2 Co 1:3; 11:31; Eph 1:3-14; 3:20-21; Php 3:1; 4:4; 4:20; Col 3:16; Heb 13:15-16; 1 Pe 1:2-3; 4:16; 5:11; 2 Pe 3:18; Jude 24-25

C. *Thanksgiving*
Ge 8:20; 12:7-8; 16:13; 26:25; 35:7; Nu 31:48-54; Dt 26:5-10; Jos 8:30-31; 1 Sa 9:13; 1 Ch 16:8-36; Ps 18:1-50; 30:1-12; 34:1-22; 65:1-13; 73:1-28; 75:1-10; 105:1-45; 107:1-43; 116:1-19; 118:1-19; 136:1-26; 138:1-8; Isa 12:1-6; 25:1-12; 38:9-20; Jer 31:9; Mt 14:19; 15:36; 26:26-27; Mk 6:41; 8:6-7; 14:22-23; Lk 2:28-35; 2:36-38; 9:16; 17:16-19; 22:19-20; 24:30; Jn 6:11; Ac 27:35; 28:15; Ro 1:8; 7:25; 14:6; 1 Co 10:30; 11:24; 15:57; 2 Co 2:14; 4:15; 8:16; 9:11; Eph 5:4; 5:19-20; Php 1:3; Col 1:3; 2:7; 3:15; 1 Th 1:2-3; 2:13; 3:9; 2 Th 1:3; 2:13; 1 Ti 1:12-13; Phm 4-5

D. *Petition*
Ge 4:26; 9:24-27; 24:12-27; 25:22-23; Ex 3:13-14; 15:25; 17:4-6; Nu 27:5-7; Dt 10:10-11; Jos

10:12-14; 18:6; 19:51; Jdg 1:1; 3:9; 4:3; 6:6-8; 10:10-16; 15:18; 16:28; 20:1; Ru 1:8-9; 1 Sa 2:20-21; 8:6-22; 10:19-22; 12:10; 12:17-23; 22:10; 23:2; 24:12-15; 30:7; 2 Sa 5:19; 5:23; 14:17; 1 Ki 3:5-14; 17:19-21; 22:8-17; 2 Ki 3:11; 13:4; 20:3; 22:13-14; 1 Ch 14:10,14; 22:11-12; 2 Ch 1:8-11; 18:6; 32:24; Ne 5:19; 6:9; 13:14,22,29,30; Ps 26:1-12; 27:1-4; 41:1-12; 85:1-13; 126:1-6; 144:1-15; Jer 10:23-25; 14:7-11; Jnh 2:1-9; Mt 24:20; 26:36-44; 26:40-41; 27:46; Mk 13:18; 14:32-39; 14:37-38; 15:34; Lk 21:36; 22:31-32; 22:40,46; Ac 1:24-26; 4:24-31; 9:40; 28:8; Php 4:6; Rev 22:20-21

E. *Intercession*

Ge 20:17; 25:21; Ex 5:22-23; 32:11-14; 32:32; Nu 11:2; 12:10-14; Ru 2:12; 2:20; 3:10; 4:11; 1 Sa 7:5-11; 2 Sa 21:1; 24:17; 24:24; 1 Ki 1:36-37; 13:6; 17:7-16; 2 Ki 2:21-22; 5:9-15; 6:17; Job 1:5; 42:8-10; Ps 45:1-17; 91:1-16; Isa 53:12; Jer 14:19—15:9; Eze 14:12-20; Da 2:18-19; Joel 2:17; Am 7:1-9; Mt 5:44-45; Lk 6:28; 23:34; Jn 17:1-26; Ac 8:14-17; 8:18-24; 26:29; Ro 8:34; 15:30-32; 2 Co 13:7; Eph 1:15-19; 3:14-19; 6:18-20; Php 1:4-11; 1:19; Col 1:9-12; 4:2-4; 4:12; 1 Th 3:12-13; 2 Th 1:11-12; 3:1-5; 1 Ti 2:1-3; 2 Ti 1:16-18; Phm 6; Heb 13:18-19; 1 Jn 5:16-17; 3 Jn 2

F. *Commitment*

Ru 1:17; 2 Sa 5:3; 23:16-17; 1 Ki 8:22-53; 2 Ki 23:3; 1 Ch 11:3; 11:18; 15:12-14; 18:11; 2 Ch 2:4; 7:5; Ne 4:9; 5:12-13; Ps 62:1-12; 63:1-11; 101:1-8; 123:1-4; Lk 2:22-24; 23:46; Ac 9:11; 14:23

G. For *Forgiveness*

Nu 14:13-24; Mt 6:14-15

H. *Confidence*

Ps 121:1-8

V. MODES OF PRAYING

A. *Worship*

Ge 33:20; Ex 23:19; 30:1,7; 30:34-36; Lev 1:9; 2:2; 3:1-5; 17:6; 23:40; Dt 12:5; 12:7,12; 14:26; 16:11; 16:16-17; 26:2; 26:11; 27:7; Jos 22:26-28; Jdg 7:15; 1 Sa 1:26-28; 6:15; 7:17; 10:8; 2 Sa 6:5; 6:14-23; 8:11-12; 12:20; 1 Ki 9:25; 1 Ch 6:49; 13:8; 15:16-28; 16:1; 16:4-6; 16:37-42; 29:6-9; 2 Ch 33:16; 35:16-18; Ezr 2:68-69; 6:21-22; Ne 8:6; 11:17; 12:24; 12:27-43; Job 1:20-21; Ps 20:1-9; 68:1-35; Am 5:21-24; Mt 2:11; 4:10; 28:9; Lk 4:8; Jn 4:23-24; Ro 12:1; Php 4:18; Heb 12:28-29; Rev 5:8-14; 7:9-12; 12:12; 14:3; 14:7; 16:7; 19:10; 22:8-9

B. *Blessing*

Ge 14:18-20; 48:15-20; 49:1-28; Nu 6:22-27; Dt 28:1-14; 33:1-29; 2 Sa 13:25; 1 Ki 1:47-48; 8:14-21; 8:55-65; 1 Ch 16:2; 2 Ch 6:3; Ps 67:1-7; Mt 19:13-15; 23:39; Mk 10:13-16; Lk 13:35; 18:15-17; 24:50-51; Ac 20:36; Ro 1:7; 15:33; 1 Co 1:3-4; 16:22-24; 2 Co 1:2; 13:11,14; Gal 1:3-5; 6:18; Eph 1:2; 6:23-24; Php 1:2; 4:23; Col 1:2; 4:18; 1 Th 1:1; 5:23-28; 2 Th 1:2; 2:16-17; 3:16-18; 1 Ti 1:2; 6:21; 2 Ti 1:2; 4:22; Tit 1:4; 3:15; Phm 3; 25; Heb 13:20-21; 13:25; 1 Pe 5:14; 2 Jn 3; Jude 2; Rev 1:4-6

C. *Curse*

2 Sa 3:29; 2 Ki 1:10,12; 2:24; Ne 4:4-5; 6:14; 10:28-29; Job 3:3-19; 6:8-10; Ps 5:10; 35:1-28; 52:1-9; 129:1-8; 137:1-9; Jer 11:18-23; 18:18-23; La 3:55-66; Jnh 4:1-11

D. *Oath*

2 Sa 19:7; 19:13; 1 Ki 2:23-24

E. *Vow*

Ge 28:20-21; Lev 9:22; Jdg 11:30; 1 Sa 23:18; 24:21-22; 2 Sa 3:39; 1 Ki 1:13; 2:42-43; 2 Ki 2:4

F. *Lament*

2 Sa 3:33-35; Job 7:7-21; 9:1—10:22; Ps 3:1-8; 4:1-8; 10:1-18; 12:1-8; 17:1-15; 22:1-31; 25:1-22; 28:1-9; 31:1-24; 42:1—43:5; 44:1-26; 54:1-7; 55:1-23; 56:1-13; 57:1-11; 59:1-17; 60:1-12; 61:1-8; 64:1-10; 69:1-36; 70:1-5; 71:1-24; 74:1-23; 77:1-20; 79:1-13; 80:1-19; 82:1-8; 86:1-17; 88:1-18; 89:1-51; 94:1-23; 102:1-28; 109:1-31; 120:1-7; 139:1-24; 140:1-13; 141:1-10; 142:1-7; 143:1-12; Isa 32:9-15; 38:2-7; 63:7—64:12; Jer 15:10-21; 20:7-18; La 1:1—5:22; Mt 9:14-15; Mk 2:18-20; Lk 5:33-35; Rev 6:9-11

G. *Music*

2 Ki 3:15-18

VI. BIBLICAL PRINCIPLES IN PRAYING

A. *Hindrances* in praying

Nu 11:10-15; 16:15; Dt 3:23-27; Jos 9:14; 1 Sa 4:3-11; 14:41-45; 23:21; 28:6; 2 Sa 12:13-16; 15:12; 1 Ki 1:9-10; 3:3; 18:26-29; 19:4; 2 Ch 16:12; 29:5-36; Job 5:1; Pr 1:28-29; 15:8; Isa 59:1-2; La 3:8; 3:44; Eze 8:18; Zec 7:13; Mal 1:9; 2:11-14; Mt 6:5-8; 8:26; 17:17-21; Mk 4:40; 5:18-19; 9:19-29; Lk 8:25; 8:38-39; 9:41; 12:13-15; 16:19-29; 18:9-14; Jas 4:2-3

B. Praying *In Jesus' Name*

Jn 14:13-14; 15:7; 15:16; 16:23-24; 1 Co 1:2

C. Proper Attitudes in Praying

1. *Faith*

Ge 15:2-3; 17:17-18; Jdg 11:27; 2 Ki 2:14; 4:44; Ps 11:1-7; 13:1-6; 46:1-11; 125:1-5; Jer 32:16-27; Hab 3:1-19; Mt 7:7-11; 8:10-13; 9:20-22; 11:22-24; 20:29-34; 21:19-22; Mk 5:25-34; 10:27; 10:51-52; Lk 8:48; 11:9-12; 17:5-6; 18:27; Jn 9:35-38; 11:22; Jas 1:5-8

2. *Humility*

Ge 17:3,17; Ex 34:28; Dt 9:18-19; 2 Sa 1:12; 2:5-6; 2 Ch 33:12-13; Est 4:3; Ps 131:1-3; Ecc 5:2; Hos 6:6; Am 5:4-6,14; Mt 9:18; Mk 11:25; Lk 7:4-10; 8:41; 1 Co 11:4-5; 11:13

3. *Sincerity* and Earnestness

Ge 32:24; Jdg 20:23; 20:26-27; 2 Ch 20:1-12; 30:18-27; Est 4:16; Ps 39:1-13; Isa 1:10-17; Hos 12:3-4; Joel 1:14; 1:19; Mt 9:13; Mk 5:23; 12:40; Lk 20:45-47; 22:39-45; Ro 9:3; 10:1; Col 2:1; Heb 13:3; Jas 5:17-18

4. *Repentance*

Ex 34:5-9; Ps 19:1-14; 38:1-22; 130:1-8; Lk 13:2-5

5. ***Responsiveness***

Ex 3:4

D. Procedures in Praying

1. **Regular and continuous *Persistence***

Ge 18:23-32; 1 Ch 23:30-31; Ne 2:4,8; Ps 83:1-18; Da 6:10-11; 10:13; Mt 15:21-28; Mk 7:25-30; Lk 11:5-13; 18:1-8; Ac 10:2-6; Ro 12:12; 1 Th 3:10-11; 5:17-18; 2 Ti 1:3; 1 Pe 4:7

2. ***Ordered* prayer**

Ps 5:1-12; Ac 3:1; 10:30

VII. PERSONAL AND COMMUNITY PRAYER

A. *Personal* prayer

Ge 29:35; Ex 33:11-17; 33:18-23; Dt 34:10; Jdg 13:8-25; Ru 2:4; 1 Sa 1:10-17; 1:23; 2 Sa 3:9-10; 14:11

B. *Family* prayer

1 Co 7:5; 1 Pe 3:7

C. *Corporate* prayer

Ex 4:31; Nu 8:5-22; Dt 27:12-26; Jos 8:33-34; 24:1,16-18,21-25; Jdg 11:11; 21:2-4; 1 Ch 29:10-22; Est 9:30-31; Ps 40:1-17; 41:13; 50:1-23; 81:1-16; 89:52; 106:48; 114:1-8; Hab 3:1,19; Mt 18:18-20; 21:13; Mk 11:17; Lk 1:10; Ac 1:14; 12:5-12; 13:2-3; 16:13; 16:16; 1 Co 14:1-19; 2 Co 1:10-11; Jas 5:16

D. *Church* prayers

Lk 19:46

CHURCH LEADERS

I. AUTHORITY OF CHURCH LEADERS

Mt 18:18; 20:25-28; 23:8-10; Ro 12:3-8; 1 Co 9:1-15; 2 Co 1:24; 4:2; Gal 2:6; Eph 4:11-12; Php 4:2-3; 1 Th 5:12-15; Heb 13:7; 13:17; 3 Jn 9-10

II. ORDINATION

Nu 27:18-23; Ac 6:6; 13:3; 1 Ti 4:14; 5:22

III. EARLIEST LEADERS

A. *The Twelve*

Mt 10:1; Mk 6:30; Lk 6:13; Jn 6:70; Ac 1:2-5

B. *Apostle* as Eye Witness

Ac 1:21-22; Ro 1:1; 1 Co 15:7-9; 2 Co 13:10; Gal 2:8; Eph 2:20; Php 2:25

C. *Disciple*

Lk 6:17

D. *Prophet*

Ac 2:17; 13:1; 21:9-11; 1 Co 12:28-29; 14:3-5; Eph 2:20; 3:5; 1 Th 5:20; 1 Jn 4:1

IV. CHURCH OFFICERS

A. *Pastor and Overseer*

Ac 20:28; 2 Co 4:5; Php 1:1; 1 Ti 3:1-7; Tit 1:5-9; 1 Pe 5:1-5

B. *Elder*

Ac 11:30; 14:23; 20:17; 1 Ti 4:14; 5:17-18; Jas 5:14; 2 Jn 1

C. *Deacon*

Ac 6:1-6; Ro 16:1-2; Php 1:1; Col 1:7; 1 Ti 3:8-12

D. *Teacher*

1 Co 12:28-29; Gal 6:6; Eph 4:11; 2 Th 2:15; 2 Ti 2:15; 4:3; Jas 3:1

E. *Evangelist*

Ac 21:8; 2 Ti 4:5

F. *Widow*

Ac 9:36-39; 1 Ti 5:9-15

G. *Minister*

Phm 1

H. *Priest*

Ac 6:7

V. LEADERS OF OPPOSITION

A. *False Apostle*

2 Co 11:13

B. *False Prophet*

Mt 7:15; Mk 13:22; 2 Pe 2:1-3

EDUCATION

I. WHY EDUCATION?

A. *Commanded*

Dt 4:9-10,14; 31:12-13

B. *Essential* to wholeness

Hos 4:6

C. *Qualified Teachers*

1 Ti 5:17; 2 Ti 2:2; 2:23-26; Tit 2:7; Heb 5:12—6:3

II. TEACHERS IN THE BIBLE

A. *God* as teacher

Job 36:22; Ps 25:4-9; 27:11; 32:8; 94:10-12; Isa 2:3; Jer 32:33; Hos 11:3; Mic 4:2; Jn 7:16-17; Jas 1:5

B. *Moses* as teacher

Ex 10:2; Dt 32:2

C. *Law* as teacher

Ex 24:12; Ps 19:7-11; Pr 13:14

D. *Priests* as teachers

Lev 10:11; Dt 33:10; 2 Ch 17:7-9; 35:3; Eze 44:23; Mic 3:11; Hag 2:11-13; Mal 2:6-8

E. *Prophets* as teachers

Ac 13:1

F. *Parents* as teachers

Ge 18:19; Dt 6:1-10; Ps 78:1-6; Pr 1:8-9; 31:26; Eph 6:4; 1 Ti 4:6

G. *Jesus* as teacher

Mt 4:23; 5:2; 7:28-29; 9:35; 13:54; 22:24,36; 23:8; Mk 1:21-22; 1:25-27; 2:13; 6:6; 10:1; 12:14,32; 14:14; Lk 4:14-15; 4:31-32; 13:22; 20:21,28,39; 22:11; 24:13-27,45; Jn 1:38; 11:28; 13:13; 20:16

H. *Disciples* as teachers

Mt 13:52; Ac 2:42

I. *Evangelists* as teachers

Ac 4:1-4; 5:25-28; 8:34-35

J. *Missionaries* as teachers

Ac 15:35; 17:2; 17:22-31; 18:11; 18:19; 19:8-10; 20:20-21; 28:31; 2 Ti 1:11

K. The *Spirit* as teacher

Jn 16:13-15

L. *Scribes and Pharisees* as teachers

Mk 12:38-40; Lk 20:45-47; Jn 3:10

M. *Pastors* as teachers

Ac 11:26; Eph 4:11-16; 2 Ti 1:13-14

N. *Christians* as teachers
Ac 5:42; 18:24-26; Ro 15:14; Gal 6:6; Col 3:16
O. *False Teachers* as teachers
Jer 9:14; Mt 23:25-26; 1 Ti 1:3-7; 4:1-2; 6:3-6; 2 Ti 2:15-18; 4:2-4; 2 Pe 2:1-3; 2 Jn 10-11; Rev 2:20

III. AIMS OF EDUCATION
A. *Wisdom*
Job 28:28; Pr 1:7; 8:1-7,11; 9:9; 15:14; Jas 3:17-18
B. *Guidance* for living
2 Ki 12:2; Ps 86:11; 119:9-11
C. *Happiness*
Pr 3:13-18
D. *Correction*
Col 2:6-8; Tit 1:9-16; 2 Pe 3:16
E. *Social Order*
2 Ki 17:27-28
F. *Spiritual Renewal*
Ne 8:1-9; Ro 12:2; 1 Co 1:18-31
G. *Moral Purity*
Pr 7:1-5; 29:3; 2 Th 3:6
H. To communicate *Tradition*
1 Co 15:3
I. *Effective Witnessing*
1 Pe 3:15
J. *Self-preservation*
Pr 29:1

IV. EDUCATIONAL METHODS
A. *Discipline*
Job 6:24; Pr 4:1-10; 15:31-33; 17:10; 19:18; 22:17
B. *Example*
Pr 13:20; 22:24-25; Lk 6:39-40; Jn 13:14-15; Ro 2:19-24; 1 Co 4:17; 2 Ti 3:10
C. *Instruction*
1 Co 14:19
D. *Object Lessons*
Jos 4:4-7
E. *Parables*
Mk 4:2
F. *Questions*
Lk 2:46
G. *Scripture Study*
Lk 24:27; 2 Ti 3:14-17
H. *Symbolism*
Ex 12:24-27
I. *Repetition*
Isa 28:9-10
J. *Participation*
Php 4:8-9
K. *Obedience*
Ps 119:99-102; Isa 29:13

FAMILY

I. GOD'S PREPARATION FOR FAMILY
A. Creation of *Personhood*
Ge 1:27
B. Creation of *Sexual Nature*
Ge 1:27-28
C. Creation of *Social Persons*
Ge 2:18
D. Creation of *Environment* for living
Ge 2:4-17
E. Goodness of *Creation*
1 Ti 4:3-5

II. GOD'S PURPOSES FOR MARRIAGE AND FAMILY
A. *Companionship*: mutual submission
Ge 2:18-24
B. Sexual fulfillment: *One Flesh*
Ge 2:24; 1 Co 6:15-17
C. *Childbearing*
Ge 4:1-2; Ps 127:3-5; 128:3-6; Lk 1:24-25
D. *Education* and discipline
Ge 14:14; Jdg 13:8; Pr 12:1
E. *Economic Support*
2 Co 12:14
F. *Symbolic Nature* for faith
Pr 1:8-9; Jer 2:1-3; Eze 16:8-9; Hos 1:1-8; 2 Co 11:2
G. *Temporal* not eternal
Mt 22:23-32; Mk 12:18-27
H. *Single*
Mt 19:10-12; 1 Co 7:1,7-9

III. HUMAN FAILURE TO FULFILL GOD'S PLAN
A. *Disobedience* to God
Ge 38:1-10
B. *Female Subordination*
Ge 3:16; Est 1:10-22
C. *Intermarriage*
Dt 7:3-4; Jdg 3:5-6; Ezr 9:1—10:17; Ne 10:28-30; 13:23-27; 13:23-27; Mal 2:10-12; 1 Co 7:12-16; 2 Co 6:14-18
D. *Parental Failure*
1 Sa 2:12-17,22-25; 8:1-3; 1 Ki 1:6
E. Family favoritism, deceit, *Conflict*
Ge 25:19-34; Jdg 16:4-22; 2 Sa 6:16,20-23; 1 Ch 15:29; Mic 7:5-6
F. *Rejecting Parents*
Dt 21:18-21
G. Destructive *Sexual Sin*
Ge 34:1-31; Lev 18:6-20; Dt 22:13-28; 2 Sa 11:2—12:13; Pr 6:20-35; Eze 22:6-11; Mt 5:27-30; Ro 1:26-28; 1 Co 5:1-5; 2 Co 2:5-11
H. *Violence* in family relationships
2 Ch 21:1-8
I. Polygamy and concubines: *Multiple Wives*
Ge 16:1-16; 1 Sa 25:43-44; 1 Ki 11:1-9; 2 Ch 11:18-21
J. *Divorce*
Dt 24:1-4; Mal 2:13-16; Mt 1:18-19; 5:31-32; 19:3-9; Mk 6:17-18; 10:2-12; 1 Co 7:10-11
K. *God's Judgment* on families for sin
Jer 9:13-16; 44:25-28; Ac 5:1-11

IV. HUMAN FULFILLMENT OF GOD'S PLAN
A. *Accepting Covenant* relationship
Ge 7:1,7; 9:1-2; Jos 24:14-15; Ru 3:1—4:12; Isa 65:20-23; Lk 1:59
B. *Covenant Marriage*
Ge 24:1-67
C. *New Selfhood* in Christ
Ro 5:12-21; Gal 3:26-29; Eph 4:22-24

D. Healthy *Sexual Fulfillment*
Pr 5:15-23; SS 2:3-6; 4:1-7; 5:10-16; 7:1-9; Heb 13:4
E. Fulfilling family *Role Relationships*
Ex 20:12; Nu 30:1-15; Jdg 11:30-40; 1 Sa 14:27-45; Pr 12:4; 31:10-31; Mt 15:3-6; Mk 7:9-13; Lk 10:38-42; Jn 11:1-44; Eph 5:21; 5:22—6:4; Col 3:18-21; Tit 2:2-10; 1 Pe 3:1-7
F. *Social Concern* for others
Ro 12:13; Gal 6:9-10
G. *Mutual Respect*
Ro 12:10
H. *Continuing Growth*
Php 1:9-11

V. QUALITIES OF MATURITY
A. Perspective on *Priorities*
Dt 24:5; Mt 10:21,34-39; Mk 3:21,31-35; 13:12; Lk 9:59-62; 12:49-53; 14:25-27; Jn 7:2-5; 1 Co 7:8,25-28,32-40; 7:36-38
B. Mutual *Need Fulfillment*
1 Co 7:2-7
C. *Accepted Grace*
Eph 2:8-10,19-20

VI. ESSENTIAL FACTORS IN STRONG FAMILIES
A. *Bible Study*
Dt 6:4-9; Ps 78:1-8; Isa 38:19
B. Family *Worship*
Ex 12:3-4; Dt 12:7; 1 Sa 1:9-28; 2:18-21,26; Job 1:5; Lk 2:41-42
C. Commitment to effective *Communication*
Pr 15:1,4,23; 18:2,13,17; 24:26; 26:18-19; 27:5; Eph 4:15,25,29-31; Col 3:8-10
D. Practicing principles of *Conflict Resolution*
Ge 32:3—33:17; Mt 18:15-17; Eph 4:26-27
E. Developing *Friendships*
1 Sa 18:1-4; Pr 27:10; Jn 15:13-15
F. *Authentic Love*
Ru 1:15-18; SS 8:6-7; Ro 12:9
G. *Forgiveness*
Lk 17:3-4
H. *Shared Joy*
Job 1:4; Jn 15:11

THE CHURCH AND THE WORLD

EVANGELISM

I. THE MEANING OF EVANGELISM
A. As seen in the *Gospel*
Ps 71:14-18; 105:1-45; Mt 13:1-23; Mk 4:26-29; Ac 13:16-43; 17:10-12; 1 Co 1:21-25; 1 Jn 5:10; Rev 14:6
B. *God's Provision* of Salvation
Ge 12:1-7; 17:16,21; Ps 46:10; Jer 33:6-9; 48:47; 49:6; 49:39; Zec 8:13; Lk 1:16-17; 3:6; Ac 3:25; Gal 3:8-14
C. *Universality* For all People
Isa 42:10-12; 45:6; 49:1-6; 56:3-8; 60:1-14; 66:17-24; Zep 3:9-10; Zec 2:11; Mal 1:11; Mt 12:21; Lk 24:45-49; Ac 8:4-8; 8:25; 8:26-40; 10:1-48; 13:46-48; Ro 3:29-31; 10:12-15; 15:7-12; 16:26; 1 Co 7:18-20; Rev 7:9; 15:4

II. THE MOTIVES OF EVANGELISM
A. God's *Call to Evangelize*
Mt 4:19; 10:5-10; 28:18-20; Mk 1:17-18; Lk 9:1-6; 10:1-24; Jn 17:18-19; 20:21-23; Ac 1:8; 9:15; 13:1-3; 22:20-21; 23:11; Eph 3:8; Col 1:23-29
B. Give *Glory to God*
Ex 7:5; 14:4,18,25; 1 Ki 8:59-60; 2 Ki 19:19; Isa 24:14-16; 1 Co 10:31-33
C. *Love* for People
Ps 51:7-13; Ro 9:1-3; 10:1; 2 Co 5:14
D. *Obedience* to Christ
1 Sa 3:1-19; 1 Ki 19:19-21; Ps 76:11; 145:3-13; Isa 6:8; 12:4-6; Jer 1:5-10; Jnh 1:1—4:11; Mal 1:14; 2 Ti 4:5; Jude 21-23
E. Eternal *Rewards* Promised
Da 12:3; Mk 10:29-31

III. THE REASONS FOR EVANGELISM
A. *Lostness* of Humanity
Ex 9:20-21,25,30; Isa 64:1-12; Mk 2:15-17; Ro 6:23
B. *Christ*, Humanity's Only *Hope*
Lk 2:30-32; 1 Jn 1:1-4
C. God's *Salvation* of People
Ps 67:1-2; 72:17; 102:15; Isa 25:3; 52:10
D. God *Involves* His People
Ex 3:1—4:31; Isa 42:6-7; 54:1-5; 61:6; 1 Co 3:5; 2 Co 2:14-16; 5:20; 10:12-18; Eph 4:11-16

IV. THE THEOLOGY OF EVANGELISM
A. Based in the *Work of Christ*
Ac 2:17-40; 3:15; 4:12; Ro 5:8; Gal 1:11—2:15; 4:12-20
B. God's *Judgment* on Sin
Ex 10:3-7; Isa 49:26; Jer 8:20-22; 12:14-17; Am 4:12; Zep 2:11; Zec 14:16-21; Lk 16:27-31
C. The *Call to Salvation* through Repentance and Faith
Ge 3:9-20; Ps 86:8-10; Isa 45:22-24; 55:1-13; Jer 4:1-2; Mt 7:13-14; 9:12-13; Jn 1:12; 20:31; Ac 10:34-48; 20:17-21; 2 Co 6:1-2; Eph 2:8-9; Rev 22:17
D. *Results* of Salvation
Ge 18:18-19; 22:18; 26:4; Ps 19:1-4; Eze 3:5-11; Hab 2:14; Mt 10:32-33; Lk 7:1-10; Jn 15:1-8; 16:27; 17:20-23; Ac 17:34; Ro 15:18; Eph 3:6; Col 1:6; 3:11; 1 Th 2:19-20; 2 Th 1:10; Jas 5:19-20
E. Includes *Follow-up*
Ac 14:21-28; 1 Th 3:2

V. EXAMPLES OF EVANGELISM
A. *Mass* Evangelism
Ex 12:38,48; 2 Ki 17:24-28; Ps 26:7; 47:1; Eze 38:16; 47:22; Da 6:26; Zec 8:20-23; Mt 9:26; 9:31; 24:14; Ac 2:41
B. *Personal* Evangelism
2 Ch 6:32-33; Ps 35:28; Isa 43:10-13; 44:8; Jer 51:10; Mt 23:15; Lk 2:17; Jn 1:7-9; 1:41; 4:1-42; Ac 28:23-31; 1 Co 9:19-23; 1 Th 2:1-9; 2 Ti 1:8; Phm 6

C. *Social Action* in Evangelism
Mt 4:23-25; Lk 8:36; Ac 5:12-14
D. *Teaching* Evangelism
Isa 2:3; Jer 16:19-21; Mic 4:2; 1 Ti 2:7

VI. HOW EVANGELISM IS PRACTICED
A. *In the Church*
Ac 2:47; 15:3; 2 Ti 2:2
B. Through *Worship* experiences
Ps 9:11; 48:9; 66:1; 113:1-9; Mk 11:17; Ac 14:1-2; 16:13-15; 17:1-4
C. *In the Marketplace*
Ps 2:10; 18:49; Mt 10:11-20; 18:10-14; Ac 16:16-17; 19:9-10
D. *In the Home*
Ru 1—4:22; 2 Ki 5:1-8; Mk 5:19-20; Lk 8:39
E. Through *Confrontation*
Ac 18:6
F. Through Personal *Testimony*
Ps 40:3; Jn 12:17-19; 19:35; Ac 24:10-21; 26:1-20; 1 Co 1:6; Col 4:5-6; 1 Th 1:6-8; Rev 12:11; 19:10
G. Through *Persecution*
Mt 5:11-12; Mk 13:9-10; Lk 21:13-15; Ac 16:25-34; 1 Th 2:15-16; Rev 2:13; 6:9; 12:17; 17:6; 20:4

VII. SUPPORT FOR EVANGELISM
A. *Power* of God
2 Ch 7:13-14; 30:6-9; Ps 138:4; Eze 38:23; 39:7; 39:27; Jn 5:31-40; Ac 4:1-4; 6:7; 11:21; 11:22-25; 12:24; 16:5; 2 Ti 4:16-17
B. Power of the *Holy Spirit*
Ac 2:1-13; 5:29-32; 9:31; 13:6-12; 2 Co 2:12-13; 1 Th 1:5
C. Power of *Holy Life*
Jdg 13:1-7; 2 Ch 33:16; Ps 85:4-7; Eze 37:28; Jn 3:30; Ro 1:13-17; 1 Pe 2:12; 3:1
D. Power of *Prayer*
Mt 9:37-38; 2 Th 3:1

MISSIONS

I. GOD IS THE *SOURCE* OF MISSIONS
Ge 12:1-3; Jnh 4:11; Jn 14:11-12

II. HUMANITY IS THE *SCOPE* OF MISSIONS
Ge 18:16-33; 2 Ch 6:32-33; Ps 67:1-7; Ac 10:42-48; Gal 3:8; Eph 3:6; 3:8

III. REDEMPTION IS THE PURPOSE OF MISSIONS
A. A biblical *Command*
Mt 28:18-20; Jn 20:21
B. Consistent with God's *Call*
Isa 6:1-8; Jnh 1:1-3; Mt 28:6-7
C. On the risen Lord's *Authority*
Ex 9:16
D. Based on the gospel *Message*
Lk 24:44-49
E. Given *Power* by the Holy Spirit
Ac 1:6-8
F. *Nature* found in reconciliation, ministry, fellowship
Ge 22:16-18; Isa 61:1-3; Rev 22:17

IV. MESSENGERS ARE THE INSTRUMENTS OF MISSIONS
A. *Sending* Messengers is God's Work
Isa 66:19-23; Mt 9:35-38; Ac 13:2-5
B. Early missionaries and churches are *Examples*
Mt 10:5-15; Lk 10:1-18; Ac 8:26-40; 1 Th 1:8
C. Human *Means* are needed in missions
Ex 19:3-6; Ro 10:10-15

V. MISSIONS YIELD HISTORICAL AND ETERNAL *RESULTS*
Ps 67:3-4; Mt 13:18-23; Rev 7:9

A Concordance

to the

NEW INTERNATIONAL VERSION

Introduction to the NIV Concordance

(Mini-Concordance)

The NIV Concordance, created by Edward W. Goodrick and John R. Kohlenberger III, has been developed specifically for use with the New International Version. Like all concordances, it is a special index which contains an alphabetical listing of words used in the Bible text. By looking up key words, readers can find verses and passages for which they remember a word or two but not their location.

This concordance contains nearly 5,000 word entries, with some 35,000 Scripture references. Each word entry is followed by the Scripture references in which that particular word is found, as well as by a brief excerpt from the surrounding context. The first letter of the entry word is italicized to conserve space and to allow for a longer context excerpt. Variant spellings due to number and tense and compound forms follow the entry in parentheses, and direct the reader to check other forms of that word in locating a passage.

This concordance contains a number of "block entries," which highlight some of the key events and characteristics in the lives of certain Bible figures. The descriptive phrases replace the brief context surrounding each occurrence of the name. In those instances where more than one Bible character has the same name, that name is placed under one block entry, and each person is given a number (1), (2), etc. Insignificant names are not included.

Word or block entries marked with an asterisk (*) list every verse in the Bible in which the word appears.

This concordance is a valuable tool for Bible study. While one of its key purposes is to help the reader find forgotten references to verses, it can also be used to do word studies and to locate and trace biblical themes. Be sure to use this concordance as more than just a verse finder. Whenever you look up a verse, aim to discover the intended meaning of the verse in context. Give special attention to the flow of thought from the beginning of the passage to the end.

ABBREVIATIONS FOR THE BOOKS OF THE BIBLE

Genesis	Ge
Exodus	Ex
Leviticus	Lev
Numbers	Nu
Deuteronomy	Dt
Joshua	Jos
Judges	Jdg
Ruth	Ru
1 Samuel	1Sa
2 Samuel	2Sa
1 Kings	1Ki
2 Kings	2Ki
1 Chronicles	1Ch
2 Chronicles	2Ch
Ezra	Ezr
Nehemiah	Ne
Esther	Est
Job	Job
Psalms	Ps
Proverbs	Pr
Ecclesiastes	Ecc
Song of Songs	SS
Isaiah	Isa
Jeremiah	Jer
Lamentations	La
Ezekiel	Eze
Daniel	Da
Hosea	Hos
Joel	Joel
Amos	Am
Obadiah	Ob
Jonah	Jnh
Micah	Mic
Nahum	Na
Habbakuk	Hab
Zephaniah	Zep
Haggai	Hag
Zechariah	Zec
Malachi	Mal
Matthew	Mt
Mark	Mk
Luke	Lk
John	Jn
Acts	Ac
Romans	Ro
1 Corinthians	1Co
2 Corinthians	2Co
Galatians	Gal
Ephesians	Eph
Philippians	Php
Colossians	Col
1 Thessalonians	1Th
2 Thessalonians	2Th
1 Timothy	1Ti
2 Timothy	2Ti
Titus	Tit
Philemon	Phm
Hebrews	Heb
James	Jas
1 Peter	1Pe
2 Peter	2Pe
1 John	1Jn
2 John	2Jn
3 John	3Jn
Jude	Jude
Revelation	Rev

AARON

Priesthood of (Ex 28:1; Nu 17; Heb 5:1-4; 7), garments (Ex 28; 39), consecration (Ex 29), ordination (Lev 8).

Spokesman for Moses (Ex 4:14-16, 27-31; 7:1-2). Supported Moses' hands in battle (Ex 17:8-13). Built golden calf (Ex 32; Dt 9:20). Talked against Moses (Nu 12). Priesthood opposed (Nu 16); staff budded (Nu 17). Forbidden to enter land (Nu 20:1-12). Death (Nu 20:22-29; 33:38-39).

ABANDON

Dt 4:31 he will not *a* or destroy you
1Ti 4: 1 in later times some will *a* the faith

ABBA

Ro 8:15 And by him we cry, "*A*, Father."
Gal 4: 6 the Spirit who calls out, "*A*, Father

ABEL

Second son of Adam (Ge 4:2). Offered proper sacrifice (Ge 4:4; Heb 11:4). Murdered by Cain (Ge 4:8; Mt 23:35; Lk 11:51; 1Jn 3:12).

ABHORS

Pr 11: 1 The LORD *a* dishonest scales,

ABIGAIL

Wife of Nabal (1Sa 25:30); pled for his life with David (1Sa 25:14-35). Became David's wife (1Sa 25:36-42).

ABIJAH

Son of Rehoboam; king of Judah (1Ki 14:31-15:8; 2Ch 12:16-14:1).

ABILITY (ABLE)

Ezr 2:69 According to their *a* they gave
2Co 1: 8 far beyond our *a* to endure,
8: 3 were able, and even beyond their *a*.

ABIMELECH

1. King of Gerar who took Abraham's wife Sarah, believing her to be his sister (Ge 20). Later made a covenant with Abraham (Ge 21:22-33).

2. King of Gerar who took Isaac's wife Rebekah, believing her to be his sister (Ge 26:1-11). Later made a covenant with Isaac (Ge 26:12-31).

ABLE (ABILITY ENABLE ENABLED ENABLES)

Eze 7:19 and gold will not be *a* to save them
Da 3:17 the God we serve is *a* to save us
Ro 8:39 will be *a* to separate us
14: 4 for the Lord is *a* to make him stand
16:25 to him who is *a* to establish you
2Co 9: 8 God is *a* to make all grace abound
Eph 3:20 him who is *a* to do immeasurably
2Ti 1:12 and am convinced that he is *a*
3:15 which are *a* to make you wise
Heb 7:25 he is *a* to save completely
Jude :24 To him who is *a* to keep you
Rev 5: 5 He is a to open the scroll

ABOLISH

Mt 5:17 that I have come to *a* the Law

ABOMINATION

Da 11:31 set up the *a* that causes desolation.

ABOUND (ABOUNDING)

2Co 9: 8 able to make all grace *a* to you,
Php 1: 9 that your love may *a* more

ABOUNDING (ABOUND)

Ex 34: 6 slow to anger, *a* in love
Ps 86: 5 *a* in love to all who call to you.

ABRAHAM

Covenant relation with the LORD (Ge 12:1-3; 13:14-17; 15; 17; 22:15-18; Ex 2:24; Ne 9:8; Ps 105; Mic 7:20; Lk 1:68-75; Ro 4; Heb 6:13-15).

Called from Ur, via Haran, to Canaan (Ge 12:1; Ac 7:2-4; Heb 11:8-10). Moved to Egypt, nearly lost Sarah to Pharoah (Ge 12:10-20). Divided the land with Lot (Ge 13). Saved Lot from four kings (Ge 14:1-16); blessed by Melchizedek (Ge 14:17-20; Heb 7:1-20). Declared righteous by faith (Ge 15:6; Ro 4:3; Gal 3:6-9). Fathered Ishmael by Hagar (Ge 16).

Name changed from Abram (Ge 17:5; Ne 9:7). Circumcised (Ge 17; Ro 4:9-12). Entertained three visitors (Ge 18); promised a son by Sarah (Ge 18:9-15; 17:16). Moved to Gerar; nearly lost Sarah to Abimelech (Ge 20). Fathered Isaac by Sarah (Ge 21:1-7; Ac 7:8; Heb 11:11-12); sent away Hagar and Ishmael (Ge 21:8-21; Gal 4:22-30). Tested by offering Isaac (Ge 22; Heb 11:17-19; Jas 2:21-24). Sarah died; bought field of Ephron for burial (Ge 23). Secured wife for Isaac (Ge 24). Death (Ge 25:7-11).

ABSALOM

Son of David by Maacah (2Sa 3:3; 1Ch 3:2). Killed Amnon for rape of his sister Tamar; banished by David (2Sa 13). Returned to Jerusalem; received by David (2Sa 14). Rebelled against David; seized kingdom (2Sa 15-17). Killed (2Sa 18).

ABSTAIN (ABSTAINS)

1Pe 2:11 to *a* from sinful desires,

ABSTAINS* (ABSTAIN)

Ro 14: 6 thanks to God; and he who *a*,

ABUNDANCE (ABUNDANT)

Lk 12:15 consist in the *a* of his possessions."
Jude : 2 peace and love be yours in *a*.

ABUNDANT (ABUNDANCE)

Dt 28:11 will grant you *a* prosperity—
Ps 145: 7 will celebrate your *a* goodness
Pr 28:19 works his land will have *a* food,
Ro 5:17 who receive God's *a* provision

ACCEPT (ACCEPTED ACCEPTS)

Ex 23: 8 "Do not *a* a bribe,
Pr 10: 8 The wise in heart *a* commands,
19:20 Listen to advice and *a* instruction,
Ro 15: 7 *A* one another, then, just
Jas 1:21 humbly *a* the word planted in you,

ACCEPTED (ACCEPT)

Lk 4:24 "no prophet is *a* in his hometown.

ACCEPTS (ACCEPT)

Ps 6: 9 the LORD *a* my prayer.
Jn 13:20 whoever *a* anyone I send *a* me;

ACCOMPANY

Mk 16:17 these signs will *a* those who believe
Heb 6: 9 your case—things that *a* salvation.

ACCOMPLISH

Isa 55:11 but will *a* what I desire

ACCORD

Nu 24:13 not do anything of my own *a*,
Jn 10:18 but I lay it down of my own *a*.
12:49 For I did not speak of my own *a*,

ACCOUNT (ACCOUNTABLE)

Mt 12:36 to give *a* on the day of judgment
Ro 14:12 each of us will give an *a* of himself
Heb 4:13 of him to whom we must give *a*.

ACCOUNTABLE (ACCOUNT)

Eze 33: 6 but I will hold the watchman *a*
Ro 3:19 and the whole world held *a* to God.

ACCUSATION (ACCUSE)

1Ti 5:19 Do not entertain an *a*

ACCUSATIONS (ACCUSE)

2Pe 2:11 do not bring slanderous *a*

ACCUSE (ACCUSATION ACCUSATIONS)

Pr 3:30 Do not *a* a man for no reason—
Lk 3:14 and don't *a* people falsely—

ACHAN*

Sin at Jericho caused defeat at Ai; stoned (Jos 7; 22:20; 1Ch 2:7).

ACHE*

Pr 14:13 Even in laughter the heart may *a*,

ACKNOWLEDGE

Mt 10:32 *a* him before my Father in heaven.
1Jn 4: 3 spirit that does not *a* Jesus is not

ACQUIT

Ex 23: 7 to death, for I will not *a* the guilty.

ACTION (ACTIONS ACTIVE ACTS)

Jas 2:17 if it is not accompanied by *a*,
1Pe 1:13 minds for *a*; be self-controlled;

ACTIONS (ACTION)

Mt 11:19 wisdom is proved right by her *a*."
Gal 6: 4 Each one should test his own *a*.
Tit 1:16 but by their *a* they deny him.

ACTIVE (ACTION)

Heb 4:12 For the word of God is living and *a*

ACTS (ACTION)

Ps 145: 12 all men may know of your mighty *a*
150: 2 Praise him for his *a* of power;
Isa 64: 6 all our righteous *a* are like filthy
Mt 6: 1 not to do your '*a* of righteousness'

ADAM

First man (Ge 1:26-2:25; Ro 5:14; 1Ti 2:13). Sin of (Ge 3; Hos 6:7; Ro 5:12-21). Children of (Ge 4:1-5:5). Death of (Ge 5:5; Ro 5:12-21; 1Co 15:22).

ADD

Dt 12:32 do not *a* to it or take away from it.
Pr 30: 6 Do not *a* to his words,
Lk 12:25 by worrying can *a* a single hour
Rev 22:18 God will *a* to him the plagues

ADMIRABLE*

Php 4: 8 whatever is lovely, whatever is *a*—

ADMONISH

Col 3:16 and *a* one another with all wisdom,

ADOPTED (ADOPTION)

Eph 1: 5 In love he predestined us to be *a*

ADOPTION (ADOPTED)

Ro 8:23 as we wait eagerly for our *a* as sons,

ADORE*
SS 1: 4 How right they are to *a* you!

ADORNMENT* (ADORNS)
1Pe 3: 3 should not come from outward *a,*

ADORNS (ADORNMENT)
Ps 93: 5 holiness *a* your house

ADULTERY
Ex 20: 14 "You shall not commit *a.*
Mt 5: 27 that it was said, 'Do not commit *a.'*
5: 28 lustfully has already committed *a*
5: 32 the divorced woman commits *a.*
15: 19 murder, *a,* sexual immorality, theft

ADULTS*
1Co 14: 20 but in your thinking be *a.*

ADVANCED
Job 32: 7 *a* years should teach wisdom.'

ADVANTAGE
Ex 22: 22 "Do not take *a* of a widow.
Dt 24: 14 Do not take *a* of a hired man who is
1Th 4: 6 should wrong his brother or take *a*

ADVERSITY
Pr 17: 17 and a brother is born for *a.*

ADVICE
1Ki 12: 8 rejected the *a* the elders
12: 14 he followed the *a* of the young men
Pr 12: 5 but the *a* of the wicked is deceitful.
12: 15 but a wise man listens to *a.*
19: 20 Listen to *a* and accept instruction,
20: 18 Make plans by seeking *a;*

AFFLICTION
Ro 12: 12 patient in *a,* faithful in prayer.

AFRAID (FEAR)
Ge 26: 24 Do not be *a,* for I am with you;
Ex 3: 6 because he was *a* to look at God.
Ps 27: 1 of whom shall I be *a?*
56: 3 When I am *a,* / I will trust in you.
Pr 3: 24 lie down, you will not be *a;*
Jer 1: 8 Do not be *a* of them, for I am
Mt 8: 26 You of little faith, why are you so *a*
10: 28 be *a* of the One who can destroy
10: 31 So don't be *a;* you are worth more
Mk 5: 36 "Don't be *a;* just believe."
Jn 14: 27 hearts be troubled and do not be *a.*
Heb 13: 6 Lord is my helper; I will not be *a.*

AGED
Job 12: 12 Is not wisdom found among the *a?*
Pr 17: 6 children are a crown to the *a,*

AGREE
Mt 18: 19 on earth *a* about anything you ask
Ro 7: 16 want to do, I *a* that the law is good.
Php 4: 2 with Syntyche to *a* with each other

AHAB
Son of Omri; king of Israel (1Ki 16:28-22:40), husband of Jezebel (1Ki 16:31). Promoted Baal worship (1Ki 16:31-33); opposed by Elijah (1Ki 17:1; 18; 21), a prophet (1Ki 20:35-43), Micaiah (1Ki 22:1-28). Defeated Ben-Hadad (1Ki 20). Killed for failing to kill Ben-Hadad and for murder of Naboth (1Ki 20:35-21:40).

AHAZ
Son of Jotham; king of Judah, (2Ki 16; 2Ch 28; Isa 7).

AHAZIAH
1. Son of Ahab; king of Israel (1Ki 22:51-2Ki 1:18; 2Ch 20:35-37).
2. Son of Jehoram; king of Judah (2Ki 8:25-29; 9:14-29), also called Jehoahaz (2Ch 21:17-22:9; 25:23).

AIM
1Co 7: 34 Her *a* is to be devoted to the Lord
2Co 13: 11 *A* for perfection, listen

AIR
Mt 8: 20 and birds of the *a* have nests,
1Co 9: 26 not fight like a man beating the *a.*
Eph 2: 2 of the ruler of the kingdom of the *a,*
1Th 4: 17 clouds to meet the Lord in the *a.*

ALABASTER
Mt 26: 7 came to him with an *a* jar

ALERT
Jos 8: 4 All of you be on the *a.*
Mk 13: 33 Be *a!* You do not know
Eph 6: 18 be *a* and always keep on praying
1Th 5: 6 but let us be *a* and self-controlled.

ALIEN (ALIENATED)
Ex 22: 21 "Do not mistreat an *a*

ALIENATED (ALIEN)
Gal 5: 4 by law have been *a* from Christ;

ALIVE (LIVE)
Ac 1: 3 convincing proofs that he was *a.*
Ro 6: 11 but *a* to God in Christ Jesus.
1Co 15: 22 so in Christ all will be made *a.*

ALMIGHTY (MIGHT)
Ge 17: 1 "I am God *A;* walk before me
Job 11: 7 Can you probe the limits of the *A?*
33: 4 the breath of the *A* gives me life.
Ps 91: 1 will rest in the shadow of the *A.*
Isa 6: 3 "Holy, holy, holy is the LORD *A;*

ALTAR
Ge 22: 9 his son Isaac and laid him on the *a,*
Ex 27: 1 "Build an *a* of acacia wood,
1Ki 18: 30 and he repaired the *a* of the LORD
2Ch 4: 1 made a bronze *a* twenty cubits
4: 19 the golden *a;* the tables

ALWAYS
Ps 16: 8 I have set the LORD *a* before me.
51: 3 and my sin is *a* before me.
Mt 26: 11 The poor you will *a* have with you,
28: 20 And surely I will be with you *a,*
1Co 13: 7 *a* protects, *a* trusts, *a* hopes, *a*
Php 4: 4 Rejoice in the Lord *a.*
1Pe 3: 15 *A* be prepared to give an answer

AMAZIAH
Son of Joash; king of Judah (2Ki 14; 2Ch 25).

AMBASSADORS
2Co 5: 20 We are therefore Christ's *a,*

AMBITION
Ro 15: 20 It has always been my *a*
1Th 4: 11 Make it your a to lead a quiet life,

AMON
Son of Manasseh; king of Judah (2Ki 21:18-26; 1Ch 3:14; 2Ch 33:21-25).

ANANIAS
1. Husband of Sapphira; died for lying to God (Ac 5:1-11).
2. Disciple who baptized Saul (Ac 9:10-19).
3. High priest at Paul's arrest (Ac 22:30-24:1).

ANCHOR
Heb 6: 19 We have this hope as an *a*

ANCIENT
Da 7: 9 and the *A* of Days took his seat.

ANDREW*
Apostle; brother of Simon Peter (Mt 4:18; 10:2; Mk 1:16-18, 29; 3:18; 13:3; Lk 6:14; Jn 1:35-44; 6:8-9; 12:22; Ac 1:13).

ANGEL (ANGELS ARCHANGEL)
Ps 34: 7 The *a* of the LORD encamps
Ac 6: 15 his face was like the face of an *a.*
2Co 11: 14 Satan himself masquerades as an *a*
Gal 1: 8 or an *a* from heaven should preach

ANGELS (ANGEL)
Ps 91: 11 command his *a* concerning you
Mt 18: 10 For I tell you that their *a*
25: 41 prepared for the devil and his *a.*
Lk 20: 36 for they are like the *a.*
1Co 6: 3 you not know that we will judge *a?*
Heb 1: 4 as much superior to the *a*
1: 14 Are not all *a* ministering spirits
2: 7 made him a little lower than the *a;*
13: 2 some people have entertained *a*
1Pe 1: 12 Even *a* long to look
2Pe 2: 4 For if God did not spare *a*

ANGER (ANGERED ANGRY)
Ex 32: 10 alone so that my *a* may burn
34: 6 slow to *a,* abounding in love
Dt 29: 28 In furious *a* and in great wrath
2Ki 22: 13 Great is the LORD's *a* that burns
Ps 30: 5 For his *a* lasts only a moment,
Pr 15: 1 but a harsh word stirs up *a.*
29: 11 A fool gives full vent to his *a,*

ANGERED (ANGER)
Pr 22: 24 do not associate with one easily *a,*
1Co 13: 5 it is not easily *a,* it keeps no record

ANGRY (ANGER)
Ps 2: 12 Kiss the Son, lest he be *a*
Pr 29: 22 An *a* man stirs up dissension,
Jas 1: 19 slow to speak and slow to become *a*

ANGUISH
Ps 118: 5 In my *a* I cried to the LORD,

ANOINT
Ps 23: 5 You *a* my head with oil;
Jas 5: 14 and *a* him with oil in the name

ANT*
Pr 6: 6 Go to the *a,* you sluggard;

ANTICHRIST
1Jn 2: 18 have heard that the *a* is coming,
2Jn : 7 person is the deceiver and the *a.*

ANTIOCH
Ac 11: 26 were called Christians first at *A.*

ANXIETY (ANXIOUS)
1Pe 5: 7 Cast all your *a* on him

ANXIOUS (ANXIETY)
Pr 12: 25 An *a* heart weighs a man down,

Php 4: 6 Do not be *a* about anything,

APOLLOS*

Christian from Alexandria, learned in the Scriptures; instructed by Aquila and Priscilla (Ac 18:24-28). Ministered with Paul at Corinth (Ac 19:1; 1Co 1:12; 3; Tit 3:13).

APOSTLES

See also Andrew, Bartholomew, James, John, Judas, Matthew, Nathanael, Paul, Peter, Philip, Simon, Thaddaeus, Thomas.
Mk 3: 14 twelve—designating them *a*—
Ac 1: 26 so he was added to the eleven *a.*
2: 43 signs were done by the *a.*
1Co 12: 28 God has appointed first of all *a,*
15: 9 For I am the least of the *a*
2Co 11: 13 masquerading as *a* of Christ.
Eph 2: 20 built on the foundation of the *a*

APPEAR (APPEARANCE APPEARING)

Mk 13: 22 false prophets will *a* and perform
2Co 5: 10 we must all *a* before the judgment
Col 3: 4 also will *a* with him in glory.
Heb 9: 24 now to *a* for us in God's presence.
9: 28 and he will *a* a second time,

APPEARANCE (APPEAR)

1Sa 16: 7 Man looks at the outward *a,*
Gal 2: 6 God does not judge by external *a*—

APPEARING (APPEAR)

2Ti 4: 8 to all who have longed for his *a.*
Tit 2: 13 the glorious *a* of our great God

APPLY

Pr 22: 17 *a* your heart to what I teach,
23: 12 *A* your heart to instruction

APPROACH

Eph 3: 12 in him we may *a* God with freedom
Heb 4: 16 Let us then *a* the throne of grace

APPROVED

2Ti 2: 15 to present yourself to God as one *a,*

AQUILA*

Husband of Priscilla; co-worker with Paul, instructor of Apollos (Ac 18; Ro 16:3; 1Co 16:19; 2Ti 4:19).

ARARAT

Ge 8: 4 came to rest on the mountains of *A.*

ARCHANGEL* (ANGEL)

1Th 4: 16 with the voice of the *a*
Jude : 9 *a* Michael, when he was disputing

ARCHITECT*

Heb 11: 10 whose *a* and builder is God.

ARK

Ge 6: 14 So make yourself an *a*
Dt 10: 5 put the tablets in the *a* I had made,
2Ch 35: 3 "Put the sacred *a* in the temple that
Heb 9: 4 This *a* contained the gold jar

ARM (ARMY)

Nu 11: 23 "Is the LORD's *a* too short?
1Pe 4: 1 *a* yourselves also with the same

ARMAGEDDON*

Rev 16: 16 that in Hebrew is called *A.*

ARMOR (ARMY)

1Ki 20: 11 on his *a* should not boast like one
Eph 6: 11 Put on the full *a* of God
Eph 6: 13 Therefore put on the full *a* of God,

ARMS (ARMY)

Dt 33: 27 underneath are the everlasting *a.*
Ps 18: 32 It is God who *a* me with strength
Pr 31: 20 She opens her *a* to the poor
Isa 40: 11 He gathers the lambs in his *a*
Mk 10: 16 And he took the children in his *a,*

ARMY (ARM ARMOR ARMS)

Ps 33: 16 No king is saved by the size of his *a*
Rev 19: 19 the rider on the horse and his *a.*

AROMA

2Co 2: 15 For we are to God the *a* of Christ

ARRAYED*

Ps 110: 3 *A* in holy majesty,
Isa 61: 10 and *a* me in a robe of righteousness

ARROGANT

Ro 11: 20 Do not be *a,* but be afraid.

ARROWS

Eph 6: 16 you can extinguish all the flaming *a*

ASA

King of Judah (1Ki 15:8-24; 1Ch 3:10; 2Ch 14-16).

ASCENDED

Eph 4: 8 "When he *a* on high,

ASCRIBE

1Ch 16: 28 *a* to the LORD glory and strength,
Job 36: 3 I will *a* justice to my Maker.
Ps 29: 2 *A* to the LORD the glory due his

ASHAMED (SHAME)

Lk 9: 26 If anyone is *a* of me and my words,
Ro 1: 16 I am not *a* of the gospel,
2Ti 1: 8 So do not be *a* to testify about our
2: 15 who does not need to be *a*

ASSIGNED

Mk 13: 34 with his *a* task, and tells the one
1Co 3: 5 as the Lord has *a* to each his task.
7: 17 place in life that the Lord *a* to him

ASSOCIATE

Pr 22: 24 do not *a* with one easily angered,
Ro 12: 16 but be willing to *a* with people
1Co 5: 11 am writing you that you must not *a*
2Th 3: 14 Do not *a* with him,

ASSURANCE

Heb 10: 22 with a sincere heart in full *a* of faith

ASTRAY

Pr 10: 17 ignores correction leads others *a.*
Isa 53: 6 We all, like sheep, have gone *a,*
Jer 50: 6 their shepherds have led them *a*
Jn 16: 1 you so that you will not go *a.*
1Pe 2: 25 For you were like sheep going *a,*
1Jn 3: 7 do not let anyone lead you *a.*

ATHALIAH

Evil queen of Judah (2Ki 11; 2Ch 23).

ATHLETE*

2Ti 2: 5 if anyone competes as an *a,*

ATONEMENT

Ex 25: 17 "Make an *a* cover of pure gold—
30: 10 Once a year Aaron shall make *a*
Lev 17: 11 it is the blood that makes *a*
23: 27 this seventh month is the Day of *A.*
Nu 25: 13 and made *a* for the Israelites."
Ro 3: 25 presented him as a sacrifice of *a,*
Heb 2: 17 that he might make *a* for the sins

ATTENTION

Pr 4: 1 pay *a* and gain understanding.
5: 1 My son, pay *a* to my wisdom,
22: 17 Pay *a* and listen to the sayings
Tit 1: 14 and will pay no *a* to Jewish myths

ATTITUDE (ATTITUDES)

Eph 4: 23 new in the *a* of your minds;
Php 2: 5 Your *a* should be the same
1Pe 4: 1 yourselves also with the same *a,*

ATTITUDES (ATTITUDE)

Heb 4: 12 it judges the thoughts and *a*

ATTRACTIVE

Tit 2: 10 teaching about God our Savior *a.*

AUTHORITIES (AUTHORITY)

Ro 13: 5 it is necessary to submit to the *a,*
13: 6 for the *a* are God's servants,
Tit 3: 1 people to be subject to rulers and *a,*
1Pe 3: 22 *a* and powers in submission to him.

AUTHORITY (AUTHORITIES)

Mt 7: 29 because he taught as one who had *a*
9: 6 the Son of Man has *a* on earth
28: 18 "All *a* in heaven and on earth has
Ro 13: 1 for there is no *a* except that which
13: 2 rebels against the *a* is rebelling
1Co 11: 10 to have a sign of *a* on her head.
1Ti 2: 2 for kings and all those in *a,*
2: 12 to teach or to have *a* over a man;
Heb 13: 17 your leaders and submit to their *a.*

AVENGE (VENGEANCE)

Dt 32: 35 It is mine to *a;* I will repay.

AVOID

Pr 20: 3 It is to a man's honor to *a* strife,
20: 19 so *a* a man who talks too much.
1Th 4: 3 you should *a* sexual immorality;
5: 22 *A* every kind of evil.
2Ti 2: 16 *A* godless chatter, because those
Tit 3: 9 But *a* foolish controversies

AWAKE

Ps 17: 15 when I *a,* I will be satisfied

AWE (AWESOME)

Job 25: 2 "Dominion and *a* belong to God;
Ps 119: 120 I stand in *a* of your laws.
Ecc 5: 7 Therefore stand in *a* of God.
Isa 29: 23 will stand in *a* of the God of Israel.
Jer 33: 9 they will be in *a* and will tremble
Hab 3: 2 I stand in *a* of your deeds,
Mal 2: 5 and stood in *a* of my name.
Mt 9: 8 they were filled with *a;*
Lk 7: 16 They were all filled with *a*
Ac 2: 43 Everyone was filled with *a,*
Heb 12: 28 acceptably with reverence and *a,*

AWESOME (AWE)

Ge 28: 17 and said, "How *a* is this place!
Ex 15: 11 *a* in glory,
Dt 7: 21 is among you, is a great and *a* God.
10: 17 the great God, mighty and *a,*
28: 58 revere this glorious and *a* name—
Jdg 13: 6 like an angel of God, very *a.*
Ne 1: 5 of heaven, the great and *a* God,
9: 32 the great, mighty and *a* God,
Job 10: 16 again display your *a* power
37: 22 God comes in *a* majesty.
Ps 45: 4 let your right hand display *a* deeds.
47: 2 How *a* is the LORD Most High,

Ps 66: 5 how *a* his works in man's behalf!
68:35 You are *a*, O God,
89: 7 he is more *a* than all who surround
99: 3 praise your great and *a* name—
111: 9 holy and *a* is his name.
145: 6 of the power of your *a* works,
Da 9: 4 "O Lord, the great and *a* God,

BAAL

1Ki 18:25 Elijah said to the prophets of *B*,

BAASHA

King of Israel (1Ki 15:16-16:7; 2Ch 16:1-6).

BABIES (BABY)

Lk 18:15 also bringing *b* to Jesus
1Pe 2: 2 Like newborn *b*, crave pure

BABY (BABIES)

Isa 49:15 "Can a mother forget the *b*
Lk 1:44 the *b* in my womb leaped for joy.
2:12 You will find a *b* wrapped in strips
Jn 16:21 but when her *b* is born she forgets

BABYLON

Ps 137: 1 By the rivers of *B* we sat and wept

BACKSLIDING

Jer 3:22 I will cure you of *b*."
14: 7 For our *b* is great;
Eze 37:23 them from all their sinful *b*,

BALAAM

Prophet who attempted to curse Israel (Nu 22-24; Dt 23:4-5; 2Pe 2:15; Jude 11). Killed (Nu 31:8; Jos 13:22).

BALM

Jer 8:22 Is there no *b* in Gilead?

BANISH

Jer 25:10 I will *b* from them the sounds of joy

BANQUET

SS 2: 4 He has taken me to the *b* hall,
Lk 14:13 when you give a *b*, invite the poor,

BAPTIZE (BAPTIZED)

Mt 3:11 He will *b* you with the Holy Spirit
Mk 1: 8 he will *b* you with the Holy Spirit."
1Co 1:17 For Christ did not send me to *b*,

BAPTIZED (BAPTIZE)

Mt 3: 6 they were *b* by him in the Jordan
Mk 1: 9 and was *b* by John in the Jordan.
10:38 or be *b* with the baptism I am
16:16 believes and is *b* will be saved,
Jn 4: 2 in fact it was not Jesus who *b*,
Ac 1: 5 but in a few days you will be *b*

BARABBAS

Mt 27:26 Then he released *B* to them.

BARBS*

Nu 33:55 allow to remain will become *b*

BARE

Heb 4:13 and laid *b* before the eyes of him

BARNABAS*

Disciple, originally Joseph (Ac 4:36), prophet (Ac 13:1), apostle (Ac 14:14). Brought Paul to apostles (Ac 9:27), Antioch (Ac 11:22-29; Gal 2:1-13), *on the first missionary* journey (Ac 13-14). Together at Jerusalem Council, they separated over John Mark (Ac 15). Later co-workers (1Co 9:6; Col 4:10).

BARREN

Ps 113: 9 He settles the *b* woman

BARTHOLOMEW*

Apostle (Mt 10:3; Mk 3:18; Lk 6:14; Ac 1:13). Possibly also known as Nathanael (Jn 1:45-49; 21:2).

BATH

Jn 13:10 person who has had a *b* needs only

BATHSHEBA

Wife of Uriah who committed adultery with and became wife of David (2Sa 11), mother of Solomon (2Sa 12:24; 1Ki 1-2; 1Ch 3:5).

BATTLE

2Ch 20:15 For the *b* is not yours, but God's.
Ps 24: 8 the LORD mighty in *b*.
Ecc 9:11 or the *b* to the strong,

BEAR (BEARING BIRTH BIRTHRIGHT BORN FIRSTBORN NEWBORN)

Ge 4:13 punishment is more than I can *b*.
Ps 38: 4 like a burden too heavy to *b*.
Isa 53:11 and he will *b* their iniquities.
Da 7: 5 beast, which looked like a *b*.
Mt 7:18 A good tree cannot *b* bad fruit,
Jn 15: 2 branch that does *b* fruit he prunes
15:16 and appointed you to go and *b* fruit—
Ro 15: 1 ought to *b* with the failings
1Co 10:13 tempted beyond what you can *b*.
Col 3:13 *B* with each other and forgive

BEARING (BEAR)

Eph 4: 2 *b* with one another in love.
Col 1:10 *b* fruit in every good work,

BEAST

Rev 13:18 him calculate the number of the *b*,

BEAT (BEATING)

Isa 2: 4 They will *b* their swords
Joel 3:10 *B* your plowshares into swords
1Co 9:27 I *b* my body and make it my slave

BEATING (BEAT)

1Co 9:26 I do not fight like a man *b* the air.
1Pe 2:20 if you receive a *b* for doing wrong

BEAUTIFUL (BEAUTY)

Ge 6: 2 that the daughters of men were *b*,
12:11 "I know what a *b* woman you are.
12:14 saw that she was a very *b* woman.
24:16 The girl was very *b*, a virgin;
26: 7 of Rebekah, because she is *b*."
29:17 Rachel was lovely in form, and *b*.
Job 38:31 "Can you bind the *b* Pleiades?
Pr 11:22 is a *b* woman who shows no
Ecc 3:11 He has made everything *b*
Isa 4: 2 of the LORD will be *b*
52: 7 How *b* on the mountains
Eze 20: 6 and honey, the most *b* of all lands.
Zec 9:17 How attractive and *b* they will be!
Mt 23:27 which look *b* on the outside
26:10 She has done a *b* thing to me.
Ro 10:15 "How *b* are the feet
1Pe 3: 5 in God used to make themselves *b*.

BEAUTY (BEAUTIFUL)

Ps 27: 4 to gaze upon the *b* of the LORD
45:11 The king is enthralled by your *b*;
Pr 31:30 is deceptive, and *b* is fleeting;
Isa 33:17 Your eyes will see the king in his *b*
53: 2 He had no *b* or majesty
61: 3 to bestow on them a crown of *b*
Eze 28:12 full of wisdom and perfect in *b*.

1Pe 3: 4 the unfading *b* of a gentle

BED

Heb 13: 4 and the marriage *b* kept pure,

BEELZEBUB

Lk 11:15 "By *B*, the prince of demons,

BEER

Pr 20: 1 Wine is a mocker and *b* a brawler;

BEERSHEBA

Jdg 20: 1 all the Israelites from Dan to *B*

BEGINNING

Ge 1: 1 In the *b* God created the heavens
Ps 102: 25 In the *b* you laid the foundations
111: 10 of the LORD is the *b* of wisdom;
Pr 1: 7 of the LORD is the *b* of knowledge
Jn 1: 1 In the *b* was the Word,
1Jn 1: 1 That which was from the *b*,
Rev 21: 6 and the Omega, the *B* and the End.

BEHAVE

Ro 13:13 Let us *b* decently, as in the daytime

BELIEVE (BELIEVED BELIEVER BELIEVERS BELIEVES BELIEVING)

Mt 18: 6 one of these little ones who *b* in me
21:22 If you *b*, you will receive whatever
Mk 1:15 Repent and *b* the good news!"
9:24 "I do *b*; help me overcome my
16:17 signs will accompany those who *b*:
Lk 8:50 just *b*, and she will be healed."
24:25 to *b* all that the prophets have
Jn 1: 7 that through him all men might *b*.
3:18 does not *b* stands condemned
6:29 to *b* in the one he has sent."
10:38 you do not *b* me, *b* the miracles,
11:27 "I *b* that you are the Christ,
14:11 *B* me when I say that I am
16:30 This makes us *b* that you came
16:31 "You *b* at last!" Jesus answered.
17:21 that the world may *b* that you have
20:27 Stop doubting and *b*."
20:31 written that you may *b* that Jesus is
Ac 16:31 They replied, "*B* in the Lord Jesus,
24:14 I *b* everything that agrees
Ro 3:22 faith in Jesus Christ to all who *b*.
4:11 he is the father of all who *b*
10: 9 *b* in your heart that God raised him
10:14 And how can they *b* in the one
16:26 so that all nations might *b*
1Th 4:14 We *b* that Jesus died and rose again
2Th 2:11 delusion so that they will *b* the lie
1Ti 4:10 and especially of those who *b*.
Tit 1: 6 a man whose children *b*
Heb 11: 6 comes to him must *b* that he exists
Jas 2:19 Even the demons *b* that—
1Jn 4: 1 Dear friends, do not *b* every spirit,

BELIEVED (BELIEVE)

Ge 15: 6 Abram *b* the LORD, and he
Jnh 3: 5 The Ninevites *b* God.
Jn 1:12 to those who *b* in his name,
2:22 Then they *b* the Scripture
3:18 because he has not *b* in the name
20: 8 He saw and *b*.
20:29 who have not seen and yet have *b*."
Ac 13:48 were appointed for eternal life *b*.
Ro 4: 3 Scripture say? "Abraham *b* God,
10:14 call on the one they have not *b* in?

1Co 15: 2 Otherwise, you have *b* in vain.
Gal 3: 6 Consider Abraham: "He *b* God,
2Ti 1: 12 because I know whom I have *b*,
Jas 2: 23 that says, "Abraham *b* God,

BELIEVER (BELIEVE)

1Co 7: 12 brother has a wife who is not a *b*
2Co 6: 15 What does a *b* have in common

BELIEVERS (BELIEVE)

Ac 4: 32 All the *b* were one in heart
5: 12 And all the *b* used to meet together
1Co 6: 5 to judge a dispute between *b*?
1Ti 4: 12 set an example for the *b* in speech,
1Pe 2: 17 Love the brotherhood of *b*,

BELIEVES (BELIEVE)

Pr 14: 15 A simple man *b* anything,
Mk 9: 23 is possible for him who *b*."
11: 23 *b* that what he says will happen,
16: 16 Whoever *b* and is baptized will be
Jn 3: 16 that whoever *b* in him shall not
3: 36 Whoever *b* in the Son has eternal
5: 24 *b* him who sent me has eternal life
6: 35 and he who *b* in me will never be
6: 40 and *b* in him shall have eternal life,
6: 47 he who *b* has everlasting life.
7: 38 Whoever *b* in me, as the Scripture
11: 26 and *b* in me will never die.
Ro 1: 16 for the salvation of everyone who *b*
10: 4 righteousness for everyone who *b*.
1Jn 5: 1 Everyone who *b* that Jesus is
5: 5 Only he who *b* that Jesus is the Son

BELIEVING (BELIEVE)

Jn 20: 31 and that by *b* you may have life

BELONG (BELONGS)

Dt 29: 29 The secret things *b*
Job 25: 2 "Dominion and awe *b* to God;
Ps 47: 9 for the kings of the earth *b* to God;
95: 4 and the mountain peaks *b* to him.
Jn 8: 44 You *b* to your father, the devil,
15: 19 As it is, you do not *b* to the world,
Ro 1: 6 called to *b* to Jesus Christ.
7: 4 that you might *b* to another,
14: 8 we live or die, we *b* to the Lord.
Gal 5: 24 Those who *b* to Christ Jesus have
1Th 5: 8 But since we *b* to the day, let us be

BELONGS (BELONG)

Job 41: 11 Everything under heaven *b* to me.
Ps 111: 10 To him *b* eternal praise.
Eze 18: 4 For every living soul *b* to me,
Jn 8: 47 He who *b* to God hears what God
Ro 12: 5 each member *b* to all the others.

BELOVED (LOVE)

Dt 33: 12 "Let the *b* of the LORD rest secure

BELT

Isa 11: 5 Righteousness will be his *b*
Eph 6: 14 with the *b* of truth buckled

BENEFIT (BENEFITS)

Ro 6: 22 the *b* you reap leads to holiness,
2Co 4: 15 All this is for your *b*,

BENEFITS (BENEFIT)

Ps 103: 2 and forget not all his *b*.
Jn 4: 38 you have reaped the *b* of their labor

BENJAMIN

Twelfth son of Jacob by Rachel (Ge 35:16-24; 46:19-21; 1Ch 2:2). Jacob refused to send him to Egypt, but relented (Ge 42-45).

BEREANS*

Ac 17: 11 the *B* were of more noble character

BESTOWS

Ps 84: 11 the LORD *b* favor and honor;

BETHLEHEM

Mt 2: 1 After Jesus was born in *B* in Judea,

BETRAY

Pr 25: 9 do not *b* another man's confidence,

BIND (BINDS)

Dt 6: 8 and *b* them on your foreheads.
Pr 6: 21 *B* them upon your heart forever;
Isa 61: 1 me to *b* up the brokenhearted,
Mt 16: 19 whatever you *b* on earth will be

BINDS (BIND)

Ps 147: 3 and *b* up their wounds.
Isa 30: 26 when the LORD *b* up the bruises

BIRDS

Mt 8: 20 and *b* of the air have nests,

BIRTH (BEAR)

Ps 58: 3 Even from *b* the wicked go astray;
Mt 1: 18 This is how the *b* of Jesus Christ
1Pe 1: 3 great mercy he has given us new *b*

BIRTHRIGHT (BEAR)

Ge 25: 34 So Esau despised his *b*.

BLAMELESS

Ge 17: 1 walk before me and be *b*.
Job 1: 1 This man was *b* and upright;
Ps 84: 11 from those whose walk is *b*.
119: 1 Blessed are they whose ways are *b*,
Pr 19: 1 Better a poor man whose walk is *b*
1Co 1: 8 so that you will be *b* on the day
Eph 5: 27 any other blemish, but holy and *b*.
Php 2: 15 so that you may become *b* and pure
1Th 3: 13 hearts so that you will be *b*
5: 23 and body be kept *b* at the coming
Tit 1: 6 An elder must be *b*, the husband of
Heb 7: 26 *b*, pure, set apart from sinners,
2Pe 3: 14 effort to be found spotless, *b*

BLASPHEMES

Mk 3: 29 whoever *b* against the Holy Spirit

BLEMISH

1Pe 1: 19 a lamb without *b* or defect.

BLESS (BLESSED BLESSING BLESSINGS)

Ge 12: 3 I will *b* those who *b* you,
Ro 12: 14 Bless those who persecute you; *b*

BLESSED (BLESS)

Ge 1: 22 God *b* them and said, "Be fruitful
2: 3 And God *b* the seventh day
22: 18 nations on earth will be *b*,
Ps 1: 1 *B* is the man
2: 12 *B* are all who take refuge in him.
33: 12 *B* is the nation whose God is
41: 1 *B* is he who has regard for the weak
84: 5 *B* are those whose strength is
Ps 106: 3 *B* are they who maintain justice,
112: 1 *B* is the man who fears the LORD,
118: 26 *B* is he who comes in the name
Pr 29: 18 but *b* is he who keeps the law.
31: 28 Her children arise and call her *b*;
Mt 5: 3 saying: "*B* are the poor in spirit,
5: 4 *B* are those who mourn,
5: 5 *B* are the meek,
5: 6 *B* are those who hunger
5: 7 *B* are the merciful,
5: 8 *B* are the pure in heart,
5: 9 *B* are the peacemakers,
5: 10 *B* are those who are persecuted
5: 11 "*B* are you when people insult you,
Lk 1: 48 on all generations will call me *b*,
Jn 12: 13 "*B* is he who comes in the name
Ac 20: 35 'It is more *b* to give than to receive
Tit 2: 13 while we wait for the *b* hope—
Jas 1: 12 *B* is the man who perseveres
Rev 1: 3 *B* is the one who reads the words
22: 14 "*B* are those who wash their robes,

BLESSING (BLESS)

Eze 34: 26 there will be showers of *b*.

BLESSINGS (BLESS)

Pr 10: 6 *B* crown the head of the righteous,

BLIND

Mt 15: 14 a *b* man leads a *b* man, both will fall
23: 16 "Woe to you, *b* guides! You say,
Jn 9: 25 I was *b* but now I see!"

BLOOD

Ge 9: 6 "Whoever sheds the *b* of man,
Ex 12: 13 and when I see the *b*, I will pass
24: 8 "This is the *b* of the covenant that
Lev 17: 11 For the life of a creature is in the *b*,
Ps 72: 14 for precious is their *b* in his sight.
Pr 6: 17 hands that shed innocent *b*,
Mt 26: 28 This is my *b* of the covenant,
Ro 3: 25 of atonement, through faith in his *b*
5: 9 have now been justified by his *b*,
1Co 11: 25 cup is the new covenant in my *b*;
Eph 1: 7 we have redemption through his *b*,
2: 13 near through the *b* of Christ.
Col 1: 20 by making peace through his *b*,
Heb 9: 12 once for all by his own *b*,
9: 22 of *b* there is no forgiveness.
1Pe 1: 19 but with the precious *b* of Christ,
1Jn 1: 7 and the *b* of Jesus, his Son,
Rev 1: 5 has freed us from our sins by his *b*,
5: 9 with your *b* you purchased men
7: 14 white in the *b* of the Lamb.
12: 11 him by the *b* of the Lamb

BLOT (BLOTS)

Ex 32: 32 then *b* me out of the book you have
Ps 51: 1 *b* out my transgressions.
Rev 3: 5 I will never *b* out his name

BLOTS (BLOT)

Isa 43: 25 "I, even I, am he who *b* out

BLOWN

Eph 4: 14 and *b* here and there by every wind
Jas 1: 6 doubts is like a wave of the sea, *b*

BOAST

1Ki 20: 11 armor should not *b* like one who
Ps 34: 2 My soul will *b* in the LORD;
44: 8 In God we make our *b* all day long,
Pr 27: 1 Do not *b* about tomorrow,

1Co 1:31 Let him who boasts *b* in the Lord."
Gal 6:14 May I never *b* except in the cross
Eph 2:9 not by works, so that no one can *b*.

BOAZ

Wealthy Bethlehemite who showed favor to Ruth (Ru 2), married her (Ru 4). Ancestor of David (Ru 4:18-22; 1Ch 2:12-15), Jesus (Mt 1:5-16; Lk 3:23-32).

BODIES (BODY)

Ro 12:1 to offer your *b* as living sacrifices,
1Co 6:15 not know that your *b* are members
Eph 5:28 to love their wives as their own *b*.

BODY (BODIES)

Zec 13:6 What are these wounds on your *b*?'
Mt 10:28 afraid of those who kill the *b*
26:26 saying, "Take and eat; this is my *b*
26:41 spirit is willing, but the *b* is weak."
Jn 13:10 wash his feet; his whole *b* is clean.
Ro 6:13 Do not offer the parts of your *b*
12:4 us has one *b* with many members,
1Co 6:19 not know that your *b* is a temple
11:24 "This is my *b*, which is for you;
12:12 The *b* is a unit, though it is made up
Eph 5:30 for we are members of his *b*.

BOLD (BOLDNESS)

Ps 138:3 you made me *b* and stouthearted.
Pr 21:29 A wicked man puts up a *b* front,
28:1 but the righteous are as *b* as a lion.

BOLDNESS* (BOLD)

Ac 4:29 to speak your word with great *b*.

BONDAGE

Ezr 9:9 God has not deserted us in our *b*.

BOOK (BOOKS)

Jos 1:8 Do not let this *B* of the Law depart
Ne 8:8 They read from the *B* of the Law
Jn 20:30 which are not recorded in this *b*.
Php 4:3 whose names are in the *b* of life.
Rev 21:27 written in the Lamb's *b* of life.

BOOKS (BOOK)

Ecc 12:12 Of making many *b* there is no end,

BORN (BEAR)

Isa 9:6 For to us a child is *b*,
Jn 3:7 at my saying, 'You must be *b* again
1Pe 1:23 For you have been *b* again,
1Jn 4:7 Everyone who loves has been *b*
5:1 believes that Jesus is the Christ is *b*

BORROWER

Pr 22:7 and the *b* is servant to the lender.

BOUGHT

Ac 20:28 which he *b* with his own blood.
1Co 6:20 You are not your own; you were *b*
7:23 You were *b* at a price; do not
2Pe 2:1 the sovereign Lord who *b* them—

BOW

Ps 95:6 Come, let us *b* down in worship,
Isa 45:23 Before me every knee will *b*;
Ro 14:11 'every knee will *b* before me;
Php 2:10 name of Jesus every knee should *b*,

BRANCH (BRANCHES)

Isa 4:2 In that day the *B* of the LORD will
Jer 33:15 I will make a righteous *B* sprout

BRANCHES (BRANCH)

Jn 15:5 "I am the vine; you are the *b*.

BRAVE

2Sa 2:7 Now then, be strong and *b*,

BREAD

Dt 8:3 that man does not live on *b* alone
Pr 30:8 but give me only my daily *b*.
Ecc 11:1 Cast your *b* upon the waters,
Isa 55:2 Why spend money on what is not *b*
Mt 4:4 'Man does not live on *b* alone,
6:11 Give us today our daily *b*.
Jn 6:35 Jesus declared, "I am the *b* of life.
21:13 took the *b* and gave it to them,
1Co 11:23 took *b*, and when he had given

BREAK (BREAKING BROKEN)

Nu 30:2 he must not *b* his word
Jdg 2:1 'I will never *b* my covenant
Isa 42:3 A bruised reed he will not *b*,
Mt 12:20 A bruised reed he will not *b*,

BREAKING (BREAK)

Jas 2:10 at just one point is guilty of *b* all

BREASTPIECE (BREASTPLATE)

Ex 28:15 Fashion a *b* for making decisions—

BREASTPLATE* (BREASTPIECE)

Isa 59:17 He put on righteousness as his *b*,
Eph 6:14 with the *b* of righteousness in place
1Th 5:8 putting on faith and love as a *b*,

BREATHED (GOD-BREATHED)

Ge 2:7 *b* into his nostrils the breath of life,
Jn 20:22 And with that he *b* on them

BREEDS*

Pr 13:10 Pride only *b* quarrels,

BRIBE

Ex 23:8 "Do not accept a *b*,
Pr 6:35 will refuse the *b*, however great it

BRIDE

Rev 19:7 and his *b* has made herself ready,

BRIGHTER (BRIGHTNESS)

Pr 4:18 shining ever *b* till the full light

BRIGHTNESS (BRIGHTER)

2Sa 22:13 Out of the *b* of his presence
Da 12:3 who are wise will shine like the *b*

BROAD

Mt 7:13 and *b* is the road that leads

BROKEN (BREAK)

Ps 51:17 The sacrifices of God are a *b* spirit;
Ecc 4:12 of three strands is not quickly *b*.
Jn 10:35 and the Scripture cannot be *b*—

BROKENHEARTED* (HEART)

Ps 34:18 The LORD is close to the *b*
109:16 and the needy and the *b*.
147:3 He heals the *b*
Isa 61:1 He has sent me to bind up the *b*,

***BROTHER* (BROTHER'S BROTHERS)**

Pr 17:17 and a *b* is born for adversity.
18:24 a friend who sticks closer than a *b*.
27:10 neighbor nearby than a *b* far away.
Mt 5:24 and be reconciled to your *b*;
18:15 "If your *b* sins against you,
Mk 3:35 Whoever does God's will is my *b*
Lk 17:3 "If your *b* sins, rebuke him,
1Co 8:13 if what I eat causes my *b* to fall
1Jn 2:10 Whoever loves his *b* lives
4:21 loves God must also love his *b*.

BROTHER'S (BROTHER)

Ge 4:9 "Am I my *b* keeper?" The LORD

BROTHERS (BROTHER)

Ps 133:1 is when *b* live together in unity!
Pr 6:19 who stirs up dissension among *b*.
Mt 25:40 one of the least of these *b* of mine,
Mk 10:29 or *b* or sisters or mother or father
Heb 13:1 Keep on loving each other as *b*.
1Pe 3:8 be sympathetic, love as *b*,
1Jn 3:14 death to life, because we love our *b*.

BUILD (BUILDING BUILDS BUILT)

Mt 16:18 and on this rock I will *b* my church,
Ac 20:32 which can *b* you up and give you
1Co 14:12 excel in gifts that *b* up the church.
1Th 5:11 one another and *b* each other up,

BUILDING (BUILD)

1Co 3:9 you are God's field, God's *b*.
2Co 10:8 us for *b* you up rather
Eph 4:29 helpful for *b* others up according

BUILDS (BUILD)

Ps 127:1 Unless the LORD *b* the house,
1Co 3:10 one should be careful how he *b*.
8:1 Knowledge puffs up, but love *b* up.

BUILT (BUILD)

Mt 7:24 is like a wise man who *b* his house
Eph 2:20 *b* on the foundation of the apostles
4:12 the body of Christ may be *b* up

BURDEN (BURDENED BURDENS)

Ps 38:4 like a *b* too heavy to bear.
Mt 11:30 my yoke is easy and my *b* is light."

BURDENED (BURDEN)

Gal 5:1 do not let yourselves be *b* again

BURDENS (BURDEN)

Ps 68:19 who daily bears our *b*.
Gal 6:2 Carry each other's *b*,

BURIED

Ro 6:4 *b* with him through baptism
1Co 15:4 that he was *b*, that he was raised

BURNING

Lev 6:9 the fire must be kept *b* on the altar.
Ro 12:20 you will heap *b* coals on his head."

BUSINESS

Da 8:27 and went about the king's *b*.
1Th 4:11 to mind your own *b* and to work

BUSY

1Ki 20:40 While your servant was *b* here
2Th 3:11 They are not *b*; they are
Tit 2:5 to be *b* at home, to be kind,

CAESAR

Mt 22:21 "Give to *C* what is Caesar's,

CAIN

Firstborn of Adam (Ge 4:1), murdered brother Abel (Ge 4:1-16; 1Jn 3:12).

CALEB

Judahite who spied out Canaan (Nu 13:6); allowed to enter land because of faith (Nu 13:30-14:38; Dt 1:36). Possessed Hebron (Jos 14:6-15:19).

CALF

Ex 32: 4 into an idol cast in the shape of a *c,*
Lk 15:23 Bring the fattened *c* and kill it.

CALL (CALLED CALLING CALLS)

Ps 105: 1 to the LORD, *c* on his name;
145: 18 near to all who *c* on him,
Pr 31:28 children arise and *c* her blessed;
Isa 5:20 Woe to those who *c* evil good
55: 6 *c* on him while he is near.
65:24 Before they *c* I will answer;
Jer 33: 3 '*C* to me and I will answer you
Mt 9:13 come to *c* the righteous,
Ro 10:12 and richly blesses all who *c* on him,
11:29 gifts and his *c* are irrevocable.
1Th 4: 7 For God did not *c* us to be impure,

CALLED (CALL)

1Sa 3: 5 and said, "Here I am; you *c* me."
2Ch 7:14 if my people, who are *c*
Ps 34: 6 This poor man *c,* and the LORD
Mt 21:13 " 'My house will be *c* a house
Ro 8:30 And those he predestined, he also *c*
1Co 7:15 God has *c* us to live in peace.
Gal 5:13 You, my brothers, were *c* to be free
1Pe 2: 9 of him who *c* you out of darkness

CALLING (CALL)

Jn 1:23 I am the voice of one *c* in the desert
Ac 22:16 wash your sins away, *c* on his name
Eph 4: 1 worthy of the *c* you have received.
2Pe 1:10 all the more eager to make your *c*

CALLS (CALL)

Joel 2:32 And everyone who *c*
Jn 10: 3 He *c* his own sheep by name
Ro 10:13 "Everyone who *c* on the name

CAMEL

Mt 19:24 it is easier for a *c* to go
23:24 strain out a gnat but swallow a *c.*

CANAAN

1Ch 16:18 "To you I will give the land of *C*

CANCELED

Lk 7:42 so he *c* the debts of both.
Col 2:14 having *c* the written code,

CAPITAL

Dt 21:22 guilty of a *c* offense is put to death

CAPSTONE (STONE)

Ps 118: 22 has become the *c;*
1Pe 2: 7 has become the *c,"*

CARE (CAREFUL CARES CARING)

Ps 8: 4 the son of man that you *c* for him?
Pr 29: 7 The righteous *c* about justice
Lk 10:34 him to an inn and took *c* of him.
Jn 21:16 Jesus said, "Take *c* of my sheep."
Heb 2: 6 the son of man that you *c* for him?
1Pe 5: 2 of God's flock that is under your *c,*

CAREFUL (CARE)

Ex 23:13 "Be *c* to do everything I have said
Dt 6: 3 be *c* to obey so that it may go well
Jos 23: 6 be *c* to obey all that is written
23:11 be very *c* to love the LORD your

Pr 13:24 he who loves him is *c*
Mt 6: 1 "Be *c* not to do your 'acts
Ro 12:17 Be *c* to do what is right in the eyes
1Co 3:10 each one should be *c* how he builds
8: 9 Be *c,* however, that the exercise
Eph 5:15 Be very *c,* then, how you live—

CARELESS

Mt 12:36 for every *c* word they have spoken.

CARES (CARE)

Ps 55:22 Cast your *c* on the LORD
Na 1: 7 He *c* for those who trust in him,
Eph 5:29 but he feeds and *c* for it, just
1Pe 5: 7 on him because he *c* for you.

CARING* (CARE)

1Th 2: 7 like a mother *c* for her little
1Ti 5: 4 practice by *c* for their own family

CARRIED (CARRY)

Ex 19: 4 and how I *c* you on eagles' wings
Isa 53: 4 and *c* our sorrows,
Heb 13: 9 Do not be *c* away by all kinds
2Pe 1:21 as they were *c* along by the Holy

CARRIES (CARRY)

Dt 32:11 and *c* them on its pinions.
Isa 40:11 and *c* them close to his heart;

CARRY (CARRIED CARRIES)

Lk 14:27 anyone who does not *c* his cross
Gal 6: 2 *C* each other's burdens,
6: 5 for each one should *c* his own load.

CAST

Ps 22:18 and *c* lots for my clothing.
55:22 *C* your cares on the LORD
Ecc 11: 1 *C* your bread upon the waters,
Jn 19:24 and *c* lots for my clothing."
1Pe 5: 7 *C* all your anxiety on him

CATCH (CAUGHT)

Lk 5:10 from now on you will *c* men."

CATTLE

Ps 50:10 and the *c* on a thousand hills.

CAUGHT (CATCH)

1Th 4:17 and are left will be *c* up together

CAUSE (CAUSES)

Pr 24:28 against your neighbor without *c,*
Ecc 8: 3 Do not stand up for a bad *c,*
Mt 18: 7 of the things that *c* people to sin!
Ro 14:21 else that will *c* your brother
1Co 10:32 Do not *c* anyone to stumble,

CAUSES (CAUSE)

Isa 8:14 a stone that *c* men to stumble
Mt 18: 6 if anyone *c* one of these little ones

CAUTIOUS*

Pr 12:26 A righteous man is *c* in friendship,

CEASE

Ps 46: 9 He makes wars *c* to the ends

CENSER

Lev 16:12 is to take a *c* full of burning coals

CENTURION

Mt 8: 5 had entered Capernaum, a *c* came

CERTAIN (CERTAINTY)

2Pe 1:19 word of the prophets made more *c,*

CERTAINTY* (CERTAIN)

Lk 1: 4 so that you may know the *c*

Jn 17: 8 They knew with *c* that I came

CHAFF

Ps 1: 4 They are like *c*

CHAINED

2Ti 2: 9 But God's word is not *c.*

CHAMPION

Ps 19: 5 like a *c* rejoicing to run his course.

CHANGE (CHANGED)

1Sa 15:29 of Israel does not lie or *c* his mind;
Ps 110: 4 and will not *c* his mind:
Jer 7: 5 If you really *c* your ways
Mal 3: 6 "I the LORD do not *c.*
Mt 18: 3 unless you *c* and become like little
Heb 7:21 and will not *c* his mind:
Jas 1:17 who does not *c* like shifting

CHANGED (CHANGE)

1Co 15:51 but we will all be *c*—in a flash,

CHARACTER

Ru 3:11 that you are a woman of noble *c.*
Pr 31:10 A wife of noble *c* who can find?
Ro 5: 4 perseverance, *c;* and *c,* hope.
1Co 15:33 "Bad company corrupts good *c."*

CHARGE

Ro 8:33 Who will bring any *c*
2Co 11: 7 the gospel of God to you free of *c?*
2Ti 4: 1 I give you this *c:* Preach the Word;

CHARIOTS

2Ki 6:17 and *c* of fire all around Elisha.
Ps 20: 7 Some trust in *c* and some in horses,

CHARM

Pr 31:30 *C* is deceptive, and beauty is

CHASES

Pr 12:11 he who *c* fantasies lacks judgment.

CHATTER* (CHATTERING)

1Ti 6:20 Turn away from godless *c*
2Ti 2:16 Avoid godless *c,* because those

CHATTERING* (CHATTER)

Pr 10: 8 but a *c* fool comes to ruin.
10:10 and a *c* fool comes to ruin.

CHEAT* (CHEATED)

Mal 1:14 "Cursed is the *c* who has
1Co 6: 8 you yourselves *c* and do wrong,

CHEATED (CHEAT)

Lk 19: 8 if I have *c* anybody out of anything,
1Co 6: 7 Why not rather be *c?* Instead,

CHEEK

Mt 5:39 someone strikes you on the right *c,*

CHEERFUL* (CHEERS)

Pr 15:13 A happy heart makes the face *c,*
15:15 but the *c* heart has a continual feast
15:30 A *c* look brings joy to the heart,
17:22 A *c* heart is good medicine,
2Co 9: 7 for God loves a *c* giver.

CHEERS (CHEERFUL)

Pr 12:25 but a kind word *c* him up.

CHILD (CHILDISH CHILDREN)

Pr 20:11 Even a *c* is known by his actions,
22: 6 Train a *c* in the way he should go,
22:15 Folly is bound up in the heart of a *c*

Pr 23: 13 not withhold discipline from a *c;*
29: 15 *c* left to himself disgraces his mother.
Isa 7: 14 The virgin will be with *c*
9: 6 For to us a *c* is born,
11: 6 and a little *c* will lead them.
66: 13 As a mother comforts her *c,*
Mt 1: 23 "The virgin will be with *c*
18: 2 He called a little *c* and had him
Lk 1: 42 and blessed is the *c* you will bear!
1: 80 And the *c* grew and became strong
1Co 13: 11 When I was a *c,* I talked like a *c,*
1Jn 5: 1 who loves the father loves his *c*

CHILDISH* (CHILD)

1Co 13: 11 When I became a man, I put *c* ways

CHILDREN (CHILD)

Dt 4: 9 Teach them to your *c*
11: 19 them to your *c,* talking about them
Ps 8: 2 From the lips of *c* and infants
Pr 17: 6 Children's *c* are a crown
31: 28 Her *c* arise and call her blessed;
Mt 7: 11 how to give good gifts to your *c,*
11: 25 and revealed them to little *c.*
18: 3 you change and become like little *c*
19: 14 "Let the little *c* come to me,
21: 16 " 'From the lips of *c* and infants
Mk 9: 37 one of these little *c* in my name
10: 14 "Let the little *c* come to me,
10: 16 And he took the *c* in his arms,
13: 12 *C* will rebel against their parents
Lk 10: 21 and revealed them to little *c.*
18: 16 "Let the little *c* come to me,
Ro 8: 16 with our spirit that we are God's *c.*
2Co 12: 14 parents, but parents for their *c.*
Eph 6: 1 *C,* obey your parents in the Lord,
6: 4 do not exasperate your *c;* instead,
Col 3: 20 *C,* obey your parents in everything,
3: 21 Fathers, do not embitter your *c,*
1Ti 3: 4 and see that his *c* obey him
3: 12 and must manage his *c* and his
5: 10 bringing up *c,* showing hospitality,
1Jn 3: 1 that we should be called *c* of God!

CHOOSE (CHOOSES CHOSE CHOSEN)

Dt 30: 19 Now *c* life, so that you
Jos 24: 15 then *c* for yourselves this day
Pr 8: 10 *C* my instruction instead of silver,
16: 16 to *c* understanding rather
Jn 15: 16 You did not *c* me, but I chose you

CHOOSES (CHOOSE)

Jn 7: 17 If anyone *c* to do God's will,

CHOSE (CHOOSE)

Ge 13: 11 So Lot *c* for himself the whole plain
Ps 33: 12 the people he *c* for his inheritance.
Jn 15: 16 but I *c* you and appointed you to go
1Co 1: 27 But God *c* the foolish things
Eph 1: 4 he *c* us in him before the creation
2Th 2: 13 from the beginning God *c* you

CHOSEN (CHOOSE)

Isa 41: 8 Jacob, whom I have *c,*
Mt 22: 14 For many are invited, but few are *c*
Lk 10: 42 Mary has *c* what is better,
23: 35 the Christ of God, the *C* One."
Jn 15: 19 but I have *c* you out of the world.
1Pe 1: 20 He was *c* before the creation
2: 9 But you are a *c* people, a royal

CHRIST (CHRIST'S CHRISTIAN CHRISTS)

Mt 1: 16 was born Jesus, who is called *C.*
16: 16 Peter answered, "You are the *C,*
22: 42 "What do you think about the *C?*
Jn 1: 41 found the Messiah" (that is, the *C).*
20: 31 you may believe that Jesus is the *C,*
Ac 2: 36 you crucified, both Lord and *C."*
5: 42 the good news that Jesus is the *C.*
9: 22 by proving that Jesus is the *C.*
17: 3 proving that the *C* had to suffer
18: 28 the Scriptures that Jesus was the *C.*
26: 23 that the *C* would suffer and,
Ro 3: 22 comes through faith in Jesus *C*
5: 6 we were still powerless, *C* died
5: 8 While we were still sinners, *C* died
5: 17 life through the one man, Jesus *C.*
6: 4 as *C* was raised from the dead
8: 1 for those who are in *C* Jesus,
8: 9 Spirit of *C,* he does not belong to *C.*
8: 35 us from the love of *C?*
10: 4 *C* is the end of the law
14: 9 *C* died and returned to life
15: 3 For even *C* did not please himself
1Co 1: 23 but we preach *C* crucified:
2: 2 except Jesus *C* and him crucified.
3: 11 one already laid, which is Jesus *C.*
5: 7 For *C,* our Passover lamb,
8: 6 and there is but one Lord, Jesus *C,*
10: 4 them, and that rock was *C.*
11: 1 as I follow the example of *C.*
11: 3 the head of every man is *C,*
12: 27 Now you are the body of *C,*
15: 3 that *C* died for our sins according
15: 14 And if *C* has not been raised,
15: 22 so in *C* all will be made alive.
15: 57 victory through our Lord Jesus *C.*
2Co 3: 3 show that you are a letter from *C,*
4: 5 not preach ourselves, but Jesus *C*
5: 10 before the judgment seat of *C,*
5: 17 Therefore, if anyone is in *C,*
11: 2 you to one husband, to *C,*
Gal 2: 20 I have been crucified with *C*
3: 13 *C* redeemed us from the curse
6: 14 in the cross of our Lord Jesus *C,*
Eph 1: 3 with every spiritual blessing in *C.*
3: 8 the unsearchable riches of *C,*
4: 13 measure of the fullness of *C.*
5: 2 as *C* loved us and gave himself up
5: 23 as *C* is the head of the church,
5: 25 just as *C* loved the church
Php 1: 21 to live is *C* and to die is gain.
1: 27 worthy of the gospel of *C.*
4: 19 to his glorious riches in *C* Jesus.
Col 1: 27 which is *C* in you, the hope of glory
1: 28 may present everyone perfect in *C.*
2: 6 as you received *C* Jesus as Lord,
2: 17 the reality, however, is found in *C.*
3: 15 Let the peace of *C* rule
2Th 2: 1 the coming of our Lord Jesus *C*
1Ti 1: 15 *C* Jesus came into the world
2: 5 the man *C* Jesus, who gave himself
2Ti 2: 3 us like a good soldier of *C* Jesus.
3: 15 salvation through faith in *C* Jesus.
Tit 2: 13 our great God and Savior, Jesus *C,*
Heb 3: 14 to share in *C* if we hold firmly
9: 14 more, then, will the blood of *C,*
9: 15 For this reason *C* is the mediator
9: 28 so *C* was sacrificed once
10: 10 of the body of Jesus *C* once for all.
13: 8 Jesus *C* is the same yesterday
1Pe 1: 19 but with the precious blood of *C,*
2: 21 because *C* suffered for you,
1Pe 3: 18 For *C* died for sins once for all,
4: 14 insulted because of the name of *C,*
1Jn 2: 22 man who denies that Jesus is the *C.*
3: 16 Jesus *C* laid down his life for us.
5: 1 believes that Jesus is the *C* is born
Rev 20: 4 reigned with *C* a thousand years.

CHRIST'S (CHRIST)

2Co 5: 14 For *C* love compels us,
5: 20 We are therefore *C* ambassadors,
12: 9 so that *C* power may rest on me.

CHRISTIAN (CHRIST)

1Pe 4: 16 as a *C,* do not be ashamed,

CHRISTS (CHRIST)

Mt 24: 24 For false *C* and false prophets will

CHURCH

Mt 16: 18 and on this rock I will build my *c,*
18: 17 if he refuses to listen even to the *c,*
Ac 20: 28 Be shepherds of the *c* of God,
1Co 5: 12 of mine to judge those outside the *c*
14: 4 but he who prophesies edifies the *c.*
14: 12 to excel in gifts that build up the *c.*
14: 26 done for the strengthening of the *c.*
Eph 5: 23 as Christ is the head of the *c,*
Col 1: 24 the sake of his body, which is the *c.*

CIRCUMCISED

Ge 17: 10 Every male among you shall be *c.*

CIRCUMSTANCES

Php 4: 11 to be content whatever the *c.*
1Th 5: 18 continually; give thanks in all *c,*

CITIZENS (CITIZENSHIP)

Eph 2: 19 but fellow *c* with God's people

CITIZENSHIP (CITIZENS)

Php 3: 20 But our *c* is in heaven.

CITY

Mt 5: 14 A *c* on a hill cannot be hidden.
Heb 13: 14 here we do not have an enduring *c,*

CIVILIAN*

2Ti 2: 4 a soldier gets involved in *c* affairs—

CLAIM (CLAIMS)

Pr 25: 6 do not *c* a place among great men;
1Jn 1: 6 If we *c* to have fellowship
1: 8 If we *c* to be without sin, we
1: 10 If we *c* we have not sinned,

CLAIMS (CLAIM)

Jas 2: 14 if a man *c* to have faith
1Jn 2: 6 Whoever *c* to live in him must walk
2: 9 Anyone who *c* to be in the light

CLAP

Ps 47: 1 *C* your hands, all you nations;
Isa 55: 12 will *c* their hands.

CLAY

Isa 45: 9 Does the *c* say to the potter,
64: 8 We are the *c,* you are the potter;
Jer 18: 6 "Like *c* in the hand of the potter,
La 4: 2 are now considered as pots of *c,*
Da 2: 33 partly of iron and partly of baked *c.*
Ro 9: 21 of the same lump of *c* some pottery

2Co 4: 7 we have this treasure in jars of *c*
2Ti 2: 20 and *c;* some are for noble purposes

CLEAN

Lev 16: 30 you will be *c* from all your sins.
Ps 24: 4 He who has *c* hands and a pure
Mt 12: 44 the house unoccupied, swept *c*
23: 25 You *c* the outside of the cup
Mk 7: 19 Jesus declared all foods *"c.")*
Jn 13: 10 to wash his feet; his whole body is *c*
15: 3 are already *c* because of the word
Ac 10: 15 impure that God has made *c."*
Ro 14: 20 All food is *c,* but it is wrong

CLING (CLINGS)

Ro 12: 9 Hate what is evil; *c* to what is good.

CLINGS (CLING)

Ps 63: 8 My soul *c* to you;

CLOAK

2Ki 4: 29 "Tuck your *c* into your belt,

CLOSE (CLOSER)

Ps 34: 18 LORD is *c* to the brokenhearted
Isa 40: 11 and carries them *c* to his heart;
Jer 30: 21 himself to be *c* to me?'

CLOSER (CLOSE)

Ex 3: 5 "Do not come any *c,"* God said.
Pr 18: 24 there is a friend who sticks *c*

CLOTHE (CLOTHED CLOTHES CLOTHING)

Ps 45: 3 *c* yourself with splendor
Isa 52: 1 *c* yourself with strength.
Ro 13: 14 *c* yourselves with the Lord Jesus
Col 3: 12 *c* yourselves with compassion,
1Pe 5: 5 *c* yourselves with humility

CLOTHED (CLOTHE)

Ps 30: 11 removed my sackcloth and *c* me
Pr 31: 25 She is *c* with strength and dignity;
Lk 24: 49 until you have been *c* with power

CLOTHES (CLOTHE)

Mt 6: 25 the body more important than *c?*
6: 28 "And why do you worry about *c?*
Jn 11: 44 Take off the grave *c* and let him go

CLOTHING (CLOTHE)

Dt 22: 5 A woman must not wear men's *c,*
Mt 7: 15 They come to you in sheep's *c,*

CLOUD (CLOUDS)

Ex 13: 21 them in a pillar of *c* to guide them
Isa 19: 1 See, the LORD rides on a swift *c*
Lk 21: 27 of Man coming in a *c* with power
Heb 12: 1 by such a great *c* of witnesses,

CLOUDS (CLOUD)

Ps 104: 3 He makes the *c* his chariot
Da 7: 13 coming with the *c* of heaven.
Mk 13: 26 coming in *c* with great power
1Th 4: 17 with them in the *c* to meet the Lord

CO-HEIRS* (INHERIT)

Ro 8: 17 heirs of God and *c* with Christ,

COALS

Pr 25: 22 you will heap burning *c* on his head
Ro 12: 20 you will heap burning *c* on his head

COLD

Pr 25: 25 Like *c* water to a weary soul
Mt 10: 42 if anyone gives even a cup of *c* water

Mt 24: 12 the love of most will grow *c,*

COMFORT (COMFORTED COMFORTS)

Ps 23: 4 rod and your staff, they *c* me.
119: 52 and I find *c* in them.
119: 76 May your unfailing love be my *c,*
Zec 1: 17 and the LORD will again *c* Zion
1Co 14: 3 encouragement and *c.*
2Co 1: 4 so that we can *c* those
2: 7 you ought to forgive and *c* him,

COMFORTED (COMFORT)

Mt 5: 4 for they will be *c.*

COMFORTS* (COMFORT)

Job 29: 25 I was like one who *c* mourners.
Isa 49: 13 For the LORD *c* his people
51: 12 "I, even I, am he who *c* you.
66: 13 As a mother *c* her child,
2Co 1: 4 who *c* us in all our troubles,
7: 6 But God, who *c* the downcast,

COMMAND (COMMANDED COMMANDING COMMANDENT COMMANDMENTS COMMANDS)

Ex 7: 2 You are to say everything I *c* you,
Nu 24: 13 to go beyond the *c* of the LORD—
Dt 4: 2 Do not add to what I *c* you
30: 16 For I *c* you today to love
32: 46 so that you may *c* your children
Ps 91: 11 For he will *c* his angels concerning
Pr 13: 13 but he who respects a *c* is rewarded
Ecc 8: 2 Obey the king's *c,* I say,
Joel 2: 11 mighty are those who obey his *c.*
Jn 14: 15 love me, you will obey what I *c.*
15: 12 My *c* is this: Love each other
1Co 14: 37 writing to you is the Lord's *c.*
Gal 5: 14 law is summed up in a single *c:*
1Ti 1: 5 goal of this *c* is love, which comes
Heb 11: 3 universe was formed at God's *c,*
1Jn 3: 23 this is his *c:* to believe in the name
2Jn : 6 his *c* is that you walk in love.

COMMANDED (COMMAND)

Ps 33: 9 he *c,* and it stood firm.
148: 5 for he *c* and they were created.
Mt 28: 20 to obey everything I have *c* you.
1Co 9: 14 Lord has *c* that those who preach
1Jn 3: 23 and to love one another as he *c* us.

COMMANDING (COMMAND)

2Ti 2: 4 he wants to please his *c* officer.

COMMANDMENT (COMMAND)

Jos 22: 5 But be very careful to keep the *c*
Mt 22: 38 This is the first and greatest *c.*
Jn 13: 34 "A new *c* I give you: Love one
Ro 7: 12 and the *c* is holy, righteous
Eph 6: 2 which is the first *c* with a promise

COMMANDMENTS (COMMAND)

Ex 20: 6 who love me and keep my *c.*
34: 28 of the covenant—the Ten *C.*
Ecc 12: 13 Fear God and keep his *c,*
Mt 5: 19 one of the least of these *c*
22: 40 the Prophets hang on these two *c."*

COMMANDS (COMMAND)

Dt 7: 9 those who love him and keep his *c.*
11: 27 the blessing if you obey the *c*
Ps 112: 1 who finds great delight in his *c.*
119: 47 for I delight in your *c*
119: 86 All your *c* are trustworthy;
119: 98 Your *c* make me wiser
119: 127 Because I love your *c*
119: 143 but your *c* are my delight.
119: 172 for all your *c* are righteous.
Pr 3: 1 but keep my *c* in your heart,

Pr 6: 23 For these *c* are a lamp,
10: 8 The wise in heart accept *c,*
Da 9: 4 all who love him and obey his *c,*
Mt 5: 19 teaches these *c* will be called great
Jn 14: 21 Whoever has my *c* and obeys them,
Ac 17: 30 but now he *c* all people everywhere
1Co 7: 19 Keeping God's *c* is what counts.
1Jn 5: 3 And his *c* are not burdensome,
5: 3 This is love for God: to obey his *c.*

COMMEND (COMMENDED COMMENDS)

Ecc 8: 15 So I *c* the enjoyment of life,
Ro 13: 3 do what is right and he will *c* you.
1Pe 2: 14 and to *c* those who do right.

COMMENDED (COMMEND)

Heb 11: 39 These were all *c* for their faith,

COMMENDS (COMMEND)

2Co 10: 18 not the one who *c* himself who is

COMMIT (COMMITS COMMITTED)

Ex 20: 14 "You shall not *c* adultery.
Ps 37: 5 *C* your way to the LORD;
Mt 5: 27 that it was said, 'Do not *c* adultery.'
Lk 23: 46 into your hands I *c* my spirit."
Ac 20: 32 I *c* you to God and to the word
1Co 10: 8 We should not *c* sexual immorality,
1Pe 4: 19 to God's will should *c* themselves

COMMITS (COMMIT)

Pr 6: 32 man who *c* adultery lacks
29: 22 a hot-tempered one *c* many sins.
Mt 19: 9 marries another woman *c* adultery

COMMITTED (COMMIT)

Nu 5: 7 and must confess the sin he has *c.*
1Ki 8: 61 But your hearts must be fully *c*
2Ch 16: 9 those whose hearts are fully *c*
Mt 5: 28 lustfully has already *c* adultery
2Co 5: 19 And he has *c* to us the message
1Pe 2: 22 "He *c* no sin,

COMMON

Pr 22: 2 Rich and poor have this in *c:*
1Co 10: 13 has seized you except what is *c*
2Co 6: 14 and wickedness have in *c?*

COMPANION (COMPANIONS)

Pr 13: 20 but a *c* of fools suffers harm.
28: 7 a *c* of gluttons disgraces his father.
29: 3 *c* of prostitutes squanders his

COMPANIONS (COMPANION)

Pr 18: 24 A man of many *c* may come to ruin

COMPANY

Pr 24: 1 do not desire their *c;*
Jer 15: 17 I never sat in the *c* of revelers,
1Co 15: 33 "Bad *c* corrupts good character."

COMPARED (COMPARING)

Eze 31: 2 Who can be *c* with you in majesty?
Php 3: 8 I consider everything a loss *c*

COMPARING* (COMPARED)

Ro 8: 18 present sufferings are not worth *c*
2Co 8: 8 the sincerity of your love by *c* it
Gal 6: 4 without *c* himself to somebody else

COMPASSION (COMPASSIONATE COMPASSIONS)

Ex 33: 19 I will have *c* on whom I will have *c.*

Ne 9: 19 of your great *c* you did not
9: 28 in your *c* you delivered them time
Ps 51: 1 according to your great *c*
103: 4 and crowns you with love and *c.*
103: 13 As a father has *c* on his children,
145: 9 he has *c* on all he has made.
Isa 49: 13 and will have *c* on his afflicted ones
49: 15 and have no *c* on the child she has
Hos 2: 19 in love and *c.*
11: 8 all my *c* is aroused.
Jnh 3: 9 with *c* turn from his fierce anger
Mt 9: 36 When he saw the crowds, he had *c*
Mk 8: 2 "I have *c* for these people;
Ro 9: 15 and I will have *c* on whom I have *c*
Col 3: 12 clothe yourselves with *c,* kindness,
Jas 5: 11 The Lord is full of *c* and mercy.

COMPASSIONATE (COMPASSION)

Ne 9: 17 gracious and *c,* slow to anger
Ps 103: 8 The LORD is *c* and gracious,
112: 4 the gracious and *c* and righteous
Eph 4: 32 Be kind and *c* to one another,
1Pe 3: 8 love as brothers, be *c* and humble.

COMPASSIONS* (COMPASSION)

La 3: 22 for his *c* never fail.

COMPELLED (COMPELS)

Ac 20: 22 "And now, *c* by the Spirit,
1Co 9: 16 I cannot boast, for I am *c* to preach.

COMPELS (COMPELLED)

2Co 5: 14 For Christ's love *c* us, because we

COMPETENCE* (COMPETENT)

2Co 3: 5 but our *c* comes from God.

COMPETENT* (COMPETENCE)

Ro 15: 14 and *c* to instruct one another.
1Co 6: 2 are you not *c* to judge trivial cases?
2Co 3: 5 Not that we are *c* in ourselves
3: 6 He has made us *c* as ministers

COMPETES*

1Co 9: 25 Everyone who *c* in the games goes
2Ti 2: 5 Similarly, if anyone *c* as an athlete,
2: 5 unless he *c* according to the rules.

COMPLACENT

Am 6: 1 Woe to you who are *c* in Zion,

COMPLAINING*

Php 2: 14 Do everything without *c* or arguing

COMPLETE

Jn 15: 11 and that your joy may be *c.*
16: 24 will receive, and your joy will be *c.*
17: 23 May they be brought to *c* unity
Ac 20: 24 *c* the task the Lord Jesus has given
Php 2: 2 then make my joy *c*
Col 4: 17 to it that you *c* the work you have
Jas 1: 4 so that you may be mature and *c,*
2: 22 his faith was made *c* by what he did

CONCEAL (CONCEALED CONCEALS)

Ps 40: 10 I do not *c* your love and your truth
Pr 25: 2 It is the glory of God to *c* a matter;

CONCEALED (CONCEAL)

Jer 16: 17 nor is their sin *c* from my eyes.
Mt 10: 26 There is nothing *c* that will not be
Mk 4: 22 and whatever is *c* is meant

CONCEALS (CONCEAL)

Pr 28: 13 He who *c* his sins does not prosper,

CONCEITED

Ro 12: 16 Do not be *c.*
Gal 5: 26 Let us not become *c,* provoking
1Ti 6: 4 he is *c* and understands nothing.

CONCEIVED

Mt 1: 20 what is *c* in her is from the Holy
1Co 2: 9 no mind has *c*

CONCERN (CONCERNED)

Eze 36: 21 I had *c* for my holy name, which
1Co 7: 32 I would like you to be free from *c.*
12: 25 that its parts should have equal *c*
2Co 11: 28 of my *c* for all the churches.

CONCERNED (CONCERN)

Jnh 4: 10 "You have been *c* about this vine,
1Co 7: 32 An unmarried man is *c* about

CONDEMN (CONDEMNATION CONDEMNED CONDEMNING CONDEMNS)

Job 40: 8 Would you *c* me to justify yourself?
Isa 50: 9 Who is he that will *c* me?
Lk 6: 37 Do not *c,* and you will not be
Jn 3: 17 Son into the world to *c* the world,
12: 48 very word which I spoke will *c* him
Ro 2: 27 yet obeys the law will *c* you who,
1Jn 3: 20 presence whenever our hearts *c* us.

CONDEMNATION (CONDEMN)

Ro 5: 18 of one trespass was *c* for all men,
8: 1 there is now no *c* for those who are

CONDEMNED (CONDEMN)

Ps 34: 22 no one will be *c* who takes refuge
Mt 12: 37 and by your words you will be *c.*"
23: 33 How will you escape being *c* to hell
Jn 3: 18 Whoever believes in him is not *c,*
5: 24 has eternal life and will not be *c;*
16: 11 prince of this world now stands *c.*
Ro 14: 23 But the man who has doubts is *c*
1Co 11: 32 disciplined so that we will not be *c*
Heb 11: 7 By his faith he *c* the world

CONDEMNING (CONDEMN)

Pr 17: 15 the guilty and *c* the innocent—
Ro 2: 1 judge the other, you are *c* yourself,

CONDEMNS (CONDEMN)

Ro 8: 34 Who is he that *c*? Christ Jesus,
2Co 3: 9 the ministry that *c* men is glorious,

CONDUCT

Pr 10: 23 A fool finds pleasure in evil *c,*
20: 11 by whether his *c* is pure and right.
21: 8 but the *c* of the innocent is upright.
Ecc 6: 8 how to *c* himself before others?
Jer 4: 18 "Your own *c* and actions
17: 10 to reward a man according to his *c,*
Eze 7: 3 I will judge you according to your *c*
Php 1: 27 *c* yourselves in a manner worthy
1Ti 3: 15 to *c* themselves in God's household

CONFESS (CONFESSION)

Lev 16: 21 and *c* over it all the wickedness
26: 40 " 'But if they will *c* their sins
Nu 5: 7 must *c* the sin he has committed.
Ps 38: 18 I *c* my iniquity;
Ro 10: 9 That if you *c* with your mouth,
Php 2: 11 every tongue *c* that Jesus Christ is
Jas 5: 16 Therefore *c* your sins to each other
1Jn 1: 9 If we *c* our sins, he is faithful

CONFESSION (CONFESS)

Ezr 10: 11 Now make *c* to the LORD,
2Co 9: 13 obedience that accompanies your *c*

CONFIDENCE

Ps 71: 5 my *c* since my youth.
Pr 3: 26 for the LORD will be your *c*
11: 13 A gossip betrays a *c,*
25: 9 do not betray another man's *c,*
31: 11 Her husband has full *c* in her
Isa 32: 17 will be quietness and *c* forever.
Jer 17: 7 whose *c* is in him.
Php 3: 3 and who put no *c* in the flesh—
Heb 3: 14 till the end the *c* we had at first.
4: 16 the throne of grace with *c,*
10: 19 since we have *c* to enter the Most
10: 35 So do not throw away your *c;*
1Jn 5: 14 This is the *c* we have

CONFORM* (CONFORMED)

Ro 12: 2 Do not *c* any longer to the pattern
1Pe 1: 14 do not *c* to the evil desires you had

CONFORMED (CONFORM)

Ro 8: 29 predestined to be *c* to the likeness

CONQUERORS

Ro 8: 37 than *c* through him who loved us.

CONSCIENCE (CONSCIENCES)

Ro 13: 5 punishment but also because of *c.*
1Co 8: 7 since their *c* is weak, it is defiled.
8: 12 in this way and wound their weak *c*
10: 25 without raising questions of *c,*
10: 29 freedom be judged by another's *c*?
Heb 10: 22 to cleanse us from a guilty *c*
1Pe 3: 16 and respect, keeping a clear *c,*

CONSCIENCES* (CONSCIENCE)

Ro 2: 15 their *c* also bearing witness,
1Ti 4: 2 whose *c* have been seared
Tit 1: 15 their minds and *c* are corrupted.
Heb 9: 14 cleanse our *c* from acts that lead

CONSCIOUS*

Ro 3: 20 through the law we become *c* of sin
1Pe 2: 19 of unjust suffering because he is *c*

CONSECRATE (CONSECRATED)

Ex 13: 2 "*C* to me every firstborn male.
Lev 20: 7 " '*C* yourselves and be holy,

CONSECRATED (CONSECRATE)

Ex 29: 43 and the place will be *c* by my glory.
1Ti 4: 5 because it is *c* by the word of God

CONSIDER (CONSIDERATE CONSIDERED CONSIDERS)

1Sa 12: 24 *c* what great things he has done
Job 37: 14 stop and *c* God's wonders.
Ps 8: 3 When I *c* your heavens,
107: 43 and *c* the great love of the LORD.
143: 5 and *c* what your hands have done.
Lk 12: 24 *C* the ravens: They do not sow
12: 27 about the rest? "*C* how the lilies
Php 2: 3 but in humility *c* others better

Php 3: 8 I *c* everything a loss compared
Heb 10: 24 And let us *c* how we may spur one
Jas 1: 2 *C* it pure joy, my brothers,

CONSIDERATE* (CONSIDER)

Tit 3: 2 to be peaceable and *c*,
Jas 3: 17 then peace-loving, *c*, submissive,
1Pe 2: 18 only to those who are good and *c*,
3: 7 in the same way be *c* as you live

CONSIDERED (CONSIDER)

Job 1: 8 "Have you *c* my servant Job?
2: 3 "Have you *c* my servant Job?
Ps 44: 22 we are *c* as sheep to be slaughtered.
Isa 53: 4 yet we *c* him stricken by God,
Ro 8: 36 we are *c* as sheep to be slaughtered

CONSIDERS (CONSIDER)

Pr 31: 16 She *c* a field and buys it;
Ro 14: 5 One man *c* one day more sacred
Jas 1: 26 If anyone *c* himself religious

CONSIST

Lk 12: 15 a man's life does not *c*

CONSOLATION

Ps 94: 19 your *c* brought joy to my soul.

CONSTRUCTIVE*

1Co 10: 23 but not everything is *c*.

CONSUME (CONSUMING)

Jn 2: 17 "Zeal for your house will *c* me."

CONSUMING (CONSUME)

Dt 4: 24 For the LORD your God is a *c* fire,
Heb 12: 29 and awe, for our "God is a *c* fire."

CONTAIN

1Ki 8: 27 the highest heaven, cannot *c* you.
2Pe 3: 16 His letters *c* some things that are

CONTAMINATES*

2Co 7: 1 from everything that *c* body

CONTEMPT

Pr 14: 31 He who oppresses the poor shows *c*
17: 5 He who mocks the poor shows *c*
18: 3 When wickedness comes, so does *c*
Da 12: 2 others to shame and everlasting *c*.
Ro 2: 4 Or do you show *c* for the riches
Gal 4: 14 you did not treat me with *c*
1Th 5: 20 do not treat prophecies with *c*.

CONTEND (CONTENDING)

Jude : 3 you to *c* for the faith that was once

CONTENDING* (CONTEND)

Php 1: 27 *c* as one man for the faith

CONTENT (CONTENTMENT)

Pr 13: 25 The righteous eat to their hearts' *c*,
Php 4: 11 to be *c* whatever the circumstances
4: 12 I have learned the secret of being *c*
1Ti 6: 8 and clothing, we will be *c* with that.
Heb 13: 5 and be *c* with what you have,

CONTENTMENT (CONTENT)

1Ti 6: 6 But godliness with *c* is great gain.

CONTINUAL (CONTINUE)

Pr 15: 15 but the cheerful heart has a *c* feast.

CONTINUE (CONTINUAL)

Php 2: 12 *c* to work out your salvation
2Ti 3: 14 *c* in what you have learned
1Jn 5: 18 born of God does not *c* to sin;
Rev 22: 11 and let him who is holy *c* to be holy
22: 11 let him who does right *c* to do right;

CONTRITE*

Ps 51: 17 a broken and *c* heart,
Isa 57: 15 also with him who is *c* and lowly
57: 15 and to revive the heart of the *c*.
66: 2 he who is humble and *c* in spirit,

CONTROL (CONTROLLED SELF-CONTROL SELF-CONTROLLED)

Pr 29: 11 a wise man keeps himself under *c*.
1Co 7: 9 But if they cannot *c* themselves,
7: 37 but has *c* over his own will,
1Th 4: 4 you should learn to *c* his own body

CONTROLLED (CONTROL)

Ps 32: 9 but must be *c* by bit and bridle
Ro 8: 6 but the mind *c* by the Spirit is life
8: 8 Those *c* by the sinful nature cannot

CONTROVERSIES

Tit 3: 9 But avoid foolish *c* and genealogies

CONVERSATION

Col 4: 6 Let your *c* be always full of grace,

CONVERT

1Ti 3: 6 He must not be a recent *c*,

CONVICT

Jn 16: 8 he will *c* the world of guilt in regard

CONVINCED (CONVINCING)

Ro 8: 38 For I am *c* that neither death
2Ti 1: 12 and am *c* that he is able
3: 14 have learned and have become *c*

CONVINCING* (CONVINCED)

Ac 1: 3 and gave many *c* proofs that he was

CORNELIUS*

Roman to whom Peter preached; first Gentile Christian (Ac 10).

CORNERSTONE (STONE)

Isa 28: 16 a precious *c* for a sure foundation;
Eph 2: 20 Christ Jesus himself as the chief *c*.
1Pe 2: 6 a chosen and precious *c*,

CORRECT (CORRECTING CORRECTION CORRECTS)

2Ti 4: 2 *c*, rebuke and encourage—

CORRECTING* (CORRECT)

2Ti 3: 16 *c* and training in righteousness,

CORRECTION (CORRECT)

Pr 10: 17 whoever ignores *c* leads others
12: 1 but he who hates *c* is stupid.
15: 5 whoever heeds *c* shows prudence.
15: 10 he who hates *c* will die.
29: 15 The rod of *c* imparts wisdom,

CORRECTS* (CORRECT)

Job 5: 17 "Blessed is the man whom God *c*;
Pr 9: 7 Whoever *c* a mocker invites insult;

CORRUPT (CORRUPTS)

Ge 6: 11 Now the earth was *c* in God's sight

CORRUPTS* (CORRUPT)

Ecc 7: 7 and a bribe *c* the heart.
1Co 15: 33 "Bad company *c* good character."
Jas 3: 6 It *c* the whole person, sets

COST

Pr 4: 7 Though it *c* all you have, get
Isa 55: 1 milk without money and without *c*.
Rev 21: 6 to drink without *c* from the spring

COUNSEL (COUNSELOR)

1Ki 22: 5 "First seek the *c* of the LORD."
Pr 15: 22 Plans fail for lack of *c*,
Rev 3: 18 I *c* you to buy from me gold refined

COUNSELOR (COUNSEL)

Isa 9: 6 Wonderful *C*, Mighty God,
Jn 14: 16 he will give you another *C* to be
14: 26 But the *C*, the Holy Spirit,

COUNT (COUNTING COUNTS)

Ro 4: 8 whose sin the Lord will never *c*
6: 11 *c* yourselves dead to sin

COUNTING (COUNT)

2Co 5: 19 not *c* men's sins against them.

COUNTRY

Jn 4: 44 prophet has no honor in his own *c*.)

COUNTS (COUNT)

Jn 6: 63 The Spirit gives life; the flesh *c*
1Co 7: 19 God's commands is what *c*.
Gal 5: 6 only thing that *c* is faith expressing

COURAGE (COURAGEOUS)

Ac 23: 11 "Take *c*! As you have testified
1Co 16: 13 stand firm in the faith; be men of *c*;

COURAGEOUS (COURAGE)

Dt 31: 6 Be strong and *c*.
Jos 1: 6 and *c*, because you will lead these

COURSE

Ps 19: 5 a champion rejoicing to run his *c*.
Pr 15: 21 of understanding keeps a straight *c*.

COURTS

Ps 84: 10 Better is one day in your *c*
100: 4 and his *c* with praise;

COVENANT (COVENANTS)

Ge 9: 9 "I now establish my *c* with you
Ex 19: 5 if you obey me fully and keep my *c*,
1Ch 16: 15 He remembers his *c* forever,
Job 31: 1 "I made a *c* with my eyes
Jer 31: 31 "when I will make a new *c*
1Co 11: 25 "This cup is the new *c* in my blood;
Gal 4: 24 One *c* is from Mount Sinai
Heb 9: 15 Christ is the mediator of a new *c*,

COVENANTS (COVENANT)

Ro 9: 4 theirs the divine glory, the *c*,
Gal 4: 24 for the women represent two *c*.

COVER (COVER-UP COVERED COVERS)

Ps 91: 4 He will *c* you with his feathers,
Jas 5: 20 and *c* over a multitude of sins.

COVER-UP (COVER)
1Pe 2:16 but do not use your freedom as a *c*

COVERED (COVER)
Ps 32: 1 whose sins are *c.*
Isa 6: 2 With two wings they *c* their faces,
Ro 4: 7 whose sins are *c.*
1Co 11: 4 with his head *c* dishonors his head.

COVERS (COVER)
Pr 10:12 but love *c*over all wrongs.
1Pe 4: 8 love *c*over a multitude of sins.

COVET
Ex 20:17 You shall not *c* your neighbor's
Ro 13: 9 "Do not steal," "Do not *c,*"

COWARDLY*
Rev 21: 8 But the *c,* the unbelieving, the vile,

CRAFTINESS (CRAFTY)
1Co 3:19 "He catches the wise in their *c*";

CRAFTY (CRAFTINESS)
Ge 3: 1 the serpent was more *c* than any
2Co 12:16 *c* fellow that I am, I caught you

CRAVE
Pr 23: 3 Do not *c* his delicacies,
1Pe 2: 2 newborn babies, *c* pure spiritual

CREATE (CREATED CREATION CREATOR)
Ps 51:10 *C* in me a pure heart, O God,
Isa 45:18 he did not *c* it to be empty,

CREATED (CREATE)
Ge 1: 1 In the beginning God *c* the heavens
1:21 God *c* the great creatures of the sea
1:27 So God *c* man in his own image,
Ps 148: 5 for he commanded and they were *c*
Isa 42: 5 he who *c* the heavens and stretched
Ro 1:25 and served *c* things rather
1Co 11: 9 neither was man *c* for woman,
Col 1:16 For by him all things were *c:*
1Ti 4: 4 For everything God *c* is good,
Rev 10: 6 who *c* the heavens and all that is

CREATION (CREATE)
Mk 16:15 and preach the good news to all *c.*
Jn 17:24 me before the *c* of the world.
Ro 8:19 The *c* waits in eager expectation
8:39 depth, nor anything else in all *c,*
2Co 5:17 he is a new *c;* the old has gone,
Col 1:15 God, the firstborn over all *c.*
1Pe 1:20 chosen before the *c* of the world,
Rev 13: 8 slain from the *c* of the world.

CREATOR (CREATE)
Ge 14:22 God Most High, *C* of heaven
Ro 1:25 created things rather than the *C*—

CREATURE (CREATURES)
Lev 17:11 For the life of a *c* is in the blood,

CREATURES (CREATURE)
Ge 6:19 bring into the ark two of all living *c,*
Ps 104: 24 the earth is full of your *c.*

CREDIT (CREDITED)
Ro 4:24 to whom God will *c* righteousness
1Pe 2:20 it to your *c* if you receive a beating

CREDITED (CREDIT)
Ge 15: 6 and he *c* it to him as righteousness.
Ro 4: 5 his faith is *c* as righteousness.
Gal 3: 6 and it was *c* to him as righteousness
Jas 2:23 and it was *c* to him as righteousness

CRIED (CRY)
Ps 18: 6 I *c* to my God for help.

CRIMSON
Isa 1:18 though they are red as *c,*

CRIPPLED
Mk 9:45 better for you to enter life *c*

CRITICISM
2Co 8:20 We want to avoid any *c*

CROOKED
Pr 10: 9 he who takes *c* paths will be found
Php 2:15 children of God without fault in a *c*

CROSS
Mt 10:38 and anyone who does not take his *c*
Lk 9:23 take up his *c* daily and follow me.
Ac 2:23 to death by nailing him to the *c.*
1Co 1:17 lest the *c* of Christ be emptied
Gal 6:14 in the *c* of our Lord Jesus Christ,
Php 2: 8 even death on a *c!*
Col 1:20 through his blood, shed on the *c.*
2:14 he took it away, nailing it to the *c.*
2:15 triumphing over them by the *c.*
Heb 12: 2 set before him endured the *c,*

CROWD
Ex 23: 2 Do not follow the *c* in doing wrong.

CROWN (CROWNED CROWNS)
Pr 4: 9 present you with a *c* of splendor."
10: 6 Blessings *c* the head
12: 4 noble character is her husband's *c,*
17: 6 Children's children are a *c*
Isa 61: 3 to bestow on them a *c* of beauty
Zec 9:16 like jewels in a *c.*
Mt 27:29 then twisted together a *c* of thorns
1Co 9:25 it to get a *c* that will last forever.
2Ti 4: 8 store for me the *c* of righteousness,
Rev 2:10 and I will give you the *c* of life.

CROWNED (CROWN)
Ps 8: 5 and *c* him with glory and honor.
Pr 14:18 the prudent are *c* with knowledge.
Heb 2: 7 you *c* him with glory and honor

CROWNS (CROWN)
Rev 4:10 They lay their *c* before the throne
19:12 and on his head are many *c.*

CRUCIFIED (CRUCIFY)
Mt 20:19 to be mocked and flogged and *c.*
27:38 Two robbers were *c* with him,
Lk 24: 7 be *c* and on the third day be raised
Jn 19:18 Here they *c* him, and with him two
Ac 2:36 whom you *c,* both Lord and Christ
Ro 6: 6 For we know that our old self was *c*
1Co 1:23 but we preach Christ *c:* a stumbling
2: 2 except Jesus Christ and him *c.*
Gal 2:20 I have been *c* with Christ
5:24 Christ Jesus have *c* the sinful

CRUCIFY (CRUCIFIED CRUCIFYING)
Mt 27:22 They all answered, "*C* him!" "Why
27:31 Then they led him away to *c* him.

CRUCIFYING* (CRUCIFY)
Heb 6: 6 to their loss they are *c* the Son

CRUSH (CRUSHED)
Ge 3:15 he will *c* your head,
Isa 53:10 it was the LORD's will to *c* him
Ro 16:20 The God of peace will soon *c* Satan

CRUSHED (CRUSH)
Ps 34:18 and saves those who are *c* in spirit.
Isa 53: 5 he was *c* for our iniquities;
2Co 4: 8 not *c;* perplexed, but not in despair;

CRY (CRIED)
Ps 34:15 and his ears are attentive to their *c;*
40: 1 he turned to me and heard my *c.*
130: 1 Out of the depths I *c* to you,

CUP
Ps 23: 5 my *c* overflows.
Mt 10:42 if anyone gives even a *c* of cold water
23:25 You clean the outside of the *c*
26:39 may this *c* be taken from me.
1Co 11:25 after supper he took the *c,* saying,

CURSE (CURSED)
Dt 11:26 before you today a blessing and a *c*
21:23 hung on a tree is under God's *c.*
Lk 6:28 bless those who *c* you, pray
Gal 3:13 of the law by becoming a *c* for us,
Rev 22: 3 No longer will there be any *c.*

CURSED (CURSE)
Ge 3:17 "*C* is the ground because of you;
Dt 27:15 "*C* is the man who carves an image
27:16 "*C* is the man who dishonors his
27:17 "*C* is the man who moves his
27:18 "*C* is the man who leads the blind
27:19 *C* is the man who withholds justice
27:20 "*C* is the man who sleeps
27:21 "*C* is the man who has sexual
27:22 "*C* is the man who sleeps
27:23 "*C* is the man who sleeps
27:24 "*C* is the man who kills his
27:25 "*C* is the man who accepts a bribe
27:26 "*C* is the man who does not uphold
Ro 9: 3 I could wish that I myself were *c*
Gal 3:10 "*C* is everyone who does not

CURTAIN
Ex 26:33 The *c* will separate the Holy Place
Lk 23:45 the *c* of the temple was torn in two.
Heb 10:20 opened for us through the *c,*

CYMBAL*
1Co 13: 1 a resounding gong or a clanging *c*

DANCE (DANCING)
Ecc 3: 4 a time to mourn and a time to *d,*
Mt 11:17 and you did not *d;*

DANCING (DANCE)
Ps 30:11 You turned my wailing into *d;*
149: 3 Let them praise his name with *d*

DANGER
Pr 27:12 The prudent see *d* and take refuge,

…or (or
…me changed
…efused to eat
…preted Nebu-
…), writing on
…lion's den (Da

…nce, no deep
…e it is still *d;*
…who are in the *d,*
…ing in a *d* place,

…he light from the *d.*
…s my *d* into light.
…d *d* instead of light
…n light have with *d?*
…e once *d,* but now

…*d* into his wonderful light.
…him there is no *d* at all.
…but hates his brother is still in the *d.*

…UGHTERS

Joel 2:28 sons and *d* will prophesy,

DAVID

Son of Jesse (Ru 4:17-22; 1Ch 2:13-15), ancestor of Jesus (Mt 1:1-17; Lk 3:31).

Anointed king by Samuel (1Sa 16:1-13). Musician to Saul (1Sa 16:14-23; 18:10). Killed Goliath (1Sa 17). Relation with Jonathan (1Sa 18:1-4; 19-20; 23:16-18; 2Sa 1). Disfavor of Saul (1Sa 18:6-23:29). Spared Saul's life (1Sa 24; 26). Among Philistines (1Sa 21:10-14; 27-30). Lament for Saul and Jonathan (2Sa 1).

Anointed king of Judah (2Sa 2:1-11); of Israel (2Sa 5:1-4; 1Ch 11:1-3). Promised eternal dynasty (2Sa 7; 1Ch 17; Ps 132). Adultery with Bathsheba (2Sa 11-12). Absalom's revolt (2Sa 14-18). Last words (2Sa 23:1-7). Death (1Ki 2:10-12; 1Ch 29:28).

DAWN

Ps 37: 6 your righteousness shine like the *d,*
Pr 4:18 is like the first gleam of *d,*

DAY (DAYS)

Ge 1: 5 God called the light *"d,"*
Ex 20: 8 "Remember the Sabbath *d*
Lev 23:28 because it is the *D* of Atonement,
Nu 14:14 before them in a pillar of cloud by *d*
Jos 1: 8 meditate on it *d* and night,
Ps 84:10 Better is one *d* in your courts
96: 2 proclaim his salvation *d* after *d.*
118: 24 This is the *d* the LORD has made;
Pr 27: 1 not know what a *d* may bring forth.
Joel 2:31 and dreadful *d* of the LORD.
Ob :15 The *d* of the LORD is near
Lk 11: 3 Give us each *d* our daily bread.
Ac 17:11 examined the Scriptures every *d*
2Co 4:16 we are being renewed *d* by *d.*
1Th 5: 2 for you know very well that the *d*
2Pe 3: 8 With the Lord a *d* is like

DAYS (DAY)

Dt 17:19 he is to read it all the *d,* of his life
Ps 23: 6 all the *d* of my life,
90:10 The length of our *d* is seventy years
Ecc 12: 1 Creator in the *d* of your youth,
Joel 2:29 I will pour out my Spirit in those *d.*
Mic 4: 1 In the last *d*
Heb 1: 2 in these last *d* he has spoken to us
2Pe 3: 3 that in the last *d* scoffers will come,

DEACONS

1Ti 3: 8 *D,* likewise, are to be men worthy

DEAD (DIE)

Dt 18:11 or spiritist or who consults the *d.*
Mt 28: 7 'He has risen from the *d*
Ro 6:11 count yourselves *d* to sin
Eph 2: 1 you were *d* in your transgressions
1Th 4:16 and the *d* in Christ will rise first.
Jas 2:17 is not accompanied by action, is *d.*
2:26 so faith without deeds is *d.*

DEATH (DIE)

Nu 35:16 the murderer shall be put to *d.*
Ps 23: 4 the valley of the shadow of *d,*
116: 15 is the *d* of his saints.
Pr 8:36 all who hate me love *d."*
14:12 but in the end it leads to *d.*
Ecc 7: 2 for *d* is the destiny of every man;
Isa 25: 8 he will swallow up *d* forever.
53:12 he poured out his life unto *d,*
Jn 5:24 he has crossed over from *d* to life.
Ro 5:12 and in this way *d* came to all men,
6:23 For the wages of sin is *d,*
8:13 put to *d* the misdeeds of the body,
1Co 15:21 For since *d* came through a man,
15:55 Where, O *d,* is your sting?"
Rev 1:18 And I hold the keys of *d* and Hades
20: 6 The second *d* has no power
20:14 The lake of fire is the second *d.*
21: 4 There will be no more *d*

DEBAUCHERY

Ro 13:13 not in sexual immorality and *d,*
Eph 5:18 drunk on wine, which leads to *d.*

DEBORAH

Prophetess who led Israel to victory over Canaanites (Jdg 4-5).

DEBT (DEBTORS DEBTS)

Ro 13: 8 Let no *d* remain outstanding,
13: 8 continuing *d* to love one another,

DEBTORS (DEBT)

Mt 6:12 as we also have forgiven our *d.*

DEBTS (DEBT)

Dt 15: 1 seven years you must cancel *d.*
Mt 6:12 Forgive us our *d,*

DECAY

Ps 16:10 will you let your Holy One see *d.*
Ac 2:27 will you let your Holy One see *d.*

DECEIT (DECEIVE)

Mk 7:22 greed, malice, *d,* lewdness, envy,
1Pe 2: 1 yourselves of all malice and all *d,*
2:22 and no *d* was found in his mouth."

DECEITFUL (DECEIVE)

Jer 17: 9 The heart is *d* above all things
2Co 11:13 men are false apostles, *d* workmen,

DECEITFULNESS (DECEIVE)

Mk 4:19 the *d* of wealth and the desires
Heb 3:13 of you may be hardened by sin's *d.*

DECEIVE (DECEIT DECEITFUL DECEITFULNESS DECEIVED DECEIVES DECEPTIVE)

Lev 19:11 " 'Do not *d* one another.
Pr 14: 5 A truthful witness does not *d,*
Mt 24: 5 'I am the Christ,' and will *d* many.
Ro 16:18 and flattery they *d* the minds
1Co 3:18 Do not *d* yourselves.
Eph 5: 6 Let no one *d* you with empty words
Jas 1:22 to the word, and so *d* yourselves.
1Jn 1: 8 we *d* ourselves and the truth is not

DECEIVED (DECEIVE)

Ge 3:13 "The serpent *d* me, and I ate."
Gal 6: 7 Do not be *d:* God cannot be
1Ti 2:14 And Adam was not the one *d;*
2Ti 3:13 to worse, deceiving and being *d.*
Jas 1:16 Don't be *d,* my dear brothers.

DECEIVES (DECEIVE)

Gal 6: 3 when he is nothing, he *d* himself.
Jas 1:26 he *d* himself and his religion is

DECENCY*

1Ti 2: 9 women to dress modestly, with *d*

DECEPTIVE (DECEIVE)

Pr 31:30 Charm is *d,* and beauty is fleeting;
Col 2: 8 through hollow and *d* philosophy,

DECLARE (DECLARED DECLARING)

1Ch 16:24 *D* his glory among the nations,
Ps 19: 1 The heavens *d* the glory of God;
96: 3 *D* his glory among the nations,
Isa 42: 9 and new things I *d;*

DECLARED (DECLARE)

Mk 7:19 Jesus *d* all foods "clean.")
Ro 2:13 the law who will be *d* righteous.
3:20 no one will be *d* righteous

DECLARING (DECLARE)

Ps 71: 8 *d* your splendor all day long.
Ac 2:11 we hear them *d* the wonders

DECREED (DECREES)

La 3:37 happen if the Lord has not *d* it?
Lk 22:22 Son of Man will go as it has been *d,*

DECREES (DECREED)

Lev 10:11 Israelites all the *d* the LORD has
Ps 119:112 My heart is set on keeping your *d*

DEDICATE (DEDICATION)

Nu 6:12 He must *d* himself to the LORD
Pr 20:25 for a man to *d* something rashly

DEDICATION (DEDICATE)

1Ti 5:11 sensual desires overcome their *d*

DEED (DEEDS)

Col 3:17 you do, whether in word or *d,*

DEEDS (DEED)

1Sa 2: 3 and by him *d* are weighed.
Ps 65: 5 with awesome *d* of righteousness,
66: 3 "How awesome are your *d!*
78: 4 the praiseworthy *d* of the LORD,
86:10 you are great and do marvelous *d;*
92: 4 For you make me glad by your *d,*
111: 3 Glorious and majestic are his *d,*
Hab 3: 2 I stand in awe of your *d,* O LORD.
Mt 5:16 that they may see your good *d*
Ac 26:20 prove their repentance by their *d.*
Jas 2:14 claims to have faith but has no *d?*
2:20 faith without *d* is useless?
1Pe 2:12 they may see your good *d*

DEEP (DEPTH)

1Co 2:10 all things, even the *d* things
1Ti 3: 9 hold of the *d* truths of the faith

DEER

Ps 42: 1 As the *d* pants for streams of water,

DEFEND (DEFENSE)
Ps 74:22 Rise up, O God, and *d* your cause;
Pr 31: 9 *d* the rights of the poor and needy
Jer 50:34 He will vigorously *d* their cause

DEFENSE (DEFEND)
Ps 35:23 Awake, and rise to my *d!*
Php 1:16 here for the *d* of the gospel.
1Jn 2: 1 speaks to the Father in our *d*—

DEFERRED*
Pr 13:12 Hope *d* makes the heart sick,

DEFILE (DEFILED)
Da 1: 8 Daniel resolved not to *d* himself

DEFILED (DEFILE)
Isa 24: 5 The earth is *d* by its people;

DEFRAUD
Lev 19:13 Do not *d* your neighbor or rob him.

DEITY*
Col 2: 9 of the *D* lives in bodily form,

DELIGHT (DELIGHTS)
1Sa 15:22 "Does the LORD *d*
Ps 1: 2 But his *d* is in the law of the LORD
16: 3 in whom is all my *d.*
35: 9 and *d* in his salvation.
37: 4 *D* yourself in the LORD
43: 4 to God, my joy and my *d.*
51:16 You do not *d* in sacrifice,
119: 77 for your law is my *d.*
Pr 29:17 he will bring *d* to your soul.
Isa 42: 1 my chosen one in whom I *d;*
55: 2 and your soul will *d* in the richest
61:10 I *d* greatly in the LORD;
Jer 9:24 for in these I *d,"*
15:16 they were my joy and my heart's *d,*
Mic 7:18 but *d* to show mercy.
Zep 3:17 He will take great *d* in you,
Mt 12:18 the one I love, in whom I *d;*
1Co 13: 6 Love does not *d* in evil
2Co 12:10 for Christ's sake, I *d* in weaknesses,

DELIGHTS (DELIGHT)
Ps 22: 8 since he *d* in him."
35:27 who *d* in the well-being
36: 8 from your river of *d.*
37:23 if the LORD *d* in a man's way,
Pr 3:12 as a father the son he *d* in.
12:22 but he *d* in men who are truthful.
23:24 he who has a wise son *d* in him.

DELILAH*
Woman who betrayed Samson (Jdg 16: 4-22).

DELIVER (DELIVERANCE DELIVERED DELIVERER DELIVERS)
Ps 72:12 For he will *d* the needy who cry out
79: 9 *d* us and forgive our sins
Mt 6:13 but *d* us from the evil one.'
2Co 1:10 hope that he will continue to *d* us,

DELIVERANCE (DELIVER)
Ps 3: 8 From the LORD comes *d.*
32: 7 and surround me with songs of *d.*
33:17 A horse is a vain hope for *d;*

DELIVERED (DELIVER)
Ps 34: 4 he *d* me from all my fears.
Ro 4:25 He was *d* over to death for our sins

DELIVERER (DELIVER)
Ps 18: 2 is my rock, my fortress and my *d;*
40:17 You are my help and my *d;*
140: 7 O Sovereign LORD, my strong *d,*
144: 2 my stronghold and my *d,*

DELIVERS (DELIVER)
Ps 34:17 he *d* them from all their troubles.
34:19 but the LORD *d* him from them all
37:40 The LORD helps them and *d* them
37:40 he *d* them from the wicked

DEMANDED
Lk 12:20 This very night your life will be *d*
12:48 been given much, much will be *d;*

DEMONS
Mt 12:27 And if I drive out *d* by Beelzebub,
Mk 5:15 possessed by the legion of *d,*
Ro 8:38 neither angels nor *d,* neither
Jas 2:19 Good! Even the *d* believe that—

DEMONSTRATE (DEMONSTRATES)
Ro 3:26 he did it to *d* his justice

DEMONSTRATES* (DEMONSTRATE)
Ro 5: 8 God *d* his own love for us in this:

DEN
Da 6:16 and threw him into the lions' *d.*
Mt 21:13 you are making it a '*d* of robbers.'"

DENARIUS
Mk 12:15 Bring me a *d* and let me look at it."

DENIED (DENY)
1Ti 5: 8 he has *d* the faith and is worse

DENIES (DENY)
1Jn 2:23 No one who *d* the Son has

DENY (DENIED DENIES DENYING)
Ex 23: 6 "Do not *d* justice to your poor
Job 27: 5 till I die, I will not *d* my integrity.
La 3:35 to *d* a man his rights
Lk 9:23 he must *d* himself and take up his
Tit 1:16 but by their actions they *d* him.

DENYING* (DENY)
Eze 22:29 mistreat the alien, *d* them justice.
2Ti 3: 5 a form of godliness but *d* its power.
2Pe 2: 1 *d* the sovereign Lord who bought

DEPART (DEPARTED)
Ge 49:10 The scepter will not *d* from Judah,
Job 1:21 and naked I will *d.*
Mt 25:41 '*D* from me, you who are cursed,
Php 1:23 I desire to *d* and be with Christ,

DEPARTED (DEPART)
1Sa 4:21 "The glory has *d* from Israel"—
Ps 119:102 I have not *d* from your laws,

DEPOSIT
2Co 1:22 put his Spirit in our hearts as a *d,*
5: 5 and has given us the Spirit as a *d,*
Eph 1:14 who is a *d* guaranteeing our
2Ti 1:14 Guard the good *d* that was

DEPRAVED (DEPRAVITY)
Ro 1:28 he gave them over to a *d* mind,
Php 2:15 fault in a crooked and *d* generation,

DEPRAVITY (DEPRAVED)
Ro 1:29 of wickedness, evil, greed and *d.*

DEPRIVE
Dt 24:17 Do not *d* the alien or the fatherless
Pr 18: 5 or to *d* the innocent of justice.
Isa 10: 2 to *d* the poor of their rights
Isa 29:21 with ...
innoce...
1Co 7: 5 Do not ...

DEPTH (DEEP)
Ro 8:39 any powers, ...
11:33 the *d* of the ...

DESERT
Nu 32:13 wander in the *d* ...
Ne 9:19 you did not aband...
d.
Ps 78:19 "Can God spread a t...
78:52 led them like sheep th...
d.
Mk 1:13 and he was in the *d* fort...

DESERTED (DESERTS)
Ezr 9: 9 our God has not *d* us
Mt 26:56 all the disciples *d* him and fl...
2Ti 1:15 in the province of Asia has

DESERTING (DESERTS)
Gal 1: 6 are so quickly *d* the one who called

DESERTS (DESERTED DESERTING)
Zec 11:17 who *d* the flock!

DESERVE (DESERVES)
Ps 103: 10 he does not treat us as our sins *d*
Jer 21:14 I will punish you as your deeds *d,*
Mt 22: 8 those I invited did not *d* to come.
Ro 1:32 those who do such things *d* death,

DESERVES (DESERVE)
2Sa 12: 5 the man who did this *d* to die!
Lk 10: 7 for the worker *d* his wages.
1Ti 5:18 and "The worker *d* his wages."

DESIRABLE (DESIRE)
Pr 22: 1 A good name is more *d*

DESIRE (DESIRABLE DESIRES)
Ge 3:16 Your *d* will be for your husband,
Dt 5:21 You shall not set your *d*
1Ch 29:18 keep this *d* in the hearts
Ps 40: 6 Sacrifice and offering you did not *d*
40: 8 I *d* to do your will, O my God;
73:25 earth has nothing I *d* besides you
Pr 3:15 nothing you *d* can compare
10:24 what the righteous *d* will be
11:23 The *d* of the righteous ends only
Isa 26: 8 are the *d* of our hearts.
53: 2 appearance that we should *d* him.
55:11 but will accomplish what I *d*
Hos 6: 6 For I *d* mercy, not sacrifice,
Mt 9:13 learn what this means: 'I *d* mercy,
Ro 7:18 For I have the *d* to do what is good,
1Co 12:31 But eagerly *d* the greater gifts.
14: 1 and eagerly *d* spiritual gifts,
Php 1:23 I *d* to depart and be with Christ,
Heb 13:18 *d* to live honorably in every way.
Jas 1:15 Then, after *d* has conceived,

DESIRES (DESIRE)
Ge 4: 7 at your door; it *d* to have you,
Ps 34:12 and *d* to see many good days,
37: 4 he will give you the *d* of your heart.
103: 5 satisfies your *d* with good things,
145: 19 He fulfills the *d* of those who fear
Pr 11: 6 the unfaithful are trapped by evil *d.*
19:22 What a man *d* is unfailing love;
Mk 4:19 and the *d* for other things come in
Ro 8: 5 set on what that nature *d;*
13:14 to gratify the *d* of the sinful nature.
Gal 5:16 and you will not gratify the *d*
5:17 the sinful nature *d* what is contrary

1Ti 3: 1 an overseer, he *d* a noble task.
6: 9 and harmful *d* that plunge men
2Ti 2:22 Flee the evil *d* of youth,
Jas 1:20 about the righteous life that God *d*.
4: 1 from your *d* that battle within you?
1Pe 2:11 to abstain from sinful *d*, which war
1Jn 2:17 The world and its *d* pass away,

DESOLATE
Isa 54: 1 are the children of the *d* woman

DESPAIR
Isa 61: 3 instead of a spirit of *d*.
2Co 4: 8 perplexed, but not in *d*; persecuted,

DESPISE (DESPISED DESPISES)
Job 42: 6 Therefore I *d* myself
Pr 1: 7 but fools *d* wisdom and discipline.
3:11 do not *d* the LORD's discipline
23:22 do not *d* your mother
Lk 16:13 devoted to the one and *d* the other.
Tit 2:15 Do not let anyone *d* you.

DESPISED (DESPISE)
Ge 25:34 So Esau *d* his birthright.
Isa 53: 3 He was *d* and rejected by men,
1Co 1:28 of this world and the *d* things—

DESPISES (DESPISE)
Pr 14:21 He who *d* his neighbor sins,
15:20 but a foolish man *d* his mother.
15:32 who ignores discipline *d* himself,
Zec 4:10 "Who *d* the day of small things?

DESTINED (DESTINY)
Lk 2:34 "This child is *d* to cause the falling

DESTINY (DESTINED PREDESTINED)
Ps 73:17 then I understood their final *d*.
Ecc 7: 2 for death is the *d* of every man;

DESTITUTE
Pr 31: 8 for the rights of all who are *d*.
Heb 11:37 *d*, persecuted and mistreated—

DESTROY (DESTROYED DESTROYS DESTRUCTION)
Pr 1:32 complacency of fools will *d* them;
Mt 10:28 of the One who can *d* both soul

DESTROYED (DESTROY)
Job 19:26 And after my skin has been *d*,
Isa 55:13 which will not be *d*."
1Co 8:11 for whom Christ died, is *d*
15:26 The last enemy to be *d* is death.
2Co 5: 1 if the earthly tent we live in is *d*,
Heb 10:39 of those who shrink back and are *d*,
2Pe 3:10 the elements will be *d* by fire,

DESTROYS (DESTROY)
Pr 6:32 whoever does so *d* himself.
11: 9 mouth the godless *d* his neighbor,
18: 9 is brother to one who *d*.
28:24 he is partner to him who *d*.
Ecc 9:18 but one sinner *d* much good.
1Co 3:17 If anyone *d* God's temple,

DESTRUCTION (DESTROY)
Pr 16:18 Pride goes before *d*,
Hos 13:14 Where, O grave, is your *d*?
Mt 7:13 broad is the road that leads to *d*,
Gal 6: 8 from that nature will reap *d*;
2Th 1: 9 punished with everlasting *d*
1Ti 6: 9 that plunge men into ruin and *d*.
2Pe 2: 1 bringing swift *d* on themselves.
3:16 other Scriptures, to their own *d*.

DETERMINED (DETERMINES)
Job 14: 5 Man's days are *d*;
Isa 14:26 This is the plan *d* for the whole
Da 11:36 for what has been *d* must take place
Ac 17:26 and he *d* the times set for them

DETERMINES* (DETERMINED)
Ps 147: 4 He *d* the number of the stars
Pr 16: 9 but the LORD *d* his steps.
1Co 12:11 them to each one, just as he *d*.

DETESTABLE (DETESTS)
Pr 21:27 The sacrifice of the wicked is *d*—
28: 9 even his prayers are *d*.
Isa 1:13 Your incense is *d* to me.
Lk 16:15 among men is *d* in God's sight.
Tit 1:16 They are *d*, disobedient

DETESTS (DETESTABLE)
Dt 22: 5 LORD your God *d* anyone who
23:18 the LORD your God *d* them both.
25:16 LORD your God *d* anyone who
Pr 12:22 The LORD *d* lying lips,
15: 8 The LORD *d* the sacrifice
15: 9 The LORD *d* the way
15:26 The LORD *d* the thoughts
16: 5 The LORD *d* all the proud of heart
17:15 the LORD *d* them both.
20:23 The LORD *d* differing weights,

DEVIL (DEVIL'S)
Mt 13:39 the enemy who sows them is the *d*.
25:41 the eternal fire prepared for the *d*
Lk 4: 2 forty days he was tempted by the *d*.
8:12 then the *d* comes and takes away
Eph 4:27 and do not give the *d* a foothold.
2Ti 2:26 and escape from the trap of the *d*,
Jas 4: 7 Resist the *d*, and he will flee
1Pe 5: 8 Your enemy the *d* prowls
1Jn 3: 8 who does what is sinful is of the *d*,
Rev 12: 9 that ancient serpent called the *d*

DEVIL'S* (DEVIL)
Eph 6:11 stand against the *d* schemes.
1Ti 3: 7 into disgrace and into the *d* trap.
1Jn 3: 8 was to destroy the *d* work.

DEVOTE (DEVOTED DEVOTING DEVOTION DEVOUT)
Job 11:13 "Yet if you *d* your heart to him
Jer 30:21 for who is he who will *d* himself
Col 4: 2 *D* yourselves to prayer, being
1Ti 4:13 *d* yourself to the public reading
Tit 3: 8 may be careful to *d* themselves

DEVOTED (DEVOTE)
Ezr 7:10 For Ezra had *d* himself to the study
Ac 2:42 They *d* themselves
Ro 12:10 Be *d* to one another
1Co 7:34 Her aim is to be *d* to the Lord

DEVOTING (DEVOTE)
1Ti 5:10 *d* herself to all kinds of good deeds.

DEVOTION (DEVOTE)
1Ch 28: 9 and serve him with wholehearted *d*
Eze 33:31 With their mouths they express *d*,
1Co 7:35 way in undivided *d* to the Lord.
2Co 11: 3 from your sincere and pure *d*

DEVOUR
2Sa 2:26 "Must the sword *d* forever?
Mk 12:40 They *d* widows' houses
1Pe 5: 8 lion looking for someone to *d*.

DEVOUT (DEVOTE)
Lk 2:25 Simeon, who was righteous and *d*.

DIE (DEAD DEATH DIED DIES)
Ge 2:17 when you eat of it you will surely *d*
Ex 11: 5 Every firstborn son in Egypt will *d*,
Ru 1:17 Where you *d* I will *d*, and there I
2Ki 14: 6 each is to *d* for his own sins."
Pr 5:23 He will *d* for lack of discipline,
10:21 but fools *d* for lack of judgment.
15:10 he who hates correction will *d*.
23:13 with the rod, he will not *d*.
Ecc 3: 2 a time to be born and a time to *d*,
Isa 66:24 their worm will not *d*, nor will their
Eze 3:18 that wicked man will *d* for his sin,
18: 4 soul who sins is the one who will *d*.
33: 8 'O wicked man, you will surely *d*,'
Mt 26:52 "for all who draw the sword will *d*
Jn 11:26 and believes in me will never *d*.
Ro 5: 7 Very rarely will anyone *d*
14: 8 and if we *d*, we *d* to the Lord.
1Co 15:22 in Adam all *d*, so in Christ all will
15:31 I *d* every day—I mean that,
Php 1:21 to live is Christ and to *d* is gain.
Heb 9:27 Just as man is destined to *d* once,
Rev 14:13 Blessed are the dead who *d*

DIED (DIE)
Ro 5: 6 we were still powerless, Christ *d*
6: 2 By no means! We *d* to sin;
6: 8 if we *d* with Christ, we believe that
14:15 brother for whom Christ *d*.
1Co 8:11 for whom Christ *d*, is destroyed
15: 3 that Christ *d* for our sins according
2Co 5:14 *d* for all, and therefore all *d*.
Col 3: 3 For you *d*, and your life is now
1Th 5:10 He *d* for us so that, whether we are
2Ti 2:11 If we *d* with him,
Heb 9:15 now that he has *d* as a ransom
1Pe 3:18 For Christ *d* for sins once for all,
Rev 2: 8 who *d* and came to life again.

DIES (DIE)
Job 14:14 If a man *d*, will he live again?
Pr 11: 7 a wicked man *d*, his hope perishes;
Jn 11:25 in me will live, even though he *d*;
1Co 15:36 does not come to life unless it *d*.

DIFFERENCE (DIFFERENT)
Ro 10:12 For there is no *d* between Jew

DIFFERENT (DIFFERENCE)
1Co 12: 4 There are *d* kinds of gifts,
2Co 11: 4 or a *d* gospel from the one you

DIGNITY
Pr 31:25 She is clothed with strength and *d*;

DIGS
Pr 26:27 If a man *d* a pit, he will fall into it;

DILIGENCE (DILIGENT)
Heb 6:11 to show this same *d* to the very end

DILIGENT (DILIGENCE)
Pr 21: 5 The plans of the *d* lead to profit
1Ti 4:15 Be *d* in these matters; give yourself

DIRECT (DIRECTS)
Ps 119: 35 *D* me in the path of your

Ps 119: 133 *D* my footsteps according
Jer 10: 23 it is not for man to *d* his steps.
2Th 3: 5 May the Lord *d* your hearts

DIRECTS (DIRECT)
Ps 42: 8 By day the LORD *d* his love,
Isa 48: 17 who *d* you in the way you should

DIRGE
Mt 11: 17 we sang a *d,*

DISAPPEAR
Mt 5: 18 will by any means *d* from the Law
Lk 16: 17 earth to *d* than for the least stroke

DISAPPOINT* (DISAPPOINTED)
Ro 5: 5 And hope does not *d* us,

DISAPPOINTED (DISAPPOINT)
Ps 22: 5 in you they trusted and were not *d.*

DISASTER
Ps 57: 1 wings until the *d* has passed.
Pr 3: 25 Have no fear of sudden *d*
17: 5 over *d* will not go unpunished.
Isa 45: 7 I bring prosperity and create *d;*
Eze 7: 5 An unheard-of *d* is coming.

DISCERN (DISCERNING DISCERNMENT)
Ps 19: 12 Who can *d* his errors?
139: 3 You *d* my going out and my lying
Php 1: 10 you may be able to *d* what is best

DISCERNING (DISCERN)
Pr 14: 6 knowledge comes easily to the *d.*
15: 14 The *d* heart seeks knowledge,
17: 24 A *d* man keeps wisdom in view,
17: 28 and *d* if he holds his tongue.
19: 25 rebuke a *d* man, and he will gain

DISCERNMENT (DISCERN)
Pr 17: 10 A rebuke impresses a man of *d*
28: 11 a poor man who has *d* sees

DISCIPLE (DISCIPLES)
Mt 10: 42 these little ones because he is my *d,*
Lk 14: 27 and follow me cannot be my *d.*

DISCIPLES (DISCIPLE)
Mt 28: 19 Therefore go and make *d*
Jn 8: 31 to my teaching, you are really my *d*
13: 35 men will know that you are my *d*
Ac 11: 26 The *d* were called Christians first

DISCIPLINE (DISCIPLINED DISCIPLINES)
Ps 38: 1 or *d* me in your wrath.
39: 11 You rebuke and *d* men for their sin;
94: 12 Blessed is the man you *d,* O LORD
Pr 1: 7 but fools despise wisdom and *d.*
3: 11 do not despise the LORD's *d*
5: 12 You will say, "How I hated *d!*
5: 23 He will die for lack of *d,*
6: 23 and the corrections of *d*
10: 17 He who heeds *d* shows the way
12: 1 Whoever loves *d* loves knowledge,
13: 18 He who ignores *d* comes to poverty
13: 24 who loves him is careful to *d* him.
15: 5 A fool spurns his father's *d,*
15: 32 He who ignores *d* despises himself,
19: 18 *D* your son, for in that there is hope
22: 15 the rod of d will drive it far
23: 13 Do not withhold *d* from a child;
29: 17 *D* your son, and he will give you
Heb 12: 5 do not make light of the Lord's *d,*
12: 7 as *d;* God is treating you
Heb 12: 11 No *d* seems pleasant at the time,
Rev 3: 19 Those whom I love I rebuke and *d.*

DISCIPLINED (DISCIPLINE)
Pr 1: 3 for acquiring a *d* and prudent life,
Jer 31: 18 'You *d* me like an unruly calf,
1Co 11: 32 we are being *d* so that we will not
Tit 1: 8 upright, holy and *d.*
Heb 12: 7 For what son is not *d* by his father?

DISCIPLINES (DISCIPLINE)
Dt 8: 5 your heart that as a man *d* his son,
Pr 3: 12 the LORD *d* those he loves,
Heb 12: 6 because the Lord *d* those he loves,
12: 10 but God *d* us for our good,

DISCLOSED
Lk 8: 17 is nothing hidden that will not be *d,*

DISCOURAGED
Jos 1: 9 Do not be terrified; do not be *d,*
10: 25 "Do not be afraid; do not be *d.*
1Ch 28: 20 or *d,* for the LORD God,
Isa 42: 4 he will not falter or be *d*
Col 3: 21 children, or they will become *d.*

DISCREDITED
2Co 6: 3 so that our ministry will not be *d.*

DISCRETION*
1Ch 22: 12 May the LORD give you *d*
Pr 1: 4 knowledge and *d* to the young—
2: 11 *D* will protect you,
5: 2 that you may maintain *d*
8: 12 I possess knowledge and *d.*
11: 22 a beautiful woman who shows no *d.*

DISCRIMINATED*
Jas 2: 4 have you not *d* among yourselves

DISFIGURED
Isa 52: 14 his appearance was so *d*

DISGRACE (DISGRACEFUL DISGRACES)
Pr 11: 2 When pride comes, then comes *d,*
14: 34 but sin is a *d* to any people.
19: 26 is a son who brings shame and *d.*
Ac 5: 41 of suffering *d* for the Name.
Heb 13: 13 the camp, bearing the *d* he bore.

DISGRACEFUL (DISGRACE)
Pr 10: 5 during harvest is a *d* son.
17: 2 wise servant will rule over a *d* son,

DISGRACES (DISGRACE)
Pr 28: 7 of gluttons *d* his father.
29: 15 but a child left to itself *d* his mother

DISHONEST
Pr 11: 1 The LORD abhors *d* scales,
29: 27 The righteous detest the *d;*
Lk 16: 10 whoever is *d* with very little will
1Ti 3: 8 wine, and not pursuing *d* gain.

DISHONOR (DISHONORS)
Lev 18: 7 " 'Do not *d* your father
Pr 30: 9 and so *d* the name of my God.
1Co 15: 43 it is sown in *d,* it is raised in glory;

DISHONORS (DISHONOR)
Dt 27: 16 Cursed is the man who *d* his father

DISMAYED
Isa 28: 16 the one who trusts will never be *d.*
Isa 41: 10 do not be *d,* for I am your God.

DISOBEDIENCE (DISOBEY)
Ro 5: 19 as through the *d* of the one man
11: 32 to *d* so that he may have mercy
Heb 2: 2 and *d* received its just punishment,
4: 6 go in, because of their *d.*
4: 11 fall by following their example of *d.*

DISOBEDIENT (DISOBEY)
2Ti 3: 2 proud, abusive, *d* to their parents,
Tit 1: 6 to the charge of being wild and *d.*
1: 16 *d* and unfit for doing anything

DISOBEY (DISOBEDIENCE DISOBEDIENT)
Dt 11: 28 the curse if you *d* the commands
2Ch 24: 20 'Why do you *d* the LORD's
Ro 1: 30 they *d* their parents; they are

DISORDER
1Co 14: 33 For God is not a God of *d*
2Co 12: 20 slander, gossip, arrogance and *d.*
Jas 3: 16 there you find *d* and every evil

DISOWN
Pr 30: 9 I may have too much and *d* you
Mt 10: 33 I will *d* him before my Father
26: 35 to die with you, I will never *d* you."
2Ti 2: 12 If we *d* him,

DISPLAY (DISPLAYS)
Eze 39: 21 I will *d* my glory among the nations
1Ti 1: 16 Christ Jesus might *d* his unlimited

DISPLAYS (DISPLAY)
Isa 44: 23 he *d* his glory in Israel.

DISPUTE (DISPUTES)
Pr 17: 14 before a *d* breaks out.
1Co 6: 1 If any of you has a *d* with another,

DISPUTES (DISPUTE)
Pr 18: 18 Casting the lot settles *d*

DISQUALIFIED
1Co 9: 27 I myself will not be *d* for the prize.

DISREPUTE*
2Pe 2: 2 will bring the way of truth into *d.*

DISSENSION*
Pr 6: 14 he always stirs up *d.*
6: 19 and a man who stirs up *d*
10: 12 Hatred stirs up *d,*
15: 18 A hot-tempered man stirs up *d,*
16: 28 A perverse man stirs up *d,*
28: 25 A greedy man stirs up *d,*
29: 22 An angry man stirs up *d,*
Ro 13: 13 debauchery, not in *d* and jealousy.

DISSIPATION*
Lk 21: 34 will be weighed down with *d,*
1Pe 4: 4 with them into the same flood of *d,*

DISTINGUISH
1Ki 3: 9 and to *d* between right and wrong.
Heb 5: 14 themselves to *d* good from evil.

DISTORT
2Co 4: 2 nor do we *d* the word of God.
2Pe 3: 16 ignorant and unstable people *d,*

DISTRESS (DISTRESSED)
Ps 18: 6 In my *d* I called to the LORD;
Jnh 2: 2 "In my *d* I called to the LORD,
Jas 1: 27 orphans and widows in their *d*

DISTRESSED (DISTRESS)
Ro 14:15 If your brother is *d*

DIVIDED (DIVISION)
Mt 12:25 household *d* against itself will not
Lk 23:34 they *d* up his clothes by casting lots
1Co 1:13 Is Christ *d?* Was Paul crucified

DIVINATION
Lev 19:26 " 'Do not practice *d* or sorcery.

DIVINE
Ro 1:20 his eternal power and *d* nature—
2Co 10: 4 they have *d* power
2Pe 1: 4 you may participate in the *d* nature

DIVISION (DIVIDED DIVISIONS DIVISIVE)
Lk 12:51 on earth? No, I tell you, but *d.*
1Co 12:25 so that there should be no *d*

DIVISIONS (DIVISION)
Ro 16:17 to watch out for those who cause *d*
1Co 1:10 another so that there may be no *d*
11:18 there are *d* among you,

DIVISIVE* (DIVISION)
Tit 3:10 Warn a *d* person once,

DIVORCE
Mal 2:16 "I hate *d,*" says the LORD God
Mt 19: 3 for a man to *d* his wife for any
1Co 7:11 And a husband must not *d* his wife.
7:27 Are you married? Do not seek a *d.*

DOCTOR
Mt 9:12 "It is not the healthy who need a *d,*

DOCTRINE
1Ti 4:16 Watch your life and *d* closely.
Tit 2: 1 is in accord with sound *d.*

DOMINION
Ps 22:28 for *d* belongs to the LORD

DOOR
Ps 141: 3 keep watch over the *d* of my lips.
Mt 6: 6 close the *d* and pray to your Father
7: 7 and the *d* will be opened to you.
Rev 3:20 I stand at the *d* and knock.

DOORKEEPER
Ps 84:10 I would rather be a *d* in the house

DOUBLE-EDGED
Heb 4:12 Sharper than any *d* sword,
Rev 1:16 of his mouth came a sharp *d* sword.
2:12 of him who has the sharp, *d* sword.

DOUBLE-MINDED (MIND)
Ps 119:113 I hate *d* men,
Jas 1: 8 he is a *d* man, unstable

DOUBT
Mt 14:31 he said, "why did you *d?*"
21:21 if you have faith and do not *d,*
Mk 11:23 and does not *d* in his heart
Jas 1: 6 he must believe and not *d,*
Jude :22 Be merciful to those who *d;*

DOWNCAST
Ps 42: 5 Why are you *d,* O my soul?
2Co 7: 6 But God, who comforts the *d,*

DRAW (DRAWING DRAWS)
Mt 26:52 "for all who *d* the sword will die
Jn 12:32 up from the earth, will *d* all men
Heb 10:22 let us *d* near to God

DRAWING (DRAW)
Lk 21:28 because your redemption is *d* near

DRAWS (DRAW)
Jn 6:44 the Father who sent me *d* him,

DREADFUL
Heb 10:31 It is a *d* thing to fall into the hands

DRESS
1Ti 2: 9 I also want women to *d* modestly,

DRINK (DRUNK DRUNKARDS DRUNKENNESS)
Pr 5:15 *D* water from your own cistern,
Lk 12:19 Take life easy; eat, *d* and be merry
Jn 7:37 let him come to me and *d.*
1Co 12:13 were all given the one Spirit to *d.*
Rev 21: 6 to *d* without cost from the spring

DRIVES
1Jn 4:18 But perfect love *d* out fear,

DROP
Pr 17:14 so *d* the matter before a dispute
Isa 40:15 Surely the nations are like a *d*

DRUNK (DRINK)
Eph 5:18 Do not get *d* on wine, which leads

DRUNKARDS (DRINK)
Pr 23:21 for *d* and gluttons become poor,
1Co 6:10 nor the greedy nor *d* nor slanderers

DRUNKENNESS (DRINK)
Lk 21:34 weighed down with dissipation, *d*
Ro 13:13 and *d,* not in sexual immorality
Gal 5:21 factions and envy; *d,* orgies,
1Pe 4: 3 living in debauchery, lust, *d,* orgies,

DRY
Isa 53: 2 and like a root out of *d* ground.
Eze 37: 4 '*D* bones, hear the word

DUST
Ge 2: 7 man from the *d* of the ground
Ps 103: 14 he remembers that we are *d.*
Ecc 3:20 all come from *d,* and to *d* all return.

DUTY
Ecc 12:13 for this is the whole *d* of man.
Ac 23: 1 I have fulfilled my *d* to God
1Co 7: 3 husband should fulfill his marital *d*

DWELL (DWELLING)
1Ki 8:27 "But will God really *d* on earth?
Ps 23: 6 I will *d* in the house of the LORD
Isa 43:18 do not *d* on the past.
Eph 3:17 so that Christ may *d* in your hearts
Col 1:19 to have all his fullness *d* in him,
3:16 the word of Christ *d* in you richly

DWELLING (DWELL)
Eph 2:22 to become a *d* in which God lives

EAGER
Pr 31:13 and works with *e* hands.
1Pe 5: 2 greedy for money, but *e* to serve;

EAGLE'S (EAGLES)
Ps 103: 5 your youth is renewed like the *e.*

EAGLES (EAGLE'S)
Isa 40:31 They will soar on wings like *e;*

EAR (EARS)
1Co 2: 9 no *e* has heard,
12:16 if the *e* should say, "Because I am

EARNED
Pr 31:31 Give her the reward she has *e,*

EARS (EAR)
Job 42: 5 My *e* had heard of you
Ps 34:15 and his *e* are attentive to their cry;
Pr 21:13 If a man shuts his *e* to the cry
2Ti 4: 3 to say what their itching *e* want

EARTH (EARTHLY)
Ge 1: 1 God created the heavens and the *e.*
Ps 24: 1 *e* is the LORD's, and everything
108: 5 and let your glory be over all the *e.*
Isa 6: 3 the whole *e* is full of his glory."
51: 6 the *e* will wear out like a garment
55: 9 the heavens are higher than the *e,*
66: 1 and the *e* is my footstool.
Jer 23:24 "Do not I fill heaven and *e?*"
Hab 2:20 let all the *e* be silent before him."
Mt 6:10 done on *e* as it is in heaven.
16:19 bind on *e* will be bound
24:35 Heaven and *e* will pass away,
28:18 and on *e* has been given to me.
Lk 2:14 on *e* peace to men
1Co 10:26 The *e* is the Lord's, and everything
Php 2:10 in heaven and on *e* and under the *e,*
2Pe 3:13 to a new heaven and a new *e,*

EARTHLY (EARTH)
Php 3:19 Their mind is on *e* things.
Col 3: 2 on things above, not on *e* things.

EAST
Ps 103: 12 as far as the *e* is from the west,

EASY
Mt 11:30 For my yoke is *e* and my burden is

EAT (EATING)
Ge 2:17 but you must not *e* from the tree
Isa 55: 1 come, buy and *e!*
65:25 and the lion will *e* straw like the ox,
Mt 26:26 "Take and *e;* this is my body."
Ro 14: 2 faith allows him to *e* everything,
1Co 8:13 if what I *e* causes my brother to fall
10:31 So whether you *e* or drink
2Th 3:10 man will not work, he shall not *e.*"

EATING (EAT)
Ro 14:17 kingdom of God is not a matter of *e*

EDICT
Heb 11:23 they were not afraid of the king's *e.*

EDIFIES
1Co 14: 4 but he who prophesies *e* the church

EFFECT
Isa 32:17 *e* of righteousness will be quietness
Heb 9:18 put into *e* without blood.

EFFORT

Lk 13: 24 "Make every *e* to enter
Ro 9: 16 depend on man's desire or *e*,
14: 19 make every *e* to do what leads
Eph 4: 3 Make every *e* to keep the unity
Heb 4: 11 make every *e* to enter that rest,
12: 14 Make every *e* to live in peace
2Pe 1: 5 make every *e* to add
3: 14 make every *e* to be found spotless,

ELAH

Son of Baasha; king of Israel (1Ki 16: 6-14).

ELDERLY* (ELDERS)

Lev 19: 32 show respect for the *e*

ELDERS (ELDERLY)

1Ti 5: 17 The *e* who direct the affairs

ELECTION

Ro 9: 11 God's purpose in *e* might stand:
2Pe 1: 10 to make your calling and *e* sure.

ELI

High priest in youth of Samuel (1Sa 1-4). Blessed Hannah (1Sa 1:12-18); raised Samuel (1Sa 2:11-26).

ELIJAH

Prophet; predicted famine in Israel (1Ki 17:1; Jas 5:17). Fed by ravens (1Ki 17:2-6). Raised Sidonian widow's son (1Ki 17:7-24). Defeated prophets of Baal at Carmel (1Ki 18: 16-46). Ran from Jezebel (1Ki 19:1-9). Prophesied death of Azariah (2Ki 1). Succeeded by Elishah (1Ki 19:19-21; 2Ki 2: 1-18). Taken to heaven in whirlwind (2Ki 2: 11-12).

Return prophesied (Mal 4:5-6); equated with John the Baptist (Mt 17:9-13; Mk 9: 9-13; Lk 1:17). Appeared with Moses in transfiguration of Jesus (Mt 17:1-8; Mk 9: 1-8).

ELISHA

Prophet; successor of Elijah (1Ki 19:16-21); inherited his cloak (2Ki 2:1-18). Miracles of (2Ki 2-6).

ELIZABETH*

Mother of John the Baptist, relative of Mary (Lk 1:5-58).

EMBITTER*

Col 3: 21 Fathers, do not *e* your children,

EMPTY

Eph 5: 6 no one deceive you with *e* words,
1Pe 1: 18 from the *e* way of life handed

ENABLE (ABLE)

Lk 1: 74 to *e* us to serve him without fear
Ac 4: 29 *e* your servants to speak your word

ENABLED (ABLE)

Lev 26: 13 *e* you to walk with heads held high.
Jn 6: 65 unless the Father has *e* him."

ENABLES (ABLE)

Php 3: 21 by the power that *e* him

ENCAMPS*

Ps 34: 7 The angel of the LORD *e*

ENCOURAGE (ENCOURAGEMENT)

Ps 10: 17 you *e* them, and you listen
Isa 1: 17 *e* the oppressed.
Ac 15: 32 to *e* and strengthen the brothers.
Ro 12: 8 if it is encouraging, let him *e*;
1Th 4: 18 Therefore *e* each other
2Ti 4: 2 rebuke and *e*—with great patience
Tit 2: 6 *e* the young men to be
Heb 3: 13 But *e* one another daily, as long
10: 25 but let us *e* one another—

ENCOURAGEMENT (ENCOURAGE)

Ac 4: 36 Barnabas (which means Son of *E*),
Ro 15: 4 *e* of the Scriptures we might have
15: 5 and *e* give you a spirit of unity
1Co 14: 3 to men for their strengthening, *e*
Heb 12: 5 word of *e* that addresses you

END

Ps 119: 33 then I will keep them to the *e*.
Pr 14: 12 but in the *e* it leads to death.
19: 20 and in the *e* you will be wise.
23: 32 In the *e* it bites like a snake
Ecc 12: 12 making many books there is no *e*,
Mt 10: 22 firm to the *e* will be saved.
Lk 21: 9 but the *e* will not come right away
Ro 10: 4 Christ is the *e* of the law
1Co 15: 24 the *e* will come, when he hands

ENDURANCE (ENDURE)

Ro 15: 4 through *e* and the encouragement
15: 5 May the God who gives *e*
2Co 1: 6 which produces in you patient *e*
Col 1: 11 might so that you may have great *e*
1Ti 6: 11 faith, love, *e* and gentleness.
Tit 2: 2 and sound in faith, in love and in *e*.

ENDURE (ENDURANCE ENDURES)

Ps 72: 17 May his name *e* forever;
Pr 12: 19 Truthful lips *e* forever,
27: 24 for riches do not *e* forever,
Ecc 3: 14 everything God does will *e* forever;
Mal 3: 2 who can *e* the day of his coming?
2Ti 2: 3 *E* hardship with us like a good
2: 12 if we *e*, / we will also reign
Heb 12: 7 *E* hardship as discipline; God is
Rev 3: 10 kept my command to *e* patiently,

ENDURES (ENDURE)

Ps 112: 9 his righteousness *e* forever;
136: 1 *His love e forever.*
Da 9: 15 made for yourself a name that *e*

ENEMIES (ENEMY)

Ps 23: 5 in the presence of my *e*.
Mic 7: 6 a man's *e* are the members
Mt 5: 44 Love your *e* and pray
Lk 20: 43 hand until I make your *e*

ENEMY (ENEMIES ENMITY)

Pr 24: 17 Do not gloat when your *e* falls;
25: 21 If your *e* is hungry, give him food
27: 6 but an *e* multiplies kisses.
1Co 15: 26 The last *e* to be destroyed is death.
1Ti 5: 14 and to give the *e* no opportunity

ENJOY (JOY)

Dt 6: 2 and so that you may *e* long life.
Eph 6: 3 and that you may *e* long life
Heb 11: 25 rather than to *e* the pleasures of sin

ENJOYMENT (JOY)

Ecc 4: 8 and why am I depriving myself of *e*
1Ti 6: 17 us with everything for our *e*.

ENLIGHTENED* (LIGHT)

Eph 1: 18 that the eyes of your heart may be *e*
Heb 6: 4 for those who have once been *e*,

ENMITY* (ENEMY)

Ge 3: 15 And I will put *e*

ENOCH

Walked with God and taken by him (Ge 5:18-24; Heb 11:5). Prophet (Jude 14).

ENTANGLED (ENTANGLES)

2Pe 2: 20 and are again *e* in it and overcome,

ENTANGLES* (ENTANGLED)

Heb 12: 1 and the sin that so easily *e*,

ENTER (ENTERED ENTERS ENTRANCE)

Ps 100: 4 *E* his gates with thanksgiving
Mt 5: 20 will certainly not *e* the kingdom
7: 13 "*E* through the narrow gate.
18: 8 It is better for you to *e* life maimed
Mk 10: 15 like a little child will never *e* it."
10: 23 is for the rich to *e* the kingdom

ENTERED (ENTER)

Ro 5: 12 as sin *e* the world through one man,
Heb 9: 12 but he *e* the Most Holy Place once

ENTERS (ENTER)

Mk 7: 18 you see that nothing that *e* a man
Jn 10: 2 The man who *e* by the gate is

ENTERTAIN

1Ti 5: 19 Do not *e* an accusation
Heb 13: 2 Do not forget to *e* strangers,

ENTHRALLED*

Ps 45: 11 The king is *e* by your beauty;

ENTHRONED (THRONE)

1Sa 4: 4 who is *e* between the cherubim.
Ps 2: 4 The One *e* in heaven laughs;
102: 12 But you, O LORD, sit *e* forever;
Isa 40: 22 He sits *e* above the circle

ENTICE

Pr 1: 10 My son, if sinners *e* you,
2Pe 2: 18 they *e* people who are just escaping

ENTIRE

Gal 5: 14 The *e* law is summed up

ENTRUSTED (TRUST)

1Ti 6: 20 guard what has been *e* to your care.
2Ti 1: 12 able to guard what I have *e* to him
1: 14 Guard the good deposit that was *e*
Jude : 3 once for all *e* to the saints.

ENVY

Pr 3: 31 Do not *e* a violent man
14: 30 but *e* rots the bones.
1Co 13: 4 It does not *e*, it does not boast,

EPHRAIM

1. Second son of Joseph (Ge 41:52; 46: 20). Blessed as firstborn by Jacob (Ge 48).
2. Synonymous with Northern Kingdom (Isa 7:17; Hos 5).

EQUAL

Isa 40: 25 who is my *e*?" says the Holy One.
Jn 5: 18 making himself *e* with God.
1Co 12: 25 that its parts should have *e* concern

EQUIP* (EQUIPPED)

Heb 13: 21 *e* you with everything good

EQUIPPED (EQUIP)

2Ti 3: 17 man of God may be thoroughly *e*

ERROR

Jas 5:20 Whoever turns a sinner from the e

ESAU

Firstborn of Isaac, twin of Jacob (Ge 25:21-26). Also called Edom (Ge 25:30). Sold Jacob his birthright (Ge 25:29-34); lost blessing (Ge 27). Reconciled to Jacob (Gen 33).

ESCAPE (ESCAPING)

Ro 2: 3 think you will e God's judgment?
Heb 2: 3 how shall we e if we ignore such

ESCAPING (ESCAPE)

1Co 3:15 only as one e through the flames.

ESTABLISH

Ge 6:18 But I will e my covenant with you,
1Ch 28: 7 I will e his kingdom forever
Ro 10: 3 God and sought to e their own,

ESTEEMED

Pr 22: 1 to be e is better than silver or gold.
Isa 53: 3 he was despised, and we e him not.

ESTHER

Jewess who lived in Persia; cousin of Mordecai (Est 2:7). Chosen queen of Xerxes (Est 2:8-18). Foiled Haman's plan to exterminate the Jews (Est 3-4; 7-9).

ETERNAL (ETERNALLY ETERNITY)

Ps 16:11 with e pleasures at your right hand.
111: 10 To him belongs e praise.
119: 89 Your word, O LORD, is e;
Isa 26: 4 LORD, the LORD, is the Rock e.
Mt 19:16 good thing must I do to get e life?"
25:41 into the e fire prepared for the devil
25:46 they will go away to e punishment,
Jn 3:15 believes in him may have e life.
3:16 him shall not perish but have e life.
3:36 believes in the Son has e life,
4:14 spring of water welling up to e life."
5:24 believes him who sent me has e life
6:68 You have the words of e life.
10:28 I give them e life, and they shall
17: 3 this is e life: that they may know
Ro 1:20 his e power and divine nature—
6:23 but the gift of God is e life
2Co 4:17 for us an e glory that far outweighs
4:18 temporary, but what is unseen is e.
1Ti 1:16 believe on him and receive e life.
1:17 Now to the King e, immortal,
Heb 9:12 having obtained e redemption.
1Jn 5:11 God has given us e life,
5:13 you may know that you have e life.

ETERNALLY (ETERNAL)

Gal 1: 8 let him be e condemned! As we

ETERNITY (ETERNAL)

Ps 93: 2 you are from all e.
Ecc 3:11 also set e in the hearts of men;

ETHIOPIAN

Jer 13:23 Can the E change his skin

EUNUCHS

Mt 19:12 For some are e because they were

EVANGELIST (EVANGELISTS)

2Ti 4: 5 hardship, do the work of an e,

EVANGELISTS* (EVANGELIST)

Eph 4:11 some to be prophets, some to be e,

EVE

2Co 11: 3 as E was deceived by the serpent's
1Ti 2:13 For Adam was formed first, then E

EVEN-TEMPERED*

Pr 17:27 and a man of understanding is e.

EVER (EVERLASTING FOREVER)

Ex 15:18 LORD will reign for e and e."
Dt 8:19 If you e forget the LORD your
Ps 5:11 let them e sing for joy.
10:16 The LORD is King for e and e;
25: 3 will e be put to shame,
26: 3 for your love is e before me,
45: 6 O God, will last for e and e;
52: 8 God's unfailing love for e and e.
89:33 nor will I e betray my faithfulness.
145: 1 I will praise your name for e and e.
Pr 4:18 shining e brighter till the full light
5:19 may you e be captivated
Isa 66: 8 Who has e heard of such a thing?
Jer 31:36 the descendants of Israel e cease
Da 7:18 it forever—yes, for e and e.'
12: 3 like the stars for e and e.
Mk 4:12 e hearing but never understanding;
Jn 1:18 No one has e seen God,
Rev 1:18 and behold I am alive for e and e!
22: 5 And they will reign for e and e.

EVER-INCREASING* (INCREASE)

Ro 6:19 to impurity and to e wickedness,
2Co 3:18 into his likeness with e glory,

EVERLASTING (EVER)

Dt 33:27 and underneath are the e arms.
Ne 9: 5 your God, who is from e to e."
Ps 90: 2 from e to e you are God.
139: 24 and lead me in the way e.
Isa 9: 6 E Father, Prince of Peace.
33:14 Who of us can dwell with e burning
35:10 e joy will crown their heads.
45:17 the LORD with an e salvation;
54: 8 but with e kindness
55: 3 I will make an e covenant with you,
63:12 to gain for himself e renown,
Jer 31: 3 "I have loved you with an e love;
Da 9:24 to bring in e righteousness,
12: 2 some to e life, others to shame
Jn 6:47 the truth, he who believes has e life.
2Th 1: 9 punished with e destruction
Jude : 6 bound with e chains for judgment

EVER-PRESENT*

Ps 46: 1 an e help in trouble

EVIDENCE (EVIDENT)

Jn 14:11 on the e of the miracles themselves.

EVIDENT (EVIDENCE)

Php 4: 5 Let your gentleness be e to all.

EVIL

Ge 2: 9 of the knowledge of good and e.
Job 1: 1 he feared God and shunned e.
1: 8 a man who fears God and shuns e."
34:10 Far be it from God to do e,
Ps 23: 4 I will fear no e,
34:14 Turn from e and do good;
51: 4 and done what is e in your sight,
97:10 those who love the LORD hate e,
101: 4 I will have nothing to do with e.
Pr 8:13 To fear the LORD is to hate e;
10:23 A fool finds pleasure in e conduct,
11:27 e comes to him who searches for it.
24:19 Do not fret because of e men
24:20 for the e man has no future hope,
Isa 5:20 Woe to those who call e good
13:11 I will punish the world for its e,
55: 7 and the e man his thoughts.
Hab 1:13 Your eyes are too pure to look on e;
Mt 5:45 He causes his sun to rise on the e
6:13 but deliver us from the e one.'
7:11 If you, then, though you are e,
12:35 and the e man brings e things out
Jn 17:15 you protect them from the e one.
Ro 2: 9 for every human being who does e:
12: 9 Hate what is e; cling
12:17 Do not repay anyone e for e.
16:19 and innocent about what is e.
1Co 13: 6 Love does not delight in e
14:20 In regard to e be infants,
Eph 6:16 all the flaming arrows of the e one.
1Th 5:22 Avoid every kind of e.
1Ti 6:10 of money is a root of all kinds of e.
2Ti 2:22 Flee the e desires of youth,
Jas 1:13 For God cannot be tempted by e,
1Pe 2:16 your freedom as a cover-up for e;
3: 9 Do not repay e with e or insult

EXACT

Heb 1: 3 the e representation of his being,

EXALT (EXALTED EXALTS)

Ps 30: 1 I will e you, O LORD,
34: 3 let us e his name together.
118: 28 you are my God, and I will e you.
Isa 24:15 e the name of the LORD, the God

EXALTED (EXALT)

2Sa 22:47 E be God, the Rock, my Savior!
1Ch 29:11 you are e as head over all.
Ne 9: 5 and may it be e above all blessing
Ps 21:13 Be e, O LORD, in your strength;
46:10 I will be e among the nations,
57: 5 Be e, O God, above the heavens;
97: 9 you are e far above all gods.
99: 2 he is e over all the nations.
108: 5 Be e, O God, above the heavens,
148: 13 for his name alone is e;
Isa 6: 1 e, and the train of his robe filled
12: 4 and proclaim that his name is e.
33: 5 The LORD is e, for he dwells
Eze 21:26 The lowly will be e and the e will be
Mt 23:12 whoever humbles himself will be e.
Php 1:20 always Christ will be e in my body,
2: 9 Therefore God e him

EXALTS (EXALT)

Ps 75: 7 He brings one down, he e another.
Pr 14:34 Righteousness e a nation,
Mt 23:12 For whoever e himself will be

EXAMINE (EXAMINED)

Ps 26: 2 e my heart and my mind;
Jer 17:10 and e the mind,
La 3:40 Let us e our ways and test them,
1Co 11:28 A man ought to e himself
2Co 13: 5 E yourselves to see whether you

EXAMINED (EXAMINE)

Ac 17:11 e the Scriptures every day to see

EXAMPLE (EXAMPLES)

Jn 13:15 have set you an e that you should
1Co 11: 1 Follow my e, as I follow

1Ti 4:12 set an e for the believers in speech,
Tit 2: 7 In everything set them an e
1Pe 2:21 leaving you an e, that you should

EXAMPLES* (EXAMPLE)
1Co 10: 6 Now these things occurred as e
10:11 as e and were written down
1Pe 5: 3 to you, but being e to the flock.

EXASPERATE*
Eph 6: 4 Fathers, do not e your children;

EXCEL (EXCELLENT)
1Co 14:12 to e in gifts that build up the church
2Co 8: 7 But just as you e in everything—

EXCELLENT (EXCEL)
1Co 12:31 now I will show you the most e way
Php 4: 8 if anything is e or praiseworthy—
1Ti 3:13 have served well gain an e standing
Tit 3: 8 These things are e and profitable

EXCHANGED
Ro 1:23 e the glory of the immortal God
1:25 They e the truth of God for a lie,

EXCUSE (EXCUSES)
Jn 15:22 they have no e for their sin.
Ro 1:20 so that men are without e.

EXCUSES* (EXCUSE)
Lk 14:18 "But they all alike began to make e.

EXISTS
Heb 2:10 and through whom everything e,
11: 6 to him must believe that he e

EXPECT (EXPECTATION)
Mt 24:44 at an hour when you do not e him.

EXPECTATION (EXPECT)
Ro 8:19 waits in eager e for the sons
Heb 10:27 but only a fearful e of judgment

EXPEL*
1Co 5:13 E the wicked man from among you

EXPENSIVE
1Ti 2: 9 or gold or pearls or e clothes,

EXPLOIT
Pr 22:22 Do not e the poor because they are
2Co 12:17 Did I e you through any

EXPOSE
1Co 4: 5 will e the motives of men's hearts.
Eph 5:11 of darkness, but rather e them.

EXTENDS
Pr 31:20 and e her hands to the needy.
Lk 1:50 His mercy e to those who fear him,

EXTINGUISHED
2Sa 21:17 the lamp of Israel will not be e."

EXTOL*
Job 36:24 Remember to e his work,
Ps 34: 1 I will e the LORD at all times;
68: 4 e him who rides on the clouds—
95: 2 and e him with music and song.
109: 30 mouth I will greatly e the LORD;
111: 1 I will e the LORD with all my heart
115: 18 it is we who e the LORD,
117: 1 e him, all you peoples.
145: 2 and e your name for ever.
Ps 145: 10 your saints will e you.
147: 12 E the LORD, O Jerusalem;

EXTORT*
Lk 3:14 "Don't e money and don't accuse

EYE (EYES)
Ex 21:24 you are to take life for life, e for e,
Ps 94: 9 Does he who formed the e not see?
Mt 5:29 If your right e causes you to sin,
5:38 'E for e, and tooth for tooth.'
7: 3 of sawdust in your brother's e
1Co 2: 9 "No e has seen,
Col 3:22 not only when their e is on you
Rev 1: 7 and every e will see him,

EYES (EYE)
Nu 33:55 remain will become barbs in your e
Jos 23:13 on your backs and thorns in your e,
2Ch 16: 9 For the e of the LORD range
Job 31: 1 "I made a covenant with my e
36: 7 He does not take his e
Ps 119: 18 Open my e that I may see
121: 1 I lift up my e to the hills—
141: 8 But my e are fixed on you,
Pr 3: 7 Do not be wise in your own e;
4:25 Let your e look straight ahead,
15: 3 The e of the LORD are everywhere
Isa 6: 5 and my e have seen the King,
Hab 1:13 Your e are too pure to look on evil;
Jn 4:35 open your e and look at the fields!
2Co 4:18 So we fix our e not on what is seen,
Heb 12: 2 Let us fix our e on Jesus, the author
Jas 2: 5 poor in the e of the world to be rich
1Pe 3:12 For the e of the Lord are
Rev 7:17 wipe away every tear from their e."
21: 4 He will wipe every tear from their e

EZEKIEL

Priest called to be prophet to the exiles (Eze 1-3).

EZRA

Priest and teacher of the Law who led a return of exiles to Israel to reestablish temple and worship (Ezr 7-8). Corrected intermarriage of priests (Ezr 9-10). Read Law at celebration of Feast of Tabernacles (Neh 8).

FACE (FACES)
Ge 32:30 "It is because I saw God f to f,
Ex 34:29 was not aware that his f was radiant
Nu 6:25 the LORD make his f shine
1Ch 16:11 seek his f always.
2Ch 7:14 and seek my f and turn
Ps 4: 6 Let the light of your f shine upon us
27: 8 Your f, LORD, I will seek.
31:16 Let your f shine on your servant;
105: 4 seek his f always.
119:135 Make your f shine
Isa 50: 7 Therefore have I set my f like flint,
Mt 17: 2 His f shone like the sun,
1Co 13:12 mirror; then we shall see f to f.
2Co 4: 6 the glory of God in the f of Christ.
1Pe 3:12 but the f of the Lord is
Rev 1:16 His f was like the sun shining

FACES (FACE)
2Co 3:18 who with unveiled f all reflect

FACTIONS
Gal 5:20 selfish ambition, dissensions, f

FADE
1Pe 5: 4 of glory that will never f away.

FAIL (FAILING FAILINGS FAILS)
1Ch 28:20 He will not f you or forsake you
2Ch 34:33 they did not f to follow the LORD,
Ps 89:28 my covenant with him will never f.
Pr 15:22 Plans f for lack of counsel,
Isa 51: 6 my righteousness will never f.
La 3:22 for his compassions never f.
2Co 13: 5 unless, of course, you f the test?

FAILING (FAIL)
1Sa 12:23 sin against the LORD by f to pray

FAILINGS (FAIL)
Ro 15: 1 ought to bear with the f of the weak

FAILS (FAIL)
1Co 13: 8 Love never f.

FAINT
Isa 40:31 they will walk and not be f.

FAIR
Pr 1: 3 doing what is right and just and f;
Col 4: 1 slaves with what is right and f,

FAITH (FAITHFUL FAITHFULLY FAITHFULNESS FAITHLESS)
2Ch 20:20 Have f in the LORD your God
Hab 2: 4 but the righteous will live by his f—
Mt 9:29 According to your f will it be done
17:20 if you have f as small as a mustard
24:10 many will turn away from the f
Mk 11:22 "Have f in God," Jesus answered.
Lk 7: 9 I have not found such great f
12:28 will he clothe you, O you of little f!
17: 5 "Increase our f!" He replied,
18: 8 will he find f on the earth?"
Ac 14: 9 saw that he had f to be healed
14:27 the door of f to the Gentiles.
Ro 1:12 encouraged by each other's f.
1:17 is by f from first to last,
1:17 "The righteous will live by f."
3: 3 What if some did not have f?
3:22 comes through f in Jesus Christ
3:25 a sacrifice of atonement, through f
4: 5 his f is credited as righteousness.
5: 1 we have been justified through f,
10:17 f comes from hearing the message,
14: 1 Accept him whose f is weak,
14:23 that does not come from f is sin.
1Co 13: 2 and if I have a f that can move
13:13 And now these three remain: f,
16:13 stand firm in the f; be men
2Co 5: 7 We live by f, not by sight.
13: 5 to see whether you are in the f;
Gal 2:16 Jesus that we may be justified by f
2:20 I live by f in the Son of God,
3:11 "The righteous will live by f."
3:24 that we might be justified by f.
Eph 2: 8 through f—and this not
4: 5 one Lord, one f, one baptism;
6:16 to all this, take up the shield of f,
Col 1:23 continue in your f, established
1Th 5: 8 on f and love as a breastplate,
1Ti 2:15 if they continue in f, love
4: 1 later times some will abandon the f
5: 8 he has denied the f and is worse
6:12 Fight the good fight of the f.
2Ti 3:15 wise for salvation through f
4: 7 finished the race, I have kept the f.
Phm : 6 may be active in sharing your f,
Heb 10:38 But my righteous one will live by f.

Heb 11: 1 *f* is being sure of what we hope for
11: 3 By *f* we understand that
11: 5 By *f* Enoch was taken from this life
11: 6 And without *f* it is impossible
11: 7 By *f* Noah, when warned about
11: 8 By *f* Abraham, when called to go
11:17 By *f* Abraham, when God tested
11:20 By *f* Isaac blessed Jacob
11:21 By *f* Jacob, when he was dying,
11:22 By *f* Joseph, when his end was near
11:24 By *f* Moses, when he had grown up
11:31 By *f* the prostitute Rahab,
12: 2 the author and perfecter of our *f*,
Jas 2:14 if a man claims to have *f*
2:17 In the same way, *f* by itself,
2:26 so *f* without deeds is dead.
2Pe 1: 5 effort to add to your *f* goodness;
1Jn 5: 4 overcome the world, even our *f*.
Jude : 3 to contend for the *f* that was once

FAITHFUL (FAITH)

Nu 12: 7 he is *f* in all my house.
Dt 7: 9 your God is God; he is the *f* God,
32: 4 A *f* God who does no wrong,
2Sa 22:26 "To the *f* you show yourself *f*,
Ps 25:10 of the LORD are loving and *f*
31:23 The LORD preserves the *f*,
33: 4 he is *f* in all he does.
37:28 and will not forsake his *f* ones.
97:10 for he guards the lives of his *f* ones
145: 13 The LORD is *f* to all his promises
146: 6 the LORD, who remains *f* forever.
Pr 31:26 and *f* instruction is on her tongue.
Mt 25:21 'Well done, good and *f* servant!
Ro 12:12 patient in affliction, *f* in prayer.
1Co 4: 2 been given a trust must prove *f*.
10:13 And God is *f*; he will not let you be
1Th 5:24 The one who calls you is *f*
2Ti 2:13 he will remain *f*,
Heb 3: 6 But Christ is *f* as a son
10:23 for he who promised is *f*.
1Pe 4:19 themselves to their *f* Creator
1Jn 1: 9 he is *f* and just and will forgive us
Rev 1: 5 who is the *f* witness, the firstborn
2:10 Be *f*, even to the point of death,
19:11 whose rider is called *F* and True.

FAITHFULLY (FAITH)

Dt 11:13 if you *f* obey the commands I am
1Sa 12:24 and serve him *f* with all your heart;
1Ki 2: 4 and if they walk *f* before me
1Pe 4:10 *f* administering God's grace

FAITHFULNESS (FAITH)

Ps 57:10 your *f* reaches to the skies.
85:10 Love and *f* meet together;
86:15 to anger, abounding in love and *f*.
89: 1 mouth I will make your *f* known
89:14 love and *f* go before you.
91: 4 his *f* will be your shield
117: 2 the *f* of the LORD endures forever.
119: 75 and in *f* you have afflicted me.
Pr 3: 3 Let love and *f* never leave you;
Isa 11: 5 and *f* the sash around his waist.
La 3:23 great is your *f*.
Ro 3: 3 lack of faith nullify God's *f*?
Gal 5:22 patience, kindness, goodness, *f*,

FAITHLESS (FAITH)

Ps 119:158 I look on the *f* with loathing,
Jer 3:22 "Return, *f* people;
Ro 1:31 they are senseless, *f*, heartless,
2Ti 2:13 if we are *f*,

FALL (FALLEN FALLING FALLS)

Ps 37:24 though he stumble, he will not *f*,
55:22 he will never let the righteous *f*.
69: 9 of those who insult you *f* on me.
Pr 11:28 Whoever trusts in his riches will *f*,
Lk 11:17 a house divided against itself will *f*.
Ro 3:23 and *f* short of the glory of God,
Heb 6: 6 if they *f* away, to be brought back

FALLEN (FALL)

2Sa 1:19 How the mighty have *f*!
Isa 14:12 How you have *f* from heaven,
1Co 15:20 of those who have *f* asleep.
Gal 5: 4 you have *f* away from grace.
1Th 4:15 precede those who have *f* asleep.

FALLING (FALL)

Jude :24 able to keep you from *f*

FALLS (FALL)

Pr 24:17 Do not gloat when your enemy *f*;
Jn 12:24 a kernel of wheat *f* to the ground
Ro 14: 4 To his own master he stands or *f*.

FALSE (FALSEHOOD FALSELY)

Ex 20:16 "You shall not give *f* testimony
23: 1 "Do not spread *f* reports.
Pr 13: 5 The righteous hate what is *f*,
19: 5 A *f* witness will not go unpunished,
Mt 7:15 "Watch out for *f* prophets.
19:18 not steal, do not give *f* testimony,
24:11 and many *f* prophets will appear
Php 1:18 whether from *f* motives or true,
1Ti 1: 3 not to teach *f* doctrines any longer
2Pe 2: 1 there will be *f* teachers among you.

FALSEHOOD (FALSE)

Ps 119:163 I hate and abhor *f*
Pr 30: 8 Keep *f* and lies far from me;
Eph 4:25 each of you must put off *f*

FALSELY (FALSE)

Lev 19:12 " 'Do not swear *f* by my name
Lk 3:14 and don't accuse people *f*—
1Ti 6:20 ideas of what is *f* called knowledge,

FALTER*

Pr 24:10 If you *f* in times of trouble,
Isa 42: 4 he will not *f* or be discouraged

FAMILIES (FAMILY)

Ps 68: 6 God sets the lonely in *f*,

FAMILY (FAMILIES)

Pr 15:27 greedy man brings trouble to his *f*,
31:15 she provides food for her *f*
Lk 9:61 go back and say good-by to my *f*."
12:52 in one *f* divided against each other,
1Ti 3: 4 He must manage his own *f* well
3: 5 how to manage his own *f*,
5: 4 practice by caring for their own *f*
5: 8 and especially for his immediate *f*,

FAMINE

Ge 41:30 seven years of *f* will follow them.
Am 8:11 but a *f* of hearing the words
Ro 8:35 or persecution or *f* or nakedness

FAN*

2Ti 1: 6 you to *f* into flame the gift of God,

FAST

Dt 13: 4 serve him and hold *f* to him.
Jos 22: 5 to hold *f* to him and to serve him
23: 8 to hold *f* to the LORD your God,
Ps 119: 31 I hold *f* to your statutes, O LORD;
139: 10 your right hand will hold me *f*.
Mt 6:16 "When you *f*, do not look somber
1Pe 5:12 Stand *f* in it.

FATHER (FATHER'S FATHERLESS FATHERS FOREFATHERS)

Ge 2:24 this reason a man will leave his *f*
17: 4 You will be the *f* of many nations.
Ex 20:12 "Honor your *f* and your mother,
21:15 "Anyone who attacks his *f*
21:17 "Anyone who curses his *f*
Lev 18: 7 " 'Do not dishonor your *f*
19: 3 you must respect his mother and *f*,
Dt 5:16 "Honor your *f* and your mother,
21:18 son who does not obey his *f*
Ps 27:10 Though my *f* and mother forsake
68: 5 A *f* to the fatherless, a defender
Pr 10: 1 A wise son brings joy to his *f*,
17:21 there is no joy for the *f* of a fool.
23:22 Listen to your *f*, who gave you life,
23:24 *f* of a righteous man has great joy;
28: 7 of gluttons disgraces his *f*.
29: 3 loves wisdom brings joy to his *f*,
Isa 9: 6 Everlasting *F*, Prince of Peace.
Mt 6: 9 " 'Our *F* in heaven,
10:37 "Anyone who loves his *f*
15: 4 'Honor your *f* and mother'
19: 5 this reason a man will leave his *f*
Lk 12:53 *f* against son and son against *f*,
23:34 Jesus said, "*F*, forgive them,
Jn 6:44 the *F* who sent me draws him,
6:46 No one has seen the *F*
8:44 You belong to your *f*, the devil,
10:30 I and the *F* are one."
14: 6 No one comes to the *F*
14: 9 who has seen me has seen the *F*.
Ro 4:11 he is the *f* of all who believe
2Co 6:18 "I will be a *F* to you,
Eph 6: 2 "Honor your *f* and mother"—
Heb 12: 7 what son is not disciplined by his *f*?

FATHER'S (FATHER)

Pr 13: 1 A wise son heeds his *f* instruction,
15: 5 A fool spurns his *f* discipline,
19:13 A foolish son is his *f* ruin,
Lk 2:49 had to be in my *F* house?"
Jn 2:16 How dare you turn my *F* house
10:29 can snatch them out of my *F* hand.
14: 2 In my *F* house are many rooms;

FATHERLESS (FATHER)

Dt 10:18 He defends the cause of the *f*
24:17 Do not deprive the alien or the *f*
24:19 Leave it for the alien, the *f*
Ps 68: 5 A father to the *f*, a defender
Pr 23:10 or encroach on the fields of the *f*,

FATHERS (FATHER)

Ex 20: 5 for the sin of the *f* to the third
Lk 11:11 "Which of you *f*, if your son asks
Eph 6: 4 *F*, do not exasperate your children;
Col 3:21 *F*, do not embitter your children,

FATHOM*

Job 11: 7 "Can you *f* the mysteries of God?
Ps 145: 3 his greatness no one can *f*.
Ecc 3:11 yet they cannot *f* what God has
Isa 40:28 and his understanding no one can *f*
1Co 13: 2 and can *f* all mysteries and all

FAULT (FAULTS)

Mt 18:15 and show him his *f*, just
Php 2:15 of God without *f* in a crooked
Jas 1: 5 generously to all without finding *f*,
Jude :24 his glorious presence without *f*

FAULTFINDERS*

Jude :16 These men are grumblers and *f*;

FAULTS (FAULT)

Ps 19:12 Forgive my hidden *f*.

FAVORITISM*
Ex 23: 3 and do not show *f* to a poor man
Lev 19:15 to the poor or *f* to the great,
Ac 10:34 true it is that God does not show *f*
Ro 2:11 For God does not show *f*.
Eph 6: 9 and there is no *f* with him.
Col 3:25 for his wrong, and there is no *f*.
1Ti 5:21 and to do nothing out of *f*.
Jas 2: 1 Lord Jesus Christ, don't show *f*.
2: 9 But if you show *f*, you sin

FEAR (AFRAID FEARS)
Dt 6:13 *F* the LORD your God, serve him
10:12 but to *f* the LORD your God,
31:12 and learn to *f* the LORD your God
Ps 19: 9 The *f* of the LORD is pure,
23: 4 I will *f* no evil,
27: 1 whom shall I *f*?
91: 5 You will not *f* the terror of night,
111: 10 *f* of the LORD is the beginning
Pr 8:13 To *f* the LORD is to hate evil;
9:10 *f* of the LORD is the beginning
10:27 The *f* of the LORD adds length
14:27 The *f* of the LORD is a fountain
15:33 *f* of the LORD teaches a man
16: 6 through the *f* of the LORD a man
19:23 The *f* of the LORD leads to life:
29:25 *F* of man will prove to be a snare,
Isa 11: 3 delight in the *f* of the LORD.
41:10 So do not *f*, for I am with you;
Lk 12: 5 I will show you whom you should *f*:
Php 2:12 to work out your salvation with *f*
1Jn 4:18 But perfect love drives out *f*,

FEARS (FEAR)
Job 1: 8 a man who *f* God and shuns evil."
Ps 34: 4 he delivered me from all my *f*.
Pr 31:30 a woman who *f* the LORD is
1Jn 4:18 The one who *f* is not made perfect

FEED
Jn 21:15 Jesus said, "*F* my lambs."
21:17 Jesus said, "*F* my sheep.
Ro 12:20 "If your enemy is hungry, *f* him;
Jude :12 shepherds who *f* only themselves.

FEET (FOOT)
Ps 8: 6 you put everything under his *f*:
22:16 have pierced my hands and my *f*.
40: 2 he set my *f* on a rock
110: 1 a footstool for your *f*."
119:105 Your word is a lamp to my *f*
Ro 10:15 "How beautiful are the *f*
1Co 12:21 And the head cannot say to the *f*,
15:25 has put all his enemies under his *f*.
Heb 12:13 "Make level paths for your *f*,"

FELLOWSHIP
2Co 6:14 what *f* can light have with darkness
13:14 and the *f* of the Holy Spirit be
Php 3:10 the *f* of sharing in his sufferings,
1Jn 1: 6 claim to have *f* with him yet walk
1: 7 we have *f* with one another,

FEMALE
Ge 1:27 male and *f* he created them.
Gal 3:28 *f*, for you are all one in Christ Jesus

FERVOR
Ro 12:11 but keep your spiritual *f*, serving

FIELD (FIELDS)
Mt 6:28 See how the lilies of the *f* grow.
13:38 *f* is the world, and the good seed
1Co 3: 9 you are God's *f*, God's building.

FIELDS (FIELD)
Lk 2: 8 were shepherds living out in the *f*
Jn 4:35 open your eyes and look at the *f*!

FIG (FIGS)
Ge 3: 7 so they sewed *f* leaves together

FIGHT (FOUGHT)
Ex 14:14 The LORD will *f* for you; you need
Dt 1:30 going before you, will *f* for you,
3:22 the LORD your God himself will *f*
Ne 4:20 Our God will *f* for us!"
Ps 35: 1 *f* against those who *f* against me.
Jn 18:36 my servants would *f*
1Co 9:26 I do not *f* like a man beating the air.
2Co 10: 4 The weapons we *f*
1Ti 1:18 them you may *f* the good *f*,
6:12 Fight the good *f* of the faith.
2Ti 4: 7 fought the good *f*, I have finished

FIGS (FIG)
Lk 6:44 People do not pick *f*

FILL (FILLED FILLS FULL FULLNESS FULLY)
Ge 1:28 and increase in number; *f* the earth
Ps 16:11 you will *f* me with joy
81:10 wide your mouth and I will *f* it.
Pr 28:19 who chases fantasies will have his *f*
Hag 2: 7 and I will *f* this house with glory,'
Jn 6:26 you ate the loaves and had your *f*.
Ac 2:28 you will *f* me with joy
Ro 15:13 the God of hope *f* you with all joy

FILLED (FILL)
Ps 72:19 may the whole earth be *f*
119: 64 The earth is *f* with your love,
Eze 43: 5 the glory of the LORD *f* the temple
Hab 2:14 For the earth will be *f*
Lk 1:15 and he will be *f* with the Holy Spirit
1:41 and Elizabeth was *f* with the Holy
Jn 12: 3 the house was *f* with the fragrance
Ac 2: 4 All of them were *f*
4: 8 Then Peter, *f* with the Holy Spirit,
9:17 and be *f* with the Holy Spirit."
13: 9 called Paul, *f* with the Holy Spirit,
Eph 5:18 Instead, be *f* with the Spirit.
Php 1:11 *f* with the fruit of righteousness

FILLS (FILL)
Nu 14:21 of the LORD *f* the whole earth,
Ps 107: 9 and *f* the hungry with good things.
Eph 1:23 fullness of him who *f* everything

FILTHY
Isa 64: 6 all our righteous acts are like *f* rags;
Col 3: 8 and *f* language from your lips.
2Pe 2: 7 by the *f* lives of lawless men

FIND (FINDS FOUND)
Nu 32:23 be sure that your sin will *f* you out.
Dt 4:29 you will *f* him if you look for him
1Sa 23:16 and helped him *f* strength in God.
Ps 36: 7 *f* refuge in the shadow
91: 4 under his wings you will *f* refuge;
Pr 14:22 those who plan what is good *f* love
31:10 A wife of noble character who can *f*
Jer 6:16 and you will *f* rest for your souls.
Mt 7: 7 seek and you will *f*; knock
11:29 and you will *f* rest for your souls.
16:25 loses his life for me will *f* it.
Lk 18: 8 will he *f* faith on the earth?"
Jn 10: 9 come in and go out, and *f* pasture.

FINDS (FIND)
Ps 62: 1 My soul *f* rest in God alone;
112: 1 who *f* great delight
119:162 like one who *f* great spoil.
Pr 18:22 He who *f* a wife *f* what is good
Mt 7: 8 he who seeks *f*; and to him who
10:39 Whoever *f* his life will lose it,
Lk 12:37 whose master *f* them watching
15: 4 go after the lost sheep until he *f* it?

FINISH (FINISHED)
Jn 4:34 him who sent me and to *f* his work.
5:36 that the Father has given me to *f*,
Ac 20:24 if only I may *f* the race
2Co 8:11 Now *f* the work, so that your eager
Jas 1: 4 Perseverance must *f* its work

FINISHED (FINISH)
Ge 2: 2 seventh day God had *f* the work he
Jn 19:30 the drink, Jesus said, "It is *f*."
2Ti 4: 7 I have *f* the race, I have kept

FIRE
Ex 13:21 in a pillar of *f* to give them light,
Lev 6:12 *f* on the altar must be kept burning;
Isa 30:27 and his tongue is a consuming *f*.
Jer 23:29 my word like *f*," declares
Mt 3:11 you with the Holy Spirit and with *f*.
5:22 will be in danger of the *f* of hell.
25:41 into the eternal *f* prepared
Mk 9:43 where the *f* never goes out.
Ac 2: 3 to be tongues of *f* that separated
1Co 3:13 It will be revealed with *f*,
1Th 5:19 Do not put out the Spirit's *f*;
Heb 12:29 for our "God is a consuming *f*."
Jas 3: 5 set on *f* by a small spark.
2Pe 3:10 the elements will be destroyed by *f*,
Jude :23 snatch others from the *f*
Rev 20:14 The lake of *f* is the second death.

FIRM
Ex 14:13 Stand *f* and you will see
2Ch 20:17 stand *f* and see the deliverance
Ps 33:11 of the LORD stand *f* forever,
37:23 he makes his steps *f*;
40: 2 and gave me a *f* place to stand.
89: 2 that your love stands *f* forever,
119: 89 it stands *f* in the heavens.
Pr 4:26 and take only ways that are *f*.
Zec 8:23 nations will take *f* hold of one Jew
Mk 13:13 he who stands *f* to the end will be
1Co 16:13 on your guard; stand *f* in the faith;
2Co 1:24 because it is by faith you stand *f*.
Eph 6:14 Stand *f* then, with the belt
Col 4:12 that you may stand *f* in all the will
2Th 2:15 stand *f* and hold to the teachings
2Ti 2:19 God's solid foundation stands *f*,
Heb 6:19 an anchor for the soul, *f* and secure
1Pe 5: 9 Resist him, standing *f* in the faith,

FIRST
Isa 44: 6 I am the *f* and I am the last;
48:12 I am the *f* and I am the last.
Mt 5:24 *F* go and be reconciled
6:33 But seek *f* his kingdom
7: 5 *f* take the plank out
20:27 wants to be *f* must be your slave—
22:38 This is the *f* and greatest
23:26 *F* clean the inside of the cup
Mk 13:10 And the gospel must *f* be preached
Ac 11:26 disciples were called Christians *f*
Ro 1:16 *f* for the Jew, then for the Gentile.
1Co 12:28 in the church God has appointed *f*
2Co 8: 5 they gave themselves *f* to the Lord
1Ti 2:13 For Adam was formed *f*, then Eve.
Jas 3:17 comes from heaven is *f* of all pure;

1Jn 4:19 We love because he *f* loved us.
3Jn :9 but Diotrephes, who loves to be *f*,
Rev 1:17 I am the *F* and the Last.
2:4 You have forsaken your *f* love.

FIRSTBORN (BEAR)
Ex 11:5 Every *f* son in Egypt will die,

FIRSTFRUITS
Ex 23:19 "Bring the best of the *f* of your soil

FISHERS
Mk 1:17 "and I will make you *f* of men."

FITTING*
Ps 33:1 it is *f* for the upright to praise him.
147:1 how pleasant and *f* to praise him!
Pr 10:32 of the righteous know what is *f*,
19:10 It is not *f* for a fool to live in luxury
26:1 honor is not *f* for a fool.
1Co 14:40 everything should be done in a *f*
Col 3:18 to your husbands, as is *f* in the Lord
Heb 2:10 sons to glory, it was *f* that God,

FIX
Dt 11:18 *F* these words of mine
Pr 4:25 *f* your gaze directly before you.
2Co 4:18 we *f* our eyes not on what is seen,
Heb 3:1 heavenly calling, *f* your thoughts
12:2 Let us *f* our eyes on Jesus,

FLAME (FLAMES FLAMING)
2Ti 1:6 you to fan into *f* the gift of God,

FLAMES (FLAME)
1Co 3:15 only as one escaping through the *f*.
13:3 and surrender my body to the *f*,

FLAMING (FLAME)
Eph 6:16 you can extinguish all the *f* arrows

FLASH
1Co 15:52 in a *f*, in the twinkling of an eye,

FLATTER (FLATTERING FLATTERY)
Job 32:21 nor will I *f* any man;
Jude :16 *f* others for their own advantage.

FLATTERING (FLATTER)
Ps 12:2 their *f* lips speak with deception.
12:3 May the LORD cut off all *f* lips
Pr 26:28 and a *f* mouth works ruin.

FLATTERY (FLATTER)
Ro 16:18 and *f* they deceive the minds
1Th 2:5 You know we never used *f*,

FLAWLESS*
2Sa 22:31 the word of the LORD is *f*.
Job 11:4 You say to God, 'My beliefs are *f*
Ps 12:6 And the words of the LORD are *f*,
18:30 the word of the LORD is *f*.
Pr 30:5 "Every word of God is *f*;
SS 5:2 my dove, my *f* one.

FLEE
Ps 139:7 Where can I *f* from your presence?
1Co 6:18 *F* from sexual immorality.
10:14 my dear friends, *f* from idolatry.
1Ti 6:11 But you, man of God, *f* from all this
2Ti 2:22 *F* the evil desires of youth,
Jas 4:7 Resist the devil, and he will *f*

FLEETING
Ps 89:47 Remember how *f* is my life.
Pr 31:30 Charm is deceptive, and beauty is *f*

FLESH
Ge 2:23 and *f* of my *f*;
2:24 and they will become one *f*.
Job 19:26 yet in my *f* I will see God;
Eze 11:19 of stone and give them a heart of *f*.
36:26 of stone and give you a heart of *f*.
Mk 10:8 and the two will become one *f*.'
Jn 1:14 The Word became *f* and made his
6:51 This bread is my *f*, which I will give
1Co 6:16 "The two will become one *f*."
Eph 5:31 and the two will become one *f*."
6:12 For our struggle is not against *f*

FLOCK (FLOCKS)
Isa 40:11 He tends his *f* like a shepherd:
Eze 34:2 not shepherds take care of the *f*?
Zec 11:17 who deserts the *f*!
Mt 26:31 the sheep of the *f* will be scattered.'
Ac 20:28 all the *f* of which the Holy Spirit
1Pe 5:2 Be shepherds of God's *f* that is

FLOCKS (FLOCK)
Lk 2:8 keeping watch over their *f* at night.

FLOG
Ac 22:25 to *f* a Roman citizen who hasn't

FLOODGATES
Mal 3:10 see if I will not throw open the *f*

FLOURISHING
Ps 52:8 *f* in the house of God;

FLOW (FLOWING)
Nu 13:27 and it does *f* with milk and honey!
Jn 7:38 streams of living water will *f*

FLOWERS
Isa 40:7 The grass withers and the *f* fall,

FLOWING (FLOW)
Ex 3:8 a land *f* with milk and honey—

FOLDING
Pr 6:10 a little *f* of the hands to rest—

FOLLOW (FOLLOWING FOLLOWS)
Ex 23:2 Do not *f* the crowd in doing wrong.
Lev 18:4 and be careful to *f* my decrees.
Dt 5:1 Learn them and be sure to *f* them.
Ps 23:6 Surely goodness and love will *f* me
Mt 16:24 and take up his cross and *f* me.
Jn 10:4 his sheep *f* him because they know
1Co 14:1 *F* the way of love and eagerly
Rev 14:4 They *f* the Lamb wherever he goes.

FOLLOWING (FOLLOW)
1Ti 1:18 by *f* them you may fight the good

FOLLOWS (FOLLOW)
Jn 8:12 Whoever *f* me will never walk

FOOD (FOODS)
Pr 20:13 you will have *f* to spare.
22:9 for he shares his *f* with the poor.
25:21 If your enemy is hungry, give him *f*
31:15 she provides *f* for her family
Da 1:8 to defile himself with the royal *f*
Jn 6:27 Do not work for *f* that spoils,
Ro 14:14 fully convinced that no *f* is unclean
1Co 8:8 But *f* does not bring us near to God
1Ti 6:8 But if we have *f* and clothing,
Jas 2:15 sister is without clothes and daily *f*.

FOODS (FOOD)
Mk 7:19 Jesus declared all *f* "clean.")

FOOL (FOOLISH FOOLISHNESS FOOLS)
Ps 14:1 The *f* says in his heart,
Pr 15:5 A *f* spurns his father's discipline,
17:28 Even a *f* is thought wise
18:2 A *f* finds no pleasure
26:5 Answer a *f* according to his folly,
28:26 He who trusts in himself is a *f*,
Mt 5:22 But anyone who says, 'You *f*!'

FOOLISH (FOOL)
Pr 10:1 but a *f* son grief to his mother.
17:25 A *f* son brings grief to his father
Mt 7:26 practice is like a *f* man who built
25:2 of them were *f* and five were wise.
1Co 1:27 God chose the *f* things of the world

FOOLISHNESS (FOOL)
1Co 1:18 of the cross is *f* to those who are
1:25 For the *f* of God is wiser
2:14 for they are *f* to him, and he cannot
3:19 of this world is *f* in God's sight.

FOOLS (FOOL)
Pr 14:9 *F* mock at making amends for sin,
1Co 4:10 We are *f* for Christ, but you are

FOOT (FEET FOOTHOLD)
Jos 1:3 every place where you set your *f*,
Isa 1:6 From the sole of your *f* to the top
1Co 12:15 If the *f* should say, "Because I am

FOOTHOLD (FOOT)
Eph 4:27 and do not give the devil a *f*.

FORBEARANCE*
Ro 3:25 because in his *f* he had left the sins

FORBID
1Co 14:39 and do not *f* speaking in tongues.

FOREFATHERS (FATHER)
Heb 1:1 spoke to our *f* through the prophets

FOREKNEW* (KNOW)
Ro 8:29 For those God *f* he
11:2 not reject his people, whom he *f*.

FOREVER (EVER)
1Ch 16:15 He remembers his covenant *f*,
16:34 his love endures *f*.
Ps 9:7 The LORD reigns *f*;
23:6 dwell in the house of the LORD *f*.
33:11 the plans of the LORD stand firm *f*
86:12 I will glorify your name *f*.
92:8 But you, O LORD, are exalted *f*.
110:4 "You are a priest *f*,
119:111 Your statutes are my heritage *f*;
Jn 6:51 eats of this bread, he will live *f*.
14:16 Counselor to be with you *f*—
1Co 9:25 it to get a crown that will last *f*.
1Th 4:17 And so we will be with the Lord *f*.
Heb 13:8 same yesterday and today and *f*.
1Pe 1:25 but the word of the Lord stands *f*."
1Jn 2:17 who does the will of God lives *f*.

FORFEIT
Lk 9:25 and yet lose or *f* his very self?

FORGAVE (FORGIVE)
Ps 32:5 and you *f*
Eph 4:32 just as in Christ God *f* you.
Col 2:13 He *f* us all our sins, having
3:13 Forgive as the Lord *f* you.

FORGET (FORGETS FORGETTING)
Dt 6:12 that you do not f the LORD,
Ps 103: 2 and f not all his benefits.
137: 5 may my right hand f ⌊its skill⌋.
Isa 49:15 "Can a mother f the baby
Heb 6:10 he will not f your work

FORGETS (FORGET)
Jn 16:21 her baby is born she f the anguish
Jas 1:24 immediately f what he looks like.

FORGETTING (FORGET)
Php 3:13 F what is behind and straining

FORGIVE (FORGAVE FORGIVENESS FORGIVING)
2Ch 7:14 will f their sin and will heal their
Ps 19:12 F my hidden faults.
Mt 6:12 F us our debts,
6:14 For if you f men when they sin
18:21 many times shall I f my brother
Mk 11:25 in heaven may f you your sins."
Lk 11: 4 F us our sins,
23:34 Jesus said, "Father, f them,
Col 3:13 F as the Lord forgave you.
1Jn 1: 9 and just and will f us our sins

FORGIVENESS (FORGIVE)
Ps 130: 4 But with you there is f;
Ac 10:43 believes in him receives f of sins
Eph 1: 7 through his blood, the f of sins,
Col 1:14 in whom we have redemption, the f
Heb 9:22 the shedding of blood there is no f.

FORGIVING (FORGIVE)
Ne 9:17 But you are a f God, gracious
Eph 4:32 to one another, f each other,

FORMED
Ge 2: 7 And the LORD God f man
Ps 103: 14 for he knows how we are f,
Isa 45:18 but f it to be inhabited—
Ro 9:20 "Shall what is f say to him who f it,
1Ti 2:13 For Adam was f first, then Eve.
Heb 11: 3 understand that the universe was f

FORSAKE (FORSAKEN)
Jos 1: 5 I will never leave you nor f you.
24:16 "Far be it from us to f the LORD
2Ch 15: 2 but if you f him, he will f you.
Ps 27:10 Though my father and mother f me
Isa 55: 7 Let the wicked f his way
Heb 13: 5 never will I f you."

FORSAKEN (FORSAKE)
Ps 22: 1 my God, why have you f me?
37:25 I have never seen the righteous f
Mt 27:46 my God, why have you f me?"
Rev 2: 4 You have f your first love.

FORTRESS
Ps 18: 2 The LORD is my rock, my f
71: 3 for you are my rock and my f.

FOUGHT (FIGHT)
2Ti 4: 7 I have f the good fight, I have

FOUND (FIND)
1Ch 28: 9 If you seek him, he will be f by you;
Isa 55: 6 Seek the LORD while he may be f;
Da 5:27 on the scales and f wanting.
Lk 15: 6 with me; I have f my lost sheep.'
15: 9 with me; I have f my lost coin.'
Ac 4:12 Salvation is f in no one else,

FOUNDATION
Isa 28:16 a precious cornerstone for a sure f;
1Co 3:11 For no one can lay any f other
Eph 2:20 built on the f of the apostles
2Ti 2:19 God's solid f stands firm,

FOXES
Mt 8:20 "F have holes and birds

FRAGRANCE
2Co 2:16 of death; to the other, the f of life.

FREE (FREED FREEDOM FREELY)
Ps 146: 7 The LORD sets prisoners f,
Jn 8:32 and the truth will set you f."
Ro 6:18 You have been set f from sin
Gal 3:28 slave nor f, male nor female,
1Pe 2:16 f men, but do not use your freedom

FREED (FREE)
Rev 1: 5 has f us from our sins by his blood,

FREEDOM (FREE)
Ro 8:21 into the glorious f of the children
2Co 3:17 the Spirit of the Lord is, there is f.
Gal 5:13 But do not use your f to indulge
1Pe 2:16 but do not use your f as a cover-up

FREELY (FREE)
Isa 55: 7 and to our God, for he will f pardon
Mt 10: 8 Freely you have received, f give.
Ro 3:24 and are justified f by his grace
Eph 1: 6 which he has f given us

FRIEND (FRIENDS)
Ex 33:11 as a man speaks with his f.
Pr 17:17 A f loves at all times,
18:24 there is a f who sticks closer
27: 6 Wounds from a f can be trusted,
27:10 Do not forsake your f and the f
Jas 4: 4 Anyone who chooses to be a f

FRIENDS (FRIEND)
Pr 16:28 and a gossip separates close f.
Zec 13: 6 given at the house of my f.'
Jn 15:13 that he lay down his life for his f.

FRUIT (FRUITFUL)
Ps 1: 3 which yields its f in season
Pr 11:30 The f of the righteous is a tree
Mt 7:16 By their f you will recognize them.
Jn 15: 2 branch in me that bears no f,
Gal 5:22 But the f of the Spirit is love, joy,
Rev 22: 2 of f, yielding its f every month.

FRUITFUL (FRUIT)
Ge 1:22 "Be f and increase in number
Ps 128: 3 Your wife will be like a f vine
Jn 15: 2 prunes so that it will be even more f.

FULFILL (FULFILLED FULFILLMENT)
Ps 116: 14 I will f my vows to the LORD
Mt 5:17 come to abolish them but to f them.
1Co 7: 3 husband should f his marital duty

FULFILLED (FULFILL)
Pr 13:19 A longing f is sweet to the soul,
Mk 14:49 But the Scriptures must be f."
Ro 13: 8 loves his fellowman has f the law.

FULFILLMENT (FULFILL)
Ro 13:10 Therefore love is the f of the law.

FULL (FILL)
Ps 127: 5 whose quiver is f of them.
Pr 31:11 Her husband has f confidence
Isa 6: 3 the whole earth is f of his glory."
11: 9 for the earth will be f
Jn 10:10 may have life, and have it to the f.
Ac 6: 3 known to be f of the Spirit

FULLNESS (FILL)
Col 1:19 to have all his f dwell in him,
2: 9 in Christ all the f of the Deity lives

FULLY (FILL)
1Ki 8:61 your hearts must be f committed
2Ch 16: 9 whose hearts are f committed
Ps 119: 4 that are to be f obeyed.
119:138 they are f trustworthy.
1Co 15:58 Always give yourselves f

FUTURE
Ps 37:37 there is a f for the man of peace.
Pr 23:18 There is surely a f hope for you,
Ro 8:38 neither the present nor the f,

GABRIEL*
Angel who interpreted Daniel's visions (Da 8:16-26; 9:20-27); announced births of John (Lk 1:11-20), Jesus (Lk 1:26-38).

GAIN (GAINED)
Ps 60:12 With God we will g the victory,
Mk 8:36 it for a man to g the whole world,
1Co 13: 3 but have not love, I g nothing.
Php 1:21 to live is Christ and to die is g.
3: 8 that I may g Christ and be found
1Ti 6: 6 with contentment is great g.

GAINED (GAIN)
Ro 5: 2 through whom we have g access

GALILEE
Isa 9: 1 but in the future he will honor G

GALL
Mt 27:34 mixed with g; but after tasting it,

GAP
Eze 22:30 stand before me in the g on behalf

GARDENER
Jn 15: 1 true vine, and my Father is the g.

GARMENT (GARMENTS)
Ps 102: 26 they will all wear out like a g.
Mt 9:16 of unshrunk cloth on an old g,
Jn 19:23 This g was seamless, woven

GARMENTS (GARMENT)
Ge 3:21 The LORD God made g of skin
Isa 61:10 me with g of salvation
63: 1 with his g stained crimson?
Jn 19:24 "They divided my g among them

GATE (GATES)
Mt 7:13 For wide is the g and broad is
Jn 10: 9 I am the g; whoever enters

GATES (GATE)
Ps 100: 4 Enter his g with thanksgiving
Mt 16:18 the g of Hades will not overcome it

GATHER (GATHERS)
Zec 14: 2 I will g all the nations to Jerusalem
Mt 12:30 he who does not g with me scatters
23:37 longed to g your children together,

GATHERS (GATHER)
Isa 40:11 He g the lambs in his arms
Mt 23:37 a hen g her chicks under her wings,

GAVE (GIVE)
Ezr 2:69 According to their ability they g
Job 1:21 LORD g and the LORD has taken
Jn 3:16 so loved the world that he g his one
2Co 8: 5 they g themselves first to the Lord
Gal 2:20 who loved me and g himself for me

1Ti 2: 6 who *g* himself as a ransom

GAZE

Ps 27: 4 to *g* upon the beauty of the LORD
Pr 4: 25 fix your *g* directly before you.

GENEALOGIES

1Ti 1: 4 themselves to myths and endless *g.*

GENERATIONS

Ps 22: 30 future *g* will be told about the Lord
102: 12 your renown endures through all *g.*
145: 13 dominion endures through all *g.*
Lk 1: 48 now on all *g* will call me blessed,
Eph 3: 5 not made known to men in other *g*

GENEROUS

Ps 112: 5 Good will come to him who is *g*
Pr 22: 9 A *g* man will himself be blessed,
2Co 9: 5 Then it will be ready as a *g* gift,
1Ti 6: 18 and to be *g* and willing to share.

GENTILE (GENTILES)

Ro 1: 16 first for the Jew, then for the *G.*
10: 12 difference between Jew and *G*—

GENTILES (GENTILE)

Isa 42: 6 and a light for the *G,*
Ro 3: 9 and *G* alike are all under sin.
11: 13 as I am the apostle to the *G,*
1Co 1: 23 block to Jews and foolishness to *G,*

GENTLE (GENTLENESS)

Pr 15: 1 A *g* answer turns away wrath,
Zec 9: 9 *g* and riding on a donkey,
Mt 11: 29 for I am *g* and humble in heart,
21: 5 *g* and riding on a donkey,
1Co 4: 21 or in love and with a *g* spirit?
1Pe 3: 4 the unfading beauty of a *g*

GENTLENESS* (GENTLE)

2Co 10: 1 By the meekness and *g* of Christ,
Gal 5: 23 faithfulness, *g* and self-control.
Php 4: 5 Let your *g* be evident to all.
Col 3: 12 kindness, humility, *g* and patience.
1Ti 6: 11 faith, love, endurance and *g.*
1Pe 3: 15 But do this with *g* and respect,

GETHSEMANE

Mt 26: 36 disciples to a place called *G,*

GIDEON*

Judge, also called Jerub-Baal; freed Israel from Midianites (Jdg 6-8; Heb 11:32). Given sign of fleece (Jdg 8:36-40).

GIFT (GIFTS)

Pr 21: 14 A *g* given in secret soothes anger,
Mt 5: 23 if you are offering your *g*
Ac 2: 38 And you will receive the *g*
Ro 6: 23 but the *g* of God is eternal life
1Co 7: 7 each man has his own *g* from God;
2Co 8: 12 the *g* is acceptable according
9: 15 be to God for his indescribable *g!*
Eph 2: 8 it is the *g* of God—not by works,
1Ti 4: 14 not neglect your *g,* which was
2Ti 1: 6 you to fan into flame the *g* of God,
Jas 1: 17 and perfect *g* is from above,
1Pe 4: 10 should use whatever *g* he has

GIFTS (GIFT)

Ro 11: 29 for God's *g* and his call are
12: 6 We have different *g,* according
1Co 12: 4 There are different kinds of *g,*
12: 31 But eagerly desire the greater *g.*
14: 1 and eagerly desire spiritual *g,*
14: 12 excel in *g* that build up the church.

GILEAD

Jer 8: 22 Is there no balm in *G?*

GIVE (GAVE GIVEN GIVER GIVES GIVING)

Nu 6: 26 and *g* you peace." '
1Sa 1: 11 then I will *g* him to the LORD
2Ch 15: 7 be strong and do not *g* up,
Pr 21: 26 but the righteous *g* without sparing
23: 26 My son, *g* me your heart
30: 8 but *g* me only my daily bread.
31: 31 *G* her the reward she has earned,
Isa 42: 8 I will not *g* my glory to another
Eze 36: 26 I will *g* you a new heart
Mt 6: 11 *G* us today our daily bread.
10: 8 Freely you have received, freely *g.*
22: 21 "*G* to Caesar what is Caesar's,
Mk 8: 37 Or what can a man *g* in exchange
Lk 6: 38 *G,* and it will be given to you.
11: 13 Father in heaven *g* the Holy Spirit
Jn 10: 28 I *g* them eternal life, and they shall
13: 34 "A new commandment I *g* you:
Ac 20: 35 blessed to *g* than to receive.' "
Ro 12: 8 let him *g* generously;
13: 7 *G* everyone what you owe him:
14: 12 each of us will *g* an account
2Co 9: 7 Each man should *g* what he has
Rev 14: 7 "Fear God and *g* him glory,

GIVEN (GIVE)

Nu 8: 16 are to be *g* wholly to me.
Ps 115: 16 but the earth he has *g* to man.
Isa 9: 6 to us a son is *g,*
Mt 6: 33 and all these things will be *g* to you
7: 7 "Ask and it will be *g* to you;
Lk 22: 19 saying, "This is my body *g* for you;
Jn 3: 27 man can receive only what is *g* him
Ro 5: 5 the Holy Spirit, whom he has *g* us.
1Co 4: 2 those who have been *g* a trust must
12: 13 we were all *g* the one Spirit to drink
Eph 4: 7 to each one of us grace has been *g*

GIVER* (GIVE)

Pr 18: 16 A gift opens the way for the *g*
2Co 9: 7 for God loves a cheerful *g.*

GIVES (GIVE)

Ps 119: 130 The unfolding of your words *g* light;
Pr 14: 30 A heart at peace *g* life to the body,
15: 30 good news *g* health to the bones.
28: 27 He who *g* to the poor will lack
Isa 40: 29 He *g* strength to the weary
Mt 10: 42 if anyone *g* even a cup of cold water
Jn 6: 63 The Spirit *g* life; the flesh counts
1Co 15: 57 He *g* us the victory
2Co 3: 6 the letter kills, but the Spirit *g* life.

GIVING (GIVE)

Ne 8: 8 *g* the meaning so that the people
Ps 19: 8 *g* joy to the heart.
Mt 6: 4 so that your *g* may be in secret.
2Co 8: 7 also excel in this grace of *g.*

GLAD (GLADNESS)

Ps 31: 7 I will be *g* and rejoice in your love,
46: 4 whose streams make *g* the city
97: 1 LORD reigns, let the earth be *g;*
118: 24 let us rejoice and be *g* in it.
Pr 23: 25 May your father and mother be *g;*
Zec 2: 10 and be *g,* O Daughter of Zion.
Mt 5: 12 be *g,* because great is your reward

GLADNESS (GLAD)

Ps 45: 15 They are led in with joy and *g;*
51: 8 Let me hear joy and *g;*
100: 2 Serve the LORD with *g;*
Jer 31: 13 I will turn their mourning into *g;*

GLORIFIED (GLORY)

Jn 13: 31 Son of Man *g* and God is *g* in him.
Ro 8: 30 those he justified, he also *g.*
2Th 1: 10 comes to be *g* in his holy people

GLORIFY (GLORY)

Ps 34: 3 *G* the LORD with me;
86: 12 I will *g* your name forever.
Jn 13: 32 God will *g* the Son in himself,
17: 1 *G* your Son, that your Son may

GLORIOUS (GLORY)

Ps 45: 13 All *g* is the princess
111: 3 *G* and majestic are his deeds,
145: 5 of the *g* splendor of your majesty,
Isa 4: 2 the LORD will be beautiful and *g,*
12: 5 for he has done *g* things;
42: 21 to make his law great and *g.*
63: 15 from your lofty throne, holy and *g.*
Mt 19: 28 the Son of Man sits on his *g* throne,
Lk 9: 31 appeared in *g* splendor, talking
Ac 2: 20 of the great and *g* day of the Lord.
2Co 3: 8 of the Spirit be even more *g?*
Php 3: 21 so that they will be like his *g* body.
4: 19 to his *g* riches in Christ Jesus.
Tit 2: 13 the *g* appearing of our great God
Jude : 24 before his *g* presence without fault

GLORY (GLORIFIED GLORIFY GLORIOUS)

Ex 15: 11 awesome in *g,*
33: 18 Moses said, "Now show me your *g.*"
1Sa 4: 21 "The *g* has departed from Israel"—
1Ch 16: 24 Declare his *g* among the nations,
16: 28 ascribe to the LORD *g*
29: 11 and the *g* and the majesty
Ps 8: 5 and crowned him with *g* and honor
19: 1 The heavens declare the *g* of God;
24: 7 that the King of *g* may come in.
29: 1 ascribe to the LORD *g*
72: 19 the whole earth be filled with his *g.*
96: 3 Declare his *g* among the nations,
Pr 19: 11 it is to his *g* to overlook an offense.
25: 2 It is the *g* of God to conceal
Isa 6: 3 the whole earth is full of his *g.*"
48: 11 I will not yield my *g* to another.
Eze 43: 2 and the land was radiant with his *g.*
Mt 24: 30 of the sky, with power and great *g.*
25: 31 the Son of Man comes in his *g,*
Mk 8: 38 in his Father's *g* with the holy
13: 26 in clouds with great power and *g.*
Lk 2: 9 and the *g* of the Lord shone
2: 14 saying, "*G* to God in the highest,
Jn 1: 14 We have seen his *g,* the *g* of the One
17: 5 presence with the *g* I had with you
17: 24 to see my *g,* the *g* you have given
Ac 7: 2 The God of *g* appeared
Ro 1: 23 exchanged the *g* of the immortal
3: 23 and fall short of the *g* of God,
8: 18 with the *g* that will be revealed
9: 4 theirs the divine *g,* the covenants,
1Co 10: 31 whatever you do, do it all for the *g*
11: 7 but the woman is the *g* of man.

1Co 15:43 it is raised in g; it is sown
2Co 3:10 comparison with the surpassing g.
3:18 faces all reflect the Lord's g,
4:17 us an eternal g that far outweighs
Col 1:27 Christ in you, the hope of g.
3:4 also will appear with him in g.
1Ti 3:16 was taken up in g.
Heb 1:3 The Son is the radiance of God's g
2:7 you crowned him with g and honor
1Pe 1:24 and all their g is like the flowers
Rev 4:11 to receive g and honor and power,
21:23 for the g of God gives it light,

GLUTTONS

Tit 1:12 always liars, evil brutes, lazy g."

GNASHING

Mt 8:12 where there will be weeping and g

GNAT*

Mt 23:24 You strain out a g but swallow

GOAL

2Co 5:9 So we make it our g to please him,
Gal 3:3 to attain your g by human effort?
Php 3:14 on toward the g to win the prize

GOAT (GOATS SCAPEGOAT)

Isa 11:6 the leopard will lie down with the g

GOATS (GOAT)

Nu 7:17 five male g and five male lambs

GOD (GOD'S GODLINESS GODLY GODS)

Ge 1:1 In the beginning G created
1:2 and the Spirit of G was hovering
1:26 Then G said, "Let us make man
1:27 So G created man in his own image
1:31 G saw all that he had made,
2:3 And G blessed the seventh day
2:22 Then the LORD G made a woman
3:21 The LORD G made garments
3:23 So the LORD G banished him
5:22 Enoch walked with G 300 years
6:2 sons of G saw that the daughters
9:16 everlasting covenant between G
17:1 "I am G Almighty; walk before me
21:33 name of the LORD, the Eternal G.
22:8 "G himself will provide the lamb
28:12 and the angels of G were ascending
32:28 because you have struggled with G
32:30 "It is because I saw G face to face,
35:10 G said to him, "Your name is Jacob
41:51 G has made me forget all my
50:20 but G intended it for good
Ex 2:24 G heard their groaning
3:6 because he was afraid to look at G.
6:7 own people, and I will be your G.
8:10 is no one like the LORD our G.
13:18 So G led the people
15:2 He is my G, and I will praise him,
17:9 with the staff of G in my hands."
19:3 Then Moses went up to G,
20:2 the LORD your G, who brought
20:5 the LORD your G, am a jealous G,
20:19 But do not have G speak to us
22:28 "Do not blaspheme G
31:18 inscribed by the finger of G.
34:6 the compassionate and gracious G,
34:14 name is Jealous, is a jealous G.
Lev 18:21 not profane the name of your G.
Lev 19:2 the LORD your G, am holy.
26:12 walk among you and be your G,
Nu 22:38 I must speak only what G puts
23:19 G is not a man, that he should lie,
Dt 1:17 for judgment belongs to G.
3:22 LORD your G himself will fight
3:24 For what g is there in heaven
4:24 is a consuming fire, a jealous G.
4:31 the LORD your G is a merciful G;
4:39 heart this day that the LORD is G
5:11 the name of the LORD your G,
5:14 a Sabbath to the LORD your G.
5:26 of the living G speaking out of fire,
6:4 LORD our G, the LORD is one.
6:5 Love the LORD your G
6:13 the LORD your G, serve him only
6:16 Do not test the LORD your G
7:9 your G is G; he is the faithful G,
7:12 the LORD your G will keep his
7:21 is a great and awesome G.
8:5 the LORD your G disciplines you.
10:12 but to fear the LORD your G,
10:14 the LORD your G belong
10:17 For the LORD your G is G of gods
11:13 to love the LORD your G
13:3 The LORD your G is testing you
13:4 the LORD your G you must
15:6 the LORD your G will bless you
19:9 to love the LORD your G
25:16 the LORD your G detests anyone
29:29 belong to the LORD our G,
30:2 return to the LORD your G
30:16 today to love the LORD your G,
30:20 you may love the LORD your G,
31:6 for the LORD your G goes
32:3 Oh, praise the greatness of our G!
32:4 A faithful G who does no wrong,
33:27 The eternal G is your refuge,
Jos 1:9 for the LORD your G will be
14:8 the LORD my G wholeheartedly.
22:5 to love the LORD your G,
22:34 Between Us that the LORD is G.
23:11 careful to love the LORD your G.
23:14 the LORD your G gave you has
Jdg 16:28 O G, please strengthen me just
Ru 1:16 be my people and your G my G.
1Sa 2:2 there is no Rock like our G.
2:3 for the LORD is a G who knows,
2:25 another man, G may mediate
10:26 men whose hearts G had touched.
12:12 the LORD your G was your king.
17:26 defy the armies of the living G?"
17:46 world will know that there is a G
30:6 strength in the LORD his G.
2Sa 14:14 But G does not take away life;
22:3 my G is my rock, in whom I take
22:31 "As for G, his way is perfect;
1Ki 4:29 G gave Solomon wisdom
8:23 there is no G like you in heaven
8:27 "But will G really dwell on earth?
8:61 committed to the LORD our G,
18:21 If the LORD is G, follow him;
18:37 are G, and that you are turning
20:28 a g of the hills and not a g
2Ki 19:15 G of Israel, enthroned
1Ch 16:35 Cry out, "Save us, O G our Savior;
28:2 for the footstool of our G,
28:9 acknowledge the G of your father,
29:10 G of our father Israel,
29:17 my G, that you test the heart
2Ch 2:4 for the Name of the LORD my G
5:14 of the LORD filled the temple of G
6:18 "But will G really dwell on earth
18:13 I can tell him only what my G says
20:6 are you not the G who is in heaven?
25:8 for G has the power to help
30:9 for the LORD your G is gracious
33:12 the favor of the LORD his G
Ezr 8:22 "The good hand of our G is
Ezr 9:6 "O my G, I am too ashamed
9:13 our G, you have punished us less
Ne 1:5 the great and awesome G,
8:8 from the Book of the Law of G,
9:17 But you are a forgiving G,
9:32 the great, mighty and awesome G,
Job 1:1 he feared G and shunned evil.
2:10 Shall we accept good from G,
4:17 a mortal be more righteous than G?
5:17 is the man whom G corrects;
11:7 Can you fathom the mysteries of G
19:26 yet in my flesh I will see G;
22:13 Yet you say, 'What does G know?
25:4 can a man be righteous before G?
33:14 For G does speak—now one way,
34:12 is unthinkable that G would do
36:26 is G—beyond our understanding!
37:22 G comes in awesome majesty.
Ps 18:2 my G is my rock, in whom I take
18:28 my G turns my darkness into light.
19:1 The heavens declare the glory of G;
22:1 G, my G, why have you forsaken
29:3 the G of glory thunders,
31:14 I say, "You are my G."
40:3 a hymn of praise to our G.
40:8 I desire to do your will, O my G;
42:2 thirsts for G, for the living G.
42:11 Put your hope in G,
45:6 O G, will last for ever and ever;
46:1 G is our refuge and strength,
46:10 "Be still, and know that I am G;
47:7 For G is the King of all the earth;
50:3 Our G comes and will not be silent;
51:1 Have mercy on me, O G,
51:10 Create in me a pure heart, O G,
51:17 O G, you will not despise.
62:7 my honor depend on G;
65:5 O G our Savior,
66:1 Shout with joy to G, all the earth!
66:16 listen, all you who fear G;
68:6 G sets the lonely in families,
71:17 my youth, O G, you have taught
71:19 reaches to the skies, O G,
71:22 harp for your faithfulness, O my G;
73:26 but G is the strength of my heart
77:13 What g is so great as our God?
78:19 Can G spread a table in the desert?
81:1 Sing for joy to G our strength;
84:2 out for the living G.
84:10 a doorkeeper in the house of my G
86:12 O Lord my G, with all my heart;
89:7 of the holy ones G is greatly feared;
90:2 to everlasting you are G.
91:2 my G, in whom I trust."
95:7 for he is our G
100:3 Know that the LORD is G.
108:1 My heart is steadfast, O G;
113:5 Who is like the LORD our G,
139:23 Search me, O G, and know my
Pr 3:4 in the sight of G and man.
25:2 of G to conceal a matter;
30:5 "Every word of G is flawless;
Ecc 3:11 cannot fathom what G has done
11:5 cannot understand the work of G,
12:13 Fear G and keep his
Isa 9:6 Wonderful Counselor, Mighty G,
37:16 you alone are G over all
40:3 a highway for our G.
40:8 the word of our G stands forever."
40:28 The LORD is the everlasting G,
41:10 not be dismayed, for I am your G.
44:6 apart from me there is no G.
52:7 "Your G reigns!"

Isa 55: 7 to our *G*, for he will freely pardon.
57: 21 says my *G*, "for the wicked."
59: 2 you from your *G*;
61: 10 my soul rejoices in my *G*.
62: 5 so will your *G* rejoice over you.
Jer 23: 23 "Am I only a *G* nearby,"
31: 33 I will be their *G*,
32: 27 "I am the LORD, the *G*
Eze 28: 13 the garden of *G*;
Da 3: 17 the *G* we serve is able to save us
9: 4 O Lord, the great and awesome *G*,
Hos 12: 6 and wait for your *G* always.
Joel 2: 13 Return to the LORD your *G*,
Am 4: 12 prepare to meet your *G*, O Israel."
Mic 6: 8 and to walk humbly with your *G*.
Na 1: 2 LORD is a jealous and avenging *G*;
Zec 14: 5 Then the LORD my *G* will come,
Mal 3: 8 Will a man rob *G*? Yet you rob me.
Mt 1: 23 which means, "*G* with us."
5: 8 for they will see *G*.
6: 24 You cannot serve both *G*
19: 6 Therefore what *G* has joined
19: 26 but with *G* all things are possible."
22: 21 and to *G* what is God's."
22: 37 " 'Love the Lord your *G*
27: 46 which means, "My *G*, my *G*,
Mk 12: 29 the Lord our *G*, the Lord is one.
16: 19 and he sat at the right hand of *G*.
Lk 1: 37 For nothing is impossible with *G*."
1: 47 my spirit rejoices in *G* my Savior,
10: 9 'The kingdom of *G* is near you.'
10: 27 " 'Love the Lord your *G*
18: 19 "No one is good—except *G* alone.
Jn 1: 1 was with *G*, and the Word was *G*.
1: 18 seen *G*, but *G* the One and Only,
3: 16 "For *G* so loved the world that he
4: 24 *G* is spirit, and his worshipers must
14: 1 Trust in *G*; trust also in me.
20: 28 "My Lord and my *G*!"
Ac 2: 24 But *G* raised him from the dead,
5: 4 You have not lied to men but to *G*
5: 29 "We must obey *G* rather than men!
7: 55 to heaven and saw the glory of *G*,
17: 23 TO AN UNKNOWN *G*.
20: 27 to you the whole will of *G*.
20: 32 "Now I commit you to *G*
Ro 1: 17 a righteousness from *G* is revealed,
2: 11 For *G* does not show favoritism.
3: 4 Let *G* be true, and every man a liar.
3: 23 and fall short of the glory of *G*,
4: 24 to whom *G* will credit
5: 8 *G* demonstrates his own love for us
6: 23 but the gift of *G* is eternal life
8: 28 in all things *G* works for the good
11: 22 the kindness and sternness of *G*:
14: 12 give an account of himself to *G*.
1Co 1: 20 Has not *G* made foolish
2: 9 what *G* has prepared
3: 6 watered it, but *G* made it grow.
6: 20 Therefore honor *G* with your body.
7: 24 each man, as responsible to *G*,
8: 8 food does not bring us near to *G*;
10: 13 *G* is faithful; he will not let you be
10: 31 do it all for the glory of *G*.
14: 33 For *G* is not a *G* of disorder
15: 28 so that *G* may be all in all.
2Co 1: 9 rely on ourselves but on *G*,
2: 14 be to *G*, who always leads us
3: 5 but our competence comes from *G*.
4: 7 this all-surpassing power is from *G*
5: 19 that *G* was reconciling the world
5: 21 *G* made him who had no sin
6: 16 we are the temple of the living *G*.
9: 7 for *G* loves a cheerful giver.
9: 8 *G* is able to make all grace abound
Gal 2: 6 *G* does not judge by external
6: 7 not be deceived: *G* cannot be
Eph 2: 10 which *G* prepared in advance for us
4: 6 one baptism; one *G* and Father
5: 1 Be imitators of *G*, therefore,
Php 2: 6 Who, being in very nature *G*,
4: 19 And my *G* will meet all your needs
1Th 2: 4 trying to please men but *G*,
4: 7 For *G* did not call us to be impure,
4: 9 taught by *G* to love each other.
5: 9 For *G* did not appoint us
1Ti 2: 5 one mediator between *G* and men,
4: 4 For everything *G* created is good,
5: 4 for this is pleasing to *G*.
Tit 2: 13 glorious appearing of our great *G*
Heb 1: 1 In the past *G* spoke
4: 12 For the word of *G* is living
6: 10 *G* is not unjust; he will not forget
10: 31 to fall into the hands of the living *G*
11: 6 faith it is impossible to please *G*,
12: 10 but *G* disciplines us for our good,
12: 29 for our "*G* is a consuming fire."
13: 15 offer to *G* a sacrifice of praise—
Jas 1: 13 For *G* cannot be tempted by evil,
2: 19 You believe that there is one *G*.
2: 23 "Abraham believed *G*,
4: 4 the world becomes an enemy of *G*.
4: 8 Come near to *G* and he will come
1Pe 4: 11 it with the strength *G* provides,
2Pe 1: 21 but men spoke from *G*
1Jn 1: 5 *G* is light; in him there is no
3: 20 For *G* is greater than our hearts,
4: 7 for love comes from *G*.
4: 9 This is how *G* showed his love
4: 11 Dear friends, since *G* so loved us,
4: 12 No one has ever seen *G*;
4: 16 *G* is love.
Rev 4: 8 holy is the Lord *G* Almighty,
7: 17 *G* will wipe away every tear
19: 6 For our Lord *G* Almighty reigns.

GOD-BREATHED* (BREATHED)

2Ti 3: 16 All Scripture is *G* and is useful

GOD'S (GOD)

2Ch 20: 15 For the battle is not yours, but *G*.
Job 37: 14 stop and consider *G* wonders.
Ps 52: 8 I trust in *G* unfailing love
69: 30 I will praise *G* name in song
Mk 3: 35 Whoever does *G* will is my brother
Jn 7: 17 If anyone chooses to do *G* will,
10: 36 'I am *G* Son'? Do not believe me
Ro 2: 3 think you will escape *G* judgment?
2: 4 not realizing that *G* kindness leads
3: 3 lack of faith nullify *G* faithfulness?
7: 22 in my inner being I delight in *G* law
9: 16 or effort, but on *G* mercy.
11: 29 for *G* gifts and his call are
12: 2 and approve what *G* will is—
12: 13 Share with *G* people who are
13: 6 for the authorities are *G* servants,
1Co 7: 19 Keeping *G* commands is what
2Co 6: 2 now is the time of *G* favor,
Eph 1: 7 riches of *G* grace that he lavished
1Th 4: 3 It is *G* will that you should be
5: 18 for this is *G* will for you
1Ti 6: 1 so that *G* name and our teaching
2Ti 2: 19 *G* solid foundation stands firm,
Tit 1: 7 overseer is entrusted with *G* work,
Heb 1: 3 The Son is the radiance of *G* glory
9: 24 now to appear for us in *G* presence.
11: 3 was formed at *G* command,
1Pe 2: 15 For it is *G* will that
3: 4 which is of great worth in *G* sight.
1Jn 2: 5 *G* love is truly made complete

GODLINESS (GOD)

1Ti 2: 2 and quiet lives in all *g* and holiness.
4: 8 but *g* has value for all things,
6: 6 *g* with contentment is great gain.
6: 11 and pursue righteousness, *g*, faith,

GODLY (GOD)

Ps 4: 3 that the LORD has set apart the *g*
2Co 7: 10 *G* sorrow brings repentance that
11: 2 jealous for you with a *g* jealousy.
2Ti 3: 12 everyone who wants to live a *g* life
2Pe 3: 11 You ought to live holy and *g* lives

GODS (GOD)

Ex 20: 3 "You shall have no other *g*
Ac 19: 26 He says that man-made *g* are no *g*

GOLD

Job 23: 10 tested me, I will come forth as *g*.
Ps 19: 10 They are more precious than *g*,
119: 127 more than *g*, more than pure *g*,
Pr 22: 1 esteemed is better than silver or *g*.

GOLGOTHA

Jn 19: 17 (which in Aramaic is called *G*).

GOLIATH

Philistine giant killed by David (1Sa 17; 21:9).

GOOD

Ge 1: 4 God saw that the light was *g*,
1: 31 he had made, and it was very *g*.
2: 18 "It is not *g* for the man to be alone.
50: 20 but God intended it for *g*
Job 2: 10 Shall we accept *g* from God,
Ps 14: 1 there is no one who does *g*.
34: 8 Taste and see that the LORD is *g*;
37: 3 Trust in the LORD and do *g*;
84: 11 no *g* thing does he withhold
86: 5 You are forgiving and *g*, O Lord
103: 5 satisfies your desires with *g* things,
119: 68 You are *g*, and what you do is *g*;
133: 1 How *g* and pleasant it is
147: 1 How *g* it is to sing praises
Pr 3: 4 you will win favor and a *g* name
11: 27 He who seeks *g* finds *g* will,
17: 22 A cheerful heart is *g* medicine,
18: 22 He who finds a wife finds what is *g*
22: 1 A *g* name is more desirable
31: 12 She brings him *g*, not harm,
Isa 5: 20 Woe to those who call evil *g*
52: 7 the feet of those who bring *g* news,
Jer 6: 16 ask where the *g* way is,
32: 39 the *g* of their children after them.
Mic 6: 8 has showed you, O man, what is *g*.
Mt 5: 45 sun to rise on the evil and the *g*,
7: 17 Likewise every *g* tree bears *g* fruit,
12: 35 The *g* man brings *g* things out
19: 17 "There is only One who is *g*.
25: 21 'Well done, *g* and faithful servant!
Mk 3: 4 lawful on the Sabbath: to do *g*
8: 36 What *g* is it for a man
Lk 6: 27 do *g* to those who hate you,
Jn 10: 11 "I am the *g* shepherd.
Ro 8: 28 for the *g* of those who love him,
10: 15 feet of those who bring *g* news!"

Ro 12: 9 Hate what is evil; cling to what is g.
1Co 10:24 should seek his own g, but the g
15:33 Bad company corrupts g character
2Co 9: 8 you will abound in every g work.
Gal 6: 9 us not become weary in doing g,
6:10 as we have opportunity, let us do g
Eph 2:10 in Christ Jesus to do g works,
Php 1: 6 that he who began a g work
1Th 5:21 Hold on to the g.
1Ti 3: 7 have a g reputation with outsiders,
4: 4 For everything God created is g,
6:12 Fight the g fight of the faith.
6:18 them to do g, to be rich in g deeds,
2Ti 3:17 equipped for every g work.
4: 7 I have fought the g fight, I have
Heb 12:10 but God disciplines us for our g,
1Pe 2: 3 you have tasted that the Lord is g.
2:12 Live such g lives among the pagans

GOSPEL
Ro 1:16 I am not ashamed of the g,
15:16 duty of proclaiming the g of God,
1Co 1:17 to preach the g—not with words
9:16 Woe to me if I do not preach the g!
15: 1 you of the g I preached to you,
Gal 1: 7 a different g—which is really no g
Php 1:27 in a manner worthy of the g

GOSSIP
Pr 11:13 A g betrays a confidence,
16:28 and a g separates close friends.
18: 8 of a g are like choice morsels;
26:20 without g a quarrel dies down.
2Co 12:20 slander, g, arrogance and disorder.

GRACE (GRACIOUS)
Ps 45: 2 lips have been anointed with g,
Jn 1:17 g and truth came through Jesus
Ac 20:32 to God and to the word of his g,
Ro 3:24 and are justified freely by his g
5:15 came by the g of the one man,
5:17 God's abundant provision of g
5:20 where sin increased, g increased all
6:14 you are not under law, but under g.
11: 6 if by g, then it is no longer by works
2Co 6: 1 not to receive God's g in vain.
8: 9 For you know the g
9: 8 able to make all g abound to you,
12: 9 "My g is sufficient for you,
Gal 2:21 I do not set aside the g of God,
5: 4 you have fallen away from g.
Eph 1: 7 riches of God's g that he lavished
2: 5 it is by g you have been saved.
2: 7 the incomparable riches of his g,
2: 8 For it is by g you have been saved,
Php 1: 7 all of you share in God's g with me.
Col 4: 6 conversation be always full of g,
2Th 2:16 and by his g gave us eternal
2Ti 2: 1 be strong in the g that is
Tit 2:11 For the g of God that brings
3: 7 having been justified by his g,
Heb 2: 9 that by the g of God he might taste
4:16 find g to help us in our time of need
4:16 the throne of g with confidence,
Jas 4: 6 but gives g to the humble."
2Pe 3:18 But grow in the g and knowledge

GRACIOUS (GRACE)
Nu 6:25 and be g to you;
Pr 22:11 a pure heart and whose speech is g
Isa 30:18 Yet the LORD longs to be g to you

GRAIN
1Co 9: 9 ox while it is treading out the g."

GRANTED
Php 1:29 For it has been g to you on behalf

GRASS
Ps 103:15 As for man, his days are like g,
1Pe 1:24 "All men are like g,

GRAVE (GRAVES)
Pr 7:27 Her house is a highway to the g,
Hos 13:14 Where, O g, is your destruction?

GRAVES (GRAVE)
Jn 5:28 are in their g will hear his voice
Ro 3:13 "Their throats are open g;

GREAT (GREATER GREATEST GREATNESS)
Ge 12: 2 "I will make you into a g nation
Dt 10:17 the g God, mighty and awesome,
2Sa 22:36 you stoop down to make me g.
Ps 19:11 in keeping them there is g reward.
89: 1 of the LORD's g love forever;
103: 11 so g is his love for those who fear
107: 43 consider the g love of the LORD.
108: 4 For g is your love, higher
119:165 G peace have they who love your
145: 3 G is the LORD and most worthy
Pr 23:24 of a righteous man has g joy;
Isa 42:21 to make his law g and glorious.
La 3:23 g is your faithfulness.
Mk 10:43 whoever wants to become g
Lk 21:27 in a cloud with power and g glory.
1Ti 6: 6 with contentment is g gain.
Tit 2:13 glorious appearing of our g God
Heb 2: 3 if we ignore such a g salvation?
1Jn 3: 1 How g is the love the Father has

GREATER (GREAT)
Mk 12:31 There is no commandment g
Jn 1:50 You shall see g things than that."
15:13 G love has no one than this,
1Co 12:31 But eagerly desire the g gifts.
Heb 11:26 as of g value than the treasures
1Jn 3:20 For God is g than our hearts,
4: 4 is in you is g than the one who is

GREATEST (GREAT)
Mt 22:38 is the first and g commandment.
Lk 9:48 least among you all—he is the g."
1Co 13:13 But the g of these is love.

GREATNESS (GREAT)
Ps 145: 3 his g no one can fathom.
150: 2 praise him for his surpassing g.
Isa 63: 1 forward in the g of his strength?
Php 3: 8 compared to the surpassing g

GREED (GREEDY)
Lk 12:15 on your guard against all kinds of g
Ro 1:29 kind of wickedness, evil, g
Eph 5: 3 or of any kind of impurity, or of g,
Col 3: 5 evil desires and g, which is idolatry
2Pe 2:14 experts in g—an accursed brood!

GREEDY (GREED)
Pr 15:27 A g man brings trouble
1Co 6:10 nor thieves nor the g nor drunkards
Eph 5: 5 No immoral, impure or g person—
1Pe 5: 2 not g for money, but eager to serve;

GREEN
Ps 23: 2 makes me lie down in g pastures,

GREW (GROW)
Lk 2:52 And Jesus g in wisdom and stature,
Ac 16: 5 in the faith and g daily in numbers.

GRIEF (GRIEVE)
Ps 10:14 O God, do see trouble and g;
Pr 14:13 and joy may end in g.
La 3:32 Though he brings g, he will show
Jn 16:20 but your g will turn to joy.
1Pe 1: 6 had to suffer g in all kinds of trials.

GRIEVE (GRIEF)
Eph 4:30 do not g the Holy Spirit of God,
1Th 4:13 or to g like the rest of men,

GROUND
Ge 3:17 "Cursed is the g because of you;
Ex 3: 5 where you are standing is holy g."
Eph 6:13 you may be able to stand your g,

GROW (GREW)
Pr 13:11 by little makes it g.
1Co 3: 6 watered it, but God made it g.
2Pe 3:18 But g in the grace and knowledge

GRUMBLE (GRUMBLING)
1Co 10:10 And do not g, as some of them did
Jas 5: 9 Don't g against each other,

GRUMBLING (GRUMBLE)
Jn 6:43 "Stop g among yourselves,"
1Pe 4: 9 to one another without g.

GUARANTEE (GUARANTEEING)
Heb 7:22 Jesus has become the g

GUARANTEEING (GUARANTEE)
2Co 1:22 as a deposit, g what is to come.
Eph 1:14 who is a deposit g our inheritance

GUARD (GUARDS)
Ps 141: 3 Set a g over my mouth, O LORD;
Pr 4:23 Above all else, g your heart,
Isa 52:12 the God of Israel will be your rear g
Mk 13:33 Be on g! Be alert! You do not know
1Co 16:13 Be on your g; stand firm in the faith
Php 4: 7 will g your hearts and your minds
1Ti 6:20 g what has been entrusted

GUARDS (GUARD)
Pr 13: 3 He who g his lips g his life,
19:16 who obeys instructions g his life,
21:23 He who g his mouth and his tongue
22: 5 he who g his soul stays far

GUIDE
Ex 13:21 of cloud to g them on their way
15:13 In your strength you will g them
Ne 9:19 cease to g them on their path,
Ps 25: 5 g me in your truth and teach me,
43: 3 let them g me;
48:14 he will be our g even to the end.
67: 4 and g the nations of the earth.
73:24 You g me with your counsel,
139: 10 even there your hand will g me,
Pr 4:11 I g you in the way of wisdom
6:22 When you walk, they will g you;
Isa 58:11 The LORD will g you always;
Jn 16:13 comes, he will g you into all truth.

GUILTY
Ex 34: 7 does not leave the g unpunished;
Jn 8:46 Can any of you prove me g of sin?
Heb 10:22 to cleanse us from a g conscience
Jas 2:10 at just one point is g of breaking all

HADES
Mt 16:18 the gates of *H* will not overcome it.

HAGAR
Servant of Sarah, wife of Abraham, mother of Ishmael (Ge 16:1-6; 25:12). Driven away by Sarah while pregnant (Ge 16:5-16); after birth of Isaac (Ge 21:9-21; Gal 4:21-31).

HAGGAI*
Post-exilic prophet who encouraged rebuilding of the temple (Ezr 5:1; 6:14; Hag 1-2).

HAIR (HAIRS)
Lk 21:18 But not a *h* of your head will perish
1Co 11: 6 for a woman to have her *h* cut

HAIRS (HAIR)
Mt 10:30 even the very *h* of your head are all

HALLELUJAH*
Rev 19: 1 3,4,6.

HALLOWED (HOLY)
Mt 6: 9 *h* be your name,

HAND (HANDS)
Ps 16: 8 Because he is at my right *h*,
37:24 the LORD upholds him with his *h*.
139: 10 even there your *h* will guide me,
Ecc 9:10 Whatever your *h* finds to do,
Mt 6: 3 know what your right *h* is doing,
Jn 10:28 one can snatch them out of my *h*.
1Co 12:15 I am not a *h*, I do not belong

HANDS (HAND)
Ps 22:16 they have pierced my *h*
24: 4 He who has clean *h* and a pure
31: 5 Into your *h* I commit my spirit;
31:15 My times are in your *h*;
Pr 10: 4 Lazy *h* make a man poor,
31:20 and extends her *h* to the needy.
Isa 55:12 will clap their *h*.
65: 2 All day long I have held out my *h*
Lk 23:46 into your *h* I commit my spirit."
1Th 4:11 and to work with your *h*,
1Ti 2: 8 to lift up holy *h* in prayer,
5:22 hasty in the laying on of *h*,

HANNAH*
Wife of Elkanah, mother of Samuel (1Sa 1). Prayer at dedication of Samuel (1Sa 2:1-10). Blessed (1Sa 2:18-21).

HAPPY
Ps 68: 3 may they be *h* and joyful.
Pr 15:13 A *h* heart makes the face cheerful,
Ecc 3:12 better for men than to be *h*
Jas 5:13 Is anyone *h*? Let him sing songs

HARD (HARDEN HARDSHIP)
Ge 18:14 Is anything too *h* for the LORD?
Mt 19:23 it is *h* for a rich man
1Co 4:12 We work *h* with our own hands.
1Th 5:12 to respect those who work *h*

HARDEN (HARD)
Ro 9:18 he hardens whom he wants to *h*.
Heb 3: 8 do not *h* your hearts

HARDHEARTED* (HEART)
Dt 15: 7 do not be *h* or tightfisted

HARDSHIP (HARD)
Ro 8:35 Shall trouble or *h* or persecution
2Ti 2: 3 Endure *h* with us like a good
4: 5 endure *h*, do the work
Heb 12: 7 Endure *h* as discipline; God is

HARM
Ps 121: 6 the sun will not *h* you by day,
Pr 3:29 not plot *h* against your neighbor,
31:12 She brings him good, not *h*,
Ro 13:10 Love does no *h* to its neighbor.
1Jn 5:18 and the evil one cannot *h* him.

HARMONY
Ro 12:16 Live in *h* with one another.
2Co 6:15 What *h* is there between Christ
1Pe 3: 8 live in *h* with one another;

HARVEST
Mt 9:37 *h* is plentiful but the workers are
Jn 4:35 at the fields! They are ripe for *h*.
Gal 6: 9 at the proper time we will reap a *h*
Heb 12:11 it produces a *h* of righteousness

HASTE (HASTY)
Pr 21: 5 as surely as *h* leads to poverty.
29:20 Do you see a man who speaks in *h*?

HASTY* (HASTE)
Pr 19: 2 nor to be *h* and miss the way.
Ecc 5: 2 do not be *h* in your heart
1Ti 5:22 Do not be *h* in the laying

HATE (HATED HATES HATRED)
Lev 19:17 " 'Do not *h* your brother
Ps 5: 5 you *h* all who do wrong.
45: 7 righteousness and *h* wickedness;
97:10 those who love the LORD *h* evil,
139: 21 Do I not *h* those who *h* you,
Pr 8:13 To fear the LORD is to *h* evil;
Am 5:15 *H* evil, love good;
Mal 2:16 "I *h* divorce," says the LORD God
Mt 5:43 your neighbor and *h* your enemy.'
10:22 All men will *h* you because of me,
Lk 6:27 do good to those who *h* you,
Ro 12: 9 *H* what is evil; cling to what is good

HATED (HATE)
Ro 9:13 "Jacob I loved, but Esau I *h*."
Eph 5:29 no one ever *h* his own body,
Heb 1: 9 righteousness and *h* wickedness;

HATES (HATE)
Pr 6:16 There are six things the LORD *h*,
13:24 He who spares the rod *h* his son,
Jn 3:20 Everyone who does evil *h* the light,
1Jn 2: 9 *h* his brother is still in the darkness.

HATRED (HATE)
Pr 10:12 *H* stirs up dissension,
Jas 4: 4 with the world is *h* toward God?

HAUGHTY
Pr 16:18 a *h* spirit before a fall.

HAY
1Co 3:12 costly stones, wood, *h* or straw,

HEAD (HEADS HOTHEADED)
Ge 3:15 he will crush your *h*,
Ps 23: 5 You anoint my *h* with oil;
Pr 25:22 will heap burning coals on his *h*,
Isa 59:17 and the helmet of salvation on his *h*
Mt 8:20 of Man has no place to lay his *h*."
Ro 12:20 will heap burning coals on his *h*."
1Co 11: 3 and the *h* of Christ is God.
12:21 And the *h* cannot say to the feet,
Eph 5:23 For the husband is the *h* of the wife
2Ti 4: 5 keep your *h* in all situations,
Rev 19:12 and on his *h* are many crowns.

HEADS (HEAD)
Lev 26:13 you to walk with *h* held high.
Isa 35:10 everlasting joy will crown their *h*.

HEAL (HEALED HEALING HEALS)
2Ch 7:14 their sin and will *h* their land.
Ps 41: 4 *h* me, for I have sinned against you
Mt 10: 8 *H* the sick, raise the dead,
Lk 4:23 to me: 'Physician, *h* yourself!
5:17 present for him to *h* the sick.

HEALED (HEAL)
Isa 53: 5 and by his wounds we are *h*.
Mt 9:22 he said, "your faith has *h* you."
14:36 and all who touched him were *h*.
Ac 4:10 this man stands before you *h*.
14: 9 saw that he had faith to be *h*
Jas 5:16 for each other so that you may be *h*
1Pe 2:24 by his wounds you have been *h*.

HEALING (HEAL)
Eze 47:12 for food and their leaves for *h*."
Mal 4: 2 rise with *h* in its wings.
1Co 12: 9 to another gifts of *h*
12:30 Do all have gifts of *h*? Do all speak
Rev 22: 2 are for the *h* of the nations.

HEALS (HEAL)
Ex 15:26 for I am the LORD, who *h* you."
Ps 103: 3 and *h* all your diseases;
147: 3 He *h* the brokenhearted

HEALTH (HEALTHY)
Pr 3: 8 This will bring *h* to your body
15:30 and good news gives *h* to the bones

HEALTHY (HEALTH)
Mk 2:17 "It is not the *h* who need a doctor,

HEAR (HEARD HEARING HEARS)
Dt 6: 4 *H*, O Israel: The LORD our God,
31:13 must *h* it and learn
2Ch 7:14 then will I *h* from heaven
Ps 94: 9 he who implanted the ear not *h*?
Isa 29:18 that day the deaf will *h* the words
65:24 while they are still speaking I will *h*
Mt 11:15 He who has ears, let him *h*.
Jn 8:47 reason you do not *h* is that you do
2Ti 4: 3 what their itching ears want to *h*.

HEARD (HEAR)
Job 42: 5 My ears had *h* of you
Isa 66: 8 Who has ever *h* of such a thing?
Mt 5:21 "You have *h* that it was said
5:27 "You have *h* that it was said,
5:33 you have *h* that it was said
5:38 "You have *h* that it was said,
5:43 "You have *h* that it was said,
1Co 2: 9 no ear has *h*,
1Th 2:13 word of God, which you *h* from us,
2Ti 1:13 What you *h* from me, keep
Jas 1:25 not forgetting what he has *h*,

HEARING (HEAR)
Ro 10:17 faith comes from *h* the message,

HEARS (HEAR)
Jn 5:24 whoever *h* my word and believes
1Jn 5:14 according to his will, he *h* us.
Rev 3:20 If anyone *h* my voice and opens

HEART (BROKENHEARTED HARDHEARTED HEARTS WHOLEHEARTEDLY)
Ex 25: 2 each man whose *h* prompts him
Lev 19:17 Do not hate your brother in your *h*.
Dt 4:29 if you look for him with all your *h*

Dt 6: 5 LORD your God with all your *h*
10: 12 LORD your God with all your *h*
15: 10 and do so without a grudging *h;*
30: 6 you may love him with all your *h*
30: 10 LORD your God with all your *h*
Jos 22: 5 and to serve him with all your *h*
1Sa 13: 14 sought out a man after his own *h*
16: 7 but the LORD looks at the *h.*"
2Ki 23: 3 with all his *h* and all his soul,
1Ch 28: 9 for the LORD searches every *h*
2Ch 7: 16 and my *h* will always be there.
Job 22: 22 and lay up his words in your *h.*
37: 1 "At this my *h* pounds
Ps 14: 1 The fool says in his *h,*
19: 14 and the meditation of my *h*
37: 4 will give you the desires of your *h.*
45: 1 My *h* is stirred by a noble theme
51: 10 Create in me a pure *h,* O God,
51: 17 a broken and contrite *h,*
66: 18 If I had cherished sin in my *h,*
86: 11 give me an undivided *h,*
119: 11 I have hidden your word in my *h*
119: 32 for you have set my *h* free.
139: 23 Search me, O God, and know my *h*
Pr 3: 5 Trust in the LORD with all your *h*
4: 21 keep them within your *h;*
4: 23 Above all else, guard your *h,*
7: 3 write them on the tablet of your *h.*
13: 12 Hope deferred makes the *h* sick,
14: 13 Even in laughter the *h* may ache,
15: 30 A cheerful look brings joy to the *h,*
17: 22 A cheerful *h* is good medicine,
24: 17 stumbles, do not let your *h* rejoice,
27: 19 so a man's *h* reflects the man.
Ecc 8: 5 wise *h* will know the proper time
SS 4: 9 You have stolen my *h,* my sister,
Isa 40: 11 and carries them close to his *h;*
57: 15 and to revive the *h* of the contrite.
Jer 17: 9 The *h* is deceitful above all things
29: 13 when you seek me with all your *h.*
Eze 36: 26 I will give you a new *h*
Mt 5: 8 Blessed are the pure in *h,*
6: 21 treasure is, there your *h* will be
12: 34 of the *h* the mouth speaks.
22: 37 the Lord your God with all your *h*
Lk 6: 45 overflow of his *h* his mouth speaks.
Ro 2: 29 is circumcision of the *h,*
10: 10 is with your *h* that you believe
1Co 14: 25 the secrets of his *h* will be laid bare.
Eph 5: 19 make music in your *h* to the Lord,
6: 6 doing the will of God from your *h.*
Col 3: 23 work at it with all your *h,*
1Pe 1: 22 one another deeply, from the *h.*

HEARTS (HEART)

Dt 11: 18 Fix these words of mine in your *h*
1Ki 8: 39 for you alone know the *h* of all men
8: 61 your *h* must be fully committed
Ps 62: 8 pour out your *h* to him,
Ecc 3: 11 also set eternity in the *h* of men;
Jer 31: 33 and write it on their *h.*
Lk 16: 15 of men, but God knows your *h.*
24: 32 "Were not our *h* burning within us
Jn 14: 1 "Do not let your *h* be troubled.
Ac 15: 9 for he purified their *h* by faith.
Ro 2: 15 of the law are written on their *h,*
2Co 3: 2 written on our *h,* known
3: 3 but on tablets of human *h.*
4: 6 shine in our *h* to give us the light
Eph 3: 17 dwell in your *h* through faith.
Col 3: 1 set your *h* on things above,
Heb 3: 8 do not harden your *h*
10: 16 I will put my laws in their *h,*
1Jn 3: 20 For God is greater than our *h,*

HEAT

2Pe 3: 12 and the elements will melt in the *h.*

HEAVEN (HEAVENLY HEAVENS)

Ge 14: 19 Creator of *h* and earth.
1Ki 8: 27 the highest *h,* cannot contain you.
2Ki 2: 1 up to *h* in a whirlwind,
2Ch 7: 14 then will I hear from *h*
Isa 14: 12 How you have fallen from *h,*
66: 1 "*H* is my throne,
Da 7: 13 coming with the clouds of *h.*
Mt 6: 9 " 'Our Father in *h,*
6: 20 up for yourselves treasures in *h,*
16: 19 bind on earth will be bound in *h,*
19: 23 man to enter the kingdom of *h.*
24: 35 *H* and earth will pass away,
26: 64 and coming on the clouds of *h.*"
28: 18 "All authority in *h*
Mk 16: 19 he was taken up into *h*
Lk 15: 7 in *h* over one sinner who repents
18: 22 and you will have treasure in *h.*
Ro 10: 6 'Who will ascend into *h?*' "(that is,
2Co 5: 1 an eternal house in *h,* not built
12: 2 ago was caught up to the third *h.*
Php 2: 10 *h* and on earth and under the earth,
3: 20 But our citizenship is in *h.*
1Th 1: 10 and to wait for his Son from *h,*
Heb 8: 5 and shadow of what is in *h.*
9: 24 he entered *h* itself, now to appear
2Pe 3: 13 we are looking forward to a new *h*
Rev 21: 1 Then I saw a new *h* and a new earth

HEAVENLY (HEAVEN)

Ps 8: 5 him a little lower than the *h* beings
2Co 5: 2 to be clothed with our *h* dwelling,
Eph 1: 3 in the *h* realms with every spiritual
1: 20 at his right hand in the *h* realms,
2Ti 4: 18 bring me safely to his *h* kingdom.
Heb 12: 22 to the *h* Jerusalem, the city

HEAVENS (HEAVEN)

Ge 1: 1 In the beginning God created the *h*
1Ki 8: 27 The *h,* even the highest heaven,
2Ch 2: 6 since the *h,* even the highest
Ps 8: 3 When I consider your *h,*
19: 1 The *h* declare the glory of God;
102: 25 the *h* are the work of your hands.
108: 4 is your love, higher than the *h;*
119: 89 it stands firm in the *h.*
139: 8 If I go up to the *h,* you are there;
Isa 51: 6 Lift up your eyes to the *h,*
55: 9 "As the *h* are higher than the earth,
65: 17 new *h* and a new earth.
Joel 2: 30 I will show wonders in the *h*
Eph 4: 10 who ascended higher than all the *h,*
2Pe 3: 10 The *h* will disappear with a roar;

HEBREW

Ge 14: 13 and reported this to Abram the *H.*

HEEDS

Pr 13: 1 wise son *h* his father's instruction,
13: 18 whoever *h* correction is honored.
15: 5 whoever *h* correction shows
15: 32 whoever *h* correction gains

HEEL

Ge 3: 15 and you will strike his *h.*"

HEIRS (INHERIT)

Ro 8: 17 then we are *h*— *h* of God
Gal 3: 29 and *h* according to the promise.

Eph 3: 6 gospel the Gentiles are *h* together
1Pe 3: 7 as *h* with you of the gracious gift

HELL

Mt 5: 22 will be in danger of the fire of *h.*
Lk 16: 23 In *h,* where he was in torment,
2Pe 2: 4 but sent them to *h,* putting them

HELMET

Isa 59: 17 and the *h* of salvation on his head;
Eph 6: 17 Take the *h* of salvation
1Th 5: 8 and the hope of salvation as a *h.*

HELP (HELPED HELPER HELPING HELPS)

Ps 18: 6 I cried to my God for *h.*
30: 2 my God, I called to you for *h*
46: 1 an ever-present *h* in trouble.
79: 9 *H* us, O God our Savior,
121: 1 where does my *h* come from?
Isa 41: 10 I will strengthen you and *h* you;
Jnh 2: 2 depths of the grave I called for *h,*
Mk 9: 24 *h* me overcome my unbelief!"
Ac 16: 9 Come over to Macedonia and *h* us
1Co 12: 28 those able to *h* others, those

HELPED (HELP)

1Sa 7: 12 "Thus far has the LORD *h* us."

HELPER (HELP)

Ge 2: 18 I will make a *h* suitable for him."
Ps 10: 14 you are the *h* of the fatherless.
Heb 13: 6 Lord is my *h;* I will not be afraid.

HELPING (HELP)

Ac 9: 36 always doing good and *h* the poor.
1Ti 5: 10 *h* those in trouble and devoting

HELPS (HELP)

Ro 8: 26 the Spirit *h* us in our weakness.

HEN

Mt 23: 37 as a *h* gathers her chicks

HERITAGE (INHERIT)

Ps 127: 3 Sons are a *h* from the LORD,

HEROD

1. King of Judea who tried to kill Jesus (Mt 2; Lk 1:5).

2. Son of 1. Tetrarch of Galilee who arrested and beheaded John the Baptist (Mt 14:1-12; Mk 6:14-29; Lk 3:1, 19-20; 9:7-9); tried Jesus (Lk 23:6-15).

3. Grandson of 1. King of Judea who killed James (Ac 12:2); arrested Peter (Ac 12:3-19). Death (Ac 12:19-23).

HERODIAS

Wife of Herod the Tetrarch who persuaded her daughter to ask for John the Baptist's head (Mt 14:1-12; Mk 6:14-29).

HEZEKIAH

King of Judah. Restored the temple and worship (2Ch 29-31). Sought the LORD for help against Assyria (2Ki 18-19; 2Ch 32:1-23; Isa 36-37). Illness healed (2Ki 20:1-11; 2Ch 32:24-26; Isa 38). Judged for showing Babylonians his treasures (2Ki 20:12-21; 2Ch 32:31; Isa 39).

HID (HIDE)

Ge 3: 8 and they *h* from the LORD God
Ex 2: 2 she *h* him for three months.
Jos 6: 17 because she *h* the spies we sent.
Heb 11: 23 By faith Moses' parents *h* him

HIDDEN (HIDE)

Ps 19: 12 Forgive my *h* faults.
119: 11 I have *h* your word in my heart
Pr 2: 4 and search for it as for *h* treasure,

Isa 59: 2 your sins have *h* his face from you,
Mt 5: 14 A city on a hill cannot be *h.*
13: 44 of heaven is like treasure *h*
Col 1: 26 the mystery that has been kept *h*
2: 3 in whom are *h* all the treasures
3: 3 and your life is now *h* with Christ

HIDE (HID HIDDEN)

Ps 17: 8 *h* me in the shadow of your wings
143: 9 for I *h* myself in you.

HILL (HILLS)

Mt 5: 14 A city on a *h* cannot be hidden.

HILLS (HILL)

Ps 50: 10 and the cattle on a thousand *h.*
121: 1 I lift up my eyes to the *h*—

HINDER (HINDERS)

1Sa 14: 6 Nothing can *h* the LORD
Mt 19: 14 come to me, and do not *h* them,
1Co 9: 12 anything rather than *h* the gospel
1Pe 3: 7 so that nothing will *h* your prayers.

HINDERS (HINDER)

Heb 12: 1 let us throw off everything that *h*

HINT*

Eph 5: 3 even a *h* of sexual immorality,

HOLD

Ex 20: 7 LORD will not *h* anyone guiltless
Lev 19: 13 " 'Do not *h* back the wages
Jos 22: 5 to *h* fast to him and to serve him
Ps 73: 23 you *h* me by my right hand.
Pr 4: 4 "Lay *h* of my words
Isa 54: 2 do not *h* back;
Mk 11: 25 if you *h* anything against anyone,
Php 2: 16 as you *h* out the word of life—
3: 12 but I press on to take *h* of that
Col 1: 17 and in him all things *h* together.
1Th 5: 21 *H* on to the good.
1Ti 6: 12 Take *h* of the eternal life
Heb 10: 23 Let us *h* unswervingly

HOLINESS (HOLY)

Ex 15: 11 majestic in *h,*
Ps 29: 2 in the splendor of his *h.*
96: 9 in the splendor of his *h;*
Ro 6: 19 to righteousness leading to *h.*
2Co 7: 1 perfecting *h* out of reverence
Eph 4: 24 God in true righteousness and *h.*
Heb 12: 10 that we may share in his *h.*
12: 14 without *h* no one will see the Lord.

HOLY (HALLOWED HOLINESS)

Ex 19: 6 kingdom of priests and a *h* nation.
20: 8 the Sabbath day by keeping it *h.*
Lev 11: 44 and be *h,* because I am *h.*
20: 7 " 'Consecrate yourselves and be *h,*
20: 26 You are to be *h* to me because I,
21: 8 Consider them *h,* because I
22: 32 Do not profane my *h* name.
Ps 16: 10 will you let your *H* One see decay.
24: 3 Who may stand in his *h* place?
77: 13 Your ways, O God, are *h.*
99: 3 he is *h.*
99: 5 he is *h.*
99: 9 for the LORD our God is *h.*
111: 9 *h* and awesome is his name.
Isa 5: 16 the *h* God will show himself *h*
6: 3 *H, h, h* is the LORD Almighty;
40: 25 who is my equal?" says the *H* One.
57: 15 who lives forever, whose name is *h:*
Eze 28: 25 I will show myself *h* among them
Da 9: 24 prophecy and to anoint the most *h.*

Hab 2: 20 But the LORD is in his *h* temple;
Ac 2: 27 will you let your *H* One see decay.
Ro 7: 12 and the commandment is *h,*
12: 1 as living sacrifices, *h* and pleasing
Eph 5: 3 improper for God's *h* people.
2Th 1: 10 to be glorified in his *h* people
2Ti 1: 9 saved us and called us to a *h* life—
3: 15 you have known the *h* Scriptures,
Tit 1: 8 upright, *h* and disciplined.
1Pe 1: 15 But just as he who called you is *h,*
1: 16 is written: "Be *h,* because I am *h.*"
2: 9 a royal priesthood, a *h* nation,
2Pe 3: 11 You ought to live *h* and godly lives
Rev 4: 8 *"H, h, h* is the Lord God

HOME (HOMES)

Dt 6: 7 Talk about them when you sit at *h*
Ps 84: 3 Even the sparrow has found a *h,*
Pr 3: 33 but he blesses the *h* of the righteous
Mk 10: 29 "no one who has left *h* or brothers
Jn 14: 23 to him and make our *h* with him.
Tit 2: 5 to be busy at *h,* to be kind,

HOMES (HOME)

Ne 4: 14 daughters, your wives and your *h.*"
1Ti 5: 14 to manage their *h* and to give

HOMOSEXUAL*

1Co 6: 9 male prostitutes nor *h* offenders

HONEST

Lev 19: 36 Use *h* scales and *h* weights,
Dt 25: 15 and *h* weights and measures,
Job 31: 6 let God weigh me in *h* scales
Pr 12: 17 truthful witness gives *h* testimony,

HONEY

Ex 3: 8 a land flowing with milk and *h*—
Ps 19: 10 than *h* from the comb.
119: 103 sweeter than *h* to my mouth!

HONOR (HONORABLE HONORABLY HONORED HONORS)

Ex 20: 12 *"H* your father and your mother,
Nu 25: 13 he was zealous for the *h* of his God
Dt 5: 16 *"H* your father and your mother,
1Sa 2: 30 Those who *h* me I will *h,*
Ps 8: 5 and crowned him with glory and *h.*
Pr 3: 9 *H* the LORD with your wealth,
15: 33 and humility comes before *h.*
20: 3 It is to a man's *h* to avoid strife,
Mt 15: 4 *'H* your father and mother'
Ro 12: 10 *H* one another above yourselves.
1Co 6: 20 Therefore *h* God with your body.
Eph 6: 2 *"H* your father and mother"—
1Ti 5: 17 well are worthy of double *h,*
Heb 2: 7 you crowned him with glory and *h*
Rev 4: 9 *h* and thanks to him who sits

HONORABLE (HONOR)

1Th 4: 4 body in a way that is holy and *h,*

HONORABLY (HONOR)

Heb 13: 18 and desire to live *h* in every way.

HONORED (HONOR)

Ps 12: 8 when what is vile is *h* among men.
Pr 13: 18 but whoever heeds correction is *h.*
1Co 12: 26 if one part is *h,* every part rejoices
Heb 13: 4 Marriage should be *h* by all,

HONORS (HONOR)

Ps 15: 4 but *h* those who fear the LORD,
Pr 14: 31 to the needy *h* God.

HOOKS

Isa 2: 4 and their spears into pruning *h.*
Joel 3: 10 and your pruning *h* into spears.

HOPE (HOPES)

Job 13: 15 Though he slay me, yet will I *h*
Ps 42: 5 Put your *h* in God,
62: 5 my *h* comes from him.
119: 74 for I have put my *h* in your word.
130: 7 O Israel, put your *h* in the LORD,
147: 11 who put their *h* in his unfailing love
Pr 13: 12 *H* deferred makes the heart sick,
Isa 40: 31 but those who *h* in the LORD
Ro 5: 4 character; and character, *h.*
8: 24 But *h* that is seen is no *h* at all.
12: 12 Be joyful in *h,* patient in affliction,
15: 4 of the Scriptures we might have *h.*
1Co 13: 13 now these three remain: faith, *h*
15: 19 for this life we have *h* in Christ,
Col 1: 27 Christ in you, the *h* of glory.
1Th 5: 8 and the *h* of salvation as a helmet.
1Ti 6: 17 but to put their *h* in God,
Tit 2: 13 while we wait for the blessed *h*—
Heb 6: 19 We have this *h* as an anchor
11: 1 faith is being sure of what we *h* for
1Jn 3: 3 Everyone who has this *h*

HOPES (HOPE)

1Co 13: 7 always *h,* always perseveres.

HORSE

Ps 147: 10 not in the strength of the *h,*
Pr 26: 3 A whip for the *h,* a halter
Zec 1: 8 before me was a man riding a red *h*
Rev 6: 2 and there before me was a white *h!*
6: 4 Come!" Then another *h* came out,
6: 5 and there before me was a black *h!*
6: 8 and there before me was a pale *h!*
19: 11 and there before me was a white *h,*

HOSANNA

Mt 21: 9 *"H* in the highest!"

HOSHEA

Last king of Israel (2Ki 15:30; 17:1-6).

HOSPITABLE* (HOSPITALITY)

1Ti 3: 2 self-controlled, respectable, *h,*
Tit 1: 8 Rather he must be *h,* one who loves

HOSPITALITY (HOSPITABLE)

Ro 12: 13 Practice *h.*
1Ti 5: 10 as bringing up children, showing *h,*
1Pe 4: 9 Offer *h* to one another

HOSTILE

Ro 8: 7 the sinful mind is *h* to God.

HOT

1Ti 4: 2 have been seared as with a *h* iron.
Rev 3: 15 that you are neither cold nor *h.*

HOT-TEMPERED

Pr 15: 18 A *h* man stirs up dissension,
19: 19 A *h* man must pay the penalty;
22: 24 Do not make friends with a *h* man,
29: 22 and a *h* one commits many sins.

HOTHEADED (HEAD)
Pr 14:16 but a fool is *h* and reckless.

HOUR
Ecc 9:12 knows when his *h* will come:
Mt 6:27 you by worrying can add a single *h*
Lk 12:40 the Son of Man will come at an *h*
Jn 12:23 The *h* has come for the Son of Man
12:27 for this very reason I came to this *h*

HOUSE (HOUSEHOLD STOREHOUSE)
Ex 20:17 shall not covet your neighbor's *h*.
Ps 23:6 I will dwell in the *h* of the LORD
84:10 a doorkeeper in the *h* of my God
122:1 "Let us go to the *h* of the LORD."
127:1 Unless the LORD builds the *h*,
Pr 7:27 Her *h* is a highway to the grave,
21:9 than share a *h* with a quarrelsome
Isa 56:7 a *h* of prayer for all nations."
Zec 13:6 given at the *h* of my friends.'
Mt 7:24 is like a wise man who built his *h*
12:29 can anyone enter a strong man's *h*
21:13 My *h* will be called a *h* of prayer,'
Mk 3:25 If a *h* is divided against itself,
Lk 11:17 a *h* divided against itself will fall.
Jn 2:16 How dare you turn my Father's *h*
12:3 the *h* was filled with the fragrance
14:2 In my Father's *h* are many rooms;
Heb 3:3 the builder of a *h* has greater honor

HOUSEHOLD (HOUSE)
Jos 24:15 my *h*, we will serve the LORD."
Mic 7:6 are the members of his own *h*.
Mt 10:36 will be the members of his own *h*.'
12:25 or *h* divided against itself will not
1Ti 3:12 manage his children and his *h* well.
3:15 to conduct themselves in God's *h*,

HUMAN (HUMANITY)
Gal 3:3 to attain your goal by *h* effort?

HUMANITY* (HUMAN)
Heb 2:14 he too shared in their *h* so that

HUMBLE (HUMBLED HUMBLES HUMILIATE HUMILITY)
2Ch 7:14 will *h* themselves and pray
Ps 25:9 He guides the *h* in what is right
Pr 3:34 but gives grace to the *h*.
Isa 66:2 he who is *h* and contrite in spirit,
Mt 11:29 for I am gentle and *h* in heart,
Eph 4:2 Be completely *h* and gentle;
Jas 4:10 *H* yourselves before the Lord,
1Pe 5:6 *H* yourselves,

HUMBLED (HUMBLE)
Mt 23:12 whoever exalts himself will be *h*,
Php 2:8 he *h* himself

HUMBLES (HUMBLE)
Mt 18:4 whoever *h* himself like this child is
23:12 whoever *h* himself will be exalted.

HUMILIATE* (HUMBLE)
Pr 25:7 than for him to *h* you
1Co 11:22 and *h* those who have nothing?

HUMILITY (HUMBLE)
Pr 11:2 but with *h* comes wisdom.
15:33 and *h* comes before honor.
Php 2:3 but in *h* consider others better
Tit 3:2 and to show true *h* toward all men.
1Pe 5:5 clothe yourselves with *h*

HUNGRY
Ps 107:9 and fills the *h* with good things.
146:7 and gives food to the *h*.
Pr 25:21 If your enemy is *h*, give him food
Eze 18:7 but gives his food to the *h*
Mt 25:35 For I was *h* and you gave me
Lk 1:53 He has filled the *h* with good things
Jn 6:35 comes to me will never go *h*,
Ro 12:20 "If your enemy is *h*, feed him;

HURT (HURTS)
Ecc 8:9 it over others to his own *h*.
Mk 16:18 deadly poison, it will not *h* them
Rev 2:11 He who overcomes will not be *h*

HURTS* (HURT)
Ps 15:4 even when it *h*,
Pr 26:28 A lying tongue hates those it *h*,

HUSBAND (HUSBAND'S HUSBANDS)
1Co 7:3 The *h* should fulfill his marital duty
7:10 wife must not separate from her *h*.
7:11 And a *h* must not divorce his wife.
7:13 And if a woman has a *h* who is not
7:39 A woman is bound to her *h* as long
2Co 11:2 I promised you to one *h*, to Christ,
Eph 5:23 For the *h* is the head of the wife
5:33 and the wife must respect her *h*.
1Ti 3:2 the *h* of but one wife, temperate,

HUSBAND'S (HUSBAND)
Pr 12:4 of noble character is her *h* crown,
1Co 7:4 the *h* body does not belong

HUSBANDS (HUSBAND)
Eph 5:22 submit to your *h* as to the Lord.
5:25 *H*, love your wives, just
Tit 2:4 the younger women to love their *h*
1Pe 3:1 same way be submissive to your *h*
3:7 *H*, in the same way be considerate

HYMN
1Co 14:26 everyone has a *h*, or a word

HYPOCRISY (HYPOCRITE HYPOCRITES)
Mt 23:28 but on the inside you are full of *h*
1Pe 2:1 *h*, envy, and slander of every kind.

HYPOCRITE (HYPOCRISY)
Mt 7:5 You *h*, first take the plank out

HYPOCRITES (HYPOCRISY)
Ps 26:4 nor do I consort with *h*;
Mt 6:5 when you pray, do not be like the *h*

HYSSOP
Ps 51:7 with *h*, and I will be clean;

IDLE (IDLENESS)
1Th 5:14 those who are *i*, encourage
2Th 3:6 away from every brother who is *i*
1Ti 5:13 they get into the habit of being *i*

IDLENESS* (IDLE)
Pr 31:27 and does not eat the bread of *i*.

IDOL (IDOLATRY IDOLS)
Isa 44:17 From the rest he makes a god, his *i*;
1Co 8:4 We know that an *i* is nothing at all

IDOLATRY (IDOL)
Col 3:5 evil desires and greed, which is *i*.

IDOLS (IDOL)
1Co 8:1 Now about food sacrificed to *i*:

IGNORANT (IGNORE)
1Co 15:34 for there are some who are *i* of God
Heb 5:2 to deal gently with those who are *i*
1Pe 2:15 good you should silence the *i* talk
2Pe 3:16 which *i* and unstable people distort

IGNORE (IGNORANT IGNORES)
Dt 22:1 do not *i* it but be sure
Ps 9:12 he does not *i* the cry of the afflicted
Heb 2:3 if we *i* such a great salvation?

IGNORES (IGNORE)
Pr 10:17 whoever *i* correction leads others
15:32 He who *i* discipline despises

ILLUMINATED*
Rev 18:1 and the earth was *i* by his splendor.

IMAGE
Ge 1:26 "Let us make man in our *i*,
1:27 So God created man in his own *i*,
1Co 11:7 since he is the *i* and glory of God;
Col 1:15 He is the *i* of the invisible God,
3:10 in knowledge in the *i* of its Creator.

IMAGINE
Eph 3:20 more than all we ask or *i*,

IMITATE (IMITATORS)
1Co 4:16 Therefore I urge you to *i* me.
Heb 6:12 but to *i* those who through faith
13:7 of their way of life and *i* their faith.
3Jn :11 do not *i* what is evil but what is

IMITATORS* (IMITATE)
Eph 5:1 Be *i* of God, therefore,
1Th 1:6 You became *i* of us and of the Lord
2:14 became *i* of God's churches

IMMANUEL
Isa 7:14 birth to a son, and will call him *I*.
Mt 1:23 and they will call him *I*"—

IMMORAL* (IMMORALITY)
Pr 6:24 keeping you from the *i* woman,
1Co 5:9 to associate with sexually *i* people
5:10 the people of this world who are *i*,
5:11 but is sexually *i* or greedy,
6:9 Neither the sexually *i* nor idolaters
Eph 5:5 No *i*, impure or greedy person—
Heb 12:16 See that no one is sexually *i*,
13:4 the adulterer and all the sexually *i*.
Rev 21:8 the murderers, the sexually *i*,
22:15 the sexually *i*, the murderers,

IMMORALITY (IMMORAL)
1Co 6:13 The body is not meant for sexual *i*,
6:18 Flee from sexual *i*.
10:8 We should not commit sexual *i*,
Gal 5:19 sexual *i*, impurity and debauchery;
Eph 5:3 must not be even a hint of sexual *i*,
1Th 4:3 that you should avoid sexual *i*;
Jude :4 grace of our God into a license for *i*

IMMORTAL* (IMMORTALITY)
Ro 1:23 glory of the *i* God for images made
1Ti 1:17 Now to the King eternal, *i*,
6:16 who alone is *i* and who lives

IMMORTALITY (IMMORTAL)
Ro 2:7 honor and *i*, he will give eternal life
1Co 15:53 and the mortal with *i*.
2Ti 1:10 and *i* to light through the gospel.

IMPERISHABLE
1Pe 1:23 not of perishable seed, but of *i*,

IMPORTANCE* (IMPORTANT)
1Co 15:3 passed on to you as of first *i*:

IMPORTANT (IMPORTANCE)
Mt 6:25 Is not life more *i* than food,
23:23 have neglected the more *i* matters
Mk 12:29 "The most *i* one," answered Jesus,
12:33 as yourself is more *i* than all burnt
Php 1:18 The *i* thing is that in every way,

IMPOSSIBLE
Mt 17:20 Nothing will be *i* for you."
Lk 1:37 For nothing is *i* with God."
18:27 "What is *i* with men is possible
Heb 6:18 things in which it is *i* for God to lie,
11:6 without faith it is *i* to please God,

IMPROPER*
Eph 5:3 these are *i* for God's holy people.

IMPURE (IMPURITY)
Ac 10:15 not call anything *i* that God has
Eph 5:5 No immoral, *i* or greedy person—
1Th 4:7 For God did not call us to be *i*,
Rev 21:27 Nothing *i* will ever enter it,

IMPURITY (IMPURE)
Ro 1:24 hearts to sexual *i* for the degrading
Eph 5:3 or of any kind of *i*, or of greed,

INCENSE
Ex 40:5 Place the gold altar of *i* in front
Ps 141:2 my prayer be set before you like *i*;
Mt 2:11 him with gifts of gold and of *i*

INCOME
Ecc 5:10 wealth is never satisfied with his *i*.
1Co 16:2 sum of money in keeping with his *i*,

INCOMPARABLE*
Eph 2:7 ages he might show the *i* riches

INCREASE (EVER-INCREASING INCREASED INCREASES INCREASING)
Ge 1:22 "Be fruitful and *i* in number
Ps 62:10 though your riches *i*,
Isa 9:7 Of the *i* of his government
Lk 17:5 said to the Lord, "*I* our faith!"
1Th 3:12 May the Lord make your love *i*

INCREASED (INCREASE)
Ac 6:7 of disciples in Jerusalem *i* rapidly,
Ro 5:20 But where sin *i*, grace *i* all the more

INCREASES (INCREASE)
Pr 24:5 and a man of knowledge *i* strength;

INCREASING (INCREASE)
Ac 6:1 when the number of disciples was *i*,
2Th 1:3 one of you has for each other is *i*.

2Pe 1:8 these qualities in *i* measure,

INDEPENDENT*
1Co 11:11 however, woman is not *i* of man,
11:11 of man, nor is man *i* of woman.

INDESCRIBABLE*
2Co 9:15 Thanks be to God for his *i* gift!

INDISPENSABLE*
1Co 12:22 seem to be weaker are *i*,

INEFFECTIVE*
2Pe 1:8 they will keep you from being *i*

INEXPRESSIBLE*
2Co 12:4 He heard *i* things, things that man
1Pe 1:8 are filled with an *i* and glorious joy,

INFANTS
Mt 21:16 " 'From the lips of children and *i*
1Co 14:20 In regard to evil be *i*,

INFIRMITIES
Isa 53:4 Surely he took up our *i*

INHERIT (CO-HEIRS HEIRS HERITAGE INHERITANCE)
Ps 37:11 But the meek will *i* the land
37:29 the righteous will *i* the land
Mt 5:5 for they will *i* the earth.
Mk 10:17 "what must I do to *i* eternal life?"
1Co 15:50 blood cannot *i* the kingdom of God

INHERITANCE (INHERIT)
Dt 4:20 to be the people of his *i*,
Pr 13:22 A good man leaves an *i*
Eph 1:14 who is a deposit guaranteeing our *i*
5:5 has any *i* in the kingdom of Christ
Heb 9:15 receive the promised eternal *i*—
1Pe 1:4 and into an *i* that can never perish,

INIQUITIES (INIQUITY)
Ps 78:38 he forgave their *i*
103:10 or repay us according to our *i*.
Isa 59:2 But your *i* have separated
Mic 7:19 and hurl all our *i* into the depths

INIQUITY (INIQUITIES)
Ps 51:2 Wash away all my *i*
Isa 53:6 the *i* of us all.

INJUSTICE
2Ch 19:7 the LORD our God there is no *i*

INNOCENT
Pr 17:26 It is not good to punish an *i* man,
Mt 10:16 shrewd as snakes and as *i* as doves.
27:4 "for I have betrayed *i* blood."
1Co 4:4 but that does not make me *i*.

INSCRIPTION
Mt 22:20 And whose *i*?" "Caesar's,"

INSOLENT
Ro 1:30 God-haters, *i*, arrogant

INSTITUTED
Ro 13:2 rebelling against what God has *i*,
1Pe 2:13 to every authority *i* among men:

INSTRUCT (INSTRUCTION)
Ps 32:8 I will *i* you and teach you
Pr 9:9 *I* a wise man and he will be wiser
Ro 15:14 and competent to *i* one another.
2Ti 2:25 who oppose him he must gently *i*,

INSTRUCTION (INSTRUCT)
Pr 1:8 Listen, my son, to your father's *i*
4:1 Listen, my sons, to a father's *i*;
4:13 Hold on to *i*, do not let it go;
8:10 Choose my *i* instead of silver,
8:33 Listen to my *i* and be wise;
13:1 A wise son heeds his father's *i*,
13:13 He who scorns *i* will pay for it,
16:20 Whoever gives heed to *i* prospers,
16:21 and pleasant words promote *i*.
19:20 Listen to advice and accept *i*,
23:12 Apply your heart to *i*
1Co 14:6 or prophecy or word of *i*?
14:26 or a word of *i*, a revelation,
Eph 6:4 up in the training and *i* of the Lord.
1Th 4:8 he who rejects this *i* does not reject
2Th 3:14 If anyone does not obey our *i*
1Ti 1:18 I give you this *i* in keeping
6:3 to the sound *i* of our Lord Jesus
2Ti 4:2 with great patience and careful *i*.

INSULT
Pr 9:7 corrects a mocker invites *i*;
12:16 but a prudent man overlooks an *i*.
Mt 5:11 Blessed are you when people *i* you,
Lk 6:22 when they exclude you and *i* you
1Pe 3:9 evil with evil or *i* with *i*,

INTEGRITY
1Ki 9:4 if you walk before me in *i* of heart
Job 2:3 And he still maintains his *i*,
27:5 till I die, I will not deny my *i*.
Pr 10:9 The man of *i* walks securely,
11:3 The *i* of the upright guides them,
29:10 Bloodthirsty men hate a man of *i*
Tit 2:7 your teaching show *i*, seriousness

INTELLIGENCE
Isa 29:14 the *i* of the intelligent will vanish."
1Co 1:19 *i* of the intelligent I will frustrate."

INTELLIGIBLE
1Co 14:19 I would rather speak five *i* words

INTERCEDE (INTERCEDES INTERCESSION)
Heb 7:25 he always lives to *i* for them.

INTERCEDES (INTERCEDE)
Ro 8:26 but the Spirit himself *i* for us

INTERCESSION* (INTERCEDE)
Isa 53:12 and made *i* for the transgressors.
1Ti 2:1 *i* and thanksgiving be made

INTERESTS
1Co 7:34 his wife—and his *i* are divided.
Php 2:4 only to your own *i*, but also to the *i*
2:21 everyone looks out for his own *i*,

INTERMARRY (MARRY)
Dt 7:3 Do not *i* with them.

INVENTED*
2Pe 1:16 We did not follow cleverly *i* stories

INVESTIGATED
Lk 1:3 I myself have carefully *i* everything

INVISIBLE
Ro 1:20 of the world God's *i* qualities—
Col 1:15 He is the image of the *i* God,
1Ti 1:17 immortal, *i*, the only God,

INVITE (INVITED INVITES)
Lk 14:13 you give a banquet, *i* the poor,

INVITED (INVITE)
Mt 22:14 For many are *i*, but few are chosen

Mt 25:35 I was a stranger and you *i* me in,

INVITES (INVITE)

1Co 10:27 If some unbeliever *i* you to a meal

INVOLVED

2Ti 2: 4 a soldier gets *i* in civilian affairs—

IRON

1Ti 4: 2 have been seared as with a hot *i*.
Rev 2:27 He will rule them with an *i* scepter;

IRREVOCABLE*

Ro 11:29 for God's gifts and his call are *i*.

ISAAC

Son of Abraham by Sarah (Ge 17:19; 21:1-7; 1Ch 1:28). Offered up by Abraham (Ge 22; Heb 11:17-19). Rebekah taken as wife (Ge 24). Fathered Esau and Jacob (Ge 25:19-26; 1Ch 1:34). Tricked into blessing Jacob (Ge 27). Father of Israel (Ex 3:6; Dt 29:13; Ro 9:10).

ISAIAH

Prophet to Judah (Isa 1:1). Called by the LORD (Isa 6).

ISHMAEL

Son of Abraham by Hagar (Ge 16; 1Ch 1:28). Blessed, but not son of covenant (Ge 17:18-21; Gal 4:21-31). Sent away by Sarah (Ge 21:8-21).

ISRAEL (ISRAELITES)

1. Name given to Jacob (see JACOB).
2. Corporate name of Jacob's descendants; often specifically Northern Kingdom.
Dt 6: 4 Hear, O *I*: The LORD our God,
1Sa 4:21 "The glory has departed from *I*"—
Isa 27: 6 *I* will bud and blossom
Jer 31:10 'He who scattered *I* will gather
Eze 39:23 of *I* went into exile for their sin,
Mk 12:29 'Hear, O *I*, the Lord our God,
Lk 22:30 judging the twelve tribes of *I*.
Ro 9: 6 all who are descended from *I* are *I*.
11:26 And so all *I* will be saved,
Eph 3: 6 Gentiles are heirs together with *I*,

ISRAELITES (ISRAEL)

Ex 14:22 and the *I* went through the sea
16:35 The *I* ate manna forty years,
Hos 1:10 "Yet the *I* will be like the sand
Ro 9:27 the number of the *I* be like the sand

ITCHING*

2Ti 4: 3 to say what their *i* ears want to hear

JACOB

Second son of Isaac, twin of Esau (Ge 26:21-26; 1Ch 1:34). Bought Esau's birthright (Ge 26:29-34); tricked Isaac into blessing him (Ge 27:1-37). Abrahamic covenant perpetuated through (Ge 28:13-15; Mal 1:2). Vision at Bethel (Ge 28:10-22). Wives and children (Ge 29:1-30:24; 35:16-26; 1Ch 2-9). Wrestled with God; name changed to Israel (Ge 32:22-32). Sent sons to Egypt during famine (Ge 42-43). Settled in Egypt (Ge 46). Blessed Ephraim and Manasseh (Ge 48). Blessed sons (Ge 49:1-28; Heb 11:21). Death (Ge 49:29-33). Burial (Ge 50:1-14).

JAMES

1. Apostle; brother of John (Mt 4:21-22; 10:2; Mk 3:17; Lk 5:1-10). At transfiguration (Mt 17:1-13; Mk 9:1-13; Lk 9:28-36). Killed by Herod (Ac 12:2).
2. Apostle; son of Alphaeus (Mt 10:3; Mk 3:18; Lk 6:15).
3. Brother of Jesus (Mt 13:55; Mk 6:3; Lk 24:10; Gal 1:19) and Judas (Jude 1). With believers before Pentecost (Ac 1:13). Leader of church at Jerusalem (Ac 12:17; 15; 21:18; Gal 2:9, 12). Author of epistle (Jas 1:1).

JAPHETH

Son of Noah (Ge 5:32; 1Ch 1:4-5). Blessed (Ge 9:18-28).

JARS

2Co 4: 7 we have this treasure in *j* of clay

JEALOUS (JEALOUSY)

Ex 20: 5 the LORD your God, am a *j* God,
34:14 whose name is Jealous, is a *j* God.
Dt 4:24 God is a consuming fire, a *j* God.
Joel 2:18 the LORD will be *j* for his land
Zec 1:14 I am very *j* for Jerusalem and Zion,
2Co 11: 2 I am *j* for you with a godly jealousy

JEALOUSY (JEALOUS)

1Co 3: 3 For since there is *j* and quarreling
2Co 11: 2 I am jealous for you with a godly *j*.
Gal 5:20 hatred, discord, *j*, fits of rage,

JEHOAHAZ

1. Son of Jehu; king of Israel (2Ki 13:1-9).
2. Son of Josiah; king of Judah (2Ki 23:31-34; 2Ch 36:1-4).

JEHOASH

Son of Jehoahaz; king of Israel (2Ki 13-14; 2Ch 25).

JEHOIACHIN

Son of Jehoiakim; king of Judah exiled by Nebuchadnezzar (2Ki 24:8-17; 2Ch 36:8-10; Jer 22:24-30; 24:1). Raised from prisoner status (2Ki 25:27-30; Jer 52:31-34).

JEHOIAKIM

Son of Jehoahaz; king of Judah (2Ki 23:34-24:6; 2Ch 36:4-8; Jer 22:18-23; 36).

JEHORAM

Son of Jehoshaphat; king of Judah (2Ki 8:16-24).

JEHOSHAPHAT

Son of Asa; king of Judah (1Ki 22:41-50; 2Ki 3; 2Ch 17-20).

JEHU

King of Israel (1Ki 19:16-19; 2Ki 9-10).

JEPHTHAH

Judge from Gilead who delivered Israel from Ammon (Jdg 10:6-12:7). Made rash vow concerning his daughter (Jdg 11:30-40).

JEREMIAH

Prophet to Judah (Jer 1:1-3). Called by the LORD (Jer 1). Put in stocks (Jer 20:1-3). Threatened for prophesying (Jer 11:18-23; 26). Opposed by Hananiah (Jer 28). Scroll burned (Jer 36). Imprisoned (Jer 37). Thrown into cistern (Jer 38). Forced to Egypt with those fleeing Babylonians (Jer 43).

JEROBOAM

1. Official of Solomon; rebelled to become first king of Israel (1Ki 11:26-40; 12:1-20; 2Ch 10). Idolatry (1Ki 12:25-33); judgment for (1Ki 13-14; 2Ch 13).
2. Son of Jehoash; king of Israel (1Ki 14:23-29).

JERUSALEM

2Ki 23:27 and I will reject *J*, the city I chose,
2Ch 6: 6 now I have chosen *J* for my Name
Ne 2:17 Come, let us rebuild the wall of *J*,
Ps 122: 6 Pray for the peace of *J*:
125: 2 As the mountains surround *J*,
137: 5 If I forget you, O *J*,
Isa 40: 9 You who bring good tidings to *J*,
65:18 for I will create *J* to be a delight
Joel 3:17 *J* will be holy;
Zep 3:16 On that day they will say to *J*,
Zec 2: 4 '*J* will be a city without walls
8: 8 I will bring them back to live in *J*;
14: 8 living water will flow out from *J*,
Mt 23:37 "O *J*, *J*, you who kill the prophets
Lk 13:34 die outside *J*!"O *J*, *J*,
21:24 *J* will be trampled
Jn 4:20 where we must worship is in *J*."
Ac 1: 8 and you will be my witnesses in *J*,
Gal 4:25 corresponds to the present city of *J*
Rev 21: 2 I saw the Holy City, the new *J*,

JESUS

LIFE: Genealogy (Mt 1:1-17; Lk 3:21-37). Birth announced (Mt 1:18-25; Lk 1:26-45). Birth (Mt 2:1-12; Lk 2:1-40). Escape to Egypt (Mt 2:13-23). As a boy in the temple (Lk 2:41-52). Baptism (Mt 3:13-17; Mk 1:9-11; Lk 3:21-22; Jn 1:32-34). Temptation (Mt 4:1-11; Mk 1:12-13; Lk 4:1-13). Ministry in Galilee (Mt 4:12-18:35; Mk 1:14-9:50; Lk 4:14-13:9; Jn 1:35-2:11; 4; 6), Transfiguration (Mt 17:1-8; Mk 9:2-8; Lk 9:28-36), on the way to Jerusalem (Mt 19-20; Mk 10; Lk 13:10-19:27), in Jerusalem (Mt 21-25; Mk 11-13; Lk 19:28-21:38; Jn 2:12-3:36; 5; 7-12). Last supper (Mt 26:17-35; Mk 14:12-31; Lk 22:1-38; Jn 13-17). Arrest and trial (Mt 26:36-27:31; Mk 14:43-15:20; Lk 22:39-23:25; Jn 18:1-19:16). Crucifixion (Mt 27:32-66; Mk 15:21-47; Lk 23:26-55; Jn 19:28-42). Resurrection and appearances (Mt 28; Mk 16; Lk 24; Jn 20-21; Ac 1:1-11; 7:56; 9:3-6; 1Co 15:1-8; Rev 1:1-20).

MIRACLES. Healings: official's son (Jn 4:43-54), demoniac in Capernaum (Mk 1:23-26; Lk 4:33-35), Peter's mother-in-law (Mt 8:14-17; Mk 1:29-31; Lk 4:38-39), leper (Mt 8:2-4; Mk 1:40-45; Lk 5:12-16), paralytic (Mt 9:1-8; Mk 2:1-12; Lk 5:17-26), cripple (Jn 5:1-9), shriveled hand (Mt 12:10-13; Mk 3:1-5; Lk 6:6-11), centurion's servant (Mt 8:5-13; Lk 7:1-10), widow's son raised (Lk 7:11-17), demoniac (Mt 12:22-23; Lk 11:14), Gadarene demoniacs (Mt 8:28-34; Mk 5:1-20; Lk 8:26-39), woman's bleeding and Jairus' daughter (Mt 9:18-26; Mk 5:21-43; Lk 8:40-56), blind man (Mt 9:27-31), mute man (Mt 9:32-33), Canaanite woman's daughter (Mt 15:21-28; Mk 7:24-30), deaf man (Mk 7:31-37), blind man (Mk 8:22-26), demoniac boy (Mt 17:14-18; Mk 9:14-29; Lk 9:37-43), ten lepers (Lk 17:11-19), man born blind (Jn 9:1-7), Lazarus raised (Jn 11), crippled woman (Lk 13:11-17), man with dropsy (Lk 14:1-6), two blind men (Mt 20:29-34; Mk 10:46-52; Lk 18:35-43), Malchus' ear (Lk 22:50-51). Other Miracles: water to wine (Jn 2:1-11), catch of fish (Lk 5:1-11), storm stilled (Mt 8:23-27; Mk 4:37-41; Lk 8:22-25), 5,000 fed (Mt 14:15-21; Mk 6:35-44; Lk 9:10-17; Jn 6:1-14), walking on water (Mt 14:25-33; Mk 6:48-52; Jn 6:15-21), 4,000 fed (Mt 15:32-39; Mk 8:1-9), money from fish (Mt 17:24-27), fig tree cursed (Mt 21:18-22; Mk 11:12-14), catch of fish (Jn 21:1-14).

MAJOR TEACHING: Sermon on the Mount (Mt 5-7; Lk 6:17-49), to Nicodemus (Jn 3), to Samaritan woman (Jn 4), Bread of Life (Jn 6:22-59), at Feast of Tabernacles (Jn 7-8), woes to Pharisees (Mt 23; Lk 11:37-54), Good Shepherd (Jn 10:1-18), Olivet Discourse (Mt 24-25; Mk 13; Lk 21:5-36), Upper Room Discourse (Jn 13-16).

PARABLES: Sower (Mt 13:3-23; Mk 4:

3-25; Lk 8:5-18), seed's growth (Mk 4:26-29), wheat and weeds (Mt 13:24-30, 36-43), mustard seed (Mt 13:31-32; Mk 4:30-32), yeast (Mt 13:33-35; Mk 4:33-34), hidden treasure (Mt 13:44), valuable pearl (Mt 13:45-46), net (Mt 13:47-51), house owner (Mt 13:52), good Samaritan (Lk 10:25-37), unmerciful servant (Mt 18:15-35), lost sheep (Mt 18:10-14; Lk 15:4-7), lost coin (Lk 15:8-10), prodigal son (Lk 15:11-32), dishonest manager (Lk 16:1-13), rich man and Lazarus (Lk 16:19-31), persistent widow (Lk 18:1-8), Pharisee and tax collector (Lk 18:9-14), payment of workers (Mt 20:1-16), tenants and the vineyard (Mt 21:28-46; Mt 12:1-12; Lk 20:9-19), wedding banquet (Mt 22:1-14), faithful servant (Mt 24:45-51), ten virgins (Mt 25:1-13), talents (Mt 25:1-30; Lk 19:12-27).

DISCIPLES see APOSTLES. Call of (Jn 1:35-51; Mt 4:18-22; 9:9; Mk 1:16-20; 2:13-14; Lk 5:1-11, 27-28). Named Apostles (Mk 3:13-19; Lk 6:12-16). Twelve sent out (Mt 10; Mk 6:7-11; Lk 9:1-5). Seventy sent out (Lk 10:1-24). Defection of (Jn 6:60-71; Mt 26:56; Mk 14:50-52). Final commission (Mt 28:16-20; Jn 21:15-23; Ac 1:3-8).

Ac 2:32 God has raised this *J* to life,
9:5 "I am *J*, whom you are persecuting
15:11 of our Lord *J* that we are saved,
16:31 "Believe in the Lord *J*,
Ro 3:24 redemption that came by Christ *J*.
5:17 life through the one man, *J* Christ.
8:1 for those who are in Christ *J*,
1Co 2:2 except *J* Christ and him crucified.
8:6 and there is but one Lord, *J* Christ,
12:3 and no one can say, "*J* is Lord,"
2Co 4:5 not preach ourselves, but *J* Christ
Gal 2:16 but by faith in *J* Christ.
3:28 for you are all one in Christ *J*.
5:6 in Christ *J* neither circumcision
Eph 2:10 created in Christ *J*
2:20 with Christ *J* himself as the chief
Php 1:6 until the day of Christ *J*.
2:5 be the same as that of Christ *J*:
2:10 name of *J* every knee should bow,
Col 3:17 do it all in the name of the Lord *J*,
2Th 2:1 the coming of our Lord *J* Christ
1Ti 1:15 Christ *J* came into the world
2Ti 3:12 life in Christ *J* will be persecuted,
Tit 2:13 our great God and Savior, *J* Christ,
Heb 2:9 But we see *J*, who was made a little
3:1 fix your thoughts on *J*, the apostle
4:14 through the heavens, *J* the Son
7:22 *J* has become the guarantee
7:24 but because *J* lives forever,
12:2 Let us fix our eyes on *J*, the author
2Pe 1:16 and coming of our Lord *J* Christ,
1Jn 1:7 and the blood of *J*, his Son,
2:1 *J* Christ, the Righteous One.
2:6 to live in him must walk as *J* did.
4:15 anyone acknowledges that *J* is
Rev 22:20 Come, Lord *J*.

JEW (JEWS JUDAISM)

Zec 8:23 of one *J* by the edge of his robe
Ro 1:16 first for the *J*, then for the Gentile.
10:12 there is no difference between *J*
1Co 9:20 To the Jews I became like a *J*,
Gal 3:28 There is neither *J* nor Greek,

JEWELRY (JEWELS)

1Pe 3:3 wearing of gold *j* and fine clothes.

JEWELS (JEWELRY)

Isa 61:10 as a bride adorns herself with her *j*.
Zec 9:16 like *j* in a crown.

JEWS (JEW)

Mt 2:2 who has been born king of the *J*?
27:11 "Are you the king of the *J*?" "Yes,
Jn 4:22 for salvation is from the *J*.
Ro 3:29 Is God the God of *J* only?
1Co 1:22 *J* demand miraculous signs
9:20 To the *J* I became like a Jew,
12:13 whether *J* or Greeks, slave or free
Gal 2:8 of Peter as an apostle to the *J*,
Rev 3:9 claim to be *J* though they are not,

JEZEBEL

Sidonian wife of Ahab (1Ki 16:31). Promoted Baal worship (1Ki 16:32-33). Killed prophets of the LORD (1Ki 18:4, 13). Opposed Elijah (1Ki 19:1-2). Had Naboth killed (1Ki 21). Death prophesied (1Ki 21:17-24). Killed by Jehu (2Ki 9:30-37).

JOASH

Son of Ahaziah; king of Judah. Sheltered from Athaliah by Jehoiada (2Ki 11; 2Ch 22:10-23:21). Repaired temple (2Ki 12; 2Ch 24).

JOB

Wealthy man from Uz; feared God (Job 1:1-5). Righteousness tested by disaster (Job 1:6-22), personal affliction (Job 2). Maintained innocence in debate with three friends (Job 3-31), Elihu (Job 32-37). Rebuked by the LORD (Job 38-41). Vindicated and restored to greater stature by the LORD (Job 42). Example of righteousness (Eze 14:14, 20).

JOHN

1. Son of Zechariah and Elizabeth (Lk 1). Called the Baptist (Mt 3:1-12; Mk 1:2-8). Witness to Jesus (Mt 3:11-12; Mk 1:7-8; Lk 3:15-18; Jn 1:6-35; 3:27-30; 5:33-36). Doubts about Jesus (Mt 11:2-6; Lk 7:18-23). Arrest (Mt 4:12; Mk 1:14). Execution (Mt 14:1-12; Mk 6:14-29; Lk 9:7-9). Ministry compared to Elijah (Mt 11:7-19; Mk 9:11-13; Lk 7:24-35).

2. Apostle; brother of James (Mt 4:21-22; 10:2; Mk 3:17; Lk 5:1-10). At transfiguration (Mt 17:1-13; Mk 9:1-13; Lk 9:28-36). Desire to be greatest (Mk 10:35-45). Leader of church at Jerusalem (Ac 4:1-3; Gal 2:9). Elder who wrote epistles (2Jn 1; 3Jn 1). Prophet who wrote Revelation (Rev 1:1; 22:8).

3. Cousin of Barnabas, co-worker with Paul, (Ac 12:12-13:13; 15:37), see MARK.

JOIN (JOINED)

Pr 23:20 Do not *j* those who drink too much
24:21 and do not *j* with the rebellious,
Ro 15:30 to *j* me in my struggle by praying
2Ti 1:8 *j* with me in suffering for the gospel

JOINED (JOIN)

Mt 19:6 Therefore what God has *j* together,
Mk 10:9 Therefore what God has *j* together,
Eph 2:21 him the whole building is *j* together
4:16 *j* and held together

JOINTS

Heb 4:12 even to dividing soul and spirit, *j*

JOKING

Eph 5:4 or coarse *j*, which are out of place,

JONAH

Prophet in days of Jeroboam II (2Ki 14:25). Called to Nineveh; fled to Tarshish (Jnh 1:1-3). Cause of storm; thrown into sea (Jnh 1:4-16). Swallowed by fish (Jnh 1:17). Prayer (Jnh 2). Preached to Nineveh (Jnh 3). Attitude reproved by the LORD (Jnh 4). Sign of (Mt 12:39-41; Lk 11:29-32).

JONATHAN

Son of Saul (1Sa 13:16; 1Ch 8:33). Valiant warrior (1Sa 13-14). Relation to David (1Sa 18:1-4; 19-20; 23:16-18). Killed at Gilboa (1Sa 31). Mourned by David (2Sa 1).

JORAM

1. Son of Ahab; king of Israel (2Ki 3; 8-9; 2Ch 22).

JORDAN

Nu 34:12 boundary will go down along the *J*
Jos 4:22 Israel crossed the *J* on dry ground.'
Mt 3:6 baptized by him in the *J* River.

JOSEPH

1. Son of Jacob by Rachel (Ge 30:24; 1Ch 2:2). Favored by Jacob, hated by brothers (Ge 37:3-4). Dreams (Ge 37:5-11). Sold by brothers (Ge 37:12-36). Served Potiphar; imprisoned by false accusation (Ge 39). Interpreted dreams of Pharaoh's servants (Ge 40), of Pharaoh (Ge 41:4-40). Made greatest in Egypt (Ge 41:41-57). Sold grain to brothers (Ge 42-45). Brought Jacob and sons to Egypt (Ge 46-47). Sons Ephraim and Manas-Zseh blessed (Ge 48). Blessed (Ge 49:22-26;ZDt 33:13-17). Death (Ge 50:22-26; Ex 13:19;ZHeb 11:22). 12,000 from (Rev 7:8).

2. Husband of Mary, mother of Jesus (Mt 1:16-24; 2:13-19; Lk 1:27; 2; Jn 1:45).

3. Disciple from Arimathea, who gave his tomb for Jesus' burial (Mt 27:57-61; Mk 15:43-47; Lk 24:50-52).

4. Original name of Barnabas (Ac 4:36).

JOSHUA

1. Son of Nun; name changed from Hoshea (Nu 13:8, 16; 1Ch 7:27). Fought Amalekites under Moses (Ex 17:9-14). Servant of Moses on Sinai (Ex 24:13; 32:17). Spied Canaan (Nu 13). With Caleb, allowed to enter land (Nu 14:6, 30). Succeeded Moses (Dt 1:38; 31:1-18; 33:9).

Charged Israel to conquer Canaan (Jos 1). Crossed Jordan (Jos 3-4). Circumcised sons of wilderness wanderings (Jos 5). Conquered Jericho (Jos 6), Ai (Jos 7-8), five kings at Gibeon (Jos 10:1-28), southern Canaan (Jos 10:29-43), northern Canaan (Jos 11-12). Defeated at Ai (Jos 7). Deceived by Gibeonites (Jos 9). Renewed covenant (Jos 8:30-35; 24:1-27). Divided land among tribes (Jos 13-22). Last words (Jos 23). Death (Jos 24:28-31).

2. High priest during rebuilding of temple (Hag 1-2; Zec 3:1-9; 6:11).

JOSIAH

Son of Amon; king of Judah (2Ki 22-23; 2Ch 34-35).

JOTHAM

Son of Azariah (Uzziah); king of Judah (2Ki 15:32-38; 2Ch 26:21-27:9).

JOY (ENJOY ENJOYMENT JOYFUL OVERJOYED REJOICE REJOICES REJOICING)

Dt 16:15 and your *j* will be complete.
1Ch 16:27 strength and *j* in his dwelling place.
Ne 8:10 for the *j* of the LORD is your
Est 9:22 their sorrow was turned into *j*
Job 38:7 and all the angels shouted for *j*?
Ps 4:7 have filled my heart with greater *j*
21:6 with the *j* of your presence.
30:11 sackcloth and clothed me with *j*,

Ps 43: 4 to God, my *j* and my delight.
51: 12 to me the *j* of your salvation
66: 1 Shout with *j* to God, all the earth!
96: 12 the trees of the forest will sing for *j*;
107: 22 and tell of his works with songs of *j*
119: 111 they are the *j* of my heart.
Pr 10: 1 A wise son brings *j* to his father,
10: 28 The prospect of the righteous is *j*,
12: 20 but *j* for those who promote peace.
Isa 35: 10 everlasting *j* will crown their heads
51: 11 Gladness and *j* will overtake them,
55: 12 You will go out in *j*
Lk 1: 44 the baby in my womb leaped for *j*.
2: 10 news of great *j* that will be
Jn 15: 11 and that your *j* may be complete.
16: 20 but your grief will turn to *j*.
2Co 8: 2 their overflowing *j* and their
Php 2: 2 then make my *j* complete
4: 1 and long for, my *j* and crown,
1Th 2: 19 For what is our hope, our *j*,
Phm : 7 Your love has given me great *j*
Heb 12: 2 for the *j* set before him endured
Jas 1: 2 Consider it pure *j*, my brothers,
1Pe 1: 8 with an inexpressible and glorious *j*
2Jn : 4 It has given me great *j* to find some
3Jn : 4 I have no greater *j*

JOYFUL (JOY)

Ps 100: 2 come before him with *j* songs.
Hab 3: 18 I will be *j* in God my Savior.
1Th 5: 16 Be *j* always; pray continually;

JUDAH

1. Son of Jacob by Leah (Ge 29:35; 35:23; 1Ch 2:1). Tribe of blessed as ruling tribe (Ge 49:8-12; Dt 33:7).

2. Name used for people and land of Southern Kingdom.

Jer 13: 19 All *J* will be carried into exile,
Zec 10: 4 From *J* will come the cornerstone,
Heb 7: 14 that our Lord descended from *J*,

JUDAISM (JEW)

Gal 1: 13 of my previous way of life in *J*,

JUDAS

1. Apostle (Lk 6:16; Jn 14:22; Ac 1:13). Probably also called Thaddaeus (Mt 10:3; Mk 3:18).

2. Brother of James and Jesus (Mt 13:55; Mk 6:3), also called Jude (Jude 1).

3. Apostle, also called Iscariot, who betrayed Jesus (Mt 10:4; 26:14-56; Mk 3:19; 14:10-50; Lk 6:16; 22:3-53; Jn 6:71; 12:4; 13:2-30; 18:2-11). Suicide of (Mt 27:3-5; Ac 1:16-25).

JUDGE (JUDGED JUDGES JUDGING JUDGMENT)

Ge 18: 25 Will not the *J* of all the earth do
1Ch 16: 33 for he comes to *j* the earth.
Ps 9: 8 He will *j* the world in righteousness
Joel 3: 12 sit to *j* all the nations on every side.
Mt 7: 1 Do not *j*, or you too will be judged.
Jn 12: 47 For I did not come to *j* the world,
Ac 17: 31 a day when he will *j* the world
Ro 2: 16 day when God will *j* men's secrets
1Co 4: 3 indeed, I do not even *j* myself.
6: 2 that the saints will *j* the world?
Gal 2: 6 not *j* by external appearance—
2Ti 4: 1 who will *j* the living and the dead,
4: 8 which the Lord, the righteous *J*,
Jas 4: 12 There is only one Lawgiver and *J*,
Jas 4: 12 who are you to *j* your neighbor?
Rev 20: 4 who had been given authority to *j*.

JUDGED (JUDGE)

Mt 7: 1 "Do not judge, or you too will be *j*.
1Co 11: 31 But if we *j* ourselves, we would not
Jas 3: 1 who teach will be *j* more strictly.
Rev 20: 12 The dead were *j* according

JUDGES (JUDGE)

Jdg 2: 16 Then the LORD raised up *j*,
Ps 58: 11 there is a God who *j* the earth."
Heb 4: 12 it *j* the thoughts and attitudes
Rev 19: 11 With justice he *j* and makes war.

JUDGING (JUDGE)

Mt 19: 28 *j* the twelve tribes of Israel.
Jn 7: 24 Stop *j* by mere appearances,

JUDGMENT (JUDGE)

Dt 1: 17 of any man, for *j* belongs to God.
Ps 1: 5 the wicked will not stand in the *j*,
119: 66 Teach me knowledge and good *j*,
Pr 6: 32 man who commits adultery lacks *j*;
12: 11 but he who chases fantasies lacks *j*.
Ecc 12: 14 God will bring every deed into *j*,
Isa 66: 16 the LORD will execute *j*
Mt 5: 21 who murders will be subject to *j*.'
10: 15 on the day of *j* than for that town.
12: 36 have to give account on the day of *j*
Jn 5: 22 but has entrusted all *j* to the Son,
7: 24 appearances, and make a right *j*."
16: 8 to sin and righteousness and *j*:
Ro 14: 10 stand before God's *j* seat.
14: 13 Therefore let us stop passing *j*
1Co 11: 29 body of the Lord eats and drinks *j*
2Co 5: 10 appear before the *j* seat of Christ,
Heb 9: 27 to die once, and after that to face *j*,
10: 27 but only a fearful expectation of *j*
1Pe 4: 17 For it is time for *j* to begin
Jude : 6 bound with everlasting chains for *j*

JUST (JUSTICE JUSTIFICATION JUSTIFIED JUSTIFY JUSTLY)

Dt 32: 4 and all his ways are *j*.
Ps 37: 28 For the LORD loves the *j*
111: 7 of his hands are faithful and *j*;
Pr 1: 3 doing what is right and *j* and fair;
2: 8 for he guards the course of the *j*
Da 4: 37 does is right and all his ways are *j*.
Ro 3: 26 as to be *j* and the one who justifies
Heb 2: 2 received its *j* punishment,
1Jn 1: 9 and *j* and will forgive us our sins
Rev 16: 7 true and *j* are your judgments."

JUSTICE (JUST)

Ex 23: 2 do not pervert *j* by siding
23: 6 "Do not deny *j* to your poor people
Job 37: 23 in his *j* and great righteousness,
Ps 9: 8 he will govern the peoples with *j*.
9: 16 The LORD is known by his *j*;
11: 7 he loves *j*;
45: 6 a scepter of *j* will be the scepter
101: 1 I will sing of your love and *j*;
106: 3 Blessed are they who maintain *j*,
Pr 21: 15 When *j* is done, it brings joy
28: 5 Evil men do not understand *j*,
29: 4 By *j* a king gives a country stability
29: 26 from the LORD that man gets *j*.
Isa 9: 7 it with *j* and righteousness
28: 17 I will make *j* the measuring line
30: 18 For the LORD is a God of *j*.
42: 1 and he will bring *j* to the nations.
42: 4 till he establishes *j* on earth.
Isa 56: 1 "Maintain *j*
61: 8 "For I, the LORD, love *j*;
Jer 30: 11 I will discipline you but only with *j*;
Eze 34: 16 I will shepherd the flock with *j*.
Am 5: 15 maintain *j* in the courts.
5: 24 But let *j* roll on like a river,
Zec 7: 9 'Administer true *j*; show mercy
Lk 11: 42 you neglect *j* and the love of God.
Ro 3: 25 He did this to demonstrate his *j*,

JUSTIFICATION (JUST)

Ro 4: 25 and was raised to life for our *j*.
5: 18 of righteousness was *j* that brings

JUSTIFIED (JUST)

Ac 13: 39 him everyone who believes is *j*
Ro 3: 24 and are *j* freely by his grace
3: 28 For we maintain that a man is *j*
5: 1 since we have been *j* through faith,
5: 9 Since we have now been *j*
8: 30 those he called, he also *j*; those he *j*,
1Co 6: 11 you were *j* in the name
Gal 2: 16 observing the law no one will be *j*.
3: 11 Clearly no one is *j* before God
3: 24 to Christ that we might be *j* by faith
Jas 2: 24 You see that a person is *j*

JUSTIFY (JUST)

Gal 3: 8 that God would *j* the Gentiles

JUSTLY (JUST)

Mic 6: 8 To act *j* and to love mercy

KEEP (KEEPER KEEPING KEEPS KEPT)

Ge 31: 49 "May the LORD *k* watch
Ex 20: 6 and *k* my commandments.
Nu 6: 24 and *k* you;
Ps 18: 28 You, O LORD, *k* my lamp burning
19: 13 *K* your servant also from willful
119: 9 can a young man *k* his way pure?
121: 7 The LORD will *k* you
141: 3 *k* watch over the door of my lips.
Pr 4: 24 *k* corrupt talk far from your lips.
Isa 26: 3 You will *k* in perfect peace
Mt 10: 10 for the worker is worth his *k*.
Lk 12: 35 and *k* your lamps burning,
Gal 5: 25 let us *k* in step with the Spirit.
Eph 4: 3 Make every effort to *k* the unity
1Ti 5: 22 *K* yourself pure.
2Ti 4: 5 *k* your head in all situations,
Heb 13: 5 *K* your lives free from the love
Jas 1: 26 and yet does not *k* a tight rein
2: 8 If you really *k* the royal law found
Jude : 24 able to *k* you from falling

KEEPER (KEEP)

Ge 4: 9 I my brother's *k*?" The LORD

KEEPING (KEEP)

Ex 20: 8 the Sabbath day by *k* it holy.
Ps 19: 11 in *k* them there is great reward.
Mt 3: 8 Produce fruit in *k* with repentance.
Lk 2: 8 *k* watch over their flocks at night.
1Co 7: 19 *K* God's commands is what counts.
2Pe 3: 9 Lord is not slow in *k* his promise,

KEEPS (KEEP)

Pr 17: 28 a fool is thought wise if he *k* silent,
Am 5: 13 Therefore the prudent man *k* quiet
1Co 13: 5 is not easily angered, it *k* no record
Jas 2: 10 For whoever *k* the whole law

KEPT (KEEP)

Ps 130: 3 If you, O LORD, *k* a record of sins,

2Ti 4: 7 finished the race, I have *k* the faith.
1Pe 1: 4 spoil or fade—*k* in heaven for you,

KEYS

Mt 16:19 I will give you the *k* of the kingdom

KILL (KILLS)

Mt 17:23 They will *k* him, and on the third

KILLS (KILL)

Lev 24:21 but whoever *k* a man must be put
2Co 3: 6 for the letter *k*, but the Spirit gives

KIND (KINDNESS KINDS)

Ge 1:24 animals, each according to its *k*."
2Ch 10: 7 "If you will be *k* to these people
Pr 11:17 A *k* man benefits himself,
12:25 but a *k* word cheers him up.
14:21 blessed is he who is *k* to the needy.
14:31 whoever is *k* to the needy honors
19:17 He who is *k* to the poor lends
Da 4:27 by being *k* to the oppressed.
Lk 6:35 because he is *k* to the ungrateful
1Co 13: 4 Love is patient, love is *k*.
15:35 With what *k* of body will they
Eph 4:32 Be *k* and compassionate
1Th 5:15 but always try to be *k* to each other
2Ti 2:24 instead, he must be *k* to everyone,
Tit 2: 5 to be busy at home, to be *k*,

KINDNESS (KIND)

Ac 14:17 He has shown *k* by giving you rain
Ro 11:22 Consider therefore the *k*
Gal 5:22 peace, patience, *k*, goodness,
Eph 2: 7 expressed in his *k* to us
2Pe 1: 7 brotherly *k*; and to brotherly *k*,

KINDS (KIND)

1Co 12: 4 There are different *k* of gifts,
1Ti 6:10 of money is a root of all *k* of evil.

KING (KINGDOM KINGS)

1. Kings of Judah and Israel: see Saul, David, Solomon.
2. Kings of Judah: see Rehoboam, Abijah, Asa, Jehoshaphat, Jehoram, Ahaziah, Athaliah (Queen), Joash, Amaziah, Uzziah, Jotham, Ahaz, Hezekiah, Manasseh, Amon, Josiah, Jehoahaz, Jehoiakim, Jehoiachin, Zedekiah.
3. Kings of Israel: see Jeroboam I, Nadab, Baasha, Elah, Zimri, Tibni, Omri, Ahab, Ahaziah, Joram, Jehu, Jehoahaz, Jehoash, Jeroboam II, Zechariah, Shallum, Menahem, Pekah, Pekahiah, Hoshea.

Jdg 17: 6 In those days Israel had no *k*;
1Sa 12:12 the LORD your God was your *k*.
Ps 24: 7 that the *K* of glory may come in.
Isa 32: 1 See, a *k* will reign in righteousness
Zec 9: 9 See, your *k* comes to you,
1Ti 6:15 the *K* of kings and Lord of lords,
1Pe 2:17 of believers, fear God, honor the *k*.
Rev 19:16 *K*OF KINGS AND LORD

KINGDOM (KING)

Ex 19: 6 you will be for me a *k* of priests
1Ch 29:11 Yours, O LORD, is the *k*;
Ps 45: 6 justice will be the scepter of your *k*.
Da 4: 3 His *k* is an eternal *k*;
Mt 3: 2 Repent, for the *k* of heaven is near
5: 3 for theirs is the *k* of heaven.
6:10 your *k* come,
6:33 But seek first his *k* and his
7:21 Lord,' will enter the *k* of heaven,
11:11 least in the *k* of heaven is greater
Mt 13:24 "The *k* of heaven is like a man who
13:31 *k* of heaven is like a mustard seed,
13:33 "The *k* of heaven is like yeast that
13:44 *k* of heaven is like treasure hidden
13:45 the *k* of heaven is like a merchant
13:47 *k* of heaven is like a net that was let
16:19 the keys of the *k* of heaven;
18:23 the *k* of heaven is like a king who
19:24 for a rich man to enter the *k* of God
24: 7 rise against nation, and *k* against *k*.
24:14 gospel of the *k* will be preached
25:34 the *k* prepared for you
Mk 9:47 better for you to enter the *k* of God
10:14 for the *k* of God belongs to such
10:23 for the rich to enter the *k* of God!"
Lk 10: 9 'The *k* of God is near you.'
12:31 seek his *k*, and these things will be
17:21 because the *k* of God is within you
Jn 3: 5 no one can enter the *k* of God
18:36 "My *k* is not of this world.
1Co 6: 9 the wicked will not inherit the *k*
15:24 hands over the *k* to God the Father
Rev 1: 6 has made us to be a *k* and priests
11:15 of the world has become the *k*

KINGS (KING)

Ps 2: 2 The *k* of the earth take their stand
72:11 All *k* will bow down to him
Da 7:24 ten horns are ten *k* who will come
1Ti 2: 2 for *k* and all those in authority,
Rev 1: 5 and the ruler of the *k* of the earth.

KINSMAN-REDEEMER (REDEEM)

Ru 3: 9 over me, since you are a *k*."

KISS

Ps 2:12 *K* the Son, lest he be angry
Pr 24:26 is like a *k* on the lips.
Lk 22:48 the Son of Man with a *k*?"

KNEE (KNEES)

Isa 45:23 Before me every *k* will bow;
Ro 14:11 'every *k* will bow before me;
Php 2:10 name of Jesus every *k* should bow,

KNEES (KNEE)

Isa 35: 3 steady the *k* that give way;
Heb 12:12 your feeble arms and weak *k*.

KNEW (KNOW)

Job 23: 3 If only I *k* where to find him;
Jnh 4: 2 I *k* that you are a gracious
Mt 7:23 tell them plainly, 'I never *k* you.

KNOCK

Mt 7: 7 *k* and the door will be opened
Rev 3:20 I am! I stand at the door and *k*.

KNOW (FOREKNEW KNEW KNOWING KNOWLEDGE KNOWN KNOWS)

Dt 18:21 "How can we *k* when a message
Job 19:25 I *k* that my Redeemer lives,
42: 3 things too wonderful for me to *k*.
Ps 46:10 "Be still, and *k* that I am God;
139: 1 and you *k* me.
139: 23 Search me, O God, and *k* my heart;
Pr 27: 1 for you do not *k* what a day may
Jer 24: 7 I will give them a heart to *k* me,
31:34 his brother, saying, '*K* the LORD,'
Mt 6: 3 let your left hand *k* what your right
24:42 you do not *k* on what day your
Lk 1: 4 so that you may *k* the certainty
Jn 3:11 we speak of what we *k*,
4:22 we worship what we do *k*,
9:25 One thing I do *k*.
10:14 I *k* my sheep and my sheep *k* me—
17: 3 that they may *k* you, the only true
21:24 We *k* that his testimony is true.
Ac 1: 7 "It is not for you to *k* the times
Ro 6: 6 For we *k* that our old self was
7:18 I *k* that nothing good lives in me,
8:28 we *k* that in all things God works
1Co 2: 2 For I resolved to *k* nothing
6:15 Do you not *k* that your bodies are
6:19 Do you not *k* that your body is
13:12 Now I *k* in part; then I shall *k* fully,
15:58 because you *k* that your labor
Php 3:10 I want to *k* Christ and the power
2Ti 1:12 because I *k* whom I have believed,
Jas 4:14 *k* what will happen tomorrow.
1Jn 2: 4 The man who says, "I *k* him,"
3:14 We *k* that we have passed
3:16 This is how we *k* what love is:
5: 2 This is how we *k* that we love
5:13 so that you may *k* that you have

KNOWING (KNOW)

Ge 3: 5 and you will be like God, *k* good
Php 3: 8 of *k* Christ Jesus my Lord,

KNOWLEDGE (KNOW)

Ge 2: 9 the tree of the *k* of good and evil.
Job 42: 3 obscures my counsel without *k*?'
Ps 19: 2 night after night they display *k*.
73:11 Does the Most High have *k*?"
139: 6 Such *k* is too wonderful for me,
Pr 1: 7 of the LORD is the beginning of *k*,
10:14 Wise men store up *k*,
12: 1 Whoever loves discipline loves *k*,
13:16 Every prudent man acts out of *k*,
19: 2 to have zeal without *k*,
Isa 11: 9 full of the *k* of the LORD
Hab 2:14 filled with the *k* of the glory
Ro 11:33 riches of the wisdom and *k* of God!
1Co 8: 1 *K* puffs up, but love builds up.
8:11 Christ died, is destroyed by your *k*.
13: 2 can fathom all mysteries and all *k*,
2Co 2:14 everywhere the fragrance of the *k*
4: 6 light of the *k* of the glory of God
Eph 3:19 to know this love that surpasses *k*
Col 2: 3 all the treasures of wisdom and *k*.
1Ti 6:20 ideas of what is falsely called *k*,
2Pe 3:18 grow in the grace and *k* of our Lord

KNOWN (KNOW)

Ps 16:11 You have made *k* to me the path
105: 1 make *k* among the nations what he
Isa 46:10 *k* the end from the beginning,
Mt 10:26 or hidden that will not be made *k*.
Ro 1:19 since what may be *k* about God is
11:34 "Who has *k* the mind of the Lord?
15:20 the gospel where Christ was not *k*,
2Co 3: 2 written on our hearts, *k*
2Pe 2:21 than to have *k* it and then

KNOWS (KNOW)

1Sa 2: 3 for the LORD is a God who *k*,
Job 23:10 But he *k* the way that I take;
Ps 44:21 since he *k* the secrets of the heart?
94:11 The LORD *k* the thoughts of man;
Ecc 8: 7 Since no man *k* the future,
Mt 6: 8 for your Father *k* what you need
24:36 "No one *k* about that day or hour,
Ro 8:27 who searches our hearts *k* the mind
1Co 8: 2 who thinks he *k* something does
2Ti 2:19 The Lord *k* those who are his," and

LABAN

Brother of Rebekah (Ge 24:29-51), father of Rachel and Leah (Ge 29-31).

LABOR

Ex 20: 9 Six days you shall *l* and do all your
Isa 55: 2 and your *l* on what does not satisfy
Mt 6:28 They do not *l* or spin.
1Co 3: 8 rewarded according to his own *l.*
15:58 because you know that your *l*

LACK (LACKING LACKS)

Pr 15:22 Plans fail for *l* of counsel,
Ro 3: 3 Will their *l* of faith nullify God's
Col 2:23 *l* any value in restraining sensual

LACKING (LACK)

Ro 12:11 Never be *l* in zeal, but keep your
Jas 1: 4 and complete, not *l* anything.

LACKS (LACK)

Pr 6:32 who commits adultery *l* judgment;
12:11 he who chases fantasies *l* judgment
Jas 1: 5 any of you *l* wisdom, he should ask

LAID (LAY)

Isa 53: 6 and the LORD has *l* on him
1Co 3:11 other than the one already *l,*
1Jn 3:16 Jesus Christ *l* down his life for us.

LAKE

Rev 19:20 into the fiery *l* of burning sulfur.
20:14 The *l* of fire is the second death.

LAMB (LAMB'S LAMBS)

Ge 22: 8 "God himself will provide the *l*
Ex 12:21 and slaughter the Passover *l.*
Isa 11: 6 The wolf will live with the *l,*
53: 7 he was led like a *l* to the slaughter,
Jn 1:29 *L* of God, who takes away the sin
1Co 5: 7 our Passover *l,* has been sacrificed.
1Pe 1:19 a *l* without blemish or defect.
Rev 5: 6 Then I saw a *L,* looking
5:12 "Worthy is the *L,* who was slain,
14: 4 They follow the *L* wherever he

LAMB'S (LAMB)

Rev 21:27 written in the *L* book of life.

LAMBS (LAMB)

Lk 10: 3 I am sending you out like *l*
Jn 21:15 Jesus said, "Feed my *l.*"

LAMENT

2Sa 1:17 took up this *l* concerning Saul

LAMP (LAMPS)

2Sa 22:29 You are my *l,* O LORD;
Ps 18:28 You, O LORD, keep my *l* burning;
119:105 Your word is a *l* to my feet
Pr 31:18 and her *l* does not go out at night.
Lk 8:16 "No one lights a *l* and hides it
Rev 21:23 gives it light, and the Lamb is its *l.*

LAMPS (LAMP)

Mt 25: 1 be like ten virgins who took their *l*
Lk 12:35 for service and keep your *l* burning,

LAND

Ge 1:10 God called the dry ground "*l,*"
1:11 "Let the *l* produce vegetation:
12: 7 To your offspring I will give this *l.*"
Ex 3: 8 a *l* flowing with milk and honey—
Nu 35:33 Do not pollute the *l* where you are.
Dt 34: 1 LORD showed him the whole *l*—
Jos 13: 2 "This is the *l* that remains:
14: 4 Levites received no share of the *l*
2Ch 7:14 their sin and will heal their *l.*
7:20 then I will uproot Israel from my *l,*
Eze 36:24 and bring you back into your own *l.*

LANGUAGE

Ge 11: 1 Now the whole world had one *l*
Ps 19: 3 There is no speech or *l*
Jn 8:44 When he lies, he speaks his native *l*
Ac 2: 6 heard them speaking in his own *l.*
Col 3: 8 slander, and filthy *l* from your lips.
Rev 5: 9 from every tribe and *l* and people

LAST (LASTING LASTS LATTER)

2Sa 23: 1 These are the *l* words of David:
Isa 44: 6 I am the first and I am the *l;*
Mt 19:30 But many who are first will be *l,*
Mk 10:31 are first will be *l,* and the *l* first."
Jn 15:16 and bear fruit—fruit that will *l.*
Ro 1:17 is by faith from first to *l,*
2Ti 3: 1 will be terrible times in the *l* days.
2Pe 3: 3 in the *l* days scoffers will come,
Rev 1:17 I am the First and the *L.*
22:13 the First and the *L,* the Beginning

LASTING (LAST)

Ex 12:14 to the LORD—a *l* ordinance.
Lev 24: 8 of the Israelites, as a *l* covenant.
Nu 25:13 have a covenant of a *l* priesthood,
Heb 10:34 had better and *l* possessions.

LASTS (LAST)

Ps 30: 5 For his anger *l* only a moment,
2Co 3:11 greater is the glory of that which *l!*

LATTER (LAST)

Job 42:12 The LORD blessed the *l* part

LAUGH (LAUGHS)

Ecc 3: 4 a time to weep and a time to *l,*

LAUGHS (LAUGH)

Ps 2: 4 The One enthroned in heaven *l;*
37:13 but the Lord *l* at the wicked,

LAVISHED

Eph 1: 8 of God's grace that he *l* on us
1Jn 3: 1 great is the love the Father has *l*

LAW (LAWS)

Dt 31:11 you shall read this *l* before them
31:26 "Take this Book of the *L*
Jos 1: 8 of the *L* depart from your mouth;
Ne 8: 8 from the Book of the *L* of God,
Ps 1: 2 and on his *l* he meditates day
19: 7 The *l* of the LORD is perfect,
119: 18 wonderful things in your *l.*
119: 72 *l* from your mouth is more precious
119: 97 Oh, how I love your *l!*
119:165 peace have they who love your *l,*
Isa 8:20 To the *l* and to the testimony!
Jer 31:33 "I will put my *l* in their minds
Mt 5:17 that I have come to abolish the *L*
7:12 sums up the *L* and the Prophets.
22:40 All the *L* and the Prophets hang
Lk 16:17 stroke of a pen to drop out of the *L.*
Jn 1:17 For the *l* was given through Moses;
Ro 2:12 All who sin apart from the *l* will
2:15 of the *l* are written on their hearts,
5:13 for before the *l* was given,
5:20 *l* was added so that the trespass
6:14 because you are not under *l,*
7: 6 released from the *l* so that we serve
Ro 7:12 *l* is holy, and the commandment is
8: 3 For what the *l* was powerless to do
10: 4 Christ is the end of the *l*—
13:10 love is the fulfillment of the *l.*
Gal 3:13 curse of the *l* by becoming a curse
3:24 So the *l* was put in charge to lead us
5: 3 obligated to obey the whole *l.*
5: 4 justified by *l* have been alienated
5:14 The entire *l* is summed up
Heb 7:19 (for the *l* made nothing perfect),
10: 1 The *l* is only a shadow
Jas 1:25 intently into the perfect *l* that gives
2:10 For whoever keeps the whole *l*

LAWLESSNESS*

2Th 2: 3 and the man of *l* is revealed,
2: 7 power of *l* is already at work;
1Jn 3: 4 sins breaks the law; in fact, sin is *l.*

LAWS (LAW)

Lev 25:18 and be careful to obey my *l,*
Ps 119: 30 I have set my heart on your *l.*
119:120 I stand in awe of your *l.*
Heb 8:10 I will put my *l* in their minds
10:16 I will put my *l* in their hearts,

LAY (LAID LAYING)

Job 22:22 and *l* up his words in your heart.
Isa 28:16 "See, I *l* a stone in Zion,
Mt 8:20 of Man has no place to *l* his head."
Jn 10:15 and I *l* down my life for the sheep.
15:13 that he *l* down his life
1Co 3:11 no one can *l* any foundation other
1Jn 3:16 And we ought to *l* down our lives
Rev 4:10 They *l* their crowns

LAYING (LAY)

1Ti 5:22 Do not be hasty in the *l* on of hands
Heb 6: 1 not *l* again the foundation

LAZARUS

1. Poor man in Jesus' parable (Lk 16: 19-31).

2. Brother of Mary and Martha whom Jesus raised from the dead (Jn 11:1-12:19).

LAZY

Pr 10: 4 *L* hands make a man poor,
Heb 6:12 We do not want you to become *l,*

LEAD (LEADERS LEADERSHIP LEADS LED)

Ex 15:13 "In your unfailing love you will *l*
Ps 27:11 *l* me in a straight path
61: 2 *l* me to the rock that is higher
139: 24 and *l* me in the way everlasting.
143: 10 *l* me on level ground.
Ecc 5: 6 Do not let your mouth *l* you
Isa 11: 6 and a little child will *l* them.
Da 12: 3 those who *l* many to righteousness,
Mt 6:13 And *l* us not into temptation,
1Jn 3: 7 do not let anyone *l* you astray.

LEADERS (LEAD)

Heb 13: 7 Remember your *l,* who spoke
13:17 Obey your *l* and submit

LEADERSHIP (LEAD)

Ro 12: 8 if it is *l,* let him govern diligently;

LEADS (LEAD)

Ps 23: 2 he *l* me beside quiet waters,
Pr 19:23 The fear of the LORD *l* to life:
Isa 40:11 he gently *l* those that have young.
Mt 7:13 and broad is the road that *l*
15:14 If a blind man *l* a blind man,

Jn 10: 3 sheep by name and l them out.
Ro 14: 19 effort to do what l to peace
2Co 2: 14 always l us in triumphal procession

LEAH

Wife of Jacob (Ge 29:16-30); bore six sons and one daughter (Ge 29:31-30:21; 34:1; 35:23).

LEAN

Pr 3: 5 l not on your own understanding;

LEARN (LEARNED LEARNING)

Isa 1: 17 l to do right!
Mt 11: 29 yoke upon you and l from me,

LEARNED (LEARN)

Php 4: 11 for I have l to be content whatever
2Ti 3: 14 continue in what you have l

LEARNING (LEARN)

Pr 1: 5 let the wise listen and add to their l,
2Ti 3: 7 always l but never able

LED (LEAD)

Ps 68: 18 you l captives in your train;
Isa 53: 7 he was l like a lamb to the slaughter
Am 2: 10 and I l you forty years in the desert
Ro 8: 14 those who are l by the Spirit
Eph 4: 8 he l captives in his train

LEFT

Jos 1: 7 turn from it to the right or to the l,
Pr 4: 27 Do not swerve to the right or the l;
Mt 6: 3 do not let your l hand know what
25: 33 on his right and the goats on his l.

LEGION

Mk 5: 9 "My name is L," he replied,

LEND (LENDS)

Dt 15: 8 freely l him whatever he needs.
Ps 37: 26 are always generous and l freely;
Lk 6: 34 if you l to those from whom you

LENDS (LEND)

Pr 19: 17 to the poor l to the LORD,

LENGTH (LONG)

Ps 90: 10 The l of our days is seventy years—
Pr 10: 27 The fear of the LORD adds l to life

LEPROSY

2Ki 7: 3 men with l at the entrance

LETTER (LETTERS)

Mt 5: 18 not the smallest l, not the least
2Co 3: 2 You yourselves are our l, written
3: 6 for the l kills, but the Spirit gives
2Th 3: 14 not obey our instruction in this l,

LETTERS (LETTER)

2Co 3: 7 which was engraved in l on stone,
10: 10 "His l are weighty and forceful,"
2Pe 3: 16 His l contain some things that are

LEVEL

Ps 143: 10 lead me on l ground.
Pr 4: 26 Make l paths for your feet
Isa 26: 7 The path of the righteous is l;
Heb 12: 13 "Make l paths for your feet,"

LEVI (LEVITES)

1. Son of Jacob by Leah (Ge 29:34; 46:11; 1Ch 2:1). Tribe of blessed (Ge 49:5-7; Dt 33:8-11), chosen as priests (Nu 3-4), numbered (Nu 3:39; 26:62), allotted cities, but not land (Nu 18; 35; Dt 10:9; Jos 13:14; 21), land (Eze 48:8-22), 12,000 from (Rev 7:7).
2. See MATTHEW.

LEVITES (LEVI)

Nu 1: 53 The L are to be responsible
8: 6 "Take the L from among the other
18: 21 I give to the L all the tithes in Israel

LEWDNESS

Mk 7: 22 malice, deceit, l, envy, slander,

LIAR (LIE)

Pr 19: 22 better to be poor than a l.
Jn 8: 44 for he is a l and the father of lies.
Ro 3: 4 Let God be true, and every man a l.

LIBERATED*

Ro 8: 21 that the creation itself will be l

LIE (LIAR LIED LIES LYING)

Lev 19: 11 " 'Do not l.
Nu 23: 19 God is not a man, that he should l,
Dt 6: 7 when you l down and when you get
Ps 23: 2 me l down in green pastures,
Isa 11: 6 leopard will l down with the goat,
Eze 34: 14 they will l down in good grazing
Ro 1: 25 exchanged the truth of God for a l,
Col 3: 9 Do not l to each other,
Heb 6: 18 which it is impossible for God to l,

LIED (LIE)

Ac 5: 4 You have not l to men but to God."

LIES (LIE)

Ps 34: 13 and your lips from speaking l.
Jn 8: 44 for he is a liar and the father of l.

LIFE (LIVE)

Ge 2: 7 into his nostrils the breath of l,
2: 9 of the garden were the tree of l
9: 11 Never again will all l be cut
Ex 21: 23 you are to take l for l, eye for eye,
Lev 17: 14 the l of every creature is its blood.
24: 18 must make restitution—l for l.
Dt 30: 19 Now choose l, so that you
Ps 16: 11 known to me the path of l;
23: 6 all the days of my l,
34: 12 Whoever of you loves l
39: 4 let me know how fleeting is my l.
49: 7 No man can redeem the l
104: 33 I will sing to the LORD all my l;
Pr 1: 3 a disciplined and prudent l,
6: 23 are the way to l,
7: 23 little knowing it will cost him his l.
8: 35 For whoever finds me finds l
11: 30 of the righteous is a tree of l,
21: 21 finds l, prosperity and honor.
Jer 10: 23 that a man's l is not his own;
Eze 37: 5 enter you, and you will come to l.
Da 12: 2 some to everlasting l, others
Mt 6: 25 Is not l more important than food,
7: 14 and narrow the road that leads to l,
10: 39 Whoever finds his l will lose it,
16: 25 wants to save his l will lose it,
20: 28 to give his l as a ransom for many."
Mk 10: 45 to give his l as a ransom for many."
Lk 12: 15 a man's l does not consist
12: 22 do not worry about your l,
14: 26 even his own l—he cannot be my
Jn 1: 4 In him was l, and that l was
3: 15 believes in him may have eternal l.
3: 36 believes in the Son has eternal l,
4: 14 of water welling up to eternal l."
5: 24 him who sent me has eternal l
6: 35 Jesus declared, "I am the bread of l
6: 47 he who believes has everlasting l.
6: 68 You have the words of eternal l.
10: 10 I have come that they may have l,
10: 15 and I lay down my l for the sheep.
10: 28 I give them eternal l, and they shall
11: 25 "I am the resurrection and the l.
14: 6 am the way and the truth and the l.
15: 13 lay down his l for his friends.
20: 31 that by believing you may have l
Ac 13: 48 appointed for eternal l believed.
Ro 4: 25 was raised to l for our justification.
6: 13 have been brought from death to l;
6: 23 but the gift of God is eternal l
8: 38 convinced that neither death nor l,
1Co 15: 19 If only for this l we have hope
2Co 3: 6 letter kills, but the Spirit gives l.
Gal 2: 20 The l I live in the body, I live
Eph 4: 1 I urge you to live a l worthy
Php 2: 16 as you hold out the word of l—
Col 1: 10 order that you may live a l worthy
1Th 4: 12 so that your daily l may win
1Ti 4: 8 for both the present l and the l
4: 16 Watch your l and doctrine closely.
6: 19 hold of the l that is truly l.
2Ti 3: 12 to live a godly l in Christ Jesus will
Jas 1: 12 crown of l that God has promised
3: 13 Let him show it by his good l,
1Pe 3: 10 "Whoever would love l
2Pe 1: 3 given us everything we need for l
1Jn 3: 14 we have passed from death to l,
5: 11 has given us eternal l, and this l is
Rev 13: 8 written in the book of l belonging
20: 12 was opened, which is the book of l.
21: 27 written in the Lamb's book of l.
22: 2 side of the river stood the tree of l,

LIFT (LIFTED)

Ps 121: 1 I l up my eyes to the hills—
134: 2 L up your hands in the sanctuary
La 3: 41 Let us l up our hearts and our
1Ti 2: 8 everywhere to l up holy hands

LIFTED (LIFT)

Ps 40: 2 He l me out of the slimy pit,
Jn 3: 14 Moses l up the snake in the desert,
12: 32 when I am l up from the earth,

LIGHT (ENLIGHTENED)

Ge 1: 3 "Let there be l," and there was l.
2Sa 22: 29 LORD turns my darkness into l.
Job 38: 19 "What is the way to the abode of l?
Ps 4: 6 Let the l of your face shine upon us
19: 8 giving l to the eyes.
27: 1 LORD is my l and my salvation—
56: 13 God in the l of life.
76: 4 You are resplendent with l,
104: 2 He wraps himself in l
119: 105 and a l for my path.
119: 130 The unfolding of your words gives l;
Isa 2: 5 let us walk in the l of the LORD.
9: 2 have seen a great l;
49: 6 also make you a l for the Gentiles,
Mt 4: 16 have seen a great l;
5: 16 let your l shine before men,
11: 30 yoke is easy and my burden is l."
Jn 3: 19 but men loved darkness instead of l
8: 12 he said, "I am the l of the world.
2Co 4: 6 made his l shine in our hearts

2Co 6:14 Or what fellowship can *l* have
11:14 masquerades as an angel of *l*.
1Ti 6:16 and who lives in unapproachable *l*,
1Pe 2:9 of darkness into his wonderful *l*.
1Jn 1:5 God is *l*; in him there is no
1:7 But if we walk in the *l*,
Rev 21:23 for the glory of God gives it *l*,

LIGHTNING
Da 10:6 his face like *l*, his eyes like flaming
Mt 24:27 For as the *l* that comes from the east
28:3 His appearance was like *l*,

LIKENESS
Ge 1:26 man in our image, in our *l*,
Ps 17:15 I will be satisfied with seeing your *l*
Isa 52:14 his form marred beyond human *l*—
Ro 8:3 Son in the *l* of sinful man
8:29 to be conformed to the *l* of his Son,
2Co 3:18 his *l* with ever-increasing glory,
Php 2:7 being made in human *l*.
Jas 3:9 who have been made in God's *l*.

LILIES
Lk 12:27 "Consider how the *l* grow.

LION
Isa 11:7 and the *l* will eat straw like the ox.
1Pe 5:8 around like a roaring *l* looking
Rev 5:5 See, the *L* of the tribe of Judah,

LIPS
Ps 8:2 From the *l* of children and infants
34:1 his praise will always be on my *l*.
119:171 May my *l* overflow with praise,
Pr 13:3 He who guards his *l* guards his life,
27:2 someone else, and not your own *l*.
Isa 6:5 For I am a man of unclean *l*,
Mt 21:16 " 'From the *l* of children
Col 3:8 and filthy language from your *l*.

LISTEN (LISTENING LISTENS)
Dt 30:20 *l* to his voice, and hold fast to him.
Pr 1:5 let the wise *l* and add
Jn 10:27 My sheep *l* to my voice; I know
Jas 1:19 Everyone should be quick to *l*,
1:22 Do not merely *l* to the word,

LISTENING (LISTEN)
1Sa 3:9 Speak, LORD, for your servant is *l*
Pr 18:13 He who answers before *l*—

LISTENS (LISTEN)
Pr 12:15 but a wise man *l* to advice.

LIVE (ALIVE LIFE LIVES LIVING)
Ex 20:12 so that you may *l* long
33:20 for no one may see me and *l*."
Dt 8:3 to teach you that man does not *l*
Job 14:14 If a man dies, will he *l* again?
Ps 119:175 Let me *l* that I may praise you,
Isa 55:3 hear me, that your soul may *l*.
Eze 37:3 can these bones *l*?" I said,
Hab 2:4 but the righteous will *l* by his faith
Mt 4:4 'Man does not *l* on bread alone,
Ac 17:24 does not *l* in temples built by hands
17:28 'For in him we *l* and move
Ro 1:17 "The righteous will *l* by faith."
2Co 5:7 We *l* by faith, not by sight.
Gal 2:20 The life I *l* in the body, I *l* by faith
5:25 Since we *l* by the Spirit, let us keep
Php 1:21 to *l* is Christ and to die is gain.
1Th 5:13 *L* in peace with each other.
2Ti 3:12 who wants to *l* a godly life
Heb 12:14 Make every effort to *l* in peace
1Pe 1:17 *l* your lives as strangers here

LIVES (LIVE)
Job 19:25 I know that my Redeemer *l*,
Isa 57:15 he who *l* forever, whose name is
Da 3:28 to give up their *l* rather than serve
Jn 14:17 for he *l* with you and will be in you.
Ro 7:18 I know that nothing good *l* in me,
14:7 For none of us *l* to himself alone
1Co 3:16 and that God's Spirit *l* in you?
Gal 2:20 I no longer live, but Christ *l* in me.
Heb 13:5 Keep your *l* free from the love
2Pe 3:11 You ought to live holy and godly *l*
1Jn 3:16 to lay down our *l* for our brothers.
4:16 Whoever *l* in love *l* in God,

LIVING (LIVE)
Ge 2:7 and man became a *l* being.
Jer 2:13 the spring of *l* water,
Mt 22:32 the God of the dead but of the *l*."
Jn 7:38 streams of *l* water will flow
Ro 12:1 to offer your bodies as *l* sacrifices,
Heb 4:12 For the word of God is *l* and active.
10:31 to fall into the hands of the *l* God.
Rev 1:18 I am the *L* One; I was dead,

LOAD
Gal 6:5 for each one should carry his own *l*.

LOCUSTS
Mt 3:4 His food was *l* and wild honey.

LOFTY
Ps 139:6 too *l* for me to attain.
Isa 57:15 is what the high and *l* One says—

LONELY
Ps 68:6 God sets the *l* in families,

LONG (LENGTH LONGED LONGING LONGS)
1Ki 18:21 "How *l* will you waver
Jn 9:4 As *l* as it is day, we must do
Eph 3:18 to grasp how wide and *l* and high
1Pe 1:12 Even angels *l* to look

LONGED (LONG)
Mt 13:17 righteous men *l* to see what you see
23:37 how often I have *l*
2Ti 4:8 to all who have *l* for his appearing.

LONGING (LONG)
Pr 13:19 A *l* fulfilled is sweet to the soul,
2Co 5:2 *l* to be clothed with our heavenly

LONGS (LONG)
Isa 30:18 Yet the LORD *l* to be gracious

LOOK (LOOKING LOOKS)
Dt 4:29 you will find him if you *l* for him
Job 31:1 not to *l* lustfully at a girl.
Ps 34:5 Those who *l* to him are radiant;
Pr 4:25 Let your eyes *l* straight ahead,
Isa 60:5 Then you will *l* and be radiant,
Hab 1:13 Your eyes are too pure to *l* on evil;
Zec 12:10 They will *l* on me, the one they
Mk 13:21 '*L*, here is the Christ!' or, '*L*,
Lk 24:39 *L* at my hands and my feet.
Jn 1:36 he said, "*L*, the Lamb of God!"
4:35 open your eyes and *l* at the fields!
19:37 "They will *l* on the one they have
Jas 1:27 to *l* after orphans and widows
1Pe 1:12 long to *l* into these things.

LOOKING (LOOK)
2Co 10:7 You are *l* only on the surface
Rev 5:6 I saw a Lamb, *l* as if it had been

LOOKS (LOOK)
1Sa 16:7 Man *l* at the outward appearance,
Lk 9:62 and *l* back is fit for service
Php 2:21 For everyone *l* out

LORD† (LORD'S† LORDING)
Ne 4:14 Remember the *L*, who is great
Job 28:28 'The fear of the *L*—that is wisdom,
Ps 54:4 the *L* is the one who sustains me.
62:12 and that you, O *L*, are loving.
86:5 You are forgiving and good, O *L*,
110:1 The LORD says to my *L*:
147:5 Great is our *L* and mighty in power
Isa 6:1 I saw the *L* seated on a throne,
Da 9:4 "O *L*, the great and awesome God,
Mt 3:3 'Prepare the way for the *L*,
4:7 'Do not put the *L* your God
7:21 "Not everyone who says to me, '*L*,
22:37 " 'Love the *L* your God
22:44 For he says, " 'The *L* said to my *L*:
Mk 12:11 the *L* has done this,
12:29 the *L* our God, the *L* is one.
Lk 2:9 glory of the *L* shone around them,
6:46 "Why do you call me, '*L*, *L*,'
10:27 " 'Love the *L* your God
Ac 2:21 on the name of the *L* will be saved.'
16:31 replied, "Believe in the *L* Jesus,
Ro 10:9 with your mouth, "Jesus is *L*,"
10:13 on the name of the *L* will be saved
12:11 your spiritual fervor, serving the *L*.
14:8 we live to the *L*; and if we die,
1Co 1:31 Let him who boasts boast in the *L*."
3:5 the *L* has assigned to each his task.
7:34 to be devoted to the *L* in both body
10:9 We should not test the *L*,
11:23 For I received from the *L* what I
12:3 "Jesus is *L*," except by the Holy
15:57 victory through our *L* Jesus Christ.
16:22 If anyone does not love the *L*—
2Co 3:17 Now the *L* is the Spirit,
8:5 they gave themselves first to the *L*
10:17 Let him who boasts boast in the *L*."
Gal 6:14 in the cross of our *L* Jesus Christ,
Eph 4:5 one *L*, one faith, one baptism;
5:10 and find out what pleases the *L*.
5:19 make music in your heart to the *L*,
Php 2:11 confess that Jesus Christ is *L*,
3:1 my brothers, rejoice in the *L*!
4:4 Rejoice in the *L* always.
Col 2:6 as you received Christ Jesus as *L*,
3:17 do it all in the name of the *L* Jesus,
3:23 as working for the *L*, not for men,
4:17 work you have received in the *L*."
1Th 3:12 May the *L* make your love increase
5:2 day of the *L* will come like a thief
5:23 at the coming of our *L* Jesus Christ.
2Th 2:1 the coming of our *L* Jesus Christ
2Ti 2:19 "The *L* knows those who are his,"
Heb 12:14 holiness no one will see the *L*.
13:6 *L* is my helper; I will not be afraid.
Jas 4:10 Humble yourselves before the *L*,
1Pe 1:25 the word of the *L* stands forever."
2:3 you have tasted that the *L* is good.
3:15 in your hearts set apart Christ as *L*.
2Pe 1:16 and coming of our *L* Jesus Christ,
2:1 the sovereign *L* who bought

†This entry represents the translation of the Hebrew name for God, *Yahweh*, always indicated in the NIV by LORD. For Lord, see the concordance entries **LORD†** and **LORD'S†**.

2Pe 3:9 The L is not slow in keeping his
Jude :14 the L is coming with thousands
Rev 4:8 holy, holy is the L God Almighty,
4:11 "You are worthy, our L and God,
17:14 he is L of lords and King of kings—
22:20 Come, L Jesus.

LORD'S† (LORD†)

Ac 21:14 and said, "The L will be done."
1Co 10:26 "The earth is the L, and everything
11:26 you proclaim the L death
2Co 3:18 faces all reflect the L glory,
2Ti 2:24 And the L servant must not quarrel
Jas 4:15 you ought to say, "If it is the L will,

LORDING* (LORD†)

1Pe 5:3 not l it over those entrusted to you,

LORD‡ (LORD'S‡)

Ge 2:4 When the L God made the earth
2:7 the L God formed the man
3:21 The L God made garments of skin
7:16 Then the L shut him in.
15:6 Abram believed the L,
18:14 Is anything too hard for the L?
31:49 "May the L keep watch
Ex 3:2 the angel of the L appeared to him
9:12 the L hardened Pharaoh's heart
14:30 That day the L saved Israel
20:2 "I am the L your God, who
33:11 The L would speak to Moses face
40:34 glory of the L filled the tabernacle.
Lev 19:2 'Be holy because I, the L your God,
Nu 8:5 L said to Moses: "Take the Levites
14:21 glory of the L fills the whole earth,
Dt 2:7 forty years the L your God has
5:9 the L your God, am a jealous God,
6:4 The L our God, the L is one.
6:5 Love the L your God
6:16 Do not test the L your God
10:14 To the L your God belong
10:17 For the L your God is God of gods
11:1 Love the L your God and keep his
28:1 If you fully obey the L your God
30:16 today to love the L your God,
30:20 For the L is your life, and he will
31:6 for the L your God goes with you;
Jos 22:5 to love the L your God, to walk
24:15 my household, we will serve the L
1Sa 1:28 So now I give him to the L.
2:2 "There is no one holy like the L;
7:12 "Thus far has the L helped us."
12:22 his great name the L will not reject
15:22 "Does the L delight
2Sa 22:2 "The L is my rock, my fortress
1Ki 2:3 and observe what the L your God
8:11 the glory of the L filled his temple.
8:61 fully committed to the L our God,
18:21 If the L is God, follow him;
2Ki 13:23 But the L was gracious to them
1Ch 16:8 Give thanks to the L, call
16:23 Sing to the L, all the earth;
28:9 for the L searches every heart
29:11 O L, is the greatness and the power
2Ch 5:14 the glory of the L filled the temple
16:9 of the L range throughout the earth
19:6 judging for man but for the L,
30:9 for the L your God is gracious
Ne 1:5 Then I said: "O L, God of heaven,
Job 1:21 L gave and the L has taken away;
Job 38:1 the L answered Job out
42:9 and the L accepted Job's prayer.
Ps 1:2 But his delight is in the law of the L
9:9 The L is a refuge for the oppressed,
12:6 And the words of the L are flawless
16:8 I have set the L always before me.
18:30 the word of the L is flawless.
19:7 The law of the L is perfect,
19:14 O L, my Rock and my Redeemer.
23:1 The L is my shepherd, I shall not be
23:6 I will dwell in the house of the L
27:1 The L is my light and my salvation
27:4 to gaze upon the beauty of the L
29:1 Ascribe to the L, O mighty ones,
32:2 whose sin the L does not count
33:12 is the nation whose God is the L,
33:18 But the eyes of the L are
34:3 Glorify the L with me;
34:7 The angel of the L encamps
34:8 Taste and see that the L is good;
34:18 The L is close to the brokenhearted
37:4 Delight yourself in the L
40:1 I waited patiently for the L;
47:2 How awesome is the L Most High,
48:1 Great is the L, and most worthy
55:22 Cast your cares on the L
75:8 In the hand of the L is a cup
84:11 For the L God is a sun and shield;
86:11 Teach me your way, O L,
89:5 heavens praise your wonders, O L,
91:2 I will say of the L, "He is my refuge
95:1 Come, let us sing for joy to the L;
96:1 Sing to the L a new song;
98:4 Shout for joy to the L, all the earth,
100:1 Shout for joy to the L, all the earth.
103:1 Praise the L, O my soul;
103:8 The L is compassionate
104:1 O L my God, you are very great;
107:8 to the L for his unfailing love
110:1 The L says to my Lord:
113:4 L is exalted over all the nations,
115:1 Not to us, O L, not to us
116:15 Precious in the sight of the L
118:1 Give thanks to the L, for he is good
118:24 This is the day the L has made;
121:2 My help comes from the L,
121:5 The L watches over you—
125:2 so the L surrounds his people
127:1 Unless the L builds the house,
127:3 Sons are a heritage from the L,
130:3 If you, O L, kept a record of sins,
135:6 The L does whatever pleases him,
136:1 Give thanks to the L, for he is good
139:1 O L, you have searched me
144:3 O L, what is man that you care
145:3 Great is the L and most worthy
145:18 The L is near to all who call on him
Pr 1:7 The fear of the L is the beginning
3:5 Trust in the L with all your heart
3:9 Honor the L with your wealth,
3:12 the L disciplines those he loves,
3:19 By wisdom the L laid the earth's
5:21 are in full view of the L,
6:16 There are six things the L hates,
10:27 The fear of the L adds length to life
11:1 The L abhors dishonest scales,
12:22 The L detests lying lips,
14:26 He who fears the L has a secure
15:3 The eyes of the L are everywhere,
Pr 16:2 but motives are weighed by the L.
16:4 The L works out everything
16:9 but the L determines his steps.
16:33 but its every decision is from the L.
18:10 The name of the L is a strong tower
18:22 and receives favor from the L.
19:14 but a prudent wife is from the L.
19:17 to the poor lends to the L,
21:3 to the L than sacrifice.
21:30 that can succeed against the L.
21:31 but victory rests with the L.
22:2 The L is the Maker of them all.
24:18 or the L will see and disapprove
31:30 a woman who fears the L is
Isa 6:3 holy, holy is the L Almighty;
11:2 The Spirit of the L will rest on him
11:9 full of the knowledge of the L
12:2 The L, the L, is my strength
24:1 the L is going to lay waste the earth
25:8 The Sovereign L will wipe away
29:15 to hide their plans from the L,
33:6 the fear of the L is the key
35:10 the ransomed of the L will return.
40:5 the glory of the L will be revealed,
40:7 the breath of the L blows on them.
40:10 the Sovereign L comes with power,
40:28 The L is the everlasting God,
40:31 but those who hope in the L
42:8 "I am the L; that is my name!
43:11 I, even I, am the L,
44:24 I am the L,
45:5 I am the L, and there is no other;
45:21 Was it not I, the L?
51:11 The ransomed of the L will return.
53:6 and the L has laid on him
53:10 and the will of the L will prosper
55:6 Seek the L while he may be found;
58:8 of the L will be your rear guard.
58:11 The L will guide you always;
59:1 the arm of the L is not too short
61:3 a planting of the L
61:10 I delight greatly in the L;
Jer 1:9 Then the L reached out his hand
9:24 I am the L, who exercises kindness,
16:19 O L, my strength and my fortress,
17:7 is the man who trusts in the L,
La 3:40 and let us return to the L.
Eze 1:28 of the likeness of the glory of the L.
Hos 1:7 horsemen, but by the L their God."
3:5 They will come trembling to the L
6:1 "Come, let us return to the L.
Joel 2:1 for the day of the L is coming.
2:11 The day of the L is great;
3:14 For the day of the L is near
Am 5:18 long for the day of the L?
Jnh 1:3 But Jonah ran away from the L
Mic 4:2 up to the mountain of the L,
6:8 And what does the L require of you
Na 1:2 The L takes vengeance on his foes
1:3 The L is slow to anger
Hab 2:14 knowledge of the glory of the L,
2:20 But the L is in his holy temple;
Zep 3:17 The L your God is with you,
Zec 1:17 and the L will again comfort Zion
9:16 The L their God will save them
14:5 Then the L my God will come,
14:9 The L will be king
Mal 4:5 and dreadful day of the L comes.

LORD'S‡ (LORD‡)

Ex 34:34 he entered the L presence
Nu 14:41 you disobeying the L command?

‡This entry represents the translation of the Hebrew name for God, *Yahweh*, always indicated in the NIV by LORD. For Lord, see the concordance entries **LORD†** and **LORD'S†**.

Dt 6:18 is right and good in the *L* sight,
32: 9 For the *L* portion is his people,
Jos 21:45 Not one of all the *L* good promises
Ps 24: 1 The earth is the *L*, and everything
32:10 but the *L* unfailing love
89: 1 of the *L* great love forever;
103: 17 *L* love is with those who fear him,
Pr 3:11 do not despise the *L* discipline
Isa 24:14 west they acclaim the *L* majesty.
62: 3 of splendor in the *L* hand,
Jer 48:10 lax in doing the *L* work!
La 3:22 of the *L* great love we are not
Mic 4: 1 of the *L* temple will be established

LOSE (LOSES LOSS LOST)

1Sa 17:32 "Let no one *l* heart on account
Mt 10:39 Whoever finds his life will *l* it,
Lk 9:25 and yet *l* or forfeit his very self?
Jn 6:39 that I shall *l* none of all that he has
Heb 12: 3 will not grow weary and *l* heart.
12: 5 do not *l* heart when he rebukes you

LOSES (LOSE)

Mt 5:13 But if the salt *l* its saltiness,
Lk 15: 4 you has a hundred sheep and *l* one
15: 8 has ten silver coins and *l* one.

LOSS (LOSE)

Ro 11:12 and their *l* means riches
1Co 3:15 he will suffer *l*; he himself will be
Php 3: 8 I consider everything a *l* compared

LOST (LOSE)

Ps 73: 2 I had nearly *l* my foothold.
Jer 50: 6 "My people have been *l* sheep;
Eze 34: 4 the strays or searched for the *l*.
34:16 for the *l* and bring back the strays.
Mt 18:14 any of these little ones should be *l*.
Lk 15: 4 go after the *l* sheep until he finds it?
15: 6 with me; I have found my *l* sheep.'
15: 9 with me; I have found my *l* coin.'
15:24 is alive again; he was *l* and is found
19:10 to seek and to save what was *l*."
Php 3: 8 for whose sake I have *l* all things.

LOT (LOTS)

Nephew of Abraham (Ge 11:27; 12:5). Chose to live in Sodom (Ge 13). Rescued from four kings (Ge 14). Rescued from Sodom (Ge 19:1-29; 2Pe 2:7). Fathered Moab and Ammon by his daughters (Ge 19:30-38).

Est 3: 7 the *l*) in the presence of Haman
9:24 the *l*) for their ruin and destruction.
Pr 16:33 The *l* is cast into the lap,
18:18 Casting the *l* settles disputes
Ecc 3:22 his work, because that is his *l*.
Ac 1:26 Then they drew lots, and the *l* fell

LOTS (LOT)

Ps 22:18 and cast *l* for my clothing.
Mt 27:35 divided up his clothes by casting *l*.

LOVE (BELOVED LOVED LOVELY LOVER LOVERS LOVES LOVING)

Ge 22: 2 your only son, Isaac, whom you *l*,
Ex 15:13 "In your unfailing *l* you will lead
20: 6 showing *l* to a thousand generations
20: 6 of those who *l* me
34: 6 abounding in *l* and faithfulness,
Lev 19:18 but *l* your neighbor as yourself.
19:34 *L* him as yourself,
Nu 14:18 abounding in *l* and forgiving sin
Dt 5:10 showing *l* to a thousand generations
5:10 of those who *l* me
Dt 6: 5 *L* the LORD your God
7:13 He will *l* you and bless you
10:12 to walk in all his ways, to *l* him,
11:13 to *l* the LORD your God
13: 6 wife you *l*, or your closest friend
30: 6 so that you may *l* him
Jos 22: 5 to *l* the LORD your God, to walk
1Ki 3: 3 Solomon showed his *l*
8:23 you who keep your covenant of *l*
2Ch 5:13 his *l* endures forever."
Ne 1: 5 covenant of *l* with those who *l* him
Ps 18: 1 I *l* you, O LORD, my strength.
23: 6 Surely goodness and *l* will follow
25: 6 O LORD, your great mercy and *l*,
31:16 save me in your unfailing *l*.
32:10 but the LORD's unfailing *l*
33: 5 the earth is full of his unfailing *l*.
33:18 whose hope is in his unfailing *l*,
36: 5 Your *l*, O LORD, reaches
36: 7 How priceless is your unfailing *l*!
45: 7 You *l* righteousness and hate
51: 1 according to your unfailing *l*;
57:10 For great is your *l*, reaching
63: 3 Because your *l* is better than life,
66:20 or withheld his *l* from me!
70: 4 may those who *l* your salvation
77: 8 Has his unfailing *l* vanished forever
85: 7 Show us your unfailing *l*, O LORD
85:10 *L* and faithfulness meet together;
86:13 For great is your *l* toward me;
89: 1 of the LORD's great *l* forever;
89:33 but I will not take my *l* from him,
92: 2 to proclaim your *l* in the morning
94:18 your *l*, O LORD, supported me.
100: 5 is good and his *l* endures forever;
101: 1 I will sing of your *l* and justice;
103: 4 crowns you with *l* and compassion.
103: 8 slow to anger, abounding in *l*.
103: 11 so great is his *l* for those who fear
107: 8 to the LORD for his unfailing *l*
108: 4 For great is your *l*, higher
116: 1 I *l* the LORD, for he heard my
118: 1 his *l* endures forever.
119: 47 because I *l* them.
119: 64 The earth is filled with your *l*,
119: 76 May your unfailing *l* be my
119: 97 Oh, how I *l* your law!
119:119 therefore I *l* your statutes.
119:124 your servant according to your *l*
119:132 to those who *l* your name.
119:159 O LORD, according to your *l*.
119:163 but I *l* your law.
119:165 peace have they who *l* your law,
122: 6 "May those who *l* you be secure.
130: 7 for with the LORD is unfailing *l*
136: 1 -26 *His l endures forever.*
143: 8 of your unfailing *l*,
145: 8 slow to anger and rich in *l*.
145: 20 over all who *l* him,
147: 11 who put their hope in his unfailing *l*
Pr 3: 3 Let *l* and faithfulness never leave
4: 6 *l* her, and she will watch over you.
5:19 you ever be captivated by her *l*.
8:17 I *l* those who *l* me,
9: 8 rebuke a wise man and he will *l* you
10:12 but *l* covers over all wrongs.
14:22 those who plan what is good find *l*
15:17 of vegetables where there is *l*
17: 9 over an offense promotes *l*,
19:22 What a man desires is unfailing *l*;
20: 6 claims to have unfailing *l*,
20:13 Do not *l* sleep or you will grow
20:28 through *l* his throne is made secure
21:21 who pursues righteousness and *l*
27: 5 rebuke than hidden *l*.
Ecc 9: 6 Their *l*, their hate
9: 9 life with your wife, whom you *l*,
SS 2: 4 and his banner over me is *l*.
8: 6 for *l* is as strong as death,
8: 7 Many waters cannot quench *l*;
8: 7 all the wealth of his house for *l*,
Isa 5: 1 I will sing for the one I *l*
16: 5 In *l* a throne will be established;
38:17 In your *l* you kept me
54:10 yet my unfailing *l* for you will not
55: 3 my faithful *l* promised to David.
61: 8 "For I, the LORD, *l* justice;
63: 9 In his *l* and mercy he redeemed
Jer 5:31 and my people *l* it this way.
31: 3 you with an everlasting *l*;
32:18 You show *l* to thousands
33:11 his *l* endures forever."
La 3:22 of the LORD's great *l* we are not
3:32 so great is his unfailing *l*.
Eze 33:32 more than one who sings *l* songs
Da 9: 4 covenant of *l* with all who *l* him
Hos 2:19 in *l* and compassion.
3: 1 Go, show your *l* to your wife again,
11: 4 with ties of *l*;
12: 6 maintain *l* and justice,
Joel 2:13 slow to anger and abounding in *l*,
Am 5:15 Hate evil, *l* good;
Mic 3: 2 you who hate good and *l* evil;
6: 8 To act justly and to *l* mercy
Zep 3:17 he will quiet you with his *l*,
Zec 8:19 Therefore *l* truth and peace."
Mt 3:17 "This is my Son, whom I *l*;
5:44 *L* your enemies and pray
6:24 he will hate the one and *l* the other,
17: 5 "This is my Son, whom I *l*;
19:19 and '*l* your neighbor as yourself.' "
22:37 " '*L* the Lord your God
Lk 6:32 Even 'sinners' *l* those who *l* them.
7:42 which of them will *l* him more?"
20:13 whom I *l*; perhaps they will respect
Jn 13:34 I give you: *L* one another.
13:35 disciples, if you *l* one another."
14:15 "If you *l* me, you will obey what I
15:13 Greater *l* has no one than this,
15:17 This is my command: *L* each other.
21:15 do you truly *l* me more than these
Ro 5: 5 because God has poured out his *l*
5: 8 God demonstrates his own *l* for us
8:28 for the good of those who *l* him,
8:35 us from the *l* of Christ?
8:39 us from the *l* of God that is
12: 9 *L* must be sincere.
12:10 to one another in brotherly *l*.
13: 8 continuing debt to *l* one another,
13: 9 "*L* your neighbor as yourself."
13:10 Therefore *l* is the fulfillment
13:10 *L* does no harm to its neighbor.
1Co 2: 9 prepared for those who *l* him"—
8: 1 Knowledge puffs up, but *l* builds up
13: 1 have not *l*, I am only a resounding
13: 2 but have not *l*, I am nothing.
13: 3 but have not *l*, I gain nothing.
13: 4 Love is patient, *l* is kind.
13: 4 *L* is patient, love is kind.
13: 6 *L* does not delight in evil
13: 8 *L* never fails.
13:13 But the greatest of these is *l*.
13:13 three remain: faith, hope and *l*.
14: 1 way of *l* and eagerly desire spiritual
16:14 Do everything in *l*.
2Co 5:14 For Christ's *l* compels us,
8: 8 sincerity of your *l* by comparing it
8:24 show these men the proof of your *l*
Gal 5: 6 is faith expressing itself through *l*.
5:13 rather, serve one another in *l*.
5:22 But the fruit of the Spirit is *l*, joy,
Eph 1: 4 In *l* he predestined us
2: 4 But because of his great *l* for us,

Eph 3: 17 being rooted and established in *l*,
3: 18 and high and deep is the *l* of Christ,
3: 19 and to know this *l* that surpasses
4: 2 bearing with one another in *l*.
4: 15 Instead, speaking the truth in *l*,
5: 2 loved children and live a life of *l*,
5: 25 *l* your wives, just as Christ loved
5: 28 husbands ought to *l* their wives
5: 33 each one of you also must *l* his wife
Php 1: 9 that your *l* may abound more
2: 2 having the same *l*, being one
Col 1: 5 *l* that spring from the hope that is
2: 2 in heart and united in *l*,
3: 14 And over all these virtues put on *l*,
3: 19 *l* your wives and do not be harsh
1Th 1: 3 your labor prompted by *l*,
4: 9 taught by God to *l* each other.
5: 8 on faith and *l* as a breastplate,
2Th 3: 5 direct your hearts into God's *l*
1Ti 1: 5 The goal of this command is *l*,
2: 15 *l* and holiness with propriety.
4: 12 in life, in *l*, in faith and in purity.
6: 10 For the *l* of money is a root
6: 11 faith, *l*, endurance and gentleness.
2Ti 1: 7 of power, of *l* and of self-discipline.
2: 22 and pursue righteousness, faith, *l*
3: 10 faith, patience, *l*, endurance,
Tit 2: 4 women to *l* their husbands
Phm : 9 yet I appeal to you on the basis of *l*.
Heb 6: 10 and the *l* you have shown him
10: 24 may spur one another on toward *l*
13: 5 free from the *l* of money
Jas 1: 12 promised to those who *l* him.
2: 5 he promised those who *l* him?
2: 8 "*L* your neighbor as yourself,"
1Pe 1: 22 the truth so that you have sincere *l*
1: 22 *l* one another deeply,
2: 17 *L* the brotherhood of believers,
3: 8 be sympathetic, *l* as brothers,
3: 10 "Whoever would *l* life
4: 8 Above all, *l* each other deeply,
4: 8 *l* covers over a multitude of sins.
5: 14 Greet one another with a kiss of *l*.
2Pe 1: 7 and to brotherly kindness, *l*.
1: 17 "This is my Son, whom I *l*;
1Jn 2: 5 God's *l* is truly made complete
2: 15 Do not *l* the world or anything
3: 1 How great is the *l* the Father has
3: 10 anyone who does not *l* his brother.
3: 11 We should *l* one another.
3: 14 Anyone who does not *l* remains
3: 16 This is how we know what *l* is:
3: 18 let us not *l* with words or tongue
3: 23 to *l* one another as he commanded
4: 7 Dear friends, let us *l* one another,
4: 7 for *l* comes from God.
4: 8 Whoever does not *l* does not know
4: 9 This is how God showed his *l*
4: 10 This is *l*: not that we loved God,
4: 11 we also ought to *l* one another.
4: 12 and his *l* is made complete in us.
4: 16 God is *l*.
4: 16 Whoever lives in *l* lives in God,
4: 17 *l* is made complete among us
4: 18 But perfect *l* drives out fear,
4: 19 We *l* because he first loved us.
4: 20 If anyone says, "I *l* God,"
4: 21 loves God must also *l* his brother.
5: 2 we know that we *l* the children
5: 3 This is *l* for God: to obey his
2Jn : 5 I ask that we *l* one another.
: 6 his command is that you walk in *l*.
: 6 this is *l*: that we walk in obedience
Jude : 12 men are blemishes at your *l* feasts,
: 21 Keep yourselves in God's *l*
Rev 2: 4 You have forsaken your first *l*.
3: 19 Those whom I *l* I rebuke
12: 11 they did not *l* their lives so much

LOVED (LOVE)

Ge 24: 67 she became his wife, and he *l* her;
29: 30 and he *l* Rachel more than Leah.
37: 3 Now Israel *l* Joseph more than any
Dt 7: 8 But it was because the LORD *l* you
1Sa 1: 5 a double portion because he *l* her,
20: 17 because he *l* him as he *l* himself.
Ps 44: 3 light of your face, for you *l* them.
Jer 2: 2 how as a bride you *l* me
31: 3 "I have *l* you with an everlasting
Hos 2: 23 to the one I called 'Not my *l* one.'
3: 1 though she is *l* by another
9: 10 became as vile as the thing they *l*.
11: 1 "When Israel was a child, I *l* him,
Mal 1: 2 "But you ask, 'How have you *l* us?'
Mk 12: 6 left to send, a son, whom he *l*.
Jn 3: 16 so *l* the world that he gave his one
3: 19 but men *l* darkness instead of light
11: 5 Jesus *l* Martha and her sister
12: 43 for they *l* praise from men more
13: 1 Having *l* his own who were
13: 23 the disciple whom Jesus *l*,
13: 34 As I have *l* you, so you must love
14: 21 He who loves me will be *l*
15: 9 the Father has *l* me, so have I *l* you.
15: 12 Love each other as I have *l* you.
19: 26 the disciple whom he *l* standing
Ro 8: 37 conquerors through him who *l* us.
9: 13 "Jacob I *l*, but Esau I hated."
9: 25 her 'my *l* one' who is not my *l* one,"
11: 28 they are *l* on account
Gal 2: 20 who *l* me and gave himself for me.
Eph 5: 2 as Christ *l* us and gave himself up
5: 25 just as Christ *l* the church
2Th 2: 16 who *l* us and by his grace gave us
2Ti 4: 10 for Demas, because he *l* this world,
Heb 1: 9 You have *l* righteousness
1Jn 4: 10 This is love: not that we *l* God,
4: 11 Dear friends, since God so *l* us,
4: 19 We love because he first *l* us.

LOVELY (LOVE)

Ps 84: 1 How *l* is your dwelling place,
SS 2: 14 and your face is *l*.
5: 16 he is altogether *l*.
Php 4: 8 whatever is *l*, whatever is

LOVER (LOVE)

SS 2: 16 *Beloved* My *l* is mine and I am his;
7: 10 I belong to my *l*,
1Ti 3: 3 not quarrelsome, not a *l* of money.

LOVERS (LOVE)

2Ti 3: 2 People will be *l* of themselves,
3: 3 without self-control, brutal, not *l*
3: 4 *l* of pleasure rather than *l* of God—

LOVES (LOVE)

Ps 11: 7 he *l* justice;
33: 5 The LORD *l* righteousness
34: 12 Whoever of you *l* life
91: 14 Because he *l* me," says the LORD,
127: 2 for he grants sleep to those he *l*.
Pr 3: 12 the LORD disciplines those he *l*,
12: 1 Whoever *l* discipline *l* knowledge,
13: 24 he who *l* him is careful
17: 17 A friend *l* at all times,
17: 19 He who *l* a quarrel *l* sin;
22: 11 He who *l* a pure heart and whose
Ecc 5: 10 whoever *l* wealth is never satisfied
Mt 10: 37 anyone who *l* his son or daughter
Lk 7: 47 has been forgiven little *l* little."
Jn 3: 35 Father *l* the Son and has placed
10: 17 reason my Father *l* me is that I lay
12: 25 The man who *l* his life will lose it,
14: 21 obeys them, he is the one who *l* me.
14: 23 Jesus replied, "If anyone *l* me,
Ro 13: 8 for he who *l* his fellowman has
2Co 9: 7 for God *l* a cheerful giver.
Eph 5: 28 He who *l* his wife *l* himself.
5: 33 must love his wife as he *l* himself,
Heb 12: 6 the Lord disciplines those he *l*,
1Jn 2: 10 Whoever *l* his brother lives
2: 15 If anyone *l* the world, the love
4: 7 Everyone who *l* has been born
4: 21 Whoever *l* God must also love his
5: 1 who *l* the father *l* his child
3Jn : 9 but Diotrephes, who *l* to be first,
Rev 1: 5 To him who *l* us and has freed us

LOVING (LOVE)

Ps 25: 10 All the ways of the LORD are *l*
62: 12 and that you, O Lord, are *l*.
145: 17 and *l* toward all he has made.
Heb 13: 1 Keep on *l* each other as brothers.
1Jn 5: 2 by *l* God and carrying out his

LOWLY

Job 5: 11 The *l* he sets on high,
Pr 29: 23 but a man of *l* spirit gains honor.
Isa 57: 15 also with him who is contrite and *l*
Eze 21: 26 *l* will be exalted and the exalted
1Co 1: 28 He chose the *l* things of this world

LUKE*

Co-worker with Paul (Col 4:14; 2Ti 4:11; Phm 24).

LUKEWARM*

Rev 3: 16 So, because you are *l*—neither hot

LUST

Pr 6: 25 Do not *l* in your heart
Col 3: 5 sexual immorality, impurity, *l*,
1Th 4: 5 not in passionate *l* like the heathen,
1Jn 2: 16 the *l* of his eyes and the boasting

LYING (LIE)

Pr 6: 17 a *l* tongue,
26: 28 A *l* tongue hates those it hurts,

MACEDONIA

Ac 16: 9 "Come over to *M* and help us."

MADE (MAKE)

Ge 1: 16 He also *m* the stars.
1: 25 God *m* the wild animals according
2: 22 Then the LORD God *m* a woman
2Ki 19: 15 You have *m* heaven and earth.
Ps 95: 5 The sea is his, for he *m* it,
100: 3 It is he who *m* us, and we are his;
118: 24 This is the day the LORD has *m*;
139: 14 I am fearfully and wonderfully *m*;
Ecc 3: 11 He has *m* everything beautiful
Mk 2: 27 "The Sabbath was *m* for man,
Jn 1: 3 Through him all things were *m*;
Ac 17: 24 "The God who *m* the world
Heb 1: 2 through whom he *m* the universe.
Rev 14: 7 Worship him who *m* the heavens,

MAGI

Mt 2: 1 *M* from the east came to Jerusalem

MAGOG

Eze 38: 2 of the land of *M,* the chief prince
39: 6 I will send fire on *M*
Rev 20: 8 and *M*—to gather them for battle.

MAIDEN

Pr 30: 19 and the way of a man with a *m.*
Isa 62: 5 As a young man marries a *m,*
Jer 2: 32 Does a *m* forget her jewelry,

MAIMED

Mt 18: 8 It is better for you to enter life *m*

MAJESTIC (MAJESTY)

Ex 15: 6 was *m* in power.
15: 11 *m* in holiness,
Ps 8: 1 how *m* is your name in all the earth
29: 4 the voice of the LORD is *m.*
111: 3 Glorious and *m* are his deeds,
SS 6: 10 *m* as the stars in procession?
2Pe 1: 17 came to him from the *M* Glory,

MAJESTY (MAJESTIC)

Ex 15: 7 In the greatness of your *m*
Dt 33: 26 and on the clouds in his *m.*
1Ch 16: 27 Splendor and *m* are before him;
Est 1: 4 the splendor and glory of his *m.*
Job 37: 22 God comes in awesome *m.*
40: 10 and clothe yourself in honor and *m*
Ps 45: 4 In your *m* ride forth victoriously
93: 1 The LORD reigns, he is robed in *m*
110: 3 Arrayed in holy *m,*
145: 5 of the glorious splendor of your *m,*
Isa 53: 2 or *m* to attract us to him,
Eze 31: 2 can be compared with you in *m?*
2Pe 1: 16 but we were eyewitnesses of his *m.*
Jude : 25 only God our Savior be glory, *m,*

MAKE (MADE MAKER MAKES MAKING)

Ge 1: 26 "Let us *m* man in our image,
2: 18 I will *m* a helper suitable for him."
12: 2 "I will *m* you into a great nation
Ex 22: 3 thief must certainly *m* restitution,
Nu 6: 25 the LORD *m* his face shine
Ps 108: 1 *m* music with all my soul.
Isa 14: 14 I will *m* myself like the Most High
29: 16 "He did not *m* me"?
Jer 31: 31 "when I will *m* a new covenant
Mt 3: 3 *m* straight paths for him.' "
28: 19 and *m* disciples of all nations,
Mk 1: 17 "and I will *m* you fishers of men."
Lk 13: 24 "*M* every effort to enter
14: 23 country lanes and *m* them come in,
Ro 14: 19 *m* every effort to do what leads
2Co 5: 9 So we *m* it our goal to please him,
Eph 4: 3 *M* every effort to keep the unity
Col 4: 5 *m* the most of every opportunity.
1Th 4: 11 *M* it your ambition
Heb 4: 11 *m* every effort to enter that rest,
12: 14 *M* every effort to live in peace
2Pe 1: 5 *m* every effort to add
3: 14 *m* every effort to be found spotless,

MAKER (MAKE)

Job 4: 17 Can a man be more pure than his *M*
36: 3 I will ascribe justice to my *M.*
Ps 95: 6 kneel before the LORD our *M;*
Pr 22: 2 The LORD is the *M* of them all.
Isa 45: 9 to him who quarrels with his *M,*
54: 5 For your *M* is your husband—
Jer 10: 16 for he is the *M* of all things,

MAKES (MAKE)

1Co 3: 7 only God, who *m* things grow.

MAKING (MAKE)

Ps 19: 7 *m* wise the simple.
Ecc 12: 12 Of *m* many books there is no end,
Jn 5: 18 *m* himself equal with God.
Eph 5: 16 *m* the most of every opportunity,

MALE

Ge 1: 27 *m* and female he created them.
Gal 3: 28 slave nor free, *m* nor female,

MALICE (MALICIOUS)

Ro 1: 29 murder, strife, deceit and *m.*
Col 3: 8 *m,* slander, and filthy language
1Pe 2: 1 rid yourselves of all *m*

MALICIOUS (MALICE)

Pr 26: 24 A *m* man disguises himself
1Ti 3: 11 not *m* talkers but temperate
6: 4 *m* talk, evil suspicions

MAN (MEN WOMAN WOMEN)

Ge 1: 26 "Let us make *m* in our image,
2: 7 God formed the *m* from the dust
2: 18 for the *m* to be alone
2: 23 she was taken out of *m.*
9: 6 Whoever sheds the blood of *m,*
Dt 8: 3 *m* does not live on bread
1Sa 13: 14 a *m* after his own heart
15: 29 he is not a *m* that he
Job 14: 1 *M* born of woman is of few
14: 14 If a *m* dies, will he live
Ps 1: 1 Blessed is the *m* who does
8: 4 what is *m* that you are
119: 9 can a young *m* keep his
127: 5 Blessed is the *m* whose quiver
Pr 14: 12 that seems right to a *m,*
30: 19 way of a *m* with a maiden.
Isa 53: 3 a *m* of sorrows,
Mt 19: 5 a *m* will leave his father
Mk 8: 36 What good is it for a *m*
Lk 4: 4 '*M* does not live on bread
Ro 5: 12 entered the world through one *m*
1Co 7: 2 each *m* should have his own
11: 3 head of every *m* is Christ,
11: 3 head of woman is *m*
13: 11 When I became a *m,*
Php 2: 8 found in appearance as a *m,*
1Ti 2: 5 the *m* Christ Jesus,
2: 11 have authority over a *m;*
Heb 9: 27 as *m* is destined to die

MANAGE

Jer 12: 5 how will you *m* in the thickets
1Ti 3: 4 He must *m* his own family well
3: 12 one wife and must *m* his children
5: 14 to *m* their homes and to give

MANASSEH

1. Firstborn of Joseph (Ge 41:51; 46:20). Blessed (Ge 48).

2. Son of Hezekiah; king of Judah (2Ki 21:1-18; 2Ch 33:1-20).

MANGER

Lk 2: 12 in strips of cloth and lying in a *m.*"

MANNA

Ex 16: 31 people of Israel called the bread *m.*
Dt 8: 16 He gave you *m* to eat in the desert,
Jn 6: 49 Your forefathers ate the *m*
Rev 2: 17 I will give some of the hidden *m.*

MANNER

1Co 11: 27 in an unworthy *m* will be guilty
Php 1: 27 conduct yourselves in a *m* worthy

MARITAL* (MARRY)

Ex 21: 10 of her food, clothing and *m* rights.
Mt 5: 32 except for *m* unfaithfulness,
19: 9 except for *m* unfaithfulness,

1Co 7: 3 husband should fulfill his *m* duty

MARK (MARKS)

Cousin of Barnabas (Col 4:10; 2Ti 4:11; Phm 24; 1Pe 5:13), see JOHN.

Ge 4: 15 Then the LORD put a *m* on Cain
Rev 13: 16 to receive a *m* on his right hand

MARKS (MARK)

Jn 20: 25 Unless I see the nail *m* in his hands
Gal 6: 17 bear on my body the *m* of Jesus.

MARRED

Isa 52: 14 his form *m* beyond human likeness

MARRIAGE (MARRY)

Mt 22: 30 neither marry nor be given in *m;*
24: 38 marrying and giving in *m,*
Ro 7: 2 she is released from the law of *m.*
Heb 13: 4 by all, and the *m* bed kept pure,

MARRIED (MARRY)

Ro 7: 2 by law a *m* woman is bound
1Co 7: 27 Are you *m?* Do not seek a divorce.
7: 33 But a *m* man is concerned about
7: 36 They should get *m.*

MARRIES (MARRY)

Mt 5: 32 and anyone who *m* the divorced
19: 9 and *m* another woman commits
Lk 16: 18 the man who *m* a divorced woman

MARRY (INTERMARRY MARITAL MARRIAGE MARRIED MARRIES)

Mt 22: 30 resurrection people will neither *m*
1Co 7: 1 It is good for a man not to *m.*
7: 9 control themselves, they should *m,*
1Ti 5: 14 So I counsel younger widows to *m,*

MARTHA*

Sister of Mary and Lazarus (Lk 10:38-42; Jn 11; 12:2).

MARVELED

Lk 2: 33 mother *m* at what was said about

MARY

1. Mother of Jesus (Mt 1:16-25; Lk 1:27-56; 2:1-40). With Jesus at temple (Lk 2:41-52), at the wedding in Cana (Jn 2:1-5), questioning his sanity (Mk 3:21), at the cross (Jn 19:25-27). Among disciples after Ascension (Ac 1:14).

2. Magdalene; former demoniac (Lk 8:2). Helped support Jesus' ministry (Lk 8:1-3). At the cross (Mt 27:56; Mk 15:40; Jn 19:25), burial (Mt 27:61; Mk 15:47). Saw angel after resurrection (Mt 28:1-10; Mk 16:1-9; Lk 24:1-12); also Jesus (Jn 20:1-18).

3. Sister of Martha and Lazarus (Jn 11). Washed Jesus' feet (Jn 12:1-8).

MASQUERADES*

2Co 11: 14 for Satan himself *m* as an angel

MASTER (MASTERED MASTERS)

Mt 10: 24 nor a servant above his *m.*
23: 8 for you have only one *M*
24: 46 that servant whose *m* finds him
25: 21 "His *m* replied, 'Well done,
Ro 6: 14 For sin shall not be your *m,*
14: 4 To his own *m* he stands or falls.
2Ti 2: 21 useful to the *M* and prepared

MASTERED* (MASTER)

1Co 6: 12 but I will not be *m* by anything.
2Pe 2: 19 a slave to whatever has *m* him.

MASTERS (MASTER)
Mt 6:24 "No one can serve two *m*.
Eph 6:5 obey your earthly *m* with respect
6:9 And *m*, treat your slaves
Tit 2:9 subject to their *m* in everything,

MATTHEW*
Apostle; former tax collector (Mt 9:9-13; 10:3; Mk 3:18; Lk 6:15; Ac 1:13). Also called Levi (Mk 2:14-17; Lk 5:27-32).

MATURE (MATURITY)
Eph 4:13 of the Son of God and become *m*,
Php 3:15 of us who are *m* should take such
Heb 5:14 But solid food is for the *m*,
Jas 1:4 work so that you may be *m*

MATURITY* (MATURE)
Heb 6:1 about Christ and go on to *m*,

MEAL
Pr 15:17 Better a *m* of vegetables where
1Co 10:27 some unbeliever invites you to a *m*
Heb 12:16 for a single *m* sold his inheritance

MEANING
Ne 8:8 and giving the *m* so that the people

MEANS
1Co 9:22 by all possible *m* I might save some

MEAT
Ro 14:6 He who eats *m*, eats to the Lord,
14:21 It is better not to eat *m*

MEDIATOR
1Ti 2:5 and one *m* between God and men,
Heb 8:6 of which he is *m* is superior
9:15 For this reason Christ is the *m*
12:24 to Jesus the *m* of a new covenant,

MEDICINE*
Pr 17:22 A cheerful heart is good *m*,

MEDITATE (MEDITATES MEDITATION)
Jos 1:8 from your mouth; *m* on it day
Ps 119:15 I *m* on your precepts
119:78 but I will *m* on your precepts.
119:97 I *m* on it all day long.
145:5 I will *m* on your wonderful works.

MEDITATES* (MEDITATE)
Ps 1:2 and on his law he *m* day and night.

MEDITATION* (MEDITATE)
Ps 19:14 of my mouth and the *m* of my heart
104:34 May my *m* be pleasing to him,

MEDIUM
Lev 20:27 " 'A man or woman who is a *m*

MEEK (MEEKNESS)
Ps 37:11 But the *m* will inherit the land
Mt 5:5 Blessed are the *m*,

MEEKNESS* (MEEK)
2Co 10:1 By the *m* and gentleness of Christ,

MEET (MEETING)
Ps 85:10 Love and faithfulness *m* together;
Am 4:12 prepare to *m* your God, O Israel."
1Th 4:17 them in the clouds to *m* the Lord

MEETING (MEET)
Heb 10:25 Let us not give up *m* together,

MELCHIZEDEK
Ge 14:18 *M* king of Salem brought out bread
Ps 110:4 in the order of *M*."
Heb 7:11 in the order of *M*, not in the order

MELT
2Pe 3:12 and the elements will *m* in the heat.

MEMBERS
Mic 7:6 a man's enemies are the *m*
Ro 7:23 law at work in the *m* of my body,
12:4 of us has one body with many *m*,
1Co 6:15 not know that your bodies are *m*
12:24 But God has combined the *m*
Eph 4:25 for we are all *m* of one body.
Col 3:15 as *m* of one body you were called

MEN (MAN)
Mt 4:19 will make you fishers of *m*
5:16 your light shine before *m*
12:36 *m* will have to give account
Jn 12:32 will draw all *m* to myself
Ac 5:29 obey God rather than *m*!
Ro 1:27 indecent acts with other *m*,
5:12 death came to all *m*,
1Co 9:22 all things to all *m*
2Co 5:11 we try to persuade *m*.
1Ti 2:4 wants all *m* to be saved
2Ti 2:2 entrust to reliable *m*
2Pe 1:21 but *m* spoke from God

MENAHEM
King of Israel (2Ki 15:17-22).

MERCIFUL (MERCY)
Dt 4:31 the LORD your God is a *m* God;
Ne 9:31 for you are a gracious and *m* God.
Mt 5:7 Blessed are the *m*,
Lk 6:36 Be *m*, just as your Father is *m*.
Heb 2:17 in order that he might become a *m*
Jude :22 Be *m* to those who doubt; snatch

MERCY (MERCIFUL)
Ex 33:19 *m* on whom I will have *m*,
Ps 25:6 O LORD, your great *m* and love,
Isa 63:9 and *m* he redeemed them;
Hos 6:6 For I desire *m*, not sacrifice,
Mic 6:8 To act justly and to love *m*
Hab 3:2 in wrath remember *m*.
Mt 12:7 'I desire *m*, not sacrifice,' you
23:23 justice, *m* and faithfulness.
Ro 9:15 "I will have *m* on whom I have *m*,
Eph 2:4 who is rich in *m*, made us alive
Jas 2:13 *M* triumphs over judgment!
1Pe 1:3 In his great *m* he has given us new

MESSAGE
Isa 53:1 Who has believed our *m*
Jn 12:38 "Lord, who has believed our *m*
Ro 10:17 faith comes from hearing the *m*,
1Co 1:18 For the *m* of the cross is
2Co 5:19 to us the *m* of reconciliation.

MESSIAH*
Jn 1:41 "We have found the *M*" (that is,
4:25 "I know that *M*" (called Christ) "is

METHUSELAH
Ge 5:27 Altogether, *M* lived 969 years,

MICHAEL
Archangel (Jude 9); warrior in angelic realm, protector of Israel (Da 10:13, 21; 12:1; Rev 12:7).

MIDWIVES
Ex 1:17 The *m*, however, feared God

MIGHT (ALMIGHTY MIGHTY)
Jdg 16:30 Then he pushed with all his *m*,
2Sa 6:14 before the LORD with all his *m*,
Ps 21:13 we will sing and praise your *m*.
Zec 4:6 'Not by *m* nor by power,
1Ti 6:16 To him be honor and *m* forever.

MIGHTY (MIGHT)
Ex 6:1 of my *m* hand he will drive them
Dt 7:8 he brought you out with a *m* hand
2Sa 1:19 How the *m* have fallen!
23:8 the names of David's *m* men:
Ps 24:8 The LORD strong and *m*,
50:1 The *M* One, God, the LORD,
89:8 You are *m*, O LORD,
136:12 with a *m* hand and outstretched
147:5 Great is our Lord and *m* in power;
Isa 9:6 Wonderful Counselor, *M* God,
Zep 3:17 he is *m* to save.
Eph 6:10 in the Lord and in his *m* power.

MILE*
Mt 5:41 If someone forces you to go one *m*,

MILK
Ex 3:8 a land flowing with *m* and honey—
Isa 55:1 Come, buy wine and *m*
1Co 3:2 I gave you *m*, not solid food,
Heb 5:12 You need *m*, not solid food!
1Pe 2:2 babies, crave pure spiritual *m*,

MILLSTONE (STONE)
Lk 17:2 sea with a *m* tied around his neck

MIND (DOUBLE-MINDED MINDFUL MINDS)
1Sa 15:29 Israel does not lie or change his *m*;
1Ch 28:9 devotion and with a willing *m*,
Ps 26:2 examine my heart and my *m*;
Isa 26:3 him whose *m* is steadfast,
Mt 22:37 all your soul and with all your *m*.'
Ac 4:32 believers were one in heart and *m*.
Ro 7:25 I myself in my *m* am a slave
8:7 the sinful *m* is hostile to God.
12:2 by the renewing of your *m*.
1Co 2:9 no *m* has conceived
14:14 spirit prays, but my *m* is unfruitful.
2Co 13:11 be of one *m*, live in peace.
Php 3:19 Their *m* is on earthly things.
1Th 4:11 to *m* your own business
Heb 7:21 and will not change his *m*:

MINDFUL* (MIND)
Ps 8:4 what is man that you are *m* of him,
Lk 1:48 God my Savior, for he has been *m*
Heb 2:6 What is man that you are *m* of him,

MINDS (MIND)
Ps 7:9 who searches *m* and hearts,
Jer 31:33 "I will put my law in their *m*
Eph 4:23 new in the attitude of your *m*;
Col 3:2 Set your *m* on things above,
Heb 8:10 I will put my laws in their *m*
Rev 2:23 I am he who searches hearts and *m*,

MINISTERING (MINISTRY)
Heb 1:14 Are not all angels *m* spirits sent

MINISTRY (MINISTERING)
Ac 6:4 to prayer and the *m* of the word."
2Co 5:18 gave us the *m* of reconciliation:
2Ti 4:5 discharge all the duties of your *m*.

MIRACLES (MIRACULOUS)
1Ch 16:12 his *m*, and the judgments he
Ps 77:14 You are the God who performs *m*;
Mt 11:20 most of his *m* had been performed,
11:21 If the *m* that were performed
24:24 and perform great signs and *m*
Mk 6:2 does *m*! Isn't this the carpenter?
Jn 10:32 "I have shown you many great *m*
14:11 the evidence of the *m* themselves.
Ac 2:22 accredited by God to you by *m*,
19:11 God did extraordinary *m*
1Co 12:28 third teachers, then workers of *m*,
Heb 2:4 it by signs, wonders and various *m*,

MIRACULOUS (MIRACLES)
Jn 3:2 could perform the *m* signs you are
9:16 "How can a sinner do such *m* signs
20:30 Jesus did many other *m* signs
1Co 1:22 Jews demand *m* signs and Greeks

MIRE
Ps 40:2 out of the mud and *m*;
Isa 57:20 whose waves cast up *m* and mud.

MIRIAM
Sister of Moses and Aaron (Nu 26:59). Led dancing at Red Sea (Ex 15:20-21). Struck with leprosy for criticizing Moses (Nu 12). Death (Nu 20:1).

MIRROR
Jas 1:23 a man who looks at his face in a *m*

MISERY
Ex 3:7 "I have indeed seen the *m*
Jdg 10:16 he could bear Israel's *m* no longer.
Hos 5:15 in their *m* they will earnestly seek
Ro 3:16 ruin and *m* mark their ways,
Jas 5:1 of the *m* that is coming upon you.

MISLED
1Co 15:33 Do not be *m*: "Bad company

MISS
Pr 19:2 nor to be hasty and *m* the way.

MIST
Hos 6:4 Your love is like the morning *m*,
Jas 4:14 You are a *m* that appears for a little

MISUSE*
Ex 20:7 "You shall not *m* the name
Dt 5:11 "You shall not *m* the name
Ps 139:20 your adversaries *m* your name.

MOCK (MOCKED MOCKER MOCKERS MOCKING)
Ps 22:7 All who see me *m* me;
Pr 14:9 Fools *m* at making amends for sin,
Mk 10:34 who will *m* him and spit on him,

MOCKED (MOCK)
Mt 27:29 knelt in front of him and *m* him.
27:41 of the law and the elders *m* him.
Gal 6:7 not be deceived: God cannot be *m*.

MOCKER (MOCK)
Pr 9:7 corrects a *m* invites insult;
9:12 if you are a *m*, you alone will suffer
20:1 Wine is a *m* and beer a brawler;
22:10 Drive out the *m*, and out goes strife

MOCKERS (MOCK)
Ps 1:1 or sit in the seat of *m*.

MOCKING (MOCK)
Isa 50:6 face from *m* and spitting.

MODEL*
Eze 28:12 " 'You were the *m* of perfection,
1Th 1:7 And so you became a *m*
2Th 3:9 to make ourselves a *m* for you

MOMENT
Job 20:5 the joy of the godless lasts but a *m*.
Ps 30:5 For his anger lasts only a *m*,
Isa 66:8 or a nation be brought forth in a *m*?
Gal 2:5 We did not give in to them for a *m*,

MONEY
Ecc 5:10 Whoever loves *m* never has *m*
Isa 55:1 and you who have no *m*,
Mt 6:24 You cannot serve both God and *M*.
Lk 9:3 no bread, no *m*, no extra tunic.
1Co 16:2 set aside a sum of *m* in keeping
1Ti 3:3 not quarrelsome, not a lover of *m*.
6:10 For the love of *m* is a root
2Ti 3:2 lovers of *m*, boastful, proud,
Heb 13:5 free from the love of *m*
1Pe 5:2 not greedy for *m*, but eager to serve

MOON
Ps 121:6 nor the *m* by night.
Joel 2:31 and the *m* to blood
1Co 15:41 *m* another and the stars another;

MORNING
Ge 1:5 and there was *m*—the first day.
Dt 28:67 In the *m* you will say, "If only it
Ps 5:3 In the *m*, O LORD,
2Pe 1:19 and the *m* star rises in your hearts.
Rev 22:16 of David, and the bright *M* Star."

MORTAL
1Co 15:53 and the *m* with immortality.

MOSES
Levite; brother of Aaron (Ex 6:20; 1Ch 6:3). Put in basket into Nile; discovered and raised by Pharaoh's daughter (Ex 2:1-10). Fled to Midian after killing Egyptian (Ex 2:11-15). Married to Zipporah, fathered Gershom (Ex 2:16-22).

Called by the LORD to deliver Israel (Ex 3-4). Pharaoh's resistance (Ex 5). Ten plagues (Ex 7-11). Passover and Exodus (Ex 12-13). Led Israel through Red Sea (Ex 14). Song of deliverance (Ex 15:1-21). Brought water from rock (Ex 17:1-7). Raised hands to defeat Amalekites (Ex 17:8-16). Delegated judges (Ex 18; Dt 1:9-18).

Received Law at Sinai (Ex 19-23; 25-31; Jn 1:17). Announced Law to Israel (Ex 19:7-8; 24; 35). Broke tablets because of golden calf (Ex 32; Dt 9). Saw glory of the LORD (Ex 33-34). Supervised building of tabernacle (Ex 36-40). Set apart Aaron and priests (Lev 8-9). Numbered tribes (Nu 1-4; 26). Opposed by Aaron and Miriam (Nu 12). Sent spies into Canaan (Nu 13). Announced forty years of wandering for failure to enter land (Nu 14). Opposed by Korah (Nu 16). Forbidden to enter land for striking rock (Nu 20:1-13; Dt 1:37). Lifted bronze snake for healing (Nu 21:4-9; Jn 3:14). Final address to Israel (Dt 1-33). Succeeded by Joshua (Nu 27:12-23; Dt 34). Death (Dt 34:5-12).

"Law of Moses" (1Ki 2:3; Ezr 3:2; Mk 12:26; Lk 24:44). "Book of Moses" (2Ch 25:12; Ne 13:1). "Song of Moses" (Ex 15:1-21; Rev 15:3). "Prayer of Moses" (Ps 90).

MOTH
Mt 6:19 where *m* and rust destroy,

MOTHER (MOTHER'S)
Ge 2:24 and *m* and be united to his wife,
3:20 because she would become the *m*
Ex 20:12 "Honor your father and your *m*,
Lev 20:9 " 'If anyone curses his father or *m*,
Dt 5:16 "Honor your father and your *m*,
21:18 who does not obey his father and *m*
27:16 who dishonors his father or his *m*."
1Sa 2:19 Each year his *m* made him a little
Ps 113:9 as a happy *m* of children.
Pr 23:25 May your father and *m* be glad;
29:15 child left to himself disgraces his *m*.
31:1 an oracle his *m* taught him:
Isa 49:15 "Can a *m* forget the baby
66:13 As a *m* comforts her child,
Mt 10:37 or *m* more than me is not worthy
15:4 'Honor your father and *m*'
19:5 and *m* and be united to his wife,
Mk 7:10 'Honor your father and your *m*,'
10:19 honor your father and *m*.' "
Jn 19:27 to the disciple, "Here is your *m*."

MOTHER'S (MOTHER)
Job 1:21 "Naked I came from my *m* womb,
Pr 1:8 and do not forsake your *m* teaching

MOTIVES*
Pr 16:2 but *m* are weighed by the LORD.
1Co 4:5 will expose the *m* of men's hearts.
Php 1:18 whether from false *m* or true,
1Th 2:3 spring from error or impure *m*,
Jas 4:3 because you ask with wrong *m*,

MOUNTAIN (MOUNTAINS)
Mic 4:2 let us go up to the *m* of the LORD,
Mt 17:20 say to this *m*, 'Move from here'

MOUNTAINS (MOUNTAIN)
Isa 52:7 How beautiful on the *m*
55:12 the *m* and hills
1Co 13:2 if I have a faith that can move *m*,

MOURN (MOURNING)
Ecc 3:4 a time to *m* and a time to dance,
Isa 61:2 to comfort all who *m*,
Mt 5:4 Blessed are those who *m*,
Ro 12:15 *m* with those who *m*.

MOURNING (MOURN)
Jer 31:13 I will turn their *m* into gladness;
Rev 21:4 There will be no more death or *m*

MOUTH
Jos 1:8 of the Law depart from your *m*;
Ps 19:14 May the words of my *m*
40:3 He put a new song in my *m*,
119:103 sweeter than honey to my *m*!
Pr 16:23 A wise man's heart guides his *m*,
27:2 praise you, and not your own *m*;
Isa 51:16 I have put my words in your *m*
Mt 12:34 overflow of the heart the *m* speaks.
15:11 into a man's *m* does not make him
Ro 10:9 That if you confess with your *m*,

MUD
Ps 40:2 out of the *m* and mire;
Isa 57:20 whose waves cast up mire and *m*.
2Pe 2:22 back to her wallowing in the *m*."

MULTITUDE (MULTITUDES)
Isa 31:1 who trust in the *m* of their chariots

PIECES
Ge 15:17 and passed between the *p*.
Jer 34:18 and then walked between its *p*.

PIERCED
Ps 22:16 they have *p* my hands and my feet.
Isa 53: 5 But he was *p* for our transgressions,
Zec 12:10 look on me, the one they have *p*,
Jn 19:37 look on the one they have *p*."

PIGS
Mt 7: 6 do not throw your pearls to *p*.

PILATE
Governor of Judea. Questioned Jesus (Mt 27:1-26; Mk 15:15; Lk 22:66-23:25; Jn 18:28-19:16); sent him to Herod (Lk 23: 6-12); consented to his crucifixion when crowds chose Barabbas (Mt 27:15-26; Mk 15:6-15; Lk 23:13-25; Jn 19:1-10).

PILLAR
Ge 19:26 and she became a *p* of salt.
Ex 13:21 ahead of them in a *p* of cloud
1Ti 3:15 the *p* and foundation of the truth.

PIT
Ps 40: 2 He lifted me out of the slimy *p*,
103: 4 who redeems your life from the *p*
Mt 15:14 a blind man, both will fall into a *p*."

PITIED
1Co 15:19 we are to be *p* more than all men.

PLAGUE
2Ch 6:28 "When famine or *p* comes

PLAIN
Ro 1:19 what may be known about God is *p*

PLAN (PLANNED PLANS)
Job 42: 2 no *p* of yours can be thwarted.
Pr 14:22 those who *p* what is good find love
Eph 1:11 predestined according to the *p*

PLANK
Mt 7: 3 attention to the *p* in your own eye?
Lk 6:41 attention to the *p* in your own eye?

PLANNED (PLAN)
Ps 40: 5 The things you *p* for us
Isa 46:11 what I have *p*, that will I do.
Heb 11:40 God had *p* something better for us

PLANS (PLAN)
Ps 20: 4 and make all your *p* succeed.
33:11 *p* of the LORD stand firm forever,
Pr 20:18 Make *p* by seeking advice;
Isa 32: 8 But the noble man makes noble *p*,

PLANTED (PLANTS)
Ps 1: 3 He is like a tree *p* by streams
Mt 15:13 Father has not *p* will be pulled
1Co 3: 6 I *p* the seed, Apollos watered it,

PLANTS (PLANTED)
1Co 3: 7 So neither he who *p* nor he who
9: 7 Who *p* a vineyard and does not eat

PLATTER
Mk 6:25 head of John the Baptist on a *p*."

PLAYED
Lk 7:32 " 'We *p* the flute for you,
1Co 14: 7 anyone know what tune is being *p*

PLEADED
2Co 12: 8 Three times I *p* with the Lord

PLEASANT (PLEASE)
Ps 16: 6 for me in *p* places;
133: 1 How good and *p* it is
147: 1 how *p* and fitting to praise him!
Heb 12:11 No discipline seems *p* at the time,

PLEASE (PLEASANT PLEASED PLEASES PLEASING PLEASURE PLEASURES)
Pr 20:23 and dishonest scales do not *p* him.
Jer 6:20 your sacrifices do not *p* me."
Jn 5:30 for I seek not to *p* myself
Ro 8: 8 by the sinful nature cannot *p* God.
15: 2 Each of us should *p* his neighbor
1Co 7:32 affairs—how he can *p* the Lord.
10:33 I try to *p* everybody in every way.
2Co 5: 9 So we make it our goal to *p* him,
Gal 1:10 or of God? Or am I trying to *p* men
1Th 4: 1 how to live in order to *p* God,
2Ti 2: 4 wants to *p* his commanding officer.
Heb 11: 6 faith it is impossible to *p* God,

PLEASED (PLEASE)
Mt 3:17 whom I love; with him I am well *p*
1Co 1:21 God was *p* through the foolishness
Col 1:19 For God was *p* to have all his
Heb 11: 5 commended as one who *p* God.
2Pe 1:17 whom I love; with him I am well *p*

PLEASES (PLEASE)
Ps 135: 6 The LORD does whatever *p* him,
Pr 15: 8 but the prayer of the upright *p* him.
Jn 3: 8 The wind blows wherever it *p*.
8:29 for I always do what *p* him."
Col 3:20 in everything, for this *p* the Lord.
1Ti 2: 3 This is good, and *p* God our Savior,
1Jn 3:22 his commands and do what *p* him.

PLEASING (PLEASE)
Ps 104: 34 May my meditation be *p* to him,
Ro 12: 1 *p* to God—which is your spiritual
Php 4:18 an acceptable sacrifice, *p* to God.
Heb 13:21 may he work in us what is *p* to him,

PLEASURE (PLEASE)
Ps 5: 4 You are not a God who takes *p*
147:10 His *p* is not in the strength
Pr 21:17 He who loves *p* will become poor;
Eze 18:32 For I take no *p* in the death
Eph 1: 5 in accordance with his *p* and will—
1: 9 of his will according to his good *p*,
2Ti 3: 4 lovers of *p* rather than lovers

PLEASURES (PLEASE)
Ps 16:11 with eternal *p* at your right hand.
Heb 11:25 rather than to enjoy the *p* of sin
2Pe 2:13 reveling in their *p* while they feast

PLENTIFUL
Mt 9:37 harvest is *p* but the workers are

PLOW (PLOWSHARES)
Lk 9:62 "No one who puts his hand to the *p*

PLOWSHARES (PLOW)
Isa 2: 4 They will beat their swords into *p*
Joel 3:10 Beat your *p* into swords

PLUNDER
Ex 3:22 And so you will *p* the Egyptians."

POINT
Jas 2:10 yet stumbles at just one *p* is guilty

POISON
Mk 16:18 and when they drink deadly *p*,
Jas 3: 8 It is a restless evil, full of deadly *p*.

POLLUTE* (POLLUTED)
Nu 35:33 " 'Do not *p* the land where you are.
Jude : 8 these dreamers *p* their own bodies,

POLLUTED* (POLLUTE)
Ezr 9:11 entering to possess is a land *p*
Pr 25:26 Like a muddied spring or a *p* well
Ac 15:20 to abstain from food *p* by idols,
Jas 1:27 oneself from being *p* by the world.

PONDER
Ps 64: 9 and *p* what he has done.
119: 95 but I will *p* your statutes.

POOR (POVERTY)
Dt 15: 4 there should be no *p* among you,
15:11 There will always be *p* people
Ps 34: 6 This *p* man called, and the LORD
82: 3 maintain the rights of the *p*
112: 9 scattered abroad his gifts to the *p*,
Pr 10: 4 Lazy hands make a man *p*,
13: 7 to be *p*, yet has great wealth.
14:31 oppresses the *p* shows contempt
19: 1 Better a *p* man whose walk is
19:17 to the *p* lends to the LORD,
22: 2 Rich and *p* have this in common:
22: 9 for he shares his food with the *p*.
28: 6 Better a *p* man whose walk is
31:20 She opens her arms to the *p*
Isa 61: 1 me to preach good news to the *p*.
Mt 5: 3 saying: "Blessed are the *p* in spirit,
11: 5 the good news is preached to the *p*.
19:21 your possessions and give to the *p*,
26:11 The *p* you will always have
Mk 12:42 But a *p* widow came and put
Ac 10: 4 and gifts to the *p* have come up
1Co 13: 3 If I give all I possess to the *p*
2Co 8: 9 yet for your sakes he became *p*,
Jas 2: 2 and a *p* man in shabby clothes

PORTION
Dt 32: 9 For the LORD's *p* is his people,
2Ki 2: 9 "Let me inherit a double *p*
La 3:24 to myself, "The LORD is my *p*;

POSSESS (POSSESSING POSSESSION POSSESSIONS)
Nu 33:53 for I have given you the land to *p*.
Jn 5:39 that by them you *p* eternal life.

POSSESSING* (POSSESS)
2Co 6:10 nothing, and yet *p* everything.

POSSESSION (POSSESS)
Ge 15: 7 to give you this land to take *p* of it
Nu 13:30 "We should go up and take *p*
Eph 1:14 of those who are God's *p*—

POSSESSIONS (POSSESS)
Lk 12:15 consist in the abundance of his *p*."
2Co 12:14 what I want is not your *p* but you.
1Jn 3:17 If anyone has material *p*

POSSIBLE
Mt 19:26 but with God all things are *p.*"
Mk 9:23 "Everything is *p* for him who
10:27 all things are *p* with God."
Ro 12:18 If it is *p,* as far as it depends on you,
1Co 9:22 by all *p* means I might save some.

POT (POTSHERD POTTER POTTERY)
2Ki 4:40 there is death in the *p!*"
Jer 18:4 But the *p* he was shaping

POTSHERD (POT)
Isa 45:9 a *p* among the potsherds

POTTER (POT)
Isa 29:16 Can the pot say of the *p,*
45:9 Does the clay say to the *p,*
64:8 We are the clay, you are the *p;*
Jer 18:6 "Like clay in the hand of the *p,*
Ro 9:21 Does not the *p* have the right

POTTERY (POT)
Ro 9:21 of clay some *p* for noble purposes

POUR (POURED)
Ps 62:8 *p* out your hearts to him,
Joel 2:28 I will *p* out my Spirit on all people.
Mal 3:10 *p* out so much blessing that you
Ac 2:17 I will *p* out my Spirit on all people.

POURED (POUR)
Ac 10:45 of the Holy Spirit had been *p* out
Ro 5:5 because God has *p* out his love

POVERTY (POOR)
Pr 14:23 but mere talk leads only to *p.*
21:5 as surely as haste leads to *p.*
30:8 give me neither *p* nor riches,
Mk 12:44 out of her *p,* put in everything—
2Co 8:2 and their extreme *p* welled up
8:9 through his *p* might become rich.

POWER (POWERFUL POWERS)
1Ch 29:11 LORD, is the greatness and the *p*
2Ch 32:7 for there is a greater *p* with us
Job 36:22 "God is exalted in his *p.*
Ps 63:2 and beheld your *p* and your glory.
68:34 Proclaim the *p* of God,
147:5 Great is our Lord and mighty in *p;*
Pr 24:5 A wise man has great *p,*
Isa 40:10 the Sovereign LORD comes with *p*
Zec 4:6 nor by *p,* but by my Spirit,'
Mt 22:29 do not know the Scriptures or the *p*
24:30 on the clouds of the sky, with *p*
Ac 1:8 you will receive *p* when the Holy
4:33 With great *p* the apostles
10:38 with the Holy Spirit and *p,*
Ro 1:16 it is the *p* of God for the salvation
1Co 1:18 to us who are being saved it is the *p*
15:56 of death is sin, and the *p*
2Co 12:9 for my *p* is made perfect
Eph 1:19 and his incomparably great *p*
Php 3:10 and the *p* of his resurrection
Col 1:11 strengthened with all *p* according
2Ti 1:7 but a spirit of *p,* of love
Heb 7:16 of the *p* of an indestructible life.
Rev 4:11 to receive glory and honor and *p,*
19:1 and glory and *p* belong to our God,
20:6 The second death has no *p*

POWERFUL (POWER)
Ps 29:4 The voice of the LORD is *p;*
Lk 24:19 *p* in word and deed before God
2Th 1:7 in blazing fire with his *p* angels.
Heb 1:3 sustaining all things by his *p* word.
Jas 5:16 The prayer of a righteous man is *p*

POWERLESS
Ro 5:6 when we were still *p,* Christ died
8:3 For what the law was *p* to do

POWERS (POWER)
Ro 8:38 nor any *p,* neither height nor depth
1Co 12:10 to another miraculous *p,*
Col 1:16 whether thrones or *p* or rulers
2:15 And having disarmed the *p*

PRACTICE
Lev 19:26 " 'Do not *p* divination or sorcery.
Mt 23:3 for they do not *p* what they preach.
Lk 8:21 hear God's word and put it into *p.*"
Ro 12:13 *P* hospitality.
1Ti 5:4 to put their religion into *p* by caring

PRAISE (PRAISED PRAISES PRAISING)
Ex 15:2 He is my God, and I will *p* him,
Dt 32:3 Oh, *p* the greatness of our God!
Ru 4:14 said to Naomi: "*P* be to the LORD,
2Sa 22:47 The LORD lives! *P* be to my Rock
1Ch 16:25 is the LORD and most worthy of *p;*
2Ch 20:21 and to *p* him for the splendor
Ps 8:2 you have ordained *p*
33:1 it is fitting for the upright to *p* him.
34:1 his *p* will always be on my lips.
40:3 a hymn of *p* to our God.
48:1 the LORD, and most worthy of *p,*
68:19 *P* be to the Lord, to God our Savior
89:5 The heavens *p* your wonders,
100:4 and his courts with *p;*
105:2 Sing to him, sing *p* to him;
106:1 *P* the LORD.
119:175 Let me live that I may *p* you,
139:14 I *p* you because I am fearfully
145:21 Let every creature *p* his holy name
146:1 *P* the LORD, O my soul.
150:2 *p* him for his surpassing greatness.
150:6 that has breath *p* the LORD.
Pr 27:2 Let another *p* you, and not your
27:21 man is tested by the *p* he receives.
31:31 let her works bring her *p*
Mt 5:16 and *p* your Father in heaven.
21:16 you have ordained *p*'?"
Jn 12:43 for they loved *p* from men more
Eph 1:6 to the *p* of his glorious grace,
1:12 might be for the *p* of his glory.
1:14 to the *p* of his glory.
Heb 13:15 offer to God a sacrifice of *p*—
Jas 5:13 happy? Let him sing songs of *p.*

PRAISED (PRAISE)
1Ch 29:10 David *p* the LORD in the presence
Ne 8:6 Ezra *p* the LORD, the great God;
Da 2:19 Then Daniel *p* the God of heaven
Ro 9:5 who is God over all, forever *p!*
1Pe 4:11 that in all things God may be *p*

PRAISES (PRAISE)
2Sa 22:50 I will sing *p* to your name.
Ps 47:6 Sing *p* to God, sing *p;*
147:1 How good it is to sing *p* to our God,
Pr 31:28 her husband also, and he *p* her:

PRAISING (PRAISE)
Ac 10:46 speaking in tongues and *p* God.
1Co 14:16 If you are *p* God with your spirit,

PRAY (PRAYED PRAYER PRAYERS PRAYING)
Dt 4:7 is near us whenever we *p* to him?
1Sa 12:23 the LORD by failing to *p* for you.
2Ch 7:14 will humble themselves and *p*
Job 42:8 My servant Job will *p* for you,
Ps 122:6 *P* for the peace of Jerusalem:
Mt 5:44 and *p* for those who persecute you,
6:5 "And when you *p,* do not be like
6:9 "This, then, is how you should *p:*
26:36 Sit here while I go over there and *p*
Lk 6:28 *p* for those who mistreat you.
18:1 them that they should always *p*
22:40 "*P* that you will not fall
Ro 8:26 do not know what we ought to *p,*
1Co 14:13 in a tongue should *p* that he may
1Th 5:17 Be joyful always; *p* continually;
Jas 5:13 one of you in trouble? He should *p.*
5:16 *p* for each other so that you may be

PRAYED (PRAY)
1Sa 1:27 I *p* for this child, and the LORD
Jnh 2:1 From inside the fish Jonah *p*
Mk 14:35 *p* that if possible the hour might

PRAYER (PRAY)
2Ch 30:27 for their *p* reached heaven,
Ezr 8:23 about this, and he answered our *p.*
Ps 6:9 the LORD accepts my *p.*
86:6 Hear my *p,* O LORD;
Pr 15:8 but the *p* of the upright pleases him
Isa 56:7 a house of *p* for all nations."
Mt 21:13 house will be called a house of *p,*'
Mk 11:24 whatever you ask for in *p,*
Jn 17:15 My *p* is not that you take them out
Ac 6:4 and will give our attention to *p*
Php 4:6 but in everything, by *p* and petition
Jas 5:15 *p* offered in faith will make the sick
1Pe 3:12 and his ears are attentive to their *p,*

PRAYERS (PRAY)
1Ch 5:20 He answered their *p,* because they
Mk 12:40 and for a show make lengthy *p.*
1Pe 3:7 so that nothing will hinder your *p.*
Rev 5:8 which are the *p* of the saints.

PRAYING (PRAY)
Mk 11:25 And when you stand *p,*
Jn 17:9 I am not *p* for the world,
Ac 16:25 and Silas were *p* and singing hymns
Eph 6:18 always keep on *p* for all the saints.

PREACH (PREACHED PREACHING)
Mt 23:3 they do not practice what they *p.*
Mk 16:15 and *p* the good news to all creation.
Ac 9:20 At once he began to *p*
Ro 10:15 how can they *p* unless they are sent
15:20 to *p* the gospel where Christ was
1Co 1:17 to *p* the gospel—not with words
1:23 wisdom, but we *p* Christ crucified:
9:14 that those who *p* the gospel should
9:16 Woe to me if I do not *p* the gospel!
2Co 10:16 so that we can *p* the gospel
Gal 1:8 from heaven should *p* a gospel
2Ti 4:2 I give you this charge: *P* the Word;

PREACHED (PREACH)
Mk 13:10 And the gospel must first be *p*
Ac 8:4 had been scattered *p* the word
1Co 9:27 so that after I have *p* to others,
15:1 you of the gospel I *p* to you,

2Co 11: 4 other than the Jesus we *p,*
Gal 1: 8 other than the one we *p* to you,
Php 1: 18 false motives or true, Christ is *p.*
1Ti 3: 16 was *p* among the nations,

PREACHING (PREACH)
Ro 10: 14 hear without someone *p* to them?
1Co 9: 18 in *p* the gospel I may offer it free
1Ti 4: 13 the public reading of Scripture, to *p*
5: 17 especially those whose work is *p*

PRECEPTS
Ps 19: 8 The *p* of the LORD are right,
111: 7 all his *p* are trustworthy.
111: 10 who follow his *p* have good
119: 40 How I long for your *p!*
119: 69 I keep your *p* with all my heart.
119: 104 I gain understanding from your *p;*
119: 159 See how I love your *p;*

PRECIOUS
Ps 19: 10 They are more *p* than gold,
116: 15 *P* in the sight of the LORD
Pr 8: 11 for wisdom is more *p* than rubies,
Isa 28: 16 a *p* cornerstone for a sure
1Pe 1: 19 but with the *p* blood of Christ,
2: 6 a chosen and *p* cornerstone,
2Pe 1: 4 us his very great and *p* promises,

PREDESTINED* (DESTINY)
Ro 8: 29 *p* to be conformed to the likeness
8: 30 And those he *p,* he also called;
Eph 1: 5 In love he *p* us to be adopted
1: 11 having been *p* according

PREDICTION*
Jer 28: 9 only if his *p* comes true."

PREPARE (PREPARED)
Ps 23: 5 You *p* a table before me
Am 4: 12 *p* to meet your God, O Israel."
Jn 14: 2 there to *p* a place for you.
Eph 4: 12 to *p* God's people for works

PREPARED (PREPARE)
Mt 25: 34 the kingdom *p* for you
1Co 2: 9 what God has *p* for those who love
Eph 2: 10 which God *p* in advance for us
2Ti 4: 2 be *p* in season and out of season;
1Pe 3: 15 Always be *p* to give an answer

PRESENCE (PRESENT)
Ex 25: 30 Put the bread of the *P* on this table
Ezr 9: 15 one of us can stand in your *p."*
Ps 31: 20 the shelter of your *p* you hide them
89: 15 who walk in the light of your *p,*
90: 8 our secret sins in the light of your *p*
139: 7 Where can I flee from your *p?*
Jer 5: 22 "Should you not tremble in my *p?*
Heb 9: 24 now to appear for us in God's *p.*
Jude : 24 before his glorious *p* without fault

PRESENT (PRESENCE)
2Co 11: 2 so that I might *p* you as a pure
Eph 5: 27 and to *p* her to himself
2Ti 2: 15 Do your best to *p* yourself to God

PRESERVES
Ps 119: 50 Your promise *p* my life.

PRESS (PRESSED PRESSURE)
Php 3: 14 I *p* on toward the goal

PRESSED (PRESS)
Lk 6: 38 *p* down, shaken together

PRESSURE (PRESS)
2Co 1: 8 We were under great *p,* far
11: 28 I face daily the *p* of my concern

PREVAILS
1Sa 2: 9 "It is not by strength that one *p;*

PRICE
Job 28: 18 the *p* of wisdom is beyond rubies.
1Co 6: 20 your own; you were bought at a *p.*
7: 23 bought at a *p;* do not become slaves

PRIDE (PROUD)
Pr 8: 13 I hate *p* and arrogance,
16: 18 *P* goes before destruction,
Da 4: 37 And those who walk in *p* he is able
Gal 6: 4 Then he can take *p* in himself,
Jas 1: 9 ought to take *p* in his high position.

PRIEST (PRIESTHOOD PRIESTS)
Heb 4: 14 have a great high *p* who has gone
4: 15 do not have a high *p* who is unable
7: 26 Such a high *p* meets our need—
8: 1 We do have such a high *p,*

PRIESTHOOD (PRIEST)
Heb 7: 24 lives forever, he has a permanent *p.*
1Pe 2: 5 into a spiritual house to be a holy *p,*
2: 9 you are a chosen people, a royal *p,*

PRIESTS (PRIEST)
Ex 19: 6 you will be for me a kingdom of *p*
Rev 5: 10 to be a kingdom and *p*

PRINCE
Isa 9: 6 Everlasting Father, *P* of Peace.
Jn 12: 31 now the *p* of this world will be
Ac 5: 31 as *P* and Savior that he might give

PRISON (PRISONER)
Isa 42: 7 to free captives from *p*
Mt 25: 36 I was in *p* and you came to visit me
1Pe 3: 19 spirits in *p* who disobeyed long ago
Rev 20: 7 Satan will be released from his *p*

PRISONER (PRISON)
Ro 7: 23 and making me a *p* of the law of sin
Gal 3: 22 declares that the whole world is a *p*
Eph 3: 1 the *p* of Christ Jesus for the sake

PRIVILEGE*
2Co 8: 4 pleaded with us for the *p* of sharing

PRIZE
1Co 9: 24 Run in such a way as to get the *p.*
Php 3: 14 on toward the goal to win the *p*

PROCLAIM (PROCLAIMED PROCLAIMING)
1Ch 16: 23 *p* his salvation day after day.
Ps 19: 1 the skies *p* the work of his hands.
50: 6 the heavens *p* his righteousness,
68: 34 *P* the power of God,
118: 17 will *p* what the LORD has done.
Zec 9: 10 He will *p* peace to the nations.
Ac 20: 27 hesitated to *p* to you the whole will
1Co 11: 26 you *p* the Lord's death

PROCLAIMED (PROCLAIM)
Ro 15: 19 I have fully *p* the gospel of Christ.
Col 1: 23 that has been *p* to every creature

PROCLAIMING (PROCLAIM)
Ro 10: 8 the word of faith we are *p:*

PRODUCE (PRODUCES)
Mt 3: 8 *P* fruit in keeping with repentance.
3: 10 tree that does not *p* good fruit will

PRODUCES (PRODUCE)
Pr 30: 33 so stirring up anger *p* strife."
Ro 5: 3 that suffering *p* perseverance;
Heb 12: 11 it *p* a harvest of righteousness

PROFANE
Lev 22: 32 Do not *p* my holy name.

PROFESS*
1Ti 2: 10 for women who *p* to worship God.
Heb 4: 14 let us hold firmly to the faith we *p.*
10: 23 unswervingly to the hope we *p,*

PROMISE (PROMISED PROMISES)
1Ki 8: 20 The LORD has kept the *p* he made
Ac 2: 39 The *p* is for you and your children
Gal 3: 14 that by faith we might receive the *p*
1Ti 4: 8 holding *p* for both the present life
2Pe 3: 9 Lord is not slow in keeping his *p,*

PROMISED (PROMISE)
Ex 3: 17 And I have *p* to bring you up out
Dt 26: 18 his treasured possession as he *p,*
Ps 119: 57 I have *p* to obey your words.
Ro 4: 21 power to do what he had *p.*
Heb 10: 23 for he who *p* is faithful.
2Pe 3: 4 "Where is this 'coming' he *p?*

PROMISES (PROMISE)
Jos 21: 45 one of all the LORD's good *p*
Ro 9: 4 the temple worship and the *p.*
2Pe 1: 4 us his very great and precious *p,*

PROMPTED
1Th 1: 3 your labor *p* by love, and your
2Th 1: 11 and every act *p* by your faith.

PROPHECIES (PROPHESY)
1Co 13: 8 where there are *p,* they will cease;
1Th 5: 20 do not treat *p* with contempt.

PROPHECY (PROPHESY)
1Co 14: 1 gifts, especially the gift of *p.*
2Pe 1: 20 you must understand that no *p*

PROPHESY (PROPHECIES PROPHECY PROPHESYING PROPHET PROPHETS)
Joel 2: 28 Your sons and daughters will *p,*
Mt 7: 22 Lord, did we not *p* in your name,
1Co 14: 39 my brothers, be eager to *p,*

PROPHESYING (PROPHESY)
Ro 12: 6 If a man's gift is *p,* let him use it

PROPHET (PROPHESY)
Dt 18: 18 up for them a *p* like you
Am 7: 14 "I was neither a *p* nor a prophet's
Mt 10: 41 Anyone who receives a *p*
Lk 4: 24 "no *p* is accepted in his hometown.

PROPHETS (PROPHESY)
Ps 105: 15 do my *p* no harm."
Mt 5: 17 come to abolish the Law or the *P;*
7: 12 for this sums up the Law and the *P.*
24: 24 false Christs and false *p* will appear
Lk 24: 25 believe all that the *p* have spoken!
Ac 10: 43 All the *p* testify about him that
1Co 12: 28 second *p,* third teachers, then
14: 32 The spirits of *p* are subject

Eph 2:20 foundation of the apostles and *p*,
Heb 1: 1 through the *p* at many times
1Pe 1:10 Concerning this salvation, the *p*,
2Pe 1:19 word of the *p* made more certain,

PROSPER (PROSPERITY PROSPERS)

Pr 28:25 he who trusts in the LORD will *p*.

PROSPERITY (PROSPER)

Ps 73: 3 when I saw the *p* of the wicked.
Pr 13:21 but *p* is the reward of the righteous.

PROSPERS (PROSPER)

Ps 1: 3 Whatever he does *p*.

PROSTITUTE (PROSTITUTES)

1Co 6:15 of Christ and unite them with a *p*?

PROSTITUTES (PROSTITUTE)

Lk 15:30 property with *p* comes home,
1Co 6: 9 male *p* nor homosexual offenders

PROSTRATE

Dt 9:18 again I fell *p* before the LORD

PROTECT (PROTECTS)

Ps 32: 7 you will *p* me from trouble
Pr 2:11 Discretion will *p* you,
Jn 17:11 *p* them by the power of your name

PROTECTS (PROTECT)

1Co 13: 7 It always *p*, always trusts,

PROUD (PRIDE)

Pr 16: 5 The LORD detests all the *p*
Ro 12:16 Do not be *p*, but be willing
1Co 13: 4 it does not boast, it is not *p*.

PROVE

Ac 26:20 *p* their repentance by their deeds.
1Co 4: 2 been given a trust must *p* faithful.

PROVIDE (PROVIDED PROVIDES)

Ge 22: 8 "God himself will *p* the lamb
Isa 43:20 because I *p* water in the desert
1Ti 5: 8 If anyone does not *p*

PROVIDED (PROVIDE)

Jnh 1:17 But the LORD *p* a great fish
4: 6 Then the LORD God *p* a vine
4: 7 dawn the next day God *p* a worm,
4: 8 God *p* a scorching east wind,

PROVIDES (PROVIDE)

1Ti 6:17 who richly *p* us with everything
1Pe 4:11 it with the strength God *p*,

PROVOKED

Ecc 7: 9 Do not be quickly *p* in your spirit,

PRUDENT

Pr 14:15 a *p* man gives thought to his steps.
19:14 but a *p* wife is from the LORD.
Am 5:13 Therefore the *p* man keeps quiet

PRUNING

Isa 2: 4 and their spears into *p* hooks.
Joel 3:10 and your *p* hooks into spears.

PSALMS

Eph 5:19 Speak to one another with *p*,
Col 3:16 and as you sing *p*, hymns

PUBLICLY

Ac 20:20 have taught you *p* and from house
1Ti 5:20 Those who sin are to be rebuked *p*,

PUFFS

1Co 8: 1 Knowledge *p* up, but love builds up

PULLING

2Co 10: 8 building you up rather than *p* you

PUNISH (PUNISHED PUNISHES)

Ex 32:34 I will *p* them for their sin."
Pr 23:13 if you *p* him with the rod, he will
Isa 13:11 I will *p* the world for its evil,
1Pe 2:14 by him to *p* those who do wrong

PUNISHED (PUNISH)

La 3:39 complain when *p* for his sins?
2Th 1: 9 be *p* with everlasting destruction
Heb 10:29 to be *p* who has trampled the Son

PUNISHES (PUNISH)

Heb 12: 6 and he *p* everyone he accepts

PURE (PURIFIES PURIFY PURITY)

2Sa 22:27 to the *p* you show yourself *p*,
Ps 24: 4 who has clean hands and a *p* heart,
51:10 Create in me a *p* heart, O God,
119: 9 can a young man keep his way *p*?
Pr 20: 9 can say, "I have kept my heart *p*;
Isa 52:11 Come out from it and be *p*,
Hab 1:13 Your eyes are too *p* to look on evil;
Mt 5: 8 Blessed are the *p* in heart,
2Co 11: 2 I might present you as a *p* virgin
Php 4: 8 whatever is *p*, whatever is lovely,
1Ti 5:22 Keep yourself *p*.
Tit 1:15 To the *p*, all things are *p*,
2: 5 to be self-controlled and *p*,
Heb 13: 4 and the marriage bed kept *p*,
1Jn 3: 3 him purifies himself, just as he is *p*.

PURGE

Pr 20:30 and beatings *p* the inmost being.

PURIFIES* (PURE)

1Jn 1: 7 of Jesus, his Son, *p* us from all sin.
3: 3 who has this hope in him *p* himself,

PURIFY (PURE)

Tit 2:14 to *p* for himself a people that are
1Jn 1: 9 and *p* us from all unrighteousness.

PURITY (PURE)

2Co 6: 6 in *p*, understanding, patience
1Ti 4:12 in life, in love, in faith and in *p*.

PURPOSE

Pr 19:21 but it is the LORD's *p* that prevails
Isa 55:11 and achieve the *p* for which I sent it
Ro 8:28 have been called according to his *p*.
Php 2: 2 love, being one in spirit and *p*.

PURSES

Lk 12:33 Provide *p* for yourselves that will

PURSUE

Ps 34:14 seek peace and *p* it.
2Ti 2:22 and *p* righteousness, faith,
1Pe 3:11 he must seek peace and *p* it.

QUALITIES (QUALITY)

2Pe 1: 8 For if you possess these *q*

QUALITY (QUALITIES)

1Co 3:13 and the fire will test the *q*

QUARREL (QUARRELSOME)

Pr 15:18 but a patient man calms a *q*.
17:14 Starting a *q* is like breaching a dam;
Pr 17:19 He who loves a *q* loves sin;
2Ti 2:24 And the Lord's servant must not *q*;

QUARRELSOME (QUARREL)

Pr 19:13 a *q* wife is like a constant dripping.
1Ti 3: 3 not violent but gentle, not *q*,

QUICK-TEMPERED

Tit 1: 7 not *q*, not given to drunkenness,

QUIET (QUIETNESS)

Ps 23: 2 he leads me beside *q* waters,
Zep 3:17 he will *q* you with his love,
Lk 19:40 he replied, "if they keep *q*,
1Ti 2: 2 we may live peaceful and *q* lives
1Pe 3: 4 beauty of a gentle and *q* spirit,

QUIETNESS (QUIET)

Isa 30:15 in *q* and trust is your strength,
32:17 the effect of righteousness will be *q*
1Ti 2:11 A woman should learn in *q*

QUIVER

Ps 127: 5 whose *q* is full of them.

RACE

Ecc 9:11 The *r* is not to the swift
1Co 9:24 that in a *r* all the runners run,
2Ti 4: 7 I have finished the *r*, I have kept
Heb 12: 1 perseverance the *r* marked out

RACHEL

Daughter of Laban (Ge 29:16); wife of Jacob (Ge 29:28); bore two sons (Ge 30:22-24; 35:16-24; 46:19).

RADIANCE (RADIANT)

Heb 1: 3 The Son is the *r* of God's glory

RADIANT (RADIANCE)

Ex 34:29 he was not aware that his face was *r*
Ps 34: 5 Those who look to him are *r*;
SS 5:10 *Beloved* My lover is *r* and ruddy,
Isa 60: 5 Then you will look and be *r*,
Eph 5:27 her to himself as a *r* church,

RAIN (RAINBOW)

Mt 5:45 and sends *r* on the righteous

RAINBOW (RAIN)

Ge 9:13 I have set my *r* in the clouds,

RAISED (RISE)

Ro 4:25 was *r* to life for our justification.
10: 9 in your heart that God *r* him
1Co 15: 4 that he was *r* on the third day

RAN (RUN)

Jnh 1: 3 But Jonah *r* away from the LORD

RANSOM

Mt 20:28 and to give his life as a *r* for many."
Heb 9:15 as a *r* to set them free

RAVENS

1Ki 17: 6 The *r* brought him bread
Lk 12:24 Consider the *r*: They do not sow

READ (READS)

Jos 8:34 Joshua *r* all the words of the law—
Ne 8: 8 They *r* from the Book of the Law
2Co 3: 2 known and *r* by everybody.

READS (READ)

Rev 1: 3 Blessed is the one who *r* the words

REAL (REALITY)

Jn 6:55 is *r* food and my blood is *r* drink.

REALITY* (REAL)
Col 2:17 the *r,* however, is found in Christ.

REAP (REAPS)
Job 4:8 and those who sow trouble *r* it.
2Co 9:6 generously will also *r* generously.

REAPS (REAP)
Gal 6:7 A man *r* what he sows.

REASON
Isa 1:18 "Come now, let us *r* together,"
1Pe 3:15 to give the *r* for the hope that you

REBEKAH
Sister of Laban, secured as bride for Isaac (Ge 24). Mother of Esau and Jacob (Ge 25:19-26). Taken by Abimelech as sister of Isaac; returned (Ge 26:1-11). Encouraged Jacob to trick Isaac out of blessing (Ge 27:1-17).

REBEL
Mt 10:21 children will *r* against their parents

REBUKE (REBUKED REBUKING)
Pr 9:8 *r* a wise man and he will love you.
27:5 Better is open *r*
Lk 17:3 "If your brother sins, *r* him,
2Ti 4:2 correct, *r* and encourage—
Rev 3:19 Those whom I love I *r*

REBUKED (REBUKE)
1Ti 5:20 Those who sin are to be *r* publicly,

REBUKING (REBUKE)
2Ti 3:16 *r,* correcting and training

RECEIVE (RECEIVED RECEIVES)
Ac 1:8 you will *r* power when the Holy
20:35 'It is more blessed to give than to *r*
2Co 6:17 and I will *r* you."
Rev 4:11 to *r* glory and honor and power,

RECEIVED (RECEIVE)
Mt 6:2 they have *r* their reward in full.
10:8 Freely you have *r,* freely give.
1Co 11:23 For I *r* from the Lord what I
Col 2:6 just as you *r* Christ Jesus as Lord,
1Pe 4:10 should use whatever gift he has *r*

RECEIVES (RECEIVE)
Mt 7:8 everyone who asks *r;* he who seeks
10:40 he who *r* me *r* the one who sent me.
Ac 10:43 believes in him *r* forgiveness of sins

RECKONING
Isa 10:3 What will you do on the day of *r,*

RECOGNIZE (RECOGNIZED)
Mt 7:16 By their fruit you will *r* them.

RECOGNIZED (RECOGNIZE)
Mt 12:33 for a tree is *r* by its fruit.
Ro 7:13 in order that sin might be *r* as sin,

RECOMPENSE
Isa 40:10 and his *r* accompanies him.

RECONCILE (RECONCILED RECONCILIATION)
Eph 2:16 in this one body to *r* both of them

RECONCILED (RECONCILE)
Mt 5:24 First go and be *r* to your brother;
Ro 5:10 we were *r* to him through the death
2Co 5:18 who *r* us to himself through Christ

RECONCILIATION* (RECONCILE)
Ro 5:11 whom we have now received *r.*
11:15 For if their rejection is the *r*
2Co 5:18 and gave us the ministry of *r:*
5:19 committed to us the message of *r.*

RECORD
Ps 130:3 If you, O LORD, kept a *r* of sins,

RED
Isa 1:18 though they are *r* as crimson,

REDEEM (KINSMAN-REDEEMER REDEEMED REDEEMER REDEMPTION)
2Sa 7:23 on earth that God went out to *r*
Ps 49:7 No man can *r* the life of another
Gal 4:5 under law, to *r* those under law,

REDEEMED (REDEEM)
Gal 3:13 Christ *r* us from the curse
1Pe 1:18 or gold that you were *r*

REDEEMER (REDEEM)
Job 19:25 I know that my *R* lives,

REDEMPTION (REDEEM)
Ps 130:7 and with him is full *r.*
Lk 21:28 because your *r* is drawing near."
Ro 8:23 as sons, the *r* of our bodies.
Eph 1:7 In him we have *r* through his blood
Col 1:14 in whom we have *r,* the forgiveness
Heb 9:12 having obtained eternal *r.*

REFLECT
2Co 3:18 unveiled faces all *r* the Lord's

REFUGE
Nu 35:11 towns to be your cities of *r,*
Dt 33:27 The eternal God is your *r,*
Ru 2:12 wings you have come to take *r.*"
Ps 46:1 God is our *r* and strength,
91:2 "He is my *r* and my fortress,

REHOBOAM
Son of Solomon (1Ki 11:43; 1Ch 3:10). Harsh treatment of subjects caused divided kingdom (1Ki 12:1-24; 14:21-31; 2Ch 10-12).

REIGN
Ex 15:18 The LORD will *r*
Ro 6:12 Therefore do not let sin *r*
1Co 15:25 For he must *r* until he has put all
2Ti 2:12 we will also *r* with him.
Rev 20:6 will *r* with him for a thousand years

REJECTED (REJECTS)
Ps 118:22 The stone the builders *r*
Isa 53:3 He was despised and *r* by men,
1Ti 4:4 nothing is to be *r* if it is received
1Pe 2:4 *r* by men but chosen by God
2:7 "The stone the builders *r*

REJECTS (REJECTED)
Lk 10:16 but he who *r* me *r* him who sent me
Jn 3:36 whoever *r* the Son will not see life,

REJOICE (JOY)
Ps 2:11 and *r* with trembling.
66:6 come, let us *r* in him.
118:24 let us *r* and be glad in it.
Pr 5:18 may you *r* in the wife of your youth
Lk 10:20 but *r* that your names are written
15:6 '*R* with me; I have found my lost
Ro 12:15 Rejoice with those who *r;* mourn
Php 4:4 *R* in the Lord always.

REJOICES (JOY)
Isa 61:10 my soul *r* in my God.
Lk 1:47 and my spirit *r* in God my Savior,
1Co 12:26 if one part is honored, every part *r*
13:6 delight in evil but *r* with the truth.

REJOICING (JOY)
Ps 30:5 but *r* comes in the morning.
Lk 15:7 in the same way there will be more *r*
Ac 5:41 *r* because they had been counted

RELIABLE
2Ti 2:2 witnesses entrust to *r* men who will

RELIGION
1Ti 5:4 all to put their *r* into practice
Jas 1:27 *R* that God our Father accepts

REMAIN (REMAINS)
Nu 33:55 allow to *r* will become barbs
Jn 15:7 If you *r* in me and my words
Ro 13:8 Let no debt *r* outstanding,
1Co 13:13 And now these three *r:* faith,
2Ti 2:13 he will *r* faithful,

REMAINS (REMAIN)
Ps 146:6 the LORD, who *r* faithful forever.
Heb 7:3 Son of God he *r* a priest forever.

REMEMBER (REMEMBERS REMEMBRANCE)
Ex 20:8 "*R* the Sabbath day
1Ch 16:12 *R* the wonders he has done,
Ecc 12:1 *R* your Creator
Jer 31:34 and will *r* their sins no more."
Gal 2:10 we should continue to *r* the poor,
Php 1:3 I thank my God every time I *r* you.
Heb 8:12 and will *r* their sins no more."

REMEMBERS (REMEMBER)
Ps 103:14 he *r* that we are dust.
111:5 he *r* his covenant forever.
Isa 43:25 and *r* your sins no more.

REMEMBRANCE (REMEMBER)
1Co 11:24 which is for you; do this in *r* of me

REMIND
Jn 14:26 will *r* you of everything I have said

REMOVED
Ps 30:11 you *r* my sackcloth and clothed me
103:12 so far has he *r* our transgressions
Jn 20:1 and saw that the stone had been *r*

RENEW (RENEWED RENEWING)
Ps 51:10 and *r* a steadfast spirit within me.
Isa 40:31 will *r* their strength.

RENEWED (RENEW)
Ps 103:5 that your youth is *r* like the eagle's.
2Co 4:16 yet inwardly we are being *r* day

RENEWING (RENEW)
Ro 12:2 transformed by the *r* of your mind.

RENOUNCE (RENOUNCES)
Da 4:27 *R* your sins by doing what is right,

RENOUNCES (RENOUNCE)
Pr 28:13 confesses and *r* them finds

RENOWN
Isa 63:12 to gain for himself everlasting *r,*
Jer 32:20 have gained the *r* that is still yours.

REPAID (PAY)
Lk 14:14 you will be *r* at the resurrection
Col 3:25 Anyone who does wrong will be *r*

REPAY (PAY)
Dt 32:35 It is mine to avenge; I will *r*.
Ru 2:12 May the LORD *r* you
Ps 116:12 How can I *r* the LORD
Ro 12:19 "It is mine to avenge; I will *r*,"
1Pe 3:9 Do not *r* evil with evil

REPENT (REPENTANCE REPENTS)
Job 42:6 and *r* in dust and ashes."
Jer 15:19 "If you *r*, I will restore you
Mt 4:17 "*R*, for the kingdom of heaven is
Lk 13:3 unless you *r*, you too will all perish.
Ac 2:38 Peter replied, "*R* and be baptized,
17:30 all people everywhere to *r*.

REPENTANCE (REPENT)
Lk 3:8 Produce fruit in keeping with *r*.
5:32 call the righteous, but sinners to *r*."
Ac 26:20 and prove their *r* by their deeds.
2Co 7:10 Godly sorrow brings *r* that leads

REPENTS (REPENT)
Lk 15:10 of God over one sinner who *r*."
17:3 rebuke him, and if he *r*, forgive him

REPROACH
1Ti 3:2 Now the overseer must be above *r*,

REPUTATION
1Ti 3:7 also have a good *r* with outsiders,

REQUESTS
Ps 20:5 May the LORD grant all your *r*.
Php 4:6 with thanksgiving, present your *r*

REQUIRE
Mic 6:8 And what does the LORD *r* of you

RESCUE (RESCUES)
Da 6:20 been able to *r* you from the lions?"
2Pe 2:9 how to *r* godly men from trials

RESCUES (RESCUE)
1Th 1:10 who *r* us from the coming wrath.

RESIST
Jas 4:7 *R* the devil, and he will flee
1Pe 5:9 *R* him, standing firm in the faith,

RESOLVED
Ps 17:3 I have *r* that my mouth will not sin.
Da 1:8 But Daniel *r* not to defile himself
1Co 2:2 For I *r* to know nothing while I was

RESPECT (RESPECTABLE)
Lev 19:3 " 'Each of you must *r* his mother
19:32 show *r* for the elderly and revere
Pr 11:16 A kindhearted woman gains *r*,
Mal 1:6 where is the *r* due me?" says
1Th 4:12 so that your daily life may win the *r*
5:12 to *r* those who work hard
1Ti 3:4 children obey him with proper *r*.
1Pe 2:17 Show proper *r* to everyone:
3:7 them with *r* as the weaker partner

RESPECTABLE* (RESPECT)
1Ti 3:2 self-controlled, *r*, hospitable,

REST
Ex 31:15 the seventh day is a Sabbath of *r*,
Ps 91:1 will *r* in the shadow

Jer 6:16 and you will find *r* for your souls.
Mt 11:28 and burdened, and I will give you *r*.

RESTITUTION
Ex 22:3 "A thief must certainly make *r*,
Lev 6:5 He must make *r* in full, add a fifth

RESTORE (RESTORES)
Ps 51:12 *R* to me the joy of your salvation
Gal 6:1 are spiritual should *r* him gently.

RESTORES (RESTORE)
Ps 23:3 he *r* my soul.

RESURRECTION
Mt 22:30 At the *r* people will neither marry
Lk 14:14 repaid at the *r* of the righteous."
Jn 11:25 Jesus said to her, "I am the *r*
Ro 1:4 Son of God by his *r* from the dead:
1Co 15:12 some of you say that there is no *r*
Php 3:10 power of his *r* and the fellowship
Rev 20:5 This is the first *r*.

RETRIBUTION
Jer 51:56 For the LORD is a God of *r*;

RETURN
2Ch 30:9 If you *r* to the LORD, then your
Ne 1:9 but if you *r* to me and obey my
Isa 55:11 It will not *r* to me empty,
Hos 6:1 "Come, let us *r* to the LORD.
Joel 2:12 "*r* to me with all your heart,

REVEALED (REVELATION)
Dt 29:29 but the things *r* belong to us
Isa 40:5 the glory of the LORD will be *r*,
Mt 11:25 and *r* them to little children.
Ro 1:17 a righteousness from God is *r*,
8:18 with the glory that will be *r* in us.

REVELATION (REVEALED)
Gal 1:12 I received it by *r* from Jesus Christ.
Rev 1:1 *r* of Jesus Christ, which God gave

REVENGE (VENGEANCE)
Lev 19:18 " 'Do not seek *r* or bear a grudge
Ro 12:19 Do not take *r*, my friends,

REVERE (REVERENCE)
Ps 33:8 let all the people of the world *r* him

REVERENCE (REVERE)
Lev 19:30 and have *r* for my sanctuary.
Ps 5:7 in *r* will I bow down
Col 3:22 of heart and *r* for the Lord.
1Pe 3:2 when they see the purity and *r*

REVIVE (REVIVING)
Ps 85:6 Will you not *r* us again,
Isa 57:15 to *r* the spirit of the lowly

REVIVING (REVIVE)
Ps 19:7 *r* the soul.

REWARD (REWARDED)
Ps 19:11 in keeping them there is great *r*.
127:3 children a *r* from him.
Pr 19:17 he will *r* him for what he has done.
25:22 and the LORD will *r* you.
31:31 Give her the *r* she has earned,
Jer 17:10 to *r* a man according to his conduct
Mt 5:12 because great is your *r* in heaven,
6:5 they have received their *r* in full.
16:27 and then he will *r* each person
1Co 3:14 built survives, he will receive his *r*.
Rev 22:12 I am coming soon! My *r* is with me

REWARDED (REWARD)
Ru 2:12 May you be richly *r* by the LORD,
Ps 18:24 The LORD has *r* me according
Pr 14:14 and the good man *r* for his.
1Co 3:8 and each will be *r* according

RICH (RICHES)
Pr 23:4 Do not wear yourself out to get *r*;
Jer 9:23 or the *r* man boast of his riches,
Mt 19:23 it is hard for a *r* man
2Co 6:10 yet making many *r*; having nothing
8:9 he was *r*, yet for your sakes he
1Ti 6:17 Command those who are *r*

RICHES (RICH)
Ps 119:14 as one rejoices in great *r*.
Pr 30:8 give me neither poverty nor *r*,
Isa 10:3 Where will you leave your *r*?
Ro 9:23 to make the *r* of his glory known
11:33 the depth of the *r* of the wisdom
Eph 2:7 he might show the incomparable *r*
3:8 to the Gentiles the unsearchable *r*
Col 1:27 among the Gentiles the glorious *r*

RID
Ge 21:10 "Get *r* of that slave woman
1Co 5:7 Get *r* of the old yeast that you may
Gal 4:30 "Get *r* of the slave woman

RIGHT (RIGHTS)
Ge 18:25 the Judge of all the earth do *r*?"
Ex 15:26 and do what is *r* in his eyes,
Dt 5:32 do not turn aside to the *r*
Ps 16:8 Because he is at my *r* hand,
19:8 The precepts of the LORD are *r*,
63:8 your *r* hand upholds me.
110:1 "Sit at my *r* hand
Pr 4:27 Do not swerve to the *r* or the left;
14:12 There is a way that seems *r*
Isa 1:17 learn to do *r*!
Jer 23:5 and do what is just and *r* in the land
Hos 14:9 The ways of the LORD are *r*;
Mt 6:3 know what your *r* hand is doing,
Jn 1:12 he gave the *r* to become children
Ro 9:21 Does not the potter have the *r*
12:17 careful to do what is *r* in the eyes
Eph 1:20 and seated him at his *r* hand
Php 4:8 whatever is *r*, whatever is pure,
2Th 3:13 never tire of doing what is *r*.

RIGHTEOUS (RIGHTEOUSNESS)
Ps 34:15 The eyes of the LORD are on the *r*
37:25 yet I have never seen the *r* forsaken
119:137 *R* are you, O LORD,
143:2 for no one living is *r* before you.
Pr 3:33 but he blesses the home of the *r*.
11:30 The fruit of the *r* is a tree of life,
18:10 the *r* run to it and are safe.
Isa 64:6 and all our *r* acts are like filthy rags
Hab 2:4 but the *r* will live by his faith—
Mt 5:45 rain on the *r* and the unrighteous.
9:13 For I have not come to call the *r*,
13:49 and separate the wicked from the *r*
25:46 to eternal punishment, but the *r*
Ro 1:17 as it is written: "The *r* will live
3:10 "There is no one *r*, not even one;
1Ti 1:9 that law is made not for the *r*
1Pe 3:18 the *r* for the unrighteous,
1Jn 3:7 does what is right is *r*, just as he is *r*.
Rev 19:8 stands for the *r* acts of the saints.)

RIGHTEOUSNESS (RIGHTEOUS)
Ge 15:6 and he credited it to him as *r*.
1Sa 26:23 LORD rewards every man for his *r*
Ps 9:8 He will judge the world in *r*;
23:3 He guides me in paths of *r*

Ps 45: 7 You love *r* and hate wickedness;
85: 10 *r* and peace kiss each other.
89: 14 *R* and justice are the foundation
111: 3 and his *r* endures forever.
Pr 14: 34 *R* exalts a nation,
21: 21 He who pursues *r* and love
Isa 5: 16 will show himself holy by his *r.*
59: 17 He put on *r* as his breastplate,
Eze 18: 20 The *r* of the righteous man will be
Da 9: 24 to bring in everlasting *r,*
12: 3 and those who lead many to *r,*
Mal 4: 2 the sun of *r* will rise with healing
Mt 5: 6 those who hunger and thirst for *r,*
5: 20 unless your *r* surpasses that
6: 33 But seek first his kingdom and his *r*
Ro 4: 3 and it was credited to him as *r.*"
4: 9 faith was credited to him as *r.*
6: 13 body to him as instruments of *r.*
2Co 5: 21 that in him we might become the *r*
Gal 2: 21 for if *r* could be gained
3: 6 and it was credited to him as *r.*"
Eph 6: 14 with the breastplate of *r* in place,
Php 3: 9 not having a *r* of my own that
2Ti 3: 16 correcting and training in *r,*
4: 8 is in store for me the crown of *r,*
Heb 11: 7 became heir of the *r* that comes
2Pe 2: 21 not to have known the way of *r,*

RIGHTS (RIGHT)
La 3: 35 to deny a man his *r*
Gal 4: 5 that we might receive the full *r*

RISE (RAISED)
Isa 26: 19 their bodies will *r.*
Mt 27: 63 'After three days I will *r* again.'
Jn 5: 29 those who have done good will *r*
1Th 4: 16 and the dead in Christ will *r* first.

ROAD
Mt 7: 13 and broad is the *r* that leads

ROBBERS
Jer 7: 11 become a den of *r* to you?
Mk 15: 27 They crucified two *r* with him,
Lk 19: 46 but you have made it 'a den of *r.*'"
Jn 10: 8 came before me were thieves and *r,*

ROCK
Ps 18: 2 The LORD is my *r,* my fortress
40: 2 he set my feet on a *r*
Mt 7: 24 man who built his house on the *r.*
16: 18 and on this *r* I will build my church
Ro 9: 33 and a *r* that makes them fall,
1Co 10: 4 the spiritual *r* that accompanied

ROD
Ps 23: 4 your *r* and your staff,
Pr 13: 24 He who spares the *r* hates his son,
23: 13 if you punish him with the *r,*

ROOM (ROOMS)
Mt 6: 6 But when you pray, go into your *r,*
Lk 2: 7 there was no *r* for them in the inn.
Jn 21: 25 the whole world would not have *r*

ROOMS (ROOM)
Jn 14: 2 In my Father's house are many *r;*

ROOT
Isa 53: 2 and like a *r* out of dry ground.
1Ti 6: 10 of money is a *r* of all kinds of evil.

ROYAL
Jas 2: 8 If you really keep the *r* law found
1Pe 2: 9 a *r* priesthood, a holy nation,

RUBBISH*
Php 3: 8 I consider them *r,* that I may gain

RUDE*
1Co 13: 5 It is not *r,* it is not self-seeking,

RUIN (RUINS)
Pr 18: 24 many companions may come to *r,*
1Ti 6: 9 desires that plunge men into *r*

RUINS (RUIN)
Pr 19: 3 A man's own folly *r* his life,
2Ti 2: 14 and only *r* those who listen.

RULE (RULER RULERS RULES)
1Sa 12: 12 'No, we want a king to *r* over us'—
Ps 2: 9 You will *r* them with an iron
119: 133 let no sin *r* over me.
Zec 9: 10 His *r* will extend from sea to sea
Col 3: 15 the peace of Christ *r* in your hearts,
Rev 2: 27 He will *r* them with an iron scepter;

RULER (RULE)
Ps 8: 6 You made him *r* over the works
Eph 2: 2 of the *r* of the kingdom of the air,
1Ti 6: 15 God, the blessed and only *R,*

RULERS (RULE)
Ps 2: 2 and the *r* gather together
Col 1: 16 or powers or *r* or authorities;

RULES (RULE)
Ps 103: 19 and his kingdom *r* over all.
Lk 22: 26 one who *r* like the one who serves.
2Ti 2: 5 he competes according to the *r.*

RUMORS
Mt 24: 6 You will hear of wars and *r* of wars,

RUN (RAN)
Isa 40: 31 they will *r* and not grow weary,
1Co 9: 24 *R* in such a way as to get the prize.
Heb 12: 1 let us *r* with perseverance the race

RUST
Mt 6: 19 where moth and *r* destroy,

RUTH*

Moabitess; widow who went to Bethlehem with mother-in-law Naomi (Ru 1). Gleaned in field of Boaz; shown favor (Ru 2). Proposed marriage to Boaz (Ru 3). Married (Ru 4:1-12); bore Obed, ancestor of David (Ru 4:13-22), Jesus (Mt 1:5).

SABBATH
Ex 20: 8 "Remember the *S* day
Dt 5: 12 "Observe the *S* day
Col 2: 16 a New Moon celebration or a *S* day

SACKCLOTH
Mt 11: 21 would have repented long ago in *s*

SACRED
Mt 7: 6 "Do not give dogs what is *s;*
1Co 3: 17 for God's temple is *s,* and you are

SACRIFICE (SACRIFICED SACRIFICES)
Ge 22: 2 *S* him there as a burnt offering
Ex 12: 27 'It is the Passover *s* to the LORD,
1Sa 15: 22 To obey is better than *s,*
Hos 6: 6 For I desire mercy, not *s,*
Mt 9: 13 this means: 'I desire mercy, not *s.*'
Heb 9: 26 away with sin by the *s* of himself.
13: 15 offer to God a *s* of praise—
1Jn 2: 2 He is the atoning *s* for our sins,

SACRIFICED (SACRIFICE)
1Co 5: 7 our Passover lamb, has been *s.*
8: 1 Now about food *s* to idols:
Heb 9: 28 so Christ was *s* once

SACRIFICES (SACRIFICE)
Ps 51: 17 The *s* of God are a broken spirit;
Ro 12: 1 to offer your bodies as living *s,*

SADDUCEES
Mk 12: 18 *S,* who say there is no resurrection,

SAFE (SAVE)
Ps 37: 3 in the land and enjoy *s* pasture.
Pr 18: 10 the righteous run to it and are *s.*

SAFETY (SAVE)
Ps 4: 8 make me dwell in *s.*
1Th 5: 3 people are saying, "Peace and *s,*"

SAINTS
Ps 116: 15 is the death of his *s.*
Ro 8: 27 intercedes for the *s* in accordance
Eph 1: 18 of his glorious inheritance in the *s,*
6: 18 always keep on praying for all the *s*
Rev 5: 8 which are the prayers of the *s.*
19: 8 for the righteous acts of the *s.*

SAKE
Ps 44: 22 Yet for your *s* we face death all day
Php 3: 7 loss for the *s* of Christ.
Heb 11: 26 He regarded disgrace for the *s*

SALT
Ge 19: 26 and she became a pillar of *s.*
Mt 5: 13 "You are the *s* of the earth.

SALVATION (SAVE)
Ex 15: 2 he has become my *s.*
1Ch 16: 23 proclaim his *s* day after day.
Ps 27: 1 The LORD is my light and my *s*—
51: 12 Restore to me the joy of your *s*
62: 2 He alone is my rock and my *s;*
85: 9 Surely his *s* is near those who fear
96: 2 proclaim his *s* day after day.
Isa 25: 9 let us rejoice and be glad in his *s.*"
45: 17 the LORD with an everlasting *s;*
51: 6 But my *s* will last forever,
59: 17 and the helmet of *s* on his head;
61: 10 me with garments of *s*
Jnh 2: 9 *S* comes from the LORD."
Zec 9: 9 righteous and having *s,*
Lk 2: 30 For my eyes have seen your *s,*
Jn 4: 22 for *s* is from the Jews.
Ac 4: 12 *S* is found in no one else,
13: 47 that you may bring *s* to the ends
Ro 11: 11 *s* has come to the Gentiles
2Co 7: 10 brings repentance that leads to *s*
Eph 6: 17 Take the helmet of *s* and the sword
Php 2: 12 to work out your *s* with fear
1Th 5: 8 and the hope of *s* as a helmet.
2Ti 3: 15 wise for *s* through faith
Heb 2: 3 escape if we ignore such a great *s?*
6: 9 case—things that accompany *s.*
1Pe 1: 10 Concerning this *s,* the prophets,
2: 2 by it you may grow up in your *s,*

SAMARITAN
Lk 10: 33 But a *S,* as he traveled, came where

SAMSON

Danite judge. Birth promised (Jdg 13). Married to Philistine (Jdg 14). Vengeance on Philistines (Jdg 15). Betrayed by Delilah (Jdg 16:1-22). Death (Jdg 16:23-31). Feats of strength: killed lion (Jdg 14:6), 30 Philistines (Jdg 14:19), 1,000 Philistines with jawbone (Jdg 15:13-17), carried off gates of Gaza (Jdg 16:3), pushed down temple of Dagon (Jdg 16:25-30).

SAMUEL

Ephraimite judge and prophet (Heb 11:32). Birth prayed for (1Sa 1:10-18). Dedicated to temple by Hannah (1Sa 1:21-28). Raised by Eli (1Sa 2:11, 18-26). Called as prophet (1Sa 3). Led Israel to victory over Philistines (1Sa 7). Asked by Israel for a king (1Sa 8). Anointed Saul as king (1Sa 9-10). Farewell speech (1Sa 12). Rebuked Saul for sacrifice (1Sa 13). Announced rejection of Saul (2Sa 15). Anointed David as king (1Sa 16). Protected David from Saul (1Sa 19:18-24). Death (1Sa 25:1). Returned from dead to condemn Saul (1Sa 28).

SANCTIFIED (SANCTIFY)

Ac 20:32 among all those who are *s.*
Ro 15:16 to God, *s* by the Holy Spirit.
1Co 6:11 But you were washed, you were *s,*
7:14 and the unbelieving wife has been *s*
Heb 10:29 blood of the covenant that *s* him,

SANCTIFY (SANCTIFIED SANCTIFYING)

1Th 5:23 *s* you through and through.

SANCTIFYING (SANCTIFY)

2Th 2:13 through the *s* work of the Spirit

SANCTUARY

Ex 25: 8 "Then have them make a *s* for me,

SAND

Ge 22:17 and as the *s* on the seashore.
Mt 7:26 man who built his house on *s.*

SANDALS

Ex 3: 5 off your *s,* for the place where you
Jos 5:15 off your *s,* for the place where you

SANG (SING)

Job 38: 7 while the morning stars *s* together
Rev 5: 9 And they *s* a new song:

SARAH

Wife of Abraham, originally named Sarai; barren (Ge 11:29-31; 1Pe 3:6). Taken by Pharaoh as Abraham's sister; returned (Ge 12:10-20). Gave Hagar to Abraham; sent her away in pregnancy (Ge 16). Name changed; Isaac promised (Ge 17:15-21; 18:10-15; Heb 11:11). Taken by Abimelech as Abraham's sister; returned (Ge 20). Isaac born; Hagar and Ishmael sent away (Ge 21:1-21; Gal 4:21-31). Death (Ge 23).

SATAN

Job 1: 6 and *S* also came with them.
Zec 3: 2 said to *S,* "The LORD rebuke you,
Mk 4:15 *S* comes and takes away the word
2Co 11:14 for *S* himself masquerades
12: 7 a messenger of *S,* to torment me.
Rev 12: 9 serpent called the devil, or *S,*
20: 2 or *S,* and bound him for a thousand
20: 7 *S* will be released from his prison

SATISFIED (SATISFY)

Isa 53:11 he will see the light ˪of life˩ and be *s*

SATISFIES (SATISFY)

Ps 103: 5 who *s* your desires with good things,

SATISFY (SATISFIED SATISFIES)

Isa 55: 2 and your labor on what does not *s?*

SAUL

1. Benjamite; anointed by Samuel as first king of Israel (1Sa 9-10). Defeated Ammonites (1Sa 11). Rebuked for offering sacrifice (1Sa 13:1-15). Defeated Philistines (1Sa 14). Rejected as king for failing to annihilate Amalekites (1Sa 15). Soothed from evil spirit by David (1Sa 16:14-23). Sent David against Goliath (1Sa 17). Jealousy and attempted murder of David (1Sa 18:1-11). Gave David Michal as wife (1Sa 18:12-30). Second attempt to kill David (1Sa 19). Anger at Jonathan (1Sa 20:26-34). Pursued David: killed priests at Nob (1Sa 22), went to Keilah and Ziph (1Sa 23), life spared by David at En Gedi (1Sa 24) and in his tent (1Sa 26). Rebuked by Samuel's spirit for consulting witch at Endor (1Sa 28). Wounded by Philistines; took his own life (1Sa 31; 1Ch 10).

2. See PAUL

SAVE (SAFE SAFETY SALVATION SAVED SAVIOR)

Isa 63: 1 mighty to *s."*
Da 3:17 the God we serve is able to *s* us
Zep 3:17 he is mighty to *s.*
Mt 1:21 he will *s* his people from their sins
16:25 wants to *s* his life will lose it,
Lk 19:10 to seek and to *s* what was lost."
Jn 3:17 but to *s* the world through him.
1Ti 1:15 came into the world to *s* sinners—
Jas 5:20 of his way will *s* him from death

SAVED (SAVE)

Ps 34: 6 he *s* him out of all his troubles.
Isa 45:22 "Turn to me and be *s,*
Joel 2:32 on the name of the LORD will be *s;*
Mk 13:13 firm to the end will be *s.*
16:16 believes and is baptized will be *s,*
Jn 10: 9 enters through me will be *s.*
Ac 4:12 to men by which we must be *s."*
16:30 do to be *s?"* They replied,
Ro 9:27 only the remnant will be *s.*
10: 9 him from the dead, you will be *s.*
1Co 3:15 will suffer loss; he himself will be *s,*
15: 2 By this gospel you are *s,*
Eph 2: 5 it is by grace you have been *s.*
2: 8 For it is by grace you have been *s,*
1Ti 2: 4 who wants all men to be *s*

SAVIOR (SAVE)

Ps 89:26 my God, the Rock my *S.'*
Isa 43:11 and apart from me there is no *s.*
Hos 13: 4 no *S* except me.
Lk 1:47 and my spirit rejoices in God my *S,*
2:11 of David a *S* has been born to you;
Jn 4:42 know that this man really is the *S*
Eph 5:23 his body, of which he is the *S.*
1Ti 4:10 who is the *S* of all men,
Tit 2:10 about God our *S* attractive.
2:13 appearing of our great God and *S,*
3: 4 and love of God our *S* appeared,
1Jn 4:14 Son to be the *S* of the world.
Jude :25 to the only God our *S* be glory,

SCALES

Lev 19:36 Use honest *s* and honest weights,
Da 5:27 You have been weighed on the *s*

SCAPEGOAT (GOAT)

Lev 16:10 by sending it into the desert as a *s.*

SCARLET

Isa 1:18 "Though your sins are like *s,*

SCATTERED

Jer 31:10 'He who *s* Israel will gather them
Ac 8: 4 who had been *s* preached the word

SCEPTER

Rev 19:15 "He will rule them with an iron *s."*

SCHEMES

2Co 2:11 For we are not unaware of his *s.*
Eph 6:11 stand against the devil's *s.*

SCOFFERS

2Pe 3: 3 that in the last days *s* will come,

SCORPION

Rev 9: 5 sting of a *s* when it strikes a man.

SCRIPTURE (SCRIPTURES)

Jn 10:35 and the *S* cannot be broken—
1Ti 4:13 yourself to the public reading of *S,*
2Ti 3:16 All *S* is God-breathed
2Pe 1:20 that no prophecy of *S* came about

SCRIPTURES (SCRIPTURE)

Lk 24:27 said in all the *S* concerning himself.
Jn 5:39 These are the *S* that testify about
Ac 17:11 examined the *S* every day to see

SCROLL

Eze 3: 1 eat what is before you, eat this *s;*

SEA

Ex 14:16 go through the *s* on dry ground.
Isa 57:20 the wicked are like the tossing *s,*
Mic 7:19 iniquities into the depths of the *s.*
Jas 1: 6 who doubts is like a wave of the *s,*
Rev 13: 1 I saw a beast coming out of the *s.*

SEAL (SEALS)

Jn 6:27 God the Father has placed his *s*
2Co 1:22 set his *s* of ownership on us,
Eph 1:13 you were marked in him with a *s,*

SEALS (SEAL)

Rev 5: 2 "Who is worthy to break the *s*
6: 1 opened the first of the seven *s.*

SEARCH (SEARCHED SEARCHES SEARCHING)

Ps 4: 4 *s* your hearts and be silent.
139: 23 *S* me, O God, and know my heart;
Pr 2: 4 and *s* for it as for hidden treasure,
Jer 17:10 "I the LORD *s* the heart
Eze 34:16 I will *s* for the lost and bring back
Lk 15: 8 and *s* carefully until she finds it?

SEARCHED (SEARCH)

Ps 139: 1 O LORD, you have *s* me

SEARCHES (SEARCH)

Ro 8:27 And he who *s* our hearts knows
1Co 2:10 The Spirit *s* all things,

SEARCHING (SEARCH)

Am 8:12 *s* for the word of the LORD,

SEARED

1Ti 4: 2 whose consciences have been *s*

SEASON

2Ti 4: 2 be prepared in *s* and out of *s;*

SEAT (SEATED SEATS)

Ps 1: 1 or sit in the *s* of mockers.
Da 7: 9 and the Ancient of Days took his *s.*
2Co 5:10 before the judgment *s* of Christ,

SEATED (SEAT)

Ps 47: 8 God is *s* on his holy throne.

Isa 6: 1 I saw the Lord *s* on a throne,
Col 3: 1 where Christ is *s* at the right hand

SEATS (SEAT)
Lk 11: 43 you love the most important *s*

SECRET (SECRETS)
Dt 29: 29 The *s* things belong
Jdg 16: 6 Tell me the *s* of your great strength
Ps 90: 8 our *s* sins in the light
Pr 11: 13 but a trustworthy man keeps a *s*.
Mt 6: 4 so that your giving may be in *s*.
2Co 4: 2 we have renounced *s* and shameful
Php 4: 12 I have learned the *s*

SECRETS (SECRET)
Ps 44: 21 since he knows the *s* of the heart?
1Co 14: 25 the *s* of his heart will be laid bare.

SECURE (SECURITY)
Ps 112: 8 His heart is *s*, he will have no fear;
Heb 6: 19 an anchor for the soul, firm and *s*.

SECURITY (SECURE)
Job 31: 24 or said to pure gold, 'You are my *s*,'

SEED (SEEDS)
Lk 8: 11 of the parable: The *s* is the word
1Co 3: 6 I planted the *s*, Apollos watered it,
2Co 9: 10 he who supplies *s* to the sower
Gal 3: 29 then you are Abraham's *s*,
1Pe 1: 23 not of perishable *s*,

SEEDS (SEED)
Jn 12: 24 But if it dies, it produces many *s*.
Gal 3: 16 Scripture does not say "and to *s*,"

SEEK (SEEKS SELF-SEEKING)
Dt 4: 29 if from there you *s* the LORD your
1Ch 28: 9 If you *s* him, he will be found
2Ch 7: 14 themselves and pray and *s* my face
Ps 119: 10 I *s* you with all my heart;
Isa 55: 6 *S* the LORD while he may be
65: 1 found by those who did not *s* me.
Mt 6: 33 But *s* first his kingdom
Lk 19: 10 For the Son of Man came to *s*
Ro 10: 20 found by those who did not *s* me;
1Co 7: 27 you married? Do not *s* a divorce.

SEEKS (SEEK)
Jn 4: 23 the kind of worshipers the Father *s*.

SEER
1Sa 9: 9 of today used to be called a *s*.)

SELF-CONTROL (CONTROL)
1Co 7: 5 you because of your lack of *s*.
Gal 5: 23 faithfulness, gentleness and *s*.
2Pe 1: 6 and to knowledge, *s*; and to *s*,

SELF-CONTROLLED* (CONTROL)
1Th 5: 6 are asleep, but let us be alert and *s*.
5: 8 let us be *s*, putting on faith and love
1Ti 3: 2 *s*, respectable, hospitable,
Tit 1: 8 who is *s*, upright, holy
2: 2 worthy of respect, *s*, and sound
2: 5 to be *s* and pure, to be busy at home
2: 6 encourage the young men to be *s*.
2: 12 to live *s*, upright and godly lives
1Pe 1: 13 prepare your minds for action; be *s*;
4: 7 and *s* so that you can pray.
5: 8 Be *s* and alert.

SELF-INDULGENCE
Mt 23: 25 inside they are full of greed and *s*.

SELF-SEEKING (SEEK)
1Co 13: 5 it is not *s*, it is not easily angered,

SELFISH*
Ps 119: 36 and not toward *s* gain.
Pr 18: 1 An unfriendly man pursues *s* ends;
Gal 5: 20 fits of rage, *s* ambition, dissensions,
Php 1: 17 preach Christ out of *s* ambition,
2: 3 Do nothing out of *s* ambition
Jas 3: 14 and *s* ambition in your hearts,
3: 16 you have envy and *s* ambition,

SEND (SENDING SENT)
Isa 6: 8 *S* me!" He said, "Go and tell this
Mt 9: 38 to *s* out workers into his harvest
Jn 16: 7 but if I go, I will *s* him to you.

SENDING (SEND)
Jn 20: 21 Father has sent me, I am *s* you."

SENSES*
Lk 15: 17 "When he came to his *s*, he said,
1Co 15: 34 Come back to your *s* as you ought,
2Ti 2: 26 and that they will come to their *s*

SENSUAL
Col 2: 23 value in restraining *s* indulgence.

SENT (SEND)
Isa 55: 11 achieve the purpose for which I *s* it.
Mt 10: 40 me receives the one who *s* me.
Jn 4: 34 "is to do the will of him who *s* me
Ro 10: 15 can they preach unless they are *s*?
1Jn 4: 10 but that he loved us and *s* his Son

SEPARATE (SEPARATED SEPARATES)
Mt 19: 6 has joined together, let man not *s*."
Ro 8: 35 Who shall *s* us from the love
1Co 7: 10 wife must not *s* from her husband.
2Co 6: 17 and be *s*, says the Lord.

SEPARATED (SEPARATE)
Isa 59: 2 But your iniquities have *s*

SEPARATES (SEPARATE)
Pr 16: 28 and a gossip *s* close friends.

SERPENT
Ge 3: 1 the *s* was more crafty than any
Rev 12: 9 that ancient *s* called the devil

SERVANT (SERVANTS)
1Sa 3: 10 "Speak, for your *s* is listening."
Mt 20: 26 great among you must be your *s*,
25: 21 'Well done, good and faithful *s*!
Lk 16: 13 "No *s* can serve two masters.
Php 2: 7 taking the very nature of a *s*,
2Ti 2: 24 And the Lord's *s* must not quarrel;

SERVANTS (SERVANT)
Lk 17: 10 should say, 'We are unworthy *s*;
Jn 15: 15 longer call you *s*, because a servant

SERVE (SERVICE SERVING)
Dt 10: 12 to *s* the LORD your God
Jos 22: 5 and to *s* him with all your heart
24: 15 this day whom you will *s*,
Mt 4: 10 Lord your God, and *s* him only.' "
6: 24 "No one can *s* two masters.
20: 28 but to *s*, and to give his life
Eph 6: 7 *S* wholeheartedly,

SERVICE (SERVE)
1Co 12: 5 There are different kinds of *s*,
Eph 4: 12 God's people for works of *s*,

SERVING (SERVE)
Ro 12: 11 your spiritual fervor, *s* the Lord.
Eph 6: 7 as if you were *s* the Lord, not men,
Col 3: 24 It is the Lord Christ you are *s*.
2Ti 2: 4 No one *s* as a soldier gets involved

SEVEN (SEVENTH)
Ge 7: 2 Take with you *s* of every kind
Jos 6: 4 march around the city *s* times,
1Ki 19: 18 Yet I reserve *s* thousand in Israel—
Pr 6: 16 *s* that are detestable to him:
24: 16 a righteous man falls *s* times,
Isa 4: 1 In that day *s* women
Da 9: 25 comes, there will be *s* 'sevens,'
Mt 18: 21 Up to *s* times?" Jesus answered,
Lk 11: 26 takes *s* other spirits more wicked
Ro 11: 4 for myself *s* thousand who have not
Rev 1: 4 To the *s* churches in the province
6: 1 opened the first of the *s* seals.
8: 2 and to them were given *s* trumpets.
10: 4 And when the *s* thunders spoke,
15: 7 to the *s* angels *s* golden bowls filled

SEVENTH (SEVEN)
Ge 2: 2 By the *s* day God had finished
Ex 23: 12 but on the *s* day do not work,

SEXUAL (SEXUALLY)
1Co 6: 13 body is not meant for *s* immorality,
6: 18 Flee from *s* immorality.
10: 8 should not commit *s* immorality,
Eph 5: 3 even a hint of *s* immorality,
1Th 4: 3 that you should avoid *s* immorality

SEXUALLY (SEXUAL)
1Co 5: 9 to associate with *s* immoral people
6: 18 he who sins *s* sins against his own

SHADOW
Ps 23: 4 through the valley of the *s* of death,
36: 7 find refuge in the *s* of your wings.
Heb 10: 1 The law is only a *s*

SHALLUM
King of Israel (2Ki 15:10-16).

SHAME (ASHAMED)
Ps 34: 5 their faces are never covered with *s*
Pr 13: 18 discipline comes to poverty and *s*,
Heb 12: 2 endured the cross, scorning its *s*,

SHARE (SHARED)
Ge 21: 10 that slave woman's son will never *s*
Lk 3: 11 "The man with two tunics should *s*
Gal 4: 30 the slave woman's son will never *s*
6: 6 in the word must *s* all good things
Eph 4: 28 something to *s* with those in need.
1Ti 6: 18 and to be generous and willing to *s*.
Heb 12: 10 that we may *s* in his holiness.
13: 16 to do good and to *s* with others,

SHARED (SHARE)
Heb 2: 14 he too *s* in their humanity so that

SHARON
SS 2: 1 I am a rose of *S*,

SHARPER*
Heb 4: 12 *S* than any double-edged sword,

SHED (SHEDDING)
Ge 9: 6 by man shall his blood be *s;*
Col 1: 20 through his blood, *s* on the cross.

SHEDDING (SHED)
Heb 9: 22 without the *s* of blood there is no

SHEEP
Ps 100: 3 we are his people, the *s*
119: 176 I have strayed like a lost *s.*
Isa 53: 6 We all, like *s,* have gone astray,
Jer 50: 6 "My people have been lost *s;*
Eze 34: 11 I myself will search for my *s*
Mt 9: 36 helpless, like *s* without a shepherd.
Jn 10: 3 He calls his own *s* by name
10: 15 and I lay down my life for the *s.*
10: 27 My *s* listen to my voice; I know
21: 17 Jesus said, "Feed my *s.*
1Pe 2: 25 For you were like *s* going astray,

SHELTER
Ps 61: 4 take refuge in the *s* of your wings.
91: 1 in the *s* of the Most High

SHEM
Son of Noah (Ge 5:32; 6:10). Blessed (Ge 9:26). Descendants (Ge 10:21-31; 11:10-32).

SHEPHERD (SHEPHERDS)
Ps 23: 1 LORD is my *s,* I shall not be in want.
Isa 40: 11 He tends his flock like a *s:*
Jer 31: 10 will watch over his flock like a *s.'*
Eze 34: 12 As a *s* looks after his scattered
Zec 11: 17 "Woe to the worthless *s,*
Mt 9: 36 and helpless, like sheep without a *s.*
Jn 10: 11 The good *s* lays down his life
10: 16 there shall be one flock and one *s.*
1Pe 5: 4 And when the Chief *S* appears,

SHEPHERDS (SHEPHERD)
Jer 23: 1 "Woe to the *s* who are destroying
Lk 2: 8 there were *s* living out in the fields
Ac 20: 28 Be *s* of the church of God,
1Pe 5: 2 Be *s* of God's flock that is

SHIELD
Ps 28: 7 LORD is my strength and my *s;*
Eph 6: 16 to all this, take up the *s* of faith,

SHINE (SHONE)
Ps 4: 6 Let the light of your face *s* upon us,
80: 1 between the cherubim, *s* forth
Isa 60: 1 "Arise, *s,* for your light has come,
Da 12: 3 are wise will *s* like the brightness
Mt 5: 16 let your light *s* before men,
13: 43 the righteous will *s* like the sun
2Co 4: 6 made his light *s* in our hearts
Eph 5: 14 and Christ will *s* on you."

SHIPWRECKED*
2Co 11: 25 I was stoned, three times I was *s,*
1Ti 1: 19 and so have *s* their faith.

SHONE (SHINE)
Mt 17: 2 His face *s* like the sun,
Lk 2: 9 glory of the Lord *s* around them,
Rev 21: 11 It *s* with the glory of God,

SHORT
Isa 59: 1 of the LORD is not too *s* to save,
Ro 3: 23 and fall *s* of the glory of God,

SHOULDERS
Isa 9: 6 and the government will be on his *s*
Lk 15: 5 he joyfully puts it on his *s*

SHOWED
1Jn 4: 9 This is how God *s* his love

SHREWD
Mt 10: 16 Therefore be as *s* as snakes and

SHUN*
Job 28: 28 and to *s* evil is understanding.' "
Pr 3: 7 fear the LORD and *s* evil.

SICK
Pr 13: 12 Hope deferred makes the heart *s,*
Mt 9: 12 who need a doctor, but the *s.*
25: 36 I was *s* and you looked after me,
Jas 5: 14 of you *s?* He should call the elders

SICKLE
Joel 3: 13 Swing the *s,*

SIDE
Ps 91: 7 A thousand may fall at your *s,*
124: 1 If the LORD had not been on our *s*
2Ti 4: 17 But the Lord stood at my *s*

SIGHT
Ps 90: 4 For a thousand years in your *s*
116: 15 Precious in the *s* of the LORD
2Co 5: 7 We live by faith, not by *s.*
1Pe 3: 4 which is of great worth in God's *s.*

SIGN (SIGNS)
Isa 7: 14 the Lord himself will give you a *s:*

SIGNS (SIGN)
Mk 16: 17 these *s* will accompany those who
Jn 20: 30 Jesus did many other miraculous *s*

SILENT
Pr 17: 28 a fool is thought wise if he keeps *s,*
Isa 53: 7 as a sheep before her shearers is *s,*
Hab 2: 20 let all the earth be *s* before him."
1Co 14: 34 women should remain *s*
1Ti 2: 12 over a man; she must be *s.*

SILVER
Pr 25: 11 is like apples of gold in settings of *s.*
Hag 2: 8 'The *s* is mine and the gold is mine,'
1Co 3: 12 *s,* costly stones, wood, hay or straw

SIMON
1. See PETER.
2. Apostle, called the Zealot (Mt 10:4; Mk 3:18; Lk 6:15; Ac 1:13).
3. Samaritan sorcerer (Ac 8:9-24).

SIN (SINFUL SINNED SINNER SINNERS SINNING SINS)
Nu 5: 7 and must confess the *s* he has
32: 23 be sure that your *s* will find you
Dt 24: 16 each is to die for his own *s.*
1Ki 8: 46 for there is no one who does not *s*
2Ch 7: 14 and will forgive their *s* and will heal
Ps 4: 4 In your anger do not *s;*
32: 2 whose *s* the LORD does not count
32: 5 Then I acknowledged my *s* to you
51: 2 and cleanse me from my *s.*
66: 18 If I had cherished *s* in my heart,
119: 11 that I might not *s* against you.
119: 133 let no *s* rule over me.
Isa 6: 7 is taken away and your *s* atoned
Mic 7: 18 who pardons *s* and forgives
Mt 18: 6 little ones who believe in me to *s,*
Jn 1: 29 who takes away the *s* of the world!
8: 34 everyone who sins is a slave to *s.*
Ro 5: 12 as *s* entered the world
5: 20 where *s* increased, grace increased
6: 11 count yourselves dead to *s*
6: 23 For the wages of *s* is death,
14: 23 that does not come from faith is *s.*
2Co 5: 21 God made him who had no *s* to be *s*
Gal 6: 1 if someone is caught in a *s,*
Heb 9: 26 to do away with *s* by the sacrifice
11: 25 the pleasures of *s* for a short time.
12: 1 and the *s* that so easily entangles,
1Pe 2: 22 "He committed no *s,*
1Jn 1: 8 If we claim to be without *s,*
3: 4 in fact, *s* is lawlessness.
3: 5 And in him is no *s.*
3: 9 born of God will continue to *s,*
5: 18 born of God does not continue to *s;*

SINCERE
Ro 12: 9 Love must be *s.*
Heb 10: 22 near to God with a *s* heart

SINFUL (SIN)
Ps 51: 5 Surely I was *s* at birth
51: 5 *s* from the time my mother
Ro 7: 5 we were controlled by the *s* nature,
8: 4 not live according to the *s* nature
8: 9 are controlled not by the *s* nature
Gal 5: 19 The acts of the *s* nature are obvious
5: 24 Jesus have crucified the *s* nature
1Pe 2: 11 abstain from *s* desires, which war

SING (SANG SINGING SONG SONGS)
Ps 30: 4 *S* to the LORD, you saints of his;
47: 6 *S* praises to God, *s* praises;
59: 16 But I will *s* of your strength,
89: 1 I will *s* of the LORD's great love
101: 1 I will *s* of your love and justice;
Eph 5: 19 *S* and make music in your heart

SINGING (SING)
Ps 63: 5 with *s* lips my mouth will praise
Ac 16: 25 Silas were praying and *s* hymns

SINNED (SIN)
2Sa 12: 13 "I have *s* against the LORD."
Job 1: 5 "Perhaps my children have *s*
Ps 51: 4 Against you, you only, have I *s*
Da 9: 5 we have *s* and done wrong.
Mic 7: 9 Because I have *s* against him,
Lk 15: 18 I have *s* against heaven
Ro 3: 23 for all have *s* and fall short
1Jn 1: 10 claim we have not *s,* we make him

SINNER (SIN)
Ecc 9: 18 but one *s* destroys much good.
Lk 15: 7 in heaven over one *s* who repents
18: 13 'God, have mercy on me, a *s.'*
1Co 14: 24 convinced by all that he is a *s*
Jas 5: 20 Whoever turns a *s* from the error
1Pe 4: 18 become of the ungodly and the *s?"*

SINNERS (SIN)
Ps 1: 1 or stand in the way of *s*
Pr 23: 17 Do not let your heart envy *s,*
Mt 9: 13 come to call the righteous, but *s."*
Ro 5: 8 While we were still *s,* Christ died
1Ti 1: 15 came into the world to save *s*—

SINNING (SIN)
Ex 20: 20 be with you to keep you from *s."*
1Co 15: 34 stop *s;* for there are some who are
Heb 10: 26 If we deliberately keep on *s*
1Jn 3: 6 No one who lives in him keeps on *s*

1Jn 3: 9 go on *s*, because he has been born

SINS (SIN)

2Ki 14: 6 each is to die for his own *s*."
Ezr 9: 6 our *s* are higher than our heads
Ps 19: 13 your servant also from willful *s*;
32: 1 whose *s* are covered.
103: 3 who forgives all your *s*
130: 3 O LORD, kept a record of *s*,
Pr 28: 13 who conceals his *s* does not
Isa 1: 18 "Though your *s* are like scarlet,
43: 25 and remembers your *s* no more.
59: 2 your *s* have hidden his face
Eze 18: 4 soul who *s* is the one who will die.
Mt 1: 21 he will save his people from their *s*
18: 15 "If your brother *s* against you,
Lk 11: 4 Forgive us our *s*,
17: 3 "If your brother *s*, rebuke him,
Ac 22: 16 be baptized and wash your *s* away,
1Co 15: 3 died for our *s* according
Eph 2: 1 dead in your transgressions and *s*,
Col 2: 13 us all our *s*, having canceled
Heb 1: 3 he had provided purification for *s*,
7: 27 He sacrificed for their *s* once for all
8: 12 and will remember their *s* no more
10: 12 for all time one sacrifice for *s*,
Jas 4: 17 ought to do and doesn't do it, *s*.
5: 16 Therefore confess your *s*
5: 20 and cover over a multitude of *s*.
1Pe 2: 24 He himself bore our *s* in his body
3: 18 For Christ died for *s* once for all,
1Jn 1: 9 If we confess our *s*, he is faithful
Rev 1: 5 has freed us from our *s* by his blood

SITS

Ps 99: 1 *s* enthroned between the cherubim,
Isa 40: 22 He *s* enthroned above the circle
Mt 19: 28 of Man *s* on his glorious throne,
Rev 4: 9 thanks to him who *s* on the throne

SKIN

Job 19: 20 with only the *s* of my teeth.
19: 26 And after my *s* has been destroyed,
Jer 13: 23 Can the Ethiopian change his *s*

SLAIN (SLAY)

Rev 5: 12 "Worthy is the Lamb, who was *s*,

SLANDER (SLANDERED SLANDERERS)

Lev 19: 16 " 'Do not go about spreading *s*
1Ti 5: 14 the enemy no opportunity for *s*.
Tit 3: 2 to *s* no one, to be peaceable

SLANDERED (SLANDER)

1Co 4: 13 when we are *s*, we answer kindly.

SLANDERERS (SLANDER)

Ro 1: 30 They are gossips, *s*, God-haters,
1Co 6: 10 nor the greedy nor drunkards nor *s*
Tit 2: 3 not to be *s* or addicted

SLAUGHTER

Isa 53: 7 he was led like a lamb to the *s*,

SLAVE (SLAVERY SLAVES)

Ge 21: 10 "Get rid of that *s* woman
Mt 20: 27 wants to be first must be your *s*—
Jn 8: 34 everyone who sins is a *s* to sin.
1Co 12: 13 whether Jews or Greeks, *s* or free
Gal 3: 28 *s* nor free, male nor female,
4: 30 Get rid of the *s* woman and her son
2Pe 2: 19 a man is a *s* to whatever has

SLAVERY (SLAVE)

Ro 6: 19 parts of your body in *s* to impurity
Gal 4: 3 were in *s* under the basic principles

SLAVES (SLAVE)

Ro 6: 6 that we should no longer be *s* to sin
6: 22 and have become *s* to God,

SLAY (SLAIN)

Job 13: 15 Though he *s* me, yet will I hope

SLEEP (SLEEPING)

Ps 121: 4 will neither slumber nor *s*.
1Co 15: 51 We will not all *s*, but we will all be

SLEEPING (SLEEP)

Mk 13: 36 suddenly, do not let him find you *s*.

SLOW

Ex 34: 6 and gracious God, *s* to anger,
Jas 1: 19 *s* to speak and *s* to become angry,
2Pe 3: 9 The Lord is not *s* in keeping his

SLUGGARD

Pr 6: 6 Go to the ant, you *s*;
20: 4 A *s* does not plow in season;

SLUMBER

Ps 121: 3 he who watches over you will not *s*;
Pr 6: 10 A little sleep, a little *s*,
Ro 13: 11 for you to wake up from your *s*,

SNAKE (SNAKES)

Nu 21: 8 "Make a *s* and put it up on a pole;
Pr 23: 32 In the end it bites like a *s*
Jn 3: 14 Moses lifted up the *s* in the desert,

SNAKES (SNAKE)

Mt 10: 16 as shrewd as *s* and as innocent
Mk 16: 18 they will pick up *s* with their hands;

SNATCH

Jn 10: 28 no one can *s* them out of my hand.
Jude : 23 *s* others from the fire and save

SNOW

Ps 51: 7 and I will be whiter than *s*.

SOAR

Isa 40: 31 They will *s* on wings like eagles;

SODOM

Ge 19: 24 rained down burning sulfur on *S*
Ro 9: 29 we would have become like *S*,

SOIL

Ge 4: 2 kept flocks, and Cain worked the *s*.
Mt 13: 23 on good *s* is the man who hears

SOLDIER

1Co 9: 7 as a *s* at his own expense?
2Ti 2: 3 with us like a good *s* of Christ Jesus

SOLE

Dt 28: 65 place for the *s* of your foot.
Isa 1: 6 From the *s* of your foot to the top

SOLID

2Ti 2: 19 God's *s* foundation stands firm,
Heb 5: 12 You need milk, not *s* food!

SOLOMON

Son of David by Bathsheba; king of Judah (2Sa 12:24; 1Ch 3:5, 10). Appointed king by David (1Ki 1); adversaries Adonijah, Joab, Shimei killed by Benaiah (1Ki 2). Asked for wisdom (1Ki 3; 2Ch 1). Judged between two prostitutes (1Ki 3:16-28). Built temple (1Ki 5-7; 2Ch 2-5); prayer of dedication (1Ki 8; 2Ch 6). Visited by Queen of Sheba (1Ki 9; 2Ch 9). Wives turned his heart from God (1Ki 11:1-13). Jeroboam rebelled against (1Ki 11:26-40). Death (1Ki 11:41-43; 2Ch 9:29-31).

Proverbs of (1Ki 4:32; Pr 1:1; 10:1; 25:1); psalms of (Ps 72; 127); song of (SS 1:1).

SON (SONS)

Ge 22: 2 "Take your *s*, your only *s*, Isaac,
Ex 11: 5 Every firstborn *s* in Egypt will die,
Dt 21: 18 rebellious *s* who does not obey his
Ps 2: 7 He said to me, "You are my *S*;
2: 12 Kiss the *S*, lest he be angry
Pr 10: 1 A wise *s* brings joy to his father,
13: 24 He who spares the rod hates his *s*,
29: 17 Discipline your *s*, and he will give
Isa 7: 14 with child and will give birth to a *s*,
Hos 11: 1 and out of Egypt I called my *s*.
Mt 2: 15 "Out of Egypt I called my *s*."
3: 17 "This is my *S*, whom I love;
11: 27 one knows the *S* except the Father,
16: 16 "You are the Christ, the *S*
17: 5 "This is my *S*, whom I love;
20: 18 and the *S* of Man will be betrayed
24: 30 They will see the *S* of Man coming
24: 44 the *S* of Man will come at an hour
27: 54 "Surely he was the *S* of God!"
28: 19 and of the *S* and of the Holy Spirit,
Mk 10: 45 even the *S* of Man did not come
14: 62 you will see the *S* of Man sitting
Lk 9: 58 but the *S* of Man has no place
18: 8 when the *S* of Man comes,
19: 10 For the *S* of Man came to seek
Jn 3: 14 so the *S* of Man must be lifted up,
3: 16 that he gave his one and only *S*,
17: 1 Glorify your *S*, that your *S* may
Ro 8: 29 conformed to the likeness of his *S*,
8: 32 He who did not spare his own *S*,
1Co 15: 28 then the *S* himself will be made
Gal 4: 30 rid of the slave woman and her *s*,
1Th 1: 10 and to wait for his *S* from heaven,
Heb 1: 2 days he has spoken to us by his *S*,
10: 29 punished who has trampled the *S*
1Jn 1: 7 his *S*, purifies us from all sin.
4: 9 only *S* into the world that we might
5: 5 he who believes that Jesus is the *S*
5: 11 eternal life, and this life is in his *S*.

SONG (SING)

Ps 40: 3 He put a new *s* in my mouth,
96: 1 Sing to the LORD a new *s*;
149: 1 Sing to the LORD a new *s*,
Isa 49: 13 burst into *s*, O mountains!
55: 12 will burst into *s* before you,
Rev 5: 9 And they sang a new *s*:
15: 3 and sang the *s* of Moses the servant

SONGS (SING)

Job 35: 10 who gives *s* in the night,
Ps 100: 2 come before him with joyful *s*.
Eph 5: 19 with psalms, hymns and spiritual *s*.
Jas 5: 13 Is anyone happy? Let him sing *s*

SONS (SON)

Joel 2: 28 Your *s* and daughters will prophesy
Jn 12: 36 so that you may become *s* of light."
Ro 8: 14 by the Spirit of God are *s* of God.
2Co 6: 18 and you will be my *s* and daughters

Gal 4: 5 we might receive the full rights of *s.*
Heb 12: 7 discipline; God is treating you as *s.*

SORROW (SORROWS)

Jer 31: 12 and they will *s* no more.
Ro 9: 2 I have great *s* and unceasing
2Co 7: 10 Godly *s* brings repentance that

SORROWS (SORROW)

Isa 53: 3 a man of *s,* and familiar

SOUL (SOULS)

Dt 6: 5 with all your *s* and with all your
10: 12 all your heart and with all your *s,*
Jos 22: 5 with all your heart and all your *s."*
Ps 23: 3 he restores my *s.*
42: 1 so my *s* pants for you, O God.
42: 11 Why are you downcast, O my *s?*
103: 1 Praise the LORD, O my *s;*
Pr 13: 19 A longing fulfilled is sweet to the *s,*
Isa 55: 2 your *s* will delight in the richest
Mt 10: 28 kill the body but cannot kill the *s.*
16: 26 yet forfeits his *s?* Or what can
22: 37 with all your *s* and with all your
Heb 4: 12 even to dividing *s* and spirit,

SOULS (SOUL)

Pr 11: 30 and he who wins *s* is wise.
Jer 6: 16 and you will find rest for your *s.*
Mt 11: 29 and you will find rest for your *s.*

SOUND

1Co 14: 8 if the trumpet does not *s* a clear call
15: 52 the trumpet will *s,* the dead will
2Ti 4: 3 men will not put up with *s* doctrine.

SOVEREIGN

Da 4: 25 that the Most High is *s*

SOW (SOWS)

Job 4: 8 and those who *s* trouble reap it.
Mt 6: 26 they do not *s* or reap or store away
2Pe 2: 22 and, "A *s* that is washed goes back

SOWS (SOW)

Pr 11: 18 he who *s* righteousness reaps a sure
22: 8 He who *s* wickedness reaps trouble
2Co 9: 6 Whoever *s* sparingly will
Gal 6: 7 A man reaps what he *s.*

SPARE (SPARES)

Ro 8: 32 He who did not *s* his own Son,
11: 21 natural branches, he will not *s* you

SPARES (SPARE)

Pr 13: 24 He who *s* the rod hates his son,

SPEARS

Isa 2: 4 and their *s* into pruning hooks.
Joel 3: 10 and your pruning hooks into *s.*
Mic 4: 3 and their *s* into pruning hooks.

SPECTACLE

1Co 4: 9 We have been made a *s*
Col 2: 15 he made a public *s* of them,

SPIN

Mt 6: 28 They do not labor or *s.*

SPIRIT (SPIRIT'S SPIRITS SPIRITUAL SPIRITUALLY)

Ge 1: 2 and the *S* of God was hovering
6: 3 "My *S* will not contend
2Ki 2: 9 inherit a double portion of your *s,"*
Job 33: 4 The *S* of God has made me;
Ps 31: 5 Into your hands I commit my *s;*
51: 10 and renew a steadfast *s* within me.
51: 11 or take your Holy *S* from me.
51: 17 sacrifices of God are a broken *s;*
139: 7 Where can I go from your *S?*
Isa 57: 15 him who is contrite and lowly in *s,*
63: 10 and grieved his Holy *S.*
Eze 11: 19 an undivided heart and put a new *s*
36: 26 you a new heart and put a new *s*
Joel 2: 28 I will pour out my *S* on all people.
Zec 4: 6 but by my *S,* 'says the LORD
Mt 1: 18 to be with child through the Holy *S*
3: 11 will baptize you with the Holy *S*
3: 16 he saw the *S* of God descending
4: 1 led by the *S* into the desert
5: 3 saying: "Blessed are the poor in *s,*
26: 41 *s* is willing, but the body is weak."
28: 19 and of the Son and of the Holy *S,*
Lk 1: 80 child grew and became strong in *s;*
11: 13 Father in heaven give the Holy *S*
Jn 4: 24 God is *s,* and his worshipers must
7: 39 Up to that time the *S* had not been
14: 26 But the Counselor, the Holy *S,*
16: 13 But when he, the *S* of truth, comes,
20: 22 and said, "Receive the Holy *S.*
Ac 1: 5 will be baptized with the Holy *S."*
2: 4 of them were filled with the Holy *S*
2: 38 will receive the gift of the Holy *S.*
6: 3 who are known to be full of the *S*
19: 2 "Did you receive the Holy *S*
Ro 8: 9 And if anyone does not have the *S*
8: 26 the *S* helps us in our weakness.
1Co 2: 10 God has revealed it to us by his *S.*
2: 14 man without the *S* does not accept
6: 19 body is a temple of the Holy *S,*
12: 13 baptized by one *S* into one body—
2Co 3: 6 the letter kills, but the *S* gives life.
5: 5 and has given us the *S* as a deposit,
Gal 5: 16 by the *S,* and you will not gratify
5: 22 But the fruit of the *S* is love, joy,
5: 25 let us keep in step with the *S.*
Eph 1: 13 with a seal, the promised Holy *S,*
4: 30 do not grieve the Holy *S* of God,
5: 18 Instead, be filled with the *S.*
6: 17 of salvation and the sword of the *S,*
2Th 2: 13 the sanctifying work of the *S*
Heb 4: 12 even to dividing soul and *s,*
1Pe 3: 4 beauty of a gentle and quiet *s,*
2Pe 1: 21 carried along by the Holy *S.*
1Jn 4: 1 Dear friends, do not believe every *s*

SPIRIT'S (SPIRIT)

1Th 5: 19 not put out the *S* fire; do not treat

SPIRITS (SPIRIT)

1Co 12: 10 to another distinguishing between *s,*
14: 32 The *s* of prophets are subject
1Jn 4: 1 test the *s* to see whether they are

SPIRITUAL (SPIRIT)

Ro 12: 1 this is your *s* act of worship.
12: 11 but keep your *s* fervor, serving
1Co 2: 13 expressing *s* truths in *s* words.
3: 1 I could not address you as *s* but
12: 1 Now about *s* gifts, brothers,
14: 1 of love and eagerly desire *s* gifts,
15: 44 a natural body, it is raised a *s* body.
Gal 6: 1 you who are *s* should restore him
Eph 1: 3 with every *s* blessing in Christ.
5: 19 with psalms, hymns and *s* songs.
6: 12 and against the *s* forces of evil
1Pe 2: 2 newborn babies, crave pure *s* milk,
2: 5 are being built into a *s* house

SPIRITUALLY (SPIRIT)

1Co 2: 14 because they are *s* discerned.

SPLENDOR

1Ch 16: 29 the LORD in the *s* of his holiness.
29: 11 the glory and the majesty and the *s,*
Job 37: 22 of the north he comes in golden *s;*
Ps 29: 2 in the *s* of his holiness.
45: 3 clothe yourself with *s* and majesty.
96: 6 *S* and majesty are before him;
96: 9 in the *s* of his holiness;
104: 1 you are clothed with *s* and majesty.
145: 5 of the glorious *s* of your majesty,
Isa 61: 3 the LORD for the display of his *s.*
63: 1 Who is this, robed in *s,*
Lk 9: 31 appeared in glorious *s,* talking
2Th 2: 8 and destroy by the *s* of his coming.

SPOIL

Ps 119: 162 like one who finds great *s.*

SPOTLESS

2Pe 3: 14 make every effort to be found *s,*

SPREAD (SPREADING)

Ac 12: 24 of God continued to increase and *s.*
19: 20 the word of the Lord *s* widely

SPREADING (SPREAD)

1Th 3: 2 God's fellow worker in *s* the gospel

SPRING

Jer 2: 13 the *s* of living water,
Jn 4: 14 in him a *s* of water welling up
Jas 3: 12 can a salt *s* produce fresh water.

SPUR*

Heb 10: 24 how we may *s* one another

SPURNS*

Pr 15: 5 A fool *s* his father's discipline,

STAFF

Ps 23: 4 your rod and your *s,*

STAKES

Isa 54: 2 strengthen your *s.*

STAND (STANDING STANDS)

Ex 14: 13 *S* firm and you will see
2Ch 20: 17 *s* firm and see the deliverance
Ps 1: 5 Therefore the wicked will not *s*
40: 2 and gave me a firm place to *s.*
119: 120 I *s* in awe of your laws.
Eze 22: 30 *s* before me in the gap on behalf
Zec 14: 4 On that day his feet will *s*
Mt 12: 25 divided against itself will not *s.*
Ro 14: 10 we will all *s* before God's judgment
1Co 10: 13 out so that you can *s* up under it.
15: 58 Therefore, my dear brothers, *s* firm
Eph 6: 14 *S* firm then, with the belt
2Th 2: 15 *s* firm and hold to the teachings we
Jas 5: 8 You too, be patient and *s* firm,
Rev 3: 20 Here I am! I *s* at the door

STANDING (STAND)
Ex 3: 5 where you are *s* is holy ground."
Jos 5: 15 the place where you are *s* is holy."
1Pe 5: 9 Resist him, *s* firm in the faith,

STANDS (STAND)
Ps 89: 2 that your love *s* firm forever,
119: 89 it *s* firm in the heavens.
Mt 10: 22 but he who *s* firm to the end will be
2Ti 2: 19 God's solid foundation *s* firm,
1Pe 1: 25 but the word of the Lord *s* forever

STAR (STARS)
Nu 24: 17 A *s* will come out of Jacob;
Rev 22: 16 and the bright Morning *S*."

STARS (STAR)
Da 12: 3 like the *s* for ever and ever.
Php 2: 15 in which you shine like *s*

STATURE
Lk 2: 52 And Jesus grew in wisdom and *s*,

STEADFAST
Ps 51: 10 and renew a *s* spirit within me.
Isa 26: 3 him whose mind is *s*,
1Pe 5: 10 and make you strong, firm and *s*.

STEAL
Ex 20: 15 "You shall not *s*.
Mt 19: 18 do not *s*, do not give false
Eph 4: 28 has been stealing must *s* no longer,

STEP (STEPS)
Gal 5: 25 let us keep in *s* with the Spirit.

STEPS (STEP)
Pr 16: 9 but the LORD determines his *s*.
Jer 10: 23 it is not for man to direct his *s*.
1Pe 2: 21 that you should follow in his *s*.

STICKS
Pr 18: 24 there is a friend who *s* closer

STIFF-NECKED
Ex 34: 9 Although this is a *s* people,

STILL
Ps 46: 10 "Be *s*, and know that I am God;
Zec 2: 13 Be *s* before the LORD, all mankind

STIRS
Pr 6: 19 and a man who *s* up dissension
10: 12 Hatred *s* up dissension,
15: 1 but a harsh word *s* up anger.
15: 18 hot-tempered man *s* up dissension,
16: 28 A perverse man *s* up dissension,
28: 25 A greedy man *s* up dissension,
29: 22 An angry man *s* up dissension,

STONE (CAPSTONE CORNERSTONE MILLSTONE)
1Sa 17: 50 the Philistine with a sling and a *s*;
Isa 8: 14 a *s* that causes men to stumble
Eze 11: 19 remove from them their heart of *s*
Mk 16: 3 "Who will roll the *s* away
Lk 4: 3 tell this *s* to become bread."
Jn 8: 7 the first to throw a *s* at her."
2Co 3: 3 not on tablets of *s* but on tablets

STOOP
2Sa 22: 36 you *s* down to make me great.

STORE
Pr 10: 14 Wise men *s* up knowledge,
Mt 6: 19 not *s* up for yourselves treasures

STOREHOUSE (HOUSE)
Mal 3: 10 Bring the whole tithe into the *s*,

STRAIGHT
Pr 3: 6 and he will make your paths *s*.
4: 25 Let your eyes look *s* ahead,
15: 21 of understanding keeps a *s* course.
Jn 1: 23 'Make *s* the way for the Lord.' "

STRAIN
Mt 23: 24 You *s* out a gnat but swallow

STRANGER (STRANGERS)
Mt 25: 35 I was a *s* and you invited me in,
Jn 10: 5 But they will never follow a *s*;

STRANGERS (STRANGER)
1Pe 2: 11 as aliens and *s* in the world,

STREAMS
Ps 1: 3 He is like a tree planted by *s*
46: 4 is a river whose *s* make glad
Ecc 1: 7 All *s* flow into the sea,
Jn 7: 38 *s* of living water will flow

STRENGTH (STRONG)
Ex 15: 2 The LORD is my *s* and my song;
Dt 6: 5 all your soul and with all your *s*.
2Sa 22: 33 It is God who arms me with *s*
Ne 8: 10 for the joy of the LORD is your *s*."
Ps 28: 7 The LORD is my *s* and my shield;
46: 1 God is our refuge and *s*,
96: 7 ascribe to the LORD glory and *s*.
118: 14 The LORD is my *s* and my song;
147: 10 not in the *s* of the horse,
Isa 40: 31 will renew their *s*.
Mk 12: 30 all your mind and with all your *s*.'
1Co 1: 25 of God is stronger than man's *s*.
Php 4: 13 through him who gives me *s*.
1Pe 4: 11 it with the *s* God provides,

STRENGTHEN (STRONG)
2Ch 16: 9 to *s* those whose hearts are fully
Ps 119: 28 *s* me according to your word.
Isa 35: 3 *S* the feeble hands,
41: 10 I will *s* you and help you;
Eph 3: 16 of his glorious riches he may *s* you
2Th 2: 17 and *s* you in every good deed
Heb 12: 12 *s* your feeble arms and weak knees.

STRENGTHENING (STRONG)
1Co 14: 26 done for the *s* of the church.

STRIFE
Pr 20: 3 It is to a man's honor to avoid *s*,
22: 10 out the mocker, and out goes *s*;

STRIKE (STRIKES)
Ge 3: 15 and you will *s* his heel."
Zec 13: 7 "*S* the shepherd,
Mt 26: 31 " 'I will *s* the shepherd,

STRIKES (STRIKE)
Mt 5: 39 If someone *s* you on the right

STRONG (STRENGTH STRENGTHEN STRENGTHENING)
Dt 31: 6 Be *s* and courageous.
1Ki 2: 2 "So be *s*, show yourself a man,
Pr 18: 10 The name of the LORD is a *s* tower
31: 17 her arms are *s* for her tasks.
SS 8: 6 for love is as *s* as death,
Lk 2: 40 And the child grew and became *s*;
Ro 15: 1 We who are *s* ought to bear
1Co 1: 27 things of the world to shame the *s*.
16: 13 in the faith; be men of courage; be *s*
2Co 12: 10 For when I am weak, then I am *s*.
Eph 6: 10 be *s* in the Lord and in his mighty

STRUGGLE
Ro 15: 30 me in my *s* by praying to God
Eph 6: 12 For our *s* is not against flesh
Heb 12: 4 In your *s* against sin, you have not

STUDY
Ezr 7: 10 Ezra had devoted himself to the *s*
Ecc 12: 12 and much *s* wearies the body.
Jn 5: 39 You diligently *s* the Scriptures

STUMBLE (STUMBLING)
Ps 37: 24 though he *s*, he will not fall,
119: 165 and nothing can make them *s*.
Isa 8: 14 a stone that causes men to *s*
Jer 31: 9 a level path where they will not *s*,
Eze 7: 19 for it has made them *s* into sin.
1Co 10: 32 Do not cause anyone to *s*,
1Pe 2: 8 and, "A stone that causes men to *s*

STUMBLING (STUMBLE)
Ro 14: 13 up your mind not to put any *s* block
1Co 8: 9 freedom does not become a *s* block
2Co 6: 3 We put no *s* block in anyone's path,

SUBDUE
Ge 1: 28 in number; fill the earth and *s* it.

SUBJECT (SUBJECTED)
1Co 14: 32 of prophets are *s* to the control
15: 28 then the Son himself will be made *s*
Tit 2: 5 and to be *s* to their husbands,
2: 9 slaves to be *s* to their masters
3: 1 Remind the people to be *s* to rulers

SUBJECTED (SUBJECT)
Ro 8: 20 For the creation was *s*

SUBMISSION (SUBMIT)
1Co 14: 34 but must be in *s*, as the Law says.
1Ti 2: 11 learn in quietness and full *s*.

SUBMISSIVE (SUBMIT)
Jas 3: 17 then peace-loving, considerate, *s*,
1Pe 3: 1 in the same way be *s*
5: 5 in the same way be *s*

SUBMIT (SUBMISSION SUBMISSIVE SUBMITS)
Ro 13: 1 Everyone must *s* himself
13: 5 necessary to *s* to the authorities,
1Co 16: 16 to *s* to such as these
Eph 5: 21 *S* to one another out of reverence
Col 3: 18 Wives, *s* to your husbands,
Heb 12: 9 How much more should we *s*
13: 17 Obey your leaders and *s*
Jas 4: 7 *S* yourselves, then, to God.
1Pe 2: 18 *s* yourselves to your masters

SUBMITS* (SUBMIT)
Eph 5: 24 Now as the church *s* to Christ,

SUCCESSFUL
Jos 1: 7 that you may be *s* wherever you go.
2Ki 18: 7 he was *s* in whatever he undertook.
2Ch 20: 20 in his prophets and you will be *s*."

SUFFER (SUFFERED SUFFERING SUFFERINGS SUFFERS)
Isa 53: 10 to crush him and cause him to *s*,
Mk 8: 31 the Son of Man must *s* many things
Lk 24: 26 the Christ have to *s* these things
24: 46 The Christ will *s* and rise
Php 1: 29 to *s* for him, since you are going
1Pe 4: 16 However, if you *s* as a Christian,

SUFFERED (SUFFER)
Heb 2: 9 and honor because he *s* death,
2: 18 Because he himself *s*
1Pe 2: 21 Christ *s* for you, leaving you

SUFFERING (SUFFER)
Isa 53: 3 of sorrows, and familiar with *s.*
Ac 5:41 worthy of *s* disgrace for the Name.
2Ti 1: 8 But join with me in *s* for the gospel,
Heb 2:10 of their salvation perfect through *s.*

SUFFERINGS (SUFFER)
Ro 8:17 share in his *s* in order that we may
8:18 that our present *s* are not worth
2Co 1: 5 as the *s* of Christ flow
Php 3:10 the fellowship of sharing in his *s,*

SUFFERS (SUFFER)
Pr 13:20 but a companion of fools *s* harm.
1Co 12:26 If one part *s,* every part *s* with it;

SUFFICIENT
2Co 12: 9 said to me, "My grace is *s* for you,

SUITABLE
Ge 2:18 I will make a helper *s* for him."

SUN
Ecc 1: 9 there is nothing new under the *s.*
Mal 4: 2 the *s* of righteousness will rise
Mt 5:45 He causes his *s* to rise on the evil
17: 2 His face shone like the *s,*
Rev 1:16 His face was like the *s* shining
21:23 The city does not need the *s*

SUPERIOR
Heb 1: 4 he became as much *s* to the angels
8: 6 ministry Jesus has received is as *s*

SUPERVISION
Gal 3:25 longer under the *s* of the law.

SUPREMACY* (SUPREME)
Col 1:18 in everything he might have the *s.*

SUPREME (SUPREMACY)
Pr 4: 7 Wisdom is *s;* therefore get wisdom.

SURE
Nu 32:23 you may be *s* that your sin will find
Dt 6:17 Be *s* to keep the commands
14:22 Be *s* to set aside a tenth
Isa 28:16 cornerstone for a *s* foundation;
Heb 11: 1 faith is being *s* of what we hope for
2Pe 1:10 to make your calling and election *s.*

SURPASS* (SURPASSES SURPASSING)
Pr 31:29 but you *s* them all."

SURPASSES (SURPASS)
Mt 5:20 unless your righteousness *s* that
Eph 3:19 to know this love that *s* knowledge

SURPASSING* (SURPASS)
Ps 150: 2 praise him for his *s* greatness.
2Co 3:10 in comparison with the *s* glory.
9:14 of the *s* grace God has given you.
Php 3: 8 the *s* greatness of knowing Christ

SURROUNDED
Heb 12: 1 since we are *s* by such a great cloud

SUSPENDS*
Job 26: 7 he *s* the earth over nothing.

SUSTAINING* (SUSTAINS)
Heb 1: 3 *s* all things by his powerful word.

SUSTAINS (SUSTAINING)
Ps 18:35 and your right hand *s* me;
146: 9 and *s* the fatherless and the widow,
147: 6 The LORD *s* the humble
Isa 50: 4 to know the word that *s* the weary.

SWALLOWED
1Co 15:54 "Death has been *s* up in victory."
2Co 5: 4 so that what is mortal may be *s* up

SWEAR
Mt 5:34 Do not *s* at all: either by heaven,

SWORD (SWORDS)
Ps 45: 3 Gird your *s* upon your side,
Pr 12:18 Reckless words pierce like a *s,*
Mt 10:34 come to bring peace, but a *s.*
26:52 all who draw the *s* will die by the *s.*
Lk 2:35 a *s* will pierce your own soul too."
Ro 13: 4 for he does not bear the *s*
Eph 6:17 of salvation and the *s* of the Spirit,
Heb 4:12 Sharper than any double-edged *s,*
Rev 1:16 came a sharp double-edged *s.*

SWORDS (SWORD)
Isa 2: 4 They will beat their *s*
Joel 3:10 Beat your plowshares into *s*

SYMPATHETIC*
1Pe 3: 8 in harmony with one another; be *s,*

SYNAGOGUE
Lk 4:16 the Sabbath day he went into the *s,*
Ac 17: 2 custom was, Paul went into the *s,*

TABERNACLE
Ex 40:34 the glory of the LORD filled the *t.*

TABLE (TABLES)
Ps 23: 5 You prepare a *t* before me

TABLES (TABLE)
Ac 6: 2 word of God in order to wait on *t.*

TABLET (TABLETS)
Pr 3: 3 write them on the *t* of your heart.
7: 3 write them on the *t* of your heart.

TABLETS (TABLET)
Ex 31:18 he gave him the two *t*
Dt 10: 5 and put the *t* in the ark I had made,
2Co 3: 3 not on *t* of stone but on *t*

TAKE (TAKEN TAKES TAKING TOOK)
Dt 12:32 do not add to it or *t* away from it.
31:26 "*T* this Book of the Law
Job 23:10 But he knows the way that I *t;*
Ps 49:17 for he will *t* nothing with him
51:11 or *t* your Holy Spirit from me.
Mt 10:38 anyone who does not *t* his cross
11:29 *T* my yoke upon you and learn
16:24 deny himself and *t* up his cross

TAKEN (TAKE)
Lev 6: 4 must return what he has stolen or *t*
Isa 6: 7 your guilt is *t* away and your sin
Mt 24:40 one will be *t* and the other left.
Mk 16:19 he was *t* up into heaven
1Ti 3:16 was *t* up in glory.

TAKES (TAKE)
1Ki 20:11 should not boast like one who *t* it
Ps 5: 4 You are not a God who *t* pleasure
Jn 1:29 who *t* away the sin of the world!
Rev 22:19 And if anyone *t* words away

TAKING (TAKE)
Ac 15:14 by *t* from the Gentiles a people
Php 2: 7 *t* the very nature of a servant,

TALENT
Mt 25:15 to another one *t,* each according

TAME*
Jas 3: 8 but no man can *t* the tongue.

TASK
Mk 13:34 each with his assigned *t,*
Ac 20:24 complete the *t* the Lord Jesus has
1Co 3: 5 the Lord has assigned to each his *t.*
2Co 2:16 And who is equal to such a *t?*

TASTE (TASTED)
Ps 34: 8 *T* and see that the LORD is good;
Col 2:21 Do not *t!* Do not touch!"?
Heb 2: 9 the grace of God he might *t* death

TASTED (TASTE)
1Pe 2: 3 now that you have *t* that the Lord

TAUGHT (TEACH)
Mt 7:29 he *t* as one who had authority,
1Co 2:13 but in words *t* by the Spirit,
Gal 1:12 nor was I *t* it; rather, I received it

TAXES
Mt 22:17 Is it right to pay *t* to Caesar or not
Ro 13: 7 If you owe *t,* pay *t;* if revenue,

TEACH (TAUGHT TEACHER TEACHERS TEACHES TEACHING)
Ex 33:13 *t* me your ways so I may know you
Dt 4: 9 *T* them to your children
8: 3 to *t* you that man does not live
11:19 *T* them to your children, talking
1Sa 12:23 I will *t* you the way that is good
Ps 32: 8 *t* you in the way you should go;
51:13 I will *t* transgressors your ways,
90:12 *T* us to number our days aright,
143:10 *T* me to do your will,
Jer 31:34 No longer will a man *t* his neighbor
Lk 11: 1 said to him, "Lord, *t* us to pray,
Jn 14:26 will *t* you all things and will remind
1Ti 2:12 I do not permit a woman to *t*
3: 2 respectable, hospitable, able to *t,*
Tit 2: 1 You must *t* what is in accord
Heb 8:11 No longer will a man *t* his neighbor
Jas 3: 1 know that we who *t* will be judged
1Jn 2:27 you do not need anyone to *t* you.

TEACHER (TEACH)
Mt 10:24 "A student is not above his *t,*
Jn 13:14 and *T,* have washed your feet,

TEACHERS (TEACH)
1Co 12:28 third *t,* then workers of miracles,
Eph 4:11 and some to be pastors and *t,*
Heb 5:12 by this time you ought to be *t,*

TEACHES (TEACH)
1Ti 6: 3 If anyone *t* false doctrines

TEACHING (TEACH)
Pr 1: 8 and do not forsake your mother's *t.*
Mt 28:20 *t* them to obey everything I have
Jn 7:17 whether my *t* comes from God or
14:23 loves me, he will obey my *t.*
1Ti 4:13 of Scripture, to preaching and to *t.*
2Ti 3:16 is God-breathed and is useful for *t,*
Tit 2: 7 In your *t* show integrity,

TEAR (TEARS)
Rev 7:17 God will wipe away every t

TEARS (TEAR)
Ps 126: 5 Those who sow in t
Php 3:18 and now say again even with t,

TEETH (TOOTH)
Mt 8:12 will be weeping and gnashing of t."

TEMPERATE*
1Ti 3: 2 t, self-controlled, respectable,
3:11 not malicious talkers but t
Tit 2: 2 Teach the older men to be t,

TEMPEST
Ps 55: 8 far from the t and storm."

TEMPLE (TEMPLES)
1Ki 8:27 How much less this t I have built!
Hab 2:20 But the LORD is in his holy t;
1Co 3:16 that you yourselves are God's t
6:19 you not know that your body is a t
2Co 6:16 For we are the t of the living God.

TEMPLES (TEMPLE)
Ac 17:24 does not live in t built by hands.

TEMPT (TEMPTATION TEMPTED)
1Co 7: 5 again so that Satan will not t you

TEMPTATION (TEMPT)
Mt 6:13 And lead us not into t,
26:41 pray so that you will not fall into t.
1Co 10:13 No t has seized you except what is

TEMPTED (TEMPT)
Mt 4: 1 into the desert to be t by the devil.
1Co 10:13 he will not let you be t
Heb 2:18 he himself suffered when he was t,
4:15 but we have one who has been t
Jas 1:13 For God cannot be t by evil,

TEN (TENTH TITHE TITHES)
Ex 34:28 covenant—the T Commandments.
Ps 91: 7 t thousand at your right hand,
Mt 25:28 it to the one who has the t talents.
Lk 15: 8 suppose a woman has t silver coins

TENTH (TEN)
Dt 14:22 Be sure to set aside a t

TERRIBLE (TERROR)
2Ti 3: There will be t times

TERROR (TERRIBLE)
Ps 91: 5 You will not fear the t of night,
Lk 21:26 Men will faint from t, apprehensive
Ro 13: 3 For rulers hold no t

TEST (TESTED TESTS)
Dt 6:16 Do not t the LORD your God
Ps 139: 23 t me and know my anxious
Ro 12: 2 Then you will be able to t
1Co 3:13 and the fire will t the quality
1Jn 4: 1 t the spirits to see whether they are

TESTED (TEST)
Ge 22: 1 Some time later God t Abraham.
Job 23:10 when he has t me, I will come forth
Pr 27:21 man is t by the praise he receives.
1Ti 3:10 They must first be t; and then

TESTIFY (TESTIMONY)
Jn 5:39 are the Scriptures that t about me,
2Ti 1: 8 ashamed to t about our Lord,

TESTIMONY (TESTIFY)
Isa 8:20 and to the t! If they do not speak
Lk 18:20 not give false t, honor your father

TESTS (TEST)
Pr 17: 3 but the LORD t the heart.
1Th 2: 4 but God, who t our hearts.

THADDAEUS
Apostle (Mt 10:3; Mk 3:18); probably also known as Judas son of James (Lk 6:16; Ac 1:13).

THANKFUL (THANKS)
Heb 12:28 let us be t, and so worship God

THANKS (THANKFUL THANKSGIVING)
1Ch 16: 8 Give t to the LORD, call
Ne 12:31 assigned two large choirs to give t.
Ps 100: 4 give t to him and praise his name.
1Co 15:57 t be to God! He gives us the victory
2Co 2:14 t be to God, who always leads us
9:15 T be to God for his indescribable
1Th 5:18 give t in all circumstances,

THANKSGIVING (THANKS)
Ps 95: 2 Let us come before him with t
100: 4 Enter his gates with t
Php 4: 6 by prayer and petition, with t,
1Ti 4: 3 created to be received with t

THIEF (THIEVES)
Ex 22: 3 A t must certainly make restitution
1Th 5: 2 day of the Lord will come like a t
Rev 16:15 I come like a t! Blessed is he who

THIEVES (THIEF)
1Co 6:10 nor homosexual offenders nor t

THINK (THOUGHT THOUGHTS)
Ro 12: 3 Do not t of yourself more highly
Php 4: 8 praiseworthy—t about such things

THIRST (THIRSTY)
Ps 69:21 and gave me vinegar for my t.
Mt 5: 6 Blessed are those who hunger and t
Jn 4:14 the water I give him will never t.

THIRSTY (THIRST)
Isa 55: 1 "Come, all you who are t,
Jn 7:37 "If anyone is t, let him come to me
Rev 22:17 Whoever is t, let him come;

THOMAS
Apostle (Mt 10:3; Mk 3:18; Lk 6:15; Jn 11:16; 14:5; 21:2; Ac 1:13). Doubted resurrection (Jn 20:24-28).

THONGS
Mk 1: 7 t of whose sandals I am not worthy

THORN (THORNS)
2Co 12: 7 there was given me a t in my flesh,

THORNS (THORN)
Nu 33:55 in your eyes and t in your sides.
Mt 27:29 then twisted together a crown of t
Heb 6: 8 But land that produces t

THOUGHT (THINK)
Pr 14:15 a prudent man gives t to his steps.
1Co 13:11 I talked like a child, I t like a child,

THOUGHTS (THINK)
Ps 94:11 The LORD knows the t of man;
Ps 139: 23 test me and know my anxious t.
Isa 55: 8 "For my t are not your t,
Heb 4:12 it judges the t and attitudes

THREE
Ecc 4:12 of t strands is not quickly broken.
Mt 12:40 t nights in the belly of a huge fish,
18:20 or t come together in my name,
27:63 'After t days I will rise again.'
1Co 13:13 And now these t remain: faith,
14:27 or at the most t—should speak,
2Co 13: 1 testimony of two or t witnesses."

THRESHING
2Sa 24:18 an altar to the LORD on the t floor

THRONE (ENTHRONED)
2Sa 7:16 your t will be established forever
Ps 45: 6 Your t, O God, will last for ever
47: 8 God is seated on his holy t.
Isa 6: 1 I saw the Lord seated on a t,
66: 1 "Heaven is my t
Heb 4:16 Let us then approach the t of grace
12: 2 at the right hand of the t of God.
Rev 4:10 They lay their crowns before the t
20:11 Then I saw a great white t
22: 3 t of God and of the Lamb will be

THROW
Jn 8: 7 the first to t a stone at her."
Heb 10:35 So do not t away your confidence;
12: 1 let us t off everything that hinders

THWART*
Isa 14:27 has purposed, and who can t him?

TIBNI
King of Israel (1Ki 16:21-22).

TIME (TIMES)
Est 4:14 come to royal position for such a t
Da 7:25 to him for a t, times and half a t.
Hos 10:12 for it is t to seek the LORD,
Ro 9: 9 "At the appointed t I will return,
Heb 9:28 and he will appear a second t,
10:12 for all t one sacrifice for sins,
1Pe 4:17 For it is t for judgment to begin

TIMES (TIME)
Ps 9: 9 a stronghold in t of trouble.
31:15 My t are in your hands;
62: 8 Trust in him at all t, O people;
Pr 17:17 A friend loves at all t,
Am 5:13 for the t are evil.
Mt 18:21 how many t shall I forgive my
Ac 1: 7 "It is not for you to know the t
Rev 12:14 t and half a time, out

TIMIDITY*
2Ti 1: 7 For God did not give us a spirit of t

TIMOTHY
Believer from Lystra (Ac 16:1). Joined Paul on second missionary journey (Ac 16-20). Sent to settle problems at Corinth (1Co 4:17; 16:10). Led church at Ephesus (1Ti 1:3). Co-writer with Paul (1Th 1:1; 2Th 1:1; Phm 1).

TIRE (TIRED)
2Th 3:13 never t of doing what is right.

TIRED (TIRE)
Ex 17:12 When Moses' hands grew t,
Isa 40:28 He will not grow t or weary,

TITHE (TEN)
Lev 27:30 " 'A t of everything from the land,
Dt 12:17 eat in your own towns the t
Mal 3:10 the whole t into the storehouse,

TITHES (TEN)
Mal 3: 8 'How do we rob you?' "In t

TITUS
Gentile co-worker of Paul (Gal 2:1-3; 2Ti 4:10); sent to Corinth (2Co 2:13; 7-8; 12:18), Crete (Tit 1:4-5).

TODAY
Mt 6: 11 Give us t our daily bread.
Lk 23: 43 t you will be with me in paradise."
Heb 3: 13 daily, as long as it is called T,
13: 8 Christ is the same yesterday and t

TOIL
Ge 3: 17 through painful t you will eat of it

TOLERATE
Hab 1: 13 you cannot t wrong.
Rev 2: 2 that you cannot t wicked men,

TOMB
Mt 27: 65 make the t as secure as you know
Lk 24: 2 the stone rolled away from the t,

TOMORROW
Pr 27: 1 Do not boast about t,
Isa 22: 13 "for t we die!"
Mt 6: 34 Therefore do not worry about t,
Jas 4: 13 "Today or t we will go to this

TONGUE (TONGUES)
Ps 39: 1 and keep my t from sin;
Pr 12: 18 but the t of the wise brings healing.
1Co 14: 2 speaks in a t does not speak to men
14: 4 He who speaks in a t edifies himself
14: 13 in a t should pray that he may
14: 19 than ten thousand words in a t.
Php 2: 11 every t confess that Jesus Christ is
Jas 1: 26 does not keep a tight rein on his t,
3: 8 but no man can tame the t.

TONGUES (TONGUE)
Isa 28: 11 with foreign lips and strange t
66: 18 and gather all nations and t,
Mk 16: 17 in new t; they will pick up snakes
Ac 2: 4 and began to speak in other t
10: 46 For they heard them speaking in t
19: 6 and they spoke in t and prophesied
1Co 12: 30 Do all speak in t? Do all interpret?
14: 18 speak in t more than all of you.
14: 39 and do not forbid speaking in t.

TOOK (TAKE)
1Co 11: 23 the night he was betrayed, t bread,
Php 3: 12 for which Christ Jesus t hold of me.

TOOTH (TEETH)
Ex 21: 24 eye for eye, t for t, hand for hand,
Mt 5: 38 'Eye for eye, and t for t.'

TORMENTED
Rev 20: 10 They will be t day and night

TORN
Gal 4: 15 you would have t out your eyes
Php 1: 23 I do not know! I am t

TOUCH (TOUCHED)
Ps 105: 15 "Do not t my anointed ones;
Lk 24: 39 It is I myself! T me and see;
2Co 6: 17 T no unclean thing,
Col 2: 21 Do not taste! Do not t!"?

TOUCHED (TOUCH)
1Sa 10: 26 men whose hearts God had t.
Mt 14: 36 and all who t him were healed.

TOWER
Ge 11: 4 with a t that reaches to the heavens
Pr 18: 10 of the LORD is a strong t;

TOWNS
Nu 35: 2 to give the Levites t to live
35: 15 These six t will be a place of refuge

TRACING*
Ro 11: 33 and his paths beyond t out!

TRADITION
Mt 15: 6 word of God for the sake of your t.
Col 2: 8 which depends on human t

TRAIN (TRAINING)
Pr 22: 6 T a child in the way he should go,
Eph 4: 8 he led captives in his t

TRAINING (TRAIN)
1Co 9: 25 in the games goes into strict t.
2Ti 3: 16 correcting and t in righteousness,

TRAMPLED
Lk 21: 24 Jerusalem will be t
Heb 10: 29 to be punished who has t the Son

TRANCE
Ac 10: 10 was being prepared, he fell into a t.

TRANSCENDS*
Php 4: 7 which t all understanding,

TRANSFIGURED
Mt 17: 2 There he was t before them.

TRANSFORM* (TRANSFORMED)
Php 3: 21 will t our lowly bodies

TRANSFORMED (TRANSFORM)
Ro 12: 2 be t by the renewing of your mind.
2Co 3: 18 are being t into his likeness

TRANSGRESSION (TRANSGRESSIONS TRANSGRESSORS)
Isa 53: 8 for the t of my people he was
Ro 4: 15 where there is no law there is no t.

TRANSGRESSIONS (TRANSGRESSION)
Ps 32: 1 whose t are forgiven,
51: 1 blot out my t.
103: 12 so far has he removed our t from us
Isa 53: 5 But he was pierced for our t,
Eph 2: 1 you were dead in your t and sins,

TRANSGRESSORS (TRANSGRESSION)
Ps 51: 13 Then I will teach t your ways,
Isa 53: 12 and made intercession for the t.
53: 12 and was numbered with the t.

TREADING
Dt 25: 4 an ox while it is t out the grain.
1Co 9: 9 an ox while it is t out the grain."

TREASURE (TREASURED TREASURES)
Isa 33: 6 of the LORD is the key to this t.
Mt 6: 21 For where your t is, there your
2Co 4: 7 But we have this t in jars of clay

TREASURED (TREASURE)
Dt 7: 6 to be his people, his t possession.
Lk 2: 19 But Mary t up all these things

TREASURES (TREASURE)
Mt 6: 19 up for yourselves t on earth,
Col 2: 3 in whom are hidden all the t
Heb 11: 26 of greater value than the t of Egypt,

TREAT
Lev 22: 2 sons to t with respect the sacred
1Ti 5: 1 T younger men as brothers,
1Pe 3: 7 and t them with respect

TREATY
Dt 7: 2 Make no t with them, and show

TREE
Ge 2: 9 and the t of the knowledge of good
2: 9 of the garden were the t of life
Dt 21: 23 hung on a t is under God's curse.
Ps 1: 3 He is like a t planted by streams
Mt 3: 10 every t that does not produce good
12: 33 for a t is recognized by its fruit.
Gal 3: 13 is everyone who is hung on a t."
Rev 22: 14 they may have the right to the t

TREMBLE (TREMBLING)
1Ch 16: 30 T before him, all the earth!
Ps 114: 7 T, O earth, at the presence

TREMBLING (TREMBLE)
Ps 2: 11 and rejoice with t.
Php 2: 12 out your salvation with fear and t,

TRESPASS
Ro 5: 17 For if, by the t of the one man,

TRIALS
1Th 3: 3 one would be unsettled by these t.
Jas 1: 2 whenever you face t of many kinds,
2Pe 2: 9 how to rescue godly men from t

TRIBES
Ge 49: 28 All these are the twelve t of Israel,
Mt 19: 28 judging the twelve t of Israel.

TRIBULATION*
Rev 7: 14 who have come out of the great t;

TRIUMPHAL* (TRIUMPHING)
Isa 60: 11 their kings led in t procession.
2Co 2: 14 us in t procession in Christ

TRIUMPHING* (TRIUMPHAL)
Col 2: 15 of them, t over them by the cross.

TROUBLE (TROUBLED TROUBLES)
Job 14: 1 is of few days and full of t.
Ps 46: 1 an ever-present help in t.
107: 13 they cried to the LORD in their t,
Pr 11: 29 He who brings t on his family will
24: 10 If you falter in times of t,
Mt 6: 34 Each day has enough t of its own.
Jn 16: 33 In this world you will have t.
Ro 8: 35 Shall t or hardship or persecution

TROUBLED (TROUBLE)
Jn 14: 1 "Do not let your hearts be t.
14: 27 Do not let your hearts be t

TROUBLES (TROUBLE)
1Co 7: 28 those who marry will face many t
2Co 1: 4 who comforts us in all our t,
4: 17 and momentary t are achieving

TRUE (TRUTH)
Dt 18: 22 does not take place or come t,
1Sa 9: 6 and everything he says comes t.
Ps 119: 160 All your words are t;
Jn 17: 3 the only t God, and Jesus Christ,
Ro 3: 4 Let God be t, and every man a liar.
Php 4: 8 whatever is t, whatever is noble,
Rev 22: 6 These words are trustworthy and t.

TRUMPET

1Co 14: 8 if the *t* does not sound a clear call,
15: 52 For the *t* will sound, the dead will

TRUST (ENTRUSTED TRUSTED TRUSTS TRUSTWORTHY)

Ps 20: 7 we *t* in the name of the LORD our
37: 3 *T* in the LORD and do good;
56: 4 in God I *t;* I will not be afraid.
119: 42 for I *t* in your word.
Pr 3: 5 *T* in the LORD with all your heart
Isa 30: 15 in quietness and *t* is your strength,
Jn 14: 1 *T* in God; *t* also in me.
1Co 4: 2 been given a *t* must prove faithful.

TRUSTED (TRUST)

Ps 26: 1 I have *t* in the LORD
Isa 25: 9 we *t* in him, and he saved us.
Da 3: 28 They *t* in him and defied the king's
Lk 16: 10 *t* with very little can also be *t*

TRUSTS (TRUST)

Ps 32: 10 surrounds the man who *t* in him.
Pr 11: 28 Whoever *t* in his riches will fall,
28: 26 He who *t* in himself is a fool,
Ro 9: 33 one who *t* in him will never be put

TRUSTWORTHY (TRUST)

Ps 119: 138 they are fully *t.*
Pr 11: 13 but a *t* man keeps a secret.
Rev 22: 6 "These words are *t* and true.

TRUTH (TRUE TRUTHFUL TRUTHS)

Ps 51: 6 Surely you desire *t*
Isa 45: 19 I, the LORD, speak the *t;*
Zec 8: 16 are to do: Speak the *t* to each other,
Jn 4: 23 worship the Father in spirit and *t,*
8: 32 Then you will know the *t,*
8: 32 and the *t* will set you free."
14: 6 I am the way and the *t* and the life.
16: 13 comes, he will guide you into all *t.*
18: 38 "What is *t?*" Pilate asked.
Ro 1: 25 They exchanged the *t* of God
1Co 13: 6 in evil but rejoices with the *t.*
2Co 13: 8 against the *t,* but only for the *t.*
Eph 4: 15 Instead, speaking the *t* in love,
6: 14 with the belt of *t* buckled
2Th 2: 10 because they refused to love the *t*
1Ti 2: 4 to come to a knowledge of the *t.*
3: 15 the pillar and foundation of the *t.*
2Ti 2: 15 correctly handles the word of *t.*
3: 7 never able to acknowledge the *t.*
Heb 10: 26 received the knowledge of the *t,*
1Pe 1: 22 by obeying the *t* so that you have
2Pe 2: 2 the way of *t* into disrepute.
1Jn 1: 6 we lie and do not live by the *t.*
1: 8 deceive ourselves and the *t* is not

TRUTHFUL (TRUTH)

Pr 12: 22 but he delights in men who are *t.*
Jn 3: 33 it has certified that God is *t.*

TRUTHS (TRUTH)

1Co 2: 13 expressing spiritual *t*
1Ti 3: 9 hold of the deep *t* of the faith
Heb 5: 12 to teach you the elementary *t*

TRY (TRYING)

Ps 26: 2 Test me, O LORD, and *t* me,
Isa 7: 13 enough to *t* the patience of men?
1Co 14: 12 *t* to excel in gifts that build up
2Co 5: 11 is to fear the Lord, we *t*
1Th 5: 15 always *t* to be kind to each other

TRYING (TRY)

2Co 5: 12 We are not *t* to commend ourselves
1Th 2: 4 We are not *t* to please men but God

TUNIC

Lk 6: 29 do not stop him from taking your *t.*

TURN (TURNED TURNS)

Ex 32: 12 *T* from your fierce anger; relent
Dt 5: 32 do not *t* aside to the right
28: 14 Do not *t* aside from any
Jos 1: 7 do not *t* from it to the right
2Ch 7: 14 and *t* from their wicked ways,
30: 9 He will not *t* his face from you
Ps 78: 6 they in *t* would tell their children.
Pr 22: 6 when he is old he will not *t* from it.
Isa 29: 16 You *t* things upside down,
30: 21 Whether you *t* to the right
45: 22 "*T* to me and be saved,
55: 7 Let him *t* to the LORD,
Eze 33: 11 *T! T* from your evil ways!
Mal 4: 6 He will *t* the hearts of the fathers
Mt 5: 39 you on the right cheek, *t*
10: 35 For I have come to *t*
Jn 12: 40 nor *t*—and I would heal them."
Ac 3: 19 Repent, then, and *t* to God,
26: 18 and *t* them from darkness to light,
1Ti 6: 20 *T* away from godless chatter
1Pe 3: 11 He must *t* from evil and do good;

TURNED (TURN)

Ps 30: 11 You *t* my wailing into dancing;
40: 1 he *t* to me and heard my cry.
Isa 53: 6 each of us has *t* to his own way;
Hos 7: 8 Ephraim is a flat cake not *t* over.
Joel 2: 31 The sun will be *t* to darkness
Ro 3: 12 All have *t* away,

TURNS (TURN)

2Sa 22: 29 the LORD *t* my darkness into light
Pr 15: 1 A gentle answer *t* away wrath,
Isa 44: 25 and *t* it into nonsense,
Jas 5: 20 Whoever *t* a sinner from the error

TWELVE

Ge 49: 28 All these are the *t* tribes of Israel,
Mt 10: 1 He called his *t* disciples to him

TWINKLING*

1Co 15: 52 in a flash, in the *t* of an eye,

UNAPPROACHABLE*

1Ti 6: 16 immortal and who lives in *u* light,

UNBELIEF (UNBELIEVER UNBELIEVERS UNBELIEVING)

Mk 9: 24 help me overcome my *u!*"
Ro 11: 20 they were broken off because of *u,*
Heb 3: 19 able to enter, because of their *u.*

UNBELIEVER* (UNBELIEF)

1Co 7: 15 But if the *u* leaves, let him do so.
10: 27 If some *u* invites you to a meal
14: 24 if an *u* or someone who does not
2Co 6: 15 have in common with an *u?*
1Ti 5: 8 the faith and is worse than an *u.*

UNBELIEVERS (UNBELIEF)

1Co 6: 6 another—and this in front of *u!*
2Co 6: 14 Do not be yoked together with *u.*

UNBELIEVING (UNBELIEF)

1Co 7: 14 For the *u* husband has been
Rev 21: 8 But the cowardly, the *u,* the vile,

UNCERTAIN*

1Ti 6: 17 which is so *u,* but to put their hope

UNCHANGEABLE*

Heb 6: 18 by two *u* things in which it is

UNCIRCUMCISED

1Sa 17: 26 Who is this *u* Philistine that he
Col 3: 11 circumcised or *u,* barbarian,

UNCIRCUMCISION

1Co 7: 19 is nothing and *u* is nothing.
Gal 5: 6 neither circumcision nor *u* has any

UNCLEAN

Isa 6: 5 ruined! For I am a man of *u* lips,
Ro 14: 14 fully convinced that no food is *u*
2Co 6: 17 Touch no *u* thing,

UNCONCERNED*

Eze 16: 49 were arrogant, overfed and *u;*

UNCOVERED

Heb 4: 13 Everything is *u* and laid bare

UNDERSTAND (UNDERSTANDING UNDERSTANDS)

Job 42: 3 Surely I spoke of things I did not *u,*
Ps 73: 16 When I tried to *u* all this,
119: 125 that I may *u* your statutes.
Lk 24: 45 so they could *u* the Scriptures.
Ac 8: 30 "Do you *u* what you are reading?"
Ro 7: 15 I do not *u* what I do.
1Co 2: 14 and he cannot *u* them,
Eph 5: 17 but *u* what the Lord's will is.
2Pe 3: 16 some things that are hard to *u,*

UNDERSTANDING (UNDERSTAND)

Ps 119: 104 I gain *u* from your precepts;
147: 5 his *u* has no limit.
Pr 3: 5 and lean not on your own *u;*
4: 7 Though it cost all you have, get *u.*
10: 23 but a man of *u* delights in wisdom.
11: 12 but a man of *u* holds his tongue.
15: 21 a man of *u* keeps a straight course.
15: 32 whoever heeds correction gains *u.*
23: 23 get wisdom, discipline and *u.*
Isa 40: 28 and his *u* no one can fathom.
Da 5: 12 a keen mind and knowledge and *u,*
Mk 4: 12 and ever hearing but never *u;*
12: 33 with all your *u* and with all your
Php 4: 7 of God, which transcends all *u,*

UNDERSTANDS (UNDERSTAND)

1Ch 28: 9 and *u* every motive
1Ti 6: 4 he is conceited and *u* nothing.

UNDIVIDED*

1Ch 12: 33 to help David with *u* loyalty—
Ps 86: 11 give me an *u* heart,
Eze 11: 19 I will give them an *u* heart
1Co 7: 35 way in *u* devotion to the Lord.

UNDOING

Pr 18: 7 A fool's mouth is his *u,*

UNDYING*

Eph 6: 24 Lord Jesus Christ with an *u* love.

UNFADING*

1Pe 3: 4 the *u* beauty of a gentle

UNFAILING

Ps 33: 5 the earth is full of his *u* love.
119: 76 May your *u* love be my comfort,
143: 8 bring me word of your *u* love,
Pr 19: 22 What a man desires is *u* love;
La 3: 32 so great is his *u* love.

UNFAITHFUL (UNFAITHFULNESS)

Lev 6: 2 is *u* to the LORD by deceiving his
1Ch 10: 13 because he was *u* to the LORD;
Pr 13: 15 but the way of the *u* is hard.

UNFAITHFULNESS (UNFAITHFUL)
Mt 5:32 except for marital *u,* causes her
19: 9 for marital *u,* and marries another

UNFOLDING
Ps 119:130 the *u* of your words gives light;

UNGODLINESS
Tit 2:12 It teaches us to say "No" to *u*

UNIT
1Co 12:12 body is a *u,* though it is made up

UNITED (UNITY)
Ro 6: 5 If we have been *u* with him
Php 2: 1 from being *u* with Christ,
Col 2: 2 encouraged in heart and *u* in love,

UNITY (UNITED)
Ps 133: 1 is when brothers live together in *u!*
Ro 15: 5 a spirit of *u* among yourselves
Eph 4: 3 effort to keep the *u* of the Spirit
4:13 up until we all reach *u* in the faith
Col 3:14 them all together in perfect *u.*

UNIVERSE
Php 2:15 which you shine like stars in the *u*
Heb 1: 2 and through whom he made the *u.*

UNKNOWN
Ac 17:23 TO AN *U* GOD.

UNLEAVENED
Ex 12:17 "Celebrate the Feast of *U* Bread,

UNPROFITABLE
Tit 3: 9 because these are *u* and useless.

UNPUNISHED
Ex 34: 7 Yet he does not leave the guilty *u;*
Pr 19: 5 A false witness will not go *u,*

UNREPENTANT*
Ro 2: 5 stubbornness and your *u* heart,

UNRIGHTEOUS*
Zep 3: 5 yet the *u* know no shame.
Mt 5:45 rain on the righteous and the *u.*
1Pe 3:18 the righteous for the *u,* to bring you
2Pe 2: 9 and to hold the *u* for the day

UNSEARCHABLE
Ro 11:33 How *u* his judgments,
Eph 3: 8 preach to the Gentiles the *u* riches

UNSEEN
2Co 4:18 on what is seen, but on what is *u.*
4:18 temporary, but what is *u* is eternal.

UNSTABLE*
Jas 1: 8 he is a double-minded man, *u*
2Pe 2:14 they seduce the *u;* they are experts
3:16 ignorant and *u* people distort,

UNTHINKABLE*
Job 34:12 It is *u* that God would do wrong,

UNVEILED*
2Co 3:18 with *u* faces all reflect the Lord's

UNWORTHY
Job 40: 4 "I am *u*—how can I reply to you?
Lk 17:10 should say, 'We are *u* servants;

UPRIGHT
Job 1: 1 This man was blameless and *u;*
Pr 2: 7 He holds victory in store for the *u,*
Pr 15: 8 but the prayer of the *u* pleases him.
Tit 1: 8 who is self-controlled, *u,* holy
2:12 *u* and godly lives in this present

UPROOTED
Jude :12 without fruit and *u*—twice dead.

USEFUL
2Ti 2:21 *u* to the Master and prepared
3:16 Scripture is God-breathed and is *u*

USELESS
1Co 15:14 our preaching is *u*
Jas 2:20 faith without deeds is *u?*

USURY
Ne 5:10 But let the exacting of *u* stop!

UTTER
Ps 78: 2 I will *u* hidden things, things from of

UZZIAH
Son of Amaziah; king of Judah also known as Azariah (2Ki 15:1-7; 1Ch 6:24; 2Ch 26).

VAIN
Ps 33:17 A horse is a *v* hope for deliverance;
Isa 65:23 They will not toil in *v*
1Co 15: 2 Otherwise, you have believed in *v.*
15:58 labor in the Lord is not in *v.*
2Co 6: 1 not to receive God's grace in *v.*

VALLEY
Ps 23: 4 walk through the *v* of the shadow
Isa 40: 4 Every *v* shall be raised up,
Joel 3:14 multitudes in the *v* of decision!

VALUABLE (VALUE)
Lk 12:24 And how much more *v* you are

VALUE (VALUABLE)
Mt 13:46 When he found one of great *v,*
1Ti 4: 8 For physical training is of some *v,*
Heb 11:26 as of greater *v* than the treasures

VEIL
Ex 34:33 to them, he put a *v* over his face.
2Co 3:14 for to this day the same *v* remains

VENGEANCE (AVENGE REVENGE)
Isa 34: 8 For the LORD has a day of *v,*

VICTORIES (VICTORY)
Ps 18:50 He gives his king great *v;*
21: 1 great is his joy in the *v* you give!

VICTORIOUSLY* (VICTORY)
Ps 45: 4 In your majesty ride forth *v*

VICTORY (VICTORIES VICTORIOUSLY)
Ps 60:12 With God we will gain the *v,*
1Co 15:54 "Death has been swallowed up in *v*
15:57 He gives us the *v* through our Lord
1Jn 5: 4 This is the *v* that has overcome

VINDICATED
1Ti 3:16 was *v* by the Spirit,

VINE
Jn 15: 1 "I am the true *v,* and my Father is

VINEGAR
Mk 15:36 filled a sponge with wine *v,*

VIOLATION
Heb 2: 2 every *v* and disobedience received

VIOLENCE
Isa 60:18 No longer will *v* be heard
Eze 45: 9 Give up your *v* and oppression

VIPERS
Ro 3:13 "The poison of *v* is on their lips."

VIRGIN
Isa 7:14 The *v* will be with child
Mt 1:23 "The *v* will be with child
2Co 11: 2 that I might present you as a pure *v*

VIRTUES*
Col 3:14 And over all these *v* put on love,

VISION
Ac 26:19 disobedient to the *v* from heaven.

VOICE
Ps 95: 7 Today, if you hear his *v,*
Isa 30:21 your ears will hear a *v* behind you,
Jn 5:28 are in their graves will hear his *v*
10: 3 and the sheep listen to his *v.*
Heb 3: 7 "Today, if you hear his *v,*
Rev 3:20 If anyone hears my *v* and opens

VOMIT
Pr 26:11 As a dog returns to its *v,*
2Pe 2:22 "A dog returns to its *v,*" and,

VOW
Nu 30: 2 When a man makes a *v*

WAGES
Lk 10: 7 for the worker deserves his *w.*
Ro 4: 4 his *w* are not credited to him
6:23 For the *w* of sin is death,

WAILING
Ps 30:11 You turned my *w* into dancing;

WAIST
2Ki 1: 8 with a leather belt around his *w.*"
Mt 3: 4 he had a leather belt around his *w.*

WAIT (WAITED WAITS)
Ps 27:14 *W* for the LORD;
130: 5 I *w* for the LORD, my soul waits,
Isa 30:18 Blessed are all who *w* for him!
Ac 1: 4 *w* for the gift my Father promised,
Ro 8:23 as we *w* eagerly for our adoption
1Th 1:10 and to *w* for his Son from heaven,
Tit 2:13 while we *w* for the blessed hope—

WAITED (WAIT)
Ps 40: 1 I *w* patiently for the LORD;

WAITS (WAIT)
Ro 8:19 creation *w* in eager expectation

WALK (WALKED WALKS)
Dt 11:19 and when you *w* along the road,
Ps 1: 1 who does not *w* in the counsel
23: 4 Even though I *w*
89:15 who *w* in the light of your presence
Isa 2: 5 let us *w* in the light of the LORD.
30:21 saying, "This is the way; *w* in it."
40:31 they will *w* and not be faint.
Jer 6:16 ask where the good way is, and *w*
Da 4:37 And those who *w* in pride he is able
Am 3: 3 Do two *w* together
Mic 6: 8 and to *w* humbly with your God.
Mk 2: 9 'Get up, take your mat and *w*'?
Jn 8:12 Whoever follows me will never *w*
1Jn 1: 7 But if we *w* in the light,
2Jn : 6 his command is that you *w* in love.

WALKED (WALK)
Ge 5:24 Enoch *w* with God; then he was no
Jos 14: 9 which your feet have *w* will be your
Mt 14:29 *w* on the water and came toward

WALKS (WALK)
Pr 13:20 He who *w* with the wise grows wise

WALL
Jos 6:20 *w* collapsed; so every man charged
Ne 2:17 let us rebuild the *w* of Jerusalem,
Rev 21:12 It had a great, high *w*

WALLOWING
2Pe 2:22 back to her *w* in the mud."

WANT (WANTED WANTING WANTS)
1Sa 8:19 "We *w* a king over us.
Ps 23: 1 is my shepherd, I shall not be in *w*.
Lk 19:14 'We don't *w* this man to be our king
Ro 7:15 For what I *w* to do I do not do,
Php 3:10 I *w* to know Christ and the power

WANTED (WANT)
1Co 12:18 of them, just as he *w* them to be.

WANTING (WANT)
Da 5:27 weighed on the scales and found *w*.
2Pe 3: 9 with you, not *w* anyone to perish,

WANTS (WANT)
Mt 20:26 whoever *w* to become great
Mk 8:35 For whoever *w* to save his life will
Ro 9:18 he hardens whom he *w* to harden.
1Ti 2: 4 who *w* all men to be saved

WAR (WARS)
Isa 2: 4 nor will they train for *w* anymore.
Da 9:26 *W* will continue until the end,
2Co 10: 3 we do not wage *w* as the world does
Rev 19:11 With justice he judges and makes *w*

WARN (WARNED WARNINGS)
Eze 3:19 But if you do *w* the wicked man
33: 9 if you do *w* the wicked man to turn

WARNED (WARN)
Ps 19:11 By them is your servant *w*;

WARNINGS (WARN)
1Co 10:11 and were written down as *w* for us,

WARS (WAR)
Ps 46: 9 He makes *w* cease to the ends
Mt 24: 6 You will hear of *w* and rumors of *w*,

WASH (WASHED WASHING)
Ps 51: 7 *w* me, and I will be whiter
Jn 13: 5 and began to *w* his disciples' feet,
Ac 22:16 be baptized and *w* your sins away,
Rev 22:14 Blessed are those who *w* their robes

WASHED (WASH)
1Co 6:11 you were *w*, you were sanctified,
Rev 7:14 they have *w* their robes

WASHING (WASH)
Eph 5:26 cleansing her by the *w* with water
Tit 3: 5 us through the *w* of rebirth

WATCH (WATCHES WATCHING WATCHMAN)
Ge 31:49 "May the LORD keep *w*
Jer 31:10 will *w* over his flock like a shepherd
Mt 24:42 "Therefore keep *w*, because you do
26:41 *W* and pray so that you will not fall
Lk 2: 8 keeping *w* over their flocks at night
1Ti 4:16 *W* your life and doctrine closely.

WATCHES (WATCH)
Ps 1: 6 For the LORD *w* over the way
121: 3 he who *w* over you will not slumber

WATCHING (WATCH)
Lk 12:37 whose master finds them *w*

WATCHMAN (WATCH)
Eze 3:17 I have made you a *w* for the house

WATER (WATERED WATERS)
Ps 1: 3 like a tree planted by streams of *w*,
22:14 I am poured out like *w*,
Pr 25:21 if he is thirsty, give him *w* to drink.
Isa 49:10 and lead them beside springs of *w*.
Jer 2:13 broken cisterns that cannot hold *w*.
Zec 14: 8 On that day living *w* will flow out
Mk 9:41 anyone who gives you a cup of *w*
Jn 4:10 he would have given you living *w*."
7:38 streams of living *w* will flow
Eph 5:26 washing with *w* through the word,
1Pe 3:21 this *w* symbolizes baptism that now
Rev 21: 6 cost from the spring of the *w* of life.

WATERED (WATER)
1Co 3: 6 I planted the seed, Apollos *w* it,

WATERS (WATER)
Ps 23: 2 he leads me beside quiet *w*,
Ecc 11: 1 Cast your bread upon the *w*,
Isa 58:11 like a spring whose *w* never fail.
1Co 3: 7 plants nor he who *w* is anything,

WAVE (WAVES)
Jas 1: 6 he who doubts is like a *w* of the sea,

WAVES (WAVE)
Isa 57:20 whose *w* cast up mire and mud.
Mt 8:27 Even the winds and the *w* obey him
Eph 4:14 tossed back and forth by the *w*,

WAY (WAYS)
Dt 1:33 to show you the *w* you should go.
2Sa 22:31 "As for God, his *w* is perfect;
Job 23:10 But he knows the *w* that I take;
Ps 1: 1 or stand in the *w* of sinners
37: 5 Commit your *w* to the LORD;
119: 9 can a young man keep his *w* pure?
139: 24 See if there is any offensive *w* in me
Pr 14:12 There is a *w* that seems right
16:17 he who guards his *w* guards his life.
22: 6 Train a child in the *w* he should go,
Isa 30:21 saying, "This is the *w*; walk in it."
53: 6 each of us has turned to his own *w*;
Isa 55: 7 Let the wicked forsake his *w*
Mt 3: 3 'Prepare the *w* for the Lord,
Jn 14: 6 "I am the *w* and the truth
1Co 10:13 also provide a *w* out so that you can
12:31 will show you the most excellent *w*.
Heb 4:15 who has been tempted in every *w*,
9: 8 was showing by this that the *w*
10:20 and living *w* opened for us

WAYS (WAY)
Ex 33:13 teach me your *w* so I may know
Ps 25:10 All the *w* of the LORD are loving
51:13 I will teach transgressors your *w*,
Pr 3: 6 in all your *w* acknowledge him,
Isa 55: 8 neither are your *w* my *w*,"
Jas 3: 2 We all stumble in many *w*.

WEAK (WEAKER WEAKNESS)
Mt 26:41 spirit is willing, but the body is *w*."
Ro 14: 1 Accept him whose faith is *w*,
1Co 1:27 God chose the *w* things
8: 9 become a stumbling block to the *w*.
9:22 To the *w* I became *w*, to win the *w*.
2Co 12:10 For when I am *w*, then I am strong.
Heb 12:12 your feeble arms and *w* knees.

WEAKER (WEAK)
1Co 12:22 seem to be *w* are indispensable,
1Pe 3: 7 them with respect as the *w* partner

WEAKNESS (WEAK)
Ro 8:26 the Spirit helps us in our *w*.
1Co 1:25 and the *w* of God is stronger
2Co 12: 9 for my power is made perfect in *w*
Heb 5: 2 since he himself is subject to *w*.

WEALTH
Pr 3: 9 Honor the LORD with your *w*,
Mk 10:22 away sad, because he had great *w*.
Lk 15:13 and there squandered his *w*

WEAPONS
2Co 10: 4 The *w* we fight with are not

WEARIES (WEARY)
Ecc 12:12 and much study *w* the body.

WEARY (WEARIES)
Isa 40:31 they will run and not grow *w*,
Mt 11:28 all you who are *w* and burdened,
Gal 6: 9 Let us not become *w* in doing good,

WEDDING
Mt 22:11 who was not wearing *w* clothes.
Rev 19: 7 For the *w* of the Lamb has come,

WEEP (WEEPING WEPT)
Ecc 3: 4 a time to *w* and a time to laugh,
Lk 6:21 Blessed are you who *w* now,

WEEPING (WEEP)
Ps 30: 5 *w* may remain for a night,
126: 6 He who goes out *w*,
Mt 8:12 where there will be *w* and gnashing

WELCOMES
Mt 18: 5 whoever *w* a little child like this
2Jn :11 Anyone who *w* him shares

WELL
Lk 17:19 your faith has made you *w*."
Jas 5:15 in faith will make the sick person *w*

WEPT (WEEP)
Ps 137: 1 of Babylon we sat and w
Jn 11:35 Jesus w.

WEST
Ps 103: 12 as far as the east is from the w,

WHIRLWIND (WIND)
2Ki 2: 1 to take Elijah up to heaven in a w,
Hos 8: 7 and reap the w.
Na 1: 3 His way is in the w and the storm,

WHITE (WHITER)
Isa 1:18 they shall be as w as snow;
Da 7: 9 His clothing was as w as snow;
Rev 1:14 hair were w like wool, as w as snow,
3: 4 dressed in w, for they are worthy.
20:11 Then I saw a great w throne

WHITER (WHITE)
Ps 51: 7 and I will be w than snow.

WHOLE
Mt 16:26 for a man if he gains the w world,
24:14 will be preached in the w world
Jn 13:10 to wash his feet; his w body is clean
21:25 the w world would not have room
Ac 20:27 proclaim to you the w will of God.
Ro 3:19 and the w world held accountable
8:22 know that the w creation has been
Gal 3:22 declares that the w world is
5: 3 obligated to obey the w law.
Eph 4:13 attaining to the w measure
Jas 2:10 For whoever keeps the w law
1Jn 2: 2 but also for the sins of the w world.

WHOLEHEARTEDLY (HEART)
Dt 1:36 because he followed the LORD w
Eph 6: 7 Serve w, as if you were serving

WICKED (WICKEDNESS)
Ps 1: 1 walk in the counsel of the w
1: 5 Therefore the w will not stand
73: 3 when I saw the prosperity of the w.
Pr 10:20 the heart of the w is of little value.
11:21 The w will not go unpunished,
Isa 53: 9 He was assigned a grave with the w
55: 7 Let the w forsake his way
57:20 But the w are like the tossing sea,
Eze 3:18 that w man will die for his sin,
18:23 pleasure in the death of the w?
33:14 to the w man, 'You will surely die,'

WICKEDNESS (WICKED)
Eze 28:15 created till w was found in you.

WIDE
Isa 54: 2 stretch your tent curtains w,
Mt 7:13 For w is the gate and broad is
Eph 3:18 to grasp how w and long and high

WIDOW (WIDOWS)
Dt 10:18 cause of the fatherless and the w,
Lk 21: 2 saw a poor w put in two very small

WIDOWS (WIDOW)
Jas 1:27 look after orphans and w

WIFE (WIVES)
Ge 2:24 and mother and be united to his w,
24:67 she became his w, and he loved her;
Ex 20:17 shall not covet your neighbor's w,
Dt 5:21 shall not covet your neighbor's w.
Pr 5:18 in the w of your youth.
12: 4 w of noble character is her
18:22 He who finds a w finds what is
19:13 quarrelsome w is like a constant
31:10 w of noble character who can find?
Mt 19: 3 for a man to divorce his w for any
1Co 7: 2 each man should have his own w,
7:33 how he can please his w—
Eph 5:23 the husband is the head of the w
5:33 must love his w as he loves himself,
1Ti 3: 2 husband of but one w, temperate,
Rev 21: 9 I will show you the bride, the w

WILD
Lk 15:13 squandered his wealth in w living.
Ro 11:17 and you, though a w olive shoot,

WILL (WILLING WILLINGNESS)
Ps 40: 8 I desire to do your w, O my God;
143: 10 Teach me to do your w,
Isa 53:10 Yet it was the LORD's w
Mt 6:10 your w be done
26:39 Yet not as I w, but as you w."
Jn 7:17 If anyone chooses to do God's w,
Ac 20:27 to you the whole w of God.
Ro 12: 2 and approve what God's w is—
1Co 7:37 but has control over his own w,
Eph 5:17 understand what the Lord's w is.
Php 2:13 for it is God who works in you to w
1Th 4: 3 God's w that you should be
5:18 for this is God's w for you
Heb 9:16 In the case of a w, it is necessary
10: 7 I have come to do your w, O God
Jas 4:15 "If it is the Lord's w,
1Jn 5:14 we ask anything according to his w,
Rev 4:11 and by your w they were created

WILLING (WILL)
Ps 51:12 grant me a w spirit, to sustain me.
Da 3:28 were w to give up their lives rather
Mt 18:14 Father in heaven is not w that any
23:37 her wings, but you were not w.
26:41 The spirit is w, but the body is weak

WILLINGNESS (WILL)
2Co 8:12 For if the w is there, the gift is

WIN (WINS)
Php 3:14 on toward the goal to w the prize
1Th 4:12 your daily life may w the respect

WIND (WHIRLWIND)
Jas 1: 6 blown and tossed by the w.

WINE
Pr 20: 1 W is a mocker and beer a brawler;
Isa 55: 1 Come, buy w and milk
Mt 9:17 Neither do men pour new w
Lk 23:36 They offered him w vinegar
Ro 14:21 not to eat meat or drink w
Eph 5:18 on w, which leads to debauchery.

WINESKINS
Mt 9:17 do men pour new wine into old w.

WINGS
Ru 2:12 under whose w you have come
Ps 17: 8 hide me in the shadow of your w
Isa 40:31 They will soar on w like eagles;
Mal 4: 2 rise with healing in its w.
Lk 13:34 hen gathers her chicks under her w,

WINS (WIN)
Pr 11:30 and he who w souls is wise.

WIPE
Rev 7:17 God will w away every tear

WISDOM (WISE)
1Ki 4:29 God gave Solomon w and very
Ps 111: 10 of the LORD is the beginning of w;
Pr 31:26 She speaks with w,
Jer 10:12 he founded the world by his w
Mt 11:19 But w is proved right by her actions
Lk 2:52 And Jesus grew in w and stature,
Ro 11:33 the depth of the riches of the w
Col 2: 3 are hidden all the treasures of w
Jas 1: 5 of you lacks w, he should ask God,

WISE (WISDOM WISER)
1Ki 3:12 give you a w and discerning heart,
Job 5:13 He catches the w in their craftiness
Ps 19: 7 making w the simple.
Pr 3: 7 Do not be w in your own eyes;
9: 8 rebuke a w man and he will love
10: 1 A w son brings joy to his father,
11:30 and he who wins souls is w.
13:20 He who walks with the w grows w,
17:28 Even a fool is thought w
Da 12: 3 Those who are w will shine like
Mt 11:25 hidden these things from the w
1Co 1:27 things of the world to shame the w;
2Ti 3:15 able to make you w for salvation

WISER (WISE)
1Co 1:25 of God is w than man's wisdom,

WITHER (WITHERS)
Ps 1: 3 and whose leaf does not w.

WITHERS (WITHER)
Isa 40: 7 The grass w and the flowers fall,
1Pe 1:24 the grass w and the flowers fall,

WITHHOLD
Ps 84:11 no good thing does he w
Pr 23:13 Do not w discipline from a child;

WITNESS (WITNESSES)
Jn 1: 8 he came only as a w to the light.

WITNESSES (WITNESS)
Dt 19:15 by the testimony of two or three w.
Ac 1: 8 and you will be my w in Jerusalem,

WIVES (WIFE)
Eph 5:22 W, submit to your husbands
5:25 love your w, just as Christ loved
1Pe 3: 1 words by the behavior of their w,

WOE
Isa 6: 5 "W to me!" I cried.

WOLF
Isa 65:25 w and the lamb will feed together,

WOMAN (MAN)
Ge 2:22 God made a w from
3:15 between you and the w,
Lev 20:13 as one lies with a w,
Dt 22: 5 w must not wear men's
Ru 3:11 a w of noble character
Pr 31:30 a w who fears the LORD
Mt 5:28 looks at a w lustfully
Jn 8: 3 a w caught in adultery.
Ro 7: 2 a married w is bound to
1Co 11: 3 the head of the w is man,
11:13 a w to pray to God with
1Ti 2:11 A w should learn in

Ps 90: 10 The length of our days is seventy *y*
2Pe 3: 8 the Lord a day is like a thousand *y*,
Rev 20: 2 and bound him for a thousand *y*.

YESTERDAY

Heb 13: 8 Jesus Christ is the same *y*

YOKE (YOKED)

Mt 11: 29 Take my *y* upon you and learn

YOKED (YOKE)

2Co 6: 14 Do not be *y* together

YOUNG (YOUTH)

Ps 119: 9 How can a *y* man keep his way
1Ti 4: 12 down on you because you are *y*,

YOUTH (YOUNG)

Ps 103: 5 so that your *y* is renewed like
Ecc 12: 1 Creator in the days of your *y*,
2Ti 2: 22 Flee the evil desires of *y*,

ZEAL

Pr 19: 2 to have *z* without knowledge,
Ro 12: 11 Never be lacking in *z*,

ZECHARIAH

1. Son of Jeroboam II; king of Israel (2Ki 15:8-12).

2. Post-exilic prophet who encouraged rebuilding of temple (Ezr 5:1; 6:14; Zec 1:1).

ZEDEKIAH

Mattaniah, son of Josiah (1Ch 3:15), made king of Judah by Nebuchadnezzar (2Ki 24:17-25:7; 2Ch 36:10-14; Jer 37-39; 52: 1-11).

ZERUBBABEL

Descendant of David (1Ch 3:19; Mt 1:3). Led return from exile (Ezr 2-3; Ne 7:7; Hag 1-2; Zec 4).

ZIMRI

King of Israel (1Ki 16:9-20).

ZION

Ps 137: 3 "Sing us one of the songs of *Z*!"
Jer 50: 5 They will ask the way to *Z*
Ro 9: 33 I lay in *Z* a stone that causes men
11: 26 "The deliverer will come from *Z*;

MAP INDEX

A

B

C

D

E

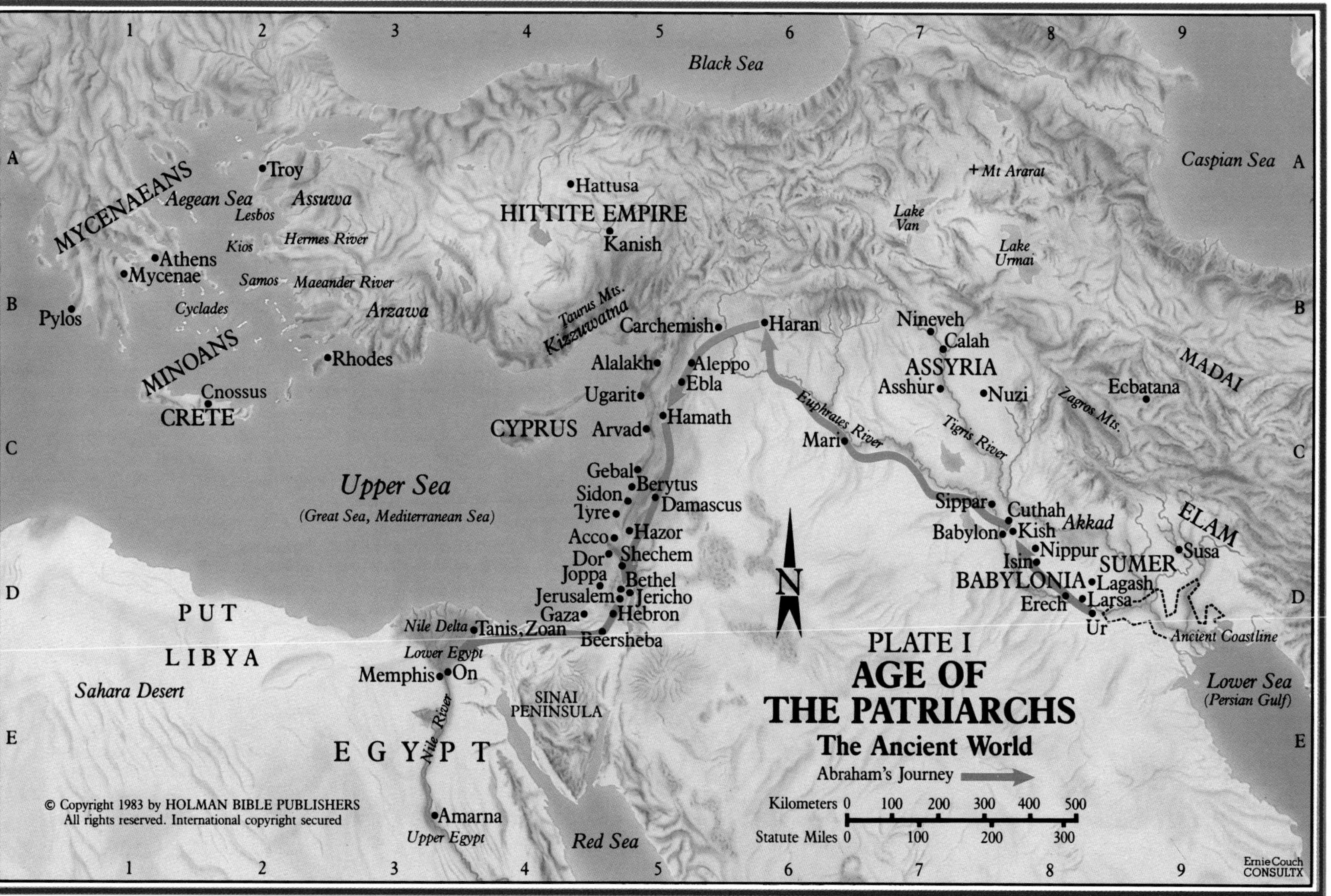
PLATE I
AGE OF THE PATRIARCHS
The Ancient World
Abraham's Journey
Kilometers 0 100 200 300 400 500
Statute Miles 0 100 200 300
Black Sea
Caspian Sea
Upper Sea
(Great Sea, Mediterranean Sea)
Lower Sea
(Persian Gulf)
Red Sea
MYCENAEANS
Aegean Sea
Lesbos
Kios
Samos
Cyclades
Troy
Assuwa
Hermes River
Maeander River
Arzawa
Athens
Mycenae
Pylos
MINOANS
Cnossus
CRETE
Rhodes
HITTITE EMPIRE
Hattusa
Kanish
Taurus Mts.
Kizzuwatna
Carchemish
Haran
Alalakh
Aleppo
Ebla
Ugarit
Hamath
CYPRUS
Arvad
Gebal
Berytus
Sidon
Tyre
Damascus
Hazor
Acco
Shechem
Dor
Joppa
Bethel
Jerusalem
Jericho
Gaza
Hebron
Beersheba
Nile Delta
Tanis, Zoan
Lower Egypt
Memphis
On
Nile River
EGYPT
Amarna
Upper Egypt
SINAI PENINSULA
PUT
LIBYA
Sahara Desert
Euphrates River
Mari
Tigris River
Lake Van
Lake Urmai
Mt Ararat
Nineveh
Calah
ASSYRIA
Asshur
Nuzi
Zagros Mts.
Ecbatana
MADAI
Sippar
Cuthah
Akkad
Babylon
Kish
Nippur
Isin
SUMER
BABYLONIA
Lagash
Erech
Larsa
Ur
ELAM
Susa
Ancient Coastline
N
Ernie Couch CONSULTX

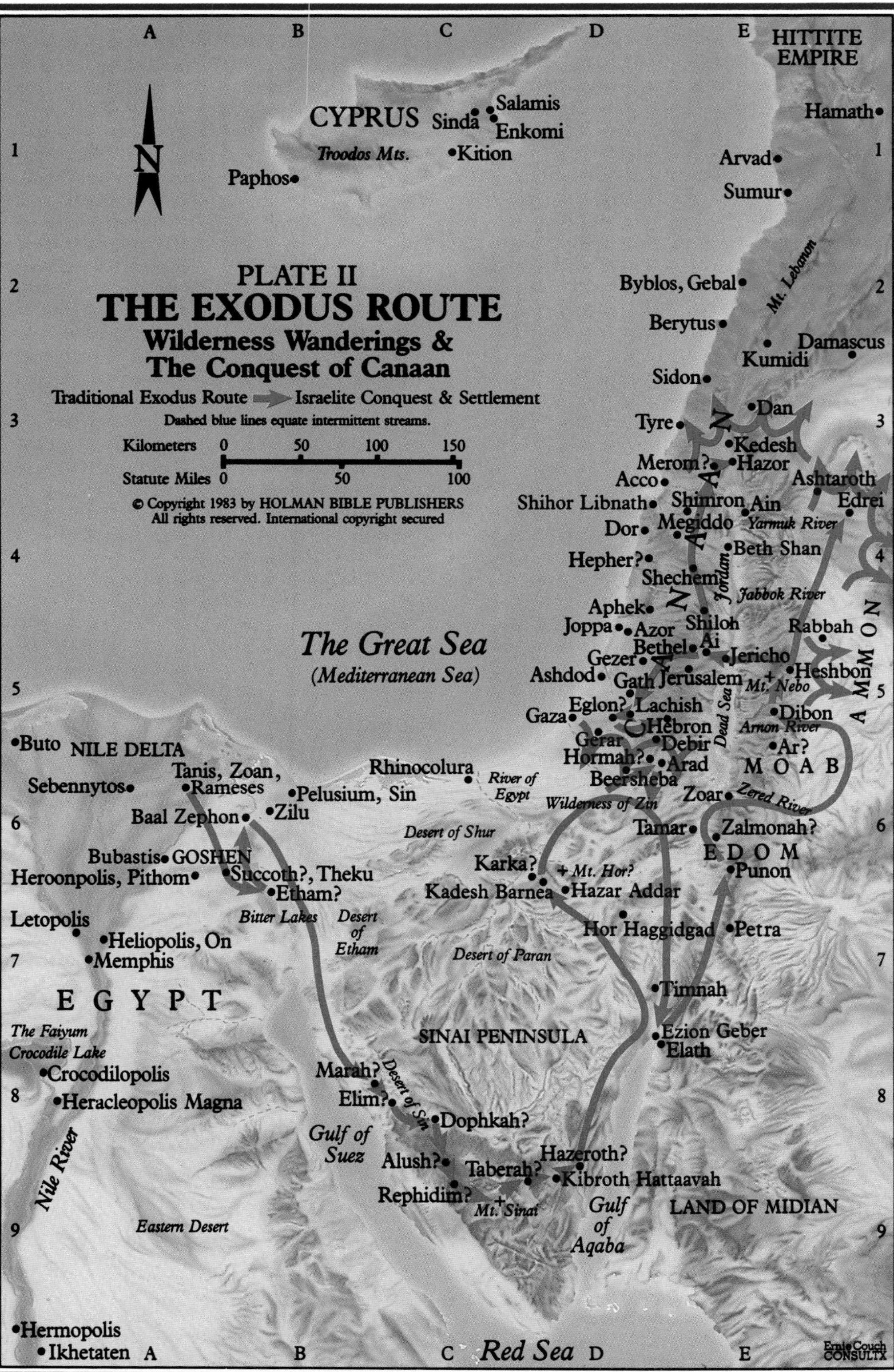
PLATE II
THE EXODUS ROUTE
Wilderness Wanderings &
The Conquest of Canaan
Traditional Exodus Route
Israelite Conquest & Settlement
Dashed blue lines equate intermittent streams.
Kilometers 0 50 100 150
Statute Miles 0 50 100
© Copyright 1983 by HOLMAN BIBLE PUBLISHERS
All rights reserved. International copyright secured
HITTITE EMPIRE
CYPRUS
Salamis
Sinda
Enkomi
Troodos Mts.
Kition
Paphos
Hamath
Arvad
Sumur
Byblos, Gebal
Mt. Lebanon
Berytus
Damascus
Kumidi
Sidon
Tyre
Dan
Kedesh
Merom?
Hazor
Acco
Ashtaroth
Shihor Libnath
Shimron
Ain
Edrei
Dor
Megiddo
Yarmuk River
Beth Shan
Hepher?
Shechem
Jordan
Jabbok River
Aphek
Shiloh
Joppa
Azor
Rabbah
Bethel
Ai
Gezer
Jericho
Heshbon
Ashdod
Gath
Jerusalem
Mt. Nebo
Dead Sea
Gaza
Eglon?
Lachish
Dibon
Hebron
Arnon River
Gerar
Debir
Ar?
Hormah?
Arad
Beersheba
CANAAN
AMMON
MOAB
Zoar
Zered River
Wilderness of Zin
Tamar
Zalmonah?
EDOM
Punon
The Great Sea
(Mediterranean Sea)
Buto
NILE DELTA
Sebennytos
Tanis, Zoan,
Rameses
Rhinocolura
River of Egypt
Pelusium, Sin
Baal Zephon
Zilu
Desert of Shur
Bubastis
GOSHEN
Heroonpolis, Pithom
Succoth?, Theku
Etham?
Karka?
Mt. Hor?
Kadesh Barnea
Hazar Addar
Letopolis
Bitter Lakes
Desert of Etham
Hor Haggidgad
Petra
Heliopolis, On
Memphis
Desert of Paran
Timnah
EGYPT
The Faiyum
Crocodile Lake
SINAI PENINSULA
Ezion Geber
Elath
Crocodilopolis
Heracleopolis Magna
Marah?
Desert of Sin
Elim?
Dophkah?
Gulf of Suez
Alush?
Taberah?
Hazeroth?
Kibroth Hattaavah
Rephidim?
Mt. Sinai
Gulf of Aqaba
LAND OF MIDIAN
Nile River
Eastern Desert
Hermopolis
Ikhetaten
Red Sea
Ernie Couch
CONSULTX

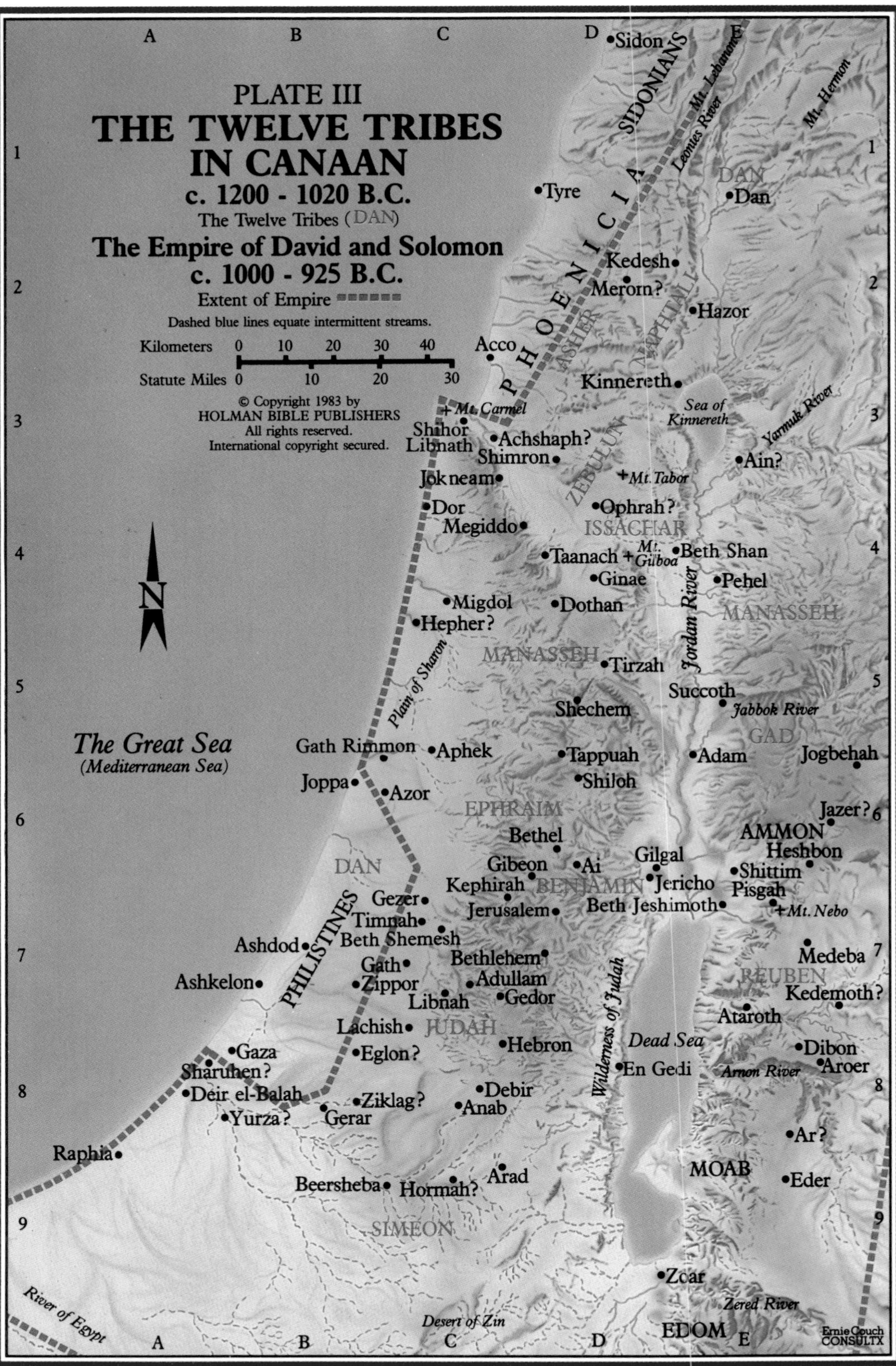
PLATE III
THE TWELVE TRIBES IN CANAAN
c. 1200 - 1020 B.C.
The Twelve Tribes (DAN)
The Empire of David and Solomon
c. 1000 - 925 B.C.
Extent of Empire
Dashed blue lines equate intermittent streams.
Kilometers 0 10 20 30 40
Statute Miles 0 10 20 30
© Copyright 1983 by HOLMAN BIBLE PUBLISHERS
All rights reserved.
International copyright secured.
The Great Sea
(Mediterranean Sea)
N
Sidon
SIDONIANS
Mt. Lebanon
Leonies River
Mt. Hermon
PHOENICIA
Tyre
DAN
Dan
Kedesh
Merom?
NAPHTALI
ASHER
Hazor
Acco
Kinnereth
Sea of Kinnereth
Yarmuk River
Mt. Carmel
Shihor Libnath
Achshaph?
Shimron
ZEBULUN
Ain?
Jokneam
Mt. Tabor
Dor
Ophrah?
Megiddo
ISSACHAR
Taanach
Mt. Gilboa
Beth Shan
Ginae
Pehel
Migdol
Dothan
Jordan River
Hepher?
MANASSEH
Plain of Sharon
Tirzah
Succoth
Jabbok River
Shechem
GAD
Gath Rimmon
Aphek
Tappuah
Adam
Jogbehah
Joppa
Shiloh
Azor
EPHRAIM
Jazer?
AMMON
Bethel
Heshbon
DAN
Gibeon
Ai
Gilgal
Shittim
Kephirah
BENJAMIN
Jericho
Pisgah
Gezer
Jerusalem
Beth Jeshimoth
Mt. Nebo
PHILISTINES
Timnah
Ashdod
Beth Shemesh
Medeba
Gath
Bethlehem
Ashkelon
Zippor
Adullam
REUBEN
Libnah
Gedor
Kedemoth?
Wilderness of Judah
Ataroth
Lachish
JUDAH
Dead Sea
Gaza
Eglon?
Hebron
Dibon
Sharuhen?
En Gedi
Arnon River
Aroer
Deir el-Balah
Debir
Ziklag?
Anab
Yurza?
Gerar
Ar?
Raphia
Arad
MOAB
Eder
Beersheba
Hormah?
SIMEON
Zoar
Zered River
River of Egypt
Desert of Zin
EDOM
Ernie Couch CONSULTX

PLATE IV
THE DIVIDED KINGDOM
Judah and Israel
Dashed blue lines equate intermittent streams.
© Copyright 1983 by HOLMAN BIBLE PUBLISHERS
All rights reserved. International copyright secured
Sidon
Zarephath
SIDONIANS
Mt. Lebanon
Leontes River
Mt. Hermon
Tyre
Dan
PHOENICIA
ARAM (Syrians)
Kedesh
Merom?
Bashan
Hazor
Acco
Kinnereth
Geshur
Ashtaroth
Sea of Kinnereth
Aphek
Mt. Carmel
Shihor Libnath
Achshaph?
Yarmuk River
Shimron
Ain?
Mt. Tabor
Havvoth Jair
Plain of Jezreel
Dor
Ophrah?
Lo Debar
Megiddo
Jezreel
Taanach
Mt. Gilboa
Beth Shan
Ginae
Jabesh Gilead
Migdol
Dothan
Tishbe
Hepher?
ISRAEL
Jordan River
Socoh
Plain of Sharon
Samaria
Tirzah
Mt. Ebal
Zarethan
Succoth
Mahanaim
Shechem
Jabbok River
The Great Sea
(Mediterranean Sea)
Gath Rimmon
Aphek
Tappuah
Adam
Jogbehah
Joppa
Azor
Gilead
Jazer?
AMMON
Jabneel
Beth Horon
Bethel
Heshbon
Lod
Gibeon
Ai
Gilgal
Shittim
Gezer
Kephirah
Jericho
Pisgah
PHILISTINES
Ekron
Jerusalem
Beth Jeshimoth
Mt. Nebo
Timnah
Beth Shemesh
Ashdod
Bethlehem
Medeba
Gath
Wilderness of Judah
Ashkelon
Zippor
Adullam
Kedemoth?
Libnah?
Gedor
Ataroth
Lachish
Gaza
Hebron
Dead Sea
Dibon
Sharuhen?
Eglon?
Ziph
En Gedi
Arnon River
Aroer
Deir el-Balah
Debir
Ziklag?
Anab
Yurza?
Gerar
JUDAH
Ar?
Raphia
Arad
MOAB
Beersheba
Hormah?
Eder
Kir Hareseth
Tamar
Valley of Salt
Zoar
Zered River
River of Egypt
Desert of Zin
EDOM
Ernie Couch CONSULTX
A
B
C
D
E
1
2
3
4
5
6
7
8
9

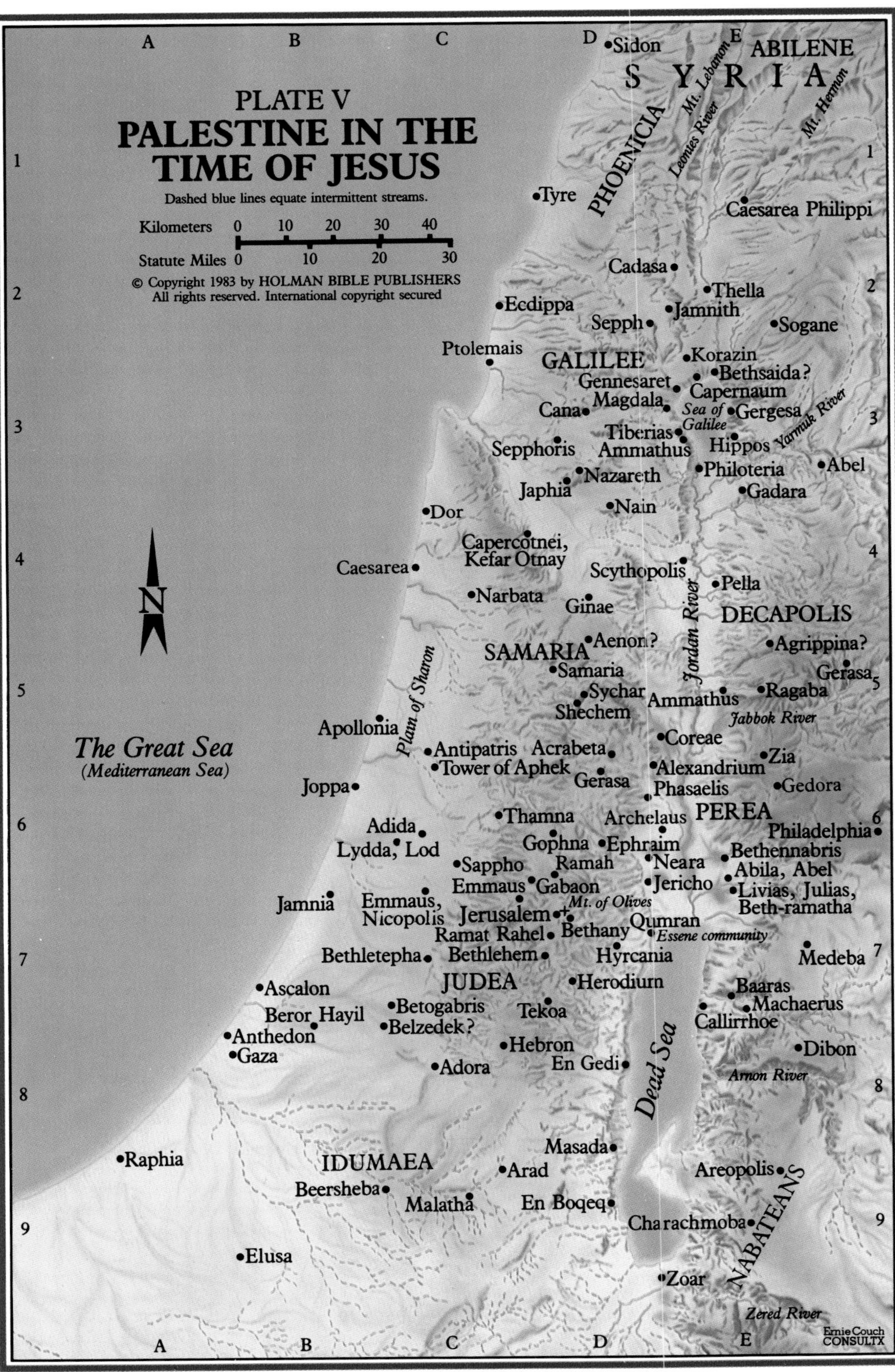
PLATE V
PALESTINE IN THE TIME OF JESUS
Dashed blue lines equate intermittent streams.
Kilometers 0 10 20 30 40
Statute Miles 0 10 20 30
© Copyright 1983 by HOLMAN BIBLE PUBLISHERS
All rights reserved. International copyright secured
A B C D E
1 2 3 4 5 6 7 8 9
N
The Great Sea
(Mediterranean Sea)
Sidon
ABILENE
SYRIA
Mt. Lebanon
Leontes River
Mt. Hermon
PHOENICIA
Tyre
Caesarea Philippi
Cadasa
Thella
Ecdippa
Jamnith
Sepph
Sogane
Ptolemais
GALILEE
Korazin
Bethsaida?
Gennesaret
Capernaum
Magdala
Cana
Sea of Galilee
Gergesa
Yarmuk River
Tiberias
Ammathus
Hippos
Sepphoris
Nazareth
Philoteria
Abel
Japhia
Gadara
Dor
Nain
Capercotnei,
Kefar Otnay
Caesarea
Scythopolis
Pella
Narbata
Ginae
Jordan River
DECAPOLIS
SAMARIA
Aenon?
Agrippina?
Samaria
Gerasa
Plain of Sharon
Sychar
Shechem
Ammathus
Ragaba
Jabbok River
Apollonia
Coreae
Antipatris
Acrabeta
Zia
Tower of Aphek
Alexandrium
Gerasa
Joppa
Phasaelis
Gedora
Thamna
Archelaus
PEREA
Adida
Philadelphia
Lydda, Lod
Gophna
Ephraim
Bethennabris
Sappho
Ramah
Neara
Abila, Abel
Emmaus
Gabaon
Jericho
Jamnia
Emmaus,
Nicopolis
Livias, Julias,
Beth-ramatha
Jerusalem
Mt. of Olives
Qumran
Ramat Rahel
Bethany
Essene community
Bethletepha
Bethlehem
Hyrcania
Medeba
JUDEA
Ascalon
Herodium
Baaras
Beror Hayil
Betogabris
Machaerus
Tekoa
Callirrhoe
Anthedon
Belzedek?
Gaza
Hebron
Dibon
En Gedi
Adora
Dead Sea
Arnon River
Masada
Raphia
IDUMAEA
Arad
Areopolis
Beersheba
Malatha
En Boqeq
Charachmoba
NABATEANS
Elusa
Zoar
Zered River
Ernie Couch
CONSULTX

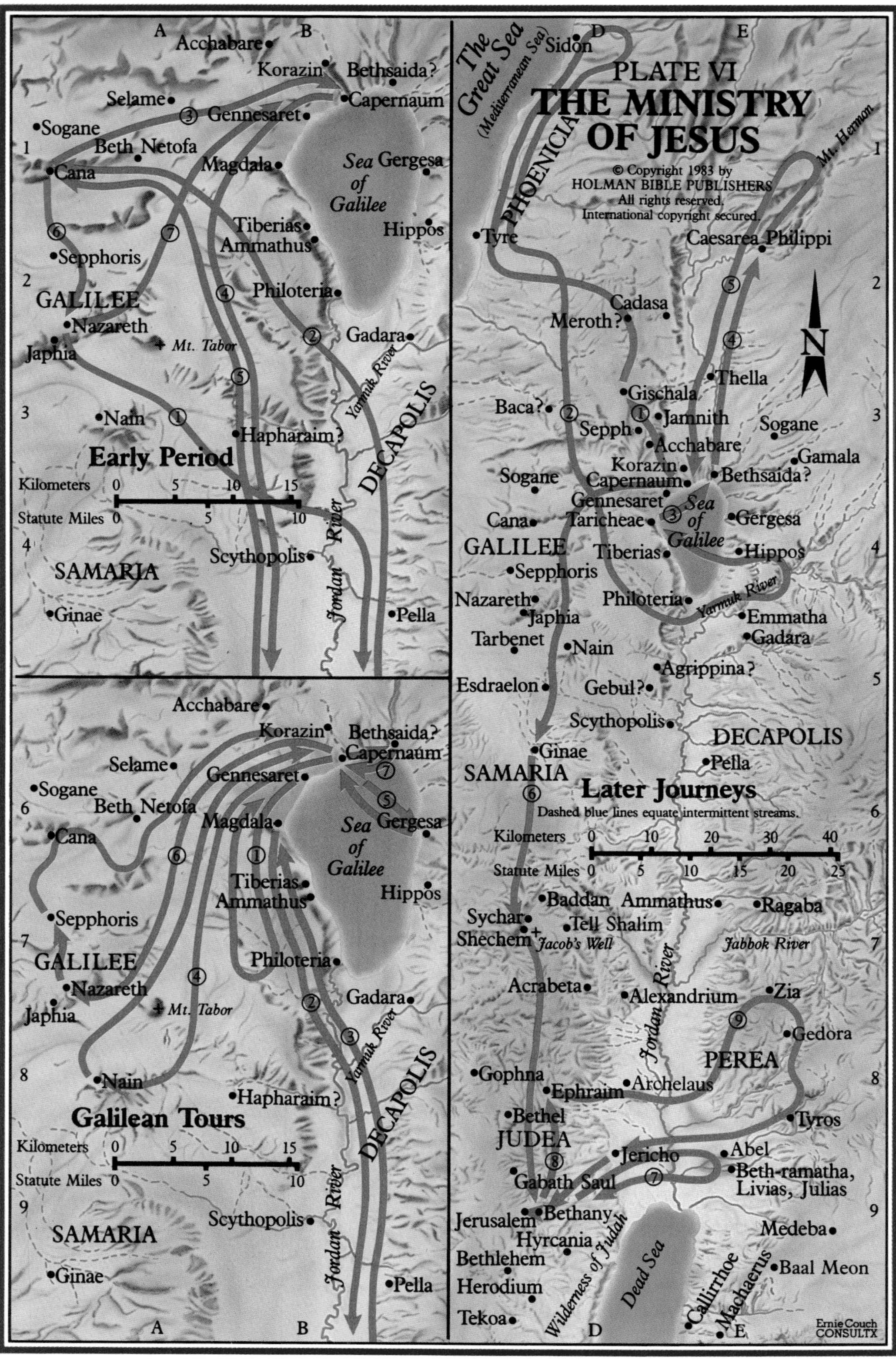
PLATE VI
THE MINISTRY OF JESUS
© Copyright 1983 by HOLMAN BIBLE PUBLISHERS
All rights reserved.
International copyright secured.
Early Period
Galilean Tours
Later Journeys
Dashed blue lines equate intermittent streams.
Kilometers 0 5 10 15
Statute Miles 0 5 10
Kilometers 0 10 20 30 40
Statute Miles 0 5 10 15 20 25
A
B
D
E
1
2
3
4
5
6
7
8
9
The Great Sea
(Mediterranean Sea)
PHOENICIA
GALILEE
SAMARIA
DECAPOLIS
PEREA
JUDEA
Sea of Galilee
Dead Sea
Jordan River
Yarmuk River
Jabbok River
Wilderness of Judah
Mt. Tabor
Mt. Hermon
Jacob's Well
N
Acchabare
Korazin
Bethsaida?
Capernaum
Selame
Gennesaret
Sogane
Beth Netofa
Cana
Magdala
Gergesa
Tiberias
Ammathus
Hippos
Sepphoris
Philoteria
Nazareth
Japhia
Gadara
Nain
Hapharaim?
Scythopolis
Ginae
Pella
Sidon
Tyre
Caesarea Philippi
Cadasa
Meroth?
Thella
Gischala
Baca?
Jamnith
Sepph
Gamala
Taricheae
Emmatha
Tarbenet
Agrippina?
Esdraelon
Gebul?
Baddan
Ragaba
Sychar
Tell Shalim
Shechem
Acrabeta
Alexandrium
Zia
Gedora
Gophna
Archelaus
Ephraim
Bethel
Tyros
Jericho
Abel
Beth-ramatha, Livias, Julias
Gabath Saul
Jerusalem
Bethany
Medeba
Hyrcania
Bethlehem
Baal Meon
Herodium
Callirrhoe
Machaerus
Tekoa
Ernie Couch CONSULTX